THE NAZI HUNTERS WANTED LIST

War Criminals and Security Suspects

CROWCASS

1947

THE NAZI HUNTERS WANTED LIST

War Criminals and Security Suspects

CROWCASS

PART 1

GERMANS ONLY (A–L)

GERMANS ONLY (M–Z)

MARCH 1947

PART 2

NON-GERMANS ONLY

MARCH 1947

SUPPLEMMENTARY WANTED LIST NO.2

PART 1 GERMANS

PART 2 NON GERMANS

SEPTEMBER 1947

Reproduced by The Naval & Milkitary Press in facsimile
from original documents housed at The National Archives

The Naval & Military Press Ltd

Published by

The Naval & Military Press Ltd
Unit 5 Riverside, Brambleside
Bellbrook Industrial Estate
Uckfield, East Sussex
TN22 1QQ England

Tel: +44 (0)1825 749494

www.naval-military-press.com
www.nmarchive.com

This edition © The Naval & Military Press Ltd 2024

ACKNOWLEDGEMENT

Images reproduced by permission of
The National Archives, London, England
www.nationalarchives.gov.uk

The National Archives give no warranty as to the accuracy,
completeness or fitness for the purpose of the information provided.

Images may be used only for purposes of research, private study or education.
Applications for any other use should be made to:
The National Archives Image Library, Kew, Richmond, Surrey TW9 4DU.
Infringement of the above condition may result in legal action.

*In reprinting in facsimile from the original, any imperfections are inevitably reproduced
and the quality may fall short of modern type and cartographic standards.*

THE CENTRAL REGISTRY OF WAR CRIMINALS AND SECURITY SUSPECTS

CONSOLIDATED WANTED LIST – PART 1 (A–L)

GERMANS ONLY

NOTE: ALL PREVIOUS CROWCASS WANTED LISTS SHOULD BE DESTROYED

CROWCASS
ALLIED CONTROL AUTHORITY
APO 742,
U.S. ARMY

TELEPHONE: BERLIN (TEMPELHOF) 5336, 5775
TELEPRINTER: BERLIN / STATION DHBP.

MARCH 1947

CONSOLIDATED WANTED LIST (PART I - GERMANS)

IT IS IMPORTANT THAT YOU READ THIS!

1. This List is the first part of the Consolidation of the names of all persons in CROWCASS Records who are wanted in connection with War Crimes and includes all Wanted Reports received up to 31 Jan.1947 plus a few additional names not published in previous lists.

2. This list contains the names of all persons stated to be of German nationality who according to the information passed to CROWCASS are still wanted by the Allied Nations in connection with War Crimes. Persons who are stated to be of nationality other than German will be listed in the second part of this Consolidated List, which is in course of preparation and will be distributed shortly. All persons of UNKNOWN name will also be included in the second part.

3. This list also includes the names of all persons stated to be of German nationality who have been listed in the United Nations War Crimes Commission Lists Nos. 1 - 50 who, so far as CROWCASS is aware, are still wanted.

4. It is considered probable that some of the persons listed have been detained, some tried, some sentenced and others may be no longer wanted. If that is so, CROWCASS has not been informed and the various Allied Authorities who can supply such information are requested to do so immediately in order that CROWCASS Records may be adjusted. It is also possible that some Wanted Reports went astray during the move of CROWCASS from Paris to Berlin and the names are therefore not included in this list. If such is the case new Wanted Reports should be submitted immediately and the names will be published in a supplementary List.

5. Names of persons known to be detained, and where the Wanting Authority has been informed accordingly, are not included in this list.

6. It is hoped that by now all authorities receiving a copy of this List will also have received and read the pamphlet entitled "What is CROWCASS?" in order that a better understanding may be reached concerning the functions of this organization and the service given to and required from all using agencies.

7. All recipients of this List are reminded of the following requirements as previously set out in the frontispieces of CROWCASS Wanted Lists:

    (i) If any person listed should be located and detained the CROWCASS Detention Report (to be invariably submitted in respect of all Detainees) should be completed showing Reason for Arrest as "CROWCASS Consolidated Wanted List (Part I) CR.NO. ..." or "Possibly CROWCASS Consolidated Wanted List (Part I) CR.NO. ...". If a Wanted Person is located only and not detained as full a description as possible of the person located should be set out in letter form and forwarded to CROWCASS including the reason for non-detention.

    (ii) In the event of CROWCASS thus receiving information of a match or possible match between a Wanted Person and a Detained or located Person the wanting nation is immediately informed, even although the Detainee may be held in the custody of that nation. In some cases where the persons name has not been listed by the UNWCC and where extradition is applied for considerable delay may be unavoidable. (See page (ii)). If and when the extradition of a CROWCASS Wanted Personality has taken place CROWCASS should be informed immediately.

    (iii) If a Detaining Authority receives instructions to Release or Transfer any Detainee who is possibly or definitely a CROWCASS Wanted Personality a check should first be made with that Authority's War Crimes Group HQ. and a copy of the communication endorsed to CROWCASS.

    (iv) The information given in this list about each person is all that is contained on the Wanted Reports filed with CROWCASS. The descriptions given are not summaries.

8. It is particularly requested that the War Crimes HQ.'s of all the Allied Nations endeavour to make special arrangements to have this List distributed to all Detaining Authorities, Prisoner of War Information Bureaus (or the equivalent) and all other HQ.'s or Formations which may be able to assist in locating the persons listed.

9. No doubt the Inter-Allied National policy as regards the probable duration of the Investigation of War Crimes will depend to quite a considerable extent upon the number of Alleged War Criminals "still at large" in the sense of not being in the custody of the nation who wants them. To help to reduce this period of duration and the enormous expenditure and man power involved all Allied Nations are again requested to exploit every means within their power to reduce this List as quickly as possible.

10. Pages 266 to 271 of Volume A-L include the names of persons (also A-L), especially listed under different headings owing to a lack of detailed information suitable for listing under the normal headings.

11. At Appendix "A" of Volume M-Z will be found a table showing the total number of persons included in this List who are wanted by each of the Allied Nations.

12. At Appendix "B" of Volume M-Z will be found a list of persons (herein listed as wanted) regarding whom Detention Reports have been received since the preparation of this List for publication was commenced.

13. CROWCASS has a teleprinter station in its office. It is "Station DHBP - Berlin". Using agencies are requested to make use of it as it greatly speeds up replies to requests for information.

14. CROWCASS holds large stocks of Blank Wanted and Detention Reports and they can be had on application by TPM, Signal or letter.

15. Whilst every effort has been made to eliminate error from this List there may still be left a few discrepancies which although unavoidable are regretted.

(ii)

CONCERNING THE UNITED NATIONS WAR CRIMES COMMISSION.

The following is quoted from Section X of Information Paper No. 1 issued by the Reference Division of the United Nations Information Organisation, London:

INTER-ALLIED DECLARATION OF DECEMBER 17, 1942

On December 17, 1942, a Declaration was made simultaneously in London, Moscow, and Washington in connection with reports that the German authorities were engaged in exterminating the Jewish people in Europe. In this Declaration, the Governments of Belgium, Czechoslovakia, Greece, Luxembourg, the Netherlands, Norway, Poland, the United States of America, the United Kingdom, the Soviet Union and Yugoslavia and the French National Committee reaffirmed their solemn resolution that those responsible should not escape retribution and their intention to press on with the necessary practical measures to that end.

There was some delay in setting up the United Nations War Crimes Commission, but it was eventually brought into being by a meeting of Government representatives at the British Foreign Office on October 20, 1943.

COMPOSITION OF THE COMMISSION

The Commission consists of seventeen members: the representatives of the Governments of Australia, Belgium, Canada, China, Czechoslovakia, Denmark, France, Greece, India, Luxembourg, the Netherlands, New Zealand, Norway, Poland, the United Kingdom, the United States of America and Yugoslavia. The representatives are all distinguished lawyers or diplomats.

If a representative is unable to act, or for some other special reason, he may be replaced.

The Commission may hear experts.

The first Chairman was the United Kingdom representative, Sir Cecil Hurst, Vice-President of the Permanent Court of International Justice, formerly legal Adviser to the Foreign Office. After his resignation on account of illhealth, he was replaced by the Right Hon. Lord Wright, Lord of Appeal in Ordinary, who represents Australia on the Commission. Lord Wright has been Chairman since January 31, 1945.

TERMS OF REFERENCE OF THE COMMISSION

The Commission has limited functions. It is primarily a fact-finding body, though it has also advisory functions.

Its terms of reference were defined in the Lord Chancellor's statement of October 7, 1942. Its purpose, he said is to investigate war crimes committed against nationals of the United Nations, recording the testimony available, and to report from time to time to the Governments of those nations cases in which such crimes appear to have been committed, naming and identifying wherever possible the persons responsible.

After its creation, it was entrusted with advisory functions, namely to make recommendations to the Governments on the methods to be adopted to ensure the surrender or capture of the persons wanted for trial as war criminals and on the tribunals by which they should be tried.

HOW THE COMMISSION OPERATES

The United Nations War Crimes Commission prepares lists of war criminals on the basis of evidence submitted by National War Crimes Offices which have been set up to detect, investigate and record evidence of war crimes committed against the citizens or subjects of their own countries.

The lists are furnished to the apprehending authorities - at present the military authorities - in order that the persons accused of crimes against people or property may be sent back to the country against which they have offended. This was the procedure contemplated in the Moscow Declaration on Atrocities by President Roosevelt, Mr. Winston Churchill and Marshal Stalin which was issued on November 1, 1943 and by the Foreign Secretaries of their three countries, who had been attending the Moscow Conference of October 16 to 30.

After referring to the atrocities, massacres and mass executions which were being perpetrated by the Hitlerite forces, the Declaration said:

"The United Kingdom, the United States and the Soviet Union ....

"... speaking in the interests of the thirty-two United Nations ... solemnly declare and give full warning of their declaration as follows· At the time of the granting of any armistice to any Government which may be set up in Germany, those German officers and men and members of the Nazi Party who have been responsible for or who have taken a consenting part in the above atrocities, massacres and executions will be sent back to the countries in which their abominable deeds were done in order that they many be judged and punished according to the laws of these liberated countries and of the Free Governments which will be erected therein. Lists will be compiled in all possible detail from all these countries ..."

Offences against members of the Allied armed forces will be dealt with summarily by military courts, in accordance with international custom.

The following is a Statement issued by UNWCC especially for incorporation in this Consolidated Wanted List:

"All Allied Authorities concerned are reminded that in order to secure extradition they should submit to the United Nations "War Crimes Commission in London dossiers with charges concerning the offences committed by persons wanted. The United "Nations War Crimes Commission in accordance with its terms of reference decides whether there appears to be either prima "facie evidence sufficient to justify the handing over for trial of individuals accused of War Crimes or else sufficient "ground to consider the wanted persons as suspects or material witnesses"

AAH -ADA

NAME	C.R.FILE NUMBER	SEX	NATIO-NALITY	DATE OF BIRTH	RANK OCCUPATION UNIT PLACE AND DATE OF CRIME	REASON WANTED	WANTED BY
AAHRING, Werner	72222	M			Sgt., Army, Redon (Fr.) 44	MURDER	FR.
ABBE	131778	M			Oberscharfhr., SS, C.C. Flossenburg (Ger.)	MURDER	U.S.
ABBE	132047	M		07	SS-Rottenfhr.	TORTURE	U.S.
ABDALA	192154	M	Ger.		Dr., C.C. Falkenser (Ger.)	MURDER	BEL.
ABEL	122860	M	Ger.		Sgt., Army, C.C. Stammlag. XII A (Ger.)	MURDER	U.S.
ABEL	167664	M	Ger.		Prof., Stationer Office, Ostgebietsministerium, Einsatzstab "Rosenberg", Berlin (Ger.) 40-44	PILLAGE	FR.
ABEL	172892	M	Ger.		Lt.Col., 74. Sicherungs-Regt., Claviere (Fr.) 6.44	MURDER	FR.
ABEL, Christian	250006	M		05	Flyer, Camp Ellrich, Nordhausen (Ger.)	MURDER	U.S.
ABEL, Otto	300001	M	Ger.	3.12.13	Oberfeldmeister, 2-370 RAD, Flak-Btty., Bemerode (Ger.) 4.45	MURDER	U.K.
ABEL, Richard	259057	M	Ger.		SS-Pvt., SS, Mühldorf area (Ger.)	MURDER	U.S.
ABELE, Otto	121032	M		95	Member of Gestapo, Civ.Director, Busenbach, Neurod, Karlsruhe (Ger.) 43-45	TORTURE	FR.
ABELE, Willi	168626	M	Ger.		Kapo, C.C. Sachsenhausen-Oranienburg (Ger.) 39-45	MURDER	POL.
ABENDROTH	189523	M	Ger.		Usturmfhr., SS, Gestapo, Lons le Saunier, Lyon (Fr.) 9.44	MURDER	FR.
ABENDSCHOEN, Willy (aliases: GROSSMANN, Willy)	257315	M	Ger.	27. 8.05	Chief secret., Crim.Pol., SS-Sturmfhr., Gestapo, Prague (Czech.)41-45	MISC.CRIMES	CZECH.
ABERG, Erich	300160	M	Ger.		Capt., Verbindungsstab 802, Rodez, Aveyron, Herault and Gard 8.44	MURDER	FR.
ABETZ, Otto	62144	M			Standartenfhr., NSDAP (Fr.)	MURDER	UNWCC
ABLGRIMM, Franz	257335	M	Ger.		SS-Sturmfhr., SS, Slave Labour Camp, Beisfjord-Narvik (Nor.) 6.-11.42	MISC.CRIMES	YUGO.
ABNIK, Johann	250003	M			Sturmmann, C.C. Nordhausen (Ger.)	MURDER	U.S.
ABRAHAM	9622	M	Ger.		Scharfhr., SS, Buchenwald (Ger.) 44	MURDER	CZECH.,NOR.,BEL.
ABRAHAM	31528	M			Scharfhr., Waffen-SS, Maidanek (Pol.)	MURDER	POL.
ABRAHAM	194811	M	Ger.		SS-Hptscharfhr., SS, C.C. Lublin (Pol.) 40-44	MURDER	POL.
ABRAHAM, Herbert	142404	M		14	Oschafhr., Waffen-SS, Totenkopf-Standarte, C.C.Buchenwald (Ger.) 39-44	TORTURE	U.S., FR.
ABRAHAM, Willy	254923	M	Ger.		Cook, Army, Heusden (Neth.) 11.44	PILLAGE	NETH.
ABRAHAMCZYK	192635	M	Ger.		Cpl., Kgf.Arb.Bn. 190, Karasjok (Nor.) 8.43	MURDER	NOR.
ABRECHT	31527	M			Gen., Army, St.Die (Fr.)	LOOTING	FR.
ABS, Hermann	260214	M	Ger.	02	Counsellor, German Reichsbank, Vorstand Deutsche Bank,Berlin (Ger.)	MISC.CRIMES	U.K.
ABS, Otto	142405	M	Ger.		Oberscharfhr., SS and SD, C.C.Mielheim-Ruhr (Ger.) 43	TORTURE	U.S.
ABSALON	172891	M	Ger.		Hptsturmfhr., SS, Krim.Kommsser, Kripo, C.C. Stalag Luft III (Ger.) 3.44	MURDER	U.K.
ABSOLOM	36658	M			Hptsturmfhr., SS - Prevention of escapes of prisoners of war - KL Stalag Luft III (Ger.) 44	MURDER	U.K.
ABT, Hugo	195580	M		17. 7.95	Reichsprotektor, Bratislava (Czech.) 39-45	TORTURE	CZECH.
ABTERLANDT	72207	M			Lt., Army, Montmoudist (Fr.)	TORTURE	FR.
ABUER	122487	M	Ger.		Officer, Stalag 317, Markt-Pongau	MISC.CRIMES	U.K.
ACHAMER-PFRADER	62145	M	Ger.		SS-Obersturmfhr., SS	TORTURE	UNWCC
ACHAMER-PIFFRADER (see PFIFRATER)	301594	M	Ger.		Dr., SS-Lt., stationed at C.C. Mauthausen (Austria) 40-45	MURDER	BEL.
ACHENBACH	157157	M	Ger.		Manufacturer, Civ., Plettenberg, Ohle (Ger.) 4.45	TORTURE	U.S.
ACHERMANN	12425	M	Ger.		Scharfhr., SS Panz.Gren.Regt., 10.Coy. "Hohenstaufen", Arnheim (Neth.)44	MURDER	U.K.
ACHERMANN (see ACKERMANN)	31999						
ACHILLES	140341	M		10	Civilian	LOOTING	FR.
ACHINGER	121033	M	Ger.		Sgt., Army, 515. Inf.Bn., 12.Coy., (Pol.)	TORTURE	U.K.
ACHINGER	122486	M	Ger.		Feldw., Army, 515. Bn., near Koeniggraetz.	MURDER	U.K.
ACHKE	126522	M	Ger.		Civ., Kgf.-Arbeitskommando, Guard, Kohlscheid (Ger.) 41-44	TORTURE	U.S.
ACHMUND (see LACKMUD)	151961						
ACHSTE	140342	M			Civilian, Stuttgart (Ger.)	TORTURE	FR.
ACHTELICK	192598	M	Ger.	20	Untersturmfhr., Political Dept., C.C. Buchenwald (Ger.)40-44	MURDER	U.S.
ACHTELINK, Willi	250002	M	Ger.		SS-Oschafhr., C.C. Buchenwald (Ger.)	TORTURE	BEL.
ACHTENBERG, Erna	135144	F	Ger.		Guard, Civ. C.C. Helmbrechts (Ger.) 7.44-4.45	WITNESS	U.S.
ACHTER	189143	M	Ger.		Member of Gestapo, C.C. Dachau (Ger.)	MURDER	BEL.
ACHTER, Franz	260494	M	Ger.	30.10.09	Pvt., Panzer Army School (Huta Arbeitskommando) - Civ.photographer - C.C.Auschwitz (Pol.) 41-44	MURDER	POL.
ACHTMUELLER, Heinrich	135140	M	Ger.	10	Capt., Betriebsobmann of Fortuna Nord , Niederausum (Ger.)	TORTURE	U.S.
ACK	307026	M	Ger.		SS Pol., Falstad Slave Labour Camp (Nor.) 42 and 43	MURDER	YUGO.
ACKE	72213	M			Oberleutnant, Army, Nimes (Fr.)	MURDER	FR.
ACKEL (or ACKERL)	168573	M	Ger.	06	Civ. Chief of Barracks 13, C.C.Mauthausen (Austria) 41-45	MURDER	U.S.
ACKENHAUSEN	250008	M	Ger.		Sgt., Army, 6.Div. Paratroopers, 17.Regt., Nieuwoul (Neth.) 1.45	WITNESS	NETH.
ACKER	258130	M	Ger.		Prof., C.C. Natzweiler (Fr.)	SUSPECT	BEL.
ACKER	261768	M	Ger.		Pvt., Gend., Romilly-sur-Seine (Fr.) 6.44	MISC.CRIMES	FR.
ACKER, Anton	196170	M	Ger.	6. 2.99	Oberwachtmeister, Gend., Sierentz (Fr.) 10.44	MURDER	FR.
ACKER, Willy	129161	M	Ger.		C.C. Mauthausen (Austria) 41-45	MURDER	U.S.
ACKERE (or ACKERT, ECKERT)	187835	M			Zahlmeister (Cpl.), Army, Ers.Art.Bn., St.Andries, Varsenare, Les, B.Roges (Bel.)	MURDER	BEL.
ACKERL	129160	M	Ger.		Officer, C.C. Mauthausen (Austria) 41-45	MURDER	U.S.
ACKERL (see ACKEL)	168573						
ACKERMANN (or ACHERMANN)	31999	M	Ger.		Army, Member of NSKK, Noailles-Parisis (Fr.) 8.44	MURDER	FR.
ACKERMANN	108862	M	Ger.		Techn.Sgt., SS, 9.Panz.Div. "Hohenstaufen", 19.Panz.Gren.Regt., 10.Coy. (Ger.)	MISC.CRIMES	U.S.
ACKERMANN	196169	M	Ger.		Pvt., Noailles (Fr.) 8.44	WITNESS	FR.
ACKERMANN	250004	M	Ger.		Lt., Detachment for reprisal, Chateauvillain (Fr.) 8.44	TORTURE	FR.
ACKERMANN	262203	M	Ger.		Pvt., 5-I. N.Regt.211, 139.Arbeitsbereich "Liane", Alleur-lez-Liege (Bel.) 9.44	MURDER	BEL.
ACKERMANN, Emj	193932	M	Ger.		Kapo, C.C. "Gustloff", Weimar, Buchenwald (Ger.)	TORTURE	U.S.
ACKERMANN, Hugo	192047	M	Ger.		Civ., Didier-Werke, Belgrad (Yugo.) 42-44	MURDER	YUGO.
ACKERMANN, Karl	259755	M	Ger.		Architect, Civ., Luxemburg (Lux.) 40-45	PILLAGE	LUX.
ACKERMANN, Kurt	140344	M	Ger.	4. 7.23	Sgt., Air Force, Dienststelle Sete (Fr.)	MURDER	FR.
ACKERMANN, Kurt	259410	M	Ger.		Pvt., Gestapo Poitiers, Antenne of Rochelle, Poitiers area (Fr.)40-45	MISC.CRIMES	FR.
ACKERMANN, Werner	1096	M	Ger.		SS-Oberscharfhr., 9.SS Panzer Div. "Hohenstaufen", 3.Bn., 10.Coy., Arnheim, Petite Langlir (Neth., Bel.) 44-1.45	MISC.CRIMES	U.S., U.K.
ACKERMANN, Wilhelm	195770	M	Ger.	11	Uscharfhr., C.C. Struthof-Natzweiler (Fr.) 42-44	MURDER	FR.
ACKERT (see ACKERE)	187835						
ACKMANN	142406	M	Ger.	05	Civilian, Nuernberg (Ger.) 40-45	TORTURE	U.S.
ADALBERT	147031	M	Ger.		Obersturmfhr., SS Panz.Div. "Das Reich", Montauban (Fr.) 44	MURDER	FR.
ADAM	69841	M	Ger.		Army, Malestrait	MURDER	FR.

ADA-AHS

-2-

NAME	C.R.FILE NUMBER	SEX	NATIO- NALITY	DATE OF BIRTH	RANK OCCUPATION UNIT PLACE AND DATE OF CRIME	REASON WANTED	WANTED BY
ADAM	140349	M	Ger.	00	Member, S.A., C.C. Aurigny (Fr.) 43-5.44	TORTURE	FR.
ADAM	139843	M	Ger.		Major, Stalag X B, Sandbostel (Ger.) 1.-5.45	TORTURE	U.S.
ADAM	140350	M	Ger.	00	Member, SS, C.C. Norderney (Ger.)	MURDER	FR.
ADAM	178334	M	Ger.		Hptsturmfhr., SS, C.C. Flossenburg (Ger.) 11.44-45	MURDER	FR.,U.S.,BEL
ADAM	186472	M	Ger.		Member, Gestapo, Brieux (Fr.)	TORTURE	FR.
ADAM	187667	M	Ger.	95	Dr., Hptsturmbannfhr., SS, C.C. Oranienburg, Sachsenhausen (Ger.)	MURDER	U.K.
ADAM	188463	M	Ger.		Lt., Pz.Armee, Melestroit (Fr.) 3.44	MURDER	FR.
ADAM	189458	M	Ger.		Lt., Army, Vlissingen (Neth.) 9.44	MURDER	NETH.
ADAM	250028	M	Ger.		Dr., cmdt., 27 732 B, SS, Mondrepuis (Fr.) 6.44	MISC.CRIMES	FR.
ADAM	301541	M			Warder, C.C. Gusen, C.C. Mauthausen (Aust.) 40-45	MURDER	BEL
ADAM, Georg	69847	M			Sturmscharfhr., Gestapo, H.Q., Fredrikstad (Nor.)	TORTURE	NOR.
ADAM, Hans	140348	M	Ger.	01	Group-leader, N.S.D.A.P., C.C. Geiserbrunn (Ger.)	TORTURE	FR.
ADAM, Heinrich	187391	M	Ger.	22. 5.07	Asst., S.D., Gestapo, Brno (Czech.) 39-45	MURDER	CZECH.
ADAM, Hermann	192279	M	Ger.		Pvt., 4 SS-Pz.Gren.A.u.E.Bn.2, Yves - Gome zee (Bel.)	MURDER	BEL.
ADAM, Karl	148431	M	Ger.		Crim.secret., member, Crim.Police, Gestapo, S.D., Henningsdorf, Brno (Ger., Czech.) 39-45	TORTURE	U.K.,CZECH.
ADAM, Karl Richard	250027	M	Ger.	3. 3.99	Kreisleiter, N.S.D.A.P., Chomitov, Prague (Czech.) 39-45	MISC. CRIMES	CZECH.
ADAM, Valentin	134720	M		24.10.03	Cpl., guard, 4 SS-Totenkopfsturmbann, W-SS, C.C. Nordhausen (Ger.) 43-45	MURDER	U.S.
ADAM, Willi	28	M	Ger.		Cpl., Army, Greville - Hague (Fr.) 5.44	WITNESS	FR.
ADAM, Willy	175673	M	Ger.		Civilian, Iserbrook near Osdorf (Ger.) 6.44	TORTURE	U.S.
ADAMDWITSCH	173647	M			Org.Todt, Labour Camp, Mühldorf, Ampfing (Ger.) 6.44-4.45	MURDER	U.S.
ADAMOWSKI	134721	M			Cpl., 4 SS-Totenkopfsturmbann, Nordhausen (Ger.) 43-45	MURDER	U.S.
ADAMS	140356	M	Ger.		Overseer, C.C. Elsch (Ger.)	TORTURE	FR.
ADAMS, Reinhold	231972	M	Ger.	12	Pvt., Nachr.Regt.506 (D.A.U.A.), Bad Wildungen (Ger.) 45	MISC.CRIMES	U.S.
ADDLER	140357	M	Ger.		Civilian, Waiblingen (Ger.)	TORTURE	FR.
ADEER	121096	M			Lt., C.C. Neuengamme (Ger.) 42	MURDER	BEL.
ADELHARDT, Johann	187634	M	Ger.	22. 1.02	Member, S.A., Dachsbach (Ger.)	TORTURE	POL.
ADELMANN	162878	M	Ger.		Pvt., 10 SS-Pz.Div. "Frundsberg", Revin (Fr.) 6.44	MURDER	FR.
ADELSBERGER	132168	M	Ger.	10	Pvt., Army, Stalag 21 D, near Ostrowo (Pol.) 7.43	MISC.CRIMES	U.K.
ADENAU, Eifel	132596	M	Ger.		Waffen-SS, Arenberg (Ger.)	BRUTALITY	FR.
ADERMANN	31519	M			Pvt., Pz.Gren.Div., Gourdon (Fr.)	MURDER	FR.
ADLER	36678	M	Ger.		N.C.O., Landesschuetzen-Bn.714, Stalag XX A, Obklas (Ger.)	MURDER	U.K.
ADLER	36679	M	Ger.		S-Sgt., Army, Stalag VIII A, 2.45	MURDER	SOV.UN.
ADLER or ALDINE	189416	M			Sgt., Landesschuetzen-Bn.714, Stalag XX A, Thorn (Pol.) 3.44	TORTURE	U.K.
ADLER	192597	M	Ger.		Usturmfhr., SS, C.C. Buchenwald (Ger.) 42-45	MISC.CRIMES	U.S.
ADLER	250030	M	Ger.		Sturmmann, member, S.D., Toulouse (Fr.) 11.42-8.44	MISC.CRIMES	FR.
ADLER	250031	M	Ger.		Osturmfhr., SS, C.C. Neuengamme (Ger.)	TORTURE	BEL.
ADLER	300002	M			Uscharfhr., SS, S.D., Pontivy, Morbihan, 4.-8.44	MISC.CRIMES	FR.
ADLER, Adam	172893	M	Ger.	00	Cmdt. Police, Reichelsheim (Ger.) 40-45	TORTURE	POL.
ADLER, Adam	121035	M	Ger.	05	Lt., SS, Org.Todt, Camp II Norderney, Ile d'Aurigny (U.K.) 43-44	TORTURE	FR.
ADLER, Adam	195800	M	Ger.		Osturmfhr., cmdt., W-SS, Camp Alderney Channel, 7.43	TORTURE	FR.
ADLER, Ewald	185288	M	Ger.		Sturmscharfhr., SS, Crim.Secret., S.D., Gestapo, Pilsen (Czech.)	MURDER	CZECH.
ADLER, Fritz	146096	M	Ger.		Group-leader, N.S.D.A.P., Gardelegen (Ger.) 4.45	MURDER	U.S.
ADLER, Michel	131781	M	Ger.		Member, N.S.D.A.P., Karlsruhe (Ger.)	MISC.CRIMES	U.S.
ADLER, Rudolf	187633	M	Ger.	15. 2.14	Member, Gestapo, S.D., Valasske Klobouky (Czech.) 39-45	MURDER	CZECH.
ADLER, Valeska, Hedwig	187632	F	Ger.	3.12.15	C.C. Valasske Klobouky (Czech.) 39-45	MURDER	CZECH.
ADOLF	133734	M			Dr., SS, C.C. Buchenwald-Weimar (Ger.)	TORTURE	U.S.
ADOLF	186569	M	Ger.		1 Pz.Div."A.H.", 1 SS Rec.Bn., Parpondruy, Stavelot (Bel.) 12.44	MURDER	U.S.
ADOLF	186574	M	Ger.		Pvt., Army, guard post, Vasiliki (Gre.) 44	MURDER	GRC.
ADOLPH	29	M			Major, General, Field-Cmdt., Feldkommandantur 755, Le Mans (Fr.) 6.40-8.44	WITNESS	FR.
ADOLPHE	196455	M	Ger.		Capt., Le Lonzac (Fr.)	SUSPECT	FR.
ADRAMANOFF	30	M	Ger.		Flyer, Air force, Baudrigues (Fr.) 8.44	MURDER	FR.
ADRIAN, Erich	259395	M	Ger.	19. 4.89	Agent, Gestapo, Antenne of Rochelle, area Poitiers (Fr.) Police-commissar, Elberfeld (Ger.)	MISC.CRIMES	FR.
ADRIAN, Peter	250023	M	Ger.	12	Pvt., 3 Inf.Ers.Bn.352, Koolskamp (Bel.) 9.44	WITNESS	BEL
ADRIANSEN	255253	M	Ger.		Staffelmann, Abt. II C 3, Sipo, Bruessel (Bel.)	INTERR.	BEL
ADRIANT	185997	M	Ger.		Lt., Army, Lamothe Montravel, Montcaret (Fr.) 5.44	TORTURE	FR.
AESZEIBAUM, Rosza	131788	F			SS-girl, C.C., vicinity of Erfurt (Ger.) 44	TORTURE	U.S.
AGATHE	250026	M			Overseer, SS, C.C. Ravensbrueck (Ger.)	BRUTALITY	FR.
AGER	194730	M	Ger.		Guard, Stalag II A, Roggensdorf (Ger.) 9.44	TORTURE	FR.
AGERT, Emil	166883	M	Ger.		N.C.O., Army, Cheveuges (Fr.) 6.42	WITNESS	FR.
AGESS, Friedrich, Wilhelm	134744	M	Ger.		Sturmmann, W-SS, C.C. Buchenwald (Ger.) 41-45	MURDER	U.S.
AGSTEN or AXTEN	257568	M			Crim.secret., State Service, Pol., Ingersheim (Fr.) 1.44	MISC.CRIMES	FR.
AHEGRIM, Wilhelm see ALLGRIM	250600						
AHLERS	136992	M	Ger.		Capt., 21 Pz.Div., 200 A Tk.Bn., Sessenheim (Fr.) 1.45	MURDER	U.S.
AHLERS, Kurt	188429	M	Ger.	13	Capt., 29 Gren.Regt., II Bn., St. Mauro (It.)	MURDER	U.K.
AHLERT	261228	M	Ger.	10	Capt., Army, SS, G.F.P., area Auezzano (It.)	INTERR.	U.K.
AHMANN	11201	M			Cmdt., Major, 157 Ers.Div., Grenoble (Fr.) 11.43	MISC.CRIMES	U.K.
AHMANN, Walter	262013	M	Ger.	17. 4.11	SS-Mann, W-SS, Gren.Div.36 "Dirlewanger-Bde.", Warschau (Pol.) 40-44	MURDER	POL.
AHNA, V.	126753	M	Ger.		Cmdt., leichte Flak, C.C. Oflag IV C, Koenigstein (Ger.) 42	MISC.CRIMES	FR.
AHRENDT	31	M			Hptsturmfhr., 12 SS-Pz.Gren.Div."Hitler-Jugend", (Fr.) 4.44	MURDER	FR.
AHRENDT	140747	M			Oberstabsrichter, Justice Ministerium, Leipzig (Ger.)	MURDER	U.S.
AHRENS	194107	M	Ger.		Chief, Custom, Blaye (Fr.) 6.44	TORTURE	FR.
AHRENS see ARENS	250935						
AHRENS	300982	M	Ger.		Member of Staff, C.C. Struthof-Natzweiler (Fr.) 42-44	MURDER	FR.
AHRENS	301249	M	Ger.		Employee, Abt.III C, Kulturelle Gebiete, S.D., Bruessel (Bel.) 40-44	MURDER	BEL
AHRENS, Erwin	196168	M	Ger.	25. 9.12	Member, Green Police, 3 Coy., Arnheim (Neth.) 3.45	MURDER	NETH.
AHRENS, Ludwig, Philip, Hubert	310161	M	Ger.	11. 8.09	Uscharfhr., Sipo, SS, Rotterdam (Neth.) 40-5.45	INTERR.	NETH.
AHRENTZ	257569	M			M.Pol.Chief, Foreign Espionage, Amsterdam (Neth.) 10.44-2.45	INTERR.	NETH.
AHRENZ	32	M	Ger.		Lt., Flak-Regt.738, 2 Bn. or Coy., (Yugo.) 7.43	MURDER	YUGO.
AHRENZ	134745	M	Ger.		Oscharfhr., C.C. Cmdt., Mannheim (Ger.) 1.45	MURDER	U.S.
AHRUNO	33	M	Ger.		Sgt., Feldgendarmerie, Locmine (Fr.) 7.,8.44	MURDER	FR.
AHSMANN, Ferdinand	146482	M	Ger.		Usturmfhr., C.C. Wulfen (Ger.) 3.45	MURDER	U.S.

AIC - ALE

NAME	C.R.FILE NUMBER	SEX	NATIO-NALITY	DATE OF BIRTH	RANK OCCUPATION UNIT PLACE AND DATE OF CRIME	REASON WANTED	WANTED BY
AICHELBURG, Alois	300354	M	Ger.	5.6.88	Lt., Inspector, Gendarmerie, Warsaw, Koclow, Lascy (Pol.) 43	MURDER	POL.
AICHELER	305813	M	Ger.		Pvt., 1 Aufkl.Abt.3 Coy XV Div.Afrika Corps, St.-Leger (Arlon) 9.44	MISC.CRIMES	BEL.
AICHELER, Adolf	306327	M	Ger.	24.1.08	Rottfhr., SS, C.C.Buchenwald (Ger.) 5.38-10.43	MURDER	BEL.
AICHER	142407	M	Ger.		Oschfhr., Waffen SS Totenkopf Standarte C.C.Berga-Elster (Ger.) 3.45	MURDER	U.S.
AICHHOLZER	129652	M		15	Rottfhr., SS, Hohenrhein, Plattling (Ger.) 2.-5.45	MURDER	U.S.
AICHON	141951	M	Ger.		Guard, SS Waldlager V and VI, Ampfing, Muhldorf, Meltenheim (Ger.) 44-45	TORTURE	U.S.
AIFFULDISCH, Hans	129159	M			Osturmfhr., SS, Mauthausen (Aust.) 41-45	MURDER	U.S.
AIGEL	142408	M			Major, Stalag 17 B, Krems (Aust.) 11.44	TORTURE	U.S.
AIGELMANN, Paul (or EGELMANN)	186464	M	Ger.		C.C.official, Chief, C.C.Kradischko, Flossenburg (Ger.)	TORTURE	U.K.
AIGNER	72223	M			Army, Oberfeldwebel, Montfeerier (Fr.) 44	MURDER	FR.
AIGNER	148424	M		12	SS-Osturmfhr., C.C.Sachsenhausen, Oranienburg (Ger.)	MURDER	U.K.
AIGNER, Karl	195315	M		12.7.96	Policeman, Rowno (Pol.) 11.41-4.42	MURDER	POL.
AIGNER, Leo	254267	M		28.12.06	Civilian-teacher, Dl.Ves (Czech.) 43	MISC.CRIMES	CZECH
AIME, Julie	131782	F			Civilian (Ger.) 12.44	MISC.CRIMES	U.S.
AISTLEITNER, Josef	195677	M	Ger.		Sturmmann, 1 SS Panz.Div.Leibst.A.H.,3 Pi.Coy, Ligneuville (Bel.) 12.44	MURDER	U.S.
AIX, Albert	301675	M	Ger.		E.M.Luftpark, Cambrai, Nord (Fr.) 40-41	PILLAGE	FR.
AKKERMANN, Jan J.	306733	M	Ger.		Civilian, Borkum, Island (Ger.) 8.44	MURDER	U.S.
ALARICH	1282	M			Pvt., Army, 2 Fl. 194 Gr.	MISC.CRIMES	U.S.
ALATENS	192796	M	Ger.		Wachtmeister, Schupo, C.C.Falstadt, Stalag (Nor.) 41-44	MURDER	NOR.
ALBANI	300003	M	Ger.		Member, Sipo, Utrecht, Hoogland near Amersfoort (Neth.) 9.44	MURDER	NETH.
ALBANI	300162	M	Ger.		S.D.-Mann in Utrecht (Neth.) 44	MURDER	NETH.
ALBAROUS	134739	M			Member of Crew, German Navy, Pointe de Mousterlin (Fr.) 6.44	MURDER	U.S.
ALBATH, Walter Hugo	194008	M	Ger.	7.12.04	Oberregierungsrat, Standartenfhr., Gestapo, SS, SD, Enschede, Duesseldorf (Ger.) 11.44	MURDER	U.K.
ALBERS	124342	M			Capt., Wehrkreis X H.Q.(Abt.Kgf.)	MISC.CRIMES	U.K.
ALBERS, August	133733	M			Member, NSDAP, Moers (Ger.)	TORTURE	U.S.
ALBERST	29822	M			Oberfeldwebel, 12 Feldgendarmerie, Fallschirmjg., Abbeville (Fr.) 8.44	MURDER	FR.
ALBERT	35	M	Ger.		Gestapo Officer, Amsterdam (Neth.) 10.44	MURDER	NETH.
ALBERT	147204	M	Ger.		Capt., 11 Panz.Div. (Fr.) 44	MURDER	FR.
ALBERT	168571	M			Bdefhr., SS (Pol.) 42	MURDER	U.S.
ALBERT (see: VON BERTHOLDI, Herbert)	257903 85	M			Lt., Adj.to Musclus, 150 Pz.Bde., Meuse Bridge-Antwerp (Bel.) 12.44	MISC.CRIMES	U.S.
ALBERT, Karl	250610	M	Ger.	9.6.82	Abwehrbeauftragter, Civilian, Pilsen (Czech.) 39-45	MISC.CRIMES	CZECH.
ALBERT, Kurt	164052	M	Ger.		Capt., Waffen SS, Totenkopf, C.C.Buchenwald, Weimar (Ger.)	TORTURE	U.S.
ALBERT, Otto	187631	M	Ger.	92	Civ.-Administrative-Asst., Prison, C.C.Nuernberg (Ger.) 34-45	WITNESS	CZECH.
ALBERT, Otto	250611	M	Ger.		Cpl., Field-police, Argonnex (Fr.) 12.43	MISC.CRIMES	FR.
ALBERT, Post	134746	M			Civilian, Budesheim (Ger.) 6.44	MISC.CRIMES	U.S.
ALBERT, Wilhelm	221236	M	Ger.	8.9.98	Dr., Regierungspraesident, Public official, Inowroclaw (Pol.) 11.44	MURDER	U.S.
ALBERTS	35261	M			Generaldirektor of Bochumer Verein, Civilian	MISC.CRIMES	U.S.
ALBERTS	167663	M	Ger.		Lt., Abwehr Kdo.343, Landerau (Fr.) 4.-8.44	MURDER	FR.
ALBERTS	191701	M	Ger.		Lt., Work Kdo.343, Landerau (Fr.) 4.-8.44	MURDER	FR.
ALBICHSHAUSEN (or ALBIGSHAUSEN)	142409	M			Leader, SA and Volkssturm, Koeln (Ger.) 11.44	MURDER	U.S.
ALBIDZ, Ferenc	176597	M			SS-Mann, Hungarian SS, Kampfgruppe Ney, near Suhr (Hung.)	MURDER	U.S.
ALBIGSHAUSEN (see: ALBICHSHAUSEN)	142409						
ALBINGHAUS	142410	M	Ger.		NSDAP, Ortsgruppenleiter, Koeln-Bickendorf (Ger.)	MURDER	U.S.
ALBORN, Otto	142411	M			Rottfhr., SS 1 Panz.Div.2 Panz.Gren.Rgt.3 Bn.12 Coy, Stavelot-Malmedy (Bel.) 12.44	MURDER	U.S.
ALBRECHT	28721	M	Ger.		Sturmbannfhr., SS, Finnmark (Nor.) 44	MURDER	NOR.
ALBRECHT	131783	M			Usturmfhr., SS, Gestapo, Tabor (Czech.) 39-45	MURDER	CZECH.
ALBRECHT	135141	M	Ger.		Gendarmerie Kreis Chief, Wurzburg (Ger.) 44	MURDER	U.S.
ALBRECHT	165931	M			Pvt., SS Panz.Div.,"Das Reich", Tulle (Fr.) 44	MURDER	FR.
ALBRECHT	174908	M			Civilian, Tyez (Fr.) 7.44	MURDER	FR.
ALBRECHT	194930	M			Hptsturmfhr., SD Einsatz Kdo.2 BV 6 St.Die (Fr.) 44	MURDER	U.K.
ALBRECHT	196166	M		15	Lt., Mil.Sec.Police, Forno, Cavanese (It.) 12.43	INTERR.	U.K.
ALBRECHT	250013	M			Chief of Civil Control Service, C.C.Buchenwald (Ger.)	INTERR.	FR.
ALBRECHT	255254	M			Crim.Sec., Abt.V B Sipo, Bruessel (Bel.)	MISC.CRIMES	BEL.
ALBRECHT	306450	M			Engineer, Chief of Control Section at Rochlitz Mech.Wks.Wansleben am See nr.Buchenwald (Ger.) 43-45	MURDER	FR.
ALBRECHT, Anton Hermann	131784	M	Ger.	6.8.06	City Police, Frankfurt-Main	TORTURE	U.S.
ALBRECHT, Arthur	193559	M	Ger.		Hptschfhr., SD, Leeuwarden (Neth.)	MURDER	NETH.
ALBRECHT, Bernhard	250609	M	Ger.	15.1.15	Flyer, C.C.Ellrich, Nordhausen (Ger.)	MURDER	U.S.
ALBRECHT, Erwin	173649	M	Ger.	21.2.00	Councellor of County Court, Occ.territories, Prague, Bohemia (Czech.) 41-45	MURDER	CZECH.
ALBRECHT, Josef	9623	M	Ger.	29.11.02	Usturmfhr., SS, Gestapo, Crim.Police, Tabor (Czech.) 3.39-5.41	TORTURE	CZECH.
ALBRECHT, Josef	193579	M	Ger.		Kapo, Block 3 C.C.Flossenburg (Ger.)	TORTURE	BEL.
ALBRECHT, Joseph	142323	M			Col., SS, C.C.Flossenburg (Ger.)	TORTURE	U.S.
ALBRECHT, Kurt	174911	M	Ger.		Lt., Marine Art., St.Andre Deseaux, Reneguy (Fr.) 1.44	MISC.CRIMES	FR.
ALBRECHT, Otto	199391	M			Major, Chief staff to Prisoner of War Bezirkskommandantur, Oslo (Nor.) 45	TORTURE	U.K.
ALBRECHT, Richard	306139	M	Ger.		Hptsturmfhr., SS, St.Die (Fr.) 9.44	MURDER	U.K.
ALBRECHT, Ruppert	187389	M	Ger.		Asst., SD, Gestapo, Brno (Czech.) 39-45	MURDER	CZECH.
ALBRECHT, Siegfried Sigmund	161637	M		02	Schuetze, Army 3 Coy 188 KGF Arb.Bn., Herdla (Nor.)	MURDER	NOR.
ALBRECHTS	250606	M			Usturmfhr., Army, SD, Arnheim (Neth.) 5.44	BRUTALITY	NETH.
ALBRET	167662	M			Cpl., Georgien Batt. 1 Coy, Tulle (Fr.) 4.44	MISC.CRIMES	FR.
ALBURG	191337	M			Cpl., Festungs Bn.999, Kato Achai (Gre.) 2.44	MURDER	U.K.
ALDENDORF, Karl	250605	M			Sgt., C.C.Nordhausen (Ger.)	MURDER	U.S.
ALDINE	131072	M	Ger.	19	Cpl., 714 Ldsch.Bn., Oberwalden	TORTURE	U.K.
ALDINE (see: ADLER)	189416						
ALDINGER	188666	M	Ger.		Inspector, Ruestungsamt, Belfort (Fr.) 11.45	PILLAGE	FR.
ALDRIAN, Eduard	260638	M			Lt.General	WITNESS	U.S.
ALEKS (see: ALEX)	174910						
ALEKS (or ALEX)	250603	M			Pvt., Camp Rottleberode, Nordhausen (Ger.)	MURDER	U.S.
ALEX	174910	M			Adj., Detachm.Voluntary Ukraine, Donchery, Bois de Banel (Fr.) 6.44	MURDER	FR.
ALEX, Paul Otto	250604	M	Ger.	8.6.02	C.C.78 Ludwigsburg, Sennewitz (Ger.) 40-44	MISC.CRIMES	POL.
ALEXANDER	188466	M	Ger.		Interpreter, Maison, Lafitte (Fr.) 7.-8.43	TORTURE	CZECH.
ALEXANDER	260058	M	Ger.		Adj., Navy, Sore Landes (Fr.) 7.44	MURDER	FR.
ALEXEEFF	162737	M		19	Lt., Cossack Bn., Warsaw (Pol.) 44	MURDER	U.S.
ALEXI, Alfred	173650	M			SS Labor Camp, Muhldorf Ampfing (Ger.) 6.44-4.45	MURDER	U.S.

ALF - ALV

NAME	C.R.FILE NUMBER	SEX	NATIO- NALITY	DATE OF BIRTH	RANK OCCUPATION UNIT PLACE AND DATE OF CRIME	REASON WANTED	WANTED BY
ALF	124541	M	Ger.	21	Osturmfhr.,Waffen-SS,Hitler Jugend,Chateau,D' Audrieu(Fr.)6.44	MURDER	U.K.
ALFKEN	72239	M		97	Capt.,Gestapo-Capt.,Lons le Saunier (Fr.) 44	TORTURE	FR.
ALFONS	250602	M			Pvt., Camp Ellrich, Nordhausen (Ger.)	MURDER	U.S.
ALFRED	192201	M	Ger.		Blockmann, C.C. Flossenburg (Ger.)	MURDER	FR.
ALFRED	250007	M	Ger.		Kapo, C.C. Buchenwald (Ger.)	BRUTALITY	FR.
ALFRED,Franz	257961	M			150 Pz.Bde., Meusebridge, Antwerpen (Bel.) 12.44	MISC.CRIMES	U.S.
ALFULISCH	301542	M			Lt., SS-Lagerfuehrer,C.C.Mauthausen (Aust.) 40-45	MURDER	BEL.
ALI	174909	M	Ger.		Kapo, Camp official Laura (Ger.) 44	MURDER	FR.
ALI	300334	M	Ger.		Medical officer,Bad Oeynhausen,Kdo.409,Stalag 326,VI K, Gohfeld-Westfalen (Ger.) 44	BRUTALITY	FR.
ALIS,Hermann	121040	M			Civ.,C.C.,Kriegsgefangenen-Lager XVII A	TORTURE	BEL.
ALISCH	31578	M			Cpl., SS, Struthof (Fr.)	MURDER	FR.
ALISCHSKI,Herbert	174554	M	Ger.	07	Pvt.,6 Coy., 337 Lässchtz.Bn.,C.C.,Stalag 8 B,Schoppinitz-Moosburg (Ger.) 1.-4.45	TORTURE	U.K.
ALITSKI,Herbert	72202	M	Ger.		Pvt.,Army, 6-337 Coy., H.Q.Kattowitz,Gratz (Czech.)	TORTURE	U.K.
ALKER	1281	M			Inspector,Navy Supply	MISC.CRIMES	U.K.
ALKERMANN	232028	M	Ger.		Capt.,Lt.,(D.A.U.A.) Nachr.-Regt.506,Bad Wildungen (Ger.) 45	MISC.CRIMES	U.S.
ALKIN	134735	M			Oschfhr.,SS,Tooper,Company Commander,Mannheim(Ger.) 1.45	MURDER	U.S.
ALLENDORF,Ludwig	124289	M	Ger.	00	Oberfw.,Member of Guard det of Prison,C.C. Portiers(Fr.) 43-11.44	MURDER	U.S.
ALLER	36	M	Ger.		S.D.Chief, Guingamp (Fr.) 7.44	MURDER	FR.
ALLERS	188274	M	Ger.		Osturmfhr., SA (Ger.) 40-45	MURDER	CZECH.
ALLES	38	M			Lager-Sgt.,Caen(Fr.) 6.44	MURDER	FR.
ALLGEIER,Rudolf	188048	M	Ger.	11. 3.01	Geubereichsleiter, NSDAP, Strassburg (Fr.) 44	MISC.CRIMES	FR.
ALLGRIM,Wilhelm (or AHEGRIM)	250600	M		29. 1.97	N.C.O.,C.C.Ellrich,Nordhausen (Ger.)	MURDER	U.S.
ALLHAS,Kurt (or AHLERS)	188429	M	Ger.	13	Capt.,Army, 2 Bn.,29 Gren.Regt.St.Mauro(Ital.)	MURDER	U.K.
ALLIMAN	257468	M			Volkswagenwerk,Sochaux (Fr.) 40-44	BRUTALITY	FR.
ALLNER	146092	M			Civ.,Ottmannshausen (Ger.) 8.44	MURDER	U.S.
ALLWART,Hans	172843	M		26. 5.98	Kreishauptstellenleiter,NSDAP, Railway official,Strassburg (Fr.)	MISC.CRIMES	FR.
ALMER,Josef	306328	M	Ger.	11. 3.12	SS-Sgt.,C.C.Buchenwald (Ger.) 5.38-10.43	MURDER	BEL.
ALMERS	173328	M	Ger.		Commander, 125 Pz.Gren.Regt., Serbia (Yugo.)9.-12.41	MURDER	YUGO.
ALMEYER	129244	M	Ger.		L.Beckewerth(Ger.)	TORTURE	BEL.
ALOIS	300334	M	Ger.		Medical officer,Bad Oeynhausen, Kdo.409, Stalag 326 VI K, Gohfeld (Westfalen),(Ger.) 44	BRUTALITY	FR.
ALPHONSE	196456	M	Ger.		Interpreter,Gestapo Tulle, Le Lonzag (Fr.) 5.44	MISC.CRIMES	FR.
ALPHONSE	300355	M	Ger.		Staff at Buchenwald,C.C. (Ger.) 42-45	MURDER	FR.
ALQUEN,Guenther	140858	M	Ger.		Capt.,SS,Head of Kurt Eggers,Organisation	WITNESS	U.K.
ALSCHER	193578	M	Ger.		Inspector,Geujugendamt,Posen,Lidice (Czech.)	WITNESS	CZECH.
ALSCHER,Paul	301250	M	Ger.		Crim.secr., Abt.IV B 1, S.D.,Bruessel (Bel.) 6.40-9.44	MURDER	BEL.
ALT (or ARLT)	300550	M	Ger.		Untersuchungsfuehrer, worked with Dr.Schoengarth, General der Polizei,Amsterdam (Neth.) 10.44	MURDER	NETH.
ALT	305882	M	Ger.		Osturmfhr.,SS, S.D., Oswiecim, C.C.Birkenau (Pol.) 39-45	MURDER	CZECH.
ALTEKRUSE	186573	M			Flak-Bn. Light AAA Assault Bn.84, Malmedy (Bel.) 12.44	MURDER	U.S.
ALTEMEIER (see ALTEMEYER)	168612						
ALTEMEYER (or ALTEMEIER)	168612	M	Ger.	20	Stabsleiter,SS, Riga (Latv.) 12.41	MURDER	U.N.W.C.C.
ALTNA,Friedrich	135143	M	Ger.	9. 7.01	Osturmfhr.,SS, Saulgau (Ger.) 8.45	MURDER	U.S.
ALTNA,Wilhelm	260824	M	Ger.	02 or 96	Sturmbannfhr., SS, Stapelburg (Ger.) 8.45	MURDER	U.S.
ALTENBERG	250597	M	Ger.		Capt.,Field-police,All parts of Serbia (Yugo.) 43	MISC.CRIMES	YUGO.
ALTENBRUNN,Hans	187387	M	Ger.	29. 9.09	Official, Inspector, S.D.,Gestapo, Bruenn (Czech.) 39-45	MURDER	CZECH.
ALTENBRUNNER, E.	4667	M			Obergruppenfhr.,SS,Reichssicherheitshauptamt	TORTURE	BEL.
ALTENDORF,Ilse	187422	F	Ger.	31.10.16	Employee,Gestapo, Bruenn (Czech.) 39-45	WITNESS	CZECH.
ALTNDORF,Wilhelm	250446	M			Sgt., C.C.Ellrich, Nordhausen (Ger.)	MURDER	U.S.
ALTENHOFER	146097	M			Hptschfhr.,4 SS-Baubrigade Totenkopf,Ellrich,Gardelegen (Ger.) 4.45	MURDER	U.S.
ALTENHOFER(see ALTENHOHER)Max	166882						
ALTENHOFF	142414	M			Civ., Farmer, Kamperbruck (Ger.) 3.43	MURDER	U.S.
ALTENHOHER,Max(or ALTENHOFER)	166882	M	Ger.		Capt.,Army, Heining (Fr.) 11.44	LOOTING	FR.
ALTENKRUGER	124316	M	Ger.		Civ.,Criminal Magistrate, C.C. Oberdorfelden (Ger.) 2.42-3.45	MURDER	U.S.
ALTENLOH	196164	M	Ger.		Physician, Compiegne (Fr.) 41-44	MISC.CRIMES	FR.
ALTER, Eugen	194983	M	Ger.		Pvt., 111 Pz.Gren.Div., Albine (Fr.) 6.44	MURDER	FR.
ALTFULDISCH,Hans	182566	M		11	Osturmfhr., SS, C.C. Mauthausen (Aust.)	MURDER	U.S.
ALTGAYER, Branimir	259578	M	Ger.	9.11.97	Col.,leader of German Volksgruppe (Crotia),Member of the Quisling Croat.Parliament (Sabor) believed to be in the 373 P.o.W.-Camp at Kerten (Yugo.) 4.42-12.42	SUSPECT	YUGO.
ALTHAMER, Alois	187388	M	Ger.		Regensburg (Ger.) 41-45	TORTURE	U.S.
ALTHAMMER, Eduard	190420	M	Ger.		Driver,Civ.,SS,Gaienhofen or Oehningen (Ger.) 7.44	MURDER	U.S.
ALTHANSBERGER,M	11203	M	Ger.		Pvt.,111.Pz.Gren.Regt.,N.C.O., Albine (Fr.) 44	MURDER	FR.
ALTHAUS,Luzi	250598	F	Ger.		Civ.,Member,Admin. (G.Z.A.),S.D., Toulouse(Fr.) 11.42-8.44	MISC.CRIMES	FR.
ALTHERR, Eduard (or ALTMER)	162876	M	Ger.	17. 5.22	N.C.O.,10 Pz.Div."Frundsberg", Revin (Fr.) 6.44	MURDER	FR.
ALTHOFF	148716	M			Major,O.K.W. Subsection V PW Affairs	MISC.CRIMES	U.S.
ALTKRUEGER	191338	M			Uschfhr.,1 Pz.Div.3 Pio.Coy.Leibst.Ad.Hitler,Stoumont,Ligneuville(Bel) 12.44	SUSPECT	U.S.
ALTMANN	121039	M		00	Agent,Gestapo, Belfort (Fr.)	WITNESS	FR.
ALTMANN (see LANGENBACH)	136223	M		00	Hptsturmfhr., S.D.,Labourbouble,Le Mont-Dore (Fr.)	MURDER	FR.
ALTMANN, Helmut	259828	M	Ger.	97	Capt., Commander of guard at Laterina (Ital.) 6.44	MURDER	U.S.
ALTMANN,Karl	194810	M	Ger.		Civ. (Ger.)	MISC.CRIMES	U.S.
ALTMAYER	195945	M	Ger.		Head,Navy,Schiffstamm-Abtl.,Digne (Fr.)	MISC.CRIMES	FR.
ALTMEIER (or ALTMEYER)	250012	M	Ger.		W.O., 98 Regt.,Jaeger-Bn.,Aignebelle (Fr.) 6.44	INTERR.	FR.
ALTMKLER (or ALTMAYER)	72237	M			Director,Pynami Aktiengesellschaft, Krumel (Ger.) 44	MISC.CRIMES	FR.
ALTMER (see ALTHERR)	162876						
ALTMEYER	261117	M	Ger.		Councillor,Ministry of Justice,Reich Justice Examination Office	MURDER	U.S.
ALTMEYER (see ALTMAYER)	250012	M	Ger.				
ALTNEIER	250599				SS,Camp Rottleberode,Nordhausen (Ger.)	MURDER	U.S.
ALTOFF	149171	M	Ger.		C.C. Kaisergarten (Ger.) 44-45	MURDER	BEL.
ALTSTAEDTER,Michael	134722	M	Ger.		Pv.,4 SS-Totenkopfsturmbann,Nordhausen (Ger.)43-45	MURDER	U.S.
ALTVATER,Heinrich	142415	M	Ger.	00	Agent,Gestapo and NSDAP, Bremen,Lesum (Ger.)	TORTURE	U.S.
ALVARO (or NOVARO, A)	72238	M			Civilian, St.Ouis les Roches (Fr.) 44	MURDER	FR.

AMA-AND

NAME	C.R.FILE NUMBER	SEX	NATIO-NALITY	DATE OF BIRTH	RANK OCCUPATION UNIT PLACE AND DATE OF CRIME	REASON WANTED	WANTED BY
AMANN	11204	M	Ger.		Capt.,110.Pz.Gren.Rgt.,Gourdon,(Fr.) 44	MURDER	FR.
AMANN	166881	M	Ger.		Gendarme,Gendarmerie,Hangienbieten (Fr.) 14.8.44	MURDER	FR.
AMANN	256685	M	Ger.		Chief of the Bde.,Gendarmerie,Seltz (Fr.) 4.3.44	MISC.CRIMES	FR.
AMANN	260057	M	Ger.		Major,157.Res.Div.Bayern,Massif of Vercors,Isere,Drome (Fr.)20.7.-8.44	SUSPECT	FR.
AMANN	260957	M	Ger.		Mann,SS,3.Coy.,1.Bn.Rgt."Der Fuehrer",Div."Das Reich",Oradour sur Glane,Hte.Vienne (Fr.) 10.6.44	INCENDIARISM	FR.
AMANN	305814	M	Ger.		Pvt.,1.Aufkl.Abt.,3.Coy.,XV.Div.,Afrika Korps,St.Leger (Arlon) 5.9.44	MISC.CRIMES	BEL.
AMANN, Alwine	260839	F			Resides at Moltke-Strasse 8,Trier,Schweich-Mosel (Ger.)15.1.45 L.O.D.N.A.O.D.	WITNESS	U.S.
AMANN, Willy	188433	M	Ger.		Policeman,Pol. Burg near Solingen (Ger.) 5.11.44	MURDER	FR.
AMBACH (or AMBACHER) Paul	261328	M	Ger.	25. 6.02	Cpl.,SS Art.,3.Bn.,12.Rgt.,Tourcuvre (Fr.) 13.8.44	MURDER	FR.
AMBERG	187423	M	Ger.		Cpl.SS Guard,CC.,Ravensbrueck (Ger.) 42-43	MURDER	U.S.
AMBERG	195943	M	Ger.		Oberwachtmeister,Schutzpolizei,Westerbork (Neth.) 9.44	MURDER	NETH.
AMBERG, Anton	11205	M	Ger.		Pvt.,Pz.Gren.Rgt.111,Albine (Fr.) 44	MURDER	FR.
AMBERGE, Heinz	168610	M	Ger.		Cpl.,9.Gren.Ers.Rgt.,1.Coy.,Rechnungsfhr.,Magny d' Anigon,(Fr.)18.9.44	MURDER	FR.
AMBERGER	173310	M	Ger.		SS Fuehrer,Alsace (Fr.) 44	TORTURE	FR.
AMBERGER, Hans	187430	M	Ger.		Manager,Civilian,Camp Regensburg (Ger.) 41-45	MURDER	U.S.
AMBERGER, Karl	174369	M		11	Sgt.,Air-force,near Einhof-Hopsten (Ger.) 21.3.45	MURDER	U.K.
AMBROS, Otto	260215	M	Ger.	19. 5.01	Mem Vorstand,I.G.Farbenindustrie A.G.,Frankfurt-Main,(Ger.)	MISC.CRIMES	U.S.
AMBROSI, Gustav	262014	M	Ger.	14. 8.95	Mann,Waffen SS,Gren.Div.36,Dirlewanger Bde.,Warschau and other,(Pol.) 40-44	MURDER	POL.
AMBS, Ernest	191320	M	Ger.		Lt.,Army,Kervicherne,Merlevenez (Fr.) 28.4.45	MURDER	FR.
AMBURGER, Karl	306257	M			Sgt.,Unit IG 27,No.1,Group Dreierwalde,Aerodrome, 3.45	MURDER	U.K.
AMELINCKX, Franz Alois	10002	M	Ger.		Camp,Breendonck, 40-44	TORTURE	BEL.
AMEND, Alois	250947	M			Flyer, Camp Ellrich (Ger.)	MURDER	U.S.
AMENT, Jakob	129158	M			Rottfhr.,SS Standarte Totenkopf,Mauthausen (Aust.) 1.44-5.45	MURDER	U.S.
AMLACHER, Gerhard	261931	M	Ger.		Beauftragter fuer das Gerichtswesen, Lower Styria (Yugo.) 41	SUSPECT	YUGO.
AMMEL	174907	M			SS,C.C.,Calais,Arras,Bz.Thune,Boulogne s,Mer,Berck-Plage,St.Pol, Belamont,St.Omer (Fr.) 43	TORTURE	FR.
AMMEL	184586	M	Ger.		Camp Chief C.C.,Sachsenhausen (Ger.)	TORTURE	FR.
AMMER, Josef	250948	M	Ger.	20.10.95	Civilian,Mutenice near Hedonin (Czech.) 44	MURDER	CZECH.
AMMER	140748	M			Stabsschfr.,SS C.C.,Amfing (Ger.)	MURDER	U.S.
AMMERSBACH, Erich	172899	M	Ger.	79	Medicin Chief,Stalag XII A,Limburg (Ger.) 41	MISC.CRIMES	FR.
AMMLER, Filomena	189142	M	Ger.		Camp leader,SS,Textil-Plant:Gebr.Walzel O.G.,Parschwitz	TORTURE	POL.
AMMON	257842	M	Ger.		Rottfhr.,Waffen SS,37.Rgt.,Div."Goetz v.Berlichingen",St.Eny (Fr.)7.44	WITNESS	U.S.
AMNORN	163437	M	Ger.		Civilian,Kreigsheim (Ger.)	MURDER	FR.
AMON, Stefan	134723	M			Pvt.,4.SS Totenkopfsturmbann,Nordhausen (Ger.) 43-45	MURDER	U.S.
AMPLETZER	193935	M			Kriminalrat,SIPO,Progen,Meckel (Ger.)	MURDER	U.S.
AMSEL	134726	M			Pvt.,4.SS Totenkopfsturmbann,Nordhausen (Ger.) 43-45	MURDER	U.S.
AMSTAETTER, Franz	196451	M	Ger.	5.10.19	Mann,SS,C.C.,Dachau (Ger.)	MURDER	CZECH.
AMTGOR	133732	M	Ger.		Sgt.,SS,C.C.,Dessau (Ger.) 14.4.45	MURDER	U.S.
AMTHOR, Rudolf	121038	M			Police,C.C.,Untermassfeld (Ger.)	MURDER	BEL.
AMTMANN, Kaspar	189032	M		09- 11	Capt.,Army,near Shio (It.) 1.45	TORTURE	BEL.
ANACKER	172900	M	Ger.		Wagon Keeper, Civilian,Steinbach (Ger.) 2.44	WITNESS	U.S.
ANACKER	250949	M			Pvt.,Camp Ellrich Nordhausen (ger.)	MURDER	U.S.
ANCKE, Philippe	300005	M	Ger.		Hptschfhr.,SS,C.C.,Mauthausen (Aust.) 11.42-5.45	MISC.CRIMES	FR.
ANCKER	167003	M			Doctor,SD,RSHA,(Ger.) 43	MURDER	U.S.
ANDEL, Franz	142436	M			Army officer,Elven (Fr.)	MURDER	U.S.
ANDERHEIDEN	152500	M	Ger.		Cpl.,Landesschuetzen Bn.788 (Ger.) 15.10.41-11.42	WITNESS	U.K.
ANDERLE, Josef	255089	M	Ger.	16.10.94	Civilian,Podbreyna,(Czech.) 40-45	MURDER	CZECH.
ANDERMANN, Wilhelm	254921	M	Ger.	23.11.98	Railway-worker, Civilian,Luzice (Czech.) 44	MURDER	CZECH.
ANDERS	166633	M	Ger.		Civilian, (Aust.) 38-45	WITNESS	U.S.
ANDERS	187565	M		90	Lt.,Kriegsgef.Arbeits Bn.,Posen (Pol.)	TORTURE	U.K.
ANDERS	259996	M	Ger.		Agent,Act.member of Gestapo,Poitiers area (Fr.)Hairdresser in Schweidnitz, 40-45	MISC.CRIMES	FR.
ANDERS, Gustav	261329	M	Ger.		Wachtmeister,Commander Paulare Gend.,Udine (It.) 4.4.45	WITNESS	U.S.
ANDERS, Paul	196124	M	Ger.		Feldgendarme,Feldgendarmerie Tourcoing,Unit 43-800 (Fr.) 2.9.44	MURDER	FR.
ANDERSCH	28728	M			Lt.,Armee,Oberkommando 20,Finmark (Nor.) 44	MURDER	NOR.
ANDERSEN	194234	M	Ger.	20	Osturmfhr.,12.SS Pz.Gren.Div.,Hitler-Jugend 26.SS Pz.Gren.,Caen (Fr.)	TORTURE	CAN.
ANDERSEN	196162	M	Ger.		Guard,Camp,Compiegne (Fr.) 41-44	MISC.CRIMES	FR.
ANDERSEN	195675	M	Ger.	03	Feldgendarmerie,Voorburg (Neth.) 14.2.43	MISC.CRIMES	NETH.
ANDERSON	108959	M			Lt.,SS,town commander of Lyons Laforet,Falaise (Fr.) 15.-20.8.44	WITNESS	U.S.
ANDHOL	174906	M			Cpl.,Army,St.Barthelemy de Lun (Fr.) 27.-30.7.44	MURDER	FR.
ANDING	106969	M		01	Policeman,Police,	MURDER	U.S.
ANDING, Wilhelm	149172	M	Ger.	92	Auxiliary Policeman,Clerk,Schwickhausen (ger.) 9.44	MURDER	U.S.
ANDOHR, Josef	173651	M			SS Labor Camps,Mühldorf,Ampfing (Ger.) 6.44-4.45	MURDER	U.S.
ANDORE	1516	M	Ger.		Lt.,Army,Chassar,Tefaa,Tunis (Fr.) 1.2.43	MURDER	FR.
ANDORFER	194809	M	Ger.	11	Lt.,Army,SS on staff of Gen.Brunner,Marte,Grappa (It.) 25.9.44	WITNESS	U.K.
ANDRA	168572	M			General,Army, (Gre.)41	MURDER	U.S.
ANDRE	130084	M			C.C.,Dora Mittelbau,Nordhausen (Ger.)	MURDER	U.S.
ANDRE	196163	M	Ger.		Pvt.,Compiegne (Fr.) 41-44	MISC.CRIMES	FR.
ANDRE, Katharina	186575	F	Ger.	7. 3.07	Civilian (Nazi) Maulusmuehle (Lux.) 25.12.44	MISC.CRIMES	LUX.
ANDREAS, Waldemar	259030	M	Ger.	90	General der Flieger,Air-force	WITNESS	U.S.
ANDREAS	126829	M	Ger.		Civilian,Bleicherode-Harz (Ger.) 6.43-45	TORTURE	U.K.
ANDREAS, Bernhard	186244	M	Ger.		Uschfhr.,SS Leibstandarte "Adolf Hitler",Stavelot (Bel.)	MURDER	BEL.
ANDREAS, Berthold	178333	M	Ger.		Cpl.,2.Pz.Gr.Rgt.,10.Coy.,3.Bn.,L.A.H.,Malmedy (Bel.) 17.12.44	MURDER	U.S.
ANDREAS, Friedrich	166632	M	Ger.	93	Policeman,Police,Aachen (Ger.) 3.44	TORTURE	U.S.
ANDREAS, Otto	174905	M		89	Civilian,Jeserig (Ger.) 40	TORTURE	FR.
ANDREAS, Walter	190449	M	Ger.	16. 6.97	Head,Gendarmerie,Longeville,Les-Saint Avold (Fr.) 29.11.44	MURDER	FR.
ANDREAS, Werner	250942	M			Cpl.,Camp Ellrich Nordhausen (ger.)	MURDER	U.S.
ANDRERS, Hans	195801	M			Uschfhr.,C.C.,Auschwitz (Ger.)	MURDER	FR.
ANDRES	157158	M			Hirwachtmeister,C.C.,Parzymiecki (Pol.) 41-44	MURDER	U.S.
ANDRES	305872	M	Ger.		Osturmfhr.,C.C.,Oranienburg (Ger.) 39-45	MURDER	GERM.
ANDRES, Ernest	40	M	Ger.		Lt.,Luftwaffe,Thiebis-Marne (Fr.) 22.8.44	MURDER	FR.
ANDRES, Fritz	192596	M	Ger.		Sturmmann,SS Totenkopfverband,C.C.,Buchenwald (Ger.) 42-45	MISC.CRIMES	U.S.

AND - APP

NAME	C.R.FILE NUMBER	SEX	NATIO-NALITY	DATE OF BIRTH	RANK OCCUPATION UNIT PLACE AND DATE OF CRIME	REASON WANTED	WANTED BY
ANDRES, Hans	250943	M	Ger.		Uscharfhr., SS, C.C. Auschwitz-Birkenau (Pol.) 11.42	MURDER	YUGO.
ANDRES, Nicolaus	162877	M		13. 2.02	Montigny en Metz (Fr.)	MISC.CRIMES	FR.
ANDRES, Otto	41	M	Ger.		Gauleiter, NSDAP, Danzig 9.39-42	MURDER	POL.
ANDRESS, Fritz	194729	M	Ger.	21	Dr., Sanitaets-Abt., Vaux Andigny (Fr.)	WITNESS	FR.
ANDRESS, Walter	136320	M	Ger.	97	Gendarmeriemstr.,Feldgendarmerie,Longeville les St.Avold (Fr.)11.44	MURDER	FR.
ANDROSZOWSKI	250944	M	Ger.		Major, Army, Enschede (Neth.) 9.-10.44	PILLAGE	NETH.
ANESINI, Ankai	148425	M			General, Army, Hung.Troops, Aust.,South-Voklabruck,Ujvidek (Hung.)	MURDER	U.S.
ANGELS see ENGELS, Henri or August	250717						
ANGEMANN	305815	M	Ger.		Pvt., 1 Aufkl.Abt., 3 Coy,XV Div.Afrika Corps,St.Leger(Arlon) 9.44	MISC.CRIMES	BEL.
ANGENENT	72201	M			Lt.,Adjutant Stalag VI a, Duisdorf (Ger.)	TORTURE	U.S.
ANGER	134695	M	Ger.		Commander of PWS Wehrkreis XIII (Ger.) 44	WITNESS	U.S.
ANGER	188130	M		09	Oscharfhr.-SS,Member,Gestapo, Sosnowice(Pol.) 43	MURDER	POL.
ANGER, Franz	162086	M			29 Flak Rgt.,Lt., between Hausen and Ginnheim (Ger.)	WITNESS	U.S.
ANGERHAUER, Friedrich alias MALINA, Rudolf-Engelmann Fritz	196158	M	Ger.	9. 1.06	Employee, SD, Pilsen (Czech.)	MURDER	CZECH.
ANGERER	168619	M	Ger.		Interpreter, Gestapo (Nor.) 4.40	TORTURE	YUGO.
ANGERER, Franz	301918	M	Ger.		Agent, Member, Sipo, Gestapo, Sosnowiec (Pol.) 43	INTERR.	POL.
ANGERER, Herbert	250945	M			1 SS-Coy, 1 SS-Pz.Rgt.,) Div., Malmedy (Bel.) 12.44	MISC.CRIMES	U.S.
ANGERER, Sepp	129654	M	Ger.		Civ., to be confined Dealer in Looted Art., Berlin (Ger.) 41-45	PILLAGE	U.S.
ANGERMAIER, Josef	250928	M			Pvt., Camp Ellrich, Nordhausen (ger.)	MURDER	U.S.
ANGERMANN	186681	M	Ger.	95	Hptscharfhr., SS, C.C. Zwieberge (Ger.)	MURDER	U.K.
ANGRER	28724	M	Ger.		Major, Geb.Jg.Rgt.206, Finmark (Nor.) 44	MURDER	NOR.
ANGST	257366	M	Ger.		SS-Cpl., slave Labour Camp, Beisfjord-Narvik (Nor.) 6.-11.42	BRUTALITY	YUGO.
ANGST, Karl	250929	M		30. 8.07	Pvt., Camp Ellrich, Nordhausen (Ger.)	MURDER	U.S.
ANHAEUSER see AUFHAESER	307028	M	Ger.		Commissar, Gestapo Prague (Czech.) 38-45	INTERR.	CZECH.
ANHALT, Bernard	106968	M			Lt., Waffen-SS,Sonder-Kdo.Langenbach,Tal,Hohenlichte,Suttrop (Ger.) 3.45	MURDER	U.S.
ANHORN, Arthur	168611	M	Ger.		Pvt., 9 Gren.Ers.Rgt.,1 Coy, Magny d'Anigon (Fr.) 9.44	MURDER	FR.
ANKE, Hermann	187429	M	Ger.	1.11.09	Employee, SS, SD and Gestapo, Brno (Czech.) 39-45	MURDER	CZECH.
ANKERS	256977	M			Officer, Kreis-Kdtr.Polit.Department,Gruza,Kragujevak (Yugo.)42-44	MURDER	YUGO.
ANKONIA, K.	168581	M	Ger.		Oscharfhr., SS, C.C. Struthof-Natzweiler (Fr.) 42-44	MURDER	FR.
ANNAN	173652	M			Oscharfhr., SS, Labour Camp,Muhldorf-Ampfing (Ger.) 6.44-4.45	MURDER	U.S.
ANNAN	256686	M			Oscharfhr., C.C. Muhldorf-Dachau (ger.)	INTERR.	U.S.
ANNERUBES, Solfe	72162	M			Civilian, Greville-Hague (Fr.)	MURDER	FR.
ANNIA	142138	F	Ger.		Overseer, C.C. Ravensbruck (Ger.)	MISC.CRIMES	FR.
ANRAV, Horst	48622	M	Ger.	16	Lt., 12 Coy,23 Gren.Rgt.,Communanza (It.)	WITNESS	U.K.
ANRAU, Horst see UNRAU	1342						
ANSELM, Oscar	186245	M	Ger.	12	Army, Oberweier (Ger.) 7.44	MURDER	CAN.
ANSORGE	140040	M	Ger.		Uscharfhr., SS, C.C. Struthof (Fr.)	MISC.CRIMES	FR.
ANSORGE	191699	M	Ger.		Cpl., SS-Hauptamt, C.C. Struthof-Natzweiler(Fr.) 42-44	MURDER	FR.
ANTALKE	250930	M			Pvt., Camp Ellrich, Nordhausen (Ger.)	MURDER	U.S.
ANTHOESS	42	M	Ger.		CC -Officer(Cmdt.), C.C. Oswiecim (pol.)	MURDER	YUGO.
ANTHOESS see HOESS	392						
ANTHON, Rudolf see AMTHOR	121038						
ANTKOVIAK, Johann	165534	M	Ger.	98	Oscharfhr., SS, C.C. Natzweiler-Struthof (Fr.)	PILLAGE	BEL.
ANTON	62279	M	Ger.	95	Sgt., Stalag, Simonsdorf (Pol.) 11.40	TORTURE	U.K.
ANTON	172901	M	Ger.		Policeman, Police, Ladung (Czech.) 445	MURDER	U.S.
ANTON	254266	M	Ger.		Pvt., SD, Toulouse (Fr.) 11.42-8.44	INTERR.	FR.
ANTONI, Rudolf	192636	M	Ger.	00	Sgt., Reichsjustizministerium, Strafgefangenenlager Nord Finmark (Nor.) 6.42-45	MISC.CRIMES	NOR.
ANTONO	1678	M			Inf.Rgt. 959 (Fr.) 44	MURDER	U.K.
ANPONYSCHIN	131787	M		21	Guard, SS, C.C.Hohenheim near Plattling(Ger.) 2.-5.45	MURDER	U.S.
ANTOUAN, Court	186578	M	Ger.		Cpl., Army, Voutes (Grc.) 3.44	MURDER	GRC.
ANTROPOFF, Andreas	40291	M	Ger.		SS-Osturmfhr.,Prof.Dr.,Bonn (Ger.) 44	MURDER	U.S.
ANTUSCH, Rudolf	250931	M			Pvt., Camp Ellrich, Nordhausen (Ger.)	MURDER	U.S.
ANUSCH see ANUCH or HANOSCH	196157	M	Ger.	08 - 15	559 Coy, Landesschs.Bn, Domstadtl (Ger.) 11.41	MURDER	U.K.
ANWEILER	261769	M	Ger.		Cpl., Gend., Romilly sur Seine (Fr.) 6.44	MISC.CRIMES	FR.
ANZINGER, Georges	126734	M	Ger.		Lt., Gestapo, Trondes, Bousq, Menil la Tour (Fr.) 8.44	MURDER	FR.
ANZIGER	126734	M	Ger.	95	Lt., SD, Trondes, Bousq,Menil la Tour (Fr.) 8.44	TORTURE	FR.
APALLNER, Johann	259809	M	Ger.	4.14	Rottenfhr., SS, 1 Zug, 2 Group, probably stationed at Bergeyk, Schnellf.Gewehr, Noord Brabant (Neth.) 9.44	MURDER	NETH.
APACHOWSKI	167661	M	Ger.		Capt., Georgian Bn, 4 Coy, Tulle (Fr.) 4.44	MISC.CRIMES	BEL.
APELT, Kurt	262253	M	Ger.	15. 8. ?	Uscharfhr., SS, Gestapo, Rennes (Fr.) 43-44	MISC.CRIMES	FR.
APENBURG	190023	M	Ger.	07	Leader, SD, C.C. Neuengamme (Ger.) 43	MURDER	YUGO.
APEREN	189779	M	Dutch		SD, C.C. Vughte (Neth.) 6.44	MURDER	NETH.
APETZ	301227	M	Ger.		Oberrat, Army-administration, Brussels (Bel.) 41-44	MURDER	BEL.
APHACHOWSKI	191698	M	Ger.		Capt., 4 Coy, Georgian Bn, Tulle (Fr.) 4.44	MISC.CRIMES	FR.
APIARY nee WALIAN, Anna	256689	F	Ger.	20.12.19	Clerk, Civilian, Kladovy (Czech.) 42	MURDER	CZECH.
APIARY, Stephan	256688	M	Ger.	31. 7.19	Civ., Gestapo, Klatovy (Czech.) 42	MURDER	CZECH.
APITZ, Kurt	250998	M			Pvt., Camp Ellrich, Nordhausen (ger.)	MURDER	U.S.
APPAN	301543	M	Ger.		Staff at C.C. Mauthausen (Aust.) 40-45	MURDER	BEL.
APPEHEUSER	72209	M	Ger.		Prison-guard, SS, Hintzert (Ger.) 43	TORTURE	U.S.
APPEL	11206	M			Lt., Hauptverbindungsstab Nr.588, Oradour (Fr.) 6.44	MURDER	FR.
APPEL	301676	M			05-243 Mongolian "Oberland" Unit, St.Nazaire-Drôme (fr.) 7.-8.44	MURDER	FR.
APPEL, Emil	72168	M			Lt., SS, Adjutant, Clermond-Ferrand (Fr.)	MURDER	FR.
APPEL, Victor	130083	M			Civilian, C.C. Dora Mittelbau, Nordhausen (Ger.)	MURDER	U.S.
APRELL	250939	M			Sturmmann, Camp Rottleberode, Nordhausen (Ger.)	MURDER	U.S.
APPELSBACH, Alfons	172914	M	Ger.		Sgt., Army, 6 Coy, Wertalarm-Bn, Kermassonet en Karvignat (Fr.)8.44	MURDER	FR.
APPELT	250940	M			Gestapo, C.C. Dora, Nordhausen (Ger.)	MURDER	U.S.
APPELT, August	195674	M		1. 3.86	Civilian, Manager of Factory, Petrovice (Czech.) 45	PILLAGE	CZECH.
APPERMANN	134725	M			Cpl., SS-Rottenfhr., Totenkopfsturmbann, Nordhausen (Ger.) 43-45	MURDER	U.S.

APP-ARR

NAME	C.R.FILE NUMBER	SEX	NATIO- NALITY	DATE OF BIRTH	RANK OCCUPATION UNIT PLACE AND DATE OF CRIME	REASON WANTED	WANTED BY
APPONYI, George	148426	M			Member of Parliament for the Hung.Liberal party,Ujvider(Hung.)	MURDER	U.S.
APT	155885	M			S-Sgt., Army, Woroschilowgrad (Russ.) 11.42	MURDER	U.S.
APTH	196453	M	Ger.		Gendarm,Feldgendarmerie d'Argentan,St.Evroult Notre Dame du Bois(Fr.)44	INTERR.	FR.
ARABIN, Erich	250941	M	Ger.	21.3.18	Sgt., Camp Ellrich, Nordhausen(Ger.)	MURDER	U.S.
ARANCEM, Alex	250934	M	Ger.	16.3.23	Lt.,Baracks Foch,Colonne Russia-Germany,Chaumont, L'Ain, La Ferte (Fr.) 6.u.7.44	MISC.CRIMES	FR.
ARBOGAST	157154	M			Oschfhr., SS, Ensisheim (Fr.)	TORTURE	FR.
ARBOGAST, August	72169	M			SS-Rottfhr., KL. Struthof(Fr.)	TORTURE	FR.
ARDEN	192797	M	Ger.		SS-Major, SS, Stalag, Falstad (Nor.)41-44	MURDER	NOR.
ARDET	25005	M	Ger.		Major,Sicherheitspolizei-Commander,Hengelo(Neth.)4.43	MURDER	NETH.
ARDREE	257675	M	Ger.		Schfhr.,Camp Dora, Nordhausen(Ger.)	MURDER	U.S.
ARENDS	257904	M	Ger.		Waffen-Insp.,150 Panzer-Bde.,Meuse Bridge Antwerpen(Bel.)12.44	MISC.CRIMES	U.S.
ARENDT	147209	M	Ger.		Capt.,11 Panz.Div. (Fr.) 44	MURDER	FR.
ARENDT	261771	M	Ger.		Kapo, C.C. Dora, Nordhausen(Ger.)	MURDER	FR.
ARENS	23911	M	Ger.		Hauptfeldwebel and Guard, C.C., Rheinbach(Ger.)42-44	TORTURE	U.S.
AHRNS	157145	M			Pvt., Wehrmacht Gren.Regt.1222	MURDER	U.K.
AHENS or AHRENS	250935	M			Cpl., Camp Ellrich, Nordhausen(Ger.)	MURDER	U.S.
ARENSMANN (EISERMANN)	305690	M			Sturmschfhr., Sicherheitspolice at Tromsoe,Toftefjord,Tromsoe (Nor.)4.43	MURDER	NOR.
ARENTZ	300165	M			Kapo- common law prisoner, C.C. Flossenburg(Ger.)42-45	MURDER	FR.
ARENZ, Franz	256001	M			Kapo, C.C. Flossenburg(Ger.)	BRUTALITY	FR.
ARENZMANN, Willy	256945	M		10	Schfhr., SD, Tromsoe (Nor.)44	MURDER	NOR.
ARESTA see TISANI	194290						
ARETZ	250936	M			Lt.,Chief of section SS Poliz.Regt.Todt,10 Coy.,3 Bn., Mont Saxonnex(Fr.)	MURDER	FR.
ARHEIT, Alfred	194808	M			SS-Member, Gestapo, SS,Colmar-Berg(Lux.)	MISC.CRIMES	LUX.
ARIANS	1283	M	Ger.		Store Keeper, Navy	MISC.CRIMES	U.K.
ARJES, Reinhard	192281	M			Pvt., Army	WITNESS	POL.
ARKAPIN	72171	M			SS-Uschfhr., SS, Paris(Fr.)	TORTURE	FR.
ARKEN	196452	M		10	Cpl., H.K.P.664, Laloubere(Fr.)8.44	MURDER	FR.
ARLAUTSKI	185995	M		26.1.97	Gendarm, Gendarmerie Bouzonville(Fr.)10.44	MURDER	FR.
ARLEDTER, Fritz	195803	M	Ger.		SS-Rottfhr., W-SS, C.C., Auschwitz-Birkenau(Pol.)40-1.43	MURDER	YUGO.,FR.
ARLT	259409	M			Leader, C.C., Auschwitz(Pol.)	MURDER	FR.
ARLT (see ALT)	300550	M	Ger.				
ARLT, Fritz	168627	M	Ger.		Stabsfuehrer,Beauftragter Reichskommissar fuer die Festigung des Deutschtums, Krakow(Pol.)39-44	PILLAGE	POL.
ARMADA	301294	M	Ger.		Member Gestapo at Trencin, C.C. Oswiecim-Birkenau(Pol.)39-45	MURDER	CZECH.
ARMAND	298233	M	Ger.		Pvt., Abwehr-Official Feldgend.,Abbenville(Fr.)8.44	MURDER	FR.
ARMBRECHT	250925	M	Ger.		Chief of section 4 Gestapo, Bruenn(Czech.)43-45	TORTURE	CZECH.
ARMBRUESTER, Philipp	194807	M		99	Amts-Buergermeister,Public Official,Petange(Lux.)	MISC.CRIMES	LUX.
ARMBRUSTER	142139	M	Ger.		Civilian, Odsbach(Ger.)	MISC.CRIMES	FR.
ARMBRUSTER	179124	M	Ger.		C.C,Schirmeck,Rotenfels,Gaggenau(Fr.,Ger.)	INTERR.	U.K.
ARMBRUSTER	173930	M	Ger.		Governor, C.C., Celje(Yugo.)4.41-44	MURDER	YUGO.
ARMBRUSTER, M.	193749	M	Ger.		SS-Uschfhr., C.C. Buchenwald(Ger.)	TORTURE	U.S.
ARMBRUSTER, Otto	250926	M			Flyer, Camp Ellrich, Nordhausen(Ger.)	MURDER	U.S.
ARMBRUSTER, Willie	162879	M			W.O., Army, Moulins(Fr.)	TORTURE	FR.
ARMDT, Karl	250927				377 Jaeger Regt.,10 Coy., Vinkt Meigem(Bel.)	MURDER	BEL.
ARNAUD	174916	M	Ger.		Sturmschfhr., SS, Hirson(Fr.)	MURDER	FR.
ARNDT	134724				Scharfhr., 4 SS Totenkopfsturmbann,Nordhausen(Ger.) 43-45	MURDER	U.S.
ARNDT	195145	M	Ger.		Guard, Civilian KL.Helinbrechts(Ger.)7.44-4.45	WITNESS	U.S.
ARNDT	174917	M			Capt.,Gestapo, Metz(Fr.)	MURDER	FR.
ARNDT	182568	M			SS-Usturmfhr.,SD-Official,SS,SD,Reichssicherheitshauptamt, C.C. Mauthausen(Aust.)45	MURDER	U.S.
ARNDT	189487	M			Oberwachtmeister,Police,C.C. Oswiecim (Pol.)	MURDER	POL.
ARNDT, Felix	142421	M	Ger.	97	Feldw., Army, Augsburg(Ger.)40-4.45	MURDER	U.S.
ARNDT, Hans	172902	M	Ger.	6.7.20	SS-Rottfhr., SS, C.C. Flossenburg(Ger.)44-45	TORTURE	U.S.
ARNDT, Karl	189522	M			Lt.-Gen., arrived at Perigeux with Cossack Troops from East Prussia, Perigeux(Fr.)6.-8.44	MURDER	FR.,U.S.
ARNDT, Paul	168615	M	Ger.		Treuhaender, General-Government Poland, Posen(Pol.)9.39-12.44	MISC.CRIMES	FR.,POL.
ARNDT, Robert	29824	M			Gen., Army, Perigeux(Fr.)6.-7.44	MURDER	FR.
ARNDT, Wilhelm	1889	M			C.C. Ravensbrueck(Ger.)12.44	MURDER	U.S.
ARNEMANN	133744	M			SD and Local Police,Polangen(Lith.)	WITNESS	U.S.
ARNEMANN, Christ.Friedr.	129840	M	Ger.		Lt.,Fallschirmjaeger-Div.5 Air Force,Buch and Tegel-Berlin(Ger.), Polangen,Starya Russia(Russ.)7.41,11.43-5.44	WITNESS	U.S.
ARNO	186572	M	Ger.		Pvt., Army,Vasiliki(Gre.)43-44	MURDER	GRC.
ARNOD	157146	M	Ger.		Director,Civilian,Jagen(Ger.)4.44-45	MISC.CRIMES	U.K.
ARNOLD	251950	M	Ger.		Scharfhr., Gestapo, Le Chablais(Fr.)5.44	MISC.CRIMES	FR.
ARNOLD	166879	M	Ger.		Member,Feldgendarmerie,Laroshemillay(Fr.)	PILLAGE	FR.
ARNOLD	132549	M	Ger.		Sturmmann, SS, Hallein(Ger.)	TORTURE	FR.
ARNOLD	138285	M	Ger.		Scharfhr.,SS,Gestapo Lyon(Fr.)	MURDER	FR.
ARNOLD	185994	M	Ger.		Employee, Gestapo, Sarrebruck(Ger.)	PILLAGE	FR.
ARNOLD	187035	M	Ger.		Cpl.,Feldgendarmerie of Vesoul, Montignyen Vesoul(Fr.)7.44	MURDER	FR.
ARNOLD (maybe family or christian name)	259150	M	Ger.		Kommandofuehrer, 2 Coy., 607 Landesschuetzen-Bn., Arbeits-Kdo., Allendorf(Ger.)3.43	MURDER	YUGO.
ARNOLD, Adolf	300166	M	Ger.		Sgt.,Truppe 533,Feldgendarmerie,Troyes and region(Fr.)10.43-8.44	MURDER	FR.
ARNOLD, Albert	194806	M	Ger.		Verlagsleiter und Betriebsfuehrer(Lux.)	MISC.CRIMES	LUX.
ARNOLD, Heinz	251947	M			Flyer, Nordhausen(Ger.)	MURDER	U.S.
ARNOLD, Karl	124317	M	Ger.	18	Hptschfhr.,Waffen-SS,Leibstand.Adolf Hitler,Rosbach(Ger.)3.45	MURDER	U.S.
ARNOLD, Stefan	251949	M	Ger.		Pvt., Kragujevao(Yugo.)10.41	MURDER	YUGO.
ARNOOL	196159	M	Ger.		Head of police, Arnstadt(Ger.)	MISC.CRIMES	FR.
ARNS	192798	M	Ger.		Wachtmeister,Schupo,C.C.Falstad-Stalag,Falstad(Nor.)41-44	MURDER	NOR.
ARNT, Bruno	195802	M	Ger.		Rottfhr.,Waffen-SS,Staff, C.C., Auschwitz-Birkenau(Pol.)40	MURDER	FR.,YUGO.
ARP, Max	261878	M			Cpl., 1 Coy.,377 Jaeger-Regt.,Vinkt-Meigem and district(Bel.)5.40	WITNESS	BEL.
ARQUART	251954	M			SS-Blockfuehrer, C.C. Neuengamme(Ger.)	MURDER	BEL.
ARRESLEITHER, Max	188665	M			Army, 18 Bn., Busset(Fr.)8.44	MURDER	FR.

ARR - AUF

NAME	C.R.FILE NUMBER	SEX	NATIO- NALITY	DATE OF BIRTH	RANK	OCCUPATION UNIT PLACE AND DATE OF CRIME	REASON WANTED	WANTED BY
ARRNEGER, Josef	150767	M	Ger.			Cultivateur, Civilian, KL.Untereschach, Stalag VB(Ger.)	TORTURE	FR.
ARTHABER, Leopold	251955	M	Ger.	16	Pvt.,192 Signals Bn., 92 Inf.Div., Farnese (Italy) 6.44		INTERR.	U.K.
ARTIG, Oskar	173653	M				Pit overseer,Org.Todt Labour Camp,Mühldorf-Ampfing(Ger.)6.44-4.45	MURDER	U.S.
ARTL, Adolf	187424	M	Ger.			Criminalsecretary, Gestapo and SD, Brno (Czech.) 39-45	MURDER	CZECH.
ARTMANN	72177	M			Sgt.,D.C.A.Armee,F.P.Nr.55099,Villemur (France)		TORTURE	FR.
ARTMANN	173655	M				Civilian, Org.Todt, Labour Camp, Mühldorf-Ampfing(Ger.) 6.44-4.45	MURDER	U.S.
ARTNER	126523	M	Ger.			9 Pdnz.Div.,1 Regt. Obgfr.	MURDER	U.S.
ARTNER, Max	174290	M				SS-Sturmbannfhr., SS, C.C., Mühldorf-Ampfing(Ger.) 6.44-4.45	MURDER	U.S.
ARWEYDEN	44	M	Ger.			Lt.,Army, Clermont-Ferrand (France) 2.-7.44	MURDER	FR.
ASBECK or ASBECH	174099	M				Civilian, Org. Todt, C.C., Mühldorf-Ampfing(Ger.) 6.44-4.45	MURDER	U.S.
ASBOECK, Leopold	196156	M				Ortsgruppenleiter, 375 Gren.-Regt., Amstetten (Austria) 3.45	MISC.CRIMES	U.S.
ASCH	148715	M				Stabsintendant, O.K.W.Subsection IV P.W.Affairs	MISC.CRIMES	U.S.
ASCH	251956	M	Ger.			W.O.-Cmdt., Air Force, Seguret-Vaison (France) 6.44	MISC.CRIMES	FR.
ASCHAUER, Franz	187428	M	Ger.			Kriminalobersekretaer, Gestapo, SD, Brno (Czech.) 39-45	MURDER	CZECH.
ASCHAUER, Willi	307090	M	Ger.			Hptschfhr. 13 SS"Handzar"-Div., Brem and Bosnia(Yugo.) 3.-9.44	MURDER	YUGO.
ASCHE	149528	M				Cpl.-Chief, Stalag 6 C.	TORTURE	FR.
ASCHE, Kurt	255255	M	Ger.			Lt.,SS Abt. IV B, Bruessels (Belgium)	INTERR.	BEL.
ASCHENBACH	173311	M				Pvt., Stalag IX C.C., Bad Sulza (Ger.) 44-45	MURDER	FR.
ASCHENBERG	251958	M				Cpl., Camp Ellrich, Nordhausen (Ger.)	MURDER	U.S.
ASCHENBRENNER	199127	M	Ger.	00	Civilian, Kutno (Poland) 42		WITNESS	U.S.
ASCHENBRENNER, Heinrich	251951	M	Ger.	6.12.18	Employee, Gestapo, Pardubice (Czech.) 39-45		INTERR.	CZECH.
ASCHMANN, Franz Josef	194727	M	Ger.	28.11.00	Civilian Manager, Brno (Czech.) 43-44		SUSPECT	CZECH.
ASCHMITAT, Fritz	124397	M	Ger.	20	Pvt., A.Gren.Inf.Regt., Longueil (France) 6.44		MURDER	U.S.
ASCHMUSSON, Christian	251952	M	Ger.	08	Pvt., 377 Jaeger Regt. 12 Coy., Vinkt Meigem (Belgium)		MURDER	BEL.
ASCHNER, Thomas	251461	M				Rottfhr., SS, Radolfzell (Germany) 7.44	MURDER	U.S.
ASCHOFF	45	M				Gestapo-Col., Tunis (Tunesia)	LOOTING	FR.
ASEL	251953	M	Ger.			N.C.O., Pepingen (Belgium)	WITNESS	BEL.
ASHAUER, Karl	262015	M	Ger.	1. 5.06	SS-Mann,Waffen-SS,Gren.Div.36"Dirlewanger-Bde."Warschau and other(Pol.)-44 MURDER			POL.
ASKAMP, Bernard	261767	M	Ger.			Agent, Gestapo-Amiens, Gentelles (France) 6.-8.44	MURDER	FR.
ASMAS	121031	M	Ger.			Sgt. Major, C.C. Brux Lager 22a (Czech.) 5.44	MURDER	U.K.
ASMER	124838	M	Ger.	05	Sgt., Stalag IVC, Bruex (Germany) 3.45		MURDER	U.K.
ASMUS	121030	M	Ger.			Sgt., C.C., Brüx Stalag IVC (Czech.) 2.45	BRUTALITY	U.K.
ASMUS	148239	M				Arbeitskommando Rodelheim (Germany) 43-44	TORTURE	FR.
ASMUS, Gisela	257674	F	Ger.	17. 6.05	Dr., Clerk, National Museum, Brno (Czech.) 42-45		WITNESS	CZECH.
ASMUS, Karl (junior)	190466	M	Ger.			Civilian, Beckendorf (Germany) 10.44	WITNESS	U.S.
ASMUSS	190683	M	Ger.			Pvt.,Eis.Art.Bn.717, St.Andries,Varsenare,Les Bruges(Belgium)	MURDER	BEL.
ASMUSSEN	11870	M	Ger.			Abwehr-Official Paris.	MURDER	FR.
ASMUTH, Friedrich	46	M				Army,Feldpolizei,Staff Officer, Vesoul (France) 11.43-7.44	MURDER	FR.
ASSCHE	155887	M				Civilian, KL.Gardelegen (Germany) 4.45	WITNESS	U.S.
ASSERH	166884	M	Ger.			Doctor-Oberarzt,Kommandantur Army,Obercommando, La Rochette,Crest(Fr.)44	INTERR.	FR.
ASSMAN, Helmut	301083	M	Ger.			Pvt., Vendeuvre,Aube (France) 8.44	PILLAGE	FR.
ASSMAN, Kurt Victor	260635	M				Vice-Admiral, Navy.	WITNESS	U.S.
ASSMANN	194931	M	Ger.			Uschfhr., SD, Corsell Beck (Netherlands)	MURDER	NETH.
ASSMIS	157147	M	Ger.	97	Wehrmacht 379 Landschuetz.Bn., Bruex (Czech.) 5.44-5.45		TORTURE	U.K.
ASSMUSSEN, Werner	306569	M	Ger.			Sgt., Varrelbusch Air Field nr.Boesel, Oldenburg, member of Volkssturm, Boesel, Oldenburg (Germany) 4.45	MURDER	U.K.
AST, Paul	71185	M			Capt., Army.		MISC.CRIMES	U.K.
ASTEL, Karl	133966	M	Ger.	26. 2.98	Dr.,Civilian, C.C.,Weimar-Buchenwald (Germany)		MISC.CRIMES	U.S.
ASTHALTER	108970	M	Ger.	05	SS-Osturmfhr.,Blutordenstraeger,with SD (Security Service) of Berlin, Beresina (Russia)		MURDER	BEL.
ASTRATH, Henrich	142424	M	Ger.			Civilian, Kalme (Germany) 1.44	TORTURE	U.S.
ATTINGER	195673	M	Ger.			Sgt., Gendarmerie, Mizocz (Poland) 10.42	MURDER	POL.
ATZRODT, Waldemar	261985	M	Ger.	22. 1.07	SS-Mann, Dirlewanger-Bde., Waffen-SS,Gren.Div.36,Warsaw and other(Pol.)-44 MURDER			POL.
AUBRECHT, Franz	254920	M	Ger.	96	Employee, Gestapo, Kolin (Czech.) 39-45		MURDER	CZECH.
AUCH	257960	M				Major, SS-Jagdv. 150 Pz.Bde.,Meusebridge Antwerpen(Belgium) 12.44	MISC.CRIMES	U.S.
AUCHAPT, Roland	142140	M				Civilian, Karlsbad (Czech.) 9.43	MISC.CRIMES	FR.
AUDOERSCH	260634	M				Col., Army.	WITNESS	U.S.
AUE	152501	M	Ger.	02	Cpl.,Waffen-SS, C.C. Buchenwald (Germany)		MISC.CRIMES	U.S.
AUKLINE	173313	M	Ger.			Agent, Gestapo, Chamalieres (France) 6.44	PILLAGE	FR.
AUER	23907	M				Lt., Army, Champagney (France)	TORTURE	FR.
AUER	140750	M	Ger.	10	Oschfhr. SS, KL. Mühldorf & Ampfing (Germany) 44-45		MURDER	U.S.
AUER	185163	M	Ger.			Chief de dortoir, SS, C.C. Dachau (Germany)	TORTURE	FR.
AUER	251937	M				Rottfhr., C.C. Dora, Nordhausen (Germany)	MURDER	U.S.
AUER	257570	M	Ger.			Gendarm, Gendarmerie Seltz,Schaffhouse et Eberbach(Fr.) 43-44	MISC.CRIMES	FR.
AUER	259205	M				Lagerfuehrer, Sprengshemie Plant, Mühldorf Area (Germany)	MURDER	U.S.
AUER, Erwin	185286	M	Ger.	21.11.09	SS-Hptschfhr.,Criminal-Assistant, SD,Gestapo, Praha(Czech.) 39-43		MURDER	CZECH.
AUER, Ferdinand	174097	M				Leader, Org.Todt, C.C. Mühldorf-Ampfing (Germany) 6.44-4.45	MURDER	U.S.
AUER, Otto	10730	M	Ger.	05	Capt., Feldgendarmerie, Laferte Aube Chaumont (France) 4.44-6.44		TORTURE	FR.
AUERBACH	259201	M				SS-Capt.,SS Div."Prinz Eugen", Niksic, Montenegro (Yugo.) 5.-6.43	MISC.CRIMES	YUGO.
AUERBECK	187425	M	Ger.			Pvt.,4 Coy.,Landesschuetzen Bn.829, Obertraubling (Germany) 1.45	MURDER	U.S.
AUERRUEFER	205321A	M				Civilian, Gensbach (Germany)	MURDER	U.S.
AUERSWALD	129157	M				Orpo Kriminalobersekretaer, Mauthausen (Austria) 41-45	MURDER	U.S.
AUF DER HEIDE, Joseph	148430	M	Ger.			Guard, Mines, Erkenschwik (Germany)	TORTURE	U.S.
AUFER or HOFFER	189576	M	Ger.			Lt., Army, Cotes Du Nord (France)	MURDER	FR.
AUFFENBERG	257938	M				Lt., Panzer-Bde. 150, Meusebridge Antwerpen (Belgium) 12.44	MISC.CRIMES	U.S.
AUFFERMANN, Wilhelm	257997	M				Lt., Panzer-Bde. 150, Meusebridge Antwerpen (Belgium) 12.44	MISC.CRIMES	U.S.
AUFFSTEIN, Jack	167660	M	Ger.			Sgt., Warder at Prison C.C., St. Lo (France) 6.44	MURDER	FR.
AUFHAEUSER see ANHAEUSER	307028	M	Ger.			Commissar, Gestapo Prague, Prague (Czech.)	INTERR.	CZECH.

AUF-BAC

NAME	C.R.FILE NUMBER	SEX	NATIO-NALITY	DATE OF BIRTH	RANK OCCUPATION UNIT PLACE AND DATE OF CRIME	REASON WANTED	WANTED BY
AUFMAYER (or AUFLEYER)	47	M	Ger.		SS Hauptsturmfhr., C.C. Oswiecim (Pol.)	MURDER	POL., BEL., FR.
AUFHASSEN, Heinz	196454	M	Ger.		Pvt., Afrika-Corps, Aube (Fr.)	MURDER	FR.
AUGEL, Nikolas	192634	M	Ger.	05	Leader, Organisation Todt, Trondenes (Nor.) 42-43	MISC.CRIMES	NOR.
AUGELLANG, Matheus	192799	M	Ger.		Schupo, C.C. Falstad, Stalag (Nor.) 41-44	TORTURE	NOR.
AUGINGER, Rudulf	306735	M	Ger.		Moetzing nr. Regensburg (Ger.) 6.44	BRUTALITY	U.S.
AUGUST	190682	M			Pvt., Els.Art.Bn. 717, St.Andries,Varsenhare,Les Bruges (Bel.)	MURDER	BEL.
AUGUST	192800	M	Ger.		Wachtmeister, Schupo, C.C. Falstad, Stalag (Nor.) 41-44	MURDER	NOR.
AUGUST	251938	M	Ger.		Attached to SD Police, Fiume (It.) 3.45	INTERR.	YUGO.
AUGUST, Oskar, Hugo	260472	M	Ger.	14.12.86	Major, Civ.-Administration, Local, Kiejska Gorka (Pol.) 39-45	MISC.CRIMES	POL.
AUGUSTE, Antoine	189571	M	Ger.	02	Cpl., SS Div. "Das Reich", Flamarens (Fr.) 7.44	MURDER	FR.
AUGUSTI	192633	M	Ger.		Major, Inf.Div.230, C.C. Drag (Nor.) 44-45	TORTURE	NOR.
AUGUSTIN, Alfons	251939	M	Ger.	13. 5.13	Employee, Gestapo, Breclav (Czech.) 39-45	INTERR.	CZECH.
AUGUSTIN, Erich	187426	M	Ger.	04	SS-Usturmfhr., leader, Gestapo, Krasnik, Kurpilowka (Pol.) 43-44	MURDER	POL.
AUGUSTIN, Fritz	134729	M	Ger.	28.10.95	Sgt. of the Guard, SS Hauptscharfhr.,4.SS-Totenkopfsturmbann, Nordhausen (Ger.) 43-45	WITNESS	U.S.
AUHORN	139129	M			Civilian, Dresden (Ger.) 3.45	MURDER	U.S.
AUL	255088	M			Uschfhr., C.C. Buchenwald (Ger.)	MURDER	U.S.
AULHILA	252849	M		16	Lt., now employed as engineer in British Textil Plant,Gerard Mer. (Fr.) 5.44	WITNESS	U.S.
AULAIER (or AULMAYER), Hans	131789	M			Hauptsturmfhr., SS, Kl.Flossenburg (Ger.)	MURDER	U.S.
AULANN	259472	M			Lt.Colonel, plaster Factory Spaeth,Windsheim, Illiesheim (Ger.)12.43	MURDER	U.S.
AULMANN, Karl	251940	M	Ger.		Guard, C.C. Lahde-Westf. (Ger.)	INTERR.	BEL.
AULMAYER	131029	M	Ger.		Lagerfhr., SS-C.C. Auschwitz	MURDER	FR.
AULMAYER (see AULAIER), Hans	131789	M					
AULMAYER	251941	M	Ger.		Inspector, Ger. Reichseisenbahn, Hauptverkehrsdir., Romilly (Fr.)8.44	PILLAGE	FR.
AULMAYER	252942	M	Ger.		Ogruppenfhr., C.C.,Waffen SS, Auschwitz-Birkenau (Ger.) 42-45	MISC.CRIMES	YUGO.
AULEIER	193577	M	Ger.		SS Osturmbannfhr., C.C. Flossenburg (Ger.)	MURDER	BEL.
AULMEIER, Wolfgang	261986	M	Ger.	17. 9.11	Pvt., Waffen SS Gren.Div.36 Dirlewanger Bde.,Warsaw (Pol.)40-44	MURDER	POL.
AULMEINEA	251948	M		05	SS Hauptsturmfhr.,Waffen SS,C.C. Auschwitz-Birkenau (Ger.)42-45	MISC.CRIMES	YUGO.
AURDZIEJ, Antoni	306330	M	Ger.		Pvt., SS, C.C. Bergen-Belsen (Ger.) 40-45	MURDER	BEL.
AURIN	36675	M	Ger.		Pvt., Army 596 Landschtz.Bn.,Nordhausen (Ger.) 11.42	BRUTALITY	U.K.
AUSBERGER, Johann-Josef	193256	M	Ger.	17. 4.24	SS Rottenfhr., Bohemia (Czech.)	MISC.CRIMES	CZECH.
AUS DEM BRUCH	149651	M			Sgt., SS C.C. Schamberg (Ger.)	TORTURE	U.K.
AUS DEM BRUCH, Kurt	72192	M	Ger.	17	Dr., SS Capt., C.C. Struthof-Natzweiler (Fr.) 9.44	MURDER	U.K.
AUS DER FUENTE	48	M	Ger.	05	SS Osturmfhr., Amsterdam (Neth.) 40-43	MISC.CRIMES	NETH.
AUSPERGER	261349	M	Ger.		Sgt., Police, Lask (Pol.) 8.42	MURDER	POL.
AUSPITZ	132560	M	Ger.		Guard, C.C. Ravensbrueck (Ger.)	MURDER	FR.
AUST	251945	M	Ger.		Trossfhr., Unit 11.165 B, Coufty (Fr.) 8.44	MISC.CRIMES	FR.
AUST, Reinnold, Paul	195220	M		25. 1.88	Crim.Commissar, SS Gestapo, Niederdorfelden (Ger.) 42	MURDER	POL.
AUSTEN, Konrad	165935	M	Ger.		SS Rottenfhr., SS Pz.Div."Das Reich", Moissac (Fr.) 44	MURDER	FR.
AUSTERMANN, Hans	300008	M	Ger.		Capt. 16 Inf.Rgt., 1 Bn. 1 Coy., Crete (Grc.) 9.43	MISC.CRIMES	GRC.
AUSTREICH	67701	M	Ger.		Sgt., Major, C.C. Graudenz (Pol.)	MURDER	U.K.
AUSWITZ	195835	M	Ger.		C.C. Staff, Auschwitz (Pol.) 40-45	MURDER	FR.
AVELINE	132597	M	Ger.		Pvt., Gestapo, Chamaliers (Fr.) 6.45	RAPE	FR.
AVERDUNG, Georg	164931	M	Ger.		Schfhr., SD, Strassburg (Fr.) 40	WITNESS	U.N.W.C.C.
AWISZUS, Erich	108957	M			Pvt., Army 34.Fortress machine gun Bat., Aachen (Ger.) 9.44	MURDER	U.S.
AUCH	188436	F	Ger.		C.C. Female Guard, C.C. Ravensbrueck (Ger.)	MURDER	FR.
AXE	162714	M			N.C.O., Army, KGF.Arb.Bn.184, Coy.4 Basis Tunnel nr.Kobbelveid, Botn. (Nor.) 4.44	MURDER	NOR.
AXMANN, Arthur	62148	M	Ger.		Leader of Hitler Youth	MURDER	U.N.W.C.C.
AXT	150768	M	Ger.		Cpl., Landesschtz.Coy., Boehlen (Ger.) 2.-4.45	TORTURE	U.K.
AXTEN (see AGSTEN)	257568						
AXTHELL, Arthur	261984	M		10. 5.12	Pvt., Dirlewanger Bde., Waffen SS,Gren.Div.36,Warsaw (Pol.)40-44	MURDER	POL.
AYS, Franz	174096	M			SS Oschfhr., C.C. Muehldorf, Ampfing (Ger.) 6.44-4.45	MURDER	U.S.
AZP, Joseph	142429	M	Ger.		Civilian, Eichelstadt nr. Wuerzburg (Ger.) 5.45	MURDER	U.S.
BAAB, Heinrich	188430	M		11	Crim.Secretary, Gestapo, Frankfurt (Ger.) 5.43	TORTURE	U.K.
BAACK	72724	M			Lt., SS Chief, Postaussenkommando, Vannes (Fr.) 44	MURDER	FR.
BAADE, Conrad	250641	M	Ger.		Capt., 377.Jaeger Rgt., Vinkt (Bel.) 5.40	MURDER	BEL.
BAADER	255980	M	Ger.		Osturmfhr., Elten, Rotterdam (Neth.) 11.44	MISC.CRIMES	NETH.
BAAKE	250018	M			SS Hauptschfhr., SS	INTERR.	BEL.
BAALMAN	306672	M	Ger.		331 Pionier Bn. 331 Inf.Div., Mijnheerenland (Neth.) 5.45	PILLAGE	NETH.
BAAR, Hans	187454	M	Ger.	20.10.13	Employee, Gestapo, SD, Brno (Czech.) 39-45	MURDER	CZECH.
BAAR, Karl	258096	M	Ger.	12. 1.04	Informer, Clerk, Gestapo, State Service, C.Budejovice (Czech.)42	MURDER	CZECH.
BAARFUS, (or BARFUSS)	250640	M			Pvt., Camp Ellrich, Nordhausen (Ger.)	MURDER	U.S.
BAASNER	300953	M	Ger.		SS Oschfhr., Official of SD,Leitabschnitt, Prague, Oswiecim-Birkenau (Pol.) 39-45	MURDER	CZECH.
BAATZ	255979	M	Ger.		Lt., Gouda (Neth.) 45	SUSPECT	NETH.
BABEL, Rudolf, Maximilian	261894	M	Ger.	9. 8.01	Informer, Gestapo, Prague (Czech.) 8.44	MURDER	CZECH.
BABL, Ludwig	192282	M	Ger.	12	Camp Guard, C.C. Bayreuth (Ger.) 6.42	MURDER	FR.
BABOR, Karl	306216	M	Ger.		Dr., Medical Officer, C.C. Struthof-Natzweiler (Fr.) 42-44	MURDER	YUGO.,U.S.
BABOV	190488	M	Ger.		SS Usturmfhr., Dr. Asst., C.C. Dachau (Ger.) 42	TORTURE	U.S.
BABRISCHEK (or BACRISCHEK)	142325	M			Sgt., SS, C.C. Flossenburg (Ger.)	MURDER	U.S.
BABSKI	250637	M			Pvt., Camp Ellrich (Ger.)	MURDER	FR.
BACH	49	M	Ger.		Cpl., Stalag 194,-Mouzay, Nancy (Fr.) 3.43	MURDER	FR.
BACH	72246	M			Colonel,Major, Chief Kdo. 3-769, Mouzay (Fr.) 3.43	MURDER	U.S.
BACH	124382	M		00	Hauptsturmfhr., Kriminalrat, SS, Gestapo Kdo. 16 z.b.V.	MURDER	U.K.
BACH	158336	M	Ger.		Staff-Sgt., Army, 714 Coy., Mielub-Briesen (Ger.) 6.44	MURDER	POL., BEL., FR., YUGO.
BACH	185162	M	Ger.		Officer, Hauptscharfhr., SS, Gestapo, C.C. Dachau (Ger.) 42-45	MURDER	
BACH	185411	M			Uschfhr., SS, C.C. Mauthausen (Aust.)	TORTURE	U.S.
BACH	260126	M	Ger.		Gendarm, Div. Oberland, Unity Russia-Ger., Massif du Vercors (Fr.) 7.-8.44	SUSPECT	FR.

BAC-BAD

-10-

NAME	C.R.FILE NUMBER	SEX	NATIO- NALITY	DATE OF BIRTH	RANK OCCUPATION UNIT PLACE AND DATE OF CRIME	REASON WANTED	WANTED BY
BACH, Alois	260365	M	Ger.		W.O.,23 Uhland Stand,Harbacq,Somme (Fr.) 5.40	WITNESS	BEL.
BACH, Andre	192158	M	Ger.	88	Member,Gestapo,Liege,Monsand Namur (Bel.)	TORTURE	BEL.
BACH, Franz	196155	M	Ger.	00	Sgt.,Air Force,Member of Guard at Bruttig Tunnel (Ger.) 44	MURDER	U.S.
BACH, Hans	250638	M	Ger.		Inspector,SD,Arpavon (Fr.) 6.44	MISC.CRIMES	FR.
BACH, Peter	250080	M	Ger.		Civilian,Preist (Ger.) 8.44	MURDER	U.S.
BACH, Willi	124502	M	Ger.	09	Oschfhr.,SS,C.C.Dachau (Ger.) 39-45	MURDER	U.K.
BACHAUS (or BARKHOUS,BARKHAUS, BACHOUS)	250081	M	Ger.		Commandant,Marlag and Milag Nord,Westertimke near Bremen (Ger.)	INTERR.	U.K.
BACHE, Fritz	250079	M	Ger.		Member,Gestapo,Lille (Fr.) 40-44	MISC.CRIMES	FR.
BACHE, Hannes	189033	M	Ger.	22	Pvt.,Army,Santa Lucia near Piedemonte (It.) 44	MURDER	U.K.
BACHEMAIER	125120	M	Ger.		Capt.,Army,Chenebier (Fr.) 9.44	MURDER	FR.
BACHER, Maximilian	257754	M	Ger.	9.08	Geh.Feld Pol.,Bergen (Nor.) 44	MURDER	NOR.
BACHER, Pius	173126	M			Cook,C.C.Schirmeck,Gaggenau (Fr.,Ger.) 44	INTERR.	U.K.
BACHHUBER, Moritz	29838	M	Ger.		Sgt.,Army,Lanthenay (Fr.) 44	MURDER	FR.
BACHINGER, Johann	157128	M			Stabsgefr.,Armee Oberkdo.1,1 Flat.4 Coy Sturmbn.AOK 1,Courcelles sur Nied (Fr.) 11.44	MURDER	U.S.
BACHMAIER	141449	M	Ger.		Capt.,Army,Chenebier-Etobon (Fr.) 9.44	MURDER	FR.
BACHMAN, Eugen	187216	M	Ger.	98	Uschfhr.,SD,C.C.Metz Woippy (Fr.) 6.-7.44	MISC.CRIMES	CAN.
BACHMAN, Heinrich	129838	M	Ger.	85-95	Volkssturm,Altengrebow Stalag 2 A (Ger.) 3.45	MURDER	U.S.
BACHMAN, Sepp	157150	M	Ger.	05	Electrician,Civilian,Ebensee (Aust.) 44-45	MURDER	U.S.
BACHMANN	11207	M	Ger.		SS Das Reich BZ Div.Adjoint to Lt.Philippe,Castelmaurou (Fr.) 6.44	MURDER	FR.
BACHMANN	187216	M		98	Uschfhr.,SS,C.C.Woippy (SD) Moselle (Bel.,Fr.) 6.-7.44	TORTURE	BEL.,FR.
BACHMANN	196607	M	Ger.		W.O.,157 Div.Chasseurs de montagne de Res.,Glieres (Fr.) 3.-4.44	WITNESS	FR.
BACHMANN, Heinrich	135121	M	Ger.		Civilian,Police Secr.,Wuerzburg (Ger.) 44	WITNESS	U.S.
BACHMANN, Hermann	151711	M	Ger.		Cpl.,Army-Art.,2 Army 503 Bde.10 Btty.,Hilden (Ger.) 4.45	WITNESS	U.S.
BACHMANN, U.	168616	M	Ger.		Civilian,Commissary Administrator,Lipno (Danzig) 9.39-44	MISC.CRIMES	POL.
BACHMAYER	136187	M	Ger.		Chief du Camp,C.C.Mauthausen (Aust.)	MURDER	FR.
BACHMAYER	173644	M	Ger.		Civilian,Asst.commander,C.C.Mauthausen (Aust.)	MURDER	U.S.
BACHMAYER (or DACHMAYER)	265848	M	Ger.		Lt.,Air Force,Chenoise (Fr.) 8.44	MURDER	FR.
BACHMAYER (see BACHMEYER)	132169						
BACHMAYR (see BACHMEYER)	132169						
BACHMEIER	168594	M		11	Sturmbannfhr.,SS,C.C.Mauthausen (Aust.)	WITNESS	U.S.
BACHMEIER (see BACHMEYER)	132169						
BACHMEIER, Andreas	250083	M		1. 2.00	Pvt.,Army,Nordhausen (Ger.)	MURDER	U.S.
BACHMEYER (or BACHMAYER or BACHMEIER or BACHMAYR)	132169	M	Ger.	11	SS-Sturmbannfhr.,Adj.Camp Commander,C.C.Mauthausen (Aust.)	SUSPECT	U.S.,BEL., FR.,U.K.
BACHOR, Liesel	305990	F	Ger.		Nursing sister,Member of staff of Baby Clinic,Wolfsburg and Ruehen (Ger.)	MURDER	U.K.
BACHOUS (see BACHAUS)	250081						
BACHTKE	125127	M	Ger.		Waffen SS,F.P.Nr.48963 B,St.Sulpice,Montmusson,Chateau-Gontier (Fr.)44	MURDER	FR.
BACK	166948	M	Ger.		Lt.,Army,Plachy Buyon (Fr.) 8.-9.44	WITNESS	FR.
BACK	188432	M			Generalmajor,16 Panz.Div.,Salermo (It.) 9.44	MISC.CRIMES	U.K.
BACK, Alphonse	250082	M	Ger.	23. 1.25	Pvt.,558 Gren.Rgt.13 Coy,Brusy en Artois (Fr.) 9.44	INTERR.	FR.
BACK, Anne Elisabeth	260862	F		24	Member,NSDAP,Resides at Johannstr.44,Trier (Ger.),L.O.D.N.A.O.D., Schweich (Ger.) 1.45	WITNESS	U.S.
BACK, Peter	121065	M	Ger.	09-10	Tailor,Civilian,Preist (Ger.) 8.44	MURDER	U.S.
BACKA	72669	M		10	Cpl.and employee,Army and Civilian,C.C.BE 2 Bitterfeld (Ger.)10.43-45	TORTURE	U.K.
BACKAUS, Helmut	260395	M	Ger.		Pvt.,157 Bavarian Res.Div.,Massif du Vercors,Isere Drome (Fr.) 7.-8.44	MISC.CRIMES	FR.
BACKAUSEN	196154	F			Doctor,Institut of Anatomie,Strasbourg (Fr.) 40-44	MISC.CRIMES	FR.
BACKE, Hans	301921	M	Ger.		Kapo,C.C.Auschwitz (Pol.) 41-45	BRUTALITY	POL.
BACKF, Hermann	136564	M			Formely Secr.of State,Public official Ministry of Economics,Berlin (Ger.)	MURDER	U.K.
BACKENHOFF	166947	M	Ger.		Cpl.,Feldgendarmerie,Montigny en Vesoul (Fr.) 7.44	MURDER	FR.
BACKENHUS, Johann Georg	307031	M	Ger.		Crim.-asst.,Staatspolizei Oldenburg from 6.3.37 until arrest on 1.6.45 Oldenburg (Ger.) 9.39-5.45	TORTURE	POL.
BACKER	157134	M	Ger.		Oberschrfuehrer SS,C.C.Buchenwald (Ger.) 4.44	TORTURE	U.K.
BACKER	166946	M			Sgt.,A.O.K.,La Rochette (Fr.) 8.44	MURDER	FR.
BACTER	168614	M			Adj.,Commandantur,Crest,Drome (Fr.)	MURDER	FR.
BACKER, Franz	125126	M	Ger.		Rottfhr.,SS,C.C.Bitterfeld-Railway (Ger.) 12.43	TORTURE	U.K.
BACKER, Heinrich	134737	M	Ger.		Baker,Civilian (Ger.)	TORTURE	U.S.
BACKER, Otto	148527	M			Civilian Chief Guard Rheinhausen (Ger.)	MURDER	U.S.
BACKHAUS	196081	M			Adj.,11 Pz.Div.F.P.Nr.24259 and 38260,Southof Turnes (Fr.)	MURDER	FR.
BACKHAUS, Erich Hermann	257586	M	Ger.		Employee,C.C.Nordhausen (Ger.)	MURDER	U.S.
BACKHOLTZ	259614	M	Ger.	06	Principal:Inspector,Railway:at Agen (Lot and Garonne),Aude,Herault, Gard (Fr.) 8.44	MISC.CRIMES	FR.
BACKIN, Steffan	72666	M			SS Totenkopf,C.C.Struthof (Fr.)	TORTURE	FR.
BACKLAUS, Gustav	250071	M	Ger.	04	Pvt.,Juvisy-Seine (Fr.) 8.44	INTERR.	FR.
BACKLAUS, Helmut	166945	M	Ger.		Cpl.-chief,197 D.A.,Vercheny la Plaine (Fr.) 7.44	MURDER	FR.
BACKLER	300009		Ger.		Member,SD,Groningen,Drente (Neth.) 43-45	MISC.CRIMES	NETH.
BACKMEYER	257587	M	Ger.		SS-Adj.,C.C.Mauthausen (Aust.) 9.42	MURDER	BEL.
BACRISCHECK (or BABRISCHECK)	142325	M			SS-Stabsgefreiter	TORTURE	U.S.
BADAEUS	250074	M	Ger.		Lt.,12 Div.SS Hitler Jugend,Ascyu (Fr.) 4.44	INTERR.	FR.
BADE	29751	M	Ger.		Ogefr.,Feldgendarmerie,Gestapo,Josselin (Fr.) 7.-8.44	MURDER	FR.
BADE	139827	M	Ger.		Capt.,Stalag X B,Sandbostel (Ger.) 5.45	MISC.CRIMES	U.S.
BADEN	176557	M	Ger.		Officer,C.C.,SS,Sachsenhausen (Ger.)	TORTURE	FR.
BADEN	300983	M	Ger.		N.C.O.,Camp III,S.S.Oranienburg-Sachsenhausen (Ger.) 42-45	MURDER	FR.
BADENTH, Anton	257755	M			Schfhr.,SD,Tromsoe (Nor.) 44	MURDER	NOR.
BADER	50	M	Ger.		Lt.General,9C Div.Mot.Inf.,Savoie (Fr.) 8.44	MURDER	FR.
BADER	141346	M	Ger.		Lt.,Stalag 357,C.C.Fallingbostel (Ger.) 4.45	MISC.CRIMES	U.K.
BADER	143320	M			Hptsturmfhr.,SS Totenkopf,Buchenwald (Ger.) 44	BRUTALITY	FR.
BADER	257588	M			Rottfhr.,SS,C.C.Dachau,Muehldorf (Ger.)	MURDER	U.S.
BADER	260358	M	Ger.		SS-Guard,SS,slave labour camp,Botn near Rognan (Nor.) 8.42-45	MURDER	YUGO.

BAD-BAK

NAME	C.R.FILE NUMBER	SEX	NATIO-NALITY	DATE OF BIRTH	RANK OCCUPATION UNIT PLACE AND DATE OF CRIME	REASON WANTED	WANTED BY
BADER,Ernst	193970	M	Ger.		Police-inspector,SS-Hptsturmfhr.,Gestapo,SD,Prag (Czech.) 39-45	MURDER	CZECH.
BADER,O.	300010	M	Ger.		Purchaser of factory "De Amstel",Waalwijk and Heusden (Neth.) 3.43-10.44	PILLAGE	NETH.
BADER,Paul	51	M	Ger.		Army,Artillery,General der Artl.Serbien,Beograd and Valjevo (Serb.) 41-43	MURDER	YUGO.
BADER,Rudolph	128027	M			Kampfgruppe officer	MURDER	U.S.
BADSTDT,Adolph	196153	M	Ger.		Commandant,Jard sur Mer (Fr.) 1.44	WITNESS	FR.
BADING	124503	M	Ger.	10	Lt.,Parachute-Regt.,(Fr.) 12.44	MISC.CRIMES	U.S.
BAIMANN	194805	M	Ger.		SS-Obersturmfhr.,C.C.Lublin (Pol.) 40-44	MURDER	POL.
BADSTUBNER,R.	192801	M	Ger.		Schupo,Stalag,Falstad (Nor.) 41-44	MURDER	NOR.
BAECHLER,Alois	139841	M	Ger.	04	Pvt.,Medical-corps,near Heilbronn (Ger.) 3.45	WITNESS	U.S.
BAECKER	259176	M	Ger.	85	SS-Hptsturmfhr.,commandant,C.C.Dachau (Ger.) 42-45	MISC.CRIMES	YUGO.
BAECKER,Ilse	301922	F	Ger.		Private secretary,Fa.Franz Reible,N.J.Menko & Coy.Ltd.,"Twentse Textil maatschappij",M.van Dam en Zonen ,Textilfabriken, Enschede (Neth.) 41-45	PILLAGE	NETH.
BAECKERS	126524		Ger.		Civilian,Kriegsgefangenen-Arbeitskdo.,C.C.Kohlscheid (Ger.) 41-44	TORTURE	U.S.
BAEDTKE	133763	M	Ger.		Sgt.,Military,guard,prison-camp,Berlin-Tegel (Ger.) 11.43-5.44	TORTURE	U.S.
BAEHR	168628	M	Ger.		SS-Sturmfhr.,C.C.Oranienburg (Ger.) 39-44	MURDER	POL.
BAEHR	172912	M	Ger.		Pvt.,Inf.Landesschuetzen-Bn.789,Sinzig (Ger.) 12.41	TORTURE	U.S.
BAEHREL,August	250072	M	Ger.	12.12.25	Pvt.,558 Gren.Regt.,13 Coy.,Bruay-en-Artois (Fr.) 9.44	INTERR.	FR.
BAEHSLER	259686	M	Ger.		Maj.-Gen.,242 Inf.Div.,Panteves Var (Fr.) 7.44	MURDER	FR.
BAEKER	36674	M	Ger.		Cpl.,Army,Stalag XX A,Thorn (Pol.)	BRUTALITY	U.K.
BAENENER	250019	M	Ger.		Member,G.F.P.of Lille Nord (Fr.) 40-44	MURDER	FR.
BAENSCH,Otto	131143	M	Ger.	17. 4.13	Pvt.,Stabs-Coy.Wolga Tataren-Bn.627,Quaregnon (Bel.) 9.44	MURDER	BEL.
BAER	125122	M			Sturmbannfhr.,SS,C.C.Auschwitz (Pol.) 42-44	TORTURE	U.S.,FR.
BAER	125123	M	Ger.		Gen.,Army,Oberkdo.,Dax (Fr.) 6.44	MURDER	FR.
BAER	125125	M	Ger.		Cmdt.,Stalag Luft VII,Bankau (Ger.) 12.44	MURDER	U.K.
BAER	130098	M			Usturmfhr.,SS,C.C.Dora Mittelbau,Nordhausen (Ger.)	MURDER	U.S.
BAER	157131	M	Ger.	15	Member,Gestapo,Innsbruck (Aust.) 4.45	MURDER	U.S.
BAER	162262	M	Ger.		Cpl.,Stalag 383,Hohenfels (Ger.)	MISC.CRIMES	U.K.
BAER	196152	M	Ger.	11 - 17	Osturmfhr.,SS,Bruttig-Treis (Ger. 3.-5.44	MURDER	U.S.
BAER	231069	M	Ger.	00	SS-Hptscharfhr.,SD-Aussenstelle,Zweibruecken (Ger.)	MISC.CRIMES	bOV.UN.
BAER	305873	M	Ger.		Usturmfhr.,C.C.Oranienburg (Ger.) 39-45	MURDER	CZECH.
BAER,Karl	191901	M	Ger.		Male-nurse,Army,St.Hilaire und St.Mesnier (Fr.) 8.44	MURDER	FR.
BAER,Richard	196151	M	Ger.		Osturmfhr.,C.C.Neuengamme (Ger.)	TORTURE	BEL.
BAER,Walter	195886	M	Ger.		Camp-cmdt.,C.C.,Schirmeck (Ger.) 40-44	MISC.CRIMES	FR.
BAERENS,Peter	140775	M	Ger.	13	Civilian,C.C.Mauthausen (Aust.)	MURDER	U.S.
BAERTHEL,Fritz	187451	M	Ger.		Mayor,public official,Meinheim near Gunzenhausen (Ger.)	TORTURE	BEL.
BAESCHEL,Ludwig	250020	M	Ger.		Inspector,SD,Alencon (Fr.) 40-44	MISC.CRIMES	FR.
BAESE	176424	M		09	Scharfhr.,SS,C.C.Dora,Nordhausen (Ger.) 45	MURDER	FR.
BAEUML,Ernst	261972	M	Ger.		Member,N.S.D.A.P.and Allg.SS,merchant,Bratislava (Czech.) 4.42 and 8.44-4.45	MURDER	CZECH.
BAEUML,Josef	193969	M	Ger.	3. 5.11	Member,Gestapo,Cheb (Czech.) 39-45	TORTURE	CZECH.
BAGANZ	250069	M	Ger.		Capt.,Geheime Feldpolizei,Lille (Fr.) 40-44	MISC.CRIMES	FR.
BAGANZ,Karl	250068	M		6. 9.23	Pvt.,Camp Ellrich,Nordhausen (Ger.)	MURDER	U.S.
BAHL	6288	M	Ger.	00	Sgt.,Hptwachtmeister,Feldstraflager,Reichsjustizministerium (Nor.)	MISC.CRIMES	NOR.,YUGO.
BAHLINGER	250070	M	Ger.		Hptscharfhr.,Gestapo,Limoges (Fr.)	INTERR.	FR.
BAHLKE	185619	M	Ger.		Sgt.,Feldgendarmerie,Lyon (Fr.)	MURDER	FR.
BAHNE,Fritz	300565	M	Ger.		Bandsman,Army,377 Inf.Regt.,Vinct-Meigem (Bel.) 5.40	MISC.CRIMES	BEL
BAHNER	135575	M	Ger.		Dr.,Arbeitskdo.119,Mankendorf (Ger.)	TORTURE	U.K.
BAHNER	169451	M	Ger.	95	Dr.,civilian,Odrau (Ger.)	TORTURE	U.K.
BAHNES,Willi	250059	M			SS-Uscharfhr.,1 Coy.,1 Regt.,1 SS-Pz.Div.,Malmedy (Bel.) 12.44	MURDER	U.S.
BAHNHOF	121066	F	Ger.	15	SS-Woman,overseer,Arbeitslager 101 Polte Department, C.C.Buchenwald (Ger.) 44-45	MISC.CRIMES	U.S.
BAHNMUELLER,Arnold	53	M	Ger.	08	SS-Osturmfhr.,II SS-Pz.Div.,Kampfgruppe "Wilde",Albine Montmorency (Fr.) 7.-8.44	MURDER	FR.
BAHNSEN,Hans	72660	M		18. 4.14	Osturmfhr.,Waffen-SS,15 Bde.,10 Pion.Coy.,Troytes (Fr.) 8.44	MURDER	FR.
BAHR	72679	M			Sturmfhr.,Waffen-SS,Schirmeck (Fr.)	TORTURE	FR.
BAHR	125128	M	Ger.		Uscharfhr.,SS,Neuengamme (Ger.)	MURDER	BEL
BAHR	189958	M	Ger.		SD,Lyon (Fr.)	MISC.CRIMES	FR.
BAHR,Willy	305991	M			Member of staff at C.C.Neuengamme (Ger.) 6.40-5.45	MURDER	U.Y.
BAHRE,Fritz	250061	M	Ger.		377.Jaeger-Regt.,Vinkt (Bel.)	INTERR.	BEL
BAIDNER,M.	192802	M	Ger.		Schupo,Stalag,Falstad near Drontheim (Nor.) 41-44	MURDER	NOR.
BAIER	133761	M		85	SS-Oscharfhr.,C.C.Buchenwald (Ger.)	MURDER	U.S.
BAIER	133762	M		14 or 15	SS-Hptscharfhr.,C.C.Buchenwald (Ger.)	TORTURE	U.S.
BAIER	185160	M	Ger.		Chief,SS,C.C.Sachsenhausen (Ger.)	MURDER	FR.
BAIER or BAYER	250062	M			Rottenfhr.,C.C.Dora,Nordhausen (Ger.)	MURDER	U.S.
BAIER	307034	M	Ger.		Capt.,member of Standgericht,1 Bn.,24 Regt.Fallschirmjaeger Hubner, 7 Div.Gen.Maj.Erdmann,Roermond (Neth.) 12.44-1.45	MURDER	NETH.
BAIER,Alfons	257543	M	Ger.		Senior of block,Camp Muehldorf (Ger.)	MURDER	U.S.
BAIER,Ernst	157129	M	Ger.	90	Oscharfhr.,Waffen-SS,C.C.Buchenwald (Ger.) 39-45	WITNESS	U.S.
BAIER or BAYER,Josef	250063	M		9. 9.23	Pvt.,Camp Ellrich,Nordhausen (Ger.)	MURDER	U.S.
BAIER,Kurt	176433	M	Ger.		N.C.O.,Lageraeltester,SS,C.C.Sachsenhausen (Ger.) 43-45	MURDER	FR.
BAIER,Otto	260466	M	Ger.	9. 1.08	Member,Gestapo,Abwehrstelle,Army,Counter-Intelligence-Kampfgruppe, Prag (Czech.) 40-45	MISC.CRIMES	CZECH.
BAIERL,Wilhelm	72659	M	Ger.		Adjutant,Army,Carcassone (Fr.)	MURDER	FR.
BAIERLEIN	9625	M	Ger.		Oscharfhr.,SS-supplies and feeding,C.C.Natzweiler (Fr.) 42	TORTURE	CZECH.
BAIERSDORF	261479	M	Ger.		Scharfhr.,SS,police-forces,Sluck (Pol.) 40-44	MURDER	POL
BAIL see BAYL							
BAILDON,Arthur	252096	M	Ger.	about 05	Capt.,Army,POW-camp,Bologna (It.) 6.44	MURDER	U.S.
BAILLER	261369	M			Capt.,19 SS-Regt.,Limoges Dijon (Fr.) 10.44	MURDER	FR.
BAILOR	149717	M			Hptsturmfhr.,SS,19 SS-Polizei-Regt.,Oberkrain (Yugo.) 5.41-3.44	MURDER	U.S.
BAISCH,Gerhard	135119	M			Toulouse,Compiègne,Tulle (Fr.) 3.-10.44	WITNESS	U.S.
BAKALA,Emil	261370	M			SS-Uscharfhr.,near Pfundres (It.) 6.44	MURDER	CZECH.
BAKER	306075	M			Member of staff Hamburg,C.C.Neuengamme (Ger.) 45	BRUTALITY	BEL.
BAKERSXI	250066	M	Ger.		Guard,prison,Hagen (Ger.)	MISC.CRIMES	NOR.
	12647	M	Ger.		SS-Osturmfhr.,SD-official,Finmark (Nor.) 11.44		

BAK - BAR

NAME	C.R.FILE NUMBER	SEX	NATIO-NALITY	DATE OF BIRTH	RANK	OCCUPATION	UNIT	PLACE AND DATE OF CRIME	REASON WANTED	WANTED BY
BAKHOUS	905654	M	Ger.		Cmdt., Marlag.POW.Camp, C.C.Bremen-Farge (Ger.) 1.43-4.45				MURDER	U.K.
BAKKA	185827	M	Ger.	98	Sgt., Gendarmerie, Luxembourg, Grand-Duchy, 40-45				MURDER	LUX.
BAKOLO, Paul	250067	M			Camp Harzungen, Nordhausen Harzungen (Ger.)				MURDER	U.S.
BAKOSCH	195885	M	Ger.		Staff-Member, C.C. Struthof-Natzweiler (Fr.) 40-44				MURDER	FR.
BALBACH, Ernst	196608	M	Ger.	15.11.07	Crim.Secret., Crim.Pol., Kaiserslautern (Ger.) 11.44				TORTURE	U.S.
BALCAR, Hugo	255572	M			Member, SS, Gestapo, Bratislava (Czech.) 44				MURDER	CZECH.
BALCAR, Josefina (nee PIPKA)	255502	F	Ger.		Member, Gestapo, Bratislava (Czech.) 44				TORTURE	CZECH.
BALDAUF, Arthur	150758	M	Ger.		Unterscharf., SS-Totenkopf-Standarte, C.C.Buchenwald-Weimar (Ger.)				TORTURE	U.S.
BALDERMAN	196255	M	Ger.		Lt., 1.Brandenburg-Regt., 16.Coy.				MISC.CRIMES	U.S.
BALDES	256980	M	Ger.		Cpl.,Military, 2.Nachr.Coy., Bolnes (Neth.) 5.45				INTERR.	NETH.
BALDEWEG	196597	M	Ger.		Sturmscharf., Gestapo of Lyon, Glieres (Fr.) 3.-4.44				WITNESS	FR.
BALDUF	250017	M	Ger.		Lt., Army, Montjean et Mesnil-Vallee (Fr.) 10.40				INTERR.	FR.
BALG, Johann	255087	M	Ger.	12. 2.98	Grenadier, SS, Nordhausen (Ger.)				MURDER	U.S.
BALIERSTADT	150756	M	Ger.		Lt.-Col., C.C. Altengrabe (Ger.) 4.45				MURDER	U.S.
BALINSKI, Wilhelm	134783	M			Cpl., 4.SS-Totenkopfsturmbann, C.C.Nordhausen Dora-Mittelbau (Ger.)43				WITNESS	U.S.
BALKE	162321	M	Ger.		Stabsintendant, SS, Lorient (Fr.) 44				MURDER	FR.
BALKE	196149	M			Lt., 3.Brandenburg-Regt.				SUSPECT	FR.
BALKE	261371	M	Ger.		Oberkapo, SS, C.C.Auschwitz (Pol.) 40-45				MURDER	POL.
BALLAENGER, Fritz	72655	M			Adjutant-Chef Artificier, Army, Roullens (Fr.) 8.44				TORTURE	FR.
BALLAORST	906451	M	Ger.		Oberscharf., SS, Kommandostab, C.C.Mauthausen (Aust.) 11.42-5.45				MURDER	U.S.
BALLAS	124286	M		99	Lt.-Col., Stalag 3 B Asst.C.D., C.C. Fuerstenberg (Oder) (Ger.) 44-45				MURDER	U.S.
BALLAUF, Werner	250014	M	Ger.		Standartenf., Chief of SS, Prag (Czech.) 11.39				INTERR.	CZECH.
BALLE	148241	M			Arbeitskommando, Rodelheim (Ger.) 43-44				TORTURE	FR.
BALLENDOWICZ	250015	M			Pvt., Camp Ellrich, Nordhausen (Ger.)				MURDER	U.S.
BALLER, Dietrich	257753	M	Ger.		Lt., Angouleme (Fr.) 44				MURDER	FR.
BALLNOV, Guenther	256894	M	Ger.	19. 1.23	Oberstandartenjunker, SS, Benesov (Czech.) 5.45				MURDER	CZECH.
BALLREICH	168629	M	Ger.		Leader, General Government, Abt.Treuhandwesen, Warsow (Pol.) 39-44				PILLAGE	POL.
BALLSTEDT, Paul	250016	M		18. 8.02	Rottenf., C.C.Harzungen, Nordhausen Harzungen (Ger.)				MURDER	U.S.
BALONIJ	131793	M		22	Sturmmann, SS, C.C.Hohrenheim (Ger.) 2.-5.45				MURDER	U.S.
BALOUSCHECK	250050	M	Ger.		Aspirant, Luftwaffe, Entzheim (Fr.) 42-44				TORTURE	FR.
BALS	250051	M	Ger.		Capt., Kreiskommandantur, Kragujevac (Yugo.) 10.41				TORTURE	YUGO.
BALS, Josef	187839	M			Sgt., Coastal defence, Oost-Duinkerke (Bel.)				MURDER	BEL.
BALSDORF (see BAZEDOW)	132603									
BALTES	192202	M	Ger.		Unterscharf., 9.SS-Panz.Div.Hohenstaufen, 4.Feld-Ers.-Bn., Neuville-les-Bois (Fr.) 8.44				MURDER	FR.
BALTRUSCH, Fritz	193968	M	Ger.	18. 4.96	Untersturmf., SS, C.C.Terezin (Czech.) 39-45				TORTURE	CZECH.
BALUK	29818	M	Ger.		Hauptscharf., SS, C.C.Buchenwald (Ger.)				TORTURE	BEL.
BALZ	124340	M	Ger.	03	Hauptscharf., SS, C.C.Belsen (Ger.) 3.45				MURDER	U.K.
BALZ	135217	M	Ger.		Major, Engineer-corps, Egersund (Nor.) 11.42				MURDER	U.K.
BALZ, Helmuth	141952	M	Ger.		Civilian, Heilbronn (Ger.)				MISC.CRIMES	U.S.
BALZER	54	M	Ger.		Major, Army, Panzer-Abtlg., Issy Les Moulineaux (Fr.) 8.44				MURDER	FR.
BALZER	124504	M	Ger.		Lt., C.C. Varaville (Fr.) 7.-8.44				MURDER	U.K.
BALZER	137738	L.	Ger.		Lt., 15.Panz.Gren.Regt.				WITNESS	U.S.
BALZER, Johannes	250052	M	Ger.		Capt., 607.Landessch.Bn., 2.Coy., Allendorf, Marburg (Ger.) 3.43-45				MURDER	YUGO.
BAMBA (see BAMBACH)	125130	M			Major, Fliegerhorst, Gerzat-Aulnat (Fr.) 7.44				MISC.CRIMES	FR.
BAMBER	72651	M			Col., Army, Abwehr, Special-Eds.,(CE)				TORTURE	FR.
BAMBERGER	1284	M	Ger.		Obersturmfuehrer, SS,				MURDER	U.K.
BAMBERGER	125101	M	Ger.		Obergefreiter, 877.Land.Schtz.Bn., Schladming-Steiermark,Leizen(Ger.)				TORTURE	U.K.
BAMBULA, Anton	255504	M		18. 8.06	SS-Scharfuehrer, Gestapo, Prag (Czech.) 39-45				MISC.CRIMES	CZECH.
BAMM	176373	M			Feldgendarmerie, (Fr.)				MISC.CRIMES	FR.
BAMME	250053	M	Ger.		Sgt., Field-police 924 of Bourgon, La Folatiere (Fr.) 6.44				MURDER	FR.
BAMSTEIN	192153	M	Ger.		Kommandantur, C.C. Antwerp.(Bel.) 42				TORTURE	BEL.
BAN, Josef	301661	M	Ger.		Baker's Asst., Neusiersberg near Mostar, 44				MURDER	YUGO.
BANA	150930	M	Ger.	95	Cpl., SS, C.C.Buchenwald (Ger.)				MURDER	FR.
BANACH	28728	M	Ger.		Major, 20.Army, Finmark (Nor.) 44				MURDER	NOR.
BANASCHEWSKI, Bruno	29750	M	Ger.		Feldgendarmerie und Gestapo, Josselin (Fr.) 7.44				MURDER	U.S.
BANCHWIEB, Helmuth	176376	M	Ger.		Capt., Ers.Bn.181, Bouchaux (Fr.)				PILLAGE	FR.
BANDERMANN, Heinz	131156	M	Ger.		Camp Personnel, C.C.Mauthausen (Aust.) 44-45				MURDER	U.S.
BANDISCH	190025	M			Cpl., Kreiskommandantur, Kragujevac (Yugo.)				MURDER	YUGO.
BANDLE, Franz	173645	M			SS, C.C.Muehldorf-Ampfing (Ger.) 6.44-4.45				MURDER	U.S.
BANEK	168630	M	Ger.		Public Official, Stellvertretender Reg.Praes., Inowroclaw (Pol.)				MISC.CRIMES	POL.
BANER	176974	M			Sgt., Fallsch.Jg.Regt. 2.Bn., Plouzane (Fr.)				MURDER	FR.
BANERE (nee RENTEEO)	250054	F	Ger.		Agent, S.D., Toulouse (Fr.) 11.42-8.44				MISC.CRIMES	FR.
BANES	173646	M			Oberscharf., SS, Labour Camp, Muehldorf-Ampfing (Ger.)				MURDER	U.S.
BANG	168691	M	Ger.		Dr., High Official, Umsiedlungs-Treuhand-Ges., Posen (Pol.) 44				MISC.CRIMES	POL.
BANGER, Karl	55	M	Ger.		Sgt., Army, Baudrigues (Fr.) 8.44				MURDER	FR.
BANGERT, Adolf	192152	M	Ger.		Oberpolier, Org.Todt, Firma Otto Menzel of Bittburg, 6.40 Alle-Sur-Semois (Bel.)				PILLAGE	BEL.
BANGHOFF	195810	M	Ger.		Cmdt. or Col., Georgian Legion,(Fr.) Mont Ferrier, 8.44				MURDER	FR.
BANHARDT	194932	M	Ger.		Rottenf., SS, S.D., Gorssel (Neth.) 9.44				WITNESS	NETH.
BANK	148242	M	Ger.		Agent, Gestapo, Stalag VI, C.C.Jegraf (Fr.)				MURDER	FR.
BANKEN, Robert	259728	M	Ger.		Teacher, Member, Gestapo, area Angers,Meine and Loire (Fr.) 42-44				MISC.CRIMES	FR.
BANNACH	250055	M			Lt., Nordhausen (Ger.)				MURDER	U.S.
BANNECK	1285	M	Ger.		N.C.O., S.D. Aussenkommando				MISC.CRIMES	U.K.
BANNERTH	301613	M	Ger.		Interpreter, Hindoustani, PG.H.Q. Poitiers, Vienne and Charente, 8.44				MURDER	FR.
BANNEWALD	250056	M	Ger.		Col., C.C.Buchenwald (Ger.)				BRUTALITY	FR.
BANNEWALD	300357	M	Ger.		Standartenf., C.C. Buchenwald (Ger.) 42-45				MURDER	FR.
BANNING	250057	M			Sgt., Camp Ellrich, Nordhausen (Ger.)				MURDER	U.S.,BEL.
BANSEN	250046	M	Ger.	13	Capt., Army, Brandenburg-Regt., (It.)				INTERR.	U.K.
BANTEL, Ernst	140776	M	Ger.	31.12.93	Verkaeufer, NSDAP, Kreisleiter, Welzheim (Ger.)				MISC.CRIMES	U.S.
BANTES	131141	M	Ger.		Supervisor, Strafgefangenenlager Rhein.Zellwolle A.G., Siegburg (Ger.)42				TORTURE	BEL.
BAPLICK or BABLIC	157130	M	Ger.	20	Unterscharf., Waffen-SS, C.C. Chrdruf-Buchenwald (Ger.) 4.45				WITNESS	U.S.
BAR or BEHR	306932		Ger.		Sturmbahnf., Head of Camp, C.C. Dora-Nordhausen (Ger.) 40-45				MURDER	BEL.
BARABAS, Karl	250047	M			Pvt., C.C.Ellrich, Nordhausen (Ger.)				MURDER	U.S.

NAME	C.R.FILE NUMBER	SEX	NATIO- NALITY	DATE OF BIRTH	RANK OCCUPATION UNIT PLACE AND DATE OF CRIME	REASON WANTED	WANTED BY
BARAN, Stanislas	150755	M			Civilian, Lauf (Ger.)	WITNESS	U.S.
BARANOWSKI, Hermann	56	M	Ger.		SS-Osturmfhr., C.C.Dachau, Sachsenhausen (Ger.) 40-43	PILLAGE	FR.
BARBARINO, Friedrich (or BARBA-RENO)	140774	M	Ger.		Oberstlt., Army, (It.)	MISC.CRIMES	U.S.
BARBE (see MEYER, Josef)	254684						
BARBI	256982		Ger.		Leader of the Crim.Secr., Sipo, Amsterdam (Neth.) 2.45	SUSPECT	NETH.
BARBIE (see BARBIER)	57						
BARBIER, Klaus (or BARBIE or BARBY or MAYER or KLEIN or FREITZ)	57	M	Ger.	04.09.15	Hptsturmfhr.or Osturmbannfhr., Gestapo-official (SD) Leiter of Abt. IV and E.K. (Aktion Jerzy Fichte), Lyon, Strassburg, Rhone, Paris (Fr.) 43-44	MURDER	FR.
BARBILON (or BARBION) Friedrich	262154	M	Ger.		Pvt., Unit L 50656 A, Steene (Fr.) 5.44	MURDER	FR.
BARBY (see BARBIER)	57						
BARCZYK, Georg	131275	M			C.C.Kapo, Jewischowitz, Auschwitz (Pol.) 43-44	MURDER	U.S.
BARD	260044	M	Ger.		Gendarm, Unit Russia-Germany Div. "Oberland", Massif du Vercors, Isere and Drome (Fr.) 7.-8.44	SUSPECT	FR.
BARDAS, Friedrich	250042	M	Ger.	21.1.14	Civilian, Member, SD, Olomouc (Czech.) 38-45	BRUTALITY	CZECH.
BARDIG	36673	M	Ger.		Gefr., Ldsch.Bn.714, Falkenberg, Modlin, Bromberg (Ger.) 6.43-1.44	MURDER	U.K.
BARDHOFF, Anton	157132	M			Civilian, Bad Neustadt (Ger.) 9.44	WITNESS	U.S.
BAREIS	257367	M	Ger.		Guard, Sgt., SS slave labour camp, Beisfjord, Narvik (Nor.) 6.-11.42	BRUTALITY	YUGO.
BARENS, Peter	131157	M	Ger.		Member of Camp Personnel, Mauthausen (Aust.) 41-45	MURDER	FR.
BARETSKI	195809	M	Ger.		Pvt., Blockfhr., SS, C.C.Auschwitz (Pol.) 40	MURDER	FR.
BARFUSS	132535	M	Ger.		Oberlt., Army, Ville-le-Marclet (Fr.) 8.44	MURDER	FR.
BARFUSS (or BAARFUS)	250640	M			Pvt., Camp Ellrich, Nordhausen (Ger.)	MURDER	U.S.
BARHRMANN, Max	72641	M			LNS 2 Coy, Lyon (Fr.) 8.44	MURDER	FR.
BARIEKERS	256861	M	Ger.		Schfhr., SD, Pontivy (Fr.) 44	MISC.CRIMES	FR.
BARIS (see BAROS)	258215						
BARITZ (see BAROS)	258215						
BARK (or BORK)	168692	M	Ger.		Leader, Abt.Forsten, Amt des Gouverneurs, Lwow, Galizia (Pol.)	MISC.CRIMES	POL.
BARK	300011	M	Ger.		Member, SD, Groningen Drente (Neth.) 43-45	MISC.CRIMES	NETH.
BARKE	72698	M	Ger.		Lt., Army, Coy Brandenburg, Pont St.Esprit (Fr.) 3.44	MURDER	FR.
BARKE (alias: BARKER)	261473			07	Senior W.O., Waffen SS 02836 D, near Libourne and Castillon, Dordogne (Fr.) 9. and 11.43	MURDER	FR.
BARKER (see BECKE)	178767						
BARKER	185399	M	Ger.		Lt.Col., Army, Art.Rgt., Boukola (Grc.) 2.44	MURDER	GRC.
BARKER	196146	M	Ger.		Adj., Waffen SS, Vercoiran (Fr.) 3.44	MURDER	FR.
BARKHAUS (see BACHAUS)	250081						
BARKHAUSEN	62149	M	Ger.		Lt.General, Army, War Economics Board	MISC.CRIMES	U.N.W.C.C.
BARKHOUS (see BACHAUS)	250081						
BARKOW	121068	M	Ger.		Capt., Army, C.C.Wulfen (Ger.) 3.45	MURDER	U.S.
BARLAN	250092	M			Sturmmann, Camp Rottleberode, Nordhausen (Ger.)	MURDER	U.S.
BARNAK	166944	M	Ger.		Staff Pvt., Army, Bechivillers (Fr.) 8.44	WITNESS	FR.
BARNARD	174551	M	Ger.	95	Capt., 354 Ldsch.Bn., C.C.Stg.XX A, Kleine Bartelsee (Pol.) 2.43	WITNESS	U.K.
BARNBECK (or BARMBECK)	194933	M	Ger.		Schfhr., SA, C.C.Epe and Vreden (Ger.) 10.44-2.45	TORTURE	NETH.
BARNEKERS	300012	M	Ger.		Sonderfhr., SD Pontivy, Morbihan, 4.-8.44	MISC.CRIMES	FR.
BARNETALD (see BARNEWALD)							
BARNEWALD	131158	M			Hptsturmfhr., SS, C.C.Mauthausen (Aust.) 41-45	MURDER	U.S.
BARNEWALD (or PARNAWALD)	133760	M			Sturmbannfhr., SS, C.C.Buchenwald (Ger.)	TORTURE	U.S.
BARNEWALD	131794	M	Ger.	87	Sturmbannfhr., SS, KL S III Thueringen (Ger.)	TORTURE	U.S.
BARNICKEL	193675	M	Ger.		Lt., Army, Sulmona (It.) 9.45	MURDER	U.K.
BARNICKEL	305816	M	Ger.		Lt.1 Aufkl.Abt.3 Coy 2 Col.XV Afrika Corps, St.Leger (Arlon) 9.44	MISC.CRIMES	BEL.
BARNICKEL, Paul	261115	M	Ger.	5.85	Senior Public Prosecutor, People's Court, Supreme Court, Berlin, Leipzig (Ger.)	SUSPECT	U.S.
BAROFSKY, Paul	162933	M	Ger.		Civilian, Ostend (Bel.)	PILLAGE	BEL.
BARON	307036	M	Ger.		Oschfhr., Serving at the Sub-Section of Gestapo Niort, Chatellerault, Charente (Fr.) 40-45	MURDER	FR.
BARON, Johann	173332	M	Ger.		Volksgruppenfhr., Zentral Abt.Kultur, Maribor (Yugo.) 4.41-44	MURDER	YUGO.
BARON, Michael	250033	M			Pvt., C.C.Bodungen, Nordhausen (Ger.)	MURDER	U.S.
BARONYCK	124505	M	Ger.		Pvt., Ldsch.Bn.439, Coselhsuen (Ger.) 1.45	TORTURE	U.K.
BAROS (or BARTIS, BARITZ, BARIS)	258215	M		01	Member, Caucasian Volunteer Bde., Udine (It.) 4.45	MURDER	U.S.
BAROW	259408	M	Ger.		SS-Oschfhr., Gestapo Poitiers, Antenne of Niort, (Fr.) 40-45	MISC.CRIMES	FR.
BARR	72634	M		14	Lt., SS, Schirmeck, Bierwart-Namur, (Bel., Fr.) 41 and 9.44	TORTURE	FR., BEL.
BARSA	300359	M	Ger.		Schreiber, C.C.Buchenwald (Ger.) 42-45	MURDER	FR.
BARSDORFF	301379	M	Ger.		Crim.O.Asst., Oslo (Nor.) 5.42	MURDER	NOR.
BARSTUHLE	121069	M	Ger.		Cpl., SS, C.C.Thekla (Ger.)	MURDER	U.S.
BART	157152				SS Das Reich 4 Rgt., Ustumfhr., Gradour-Glane (Fr.)	MURDER	FR.
BART (or BARTH)	188439	M	Ger.		Osturmfhr., SS Div. "Das Reich" "Der Fuehrer" 3 Coy, Gradour-Glane, 6.44 (Fr.)	MURDER	FR.
BARTE	165937	M	Ger.		Officer, Landwacht, Capestang (Fr.) 44	MISC.CRIMES	FR.
BARTE, Adolf	187452	M	Ger.	11.11.08	Employee, SD and Gestapo, Brno (Czech.) 39-45	MURDER	CZECH.
BARTECZKO	58	M	Ger.		Lager Deputy Commandant, C.C.Belzec (Pol.) 42-43	MURDER	POL.
BARTEL	198305	M	Ger.		Uschfhr., SS, Gestapo, Lyon (Fr.)	MURDER	FR.
BARTEL	173344	M	Ger.		Lt., Army, C.C.Graudenz (Pol.) 7.44	PILLAGE	U.K.
BARTEL	250646	M	Ger.		Osturmfhr., 84 Rgt.Landsturm, Rhenen (Neth.)	PILLAGE	NETH.
BARTEL, Erich	157133	M	Ger.		SS-Pvt., SS Arbeitskdo.418, Kl.Stangendorf, Marienwerder (Ger., Pol.)	TORTURE	U.K.
BARTEL, Johann	250648	M		30.1.99	Pvt., Camp Ellrich, Nordhausen (Ger.)	MURDER	U.S.
BARTELES	157135	M	Ger.		Capt., Gestapo, Brive (Fr.) 44	MURDER	FR.
BARTELL	125115	M	Ger.		Lt., Army, Inf., Graudenz (Pol.)	MURDER	U.K.
BARTELL, Heinz	166277	M	Ger.		Arbeitskdo., Stalag II B, C.C.Grspitz (Ger.) 8.43	MURDER	U.S.
BARTELS	20610	M	Ger.	09	SS-Uschfhr., Crini (Nor.)	TORTURE	NOR.
BARTELS, Otto	149357	M	Ger.		Civilian, Dornbusch (Ger.)	TORTURE	FR.
BARTELS, Rolf Ludwig August	185284	M	Ger.	29.12.07	SS-Mann, Quartermaster, C.C., Terecin (Czech.) 39-45	WITNESS	CZECH.

BAR - BAS

NAME	C.R.FILE NUMBER	SEX	NATIO-NALITY	DATE OF BIRTH	RANK OCCUPATION UNIT PLACE AND DATE OF CRIME	REASON WANTED	WANTED BY
BARTELOCHEN	257483	M	Ger.		Capt.,Kreiskommandant at Nis,Gradetin and Nis(Yugo.) 7.43	INTERR.	YUGO.
BARTENSTEIN	121070	M	Ger.		Civilian Kiew Institute Doctor, Kiew(Pol.)6.41-3.42	MURDER	U.S.
BARTESS	649726	M			Gestapo-Agent Berlin-Tempelhof(Ger.) 44	MISC.CRIMES	FR.
BARTFELD	256007	M	Ger.	05	Sgt., Feld-Kommandantur, Marseille(Fr.) 43-44	PILLAGE	FR.
BARTH	39632		Ger.		N.C.O.,Standort-Kommandantur de Chateau-Gontier(Fr.) 8.44	MISC.CRIMES	FR.
BARTH	124790	M	Ger.		Capt., Army, Laufen(Ger.) 12.44	MURDER	U.S.
BARTH	185400	M	Ger.		Blockfuehrer, SS, C.C. Gross-Rosen(Ger.) 42	MURDER	U.S.
BARTH	188062	M			Feldpost-Nr. 57205 E, Ugine(Fr.) 6.44	MURDER	FR.
BARTH (see BART)	188439						
BARTH	250042	M			Sturmmann, I SS Panzer-Regt.,9 Pz.Pi.Coy., Malmedy(Bel.) 12.44	MURDER	U.S.
BARTH	250644				Rottfhr., Camp Nixei, Nordhausen(Ger.)	MURDER	U.S.
BARTH	250650	M	Ger.		(Bel.)	MISC.CRIMES	BEL.
BARTH	259651	M	Ger.		Lt.,Clerk, Justice,Paris(Fr.) 6.42	WITNESS	FR.
BARTH, Ernest	250649	M	Ger.		Member, German Police, Ugine(Fr.) 6.44	MURDER	FR.
BARTH, Franz	256797	M	Ger.	11	Lt., Lidice(Czech.) 6.42	MURDER	CZECH.
BARTH, Georg	157136	M	Ger.		Staff-Sgt.,3 Coy. Kriegsgefangenenarbeits Bn.188,Brattholm(Nor.) 3.43	MURDER	NOR.
BARTH, Heinz	250645	M			Pvt., Camp Ellrich, Nordhausen(Ger.)	MURDER	U.S.
BARTH, Joseph	60	M	Ger.	17. 5.17	SS-Oschfhr., C.C. Maidanek(Pol.) 40-4.44	MURDER	POL.
BARTH, Margarethe	250643	F	Ger.	28. 2.92	SS-Helferin,State Service SS,Geisenheim(Ger.) 12.44-4.45	TORTURE	POL.
BARTH, Markus	148446	M	Ger.		Civilian,Ludwigshafen(Ger.)	MURDER	FR.
BARTH, Rudolf	150757	M	Ger.	2. 7.98	Oberfeldwebel,Army Landesschuetzen Ersatz-Bn.24,KL.Augsburg(Ger.)40-445	MURDER	U.S.
BARTH, Rudolf	255083	M	Ger.	2. 2.97	Oschfhr.,4 SS Totenkopfsturmbann,SS Camp-Sgt. of the Guard C.C.Dora (Mittelbau), Nordhausen(Ger.) 43-45	WITNESS	U.S.
BARTHE	196145	M	Ger.		Police Man, SD-Kdo."Wenger",Baccarat & E(Fr.) 44	MURDER	U.K.
BARTHEL, Herbert	124839	M	Ger.	21	Stalag IV F, Chemnitz 10.43-3.45	TORTURE	U.K.
BARTHEL, Konrad	1288				Hauptfeldwebel, Army,194 Gr.,1 Coy.	MURDER	U.K.
BARTHEL, Wilhelm	11209	M	Ger.		Pvt., Ersatz-Abt.,1 Art.Regt., St.Jean Au Doigt(Fr.) 6.44	RAPE	FR.
BARTHELMES, Erich	72621	M	Ger.	15	Hptschfhr.,SS, SD,Section IVB Anti Jews,Lyon(Fr.) 6.-8.44	MISC.CRIMES	FR.
BARTHELEMY	72623	M			W.O.,Base Aerienne Cie aerienne III-90,Salon(Fr.)	MURDER	FR.
BARTHELL	194108		Ger.		Capt.,5 Bn.,Land.Schuetzen 396 Stalag 4A, Kdo.948, C.C. Ottendorf, Okrilla(Ger.)	MURDER	FR.
BARTHELMESS	131795	M	Ger.		Major, Army Oflag XIIIB, KL.Hammelburg(Ger.)	MURDER	U.S.
BARTHELMOS	61	M			Hptsturmfhr.,SD, Gestapo,Lyon(Fr.) 7.44	MURDER	FR.
BARTHELMUS, Erich	225166	M	Ger.	15	SS-Hptschfhr., Member SS,SD-Gestapo. 44	MURDER	U.S.
BARTHEIS	62	M			Dr., SS-Hptsturmfhr., SS-Polizei Regt.Todt, Payzac(Fr.) 2.44	MURDER	FR.
BARTHEIS	138234	M	Ger.	02	Sturmbannfhr.,SD, Massidan(Fr.) 2.44	MURDER	FR.
BARTHEIS	250691	F	Ger.		Member Gestapo,Limoges(Fr.)	MISC.CRIMES	FR.
BARTHEIS	300438	F	Ger.		Wife of Dr.Barthels, Gestapo Limoges,Hte.Vienne-Gironde(Fr.) 40-45	MISC.CRIMES	FR.
BARTHOLD	188431	M		94	Capt.,5 Coy.,Landesschuetzen Bn.396,Stalag IVA,Dresden(Ger.) 3.45	MURDER	CAN.
BARTHOLOMAEI	172870	M	Ger.		SS-Sturmbannfhr.,19 SS Pz.Gren.Regt.,Palmersheim(Ger.) 12.44	MURDER	U.S.
BARTHOLOMAI	126729	M	Ger.		SS-Omdt.,9 SS Panzer-Gren.-Div.Hohenstaufen,Neuville-Les-Hois (Fr.) 8.44	MURDER	FR.
BARTHUFF, Karl	72731	M	Ger.		Pvt., Army,Waffen-SS,6 Mtn.Div. Bakery Coy.	TORTURE	U.S.
BARTIG	63	M	Ger.		Army Lance Cpl. Stalag 2XA. 4-6.43	MURDER	U.K.
BARTIS (see Baros)	258215						
BARTITSCH	124956	M	Ger.		Wachtmeister, Police C.C.Bremen-Farge(Ger.) 6.43	TORTURE	U.K.
BARTL, Alois	258095	M	Ger.	24. 2.10	Employee, Gestapo, Olomouc(Czech.) 42-45	MURDER	CZECH.
BARTLE	178282	M	Ger.	00	Obersteiger,Stalag VIIIB,Beuthen(Ger.) 41	TORTURE	U.K.
BARTLE	259696	M	Ger.		Gendarm, Bde. of Oberhergheim Haut-Rhin(Fr.) 40-45	BRUTALITY	FR.
BARTLER	123924	M	Ger.		Lt., Camp Graudenz(Pol.) 7.44	MURDER	U.K.
BARTLING	120566	M	Ger.		NSDAP-Member Gniezno,Oleszyn(Pol.)	LOOTING	POL.
BARTLING	186482	M	Ger.		Sturmbannfhr., Cmdt.,12 SS Panz.Div."Hitler Jugend", near Caen, Tourouvre (Fr.)6.-8.44	TORTURE	CAN.,FR.
BARTMANN, Ernst	250630	M	Ger.	28. 1.79	Clerk, Civ.Factory, N.Etynk(Czech.) 5.45	PILLAGE	CZECH.
BARTMANN, Josef	116709	M			Civilian, C.C.Flossenburg(Ger.) 44-45	MURDER	U.S.
BARTOLEIT	196132	M	Ger.		Chief, NSDAP, Barcelona(Spain.) 43-44	MISC.CRIMES	BEL.
BARTOLOMAE	121071	M			Major, Army SS 9 Pz.Div.,Arnheim,Pz.Gren.Regt.,Arnheim(Neth.)	MURDER	U.S.
BARTON, Paul	140872	M	Ger.	8. 6.91	Gendarmerie Elten(Ger.) 9.44	MURDER	CAN.
BARTOSCH, Josef	250633	M	Ger.	18.12.11	Civ.-Employee, Gestapo, Breclav(Czech.) 39-45	MISC.CRIMES	CZECH.
BARTOSZYNSKI, Joseph	191241	M	Ger.		Pvt.,9 Gren.Res.Regt., Magny-Danigon(Fr.)	MURDER	FR.
BARTOWITSCH, Hans	186249	M	Ger.		SS-Pvt., SS Leibstand."Adolf Hitler",Stavelot(Bel.)	MURDER	BEL.
BARTSCH	28729	M			Army-Pfarrer,Army Church Finmark(Nor.) 11.44	MURDER	NOR.
BARG	62368	M			Sturmmann,SS Panzer Abt.17,1 Coy.,St.Aubin Duperron(Fr.) 6.44	MISC.CRIMES	U.S.
BARTSCH	250632	M			Sgt.,Gendarmerie 924 of Bourjon, La Folatiere(Fr.) 6.44	MISC.CRIMES	FR.
BARTSCH	300980	M	Ger.		Capt.,Camp-Omdt. Oflag VI-C, Osnabrueck-Ewersheide(Ger.) 41-44	MURDER	YUGO.
BARTSCH	305817	M	Ger.		Pvt.,1 Aufkl. Abt.,9 Coy., 2 Col., XV Div. Afrika Korps, St.Leger(Arlon) 9.44	MISC.CRIMES	BEL.
BARTSCH, Erich	194935	M	Ger.	11	Bezirksoberwachtmeister, Police, Bressanone(It.)	MURDER	U.K.
BARTSCH, Hans	168633	M			C.C.-Warder, C.C. Sachsenhausen and Oranienburg(Ger.)	MISC.CRIMES	POL.
BARTSCH, Heinrich	162483	M			Gestapo, Bretagne-Morbihan,Hennebont(Fr.) 44	MURDER	FR.
BARTSCH, Werner	306931	M	Ger.		SS-Opl., C.C. Buchenwald(Ger.) 5.38-10.43	MURDER	BEL.
BARTZ	193390	M	Ger.		Pvt., 2 Coy.,PW, Werk Btty.206, Mosjoen(Nor.) 4.45	WITNESS	NOR.
BARTZ	250628	M			Rottfhr.,Camp Dora, Nordhausen(Ger.)	MURDER	U.S.
BARUSSEL	21402				SS 9 Div."Das Reich",Viensses-Barthes et Montastrui(Fr.) 7.44	MURDER	FR.
BARVITCH	193389	M			Capt.,Kriegsgefang.Arb.Bn.41 C.C.Nerlandsdal Christiansund(Nor.)41-45	TORTURE	NOR.
BARZ, H.	1287				Capt., H.G.Div.(16 Tp. 3 H.G.Div.)	MURDER	U.K.
BASCH	250626	M			Pvt., Camp Ellrich, Nordhausen(Ger.)	MURDER	U.S.
BASCHE, Dr.	250627	M			Civilian,Malomerice near Brno(Czech.) 39	MISC.CRIMES	CZECH.
BASEDO, Fritz alias:dit"Charly"	194725	M	Ger.	01	Member Gestapo, Savigny en Septaine(Fr.) 7.-8.44	MURDER	FR.
BASEDOW, Hans	194785	M	Ger.	04	Agent Gestapo, Savigny en Septaine(Fr.) 7.-8.44	MURDER	FR.
BASENKO	134785	M			SS-Scharfhr.,4 SS Totenkopfsturmbann, Dora Mittelbau,Nordhausen(Ger.)-45	WITNESS	U.S.
BASHOF	260045		Ger.		Chief, C.C. Dachau(Ger.) 42	MURDER	FR.
BASNER, Fritz	261983	M	Ger.	14. 2.11	SS-Mann,Dirlewanger-Bde.,Waffen-SS,Gren.Div.36,Warsaw and other(Pol.)-44	MURDER	POL.

BAS-BAU

NAME	C.R.FILE NUMBER	SEX	NATIO-NALITY	DATE OF BIRTH	RANK OCCUPATION UNIT PLACE AND DATE OF CRIME	REASON WANTED	WANTED BY
BASPT	21406	M			CC Madjanck (Pol.) 11.43	MURDER	FR.
BASQUITO (see TIERNEY, Jon)	39703						
BASSA, Wladislaus	132170	M			Pvt, Army, 922 Inf.Rgt., 4 Coy, Valognes (Fr.) 6.44	WITNESS	U.S.
BASSLER, Hans	31989	M	Ger.		Senatspraesident, Pub.Of., Dr., Litomerice (Czech.) 2.40	MURDER	CZECH.
BASSMAN	250635	M	Ger.		Dr., foundling home for Polish children, Laberweinting (Ger.)8.44-4.45	MURDER	POL.
BASSONPIERPE	151713	M	Ger.		Kommandantur Col., La Parade et Badaroux (Fr.) 5.44	WITNESS	FR.
BAST	196603	M	Ger.		Capt, Abergement de Varey (Fr.) 7.44	WITNESS	FR.
BAST, Walter	179796	M	Ger.	15	Uschfhr, SS Totenkopfverband, CC Gusen (Aust.) 44	WITNESS	U.S.
BAST, Willi	131159	M			SS Oschfhr, CC Gusen Mauthausen (Aust. (7.44)	MURDER	U.S.
BASTEIN	176430	M	Ger.		Hptschfhr, SS, Hirson (Fr.)	MURDER	FR.
BASTEK, Richard	133759	M			2 Army, 503 Bde, 10 Bttr., Hilden (Ger.) 4.45	WITNESS	U.S.
BASTIAN	191147	M	Ger.		Oberwachtmstr, Police, CC Kaisheim (Ger.)	MURDER	BEL.,CZECH,FR.
BASTIAN	189627	M	Ger.		Admiral (Praesident) Reichs-Kriegsgericht (Military Tribunal), Torgau (Ger.) 5.40- 43, 45	MURDER	FR.
BASTOBRE	250634	M	Ger.		Sgt, Pepingen (Bel.)	PILLAGE	BEL.
BASTUK	305818	M	Ger.		Cpl., 1 Aufkl.Abt., 3 Coy, 2 Col, XV Div. Afrika Korps, St.Leger (Arlon) 9.44	MISC.CRIMES	BEL.
BATENBROCK	257482	M	Ger.	14.10.09	Kapo, CC Dora, Nordhausen (Ger.)	BRUTALITY	FR.
BATHEL, Konrad	1288	M	Ger.		Inf.Rgt.194, Officer	MURDER	U.K.
BATLINER, Hans	21397	M		26. 6.16	K.D. Fl.H. Ber. 1,8, Aude (Fr.) 44	MURDER	FR.
BATTE	175704	M	Ger.		Officer, Stg.VI A, CC Hemer, (Ger.) 41-45	TORTURE	U.S.
BATTEL	125078	M			N.C.O. Arbeits-Kdo., Beuthen (Ger.) 42	TORTURE	U.K.
BATTENBROCK, Heinrich	194735	M	Ger.		Kapo, Blockaeltester, CC Mauthausen (Aust.)	TORTURE	FR.
BATZ (see BETZ)	307037				SS Wachtmstr, Falstad Slave Labour Camp Norway 42-43	MURDER	YUGO.
BATZER, Paul	232303	M	Ger.	00	Obersturmbannfhr, Fuehrungsnachrichten Rgt.500 SA, Zoppot (Pol.) 39	MISC.CRIMES	U.S.
BAUCH	72746	M		96	Adjutant, SA, Grenzpolizei, Roermond (Neth.) 9.44-10.44	MISC.CRIMES	U.S., NETH.
BAUCH	191832	M			Capt, SS, Gestapo, Paris (Fr.)	TORTURE	FR.
BAUCH	257480	M	Ger.	95	Plant Manager, Plant 2 Ghetto, Warsaw, Treblinka, Poniatowo(Pol.) 41-45	MURDER	POL.
BAUCH, Erich	134782	M			Pvt, 4 SS Totenkopfsturmbann, CC Nordhausen, Dora-Mittelbau(Ger)43-45	WITNESS	U.S.
BAUCHSPIES	142326	M			Sgt., SS, CC Flossenburg (Ger.)	TORTURE	U.S.
BAUCHWIEG, Helmut	169117	M	Ger.		Capt, Army, Les Bachaux (Fr.) 8.44	MURDER	FR.
BAUCKE, Rudolf	187446	M	Ger.		Crim.Secretary, SD and Gestapo, Brno (Czech.) 39-45	MURDER	CZECH.
BAUCKLE, Georg (or BUCKLEY, or BRUCKLE)	160232	M	Ger.	1905- 15	Osturmfhr,Chief,Gestapo,Tours,Angers (Fr.) 42-44	MURDER	FR.
BAUCKLOW, Fritz	163249	M	Ger.		Hptsturmfhr, Gestapo, St.Quentin, Rouvrew (Fr.) 7.-8.44	MURDER	FR.
BAUDACH	21395	M			Capt, Feld-Gend.(Commune de Moussouc) Fce., La Baffe (Fr.)	MURDER	FR.
BAUDACH	195824	M	Ger.		W.O., Army SS, Izon la Bruisse, Sederen (Fr.) 2.44	MURDER	FR.
BAUER	64	M	Ger.		Pvt, Army, L 20.368, Baudrigues (Fr.) 8.44	MURDER	FR.
BAUER	65	M	Ger.	93	Capt, Gestapo, Organisation Todt, Hazibrouck (Fr.) 8.44	MURDER	FR.
BAUER	66	M	Ger.		Sgt, Army, Tank Div., Issy les Moulineaux (Fr.) 8.41	MURDER	FR.
BAUER	67	M			Army Major, Field Kommandantur 755, Le Mans (Fr.) 40-44	LOOTING	FR.
BAUER	68	M	Ger.		Frontfuehrer, Organisation Todt official, Hazebrouck (Fr.) 5.44	MURDER	FR.
BAUER	1289	M	Ger.		Company Sergeant Major,11.Coy. 3.Bn.,999	MURDER	U.K.
BAUER	12983	M	Ger.		Crim.Asst. member of Dept.Staatspolizeileitstelle,Prague(Czech.)10.39	MURDER	CZECH.
BAUER	12419	M	Ger.		Chef der Gend., Munster (Fr.) 9.44	MURDER	FR.
BAUER	12420	M	Ger.		Lt, SS Charge Deportation Trani (Fr.) 7.-8.44	TORTURE	FR.
BAUER	21982	M			Sgt., 7 Army, 1 Coy, St.Die (Fr.)	LOOTING	FR.
BAUER	21989	M			Lt., SS, Sarrebrul (Ger.)	MURDER	FR.
BAUER	21992	M			Schfhr, "Das Reich", SS Div.2, Valence d'Ogen (Fr.)	MURDER	FR.
BAUER	28730	M	Ger.		Obersturmfhr, SS, 20 Army, Finmark (Nor.) 11.44	MURDER	NOR.
BAUER	29826	M	Ger.		Cmdt, Head of Aviation, Mont de Marsan (Fr.) 44	MURDER	FR.
BAUER	45568	M	Ger.		Engineer, Arbeitskommando, Muenchen (Ger.) 41-45	MURDER	FR.
BAUER	62153	M	Ger.		Dr., Chief, Ostgebietsministerium, Einsatzstab Rosenberg, Berlin (Ger.) 40-44	PILLAGE	U.S., FR.
BAUER	62367	M	Ger.		Lt., 497 Inf.Rgt (Germany)	MISC.CRIMES	U.S.
BAUER	124679	M	Ger.	00	Cmdt, Stalag III, Prague (Czech.), Sagan (Ger.) 3.44; 39-45	MURDER	U.K.
BAUER	125193	M	Ger.		Lt., Inf.Rgt. 497, Sars la Bruyere (Bel.) 9.44	MURDER	BEL.
BAUER	131160	M			Oschfhr, SS Pz.Div. Totenkopf, CC Mauthausen (Aust.) 41-45	MURDER	U.S.
BAUER	133757	M			SS-Trooper, CC Oetheim (Ger.)	TORTURE	U.S.
BAUER	134008	M	Ger.		Lt.,SS "Das Reich", Marcheken Famenne (Bel.) 9.44	MURDER	BEL.
BAUER	136184	M	Ger.		N.C.O., Feld-Gend., Verdun, Stenay (Fr.) 44	MURDER	FR.
BAUER	141847	M	Ger.		Pvt., 2,397 Lds.Schtz.Bn., Tiege (Ger.) 7.41	MURDER	U.K.
BAUER	144620	M		95	Contre Maitre, Organisation Todt	MISC.CRIMES	FR.
BAUER	144668	M			Wittersburg (Ger.)	MURDER	FR.
BAUER	147199	M	Ger.		Kampfgruppe "Wilde", 11 Pz.Div., South-West France 44	MURDER	FR.
BAUER	149633	M		13	Gestapo, Cannes (Fr.)	MURDER	FR.
BAUER	149636	M			Sgt, Army, SS Rgt."Der Fuehrer", 1 Bn, Lot (Fr.)	TORTURE	FR.
BAUER	149637	M			Chef, Gend. Munster (Ger.) 8.44	MURDER	FR.
BAUER	149639	M			Cmdt, Air Force, Fliegerhorst-Kdtr.40,XIII, Cere-Grenade s-Adout(Fr.) 6.-8.44	MURDER	FR.
BAUER (see BAUES)	157143						
BAUER	166943	M	Ger.		Oberjaeger, Jaeger-Rgt., Bachivillers (Fr.) 8.44	WITNESS	FR.
BAUER	167631	F	Ger.		Civilian, Einsatzstab Rosenberg, Paris (Fr.) 44	PILLAGE	FR.
BAUER	167632	M	Ger.		Untersturmbefehlshaber, Sipo, Marseille (Fr.) 44	PILLAGE	FR.
BAUER	173112	M			CC Schirmeck, Rotenfels (Fr.)	MURDER	U.K.
BAUER	176427	M	Ger.		Blockaeltester, CC Sachsenhausen (Ger.) 43-45	MURDER	FR.
BAUER	176428	M			Lt., Uschfhr, SS, Hirson (Fr.)	MURDER	FR.
BAUER	185159	M			Sgt., Army, Condom (Fr.)	MURDER	FR.
BAUER	185622	M			Col., Army, Quatre-Vent (Fr.) 9.44	MURDER	FR.
BAUER	185834	M	Ger.		Engineer, firm of Dr.Hans Heymann, Hochstetten (Ger.)	TORTURE	GRC.
BAUER	187447	M	Ger.		Capt, Air Force, Air Port, De Mok near Den Burg (Neth.) 4.45	MURDER	NETH.
BAUER	188061	M			Lt., SS, 8.44	TORTURE	FR.
BAUER	191740	M			Hptsturmfhr, SS Div."Das Reich", Marche and Famenne (Bel.) 9.44	MURDER	BEL.
BAUER	191846	M			Sturmscharfhr, SS Gestapoamt 43	TORTURE	NOR.
BAUER	193387	M			Bauleiter Organisation Todt, Drag (Nor.)	TORTURE	NOR.

BAU-BAU

NAME	C.R.FILE NUMBER	SEX	NATIO-NALITY	DATE OF BIRTH	RANK OCCUPATION UNIT PLACE AND DATE OF CRIME	REASON WANTED	WANTED BY
BAUER	194109	M	Ger.		Lt., Army, Loire and Ampuis (Fr.) 8.44	MURDER	FR.
BAUER	194721	M	Ger.		Pvt.,Feldgendarmerie, Ploermel (Fr.) 6.44	TORTURE	FR.
BAUER	194803	M	Ger.		Lt., Army Abwehr - Funkabwehr, Averoff Prison Athens (Grc.) 43-44	MISC.CRIMES	U.K.
BAUER	195881	M	Ger.		Sturmfhr., SS, chief of Convoy, Royallieu (Fr.) 41-45	MURDER	FR.
BAUER	195882	M	Ger.		Capt., S.D., assistent to Capt. Knorr, Amsterdam (Neth.) 12.40	MISC.CRIMES	NETH.
BAUER	250623	M	Ger.		Sgt., Glageon (Fr.) 9.44	WITNESS	FR.
BAUER	250625	M	Ger.		Sgt., Pepingen (Bel.) 2.44-9.44	PILLAGE	BEL.
BAUER	255563	M	Ger.		Lt., 25.Div. Coy.stat.at La Roche, Calsis, Servanches (Fr.) 3.44	BRUTALITY	FR.
BAUER	262147	M	Ger.		Capt., Horsching (Aust.) (L.O.D.N.A.O.D.) 4.45	SUSPECT	U.S.
BAUER	300169	M	Ger.		Lt.,1.Russo-Ger.Unit at Chaumont Haute-Marne,Ain-Departm.(Fr.) 7.44	MURDER	FR.
BAUER	301924	M	Ger.		Capt.Lt., 3-10 M.K.A. 8.Zug, Texel (Neth.) 4.45	MURDER	NETH.
BAUER	305819	M	Ger.		Cpl., 1.Aufkl.Abt. 3. Coy. 2.Col. XV.Div. Afrika-Korps, St.Leger (Arlon) 9.44	MISC.CRIMES	BEL.
BAUER	306856	M	Ger.	about 13	Pvt. Guard, in charge on 16.7.41 of Tiege Labour Coy. at Marienburg, Stalag XX B, Marienburg (Ger.) 7.41	MURDER	U.K.
BAUER	307038	M	Ger.		SS-Osturmbannfhr.,Falstad Slave Labour Camp (Nor.) 42-43	MURDER	YUGO.
BAUER, Adolphe	166942	M	Ger.		Feldgendarm, Feldgendarmerie, Maix (Fr.) 8.44	MURDER	U.K.
BAUER, Alfred	192803	M	Ger.		Schupo, Stalag, C.C. Falestad nr.Drontheim (Nor.) 41-44	MURDER	NOR.
BAUER, Alois	131797	M	Ger.		Buergermeister Civ., Vicinity of Nammering (Ger.) 4.45	WITNESS	U.S.
BAUER, Emil	261982	M	Ger.	14..8.97	SS-Mann, Waffen SS,Gren.Div.36, Dirlewanger-Bde., Warsaw and other, (Pol.) 40-44	MURDER	POL.
BAUER, Esau	141345	M	Ger.		Army, Kazemark Krs. Danzig (Pol.)	MISC.CRIMES	U.K.
BAUER, Felix (see LANGELOH, Wilh.)	256590						
BAUER, Franz	21390	M		22	Army, 1.Coy. 1.Section, Condom, Oradour (Fr.)	MURDER	FR.
BAUER, Franz	131796	M		91	Gestapo, Pelhrimov (Czech.) 39-45	MISC.CRIME	CZECH.
BAUER, Franz	140770	M	Ger.		Blockleiter,Kriegsgefangenen-Arbeitskommando Guard,Nuernberg (Ger.)	TORTURE	U.S.
BAUER, Franz	167633	M	Ger.		SS-Adjutant,1.Pz.Div."Das Reich",1.Bn. 1.Coy.,Cradour-Glane (Fr.) 6.44	MURDER	FR.
BAUER, Franz	192283	M		6. 8.14	Fondateur, NSDAP, Vetrni Distr.Cesky Krumlov (Czech.) 39-45	MISC.CRIMES	CZECH.
BAUER, Frayer	139107	M	Ger.		Blockleiter, foreman, NSDAP, wholesale, Nuernberg (Ger.)	TORTURE	U.S.
BAUER, Friedrich	150762	M		27.11.88	Civ. Member NSDAP, Welzheim (Ger.) 8.44	TORTURE	U.S.
BAUER, Friedrich	185282	M	Ger.	12	SS-Usturmfhr., Crim.Commissar, S.D., Gestapo, Prague (Czech.) 39-44	MURDER	CZECH.
BAUER, Hans	187629	M	Ger.	14	Flakeinheiten Anti-aircraft Wehrmacht Camp, Kreis St.Goar (Ger.) 12.44	MURDER	U.S.
BAUER, Heinz see BUCKO,Heinr.	260495						
BAUER, Helmut	192687	M	Ger.	14.11.20	Reichs-Justizministerium,Strafgefangenenlager Nord, Finnmark (Nor.)	MURDER	NOR.
BAUER, Jacob	134781	M		29. 2.08	Pvt.Guard,4.SS-Totenk.Sturmb.CC.Nordhausen Dora-Mittelbau (Ger.) 43-45	WITNESS	U.S.
BAUER, Jan	187449	M	Ger.		Kriminalkommissar, Gestapo and S.D., Brno (Czech.) 39-45	MURDER	CZECH.
BAUER, Jenny	261235	M	Ger.		Flyer, C.C. camp Ellrich Nordhausen (Ger.)	MURDER	U.S.
BAUER, Johann	192284	M		24. 4.13	Founder NSDAP, Vetrni Distr.Cesky Krumlov (Czech.) 39-45	MISC.CRIMES	CZECH.
BAUER, Johann	192526	M	Ger.	25. 3.93	Civ., Schussbach (Ger.) 3.45	TORTURE	U.K.
BAUER, Josef	172911	M	Ger.		Pvt., Army, Haussenstamm (Ger.) 2.45	MURDER	U.S.
BAUER, Josef	261234	M			Sgt., C.C. Camp Ellrich, Nordhausen (Ger.)	MURDER	U.S.
BAUER, Joseph	176559	M			Uscharfhr., SS, C.C. Schoerzingen (Ger.)	BRUTALITY	FR.
BAUER, Karl	31990	M	Ger.		Oberlandgerichtsrat, Public off., Litomerice (Czech.) 2.40	MURDER	CZECH.
BAUER, Karl	179154	M			Civ., Organisation Todt, C.C. Muehldorf, Ampfing (Ger.) 6.44-4.45	MURDER	U.S.
BAUER, Karl	253595	M			Flyer, Camp Ellrich, Nordhausen (Ger.)	MURDER	U.S.
BAUER, Karl	262020	M		3. 3.08	SS Mann, Waffen-SS,Gren.Div.36 Dirlewanger-Bde.,Warschau and other, (Pol.) 40-44	MURDER	POL.
BAUER, Krt.(or BOUWER)	306675	M	Ger.		Pvt. 331.Pion.Bn., 331.Inf.Div.,Mijnheerenland (Neth.) 5.45	PILLAGE	NETH.
BAUER, Kurt	150765	M			Civ., Aufhausen (Ger.) 7.44	WITNESS	U.S.
BAUER, Kurt	190681	M	Ger.		Oberfeldwebel, Army, St.Andries,Varsenare,Bruegge (Bel.) 9.44	MURDER	BEL.
BAUER, Leo	250622	M	Ger.		Unit "Birkerdorff", St.Laurent (Fr.) 8.44	TORTURE	FR.
BAUER, Otto	167680	M			Stellvertreter d.Gouverneurs, Publ.off., Lwow (Pol.) 39-44	MISC.CRIMES	POL.
BAUER, Otto	259697	M	Ger.	about 99	SS-Oscharfhr., Gestapo, Area of Angers, Maine and Loire (Fr.) 42-44	MISC.CRIMES	FR.
BAUER, Paul	173353	M	Ger.		Pvt., 12.Pz.Gren.Ausb. u.Ers.Bn., Anhee, Meuse (Fr.)	MURDER	BEL.
BAUER, Robert	250624	M	Ger.	7. 5.18	Pvt., 558.Gren.Rgt. 13.Coy., Bruay (Fr.) 9.44	MURDER	FR.
BAUER, Siegfried	195883	M	Ger.		Cdo.-chief, SS Arbeitskommando, Member NSDAP, Flossenburg (Ger.)	TORTURE	FR.
BAUER, Wilhelm	147200	M	Ger.		11. Pz.Div. (Fr.) 44	MURDER	U.S.
BAUER, Willy	29825	M		11	Gestapo, Cannes (Fr.) 44	INTERR.	FR.
BAUER, Willy	157142	M	Ger.		SS-Mann, SS Deutschland, Das Reich Div. 3.Rgt., Aiguillon (Fr.) 6.44	WITNESS	FR.
BAUER, Willy	194723	M	Ger.	12	Member, Gestapo, Mougins (Fr.) 7.44	MURDER	FR.
BAUERD	250612	M			Sgt., Stalag Luft IV, Gross-Tychow (Pol.) 6.44	WITNESS	U.S.
BAUERLEIN	250613	M			Flyer, Camp Ellrich, Nordhausen (Ger.)	MURDER	U.S.
BAUERMANN, Helmut	250614	M			Pvt., Camp Ellrich, Nordhausen (Ger.)	MURDER	U.S.
BAUERNFEIND	192285	M			Member NSDAP, C.C. Flossenburg (Ger.) 44-45	MURDER	U.S.
BAUERZWEID	250615	M	Ger.		Cpl., Army, Ihlowerfehn Distr. of Aurich (Ger.) 44	MURDER	YUGO.
BAUES or BAUER	157143	M		07	Lt., Gestapo, d'Angers (Fr.)	MURDER	FR.
BAUES	257481	M			Oscharfhr., SS, Muehldorf (Ger.)	WITNESS	U.S.
BAUESCHERT, Hans	172972	M	Ger.	12.12.01	Civ., Farm-worker, Sommerhausen (Ger.) 3.45	WITNESS	U.S.
BAUGER, Karl	157141	M			Adjudant, Army, Rouelens (Fr.) 8.44	MURDER	FR.
BAUGNER, Karl	149631	M			Adjudant-chief, Army	TORTURE	FR.
BAUHAM	131798	M	Ger.		SS, C.C. Vicinity of Erfurt (Ger.) summer 44	TORTURE	U.S.
BAUHOFER	135219	M			SS-Osturmfhr., S.D.	MURDER	U.K.
BAUHOFER	144682	M			Feldwebel, Feldgendarmerie Besancon (Fr.)	MURDER	FR.
BAUHOFER	177344	M	Ger.	12	Zugwachtmeister, Schutzpolizei, Elven (Nor.) 7.43	MURDER	NOR.
BAUKLOH or BAUKOH	69	M	Ger.		Capt., Gestapo, St.Quentin (Fr.) 10.43	MURDER	FR.
BAUNENECHT	144685	M			Gefreiter, Army, Unit 15258 B, Monthem (Bel.) 9.44	MURDER	BEL.
BAUNENECHT, Franz	250616	M			Rottfhr., Camp Ellrich, Nordhausen (Ger.)	MURDER	U.S.
BAUKOH (see BAUKLOH)	69						
BAUKOTTER, Heinz	194720	M	Ger.		SS-Lt., C.C. Mauthausen (Aust.)	MISC.CRIMES	FR.
BAUL	195879	M	Ger.		Member of staff, C.C. Struthof-Natzweiler (Fr.) 40-44	MURDER	FR.
BAULIG, Max	157139	M	Ger.	90	Uscharfhr., Waffen SS, Buchenwald (Ger.) 41-45	TORTURE	U.S.
BAULITZ	194780	M	Ger.		Lt., SS-Fuehrungsstab C.C. Nordhausen Dora-Mittelbau (Ger.) 43-45	WITNESS	U.S.
BAUM	144696	M			General, Beauftragter, Army, Breiy (Fr.) 8.44	MURDER	FR.
BAUM	250962	M	Ger.		Pvt. Military F.P. 24945, Maasbracht (Neth.) 12.44	MURDER	NETH.

NAME	C.R.FILE NUMBER	SEX	NATIO-NALITY	DATE OF BIRTH	RANK OCCUPATION UNIT PLACE AND DATE OF CRIME	REASON WANTED	WANTED BY
BAUM, Karl	259487	M	Ger.	30. 9.00	Chief of Admin and Crim.Reporter, Staff of BDS, Alsace, Cripo.-section, Wolfisheim Alsace (Fr.) 8.1944	MURDER	FR.
BAUM, Willy	144697	M			Cerisay (Fr.)	MURDER	FR.
BAUM, Willy	259407	M	Ger.		Unterscharfhr., Gestapo, Poitiers antenne of Niort (Fr.) 1940	MISC.CRIMES	FR.
BAUMANN	71	M	Ger.	12	Guard, C.C., Unterbuchsbau (Pol.) 9.39-10.39	MURDER	POL.
BAUMANN	1290	M			Lt., Police, 3.Bn.	MISC.CRIMES	U.K.
BAUMANN	12364	M	Ger.		Cpl., SS, C.C., Natzweiler (Fr.) 3.42-8.42	TORTURE	CZECH.
BAUMANN	137739	M			Lt., 15.Pz.Gren.Rgt.	WITNESS	U.S.
BAUMANN (see SIGFRIED)	152106						
BAUMANN	173111	M	Ger.		Staff of C.C., Schirmeck, Rotenfels (Fr.)	MURDER	U.K.
BAUMANN	174762	M			Pvt., P.o.W.-Arb.Bn.185, C.C., Aspfjord (Nor.)	TORTURE	NOR.
BAUMANN	176377	M			Professor, 7.Rgt.Artillerie, Res., Tours et Albertville (Fr.) 6.44	MURDER	FR.
BAUMANN	190026	M			Sonderfhr., Gestapo, Pozarevac (Yugo.) 1941-43	MURDER	YUGO.
BAUMANN	192196	M	Ger.		2.Coy., 3.Inf.Rgt., Navy, Queven (Fr.)	MURDER	FR.
BAUMANN (or MADERA)	250620	M	Ger.		Member, Gestapo, Liberec (Czech.) 1942	TORTURE	CZECH.
BAUMANN	306941	M	Ger.		Probably Waffen-SS, OFK 670, Gebiet Maubenge (Bel.) 1941-45	BRUTALITY	BEL.
BAUMANN, Charles	186471	M			Adjutant, Army, Ussel (Fr.) 10.44	MURDER	FR.
BAUMANN, Emil	72722	M	Ger.		Pvt., Waffen-SS, C.C., Struthof (Fr.)	MISC.CRIMES	FR.
BAUMANN, Erich	72726	M	Ger.		Sturmfhr., Waffen-SS, Struthof (Fr.) 44	MURDER	FR.
BAUMANN, Georg	255364	M	Ger.	02	Civilian, Essfeld near Wuerzburg (Ger.) 42-45	TORTURE	POL., FR.
BAUMANN, Georges	135933	M	Ger.	99	Secretary, Gestapo, Ruppertshutten, Wuerzburg (Ger.) 9.44	MURDER	U.S.
BAUMANN, Hans	187445	M	Ger.	17. 1.16	Employee, SD and Gestapo, Brno (Czech.) 39-45	MURDER	CZECH.
BAUMANN, Heinrich	135212	M		10	Secretary, Kripo, Ruppertshutten (Ger.) 9.44	MURDER	U.S.
BAUMANN, Hilde	257238	F	Ger.	21	Typist, Sipo, SD, Abt. IV B, Anvers (Bel.) 40	SUSPECT	BEL.
BAUMANN, Johann	250619	M		3. 6.03	Rottfhr., Camp Harzungen, Nordhausen (Ger.)	MURDER	U.S.
BAUMANN, Siegfried	195807	M	Ger.		Lt., Pressnig 169.V.B.R., Etobon (Fr.) 9.44	MURDER	FR.
BAUMANN, Walter	11211	M	Ger.		Pvt., Panzer-Gren.Rgt.111, Albine (Fr.) 6.44	MURDER	FR.
BAUMAST, Hans	151716	M	Ger.	16	Civilian, near Ebensee (Aust.)	WITNESS	U.S.
BAUMBACH	250923	M			Lt. Colonel, Stalag Luft IV, Gross-Tychow (Pol.) 6.44	WITNESS	U.S.
BAUMBACH, August	193258	M	Ger.	28. 5.09	Sturmmann, SS, C.C., Thekla (Ger.) 4.45	MURDER	POL., U.S.
BAUMEISTER	132599	M			Revier-Chef, C.C., Buchenwald (Ger.)	MURDER	FR.
BAUMEISTER (or BRAUER)	221413	M	Ger.	13	Pvt., Abwehr-Nachr.Rgt.506, Bad Wildungen (Ger.) 45	MISC.CRIMES	U.S.
BAUMEISTER	250618	M	Ger.	95	Sgt., Nuernberg (Ger.)	MISC.CRIMES	FR.
BAUMEISTER, Heinrich	250621	M		31. 1.05	Flyer, Camp Wolffleben-Harz, Nordhausen (Ger.)	MURDER	U.S.
BAUMEISTER, Heinz	157138	M	Ger.	03	Civilian, C.C., Buchenwald (Ger.)	WITNESS	U.S.
BAUMEISTER, Joseph (or BURMEOSTER)	179571	M	Ger.	13	Official, Gestapo, Sect.IV, Bensheim and Muenchen (Ger.) 44	TORTURE	U.S.
BAUMEISTER, Liselotte	262155	F	Ger.		Secretary, Gestapo, Section IV, Rennes (Fr.) 43-44	SUSPECT	FR.
BAUMER (or BOMMER)	189120	M			Hptscharfhr., SS, C.C., Dachau (Ger.)	MURDER	BEL.
BAUMERT	250961	M			Cpl., C.C. Ellrich, Nordhausen (Ger.)	MURDER	U.S.
BAUMGAERTEL	134778	M			Pvt.,Guard,4.SS-Totenkopf-Sturmbann, Conc.Camp, Dora-Mittelbau, Nordhausen (Ger.) 43-45	WITNESS	U.S.
BAUMGAERTNER	137000	M	Ger.	1. 9.10	W.O., Osturmfhr., SS, C.C., Flossenburg (Ger.) 42	TORTURE	U.S., FR.
BAUMGAERTNER	144701	M			Lt., (Cosaques) 360.Gr.Rgt., St.Laurent (Fr.)	TORTURE	FR.
BAUMGARD	195224	M	Ger.		Lt.Colonel, SS, C.C., Flossenburg (Ger.) 40-45	MURDER	POL.
BAUMGARGNER (see BAUMGARTNER)	62366						
BAUMGART	250959	M			Pvt., Conc.Camp Ellrich, Nordhausen (Ger.)	MURDER	U.S.
BAUMGART, Peter	190411	M	Ger.		Civilian, Wiesbaden (Ger.) 43-45	WITNESS	U.S.
BAUMGARTEN	129835	M			Kapitaen-Lt., Marine-Kuesten-Art.262, 5.Btty., Brest (Fr.) 9.44	MISC.CRIMES	U.S.
BAUMGARTEN	144702	M			Major, Freiw.Cosaquen Stamm-Rgt., Langres (Fr.)	MURDER	FR.
BAUMGARTEN	149340	M	Ger.		Capt., Abwehr, Stg.369, Kobierzyn (Pol.) 8.44	TORTURE	FR.
BAUMGARTEN	173333	M	Ger.		Director, Zentral-Abt. Kultur, Maribor (Yugo.) 4.41-44	MURDER	YUGO.
BAUMGARTEN	191882	M	Ger.	4.95 - 96	Capt., Stalag VIII A, C.C., rear Stalag VIII A (Ger.)	MURDER	U.S.
BAUMGARTEN	257589	M	Ger.		Camp-Leader, C.C. Dora, Nordhausen (Ger.)	BRUTALITY	FR.
BAUMGARTEN, Franz-Wilhelm	134779	M			Pvt.,Guard,4.SS-Totenkopf-Sturmbann, Conc.Camp, Dora-Mittelbau, Nordhausen (Ger.) 43-45	MURDER	U.S.
BAUMGARTEN, Wilhelm	167679	M			Upper-Forest-Master, Section-leader,Office of the Gen.Gouverneur 39-44	MISC.CRIMES	POL.
BAUMGARTEN, Willy	176423	M	Ger.		Waffen-SS, C.C., Dachau (Ger.) 44	MURDER	FR.
BAUMGARTI	172869	M			Pvt., Army, C.C. Leipzig - Torgau (Ger.)	TORTURE	U.S.
BAUMGARTL	176560	M	Ger.		Osturmfhr., SS, Bavaria (Ger.) 44-45	MURDER	CZECH.
BAUMGARTNER (or BAUMGARGNER)	62366	M	Ger.	95	Gend., Gendarmerie, Gernsbach (Ger.) 6.44	MURDER	U.S.
BAUMGARTNER	124506	M	Ger.	11	Osturmfhr., SS, C.C., Flossenburg (Ger.) 3.45	MURDER	U.K.
BAUMGARTNER	176149	M			Lt., Art.Rgt.7, Kommandantur, Tours and Albertville (Fr.) 6.44	MURDER	FR.
BAUMGARTNER	189112	M	Ger.		Hptscharfhr., SS, C.C., Dachau (Ger.)	MURDER	BEL.
BAUMGARTNER	191333	M	Ger.	00	Stabsfeldw., Feldzeug.Coy.51, Olga Troems Camp (Nor.) 3.45	MURDER	U.K.
BAUMGARTNER	192688	M	Ger.		Staff-Sgt., Army (Nor.)	MURDER	NOR.
BAUMGARTNER (see BUUMGARTNER)	254461	M					
BAUMGARTNER	261216	M			Cpl., 139.Arbeitsbereich Liège, 5.Ln.Rgt.211, Alleur-Lez-Liegev (Bel.) 9.44	MURDER	BEL.
BAUMGARTNER, Franz	250960	M	Ger.		Sgt., Gendarmerie (Bel.)	INTERR.	BEL.
BAUMGARTNER, Hans	193967	M	Ger.		Oscharfhr., SS, C.C., Terezin (Czech.)	TORTURE	CZECH.
BAUMGARTNER, Josef	157140	M	Ger.	30. 6.12	Civilian Policeman, Sgt., Rosenhein,Schlossberg (Ger.) 4.45	WITNESS	U.S.
BAUMGARTNER, Peter	11212	M	Ger.		Pvt., Panz.Gren.Rgt.111, Albine (Fr.) 6.44	MURDER	FR.
BAUMGARTNER, Stefan	144557	M		23. 1.22	Sturmmann, Geyer-SS-Div.8, Singen (Ger.)	MISC.CRIMES	FR.-
BAUMKETTER	185158	M	Ger.		Medicin-Chief, SS, C.C., Sachsenhausen (Ger.)	MURDER	FR.
BAUMKOTTER, Heinz	305781	M	Ger.		Hptsturmfhr., Sen.Medical-Officer, C.C., Sachsenhausen (Ger.) 1.40-4.45	MURDER	U.K.
BAUMKOTTNER	187668	M	Ger.	10	Osturmfhr., SS, C.C., Oranienburg Sachsenhausen (Ger.)	MURDER	U.K.
BAUMLER	166941	M	Ger.		Member, Fieldgend., Larochemiliay (Fr.) 8.44	PILLAGE	FR.
BAUMLER, Ernest	260436	M	Ger.	24. 8.02	Member, Freiw.Schutzstaff.in Slovakia, Leader, Deutsche Partei in Slovakia (Czech.) 9.42, 8.44-4.45	MISC.CRIMES	CZECH.
BAUQUELLAU	144703	M			Capt., SD, St.Quentin (Fr.) 44	MURDER	FR.
BAUR	195805	M	Ger.		H.S.F., C.C., Auschwitz (Pol.) 40	MURDER	FR.
BAUR	195806	M	Ger.		Member of Rum.Kdo., Gestapo, Vichy (Fr.) 10.43-9.44	MURDER	FR.
BAUR, Alb	141450	M	Ger.		Entreprise de Pillage des Biens des Juifs Chef D'entreprise 42-44	LOOTING	U.S.
BAUR, Oskar	144558	M			Blockchef, C.C., Buchenwald (Ger.) 44	MISC.CRIMES	FR.

BAU-BEC

NAME	C.R.FILE NUMBER	SEX	NATIO-NALITY	DATE OF BIRTH	RANK OCCUPATION UNIT	PLACE AND DATE OF CRIME	REASON WANTED	WANTED B
BAUR, William	196129	M	Ger.		Cpl.,3 Brandenburg Rgt.,Communanza (It.) 5.44		MISC.CRIMES	U.K.
BAUPAT	130088				Member,SS Planning Staff,C.C.Dora Mittelbau,Nordhausen (Ger.)		MURDER	U.S.
BAUROCHSE	134777	M			Cpl.,4 SS Totenkopfsturmbann,C.C.Dora Mittelbau,Nordhausen (Ger.)43-45		WITNESS	U.S.
BAUS (or BAUTZ)	162482	M	Ger.		Cpl.,263 Inf.Div.Arbeitslager Kommando 343,Landerneau (Fr.)6.44-8.44		MURDER	FR.
BAUS	192649	M	Ger.		Staff-Sgt.,Army,C.C.Buchenwald (Ger.) 42-45		TORTURE	U.S.
BAUSCH,Wilhelm	125170	M	Ger.	07	Civilian,Erbach (Ger.) 9.44		TORTURE	U.S.
BAUSELER	139118	M	Ger.		Capt.,Flughafenbereich,Kittorf (Ger.)		MURDER	U.S.
BAUSENACK	250955	M	Ger.		Sturmschfhr.,Gestapo,Limoges (Fr.) 40-45		MISC.CRIMES	FR.
BAUSENEICH	144681	M			Army,Prey d'Eymoutiers (Fr.) 3.44		MURDER	FR.
BAUSENEICK,Heinrich	250956	M	Ger.		Member,Gestapo,Limoges (Fr.)		MISC.CRIMES	FR.
BAUSENHAFT,Walter	72	M			Polizeidirektor,Police,Warschau (Pol.) 9.41		MURDER	POL.
BAUSTAEDT	9627		Ger.		Osturmbannfhr.,Waffen SS,Pilsen (Czech.) 39		TORTURE	CZECH.
BAUSTAEDT	134253	M	Ger.		Osturmbannfhr.,SS, 40		TORTURE	U.S.
BAUSTAEDT	144683	M			Oberkriegsrat,Public official,Charleville (Fr.)		MURDER	FR.
BAUTZ (see BAUS)	162482							
PAUTZ	189169	M	Ger.		Hptschfhr.,SS,C.C.Dachau (Ger.)		MURDER	BEL.
BAUZ	144684	M			SS-Hptschfhr.,C.C.Struthof (Fr.)		MURDER	FR.
BAUZ,Alex	168577	M		05	SS-Oschfhr.,C.C.Natzweiler,Struthof (Fr.) 43-44		MURDER	FR.
BAUZ,Max	195804	M	Ger.		Oschfhr.,C.C.Struthof,Natzweiler (Fr.) 42-44		MURDER	FR.
BAXMANN,Willi	196127	M	Ger.	28.2.09	Manufacturer,Grand-Duchy of Luxemburg (Lux.) 45		INTERR.	LUX.
BAYER	1291	M	Ger.		Cpl.,Army,11 Coy 3 Bn.-999		MISC.CRIMES	U.K.
BAYER	39577	M	Ger.		Lt.,Army,Gilly s.-Isere 3 Coy 179 Bn., (Fr.) 8.44		MURDER	FR.
BAYER	120567	M			Rottfhr.,SS,C.C.Oswiecim (Pol.) 6.40-1.45		MURDER	POL.
BAYER	147725	M	Ger.		Civilian,Buchenwald,Bergen-Belsen (Ger.)		MURDER	FR.
BAYER	150770	M	Ger.	95	Col.,Oberstabsarzt,Medical corps,Neubukow and Rerik (Ger.) 3.44		WITNESS	U.S.
BAYER	167637	M	Ger.		Officer,Gestapo,Lyon (Fort Montluc) (Fr.) 7.43		MURDER	FR.
BAYER	174758	M			Sturmschfhr.,SS,C.C.Muhldorf,Ampfing (Ger.) 6.44-4.45		MURDER	U.S.
BAYER	189034	M	Ger.	20	Pvt.,3 Coy 714 Ldsch.Bn.,Area of Espe (Pol.) 10.44		TORTURE	U.K.
BAYER	189168	M	Ger.		Crim.-Insp.,Gestapo,C.C.Dachau (Ger.)		MURDER	BEL.
BAYER	194228	M	Ger.		Lt.,12 SS Panz.Div.Hitler Jugend 26 Panz.Gren.Rgt.15 Coy,Caen (Fr.) 6.-7.44		TORTURE	CAN.
BAYER (or BEIR)	196128	M		14	Lt.,Army		MISC.CRIMES	U.S.
BAYER (see BAIER)	250062							
BAYER	250958	M			Pvt.,C.C.Ellrich,Nordhausen (Ger.)		MURDER	U.S.
BAYER	260178	M	Ger.		Lt.,157 bavarian Div.d.Res.,Massif du Vercors,Isere et Drome (Fr.) 7.-8.44		SUSPECT	FR.
BAYER	301544	M	Ger.		Crim.Insp.,Gestapo at Munich,C.C.Dachau (Ger.) 40-45		MURDER	BEL.
BAYER	306856	M	Ger.	10-15	Pvt.,Guard in charge an 16.7.41 of Tiege Labour Coy at Marienburg Stalag XX B (Ger.) 7.41		MURDER	U.K.
BAYER,Albert	301878	M	Ger.		Hptschfhr.,Crim.-Asst.,attached to Gestapo in Norway 4.40		TORTURE	NOR.
BAYER,Franz	31991	M	Ger.		Landgerichtsrat,Public-official,Cheb (Czech.) 3.40		MURDER	CZECH.
BAYER,Hans	301295	M	Ger.		Member,Gestapo at Trencin,Oswiecim-Birkenau (Pol.) 39-45		MURDER	CZECH.
BAYER,Josef (see BAIER)	250063	M		23				
BAYER,Joseph	195877	M	Ger.		Crim.-Asst.,Gestapo (Dworschak),Prag (Czech.)		MURDER	CZECH.
BAYER,Kurt	193575	M	Ger.	18.3.12	Official,Member,Reichsprotector,NSDAP,Prag (Czech.) 38-45		MISC.CRIMES	CZECH.
BAYER,Ludwig	262019	M	Ger.	12.1.08	SS-Mann,Waffen SS,Gren.Div.36 "Dirlewanger Bde.",Warschau and other Towns (Pol.) 40-44		MURDER	POL.
BAYER,Max	259996	M	Ger.	09	SS-Uschfhr.,Crim.-Asst.,Gestapo,Trencin Slovenia (Czech.) 11.44-4.45		MURDER	CZECH.
BAYER,Paul	133824	M		83	Hptschfhr.,SS,Buchenwald-Weimar (Ger.)		MURDER	U.S.
BAYER,Varli	175703	M	Ger.		Medical-officer,Army,C.C.Hemer (Ger.) 43-45		MURDER	U.S.
BAYER,Xavier	144686	M			Asst.,Customs,St.Gaudens,St.Girons-Rimont (Fr.)		MURDER	FR.
BAYER.	176425	M	Ger.		Sgt.,Army, (Russ.) 44		TORTURE	FR.
BAYERL,Josef	258094	M		26.11.94	Group-leader,NSDAP,Civilian (Czech.), Stribro,44		MURDER	CZECH.
BAYERLE	173347	M			Inspector,Occupied territories,C.C.Oswiecim-Birkenau,Bruenn (Pol., Czech.) 43		MURDER	CZECH.
BAYERLE	260043	M	Ger.		Cpl.,217 Gren.Bn.d.Res.(G.A.P.),Massif du Vercors,Drome Isere (Fr.) 7.-8.44		SUSPECT	FR.
BAYERLEIN,Fritz	140759	M			General,130 Pz.Tchr.Div.,Wardin (Bel.) 12.44		MURDER	U.S.
BAYL (or BAIL)	252036	M		05	Hptsturmfhr.,SS,Saint Antonin (Fr.) 6.44		MISC.CRIMES	FH.
BAZATA,Robert	195668	M	Ger.	13	Agent,Gestapo,Ceske,Budejovice,Blatna (Czech.) 41-45		MISC.CRIMES	CZECH.
BAZEDOW (or BALSDORF)	132603	M	Ger.	00	Gestapo S-Chef de Bourges,Savigny en Septaine (Fr.) 7.44		MURDER	FR.
BEAR	306856	M	Ger.	10-15	Pvt.,Guard,in charge on 16.7.41 of Tiege Labour Coy at Marienburg, Stalag XX B (Ger.) 7.41		MURDER	U.K.
BEAUFRENOT	144688	M			Coy Brandenburg Legionnaire,Pont St.Esprit (Fr.)		MURDER	FR.
BECH,Walter	158346	M	Ger.		Civilian,Army,Wilhelmshaven (Ger.)		MURDER	U.K.
BECHE	193299	M	Ger.	90	Prison Guard,Frison Freumgesheim,Frankfurt-Main (Ger.) 7.-10.44		TORTURE	U.K.
BECHELIN	305598	M	Ger.	00	Hptschfhr.,I-C Construction L.K.,C.C.Natzweiler (Fr.) 40		MURDER	BEL.
BECHER	133378	M	Ger.	85	Oб.,Schutzbereichskommandeur,Army,Fassau (Ger.) 4.45		MURDER	U.S.
BECHER,Hans	167678	M	Ger.		Wirtschaftleiter,Abt.Wirtschaft Amt des Gouverneurs,Lublin (Pol.) 44		MISC.CRIMES	POL.
BECHER,Hermann	158371	M	Ger.		Civ.,Stalag IX,Niederorschel (Ger.) 1.43		TORTURE	U.K.
BECHER,Kurt	137737	M			Oschfhr.,Allg.SS, 4.45		MURDER	U.S.
BECHER,Kurt	221259	M	Ger.	09	Standartenfhr.,SS Ausb-Stab,SA Fuehrungshauptamt,Budapest,Mauthausen, (Hung.,Aust.) 43-45		TORTURE	U.S.
BECHER,Sofie	139121	F	Ger.	15	Teacher,Civilian,Ruppertshutten (Ger.) 9.44		WITNESS	U.S.
BECHEREK,Georges	168574	M	Ger.		Cpl.,Feldgend.de Langes,Flagey Coiffey,Auberive,Chalency (Fr.) 4.-44		MURDER	FR.
BECHETLER	11213	M	Ger.		Pvt.,111 Pz.Gren.Rgt.,N.C.O.,Albine (Fr.) 6.44		MURDER	FR.
BECHIN	194110	M	Ger.		Sicherungs Rgt.95 B or 13 Coy,Tulle (Fr.) 6.44		MURDER	FR.
BECHLER,Renatus	192689	M		1.5.10	Reichsjustizministerium,Strafgef.Lager Nord,Finmark (Nor.)		WITNESS	NOR.
BECHLIN (or BECKLIN)	258128	M	Ger.		SS-Hptschfhr.,C.C.Natzweiler (Fr.) 42		MISC.CRIMES	BEL.
BECHMANN	257334	M	Ger.		Rottfhr.,SS slave labour camp,Jasen (Nor.) 6.42-3.43		MURDER	YUGO.
BECHT	260969	M	Ger.	07	District Pres.and Kreisleiter,SS-Lt.,State Service,SS,Kolo(Pol.)42-45		MURDER	POL.
BECHTENHOLZ	136183	M	Ger.	16	Sgt.,Army,C.C.Marseille (Fr.) 44		WITNESS	FR.
BECHTEL (see BOCHTEL) Heinrich	140361							
BECHTELER	11213	M			Pvt.,110 Pz.Gren.Rgt.2 Coy,Albine (Fr.) 6.44		MURDER	FR.
BECHTOLD	193574	M		08	Oberzahlmeister,Dulag 377,Gerolstein (Ger.) 12.44-2.45		TORTURE	U.S.

BEC-BEC

NAME	C.R.FILE NUMBER	SEX	NATIO-NALITY	DATE OF BIRTH	RANK OCCUPATION UNIT	PLACE AND DATE OF CRIME	REASON WANTED	WANTED BY
BECK	188057	M			Sgt.Army,Valdahon(Fr.)		MURDER	FR.
BECK	11214	M	Ger.		Adjutant,CC Valdahon(Fr.)8.44		MURDER	FR.
BECK	28751	M			Dr.,Oberfeldarzt,IVb 163 Inf.Div.Staff 20 Army,Finmark(Nor.)11.44		MURDER	NOR.
BECK	121078	M	Ger.	98	Teacher,Civilian,school,Muehlheim,Dietesheim(Ger.)2.45		MURDER	U.S.
BECK	163118	M			SS Pvt.I Camp,34 Pz.Regt.SS Pz.Div.,Revin(Fr.)6.44		MURDER	FR.
BECK	166940	M			Capt.Oflag XIII A,CC Nuernberg(Ger.)7.41		MISC.CRIMES	FR.
BECK	185822	M	Ger.		Ordensjunker Waffen SS,CC Rovno(Pol.)41-42		MURDER	U.S.
BECK	188673	M	Ger.		Oberlt.(Lt.Col.)Dienststelle Mehun-Yevre(Fr.)8.44		WITNESS	FR.
BECK	189167	M	Ger.		Sturmfhr.Oberreg.Rat,SS Gestapo,CC Dachau(Ger.)		MURDER	BEL.
BECK	192289	M	Ger.		2nd Lt.116 Panz.Div.1 Bn.Schwere Werfer Abt.,Rabozee,Herstal(Bel.)		MURDER	BEL.
BECK	192290	M			Hauptscharfhr.SS CC Flossenburg(Ger.)44-45		MURDER	U.S.
BECK	194984	M	Ger.		Adjutant,Army,Valdahou(Fr.)8.44		MURDER	FR.
BECK	195315	M	Ger.		Reich-Official-Ordensjunker,Deputy Gebietskommissar in charge of the distr.Governor General,Rowno(Pol.)11.41-7.43		MURDER	POL.
BECK	196139	M	Ger.		Lt.SS CC Gusen(Ger.)		MISC.CRIMES	BEL.
BECK	255564	M	Ger.		SS Officer,CC Mauthausen(Ger.)		BRUTALITY	FR.
BECK	301545	M	Ger.		SS Lt.Lagerfhr.1,Camp guard at CC Gusen,Mauthausen(Aust.)40-45		MURDER	BEL.
BECK	306857	M	Ger.		Cpl.staff of Stalag VII A at Moosburg(Ger.)8.-9.44		MISC.CRIMES	U.K.
BECK	260720	M	Ger.	22. 2.85	Osturmbannfhr.SA,Oprodno(Czech.)39-40		MURDER	CZECH.
BECK, Gunther	168599	M	Ger.		Pvt.9 Ers.Gren.Regt.1 Coy.,Magny d'Anigon(Fr.)9.44		MURDER	FR.
BECK, Hans	193573	M	Ger.		Civilian,Solz(Ger.)10.44		MURDER	U.S.
BECK, J.Ignaz	173994	M			SS member,CC Muehldorf,Ampfing(Ger.)1.44-4.45		MURDER	U.S.
BECK, Jan	255565	M			Lagerfhr.CC Mauthausen(Ger.)		INTERR	FR.
BECK, Johann	134738	M	Ger.		Ortsgruppenlt.Buergermeister,SS Public official NSDAP,Poelling(Ger.)		MURDER	U.S.
BECK, Johann	172943	M	Ger.		SA Oberscharfhr.SA,NSDAP,43-44		MURDER	U.S.
BECK, Julius or BECKE	121077	M	Ger.	1. 2.00	Dr.,Cpl.Army,KL.Mosburg Stalag VIII A,Muehldorf(Ger.)9.39,6.44,4.45		MISC.CRIMES	U.K.
BECK, Ludwig	150747	M	Ger.		Member SA,Muehlberg(Ger.)3.42		MURDER	U.S.
BECK, Karl	196134	M	Ger.	15. 7.96	Wachtmeister,Schutzpolizei,Geggenau(Fr.)Autumn 44		MISC.CRIMES	U.K.
BECK, Paul	131162	M			Cripo Obersekretaer		MURDER	U.S.
BECK, Paul	149743	M			Kapo,CC Mauthausen(Aust.)41-45		MURDER	U.S.
BECK, Reinhard	306796	M	Ger.		Civilian,Nenterhaus(Ger.)9.44		MURDER	U.S.
BECK, Samuel	258382	M			Guard,Ohrdruf(Ger.)12.44-4.45		MURDER	U.S.
BECK, Werner	305651	M	Ger.	15	Dr.Former Asst.Head of the Institute of Forensic Medicine at Wroclaw (Breslau)and the University of Cracow(Pol.)4.40-45		MISC.CRIMES	POL.
BECKE see BECK	121077							
BECKE or BECKER or BARKER	178767	M.	Ger.		Capt.3 Coy.610 Inf.Bn.Stalag XXB,Elbing,Halberstadt(Ger.)		TORTURE	U.K.
BECKE, Ignatz or Julius see BECK, Julius	121077							
BECKELMAN, Otto	149730	M	Ger.	30. 5.93	Adjutant,Volkssturm 1 Bn.,Gerdelingen(Ger.)4.45		MURDER	U.S.
BECKENHEUSER	185823	M	Ger.		Sturmbannfhr.5 SS Totenkopf Regt.,Plock(Pol.)2.-4.41		MURDER	POL.
BECKER	73	M	Ger.		SS Unterscharfhr.,Rotterdam(Neth.)42		MISC.CRIMES	NETH.
BECKER	74	M	Ger.		SD Officer,Apeldoorn(Neth.)12.42		TORTURE	NETH.
BECKER	75	M	Ger.		SS Lt.Div.Das Reich,Regt.Der Fuehrer,Buzet S/Tarn(Fr.)7.44		MURDER	FR.
BECKER	76	M	Ger.		O.R.P.O,Befehlshaber,(Pol.)39		MURDER	(POL.)
BECKER	28732	M	Ger.		Major,20 Army,Finmark(Nor.)11.44		MURDER	NOR.
BECKER see BECKERT	31532							
BECKER	31561	M	Ger.	15	SS Obersturmfhr.? SS Pz.Gren.Div.Das Reich		MURDER	FR.
BECKER	36672	M	Ger.		1st Lt.Army,KL.Sagen(Ger.)		MISC.CRIMES	U.K.
BECKER	120077	M	Ger.		Pvt.Stalag		MISC.CRIMES	U.K.
BECKER	136192	M	Ger.	16	Oberlt.SS Panz.Div.Das Reich,Der Fuehrer,Buzet-sur-Tarn et St-Laurent-de-Neste(Fr.)7.-8.44		MURDER	FR.
BECKER	136996	M	Ger.		Major,21 Pz.Div.Hgrs(Wissembourg),Sessenheim(Fr.)1.45		MURDER	U.S.
BECKER	141932	M	Ger.		SS Bdefhr.,Dulag-Luft/Brandenburg(Ger.)5.43		MURDER	U.K.
BECKER	144693	M			Capt.Army,Gannat(Fr.)7.44		MURDER	FR.
BECKER	144495	M		17	Lt.SS Div.Das Reich,Viensses,Barthes,Montastrug(Fr.)7.44		MURDER	FR.
BECKER	146647	M	Ger.	-	Director,Civilian,Deutz(Ger.)		TORTURE	FR.
BECKER	146919	M			Lt.SS,49 Bde.Blindee,Groupe de Art.,Montmirail(Fr.)		MURDER	FR.
BECKER	147197	M			Cpl.SS Scandinavian Leg.,Montferrier(Fr.)44		LOOTING	FR.
BECKER	147198	M			Lt.Col.11 Panz.Div.S.W.of France		MURDER	FR.
BECKER	148526	M			SS Guard,SS Totenkopf Div.4 SS Baubde.CC Ellrich(Ger.)4.45		MURDER	U.S.
BECKER	149336	M	Ger.		CC Flossenburg(Ger.)		MURDER	FR.
BECKER	150750	M			Dr.,Oberstlt.,Army,KL.Altdrewitz,Stalag IIIC(Ger.)9.44-2.45		MISC.CRIMES	U.S.
BECKER	158351	M			Capt.Army,CC Leipzig(Ger.)12.43		TORTURE	U.K.
BECKER	158368	M			Cpl.Stalag IIIC near Kuestrin(Ger.)1.45		MURDER	FR.
BECKER	158370	M	Ger.		Adjudant,Railway,Lyon(Fr.)5.44		MURDER	FR.
BECKER	166929	M	Ger.		Major,Parachutiste,May sur Aisne(Fr.)8.44-9.44		PILLAGE	FR.
BECKER	166938	M			1st.Lt.Paratroops,Bellegarde(Fr.)		WITNESS	FR.
BECKER see RECKER	167139							
BECKER	173110	M	Ger.		Capt.Stalag VIA,Hemer(Ger.)41-45		TORTURE	U.S.
BECKER	176375	M			Capt/Feldgendarmerie,Gaunat(Fr.)		MURDER	FR.
BECKER	176561	M	Ger.		Kommandant(Sturmbannfhr.),SS Totenkopf,Roumania,Hung.Aust.		MURDER	U.K.
BECKER	178330	M	Ger.		1st.Lt.StalagVIIIC,Sagan(Ger.)		TORTURE	U.K.
BECKER see BECKE	178767							
BECKER	185624	M	Ger.		Stadtkommandantur,Metz(Fr.)42-44		MISC.CRIMES	FR.
BECKER	187008	F	Ger.		Wardress,CC Flossenburg(Ger.)42-45		MURDER	FR.
BECKER	187009	M	Ger.		Sgt.-Stabsfeldwebel,Feldgendarmerie Trupp 626,Peronne,Licourt(Fr.)8.44		MURDER	FR.
BECKER	188275	M	Ger.		SS Officer,JS CC Beelitz(Ger.)40-45		MURDER	CZECH.UNWCC
BECKER	189468	M	Ger.		Major,XIX Geb.Corps Staff 20 Army,Finmark(Nor.)11.44		MURDER	NOR.
BECKER	189649	M	Ger.		NCO,Army,Lyon,Perrache(Fr.)5.45		MURDER	FR.
BECKER	190077	M	Ger.		Chief,Abwehr official,Arnheim,Apeldoorn(Neth.)12.42		TORTURE	NETH.
BECKER	192292	M	Ger.	95	Sgt.Army,CC Forst Zinna,Torgau(Ger.)		MURDER	U.S.
BECKER	193384	M	Ger.		Sgt.Kriegsgef.Arb.Bn.184,CC Vasmo(Nor.)		TORTURE	NOR.
BECKER	193385	M	Ger.		Cpl.Army,Sunndalsora(Nor.)9.42		MURDER	NOR.
BECKER	193386	M	Ger.		Sgt.3 Kriegsgef.Arb.Bn.206,Heimdal,Drontheim(Nor.)2.45		WITNESS	NOR.
BECKER	195041	M	Ger.		Obersturmfhr.(Lt.)E.M.Div.SS,Buzet(Fr.)7.44-8.44		MURDER	UNWCC
BECKER	195669	M	Ger.		Inspector,Railway,Zdolbunow(Pol.)42-43		TORTURE	POL.

BEC-BEC

NAME	C.R.FILE NUMBER	SEX	NATIO-NALITY	DATE OF BIRTH	RANK OCCUPATION UNIT PLACE AND DATE OF CRIME	REASON WANTED	WANTED BY
BECKER	195735	M	Ger.		Chief,Gestapo, Arnheim(Neth.)	TORTURE	NETH.
BECKER	195736	M	Ger.		Gen.-Major,Befehlshaber der Ordnung fuer General-Government 39-40	MURDER	POL.
BECKER	196107	M	Aust.		SS-Pvt.,SS, C.C. Krispl(Aust.)	TORTURE	NETH.
BECKER see BRAGART	222613					MISC.CRIMES	
BECKER (or BEKER)	250950	M	Ger.		Cpl.,Navy,Erquy(Fr.) 6.44	MISC.CRIMES	FR.
BECKER	250951	M	Ger.		Major,Seguret and Vaison(Fr.) 6.44	MURDER	FR.
BECKER	250952	M	Ger.		Funktionaer Civil,Member, SD-Gestapo,Toulouse(Fr.) 42-44	MURDER	FR.
BECKER	250953	M			Capt., Arty,Torgau(Ger.) 43-45	MURDER	U.S.
BECKER	250954	M			S.T.Mann,Member SD-Gestapo,Toulouse(Fr.) 11.42-8.44	MISC.CRIMES	FR.
BECKER	251982	M			Employee,Zipo VB,Bruessels(Bel.)	INTERR.	BEL.
BECKER	252098	M			Ortsgruppenleiter Civilian,Duisburg(Ger.)	MURDER	U.S.
BECKER	256064	M			Cmdt. of "Sonderstab Becker"Navy,Werkendam(Neth.) 4.45	MURDER	NETH.
BECKER	257417	M	Ger.		SS-Osturmfhr.,SS slave labour camp,Beisfjord-Narvik(Nor.)6.-11.42	MURDER	YUGO.
BECKER	258223	M			SS-Officer,Waffen-SS,Member NSDAP	SUSPECT	BEL.
BECKER	259060	M			A Dulag Luft (Ger.) 43-4.45	BRUTALITY	U.S.
BECKER	260835	M			Lt.,Chief of the police staff,Kassel Area(Ger.) 44	MURDER	U.S.
BECKER	261046	M			Major,Orts-Cmdt.,17 Panzer-Div.,Amiens(Fr.) 5.-6.40	INCENDIARISM	FR.
BECKER	261351	M			Capt.,armament command,Nancy(Fr.) 9.44	INCENDIARISM	FR.
BECKER	261863	M	Ger.		Osturmfhr.,SS Commanding Staff in P.O.W.Camp,Beisfjord and Korgen (Nor.) 7.42-45	MURDER	YUGO.
BECKER	261955	M	Ger.		Crim.Assist.,Cripo(Gestapo),Various Places in Slovenia(Yugo.) 41-45	MISC.CRIMES	YUGO.
BECKER	300015	M	Ger.		Osturmfhr.,SS,Camp at Beisfjord near Narvik(Nor.) 6.-11.42	MISC.CRIMES	YUGC.
BECKER	300985	M	Ger.		Customs Official at Tardets,Esquiule,Basses-Pyrenees(Fr.) 7.44	PILLAGE	FR.
BECKER	301187	M	Ger.		Standartenfhr.,Huchenfeld(Ger.) 3.45	MURDER	U.K.
BECKER	301677	M	Ger.		OB/243 Mongolian"Oberland"Unit,St.Nazaire En Royans(Drome)(Fr.)7.8.44	MURDER	FR.
BECKER	301925		Ger.		Member SD,Enschede(Neth.) 44	MURDER	NETH.
BECKER	306452	M	Ger.		Warder C.C.Vaihingen nr.Stuttgart(Ger.) 42-45	TORTURE	FR.
BECKER	306673	M	Ger.		Sgt.,331 St. Pioneer Bn., 331 St. Inf. Div., Mijnheeren Land (Neth.) 5.45	PILLAGE	NETH.
BECKER	306944	M	Ger.		SS-Uschfhr., SS-Cmdt.,Rotterdam(Neth.) 42	BRUTALITY	NETH.
BECKER, Adolf	144675	M	Ger.		SS-Rottfhr.,KL.Struthof,Struthof-Natzweiler(Fr.) 42-44	MURDER	FR.
BECKER, Adolf Jacob	260528	M	Ger.	7.12.08	SS-Hptschfhr.,Allg. SS,Auschwitz(Pol.) 41-45	BRUTALITY	POL.
BECKER, Bruno,Dr.	167677	M	Ger.		Leader,Economy,Gouvernement Abt.Wirtschaft,Lublin(Pol.) 39-44	MISC.CRIMES	POL.
BECKER, Carl	188132	M	Ger.		Civilian,Muhlheim(Ger.) 2.43 or 45	MURDER	U.S.
BECKER, Erich	151743	M	Ger.	15	Hptschfhr.,Waffen-SS-Totenkopf-Stand.,Buchenwald-Weimar(Ger.)	TORTURE	U.S.,FR.,B
BECKER, Felix	124587	M	Ger.		Camp Hannover-Limmer(Ger.)	MISC.CRIMES	BEL.
BECKER, Fritz	146355	M	Ger.	8. 2.98	Int.Officer,SD,Marseille(Fr.) 11.43-44	INTERR.	FR.
BECKER (BECKER), Fritz M.K.	190491	M			Capt.,C.C.Dachau(Ger.)	MURDER	U.S.
BECKER, Fritz	260408	M	Ger.	14. 2.19	Pvt.,11 Coy.,3 Bn.,487 Regt.,267 Inf.Div.,Beograd,Nis,Zagreb (Yugo.) 4.42-10.42	MURDER	YUGO.
BECKER, Georg	188056	M			Army, C.C. of Foy(Fr.)	MURDER	FR.
BECKER, Gert Joachim	256895	M	Ger.	3.12.25	Hptsturmfhr., SS,St.Nay(Fr.)	MURDER	U.S.
BECKER, Hans	133056	M	Ger.	4. 5.11	Uschfhr.,SS-Totenkopfsturmbann,Buchenwald(Ger.)	TORTURE	U.S.
BECKER, Hans	187444	M	Ger.		Kriminalsekretaer,SD,Gestapo,Brno(Czech.) 39-45	MURDER	CZECH.
BECKER, Heinrich	72739	M	Ger.		Cpl.,SS ,C.C.,Struthof(Fr.)	MISC.CRIMES	FR.
BECKER, Heinrich	191690	M	Ger.		Cpl.,C.C.,SS, Struthof(Fr.) 42-44	MURDER	FR.
BECKER, Heinz	192291	M	Ger.	29	Member,Landwacht,C.C.,Schlossberg,Petershausen(Ger.) 10.43	MURDER	BEL.
BECKER, Helene	185278	F	Ger.	10. 9.06	Angestellte,Gestapo,Praha(Czech.) 39-45	MURDER	CZECH.
BECKER, Helmar or Herke	170076	M		06	Lt.,SS Div.Hohenstaufen,Buzet(Fr.) 7.44-8.44	MURDER	FR.
BECKER, Helmut	131274	M	Ger.		Capo,Kasernierte Police,C.C. Gusen(Aust.)	MURDER	U.S.
BECKER, Herbert Paul	76	M	Ger.	13. 3.87	Gen.-Major,Cmdt.und Befehlshaber d.Police(Pol.) 39-40	MURDER	POL.
BECKER, Hermann	137622	M	Ger.		Cpl.,Stalag 20 A,(4) Fort 14,Kl.Thorn(Pol.)40-6.41	TORTURE	U.K.
BECKER, Hugo	151744	M			Civilian,Ginnheim(Ger.) 11.44	WITNESS	U.S.
BECKER, Jochen	134908	M		08	Member SA, C.C.Hartheim(Aust.) 40-44	MURDER	U.S.
BECKER, Johann	258983	M			SS-Sturmmann,SS,C.C.Ohrdruf(Ger.) 12.44-4.45	MURDER	U.S.
BECKER, Josef	232226	M	Ger.	24	Pvt.,6 Coy.Nachr.Regt.506,Abwehr Official,Bad Wildungen(Ger.) 44-45	MISC.CRIMES	U.S.
BECKER, Josef	305579	M	Ger.		Member,C.C.Personel,C.C.Flossenburg,Hersbruck,Wolkenburg,Ganacker and Leitmeritz(Ger.and Czech.) 1.42 and 5.45	MURDER	U.S.
BECKER, Karl	185277	M	Ger.	05	SS-Sturmschfhr., Secretary,SD-Gestapo,Praha(Czech.) 43-45	MURDER	CZECH.
BECKER, Nikolaus	252393	M			N.C.O.,Camp Harzungen,Nordhausen(Ger.)	MURDER	U.S.
BECKER, Otto	139117	M	Ger.	24. 1.92	Member NSDAP,Civilian,Ebendorf(Ger.) 4.43	TORTURE	U.S.
BECKER, Paul	158941	M			Saddler,Civilian,Daasdorf and Guthmannshausen(Ger.) 7.-8.44	MURDER	U.S.
BECKER, Paul	195876	M	Ger.		Sgt.,116 Inf.Regt.,2 Coy.,Feldausbildungs-Bn.,Lanagistere(Fr.) 8.44	MURDER	FR.
BECKER, Paul	252391	M			Rottfhr., C.C. Dora, Nordhausen(Ger.)	MURDER	U.S.
BECKER, Rudolf	255079	M	Ger.		Civilian,Gossengrun(Czech.)	INTERR.	CZECH.
BECKER, Theodor Wilhelm	305763	M	Ger.	20.11.11	Hptschfhr.,Ob.-Assist.,S.Polizei Oslo(Nor.) 4.43-5.45	MURDER	NOR.
BECKER, Walter	257544	M	Ger.	14. 2.11	C.C.Nordhausen(Ger.)	MURDER	U.S.
BECKER, Wilhelm	149714	M	Ger.	92	C.O. Volkssturm,3 Coy.,1 Bn., Gardelegen(Ger.) 4.45	MURDER	U.S.
BECKERER	133980	M	Ger.		SS-Official, C.C.Brunswick Vighen(Ger.) 40-42.44-45	MURDER	U.S.
BECKERS	306674	M	Ger.		Pvt., 331 St.Pioneer Bn., 331 Inf.Div., Mijnheeren Land(Neth.) 5.45	PILLAGE	NETH.
BECKERT or BECKER	31532	M	Ger.		Capt.,SS Army,Gannat Lourouv de Bouble(Fr.) 6.-7.44	MURDER	FR.
BECKERT	146922	M			Col.,Army 16 Div.Inf.,St.Gemmes(Fr.)	MURDER	FR.
BECKERT, Hugo	149746	M	Ger.	92	Funkstellenleiter,Kreisltr.,Regional Official,Gardelegen(Ger.) 4.45	MURDER	U.S.
BECKHOFF, Friedrich	258978	M	Ger.	8. 9.06	Ceske Budejovice(Czech.) 39-45	MISC.CRIMES	CZECH.
BECKLER	251983	M	Ger.		Lt.,Pleucadeux and St.Marsel(Fr.) 6.44	MISC.CRIMES	FR.
BECKLIN (see BECHLIN)	258128						
BECKMAN, Anni	150752	F	Ger.		SS-Woman-Guard, KL.Ravensbruack(Ger.)	MISC.CRIMES	U.S.
BECKMANN	166939	M	Ger.		Pvt.,21 Panzer-Div.,125 Escadron,Reberrey(Fr.) 10.44	MURDER	FR.
BECKMANN	192199	M	Ger.		Pvt.,9 SS Pz.Div.Hohenstaufen,Neuville les Bois(Fr.) 8.44	MURDER	FR.
BECKMANN	251984	M	Ger.		Physician,Military Air Force, Uden(Neth.) 8.44	INTERR.	NETH.
BECKMANN	252392	M			Hptschfhr.,C.C. Dora, Nordhausen(Ger.)	MURDER	U.S.
BECKMANN	261389	M	Ger.		Cpl.,Unit L.52511,Pau,Soumoulon,Narp,Lescar(Fr.) 6.and 8.44	MURDER	FR.

NAME	C.R.FILE NUMBER	SEX	NATIO- NALITY	DATE OF BIRTH	RANK OCCUPATION UNIT PLACE AND DATE OF CRIME	REASON WANTED	WANTED BY
BECKMANN	307042	M	Ger.		Member of NSDAP, Head of Camp Huize Mooiland, Heelsum, Oosterbeek, Heelsum (Neth.) 11.44-4.45	MURDER	NETH.
BECKMANN, Ernst	187460	M	Ger.	10	Hptscharfhr., SS Sonderkommando RSHA, Sachsenhausen (Ger.) 44	MURDER	POL.
BECKMANN, Gerhard	158384	M	Ger.	08	Hptscharfhr., SS, C.C.Buchenwald (Ger.) 39-40	TORTURE	U.S.
BECKMANN, Heinrich	131273	M			SS-Leader (Officer), C.C.Arnstadt-Thueringen (Ger.)	MURDER	U.S.
BECKMANN, Heinrich	260879	M	Ger.		Officer, Field Pol., Avallon (Fr.) 3.44	MURDER	FR.
BECKMANN, Johann	257545	M		3.3.07	Worked Bloc 113 C.C. Nordhausen (Ger.)	MURDER	U.S.
BECKMANN, Otto	301614	M			Cpl., Feldgend. Chateaubriant (Loire-Inf.), St.Julien en Mouvantes (Fr.)44	MURDER	FR.
BECKMANS	251985	M	Ger.		Sippenforscher. Sipo Abt. IV B., Brussels (Bel.)	INTERR.	BEL.
BECL	166936	M			Member of Feldgend., Larochemillay (Fr.) 8.44	PILLAGE	FR.
BEDARF, Josef	134776	M			Pvt., 4.SS Totenkopf-Sturmbann, C.C. Dora-Mittelbau,Nordhausen (Ger.)43	WITNESS	U.S.
BEDARF, Walter	252261	M	Ger.		SS-Sturmmann, C.C. Auschwitz-Birkenau (Pol.) 1.43	MURDER	YUGO.
BEDOL	185625	M	Ger.		Capt., Feldkommandantur, St.Germain Les Corbeilles (Fr.) 8.44	MURDER	FR.
BEDRICH, Karl Heinz	301055	M			Arbeitsfhr., RAD Marianske, Lazne, Bohemia (Czech.) 42-44	INTERR.	CZECH.
BEDURKE	166935	M	Ger.		Pvt., Army, Etreux (Fr.) 9.44	WITNESS	FR.
BEECK	158348	M	Ger.	92	Oschafhr., SS, Enschede (Neth.)	MURDER	U.K.
BEEK (or BEECK)	174555	M	Ger.	93	SS Obersturmfhr., SS, Enschede (Neth.)	MURDER	U.K.
BEEKE	137001	M	Ger.		SS-Cmdt, Cologne (Ger.) 10.44	MURDER	U.S.
BEEKMAN	301926	M	Ger.		Member, SS and S.D., Leeuwarden (Neth.) 10.44	TORTURE	NETH.
BEEKMANS	301252	M	Ger.		Sippenforscher. Abt.IV B 1, S.D., Brussels (Bel.) 6.40-9.44	MURDER	BEL.
BEEL	176562	M	Ger.		Lt., Ersatz-Regt.1, Stolpee near Minsk (Russia) 8.43	MURDER	FR.
BEELAND	252276	M	Ger.		Capt., Army, near Schouwen-Duiveland (Neth.) 8.43	MISC.CRIMES	NETH.
BEER	125113	M	Ger.		Pvt., C.C. XX B, Marienburg (Ger.) 42	MURDER	U.K.
BEER	132013	M	Ger.		Sgt., Kraftfahrpark, Wuerzburg (Ger.)	WITNESS	U.S.
BEER	158338	M	Ger.		Lt., Sipo, Skriweri (Latvia) 44	MURDER	U.S.
BEER	176563	M	Ger.		Sonderfhr., Reichs-Propaganda-Abt., Paris (Fr.) 41-44	TORTURE	FR.
BEER	185826	M		12	Gebietskommissar Poland, Rowno (Pol.) 41-42	MURDER	U.S.
BEER	192293	M			S.A.-Sturmfhr., C.C. Flossenburg (Ger.) 44-45	MURDER	U.S.
BEER	195317	M	Ger.	05	Governor General of Poland, Dr., Rowno (Pol.)	MURDER	POL.
BEER	196135	M	Ger.		Lt., C.C. Ravensbrueck (Ger.)	MISC.CRIMES	BEL.
BEERBAUM	196136	M	Ger.		Lt., C.C. Neuengamme (Ger.) 40-44	MISC.CRIMES	BEL.
BEERBAUM	196922	M	Ger.		Uschafhr., SS, Neuengamme, Hamburg (Ger.) 40-44	MURDER	BEL.
BEERENBRUECK, Martin	252265	M	Ger.		Bisingen (Fr.)	BRUTALITY	FR.
BEESE, Heinz	252091	M	Ger.		SS-Mann, 12.SS Panzer Div. Spach, St.Sulpice (Fr.)	WITNESS	U.S.
BEESKOW	252850	M			Flyer, Camp Woffleben, Nordhausen (Ger.)	MURDER	U.S.
BEEST	195130	M			SS-Kommissar, Gestapo H.Q.S., Koeln (Ger.)	MURDER	U.S.
BEETZ, Konrad or Conrad	133379	M	Ger.	05	Usturmfhr., SS-R.S.H.A., Crim.Secr., Gestapo, Langenzenn-Nuernberg (Ger.) 43-45	MURDER	U.S.
BEETZ, Peter	176151	M	Ger.		SS-Oschafhr., SS, betw.Osterode and Seesen (Ger.)	MURDER	FR.
BEEWEN, Paul	256841	M	Ger.	5.9.09	Employee, C.C. Nordhausen (Ger.)	MURDER	U.S.
BEGE, Robert	252266	M	Ger.		Capt., Kreis-Cmdt., Army, Rocsvag (Serbia) 4.43	MURDER	YUGO.
BEGEN (see BEKEN)	172909						
BEGER	259353	M	Ger.		Rottenfhr., Gestapo of Poitiers, Antenne of Saintes, area Poitiers (Fr.) 40-45	MISC.CRIMES	FR.
BEGGER, Hermann	131163	M			Special Reservation foreman at C.C. Mauthausen (Austria) 41-45	MURDER	U.S.
BEGING	189651	M			Landwachtmann, Landwacht, Burg a.d.Wupper (Ger.) 11.44	MURDER	FR.
BEGLER	173335	M	Ger.		Lt., Army, Cmdt. of a punitive expedition 8.41-1.42	MURDER	YUGO.
BEHEING (see WEBER)	994						
BEHLE	124507	M	Ger.		Lt., Army, 1049. Regt., La Grandville (Fr.) 6.44	MURDER	U.K.
BEHLEN	306530	M			Sgt., Acting District Commander at Woudrichem (Neth.) 5.45	MURDER	NETH.
BEHLENDORF	253583	M	Ger.		Sgt., 2.Coy of Kampfgruppe "Oberst Mietsch", Crosaac (Fr.) 3.45	INTERR.	FR.
BEHLERT	163098	M			Uschafhr., 36.Panz.Regt. 10.Pans.Div., Revin (Fr.) 6.44	MURDER	FR.
BEHLERT, Hubert	259740	M	Ger.		Pvt., F.P. 150.831 LGPA Paris, St.Pierre de Semilly-Marche (Fr.) 9.42	WITNESS	FR.
BEHLING	305820	M			Pvt., 1.Aufkl.Abt. 3.Coy., 2.Col. XV. Div.Afrika Korps, St.Leger (Arlon) 9.44	MISC.CRIMES	BEL.
BEHLING, Karstien	221296	M	Ger.		Agent, Sipo (Neth.) 9.44	MISC.CRIMES	U.S.
BEHLKE, Kurt	262021	M	Ger.	10.7.05	SS-Mann, Waffen-SS, Gren.Div.36, "Dirlewanger-Bde", Warsaw and other towns" (Pol.) 40-44	MURDER	POL.
BEHME, Otto	125171	M	Ger.		Buergermeister, Public Official, Helm 5.44	TORTURE	U.S.
BEHMIG (or BOEHMIG)	129824	M			Civilian, C.C. Buchenwald (Ger.)	BRUTALITY	U.S.
BEHMIG (see BORMING)	192578	M	Ger.				
BEHN, Helmut	255078	M		29	Civ. (may live in Goeddenstedt), Goeddenstedt (Ger.) 3.45	WITNESS	U.S.
BEHNCKE	148500	M			Agent, Camp Hamburg-Wilhelmsburg (Ger.) 43-44	MISC.CRIMES	FR.
BEHNKE	121079	M			Dr. Civ. Institute "Kiew", Kiew (Russia) 6.41-9.42	MURDER	U.S.
BEHNKE	305821	M			Pvt., 1.Aufkl.Abt. 3.Coy., 2.Col. XV. Div. Afrika Korps,St.Leger (Arlon) 9.44	MISC.CRIMES	BEL.
BEHR	28733	M			Major, 20. Army, Finmark (Nor.) 11.44	MURDER	NOR.
BEHR	125112	M	Ger.	00	Col., Stalag Luft VII, near Breslau (Ger.) 12.44	MISC.CRIMES	U.K.
BEHR, Baron	151712	M			Gen., Army, Pz.Gren.Regt., St.Pierre, St.Allean (Fr.) 9.44	MURDER	U.S.
BEHR	167676	M			Leader, Gen.Government of Poland, Krakau (Pol.) 39-44	MISC.CRIMES	POL.
BEHR (or BAR)	306332	M	Ger.		SBF, Head of Camp,C.C. Dora, Nordhausen (Ger.) 40-45	MURDER	BEL.
BEHR, Willy	158369	M	Ger.		Gestapo, Argeles-Gazost (Fr.) 43	TORTURE	FR.
BEHR, Wilhelm	262022	M		6.12.11	SS-Mann, Waffen-SS, Gren.Div.36 "Dirlewanger-Bde.", Warsaw and other towns (Pol.) 40-44	MURDER	POL.
BEHREM (BEHRENDS or BEHRENS)	146471			05	Osturmbannfhr., SS, Prevention of escapes of prisoners of war, Stalag Luft III 3.44	MURDER	U.K.
BEHREND	191834		Ger.	.13	Lt., Army, Stalag IX B, Fischau or Sommerau 40,	TORTURE	U.K.
BEHREND	192690	M	Ger.	05	Oberwachtmeister, Sgt., Reichsjustizministerium, Strafgefangenen-Lager Nord, C.C. Finmark (Nor.) 6.42-45	MISC.CRIMES	NOR.
BEHREND, Emil	151718	M			Arbeitslager-Guard, C.C.Leipzig and Celle (Ger.)	TORTURE	U.S.
BEHREND, Eugen	252457	M			Pvt., Camp Ellrich, Nordhausen (Ger.)	MURDER	U.S.
BEHREND, Kurt	136182	M	Ger.		Pvt., Army, Ville-le-Marclet 8.44	WITNESS	FR.
BEHRENDS (BEHRENS or BEHREM)	146471	M	Ger.	05	Osturmbannfhr., SS, Prevention of escapes of prisoners of war, Stalag Luft III. 3.44	MURDER	U.K.
BEHRENDS	196137	M	Ger.		Col., Stalag VI C, Bathorn (Ger.) 43-44	MISC.CRIMES	FR.
BEHRENDT	149526	M			Col., Camp-Cmdt., Stalag 4 C (Ger.) 43-44	TORTURE	FR.

BEH - BEL

NAME	C.R.FILE NUMBER	SEX	NATIO-NALITY	DATE OF BIRTH	RANK OCCUPATION UNIT PLACE AND DATE OF CRIME	REASON WANTED	WANTED BY
BEHRENDT	252905	M	Ger.		Sturmschfhr. S.D., Toulouse (Fr.) 11.42-8.44	MISC.CRIMES	FR.
BEHRENDT	305822	M	Ger.		Pvt., 1.Aufkl.Abt. 3. Coy. 2. Col. XV.Div. Afrika-Korps, St.Leger (Arlon) 9.44	MISC.CRIMES	BEL.
BEHRLNE, Fritz	190092	M			SS, C.C. Dora-Mittelbau, Nordhausen (Ger.)	MURDER	U.S.
BEHRENS see Berens	81	M					
BEHRENS (BEHRNDS or BEHREM)	146471	M	Ger.	05	Osturmbannfhr., Prevention of escapes of prisoners of war, SS, Stalag Luft III (Ger.) 3.44	MURDER	U.K.
BEHRENS	158343	M	Ger.		Pvt., 1.SS Pz.Div. "Adolf Hitler" 1.Bn. II.Zug,Parfondruy Stavelot (Bel.) 12.44	TORTURE	U.S. BEL.
BEHRENS	173314	M	Ger.		Commander, S.D., Strasbourg (Fr.) 44	TORTURE	FR.
BEHRENS	188674	M	Ger.		Pvt., Geh.Feldpolizei, Morbihan (Fr.)	WITNESS	FR.
BEHRENS	188943	M	Ger.	96	Navy, Luneberg (Ger.) 4.45	MURDER	U.K.
BEHRENS	256916	M	Ger.		Osturmfhr., SS-Camp Leader Wieda, Nordhausen (Ger.)	MURDER	U.S.
BEHRENS or REHRENS	260429	M	Ger.		Capt. Commandant, Schutzpolizei 309.Btty. 221.SS-Div., Okolniki (Pol.)41	MURDER	POL.
BEHRENS	261772	M	Ger.		Cpl., Art.H.D.V. 199-2235 H.D.F. No.of S.P.27.046 C.,Lorgies (Fr.)9.44	MURDER	FR.
BEHRENS, Arnold	134909	M	Ger.	05	Civ., C.C. Hartheim (Aust.) 40-44	MURDER	U.S.
BEHRENS, Ewald	258216	M	Ger.		Dr. phil., Institut fuer Deutsche Ostarbeiter,Cracow (Pol.) 41-43	MISC.CRIMES	POL.
BEHRENS, Fritz	148529	M	Ger.		Osturmfhr.,Engineer, 3.SS-Bau-Bde. C.C. Wieda or Gardelegen (Ger.)4.45	MURDER	U.S.
BEHRENS, Gustav	260216	M	Ger.	89	Deputy Reich Farm Leader (Reichsobmann des Reichsnaehrstandes) SS-Bde.-Fhr., Reich Food Estate, SS	INTER.	U.S.
BEHRENS, Johann	262023	M	Ger.	17. 1.11	SS-Mann, Waffen-SS,Gren.Div.36, Dirlewanger-Bde., Warsaw and other towns (Pol.) 40-44	MURDER	POL.
BEHRENS, Paul	256908	M	Ger.		Employee, C.C. Nordhausen (Ger.)	MURDER	U.S.
BEHRENS, Rudolf	121080	M	Ger.		Civ., Aderstedt (Ger.) 9.44	MURDER	U.S.
BEHRENS, Willi	252456	M		2. 3.00	N.C.O., Camp Harzungen, Nordhausen (Ger.)	MURDER	U.S.
BEHRHARD, Hans see BERNHARDT	185272						
BEHRHARD	192648	M	Ger.	20	Uschrfhr., SS, C.C. Buchenwald (Ger.)	MURDER	U.S.
BEHRING	136181	M		00	Adjudant, SS, C.C. Marseille (Fr.)	TORTURE	FR.
BEHRING	148528	M			SS 3.Bann-Bde., Camp-commander, C.C. Wieda-Gardelegen	MURDER	U.S.
BEHRINGER	174757	M			Rottfhr., SS C.C. Muehldorf-Ampfing (Ger.) 6.44-4.45	MURDER	U.S.
BEHRINGER, Heinrich	176145	M	Ger.	9.11.95	Cpl., Army, C.C. Vannes (Fr.) 42-44	TORTURE	FR.
BEHRINGER, Joseph	166934	M			Feldgendarm, Feldgendarmerie, Luneville Maixe (Fr.) 8.44	MURDER	FR.
BEHRNDT	141850	M	Ger.		Cpl., Pz.Jaeger-Abt. I, Normandy (Fr.) 6.-7.44	WITNESS	U.K.
BEHRSINGER	252455	M			Camp Rottleberode, Nordhausen (Ger.)	MURDER	U.S.
BEHTMANN	173336	M	Ger.		Lt. Col., Army, German punitive Expedition, Serbia-Yugo. 9.-12.41	MURDER	YUGO.
BEICK, Paul	191917	M	Ger.		Civ., Burg a.d.Wupper (Ger.) 11.44	MURDER	FR.
BEICKERT or BUICKERT	253571	M	Ger.		Col., 16. D.I., St. Gemme (Fr.) 8.44	INTER.	FR.
BEIER	192647	M	Ger.		SS-Sgt., Hptschfhr., C.C. Buchenwald (Ger.) 42-45	TORTURE	U.S.
BEIER	195043	M	Ger.		Wehrmachtsgefaengnis, Caen (Fr.) 6.44	MURDER	FR.
BEIER, Walter	253573	M	Ger.		Employee, Abt. V B, Brussels (Bel.)	INTER.	BEL.
BFIER	258112	M	Ger.	2. 8.01	School-master, State service, C.C.Budjovice (Czech.) 4.45	PILLAGE	CZECH.
BEIERLE	305874	M	Ger.		Uschfhr., C.C. Oranienburg (Ger.) 39-45	MURDER	CZECH.
BEIGMANN	306235	M	Ger.	05	Paymaster, 1-602 Schnelle Abt. F.P.No. 27 690 A, Chambord (Fr.) 8.44	MURDER	FR.
BEIHER	192645	M	Ger.		Stabsarzt, Airforce Sanit.Abt. C.C. Buchenwald, Dora (Ger.) 42-45	TORTURE	U.S.
BEIHSMANN, Franz	176566	M			Arbeitslager C.C. Grambk nr. Bremen (Ger.) 41-42	TORTURE	U.S. FR.
BEIHSMANN, H.	194936	M	Ger.		Foreman, Civ., Arnheim (Neth.) 9.44-4.45	PILLAGE	NETH.
BEIL	252453	M			Oschfhr., Gestapo C.C. Dora Nordhausen (Ger.)	MURDER	U.S.
BEIL, Hans	158361	M	Ger.		Blockaeltester, C.C. Jawitschwitz (Pol.) 8.23	TORTURE	FR.
BEIL, Otto Friedrich	301927	M	Ger.	31. 9.99	Guard, Labour Education camp, Lahde-Weser (Ger.) 5.43-4.45	BRUTALITY	U.K.
BEILNER, Arnost	187462	M		5.10.01	Guard SS, Czech. 44	MURDER	CZECH.
BEINACH, Oscar	125110	M		00	Camp-commandant of 149 L C.C. Buchberg (Ger.)	TORTURE	U.K.
BEINLICH	260042	M			Rottfhr., SS, Nor. 8.42-3.43 and 4.43-45	TORTURE	YUGO.
BEINSEN, Theodor	139120	M	Ger.		Farmer, Civ., Ger.	TORTURE	U.S.
BEINZ, Thea	140266	F		20	SS Overseer, chief, C.C.Ravensbrueck (Ger.)	MURDER	U.K.
BEIR	158353	M	Ger.		Capt., Army, Silesia (Ger.) 1.45	MURDER	U.K.
BEIR see BAYER	196128						
BEISCHROT, Adam	172319	M		1.24	SS-Mann, SS-Totenkopfsturmbann 1.Coy. C.C.Auschwitz (Pol.)	MISC.CRIMES	U.S.
BEISECKER, Rudi	124299	M			SS 1.Pz.Div. 1.Pz.Rgt., Malmedy (Bel.) 12.44	MURDER	U.S.
BEISLER	132602	M	Ger.		Lt. SS, Ile de Djerba (Tun.) 2.43	PILLAGE	FR.
BEISNER	190028	M			SS Sturmbannfhr., Liaison officer of the Military commander of the German Embassy at Zagreb,Ljudhljana (Yugo.) 41-44	MURDER	YUGO.
BEISSE, F.	301928	M	Ger.		Sgt. Feldgendarmerie Utrecht, Baarn (Neth.) 12.43	PILLAGE	NETH.
BEISSMAN, Jean	176568	M		15	Sgt., Army, I.R. 87, Mailley le camp (Fr.) 4.44	MURDER	FR.
BEISSNER	132548	M	Ger.	24	Rottfhr., SS, Hallein (Ger.)	MURDER	FR.
BEISSWENGER, Walter	144568	M		21.10.22	SS Osturmfhr., SS Freiwilligen-Bde. 15, Budmera, Cernay,Troyes (Fr.)	MURDER	FR.
BEISTEINER	252454	M			Pvt., Camp Ellrich Nordhausen (Ger.)	MURDER	U.S.
BEISWANGER see BEISWENGER	252463						
BEISWENGER, Eugen or BEISWANGER	252463	M		29. 1.14	Airman, Camp Ellrich Nordhausen (Ger.)	MURDER	U.S.
BEITSVINGER	131136	M			Guard C.C. Oberdingen (Ger.)	TORTURE	BEL.
BEIXNER, Wilhelm	187463	M	Ger.	77	Reichsleiter NSDAP, Praha (Czech.)	MISC.CRIMES	CZECH.
BEKATSCH	144566	M			SS Oscharfhr.	TORTURE	FR.
BEKEN or BEGEN	172909	M	Ger.		Capt., Oflag X D C.C. Fischbeck (Ger.) 6.42	MISC.CRIMES	FR.
BEKER see BECKER	250950						
BEKER, Hans	196138	M	Ger.		Lt. 52.Coy. Parachut S.P.L.G.P.A. Paris 3-268 C. Bessancourt (Fr.)8.44	WITNESS	FR.
BELAU, Guenther	221412	M		19	Pvt. Abwehr Nachr Rgt. 506, Bad Wildungen (Ger.) 45	MISC.CRIMES	U.S.
BELDER, Pierre	163655	M	Ger.		Gestapo, Dun les places (Fr.)	MURDER	FR.
BELER, Danilo	258426	M			SS-Mann, Guard, SS C.C. Ohrdruf (Ger.) 12.44-4.45	MURDER	U.S.
BELIESITZ, Johann	258477	M			Sturmmann SS, C.C. Ohrdruf (Ger.) 12.44-4.45	MURDER	U.S.
BELIMER	188942	M	Ger.		SD Hptsturmfhr., Gestapo, C.C. Westerbork Groningen (Neth.)	MURDER	NETH.
BELING, Otto	262059	M	Ger.	26. 3.14	SS-Mann, Waffen SS Gren.Div.36 Dirlewanger-Bde.Warschau and other (Pol.) 40-44	MURDER	POL.
BELISTEDT	257947	M			Lt. z.See, 150. Pz.Bde.,Operation Grief, 12.44	MISC.CRIMES	U.S.
BELITZ, Otto	306333	M	Ger.		SS-Scharfhr., C.C. Buchenwald (Ger.) 5.38 and 10.43	MURDER	BEL.

BEL-BEN

NAME	C.R.FILE NUMBER	SEX	NATIONALITY	DATE OF BIRTH	RANK OCCUPATION UNIT PLACE AND DATE OF CRIME	REASON WANTED	WANTED BY
BELKE, Erich	262060	M	Ger.	31.12.06	SS-Mann, Waffen-SS,Gren.Div.36, "Dirlewanger Bde" Warschau and other (Pol.) 40-45	MURDER	POL.
BELL	306334	M	Ger.	7. 1.09	Sgt., SS, C.C. Buchenwald (Ger.) 5.38-10.43	MURDER	BEL.
BELL, Adam	252904	M	Ger.		SS-Mann, SD, Toulouse (Fr.) 11.42-8.44	MISC.CRIMES	FR.
BELL, Alfons	252388	M	Ger.		Lt., 264 Div., 893 Inf.Rgt., Primosten (Yugo.)	MURDER	YUGO.
BELL, Walter	256909	M	Ger.	5. 9.21	Employee, C.C. Nordhausen (Ger.)	MURDER	U.S.
BELLA	226589	M	Ger.		Oberwachtmstr., guard, C.C. Esterwegen (Ger.) 45	MURDER	U.S.
BELLER, Fritz-Fidelius	174759	M			Oschfhr., SS, C.C. Muehldorf, Ampfing (Ger.) 6.44-4.45	MURDER	U.S.
BELLER, Otto	174760	M		28	Pvt., Army, Gollheim (Ger.) 9.44	MURDER	U.S.
BELLIEN, Valentina	305992	F	Ger.		Woman in charge of children in Velpke Clinic (Ger.) 5.44-12.44	MURDER	U.K.
BELLIER	144563	M			Adjutant, Milice Rennes (Fr.)	MURDER	FR.
BELLIN, Emmie	151721	F	Ger.		Civilian, C.C. Hadamar (Ger.) 6.44-5.45	WITNESS	U.S.
BELLITZ	301546	M	Ger.		Employee, Customs official, Franco-Belgian frontier in particulars at Vieux-Conde, Peruwelz,Bon-Secours (Hainaut) 5.-6.43	MISC.CRIMES	BEL.
BELLMAN	166933	M	Ger.		Medician, C.C. Olbernhau-Gruenthal (Ger.) 4.45	MURDER	FR.
BELLMANN, Emil see BILLEMANS	131145						
BELLNIDT	253574		Ger.		SS, C.C. Buchenwald (Ger.)	INTERR.	FR.
BELLO	124789	M	Ger.		Scharfhr., SS, C.C. Sachsenhausen (Ger.)	MURDER	U.S.
BELLWIDT	49246	M	Ger.		Sturmbannfhr., SS Totenkopfstandarte, C.C. Buchenwald (Ger.) 42-45	TORTURE	U.S.
BELMER	194937	M	Ger.		Custom field guard, Zijldijk (Neth.) 3.45	PILLAGE	NETH.
BELOW	260883	M	Ger.		Col., Airforce	WITNESS	U.S.
BELS	253575	M	Ger.		Osturmfhr., SS, 5 Ers.Coy, Leibstandarte "A.H.", Berlin-Lichterfelde (Ger.) 11.42	MISC.CRIMES	POL.
BELSCHNER, Clemens Werner Philipp	305760	M	Ger.		Cashier, NSDAP, Raeumungskommissar for Zuid-Neth., Bezuidenhout District,Reichskommissariat,The Hague (Neth.) 43-44	PILLAGE	NETH.
BELSNER, Karl	252464	M			Flyer, Camp Ellrich, Nordhausen (Ger.)	MURDER	U.S.
BELTZ,	131807	M	Ger.		Public official Ministerialrat, Prague (Czech.) 39-41	TORTURE	CZECH.
BELZ, Helmut	172907	M			Abwehr, Dienststelle Kern, Sachsenburg (Ger.) 3.45	WITNESS	U.K.
BELZER	261233	M	Ger.		Employee, Sipo, Section II B, Bruessel (Bel.) 40-45	SUSPECT	BEL.
BEMANN	130182	M	Ger.		Capt., Army, Oflag (Ger.) 10.41-10.42	MISC.CRIMES	U.K.
BENATZKY	167641	M	Ger.		Dr., Civ., Einsatzstab Rosenberg, Office for Supervision of Literature, Paris (Fr.) 44	PILLAGE	FR.
BENCKEN, Jacob	261232	M	Gen.		Sgt., 1 Coy, 377 Jg.Rgt., Rgt.-B,Vinkt,Meigem Area (Bel.)5.40	SUSPECT	BEL.
BEND, Sunkel	131167	M			SS, C.C., asst. Med.Sec. Camp Mauthausen (Aust.) 41-45	MURDER	U.S.
BENDA, Robert	126526	M	Ger.	96	Mayor and Groupleader, Public official, Halchter (Ger.) 9.44	MURDER	U.S.
BENDAK	185824	M			Lt.Gen., Army, Gavalochori (Grc.) 5.45	MURDER	GRC.
BENDE, Wilhelm	188133	M	Ger.	12	Farmer, Member, NSDAP,civilian,Hof Ebental (Ger.) 40-42	TORTURE	POL.
BENDEL	253567				Senior W.O., Feldgendarmerie, Perigueux, Boulazac (Fr.) 6.44	INTERR.	FR.
BENDELE, Anton	128595	M			Osturmfhr., SS, C.C. Mauthausen (Aust.) 41-45	MURDER	U.S.
BENDELE	190029	M			SS-Osturmfhr., Verwaltungsfuehrer C.C. Neuengamme (Ger.) 43	MURDER	YUGO.
BENDER	131150	M			5 Parachut-Rgt., Nachrichtenzug,Auregnon,Jemappes-Chlin(Bel.) 9.44	MURDER	BEL.
BENDER	252918	M	Ger.		Paymaster, Airforce (Dana) Kitzingen (Ger.) 3.45	MURDER	U.K.
BENDER	252919	M		05	Dr., Civ., Stalag Luft IV, Gross-Tychow (Pol.) 6.44	WITNESS	U.S.
BENDER	305823	M	Ger.		Pvt. 1 Aufkl.Abt., 3 Coy, 2 Col., XV Div. Afrika Corps, St. Leger Distr.Arlon (Bel.) 9.44	MISC.CRIMES	BEL.
BENDHORF	196123	M	Ger.		Master, C.C. Dachau (Ger.)	TORTURE	FR.
BENDIG	172908	M	Ger.		Capt., Baupionier-Bn, on Board "Gotha" Trondelhog (Nor.) 4.45	MURDER	NOR.
BENDL	256910	M	Ger.		Employee, Mittelwerk G.m.b.H., Head of Sub.Sec.,Nordhausen (Ger.)	MURDER	U.S.
BENDLER	149732	M			Gestapo, Cherbourg, St.Lo Toutlaville (Fr.)	MURDER	FR.
BENDLER	301254	M	Ger.		SS-Sturmscharfhr., Crim.secr.,Ltr. der Abt.V.D. Erkennungsdienst, Crim.techn.Untersuchungsstelle Bruessel (Bel.) 6.40-9.44	MURDER	BEL.
BENDORF	62365	M		03 or 01	Col., Army, CO PW Enclosure Gneisenau Kaserne,Ehrenbreitstein (Ger.) Plauen (Ger.)	MURDER	U.S.
BENDRESCH, P.	252920	M	Ger.			MURDER	U.S.
BENECKE, Arnost	187461	M	Ger.	20. 4.12	Kriminalkommissar, SD, Gestapo, Brno (Czech.) 39-45	MURDER	CZECH.
BENEKE, Willy	261231	M			Pvt., 377 Jg.Rgt., Vinkt, Meigem Area (Bel.) 5.40	SUSPECT	BEL.
BENEDICT	195821	M			Lt., SS, Neuengamme (Ger.)	MURDER	BEL.
BENEDICTS	158355	M		95	Capt., C.C. B 2, Bitterfeld (Ger.) 10.43-5.45	TORTURE	U.K.
BENEDIKT	176959	M			Crim.Inspect., Gestapo, Stuttgart (Ger.)	MISC.CRIMES	FR.
BENESCH	166278	M	Ger.	05	Major, Army, (Serb.) 44	TORTURE	U.S.
BENEWITZ	257794	M			Chief of Gestapo Przemysl (Pol.) 42	MISC.CRIMES	POL.
BENFELS, Wilhelm	130078	M			Cpl., 8 Flug-Sich.Coy, Luftnachrichten-Rgt.35, C.C.Hamburg-Altona (Ger.) 8.44	MISC.CRIMES	U.S.
BENGER	173315	M	Ger.		Col., Feldkdtr., St.Aubin-D'Aprenai (Fr.) 6.44	PILLAGE	FR.
BENGNER, Alfred	158359	M		85	Civilian, Cracow (Pol.)	TORTURE	U.K.
BENGS	185779	M			N.C.O., Liege (Bel.)	TORTURE	BEL.
BENGSON	62364	M	Ger.		Obermaat, Navy, 2 Btty, Mar.Flak 810, Walcheren (Neth.) 10.44	MURDER	U.S.
BENIDER, Wichlem	257624	M	Ger.		Lt., Feldgendarmerie, Zajecar (Yugo.) 11-44	MURDER	YUGO.
BENISCH, Karl or BENSCH	194938	M	Ger.	03	Sgt., 2 Coy, 877 Landesschz.Bn, C.C. Veitsch (Aust.) 10.42	TORTURE	U.K.
BENK, Hermann	252917	M			Flyer, Camp Ellrich, Nordhausen (Ger.)	MURDER	U.S.
BENKER, Wilhelm	252921	M	Ger.	25. 4.13	Pvt., 13 Coy, 558 Gren.Rgt., Bruay en Artois (Fr.) 9.44	MURDER	FR.
BENN	125109	M			Civilian, Canteen manager, Milk Factory, Obermassfeld (Ger.) 2.41	TORTURE	U.K.
BENNE, Ernst	193383	M			Pvt., Landes-Schz.Ers.Bn 11, C.C. Brenne Nor.) 7.44	TORTURE	NOR.
BENNER	175670	M			Officer, Stalag VI A, Hemer (Ger.) 41-45	TORTURE	U.S.
BENNER or BRENNER	196140	M			Capt., Ger.Field Pol., Chimay, St.Remy (Bel.) 4.44	MURDER	BEL.
BENNER	252262	M	Ger.		Pvt., 607 Landes-Schz.Bn, 2 Coy, Allendorf (Ger.) 3.43	MURDER	YUGO.
BENNETZ	301879	M	Ger.		Crim.asst., Gestapo Nor. since 4.40	TORTURE	NOR.
BENNEWITZ	305895	M			Prison guard, C.C.Theresienstadt(Terezin) Prison Small Fortress, (Czech.) 10.38-44	MURDER	CZECH.
BENNI	195821	M	Ger.		Personnel C.C. Struthof-Natzweiler (Fr.) 40-44	MURDER	FR.
BENNIBLER, Oskar	126527	M	Ger.		Cpl., 9 Pz.Div., I Rgt., Fuerth (Ger.) 9.44	MURDER	U.S.
BENNING, Theodor	252916	M		13.11.94	Sgt., Camp Ellrich, Nordhausen (Ger.)	MURDER	U.S.
BENNINGHAUSEN	141955	M			Pvt., Stalag VIII C, guard, Goerlitz (Ger.) 5.-8.40	TORTURE	FR.
BENNO	149360	M			Civilian	TORTURE	FR.
"BENNY" (known as)	253568	M		01	Foreman of Kostermann, (D.A.U.A.) Civilian Coalyard,Muenchen(Ger.)6.44	MURDER	U.S.
BENSCH	120625			10	Sgt., Army, 559 Lds.Schz.Bn,4 Coy, Schischitz (Czech.) 3.45	MISC.CRIMES	U.K.
BENSCH	124296		Ger.	18	Civilian Gardelegen (Ger.) 4.45	MURDER	U.S.
BENSCH	306217				Employee, Office for registration of deaths, C.C. Struthof-Natzweiler (Fr.) 42-44	MURDER	FR.

BEN - BER   -24-

NAME	C.R.FILE NUMBER	SEX	NATIO-NALITY	DATE OF BIRTH	RANK	OCCUPATION	UNIT	PLACE AND DATE OF CRIME	REASON WANTED	WANTED BY
BENSCH, Georg	149712	M		08	Wachtmeister, Airforce, 4 Coy., A.A. Btty., Gardelegen (Ger.) 4.45				MURDER	U.S.
BENSCH, Karl see BENISCH	194938									
BENSCH, Richard	300017	M	Ger.		Worker, Lohman-works, Pabianice, Herford, Sundern, 6.40-8.44, 4.45				MISC.CRIMES	POL.
BENSCH, Willy	168580	M	Ger.	11	SS-Hptscharfhr., C.C.Struthof-Natzweiler (Fr.)				MURDER	FR.
BENSCH-GINRICH	139829	M	Ger.		Maj., Dr., Stalag X B, Sandbostel (Ger.) 1.-5.45				MISC.CRIMES	U.S.
BENSKIEWITZ see BENYSKIEWICZ	252914									
BENTEL	261230	M			Rottenfhr., C.C. Buchenwald (Ger.)				MURDER	U.S.
BENTIN	189579	M	Ger.		Head-pay-master, Zentral-Ersatzteillager 206, Paris (Fr.) 8.44				MURDER	FR.
BENTIN	257799	M			SS-Mann, cmdt. of the C.C. Przemysl (Pol.) 42				MURDER	POL.
BENTLER	252915	M			Pvt., Camp Ellrich, Nordhausen (Ger.)				MURDER	U.S.
BENTLIN	166992	M	Ger.		Officer, Obsturmfhr., SS-Pz.Div., Leibst. Adolf Hitler, Troussencour - Oise (Fr.) 8.44				WITNESS	FR.
BENTMANN	140850	M	Ger.	10	Capt., Army, Artl.				WITNESS	U.K.
BENTROP	195874	M	Ger.		Pay-master, Stalag VI C, Bathorn (Ger.) 1.-7.42				MURDER	FR.
BENTZ	141451	M	Ger.		Chief, C.C. Grossbeeren (Ger.)				MURDER	FR.
BENTZ	166931	M	Ger.		Army, Lixheim (Fr.) 9.44				MURDER	FR.
BENTZ	261266	M	Ger.		Lt., 2 Tank-Div., Bergerac, Issigeac, Gardonne, Dordogne (Fr.) 6.44				MISC.CRIMES	FR.
BENTZ	261267	M	Ger.		Lt., Feldzensur-Stab 46, Corminville, Eure-et-Loire(Fr.) 8.44				MURDER	FR.
BENYSKIEWICZ see BENSKIEWITZ	252914	M			Rottenfhr., Camp Dora, Nordhausen (Ger.)				MURDER	U.S.
BENZ	146787	F			Guard,Administration Penitentiary,C.C.Ravensbrueck(Ger.)				TORTURE	FR.
BENZ	146789	M			Wachtmeister, SS-Pol.Regt.Todt				MURDER	FR.
BENZ	151720	M	Ger.		Civilian, supervisor, C.C., Bamberg(Ger.)				TORTURE	U.S.,U.K.
BENZ	158347	M	Ger.		Col., Stalag 13 D, C.C., Nuernberg (Ger.) 5.44				TORTURE	U.K.
BENZ, Heinrich	251967	M	Ger.	00	Sgt., 532 Gendarmerie, Nave (It.) 8.44				INTERR.	U.K.
BENZ	252397	M	Ger.		Landholder,civilian, Ihlowerfehn (Ger.) 44				INTERR.	YUGO.
BENZ, Peter	176958	M	Ger.		Prison-guard, C.C., (Lux.)				TORTURE	FR.
BENZE	189467	M			Maj., Army, 36 Geb.Korps, staff 20, Finmark (Nor.)				MURDER	NOR.
BENZEL	1680	M	Ger.		Capt., Regt. 752-I. 7.44				MURDER	U.K.
BENZLER	190030	M			Reichsministerium for the Ostgebiete, German minister in Zagreb,Dr., Ljubljana, Zagreb (Yugo.) 4.41-44				MURDER	YUGO.
BERAN	142043	M	Ger.		Capt., N.S.D.A.P., Stalag 17, C.C., Kaisersteinbruch (Aust.) 5.43				TORTURE	U.S.
BERAN-OVA, Marie	187464				See:Part.II,Nation.:Czech.					
BERBIN see DERBIN,Franz	188172									
BERCE, Jean	189654	M			Worker, civilian, St.Ruprecht (Aust.)				TORTURE	U.S.
BECHERT, Rudi	80	M	Ger.		Chief of Gestapo, Velmanya (Fr.) 8.-9.43				TORTURE	FR.
					SS-Sturmbann, civilian in a camp, Bebogingta at C.C. Oswiecim-Birkenau (Pol.) 42-44				MURDER	FR.,BEL.,YUGO
BECK, Adolphe	166930	M	Ger.		Gendarm, Feldgendarmerie, Luneville Maisce (Fr.) 8.44				MURDER	FR.
BECK, Jean	132598	M	Ger.		Chief of the Gestapo, Velmanya (Fr.)				TORTURE	FR.
BECKFELD	256678	M	Ger.		Employee, civilian, camp Dora, Nordhausen (Ger.)				INTERR.	FR.
BERDEISMAN	151729	M			SS-Osturmfhr., SS-E.A.Bn.II, Graz-Wenzeldorf (Aust.) 2.45				MURDER	U.S.
BERDEISMANN	128597	M			Obersturmfhr., SS, Mauthausen (Aust.)				MURDER	U.S.
BEREUX	167642	M	Ger.		SS-Sonderfhr., SS, Chateaubriant (Fr.) 10.-12.41				MURDER	FR.
BERECEM see BEREGEN,Joseph	146914									
BERECZEN see BEREGEN,Joseph	146914									
BEREGEN,Joseph or BERRESSEN or BERRENSSEN or BERECEM or BERRESSEM or BERECZEN	146914	M	Ger.		Lt., C.O., 54 Airforce-Regt., 9 Coy., Camp Finistere, place Plougasnou (Fr.) 7.44				MURDER	FR.
BEREND	159411	M			Sturmbannfhr., Waffen-SS, Ploc (Pol.) 8.42				MURDER	U.S.
BERES or BEHRENS or BIERES	81	M	Ger.		Interpreter, Geheime Feldpolizei, Locmine (Fr.) 7.-8.44				TORTURE	FR.
BERES	257901	M			Capt., Panzer-Bde., Meuse-Bridge, Antwerpen (Bel.) 12.44				MISC.CRIMES	U.S.
BERENS,Joseph	176957	M	Ger.		Pvt., Army-Kdo., C.C. Michahrweiler (Ger.) 44-45				TORTURE	FR.
BERENS,Paul	257799	M	Ger.	1. 9.96	Employee, Camp Nordhausen (Ger.)				MURDER	U.S.
BERENZ	139833	M			Uscharfhr., SS				MURDER	U.S.
BERG	82	M	Ger.		Camp-official, C.C. Leusderheide (Neth.) 5.42				TORTURE	NETH.
BERG	10171	M	Ger.		Lt., Army				TORTURE	U.S.
BERG	62362	M	Ger.		SS-Scharfhr., SS, C.C. Amersfoort (Neth.) 42				MURDER	U.S.
BERG see BERGER	146653									
BERG	172906	M	Ger.		Custom-house-officer, customs-exercises Fitlinges-Concises Rives (Fr.) 3.44-8.44				MURDER	FR.
BERG	185776	M	Ger.		SS-Rottenfhr., SS-Leibst.Adolf Hitler, Renardmaut, Stavelot (Bel.)				MURDER	BEL.
BERG	187007	M	Ger.		Cmdt., 21 Inf.Regt. Bavarois, Aulnay (Fr.) 8.44				MURDER	FR.
BERG	189580	M	Ger.		Adjutant, Zollgrenzschutz, Cousises (Fr.) 6.44				MURDER	FR.
BERG	195873	M	Ger.		Guard, C.C. Struthof-Natzweiler (Fr.) 40-44				TORTURE	FR.
BERG	253562	M	Ger.		Hptsturmfhr., SS, (Ger.)				MURDER	U.S.
BERG	255080	M			Oscharfhr., C.C. Buchenwald (Ger.)				MURDER	U.S.
BERG	300987	M	Ger.		Member of staff C.C. Struthof-Natzweiler (Fr.) 42-44				MURDER	FR.
BERG,Franz	305782	M	Ger.		Member of staff C.C. Struthof-Natzweiler (Fr.) 7. or 8.44				MURDER	U.K.
BERG,Friedrich	192691	M	Ger.	13. 7.02	Oberwachtmeister, Reichsjustizministerium, Strafgefangenenlager Nord, C.C. Finmark (Nor.)				MURDER	NOR.
BERG,Guenther	196142	M	Ger.		Sgt., Feldpost-Nr. 03429, Selles s.Mer(Fr.)8.44				WITNESS	FR.
BERG,Heinrich	151736	M	Ger.	18. 5.99	Civilian, tax-collector, Simmern (Ger.) 8.44				TORTURE	U.S.
BERG,Rudolf	252396	M	Ger.		Capt., Gestapo, Kragujevac (Yugo.) 10.41				MURDER	YUGO.
BERGA,Karl	132573	M	Ger.		Gendarm, Feldgendarmerie 958, Sisteron (Fr.) 6.44				MURDER	FR.
BERGBAUER,Sepp or Josef aliases BERGHAUER or BERGAUER	261900	M	Ger.	6. 1.13	Employee-chief, Gestapo, jewish-section, Moravska, Ostrava (Czech.) 40-45				SUSPECT	CZECH.
BERGDORF,Karl	187465	M	Ger.		Stalag XIII D, Meinheim near Gunzenhausen (Ger.)				TORTURE	BEL.
BERGEL,Karl	193998	M	Ger.	21. 3.02	Osturmfhr., SS, C.C. Terezin (Czech.) 39-45				TORTURE	CZECH.
BERGMANN	72670	M	Ger.		Scharfhr., Waffen-SS, C.C. Struthof (Fr.) 9.44				MISC.CRIMES	FR.
BERGMANN	148760	M	Ger.		Crim.comm., Police, Aachen (Ger.) 8.44				WITNESS	U.S.
BERGMANN see BERGMANN	173108									
BERGMANN	253569	M	Ger.		Hptscharfhr., SS, C.C. Buchenwald (Ger.)				INTERR.	FR.
BERGMANN,Horst	253565	M	Ger.	about 23	Lt., German Army, Inf., Bn."Draumburg", Bilt (Utrecht) (Neth.) 3.41				MURDER	NETH.

BER-BER

NAME	C.P.FILE NUMBER	SEX	NATIO-NALITY	DATE OF BIRTH	RANK OCCUPATION UNIT PLACE AND DATE OF CRIME	REASON WANTED	WANTED BY
BERGEMANN, Otto	151737	M	Ger.		Uschfhr, W-SS, Totenkopf Standarte, CC Buchenwald, Weimar	TORTURE	U.S.
BERGENTZLE	11215	M	Ger.		Pvt, 110 Pz. Gren.Rgt., N.C.O., Albine (Fr.) 6.44	MURDER	FR.
BERGER	1293	M	Ger.		Civilian Jaeger Div. Rgt.114 Col	MURDER	U.K., U.S.
BERGER	72749	M			Pvt., Interpreter, Dulag 377, 1.45	TORTURE	U.S.
BERGER	125097	M	Ger.		Cpl., Lds.Schtz.Br.559, Boelton (Ger.) 12.42	TORTURE	U.K.
BERGER	126297	M		00	SS Obersturmbannfhr, Head of Gestapo, Klagenfurt (Aust.)	MISC.CRIMES	U.S.
BERGER	131812	M			Dr., Chief of Gestapo, CC Tarnow (Pol.)	MURDER	U.S.
BERGER (or BERG, or BERTEL)	146653	M	Ger.		SS Oschfhr., CC Buchenwald, Weimar (Ger.)	MURDER	U.S.
BERGER	157153	M	Ger.		Civilian, Brux (Czech.) 5.44-5.45	TORTURE	U.K.
BERGER	158360	M	Ger.	1903 - 05	Cpl., Stalag 8 A, Goerlitz and Mellingen (Ger.) 2.45	TORTURE	U.K.
BERGER	163245	M	Ger.	15	Bannfhr, Hitler Jugend, Hunspach (Fr.) 2.44	MURDER	FR.
BERGER	176372	M			Col., Feldkommandantur, Alencon (Fr.)	PILLAGE	FR.
BERGER	179764	M	Ger.	90	Lt.Col., 721 Jg.Rgt., Bubbio Sansefolcro (It.) 6.44	MURDER	U.K.
BERGER	188669	M	Ger.		Feld-Gend., Bar le Duc (Fr.) 8.44	MURDER	FR.
BERGER	189681	M			Civilian, firm of A.Niklas Waters Engineers, Teplitz-Schoenau (Czech.) 5.44-5.45	TORTURE	U.K.
BERGER	191900	M	Ger.	13	Camp Chief (Bauleiter), CC Camiers (Fr.) 41-44	TORTURE	FR.
BERGER	192195	M	Ger.		Col., Feld-Kdtr. Alencon, St.Aubin d'Appenai (Fr.) 6.44	PILLAGE	FR.
BERGER	192294	M			SS, CC Flossenburg (Ger.) 44-45	MURDER	U.S.
BERGER	196143	M	Ger.		Osturmfhr., CC Ravensbrueck (Ger.)	TORTURE	BEL.
BERGER	196387	M	Ger.		9 Brandenburg Rgt.	MISC.CRIMES	U.S.
BERGER	255081	M			Uschfhr, CC Buchenwald (Ger.)	MURDER	U.S.
BERGER (or BOERGER)	257948	M			Oberregierungsrat, Staatsrat Orator, 150 Pz.Bde., Meuse Bridge Antwerpen (Bel.) 12.44	MISC.CRIMES	U.S.
BERGER	260699	M	Ger.		Hptwachtmstr, W-SS, Straf-Gefangenen-Lager, North Norway 6.42-5.45	MURDER	YUGO.
BERGER	301387	M	Ger.		SS Inspector, General of PoW-Camps, Freystadt, Bitterfeld (Ger.) 1.45-4.45	BRUTALITY	U.K.
BERGER	306062	M	Ger.		Sgt, Stalag IX-D, PoW-Camp Stalag XII D, Trier (Ger.) 41-43	MISC.CRIMES	YUGO.
BERGER	306074	M	Ger.		Town Mayor, St.Josephs Hospital, Diest (Bel.) 4.44	TORTURE	CAN.
BERGER, Alex	151727	M			Civilian, CC Lenzing (Aust.)	MURDER	U.S.
BERGER, Alfred	124904	M			Pvt, 1 SS Pz.Div., 1 SS Pz.Rgt., 2 Coy, Malmedy (Bel.) 12.44	MURDER	U.K.
BERGER, Alfred	190347	M	Ger.		Cpl., Army, Gross-Rohrheim (Ger.) 3.45	WITNESS	CAN.
BERGER, Emil	72683	M	Ger.		Civilian Employee, CC BE 2, Bitterfeld (Ger.) 10.43-4.45	MISC.CRIMES	U.S., U.K.
BERGER, Emil	194939	M	Ger.		Dr., Arbeits-Kdo, CC Pottenbrun (Ger.) 44-45	TORTURE	U.K.
BERGER, Franz	252851	M			Uschfhr, CC Harzungen, Ellrich, Nordhausen (Ger.)	MURDER	U.S.
BERGER, Franz	305580	M	Ger.		SS-Mann, CC Flossenburg, Hersbruck, Wolkenburg, Ganacker and Leitmeritz (Ger. and Czech.) 1.42 and 5.45	MURDER	U.S.
BERGER, Friedrich	132591	M	Ger.		Chef, Gestapo, Paris (Fr.)	MURDER	FR.
BERGER, Georg	192692	M			Sgt, Reichs-Justiz-Ministerium, Straf-Gef.Lager Nord, Finmark (Nor.) 45	MISC.CRIMES	NOR.
BERGER, Georges	176146	M	Ger.		Cpl., 7 Coy, SS Formation "Germania", Jussey (Fr.) 4.41	MURDER	FR.
BERGER, Gottlieb	135135	M	Ger.		Obergruppenfhr, SS, Germany, 1.45	TORTURE	U.S.
BERGER, Gottlieb	62156	M	Ger.		Lt. General, SS Chief for Railways and Broadcast	TORTURE	U.N.W.C.C.
BERGER, Heinrich	192106	M	Ger.		Camp Guard, CC Brno (Czech.)	TORTURE	CZECH.
BERGER, Helmuth	252459	M	Ger.		Chief de Chantier of work party, Mauthausen (Aust.) 45	TORTURE	FR.
BERGER, Helmuth	300175	M	Ger.		Foreman, CC Neuengamme (Ger.)	TORTURE	FR.
BERGER, Hermann	189521	M	Ger.		Coy 62852, Noaille Parisis Fontaine (Fr.)	MURDER	FR.
BERGER, Hy	301725	M	Ger.	about 17	Bannfhr, operating with Gend. Aschbach	MURDER	FR.
BERGER, Joseph	173107	M			Oschfhr, SS Lager M-I, CC Muehldorf-Ampfing (Ger.) 6.44-4.45	MURDER	U.S.
BERGER, Karl	151726	M	Ger.	5.12.01	SS-Pvt, 65 Totenkopf-Standarte, CC Korczyn and Chmielanik (Pol.)42	MURDER	U.S.
BERGER, Karl	187003	M		12	Feldgendarm, Feld-Gend.958, Sisteron (Fr.) 6.44	MURDER	FR.
BERGER, Karl	253566	M	Ger.	15. 6.13	Sgt, z.b.V. Kdo.31, Valasske Mezirici (Czech.) 2.-5.45	TORTURE	CZECH.
BERGER, Kurt	290308	M	Ger.	12. 2.01	Agent, SD	MISC.CRIMES	U.S.
BERGER, LtD, Heinrich	185829	M	Ger.		SS-Obersturmbannfhr, Gestapo, SD, Prag	MURDER	CZECH.
BERGER, Otto (see BURGER)	158378						
BERGER, Paul	36671	M	Ger.	about 07	N.C.O., Posten Schlindler, Boelton (Sudetenland) 7.41-43	MISC.CRIMES	U.K.
BERGER, Paul	131811	M	Ger.		Factory Worker, Working Camp, Duisburg (Ger.)	TORTURE	U.S.
BERGER, Paul	301988	M	Ger.		N.C.O., 2 Coy, 559 Lds.Schtz.Bn. in charge of ARB, Kdo. E 540, attached to Stalag VIII-B at Bolten, Boeltonor St.Bolten(Sudetenld)42	BRUTALITY	U.K.
BERGER, Walter	253557	M	Ger.		Pvt., 377 Jaeger Rgt., Vinkt (Bel.)	INTERR.	BEL.
BERGER, Werner	133753	M			Oschfhr, SS, CC Buchenwald - Weimar (Ger.)	MURDER	FR.
BERGERMAN	149729	M			Hptschfhr, SS, Natzweiler (Fr.) 8.44-45	MURDER	FR., U.S.
BERGERT, Kurt	306335	M	Ger.		SS-Scharfhr, CC Buchenwald (Ger.) 5.38 und 10.43	MURDER	BEL.
BERGET (alias PEPE)	176371	M	Ger.	15	Civilian	MURDER	FR.
BERGFELD	127072	M			Meister des Haeftlingseinsatzes, CC Dora, Nordhausen (Ger.)	MURDER	FR., BEL.
BERGFELD	256864	M			Mittelwerk GmbH., Labor Asst, CC Nordhausen (Ger.)	MURDER	U.S.
BERGHAUS	11216	M			Lt., Army, Pz.Gren.Rgt.III, Gourdon (Fr.)	MURDER	FR.
BERGHAUS, Bernhard	258118	M		31. 7.96	Civilian, Industrialist, Luebeck (Ger.)	INTERR.	U.S.
BERGHAUS, Guenther	253558	M			Uschfhr., 10 Coy, 2 Pz.Gren.Rgt., Malmedy (Bel.)	MURDER	U.S.
BERGHAUSER	194801	M	Ger.		Civilian, Weiterode, Galgenkopf (Ger.) 2.45	MURDER	U.S.
BERGIEHNER, M.	11217	M			Pvt., Pz.Gren.Rgt. III, N.C.O., Albine (Fr.) 6.44	MURDER	FR.
BERGLER	192295	M			Sturmbannfhr, SS, CC Flossenburg (Ger.) 44-45	MURDER	U.S.
BERGMAN	148590	M		05	Camp Guard, CC Gardelegen (Ger.) 4.45	MURDER	U.S.
BERGMANN	49556	M	Ger.		Prof. Dr.,Civilian, Charite, Berlin (Ger.)	WITNESS	U.S.
BERGMANN (or BERGEMANN)	173108	M	Ger.		Hptscharfhr, SS, CC Natzweiler (Fr.) 9.44	MURDER	U.K.
BERGMANN	185460	M	Ger.	07	SS Obersturmbannfhr., SD, Praha (Czech.)	MURDER	CZECH.
BERGMANN	186714	M		about .91	Lt., Army, Elten (Ger.) 9.44	WITNESS	U.K.
BERGMANN	191739	M			Lt, Army, Inf., 77 Bn, 4 Coy, Foret Liege (Bel.) 9.44	MURDER	BEL.
BERGMANN	196122	M		05	Officer, Schnelle Abt.602, Chambord (Fr.) 8.44	MURDER	FR.
BERGMANN	252854	M			CC Nordhausen (Ger.)	MURDER	U.S.
BERGMANN	256332	M	Ger.		Sgt., Army, Trier (Ger.)	MISC.CRIMES	YUGO.
BERGMANN	257773	M	Ger.		Cmdt, Feld-Gend., Amsterdam (Neth.) 10.44	MURDER	NETH.
BERGMANN	259602	M	Ger.		Capt, Commander, Coy, E.M. of 3 Rgt.of Voluntary Ukraine, Saint-Loup, Rhone (Fr.) 8.44	MURDER	FR.
BERGMANN, Lothar	124305	M			Oschfhr, 1 SS Pz.Div, 2 Pz.Gr.Rgt.,9 Coy, Malmedy (Bel.) 12.44	MURDER	U.S.
BERGMANN, Max	141347	M	Ger.		Pvt, Army, Ldschtz.Bn.178 Lager Coy, CC Halberstadt (Ger.)	TORTURE	U.K.
BERGMANN, Rudolf	256334	M	Ger.		Pvt, 2 Coy, St. Gildas des Bois (Fr.) 10.44	INTERR.	FR.

BER-BER

NAME	C.R.FILE NUMBER	SEX	NATIO-NALITY	DATE OF BIRTH	RANK OCCUPATION UNIT PLACE AND DATE OF CRIME	REASON WANTED	WANTED BY
BERGMEIER	192644	M			Untersturmfhr.,SS,C.C.Buchenwald (Ger.) 1942-45	TORTURE	U.S.
BERGMEIER, Anton	151728	M	Ger.	9.12.13	Obscharfhr.,SS-Totenkopf-Standarte,C.C. Buchenwald,Luetzkendorf	TORTURE	U.S.
BERGMEYER	133751	M			Obscharfhr.,SS,C.C. Buchenwald-Weimar (Ger.)	TORTURE	U.S.
BERGMUELLER, Josef	131813	M	Ger.		Unterscharfhr.,Guard,C.C.Flossenburg (Ger.) 42-45	TORTURE	BEL.
BERGNER	258127	M	Ger.		SS-Officer, physician,C.C.Natzweiler (Fr.)	MURDER	BEL.
BERGNER, Emil	153356	M		90	Official,Railway,C.C.Bitterfeld (Ger.) 43-45	TORTURE	U.K.
BERGS	252852	M			Pvt.,C.C.Ellrich,Nordhausen (Ger.)	MURDER	U.S.
BERGS	305824	M	Ger.		Pvt.,1 Aufkl.Abt.3.Coy.2 Col.XV Div.Afrika Korps,St.Leger (Arlon) 5.9.44	MISC.CRIMES	BEL.
BERGS, Gerhard	191881	M	Ger.	30.12.00	Manager,Civilian,Dillingen (Ger.) 11.5.44	PILLAGE	U.S.
BERGSTALLER	252853	M			N.C.O.,C.C.Ellrich,Nordhausen (Ger.)	MURDER	U.S.
BERGT, Helmuth	151734	M	Ger.	6.10.11	Obscharfhr.,SS-Totenkopf-Standarte,C.C. Buchenwald-Weimar (Ger.)	TORTURE	U.S.
BERHARDT	128596	M			Hauptscharfhr.,SS-Panzer Div.Totenkopf,C.C.Mauthausen (Aust.)41-45	MURDER	U.S.
BERHARDT	196604	M	Ger.		Gend.No.11866,Valence (Fr.)	PILLAGE	FR.
BERINGER, Annie	176962	F	Ger.		Camp-Secretary,C.C.Vannes (Fr.) 44	TORTURE	FR.
BERINGER, Victor	11218	M			Pvt.,Panzer Gren.Regt. III,Albine (Fr.) 29.6.44	MURDER	FR.
BERINGER	131702	M			Col.,Judge,Reich Military Court,Berlin-Torgau (Ger.) 40-45	MURDER	FR.
BERINGER	300400	M	Ger.		Oberkraegsgerichtsrat,Halle (Ger.) 4.2.44	MISC.CRIMES	FR.
BE INGER, Rudolph	153345	M		10	Civ.Leader,Gestapo,Innsbruck (Aust.)	MURDER	U.S.
BERK, Guenther	195764	M	Ger.		SS-Pvt.,1.Panzer Div. "Adolf Hitler",St.Avelot (Bel.) 44	MURDER	BEL.
BERKEMEYER	185273	M			Civilian,Herkemissen (Ger.) 44	MURDER	U.S.
BERKER	158380	M	Ger.		Agent,Gestapo,Bourg-Madame (Fr.) 43-44	LOOTING	FR.
BERKER	174421	M	Ger.	17	Civilian,Penemoult,Penencoult s.mer Baltique (Fr.) 45	TORTURE	FR.
BERKER	185156	M			C.C.Dachau (Ger.)	MURDER	FR.
BERKER, Gaston	127117	M			Lagerfhr.,C.C. Erfurt,Hochheim-Grunestahl (Ger.)	MURDER	FR.
BERKHOF	36670	M			Capt.,Army,Stalag VIII B,Lamsdorf (Ger.) 43	BRUTALITY	U.K.
BERKHOFF	141853	M	Ger.	05	Major,Stalag VIII B,Lamsdorf (Ger.) 41-42	TORTURE	U.K.
BERKMANN, Martin	151790	M			Civilian,Borkum (Ger.) 44	MURDER	U.S.
BERKNER	300362	M	Ger.		Adjutant,Feldgendarmerie,Chaumont,Chateauvillain,Haute-Marne (Fr.)	MURDER	FR.
BERLETH	174225	M			Lager I,C.C.Muehldorf-Ampfing (Ger.) 44-45	MURDER	U.S.
BERLICHINGER	136994	M	Ger.		Capt.,21 Panzer Div.,HQrs,Sessenheim (Fr.) 45	MURDER	U.C.
BERLIN, Wilhelm	158366	M		79	Mayor,Civ.,Public Official,Gardelegen (Ger.) 45	MURDER	U.S.
BERLING	36646	M			C.C.Bodungen,Osterode (Ger.)	MURDER	FR.,POL.
BERLING	124840	M		05	Civilian,Carpenter,Nentershausen (Ger.) 44	PILLAGE	U.S.
BERLINGER, Emil	207044	M	Ger.		SS-Untersturmfhr.,C.C.Northern,Karasjok (Nor.) 42	MURDER	YUGO.
BERLINGHOF	195872	M			Guard,C.C.Struthof-Natzweiler (Fr.) 40-44	TORTURE	FR.
BERLINGHOFF	194800	M	Ger.		SS-Hauptscharfhr.,SS,C.C.Lublin (Pol.) 40-43	MURDER	POL.
BERMEISTER (or BURMEISTER)	121119						
BIRKEL, Friedrich	253559	M	Ger.	23.10.02	Official,Civ.,Labour-Office,Hradec,Kralove (Czech.) 39-45	MISC.CRIMES	CZECH.
BERN, Josef	190408	M	Ger.		Civilian,Wiesbaden (Ger.) 43-45	PILLAGE	U.S.
BERNAERT	163099	M	Ger.		Inspector,Reichsbahn-Direction,Karlsruhe,Chantilly (Fr.) 44	PILLAGE	FR.
BERNARD	199657	M	Ger.		Lt.,SS Panzer Div.24,9 mot.Coy.,Port St.Foy, La Fleix (Fr.) 44	MURDER	FR.
BERNARD	83	M	Ger.		Hauptscharfhr.,C.C.Loos (Ger.)	TORTURE	U.K.
BERNARD	96660	M	Ger.		Agent,Gestapo,Loos (Ger.)	BRUTALITY	U.K.
BERNARD	121083	M		05	Stabsscharfhr.,SS,Gestapo,Lille (Fr.) 40	BRUTALITY	U.K.
BERNARD	125111	M			Kreisleiter,NSDAP,Landeck Tirol, (Aust.) 45	MISC.CRIMES	U.K.
BERNARD	141382	M			Lt.,28 Inf.Regt.,116 Bn.,Lehr.Coy.,Maubourguet (Fr.) 44	MURDER	FR.
BERNARD	176960	M		10	SS-Commandant,SS-Panzer Gren.Div.24, Port St.Foy (Fr.) 18.6.44	MURDER	FR.
BERNARD	189658	M			N.C.O., 116 Inf.Bn.,1.Coy. Sombrun (Fr.) 44	MURDER	FR.
BERNARD	258126	M	Ger.		Kommandofhr.,C.C.Dachau (Ger.)	SUSPECT	BEL.
BERNARDI, Michael	193458	M	Ger.	13.2.03	Civilian,Servant,Obwachtmeister,Reichsjustizministerium,Strafgefangenenlager Nord,C.C.Finnmark (Nor.) 6.42	TORTURE	NOR.
BERNARDT, Carlo (or CARLOS Bernardt)	194799	M	Ger.		Sgt.,Army,Carpi (It.) 9.43	MURDER	U.K.
BERNARDY, Heinrich	134789	M	Ger.		Civilian,Efforen (Ger.) 10.44	PILLAGE	U.S.
BERND	151732	M	Ger.		Sturmbannfhr.,Major,SS,C.C.Dachau (Ger.) 42-45	TORTURE	U.S.
BERND	158349	M	Ger.		Hauptsturmfhr.,SS,SD,Segeletz (Ger.)	MURDER	U.S.
BERNDT	72734	M			Brigade Leader,SD Office Berlin,Segeletz (Ger.) 5.44	MURDER	U.K.,U.S.
BERNDT	121084	M	Ger.		Civilian,Kiew (Russia) 41-42	MURDER	U.S.
BERNDT	125096	M	Ger.	85	Col.,Commandant de l'Oflag X C. Luebeck (Ger.) 44	MURDER	FR.
BERNDT	151731	M			Rottenfhr.,SS,2 Panzer Gren.Regt.2 Coy.,Stavelot-Malmedy (Bel.)44	MURDER	U.S.
BERNDT	194798	M	Ger.		Ortsgruppenleiter,Territories Occupies,Luxembourg	LOOTING	LUX.
BERNDT, Hans	258221	M			Sgt.,"Teufel"Div. Sarajevo (Yugo.) 44	INTERR.	YUGO.
BERNDT, Helmut	187459	M	Ger.	08	Ortsgruppenleiter,N.S.V., Bad Neuenahr (Ger.) 39-44	MURDER	U.S.
BERNDT, Helmuth	195320	M	Ger.		Prisoner-Secretary,C.C.Auschwitz (Pol.)	BRUTALITY	BEL.
BERNEC, Viktor	168600	M	Ger.		Pvt.,9 Gren.Ers.Regt., 1 Coy.,Magny D'Anigon (Fr.) 9.44	MURDER	FR.
BERNECHNER	189165	F	Ger.		Member,Gestapo,C.C.Dachau (Ger.) 40-45	MURDER	BEL.
BERNELSCH, Theo	188670	M			Civilian	MURDER	FR.
BERNER	300177	M			Town Mayor,Police, SS Police Geb.Jg.Regt.,18 of Livadia,Vrestamites Near Livadia,Beotia. 7.44	PILLAGE	GRC.
BERNER, Alma	195417	F	Ger.	05	Head-Guard,C.C. Bremen,Oslebshausen (Ger.)	TORTURE	POL.
BERNERT, Erich	84	M	Ger.		Obscharfhr.,Gestapo,Crimassistent,Abt.IV Ref.r 2 Oslo (Nor.)40-45	TORTURE	NOR.
BERNETTE (or WERNETTE)	196270	M			Interpreter,Sicherungstruppen St.Flour,93 Inf.Regt., 2 Sec.Coy. St.Flour (Fr.) 44	MURDER	FR.
BERNHARD	1294	M	Ger.		Pvt.,Army,194 Gr. 2 Pl. 4 See	MISC.CRIMES	U.K.
BERNHARD	185626	M			Lt.,Feldgendarmerie,Baume Cornillane, (Fr.)	MURDER	FR.
BERNHARD	185771	M			SS-Obersturmfhr.,SS-Leibstandarte "Adolf Hitler" 1 Pz.Gren.Div. Stavelot (Bel.) 12.44	MURDER	BEL.
BERNHARD	192193				SS-Untersturmfhr.,SS-Div."Das Reich",SS-Rgt. "Der Fuehrer" FP 15 807, Frayssmet le Gelat (Fr.) 5.44	MURDER	FR.
BERNHARD	192648	M	Ger.	20	SS-Unterscharfhr., C.C.Buchenwald (Ger.)	MURDER	U.S.
BERNHARD, Walter	173305	M	Ger.		Cpl., Army,Brignon (Fr.) 8.44	MURDER	FR.
BERNHARD, Wilhelm	259354	M	Ger.		Sturmbannfhr.,Gestapo of Poitiers (Fr.) 40-45	MISC.CRIMES	FR.
BERNHARDT	62361	M	Ger.		SS-Cpl.,12 SS Panzer Div."Hitler Jugend"	MISC.CRIMES	CAN.
BERNHARDT	124511	M	Ger.		Unterscharfhr., Inf.Regt. 25 Rots (Fr.) 6.44	TORTURE	U.K.
BERNHARDT	127174	M	Ger.		Hauptmann-Adjutant, du Cdt. Camp Oflag X C,C.C.Luebeck (Ger.) 44	MURDER	FR.

BER-BES

NAME	C.R.FILE NUMBER	SEX	NATIO- NALITY	DATE OF BIRTH	RANK OCCUPATION UNIT PLACE AND DATE OF CRIME	REASON WANTED	WANTED BY
BERNHARDT	252264	M	Ger.		Leader of G.F.P.-Gestapo, Lille (Fr.) 40-44	MISC.CRIMES	FR.
BERNHARDT, Adolf	252927	M	Ger.		13. SS-Polizei-Regt., Ferlach (Aust.) 44-45	MURDER	YUGO.
BERNHARDT, Carlos (see Carlos Bernhardt)	194799	M	Ger.		Sgt., Army, Capri (Ital.)	MURDER	U.K.
BERNHARDT, Ehregott	306766	M	Ger.		Civilian, Borsdorf (Ger.) 8.44	BRUTALITY	U.S.
BERNHARDT, Hans (or BEHRHARD)	185272	M	Ger.	27. 7.21	Uschfhr., SS, Buchenwald (Ger.) 42-45	MURDER	U.S.
BERNHARDT, Heinz	252928	M			Uschfhr., C.C.Nordhausen (Ger.)	MURDER	U.S.
BERNHARDT, Theodor	306337	M	Ger.		SS-Cpl., C.C.Buchenwald (Ger.) 5.38-10.43	MURDER	BEL.
BERNHART, Josef	173127	M	Ger.		Zugwachtmeister, C.C.Schirmeck-Rotenfels (Fr.)	INTERR.	U.K.
BERNHART, Karl	253561	M	Ger.	15.10.78	Civ.,Gravedigger, Breclav (Czech.) 1.45	MURDER	CZECH.
BERNHAUER	173128	M			C.C.Schirmeck, Rotenfels, Gaggenau (Fr.-Ger.)	INTERR.	U.K.
BERNICKE	306142	M	Ger.		Col.,Heereszeugamt Glince,Osteinbek bei Glinde (Ger.) 3.45	MURDER	U.K.
BERNOTAT, Fritz	121085	M	Ger.		Head of Physicians Hadamar-Institute,Hadamar (Ger.)	MURDER	U.S.
BERNOTH	305825	M	Ger.		Pvt.,1.Aufkl.Abt., 3 Coy.,2 Column, XV.Div. Afrika-Corps, St. Leger (Arlon) 9.44	MISC.CRIMES	BEL.
BERNS, Jean	252906	M	Ger.	22. 4.13	Pvt.,13. Coy.553 Gren.Regt., Bruay en Artois (Fr.) 9.44	MURDER	FR.
BERNSCHEIN, Wilhelm	306338	M	Ger.		SS-Sgt.,C.C.Buchenwald (Ger.) 5.38 and 10.43	MURDER	BEL.
BERNSDORF	261607	M	Ger.		Sgt., Waffen-SS "Dirlewanger-Brigade",Warschau and Sluck (Pol.)40-44	MURDER	POL.
BERNSDORFF	149745	M	Ger.		Stendartenfhr.,Sturmbannfhr.,Official SS-Regt.,C.C.Gardelegen(Ger.)45	MURDER	U.S.
BERNSTEIN	190680	M	Ger.		Pvt., Eis.Bn.717,St.Andries, Versenare, Les Bruges (Bel.)	MURDER	BEL.
BERNSTEIN	194797	M	Ger.		SS-Lt., C.C.Lublin (Pol.) 40-44	SUSPECT	POL.
BERNSTEIN	255082	M			Sturmfhr.,C.C. Buchenwald (Ger.)	MURDER	U.S.
BERNSTEIN, Hans	151733	M	Ger.	13	Usturmfhr.,SS, C.C.Lublin (Pol.)	TORTURE	U.S.
BERNSTORFF, Graf, Andreas Peter	257899	M	Ger.		Lt.,150 Pz.Bds., Jagdverband,Meuse Bridge,Antwerpen (Bel.) 12.44	MISC.CRIMES	U.S.
BERNT	255566	M	Ger.	10	Lt.,Navy,Pioniergruppe, Heusden (Neth.) 1.44	PILLAGE	NETH.
BERNTH	301074	M	Ger.		Crim.secr., leader S.D.,R.S.D. of Ordenspol., Aalborg, Copenhagen, Boulevarden 27 Prison in Sect.Hansgade (Denmark) 9.43-44	TORTURE	DEN.
BERNTHAUSEL	252907	M	Ger.		Sgt.,Gend.Trupp 694,Lancon (Fr.) 6.44	MURDER	FR.
BERRE	253563	M	Ger.		Interpreter, Sipo, Abt.IV D,Bruessel (Bel.)	INTERR.	BEL.
BERREND	139825	M		95	Cpl.,Waffen-SS,Arbeitskdo. A-6 (Ger.)	MURDER	U.S.
BERRENSSEN (see BEREGEN)Joseph	146914						
BERRESSEM (see BEREGEN) Joseph	146914						
BERRESSEN (see BEREGEN) Joseph	146914						
BERREVOETS	253560	M	Ger.		Section-leader,Sipo,Bruessel (Bel.)	INTERR.	BEL.
BERRON	176420	M			Interpreter,Army,Troissereúx (Fr.)	MURDER	FR.
BERS,	173337	M	Ger.		Dr.,Lt.,Army,Fieldpost 22372, Macva Sabac (Yugo.)41	MURDER	YUGO.
BERSCH	130097				Civ., Business-manager of plant at C.C.Dora,Mittelbau Nordhausen(Ger.)	MURDER	U.S.
BERSCH, Erich	256865	M	Ger.		Scharfhr., SS-Medical,Attendant, C.C.Dora Nordhausen (Ger.)	MURDER	U.S.
BERSCHAOUT	121087	M	Ger.		Lt.,NSDAP,Army,Stalag VIII B,Lamsdorf (Ger.) 10.42-2.43	BRUTALITY	U.K.
BERSIN	62360	M			Cpl., SS,Army,1.SS-Pz.Div."Hitler Jugend", 1.Pz.-Regt., 2 or 3 Coy., Malmedy (Bel.) 12.44	MURDER	U.S.
BERT (see Best)	252913	M			Organisation Todt,C.C.Muhldorf,Ampfing (Ger.) 6.44-4.45	MURDER	U.S.
BERTAGNOLLI	173987	M					
BERTEL (see BERGER)	146653						
BERTEL	189659	M	Ger.		N.C.O.,SS, Paris (Fr.) 7.44	TORTURE	FR.
BERTEL, Werner	133753	M	Ger.		Oschfhr.,SS,C.C.Buchenwald,Weimar (Ger.)	MURDER	U.S.
BERTELS	156824	M	Ger.		Cpl.,Army,6 Para-Artillery-Regt.1 Btty.,Xanten(Ger.) 3.45	MURDER	CAN.
BERTELSMANN	120539	M	Ger.		Dr.,Civ., Physician,Kiew-Institute,Kiew (Russ.) 41-42	MURDER	U.S.
BERTHEL, Arno	134790	M		28. 2.03	Pvt.,4 Waffen-SS,Tot.Kopf-Sturmbann,C.C.Dora Mittelbau,Nordhausen (Ger.) 43-45	WITNESS	U.S.
BERTHLING, Ernest	260626	M	Ger.		SP. 08291, Neuville en Ferrain (Fr.) 9.44	SUSPECT	FR.
BERTHOLD	128741	M	Ger.		Ob.Gefr.,Ldsschtz.-Bn.299,H.Q.Rochlitz, C.C. Penig (Ger.)11.43-44	TORTURE	U.K.
BERTHOLD	139831	M	Ger.		Lt.,Stalag X B,Sandbostel (Ger.) 5.45	MISC.CRIMES	U.S.
BERTHOLD, Mathias	196386	M		25	Pvt., SS-Menn,Malmedy (Bel.) 12.44	MURDER	U.S.
BERTL	187542	M	Ger.		Usturmfhr.,SS,C.C.Mecklenburg (Ger.)	MURDER	U.S.
BERTL	255513	M			Sgt., C.C.Buchenwald (Ger.)	MURDER	U.S.
BERTOG, Herbert	194391	M	Ger.	23	Member,SS	MURDER	U.S.
BERTOLACCINI	188671	M			Civilian,Lyon (Fr.) 8.44	MURDER	FR.
BERTOLD, Paul	252389	M	Ger.	23	Cpl.,on anti-partisan duties,Mesola,Ariano Polesine (Ital.) 12.44	TORTURE	U.K.
BERTRAM	86	M	Ger.		Lt.General,Army,Oberfeldkommandantur,Liege (Bel.) 42-43	MURDER	BEL.
BERTRAM	124512	M	Ger.		Oberleutnant,Inf.Regt.855 (Fr.) 7.44	MURDER	U.K.
BERTRAM	139123	M	Ger.	10	Oschfhr.,Waffen-SS,286 Div.,1200 Regt.,7 Coy.,Anzegem (Bel.) 9.44	MURDER	U.S.
BERTRAM	162721	M	Ger.		Oberfeldkommandantur,Oberfeldkommendant Liege (Bel.)	MURDER	BEL.
BERTRAM	261773	M	Ger.		Cpl., Art.H.D.V.199-2235 H.D.F.N. of S.P.27046 C,Lorgies (Fr.) 9.44	MURDER	FR.
BERTRAM, Albert	158385	M	Ger.		Lt.,788 Ldsschtz.Bn.,1 Coy.,Marienau (Ger.)	WITNESS	U.K.
BERTRAM, Albert	255573	M		95	Lt.Col.,Stalag XII A,Limburg (Ger.)	MURDER	U.S.
BERTRAM, Elrich	261918	M			Building-leader, Engineer,Civ., Hamm and Kirchlengern (Ger.) 40-45	BRUTALITY	NETH.
BERTRAM, Georg	258967	M	Ger.		Lt.General	WITNESS	U.S.
BERTRAM, Hans	252908	M			Lt.Commandant, Unit 33743 E,Berck-Plage (Fr.)	INTERR.	FR.
BERTRAM, Hermann	158344	M		1. 7.87	Member of Special Police at Ullnitz,Gloethe(Ger.) 7.44	MURDER	U.S.
BERTRAND, Albert	36668	M	Ger.		Lt.,Army,C.C. (Ger.) 3.45	BRUTALITY	U.K.
BERTSCH, Walter	9630	M	Ger.		Dr.,Pol.Chief,State Minister,Staatsministerium,Bohemia-Moravia,Prag (Czech.) 42-45	MISC.CRIMES	CZECH.
BERWICK, Josef	253564	M	Ger.		Cpl.-Chief,Plouguiel (Fr.) 8.44	INTERR.	FR.
BESATI, Gerard (see GILLARDO, Jean)	259369						
BESCH	163634	M			Lt.,Totenkopf-Standarte,Waffen-SS,C.C.Buchenwald,Weimar (Ger.)	TORTURE	U.S.
BESCH	252929	M			Uschfhr., Camp Osterhagen, Nordhausen(Ger.)	MURDER	U.S.
BESCH, Joseph	195397	M			Civilian, Aachen (Ger.) 8.44	TORTURE	U.S.
BESCH, Walter	176419	M	Ger.		SS-Osturmfhr.,SS,C.C.Neuengamme,Wilhelmshaven (Ger.) 44-45	MURDER	FR.-U.K.
BESCH, Walter	252935	M	Ger.		Blockaeltester,C.C.Neuengamme (Ger.) 44	MURDER	FR.
BESCHEERER, Rudolf	134751	M		22. 6.04	Uschfhr., Sgt. of the Guard,SS, Camp Nordhausen (Ger.) 43-45	WITNESS	U.S.
BESCHTEL	49793	M			Member of Gestapo,Chateau,Gaillard and Saintes (Fr.) 8.45	MURDER	FR.
BESCHTEL	301615	M			Chief,S.D. at Saintes,Commune of Juicq Saintes (Fr.) 8.44	MURDER	FR.
BESENBRUCH	151723	M		25	Navy Co.Stielau Musculus,Gravenwoehr (Ger.) 11.-12.44	MISC.CRIMES	U.S.
BESKEN	173986	M	Ger.		Cpl.,Stalag VI A,C.C.Hemer (Ger.) 42-45	TORTURE	U.S.

BES - BHO

NAME	C.R.FILE NUMBER	SEX	NATIO-NALITY	DATE OF BIRTH	RANK OCCUPATION UNIT	PLACE AND DATE OF CRIME	REASON WANTED	WANTED BY
BESNECH	260056	M	Ger.		Gendarm,Div.Oberland,Isere,Drome(Fr.)7.-8.44		SUSPECT	FR.
BESSEMER	256653	M			Employee,CC Muehldorf(Ger.)		MURDER	U.S.
BESSINGER	169468	M	Ger.	92	Col.Army,Oflag VIIB,Artillery,Eichstaett(Ger.)4.45		MURDER	U.K.
BESSMANN	151724	M			Untersturmfhr.SS 2 Pz.Div.Das Reich,2 Coy.Recce Bn.,Tulle(Fr.)5.44		MURDER	U.S.
BEST	87	M	Ger.		Gestapo Commandant,SS Osturmbannfhr.,Sousse(Tunisia)43		MISC.CRIMES	FR.
BEST or BERT	252913	M			CC Dora,Nordhausen(Ger.)		INTERR.	U.S.
BEST, Erich	190249	M	Ger.		Gestapo H.G.,Koeln(Ger.)43-45		MURDER	U.K.
BEST, Melchiados	255569	M			Lt.Control of the powder-magazine,Bergerac,Perigueux(Fr.)6.-7.44		TORTURE	FR.
BEST, Werner	195695	M			Dr.,SS Lt.Gen./official,Auswaertiges Amt,Administr.42		MISC.CRIMES	U.S.
BESTAHN	138252	M	Ger.		Lt.4 Coy.SS Formation Walker,Gambsheim(Fr.)12.44-1.45		MURDER	FR.
BESTEL	195827	M			Kapo,Bruno works,Auschwitz(Ger.)40-45		MURDER	FR.
BESTEMAN, Peter	307045	M	Ger.		Member,Sonderkdo.Feldmeier,Apeldoorn,Arnhem,Wangeningen(Neth.)10.43-44		MURDER	NETH.
BESTMANN	88	M	Ger.	09	Navy,Marinearzt,Dr.,Trondheim Asst.Surgeon(Nor.)2.42		MURDER	NOR.
BETCHER, Max	252910	M	Ger.		Overseer,CC Ravensbrueck(Ger.)		BRUTALITY	FR.
BETCHERER	306299	M			Lt.attached at St.Malo,Ille,Vilaine(Fr.)8.44		PILLAGE	FR.
BETHE, Walter	260544	M	Ger.	4. 8.11	SS Rottfhr.SS Totenkopf CC Auschwitz(Pol.)44-45		BRUTALITY	POL.
BETHKE	135132	M	Ger.		SS Kommissar,SS Member,Gestapo Hqs,Koeln(Ger.)		MURDER	U.S.
BETHKE	176370	M			469 Inf.Regt.2 Bn.,Le Tholy(Fr.)11.44		PILLAGE	FR.
BETHKE, Willy	173135	M	Ger.		Kapo,CC Gaggenau,Natzweiler(Ger.Fr.)42-43		MURDER	U.K.
BETKE	185752	M	Ger.		Waffen SS Adolf Hitler,1 Pz.Div.Zugaufstellung II,1 SS Recon.Bn. Parfondruy,Stavelot(Bel.)		MURDER	U.S.
BETKE	193991	M	Ger.		SS Sturmmann,Stavelot(Bel.)12.44		MURDER	BEL.
BETKOW, Fritz	252465	M			Pvt.Camp Ellrich,Nordhausen(Ger.)		MURDER	U.S.
BETLJEWSKI, Kazimierz	151719	M			Civilian,Ploc(Pol.)42		WITNESS	U.S.
BETMAN	300021	M	Ger.		Col.,Crete(Grc.)9.43		MISC.CRIMES	GRC.
BETOW	192805	M	Ger.		SS Oscharfhr.CC Stalag,Falstad near Trondheim(Nor.)41-44		WITNESS	NOR.
BETRAOURI	167643	M			Sgt.Georgian Bn.1 Coy.,Tulle(Fr.)4.44		MISC.CRIMES	FR.
BETSCH, Georg	258422	M			SS Mann,guard,CC Ohrdruf(Ger.)12.44-4.45		MURDER	U.S.
BETTCHER, Heinz	196120	M	Ger.		Feldgendarm,Feldgendarmerie Unit.43800,Tourcoing(Fr.)9.44		MURDER	FR.
BETTENHAUSEN, J.	168617	M	Ger.		Treuhaender,firm Ksiegarnia Ruch,Warschau(Pol.)9.39-44		MISC.CRIMES	POL.
BETTGES, Berthe	261066	F	Ger.		Secretary,NSDAP,Le Creusot(Fr.)3.44		INTERR.	FR.
BETTGES, Willy	261065	M	Ger.		Member,German Mission,detailed at Schneider's Works,Le Creusot(Fr.) Civ.Occ.Engineer,Schwarzkopf A.G.,2.44		INTERR.	FR.
BETTINI	195871	M	Ger.		Personnel CC Struthof-Natzweiler(Fr.)40-44		TORTURE	FR.
BETTKER	142044	M		95	Sturmscharfhr.SS CC Dachau(Ger.)40-45		MURDER	U.S.POL.
BETTRAM	133956	M		05	SS Obsturmfhr.CC Buchenwald(Ger.)		MURDER	U.S.
BETZ	192806	M	Ger.		Wachtmeister,Schupo,CC-Stalag Falstad near Trondheim(Nor.)41-44		MURDER	NOR.
BATZ see BATZ	307037							
BETZ, Sebastian	158342	M	Ger.	94	Dr.med.,Physician,Civilian,Schlossberg Krs.Rosenheim(Ger.)4.45		WITNESS	U.S.
BETZ, Wilhelm	261368	M	Ger.	8. 5.13	Cpl.Waffen SS,3 Bn.Art.Regt.12,Tourouvre(Fr.)8.44		MURDER	FR.
BETZE	256866	M			Scharfhr.SS CC Nordhausen(Ger.)		MURDER	U.S.
BETZE, Anton	252466	M			Rottfhr.Camp Harzungen,Nordhausen(Ger.)		MURDER	U.S.
BETZEE, Anton	257782	M	Ger.		SS Scharfhr.Camp Wieda,Nordhausen(Ger.)		MURDER	U.S.
BETZOLD, Johann	192807	M			Schupo,CC Stalag,Falstad,Trondheim(Nor.)41-45		MURDER	NOR.
BEUCHR	256867	M			Mittelwerk GmbH.Head of Sub-Sec.CC Nordhausen(Ger.)		MURDER	U.S.
BEULE	125022	M	Ger.	10	Inspektor,Verwaltungs Police,Charleville(Fr.)		TORTURE	FR.
BEULKE	188672	M	Ger.		Army Inspector,Commandant,Ruestungsamt-Ruestungsinspection Aussenstelle Belfort(Fr.)11.44		PILLAGE	FR.
BEULWITZ	252911	M	Ger.		Major,Chief of SS,Brianza,Atha,Milano(It.)8.44		INTERR.	U.K.
BEUMANN	196384	M	Ger.		W.O.,Fallschirm-Pion.Bn.8,St.Amand-Montrond(Fr.)6.44		INTERR.	FR.
BEUS, Magdalene	188135	F	Ger.	12.10.29	Civilian,Aachen(Ger.)44		TORTURE	U.S.
BEUSZ, Paul	261879	M	Ger.		N.C.O.,Army 1 Coy.377 Jaeg.Regt.,Vinkt-Meigem,Environs(Bel.)5.40		WITNESS	BEL.
BEUTCHER	189583	M	Ger.		Chief,Lt.SS Gestapo,Rodez(Fr.)5.44		MURDER	FR.
BEUTE	258476	M			Blockfhr.Sturmmann,SS CC Ohrdruf(Ger.)12.44-4.45		MURDER	U.S.
BEUTEL	258898	M		24. 8.05	Block-Chief,SS,Ohrdruf(Ger.)44-45		MURDER	FR.
BEUTEL, Hans	261627	M	Ger.	24.12.25	SS Mann,CC Ohrdruf(Ger.)44-45		MURDER	FR.
BEUTHORN alias BUETHORN	160214	M			Pvt.Army,12 Volksgrend.Div.27,Fires Regt.,Languille(Bel.)		WITNESS	U.S.
BEUTL, Otto	194796	M		29. 7.24	SS Cpl.,Waffen SS,9 Coy.Pz.Gren.Regt.2,Malmedy(Bel.)12.44		SUSPECT	U.S.
BEUTLER alias DEUTLER	172946	M	Ger.		Capt.Stalag IX B,CC Bad Orb(Ger.)44		MURDER	U.S.
BEUTLER, Fritz	260625	M	Ger.		Lt.Col.		WITNESS	U.S.
BEWERSDORF	252912	M	Ger.		Cpl.Gend.Troop 535,Annecy,le Chablais(Fr.)5.44		MISC.CRIMES	FR.
BEWOAK	187335	M	Ger.		Lt.General,Occupied Territory,Crete(Crete/Grc.)3.43		MURDER	GRC.
BEXEL see BEYER	193592							
BEXEL	251977	M	Ger.		W.O.,2 Coy.Bn.Heptin,Le Clion sur mer(Fr.)9.44		TORTURE	FR.
BEXO	301296	M	Ger.		Member,Gestapo at Trencin,CC Oswiecim-Birkenau(Pol.)39-45		MURDER	CZECH.
BEYER	1295	M	Ger.		Officer,Naval supply		MISC.CRIMES	U.K.
BEYER	62359	M	Ger.		Capt.Paratroops,Roermond(Neth.)11.44-1.45		MURDER	U.S.NETH.
BEYER	141348	M	Ger.		Sgt.Army,Kundorf/Posen(Pol.)5.41		TORTURE	U.K.
BEYER see BEXEL	193592							
BEYER	252467	M			Rottfhr.Camp Osterhagen,Nordhausen(Ger.)		MURDER	U.S.
BEYER, Ernst	151725	M	Ger.	20. 3.91	SS Totenkopf Standarte,KL Buchenwald-Weimar(Ger.)39-45		MURDER	U.S.
BEYER, Jerrie (BYER)	123418	M			Civilian		TORTURE	U.K.
BEYERLE (see BEYERLE)	90						MURDER	FR.
BEYERLE	195048	M	Ger.		Gestapo official,Lyon(Fr.)7.44		MURDER	FR.
BEYERLE, Fritz	301189	M	Ger.		Rottfhr.SA Volkssturm,Huchenfeld(Ger.)3.45		MURDER	U.K.
BEYERLE, Johann	258384	M	Ger.		Guard,SS CC Ohrdruf(Ger.)12.44-4.45		MURDER	U.S.
BEZZENBERGER or BITZENBERGER	252458	M	Ger.		Lt.Unit L.N.S.4,L'Ain(Fr.)7.44		MISC.CRIMES	FR.
BGRUKOGEMANN, Otto	192693	M	Ger.	18. 9.02	Sgt.Reichsjustiz-Ministerium,Strafgefangenlager Nord,CC Finmark(Nor.)		MISC.CRIMES	NOR.
BHIEL	147196	M	Ger.		Ob.Lt.,11 Pz.Div.(Fr.)44		MURDER	FR.
BHOLE see BOHLE	300030							

BIA-BIL

NAME	C.R.FILE NUMBER	SEX	NATIO-NALITY	DATE OF BIRTH	RANK OCCUPATION UNIT PLACE AND DATE OF CRIME	REASON WANTED	WANTED BY
BIAGOCH or BIAGOFF	253597	M	Ger.		Capt., Col., Langres Kaserne Turenne, L'Ain (Fr.) 7.44	MURDER	FR.
BIALAS	301678	M	Ger.		Bde.-Chief, Mongolian "Oberland" Unit, St.Nazaire en Royans (Fr.) 8.44	MURDER	FR.
BIALKOWSKI	91	M	Ger.		Sturmbannf., SS, C.C. Dachau (Ger.) 40-43	MURDER	FR.
BIALOWANS	159406	M			Untersturmf., S.D.-Chief, Creil (Fr.) 43	MISC.CRIMES	FR.
BIASOLO, Arthur	147210	M	Ger.		Interpreter, Feldgendarmerie, Charlercy (Bel.)	TORTURE	BEL.
BIBLENSKI	188676	M	Ger.		Oberscharf., SS, S.D., Chembery (Fr.)	MURDER	FR.
BIBOW	173984	M	Ger.		Member, SS, Zdunska, Wola and Lodz (Pol.) 8.42-8.43	MURDER	POL.
BIBOWSKY	151763	M			Dr., Oberstabsarzt, OKW, Chief of PW Affairs	MISC.CRIMES	U.S.
BICHEL	188677	M	Ger.		Feldgendarmerie, Bar le Duc (Fr.)	MURDER	FR.
BICHEL, Johann	253589	M			Unterscharf., Camp Harzungen, Nordhausen (Ger.)	MURDER	U.S.
BICHKA	159410	M	Ger.	10	Pvt., Stalag XX.A, Nesseu (Pol.) 44	TORTURE	U.K.
BICK	253576	M			Unterscharf., Camp Ellrich, Nordhausen (Ger.)	MURDER	U.S.
BICKART or BICKHART	172944	M		11	Pvt., Stalag IX.C, Kdo.625, C.C. Berga (Ger.) 2.-4.45	MURDER	U.S.
BICKEL or BIRKEL	185629	M	Ger.		Festungs-Kommandant, Fort du Hâ (Fr.) 44-45	MURDER	FR.
BICKENBACH, Otto	196982	M	Ger.	2. 3.01	Professor, Institute of Anatomie, Strassburg (Fr.) 40-44	MURDER	FR.
BICKERICH, Wolfgang	168597	M	Ger.		Pastor, Official, C.C. Leszno (Pol.)	WITNESS	POL.
BICKERT (see BICKLER)	159405						
BICKETT	151757	M			Pvt., Inf.Regt., (K-Coy., 423.Inf.) C.C. Berga (Ger.) 4.45	TORTURE	U.S.
BICKHART (see BICKART)	172944						
BICKLER or BICKERT	159405	M	Ger.		SS-Standertenfuehrer, Sicherheits-Polizei, Paris Chief of Section VI, Paris, 11, Boulevard Flondrin (Fr.) 6.44	TORTURE	FR.
BICKLER	196605	M			Lt., 157.Div., Mountain-Regt. (Res.), Plateau des Glieres (Fr.) 3.44	WITNESS	FR.
BIDGER (see BOGER)	252007						
BIDON, Johann	72735	M	Ger.		Pvt., Paratrooper, Roermond (Neth.) 11.44-1.45	TORTURE	U.S.
BIEBER, Otto	135123	M	Ger.		Pvt., 709.Inf.Div., Bakery-Coy., Cherbourg (Fr.) 6.44	MURDER	U.S.
BIEBERBICK	151767	M			Cmdt.-Chief, Gestapo, Service Central Gestapo de Paris Cannes (Fr.) 44	LOOTING	FR.
BIERICHT	207694	M	Ger.		Obersturmbannfuehrer, S.D., Gestapo, Dijon (Fr.) 44	TORTURE	U.K.
BIEDERBICH	252559	M	Ger.		Sturmbannfuehrer, SS, Abt. III, Sicherheits-Polizei Brussel (Bel.)	MURDER	BEL.
BIEFLECK or BIELECK	133752	M			Rottenfuehrer, SS, C.C. Buchenwald (Ger.)	MISC.CRIMES	U.S.
BIEG, Otto	92	M	Ger.		Pioneer-Chief, Caen (Fr.) 3.43	MURDER	FR.
BIEGI, George	259430	M			Farmer, Bechtheim (Ger.) 10.44	MURDER	U.S.
BIEHLE, Heine	193561	M	Ger.		Cpl., S.D., Sipo, Leeuwarden (Neth.) 9.44-4.45	MURDER	NETH.
BIEHLER	174845	M	Ger.		Crim.Secret., Gestapo, Searburg (Ger.)	MURDER	U.S.
BIEHLCHLAVEK, Richard	187541	M			Employee, S.D. and Gestapo, Brno (Czech.) 39-45	MURDER	CZECH.
BIEHRS	191315	M			Civilian, Reneuy (Fr.) 1.44	MURDER	FR.
BIEKEL	256987	M			Cpl., Army, Kreiskommandantur - Iol. Department, Kragujevac, Orasac, Gruza (Yugo.) 42-44	MURDER	YUGO.
BIEKER, Frantz	167644	M	Ger.		Cpl., Dienststelle, Gruppe Verwaltung, Biache, St. Vaast (Fr.) 8.44	MURDER	FR.
BIELECK (see BIEFLECK)	133752						
BIELECK	193929	M			Rottenfuehrer, SS, C.C. Buchenwald (Ger.)	TORTURE	U.S.
BIELITZ, Karl (Otto)	159401	M	Ger.	03	Oberwachtmeister, Reserve, Police, C.C.Ohrdruf - Buchenwald (Ger.)	WITNESS	U.S.
BIELL, Hans	131272	M	Ger.		Kapo, Block-Aeltester, C.C. Jawischowitz/Auschwitz (Pol.) 43-44	MURDER	U.S.
BIELSKI	147195	M	Ger.		Pvt., 11.Panz.Div., I.Grp. of Kampfgruppe "Wilde", (Fr.) 44	MURDER	FR.
BIENECK, Johannes	159407	M		29	Hitler Jugend, Javenitz, C.C.Gardelegen (Ger.) 4.45	MURDER	U.S.
BIENERT	173983	M			Capt., Police, Brest-Litowsk (Pol.) 10.-11.42	MURDER	POL.
BIENERT, Otto	72736	M	Ger.		Pvt., Fallschirmjaeger-Bn., Roermond (Neth.) 11.44- 1.45	TORTURE	U.S.
BIENKOWSKI, Michael	253579	M			Pvt., Camp Harzungen, Nordhausen (Ger.)	MURDER	U.S.
BIENSKY	261380	M			Lt., San Vittoria (South of Ancona near Aso River) (It.) 3.44	MURDER	U.K.
BIER	137659	M	Ger.		Capt., German Army, Official Arbeitskommando E 51, Klausberg (Ger.) 1.45	MURDER	U.K.
BIER, Erich	189791	M	Ger.	16	Pvt., Army, Demmin (Ger.) 2.45	MURDER	U.K.
BIER, Francois (Franz)	306788	M	Ger.	27.11.06	Employee, Gestapo,Vichy previously from 1.10.40- end of Jan.44 Interpreter at H.U.V. Paris (Fr.) 10.43-9.44	MURDER	FR.
BIERER, Hermann	149740	M			Unterscharf., SS, C.C.Mauthausen (Aust.) 41-45	MURDER	U.S.
BIERES (see BERENS)	195045	M			Feldgendarm, Loomine (Fr.) 7.-8.44	MURDER	FR.
BIERGER	148537	M			Capt., Neus P.Z.M. 6326, Chanas (Fr.) 44	MURDER	FR.
BIERKAMP, Walter	93	M	Ger.		Oberfuehrer, SS, Commander of Sipo, Kracow (Pol.) 40-45	INTERR.	POL.,U.S.
BIERLING	253599	M			Oberscharfuehrer, SS, "Das Reich", "Der Fuehrer", 3.Coy., 1.Bn., Oradour sur Glane (Fr.) 6.44	MISC.CRIMES	U.K.
BIERMANN	1297	M	Ger.		Capt., Army, 331.Eng.Bde., 3.Coy.,	MURDER	U.N.W.C.C.
BIERMANN	187577	M	Ger.		Sturmfuehrer, SS, Wkr. VIII, Col.	MURDER	U.K.
BIERMANN, Otto	197718	M	Ger.	00	Marine-Art., C.C.Lueneburg, Wilhelmshaven (Ger.)	WITNESS	FR.
BIERNAT, Georges	185627	M			Army, Cantal Puy-de-Dome (Fr.)	MURDER	U.S.
BIERS	151764	M		95	Sgt., Army, C.C.Stalag III.B III.A, 2.45	MURDER	U.S.
BIERSACK, Martin	139115	M	Ger.		Foreman, Civilian, Armamentworks, Mauthausen (Aust.)	MURDER	U.S.
BIERWIRTH, Eduard	253580	M	Ger.		Rottenfuehrer, Camp Harzungen, Nordhausen (Ger.)	MURDER	FR.
BIESE, Hermann	176952	M			Officer, Kommando 419 S, Kassel (Ger.) 11.41	MURDER	U.S.
BIESOLD	253581	M			Pvt., Camp Ellrich, Nordhausen (Ger.)	MURDER	U.S.
BIETA	253582	M			Pvt., Camp Rottleberode, Nordhausen (Ger.)	MURDER	U.S.
BIETAU, Gerhard	72737	M			Sgt., Waffen-SS, Chabrehez (Bel.) 2.45	MURDER	FR.
BIETHES or BIETLER	176953	M			Col., Army, (Fr.)	MURDER	FR.
BIETZ	189664	F	Ger.		C.C.Chief of female wardens, Ravensbrueck (Ger.) 42-45	MURDER	BEL.
BIETZSCHKE or FIETZSCHKE, Kurt	162488	M	Ger.		Cpl., 263. Inf.Div., Landerneau (Fr.) 44	MURDER	NOR.
BIGNIAK, W.	131149	M	Ger.	27	Navy, Jemappes (Ger.) 9.44	TORTURE	FR.
BIGUS, Konrad	162720	M		17. 1.18	N.C.O., Army, Regt. Stabs-Coy., 27 (174), Bodoe (Nor.)	MURDER	HUNG,FR.
BILAIR	136179	M	Ger.	95	Secretary, NSDAP, Sterbflitz (Ger.) 41-45	MURDER	FR.
BILAKOWA, Martha	167645	F	Ger.		Prison-guard, St.Lo (Fr.) 44	MURDER	BEL.
BILANG	127116	M	Ger.	05	Member, Gestapo at Karlsruhe, C.C. Anrath (Ger.)	MURDER	FR.
BILEB, Paul	252704	M	Ger.	18. 7.20	Civilian, Neuvy au Hculme (Fr.) 7.43 Pvt. SS, C.C.Buchenwald (Ger.) 5.38-10.43	TORTURE	FR.
BILEK, Hans	306339	M	Ger.		Member, NSDAP, foreign labourers, C.C.Moers (Ger.)	MURDER	U.S.
BILEN, Henrik	129828	M	Ger.		Cpl., Unit No.39817 B, Neuvy au Hculme (Fr.) 7.43	MURDER	FR.
BILER, Paul	253596	M			Oberscharf., Camp Ellrich, Nordhausen (Ger.)	MURDER	U.S.
BILGER	253585	M			Unterscharf., SS, C.C. Struthof-Natzweiler (Fr.) 42-44	MURDER	FR.
BILGER, Eugen	176981	M	Ger.				

BIL-BIR

NAME	C.R.FILE NUMBER	SEX	NATIO-NALITY	DATE OF BIRTH	RANK OCCUPATION UNIT PLACE AND DATE OF CRIME	REASON WANTED	WANTED BY
BILK, Josef	168601	M	Ger.		Cpl., 9.Gren.Ers.Regt. I.Coy., Magny d'Anigon (Fr.) 9.44	MURDER	FR.
BILL	251306	M	Ger.		Lt.-Cmdt., Btty.-Art., Berck-Plage (Fr.) 9.44	PILLAGE	FR.
BILL	252847	M	Ger.	15	Lageraeltester, C.C. Auschwitz (Pol.)	INTERR.	FR.
BILL	306454	M	Ger.		W.O., 10 Motor Coy. CA 2-98 Bn., Grotto of Luire, Vercors (Drôme) (Fr.)44	MURDER	FR.
BILLART	11219	M	Ger.		Pvt., Marine Art. Bn.4, Quiberon (Fr.) 44	MURDER	FR.
BILLAU	176416	M	Ger.		SS-Rottenfhr., SS, Barth (Ger.) 43-45	MURDER	FR.
BILLAU	195870	M	Ger.		Personnel, C.C. Struthof-Natzweiler (Fr.) 40-44	TORTURE	FR.
BILLEMANS, Emil (or BILLEMANN, BOLLMANN)	131145	M	Ger.		N.C.O., Feldpost Nr.22380 (Bn.717), St.Andre and Varsenare (Bel.) 9.44	MURDER	BEL.
BILLIMEYER (see BILLMEYER)	259774						
BILLINGER	147084	M	Ger.		Guard, SS, Begunje (Yugo.) 43	MURDER	YUGO.
BILLMEYER (or BILLIMEYER)	259774	M	Ger.	96 or 99	Cpl., Army, Landesschuetzen Bn.483, Camp E 173, Setzdorf (Czedh.) 44	BRUTALITY	U.K.
BILLOSCHETSKY, Willie	195672	M	Ger.		Pvt., 1.SS-Panz.Div."Leibstandarte Adolf Hitler", Ligneuville (Bel.)12.44	MURDER	U.S.
BILSHAUSEN, Herbert	257827	M	Ger.		Lt. zur See, German Navy, Honseidet (Nor.) 5.45	INTERR.	NOR.
BINAR, Erich	301056	M	Ger.		Commissar, Government, Tisnov-Moravia (Czech.) 3.45	INTERR.	CZECH.
BINDE	141956	M	Ger.	95	Hptscharfhr., Guard-Waldlager V and VI, Ampfing, Mühldorf, Nettenheim (Ger.) 44-45	TORTURE	U.S.
BINDEL, Horst	221411	M	Ger.	25	SS-Oberfhr., Nachr.Regt.506, Abwehr, Bad Wildungen (Ger.) 45	MISC.CRIMES	U.S.
BINDEN	1224	M	Ger.		Public official, Judge, Oberkriegsgerichtsrat, Eisenstadt (Austria)	TORTURE	U.S.
BINDER	166928	M	Ger.		Capt., Abwehr, C.C. Nuernberg (Ger.)	MISC.CRIMES	FR.
BINDER	173226	M	Ger.	07	Sgt.- Major, Stalag XVIII A, C.C. Klausberg (Ger.) 7.43	INTERR.	U.K.
BINDER	146493	M	Ger.	00 or 10	SS-Mann, C.C. Ravensbrueck (Ger.) 8.42-4.45	MURDER	FR., BEL.
BINDER	252472	M	Ger.		SS-Rottenfhr., 3.Coy., 1.Bn. "Das Reich", "Der Fuehrer", Oradour sur Glave (Fr.) 6.44	MURDER	FR.
BINDER (or MINDER)	256808	M			Hptscharfhr., Waffen-SS.	MURDER	U.S.
BINDER	256993	M	Ger.		Major, Army, 5.Schupo-Regt., 332. Bn., Kragujevac, Gruza, Ovasac (Yugo.) 42-44	MURDER	YUGO.
BINDER, August	172904	M	Ger.		Dr., SS-Stubannfhr., Waffen-SS,Totenkopf-Standarte, C.C.Buchenwald-Weimar (Ger.)	TORTURE	U.S.
BINDER, Paula	141453	F	Ger.		Subject took the property of the Jewish employees.	PILLAGE	FR.
BINDGES	197741	M	Ger.		SS-Hptscharfhr., C.C. Buchenwald (Ger.)	TORTURE	U.S.
BINDZUS	196299	M	Ger.		SS-Rottenfhr., C.C. Mauthausen (Austria)	TORTURE	BEL.
BINECK, Richard	185633	M	Ger.		Sgt., Army, Semoussac (Fr.) 9.44	MURDER	FR.
BINERT	128593	M	Ger.	16	Uschafhr., SS, C.C. Mauthausen (Austria) 41-45	MURDER	U.S.
BING, Otto	159409	M	Ger.		Sturmscharfhr., SS-Gestapo Saarebruck, Folkling (Ger.) 11.44	MURDER	FR.
BINGEL	306573	M	Ger.		Blockfuehrer, C.C. Wilhelmshaven (Ger.) 3.44	MURDER	U.K.
BINGEN	172873	M	Ger.		Untersturmfhr., SS, Chatillon Coligny (Fr.) 3.-7.44	WITNESS	FR.
BINING	258899	M	Ger.		Dr., SS-Osturmfhr., Chief of Block 10, Auschwitz (Pol.) 40-45	TORTURE	FR.
BINKE	151761	M	Ger.	05	Uscharfhr., SS 2.Panz.Gren.Regt. 3.Bn. 12.Coy., Stavelot (Bel.) 12.44	MURDER	U.S.
BINNA, Theodor	137742	M			Civilian	WITNESS	U.S.
BINNEFELD	185630	F	Ger.		CC-Aufseherin, C.C.Koenigsberg-Oder (Ger.)	TORTURE	FR.
BINNS	62356	M	Ger.		SS Women Guard, Waffen-SS, C.C. Ravensbrueck (Ger.)	MURDER	U.K.
BINS	124588	M	Ger.	20	Officer, S.S. Ravensbrueck (Ger.) 4.42-4.45	MISC.CRIMES	BEL.
BINTZ (see BINZ)	146681						
BINTZ	196298	F	Ger.		Woman head of supervisors, C.C.Ravensbrueck (Ger.)	TORTURE	BEL.
BINTZIK, Heinrich	147194	M	Ger.		Cpl., 11.Panz.Div. (Fr.) 44	MURDER	FR.
BINZ	141954	M			Oberlagerfuehrer, Camp Kala, Rudolstadt (Ger.)	TORTURE	U.S.
BINZ (or BINTZ)	146681	F	Ger.	21	SS-Oberaufseherin, C.C. Ravensbrueck (Ger.)	TORTURE	FR.
BINZ	163495	M	Ger.		Chief, C.C. Kala, Rudolstadt (Ger.) 44-45	TORTURE	FR.
BINZ	172872	M	Ger.	93	SS-Major, 4.Police Bn., Minsk (Russia) 42-44	MURDER	U.S.
BINZ, Moriz	176417	M	Ger.	05	C.C.Dora, Nordhausen (Ger.) 4.45	TORTURE	FR.
BINZINGER, Franz	261085	M	Ger.	22.12.99	SS-Mann, Waffen-SS, Gren.Div.36 "Dirlewanger-Bde", Warsaw and other towns (Pol.) 40-44	MURDER	POL.
BIOTTA	252415	M			SS-Uschafhr., 9.Panz.Pion.Coy., 1.SS Panz.Regt., Malmedy (Bel.)	INTERR.	U.S.
BIPP, Fritz	255570	M	Ger.		Civilian, Mauthausen (Austria)	BRUTALITY	FR.
BIRBAM	251305	M	Ger.		Member, S.D., Toulouse (Fr.) 11.42-8.44	MISC.CRIMES	FR.
BIRCH	141349	M	Ger.		Lt., Army, Pomeranja (Ger.) 2.45	TORTURE	U.K.
BIRCHWALD	191833	M	Ger.	95	Civ. Servant, Railway, Ilnau (Ger.) 6.44	TORTURE	U.K.
BIRGS	194731	M	Ger.		Cpl., Army, Cressonsacq (Fr.) 6.40	WITNESS	FR.
BIRIBI (see DIEDRICH)	150929						
BIRKE, Josef	124517	M	Ger.		Hptscharfhr., SS, C.C. Oranienburg-Sachsenhausen (Ger.) 39-45	MURDER	U.K.
BIRKE	137062	M	Ger.		Civ. Coal-Mine foreman	TORTURE	U.S.
BIRKEL	141454	M	Ger.		Cmdt., Army, Fort de Bordeaux (Fr.) 4.44	MURDER	FR.
BIRKEL (see BICKEL)	185629						
BIRKENBACH	176418	M	Ger.		Capt., Army, Royallieu (Fr.) 41-44	MURDER	FR.
BIRKENBAUL, Werner	11220	M	Ger.		Pvt., Panz.Gren.Regt.III, Albine (Fr.) 6.44	MURDER	FR.
BIRKENDAHL	186484	M	Ger.	21	SS-Usturmfhr., 12.SS Panz.Div."Hitler Jugend", near Caen (Fr.) 6.44	TORTURE	CAN.
BIRKENFELD, Willi (see GERSBACH, Werner)	174790						
BIRKENHAGEN	141849	M	Ger.		Capt., 214.Div. 355.Regt., 12.Coy., Sletteb (Nor.) 12.42	WITNESS	U.K.
BIRKENMEIER	253587	M			Camp Dora, Nordhausen (Ger.)	MURDER	U.S.
BIRKENSTOCK, Edward	192296	M			C.C. Flossenburg (Ger.) 44-45	MURDER	U.S.
BIRKER	139836	F	Ger.		Women-Guard, Waffen-SS, Arbeitslager 101 (Buchenwald), Magdeburg (Ger.) 44-45	TORTURE	U.S.
BIRKHOFF (see BERSCHAOUF)	121087						
BIRKHOLZ, Erwin	252845	M	Ger.	25. 9.04	Employee, Gestapo, Vsetin (Czech.) 39-45	MURDER	CZECH.
BIRKL	260723	M			SS-Uschafhr., C.C. Hallein (Austria)	MURDER	U.S.
BIRKOFF	120607	M	Ger.		Major, Stalag VIII B, Lamsdorf. Niesky-Stalag VIII B (Ger.) 4.43	TORTURE	U.K.
BIRLENBACH, Willy	187004	M	Ger.		Feldgen., Feldgendarmerie-Truppe 626, Peronne Licourt (Fr.) 8.44	MURDER	FR.
BIRLI	173982	M			Civilian, Labour Camp, Lager M 1, Mühldorf, Ampfing (Ger.) 6.44-4.45	MURDER	U.S.
BIRLO	253598	M			Capt., Bonn (Ger.) 43-45	WITNESS	U.S.
BIRMANN	1682		Ger.		Capt., Commanding officer, 148.Inf.Regt. 2.Bn., Amiens (Fr.)6.44	TORTURE	U.K.

NAME	C.R.FILE NUMBER	SEX	NATIO-NALITY	DATE OF BIRTH	RANK	OCCUPATION	UNIT	PLACE AND DATE OF CRIME	REASON WANTED	WANTED BY
BIRMAN see BOLTE	256938									
BIRNBREIER	168591	M	Ger.					Ubach (Ger.)	MURDER	U.S.
BIRNEBACH, Karl	259810	M	Ger.	about 06		Civ., engine-driver, German railways, betw. Dortrecht-Gouda (Neth.) 10.44			BRUTALITY	NETH.
BIRNER	185840	M	Ger.		Lt., Kommandantur, Kissamou at Kastelliou (Crete) (Grc.) 9.44				MURDER	GRC.
BIRNKOTT, Heinrich dit Harry	132726	M	Ger.		Lagerkapo "Dora", Buchenwald (Ger.) 4.43-45				MURDER	FR.
BIRO, Anton O.	255259	M	Ger.		Engineer, Civ., Podbrezova (Czech.) 40-45				MISC.CRIMES	CZECH.
BIR, Wilhelm	125108	M	Ger.		Foreman Civ., Stalag IV C, Bruex (Sud.) (Ger.) 44-45				BRUTALITY	U.K.
BIRTH, Kurt	256851	M	Ger.	30.10.18	Employee, C.C. Nordhausen (Ger.)				MURDER	U.S.
BIRTS	190492	M			Dr., physician, Civ., Dachau (Ger.)				MURDER	U.S.
BIRZE	305876	M	Ger.		Osturmfhr., C.C. Oranienburg (Ger.) 39-45				MURDER	CZECH.
BISACZUCK	179981	M			Army, Labour-camp at Waldlager 5, Muehldorf-Ampfing (Ger.) 6.44-4.45				MURDER	U.S.
BISBORGT	192151	M	Ger.	96	Officer, Geheime Feldpolizei, Brussels (Bel.)				TORTURE	BEL.
BISCHHOF, Karl	148533	M	Ger.		SS Sturmbannfhr., C.C. Auschwitz (Pol.)				TORTURE	U.S.
BISCHOF see BISSHOF	190090									
BISCHOF	173348	M	Ger.		Sturmbannfhr., C.C. Oswiecim-Birkenau (Pol.) 39-45				MURDER	CZECH.
BISCHOF	253577	M	Ger.		Lt. Col. Army, Nuernberg (Ger.) 41-45				MISC.CRIMES	YUGO.
BISCHOF, Heinz	131271	M	Ger.		SS Sturmmann C.C. Jawischowitz-Auschwitz (Pol.)				MURDER	U.S.
BISCHOF, Karl	148490	M			SS Sturmbannfhr., C.C. Auschwitz (Pol.) 43-44				TORTURE	U.S.
BISCHOFF	94	M	Ger.		Gestapo-Leiter Poznan (Pol.)				MURDER	POL.
BISCHOFF	1061	M	Ger.		SS Scharfhr., S.D., Chalons-Marne (Fr.)				MURDER	FR.
BISCHOFF	1298	M	Ger.		Lt., Army, 44.Div. 1.Coy. 8.Bn. (Eng.)				MISC.CRIMES	U.K.
BISCHOFF	128742	M	Ger.		Civ., Falkenburg (Ger.) 6.44-4.45				MISC.CRIMES	U.K.
BISCHOFF	132171	M	Ger.	about 18	Interrogator, Gestapo, Paris (Fr.) 8.42				TORTURE	U.K.
BISCHOFF	159402	M	Ger.	03	Uscharfhr., SS, C.C. Buchenwald (Ger.)				WITNESS	U.S.
BISCHOFF	159403	M	Ger.	00	Lt. Col., Gestapo C.C.Ohrdruf, Nordhausen, Buchenwald (Ger.)				WITNESS	U.S.
BISCHOFF	187038	M	Ger.	00	SA Sturmfhr., Reichsbahn-Direction, Falkenburg (Ger.) 10.43-5.45				TORTURE	U.K.
BISCHOFF	192200	M	Ger.		Cpl., Army, Feldpost-No. 26033 E, Soissons (Fr.) 8.44				WITNESS	FR.
BISCHOFF	259741	M	Ger.		Capt., F.P. No. 41498, Pierre de Semilly - Manche (Fr.) 9.44				WITNESS	FR.
BISCHOFF	901616	M	Ger.		Cpl., Feldgendarmerie Chateaubriant (Loire-Inf.) St.Julian de Mouvautes (Fr.) 7.44				MURDER	FR.
BISCHOFF	901931	M	Ger.		Cpl., Geh. Feldpolizei, Velp, Arnheim (Neth.) 1.45				BRUTALITY	NETH.
BISCHOFF, Emil	191314	M	Ger.		Gendarm, Feldgendarmerie, Kerviherne, Merlevenez (Fr.) 4.45				MURDER	FR.
BISCHOFF, Franz	262005	M	Ger.	1.12.09	SS-Mann, Waffen-SS,Gren.Div.36 Dirlewanger-Bde.,Warschau and other (Pol.) 40-44				MURDER	POL.
BISCHOFF, Heinrich	261113	M	Ger.	21. 6.98	Rottfhr.,Guard, SS Wachbn. 14 C.C.Terezin, Mala Pevnost (Czech.) 43				MISC.CRIMES	CZECH.
BISCHOFF, Helmut or Fritz	240090	M	Ger.	97	SS Osturmbannfhr., Inspector d.SIPO, S.D., Regierungsrat, Braunschweig (Ger.) 44				TORTURE	U.S.
BISEMNIUS, Leo or DUBOIS,Jean	189665	M	Ger.		Member S.D., La Bourboule, Le Mont d'Or (Fr.) 4.44				MISC.CRIMES	FR.
BISEMNIUS, Leo or DUBOIS,Jean	189665	M	Ger.		Oscharfhr., S.D., Chalons (Fr.)				MURDER	FR.
BISHOFF	1061	M	Ger.	05	Pvt., AF Lafayette Prison, Nantes (Fr.) 44				MURDER	FR.
BISKUPP, Gerhardt	29829	M			Osturmbannfhr., SS, Doro-Mittelbau Nordhausen C.C. (Ger.)				MURDER	U.S.
BISSHOF or BISCHOF	190090	M	Ger.		Civ., Burg a.d.Wupper (Ger.) 11.44				MURDER	FR.
BISTER, Otto	191313	M	Ger.	15	Inf.Div. Rgt. 13.Bn.				MURDER	U.S.
BITCH, David	124297	M	Ger.		Auslaendischer Col., Army official Bn.634, Riel sur Below (Fr.) 8.44				MURDER	FR.
BITCHEROV	95	M			Cmdt. H.K.P. 668, Voiron (Fr.) 3.44				WITNESS	FR.
BITNER	196964	M			Org.Todt, C.C. Muehldorf-Ampfing (Ger.) 6.44-4.45				MURDER	U.S.
BITSCH	173980	M			Pvt., Army Unit L 20368, Bandrignes (Fr.) 8.44				MURDER	FR.
BITTALIS	96	M	Ger.		Lt., Wehrkreis-Kdo. X				MISC.CRIMES	U.K.
BITTEL	124343	M			Pvt., Camp Ellrich Nordhausen (Ger.)				MURDER	U.S.
BITTEL, Herbert	253587	M			Dr., civ. in a camp, Hagen (Ger.) 40-45				MURDER	U.S.
BITTER, Heinrich	126528	M	Ger.		Member, Feldgendarmerie, Bel.				INTERR.	BEL.
BITTERLING	252387	M	Ger.		Pvt., 2.Coy., PW-work-Bn. 206, Rovanimie, Kresmenes, Mosjoen (Finl.to Nor. Ger.)				MURDER	NOR.
BITTERMANN	193382	M	Ger.		Civ. working for army, Oflag XI A, Wlodlzimierez (Sov.Un.) 41				WITNESS	U.S.
BITTINS	142330	M			Uscharfhr. SS, Hamburg C.C.Neuengamme (Ger.) up to 45				MURDER	CZECH.
BITTMANN	306076	M			Warder of Prison, Caen (Fr.) 6.44				MURDER	FR.
BITNER	97	M			SS Oscharfhr., C.C. Hutten (Ger.) 3.45				TORTURE	FR.
BITNER	176980	M			Dr., Member NSDAP, S.D., Gestapo, Pilzen (Czech.) 39-45				MURDER	CZECH.
BITNER	185250	M	Ger.	15. 5.15	Manager, Civ. factory, Zlin (Czech.) 43-45				PILLAGE	CZECH.
BITTNER, Maximilian	252717	M	Ger.		Guard, Cpl., Army, C.C. Caen (Fr.) 6.44				MURDER	FR.
BITTNER, Paul	97	M	Ger.		Matr.Gefreiter, Navy, Hopseidet (Nor.) 5.45				MURDER	NOR.
BITTNER, Werner	257828	M	Ger.		Commander, Oberfhr., 8.Rgt. "Grossdeutschland", Alibunar (Yugo.) 4.41				MURDER	YUGO.
BITTRICH, Wilhelm	261965	M	Ger.		SS-Gruppenfhr., 9. SS Pz.Div., Vaucluse (Fr.) 3.44				MURDER	FR.
BITTRICH, Willi	98	M								
BITZER, Georg see BITZER	253588									
BITZEN	192808	M			SS-Hptscharfhr., C.C. Stalag Falstad, Trondheim (Nor.) 41-44				WITNESS	NOR.
BITZENBERGER see BEZZENBERGER	252458									
BITZER, Georg or BITZEL	253588	M			Uscharfhr., Camp Dora Nordhausen (Ger.)				MURDER	U.S.
BIZWANG, Karl	192809	M	Ger.		Member Schupo, C.C. Falstad, Trondheim (Nor.) 41-45				MURDER	NOR.
BJUN	256809	M			Pvt., C.C. Muehldorf, Dachau (Ger.)				MURDER	U.S.
BLAASBERG	192301	M	Ger.		Leg.official, Verwaltungsgericht, Brussels (Bel.) 40-45				MURDER	BEL.
BLACHE	191815	M			Oscharfhr., SS, C.C. Tarnoff (Pol.)				MURDER	U.S.
BLACK	189281	M	Ger.		Uscharfhr., SS, C.C. Dachau (Ger.) 40-45				MURDER	BEL.
BLAECKER, Anton	307049	M			Reichsbahn official, Employee, Fernmeldemeisterei, Amersfoort (Neth.) betw. 10.44 and 5.45				PILLAGE	NETH.
BLAEKE	195869	M			Civ. C.C.Struthof-Natzweiler (Fr.) 40-44				TORTURE	FR.
BLAENECK	149354	M		05	Police chief, Berlin (Ger.)				MISC.CRIMES	FR.
BLAESER, Arnold	157137	M			Civ., Daasdorf, Guthmannshausen (Ger.) 7.-8.44				WITNESS	U.S.
BLAESER, Erwin	131118	M	Ger.	25. 8.26	Kriegsmarine Jemappes (Bel.) 9.44				MURDER	BEL.
BLAESKE, Wilhelm see BLESKE	185404									
BLAGDAROW, Konstantin	134775	M			SS Guard, 4.SS Totenkopfsturmbann C.C.Dora Mittelbau Nordhausen (Ger.) 43-45				WITNESS	U.S.
BLAHA, Adolf	252703	M	Ger.	17. 6.04	Engineer, Civ. factory, Bruenn (Czech.) 5.45				PILLAGE	CZECH.
BLAICH, Friedrich	253601	M	Ger.		Sgt., Unit 90973 398.Div., La Bresse (Fr.) 9.-11.44				MISC.CRIMES	FR.
BLAIZER	29830	M	Ger.		Adjudant-chief, 12.Feldgendarmerie Parachutiste, Abbeville (Fr.) 8.44				MURDER	FR.
BLANCHE, Max	306218	M	Ger.		Dr., Medical officer, C.C. Struthof-Natzweiler (Fr.) 42-44				MURDER	FR.

BLA - BLE

NAME	C.R.FILE NUMBER	SEX	NATIO-NALITY	DATE OF BIRTH	RANK OCCUPATION UNIT PLACE AND DATE OF CRIME	REASON WANTED	WANTED BY
BLANCK, Walter	300022	M	Ger.		Capt., Customs, Luz St.-Sauveur, Htes.-Pyrenees (Fr.) 8.44	PILLAGE	FR.
BLANCKE, Max	173129	M	Ger.		Dr., C.C., Struthof-Natzweiler (Fr.) 43	MURDER	U.K.
BLANK	10888	M			Hptscharfhr., SS	MURDER	U.S.
BLANK	149736	M			Hptscharfhr., SS, C.C., Mauthausen (Aust.) 41-45	MURDER	U.S.
BLANK	151/54	M			Hptscharfhr., SS, C.C., Weimar-Buchenwald (Ger.)	TORTURE	U.S.
BLANK	259681	M	Ger.		Lt.Col., 242.Inf.Div., Chief by Gen.Staff, Ponteves,Var (Fr.) 7.44	MURDER	FR.
BLANKE	99	M	Ger.		Dr., Hptsturmfhr., SS, Physician, C.C., Maidanek (Pol.) 40-4.44	MURDER	POL.
BLANKE	100	M	Ger.		Hptsturmfhr., SS, C.C., Maidanek (Pol.)	MURDER	POL., FR.
BLANKE	1299	M	Ger.		Storeman, Navy Supply	MISC.CRIMES	U.K.
BLANKE	72248	M	Ger.		Dr.med., Capt., Waffen-SS, C.C., Struthof (Fr.) 5.38-10.43	MISC.CRIMES	FR., BEL.
BLANKE	192300	M	Ger.		Hptsturmfhr., SS, C.C., Flossenburg (Ger.) 44-45	MURDER	U.S.
BLANKE, Gertrud	134910	F	Ger.	90	Nurse, C.C., Hartheim (Ger.) 40-44	MURDER	U.S.
BLANKE, Karl	11194	M	Ger.		Pvt., SS-Panz.Gren.Rgt.110	MURDER	FR.
BLANKE, Max	158377	M	Ger.	08	Hptsturmfhr., SS, C.C., Buchenwald (Ger.) 42	TORTURE	U.S.
BLANKE, Werner	300443	M	Ger.		Lt., 784.Turkestan-Bn., commanding fortress of Tonneins, Clairac (Fr.) 8.44	MISC.CRIMES	FR.
BLANKEN	194940	M	Ger.	10	Cpl., 515.Lds.Schtz.Bn., C.C., Sosnowitz (Pol.) 42-44	TORTURE	U.K.
BLANKENAGEL	155890	M	Ger.	95	Oscharfhr., SS, Enschede (Neth.)	MURDER	U.K.
BLANKENBURG	131816	M	Ger.		Dr., Col.-Reichsminister, SS, Ministerium des Innern, Kaufbeuren (Ger.)	MURDER	U.S.
BLANKENBURG, Werner	134911	M	Ger.	05	SA-Oberfuehrer, C.C., Hartheim (Ger.) 40-44	MURDER	U.S.
BLANKLEY	188426	M	Ger.	10	Cpl., Lds.Schtz.Bn.515, Stalag 344, Sosnowitz (Pol.) 43	TORTURE	U.K.
BLANRE	127075	M	Ger.		SS-Medecin chief and Kapo-Chief,C.C.,Landsberg (Ger.)	TORTURE	FR.
BLARCYK, Frank	11222	M	Ger.		Pvt., Army, Feldpost-Nr.47 648c, Divion (Fr.) 4.44	MURDER	FR.
BLASCHEK, Hans	10172	M	Ger.	24. 4.07	Dr., Oberlandrat, Ministry of Justice Boehmen und Maehren, Budejovice (Czech.) 39-45	MURDER	CZECH.
BLASCHIS, Bedor	168602	M	Ger.		Pvt., 9.Gren.Res.Rgt., 1.Coy., Magny d'Anigon (Fr.) 9.44	MURDER	FR.
BLASCHKE, Otto	260921	M	Ger.	24. 9.08	Dr., Osturmfhr., Waffen-SS, C.C., Auschwitz, Flossenburg, Ravensbrueck, Oranienburg, Mauthausen (Pol., Ger.) 40-42	BRUTALITY	POL.
BLASCHKE, Otto	301547	M	Ger.		Scharfhr., SS, C.C., Mauthausen (Aust.) 40-45	MURDER	BEL.
BLASCHKE, Robert	151755	M	Ger.		Civilian, Kapo, C.C., Flossenburg and Buchenwald (Ger.) 44-45	MURDER	U.S.
BLASCHTOWITSCH, Kurt	9633	M	Ger.		Public Prosecutor, Public Official, Prague (Czech.) 40	MURDER	CZECH.
BLASCHTOWITSCHKA, Anton	31993	M	Ger.		Senatspraesident, Dr., Public Official, Litomerice (Czech.) 2.40	MURDER	CZECH.
BLASCYK, Stephan	185251	M	Ger.	14.12.12	Chief, SD, Gestapo, C.C., Benesou Prison (Czech.) 39-45	MURDER	CZECH.
BLASE	173993	M			Sturmscharfhr., SS, C.C., Muhldorf Ampfing (Ger.) 6.44-4.45	MURDER	U.S.
BLASS (see PLASS)	192160						
BLASS, Anton	301548	M		05	Sgt., Inspector, G.F.P.632, C.C., Flossenburg (Ger.) 2.45-3.45	TORTURE	BEL.
BLASY	257622	M		92	Sgt., C.C., Muhldorf (Ger.)	MURDER	U.S.
BLASYCK, Stephan (see BLASCYK)	185251						
BLASZCYK, Margarete	124589	F	Ger.		Conc.Camp, Hannover-Limmer (Ger.)	TORTURE	BEL.
BLATT	163101	M	Ger.		Lt., Commandant, Nachr.Rgt.34304, Lamanon (Fr.) 6.44	WITNESS	FR.
BLATT	253606	M			Cpl., C.C. Ellrich, Nordhausen (Ger.)	MURDER	U.S.
BLATT, Jakob (see DIETZSCH, Arthur)	133771						
BLATT, Karl	305994	M	Ger.		Member, SS, Staff, C.C., Sasel (Ger.) 10.44-4.45	TORTURE	U.K.
BLATTERBAUER	72692	M			Lt.Col., Commandant, Oflag 7 B (Ger.)	TORTURE	U.K.
BLATTERSPIEL	151753	M			Hptschfhr., SS, Totenkopf, Riga (Latv.), Auschwitz (Pol.) 41-43	MURDER	U.S.
BLAU	153564	M	Ger.	85	Col., Stalag III B, Fuerstenberg-Oder (Ger.) 43-45	TORTURE	U.S.
BLAU	172882	M	Ger.	19	Sturmfhr., SS, C.C., Buchenwald (Ger.) 43	MURDER	POL.
BLAU	179783	M	Ger.		Col., PW.Arbeits-Kdo, Stalag III B, Trattendorf b.Spremberg (Ger.) 9.43-7.44	TORTURE	U.S.
BLAU	252574	M			Col.-Cmdt., Stalag XX A, Marienburg (Ger.)	MURDER	U.S.
BLAU	257902	M			Col., 150.Pz.Bde., Meuse-Bridge,Antwerp.12.44	MISC.CRIMES	U.S.
BLAU, Willy	262004	M	Ger.	5. 7.99	SS-Mann, Waffen-SS, Gren.Div.36, Dirlewanger-Bde.,Warsaw (Pol.) 40-44	MURDER	POL.
BLAUE	196614	M	Ger.		Lt., 157.Div. Mountain Leg.(Res.), Plateau des Glieres (Fr.) 3.44-4.44	WITNESS	FR.
BLAUE	197742	M	Ger.		Sturmfhr., SS, C.C., Buchenwald (Ger.)	MURDER	U.S.
BLAUEL (or PLAUEL)	139750	M		05 - 12	Scharfhr., SS, or Osturmbannfhr. or Osturmfhr.,C.C.,Buchenwald (Ger.)	TORTURE	U.S.
BLAUEL, Adolf (see SCHMIDT, Kurt)	254013						
BLAUENSTEINER, Franz	300183	M	Ger.		Vormann, RAD, Schulzen am Gebirge, distr.Eisenstadt (Aust.) 2.45	MURDER	U.S.
BLAUFUCHS, Werner	131169				Personnel of Camp,Mauthausen (Aust.) 41-45	MURDER	U.S.
BLAUHORN, Karl	193460	M		31. 3.02	Sgt., Reichsjustiz-Ministerium,Strafgef.Lager Nord,Finnmark (Nor.)	TORTURE	NOR.
BLAUM	121757	M			Officer, Conc.Camp	MURDER	FR.
BLAUMANN, Paul	301617	M	Ger.		Lt., Fieldgend., Lannion, Cotes-du-Nord (Fr.) 6.44	TORTURE	FR.
BLAUROCH	149341	M	Ger.		Capt., Abwehr, Stg.369, Kobierzyn (Pol.) 8.44	TORTURE	FR.
BLAVATT, Georg	176979	M			Oschfhr., SS, C.C., Schoerzingen (Ger.)	TORTURE	FR.
BLAZATON	301297	M	Ger.		Member, Gestapo at Nove Mesto n.Vahom, C.C., Oswiecim-Birkenau (Pol.) 39-45	MURDER	CZECH.
BLECHSCHMID, Ferdinand	179765	M	Ger.		Capt., 611.Transportbegleit-Bn., Partina (It.) 4.44	MURDER	U.K.
BLECHSCHMIDT, Fritz	193463	M	Ger.	30. 5.13	Ex-convict,Reichsjust.-Minist.,Strafgef.Lager, Finnmark (Nor.) 3.45	WITNESS	NOR.
BLECKMANN, Fritz	262003	M	Ger.	14. 8.12	SS-Mann, Waffen-SS, Dirlewanger-Bde., Warsaw (Pol.) 40-44	MURDER	POL.
BLECKWEN (or BLECKUENN)	6110	M	Ger.		Col., 708.Volks-Gren.Div., Alsace (Fr.) 11.44-12.44	MISC.CRIMES	FR.
BLEIBOHM	305826	M	Ger.		Pvt., 1.Aufkl.Abt., 3.Coy., 2.Column, XV.Div.Afrika-Korps, St.Leger (Arlon) 9.44	MISC.CRIMES	BEL.
BLEICH	102	M	Ger.		Prison Vollan Governor, C.C., Vollan (Nor.) 41-42	TORTURE	NOR., U.S.
BLEICH	125753	M	Ger.		Postman, Stalag XX B, strong Nazi, Rosenberg (Pol.) 1.43-2.44	TORTURE	U.K.
BLEICHER	253592	M	Ger.		Guard, Prison, Hagen (Ger.)	BRUTALITY	BEL.
BLEIER, Waldemar	168590	M		14.10.10	Civilian, Army, Physician in Latv., Rositten (Latv.) 42	WITNESS	U.S.
BLEILE, Adolf	253607	M			Pvt., Conc.Camp Ellrich, Nordhausen (Ger.)	MURDER	U.S.
BLEIMEYER, George	192299	M			Conc.Camp, Flossenburg (Ger.) 44-45	MURDER	U.S.
BLEININENFELD	138354	M	Ger.		W.O., SS, Gestapo, Lyon (Fr.)	MURDER	FR.
BLEISNER	192642	M	Ger.		Oschfhr., SS, C.C., Buchenwald (Ger.) 42-45	MURDER	U.S.
BLEISNER, Emil (see PLEISNER)	129872						
BLEISS	190031	M			Capt., Kreiskommandantur, Kragujevak (Yugo.) 10.41	MURDER	YUGO.

BLE-BLU

NAME	C.R.FILE NUMBER	SEX	NATIO-NALITY	DATE OF BIRTH	RANK OCCUPATION UNIT PLACE AND DATE OF CRIME	REASON WANTED	WANTED BY
BLEISTEIN, Wilh.	140756	M	Ger.		Hilfsmeister,Arbeits-Kdo. KL.Ludwigshafen(Ger.) 1.45	TORTURE	U.S.
BLEITCHER	301091	M	Ger.		Warder Prison,Hagen(Ger.)	MISC.CRIMES	BEL.
BLEKER	158374	M			Rottfhr.,SS,Aschendorfer Moor(Ger.)	TORTURE	U.S.
BLENSKY	196277	M			Lt.,6-3 Brandenburg Regt.	MISC.CRIMES	U.S.
BLESKE, Wilhem (or BLAESKE)	185404	M	Ger.		Lt.,Gendarmerie,Grand Duchy(Lux.)	MURDER	LUX.
BLESSEMANN	165732	M	Ger.		Member,Criminal-Secretary,NSDAP,Kripo,Bruhl(Ger.) 1.45	TORTURE	U.S.
BLESSING	193462	M			Sgt.,Army, C.C. Bonnes	TORTURE	NOR.,YUGO.
BLESSING	260180	M	Ger.		Cpl.,SS slave labour camp,Botn near Rognan(Nor.) 8.42-3.43,4.43-5.45	BRUTALITY	YUGO.
BLESSING, Karl	260695	M	Ger.		Manager,Civ.Firm:Margarine-Verkaufs-Union,Reichsbank-Official,R.W.M.	MISC.CRIMES	U.S.
BLEYER	1300	M	Ger.	21	Cpl.,3 Pl.,2 Coy.,334 Eng.Bn.,L Vigne. 8.44	MURDER	U.K.
BLHUM (see BLUHM)	253591						
BLEUM	306178	M	Ger.		Sturmbannfhr.,C.C. Kahla(Ger.) 40-45	MURDER	BEL.
BLICHT	127327			19	Uschfhr.,SS,C.C.Weimar-Buchenwald(Ger.)	MURDER	U.S.
BLICHT, Hans (see PLICHT,Hans)	137571						
BLICK	192641	M	Ger.		Officer,C.C. ,SS,Buchenwald(Ger.) 42-45	MURDER	U.S.
BLICKE	252590	M	Ger.		Employee,Sipo -Abt.IVB,Bruessel(Bel.)	INTERR.	BEL.
BLIECK	131166	M			Guard,SS,N.C.O.,Buchenwald(Ger.)	TORTURE	BEL.
BLIEFS, Ludwig	158376	M	Ger.	90	Stand.-Fhr.,SS,C.C.Buchenwald(Ge) 39-44	TORTURE	U.S.
BLIES	163636	M			Capt.,Totenkopf-Stand.,Waffen-SS, C.Buchenwald,Weimar(Ger.)	TORTURE	U.S.
BLIESENER	176978	M			Hptsturmfhr.,SS-Officer of Karlsruhe,Loerrach(Ger.)	TORTURE	FR.
BLIESS	192640	M	Ger.		Doctor,SS-Uschfhr.,C.C.Buchenwald(Ger.) 42-45	MURDER	U.S.
BLIESSNER	124303	M			Oschfhr.,1 Pz.Div,SS,2 Pz.Regt.SS,9 Coy.,Malmedy(Bel.) 12.44	MURDER	U.S.
BLINCKE	135118	M			Major,Army,19 SS Police Regt.,Tulle Vigaun, Oberkrain(Yugo.)5.41-2.44, Toulouse,Compiegne(Fr.) 3.-10.44	MURDER	U.S.
BLINLENHOLFER, Hans	150582	M	Ger.		Gestapo,Rodelheim(Ger.) 43-44	TORTURE	FR.
BLINESORG, Peter	166281	M		21	Lt.,Ustumfhr.,Navy,SS,Liez(Fr.) 8.44	MURDER	U.S.
BLINN, Alois	172871	M	Ger.		Sub-Foreman,Arbeits-Kdo.at Adolf Mine,Merkstein(Ger.) 42-44	MURDER	U.S.
BLISS	253604	M	Ger.		Lt.,SS Police-Regt.Todt,2 Coy.,3 Bn.,Annecy,St.Martin-Bellevue(Fr.)1.44	MISC.CRIMES	FR.
BLITTNER	195865	M	Ger.		Personnel C.C.Struthof-Natzweiler(Fr.) 40-44	MURDER	FR.
BLOCH	257623	M		18	SS-Schfhr. C.C. Mühldorf Area(Ger.)	MURDER	U.S.
BLOCH, Arthur	306209	M	Ger.		Guard-Rottfhr.,C.C.(Alsace) Struthof-Natzweiler(Fr.) 42-44	MURDER	U.S.
BLOCH, Kurt	72738	M	Ger.		Pvt.,Fallsch.Jg.Bn.,Roermond(Neth.) 11.44-1.45	TORTURE	U.S.
BLOCHWITZ	256831	M			Employee,Bereitstellungslager,Nordhausen(Ger.)	MURDER	U.S.
BLOCK	141852	M	Ger.	00	Major,Stalag VIIIC,Nuernberg.45	TORTURE	U.K.
BLOCK	155889	M	Ger.		N.C.O.,Army,Stalag Luft VI,IV,KL.Gross Tichow(Ger.) 7.44	TORTURE	U.K.
BLOCK, Ernst	193461	M			Pvt.,Army (Nor.)	MURDER	NOR.
BLOCK, Hans	262244	M		8. 3.	Dr.,Oschfhr.,Gestapo,Rennes(Fr.) 43-44	MURDER	FR.
BLOCK, Karl	62357	M	Ger.		Civilian,Beltershain(Ger.) 12.44	MURDER	U.S.
BLOCK, Walter	191910	M	Ger.		Kapo,C.C.Nordhausen(Ger.) 1.-4.45	MURDER	FR.
BLOCK, Walter	257625	M	Ger.		Kapo,C.C.Neuengamme(Ger.)	MURDER	BEL.
BLOEDMANN	162719	M	Ger.		SS,Adolf Hitler,Odet(Bel.) 9.44	MURDER	BEL.
BLOEK or BLOK, Ernst Adolf	260465	M	Ger.	29.12.05	SS-Oschfhr.,SS Guard,Danzig-Matzkau(Pol.) 40-45	BRUTALITY	POL.
BLOEMERS, Karl	221410	M		10	Pvt.,Nachr.Regt.506 Abwehr,Bad Wildungen(Ger.) 41-45	MISC.CRIMES	U.S.
BLOENER	261386	M			SS-Sturmsohfhr.,Gestapo,Mende,Loezere(Fr.) 43-44	SUSPECT	FR.
BLOENNER, Alexander	155888	M	Ger.		Civilian,Le Roc(Fr.) 6.44	MURDER	FR.
BLOESSER	149710	M			SS,4 Bau-Bde.,Guard Totenkopf-Div.,Alrich Gardelegen(Ger.) 4.45	MURDER	U.S.
BLOHM	187005	M			Major,Charentes Maritimes. 8.44	WITNESS	FR.
BLOHM, Rudolf	260406	M		2. 9.85	Pers.Liable Partner Firm:Blohm & Voss,Hamburg(Ger.)	MISC.CRIMES	U.S.
BLOK (see BLOEK,Ernst Adolf)	260465						
BLOK, Walter	191910	M	Ger.		Camp-Kapo,C.C. Nordhausen(Ger.)	MURDER	FR.
BLOMBERG	12648				SS Lt.-Col.,SS,Employed Gestapo H.Q.,Bergen(Nor.) 41	TORTURE	NOR.
BLOMBERG, Willi	256943	M	Ger.		Schfhr.,Waffen-SS,C.C. Nordhausen(Ger.)	MURDER	U.S.
BLOMBINK	253608	M			Pvt.,Camp Dora, Nordhausen(Ger.)	MURDER	U.S.
BLOMBINK, Willi	130101	M			Blockfuehrer,SS,C.C.Dora Mittelbau,Nordhausen(Ger.)	MURDER	U.S.
BLOME, Fritz	124999	M	Ger.		Gestapo, C.C.Hannau Oberdorfelden(Ger.) 2.42-9.45	MURDER	U.S.
BLOMER	261774	M			Cpl.,Art.H.D.V. 199-2235 H.D.F.No.of S.P.270460,Lorgies(Fr.) 9.44	MURDER	FR.
BLOODY, Alois	192298	M			C.C.,Flossenburg(Ger.) 44-45	MURDER	U.S.
BLOSKEVITCH, Vallik	306907	M	Ger.	33	Polish boy,Gut Freydeck(Ger.) 45	MURDER	U.K.
BLOSYT	301298	M			Member,Gestapo at Nove Mesto n.Vahom,C.C.Oswiecim-Birkenau(Pol.)39-45	MURDER	CZECH.
BLUCAK	190092	M		07	Major,Schupo,Vidrovac(Yugo.) 6.44	MURDER	YUGO.
BLUEMEL, Walter	260430	M			SS-Uschfhr.,SS,SD,Lublin(Pol.) 42	MISC.CRIMES	POL.
BLUEMLEIN, Hans	173978	M	Ger.	07	Foreman,Arbeits-Kdo.,C.C.Feucht(Ger.) 40-45	TORTURE	U.S.
BLUHM	29831	M	Ger.	03	Kriminalkommissar,Police,Perigueux(Fr.) 6.-8.44	MURDER	FR.
BLUHM or BLHUM	253591	M			Agent,Gestapo,Limoges(Fr.)	TORTURE	FR.
BLUHM, Helmut (see BLUM)	129827	M	Ger.	10	Uschfhr.,Kraftfahrer,Sipo,SS		
BLUHME, Knud	306115	M	Ger.		Lt.,Army,Abwehr-Abt.IIIF Aarhus Examining Judge,Viborg Prison. 8.43	TORTURE	DEN.
BLUHMER	253603	M	Ger.		Secretary,Gestapo,Region Limoges(Fr.) 40-44	INTERR.	FR.
BLUM	11223	M			Pvt.,Panzer Gren.Regt.111,Gourdon(Fr.) 6.44	MURDER	FR.
BLUM	29832	M			Geheime Feldpolizei(Air Force) Quimperle(Fr.) 44	MURDER	FR.
BLUM	125107	M			Feldw.,Army,Stalag Luft III,Mouskau(Ger.) 2.45	BRUTALITY	U.K.
BLUM	125172	M			Custom-Official,Zollgrenzschutz,Creach'Maout (Fr.) 8.44	MURDER	FR.
BLUM	129827	M		10	Cpl.,driver at the Sipo,Waffen-SS,3 Pl.of Kommando 16 z.v.B., Bad Neuenahr, Bruessel(Russ.-Bel.)	MURDER	U.S.,BEL.
BLUM	141455	M	Ger.		Capt.,Army,Chenebier-Etobon(Fr.) 9.44	MURDER	FR.
BLUM	165940	M	Ger.		Sgt.,Army,Munich. 7.44	MURDER	U.S.
BLUM	185155	M			Sgt.,Sicherungs-Regt.192,Foret des Colettes et bois de Jevimat(Fr.)7.44	MURDER	FR.
BLUM	189161	M			Osturmfhr.,SS,CC,Dachau(Ger.)	MURDER	BEL.
BLUM	195772	M			Chief of building 14 Polte II,Arnstadt(Ger.)	MISC.CRIMES	U.S.
BLUM	196118	M	Ger.		Zollbeamter,Zollgrenzschutz,Semaphore de Creach Maout(Fr.) 8.44	MURDER	FR.
BLUM	258124	M	Ger.		Gen. German Army,Breendonck(Bel.)	MURDER	BEL.
BLUM	259076	M			Gen.	WITNESS	U.S.
BLUM, Gerhard	194917	M	Ger.	28.10.08	Member,Gestapo,Kolin(Czech.) 39-45	MURDER	CZECH.
BLUM, Helmuth	121091	M	Ger.	17	SS-Schfhr.,SS,Stalingrad(Russ.)	MURDER	U.S.
BLUM, Josef	253594	M	Ger.		Birkendorff,Feldpost No.18810,Saint Laurent(Fr.) 8.44	TORTURE	FR.

BLU-BOC

NAME	C.R.FILE NUMBER	SEX	NATIO-NALITY	DATE OF BIRTH	RANK OCCUPATION UNIT PLACE AND DATE OF CRIME	REASON WANTED	WANTED BY
BLUM, Karl Wilhelm Ludwig	195670	M	Ger.	9. 4.05	Lt., Air-Raid shelter Police, Offenbach (Ger.) 2.45	MURDER	U.S.
BLUM, Kurt	253593	M	Ger.	17	Sgt.,29 Rgt.Art.6 Btty.,Physhiki (Russ.) 7.44	MURDER	FR.
BLUM, Matheas	134791	M	Ger.		Civilian, Efferen (Ger.) 10.44	WITNESS	U.S.
BLUM, Willybald	124291	M	Ger.		Civilian, Oberndorf (Pfalz) (Ger.)	MURDER	U.S.
BLUMBERG, Paul	185253	M	Ger.	96	SS-Usturmfhr.,Crim.O.Secr.,SD,Gestapo,Praha (Czech.) 39-45	MURDER	CZECH.
BLUME	158375	M	Ger.		Police-chief,Standfhr.,Sipo,SS, (Grc.) 43-44	MURDER	U.S.
BLUME	168589	M	Ger.	00	SS-Standfhr., Athen (Grc.)	MURDER	U.S.
BLUME	176414	M			Capt.,Army,Verdun (Fr.) 44	MURDER	FR.
BLUME	187566	M	Ger.		Lt.,65 Inf.Div.,Cisa Pass Genoa-Spezia (It.) 10.45	WITNESS	U.K.
BLUME	190033	M			Capt.,Kommandantur,Sibenik Zablsc (Yugo.) 5.-6.44	MURDER	YUGO.
BLUME, Walter	218414	M	Ger.	23. 7.06	Dr.,SS-Sturmbannfhr.,Inspector,SD,Sipo,Athens (Grc.) 44	MURDER	U.S.
BLUMEL	261775	M	Ger.		Pvt.,Nord-Verlinghem (Fr.) 40-41	INTERR.	FR.
BLUMENAU	253602	M			Lt.,F.P.Nr.50909,Romilly s-Seine (Fr.) 8.44	PILLAGE	FR.
BLUMENKAMM	29452	M			Capt.,Army,Gestapo,St.Die (Fr.) 11.44	MURDER	FR.
BLUMENKAMP, Paul	11224	M			SD,Sicherheitspolizei,Clemont-Ferrand (Fr.) 43-44	TORTURE	FR.
BLUMENKAMPF	189582	M	Ger.		Usturmfhr.,SD,Region Lyonaise (Fr.)	MISC.CRIMES	FR.
BLUMENROTH	192698	M	Ger.		Staff-Sgt.,SS,C.C.Buchenwald (Ger.) 42-43	MURDER	U.S.
BLUMLE	173992	M			Leader,C.C.Bad Durrenberg (Ger.) 5.44	TORTURE	U.S.
BLUMMER	257336	M			Sturmfhr.,SS lave labour camp,Beisfjord near Narvik (Nor.) 6.-11.42	MISC.CRIMES	YUGO.
BLUMMES	39633	M	Ger.		Pvt.,Army,Coudes (Fr.) 7.44	MURDER	FR.
BLUMUT	151756	M			Civilian,Inspector of a Mine,C.C.Klusenstein (Ger.) 1.-4.45	TORTURE	U.S.
BLUNK, Johannes	185403	M	Ger.	25. 9.11	Manager,Leader,armament-works,Brno (Czech.) 39-45	PILLAGE	CZECH.
BLUTBLASE	158373	M		10	Guard,SS,C.C.Aschendorfermoor (Ger.) 40-41	TORTURE	U.S.
BLUTIGEL	158372	M		23	SS,C.C.Aschendorfermoor (Ger.) 40-41	TORTURE	U.S.
BOAL	300025	M	Ger.		Capt.,Waalwijk,Heusden, 5.43-10.44	PILLAGE	NETH.
BOBARDT	305827	M	Ger.		Pvt.,1 Aufkl.Abt.3 Coy 2 Col.XV Div.Afrika Corps,St.Leger (Arlon)	MISC.CRIMES	BEL.
BOBON, Emil	196587	M	Ger.		Kdo.-Fuehrer,740 Ldsch.Bn.1 Cor.Kdo.102-3,Bodendorf (Ger.) 10.44	WITNESS	FR.
BOBRICHE	188678	M	Ger.		Insp.,Lt.,Ruestungsamt,Army,Belfort (Fr.) 10.-11.44	PILLAGE	FR.
BOBS	301550	M	Ger.		Lagerealtester,C.C.Neuengamme (Ger.) 40-45	MURDER	BEL.
BOBY (see FOLKER)	138222						
BOCH	1301	M	Ger.		Cpl.,Army (194 Gr.) (L.Pl.)	MISC.CRIMES	U.K.
BOCH (see BOCK)	139838	M					
BOCH	251974	M	Ger.		Crim.O.Asst.,Abt.IV D Sipo,Brussels (Bel.)	INTERR.	BEL.
BOCH (see BOCK)	252008						
BOCH (see BOCK)	252017						
BOCHART	132607	M	Ger.	10	Agent,Gestapo	MISC.CRIMES	FR.
BOCHBERGER	146347	M	Ger.	05	Officer,Army,Chambery (Fr.)	MURDER	FR.
BOCHERER	140360	M	Ger.		Chief,Guard,C.C.Vaihingen-Enz (Ger.)	TORTURE	FR.
BOCHERT, Kurt	191847	M	Ger.	40	Pvt.,Army,Weimar (Ger.) 9.-10.40	TORTURE	U.K.
BOCHMANN	187578	M			SS-Ostumfhr.,SS-Fuehrerschule	MURDER	U.N.W.C.C.
BOCHNER	185637	M	Ger.		SS,C.C.II Linz Mauthausen (Aust.) 11.42-5.45	TORTURE	FR.
BOCHNIK, Bernhard	252018	M	Ger.		Flyer,Camp Ellrich,Nordhausen (Ger.)	MURDER	U.S.
BOCHTEL, Heinrich dit Henry	31310	M	Ger.		Chef de la Gestapo,Schfhr.,Saintes,Ternant (Fr.) 7.44	MISC.CRIMES	FR.
BOCK	105	M	Ger.		Camp official Guard,C.C.Rajsko,Oswiecim (Pol.) 6.40-43	MURDER	POL.,BEL.
BOCK (or BOCH)	139838	M	Ger.	00	Foreman,Organ.Todt,C.C.Mahldorf (Ger.) 44-45	MURDER	U.S.
BOCK	140364	M	Ger.		Capt.,Stalag 369,Ziegenhain (Ger.)	TORTURE	FR.
BOCK	140365	M	Ger.		Lt.,SS-Todt,3 Bn.12 Coy,Faverges et Glieres (Fr.) 2.44	MURDER	FR.
BOCK	140367	M	Ger.		Sturmbannfhr.,SS,Smolensk (Russ.)	TORTURE	FR.
BOCK	140368	M	Ger.		Prof.Dr.med.,Col.,C.C.Hohenlychen (Ger.) 5.44	TORTURE	FR.
BOCK	140903	M	Ger.	11	Cpl.,Army,C.C.Breendonck (Bel.)	TORTURE	BEL.
BOCK	141456	M	Ger.		Capt.,Stalag IV A,Ziegenhain (Ger.)	MURDER	FR.
BOCK	162516	M	Ger.		Lt.,Kampfgruppe,Saillans (Fr.) 7.-8.44	PILLAGE	FR.
BOCK	167647	F	Ger.		Einsatzstab Rosenberg Pay Section,Paris (Fr.) 44	PILLAGE	FR.
BOCK	193937	M	Ger.		Chief,Stalag IX C,Bad Sulze (Ger.)	MURDER	FR.
BOCK	187848	M			Cpl.,Army,C.C.Breendonck (Ger.) 40-44	MURDER	BEL.
BOCK	191682	F	Ger.		Civ.Serv.,Ostgebietsministerium,Einsatzstab Rosenberg,Paris (Fr.) 40-44	PILLAGE	FR.
BOCK	194986	M	Ger.		Kapo,C.C. Oswiecim-Birkenau,Raysko (Ger.,Pol.) 43-5.44	TORTURE	POL.,BEL.
BOCK	195743				Kapo,C.C.Birkenau (Pol.) 40-43	MURDER	POL.
BOCK	196615	M	Ger.		Lt.,157 Div.Mountain Leg.(Res.),Plateau des Glieres (Fr.) 3.-4.44	WITNESS	FR.
BOCK (or BOCH)	252008	M	Ger.		Oschfhr.,Camp Wieda,Nordhausen (Ger.)	MURDER	U.S.
BOCK (or BOCH)	252017	M			Flyer,Camp Ellrich,Nordhausen (Ger.)	MURDER	U.S.
BOCK	258928	M	Ger.		Lt.,Police Rgt.Fort d'Annecy,St.Francois Haute Savoie (Fr.) 3.45	MURDER	FR.
BOCK	260186	M	Ger.		Lt.,Kampfgruppe Kaiser,Massif du Vercors,Isere et Drome (Fr.)7.-8.44	SUSPECT	FR.
BOCK	300184	M	Ger.		Dir.,Political Affairs Department,Patras,Calavrita,Mega Apileon Aghia Lavra, 42-44	MURDER	YUGO.
BOCK	306455	M	Ger.		Member,SD Montlucon,Chappes,Louroux-Hodement (Allier) (Fr.) 7.44	MURDER	FR.
BOCK, Helmut	307051	M	Ger.	18. 6.17	On staff of Town Hospital Lueneburg (Ger.) 1.43-4.45	MURDER	YUGO.
BOCH, Herbert	29833	M	Ger.		Betriebsdir.,Pvt.,Public official,Mines at Bazeilles (Fr.) 44	MISC.CRIMES	FR.
BOCK, Johann	72740	M	Ger.		Oberwachtmeister,Schupo,C.C.Hinzert (Ger.)	TORTURE	FR.
BOCK, Karl	187539	M	Ger.		Police Constable,Halchter (Ger.) 9.44	MISC.CRIMES	CZECH.
BOCK, Willy	139837	M	Ger.	86	Reichsleiter,NSDAP,Praha (Czech.)	MURDER	U.S.
BOCKE	133749	M		85	Civilian,C.C.Buchenwald (Ger.)	TORTURE	U.S.
BOCKEL, Heinrich	252025	M			Cpl.,Camp Ellrich,Nordhausen (Ger.)	MURDER	U.S.
BOCKELMANN	257963	M	Ger.		N.C.O.,6 Army,Vinckt-Meigem (Bel.)	MURDER	BEL.
BOCKELMANN	176977	M			Commandant,Major,Armee Oberkommando of Annecy,Glieres (Fr.)	MURDER	FR.
BOCKER	125164				SS,C.C.Schlesiersee (Ger.)	TORTURE	FR.
BOCKHARDT, Xaver	149723	M	Ger.		Driver,Civilian,Lublin (Pol.)	MURDER	FR.
BOCKHOLDT, Willi	154763	M	Ger.	97	Sgt.,SS-Guard,C.C.Dora-Nordhausen (Ger.) 43-45	WITNESS	U.S.
BOCKL	151168	M			SS-Hptschfhr.,SS Pz.Div.Totenkopf,C.C.Mauthausen (Aust.) 41-45	MURDER	U.S.
BOCKL	300028	M	Ger.		Usturmfhr.,Deputy commanding officer,SS,Garrison,Levadia, 9.43	MISC.CRIMES	GRC.
BOCKS, Berthold	256882	M	Ger.	22. 5.10	Employee,C.C.Nordhausen (Ger.)	MURDER	U.S.
BOCK VON WUELFINGEN, Ferdinand	196911	M	Ger.		Major-General,Army (Fr.)	INTERR.	FR.
BOCKWOLD	140371	M	Ger.		Civilian,C.C.Hessen (Ger.)	MURDER	FR.

BOC-BOE

NAME	C.R.FILE NUMBER	SEX	NATIO-NALITY	DATE OF BIRTH	RANK OCCUPATION UNIT PLACE AND DATE OF CRIME	REASON WANTED	WANTED BY
BOCZAR	140370	M	Ger.		Uscharfhr., SS, C.C. Auschwitz (Pol.)	TORTURE	FR.
BOCZKI, Edgar	262007	M	Ger.	15.11.12	SS-Mann, Dirlewanger Bde, Waffen-SS,Gren.Div.36,Warsaw (Pol.) 40-44	MURDER	POL.
BODDEN	140372	M	Ger.		Ortsbauernfuehrer, Niederzier b.Dueren (Ger.)	TORTURE	FR.
BODE	27758	M			Cmdt., Army, Bergerac (Fr.) 6.-7.44	MISC.CRIMES	FR.
BODE	36665	M	Ger.		Pvt., Stalag XX B, 610 Bn, Stalag. 6.44	TORTURE	U.K.
BODE	62163	M	Ger.		Col., Chief of Staff (Serb.)	TORTURE	UNWCC
BODE	140374	M	Ger.		Major, Div. Blindee "Das Reich", Bergerac (Fr.) 6.44	MURDER	FR.
BODE	149711	M			Uscharfhr., SS, 4 Baubde Totenkopf, Elrich b.Gardelegen (Czech.)	MURDER	U.S.
BODE	159356	M			Osturmfhr., SS, 2 Pz.Div. "Das Reich", Tulle (Fr.) 5.44	MURDER	U.S.
BODE	173317	M	Ger.		Districtleader, NSDAP, Schlettstadt (Fr.) 44	TORTURE	FR.
BODE	187579	M			Col., Army Staff (Serb.)	MURDER	UNWCC
BODE	190034	M			Dr., Head of Gestapo, Belgrad, Neuengamme (Yugo.,Ger.) 41-45	MURDER	YUGO.
BODE, Adolf	185254	M	Ger.	26. 4.02	SS-Usturmfhr., SD, Gestapo, Praha and Mlada Boleslau (Czech.) 41-45	MURDER	CZECH.
BODE, Friedel	195671	M	Ger.		Uscharfhr., I SS-Pz.Div."LAH", 3 Pio.Coy, Stoumont, Ligneville (Bel.) 12.44	MURDER	U.S.
BODE, Hans	221409	M	Ger.		Sgt., SD, Cattinava (It.) 43-44	MURDER	U.S.
BODE, Otto	262226	M	Ger.		Civ., Cramme (Ger.) 9.44 (L.O.D.N.A.O.D.)	WITNESS	U.S.
BODEN	193992	M	Ger.	92	Crim.sec.,Sturmscharfhr., Gestapo, SS, C.C. Malines (Bel.)	MURDER	BEL.
BODEN	260139	M	Ger.		Osturmfhr., SS, Belgrad (Yugo.) 1.-9.44	MURDER	YUGO.
BODEN, Erich	306342	M	Ger.		SS-Scharfhr. (Nr.242486), C.C. Buchenwald (ger.) 5.38-10.43	MURDER	BEL.
BODEN, Fritz	251964	M	Ger.		Sgt., 377 Jg.Rgt., 10 Coy, Vinkt, Meigem (Bel.)	INTERR.	BEL.
BODEN, Wilhelm	185255	M	Ger.	30.11.11	Sturmbannfhr., SS, Hradistka Distr.Jilove (Czech.) 42-45	MURDER	CZECH.
BODENBURG	159378	M	Ger.		Rottenfhr., 1 SS-Pz.Div.,2 Pz.Gren.Rgt.,3 Bn,12 Coy,Stavelot-Malmedy (Bel.) 12.44	MURDER	U.S.
BODENSCHATZ, Karl Martin	261247	M	Ger.	90		WITNESS	U.S.
BODENSIERNEN	106	M	Ger.		Hptsturmfhr., SS, C.C. Oswiecim-Birkenau (Pol.) 40	MURDER	FR.
BODENSTEIN	1302	M			N.C.O., SD, Aussen-Kdo.	MISC.CRIMES	U.K.
BODENSTEIN	240133	M	Ger.		SS-Oscharfhr., SD official Sipo,SD Einsatzkdo,Rome (It.) 44	TORTURE	U.S.
BODENSTEIN, Werner	260624					MISC.CRIMES	U.S.
BODESHEIM	27764				Lt., Army, Brommat (Fr.) 7.44	MURDER	FR.
BODESHEIM	164373	M	Ger.	00	Fuehrer, NSKK, Waltershausen (Ger.) 45	PILLAGE	UNWCC
BODET, Heinrich	192936	M		94	C.C. Flossenburg (Ger.) 44-45	WITNESS	U.S.
BODF	192637	M	Ger.		SS-Scharfhr., C.C. Buchenwald (Ger.) 42-45	MURDER	U.S.
BODMANN	190035	M		10	Dr., SS-Hptsturmfhr., C.C. Neuengamme (ger.)	MURDER	YUGO.
BODMANN, Franz	306220	M	Ger.		Dr., Medical-officer, C.C. Struthof-Natzweiler (Fr.) 42-44	MURDER	FR.
BOECK	159355	M			Uscharfhr., SS, C.C. Dachau (Ger.)	TORTURE	U.S.
BOECK	251979	M	Ger.		Employee, 1 Abt.III A Sipo, Bruessel (Bel.) 40-45	INTERR.	BEL.
BOECK, Adolf	262006	M	Ger.	10. 1.16	SS-Mann, W-SS, Gren.Div.36, Dirlewanger Bde, Warschau (Pol.) 40-45	MURDER	POL.
BOECKEL	300026	M			Capt., Levadia 9.43	MISC.CRIMES	GRC.
BOECKELMANN, Heinrich	307052	M			Serving at General Rossums H.Q., Oflag X-C Lusbeck (ger.) 4.-5.44	MURDER	FR.
BOECKEN	72741	M	Ger.		Custom secr.official, Gestapo, C.C. Klingelpuetz (Ger.)	MISC.CRIMES	U.S.
BOECKER, Ernst Ludwig Friedr.	196101	M	Ger.	04	Caretaker for few jewish shops, Dieren (Neth.)	MISC.CRIMES	NETH.
BOECKER, Reinhold	260011	M	Ger.	23. 5.08	Hpt.sturmfhr., SS, Security Reporter,Ger.official,Podbrezova (Slovakia-CSR) 9.44-4.45	MISC.CRIMES	CZECH.
BOECKLER, Walter	252029	M	Ger.		13 SS-Pol.Rgt., Ferlach (Aust.) 44-45	INTERR.	YUGO.
BOEDDEKER, Heinrich Anton Joseph	300029	M	Ger.	29. 8.02	Deputy local groupleader, head manager,president,Apeldoorn,Gelderland-district,jewish business Neth.,Ger., culture Society-NSDAP,SD, "Holland Action" Commission Apeldoorn (Neth.) 2.-9.43	MISC.CRIMES	NETH.
BOEDE	140877	M		20	Pvt., Army, Stalag XX B, Altefelde (Ger.) 6.44	TORTURE	U.S.
BOEDECKER	193381	M	Ger.		Lt., Army, C.C. Sunndalsora (Nor.) 43	MURDER	NOR.
BOEDECKER, Heinrich	168117	M				TORTURE	U.S.
BOEDEKER	186559	M		15	Lt., 2 Bn,64 Pz.Gren.Rgt., 16 Div. (It.) 8.43	MURDER	U.K.
BOEDEKER, Georg	261225	M	Ger.	11.12.13	N.C.O., G.F.P., Bruessel (Bel.) 6.41-4.43	INTERR.	BEL.
BOEDER	173977	M			Org.Todt, C.C. Muhldorf,Ampfing (Ger.) 6.44-4.45	MURDER	U.S.
BOEDICKER, Alfred	159369	M	Ger.		Chief Adjutant, Gestapo, Trondes,Bouges,Menil la Tour (Fr.) 8.44	MURDER	FR.
BOEDICKER, Alfred	166927	M	Ger.		Chief Adjutant, Sgt., Gestapo, Army, Luneville, Maixe (Fr.) 8.44	MURDER	FR.
BOEGE, Ehrenfried	258966	M	Ger.	89	Lt.Gen.	WITNESS	U.S.
BOEGENER	256830	M	Ger.		Head of Sub.sec., Mittelwerk GmbH, Nordhausen (Ger.)	MURDER	U.S.
BOEHLE, Heinz see BOHLE	130079						
BOEHLER	176411	M			Civilian, Veterinar of Loerrach	MISC.CRIMES	FR.
BOEHLER or BOHLER	140381	M	Ger.		Prof.Dr.Med.,Ober-Feldarzt,C.C. Ravensbrueck (Ger.)Hohenlychen 5.44	TORTURE	FR.
BOEHM	27768				Nogent le Rotrau (Fr.)	MISC.CRIMES	FR.
BOEHM	148708	F	Ger.		Woman guard, Civilian, C.C. Vicinity,Hirzenhain (Ger.) 3.45	WITNESS	U.S.
BOEHM	159365	M			Sturmmann, W-SS, Cantine Department I, C.C. Buchenwald (Ger.)	TORTURE	U.S.
BOEHM see BOHM	254499						
BOEHM, Alfred	31994	M	Ger.		Landgerichtsrat, Public official, Litomarice (Czech.) 40	MURDER	CZECH.
BOEHM, Arno	108	M	Ger.		Employed at C.C. Oswiecim-Birkenau (Pol.),40	MURDER	FR.,POL.,YUGO.
BOEHM, Baptist	107	M			Pvt., Army, Baudrignes (Fr.) 8.44	MURDER	FR.
BOEHM, Clemens	124787	M			Capt., Gendarmarie, Lodz (Pol.) 2.-3.45	MURDER	U.S.
BOEHM, Erhard	193465	M	Ger.		Usturmfhr., SD, Dresden (Ger.)	MURDER	NOR.
BOEHM, Friedrich Johann	194943	M	Ger.	6. 2.18	Uscharfhr., Waffen-SS, Gorssel, Enschede (Neth.) 9.44	MURDER	NETH.
BOEHM, Fritz	10062	M			Oscharfhr., SS, Enschede (Neth.) 11.44	PILLAGE	NETH.
BOEHM, Helmuth	307054				Sgt., Rotterdam (Neth.) 45		
BOEHM, Hermann	153563	M	Ger.		Gruppenfhr., Member, SA, NSDAP (Ger.) 34-45	TORTURE	U.S.
BOEHM, Hermann	176975	M	Ger.		Dr., Aerztekammer, public health official, Alt Rehse, Muenchen (Ger.)	TORTURE	FR.
BOEHM, Hermann	258965	M	Ger.	96	Admiral of the Fleet	WITNESS	U.S.
BOEHM, Josef	185402	M	Ger.	12. 4.00	Crim.employee, Gestapo and SD, Praha (Czech.) 39-45	MURDER	CZECH.
BOEHM, Josef	187538	M	Ger.		Groupleader, NSDAP, Velke,Hledsehe (Czech.) 39-45	MISC.CRIMES	CZECH.
BOEHM, Karl	139112	M	Ger.	20	Lt.,Army,replacement 7 Pz.Reconnaissance and Train.Bn, 1 Pz.Reconnaissance Coy, Freilassing (Ger.) 4.45	MURDER	U.S.
BOEHM, Ludwig	27769				SS-officer, St.Gaudens,St.Girons,Rimout (Fr.)	TORTURE	FR.
BOEHM, Wilhelm	136701	M	Ger.		Foreman, Member, NSDAP, C.C. Sachsenhausen,Oranienburg (Ger.) 39-44	TORTURE	U.K.
BOEHM, William	188215	M	Ger.		Major, Army, Dietz (Ger.) 1.45	WITNESS	U.S.
BOEHM-TETTELBACH	260705	M			Col.	MURDER	U.S.
BOEHME	136993	M	Ger.		Lt., 21 Pz.Div.Hqrs, Sessenheim (Fr.) 1.45	MURDER	U.S.
BOEHME	251959	M	Ger.		Pvt.,Kdo.-Fuehrer, Saechs.Guss-Stahlwerke,Gettersee (Ger.) 7.43	BRUTALITY	NETH.

BOE-BOG

NAME	C.R.FILE NUMBER	SEX	NATIO-NALITY	DATE OF BIRTH	RANK OCCUPATION UNIT PLACE AND DATE OF CRIME	REASON WANTED	WANTED BY
BOEHME	251961	M	Ger.		Uscharfhr., 83 Regt. Landsturm, Tiel (Neth.) spring 45	PILLAGE	NETH.
BOEHME	257186	M	Ger.	05 or 07	Lt., C.O. of Pressburg-prison at Bratislava, Theben-Neudorf (Aust.) 4.45	WITNESS	U.S.
BOEHME, Busso	124519	M	Ger.		Lt., 2 Fallschirmjaeger-Regt., 6 Bn., (Fr.) 12.44	MISC.CRIMES	U.S.
BOEHME, Horst	9634	M	Ger.		Standartenfhr., SS-Befehlshaber der Sicherheitspolizei, (Czech.)41-44	MURDER	CZECH.
BOEHME, Karl	140386	M	Ger.	13. 5.96	Capt., 28 Inf.Regt., 116 Bn., Lannesnezan, St. Laurent de Nestle (Fr.) 10.44	MURDER	FR.
BOEHMER, Karl	262001	M	Ger.	31. 7.03	SS-Mann, Dirlewanger-Bde., Waffen-SS, Gren.Div.36, Warsaw (Pol.)40-44	MURDER	POL.
BOEHMIG see BEHMIG	129834						
BOEHN, Gustav	261997	M	Ger.	30. 8.00	SS-Mann, Dirlewanger-Bde., Waffen-SS, Gren.Div.36, Warsaw (Pol.)40-44	MURDER	POL.
BOEHNE	257900	M			Lt., 150 Panzer-Bde., Meuse-Bridge, Antwerpen (Bel.) 12.44	MISC.CRIMES	U.S.
BOEHNE, Friedrich	185423	M			Police-chief, SS-Police, Kreis Celle (Ger.)	TORTURE	U.K.
BOEHNFELDT or BOEHNEFELDT	6112	M			Lt., 708 Gren. Div., 748 Gren. Regt., Faing-Elsenheim (Fr.) 11.44	MISC.CRIMES	FR.
BOEHRSCH, Norbert	31996	M			President, Dr., Country Court, Cheb (Czech.) 6.40	MURDER	CZECH.
BOEL	1303	M			Prt., 305 Div., 578 Gr., 3 Pi., 5 Coy.	MISC.CRIMES	U.K.
BOELLING	251978	M			Employee, Abt.VI, Sipo, Bruessel (Bel.)	INTERR.	BEL.
BOELLING, Paul	300186	M		27. 6.12	Cpl., guard of Army-prisoners in Vollan-prison, Trondheim (Nor.) 42	TORTURE	NOR.
BOELSEN	179766	M		85	Maj.-Gen., 26 Pz.Div., Gubbio (It.) 6.44	MURDER	U.F.
BOEMEIBURG or BOEMMEIBURG or BOEMEIBOURG	27772	M		85 or 90	Sturmbannfhr., cmdt. and chief of SD, Abt1g.IV, Vichy, Clermont, Ferrand (Fr.) 7.40, 44-45	MURDER	FR.
BOEMEIBURG, Karl	185267	M	Ger.	28.10.85	Sturmbannfhr., director, SD, Gestapo, Prag (Czech.) 39-41	MURDER	CZECH.
BOEMER or BOHMER	100420	M			Lt., Kampfgruppe Brenner, Terrasson (Fr.) 3.44-4.44	PILLAGE	FR.
BOEMER	306701	M			Keeper, Stavelot (Bel.) 9.44	MURDER	BEL.
BOEMKE	140377	M			Dozent, medical branch, surgeon, C.C. Ravensbrueck (Ger.) 6.44	TORTURE	FR.
BOEMKE	307055	M			Member, Sicherheitsdienst, Almelo district (Neth.) 9.44-2.45	MURDER	NETH.
BOEMMEIBURG or BOEMEIBURG	27772						
BOENICKE, Hermann	159380	M	Ger.		Lt.Col., C.C. Oranienburg (Ger.) 43-45	MISC.CRIMES	U.S.
BOENIG	252028	M			Chief-W.O., Gendarmerie of Gex, Thoiry (Fr.) 2.43	INTERR.	FR.
BOENIG	256991		Ger.		German Army, 2 Signal-Coy., Bolnes (Neth.) 5.45	INTERR.	NETH.
BOENIG, Otto	166926	M	Ger.		Leffinekrouke (Fr.) 44	MURDER	FR.
BOENISCH, Josef	252030	M		31.10.08	SS-Scharfhr., Gestapo, crim.police-driver, Sumperk -Moravic (Czech.) 3-45	MURDER	CZECH.
BOENNEN, Johan	307056	M		28. 2.91	Member of Sicherheitsdienst, The Hague (Neth.) 1.43	PILLAGE	NETH.
BOENNER aliases MARSCHALL	62354				800 Pz.Gren.Div."Brandenburg", Sabotage-Trupp, Josselin (Fr.) 7.44	MURDER	U.S.
BOENNER	125751	M	Ger.	01	Lt., Fallschirmjaeger-Ausb.Regt.2, C.C. Josselin (Fr.) 8.44	MURDER	U.F.
BOER	27777	M			Lt., Army, 13 Coy., Sich.Rgt.192 Dun S-Auroux (Fr.) 8.44	MURDER	FR.
BOER	251935	M	Ger.		Sgt., 377 Jaeger-Regt., 10 Coy., Vinkt (Bel.) 5.40	MISC.CRIMES	BEL
BOERE, Hendrik	307053	M	Ger.		Member, Sonderkdo.Feldmeier, Apeldoorn (Neth.) 10.43-10.44	MURDER	NETH.
BOERGER	257910	M			Sgt., 150 Panzer-Bde., Meuse-Bridge, Antwerpen (Bel.) 12.44	INTERR.	U.S.
BOERGER see BERGER	257948	M					
BOERNER	173319	M	Ger.		Prt., 3-622 Stalag IX, C.C., Bad Sulza (Ger.) 44-45	MURDER	FR.
BOERNER, Albin	189987	M			Capt., Ortskommandantur, Meckovac near Kragujevac (Yugo.) 10.41	MURDER	YUGO.
BOERs	159846	M			N.S.D.A.P.-leader, Hamburg (Ger.) 5.44	MURDER	U.S.
BOERSE, Ernst	130181	M	Ger.		Civilian, peasant, Fischbeck (Ger.) 6.44	MURDER	U.S.
BOESCHE see BOLSCHE, Karl, Ludwig	192917						
BOESE, Guenther	124307	M			1 SS-Pz.Div., 1 SS-Pz.Regt., 1 Bn., Malmedy (Bel.) 12.44	MURDER	U.S.
BOESEN, Erich	134773	M			SS-Scharfhr., 4 SS-Totenkopf-Sturmbann, C.C. Dora-Mittelbau, Nordhausen (Ger.) 43-45	WITNESS	U.S.
BOESON, Ernst	134772	M		17. 5.91	SS-Prt., 4 SS-Totenk.Stuba., C.C.Dora-Mittelbau, Nordhausen (Ger.)43	WITNESS	U.S.
BOESSEL	194795	M	Ger.		Terr.occup., Luxembourg, Murder	MURDER	LUX.
BOETCHER	185152	M	Ger.		Record-clerk, SS, C.C. Dachau (Ger.)	WITNESS	FR.
BOETCHER or BUTTCHER, Emil	251975	M	Ger.		Capt., cmdt., Calais (Fr.) 9.44	MURDER	FR.
BOETCHER, Hans	191334	M	Ger.	15	Sgt., 599 Flak-Anti-Aircraft, Schwalbach (Ger.) 8.44	TORTURE	U.S.
BOETCHER, Kurt	174850	M	Ger.		Farmer, civilian, Reichardtsdorf (Ger.) 8.-9.44	MURDER	U.S.
BOETEL or BOTEL, George	165731	M	Ger.		Mayor, civilian, Wetzlegen (Ger.) 3.45	TORTURE	U.S.
BOETSCHER	306179	M	Ger.	14	Oberfhr., C.C. Kahla (Ger.) 40-45	MURDER	BEL.
BOETSCHER, Heinz	301551	M	Ger.		SS-Scharfhr. attached to Gestapo at Arlon, 8.44 and 9.44	MURDER	BEL.
BOETTCHER	129826	M	Ger.	07	Hoeh.Polizei-Fhr., SS, Radom (Pol.) 44	MURDER	U.S.
BOETTCHER	159372	M	Ger.	00	Col., SS, district Radom (Pol.) 43-44	MURDER	U.S.
BOETTCHER	192914	M	Ger.	05	Cpl., 367 Landesschtz.Bn., camp L 91 to Stalag IV G, C.C., Gaschwitz near Leipzig, 12.43	MURDER	U.K.
BOETTCHER	301255	F	Ger.		Interpreter,Abt.III C, Kulturelle Gebiete und Abteilung Lage und Taetigkeitsberichte, SD, Bruessel (Bel.) 6.40-9.44	MURDER	BEL
BOETTCHER, Heinz	131142	M	Ger.	09	Uscharfhr., SS, Arlon	MURDER	BEL.
BOETTCHER, Victor	120	M	Ger.		SA-Oberfhr.,Regierungspraesident, Dr., Wartheland (Pol.)9.39-1.42	MURDER	POL.
BOETTEL	142328	M	Ger.		Oflag XI, civilian, Wlodzimierz (Rus.) 41	WITNESS	U.S.
BOETTGER	1304	M			Capt., Army, H.Q.-Div.	MISC.CRIMES	U.K.
BOETTGER	124520	M	Ger.	89	Hptscharfhr., Rapportfhr., SS, Gestapo, Dachau (Ger.) 42-4.45	MURDER	U.K.
BOETTICHER, Hans, Julius	107955	M	Ger.		Dr., Army, Brigadier-Gen.	TORTURE	U.S.
BOETTNER	167651	M	Ger.		Dr., office for supervision of literatur,Einsatzstab Rosenberg, Berlin (Ger.) 40-44	PILLAGE	FR.
BOG or BOY	185151	M	Ger.		SS-Mann, SS, C.C., (Kdo. Sachsenhausen), Huggelheim (Ger.)	TORTURE	FR.
BOGDAIA or BUCHTAIA or BUGDAIA	9635	M	Ger.		Hptscharfhr.,SS, C.C.Oranienburg,Sachsenhausen (Ger.) 39,42,44	MURDER	POL.,U.K.,0
BOGDAIA	140379	M	Ger.		Lt.,C.C. Sachsenhausen (Ger.)	MISC.CRIMES	BEL
BOGDAIA	168625	M	Ger.		SS-Scharfhr., SS, C.C. Oranienburg (Ger.)	MURDER	U.K.,POL.
BOGDALIA	110	M	Ger.		SS-Hptscharfhr., C.C. Dachau (Ger.) 40	MURDER	FR.
BOGE	189581	M	Ger.		Chief of Gestapo at Melun, Fontainebleau (Fr.) 44	TORTURE	FR.
BOGELSACK, Friedrich	1320	M			Civilian, detain Gendarmerie	TORTURE	U.S.
BOGEN	19 ,94	M			Col., Army, Athen (Grc.)	MISC.CRIMES	U.K.
BOGENRIEDER	2 281	M			Capt., 3 or 10 parachute-Div., Ussel (Fr.) 4.44	INTERR.	FR.
BOGENRIEDER, Alfons	1084	M	Ger.	3.10.00	Former prosecutor in the Stuttgart-Court, Stuttgart (Ger.)	MURDER	FR.
BOGER	111	M	Ger.		SS-Oscharfhr., C.C. Oswiecim-Birkenau, Rajsko (Pol.) 6.40-43	MURDER	BEL.
BOGER see BOGGER, Friedrich, Wilhelm	130099						
BOGER or BIDGER	252007	M	Ger.		Lt., 197 Div.Alpine, Vercheny la Plaine (Fr.) 7.44	MISC.CRIMES	FR.
BOGEV	73		Ger.		Osturmfhr., SS-Political-Section, Auschwitz (Pol.) 40	MURDER	FR.
BOGGER or BOGER,Friedrich, Wilhelm	130099	M			Oscharfhr., SS, C.C. Dora-Mittelbau, Nordhausen (Ger.)	MURDER	U.S.

BOG-BOK

NAME	C.R.FILE NUMBER	SEX	NATIO-NALITY	DATE OF BIRTH	RANK OCCUPATION UNIT PLACE AND DATE OF CRIME	REASON WANTED	WANTED BY
BOGNER, Josef	193464	M	Ger.	24.9.95	Oberwachtmeister,Reichsjustizministerium Strafgefangenlager Nord Finnmark(Nor.)6.42	MURDER	NOR.
BOGULA	112	M	Ger.		NSDAP Gauleiter,CC Grini(Nor.)11.42-2.43	TORTURE	NOR.
BOGUSZ	120568	M	Ger.		Cpl.SS CC Oswiecim(Pol.)6.40-1.45	MURDER	POL.
BOHATSCH, Karl	251970	M	Ger.	10.3.08	Manager,Civilian,factory,Haj(Czech.)39-45	PILLAGE	CZECH.
BOHEME	153562	M			Officer,Freiwillige Stamm Regt.2,La Parade Baradoux(Fr.)5.44	MURDER	FR.
BOHL	301894	M			Major,Comd.I/379 Gren.Regt.169 Inf.Div.20 Army(Fin.)11.44	MURDER	NOR.
BOHLAENDER, Andreas	134774	M			SS Sgt.4 SS Totenkopfsturmbann,CC Dora Mittelbau,Nordhausen(Ger.)43-45	WITNESS	U.S.
BOHLE or BHOLE or BOJE	300030	M	Ger.		Cmdt,Front.supervis.office,Usquert,Warffum,Breede,Baflo.4.45	MURDER	NETH.
BOHLE, Anna	262243	F	Ger.	26.9.	Secretary,Gestapo section IV,Rennes(Fr.)43-44	SUSPECT	FR.
BOHLE, Ernst Wilhelm	62353		Ger.		SS Lt.General,Gauleiter,Waffen SS,Head of Foreign Section NSDAP, Berlin(Ger.)44	MISC.CRIMES	UNWCC
BOHLE, Hans see BOUHLER	17513						
BOHLE, Heinz	189529	M		05	Feldwebel,Guard at P.G.52,Chiavari(It.)9-43	TORTURE	U.K.
BOHLE, Willi	159392	M	Ger.		Pvt.214 Div.Inf.Regt.355,12 M.G.Coy.,Egersund(Nor.)42-43	MURDER.	NOR.
BOHLE or BOEHLE, Heinz	130079	M		02	Feldwebel,Wehrmacht 65,Inf.Div.146 Gren.Regt.7 Coy.CIE,CC 52,Chaivari(It.)9.43	MURDER	U.K.
BOHLENDER, Kurt	134912	M		12	SS CC Hartheim(Aust.)40-44	MURDER	U.S.
BOHLER	27782	M	Ger.		1st Lt.Army,Chief 1st Unit,3 techn.Bn.(mot.)23,Belfort(Fr.)44	INTERR.	FR.
BOHLER	149359	M			Civilian,Fa.Burmeister(Fr.)	MISC.CRIMES	FR.
BOHLER see BOEHLER	140581						
BOHLITZ, Bankhart	159371	M	Ger.		Doctor for Medicin,Physician in control of Camp Hospital,controlled by "Fum Korting and Matheison"of Franc,Flemming,Strasse,Leipzig(Ger.)2.45	MURDER	FR.
BOHLMAN	176410	M	Ger.	85	Civilian,Haimar Kr.Burgdorf(Ger.)	TORTURE	FR.
BOHM	11225	M	Ger.		Pvt.Army,Ugine(Fr.)44	MURDER	FR.
BOHM	125167	M			Obfhr.SS,Koenigsberg(Ger.)44-45	MURDER	U.S.
BOHM	140758	M			Capt.902 Panz.Gren.Regt.2 Bn.,Wardin(Bel.)12.44	MURDER	U.S.
BOHM	159391	M		15	Obscharfhr.SS,Enschede(Neth.)	MURDER	U.K.
BOHM	168620	M	Ger.		Sturmfhr.SS Gestapo(Nor.)4,40	TORTURE	NOR.
BOHM	188051	M			Pvt.,Ugines(Fr.)	MURDER	FR.
BOHM	192810	M			Member,Schupo,CC Falstad,Trondheim(Nor.)41-45	MURDER	NOR.
BOHM or BOEHM	254493	M	Ger.		Capt.Unit 59029A,Bourgeauville(Fr.)6.44	INTERR.	FR.
BOHM, Edgar	31995	M			Dr.,Landgerichtsrat,Public official,Litomerice(Czech.)1940	MURDER	CZECH.
BOHM, Joseph	140382	M			Civilian,Wuestenswchsen Krs.Fulda(Ger.)	TORTURE	FR.
BOHM, Karl	132011	M		19	Lt.7 Panz.Reconnaissance Coy.,Freilassing(Ger.)4.45	MURDER	U.S.
BOHME	251980	M	Ger.		Crim.secretary,Sipo VB,Brussels(Bel.)	INTERR	BEL.
BOHME	252035	M			Interpreter,Feldgendarmerie 924 Bourjon,La Folatiere(Fr.)6.44	MURDER	FR.
BOHME, Franz	62165	M			Gen.der Inf.Chief of Staff Praesident of Armistice Commission(Fr.)	TORTURE	UNWCC
BOHME, Horst	113	M			SS Standartenfhr.SD official,Befehlshaber der Sipo and SD,Prag(Czech.) 7.42	MURDER	CZECH.
BOHME, Karl	193995	M	Ger.		Sipo,Dorgen(Meckl/Ger.)5.or 6.44	WITNESS	U.S.
BOHMER	27788	M		95 or 00	Inspector,Police,Rheinbach(Ger.)	TORTURE	FR.
BOHMER see BOEMER	100420						
BOHMER	176143	M	Ger.		Col.,Feldkommandantur,Tours(Fr.)	TORTURE	FR.
BOHMICHEN, Karl	128600	M			Hptsturmfhr.SS CC Mauthausen(Aust.)42-44	MURDER	U.S.
BOHMIG see BORMING	192578						
BOHMLER	259739				Commandant,Unit F.P.VL OS-811,St.Pierre de Semilly(Manche/Fr.(9.42	WITNESS	FR.
BOHN	195867	M	Ger.		Hptscharfhr.Sicherheitspolizei,Westerbork(Neth.)9.-12.44	MURDER	NETH.
BOHN, Conrad	259355	M	Ger.		Unterscharfhr.Gestapo of Poitiers(Fr.)40-44	MISC.CRIMES	FR.
BOHN, Jakob	258387	M			Guard,CC Ohrdruf(Ger.)12.44-4.45	MURDER	U.S.
BOHN, Richard	152493	M	Ger.	23.1.84	Stalag Civilian KL Stalag Ausweiskarte(Ger.)	TORTURE	U.S.
BOHNE	252010	M	Ger.		Lt.Block-officer at Oflag XIIIB,Nuernberg,Hamelburg(Ger.)41-45	MURDER	YUGO.
BOHNE, Horst	185429	M			SS Standartenfhr.SS,SD,Prague(Czech.)	MURDER	U.S.
BOHNE see BOHRER	252006						
BOHNEL, Ehrhard	27791	M		10.4.19	Lt.SS,Montmirail(Fr.)	MURDER	FR.
BOHNEN	173976	M			Campleader,Organisation Todt,Camp Ecksberg,Muhldorf Ampfing(Ger.)44-45	MURDER	U.S.
BOHNEN	194942	M	Ger.		Capt.405 Inf.Div.St.Die(Fr.)44	MURDER	U.K.
BOHNENBERGER, Robert	251944	M			Flyer,Camp Ellrich,Nordhausen(Ger.)	MURDER	U.S.
BOHNENKAMP	140388	M	Ger.		Oberfeldarzt,Camp Ravensbrueck(Ger.)	TORTURE	FR.
BOHNENKAMP, Hans	301229	M		98	SS Hptsturmfhr.Kriminalrat,SS Sicherheitsdienst,Fremdenlegionsachen Abt.IVE,Brussels(Bel.)6.40-9.44	INTERR	BEL.
BOHNER, Alfred	132817	M	Ger.		Oblt.,Bad Soden,Mulheim/Baden(Ger.)1.-2.45	WITNESS	U.K.
BOHNER, Fritz	251466	M	Ger.		Pvt.Camp Harzungen,Nordhausen(Ger.)	MURDER	U.S.
BOHNERT	140389	M			Cpl.Chief,Landesschuetzen Bn.12 Army,Donaueschingen(Ger.)42-43	TORTURE	FR.
BOHNERT	159361	M			Oschafhr.SS,CC Flossenburg(Ger.)2.44	MURDER	U.S.
BOHNIG	140390	M	Ger.-		Civilian,Gustloffwerke,CC Weimar(Ger.)	TORTURE	FR.
BOHNKE	159962	M			Policeman,Police,KL Kunsebech(Ger.)3.45	WITNESS	U.S.
BOHNKE, Herbert	152491	M			Sgt.SD and Sipo,Toulouse,Tarbes,Agen,Cahors,Fuix,Pau,Montrebun,6.-8.44	MURDER	U.S.
BOHR	121095	M	Ger.		Civilian Kiew Institute Physician,Kiew(Russ.)41-42	TORTURE	U.S.
BOER, Franz	171956	M			Civilian,Saarbuten,Hostenbach(Ger.)9.44	MURDER	U.S.
BOHRER or BOHNE	252006	M			Rottfhr., Camp Dora,Nordhausen (Ger.)	TORTURE	U.S.
BOHRER, Adolph	72742	M	Ger.		Pvt.Fallschirm-Jaeger Bn.,Roermond(Neth.)11.44-1.45	MURDER	FR.
BOHRING,Schulte	256785	M			Hptscharfhr.SD,Foix(Fr.)11.42-8.44	INTERR	U.S.
BOHRMANN, Hermann	251968	M	Ger.	3.8.91	Polizeimeister,5 Police District,Saarbruecken-Burbach(Ger.)8.44	MURDER	CZECH.
BOHRN, Arnost	187536	M			Employee,SD and Gestapo,Bruenn(Czech.)39-45	MURDER	FR.
BOHRNING-SCHULTE	300185	M			SS Hptscharfhr.Deputy Chief,SD,Grenzkommissariat Foix(Fr.)11.42&.44	MISC.CRIMES	CZECH.
BOHRSCH, Herbert	255260	M	Ger.	26.4.13	Dr.Civilian,Bratislava(Czech.)44		
BOHUM see BOHAN	186704						
BOJAHR	176976	M	Ger.		Oberjaeger(Cpl.)Kampfgruppe,Le Temple(Fr.)8.44	MURDER	FR.
BOJE see BOHLE	300030						
BOJE	301628				Member SS,Renardmont,Stavelot(Bel.)12.44	MURDER	BEL.
BOJETUL, Michael	260920	M	Ger.	9.11.25	St.Mann,SS guard,CC Auschwitz,Gross-Rosen(Pol.Ger.)43-45	BRUTALITY	POL.
BOJKO	72745	M			Capt.SD,CC Theresienstadt(Pol.)12.41	TORTURE	U.S.
BOKEMEIER, Gusta	124298	M	Ger.	97	Soldier,Army	MISC.CRIMES	U.K.
BOKER	1305				Lt.Army 112 Div.721 Tayer Regt.	MISC.CRIMES	U.K.
BOKER	179761	M		13	Sec.Lt.721 Jg.Regt.114 Div.,Sansepolcro(It.)8.44	MURDER	U.K.
BOKKI	195866	M			Block-Foreman,"Rijka"Art.silk factory,Anrath(Ger.)1.42-3.44	WITNESS	NETH.
BOKLE	27794	M			Commandant,Gestapo,St.Quentin(Fr.)	TORTURE	FR.

BOL-BON

NAME	C.R.FILE NUMBER	SEX	NATIONALITY	DATE OF BIRTH	RANK OCCUPATION UNIT PLACE AND DATE OF CRIME	REASON WANTED	WANTED BY
BOLANZ	251965	M	Ger.		Civ., Loerrach (Ger.)	INTERR	BEL.
BOLBACH (or HOLBACH)	138281	M	Ger.		SS-Usturmfhr., W.O., SS-Gestapo, Lyon (Fr.) 44	MURDER	FR.
BOLBINSKI	134786	M			Pvt., 4.Waffen-SS, Totenkopf-Sturmbann, C.C. Dora-Mittelbau, Nordhausen (Ger.) 43-45	WITNESS	U.S.
BOLCHERT Paul	27795	M		22	SS	TORTURE	FR.
BOLCHETZ	27796	M			Pvt., SS Div. "Das Reich".	MISC.CRIMES	FR.
BOLCHSET	193380	M	Ger.		Capt., Army, C.C. Sunndalsora (Nor.) 6.42	MURDER	NOR.
BOLDEL	140391	M	Ger.		Sturmbannfuhr., SS, Reval (Esth.)	MURDER	FR.
BOLDT	159389	F			Stalag II D, Stargard (Ger.)	TORTURE	U.S.,U.K.
BOLECEK, Theodor	196293	M		18. 9.16	Member, State Service S.D. (Czech.)	MURDER	CZECH.
BOLESLAWSKI	27798	M	Ger.		Lt., Army, Rosguveo (Fr.) 6.-7.44	MURDER	FR.
BOLHACHEN	196296				Physician, C.C. Mauthausen (Austria)	TORTURE	BEL.
BOLIAHAN	125750	M	Ger.		Civ.Kreishandwerksmeister, Rosenberg (Pol.) 1.43-2.44	MISC.CRIMES	U.K.
BOLICK	140392	M	Ger.		Chief, Gestapo, C.C. Butzow (Ger.) 10.43	MURDER	FR.
BOLI	166925	M			Chief, Gend., Reichschaffen (Fr.) 44-45	TORTURE	FR.
BOLL	252271	M			Pvt., Camp Dora, Nordhausen (Ger.)	MURDER	U.S.
BOLL, Hermann	140393	M	Ger.		Home address formerly Finkenwaerder, Endenstr.23. Prison at Altona	MURDER	FR.
BOLLAND	300364	M	Ger.		Member of the Sicherheitsdienst The Hague, Driebergen, Rotterdam (Neth.) 10.43	MISC.CRIMES	NETH.
BOLLANDER, Fritz	27799	M			W.O.-Chief, Army, Beaudrigue, Carcassone (Fr.)	TORTURE	FR.
BOLLE	28000	M			Hptsturmfhr., SS, Paris (Fr.)	MISC.CRIMES	FR.
BOLLE	152492	M		00 or 05	Sturmbannfhr., Kriminalrat, S.D. and Sipo, Toulouse,Foix, Tarbes.8.44	MURDER	U.S.
BOLLE	252016	M	Ger.		Kapo, Meigem (Bel.) 45	INTERR.	BEL.
BOLLE	254282	M	Ger.		Capt., Gestapo, Paris (Fr.) 41-44	TORTURE	FR.
BOLLER	252270	M			Pvt., Camp Ellrich, Nordhausen (Ger.)	MURDER	U.S.
BOLLET	173133	M	Ger.		Wachtmeister, C.C. Gaggenau, Schirmeck-Rotenfels (Ger.)	INTERR.	U.K.
BOLLINGER, Werner	126999				Switzerland Gestapo, Delle (Fr.) 7.44	MURDER	FR.
BOLLMACHER	140399	M	Ger.		SS, C.C. Naumburg-Saale (Ger.)	TORTURE	FR.
BOLLMAN	114				Col., Kl. Stalag 20 B, Cmdt. POW-Camp. 4.41-8.42	MISC.CRIMES	U.K.
BOLLMAN	121096	M			Col., Stalag XX B, Marienburg (Pol.) 40-42	BRUTALITY	U.K.
BOLLMANN	193467	M			Col., Stabs Pionier Regt. 664. 42	MISC.CRIMES	NOR.
BOLL-WEBER	177742	M	Ger.		Custom-officer, Zollgrenzschutz, Badiau, Thoiry (Fr.) 4.44	MURDER	FR.
BOLMO, Walter	260076	M	Ger.		Oberwachtmeister, SS-Strafgefangenen-Lager, Nord-Norway (Nor.) 6.42-45	SUSPECT	YUGO.
BOLSCHE, Karl Ludwig (see BOESCHE)	192917	M	Ger.	95	Major, 12.Pol.Regt. III. Bn., Montorio, San Michele (Italy) 11.43	MURDER	U.K.
BOLTE	261182	M	Ger.		Member of Staff of C.C. Ravensbrueck (Ger.)	SUSPECT	BEL.
BOLTE, Hermann (aliases. BIERMAN)	256938	M		90	Lt., Abwehr, Nebenstelle, Navy, Bergen (Nor.) 41-42	WITNESS	NOR.
BOLTZ	194740	M	Ger.		SS-Polizeifuehrer, SS, Chelmno (Pol.) 42	MURDER	POL.
BOLZ	116	M			Official (Sgt.), Gestapo, Perpignan (Fr.) 3.-8.44	MURDER	FR.
BOLZ	156748	M			Cmit., C.C. Aschendorfer-Moor (Ger.)	TORTURE	FR.
BOMBA	36662	M			Cmit., Army, Marburg, Heyderug-Swinemuende (Ger.) 42-44	MURDER	U.K.
BOMBACH	12197	M		06	Lt.Col., Camp-Cmdt., Stalag-Luft 4, Kief-Hyde	MURDER	U.S.
BOMBER	10060	M			Col., Army, C.C.-Cmdt., Stalag-Luft 4, Pommern (Ger.) 7.44	MURDER	U.K.
BOMBERGER, Franz	185414	M	Ger.		Civilian, Weferting (Ger.) 4.45	MURDER	U.S.
BOMBSCHLIT, Heinz	252462	M	Ger.		Pvt., Dulag-Luft, Frankfurt (Ger.) 9.44	MURDER	U.S.
BOMDONER, Max	176407	M			C.C. Siemensstadt (Ger.) 44	TORTURE	FR.
BOMELBURG	254283	M	Ger.		Osturmfhr., Gestapo, Paris (Fr.) 41-44	TORTURE	FR.
BOMM	251962	M			Lt., Westen Schouwen (Neth.) 8.43	INTERR.	NETH.
BOMMER (see BAUMER)	189120						
BOMMER, Berta	252460	F	Ger.		Guard, SS, Women-C.C. Geislingen (Ger.) 40-45	INTERR.	POL.
BOMMERSHIN	140400	M	Ger.		Kriegsgef.Arbeitskdo., C.C. Roedelheim (Ger.)	TORTURE	FR.
BONCZECK (see BONEZEK)	196117						
BOND	159396	M			Civ., Bond's Restaurant, Estedt, Germany. Vicinity of Gardelegen (Ger.) 4.45	WITNESS	U.S.
BONDARENTO, Fedor	31304	M		1. 7.24	N.C.O., Army.	MURDER	FR.
BONDE	140401	M	Ger.		Capt., Police, Oflag X C, Luebeck (Ger.) 4.44	MURDER	FR.
BONDER, Hermann	261776	M	Ger.	96	Sgt., Gend. of Peray le Moniel, Bragny-Charollais (Fr.) 7.44	INCENDIARISM	FR.
BONDERENKO, Ivan	159354	M			Civilian, Mariandorf near Eschweiler (Ger.) 42-44	TORTURE	U.S.
BONDERENKO, Nikolai (aliases. NICKOLAI BOTHAROV)	159418	M	Ger.		Civilian, C.C.Eschweiler-Bruchweiden, Mariandorf-Eschweiler (Ger.) 42-44	TORTURE	U.S.
BONDZIO, Fritz	187534	M		11	Miner, Adolf Mine, Merkstein (Ger.) 43	WITNESS	U.S.
BONEZEK (or BONCZECK)	196117	M	Ger.		Cpl., Army, 158.Div.de la Rochelle,223.Regt., La Franche s.Mer(Fr.)9.44	MURDER	FR.
BONGARD	252026	M			Rottenfhr., C.C. Mackenrode, Nordhausen (Ger.)	MURDER	U.S.
BONGART, Henri or Heinrich	251976	M	Ger.	7. 2.14	Pvt., 558. Gren.Regt., 13.Coy., Bruay en Artois (Fr.) 9.44	MURDER	FR.
BONGARTZ	147955	M		95	Member, NSKK.	PILLAGE	FR.
BONGARTZ, Johann	190487	M			C.C. Dachau (Ger.)	MURDER	U.S.
BONGARTZ, Philipp	256807	M		26	Cpl., 10. Flottille (Navy), Guilligomarch (Fr.) 7.44	MURDER	FR.
BONGER	186017	M			Pvt., 3.Sich.Regt. 16 (Bel.) 44	MURDER	BEL.
BONGERS, Carl	187847	M			Hauptwachtmeister, Heereskuesten-Art.Abt.1240, Oostduin (Ger.) 9.44	MURDER	BEL.
BONGREUBER	252009	M	Ger.		Major, Army, 443. Jaeger Regt., Belgrad (Yugo.) 10.-12.41	MURDER	YUGO.
BONHAGE	127066	M	Ger.		SS-Scharfhr., SS Panz.Div."Das Reich" (South-West-France)	MURDER	FR.
BONICKE, Hermann	159398	M			Member, Civ., C.C. Gardelegen (Ger.)	MURDER	U.S.
BONISCH	193468	M	Ger.		Cpl., Kriegsgefangenen-Arbeits-Bn.190, Karasjok. 8.43	TORTURE	NOR.
BONKOWSKI, Walter	134761	M	Ger.	18. 6.05	Sgt. of the Guard, SS, Thueringen (Ger.) 43-45	WITNESS	U.S.
BONN	1063	M			N.C.O., Feldgend., Vitry le François (Fr.)	MISC.CRIMES	FR.
BONN	127329	M			Cmit., C.C. Roermond (Neth.) 11.44	MURDER	U.S.
BONN	159390	M			Crim.Commissar, Gestapo, C.C. Graudenz (Pol.) 44	TORTURE	U.K.
BONN	261180	M	Ger.		Cmit., Angleur (Bel.) 5.40	SUSPECT	BEL.
BONN, Emil	130089	M			Obersturmfhr., S.A., C.C. Nordhausen (Ger.)	MURDER	U.S.
BONN, Karl	149722	M	Ger.		Chief, Bloc 5, C.C. Schirmeck (Fr.) 41-43	TORTURE	FR.
BONN, William	121098	M	Ger.	00	Major, Army, C.C. Stalag XII (A) or B (Ger.) 1.45	BRUTALITY	U.S.
BONNEMAN	121099	M	Ger.		Lt., worked for the Sonder-Kommando at Suttrop, Langenbach, Warstein, Arnsberg, Suttrop, Lippstadt (Ger.) 3.45	MURDER	U.S.
BONNER	305784	M	Ger.				
BONNET	27728	M			Pvt., near St.Die (Fr.) 9.44	MURDER	U.K.
BONNGARTZ	185150	M	Ger.	09	Flieger Regt. 71, 8.Coy., Carcassone,Limoux,Ledern,Rabassier (Fr.) 7.44	PILLAGE	FR.
BONNING, Bruno	193589	M	Ger.	22. 5.09	SS-Mann, SS, C.C. Dachau (Ger.)	MURDER	FR.
					C.C. Flossenburg (Ger.)	WITNESS	BEL.

NAME	C.R.FILE NUMBER	SEX	NATIO-NALITY	DATE OF BIRTH	RANK OCCUPATION UNIT PLACE AND DATE OF CRIME	REASON WANTED	WANTED BY
BONNSELS	191680	M	Ger.		Lt.,Army,Vienne la Tricherie (Fr.)	MURDER	FR.
BONS (or BRUNS)	62352	M	Ger.	00 - 02	Capt.,Army,18 Volks Gren.Div.293 Regt.,2 Bn. Ger. Bel. 12.44	MURDER	U.S.
BONSE	27726	M			Lt.,Army	INCENDIARISM	FR.
BONSHEIM	36661	M	Ger.		Pvt., Army,C.C.,Stalag IX C	MURDER	U.K.
BONTE	188679	M	Ger.		Lt.,28 Res.Gren.Rgt., Puydarrieux (Fr.) 6.44	MURDER	FR.
BONUS, Joseph	221406	M	Ger.	18	Pvt.,Nachr.Rgt. 506,Abwehr-Official,Bad Wildungen (Ger.)	MISC.CRIMES	U.S.
BONY	166924	M			Officer,SD,Verviere Grandeyolles (Fr.) 8.44	PILLAGE	FR.
BOOCHS	166923	M			Secretary,Public-Official,Wissembourg (Fr.) 12.44	MURDER	FR.
BOOK, Kurt	305000	M	Ger.		Administrator, Enschede (Neth.) 43-45	PILLAGE	NETH.
BOON	159399	M			Civilian, political prisoner interned near Hannover. (Ger.) 4.45	WITNESS	U.S.
BOONEN	192156	M	Ger.		Member, Geheime Feldpolizei,Brussels (Bel.)	MISC.CRIMES	BEL.
BOORBERG	72743	M	Ger.		Sonderfhr.,Volksgren.,246 Div., G 2 Sect.	TORTURE	U.S.
BOOS	141458	M			Unterscharfhr.,SS-Div."Das Reich"Rgt."Der Fuehrer"20 Coy,1 Bn. Oradour sur Glane (Fr.) 6.44	TORTURE	FR.
BOOS	251969	M	Ger.		N.C.O.,"Das Reich" 3 Coy. St.Junien (Fr.) 6.44	MURDER	FR.
BOOS, Anne-Lise	176408	F	Ger.	13	Civilian, Harber (Ger.)	TORTURE	FR.
BOOS, Hermann	189669	M	Ger.		SS-Unterscharfhr.,SS-Div."Das Reich" Oradour Glane (Fr.) 6.44	MURDER	FR.
BOPP	163100	M	Ger.		Cpl.Chief,Group of Transmission 34304,Lamanon (Fr.) 6.44	WITNESS	FR.
BOPP	251981	M	Ger.		Interpreter,SD,Abt. VI,Nachrichten,Brussels (Bel.) 40-44	INTERR.	BEL.
BOPP, Alfred	168603	M	Ger.		Pvt.,9 Gren.Ers.Rgt., Magny D'Avignon (Fr.)	MURDER	FR.
BOR	27724	M			Capt.,12 S^e Panzer Div."Hitler Jugend"Tourouvres (Fr.)	MURDER	FR.
BORBECK	166922	M			SS-Hauptsturmfhr.,SS,C.C.Braunschweig (Ger.) 6.44	TORTURE	FR.
BORCH, Johann (see BORSCH)	174849	M					
BORCHARDT, Werner	251877	M	Ger.		Crim.Commissar,SS-Obsturmfhr.,Gestapo,Chef of Abt.IV B,Sipo Brussels (Bel.)	INTERR.	BEL.
BORCHARR	189670	M	Ger.		Member,C.C.Ravensbrueck (Ger.)	MURDER	FR.
BORCHART	132607	M	Ger.	10	Agent,Gestapo, C.C.Ravensbrueck (Ger.)	MISC.CRIMES	FR.
BORCHART	260694	M	Ger.		SS-Obersturmfhr., Waffen-SS,Belgrade (Yugo.) 9.44	MURDER	YUGO.
BORCHERS, Walter	167650	M	Ger.		Dr., civilian,Expert, Einsatzstab Rosenberg,(Fr.) 44	PILLAGE	FR.
BORCHERT	1683	M	Ger.		NSDAP	TORTURE	U.K.
BORCHERT	62322	M	Ger.	90	Civilian,Miller,NSDAP,Gestapo,Grossgarten,Angerburg (Ger.)	TORTURE	U.S.
BORCHERT	141418	M	Ger.		Sgt.,127 Rgt.,d'Inf.Crapux (Fr.) 8.44	WITNESS	FR.
BORCHERT	252005	M			Rottenfhr.,C.C.Rottleberode, Nordhausen (Ger.)	MURDER	U.S.
BORCHERTS	159374	M		10	Cpl.,C.C.Landshut,Sachsenhausen,Guard at Loibersdorf (Ger.)5.45	WITNESS	U.S.
BORCHMANN	255291	M			Pvt.,C.C.Dora, Nordhausen (Ger.)	MURDER	U.S.
BORCK	12110	M			Col.,Army, Stammlager Limburg XII A (Ger.)	MURDER	U.S.
BORD, Fritz	196291	M	Ger.		Kapo,C.C.Dachau (Ger.) 44	TORTURE	POL.
BORDELMANN	134787	M			Cpl.,4 Waffen-SS Totenkopf Sturmbann C.C.Nordhausen,Dora Mittelbau (Ger.) 43-45	WITNESS	U.S.
BORDON	260981	M			Unterscharfhr., SS,C.C.Vaihingen (Ger.) 44-45	MURDER	U.S.
BORELL	139834	M			Lt.,Waffen-SS,Arbeitslager 101,Buchenwald,Magdeburg (Ger.) 44-45	TORTURE	U.S.
BORELL	194792	M	Ger.		SS-Lt. C.C.Lublin (Pol.) 40-42	MURDER	POL.
BORELL, Gustav	159854	M	Ger.	98	SS-Obersturmfhr.,Waffen-SS Arbeitslager 101,Camp Staff,HQ Coy. C.C.Schoenbeck (Ger.)	TORTURE	U.S.
BORER	159388	M	Ger.		Cpl., SS "Das Reich" Rgt.,"Der Fuehrer" 3 Coy.1 Bn.,Oradour sur Glane (Fr.) 6.44	MURDER	FR.
BORERSCHRIVER	130086	M			Hauptscharfhr.,SS,C.C.Dora Mittelbau,Nordhausen (Ger.)	MURDER	U.S.
BORG, Auguste	185149	M	Ger.		Medicin chief,C.C.Sachsenhausen (Ger.) 43	MURDER	FR.
BORGER	252274	M			Oberscharfhr.,Pol.Abt. C.C.Auschwitz Nordhausen (Ger.)	MURDER	U.S.
BORGERMANN, Heinrich	168604	M	Ger.		Pvt.,9 Gren.Ers.Rgt., 1 Coy. Magny D'Avignon (Fr.) 9.44	MURDER	FR.
BORGERS, Sander	300366	M			Member,SS belonged to Sonderkommando Feldmeyer,Blaricum-Beemster (Neth.) 43-44	MURDER	NETH.
BORGL	192577	M	Ger.		SS-C.C.Buchenwald (Ger.) 42-45	MURDER	U.S.
BORGMANN	27717	M	Ger.		Lt.Col.,Inf.Rgt.,93,St.Flour, Cantal (Fr.) 6.44	MURDER	FR.
BORGMANN	159387	M	Ger.		Col.,Commandant of Aurillier,Lavissiere (Fr.) 8.44	MURDER	FR.
BORGMANN, Adolphe	27719	M	Ger.	9. 2.17	Annonay,La Ciotat (Fr.)	MURDER	FR.
BORGRAF, Alois	252273	M			Flyer,Camp Ellrich,Nordhausen (Ger.)	MURDER	U.S.
BORGSTEDT	251973	M	Ger.		Hauptscharfhr., SS,Sipo Abt.III C 3,Brussels (Bel.)	INTERR.	BEL.
BOHM	27718	M			Lt., Army, Le Tholy (Fr.)	INCENDIARISM	FR.
BORIS, Wilhelm	252272	M			Pvt.,Camp Ellrich, Nordhausen (Ger.)	MURDER	U.S.
BORK (see BARK)	168632	M					
BORKELOH, Richard, Joseph	27715	M	Ger.	80	Chief,Gestapo,Paris (Fr.)	MISC.CRIMES	FR.
BORKOTT	252269	M			Rottenfhr., Camp Rottleberode,Nordhausen (Ger.)	MURDER	U.S.
BORMANN	159386	M	Ger.		Dr.,Organis.-leader, SS,Ensisheim,Arrest-House, (Fr.) 43	MURDER	FR.
BORMANN, Juana	173307	F	Ger.		SS-Woman,SS,C.C.Bergem-Belsen, Auschwitz (Ger.-Pol.)	MURDER	UNWCC
BORMANN, Martin	118	M	Ger.	17. 5.00	Sb-Obergr.-Fhr.,Reichsleit.,NSDAP,leader of the party,Munich,39-43	MISC.CRIMES	POL.BEL.U.S.
BORMING (or BOHMIG) (or BEHMIG)	192578	M	Ger.		Foreman,Civilian,C.C.Buchenwald (Ger.) 42-45	MURDER	U.S.
BORN	141911	M		08	Sgt.,Fliegerhorst Kommandantur 208,Hobsten (Ger.) 3.44	WITNESS	U.K.
BORN	187006	M	Ger.		Pvt., Army,Hennebont (Fr.) 8.44	MURDER	FR.
BORN	252015	M	Ger.	06	Sgt.,Army,Hopster (Ger.)	MURDER	U.S.
BORN	256806	M	Ger.		Lt., Formation Bode,St.Pierre,Pressignac,St.Avil (Fr.) 7.44	MURDER	FR.
BORN, August	176404	M	Ger.	00	Civilian,C.C.Sachsenhausen (Ger.) 43-45	MURDER	FR.
BORNECIN, Johann	140754	M			Civilian	MURDER	U.S.
BORNEMANN	306180	M	Ger.		Lt.,C.C.Kahla (Ger.) 40-45	MURDER	BEL.
BORNEMANN	121102	M	Ger.		General,Army Wehrkreiskommando XIII,Ochsenfurt, (Ger.) 8.44	MURDER	U.S.
BORNEMANN (or MINSINGER or POSCHINGER)	190092	M	Ger.		Lt.Col.Stalag V III B	MURDER	U.K.
BORNEMANN, Heinrich	196290	M	Ger.	22. 3.20	Guard,civil Labourer,Terezin (Czech.)	TORTURE	CZECH.
BORNFANN, Heinrich	252268	M			Rottenfhr., Camp Harzungen,Nordhausen (Ger.)	MURDER	U.S.
BORNER	137082	M	Ger.	03	Sgt.,610 Landesschuetzen Bn. 1 Coy.Stalag XX B Christburg (Ger.)5.43	MURDER	U.K.POL.
BORNER	188073	M	Ger.		Capt.,110 Panzer Gren.Rgt. Courdon (Fr.)	MURDER	FR.
BORNER	189671	M	Ger.		Cpl.,SS-Div."Das Reich" Oradour Glane (Fr.)	MURDER	FR.
BORHOEFT	186496	M	Ger.		Capt.,POW work Bn. 184, 3 Coy.,Kraakmoen (Nor.)	MURDER	NOR.
BORNS	261766	M	Ger.		Supervisor,C.C.Dora, Nordhausen (Ger.)	MURDER	FR.
BORNSCHEIN	125102	M			Pvt.,Army,Pothen,Thueringen (Ger.)	WITNESS	U.K.
BORNSCHEIN	252275	M			Unterscharfhr., C.C.Ellrich,Dora,Nordhausen (Ger.)	MURDER	U.S.

BOR - BOU

NAME	C.R.FILE NUMBER	SEX	NATIO-NALITY	DATE OF BIRTH	RANK OCCUPATION UNIT PLACE AND DATE OF CRIME	REASON WANTED	WANTED BY
BORNSCHEIN, Theodor	306344	M	Ger.	9.9.05	SS-Pvt.,C.C.Buchenwald (Ger.) 5.38-10.43	MURDER	BEL.
BORNSCHEIN-SCHMIDT	306258	M	Ger.	10	Pvt.,Army,622 Ldschtz.Bn.,Poethen Salt Mine (U.K.) 5.43	MURDER	U.K.
BOROVSKI	189988	M			General,Army,Pozarevac (Serbia-Yugo.) 41-43	MURDER	YUGO.
BORR	195864	M	Ger.		Capt.,SS,12 Regt.Art.,Tourouvres (Fr.) 8.44	MURDER	FR.
BORREK	28736	M			Capt.,SS,Geb.Div.Nord,Finmark (Norway) 11.44	MURDER	NOR.
BORS, Ernst	124292	M	Ger.		Civilian, Neu-Wuhmsdorf (Ger.) 6.44	MURDER	U.S.
BORSCH (BOSCH)(BORCH),Johann	174849	M			Police-man,Police,Weissenbach,Gernsbach (Ger.)	MURDER	U.S.
BORSCHERT,Heinz(or BORSCHEN)	176403	M	Ger.		Sturmmann,SS-Pz.Gren.Div."Goetz v.Berlichingen",Raids (Fr.) 6.-7.44	MURDER	U.S.
BORSDORF, Heinz	300188	M	Ger.		Sgt.,749 Regt.,1 Coy.,Calavrita,Mega,Apileon,Aghia,Lavra, 12.43	MURDER	GRC.
BORSIG, Hans Joachim	260621	M	Ger.	20.5.20	Off.CadetCoy., Anti-Terroriste "Siegfried", Ampus (Fr.) 7.44	MURDER	FR.
BORST, Alfons	159400	M			Civ.,NSDAP,Ortsgruppenleiter,Bad Neustadt (Ger.) 9.44	WITNESS	U.S.
BORSTELMANN	190679	M	Ger.		Pvt.,Ers.Bn.717,St.Andries,Varsenare,Les Bruges (Bel.)	MURDER	BEL.
BORYS, Regina	301935	F	Ger.	12	Lageraelteste,C.C.Eberswalde (Ger.) 44	BRUTALITY	POL.
BOSBACH, Hans	258780	M			Mechanist,Airfield,Wieseck(Ger.) 3.-4.44	WITNESS	U.S.
BOSBACH, Robert	260863	M			Chief,Police,Schweich (Ger.) 1.45	WITNESS	U.S.
BOSCH	305828	M	Ger.		Pvt.,1.Aufkl.-Abt.,3 Coy.,2 Column,XV Div.,Afrika-Corps, St.Leger (Arlon) 9.44	MISC.CRIMES	BEL.
BOSCH (see BORSCH) Johann	174849						
BOSCH, Willy	259698	M	Ger.	95 or 00	Hptschfhr.,SS,Gestapo, Area of Angers (Fr.) 42-44	MISC.CRIMES	FR.
BOSCHE	62321	M	Ger.		Gendarm,Gendarmerie,Baden 6.44	MURDER	U.S.
BOSCHE	192579	M			U-Fuehrer,SS,C.C.Buchenwald (Ger.) 42-45	MURDER	U.S.
BOSCHERER	195863	M			C.C.Personnel,Struthof,Natzweiler (Fr.) 40-44	TORTURE	FR.
BOSCHERER	261005	M			Oberwachtmeister (Pol.-Sgt.),SS,C.C.Vaihingen(Ger.) 8.44-4.45	MURDER	U.S.
BOSCHNER	173321	M	Ger.		Rottfhr.,SS,C.C.Struthof (Fr.) 6.44	MURDER	FR.
BOSE	181256	M	Ger.		SS-Leibstandarte "Adolf Hitler", 1.Pz.Gr.Div.,Stavelot (Bel.)12.44	MURDER	BEL.
BOSE	192918	M		10	Cpl.,Army,Police,3 Bn.,12 Pol.-Regt.,Monterio,San Michele(Ital.)11.43	MURDER	U.K.
BOSE	300189	M			Sec.Lt.,Officer Commanding,Gestapo,Tripolis, 3.44	MURDER	GRC.
BOSEL	196588	M	Ger.		Overseer,Generac Grosswerke Factory,Neusalz (Ger.) 44	TORTURE	FR.
BOSEL, Hans	252019	M			Pvt.,C.C.Ellrich,Nordhausen(Ger.)	MURDER	U.S.
BOSOTTE	133748	M			SS,C.C.Buchenwald (Ger.)	TORTURE	U.S.
BOSS	119	M			Army,Private	MURDER	FR.
BOSS	195020	M	Ger.		Adjutant,Army,Le Kernic (Fr.)	MURDER	FR.
BOSS, Willy	168582	M	Ger.		Sgt.,Feldgendarmerie de Langes,Coiffey,Aubevive,Flagey,Chalencey (Fr.) 43-44	MURDER	FR.
BOSS, Karl	188137	M	Ger.	02	SA-Mann,SA,NSDAP,Vic,Ettinghausen,Harbach (Ger.) 9.44	MURDER	U.S.
BOSS, Karl	252033	M	Ger.		Pvt.,Unit L.06459,Romilly (Fr.) 8.44	PILLAGE	FR.
BOSS, Walter	220477	M	Ger.		Inspector,Gestapo,Gruppe 7-2 G.F.P.,Antwerpen (Bel.) 41	MURDER	U.S.
BOSSE	27731	M			Cosne (Fr.)	MISC.CRIMES	FR.
BOSSE	141459	M	Ger.		Lt.,Kommandantur,Pionierschule,Cosne (Fr.) 7.44	MURDER	FR.
BOSSE	159368	M	Ger.		Osturmfhr.,SS,Kdo.394,L 19,Neusalz,C.C. (Ger.) 44	TORTURE	FR.
BOSSE, Friedrich	301057	M	Ger.		Arbeitsfhr.,Reichsarbeitsdienst,Marianske,Lazne,Bohemia(Czech.)42-44	TORTURE	CZECH.
BOSSE	252020	M	Ger.		Pvt.,C.C.Ellrich,Nordhausen (Ger.)	MURDER	U.S.
BOSSL	187650	M	Ger.		Oberfw.,Feldgendarmerie,Goudriaan (Neth.) 5.44	MURDER	U.K.
BOSSLE	172877	M	Ger.		Lt.,Stalag XIII C,Ldsschtz.-Bn.,Kitzingen (Ger.) 3.45	MURDER	U.K.
BOSSMANN, Ernst	307057	M	Ger.	11.5.93	Ortsobmann,Oss (Neth.) 41-45	PILLAGE	NETH.
BOSSOW	27730	M			Major,Army,Aire s/Adour (Fr.) 8.44	PILLAGE	FR.
BOST	159366	M	Ger.		Agent,Gestapo,Region of Angers (Fr.) 42-44	MURDER	FR.
BOTCHAROW, Nickolai	159418	M			Civilian,Mariandorf near Eschweiler (Ger.) 42-44	TORTURE	U.S.
BOTCHER (see BOTKER)	174769						
BOTEL (see BOETEL),George	165731						
BOTGERS, Johann	252013	M	Ger.		Sgt.,197 Div.Alpine,Vercheny la Plaine (Fr.) 7.44	INTERR.	FR.
BOTH, Norbert	159358	M			S.D. Official	MURDER	U.S.
BOTHEN	192580	M	Ger.		Scharfhr.,SS,C.C.Buchenwald (Ger.) 42-45	MURDER	U.S.
BOTHHAROV,Nickolai (see BONDERENKO)	159418						
BOTMANN	221405	M		07	Hptsturmfhr.,SS,C.C.Poland (Pol.)	MURDER	U.S.
BOTNIK (or BOTTNICK or BOTWIK)	255567	M	Ger.	10	Sgt.,Pion.Troops,Heusden (Neth.) 11.44	PILLAGE	NETH.
BOTT	27737	M			Capt.,Army,Chateauroux	MISC.CRIMES	FR.
BOTT, Karl	194790	M	Ger.		Sgt.,SS-Guard,C.C.Lublin (Pol.) 40-44	MURDER	POL.
BOTTCHE (or BOTTKE,Otto)	194944	M			SS-Scharfhr.,S.D.Einsatz-Kdo.,St.Die (Fr.) 44	MURDER	U.K.
BOTTCHER	252024	M			Pvt.,C.C.Ellrich,Nordhausen (Ger.)	MURDER	U.S.
BOTTCHER	159376	M			Lt.Col.,Oberkommando,Wehrmacht,Subsection III,P.W.Affairs	INTERR.	U.S.
BOTTCHER	159394	M	Ger.		Medical Orderly,Arbeitskommando E 1 101 E,Eisleben (Ger.) 8.44	TORTURE	U.K.
BOTTCHER	181257	M	Ger.		1 SS-Pz.Div."Adolf Hitler",1.Ers.Bn.,2 Zug,Parfondruy(Bel.)12.44	MURDER	U.S.
BOTTCHER	193990	M	Ger.		Pvt.,SS,Stavelot (Bel.) 12.44	MURDER	BEL.
BOTTCHER, Friedrich Johann	152489	M	Ger.		Wachfhr.,Punishment Coy,C.C.Oldenburg(Ger.) 44-45	TORTURE	NETH.
BOTTCHER, Hermann	168605	M	Ger.		Pvt.,9 Gr.Ers.Regt.,1 Coy.,Megny d' Anigon (Fr.) 9.44	MURDER	FR.
BOTTCHER, Victor	194741	M	Ger.		SS-Oberfuehrer,Regierungspraesident,Gau Wartheland, 39-42	MURDER	POL.
BOTTE	159367	M	Ger.		Agent,Gestapo,II.Section,Angers(Fr.)	MURDER	FR.
BOTTE, Fritz	11227	M			N.C.O.,Pz.Gren.Regt.111 or 110,Albi (Fr.) 6.44	MURDER	FR.
BOTTGER	62320	M			Record.Officer C.C.Dachau (Ger.)	MURDER	U.S.
BOTTGER	259615	M	Ger.	95 - 05	Member,Gestapo,Area of Angers (Fr.) 42-44	MISC.CRIMES	FR.
BOTTKE (see BOTTCHE,Otto)	252024						
BOTTLE	252034	M	Ger.	06	Capt.,784 Bn.,Clairac,Marmande (Fr.) 44	MISC.CRIMES	FR.
BOTTNER	148951	M	Ger.		Record-clerk, C.C.Dachau (Ger.)	TORTURE	FR.
BOTTNICK (see BOTNIK)	255567						
BOTTSCAER	159377	M			Stabsintendant,Oberkommando,Wehrmacht,Subsection IV P.W.Affairs	INTERR.	U.S.
BOTWIK (see BOTNIK)	255567						
BOTZ	27742	M			Lt.,Feldgendarmerie,Quinssaines near Montlucon (Fr.) 8.44	MURDER	FR.
BOUCART (see BOUCARD)	27744						
BOUCHAL, Antonin	194733	M	Ger.	31.1.10	Agent,Gestapo,Pilsen (Czech.) 40-45	SUSPECT	CZECH.
BOUCHER, Francois (see SCHENK)	173546						

BOU-BRA

NAME	C.R.FILE NUMBER	SEX	NATIO-NALITY	DATE OF BIRTH	RANK OCCUPATION UNIT PLACE AND DATE OF CRIME	REASON WANTED	WANTED BY
"BOUDIN BLANC" (see KASTENING, Wilhelms)	194715						
BOUHLER, Philipp	17513	M	Ger.	11. 9.99	SS-Gruppenfhr.,SS Reichsleiter NSDAP	MURDER	U.N.W.C.C.
BOUILLON	185422	M	Ger.		Capt.,Occ.territ.,Chief of the Department for Sabotage,Athens (Grc.)	TORTURE	GRC.
BOUILLON	260075	M	Ger.		Capt.,157 bavarian Div.of Res.,Massif du Vercors (Fr.) 7.-8.44	SUSPECT	FR.
BOUL (or BUHL)	172878	M	Ger.	00	Pvt.,Army,Samwitz,Graefenhainichen (Ger.) 2.-4.45	MURDER	U.K.
BOULAGNI	124293	M		10	Hptsturmfhr.,Polizeigericht,Waffen SS,Hague (Neth.)	MURDER	U.S.
BOULANGER	252027	M			Member,SS Dr.Presid. of a court,Hengelo (Neth.) 5.45	MURDER	NETH.
BOULER, Phillip	174855	M			Reichsfuehrer,SS,Hartheim Castle and Alkoven (Aust.) 40-44	MURDER	U.S.
BOULKEY, Ferdinand	136165	M	Ger.		Sgt.,Army,	MURDER	FR.
BOULKEY, Ferdinand (see MICKEY)	136176						
BOUMGARTNER (aliases: BAUMGARTner)	252461	M			Sgt.,Army,Hohenlinden (Ger.) 9.44	MURDER	U.S.
BOURNE	162308	M	Ger.		Sgt.,299 Ldsch.Bn.,Kunrow (Pol.) 5.42	MURDER	U.K.
BOURSAVA	221703	M	Ger.		Lt.,Gestapo,Troyes Rennes (Fr.) 44	TORTURE	U.S.
BOUTZ, Limilius	185205	M	Ger.		N.C.O.,Police,Crete (Grc.)	TORTURE	GRC.
BOUWER Krt. (see BAUER)	306675						
BOVENSCHEN, Heinrich	252023	M			Flyer,Camp Ellrich,Nordhausen (Ger.)	MURDER	U.S.
BOVENSIEBEN	187582	M	Ger.		Osturmfhr.,SS,WKR IX	MURDER	U.N.W.C.C.
BOVON, Paul Golker	172876	M	Ger.		Feldgendarm,Feldgendarmerie,St.Geraud-le-Puy (Fr.) 43-44	PILLAGE	FR.
BOX, Emil (or BOZ)	185420	M	Ger.		Cpl.,Feldgendarmerie,Crete (Grc.)	MURDER	GRC.
BOY (see BOG)	185151						
BOYSEN, Erich	252022	M			Oschfhr.,C.C.Dora,Nordhausen,Auschwitz (Ger.,Pol.)	MURDER	U.S.
BOYSEN, Ernst	252021	M			Pvt.,C.C.Auschwitz,Nordhausen (Pol.,Ger.)	MURDER	U.S.
BOZ, Emil (see BOX)	185420						
BRAAG, Egle	253826	M	Ger.		Pvt.,Lombartzyde (Bel.) 9.44	MURDER	BEL.
BRABANGER	192484	M			Generallt.,270 Inf.Div.,(Nor.)	TORTURE	NOR.
BRACHMAYER	185643	M	Ger.	10	SS-Sturmbannfhr.,C.C.Mauthausen (Aust.)	MURDER	FR.
BRACHT	185397	M	Ger.		SS-Osturmfhr.,SS Unterfuehrerschule,Prague (Czech.) 5.45	MURDER	CZECH.
BRACHT	301860	M	Ger.		Ogruppenfhr.,Oberpraesident,SS,C.C.Oswiecim-Birkenau (Pol.) 39-45	MURDER	CZECH.
BRACHT, Friedrich	158358	M	Ger.		District-leader,SS, (Ger.,Pol.) 42	PILLAGE	U.S.
BRACHT, Willi	261998	M	Ger.	10. 3.12	SS-Mann,Dirlewanger Bde.,Waffen SS Gren.Div.36,Warsaw and other (Pol.) 40-44	MURDER	POL.
BRACHTEL (or BRACHTL)	9638	M			C.C.Dachau (Ger.)	MURDER	U.S.
BRACHTEL	196925	M	Ger.		Doctor,SS,C.C.Auschwitz,Dachau (Pol.,Ger.)	BRUTALITY	BEL.
BRACHTEL, Rudolf	185547	M	Ger.	22. 4.09	Dr.,SS-Hptsturmfhr.,C.G.Dachau,(Ger.), Asch(Czech.) 38-43	MURDER	CZECH.
BRACHTL (see BRACHTEL)	9638						
BRACK, Victor (or JENNERWEIN)	134913	M		03	Oberfhr.,SA,C.C.Hartheim (Aust.)	MURDER	U.S.
BRACK, Viktor	188277	M	Ger.		Oberreichsleiter,Inspector,7 SS Geb.Div.Prinz Eugen,Beelitz-Heilstaetten (Ger.)	MISC.CRIMES	U.N.W.C.C., CZECH.,BEL.
BRACKE	159812	M	Ger.	06	SS-Uschfhr.,C.C.Neuengamme (Ger.)	TORTURE	U.K.
BRACKHAUSER	173963	M			Pvt.,SS,Guard,C.C.Muhldorf Ampfing (Ger.) 6.44-4.45	MURDER	U.S.
BRADFISCH	250617	M	Ger.		Osturmbannfhr.,Waffen SS,Police,Lodz (Pol.) 43-44	MURDER	POL.
BRADFISCH, Otto	261026	M	Ger.		Doctor,Reg.Ret,Chief,Leader,Gestapo,Neustadt (Ger.) 40-42	MURDER	FR.
BRADLYETZ	186018	M	Ger.		Officer,SA,Wittenberg (Ger.)	MURDER	U.S.
BRADWOLF	173962	M			Sturmmann,SS,C.C.Mühldorf Ampfing (Ger.) 6.44-4.45	MURDER	U.S.
BRAEDER	194945	M	Ger.	19	Pvt.,890 Ldsch.Bn.,Stalag XVII B,Pottenbrun (Aust.) 44-45	TORTURE	U.K.
BRAEM, Harry	261999	M	Ger.	1. 2.19	SS-Mann,Dirlewanger Bde.,Waffen SS Gren.Div.Nr.36,Warsaw and other (Pol.) 40-44	MURDER	POL.
BRAENIERE	26684	M			Major,Army (Fr.)	MURDER	FR.
BRAEUER	126	M	Ger.		Abwehr General,Crete (Grc.) 5.-7.43	MURDER	U.K.
BRAEUNING	192591	M	Ger.		Oschfhr.,SS,Thueringen (Ger.) 42-45	TORTURE	U.S.
BRAEUNING	195861	M			Rev.Oberwachtmeister,Sipo,Groningen,Westerbork (Neth.) 9.-12.44	MURDER	NETH.
BRAEUNING	255512	M			SS-Hptsturmfhr.,C.C.Buchenwald (Ger.)	MURDER	U.S.
BRAEUNING, Edmund	159807	M	Ger.		Hptsturmfhr.,Waffen SS Totenkopf,C.C.Buchenwald (Ger.) 39	TORTURE	U.S.
BRAEUNING, Eduard	131832	M	Ger.	98	Hptsturmfhr.,Camp leader,Ohrdruf S III Buchenwald (Ger.) 45	MISC.CRIMES	U.S.
BRAGART (alias: BECKER,Dr.)	222613	M	Ger.	97	Dr.,official,Abwehr,Bad Wildungen (Ger.) 45	MISC.CRIMES	U.S.
BRAIDA	301937		Ger.		Gosselies, 8.44	MURDER	BEL.
BRAIN, Maximilian	167670	M			Abteilungsleiter,Generalgovernment of Poland, 39-44	MISC.CRIMES	POL.
BRAKE, Arno	149733	M	Ger.	01	Member,Volkssturm 1 Bn.3 Coy,Gardelegen (Ger.) 4.45	MURDER	U.S.
BRALENSKY	128745	M	Ger.		Sgt.,Ldsch.Bn.565,Silesia,Sudetenland (Ger.) 1.-3.45	MISC.CRIMES	U.K.
BRALINROTH, Joachim (or BRAUNROTH)	178329	M	Ger.		SS-Oschfhr.,SS Leibstandarte Adolf Hitler,Malmedy (Bel.) 12.44	MURDER	U.S.
BRAMBECK (see BARNBECK)	194933						
BRAMHOFF, Martha	159803	F	Ger.		Civilian Dietician in Prison C.C.Bielefeld (Ger.) 9.44	MURDER	U.S.
BRAMME	132016	M	Ger.	05	Sturmbannfhr.,SS	MURDER	U.S.
BRAND	188941	M	Ger.		Chief,Gestapo,Stanislawow (Pol.) 41-10.42	MURDER	POL.
BRAND	196175	M	Ger.		Lt.,Art.Rgt.352 4 Btty.,Morsang sur Orge (Fr.) 8.44	WITNESS	FR.
BRAND	254054	M	Ger.		Pvt.,Unit L 39079 (Fr.) 8.44	MURDER	FR.
BRAND	300191	M	Ger.		Quartiermeister,Fourier,green police at Driebergen-Rijsenburg 43 and 9.44	PILLAGE	NETH.
BRAND (alias: BRANDT)	257222	M	Ger.	07	SS-Capt.,SD,chief of IV Section,Gestapo Beograd and C.C.Banjica(Serb.) 41-44	MURDER	YUGO.
BRAND, Andreas	255978	M	Ger.	6. 9.11	Manufacturer,Utrechtsche machinale stoel-Meubelfabriek,Utrecht (Neth.)	INTERR.	NETH.
BRAND, Hans	172880	M	Ger.	3. 9.10	Civilian,Quarry owner,Sommerhausen (Ger.) 3.45	WITNESS	U.S.
BRAND, Helmuth	300192	M	Ger.		Kapo,C.C.Flossenburg (Ger.) 42-45	MURDER	FR.
BRAND, Marianne	139105	F	Ger.		Guard,SS Germ.Prison Camps Valory (Czech.) 41-45	MURDER	U.S.
BRAND, Max	194946	M	Ger.		Schfhr.,SA,Dorsten (Ger.) 10.44-2.45	TORTURE	NETH.
BRAND, Paul	149720	M	Ger.	15	Osturmfhr.,SS,Lublin (Pol.) 42-45	MURDER	FR.
BRAND, Rudi	168587	M	Ger.		Dr.,Standartenfhr.,SS, (Pol.) 40	INTERR.	U.S.
BRAND, Walter	196589	M	Ger.	23.11.07	Dr.,Private-secr.,Civilian,Prag (Czech.) 39-45	WITNESS	CZECH.
BRANDAL	211165	M	Ger.		Capt.,Coy Com.Ldsch.Coy Steinach,Stalag 18 A,Leizen (Aust.) 8.44	TORTURE	U.K.
BRANDAUER, Joseph	72727	M	Ger.		Schfhr.,Waffen SS,C.C.Struthof (Fr.) 42-44	MISC.CRIMES	FR.
BRANDECKER	193379	M	Ger.		Cpl.,Kriegsgef.Arb.Bn.184,Kalvik (Nor.) 6.-7.44	MURDER	NOR.
BRANDECKER, Nikolaus	134771	M			Pvt.,SS Totenkopf Sturmbann,C.C.Dora Mittelbau,Nordhausen (Ger.)	WITNESS	U.S.

BRA - BRA

NAME	C.R.FILE NUMBER	SEX	NATIO-NALITY	DATE OF BIRTH	RANK OCCUPATION UNIT PLACE AND DATE OF CRIME	REASON WANTED	WANTED BY
BRANDEL	124957	M	Ger.		Capt., Army	TORTURE	U.K.
BRANDEL	139839	F	Ger.	05	Woman-Guard, Waffen-SS, Waldlager VI, C.C., Muhldorf (Ger.) 44-45	MURDER	U.S.
BRANDEL	189162	M		00	Sturmscharfhr., SS, Crim.Secr., Colmar (Fr.) 1.45	TORTURE	U.S.
BRANDEL	305708	F	Ger.		Deputy Cmdt., SS-Woman, Female Camp, C.C., Birkenau-Auschwitz (Pol.) 42-45	MURDER	YUGO.
BRANDEL, Andreas	255261	M	Ger.	2. 4.10	Oschfhr., SS, Opava and Novy Jicin (Czech.) 39-45	MISC.CRIMES	CZECH.
BRANDEL, Kurt	160233	M	Ger.		Gestapo, Bretagne Poitou Anjou (Fr.)	MURDER	FR.
BRANDEL, Therese or Resi (or BRANDL)	139839	F		1. 2.09	SS-Record-clerk, CC Birkenau(Pol.) 40-45	MURDER	POL., YU
BRANDELL	125106	M	Ger.		Capt., Army, 877.Inf.Bn., 3.Coy., Liezen 180 GW (Ger.) 44-45	BRUTALITY	U.K.
BRANDELL, Karl	149719	M	Ger.		Oschfhr., SS, Floha Camp (Ger.) 44	MURDER	FR.
BRANDENBERGER, Erich	259024	M	Ger.	92	General	WITNESS	U.S.
BRANDENBURG	253648	M			Rottfhr., Camp Dora, Nordhausen (Ger.)	MURDER	U.S.
BRANDENBURGER, Paul	192485	M	Ger.	05	Hptwachtmstr., Reichsjustiz-Ministerium, Strafgefangenen-Lager Nord (Nor.)	MISC.CRIMES	NOR.
BRANDES	26677	M			Pvt., Army, II.Panz.Div., Albine and Bergerae (Fr.) 44	MURDER	FR.
BRANDES	124285	M		93	SA, (Neth.)	MURDER	U.S.
BRANDES	192811	M	Ger.		Sturmscharfhr., SS, C.C., Falstad, Trondheim (Nor.) 41-44	WITNESS	NOR.
BRANDES, Fritz	257821	M	Ger.	10	Sturmscharfhr., SS, SD, Trondheim (Nor.)	MURDER	NOR.
BRANDES, Karl	256787	M	Ger.		Lt., Fieldgend., Zajecar (Yugo.) 41-44	MURDER	YUGO.
BRANDHORST	260113	M	Ger.		Lt., 7.Pion.Rgt. of Grenoble, Massif du Vercors (Fr.) 7.44-8.44	SUSPECT	FR.
BRANDI	129136	M	Ger.	03	Lt., Dulag, Oberursel (Ger.)	TORTURE	U.K.
BRANDL	253572	M	Ger.		Cpl., 738.Rgt. 118.Alpen-Jaeg.Div., Bosnia-Herzegovina (Yugo.)7.43-1.44	MISC.CRIMES	YUGO.
BRANDL, Josef	253827	M	Ger.	12. 1.03	Informer, SD, Prague (Czech.) 42-45	MISC.CRIMES	CZECH.
BRANDL, Joseph	167671	M	Ger.		Dr., Leader, Occupied Territories, Krakau, Lwow (Pol.) 39-44	PILLAGE	POL.
BRANDL, Gustav	300954	M	Ger.		Osturmfhr., SS, Official of SD, Oswiecim-Birkenau (Pol.) 39-45	MURDER	CZECH.
BRANDL, Therese or Resi (see BRANDEL)	139839						
BRANDMEYER	260112	M	Ger.		Cpl., Vincennes (Fr.) 8.44	MURDER	FR.
BRANDMEYER	305602	M	Ger.		N.C.O., Cartridge Factory, Chateau de Vincennes, Seine (Fr.) 8.44	MURDER	FR.
BRANDNER, Willi	194625	M	Ger.		Oberfhr., SS, Liberec (Czech.) 9.38	MURDER	CZECH.
BRANDS, Heinrich	26676	M			Lt., Gr.Regt.1212, Pontaumur Aubusson (Fr.)	MURDER	FR.
BRANDS, Heinrich	192486	M	Ger.	22. 8.07	Oberwachtmstr., Reichsjustiz-Ministerium, SS, Finnmark (Nor.) 42-45	MURDER	NOR.
BRANDS, Heinrich	253947	M	Ger.	7. 1.09	Lt., 6.Coy., 2.Bn. 1000.Rgt., S.P.43661 C, St.Donat (Fr.) 6.44	INTERR	FR.
BRANDSTAEDTER, Fritz	185548	M	Ger.	19. 9.07	Hptsturmfhr., SS, Gestapo, Pol.Oberinspektor, Prague (Czech.) 40-45	MURDER	CZECH.
BRANDSTAETTER, Anton (see BRANDTSTAETTER)	159810						
BRANDSTAETTER, Stefania	307058	F	Ger.		Agent, Gestapo, Cracow (Pol.) 42	INTERR	POL.
BRANDT	124	M	Ger.		Gen.Lt., Army, Oberschlesien (Ger.)	MURDER	POL.
BRANDT	1307	M	Ger.		Sturmscharfhr., SD, Aussenkommando	MISC.CRIMES	U.K.
BRANDT	12422	F	Ger.		Sipo, Clermont-Ferrand (Fr.) 11.43-12.43	MISC.CRIMES	FR.
BRANDT	63319	M	Ger.	05	Stabsfw., Army, KL-Stalag II A, 718.Lds.Schtz.Bn., Gross-Schierstedt (Ger.) 12.44-4.45	MISC.CRIMES	U.S.
BRANDT	72694	M	Ger.	90	Stabsfw., Cmdt. Arb.Cmdo.340, Stalag 2 A (Ger.) 1.45-4.45	TORTURE	U.K.
BRANDT	136997	M	Ger.		Capt., 21.Panz.Div., 21.Pz.Recce Bn., Sessenheim (Fr.) 1.45	MURDER	U.S.
BRANDT	159896	M	Ger.		Capt., Airforce, Gardelegen (Ger.) 3.45	TORTURE	U.K.
BRANDT	159853	M	Ger.		Sturmbannfhr., SS Standarte Rgt. Thueringen, Buchenwald (Ger.) 42-45	MISC.CRIMES	U.S.
BRANDT	160231	M	Ger.		Gend., Fieldgend., Folkling (Fr.) 11.44	MURDER	FR.
BRANDT	160237	M	Ger.		Capt., 635.Lds.Schtz.Bn., KL-Stalag IX C, Niederorschel (Ger.) 1.43	TORTURE	U.K.
BRANDT	162323	M	Ger.		Senior W.O., Feldgendarmerie, Manlay (Fr.) 7.44	PILLAGE	FR.
BRANDT	166402	M			Usturmfhr., SD, H.Q., Campomolon (It.) 2.45	MURDER	U.K.
BRANDT	168586	M	Ger.		Usturmfhr., SD,	WITNESS	U.S.
BRANDT	176402	M			Pvt., Army, Royallieu (Fr.)	TORTURE	FR.
BRANDT	189673	M	Ger.		Oberwachtmstr., W.O., Fieldgend., Beaune-Manley (Fr.)	TORTURE	FR.
BRANDT	189787	M	Ger.		Lt.Col., Aufkl.Abt., Heumen Malden (Neth.) 5.40	MISC.CRIMES	NETH.
BRANDT	189989	M			Head, Gestapo, Banjica (Yugo.)	MURDER	YUGO.
BRANDT	191312	M	Ger.		N.C.O., Interpreter, Army, Cuves, St.Laurent (Fr.) 7.44	MURDER	FR.
BRANDT	192594	M	Ger.		Uschfhr., SS, C.C., Buchenwald (Ger.) 42-45	MISC.CRIMES	U.S.
BRANDT	196116	M	Ger.		Guard, C.C., Ravensbruack (Ger.)	TORTURE	FR.
BRANDT	196172	M	Ger.		Medicin-Gen., Strassburg (Fr.) 40-44	TORTURE	FR.
BRANDT	253811	M	Ger.		Dr., Standartenfhr., SS (Ger.)	INTERR	U.S.
BRANDT	253812	M	Ger.		Usturmfhr., SS, Meldekorps 4, Borgo (It.) 12.44	INTERR	U.K.
BRANDT	256791	M	Ger.		Sgt., Kriegsmarine, Beaucroissant (Fr.) 7.44	MURDER	FR.
BRANDT (or BRAND)	257222	M	Ger.	07	Hptsturmfhr., SS, Gestapo-Chief of IV Section-Gestapo-Beograd and Banjica C.C. (Serbia) 41-44	MURDER	YUGO.
BRANDT	261006	M			Oscharfhr., SS, C.C., Vaihingen (Ger.) 8.44-4.45	MURDER	U.S.
BRANDT	301618	M	Ger.		Cpl., St.Andrèle Gaz. and St.Marcel bel Accueil (Fr.) 7.44	MURDER	FR.
BRANDT	306921	M	Ger.		Senior W.O., Gend., Beaune, Manlay (Fr.) 7.44	BRUTALITY	FR.
BRANDT, Alfred	124786	M			Oberfhr., SC, Lodz (Pol.) 2.40-3.40	MURDER	U.S.
BRANDT, Ambrosius	254311	M			Pvt., Camp Ellrich, Nordhausen)Ger.)	MURDER	U.S.
BRANDT, Arthur	259080	M			Gen.Lt.	WITNESS	U.S.
BRANDT, Bruno	187531	M	Ger.		Riestedt (Ger.) 7.44	TORTURE	U.S.
BRANDT, Edu Steward	194392	M	Ger.	22	Member, SS	WITNESS	U.S.
BRANDT, Gustav	262002	M	Ger.	16. 6.20	SS-Mann, Waffen-SS, Gren.Div.36, Dirlewanger-Bde., Warsaw and other (Pol.) 40-44	MURDER	POL.
BRANDT, Hans	187532	M	Ger.	20. 2.07	Employee, SD and Gestapo, Brno (Czech.) 39-45	MURDER	CZECH.
BRANDT, Hermann	124785	M			Miscellaneous, Lodz (Pol.) 2.-3.40	MURDER	U.S.
BRANDT, Hermann	129824	M			Sgt., Bau-Pion.Ers.and Ausb.Bn.4 (Pol.,Russ.,Yugo.) 40-42	MURDER	U.S.
BRANDT, Hermann	159853	M	Ger.	11	Sturmbannfhr., Waffen-SS, Standarte "Thueringen", C.C., Buchenwald (Ger.) 39	TORTURE	U.S.
BRANDT, Hermann	163248	M	Ger.		9.Coy., 36.Pz.Rgt.SS, Revin (Fr.) 6.44	MURDER	FR.
BRANDT, Karl	121103	M			Sturmbannfhr., Waffen-SS, Bielitz (Pol.)	WITNESS	U.S.
BRANDT, Karl	188276	M	Ger.		Obergruppenfhr., SS, C.C. (Ger.)	MISC.CRIMES	CZECH
BRANDT, Mohr	305829	M	Ger.		Pvt., 377.Inf.Rgt. under Capt.Lohmann, F.P.No.34430, Vinkt-Meigem (Bel.) 5.40-6.40	MURDER	BEL.

BRA-BRA

NAME	C.R.FILE NUMBER	SEX	NATIO-NALITY	DATE OF BIRTH	RANK OCCUPATION UNIT PLACE AND DATE OF CRIME	REASON WANTED	WANTED BY
BRANDT, Olf	128604	M		93	Dental-specialist, Mauthausen (Aust.) 41	MURDER	U.S.
BRANDT, Paul	253808	M	Ger.		Sgt., 10 Coy., 377 Jaeger-Regt., Vinkt (Bel.)	MISC.CRIMES	BEL.
BRANDT, Reinhard	306345	M	Ger.	29.10.92	SS-W.O., C.C. Buchenwald (Ger.) 5.38+10.43	MURDER	BEL.
BRANDT, Rudy	159809	M	Ger.		Merchant, Civilian, Hordel (Ger.)	WITNESS	U.S.
BRANDT, Siegfried	257826	M	Ger.		Krft.Mt., German Navy, Hopseidet (Nor.) 5.45	MURDER	NOR.
BRANDT, Ursula ("La Panthere")	177743	F	Ger.		Member, Gestapo, Vichy (Fr.)	MURDER	U.N.W.C.C.
BRANDT, Wilhelm	134770	M			Scharfhr., 4 SS-Totenk.Stuba.,C.C.Dora-Mittelbau,Nordhausen(Ger.)43-45	WITNESS	U.S.
BRANDT DE ESTERWEGEN, Paul	178204	M	Ger.		Uscharfhr., SS, C.C. Sachsenhausen, Bethune, Calais, St.Paul (Fr.) 43	TORTURE	FR.
BRANDSTAETTER, Anton or BRANDSTAETTER	159810	M	Ger.-Aust.	10. 1.01	SS-Sturmmann, SS-Totenkopf, Dest (Ger.) 39	WITNESS	U.S.
BRANDY	121104		Ger.		Lt., Airforce, Dulag Luft, Klosterwald (Ger.)	BRUTALITY	U.K.
BRANEK or KRANEK	137058	M	Ger.		Capt., 125 Pz.Gren.Regt., 1 Bn., Sessheim (Fr.) 1.45	MURDER	FR.
BRANER, Leonard Leo	173961	M	Ger.	19	Member, Gestapo, Giessen (Ger.) 10.44	MURDER	U.S.
BRANGS	26670	M			Ingenieur, civilian, Rochefort (Fr.) 6.-9.43	MURDER	FR.
BRANNER see BRUNNER	140						
BRANNING	255511	M			Oscharfhr., C.C. Buchenwald (Ger.)	MURDER	U.S.
BRANS	127331				Kreis Moers (Ger.)	TORTURE	U.S.
BRANS	261211	M	Ger.		Member of staff at C.C. Ravensbrueck (Ger.)	SUSPECT	BEL.
BRANSE, Rudolf	260929	M	Ger.	16. 4.21	Guard, SS-Totenkopf, C.C. Auschwitz (Pol.), C.C. Buchenwald (Ger.)	BRUTALITY	POL.
BRANTNER, Steffi nee MEIXNER	254050	F	Ger.	27. 5.12	Barber, civilian, 43-44 Clerk, civilian, Hnevotin (Czech.) 39-45	MURDER	CZECH.
BRANTZ, Karl	72728	M	Ger.		Uscharfhr., SS-Hauptamt, C.C. Struthof-Natzweiler (Fr.) 42-44	MURDER	FR.
BRASCH, Henry	178206	M	Ger.	00	Cpl., Army, C.C., Vannes, Morbihan (Fr.) 42-44	TORTURE	FR.
BRASCHNIKOW, Aleks	254312	M			Camp Harzungen, Nordhausen (Ger.)	MURDER	U.S.
BRASCHOTZ	131140	M	Ger.		Civilian in a camp	MURDER	BEL.
BRASE, Heinrich	301092	M	Ger.		Guard, labour-camp Lahde-Weser (Ger.) 43-45	MURDER	BEL.
BRASSE	26667	M			Lt., Army, Noailles (Fr.) 4.44	MURDER	FR.
BRASTOOCK, Rudolf	250078	M	Ger.		W.O.-chief, St.Étienne du Ores (Fr.) 8.44	INTERR	FR.
BRASZIO, Karl	131270	M	Ger.		Guard, Blockaeltester, C.C. Auschwitz-Jawischowitz (Pol.)	MURDER	U.S.
BRATFISCH, Karl	26666	M			SS-Sturmmann, C.C. Struthof (Fr.)	MURDER	FR.
BRATHAHN, Emil	159830	M			SS, C.C. Flossenburg (Ger.)	TORTURE	U.S.
BRATL	254049	M			Pvt., Camp Ellrich, Nordhausen (Ger.)	MURDER	U.S.
BRATO, Christian	62317	M	Ger.		Pvt., SS, Pz.Jg.Lehrg.Einh.56, Waterloo (Bel.) 9.44	MURDER	BEL.
BRAU	167652	M	Ger.	11	Adjutant-chief, Airforce, Bron near Lyon (Fr.) 8.44	MURDER	FR.
BRAUCITSCH	186019	M	Ger.		SS-Rottenfhr., Leibst.Adolf Hitler, Stavelot (Bel.)	MURDER	BEL.
BRAUCK see BRUHN	258902	M					
BRAUENREUTER	62316	M	Ger.	00	Cpl., Army, Stalag VIII B, Arbeitskdo.E 30,Oppeln,(Ger.),Rouen(Fr.)6.41	TORTURE	U.K.
BRAUER	26664	M			Capt., Army, Tarn et Garonne (Fr.) 5.44	WITNESS	FR.
BRAUER	26665	M			Lt., Army, Inf.Ers.Bn.56, Kiew (Rus.)	MURDER	FR.
BRAUER	62216	M	Ger.		Dr.,crim.-ass.,Gestapo,penitentiary,Reich-official, (Nor.) 4.40	MISC.CRIMES	U.N.W.C.C.
BRAUER	128605				Dr., SS, Steyr.Lanzing	TORTURE	U.S.
BRAUER	149738	M			Head-doctor, SS, Mauthausen (Aust.) 44-45	TORTURE	U.S.
BRAUER	168621	M			Crim.asst., Gestapo, (Nor.)	TORTURE	NOR.
BRAUER	190678	M	Ger.		Capt., Ers.Artl.Btty.717, St.Andries, Varsenare, Les Bruges (Bel.)9.44	MURDER	BEL.
BRAUER se BAUMEISTER	221413						
BRAUER, Jacob	261996	M	Ger.	16. 8.12	SS-Mann, Dirlewanger-Bde.,Waffen-SS,Gren.Div.,Warsaw and other (Pol.) 40-44	MURDER	POL.
BRAUER, W.	188541	M	Ger.		SS-Crim.secretary, member, Gestapo, Danzig (Free State)	MURDER	POL.
BRAUERS, Hans	260111	M	Ger.		Sgt., I schw.Btty., D.C.A.Nr.672, Grand Quevilly (Fr.) 8.44	PILLAGE	FR.
BRAUGITSCH	301629	M	Ger.		SS-Pvt., 10 Coy., Renardmont, Stavelot (Bel.) 12.44	MURDER	BEL.
BRAUKMILLER, Fritz	162324	M	Ger.		SS-Pvt., SS, Hennebont (Fr.) 44	MURDER	FR.
BRAUM	26661	M			Cpl., Gestapo, Cherbourg, St. Lo (Fr.)	MURDER	FR.
BRAUM	258900	M	Ger.		Inspector,Fliegerhorstkmdtr. AK-XIII, Orenade s-Adour et Cere (Fr.) 6.-8.44	MURDER	FR.
BRAUMAN	162317	M	Ger.	00	Farmer, civilian, Waldau, Pruest (Ger.) 4.44	MURDER	U.K.
BRAUMANN	1684		Ger.		SD, Amiens (Fr.)	TORTURE	U.K.
BRAUMANN	126529	M			Civilian in a camp, Asst. Werkschutzleiter, Hagen (Ger.) 40-45	MURDER	U.S.
BRAUMANN	254316	M	Ger.		Oscharfhr., C.C. Buchenwald (Ger.)	INTERR.	U.S.
BRAUMANN, Willi	134769	M		25. 1.97	SS-Pvt., 4 SS-Totenkkopf-Stuba., C.C.Dora-Mittelbau, Nordhausen (Ger.) 43-45	WITNESS	U.S.
BRAUMER	163250	M	Ger.		Sgt., Army, Braunschweig (Ger.) 4.45	MURDER	FR.
BRAUMUELLER	167653	M	Ger.		Civilian, Einsatzstab Rosenberg, administration-staff, (Fr.) 44	PILLAGE	FR.
BRAUN	11229	M	Ger.		Agent, Gestapo, Nantes (Fr.) 4.44	MURDER	FR.
BRAUN	26657	M			Sgt., Army	TORTURE	FR.
BRAUN	26658				Lt., Army, Choisy le Roi (Fr.) 8.44	MURDER	FR.
BRAUN	31946	M			Sgt., Feldgendarmerie, Gestapo, Josselin (Fr.) 7.-8.44	MURDER	FR.
BRAUN	52184	M	Ger.		SS-Osturmfhr., SS, C.C. Neuengamme (Ger.) 41-42	TORTURE	BEL.
BRAUN	121105	M			Presumable-civilian, Gernsbach (Ger.) 8.44	MURDER	U.S.
BRAUN	125169	M	Ger.	05	Capt., Gestapo, H.Q., Perpignan (Fr.) 5.44	TORTURE	U.S.
BRAUN	129823	M	Ger.		Capt., Army, Landesschtz.Bn.827, 2 Coy., Stalag 13 B, Grasseth (Czech.)	MURDER	U.S.
BRAUN	139842	M	Ger.		Col., Stalag Luft III, Sagan (Ger.) 1.45	TORTURE	U.S.
BRAUN	147713				Uscharfhr., SS, Asst.camp-cmdr., Ilfeld-Gardelegen (Ger.) 4.45	MURDER	U.S.
BRAUN	159839	M	Ger.		Capt.,Army,Arbeitskdo.,2 Coy.,827 Bn., Falkenau (Czech.)	TORTURE	U.K.,U.S.
BRAUN	160229	M	Ger.		Sgt., Gestapo, Abt.IV, Trondes,Boucq,Menil,La Tour (Fr.) 8.44	MURDER	FR.
BRAUN	172697	M		15	Pvt., Army, Thorn (Pol.) 42-45	WITNESS	U.K.
BRAUN	173324	M	Ger.		Capt., Gestapo, Baccarat, Mourthe and Moselle (Fr.) 8.-10.44	MURDER	FR.
BRAUN	173325		Ger.		Health office, Amt fuer Volksgesundheit, Strassbourg (Fr.) 44	TORTURE	FR.
BRAUN	173346	M	Ger.		Sgt., 2 Bn., 1010 motor. Regt., 8 Coy., Chillaurs aux Bois (Fr.)5.44	TORTURE	U.K.
BRAUN	173956	M			Sgt., Army, C.C. Muehldorf, Ampfing (Ger.) 6.44-4.45	WITNESS	U.S.
BRAUN	174553				SS-Uscharfhr., C.C. Flossenburg, Sachsenhausen (Ger.)	WITNESS	U.K.
BRAUN	189465	M			SS-Sturmbannfhr., SS-Geb.Div.Nord, 20 Army, Finmark (Nor.)10.-11.44	MURDER	NOR.
BRAUN	195461	M	Ger.		Dr., SS-Sturmbannfhr., SD,Waffen-SS,Mizocs (Pol.) 10.42	MURDER	POL.
BRAUN	195862	M	Ger.		Cpl., Dep. Colombier (Fr.) 10.44	MURDER	FR.
BRAUN	255977	M	Ger.		Lt.Col., 21 Regt., 7 parachute-Div., Alsace (Fr.) 2.45	MURDER	U.S.
BRAUN	256828	M	Ger.		Scharfhr., SS, Camp Ellrich, Nordhausen (Ger.)	MURDER	U.S.
BRAUN	258123	M	Ger.		SS-Hptsturmfhr., Waffen-SS, C.C. Natzweiler (Fr.) 42	MURDER	BEL.

BRA-BRE

NAME	C.R.FILE NUMBER	SEX	NATIO-NALITY	DATE OF BIRTH	RANK OCCUPATION UNIT PLACE AND DATE OF CRIME	REASON WANTED	WANTED BY
BRAUN	300193	M	Ger.	95	Local commander, Org. Todt, Rhenen, betw. 11.44 and 4.45	PILLAGE	NETH.
BRAUN	300194	M	Ger.		Oberwachtmeister, Strafgefangenenlager Nord, Northern (Nor.) 49-45	MISC.CRIMES	CZECH.
BRAUN	300955	M	Ger.		Hauptwachtmeister, C.C. Stettin-Poelitz (Ger.) 44	MISC.CRIMES	CZECH.
BRAUN	307060	M	Ger.		Member of staff of the prison, Diez-Lahn (Ger.) 40-45	MURDER	BEL.
BRAUN, Adolphe	195860	M	Ger.		Cmdt., Chief of the commandantur d·Etampes (Fr.) 8.44	WITNESS	FR.
BRAUN, Alfred	257784	M	Ger.	24. 3.04	Employee, Camp B I-H Heckbau I Nordhausen (Ger.)	MURDER	U.S.
BRAUN, Elsa	250075	F	Ger.		Funktionaerin (G.Z.A.) Member S.D., Toulouse (Fr.) 11.42-8.44	MISC.CRIMES	FR.
BRAUN, Erna	187526	F	Ger.		Employee, Gestapo and S.D., Brno (Czech.) 39-45	WITNESS	CZECH.
BRAUN, Ernst	300956	M	Ger.		SS Oscharfhr., official of S.D., Leitabschnitt Prague, Oswiecim-Birkenau (Pol.) 39-45	MURDER	CZECH.
BRAUN, Franz	186020	M	Ger.		Civ. Policeman, Steimker Berg Wolfsburg (Ger.) 6.44	WITNESS	U.S.
BRAUN, Franz	194916	M	Ger.	15	Criminal-assist., Gestapo Koeln, Kolin (Czech.) 39-45	MURDER	CZECH.
BRAUN, Frederick	172961	M	Ger.	20	SS Usturmfhr., Waffen SS, 1.SS Pz.Div.Adolf Hitler, Weissenbach (Aust.) 4.45	MURDER	U.S.
BRAUN, Fritz	120563	M	Ger.	03	Capt., Arbeitskommando, Volkssturm, C.C. Zochau (Ger.)	MISC.CRIMES	U.S.
BRAUN, Hans	186021	M	Ger.	7. 6.17	San.Sgt., Flakabteilung Bn.84, Malmedy (Bel.) 12.44	WITNESS	U.S.
BRAUN, Helmuth	185366	M	Ger.	16. 2.17	Criminal-employee, SS, S.D., Gestapo, Benesov (Czech.) 39-45	MURDER	CZECH.
BRAUN, Johann see BRAUNN	159829						
BRAUN, Josef	26714	M			Sturmmann, SS, C.C. Struthof (Fr.)	MURDER	FR.
BRAUN, Josef	189429	M	Ger.		Wachtmeister, Schupo, C.C. Falstad, Trondheim (Nor.) 42	MURDER	NOR.
BRAUN, Josef	194866	M	Ger.	20. 4.24	SS Sturmmann, Totenkopf-Stuba, C.C. Auschwitz (Pol.) 44	MISC.CRIMES	UNWCC
BRAUN, Karl	148534	M	Ger.	92	SS Hptsturmfhr., C.C. Buchenwald (Ger.)	TORTURE	U.S.
BRAUN, Konrad	254309	M			Pvt. Camp Ellrich Nordhausen (Ger.)	MURDER	U.S.
BRAUN, Kurt	173323	M	Ger.		SS Osturmbannfhr., Breslau (Ger.)	MURDER	U.K. FR.B
BRAUN, Lothar	193469	M	Ger.	08	Oberwachtmeister, Reichsjustizministerium, Finnmark (Nor.) 6.42, 12.44	MISC.CRIMES	NOR. YUGO
BRAUN, Marianne	172973	F	Ger.		Civ., Nuernberg or Fuerth-Bayern (Ger.) 2.45	TORTURE	U.S.
BRAUN, Maximilien	191187	M	Ger.		Manager, General-Government, Hauptabt. Gesetzgebung (Pol.) 9.39-44	PILLAGE	POL.
BRAUN, Paul	256792	M	Ger.	27. 1.12	Employee, Gestapo, State service, Brno (Czech.) 42-45	MURDER	CZECH.
BRAUN, Rene	187528	M	Ger.		Civ., Neckarelz (Ger.)	TORTURE	U.S. FR.
BRAUN, Stefan	254308	M			Sgt., Camp Ellrich Nordhausen (Ger.)	MURDER	U.S.
BRAUN, Wilhelm	187525	M	Ger.		Employee, S.D. and Gestapo, Brno (Czech.) 39-45	MURDER	CZECH.
BRAUN, Willy	159813	M	Ger.		Hptsturmfhr., SS, C.C. Muehldorfer Hart (Ger.)	MURDER	FR. YUGO.
BRAUNE	121106	F	Ger.		Civ., Bad Koesen (Ger.) 11.44	WITNESS	U.S.
BRAUNE	132016	M	Ger.	05	Dr., Sturmbannfhr., SS, C.C. Thekin Tiraspol (Scv.Un.,Ger.Rum.Crim.)	MURDER	U.S.
BRAUNE	135128	M	Ger.	89	Army, Col. C.C. Ger.	TORTURE	U.S.
BRAUNE	306946	M	Ger.		SS Scharfhr., C.C. Buchenwald (Ger.) betw. 5.38 and 10.43	MURDER	BEL.
BRAUNE, Werner Bruno Max	258786	M	Ger.	2. 7.01	Kriminalrat, Kripo (German Criminal Police) Lidice Lezaky (Czech.)6.42	MURDER	CZECH.
BRAUNEGG	167669	M	Ger.		Dr., Leader, administration of occupied territories, Krakau (Pol.) 39-44	MISC.CRIMES	POL.
BRAUNER	1226	M	Ger.		Kreisleiter NSDAP, Public official, Eisenstadt, (Aust.)	MISC.CRIMES	U.S.
BRAUNER	150754	M	Ger.		Kreisleiter NSDAP, Oedenburg (Hung.) 10-11.44	MURDER	U.S.
BRAUNER	159842	M			SS Uscharfhr., Arb.Lg.101 C.C. Magdeburg (Ger.) 10.44-4.45	TORTURE	U.S.
BRAUNER, Ferdinand	253676	M	Ger.		SS-Mann, SS-Hospital-Stab, Auschwitz-Birkenau (Pol.) 1.43	MURDER	YUGO.
BRAUNER, Josef	173341	M	Ger.		Major-General, Army, Commander of Group "West", Yugo. 43	MURDER	YUGO.
BRAUNER, Josef Oskar	259077	M	Ger.		General	INTERR.	U.S.
BRAUNIG	191269	M			SS Hptsturmfhr., SS Adjutant, C.C. Ravensbrueck (Ger.) 41-45	MURDER	U.S.
BRAUNING	131832	M			Sgt. C.C. Buchenwald (Ger.)	TORTURE	U.S.
BRAUNING	149708	M			Hptscharfhr., Rottleberode, Gardelegen 4.45	MURDER	U.S.
BRAUNING	254310	M			Pvt., Camp Wolffleben Nordhausen (Ger.)	MURDER	U.S.
BRAUNING, Eduard or BRAEUNING	131832	M	Ger.	about 97	Hptsturmfhr., SS, C.C. Ohrdruf, Buchenwald (Ger.) 44-45	TORTURE	U.S.
BRAUNING, Ewald	187524	M	Ger.		Prison-guard, S.D., C.C. Brno (Czech.) 39-45	MURDER	CZECH.
BRAUNN	125665	M	Ger.		Capt., Army, Burg Lastic (Fr.) 7.44	MURDER	FR
BRAUNN, Adolphe	306236	M	Ger.		Cmdt., Etampes (Fr.) 8.44	MURDER	FR.
BRAUNN, Johann or BRAUN	159829	M	Ger.		Work boss in saw mill, Civ., Holzkirchen (Ger.)	TORTURE	U.S.
BRAUNROTH see BRALINROTH	178929						
BRAUNS	131137	M	Ger.		Lagerfuehrer, C.C. Ilsenburg (Ger.) 44	TORTURE	BEL.
BRAUNSDORFF	253946	M	Ger.		Secretary, 13. SS Pol.Rgt., Ferlach (Aust.) 44-45	MURDER	YUGO.
BRAUNSTEIN	127	F	Ger.		SS warden, C.C. Maidanek (Pol.) 40-4.44	MURDER	POL.
BRAUNTMAYER, Fritz	192276	M	Ger.		Local official, Verwaltungsgericht, Brussels (Bel.)	MURDER	BEL.
BRAUNY	192590	M	Ger.		Scharfhr., SS, C.C. Buchenwald (Ger.) 42-45	TORTURE	U.S.
BRAUSCHKE, Herbert	253952	M			Uscharfhr., Malmedy (Bel.) 12.44	MURDER	U.S.
BRAUSE, Gustav	185148	M	Ger.		Uscharfhr., SS, C.C. Sachsenhausen (Ger.)	TORTURE	FR.
BRAUSS, Gustave	178207	M			Uscharfhr., SS, C.C., Calais, St.Pol, Berlement, Boulogne s.M., St.Omer, Berck, Plage, Arras, Bethune (Fr.) 43	TORTURE	FR.
BRAUTIGAM	72744	M	Ger.		Pvt., Fallschirmjaeger-Bn., Roermond (Neth.) 11.44-1.45	TORTURE	U.S.
BRAUTIGAM, Otto	254053	M	Ger.	4. 7.04	Hairdresser, Kommandantur Cambrai, Niergnies and Cambrai (Fr.) 8.44	TORTURE	FR.
BRAUTSCH	253645	M	Ger.	about 06	Capt., 392. Blue Div., Lika (Yugo.) 44-45	INTER.	YUGO.
BRAXATOR	135129	M	Ger.	88	Col., Army, C.C. Ger. 1.45	TORTURE	U.S.
BRECHENMACHER	259817	M			Cpl., 2.Coy. 438.Land.Schuetz.Bn. Kommando F 204 Stalag 344, Schmagersdorf (Ger.) 9.44	MURDER	FR.
BRECHLO	129822	M			Member NSDAP, Moers (Ger.)	TORTURE	U.S.
BRECHT	148532	M	Ger.		Hptsturmfhr., SS, Auschwitz (Pol.) 43-44	TORTURE	U.S.
BRECHT, Alois	253953	M			Rottfhr., 10.Coy. 2.Panz.Gren.Rgt., Malmedy (Bel.) 12.44	MURDER	U.S.
BRECKEL	26690	M	Ger.		Army, Prigourieux (Fr.)	MURDER	FR.
BRECKMACKER	196287	M			Cpl., Airkorps, Bernay (Fr.) 1.43	MISC.CRIMES	FR.
BRECKNER	253810	M			Capt., Gestapo Angers, Savannes (Fr.) 8.44	MURDER	FR.
BREDDIN, Bruno	161642	M	Ger.		Army, H.K.A.Rgt. 97737 Btty., Ramsoy (Nor.)	WITNESS	NOR.
BREDE, Albert	193987	M			SA-Member, C.C. Gudensberg (Ger.) 41-45	TORTURE	POL.
BREDE, Georg	193988	M			Member, SA, C.C. Gudensberg (Ger.) 41-45	TORTURE	POL.
BREDEL, Adolf	253942	M			Chief of Block 7, C.C. Neuengamme (Ger.) 44	TORTURE	FR.
BREDEMAIER, Ferdinand	120569	M			Abwehr German Settler, Oleksyzn (Pol.)	PILLAGE	POL.
BREDEMEYER, Hermann	196273	M			Sgt., 755.Rgt., 334.Inf.Rgt., Ger.	MISC.CRIMES	U.S.
BREDENDIJK	259807	M	Ger.		N.C.O., 377.Jaeg.Rgt., Vinkt (Bel.)	INTERR.	BEL.

BRE-BRE

NAME	C.R.FILE NUMBER	SEX	NATIO-NALITY	DATE OF BIRTH	RANK	OCCUPATION	UNIT	PLACE AND DATE OF CRIME	REASON WANTED	WANTED BY
BREDER, Reinhard	178328	M		13	Regierungsrat. Stubannfhr., Gestapo, SS, Frankfurt (Ger.) 43-45				TORTURE	U.K.
BREDLOW	253948	M	Ger.		13. SS.Pol. Regt., Ferlach (Austria) 44-45				MURDER	YUGO.
BREDTSCHNEIDER (see BRETSCHNEIDER)	133747									
BREEM	190075	M	Ger.		Wachtmeister, Pol. C.C.Falstad (Nor.) 42				TORTURE	NOR.
BREER	173306	M	Ger.		Feldgend., Chateaudun-Logron (Fr.) 8.44				TORTURE	FR.
BREFORD-TECHNER, August	301391	M	Ger.		Farmer, Bohmte (Ger.) 2.45				MURDER	U.K.
BREGANT, Nicholas	260980	M			SS-Mann, SS, C.C. Vaihingen a.d.Enz (Ger.)8.44-4.45				MURDER	U.S.
BREHM	128	M	Ger.		Wachtmeister, Pol., C.C.Falstad (Nor.) 42				TORTURE	NOR.
BREHM	159845	M	Ger.		(Lt.Col.) Osturmbannfhr., SS, Kattowitz (Pol.) 42				LOOTING	U.S.
BREHM, Bernhardt	192813	M	Ger.		Schupo, Stalag Falstad, Drontheim (Nor.) 41-45				MURDER	NOR.
BREHM, Eduard	31997	M	Ger.		Dr.,Oberlandger.-Rat,Public Official, Litomerice (Czech.) 40				MURDER	CZECH.
BREHM, Fritz	254317	M			Cpl., Camp Harzungen, Nordhausen (Ger.)				MURDER	U.S.
BREHM, Hans	187630	M	Ger.	14. 7.00	Member, NSDAP, Dachsbach (Ger.) 43-45				TORTURE	POL.
BREHM, Hans	256789	M			SS, C.C. Muhldorf-Dachau (Ger.)				MURDER	U.S.
BREHM, Otto	125168	M	Ger.	90	Ortsgruppenleiter, NSDAP, Erbach (Ger.) 9.44				MURDER	U.S.
BREICHFEL	253943	M			Lt., 2.Coy., 99.Bn. 157.Inf.Div.d.Res., Massif du Vercors (Fr.)7.-8.44				MISC.CRIMES	FR.
BREIER	72674	M			Gutsverwalter and Guard, Waffen-SS, C.C. Hinzert (Ger.),Lublin (Pol.) 42-44				TORTURE	U.S.
BREIER	151710	M			Col., Army, P.W. Affairs.				MISC.CRIMES	U.S.
BREIER, Josef	306347	M	Ger.	27.11.19	SS Cpl., C.C. Buchenwald (Ger.) betw. 5.38 and 10.43				MURDER	BEL.
BREIG	196106	M	Ger.		Sgt., SS Div."Das Reich", SS-Regt."Deutschland" 9.Coy."iremont (Fr.)6.44				MURDER	FR.
BREIHOLZ, Heinz	179813	M		22	Usturmfhr., 12.SS Panz.Div. "Hitler Jugend" H.Q.25.SS PGR., Abbaye-Ardenne near Caen (Fr.) 6.-7.44				TORTURE	CAN.
BREILER	187521	M		18	Cpl., Army, 379.Landesschuetzen-Bn., Schwaz (Aust.) 10.43				MURDER	U.K.
BREIMEIER	185990	M			SS-Stubannfhr., Cmdt., SS Div. "Prinz Eugen", Sinj Drasnica (Yugo.)43-44				MURDER	YUGO.
BREIN, Arthur	256333	M			SJ-Rottenfhr., SS, C.C. Auschwitz-Birkenau (Pol.) 10.42				MURDER	YUGO.
BREINCKER	26688	M			Usturmfhr., SS Div. "Das Reich", Montastrug and Viennases Barthes (Fr.) 7.44				MURDER	FR.
BREINDEL (see BRENDEL)	253818									
BREINTWIESEN, Arthur	300559	M	Ger.		Rottenfhr., SS, C.C.Auschwitz-Birkenau (Pol.) 10.42				MISC.CRIMES	YUGO.
BREITEGGER	160236	M	Ger.		Official, NSDAP, Gross-Leoben (Austria)				TORTURE	U.K.
BREITENBACH	26706	M			Major, Army. (Russia)				MURDER	U.S.
BREITENBACH, Ewald	306348	M	Ger.		SS-Mann, C.C.Buchenwald (Ger.) betw.5.38 and 10.43				MURDER	BEL.
BREITENBACH, Friedrich	187899	M	Ger.		Manager of Harbour, Stalag Regensburg (Ger.) 41-45				MURDER	U.S.
BREITENBERGER	191899	M	Ger.	14	Usturmfhr., SS Leibstandarte "Adolf Hitler" Div., Amfraville Les Champs (Fr.) 5.40				MURDER	FR.
BREITER, Willi	261995	M	Ger.	15. 8.11	SS-Mann, Waffen-SS, Gren.Div.36 - "Dirlewanger-Bde.",Warsaw and other towns (Pol.) 40-44				MURDER	POL.
BREITHAUPT	195859	M	Ger.		Corvette Capt., Naval Sect. Schiffsstamm-Abt.,Montceau les Mines (Fr.)				MISC.CRIMES	FR.
BREITHAUPT, Franz	62218	M		80	Ob.Gruppenfhr., Waffen-SS, Legal Dept.				TORTURE	UNWCC
BREITHOFER, Emil	149709	M			District Staff Leader, Regional Official, Gardelegen (Ger.) 4.45				MURDER	U.S.
BREITREUCH	124294	M			Oschafhr., 2.Panzer Gren.Regt., 1.Panz.Div.12.Coy., Malmedy (Bel.)12.44				MURDER	U.S.
BREITSCHAFFER	186677	M	Ger.		Director of Factory, Ruestung-Kriegsproduktion, Clichy (Fr.) 40-44				MISC.CRIMES	FR.
BREITSCHER	189572	M	Ger.		S.D., Region Lyonnaise (Fr.)				MISC.CRIMES	FR.
BREITUNG, Kurt	131144	M	Ger.	24. 7.11	N.C.O., 11.Inf.Regt. 983, Chlin, Quaregnon-Jemappes (Bel.) 9.44				MURDER	BEL.
BREKAU, Walter	254320	M			Pvt., Camp Ellrich, Nordhausen (Ger.)				MURDER	U.S.
BREKER, Arno	125019	M	Ger.		Civilian. Sculpteur. (Fr.) 40-44				LOOTING	FR.
BRELL, Arthur	256333	M			SS-Mann, 9.SS Totenkopf-Sturmbann, Auschwitz-Birkenau (Pol.) 10.42				MURDER	YUGO.
BRELLMANN, Karl	254055	M	Ger.							
BREMA, Karl	185820	M	Ger.	00	Buergermeister, Public Official. Oberhub near Regensburg (Ger.) 43-45				TORTURE	U.S.
BREMA, Paul	162327	M	Ger.	97	Sgt., 3.Coy.Landesschuetzen-Bn.877, Stalag 18 A, C.C. Liezen(Aust.)44-45				TORTURE	U.K.
BREMEKAMP	305830	M	Ger.		Pvt., 1.Aufkl.Abt. 3.Coy.XV.Div. Afrika Corps, St.Leger (Arlon) 9.44				MISC.CRIMES	BEL.
BREMEN, Hubert	121107	M	Ger.		Gestapo, Westerode (Ger.)				WITNESS	U.S.
BREMEN, Hibert	192814	M	Ger.		SS-Scharfhr., Stalag C.C.Falstad, Drontheim (Nor.) 41-45				WITNESS	NOR.
BREMER	12327	M	Ger.		Lt., Cmdt., SS, 12.Panz.Div."Hitler Jugend", Fains (Fr.) 6.44				MURDER	U.K., U.S.,FR.
BREMER	26703	M			Cmdt., SS, Cherenvilliers (Fr.) 8.44				MURDER	FR.
BREMER	253822	M	Ger.		Cmdt., Staff Paymaster, Air Force, Unit 34505, Berre-L, Atang (Fr.)8.44				MURDER	FR.
BREMER, Gerhardt	62315	M	Ger.		Major, Army, 12.SS Panz.Div."Hitler Jugend".				MISC.CRIMES	CAN.
BREMER, Gerhardt	261762	M	Ger.		Pvt., F.P.No.36595 E, Villers near Mer (Fr.) 7.40				PILLAGE	FR.
BREMER, Paul	125103	M	Ger.		Feldwebel, 3.Coy. 877.Bn., Steiermark (Austria) 12.44-4.45				MISC.CRIMES	U.K.
BREMER, Wilhelm	121109	M	Ger.		Civilian, Wackersleben (Ger.) 4.45				TORTURE	U.S.
BREMM, Joseph	195286	M	Ger.		Cpl., 8.Bn.1.Art.Regt.3.Sect. S.P.21309 D.,Monterre-Sylly (Fr.) 6.40				MURDER	FR.
BREMMER, Paul	142019	M	Ger.		Sgt., C.C. Leizen (Austria) 4.44-4.45				MISC.CRIMES	U.K.
BREMMER, Walter	159851	M	Ger.	10	Hptsturmfhr., Waffen-SS, Sect.V, Med.Dept., Buchenwald (Ger.) 41				TORTURE	U.K.
BREMS	159823	M	Ger.		SS-Uschafhr., C.C. Neuengamme (Ger.)				MURDER	U.K.
BRENDEL	11230	M	Ger.	15	SS-Sturmmann, 16.Panz.Div.SS "Reichsfuehrer", Strettoia (Italy) 9.44				MURDER	FR.
BRENDEL, Joseph	72242	M	Ger.	05	Oschafhr., SS, C.C. Hinzert (Ger.) 41-43				MISC.CRIMES	U.S.
BRENDER, Emil	254319	M			Pvt., Camp Ellrich, Nordhausen (Ger.)				MURDER	U.S.
BRENDKOWSKY	188675	M	Ger.		Stabsarzt, Sanitaets-Abt., Dury les Amiens (Fr.) 44				WITNESS	FR.
BRENDLER	194788	M	Ger.		Lt., SS,-C.C. Lublin (Pol.) 40-44				SUSPECT	POL.
BRENECK	196592	M	Ger.		Sgt., Formation Station, Malissard,Beaumont Les Valence. 6.44				WITNESS	FR.
BRENER, Klernius	196591	M	Ger.		Chief of Camp XIV A, Kommando, Thorn (Pol.) 11.42				MURDER	FR.
BRENIERE	194704	M	Ger.		Cmdt., Army, St.Laurent sur Manoir (Fr.) 8.44				MURDER	FR.
BRENNDOERFER	134765	M			Guard, 4.SS Totenkopf-Sturmbann, C.C.Dora-Mittelbau,Nordhausen(Ger.) 43-45				WITNESS	U.S.
BRENNEIS, Max	254302	M			Flyer, C.C. Ellrich, Nordhausen (Ger.)				MURDER	U.S.
BRENNEIS, Otto	52389	M	Ger.	00	SS-Capt., SS, C.C. Flossenburg (Ger.)				TORTURE	U.S.
BRENNEISEN	62314	M	Ger.		Capt., 3.Coy., 71.Pion.Bau-Bn., Chartres (Fr.),Dueren, Obermaubach (Ger.)11.44				TORTURE	U.K.
BRENNER	28829	M	Ger.		General, O.C. SS Panz.Div."Das Reich", Gestapo, Parigueux (Fr.) 6.-8.44				MURDER	FR., U.S.
BRENNER	159837	M	Ger.		Arbeitskommando, C.C. Adorf (Ger.)				TORTURE	U.K., Sov.Un.
BRENNER	173970	M			Supervisor of Women, Labour Camp, C.C.Muhldorf, Ampfing (Ger.) 6.44-4.45				MURDER	U.S.
BRENNER	189991	M			Member of Gestapo, C.C. Banjica (Yugo.)				MURDER	YUGO.
BRENNER	301843	M	Ger.		SS-Sturmfhr., Bttr. Kommandeur, SS, "Prinz Eugen" Div. Split, Mostar, Sinj, Drasnica (Yugo.) 11.43,4.44				MURDER	YUGO.
BRENNER (see BRUNNER)	140									
BRENNER (see BENNER)	196140									

BRE-BRI

NAME	C.R.FILE NUMBER	SEX	NATIO-NALITY	DATE OF BIRTH	RANK OCCUPATION UNIT PLACE AND DATE OF CRIME	REASON WANTED	WANTED BY
BRENNER, Ernestine (Erna)	261388	F	Ger.		Guard, SS, C.C. Auschwitz (Pol.) 41-45	BRUTALITY	POL.
BRENNER, Gustav	301191	M	Ger.		Rottenfhr., Huchenfeld (Ger.) 3.45	MURDER	U.K.
BRENNER, Karl	133746	M		01	Inspector, Geh.Feld-Pol.,Grp.713 (Russia)	MURDER	U.S.
BRENNER, Karl	196288	M	Ger.		Col., Schutzpol., Warschau (Pol.) 39-40	MURDER	POL.
BRENNER, Peter	194791	M		31. 5.07	Kreisbauernfuehrer, occupied terrotories official,Luxemburg (Lux.)	MISC.CRIMES	LUX.
BRENNER, Simon	254301	M			Flyer, Airforce,C.C. Harzungen, Nordhausen (Ger.)	MURDER	U.S.
BRENNING	137740	M			Lt., 15 Pz.Gren.Rgt.	WITNESS	U.S.
BRENNINGER, Andreas	253815	M			Sgt., Feldgendarmerie 924, La Folatiere (Fr.) 6.44	MURDER	FR.
BRRONING	125116	M			Hptscharfhr.,SS, C.C. Buchenwald (Ger.)	TORTURE	FR.
BRENSCHEID, Hugo	139111	M			Pvt., Army,	WITNESS	U.S.
BRENTNER or BRINTZLER or BRINKELN	187564	M	Ger.	15	Cpl., Thuringian Art.Rgt., Oflag IV C, C.C. Colditz (Ger.) 9.43	MURDER	U.K.
BRESCHER, Nikolaus	254300	M			Pvt., C.C. Ellrich, Nordhausen (Ger.)	MURDER	U.S.
BRESEMANN, Herbert	105953	M	Ger.		Army, SS, 9 Pz.Div.,19 Pz.Gren.Rgt.,10 Coy,Arnheim (Neth.)	WITNESS	U.S.
BRESKOTT, Joseph	168606	M	Ger.		Pvt., 9 Gren.Ers.Rgt., Magny D'Anigon (Fr.) 9.44	MURDER	FR.
BRESLER	141933	M	Ger.		Funkmeister, 2 TP Art.Rgt.191, Caranten (Fr.) 6.44	WITNESS	U.S.
BRESSER, Josef	192581	M	Ger.		Oscharfhr., SS, Motor Pool, Buchenwald (Ger.) 43-45	MISC.CRIMES	U.S.
BRESSON	144559	M			Member, Gestapo, Clermont-Ferrand Claveix (Fr.)	MURDER	FR.
BRETHAUER	167654	M	Ger.		Civ., Einsatzstab Rosenberg, administrative Staff (Fr.) 44	PILLAGE	FR.
BRETNER	124957	M			Wachtmstr., SS or Gestapo, Bremen-Farge (Ger.)	MURDER	U.K.
BRETSCHNEIDER or BREDTSCHNEIDER	133747	M			Scharfhr., SS, C.C. Buchenwald (Ger.)	MISC.CRIMES	U.S.
BRETT, Andreas	168576	M	Ger.		C.C. Natzweiler-Struthof (Fr.) 43-44	MURDER	FR.
BRETTAG	129	M			Pvt., Army, Baudrigues (Fr.)	MURDER	FR., UNWCC
BRETTINAGHER	195011	M			Lt., Airforce, Rodez (Fr.) 8.44	MURDER	FR.
BRETTMEISTER, Stefan	261994	M		10.12.13	SS-Mann,W-SS,Gren.Div.36,Dirlewanger Bde.Warsaw a.other pl.(Pol.)40-44	MURDER	POL.
BRETTNACHER	130	M			Lt., Airforce, Rodez (Fr.) 8.44	MURDER	FR.
BRETTNACHER, Josef	179763	M		22	Lt., 590 Pz.Jg.Abt., Ponte Buggianese (It.) 7.-8.44	MURDER	U.K.
BRETTSCHNEIDER	131	M	Ger.		Usturmfhr., SS, C.C. Boten (Nor.) 3.42-43	MURDER	YUGO.,NOR.
BRETTSCHNEIDER, Horst	254299	M			Pvt., C.C. Ellridh, Nordhausen (Ger.)	MURDER	U.S.
BRETTSCHNEIDER, Siegfried	192480	M			Reichsministry of Justice, Strafgefangenenlager Nord,Finnmark (Nor.)	WITNESS	NOR.
BRETTUS	253814	M	Ger.		Sgt., Straf-Coy STG 3 B, Fuerstenberg-Oder (Ger.) 7.42	BRUTALITY	FR.
BRETZ, Georges	168575	M		09	SS-Sturmmann, C.C. Struthof-Natzweiler (Fr.) 43-44	MURDER	FR.
BREUER	9637	M			Prof., Psychiatrist, C.C. Dachau (Ger.) 39-44	TORTURE	CZECH.,BEL.
BREUER	156737	M		07	Lt., SS-Pol.,Sicherheits-Cdo 11 B, C.C. Therina,Tiraspol (Rum.Russ.)41	MURDER	U.S.
BREUER	172917	M			Oscharfhr., SS, C.C. Weimar (Ger.) 45	MURDER	U.S.
BREUER, Adolf	300988	M		5. 1.13	Member, Gestapo Rennes (Fr.) 40-45	TORTURE	FR.
BREUER, Erich	130100	M			SS, C.C. Dora-Mittelbau, Nordhausen (Ger.)	MURDER	U.S.
BREUER, Joseph	253821	M	Ger.	19. 4.14	Pvt., Army, 558 Gren.Rgt., 13 Coy, Bruay-Artois (Fr.) 9.44	INTERR.	FR.
BREUER, Richard	172916	M	Ger.	02 - 03	Civilian, Overseer, Russian POW on Siegfried Line,Merkstein, Nivelstein (Ger.) 41	MURDER	U.S.
BREUING, Theodor	253944	M			Hptsturmfhr., SS, Neuengamme (Ger.) 44	INTERR.	FR.
BREUNECKE, Hermann	255571	M			Pvt., SS, Folembray (Fr.) 8.44	INTERR.	FR.
BREUNING	127332	M			Hptsturmfhr., Pz.Div. SS Totenkopf,C.C.Ohrdruf (Ger.)	MURDER	U.S.
BRAUNING	148357	M			SS, CC Buchenwald (Ger.)	TORTURE	FR.
BREUNING	159824	M	Ger.		Uscharfhr., SS, C.C. Neuengamme (Ger.)	TORTURE	U.K.
BREUNING	196285	M	Ger.		Osturmfhr., C.C. Ravensbrueck (Ger.)	TORTURE	BEL.
BREUSSER	261013	M			Uscharfhr., SS, C.C. Vaihingen (Ger.) 8.44-4.45	MURDER	U.S.
BREVER, Kurt	160239	M		12	Major, Air Corps, C.C. Buchenwald, Ohrdruf (Ger.)	TORTURE	U.S.
BREVES	196115	M			Custom official, Custom field guard, Creach Maout (Fr.) 8.44	MURDER	FR.
BREWKO	124513	M		20	Lt.,2 Fallschirm-Jg.Rgt.,5 Bn (Fr.) 12.44	MISC.CRIMES	U.S.
BREY	144560	M			Lt.,Garde du Port (Hafenpol.) Marseille (Fr.) 44	MURDER	FR.
BREYER, Arpad	261882	M	Ger.	15	Dr., Member, NSDAP, leader Staff of DP-Fraction in Slovakia, Bratislava, Racisdorf (Czech.) 3.-9.42,8.44-4.45	MURDER	CZECH.
BRICA	194113	F	Ger.		Oberschwester, C.C. Ravensbrueck (Ger.)	TORTURE	FR.
BRICKNER	130080	M	Ger.		Cpl., Civilian, Jungbunzlow (Ger.) 5.45	MURDER	FR.
BRICKNER, Fritz	159416	M	Ger.	97	Guard, C.C. Jawischowitz (Pol.)	MURDER	U.K.
BRIEGER, K.	11231	M			Pvt., Pz.Gren.Rgt.111, Albine (Fr.) 6.44	MURDER	FR.
BRIEL, Peter	146966	M			Oberjaeger, Gren.Bn 47, Stamm Rgt.4, Dun les Plages (Fr.) 6.44	MURDER	FR.
BRIELER, Johann	256852	M	Ger.	17. 3.03	Employee, Block 1,8 C.C.Nordhausen(Ger.)	MURDER	U.S.
BRIENBRICKEN, Conrad	192150	M			Pvt., Member, Geh.Feldpol., L.G.P.A. (07814) Bruessel (Bel.)	MURDER	BEL.
BRIER	260652	M	Ger.		Col., Chief, PW affaires, 42-44	WITNESS	U.S.
BRIES	162777	M			Employee, Security Police, D'Agen (Fr.)	MURDER	FR.
BRIESMEISTER, Kurt	195661	M	Ger.		Cpl., 1 SS-Pz.Coy, Ligneuville (Bel.) 12.44	MURDER	U.S.
BRIGULLA	189674	M	Ger.		Cadet-officer, Army, Toulon (Fr.) 8.44	MURDER	FR.
BRILL	300196	M	Ger.		Oberwachtmstr., Strafgefangenenlager Nord, Northern (Nor.) 43-45	MISC.CRIMES	CZECH.
BRINCKMANN, Walter	256004	M	Ger.		Chief of the room, C.C. Flossenburg (Ger.)	BRUTALITY	FR.
BRINDEL	256005	M	Ger.		W.O., SS, C.C. Flossenburg (Ger.)	MURDER	FR.
BRINER	159822	M			Capt., in Stalag, Luft 4, C.C. Kiefheide (Ger.) 2.-5.45	TORTURE	U.S.
BRINGER	254321	M			Pvt., C.C. Ellrich, Nordhausen (Ger.)	MURDER	U.S.
BRINGEWALD, Emil	159827	M	Ger.		Civilian, C.C. Liebanau	TORTURE	U.S.
BRINK	191330	M		90	Oberfeldarzt, 270 Inf.Rgt., Soerreisa (Nor.) 3.-5.45	MURDER	NOR.
BRINK, Walter	166279	M	Ger.		Airforce, Stabsbild-Abt., Avignon (Fr.) 8.44	MURDER	U.S.
BRINKELN see BRENTNER	187564						
BRINKER, Karl	257783	M	Ger.	6.12.99	Worked Block 104, C.C. Nordhausen (Ger.)	MURDER	U.S.
BRINKHORST, Peze	307062	M	Ger.		Standortleiter, Ger.SS Arnhem, Apeldoorn, Wageningen (Neth.)10.43-44	MURDER	NETH.
BRINKMANN	124300	M			Uscharfhr.,1 SS-Pz.Div.,1 SS-Pz.Rgt.,Penal Unit of 9 Coy(Engineers) Malmedy (Bel.) 12.44	MURDER	U.S.
BRINKMANN	20722	M	Ger.		Lt.Col.SS,Bernhard Heydrich Rgt.	MURDER	U.S.
BRINKMANN	28722	M			Osturmfhr., SS,Fallschirm-Jg.Rgt.5,Nachrichtenzug,6 SS Geb.Div.Nord, 20 Army, Abfkl.Abt.,Quergnon-Jemappes,Czein-Finnmark(Nor.,Bel.)44	MURDER	NOR.
BRINKMANN	124514	M	Ger.		Uscharfhr(Hptscharfhr.) SS, SD,C.C. Oranienburg,Sachsenhausen (Ger.)42	MURDER	BEL.,NOR. U.K.,FR.,N

NAME	C.R.FILE NUMBER	SEX	NATIO-NALITY	DATE OF BIRTH	RANK OCCUPATION UNIT PLACE AND DATE OF CRIME	REASON WANTED	WANTED BY
BRINKMAN	127333	M	Ger.	10	Hauptscharf., SS, C.C. Weimar-Buchenwald (Ger.) 39-41	TORTURE	U.S.
BRINKMAN	149734	M			Oberscharf., SS, Guard, C.C. Dora, Gardelagen (Ger.) 4.45	MURDER	U.S.
BRINKMANN	141460	M	Ger.	10	Hauptscharf., SS, C.C. Ellrich (Ger.)	BRUTALITY	FR.
BRINKMANN	188425	M	Ger.	20	Lt., Panz.Art.Regt. 16, Salerno (It.) 9.43	WITNESS	U.K.
BRINKMANN	131151	M	Ger.		Parachute Reg.5	MURDER	BEL.
BRINKMANN	164348	M			Oberstudiendirektor, Public official, Andernach (Ger.)	MURDER	U.N.W.C.C.
BRINKMANN	178209	M			Unterscharf., SS, Camp No.3, C.C.Berlemont, Boulogne sur Mer, Calais, Arras, Bethune, Berck-Plage, St.Pol (Fr.) 43	TORTURE	FR.
BRINKMANN	187522	M	Ger.		Hauptscharf., SS, C.C.Ellrich (Ger.)	MURDER	U.S.
BRINKMANN	254052	M	Ger.		Hauptscharf., SS, C.C.Neuengamme (Ger.)	MURDER	BEL.
BRINKMANN, A.	300680	M	Ger.		Hauptscharf., Poststellenleiter, C.C.Neuengamme (Ger.) 40	MISC.CRIMES	BEL.
BRINKMANN, Heinrich	137060	M	Ger.	8. 5.02	Cpl., Gren.Ers.Bn.302, Budweis (Czech.),Aken (Ger.) 3.44	MURDER	U.S.
BRINKMANN, Otto	306950	M	Ger.		Scharf., SS, C.C. Buchenwald (Ger.) 5.38-10.43	MURDER	BEL.
BRINKMANI, Wilhelm	176399	M	Ger.	01	Guard, C.C.Bunzlau (Ger.) 43-45	MURDER	FR.
BRINKMANN, Wilhelm	196284	M	Ger.		Capt., Schutzpolizei, near Arnheim (Neth.) 3.45	MURDER	NETH.
BRINKMAYER, Fritz	185361	M	Ger.	2.12.10	Leader, Manager of factory, Brno, Moravia (Czech.) 39-45	PILLAGE	CZECH.
BRINKNER, Alfred	169465	M	Ger.	26	Pvt., Army, 337.Coy., Troppau (Czech.) 2.45	MURDER	U.S.
BRINKORT	305982	M	Ger.		Col., Cmdt., Camp Oflag VI-B, Doessel near Warburg (Ger.) 39	MURDER	POL.
BRINSK-HAUSS	261763	M	Ger.		Sgt., St.Pol, De-Leona, Morlaix (Fr.) 8.44	SUSPECT	FR.
BRINTZLER (see BRENTNER)	187564						
BRIS	124301	M			Unterscharf., 1.SS-Panz.Div.,1.SS-Panz.Regt.,9.Bn., Headquarters-Coy., Malmedy (Bel.) 12.44	MURDER	U.S.
BRISACH, Karl	178210	M	Ger.		Zollbeamter, Zollamt Challex/Ain, Badien, Commune of Thoiry (Fr.) 4.44	MURDER	FR.
BRISBALD	256860	M	Ger.		Lt., Henrichemont (Fr.) 9.40-9.41	PILLAGE	FR.
BRISEMEISTER	124302	M			N.C.O., Leibstandarte SS "Adolf Hitler", 1.Panz.Div. (Tank-Commander) Malmedy (Bel.) 12.44	MURDER	U.S.
BRISQHUET, Cister, Walter	256008	M	Ger.		Cpl., Mauthausen (Aust.)	MISC.CRIMES	FR.
BRIST	160238	M			Pvt., Div."Das Reich" 3.SS Pz.Gren.Regt., Aiguillon (Fr.) 6.44	MURDER	FR.
BRITENBACH	190103	M			SS, C.C. Dora Mittelbau Nordhausen (Ger.)	MURDER	U.S.
BRITZA, Willy	250077	M	Ger.		Agent, Gestapo, Limoges (Fr.) 6.44	INTERR.	FR.
BRIX	131152	M	Ger.		Fallschirmjaeger-Regt.5, Nachrichten Zug, Quaregnon,Jemappes-Chlin (BEL.) 9.44	MURDER	BEL.
BRIX	167668	M	Ger.		Dr., Regierungspraes., Public official, Bialystok (Pol.) 39-44	MISC.CRIMES	POL.
BRIX	254315	M	Ger.		SA, C.C. Buchenwald (Ger.)	INTERR.	FR.
BRIX, Karl	185360	M	Ger.	12. 9.15	Crim.Asst., S.D., Gestapo, Praha, Benesov (Czech.) 39-45	MURDER	CZECH.
BRIXNER, Friedrich	148524	M	Ger.	31. 1.15	Sgt., Wehrmacht-Kommandantur, Milhouse (Fr.)	TORTURE	FR.
BRNICKY, Franz	194701	M	Ger.	15. 5.11	Scharf., SS, Agent, S.D., Gestapo, Kolin (Czech.) 39-45	SUSPECT	CZECH.
BROAD	300769	M	Ger.		Obersturmf., C.C. Auschwitz-Birkenau (Pol.) 40	MURDER	FR.
BROBECKER	259619	M			Policeman, Fieldpolice of the Bde., Oberhergheim, Haut Rhin (Fr.) 7.41	BRUTALITY	FR.
BROCH	259207	M			Unterscharf., C.C. Auschwitz (Pol.)	TORTURE	FR.
BROCHE, Albert	260114	M	Ger.		Sgt., Unit: Russian-German,Div."Oberland",Massif du Vercors(Fr.)7.-8.44	SUSPECT	FR.
BROCHMAYER	196927	M			Scharf., SS, Hannover (Ger.)	MURDER	BEL.
BROCHTEL	9698	M			Dr., Hauptsturmbannf., SS, medical officer, C.C.Dachau (Ger.) 39	TORTURE	CZECH.
BROCK	259616	M	Ger.	10	SS-Oberscharf., Gestapo, area of Angers, Maine and Loire (Fr.) 42-44	MISC.CRIMES	FR.
BROCK	147193	M	Ger.		Dr., Ob.Arzt, 11.Panz.Div. (Fr.) 44	MURDER	FR.
BROCK	160234	M	Ger.		Cpl., Gestapo, Bretagne, Anjou (Fr.)	MURDER	FR.
BROCK (ZUM), Heinrich	144939	M			Rottenf., SS, C.C. Struthof (Fr.)	MURDER	FR.
BROCKAMP	178217	M			Sgt., Fallschirmjaeger-Regt., 2.Bn., Plouzane (Fr.) 44	MURDER	FR.
BROCKDORF	254313	M	Ger.		Rottenf., C.C. Buchenwald (Ger.)	INTERR.	FR.
BROCKE	168595	M	Ger.		Head warder, Camp official, C.C. Siegburg (Ger.)	TORTURE	BEL.
BROCKELMAN	31371	M			Major, Army (Nor.) 10.-11.44	MURDER	NOR.
BROCKENOFF	253940	M	Ger.	16	Cpl., Ger.Army, Guard at Stalag 6 B, Flammersheim (Ger.) 1.45	MISC.CRIMES	U.S.
BROCKER	131139	M		3. 9.82	Camp Siegburg (Ger.)	MURDER	BEL.
BROCKHAUSEN	159817	M			Civilian in a Camp, C.C. Braunschweig (Ger.)	TORTURE	BEL.
BROCKHOFF	185147	M	Ger.		Guard, SS, C.C. Sachsenhausen (Ger.)	TORTURE	FR.
BROCKHOFF, Karl	178218	M	Ger.		SS-Guard, Omer, Berlemont,Boulogne s.M.,Berck,St.P ol,Calais,Arras,Bethune	TORTURE	FR.
BROCKHOP	144671	M			Lt., Army, Lamotte Beuvron (Fr.)	TORTURE	FR.
BROCKMANN	132	M	Ger.		Stabsgefreiter, Abwehr official, Baudrigues (Fr.) 8.44	MURDER	FR.
BROCKMANN	144673	M			Stabsgefreiter, Unit 220368, Domaine de Baudrigues Rouliencs, 8.44	TORTURE	U.K.
BROCKMANN, Hugo	137621	M	Ger.		Gefreiter, Inf.Regt.662 or 602, Fort Kauch (Posen), Pol., 1944	MURDER	U.K.
BROCKMEIER	194789	M	Ger.		Kreisbauernf., occupied territories official, Luxemburg (Lux.)	MISC.CRIMES	LUX.
BROCKMEYER, Adolph	159802	M			Civilian, Bad Oeynhausen (Ger.) 41-45	TORTURE	U.S.,FR.
BROCKMON	36624	M			N.C.O., Army, Jitchin (Ditkau) Czech. 3.45	TORTURE	U.K.
BROCKS, Hans	253825	M	Ger.	9.11.07	Pvt., 13.Coy., 558.Gren.Regt., Bruey en Artois (Fr.) 9.44	INTERR.	FR.
BRODA, Valentin	168697	M	Ger.		Pvt., 9.Gren.Ers.Regt., 1.Coy., Magny d'Anigon (Fr.) 9.44	MURDER	FR.
BRODE or BRODER (see BROTE)	128607						
BRODE, Paul	300197		Ger.		Oberwachtmeister, Strafgef.Lg.Nord, Northern (Nor.) 43 - 45	BRUTALITY	CZECH.
BRODER	128865	M			N.C.O., Landessch., C.C. Mankendorf (Ger.) 1.43	TORTURE	U.K.
BRODIHUM, Josef	168608	M			Pvt., 9.Gren.Ers.Regt., 1.Coy., Magny d'Anigon (Fr.) 9.44	MURDER	FR.
BRODINGEN	31372	M			Army, Nor. 10.-11.44	MURDER	NOR.
BRODMAN	133377	M			Lt., W-SS, 2.Picn.Ausb.Bn., Passau (Ger.) 4.45	MURDER	U.S.
BRODNIEWIECZ, Bruno	120570	M	Ger.		Cpl., Army, C.C. Oswiecim (Pol.) 40-45	MURDER	POL.
BROECKEL	186022	M	Ger.		SS Leibstandarte "A.Hitler" Stabs-Coy., Roermond (Neth.),Stavelot(Bel.)	MURDER	BEL.
BROEGGERMANN, Otto	260074	M	Ger.		Oberwachtmeister, SS, Strafgef.Lg.Nord (Nor.) 6.42-45	SUSPECT	NOR.
BROEHMER	131146	M	Ger.		C.C. Kaisheim (Ger.)	TORTURE	BEL.
BROHL	162718	M			Org.Todt, Dunderland (Nor.)	MURDER	NOR.
BROICHGANS	11232	M			Pvt., Pz.Gren.Regt. III, Gourdon (Fr.) 6.44	MURDER	CAN.
BROICHHAUS, Hubert	306193	M	Ger.		Pvt., Volkssturm, Opladen (Ger.) 3.45	MURDER	FR.
BROKATE or BROKATZ, Anna	195858	F	Ger.	94	Interpreter, Gestapo, Maisons-Laffitte (Fr.) 12.41-6.44	MISC.CRIMES	FR.
BROKER	139116	M			Hauptwachtmeister, Police, C.C.Siegburg (Ger.)	TORTURE	U.S.
BROMBACHER, Ernst or BROMBERGER	149608	M			Scharf., SS, Guard, C.C. Struthof (Fr.)	MURDER	FR.
BROMBERGER, Ernst or BROMBACHER	149608						
BROMBERGER	300989	M	Ger.		Member of Staff, C.C.Struthof - Natzweiler (Fr.) 42-44	MURDER	FR.

BRO-BRU

NAME	C.R.FILE NUMBER	SEX	NATIO-NALITY	DATE OF BIRTH	RANK OCCUPATION UNIT PLACE AND DATE OF CRIME	REASON WANTED	WANTED BY
BROMBY	128606	M			Oschfhr, SS Pz.Div.Totenkopf, CC Mauthausen (Aust.) 41-45	MURDER	U.S.
BROMER	149645	M			Agent, Gestapo, CC Struthof (Fr.)	TORTURE	FR.
BROMM	62312	M			Stabsfeldwebel, Army, Abwehr Off., P.W.Encl.Gneisenaukaserne, Ehrenbreitstein (Ger.)	MURDER	U.S.
BROMM, Fritz	195817	M	Ger.		Asst, CC Dachau (Ger.) 3.42	BRUTALITY	BEL.
BROMMER, Karl	11233	M	Ger.		Feldpolizei Inspektor, Abwehr Official, Gestapo of Jesselin, Feldpolizei Inspektor, Locmine (Fr.) 44	MURDER	FR.
BROMMOND	195825	M	Ger.		Schfhr, Auschwitz (Pol.) 40	MURDER	FR.
BROMPS	129821	M			Station-Master, Civilian, Black Forest (Ger.)	MURDER	U.S.
BROMHOLD	259618	M	Ger.		SS Hptschfhr, Aussendienststellen of SD, Area Tarbes, Hte.Pyrénées (Fr.) 11.42-8.44	MISC.CRIMES	FR.
BRONTY (or BRONN)	139119	M	Ger.		Sgt, 150 Pz.Bde., Malmedy, Liege Stavelot (Bel.) 1.45	MISC.CRIMES	U.S.
BRONSTRUP née HUSEMANN	260018	F	Ger.	19.10.21	Helper, Red Cross, Lengerich (Ger.) 8.44	WITNESS	U.S.
BROOCHLE (or BRUCKLE)	160235	M	Ger.		Lt., Gestapo Angers, Bretagne, Poitou, Anjou (Fr.)	MURDER	FR.
BROOSMANN (see BROSSMANN)	120557						
BROOTHERS (see HUBERT)	12399						
BROOTMEYER	192149	M	Ger.	96	Member of Geheime Feld-Polizei, Brussels (Bel.)	TORTURE	BEL.
BROSCH	187517	M	Ger.	95	Doctor, Public Health, Channel Islands 2.43	MISC.CRIMES	U.K.
BROSCH	193378	M	Ger.		Sgt, 1 PoW-Working Bn.41, CC Nerlandsdal, Kristiansund (Nor.) 41-45	TORTURE	NOR.
BROSCHHAEUSER, Josef	173957	M			Camp Guard, SS, CC Muhldorf Ampfing (Ger.) 6.44-4.45	MURDER	U.S.
BROSE	301939	M			Crim.Secretary, Political Department, CC Auschwitz (Pol.) 44	MURDER	POL.
BROSIAN	162716	M	Ger.		Officer of Secret Field Police, Brussels (Bel.)	TORTURE	BEL.
BROSINSKI	159820	M	Ger.		Uschfhr, SS, 1 Pz.Div., 2 Pz.Rgt., 3 Bn, 12 Coy, Stavelot, Malmedy (Bel.) 12.44	MURDER	U.S.
BROSIS	133	M	Ger.		Senior W.O., Feld-Gend., Darracq (Fr.)	TORTURE	FR.
BROSIUS	193377	M	Ger.		Pvt., 2 Coy, PoW Working Bn.206, Finland Mosjoen (Nor., Finl.)	WITNESS	NOR.
BROSSMANN	129820	M	Ger.		Hptsturmfhr, Allg.SS, Totenkopfstandarte Wien, CC Norowitz, CC Dora, Nordhausen (Ger.)	MURDER	U.S.
BROSSNAN (or BROOSMANN)	120557	M			Capt, SS Hptsturmfhr, Gleiwitz (Ger.)	MURDER	U.S.
BROSTERMANN (see BROXTERMANN)	253504						
BROSZINSKI	159821	M	Ger.		Dr., Civilian in CC Spangenberg (Ger.)	TORTURE	U.S.
BROTE (or BRODE, or BRODER)	128607	M		19	Osturmfhr, SS, CC Mauthausen (Aust.) 41-45	MURDER	U.S.
BROTTEUFEL	137061	M	Ger.		SA-Mann, Cologne (Ger.) 10.44	MURDER	U.S.
BROUER	185408	M			General, Army, Officer in Charge of Crete, Heraklion (Grc.) 5.44	MURDER	GRC.
BROUNDT	31998	M	Ger.		Lt., Secret Field Police, Quimperle (Fr.) 44	MURDER	FR.
BROUNDT	149649	M			Lt., Army, Rosquee (Fr.) 6.44, 7.44	MURDER	FR.
BROWING (or BROWNING)	187846	M			Guard, Official, CC Ravensbrueck (Ger.) 42-45	MURDER	BEL.
BROXTERMANN (or BROSTERMANN)	253504	M			Cpl., CC Ellrich, Nordhausen (Ger.)	MURDER	U.S.
BROZIS	125192	M	Ger.		Senior W.O., Army, Dax (Fr.)	MURDER	FR.
BROZKIO, Karl	159414	M	Ger.		Blockaeltester, CC Sawischowitz (Pol.)	MURDER	FR.
BRTNICKY, Franz	253813	M	Ger.	10	Hptschfhr, Employee, SS, SD Kolin (Czech.) 39-45	MISC.CRIMES	CZECH.
BRUAN	300198	M			W.O., at Calavrita, Mega Apileon, Aghia Lavra	MURDER	GRC.
BRUCH	139826	M	Ger.	05	Plant-Manager, W-SS, Arbeitskommando Georgenschacht (Ger.)	TORTURE	U.S.
BRUCH	149641	M			Army Faehnrich	TORTURE	FR.
BRUCH	178219	M	Ger.		Director, Arbeitslager, CC Wansleben a-See (Ger.) 43-45	TORTURE	FR.
BRUCH (or BRUCK), Johann	254294	M			Pvt., CC Nordhausen (Ger.)	MURDER	U.S.
BRUCH, Kurt	128608	M		11	Hptschfhr, CC Mauthausen (Aust.) -4.44	MURDER	U.S.
BROCHENTZIER	11234	M			W.O., SS Div. "Der Fuehrer" 6.44	MURDER	FR.
BRUCHLOS, Adolf	11235	M		15	Lt., III Pz.Gren.Rgt., Gourdon (Fr.) 6-8.44	MURDER	FR.
BRUCHMUELLER	305003	M	Ger.		Special command branch office, L.G.P.A. Amsterdam and Bentheim, Hermann-Goering-Div., Noordwijk 9.44	TORTURE	NETH.
BRUCHNER	196593	M	Ger.		Major, Ortskommandant, Pont de Veyle (Fr.) 8.44	WITNESS	FR.
BRUCK	147192	M	Ger.		Lt., 11 Pz.Div. France 44	MURDER	FR.
BRUCK (see BRUCH)	254294						
BRUCK	149751	M			Lt., Army, Pz.Aufklaerungsabteilung II, Albine (Fr.) 8.44	LOOTING	FR.
BRUCK (see BRUHN)	258902						
BRUCKENWAGEN, Herbert	31947	M	Ger.		Feldwebel, Abwehr Official, Bannalec (Fr.) 8.44	MURDER	FR.
BRUCKER	194114	M	Ger.		Capt., Army, Ioire and Ampuis (Fr.) 8.44	MURDER	FR.
BRUCKER, August	165271	M	Ger.	28.11.90	Agent, SD, Sipo, Strassburg (Fr.) 42	PILLAGE	U.N.W.C.C.
BRUCKER, Josef	173960	M			Pvt., CC Muhldorf- Ampfing (Ger.), Org.Todt, 6.44-4.45	MURDER	U.S.
BRUCKER, Thomas	259136	M			SS Guard, Muhldorf Area (Ger.)	MURDER	U.S.
BRUCKL, Alfons	151709	M	Ger.		CC Centerenkeeper, Muenchen (Ger.) 9.44	WITNESS	U.S.
BRUCKLE (see BROOCHLE)	160235						
BRUCKLE	253816	M	Ger.		Oschfhr, Gestapo, Savannes (Fr.)	MURDER	FP.
BRUCKLER, Adolph	126931	M	Ger.	15	Gespenst.Div. 02, Lt.	MURDER	FR.
BRUCKLOS (or BRUSCHLOFF) Adolph	301619	M	Ger.		Lt., commanding 2 Coy, A A 7, II Pz.Div., Les Verreriesde Moussans (Fr.) 11.43	MURDER	FR.
BRUCKMANN	260108	M	Ger.		Lt, Kommandantur Cavaillon Vaucluse (Fr.) 11.43	INCENDIARISM	FR.
BRUCKMAYER, Georg	159818	M	Ger.	2.12.98	Doctor, Civilian, Kreis Vilsbiburg, Seyboldsdorf (Ger.) 4.45	WITNESS	U.S.
BRUCKMOELLER	256868	M	Ger.		Military Security Police, Amsterdam (Neth.) 10.44	MURDER	NETH.
BRUCKMUELLER, Johann	196590	M	Ger.		Guard, CC Auschwitz (Pol.) 42-45	MISC.CRIMES	CZECH.
BRUCKNER	137	M			Schfhr, SS, CC Pithiviers, Compiegne, Drancy (Fr.)	MURDER	FR.
BRUCKNER	128609	M			Uschfhr, SS Pz.Div. Totenkopf, CC Mauthausen (Aust.) 41 - 45	MURDER	U.S.
BRUCKNER	160230	M	Ger.		SS Sturmfhr, Gestapo, Tours (Fr.) 42 - 43	MURDER	FR.
BRUCKNER	190058	M	Ger.		N.C.O., Stalag XVIII A,3 Coy, 89 Lds.Schtz.Bn. 2.44	MURDER	U.K.
BRUCKNER	191898	M	Ger.		Lt., Army, St.Hilaire, St.Mesmin (St.Laurent des Faux) France 8.44	MURDER	FR.
BRUCKNER	196594	M	Ger.		Major, CDT, La Place de Macon St.Laurent (Fr.) 41-45	MISC.CRIMES	FR.
BRUCKNER (or BRUCKNERT)	12423	M	Ger.		Capt. or Major, Lyon Command, St.Dié (Fr.) 11.44	TORTURE	FR.

NAME	C.R.FILE NUMBER	SEX	NATIO-NALITY	DATE OF BIRTH	RANK	OCCUPATION	UNIT	PLACE AND DATE OF CRIME	REASON WANTED	WANTED BY
BRUCKNER see BRINKNER	186558									
BRUCKNER, Georg	159847	M			Pvt.Wehrmacht,KL Saal/Danube(Ger.)12.44-4.45				MURDER	U.S.
BRUCKNER-OVA, Ellen Ruth	187516	F	Ger.	10.12.21	Employee,Gestapo and S.D.,Brno(Czech.)39-45				WITNESS	CZECH.
BRUCKNER, Rudolph	128610	M			SS,Mauthausen(Aust.)41-45				MURDER	U.S.
BRUCKNERT see BRUCKNER	12423									
BRUDA or BRUDER	148525	M			Kreisstabsleiter,Volkssturm & Civilian Regional Official,Vicinity of Gardelegen(Ger.)4.45				MURDER	U.S.
BRUDER see BRUDA	148525									
BRUDER	254303				Flyer,CC Ellrich,Nordhausen(Ger.)				MURDER	U.S.
BRUECK, Karl	140765	M	Ger.	13 or 16	Civilian,Gross-Linden,Beltershain (Ger.)				MURDER	U.S.
BRUECK, Karl	306434	M	Ger.		Kreisleiter,Giessen(Ger.)9.44				MURDER	U.S.
BRUECKER, Josef	173959	M			Member SS in CC Muehldorf Ampfing(Ger.)6.44-4.45				MURDER	U.S.
BRUECKER, Thomas	173958	M			Guard SS in CC Muehldorf Ampfing(Ger.)6.44-4.45				MURDER	U.S.
BRUECKLE, Georg	134703	M	Ger.		Oberscharfhr.SS,Tours(Fr.)42				TORTURE	U.S.
BRUECKLE, Georg	195120	M	Ger.	10	SS Oberscharfhr.S.D.Einsatz Kdo.z.b.V.6,St.Dié(Fr.)Autumn 44				MURDER	U.K.
BRUECKMANN	141461	M	Ger.		Capt.Oflag IID,Gross Born(Ger.)41				MURDER	FR.
BRUECKNER	138314	M			SS Interpreter,SS and Gestapo,Lyon(Fr.)7.-8.44				MURDER	FR.
BRUECKNER, Anna	148950	F	Ger.	05	Overseer,CC Ravensbrueck(Ger.)				LOOTING	FR.
BRUECKNER, Friedrich	254056	M	Ger.	23.12.02	SS Sturmscharfhr.Waffen SS,Sumperk(Czech.)3.45				MURDER	CZECH.
BRUECKNER, Josef	192275	M	Ger.	12. 8.93	Civilian,Falkenau(Czech.)10.44				WITNESS	CZECH.
BRUECKNER, Martin	300199	M	Ger.	00 or 05	Oberfhr.and Commander,Straflager,Hamm/Westf.(Ger.)12.44				MISC.CRIMES	NETH.
BRUEGGEMANN	306077	M	Ger.		Hptscharfhr.SS,Hamburg-Neuengamme(Ger.)45				MURDER	CZECH.
BRUEGGEMANN, Gerhard	124306	M			Pvt.1 SS Pz.Div.2 Pz.Gr.Regt.9 Coy.,Malmedy(Bel.)12.44				MURDER	U.S.
BRUEGNER	131143A	M	Ger.	13	Volgatartaslegion 627,Pvt.				MURDER	BEL.
BRUEHN or Nicko BRUHN	253950	M			Probable 377 Jaeg.Regt.,Vinkt Meigen(Bel.)				MISC.CRIMES	BEL.
BRUELL, Walter	124842	M	Ger.	08	Civilian,Landwirtverwalter,Mentershausen(Ger.)9.44				MISC.CRIMES	U.S.
BRUELLS, Fritz	139	M	Ger.	27. 2.07	SS Sturmmann,CC Maidanek(Pol.)40-4.44				MURDER	BEL.
BRUENING	305878	M	Ger.		Organiser,General-Administrator,NSDAP,Aricultural Production Firm "Amylon"at Ronov on Sez,Bohemia(Czech.)45				SUSPECTS	CZECH.
BRUENING, Werner	300957	M			SS Hptsturmfhr.official of S.D.Leitabschnitt,Prague,Oswiecim-Birkenau (Pol.)39-45				MURDER	CZECH.
BRUENINGSEN	159801	M		00	Zugfhr.CC Emsland(Ger.)				MURDER	U.S.
BRUENNE, Erwin	173971	M	Ger.	04	Oberstrumfhr.Policeman,SS Police,CC Langenzenn(Ger.)43-45				MURDER	U.S.
BRUENNING	135137	M	Ger.	10	SS Hptsturmfhr.SS Sipo,Director of Security Police,Oedenburg-Sapron (Hung.)3.45				WITNESS	U.S.
BRUENNING	300201	M	Ger.		Hptwachtmeister,Trondeness Camp(Northern)Nor.1.45				MISC.CRIMES	CZECH.
BRUENNING, Willi	261993	M	Ger.	26. 9.05	SS Mann,Waffen SS,Gren.Div.No.36,Dirlewanger Bde.,Warsaw and other towns(Pol.)40-44				MURDER	POL.
BRUESSELER or BRUESSELEIN	149530	M			CC Sonneberg sous camp Buchenwald(Ger.)				MURDER	FR.
BRUEX	187845	M			Pvt.Heereskuesten Art.Abt.1240,CC Buchenwald(Ger.)				MURDER	BEL.
BRUFACH, Peter	254295	M			Pvt.CC Bodungen,Nordhausen(Ger.)				MURDER	U.S.
BRUGARD	253820	M	Ger.		SS Scharfhr.S.D.Toulouse(Fr.)11.42-8.44				MISC.CRIMES	FR.
BRUGGEMAN	192205	M	Ger.		Kraftfahrer,Army,Chatou(Fr.)8.44				WITNESS	FR.
BRUGGEMANN	254305	M			Sgt.CC Ellrich,Nordhausen(Ger.)				MURDER	U.S.
BRUGGEMANN, Waren	136999	M			Oberwachtmstr.Police,Civilian,Poppentin(Ger.)7.-8.44				MURDER	U.S.
BRUGGMANN, Adolf	255976	M			Pvt.CC Ellrich,Nordhausen(Ger.)				MURDER	U.S.
BRUGMANN	301033	M	Ger.		Hptscharfhr.Guard,CC Erich,Ellrich(Ger.)				MURDER	BEL.
BRUHL	301824	M	Ger.		Dr..Stabsarzt,Luftfahrtministerium Berlin,CC Dachau,Auschwitz(Ger.Pol.) 3.42-2.43				TORTURE	BEL.
BRUHN or BRAUCK or BRUCK	258902	M	Ger.		Capt.Army,Feldkommandantur 651,De Niort,St.Martin,D'Entraignes(Fr.)8.44				MURDER	FR.
BRUHN, Nicko see BRUEHN	253950									
BRUK	11236	M	Ger.		Sec.Lt.Abwehr official 110 or 111 Pz.Gren.Regt.,Gourdon(Fr.)6.44				MURDER	FR.
BRUKNACH	186679	M	Ger.	00	2nd Lt.Army,CC Flossenburg(Ger.)				TORTURE	FR.
BRUESCH	138	M	Ger.	02 or 03	Pvt.Lager Private KL Stalag XXB,397 Land.Schtz.Bn.,Neudorf(Ger.)4.42				MURDER	U.K.
BRULH, Wilhelm	300200	M	Ger.		Cpl.Turkestan Legion,1 Regt.of Turkestan Volunteers,Albi,Tarn,8.44				MURDER	FR.
BRUM	9639	M	Ger.		Sturmfhr.Member of Camp Guards,CC Oranienburg(Ger.)39-45				MURDER	CZECH.POL.
BRUM	195202	M	Ger.		SS Unterstrumfhr.CC Sachsenhausen(Ger.)				MURDER	BEL.
BRUMM	130095	M			Hptscharfhr.CC Sachsenhausen(Ger.)				MURDER	U.S.
BRUMM, Kurt	254296	M			Hptscharfhr.CC Sachsenhausen,Nordhausen(Ger.)				MURDER	U.S.
BRUN	137619	M	Ger.		Lt.Col., Stalag Luft III,Belaria(Ger.)				MISC.CRIMES	U.K.
BRUNCKHORST, Fritz	256790	M	Ger.	15	Pvt.Head of Abwehr,Kristiansand(Nor.)43-44				WITNESS	NOR.
BRUNDT	159840	M			Civilian,Gardelegen(Ger.)4.43				MURDER	U.S.
BRUNE	159841	M			Civilian near Gardelegen(Ger.)4.45				MURDER	U.S.
BRUNE	159814	M			Rapportfhr.KL Mauthausen(Ger.Aust.)41-45				MURDER	U.S.
BRUNER, Philipp	173303	M	Ger.		Obscharfhr.NSKK, Organisation Todt,Sarthe la Fleche(Fr.)7.44				WITNESS	FR.
BRUNES	126893	M	Ger.		Civilian,Bleicherode/Harz(Ger.)6.43-45				TORTURE	U.K.
BRUNKE	253951	M			Wachtmeister,Army,377 Jaeger Regt.,Vinkt-Meigen(Bel.)				MURDER	BEL.
BRUNNACKER, Stefan	254298	M			Flyer,CC Ellrich,Nordhausen(Ger.)				MURDER	U.S.
BRUNNE	141848	M			Capt.Lagerofficer Stalag XIII,Nuernberg(Ger.)45				TORTURE	U.K.
BRUNNER or BRENNER	140	M			SS Hptsturmfhr.KL Drancy,Pithiviers Compiegne(Fr.)7.43				TORTURE	FR.
BRUNNER	127093	M			Member Gestapo Karlsruhe,Anrath(Ger.)				MURDER	FR.
BRUNNER	148516	M			SS Hptsturmfhr.S.D.CC Drancy(Fr.)44				TORTURE	FR.
BRUNNER	159848	M		20	Driver,NCO,Sgt.SS Kl.Fahrbereitsch.(Motor-pool)Sec.I,Buchenwald(Ger.)				TORTURE	U.S.
BRUNNER	173972	M			Organisation Todt,CC Muehldorf Ampfing(Ger.)6.44-4.45				MURDER	U.S.
BRUNNER	189549	M			Capt.Agent,Gestapo,Grenoble(Fr.)				INTERR.	FR.
BRUNNER	253675	M	Ger.		Agent Gestapo,Offenburg(Ger.)11.44				BRUTALITY	FR.
BRUNNER	256010	M	Ger.		Sgt.(Oschfhr.)CC Mauthausen(Ger.)				TORTURE	U.S.
BRUNNER	258560	M			Doctor,Hohenlychen(Ger.)40-45				TORTURE	U.S.
BRUNNER	301230	M	Ger.		Dr..Militaerverwaltungs-Oberrat,Brussels(Bel.)40-44				MURDER	BEL.
BRUNNER, Franz	257337	M	Ger.		SS Hptwachtmeister,SS-slave labour camp,Beisfjord,Narvik(Nor.)6.-11.42				BRUTALITY	YUGO.
BRUNNER, Josef	254297	M			Pvt.CC Woffleben,Nordhausen(Ger.)				MURDER	U.S.
BRUNNER, Josef	257380	M	Ger.		SS Guard,Sgt.SS-slave labour camp,Beisfjord,Nervik(Nor.)6.-11.42				BRUTALITY	YUGO.
BRUNNER, Karl	187979	M		26. 7.00	Police Fhr.SS Police,Bolzano(It.)3.45				MURDER	U.S.U.K.
BRUNNER, Louise	148949	F		15	Chief-overseer,CC Ravensbrueck,Auschwitz(Ger.Pol.)45				TORTURE	FR.

BRU - BUC

NAME	C.R.FILE NUMBER	SEX	NATIO-NALITY	DATE OF BIRTH	RANK OCCUPATION UNIT PLACE AND DATE OF CRIME	REASON WANTED	WANTED BY
BRUNNER, Loys	125183	M	Ger.	22	Hptsturmfhr.,SS (Fr.) 43	MURDER	FR.
BRUNNER, Martin	261990	M		17.12.06	Pvt.,Inf.Ers.Bn.902,Guardian of Kdo.2522 Stalag XIIID,Noerdlingen (Ger.) 7.5.45	MURDER	FR.
BRUNNER, Reinhardt	169449	M	Ger.		Kriminal-Sekretaer,Gestapo Strassburg,Saales and Schirmeck(Fr.)9.-11.44	TORTURE	U.K.
BRUNNER, Rudolf	185405	M	Ger.		Civilian,Cham(Ger.) 42	MURDER	U.S.
BRUNNER, Rudolf	195660	M	Ger.		Schulungsleiter NSDAP,Sachenberg(Ger.) 42	MURDER	POL.
BRUNNER, Vaclav Venzel	260089	M	Ger.	10	Member,Gestapo,Drietoma distr.Trencin(Slovakia-Czech.) 4.45	MURDER	CZECH.
BRUNNHUBER	257381	M	Ger.		SS-Guard,Scharfhr.,SS-slave labour camp,Beisfjord-Narvik(Nor.)6.-11.42	BRUTALITY	YUGO.
BRUNNIKHAUS	254304	M			Pvt.,Camp Ellrich,Nordhausen(Ger.)	MURDER	U.S.
BRUNNIN	147191	M	Ger.		Cpl.-Chief,11 Panzer-Div.(Fr.) 44	MURDER	FR.
BRUNNING	136189	M			Pvt.,II Pz.Div.,2 Coy.A A7,Albine(Fr.) 3.44	MURDER	FR.
BRUNNING, Albert	192482	M		06	Sgt.,Reichsjustizministerium Strafgefangenenlager Nord,Finmark(Nor.)45	TORTURE	NOR.
BRUNO	130087	M			Osturmfhr.,SS,C.C.Dora Mittelbau,Nordhausen	MURDER	U.S.
BRUNO	148496	M			KL.-Lageraeltester,KL.Baumesheim near Donauwoerth(Ger.)	MURDER	FR.
BRUNO	173327	M	Ger.		SS-Guard,SS,C.C.Neekarelz(Ger.)	TORTURE	FR.
BRUNO, Dany	172974	M			Pvt.,Landesschuetzen-Bn.Stolp Coy.,Dresow(Ger.) 1.-9.44	MISC.CRIMES	U.S.
BRUNO, Dick	159417	M	Ger.		Overseer,SA Seubersdorf Stalag XXB(Ger.) 40-42	TORTURE	U.K.
BRUNO, Ludwig	146342	M	Ger.		Gestapo,Perpignan(Fr.)	MURDER	FR.
BRUNO DE MASQUIT (or JEMESKY)	189644	M	Ger.		Sgt.,Army Unite 40539,Cotes Du Nord(Fr.)	PILLAGE	FR.
BRUNS	149342	M	Ger.		Police-Officer,Bremen(Ger.)	MISC.CRIMES	FR.
BRUNS (see BONS)	62352						
BRUNS, C.	126305	M	Ger.		Civilian	TORTURE	U.S.
BRUNS, Carl	166282	M			Fallingbostel(Ger.)	MURDER	U.S.
BRUNS, Carl	168584	M			Pvt.,Major of Lauenan(Ger.) 11.44	TORTURE	U.S.
BRUNS, Emil	305996	M	Ger.		SS-Member of the staff at C.C.Sasel(Ger.) 10.44-4.45	TORTURE	U.K.
BRUNS, Karl	254314	M			Pvt.,Army,3 Regt.,3 Dara Div.,Locmaria-Berrien(Fr.)	INTERR.	FR.
BRUNS, Richard	168623	M			SS-Usturmfhr.,Gestapo,Head of Section IVB (Nor.) 4.40	TORTURE	NOR.
BRUNS, Walter	168596	M			SS-Bde.-Fhr.,Waffen-SS	MURDER	UNWCC
BRUNS, Wilhelm	195815	M	Ger.	95	Oberwachtmeister,Police,Lahde-Weser(Ger.) 43-45	MURDER	BEL.
BRUNS, Wilhelm	19259?	M	Ger.		Rottfhr.,SS-Guard,Buchenwald(Ger.) 42-45	TORTURE	U.S.
BRUNSWICH	195879	M			SS-Scharfhr.,Leibstand.Adolf Hitler,Bierwart(Bel.)	PILLAGE	BEL.
BRUNSWICK	162313	M			Uschfhr.,SS-Leibstand.Adolf Hitler Tank 174-95B,Bierwart(Bel.)-9.44	PILLAGE	U.K.
BRUNSWICK, Hans	120608	M	Ger.		Feldwebel,Army,Camp 27627 G-W(Ger.) 44-45	MISC.CRIMES	U.K.
BRUO	125165	F			SS,Auschwitz(Pol.)	MURDER	U.S.
BRUSCH, Wilhelm	305582	M	Ger.		Member of C.C.Personnel, C.C.Flossenburg,Hersbruck,Wolkenburg, Ganacker and Leitmeritz(Ger. and Czech.) 1.42-5.45	MURDER	U.S.
BRUSCHLOFF,Adolph(see BRUCKLOS)	301619						
BRUSKNER	260162	M	Ger.		Lt.,7 Res.Art.Regt.,Massif of Vercors,Isere et Drome(Fr.)7.-8.44	SUSPECT	FR.
BRUSER	141	M			Cpl.,Sgt.,Geheime Feldpolizei,Army,Locmine(Fr.) 7.-8.44	TORTURE	FR.
BRUSHEWITZ, Franz	124707	M			Sgt.,Air defense detachment,Arsimont(Bel.) 7.42	TORTURE	BEL.
BRUSSKLEIN (see BRUESSKLER)	149530	M					
BRUST	185409	M			Oschfhr.,SS,C.C.Mauthausen(Aust.)	MURDER	U.S.
BRUST	196183		Ger.		SS-Scharfhr.,SS,C.C.Gusen(Ger.)	MISC.CRIMES	BEL.
BRUYN	141953	M			Dr.,Camp-Doktor KL.Rudolstadt(Ger.)	MISC.CRIMES	U.S.
BRUZ	256011	M	Ger.		Cpl.,10 Div. Pz.SS-Frundsberg,2 Bn.,Louveciennes and Marly(Fr.)8.44	MURDER	FR.
BRZEZISKI, Johann	254051	M			Pvt.,Ers.Bn.24,Wervick(Bel.)	INTERR.	BEL.
BUBE	192815	M	Ger.		Sgt.,Schupo,C.C.Falstaf-Drontheim(Nor.) 41-45	MURDER	NOR.
BUBELER or KUBLER	192272	M			SS-Scharfr.,C.C.Flossenburg(Ger.) 44-45	MURDER	FR.
BUBENHAGEN	255505	M			Pvt.,C.C.Dora,Nordhausen(Ger.)	MURDER	U.S.
BUBER	188680	M	Ger.		Pvt.,Army, Dammerie Les Lips(Fr.) 3.41	MURDER	FR.
BUBIK, Gertrude	187514	F	Ger.	4.5.08	Employee, SD and Gestapo, Brno(Czech.) 39-45	WITNESS	CZECH.
BUBLIK	301299	M			Member of the Gestapo at Trencin,C.C.Oswiecim-Birkenau(Pol.) 39-45	MURDER	CZECH.
BUBY (see HOLZ)	254947						
BUCH	191897	M	Ger.		Doctor,Stalag XII D,Thillez Les Groselles(Fr.)	MURDER	FR.
BUCH	193039	M			Lagerfhr.-Guard at Todt Camp,Villach(Aust.) 5.45	MURDER	U.K.
BUCH	254278	M		95	Col.,15 German Police Regt.H.Q.,Vercelli-Crescentino(Ital.) 9.44	INTERR.	U.K.
BUCH, Luise nee NITKA	254479	F	Ger.		Camp-Supervisor,C.C. Ravensbrueck(Ger.) 42-44	MISC.CRIMES	POL.
BUCH, Nicolaus	178211	M		98	SS-Oschfhr.,SS,C.C.Schonberg(Ger.) 43	MURDER	FR.
BUCH, Paul	129818	M			Pvt.,P.O.W.Camp,Altengrabow Stalag 2A(Ger.) 3.45	MURDER	U.S.
BUCH, Wilhelm	11237	M			Senior W.O.,Fallschirmjaeger-Regt.,St.Menehould(Fr.) 44	MURDER	FR.
BUCH, Wilhelm	146346	M			W.O.,Army,Unit L.G.PA.Paris 55582,Somme-Tourbe,St.Menehould(Fr.)	MURDER	FR.
BUCH, Wilhelm	188068	M			Sgt.,Fallschirmjaeger-Abt.,Menehould(Fr.) 8.44	MURDER	FR.
BUCHACKER	160221	M			Pvt.,Luftnachrichten-Coy.21,Marseille(Fr.) 8.44	MURDER	FR.
BUCHAL, Heinz	148504	M			SS-Osturmfhr.,C.C. Lublin(Pol.) 42-45	MURDER	FR.
BUCHALIK	255506	M			Uscharfhr.,C.C.Nordhausen(Ger.)	MURDER	U.S.
BUCHALIK	256796	M	Ger.		Block-Leader,Boelke-Kaserne,Nordhausen(Ger.)	MURDER	U.S.
BUCHALSKI, Alex (see MICHALSKI)	261992	M	Ger.	18.7.08	SS-Mann,Waffen-SS Gren.Div.36 Dirlewanger-Bde.,Warsaw and other(Pol.) 40-44	MURDER	POL.
BUCHARDT	254293				SS-Obersturmbannfhr.,SD and Waffen-SS,Lodz(Pol.) 41-43	INTERR.	POL.
BUCHART, Karl-Heinz	255497	M		3.6.22	Pvt.,C.C.Ellrich,Nordhausen(Ger.)	MURDER	U.S.
BUCHBERGER	146347	M		05	Officer,Army,Gestapo,Chambery,Challes Les Eaux(Fr.)	MURDER	FR.
BUCHBERGER, Fritz	188575	M		06	Official,Gestapo,Biollay Chambery(Fr.)	MURDER	FR.
BUCHEDER, Johann	179787	M			Civilian, Alt Irding(Aust.) 3.45	TORTURE	U.S.
BUCHKL, Heinrich	254292	M			Pvt.,Army,Villmar(Ger.) 6.-8.44	WITNESS	U.S.
BUCHENAU	141953A	M			Officer,POW Labour Camp	MISC.CRIMES	U.S.
BUCHENTAL, Theodor	148503	M			Chief,C.C.Lustboekel near Soeltau(Ger.) 42	MISC.CRIMES	FR.
BUCHER	125105	M	Ger.		Lagerfuehrer,Arbeits-Kdo.,Member NSDAP,C.C.Graz 107 G.W.	TORTURE	U.K.
BUCHER	195856	M			C.C.Schirmeck(Fr.) 40-44	MISC.CRIMES	FR.
BUCHER	254483	M	Ger.		Col.,Ger.Army Oflag XIIIB,Neuernberg-Langwasser(Ger.) 41-45	INTERR.	Yugo.
BUCHER	254489	M	Ger.		Cpl.,C.C.Neuengamme(Ger.)	INTERR.	BEL.

BUC-BUC

NAME	C.R.FILE NUMBER	SEX	NATIO- NALITY	DATE OF BIRTH	RANK OCCUPATION UNIT PLACE AND DATE OF CRIME	REASON WANTED	WANTED BY
BUCHER	254500	M	Ger.		Crim.Asst., Sipo-Abt.4 A, Brussels (Bel.)	INTERR.	BEL.
BUCHER (see BUCHNER)	255498						
BUCHER	305831	M	Ger.		Pvt., 1.Aufkl.Abt., 3.Coy., 2.Col., XV.Div. Afrika-Korps, St.Léger (Arlon) 9.44	MISC.CRIMES	BEL.
BUCHER, Alphonse	166919	M	Ger.		Kreisamtsleiter, NSDAP, Aschbach (Fr.) 44	MURDER	FR.
BUCHER, Arno	189992	M		98	Osturmfhr., SS, C.C., Neuengamme (Ger.) 43	MURDER	YUGO.
BUCHER, Carl	132476	M			Mayor, Public Official, St.Gallen (Aust.) 8.44	MURDER	U.K.
BUCHER, Johann	172940	M			Civilian, Builder (Ger.)	WITNESS	U.S.
BUCHERT	193996	M	Ger.		Hptsturmfhr., SS, Kommissar, SS Gestapo, Droegen-Mecklenburg (Ger.) 5.44 or 6.44	MURDER	U.S.
BUCHERT	256012	M	Ger.		Chief of block 13, C.C., Mauthausen (Aust.)	TORTURE	FR.
BUCHHEIM (or BUCHSEIN)	186557	M		17	Osturmfhr., SS, 12.Pz.Div.Hitler-Jugend,12.SS Recce Bn.,Caen (Fr.) 7.44	TORTURE	CAN.
BUCHHEISTER	131153	M	Ger.		Fallschirmjaeger-Rgt.5, Nachrichtenzug, Quregnon-Jemappes-Chlin (Bel.) 9.44	MURDER	BEL.
BUCHHIEM, Heinz	254277	M			SS H.Q.'s. Coy., 1.Bn., Malmedy (Bel.) 12.44	MURDER	U.S.
BUCHHOLTZ, Graf	146350	M	Ger.		Agent, Gestapo, Monte-Carlo, Nice (Fr.)	MURDER	FR.
BUCHHOLTZ	261038	M	Ger.		Col., Oberfeldkommandantur 670, Lille and District (Fr.) 42-43	MURDER	FR.
BUCHHOLZ	258472	M			Oschfhr., SS, C.C., Ohrdruf (Ger.) 12.44-4.45	MURDER	U.S.
BUCHHOLZ	261777	M	Ger.		Cpl., Art.H.D.V.199, 2235 N.D.F. No. F.P.27046 C, Lorgies (Fr.) 9.44	MURDER	FR.
BUCHHOLZ, Herbert	196181	M			Civilian, Berlin-Reinickendorf-West (Ger.) 6.44	WITNESS	U.S.
BUCHHOLZ, Max	255499	M			Cpl., C.C. Ellrich, Nordhausen (Ger.)	MURDER	U.S.
BUCHHOLZ, Walter	167655	M	Ger.		Pvt., Pz.Ausb.Res.Rgt., 3.Coy.,St.Ouen de Thouberuille (Fr.) 8.44	PILLAGE	FR.
BUCHHOLZER	149358	M			Civilian, Pontoise (Fr.)	LOOTING	FR.
BUCHLEITER	254494	M	Ger.		Cpl., Field-Pol. Trupp 533, D'Annecy, Le Chablais (Fr.) 5.44	INTERR.	FR.
BUCHLER, Hermann	128611	M			Civilian, C.C., Mauthausen (Aust.) 11.41-42	MURDER	U.S.
BUCHLOR, Wilhelm August	140777	M	Ger.		School-teacher, Civilian	MISC.CRIMES	U.S.
BUCHMANN	62311	M	Ger.		Civilian, Owner of a vegetable Drying-Factory, Aschersleben (Ger.) 3.45-4.45	TORTURE	U.S.
BUCHMANN	128613	M			Hptscharfhr., SS-Totenkopf-Panz.Div.	MURDER	U.S.
BUCHMANN	129817	M	Ger.		Major, Military 3.SS-Panz.Div."Totenkopf", Retreat from Russia	MURDER	U.S.
BUCHMANN	146348	M			Sgt., Navy, Corcieux (Fr.) 6.44	MURDER	FR.
BUCHMANN	147189	M	Ger.	14	Lt., 11.Panz.Div. (Fr.) 44	MURDER	FR.
BUCHMANN	147190	M	Ger.		Lt., 11.Panz.Div., Pz.Aufkl.Abt.II (Fr.) 44	MURDER	FR.
BUCHMANN	194115	M	Ger.		Lt., Army, Essay (Fr.) 9.44	WITNESS	FR.
BUCHMANN	255493	M			Cpl., Camp Osterhagen,, Nordhausen (Ger.)	MURDER	U.S.
BUCHMANN	256795	M	Ger.		Oscharfhr., SS, C.C., Nordhausen (Ger.)	MURDER	U.S.
BUCHMANN	301889	M	Ger.	15	Lt., Etat-Major of Lt.Col.Wilde,11.Pz.Div.(F.P.No.24253 and 38260) in South-West-France,44	MURDER	FR.
BUCHMANN, Anna-Marie	256737	F	Ger.		Interpreter, SD, Foix (Fr.) 11.42-8.44	MURDER	FR.
BUCHMANN, Leohard	191311	M	Ger.		Civilian, Foix (Fr.) 6.44	MURDER	FR.
BUCHMANN, Paul	255366	M	Ger.		Rapportfhr., C.C., Mauthausen (Aust.)	MURDER	FR.
BUCHMANN, Rudolf	134768	M	Ger.		Sgt., 4.SS-Totenkopfsturmbann, C.C. Dora-Mittelbau, Nordhausen (Ger.) 43-45	WITNESS	U.S.
BUCHMANN, Walter	160199	M	Ger.		Interpreter, Gestapo, Foix (Fr.) 6.44	MURDER	FR.
BUCHMANN, Walter	167656	M	Ger.		Interpreter, Gestapo, Puivert (Fr.) 6.44	MURDER	FR.
BUCHMANN, Walter	256724	M	Ger.	06 - 10	Osturmfhr., SD, Foix (Fr.) 11.42	MURDER	FR.
BUCHMATTOSKI	179762	M			Major, 114. Jg.Div., Gubbio (It.) 6.44	MURDER	U.K.
BUCHMAYER, Walter	255500	M		4. 9.15	Sgt., Camp Ellrich, Nordhausen (Ger.)	MURDER	U.S.
BUCHMEIER, Arnold	172941	M	Ger.	05	Judge, Justiz-Ministerium,Public-Official, Leipzig (Ger.) 10.44	MURDER	U.S.
BUCHNER	254181	M	Ger.		Agent of Service, Gestapo, Offenburg (Ger.) 11.44	INTERR.	FR.
BUCHNER (or BUCHER)	255498	M			Lt., Camp Plaszow, Nordhausen (Ger.)	MURDER	U.S.
BUCHNER, Friedrich	188067	M			Pvt., 110.Pz.Gren.Rgt.and Coy., Albine (Fr.)	MURDER	FR.
BUCHNER, Margaret	160215	F	Ger.		Civilian, Ermsleben (Ger.)	WITNESS	U.S.
BUCHNER, Wilhelm	12587	M	Ger.		Pvt., 110.or 111.Pz.Gren.Rgt.,2.Coy., Albine (Fr.) 6.44	MURDER	FR.
BUCHOCLIK	174851	M	Ger.		Civilian, C.C., Nordhausen (Ger.) 43-44	TORTURE	U.S.
BUCHOLT	254480	M	Ger.		Capt., 392.Inf. Blue-Div., Lika (Yugo.) 44-45	INTERR.	YUGO.
BUCHOLTZ	195855	M			Asst., to Pils, Anrath-Krefeld (Ger.) 1.42-3.44	WITNESS	NETH.
BUCHOLZER, Josef	193376	M	Ger.		O.T.Master, Army, Organ.Todt, C.C., Moersry (Nor.) 44	MURDER	NOR.
BUCHOWSKY	132600	M	Ger.		Kapo, C.C., Buchenwald (Ger.)	MURDER	FR.
BUCHROITHNER, Josef	254290	M		21. 1.03	Civilian, Besiny (Czech.) 5.42	INTERR.	CZECH.
BUCHS	143318	M			Engineer, Army, Rochefort (Fr.) 6.45-9.45	MURDER	FR.
BUCHSBAUM, Hans	187510	M	Ger.	1. 7.07	Crim.Secr., Gestapo and SD, Brno (Czech.) 39-45	MURDER	CZECH.
BUCHSEIN (see BUCHHEIM)	186557						
BUCHSENSCHUTZ, Friedrich	255494	M			Pvt., Camp Osterode, Nordhausen (Ger.)	MURDER	U.S.
BUCHTA, Eugen	254273	M	Ger.	8. 8.87	Civilian, Barrister, Bruenn (Czech.) 39-45	MISC.CRIMES	CZECH.
BUCHTALA (see BOGDALA)	9635						
BUCHTALA	124515	M	Ger.		Hptscharfhr., SS, C.C., Oranienburg and Sachsenhausen (Ger.) 42	MURDER	U.K.
BUCHWALD	173968	M			SS-Mann, C.C., Muhldorf-Ampfing (Ger.) 6.44-4.45	MURDER	U.S.
BUCHWALD (see BUCKWALD)	255258						
BUCHWALD	255501	M			Pvt., Camp Dora, Nordhausen (Ger.)	MURDER	U.S.
BUCHWALD, Siegfried	306351	M	Ger.		Uschfhr., SS, C.C., Buchenwald (Ger.) 5.38-10.43	MURDER	BEL.
BUCK	39568	M	Ger.		Sturmbannfhr., Director of Vulkanlager (Ger.) 44-45	MURDER	SOV.UN., U.S.
BUCK	141930	M	Ger.		Sgt., 921.Gren.Bde., GSGS 4250-6 F -3- 34 1538 (Fr.) 7.44	WITNESS	U.S.
BUCK	173966	M	Ger.		Camp Chief, St.6 A, C.C., Hemers (Fr.) 41-42	MISC.CRIMES	U.S.
BUCK	178212	M			Oschfhr., SS, C.C., Schorzingen (Fr.)	MISC.CRIMES	FR.
BUCK	259617	M	Ger.		Lt., Unit F.P.No.07382, Villequiers Cher (Fr.) 7.40-6.41	INCENDIARISM	FR.
BUCK, Karl	146896	M			Hptsturmfhr., Agent, Gestapo, C.C., Struthof (Fr.)	MURDER	FR.
BUCK, Karl	173967	M	Ger.		Hptsturmfhr., SS, C.C., Gaggenau (Ger.) 11.44	MURDER	U.S.
BUCK, Karl	174464	M	Ger.		Guard, C.C., Schirmeck (Fr.)	MURDER	FR.
BUCK, Rudi	142	M	Ger.		N.C.O., Army, Paratroop-Coy., Saint Segal (Fr.) 7.44	MURDER	FR.
BUCKALLER	1311	M	Ger.		Pvt., 305.Div., 578.Gr., 3.Pl., 5.Coy.	MISC.CRIMES	U.K.
BUCKER	195853	M	Ger.		Employee, C.C., Struthof-Natzweiler, Bas-Rhin (Fr.) 40-44	TORTURE	FR.
BUCKERT	258908	M	Ger.		Inspector, Aktions-Kommando of Custom-house, Lourdes (Fr.) 1.44-8.44	MURDER	FR.
BUCKHART	160220	M	Ger.		Gefaengnis-Dir., C.C., Ensisheim (Fr.)	MURDER	FR.
BUCKMANN	141462	M	Ger.		Lt., Oflag 83, C.C., Wetzendorf (Ger.)	MURDER	FR.

BUC -BUE

NAME	C.R.FILE NUMBER	SEX	NATIO-NALITY	DATE OF BIRTH	RANK OCCUPATION UNIT PLACE AND DATE OF CRIME	REASON WANTED	WANTED BY
BUCKO, Heinrich (Alias BAUER, Heinz)	260495	M	Ger.	29. 5.12	SS-Oberscharfhr.,Waffen-SS,Guard,C.C.Auschwitz (Pol.) 40-41	BRUTALITY	POL.
BUCKMANN, Willy	192054	M	Ger.		Cpl.,820 Marine Artill.Rgt.,La Baule,St.Nazaire,Chantiers-de-Penhoet (Fr.) 41-44	MURDER	FR.
BUCKNER	169466	M	Ger.	09	Pvt.,Army,4 Coy,62' L S Bn.,Stalag IX C,Ilmenau (Ger.) 43	TORTURE	U.K.
BUCKSER	128614	M		17	SS-Oscharfr.,C. Mauthausen (Aust.) 41-45	MURDER	U.S.
BUCKWALD (or BUCHWALD)	255258	M			Sgt.,C.C.Buchenwald (Ger.)	MURDER	U.S.
BUDAU	305832	M	Ger.		Pvt.,1 Aufkl.Abt. 3 Coy. 2 Col. XV Div. Afrika Korps,St.Leger Arlon,5.9.44	MISC.CRIMES	BEL.
BUDDE	160195	M	Ger.	97	Sturmbannfhr.,Army,Hitler Army HQ's., Ohrdruf (Ger.)	TORTURE	U.S.
BUDDE	255257	M			Cpl.,Unterscharfhr.,C.C.Buchenwald (Ger.)	MURDER	U.S.
BUDILE	192583	M	Ger.		Unterscharfhr.,C.C.Buchenwald (Ger.) 42-45	MISC.CRIMES	U.S.
BUDE, Paul	134754	M			Pvt., 4 SS-Totenkopfsturmbann,Dora Mittelbau, Nordhausen (Ger.) 43-45	WITNESS	U.S.
BUDEFELDT	173342	M	Ger.		Central Abt.Cultur,Maribor (Yugo.) 4.41-44	MURDER	YUGO.
BUDENA	256738	M	Ger.		SS-Cpl., command Staff Harzungen,Nordhausen (Ger.)	MURDER	U.S.
BUDENSTEIN, Richard	132818	M	Ger.		Sgt.,Army,Brackel-Lueneburg (Ger.) 21.1.45	WITNESS	U.S.
BUDER, Hermann	194722	M	Ger.		Guard,334 Ld.-Schtz.-Bn.,Stalag III A.Cdo 726 C,Ebensdorf(Ger.)9.45	MURDER	FR.
BUDIG, Max	185837	M	Ger.	92	Leading Member,NSDAP,Prag (Czech.)	MISC.CRIMES	CZECH.
BUDIN, Paul	260207	M	Ger.	4.12.92	Ch.Vorstand,Hugo Schneider AG,Mem.Ar.,Allgemeine Creditanstalt Leipzig (Ger.)	MISC.CRIMES	U.S.
BUDINA	255492	M			Pvt.,C.C.Harzungen,Nordhausen (Ger.)	MURDER	U.S.
BUDNICK	160194	M	Ger.	93	Sturmbannfhr.,Army,Hitler Army HQ's., Army Gen.HQ., Ohrdruf (Ger.)	TORTURE	U.S.
BUDNIK, Walter	261991	M	Ger.	11. 5.10	SS-Mann,Waffen-SS,Gren.Div. 36,Dirlewanger Brig.,Warschau and other, (Pol.) 40-44	MURDER	POL.
BUDSCH, Karl	306415	M	Ger.		Employee,Firma Schaler & Sohn,Erbach near Amberg (Ger.) 45	MURDER	CZECH.
BUDZAN	192584	M	Ger.		Pvt.,Billeting Dept.,Buchenwald (Ger.) 42-45	TORTURE	U.S.
BUECHELE	257893	M			Sgt.,150 Pz.Bde., Operation Grief, 44	MISC.CRIMES	U.S.
BUECHES, Emil	254291	M	Ger.	82	Obersturmbannfhr., Waffen-SS, Javoricko (Czech.) 45	MURDER	CZECH.
BUEGHS, Gerhardt	261136	M			Major,Army,	WITNESS	U.S.
BUECHER	134766	M	Ger.		Lt.,SS-Fuehrungsstab,C.C.Dora Mittelbau,Nordhausen (Ger.) 43-45	WITNESS	U.S.
BUECHER, Arno	127334	M	Ger.		Obersturmfhr.,Lt.,SS-Totenkopf,C.C.Neuengamme (Ger.)	MURDER	U.S.
BUECHER, Hermann	62220	M	Ger.		Hauptamt,SS-Gericht,Obersturmbannfhr.,	TORTURE	UNWCC.
BUECHER, Hermann	187583	M	Ger.		General Inspector,President,Wasser und Energie,A.E.G.	TORTURE	UNWCC.
BUECHNER	135537	M	Ger.	11	Army,Stalag IX,C.C.Ilmenau (Ger.) 1.6.43	TORTURE	U.K.
BUECHNER, Fritz	255514	M	Ger.	7. 5.08	Crim.Secretary,Gestapo,Opava (Czech.) 40-45	MISC.CRIMES	CZECH.
BUECHSENSCHUTZ, Friedrich	134753	M			SS-Camp-Guard,4 SS Totenkopfsturmbann,Dora,Nordhausen (Ger.) 43-45	WITNESS	U.S.
BUECKENBRING	169499	M	Ger.	07	Pvt.,Guard,L-S Bn.383,Stalag IV D,C.C.Lauchhammer(Ger.) 44	MURDER	U.K.
BUECKER	254482	M	Ger.		Hauptsturmfhr.,C.C.Dachau (Ger.) 42	MURDER	YUGO.
BUEHLER see BUHL	146775	M					
BUEHLER	160206	M			Civilian,Werk Horde (Ger.) Doctor	TORTURE	U.S.
BUEHLER	173131	M	Ger.		Staff,C.C.Gaggenau,Schirmeck,Rotenfels (Ger.) (Fr.)	INTERR.	U.K.
BUEHLER, Max	258969	M	Ger.	11.12.11	Untersturmfhr.,SS,NSDAP,30.1.42	INTERR.	U.S.
BUEHLER, Robert	186528	M	Ger.		Civilian,Wolfsburg,Steinker-Berg (Ger.) 29.6.44	MURDER	U.S.
BUEHN, Edmund	193984	M	Ger.	13.12.06	SS-Pvt.,Zellenleiter,SS,NSDAP,Lostice (Czech.) 38-45	MISC.CRIMES	CZECH.
BUEHNING, August,Friedrich	301392	M	Ger.		Painter and Glazier,Bohmte (Ger.) 28.2.45	MURDER	U.K.
BUEHNING, Friedrich	301394	M	Ger.		Ortsgruppenleiter,NSDAP,Bohmte (Ger.) 28.2.45	MURDER	U.K.
BUEHRMANN	167666	M	Ger.		Leader,Army,Brig.General,Beauftragter fuer den Vierjahresplan, Cracow (Pol.) 39-44	MISC.CRIMES	POL.
BUEKA (or BYKER)	120609	M	Ger.	00 - 05	Pvt.,718 Landesschuetzen Bn.,Stalag II A,Gross-Schierstedt,Aschersleben (Ger.) 44-45	TORTURE	U.K.
BUELTE	160207	M			Untersturmfhr.,2 SS-Pz.Div. "Das Reich",1 Reace Bn.,Tulle (Fr.)5.44	MURDER	U.S.
BUENEMANN	256829	M			Employee,Mittelwork GMBH,Nordhausen (Ger.)	MURDER	U.S.
BUENGELER, Heinz	160193	M	Ger.	14	SS-Hauptsturmfhr.,Waffen-SS,Staff,C.C.Buchenwald (Ger.) 40-41	MURDER	U.S.
BUENGER	192479	M	Ger.	05	Guard,Strafgefangenenlager Nord,Finnmark (Nor.) 42-45	MISC.CRIMES	YUGO.,NOR.
BUENING	148461	M	Ger.		Doctor,,Inspector,Public Official,Arbeits Ministerium	MURDER	UNWCC.
BUENING	254490	M	Ger.		Unterscharfhr.,C.C.Neuengamme (Ger.) 40	INTERR.	BEL.
BUENNING	193587	M		15	Major,12 Coy.,3 Bn.,10 SS Div "Frundsberg" 3 Bttn.,Caen (Fr.) 7.44	MURDER	U.S.
BUERA, Herta	139106	F	Ger.		SS-Guard,Gem.Prison Camps,Volary (Czech.) 41-45	MURDER	U.S.
BUERCKEL, Josef	11186	M		30. 3.95	Gauleiter,SS-Obergruppenfhr.,NSDAP,SS,Saarbruecken,Neustadt a.d.W. Lorraine (Fr.) 40-44	MISC.CRIMES	UNWCC.
BUERCKLE	173965	M	Ger.	85	Oberlandesgerichts-President,Administration of Boheme and Moravie,Prague (Czech)	MURDER	CZECH.
BUEREL	192586	M	Ger.		Obersturmfhr.,Waffen-SS-SS-Totenkopfsturmbann,Buchenwald (Ger.)42-45	TORTURE	U.S.
BUERGENGRUBER	257338	M	Ger.		SS-Oberwachtmeister,SS-Slave Labour Camp,Beisfjord near Narvik (Nor.) 6.11.42	BRUTALITY	YUGO.
BUERGER, Heinrich	160211	M	Ger.		Abwehrbeauftragter,Eckardtwerke,Gestapo,Fuerth,Roethenbach (Ger.)	TORTURE	U.S.
BUERTEL, Hans	254498	M	Ger.		Factory "Deutsche Werke",Spaichingen-Tuttlingen (Ger.)	TORTURE	FR.
BUESCHENEDER	189310	M		21	SS-Guard,C.C.Mauthausen (Aust.)	MURDER	U.S.
BUESCHER	301058	M	Ger.		SS-Obersturmfhr.,first deputy to the Campleader,C.C.Hamburg-Neuengamme (Ger.) 45	MURDER	CZECH.
BUESS, Ralph (or BUSE)	192203	M	Ger.		Lt.,Army,Saffre (Fr.) 6.44	MURDER	FR.
BUESING	139835	M		27	Member,R.A.D.,Rosche (Ger.) 18.3.45	WITNESS	U.S.
BUETEFUER	160224	M	Ger.		Lt.,Army,Anti Aircraft, near Weseke (Ger.)	MURDER	U.K.
BUETGEN	149737	M	Ger.	27	Agent,Gestapo,Mauthausen (Aust.) 41-45	MURDER	U.S.
BUETGENBACH, Hans	257752	M	Ger.	13.10.18	Employee,C.C.Nordhausen (Ger.)	MURDER	U.S.
BUETH	108424	M	Ger.	07	Crim.Commissar,Stapostelle,Frankfurt-Main (Ger.) 5.43	TORTURE	U.K.
BUTNER	10061	M			Stabsintendant,Oberzahlmeister,Army Hesepe (Ger.) 24.3.45	MURDER	U.K.
BUETTNER	153971	M	Ger.		Hauptsturmfhr.,SS,C.C.Sachsenhausen (Ger.)	TORTURE	UNWCC.
BUETTNER	254268	M	Ger.		Army, 13 SS Pol.Rgt.,Ferlach (Aust.) 44-45	MURDER	YUGO.
BUETTNER	257750	M			Employee,Askaniestelle 12,C.C.Nordhausen (Ger.)	MURDER	U.S.
BUETTNER, Karl	260979	M			SS-Oberscharfhr.,SS,C.C.Vaihingen a.d.Enz,(Ger.) 44-45	MURDER	U.S.

BUE-BUN

NAME	C.R.FILE NUMBER	SEX	NATIO-NALITY	DATE OF BIRTH	RANK OCCUPATION UNIT PLACE AND DATE OF CRIME	REASON WANTED	WANTED BY
BUETTNER, Rudolf	261987	M	Ger.	25. 9.13	SS-Mann, Waffen SS Gren.Div.36,Dirlewanger-Bde.,Warschau and other (Pol.) 40-44	MURDER	POL.
BUFF	193375	M	Ger.		Baurat, Airforce C.C. Uthaug, Orlander (Nor.) 9.41-42	WITNESS	NOR.
BUFCJAGER, Georges	125622	M	Ger.		Gendarmerie, Bourg-Lastic (Fr.) 7.44	MURDER	FR.
BUGAR, Alexander	134764	M			Member, 4.SS-Totenkopf-Stuba C.C. Dora-Nordhausen (Ger.) 43-45	WITNESS	U.S.
BUGATTI, Giovanni	48622	M	Ger.	16	Lt., 12.Coy. 29.Gren.Rgt., Communanza (It.)	WITNESS	U.K.
BUGDALA see BOGDALA	9635						
BUGDALA	127335	M			Hangman and Executioner C.C. Sachsenhausen (Ger.)	MURDER	U.S.
BUGDALLA	160204	M	Ger.	about 11	Oscharfhr., SS, C.C. Sachsenhausen, Oranienburg (Ger.)	TORTURE	U.K.
BUGDAILA	195334	M	Ger.	12	Scharfhr. (Rapportfuehrer) SS, C.C. Sachsenhausen,Oranienburg (Ger.)	MISC.CRIMES	U.K.
BUGDALLE	195891	M	Ger.		Blockfuehrer, SS, Neuengamme (Ger.) 40-44	MURDER	BEL.
BUGGE	160225	M	Ger.	08	Pvt., 610.Landesschuetzen-Bn.,Stalag XX B, Schonweise (Ger.) 4.42	MURDER	U.K.
BUGGE	192148	M	Ger.	11	Member, Geh.Feldpolizei, Brussels (Bel.)	TORTURE	BEL.
BUGGE, Wilhelm	255495	M		23. 1.11	Sgt., Camp Ellrich, Nordhausen (Ger.)	MURDER	U.S.
BUGHARD	72696	M			Lt., Airforce 12.Nachtjagdcorps 205.Nachr.Rgt., 5.or 6.44	MISC.CRIMES	U.S.
BUH	131198	M	Ger.		Osturmfhr. SS	MURDER	BEL.
BUHL or BUHLER	146775	M			Chief, S.D., St.Etienne (Fr.)	INTERR.	FR.
BUHL see BOUL	172878						
BUHL	188423	M	Ger.	05	Camp-official, Stalag 344, C.C. Sosnowitz (Pol.) 42-45	TORTURE	U.K.
BUHL	306144	M	Ger.		Pvt., Guard, C.C. B.E.12, Stalag IV D, Bitterfeld, Samwitz (Ger.) 2., 3., 4.45	MURDER	U.K.
BUHL, Erich	306143	M	Ger.	05	Civ. Supervisor, Graf Rennard Colliery (Kommando E.538 Att.Stalag VIII B), Sosnowitz (Pol.) 42-44	BRUTALITY	U.K.
BUHLE, Walter	260693	M			Lt.Gen., Army	WITNESS	U.S.
BUHLER	12588	M	Ger.		SIPO, S.D., Clermont-Ferrand (Fr.) 11.43, 8.44	TORTURE	FR.
BUHLER	146775	M	Ger.	10	Uscharfhr., S.D., Vichy (Fr.)	INTERR.	FR.
BUHLER	196450	M	Ger.		W.O., Army, Geb.Jaeg. 157.Div., Plateau Glieres (Fr.) 3.-4.44	TORTURE	FR.
BUHLER, Emil	172942	M	Ger.	24. 9.05	Pvt., Stg. Luft I, C.C. Barth (Ger.) 3.45	MURDER	U.S.
BUHLER, Hermann	41137	M	Ger.	10	Uscharfhr., S.D. Vichy, Member d.Abt. 4 a,Bourg-Lastic, Clermont-Ferrand (Fr.) 12.43, 7.44	MURDER	FR.
BUHLER, Hermann	148505	M		about 03	Agent, Gestapo, Clermont-Ferrand (Fr.)	TORTURE	FR.
BUHLER, Hermann	189969	M	Ger.		SS-Uscharfhr., Gestapo, Bourg-Last.,Vichy (Fr.) 7.44	MURDER	FR.
BUHLER, Otto Gustav	192271	M	Ger.		C.C. Flossenburg (Ger.) 44-45	MURDER	U.S.
BUHLMANN	136190	M	Ger.		Lt., Army, 28.Infanterie-Rgt. 116.Bn. 4.Coy., Aspin (Fr.) 7.44	MURDER	FR.
BUHLMANN see BULLMANN	193586						
BUHNE, Heimkn.	160217	M		05	Oscharfhr., SS, employed at camp Duesseldorf (Ger.) 1.45	TORTURE	U.S.
BUHNER	148484	M			Uscharfhr. (Sgt.) SS, C.C. Mauthausen (Aust.) 41-45	TORTURE	U.S.
BUHNER	185645	M	Ger.		Uscharfhr., SS, C.C. Mauthausen (Aust.)	MURDER	FR.
BUHNER	185646	M	Ger.		SS Osturmfhr., C.C. Ebensee, Mauthausen (Aust.) 5.44	TORTURE	FR.
BUHNER, Hans	141373	M	Ger.		SS Uscharfhr., C.C. Mauthausen (Aust.)	MURDER	FR.
BUHR	195852	M	Ger.		Civ. C.C. Struthof-Natzweiler (Fr.) 40-44	MISC.CRIMES	FR.
BUHR	301059	M	Ger.		Oscharfhr., Chief of the work parties, C.C.Oranienburg (Ger.) 39-45	MURDER	CZECH.
BUHRDORF	195201	M	Ger.	9.10.08	Kriminal-Assistent, Gestapo, Bruessel (Bel.) 9.40-autumn 42	MISC.CRIMES	BEL.
BUERING	130991	M	Ger.	09	Oscharfhr., SS, C.C. Dora-Mittelbau, Nordhausen (Ger.)	MURDER	U.S.
BUHRMANN, Heini	222612	M	Ger.	06	Usturmfhr., S.D., Paris (Fr.) 44	MURDER	U.S.
BUERMANN, Otto	193983	M	Ger.		SS Sturmbannfhr., Krim.Director, S.D. Gestapo, Prag (Czech.)	MURDER	CZECH.
BUHRMEISTER	130075	M	Ger.		Pvt., Stalag VI G, Berg Neustadt, 2.45	TORTURE	U.K.
BUHRMEISTER	193582	M		15	Pvt., Interpreter at Stalag VI G, Duisdorf (Ger.) 2.45	TORTURE	U.S.
BUHSE	254182	M			Capt., Navy, Lille, Bonne (Fr.) 2.43	INTERR.	FR.
BUICKERT see BEICKERT	124957						
BUICKERT	148495	M		about 05	South-west France, Dr., Dr.	MURDER	FR.
BUJACK, Guenther	255496	M			Pvt., Camp Ellrich, Nordhausen (Ger.)	MURDER	U.S.
BUJNOCH, Leo	9640	M	Ger.		Dr., Public prosecutor, County court, Opava (Czech.) 40	MURDER	CZECH.
BUJNOCH, Rudolf	31984	M	Ger.		Dr., Landgerichtsrat, Public official, Brno (Czech.) 40	MURDER	CZECH.
BUKALL	261779	M	Ger.		Cpl., Geldgendarmerie, Romilly sur Seine (Fr.) 6.44	MISC.CRIMES	FR.
BUKARZ, Josef	255487	M		1. 8.11	Pvt., Camp Ellrich Nordhausen (Ger.)	MURDER	U.S.
BUKAS	301300	M	Ger.		Member Gestapo at Nove Mesto n.Vahom, C.C. Oswiecim-Birkenau (Pol.) 39-45	MURDER	CZECH.
BUKOWSKI	134767	M			Pvt.,Guard, 4.SS-Totenkopf-Stuba C.C.Dora-Mittelbau Nordhausen (Ger.)	WITNESS	U.S.
BUKOWSKY	148494	M			Civ. C.C. Buchenwald (Ger.) 44-45	MURDER	FR.
BULACH, Hans or BULLACH	162303	M	Ger.	20	SS Scharfhr., Interpreter, Gestapo Abt. IV, Brussels (Bel.)	WITNESS	BEL.
BULAJ see BULEN, Erich	254486						
BULAU	199828	M	Ger.		Capt.,Stalag X B, Sandbostel (Ger.) 5.45	MISC.CRIMES	U.S.
BULAUT	173964	M			Oscharfhr., SS, C.C. Muehldorf-Ampfing (Ger.) 6.44-4.45	MURDER	U.S.
BULEN, Erich aliases BULAJ	254486	M			Geh. Feldpolizei, Kragujevac (Yugo.) 10.41	BRUTALITY	YUGO.
BULGUS, Hans	192483	M	Ger.	07	Ex-convict, Reichministry of justice, Strafgefangenenlager Nord, Finnmark (Nor.) 42-45	WITNESS	NOR.
BULHAU	186530	M	Ger.		Blockfuehrer, SS, C.C. Dora-Mittelbau Nordhausen (Ger.)	MURDER	BEL.
BULL, Walter	1912	M	Ger.		Feldwebel, Army, 194. GR. 1.Coy.	MISC.CRIMES	U.K.
BULLACH, Hans see BULACH	162303						
BULLER	256799	M	Ger.		Lt., Formation Bode, St.Pierre (Fr.) 7.44	MURDER	FR.
BULLET, Joseph	160213	M			Ortsgruppenfuehrer NSDAP, Bickendorf (Ger.) 9.44	MURDER	U.S.
BULLIN nee Hoffmann, Paula	187512	F	Ger.	22. 5.02	Employee, Gestapo and S.D., Brno (Czech.) 39-45	WITNESS	CZECH.
BULLING	254279	M	Ger.	05	Lt., Ger.Pol.15.Pol.Rgt. H.Q. at Vercelli under Col.Buch,Cesentino (It.) 9.44	INTERR.	U.K.
BULLINGER, Max	121115	M	Ger.	21. 4.11	Civ., District-leader Gadjatsch and Uman, Kiew (Ukr.)	MURDER	U.S.
BULLMANN or BUHLMANN	193586	M	Ger.	00	SS Oscharfhr., Waffen SS, Staff-Coy.,Wallrabenstein (Ger.) 3.45	MURDER	U.S.
BULLOCH	173225	M	Ger.	88	Overseer, Scholse Cellulose Factory, Gestapo, Maltsch-Oder (Ger.)9.44	TORTURE	U.K.
BULSKI, Maryszo	254184	M			Civ., Fuerth (Ger.) 4.45	MURDER	U.S.
BULSKI, Tadeusz	254185	M			Civ., Fuerth (Ger.) 4.45	MURDER	U.S.
BUMBERGER, Josef	255488	M		9. 3.18	Pvt., Camp Nordhausen (Ger.)	MURDER	U.S.
BUMETTERT	195851	M	Ger.		Sgt., C.C. Struthof-Natzweiler (Fr.) 40-44	TORTURE	FR.
BUMKE, Oswald	178216	M	Ger.		Professor, Director, Public Health official for hospital, Muenchen-Ger.	TORTURE	FR.
BUNACHER	160196	M	Ger.		Lt., I 4653 A, Entrevaux (Fr.) 7.44	MURDER	FR.
BUNEK, Josef	255489	M		13. 7.02	Pvt., Camp Harzungen, Nordhausen (Ger.)	MURDER	U.S.
BUNGE, Klaus	160191	M	Ger.		Scharfhr., SS, C.C. Reichenau (Aust.) 44	MURDER	U.S.

- 53 -

BUN - BUR

NAME	C.R.FILE NUMBER	SEX	NATIO-NALITY	DATE OF BIRTH	RANK OCCUPATION UNIT PLACE AND DATE OF CRIME	REASON WANTED	WANTED BY
BUNGE, Robert	132172	M	Ger.		Sgt., Army 310, Landesschuetzen-Bn.,4 Coy.,Dueren-Rolsdorf (Ger.) 44	WITNESS	U.K.-U.S.
BUNGE, Willi	185247	M	Ger.	05	Obersturmfhr.,Crim.Secr.,S.D. and Gestapo,Prag (Czech.)	MURDER	CZECH.
BUNGERT, Friedrich	261990	M	Ger.	14. 4.08	SS-Mann,Waffen-SS,Gren.Div.36,Dirlewanger-Bde.,Warschau and other (Pol.) 40-44	MURDER	POL.
BUNKE, Erich	301077	M	Ger.		Crim.Rat,Hauptsturmfhr.,SS,Chief of R.S.D.,Leiter der Hilfspolizei, Copenhagen,Shellhuset (Den.) 8.44	MURDER	DEN.
BUNNER	255365	M			Cpl.,C.C.Mauthausen (Aust.)	INTERR.	FR.
BUNNIG	190486	M			Civilian,Bohmte (Ger.) 2.45	MURDER	U.S.
BUNZ, Heinrich	121117	M			Pvt.,34 Fortress Maschine Gun.Bn.,Aachen (Ger.) 9.44	MURDER	U.S.
BURAK	195823	M			Rottfhr.,Blockfhr.,C.C.Auschwitz (Pol.) 40	MURDER	FR.
BURANT	148517	M			Civilian,Nimes (Fr.) 7.44	MURDER	FR.
BURBA, Heinrich	196178	M			Polizei-Waffenschule 3, 4 Coy.,Arnhem (Neth.) 3.45	MURDER	NETH.
BURBECK	187844	M			Hptsturmfhr.,SS,C.C.Buchenwald (Ger.)	MURDER	BEL.
BURCHAARDT, Forster (or BURCHARDT)	148502	M	Ger.		Kapo,C.C.Floha,Flossenburg (Ger.) 44	MURDER	FR.
BURCHINSKI, Albert	192476	M	Ger.		Pvt.,Kgf.Arb.Bn.190,Sundbi (Nor.) 10.44	MURDER	NOR.
BURCKART (or BURKART)	148521	M			Capt.,19 Sich.Regt.192, Chappes (Fr.) 7.-8.44	MURDER	FR.
BURCKEL	168583	M	Ger.		Civ.,Administrator,Chief,Loraine (Fr.) 40-45	TORTURE	U.S.
BURCKHARDT	195850	M	Ger.		Uschfhr.,C.C.Struthof,Natzweiler (Fr.) 40-44	MISC.CRIMES	FR.
BURCKHARDT, Erwin	132609	M		97	Schfhr.,SS,C.C.Schirmeck (Fr.)	MURDER	FR.
BURCKSTALLER	255490	M	Ger.		Flyer,C.C.Ellrich,Nordhausen (Ger.)	MURDER	U.S.
BURD	254286	M			Foreman,State farm Golsdorf,Kdo.508,Stalag III B,Golsdorf(Ger.)42-44	BRUTALITY	FR.
BURDA, Alfred	258340	M		2.12.04	Guard,Prison,State Service,Gestapo,Pilsen (Czech.)40-42	TORTURE	CZECH.
BURES, Karl	187513	M		31. 5.91	Employee,Gestapo and S.D.,Bruenn (Czech.) 39-45	MURDER	CZECH.
BURFFEL, Walter	254183	M			Cpl.,11.Pz.Div.,Unit 36-185,Lautrec (Fr.) 8.44	MURDER	FR.
BURG	127336	M	Ger.		Hptsturmfhr.,SS-Totenkopf-Div.,Neuengamme (Ger.)	MURDER	U.S.
BURG, Johann	257382	M			Organisation Todt "Schutzkommando", Slave labour camps, Erlandet, Oeusand, Trola (Norway) 6.42-45	MURDER	YUGO.
BURGAARDT	167657	M			Lt.,2 SS-Div."Das Reich",1 Bn.,1 Coy.,Cradour-Glane (Fr.) 6.44	MURDER	FR.
BURGARDT	126958	M			Usturmfhr.,SS-Pz.Div."Das Reich" (Fr.) 44	MURDER	FR.
BURGARDT	149747	M			Usturmfhr.,SS-Regt.,1 Bn. (Fr.)	MURDER	FR.
BURGARDT, Otto	149748	M		18	Lt.,Armee,1 Coy.,2 Abt.,Condom (Fr.)	MURDER	FR.
BURGART, Johann	149749	M			Sturmfhr.,SS	TORTURE	FR.
BURGEL, Johann	133745	M			SS-Uschfhr.,C.C.Buchenwald (Ger.)	TORTURE	U.S.
BURGER	20167	M		89	Col.,Camp-Commandant,Stalag 7 A,Moosburg (Ger.) 8.44-4.45	TORTURE	U.S.
BURGER	135122	M	Ger.		Lt.,Pol.Gendarmerie,Kreis Gendarmerie Neustadt (Germany), Bad Neustadt (Ger.) 9.44	MURDER	U.S.
BURGER	173343	M	Ger.		Oberbaurat,Organisation Todt,Donja, Bela, Reka, District Bor-Serbia (Yugo.) 2.43	MURDER	YUGO.
BURGER	173351	M	Ger.		Sturmbannfhr.,SS,C.C.Oswiecim,Birkenau (Pol.) 39-45	MURDER	CZECH.
BURGER	178214	M			Oschfhr.,SS,C.C.Auschwitz (Pol.)	TORTURE	U.S.
BURGER	189585	M	Ger.		Sgt.,Feldgendarmerie,Meuring (Fr.) 4.44	MURDER	FR.
BURGER	190677	M	Ger.		N.C.O.,Eis.Art.Bn.717,St.Andries,Varsenare, les Bruges (Bel.) 9.44	MURDER	BEL.
BURGER	196449	M	Ger.		Sgt.,Geb.Jaeger,157 Div.,Plateau des Glieres (Fr.) 3.-4.44	MISC.CRIMES	FR.
BURGER	253590	M	Ger.		Sturmbannfhr.,Hptsturmfhr.,SS,Staff of Garrison,C.C.Auschwitz, Birkenau (Pol.) 7.42	INTERR.	YUGO.
BURGER	255077	M	Ger.		S.T.Mann,S.D.,Toulouse (Fr.)8.-11.42	MISC.CRIMES	FR.
BURGER	256842	M	Ger.		Osturmfhr.,C.C.Radom (Pol.)	MURDER	POL.
BURGER	301632	M	Ger.		Hptwachtmeister,Ebrach near Amberg (Ger.) 45	MURDER	CZECH.
BURGER	305544	M	Ger.		Cpl.,Guard from Stalag VIII A,Muhlhausen,Frankfurt a.M.(Ger.)1.-3.45	MURDER	U.K.
BURGER, Alexander	134755	M			4 SS-Totenkopf-Sturmbann Dora,Mittelbau Nordhausen,Thuer. (Ger.)43-45	WITNESS	U.S.
BURGER, Anton	193997	M	Ger.	19.11.11	SS-Osturmfhr.,S.D.,R.S.H.A.,C.C.Terezin (Czech.) 39-45	TORTURE	CZECH.
BURGER, Franz	135131	M		90	Civ.,Camp Lintfort (Ger.) 10.-11.44	WITNESS	U.S.
BURGER, Gunther	9641	M	Ger.		SA-Sturmfhr.,SS,Official in the Judenfrage,Prague (Czech.) 44	MURDER	CZECH.
BURGER, Josef	255491	M		04	Flyer,Camp Ellrich,Nordhausen (Ger.)	MURDER	U.S.
BURGER, Marian	185228	M	Ger.	24. 8.04	Member,Gestapo and S.D.,Benesov (Czech.) 39-45	MURDER	CZECH.
BURGER (or BERGER), Otto	131950	M	Ger.	20.10.88	Col., Army,Stalag 7 A,Gren.Regt.63,C.C.Moosberg,Muenchen(Ger)44-45	TORTURE	U.S.
BURGER, Otto	160205	M	Ger.		Usturmfhr.,SS,C.C.Buchenwald,Dachau (Ger.)	MURDER	U.S.
BURGER, Philip	135122	M			Lt.,Gendarmerie,Bad Neustadt (Ger.) 9.44	MURDER	U.S.
BURGER, Rudolf	257774	M		22. 8.12	SS-Anw.,State Service,Prague (Czech.) 39-45	MURDER	CZECH.
BURGER, Wilhelm	258562	M		04	Sturmbannfhr.,SS,W.V.H.A. (Ger.) 40-45	BRUTALITY	U.S.
BURGER, Willy	159413	M		98	Major,SS,Wirtschafts-Verwaltungs-Hauptamt,Amtsgruppe D,Buchenwald (Ger.) 42-43	WITNESS	U.S.
BURGERMEISTER	259314	M			Agent,Active Member,Gestapo, Antenne of Rochelle,Area Poitiers(Fr)40-45	MISC.CRIMES	FR.
BURGERMEISTER	307063	M	Ger.		Serving in Subsection of Gestapo,la Rochelle,Charente(Fr.)40-45	MURDER	FR.
BURGERMEISTER, Stefan	255086	M	Ger.	19. 3.95	Schuetze,Waffen-SS,Nordhausen (Ger.)	MURDER	U.S.
BURGGRAF	132569	M			Lt.,Army,Barjec (Fr.) 8.44	MURDER	FR.
BURGGRAF	192587	M			Hptschfhr.,SS Staff,Medical-Ward,Buchenwald (Ger.)	MURDER	U.S.
BURGGRAF, Edgar	159412	M		15	Uschfhr.,SS,C.C.Buchenwald (Ger.)	WITNESS	U.S.
BURGHARD, Heinz	186543	M		19	Lt.,Signal-Corps,205 Signal-Regt.,12 Nachtjagd-Corps,Darmstadt(Ger)44	TORTURE	U.S.
BURGHARDT	254488	M			Pvt.,Camp Mackenrode,Nordhausen (Ger.)	MURDER	U.S.
BURGIN, Jakob	300202	M	Ger.		Civ.,Buchenfeld,Pforzheim (Ger.) 2.45	MISC.CRIMES	U.K.
BURGL, Johann	162304	M	Ger.	95	Cpl.,Waffen-SS,C.C.Buchenwald (Ger.) 44-45	TORTURE	U.S.
BURGMANN	266632	M	Ger.		Capt.,Abwehr,Oflag II D,Gross-Born (Ger.) 2.42	MURDER	FR.
BURGRAFF	194116	M	Ger.	04	Major,19 Legion,Chambrai,Chanac (Fr.) 40-41,8.44	PILLAGE	FR.
BURGWINKEL, Peter	254499	M	Ger.	15. 4.88	C.C.Mauthausen (Austr.)	BRUTALITY	FR.
BURIAN, Franz	254272	M		14. 7.96	Blockleiter,NSDAP,State Service,Blatna (Czech.) 39-45	MISC.CRIMES	CZECH.
BURIAN, Rudolf	193561	M		19.12.11	Sgt.,SS-Police guard,C.C. Terezin (Czech.) 40-45	MURDER	CZECH.
BURING	130102	M			Uschfhr.,SS,C.C.Dore Mittelbau,Nordhausen(Ger.)	MURDER	U.S.
BURK	149751	M			Lt.,Army,Pz.Aufkl.-Abtlg.,II,Albins (Fr.) 8.44	LOOTING	FR.
BURKART	189584	M			Capt.,Sicherungs-Regt.192,Region de la Foret de Yaix(Fr.) 7.44	MURDER	FR.
BURKART (see BURCKART)	148521						
BURKART, Odilo	261835	M	Ger.	29. 8.99	Civ.,Firm,steel companies by Friedrich Flick,Mitteldeutsche Stahl-werke (Ger.-Fr.-Russ.)	MISC.CRIMES	U.S.

BUR - BUS

NAME	C.R.FILE NUMBER	SEX	NATIO-NALITY	DATE OF BIRTH	RANK OCCUPATION UNIT PLACE AND DATE OF CRIME	REASON WANTED	WANTED BY
BURKER	121118	M	Ger.		Civilian, CC, Stammlager XII A, Limburg (Ger.)	MURDER	U.S.
BURKERT, Heinz	185233	M	Ger.		SS Oschfhr, Gestapo, Praha (Czech.)	MURDER	CZECH.
BURKHARDT	147	M	Ger.		Dr., Public Official, Regierungspraesident, Inowroclaw (Pol.)9.39-1.42	MURDER	POL.
BURKHARDT	149752	M			Dr., Kriegsgerichtsrat, Epinal (Fr.)	MURDER	FR.
BURKHARDT	259680	M	Ger.	07	Rottfhr, Gestapo, area of Angers, Maine and Loire (Fr.) 42-44	MISC.CRIMES	FR.
BURKHARDT, Erwin	166917	M		97	SS Oschfhr, CC Schirmeck (Fr.)	MURDER	FR.
BURKHARDT, Henri Willy	259493	M		13. 4.04	Police Asst, Gestapo Strasbourg, Wolfisheim (Fr.) 8.44	MURDER	U.S.
BURKHARDT, Jakob	254481	M		1.10.99	Cpl., Camp Ellrich, Nordhausen (Ger.)	MURDER	U.S.
BURKHARDT, Karl	135139	M	Ger.	17. 7.00	Osturmfhr, SS-Mann, Bruttig (Ger.), Party No.44728, SS Nr.52909	TORTURE	U.S.
BURKHARDT, Karl	163637	M	Ger.		Sturmfhr.Totenkopf-Standarte, W-SS, CC Buchenwald, Weimar (Ger.)	MISC.CRIMES	FR.
BURKHARST	149753	M			Hptsturmfhr., Gestapo, Paris (Fr.)	WITNESS	BEL.
BURKHAUS	162305	M	Ger.		Sturmfhr, SS, Falignoul (Bel.)	MISC.CRIMES	FR.
BURKLE, Walter	254274	M	Ger.	96	Former, Guard, P.W.C. Oberndorf (Ger.)	TORTURE	U.K.
BURKOFF	36655	M	Ger.		Major, Stalag VIII B, Lamsdorf (Ger.) 10.42-7.43	MISC.CRIMES	FR.
BURLACH, Ewald	149754	M			Agent, Gestapo, Chambery (Fr.)	INTERR.	YUGO.
BURLEIN	254487	M	Ger.		Member of Abwehr, Oflag XIII-B, Nuernberg (Ger.) 41-45	TORTURE	U.N.W.C.C.
BURMEISTER	62224	M	Ger.		SS Oberbannfhr, High Official of Hauptamt SS	MISC.CRIMES	U.S.
BURMEISTER	72249	M			Pvt., Sonderfhr, Army, Interpreter Coy, Flamersheim (Ger.) 2.45	MISC.CRIMES	U.S.
BURMEISTER	199830	M	Ger.		Officer, Stalag X-B, Sandbostel (Ger.) 1.-5.45	LOOTING	FR.
BURMEISTER	149356	M			Civilian, Pontoise (Fr.)	MURDER	U.N.W.C.C.
BURMEISTER	187585	M			SS Obersturmbannfhr, SS Hauptamt Gericht	TORTURE	
BURMOSTER, Joseph (alias BAUMEISTER)	219914	M	Ger.	13	Official, Gestapo, Sect.IV, Bensheim and Muenchen (Ger.) 44	WITNESS	U.S.
BURTEL, Heinrich	135117	M	Ger.	93	Civilian, Camp Lintforst (Ger.)	MURDER	FR.
BURTELL	300990	M	Ger.		Member of Staff, CC Struthof-Natzweiler (Fr.) 42-44	TORTURE	FR.
BURTSCHKIR, Felix	178215	M		.04	SS Gestapo, Eisengiesserei, Danzig	WITNESS	U.S.
BURY, Ruediger	190421	M			Civilian, Gaienhofen and Oehningen (Ger.) 7.44	MURDER	FR.
BURZIAFF, Arthur	149757	M		17. 1.11	Hptsturmfhr, SS Pz.Gren.Br.49, Montmirail (Fr.)		
BUS, Peter	192157	M			Zimmerpolier, Org.Todt, Firma Otto Menzel, Bittburg, Alle sur Semois (Bel.) 5.-6.40	PILLAGE	BEL.
BUSCH	127067	M			SS Pz.Div. "Das Reich", South West France	MURDER	FR.
BUSCH	160198	M	Ger.		Lt., Legion Tartare, Saint Paulien (Fr.) 8.44	MURDER	FR.
BUSCH	160219	M	Ger.		SS Uschfhr, CC Voeght (Neth.)	TORTURE	FR.
BUSCH	178213	M			SS Oschfhr, CC Schorzingen (Ger.)	MISC.CRIMES	FR.
BUSCH	194925	M	Ger.		Cmdt, Org. Todt, Assen (Neth.) 12.44	MURDER	NETH.
BUSCH	194961	M	Ger.		Obersturmfhr, Oberst, Army, Groppenstein (Aust.) 42	MURDER	U.K.
BUSCH	195849	M	Ger.		Employee, CC Struthof and Natzweiler, Bas-Rhin (Fr.) 40-44	TORTURE	FR.
BUSCH	196114	M	Ger.		Adjutant, SS Div."Das Reich", SS Rgt."Deutschland", Miremont (Fr.)	MURDER	FR.
BUSCH	254280	M			Lt., Pas de Calais, Esquerdes (Fr.) 1., 2.43	INTERR.	FR.
BUSCH	254491	M			SS-Mann, Camp Mackenrode, Nordhausen (Ger.)	MURDER	U.S.
BUSCH	254495	M	Ger.		Sgt., Sicherheits-Pol., Raon l'Etape (Fr.) 9.44	MURDER	FR.
BUSCH	300447	M	Ger.		Senior N.C.O., Redzek-Detachment, Raon l'Etape(Fr.)9.44	MURDER	FR.
BUSCH	300991	M	Ger.		Member of Staff, CC Struthof-Natzweiler (Fr.) 42-44	MURDER	FR.
BUSCH	301895	M	Ger.		Major, II,169 Inf.Div.Staff, 20 Army, Finmark (Nor.) 10.-11.44	MURDER	NOR.
BUSCH, Ernst	139832	M		98	SS-Mann	MURDER	U.S.
BUSCH, Friedrich	160197	M	Ger.	00 - 05	Oschfhr, Gestapo, d'Angers (Fr.) 42-44	MURDER	FR.
BUSCH, Friedrich	307065	M	Ger.		SS Obersturmfhr, or SS Hptsturmfhr, Angers Gestapo, Maine et'Loire, Sarthe-et-Mayenne (Fr.) 42-8.44	MURDER	FR.
BUSCH, Fritz	194700	M	Ger.		SS Hptsturmfhr, Paris (Fr.) 42	TORTURE	U.S.
BUSCH, Hans	194928	M	Ger.		Uschfhr, SD Einsatz Kdo. Retschek, Celles St.Plaine (Fr.) 44	MURDER	FR.
BUSCH, Heinz	194913	M	Ger.	10	Member, Gestapo, Kolin (Czech.) 39-45	TORTURE	CZECH.
BUSCHBAUM	254496	M	Ger.		Capt., 2 Rgt.Inf. 1 Air Coy of Bruley, Boucq-Trondes Menil la Tour (Fr.) 8.44	MURDER	FR.
BUSCHBAUM, Friedrich	258903	M	Ger.	14. 9.04	Guard, State Service, W-SS, Totenkopfsturmbann, Majdanek, Warschau (Pol.) 42-45	INTERR.	POL.
BUSCHE	301620	M	Ger.		Lt. of the Volga Bn. Tartar Legion, Ruines (Cantal) 6.44	MURDER	FR.
BUSCHE, Heinz	256978	M	Ger.		Lt., 5 Pol.Rgt., 322 Bn, Orasac, Gruza, Kragujevac (Yugo.) 42-44	MURDER	YUGO.
BUSCHENDORFF	192588	M	Ger.		Officer, SS, Buchenwald (Ger.) 42	MISC.CRIMES	U.S.
BUSCHENHAGEN, Erich	260628	M		95	General	WITNESS	U.S.
BUSCHER	301884	M	Ger.	21. 2.00	Employed at German Railway, Brussels-Lille, operating at Busigny Nord (Fr.) 2.9.44	MURDER	FR.
BUSCHER, Arnold	162309	M	Ger.	02	Obersturmfhr, CC Ohrdruf (Ger.) 42-45	TORTURE	U.S.
BUSCHHAUS, Gregor	124284	M			Pvt.,246.Inf.Div.6.Coy.,Bastogne (Bel.) 12.44	MURDER	U.S.
BUSCHHAUS, Heinrich	160218	M	Ger.		Civ., Factory Policeman in Brick-Factory Schade,Plettenberg(Ger.)	TORTURE	U.S.
BUSCHLING	149759	M			Osturmfhr, Service de TP des SS, Struthof (Fr.)	TORTURE	FR.
BUSCHMANN	177161	M	Ger.	25	SS-Mann, 12 Pz.Div.Hitler Jugend, HQ 26, HQ-Coy, near Caen (Fr.)6-7.44	TORTURE	CAN.
BUSCHMANN	187649	M			Sgt.,Feld-Gend.Stab,Boodriaan (Neth.) 5.44	MURDER	U.K.
BUSCHMANN	254288	M			Hptscharfhr, SD, Amsterdam (Neth.) 3.45	MURDER	NETH.
BUSCHMANN	254484	M	Ger.		Lt., Unit F.P.No.38789, Montbeugny (Fr.) 9.44	MURDER	FR.
BUSCHMANN, Ernst	259722	M			Chief of Culture, Jeantes, Aisne (Fr.) 41-43	INCENDIARISM	FR.
BUSCHMANN, Gustav	254477	M			Cpl., Camp Ellrich, Nordhausen (Ger.)	MURDER	U.S.
BUSCHMEYER (or BUSCHMEIER, or BUSCHMEIERL)	194786	M	Ger.	04	Capt, Ukraine Bn, Monte Grappa (It.) 9.44	WITNESS	U.K.
BUSE, Ralph (see BUESE)	192203						
BUSH	162306	M	Ger.		Sturmfhr, SS Wirtschafts-Verwaltungs-Hauptamt, Ohrdruf (Ger.)42-45	TORTURE	U.S.
BUSIEK	168609	M	Ger.		Pvt., 9 Gren.Ers.Rgt., 1 Coy, Nagny d'Anigon (Fr.) 9.44	MURDER	FR.
BUSING, Wilhelm	168578	M	Ger.	26. 3.07	SS Rottfhr, Natzweiler Struthof (Fr.) 43-44	MURDER	FR.
BUSKE	260977	M	Ger.		SS Uschfhr, CC Vaihingen a.d.Enz (Ger.) 8.44-4.45	MURDER	U.S.
BUSL	301621	M	Ger.		Sgt., Interpreter with the Feld-Gend. Chateaubriant (Loire-I.), St.Julien de Nouvantes (Fr.) 7.44	MURDER	FR.
BUSMANN	168624	M	Ger.		Col., 369 Inf.Div., Chief of Intelligence Section, Zagnjez-de Udora, Herzegovine (Yugo.) 7.44	MURDER	YUGO.
BUSNOCH, Rudolf	31984	M			Dr., Landgerichtsrat, Public Official, Brno (Czech.) 40	MURDER	CZECH.
BUSS	125628	M	Ger.		SS Hptschfhr, SS Pz.Aufklaerungs Coy,Div.Hitler Jugend,Asco(Fr.)4.44	MURDER	FR.
BUSS	254476	M			Rottfhr, Camp Dora, Nordhausen (Ger.)	MURDER	U.S.
BUSS, Hermann	254306	M	Ger.		Employee of Camp, Wilhelmshaven (Ger.)	INTERR.	FR.

BUS-CAP

NAME	C.R.FILE NUMBER	SEX	NATIO-NALITY	DATE OF BIRTH	RANK OCCUPATION UNIT PLACE AND DATE OF CRIME	REASON WANTED	WANTED BY
BUSS, Otto	192477	M	Ger.	06	Oberwachtmeister, Reichsjustizministerium, Strafgefangenen-Lager "Nord" Finnmark (Nor.) 3.45	MISC.CRIMES	YUGO., NO
BUSSE	135138	M	Ger.	00	Col., Liaison Officer, O.K.W., Germany, Czechoslovakia. 2.-3.45	TORTURE	U.S.
BUSSE	148499	M			Kapo, C.C. Buchenwald (Ger.) 44	MURDER	FR.
BUSSE	167665	M	Ger.		SS-Uschafhr., SS, C.C. Sachsenhausen-Oranienburg (Ger.) 4.45	MURDER	POL.
BUSSE	191548	M	Ger.		SS-Uschafhr., Waffen-SS, C.C.Sachsenhausen-Oranienburg (Ger.) 39-45	MURDER	POL.
BUSSE	255256	M			Dr., SS-Hptscharfhr., C.C. Buchenwald (Ger.)	MURDER	U.S.
BUSSE, Ernst	162310	M	Ger.	10	SS-Scharfhr., SS Totenkopf-Org. C.C. Buchenwald (Ger.) 39	WITNESS	U.S.
BUSSE, Ernst	162311	M	Ger.	99	Civilian, C.C. Buchenwald (Ger.) 45	WITNESS	U.S.
BUSSE, Theodor	259025	M	Ger.	97	General.	WITNESS	U.S.
BUSSENSCHUTT, Hermann	162307	M			Member, Gestapo, Couvin (Bel.)	TORTURE	BEL.
BUSSERATH, Hubert	160212	M			SS, C.C. Flossenburg (Ger.)	TORTURE	U.S.
BUSSMANN, Erich	261989	M	Ger.	7.10.10	SS-Mann, Waffen-SS, Gren.Div.36, Dirlewanger-Bde., Warschau and other towns (Pol.) 40-44	MURDER	POL.
BUSSY	254475	M			Pvt., Camp Ellrich, Nordhausen (Ger.)	MURDER	U.S.
BUSTA	130085	M			SS-Hptscharfhr., Nordhausen (Ger.)	MURDER	U.S.
BUSTA	132605	M			Oschafhr., SS, C.C. Dora, Nordhausen (Ger.)	MURDER	FR.
BUSTE	148501	M	Ger.		SS-Scharfhr., C.C. Lublin (Pol.) 42-45	MURDER	FR.
BUSTER	130093	M			Hptsturmfhr., SS, C.C.Dora-Mittelbau, Nordhausen (Ger.)	MURDER	U.S.
BUSTOR	254474	M			SS-Hptscharfhr., Camp Dora, Nordhausen (Ger.)	MURDER	U.S.
BUSTY (Nickname)	123923	M	Ger.		Guard at Fort 17, Stalag 20 A, Thorn (Pol.) 40	TORTURE	U.K.
BUTCHALA	168625	M	Ger.		SS-Scharfhr., SS, C.C. Oranienburg (Ger.)	MURDER	POL., U.K.
BUTEL	173132	M	Ger.		C.C. Natzweiler, Gaggenau (Fr., Ger.) 44	INTERR.	U.K.
BUTENSIEK	192270	M			SS-Hptsturmfhr., SS, C.C. Flossenburg (Ger.) 44-45	MURDER	U.S.
BUTH, Paul	178325	M			SS-Mann, 9.SS Pion.Coy.Leibstandarte "Adolf Hitler", Malmedy (Bel.) 12.44	MURDER	U.S.
BUTLER	189022	M		05	Capt., Arbeitskommando, C.C. Regensburg (Ger.)	MURDER	U.K.
BUTNER, Karl	258906	M	Ger.		Capt., Artillery, St.Hermine (Fr.) 3.41	INCENDIARISM	FR.
BUTTCHER, Emil (see BOETCHER)	251975						
BUTTERSTEIN	254497	M			Sgt., Field Pol., Vendome (Fr.) 8.44	MURDER	FR.
BUTTINGER, Josef	173973	M			Arbeitslager, C.C. Muhldorf-Ampfing (Ger.) 6.44-4.45	MURDER	U.S.
BUTTLER, Heinrich	192204	M			Pvt., Army, Chatou (Fr.) 8.44	WITNESS	FR.
BUTTNER	149	M			Lt., Army, 98.Regt. Chass.Alp. 2.Bn., St.Jean de Maurienne (Fr.)	MURDER	FR.
BUTTNER	139125	M	Ger.		Oschafhr., SS, C.C. Natzweiler (Fr.)	MURDER	U.S.
BUTTNER	167658	M	Ger.		SS-Usturmfhr., C.C. Struthof-Natzweiler (Fr.) 42-44	MURDER	FR.
BUTTNER	195218	M	Ger.		SS-Hptsturmfhr., SS, C.C. Sachsenhausen (Ger.)	MURDER	BEL.
BUTTNER, Eugen	146371	M			Oschafhr., SS, C.C. Struthof (Fr.)	TORTURE	FR.
BUTTNER, Hermann	160203	M	Ger.	07 to 08	Oschafhr., SS, C.C.Sachsenhausen-Oranienburg (Ger.)	TORTURE	U.K.
BUTTNER, Karl	305584	M	Ger.		Member (Personnel) of C.C. Flossenburg, Hersbruck, Wolkenburg, Ganacker and Leitmeritz (Ger. and Czech.) 1.42-5.45	MURDER	U.S.
BUTTOW	259672	M	Ger.		Corvette Capt., Navy Unit 09.909, Wimereux, Pas de Calais (Fr.) 40-44	INCENDIARISM	FR.
BUTZ	254473	M			Pvt., Camp Rottleberode, Nordhausen (Ger.)	MURDER	U.S.
BUTZEN, Gustav	12589	M			Pvt., 110. or 111.Panz.Gren.Regt. 2.Coy, Albine (Fr.) 6.44	MURDER	FR.
BUTZKE	185424	M	Ger.		Member, Gestapo, (Lux.)	TORTURE	LUX.
BUZELLO, Werner	192478	M			Capt., 3.Coy. Bau Pion.Bn.428, Nordmo (Nor.) 7.43	MURDER	NOR.
BYER, Jerrie	123418	M			Civilian.	TORTURE	U.K.
BYKER (see BUEKA)	120609						
BYRNE	160190	M			Pvt., Army, Pomerania (Ger.) 6.44	TORTURE	U.K.
BYSZKOWSKI, August	160189	M			Civilian, Rumelu Mevissen Mine (Ger.)	TORTURE	U.S.
BYTONSKI	259315	M			Kapo, C.C. Auschwitz (Pol.)	BRUTALITY	FR.
BYTRICH, Anton	167458	M	Ger.		Pvt., Army, 9.Gren.Ers.Regt., 1.Coy., Magny d'Anigon (Fr.) 9.44	MURDER	FR.
BZENSKY, Peter	256794	M	Ger.	19.7.11	Zug-Wachtmeister, State Service, Lidice (Czech.) 6.42	MURDER	CZECH.
CAAP, Gerardt	130104	M			Civilian, C.C. Dora-Mittelbau, Nordhausen (Ger.)	MURDER	U.S.
CACH, Franz	194318	M	Ger.		Civilian, Mayor, Member of NSDAP, Jindrichuy-Hradec (Czech.) 39-45	MURDER	CZECH.
CACZEWSKA, Jeanine	157416	F		06	Guard, C.C. Zwodem (Czech.)	PILLAGE	FR.
CADUK (aliases: KADUCK)	196013	M	Ger.		Oschafhr., SS, C.C.Auschwitz (Pol.) 40-45	MURDER	FR.
CAEL-MARQJARIT	188195	M	Ger.		Capt., Army, Busset (Fr.) 8.44	MISC.CRIMES	FR.
CAESAR, Joachim Heinrich Ferdinand	173783	M	Ger.		Dr., SS-Stubannfhr., C.C. Oswiecim-Birkenau (Pol.) 39-45	MURDER	CZECH.
CAESAR, Joachim (see also CEZAR and COESAR)	305709	M	Ger.		Osturmfhr., Dr. Med.Off., SS, C.C. Auschwitz-Birkenau (Pol.) 8.44	MURDER	YUGO.
CAHL-MARQJARIT	185609	M			SS Hptsturmfhr., SS, Busset (Fr.) 8.44	MURDER	FR.
CAHNEN	301941		Ger.		Member, S.D., Apeldoorn-District (Neth.) 9.44-4.45	MURDER	NETH.
CAINSTER	124958	M	Ger.		Member, Gestapo or Polizei, Gestapo-Lager Bremen-Farge (Ger.) 6.43	TORTURE	U.K.
CALDER	128800	M	Ger.		Dr. Civilian, Ostheim (Ger.) 7.44	MISC.CRIMES	U.K.
CALHIES	301231	M	Ger.		Dr., Oberrat, Army administration, Brussels (Bel.) 40-44	MURDER	BEL.
CALLIS	194951	M	Ger.		SS-Osturmfhr., S.D. Einsatz-Kommando-SS, Giromagny (Fr.) 44	MURDER	U.K.
CALLSEN, Walter	261988	M	Ger.	15.9.12	SS-Mann, Dirlewanger-Bde., Waffen-SS, Gren.Div.36, Warschau and other towns (Pol.) 40-44	MURDER	POL.
CALMBACH	137660	M	Ger.		Gpl., 443.Landesschuetzen-Bn. 4.Coy. Guard-Cmdt. K 780, Widenau Krs. Freiwaldau (Czech.) 2.45	MURDER	U.K.
CALMBACH, Josef	252050	M	Ger.	15 or 16	Landesschuetzen-Bn. 4-438, Velka Krase (Czech.)	MURDER	U.K.
CAMANNS, Erich	191672	M	Ger.	1.17	Sgt., Standortkommandantur, Feldkommandantur, Nantes (Fr.) 6.-8.44	MURDER	FR.
CAMINSKY	257598	M			Pvt., Army, Ile de Sein (Fr.) 8.44	INTERR.	FR.
CAMPE	142756	M	Ger.	05	Rapportfuehrer, C.C. Sachsenhausen (Ger.)	TORTURE	U.K.
CAMPE	150959	M	Ger.		Hptsturmfhr., Waffen-SS, Totenkopf-Sturmbann, C.C.Buchenwald and Dachau (Ger.) 45	TORTURE	U.S.
CAMPE (or LAMPE)	193894	M	Ger.	16	W.O., Army, Loire et Ampuis (Fr.)	MURDER	FR.
CAMPE	195324	M			SS-Usturmfhr., SS, C.C. Sachsenhausen (Ger.) 9.44	MURDER	BEL.
CAMPE	195830	M			SS-Blockfuehrer, C.C. Neuengamme-Hamburg (Ger.) 40-44	MURDER	BEL.
CAMPE, Herman	167010	M		10	SS-Usturmfhr., C.C. Natzweiler (Fr.) 43-44	MISC.CRIMES	FR.
CAMPIAN (see also: KAMPIN)	305545	M	Ger.		Guard, SS or Gestapo Staff, Bremen-Farge (Ger.) 1.43-4.43	MURDER	U.S.
CAMUS, Henri	162873	M	Ger.		N.C.O., 10. SS Panz.Div. "Frundsberg", Revin (Fr.) 6.44	MURDER	FR.
CANNON (or CANNONZ)	124249	M			Usturmfhr., Army-SS, 1.SS.Panz.Div., 9.Coy. (Engineers), Malmedy (Bel.) 12.44	MURDER	U.S.
CAP	185610	M	Ger.		Usturmfhr., S.D., Sarrebruck (Fr.)	LOOTING	FR.

CAP-CET

NAME	C.R.FILE NUMBER	SEX	NATIONALITY	DATE OF BIRTH	RANK OCCUPATION UNIT PLACE AND DATE OF CRIME	REASON WANTED	WANTED BY
CAPEK	169510	M			Oschfhr., SS Totenkopf, C.C. Mauthausen (Aust.) 41-45	MURDER	U.S.
CAPEK	258097	M	Ger.	96	Gendarm, State Service, Val.Mezirici (Czech.) 44-45	MURDER	CZECH.
CAPEL, Raymond	120009	M			Uschfhr., C.C. Struthof (Fr.)	MURDER	FR.
CAPI, Ferruccio	189905	M			Federal secretary of the Fasci di Combatimento, Spalato (Yugo.)	MURDER	YUGO.
CARL	162754	M	Ger.	08	Osturmfhr., SS, Abt. V. Gesundheitswesen, Kl. Buchenwald,2.44-45	TORTURE	U.S.
CARL	169511	M		17	N.C.O., Kdo. Camp 1669 Stalag II.B.1944,Ger.Guard, Stolp, Swinemuende (Ger.) 2.45	MURDER	U.S.
CARL	250090	M			Hptsturmfhr., C.C. Dora-Nordhausen (Ger.)	MURDER	U.S.
CARL	250663	M	Ger.	06	Employee, Gestapo, Prag (Czech.) 44-45	MURDER	CZECH.
CARLSEN, Franz	10005	M			SD. official Hilfsbeamter, C.C. Breendonck (Bel.) 40-44	TORTURE	BEL.
CARLIER, Marguerite	142762	F	Ger.	10	Employee, Labor-Office, Paris (Fr.)	MISC.CRIMES	FR.
CARLMANN, Friedrich	195157	M	Ger.		Crim. Secretary, Gestapo, Prerov (Czech.) 39-45	TORTURE	CZECH.
CARLOS, Bernhardt (alias BERNHARD, Carlos)	194799	M			Sgt., Army, Capri (It.)	MURDER	U.K.
CARLS, Rolf	259026	M	Ger.		Admiral of the fleet	WITNESS	U.S.
CARMS	148913	M	Ger.		Director, Factory, Schorau near Halle (Ger.)	MISC.CRIMES	FR.
CARO	194091	M	Ger.		Hptschfhr. SS, Dussen (Neth.) 10.44	PILLAGE	NETH.
CAROL	251988	M	Ger.	16	Kapo, C.C., Block 9, Birkenau, Auschwitz (Pol.)	MURDER	FR.
CAROLAS	155760	M	Ger.	8.06	Lt., Landesschuetzen-Bn., West Prussia, 3.45, 4.45	TORTURE	U.K.
CARRAUS	185316	M	Ger.		Sgt., Army	TORTURE	FR.
CARRET (see COUCHARD)	31341						
CARACCIOLO, Francesco	140819	M				MISC.CRIMES	U.S.
CARSTANIER, Friedrich	250654	M	Ger.	28. 7.00	SS Hptsturmfhr., Abwehr, Pilsen (Czech.) 43	BRUTALITY	CZECH.
CARSTEN (see also KARSTEN)	302053	M			Custom-secretary at Graunen, Parish of Zierikzee (Neth.) 12.44	TORTURE	NETH.
CARSTEN nee STADLER, Marie	187294	F	Ger.	2. 5.99	Employee, Gestapo, SD., Brno (Czech.) 39-45	TORTURE	CZECH.
CARSTENS	256998	M	Ger.		Major, S.Rgt. 33 Schupo Bn., Orasac Gruza Kragojevac (Yugo.) 42-44	MURDER	YUGO.
CARTENS, Hans	182744	M		10.10.09	SS Hptschfhr., IV SS Totenkopfsturmbann, Nordhausen-Mittelbau (Ger.) 43-45	WITNESS	U.S.
CASANOGO, Emilio	189866	M			Engineer, Civ. Commissioner, Crnomlje (Yugo.)	SUSPECT	YUGO.
CASAR, Joachim	169526	M	Ger.		Dr., Department-Chief, C.C. Auschwitz (Pol.)	MISC.CRIMES	FR., U.S.
CASIMIR	147954	M		89	C.C. Dresden (Ger.)	MURDER	FR.
CASPAR, Heinz	250669	M	Ger.		SS Oschfhr., SD., Toulouse (Fr.) 11.42-8.44	MISC.CRIMES	FR.
CASPAR, Wilhelm	250089	M			Sgt., C.C. Ellrich, Nordhausen (Ger.)	MURDER	U.S.
CASPARI (or CASPIRI), Otto	169512	M			Stabsschfhr. SS, NSDAP, C.C. Mauthausen (Aust.)	MURDER	U.S.
CASPERG	250091	M			Pvt., C.C. Ellrich, Nordhausen (Ger.)	MURDER	U.S.
CASPIRI (see CASPARI), Otto	169512						
CASSEBAUM	124516	M	Ger.		Dr., Stabsarzt, Air-Force Officer, Langendiebach (Ger.) 11.43	MISC.CRIMES	U.K.
CASSEL	152018	M	Ger.		Lt., Army 31286 Heeresunterkunftsverwaltung,Cahrespuies (Fr.)8.44	MURDER	FR.
CASSEL, Erich	62226	M	Ger.		Chief of Staff, NSDAP, Head-Office for Ethnological Problems	MURDER	U.N.W.C.C.
CASSEN	257385	M	Ger.		SS Oberwachmann, Guard, slave labour camp,Beisfjord,Narvik (Nor.) 6.-11.42	BRUTALITY	YUGO.
CASSERMAN	1313	M	Ger.		Lt.	MISC.CRIMES	U.K.
CASSERMAN	155762	M	Ger.		Lt., Army, Solagne (It.) 11.44	MURDER	U.K.
CASTEL, Pietro	195814	M	Ger.		Sturmbannfhr., Dr., C.C. Dachau, Auschwitz (Ger.) 42-2.43	MISC.CRIMES	BEL.
CASTELL	260072	M			Sturmfhr., SS Slave Labour Camp, Botn near Rognan (Nor.) 4.43-5.45	BRUTALITY	YUGO.
CASTELPIETRO	301792	M	Ger.		Sturmbannfhr., Dr., C.C. Dachau, Auschwitz (Pol.) 3.42	TORTURE	BEL.
CASTNER	190314	M			C.C. Dachau (Ger.)	MURDER	U.S.
CASTRUPP	250670	M	Ger.		Guard, Kdo. 601, Stalag VI C, Barduttingsdorf (Ger.) 42-43	TORTURE	FR.
CAUDAL	120591	M	Ger.	10	Agent, Abwehr, Brest (Fr.)	MISC.CRIMES	FR.
CAUMANN (or CAUMANNS) Erich	258214	M			Commanding Officer, 6.Troops,St.Herblain, La Villabeau (Fr.) 6.44	MURDER	U.S.
CAUSTER, Albert	250671	M	Ger.		Gendarm, Gendarmerie Romorantin Nr. 577, Orcay (Fr.) 8.44	MURDER	FR.
CAVAROPOL	148432	M			Major, Stalag, Rumania, Timisul de Jos (Rum.)	TORTURE	U.S.
CEASAR	185318	F			C.C. Auschwitz (Pol.) 43-45	TORTURE	FR.
CECKEL (see also CEKL)	301301	M	Ger.		Member Gestapo at Trencin,C.C. Oswiecim-Birkenau (Pol.) 39-45	MURDER	CZECH.
CEDLASEK	185320	M	Ger.		Cpl., Feldgendarmerie, Lyon (Fr.)	WITNESS	FR.
CEFRREICHART	194320	M	Ger.		Army, Inf., Rousseloy (Fr.) 8.44	MURDER	FR.
CEHLKE	261471	M			SS Hptschfhr., Chief, SD., Frontier Posts., Ax-les-Thermes (Fr.) 11.42,8.44	MURDER	FR.
CEKL (see CECKEL)	301301						
CELNO, Lad.	301302	M	Ger.		Member Gestapo at Nove Mesto n.Vahom,C.C.Oswiecim-Birkenau (Pol.) 39-45	MURDER	CZECH.
CENARI	259658	M	Ger.		Uschfhr., 3 Coy.,1 Bn.,SS-Rgt."Der Fuehrer",SS-Div."Das Reich", Cradour sur Glane, Hte.Vienne (Fr.) 6.44	MISC.CRIMES	FR.
CENSIOR	187911	M			SS Cpl., C.C. Oranienburg (Ger.)	MURDER	CZECH.
CERATO	145723	M			Sgt., Army, C.C. Zlarin (Yugo.) 43	TORTURE	YUGO.
CERFORT	148915	M	Ger.		Camp Leader, C.C. Muelheim (Ger.)	TORTURE	FR.
CERNARCK	185317	M	Ger.		Capt., Schwer.Maschinen Gewehr Ausb.Abt., 4 Coy.	MURDER	FR.
CERNATA	157413	M			Chief of Kdo., C.C. Hulperbruck (Ger.)	TORTURE	FR.
CERNE, Hugo	140820	M	Ger.		Agent, Abwehr, Linz (Ger.) 45	MISC.CRIMES	U.S.
CERNIK, Borivoj	254932	M	Ger.		Agent, Gestapo, Pribram (Czech.) 39-45	MISC.CRIMES	CZECH.
CERNIK (or CZERNIK), Johann	250096	M		30. 3.99	Staff-Sgt., C.C. Ellrich, Nordhausen (Ger.)	MURDER	U.S.
CERNY	169513	M			SS Rottfhr., C.C. Mauthausen (Aust.) 41-45	MISC.CRIMES	U.S.
CERNY, Josef	250665	M	Ger.	13. 8.13	Forester, C IV, Kladno (Czech.) 6.42	MURDER	CZECH.
CERNY, Max	187296	M	Ger.	22. 5.03	Criminaloberassistent, Gestapo, SD., Brno (Czech.) 39-45	TORTURE,MURDER	CZECH.
CERVANTES, Fernandez	191671	M	Ger.		Member SD of Gestapo, St. Lô (Fr.) 6.44	MURDER	FR.
CERVENY, Johann	250653	M		8. 6.04	Employee, Gestapo, Vsetin (Czech.) 39-45	MURDER	CZECH.
CERNINSKI	148917	M	Ger.		Commandant, C.C. Gallechau (Ger.)	MURDER	FR.
CESAR	161701	M	Ger.	12	C.C. Mauthausen (Aust.)	TORTURE	FR.
CESARE DE DOMENICO	145721	M			Centurione, Liaison Officer, 98. facist Legion "Isonzo" Division, Trebjne (Yugo.) 43	MURDER	YUGO.
CESSNER, Willi	120032	M		13. 6.19	Sous-officer, SS 51.Brig.blindee grenadiers Matricule 365794, Troyes-Bucheres (Fr.) 8.44	MURDER	FR.
CETTMER, Heinrich	262236	M	Ger.	4. 5.13	SS Hptschfhr., Art. 51.SS armoured Bde.,Bucheres, Breviandes, St. Savine, La Riviere De Corps, Troyes (Fr.) 8.44	BRUTALITY	FR.

CEY-CHR

NAME	C.R.FILE NUMBER	SEX	NATIO- NALITY	DATE OF BIRTH	RANK	OCCUPATION	UNIT	PLACE AND DATE OF CRIME	REASON WANTED	WANTED BY
CEYFERT or SEIFERT, Kurth	195323	M	Ger.		Lt.,Army,Rixensart(Bel.)				MURDER	BEL.
CEZAR, Joachim (see CAESAR)	305709									
CFRERER, Bruno	188936	M			SS,18 Bn., Busset(Fr.) 8.44				MURDER	FR.
CHAFFEN	261636	M	Ger.		Major,Flugplatz Kdo.B 63-XI,Deshy Nord(Fr.)				INTERR.	FR.
CHAFFIN	120028								MURDER	FR.
CHAFFNER, Willy	191944	M	Ger.		Sgt.,Army,Change(Fr.)				WITNESS	FR.
CHAIBLED, Karl	194319	M	Ger.		Civilian Fermier,Muenchingen(Ger.) 6.44				MURDER	FR.
CHAIQUE or SCHALK, Helmut	191670	M	Ger.		W.O.,Army,Finistere(Fr.) 6.44				MURDER	FR.
CHALESKI	155765	M			Foreman,Saturn Coal Mine,Civilian-Cheladze Stalag VIIIB(Ger.) 44				MURDER	U.K.
CHALLA	127337	M		98	Scharfhr.,Kripo,C.C.Oranienburg(Ger.) 2.45				MURDER	U.S.
CHALLEK (see SCHALLEK)	186120									
CHALQUE, Helmut or SCHALCK	39634	M	Ger.		Sgt.,Army (Fr.) 44				MURDER	FR.
CHALQUE, Helmut	120027	M			Parachutist Coy.,Carhaix(Fr.) 44				MURDER	FR.
CHAMSE	146976	M			SS Pz.Div."Das Reich", Venerque Le Vernet(Fr.) 1944				MURDER	FR.
CHAMODRAKAS, Aristides	150956	M	Ger.		Civilian,Papier and Zellwollfabrik,KL.Lenzing(Aust.)				WITNESS	U.S.
CHANKAT	185321	M	Ger.		Inspector,Zollgrenzschutz,Perpignan(Fr.) 2.43				MURDER	FR.
CHANTRAINE	250651	M			Interpreter,SD,Apeldoorn(Neth.) 10.44				MURDER	U.S.
CHAONNOF	187010	M	Ger.		Sgt., Army,Plozevet(Fr.)				MURDER	FR.
CHAPINSKI	137641	M	Ger.	07	Standortarzt,SS.				MURDER	U.K.
CHAPELLA	124518	M	Ger.		Civilian, Camp Grafenweiler(Ger.)				MISC.CRIMES	U.K.
CHAQUE, Einion	157412	M			W.O.,Fallschirmjaeger Coy.,Carhaix(Fr.)				TORTURE	FR.
CHAR, Fritz	161699	M		00	Civilian, Ingelfingen(Ger.)				MISC.CRIMES	FR.
CHARCUSKY	174037	M			SS-Rottfhr.,SS,C.C.Muhldorf,Ampfing(Ger.) 6.44-4.45				MURDER	U.S.
CHARISSE	150	M			Police Sipo,St.Quentin(Fr.) 4.43				MURDER	FR.
CHARLES, Rene	120094	M		03	Army Div."Das Reich",Viensses Barthes-Montartruc(Fr.)				MURDER	FR.
CHARLY	250672	M			Osturmfhr.,SD,Toulouse(Fr.) 11.42-8.44				MISC.CRIMES	FR.
CHARFE	261391	M	Ger.		Interpreter,Kreiskommandantur, Vire(Fr.) 7.44				INTERR.	FR.
CHASE	167009	M	Ger.		Chief,P.O.W.Arb.-Kdo.,C.C.Kempten(Ger.)				MURDER	FR.
CHASINSKY	174098	M			Civilian Todt Organisation,C.C.Muhldorf,Ampfing(Ger.) 6.44-4.45				MURDER	U.S.
CHAULMONT, Henri	120042	M			Gestapo Milicien,Lussault (Fr.) 44				MURDER	FR.
CHAULMONT, Roger	120040	M			Gestapo Milicien,Lussault(Fr.) 44				MURDER	FR.
CHAUTAIN	161700	M			W.O.,Army,Toulouse(Fr.) 1.44				TORTURE	FR.
CHAUSS, Robert	157405	M	Ger.		N.C.O.,Feldgendarmerie, Sedan(Fr.) 44				MISC.CRIMES	FR.
CHEMILEWSKI	151	M	Ger.		SS-Hptsturmfhr., C.C.Vught(Neth.) 1.-2.43				TORTURE	NETH.
CHEMINSKY	149983	M			C.C.Gardien,Bochum(Ger.)				MURDER	FR.
CHEMNITZ	137648	M	Ger.		Records Clerk,Guard C.C.Stutthof(Ger.)				MURDER	U.K.
CHEMNITZ, Arno	261728	M			Sgt.,C.C.Dora,adjoint Cmdt.Bde.,Nordhausen(Ger.)				SUSPECT	FR
CHEMNITZ, Arno	122070	M	Ger.		SS-Hptscharfhr., C.C. Buchenwald(Ger.) 42-45				MURDER	FR.
CHENY, Germain	167008	M	Ger.		Guard, C.C. Schirmeck (Fr.) during occupation				MURDER	FR.
CHERMITZA see ZCHEMITZA	196028									
CHERMNITZ, Hans	127338	M	Ger.	10	T-Sgt.,Landesschuetzen Bn.814,Wolstein(Ger.)				MURDER	U.S.
CHERNY	137083	M	Ger.		Col.,Camp-Cmdt.Stalag XIB,Fallingbostel(Ger.) 10.44				TORTURE	U.K.
CHERUBEL	194321	M	Ger.		Interpreter,Flugmelde-Regt.57,Eure Et Loire(Fr.) 8.44				PILLAGE	FR.
CHERVATOSKI	185611	M	Ger.		SS-Uscharfhr.,C.C. Dachau(Ger.)				MURDER	FR.
CHESCH	142763	M	Ger.		Gestapo, Danzig(Ger.)				TORTURE	FR.
CHEVRON, Michel	120047	M			W.O.,SS 2 Pz.Div.,3 Pz.Gr.Regt.,Tulle Souillac Gourdon,Condom Roc. Croislejac(Fr.)				MURDER	FR.
CHEWSKY	120048	M			Sgt.-Major,Army 2 Pn.Coy.,Saint die(Fr.)				SUSPECT	FR.
CHIARI	149382	M			Doctor, C.C. Ravensbrueck(Ger.)				TORTURE	FR.
CHILLI or SCHILLY, Jupp	251995	M	Ger.	10	Sgt.,8 Coy.,9 Bn.,Sich.Regt.192.(Fr.) 6.-7.44				TORTURE	FR.
CHIEBINSKY	194825	M	Ger.		SS-Osturmfhr.,SS,C.C.Lublin(Pol.) 40-44				MURDER	POL.
CHIMINSKI probably Hans	306323	M	Ger.		N.C.O., Mijnsheeren Land Oud Beverland(Neth.) 5.45				MURDER	NETH.
CHISTOFZIK, Willi	152	M	Ger.	24.3.07	Pvt.,Army,Villerupt(Fr.) 9.44				MISC.CRIMES	FR.
CHLOND, Fritz	250673	M	Ger.		Gend.,Gend."Romorantin"No.577,Orcay(Fr.) 8.44				MISC.CRIMES	FR.
CHLOOTH	174039	M			SS-Sturmmann, SS,C.C.Muhldorf,Ampfing(Ger.) 6.44-4.45				MURDER	U.S.
CHLOSER	258907	M	Ger.		Director,Mine of Passavant,Kettenbach bei Michelbach(Ger.) 10.44				SUSPECT	FR.
CHLOSTA, Bruno	260160	M	Ger.		Sgt., Cartridge Factory,Chateau de Vincennes,Seine(Fr.) 8.44				MURDER	FR.
CHMIELEWSKI	141374	M	Ger.		Chief,SS,C.C.Mauthausen(Aust.)				TORTURE	FR.
CHMIELEWSKI, B.	153	M			Hptsturmfhr.,SS,C.C.Gusen,Gusen,Sachsenhausen,Mauthausen,(Aust.) 41-45				MURDER	BEL.,U.S.
CHNADER aliase SCHENEDER	134832	M			C.O., German Navy,Gast de Ste.Marine,near Benodet,Mousterlin(Fr.) 6.44				WITNESS	IT.,U.S.
CHOBERNEZ	192239	M			SS-Osturmfhr.,Regt."Der Fuehrer",SS Div."Das Reich",1 Bn., Frayssinet-Le Gelat(Fr.) 5.44				MURDER	FR.
CHOCOLAT	142764	M			Oldest Man in Camp,C.C.Augsburg(Ger.) -44				TORTURE	FR.
CHOEFFLEIN	120052	M			Rimont(Fr.)				PILLAGE	FR.
CHOINA, Franz	170848	M			SS Camp-Leader, 3 SS Bau-Bde.,Hptscharfhr.,KL.Osterhagen Gardelegen (Ger.) 4.45				MURDER	U.S.
CHOINI	130105	M			Hptscharfhr. SS,Dora Mittelbau, Nordhausen(Ger.)				MURDER	U.S.
CHORS	57751	M			Major,Volkssturm,KL.Koenigstein-Elbe(Ger.)				WITNESS	FR.
CHREIS	155079	M	Ger.		Pvt.,1 Pz.Div.,SS (A.Hitler),Waffen-SS,II Zug,III Gruppe, Parfounduy Stavelot(Bel.) 12.44				MURDER	U.S.,BEL.
CHRISLESEN	120055	M							TORTURE	FR.
CHRIST	120707	M			Albi(Fr.)				MURDER	FR.
CHRIST	124339	M			Osturmfhr.,1 SS Pz.Div.,1 SS Pz.Regt.,C.O. 2 Coy.,Malmedy(Bel.) 12.44				MURDER	U.S.
CHRIST	149368	M			Civilian,Augsburg(Ger.)				TORTURE	FR.
CHRIST	149369	M			Capt.,Army,C.C.Ugines(Fr.)				MURDER	FR.
CHRIST	250675	M	Ger.		Auxillary Policeman,Police,Wasser Trudingen(Ger.) 3.45				WITNESS	U.S.
CHRIST, Andreas	262011	M	Ger.	20.12.07	SS-Mann,Dirlewanger Bde.,Waffen-SS Gren.Div.36,Warsow and other(Pol.)-44				MURDER	POL.
CHRIST, Bruno	254928	M	Ger.	4.8.98	Criminal Chief Secretary,Gestapo,Novy-Jicin(Czech.) 39-45				MISC.CRIMES	CZECH.
CHRIST, Willy	157409	M	Ger.		Civilian,Niederseelbach(Ger.) 10.44				MURDER	U.S.
CHRISTEL, Roland	191977	M			Inspector,German State Railway,Avignon(Fr.) 2.44				MURDER	FR.

NAME	C.R.FILE NUMBER	SEX	NATIO-NALITY	DATE OF BIRTH	RANK OCCUPATION UNIT PLACE AND DATE OF CRIME	REASON WANTED	WANTED BY
CHRISTEN, Eduard	12590	M	Ger.		Pvt., Div. Operating "Das Reich",Ordonnance of Lt.Philipp, Castelmaurov (Fr.) 6.44	MURDER	FR.
CHRISTIAN	31375	M	Ger.		Col., Army (Nor.) 10.44-11.44	MURDER	NOR.
CHRISTIAN, Eckard	260648	M			General, Army	WITNESS	U.S.
CHRISTIANSEN, Jens	252043	M	Ger.		Sgt., Mikulov (Czech.)	MURDER	CZECH.
CHRISTL	252039	M	Ger.		Col., Commander of Unternehmen "Bergzauber Moritz", Slov.(Yugo.) 10.44	MISC.CRIMES	YUGO.
CHRISTMANN	176927	M	Ger.		Dr., Osturmbannfhr., Chief, SS, Stapo-Dienstst.,Koblenz, Munich (Ger.) 9.44-2.45	MURDER	U.S.
CHRISTMANN, Bernhard	250095	M	Ger.		Rottfhr., C.C., Harzungen, Nordhausen (Ger.)	MURDER	U.S.
CHRISTMANN, Hanne nee BEYER	194824	F	Ger.	21. 1.14	Luxembourg (Lux.)	PILLAGE	LUX.
CHRISTOFE	185325	M			Cpl., Army, Chambery-Alberville (Fr.) 4.44	MURDER	FR.
CHRISTOFELDS	155	M	Ger.		Lt., Army, La Guerche (Fr.) 9.43	MURDER	FR.
CHRISTOFFERSEN	185323	M			Gestapo, Auschwitz (Pol.) 43-44	TORTURE	FR.
CHRISTOFESSEN	142766	M			Specialist Officer, Waffen-SS, C.C., Birkenau (Pol.) 45	TORTURE	FR.
CHRISTOFFERS	250667	M	Ger.		Atelier of Forge, Wilhelmshaven (Ger.)	TORTURE	FR.
CHRISTOFFERS	300208	M	Ger.		Member, Wilhelmshaven-Kmdo., C.C. Neuengamme, Wilhelmshaven (Ger.)42-45	MURDER	FR.
CHRISTOPH	185324	M		05	Uschfhr., SS, C.C., SS-Guard, Dora, Penemuende (Ger.)	MURDER	FR.
CHRISTOPH	250658	M			Uschfhr., Camp Kelbra, Nordhausen (Ger.)	MURDER	U.S.
CHRISTOPH	252046	F		20	Secretary, SD, Maisons Laffitte (Fr.) 12.41-6.44	MISC.CRIMES	FR.
CHRISTOPHE	156	M	Ger.		Cpl., Army, Gresys-Isere (Fr.) 8.44	MURDER	FR., UNWCC
CHRISTOPHELDS	195593	M	Ger.		Lt., Army, La Guerche (Fr.) 9.43	MURDER	FR.
CHRISTUKAT	185326	M			Dr., C.C., Hohenlychen-Ravensbrueck (Ger.) 5.41	TORTURE	FR.
CHROBOK	252055	M	Ger.		Lt., Dienststellenleiter, Roubaix (Fr.) 11.41-7.42	MISC.CRIMES	FR.
CHROMY, Karl	250094	M			Pvt., C.C. Ellrich, Nordhausen (Ger.)	MURDER	U.S.
CHROSE	192773	M	Ger.		Wachtmstr., Schupo, C.C., Falstad near Drontheim (Nor.) 41-44	MISC.CRIMES	NOR.
CHTATIA	167914	M	Ger.		Chief, Georgian-Bn., 1.Coy., Tulle (Fr.) 4.44	MISC.CRIMES	FR.
CHULZE	257036	M	Ger.		Member, NSDAP, Mauthausen (Aust.)	BRUTALITY	FR.
CHUN	193611	M	Ger.		Oschfhr., SS, C.C., Lidice (Czech.) 42-44	MISC.CRIMES	CZECH.
CHURENAU	167007	M	Ger.		Cpl., La Rochette (Fr.) 8.44	MURDER	FR.
CHURENAU	167925	M	Ger.		Sgt., Kommandantur, Crest (Fr.) 7.44-8.44	MURDER	FR.
CHUSTEK	185327	M			Doctor, C.C., Auschwitz (Pol.)	MURDER	FR.
CHWOJKA, Gertrude nee GROBETZ	250668	F	Ger.	4. 1.20	Clerk, Civ., Factory, Bruenn (Czech.) 5.45	PILLAGE	CZECH.
CIARZINSKY, Apolonia	185332	F		18.10.17	Guard, C.C., Buchenwald (Ger.)	TORTURE	FR.
CIATE	185331	M			Cpl., Stalag 17 A, Kaisersteinburg (Aust.)	TORTURE	FR.
CIBA, Georg	250093	M		2. 6.13	Rottfhr., C.C. Harzungen, Nordhausen (Ger.)	MURDER	U.S.
CICHON	301942	F	Ger.		SS-Guard, C.C., Auschwitz (Pol.) 42-45	MURDER	POL.
CIEPLIK, Ernst	301060	M	Ger.		Oberarbeitsfhr., RAD,Marianske,Lazne,Bohemia (Czech.) 42-44	INTERR.	CZECH.
CIESLA	157	M			Uschfhr., SS, C.C., Stutthof (Pol.) 9.39-4.41	TORTURE	POL.
CIESLAK (see CIESLOK)	250092	M					
CIESLIK, Anton	155763	M	Ger.	00	Schuetze, Army, Blechhammer (Ger.) 10.42	MURDER	U.K.
CIESLOK (or CIESLAK), Richard	250092	M			N.C.O., C.C. Ellrich, Nordhausen (Ger.)	MURDER	U.S.
CIESZLIK	130158	M		06	Cpl., SS, SD, Bruessels (Bel.) 5.44-9.44	TORTURE	U.K.
CIEVUIAK, Josef	259431	M			Labor, Mansfeld (Ger.) 3.44	WITNESS	U.S.
CIGLER	185330	F	Ger.		Guard, C.C., Cotteszell, Ludwigsburg, Schwabgmund (Ger.) 44	MISC.CRIMES	FR.
CIHANEK, Ferdinand	258090	M	Ger., Czech.	3. 5.20	Agent, Gestapo, Olomouc (Czech.) 41-44	MISC.CRIMES	CZECH.
CILIAX, Otto	259028	M	Ger.		Admiral	WITNESS	U.S.
CILL, Egon	88983	M	Ger.	10	Sturmbannfhr., Waffen-SS, Cmmd.of Conc.Camp, Dachau (Ger.) 6.42-7.42	MURDER	U.K.
CILIE	1685	M	Ger.	10	Sturmbannfhr., SS, C.C., Dachau (Ger.)	MURDER	U.K.
CIMEK	186675	M			Hptscharfhr., SS, C.C., Flossenburg (Ger.)	MURDER	FR.
CINK, Julius	252044	M	Ger.		Workman, Civ., Farm, Lubica (Czech.)	MURDER	CZECH.
CINTHER	188935	M			Agent de Train, Railway, Le Bourget Triage (Fr.) 8.44	WITNESS	FR.
CIRANOWSKI	250659	M			Pvt., Camp Mackenrode, Nordhausen (Ger.)	MURDER	U.S.
CISSEL, Josef(or KISIEL) (Nick Name UKRAINE JOE)	10063	M	Ger.	95	Cpl., Conc.Camp, Stalag 8 B, Lamsdorf (Ger.) 4.45	TORTURE	U.K.
CITOVSKY, Alois	187295	M	Ger.		Crim.Asst., SD, Gestapo, Brno (Czech.) 39-45	MURDER	CZECH.
CLAASSEN, Peter	62249	M			Ortsbauernfhr., Reichsnaehrstand, Civ. Pub.Offic.,Weiden (Ger.)	TORTURE	U.S.
CLAASZEN	135115	M			Police-President, Chief of Pol., Karlsruhe (Ger.) 3.45	MURDER	U.S.
CLAJUS	185337	M			Capt., Army, Conc.Camp Forteresse de Graudenz (Pol.)	TORTURE	FR.
CLAM	122071	M	Ger.		Capt., Gestapo, Ferryville (Tunisie) 1.43	TORTURE	FR.
CLANQET	250655	M	Ger.		Sipo, Brussels (Bel.)	MISC.CRIMES	BEL.
CLANSBERG	185612	M			Conc.Camp, Ravensbrueck (Ger.)	TORTURE	FR.
CLAR, Willy	185336	M		09	Gestapo, Altenkirchen near Coblenz (Ger.)	TORTURE	FR.
CLARA	185344	M			Sturmbannfhr., SS, C.C., Ravensbrueck, Hohenlychen (Ger.) 5.44	TORTURE	FR.
CLARCK	163771	M	Ger.		Custom-house-officer, Custom-frontier, Fillinges (Fr.) 3.44	WITNESS	FR.
CLARE, Wilhelm	108926	M	Ger.		Civilian, Aderstedt, 9.45	MURDER	U.S.
CLARIUS	252932	M	Ger.	00	Sgt., Gend. 532.Troop, Nave (It.) 8.44	INTERR.	U.K.
CLASS	195685	M	Ger.		W.O., SS, "Der Fuehrer", 2.Coy., Oradour (Fr.) 6.44	MURDER	FR.
CLASS, Konrad	259397	M	Ger.	6.11.00	Kreisleiter, NSDAP, Muenster (Haut-Rhine-Fr.) 40-44	PILLAGE	FR.
CLASSEM (Malle)	259316	F	Ger.		Typist, Gestapo of Poitiers, Area Poitiers (Fr.) 40-44	SUSPECT	FR.
CLASSEN	174040	M			N.C.O., Army, Stalag VI A, C.C., Hemer (Ger.) 4.45	TORTURE	U.S.
CLASSEN, Hans	250679	M			Dr., Altenkirchen (Ger.) 6.44	WITNESS	U.S.
CLAUBERG	185343	M			Doctor, C.C., Ravensbrueck (Ger.)	TORTURE	FR.
CLAUBERG, Karl	251994	M	Ger.		Dr., Civ. Professor, SS, C.C., Auschwitz (Pol.) 42-45	MURDER	U.K.
CLAUDIUS (see LOHSE, Rudolph)	259491						
CLAUDT, Hans	192204	M	Ger.		Pvt., Army, No. de Feldpost 23295 E, Chatou (Fr.) 8.44	WITNESS	FR.
CLAUS,	191546	M	Ger.		Dr. Leader, Occupied-Territories, Lublin (Pol.) 39-44	PILLAGE	POL.
CLAUS	306790	M	Ger.		Member, Gestapo, St.Quentin, Vraignes en Vermandors Somme (Fr.) 8.44	MURDER	FR.
CLAUS, Detller Vierth	106789	M		21	Lt., Army Ger. Medic.Corps 5.Group, East of Reibersdorf (Ger.) 4.45	MISC.CRIMES	U.S.
CLAUS, Hans	251997	M	Ger.	2.11.98	Major, Ordnungspolizei, Huellenberg (Ger.) 9.45	MURDER	U.S.
CLAUS, Vik.	130122	M	Ger.		Miscellaneous, Bockel near Nortorf (Ger.) 40-45	TORTURE	BEL.
CLAUSE	185341	M			Uschfhr., SS, Chief of Political-section, C.C.,Auschwitz (Pol.)	MISC.CRIMES	FR.
CLAUSEN	130121	M	Ger.		Fallschirm-Jg.Rgt.5, Nachrichtenzug, Quaregnon Jemappes Ghlin (Bel.) 9.44	MURDER	BEL.

CLA - CON

NAME	C.R.FILE NUMBER	SEX	NATIO-NALITY	DATE OF BIRTH	RANK OCCUPATION UNIT PLACE AND DATE OF CRIME	REASON WANTED	WANTED BY
CLAUSEN	137616	M	Ger.		Wachtmeister, Justizvollzugsanstalten, C.C.Hamburg (Ger.) 12.42	TORTURE	U.K.
CLAUSEN	173761	M	Ger.		Major, Kreiskommandantur, C.C. Pozareuas (Yugo.) 2.43	TORTURE	YUGO.
CLAUSEN, Heinrich	193793	M	Ger.	06	SS-Hauptsturmf., Chief of Economic Section, C.C. Trezin (Czech.) 39-45	TORTURE	CZECH
CLAUSEN, Helmut	250660	M		20. 5.22	Pvt., Camp Ellrich, Nordhausen (Ger.)	MURDER	U.S.
CLAUSENS	185340	M			Records-Clerk, C.C. Auschwitz (Pol.)	MISC.CRIMES	FR.
CLAUSING, Kurt	155768	M			Civilian, Daasdorf (Ger.) 8.44	MURDER	U.S.
CLAUSS	150960	M	Ger.	05	Rottenf., W-SS, Totenk.Standarte, C.C. Buchenwald and C.C. Altenburg (Ger.) 44-45	TORTURE	U.S.
CLAUSSEN	185339	M			Dr., C.C. Ravensbrueck, Hohenlychen (Ger.) 5.44	TORTURE	FR.
CLAUSSEN	257386	M	Ger.		Capt., Org.Todt, Schutzkommando, Slave labour camps, Erlandet, Ceusand, Trole (Nor.) 6.42-45	MURDER	YUGO.
CLAUSSEN, Wilhelm Edmund	301943	M			Oberscharf., 1.Records officer, C.C. Auschwitz (Pol.) 41-45	MURDER	POL.
CLAUT	121062	M			Cpl., Stalag 8-B, Landsdorf (Ger.) 1.40	TORTURE	U.K.
CLAVIEN, Friedrich	250674	M		2. 3.01	Pvt., Camp Dora, Camp Ellrich, Nordhausen (Ger.)	MURDER	U.S.
CLAYMANS	10006	M			Cook employed at Breendonck (Bel.) 40-3.44	TORTURE	BEL.
CLAYRON (see CLAYTON)	120592						
CLAYS	250656	M	Ger.		Sipo, Bruessel (Bel.)	MISC.CRIMES	BEL.
CLAYTON, Egon or CLAYRON	120592	M		00	Abwehr Agent, German Information Service, Paris (Fr.)	MISC.CRIMES	FR.
CLEMEN	251996	M	Ger.		Lt., 225. Inf.Div., Vinkt (Bel.)	MISC.CRIMES	BEL.
CLEMENS	142759	M			Major, O.K.W.,	WITNESS	U.S.
CLEMENS	185334	M			Chief, NSDAP	TORTURE	FR.
CLEMENS, Wilhelm	184276	M		12. 5.06	Hauptsturmf., S.D. and Gestapo, Prag (Czech.) 39-45	TORTURE	CZECH.
CLEMM	108925	M			Civilian, Gernsbach (Ger.) 8.44	MURDER	U.S.
CLEMM, Fritz	172890	M			Civilian, Gernsbach (Ger.) 8.44	MURDER	U.S.
CLERVERS	152014	M	Ger.		Untersturmf., SS, Gestapo, Folkling (Fr.) 11.44	MURDER	FR.
CLEVE, Fritz	174033	M	Ger.	10. 7.89	Lt., Police, Seesen (Ger.) 6.44	MURDER	U.S.
CLEVERS, Arthur	185613	M	Ger.	11. 9.11	Untersturmf., SS, Gestapo, Saarbruecken (Ger.)	MURDER	FR.
CLEVES, Erich	259674	M	Ger.	10	Oberscharf., SS, Gestapo, area of Angers, Maine and Loire (Fr.) 42-44	MISC.CRIMES	FR.
CLOMANN, Friedrich	257597	M	Ger.	12. 3.09	Employee, Block No.20, C.C. Nordhausen (Ger.)	MURDER	U.S.
CLOOS	167913	M	Ger.		Branch-Director, Einsatzstab Rosenberg, Bordeaux (Fr.) 40-44	PILLAGE	FR.
CLOOTH, Fritz	31364	M			Informing Agent, Gestapo, Chambery (Fr.)	MURDER	FR.
CLOUK OR KLUG	125413	M			Cpl., Landessch.Bn., Arbeitskdo. E 746, C.C. Landshut (Ger.)	TORTURE	U.K.
CLOVALLA	162874	M	Ger.		SS-Chief, Member, Police, Revin (Fr.) 6.44	MURDER	FR.
CLUSSMANN	193792	M	Ger.		SS-Oberscharf., C.C. Buchenwald (Ger.) 42-44	TORTURE	U.S.
CNYRIM, Hans (see CUYRIN)	261915						
COBES (see FEZ) Jacob	177588						
COBLITZ, Wilhelm	250662	M	Ger.		Director, State Service, Krakau (Pol.) 39-45	MISC.CRIMES	POL.
COCCEJUS, Herbert Richard	163	M	Ger.		Army, C.C. Caen (Fr.) 6.43	MURDER	FR.
COCCLARELLA (see COUMARELLA)	145703						
COCEK, Josef	258385	M			Guard, C.C. Ohrdruf (Ger.) 12.44-4.45	MURDER	U.S.
COCOIN (see LOQUI)	31345						
COCRIOMONT, Raymond	182755	M			SS-Mann, 4.SS-Totenkopf-Sturmbann, C.C. Nordhausen Mittelbau (Ger.) 43-45	WITNESS	U.S.
CODER	300903	M	Ger.		Major, Cmdt., 6.Div. of the Fallschirmjaeger, 17.Regt., Nieuwaal Prov.of Gelderland (Neth.) 1.45	MURDER	NETH.
COEFFERT, Henkel	138279	M	Ger.		Chauffeur, Gestapo, Lyon (Fr.)	MURDER	FR.
COENEN, Hans	252054	M	Ger.	00	Farmer, Member, SS, Luxemburg (Lux.)German occupation	MISC.CRIMES	LUX.
COERTS (Le Tueur)	185349	M			Commissar, Waithingen (Aust.)	TORTURE	FR.
COESAR (see CAESAR), Joachim	305709	M					
COFFINET, Georges	155767	M			Barber, Civilian, C.C. Gardelegen (Ger.) 4.45	WITNESS	U.S.
COHENBERG	150957	M	Ger.	92	Lt.Col., Camp Stalag 7, C.C. Laufen, Tittmoning (Ger.) 10.42-1.45	TORTURE	U.S.
COHOUN	174035	M			SS-Sturmmann, C.C. Muhldorf-Ampfing (Ger.) 6.44-4.45	MURDER	U.S.
COHRS	142760	M			Major, Oberkommando, Army.	WITNESS	U.S.
COK	185352	M		14. 4.25	Hotthusen (Ger.)	MURDER	FR.
COKCIL	162875	M	Ger.		Adjutant, Flak-Regt., Trie le Chateau (Fr.) 8.44	WITNESS	FR.
COLAS	261227	M			Member, Staff of C.C. Ravensbrueck (Ger.)	SUSPECT	BEL.
COLASIUS	162750	M	Ger.	97	Col., O.K.H. (Hauptquartier), C.C. Buchenwald (Ger.)	TORTURE	U.S.
COLBERG, Waldemar	188194	M	Ger.	2. 5.29	Cpl., Leichte Marine-Art.-Abt., Mansbos en Lanester (Fr.) 8.44	MURDER	FR.
COLBERT, Willi	192321	M		15	Member, Gestapo, Issel (Fr.) 1.45	MURDER	U.S.
COLETTE	185928	M			Civilian, Offenbach (Ger.)	MURDER	U.S.
COLIN	189518	M			Member, Gestapo, Perigueux (Fr.) 6.-8.44	MURDER	FR.
COLLBAEFER	106977	M			Lt.Col., SS Panz.Div.9, 19.Panz.Gren.Regt., Arnheim (Neth.)	MURDER	U.S.
COLLIBAY (see KOLLIBAY)	167074						
COLLING	252042	M	Ger.		16.Hubner Regt., 6.Coy., Kinrooi (Bel.)	INTERR.	BEL.
COLMORGEN, Heinrich	152019	M	Ger.		Inspector, Mensesqueville (Fr.) 44	LOOTING	FR.
COLOMBECK, Hans	258937	M		04	Obertruppf., Org.Todt, Muhldorf area (Ger.)	MURDER	U.S.
COLOMBEK	31350	M			Sgt., D.C.A., Villemur (Fr.)	MURDER	FR.
COLP	168929	M	Ger.		Lt., Feldgendarmerie, Tournai (Bel.) 11.41	MURDER	BEL.
COLRAD (or CONRAD)	167924	M	Ger.		Interpreter, Army, Chateau d'Etoile (Fr.) 7.44	MURDER	FR.
COLS (see COOLIS)	250084						
COMBIER, Kleber (alias: Rob.LIEN or PIGNAL)	62250				Orleans (Fr.) 8.44	MURDER	U.S.
COMENSKI	306676	M	Ger.		Sgt., 331.Pioneer-Bn., 331.Inf.Div., Mijn Heerenland (Neth.) 5.45	PILLAGE	NETH.
COMIS, Guido	185347	M			Member, Gestapo, Cannes (Fr.) 6.44	MURDER	FR.
COMO	122072	M	Ger.		Dr., Civilian, C.C. Grosswenkheim (Ger.) 41-42	TORTURE	U.K.
COMPOCH	152022	M	Ger.		Sgt., SS, Div."Das Reich", Pz.Gren.Regt. 3 "Deutschland" 2.Bn. Aiguillon (Fr.) 6.44		
CONRAD	174032	M		05	SS, C.C. Muhldorf, Ampfing (Ger.) 6.44-4.45	MURDER	FR.
CONRAD or KONRADT	188015	M	Ger.	06	Major, Airforce, Verona (It.) 6.44	MURDER	U.S.
CONRAD	31349	M			Obersturmf., SS Div. "Das Reich", Lot (Fr.) 44	WITNESS	U.K.
CONRAD	129974	M	Ger.		Lt. General, 4.G.A.F.Fleet, Ostrog (SOV.UN.) 9.43	TORTURE	FR.
CONRAD	126983	M	Ger.		Obersturmf., SS Pz.Div."Das Reich", Fontanilles (Fr.) 5.44	MURDER	U.S.
CONRAD (see COLRAD)	167924						FR.

CON-CRE

NAME	C.R.FILE NUMBER	SEX	NATIO-NALITY	DATE OF BIRTH	RANK OCCUPATION UNIT PLACE AND DATE OF CRIME	REASON WANTED	WANTED BY
CONRAD	307066	M	Ger.		Member, SD, Venloo, Various places in province of Limburg (Neth.) 40-44	MURDER	NETH.
CONRAD, Emil	139459	M	Ger.		Chief, C.C. La Coitat (Fr.)	MURDER	FR.
CONRAD, Hans	167912	M	Ger.		Scharfhr., SS, guard at prison St. Lô (Fr.) 6.-7.44	MURDER	FR.
CONRAD, Herbert	120069	M	Ger.	97	Major, Army,Medical Corps C.C. Gardelegen (Ger.) 4.45	MURDER	U.S.
CONRAD, Peter	193609	M	Ger.	21.11.13	Saw-mill worker, Civ., Oberkail Krs.Wittlich (Ger.) 8.44	TORTURE	U.S.
CONRADI	31348	M			Sgt., Feldgendarmerie, Billaude (Fr.)	MURDER	FR.
CONRADI	301553	M	Ger.		SS-Scharfhr., C.C. Mauthausen (Aust.) 9.42	MURDER	BEL.
CONRADI, Heinrich	250099	M	Ger.	01	Rottenfhr., SS, C.C. Harzungen-Nordhausen (Ger.)	MURDER	U.S.
CONRADY, Josef	132572	M	Ger.		Driver, Gestapo, Barcus (Fr.) 6.43	MURDER	FR.
CONRATH, George	124250	M			SS-Pz.Rgt.1, 9 Bn, Malmedy (Bel.) 12.44	MURDER	U.S.
CONRATH, Hermann	300560	M	Ger.		Lt.Gen. commanding the "Hermann Goering" Div., Fuzine Distr.(Yugo.) 10.-12.43	MISC.CRIMES	YUGO.
CONRATH, Paul	191344	M	Ger.	98	Lt.Gen., Hermann Goering Div., Messina (ITALY) 7.43	SUSPECT	U.S.
CONSBRUCH, Heinrich	185353	M	Ger.		Civilian, Berlin-Marienfelde (Ger.) 1.45	WITNESS	U.S.
CONSTANTZA, Josef	191667	M	Ger.	18.7.16	Member, Sicherheits-Pol., Marseille (Fr.) 44	PILLAGE	FR.
CONSTANZER, Ludwig	173201	M	Ger.		Wachtmstr., C.C. Schirmeck, Rotenfels (Ger.,Fr.)	MURDER	U.K.
CONTI	62227	M	Ger.		Reichsgesundheitsfhr., Gruppenfhr.,Staatsecr., leader of Ger. Physicians, SS, Buchenwald, Kiew, Hohenlychen (Ger.,Russ.) 40-45	MURDER	US.,CZECH.,FR.
CONTURIA, Otto	173202	M	Ger.		Zugwachtmstr., Staff at C.C. Schirmeck, Rotenfels (Ger.,Fr.)	INTERR.	U.K.
COOK, Karl	251131	M	Ger.		Lt., 338 Div., La Bresse (Fr.)	MURDER	FR.
COOLIS or COIS	250084	M	Ger.		Inspecteur, Gestapo, Lille (Fr.) 40-44	MISC.CRIMES	FR.
COOLS	189638	M	Ger.		Adjutant, Art.Rgt., Beziers (Fr.) 7.44	MURDER	FR.
COORS, Hermann	300568	M	Ger.		N.C.O., Army,10 Coy,377 Inf.Rgt.,Vinkt-Meigem (Bel.) 5.40	MISC.CRIMES	BEL.
COOS, Berand	31346	M			S.A., Aude (Fr.) 8.44	MISC.CRIMES	FR.
COPA, Rudolf see CUPA, Karl	39635						
COPKA	185346	F			Guard, C.C. Ravensbruck (Ger.)	TORTURE	FR.
COPP	152016	M	Ger.		Gestapo, Bourg-Madame (Fr.) 2.44	PILLAGE	FR.
COPPE	250657	M			SS-Mann, Sipo, Bruessel (Bel.)	TORTURE	BEL.
COPPIN	250677	M			Official, Sipo,Abt.I, Bruessel (Bel.)	INTERR.	BEL.
COPPRIAN, Ina	141464	F	Ger.		Civilian (Fr.)	PILLAGE	FR.
COQUI see LOQUI	39345						
COQUIS	31344	M			Lt.or Lt.Col.,Army,Montmouchet (Fr.)	MURDER	FR.
CORCILOV	189968	M			Capt., Intelligence Service, SD, Pirot (Yugo.)	MISC.CRIMES	YUGO.
CORDES	305833	M	Ger.		Cpl., 1 Aufkl.Abt., 3.Coy., 2 Col., XV Div. Afrika Corps, St.Léger Distr.Arlon (Bel.) 9.44	MISC.CRIMES	BEL.
CORDES, Hans	250968	M	Ger.		Major, 13 SS-Pol.Rgt., Ferlach (Aust.) 44-45	MURDER	YUGO.
CORDSMAIER	186468	M	Ger.		Official, Insp.Reichs-Finanzministerium,La Roche (Fr.) 8.44	PILLAGE	FR.
CORL	301832	M	Ger.		Member, Gestapo, Revin,Ardennes (Fr.) 6.44	MURDER	FR.
CORNEHL	261222	M			Pvt., 139 Arbeits-Bereich Liane,5 Coy,1 N.Rgt.211, Alleur-Lez-Liege (Bel.) 9.44	MURDER	BEL.
CORNEILLE	188367	M			Major, Heeres-Kuesten-Art.1240, Ost-Duenkirchen (Bel.)	MURDER	BEL.
CORNELIS alias KORNELIS	196010	M	Ger.		Guard, SS, Hoppstadten, 11.44	MURDER	FR.
CORNELIS	125747	M	Ger.		Osturmfhr., SS,Sonder-Kommissariat C.C. Sachsenhausen (Ger.) 44	TORTURE	U.K.
CORNELIUS, Hans	167006	M	Ger.		Pvt., Paratroops, Tourch (Fr.) 44	MURDER	FR.
CORNELLI	195322	M	Ger.		Lt., SS, C.C. Sachsenhausen (Ger.)	MURDER	BEL.
CORNEILY, Joanne	152017				Guard, Army, Cdo.774, Stalag XII D, Hoppstedten (Ger.) 3.45	MURDER	FR.
CORNSWANDT, Hans	260428	M	Ger.		Crim.secr., Gestapo, Jičin (Bohemia-Czech.) 40-45	MISC.CRIMES	CZECH.
CORTES	154493	M			Lt.Col., Stalag Luft III C, Sagan (Ger.) 9.44	MURDER	U.K.
CORTH	1314		Ger.		Capt., Army, 9 PGR, 11 Bn	MISC.CRIMES	U.K.
CORTHAUSEN	250661	M			Sgt., Field-Pol., Gand (Bel.)	TORTURE	BEL.
CORZIENI	251992	M			Pvt., 8 Pz.Rgt.,1 Pz.Div.,SS-Leibstandarte "A.H.",Malmedy (Bel.)12.44	MURDER	U.S.
COSONOWSKY	254926	M			Lt., 3 Bn,311 D.C.A., F.P. 17512 (Fr.) 8.44	MURDER	FR.
COSTIK or COSTEK	251990	M	Ger.		Guard, C.C., Auschwitz (Pol.)	MISC.CRIMES	FR.
COTCHY	185345	M	Ger.		Lt., Army, St.Barthelemy de Cun (Fr.) 7.44	MURDER	FR.
COTERLAN	141912	M	Ger.		Guard, Stalag Wineburg (Aust.) 5.42	MURDER	FR.
COTT, Alfred	306352	M	Ger.		SS-Scharfhr., C.C. Buchenwald (Ger.) 5.38-10.43	MURDER	BEL.
COTTERMAN	106975	M	Ger.		Chief of Police, Polte Munitions Factory,Magdeburg (Ger.) 44-45	TORTURE	U.S.
COTTSCHAZK, Heinz	167005	M			Leffinskrouke (Fr.) 44	MURDER	FR.
COUCHARD or CARRET	31341	M			Waffen-SS, Seyssel (Fr.)	MURDER	FR.
COURRE	28824	M	Ger.		Adjutant, 12 Feldgend., Parachutist Unit,Abbeville-Somme (Fr.) 8.44	MURDER	FR.
COURTH see KURT, Wolf	250334						
COURTS	12649	M	Ger.		Hauptwachtmstr., SS, Gestapo, Bergen (Nor.) 41	TORTURE	NOR.
"COWBOY" (Nickname)	128771	M	Ger.		Cmdt., C.C. Niederorschel (Ger.) 1.43-44	MURDER	U.K.
CRAEMER	139823	M	Ger.		Capt., Stalag X B, Sandbostel (Ger.) 1.-5.45	MISC.CRIMES	U.S.
CRAICH, Beno	252930	M			Interpreter, SD, Chimay (Bel.) 4.44	MURDER	U.S.
CRAMER	142769			92	C.C. Lublin (Pol.) 42-45	WITNESS	FR.
CRAMER, Theodor or CREMER	193681	M	Ger.	29.9.06	Sgt.,Ministry of Justice, Punishment Camp Nord,Finmark(Nor.) 3.45	MURDER	NOR.
CRAMER, Wilhelm	135116	M	Ger.		Civilian, Camp Lintford (Ger.) 10.-11.44	WITNESS	U.S.
CRAMM, Christian	106978	M	Ger.		Lt., W-SS, Sturm-Bn,AOK 1, 1 Bn, 2 Coy, Courcelles sur Nied(Fr.)11.44	WITNESS	U.S.
CRAMSER	123973	M			Osturmfhr., SS, Leibstandarte "A.H.",I Rgt.,Malmedy and Wanne (Bel.)44	MURDER	U.S.
CRAPOHL, Hans	252004	M	Ger.		Kapo, C.C. Rathenow (Ger.) 9.44	MISC.CRIMES	NETH.
CRASEMANN, Eduard	179739	M	Ger.		Major,Gen., 26 Pz.Div.,Fucecchio Marshes (It.)	MURDER	U.K.
CRAUSE	193344	M	Ger.		Sgt., 181/Div., Molde (Nor.) 10.42	WITNESS	NOR.
CRAWFORD	124523	M	Ger.		Major, Stalag 357, Fallingbostel (Ger.)	MISC.CRIMES	U.K.
CREINER	193610	M	Ger.		Osturmbannfhr., SS, Hauptamt (Czech.) 41-45	TORTURE	CZECH.
CREMER see KRAEMER	150664						
CREMER, Peter	258905	M	Ger.		Hptscharfhr., C.C. Ohrdruf (Ger.) 44-45	MURDER	FR.
CREMER, Peter	190244	M	Ger.		Gestapo H.Q., Koeln (Ger.) 43-45	MURDER	U.K.
CREMER, Theodor see CRAMER	193681			29.9.06			
CREPS	164		Ger.		Capt., Gestapo, Sousse (Tunesie) 42	MISC.CRIMES	FR.
CRESUS, Otto	252047	M	Ger.		Custom official, Customs at Cierp-Hte,Garonne,Chaum(Fr.) 3.6.44	MISC.CRIMES	FR.

CRE-DAC

NAME	C.R.FILE NUMBER	SEX	NATIO-NALITY	DATE OF BIRTH	RANK OCCUPATION UNIT PLACE AND DATE OF CRIME	REASON WANTED	WANTED BY
CREUTZ	62229	M	Ger.		Brigadefhr.,SS-chief of Commis.for Ger.Racialism.	MISC.CRIMES	U.N.W.C.C.
CRIENITZ,Walter	192566	M	Ger.		Doctor,camp,Reichsjustizministerium,Strafgef.Lager Nord, Finmark (Nor.) 42-45	WITNESS	NOR.
CRIPINSKI,Lothar	192776	M	Ger.		Schupo,C.C.Falstad (Nor.) 41-45	MURDER	NOR.
CRISELLIOS	128867	M	Ger.		Civilian in a camp,Stalag XIII C.C.Bischofsheim (Ger.)	MURDER	U.K.
CRISELLIOS see KRAZILIUS	188532						
CRIWAN	185978	M	Ger.		Sgt.,Marinetruppe,Nord-Btty.,Texel (Neth.) 4.45	MURDER	NETH.
CROCKER	141917	M	Ger.		Cpl.,hospital,Cosel (Ger.)	TORTURE	U.K.
CROIMAN	185615	M	Ger.		Oberwachtmeister,prison,C.C.Brebieres (Fr.) 9.44	MURDER	FR.
CROME,Hermann	250678	M	Ger.		Capt.,police,Landratsamt,Helmstedt (Ger.)	MURDER	U.S.
CRONRAT,Hans	31336	M			Gerardmer (Fr.) 9.44	INCENDIARISM	FR.
CROSS	252048	M	Ger.		Capt.,SS-Pz.Gren.Regt.3 "Deutschland",Div."Das Reich",3 Bn., Marsoulas, Mazeres, Betchat and Justinias (Fr.) 6.44	MURDER	FR.
CROSSMAN or KROSSMANN	188570	M			Sgt.,guard,Army,prison,Fresner (Paris) (Fr.) spring 43	TORTURE	U.K.
CRULET	147344	M	Ger.		Capt.,II Pz.-Div.,Kampfgruppe "Wilde", (Fr.) 44	MURDER	FR.
CRUSIUS	139824	M	Ger.		Capt.,Stalag X B,Sandbostel (Ger.) 1.-5.45	MISC.CRIMES	U.S.
CRUTSCHNIG,Hans	162880	M	Ger.		Member,Gestapo,Stalag 317,C.C.Markt Pongau (Aust.) 11.44	TORTURE	FR.
CSERWANSKI	31334	M	Ger.		Sgt.(Oscharfhr.),Waffen-SS,C.C.Struthof-Natzweiler (Fr.) 42-44	MURDER	FR.
CSONKA,Michael	137746	M			Civilian,C.C.Rehmeid (Ger.)	TORTURE	U.S.
CUBSCH,Othmer	188933	M	Ger.		SS,18 Bn., Busset (Fr.) 8.44	MURDER	FR.
CUCK	155770	M		19	Guard,SS,C.C.Hohenrheim (Ger.) 2.-5.45	MURDER	U.S.
CUCUEL,Marold	129137	M	Ger.	95	Maj.,Dulag Luft,Oberursel,Frankfurt-Main (Ger.)	TORTURE	U.K.
CUGNI	261385	F	Ger.		Sgt.,Bn.Spielberg,Regt.z.b.V.Col.Wolff,vicinity of Mauleon-Navarreux (Fr.) 6.-8.44	MURDER	FR.
CUHORST,Hermann	261116	M	Ger.	7.99	President,special court,chairman,penal senate of county-court, Stuttgart (Ger.)	SUSPECT	U.S.
CUJAN,Johann	250098	M			Flyer,C.C.Ellrich,Nordhausen (Ger.)	MURDER	U.S.
CUMMBACK,Josef	306740	M	Ger.		Civilian,Nenterhaus (Ger.)	MURDER	U.S.
CUNDY	254927	M	Ger.	19 or 21	Member,SS,Mauthausen (Aust.)	INTERR.	FR.
CUNO or KUHNOW	152021	M	Ger.	95	Sgt.,Stalag IV D,Arbeitskdo.L 25,Lauchhammer (Ger.) 2.44	MURDER	U.K.
CUNO or KUNO	305879	M			SS-Osturmfhr.,head of SD,Leitabschnitt Prag, C.C.Oswiecim-Birkenau (Pol.) 39-45	MURDER	CZECH.
CUNO,Karl	252049	M			SS-Osturmfhr.,SS,SD,Ceske (Czech.)	MURDER	CZECH.
CUNOW,Friedrich	137747	M	Ger.		Civilian	MISC.CRIMES	U.S.
CUNTZ	259673	M			Court martial officer,Airforce,Paris (Fr.) 6.42	INTERR.	FR.
CUNZELEIT	140905	M			Uscharfhr.,SS,C.C.Breendonck (Bel.)	TORTURE	BEL.
CUPA,Karl or COPA,Rudolf	39635	M		05	Oberwachtmeister,Adjutant,Feldpost-Nr.L.30182 L.G.P.A.Paris, Cazeaux (Fr.) 8.44	MURDER	FR.
CURLAND,Erich	252931	M	Ger.	6.12.12	Farmer,Dettum (Ger.) 9.44	WITNESS	U.S.
CUROCH	67595	M			Army,2 Div.B,Cpl.,Noailles (Fr.) 4.44	MURDER	FR.
CURSNIK	155761	M	Ger.		Pvt.,guard,Arbeitskdo.E.708,Laband (Ger.) 10.44	MURDER	U.K.
CURT	193376	M	Ger.		SS-official,Brunswick,Vighen (Ger.) 40-42 and 44-45	MURDER	U.S.
CURT	260159	M	Ger.		Station-master,railway of Lille and Cologne,Hallebecke (Bel.) 2.-9.44	MURDER	FR.
CURTEN,Edward	147045	M			Uscharfhr.,SS,medical section,C.C.Mauthausen (Aust.) 41-45	MURDER	U.S.
CURTH,Walter	9644	M			Public prosecutor,Cheb (Czech.) 40	MURDER	CZECH.
CURTIN	256066	M	Ger.		Kapo,SS-Div."Das Reich",Mauthausen (Aust.)	MURDER	FR.
CURZWELL	152015	M			Kapo,C.C.Dachau (Ger.) 10.43	TORTURE	U.K.
CUSTERMANN,Wilhelm	130124	M			Owner of the brick-kiln at Freiburg-Elbe (Ger.) 43	TORTURE	BEL.
CUYPERS,Heinrich,Heinz	157414	M		14	Oscharfhr.,SS,Kripo,crim.asst.,Bruessel (Bel.)	MISC.CRIMES	BEL.
CUYRIN,Hans or CUYRIM	261915	M	Ger.		SS,Verdenne,Marenne,Marche en Famenne (Bel.) 9.44	MURDER	BEL.
CYBULACK,Gregor	139152	M	Ger.		Strafmeister,factory,civilian,Bad Oeynhausen (Ger.) 44-45	TORTURE	U.S.
CYGAN,Fritz	169516	M	Ger.		Osturmfhr.,SS,départm.head,Rasse- und Siedlungshauptamt	MISC.CRIMES	U.S.
CYMAN,Franz	169518	M	Ger.		Public official,guard,C.C.,Dortmund (Ger.)	MURDER	U.S.
CZABER or CZABERG,Gustav	192313	M			Kapo,C.C.Flossenburg (Ger.) 5.44-4.45	MURDER	U.S.,BEL.
CZADNY,Joseph	31317	M			Oscharfhr.,SD,Drance (Fr.)	TORTURE	FR.
CZAIKA,Max	259702	M			Member,Gestapo,area of Angers Maine and Loire (Fr.) 42-44	MISC.CRIMES	FR.
CZAPLA	175904	M			SS-Scharfhr.,C.C.Auschwitz (Pol.) 42	MURDER	U.N.W.C.C.
CZAPLIK	250097				Pvt.,C.C.Dora,Nordhausen (Ger.)	MURDER	U.S.
CZARNECKI,Ignak	259344	M	Ger.		Pvt.,Btty.of D.C.A.,Longvic les Dijon,Cote d'Or (Fr.) 8.44	MURDER	FR.
CZARNULIA,Erich	250652	M	Ger.	10.4.02	Official,Gestapo,Lodz (Pol.) 40-44	MURDER	POL.
CZERWANSKI	120070	M	Ger.		SS-Scharfhr.	MISC.CRIMES	FR.
CZECH,Hubert	305880	M	Ger.		Civilian,Velke,Heraltice (Czech.) 8.44	BRUTALITY	CZECH.
CZECZOR,Erich	167920	M	Ger.		Warder,C.C.Sachsenhausen and Oranienburg (Ger.) 39-4.45	MURDER	POL.
CZEKALA or CZEKALIA	31316	M	Ger.		Pvt.,SS-Div.,St.Sulpice,Chateaugontier,Laval,Fortmusson (Fr.) 8.44	MURDER	FR.
CZEKDIA,Paul	131259	M			Crim.secretary,Orpo,Blockaeltester,Auschwitz (Pol.)	MURDER	U.S.
CZEPICZKA	163715	M			Sturmfhr.,SS-Totenkopf-Standarte,Waffen-SS,Buchenwald,Weimar (Ger.)	TORTURE	U.S.
CZERMIN	169517	M			SS-Oscharfhr.,SS-Totenkopf-Sturmbann,C.C.Mauthausen (Aust.) 41-45	MURDER	U.S.
CZERNAY,Georg	254929	M	Ger.	8.12.00	Electrician,Gossengrun-Haberspik (Czech.) 9.39	MURDER	CZECH.
CZERNER,Gerhard	137745	M			Rottenfhr.,SS-Div."Das Reich"	MURDER	U.S.
CZERNICKI,Karl or WEBER	150962	M			Member,Gestapo,police-officer,Dortmund-Hoerde (Ger.)	MURDER	U.S.
CZERNIK see CERNIK	250096						
CZERNY,Eduard	9645	M	Ger.		Public prosecutor,Cheb (Czech.) 40	MURDER	CZECH.
CZERWINSKI,Hans	257475	M		10.8.12	Employes,C.C.Nordhausen (Ger.)	MURDER	U.S.
CZERWINSKI,Heinrich	250666	M	Ger.	10	Obermaat,Navy-Artl.,Brest (Fr.) 7.-8.44	MURDER	FR.,U.S.
CZERWINSKI,Josef,Anton,Wilhelm	301165	M			Administrator,private property,Enschede (Neth.) 3.42-4.45	PILLAGE	NETH.
CZULI see SZYLI,Joseph	256741						
CZYCHELL or CZYCHOLL,Johann	261110	M	Ger.		Oberwachtmeister,SS,penitentiary Nord, (Nor.) 6.42-5.45	MURDER	YUGO.
DABBERT	261007	M			SS-Uscharfhr.,C.C.Vaihingen (Ger.) 8.44-4.45	MURDER	U.S.
DABKA	193785	M	Ger.		SS-Scharfhr.,C.C.Buchenwald (Ger.) 42-44	TORTURE	U.S.
DACHMANN,Peter	182757	M			Pvt.,4 SS-Totenkopf-Sturmbann,C.C.Nordhausen (Ger.) 43-45	WITNESS	U.S.
DACHMAYER see BACHMAYER	256848						

DAC - DAN

NAME	C.R.FILE NUMBER	SEX	NATIO-NALITY	DATE OF BIRTH	RANK OCCUPATION UNIT PLACE AND DATE OF CRIME	REASON WANTED	WANTED BY
DACHO, Alois	250693	M		18.5.97	Pvt., Camp Ellrich, Nordhausen (Ger.)	MURDER	U.S.
DACHS, Bernhard	12591	M	Ger.		Pvt.,110 Or.,111 Panz.Gren.Rgt.,2 Coy.,Albine (Fr.) 6.44	MURDER	FR.
DAEGE, Fritz	140403	M	Ger.	97	Civilian,Lommatsch (Ger.)	MISC.CRIMES	FR.
DAEGER (see SAEGER)	302121	M	Ger.		Capt., Member of the Standgericht,1 Bn.,24 Rgt.,Fallschirmjg. Huebner 7 Div.,General Major Erdmann,Roermond (Neth.) 44-45	MURDER	NETH.
DAEHNIX	306181	M	Ger.		Lt.,Air Force,Prison,Graudenz (Pol.)	MISC.CRIMES	BEL.
DAELER	253613	M	Ger.		Commander, C.C.Auschwitz (Pol.)	MISC.CRIMES	FR.
DAEMM, Woldemar	257591	M	Ger.	93	Col.,Army, Strassburg,Barkenbruegge (Ger.) 44-45	MISC.CRIMES	YUGO.
DAEWES, August	195155	M		18.2.01	Member, Employee,Gestapo,Kolin (Czech.) 39-45	MURDER	CZECH.
DAHL	196093	M			Sgt.,Wach Bn.,C.C.Royallien Oise (Fr.) 41-44	MURDER	FR.
DAHL, Theodor	185674	M		9.4.14	Factory Manager,Beauftragter fuer Ruestung und Kriegsproduction,Brno	PILLAGE	CZECH.
DAHLGRUN	185390	M			Doctor,Arbeitskommando,Hamburg-Harburg (Ger.) 40-45	MISC.CRIMES	FR.
DAHLHOFF	162137	M	Ger.		Sgt.,Army, Semaphure de Creach Maout (Fr.) 8.44	MURDER	FR.
DAHLKE, Max	196950	M			Civilian,Berlin-Reinickendorf (Ger.) 21.6.44	WITNESS	U.S.
DAHLMANN	193786	M			SS-Hptscharfhr. Chief Clerk,C.C.Buchenwald (Ger.) 44-45	TORTURE	U.S.
DAHMEN	140406	M		93	Prison-Guard,C.C.Cologne (Ger.) 44	MURDER	FR.
DAHMEN	182781	M			SS-Mann,4 SS-Totenkopf Sturmbann,C.C.Nordhausen Mittelbau (Ger.) 43-45	WITNESS	U.S.
DAHMEN, Bernhard	261909	M			Ortsgruppenleiter, Mayor,NSDAP,Welkenraedt (Bel.)	MURDER	BEL.
DAHN	135149	M	Ger.		Kommissar,SS-Gestapo HQ's, Koeln (Ger.)	MURDER	U.S.
DAHN	191983	M	Ger.		Oberlt.,Feldgendarmerie,Chateau,Briand (Fr.)	TORTURE	FR.
DAHNEM, Joseph	723541	M			Cpl.,Gestapo,Waffen-SS,C.C. Klingelpuetz (Fr.)	MISC.CRIMES	U.S.
DAHNKE, Franz	262008	M		12.6.05	SS-Mann,Dirlewanger Bde.,Waffen-SS,Gren.Div.36,Warsaw and other (Pol.)	MURDER	POL.
DAIGENESCH	193350	M			2 Coy,PW Work Bn.,206,Mosjoen,Finnland, Germany, Norway	MURDER	NOR.
DAIKER, Georg	140408	M		00	Member,DAF,Bremen (Ger.)	MURDER	U.S.
DAITZ	260647	M		84	Crimes against peace,War Crimes, Crimes against humanity,	WITNESS	U.S.
DAJDOCK	257590	M			SS-Sgt.,5 Coy. Klein Bodungen,Nordhausen (Ger.)	MURDER	U.S.
DALHAUSEN	72355	M		95	Sgt., Prison-Guard,C.C.Rheinbach (Ger.)	MISC.CRIMES	U.S.
DALHEIMER, Firmin	253620	M		10	N.C.O.,Gend. (Bel.)	INTERR.	BEL.
DALL, Friedrich,Wilhelm	252949	M	Ger.		Sgt.,Army, Parachutists 17 Rgt., Nieuwaal (Neth.) 1.45	WITNESS	NETH.
DALLMANN, Paul	258089	M	Ger.		SS-Sturmscharfhr.,Police Official,State Service,Val Mezirici (Czech.)45	MURDER	CZECH.
DALLMER, Zerbe	108723	M			Lt., Colonel, Cmdt., Staff of Military Prison,C.C.Graudenz (Pol.) 7.44	MURDER	U.K.
DALMEIER	144314	M			C.C.Kunseebeck (Ger.) 3.45	TORTURE	U.S.
DALMER, Zerbe	175680	M			Cmdt.,Col.,Army,Graudenz (Pol.) 7.44	MURDER	U.S.
DALOS	189947	M			Agent,Police, Novi Sad (Yugo.)	MURDER	YUGO.
DALUEGE	151981	M			SS,C.C.Flossenburg (Ger.)	MURDER	U.S.
DALUEGE, Karl	305010	M	Ger.		Head of Camp,POW Labour Camp No.90,Peine (Ger.) 41-45	TORTURE	POL.
DAM	261059	M	Ger.		Major,Ortskmdt.,17 Panzer Div. Amiens (Fr.)5.6.40	INCENDIARISM	FR.
DAMANN, Claus	167923	M	Ger.		Surgeon,Fahr E.s.Coy. Ausb.6 Staff,Plombirec (Fr.) 7.44	WITNESS	FR.
DAMANN, Wilhelm	182770	M		9.9.94	Unterscharfhr.,4 SS-Totenkopf Sturmbann,C.C.Nordhausen Mittelbau (Ger.)	WITNESS	U.S.
DAMASCH, Gerhard	259804	M	Ger.		Parachutist,6 Div.Paratroopers 17 Rgt., Nieuwaal (Neth.) 1.45	MURDER	NETH.
DAMASCHK, Richard,Ernst	196722	M		4.12.11	Oberwachtmeister, Pol.Waffenschule III,Apeldoorn near Arnheim (Neth.)45	MURDER	NETH.
DAMASCHKE	152001	M			Oberscharfhr., Blockleiter, C.C.Mauthausen (Aust.) 41-45	MURDER	U.S.
DAMASCHKE, Otto	182782	M		29.5.89	Scharfhr.,4 SS-Totenkopf Sturmbann,C.C. Nordhausen Mittelbau(Ger.)43-45	WITNESS	U.S.
DAMASCUS	67588	M	Ger.		Capt, Army,Fortrauch,Posen (Ger. Pol.)4.10.41	MISC.CRIMES	U.K.
DAMEN	140410	M			Civilian,Geisweid (Ger.)	TORTURE	FR.
DAMEN, Frederic	140411	M	Ger.	05	Civilian,C.C.Mauthausen (Aust.) 44	MURDER	FR.
DAMIG	174179	M			O.T.,C.C.Muehldorf-Ampfing (Ger.) 6.44-4.45	MURDER	U.S.
DAMINCHEN, Robert	196103	M			Guard,Stalag V.A.,C.C.Ludwigsburg (Ger.)	MURDER	FR.
DAMKE, Fritz	151178	M			C.O.,Volkssturm,C.C.Vicinity of Gardelegen (Ger.) 10.-14.4.45	MURDER	U.S.
DAMM	196719	M	Ger.		Lt.,Neuengamme (Ger.)	TORTURE	BEL.
DAMM	306792	F	Ger.		Secretary,Gestapo Office,Chambery (Fr.)	MURDER	FR.
DAMM, Heinrich	306767	M	Ger.		Dorheim (Ger.) 5.44 und 28.,29.7.44	BRUTALITY	U.S.
DAMM, Ludwig	251496	M		15.8.11	Official,SS,Auschwitz (Pol.) Birkenau 42-45	MURDER	YUGO.,POL.
DAMMAN, Heinrich	140414	M	Ger.		Civilian, Lippe (Ger.)	TORTURE	FR.
DAMMAN, Wilhelm	193286	M		96	Member,SS,Ruding (Ger.) 6.44	MURDER	U.K.
DAMMANN, Hermann	192311	M	Ger.		Civilian,Neu Wuhnsdorf (Ger.) 6.44	MURDER	U.S.
DAMMASCH, Franz	252940	M	Ger.		Sgt., Feld-Gendarmerie 924, La Folatière (Fr.) 6.44	MURDER	FR.
DAMMASCH, Gerhard	252950	M	Ger.		Army,Nieuwaal (Neth.) 1.45	WITNESS	NETH.
DAMMER, Ria	193886	F			C.C.Ravensbrueck (Ger.)	TORTURE	FR.
DAMMERICH, Kurt	250694	M			Oberscharfhr., 4 SS.Totenkopf Sturmbann,C.C. Nordhausen (Ger.) 43-45	WITNESS	U.S.
DAMMERMANN	72457	M			Cpl.,Army,Ers.Bn.230,Luzek (Sov.Un.)	MURDER	FR.
DAMMI	140415	M	Ger.	95	Group Leader,NSDAP,Feuerbach (Ger.) 44	MURDER	FR.
DAMMINCHEN (or DAMMINCHER)	164608	M			Kdo.Chief,1 Rgt.,422,Kdo 2036,Manufactory of Beruwerk,Ludwigsburg (Ger.) 10.43	MURDER	FR.
DAMMRICH	31376	M	Ger.		Cpt., Army,I-307 Gren.Rgt.,163 Inf.Div.,20 Army, (Nor.) 44	MURDER	NOR.
DAMMS	173200	M			C.C. Schirmeck,Saales (Fr.)	TORTURE	U.K.
DAMREMONT	28825	M		93	Lt.,Army,Command of POW, Kassar-Said (Tunesia) 1.43	MURDER	FR.
DAMUR, Ludwig	301726	M	Ger.		C.C. Auschwitz (Pol.) 40	MURDER	FR.
DANCKERS	152008	M			Civilian,Neu Wuhnsorf (Ger.) 6.44	WITNESS	U.S.
DANECKER	135146	M		05	SS-Hauptsturmfhr., SS-Pol.,Advisor on Jewish,Question to the chief of security, Ungarn Germany	WITNESS	U.S.
DANEXER	145555	M			Agent,Gestapo Paris (Fr.) 41-42	MISC.CRIMES	FR.
DANIEL, Johann	257592	M	Ger.	5.3.93	Gend. Civilian Inkeeper,State Service, Bilina (Czech.) 39-45	BRUTALITY	CZECH.
DANIEL, Wilhelm	305011	M			Cd., Military Governor,Larissa 41-44	MURDER	GRC.
DANIELZIK, Ludwig	124914	M			Supervisor,Kriegsgefangenenlager,C.C.Rhede,Bocholt (Ger.)	TORTURE	SOV.UN.
DANES	190675	M	Ger.		Pvt.,Eis.Art.Bat.717,St.Andries,Varsenare, Lez Bruges (Bel.)	MURDER	BEL.
DANIEL	166950	M			Tyez (Fr.) 7.44	MURDER	FR.
DANIEL	166951	M			Pvt.,Army,Oberkdo., La Rochette (Fr.) 8.44	MURDER	FR.
DANIEL	191501	M	Ger.		Cpl.,General Staff,Kommandantur,Crest (Fr.) 7.-8.44	MURDER	FR.

DAN - DAU

NAME	C.R.FILE NUMBER	SEX	NATIO-NALITY	DATE OF BIRTH	RANK OCCUPATION UNIT PLACE AND DATE OF CRIME	REASON WANTED	WANTED BY
DANIEL	306825	M	Ger.		Dr.,Oberfeldarzt, Dr. Raschers immediate superior and friend, C.C. Dachau, Auschwitz (Ger.,Pol.) 3.42 2.43	TORTURE	BEL.
DANIEL, Erich Albin	168	M	Ger.	3. 4.06	Kreisleiter NSDAP, Mogilno (Pol.) 10.39, 41, 43	MISC.CRIMES	POL.
DANIEL, Jacob	255968	M			SS-Mann, Nordhausen (Ger.)	MURDER	U.S.
DANIELS	28828	M	Ger.		Capt.,Army, Fallschirmjaeger O.C. 3.Coy.,Relecq,Kerhoun (Fr.) 7.-8.44	PILLAGE	FR.
DANIELS	128868	M	Ger.		Capt.,Stalag III D, C.C. Berlin (Ger.)	MISC.CRIMES	U.K.
DANISCH	12424	M	Ger.		Cpl.,Army, 110.or 111.Panz.Gren.Rgt., Gourdon (Fr.) 6.44	MURDER	FR.
DANISCH	259945	M	Ger.		Kapo (German prisoner), Auschwitz (Pol.)	MURDER	FR.
DANISCH, Gerhard	179754	M	Ger.	10	Lt., 76.Pz.Army Corps, Cavriglia (It.) 1.44	MURDER	U.K.
DANKELMAN	301944	M	Ger.		Member S.D. Kdo."Knop", Enschede (Neth.) late 44	MURDER	NETH.
DANKELMANN	169	M	Ger.	88	Airforce, General Army, Serbia	MURDER	YUGO.
DANKELMAYER, Jan	252291	M	Ger.		Employee, Gestapo, Breclav (Czech.) 39-45	MISC.CRIMES	CZECH.
DANKERT	255515	M	Ger.	07	Crim.Comm., Gestapo, Breslau (Ger.)	MURDER	U.K.
DANKI, Franz	262012	M	Ger.	19. 7.08	SS-Mann, Waffen SS,Gren.Div.36, Dirlewanger-Bde.,Warsaw and other (Pol.) 40-44	MURDER	POL.
DANKOFF, Theo	262237	M	Ger.	13. 8.15	Lt., 2.Group, 51.SS-Armoured-Bde., Breviandes, Bucheres,St.Savine, La Riviere, De Corps, Troyes (Aube) (Fr.) 8.44	BRUTALITY	FR.
DANKWART	169477	M	Ger.	96	Cpl., Army, Bitterfeld (Ger.) 2.-4.45	TORTURE	U.K.
DANNEAL	261384	M	Ger.		Lt.Col., POW-Camp, Bologna (It.) 6.44	MURDER	U.S.
DANNEBERG	164610	M	Ger.		Lt., 36.Panz.Rgt. 10.Panz.Div., Waffen SS, Revin (Fr.) 6.44	MURDER	FR.
DANNEBERG	252948	M	Ger.		Capt., Abwehr, St. 17 B, Gneixendorf (Ger.) 40-43	MISC.CRIMES	FR.
DANNEBOOM	141496	F	Ger.		Overseer, C.C. Buchenwald (Ger.) 44	TORTURE	FR.
DANNECKER	170	M	Ger.	10	Lt.,Gestapo, Drancy camp Paris (Fr.)	MURDER	FR.
DANNEKER	141499	M	Ger.	10	Oscharfhr., SS, Gestapo, Drancy (Fr.) 42-44	TORTURE	FR.
DANNEKER	196094	M	Ger.		Lt., Gestapo C.C. Royallieu Oise (Fr.) 41-44	MURDER	FR.
DANNEL	193787	M	Ger.		Usturmfhr., Political Dept. Buchenwald (Ger.) 41-42	TORTURE	U.S.
DANNENBERG	250685	M			Pvt., Camp Ellrich Nordhausen (Ger.)	MURDER	U.S.
DANNENBERG, Willi	155758	M			Pol.Prisoner, Civ., C.C. Gardelegen C.C. Wieda (Ger.) 4.45	WITNESS	U.S.
DANNER	173760	M	Ger.		Commander, Col., 737.Rgt., Yugo. 42-44	MURDER	YUGO.
DANNER, Albert	151988	M	Ger.		Civ., Munich, Pasing (Ger.)	TORTURE	U.S.
DANNERT, Heinz	250686	M		30. 3.23	Pvt. Camp Ellrich, Nordhausen (Ger.)	MURDER	U.S.
DANNHAUSEN	300216	M	Ger.		Capt., Jaeger-Bn.,Calavrita, Mega, Apileon,Aghia Lavra, 12.43	MURDER	GRC.
DANNHAUSER, Johann	186735	M	Ger.	15. 7.99	Capt., Nachschubstab, Nuernberg (Ger.) 4.45	MURDER	U.S.
DANOVSKY	12592	M	Ger.		Lt., 110.or 111.Pz.Gren.Rgt. 10.Coy., Gourdon (Fr.) 6.44	MURDER	FR.
DANSKOPF	149561	M	Ger.		Capt., Army, Ghetto de Riga (Latv.) 11.41	MURDER	FR.
DANTZ	141500	F	Ger.	10	Kommando-Fuehrerin, C.C. Malchow (Ger.) 44-45	MURDER	FR.
DANZ	31377	M	Ger.		Capt., Inf.Rgt. 378-111, 169.Inf.Div. 20.Army, Nor. 10.-11.44	MURDER	NOR.
DANZEISEN	178077	M	Ger.		Capt., Kriegsgef.Arbeits-Bn.185 2.Coy. C.C. Bod (Nor.)	MURDER	NOR.
DANZER, Georg	185980	M	Ger.		Farmer, Stalag XIII D, C.C. Woernitz, Ansbach (Ger.)	TORTURE	BEL.
DANZIG, Hans	151189	M			Lageraeltester, C.C. Mauthausen (Aust.) 41-45	MURDER	U.S.
DANZIGER	128869	M	Ger.		Sgt., Landesschtz. 565, Silesia,West-Sudetenland (Ger.) 1.-3.45	TORTURE	U.K.
DANZMAYER, Johann	187905	M	Ger.	15.11.02	Criminal-secretary, Gestapo, S.D., Brno (Czech.) 39-45	MURDER	CZECH.
DARB, Karl	261989	M	Aust.-Ger.	4. 7.08	Dr., Hptsturmfhr., Dirlewanger-Bde., SS-Gren.Div.36, Warsaw, Lublin, Sluck and other towns, (Pol.) 40-44	MURDER	POL.
DARGATZ, August	193779	M	Ger.	13. 8.01	SS Usturmfhr., Obersekretaer, SS, Gestapo, Landskroun (Czech.) 38-45	TORTURE	CZECH.
DARGEL	171	M	Ger.		Public official, Reg.Praesident, Ciechanow (Pol.) 9.39-42	MURDER	POL.
DARGEL, Walter	64874	M			Scharfhr., Gestapo H.Q., Fredrikstad (Nor.)	TORTURE	NOR.
DARGES, Fritz Willi	260646	M		13	Ogruppenfhr., Waffen SS	WITNESS	U.S.
DARMOPIL, Johann	251296	M	Ger.	20.12.08	Legal official, State service, Tisnov (Czech.) 42	INTERR.	CZECH.
DARMSTADTER	190231	M		09	Sturmscharfhr., SS, Colmar (Fr.) 1.45	TORTURE	U.S.
DARMSTAEDTER, Hermann	198225	M	Ger.		Adjudant, Cdt., C.C. Niederbuhl (Ger.)	TORTURE	FR.
DARRENBERG	174181	M			SS Oscharfhr., C.C. Muehldorf, Ampfing (Ger.) 6.44-4.45	MISC.CRIMES	U.S.
DAR VIKTOR, Heinr. see EBELING, Karl	142336						
DATTES	250684	M			Waffen SS, Camp Rottleberode, Nordhausen (Ger.)	MURDER	U.S.
DATTLER	257984	M			SS-Guard, SS slave Labour Camp, Beisfjord nr.Narvik (Nor.) 6.-11.42	BRUTALITY	YUGO.
DATZ or VON DATZ	253625	M	Ger.		Capt., 1.Bn. 376.Jaeger-Rgt., Vinkt (Bel.)	MISC.CRIMES	BEL.
DATZAR	174	M			Pvt., Warder of prison militaire, Caen (Fr.)6.44	MURDER	FR.
DATZAR	72469	M			Pvt., Army	MURDER	FR.
DAUB, Ernest	138206	M	Ger.		Civ., Pol.	MURDER	FR.
DAUBE, Karol	185677	M	Ger.		SS Department against Communism, Kokkinia-Athens (Grc.)	TORTURE	GRC.
DAUBENSCHMIDT	173759	M	Ger.		Major, Kreiskommandantur Ujice (Yugo.) 9.43	MURDER	YUGO.
DAUBER	186465	M	Ger.		Hptsturmfhr., SS, S.D., Paris-Lyss (Fr.) 5.44	MISC.CRIMES	FR.
DAUBERSCHUTZ	191665	M	Ger.		Deputy, Gestapo of Toulouse, Retseek-Pau (Fr.) 43	MURDER	FR.
DAUBS, Willy	141503	M	Ger.	09	SS-Mann, C.C. Dora-Mittelbau Nordhausen (Ger.)	PILLAGE	FR.
DAUBSCHTEIN	141504	M	Ger.		Stalag VI G, Kommando B 5 Gladbeck, Bonn (Ger.)	MURDER	FR.
DAUDA	141505	M	Ger.		Fuehrer C.C. Schwenningen (Ger.) 44	TORTURE	FR.
DAUER	108963	M	Ger.		Pvt., C.C. Marienburg (Pol.) 5.44	MURDER	POL.
DAUER	305834	M	Ger.		Pvt., 1.Aufkl.Abt. 3.Coy. 2.Col. XV.Div. Afrika-Corps, St.Léger (Arlon) 9.44	MISC.CRIMES	BEL.
DAUER, Adolf-August	252286	M	Ger.	96	Employee, Gestapo, Prag (Czech.)	MURDER	CZECH.
DAUFELDT, Helmuth	256556	M	Ger.		Hptscharfhr., S.D., Tromsoe, Trondheim (Nor.)	TORTURE	NOR.
DAUGS, Willi	256554	M	Ger.	6. 3.00	Employee, C.C. Block 2 Nordhausen (Ger.)	MURDER	U.S.
DAULMERIE	252279	M	Ger.		Hilfspolizei-Beamter, interpreter, "U-B"-Abt. SIPO, Brussels (Bel.) 40-44	INTERR.	BEL.
DAUM	175	M			Public official, Stellvertreter d.Reg.Praesid.Wartheland (Pol.) 39-42	MURDER	POL.
DAUM aliases DAIN	193193	M	Ger.		Pvt., Army, C.C. Akervika (Nor.)	MURDER	NOR.
DAUM, Theodor	133766	M	Ger.		SS Rottfhr., C.C. Buchenwald (Ger.) 45	TORTURE	U.S.
DAUMANN	72492	M	Ger.		Unit of General von Arnt, Scupples (Fr.)	MURDER	FR.
DAUMER	12593	M	Ger.		Pvt., Army, 110.or 111.Panz.Gren.Rgt. 2.Coy., Albine (Fr.) 6.44	MURDER	FR.
DAUMER	141508	M	Ger.		Agent, Gestapo, Goeppingen (Ger.)	TORTURE	FR.
DAIN see DAUM	193193						
DAIN, Josef	251300	M	Ger.		SS Rottfhr., Driver, Dept.,Gestapo, de L'aube (Fr.) 43-44	INTERR.	FR.
DAUNER	300219	M			Col., officer commanding the 737.rifle-Rgt., Tripolis, 3.44	MURDER	GRC.
DAUSKY	139131	M			Chief, Gestapo, Martuliek (Czech.) 11.44	MURDER	U.S.

DAU - DEH

NAME	C.R.FILE NUMBER	SEX	NATIO-NALITY	DATE OF BIRTH	RANK OCCUPATION UNIT PLACE AND DATE OF CRIME	REASON WANTED	WANTED BY
DAUST	189689	M	Ger.		Member Gestapo,Stanislawow(Pol.)8.41-10.42	MURDER	POL.
DAUTERE	147342	M	Ger.		Obscharfhr.1 Panz.Div.SS,3 Gruppe,Kampfgr."Wilde"(Fr.)44	MURDER	FR.
DAUTH	250695	M			Rottfhr.Camp Nixei,Nordhausen(Ger.)	MURDER	U.S.
DAUZET, Eric	72433	M			Lt.Army,Dunes(Fr.)6.44	MURDER	FR.
DAVID	167910	M	Ger.		Adjutant,Bat.of Georgians 4 Coy.,Tulle,Correze(Fr.)4.44	MISC.CRIMES	FR.
DAVID	252941	M	Ger.		Agent Gestapo,Limoges(Fr.)40-45	INTERR	FR.
DAY	141509	M	Ger.		Adjudant,Army(Fr.)	PILLAGE	FR.
DAZE	154446	M	Ger.	20	Pvt.German Army,610 Land.Schtz.Bn.,Bohnhof(Ger.)5.44	MURDER	U.K.
DAZENKO	174182	M			Member,Labour Camp,CC Muehldorf Ampfing(Ger.)6.44-4.45	MISC.CRIMES	U.S.
DEAK, Laszlo	152007	M			Major,SS 25 Hunyadi Div.,Ujvidek(Hung.)	MURDER	U.S.
DE ANGELIS, Maximilian	173329	M	Ger.	99	Generaloberst,2nd Panzerarmee(Yugo.)42-44	MURDER	YUGO.
DEECKER	162885	M	Ger.		Lt.Army,Waamuel-Mons(Bel.)9.44	MURDER	U.K.
DEBIE alias Francois DUVAL	185988	M	Ger.		SS,Charleroi,Bruessel(Bel.)40-45	MURDER	FR.
DEBLOCK, Andree	141510	M	Ger.	98	Lille(Fr.)	MISC.CRIMES	FR.
DE BODA SECKELY	151994	M		95	Col.Army Stalag IIIC,KL Altdrewitz(Ger.)9.44-2.45	TORTURE	U.S.
DEBOLT	189996	M			Wachtmeister,Police,Malce Recica(Yugo.)7.43-2.44	MURDER	YUGO.
DEBRICH, Fritz	137750	M	Ger.		Civilian,Wollendorf(Ger.)10.43	WITNESS	U.S.
DEBRODT, Hans	151176	M	Ger.	85	1 Volkssturm Bn.and Civilian Regional Official Commander,Vicinity of Gardelegen(Ger.)4.45	MURDER	U.S.
DEBROS	141512	M	Ger.		Litzell,Steiermark(Aust.)	MURDER	FR.
DE BRUYN, Arend	257939	M			Osturmfhr.150 Panz.Bde.,Operation Grieff,12.44	MISC.CRIMES	U.S.
DEBUS	108722	M		15	Osturmfhr.Kommissar,SS Gestapo Hq.(Ger.)44	MURDER	U.S.
DEBUS	129802	M		04	SS Osturmfhr.	MURDER	U.S.
DEBUS	174189	M	Ger.		Employee,Stalag VIA,CC Hemer(Ger.)41-45	TORTURE	U.S.
DEBUS, Else	194817	F	Ger.		Civilian,Wieterode Galgenkopf(Ger.)2.45	MURDER	U.S.
DECHO, Hans	258698	M	Ger.		Mechanic,Airfield,Wieseck(Ger.)4.44	WITNESS	U.S.
DECIOUS	28826	M			Lt.Army,KL Perigueux(Fr.)6.-7.44	MURDER	FR.
DECK	72440	M			Capt.Chief of Coy.Army,95 Sich.Regt.12 Coy.,Celles(Fr.)6.44	MURDER	FR.
DECK	155633	M			Capt.Army,Laveissiere(Fr.)	LOOTING	FR.
DECKE, Hans	151999	M		12. 1.21	Pvt.Army,2 Coy.Land.Schtz.Bn.24,Augsburg(Ger.)40-4.45	MURDER	U.S.
DECKER	72441	M			Oscharfhr.SS Panz.Regt.,Chaors(Fr.)	MISC.CRIMES	FR.
DECKER	141514	M	Ger.		Chief KL Unterbillig(Ger.)	TORTURE	FR.
DECKER	155750	M	Ger.		Lt.Inf.Div.16,SS Camp de Nouatre,Maille(Fr.)44	MURDER	FR.
DECKER	252939	M	Ger.		Gen.29 Regt.3 Div.Pz.Grenadier,Hogneville(Fr.)8.44	MISC.CRIMES	FR.
DECKER, Friedrich	250957	M	Ger.		Member S.D.,Toulouse(Fr.)8.44	MISC.CRIMES	FR.
DECKER, Heinz	251039	M	Ger.		Member,Oscharfhr.S.D.,Toulouse(Fr.)11.42-8.44	MISC.CRIMES	FR.
DECKER, Karl	250696	M			Uscharfhr.Camp Harzungen,Nordhausen(Ger.)	MURDER	U.S.
DECKERT	250697	M			Oscharfhr.Camp Dora/Ellrich,Nordhausen(Ger.)	MURDER	U.S.
DECKERT, Albert	174184	M			Member,Labour Camp,CC Muehldorf Ampfing(Ger.)6.44-4.45	MURDER	U.S.
DECKMANN	185393	M	Ger.		Pvt.Fallschirmjaeger Regt.2 Bn.,Plouzane(Fr.)44	MURDER	FR.
DE CLERK	162	M			Feldkommandantur 755,Sec.Lt.,Le Mans(Fr.)40-44	PILLAGE	FR.
DEDELOW	62273	M	Ger.		SS 1st Lt.17 SS Panz.Div.1 Coy.,St.Aubin du Perron(Fr.)6.44	MURDER	U.S.
DEDERDING	252944		Ger.	87	Lt.15 Pol.Regt.,Crescentino(It.)9.44	INTERR.	U.K.IT.
DEDERDING, August	192115	M	Ger.	81	Member Gestapo,Liege(Bel.)	TORTURE	BEL.
DEDETCHEK	152013	M	Ger.		Capt.Stalag,KL Stalag IVA,396 Land.Schtz.Bn.4 Coy.,Riesa(Ger.)44-45	MURDER	U.S.
DEDIEU	141516	M	Ger.		Agent,Gestapo,Toulouse(Fr.)	MURDER	FR.
DEDONCKER	162884	M	Ger.		Major,Geh.Feldpolizei,Bruessels(Bel.)	TORTURE	U.K.
DEELITZ	195471	M	Ger.	11	Capt.17 SS Div.38 Regt.,Caen(Fr.)7.44	MURDER	U.S.
DEERING	130175	M	Ger.		Oflag 64,Schusim(Pol.)2.45	TORTURE	U.S.
DEERING see DOERING	151990						
DEERINGER, Anton	151992	M		15	Oscharfhr.Waffen SS,Totenkopf Standarte,KL Buchenwald,Weimar(Ger.)	TORTURE	U.S.
DEERT, Jakobs	185675	M	Ger.	09	Hptsturmfhr.SS Art.Ausbildungs und Ersatz Regt.,Prague(Czech.)5.45	MURDER	CZECH.
DEFFLINGER or DEFTLINGER or DETFLINGER	72429	M	Ger.		Lt.Army,St.Germain des Fosses(Fr.)44	MURDER	FR.
DEFFLINGER or DELFINGE	191974	M			2nd Lt.Army,Billy(Fr.)8.44	PILLAGE	FR.
DEFFNER	72359	M	Ger.	15. 2.10	SS Rottenfhr.CC Struthof Natzweiler(Fr.)	MURDER	FR.
DEFFNER, Emil	192231	M	Ger.		Col.Fallschirmjaeger Regt.2,Guegon(Fr.)	MURDER	FR.
DEFFNER, Georg	261085	M	Ger.		SS Oscharfhr.CC Natzweiler Struthof(Fr.)41	MURDER	FR.
DEFFNERT	191975	M	Ger.		Col.Fallschirmjaeger Regt.,La Touche en Guillac(Fr.)7.44	PILLAGE	FR.
DEFNER, Liselotte	148945	F	Ger.	21	Guard,CC Grueneberg(Ger.)44	TORTURE	FR.
DEFTLINGER see DEFFLINGER	141517						
DEGARD, Claudius	72437	M			Milicien,Cusset(Fr.)6.44	MURDER	FR.
DEGE	196097	M	Ger.		Meister der Gendarmerie V.Traeger,CC Westerbork,Ordnungs Polizei (Neth.)9.-12.44	MURDER	NETH.
DEGEN	141519	M			Oscharfhr.SS KL Ravensbrueck(Ger.)	MISC.CRIMES	FR.
DEGEN	301896	M	Ger.		Stubafhr.Comd.I/SS Geb.Jaeger Regt.11/6 SS Geb.Div.Nord,20 Army Finmark(Nor.)11.44.	MURDER	NOR.
DEGEN, C.M.	252954	M		22. 5.80	Photographer,Fokker Works,Amsterdam(Neth.)9.44	PILLAGE	NETH.
DEGEN, Carl	31948	M	Ger.		Capt.Army,2 Regt.F.N.P.L.62546,Locmine(Fr.)7.44-8.44	MURDER	FR.
DEGENER	185392	M	Ger.		Hptwachtmeister,Pol.Regt.19,6 Coy.,Aurillac(Fr.)6.44	MURDER	FR.
DEGENER	193889	M	Ger.		General Army,Loire and Ampuis(Fr.)8.44	MURDER	FR.
DECENHARDT	67817	M	Ger.		Doctor,Civilian,CC Kranenburg(Ger.)9.44	MURDER	U.K.,U.S.
DEGER	1552	M			Oberfeldwebel,Lager Stalag XIA,KL Haldensleben	MISC.CRIMES	U.S.
DEGERT or DEGIERT	193348	M	Ger.		Sgt.Kriegsgefangen Arb.Bn.41 CC,Kristiansund,Nerlandsdal(Nor.)41-45	TORTURE	NOR.
DEGNER, Fritz	125692	M	Ger.	12	Oscharfhr.S.D.de Poitiers Gestapo CC.(Fr.)40-44	TORTURE	FR.
DEGNER, Georg	305586	M	Ger.		Member,CC Personnel,CC Flossenburg,Hersbruck,Wolkenburg,Ganacker and Leitmeritz(Ger.C.S.R.)1.42-5.45	MURDER	U.S.
DEGRAAF	162666	M			Political prisoner,Civilian,KL Hannover,Gardelegen(Ger.)4.45	WITNESS	U.S.
DEHLEFSEN, Margareta	307068	F			Head nurse,Town Hospital,Luenaborg(Ger.)1.43-4.45	MURDER	YUGO.
DEHLER	129803	M	Ger.	05	Lt.57 Inf.Div.,Woronesch(Russ.)7.42	MURDER	U.S.
DEHLERT	129804	M	Ger.		Lt.Sturmfhr.Military,3 SS Panz.Regt.Engr.Coy.(Russ.)	MURDER	U.S.
DEHNE, Adolf	129504	M	Ger.		Pvt.Fallschirmjaeger Regt.5,Quaregnon,Jemappes/Ghlin(Bel.)9.44	MURDER	BEL.

DEH - DEM

NAME	C.R.FILE NUMBER	SEX	NATIO-NALITY	DATE OF BIRTH	RANK OCCUPATION UNIT PLACE AND DATE OF CRIME	REASON WANTED	WANTED BY
DEHNE, Ferdinand	72452	M	Ger.		Department Dordogne (Fr.)	MURDER	FR.
DEHNE, Paul	182783	M	Ger.	18. 8.03	Rottfhr., SS,C.C.Nordhausen (Ger.) 43-45	MURDER	U.S.
DEHNER, Ernst	260645	M			Lt.General, Army, Inf.	WITNESS	U.S.
DEIBERT, Georg	196893	M			Rottfhr.,1 SS-Pz.Div."Leibst.Adolf Hitler",St.Oumont (Bel.) 12.44	INTERR.	U.S.
DEICHMULLER	147083	M	Ger.		Soldier, Army, Boten-Camp.Rognan (Norway) 43	MURDER	YUGO.
DEICHNER, Karl	182758	M			SS-Mann,4 SS-Totenkopfsturmbann,C.C.Nordhausen,Mittelbau(Ger.)43-45	WITNESS	U.S.
DEICHSEL	252280	M	Ger.		Osturmfhr.,SS,Sipo Abt.IV B 1 (Bel.)	INTERR.	BEL.
DEIDENBACH, Harry	252955	M	Ger.		Cpl.,II Bn.,18 Fallschirmjaeger-Regt."Hermann Goering", Amersfoort (Neth.) 5.45	MURDER	NETH.
DEIFEL	72360	M	Ger.		Uschfhr., Waffen-SS,C.C.Struthof (Fr.)	MISC.CRIMES	FR.
DEIGENTASCH	250682	M			Flyer,Camp.Ellrich,Nordhausen (Ger.)	MURDER	U.S.
DEIGMOLLER, Ernest George	305014	M		5. 4.97	Collaborator,Member,5 Column,NSDAP,German colony, Holland-Action,Commission,Apeldoorn(Neth.) 43	INTERR.	NETH.
DEIK	141520	M	Ger.		Industriel a Massevald (Pomeranie)	TORTURE	FR.
DEILITSCH, Richard	193784	M		03	Civilian,Leipzig (Ger.) 3.45	MURDER	U.S.
DEIMBECK	31381	M	Ger.		Hptsturmfhr.,20 Army,SS I c,6 SS-Gebirgs-Div.Nord,Staff(Nor.)10.-11.44	MURDER	NOR.
DEINER	185384	M			Civ.,Stalag XIII B,Arb.Kdo.A 2,Gresseth (Ger.) 1.-2.45	TORTURE	FR.
DEININGER	250681	M			Pvt.,Camp.Dora,Nordhausen(Ger.)	MURDER	U.S.
DEININGER, Heinz	191345	M		17	Lt.,Anti air craft (Flak) 599 AAA Unit,Schwalbach (Ger.) 8.44	WITNESS	U.S.
DEISCH	72395				Osturmfhr., Waffen-SS,Baschweiler (Ger.) 43	MURDER	FR.
DEISCHL, Erwin	122899	M			Pvt.,Pz.Lehr-Div.,Waldrach-Ruwer (Ger.) 9.44-2.45	WITNESS	U.S.
DEISSLER, Franz	191347	M	Ger.		Policeman,Police,Dillingen,Bavaria (Ger.) 40-45	SUSPECT	POL.
DEISSNER, Willi	135301	M	Ger.		C.C.	MURDER	U.S.
DEIST	141522	M	Ger.		Oberstarzt,Pol.,Hohenlychen (Ger.) 5.44	TORTURE	FR.
DEITZ	125134	M	Ger.	10 or 15	Sgt.,.,Army,Inf.(Adverb),Dulag Luft,Stalag 17 b,Frankfurt-M.(Ger)1.44	MURDER	U.S.
DEKANT, Georg	147341	M	Ger.		Soldier,11 Pz.Div.,Kampfgr."Wilde" (Fr.) 44	MURDER	FR.
DEKANY, Michael	174186	M			Member,SS,C.C.Muhldorf,Ampfing (Ger.) 6.44-4.45	MISC.CRIMES	U.S.
DEKUBANOWSKI	139821	M	Ger.		Capt.,Stalag X B,Sandbostel (Ger.) 8.45	MISC.CRIMES	U.S.
DELAGE (or DUNCKEL,or PORTEN)	141523	M	Ger.		Gestapo-Chief,Gestapo,Marseille (Fr.)	TORTURE	FR.
DELAJOIE, Annie	193888	F	Ger.		Kapo,C.C.Ravensbrueck (Ger.)	TORTURE	FR.
DE LANGE (see DOHSE)	252951	M					
DE LA TROBE	257848				Pz.-Bie.150,Meuse Bridge-Antwerp (Bel.) 12.44	MISC.CRIMES	U.S.
DE LAYE (see LEY)	156087	M					
DELBROECK	252281	M	Ger.		Interpreter,Abtl.II B,Bruessel(Bel.)40-45	INTERR.	BEL.
DELCHIAPPO, Jean	150912	M	Ger.		Dordagne (Fr.) 44	MURDER	FR.
DELFINE, Charly	150911	M		20	French milice,Wilhelmshaven (Ger.)	TORTURE	FR.
DELFINGE (see DEFFLINGER)	191974						
DELFS	257476	M	Ger.	05	Sturmschfhr., Krim.Sekr.,S.D. Abt.IV,Referat E,Oslo (Nor.)	WITNESS	NOR.
DELHASS, Johann	250683	M		18.11.04	Pvt.,Camp Harzungen,Nordhausen (Ger.)	MURDER	U.S.
DELIGA, Edith	150907	F	Ger.	29. 5.23	Overseer,C.C.Buchenwald,Schonfeld (Ger.) 44	TORTURE	FR.
DELIKAT	185394	M			Capt.,L. 3328 I,Genas (Fr.) 7.44	MURDER	FR.
DELITZ, Fritz	190313	M			Civilian,Spitalam,Semmering (Aust.) 4.44	TORTURE	U.S.
DELITZ, Helmut	256904	M	Ger.	01	Dr.,Hptsturmfhr., Waffen-SS,St.Eny (Fr.)	MURDER	U.S.
DELITZSCH	137613	M	Ger.		Arbeitskommando,Officer,C.C.Leussig (Ger.) 45	MISC.CRIMES	U.K.
DELIUS	150906	M			Dr.,C.C.Hohenlychen,Ravensbrueck (Ger.) 5.44	TORTURE	FR.
DELIUS	185387	M			Col.,Freiburg-Breisgau (Ger.)	MURDER	FR.
DELKE	196098	M	Ger.		Pvt.,Wach-Bn.,C.C.Royallien,Oise (Fr.) 41-44	MURDER	FR.
DELL, Antonia Marta	135113	F	Ger.		Woman-guard,C.C.Helmbrechts (Ger.) 7.44-4.45	WITNESS	U.S.
DELL, Johann	151183	M		93	Civ.,Obersteiger,C.C.Eschweiler (Ger.)	MURDER	U.S.
DELL-HAUSEN	150905	M	Ger.		Col.,Oflag VI D,C.C.Soest(Ger.)	TORTURE	FR.
DELLES	152025	M	Ger.		Interpreter,Gestapo,Angers (Fr.)	MURDER	FR.
DELLIAN, G.L.	72404	M			Scharfhr.,SS,Etival,Clairefontaine (Fr.) 11.44	PILLAGE	FR.
DELLIN	186733	M	Ger.		Rottfhr.,C.C.Guard,Ravensbrueck,Mecklenburg (Ger.) 43-45	TORTURE	U.S.
DELMAN, Vilim Willy	306063	M	Ger.		N.C.O.,Gestapo,Prison Karmen at Dubrovnik,Surroundings (Yugo.) 44	MURDER	YUGO.
DELMERS	250698	M			Osturmfhr.,W.O.,Camp Dora,Nordhausen (Ger.)	MURDER	U.S.
DELMONEST, Wolfert	156997	M	Ger.		Officer,Aulnois (Bel.)	MURDER	BEL.
DEL NEGRO	251181	M	Ger.		Lt.,119 Pz.Regt.,II Div.,Coufouleux (Fr.) 8.44	INTERR.	FR.
DELOBEL	185386	M			Prison	MISC.CRIMES	FR.
DELOBEL, Charles	152009	M			Civ.,C.C.Mohl (Ger.)	WITNESS	U.S.
DE LORENZIO (or DE LORENZIS)	261331	M	Ital.		General,Pietralba (Fr.) 9.43	BRUTALITY	FR.
DELTROP, Johann	250699	M			Rottfhr.,Camp Dora,Nordhausen (Ger.)	MURDER	U.S.
DELUG, Richard	145554	M	Ger.	11.11.22	Pvt.,3 SS-Gren.Div.,6 Gren.Regt.,Singen (Ger.) 45	WITNESS	FR.
DEMAN, Adolf	307069	M	Ger.		Member,German SS,Arnhem,Apeldoorn,Arnhem,Wageningen (Neth.)10.43-10.44	MURDER	NETH.
DE MARTINI	307070	M	Ger.		Engineer,SS-Osturmfhr.,Commandant,C.C.Northern,Karasjok (Nor.)6.-10.42	MURDER	YUGO.
DEMARTO	72406	M			Lt.,Brandenburg-Div.,Pont St.Esprit (Fr.)	MURDER	FR.
DE MAYE (see LEY)	156087						
DEMBECK, Bruno	162341	M	Ger.	90	Osturmfhr.,SS-Guard-Bn.,5 Guard-Coy.,C.C.Buchenwald (Ger.) 42-45	WITNESS	U.S.
DEMBON, Otto	31983	M	Ger.		Dr.,Landgerichtsrat,Ministry of Justice,Opava (Czech.) 2.40	MURDER	CZECH.
DEMCKE	305604	M			Capt.,Inspector,Criminal-Police,Cartridge Factory,Chateau de Vincennes,Seine (Fr.) 8.44	MURDER	FR.
DEMEL	260639	M	Ger.		Staff-Sgt.,"Bertha",14.081 E, Audun le Roman (Fr.) 9.44	MURDER	FR.
DEMEL, Paul	145576	M	Ger.		Civ.,NSDAP,Zwischenmeister Factory Baidombrutter,Kattowitz (Pol.)45	TORTURE	FR.
DEMELE	67587				Pvt.,Army,21 Bn.,C.C.Hydebreck (Ger.) 6.43-1.45	MISC.CRIMES	U.K.
DEMELOFF, Hermann	72407	M	Ger.		Lt.,Army,439 Gren.Regt.,132 Inf.Regt.,Witebsk (Russia) 1.-2.44	INCENDIARISM	FR.
DEMELT	192314				Usturmfhr.,SS,C.C.Flossenburg (Ger.) 44-45	MURDER	U.S.
DEMITRIO (or DIMITRIO)	196096	M	Ger.		Sturmfhr., Waffen-SS,Vercoiran (Fr.) 3.44	MURDER	FR.
DEMKE	72408	M			Inspector,Gestapo,Vincennes (Fr.) 8.44	MURDER	FR.
DEMKLER, Otto	1230	M	Ger.		C.C.Stassfurt (Ger.)	INTERR.	U.S.
DEMM	170546	M	Ger.		Col.,Army,Oflag 65,C.C.Barkenbruegge (Ger.)44-45	MURDER	YUGO.
DEMMEL	24837	M	Ger.	97	Cpl.,Army,Coy.306,Tauber-Bischofsheim,Stalag 13 G,Geroldshausen (Ger.) 4.42	TORTURE	U.K.-FR.
DEMMELHUBER	252942		Ger.		Cpl.,F.P.No.11.178,Romilly,Seine (Fr.) 8.44	PILLAGE	FR.
DEMMELING, Martin	178073	M	Ger.	17	Pvt.,Army,Minic,Rheden (Neth.) 12.44-1.45	MURDER	NETH.
DEMMER	130106	M			Oschfhr.,SS,C.C.Dora Mittelbau,Nordhausen (Ger.)	MURDER	U.S.

NAME	C.R.FILE NUMBER	SEX	NATIO-NALITY	DATE OF BIRTH	RANK OCCUPATION UNIT PLACE AND DATE OF CRIME	REASON WANTED	WANTED BY
DEMMER	154491	M			Uschfhr, SS, 3 SS Br., CC Wieda and near Gardelegen (Ger.) 4.45	MURDER	U.S.
DEMMER	182759	M			Osturmfhr, SS Fuehrungshauptamt, CC Nordhausen Mittelbau (Ger.) 43-45	WITNESS	U.S.
DEMMER, Iwan	250700	M			Uschfhr, Camp Wieda, Nordhausen (Ger.)	MURDER	U.S.
DE MONTARGNE (see RETSCHEK, Helmuth)	190576						
DEMPFWOLLF	257539	M	Ger.		Dr., Employee, CC Nordhausen (Ger.)	MURDER	U.S.
DEMUT	151191	M			Guard, 4 SS Bau-Bde. (formerly SS Div.Totenkopf), Ellrich, Gardelegen (Ger.) 4.45	MURDER	U.S.
DEMUTH	193145	M			Obersturmfhr, Comd. of Pion.Stab 10, Narvik (Nor.)	MISC.CRIMES	NOR.
DEMUTH	261406	M	Ger.		Inspector, Unit L 52511, Air Force, Pau, Sourmoulon, Narp, Lescar (Fr.) 6. and 8.44	MURDER	FR.
DENCKE (or DENEKE, J.Erich)	137661	M	Ger.		Pvt., Army, 375 Lds.Schtz.Bn, CC Stalag IV 6, Grosszchepa (Ger.) 12.43	MURDER	U.K.
DENCKE, Sepp	250971	M	Ger.		Sgt., Army, near Hamburg (Ger.)	MURDER	YUGO.
DENCKHAUSS	151977	M	Ger.		General of Police, Gestapo Secretary, Folkling (Fr.) 11.44	MURDER	FR.
DENECKE	145579	M	Ger.		Civilian, Zwischenmeister, R.A.W. Bremen Hemelingen (Ger.)	TORTURE	FR.
DENECKE, Willy	253624	M	Ger.		N.C.O., 10 Coy, 377 Jg.Rgt., Vinkt (Bel.) 5.40	MISC.CRIMES	BEL.
DENEKE, J.Erich (see DENCKE)	137661						
DE NEUZE, Hans	254791	M	Ger.		N.C.O., 377 Jg.Rgt., Vinkt, Meigem (Bel.) 5.40	MISC.CRIMES	BEL.
DENG, Felix	192777	M	Ger.		Schupo CC Falstad (Nor.) 41-45	MURDER	NOR.
DENGG	257379	M	Ger.		Guard, SS Slave Labour Camp, Beisfjord near Narvik (Nor.) 6.-11.42	BRUTALITY	YUGO.
DENGLER	12594	M			Pvt., 1-44 Pol. 19 Dienststelle, Ugine (Fr.) 6.44	MURDER	FR.
DENGLER, Albert	135153	M	Ger.	08	Untersturmfhr, Allg.SS, Winterkasten Reichelsheim, Bensheim (Ger.)	MURDER	U.S.
DENIGER, Hermann	145561	M	Ger.	17	Guard, CC Flossenburg (Ger.)	MURDER	FR.
DENINCK, Willy	300569	M	Ger.		N.C.O., Army, 10 Coy, 377 Jg.Rgt., Vinkt-Meigem (Bel.) 5.40	MISC.CRIMES	BEL.
DENISCH, Max	108721	M	Ger.		SS Pz.Div.Hitler Jugend, 12 SS Pz.Rgt., near Hellenthal (Ger.) 12.44	MISC.CRIMES	U.S.
DENK	125980	M	Ger.	09	Pvt., Arbeitskommando	MURDER	U.K.
DENK, Erhard	167921	M	Ger.		Kommissarischer Verwalter, Betriebsfinanzierung, Warsaw (Pol.)9.39-44	PILLAGE	POL.
DENK, Josef	260446	M	Ger.	31. 7.12	Usturmfhr, Allg.SS., W-SS, SD,Pilsen (Czech.) 3.39-5.45	MISC.CRIMES	CZECH.
DENKE	307072	M	Ger.		SS Sturmbannfhr, Slave Labour Camp, Falstad (Nor.) 42-43	MURDER	YUGO.
DENKER	67007	M	Ger.		Hptsturmfhr, SS, 17 Pz.Gren.Div. Goetz von Berlichingen, Sturmgesch.Abt.17, Segre Renaze (Fr.) 7.-8.44	MURDER	FR.
DENKHAUS	185599	M	Ger.		Secretary, Police, Sarrebruck (Fr.)	MURDER	FR.
DENNEBORG, Hermann (or DENNENBERG, DENNENBURG)	305015	M	Ger.	15. 5.98	Works Manager, Sgt., Qmdt., Schutzdienst Bruhgwacht, Waalwijk and Heusden (Neth.) between 5.43 and 10.44	PILLAGE	NETH.
DENNEPLEIN	145548	M	Ger.	90	Civilian, Lublin (Pol.) 42-45	MURDER	FR.
DENNERLEIN	152010	M	Ger.		Hptsturmfhr, SS and SD, CC Lublin (Pol.) 43	TORTURE	U.S.
DENNERT, Friedrich (see Dr.FISCHER)	185670						
DENNHARDT	259623	M	Ger.	14	Capt, 15 Pol. Rgt., Crescentino (It.) 9.44	INTERR.	IT.
DENNLER, Wilhelm	9647	M			Ministerialrat, Deutsches Staatsministerium, Bohemia Moravia (Czech.) 42-44	MURDER	CZECH.
DENSCH, Hermann	259014	M	Ger.		Admiral	WITNESS	U.S.
DENTZ, Henri	145562	M			Civilian, Firm Brockelmann, Herdringen (Ger.)	TORTURE	FR.
DENTZER, Julius	179	M		00	Sturmfhr, SS, CC Grini Tromsdalen (Nor.) 42-44	TORTURE	NOR.
DENYS	72414	M			Cmdt, Army, Salas (Fr.) 8.44	MURDER	FR.
DENZEL, Wolfgang	307073	M	Ger.		Railway official, Fernmeldemeisterei, Amersfoort (Neth.) 10.44-5.45	PILLAGE	NETH.
DEPENHEUER	131264	M		02	Osturmfhr, SS Hauptamt	MURDER	U.S.
DEPNER	257532	M	Ger.		Employee, Military Security Police, Amsterdam (Neth.) 10.44	SUSPECT	NETH.
DEPPE	257538	M	Ger.		Employee, CC Nordhausen (Ger.)	MURDER	U.S.
DEPPE, Wilhelm	151179	M	Ger.		Kreisbauernfhr, Group-Leader NSDAP, Civilian Farmer, Holzminden (Ger.)	TORTURE	U.S.
DEPPER	305835	M	Ger.		Pvt, 1 Aufkl.Abt., 3 Coy, 2 Col, XV Div. Afrika Korps, St.Leger (Arlon) 9.44	MISC.CRIMES	BEL.
DEPPNER, Franz (see BERBIN)	180	M	Ger.		SS Official, CC Westerbork (Neth.) 9.-10.42	TORTURE	NETH.
DERBIN, Franz (see BERBIN)	188172						
DERBOWSKI	72415	M			Gestapo, Tourlaville,Cherbourg, St.Lo (Fr.)	MURDER	FR.
DERCROSSET, Fritz	256067	M			Chief, Block 16, CC Flossenburg (Ger.)	BRUTALITY	FR.
DEREUZE (or D'HEUREUSE)	164611	M	Ger.		Capt, Feld-Gend. of Palisse (Allier), St.Gerand-le Puy (Fr.) 10.43,44	PILLAGE	FR.
DERFLINGER	31379	M	Ger.		Obersturmfhr, 20 SS Army, Comd.II SS Geb.Jg.Rgt. Norway 10.-11.44	MURDER	NOR.
DE RIEGE (or DU RIEGE)	302109	M	Ger.		Uschfhr, Gestapo, Zoelen (Neth.) 10.44	TORTURE	NETH.
DERKSEN	145564	M	Ger.		SS, Voeght (Ger.)	MURDER	FR.
DERKSEN, Hennie	252943	M	Ger.		Sturmmann, SS Unit 35250 B, St.Remy Aux Bois (Fr.) 9.44	MISC.CRIMES	FR.
DERL, Erich	250701	M		16. 1.23	Pvt., Camp Ellrich, Nordhausen (Ger.)	MURDER	U.S.
DERLE, Fritz	12595	M	Ger.		Army, 110 or 111 Pz.Gren.Rgt., Albine (Fr.) 6.44	MURDER	FR.
DERN	252856	M	Ger.		Sturmfhr, 13 SS Pol.Rgt., Ferlach (Aust.) 44-45	MURDER	YUGO.
DERN, Heinrich	305587	M	Ger.		Civilian, near Lang Gons about 3.45	MURDER	U.S.
DERNOW	250118	M			Secretary, Pol.,Gestapo,O.C.Nordhausen, Berlin (Ger.)	MURDER	U.S.
DERRENDINGER, Louis	173781	M	Ger.	07	Smith, CC Thekla Leipzig (Ger.) 4.45	TORTURE	FR.
DERRICK	141866	M	Ger.	00	Lt., Gestapo, Tours (Fr.)	WITNESS	U.K.
DERRING	135571	M	Ger.		Cpl., Army, Parlitz, on the march Goerlitz to Mellingen (Ger.)2.-3.45	TORTURE	U.K.
DERTMON	301303	M	Ger.		Member of Gestapo at Trencin, Auschwitz-Birkenau(Pol.) 39-45	MURDER	CZECH.
DERWITSCH	305018	M	Ger.		Coy Cmdr, Prof.:School Teacher, CC Brockzetel near Wilhelmshaven (Ger.) 45	MURDER	NETH.
DERZZLER	166952	M	Ger.		Agent, Gestapo, Freiburg im Breisgau (Ger.) 4.45	MURDER	FR.
DESAGA	145566	M	Ger.		Doctor, CC Ravensbrueck (Ger.) 5.44	TORTURE	FR.
DESCH	147340	M	Ger.		Col., 11 Pz.Div. South West France 44	MURDER	FR.
DESCHAUER, Franz	260451	M	Ger.	9. 5.90	Uschfhr, SS Death Head, Auschwitz and Trzebnica (Pol.) 39-45	MURDER	POL.
DESKENDT	252282	M	Ger.		Official, Hilfspol.Abt.IV D, Sipo, Brussels (Bel.)	INTERR.	BEL.
DESPARADE, Otto	136293	M	Ger.		Guard, CC Wolfenbuettel (Ger.)	MURDER	FR.
DESPICHT	189639	M	Ger.		Sgt., Army, Unit 40539, Dep. Cote du Nord (Fr.)	PILLAGE	FR.
DE SPIES (or GOTHELUCKEN)	305856	M			Sgt, 1 Coy, Reg.B, 377 Inf.Rgt. under Capt.Lohmann, Vinkt-Meigem (Bel.) 5.40	MURDER	BEL.
DESSLOCH, Otto	259015	M	Ger.	89	General	WITNESS	U.S.
DESTRADE	72427	M			Obermatrose, Navy, Quiberon (Fr.) 44	MURDER	FR.
DETAND, Helmuth (or DITAND)	306531	M	Ger.		Member SD at Meppel (Neth.) 12.44	TORTURE	NETH.
DETER	185600	M	Ger.		Lt., Army, Perigueux (Fr.)	MURDER	FR.

-67-

DEM - DET

DET - DIC

NAME	C.R.FILE NUMBER	SEX	NATIO-NALITY	DATE OF BIRTH	RANK	OCCUPATION	UNIT	PLACE AND DATE OF CRIME	REASON WANTED	WANTED BY
DETER, Richard	300099	M	Ger.		Lt.-Cmdt., 221.Stalag, Saucats (Gironde) (Fr.) 7.43				MISC.CRIMES	FR.
DETERING	254322	M	Ger.		Osturmfhr., S.D., Toulouse (Fr.) 11.42-10.43				MISC.CRIMES	FR.
DEFFLINGER (see DEFFLINGER)	72429									
DETHLEFFSEN, Lorenz	261224	M		9. 8.07	Specialist officer, Abwehrstelle Belgien, Brussels (Bel.) 6.40-11.41. Home address: Flensburg, Moltkestr.32.				SUSPECT	BEL.
DETHLEPSEN	185385	M			Scharfhr., SS.				MISC.CRIMES	FR.
DETKI, Johann	72374				SS mot.Div. Pol. 4.Coy., Annecy (Fr.)				MURDER	FR.
DETLEWSEN (DETLEVSEN)	196392	M	Ger.		Capt., Pol. Waffen-Schule, near Arnheim (Neth.) 3.45				MURDER	NETH.
DETMAR, Heibrich	259924	M	Ger.		SS-Oschfhr., SS-guard at the transport of prisoners from Bochov to Touzim, Kozlov near Zlutice (Czech.) 4.45				MURDER	CZECH.
DETMERING	135147	M	Ger.	87	Lt.General, Army (Ger.) 45				TORTURE	U.S.
DETMERS	257557				Lt., Adjutant, C.C.Dora, Nordhausen (Ger.)				MURDER	U.S.
DETTAMBEL, Peter	181	M			N.C.O., Parachuter-Regt., Saint Segal (Fr.) 7. - 8.44				MURDER	FR.
DETTLER, Richard Emil	196715	M		8. 8.88	Amtsbuergermeister, Civ. (Lux.) 40-45				INTERR.	LUX.
DETTMANN, Heinrich	193142	M		7. 8.03	Sgt.,Guard, Reichsjustizmin.Strafgefang.Lager, Finmark (Nor.) 42-45				MISC.CRIMES	NOR.YUG.
DETTMERS	151982	M			SS-Osturmfhr., C.C. Flossenburg (Ger.)				TORTURE	U.S.
DETTWER, Heinrich	72375	M		13	Sgt., Waffen-SS, 51.Panz.Bde., Troyes, Crenay, Bucheres (Fr.) 8.44				MURDER	FR.
DETZEN (von) (known as VON BARGEN)	167919	M			Hptscharfhr., SS, Member of Camp Guard, C.C. Oranienburg (Ger.) 4.39-45				MURDER	POL.
DEUBEL, Georg	261322	M	Ger.		Capt., Geh.Feldpolizei,Beograd,Obrenovac and other places (Yugo.)42-43				MURDER	YUGO.
DEUBEL, Robert	259346	M	Ger.	14. 9.00	Local group-leader, district speaker, Kaysersberg-Rhein (Fr.) 42-43				INTERR.	FR.
DEUBNER, Konrad	187306	M	Ger.	15. 5.02	Crim.secretary, Gestapo, S.D., Brno (Czech.) 39-45				MURDER	CZECH.
DEUBNER, Marie nee WEISSLEDER	187300	F	Ger.	31.12.04	Member of S.D., Gestapo, Brno (Czech.) 39-45				MISC.CRIMES	CZECH.
DEUCHT	155748	M	Ger.		Sgt., Army, Morlaix (Fr.) 44				MURDER	FR.
DEURING, Adolf (see DOERING)	133769									
DEURINGER	193238	M	Ger.		Oschfhr., SS, C.C. Buchenwald (Ger.)				MURDER	U.S.
DEURSCHMANN, Friedrich	72376	M	Ger.	10. 5.20	Uschfhr., 5.SS Panz.Gren.Bde. 6.Coy., Troyes,Bucheres,Crenay (Fr.) 8.44				MURDER	FR.
DEUSCHLE	186483	M	Ger.	21	SS-Usturmfhr., 12.SS Panz.Div. "Hitler Jugend", near Caen (Fr.) 6.6.-7.44				TORTURE	CAN.
DEUSCHLE, Charles (Karl)	132615	M	Ger.		SS-Adjutant, S.D., Drome, Grenoble et la Region (Fr.)				MISC.CRIMES	FR.
DEUTCHMANN	188625	M	Ger.		SS-Mann, SS, Pol.Regt., Gran Hameau des Ruisots (Fr.) 6.44				MURDER	FR.
DEUTINGER, Erich	12597	M	Ger.		Pvt., 110. or 111.Panz.Gren.Regt., 2.Coy., Albine (Fr.) 6.44				MURDER	FR.
DEUTLER (see BEUTLER)	172946									
DEUTSCH	29900	M	Ger.		Cmdt., Army, Breslau to Ziegenheim (Ger.)				MISC.CRIMES	U.K.
DEUTSCH	166953	M	Ger.		Med.Chief, A.O.K., La Mochette (Fr.) 8.44				MURDER	FR.
DEUTSCH	167922	M	Ger.		Dr., Kommandantur, Crest (Fr.) 7.-8.44				MURDER	FR.
DEUTSCH	193346	M	Ger.		Inspector, Air Force, Uthang Orlandet (Nor.) 9.41-42				WITNESS	NOR.
DEUTSCH	259113	M	Ger.		Principal "Kapo", C.C. Dachau (Ger.) 42-4.45				MISC.CRIMES	YUGO.
DEUTSCHLANDER	124959	M			Member of Gestapo, C.C. Gestapo-Lager Bremen-Farge (Ger.) 6.43				MURDER	U.K.
DEUTSCHLE, Karl	301122	M	Ger.		Adjutant, SS serv.with the Gestapo at Grenoble, Isere (Fr.) 43-44				MURDER	FR.
DEUTSCHMANN, Friedrich	251281	M	Ger.		Usturmfhr., Sainte Sanie (Fr.) 8.44				INTARR.	FR.
DEUTSTRMANN, Hans	151186	M			Uschfhr., SS, C.C. Mauthausen (Austria) 41-45				MURDER	U.S., FR.
DE VALERA (aliases: FELLMANN or GOUREZ)	188717	M	Ger.		Capt., Army, Gestapo, Prison S.D., Izon, Sederon, Avignon, Barret sur Liqure (Fr.) 40-45				MURDER	FR.
DAVID, Ly	184	F	Ger.		Warder, SS, C.C. Maidanek (Pol.) 40-4.44				MURDER	POL.
DEVOS, Valero	11866	M	Ger.		Employed at C.C. Breedonok (Bel.) 40-9.44				TORTURE	BEL.
DE VRIESE, Wilhelm	133375	M	Ger.	14	Lt., Staff-Officer, Waffen-SS, Pion.Ausbildungs-Bn.2, Passau (Ger.) 4.45				MURDER	U.S.
DEVRINGER	133764	M			SS-Scharfhr., C.C. Buchenwald (Ger.)				MURDER	U.S.
DEWALD	145573	M			Agent, S.D. and Kripo, Kehl (Ger.)				MISC.CRIMES	FR.
DEWALD, Max	306353	M	Ger.	31. 8.96	SS-Uschfhr., C.C. Buchenwald (Ger.) betw.5.38 and 10.43				MURDER	BEL.
DEWALD, Otto	255091	M	Ger.	10	Pvt., asst.cook, Hairdresser, Army Pion., Heusden (Neth.) 11.44				PILLAGE	NETH.
DEWALD, Willy	145574	M	Ger.		Sgt., Feldgend., Sedan (Fr.) 44				MISC.CRIMES	FR.
DE WITTE	305383	M	Ger.		Member of Sicherheitsdienst, Lille (Fr.) 40-44				MURDER	FR.
DEWOLDORF	188932	M	Ger.		Pvt., Army, Neuville en Tenain (Fr.) 9.44				WITNESS	FR.
DEWULF	252283	M	Ger.		Official, Sipo, Hilfspol. Abt.III B, Brussels (Bel.)				INTERR.	BEL.
DEYHLER	144310	M	Ger.		Restaurateur, SS, Waiblingen (Ger.)				TORTURE	FR.
DEYRER	144313	M	Ger.		Civilian, Pflug 13 B, C.C.Hammelburg (Ger.) 10.44-45				MURDER	U.S.
DEYRINGER, Alois	250113	M			Pvt., C.C. Ellrich, Nordhausen (Ger.)				MURDER	U.S.
DEYSER	31380	M	Ger.		Capt., 20.Army Nachr.Abt.11 (Nor.) 10.-11.44				MURDER	NOR.
DEZTOR	301304	M			Member of the Gestapo at Nove Mesto n-Vahom, C.C. Oswiecim-Birkenau (Pol.) 39-45				MURDER	CZECH.
DHERMANN	72348	M			Capt., Army, St.Symphorien (Fr.) 8.44				MURDER	FR.
D'HEUREUSE (see DERENZE)	164611									
DHIETRICH, Michelsen Hans	179730	M	Ger.	10	Lt., Army, 26.Panz.Div., Fucuchio marshes (Italy) 7.-8.44				MURDER	U.K.
D'HOOGE, Alfons	305019	M	Ger.		Member, S.D., Groningen and Drente (Neth.) 43-45				MISC.CRIMES	NETH.
DHOSE	145553	M	Ger.		Usturmfhr., S.D. and SS, Bordeaux (Fr.)				MISC.CRIMES	FR.
DHULLET	145552	M	Ger.		Agent, Gestapo, C.C. Trebbin Krs.Teltow (Ger.)				MURDER	FR.
DIABLIKOPF	154447	M	Ger.		SS, C.C. Leimitz (Ger.) 40-41				MURDER	U.S.
DIABO, Heinz	185669	M	Ger.		SS-Sturmscharfhr., Crim.asst., SS, Gestapo, S.D., Praha (Czech.) 39-45				MURDER	CZECH.
DIBBERN, Otto	193146	M	Ger.	08	Guard, Sgt.,Reichsjustizmin. Strafgefang.Lager, Finmark (Nor.) 42-45				MISC.CRIMES	NOR.
DIBBIG, Otto	155746	M	Ger.		Farmer, Civ., Rudneweide Krs.Stuhm (Ger.) 6.41-10.42				TORTURE	U.K.
DICAUD	145557	M	Ger.		SS-Chief, Control of airplane-factory, Waren-Mieritz (Ger.)				MURDER	FR.
DICHL-DEJON, Ludwig	196047	M	Ger.		Professor, Med., La Croixille, Mayenne (Fr.) 8.44				WITNESS	FR.
DICHMANN	72386	M	Ger.		Dr., Asst.Arzt, Air Force, C.C. Vaihingen (Ger.)				TORTURE	FR.
DICHMANN, Johann	250974	M	Ger.		Pvt. 6.Coy.II.Bn., Inf.Regt.893, 264.Inf.Div., Primosten (Yugo.) 7.44				MURDER	YUGO.
DICHT (or DICK)	137748	M			Capt., 15.Panz.Gren.Regt.				WITNESS	U.S.
DICK	151192	M			Member of Gestapo.				MISC.CRIMES	FR.
DICK	188931	M	Ger.		Pvt., Army, Le Bourget-Triage (Fr.) 8.44				MURDER	FR.
DICK, Robert	250969	M	Ger.	27. 3.03	Member z.b.V. Kommando 31, Valasske, Mezirici (Czech.) 2.-3.45				MURDER	CZECH.
DICKE	260070		Ger.		Asst. SS, Med.asst. Slave Labour Camp, Botn near Rognan (Nor.) 4.43-4.45				BRUTALITY	YUGO.
DICKERBOOM	174188				Organisation Todt, C.C. Muhldorf-Ampfing (Ger.) 6.44-4.45				MISC.CRIMES	U.S.
DICKERHOFF	196048	M	Ger.		Professor, Faculty of Strassburg (Fr.) 40-45				MURDER	FR.
DICKERMANN	174187	M			Organisation Todt, C.C. Muhldorf-Ampfing (Ger.) 6.44-4.45				MISC.CRIMES	U.S.
DICKGRABER	168935	M	Ger.		SS-Scharfhr., C.C.Sachsenhausen-Oranienburg (Ger.) 39-4.45				MURDER	POL.
DICKHART, Gustav	150896				Pvt., Army, C.C. Valence (Fr.)				TORTURE	FR.
DICKMAN, Gustav (see DIEKMANN)	188623									
DICKMANN	72389	M	Ger.		Sturmbannfhr., 2.SS Div. "Das Reich", Regt. "Der Fuehrer", Oradour (Fr.) 4.-6.44				MURDER	FR., U.S.

DIC - DIE

NAME	C.R.FILE NUMBER	SEX	NATIO-NALITY	DATE OF BIRTH	RANK OCCUPATION UNIT PLACE AND DATE OF CRIME	REASON WANTED	WANTED BY
DICKMANN	252995	M	Ger.	96	Maj.,commander,191 Gren.Regt.,Dreno (Ger.) 4.45	MURDER	FR.
DICKMANN	259577	M	Ger.		SS-Uscharfhr.,3 Pion.Coy.,Pion.Bn.,1 Pz.Div.,Leibst.Adolf Hitler, Ligneuville,Stoumont,Engeldorf (Bel.) 12.44	SUSPECT	U.S.
DICKMANN,Frederick	144442	M	Ger.	15	Civilian,C.C.Hadamar (Ger.) 6.44-3.45	WITNESS	U.S.
DICKMANN,Gustav	151228	M	Ger.	28	SS-Sturmmann,SS,Hardencourt (Fr.) 5.44	MURDER	FR.,U.N.W.C.C.
DICKMANN,Otto	150932	M	Ger.	97	Chief,N.S.D.A.P.,C.C.,Rostock (Ger.) 4.44	MURDER	FR.
DICKRABER	191540	M	Ger.		Scharfhr.,Waffen-SS,C.C.Sachsenhausen,Oranienburg (Ger.) 39-45	MURDER	POL
DICKSCHECK,Franz	262009	M	Ger.	29. 9.09	SS-Mann,Dirlewanger-Bde.,Waffen-SS,Gren.Div.36,Warsaw and other (Pol.) 40-44	MURDER	POL
DIDERICH	260161	M	Ger.		Policeman (Gendarm),Unit Russia-Germany,Div.Oberland,Massif du Vercors,Isere and Drome (Fr.) 7.-8.44	SUSPECT	FR.
DIDMAN,Otto	187563	M		10	Cpl.,Army,Arbeitskdo.41,Stalag IV G,C.C.,Waren (Ger.) 2.44	TORTURE	U.K.
DIDSZULEIT,Walter	262010	M	Ger.	7. 7.13	SS-Mann,Dirlewanger-Bde.,Waffen-SS,Gren.Div.36,Warsaw and other (Pol.) 40-44	MURDER	POL
DIEBEL,Albert	39801	M			Rottenfhr.,SS,C.C.Struthof (Fr.)	MURDER	FR.
DIEBITSCH	196947	M	Ger.	05	Col.,Div.H.Q."Friedel",Eng-works,Piave,H.Q.San Polo,Venice, Ponte di Piave (It.) 2.45	WITNESS	U.K.
DIEBOLD	72392	M			Capt.,Army,Morez (Fr.)	MURDER	FR.
DIEBOLT,Paul	192052	M			Pvt.,SS-Pz.Div."Das Reich",Oradour sur Glane (Fr.) 6.44	MURDER	FR.
DIEBUS	193239	M			Oscharfhr.,SS,C.C. Buchenwald (Ger.) 42-45	MURDER	U.S.
DIECK,Fritz	141927	M	Ger.		Beufhr.,Arbeitskdo.1015,C.C.Bischofferode (Ger.) 6.41-4.45	MISC.CRIMES	U.K.
DIECKER	72393	M			Prof.,Strasbourg (Fr.)	MISC.CRIMES	FR.
DIECKERT,Friedrich	301192	M			Ortsgruppenleiter,Buchenfeld (Ger.) 3.45	MURDER	U.K.
DIEDERICH	168931	M			Officer-cadet,4 Coy.,77 Inf.Bn.,Foret (Bel.)	MURDER	U.K.
DIEDHARDT	132612	M			Caissier de Ravensbrueck,civilian,C.C.Ravensbrueck (Ger.)	MISC.CRIMES	FR.,BEL
DIEDRICH aliases BIRIBI or JIM LA TRIQUE	150929	M		95	Cpl.,C.C.Wansleben (Ger.) 43-45	TORTURE	FR.
DIEDRICH	150930	M		95	Uscharfhr.,SS,C.C.Buchenwald (Ger.)	MURDER	FR.
DIEDRICH	150931	M		05	Dresden (Ger.)	TORTURE	FR.
DIEDRICH	300370	M			On staff of C.C.Buchenwald (Ger.) 42-45	MURDER	FR.
DIEDRICH	300570	M			Pvt.,Feldpost-Nr.30812 E,Vinkt-Meigem (Bel.) 5.40	MISC.CRIMES	BEL
DIEEM	185	M			Police-president,police,Gdynia (Pol.) 41	MURDER	POL
DIEES	151984	M			Osturmfhr.,SS,C.C.Flossenburg (Ger.)	BRUTALITY	U.S.
DIEFENBACH,Georg	182762	M	Ger.	28. 5.94	SS-Hptscharfhr.,4 SS-Totenkopf-Sturmbann,C.C.,Nordhausen (Ger.) 43-45	WITNESS	U.S.
DIEFFENBACH	72349	M			Mietesheim (Fr.)	MURDER	FR.
DIEFFENBACH,Adolf	260834	M			Address:House-No.64,Binsfeld,Krs.Wittlich (French-Zone),Schweich (Ger.),L.O.D.N.A.O.D.	WITNESS	U.S.
DIEFFENBACHER	141466	M	Ger.		Civilian,Bischwiller (Fr.) 44	MURDER	FR.
DIEFFENBACHER,Heinrich	257411	M	Ger.	96	Kreisleiter,N.S.D.A.P. of Rastatt,Bernbach (Ger.) 8.44	MURDER	U.S.
DIEGEL	300598	M	Ger.	27	Pvt.,Army,Landesschtz.Bn.,Arbeitskdo.,Allendorf (Ger.) 3.43	MURDER	YUGO.
DIEHL	107000	M			Asst.Lagerfhr.,C.C.,Weissenhasel (Ger.) 10.44	MURDER	U.S.
DIEHL	150928	M	Ger.		Crim.secretary,Gestapo,Wiesbaden (Ger.)	TORTURE	FR.
DIEHL	257880	M			Lt.,150 Pz.Bde.,Meuse-Bridge,Antwerp (Bel.) 12.44	MISC.CRIMES	U.S.
DIEHL,Heinrich	185506	M	Ger.		Dr.,Kreisleiter,N.S.D.A.P.,Luxembourg (Lux.) 40 - 45	MISC.CRIMES	LUX.
DIEHL,Karl	185602	M	Ger.		SS-Uscharfhr.,employee,SS,SD,Gestapo,Sarrebrouk (Fr.)	PILLAGE	FR.
DIEHL,Karl	196891	M	Ger.	9.12.04	Kreisfuehrer,Fire-Bde.,Luxembourg (Lux.) 40-45	MISC.CRIMES	LUX.
DIEHL,Wilhelm	72323	M			Agent,Gestapo,SS,Struthof (Fr.)	MURDER	FR.
DIEHL,Wilhelm	72361	M	Ger.		Pvt.,Waffen-SS,C.C.Struthof (Fr.)	MISC.CRIMES	FR.
DIEHL,Wilhelm see DIEL	196949						
DIEHLE	196959	M			Paratrooper,Ligneuville and Stoumont (Bel.) 12.44	SUSPECT	U.S.
DIEKER,Joseph	129658	M	Ger.		Sgt.,Verlademeister,Navy,Camp Lintfort (Ger.) 11.44	TORTURE	U.S.
DIEKMANN,Gustav or DICKMANN	188623	M	Ger.		Pz.Div.1.2.3,Hardencourt (Fr.)	MURDER	FR.,U.N.W.C.C.
DIEL,Kristian	182763	M	Ger.or Hung.	24. 9.99	SS-Mann,4 SS-Totenkopf-Sturmbann,C.C.Mittelbau,Nordhausen (Ger.) 43-44	WITNESS	U.S.
DIEL,Wilhelm or DIEHL	196949	M		26. 2.00	Sgt.,POW collecting point,A.O.K.10	TORTURE	U.S.,FR.
DIELE,Ernst	256569	M	Ger.		Lt.,head of SD,Kristiansund (Nor.) 40-41	WITNESS	NOR.
DIEMBT,Karl	193780	M			Usturmfhr.,SS-Totenkopf-Sturmbann,C.C.Buchenwald (Ger.) 42-45	TORTURE	U.S.
DIEMEL	133773	M			SS-Oscharfhr.,C.C.Buchenwald (Ger.)	TORTURE	U.S.
DIEMER-WILBODA	126754	M	Ger.		Col.,Army,Stalag,Koenigstein (Ger.) 12.42	MISC.CRIMES	FR.
DIEMER-WILRODA	305983	M	Ger.		Major,Oflag VI B,Doessel near Warburg (Ger.) 39-45	MURDER	POL
DIEMERT	257224	M	Ger.		Capt.,Army,Oflag VII A,Murnau (Ger.) 39-42	TORTURE	POL
DIENER	72380	M	Ger.		Sgt.,Army,212 Inf.Div.,321 Gren.Regt.	MURDER	FR.
DIENFFTERM,Peter	12598	M			Officer,Feldpost-Nr.L 55975,Dencourt (Fr.) 7.44	MURDER	FR.
DIENG-SCHULER	145551	M	Ger.		Lt.Col.,medicin,C.C.Buchenwald (Ger.) 44	MURDER	FR.
DIENST	173774	M			Cpl.,guard,worker-camp,Briey (Fr.) 40-45	MURDER	FR.
DIENTLE	128872	M			Col.,Stalag V B,C.C.Allmendingen (Ger.) 3.44	TORTURE	U.K.
DIERCKES,Franz	72382	M			SA-chief,Carcassonne (Fr.)	MURDER	FR.
DIERDOF,S.	28822	M	Ger.		Usturmfhr.,SS-Regt."Deutschland",Aussonne (Fr.) 5.44	MURDER	FR.
DIERENFELD	182764	M			Civilian,Biegenbruck (Ger.) 5.43	MURDER	U.S.
DIERICA	1317	M	Ger.		Col.,cmdt.Torino (It.)	MISC.CRIMES	U.K.
DIERICH	194814	M	Ger.		Lt.Col.,Artl.Regt.,Marte Grappa (It.) 9.44	WITNESS	U.K.
DIERK	149347	M	Ger.		Farmers leader,C.C.,Schaswinkel (Ger.)	TORTURE	FR.
DIERKENS,Franz	28821	M	Ger.		Specialist-Artificier,Army,Bochum-Langendreer (Ger.) 8.44	TORTURE	FR.
DIERKES	194214	M	Ger.	18	Oscharfhr.,12 SS-Pz.Div."Hitler-Jugend",26 SS-Pz.Gren.Regt.,7 Coy., Caen (Fr.) 6.-7.44	TORTURE	CAN.
DIERKES,Franz	151227	M	Ger.		Chief artificer,Kdo.Flughafenbereich,Roullens,Carcassonne,Lumoux, Couiza,Alet,Beaudrigues (Fr.) 8.44	MURDER	FR.
DIERKING,Karl	165159	M			Civilian,Fallingbostel (Ger.)	MURDER	U.S.
DIERMEYER	31382	M			Lt.Col.,20 Army staff,(Nor.) 10.-11.44	TORTURE	NOR.
DIESBURG,Kath.	72328	M			Scharfhr.,Waffen-SS,C.C.Struthof (Fr.)	MURDER	FR.
DIESEL	186732	M			Rottenfhr.,SS-guard,C.C.Ravensbrueck,Mecklenburg (Ger.) 42 - 45	MURDER	U.S.
DIESING	167909	M			Branch-director,Einsatzstab Rosenberg,Besancon (Fr.) 40-44	PILLAGE	FR.
DIESNER	72329	M			Agent,Gestapo,C.C.Struthof (Fr.)	MURDER	FR.
DIESSNER,Paul	150921	M	Ger.	95	Crim.commissar,Usturmfhr.,SD and Gestapo,Strasbourg (Fr.)	MURDER	FR.
DIESSNER,Paul	173198	M	Ger.		SS-Hptsturmfhr.,Gestapo,C.C.,Schirmeck Saales (Fr.) autumn 44	MURDER	U.K.

DIE - DIE

NAME	C.R.FILE NUMBER	SEX	NATIO-NALITY	DATE OF BIRTH	RANK OCCUPATION UNIT PLACE AND DATE OF CRIME	REASON WANTED	WANTED BY
DIESTELKAMPF	154332	M	Ger.		Cpl., Army, Oswiecim (Pol.) 40-45	MURDER	POL.
DIET, Otto	150919	M	Ger.	27	SS, Neudorf-Eltville (Ger.) 44	MURDER	FR.
DIET, Willy	150920	M	Ger.		SS, Eltville (Ger.) 44	MURDER	FR.
DIETE	168933	M			Pvt., 9 Gren.Res.Rgt.1 Coy, Magny d'Anigon (Fr.) 18.9.44	MURDER	FR.
DIETER	150917	M			Doctor, C.C. Hohenlychen (Ger.) 16.-18.5.44	TORTURE	FR.
DIETER, Karl	194308	M		10	SS-Hptschfhr., Gestapo Stelle Stuttgart, Radzyn (Pol.) 43-44	TORTURE	POL.
DIETERICH	257693	M			Klosterwerk C.C. Nordhausen (Ger.)	MURDER	U.S.
DIETGES, Karl Benno	198195	M		19.11.99	Hptsturmfhr., SS, SD, Chief Section IV, Belgrad, Pancevo (Serbia)42-44	MISC.CRIMES	YUGO.
DIETHELM	166299	M	Ger.		Mayor, Public-official, Pabianice (Pol.) 42	MURDER	U.S.
DIETICKER	253829	M			Lt.Adj., Army, Nieuwvliet (Neth.) 43-44	BRUTALITY	NETH.
DIETIMAYER, Michael	256905	M		1. 1.98	Schfhr., SS, Nordhausen (Ger.)	MURDER	U.S.
DIETL	250687	M			Pvt., Camp Ellrich, Nordhausen (Ger.)	MURDER	U.S.
DIETL, Franz	254935	M	Ger.		Pvt., Army, 1 Coy Pion.Bn.46, Budinei (Yugo.) 9.43	INTERR.	YUGO.
DIETL, Heinrich	254934	M	Ger.	27. 2.03	Special-Pleni Potentiary, State Service, Prag (Czech.) 40-45	MURDER	CZECH.
DIETL, Karl	173773	M			Sgt., Army, Clermont-Ferrand (Fr.) 13.-14.11.43	MURDER	FR.
DIETMAIER	173772	M	Ger.		Gaupresseamt, Strasbourg (Fr.) 44	TORTURE	FR.
DIETMAN	186	M			Public-official, Insp.of labour, C.C. Ravensbrueck (Ger.) 42	MURDER	POL.
DIETMANN (or DITHMANN)	188615	M	Ger.		Insp., Labor, C.C. Ravensbrueck (Ger.) 42-45	MURDER	BEL.
DIETRICH	72713	M			Lt., Grenzpolizei, Roermond (Neth.) 9.,10.44	MISC.CRIMES	U.S.
DIETRICH	72335	M			Guard, Stalag 1467, Sythen (Ger.)	MISC.CRIMES	FR.
DIETRICH	72372	M			Hptsturmfhr., 4 SS Div.,49 SS Gren.Bde., Montmirail (Fr.)	MURDER	FR.
DIETRICH	121218				Sgt., Army,	MURDER	FR.
DIETRICH	126531	M		00	Osturmbannfhr., Waffen SS, Schupo-officier, Saarbruecken (Ger.) 1.-2.45	MURDER	U.S.
DIETRICH	135155	M	Ger.		Lt., Pz.Div.2 Rgt.,8 Coy 2 Bn., Lutrebois (Bel.) 3.-10.1.45	MURDER	U.S.
DIETRICH	138214	M			SS-Sgt., SS, Gestapo, Lyon (Fr.)	MURDER	FR.
DIETRICH	139818	M			Uschfhr., Waffen SS, Arbeitskdo.Georgen Schacht, (Ger.)	TORTURE	U.S.
DIETRICH	144322	M			Lt., Army, Normandi Oflag 64 Albergund (Fr., Ger.) 6.-7.44	TORTURE	U.S.
DIETRICH	147757	M			District-leader, NSDAP, Gallenstift, Innsbruck (Aust.) 43	PILLAGE	FR.
DIETRICH	150916	M	Ger.		Lagerfhr., Stalag IV F Usine Meymer Pilz, C.C. Meuselwitz (Ger.)	MURDER	FR.
DIETRICH	150992	M	Ger.		Doctor, C.C. Hohenlychen, Ravensbrueck (Ger.)	TORTURE	U.S.
DIETRICH	151230	M			Adj., Army, Securite Militaire, Tours (Fr.) 42-43	MURDER	FR.
DIETRICH	151993	M			Waffen SS Standarte Totenkopf, Oschfhr.,, C.C. Buchenwald Weimar (Ger.)	MURDER	U.S.
DIETRICH	155757	M		05	Stabsarst, Stalag Luft 4, Stalag 357, Hannover (Ger.) 2.-4.45	TORTURE	U.S.
DIETRICH	167908	M			Hptsturmfhr., SS, Neuenberg 7.-8.44	TORTURE	FR.
DIETRICH	194310	M			Pvt., Feldgendarmerie, Ploernel (Fr.) 18.6.44	TORTURE	FR.
DIETRICH	196046	M			SS-Hptsturmfhr., C.C. Royallieu (Fr.)	MURDER	FR.
DIETRICH	251314	M			Doctor, Capt., Air Force 77 Geschw., Seguret (Fr.) 10.6.44	INTERR.	FR.
DIETRICH	252067	M			Crv.Legal Member, German Military Court for trial of prisoner of war.	TORTURE	U.K.
DIETRICH	252473	M			Cpl., Army, Department L'Ain (Fr.) 7.44	MISC.CRIMES	FR.
DIETRICH	259706	M		00	W.O., Guard-Coy, Grossenhain Stalag IV A, Riesa Saxonia (Ger.) 10.44	MURDER	FR.
DIETRICH	306950	M			SS and Policefhr., SS and Police, Lodz (Pol.) 9.39-1.42	MURDER	POL.
DIETRICH, Fritz	194813	M		00	Dr., President, Osturmbannfhr., Schupo, Waffen SS, Neunkirchen (Ger.) 1.8.44	MURDER	U.S.
DIETRICH, Heinrich	190583	M	Ger.	06	Oschfhr., Member, SD Einsatz Kdo., Gestapo, Saales and La Grande Fosse (Fr.) 15.10.44	MURDER	U.K.
DIETRICH, Maria Almas	162344	F	Ger.		Civilian, Paris (Fr.) 40	PILLAGE	U.S.
DIETRICH, Martin	141867	M	Ger.		Interpreter, Gestapo, Paris, Fresnes, Frankfurt-Main (Fr., Ger.) 5.-6.44	TORTURE	U.K.
DIETRICH, Otto	187591	M	Ger.		SS-Ogruppenfhr., Reichsleiter, NSDAP (Top-Nazi)	MURDER	U.N.W.C.C.
DIETRICH, Theophilo	151985	M			SS, C.C. Flossenburg (Ger.)	TORTURE	U.S.
DIETSCH	150999	M	Ger.		Kapo, C.C. Buchenwald (Ger.)	MURDER	FR.
DIETSCH, Paul	255092	M			Pvt., Cmdt., Air Force, Stat."De Kiek", Alphen-Riel (Neth.) 22.4.44	MURDER	NETH.
DIETSCHE	12337	M			Lt.Col.,7 SS Div."Prinz Eugen", Vrazja Divisja, 3.44	MURDER	YUGO.
DIETSCHE	259579	M			Osturmfhr., SS, Kochel (Ger.) 2.5.45	MURDER	U.S.
DIETSCHE, Otto	150995	M		31. 5.01	Member, Feldgendarmerie, Vitry le Francois (Fr.) 6.43	TORTURE	FR.
DIETZ	72340	M	Ger.		Capt., Standortkommandantur, Gerardmer (Fr.) 9.-11.44	MURDER	FR.
DIETZ	126957	M	Ger.		Kapo Block 46, C.C. Buchenwald (Ger.)	MURDER	FR.
DIETZ	151980	M			Civilian, Budisheim (Ger.) 6.44	MURDER	U.S.
DIETZ	152000	M			Civilian, Ginnheim (Ger.) 11.44	WITNESS	U.S.
DIETZ	188612	M	Ger.		Kapo, C.C. Buchenwald (Ger.) 42-45	MURDER	FR.
DIETZ	193608	M		10	Oberzahlmeister, Dulag 377, Gerolstein (Ger.) 19.12.44-5.2.45	TORTURE	U.S.
DIETZ	252934	M	Ger.		Interpreter, Gestapo, Wismar (Ger.) 42-43	BRUTALITY	FR.
DIETZ	259347	M	Ger.		Hptschfhr., Antenne of Rochelle, active member of Poitiers Gestapo, Area Poitiers (Fr.) 40-45	MISC.CRIMES	FR.
DIETZ	301872	M	Ger.		Instructor of Auxiliary police of Saarbrueck, C.C. Mauthausen (Aust.) 10.-20.4.44	MURDER	FR.
DIETZ, Max	167907	M	Ger.		Sgt., Prison Guard, St.Lo (Fr.) 6.-7.6.44	MURDER	FR.
DIETZ, Richard	182765	M			SS-Sturmmann, SS 4 Totenkopfsturmbann, C.C. Mittelbau, Nordhausen (Ger.) 43-45	WITNESS	U.S.
DIETZ, Werner	185379	M	Ger.	25	Pvt.,17 Inf.Div."Goetz v.Berlichingen",1 SS Coy, Raids (Fr.)6.or 7.7.44	MURDER	U.S.
DIETZE	132611	M	Ger.		Capitain, Standortkommandantur, Gerardmer (Fr.) 9.-11.44	MISC.CRIMES	FR.
DIETZE	252287	M	Ger.		SS-Sturmschfhr., Chief, SS, Sipo V B Bruessels (Bel.)	MURDER	BEL.
DIETZE	306677	M	Ger.		Pvt., 331 Pion.Bn., 331 Inf.Div., Mijnheerenland (Neth.) 5.45	PILLAGE	NETH.
DIETZE, Erich	250115	M		24. 8.99	N.C.O., C.C. Harzungen, Nordhausen (Ger.)	MURDER	U.S.
DIETZE, Helmut	133772	M		05-07	Sgt., Geh.Feldpolizei Gruppe 713	MISC.CRIMES	U.S.
DIETZLER, Engelbert	250114	M	Ger.	23. 4.24	Pvt., C.C. Ellrich, Nordhausen (Ger.)	MURDER	U.S.
DIETZSCH, Arthur (or BLATT, Jacob)	133771	M	Ger.	05	Kapo, C.C. Buchenwald (Ger.) 38-45	MURDER	U.S.
DIEUDONNE (or DOLLE, Gerard)	72341	M	Ger.		Lt., Parachutist, Tourc'h (Fr.) 29.2.44	MURDER	FR.
DIEWERGE, Wolfgang	62233	M	Ger.		Ministerial Director, Propaganda Ministry Reich, Goebbels Cabinet	MURDER	U.N.W.C.C.
DIEYEMANN, Franz	256934	M	Ger.	14	Osturmfhr., SD, Larvik (Nor.) 6.5.45	TORTURE	NOR.
DIEZEMANN, Franz	305628	M	Ger.	12.14	Chief, Osturmfhr., Sipo, Aussendienststelle Larvik, Telemark (Nor.) 19.-26.3.45	TORTURE	NOR.
DIEZEN	150991		Ger.		Director, Boltawerke, Nuernberg (Ger.)	TORTURE	FR.
DIEZSCH	106984	M			Dr., Asst., C.C. Buchenwald (Ger.)	MURDER	U.S.

NAME	C.R.FILE NUMBER	SEX	NATIO- NALITY	DATE OF BIRTH	RANK	OCCUPATION	UNIT	PLACE AND DATE OF CRIME	REASON WANTED	WANTED BY
DIFFENBACH	150998	M	Ger.	00	Agent, Gestapo, Kempten (Ger.) 10.44-3.45				MISC.CRIMES	FR.
DIFOUR	191595	M	Ger.		Member, SD, Gestapo, St. Lô (Fr.) 6.44				MURDER	FR.
DIGNER	193147	M			Pvt., 2.Coy. Bau-Bn.429 (K), Karasjok (Nor.)				MURDER	NOR.
DIJONG	185676	M	Ger.	5. 2.97	Germanisation of Occupied Territories, Luxembourg (Lux.)				MURDER	LUX.
DILGER, Richard	162866	M	Ger.		Capt., Army, Harbacq (Fr.)				TORTURE	BEL.
DILL	251090	M	Ger.		Lt., Dienststelle 29229, Glageon (Fr.) 9.44				INTERR.	FR.
DILL, Karl	182754	M			Sturmmann, SS, 4.Totenkopfsturmbann, C.C., Mittelbau-Nordhausen (Ger.) 43-45				WITNESS	U.S.
DILLER	150989	M	Ger.		O.F.Apotheker, Conc.Camp, Hohenlychen, Ravensbrueck (Ger.)				TORTURE	FR.
DILLER	164716	M	Ger.		Paymaster, Stalag XVIII C, Markt Pongau (Aust.)8.44				TORTURE	FR.
DILLING, Gustav	150993	M	Ger.	95	Civilian, Thurn (Ger.)				MISC.CRIMES	FR.
DILLINGS, Theo	301833	M	Ger.		Revin (Ardennes) (Bel.) 6.44				MURDER	FR.
DILLMANN (see DILMANN)	72343									
DILLY, Hans	194818	M	Ger.		Business-leader, Territ.Occupation, Luxembourg (Lux.)				PILLAGE	LUX.
DILMANN (or DILLMANN)	72343	M	Ger.		Osturmfhr., Waffen-SS, Conc.Camp, Neckarelz Struthof (Fr.) 8.43				MURDER	FR.
DILZER	173197	M	Ger.		Gestapo, Conc.Camp, Gaggenau Baden-Baden (Ger.) 44				MURDER	U.K.
DIMITRIO (see DEMITRIO)	196096									
DIMITRJI	154449	M			Civilian, Eschweiler and Bruchweiden (Ger.) 42-44				TORTURE	U.S.
DIMPER	192315	M			Member, NSDAP, Conc.Camp, Flossenburg (Ger.) 44-45				MURDER	U.S.
DIN	167506	M	Ger.		Usturmfhr., SS, Rocaro (It.)				MURDER	U.S.
DINER, Heinz	191349	M			Uscharfhr., 1.SS-Panz.Rgt. Adolf Hitler, Ligneuville and Stoumont (Bel.) 12.44				WITNESS	U.S.
DING	72345	M			Sturmbannfhr., SS, Conc.Camp, Buchenwald (Ger.)				TORTURE	FR.
DING	253610	M	Ger.		Physician, Dr., C.C., Gusen, Mauthausen (Aust.)				INTERR.	BEL.
DINGER, Alois	189	M	Ger.	05	Pvt., Airforce, Cazaux (Fr.) 8.44				MURDER	FR.
DINGER, Alois	39636	M	Ger.	17. 7.19	Administrative-officer, Public official, Unit L 30182, Cazaux (Fr.)8.44				MURDER	UNWCC
DINGES, Heinrich	181062	M	Ger.		Oschfhr., SS, Crim.Asst., Gestapo, Darmstadt Bensheim (Ger.)				MURDER	UNWCC
DINGLER, Henri	184271	M	Ger.		Employee, Conc.Camp, Block 27, Dachau (Ger.)				MURDER	FR., BEL.
DINKEL	166954	M	Ger.		Sturmfhr., SS, de Lixelm, Lischeim (Fr.) 9.44				MURDER	FR.
DINKEL	173771	M	Ger.		NSV, 44				TORTURE	FR.
DINKEL, Andreas	193783	M	Ger.	1. 8.06	Lt., Bahnschutzpolizei, Amstetten (Aust.) 3.45				TORTURE	U.S.
DINTER, George	182756	M	Ger.		Guard, SD, C.C., Frankfurt (Ger.)				TORTURE	U.S.
DIPOLDER	301668	M	Ger.		Feldgend., Gend., Stavelot (Bel.) 9.44				MURDER	BEL.
DIRCKS	187023	M	Ger.		Capt., Army, C.C., Unterluss (Ger.)				TORTURE	U.K.
DIRKINS, Heinrich	179758	M	Ger.	08	Lt., 590.Pz.Jaeger-Abt., Ponte Buggianese (It.) 7.-8.44				MURDER	U.K.
DIRKSEN	250123	M			Flyer, C.C., Woffleben, Nordhausen (Ger.)				MURDER	U.S.
DIRLEWANGER, Oskar (or DIRR- LEWANGER)	125163	M	Ger.	03	Bde.Fhr., C.O., SS, Waffen-SS, Gren.Div.36, Warsaw-Lublin, Minsk (Pol.,Sov.Un.) 40-44				SUSPECT	U.S.,.POL.
DIRMOSER, Jindrich (Heinrich)	187303	M	Ger.	25. 9.07	Superintendant, Gestapo, Gestapo Prison SD, Brno (Czech.) 39-45				MURDER	CZECH.
DIRNAGL	144320	M	Ger.		Osturmfhr., SS, Munich (Ger.) 9.44				MURDER	U.S.
DIRSCHERL	256989	M	Ger.		Cpl., 2.Nachr.Coy., Bolnes (Neth.) 5.45				INTERR.	NETH.
DISCHER, Karl	257814	M	Ger.	20. 5.88	Painter, Conc.Camp, Nordhausen (Ger.)				MURDER	U.S.
DISCHLER	72322	M			Col., Army Cmdt., Carcassone (Fr.)				MURDER	FR.
DISCHNER	190	M	Ger.		Official, C.C., Westerbork (Neth.) 9.42-10.42				TORTURE	NETH.
DISEL, Josef	252858	M	Ger.		Landwache, Ferlach (Aust.) 44-45				MURDER	YUGO.
DISSBURG	67008	M			Sgt., Waffen-SS, C.C., Struthof (Fr.)				MISC.CRIMES	FR.
DISSER, Johann	250122	M		8. 1.98	N.C.O., Camp Harzungen, Nordhausen (Ger.)				MURDER	U.S.
DISSINGER, Sani (nee WITZ)	147962	F	Ger.		Chief of Block, C.C., Ravensbrueck (Ger.)				WITNESS	FR.
DISTELKAMP	147961	M	Ger.		Oldest in Camp, C.C., Auschwitz (Pol.)				TORTURE	FR.
DITAND, Helmuth (see DETAND)	306531	M								
DITE, Annie (see FOURHMANN) Maria	194978									
DITEZ	253629	M	Ger.		Member, Gestapo, Arras, Haplin Court (Fr.) 6.44				MURDER	FR.
DITHMANN	132613	M	Ger.		SS-Chief, C.C., Ravensbrueck (Ger.)				MISC.CRIMES	FR.
DITHMANN (see DISTMANN)	188615									
DITJURKEIT, Gertrud	306768	F	Ger.		Ger.Civilian, Bad Durrenberg (Ger.) 44				BRUTALITY	U.S.
DITMAR, Joseph	191	M	Ger.		Bizerte (Tunisia) 12.42-4.43				MURDER	FR.
DITSCH (see DITZ)	255370									
DITSCHELEIN	192235	M	Ger.		Cpl., Army, Unit 26033 E Delyon, Soissons (Fr.) 8.44				WITNESS	FR.
DITTLOFF, Alfred	250688	M		14. 1.08	Sgt., Camp Ellrich, Nordhausen (Ger.)				MURDER	U.S.
DITTMANN	147963	M	Ger.		Engineer, Civilian, Muenchen (Ger.)				TORTURE	FR.
DITTMANN	67013	M	Ger.		Pvt., SS, 17.Pz.Gr.Div. "Goetz von Berlichingen", Sturmgesch.Abt.17, Segre, Renaze (Fr.) 7.44-8.44				MURDER	FR.
DITTMANN	185395	M	Ger.		Sturmfhr., SS Pol.Rgt. Todt, 10.Coy., 3.Bn.,Mont Saxonnex Berneck (Fr.) 1.44				MURDER	FR.
DITTMANN	250689	M			Pvt., Camp Dora, Nordhausen (Ger.)				MURDER	U.S.
DITTMANN	253628	M	Ger.		Sturmfhr., 9.Coy.,SS Pol.Rgt.Todt 28, Habere Lullin (Fr.) 12.43				MISC.CRIMES	FR.
DITTMANN, Alfred	256013	M	Ger.		Arbeitseinsatz, C.C., Mauthausen (Aust.)				INTERR.	FR.
DITTMANN, Fritz	145550	M		97	Oschfhr., SS, C.C., Buchenwald (Ger.)				TORTURE	FR.
DITTMAR	124524	M	Ger.		Lt., Stalag III D, Berlin (Ger.) 3.42				MISC.CRIMES	U.K.
DITTMAR, Rudolf	110067	M	Ger.		Farmer, Civ., NSDAP, C.C., Massbach (Ger.) 10.40-10.42				TORTURE	U.K.
DITTMAYER, Julius	252057	M	Ger.	00	Employee, Gestapo, Sanov (Czech.)				MURDER	CZECH.
DITTMER, Karl	257319	M	Ger.		Hptsturmfhr.,SA,Zentr.Handelsges.,Gestapo,Teplice-Sanov (Czech.)43-45				SUSPECT	CZECH.
DITTRICH	250708	M	Ger.		Rottfhr., SS, C.C., Rottleberode-Nordhausen (Ger.)				MURDER	U.S.
DITTRICH, Alois	31982	M	Ger.		Dr., Oberlandgerichtsrat, Public Off., Prague (Czech.) 40				MURDER	CZECH.
DITTRICH, Horst	306355	M	Ger.	6. 8.11	Hptschfhr., SS, C.C., Buchenwald (Ger.) 5.38-10.43				MURDER	BEL.
DITZ (or DITSCH)	255370	M	Ger.		Guard, Neckargerach (Ger.)				BRUTALITY	FR.
DITZ	300981	M	Ger.		Capt., Camp Command Oflag VI C, Osnabrueck-Ewersheide (Ger.) 42-44				MURDER	YUGO.
DITZ, Lorenz	147959	M	Ger.		Waffen-SS, Giesburg (Ger.)				TORTURE	FR.
DIVERMANN, Joseph	301658	M	Ger.		Le Bourget Triage-Gare (Fr.) 8.44				MURDER	FR.
DIWISH, Franz	108729	M	Ger.		Conc.Camp, Kowel (Sov.Un.) 6.42-9.42				WITNESS	U.S.
DIX (see DICHT)	137748									
DIX, Paul	31949	M	Ger.		Chief, Feldgend., Pont Audemer (Fr.) 7.44				MURDER	FR.
DJAPARIDZE,	72320	F			Paris (Fr.) 8.44				TORTURE	FR.
DJFOUR (see JUNGER)	191595									

DJU - DOH

NAME	C.R.FILE NUMBER	SEX	NATIO-NALITY	DATE OF BIRTH	RANK OCCUPATION UNIT PLACE AND DATE OF CRIME	REASON WANTED	WANTED BY
DJUREN (see also SUCHANEK)	305889	M	Ger.		Oschfhr.,C.C.Oranienburg(Ger.) 11.39-45	MURDER	CZECH.
DLUGOSCH, Else	147364	F	Ger.	26	Guard,C.C. Buchenwald(Ger.)	TORTURE	FR.
DLUGOSZ, Ignaz	252471	M	Ger.		Interpreter,Labour Office,Wiesbaden(Ger.) 40-45	TORTURE	POL.
DLUGOSZ, Jan	261398	M	Ger.or Pol.		SS-Mann,SS-Guard,C.C.Auschwitz(Pol.) 40-5/42	BRUTALITY	POL.
DLUHY	256935	M	Ger.		Employee,T.O.2 shift 1,C.C.Nordhausen(Ger.)	MURDER	U.S.
DMBOIS	133379A	M		07	Usturmfhr.,SS-Hauptamt	TORTURE	U.S.
DOBBELING	129807	M		12	Sgt.,Feldgend. Abt.521,Linz(Aust.)	MURDER	U.S.
DOBBENSTEIN, Leo	253622	M	Ger.		Lt.,1 Inf.Bn.,377 Jaeger-Regt.,Vinkt,Meigem(Bel.) 5.40	INTERR.	BEL.
DOBBERT	306678	M			Pvt.,331 Pioneer Bn.,331 Inf.Div.,Mijnheeren Land(Neth.) 5.45	PILLAGE	NETH.
DOBLER	256936	M			Hptsturmfhr., SD, Region de Pontivy(Fr.) 44	MISC.CRIMES	FR.
DOBE, Kurt	134834	M	Ger.		Civilian, C.C. Oranienburg(Ger.) 43-44	MURDER	U.S.
DOBELSTEIN	29898	M	Ger.		Sgt.,KL.Posen(Pol.)	MURDER	U.K.
DOBERNIGG, Louis Labush	132174	M	Ger.		Political Leader NSDAP,Gleisdorf(Aust.)	TORTURE	U.K.
DOBEY'S	147965	M	Ger.		Feldgend.,Givet(Fr.)	MISC.CRIMES	FR.
DOBLER, Karl	140874	M	Ger.		Ortsgruppenleiter NSDAP,Horsching(Ger.) 4.45	MURDER	U.S.
DOBLER, Ludwig	12599	M	Ger.		Pvt.,Pz.Gren.Regt.,Albine(Fr.)	MURDER	FR.
DOBNER, Friedrich	306356	M	Ger.	3. 7.21	SS-Mann,C.C. Buchenwald(Ger.) 5.38 and 10.43	MURDER	BEL.
DOBRATZ, Erich	262000	M	Ger.	12. 4.12	SS-Mann,Dirlewanger-Bde., Waffen-SS, Gren.-Div.36, Warsaw and other (Pol.) 40-44	MURDER	POL.
DOBRAWA	199148	M	Ger.		Pvt.,Kgf.Arb.Bn.190,Hattera(Nor.) 9.43	MURDER	NOR.
DOERITSCH	136343	M			SS-Usturmfhr.,Paris(Fr.)	PILLAGE	FR.
DOBROWOLSI	131263	M			SS-Rottfhr.(Blockfhr.),Auschwitz(Pol.) 43	MURDER	U.S.
DOBRZANSKI, Tadeus	151187	M			SS-Rottfhr.,SS,C.C.Mauthausen(Aust.)41-45	MURDER	U.S.
DOBSCHIS, Josef	901305	M	Ger.		Member Gestapo at Nove Mesto n.Vahom,C.C.Oswiecim-Birkenau(Pol.)39-45	MURDER	CZECH.
DOCEKAL, Richard	31981	M			Dr.,Landgerichtsdirektor,Ministry of Justice,Prag(Czech.) 40	MURDER	CZECH.
DOCHE or DOLCHE	147968	M	Ger.		Major,Waffen-SS, Caen(Fr.) 6.44	PILLAGE	FR.
DODTZUWEIT	256979		Ger.		Lt.,Gend. (Serbia-Yugo.) 43	MURDER	YUGO.
DOEBLER, Anton	300372	M	Ger.		Gren.Regt.694,Bourey nr.Bastogne(Lux.) 12.44	MISC.CRIMES	BEL.
DOEBRITZ	252468	M	Ger.		Doctor,Gestapo,Lille 40-44	MISC.CRIMES	FR.
DOECKER	250124				Rottfhr.,C.C.Dora,Nordhausen(Ger.)	MURDER	U.S.
DOECKER, Herta	151181	F	Ger.		SS-Guard,SS for Women Prisoners C.C. Mauthausen(Aust.) 41-45	WITNESS	U.S.
DOEDEL, Seppel	261880	M	Ger.		Pvt.,Army,6 Coy.,377 Jaeger Regt.,Vinkt(Bel.) 5.40	MURDER	BEL.
DOEDERICH, Paul	121215	M	Ger.	06	Civilian,Camp.	MURDER	FR.
DOEHERLEIN	147967	M	Ger.		Oberstarzt,C.C.Hohenlychen(Ger.) 5.44	TORTURE	FR.
DOEHLER, Karl	262016	M	Ger.	11. 9.12	SS-Mann,Waffen-SS,Gren.Div.36, "Dirlewanger-Bde.", Warschau and other (Pol.) 40-44	MURDER	POL.
DOEHLERT	252068	M	Ger.	95	Sturmfhr.,Gestapo,Briey,Meurthe et Moselle(Fr.)	TORTURE	FR.
DOEHLING, Georg	152012	M	Ger.		Pvt.,C.C. Gosen bei Linz(Aust.)	WITNESS	U.S.
DOEHN	305896	M	Ger.		Sgt., 1 Aufkl. Abt. 3 Coy.,2 Col., XV Div.Africa Corps, St.Leger (Arlon) 9.44	MISC.CRIMES	BEL.
DOEHNER	128871	M	Ger.		Sgt.,Stalag IV D,4-989 Coy., KL.Annaberg(Ger.) 1.44-4.45	MURDER	U.K.
DOEHRING, Erwin	193198	M	Ger.		Ex Convict,Reichs-Ministry of Justice Field Punishment Camp,Finmark(Nor.)	WITNESS	NOR.
DOELLER	259270	M	Ger.		Interpreter,Schleswig-Holstein Sondergericht,Kiel(Ger.) 4.43	WITNESS	NOR.
DOELLER, Albert	182767	M		2. 9.04	SS-Rottfhr.,4 SS Totenkopfsturmbann,C.C.Mauthausen(Ger.) 43-45	WITNESS	U.S.
DOELLINGER	307074	M	Ger.		on the staff Town Hospital,Lueneburg(Ger.) 1.43-4.45	MURDER	YUGO.
DOENIGER	300232	M	Ger.	05	Capt.,Commanding Officer, German Air Force, Phaleron Hassani, Skaramanga Air Fields, Athens Phaleron. 44	MISC.CRIMES	GRC.
DOEPLITZ, Oskar Hermann Ernst	132351	M	Ger.	95	Guard,SS-Oschfhr.,SS,C.C. Flossenburg(Ger.) 44-45	MURDER	U.S.
DOEPKEL	252288	M	Ger.		SS-Hptsturmfhr.,SS,Lidice(Czech.) 6.42	MURDER	CZECH.
DOEPKERL	250116				Pvt.,C.C. Ellrich-Nordhausen	MURDER	U.S.
DOERCHER, Karl	134704	M	Ger.		SSturmfhr.,SS, Nantes(Fr.) 42	MISC.CRIMES	FR.
DOERENBACH, Hubert	250117				Pvt.,C.C.Ellrich-Nordhausen(Ger.)	MURDER	U.S.
DOERENHAUS	147969	M	Ger.	00	Lt.-Col.,UKR.Voluntary-Regt.3, Cluny(Fr.) 7.44	MURDER	FR.
DOERFLER, Karl	182772	M	Ger.	9.10.20	SS-Uschfhr.,SS,4 SS Totenkopfsturmbann,C.C.Mittelbau,Nordhausen(Ger.)-45	WITNESS	U.S.
DOERING	9648	M	Ger.		Schfhr.,SS,Buchenwald(Ger.) 39-44	TORTURE	CZECH.
DOERING, Adolf (or DEURING or DOERINGER)	133769	M		9. 1.15	SS-Oschfhr.,Waffen-SS Totenkopf-Stand.,Buchenwald(Ger.) 39-45	SUSPECT	U.S.
DOERING	151990				Oflag 64,Capt.,KL.Schubin(Ger.) 12.44	PILLAGE	U.S.
DOERING or DORING	196717	M	Ger.		Sgt.,Neuengamme(Ger.)	TORTURE	BEL.
DOERINGER, Adolf see DOERING	133769						
DOERNER, Karl	257829	M	Ger.	21.10.10	Civilian,Kunstg.(Czech.) 40	MURDER	CZECH.
DOERR	192	M			Lt.,Air Force,Sousse(Tunisia) 1.43	MURDER	FR.
DOERR	91384	M	Ger.		Major,20 Army,Comd.Aufkl.Abt.99-7 Geb.Div.(Nor.) 10.-11.44	MURDER	NOR.
DOERR	96645	M	Ger.	22	SS-Totenkopf,Belsen(Ger.) 4.45	MISC.CRIMES	FR.,POL.
DOERR	261250	M	Ger.		Pvt., 2 Col., 3 Coy.,1 Aufkl.Abt.XV Div., Africa Corps, St.Leger Distr.Arlon(Bel.) 9.44	MISC.CRIMES	BEL.
DOERR, Alois	135148	M	Ger.	02	Uschfhr.,SS, KL.Helmbrechts(Ger.)7.44-4.45	TORTURE	U.S.
DOERR, Anton	187742	M	Ger.	95	Civilian,Wehrden-Saar(Ger.) 8.44	TORTURE	U.S.
DOERR, Ernst	250100	M		9. 3.14	Pvt.,C.C.Harzungen-Nordhausen(Ger.)	MURDER	U.S.
DOERR, Willy	163717	M	Ger.	22	Uschfhr.,SS,Bergen-Belsen(Ger.)	MURDER	FR.
DOERSCH	149349	M	Ger.		Civilian,Flossenburg(Ger.)	MURDER	FR.
DOERSCH, Ludwig	191348	M	Ger.	10	Gestapo, Wiesbaden and Frankfurt-M.(Ger.) 5.44	INTERR.	U.S.
DOERTSCH	250105				Uschfhr., Camp Rosela,Nordhausen(Ger.)	MURDER	U.S.
DOERTERL, Benno	262127	M	Ger.	18.12.95	(L.O.D.N.A.O.D.) Foreman,coal yard,Muenchen(Ger.)	SUSPECT	U.S.
DORTE or VOETZ	199820	M			Lt., Army,Salzburg(Aust.),Leipzig (Ger.) 4.45	MISC.CRIMES	U.S.
DOFFER	62002	M	Ger.		Army,Coy.Brandenburg,Pz.Gren.Div.800,Pont St.Esprit(Fr.)	MURDER	FR.
DOHLES, Alfons	250972	M			C.C.Ellrich-Nordhausen(Ger.)	MURDER	U.S.
DOHM	147972				Sturmschfhr.,SS,Toulouse(Fr.)	MURDER	FR.
DOHMANN	164715	M	Ger.		Judge,Ministry of Justice,Strasbourg(Fr.) 2.43	MURDER	FR.
DOHMEN	147971		Ger.		Dr.,Surgeon,Hohenlychen(Ger.) 5.44	TORTURE	FR.

NAME	C.R.FILE NUMBER	SEX	NATIO- NALITY	DATE OF BIRTH	RANK OCCUPATION UNIT PLACE AND DATE OF CRIME	REASON WANTED	WANTED BY
DOHMEN, Bernhard	162860	M	Ger.		Buergermeister, Ortsgr.Leiter, NSDAP,Herbesthal,Walkenraedt (Bel.) 40-44	MISC.CRIMES	BEL.
DOHN, Ewald	252066	M	Ger.		Sturmschfhr., Gestapo, Toulouse (Fr.) 11.42-8.44	MISC.CRIMES	FR.
DOHNDORF	250109	M			Rottfhr., C.C. "Camp Dora", Nordhausen (Ger.)	MURDER	U.S.
DOHNE	194956	M	Ger.	01	Lt., Commandant, Customs and excise, Zijldijk (Neth.) 3.45	PILLAGE	NETH.
DOHNERT	300233	M	Ger.		Warrant Officer, Geh. Feldpolice, Calavrita, Mega Apileon, Aghia Lavra, 12.43	MURDER	GRC.
DOHOVOLSKY	301945	M	Ger.		Blockfhr., SS, C.C. Auschwitz (Pol.) 44-45	MURDER	POL.
DOHRENDORF	261220	M	Ger.		Pvt., 5-In.Rgt.211,139.Arbeits Bereich Liane 5 Coy. I N.Rgt.211 Alleur-Lez-Liège (Bel.) 9.44	MURDER	BEL.
DOHRENDORF, Karl	185673	M	Ger.	3. 3.06	Factory Manager,Beauftragter,Civilian, Equipment and War Production, Brno (Czech.) 39-45	PILLAGE	CZECH.
DOHRWALDT	147973	M	Ger.		Brigadier, Kripo-Gestapo, Toulouse (Fr.)	TORTURE	FR.
DOHRWALDT, Herbert	254501	M	Ger.		Member, SD., Toulouse (Fr.) 11.42-8.44	MURDER	FR.
DOHSE (alias DE LANGE)	252951	M	Ger.		N.C.O., Administration, Maasbracht (Neth.) 12.44	MURDER	NETH.
DOHSE, Frederik	305020	M	Ger.		Osturmfhr.,Head of Sec.IV (Political Section), SS, SD, Bordeaux, La Gironne, Les Landes, Les Lasses-Pyrenees (Fr.) 42-44	MISC.CRIMES	FR., DEN.
DOHSE, Friedrich Wilhelm	301078	M	Ger.	22. 7.13	Crim.Secretary, Hptsturmfhr.,SS Head of Sicherheitspol., Cottager's School, Odense (Den.) 2.45-5.45	MURDER	DEN.
DOLCH	148942	M	Ger.		Head-Nurse, Civilian, Eisenach (Ger.)	MISC.CRIMES	FR.
DOLCHE (see DOCHE)	147968						
DOLD, Erwin	62003	M			SS Uschfhr., Struthof, Alsace (Fr.)	MURDER	FR.
DOLD, Josef	250110	M		2. 3.02	Flyer, C.C. Ellrich, Nordhausen (Ger.)	MURDER	U.S.
DOLDI	186493	M	Ger.		SS Osturmfhr., SS Pz.Div. "Hitler Jugend", near Caen (Fr.) 6.-7.44	TORTURE	CAN.
DOLES, Peter	182768	M			SS Sturmmann, 4.SS Totenkopfsturmbann,C.C.Nordhausen-Mittelbau (Ger.) 43-45	WITNESS	U.S.
DOLETSCHEK, Herbert	259938	M	Ger.	25.10.13	Employee, Gestapo, Mainz (Ger.), Zlin, Moravia (Czech.) 40-45	INTERR.	CZECH.
DOLEZAL, Frans	257881	M			Pvt., Army, 150 Pz. Bde., Meuse Bridge, Antwerp (Bel.) 12.44	MISC.CRIMES	BEL.
DOLF	194	M	Ger.		Sturmbannfhr., SS, C.C. Belzec (Pol.) 42-43	MURDER	POL.
DOLF, Hermann	257378	M	Ger.		Sturmbannfhr., SS, Slave Labour Camps,Korgen,Osen (Nor.)6.42-43	MURDER,TORTURE	YUGO.
DOLFF	194744	M	Ger.		SS Major, C.C. Belsen (Ger.) 42-43	MURDER	POL.
DOLIMITSCHRE, Rimm	193887	M	Ger.		Cpl., Army Staffs Etat Major of Crest,Drome,La Rochette (Fr.)8.44	MURDER	FR.
DOLL	129808	M			Civilian, C.C. Buchenwald (Ger.)	CRUELTY	U.S.
DOLL	159990	M	Ger.	00	Chief, Organisation Todt Fhr., Wagbern (Ger.)	TORTURE	FR.
DOLL, Helmuth	67011	M	Ger.		Adjutant Chief, Army, Damprichard (Fr.) 7.44	MURDER	FR.
DOLLA, Nikolaus	250038	M			C.C. Harzungen, Nordhausen (Ger.)	MURDER	U.S.
DOLLE (see DIEUDONNE), Gérard	72341						
DOLLE, Frans	250111	M			Pvt., C.C. Ellrich, Nordhausen (Ger.)	MURDER	U.S.
DOLLENBERG, Heinrich	134835	M	Ger.		L.O.D.N.A.O.D.	SUSPECT	U.S.
DOLLENBERG, Heinrich	185789	M	Ger.	08	Pvt., Army, SA., Gleidingen (Ger.)	TORTURE	U.S.
DOLLER	144319	M			Lt. Abwehr, Frontaufklaerungstrupp, Nowo-Rschew, Idriza-Sebesch (Sov.Un.) 43-44	MURDER	U.S.
DOLLERING, Hans	191978	M	Ger.	18	Pvt., Army, Leglantiers (Fr.) 7.44	RAPE	FR.
DOLLGARN, Oskar	182769	M			SS Rottfhr., 4. SS Totenkopfsturmbann, C.C.Mittelbau Nordhausen (Ger.) 43-45	WITNESS	U.S.
DOLLHOFER	62087	M	Ger.		Staff-Sgt., Army, Legion Azerbaidjan, Rodez (Fr.) 9.44	MURDER	FR.
DOLLHOFER, Leopold	148940	M	Ger.		Sgt., Army	TORTURE	FR.
DOLLIN	253626	M			Sgt., 29.Pz.Gren.Rgt., 3.Div.,Robert-Espagne,Gouvonges,Beurey, Hogneville (Fr.) 8.44	INTERR.	FR.
DOLLINGER	300450	M	Ger.		Capt., Unit LL-133, Brienne le Chateau (Fr.) 8.44	LOOTING	FR.
DOLLMANN, Wilhelm	186466	M	Ger.		Feldgendarm, Feldgendarmerie Trupp 626,Peronne Licourt (Fr.) 8.44	MURDER	FR.
DOLLY	253612	F	Ger.		Guard, C.C. Auschwitz (Pol.)	TORTURE	FR.
DOLPS	12338	M	Ger.		Mayor, SS Commandant, C.C. Osen, Elsfjord (Nor.) 6.42-3.43	MURDER	YUGO.
DOLRISS	189035	M	Ger.	95	Cpl., Guard at Camp 2780/Langweid near Muenchen (Ger.) 2.45	TORTURE	U.K.
DOLZANSKI	194094	M	Ger.	00	Sturmschfhr., SD.,Administrat.Personnel, Meerenveen, Crackstate Prison (Neth.) -4.45	MURDER	NETH.
DOLZER	148939	M	Ger.		Agent, Gestapo, Linz (Aust.) 2.44	MISC.CRIMES	FR.
DOLZER, Johann	252063	M	Ger.		Pvt., Straelen (Ger.) 11.44	MURDER	U.S.
DOM	192236	M	Ger.		Frontfhr., Organisation Todt, Hazebrouck (Fr.) 8.44	MURDER	FR.
DOMANSKY	148938	M	Ger.	12	Civilian, Thorn (Pol.)	TORTURE	FR.
DOMBACK	29820	M			Usturmfhr., SS, C.C. Buchenwald (Ger.) 41-45	TORTURE	BEL.
DOMBECK (or DUMBECK,DUMBOCK)	144324	M			SS Hptschfhr., C.C. Buchenwald (Ger.)	TORTURE	U.S.
DOMBOYS	257882	M			Lt., 150 Pz. Bde., Meuse Bridge, Antwerp (Bel.) 12.44	MISC.CRIMES	U.S.
DOMCK (see DOMECK)	260640						
DOMCKE	196	M	Ger.		Army, Capt.,Commander of P.O.W. Camp, C.C. Radom (Pol.) 9.,12.39	MURDER	POL.
DOMECK (or DOMCK)	260640	M	Ger.		Navy, Rgt. Clodius, Saulieu (Fr.) 9.44	MURDER	FR.
DOMENIG	147002	M	Ger.		Capt., Army, Radouljica (Yugo.) 43	MURDER	YUGO.
DOMINEK, Franz	187283	M	Ger.		Employee, Member SD., Gestapo (Brno (Czech.) 39-45	MURDER	CZECH.
DOMING	67006	M	Ger.		Pvt.,SS 17 Pz.Gren.Div."G.v.Berlichingen", Sturmgesch.Abt.17, Segre, Renase (Fr.) 7.-8.44	MURDER	FR.
DOMINIK, Paul	72712	M	Ger.	95	Crim.Inspector, Hptsturmfhr., Sipo, SS, Lublin (Pol.) 39-44	MURDER	POL.
DOMINIK	197	M	Ger.		SS Sturmbannfhr., C.C. Maidanek (Pol.)	MURDER	FR.
DOMIS, Christian	178963	M	Ger.	90	SS Usturmfhr.,Crim.Chiefsecretary, SD., Gestapo, Praha,Lidice (Czech.) 40-45	MURDER	CZECH.
DOMKE	250112	M			Pvt., C.C. Ellrich, Nordhausen (Ger.)	MURDER	U.S.
DOMKOWSKI	148936	M	Ger.		Officer, Fortress, Graudenz (Ger,)	MURDER	FR.
DOMMO, Martin	154444	M			Stabswachtmeister of school Remunt, C.C.Gardelegen (Ger.)4.45	MURDER	U.S.
DOMOGALSKI, Felix	192310	M	Ger.	10	Army, Prisoner at Ft. Zinna, Torgau (Ger.) 45	WITNESS	U.S.
DOMROS, Artur	176926	M	Ger.	15. 5.88	Railroad Employee, Prison, C.C. Langendreer (Ger.)	TORTURE	U.S.
DOMSCHKE, Georg	194352	M	Ger.	5. 1.25	SS-Mann, Leibstandarte Adolf Hitler, 1 SS Pz.Div., Malmedy (Bel.) 12.44	MURDER	U.S.
DONABAUER, Fritz	306357	M	Ger.	26. 6.22	SS-Mann, C.C. Buchenwald (Ger.) 5.38 and 10.43	MURDER	BEL.
DONAT	189998	M			Cpl., 892 Gren.Rgt. 264 Div.,Sncuraj Mus.,Imotski-Dist.(Yugo.)10.-12.43	MURDER	YUGO.
DONAT	252278	M	Ger.		Lt., Kragujevac (Yugo.) 10.41	MURDER	YUGO.
DONATH	305837	M	Ger.		Sgt.,1.Aufkl.Abt. 3 Coy,2 Col.XV Div.Afrika Korps,St.Léger, Arlon, 9.44	MISC.CRIMES	BEL.

DON - DOT

NAME	C.R.FILE NUMBER	SEX	NATIO-NALITY	DATE OF BIRTH	RANK OCCUPATION UNIT PLACE AND DATE OF CRIME	REASON WANTED	WANTED BY
DONATH	301624	M	Ger.		Cpl., Feldgendarmerie, Chateaubriant (Loire-Inferieure), St.Julien de Mouvantes (Fr.) 7.44	MURDER	FR.
DONAU	148935	M	Ger.		Blockfuehrer, NSDAP, Schoerzingen (Ger.) 44	TORTURE	FR.
DONAUBRAUER	162343	M	Ger.	18	SS-Unterscharf., C.C. Buchenwald (Ger.)	TORTURE	U.S.
DONDA, Franz	193781	M	Ger.	16. 7.90	Agent, Gestapo, Vsetin (Czech.) 39-45	MURDER	CZECH.
DONGES, Rudolph	133770	M		12	Sgt., Geheime Feldpolizei, Gruppe 713.	MURDER	U.S.
DONGUS	193617	M	Ger.	00	SS-Sturmbannf., Head office for race and settlement, Lidice (Czech.) 42	MISC.CRIMES	CZECH.
DONIEC, Wasil	126255	M			Member, SS,	MISC.CRIMES	U.S.
DONIG, Carl	194955	M	Ger.	10. 4.90	Clerk, Civilian, Arnheim (Neth.) 49-44	MISC.CRIMES	NETH.
DONIN	62009	M		98	Feldkriegsgerichtsrat, Feldkommandantur 529, Bordeaux (Fr.)	TORTURE	FR.
DONNAU, Willy	148934	M			N.C.O., SS, C.C. Mauthausen (Aust.)	TORTURE	FR.
DONNER	196716	M			SS-Rottenf., C.C. Mauthausen (Aust.)	TORTURE	BEL.
DONNER, Erich	193144	M		31.10.02	Sgt., Guard, Reichsjustizministerium, Feldstraflager, Finmark (Nor.) 42	MISC.CRIMES	NOR.,YUGO.
DONNER, Franz	151995	M	Ger.		Civilian, Gelsenkirchen (Ger.) 43-45	TORTURE	U.S.
DONNER, Ludwig	182771	M			SS-Sturmmann, 4.SS-Totenkopf-Sturmbann, C.C. Mittelbau - Nordhausen, 43	WITNESS	U.S.
DONNER, Otto (Rudolf)	193143	M	Ger.	12.12.98	Sgt., Guard, Reichsjustizministerium, Feldstraflager, Finmark (Nor.) 45	MISC.CRIMES	NOR.,YUGO.
DONNHAUSE	252469	M			Major, Freiwillige Stamm-Div., L'Ain (Fr.) 7.44	MISC.CRIMES	FR.
DONNITZ, Feslueng	252861	M			1.Aufklaerungsabtlg.,3.Coy.,15.Div.,Africa corps, St.Leger (Bel.) 9.44	PILLAGE	BEL.
DONSBACH	148925	M			Staatsanwalt, Kriegsgericht, 44	MURDER	FR.
DOORS, Erwin	185382	M			SS-Oberscharf., 17.Inf.Div., "Goetz v.Berlichingen", Raids (Fr.) 7.44	MURDER	U.S.
DOOSE, Erwin	305765	M	Ger.	31. 3.09	Oberscharf., Sipo, Aussendienststelle Drammen (Nor.) 10.44	TORTURE	NOR.
DOOSE, Otto (see DOSE)	256918	M			Civilian, Finmark (Nor.) 5.45	WITNESS	NOR.
DOPEL, Gunther	306358	M		15. 1.15	SS-Menn, C.C. Buchenwald (Ger.) 5.38-10.43	MURDER	BEL.
DOPPELREITER, Franz-Ferdinand	148933	M		7.10.22	Unterscharf., SS, C.C. Mauthausen - Gusen (Aust.)	WITNESS	U.S.,FR.
DOPPELSTEIN	10064	M		06	Sgt., Army, C.C. Stalag 31, Posen (Pol.) 4.44	MURDER	U.K.
DOPPNER	300430	M	Ger.		Obersturmf., SS, 2.Pz.Div.,H.Q., La Roche and Wibri, 1.45	MURDER	BEL.
DORBECKER, Johannes	151229	M			Sgt., Adjutant-Chief, Army, Loudon (Fr.) 9.43	MURDER	FR.
DORBS	185603	M		15	Guard, SS, C.C.Rottenburg (Ger.)	TORTURE	FR.
DORCHER	62014	M			Official, S.D., Limoges, Mont Lucon, (Fr.) 8.44	MURDER	U.S.,FR.
DORCHER	62C15	M			Officer, Army, Tourlaville, Charbourg, St.Lo (Fr.)	MURDER	FR.
DORDEL, Seppel	301946	M	Ger.		Pvt., 6.Coy., 377.Inf.Regt., Vinkt (Bel.) 5.40	MURDER	BEL.
DORE, Pierre	148932	M			Chief, C.C. Rhoninge (Ger.) 43	TORTURE	FR.
DOHENKAMP, Karl	250120	M			Rottenf., C.C. Dora, Nordhausen (Ger.)	MURDER	U.S.
DORER	261932	M	Ger.		Untersturmf., S.D., various places in Slovenia (Yugo.) 41-45	MISC.CRIMES	YUGO.
DORER, Gottfried	251498	M	Ger.	13.11.93	Bank-Manager, Civ., Bruenn (Czech.) 39-45	BRUTALITY	CZECH.
DORFEIL	196044	M			Chief of Personnel factory, Arnstadt (Ger.)	TORTURE	FR.
DOFLER, Eberhard	152002	M			Civilian, Bielefeld (Ger.) 9.44	WITNESS	U.S.
DORING	174190	M			Org.Todt, C.C. Muhldorf, Ampfing (Ger.) 6.44-4.45	MISC.CRIMES	U.S.
DORING (see DOERING)	196717	M	Ger.		Sgt., C.C. Neuengamme (Ger.)	TORTURE	BEL.
DORING	301727	M	Ger.		Dr., Surgical Block, C.C. Auschwitz (Pol.) 40-45	MURDER	FR.
DORING, Ernst	252470	M			Foreman - Architect, C.C. Neuengamme (Ger.) 45	MISC.CRIMES	FR.
DORINGER	182773	M			Rottenf., SS, C.C. Nordhausen (Ger.)	WITNESS	U.S.
DORM	129809	M		10	Oberwachtmeister, Flak, Kampfgruppe Grande, near Reims (Fr.) 7.44	MURDER	U.S.
DORMANN	28830	M	Ger.		Capt., Army, St.Leger de Balsan, St.Symphores (Fr.) 44	MURDER	FR.
DORN	260978	M	Ger.		Capt., Intelligence-officer (Abwehr), PW Camp Prenzlau, Woldenburg (Ger.) 39-44	MURDER	POL.
DORN, Otto	193345	M			Capt., I/180.PW working Bn., Strinda (Nor.) 4.45	MURDER	NOR.
DORNACHER, Hans	162342	M		15	Oberscharf., SS, C.C. Dachau, Buchenwald (Ger.) 43	TORTURE	FR.
DORNBLUT, Otto	250106	M		14. 8.19	Pvt., C.C. Ellrich, Nordhausen (Ger.)	MURDER	U.S.
DORNER, Eleonora	187284	F	Ger.	19. 9.19	Member, Employee, S.D., Gestapo, Brno (Czech.) 39-45	MISC.CRIMES	CZECH.
DORNER, Ernest	261421	M	Ger.	10	Staff-Oberscharf., Member, SS and Gestapo, Mende (Fr.) 43-44	SUSPECT	FR.
DORNER, Georg	250107	M		5. 7.98	Pvt., C.C. Ellrich, Nordhausen (Ger.)	MURDER	U.S.
DORNER, Martin	174191	M			SS-Sturmmann, C.C. Muhldorf, Ampfing (Ger.) 6.44-4.45	MISC.CRIMES	U.S.
DORNHOFER, Hans	132544	M		20	Unterscharf., SS, Hallein (Aust.)	TORTURE	FR.
DORR	36645	M		22	SS-Totenkopf-Div., near Osterode, Ger.4.45	MURDER	FR.
DORR	166956	M		91	Medicin-Lt., Stalag 12-A, C.C. Limburg (Ger.) 10.44	MISC.CRIMES	FR.
DOER	174192	M	Ger.		Capt., Stalag, C.C. Hemer (Ger.) 41-45	TORTURE	U.S.
DORR, Rudolph	124251	M			Sgt., SS Panzer-Regt., 1.Regt., 9.Coy., Malmedy (Bel.) 12.44	MURDER	U.S.
DORRENHAUS	148928	M		00	Lt.Col., Army, Macon, Cluny, Romans (Fr.) 44	MURDER	FR.
DORRING	251145	M			W.O., 10.Panz.Div., Unit: No. 36185, Lautrec (Fr.) 8.44	MURDER	FR.
DORRWALD	195574	M			N.C.O., Airforce, Rodez (Fr.) 8.44	MURDER	FR.
DORSCH	196550	M			Policeman, Police, Broichweiden, Schleibach (Ger.) 5.42	MURDER	POL.
DORSCH, Georg	154445	M		11	Hauptscharf., SS, C.C. Reichenau (Aust.) 44	MURDER	U.S.
DORSCHL	252859	M			Pvt., Heeresflak Art.Abt.276, 18.Pz.Div., Posterholt (Neth.) 11.44	MISC.CRIMES	NETH.
DORSCHT	163716	M			S.D. Montlucon, Chappes (Fr.)	MURDER	FR.
DORSEMAGEN, Karl	184272	M			Medicin-Chief, Feldlazarett, C.C. Sachsenhausen (Ger.)	MISC.CRIMES	FR.
DORST	148927	M		10	Oberscharf., SS, C.C. Dachau (Ger.)	TORTURE	FR.
DORSTEL	144323	M			SS-Sturmscharf., S.D. Aussendienststelle Mende, Baradoux (Fr.) 5.44	MURDER	FR.
DORSTER, H.	201	M			Col. (Flyer) Airforce, Andeville (Fr.) 8.44	MURDER	FR.
DORWALD, Herbert	148926	M	Ger.		Civilian,	TORTURE	FR.
DOSCH	301403	F	Ger.		Wardress, Flossenburg (Ger.) 42-45	MURDER	FR.
DOSE or DOSO	12650	M	Ger.		Part responsability for evacuations,Finmark (Nor.) 11.44	MURDER	NOR.
DOSE, Otto (DOOSE)	256918						
DOSEZAHL	128870	M	Ger.		Pvt., Stalag Luft VII, C.C. Penkam (Ger.) 1.45	MURDER	U.K.
DOSO (see DOSE)	12650						
DOSS	196045	M			Lt., parachute pioneer Bn.8, St.Amand, Montrond (Fr.) 6.44	MURDER	FR.
DOSSE	173757	M			Kreiskommandant, Abwehr Fst-368, Valjevo (Yugo.) 42-43	MURDER	YUGO.
DOSSE, Fritz	261954	M			Sturmbannf., SS, Yugo., 8.42-9.44	SUSPECT	YUGO.
DOST	195573	M			Pvt., Strafvollzug, Caen (Fr.) 6.44	MURDER	FR.
DOST	250108	M			Rottenf., C.C. Rottleberode, Nordhausen (Ger.)	MURDER	U.S.
DOST, Emil Paul	260915	M	Ger.	8. 2.00	Sturmmann, SS-Totenkopf-guard, C.C.Auschwitz (Pol.) 44-45	BRUTALITY	POL.
DOSTALIKOVA nee URBANEC, Anna	252401	F	Ger.	16.12.14	Clerk, Post office, Bruenn (Czech.) 9.42	INTERR.	CZECH.
DOSTLER	28831	M	Ger.		Cmdt., Army, Coudray en Thelle (Fr.) 44	MURDER	U.N.W.C.C.
DOTSCH, Gretel Marie	135114	F	Ger.	12	Civ., Koblens (Ger.) 44-45	TORTURE	U.S.
DOTTERL	174193	M			SS-Unterscharf., C.C. Muhldorf, Ampfing (Ger.) 6.44-4.45	MISC.CRIMES	U.S.
DOTTERMUSCH, Alfred	151991	M	Ger.	15. 2.05	Sgt., SS-Totenkopf-Standarte, C.C. Buchenwald (Ger.)	TORTURE	U.S.

DOT - DRE

NAME	C.R.FILE NUMBER	SEX	NATIO-NALITY	DATE OF BIRTH	RANK OCCUPATION UNIT PLACE AND DATE OF CRIME	REASON WANTED	WANTED BY
DOTZAUER	250101	M			Oschfhr.CC Nordhausen(Ger.)	MURDER	U.S.
DOTZAUER, Kurt	250102	M		20. 8.25	Flyer,CC Nordhausen,Ger.)	MURDER	U.S.
DOTZE, Emil	253621	M	Ger.		377 Jaeger Regt.,Vinkt(Bel.)	MISC.CRIMES	BEL.
DOUBEK, Oswald	252400	M	Ger.	31. 5.12	Employee Gestapo,Vsetin(Czech.)39-45	MISC.CRIMES	CZECH.
DOUBROWCKI	256926	M			Capt.Cdt.Navy,Beaucroissant(Fr.)7-44	MURDER	FR.
DOUGLAS	196810	M			Polizeirat,Grand Duchy(Lux.)40-44	PILLAGE	LUX.
DOUJAK	147081	M	Ger.		Kreisleiter,SS Osturmfhr.NSDAP,SS,Radouljica(Yugo.)43,Dr.	MURDER	YUGO.
DOURU	147976	M			Official,S.D.	TORTURE	FR.
DOUSENDSCHOEN	62027	M		10	Lt.Col.SS Deutschland	TORTURE	FR.
DOWIDEIT, Walter	250103	M		1. 3.03	Sgt.CC Ellrich,Nordhausen(Ger.)	MURDER	U.S.
DRABEK	250037	M			Pvt.CC Dora,Nordhausen(Ger.)	MURDER	U.S.
DRABEK, Josef	252289	M	Ger.	11. 3.06	Ortsleiter,NSDAP,Vyskow(Czech.)42	MURDER	CZECH.
DRABNER, Josef	259923	M	Ger.	05	SS Oschafhr.Chief,Crim.Asst.SS Gestapo,Trencin(Slov./CSR)2.44-4.45	MURDER	CZECH.
DRAECHSLER	251495				SS Cmdt.Women Camp, Auschwitz-Birkenau (Pol.) 42 - 45	MURDER	YUGO.
DRAEGER	252947	M	Ger.		Civilian,Employee,Landratsamt,Helmstedt(Ger.)6.-7.44	WITNESS	U.S.
DRAEGER	259705	M	Ger.	86	Major/Commander,Airforce,Villefranche(Hte. Garonne, Fr.) 8.44	MURDER	FR.
DRAEGESTEIN	188535	M	Ger.		Capt.16 Pz.Art.Regt.,Salerno(It.)9.43	MISC.CRIMES	U.K.
DRAESKE	251128	M	Ger.		Director,Frison,Rheinbach(Ger.)	INTERR.	FR.
DRAGASCHNIGG, Friedrich	193141	M			Sgt.2 Coy.Bau Bn.429(F)(Nor.)45	MURDER	NOR.
DRAGERT	157385	M			Medezinchef,Civilian,Hospital,Radolfzell,Bodensee(Ger.)4.44	MURDER	FR.
DRAGESSEP, Otto	140321	M			Pol.Anwaerter,Polizei,Wiesbaden(Ger.)2.45	MURDER	U.S.
DRACHE	191192	M	Ger.		Lt.Aufklaerungs Res.Abt.10,Koenigsbrueck(Ger.)7.44	MISC.CRIMES	U.K.
DRAGON	196041	M			Untersturmfhr.SS Dienststelle,Feldpost 23474X,Aigues Rives(Fr.)2.-3.44	PILLAGE	FR.
DRAHEIM	262255	F	Ger.		Secretary,Gestapo,Rennes(Fr.)45-44	SUSPECTS	FR.
DRAMMER	12600	M			Sec.Lt.2 SS Div.Das Reich,6 or 7 Bn.,Leborn(Fr.)6.44	MURDER	FR.
DRANDT	190470	M		96	Sgt.718 Land.Bn.Stalag XIA,Schierstedt,Aschersleben(Ger.)12.44-4.45	TORTURE	U.K.
DRANKEL	306578	M	Ger.		1st Lt.Stalag 344 at Lamsdorf Lipper Silesia,to Western(Ger.),Siebleben nr.Gotha(Ger.)3-45	MURDER	U.K.
DRANTZ, Karl	62029	M		07	SS Unterscharfhr.CC Natzweiler(Fr.)	TORTURE	FR.
DRAPP	147759	M			Vorarlberg(Aust.)43	PILLAGE	FR.
DRASCHKE	1318	M	Ger.		Lt.Army,29 PGR 3 Coy.	MURDER	U.K.
DRASCHNER, Josef	131262	M			SS Rottenfhr.,Auschwitz(Pol.)1.44	MURDER	U.S.
DRASLER or DRAZLER	260879	M			SS Wachtmeister,SS Guard,Beisfjord,Osen,Korgen(Nor.)6.-10.42	MURDER	YUGO.
DRATZLER	147978	M	Ger.		Civilian,Oflag VA,Weinberg(Ger.)	TORTURE	FR.
DRAUNER	196879	M			Civilian Staff of CC,Auschwitz(Pol.)40	MURDER	FR.
DRAVE, Walter	192237	M	Ger.		Sgt.Army Unit 26033E Delyon,Soissons(Fr.)8.44	WITNESS	FR.
DRAXELMAIS	12601	M			NCO,110 or 111 Panz.Gren.Regt.2 Coy.,Albine(Fr.)6.44	MURDER	FR.
DRAXLER, Herbert	168994	M	Ger.		Pvt.9 Res.Gren.Regt.,Magny-D'Anigon(Fr.)9.44	MURDER	FR.
DRAXLER, Josef	189693	M	Ger.	09	Employee,Gestapo,S.D.,Waffen SS,KL.Mlada Boleslav(Czech.)41-45	TORTURE	CZECH.
DRAZDIF, Rudolf	193782	M	Ger.	18. 2.10	Agent,Territ.Occ.,Pisek(Czech.)38 - 43	MURDER	CZECH.
DRAZLER	257383	M	Ger.		SS Guard,Sgt.SS-slave labour camp,Beisfjord/Narvik(Nor.)6.-11.42	BRUTALITY	YUGO.
DRAZLER see DRASLER	260879						
DREBENSTEDT	151177	M			District Farm Leader,Volkssturm,Vicinity of Gardelegen(Ger.)4.45	MURDER	U.S.
DREES, Fritz	168996	M	Ger.		Kapo or Warder,CC Sachsenhausen,Oranienburg(Ger.)39-4.45	MURDER	POL.
DRECHALER	305838	M			Pvt.1 Aufkl.Abt.3 Coy.2 Col.XV Div.Afrika Korps,St.Leger(Arlon)9.44	MISC.CRIMES	BEL.
DRECHEL	145581	F			SS Woman-Guard,CC Holleischen(Czech.)4.44-5.45	TORTURE	CZECH.
DRECHENER, Max	155759	M	Ger.		Pvt.Army,11 Coy.999 Bde.,Honsfeld(Bel.)12.44	WITNESS	U.S.
DRECHLER-	31950	M	Ger.		Capt.2 Regt.,Locmine(Fr.)7.44-8.44	MURDER	FR.
DRECHSEL, Margot see DREXLER-	124590						
DRECHSEL	139774	M		06	Pvt.Geheime Polizei Gruppe 713 Pvt.CC Kresti nr.Pskov(Russ.)41-44	MURDER	U.S.
DRECHSEL	168115	M			Asst.CC Birkenau(Pol.)	TORTURE	U.S.
DRECHSEL	173770	M			Cpl.Stammlager IX CC Bad Sulza Stalag IX(Ger.)44-45	MURDER	FR.
DRECHSLER, Margot see DREXLER	124590						
DRECHSLER or DREXLER	130107	F		10	SS Woman CC,Dora Mittelbau, Nordhausen(Ger.)	MURDER	U.S.
DRECHSLER	145556	M			CC Holleischen(Czech.)4.44-5.45	TORTURE	FR.
DRECHSLER	147981	F	Ger.	05	Camp Commandant,CC Birkenau(Pol.)42-44	MURDER	FR.
DRECHSLER, Helmut	142431	M			Hptsturmfhr.2 SS Pz.Div.Das Reich,Recce Bn.,Tulle(Fr.)5.44	MURDER	U.S.
DRECHSLER, Kaethe	195156	F	Ger.	09	Member,Employee,Gestapo,Kolin(Czech.)39-45	MURDER	CZECH.
DRECKER	62033	M		10	W.O.Army	PILLAGE	FR.
DRECKMANN, Otto	62034	M			Betriebsobmann,SS or D.A.F.	TORTURE	FR.
DREES	192317	M			SS Untersturmfhr.CC Flossenburg(Ger.)	MURDER	U.S.
DREES, Edwards	301554	M	Ger.	29. 1.01	SS Uscharfhr.No.264402,CC Flossenburg(Ger.)5.44-4.45	BRUTALITY	BEL.
DREES, Franz	152001	M	Ger.	17	Rottenfhr.Waffen SS,Leibstandarte Adolf Hitler,1 Div.Feld Ers.Bn.1, Rosbach(Ger.)3-45	WITNESS	U.S.
DREESMANN, Willy	259348	M	Ger.		Unterscharfhr.active member of Poitiers-Gestapo,Civ.Occ.Location of cars to Freiburg(Baden), Area Poitiers(Fr.)40-44	MISC.CRIMES	FR.
DREESON see DREISSEN	137007						
DREFE, Karl	149371	M	Ger.		Sgt.Army,Albi,CC Castres(Fr.)	INCENDIARSM	FR.
DREGER	151979	M	Ger.		Master,Gendarmerie,Herzfelde(Ger.)3-45	MURDER	U.S.
DREGER	196042	M			Guard CC Royallieu Compiegne(Fr.)41-44	MURDER	FR.
DREGER, Kurt	252958	M	Ger.		Hptsturmfhr.,BEKK.,Landratsamt,Helmstedt(Ger.)6.-7.44	MURDER	U.S.
DREHER	185372	M	Ger.		Hptscharfhr.SS Totenkopfverband,Sandweiler(Ger.)	TORTURE	FR.
DREIER	260846	M			Lt.,Elversberg(Ger.)7.44	WITNESS	U.S.
DREHER, Josef	62037	M			SS Sgt.KL Neckareltz-Struthof(Ger.)8.43	MURDER	FR.
DREHKOL, Willy	251494	M	Ger.		Osturmfhr.Gestapo,Jagodina(Yugo.)2.44	INTERR.	YUGO.
DREHRSAM	145559	M		10	Hptsturmfhr.SS CC Sachsenhausen(Ger.)	MISC.CRIMES	FR.
DREIER	257894	M			150 Pz.Bde.Meusebridge Antwerpen,12.44	MISC.CRIMES	U.S.
DREIMANN or DREYMANN	253619	M	Ger.		SS Records Clerk,CC Neuengamme(Ger.)	MURDER	BEL.
DREIMANN	257837	M	Ger.		SS Oscharfhr.Camp Dora,Nordhausen(Ger.)	MURDER	FR.
DREINER	151185	M		93	Rottenfhr.CC Administrative Chief,Vicinity of Hirsenhain(Ger.)3.45	MURDER	U.S.
DREINERT, Karl	261780	M	Ger.	13	Usturmfhr.S.D.de Besancon,Rioz(Haute Saone)Fr.7.44	BRUTALITY	FR.
DREIS	196391	M	Ger.		Lt.3 Coy.Green Police,near Arnheim(Neth.)3-45	MURDER	NETH.

DRE - DRI

NAME	C.R.FILE NUMBER	SEX	NATIO-NALITY	DATE OF BIRTH	RANK OCCUPATION UNIT PLACE AND DATE OF CRIME	REASON WANTED	WANTED BY
DREISBACH, Willy	194316	M	Ger.		Interpreter, Grenzpolizei, Douvaine (Fr.) 7.44	MURDER	FR.
DREISE, Willy	305884	M	Ger.		Osturmfhr.Head of Hrazec Kralove,Aussenstelle of Sicherheitsdienst, Leitabschnitt Prague, C.C. Oswiecim-Birkenau (Pol.) 43	MISC.CRIMES	CZECH.
DREISIND or DREISLING	144318	M			Osturmfhr., SS, Kraftfahr-Abt.,C.C. Loiberedorf (Ger.) 5.45	WITNESS	U.S.
DREISS	149372			95	Director, Bremen (Ger.)	TORTURE	FR.
DREISSEN alias DREESON	137007	M		22	Pvt., Landes-Schz.Bn 439, 4 Coy,Nieder Oels (Czech.) 2.45	MURDER	U.S.
DREISSER, Fridolin	169462	M	Ger.		SD, C.C. Schirmeck (Fr.) 11.44	TORTURE	U.K.
DREIUCKER or DREUKER	202	M	Ger.		Osturmfhr., SS Div. "Das Reich", Rgt. "Der Fuehrer" Buzet (Fr.) 7.44	MURDER	FR.
DREIWURST, Josef	187298	M		2. 7.21	Employee, Gestapo, SD, Brno (Czech.) 39-45	MISC.CRIMES	CZECH.
DREIZNER-BRUECKMANN, Emmy	194816	F	Ger.		Civilian, Duesseldorf (Ger.)	MISC.CRIMES	LUX.
DREKER	62035	M			Oscharfhr., C.C. Struthof (Fr.)	MURDER	FR.
DRENKEL	178062	M	Ger.		Lt., Army, C.C. Linderback (Ger.) 3.45	MURDER	U.K.
DRENT	196039	M	Ger.		Wachtmstr., Sipo, C.C. Westerbork (Neth.) 9.44	MURDER	NETH.
DREPESS	185604	M	Ger.		Crim.Commissar, Gestapo, Sarrebruck (Fr.) 11.44	MURDER	FR.
DRES, Werner	301855	M	Ger.		Crim.Asst. Dept 2 B,Stapo-Leistelle Prague(Czech.) C.C. Oswiecim-Birkenau (Pol.) 39 - 45	MURDER	CZECH.
DRESCHE alias DRESCHKE	72357	M	Ger.	94	Director, NSDAP, Prison Rheinbach (Ger.)	MISC.CRIMES	U.S.
DRESCHER	149373			10	SS, C.C. Wilhelmshaven (Ger.)	TORTURE	FR.
DRESCHER, Adolf	187307	M	Ger.	23.12.01	Member, employee, SD, Gestapo, Brno (Czech.)	MURDER	CZECH.
DRESCHER, Paulus	149374	M	Ger.		Sgt., Army, Albi (Fr.)	MURDER	FR.
DRESCHER, Peter	126532	M			Civilian in C.C. Alsdorf (Ger.) 42-44	TORTURE	U.S.
DRESCHKE	62038	M			Prison-Dir., Police, Rheinbach (Fr.)	TORTURE	FR.
DRESCHLER	141926	M	Ger.		Capt., parachuter,Ers.u.Ausb.Rgt.2, between Plumelec and Tredion (Fr.) 6.-7.44	WITNESS	U.K.
DRESCHLER	196951	F	Ger.		Guard, C.C. Ravensbruck (Ger.)	TORTURE	BEL.
DRESCHLER	253616	M			SS, 1 Coy, 1 Pz.Rgt., Malmedy (Bel.) 12.44	MISC.CRIMES	U.S.
DRESCHLER, Willy	262254	M		7. 8.?	Uscharfhr., SS, Gestapo, Rennes (Fr.) 43-44	MISC.CRIMES	FR.
DRESCHKE see DRESCHE	72357						
DRESS, Gerhard	137662	M	Ger.		Groupleader, Civilian,NSDAP, Sebnitz (Ger.) 9.44	TORTURE	U.K.
DRESSEL	67005	M	Ger.		Uscharfhr.,SS,17 Pz.Gren.Div."Goetz von Berlichingen" Sturm-Gesch.Abt.17, Segre,Renaze (Fr.) 7.-8.44	MURDER	FR.
DRESSEL	167918	M			Hptscharfhr., SS, Gestapo (Nor.) 4.40	TORTURE	NOR.
DRESSEL, Herbert	252065	M			SS-Hptscharfhr., Crim.secr.,Gestapo, Aube (Fr.) 43-44	MISC.CRIMES	FR.
DRESSEN, Hans	252402	M	Ger.	15	Officer, SS, Aachen (Ger.) 7.43	BRUTALITY	U.S.
DRESSLER	62042	M			C.C. Auschwitz (Pol.)	TORTURE	FR.
DRESSLER	72352	M			Sgt., Gestapo, Quirnbach-Helferskirchen	MURDER	U.S.
DRESSLER	162862	M			Civilian, Boussu (Bel.)	PILLAGE	BEL.
DRESSLER, Heinrich	137006	M	Ger.	01	Specialist officer in Agriculture, Army	MURDER	U.S.
DREUKER see DREIUCKER	202						
DREUNICK, Alfred	28827	M	Ger.		Senior W.O. to O.C., Army, Marmande Beaupuy (Fr.) 4.44	TORTURE	FR.
DREUSS, Hermann	250104	M		7.10.13	Sgt., C.C. Ellrich, Nordhausen (Ger.)	MURDER	U.S.
DREWS	149375	M	Ger.		Sgt.,3 Rgt.of Macon, 3 Coy, Bourg (Fr.)	MURDER	FR.
DREWFAR	139819	M			Sgt., Transportation Rgt., Stalag X B, Sandbostel (Ger.) 1.-5.45	MISC.CRIMES	U.S.
DREWO, Franz	257312	M		9. 1.20	Crim.Pol.asst., Gestapo, Crim.-Pol., Tabor (Bohemia-Czech.)11.39-5.45	MISC.CRIMES	CZECH.
DREWS	192312	M			Osturmfhr., SS, C.C. Flossenburg (Ger.) 44-45	MURDER	U.S.
DREWS, Hermann	307076	M			Officer,Custom-house, operational Cmdo. attached to Lourdes Htes-Pyrenees (Fr.) 1.-8.44	MURDER	FR.
DREXKILIEN	257291	M	Ger.		Lt., Feuerschutzpol., Wiesbaden (Ger.)	MISC.CRIMES	U.S.
DREXHAGE	250039	M			Pvt., C.C. Dora, Nordhausen (Ger.)	MURDER	U.S.
DREXL	125135	F			SS, C.C. Auschwitz (Pol.)	MURDER	U.S.
DREXLER	124527	M	Ger.		Rottenfhr., SS, Sachsenhausen (Ger.)	TORTURE	U.K.
DREXLER, Margot or DRECHER or DRECHSEL	124590	F	Ger.		Chief-woman-guard, C.C. Birkenau-Auschwitz (Pol.)	MURDER	FR.,POL.,BEL.
DREXLER see DRECHSLER	130107						
DREXLER	157381	M			Agent, Gestapo, Florang (Fr.) 9.42	MISC.CRIMES	FR.
DREXLER	253617	M			Uscharfhr., 2 Pz.Coy, 1 Pz.Rgt., Malmedy (Bel.) 12.44	MISC.CRIMES	U.S.
DREXLER, Hans	168937	M	Ger.		Rottenfhr.,SS, C.C. Sachsenhausen, Oranienburg (Ger.) 39-45	MURDER	POL.
DREXLER, Otto	62044	M		18	SS-Pz.Gren.Div.,Montmirail (Fr.)	MURDER	FR.
DREYER	67009	M	Ger.		SS-Mann, SS-Div.,F.P.Nr.48963 B, St.Sulpice,Montmusson, Chateau-Gontier (Fr.) 8.44	MURDER	FR.
DREYER	250040	M			Flyer, C.C. Ellrich, Nordhausen (Ger.)	MURDER	U.S.
DREYER	251295	M	Ger.		Officer, Interpreter, Feldgend., Thoiry (Fr.) 11.43	INTERR.	FR.
DREYER	301123	M	Ger.		Lt.Insp.Cmdt. of Customs,Ers.Cdo.,St.Girons, Chateau,Beauregard, Ariège (Fr.) 7.44	MURDER	FR.
DREYER, Hermann	185370	M	Ger.		Emmen (Ger.) 3.45	TORTURE	U.S.
DREYHAUPT	1319	M	Ger.	99	Lt., Platz-Cmdtr.II-103, asst. to Major van Werden, Polazzo del Paro (It.) 6.44	MISC.CRIMES	U.K.,IT.
DREYMANN	121220	M	Ger.		Oscharfhr., guard, C.C. Neuengamme,Hamburg (Ger.) 42	MURDER	FR.,BEL.,U.K.
DREYMANN see DREIMANN	253619						
DREYZR	62045	M			Inspect.,Custom-house,Gaudens,St.Girons,Rimont (Fr.)	MURDER	FR.
DRI, Otto	301035	M	Ger.		Medical-officer,Pforzheim works, (Ger.) 43-45	MISC.CRIMES	BEL.
DRIESSEN, Matthias	252946	M	Ger.		Flamersheim (Ger.)	MISC.CRIMES	U.S.
DRIEMEL	133767	M			Uscharfhr., SS, C.C. Buchenwald (Ger.)	TORTURE	U.S.
DRIEMEL, Alfred	162348	M	Ger.	09	Hptsturmfhr., SS, C.C. Buchenwald (Ger.)	TORTURE	U.S.
DRIER	144326	M		98	General, OKW	WITNESS	U.S.
DRIESNOCK	141310	M	Ger.	14	Pvt.,Army,Zirkelschacht,400 Bn,Landes-Schz.,Eisleben (Ger.) 6.44	MURDER	U.K.
DRIESSEN	130323	M		22	Pvt. guard,4-439 Landesschz.Bn, Working Party of E 3 of POW, Nieder-Oels (Czech.) 2.45	MURDER	U.K.
DRIESSLER	193237	M			Rottenfhr., SS Lazarett Abt. C.C. Buchenwald (Ger.) 42-45	TORTURE	U.S.
DRIESSNER	151975	M			W.O., Gestapo,Trondes,Boucq,Hemil la Tour (Fr.) 8.44	MURDER	FR.
DRIESSNER, Fritz	252933	M	Ger.		Sgt., Cmdt., Gestapo,338 Div., Bn III Sgt.school, La Bresse (Fr.)11.44	MURDER	FR.
DRIESSON, Germain Gerard	72362	M	Ger.		Army, 4 Coy, Landesschz.Bn 439, Nieder-Oels (Czech.)3.45	MURDER	U.K.
DRIFER	149377	M	Ger.		W.O., Landesschz.740 or 741 or 742,Salawedel (Ger.) 12.43	TORTURE	U.K.
DRILLER, Wilhelm	194317	M	Ger.		Feldgendarm, Feldgendarmerie Hucqueliers (Fr.)	TORTURE	FR.
DRINCK	1680	M			San.N.C.O., Army,Feldgendarmerie 664	TORTURE	U.K.
DRINCHAUS	62248	M	Ger.	04	Uscharfhr.,clerk, SS, C.C. Hinzert (Ger.)	TORTURE	U.S.

DRI-DUE

NAME	C.R.FILE NUMBER	SEX	NATIO-NALITY	DATE OF BIRTH	RANK OCCUPATION UNIT PLACE AND DATE OF CRIME	REASON WANTED	WANTED BY
DRISCHER	146190	M	Ger.		Major,Munitions-Depot Unit L.37 419 E, Bousso (Bel.) 44	INCENDIARISM	BEL.
DRISSLER	162347	M	Ger.	10	SS Rottfhr., C.C. Buchenwald (Ger.) 3.45	TORTURE	U.S.
DRIZAL, Johann	250041	M		1.11.04	Staff Sgt., Nordhausen (Ger.)	MURDER	U.S.
DROBNY see RJASANTZEN	251856						
DROCUHT	155752	M	Ger.		SS Guard, C.C. Neubrenn (Ger.) 43-44	TORTURE	FR.
DROEGE	1687	M			Usturmfhr., SS of the engineer platoon Stavout	MURDER	U.K.
DROEDER, Wilhelm	12602	M	Ger.		Pvt., 110.or 111.Panz.Gren.Rgt. 2.Coy., Albine (Fr.) 6.44	MURDER	FR.
DROESSE, Frank	149978	M	Ger.		Civ.	MISC.CRIMES	FR.
DROEZE	250975	M	Ger.		Rottfhr., C.C. Rottleberode, Nordhausen (Ger.)	MURDER	U.S.
DROGENOLLER	155747	M	Ger.		N.C.O., Army, Morlaix (Fr.) 44	MURDER	FR.
DROGOSH, E.	192318	M	Ger.		Col., O.K.L. , Florennes,Charleroi,Cerfontaine,Senzeille (Bel.)	MURDER	BEL.
DROKUR	256014	M	Ger.		S.D., Mauthausen (Ger.)	INTERR.	FR.
DROKUR or TROCKER	301427	M			SS Deputy, chief of C.C. Neubrenn-Sarre, 43-44	MISC.CRIMES	FR.
DROLL, Karl	192233	M	Ger.	08	Lt., Georgisches Feldbn. I - 9. Colayrac, St.Ciro, Prayssas (Fr.) 8.44	PILLAGE	FR.
DROLSEN	62047	M			S.A.	TORTURE	FR.
DROOMOLLER, Werner or DRUGUEMULLER	196043	M	Ger.	15	Lt., Unit 01512 K, Trebeurden (Cotes du Nord) (Fr.)	MURDER	FR.
DROSE, Alfred	262256	M	Ger.	10. 7. ?	Uscharfhr., SS Gestapo, Rennes (Fr.) 43-44	MISC.CRIMES	FR.
DROST, Paul	250976	M			Cpl., C.C. Ellrich, Nordhausen (Ger.)	MURDER	U.S.
DROSTE	62049	M			Lt. 7355, Army, Pont d'Nieppe (Fr.) 9.44	TORTURE	FR.
DROSTE	196040	M			Zugwachtmeister, Schupo, Stuetzpunkt Groningen, C.C.Westerbork (Neth.) 9.-12.44	MURDER	NETH.
DROSTE	257949	M			Lt., 150.Panz.-Bde., Meuse-Bridge Antwerp(Bel.) 12.44	MISC.CRIMES	U.S.
DROSTE, Fritz	188928	M	Ger.		Hauptwachtmeister, Army, 25 116, Carces (Fr.) 8.44	WITNESS	FR.
DROSTE, Rudolf	261236	M	Ger.		Uscharfhr., Member, SS, S.D., Toulouse (Fr.) 11.42-8.44	MURDER	FR.
DRSCHER, Erwin	187282	M	Ger.	20.12.06	Crim.asst.,Member, Gestapo S.D., Brno (Czech.) 39-45	MURDER	CZECH.
DRUBBEL, Steinz (Heinz)	301886	M	Ger.		Rottfhr., SS, K.13.Coy. Moissac (F.P.No. 03669) Panz.Div."Das Reich" beginning of 44	MURDER	FR.
DRUCKER	149980	M		17	Scharfhr., SS, C.C. Drancy (Fr.)	TORTURE	FR.
DRUCKER	253828	M	Ger.	00	O.C., C.C. Block 26 Auschwitz (Pol.)	MISC.CRIMES	FR.
DRUCKZACHE	149981	M	Ger.		Civ., Barbee (Fr.)	PILLAGE	FR.
DRUECKE	151963	M			SS	MURDER	U.S.
DRUEG, Johann	261422	M	Ger.	04	Wachtmeister, police, C.C. Auschwitz (Pol.) 41-44	BRUTALITY	POL.
DRUEMMER	161629	M	Ger.		Senior W.O., 348.Inf.Rgt.,Teupitz (Ger.)	MURDER	FR.
DRUGIES, Fritz	251288	M		06	Driver, Gestapo, Allencon (Fr.) 40-44	MISC.CRIMES	FR.
DRUGUEMULLER, Werner see DROOMOLLER	196043						
DRUMAN, Willi	306000	M			Member of staff, C.C. Neuengamme (Ger.) 6.40-5.45	MURDER	U.K.
DRUMM, Gottfried	250977	M		12. 3.01	Rottfhr., C.C. Harzungen, Nordhausen (Ger.)	MURDER	U.S.
DRUNG, Roman	256927	M		6. 8.08	Employee, Block 105 C.C. Nordhausen (Ger.)	MURDER	U.S.
DRUNK	124960	M			Member, Gestapo C.C. Bremen-Farge (Ger.) 6.43	TORTURE	U.K.
DRUNNEL	129516	M	Ger.		officer, SS, C.C. Oberg Glenne (Ger.) 44	TORTURE	BEL.
DRUSCHEL	144312	M			Second in command, C.C. Schandelah, Braunschweig (Ger.)	MURDER	BEL.
DRUSCHK see DRUSKY	259084	M					
DRUSCHKE	124529	M	Ger.		Officer, Gestapo, Assling (Ger.) 10.11.44	MURDER	U.S.
DRUSCHKE	166362	M	Ger.		Deputy chief official, S.D. SIPO, Slov. (Czech.)	MURDER	UNWCC
DRUSKY or DRUSCHK	259084	M	Ger.		Chief, Gestapo, Villach (Aust.) 11.44	MURDER	U.S.
DRYNDA, Hilde	157398	F	Ger.	20. 5.19	Woman guard, C.C. Buchenwald (Ger.) 44	MISC.CRIMES	FR.
DRZYMALA, Claus	262017	M	Ger.	23. 7.14	SS-Mann, Waffen SS,Gren.Div.36 Dirlewanger Bde., Warschau and other (Pol.) 40-44	MURDER	POL.
DSCURAEW, Mamatkul	301625	M			Légionnaire of 2.Coy. Turkestan-Legion (F.P.No. 46 330) Boussens - Htes-Garonne (Fr.) 8.44	MURDER	FR.
DUBA, Franz	260718	M	Ger.	27. 4.02	Staff-Sgt. guard, SS, well-sinker, C.C. Bruenn, Kounicovy-Koleje (Czech.) 6.42	MURDER	CZECH.
DUBBEL	185377	M			Camp-chief, C.C. Emslandsmoor, Oranienburg (Ger.)	MURDER	FR.
DUBBEL, Franz	301555	M		about 18	W.O., SS Panz.Div."Das Reich" or SS Panz.Rgt."Deutschland",operating Perwez (Prov. Namur) (Bel.) 9.44	MURDER	BEL.
DUBIL	62055	M	Ger.		Revier-Oberwachtmeister, Schupo, Annecy (Fr.)	MURDER	FR.
DUBLIN	1688	M	Ger.		Pvt., Army, Corbeil (Fr.) 8.44	MURDER	U.S. U.K.
DUBOIS	67010	F	Ger.		Civ., Dax (Fr.) 6.44	WITNESS	FR.
DUBOIS	301947	M		10	Dental officer, Arnheim (Neth.) 12.44	PILLAGE	NETH.
DUBOIS, Jean see BISEMNIUS	189665						
DUBREL	184273	M	Ger.		Chief adjutant, C.C. Sachsenhausen (Ger.)	MURDER	FR.
DUCHATEAU	190674	M			Pvt., Eis.Art.Btty. 717, St.Andries-Varsenare, Bruegge (Bel.)	MURDER	BEL.
DUCHEK, Willibald	252058	M	Ger.	04	Ing. employee, state service, Gestapo, Zlin (Czech.)	MURDER	CZECH.
DUCHENE, Katharina	187744	F	Ger.	10	Civ., administrative employee of Zellenstrasse prison, Nuernberg (Ger.) 34-45	WITNESS	CZECH.
DUCHEYNE	252284	M			Interpreter, SIPO, Abt. III B, Bruessel (Bel.)	INTERR.	BEL.
DUCHY	251211	F			Wardress, prison C.C. Auschwitz (Pol.)	BRUTALITY	FR.
DUDA, Franz	131261	M			Kapo, Orpo, crim.secr., Auschwitz (Pol.) 44	MURDER	U.S.
DUDE	185607	M	Ger.		Lt., Sichr.Rgt. 200, Region Lyonnaise (Fr.)	MURDER	FR.
DUDEY, Albert	62060	M	Ger.		Lt., Cmdt., 2.Coy.d.Panz. SS, Bergerac, Mouleydier-Pressignal (Fr.)6.44	MURDER	FR.
DUDJACKZ, Michel	256015	M	Ger.		Lt., C.C. Flossenburg (Ger.)	BRUTALITY	FR.
DUDLER, Baionette	253609	M	Ger.		C.C. Esterwegen (Ger.)	BRUTALITY	FR.
DUEMICHEN, Paul	182776	M	Ger.	31. 5.04	Sturmscharfhr., crim.secret., S.D. Gestapo, Praha, Lidice (Czech.)39-45	MURDER	CZECH.
DUEBNER, Gustav	253611	M	Ger.		Civ. Leuze-Longhamps (Bel.) 1.43	INTERR.	BEL.
DUECKER	193591	M	Ger.		SS Hptsturmfhr., physician, Lidice (Czech.) 42-44	WITNESS	CZECH.
DUEMPELMANN, Otto	262136	M	Ger.		SS, prisoner in Sachsenhausen-Oranienburg, prisoner with the 12.SS-Bau-Bde., Camp am Rhin (Ger.) 12.44-1.45	MURDER	U.S.
DUENGRAEBER	305885	M	Ger.		Oscharfhr., C.C.Oranienburg (Ger.) 11.39-45	MURDER	CZECH.
DUENKER	252475	M	Ger.		Paymaster, Feldbekleidungsamt der Luftwaffe I - II, Enschede (Neth.) 42-45	PILLAGE	NETH.
DUEPEL	151978	M	Ger.		SS Osturmfhr., Fr. 8.41	MURDER	FR.
DUEPPEL	205	M	Ger.		SS Osturmfhr., Standort-Cmdt., Conches (Fr.) 8.44	MURDER	FR.
DUERHOLT, Walter	144328	M	Ger.	16. 3.99	Member, S.D., Gestapo, Wuppertal (Ger.) 4.45	WITNESS	U.S.

DUE - DUR

NAME	C.R.FILE NUMBER	SEX	NATIO-NALITY	DATE OF BIRTH	RANK OCCUPATION UNIT PLACE AND DATE OF CRIME	REASON WANTED	WANTED BY
DUERING, Johann	262018	M		11.2.09	SS-Mann, Waffen-SS, Gren.Div. 36, Dirlewanger-Bde., Warschau and other places (Pol.) 40-44	MURDER	POL.
DUERINGER	255516	M			Oschfhr.,C.C.,Buchenwald (Ger.)	MURDER	U.S.
DUERLING, Otto	108990	M			Sonder Kdo.,C.C.,Warstein,Suttrop (Ger.) 20.-22.3.45	MURDER	U.S.
DUERR, Alois	125136	M	Ger.		Commander,SS,C.C.,Helmbrecht (Czech.)	MURDER	U.S.
DUES, Theodor	255094	M			Civilian,Owner of firm Dues et My (Cloy-factory) Wessum (Ger.) 7.44	INTERR.	NETH.
DUESBERG	252059	M	Ger.		Lt.,Coy.Fhr.,8.Coy.,2.Bn.,4.Rgt.,parachute-Div. "Herm. Goering" (Rgt.Grassmel) Helchtern (Bel.) 9.44	BRUTALITY	BEL.
DUETSBERG, Willi	192919	M	Ger.	11	Guard,SS,C.C.,Stalag XVIII,Krusdorf,Wolfsberg,Feldbach,Steiermark (Aust.) 5.5.45	MURDER	U.K.
DUETTGENS	194699	M	Ger.		Usturmfhr.,Waffen SS,Le Mans (Fr.) summer 42	MISC.CRIMES	U.S.
DUEVEL, Wilhelm	161649	M	Ger.	06	Sgt.,Air-force Luftgau,Eggemoen,Honefoss,Buskerud (Nor.)	MURDER	NOR.
DUEWERT	250704	M			Uschfhr.,C.C.,Camp Dora Nordhausen (Ger.)	MURDER	U.S.
DUFEK, Herbert	187299	M	Ger.	12.1.(2)16	Member,Crim.Asst.,SD,Gestapo,Brno,(Czech.) 39-45	MURDER	CZECH.
DUFETREL	157394	M			Member,Gestapo,Toulouse (Fr.)	TORTURE	FR.
DUFFNER	157398	M			Lt.,74.Rgt.of security motorised,1.Bn.,Clavieres (Fr.)10.6.44	MURDER	FR.
DUFOUR, Adolph	259061	M	Ger.		N.C.O.,Hospital A DULAG Luft (Ger.) 43-45	INTERR.	U.S.
DUFOUR, Alix	62962	M			Gestapo,Tourlaville St.Lô,(Fr.)	MURDER	FR.
DUFT, Michael	258473	M			SS-Mann,guard,C.C.,Ohrdruf (Ger.) 12.44-4.45	MURDER	U.S.
DUGBEN	12603	M			Lt.,C.C.,Wolfinghausen (Ger.) 10.41	TORTURE	FR.
DUGER, Herbert	301793	M	Ger.		SS-Mann,Pz.Div."Leibstandarte Adolf Hitler",Stavelot (Bel.)19.-20.12.44	MURDER	BEL.
DUGLOKINSKI	253614	M	Ger.		N.C.O.,SS,377.Jaeger Rgt.,Vinkt (Bel.)	MISC.CRIMES	BEL.
DUHL	62064	M			Clerk,interpreter,Gestapo,Vichy,Clermont,Ferrand (Fr.)	MURDER	FR.
DUHL	164612	M			SD, Montlucon,Chappes (Fr.) 28.7.44	MURDER	FR.
DUHRING	174194	M	Ger.		Sgt.,Stalag VI A,Army,C.C.,Hemer (Ger.) 41-45	TORTURE	U.S.
DUINKER	307077	M	Ger.		Fachberater,SD,Almelo (Neth.) 40-45	INTERR.	NETH.
DULAC, Jacques	62067	M			Member,Gestapo,Lons le Saunier (Fr.) 1.12.42-25.8.44	MURDER	FR.
DULBERG	185376	M	Ger.		Civilian,Wippringsen (Ger.) 4.44	TORTURE	U.S.
DULLAND, Raman	187745	M	Ger.	15.3.09	Crim.Employee,SD,Gestapo,Praha (Czech.) 39-45	MURDER	CZECH.
DULLBERG	174195	M	Ger.		N.C.O.,Stalag VI A,C.C.,Hemer (Ger.) 43-45	TORTURE	U.S.
DULLNIG	147080	M	Ger.		Osturmfhr.,SS,Kreisltr.,NSDAP,doctor,Kamnik (Yugo.) 43	MURDER	YUGO.
DUM	162069 A	M			Adjutant,Chief of Flambette near Purpan (Fr.)	MURDER	FR.
DUMBECK, Karl(see DUMBOECK)	127339						
DUMBECK (see DOMBECK)	144324						
DUMBERT, Carol (see EDLL)	185851						
DUMBOCK, Karl(see DUMBOECK)	127339						
DUMBOCK (see DOMBECK)	144324						
DUMBOECK, Karl (alias:DUMBOCK-DUMBECK)	127339	M	Ger.	19.4.06	Osturmfhr.,Waffen SS C.C., Schmiedebach,Buchenwald (Ger.) 39-45	MURDER	U.S.
DUMBOIS	144315	M	Ger.	21	Lt.,Navy,Gravenwoehr (Ger.) 2.11.-1.12.44	MISC.CRIMES	U.S.
DUMKE	196099	M	Ger.		Cpl.,Chief of Wachbn.,Camp Royallieu,Compiegne,Oise (Fr.) 41-44	MURDER	FR.
DUMMALEIN, Gresm	157393	M			Ingenieur,Civilian,Fechenheim (Ger.)	TORTURE	FR.
DUMME, Willy	149180	M		03	Sgt.,Feldgendarmerie,Tours (Fr.)	TORTURE	FR.
DUMMER, Fritz	62071	M			Sgt.,Feldgendarmerie,Vendome (Fr.) 9.8.44	MURDER	FR.,U.S.
DUMONT	151231	M	Ger.		Capt.,Kommandantur de Privas,Tournon Samilhac (Fr.) 6.6.44-21.4.45	MURDER	FR.
DUMONT	259200	M	Ger.		Usturmfhr.,SS,Div."Prinz Eugen",Niksic district Montenegro (Yugo.) 5.-6.43	MISC.CRIMES	YUGO.
DUMONT, Daisy,Gertrude	301834	F	Ger.	21 - 26	Secretary,Gestapo,Chambery (Fr.)	MURDER	FR.
DUMONT, Joseph	149181	M	Ger.		Civilian,Westico (Ger.)	TORTURE	FR.
DUMPFEL	193234	M	Ger.		Schfhr.,SS,C.C.,Buchenwald (Ger.) 42-45	TORTURE	U.S.
DUNCKEL (see DELAGE)	141523						
DUNCKEL	185375	M	Ger.		Chief,Gestapo,Metz (Fr.) 17.9.44	MURDER	FR.
DUNCKEL	301404	M	Ger.		Chief,Gestapo,Metz (Moselle) (Fr.) 17.9.44	MURDER	FR.
DUNKE	261757	M	Ger.		Pvt.,Fieldgend.,Romilly sur Seine (Fr.) 10.6.44	MISC.CRIMES	FR.
DUNKEL	124530	M	Ger.	15	N.C.O.,parachute-Rgt. 2, 6 Coy, (Fr.) 12.44	MISC.CRIMES	U.S.
DUNKEL	149196	M	Ger.		Civilian,Schorzingen (Ger.)	TORTURE	FR.
DUNKEL	193235	M	Ger.		Sturmbannfhr.,SS,C.C.,Buchenwald (Ger.) 42-45	TORTURE	U.S.
DUNKEL	252060	M	Ger.		Lt.,4.Rgt. parachute-Div. "Herman Goering", 3 Coy, 1 Bn, Rgt. "Grassmel" Helchteren (Bel.) 9.44	BRUTALITY	BEL.
DUNKEL, Alfred	193140	M	Ger.	3.7.19	Ex-Convict,Reichs Ministry of Justice,Strafgef.Lag.,Finmark(Nor.)3.45	WITNESS	NOR.
DUNKEL, Hermann	162346	M	Ger.	90	Sturmbannfhr.,SS Wirtschafts-Verwaltungs-Hauptamt,C.C.,Ohrdruf(Ger.)	MURDER	U.S.
DUNKEL, Rudolf	306001	M	Ger.		Member,SS Staff,C.C.,Sasel (Ger.) 10.44-5.45	TORTURE	U.K.
DUNKELHOFF	250978	M			Pvt.,C.C.,Ellrich Nordhausen (Ger.)	MURDER	U.S.
DUNKELMANN	250979	M			Pvt.,C.C.,Ellrich Nordhausen (Ger.)	MURDER	U.S.
DUNKELMANN, Eric	252945	M	Ger.	08	Sturmfhr.,SS,Gestapo,Paris (Fr.) 41-44	TORTURE	FR.
DUNKER	129845	M	Ger.	86	Chiefwarden,C.C.,Aachen,(Ger.) 41-44	TORTURE	U.S.
DUNKER	300239	M	Ger.		Interpreter,Gestapo,Hagen (Ger.) 3.4.45	MURDER	U.K.
DUNKER, Walter	131260	M	Ger.	9.10.04	Rottfhr.,SS,Arnstadt-Thuer. (Ger.)	MURDER	U.S.
DUNKERN	62237	M	Ger.		Major,General,Police,SS,B.F. Lothringe-Westmark	TORTURE	UNWCC
DUNKERN	187596	M	Ger.		Brigadefhr.,SS,	MURDER	UNWCC
DUNKHAASE	250690	M			Uschfhr.,C.C.,Osterhagen,Nordhausen (Ger.)	MURDER	U.S.
DUNLOP	62073	M			Medecine,Civilian,Fa.Kolch Poser	MURDER	FR.
DUNNER, Jan	250970	M	Ger.	2.5.93	Farmer,Civilian,Vranovskves (Czech.) 10.10.38	MURDER	CZECH.
DUNST	193778	M	Ger.		Civilian,Overseer in a C.C.,Svatoborice (Czech.)	MURDER	CZECH.
DUNZINGER, Karl	250691	M			Pvt.,C.C.,Ellrich,Nordhausen (Ger.)	MURDER	U.S.
DUPLITZ	141865	M	Ger.		Sgt.,Stalag XX A,Brahnau (Pol.) 19.9.42	MURDER	U.K.
DUPOND, Rene	152004	M	Ger.		Bavaria (Ger.)	WITNESS	U.S.
DUPONT	149198	M			N.C.O.,Arbeitskommando,C.C.,Hexwurtzen	TORTURE	FR.
DURAS	29896	M	Ger.		Pvt.,Army,Landesschutz,74.Bn.,1.Coy.,Stalag XX A,Thorn (Pol.) 5.5.44	MURDER	U.K.
DURBACH	193236	M	Ger.		Oschfhr.,SS,C.C.,Buchenwald (Ger.) 42-45	MURDER	U.S.
DURCH, Marier	188927	M	Ger.		1.Pz.Gren.Rgt.11,9.Pz.Div.,Mayenne (Fr.)	WITNESS	FR.
DUREK, Karl	250692	M		27.7.87	Hytschfhr.,C.C.,Harzungen , Nordhausen (Ger.)	MURDER	U.S.
DUREN, Albrecht	168938	M	Ger.		Manager,Supply Centre for War Industries,Kattowitz (Pol.) 39-44	PILLAGE	POL.

NAME	C.R.FILE NUMBER	SEX	NATIO- NALITY	DATE OF BIRTH	RANK OCCUPATION UNIT PLACE AND DATE OF CRIME	REASON WANTED	WANTED BY
DU RIEGE (or DE RIEGE)	302109	M	Ger.		Uschfhr., Gestapo, Zoelen (Neth.) 10.44	TORTURE	NETH.
DURMANN	196827	M	Ger.		Employee, C.C., Struthof-Natzweiler, Bas-Rhin (Fr.) 40-44	TORTURE	FR.
DURMANN	252069	M	Ger.		Uschfhr., SS, SD, Toulouse (Fr.) 11.42-8.44	PILLAGE	FR.
DURNER, Josef	193139	M		04	Sgt.-Guard, Reichsjustiz-Ministerium Feldstraflager, C.C.Finnmark (Nor.) 4.45	MISC.CRIMES	NOR., YUGO.
DUROCHER	157399	M	Ger.		Doctor, Conc.Camp, Mitterteich (Ger.)	MURDER	FR.
DURR, Paul or Ludwig	173199	M	Ger.		Staff at Conc.Camp, Schirmeck, Saales (Fr.)	TORTURE	U.K.
DURMANN, Walter (or THUERMANN)	169464	M	Ger.		Wachtmstr., Schupo, Conc.Camp, Schirmeck (Fr.) 9.44-11.44	TORTURE	U.K.
DURRO, Hans	155755	M	Ger.	07	Pvt., Army, Arb.Cmdo.932-6, Bde.427, Blankenburg, Farmer, Civ., Wernigerode (Ger.) 5.44	TORTURE	U.K.
DURSCHAK, Josef	250703	M		13. 4.98	Uschfhr., C.C. Harzungen, Nordhausen (Ger.)	MURDER	U.S.
DURST	190673	M			Pvt., Eis.Art.Btty.717, St.Andries, Varsenare, Bruegge (Bel.)	MURDER	BEL.
DURSTONITZ (or DURSTOVITZ)	28832	M			Lt., Jaeger-Bn., 28.Rgt., Miramond de Guesne (Fr.) 44	MURDER	FR.
DUSAK, Johann	250707	M		6. 6.21	Cpl., Conc.Camp Ellrich, Nordhausen (Ger.)	MURDER	U.S.
DUSCHA	193347	M	Ger.		Cpl., 1.P.o.W.working Bn.41, C.C., Nerlandsdal (Nor.) 41-45	TORTURE	NOR.
DUSCHA, Hans (called Paul)	307078	M	Ger.		Cmdt., Gestapo, SD, Carinthia and Carniola at Bled (Yugo.) 4.41-5.45	MURDER	YUGO.
DUSCHER	260137	M	Ger.		Lt., 157.Res.Div. Bayern, Massif du Vercors, Isere and Drome (Fr.) 20.7.44-5.8.44	SUSPECT	FR.
DUSINCHOON, Willy	185608	M			Col., SS-Div."Deutschland", 3.Pz.Gren.Rgt., Aiguillon (Fr.) 6.44	MURDER	FR.
DUSSELSCHON	157984	M			Cmdt., SS, 8.Rgt., Buzet-Blaise-Aiguillon (Fr.) 6.44	MURDER	FR.
DUTINN	157383	M	Ger.		Guard, Conc.Camp, Diez (Ger.)	TORTURE	FR.
DUTSCH	149995	M	Ger.		N.C.O, Oberfeldkommandantur, Diege (Bel.)	MISC.CRIMES	FR.
DUTTEL	62084	M			Cpl., SS, Nekareltz (Ger.)	MURDER	FR.
DUTTIG, Karl	250702	M	Ger.	15. 9.04	Rottfhr., C.C., Nordhausen (Ger.)	MURDER	U.S.
DUTTING, Karl	182777	M	Ger.	04	Rottfhr., 4.SS-Totenkopfsturmbann, Conc.Camp, Nordhausen (Ger.)	WITNESS	U.S.
DUTZMANN	250706	M			Major, Conc.Camp Dora, Nordhausen (Ger.)	MURDER	U.S.
DUTZNER	250705	M			Sturmmann, SS, Conc.Camp Rottleberode, Nordhausen (Ger.)	MURDER	U.S.
DUVAL	142334	M			Lt., Oflag XI A, Wladzimierez (Sov.Un.) 41	WITNESS	U.S.
DUVAL, Francois (see DEBIE)	185388						
DUVENDACK, Willi	252952	M	Ger.		Batman, Parachutist Unit, Nieuwaal (Neth.) 1.45	WITNESS	NETH.
DUXAGO, Herbert	124252	M			1.Panz.Div., SS-Pz.Rgt.I, H.Q.'s. Sompany, Malmedy (Bel.) 12.44	MURDER	U.S.
DUYKERS, Toni	124789	M	Ger.	10	Hptschfhr., SD, Conc.Camp Euskirchen and Lublin (Ger.,Pol.) 44	MURDER	U.S.
DVORAK, Alfred	251327	M	Ger.		Gestapo, Jigin (Czech.) 40-45	BRUTALITY	CZECH.
DVORAK, Frantisek	194315	M	Ger.	16. 8.14	Employee, Gestapo, Klotovy-Kolin (Czech.) 39-45	TORTURE	CZECH.
DWORAK, Johann	252061	M	Ger.	5.11.15	Employee, Gestapo, Vsetin (Czech.) 39-45	MURDER	CZECH.
DWORSCHAK	195877	M	Ger.		Crim.Asst., Gestapo, Prague (Czech.)	MURDER	CZECH.
DWUZET, Erich	206	M			Usturmfhr., Waffen SS Div. "Das Reich", Engineer-Coy., Valence D'Agen (Fr.) 6.44	MURDER	FR.
DYBOWSKY, Wilhelm	187024	M			Civilian, Conc.Camp, Merkstein Adolf Mine (Ger.) 8.42-10.44	TORTURE	U.S.
DYCKERHOFF	252070	M	Ger.		Dr., Major, Lebreil (Fr.)	MURDER	FR.
DYCZECK, Alois	149994	M	Ger.	11.12.12	Legion Turkestan	PILLAGE	FR.
DYGUTSCH	67585	M	Ger.		Lt., Parachutist, F.P. L 39714 D, Plouzane (Fr.) 8.44	WITNESS	FR.
DZIUBA, Guenther	185374	M	Ger.		SS-Mann, Schoerzingen, Dautmergen (Ger.)	TORTURE	FR.
DZIUBRUSKI	196037	M	Ger.		Cpl., Wacht-Bn., C.C., Royallieu, Compiegne Oise (Fr.) 41-44	MURDER	FR.
DZWIDOR	185373	M	Ger.		Army (It.) 12.44	WITNESS	U.S.
EACES	250991	M	Ger.		6.Coy., 16.Hubner-Rgt., Kinrooi (Bel.)	MISC.CRIMES	BEL.
EAMPERT, Wilhelm	251470	M	Ger.	14. 4.10	Pvt., 558.Gren.Rgt., Bruayen Artois (Fr.) 9.44	MURDER	FR.
EARST	155734	M	Ger.		Custom-Official, Custom-frontier-guard, Lommerange (Fr.) 6.44	MURDER	FR.
EBELL	189430	M			Guard, Prison, Tromscya (Nor.) 6.42	TORTURE	NOR.
EBBEN	305839	M	Ger.		Pvt., 1.Aufkl.Abt., 3.Coy., 2.Column, XV.Div.Afrika-Korps, St.Leger (Arlon) 9.44	MISC.CRIMES	BEL.
EBBINGHAUSEN, Clemens	171964	M	Ger.		Chemist, Civilian, Lengerich (Ger.) 8.44	TORTURE	U.S.
EBRECHT	1373	M			Lt., Army, 194.Gr., 1.Coy.	MISC.CRIMES	U.K.
EBCKE	305795	M	Ger.		Cmdt.Off.Prison Camp Oflag VI C, Osnabrueck-Ewersheide (Ger.) 43-45	MURDER	YUGO.
EBEL	306679	M	Ger.		Pvt., 331. Pion.Bn., 331.Inf.Div., Mijnheerenland (Neth.) 5.45	PILLAGE	NETH.
EBEL, Anton	262178	M	Ger.		Driver, SD, Gestapo, Rennes (Fr.) 43-44	SUSPECT	FR.
EBEL, Karl	250994	M	Ger.		Pvt., 6.Army, Vinkt (Bel.)	MURDER	BEL.
EBELING, Karl (or EBERLEIN, EBERLING, Dar Victor Heinr.)	142396	M	Ger.	29.11.05	Scharfhr., Waffen-SS, Totenkopf-Sturmbann, Commander-Staff, Buchenwald-Weimar (Ger.)	MURDER	U.S.
EBELING-BREDOW, Theodor	174022	M	Ger.	16. 3.17	Civilian (Lithuania) 41-44	WITNESS	U.S.
EBELMAYER	250988	M	Ger.		Oschfhr., SS, C.C. Mauthausen (Aust.)	TORTURE	BEL.
EBENRITTER, Wilhelm	186355	M	Ger.		Prison-Guard, Conc.Camp, Luxembourg (Lux.)	TORTURE	FR.
EBERHARD	189834	M	Ger.		Lt., Eis.Art.Btty.717, St.Andries Varsenare Bruges (Bel.) 9.44	MURDER	BEL.
EBERHARDT	24759	M			Army, Saverne (Ger.)	TORTURE	FR.
EBERHARDT	108730	M		10	Specialist-Officer, Dulag Luft, Conc.Camp, Klosterwald (Ger.)	TORTURE	U.K.
EBERHARDT	142432	M			Osturmfhr., Waffen-SS, Conc.Camp, Theresienstadt (Czech.) 6.43	TORTURE	U.S.
EBERHARDT, Christian	149210	M		95	Civilian, Immendingen (Ger.)	TORTURE	FR.
EBERHARDT, Kurt	251002	M		10. 5.23	Pvt. C.C. Ellrich, Nordhausen (Ger.)	MURDER	U.S.
EBERHART	36621	M			Specialist-Officer, Dulag b.Frankfurt (Ger.) 5.43	TORTURE	U.K.
EBERHART, Karl-Heinz	191350	M			Pvt., Stabs-Coy., 1.Panz.Rgt. Leibst. A.Hitler, Ligneuville Stoumont (Bel.) 12.44	MURDER	U.S.
EBERIUS	149211	M		21. 4.18	Uschfhr., SS, Conc.Camp, Mauthausen (Aust.)	TORTURE	FR.
EBERL	120525	M		07	Dr., Dr.med., Cmdt., SS-Offz.Chief, C.C. Auschwitz,Benburg (Ger. Czech.)	MURDER	FR., BEL.
EBERL (or EBERLE)	133371	M	Ger.	00	Sgt., Waffen-SS, C.C., Muehldorf (Ger.) 44-45	MURDER	U.S.
EBERL, Joseph	12604	M	Ger.		Pvt., 110. or 111.Panz.Gren.Rgt.,2.Coy., Albine (Fr.) 6.44	MURDER	FR.
EBERL, Sebastan (see EBERLE, Westel)	145360						
EBERLE	24761	M			Schfhr., SS, Conc.Camp, Struthof (Fr.)	MURDER	FR.
EBERLE	24762	M			Lt., Army-Pion.School.Abt.I.R. AK 27,Goanne,Denny Ctane (Fr.)7.44	MURDER	FR.
EBERLE (see EBERL)	133371						
EBERLE, Hans	39637	M	Ger.		Lt., Cmdt. la Place de Gosne (Nievre) Dienststelle F.P.Nr.41609 Army-Pion.School, Abt.16 Ab.27, Thauvenay (Fr.)	MURDER	FR.
EBERLE, Westel (or EBERL, Sebastian)	145360	M	Ger.	10 - 11	Hptschfhr., SS, C.C., Muehldorf (Ger.) 44-45	MURDER	U.S.

EBE - ECK

NAME	C.R.FILE NUMBER	SEX	NATIONALITY	DATE OF BIRTH	RANK OCCUPATION UNIT PLACE AND DATE OF CRIME	REASON WANTED	WANTED BY
EBERLE	149213	M	Ger.		Dr., CC Buchenwald (Ger.)	MURDER	FR.
EBERLE	149214	M	Ger.		Sgt., CC Wetzheim (Ger.)	TORTURE	FR.
EBERLE	149384	M	Ger.		Deputy Chief, Gestapo, Montbeliard, Aucincourt (Fr.)	MURDER	FR.
EBERLE	259349	M	Ger.		Interpreter, antenne of Rochelle, Gestapo Area Poitiers (Fr.) 41-45	MISC.CRIMES	FR.
EBERLE, Hans	193614	M	Ger.		Cpl., 56 Lds.Schtz.Coy, Ryglice (Pol.) 11.39	PILLAGE	POL.
EBERLEIN (see EBELING,Karl)	142336						
EBERLEIN	167134	M	Ger.	05	SA-Chief, Wissembourg (Fr.) 12.44	MURDER	FR.
EBERLEIN	257878	M			Lt, Pz.Bde., Meuse Bridge Antwerpen (12.44)	INTERR.	U.S.
EBERLEYN, Herbert	140900	M	Ger.		Lt., Verbindungsstab, Bolnes (Neth.) 5.45	MURDER	NETH.
EBERLIN	192113	M	Ger.		Guard, Cpl., Prison St.Gillis, CC Brussels (Bel.) 42	TORTURE	BEL.
EBERLING (see EBELING,Karl)	142336						
EBERLING, Max	188129	M	Ger.		Capt, 1 Coy, Sicherungs Bn.945, Ostrow Mazowiecki (Pol.) 43	MURDER	POL.
EBERLING, Otto	162827	M	Ger.	05	Oschfhr, SS Totenkopf, CC Buchenwald (Ger.)	TORTURE	U.S.
EBERLUS, Willy	192241	M	Ger.		Uschfhr, S S, CC Flossenburg (Ger.)	TORTURE	FR.
EBERSBERGER	207	M	Ger.		Major, Army, 749 Jaeg.Rgt., Greece, 12.43	MURDER	GRC.
EBERT	12323	M	Ger.		Hptsturmfhr, SS Sicherheitspolizei, Strasbourg (Fr.) 41-42	MURDER	POL.
EBERT	147399	M	Ger.		Pvt., 11 Pz.Div., 2.Gruppe, Kampfgr."Wilde" France 44	MURDER	FR.
EBERT	149386	M	Ger.		Capt., 933. Inf.Rgt., 1 Bn. Reg.d'Aubagne (Fr.) 44	MURDER	FR.
EBERT	162833	M	Ger.		Civilian, Staff-Leader, Einsatzstab Rosenberg, Paris (Fr.) 40-41	LOOTING	U.S.
EBERT	167906	M	Ger.		Prof. Dr., Stabsfuehrer, Official, Medizinalrat, Einsatzstab Rosenberg, CC Papenburg - Emsland, Berlin (Ger.) 40-45	PILLAGE	FR.
EBERT	301659	M	Ger.		Secretary of Commissary Lorz, St.Gingolph (Fr.) 7.44	MURDER	FR.
EBERT, Hermann	187286	M	Ger.		Regierungsrat, SD Official, Gestapo, Brno (Czech.) 39-45	MURDER	CZECH.
EBERT, Reinhold	251003	M			Rottfhr, Camp Dora, C.C. Nordhausen (Ger.)	MURDER	U.S.
EBERT, Richard	157358	M	Ger.		Sturmmann, SS, CC Hinzert (Ger.)	TORTURE	FR.
EBERTS, Gottfried	251506	M	Ger.	31.12.25	Pvt., 13 Coy, 353 Rgt, Bruay Artois (Fr.) 9.44	MURDER	FR.
EBERWEIN	252962	M	Ger.		SS Hptsturmfhr, SS, Apeldoorn (Neth.) 10.44	MURDER	U.S.
EBLE	193884	M	Ger.		Chief N.S.D.A.P., PoW Working Camp, Ottendorf - Okbilla (Ger.) 12.45	MURDER	FR.
EBLING	251001	M			Rottfhr, CC Mackenrode, Nordhausen (Ger.)	MURDER	U.S.
EBLING, Andreas	126315	M	Ger.		Policeman, Friedensdorf (Ger.) 10.44	MURDER	U.S.
EBNER	193612	M	Ger.		Dr.,Physician, Civilian, CC Lidice (Czech.) 42-44	MISC.CRIMES	CZECH.
EBNER	257359	M	Ger.		Guard, Hptwachtmstr, SS Slave Labour Camp, Beisfjord near Narvik (Nor.) 6.-11.42	BRUTALITY	YUGO.
EBNER, Fabian	258408	M			Guard, SS, CC Ohrdruf 12.44-4.45	MURDER	U.S.
EBNER, Fernand	208	M	Ger.		Rottenfhr, SS Div."Hitler Jugend", 419 Bn, Ascq Colmar (Fr.) 4.44	MURDER	FR.
EBNER, Otto	145963	M	Ger.		SS Gestapo, CC Welzheim (Ger.), Waiblingen (Ger.) 8.44	MURDER	U.S.
EBRACHT, Georg	62239	M	Ger.		Off., Regional Commissioner for German Racialism in Wehrkreis I	MISC.CRIMES	U.N.W.C.C.
EBSEN	138334	M	Ger.		SS Uschfhr, CC Schandelah, Neuengamme (Ger.) 44-45	MURDER	FR., BEL.
EBSEN	195326	M	Ger.		Commander, SS, CC Braunschweig-Schandelah (Ger.)	MURDER	BEL.
EBSER	141311	M	Ger.		Capt., Oflag VII B, Eichstatt (Fr.) 2.44	MURDER	U.K.
EBSER	191211	M	Ger.		Capt., Oflag VII B, Guard Coy, Germany 2.44	MURDER	U.K.
ECHARD	149387	M	Ger.		Civilian, Tselfingen (Ger.)	MISC.CRIMES	FR.
ECHASSON	24766	M			Chatillon (Fr.)	TORTURE	FR.
ECHENWALD (or ECHENWALD)	251514	M	Ger.		Inspector, Gestapo, Alencon 40-44	INTERR.	FR.
ECHOLT, Herbert	9649	M	Ger.		Dr., Oberlandrat, Justizabteilungsreferent, Pilsen (Czech.) 39-44	MURDER	CZECH.
ECHSTEIN	167336	M	Ger.		Lt, 2 Coy, Dienststelle F.P.No.13907 C, Creches s-Saone (Fr.) 8.-9.44	INTERR.	FR.
ECHTER, Rudi	250723	M	Ger.		Rottfhr, SS Lazarett at Laag Soeren (Neth.) 9.44	INTERR.	NETH.
ECK	209	M			Cmdt, PoW Camp, Major, CC Oflag 6 b 12.41	MISC.CRIMES	U.K.
ECK, Heinz	173763	M	Ger.		Kapitaenleutnant, Navy, Commander of submarine U.852 3.44	MURDER	U.K., GRC.
ECK, Josef	24767	M			Cpl., Army, Carcassonne (Fr.) 44	MURDER	FR.
ECKARD	12605	M	Ger.		Usturmfhr, SS, Chef des S.D. u. der Sicherheitspolizei, Clermont-Ferrand (Fr.) 43-44	TORTURE	FR.
ECKARDT	142142	M			Member of Gestapo, Clermont-Ferrand (Fr.)	TORTURE	FR.
ECKARDT	162817	M	Ger.		Lt., Feld-Gend. Champigny (Fr.) 4.44	MURDER	FR.
ECKARDT	193230	M	Ger.		SS Uschfhr, CC Buchenwald (Ger.) 42-45	TORTURE	U.S.
ECKARDT, Viktor (see ECKERT)	260347						
ECKART	24171	M			Gestapo Chef Seus (Fr.)		FR.
ECKART	141426	M	Ger.	15. 1.96	Capt., 26 Inf.Rgt., Menton (Fr.) 8.44	MURDER	FR.
ECKART	258192	M	Ger.		Employee, Esterwegen (Ger.) from 1940	MISC.CRIMES	BEL.
ECKARTZ	194952	M			Uschfhr, SS Unterfuehrerschule, Arnheim (Neth.) 9.44	MURDER	NETH.
ECKEL	149187	M	Ger.		Oberarzt, CC, Hohenlychen, CC Ravensbrueck (Ger.)	MURDER	FR.
ECKELMANN	173890	M			Rottenfhr, SS, CC Muehldorf-Ampfing (Ger.) 6.44-4.45	MISC.CRIMES	U.S.
ECKEN, Heinrich	191979	M	Ger.		Adjutant, Army, Vercoiran Barret (Fr.) 2.-3.44	MURDER	FR.
ECKENDORF	157372	M	Ger.	10	Uschfhr, SS Arbeitseinsatz, CC Ravensbrueck (Ger.)	TORTURE	FR.
ECKENDORF	251000	M			Pvt., Camp Dora, Nordhausen (Ger.)	MURDER	U.S.
ECKER	261933	M	Ger.		Interpreter, various places in Slovenia (Yugo.) 41-45	MISC.CRIMES	YUGO.
ECKER, Karl	142434	M	Ger.		Hptwachtmstr, Police, CC Bamberg 2.45	TORTURE	U.S.
ECKER, Karl	187292	M	Ger.	3. 6.19	Civilian, Konstanz (Ger.) 29.7. u. 3.8.44	WITNESS	U.S.
ECKERMANN	301557	M	Ger.		SS Sturmfhr, CC Mauthausen (Aust.) 40-45	MURDER	BEL.
ECKERMANN-GREINKE, Helga	191656	F	Ger.		Dr.,Civil-Servant, Ostgebietsministerium Rosenberg 40 - 44	PILLAGE	FR.
ECKERT	24773	M			Capt, Army, Rennes (Fr.) 43-44	MURDER	FR.
ECKERT (see ACKERE)	187835						
ECKERT	108734	M	Ger.		Works Manager, Salt Mine Stalag IX C, Craja near Bleicherode (Ger.) 1.40-10.44	TORTURE	U.K.
ECKERT	127111	M	Ger.		Hptsturmfhr, SS Pz.Div. "Das Reich", Nenerque-le-Vernet (Fr.)	MURDER	FR.
ECKERT	133779	M	Ger.	08	Lt., Feld-Gend., Karamischevo, Ortskommandantur	MURDER	U.S.
ECKERT	147182	M			Hptschfhr, SS Totenkopf, CC Mauthausen (Aust.) 41-45	MURDER	U.S.
ECKERT	168912	M	Ger.		Lt., 7 Air Force Festungs Bn., Belgium, near Neuhof (Ger.)	TORTURE	U.S.
ECKERT	168955	M	Ger.		Major, Army, Navy Inf.Unit 687, Commander, Le Breil near Saumur (Fr.) 8.44	MURDER	FR.
ECKERT	186499	M	Ger.		Lt., Air Force, 22 Luftnachr.Rgt.223, Hoogeveen (Neth.) 4.45	MURDER	NETH.
ECKERT	187835	M	Ger.		Cpl., Pay Master, Army, St.Andries, Varsenare les Bruges (Bel.)	MURDER	BEL.
ECKERT	190000	M	Ger.		Capt., Police Chief, Kraljevo (Yugo.) 43	MURDER	YUGO.
ECKERT	194233	M	Ger.		SS Sturmfhr, Coy Commander, 12 SS Pz.Div."Hitler Jugend" 26 SS Pz.Gren.Rgt., 1 Coy, Caen (Fr.) 6.-7.44	TORTURE	CAN.
ECKERT (or EVANS)	250793	M	Ger.		Sgt., L'Ain (Fr.) 7.44	MISC.CRIMES	FR.
ECKERT, Kurt	186727	M	Ger.		Member of Gestapo, Praha (Czech.) 39-45	MURDER	CZECH.

ECK-EGG

NAME	C.R.FILE NUMBER	SEX	NATIO-NALITY	DATE OF BIRTH	RANK OCCUPATION UNIT PLACE AND DATE OF CRIME	REASON WANTED	WANTED BY
ECKERT, Otto	149188	M	Ger.		Civilian, Pologne	MURDER	FR.
ECKERT, Rudolf (or EGGERT)	305886	M	Ger.	90	Member, Todt-Organisation, Velke, Heraltice (Czech.) 8.44	BRUTALITY	CZECH.
ECKERT, Viktor (or ECKARDT)	260347	M	Ger.		Owner and manager, SA, factory of driving-belts and technical-leather goods, Lodz (Pol.) 39-45	TORTURE	POL.
ECKES, Walter	24751	M	Ger.		Lt., 326 VG-Div.	WITNESS	U.S.
ECKFELLNER, Oskar	24775	M	Ger.		Sturmschfhr., SS, Carcessonne (Fr.) 8.44	MURDER	FR.
ECKFELNER, Hermann	155738	M	Ger.		Sturmschfhr., S.D., Roullens (Fr.) 44	MURDER	FR.
ECKHARD	255095	M	Ger.		Capt., 2 Div., Paratroops, 6 Regt., 15 Coy., Alphen and Riel (Neth.)10.44	MURDER	NETH.
ECKHARD	301948	M	Ger.		Rottfhr., SS, C.C. Auschwitz (Pol.) 41-45	MURDER	POL.
ECKHARDT	12652	M	Ger.		Scharfr., SS, Emplyee of Gestapo in H.Q., Bergen (Nor.) 41	TORTURE	NOR.
ECKHARDT	21499	M	Ger.		Usturmfhr., S.D., Vichy, Clermont-Ferrand (Fr.) 7.-8.44	TORTURE	FR.
ECKHARDT	149189	M	Ger.		Camp. Roemild (Ger.)	MURDER	FR.
ECKHARDT	173891	M	Ger.		Camp-official, Stalag VI A, C.C. Hemer (Ger.) 41-45	TORTURE	U.S.
ECKHARDT	192347	M			Member, NSDAP, C.C. Flossenburg (Ger.) 44-45	MURDER	U.S.
ECKHARDT	255095	M	Ger.		Capt., 15 Coy., Parachute, 6 Rgt., 2 Div., Alphen (Neth.) 10. 44	MURDER	NETH.
ECKHARDT, Johann Hans	261935	M	Ger.		Crim. Asst., Various Places in Slov. (Yugo.) 41-45	MISC. CRIMES	YUGO.
ECKHARDT, Karl	191346	M	Ger.		Chauffeur, Gestapo, Nentershausen (Ger.) 9.44	SUSPECT	U.S.
ECKHARDT, Maria Eva	167133	F	Ger.		Secretary of Lt. General, Org. Todt, Parigne le Polin (Fr.) 8.44	PILLAGE	FR.
ECKHARDT, Ruth	167132	F		07	SS-Helferin, S.D., Orcines, Autnat, Clermont-Ferrand (Fr.) 4.44	MURDER	FR.
ECKHERT	157370	M		95	GUARD, C.C. Kemma (Ger.)	TORTURE	FR.
ECKSTEIN	251505	M	Ger.		Sturmfhr., Wassertruchingen (Ger.) 3.45	MURDER	U.S.
ECKSTEIN, Erich	193247	M	Ger.	3. 7.19	Ex-Convict, Reichsjustizministerium, Feldstraflager, Strafgef.-Lager Nord, C.C. Finmark (Nor.) 42-45	WITNESS	NOR.
ECKSTEIN, Hans	260067	M	Ger.		Sturmfhr., SS, Slave labour camp, Botn near Rognan (Norway) 8.42 to 3.43, 4.43-45	BRUTALITY	YUGO.
EDEL	129268	M		01	Hptwachtmeister (Offizier), SS, Mainz (Ger.) 43-45	MURDER	BEL.
EDEL, Ernst	172886	M	Ger.		Farmer, Civ., Reichardtsdorf (Ger.) 8.-9.44	MURDER	U.S.
EDELKRAUT	262179	M	Ger.	5. 9. ?	Member, Gestapo, Rennes (Fr.) 43-44	MURDER	FR.
EDELMAN	307081	M	Ger.		Wachtmeister, SS, Falstad, slave labour camp (Nor.) 42-43	MURDER	YUGO.
EDELMANN	306680	M	Ger.		Pvt., 331 Pion.Bn., 331 Inf.Div., Mijnheeren-Land (Neth.) 5.45	PILLAGE	NETH.
EDELMANN, Josef	186652	M	Ger.	10	Miner, Adolf Mine, Merkstein (Ger.) 8.42-10.44	WITNESS	U.S.
EDELSBRUNNER, Karl	127340	M			Rottfhr., SS-Totenkopf-Sturmbann, Theresienstadt (Czech.)	MISC. CRIMES	U.S.
EDENHARTER, Johann	186651	M	Ger.		Employee, Arbeitskommando, Regensburg (Ger.) 41-45	TORTURE	U.S.
EDENHUBER, Anna	171960	F	Ger.	27. 2.05	Farmer's wife, Civ., C.C. Buchenwald, Seppenberg (Ger.) 45	WITNESS	U.S.
EDER	184274	M	Ger.	85	Member, NSDAP, C.C. Dachau (Ger.)	TORTURE	FR.
EDER, Heinz	188536	M	Ger.		Pvt., Pz.Aufkl.Abt., Bautzen (Ger.) 1.44	WITNESS	U.K.
EDER, Herbert	193790	M	Ger.	9. 5.98	Civ., leather goods factory, firm: Kauder and Frank, Trebechovice Pod. (Czech.) 39-45	MURDER	CZECH.
EDER, Martin	254324	M	Ger.		Agent, Gestapo, Offenburg (Ger.) 11.44	MURDER	FR.
EDLMANN	301887	M	Ger.		3 Bn., Regt. "Deutschland", SS-Panzer-Div. "Das Reich", Venerque le Vernet (Fr.) 44	MURDER	FR.
EDLMANN, Anton	147004	M	Ger.	1.11.13	Hptschfhr., SS-Div. "Das Reich", Regt. "Deutschland", SS-Pz.Div., 3 Bn., Venerque le Vernet (Fr.) 44	MURDER	FR.
EDWIN (Alias: von ERNEST)	24780	M				PILLAGE	FR.
EEBERS	24782	M			Scharfr., SS, 2. SS-Pz.Div. "Das Reich", Department Lot (Fr.) 8.44	MURDER	FR.
EEKE	23997				Oschfhr., SS, Vaihingen, Stuttgart (Ger.)	TORTURE	FR.
EFFELOSHTAZ	149191		Ger.	95	Dir., Civ., C.C. Chomalle, Meerane (Ger.)	MURDER	FR.
EFFELSBERG, Mathias	162826	M	Ger.		Gruppenfhr., SA, NSDAP, Propagandaleiter, on Westwall (Ger.) 9.44-1.45	TORTURE	U.S.
EFFENBERG	305840	M	Ger.		Cpl., 1.Aufkl.Abt., 3 Coy., 2 Column, XV Div. Afrika-Corps, St.Leger (Arlon) 9.44	MISC. CRIMES	BEL.
EFFENBERGER, Heinz	257540	M	Ger.		Chemist, C.C. Schomberg (Ger.)	INTERR.	FR.
EFFNER	250136	M	Ger.		Pvt., C.C. Dora, Nordhausen (Ger.)	MURDER	U.S.
EGDEN, Johannes	250993	M	Ger.		Cpl., 377 Jaeger-Regt., Vinkt (Bel.)	MURDER	BEL.
EGELMANN, Paul (see AJELMANN)	186464						
EGEN	193883	M	Ger.		Lt., Army, St.Martin du Mont (Fr.) 6.44	MURDER	FR.
EGEN, Friedrich	168954	M	Ger.	27. 1.03	Dr., Deput.Commandant, C.C. Radom (Pol.) 39 - 45	PILLAGE	POL.
EGENER, Franz (Alias: KUNASEK)	260719	M	Ger.	4. 8.11	Employee, Member, County Admin. office, S.D., Kamenice, Hradec, Kralove (Czech.) 40-44	MISC. CRIMES	CZECH.
EGER, Sebastien	149192	M	Ger.		Sgt., C.C. Valence (Fr.)	TORTURE	FR.
EGERER	193232	M	Ger.		Uschfhr., SS, C.C. Buchenwald (Ger.) 42-45	TORTURE	U.S.
EGERER, Engelberth	187288	M	Ger.		Treasurer, NSDAP, Ovesne Kladruby (Czech.) 39-45	MISC. CRIMES	CZECH.
EGERMANN, Ernst	31280	M	Ger.		Dr., Public official, Landgerichtsrat, Cheb (Czech.)	MURDER	CZECH.
EGERMAYER, Karl	255098	M	Ger.	3.10.14	Civilian, Haberspirk, Gossengrun (Czech.) 9.39	MURDER	CZECH.
EGERS	257185	M	Ger.	96	Lt.Col., Abwehr Offz., Camp Saxony-Province (Ger.) 2.-8.44	BRUTALITY	U.S.
EGERT	261758	M	Ger.		Sgt., Fieldgend., Romilly sur Seine (Fr.) 6.44	MISC. CRIMES	FR.
EGERT, J.A.	250722	F.	Ger.	21.12.94	Monastery at Posterholt, Effeld (Neth.)	INTERR.	NETH.
EGERTS, Franz	182778	M	Ger.or Hung.	31. 5.97	SS-Mann, 4 SS-Totenkopf-Sturmbann, C.C. Mittelbau Nordhausen (Ger.)43-45	WITNESS	U.S.
EGGAT	149193	M	Ger.	85	SS, Mannheim (Ger.)	TORTURE	FR.
EGGEL (or EGGRERS)	260138	M	Ger.		Lt., 3 Coy., Bn.100, Reserve-Geb.Jaeg.-Regt., Massif du Vercors, Isere and Drome (Fr.) 7.-8.44	SUSPECT	FR.
EGGELHOF	250735	M	Ger.		Lt., Unit L.N.S.4, L'Ain (Fr.) 7.44	MISC. CRIMES	FR.
EGGELING, Eduard	12606	M	Ger.		Pvt., 110 or 111 Pz.Gren.Regt., 2 Coy., Albine (Fr.) 6.44	MURDER	FR.
EGGELING, Joachim Albrecht	62240	M	Ger.	30.11.84	Obergruppenfhr., (Gauleiter), Oberpraesident of Halle, Merseburg. Member of Reichstag, prussian state councillor	MURDER	U.S., UNWCC
EGGENSBERGER	149195	M	Ger.	85	Civilian, Esslingen (Ger.)	MISC. CRIMES	FR.
EGGENSPERGER	166283	M	Ger.		Officer, Ministerialrat, SS, public official ministry of justice (Ger)43	MURDER	U.S.
EGGENWEBER, Joseph	167905	M	Ger.	15. 1.14	Agent, Gestapo, Saales (Fr.) 4.43	MURDER	FR.
EGGER	127110	M	Ger.		Usturmfhr., SS-Pz.Div. "Das Reich", Venerque le Vernet (Fr.)	MURDER	FR.
EGGER	180499	M	Ger.		Lt., Army (Ital.) 4.44	MURDER	U.K.
EGGER, Hans	186456	M	Ger.		Civ., Erding (Ger.) 11.-12.44	MURDER	U.S.
EGGERMANN, Ernst	31980	M	Ger.		Dr., Landgerichtsrat, Ministry of Justice, Cheb (Czech.) 40	MURDER	CZECH.
EGGERMANN-GREINKE, Helga	167904	F	Ger.		Dr., Member, Einsatzstab Rosenberg (Fr.) 40-44	PILLAGE	FR.
EGGERS (or EGGES)	128920		Ger.		Capt., Gestapo, Leiter, Paris (Fr.) 44	TORTURE	U.S.

EGG - EIC   -82-

NAME	C.R.FILE NUMBER	SEX	NATIO-NALITY	DATE OF BIRTH	RANK OCCUPATION UNIT PLACE AND DATE OF CRIME	REASON WANTED	WANTED BY
EGGERS	187989	M	Ger.	05	Pvt., guard, C.C. official, Reigersfeld (Ger.) 3.40	TORTURE	U.K.
EGGERS, Walther	149228	M	Ger.	07	Cpl.,C.C., Riga (Lat.)	PILLAGE	FR.
EGGERT	252080	M	Ger.		SS-Oscharfhr.,Sipo,Abt.III B,Bruessel (Bel.)	INTERR.	BEL.
EGGERT, Rudolf see ECKERT	305886						
EGGES see EGGERS	128920						
EGGLER, Hanna see EGLER	179892						
EGGRERS see EGGEL	260198						
EGLER, Hanna or EGGLER	179892	F			Civilian,Org.Todt,C.C.Muehldorf-Ampfing (Ger.) 6.44-4.45	MISC.CRIMES	U.S.
EGLIEN	31985	M	Ger.		Lt.,20 Army, 1 Geb.Jaeg.Regt.139,8 Geb.Div., (Nor.) 10.-11.44	MURDER	NOR.
EGLINSKI, Friedrich	174178	M	Ger.	30. 9.99	Civilian,miner,Camp Lintfort (Ger.) 11.44	TORTURE	U.S.
EGNER, Johann	182780	M	Ger.-Hung.	7. 8.95	SS-Mann,4 SS-Totenkopf-Sturmbann,C.C.Mittelbau Nordhausen (Ger.) 43-45	WITNESS	U.S.
EGNER, Peter	182736	M	Ger.-Hung.	20.12.95	SS-Mann,31 SS-Gren.Div.,2 Artl.,Waffen-SS,C.C.Dora,Nordhausen (Ger.)	WITNESS	U.S.
EGON	31951	M			Sgt.,Feldgendarmerie 577,Romorantin (Fr.) 6.43-8.44	MURDER	FR.
EGYDI, Walter	255099	M	Ger.	6. 8.07	Sturmbannfhr.,SS,Hradec Kralove Svitavy (Czech.) 39-45	INTERR.	CZECH.
EHARDH	149229	M			SS-Oscharfhr.	PILLAGE	FR.
EHBERG, Gustave	149230	M		08	Gestapo,Montreuil s-Mer (Fr.)	MISC.CRIMES	U.K.
EHEBRECHT, Fritz	192344	M	Ger.		Member,Army,C.C.Ft.Zinna,Torgau (Ger.) 45	WITNESS	U.S.
EHELEBEN	157369	M		95	Civilian,Waldau-Prust (Ger.) 4.44	MURDER	U.K.
EHERMANN, Fritz	132618	M	Ger.		Feldgendarmerie 624,Avallon (Fr.) 11.43	MURDER	FR.
EHERT	24788	M			Pvt.,Army,2 Gruppe,Gourdon (Fr.) 44	MURDER	FR.
EHERZ	12607	M	Ger.		Pvt.,110 or 111 Pz.Gren.Regt.,2 Coy.,Gourdon (Fr.) 6.44	MURDER	FR.
EHGARTNER, Franz (Linz)	261040	M			SS-Sturmmann,C.C., Vaihingen a.d.Enz (Ger.) 8.44-4.45	MURDER	U.S.
EHIMANNSTRANT	186349	M			C.C.Struthof-Natzweiler (Fr.)	MURDER	FR.
EHL	194306	M	Ger.		Cpl.,Feldgendarmerie,Ploermel (Fr.) 6.44	TORTURE	FR.
EHLER	162828	M		15	SS-Standarte Thueringen,C.C.Buchenwald (Ger.) till 9.44	TORTURE	U.S.
EHLERS	31986	M			Major,20 Army II a,163 Inf.Div.Staffel, (Nor.) 10.-11.44	MURDER	NOR.
EHLERS	162818	M			Cpl.,19 Sicherungs-Regt.192,Chappes (Fr.) 7.44	MURDER	FR.
EHLERS	174021	M			SS-Hptsturmfhr.,1 Coy.,4 SS and police Pz.Gren.Div.,Zbydniow (Pol.) 6.43	MURDER	POL.
EHLERS	250137				SS-Rottenfhr., Camp Rottleberode,Nordhausen (Ger.)	MURDER	U.S.
EHLERS	260837	M	Ger.	07	SS-Standartenfhr.,security guard-Coy.,Kassel (Ger.) 43-45	MURDER	U.S.
EHLERT	124781			10	Hptscharfhr.,Verwaltungs-Asst.,Sonderkdo. Dirlewanger,SD	MURDER	U.S.
EHLERT	250720	M	Ger.		Sturmbannfhr.,SS,Urbes (Fr.) 10.44	TORTURE	FR.
EHLERT, Herbert	140906	M	Ger.	15	Oscharfhr.,SS,C.C.Breendonck (Bel.) 44	TORTURE	BEL.
EHLERT, Willi	108732	M		10	Scharfhr.,Waffen-SS, (Rus.)	MURDER	U.S.
EHLICH	250997	M	Ger.		Cpl.,Gendarmerie,Vendome (Fr.) 8.44	MURDER	FR.
EHISCHEIDT	300453				Member,SD,Amsterdam (Neth.) 2.45	MURDER	NETH.
EHM, Elfriede	192340	F	Ger.	22.10.08	Informer,Gestapo,Textile factory proprietor,Nove Mesto (Czech.) 40-45	MURDER	CZECH.
EHRCKE, Fritz	166400	M	Ger.	06	Sturmscharfhr.,SS,C.C.Bolzano (It.) 9.44	MURDER	IT.
EHRENBERG	124591		Ger.		Camp,Hannover-Limmer (Ger.)	TORTURE	BEL.
EHRENBERG	132617	M	Ger.		Brig.Gen.,cmdt.,Oflag XVII A,Edelbach (Aust.) 9.44	MISC.CRIMES	FR.
EHRENFRIED, Hans	251503	M	Ger.	30. 7.04	Plenipotentiary,Reichsprotektor,State Service,Prag (Czech.) 6.42	MISC.CRIMES	CZECH.
EHRENOID	24792	M			Chief,C.R.-Marseille,S.R.A.,Marseille (Fr.)	INTERR.	FR.
EHRET	188619	M			Customs-officer,Grenspolizei,Fontoy-Lommerange (Fr.) 6.41	MURDER	U.N.W.C.C.
EHRET	257362	M			SS-guard,slave labour camp,Beisfjord near Narvik (Nor.) 6.-11.42	BRUTALITY	YUGO.
EHRHARDT	211	M			Member,Gestapo,Warsaw (Pol.) 42	MURDER	POL.
EHRHARDT	305841	M			Pvt.,1 Aufkl.Abt.,1 Coy.,2 Col.,XV Div.Afrika-Korps, St.Leger (Arlon) 9.44	MISC.CRIMES	BEL
EHRHARDT, Willy	168956	M	Ger.		Pvt.,9 Res.Gren.Regt.,1 Coy.,Magny d'Anigon (Fr.) 9.44	MURDER	FR.
EHRHAUPT, Horst	259211	M	Ger.		Uscharfhr.,SS,Dachau (Ger.) 11.42-45	MURDER	YUGO.
EHRHORN, Hermann	190430	M	Ger.		Chief-adjutant,Feldgendarmerie 958,Sisteron (Fr.)	MURDER	FR.
EHRKE, Guenther	221407	M	Ger.		Pvt.,Nachrichten-Regt.506,Abwehr-official,Morlupo (Frascati) (It.)	MISC.CRIMES	U.S.
EHRLE	157360	M	Ger.		Usturmfhr.,SS,Rottenburg (Ger.)	TORTURE	FR.
EHRLE	177345	M			Sgt.,Army,999 Div.	MURDER	SOV.-UNI
EHRLICH	251511	M	Ger.		Head-chief,State Service,R.S.H.A.,Berlin (Ger.) 39-45	BRUTALITY	POL
EHRLICH	260132	M	Ger.		Gendarm,Div."Oberland",Russia-Germany,Massif du Vercors Isere et Drome (Fr.) 7.-8.44	SUSPECT	FR.
EHRLICH, Karl	149500	M	Ger.		Sgt.,Gestapo,SS,(prison militaire),Toulon (Fr.)	SUSPECT	FR.
EHRLINGER	145366	M		12	SS-Oberfhr.,SD,SS,(R.S.H.A.) Amt I und Amt II,Kiew Smolensk (Rus.)	MURDER	U.S.
EHRLINGER, Erich	251510	M	Ger.		SS-Oberfhr.,Waffen-SS and police,Warsaw (Pol.) 39-40	BRUTALITY	POL.
EHRMANN	301949	M	Ger.		Lt.,1 Coy.,64 Police-Bn.,Sabac Serb. (Yugo.) 7.-9.41	MURDER	YUGO.
EHRMANNSTRAUT	9650	M	Ger.	22	SS-Rottenfhr.(Uscharfhr.),C.C.Struthof-Natzweiler (Fr.) 3.42-44	TORTURE	CZECH.,FR.,U.L
EHRSAM	195929	M			SS-Hptsturmfhr.,C.C.Sachsenhausen (Ger.)	MURDER	BEL.
EHSER, Max	162891	M	Ger.	96	Osturmfhr.,Waffen-SS,staff,C.C.Buchenwald (Ger.) 1.45	TORTURE	U.S.
EHSER, Max, Otto	261574	M	Ger.	24. 3.99	Osturmfhr.,Waffen-SS,C.C.Auschwitz (Pol.) 42-45	MURDER	POL.
EHSES, Stefan	149502	M	Ger.		Oberwachtmeister,SS-Police,Neubruecke (Ger.)	TORTURE	FR.
EIBEL	259147	M			Pvt.,9 Jaeger-Bn.,738 Regt.,Supetar (Yugo.) 3.44	MURDER	YUGO.
EIBELHUBER, Josef	187291	M	Ger.	8. 8.01	Crim.commissar,Gestapo,SD,Brno (Czech.) 39-45	MURDER	CZECH.
EIBER, Willi	193246	M	Ger.	05	Guard,Oberwachtmeister,Reichsjustizministerium,Feldstraflager,C.C., Finmark (Nor.) 42-45	MISC.CRIMES	NOR.
EIBES	194823	M	Ger.		Occupied territories,Luxembourg (Lux.)	MURDER	LUX.
EIBICH, Robert	193248	M	Ger.	28. 6.04	Guard,Oberwachtmeister,Reichsjustizministerium,Feldstraflager,C.C., Finmark (Nor.) 42-45	MISC.CRIMES	NOR.
EIBNER	149503	M	Ger.		Capt.(Hptsturmfhr.),SS, (Rus.) 41-44	MURDER	FR.
EIBNER, Elfriede	187290	F	Ger.	15. 3.11	Employee,Gestapo,SD,Brno (Czech.) 39-45	MISC.CRIMES	CZECH.
EICH	10193	M	Ger.		Capt.,Army,Sicherungs-Regt.199,Chalons sur Marne (Fr.) 44	MURDER	U.K.
EICH	198735	M		97	Wachtmeister,Gendarmerie,Schupo,Luisenhohe in Hullenberg (Ger.) 12.44	MURDER	U.S.

EIC-EIL

NAME	C.R.FILE NUMBER	SEX	NATIO-NALITY	DATE OF BIRTH	RANK OCCUPATION UNIT PLACE AND DATE OF CRIME	REASON WANTED	WANTED BY
EICH	305842	M	Ger.		Pvt.,1.Auf.d.Abt. 3 Coy. 2 Col.XV Div. Afrika Korps, St.Leger Arlon, 9.44	MASSACRE	BEL.
EICH, Conrad	108733	M	Ger.		Master of Police, Neuwied, Wollendorf (Ger.) 9.44	MURDER	U.S.
EICH, Hermann	149362	M	Ger.	13	Lt., Presse-Propaganda, Paris (Fr.)	MISC.CRIMES	FR.
EICHBERGER	12653	M	Ger.		SS Oschfhr., Gestapo, Bergen (Nor.) 41	TORTURE	NOR.
EICHBERGER	124479	M	Ger.	05	Scharfhr., SS, C.C. Dachau (Ger.) 7.44-4.45	TORTURE	U.K.
EICHEL, Kurt	250716	M	Ger.		Commissar, Chantonnay-Paris (Fr.) 6.43-1.44	INTERR.	FR.
EICHEL, Wilhelm	305025	M	Ger.	4. 5.01	Crim.Secretary, SD, Groningen, Orente (Neth.) 43-45	MISC.CRIMES	NETH.
EICHELDORFER	193944	M	Ger.		Camp-Commandant, C.C. Dachau (Ger.)	TORTURE	FR.
EICHELE	162825	M	Ger.	12	Sgt., Waffen SS, C.C. Buchenwald (Ger.) 43	WITNESS	FR.
EICHELER	196350	F	Ger.		Civilian, Zeel	TORTURE	FR.
EICHEN	250140	M			SS Rottfhr., C.C. Dora, Nordhausen (Ger.)	MURDER	U.S.
EICHHOLZ	149540	M	Ger.		Prof.Dr., Oberstabsarzt, C.C. Hohenlychen, Ravensbrueck (Ger.)5.44	TORTURE	FR.
EICHHORN	301728	M	Ger.		Uschfhr., Member, SS Institute of Hygiene,C.C.Auschwitz (Pol.)40-45	MURDER	FR.
EICHHORN, Hans	162824	M	Ger.	06	Civilian, C.C. Buchenwald (Ger.) 39-45	WITNESS	U.S.
EICHINGER	250139	M	Ger.		SS-man, C.C. Dora, Nordhausen (Ger.)	MURDER	U.S.
EICHINGER, Franz	121265	M	Ger.	05	Scharfhr., SS Div. "Das Reich", Cantillac,St.Creplin de Richemont (Fr.) 3.44	MURDER	FR.
EICHLER	212	M	Ger.		Asst.of Feldgendarmerie, Sgt., Graces (Fr.) 8.44	MURDER	FR.
EICHLER	142435	M			SS Rottfhr., Waffen SS, C.C. Flossenburg (Ger.)	MURDER	U.S.
EICHLER	148923	M			Civilian, Zwickau (Ger.) 39-40	TORTURE	FR.
EICHLER	149542	M	Ger.		Prof.Dr., Oberstabsarzt,C.C.Hohenlychen,Ravensbrueck (Ger.) 5.45	TORTURE	FR.
EICHLER	184275	M			SS Oschfhr., SS Pol.Rgt., Organisation Todt,Annemasse (Fr.) 1.44	WITNESS	FR.
EICHLER	251501	M	Ger.		Head of SD, Budejovice (Czech.) 39-45	MURDER	CZECH.
EICHLINGER, Sepp	305710	M	Ger.		Oschfhr., SS F.Stuba, C.C. Auschwitz, Birkenau (Pol.) 10.42	MURDER	YUGO.
EICHLINGER, Thomas	262335	M	Ger.	18.12.94	Guard at C.C., SS-man,SS-Totenkopf, Dachau (Ger.) (L.o.D.N.A.o.D.)	SUSPECT	U.S.
EICHMANN	24797	M			Commandant, Police-Orpo., Rennes (Fr.) 42-44	MISC.CRIMES	FR.
EICHMANN	149389	M	Ger.		SD, R.S.H.A., Drancy (Fr.)	MURDER	FR.
EICHMANN	165158	M	Ger.		Dr., SS Sturmbannfhr., Major	MURDER	U.S.
EICHMANN	186363	M			Inspector, Public Official, Bordeaux (Fr.) 43	PILLAGE	FR.
EICHMANN, Adolf	135156	M	Ger.	95	SS Osturmbannfhr.,Hungaria, Ger. Chief of Cdo. (Ger.) 44	MISC.CRIMES	U.S.
EICHMANN, Adolf	155745	M	Ger.	19. 3.00	SS Sturmbannfhr.,High and Police Official, Berlin (Ger.,Den.) 43	TORTURE	U.S.
EICHNER	133777	M			SS Hptschfhr., C.C. Buchenwald (Ger.)	TORTURE	U.S.
EICHNER	192348	M			Uschfhr., SS, C.C. Flossenburg (Ger.) 44-45	MURDER	U.S.
EICHNER, Gustav	256537	M			SS	MURDER	U.S.
EICHNER, Sepp	193231	M	Ger.		Oschfhr., SS, C.C. Buchenwald (Ger.) 42-45	TORTURE	U.S.
EICHNOFF	185967	M	Ger.		Customs-Chief, St. Jean de Luz (Fr.) 40 - 44	TORTURE	FR.
EICHOFF	148924	M			Commander, Frontier-Police Service,Basses-Pyrenees (Fr.)	MISC.CRIMES	FR.
EICHOLTZ, Dietrich	185966	M		10	Cpl., Feldgendarmerie of Briey, Mercy le Bas (Fr.) 8.44	PILLAGE	FR.
EICHORN	149390	M	Ger.		Major, Agent of SD, 323 Ers.Rgt.2.Bn., Carny (Sov.Un.)	MURDER	FR.
EICHORN	168957	M	Ger.		Inspector, SD, Saint Lo (Fr.) 6.44	MURDER	FR.
EICHORN	259633	M	Ger.	10	Lt., 242 Inf.Div., Ponteves, Var (Fr.) 7.44	MURDER	FR.
EICHSTAEDT	174197	M	Ger.		Asst., Stalag VI A, C.C. Hamer (Ger.) 41-45	TORTURE	U.S.
EICHSTAEDT, Hermann	256701	M	Ger.	4. 9.94	Crim.Oberasst., Police Official, State Service, Bilina (Czech.)39-43	MURDER	CZECH.
EICHUNGER	149391	M	Ger.		Member Gestapo, SS Oschfhr., Limoges (Fr.)	MURDER	FR.
EICKE	124782	M	Ger.		Standartenfhr., SS, C.C. Sachsenhausen (Ger.)	MURDER	U.S.
EICKE	190312	M			C.C. Dachau (Ger.)	MURDER	U.S.
EICKE	193229	M	Ger.		SS Oberstgruppenfhr., Waffen SS, C.C. Buchenwald (Ger.)	MURDER	U.S.
EICKELSCHULTS, Wilhelm	252073	M	Ger.	16. 8.07	Pvt., 13 Coy., 558 Gren.Rgt., Bruay (Fr.) 9.44	MURDER	FR.
EICKHOFF	145367	M			Major, OKW, Subsection VPW Affaire	WITNESS	U.S.
EICKHOFF, Guenther	154335	M			Member, SS, C.C. Flossenburg (Ger.)	TORTURE	U.S.
EICKHOLN, Hans	24798	M	Ger.		Dr.med., Pvt., Army, NSDAP, Pz.Jaeger Verbindungsstab, Chambery-Georges-de-Chailles (Fr.)	MURDER	FR.
EICKLER	257227	M	Ger.		Prof., Lt.Col., Army, PW-Camp-Commandant XII A, Hademar (Ger.) 4.41	SUSPECT,MURDER	POL.
EICKMANN	157355	M	Ger.		SS Reichssicherheitshauptamt, Boheme (Pol.)	SUSPECT	FR.
EICKNER	146189	M	Ger.		Sgt., Prison, Charleroi (Bel.) 44	TORTURE	BEL.
EICKNER	149392	M		10	SS Osturmfhr., C.C. Mauthausen (Ger.)	MURDER	FR.
EIDAM	257499	M	Ger.		Employee, 3.Bv. Kdo., C.C. Nordhausen (Ger.)	MURDER	U.S.
EIDMANN, Ricard	261041	M	Ger.		SS, S-Cesario sul Panaro, Castelfranco Emilia,Modena (It.) 12.44	MURDER	U.S.
EIER	149393	M	Ger.	02	Gruppenfhr., SA, Freiburg (Ger.)	MISC.CRIMES	FR.
EIER	252953	M	Ger.		Sgt., Camp A, Bonn (Ger.)	BRUTALITY	U.S.
EIERMANN	108909	M			Presumably Civilian, Gernsbach (Ger.) 8.44	MURDER	U.S.
EIGEL	128921	M			Major, Stalag Luft 17 B, Krems (Aust.) 12.43-4.45	MURDER	U.S., U.K.
EIGEN	260636	M	Ger.		C.C. Dachau, lives at 3,Sonneneck, Kaufbeuren (Ger.) 42-44	BRUTALITY	FR.
EIGENBRODT, Franz, Hans	24802	M	Ger.		Ex-Employee, Ger.Railway, Redon (Fr.)	MURDER	FR.
EIGENBROTH, Fritz	258700	M	Ger.		Oschfhr., Waffen SS, 2 Bn., 38 SS Rgt.,"Goets v. Berlichingen"-Div., Kennat (Ger.) 10.44	WITNESS	U.S.
EIGENRAUCH, Karl	129264	M	Ger.		Interpreter, Army, Quaregnon, Jemappes, Ghlin (Bel.) 9.44	MURDER	BEL.
EIGL, Johann (or EIGLE)	262058	M	Ger.	22. 9.02	SS-man, Waffen SS, Gren.Div. 36 "Dirlewanger-Bde.", Warschau and other (Pol.) 40-44	MURDER	POL.
EIGNER	173764	M	Ger.		Interpreter, Camp Official, C.C. Tripolis (Afr.) 6.41-8.41	MURDER	U.K.
EIGNER	250738	M			SS Oschfhr., Camp Dora, Nordhausen (Ger.)	MURDER	U.S.
EIGRUBER	147181	M			Distr.Leader, SS, C.C. Mauthausen (Aust.) 41-45	MURDER	U.S.
EIKE (see SCHULZ)	152149						
EIKMANN	192774	M	Ger.		Lt., SS, C.C. Falstad (Nor.) 41-44	MISC.CRIMES	NOR.
EILAND	137009	M		05	Sgt., SS Guard at Civilian Prison, Frankfurt (Ger.) 44	TORTURE	U.S.
EILENTROPP, Josef	176928	M	Ger.	4. 2.92	Civilian, Prison Guard, C.C. Langendreer (Ger.)	TORTURE	U.S.
EILERS	139779	M	Ger.		Capt., Stalag Luft III, West-Lager, Sagan (Ger.) 1.45	MISC.CRIMES	U.S.
EILERS	155735	M	Ger.		Capt., Army, Muskau (Ger.) 1.45	TORTURE	U.S.
EILERS	255372	M	Ger.		Oschfhr., C.C. Buchenwald (Ger.)	MURDER	U.S.
EILERS, Erhard	113410	M	Ger.	10	Dr., Public Official Archives, Head of Office,Warsaw (Pol.)	LOOTING	POL.
EILERS, Heinrich (Frau)	147188	F			Civilian, Borkum (Ger.) 8.44	MURDER	U.S.
EILERS, Johannes	147150	M	Ger.		Ordnance-Officer, Volkssturm-Bn., C.C. Gardelegen (Ger.) 4.45	MURDER	U.S.
EILERS, Paul, Huber	134836	M	Ger.	13	Sgt., Lt., SS, C.C. Buchenwald, Outercamp S.3 (Ger.) 39-45	MISTR.,WITNESS	U.S.

EIL-EKA

NAME	C.R.FILE NUMBER	SEX	NATIO-NALITY	DATE OF BIRTH	RANK OCCUPATION UNIT PLACE AND DATE OF CRIME	REASON WANTED	WANTED BY
EILERT, Karl	250739	M		12. 1.14	Pvt.Camp Ellrich,Nordhausen(Ger.)	MURDER	U.S.
EILST	187644	M	Ger.		Cpl.Feldgendarmerie,Goudriaan(Neth.)5.44	MURDER	U.K.
EILTS	147147	M			Civilian,Borkum(Ger.)8.44	MURDER	U.S.
EIMER, Franz	252071	M			Civilian,Popatow(Pol.)	MURDER	POL.
EIMER, Otto	147175	M	Ger.		Teacher,Ortsgruppenleiter NSDAP,10.44	MURDER	U.S.
EINENKEL, Ludwig	186319	M	Ger.	02	Foreman,Arbeitskdo.,Nuernberg(Ger.)40-45	TORTURE	U.S.
EINERT, Fritz	250736	M		25. 8.99	SS Oscharfhr.,Nordhausen(Ger.)	MURDER	U.S.
EINGARTNER, Franz Xaver	145377	M	Ger.	31. 1.96	Farmer,Seyboldsdorf,Vilsbiburg(Ger.)	WITNESS	U.S.
EINCHINGER, Franz	191777	M		05	SS Oscharfhr.,Dordogne(Fr.)3.44	MURDER	FR.
EINHAUS	300454	M	Ger.		Sgt.Major,1013 Fortress-Bn.Matre(north of Bergen)(Nor.)5.45	MURDER	NOR.
EINKOW	186329	M	Ger.		SS Member(Ger.)44	MURDER	U.S.
EINSOHN	191980	M	Ger.		Capt.Kommandantur,St.Tropez(Fr.)7.44	WITNESS	FR.
EINTEICH, J.	213	M			Lt.Army,Bomdilly(Fr.)	TORTURE	FR.
EINTEICH, Julius	155740	M	Ger.	05	Lt.Army,Poirom(Fr.)44	MURDER	FR.
EIP	149488	M			Civilian,Contremaitre a L'Usine Hokrin,Zeel(Ger.)	TORTURE	FR.
EIRENSCHMALZ, Franz	258561	M	Ger.	01	SS Standartenfhr.W.V.H.A.(Ger.)40-45	BRUTALITY	U.S.
EIRICH	255096	M	Ger.		Pvt.2 Coy.Lt.M.G.Sturm Bn.A.O.K.I.,Courselles sur Neid(Fr.)11.44	MURDER	U.S.
EIS	250729	M			SS Rottenfhr.Camp Mackenrode,Nordhausen(Ger.)	MURDER	U.S.
EISBUSCH, Christian	305590	M	Ger.		Member CC Personnel,Flossenburg,Hersbruck,Wolkenburg,Ganacker,Leitmeritz(Ger.and C.S.R.)1.42-5.45	MURDER	U.S.
EISCH, Fritz	250992	M	Ger.		Pvt.377 Jaeger Regt.,Vinkt(Bel.)	MURDER	BEL.
EISCHINGER, Franz alias Thierry	250711	M	Ger.		SS Scharfhr.Gestapo,Limoges(Fr.)40-44	INTERR.	FR.
EISEL	255097	M	Ger.		Oberstabsarzt,Army,Rotterdam(Neth.)11.44	MURDER	NETH.
EISELE, Joseph	166301	M	Ger.		Ubach/Schwarzwald(Ger.)7.44	MURDER	U.S.
EISELEN	149490	M	Ger.		Sec.Lt.Gebirgs Jaeger Regt.98,1 Coy.1 Bn.	MURDER	FR.
EISELEN	250712	M	Ger.		Lt.1/98 Mountain-Regt.157 Inf.Res.Div.,Le Chablais(Fr.)5.-7.44	MISC.CRIMES	FR.
EISELINGER see EISEMINGER, Walter	214						
EISELT	305843	M	Ger.		Pvt.1 Aufkl.Abt.3 Coy.2 Col.XV Div.Afrika Korps,St.Leger(Arlon)9.44	MURDER	BEL.
EISELT, Rigobert	187741	M	Ger.	12.10.13	Crim.Asst.Gestapo,S.D.,Brno(Czech.)39-45	MURDER	CZECH.
EISEMANN, Karl	24758	M	Ger.		Pvt.Parastrooper,Roermond(Neth.)11.44-1.45	TORTURE	U.S.
EISEMINGER or EISELINGER,Walter	214	M	Ger.		Obersturmfhr.official,S.D.Gestapo,Perpignan(Fr.)8.43	MURDER	FR.
EISENBAD	250730	M			SS Hptscharfhr.S.D.Camp Dora,Nordhausen(Ger.)	MURDER	U.S.
EISENBARTH, Ludwig	192346	M	Ger.		Lt.Army,Dillingen(Ger.)5.44	WITNESS	U.S.
EISENBURG, Franz called Krauss	259350	M	Ger.	10	Chief of jewish-section,S.D.of Nizza,Colmars(Fr.)1.44	INTERR.	FR.
EISENFELD	260071	M	Ger.		SS Hptsturmfhr.SS Slave labour camp,Bota near Rognan(Nor.)4.43	BRUTALITY	YUGO.
EISENFEST	147178	M	Ger.		Unterscharfhr.SS Totenkopf CC Mauthausen(Aust.)41-45	MURDER	U.S.
EISENHAMMER	24805	M	Ger.		Agent Gestapo,Nice(Fr.)43	MURDER	FR.
EISENHAUER or EISENHOWER, Wilhelm	24750	M	Ger.	07	Sgt.Army and Organisation Todt,Dulag 377,Gerolstein(Ger.)12.44-2.45	MURDER	U.S.
EISENHAUER	250731	M			Pvt.Camp Osterhagen,Nordhausen(Ger.)	MURDER	U.S.
EISENHOFER	142146	M			Obersturmfhr.SS,Mauthausen(Aust.)	TORTURE	FR.
EISENHOFER	147179	M			SS Oberstumer,KL Mauthausen(Aust.)	MURDER	U.S.
EISENKOPF	193295	M	Ger.	90	Leader,Justizvollzugsanst.,CC Frankfurt/M. Preungesheim (Ger.)7.-10.44	TORTURE	U.K.
EISENHOWER see EISENHAUER,Wilh.	24750						
EISENHOWER	36620	M	Ger.	20	Sgt.Army,Worms/Rhein(Ger.)12.44	MURDER	U.K.
EISENHOWER	142437	M	Ger.	95	Pvt.Marine Corps,St.Marine(Vic.)(Fr.)	MURDER	U.S.
EISENHOWER	256016	M	Ger.		Cmdt.CC Mauthausen(Aust.)	MURDER	FR.
EISENKOPF	149199	M	Ger.		Guard of prison,KL Prungesheim(Ger.)	TORTURE	U.K.
EISENLOHR, Ernst	258092	M	Ger.	12. 9.82	Ambassador,State Service,Prague(Czech.)39-40	WITNESS	CZECH.
EISENLOHR, Georg	168939	M	Ger.		Dr.,Stellvertreter des Gouverneur,General-Government Poland,Occupied territoires,Radom(Pol.)	MISC.CRIMES	POL.
EISENMANN, Andreas	12608	M	Ger.		Pvt.110 or 111 Panz.Gren.Regt.2 Coy.(Fr.)Albine,6.44	MURDER	FR.
EISENMENGER, Walter	190582	M	Ger.		SS Obersturmfhr.S.D.Einsatz Kdo.6,La Grande Fosse(Fr.)10.44	MURDER	U.K.
EISENOFFER, Heinz	305026	M	Ger.		Administrator-Accomplice of Heinz Strauss,Mauthausen(Aust.)11-12-5-45	MISC.CRIMES	FR.
EISENREICH	191332	M	Ger.		Cpl.Army,Gossen(Nor.)42-45	TORTURE	NOR.
EISENREICH, Werner	193244	M	Ger.	07	Sgt.Reichsjustizministerium Feldstraflager,CC Finmark(Nor.)42-45	MISC.CRIMES	NOR.
EISENTRAUT	301681	M	Ger.		05/243 Mongolian"Oberland"Unit,St.Nazaire en Royans(Drome)(Fr.)7.-8.44	MURDER	FR.
EISENWALDT	191443	M	Ger.		Dr.,Governor,General Government,Radom(Pol.)9.39-44	PILLAGE	POL.
EISER	185593	F	Ger.		Overseer,KL Koenigsberg/Oder(Ger.)	TORTURE	FR.
EISERMANN see ARENSMANN	305630						
EISERMEN	127977	M	Ger.		Sgt.Army,CC Neuengamme(Ger.)41-42	TORTURE	BEL.
EISFELD	195328	M	Ger.		SS Oberstumbannfhr.CC Sachsenhausen(Ger.)39	MURDER	BEL.
EISHINGER see EISMINGER	251517						
EISINGER, Martin	194954	M	Ger.	05	Pvt.3/788 Landesschtz.Bn.,Goolens Graben(Aust.)12.42	MURDER	U.K.
EISMINGER or EISHINGER	251517	M	Ger.		SS Osturmfhr./official,Gestapo,Perpignan(Fr.)4.-8.43	MURDER	FR.
EISOLD, Alfred	174198	M	Ger.	2. 5.01	Civilian,Kospa(Ger.)6.44	MURDER	U.S.
EISOLDT	193228	M	Ger.		SS Obersturmfhr.4 SS Totenkopf Sturmbann,CC Buchenwald(Ger.)42-45	TORTURE	U.S.
EISSEN	250127	M			SS Rottenfhr.Camp Dora,Nordhausen(Ger.)	MURDER	U.S.
EISSFELDT	168950	M	Ger.		Dr.,Oberlandforstmeister,Leader,Hauptabteilung Forsten,Gen.Governement (Pol.)9.39-44	MISC.CRIMES	POL.
EISTFELD	215	M	Ger.		Lager Commander,CC Oranienburg(Ger.)39-42	TORTURE	POL.
EISWALDT	216	M	Ger.		Dr.,Public official,Stellvertretender Governor,Radom(Pol.)9.39-1.42	MURDER	POL.
EITEL, Georges	254323	M	Ger.		SS Pvt.S.D.,Toulouse(Fr.)11.42-8.44	MISC.CRIMES	FR.
EITENEUR	24808	M			Army,Organisation Todt,Firm Hermann Lorient,Lochrist en Inzinzau(Fr.)	TORTURE	FR.
EITNER	168951	M	Ger.		Leader,Treuhandverwaltung fuer Privatgrundstuecke,Warschau(Pol.) 9.39-44	MISC.CRIMES	POL.
EIZENHAMMER, Peter	187945	M			Pvt.110 or 111 Panz.Gren.Regt.,Albine(Fr.)	MURDER	FR.
EJANEKE	152027	M	Ger.		Interpreter,Gestapo,Cabrespuies(Fr.)4.45	MURDER	FR.
EKART	149201	M	Ger.		Factory,Linz(Aust.)	TORTURE	FR.

EKE-END

NAME	C.R.FILE NUMBER	SEX	NATIO-NALITY	DATE OF BIRTH	RANK OCCUPATION UNIT PLACE AND DATE OF CRIME	REASON WANTED	WANTED BY
EKERSDORFF, Karl	126998	M	Ger.		Customs and excise, Delle (Fr.) 7.44	MURDER	FR.
EKEY	174949	M	Ger.	85	Group leader, commander, NSDAP, Volkssturm, Habichthorst (Ger.) 4.45	MURDER	U.S.
EKKERT, Ernst	186357	M	Ger.		C.C. Sachsenhausen (Ger.) 43-45	MURDER	FR.
ELART	10009	M	Ger.		Cpl., employed at C.C. Breendonck (Bel.) 44	TORTURE	BEL.
ELBEN	174199	M			SS Oscharfhr., C.C. Muehldorf-Ampfing (Ger.) 6.44-4.45	MURDER	U.S.
ELBERT, Ferdinand	167930	M	Ger.		Pvt., 9.Res.Gren.Rgt. 1.Coy., Magny d'Anigon (Fr.) 9.44	MURDER	FR.
ELBL, Julius	188287	M		24. 8.79	Confidential-agent, S.D., Marianske Lazne (Czech.) 39-45	MISC.CRIMES	CZECH.
ELBL, Leo	133374	M	Ger.	20	SS Mann, Waffen SS, Pion.Ausb.Bn.2 1. Coy.,Passau (Ger.) 4.45	MURDER	U.S.
ELFERS	157378	M		00	Chief, Gestapo, Ruedersdorf-Berlin (Ger.)	MURDER	FR.
ELIAS, Hans	145369	M	Ger.	3.12.98	Pvt., Guard, SS, C.C. Leibersdorf (Ger.) 5.45	WITNESS	U.S.
ELIERCH, Joseph or HERRLICH	157368	M	Ger.		Cpl., Army, 263. D.I., Finistere (Fr.) 44	MURDER	FR.
ELIERCH, Joseph see ELLIASCH	167903						
ELINGRATH, Alfred	259805				Civ. employed with Reichskommissariat Abt. Prop.,Schiedam (Neth.) 6.41	PILLAGE	NETH.
ELINGUER	194305	M			Commandant, Ortskommandantur, Gollot Plounevez, Moedec (Fr.)	MISC.CRIMES	FR.
ELIOF	217	M			Lt., Interpreter, Gestapo, St. Brieuc (Fr.) 7.44	MURDER	FR.
ELIS	149203	M		99	Chief, SS, C.C. Hannover (Ger.)	TORTURE	FR.
ELLAND, Theodore	125415	M			Capt.,Landesschuetzen Bn.877, 1.Coy., Niklasdorf (Aust.) 9.44-3.45	MISC.CRIMES	U.K.
ELLEBECK	24826	M			Agent de train, Le Bourget, Triage (Fr.) 8.44	MURDER	FR.
ELLENBECK, Ernst	149204	M	Ger.		SS Sturmbannfhr. C.C. Buchenwald (Ger.)	MURDER	FR.
ELLENBERG	162822	M		17	Lt., SS, C.C. Buchenwald (Ger.) 42	WITNESS	U.S.
ELLENBERGER, Nicolaus	142438	M	Ger.	86	Civ., Renda to Netra (Ger.)	WITNESS	U.S.
ELLEND, Theodor	194953	M	Ger.		Capt., Army, Coy.-commander at Leoben, Radmer (Aust.) 3.42	TORTURE	U.K.
ELLER	149205	M	Ger.		Civ., Karlsruhe (Ger.)	TORTURE	FR.
ELLER, Franz	142144	M		15	Civ., Lublin (Pol.)	MURDER	FR.
ELLER, Frantz	900701	M	Ger.		Aide, 5.Coy. Tank-Gren.Div. 3, combat group, Condom - Gers. (Fr.) 7.44	MISC.CRIMES	FR.
ELLERMANN	12610	M			Lt., Feldgendarmerie, St.Germain en Laye (Fr.) 8.44	MURDER	FR.
ELLERT	218	M			SS Aufseher, C.C. Maidanek (Pol.) 40-4.44	MURDER	POL.
ELLES	152025	M			Interpreter, Gestapo, Angers (Fr.)	MURDER	FR.
ELLIASCH, Josef alias ELIERCH	167903	M			Pvt., Arbeitskommando Nr. 343, Landerneau, Finistere (Fr.) 6.44-8.44	MURDER	FR.
ELLING	199885	M			Dr., Generaldirector, Kriegsgefang.Arbeits-Cmdo.,Glanzstoffwerke, Elsterberg (Ger.) 12.40	TORTURE	FR.
ELLINGER	905887	M			Hptscharfhr., C.C. Oranienburg (Ger.) 39-45	MURDER	CZECH.
ELLINGRATH, Alfred	900374	M			Member of the Schustzgruppe, Schiedam (Neth.) 6.41	PILLAGE	NETH.
ELIMEYER	905844	M	Ger.		Pvt., 1.Aufkl.Abt. 3.Coy. 2.Col. XV.Div.Afrika-Corps, St.Leger (Arlon) 9.44	MURDER	BEL.
ELLWARTH, Anton	250128	M			Pvt., Camp Ellrich, Nordhausen (Ger.)	MURDER	U.S.
ELON	256538	M	Ger.		Policeman, Civ., Frankfurt-Main (Ger.) 6.-9.44	BRUTALITY	U.S.
ELSATZ	121263	M	Ger.		Col., Luftwaffe, Luftpark, Aulat (Fr.)	TORTURE	FR.
ELSER	124253	M			Lt., Army, SS, 1.SS Pz.Div., 12.Parachute Inf.z.b.V.,12.Coy.Malmedy (Bel.) 12.44	MURDER	U.S.
ELSESSER, Johann	259922	M	Ger.		Crim.employee, Gestapo of Bruenn, Leskovec-Moravia (Czech.) 4.45	MURDER	CZECH.
ELSNER	155744	M			3.Sturmbn. A.O.K. 1, officer, Courcelles (Fr.) 11.44	MURDER	U.S.
ELSNER, Paul Hermann	252082	M	Ger.	06	Civ. official, Labour exchange, Hradec (Czech.)	PILLAGE	CZECH.
ELSTE	162883	M	Ger.		Sgt., camp official C.C. Saarbruecken (Ger.)	TORTURE	FR.
ELSTER	261759	M	Ger.		Col., Caen (Fr.) 12.41-5.42	MURDER	FR.
ELTSATZ	24813	M			Col., Army, Aulnat (Fr.) 44	MURDER	FR.
ELTZATZ	24814	M		95	Capt., Army, Luftwaffen-Basis, Aulnat (Fr.)	PILLAGE	FR.
ELTZE	108746	M	Ger.		Dr., Sanitaets-Corps, institute physician, Kiew (Russl.)6.41 - 3.42	MURDER	U.S.
EMDEN, Karl	301167	M	Ger.		Mussel-grower, Civ. at Ierseke, Zeeland, Middelburg, 10.44	MISC.CRIMES	NETH.
EMDE	133776	M			SS Scharfhr., C.C. Buchenwald (Ger.)	TORTURE	U.S.
EMDE, Fritz	250129	M			Pvt., Camp Ellrich, Nordhausen (Ger.)	MURDER	U.S.
EMERICH	220	M			SS Oscharfhr., Chef Umform.Dept.Stutthof C.C. . 9.39-4.41	TORTURE	POL.
EMERICH	251512	M	Ger.		Rapportfuehrer and RAD-Fuehrer, Auschwitz,Birkenau (Pol.)	MURDER	YUGO.
EMERIE	900455	M	Ger.		N.C.O., Astenet, 9.44	MURDER	BEL.
EMERT, Gust.	133775	M			SS Uscharfhr., C.C. Buchenwald (Ger.)	TORTURE	U.S.
EMGE	190001	M			N.C.O., C.C. Banjica (Yugo.) 41-45	MURDER	YUGO.
EMIG, Karl	167131	M	Ger.	28. 1.98	Lt., Gendarmerie, Reichshoffen (Fr.) 44-45	MISC.CRIMES	FR.
EMILE	900242	M	Ger.		Kapo, Commando Head, C.C.Neckargerach, Neckarelz, Neckar Valley,Baden Gestapo, Cmdo.of political deportees, Neckargerach,Neckarelz (Ger.)42-5	MURDER	FR.
EMKOW, Werner	195321	M	Ger.		Civ., Berlin-Reinickendorf (Ger.) 6.44	MURDER	U.S.
EMLER, Karl Heinrich	149206	M	Ger.		SS Mann, C.C. Hinzert (Ger.)	TORTURE	FR.
EMMEL	250125	M		28.11.91	SS Oscharfhr., C.C. Nordhausen (Ger.)	MURDER	U.S.
EMMERICH	149207	M	Ger.		N.C.O., Arbeitskommando, Gladbeck (Ger.)	TORTURE	FR.
EMMERICH	157976	M	Ger.		SS Sturmfhr., Altenburg (Ger.) 42-44	TORTURE	FR.
EMMERICH	191428	M	Ger.		Dr., Ministerialrat, Wirtschafts-Abt. occupied territories,Pol.	MISC.CRIMES	POL.
EMMERICH	261881	M	Ger.		C.C. Belsen (Ger.) 45	MURDER	BEL.
EMMERICH, Walter	62243	M			Dr., Ministerialrat, public official, Leiter der Hauptabt.Wirtschaft. Amt des Generalgouverneurs, Krakau (Pol.) 9.39-44	TORTURE	UNWCC
EMMERICH, Wilhelm	139456	M	Ger.		SS Oscharfhr., C.C. Bergen-Belsen, Auschwitz (Pol.)	MURDER	FR.,BEL.
EMMERLIG	162821	M		95	Civ., C.C. Buchenwald (Ger.) 42-45	WITNESS	U.S.
EMMERLING	173887	M	Ger.	87	Civ.,Foreman, Fella works, Feucht (Ger.) 40-45	TORTURE	U.S.
EMMERLING, Rudolf	134840	M	Ger.		Soldier, Guard of French prisoners	MURDER	FR.
EMMLER	130108	M			Osturmfhr., SS, C.C. Dora-Mittelbau Nordhausen	MURDER	U.S.
EMPEL, Josef	154334	M			Civ., Leppin (Ger.)	TORTURE	U.S.
EMSHAUBER	221	M	Ger.		Army (foreign legion) Lt., "Legion de l'Est", Azerbeidjans Legion, Rodez (Fr.) 8.44	MURDER	FR.
EMSPACH	186658	M			Uscharfhr., SS, C.C. Nordhausen Dora-Mittelbau (Ger.) 43-45	WITNESS	U.S.
ENZANSEN, August	255100	M	Ger.		Landowner, Bernhausen (Ger.) 1.43	TORTURE	YUGO.
ENCKE	190226	M	Ger.		SS Osturmfhr., SS, C.C. Dachau (Ger.)	MURDER	BEL.
END, Wendelin	122713	M			Oscharfhr., SS, Struthof (Fr.)	MURDER	FR.
ENDE	124477	M	Ger.		Lt., Gren.Rgt. 148 4.Coy. Neufchatel, En Braye, Rouen, 8.44	MURDER	U.S.
ENDEL	906901	M			Capt. de fregate commanding the port, St.Malo-Ille et Vilaine (Fr.)8.44	PILLAGE	FR.
ENDEL, Eduard	250126	M		19. 7.85	Pvt., Camp Harzungen, Nordhausen (Ger.)	MURDER	U.S.

END - ENG

NAME	C.R.FILE NUMBER	SEX	NATIO-NALITY	DATE OF BIRTH	RANK OCCUPATION UNIT PLACE AND DATE OF CRIME	REASON WANTED	WANTED BY
ENDEREE	173766	M	Ger.		Kreishauptamtsleiter, Abschnittsleiter, NSDAP, Offenburg (Ger.) 44	TORTURE	FR.
ENDERS	192232	M	Ger.		Unterscharfuehrer, SS-Div. "Das Reich", SS-Regt. "Der Fuehrer", 1.Bn., 4.Coy., Gelat (Fr.) 5.44	MURDER	FR.
ENDERS (see ENDRES)	250727						
ENDERS, Alois	193789	M	Ger.	6. 8.10	Member, Gestapo, Cheb (Czech.) 39-45	TORTURE	CZECH.
ENDERS, Annemarie nee Goffke	260346	F	Ger.	18	Secretary of the Gauamtsleiter, Home-adress: Mainz am Main, Schoenbornstr. 10, Danzig (Ger.) 39	BRUTALITY	POL.
ENDERS, Herman	172887	M	Ger.		Civilian, Ulrichshalben (Ger.) 7.44	TORTURE	U.S.
ENDERS, Rudolf	155739	M	Ger.	06	Manager, Major, Arbeitskommando, C.C. Falkenstein (Ger.) 1.45	TORTURE	U.K.
ENDERTINE	122715	M			Sgt., Stalag, Graudenz (Ger.) 42	TORTURE	U.K.
ENDLICHER	193616	M	Ger.		Dr., Sonderfuehrer, Army (Czech.) 40-45	MURDER	CZECH.
ENDREJATH, Wilhelmine	194821	F	Ger.	10. 3.13	Braune Schwester, Administration of Occup.Territ., Luxemburg (Lux.)	MURDER	LUX.
ENDRES	108736	M	Ger.	90	Major, motor pool, Elementary Schoolteacher, (Ger.) 8.44	MURDER	U.S.
ENDRES	151218	M	Ger.	10	SS-Oberscharf., T/Sgt., C.C. Lublin (Pol.) 42-43	TORTURE	U.S.
ENDRES	151217	M			Dr. Obersturmf., Lt., SS-Station Doctor, C.C. Meuthausen (Aust.) 41-45	MURDER	U.S.
ENDRES or ENDERS	250727	M			Pvt., Camp Ellrich, Nordhausen (Ger.)	MURDER	U.S.
ENDRES, Hans	222	M			Pvt., Army, Unit: L 20368, Braudrigues (Fr.) 8.44	MURDER	FR.
ENDRES, Norbert	90428	M		99	Asst. Kreisleiter and S.D.-Chief, NSDAP, Bad Neustadt/Saale (Ger.) 9.44	MURDER	U.S.
ENDRESS	301729	M	Ger.		Head Doctor, C.C. Auschwitz (Pol.) 40-45	MURDER	FR.
ENDT, Alfred	31978	M	Ger.		Landgerichtsrat, Public official, Litomerice (Czech.) 40	MURDER	CZECH.
ENERS	24823	M			Cmdt., Army, C.C. Aurigny (Fr.)	TORTURE	FR.
ENERT	250726	M			Cpl., Camp Ellrich, Nordhausen (Ger.)	MURDER	U.S.
ENGBERT	259941	M	Ger.		Cpl., Camp Martin (Fr.) 43	WITNESS	U.S.
ENGBROCKS	250981	M			Pvt., Pepingen (Bel.)	PILLAGE	BEL.
ENGEL	192338	M			SS-Unterscharf., C.C. Flossenburg (Ger.)	MURDER	FR.
ENGEL	193227	M	Ger.		SS-Doctor, C.C. Buchenwald (Ger.) 42-45	TORTURE	U.S.
ENGEL	258142	M			SS-Scharf., W-SS, C.C. Natzweiler (Fr.)	MURDER	BEL.
ENGEL, Edmund	167929	M	Ger.		Pvt., 9.Res.Gren.Regt., 1.Coy., Magny d'Anigon (Fr.) 9.44	MURDER	FR.
ENGEL, Frederick	250710	M	Ger.	06	Sturmbannf., SS, Genua, Bogliasco (It.) 12.44	INTERR.	U.K.
ENGEL, Friedrich Wilhelm	306579	M	Ger.	3. 4.08	Asst., Card Index Department, office of Commandant of S.D. Sipo, Trandum nr. Oslo (Nor.) 1.43	MURDER	U.K.
ENGEL, Fritz	250980	M		10	Pvt., Commando 44, Stalag IV G, Mugeln (Ger.)	WITNESS	U.S.
ENGEL, Gerhard M.	260641	M		06	Major General	WITNESS	U.S.
ENGEL, Hermann	24824	M		09	Sturmf., SS, 15.Bde., Mte.32305, 1.Platoon, 8.Coy., Bucheres Cresay (Fr.) 44	MURDER	FR.
ENGEL, Hugo	147767	M			Crim.-Insp., Crim.Pol., Sourche (Fr.) 41	PILLAGE	FR.
ENGEL, Johannes	307087	M	Ger.	1. 7.09	Civilian, Buer Resse near Gelsenkirchen (Ger.) 2.45	BRUTALITY	U.K.
ENGEL, Max	250728	M		6.10.99	Flyer, Camp Ellrich, Nordhausen (Ger.)	MURDER	U.S.
ENGEL, Paul	162819	M	Ger.	04	Oberscharf., SS, C.C. Buchenwald (Ger.)	WITNESS	U.S.
ENGEL, Rose	193571	F	Ger.		Member, S.D., Sipo, Leeuwarden (Neth.) 9.44-4.45	MISC.CRIMES	NETH.
ENGELBERT, Otto	192231	M			Sgt., 1.Coy., 229.Gren.Bn., Soissons (Fr.) 8.44	MURDER	FR.
ENGELBERTH, Johann	187289	M	Ger.		Treasurer, NSDAP, Drmouly (Czech.) 39-45	MISC.CRIMES	CZECH.
ENGELBRECH	135157	M			Capt., 19.SS Pol.Regt., C.C. Yigaun (Yugo.), Tulle (Fr.) 5.41 - 3.44 / 3.44 - 10.44	MURDER	U.S.
ENGELBRECHT	23931	M			Hauptsturmf., SS, 2.Bn., Aixe (Fr.) 44	MURDER	FR.
ENGELBRECHT	23932	M			Capt., Army, (Fr.)	TORTURE	FR.
ENGELBRECHT	251507	M	Ger.		Hauptscharf., SS, C.C. Auschwitz-Birkenau (Pol.) 9.42	MURDER	YUGO.
ENGELBRECHT	306743	M	Ger.		Former Lt., Army, Chief of Police, Rothenberg (Ger.) 2.45	BRUTALITY	U.S.
ENGELBRECHT, Erwin	90474	M			General, Kav.,	MISC.CRIMES	U.N.W.C.C.
ENGELFRIED, Kurt	194968	M	Ger.		SS-Oberscharf., S.D., Nice, St. Julien (Fr.) 6.44- 7.44	MURDER	FR.
ENGELHARD	23934	M			Sgt., 217 Bn., Gren.Gape., Barcelonette (Fr.)	MURDER	FR.
ENGELHARD, Heinrich	23933	M		09 or 13	N.C.O., Feldgendarmerie, St. Brieuc (Fr.) 44	MURDER	FR.
ENGELHARDT	306946	M	Ger.	10	Reg.Rat, Director, Zuchthaus Luethringshausen (Ger.) 41-42	TORTURE	NETH.
ENGELHARDT	257507	M		18	Sgt., Muehldorf area (Ger.)	MURDER	U.S.
ENGELHARDT	250138	M			SS-Oberscharf., Camp Dora, Nordhausen (Ger.)	MURDER	U.S.
ENGELHARDT	257873	M			Cpl., 150.Panz.Bde., Bde.-Stab Scherff, Meuse-Bridge,Antwerp.(Bel.)12.44	MISC.CRIMES	U.S.
ENGELHARDT	305592	M	Ger.		Local Head of the Volkssturm, Kuechen (Ger.) 11.44	MURDER	U.S.
ENGELHARDT, Karl	168932	M			Feldgendarmerie, Vielsalm (Bel.)	PILLAGE	BEL.
ENGELHARDT, Ludwig	165544	M	Ger.	04	Secretary, Custom-house, Hombourg (Bel.) 5.44	MURDER	BEL.
ENGELHARDT, Otto	134899	M	Ger.	24.12.95	Horse-driver, Kdtr.Stab, C.C. Dachau (Ger.)	MISC.CRIMES	U.S.
ENGELHARDT, Walter	906361	M	Ger.		SS-Pvt., C.C. Buchenwald (Ger.) 5.38-10.43	MURDER	BEL.
ENGELHART	147176	M			Obersturmf., SS, C.C. Meuthausen (Aust.) 41-45	WITNESS	U.S.
ENGELHART	151235	M	Ger.		Director, Prison C.C. Ziegenhain (Ger.)	TORTURE	FR.
ENGELHART	306902	M	Ger.		Kreis-Kdt., attached to garrison at St. Malo, Fr. 8.44	PILLAGE	FR.
ENGELHAUP	186335	M	Ger.		Civilian,	TORTURE	FR.
ENGELKE	147338	M	Ger.		Lt., II.Panzer-Div., Kampfgruppe "Wilde", 1944 (Fr.)	MURDER	FR.
ENGELKIRCHER, Arthur aliases: "John de Bastard"	36613	M	Ger.		N.C.O., Army, 5.Coy., 398. Bn. of Gleiwitz (Oberschlesien) now attached to 515 LS Bn. KL. E 727, Mechtal (Oberschlesien) (Ger.) 3.43 - 12.43	MURDER	U.K.
ENGELKIRCHER, Johann or ENGELKIRKE	154451	M		99	N.C.O., Landesschuetzen - Bn. 398, 5.Coy., Beuthen (Ger.) 3.43	MURDER	U.K.
ENGELM, August	121262	M	Ger.		Pvt., Army, Migne (Fr.) 8.44	WITNESS	FR.
ENGELMAIER, Richard	305888	M	Ger.		SS-Hauptsturmf., Head of the Zlin Aussenstelle of the S.D. Leitabschnitt Prague, Oswiecim C.C. Birkenau (Pol.) 39- 8.42	MURDER	CZECH.
ENGELMAN, Alexander or ENGELMANN	255179	M	Ger.	4. 2.73	Employee, Administrator, Buyer, Wirtsch. Pruefstelle The Hague U.M.S. Utrechtsche Machinale Stoel en Meubelfactory (Neth.) 42-2.45	MISC.CRIMES	NETH.
ENGELMANN or ENGELMANN	189690	M		95	Obermaat, Navy, C.C. Luneberg (Ger.) 4.45	MURDER	U.K.
ENGELMANN	185968	M			Dr., Army, Vienne (Fr.) 40 - 45	MURDER	FR.
ENGELMANN	23935	M			Dr., Officer, SS, Mirebeau (Fr.)	MISC.CRIMES	FR.
ENGELMANN (see ENGELMAN)	255179						
ENGELMANN, Fritz (see ANGERBAUER, Friedrich)	257874 / 196158	M			SS-Untersturmf., 150. Panzer-Bde., Meuse-Bridge, Antwerp (Bel.) 12.44	MISC.CRIMES	U.S.
ENGELMANN, Gothbold	146188	M	Ger.	95	Lt., Gestapo, Mons, Namur (Bel.) 44	RAPE	BEL.

NAME	C.R.FILE NUMBER	SEX	NATIO-NALITY	DATE OF BIRTH	RANK OCCUPATION UNIT PLACE AND DATE OF CRIME	REASON WANTED	WANTED BY
ENGELMANN, Godfried	155595	M	Ger.		Oberarzt, Army, La Roche Rosay (Fr.) 8.44	MURDER	FR.
ENGELMANN, Hans	301306	M	Ger.		Member of Gestapo at Trencin, CC Auschwitz-Birkenau (Pol.) 39-45	MURDER	CZECH.
ENGELMANN, Rudolf	194093	M	Ger.	00	Obermaat-Guard, Marine Artill., CC Lueneburg, Wilhelmshaven (Ger.)	MURDER	U.K.
ENGELMAYER-SANITZER	102273	M			Dr., Kriminalrat, Gestapo, Wien (Aust.)	MISC.CRIMES	U.N.W.C.C.
ENGELS	108751	M	Ger.		SD Hptsturmfhr, Cuxhaven (Ger.) 3.45	MURDER	U.S.
ENGELS	138217	M	Ger.		Capt, 15 Police Rgt, St.Genis Laval (Fr.) 8.44	LOOTING	FR.
ENGELS	139817	M	Ger.		Capt., Waffen-SS, Asst.Director, SD, Lemberg (Pol.) 40 - 44	MISC.CRIMES	U.S.
ENGELS (or ENGLE, ENGLER, INGLE, INGALL)	142440	M	Ger.	20	Pvt., Army, 280 Bn, CC Varzin (Ger.) 12.43	MURDER	U.S.
ENGELS	186923	M	Ger.		Sgt., 3 Sich.Rgt.16, Belgium 44	MURDER	BEL.
ENGELS	255373	M	Ger.		Capt., Pz.Zerst.Coy of 1125 Gren.Rgt., Oron (Fr.) 10., 11.44	PILLAGE	FR.
ENGELS, Erich	195330	M	Ger.	11. 5.98	SS Hptsturmfhr, Leader SS Gestapo Kassel, Niederdorfelden, Hanau(Ger.)	MURDER	POL.
ENGELS, Hans	250719	M	Ger.	08	Cpl., Serv., Air Force Nr.36116 C, Liessel (Neth.) 9.44	INTERR.	NETH.
ENGELS, Heinrich	186660	M			Miner, "Adolf Mine", Merkstein (Ger.)	WITNESS	U.S.
ENGELS (or ANGELS), Henri (or Auguste)	250717	M	Ger.		Cmdt, Unit F.P. L 596072, Haplincourt (Fr.) 6.44	MURDER	FR.
ENGELS, Kurt	194307	M	Ger.	10	SS Sturmfhr, Gestapo Leitstelle, SD, Koeln, Warsaw (Ger., Pol.) 40-44	MURDER	POL.
ENGELSCHALK, Joseph	12611	M	Ger.		Pvt., Army, 110 or 111 Pz.Gren.Rgt., 2 Coy, Albine (Fr.) 6.44	MURDER	FR.
ENGELSHOVEN, Herbert	301377	M	Ger.		SS Uschfhr., residing Rotterdam, Schiedam (Neth.) 11.-12.44	MURDER	NETH.
ENGELSKIRCHE	24757	M			N.C.O., Stalag VIII B, Mechtal O.S. (Pol.)	MURDER	U.K.
ENGE SKIRCHER	226		Ger.		Camp N.C.O., Stalag	MURDER	U.K.
ENGFLSKIRCHER, Arthur	10148	M			Cpl., Army, 5 Coy, Lds.Schtz.Bn. 398, Beuthen (Ger.) 3-43	MURDER	U.K.
ENGELSMANN	23936	M			Hptsturmfhr, B H, SS Div.17-49, Montmirail (Fr.)	MURDER	FR.
ENGERT, Karl	166284	M	Ger.	23.10.77	Officer, Ministerialdirektor, SS, Ministry of Justice, Germany 43	MURDER	U.S.
ENGESSER	261187	M			Pvt., 139 Arbeitsbereich Liane, 5 Inf.Rgt.211, Alleur-lez-Liege (Bel.) 9.44	MURDER	BEL.
ENGHOF	250133	M			SS Rottfhr, Camp Osterhagen, Nordhausen (Ger.)	MURDER	U.S.
ENGHOLM	186936	M	Ger.		Lt.Col., American Legion, Lochwiza (Russia)	MURDER	FR.
ENGLAND	186337	M	Ger.		CC Duesseldorf (Ger.)	TORTURE	FP.
ENGLANDER, Joseph	183903	M	Ger.-Hung.	21. 2.95	SS-Mann, 4 SS Totenkopf-Stuba, CC Dora, Mittelbau Nordhausen, Dachau (Ger.) 43-45	WITNESS	U.S.
ENGLE (see ENGELS)	142440						
ENGLEBERT	186938	M			Guard at Prisoners Camp, Dortmund (Ger.)	TORTURE	FR.
ENGLEHARDT	193302	M			Guard in Prison, Justizvollzugsanstalten CC Frankfurt (Main), Preungesheim (Ger.) 7.-10.44	TORTURE	U.K.
ENGLEMAN	250732	M	Ger.		13 SS Police Rgt., Ferlach (Aust.) 44-45	MURDER	YUGO.
ENGLER	23938	M			Lt., Army, Pion.Bn.225, Gerardner (Fr.) 44	LOOTING	FR.
INGLER (see ENGELS)	142440						
ENGLER	155743	M	Ger.	90	S.A. in a camp, CC Emsland (Ger.) 44	MURDER	U.S.
ENGLER	167928	M	Ger.		Capt., Feldkommandantur 595, le Breuil near Saumur (Fr.) 8.44	MURDER	FR.
ENGLER	186939	M	Ger.		Sgt., Army, La Bresse (Fr.)	PILLAGE	FR.
ENGLER	261806	M	Ger.		Cpl., Art. N.D.V. 199,2235, F.P. 27046 C, Lorgies (Fr.) 9.44	MURDER	FR.
ENGLER, Friedrich	186941	M	Ger.		Civilian	MISC.CRIMES	FR.
ENGLER, Guenter	301795	M	Ger.		SS-Mann, 1 SS Pz.Div., Leibstandarte "Adolf Hitler" at Stavelot (Bel.) 12.44	MURDER	BEL.
ENGLER, Hans	251520	M	Ger.	4. 1.13	Capt., Civ., Command.z.b.V., Police, Gestapo, Command 31, Valasske Mezirici (Czech.) 2.-5.45	TORTURE	CZECH.
ENGLERS	291274	M	Ger.		Official Gestapo, Sgt. SS., Koeln (Ger.)	MISC.CRIMES	U.S.
ENGLING, Paul	145370	M		87	SS, CC Flossenburg (Ger.)	WITNESS	U.S.
ENGLISCH, Hans	252074	M			Lt., Beernem (Bel.)	WITNESS	BEL.
ENGLMANN	186361	M	Ger.		Prof.Dr., Physician, CC Ravensbrueck, Hohenlychen (Ger.) 5.44	MURDER	FR.
ENGMANN	194304	M	Ger.		Cpl., Feld-Gend., Ploermel (Fr.) 6.44	TORTURE	FR.
ENGWER, Walter	142754	M	Ger.	27. 6.15	Prisoner, CC Buchenwald (Ger.) 6.45	MURDER	U.S.
ENKELMANN (see ENGELMANN)	189690	M					
INKMANN	1374	M	Ger.		N.C.O., Army, H.G.Div., 8 Coy, 11 Bn.	MISC.CRIMES	U.K.
ENLEWEILER	147177	M			Crim.Asst., Sipo, CC Mauthausen (Aust.) 39-45	MURDER	U.S.
ENNEN, Hermann	250995	M	Ger.		Cpl., 377 Jaeger Rgt., Vinkt (Bel.)	TORTURE	BEL.
ENO, Heinrich	250996	M	Ger.		Pvt., 377 Jaeger Rgt., Vinkt (Bel.)	MURDER	BEL.
ENORLISCH, Auguste	167747	M	Ger.	28. 8.04	SS Uschfhr., Struthof (Fr.) 43-44	MURDER	FR.
ENRICK	23942	M	Ger.		Capt. Chief, Geheim Agent C.I.E. Brandenburg, Pont St.Esprit (Fr.)	MURDER	FR.
ENSELING	186360	M	Ger.		SS Hptsturmfhr, SS Div."Das Reich", 2 Bn., Tulle (Fr.) 5.44	MURDER	FP.
ENSEN	139088	M	Ger.		Hptsturmfhr, SS, Member of Gestapo, Osnabrueck (Ger.) 44	MURDER	YUGO.
ENSER, Max	251508	M	Ger.		SS Osturmfhr, Totenkopf-Stuba, Auschwitz-Birkenau Pol.) 12.42	MURDER	YUGO.
ENSTIP, Herbert	307088	M	Ger.		Pvt. belonging to a Pz.Div., was quartered in the Dordechtsche straat weg Rotterdam (Neth.) 1.45	PILLAGE	NETH.
ENTEMANN, Helmuth	262270	M	Ger.	27. 1.16	Hptschfhr, 51 SS Armoured Bde., Art.Detachment, Bucheres, Breviandes, Ste Savine, la Riviere de Corps (Troyes) Fr. 8.44	BRUTALITY	FR.
ENTEREST	137625	M	Ger.		Obersturmfhr, SS, CC Auschwitz (Pol.)	MURDER	U.K.
ENTRESS, Karl Richard Friedrich (or ENTREST)	227	M	Ger.	8.12.14	Dr., SS Hptsturmfhr, CC Auschwitz-Birkenau, Mauthausen (Pol., Aust.) 42-44	MURDER	U.S., FR., POL., YUGO.
EOLEIN	134880	M	Ger.	15	Dr., Lt., Asst.Physician, Army, Feldlazarett, Daun (Ger.) 12.45	WITNESS	U.S.
EPPENDAHL, Adolf	186457	M	Ger.	5. 1.89	Civilian, Lomnice-Popelkou (Czech.) 43-45	MURDER	CZECH.
EPPERLEH	186359	M	Ger.	00	Capt., Gestapo, Mimingen (Ger.)	MURDER	FR.
EPPINGER, Heinrich	31969	M			Dr., Oberlandgerichtsrat, Reichsjustizministerium, Litomerice (Czech.) 40	MURDER	CZECH.
EPPINGER, Wilhelm	187737	M	Ger.	12.11.13	Crim.Asst., Member SD, Gestapo, Brno (Czech.) 39-45	MURDER	CZECH.
EPSOM	145372	M	Ger.		CC Commander, CC Schandelah, Braunschweig (Ger.)	MURDER	BEL.
EPSTEIN	186362	M	Ger.		Hospital Chief, CC Auschwitz-Birkenau (Pol.) 42-44	MURDER	FR.
ERASMUS, Antonia	142755	F	Ger.		Civilian, Hermansdorf (Aust.) 5.44	WITNESS	U.S.
ERB, Heinrich	162292	M	Ger.	94	Mayor, Public Official, Beltershain, Griessen, Gross-Linden (Ger.) 12.44, 9.44	MURDER	U.S.
ERBACHER	135158	M	Ger.		Police Chief, Lohr (Ger.) 44	MURDER	U.S.
ERBE, Otto	183902	M			SS Sturmmann, 4 SS Totenkopfsturmbann, CC Dora, Mittelbau - Nordhausen Osterode (Ger.) 43-45	WITNESS	U.S.
ERBEN	192342	M	Ger.		Civil Servant, Forest Ministry, Spindelmuehle (Ger.)	TORTURE	BEL.

ERB - ERN

NAME	C.R.FILE NUMBER	SEX	NATIO-NALITY	DATE OF BIRTH	RANK, OCCUPATION, UNIT, PLACE AND DATE OF CRIME	REASON WANTED	WANTED BY
ERBER (or ERBES	190803	M	Ger.		Lt.,Gren.Rgt.728,Torce en Charme (Fr.)	MURDER	FR.
ERBER (or HUSTEK)	306984	M	Ger.		Uschfhr.,SS Political Department,C.C.,Auschwitz (Pol.) 42-44	MURDER	POL.
ERBER, Joseph	163682	M	Ger.	16.10.97	Schfhr.,SS,C.C.,Auschwitz (Pol.) 12.44	MURDER	FR.
ERBERT (see HERBERT)	165929						
ERBERT, Georg	260642	M	Ger.	4. 6.98	Reichsamtsleiter,Civilian,Paris (Fr.) 40-44	PILLAGE	FR.
ERBES (see ERBER)	191803						
ERBIS	250721	M	Ger.	18	Usturmfhr.,SS,commander,C.C.,Buchenwald (Ger.)	MISC.CRIMES	FR.
ERBISBERGER	306580	M	Ger.		Member,SD or Gestapo,Trandum Nr.Oslo (Nor.) 19.1.43	MURDER	U.K.
ERBS	250709	M	Ger.		Interpreter,Agent,Gestapo,Limoges (Fr.) 40-45	INTERR.	FR.
ERDMANN	23946	M			Uschfhr.,SS,Struthof (Fr.)	MURDER	FR.
ERDMANN	137085	M	Ger.	18	Pvt.,4.Coy.,610 Landesschtz.Bn.,east Russia and Brunswick (Ger.)1.-3.	TORTURE	U.K.
ERDMANN	145373	M		00- 02	Agent,Gestapo,Sachsenhausen,Oranienburg (Ger.)	MURDER	U.K.
ERDMANN	188264	M	Ger.	95	Lt.,General,7.Para Div.,Gristede (Ger.) 2.-30.4.45	MURDER	CAN.,U.S.
ERDMANN	190002	M			Lt.,Police Revier,Pozarevac (Yugo.)	MURDER	YUGO.
ERDMANN	252963	M	Ger.	16	Osturmfhr.,SS,Rgt."Gross-Deutschland",Parchim,Mecklenburg (Ger.)4-45	MURDER	U.S.
ERDMANN	257875	M			Pvt.,150.Pz.Bde.,S.I.G. Meusebridge Antwerpen (Bel.) 12.44	MISC.CRIMES	U.S.
ERDMANN	300243	M	Ger.		Oberwachtmstr.,Strafgefangenenlager-Nord,Northern Norway (Nor.)43-45	MISC.CRIMES	CZECH.
ERDMANN, Anton	167748	M		03	Sturmmann,SS,C.C.,Natzweiler,Struthof (Fr.) 43-44	MURDER	FR.
ERDMANN, Eduard	193242	M		00	Guard,Reichsjustizmin.Feldstraflager,C.C.,Finmark (Nor.)	MISC.CRIMES	NOR.
ERDMAN, Fritz	147124	M		00	Capt.,SS,Brussels (Bel.)	MISC.CRIMES	POL.,CZECH.,B
ERDMANN, Joachim	142038	M			Inspektor,Air-force,Fliegerhorst,Hopsten (Ger.)	MURDER	U.K.
ERDMANN, Kurt	195935	M		01	Krim.Sekretaer,Gestapo,C.C.,Oranienburg,Sachsenhausen,(Ger.)	MISC.CRIMES	U.K.
ERDMANNSTRAUT	142145	M			Blockfhr.,SS,Natzweiler (Fr.) 44-5	TORTURE	FR.
EREGGER	151222	M			Asst to Gen.Scheer,SIPO,SD, doctor,Kiew (Sov.Un.) 15.3.42	MURDER	U.S.
ERENMEYER	152023	M			Lt.,Gestapo,Bretagne (Fr.)	MURDER	FR.
ERFUHRT, Robert	259704	M	Ger.	05	Oschfhr.,SS,Gestapo,Deputy of commerce in Mans,Area of Angers,Maine Loire (Fr.) 42-44	MISC.CRIMES	FR.
ERFURT	23948	M			Capt.,Army,St.Loup,Bayet,Jaligny,(Fr.)	TORTURE	FR.
ERFURT	186365	M		17	Civilian,Chemnitz (Ger.) 45	TORTURE	FR.
ERGEL, Hermann	262269	M	Ger.	11. 9.09	Usturmfhr.,8.Coy.,1.Platoon,51.SS Armoured Bde.,Breviandes,Bucheres, Ste Savine,La Riviere de Corps (Troyes) (Fr.) 22.-25.8.44	BRUTALITY	FR.
ERHARD	251519	M	Ger.		Cpl.,Gend.Trupp 533 d, Annecy,Le Chablais (Fr.) 19.-21.5.44	MISC.CRIMES	FR.
ERHARDT, Adolf	12612	M	Ger.		Pvt.,110.or 111.Panz.Gren.Rgt.,2.Coy,Albine (Fr.) 29.6.44	MURDER	FR.
ERHARDT, Hans	163062	M		22	Usturmfhr.,SS Junkerschule,Braunschweig (Ger.)	MURDER	UNWCC
ERHARDT, Johann	141060	M	Ger.		Guard,SS,C.C.,Natzweiler (Fr.)	WITNESS	U.K.
ERHART, Ernst	305599	M	Ger.		Civilian,Amstetten (Aust.) 20.3.45	MISC.CRIMES	U.S.
ERICH	230	F	Ger.	12	Chief-Overseer,SS C.C. for women,Ravensbrueck,Lublin,Neuengamme (Ger., Pol.) 41-44	TORTURE	U.S.,U.K.,POL
ERICH	154450	M	Ger.		Gestapo,St.Ferdin (Fr.) 15.6.44	MURDER	U.S.
ERICH	301914	F	Ger.		SS Woman,Chief warden at C.C. Maidanek (Pol.) 40-4.44	TORTURE	BEL.
ERICHSEN	108737	M	Ger.		Sanitaetscorps,Doctor,Institute physician C.C.,Kiew (Sov.Un.) 41-42	MURDER	U.S.
ERICHSEN	301080	M	Ger.		Criminaloberseekretaer,Osturmfhr.,SS,Chief of R.S.D.,Copenhagen(Den.)43	INTERR.	DEN.
ERICKE, Artur	261936	M	Ger.		Sturmschfr.,SS,Belgrad,Vamjevo,(Yugo.) 15.8.42-10.9.44	SUSPECT	YUGO.
ERIKA	186331	F	Ger.		Nurse,C.C.,Esslingen,Ravensbrueck (Ger.)	MURDER	FR.
ERINGHAUS, Erich	255101	M	Ger.		Capt.,Army,Strasbourg,Barkenbruegge,Alexisdort (Ger.) 44-45	INTERR.	YUGO.
ERKEL	23953	M	Ger.		Major,Army Wam 82,Mentone (Fr.) 44	MURDER	FR.
ERKELE	194302	M	Ger.		Member,SD,Nice (Fr.) 7.7.44	MURDER	FR.
ERKENS	24746	M			Adjutant,Army,Roermond (Neth.) 24.9.44-27.10.44	TORTURE	U.S.
ERKLEBEN	259298	M			Kreisleiter,Camp Thekla near Leipzig (Ger.) 18.4.45	MURDER	U.S.
ERLEIVEIN	251523	M	Ger.		Sgt.,Formation de chars D'assaut no.159489 B 925,St.Christophe of Chalais (Fr.) 7.44	PILLAGE	FR.
ERLEMAN	307089	M	Ger.		Reichsdeutscher from Tiel,Zoelen (Neth.) 24.10.44	TORTURE	NETH.
ERLER	185696	M	Ger.		Member,SS,Communism.Dept.,Civil.Servant,Athen (Gre.)	MURDER	GRC.
ERLINGER, Ludwig	187643	M	Ger.		Arbeitskommando,Stalag VII A,Neider,Hummel (Ger.) 23.8.44	MURDER	U.K.
ERMANN	186328	M	Ger.		Z A.A.A. 7,2.Coy.,Albine (Fr.)	RAPE	FR.
ERMEL	186326	M	Ger.		Doctor,Physician,Medicin.Aerztekammer,C.C.,Ravensbrueck,Hohenlychen (Ger.) 16.-18.5.44	MURDER	FR.
ERMERT	193225	M	Ger.		Uschfhr.,SS,C.C.,Buchenwald (Ger.) 43-45	TORTURE	U.S.
ERMINGER	186325	M	Ger.		C.C.,Obendorf (Ger.)	MURDER	FR.
ERMISCHER,Walter	250725	M	Ger.		Cpl.,Instandsetzungszug,Ol Toussus le Noble (Fr.) 11.8.44	MURDER	FR.
ERMLICH	250134	M			Cpl.,Camp Ellrich,Nordhausen (Ger.)	MURDER	U.S.
ERMMANDRAUT, Franz	186327	M		11	Uschfhr.,SS Div.Totenkopf,C.C.,Natzweiler (Fr.) 17.7.43-22.4.44	MURDER	FR.
ERNER	179888	M			Uschfhr.,SS,C.C.,Muehldorf,Ampfing (Ger.) 6.44-4.45	MISC.CRIMES	U.S.
ERNEST	29959	M			Agent,Gestapo,Troyes (Fr.)	TORTURE	FR.
ERNESTI	31988	M			Major,20.Army,Staff I a,(Nor.) 10.-11.44	TORTURE	NOR.
ERNEVIN	194303	M			Interpreter,Bar-le-Duc (Fr.) 27.11.43	MURDER	FR.
ERNS	189687	M			Doctor,C.C.,Dachau (ger.)	MURDER	BEL.
ERNSER, Josef	262271	M	Ger.	19. 4.	Uschfhr.,Gestapo,Rennes (Fr.) 43-44	MISC.CRIMES	FR.
ERNST	1375	M	Ger.		Inspektor,Naval Supply	MISC.CRIMES	U.K.
ERNST	23969	M			1st Lt., 100 Jg.Rgt. (It.) 44	MURDER	FR.
ERNST	29964	M			Lt.,Army,Maligiai,(Fr.) 44	MURDER	FR.
ERNST	131703	M		9. 8.91	Lt.Géneral,Senat President of Tribunal,Mil.Tribunal Supreme Germany, Berlin,Torgau (Ger.) 40-45	MURDER	U.K.,FR
ERNST	152024	M		05	Chief,Gestapo,Angers,Tours,Le Mans (Fr.)	MURDER	FR.
ERNST	173765	M	Ger.		Doctor,Gauamtsleiter,NSDAP (Amt fuer Volkstumfragen) 44	TORTURE	FR.
ERNST	186350	M	Ger.	13	Uschfhr.,SS,C.C.,Auschwitz (Pol.)	MURDER	FR.
ERNST	192339	M			Uschfhr.,SS,C.C.,Flossenburg (Ger.)	MURDER	U.S.
ERNST	199881	M	Ger.		Lt.,Sicherungs Rgt.194,Prads,Lajavie (Fr.) 19.8.44	TORTURE	FR.
ERNST	250713	M	Ger.		Sturmbannfhr.,SS,Einsatz Kdo.,Chief,Haut-Rhin(Fr.) 24.9.44-5.10.44	TORTURE	FR.
ERNST	250982	M	Ger.		Pvt.,3.Peloton,4.Coy.,225 Jaeger Rgt.,Vinkt,(Bel.)	MURDER	BEL.
ERNST	257978	M			Lt.,150.Pz.Bde.,Meusebridge,Antwerpen (Bel.) 12.44	MISC.CRIMES	U.S.
ERNST	300702	M	Ger.		Uschfhr.,Blockfhr.,Official Executioner,Execution Block No.11,C.C., Auschwitz,Birkenau (Pol.) 40	MISC.CRIMES	FR.
ERNST, Adam	260541	M	Ger.	14. 1.09	Guard,SS, C.C.,Natzweiler (Fr.)	SUSPECT	FR.

NAME	C.R.FILE NUMBER	SEX	NATIO-NALITY	DATE OF BIRTH	RANK OCCUPATION UNIT PLACE AND DATE OF CRIMES	REASON WANTED	WANTED BY
ERNST, Alfred	192775	M	Ger.		Oberwachtmeister,Schupo,C.C.Falstad (Nor.) 41-44	MURDER	NOR.
ERNST, Bors	123976	M	Ger.		Civilian-Farmer,Neu Wuhmsdorf (Ger.) 6.44	MURDER	U.S.
ERNST, Christian	186657	M	Ger.	13	Assistant Foreman,Adolf Mine,Merkstein (Ger.) 42-44	WITNESS	U.S.
ERNST, Dietrich	307090	M	Ger.	3.11.08	Sturmbannfhr.,Chief,Regional Gestapo,Maine-et-Loire,Indre-et-Loire,Inferieuse,Sarthe-et-Mayenne (Fr.) 42-44	MURDER	FR.
ERNST, Hans, Dietrich	116735	M	Ger.	3.11.08	Major,SS-Sipo,Paris (Fr.) 42	TORTURE	U.S.
ERNST, Josef	194820	M	Ger.	99	Oberfeldpol.Inspector,Geheime Feldpolizei,Averoff,Athens (Grc.) 43	MISC.CRIMES	U.K.
ERNST, Otto	151220	M	Ger.		Police-Leader,Police,Civilian,C.C.Wankun (Ger.)	MURDER	U.S.
ERNST, Walberga	190230	F	Ger.		Secretary,Camp Official,C.C.Dachau (Ger.)	MURDER	BEL.
ERNSTBERGER	186656	M	Ger.		Obersturmfhr.,SS,C.C.Gross-Rosen (Ger.)	TORTURE	U.K.
ERNSTBERGER, Walter	147183	M		15 - 22	Lt.,SS,C.C.Mauthausen (Aust.) 41-45	MURDER	U.S.
ERP	151219	M			Blockleader,C.C.Mauthausen (Aust.) 41-45	MURDER	U.S.
ERP, Heinrich	62276	M	Ger.		Leader,Civilian,NSDAP,Beltershain (Ger.) 12.44	MURDER	U.S.
ERPF	258159	M	Ger.		Cpl.,2 Coy.,Signal Troops,Bolnes (Neth.) 45	INTERR.	NETH.
ERSER	141311	M	Ger.		Army,Oflag 3 B,Capt.,C.C.Eichstatt (Ger.)	MURDER	U.K.
ERSTLING, Gerhard	193572	M	Ger.		Staff-Sgt.,SD,Sipo,Assen (Neth.) 40-45	TORTURE	NETH.
ERTEL	155737	M	Ger.		Capt.,Army,Morlacx,St.Pol de l a 44	MURDER	U.K.
ERTEL	199615	M	Ger.		SS-Obersturmfhr.,SS,C.C.Lidice zech.)	MISC.CRIMES	CZECH.
ERTEL de RACHATS	186353	M	Ger.		Camp-Chief,C.C.Fechenheim (Ger.	TORTURE	FR.
ERTELL	191654	M	Ger.		Member,O.T.,Civil Servant,Ponpoint (Fr.) 41	MURDER	FR.
ERTHEL, Georg	306362	M	Ger.	17. 2.91	SS-Sgt.,C.C.Buchenwald (Ger.) 38-43	MURDER	BEL.
ERTL, Walter	188170	M	Ger.	00	SS-Sturmscharfhr.,SS-Gestapo,Koblenz (Ger.)	MURDER	BEL.
ERTMANN	250984	M			Lt.General,16 Huebner Rgt.,6 Coy.,Kinrooo (Bel.)	MURDER	BEL.
ERTMANN	259079	M			Lt.General,Wanted as defendant,possibly Witness,	WITNESS	U.S.
ERVIN	23969	M			Lt.,Army,Cahraix (Fr.)	MURDER	FR.
ERWIN	251515	M	Ger.		Member,Gestapo,Alencon (Fr.) 40-44	INTERR.	FR.
ERWIN, Luck	186354	M	Ger.	05	Member,Gestapo,SD,Deville (Fr.) 6.44-7.44	MISC.CRIMES	FR.
ERZEN, Wilibald	187740	M	Ger.	10. 9.12	Employee,SD,Gestapo,Bruenn (Czech.) 39-45	MURDER	CZECH.
ESBACH, Hans	193879	M	Ger.		Adjutant,Army,Fp.No.30463 D,Blayde (Fr.) 6.44	TORTURE	FR.
ESCH	24747	M			Guard,C.C.Hinzert (Ger.) 43	TORTURE	U.S.
ESCH	31389	M			Oberst,20 Army Comd.,200 Geb.Jg.Rgt.,1 Geb.Div. 110. - 11. 44	MURDER	NOR.
ESCH	130109	M			Obersturmfhr.,SS,C.C.Nordhausen (Ger.) Dora Mittelbau	MURDER	U.S.
ESCH	154456	M			Oberscharfhr.,SS,probably 3 SS Baubde, C.C.Wieda near Gardelegen (Ger.) 45	MURDER	U.S.
ESCHEBACH	162832	M	Ger.	08	SS-Mann,SS Wirtschaft Verw.Hauptamt,Berlin,Amtsgr.C,C.C.Buchenwald (Ger.)	WITNESS	U.S.
ESCHELBACH, Willi	250130	M		28. 9.25	M.Flyer,Camp Ellrich,Nordhausen (Ger.)	MURDER	U.S.
ESCHEMANN	261201	M	Ger.		5-I,N.Rgt.,211,139 Arbeits Bereich Liane,Alleur-lez-Liege (Bel.)44	MURDER	BEL.
ESCHENBACH, Heinrich	261903	M	Ger.		Member,SS Engineers Bn.,Hradistko (Czech.) 45	SUSPECT	CZECH.
ESCHENBACHER, Rudolf	179458	M		10. 3.14	Crim.Asst.,Oberscharfhr.,Gestapo,SD,SS Leibst."Adolf Hitler", Praha (Czech.) 39-45	MURDER	CZECH.
ESCHENBERG	192337	M			C.C.Flossenburg (Ger.) 44-45	MURDER	U.S.
ESCHENBURG, Walter	189691	M	Ger.		Crim.Asst.,SD,Gestapo,SS,Mlada-Boleslav (Czech.) 45	MURDER	CZECH.
ESCHER	250990	M	Ger.		C.C.Lahde-Weser (Ger.)	INTERR.	BEL.
ESCHER, Heinrich	167927	M			Pvt.,9 Res.Gren.Rgt.,1 Coy.,Magny D'Avignon (Fr.),9.44	MURDER	FR.
ESCHERLOR, Gottfried	252961	M	Ger.	17	Employee,Gestapo,Pardubice (Czech.) 39-45	MISC.CRIMES	CZECH.
ESCHIG, Otto	305889	M	Ger.	19. 9.95	Velke,Heraltice (Czech.) 8.44	BRUTALITY	CZECH.
ESCHIMATON-TASCHMAT	23973	M			Toulouse (Fr.)	RAPE	FR.
ESCHMANN	232	M			Prison Warder,Cpl.,Camp Caen (Fr.) 6.44	MURDER	FR.
ESCHWEY, Leopold	257452	M	Ger.		Secretary, Police,Durlach (Ger.) 41	MURDER	POL.
ESELE	128873	M	Ger.		Cpl.,Camp Genova,Mantova (It.) 7.43-11.43	TORTURE	U.K.
ESER, Adolf	300457	M	Ger.		Pvt.,Interpreter,Unit 35518 D,Trebeurden,Ste-Anns-En-Tregastel (Fr.) 7.44	MISC.CRIMES	FR.
ESKIRCHEN, Gustav	186342	M			SS-Leader,Calais,Arras,Bethune,Berg-Plage,St.Pol,Berlement, Boulogne-sur-Mer,St.Omer, (Fr.) 43	TORTURE	FR.
ESKUCHEN	184278	M	Ger.		Chief,SS,C.C.Sachsenhausen (Ger.)	MURDER	FR.
ESPANOL	121261	M	Ger.		Member of NSDAP, (Ger.)44-45	BRUTALITY	U.K.
ESSEN	306078	M	Ger.		SS-Hauptscharfhr.,Hamburg-Neuengamme (Ger.) 45	MURDER	CZECH.
ISSEN, Eunny	251502	F	Ger.		Chief,Overseer,Kdo Ludwigsfeld,C.C.Ravensbrueck (Ger.)	INTERR.	FR.
ESSER	125026	M	Ger.		State Minister,Legal,Regional Level,Mayor (Fr.) 40 - 44	PILLAGE	FR.
ESSER	130188	M	Ger.		Capt.,Stalag III A,Luckenwalde (Ger.)	MISC.CRIMES	U.K.
ESSER	156602	M			Dr.,Civilian, member of photographic Staff,Einsatzstab Rosenberg (Fr.) 40 - 44	PILLAGE	FR.
ESSER, Albert	132353	M	Ger.		Camp Todt,Honsberg (Ger.) 44-45	TORTURE	U.S.
ESSER, Johannes	300246	M	Ger.	28. 3.96	Kreisleiter,NSDAP,Neus near Duesseldorf (Ger.) 12.44	MURDER	U.K.
ESSER, Lambert	250131	M		10. 1.91	SS-Unterscharfhr.,Camp Harzungen,Nordhausen (Ger.)	MURDER	U.S.
ESSER, Lucia	134838	F	Ger.		Civilian,Efferen (Ger.) 10.44	WITNESS	U.S.
ESSER, Otto	137752	M		8.12.85	Civilian,Remscheid (Ger.)	TORTURE	U.S.
ESSER, Peter	134837	M	Ger.		Civilian,Efferen (Ger.) 10.44	WITNESS	U.S.
ESSER, Trude	256699	F			Wanted as a Witness by U.S. (Ger.)	WITNESS	U.S.
ESSER, Wilhelm	257508	M	Ger.		SS-Sgt.,C.C.Nordhausen (Ger.)	MURDER	U.S.
ESSICH	257580	M			SS-T-Sgt.,Klosterwerk,Nordhausen (Ger.)	MURDER	U.S.
ESSIG	125035	M			Capt.,215 B-N,(Ger.) 1.44 - 6.44	TORTURE	U.K.
ESSIG	173269	M	Ger.	95	Capt.,427 Ld.Sch.Bn.,C.C.Oppeln (Ger.) 45	TORTURE	U.K.
ESSIG	300375	F	Ger.	25	Interpreter, Typist,Puy-de-Dome-Haute,Loire and Cantac (Fr.) 43-44	MURDER	FR.
ESSINGER	23984	M	Ger.	28. 2.08	Oberscharfhr.,SS,Gestapo,Vichy Nice (Fr.) 43-44	MISC.CRIMES	FR.
ESSINGER, Adam	305766	M	Ger.	29. 2.08	Rottenfhr.,Crim.Asst.,Si.Pol. Oslo Section IV-I-A (Nor.) 43-45	TORTURE	NOR.
ESSLER	172888	M	Ger.	20	Obersturmfhr.,SS,C.C.Buchenwald-Auschwitz (Ger. Pol.)	MURDER	U.S.
ESSLINGER, Kurt	173989	M			Work Camp,C.C.Muehldorf Ampfing (Ger.)	MISC.CRIMES	U.S.
ESSMANN	252079	M			Employee,Sipo Abt.IV D,Brussels (Bel.)	INTERR.	BEL.
ESSWEIN, Georg	305767	M		14. 5.14	Oberscharfhr.,Crim.Sec.,SS-Police,Aussendienst,Hoyanger,Sogn (Nor.) 2.45	TORTURE	NOR.
ESTNER	251524	M	Ger.		Pvt.,Alpine Troops,Feissons sur Isere (Fr.) 8.44	MURDER	FR.
ESTRICH	191982	M	Ger.		Doctor,Stalag III, Justerbog near Berlin (Ger.) 43	MURDER	FR.
ETH	162816	M	Ger.		Choir Master,Civilian,Beaulieu (Fr.) 8.44	WITNESS	FR.

ETL - FAC

NAME	C.R.FILE NUMBER	SEX	NATIO-NALITY	DATE OF BIRTH	RANK OCCUPATION UNIT PLACE AND DATE OF CRIME	REASON WANTED	WANTED BY
ETLINGER or HAAKNEUS	233	M	Ger.-Aust.	05	Hptsturmfhr.,cmdt.,C.C.Mauthausen (Aust.), Vught (Neth.) 40-43	MURDER	NETH.,BEL
ETRAUER	191981	M			Capt.,9 Inf.Div.,361 Regt. or 85 Regt.,Ius,La Croix,Haute (Fr.) 7.44	MURDER	FR.
ETRICH,Wolfgang	186333	M		30.9.08	SS-Member,Paris,Bruessel (Fr.,Bel.) 8.-11.44	PILLAGE	FR.
ETSCHEID	234	M	Ger.		Sturmfhr.,SS,Boten-Camp (Nor.) 3.42-43	MURDER	YUGO.
ETSCHEID	252078	M	Ger.		Crim.secretary,Sipo,Abt.IV E,Bruessel (Bel.)	INTERR.	BEL.
ETSCHMANN,Willi	166302	M	Ger.		Capt.,Ortskommandantur,Recaro (It.) 1.45	MURDER	U.S.
ETTEL,Hans	167926	M	Ger.		Pvt.,9 Res.Gren.Regt.,1 Coy.,Magny D'Anigon (Fr.) 9.44	MURDER	FR.
ETTER or ETTING	135538	M	Ger.		Lt.,Army,Arnheim to Zutphen (Neth.) 9.44	WITNESS	U.K.
ETTERMANN see FLEISCHMANN, Walter	254784						
ETTING see ETTER	135538						
ETTL,Josef	187739	M	Ger.	23.2.07	Crim.asst.,SD,Gestapo,Bruenn (Czech.) 39-45	MURDER	CZECH.
ETTLINGER	259634	M	Ger.		Cpl.,probably 9 Coy.,54 Regt.of the Airforce,Plougasnou Finistere (Fr.) 7.44	INTERR.	FR.
ETTRICH	301626	M	Ger.		Cpl.,Feldgendarmerie at Chateaubriant (Loire-Inferieure),Le Teillais (Loire-Inferieure) (Fr.) 7.44	MURDER	FR.
ETTRISCH	194819	M	Ger.		SS-Uscharfhr.,SS,C.C.,Lublin (Pol.) 40-43	MURDER	POL.
ETZINGER,Guenther	186320	M	Ger.		SS-Sturmmann,SS-Leibstandarte "Adolf Hitler",Stavelot (Bel.)	MURDER	BEL.
EULER	257363	M	Ger.		SS-guard,Hauptwachtmeister,SS,slave labour camp,Beisfjord near Narvik (Nor.) 6.-11.42	BRUTALITY	YUGO.
EULER,Hans	154454	M		28	Kameradschaftsfuehrer,Hitler-Jugend,C.C. near Gardelegen (Ger.) 4.45	MURDER	U.S.
EULER,Philipp	147430	M		28.3.08	Truppfhr.,Volkssturm,Habichthorst Krs.Bremen (Ger.) 4.45	MURDER	U.S.
EULHEIM	193880	M			Ordonnance,Flak-Regt."Hermann Goering",I Div.,La Bastide d'Armagnac (Fr.) 2.43	PILLAGE	FR.
EUNUK	23988	M	Ger.		Kraftfahrstellen-Fuehrer,Abwehr,Pont St.Esprit (Fr.)	MURDER	FR.
EUSTACHI	305845	M	Ger.		Pvt.,1 Aufkl.Abt.,3 Coy.,2 Col.,XV Div.Afrika-Korps, St.Leger (Arlon) 9.44	MISC.CRIMES	BEL.
EUTENEUER	261195	M	Ger.		Cpl.,5-I Regt.211,139 Arbeitsbereich Liane,Alleur-Lez-Liege (Bel.) 9.44	MURDER	BEL
EVANS see ECKERT	250733						
EVELL	125414		Ger.	95	Employee,civilian,railway,C.C.,Bitterfeld (Ger.) 12.43	MISC.CRIMES	U.K.
EVELSBERG	152026	M			Manager,command 715, (Ger.)	TORTURE	FR.
EVERS	12613	M			Camp-leader,Organisation Todt,Cherbourg (Fr.) 43	MURDER	FR.
EVERS,Alfred	260073	M	Ger.		SS-Sturmfhr.,slave labour camp,Botn near Rognan (Nor.) 8.42-3.43 and 4.43-5.45	BRUTALITY	YUGO.
EVERS,Heinrich	121228	M			N.C.O.,Organisation Todt,Ile d'Aurigny (U.K.)	TORTURE	FR.
EVERTH,Bruno	251509	M	Ger.		Rottenfhr.,SS,Auschwitz-Birkenau (Pol.) 42	MURDER	YUGO.
EWALD	23893	M			Adjutant,Army,Jaligny (Fr.) 44	MURDER	FR.
EWALD	125036		Ger.		Korvetten-Kapitaen,Navy-Regional,Termstedt,Bez.Bremen (Ger.) 2.-6.44	MISC.CRIMES	U.K.
EWALD	186348	M	Ger.		Capt.,2 Fallschirmjaeger-Div.,Fallsch.Jg.Regt.,2 Bn.,Plouzané (Fr.) 44	MURDER	FR.
EWE see LEWE	137558						
EWE,Karl	133781	M			SS-Uscharfhr.,C.C.Buchenwald (Ger.)	TORTURE	U.S.
EWERING	190003	M			Sgt.,Gestapo,C.C.,Banjica (Yugo.) 40-45	MURDER	YUGO.
EWERS	183129	M			SS-Sturmmann,4 SS-Totenkopf-Stuba.,C.C.Dora-Mittelbau,Nordhausen, Osterode (Ger.) 43-45	WITNESS	U.S.
EWERT	1376	M	Ger.	95 - 00	Lt.Col.,Army, (It.) 7.44	MISC.CRIMES	U.K.
EWERT	186321	M			SS-Gruppenfhr.,Waffen-SS,Pz.Div."Adolf Hitler",1 Ers.Bn.,2 Zug, 2 Gruppe,Stavelot Parfaudry (Bel.) 12.44	MURDER	U.S.
EWES	235	M	Ger.		Usturmfhr.,SS,Boten-Camp (Nor.) 3.42-43	MURDER	YUGO.
EXNER,Egon	301307	M	Ger.		Member of the Gestapo at Trencin,C.C.Oswiecim-Birkenau (Pol.) 39-45	MURDER	CZECH.
EXNER,Theodore	193224	M	Ger.		SS-Oscharfhr.,C.C.Buchenwald (Ger.) 42-45	TORTURE	U.S.
EYDAM,Karl	179985	M	Ger.	08	SS-Hptscharfhr.,SD,Sipo,Metz (Fr.)	MISC.CRIMES	U.N.W.C.C.
EYER,Hermann	258568	M	Ger.		Surgeon,Dr.phil.,Dr.med.,University Erlangen near Nuernberg, Cracow and Lwow (Pol.) 39-44	INTERR.	POL.
EYIARDI,Leopold	193251	M	Ger.	10.3.78	Ortsgr.Propagandaleiter,N.S.D.A.P.,Neudorf (Czech.) 38-45	MISC.CRIMES	CZECH.
EYLERS	251504	M	Ger.		SS-Osturmbannfhr.,Dr.,SS,C.-section of SD,Leitabschnitt,Prag (Czech.) 39-45	MURDER	CZECH.
EYIMANN,Karl,Heinz	252081	M	Ger.	9.11.13	Member,Gestapo,Hradec,Kralove (Czech.) 39-45	MURDER	CZECH.
EYRICH	23898	M			SS-Scharfhr.,civilian,C.C.Struthof (Fr.) 42-44	MURDER	FR.
EYRING,Helmuth	186346	M	Ger.		2 Bn.,469 Inf.Regt.,198 Inf.Div.,Le Tholy (Fr.) 11.44	PILLAGE	FR.
FABER,Fritz	258784	M	Ger.		Erkrath (Ger.) 11.44	WITNESS	U.S.
FABER,Hans	72098	M			SS-Uscharfhr.,correspondant,Reutlinger Zeitung,Struthof (Fr.)	MURDER	FR.
FABER,Johann	161742	M	Ger.		Chief,Kriegsgefangenen-Arbeitskdo.,Erkrath (Ger.) 3.42	MURDER	U.K.
FABER,Mathias	306363	M	Ger.	20.8.12	SS-Pvt.,C.C.Buchenwald (Ger.) 5.38-10.43	MURDER	BEL.
FABER,Max	250742	M			Pvt.,Camp Ellrich,Nordhausen (Ger.)	MURDER	U.S.
FABER,Werner	12614	M	Ger.		Pvt.,Army,110 or 111 Pz.Gren.Regt.,2 Coy.,Gourdon (Fr.) 6.44	MURDER	FR.
FABESCH,Heinrich	253833	M	Ger.	24.2.81	Manager,Factory at K.Dvur (Czech.) 44	INTERR.	CZECH.
FABI,Michael	256549	M	Ger.		Pvt.,SD,Foix (Fr.) 11.42-8.44	MURDER	FR.
FABIAN	166264	M	Ger.		Major,Abwehr,Warsaw (Pol.) 42	WITNESS	U.S.
FABIAN	192933	M		17 or 18	Uscharfhr.,SS,C.C.Buchenwald (Ger.)	TORTURE	U.S.
FABISCH	83260	M		16	Oscharfhr.,C.C.Sachsenhausen (Ger.)	MISC.CRIMES	FR.
FABLER	236	M	Ger.		Lt.,Army,Dax (Fr.) 44	MURDER	FR.
FABRICIUS,Hans,Eugen,Stephan	258944	M	Ger.	6.4.91	Gauamtsleiter,Oberbereichsleiter,Dr.,R.D.B.,organizer of Parliament of N.S.D.A.P.,Ambassador to Rumania	SUSPECT	U.S.
FABRIZIUS,Peter	190245	M	Ger.		Gestapo,H.Q.,Koeln (Ger.) 43-45	MURDER	U.K.
FABRY,Georges	72101	M		18.9.97	Usturmfhr.,49 Pz.Bde.,SS,Montmirail (Fr.)	MURDER	FR.
FACCHUTTAN see FALCHENTALD	147144						
FACHING	194231	M	Ger.		SS-Hptsturmfhr.,12 SS-Pz.Div."Hitler-Jugend",26 SS-Pz.Regt.,8 Coy., Caen (Fr.) 6.-7.44	TORTURE	CAN.
FACHS	254134	M	Ger.		Sgt.,29 Pz.Gren.Regt.,3 Pz.Gren.Div.,Robert-Espagne (Fr.) 8.44	MISC.CRIMES	FR.
FACHUR,Karl	72102	M			Court martial officer,Landgerichtsrat,Reichsjustizministerium	MURDER	FR.
FACK,Carl	262339	M			L.O.D.N.A.O.D.,wanted as a witness to the shooting of an unarmed American soldier,Appen (Ger.) 1.44 or 6.44	WITNESS	U.S.
FACKERT,Heinrich	195118	M	Ger.		Civilian,Luxembourg (Lux.)	MURDER	LUX.

FAC-FAR

NAME	C.R.FILE NUMBER	SEX	NATIO-NALITY	DATE OF BIRTH	RANK OCCUPATION UNIT PLACE AND DATE OF CRIME	REASON WANTED	WANTED BY
FACKLER	173416	M			Specialist Officer,Army Oberkdo.,Valence(Fr.)	TORTURE	FR.
FACOBI, Harst	256513	M	Ger.		Oschafhr.SS CC Dora,Nordhausen(Ger.)	MURDER	U.S.
FACTAKE	12615	M			Pvt.110 or 111 Panz.Gren.Regt.3 Group,Gourdon(Fr.)6.44	MURDER	FR.
FACTAKE	187943	M			Sgt.110 or 111 Panz.Gren.Regt.,Albine(Fr.)	MURDER	FR.
FADEN	305846	M			Pvt.1 Aufkl.Abt.3 Coy.2 Col.XV Div.Afrika Korps,St.Leger(Arlon)9.44	MISC.CRIMES	BEL.
FADER	122705	M	Ger.		Sgt.Army,Kreis Briesen(Pol.)	MURDER	U.K.
FADER	256512	M			Oschafhr.SS,CC Dora,Nordhausen(Ger.)	INTERR.	FR.
FAEHNLE, Erwin	253834	M	Ger.	15. 6.09	Engineer,Plant of Waldenmaien,Heidenheim(Ger.)41-45	BRUTALITY	POL.
FAENRICH, Julius	250166	M		05	SS Rottenfhr.Camp Harzungen,Nordhausen(Ger.)	MURDER	U.S.
FAERMANN, Christ.Wilh. Bernhard	134842	M		09	Civilian,Farmer,Meetschow(Ger.)	MURDER	U.S.
FAERT, Nicholas	161652	M	Ger.	06.	Sgt.Airforce Luftgau,CC Eggemoen Honefoss(Nor.)	MURDER	NOR.
FAERMANN	261937	M			Osturmfhr.SS,Gestapo,Belgrad(Yugo./Serbia)39-45	MISC.CRIMES	YUGO.
FAUSTEL, Paul	255138	M	Ger.	3. 7.99	Employee,Gestapo,State Service,Kolin,Benesov(Czech.)39-45	MURDER	CZECH.
FAFERRE or LAFEURE	155419				Major,Commandant Stalag 10B,CC Sandbostel,8.43	MURDER	U.S.
FAGAI	192066	M	Ger.	00	Pvt.Land.Schtz.Bn.,Cosel(Ger.)6.-12.40	TORTURE	U.K.
FACUT	189907	M			Lt.CC Hammerstein(Ger.)2.45	TORTURE	YUGO.
FAHL, K.	28834	M			Major,Army SS Regt.Deutschland 16 Coy.,Aussonne(Fr.)5.44	MURDER	FR.
FAHLE	305847	M			Pvt.1 Aufkl.Abt.3 Coy.2 Col.XV Div.Afrika Korps,St.Leger(Arlon)9.44	MISC.CRIMES	BEL.
FAHNBAUER	153367	M		91	Sgt.Waffen SS,CC Hohenrteim near Plattling(Ger.)2.-5.45	MURDER	U.S.
FAHNDRICH	141526	M	Ger.		Dr.,Stabsarzt,CC Hohenlychen,Ravensbrueck(Ger.)5.44	TORTURE	FR.
FAHNENJUKER, Otto Heinr.	72103	M			Adjudant-Chef,Army,Regt.71,10 Coy.,Carassonne(Fr.)	TORTURE	FR.
FAHNER	161743	M	Ger.		SS Obersturmfhr.Gestapo,Bratislava(Czech.)42-44	SUSPECTS	CZECH.
FAHNINGER	307092	M			Commander,Bn.517,Inf.Regt.Croatia,Sabac,Macva(Serbia)11.41	MURDER	YUGO.
FAHR, Adam	250165	M			Schuetze,Camp Monowitz,Nordhausen(Ger.)	MURDER	U.S.
FAHRENHALZ	124201	M			Oberwachtmeister,Polizei,Buetzow(Ger.)	TORTURE	NOR.
FAHRENHOLTZ	300542	M	Ger.		Departm.Chief,S.D.Worked with Dr.Schoengarth,General der Polizei,Amsterdam(Neth.)10.44	MURDER	NETH.
FAHRNARD or WORNOW, FARNER, VARNAR, FARNAFF, FARANOFF, VORNOF	142527	M	Ger.	00 or 05	Sgt.Guard,Stalag Luft IV,Kiefheide(Ger.)7.44	TORTURE	U.S.
FAHRNBAUER, August	305594	M	Ger.		Member,CC Personel,CC Flossenburg,Hersbruck,Wolkenburg,Ganacker,Leitmeritz(Ger.CSR)1.42-5.45	MURDER	U.S.
FAHRNLEITNER, Hermann or FARNLEITNER	307093	M	Ger.		Gestapo station Ptuj Slovenia(Yugo.)12.44	TORTURE	YUGO.
FAIK, Carol	186997	M			Army,Crete(Grc.)	MURDER	GRC.
FAKNDAHL	176715	M			SS Unterscharfhr.CC Muehldorf,Ampfing(Ger.)6.44-4.45	MURDER	U.S.
FAKTOR	250164	M			Camp Rossla,Nordhausen(Ger.)	MURDER	U.S.
FALB see FALK, Hans	161745						
FALCH, Hans	193483	M			Gruppenfhr.Organisation Todt,Firm of Stuag,Tommenes,Morsry(Nor.)	TORTURE	NOR.
FALCHENTALD or FACCHUTTAN	161744	M	Ger.		Lt.Army,Nachr.Gruppe de Transm.34304,Lamanon(Fr.)6.44	MURDER	FR.
FALCK, Otto	301407	M	Ger.		Member,SS Cpl.S.D.of Clermont Ferrand,Aulnat(Puy-de-Dome)(Fr.)6.-7.44	MURDER	FR.
FALGAS	72106	M			Inspektor,Milice Inspektor,Montpellier(Fr.)8.44	TORTURE	FR.
FALGER, Josef	142489	M	Ger.		Chief Director Civilian,Stadtwerke,CC Bielefeld(Ger.)11.43	TORTURE	U.S.
FALK	141527	M			Prof.Dr.,Oberstabsarzt,Hohenlychen,Ravensbrueck(Ger.)5.44	TORTURE	FR.
FALK, Hans or FALB	161745	M			SA Mann,2/351 Ger.Coy.,Schutzen near Vienna(Aust.)3.45	MURDER	U.S.
FALK, Heinrich	170891	M			Freiensee(Ger.)9.44	WITNESS	U.S.
FALK, Karl Heinz	301408	M			SS Sgt.CC Dachau(Ger.)4.41	MISC.CRIMES	FR.
FALK, Otto	121240	M			Member Gestapo,Clermont-Ferrand(Fr.)	WITNESS	FR.
FALKE	141528	M			Sgt.6.Coy.Land.Schtz.Bn.492,Dortmund(Ger.)	LOOTING	FR.
FALKE, Enno	141529	M			Pvt.Feldgendarmerie 585,Vendome(Fr.)	MURDER	FR.
FALKE, Erich	300958	M			SS Osturmfhr.official of S.D.Leitabschnitt Prague,Oswiecim-Birkenau (Pol.)39-45	MURDER	CZECH.
FALKENBERG or FALKENBURG	132808	M	Ger.	93	General-Practioner-Arzt,Stalag IXC,Hildburghausen(Ger.)12.40-7.43	TORTURE	U.K.
FALKENBERG, Erich	254334	M			Oschafhr.Panzer Spaeh Coy.12 SS Panz.Div.,St.Sulpice sur Risle Eure (Fr.)6.44	WITNESS	U.S.
FALKENBERG, Walther	306117	M			Crim.Asst.,Copenhagen(Den.)Autumn 43	INTERR	DEN.
FALKENBURG see FALKENBERG	132808						
FALKENSTEINBERG, Georg	141532	M			CC Dora(Ger.)43	MURDER	FR.
FALKENSTORF, Willi	260858	M			German policeman,Lt.,Malchin(Ger.)Sommer 44	MURDER	U.S.
FALLBOHMER	39693	M	Ger.		SS Kanonier,SS Div.F.P.No.48963B,St.Sulpice,Montmusson(Fr.)8.44	MURDER	FR.
FALLDORF	192941	M	Ger.		CC Kapo Buchenwald(Ger.)42-45	MURDER	U.S.
FALLENSTEIN	193951	M			SS Pvt.,Stavelot(Bel.)	MURDER	BEL.
FALLER, Hermann	121241	M			SS Rottenfhr.KL Struthof(Fr.)	TORTURE	FR.
FALLER	141533	M	Ger.		Doctor,Yawarano(Ger.)	LOOTING	FR.
FALLER, Arthur	141534	M	Ger.	95	Gendarm,Gendarmerie Schollack(Ger.)	MURDER	FR.
FALLTH	141535	M	Ger.		Chief Police,Lipperverod(Ger.)	TORTURE	FR.
FALTEN	186309	M	Ger.		2nd Lt.Army,Quatrevent(Fr.)	MURDER	FR.
FALTER, Hermann	121242	M	Ger.		Civilian,Contremaitre usine Neurod(Ger.)	TORTURE	FR.
FALTERMEYER or FALTERMAIER	155399	M	Ger.	05	Sgt.Army,Bergen(Nor.)7.43	MURDER	NOR.
FALTHAUSER, Valentin	147764	M	Ger.	28.11.76	Director,Civilian,Kaufbeuren(Ger.)8.44	MURDER	FR.
FAMMERS, Wilhelm	250741	M			Flyer,Camp Ellrich,Nordhausen(Ger.)	MURDER	U.S.
FANDRICH	135539	M	Ger.		Oberhauer,Civilian,Jaworzno(Pol.)2.43	MISC.CRIMES	U.K.
FANDRICH, Hugo	191876	M			SS Pvt.L.A.H.SS Panz.T.Regt.Stabs Coy.,Ligneuville,Stoumont(Bel.)12.44	MURDER	U.S.
FANGOHR, Ilse	188213	F	Ger.	23. 2.12	Employee,S.D.Gestapo,Brno(Czech.)39-45	WITNESS	CZECH.
FARANOFF see FAHRNARD	142527						
FARBER	129014	M			Fallschirmjaeger Regt.5,Nachrichtenzug,Hainaut(Bel.)9.44	MURDER	BEL.
FARBLE	134862	M			Guard,Military Kdo.CC 827 Bn.2 Coy.,Maria-Kulm near Falkenau(Czech.)44	MURDER	U.S.
FAREMBRUCK	261033	M			Col.Patrol-Corps,Sued-Frankreich,Vaucluse-Bouche du Prov.Rhone-Gard-Var-Bassesalpes(Fr.)44	MISC.CRIMES	FR.
FARKAN, Karl	142524	M	Ger.		Civilian,Employee,Plettenberg(Ger.)4.45	TORTURE	U.S.
FARLER see FERBER	39682						
FARLEIGH	29889	M	Ger.		Sgt.Army,KL.7.44	MISC.CRIMES	U.K.
FARMANEK, Reinhold	141538	M	Ger.			MURDER	FR.
FARMANN	72117	M			Capt.Police-Sipo,Lille(Fr.)10.43	MURDER	FR.

FAR - FEH

NAME	C.R.FILE NUMBER	SEX	NATIO-NALITY	DATE OF BIRTH	RANK	OCCUPATION	UNIT	PLACE AND DATE OF CRIME	REASON WANTED	WANTED BY
FARNAFF (see FAHRNARD)	142527									
FARNBUEHLER, Ulrich (FREIHERR ZU HEMMINGEN)	260643								WITNESS	U.S.
FARNE	29888	M	Ger.		Sgt., CC Marburg, Heydekrug, Swinemuende (Ger.) 42,44				MURDER	U.K.
FARNER (see FAHRNARD)	142527									
FARNLEITNER, Hermann (see FAHRNLEITNER)	307093									
FARR	162025	M	Ger.		Capt., 47 Feld-Gend. Bronzolo (It.) 9.43				MURDER	U.K.
FARSCH	39685	M	Ger.	11 or 12	Cpl., Army, Scheidweiler Bez.Trier, Lamsdorf (Ger.) 41				MURDER	U.K.
FARSCH, Vincent	125449	M	Ger.		Pvt., 3 Coy, 498 Lds.Schtz.Bn., Hennersdorf - Sudetenland (Ger.) 10.44				MURDER	U.K.
FASBEDERN, Johann	191949	M			Member NSDAP, Landwehr (Ger.)				MURDER	U.S.
FASCHINBAUER	171690	M	Ger.		SS Hptsturmfhr, CC Struthof Natzweiler (Fr.)				MURDER	FR.
FASCHING, Ludwig	188212	M	Ger.	11. 8.07	Crim.Secretary, SD, Gestapo, Brno (Czech.) 39-45				MURDER	CZECH.
FASCHINGBAUER	9654	M	Ger.		Osturmfhr, SS Commander of Guards, Natzweiler (Fr.) 42				TORTURE	CZECH., FR.
FASHING	167129	M	Ger.		Cpl., Feld-Gend., Montigny en Voscul (Fr.) 7.44				MURDER	FR.
FASS, Oscar	253651	M	Ger.		SS-Mann, CC Auschwitz-Birkenau Pol.) 11.42				MISC.CRIMES	YUGO.
FASSBANDER	139364	M			SS Usturmfhr, CC Flossenburg (Ger.)				TORTURE	U.S.
FASSBINDER (or ZIMMERMANN)	176707	M			Civilian, Org.Todt, CC Muhldorf (Ger.) 6.44-4.45				MURDER	U.S.
FASSE	148411	M			SS Oschfhr, CC Mauthausen (Aust.)				MURDER	U.S.
FASSEL, Eugen	162024	M	Ger.		Pvt., 3 Fusileer Army Bn., Mulheim (Ger.) 10.44				WITNESS	U.K.
FASSEL, Werner	148412	M	Ger.		Oschfhr, CC Mauthausen (Aust.) 39-45				MURDER	FR., U.S.
FASTING, Fritz	255991	M	Ger.		Lt., III,3 Funkmess-Abtl., Perigny (Fr.) 8.44				MURDER	FR.
FATTER	141882	M	Ger.	90	Capt., Stalag XX B, Willenberg, Marienburg (Ger.) 40-45				WITNESS	U.K.
FATUM, Paul	141540	M	Ger.		Rottenfhr, CC Hinzert (Ger.)				TORTURE	FR.
FAUEL (see VAUBEL)	187810									
FAUBL (see VAUBEL)	187810									
FAUDE	193484	M	Ger.		Lt., 505 Mar.Art.Abt., Karihela Kristiansund (Nor.) 43-45				TORTURE	NOR.
FAUGEL	141541	F	Ger.		Female Overseer, CC Ravensbrueck (Ger.)				TORTURE	FR.
FAUK	252091	M	Ger.		Capt., Unit L 21 228, Cormainville (Fr.) 8.44				MISC.CRIMES	FR.
FAUL	141542	M	Ger.		Civilian, Neu Ulm (Ger.) 9.43-2.45				MURDER	FR.
FAUL, Christian	250156	M			SS-Mann, CC Bodungen, Nordhausen (Ger.)				MURDER	U.S.
FAULHABER	72254	M		22. 7.14	SS Sturmbannfhr, 49 Bde, (Art.Gruppe), Montmirail (Fr.)				MURDER	FR.
FAULHABER, SON	141543	M	Ger.		Civilian, Berlin (Ger.)				MURDER	FR.
FAULHABER, Pere Senior	141544	M	Ger.		Civilian, Berlin, Engineering firm of Faulhaber, Berlin (Ger.)				MURDER	FR.
FAULK	125696	M	Ger.		Lt., or Capt., Feld-Gend., Chateaudun, Logron (Fr.) 8.44				MURDER	FR.
FAUREE (or VAN WULFFT, VAN WULFT,WULFFT,ULFFT)	305107	M			Agent, Gestapo, Driebergen and Scheveningen(Neth.) 4.-7.44				TORTURE	NETH.
FAUSEL, Albert	188211	M	Ger.	30. 4.03	Employee, Gestapo, SD, Brno (Czech.) 39-45				MURDER	CZECH.
FAUST	240	M	Ger.		Dr., Public Official, Regierungspraesident Oberschlesien (Ger.)9.39-42				MURDER	POL.
FAUST	141545	F	Ger.	15	Female Overseer, Ravensbrueck (Ger.)				TORTURE	FR.
FAUST	187942	M			110 or 111 Pz.Gren.Rgt., 2 Coy, Albine (Fr.)				MURDER	FR.
FAUST	189986	M			Frontfuehrer, Org. Todt, Pozarevac (Yugo.) 41-43				MURDER	YUGO.
FAUST	250761	M			Flyer, Camp Ellrich, Nordhausen (Ger.)				MURDER	U.S.
FAUST	261253	M	Ger.		Cpl., 2 Col., 3 Coy, 1 Aufklaer.Abt, XV Div. Africa Corps, St.Leger, District Arlon (Bel.) 9.44				MISC.CRIMES	BEL.
FAUST, Eduard	186461	M	Ger.		Interpreter, Feld-Gend., St.Jean de Luz (Fr.)				TORTURE	FR.
FAUST, Franz	140829	M	Ger.		Doctor, Civilian Camp, Hadamar (Ger.)				MISC.CRIMES	U.S.
FAUT	260964	M			SS, CC Vaihingen (Ger.) 8.44-4.45				MURDER	U.S.
FAUTH (see VAUTH)	252980									
FAUTMABER, Hermann	12617	M	Ger.		Pvt., 110 or 111 Pz.Gren.Rgt., 2 Coy, Albine (Fr.) 6.44				MURDER	FR.
FAYMONVILLE, Josef	187815	M		94	Police, CC Merkstein (Ger.) 8.-10.42				WITNESS	U.S.
FEBAY	188893	M	Ger.		Member Feld-Gend., Bar Le Duc (Fr.) 8.44				MURDER	FR.
FEBEL	144724	M		100	Oberwachtmstr, Police, CC Siegburg (Ger.)				TORTURE	FR.
FEBEL, Max	257364	M	Ger.		Org.Todt, Slave Labour Camps "Schutzkommando", Erlandet, Deusand, Trola (Nor.) 6.42-45				MURDER	YUGO.
FEBUS (see FEHMER)	134841									
FECACCIA	148320	M			Capt., CC Fermo (It.)				WITNESS	U.K.
FECHMEISTER, Wilhelm	176714	M			CC Muhldorf Ampfing (Ger.) 6.44-4.45				MURDER	U.S.
FECHNER	144723	M	Ger.		Chief of Police, Stassfurt-Leopoldshall (Ger.)				MURDER	FR.
FECHNER, Emil	192466	M	Ger.	95	Sgt., Kriegsgef.Arbeits-Bau Bn.186, Harstadt Narvik (Nor.) 42-43				MISC.CRIMES	NOR.
FECKEN, Jonny	122702	M			Guard, CC Boegermoor (Ger.)				TORTURE	U.S.
FECKER	187418	M			SS Rottenfhr, Guard, 4 SS Totenkopf Sturmbann, Camp Dora, Nordhausen, Rosen-Aslau (Ger.) 43-45				TORTURE	U.S.
FECKLER, Franz	250150	M		16. 7.95	Pvt., CC Nordhausen (Ger.)				MURDER	U.S.
FECTER, Gustav	256176	M		07	Official, Gestapo, Rzeszow (Pol.)				MISC.CRIMES	POL.
FEDERER	122503	M	Ger.	15	Lt., Army AA 503 Bde., Hilden (Ger.) 4.45				MURDER	U.S.
FEDERSELL	144722	M	Ger.	18	Uschfhr, CC Auschwitz (Ger.)				MURDER	FR.
FEDOROWICZ	260818	M			SS Oschfhr, CC Unterriexinger (Ger.) 12.44-3.45				MURDER	U.S.
FEDROWITZ	72122	M		15	SS Osturmfhr, CC Vaihingen (Ger.)				TORTURE	FR.
FEGELEIN	155414	M			Gruppenfhr, W-SS, Muenchen-Riem (Ger.) 4.?				MURDER	U.S.
FEGELEIN, Hermann	197998	M	Ger.	30.10.06	Standartenfhr, SS Kav. Bde., Lodz Warschau (Pol.) 39-42				MURDER	POL.
FEGLER, Wilhelm	142501	M	Ger.	05	Oschfhr, W-SS, Totenkopfsturmbann, Member of the Commander Staff, Bochum (Ger.)				TORTURE	U.S.
FEGELER, Wilhelm	306364	M	Ger.		SS Truppfhr, CC Buchenwald (Ger.) 5.38-10.43				MURDER	BEL.
FEHLABER	188210	M	Ger.		Crim.Asst., Gestapo, SD, Brno (Czech.) 39-45				MURDER	CZECH.
FEHLING, Hugo	160168	M	Ger.		Pvt., Inf.Rgt., 214 Div., 355 Rgt., 12 M.G.Coy, Egersund (Nor.)42-43				MURDER	NOR.
FEHLISS	166263	M	Ger.		Commander, Standartenfhr, Sipo, SS, Oslo (Nor.) 42				PILLAGE	U.S.
FEHLNER, Margarete	139137	F			SS Guard, CC Volary (Czech.) 41-45				MURDER	U.S.
FEHMAR	129965	M	Ger.		Lager Capt., CC Nuremburg (Ger.) 3.44-4.45				MISC.CRIMES	U.K.
FEHMER (or FEBUS)	134841	M		95	Capt., Army, Stalag Luft 3, Sagan (Ger.) 4.44				WITNESS	U.S.
FEHN, Gustav	260636	M		92	Lt.Col., Pz.Tr.				WITNESS	U.S.
FEHN, Paul	133786	M		05	SS Rottenfhr, CC Weimar Buchenwald (Ger.)				MISC.CRIMES	U.S.
FEHRENBERG	122676	M	Ger.		Major FA Signal Section, 466 Inf., Doerigsen (Ger.) 4.45				MURDER	U.S.
FEHRINGER, Anton	306957	M	Ger.		Kapo, CC Plaszow near Cracow (Pol.) 44				BRUTALITY	POL.
FEHRLE	129791	M	Ger.		Obersturmfhr, W-SS, Gestapo, Chief of Police, Hanau (Ger.) 3.45				MURDER	U.S.
FEHRMERS	261481	M			Major, Police PoW Camp, Bologna (It.) 6.44				MURDER	U.S.

FEH - FEL

NAME	C.R.FILE NUMBER	SEX	NATIO- NALITY	DATE OF BIRTH	RANK OCCUPATION UNIT PLACE AND DATE OF CRIME	REASON WANTED	WANTED BY
FEBE, Fritz	253631	M	Ger.		SS Rottfhr., C.C. Auschwitz,Birkenau (Pol.) 10.42	MURDER	YUGO.
FEBE, Otto	197997	M	Ger.		Cmdo.Fuehrer, Cdo. EL-76 W Stalag IV D, Langenbogen (Ger.) 9.43	WITNESS	FR.
FEICHNER, Josef	176713	M			C.C. Muehldorf,Ampfing (Ger.) 6.44-4.45	MURDER	U.S.
FEICHTNER	197996	M			W.O., Mountain-Res.Rgt., 157.Div., Plateau des Glieres (Fr.) 4.44	WITNESS	FR.
FEID	167128	M	Ger.		Lt., Div. (A.H.) 14.Rgt.Chass.Parschut.,Villey,St.Etienne (Fr.) 9.44	MURDER	FR.
FEIDER, Anni	135164	F			SS Helferin, C.C. Erfurt (Ger.) summer 44	TORTURE	U.S.
FEIERABEND	144740	M	Ger.		Uscharfhr., Neuengamme (Ger.)	MURDER	U.K.
FEIERABEND	205386	M			Kapo, official, C.C. Natzweiler (Fr.)	MURDER	U.S.
FEIERLING	144720	F	Ger.		Interpreter, Gestapo, Toulouse (Fr.) 11.42-8.44	TORTURE	FR.
FEIFFER, Walter	1689	M	Ger.		SS Oscharfhr., Dachau (Ger.)	MISC.CRIMES	U.K.
FEIGE	141378	M	Ger.		Cpl., 5.Panz. Lehert Rgt. Lager Fallingbostel, Serzy (Fr.) 8.44	WITNESS	FR.
FEIGE, Kurt	179432	M	Ger.		Sgt., 5.Pz.Lehr-Rgt.,Serzy (Fr.)	MURDER	U.S.
FEIGENSCHLAGER	125458	M	Ger.	05	Pvt., C.C. (248-GW) Peggau (Ger.) 1.45	TORTURE	U.K.
FEIGENSPAN, Walter	142495	M	Ger.		Commercial-Director, Public official, C.C.Bielefeld (Ger.) 11.43	TORTURE	U.S.
FEIGL	119406	M	Ger.		Capt., 392-169 Inf.Div. 20.Army, Nor., 10.44	MURDER	NOR.
FEIKE, Rudolf	253845	M	Ger.	4. 1.07	SS Uscharfhr., Ortsleiter NSDAP, Opava (Czech.) 45	PILLAGE	CZECH.
FEIKEL, Oskar	181563	M	Ger.	13. 4.13	Oscharfhr., Member, S.D. and Gestapo, Kolin, Kladno, Lidice (Czech.) 39-45	MURDER	CZECH.
FEIKERT	72127	M			Lt., Army	MURDER	FR.
FEIKS	192417	M			Oscharfhr., SS, C.C. Flossenburg (Ger.) 44-45	SUSPECT	U.S.
FEILER	142497	M	Ger.		Osturmfhr., SS, Gestapo, Oschatz (Hung.) 10.-11.44	MURDER	U.S.
FEILER	171691	M			Branch-director, Einsatzstab Rosenberg,Ostgebietsministerium,Orleans (Fr.) 42-44	PILLAGE	FR.
FEILMAYER	256550	M	Ger.		Oscharfhr., SS, S.D., Foix (Fr.) 11.42-8.44	MURDER	FR.
FEINDL, F.	132485	M	Ger.		Member NSDAP	TORTURE	U.K.
FEINIGER	173368	F	Ger.		Interpreter, Gestapo, Le Mans (Fr.) 12.43-1.44	WITNESS	FR.
FEINRICH	260131	M	Ger.		Gendarm, Russia-Ger. Div. "Oberland", Massif du Vercors, Isere et Drôme (Fr.) 7.-8.44	SUSPECT	FR.
FEISCHER, Hans	143398	M	Ger.	08	SS Ofhr., S.D., Gestapo, Strassbourg (Fr.) 40-43	MURDER	FR.
FEISEGGER	100010	M	Ger.		Attached to Medical-Corps C.C. Breendonck	TORTURE	BEL.
FEISTER	147337	M	Ger.		Pvt., 11.Panz.Div. Kampfgruppe "Wilde", Fr.,44	MURDER	FR.
FEISTL, Sebastian	72191	M		1.10.22	SS Oscharfhr.,51.Pz.Gren.Div. 9.Coy. 3.Platoon, Troyes (Fr.) 8.44	MURDER	FR.
FEIT or VEIDT	142046	M	Ger.	00	Sgt., Army, Ukr.,Sov.Un., 9.41-1.44	WITNESS	U.S.
FEIT	142496	M	Ger.		Regierungssekretaer, Public official, Dueren (Ger.) 6.41	WITNESS	U.S.
FEITH	177591	M	Ger.		Employee, Gestapo, Saarbruecken (Ger.)	PILLAGE	FR.
FEITLER, Josef	176712	M	Ger.		C.C. Muehldorf,Ampfing (Ger.) 6.44-4.45	MURDER	U.S.
FEIX, Carl	300067	M	Ger.		Civ. at Niedernhausen (Ger.) 10.44	BRUTALITY	U.S.
FEL, Klement	187814	M	Ger.	7. 8.90	Civ., School-inspector, Member NSDAP of District office, Marianske Lazne (Czech.)	MISC.CRIMES	CZECH.
FELBER	161398	M	Ger.		Lt., Luftwaffe III,Kampfgeschwader 100, Villandric (Fr.) 8.44	MURDER	UNWCC
FELBER, Antoine	171685	M			Sgt., Feldgendarmerie de Langes, Chalencey, Auberive, Flagen, Coiffy (Fr.) 43-44	MURDER	FR.
FELBER, Mathias	260822	M			Civ. Priest, Pastorate, Bieber (Ger.) 2.45	MURDER	U.S.
FELBINGER	250151	M			SS Uscharfhr., Camp Dora Nordhausen (Ger.)	MURDER	U.S.
FELD	121243	M	Ger.		Adjudant, Army, C.C. Stalag 122 Compiègne(Fr.) 41-44	WITNESS	FR.
FELD	186908	M	Ger.		Chief, Arbeitskommando C.C. Melk, Mauthausen (Aust.) 44	TORTURE	FR.
FELD	901084	M	Ger.		Sgt., Royallieu Camp, Compiègne Cise (Fr.) 41-44	MURDER	FR.
FELD, August	160178	M	Ger.	about 03	Uscharfhr. SS, C.C. Buchenwald (Ger.) 43	WITNESS	U.S.
FELDAUS, Heinrich	144717	M	Ger.		Member NSDAP, Helte (Ger.)	TORTURE	FR.
FELDEN	137467	M	Ger.		Osturmbannfhr. SS, Wittlich-Hinzert (Ger.) 41-43	TORTURE	U.S.
FELDER or FELNER	72075	M	Ger.		SS Assistent Chief, Klingelputz Prison (Ger.) 2.45	TORTURE	U.S.
FELDER	186659	M	Ger.	about 07	Specialist officer, SS, Stalag 10 A, Schleswig (Ger.) 5.-6.42	TORTURE	U.K.
FELDHAUS	142500	M	Ger.		Pvt., Army, Hemer (Ger.) 3.45	TORTURE	U.S.
FELDINGE	257577	M			SS Scharfhr., Sec.IV Camp Dora Nordhausen (Ger.)	MURDER	FR.
FELDINGER or FELLINGER	197995	M	Ger.		Lt., 2.Coy. 100.Bn. Mountain-Rgt., St.Germain (Fr.)7.-8.44	MURDER	FR.
FELDMAKER	142503	M			Cpl., Army, Stalag II B, C.C. Hammerstein (Ger.)	PILLAGE	U.S.
FELDMANN	253841	M	Ger.		Feldgend. Gend. Romorantin 577 F.P.22501, Orsay (Fr.) 8.44	MISC.CRIMES	FR.
FELDMANN, H.	99694	M	Ger.		SS-Mann, SS-Div., St.Salpice, Montmusson et Chateau (Fr.) 8.44	MURDER	FR.
FELDMANN, Karl	144716	M	Ger.		Rev.Oberwachtmeister, Gestapo, Toulouse (Fr.)	MURDER	FR.
FELDMANN, Paul	128854	M	Ger.	23	Pvt., Airforce, Jaeg.Rgt. 35, Jemappes, Quaregnon (Bel.) 9.44	MURDER	BEL.
FELDMAYER	12629	M	Ger.		Member, Gestapo, Cahors (Fr.) 6.44	MURDER	FR.
FELDMEYER	305619	M	Ger.		Member, SS, Amsterdam (Neth.) 10.44	MISC.CRIMES	NETH.
FELDNER see FELDER	72075						
FELDROSS	129975	M			Oscharfhr., SS Panz.Div. 2.Gren.Rgt., Malmedy (Bel.) 12.44	MURDER	U.S.
FELDSBERG, Ludwig	144726	M	Ger.		C.C. Mauthausen (Aust.) 8.44-5.45	TORTURE	FR.
FELDSCHER	165295	M	Ger.		SS, Ger.,43	MURDER	U.S.
FELDT, Christian	192465	M	Ger.		Pvt., Arb.Bau-Bn. 184, Kobbelvik (Nor.) 6.44	MURDER	NOR.
FELEN, Christiaan	195141	M	Ger.		S.A., Dorsten (Ger.) 10.44-2.45	TORTURE	NETH.
FELFER, Hans	250152	M	Ger.		SS Uscharfhr., Camp Ellrich Nordhausen (Ger.)	MURDER	U.S.
FELISOF	901908	M	Ger.		Member, Gestapo at Nove Mesto n.Vahom, C.C. Oswiecim-Birkenau (Pol.) 39-45	MURDER	CZECH.
FELIX	161746	M			Capt., SS Panz.Gren., Condorcet (Fr.) 3.44	MURDER	FR.
FELIX	250153	M			Pvt., Camp Ellrich Nordhausen (Fr.)	MURDER	U.S.
FELIXIAN, Josef	253842	M	Ger.	10. 5.23	Pvt., 13.Coy. 558.Gren.Rgt., Bruay en Artois (Fr.) 9.44	INTERR.	FR.
FELKE	144755	M	Ger.		Oberstabsarzt, Prof. Dr., C.C. Hohenlychen (Ger.) 5.44	TORTURE	FR.
FELKE, Paul	160177	M	Ger.		Volkssturm, C.C. Gardelegen (Ger.) 4.45	MURDER	U.S.
FELKEN	173372	M			Feldgend., Field-police, Germainville,Châteaudun,Logron (Fr.)	MURDER	FR.
FELKL, Anton	253656	M	Ger.	12	SS Scharfhr., Gestapo, Kolin (Czech.) 39-45	MISC.CRIMES	CZECH.
FELLECHNER, Udo	144754	M	Ger.	10	Chief, SS, Breitenstein (Ger.) 6.-11.44	TORTURE	FR.
FELLER	144752	M	Ger.		Chief, Deutz prison (Ger.)	MURDER	FR.
FELLER	252088	M	Ger.		Hauptwachtmeister, Forteresse (Fr.)	TORTURE	FR.
FELLER, Pierre	130081	M	Ger.		Now a POW having deserted from Ger.army, Allg. SS, Fr., 7.44	WITNESS	U.K.
FELLERMEIER	12620	M			Foreman, Karl Stohr, factory, Honfleur (Fr.) 5.43	MURDER	FR.
FELLINGER	72198	M			SS Mann, C.C. Struthof (Fr.)	MURDER	FR.
FELLINGER see FELDINGER	197995						
FELLINGER, Hermann	192043	M	Ger.		Civ. Geb.Reg.Rat, Vorstand d.Didier-Werke AG.,Ofenbau, Belgrade (Yugo.) 42-3.44	MURDER	YUGO.

FEL - FEU

NAME	C.R.FILE NUMBER	SEX	NATIO-NALITY	DATE OF BIRTH	RANK	OCCUPATION	UNIT	PLACE AND DATE OF CRIME	REASON WANTED	WANTED BY
FELLMANN (see DE VALERA or GOUREZ)	188717									
FELLNER, Richard	306365	M	Ger.		Uschfhr.,SS (No.321337),C.C.Buchenwald (Ger.) 5.38-10.43				MURDER	BEL.
FELLNER, Simon	176711	M			C.C.Muhldorf,Ampfing (Ger.) 6.44-4.45				MURDER	U.S.
FELMER, Wilhelm	176710	M			C.C.Muhldorf,Ampfing (Ger.) 6.44-4.45				MURDER	U.S.
FELOWEBE	130169	M	Ger.		Cpl.,Stalag 383,Hohenfels (Ger.) 10.42-4.43				MISC.CRIMES	U.K.
FELS, Hermann	252094	M	Ger.	7. or 8. 5.16	Cpl.,Parachutist, 6 Div.,17 Regt.,Nieuwaal (Neth.) 1.45				WITNESS	NETH.
FELS, Johann	173429	M	Ger.	04	Pvt.,Army,Langen Lonsheim (Ger.) 12.44				WITNESS	U.S.
FELS, Karl	257033	M			Civilian,Langen Lonsheim (Ger.) 12.44				WITNESS	U.S.
FELSBERG	144751	M			Kapo,C.C.Mauthausen(Aust.)				TORTURE	FR.
FELSKE, Willi	152198	M			Civilian,Wiewocki,Chelno (Pol.) 10.39				TORTURE	U.S.
FELTEN, Willy or Wilhelm	255993	M			Chief of the Block (Kapo),C.C.Mauthausen(Aust.)				MISC.CRIMES	FR.
FELTER, Christian	72139	M			Lt.,Pol.-Schupo,3 Bn.,49 Bde. blinde e de grenadiers,Montmirail (Fr.)				MISC.CRIMES	U.S.
FELTES, Christian	176950	M			Sturmmann,Guard,SS-Totenkopfsturmbann,C.C.Dora Nordhausen(Ger.)43-45				MURDER	U.S.
FELTES, Emil (see SAHL)	161655									
FELTIN	197994	M	Ger.	03	Hpt.Wachtmeister,Schutzpolizei,Westerbork (Neth.) 12.44				MURDER	NETH.
FELZER, Maria	254330	F	Ger.	16. 9.03	SS-Helferin,State Service-SS,Geisenheim (Ger.) 12.44-4.45				MISC.CRIMES	POL.
FEMER	124935	M			Capt.,C.C.Sagan,Stalag Luft III (Ger.) 44				WITNESS	U.K.
FENDER (or FENDA)	125702	M			SS-Obergruppenfhr.,Lt.General,C.O.of A Field-Corps and C.O. of SS-Regt. "Brandenburg"				INTERR.	U.K.
FENDNER	142502				Rottfhr.,Waffen-SS,C.C.Leipzig-Thekla(Ger.) 12.43				MURDER	U.S.
FENGLER	258707	M			Gendarmeriemeister,SS-Mann,Pol.,Metze-Hannover (Ger.) 10.-12.42				MURDER	POL.
FENGLER, Kurt	144750	M	Ger.		Civilian,Berlin (Ger.)				TORTURE	FR.
FENSKE, Paul	72093	M			Civ.,SS,C.C.Sachsenhausen (Ger.) 5.43-44				MURDER	U.S.
FENSKI	176709	M			SS-Mann,SS,C.C.Muhldorf,Ampfing (Ger.) 6.44-4.45				MURDER	U.S.
FENT	144749	M	Ger.	10	Wernigrode (Ger.)				TORTURE	FR.
FENTZLING, Wilhelm	155420	M			Civ.,Kapo,C.C.Gardelegen (Ger.) 4.45				MURDER	U.S.
FENZEL, Otto	250142	M		21. 4.07	Pvt.,C.C.Ellrich,Nordhausen (Ger.)				MURDER	U.S.
FEPKE, Hugo	122665	M	Ger.	10	N.C.O.,Army,(Formerly Teacher)				MURDER	U.S.
FERAND, Armand	144747	M		12	Civilian,Colberg (Ger.) 7.44				MURDER	FR.
FERAZICH, Karlo	253641	M	Ger.		Cook,SS,C.C.Auschwitz,Birkenau (Pol.-Ger.)41-45				MISC.CRIMES	YUGO.
FERBER (or FARLER)	39682	M			Lt.,Chief,Gendarmerie No.486,86 Corps d Armee)Cendresse(Fr.) 6.44				INCENDIARISM	FR.
FERBER, Willy	144748	M	Ger.	10. 6.03	Oschfhr.,Waffen-SS,C.C.Lublin (Pol.)				MURDER	FR.
FERCHER	161333	M			Ob.Wachtmeister,Flak Vo Messtrupp 28,Ganges (Fr.) 8.44				MURDER	FR.
FERDINAND, Hans	39692	M	Ger.		Lt., appartiendrait au regiment de securite IoIo,stationne a Pithiviers (Fr.) 4.44				WITNESS	FR.
FERDING	305796	M	Ger.		N.C.O.,Disciplinary Chief Oflag VI C,Osnabrueck,Ewersheide(Ger.)42-45				MURDER	YUGO.
FERENDSEN	119407	M	Ger.		Oberfhr.,4 B,SS-Geb.Div.Nord,20 Army,Finmark(Nor.)				MURDER	NOR.
FERFER, Hans	259366	M	Ger.		Uschfhr.,Gestapo of Poitiers Area (Fr.) 40-45				MISC.CRIMES	FR.
FERGUEN, Frank	197993	M			Cpl.,Egletons (Fr.) 3.44				INTERR.	FR.
FERLE, Michael	193056	M			Uschfhr.,Waffen-SS,C.C.Buchenwald (Ger.) 42-45				TORTURE	U.S.
FERNAND, Simon	142499	M			CampChief,C.C.Dinslaken (Ger.) 42-45				WITNESS	U.S.
FERNANDEL	144741	M	Ger.	10	SS,C.C.Natzweiler (Fr.)43-1.44				MURDER	FR.
FERNBACHER	125037	M	Ger.		Dr.,Civ.,P.O.W.-Arbeitskommando 1178,Hainsberg bei Dresden(Ger.)11.44				TORTURE	U.K.
FERNHOLZ	306958	M	Ger.		Uschfhr.,SS,C.C.Auschwitz (Pol.) 44				BRUTALITY	POL.
FERNRICH	243				Army,Lt.,Magny Darrigon (Fr.) 9.44				MURDER	FR.
FERNYDOS	250158	M			SS,Camp Rottleberode,Nordhausen (Ger.)				MURDER	U.S.
FERRACCI	190428	M			Lt.,Army,Ile d' Oleron (Fr.) 44-4.45				TORTURE	FR.
FERRANT	189984	M			Major,Army,Maribor (Yugo.)41-44				MURDER	YUGO.
FERRER, Hans	307094	M	Ger.		Uschfhr.,Gestapo at Poitiers,Chatellerault,Nirot,Angouleme,Saintes,Vienne (Fr.)				MURDER	FR.
FERRERT	144746	M	Ger.	03	Engineer,Civ.,Wuppertal,Atzfeld (Ger.)				TORTURE	FR.
FERTZEL	38936	M			Lt.,12 SS-Pz.Div.Hitler Jugend,St.Ange (Fr.) 7.-8.44				MURDER	FR.
FESCHE	130112	M			Osturmfhr.,SS,C.C.Dora Mittelbau,Nordhausen (Ger.)				MURDER	U.S.
FESLER, Helmut	188571	M	Ger.	15	Cpl.,Army,Cosel (Ger.)				MISC.CRIMES	U.K.
FESSEL, Helmut	166998	M	Ger.	20 or 21	Usturmfhr.,SS,Vipitero (Ital.) 6.45				WITNESS	U.S.
FESSER (see FISSER)	252086									
FESSLER	165562	M	Ger.		Capt.,Stammbatt.Art.Ers.Abt.,Wodecq (Bel.) 9.44				MURDER	BEL.
FESSLER	250157	M			Rottfhr.,SS,Camp Rottleberode,Nordhausen (Ger.)				MURDER	U.S.
FEST	139809	M	Ger.		Officer,W-SS,Stalag X B,Sandbostel (Ger.) 5.45				MURDER	U.S.
FEST, Anton	253642	M	Ger.	29.12.08	Osturmbannfhr.,Chief,security Police,Sarajevo (Yugo.) 9.43-4.45				MISC.CRIMES	YUGO.
FESTER	119408	M	Ger.		Major,Geb.Div., 20 Army,Com.Jg.Bn. 6-8 (Nor.) 10.44				MURDER	NOR.
FETH	1690				Oberfeldw.,Feld-Gend.Trupp 644				TORTURE	U.K.
FETH, Tony	253843	M	Ger.		W.O.,Chief,Acheux en Amienois (Fr.) 8.44				MISC.CRIMES	FR.
FETSCH, Ernst	38937	M			Sturmbannfhr.,SS-Div."Das Reich",1 Pz.Regt.,Montpezat (Fr.)				TORTURE	FR.
FETSCHER	144745	M	Ger.		Member,NSDAP,Furamoos (Ger.)				TORTURE	FR.
FETT, Bruno	160175	M	Ger.	05	SS,C.C.Buchenwald (Ger.) 41-45				WITNESS	U.S.
FETTER	254180	M	Ger.		Col.,6 Parachutist Div.,17 Regt.,Nieuwaal (Neth.) 1.45				WITNESS	NETH.
FETTERS, Else	144744	F	Ger.	25. 6.00	Guard,C.C.Buchenwald (Ger.)				TORTURE	FR.
FETZ, Jakob	252977	M	Ger.		Camp-Aeltester,SS,C.C.Neuengamme (Ger.)				INTERR.	BEL.
FETZER	142498	M	Ger.		Rottfhr.,1 Pz.Div., 2 Pz.Gren.Regt.,3 Bn.,12 Coy.,Stavelot,Malmedy (Bel.) 12.44				MURDER	U.S.
FEUCHTENSLAGER	125452	M	Ger.		Pvt.,891 Bn., 3 Coy.,Graz (Aust.) 12.44				TORTURE	U.K.
FEUCHTER	163459	M	Ger.		Guard,C.C.Berlin (Ger.)				TORTURE	FR.
FEUCHTINGER	195117	M	Ger. or Aust.		Lt.,Army,Staff "General Brunner",Treviso,Carpane,Monte Grappa(Ital) 9.44				MURDER	U.K.
FEUCHTINGER, Max Erich	192464	M	Ger.	09	Leader and Ministerialrat,Org.Todt,Einsatzgruppe,Oslo(Nor.) 43				MISC.CRIMES	NOR.
FEUCHTLENGER	167127	M	Ger.		General,Div.F,La Neuve Ville en Raon (Fr.) 9.-11.44				WITNESS	FR.
FEUCKTHUBER, Georg	176708	M	Ger.		C.C.Muhldorf,Ampfing (Ger.) 6.44-4.45				MURDER	U.S.
FEUERLEIN	173389	M	Ger.		Rottfhr.,Official,SS,Gestapo,Stavanger (Nor.)				TORTURE	NOR.
FEUERLEIN, Fritz	190051	M	Ger.		Scharfhr.,SS,C.C.Bruesa,Terezin,Gestapo (Czech.) 39-45				MURDER	CZECH.
FEUERSTEIN	163458	M	Ger.		Interpreter,Gestapo,Saone et Loire (Fr.) 43-44				MURDER	FR.
FEUERSTEIN, Charles	38940	M		91	Group-leader,NSDAP,Saverne (Fr.)				MISC.CRIMES	FR.

NAME	C.R.FILE NUMBER	SEX	NATIO-NALITY	DATE OF BIRTH	RANK OCCUPATION UNIT DATE AND PLACE OF CRIME	REASON WANTED	WANTED BY
FEUERSTEIN, Peter	191948	M	Ger.	99	Merchant, civilian, Dillingen (Ger.) 5.44	WITNESS	U.S.
FEUNG	167126	M	Ger.		Feldpolizei, Moulins, Laroche, Millay (Fr.) 8.44	PILLAGE	FR.
FEURSTEIN, Valentin	187843	M	Ger.		General, 51 mountain-corps, Cisa Pass (It.) 44	MURDER	U.K.
FEUSTEL, Fritz	195081	M	Ger.	30. 7.89	Hptsturmfhr., SS, Gestapo-chief, Kolin (Czech.) 39-45	MURDER	CZECH.
FEUSTEL, Paul	186312	M	Ger.	30. 7.99	Crim.commissar, capt., Gestapo, SD, Kolin, Benesov (Czech.) 40-45	MURDER	CZECH.
FEUVREL	144743	F			Civilian, Ulm (Ger.)		FR.
FEY	187170	M			SS-Pvt., 4 SS-Totenkopf-Sturmbann, C.C.Dora-Mittelbau, Nordhausen (Ger.) 43-45	TORTURE	U.S.
FEY	191868	M	Ger.		Civilian, Stalag IX A, Weissenhassel (Ger.) 6.41	MURDER	FR.
FEYMAYER	38944	M	Ger.		Chief, Gestapo, Cahors, Larnagol (Fr.) 4.44 and 8.44	MURDER	FR.
FEYSANG	119414	M	Ger.		Lt.Col., Abwehr, 20 Army, Finmark (Nor.) 44	MURDER	NOR.
FEZ or FREZ	72129	M	Ger.		Cpl., Army, Bn.19-548-A, Plouaret (Fr.) 8.44	MURDER	FR.
FEZ, Jacob aliases: COBES	177588	M			C.C.Neuengamme (Ger.)	TORTURE	FR.
FFOB, Rudolf	144756	M	Ger.	3. 4.08	Feldgendarmerie, Vitry le Francois (Fr.) 6.43	TORTURE	FR.
FHEWELARS see LARSEN	162072						
FHOHR, Hermann	300571	M	Ger.		Cpl., Army, 1 Coy., 377 Bn., Inf.Regt., Feldpostnr.30084, Vinkt-Meigem (Bel.) 5.40	MISC.CRIMES	BEL.
FIAIA	150316	M			Civilian, C.C.Flossenburg (Ger.)	MURDER	U.S.
FIALA, Jaroslav	258071	M		13. 9.00	Agent, Gestapo, Prag (Czech.) 40-45	MISC.CRIMES	CZECH.
FIBERG	163468	M	Ger.		Cpl., 10 Pz.Div., 36 Regt., SS, Revin (Fr.) 6.44	MURDER	FR.
FIBINGER, Josef	254331	M	Ger.	25. 9.01	Member, Gestapo, Hradec-Kralove (Czech.) 39-45	MURDER	CZECH.
FIBIOR	261608	M			SS-Uscharfhr., chief of police, Dirlewanger-Bde., Waffen-SS, Gren.Div., Sluck (Pol.) 40-44	BRUTALITY	POL.
FIBROECK	252295	M	Ger.		Pvt., 377 Jaeger-Regt., Vinkt-Meigem (Bel.)	MISC.CRIMES	BEL.
FICHEM, Wilhelm or FICHEN	252293	M	Ger.		Pvt., 377 Jaeger-Regt., Vinkt-Meigem (Bel.)	MISC.CRIMES	BEL.
FICHER	143404	M	Ger.		C.C.Auschwitz, Ravensbrueck (Pol., Ger.)	MURDER	FR.
FICHER	190427	M	Ger.		Lt., Werft-Polizei, Navy, Chautiers de Penhoet, La Baule, St.Nazaire (Fr.) 41-44	MURDER	FR.
FICHMEYER see FISCHMEYER	129004						
FICHTE	124490	M	Ger.	09	Head-paymaster, Fallschirmjaeger-Regt.z.b.V., 2 Br.Abt.IV a, Pz.Bde.150, Ardennes (Fr.) 44	MISC.CRIMES	U.S.
FICHTER	173402	M	Ger.		Mayor, public official, Fellbach (Ger.)	MURDER	FR.
FICHTL, Josef	259846	M	Ger.	14. 2.91	Major, Army, delegate to Skoda, ammunition-works, Pilsen (Czech.) 43	INTERR.	CZECH.
FICHTNER	31952	M	Ger.		Cpl., Air-Unit L.49060 B, Perigueux (Fr.)	MURDER	FR.
FICHTNER	38945	M	Ger.		Army, Feldpostnr.12816, St.Christophe de Chalieu (Fr.) 8.44	MURDER	FR.
FICHTNER	137755	M			Law-inspector, 29 Pz.Gren.Div.	WITNESS	U.S.
FICHTNER	173393	M	Ger.		Chief magistrate, occupied territories, C.C., Jihlava, Oswiecim, Birkenau (Czech., Pol.) 42	MURDER	CZECH.
FICHTNER or FUECHTNER	259941	M	Ger.		SS-Hptscharfhr., crim.secretary, SD, Gestapo; believed to be at Plattling, Trencin Slov. (Czech.) 11.44-5.45	MURDER	CZECH.
FICHTNER	301309	M	Ger.		Member, Gestapo at Trencin, C.C.Oswiecim-Birkenau (Pol.) 39-45	MURDER	CZECH.
FICK	1691	M			Osturmbannfhr., comm.of Bn.group "Goetz von Berlichingen"	MURDER	U.K.
FICK	143440	M	Ger.		Sturmbannfhr., SS, Sennheim (Fr.)	TORTURE	FR.
FICK	173156	M	Ger.		Wachtmeister, C.C.Schirmeck, Gaggenau, Rotenfels (Ger., Fr.) autumn 44	MURDER	U.K.
FICK	190672	M	Ger.		Pvt., Eis.Artl.Btty.717, St.Andries, Varsenare, Lez Bruges (Bel.) 9.44	MURDER	BEL.
FICK	197992	M	Ger.		Lt.Col., Inf.Regt., G.O. Laroserie (Fr.) 40	MURDER	U.S.
FICK	259633	M	Ger.		SS-Osturmbannfhr., cmdt., 37 Regt., 17 SS-Div., Merzig (Ger.) 9.44	MURDER	U.S.
FICK, Helmut	142485	M		8. 8.08	Capt., 4 training-Coy.in prison Zinna at Torgau (Ger.) 4.45	MURDER	U.S.
FICK, Robert	195119	M	Ger.	about 10	Employee, Gestapo, Kolin (Czech.) 39-45	TORTURE	CZECH.
FICK, Rudi	252294	M	Ger.		N.C.O., 377 Jaeger-Regt., Vinkt-Meigem (Bel.)	MISC.CRIMES	BEL.
FICKE	197991	M	Ger.		Cpl., Camp Royallieu, Compiegne (Fr.) 41-44	MISC.CRIMES	FR.
FICKE	254505	M			Capt., Gestapo, SS, SD, Bruessel (Bel.)	MURDER	BEL.
FICKER	130642	M			Hptsturmfhr., SS, C.C.Dora-Mittelbau	MURDER	U.S.
FICKER	130647	M			Oscharfhr., SS, C.C.Sachsenhausen (Ger.) 36-40	MURDER	U.S.
FICKER	250155	M			Rottenfhr., SS, C.C.Dora, Nordhausen (Ger.)	MURDER	U.S.
FICKER	254177	M	Ger.		SS-Uscharfhr., Gestapo, Paris (Fr.) 41-44	TORTURE	FR.
FICKER	306966	M	Ger.		SS-Scharfhr., C.C.Dora, Nordhausen (Ger.) 40-45	MURDER	BEL.
FICKERS	129003	M	Ger.		Rottenfhr., SS, Neuengamme (Ger.)	TORTURE	BEL.
FICKERS	152197	M	Ger.	18	Rapportfhr., SS, Hamburg (Ger.)	MURDER	U.K.
FICKERS	185264	M	Ger.		SS-officer, Arbeitsfhr., C.C.Ellrich (Ger.)	MURDER	BEL.
FICKERT	244	M	Ger.		SS-Hptscharfhr., C.C.Dachau (Ger.) 40 onward	MURDER	FR.
FICKERT	148438	M	Ger.		Cpl.(Uscharfhr.), SS, C.C.Montluc, Ellrich (Fr., Ger.) 44	MURDER	FR.
FICKERT see FIKIERT	191440						
FICKERT	195985	M	Ger.		Osturmfhr., SS, C.C.Sachsenhausen (Ger.)	MURDER	BEL.
FICKERT	197990	M			Blockfhr., C.C.Neuengamme (Ger.)	INTERR.	BEL.
FICKERT	257578		Ger.		SS-Hptscharfhr., Block-leader, Camp Dora, Nordhausen (Ger.)	MURDER	U.S.
FICKERT	259297	M			General manager of the works, Camp Thekla near Leipzig(Ger.)18.4.45	MURDER	U.S.
FICKERT, Ernst	192467	M	Ger.	12	Einsatzgruppenleiter, Org.Todt, Oslo (Nor.) 43	MISC.CRIMES	NOR.
FICKINGER	160180	M	Ger.		Director, hospital, C.C.Emsland (Ger.) 44	MURDER	U.S.
FIDDLER	128858	M	Ger.		Capt., Stalag X A, Schleswig (Ger.) 6.41-7.41	TORTURE	U.K.
FIDYKA	38946	M			Rottenfhr., SS-Div., St.Sulpice, Fortmousson, Chateau Gonthier, Laval (Fr.) 8.44	MURDER	FR.
FIEBACK, Walter	300377		Ger.		Inf.Pz.Jg.Ers.Regt.37 Plauen, Bourcy near Bastogne (Lux.) 12.44	MISC.CRIMES	BEL.
FIEBERG see WIEHBERG, Joseph	254430						
FIEBERG, Walter	171689	M	Ger.		Trustee, Gaststaette "Empire", General Governor of Poland, Poznan (Pol.) 9.39-44	MISC.CRIMES	POL.
FIEBIG	189983	M			Cmdt., Airforce, Bjelusa-Visoki Sevoina (Yugo.) 9.-12.43	MURDER	YUGO.
FIEBICH, Franz	127343	M	Ger.	93	Officier of the D.A.F., Semi-military, Cema plant Potsdam (Ger.)	TORTURE	U.S.
FIEBINGER, Josef	194043	M	Ger.	01	Employee, Gestapo, Hradec Kralove (Czech.) 38-45	MURDER	CZECH.
FIEDERLING	261202	M	Ger.		Pvt., 5-I N.Regt.211, 139 Arbeitsbereich Liane, Alleur-Lez-Liege (Bel.) 9.44	MURDER	BEL.
FIEDLER or VIEDLER	245	M	Ger.	15	Cpl., Airforce, Fornebu (Nor.)	TORTURE	NOR.

FIE - FIN

NAME	C.R.FILE NUMBER	SEX	NATIO-NALITY	DATE OF BIRTH	RANK OCCUPATION UNIT PLACE AND DATE OF CRIME	REASON WANTED	WANTED BY
FIEDLER	39681	M	Ger.		Col., Army, Monastir (Fr.) 4.43	MISC.CRIMES	FR.
FIEDLER	124489	M	Ger.		Lt.Col., Sanitaets-Abt. Bautzer Hospital, Koenigswartha (Ger.) 7.-8.44	TORTURE	U.K.
FIEDLER	137067	M	Ger.		Lt., 21.Panz.Div., Sessenheim (Fr.) 1.45	MURDER	U.S.
FIEDLER	160175	M			Mayor, Civilian, Gardelegen (Ger.) 4.45	MURDER	U.S.
FIEDLER	176706	M			Civ.,Organisation Todt, C.C. Muhldorf, Ampfing (Ger.) 6.44-4.45	MURDER	U.S.
FIEDLER	261934	M	Ger.		Bde.-Chief and Major-Gen., Polizei, SS, Belgrad and Valjevo (Yugo.) 8.42-9.44	SUSPECT	YUGO.
FIEDLER	301682	M	Ger.		Bde.-Chief, Train Mongolian "Oberland", St.Nazaire en Royans (Fr.) 7.-8.44	MURDER	FR.
FIEDLER, Anton	194962	M		17.10.04	Pvt., Levrezy, Chateau Regnault (Fr.) 4.45	WITNESS	FR.
FIEDLER, August	250162	M		27. 1.97	Rottenfhr., SS, C.C.Harzungen-Ellrich, Nordhausen (Ger.)	MURDER	U.S.
FIEDLER, Hans	257579	M	Ger.	30. 9.13	Employee, State Service (Jewish Agency), Prague (Czech.) 39-45	MISC.CRIMES	CZECH.
FIEDLER, Hermann	194044	M	Ger.	7.12.76	Civ., Leather goods factory, Trebechovice, Podorebem (Czech.) 39-45	PILLAGE	CZECH.
FIEDLER, Joachim	301061	M	Ger.		Oberarbeitsfhr., Reichsarbeitsdienst, Marianske, Lazne, Bohemia (Czech.) 42-44	INTERR.	CZECH.
FIEDLER, Joseph	133368	M	Ger.	09	Sturmscharfhr., Waffen-SS, 2.Pion.Ausb.Bn., vicinity of Passau (Ger.) 4.45	MURDER	U.S.
FIEDLER, Werner	306959	M	Ger.		Belonging to Section I, Semur en Auxois, Cote d'Or (Fr.) 8.44	MURDER	FR.
FIEDLER, Wilhelm	192109	M	Ger.		Civ. Factory Manager, Member of SS, Brno (Czech.) 45	PILLAGE	CZECH.
FIEGE	254504	M	Ger.		Employee, Sipo, Abt.III C, Brussels (Bel.)	INTERR.	BEL.
FIEGEL	143441	M	Ger.	15	Manager of Factory, Oberndorf (Ger.)	TORTURE	FR.
FIEL	143423	M	Ger.		Leader of SS, Nentershausen (Ger.) 4.45	MURDER	U.S.
FIELHER, Karl	187602	M	Ger.		Obergruppenfhr., SS, Reichsleiter, NSDAP,	MURDER	UNWCC
FIELIES	142652	M			Member of Gestapo, Kunsbeck (Ger.) 3.45	WITNESS	U.S.
FIELITZ	254332	M	Ger.		Hptsturmfhr., SS, S.D., Detachment Apeldoorn (Neth.) 10.44	MURDER	U.S.
FIELITZ, Karl	257236	M	Ger.	05 er 07	SS-Hptsturmfhr., Sipo and S.D., Anvers (Bel.) 40-45	BRUTALITY	BEL.
FIENE, Josef	166398	M		03	SS-Lt., SS, Trento, Campomolon (Italy) 2.45	MURDER	U.K.
FIENEMANN	247	M	Ger.		Hptscharfhr., Gestapo, Rodez (Fr.) 8.44-5.44	MURDER	FR.
FIENTENSE	132622	M	Ger.		Standortoff., Standortkommandantur, Gerardmer (Fr.) 9.-11.44	MISC.CRIMES	FR., U.S.
FIERKE	248	M			Police official, Kristiansund (Nor.) 42	TORTURE	NOR.
FIERS, Hubert	300994	M	Ger.		Chief, Forest Guard, Pertisau-Maurach (Austria, Tyrol) 7.44	MISC.CRIMES	FR.
FIESCHANN, Joachim	258880	M	Ger.		Lt., Army, Art., St.-Hermine (Fr.) 3.41	INCENDIARISM	FR.
FIETH (see VIETH)	72069						
FIETH, Wilhelm	191863	M	Ger.	95	Capt., 2.Coy., 190. Kriegsgef.Arb.Bn., C.C. Russanes (Nor.) 11.44-5.45	MURDER	NOR.
FIETSCH, Johann	259432	M			At present cashier, town hall, Bechtheim (Ger.) 9.-12.44	MURDER	U.S.
FIEZ, Jacob	251534	M	Ger.		Kapo, C.C. Neuengamme (Ger.) 45	INTERR.	FR.
FIEZ, Joseph	143424	M	Ger.		Cmdt., C.C. Neuengamme (Ger.) 44	MURDER	FR.
FIGEL	122701	M	Ger.		Oschfhr., SS, Quirnbach (Ger.) 3.45	MURDER	U.S.
FIGGE	306079	M	Ger.		SS-Mann, at C.C. Alderney (Channel Is) and C.C.Kortemark. 42-45	MURDER	CZECH.
FIGGE, Erwin	171686	M	Ger.		Sgt., 9. Inf.Regt., last Unit 13-Hoelzel, 9.Coy., Magny d'Avignon (Fr.) 9.44	MURDER	FR.
FIGURA	257021	M	Ger.		SS-Sturmmann, I. SS Panzer Regt. "Adolf Hitler", 1.Coy., Wanne near Stavelot (Bel.) 12.44	MURDER	BEL.
FIHNE (or FINNE)	170547	M	Ger.		Dr., Capt., Abwehr, Oflag VI C, Osnabruek (Ger.) 42-43	MISC.CRIMES	YUGO.
FIKENTSCHER	143461	M	Ger.		Dr., Prof., Oberstabsarzt, Admiral, Navy - Beelitz-Stiftung, C.C. Hohenlychen, Ravensbrueck (Ger.) 40-45	MURDER	CZECH.
FIKIERT (or FICKERT)	191440	M	Ger.		Oschfhr., SS, C.C. Oranienburg (Ger.) 39-45	MURDER	POL.
FIKUS	141957	M	Ger.		Foreman, Organisation Todt, Muhldorf, Ampfing (Ger.) 6.44-4.45	MURDER	U.S.
FILAFANG	38948	M			Guard, Stalag 1467, Sythen (Ger.)	MISC.CRIMES	FR.
FILBERT, Mathias	250163	M			Pvt., C.C. Dora, Nordhausen (Ger.)	MURDER	U.S.
FILEP	133365	M		19	Cpl., Waffen-SS, C.C.Hohenrheim near Plattling (Ger.) 2.-5.45	MURDER	U.S.
FILER	143460	M	Ger.		Kdo.-Fuehrer, Langfjord (Nor.)	MURDER	FR.
FILHAUER	251535	M	Ger.		Hauptwachtmeister, Monsheim (Ger.)	INTERR.	FR.
FILIP, Karl	300251	M	Ger.		Confidential agent, Gestapo and Sicherheitsdienst at Jicin, Bohemia (Czech.) 40-43	INTERR.	CZECH.
FILIPOWSKI	300703	M	Ger.		Rottenfhr., C.C. Auschwitz-Birkenau (Pol.) 40	MISC.CRIMES	FR.
FILIPSIK, Fritz	259844	M		25.12.25	Pvt., 13.Coy., 558.Gren.Regt., Bruay en Artois (Fr.) 9.44	MISC.CRIMES	FR.
FILLECHNER	253635	M			Kreisleiter of Munich-Freising (Ger.) 9.44	MURDER	U.S.
FILLER	160158	M	Ger.	98	Hptsturmfhr., SS, C.C. Buchenwald (Ger.) 2.45	MURDER	U.S.
FILLES	143459	M	Ger.	20	SS-Oberrottenfhr., C.C. Faulsingen (Ger.) 44	MURDER	FR.
FILLMANN	249	M	Ger.		Member of Gestapo, Rodez (Fr.) 8.44	TORTURE	FR.
FILMER	141890	M	Ger.		Foreman, Wiesenbach (Austria) 7.-9.41	TORTURE	U.K.
FILPKOWSKI	252971	M	Ger.		Rottenfhr., SS, C.C. Auschwitz (Pol.)	INTERR.	FR.
FILTINIUS	143403	M			Chief of SS, Vilbert (Ger.)	TORTURE	FR.
FILTZ	38953	M			Cpl., Gestapo-official, Tour, La Ville, St.Lo, Cherbourg (Fr.)	MURDER	FR.
FILTZER, Hans (or FLITZER)	199895	M	Ger.		Sgt., Air Force, Flugmeldemess-Regt.57, La Bazoche Gouet (Fr.) 9.44	PILLAGE	FR.
FILVE, Paul	133366	M	Ger.	00	Cpl. Guard, Waffen-SS, C.C. Hohenrheim near Plattling (Ger.) 2.-5.45	MURDER	U.S.
FILZWEISER, Erwin	126536	M	Ger.		Oschfhr., SS-Nachrichten-Ersatz-Abteilung Goslar, Tours (Fr.)	MURDER	U.S.
FINCK	38958	M		20	Army.	MISC.CRIMES	FR.
FINDENTZ	252085	M	Ger.		Capt., Cmdt., Army, Pars les Romilly (Fr.) 8.44	PILLAGE	FR.
FINEMANN, Luc.	188622	M	Ger.		Gestapo of Rodez (Fr.) 8.44	MURDER	FR.
FINEN	257365	M	Ger.		SS-Sturmfhr., SS-Slave Labour Camp, Beisfjord and Osen (Nor.) 6.-11.42	MISC.CRIMES	YUGO.
FINGAL	29885	M	Ger.		Cpl., C.C. 3.45	TORTURE	U.K.
FINGERATH, Karl	250	M	Ger.		Sgt., Army, Pion.Corps, 1.Coy., 716. District Engineer Bn., Harouvillette (Fr.) 42-44	MURDER	U.K.
FINGER	142662	M	Ger.		Dr. Apothecary , C.C. Hohenlychen, Ravensbrueck (Ger.) 5.44	MURDER	FR.
FINGER	171692	M	Ger.		Polizeimeister, Sicherheitsdienst, Metz (Fr.) 4.44	MURDER	FR.
FINGER	188832	M	Ger.		Lt., Army, St. Martin du Mont (Fr.) 6.44	MURDER	FR.
FINGER	191649	M	Ger.		Wachtmeister, Polizei, Member, Sicherheitsdienst, C.C. Mauthausen (Austria) 4.44	MURDER	FR.

NAME	C.R.FILE NUMBER	SEX	NATIO- NALITY	DATE OF BIRTH	RANK OCCUPATION UNIT PLACE AND DATE OF CRIME	REASON WANTED	WANTED BY
FINGER	301683	M	Ger.		Bde.-Chief, Train. Mongolian "Oberland", St. Nazaire en Royans (Fr.) 7.-8.44	MURDER	FR.
FINGER	305605	M	Ger.		Lt. German detachment stationed in the Chateau de la Becassiniere; in charge of the Ammunition Depot in Foret de la Rena,(Ain) Unit 15177 P Lent, Ain (Fr.) 8.44	MURDER	FR.
FINGER, Franz	188208	M	Ger.		Guard, SD and SS, Brno (Cze.)	MURDER	CZECH.
FINGERHUT	72080	M	Ger.	00	Sgt., Prison Guard KL Rheinbach (Ger.) 42-44	TORTURE	US, U.N.W.C.C.
FINGERHUX or TURJERHUT	38955	M		00	Sgt., Conc.Camp, Rheinbach (Ger.)	TORTURE	FR., US
FINK	142663	M	Ger.		Guard, KL. Johann-Georgen-Stadt (Ger.)	MURDER	FR.
FINK	142664	M	Ger.	00	Civilian, (Ger.) 43	TORTURE	FR.
FINK, Heinrich	135165	M	Ger.	17 or 18	Sgt. 1st., 709 Inf.Div., Cherbourg (Fr.)6.44	MURDER	US.
FINK, Joseph	12621	M	Ger.		110.or 111. Panz.Gren.Regt. 2. Coy., Albine (Fr.)6.44	MURDER	FR.
FINK, Zdenek	253959	M	Ger.	10.13	Agent, Gestapo, Prag Karlovy Vary (Czech.)42-45	MURDER	CZECH.
FINKE	162943	M			Lt., Kgf.Arb.Bn. 185, Mattfelldal (Nor.)	MURDER	NOR.
FINKE	250161	M			Pvt., Conc.Camp Ellrich, Nordhausen (Ger.)	MURDER	U.S.
FINKE	253636	M	Ger.		Dr., Physician, Conc.Camp Dachau (Ger.)	BRUTALITY	BEL.
FINKE	261194	M	Ger.		Pvt., 5-1 Regt. 211, 139. Arbeit.-Bereich Liane, Alleur-Lez-Liege (Bel.) 9.44	MURDER	BEL.
FINKE, Fritz	142506	M	Ger.	12.07	Labour Camp Employee, KL. Heimathof Hermans-Heide-Paderborn (Ger.) 41-42	TORTURE	U.S.
FINKEL or FINKIE or PFIGGEL	155401	M		05	Obersturmfhr., SS Verona (It.)12.43-1.44	TORTURE	U.K.
FINKELMANN, Georges	256551	M			Officer, SS, Nordhausen (Dora) (Ger.)	MURDER	FR.
FINKEN, Heinrich	253650	M	Ger.		SS-Mann, Conc.Camp Birkenau, Auschwitz (Pol.) 1.43	MISC.CRIMES	YUGO.
FINKEN, Peter	162033	M	Ger.		Foreman, Adolf Mine, Merkstein (Ger.)	TORTURE	U.S.
FINKENSTEDT, Fritz	252408	M	Ger.		Lt., 10. Coy., 377 Jaeger-Regt. Vingt Meigem (Bel.) 5.40	BRUTALITY	BEL.
FINKENZELLER, Georg	256557	M	Ger.	3.03	Employee, Bl.-Z. Hamkohl C.C. Nordhausen (Ger.)	MURDER	U.S.
FINKERS	142666	M	Ger.	10	Unterscharfhr., SS	MURDER	FR.
FINKDRUELER	124488	M	Ger.		Sgt. Conc.Camp Staff, Sachsenhausen-Oranienburg (Ger.) 42	MURDER	U.K.
FINKIE see FINKEL	155401						
FINNE Dr. see FIHNE Dr.	170547						
FINNTENSE	39692	M	Ger.		Feldjaeger Kdo., SS-Mann	TORTURE	FR.
FINOWSCHIK	192932	M			Wachtmeister, Schupo C.C. Falstad Drontheim (Nor.) 41-45	WITNESS	NOR.
FINSTERER, Willy	262305	M			Civ. Lives at: Freilassing (Ger.)4.45 L.O.D.N.A.O.D.	WITNESS	U.S.
FINSTERWALD, Matthias	170917	M	Ger.		Crim. Secretary, Gestapo Muenchen Dept. IV, Muenchen (Ger.) Tranoum (Nor.) 43	MISC.CRIMES	NOR.
FIRAZISCH or FRANZISCH, Karl	306367	M	Ger.		SS-Mann, C.C. Bergen-Belsen (Ger.) 40-45	MURDER	BEL.
FIRINGER, Sylvester	262245	M	Ger.	4.20	US-Oschfhr., 5. Coy., 4. Platoon, 51. SS Armoured-Bde. Breviandes, Bucheres, St. Savine, La Riviere de Corps (Troyes) (Fr.)44	BRUTALITY	FR.
FIRMANN, August	255995	M	Ger.		Kapo, C.C. Flossenburg (Ger.)	MURDER	FR.
FIRMENICH, Ludwig	161705	M	Ger.	92	Sturmfhr., SA 16-27 Standarte, Bingen (Ger.)	MURDER	U.S.
FIRNROHR	256555	M	Ger.		Chief of Sub-Section, C.C. Mittelwerk, Nordhausen (Ger.)	MURDER	U.S.
FISCH	142676	M		90	Civilian, Rathenow (Ger.)	TORTURE	FR.
FISCH	187168	M			SS-Oberscharfhr., 4th. SS Totenkopf Sturmbann, C.C. Nordhausen, Dora Mittelbau (Ger.) 12.43-45	TORTURE	U.S.
FISCHBACH	306547	M	Ger.		Sgt., Crim.Employee, SS,Sicherheitspolizei SD, Oslo (Nor.)8.43-4.45	MURDER	NOR.
FISCHBACH, Elfrida	142669	F	Ger.		Betriebsfuehr. Soziale DAF, Dresden (Ger.)	TORTURE	FR.
FISCHBACH, Hans	139455	M		15	Oberscharfhr., SS, Gueret (Fr.)	MURDER	FR.
FISCHBACH, Hans Karl	306581	M	Ger.		Member, SD or Gestapo, Trandum Nr. Oslo (Nor.) 1.43	MURDER	U.K.
FISCHBACH, Hermann	31904	M	Ger.		Pvt., Army, Nienburg (Ger.) 44	MURDER	FR.
FISCHBACH, Karl	252972	M	Ger.		Oberscharfhr., SS Div. 'Das Reich', Limoges (Fr.)40-45	INTERR.	FR.
FISCHBOCK	142670	M			Reichsleiter, NSDAP	TORTURE	FR.
FISCHBOCK, Hans	251	M	Ger.	95	Oberfhr., Kommissar SS fuer Finanz-u.Wirtschaft, 43	MISC.CRIMES	NETH.,U.S.
FISCHEDICK, Johannes	160159	M	Ger.	05	Oberwachtm.,police,Wirtsch.Verwalt.Hauptamt Berlin,Amtsgruppe C Ohrdruf (Ger.) 40-45	MURDER	U.S.
FISCHEMANN see FISCHERMANN	250159						
FISCHEN, Willi	171687	M	Ger.		Pvt., Army Last Unit 4-181, 9th Regt. Res.Gren.Magny D' Avignon (Fr.) 9.44	MURDER	FR.
FISCHER	252	M	Ger.	15	Oberscharfhr., SS, The Hague (Neth.) 42	MISC.CRIMES	NETH.
FISCHER	253	M	Ger.		Sturmfhr., SS, St. Brieve (Fr.)8.44	TORTURE	FR.
FISCHER	255	M	Ger.		Hauptscharfhr., SS	TORTURE	POL.
FISCHER	12388	M	Ger.		Kommissar der Gestapo, Prague (Czech.) 38-44	TORTURE	CZECH.
FISCHER	12425	M	Ger.		Sgt.1st. Hafenueberwachungstelle, Calais (Fr.) 8.44	TORTURE	FR.
FISCHER	12427	M	Ger.		N.C.O., SD Official, Section IV 3a, Toulouse (Fr.) 7.44	MURDER	FR.
FISCHER	12461	M	Ger.		Dr., Befehlshaber, SS Sicherheitspolizei, Strasbourg (Fr.) 41-42	MURDER	POL.
FISCHER	38923	M		09	Dr., SD Official, Strasbourg, Bordeaux, Auxerre (Fr.)	TORTURE	FR.
FISCHER	72262	M	Ger.		Dr.med. Hauptsturmfhr., W.-SS C.C. Maydanek, Sachsenhausen (Ger.)	TORTURE	POL.,BEL.
FISCHER	72704	M			Engineer Principal, Etat Major De L'aviation, Carcassone (Fr.)	MISC.CRIMES	FR.
FISCHER	72706	M			Lt., Navy, Eschamps (Fr.) 9.44	MURDER	FR.
FISCHER	119409	M	Ger.		Capt., Comi.Nachr. Abt. 234-163 Inf. Div. 20th Army (Fin.,Nor.)10.44	MURDER	NOR.
FISCHER	119410	M	Ger.		Major, Comi. GEB. Nebelwerf. Abt. 10th Army 44	MURDER	NOR.
FISCHER	121247	M	Ger.		N.C.O., Custom-man, Zollgrenzschutz, Creach (Fr.) 8.44	MURDER	FR.
FISCHER	123961	M	Ger.		Cpt. Landesschuetzen 610, Com. Cpt, SS, KL. Lehrbas Freydeck by Dt. Eylau (Pol.)7.44	WITNESS	U.K.
FISCHER	125038	M	Ger.		Cpl., Camp Gaschwitz Kr. Leipzig (Ger.) 11-12.44	MISC.CRIMES	U.K.
FISCHER	125453	M	Ger.		Guard, Gestapo, Wiesbaden, Frankfurt (Ger.)4.44	TORTURE	U.K.
FISCHER	127065	M	Ger.		Civilian, Frankenburg (Ger.)	TORTURE	U.S.
FISCHER	129790	M	Ger.		Capt., W.-SS C.C. Sachsenhausen (Ger.) 9.41	MURDER	U.S.
FISCHER	130644	M	Ger.	15	Obersturmfhr. SS, C.C. Nordhausen Mittelbau Dora (Ger.)	MURDER	U.S.
FISCHER	132619	M	Ger.		Praesident, Kriegsgericht, Torgau (Ger.)	MURDER	FR.
FISCHER	134889	M	Ger.		Dr., SS C.C. Erfurt (Ger.)43-44	MURDER	U.S.

NAME	C.R.FILE NUMBER	SEX	NATIO-NALITY	DATE OF BIRTH	RANK	OCCUPATION	UNIT	PLACE AND DATE OF CRIME	REASON WANTED	WANTED BY
FISCHER	137086	M	Ger.		Sgt., Arbeits-Kdo.124,Reichs-Post-Dir.,C.C. Leipzig (Ger.)				MURDER	U.K.
FISCHER	141419	M	Ger.	92	Feldkriegsgerichtsrat, Feld-Kom.529,Bordeaux, Souges (Fr.)				MURDER	FR.
FISCHER	141471	M	Ger.		Dr., Districtleader, NSDAP, Wuerzburg (Ger.)				MURDER	FR.
FISCHER	142150	M		94	Usturmfhr., SS, C.C.,Radzyn-Lublin (Pol.) 39-44				MURDER	FR.
FISCHER	142507	M		03	Guard, W-SS, Totenkopf-Sturmbann,C.C.Buchenwald-Weimar (Ger.)				TORTURE	U.S.
FISCHER	143400	M	Ger.		Cpl.,Army,Perigueux (Fr.)				MURDER	FR.
FISCHER	143401	M	Ger.		O.F.Apotheker, C.C. Hohenlychen-Ravensbrueck (Ger.)				TORTURE	FR.
FISCHER	143405	M			Member, Gestapo, Claveix,Clermont,Ferranot (Fr.)				MURDER	FR.
FISCHER	143411	M	Ger.		Gestapo, Lourdes (Fr.)				TORTURE	FR.
FISCHER	143415	M			Policeman, Gestapo, Obandorf (Ger.) 6.44				TORTURE	FR.
FISCHER	143416	M			Hptsturmfhr., SS, Monowitz (Pol.)				MURDER	FR.
FISCHER	143418	M			Agent, Gestapo, Rennes (Fr.) 5.44				TORTURE	FR.
FISCHER	143419	M	Ger.		Interpreter, Kommandantur,Perigueux (Fr.) 44				MURDER	FR.
FISCHER	143420	M	Ger.		Interpreter, Gestapo, Toulouse (Fr.)				TORTURE	FR.
FISCHER	143421	M	Ger.		Governor, Public-official, Warschau (Pol.)				MURDER	FR.
FISCHER	148402	M	Ger.		Dr., Troop-Dr.Hptsturmfhr., SS, C.C. Auschwitz (Pol.) 43-44				MURDER	U.S.
FISCHER	148423	M			Oscharfhr., SS, C.C. Mauthausen (Aust.)				MURDER	U.S.
FISCHER	160167	M	Ger.	05	Cook, Enschede (Neth.)				MURDER	U.K.
FISCHER	161749	M			Lt., 1 Bn, Art.Rgt.74, 3 Coy, Clavieres (Fr.) 6.44				MURDER	FR.
FISCHER	162051	M	Ger.		Ofhr., SS, Ensisheim (Fr.) 2.43				MISC.CRIMES	FR.
FISCHER	169469	M	Ger.		Sgt., 3 Rgt.Pion.,Chantilly (Fr.) 8.44				WITNESS	FR.
FISCHER	169470				SD, Chappes (Fr.) 7.44				MURDER	FR.
FISCHER	169481	M		15	Guard, Stalag VIII B, Army, Mankendorf (Ger.) 2.42				TORTURE	U.K.
FISCHER	171693	M	Ger.		Director, Einsatzstab Rosenberg, Troyes (Fr.) 40-44				PILLAGE	FR.
FISCHER	173356	M			SD, Montoigut le Blanc, Puy de Dome (Fr.) 4.44				PILLAGE	FR.
FISCHER	173405	M			C.C. Auschwitz (Pol.)				TORTURE	POL.
FISCHER	173417	M			Lt., Army, Pontcharra (Fr.) 6.44				MURDER	FR.
FISCHER	174777	M	Ger.	17	Lt., 2 Bn, 3 Brandenburg-Div., Communanza (It.) 5.44				WITNESS	U.K.
FISCHER	176656	M			Foreman, Org.Todt, U.C. Muehldorf-Ampfing (Ger.) 6.44-4.45				MURDER	U.S.
FISCHER	178667	M	Ger.		Sturmbannfhr., SS, C.C. Hinzert (Ger.) 44				MURDER	U.K.
FISCHER	186462	M			Member, Gestapo, St.Brieuc (Fr.)				TORTURE	FR.
FISCHER	188829	M	Ger.		Pvt., Army, Le Bourget-Triage (Fr.) 44				MURDER	FR.
FISCHER	188830	M			Lt., Army, 74 R.S.M., 3 Coy, 1 Bn, Chaudes,Aigues (Fr.) 44				MURDER	FR.
FISCHER	189358	M	Ger.		Dr., Physician and asst., C.C. Ravensbrueck (Ger.)				MURDER	FR.,POL.,BE
FISCHER	189359	F	Ger.		Camp warden, C.C. Ravensbrueck (Ger.)				MURDER	
FISCHER	190426	M	Ger.		Senat General President, Army, Berlin, Torgau (Ger.)				MURDER	FR.
FISCHER	191351	M	Ger.	10	Pvt.,2 Coy, Kgf.Arb.Bn 188,Kgf.Bezirkskommandantur,C.C.Assane, Bergen (Nor.) 42-43				TORTURE	NOR.
FISCHER	193896	M	Ger.		Custom-collector, Custom frontier guard,Semaphore du Creach Macut (Fr.) 8.44				MURDER	FR.
FISCHER	194042	M	Ger.		Scharfhr., Zugfuehrer, SS, 2 Zug, Stavelot (Bel.) 12.44				MURDER	BEL.
FISCHER	194631	M	Ger.	40	Scharfhr., SS, Reichs-Commissar,Then Hague (Neth.) 42				TORTURE	NETH.
FISCHER	194987	M	Ger.		Sgt., Hafen-Ueberwachungsstelle Calais (Fr.) 8.44				MURDER	FR.
FISCHER	195555	M	Ger.		Osturmfhr., Waffen-SS, St.Brieuc (Fr.) 8.44				TORTURE	FR.
FISCHER see FISSER	252086									
FISCHER	252403	M	Ger.		Cpl., Field-Pol.Troup, Lechablais (Fr.) 5.44				MISC.CRIMES	FR.
FISCHER	252404	M	Ger.		Lt.Col.,Pleucadeur and St.Marcel (Fr.) 6.44				MISC.CRIMES	FR.
FISCHER	252967	M	Ger.		Guard, C.C. Lahde-Weser (Ger.)				INTERR.	BEL.
FISCHER	252990	M			Chief, Dienststelle Westeur de Troyes,Maraye and other (Fr.) 5.43				PILLAGE	FR.
FISCHER	253644	M	Ger.	15	Political-chief, SS-Ger., Auschwitz-Birkenau (Pol.) 42-45				MISC.CRIMES	YUGO.
FISCHER	253647	M			Sturmfhr., SS, Brieux (Fr.) 8.44				TORTURE	FR.
FISCHER	254179	M			Lt., Army, Dienststelle Nr.67140, Enschede (Neth.) 4.45				MISC.CRIMES	NETH.
FISCHER	254328	M	Ger.		Hptscharfhr., SD, Toulouse (Fr.) 11.42-8.44				MISC.CRIMES	FR.
FISCHER	254329	M			Employee, Sipo, Abt.I m, Brussels (Bel.)				INTERR.	BEL.
FISCHER	255136	M	Ger.		Worker, Glassworks-Ruhr, Karnapp-Essen (Ger.) 44				BRUTALITY	BEL.
FISCHER	258158	M			2 Coy, Signal Troops, Bolnes (Neth.) 5.45				INTERR.	NETH.
FISCHER	258212	M			Lt., 2-3 Coy, Rgt.Brandenburg, San Vittoria (It.) 3.44				MURDER	U.S.
FISCHER	258573		Ger.		Cpl., Army, Murnau, Oflag VII A (Ger.)				BRUTALITY	POL.
FISCHER	259343	F	Ger.		Typist, Gestapo of Poitiers (Fr.) 40-44				SUSPECT	FR.
FISCHER	261920	M	Ger.		Lt., Waalwijk and Heusden (Neth.) 5.43-10.44				PILLAGE	NETH.
FISCHER	261962	M	Ger.		Hptscharfhr., SS (Yugo.) 8.42-9.44				SUSPECT	YUGO.
FISCHER	300379	M	Ger.		Supervisor,Glasswerke Ruhr, Works Karnapp,Essen (Ger.) 7.44-45				MISC.CRIMES	BEL.
FISCHER	301242	M	Ger.		Member, SD, Clermont-Ferrand, Montaigut-le-Blanc (Fr.) 4.44				TORTURE	FR.
FISCHER	301627	M	Ger.		Sgt.,Interpreter, att.Fieldgend.,Chateaubriant,le Teillais (Loire-Inferieure) (Fr.) 7.44				MURDER	FR.
FISCHER	301730	M	Ger.		Officer,Chateau de Calmont, Argues-le-Bataille (Fr.) 8.44				PILLAGE	FR.
FISCHER	301835	M	Ger.		Lt., Navy, Saulieu (Cote-d'Or) (Fr.) 9.44				MURDER	FR.
FISCHER	306313	M	Ger.	05	Fuehrer, Gestapo Rodleben near Magdeburg (Ger.) 6.44				MISC.CRIMES	U.K.
FISCHER	306532	M	Ger.		Member, SD, Meppel (Neth.) 12.44				TORTURE	NETH.
FISCHER	306960	M	Ger.		Capt.,commander of the 2 Coy,64 Pol.Rgt.Bn,Sabam,Serbian and neighbourhood (Yugo.) 7.-9.41				MURDER	YUGO.
FISCHER, Adam	250160	M	Ger.		Pvt., C.C. Bodungen, Nordhausen (Ger.)				MURDER	U.S.
FISCHER, Alfred	259342	M	Ger.		Sturmbannfhr.,active member of Poitiers-Gestapo,area Poitiers (Fr.) 40-44				MISC.CRIMES	FR.
FISCHER, Alix	171694	M	Ger.		Sgt., Pz.Jg.Abt.227,Inf.Div.Postal Section Royville (Fr.) 40-44				PILLAGE	FR.
FISCHER, Alois	173404	M	Ger.		Civilian, Strasbourg (Fr.)				MISC.CRIMES	FR.
FISCHER, Anton	140827	M	Ger.		Hptscharfhr.,3 SS-Totenkopf-Div.				MURDER	U.S.
FISCHER, Ants	186392	M	Ger.		Cpl., Army L., Floria,Crete (Grc.) 9.44				MURDER	GRC.
FISCHER, Benno	186395	M	Ger.	02	Chief, NSDAP (Czech.)				MISC.CRIMES	CZECH.
FISCHER, Erich	57228	M			Chief, Reichspresseleitung,Deputy Fritzsche Propaganda Minist.				MISC.CRIMES	UNWCC.

FIS - FIS

NAME	C.R.FILE NUMBER	SEX	NATIO-NALITY	DATE OF BIRTH	RANK OCCUPATION UNIT PLACE AND DATE OF CRIME	REASON WANTED	WANTED BY
FISCHER, Erich	121246	M	Ger.		Lt., SS-C.C. Ravensbrueck and Auschwitz (Ger.Pol.) 42-44	MURDER	FR.
FISCHER, Erich	132271	M	Ger.		Commander in Chief of Schupo, Wiesbaden (Ger.) 2.45	TORTURE	U.S.
FISCHER, Erich	142508	M	Ger.	4.12.08	Oschfhr., SS Totenkopf-Sturmbann C.C. Buchenwald Weimar (Ger.) (Member of the Commander Staff)	TORTURE	U.S.
FISCHER, Ernst	260925	M	Ger.	18. 6.06	SS Uschfhr., SS Guard, C.C.Auschwitz (Pol.) 41-45	BRUTALITY	POL.
FISCHER, Ferdinand	38911	M			Hptschfhr., SS Gestapo, Souges (Fr.)	MURDER	FR.
FISCHER, Ferdinand	256553	M	Ger.	3. 7.07	Sgt., SD., Pontivy, Bieusy, (Fr.) 44	MURDER	FR.
FISCHER, Ferdinand	258379	M	Ger.	25. 5.07	SS Standartenfhr., SS Chief of Estate Office in Prague (Czech.)39-45	MISC.CRIMES	CZECH.
FISCHER, Frans	252985	M	Ger.		SS-Osturmfhr., 83.Rgt. Landsturm Holland, Tiel (Neth.)45	INTER.	NETH.
FISCHER, Frederic	254325	M	Ger.	5. 9.10	Pvt., 13.Coy., 558.Gren.Rgt., Bruay en Artois (Fr.) 1.9.44	MURDER	FR.
FISCHER, Friedrich (or DENNERT)	185670	M			Dr., SS Bewerber Gestapo SD, Klatovy, Prague (Czech.) 39-45	MURDER	CZECH.
FISCHER, Fritz	143414	M	Ger.	2.12.99	Secr., Gestapo, Strasseburg (Fr.) 40-43	TORTURE	FR.
FISCHER, Fritz	191931	M	Ger.		Gestapo, Vosges (Fr.) 8.-10.44	MURDER	U.K.
FISCHER, Georg	176658	M	Ger.		SS Guard, C.C. Muhldorf Ampfing (Ger.) 6.44-4.45	MURDER	U.S.
FISCHER, Georges	254326	M	Ger.		Fieldgendarm, Fieldpolice, Nos.577,F.P. 22501, Orcay (Fr.) 8. 44	INTER.	FR.
FISCHER, Gerhard	301062	M	Ger.		Oberarbeitsfhr., RAD, Marjanske, Lasne, Bohemia, (Czech.)42-44	INTER.	CZECH.
FISCHER, Gustav	139140	M	Ger.		Inspector, C.C. Leader of all Guards, Harsburg (Ger.)	TORTURE	U.S.
FISCHER, Hans	192931	M	Ger.		Schupo, C.C. Falstad Drontheim (Nor.) 41-45	MURDER	NOR.
FISCHER, Hans	193627	M	Ger.	31. 3.08	Pol.Oberwachtmeister, SS Oschfhr., Police SS, Teresin (Czech.)41-45	MURDER	CZECH.
FISCHER, Hans	306368	M	Ger.	28. 3.01	SS-Hptschfhr., C.C. Buchenwald (Ger.) 16.5.38-9.10.43	MURDER	BEL.
FISCHER, Hans, Johann, Robert	260930	M	Ger.	28. 7.10	SS Rottfhr., Army SS, SS Totenkopfverband C.C. Auschwitz (Pol.)41-42	BRUTALITY	POL.
FISCHER, (Nickname GEITENKOPF)	300071	M	Ger.	circa 00	Employee, employed at Hamm, Kirchlengern, Kr.Herford .(Ger.)	TORTURE	NETH.
FISCHER, Heinz	173381	M	Ger.		Pvt., Arb.Kdo., C.C. Briex (Fr.)	MURDER	FR.
FISCHER, Hum (HERM.)	38913	M			Rgt. Police Todt., Army, Chatillon (Fr.)	TORTURE	FR.
FISCHER, Hermann	149364	M			Civilian	TORTURE	FR.
FISCHER, Hermann, (Kurt)	160157	M	Ger.	15	SS Hptschfhr., SS Abt.I Erkennungsdienst (Photography) Buchenwald (Ger.) 39-45	MURDER	U.S.
FISCHER, Hermann	173403	M			Osturmfhr., W-SS, C.C.Flossenburg (Ger.)	MURDER	FR.
FISCHER, Hermann	192468	M	Ger.	07	Oberwachtmeister, Strafgefangenenlager Nord, Finmark (Nor.)	MISC.CRIMES	NOR.
FISCHER, Jacob	176659	M			SS-Member, C.C. Flossenburg and Straufling (Ger.) 14.-20.4.45	MURDER	U.S.
FISCHER, Karl	176657	M			SS-man, C.C. Muhldorf, Ampfing (Ger.) 6.44-4.45	MURDER	U.S.
FISCHER, Johann	190052	M	Ger.		Servant, Occupied Territories Reich National Commissoner Praha, (Czech.) 39-45	MISC. CRIMES	CZECH.
FISCHER, Josef	161715	M		18	SS-Uschfhr., SS Pz.Div., Das Reich, Altenkirchen (Ger.) 13.9.44	SUSPECT	U.S.
FISCHER, K.	38907	M		11	Sturmfhr., SS Gestapo, Vichy, Moulins, Belfort (Fr.)9.44	MURDER	FR.
FISCHER, Karl	160156	M	Ger.	circa 03	Sturmmann, W-SS, C.C. Buchenwald (Ger.)	TORTURE	U.S.
FISCHER, Karl	169458	M	Ger.		Crim., Secr., Gestapo SD, Strasbourg-Saales, Schirmeck (Fr.) 8.-11.44	MURDER	U.K.
FISCHER, Karl	189062	M		16	SS-Hptschfhr., SD-Agent, Colmar, (Fr.) 21.1.45	MURDER	U.S.
FISCHER, Karl	195139	M	Ger.		Usturmfhr., SD, Sonder u.Wirtschaftskdo, Beeck, Gorssel Beck (Neth.) 23.-24.9.44	MURDER	NETH.
FISCHER, Karl	254327	M	Ger.		Fieldpoliceman, Fieldpolice of Romarantin No. 577 F.P.No. 22501 Orcay (Fr.) 8.8.44	MURDER	FR.
FISCHER, Karl	259635	M	Ger.		SS-man, Gestapo, area of Angers, Maine and Loire (Fr.) 42-44	MISC.CRIMES	FR.
FISCHER, Karl	305757	M	Ger.		Osturmfhr., Cmdt., of Chaidarico, (Grc.) 10.43-10.44	MURDER	GRC.
FISCHER, Karl, Eugen	261643	M	Ger.	12. 3.94	Engineer, Haffner Plant, Sarregueminey (Fr.) 1.8.41	PILLAGE	FR.
FISCHER, Karl, Hans	167124	M	Ger.		Adjutant, SS, Malans, (Fr.) 1.8.41	MURDER	FR.
FISCHER, Karl, Heinrich	261140	M			Major, Army	WITNESS	U.S.
FISCHER, Karl-Heins	141472	M	Ger.		Cpl.,SS Makana, (Fr.) 1.4.41	MURDER	FR.
FISCHER, Konrad	188309	M	Ger.	2. 3.96	Member, DAF, Dachsbach (Ger.) 43-45	TORTURE	POL.
FISCHER, Kurt	38916	M			Zollgrenzschutz St.Gaudens, St. Girons, Rimont, (Fr.)	MURDER	FR.
FISCHER, Kurt	38917	M			Luftwaffen-Kommandantur Beauvais (Fr.) 10.8.44	MURDER	FR.
FISCHER, Kurt	195138	M	Ger.	24	P.O.W. Guard, Army C.C. Plauen Stalag IV F, (Ger.) 1.45	MURDER	U.K.
FISCHER, Kurt	258875	M			Secr., member of Aktions Kommando, Lourdes (Fr.) 1.-8.44	MURDER	FR.
FISCHER, Lorenz	127345	M	Ger.	07	Pvt., Landesschuetzen-Bn., 814. Wolstein-Warthegau (Ger.)	MURDER	U.S.
FISCHER, Lorenz	194388	M	Ger.	26. 9.97	Police-Commission., Lichtenfels (Ger.)	MURDER	U.S.
FISCHER, Ludwig	254	M	Ger.		Public Official Governer, S.A. Gruppenfhr., Warsaw, (Pol.)39-45	MURDER	POL.
FISCHER, Ludwig	62291	M	Ger.		Oberfhr., Reichsminister, Boehmen (Czech.)	TORTURE	U.N.W.C.C.
FISCHER, Ludwig	166996	M	Ger.	95	Civ., City Official in Pforzheim, Eutingen (Ger.) 29.7.44	MURDER	U.N.W.C.C.
FISCHER, Ludwig	187601	M	Ger.		Osturmfhr., SS, Bohemia and Moravia (Czech.)	MURDER	U.N.W.C.C.
FISCHER, Ludwig	254144	M	Ger.		Orts-Cmdt., 83.Rgt. Landsturm Holland, Tiel (Neth.) 3.-4.45	PILLAGE	NETH.
FISCHER, Ludwig	257552	M	Ger.		Ob.Btsmt., Navy, Hopseidet (Nor.) 6.5.45	MURDER	NOR.
FISCHER, Max	262152	M	Ger.	27. 9.17	Chief of Group 8.Coy.,51.SS Armoured Bde.,Bréviandes, Buchères, Ste Savine, La Rivière De Corps, Troyes (Fr.) 22.-25.8.44	BRUTALITY	FR.
FISCHER, Mlle.	307096	F	Ger.		Typist, serving in Section IV Poitiers Gestapo, Chatellerault, Niort, Angouleme, Saintes (Fr.)	MURDER	FR.
FISCHER, Ph.	142509	M			Civilian, Ginnheim near Frankfurt M. (Ger.) 11.44	WITNESS	U.S.
FISCHER, Reinhold	38905	M			Pvt., W-SS, C.C. Natzweiler-Struthof (Ger.) 42-45	MURDER	FR.
FISCHER, Richard	72251	M	Ger.		Pvt., parachute, Roermond (Neth.) 11.44-1.45	TORTURE	U.S.
FISCHER, Richard	125457	M	Ger.	03	Pvt., C.C. Wildon (Aust.) 2.42	TORTURE	U.K.
FISCHER, Richard	173354	M	Ger.		SS-Stabsschfhr., SS Div.Das Reich, Totenkopf, Der Fuehrer Tulle (Fr.) 8.4.44	TORTURE	FR.
FISCHER, Rudi	301796	M	Ger.		SS-Oschfhr., 1.SS Pz.Div., Leibstandarte Adolf Hitler at Stavelot Region of Stavelot (Bel.) 19.-20.12.44	MURDER	BEL.
FISCHER, Rudolf	38920	M		21. 1.06	Lt., Bh.SS Div. 17.,49. Rgt., Montmirail (Fr.)	SEC. SUS.	FR.
FISCHER, Ruprecht	186393	M	Ger.	3. 8.00	Civ., Factory-Manager, Brno., (Czech.) 39-45	PILLAGE	CZECH.
FISCHER, Sepp	127346	M	Ger.	10	Pvt., Ld.Schuetz. Bn., 814 C.C. Wolstein Warthegau (Pol.)	MURDER	U.S.
FISCHER, Stefan	178685	M			Guard, Pvt., 4.SS Totenkopfsturmbann, Nordhausen Dora (Ger.)43-45	MURDER	U.S.
FISCHER, Walter	195137	M	Ger.		Schfhr., SD, Sonder u. Wirtschaftskdo, Beeck, Gorssel Beck (Neth.) 23.-24.9.44	MURDER	NETH.
FISCHER, Walter	301169	M	Ger.		Revier Opt., Schutzpolizei i.Bn. SS Gren.Rgt. Tiel Gelderland, Utrecht (Neth.) 45	PILLAGE	NETH.

FIS - FLE

NAME	C.R.FILE NUMBER	SEX	NATIO-NALITY	DATE OF BIRTH	RANK OCCUPATION UNIT PLACE AND DATE OF CRIME	REASON WANTED	WANTED BY
FISCHER, Wilhelm	72261	M	Ger.		Mayor, State service, Sturmbannf., SS, Schleiden (Ger.) 9.41	MURDER	U.S.
FISCHER, Wilhelm	196078	M			Major of Police, 19.SS-Police-Regt., O.C. I.Bn., St.Pierre,Albigny(Fr.)	MURDER	FR.
FISCHER, Wilhelm	260432	M	Ger.	28. 3.10	Home-address: Moerfelden, Kreis Gross-Gerau, Kirchgasse 18 Mielec by Krakow (Pol.) 42-44	MURDER	POL.
FISCHER, Willi	195136	M	Ger.		Lt., S.D., Einsatz-Kdo., Moussey (Fr.)	MURDER	U.K.
FISCHER, Willy	152196	M	Ger.	05	Gestapo, Folkling (Fr.) 11.44	MURDER	FR.
FISCHER, Willy	300378	M			Abschnittsleiter, Dienststelle Westen, Gestapo at Troyes in charge of Jewish-Affairs, Aube Marne (Fr.) 43-44	PILLAGE	FR.
FISCHER, Willy or KORDERS, Hans	307097	M	Ger.		Member of Feldgendarmerie, Dordrecht (Neth.) 11.44	MURDER	NETH.
FISCHERK	160169		Ger.	10	Sturmschaf., Gestapo, Vichy (Fr.) 44	MISC.CRIMES	FR.
FISCHERMANN	143408	M			Registrar, SS, Buchenwald (Ger.)	TORTURE	FR.
FISCHERMANN or SOEDERMAN	189431	M			Officer,C.C.Welfare at Grini (Nor.) 2.-8.43	TORTURE	NOR.
FISCHERMANN or FISCHEMANN	250159	M			Pvt., SS, C.C. Ellrich, Nordhausen (Ger.)	MURDER	U.S.
FISCHER-see FISCHINGER	173392		Ger.		Cpt., 3.Bn., 5.Pol.-Regt., 10.Coy., Todorovei (Yugo.) 7.43	MISC.CRIMES	YUGO.
FISCHINGER	143409				Hauptwachtmeister, Polica, Ludwigsburg (Ger.)	MISC.CRIMES	FR.
FISCHMEYER or FICHMEYER	129004	M	Ger.		Lagerfuehrer, "Auto-Union" works, Zwickau (Ger.) 43		
FISCHOTIER, Alouis	194963	M	Ger.	25. 5.05	SS-Hauptsturmf., Einsatz-Kdo. Gestapo, S.D., Erfurt, Lublin (Ger.,Pol.)	TORTURE	POL.
FISHER	36644	M	Ger.		Leiter, NSDAP, Rotleben, Dessau (Ger.) 4.45	TORTURE	U.K.
FISHER	124254	M			Oberscharf., Panz.Regt. 1, 1.Panz.Div., Headquarter - Coy., Malmedy (Bel.)	MURDER	U.S.
FISHER	138227	M	Ger.		Dr., SS-Obersturmbannf., C.C. Flossenburg (Ger.)	MURDER	FR.
FISHER	161359	M	Ger.		Cpl., Army, C.C. Graudenz (Pol.)	TORTURE	U.K.
FISHER, George	131277	M	Ger.	26. 5.19	Army, Eching,Freising(Ger.) 7.44	MISC.CRIMES	U.S.
FISHER, Jacob	142510	M			SS, C.C. Flossenburg (Ger.)	MURDER	U.S.
FISHER, Kurt	36619	M	Ger.		Plauen (Vogtland) (Ger.)	MURDER	U.K.
FISHER, Philipp	129792	M	Ger.		Sturmf., NSKK, Gross-Gerau (Ger.) 8.44	MURDER	U.S.
FISHER, Willy	455423	M			Former Pol.Prison, C.C. Ilfeld, Gardelegen (Ger.) 4.45	MURDER	U.S.
FISHERMAN	173389	M			SA-Mann, C.C. Buchenwald (Ger.) 42-45	MURDER	FR.
FISSCHER, Theodor	252970	M	Ger.		Military, S.D., Halfweg (Neth.) 11.44	PILLAGE	NETH.
FISSER or FESSER or FISCHER	252086	M	Ger.		W.O., SS-Pol.Regt., 2.Coy., 3.Bn., Org.Todt, St.Martin, Bellerue, Annecy (Fr.) 1.44	TORTURE	FR.
FISZKO	143410				Pvt., Army, Thiers (Fr.) 8.44	PILLAGE	FR.
FITH	139812	M	Ger.	10	Oberpolier, Org.Todt, C.C. Ampfing (Ger.) 44-45	TORTURE	U.S.
FITKAU, Elisabeth	262153	F	Ger.	21. 9.--	Secretary, Gestapo, Rennes (Fr.) 43-44	SUSPECT	FR.
FITTINGER	255996	M	Ger.		Senior W.O., Fieldpolice, Paris (Fr.) 2.43	INTERR.	FR.
FITZ	161357	M		10	Lt., Gestapo, Grenoble (Fr.) 43-44	MURDER	FR.
FITZ	1377		Ger.		Major, Army, H.G.-Div.	MISC.CRIMES	U.K.
FITZE	143406	M	Ger.		SS-Obersturmf., C.C. Auschwitz (Pol.)	TORTURE	FR.
FITZE	257885	M			Lt., Panz.-Eds., 150, Meuse-Bridge, Antwerp (Bel.) 12.44.	MISC.CRIMES	U.S.
FITZEK, Erich	253832	M	Ger.	31. 3.03	State service, concerned with ministry of agriculture, Prag (Czech.) 42	INTERR.	CZECH.
FITZER	121248	M	Ger.		Chief, SS, C.C. Yaworzno (Pol.)	MURDER	U.S.
FITZNER, Ernst	176703	M			Labour-camp, C.C. Ampfing, Mushldorf (Ger.) 6.44-4.45	MURDER	U.S.
FITZNER, Otto	260226			4. 1.88	Dir., Georg v.Giesche's Erben, Pres., Cham of Ind & Com, Breslau, Head Member, Econ Group Metal Ind. Berlin, Advisory Counsil, Handelskammer Berlin (Ger.)	MISC.CRIMES	U.S.
FITZSCHE	161249	M			Pvt., Army, Leipzig (Ger.)	TORTURE	U.S.
FIX, Joseph	254502	M	Ger.	13. 1.25	Pvt., 13.Coy., 558.Gren.Regt., Bruay, Artois (Fr.) 9.44	MURDER	FR.
FLACKER	39687	M			SS-Unterscharf., 17.Panz.Gren.Div. "G.v.B." Sturm-Gesch.Abtlg. 17 Segre-Renaze (Fr.) 8.44	MURDER	FR.
FLADIER, Heinz	190671	M	Ger.		N.C.O., Army, St. Andries, Varsenare les Bruges (Bel.) 9.44	MURDER	BEL.
FLAGEL, Alfred or FLEGEL	250740	M		5. 3.07	Pvt., Camp Ellrich, Nordhausen (Ger.)	MURDER	U.S.
FLAGGE	252974	M	Ger.		Unterscharf., SS, C.C. Auschwitz (Ger.)	INTERR.	FR.
FLAIG	144798	M	Ger.		Chief, Gestapo, Custom-house at Lourdes (Fr.) 1.-8.44	TORTURE	FR.
FLAIHSENBERGER	161750	M			Lt., Pferdetransport (mot.) Martens Silly (Fr.) 44	MURDER	FR.
FLAIG, Otto	38926	M			Secretary, Police, Custom-Admin., St. Gaudens, St.Girons (Fr.)	MURDER	FR.
FLAMA	251533	M	Ger.		Member, Gestapo, Lille (Fr.) 40-44	MISC.CRIMES	FR.
FLAMARD, Jacob	173382	M			Foreman, C.C. Dora, factory, Buchenwald (Ger.)	MURDER	FR.
FLAMBS	144712	M			Civilian, C.C. Ravensbrueck (Ger.)	MURDER	FR.
FLAME	144710	M		12	Sgt., SS, C.C. Ravensbrueck (Ger.)	TORTURE	FR.
FLAMING or FLAU	144714	M			Capt., Oflag 4-D, Benndorf (Ger.)	TORTURE	FR.
FLAMM or FLAU	144711	M			SS-Oberscharf., C.C. Ravensbrueck (Ger.)	TORTURE	FR.
FLAMME, Kurt	300072	M	Ger.		SS-Mann, Vienenburg (Ger.) 5.44	BRUTALITY	U.S.
FLANDORFER	39683	M	Ger.		Adjudant-Chief, Feldgendarmerie, Maubeuge (Fr.) 44	MURDER	FR.
FLANN	199909	M	Ger.		Chief, Arbeitseinsatz, C.C. Ravensbrueck (Ger.)	TORTURE	FR.
FLAQUIERES, Albert	173369	M	Ger.		Forester, Official, C.C. Thekla (Ger.) 4.45	WITNESS	FR.
FLARI, Paul	144713	M			Cpl., Army, Belleval near St.Die (Fr.) 10.44	MURDER	FR.
FLASCHAR	144737	M	Ger.		Sgt., C.C. Carmaux (Fr.)	TORTURE	FR.
FLASCHE	126537	M	Ger.	00	Pres., Oberf., SS, Polizei, Aachen (Ger.) 8.44	TORTURE	U.S.
FLASCHE	252973	M			Master, Station Pantin (Fr.)	INTERR.	FR.
FLASHSENBURGER, H.	39699	M			Lt., Army, FP. 21309 E, Mouterre Silly (Fr.) 6.40	MISC.CRIMES	FR.
FLAU (see FLAMM)	144711						
FLAUCHER, Willy	255997	M	Ger.		Chief, C.C. Mauthausen (Aust.)	MURDER	FR.
FLAUDECKEN	38927	M			Lt., Army, Cheronvilliers (Fr.) 8.44	MURDER	FR.
FLAUM or FLAUMR	144733	M		05	Dir., SS, C.C. Ravensbrueck (Ger.)	MURDER	FR.
FLAUMANN or PFLAUMANN	144734	M		05	Chief, C.C. Buchenwald (Ger.)	TORTURE	FR.
FLAUMR (see FLAUM)	144733						
FLAUTAU, Martin	261875	M	Ger.		Staff Sgt., Army, 1.Coy., 377.Jaeg.Regt., Vinkt (Bel.) 5.40	WITNESS	BEL.
FLAUX	132558				Chief-Comm., Kdo.Gazelle - Buchenwald (Ger.)	TORTURE	FR.
FLEBEL	300073	M	Ger.		Oldest man, in camp, Block 31, C.C. Mauthausen (Aust.) 11.42-5.45	MURDER	FR.
FLECH	161751	M	Ger.		Sgt., Arb.Komm. 238, Feldbach (Ger.) 6.40	MISC.CRIMES	U.K.
FLECHMANN	188828	M			Judge, Prison C.C. Avignon (Fr.) 40-44	WITNESS	FR.
FLECK	155404			20	SS-Hauptscharf., Signal corps "Nibelungen-Div.", Durmhart (Ger.) 4.45	MURDER	U.S.
FLECK	144732	M			Capt., Army, Heiligenbeil (Ger.) 2.45	TORTURE	FR.
FLECK	187163	M			SS-Rottenf., 4.SS-Totenkopf Sturmbann, C.C. Mittelbau - Dora Nordhausen (Ger.)	MURDER	U.S.

FLE - FLO

NAME	C.R.FILE NUMBER	SEX	NATIO- NALITY	DATE OF BIRTH	RANK OCCUPATION UNIT PLACE AND DATE OF CRIME	REASON WANTED	WANTED BY
FLECK, Emil	12622	M	Ger.		Pvt.,110 or 111 Pz.Gren.Regt.,2 Coy.,Albine (Fr.) 6.44	MURDER	FR.
FLECK, Heinrich	253836	M	Ger.	21. 3.05	Estate-manager,Kromeriz (Czech.) 39-45	INTERR.	CZECH.
FLECK, Otto	255137	M	Ger.		Veterinary,Civ.,Libaeves near Bilina (Czech.)	MISC.CRIMES	CZECH.
FLECKENSTEIN, Karl	260103	M	Ger.		Scharfhr.,SS,Strafgef.-Lager,North (Nor.)6.42-5.45	MISC.CRIMES	YUGO.
FLECKENSTEIN, Wilhelm	135214	M	Ger.	99	Teacher,Civ.,Konig (Ger.) 11.44	MURDER	U.S.
FLECKER, Harold	188237	M	Ger.	26. 7.17	Crim.-employee,Member,Gestapo,SS,S.D.,Bruenn (Czech.) 39-45	MURDER	CZECH.
FLEGEL	256100	M	Ger.		Chief of the block 31,C.C.Mauthausen (Ger.)	INTERR.	FR.
FLEGEL, Alfred (or FLAGEL)	250740						
FLEICHER	9655	M	Ger.		Dr.,Public official,Dtsch.Staatsministerium (Czech.) 42-44	TORTURE	CZECH.
FLEICK	161752	M	Ger.		Rottfhr.,SS-Leibst."Ad.Hitler",Bierwart (Bel.)	PILLAGE	BEL.
FLEIGREIL (see FLUGWEIL)	167120						
FLEISCHANGERL	39688	M	Ger.		Uschfhr.,SS,17 Pz.Gren.Div."Goetz v. Berlichingen",Sturmgeschuetz- Abt.17,Pz.Jaeg.Abtl.17,Segre, Renaze (Fr.) 7.-8.44	MURDER	FR.
FLEISCHER	173394	M	Ger.		Crim.secr.,Staatspolizeileitstelle,C.C.Oswiecim,Birkenau,Prag (Pol.-Czech.) 39-45	MURDER	CZECH.
FLEISCHER	192165	M	Ger.		Uschfhr.,SS,9 SS-Pz.Div."Hohenstaufen",Neuville les Bois (Fr.)8.44	MURDER	FR.
FLEISCHER	250763	M			Pvt.,C.C.Ellrich,Nordhausen(Ger.)	MURDER	U.S.
FLEISCHER	253658	M	Ger.	97	Uschfhr.,SS,Employee,Gestapo,Kolin (Czech.) 39-45	MISC.CRIMES	CZECH.
FLEISCHER	259793	M	Ger.		Foreman,Civ.,Aeroplane factory,A.T.G.,Leipzig,Saxonia (Ger.) 9.43	BRUTALITY	NETH.
FLEISCHER, Hans	173406	M			SS-Guard,C.C.Schoerzingen (Ger.)	TORTURE	FR.
FLEISCHER, Oskar	181565	M	Ger.	7.12.92	Usturmfhr.,Chief,S.D.,Gestapo,Praha (Czech.) 39-45	WITNESS	CZECH.
FLEISCHER, Walter	170077	M			Dr.,Asst.to Dr.Lohse,Einsatzstab Rosenberg,Paris (Fr.) 40-44	PILLAGE	FR.
FLEISCHHAUER	137756	M			Lt.,15 Pz.Gren.Regt.,29 Pz.Gren.Div.	WITNESS	U.S.
FLEISCHHAUER	173370	M	Ger.		Lt.,Air force,Regt.12,Unit L.11166,Donai (Fr.) 1.44	WITNESS	FR.
FLEISCHITZ	257551	M			Master,O.T.,Muhldorf (Ger.)	MURDER	U.S.
FLEISCHMANN	12623	M	Ger.		N.C.O.,Pz.Regt.,Albine (Fr.)	MURDER	FR.
FLEISCHMANN	119411	M	Ger.		Lt.,SS-Geb.Jaeg.Regt.11-6,SS-Geb.Div.Nord,Finmark (Nor.) 10.44	MURDER	NOR.
FLEISCHMANN	186460	M	Ger.		Dr.,Jugenieur,Agent,Gestapo,C.C.Gleiwitz (Ger.) 1.45	MURDER	FR.
FLEISCHMANN, Walter (or HETTERMANN or ETTERMANN)	254784	M	Ger.		Sgt.,Bakery-Coy.,709 Inf.Regt.,St.Sauvier,Normandy (Fr.) 6.44	MURDER	U.S.
FLEISCHMANN	252089	M			Col.,Torgau (Ger.)	MURDER	U.S.
FLEISHNER, Hermann	167123	M	Ger.	05	Chief,Gendarmerie,Solgne (Fr.)11.43	MURDER	FR.
FLEISHNER, Paul	155403	M	Ger.	14	Sgt.,Army,Pz.Jaeger-Ers.Abt.10,2 Coy.,Metting (Ger.)12.44	WITNESS	U.S.
FLEMIGE	144731	M	Ger.	97	Sturmbannfhr.,SS,W-SS,C.C.Dora Nordhausen (Ger.)	INTERR.	FR.
FLEMING, Alfred	38928	M			Cpl.,NSDAP,Carcassone (Fr.)	MURDER	FR.
FLENDER, Karl	160452	M	Ger.		Director,Civ.,Siegen (Ger.)	TORTURE	FR.
FLESCH	38930	M			Lt.,Army,1-2 Marsch-Bn.,3 Pz.Gren.Regt.8,Florenz (Ital.)	MURDER	FR.
FLESCH	171673	M			Cpl.,Feldgend.,Langes,Coiffy,Chalencey,Auberive,Flagey (Fr.) 43-44	MURDER	FR.
FLESSFEDER, Otto	186314	M			Civilian,Palleben (Ger.) 10.-11.44	WITNESS	U.S.
FLEURY	144730	M			C.C.Sebasbruck,Bremen (Ger.)	MISC.CRIMES	FR.
FLEXER, Heinrich	250762	M			Pvt.,C.C.Ellrich,Nordhausen (Ger.)	MURDER	U.S.
FLEYMANN	144715	M			(Pol.)	MURDER	FR.
FLICHT	193000	M	Ger.		Sgt.,SS,C.C.Buchenwald (Ger.)42-45	TORTURE	U.S.
FLICK	144727	M			Dr.,Civ.,C.C.Ravensbruck,Hohenlychen (Ger.) 5.44	TORTURE	FR.
FLICK, Alois	254335	M	Ger.	22.12.25	Pvt.,13 Coy.,558 Gren.Regt.,Brusy-Artois (Fr.) 9.44	MURDER	FR.
FLIEDEL, Melle	252405	M	Ger.		Agent,Gestapo,Area Limoges (Fr.)	INTERR.	FR.
FLIEGAUFF (or FLIEGAUF)	10011				Attached to Medical Corps,C.C.Breendonck, 40-44	TORTURE	BEL.
FLIEGE	160172	M	Ger.	06	Oschfhr.,SS,C.C.Buchenwald (Ger.)	WITNESS	U.S.
FLIEGE	305849	M	Ger.		Pvt.,1.Aufkl.Abt.,3 Coy.,2 Column,XV Div.Afrika Corps, St.Leger (Arlon) (Bel.) 9.44	MISC.CRIMES	BEL.
FLIEGEL	36617	M	Ger.	05	Guard,C.C.Stalag 316 (Pol.) 10.41	MURDER	SOV.UN.
FLIEGENSCHNEE, Franz	250143	M			Sturmschfhr.,SS,C.C.Dora-Ellrich,Nordhausen (Ger.)	MURDER	U.S.
FLIEGER, Heinz	62318	M	Ger.	25. 8.25	SS-Mann,SS,Waterloo (Bel.) 9.44	MURDER	BEL.
FLIEGER, Willmann	38931	M			Army,Bosc. Geffroy (Fr.)1.43	MURDER	FR.
FLIERL	250144	M			Rottfhr.,SS,C.C.Wieda,Nordhausen (Ger.)	MURDER	U.S.
FLIES (see VLIEGS)	126465						
FLIGGE	119412	M	Ger.		Major,Army,IV a,163 Inf.Div.,20 Army,Finmark (Nor.) 10.44	MURDER	NOR.
FLINCKT, Fritz	306003	M	Ger.		Charge of children in Velpke,Clinic (Ger.),5.-12.44	MURDER	U.K.
FLINT	121250	M			Lt.,438 Gren.Regt.,Hainaut (Bel.)	MURDER	BEL.
FLINT	148400	M		24	SS-Mann,SS,Mauthausen (Aust.) 41-45	MURDER	U.S.
FLINT, Wilhelm, William or Willi	132537	M	Ger.	05	Inspector,S.D.,Caen (Fr.) 42	MISC.CRIMES	FR.
FLISTER	155422	M			Leader,Volkssturm Platoon,1 Coy.,C.C.Gardelegen (Ger.)4.45	MURDER	U.S.
FLITTER, J.	160453	M			Member,Gestapo,Anjou,Poitou (Bretagne),(Fr.)	MURDER	FR.
FLITZER (see FILTZER, Hans)	193895						
FLOCHENZI	173418	M			Capt.,Army,Chamonix,Glieres (Fr.)	MURDER	FR.
FLODER	162042	M	Ger.		Capt.,Army,Morlaix,St.Pol de Leon (Fr.) 44	MURDER	FR.
FLOEDER	257	M	Ger.		Capt.,Army,Toulbouarn (Fr.) 8.44	MURDER	FR.
FLOEGEL, Gerard	173420	M	Ger.		Inspector,Stalag,C.C.Papinzia (Ger.) 11.41	MURDER	FR.
FLOERECH	173419	M	Ger.	15	Osturmfhr.,,SS,S.D.,Grenoble (Fr.) 7.44	MURDER	FR.
FLOERECK	138308	M	Ger.		Dr.,SS-Capt.,Member,SS-Gestapo,Lyon (Fr.)	MURDER	FR.
FLOHL, August	133784	M	Ger.	08	Sgt.,Civ.,Finance,office,C.C.Buchenwald (Ger.)42-45	MISC.CRIMES	U.S.-BEL.
FLOHR	144709	M			Unterarzt,C.C.Hohenlychen,Ravensbrueck (Ger.) 5.44	TORTURE	FR.
FLOHR (see FLOEH)	191869						
FLOHR, Hermann	252409	M	Ger.		N.C.O.,Regt.B,377 Jg.-Regt.,Vingt (Bel.)	BRUTALITY	BEL.
FLOR	135161	M	Ger.		Uschfhr.,SS,C.C.Wittlich,Hinzert (Ger.) 41-43	TORTURE	U.S.
FLOR, Lena	142659	F	Ger.		Civilian,C.C.Hadamar (Ger.) 6.44-5.45	WITNESS	U.S.
FLORECK	258	M	Ger.		Osturmfhr.,SS,Gestapo of Grenoble,Massif du Vercors,Isere et Drome (Fr.)7.-8.44	MURDER	FR.
FLORECK	300704	M	Ger.		Hptsturmfhr.,Chief of Subsection 4,SS,S.D.,Oyonnex,Lyon ,Attignat (Fr.)11.43 - 8.44	MISC.CRIMES	FR.
FLOEH (or FLOHR)	191869	M	Ger.		Capt.,Army,Unit 41130 A,Ortafa (Fr.) 3.-7.44	PILLAGE	FR.
FLORIAN	187122	M			Oschfhr.,SS,4 SS-Totenkopf-Sturmbann,C.C.Mittelbau Dora,Nordhausen (Ger.) 43-45	TORTURE	U.S.
FLORKOWSKI, Franz (or FROPKOWSKI)	142528	M			Civilian,Pattensen (Ger.) 3.45	WITNESS	U.S.

FLO - FOL

NAME	C.R.FILE NUMBER	SEX	NATIO-NALITY	DATE OF BIRTH	RANK OCCUPATION UNIT PLACE AND DATE OF CRIME	REASON WANTED	WANTED BY
FLORL, Karl	253654	M	Ger.		Ing.Manager,Civ.Firm.,Prag (Czech.) 39-45	PILLAGE	CZECH.
FLORSTADT, Hermann (see FLORSTEDT)	121251						
FLORSTAEDT (see FLORSTEDT)	121251						
FLORSTEDT, Heinrich	259	M	Ger.	18. 2.95	SS-Sturmbannfhr.,Commandant,C.C.Maidanek (Pol.) 43	MURDER	POL.
FLORSTLDT, Hermann (or FLUDSCHTETT or FLORSTAEDT)	121251	M	Ger.	05	SS-Sturmbannfhr.,SS,C.C.Buchenwald-Weimar,Lublin (Ger.) (Pol.)39-42	TORTURE	FR.,U.S.
FLORSTET, Emil	124777	M	Ger.	10	SS-Obersturmfhr.,SS,C.C.Berlin-Sachsenhausen (Ger.)	MURDER	U.S.
FLOS	187121	M			SS-Mann,4 SS-Totenkopf-Sturmbann,C.C.Dora,Nordhausen (Ger.) 43-45	TORTURE	U.S.
FLOSCHELER	142696	M			Sgt.,Army,Coy.Brandenburg,Pont-St.-Espril (Fr.)	MURDER	FR.
FLOSS, Herbert	306369	M	Ger.		SS-Unterscharfhr.,(No. 281582) C.C.Buchenwald (Ger.) 6.5.38-9.10.43	MURDER	BEL.
FLOTER	261760	M			Lt.,St.Pol de Leon et Morlaix (Fr.) 4.-5.8.44	SUSPECT	FR.
FLOTNER, Kurt	253637	M	Ger.		Doctor-Physician,C.C.Dachau (Ger.) 3.42	BRUTALITY	BEL.
FLOTO (or FLOTON)	250145	M			Sturmbannfhr.,SS,C.C.Dora,Nordhausen (Ger.)	MURDER	U.S.
FLOWNY	253831	M	Ger.		Chief,Labour-Office,C.C.Ravensbrueck (Ger.)	MISC.CRIMES	FR.
FLUDSCHTETT (see FLORSTEDT)	121251						
FLUEGEL	173210	M	Ger.		Driver,Police,C.C.Ravensbrueck,Rotenfels (Ger.) 6.-9.44	INTERR.	U.K.
FLUEGEL	173407	M			Hauptwachtmeister,Schupo,C.C.Zwickau (Ger.) 39-40	TORTURE	FR.
FLUEGEL, Friedrich	122700	M	Ger.	91	Kreisleiter,NSDAP,Varel-Oldenburg (Ger.) 45	TORTURE	U.S.
FLUGHEIL	167122	M			Lt.,FeldgendarmerieNancy,Luneville (Fr.) 1.8.44	PILLAGE	FR.
FLUGEL	123978	M		89	Stabsintendant,Army,C.C.Stalag III B (G),Fuerstenberg-Oder (Ger.)11.44	MISC.CRIMES	U.S.
FLUGEL	167121	M			Feldgendarmerie of Moulins,Larochemillay (Fr.) 11.8.44	PILLAGE	FR.
FLUGWEIL (or FLEIGREIL)	167120	M			Lt.,Artillery,Raville (Fr.)	MURDER	FR.
FLUM, Erwin	144729	M			Rottenfhr.,SS,C.C.Struthof (Fr.) 14	MURDER	FR.
FLUM, Max	193626	M			Crim.Assist.,Gestapo,Praha (Czech.) 39-45	MURDER	CZECH.
FOCHEM, Kurt	121251	M		1. 3.21	Adjutant,Paratroops Lehr-Rgt.,3,Goequis,Chaussee (Bel.) 3.9.44	MURDER	BEL.
FOCHER, Gustave	260623	M		00	Cpl.,SD,Besancon,Rioz,Haute Saone (Fr.) 7.44	SUSPECT	FR.
FOCK	252860	M	Ger.		N.C.O.,Pepingen (Bel.)	SUSPECT	BEL.
FOCKE	142603	M			Lt.,Army,Maubeuge (Fr.) 29.8.44	MURDER	FR.
FOCKEN	152194	M			Oberwachtmeister,Gestapo,Trondes Boucq Menil la Tour,(Fr.) 18.8.44	MURDER	FR.
FOCKEN	194104	M		15	Pvt.,Guard,Marine Artillery,C.C.Lueneburg,Wilhelmshaven (Ger.) 10.4.45	MURDER	U.K.
FOCKLICKEL	189023	M			Major,427 Ld.Sch.Bn.,Bautzen (Ger.) 3.45	MURDER	U.K.
FOEGUELET	261482	M	Ger.		Sgt.,Nancy (Fr.) 40-45	PILLAGE	FR.
FOERBOCK, Hans (see FUERBOCK)	257845						
FOERSCHNER, Otto	9656	M			Sturmbannfhr.,Waffen-SS in Charge of Administration,C.C.Buchenwald (Ger.) 44	MISC.CRIMES	CZECH.
FOERSTE, Erich	259073	M			Admiral	WITNESS	U.S.
FOERSTER	260	M			SS-Obersturmfhr.,Perpignan (Fr.) 12.43-8.44	MURDER	FR.
FOERSTER	125062	M			Pvt.,Navy, 41	MURDER	U.K.
FOERSTER	126459	M			SS-Sturmbannfhr.,SS-Wachtkommando,Salza,Ellrich (Ger.)	TORTURE	U.S.
FOERSTER	133731	M		97	SS-Obersturmbannfhr.,C.C.Buchenwald (Ger.)	MURDER	U.S.
FOERSTER	166259	M			Official,occupied territories (Pol.,Sov.Un.)40-45	PILLAGE	U.S.
FOERSTER	186001	M	Ger.		SS-Oberscharfhr.,C.C.Leonberg (Ger.)	TORTURE	FR.
FOERSTER	303303	M			Adjutant,Secretary,Member,NSDAP,Customs-Official,Veigy Foncenex Hte.Savoie (Fr.) 6.10.43	TORTURE	FR.
FOERSTER	306961	M	Ger.		Commissar,Crim.Assist.,or Secretary,Gestapo,Aix-la-Chapelle (Fr.)40	TORTURE	BEL.
FOERSTER, Friedrich	155417	M		95	Oberbuergermeister,Public-Official,Ulm (Ger.) 40-45	MURDER	U.S.
FOERSTER, Georg	211145	M			Cmdt.,Sgt.,Stalag 344,E 27,Arb.Kdo.,Lamsdorf (Ger.) 6.40	TORTURE	U.K.
FOERSTER, Karl	181567	M	Ger.	05	SS-Hauptscharfhr., C.C.Hradistko (Czech.) 42-45	MURDER	CZECH.
FOERSTER, Otto	193897	M			Custom-Secretary,Zollgrenzschutz,Veigy Foncenex (Fr.)	TORTURE	FR.
FOERSTER, Paul	300074	M	Ger.		Policemaster,Police,near Schleiden (Ger.) 17.8.43	BRUTALITY	U.S.
FOERSTL	250146	M			Pvt.,C.C.Dora,Nordhausen (Ger.)	MURDER	BEL.
FOERSTNER, Heinrich	250149	M			Pvt.,C.C.Ellrich,Nordhausen (Ger.)	MURDER	U.S.
FOES, Otto (see FOSS)	301311						
FOEST, Heinrich	166995	M	Ger.	03 - 05	SS-Major,H.Q.SS.,Vipiter (It.) 44-45	MURDER	U.S.
FOFER	301310	M			Member,Gestapo,Trencin,C.C.Oswiecim-Birkenau (Pol.)39-45	MURDER	CZECH.
FOHR	173373	M	Ger.		SS-Rottenfhr.,Official,SS,Gestapo,Le Mans (Fr.) 29.12.43-7.1.44	MURDER	FR.
FOHR	192175	M		16	Member,Geh.Feldpol.,Brussels (Bel.)	MISC.CRIMES	BEL.
FOKESBERGER	1692	M			SS-Oberscharfhr.,SS,C.C.Dachau (Ger.)	TORTURE	U.K.
FOLCHMANN	39686	M			Sturmfhr.,SS-Div.,St.Sulpice,Fort-Misson,Chateau Gonthier (Fr.)	MURDER	FR.
FOLCHMANN	142600	M	Ger.		SS-Sturmmann,Chateau (Fr.) 6.8.44	MURDER	FR.
FOLENS	254333	M	Ger.		Interpreter,Sipo Abt.,III B,Brussels (Bel.)	INTERR.	BEL.
FOLGER	257501	M	Ger.		Manager,Volkswagenwerk,Peugeot,Sochaux (Fr.) 40-44	BRUTALITY	FR.
FOLGER, Johann	142513	M			Kapo,C.C.Mauthausen (Aust.)	TORTURE	U.S.
FOLIE, Carl	174784	M	Ger.	05	Sonderfhr.,Army,Bronzolo (It.) 9.43	WITNESS	U.K.
FOLK	163046	M	Ger.		Pvt.,10 SS-Pz.Div., 96 Rgt.,Revin (Fr.) 6.44	MURDER	FR.
FOLKER, Leopold (or VOELKER or FULKER or BOBY)	138222	M	Ger.		Interpreter,Gestapo,Lyon (Fr.) 6.-8.44	MURDER	FR.
FOLKERTS, Karl	250147	M			Cpl.,C.C.Ellrich,Nordhausen (Ger.)	MURDER	U.S.
FOLKMEN	142599	M			C.C.Officer,Struthof (Fr.)	TORTURE	FR.
FOLKMER	126538	M	Ger.		Untersturmfhr.,SS,C.C.Natzweiler (Fr.)	MURDER	U.S.
FOLLET	142698	M			Adjutant-Chief,Army,11 Pz.Div.,Albine (Fr.) 1.7.-12.8.44	MURDER	FR.
FOLLMANN	160454	M	Ger.	95	Secretary,Gestapo, Poitou,Bretagne,Anjou (Fr.)	MURDER	FR.
FOLLMARING	133372	M			SS-Unterscharfhr.,	TORTURE	U.S.
FOLSCHE	261761	M	Ger.		Capt.,F.P.25982 C,Kersiroal en Locarn (Fr.) 7.8.44	MURDER	FR.
FOLTES	137466	M	Ger.		Regierungsassessor,Assist.Chief,Gestapo,Koeln (Ger.)	MURDER	U.S.
FOLTIN, Werner, Max	142658	M	Ger.	16. 4.08	SS-Hauptscharfhr.,Wuppertal (Ger.)	WITNESS	U.S.
FOLTIS, Richard	190246	M	Ger.	12	Regierungsassessor,Capt., 2 Ile Cologne,Gestapo H.Q.,Cologne (Ger.) 43-45	MURDER	U.K.
FOLTZ, Wilhelm	125528	M	Ger.		Civilian,Farmer,Oetheim (Ger.)	TORTURE	POL.

FOL-FRA

NAME	C.R.FILE NUMBER	SEX	NATIO-NALITY	DATE OF BIRTH	RANK OCCUPATION UNIT PLACE AND DATE OF CRIME	REASON WANTED	WANTED BY
FOLZ	305850	M	Ger.		Pvt.,1 Aufkl.Abt., 3 Coy, 2 Col.,XV Div. Afrika Corps St.Leger Distr.Arlon (Bel.) 9.44	MISC.CRIMES	BEL.
FONCK	28835	M	Ger.		Lt., Inf.Coy, F.P.Nr.39467 A, Ploudel-Mezeau (Fr.) 8.44	MURDER	FR.
FONHOUF	135163	M			Guard, SS, C.C. Erfurt (Ger.) summer 44	TORTURE	U.S.
FOOKS	152193	M	Ger.		Member, employee, NSDAP, Firm Hochtief, Bruex (Czech.) 6.44	TORTURE	U.K.
FOORAY	305128	M	Ger.		Member, SD Lille (Fr.) 40-44	MURDER	FR.
FORCK	171652	M	Ger.		Manager,General-Governor Poland,Auffangges. fuer Kriegsteilnehmer-betrieb des Handels, Kattowitz (Pol.) 9.39-44	MISC.CRIMES	POL.
FORDERER, Joseph	1077	M	Ger.		Sgt., Army, Feldgend., Langes (Fr.) 43-44	TORTURE	FR.
FORDERMFELDE	191870	M	Ger.		Lt., Art., Laseyne sur Mar (Fr.) 8.44	PILLAGE	FR.
FOREST	188827	M	Ger.		Agent, Reichsbahn, Le Bourget Triage (Fr.) 8.44	WITNESS	FR.
FORGE, Karl	186459	M	Ger.		Cpl.,Army, Kuesten-Art.Lehr-Abt.1280, 4 Bn, Ile d'Oleron (Fr.)	MURDER	FR.
FORSCHER	127096	M	Ger.	95	Sturmbannfhr.,SS, C.C. Dora-Nordhausen (Ger.)	TORTURE	FR.
FORSCHING	121249	M	Ger.		Feldgend.Trupp 986, St.Illide (Fr.) 3.44	PILLAGE	FR.
FORSCHNER, Otto	127096	M	Ger.	02	Sturmbannfhr., C.C. Dora, Nordhausen, Buchenwald (Ger.)	MURDER	U.S.,FR.
FORSHING	189595	M			Lt., Feldgend., Mauriac (Fr.) 4.44	MISC.CRIMES	FR.
FORST, Josef Thomas	255999	M	Ger.	18.10.91	Informer, Gestapo, Prachatice (Czech.) 39-45	INTERR.	CZECH.
FORSTEL	256707	M			Capt., North-Btty AA, Texel (Neth.) 2.45	MURDER	U.S.
FORSTER	261	M	Ger.		Osturmfhr., SS, C.C. Dachau (Ger.) 40 onwards	MURDER	FR.
FORSTER	12389	M	Ger.		Hptsturmfhr., SS reported to be at C.C. Oranienburg (Ger.) 10.39	TORTURE	CZECH.
FORSTER	72096	M	Ger.		Uscharfhr.,SS, C.C. Struthof (Fr.)	PILLAGE	FR.
FORSTER	12426	M	Ger.		Member, Gestapo Cahors (Fr.) 6.44	MURDER	FR.
FORSTER	124953	M	Ger.		Cpl., Landes-Schz.Coy, Stalag Luft III, Sagan (Ger.) 3.44	WITNESS	U.K.
FORSTER	130646	M			Hptsturmfhr., SS, C.C. Dora (Ger.)	MURDER	U.S.
FORSTER	142516	M			Dr.,Arzt, SS, C.C. Flossenburg (Ger.)	MURDER	U.S.
FORSTER	176654	M			Uscharfhr., SS, C.C. Muhldorf,Ampfing (Ger.) 6.44, 4.45	MURDER	U.S.
FORSTER	192998	M	Ger.		Lt.,SS Doctor-Standarte Thuringia, C.C. Buchenwald (Ger.) 42-45	TORTURE	U.S.
FORSTER	254130	M	Ger.		Cpl., Forst de Seclin (Fr.) 8.44	WITNESS	FR.
FORSTER	305129	M	Ger.		Major or Lt.Col.,SS-Medical-officer, Calavrita,Mega,Apileon (Grc.) 12.43	MURDER	GRC.
FORSTER, Georges	142690	M		23. 8.18	Uscharfhr., SS Goetz v.Berlichingen, 51 Bde, Troyes,Bucheres,Cresnay (Fr.) 8.44	MURDER	FR.
FORSTER, Jan	194040	M	Ger.	20.10.00	Member, NSDAP, leader of SD, Gestapo, Cheb, Eger (Czech.) 38-45	MISC.CRIMES	CZECH.
FORSTER, Josef	142512	M		24. 7.97	Camp-Kapo, C.C. Mauthausen (Aust.) 41-45	MURDER	U.S.
FORSTER, Josef	254337	M			Scharfhr., SD, Toulouse (Fr.) 11.42-8.44	MISC.CRIMES	FR.
FORSTER, Leo	192413	M	Ger.	23	Army, Prisoner, Zinna, Torgau (Ger.) 45	WITNESS	U.S.
FORSTER, Ottmer	160165	M	Ger.	12	Osturmfhr.,SS-Standarte Thuringia, Buchenwald (Ger.) 9.39 (Dr.)	TORTURE	U.S.
FORSTER, Otto	132966	M	Ger.	94	Dr.,Director, Walraff-Richartz Museum, Koeln (Ger.) 41-45	PILLAGE	U.S.
FORSTERST	191644	M	Ger.		SS-Uscharfhr.,SS-Hauptamt,C.C. Struthof-Natzweiler (Fr.)	MURDER	FR.
FORSTINAUER	263	M	Ger.		Lt.,Army,118 Jaeger-Div. (Yugo.) 7.43-1.44	MURDER	YUGO.
FORSTNER	139454	M	Ger.	95	Hptsturmfhr.,SS, C.C. Dora (Ger.)	TORTURE	FR.
FORSTNER, A. or SCHMIDT,August	261970	M	Ger.	9.10.03	Member, SD, Prag (Czech.) 44-45	SUSPECT	CZECH.
FORTSCH	160161	M			Civilian, near Ellersleben(Ger.) 7.-8.44	WITNESS	U.S.
FORTSCH, Max	142514	M	Ger.		Groupleader, NSDAP, C.C. Buchenwald (Ger.) 41-45	TORTURE	U.S.
FORWERG, Rudy	160451	M	Ger.		Sgt., Gestapo, Brive (Fr.) 44	MURDER	FR.
FORWICK	161932	M	Ger.		Contre-maitre, Civilian, Siegen Wertal (Ger.)	TORTURE	FR.
FOSKAMP	252410	M	Ger.		N.C.O.,10 Coy, 377 Jaeger-Rgt., Vinkt (Bel.)	BRUTALITY	BEL.
FOSS	39684	M	Ger.		Capt.,Army, Bn Azerbaidjan,St.Donat,Tournon (Fr.) 6.44	MURDER	FR.
FOSS, Rudolf	258156	M	Ger.		Leader, Fieldgend., Braine-le Comte (Bel.)	PILLAGE	BEL.
FOSS, Otto see FOES	301311						
FOSTER, Eugen	300726	M	Ger.		Uscharfhr., C.C. Struthof-Natzweiler (Fr.) 44	MURDER	U.K.
FOT, Ewald	137649	M	Ger.	10	Oscharfhr.,guard, C.C. Stutthof (Ger.)	MURDER	U.K.
FOTOPOLOOS, Vasilius	134843	M			Civilian	WITNESS	U.S.
FOTTER, Karl alias VOTTER	261911	M	Ger.	25. 3.07	SS-Stubafhr., Civ. Werkschutzleiter in Skoda-Works, Pilsen (Czech.) 40-41	SUSPECT	CZECH.
FOUGHT	261609	M	Ger.		SS-Mann, W-SS, Dirlewanger Bde, Warszawa (Pol.) 40-44	MURDER	POL.
FOUL, Arthur	129017	M	Ger.	20	C.C. Mainz (Ger.) 43-45	TORTURE	BEL.
FOURHMANN,Maria alias DITE Annie	194978	F	Ger.	.29	Interpreter, Gestapo,Savigny en Septaine Bourges (Fr.) 8.44	MURDER	FR.
FOURIER, Karl	261685	M	Ger.	16. 7.04	Fanatic Nazi-works in the only butchery of Poeplingen near Stuttgart Nancy and Luneville (Fr.) 40-41	PILLAGE	FR.
FOURNIER	264	M	Ger.		Major, official at Stalag 325, Oflag XVII A Kawa-Ruyka,Edelbach (Pol.,Aust.) 42-43	MURDER	FR.
FOUSTEL	9657	M	Ger.		Osturmfhr., SS, Gestapo, Kolin (Czech.) 39-45	TORTURE	CZECH.
FOUX	253830	M	Ger.		Oberwachtmstr., Siegburg-Fortress (Ger.) 11.42	MISC.CRIMES	FR.
FRAAS, Wilhelm	132273	M	Ger.		Civilian, Farmer, Sambensdorf (Ger.) 1.45	TORTURE	U.S.
FRACHT, Leni	253655	F	Ger.		Overseer, C.C. Auschwitz (Pol.)	MISC.CRIMES	FR.
FRADRICH	253849	M	Ger.		Employee, Sipo, Brussels (Bel.)	INTERR.	BEL.
FRAESER	305133	M	Ger.		Capt., Thebes (Grc.) 7.44	MISC.CRIMES	GRC.
FRAHM	138269	M	Ger.		Uscharfhr., SS, Gestapo, planton Lyon (Fr.)	MURDER	FR.
FRAHM	142649	M	Ger.		Uscharfhr., SS, C.C. Neuengamme (Ger.)	TORTURE	U.K.
FRAHM, Johann Christian	301036	M	Ger.	28. 4.01	Oscharfhr., C.C. Neuengamme (Ger.) from 11.42	TORTURE	BEL.
FRAHNKE	253848	M			Oscharfhr.,SS, Gestapo, Brussels (Bel.)	INTERR.	BEL.
FRAKASEM	129007	M			Rottenfhr., SS, C.C. Mauthausen (Aust.)	MURDER	U.S.
FRAMEN	129008	M	Ger.		Uscharfhr.,SS, Neuengamme (Ger.)	TORTURE	BEL.
FRANC	255140	M	Ger.		Capt., Army, Huyberger (Neth.) 9.44	INTERR.	NETH.
FRANCAIS, G.	301684	M	Ger.		Hauptwachtmstr.,05-243 Mongolian "Oberland" Unit, St.Nazaire en Royans (Fr.) 7.-8.44	MURDER	FR.
FRANCHMANN	190424	M	Ger.		Capt., Army,near Lesparre and St.Germain,d'Esteuil (Fr.) 7.44	MURDER	FR.
FRANCIS	72083	M			Leader, Prison room Camp Hinzert (Ger.) 43	TORTURE	U.S.
FRANCK	125695	M	Ger.		Col.,Public official,Kriegsgericht Lille (Fr.)	MURDER	FR.
FRANCK	143447	M			Civilian, defense of the factory, Siegen (Ger.)	MISC.CRIMES	FR.
FRANCK	143472	M			Camp Drancy (Fr.) 42-44	MURDER	FR.
FRANCK	143473	M		00	Obermeister, Gestapo,Heydebreck (Ger.) 43-45	TORTURE	FR.

NAME	C.R.FILE NUMBER	SEX	NATIO- NALITY	DATE OF BIRTH	RANK OCCUPATION UNIT PLACE AND DATE OF CRIME	REASON WANTED	WANTED BY
FRANCK	143474	M	Ger.		Cpl., Army, Stalag VII, Moosburg (Ger.) 9.41-9.42	MURDER	FR.
FRANCK	163460	M	Ger.		Guard, CC Berlin (Ger.)	TORTURE	FR.
FRANCK	190670	M	Ger.		Pvt., Eisenbahn Art. Btty 717, St.Andries, Varcenare les Bruges (Bel.) 9.44	MURDER	BEL.
FRANCK (see FRANK)	192164						
FRANCK (see FRANTZ)	253962						
FRANCK	254475	M	Ger.		SS Uschfhr, Gestapo, Paris (Fr.) 41-44	TORTURE	FR.
FRANCK	259660	M	Ger.		Cpl., probably 9 Coy, 54 Rgt. Air Force, Plougasnou (Fr.) 7.44	MURDER	FR.
FRANCK, Bertha	143471	F	Ger.	00	Cmdt, CC Weisswasser Breslau (Ger.) 44	TORTURE	FR.
FRANCK, Hans	306182	M	Ger.		Sturmschfhr, Successor to Schmidt as Chief, CC Malines 7.42-9.44	MISC.CRIMES	BEL.
FRANCK, Hilde	252406	F	Ger.		Agent, Gestapo. Limoges (Fr.)	INTERR.	FR.
FRANCK, Johannes	192176	M.	Ger.		Sturmschfhr, SS, Crim.Secretary, Police, Malines (Bel.) 43-44	MURDER	BEL.
FRANCK, Kurt	192470	M	Ger.	03	Hptwachtmstr, Strafgefangenenlager Nord, Finmark (Nor.) 6.42-45	MISC.CRIMES	NOR.
FRANCK, Rudolf	125016	M	Ger.	00 - 05	Senior W.O., Gestapo, Briey (Fr.)	TORTURE	FR.
FRANCK, Rudolf	251532	M		16	Army, Gerardmer (Fr.)	WITNESS	U.S.
FRANCKEN (see FRANKEN)	39696						
FRANCKEN	143475	M	Ger.		Adjutant, Army, Cerisot (Fr.) 8.44	MURDER	FR.
FRANCKEN	143476	M			Dr., Physician, Camp Velbert, Duesseldorf	MURDER	FR.
FRANCKEN	189360	M	Ger.		Adjutant, CC St.Emiland (Fr.) 8.44	MURDER	FR.
FRANCKEN	253847	M	Ger.		Interpreter, Abt.IV A, Brussels (Bel.)	INTERR.	BEL.
FRANK	12390	M	Ger.		Oberfhr, Chef des Verwaltungsamtes der SS., Berlin (Ger.) 3.39-44	TORTURE	CZECH.
FRANK	31927	M	Ger.		Capt., Army, Georgian Legion, Castres (Fr.) 44	TORTURE	U.N.W.C.C.
FRANK	122699	M	Ger.	95	Sturmschfhr.,SS	MURDER	U.S.
FRANK	128874	M			Sgt., Stalag Luft VII, CC Bankau (Ger.) 1.45	TORTURE	U.K.
FRANK	136314	M			Sgt., Feld-Gend. de Verdun, Stenay (Fr.) 40-44	MURDER	FR.
FRANK	143444	M			Asst., SS, SD, Lyon (Fr.) 43 - 9.44	MURDER	FR.
FRANK	160184	M	Ger.	85	Col., Inf., Cmdt.Stalag XIII, Hammelburg (Ger.) 44-45	TORTURE	U.K.
FRANK (see LA FOUINE)	171697						
FRANK	187376	M			SS-Mann, 4 SS Totenkopf Sturmbann, Camp Dora Mittelbau, Nordhausen (Ger.) 43-45	MURDER	U.S.
FRANK	189024	M	Ger.		SS Sturmbannfhr, Member of Gestapo, SD, Lyon (Fr.)	TORTURE	U.K.
FRANK	189453	M	Ger.		Cmdt., Sipo, The Hague, acted only upon directions of the command H.Q. of the BDS, Scheveningen (Neth.) 3.45	MURDER	NETH.
FRANK (or FRANCK)	192164	M	Ger.		Usturmfhr, SS Div."Das Reich", Rgt. "Der Fuehrer", Frayssinet le Gelat (Fr.) 5.44	MURDER	FR.
FRANK (see WIPPLER, Gerharde)	253463						
FRANK	259505	M	Ger.		Obermaat, Navy, 20 Schiffstammabteilung, Dubbeldam (Neth.) 3.45	MURDER	NETH.
FRANK	301312	M	Ger.		Member of Gestapo at Nove Mesto near Vahom, CC Auschwitz-Birkenau (Pol.) 39-45	MURDER	CZECH.
FRANK	305997	M	Ger.		Adjutant, Communist Internee, formed Communist Party secretary of Prague, CC Buchenwald (Ger.) 42-45	MURDER	FR.
FRANK, Albert	124779	M		97	Crim.Secretary, Sturmschfhr. SS, Bruessel (Bel.), Koblenz (Ger.)44-45	TORTURE	U.S.
FRANK, Anita	305890	F	Ger.		Female Overseer, SS, CC Neugraben, Tiefstak (Ger.) 44-2.45	ILL-TREATMENT	CZECH.
FRANK, August	62294	M		98	Gruppenfhr.	MURDER	U.N.W.C.C.
FRANK, Georg	148405	M	Ger.	1.12.14	Hptschfhr, W-SS, Schleissheim (Ger.) 44	MURDER	U.S.
FRANK, Hans	62295	M	Ger.		SS Gov.Gen. Ogruppenfhr, Poland	MURDER	U.S., U.N.W.C.C.
FRANK, Ignatz	250755	M			Pvt., Camp Bodungen, Nordhausen (Ger.)	MURDER	U.S.
FRANK, Jiri (Georg)	189237	M	Ger.	31. 7.88	Crim.Insp., Gestapo, Brno (Czech.) 39-45	MURDER	CZECH.
FRANK, John	301257	M			Crim. Employee, Abt.IV A, SD, Brussels (Bel.) 6.40-9.44	MURDER	BEL.
FRANK, Julius	148404	M	Ger.		Oschfhr, SS, Wlaclanek (Pol.) 44	MURDER	POL.
FRANK, Kurt	142521	M	Ger.	26	SS-Sturmmann, 1 SS Div.Leibstandarte "Adolf Hitler", Rossbach (Ger.) 3.45	MURDER	U.S.
FRANK, Ludwig	260847	M			Pvt., Army, Elversberg (Ger.) 7.44	WITNESS	U.S.
FRANK, Otto	10065	M			Civilian, State Service, Hesepe (Ger.)	MURDER	U.S.
FRANK, Peter	162167	M	Ger.		Hptsturmfhr, CC Auschwitz (Pol.) 43-44	TORTURE	U.S.
FRANK, Philippe	136313	M		08	Sgt., 11 Pz.Gespenst.Div., St.Quirin (Fr.) 9.-10.44	MURDER	FR.
FRANK, Rudolf	189298	M			Crim.Secretary, Gestapo, Brno (Czech.) 39 - 45	MURDER	CZECH.
FRANK, Theo	176653	M			Foreman, Org.Todt, CC Mhldorf, Ampfing (Ger.) 6.44, 4.44	MURDER	U.S.
FRANK, Walter	171688	M	Ger.		Pvt., Army, Last Unit G.-R. 9 Inf.Rgt., 1 Coy, Magny d'Anigon (Fr.) 9.44	MURDER	FR.
FRANK, Willi	162125	M	Ger.	15 - 17	SS Hptschfhr, Stapelberg (Ger.) 8.45 or 43	MURDER	U.S.
FRANKE	121937	M	Ger.		Lt.Col., Army, 190 Volksgrenadier Rgt., Neuhammer (Ger.) 11.44	MURDER	U.S.
FRANKE	129784	M	Ger.	99	Lt., Stalag II B	MISC.CRIMES	U.S.
FRANKE	137754	M			Lt., 29 Pz.Gren.Div.	WITNESS	U.S.
FRANKE	142523	M			Abschnittsleiter, Camp Muelhausen (Ger.) 2.45	WITNESS	U.S.
FRANKE	147336	M	Ger.		Adjutant, 10 Pz.Div. France 44	MURDER	FR.
FRANKE	186463	M	Ger.		Doctor, Army, Honfleur (Fr.) 8.44	WITNESS	FR.
FRANKE	186840	M	Ger.		II Pz.Div. Kampfgruppe Wilde (France) 41-45	TORTURE	FR.
FRANKE	190669	M	Ger.		Pvt., Eisenbahn Btty 717, St.Andries Vercenare les Bruges (Bel.)9.44	MURDER	BEL.
FRANKE	192997	M	Ger.		Guard, SS, CC Buchenwald (Ger.) 42-45	TORTURE	U.S.
FRANKE	193625	M	Ger.		Officer, CC Neuengamme	MURDER	BEL.
FRANKE	195094	M	Ger.		Pvt., Frontstalag 153 Kdo.18, St.Léger des Aubées (Fr.) 7.41	WITNESS	FR.
FRANKE	305130	M	Ger.		Lt., Sicherheitsdienst, Calavrita, Mega, Apileon, Aghia Lavra (Grc.) 12.43	MURDER	GRC.
FRANKE, Ernst	189361	M	Ger.		Sgt., 11 Pz.Div., 2 Coy 2 AA - A 7, near Bergerac Albine (Fr.)7-8.44	MURDER	FR.
FRANKE, Felix	187833	M	Ger.	30	Civilian, Riestedt (Ger.) 7.44	WITNESS	U.S.
FRANKE, Heinrich	257500	M	Ger.	23. 5.99	Farmer and Miner, Wisper und Idstein (Ger.) 3.45	MURDER	U.S.
FRANKE, Kurt	161648	M	Ger.		Cpl., Air Force, Luftgau, CC Eggemoen Honefoss (Nor.)	MURDER	NOR.
FRANKE, Paul Willy	255587	M	Ger.	29. 5.16	Confectioner, Prag (Czech.) 42	MURDER	CZECH.
FRANKE, Rigort	187892	M	Ger.		Civilian, Riestedt (Ger.) 7.44	TORTURE	U.S.
FRANKE, Rudolf	194038	M	Ger.	09	Oberwachtmstr, Member of Gestapo, SS, Landskroun (Czech.) 38-45	TORTURE	CZECH.
FRANKE, Walter	250756	M			Pvt., Camp Ellrich, Nordhausen (Ger.)	MURDER	U.S.
FRANKEL (see FRANKLE)	163462						
FRANKEN (or FRANCKEN)	39696	M	Ger.		Capt., Army, Leitungszahl L 54146, Cerisot (Fr.)	MURDER	FR.

FRA - FRA

NAME	C.R.FILE NUMBER	SEX	NATIO- NALITY	DATE OF BIRTH	RANK OCCUPATION UNIT PLACE AND DATE OF CRIME	REASON WANTED	WANTED BY
FRANKEN	192471	M	Ger.		Wachtmeister,Schupo,Drontheim(Nor.) 41-45	MURDER	NOR.
FRANKEN	252407	M	Ger.		Dr.,Kdo.1129,St.VIJ,Velbert(Ger.) 11.44	MURDER	FR.
FRANKENBERGER, Ernest	254339	M	Ger.	4. 5.11	Pvt.,13 Coy.,558 Gren.Regt.,Bruay en Atrois(Fr.) 9.44	MURDER	FR.
FRANKENBERGER, Michael	188308	M	Ger.	8.12.09	Member SA, C.C.Dachsbach(Ger.) 43-45	TORTURE	POL.
FRANKFURT	176652				SS-Oschfhr.,SS,C.C.Mühldorf-Ampfing(Ger.) 6.44-4.45	MURDER	U.S.
FRANKIE, Richard	162031	M	Ger.		Civilian,Reistedt(Ger.)	TORTURE	U.S.
FRANKL, Arnst	169461	M	Ger.		10 SS Pz.Div.,36 Regt.,Revin(Fr.) 6.44	MURDER	FR.
FRANKLE or FRANKEL Hermann Emil	169462	M		17. 9.25	Pvt., 1 Ost-Bn.447,Plouvien(Fr.) 8.44	TORTURE	FR.
FRANKOWSKI	125155	M	Ger.		Oberfeldw.,Lager XVIII,C.C.Kaernten(Aust.) 44-45	MISC.CRIMES	U.S.
FRANKS	141061	M	Ger.	10	Ger.Inf., Between Stalag 344-Goerlitz(Ger.) 1.45	WITNESS	U.K.
FRANKS, Karl	253958	M	Ger.		Interpreter, Ger.Military,Court for trials of PW's.(Ger.) 10.44	INTERR.	U.K.
FRANKTON	192174	M	Ger.		Member,Geheime Feldpolizei,Bruessels(Bel.)	MISC.CRIMES	BEL.
FRANQ, Jean	143477	M	Ger.	16.10.02	Member Waffen-SS,Vienne(Aust.) 3.44	MURDER	FR.
FRANSKE, Walter	124255	M			Pz.Regt.1,Coy.9,Malmedy(Bel.) 12.44	MURDER	U.S.
FRANSKE	195134				SA,Politischer Einsatz,Epe,Vreden(Ger.) 10.44-2.45	TORTURE	NETH.
FRANTRIN	301313	M	Ger.		Member of the Gestapo at Trencin,C.C.Oswiecim-Birkenau(Pol.) 39-45	MURDER	CZECH.
FRANTSKE	260066	M	Ger.		Officer Commanding Btty.,Res.Gebirgs Art.Gruppe 79, Massif of Vercors(Fr.)	SUSPECT	FR.
FRANTZ	138311	M	Ger.	10	SS-Schfhr.,Gestapo,SS,Lyon(Fr.) 6.-8.44	MURDER	FR.
FRANTZ	143478	M	Ger.	10	Gulzerode,Buchenwald(Ger.)	MURDER	FR.
FRANTZ	163463	M	Ger.	00	Civilian,Arbeits-Kdo.,C.C.Erzingen(Ger.)	TORTURE	FR.
FRANTZ	173410	M		00	Sturmschfhr.,SD,Paris(Fr.)	TORTURE	FR.
FRANTZ	185120	M	Ger.		Oberkapo,SS,C.C.Dachau(Ger.)	TORTURE	FR.
FRANTZ	189962	M	Ger.		Hptschfhr.,SS Unterabteilung IV(A),Place Bellecourt,Lyon(Fr.) 7.44	MURDER	FR.
FRANTZ or FRANCK	253962	M	Ger.		Sgt.,Fieldpolice,Allarmont(Fr.) 8.44	MISC.CRIMES	FR.
FRANTZ, August	173409	M	Ger.		SS-Schfhr.,Agent,Inspector,SD-Gestapo,Charleville(Fr.) 7.44	MISC.CRIMES	FR.
FRANTZ, Karl Kurt	171665	M	Ger.		Pvt.,9 Res.Gren.Regt.,Last Unit 3-57,Magny D'Anigon(Fr.) 9.44	MURDER	FR.
FRANTZ, Wilhelm	167119	M	Ger.		Civilian,Cultivator,Fechingen(Ger.)	TORTURE	FR.
FRANZ	1378				Lt.-Col.,Army-Police Regt.	MISC.CRIMES	U.K.
FRANZ	39691	M			SS-Mann,SS-Div.F.P.No.48963B,St.Sulpice Fortmiason,Arateau(Fr.) 8.44	MURDER	FR.
FRANZ	120559	M			Gen.-Maj.,Polizei,Army,former Polizei-Praesident of Hannover, Veldes(Yugo.) 42	MURDER	U.S.
FRANZ	121253	M	Ger.		Cpl.,Carcassonne(Fr.)	WITNESS	FR.
FRANZ	130643	F		20	SS-Woman C.C.Mittelbau Dora(Ger.)	MURDER	U.S.
FRANZ	192483	M	Ger.		Stromwerkstatt Cable Firm Arb.Kom.Employed,KL.Hallendorf,Brunswick (Ger.) 10.44-5.45	TORTURE	U.K.
FRANZ	142519	M	Ger.	15	Hptschfhr.,SS,Frankfurt-M.(Ger.) 7.44-3.45	MURDER	U.S.
FRANZ	142654	M	Ger.	00	Sturmschfhr.,SS,KL.Paris-Cirey(Fr.),Schirmeck(Ger.) 40-45	TORTURE	FR.
FRANZ	143425	M			Army, Roc(Fr.)	MURDER	FR.
FRANZ	143426	M			SS-Mann,Chateau Gontier(Fr.) 8.44	MURDER	FR.
FRANZ	143427	M			Officer,Gestapo,La Ferte St.Aubin(Fr.) 6.44	MURDER	FR.
FRANZ	143428	M			Uschfhr.,SS,Aude(Fr.) 44	MURDER	FR.
FRANZ	147335	M	Ger.		11 Pz.Div. (Fr.) 44	MURDER	FR.
FRANZ	148183			90	Stalag,KL.Demmin(Ger.) 44	TORTURE	FR.
FRANZ	148184	M	Ger.	97	Kapo,KL.Gunzrot(Ger.)	TORTURE	FR.
FRANZ	148920	M			Civilian, Roc(Fr.)	MURDER	FR.
FRANZ	155410	M			Civilian,Former Political Prisoner,C.C.Gardelegen(Ger.) 4.45	MURDER	U.S.
FRANZ	156713	M	Ger.		Member of Gestapo,Cahors(Fr.)	MURDER	FR.
FRANZ	161192	M	Ger.		Pvt.,Army,Arb.-Kdo.820,Ostritz(Ger.) 1.-4.43	TORTURE	U.K.
FRANZ	169459	M	Ger.	15	Head-Foreman-Civilian,Arb.-Kdo.7001,C.C.Stalag 11B,Hallendorf(Ger.)	TORTURE	U.K.
FRANZ	171699	M	Ger.		Warder,Sgt.,Prison,St.Lo(Fr.) 6.44	MURDER	FR.
FRANZ	186907	M	Ger.		Blockaelteste,Camp-Official,C.C.Mauthausen(Aust.)	TORTURE	FR.
FRANZ	186562	M	Ger.	16	Pvt.,610 Landesschuetzen Bn.,Stalag XXB,Bonin(Ger.) 6.44	MURDER	U.K.
FRANZ	186839	M	Ger.		11 Pz.Div.Kampfgruppe Wilde (Fr.)	MURDER	FR.
FRANZ	192996	M	Ger.		SS-Scharfhr.,SS,C.C.Buchenwald(Ger.) -40	TORTURE	U.S.
FRANZ	250765	M	Ger.		Rottfhr.,SS,Camp Dora,Nordhausen(Ger.)	MURDER	U.S.
FRANZ	252087	M	Ger.		Chief of Block and Camp Sud.,Mauthausen(Aust.)	TORTURE	FR.
FRANZ	252479	M	Ger.	06	Schfhr.,SS,Milano(Ital.) 5.45	INTERR.	U.K.
FRANZ	256584	F		11	Supervisor,Women-SS,C.C.Mühldorf-Dachau(Ger.)	MURDER	U.S.
FRANZ	305130	M	Ger.	95	Sgt.,Cmdt.Army,Camp Uebigau or Mebigau nr.Falkenberg(Ger.) 8.44-11.44	MISC.CRIMES	NETH.
FRANZ, Anni	306963	F	Ger.		SS-Guard,chief cook,C.C.Auschwitz(Pol.) 41-44	MURDER	POL.
FRANZ, August	143465	M			Agent,Gestapo,Charleville(Fr.)	MISC.CRIMES	FR.
FRANZ, Erich	140830	M	Ger.	16. 6.14	Oschfhr.,SS, Leader SS Lager Katzenbach,Frankfurt-M.(Ger.) 3.45	MURDER	U.S.
FRANZ, Erich	143429	M			Sgt.,Army,Struthof(Fr.)	MURDER	FR.
FRANZ, F.	173986	M	Ger.		Official,Kulturbund,Maribor(Yugo.) 4.41-44	MURDER	YUGO.
FRANZ, Franz	186311	M	Ger.	8. 3.15	SS-Oschfhr.,Kriminalangestellter,SD,Gestapo,Praha(Czech.) 39-45	MURDER	CZECH.
FRANZ, Georg	140907	M	Ger.	15	Hptschfhr.,SS,C.C.Breendonck(Bel.)	MURDER	BEL.
FRANZ, H.	125456	M			Pvt.,Army,Waldegg(Yugo.) 7.42	TORTURE	U.K.
FRANZ, Heinrich	305398	M	Ger.	29. 7.08	Oschfhr.,SD Amsterdam,Velsen,Beverwisk,Westweud,Berkhout(Neth.)4.-6.44	MURDER	NETH.
FRANZ, Hermann	192995	M	Ger.		Oschfhr.,SS Totenkopfverband,C.C.Buchenwald(Ger.) 42-45	TORTURE	U.S.
FRANZ, Joachim	188248	M	Ger.	16. 5.13	SS-Usturmfhr.,SS,C.C.Treblinki(Pol.) 42-43	MURDER	POL.
FRANZ, Kurt	306370	M	Ger.		SS-Uschfhr.,C.C.Buchenwald(Ger.) 5.38-10.43	MURDER	BEL.
FRANZ, Paul	126539	M	Ger.	95	Police Chief,C.C.Oberhausen(Ger.)	TORTURE	U.S.
FRANZ, Peter	148398	M			Camp Civilian,KL.Mauthausen(Aust.)	MURDER	U.S.
FRANZ, W.	256589	M			Bauvormann,C.C.Dachau,Mühldorf Area(Ger.)	MURDER	U.S.
FRANZ, Wilhelm	259606	M	Ger.	5. 1.04	Employee,Gestapo,Vrohovina(Czech.) 3.45	MURDER	CZECH.
FRANZ, Willi	306971	M	Ger.		SS-Sgt.(No.39367),C.C.Buchenwald(Ger.) 5.38-10.43	MURDER	BEL.
FRANZE	160155	M	Ger.	10	Stabs-Schfhr.,SS,Guard Bn., Section VII,Buchenwald(Ger.) 30-41	TORTURE	U.S.
FRANZE	192061	M	Ger.		Pvt.,Civilian Standort-Kdtr.,Gerardmer(Fr.) 9.-10.44		FR.
FRANZEL	148919	M		16	SS-Sturmmann,C.C.Dora,Nordhausen(Ger.)	LOOTING	FR.
FRANZEL, Emil	255374	M	Ger.	29. 5.01	Member Ger.Police,Prag(Czech.) 39-45	MISC.CRIMES	CZECH.

FRA - FRE

NAME	C.R.FILE NUMBER	SEX	NATIO-NALITY	DATE OF BIRTH	RANK OCCUPATION UNIT PLACE AND DATE OF CRIME	REASON WANTED	WANTED BY
FRANZEN	39680	M	Ger.		Capt., SS Army Staffelfhr, St. Sulpice, Mont Musson, Chateau-Gonthier (Fr.) 8.44	WITNESS	FR.
FRANZISCH see FIRAZISCH	306367						
FRANZOESI, Erwin	260135	M	Ger.	15	SS, Belgrad (Yugo.) 1.44-9.44	MISC.CRIMES	YUGO.
FRASCH, Erich	142522	M	Ger.		Civilian, Germany, Director of Stone Quarry	MURDER	U.S.
FRAUBER, Hans	189363	M	Ger.		Obersturmfhr., SS, Maisons Lafitte (Fr.) 8.43	TORTURE	FR.
FRAUDORFER or FRAUENDORFER, Max	267	M			Director, Administration of G.G. Leiter d. Abt. Arbeit	MURDER	POL.
FRAUENDORFER see FRAUDORFER, Max	267	M			Dr.		
FRAUENFELD	148185	M			Gestapo, KL. Drancy (Fr.) 42-44	MURDER	FR.
FRAUENFELD, Eduard Alfred	187605	M	Ger.		Propaganda-Chief, Occupied Terri Tories, Propaganda Office, Wien (Crimea)	MURDER	U.N.W.C.C.
FRAUENHOFER	139810	M			SS-Mann, W.-SS,C.C. Nordhausen, Dora (Ger.)	MURDER	U.S.
FRAUENHOFFER	143431	M			SS-Mann, Struthof (Fr.) 40-44	MURDER	FR.
FRAUNBERG	119413	M	Ger.		Major, Army Reported Com., Ivalo (Nor.) 10.44	MURDER	NOR.
FRAY	256586	M	Ger.		Oschafhr., CC Nordhausen Dora (Ger.)	MURDER	U.S.
FRECHIS	160183	M	Ger.	08	Untersturmfhr., SS-Security Service, Gestapo Section VII Pol. Thuringia (Ger.) 39-43	TORTURE	U.S.
FRED	1071	M	Ger.		Senior W.O., Army Feldgendarmerie, Bar Sur Aube (Fr.)	TORTURE	FR.
FREDAL	36643	M	Ger.		Civilian, C.C. Kdo. #. 602, Stalag IV D, Kemberg (Ger.)	TORTURE	U.K., SOV.
FREDDY	177589	M	Ger.		Police, Porteau-Poitiers (Fr.) 8.44	MURDER	FR.
FREDDY or NICOLAI	188388						
FREDERIC	174128	M	Ger.		Stalag VI A, C.C. Hemer (Ger.) 41	MISC.CRIMES	U.S.
FREDERICHS	148203	M			Chief, KL. Unterbillig (Ger.)	TORTURE	FR.
FREDERICHS	148204	M	Ger.		Civilian, Dortmund (Ger.)	MISC.CRIMES	FR.
FREDERICK	124483	M	Ger.		Civilian, Stalag VIII C, Krum (ger.) 10.41- 2.43	TORTURE	U.K.
FREDERICK, Franke	261361	M	Ger.	12	Lt., Org. Todt, Fontaniva (It.) 12.44	SUSPECT	U.S.
FREDIANI, F.	132175	M	Ger.	03	Pvt., Landesschuetz. Bn. 74, River Manocchia (It.) 11.43	MURDER	U.K.
FREDRICH	121254	M	Ger.		SS-Obersturmfhr., C.C. Buchenwald (Ger.)	TORTURE	FR.
FREDRICHS, Kurt	257892	M			Pvt., 150 Panzer Bde., Meuse-Bridge, Antwerp (Bel.) 12.44	MISC.CRIMES	U.S.
FREESE	142651	M	Ger.	20	Lt., Tank Corps First Lt., Gravenwoehr (Ger.) 11.-12.44	MISC.CRIMES	U.S.
FREESE	257927	M			First Lt., 150. Pz. Bde., Meuse-Bridge, Antwerp (Bel.) 12.44	MISC.CRIMES	U.S.
FREESER	191828	M	Ger.	15	Pvt., Stalag IV D, Eisleben (Ger.) 3.45	MURDER	U.K.
FREGLER	155411	M	Ger.		Lt., 3. SS Pz.Div. 3 RD.SS Pz.Regt., Engr.Coy. (Sov.Un.) 42-45	MURDER	U.S.
FREHN	139139	M	Ger.		Forester, Civilian	MURDER	U.S.
FREI see FRY see FREY	29879						
FREI	130115	M			Obersturmfhr., SS, C.C. Nordhausen Dora Mittelbau (Ger.)	MURDER	U.S.
FREI	148205	M			Public Official, Karlsruhe (Ger.)	MISC.CRIMES	FR.
FREI	155421	M			Sgt., SS 3rd. Bau Bde.from Wieda to Gardelegen (Ger.) 4.45	MURDER	U.S.
FREI, Hans	167118	M	Ger.		Director.Chief, Commandantur-Gestapo, Usine of Antoigne, Sainte-Jeanne (Fr.) 44	MISC.CRIMES	FR.
FREI, Karl	129010	M	Ger.	6.20	Sgt., Wolgatartaren Legion 627, Hainaut (Bel.) 2.-9.44	MURDER	BEL.
FREIBERG	148417	M			W.O., KL. Stassfurt (Ger.) 4.-5.45	MURDER	FR.
FREIBERG	254154	M			Head, evacuation of C.C. Buchenwald (Ger.)	INTERR.	FR.
FREIBERGER, Grete	148397	F			Chief, SS, Lanzing Mauthausen (Aust.) 44-45	TORTURE	U.S.
FREIBOTT	29881	M	Ger.		KL. Grosswenkheim ueb. Monnerstadt (Ger.) 5.42	TORTURE	U.K.
FREIBURG, Norbert Bernard	148216	M	Ger.	3.03	Sturmfhr., SS	MURDER	FR.
FREIDEL, Fritz	140894	M	Ger.		Lt., 2. Coy. Verbindungsstab 331, Bolnes (Neth.)5.45	MURDER	NETH.
FREIDLIN	173412	M			SD, Strasbourg-Carpach (Fr.)	TORTURE	FR.
FREIDMANN, Paul	1380	M	Ger.		Officer, SS	MISC.CRIMES	U.K.
FREIDRICH	29880	M			Pvt. 4th TM Coy. 397 BM GD 9 FR. Graudenz (Pol.) 42	TORTURE	U.K.
FREIHER	142505	M	Ger.	20	SS Sturmmann,'SS Totenkopf Sturmbann C.C. Buchenwald-Weimar (Ger.)	MURDER	U.S.
FREIHERR	132568	M	Ger.		Col., Army, Luebeck (Ger.)	TORTURE	FR.
FREIMANN, Arthur	133370	M	Ger.	20	Sgt., Air Force, Fliegerhorst Lechfeld, Neckarsulm (Ger.)3.45	WITNESS	U.S.
FREIMARK	125455	M	Ger.		Pvt., C.C. Bobrek-Beuten (Ger.) 1.45	MURDER	U.K., SOV.
FREIMARK	256654		Ger.		SS-Sgt., C.C. Nordhausen (Ger.)	MURDER	U.S.
FREIMEYER, Jakob	176651	M			Arbeitslager C.C. Muhldorf-Ampfing (Ger.) 6.44-4.45	MURDER	U.S.
FREIMULLER	260006	M	Ger.		Lt., 217th Res.Gren.Bn., Massif of Vercors, Issle and Drome (Fr.) 7.-8.44	SUSPECT	FR.
FREIMUT	176650	M			SS-Hauptsturmfhr., C.C. Muhldorf-Ampfing (Ger.) 6.44-4.45	MURDER	U.S.
FREIMUTH	256000	M			Sgt., SS, C.C. Buchenwald (Ger.)	MURDER	U.S.
FREIS	72086	M		00	SS Scharfhr., C.C. Hinzert (ger.) 42-43	TORTURE	U.S.
FREIS	130114	M			SS Obersturmfhr., C.C. Nordhausen Dora Mittelbau (Ger.)	MURDER	U.S.
FREIS	26182	M	Ger.		Oschfhr. Chief, C.C. Nordhausen Dora (Ger.)	BRUTALITY	FR.
FREISE	122664	M	Ger.	05	Sgt., Army, Inf. (Former W.O. of Renonteschule at Gardelegen) C.C. Gardelegen (Ger.)	MURDER	U.S.
FREISE	148219	M			SS Hauptsturmfhr., Portiers (Fr.) 44	MISC.CRIMES	FR.
FREISE	189063	M	Ger.		Dr., SS Sturmbannfhr., Regierungsrat, SD Gestapo, C.C. Dachau (Ger.)	MURDER	BEL.
FREISLEBEN, Augustin	253639	M	Ger.	1.05	Informer, Gestapo, Bruenn (Czech.)42	INTERR.	CZECH.
FREISLER, Karl	136565	M	Ger.		SS-Hauptsturmfhr., C.C. Buchenwald-Dachau (Ger.)	TORTURE	CAN.
FREISLER, Roland	62335	M	Ger.		Justice-Praesident, SS-Kriegsgericht, 41-43	MURDER	U.N.W.C.C.,M
FREISS	301558	M			SS-Pvt., i-c Passports, Political Dept. C.C. Dachau (Ger.) 40-45	MURDER	BEL.
FREITAG	148218	M			Oberarzt, C.C. Hohenlychen and Ravensbrueck (Ger.) 5.44	TORTURE	FR.
FREITAG	173253	M	Ger.	01	Pvt., Stalag 4 F, C.C. Chemnitz (Ger.) 10.43-3.45	TORTURE	U.K.
FREITAG	188826	M	Ger.		Stabsarzt, Army, Dury Les Amiens (Fr.)44	WITNESS	FR.
FREITAG	252989	M	Ger.		Lt.Colonel, 338 Div. Command. 3 Bn. Unteroff.-Schule L'Hieres La Bresse (Fr.) 9.-11.44	MISC.CRIMES	FR.
FREITAG, Kurt	169480	M	Ger.		Wachtmeister, C.C. Staff, Rotenfels Schirmeck (Fr.)	MURDER	U.K.
FREITAG, Kurt	256655	M	Ger.	7.03	Employee, Pfeffer I Shift II, C.C. Nordhausen (Ger.)	MURDER	U.S.
FREITAG, Ulrich	155406	M	Ger.		Hitlerjugend, Javenitz, Gardelegen (Ger.) 4.45	MURDER	U.S.
FREITARG, Joachim Friedrich	306005	M	Ger.		Dr., Hauptsturmfhr. Chief, of Gestapo at Lueneburg (Ger.) 4.45	MURDER	U.K.
FREMEL, Josef	250764	M			Pvt., Camp Harzungen-Dora, Nordhausen (Ger.)	MURDER	U.S.
FREMEREY	173384	M	Ger.		Gaufrauenschafts-Leiter, NSDAP, Strasbourg (Fr.) 44	TORTURE	FR.
FRENK, Franz	250757	M			Pvt., Camp Dora, Nordhausen (Ger.) 44	MURDER	U.S.

FRE-FRI

NAME	C.R.FILE NUMBER	SEX	NATIO-NALITY	DATE OF BIRTH	RANK OCCUPATION UNIT PLACE AND DATE OF CRIME	REASON WANTED	WANTED BY
FRENKERT, Heinrich	250141	M			Uscharfhr., SS, Camp Ellrich, Nordhausen (Ger.)	MURDER	U.S.
FRENZEL	194977	M	Ger.		Cpl., Army, Chateau Leveque (Fr.) 6.44	TORTURE	FR.
FRENZEL	143451	M			Adjutant-chief, Army, Pz.Aufkl.Abt.II, Albine (Fr.) 8.44	MISC.CRIMES	FR.
FRENZEL	148209	M		15	Kapo, C.C.Dora, Nordhausen (Ger.)	MURDER	FR.
FRENZEL	186845	M	Ger.		C.C.Flossenburg (Ger.)	MURDER	FR.
FRENZNIC	148206	M			Capt., Army, Clermont-Ferrand (Fr.) 7.44	PILLAGE	FR.
FRENZRICH	148207	M			Major, Army, Maurice Brin (Fr.)	PILLAGE	FR.
FRERICHS	192994	M			SS-Osturmfhr., SS, C.C.Buchenwald (Ger.)	TORTURE	U.S.
FRERICHS, Wilhelm	306972	M	Ger.		SS-Sturmfhr., C.C.Buchenwald (Ger.) between 5.38 and 10.43	MURDER	BEL.
FRESDORF, Otto	250758	M			Pvt., Camp Ellrich, Nordhausen (Ger.)	MURDER	U.S.
FRESE	148208	M			Public official, Faliawerke, (Ger.)	MISC.CRIMES	FR.
FRESE	165309	M	Ger.		N.S.D.A.P., Bruehl (Ger.)	TORTURE	FR.
FRESEMANN	160181	M	Ger.		Osturmfhr., SS, Standarte Eike, 12 Coy., Camp-leader of C.C.Sachsenhausen (Ger.) 3.45	MURDER	U.K.
FRESHLEADER	36642	M			Guard, Stalag, civilian, Kemberg (Ger.)	TORTURE	SOV.UN.
FRESHNER	128855	M	Ger.		Pvt., C.C.Gullins Graben, Camp Enstal Stumach, Gullins Graben (Ger.) 12.42	MURDER	U.K.
FRESIUS	259370	M	Ger.		Admiral, Bergues (Fr.)	INTERR.	FR.
FRESSLER	162019	M		05	Cpl., Army, Bau-Pi.Bn., Stalag VIII B, Cosel (Ger.) 6.-12.40	TORTURE	U.K.
FRESTICH or PHESTERER	125454	M		90	Pvt., 877 Bn., Stalag 18 C, Gullen Grabben near Worschach (Aust.) 12.42	MURDER	U.K.
FRETTON	68627	M			Foreman, civilian, C.C.	TORTURE	U.S.
FREUD, Christian	162030	M	Ger.		Uscharfhr., SS, 16 Inf.Div., Maille Naintre (Fr.) 8.44	MURDER	FR.
FREUDE	130059	M	Ger.		Foreman of the mine, Arbeitskdo., C.C.Beuthen (Ger.)	MURDER	U.K.
FREUDENBERG	163464	M			Pvt., Army, 10 Pz.Div., 36 Regt., Revin (Fr.) 6.44	MURDER	FR.
FREUDENBERGER	1559	M			Officer medical, Sanitaets-Korps, Heppenheim (Ger.)	MISC.CRIMES	U.S.
FREUDENBERGER, Fritz	134890	M		15	Pol.secretary, SS, Gestapo, Bensheim (Fr.)	WITNESS	U.S.
FREUDENFELD, Erwin	259114	M	Ger.		SS-Mann, SS, C.C.Dachau (Ger.) 11.42-45	MISC.CRIMES	YUGO.
FREUDENHAMMER, Emmy	253643	F	Ger.		C.C.Geisenheim (Ger.) 12.44-4.45	TORTURE	POL.
FREUDENREICH, Friedrich	187365	M			Rottenfhr., 4 SS-Totenkopf-Sturmbann, C.C.Dora-Mittelbau, Nordhausen (Ger.) 43-45	MURDER	FR.
FREUN	188606	M	Ger.		Adjutant-chief, SS-Standarte "Der Fuehrer", Theil of Vanne (Fr.) 8.44	MURDER	FR.
FREUND	39695	M	Ger.		SS-Sturmfhr., SS-Div., St.Sulpice Montmusson Chateau-Gonthier (Fr.) 8.44	MURDER	FR.
FREUND	171700	M	Ger.		Member, Einsatzstab Rosenberg, civil-servant, office for Supervision of Literature, Berlin (Ger.) 40-44	PILLAGE	FR.
FREUND, Paul	173408	M			Oscharfhr., Waffen-SS, Calais Arras (Fr.)	TORTURE	FR.
FREUND, Paul	185124	M	Ger.		SS-Uscharfhr., SS, C.C.Sachsenhausen (Ger.)	TORTURE	FR.
FREUNDT	166262	M	Ger.		Lt.Col., Abwehr, Warsaw (Pol.) 42	WITNESS	U.S.
FREUNDT	176702	M			SS-Uscharfhr., SS, C.C.Miehldorf-Ampfing (Ger.) 6.44-4.45	MURDER	U.S.
FREUZEL, Otto	143452	M			Adjutant, SS, Pz.Regt., Bergerac (Fr.) 6.-7.44	MISC.CRIMES	FR.
FREY see FRY see FREI	29879						
FREY	36648	M	Ger.		Dr., Lt.Col., camp-commander, Oflag VII C-H, Laufen (Ger.) 1.41	MURDER	U.K.
FREY	123642	M			SS-Uscharfhr., C.C.Gunthergrube, C.C.Oswiecim (Pol.)	MURDER	U.S.
FREY	123963	M	Ger.	91 - 93	Head-surgeon, Stalag 383, C.C.Hohenfels (Ger.) 42-4.45	BRUTALITY	U.K.
FREY	12428	M	Ger.		Sgt., Hafenueberwachungsstelle, Calais (Fr.) 44	TORTURE	FR.
FREY	147837	M			Chemist, C.C.Ravensbrueck (Ger.) 5.44	TORTURE	FR.
FREY	155407	M			Uscharfhr., SS, 3 Bau-Bde., C.C. from Weida to Gardelegen (Ger.) 4.45	MURDER	J.S.
FREY	171702	M	Ger.		Branch-director, Einsatzstab Rosenberg, Ostgebietaministerium, St.Germain (Fr.) 40-44	PILLAGE	FR.
FREY	189245	M	Ger.	92	Pvt., Navy-Artl., C.C.Luensburg (Ger.) 4.45	MURDER	U.K.
FREY	260100	M			Lt., 7 Res.Artl.Regt., Massif du Vercors Isere and Drome (Fr.) 7.-8.44	SUSPECT	FR.
FREY, Franz	143455	M			Pvt., Army, Pont de Nieppe (Fr.) 9.44	MURDER	FR.
FREY, Hans	258173	M	Ger.		Cpl., SD, Gestapo, Jezdina (Fr.) 12.42	PILLAGE	YUGO.
FREY, Jean	143454	M	Ger.		Romainville St.Germain (Fr.) 10.43	MURDER	FR.
FREY, Johann-Frederick	173428	M	Ger.	11	Pvt., 1 Flak-Regt., 17 Div., Langenlonsheim (Ger.) 12.44	WITNESS	U.S.
FREY, Karl	250744	M			Pvt., Camp Ellrich, Nordhausen (Ger.)	MURDER	U.S.
FREY, Liesel	252988	F	Ger.		Civilian, Langenlonsheim (Ger.) 12.44	WITNESS	U.S.
FREY, Otto	37968	M	Ger.		County-court-director, public official, Prag (Czech.) 39-45	MURDER	U.N.W.C.C.
FREY, Robert	147836	M			Engineer, Hadmersleben (Ger.)	TORTURE	FR.
FREY, Willy	148394	M			Camp personnel, C.C.Mauthausen (Aust.) 41-45	MURDER	FR.
FREYE, Walter	163465	M		21. 9.09	Volonteer, 1 Ost-Bn.447, Plouvien (Fr.) 8.44	TORTURE	FR.
FREYER, Kurt	160182	M	Ger.	21	Uscharfhr., SS, C.C.Buchenwald (Ger.) 40-45	TORTURE	FR.
FREYS	130111	M			Hptsturmfhr., SS, C.C.Dora-Mittelbau, Nordhausen (Ger.)	MURDER	U.S.
FREYS	135160	M	Ger.		SS-Scharfhr., C.C.Wittlich (Ger.) 41, 42 and 43	TORTURE	U.S.
FREYSANG	119414	M	Ger.		Lt.Col., 20 Army-staff, I C Abwehr, Prov.Finmark (Nor.) 10.44	MURDER	NOR.
FREYSE	259371	M	Ger.		SS-Hptsturmfhr., Gestapo of Poitiers area (Fr.) 40-45	MISC.CRIMES	FR.
FREYSINGER, Hans	258574	M	Ger.	1. 2.62	Sonderfhr., State service, Oflag VII A, Murnau (Ger.) 39-45	BRUTALITY	POL.
FREYTACT	254167	M	Ger.		Org.Todt, Rosny-Bois (Fr.) 8.44	INTERR.	FR.
FREYWALD, Willy	148364	M			Civilian, C.C.Mauthausen (Aust.)	MURDER	U.S.
FREZ see FEZ	72129						
FRIBIZ	350134	M	Ger.		Member, SS-Sicherheitsdienst, Gestapo, Rennes Troyes and region (Fr.) 10.43-8.44	MURDER	FR.
FRICH, Otto	257358	M	Ger.		SS-Sturmschfhr., SS, slave labour camp, Beisfjord near Narvik (Nor.) 6.-11.42	BRUTALITY	YUGO.
FRICHER	142633	M			Lt., Army, Troissereux (Fr.) 8.44	MURDER	FR.
FRICHKE	136915	M		20	SS-Uscharfhr., SS, C.C.Hallein (Ger.)	BRUTALITY	FR.
FRICHS, Heinrich	252411	M	Ger.		Pvt., 377 Jaeger-Regt., Vinkt (Bel.)	MISC.CRIMES	BEL.
FRICHT	148197	M			C.C.Duesseldorf (Ger.)	TORTURE	FR.
FRICK	142631	M			Lt.Col., Army, Div.405, Roppe Severans Giromagny (Fr.) 9.44	MURDER	FR.
FRICK	160163	M	Ger.		Civilian, Stalag XII D, Sohleich (Ger.)	TORTURE	FR.
FRICK	256102	M	Ger.		Farmer, Westerroch (Ger.) 2.44	MURDER	FR.
FRICK, Heinrich	163466	M	Ger.	5. 7.81	Civilian, Montigny en Metz (Fr.) 40-45	TORTURE	FR.
FRICK, Karl	252986	M	Ger.	14	Sgt., Orts-Kmdtr.91859, Vitry en Artois (Fr.) 7.44	TORTURE	U.S.

FRI-FRI

NAME	C.R.FILE NUMBER	SEX	NATIO-NALITY	DATE OF BIRTH	RANK OCCUPATION UNIT PLACE AND DATE OF CRIME	REASON WANTED	WANTED BY
FRICK, Peter	250746	M			Rottfhr., SS, Camp Nixei, Nordhausen (Ger.)	MURDER	U.S.
FRICKE	133730	M	Ger.		Hptschfhr., SS, C.C. Buchenwald (Ger.)	TORTURE	U.S.
FRICKE	139808	M		00	Hptschfhr., Waffen-SS, Arbeitskdo.A-6	MISC.CRIMES	U.S.
FRICKE	176649	M			Organ.Todt, C.C. Muhldorf, Ampfing (Ger.) 6.44-4.45	MURDER	U.S.
FRICKE	193913	M	Ger.		Lt., Feldgendarmerie, Ascq (Fr.)	WITNESS	FR.
FRICKE	194976	M	Ger.		Pvt., Army, Cressensacq (Fr.) 6.40	WITNESS	FR.
FRICKE	301170	M			N.C.O., parachute, Gorinchem (Neth.) 1.45	PILLAGE	NETH.
FRICKE, Friedrich	250745	M			Pvt., C.C. Ellrich, Nordhausen (Ger.)	MURDER	U.S.
FRICKE, Kurt	1379	M	Ger.		Pvt., Army	MISC.CRIMES	U.K.
FRICKE, Kurt	259074	M	Ger.		Admiral	WITNESS	U.S.
FRICKE, Max August	189240	M	Ger.	6. 3.02	Crim.Secr., SS, S.D., Gestapo, Mlada Boleslav Jicin (Czech.) 40-45	MURDER	CZECH.
FRICKE, Werner	142504	M	Ger.	17. 6.09 or 08	Hptschfhr.,(Member of the Commander Staff), Waffen-SS-Totenkopf-Sturmbann, C.C. Weimar, Buchenwald (Ger.) 39	TORTURE	U.S.
FRICKE, Wilhelm	252412	M	Ger.		Sgt., 377 Jaeg.Regt., Vinkt (Bel.)	MURDER	BEL.
FRICKEL, Albert	163467	M	Ger.		SS, 36 Pz.Regt., 9 Coy., Revin, Issancourt (Fr.) 6.44	MURDER	FR.
FRICKER	250747	M			Uschfhr., SS, C.C. Ellrich, Nordhausen (Ger.)	MURDER	U.S.
FRICKER, Albert	171701	M	Ger.	9. 4.20	Sicherheits-Pol., Marseille (Fr.) 4.44	PILLAGE	FR.
FRICKINGER	137758	M			Lt., 15 Pz.Gren.Regt., 29 Pz.Gren.Div.	WITNESS	U.S.
FRIDAG	148196	M			Civilian, Drensteinfurt (Ger.)	MISC.CRIMES	FR.
FRIDEL, August	193914	M	Ger.		Adjutant, Army, Blaye (Fr.)	MURDER	FR.
FRIDERICI	260838	M	Ger.		Hptsturmfhr., SS, Security Guard, Kassel (Ger.) 43-45	MURDER	U.S.
FRIDERITZI, Hans Heinrich Johannes	300076	M	Ger.		Overseer, foreign workers, Harbour of Luebeck (Ger.) 42-45	MURDER	POL.
FRIDRICH	270	M	Ger.		Major-General, Army, 8 Army, 17 Inf.Div. 9.39-10.39	MURDER	POL.
FRIEBE	250748	M			Rottfhr., SS, Camp Nixei, Nordhausen (Ger.)	MURDER	U.S.
FRIEBOCS	148195	M			Medecin, C.C. Hohenlychen, Ravensbrueck (Ger.) 5.44	TORTURE	FR.
FRIED	39640	M			Cpl., Army, 3 Coy., 179 Bn., Gilly sur Jacre (Fr.) 8.44	MURDER	FR.
FRIED	261200	M	Ger.		Pvt., 5-I N-Regt.211, 139 Arbeits-Bereich Liane, Alleur, Lez Liege (Bel.) 9.44	MURDER	BEL.
FRIED, Rudolf	188307	M	Ger.	07 or 10	Civ. Kreisleiter, NSDAP, Aachen (Ger.) 8.44	TORTURE	U.S.
FRIEDEL (or RIEDEL)	173398	M	Ger.		Cpl., 6 Coy., Landesschuetzen-Bn.400, Gross Orner, Hettstedt (Ger.)9.44	MURDER	U.S.
FRIEDEMANN, Hans	192930	M	Ger.		Schupe, C.C. Falstad (Nor.) 11.42	MURDER	NOR.
FRIEDEMANN, Paul	1380	M	Ger.		Officer, SS, Div.17 "Goetz von Berlichingen", Waffen-Grenadier-Bde.SS I E	MISC.CRIMES	U.K.
FRIEDERES, Daniel	256658	M		27. 2.05	Employee, Block3, C.C. Dora, Nordhausen (Ger.)	MURDER	U.S.
FRIEDL, Franz-Xaver	148409	M	Ger.	1. 1.87	Chief, Pol., Freising, Altenkirchen (Ger.) 6.44	MURDER	U.S.
FRIEDL, Johann	305891	M			Agent, Gestapo (Czech.) 39-45	INTERR.	CZECH.
FRIEDLER	167117	M			Feldgendarmerie of Moulins, Larochemillay (Fr.) 8.44	PILLAGE	FR.
FRIEDMANN	161358	M			Lt., Army, Chenebier, Etobon (Fr.) 9.44	MURDER	FR.
FRIEDMANN	173357	M	Ger.	10	Feldgendarmerie, Vouziers, Ardennes (Fr.)	MISC.CRIMES	FR.
FRIEDMANN	179497	M		09	Pol.-Wachtmeister, Polizei, Thorn (Pol.)	MURDER	POL.
FRIEDMANN	250749	M			Sgt., C.C. Ellrich, Nordhausen (Ger.)	MURDER	U.S.
FRIEDMANN, Heinrich	195133	M	Ger.		Director, Omnia Treuhand-Ges., Amsterdam (Neth.) 40-45	PILLAGE	NETH.
FRIEDNER, Otto	252979	M	Ger.	13	Pvt., Flak-Abt.122, Bn.91, Strijpen (Bel.)	PILLAGE	BEL.
FRIEDRICH	39690	M	Ger.		Usturmfhr., SS, SS-Div.17, Pz.Gren.Div. "Goetz v. Berlichingen", Sturm-Geschuetz-Abt.17 or Pz.Jg.-Abt.17, Segre, Renaze (Fr.) 7.-8.44	MURDER	FR.
FRIEDRICH	119415	M			Lt.Col., Comd.550 Nachr.Regt., 20 Army, Finmark (Nor.) 44	MURDER	U.N.W.C.C.-N
FRIEDRICH	133729	M			Hptschfhr., SS, C.C. Weimar, Buchenwald (Ger.)	BRUTALITY	U.S.
FRIEDRICH	141474	M			N.C.O., Gestapo, Chenebier, Etobon (Fr.) 9.44	MURDER	FR.
FRIEDRICH	148201	M		00	Dr., SA, Stalag, C.C. Wittlich (Ger.)	BRUTALITY	FR.
FRIEDRICH	189761	M	Ger.		Gendarmerie, Metzeral (Fr.) 44	MURDER	FR.
FRIEDRICH	189981	M			Gmdt., C.C. Banjica (Yugo.)	MURDER	YUGO.
FRIEDRICH	261348	F	Ger.		Lt., Bn. Spielberg, Regt.z.b.V. "Colonel Wolff", Mauleon, Navarreaux (Fr.) 6.+8.44	MURDER	FR.
FRIEDRICH	300771	M	Ger.		Member, Gestapo, Alencon and Throughout erae Department (Fr.)6.-8.44	MURDER	FR.
FRIEDRICH	306681	M			Pvt., 331 Pion.Bn., 331 Inf.Div., Mijnheerenland (Neth.) 5.45	PILLAGE	NETH.
FRIEDRICH	251538	M	Ger.		Dr., Lt., Army, District Command of, Kragujevac, Arandjelovac (Yugo.)41	MURDER	YUGO.
FRIEDRICH, Charles	62172	M	Ger.	6. 3.08	Commanding officer, Gestapo, Saales (Fr.) 4.43	MURDER	FR.
FRIEDRICH, Curt	171664	M	Ger.		Pvt., 9 Gren.Regt.d.Res., I Coy., Army, Last Unit 4-181, Melder-Coy., Magny d' Anigon (Fr.) 9.44	MURDER	FR.
FRIEDRICH, Edmond	307101	M	Ger.	5. 8.04	Head of Gendarmerie at Metzeral, Breitenbach Haut Rhin (Fr.) 11.44	MURDER	FR.
FRIEDRICH, Emil	181564	M	Ger.	14. 3.01	Kriminal-Angestellter, SS-Bewerber, S.D., Gestapo, Prag (Czech.) 39-45	MURDER	CZECH.
FRIEDRICH, Erich	250753	M			Cpl., C.C. Ellrich, Nordhausen (Ger.)	MURDER	U.S.
FRIEDRICH, Ernst	148200	M		03	Civ., C.C. Salzwedel (Ger.)	TORTURE	FR.
FRIEDRICH, Friederika	122660	F	Ger.	15	Female Overseer, SS-Arbeitslager 101, C.C. Buchenwald (Ger.) 44-45	TORTURE	U.S.
FRIEDRICH, Fritz	134709	M	Ger.	04	Osturmbannfhr., SS, Neustadt-Schweinfurt (Ger.) 2.45	MISC.CRIMES	U.S.
FRIEDRICH, Fritz	256657	M	Ger.	5. 7.13	Sgt., S.D., Larvik (Nor.) 42-45	TORTURE	NOR.
FRIEDRICH, Georg	186313	M	Ger.	25. 7.09	SS-Mann, S.D., Gestapo, Notdienstverpflichteter, Prag (Czech.) 42-45	MURDER	CZECH.
FRIEDRICH, Herbert	256099	M	Ger.		Kapo, C.C. Flossenburg (Ger.)	MURDER	FR.
FRIEDRICH, Joseph	253961	M	Ger.	26.12.25	Pvt., 13 Coy., 558 Gren.Regt., Bruay ex Artois (Fr.) 9.44	MURDER	FR.
FRIEDRICH, Karl	150502	M	Ger.	05	Krimin. Oberasst., Gestapo, (Lux.) 43	MURDER	LUX
FRIEDRICH, Karl	173209	M			Civilian, C.C. Schirmeck, Saales (Fr.) 6.44	TORTURE	U.K.
FRIEDRICH, Karl	252982	M	Ger.	26. 3.05	N.C.O., Fieldpolice, NSDAP (Bel.)	INTERR.	BEL.
FRIEDRICH, Martin	250752	M	Ger.	19.11.00	Hptschfhr., SS, C.C. Dora, Nordhausen (Ger.)	MURDER	U.S.
FRIEDRICH, Michael	250751	M			SS-Mann, SS, C.C. Bedungen, Nordhausen (Ger.)	MURDER	U.S.
FRIEDRICH, Otto	128856	M	Ger.	95	Foreman, Member, Woedtard, NSDAP, Stutzengruen (Ger.) 11.43	MISC.CRIMES	U.K.
FRIEDRICH, Otto	136316	M	Ger.	98	Army, Cpl., Flixecourt at Ville le Marclet (Fr.) 8.44	TORTURE	FR.
FRIEDRICH, Peter	192652	M	Ger.	4.10.18	SS-Guard, 4 SS-Totenkopf-Sturmbann, C.C. Dora Mittelbau, Nordhausen (Ger.) 43-45	MURDER	U.S.
FRIEDRICH, Ronald	135213	M	Ger.	29	Civilian, C.C. Lintfort (Ger.) 10.-11.41	WITNESS	U.S.
FRIEDRICH, Walter	194975	M	Ger.		Pvt., Pz.Army, Montirat (Fr.)	MURDER	FR.
FRIEDRICHS	261840	M	Ger.		Cpl., Remilly sur Seine (Fr.) 6.44	MISC.CRIMES	FR.

NAME	C.R.FILE NUMBER	SEX	NATIO- NALITY	DATE OF BIRTH	RANK OCCUPATION UNIT PLACE AND DATE OF CRIME	REASON WANTED	WANTED BY
FRIEDRICHS, Helmut	188344	M			Goerlitz(Ger.)	MURDER	BEL.
FRIEDRICHS, Willi	191836	M	Ger.	09	Capt.,Army,7 Jagd-Div.,227 Luftnachrichten-Regt.,Thanham(Ger.) 4.45	MURDER	U.S.
FRIEDRICHSEN, Konrad	142657	M	Ger.	6. 9.06	SS-Oschfhr.,SS-Wirtschaftsverwaltungshauptamt,between Seyboldsdorf-Vilsbiburg(Ger.) 4.45	WITNESS	U.S.
FRIEDSAM	139811	M		08	SG-Hptschfhr.,SS	MURDER	U.S.
FRIEDT	119416	M	Ger.		Maj.,Cmdt.6 Jaeg.Bn.,8 Geb.Div.,20 Army,Finmark(Nor.) 44	MURDER	NOR.
FRIES or FRIESE	143486	M			SS-Oschfhr.,SS,Auschwitz(Pol.)	MURDER	POL.
FRIEGER	271	M	Ger.		Capt.,Army,Jaeger Div.118.(Yugo) 7.43-1.44	MURDER	YUGO.
FRIEMEL, Siegfried	191288	M	Ger.		SS-Sturmbannfhr.,9 or 20 Gren.Regt.SS Panz.Div."Hohenstaufen" Jevigne Lierneux(Bel.) 12.44	MURDER	BEL.
FRIES	155412	M	Ger.		SS-Ogruppenfhr.,SS-3 Panz.Div.(Russ.) 42-45	MURDER	U.S.
FRIES	252476	M	Gef.		Cpl.,16 Coy.,377 Jg.Regt.	MISC.CRIMES	BEL.
FRIES, Otto	148268	M		03	C.C.,Sarre Louis(Fr.)	TORTURE	FR.
FRIESE see FRIES	143486						
FRIESE, Walter	256656	M	Ger.	3. 4.15	Civ.,Genthin(Ger.) 12.44	BRUTALITY	U.S.
FRIESS	173366	M		99	Capt., 3 Coy.,Landesschuetzen-Bn.393,Carcassone-Aude(Fr.) 44	MURDER	FR.
FRIESS, Walter	137753	M			Maj.-Gen.,29 Panz.Gren.Div.	WITNESS	U.S.
FRIESSNER, Johannes	259072	M	Ger.	92	Gen.,wanted as witness,possibly defendant	WITNESS	U.S.
FRIGGE	173385	M	Ger.		Lt.-Col.,Sicherheitsabschnitt Mitte,Cacak(Yugo.) 42-44	MURDER	YUGO.
FRIIS, Kurt or FRIESCH	256816	M	Ger.	05	Interpreter,SD,Sandefjord(Nor.)	WITNESS	NOR.
FRIKE	301836	F	Ger.		Member of St.Quentin Gestapo,Vraignes en Verman,Dois(Somme)(Fr.)8.44	MURDER	FR.
FRILL	148266	M		00	Osturmbannfhr.,Member SS,Kromag-Werke,Pol.,Hirtenberg(Ger.) 42-44	TORTURE	FR.
FRILLE, Albert	253960	M	Ger.	23. 1.07	Pvt.,13 Coy.,558 Gren.Regt.,Bruay en Artois(Fr.) 9.44	MURDER	FR.
FRINBERGER	252983	M	Ger.		Capt.,Army,Huy(Bel.) 40-45	BRUTALITY	BEL.
FRIND, Johana	31967	M			Dr.,Landgerichtsrat,Public Official,Cheb(Czech.) 40	MURDER	CZECH.
FRIND, Josef	31966	M			Dr.,Oberlandgerichtsrat,Public Official,Litomerice(Czech.) 40	MURDER	CZECH.
FRINGS	258589	M			S-Sgt.,Police,Poppentin(Ger.) 7. or 8.44	WITNESS	U.S.
FRINGS	307025	M			Pvt.,Kdr.Fest.Stamm-Tr.L XXXVIII 88 Kriegsgericht Utrecht(Neth.) 7.44	BRUTALITY	NETH.
FRINK, Engelbert	193898	M	Ger.		custom-house-officer,Zollgrenzschutz,Alos(Fr.)	MURDER	FR.
FRINTCH	194974	M	Ger.		Capt.,Kraftfahr-Coy.,Pornichet(Fr.)	PILLAGE	FR.
FRISC see FRISS	135540						
FRISCH	148222	M			Hptsturmfhr.,SS,Ellrich(Ger.) 45	MURDER	FR.
FRISCH	255143	M	Ger.		Oschfhr.,SS,Toulouse(Fr.) 11.42-8.44	MISC.CRIMES	FR.
FRISCH see FRIIS	256816						
FRISCH, Georges	173360	M	Ger.		Capt.,Standortkom.,Mezerolls-Dollens(Fr.) 8.44	MURDER	FR.
FRISCHE	189980	M	Ger.	96	Bauleiter,C.C.Neuengamme(Ger.) 43	MURDER	YUGO.
FRISCHE, Robert	301669	M			Serving with Ger.Troops,Monceau sur Sambre(Bel.) 9.44	PILLAGE	BEL.
FRISCHLER, Samuel	250759	M	Ger.		SS-Sturmmann,Camp Kelbra-Rossla SS,Nordhausen(Ger.)	MURDER	U.S.
FRISCHMANN	301394	M	Ger.		Maj.,Member of camp staff,Markt Pongau. 9.43-5.45	BRUTALITY	U.K.
FRISS or FRISC	135540	M	Ger.	05	N.C.O.,Army Stalag VIC,Land.Schuetzen Bn.622,Ilmenau(Ger.) 6.43	TORTURE	U.K.
FRISTCHE or FRITECH	148223	M	Ger.	03	Gruppenfhr.,SS,CC,Dora,Nordhausen(Ger.)	MURDER	FR.
FRITAG	67823	M	Ger.		Civilian,C.C.756,Suplingen(Ger.) 2.45	MURDER	U.K.
FRITCH see FRITSCH	275						
FRITCH	148224	M		08	CC.Altenburg(Ger.)	TORTURE	FR.
FRITCH	173359	M			Cmdt.,C.C.Ellrich,Bischofrode(Ger.)	MISC.CRIME	FR.
FRITSCHE, Hans	62337	M	Ger.		Political Controller German Broadcasting	TORTURE	UNWCC.
FRITS	273	M	Ger.		Capt.,Chief of Gestapo,Bizerta(Tunesia) 12.42-4.43	MURDER	FR.
FRITSCH	274	M	Ger.		SS-Hptsturmfhr.,Camp Leader,C.C.Oswiecim. (Pol.) 40 - 42	MURDER	FR.,POL.
FRITSCH or FRITCH	275	M	Ger.		Capt.,Feldgend.,Parachutist 8,51,910,Abbeville,Bernaville(Fr.) 8.44	MURDER	FR.
FRITSCH or FRITSCHE	122708	M	Ger.	05-10	Hptsturmfhr.,Totenkopf Unit,CC.,Ellrich(Ger.) 8.44-2.45	MURDER	U.S.,FR.,BEL.
FRITSCH	142777	M			SS-Osturmfhr.,Waffen-SS,C.C.Buchenwald(Ger.)	TORTURE	FR.
FRITSCH see FRISTCHE	148223						
FRITSCH	162028	M	Ger.		Member,Gestapo.	MURDER	U.S.
FRITSCH	177549	M	Ger.		SS-Sgt.,SD,Gestapo,Sarrebruck(Ger.)	MISC.CRIMES	FR.
FRITSCH	250754	M	Ger.		Rottfhr.,SS,Camp Ellrich,Nordhausen(Ger.)	MURDER	U.S.
FRITSCH	252084	M	Ger.		Lt.,29 Gren.Pz.Regt.,3 Gren.Pz.Div.,Couvognes, Beurey Robert Espagne (Fr.) 8.44	PILLAGE	FR.
FRITSCH	256817	M			Kapo,C.C.Miehldorf(Ger.)	MURDER	U.S.
FRITSCH, Emil	148410	M	Ger.	00	Leader,Sgt.,Hptschfhr.,SS,C.C.Hirzenhain(Ger.)	MURDER	U.S.
FRITSCH, Emil	253653	M	Ger.	24. 8.05	SS-Mann,Gestapo,C.C.Neuenbremm(Ger.)	MISC.CRIMES	FR.
FRITSCH, Hans	189368	M	Ger.		Lt.,Inf.Bn.116,28 Inf.Regt.,Lannemezan, Puydarrieux Meilhan (Fr.) 7.44	MURDER	FR.
FRITSCH, Josef	255139	M	Ger.	31. 8.13	Civilian,Gossengrun-Habersprik(Czech.) 9.39	MURDER	CZECH.
FRITSCH, Richard	194097	M	Ger.	5. 1.11	Member Gestapo,Cheb(Czech.) 39-45	MURDER	CZECH.
FRITSCHE see FRITSCH	122708						
FRITSCHE	160162	M			Butcher,Civilian,Gardelegen(Ger.) 4.45	MURDER	U.S.
FRITSCHE	251017	M			SS-Rottfhr.,Camp Mackenrode,Nordhausen(Ger.)	MURDER	U.S.
FRITSCHE	257856	M			Lt.,150 Panzer Bde.,Meuse Bridge-Antwerp(Bel.) 12.44	MISC.CRIMES	U.S.
FRITSCHE	350136	M	Ger.		SS-Gruppenfhr.,SS,C.C.Dora Camp and Buchenwald,Dora,Buchenwald(Ger.)-45	MURDER	FR.
FRITSCHE, Jobst	253840	M	Ger.	6. 9.11	Bezirkshauptmann,Vsetin(Czech.) 39-45	INTERR.	CZECH.
FRITSCHER	142775	M	Ger.		Lt.,Army,Legion Caucasienne,Tara(Fr.) 7.44	MURDER	FR.
FRITSCHING	176700	M			SS-Oschfhr.,SS,C.C.,Mühldorf-Ampfing(Ger.) 6.44-4.45	MURDER	U.S.
FRITSH	171684	M	Ger.		Arbeits-Kdo.343,C.C.Landernea(Fr.) 4.-8.44	MURDER	FR.
FRITSHGER, Volkmar	189364	M	Ger.		Lt.,Regt.I of volunteers,Labrespy,Canton de Mazomet(Fr.) 7.44	MURDER	FR.
FRITZ	1981	M	Ger.		N.C.O.,SD Aussen-Kdo.	MISC.CRIMES	U.K.
FRITZ	124482	M	Ger.		Oberstabsarzt,Civilian,C.C.Doctor Hospital Elsterhorst,Konigswartha (Ger.) 6.-7.44	TORTURE	U.K.
FRITZ	124939	M	Ger.		Cpl.,Landesschtz.Coy.4,5 or 6,C.C. Sagan Stalag Luft III(Ger.) 44	WITNESS	U.K.
FRITZ	126975	M	Ger.		Guard,Zugwachtmeister,C.C.Schirmeck(Fr.) 43-44	MURDER	FR.
FRITZ	131278	M			Block-Aeltester,CC,Pvt.,C.C.Jamischowitz-Auschwitz(Pol.) 43-45	MURDER	U.S.
FRITZ	132484	M	Ger.		Ortsgruppenleiter NSDAP,Gams-Deutschlandsberg(Aust.) 4.44	MURDER	U.S.

FRI-FRI

FRI-FRO

NAME	C.R.FILE NUMBER	SEX	NATIO- NALITY	DATE OF BIRTH	RANK OCCUPATION UNIT PLACE AND DATE OF CRIME	REASON WANTED	WANTED BY
FRITZ	142772	M			Cpl., Feldgendarmerie, Rethel (Fr.)	TORTURE	FR.
FRITZ	148213	M		00	Kapo, C.C. Bergen - Belsen (Ger.)	TORTURE	FR.
FRITZ	148214	M	Ger.		Kapo, C.C. Mauthausen (Aust.) 42-45	TORTURE	FR.
FRITZ	148269	M			C.C. Hinzert (Ger.)	MURDER	FR.
FRITZ	148271	M			Chief, C.C. Trippel (Ger.)	TORTURE	FR.
FRITZ	148272	M	Ger.		Public official, Hasbach (Ger.)	MISC.CRIMES	FR.
FRITZ	173422	M			Sgt., Fallschirmjaeger-Regt., 2.Bn., 2.Div., Plouzane (Fr.) 44	MURDER	FR.
FRITZ	186917	M	Ger.		Kapo, Camp Bad Gandersheim, C.C. Dachau (Ger.) 4.45	MURDER	FR.
FRITZ	186318	M	Ger.		Kapo-Chief, C.C. Neuengamme (Ger.)	TORTURE	FR.
FRITZ	186390	M	Ger.		Pvt., Army, Chania (Grc.) 9.44	MURDER	GRC.
FRITZ	192472	M	Ger.	05	Oberwachtmeister, Strafgef.Lager Nord, Finmark (Nor.) 6.42	MISC.CRIMES	NOR.
FRITZ	193486	M	Ger.		Pvt., Army, 1.Kgf.Arb.Bn.41, Nerlandsdal, Kristiansund (Nor.) 41-45	TORTURE	NOR.
FRITZ	252975	M	Ger.		Guard, C.C. Auschwitz (Pol.) 40	INTERR.	FR.
FRITZ	254193	M	Ger.		Head, Block 57, C.C. Buchenwald (Ger.)	TORTURE	FR.
FRITZ	259365	M	Ger.		Adjutant, Feldgendarmerie, St. Denis, Fort de Stains, Set Oise, (Fr.) 8.44	MURDER	FR.
FRITZ	300077	M	Ger.		Staff at C.C. Mauthausen (Aust.) 11.42-5.45	MURDER	FR.
FRITZ	301314	M	Ger.		Major, Member, Gestapo at Nove Mesto n. Vahom, C.C. Oswiecim - Birkenau (Pol.) 39-45	MURDER	CZECH.
FRITZ (nee STANGE)	306965	F	Ger.		SS-guard, C.C. Auschwitz (Pol.) 42-44	BRUTALITY	POL.
FRITZ	307102	M	Ger.		One of the guards at "Huize Mooiland" was later transferred to Wageningen, Heelsum (Neth.) 2.-4.45	MURDER	NETH.
FRITZ, Alfons	72088	M			Hauptscharf., SS-Totenkopf, SS-Ers.Regt. Berlin-Lichterfelde (Ger.)	TORTURE	U.S.
FRITZ, Erwin	31926	M	Ger.		Sgt., Kerlaz, La Roche, Maurice (Fr.) 44	MURDER	FR.
FRITZ, Johann	259576	M	Ger.	11	Pvt., 5.Coy., L 891, Guard, Working Camp at Peggau (Aust.) Pernegg (Aust.) 9.42	MURDER	U.K.
FRITZ, Karl	173996	M	Ger.		SS-Scharf., Staatspol., C.C. Brno, Oswiecim-Birkenau (Czech.,Pol.) 39	MURDER	CZECH.
FRITZ, Karl	259659	M	Ger.		Furniture-dealer, Lt., Etat Major of the 18. Flak-Bde., Haurincourt P.D.C. (Fr.) 6.44	MURDER	FR.
FRITZ, Leo	185127	M	Ger.		Dr., SS, C.C. Sachsenhausen, Struthof (Ger/Fr.) 40-44	MURDER	FR.
FRITZ, Leo	300995	M	Ger.		Zugwachtmeister, C.C. Struthof-Natzweiler (Fr.) 42-44	MURDER	FR.
FRITZ, Peter	193624	M	Ger.	13. 3.91	SS-Sturmbannf., Agent, Gestapo, Nove Morave (Czech.) 39-45	MURDER	CZECH.
FRITZ, Phillip	133362	M	Ger.	90 - 95	Gestapo, Lager Langenzenn, Nuernberg (Ger.) 43-4.45	TORTURE	U.S.
FRITZ, Rugio	191856	M	Ger.		Cpl., Army, 11.Coy., F.P. 06682, Bauge (Fr.)	PILLAGE	FR.
FRITZ, Walter	251016	M	Ger.		Flyer, Camp Harzungen, Nordhausen (Ger.)	MURDER	U.S.
FRITZ, Wilhelm	143485	M	Ger.		Gniezno (Pol.) 12.39	INCENDIARISM	POL.
FRITZ, Wilhelm	148273	M	Ger.		Civilian, Glatz (Ger.) 6.44-11.44	TORTURE	FR.
FRITZ, Wilhelm	171663	M	Ger.		N.C.O., 9.Gren.Regt.d.Res., last unit 4/181, 1.Coy., Magny d'Avignon (Fr.) 9.44	MURDER	FR.
FRITZE, Fritz	148274	M			C.C. Bischofsheim (Bischofsheim, Germany)	TORTURE	FR.
FRITZEN	195132	M	Ger.		Dr., Reichsbahnrat, German Railway, Neth.Railway (Ger.)(Neth.)	MISC.CRIMES	NETH.
FRITZEN, Heinrich	146883	M	Ger.		SS-Rottenf., Panz.Div. "Das Reich", 13.Coy., Moissac (Fr.) 44	MURDER	FR.
FRITZHEN, Joachim	252477	M	Ger.		377.Jg.Regt., Vinkt (Bel.)	MISC.CRIMES	BEL.
FRITZMANN	256617		Ger.		Employee, C.C. Nordhausen (Ger.)	MURDER	U.S.
FRITZOTASKI	148249	M	Ger.	95	C.C. Lanrahtte	TORTURE	FR.
FRITZSCH, Hans	173430	M	Ger.	95	SS, Langenzenn (Ger.)	WITNESS	U.S.
FRITZZ, Max	72089	M			SS-Oberscharf., SS-Totenkopf, 11.SS-Mtn.Regt., (Ger.)	TORTURE	U.S.
FROCHLIC (see FROEHLICH)	72090						
FRODL	251009	M			SS-Rottenf., Camp Nixei, Nordhausen (Ger.)	MURDER	U.S.
FROEBEL	193487	M	Ger.		Lt., Airforce, Uthaug, Orlandet (Nor.) 9.41-42	WITNESS	NOR.
FROEBEL, Fritz	140892	M	Ger.	17. 6.09	Hauptscharf., W-SS, Totenkopf, Sturmbann, C.C. Buchenwald (Ger.) 37-43	TORTURE	U.S.
FROEHDE, Kurt	127350	M	Ger.		Cpl., Land.Schtz.Bn.400, 6.Coy., Gross-Oerner (Ger.) 9.44	MURDER	U.S.
FROEHLICH	31925	M	Ger.		Lt., 7.Res.Art.Regt., St.Paul, Isere (Fr.) 6.44	MURDER	U.N.W.C.C.
FROEHLICH or FROLICH or FROCHLIC	72090	M	Ger.	20	SS-Scharfhr., C.C. Hinzert (Ger.) 42-43	MISC.CRIMES	U.S.
FROEHLICH	128857	M	Ger.		Col., Camp 319 A, Cholm (Pol.) 11.42	TORTURE	SOV.UN.
FROEHLICH	139887	M	Ger.	05 - 10	Crim.Insp., Gestapo, Germany	MURDER	U.K.
FROEHLICH	148403	M	Ger.	11	SS-Unterscharf., Guard, C.C. Innsbruck, Reichenau, 44-45	TORTURE	U.S.
FROEHLICH, Hans (see FROHLEG)	126540						
FROEHLING	148247	M			C.C. Troisdorf (Ger.) 45	MISC.CRIMES	FR.
FROELICH, Hans (see FROHLEG)	126540						
FROELICH	173423	M			Chief, Transport-Kdo., Grenoble (Fr.)	PILLAGE	FR.
FROELLE or FROELLER	221416	M	Ger.	09	SS-Oberscharf., W-SS, C.C. Dachau (Ger.) 8.44	TORTURE	U.S.
FROEMMER (see FROMMER)	188249						
FROETSCH	142494	M	Ger.	00	SS-Oberscharf., W-SS, Totenkopf-Stuba., C.C. Buchenwald and Altenburg (Ger.) 42-45	TORTURE	U.S.
FROFP	252292	M	Ger.		SS-Sturmscharf., Gestapo, Limoges (Fr.)	INTERR.	FR.
FROHANAPFEL	137612	M	Ger.		Member, S.D., Gestapo, Tilburg (Neth.) 7.44	MURDER	U.K.
FROHLE	191842	M			C.C. Dachau (Ger.)	MURDER	U.S.
FROHLEG, Hans OR Froehlich	126540	M	Ger.		SS, Vienenburg (Ger.) 5.44	MURDER	U.S.
FROHLICH	135162	M	Ger.		SS-Mann, C.C. Hinzert, Wittlich (Ger.)	TORTURE	U.S.
FROHLICH	141958	M			Lagerf., Camp Kala, Rudolstadt (Ger.)	MISC.CRIMES	U.S.
FROHLICH	148270	M			Lt., Army, 7.Res.Art.Regt., Albertville Ugine (Fr.)	MURDER	FR.
FROHLICH	254169	M	Ger.		Lt., Pioneer-Coy., Res.Bn. 15, Hossegor (Fr.) 8.44	INTERR.	FR.
FROHLING	165326	M	Ger.		SS, NSDAP, R.S.A., Berlin (Ger.) 43	MURDER	U.S.
FROHLING	253898	M	Ger.		Medical-Officer, Asst.of Chief, Siegburg (Ger.)	MISC.CRIMES	FR.
FROHLINGS, Bernh.	129019	M	Ger.	27.11.01	C.C. Siegburg (Ger.) 3.-8.42	MURDER	BEL.
FROHN	31965	M	Ger.		Dr., Landgerichtsrat, Public off., Bruenn (Czech.) 40	MURDER	CZECH.
FROHN	256618	M	Ger.		Regierungsbaurat, Official of War Office, Sochaux (Fr.) 9.-11.44	MISC.CRIMES	FR.
FROHNAPFEL, Wilhelm	300461	M	Ger.		Possibly served with the Sicherheitsdienst, Eindhoven (Neth.) 1.44	BRUTALITY	NETH.
FROHNE	148244	M	Ger.		Hauptsturmf., SS, C.C. Nordhausen (Ger.),	MURDER	FR.
FROHNER	253899	M	Ger.		SS-Unterscharfhr., Gestapo, Aube (Fr.) 43-44	INTERR.	FR.
FROHNERT, Ernst	192473	M	Ger.		Cpl., Army (Nor.) 4.45	MURDER	NOR.

FRO-FUC

NAME	C.R.FILE NUMBER	SEX	NATIO-NALITY	DATE OF BIRTH	RANK OCCUPATION UNIT PLACE AND DATE OF CRIME	REASON WANTED	WANTED BY
FROLICH (see FROEHLICH)	72090	M					
FROLICH	148283	M		12	Capt., SS-Pol.Div., Perytz-Rottenburg (Ger.)	PILLAGE	FR.
FROLLMANN	173373	M	Ger.		General-Major, Police,Ordnungspolizei, Auschwitz-Birkenau (Pol.) 41	MURDER	CZECH.
FROM	256811	M	Ger.		Dr., Leader, Police, Sarajewo (Yugo.) 43-45	MURDER	YUGO.
FROMAS	142696	M			SD, Cluses (Fr.) 7.44	MURDER	FR.
FROMBERG	148281	M			C.C., Hohenlychen, Ravensbrueck (Ger.) 5.44	TORTURE	FR.
FROME	130640	M			Hauptsturmfhr., SS, C.C.Dora, Nordhausen (Ger.)	MURDER	U.S.
FROMEL	148280	M	Ger.		Lt., 2.und 3.Panz.Div., Tulle,Gourdon, Roc Croislejac (Fr.)	MURDER	FR.
FROMM, Fritz	62338	M	Ger.		Chief of Army, Equipment with.Ger.Bekleidungsamt	TORTURE	UNWCC.
FROMMANN, Albert	142488	M			Employee, Civilian , Plettenberg (Ger.) 4.45	TORTURE	U.S.
FROMMEL	12624	M			Capt.,110.or 111.Panz.Gren.Rgt. Gourdon (Fr.) 6.44	MURDER	FR.
FROMMEL, Adolf	257832	M	Ger.		Hauptscharfhr. SD, Bergen (Nor.) 40 - 44	INTERR.	NOR.
FROMMEN	148279	M	Ger.		Arbeitskommando Kl.Brueckenbau, Dortmund (Ger.)	MURDER	FR.
FROMMER	179777	M	Ger.	20	Lt., 61.Flak-Ausb.Abt., Montemignaio (It.) 6.44	MURDER	U.K.
FROMMER (or FROEMMER)	188249	M	Ger.	85	Major, 945.Sicherungs-Bn., Mazowiecki (Pol.) 43	MURDER	POL.
FROMMHAGEN, Otto	155405	M	Ger.	32	Hitler Youth, C.C. Javenitz and Gardelegen (Ger.) 4.45	MURDER	U.S.
FRONAPFER (or FRONAPPEL or KRONAPPEL)	277	M	Ger.	11 or 12 or 15	Sturmscharfhr. SS, C.C. Dachau (Ger.) 40-45	MURDER	U.S. FR, Pol.
FRONE	252093	M	Ger.		Lt.,M.Rgt.6.Div. Paratrooper, Nieuwaal (Neth.) 1.45	WITNESS	NETH.
FROPP	300462	M			Sturmscharfhr.,attached to Section for the Repression of Partisans, at Gestapo in Limoges,Hte.Vienne,Creuse,Correze,Dordogne,Indre (Fr.)-45	MISC.CRIMES	FR.
FRORKOWSKI, Franz (see FLORKOWSKI)	142528						
FROSCH, Hubert	189242	M	Ger.	3.11.12	Criminal-Commissar, Gestapo, Bruenn (Czech.) 39-45	MURDER	CZECH.
FROSCH, Leo	142493	M			Civilian	WITNESS	U.S.
FROSCHAUER	162050	M	Ger.		Chief, SA, Kingersheim (Fr.)	MURDER	FR.
FROSCHEL	260102	M			Sgt.,217.Res.Gren.Bn.,Massif du Vercors,Isere et Drome (Fr.)7.u.8.44	SUSPECT	FR.
FROSCHER, Frederic	137063	M	Ger.		Civilian	MURDER	U.S.
FROSCHER, Karlo	257843	M	Ger.	16	Zugwachtmeister,7.Coy.322.Bn.,5.Schuetzen Rgt. Ljubljana (Yugo.)42-43	MISC.CRIMES	YUGO.
FROSER	251010	M			Pvt. C.C. Ellrich, Nordhausen (Ger.)	MURDER	U.S.
FROSSMANN	148277	M	Ger.		Cmdt., C.C. Neuengamme (Ger.)	TORTURE	FR.
FROST	257857	M			Cpl., 156.Panz.-Brigade, Meuse-Bridge-Antwerp.(Bel.) 12.44	MISC.CRIMES	U.S.
FROSTER, Eugen	142640	M			SS-Uscharfhr. C.C., Struthof (Fr.)	TORTURE	FR.
FROTSCHER	192993	M	Ger.		Uscharfhr. 3.SS-Rgt., C.C. Buchenwald (Ger.) 42-45	TORTURE	U.S.
FROTSCHER, Joachim	186389	M	Ger.		SS - Obersturmfhr., Pysely (Czech.)	TORTURE	CZECH.
FRUCHEL, Heinz	251011	M			Pvt. C.C. Ellrich, Nordhausen (Ger.)	MURDER	U.S.
FRUCHTNICHT (see FRYCHTNICHT, Heinrich)	171957						
FRUEHAUF, Fritz	260423	M	Ger.	5. 3.95	Dr.Ing., Propagandaleiter,NSDAP,Member of DAF,NSKK,Bruenn(Czech.)39-45	MISC.CRIMES	CZECH.
FRUEHAUF, Karl	147352	M			Guard, Civilian, C.C. Enkenbach (Ger.) 12.43 - 3.45	TORTURE	U.S.
FRUEHWALD, Franz	167115	M	Ger.		Pvt., Army, 5.Coy. Brand,Gmuend (Aust.) 4.43	MURDER	FR.
FRUHLING	178318	M		02	Pvt., 4.Coy.,427.Landesschuetzen Bn. Drausnhkonitz (Ger.) 4.45	MURDER	U.K.
FRUEHRBROTH	127351	M	Ger.		Sgt. C.C. Tegel (Ger.) 11.43 - 5.44	TORTURE	U.S.
FRUHBUSS, Oswald	205421	M	Ger.		Member, Gestapo, Radom (Pol.)	MURDER	POL.
FRUHLING, Kurt	178076	M			Cpl., Kgf.Arb.Bn. 184, 1.Coy., C.C. Kroken (Nor.)	WITNESS	NOR.
FRUICKER	138232	M	Ger.		Member, NSDAP, Army, Bourg-Lastic (Fr.) 7.44	MURDER	FR.
FRUKEN, Heinrich	301731	M	Ger.		Pvt., C.C. Auschwitz (Pol.) 40	MURDER	FR.
FRULICH	199912	M	Ger.		Lt., Art.Ers.Rgt. 7, 79.D.A.M.,Albertville (Fr.) 6.44	MURDER	FR.
FRUNZEL	147942	M	Ger.		Capt., Oflag IVD (Ger.)	TORTURE	FR.
FRUSKANSKAS	170832	M			Major, Lithunian Army, Vilianpole (Lith.)10.41	SUSPECT	U.S.
FRY (or FREI or FREY)	29879	M	Ger.		Commandant C.C., Oflag 7-CH, Laufen-Thorn (Pol.) 41-42	MURDER	U.K.
FRYCHTNICHT, Heinrich (alias FRUCHTNICHT)	171957	M	Ger.	29. 4.94	Civilian, Dauelsen - Verden (Ger.) 10.43	TORTURE	U.S.
FUCHE	142682				SS-Uscharfhr., Rollweith (Ger.)	MURDER	FR.
FUCHEN, Julius	132621	M	Ger.		Waffen SS, Stalag XII D, Kommando CC, Aremberg (Ger.)	TORTURE	FR.
FUCHRER, Adolph (see FIEURER)	262272	M	Ger.				
FUCHS	279	M	Ger.	92	SS-Standartenfhr.,Belgrade (Yugo.) 41-42	MURDER	YUGO.
FUCHS	31924	M	Ger.	95	SS-Untersturmfhr., Waffen SS, C.C. Natzweiler,Struthof (Fr.)42-44	MURDER	U.S. FR.
FUCHS	62340	M	Ger.	95	Dr., Lt. SS.Of.WKR.II	TORTURE	UNWCC.
FUCHS	121256	M	Ger.		Lt., Army,Corps 66.	MURDER	FR.
FUCHS	129001	M	Ger.		Fallschirmjaeger-Rgt. 5,Nachrichtenzug,Hainaut (Bel.) 3-9.44	MURDER	BEL.
FUCHS	129786	M	Ger.	05	Sturmbannfhr.,Criminal-Rat, SA or SS, Radom (Pol.) 44-45	MURDER	U.S.
FUCHS	138841	M			Civilian, Dr. Bibliotheksohutz, Paris (Fr.)44.	PILLAGE	FR.
FUCHS	139813	M	Ger.	20	Sgt., Waffen - SS, Muehldorf (Ger.) 44-45	MURDER	U.S.
FUCHS	148257	M			Lt., Army, Dijon (Fr.)	TORTURE	FR.
FUCHS	149221	M			Sturmmann, SS-Totenkopf Panzer Div.,Landweier (Ger.)	TORTURE	FR.
FUCHS	187852	M			N.C.O., Stalag Guard, C.C.Graudens, Harwerstein (Pol.,Ger.)1.45	TORTURE	BEL.
FUCHS	188166	M			SS-Oberscharfhr., Karlovy Vary (Czech.)	MURDER	U.S.
FUCHS	191871	M			Lt.,90 Inf.Div.,361.Inf.Rgt.(mot.) Luss la Croix Haute (Fr.) 7.44	MURDER	FR.
FUCHS	222562	M	Ger.	00	Kreisleiter, NSDAP, Mainz (Ger.) 1.45	TORTURE	U.S.
FUCHS	222568	M	Ger.		Dr.,SS-Col.,Agent,SD,Police,Sipo, Belgrad (Yugo.) 8.42	TORTURE	U.S.
FUCHS	251018	M	Ger.		Capt., Adjutant and Block Officer at Oflag XIII B, Nuernberg, Hamelburg (Ger.) 41-45	MURDER	YUGO.
FUCHS	251019	M	Ger.		Sgt.738.Regt.118 Alp.Jaeg.Div.,Kalinovik,Imotski,Konjic,Ostrosac(Yugo.)	MURDER	YUGO.
FUCHS	251539	M	Ger.		Gestapo, Maribor, Yugo. 45	INTERR.	YUGO.
FUCHS (or FUESCHS)	252978	M	Ger.		Empoyee , C.C. Flossenburg (Ger.)	MURDER	BEL.
FUCHS	257833	M	Ger.		Truppfhr. O.T. C.C. Muehldorf (Ger.)	MURDER	U.S.
FUCHS	257834	M	Ger.	23	Sturmmann, C.C. Muehldorf (Ger.)	MURDER	U.S.
FUCHS	300689	M	Ger.		Dr., Public Prosecutor-Head of Oberstaatsanwaltschaft,Ministry of State, Departement of Justice, Prague (Czech.) 2.40	MISC.CRIMES	CZECH.
FUCHS	301243	M	Ger.		Naval Commandant, Att.Garrison at St. Malo (Fr.)8.44	INCENDIARISM	FR.

FUC - FUN

NAME	C.R. FILE NUMBER	SEX	NATIO-NALITY	DATE OF BIRTH	RANK OCCUPATION UNIT PLACE AND DATE OF CRIME	REASON WANTED	WANTED BY
FUCHS, Adolf	132216	M	Ger.	07	Osturmfhr., Crim.Rat, SS.Crim., Councellor Sipo Prague (Cze.)	MISC.CRIMES	U.S.
FUCHS, Anton	31964	M	Ger.		Oberlandesgerichtsrat Public Official Litomerice (Cze.) 40	MURDER	CZECH.
FUCHS, Erich	170835	M	Ger.		Miscellaneous, Ulrichshalben (Ger.) 7.44	TORTURE	U.S.
FUCHS, Franz	162027	M	Ger.		Foreman, Civ., Adolf Mine, Merkstein (Ger.) 42-44	TORTURE	U.S.
FUCHS, Georg	188310	M	Ger.		Civilian, Arbeitskdo., Dachsbach (Ger.) 43-45	TORTURE	POL.
FUCHS, Johann	72258	M	Ger.		Uschfhr., W-SS C.C. Lublin (Pol.)43	TORTURE	U.S.
FUCHS, Ludwig	173397	M	Ger.		Crim., Commissar, Staatspolizeileitstelle C.C. Prague Oswiecim, Birkenau (Cze.,Pol.) 39-45	MURDER	CZECH.
FUCHS, M.	133317	M			SS-Officer	TORTURE	U.S.
FUCHS, Otto	142482	M	Ger.		Lt., Army, St.Marine (Fr.) 6.44	MURDER	U.S.
FUCHSEL, Walter	148363	M		25. 6.95	Hptschfhr., C.C. Mauthausen (Aust.) 5.44-5.45	MURDER	U.S.
FUCHSENBURG	125063	M	Ger.	95	Lt., Stalag XXID 42	BRUTALITY	U.K.
FUCHSLOCH, Josef	251012	M	Ger.		SS-Hptschfhr., Camp Harsungen (Ger.)	MURDER	U.S.
FUCHSMANN, Roman	187831	M			Civ., C.C.Merkstein (Ger.) 43	WITNESS	U.S.
FUCHTRAURE	280	M	Ger.		General, Army, Dijon, (Fr.) 41-42	MURDER	FR.
FUECHTNER (see FICHTNER)	259941						
FUCKLICKEL	306259	M	Ger.		Major, Commanding 427 Ld.Schts., Bn. (Stalag VIII B) Gogolin, U. Silesia (U.K.) 1.45-4.45	MURDER	U.K.
FUEHR, Arthur, Walter	194255	M	Ger.	27. 4.10	Driver, Gestapo, Deckenheim (Ger.) 12.44	MURDER	U.S.
FUELLER	10149	M			Sonderfhr., Welfare Stalag 344 (Ger.) 42-44	MISC.CRIMES	U.K.
FUELLER	176705	M			Civ., Org., Todt C.C. Muhldorf, Ampfing (Ger.) 6.44-4.45	MURDER	U.S.
FUER	257831	M			Pvt., C.C. Transportation Nordhausen (Ger.)	MURDER	U.S.
FUERBOCK, Hans, (Johann) (alias FOERBOCK)	257845	M	Ger.	15. 6.02	Major, Cmdt., Gendarmerie, Wolfisheim (Fr.) 44	MURDER	FR.
FUERICH, Willy	254176	M	Ger.		Pvt., Driver St.Michielsgestel (Neth.)9.44	PILLAGE	NETH.
FUERLEIN, Adolf	306745	M	Ger.		Ger., Civ., Solln-Muenich (Ger.) 7.44	BRUTALITY	U.S.
FUERST	129788	M	Ger.		Lt.Col., Army Defense Area (Brest (Fr.) 9.44	MISCELL.	U.S.
FUERST	147946	M			Sgt., Army Graudens (Pol.)	TORTURE	FR.
FUERST, Friedrich	142483	M	Ger.	90	Major-General, C.C.Altengrade (Ger.) 4.45	MURDER	U.S.
FUERST, Paul	255585	M	Ger.		Chief-W.O. Fieldpolice, Valenciennes (Fr.) 8.44	WITNESS	FR.
FUERSTL	301315	M	Ger.		Member, of the Gestapo at Trencin C.C. Oswiecim-Birkenau (Pol.)39-45	MURDER	CZECH.
FUES	133313	M			Hptschfhr., W-SS Flossenburg (Ger.)	MURDER	U.S.
FUES	133315	M		21	SS-Totenkopf Usturmfhr.,	MURDER	U.S.
FUESCHS, (see FUCHS)	252978						
FUESSL	186386	M	Ger.		SS-Guard,Sturmschfhr., C.C. Mauthausen (Aust.,)	TORTURE	U.S.
FUGAZZA	192474	M			Lt., Col., Army Engineering Unit (Nor.)	MURDER	NOR.
FUHL	161670	M	Ger.		Lt., Army, Putlitz, Mecklenburg (Pol.) 4.45	WITNESS	U.K.
FUHMANN	160170	M			Lt., Sturm Bn., AOK, 1, Courcelles sur-nied (Fr.) 11.44	MURDER	U.S.
FUHRBETH	253837	M			Lt., Army Villmar (Ger.) 7.-8.44	INTERR.	U.S.
FUHRER, Alfred	124693	M	Ger.		Pvt., Leibstand., Adolf Hitler 1. Ps.Gren.Bn., Renardmond Stavelot (Bel.) 12.44	MURDER	BEL.
FUHRHOFF	250743	M			Usturmfhr., Camp Dora Nordhausen (Ger.)	MURDER	U.S.
FUHRI Otto	161671	M			SS-Rgt., Der Fuehrer, Houyet-Dinant (Bel.) 9.44	PILLAGE	BEL.
FUHRMANN	126940	M	Ger.		Pvt., Ld.Schts., Bn., 777 C.C.Dockweiler Daun, (Ger.)2.45	MURDER	FR.
FUHRMANN	142607	M			Meister der Schupo, Gestapo, Vichy (Fr.)	MISC.CRIMES	FR.
FUHRMANN	148254	M			Pvt., Army Privas (Fr.)	MISC.CRIMES	FR.
FUHRMANN	142600	M	Ger.	12	Oschfhr., Crim. Angest., Gestapo SD, Praha, (Cze.) 40-45	MURDER	CZECH.
FUHRMANN	181566	M			Cpt., Schupo C.C.Falstad (Nor.) 41-45	WITNESS	NOR.
FUHRMANN	192929	M			Stabsfhr., 99.Alpenjg., 157.Res.Div.,Allemont (Fr.)8.44	INTERR.	FR.
FUHRMANN	255992	M			Stenographer, SD, Caen (Fr.) 42	INTERR.	FR.
FUHRMANN	257830	M			Stabsfhr., 99.Bn.,157.Bavarian Div., Isere,(Fr)8.44	INTERR.	FR.
FUHRMANN, Albert	261684	M			Landgerichtsdirector, Ministry of Justice, Cheb (Cze.) 2.40	MURDER	CZECH.
FUHRMANN, Johann	31977	M		87	Policeman, Police N.C., Niederseelbach, 10. 44	MURDER	U.S.
FUHRMANN, Josef	122710	M		89	Political-leader, Camp-leader, Siessen-Camp, Relocation Saulgau, (Ger.) L.O.D.N.A.O.D. 8.44	WITNESS	U.S.
FUHRMANN, Otto	260842	M			O-Cand., Tcn.Team"Stielau" 150.Ps.Brig.,Meuse Brig.Antwerpen (Bel.) 44	MISC.CRIMES	U.S.
FUHRMEISTER	257969	M					
FUHSL	129021	M		95	Sturmschfhr., C.C. Mauthausen (Aust.)41-45	MURDER	U.S.
FUIDE	306200		Ger.		Member of Staff Small Fortress C.C. Theresienstadt (Cze.)10.38-44	MURDER	CZECH.
FUIERER	252096	M			Lt., 1.Coy., 654.Bn. Nievre (Fr.) 6.44	PILLAGE	FR.
FUIOR	139815	M		05	Cpl., W-SS, Cracow, (Pol.) 6.42	MURDER	U.S.
FUKARI	148255	M			Army 56.Sich., Rgt., Quimper (Fr.)	MURDER	FR.
FUKNER	186316	M	Ger.		Cmdt., Camp Official, C.C. Ravensbrueck, (Ger.)	TORTURE	FR.
FULBA	142492	M			Chief Judge, Public Official, Occupied Countries of Europe(Ger.)41-42	WITNESS	U.S.
FULCHMANN (see FOLCHMANN)	142600						
FULDNER	173431	M	Ger.		Reichstreuhaender Occup.,Terr.,Civ.,Zbydniow near Debica (Pol.)6.43	MURDER	POL.
FULERER	305401	M	Ger.		Lt., 1.Coy., 654 Ostbn., Dun-Les-Places Nievres (Fr.) 6.44	MURDER	FR.
FULKER (see FOLKER)	138222						
FULKMEN (see FOLKMEN)	142599						
FULL, Hermann, Kamill	148251	M		8. 4.21	Member, Feldgend., Vitry Le Franc Ois (Fr.) 6.43	TORTURE	FR.
FULLEHR	125697	M	Ger.	03	Opl., SD, Gestapo C.C. Poitiers (Fr.) 40-44	TORTURE	FR.
FULLER	169457	M		00	Sonderfhr., Army C.C. Heydebreck (Ger.)	TORTURE	U.K.
FULLE	257968	M			Major, 150.Ps.Brig., Meuse Brigade Antwerp (Bel.) 12.44	MISC.CRIMES	U.S.
FULLGRAPP	185265	M			Osturmfhr., SS-Ps.Gren.Div., Leibstandarte A.Hitler Stavelot (Bel.)	MURDER	BEL.
FULSCHE, Heinrich	193055	M	Ger.		Sgt., W-SS, Mauthausen, Buchenwald (Aust.,Ger.) 42-45	TORTURE	U.S.
FULZER	160176	M	Ger.		Chief, Gestapo, Le Roc (Fr.) 6.44	MURDER	FR.
FUMO	148303	M			Major, 137. Fascist Legion Slovenia Croatia (Yug.)41-43	MURDER	YUG.
FUNCK	194973	M			N.C.O, Paymaster Army S.P23265 A, Chennevieres sur Marne (Fr.) 40-44	PILLAGE	FR.
FUNCK	254166	M			SS-Uschfhr., Gestapo, Paris(Fr)41-44	TORTURE	FR.
FUNCK, Heinz	17320	M			Osturmfhr., SS (Sov.Un.) 8.41	MURDER	U.K.
FUNCKT	252478	M			Officer 377.Jaeg.Rgt., Vinkt (Bel.)	MISC.CRIMES	BEL.
FUNDEL, Willie	252981	M		99	Army, Gerardmer (Fr.) 5.44	WITNESS	FR.U.S.
FUNHOFF, Theodor	192412	M			C.C. Flossenburg (Ger.) 44-45	SUSPECT	U.S.
FUNK	142491	M			Oschfhr., 1.SS.Ps.Div.,2.Ps.Gr.Rgt.,3.Bn.12.Coy. Stavelott Malmedy (Bel.) 12.44	MURDER	U.S.

FUN-GAD

NAME	C.R.FILE NUMBER	SEX	NATIO-NALITY	DATE OF BIRTH	RANK OCCUPATION UNIT PLACE AND DATE OF CRIME	REASON WANTED	WANTED BY
FUNK	148238	M	Ger.		C.C.Gut Rottenau (Ger.)	TORTURE	FR.
FUNK	148260	M			C.C.Hohenlychen,Ravensbrueck (Ger.)	TORTURE	FR.
FUNK	148261	M	Ger.		Public official,Wattenstedt,Salzgitter (Ger.)	TORTURE	FR
FUNK	253955	M	Ger.		S.D.-Mann,S.D.,Toulouse (Fr.) 11.42-8.44	MISC.CRIMES	FR.
FUNK	305402	M	Ger.		SS-Mann,Gestapo,Toulouse,Ht. Garonne, Gers, Tarn, South-West (Fr.) 11.42-8.44	MURDER	FR.
FUNK,Alphonse	147940	M			Feldgendarmerie,Sedan (Fr.) 44	PILLAGE	FR.
FUNK,Heinrich	252966	M	Ger.		Guard,SS,C.C.Lende-Weser (Bel.)	MISC.CRIMES	BEL.
FUNKE	148259	M	Ger.		Feldgendarmerie,C.C.Verfeil (Fr.)	MURDER	FR.
FUNKE	187226	M			Guard,4 SS-Totenkopf-Stuba,C.C.Dora,Nordhausen (Ger.) 43-45	WITNESS	U.S.
FUNKE	192411	M			SS-Oschfhr.,Flossenburg (Ger.) 44-45	SUSPECT	U.S.
FUNKE	252968	M	Ger.		6 Coy.,16 Hubner-Regt.,Kinrooc (Bel.)	INTERR.	BEL.
FUNKE	301892	M			Capt.,2 Regt.,(Major de Locmine) 7.-8.44	MURDER	FR.
FUNKE,Adolf	142484	M	Ger.	7. 9.97	Policeman,Police,Tiddische (Ger.) 5.44	MURDER	U.S.
FUNKE,Heinrich	187223	M		29.11.93	SS-Guard,Uschfhr.,4 Totenkopf-Sturmbann, C.C.Dora Mittelbau, Nordhausen (Ger.) 43-45	WITNESS	U.S.
FUNKE,Oskar	306373	M	Ger.		Cpl.,SS(No.206252),C.C.Buchenwald (Ger.) 5.38-10.43	MURDER	BEL.
FUNKE,Wilhelm	186844	M	Ger.		Member,Gestapo,St.Brieuc (Fr.)	TORTURE	FR.
FUNKE,Willi	10150	M		88	Guard,C.C.Falkenberg (Ger.) 6.44	TORTURE	U.K.
FUNKE,Willie	306153	M	Ger.	about 06	Foreman,Civilian,Working Kommando,Stalag IV D,Bitterfeld,B.E.2 and Falkenberg (Ger.)44-45	BRUTALITY	U.K.
FUNKER	193911	M	Ger.		G.F.P.R.,Army,Staff Etat-Major of Crest,La Rochelle (Fr.) 8.44	INTERR.	FR.
FUNKERIGG (see FUNKRIGO)	138231						
FUNKRIGO (or FUNKERIGG)	138231	M	Ger.		Member,NSDAP,Bourg-Zastic (Fr.) 7.44	MURDER	FR.
FUMTZ	251530	M			Gestapo,Lille (Fr.) 40-44	MISC.CRIMES	FR.
FUMYB	161190	M	Ger.		Capt.,Army,559 Bn.,6 Coy.,Rothenstadt (Ger.) 4.45	MISC.CRIMES	U.K.
FURBRINGER	176704	M			Sturmschfhr.,SS,C.C.Muhldorf,Ampfing (Ger.) 6.44-4.45	MURDER	U.S.
FURDUSCH	142622	M			Army,Chateauneuf du Faou (Fr.)	MURDER	FR.
FUREHT,Bruno	192410	M			C.C.Flossenburg (Ger.) 44-45	SUSPECT	U.S.
FURER	190524	M	Ger.		Lt.,Navy, Hafenpolizei, La Baule, St.Nazaire Chantiers de Penheet (Fr.) 41-44	MURDER	FR.
FURICH,Willi (or FURIG)	252090	M	Ger.		Driver,Parachutists,St.Michielsgestel (Neth.) 9.-10.44	MISC.CRIMES	NETH.
FURINGER,Christian	133312	M	Ger.		Civilian,Muhlheim-Main (Ger.) 2.45	MURDER	U.S.
FURKE,Elli	149554	F		13. 9.23	Overseer, C.C.Buchenwald (Ger.)	MISC.CRIMES	FR.
FURMAN,J.	147943	M			Civilian,Messeburg (Ger.)	TORTURE	FR.
FURSMANN	121257	M	Ger.		Interpreter,S.D.,Gestapo,Paris (Fr.)	MISC.CRIMES	FR.
FURSMANN	189365	M			Interpreter,Gestapo,C.C.Drancy (Fr.) 6.43	MURDER	FR.
FURST	142621	M			Col.,Army,St.Pol de Leon,et Morlaix (Fr.)	MURDER	FR.
FURSTER	141475	M	Ger.		Chief,Gestapo,Chenebier-Etobon (Fr.) 9.44	MURDER	FR.
FURSTER	147939	M			Lt.,Waffen-SS,C.C.Auschwitz (Pol.)	TORTURE	FR.
FURT,Paul	185128	M			Guard,C.C.Sachsenhausen,Oranienburg (Ger.)	MURDER	FR.
FURTHMANN,Rudolf	147944	M	Ger.			TORTURE	FR.
FURZINGER	178758	M	Ger.	05	Oberfhr.,SS,conscript foreign workers, Marien-Murtzal(Aust.)3.45	MURDER	U.K.
FUSER	300681	M	Ger.		German common law prisoner,Chief of service,Praezifix Camp, Kdo.,C.C.Dachau (Ger.) 43-45	MISC.CRIMES	BEL.
FUSS,Hugo	162023	M	Ger.	18	Hptwachtmeister,Ordnungspolizei,1 Krad-Schtz.-Coy.,BDO,Stavern(Nor.) 11.43	MURDER	NOR.
FUSSEL,Rudolph	167114	M	Ger.	30.12.97	Oschfhr.,SS,C.C.Natzweiler (Fr.) 42-44	MURDER	FR.
FUSST	192173	M	Ger.		Sonderfhr.,Geh.Feldpolizei SS,official,Ghent (Bel.)	MISC.CRIMES	BEL.
FUST,Rudolph	142616	M			Lt.,Army,Beclin (Fr.) 9.44	MURDER	FR.
FUST,Walter	258779	M	Ger.		Employee,Airfield,Wieseck (Ger.) 3.or 4.44	WITNESS	U.S.
FUSZ	142650	M	Ger.		Hptsturmfhr.,SS,C.C.Vught (Neth.) 43-44	MURDER	BEL.
FUTSE	147943	M			C.C.Auschwitz (Pol.)	MURDER	FR.
FUTTERER	257844	M			Boufirman,C.C.Muhldorf (Ger.)	MURDER	U.S.
FUTZ	252301	M			Cmdt.,Metallwerk,Stalag IX A,Rotenburg (Ger.) 40-44	TORTURE	FR.
FUTZER,Fritz	306374	M			Head of Block No.6,C.C.Dora,Nordhausen (Ger.) 40-45	MURDER	BEL.
FUX	167589	M			Head-Warder,Justizvollzuganstalt,Siegburg near Bonn (Ger.)	MISC.CRIMES	BEL.
FUX,Adolf	162026	M			Pvt.,Guard,C.C.Regensburg (Ger.)1.45	MURDER	U.S.
FWERHOFF	130645	M			Usturmfhr.,SS and leader,Central committe for commitment of Workers,C.C.Dora Mittelbau (Ger.)	MURDER	U.S.
GABAUER,Bernard	262141	M		95 - 00	Former inmate of C.C.Flossenburg (Ger.)	WITNESS	U.S.
GABE	145378	M			Hptsturmfhr.,SS,Gestapo,Hoerde (Ger.)	MURDER	U.S.
GABE	257594	M			Rottfhr.,SS,C.C.Dachau,Muehldorf (Ger.)	MURDER	U.S.
GABEL	132279	M	Ger.	10	Capt.,Schupo,Sicherheits-Commando 11 B,Thekina,Tiraspol(Rum.-Russ)41	MURDER	U.S.
GABELE,Gottlob	191788	M	Ger.		Pvt.,Air Force,Arles (Fr.) 8.44	PILLAGE	FR.
GABELE,Gottlob	167620	M	Ger.		Pvt.,Feldluftpark,Camp at Chanoime,Arles (Fr.) 8.44	MISC.CRIMES	FR.
GABERCKEL	256676	M			Interpreter,Air Force,Abergement de Varey (Fr.) 7.44	MURDER	FR.
GABERLE	250800	M			Dr.,Stadortarzt,Usturmfhr.,SS,C.C.Dora,Nordhausen (Ger.)	MURDER	U.S.
GABINGER	141863	M	Ger.	85 or 80	Col.,Stalag VIII E,C.C.Nuremberg (Ger.)	TORTURE	U.K.
GABLER	144764	M	Ger.	00	Dr.,SS,C.C.Sachsenhausen,Oranienburg (Ger.)	MURDER	U.K.
GABLER,Richard	259367	M	Ger.		Uschfhr.,SS,Gestapo of Poitiers Area (Fr.) 40-45	MISC.CRIMES	FR.
GABRICH,Maria	135168	F	Ger.		Woman,Civ.,Guard,C.C.Helmbrechts (Ger.) 7.43-4.45	WITNESS	U.S.
GABRIEL	12391	M			Hauptsturmfhr.,Generalstaatsanwalt,SS,Kommissar Gestapo, Prague (Czech.) 38-45	TORTURE	CZECH.
GABRIEL	250801	M			Rottfhr.,SS,C.C.Dora,Nordhausen (Ger.)	MURDER	U.S.
GABRIEL,Jean	146882	M	Ger.		Soldier,Police de Campagne,Capestang (Fr.) 44	MISC.CRIMES	FR.
GABIREL,Helmuth	174140	M	Ger.		General-Staatsanwalt,Occup.Territ.Prag (Czech.)	TORTURE	CZECH.
GABRIEL,Therese	260866	F			Civ.,C.C.Hallein (Aust.)	WITNESS	U.S.
GABRISCH	250787	M	Ger.		Staatsanwalt,Hptsturmfhr.,SS,Waffen-SS,Maribor (Yugo.) 44	MURDER	YUGO.
GABRYSH	36559	M	Ger.		Osturmfhr.,SS	MURDER	U.K.
GACHELER	147740	F		05	Woman-Guard,Waffen-SS,C.C.Ravensbrueck (Ger.)	TORTURE	FR.
GACK	257024	M			Cpl.,Fieldpolice,Romerantin No.577,Orcay (Fr.) 8.44	MURDER	FR.
GACKI,Albert	141547	M			Member,Kriegsgericht,Toulon (Fr.)	MURDER	FR.
GADABUSCH	120612	M	Ger.		Pvt.,Army,Guard at Working Camp 1006,Schiller-Schule,Freital, Gitterseer (Ger.) 4.45	TORTURE	U.K.-U.S.

GAD-GAN

NAME	C.R.FILE NUMBER	SEX	NATIO-NALITY	DATE OF BIRTH	RANK OCCUPATION UNIT PLACE AND DATE OF CRIME	REASON WANTED	WANTED BY
GADDE, Johann	252113	M	Ger.		Lt., Police, Luxemburg (Fr.) 40-45	INTERR.	LUX.
GADE, Rudolf	250782	M	Ger.		Kapo, Concerned in Deportation of Civilians, Neuengamme (Ger.) 44	TORTURE	FR.
GADNER	141548	M	Ger.	02	Oberscharfhr., SS-Totenkopf, Natzweiler,Schirmeck (Fr.) 7.43-4.44	MURDER	FR.
GADOW, Charlotte	191841	F	Ger.		Civilian, Harzfelde Niederbarnim (Ger.) 45	WITNESS	U.S.
GAEBELER	141549	F	Ger.		Aufseherin K.L., Ravensbrueck (Ger.)	MISC.CRIMES	FR.
GAEDE, Horst	190581	M	Ger.	08	Sgt., SD Einsatzkdo. z B V 6, La Grande Fosse (Fr.) 10.44	MURDER	U.K.
GAEDECKE, Walter	254111	M	Ger.		Dir., Special Tribunal, Strasbourg (Fr.) 40-44	MISC.CRIMES	FR.
GAEDERTZ, Juergen	253005	M	Ger.	9.23	Officer, "Hitler-Jugend" Div., Aufkl. Abt., Oradour-Glane, (Fr.)	MURDER	FR.
GAEDICKE, Kurt	261842	M	Ger.		Railway-councillor, Paris (Fr.) 2.44	INTERR.	FR.
GAEINER, Joseph	149258	M	Ger.	12	Lagerfhr., C.Camp Munich (Ger.)	MURDER	FR.
GAENNEL	141550	M		07	Manager, Factory, Boehmisch-Leipa (Czech.) 43-44	TORTURE	FR.
GAERTIG	193054	M			Kapo, C.C. Buchenwald (Ger.) 42-45	WITNESS	U.S.
GAERTNER	188250	M	Ger.		Civilian, Bitburg (Ger.) 7. or 8.44	MURDER	U.S.
GAERTNER	253665	M	Ger.		Employee, Sipo VI, Brussels (Bel.)	INTERR.	BEL.
GAERTNER, Lothar	262330	M		02	L.o.D.N.A.o.D., Dr., Physician, Wanted for the murder of men,women and children by the means of prison and killing by intra-muscular injections, Kaufbeuren (Ger.) 29-45	SUSPECT	U.S.
GAERTNER, Helmut	185508	M	Ger.		SS-Mann, SS Leibstand. Adolf Hitler, Stabskompanie, Aufkl.Abt. Renardmont, Stavelot (Bel.) 12.44	MURDER	BEL.
GAERTNER, R.	195549	M	Ger.		Guard, C.C. Kaufering (Ger.) 39-45	MURDER	CZECH.
GAETZ	147333	M	Ger.		Lt., 11 Pz.Div., 110. Pz.Gren.Regt., (Fr.)44	MURDER	FR.
GAETZ, Christoph	300080	M	Ger.		Policeman, Police, Lodz (Pol.) 39-44	MURDER	POL.
GAFFRON	259278	M			Crim.-Secretary, Camp Thekla near Leipzig (Ger.) 4.45	MURDER	U.S.
GAFLING, Alois	132282	M	Ger.		Wachtmeister, Prison Guard, Police C.C. Bayreuth, Amberg (Ger.)4.45	TORTURE	U.S.
GAFLITA	251546	M	Ger.		16. Hubner Regt., Kinroy (Bel.)	INTERR.	BEL.
GAGEL, Erich	187830	M	Ger.	22	Rottenfhr., 10. Pz. Div., Sobisdorf (Ger.) 4.45	MURDER	U.S.
GAGEL, Oscar	141551	M	Ger.		NSDAP, Vienne (Aust.)	MURDER	FR.
GAGER, Johann	23844	M		7.20	Chef-Fuehrer, SS Troyes-Bucheres-Cernay (Fr.) 44	MURDER	FR.
GAIDA	251549	M			Pvt., Pepingen (Bel.)		BEL.
GAIDA, Hugo	250794	M	Ger.		Commissar, Police, Maribor (Yugo.) 44	INTERR.	YUGO.
GAIDSCH	257966	M			O-Cand. 150th Pz.Bde., Meuse Bridge, Antwerp (Bel.) 12.44	MISC.CRIMES	U.S.
GAIGNER, Walter	192928	M	Ger.		Zugwachtmeister, Police, C.C. Falstad (Nor.) 5.42	TORTURE	NOR.
GAILS	161203	M	Ger.		SS-Rottenfhr., K.L. Buchenwald (Ger.)	MURDER	U.S.
GAINSTER	253090	M	Ger.		SS, Gestapo, C.C. Bremen-Farge (Ger.)	BRUTALITY	U.K.
GAISER	254113	M	Ger.		Lt., Unit Dienststelle 58.104. E, Aigues-Vives (Fr.) 43	PILLAGE	FR.
GAITH, Edward	189064	M	Ger.		Untersturmfhr., Crim.Secretary Gestapo, SD, Munich, C.C. Dachau (Ger.) 40-45	MURDER	BEL.
GAKOP, Leopold	167395	M	Ger.		Gendarm, Feldgend., Luneville Maixe, (Fr.) 8.44	MURDER	FR.
GALASCH	193629	M	Ger.		SS-Unterscharfhr., C.C., Fuenfteichen, Grossrosen (Pol.) 1.45	MURDER	POL.
GALBIERS, Guenther	250802	M			Pvt., Camp Ellrich, Nordhausen (Ger.)	MURDER	U.S.
GALDIX, Heinz	251577	M	Ger.		Cpl., Air-Force, Maubeuge (Fr.)4.42	MURDER	FR.
GALECKA, Alfred	152192	M		15	Civilian, Gestapo, Krakau (Pol.) 44	MURDER	U.K.
GALEINER	252128	M	Ger.		Obersturmfhr., SS-Dienststelle, Aigues-Vives (Fr.) 2.44	PILLAGE	FR.
GALEY	141552	M	Ger.		Capt., Pi. Bn. 21, (Sov.Un.)	MURDER	FR.
GALHICK	251576	M	Ger.		SS-Sturmfhr., Gestapo, Limoges (Fr.) 40-45	INTERR.	FR.
GALINAT	282	F	Ger.		Lager Official, Deputy Supervisor, C.C. Ravensbrueck (Ger.)	MURDER	YUGO.
GALINGER	191637	M	Ger.	06	Capt., Member, SD Gestapo, Vichy (Fr. and Ger.) 44	MURDER	FR.
GALITZ	167621	M	Ger.		Capt, Feldluftpark, Camp at Chanoine, Arles (Fr.) 8.44	MISC.CRIMES	FR.
GALL, Hans	189366	M	Ger.		Sgt., Battery DCA, Grand Quevilly (Fr.) 8.44	MURDER	FR.
GALLE	23841	M			Secretary, Police SD Administration, Tour la Ville, Cherbourg, St. Lo (Fr.) 6.44	MURDER	FR.
GALLE, Bernhard	261877	M	Ger.		Sgt., G.F.P. Group 6, Gand-Bruges-Renaix Et Courtrai (Bel.) 42-44	MURDER	BEL.
GALLENT, Wilhelm	257863	M			Ostuf. 150. Pz.Bde., Meuse Bridge, Antwerp (Bel.) 12.44	MISC.CRIMES	U.S.
GALLER, Frantz	252863	M		11.24	Pvt., 13. Coy., 558 Gren. Regt., Brusy en Artois (Fr.) 9.44	MURDER	FR.
GALLESEN	305138	M	Ger.		SS-Unterscharfhr., C.C. Neuengamme (Ger.)	MISC.CRIMES	FR.
GALLIGER see KALIGE	254967						
GALLINGER	23843	M		04	Hauptsturmfhr., Dr., Fernand, Vichy, Clermont (Fr.) 44	MURDER	FR.
GALLINGER	252103	M	Ger.	06-10	Dr., Hauptscharfhr., C.C. Compiegne (Fr.) 41-6.44	MURDER	FR.
GALLOW	121026	M	Ger.		Capt., Greville-Hague (Fr.) 5.44	WITNESS	FR.
GALLSEN	189452	M	Ger.		Commandant, 3rd SS Pol. Regt., Scheveningen (Neth.) 3.45	MURDER	NETH.
GALLUS, Georg	186422	M	Ger.		Crim.Comissar, Gestapo SD, Prague (Czech.) 39-45	MURDER	CZECH.
GALLUS, Hendrick	161898	M	Ger.		Employee, Civilian 9.42	MISC.CRIMES	U.S.
GALM, Anton, Gustav	257595	M			Polizeiwachtmstr. Viernheim (Ger.) 10.44	TORTURE	U.S.
GALMAN	67725	M	Ger.		C.C. Klausberg (Ger.) 12.41	MURDER	U.K.
GALSTER	177600	M	Ger.		Official, Reichsbaudirektion, Aulnat (Fr.)	MISC.CRIMES	FR.
GAMBE	193053	M	Ger.		Lt., W.SS, C.C. Buchenwald (Ger.) 42-45	TORTURE	U.S.
GAMINGER	23840	M	Ger.		Obersturmfhr., SS, Karelz	MISC.CRIMES	FR.
GAMMRADT	141554	M			Commandant, Deutz (Ger.) 42	TORTURE	FR.
GAMPFE or GOMPFE	195497	M	Ger.	93	Arbeitslager. Hesslar (Ger.) 43-44	TORTURE	POL.
GAMS, Kaspar	12625	M	Ger.		Pvt., 110 or 111. Pz. Gren.Regt. 2. Coy., Albine (Fr.) 6.44	MURDER	FR.
GAMSER or GANSER	23804	M			Mayor, Public official, Ferette (Fr.)	MURDER	FR.
GANCZA, Alfons	176698	M	Ger.		Betriebs-Fuehrer, C.C. Alsfeld (Adam) (Ger.)	MURDER	U.S.,U.L
GANGLHOFF, Mlle.	141555	F			Gestapo, Interprete, Tarbes (Fr.)	TORTURE	FR.
GANOS	255264	M			Cmdt., Camp Mauthausen (Ger.)	INTERR.	FR.
GANINSKI	141557	M			Chief of D.P., Chemnitz (Ger.)	TORTURE	FR.
GANN	254092	M	Ger.		Farmer, Emerding (Austr.) 4.45	INTERR.	FR.
GANNIGER	23802	M	Ger.		Oberscharfhr., SS, Struthof (Fr.)	MURDER	FR.
GANNIGER	126544	M			Cpl. K.L.	MURDER	YUGO.SOV.U
GANNINGER	261956	M	Ger.		SS Oschfhr., W.-SS, Auschwitz (Pol.) 41-44	BRUTALITY	POL.
GANS	195174	M	Ger.		SS-Oberscharfhr., K.L. Wittlich-Einzert (Ger.) 41,42,43	TORTURE	U.S.
GANSER or GAMSER	23804	M			Buergermeister, Public Offic. Ferette (Fr.)	MURDER	FR.
GANSKE	133790	M			SS-Gruppenfhr., C.C. Buchenwald (Ger.)	TORTURE	U.S.
GANEL	141560	M			Agent, SD, Strassburg (Fr.)	INTERR.	FR.
GANTENBERG	141559	M			Prof.Dr., Hohenlychen (Ger.) 5.44	TORTURE	FR.
GANTNER, Franz	161198	M	Ger.	30	Civilian, Schlossberg Krs. Rosenheim (Ger.) 4.45	WITNESS	U.S.
GANTZ	141561	M			Cmdt., W.-SS, Le Valdahon (Fr.) Zamacs Mogilex (Sov.Un.)12.41-9.44	MURDER	FR.

GAN-GAS

NAME	C.R.FILE NUMBER	SEX	NATIO-NALITY	DATE OF BIRTH	RANK OCCUPATION UNIT PLACE AND DATE OF CRIME	REASON WANTED	WANTED BY
GANTZER, Gottfried	183127	M			SS Scharfhr.4 SS Totenkopf Sturmbann,CC Nordhausen-Dora-Mittelbau Auschwitz(Pol.Ger.)43-45	WITNESS	U.S.
GANZ	284	M	Ger.		NCO,Div.Das Reich SS,Buzet(Fr.)7.44-8.44	MURDER	FR.
GANZ	129637	M	Ger.		5 parachute Rgt.,Nachrichtenzug, Quaregnon, Jemappes, Ghlin (Bel.) 9.44	MURDER	BEL.
GANZ	195548	M	Ger.		NCO,SS Div.Das Reich,Buzet(Fr.)7.44-8.44	MURDER	FR.
GANZ	305851	M	Ger.		Cpl.1 Aufkl.Abt.3 Coy.2 Col.XV Div.Afrika Korps,St.Leger(Arlon)9.44	MISC.CRIMES	BEL.
GANZ, Alfred	252999	M	Ger.		SS Sturmmann,SS Gestapo,La Chaise(Fr.)7.44	BRUTALITY	FR.
GANZ, Alfred	350139	M	Ger.		SS Sturmmann,Member SS,Dienville,Aube(Fr.)6.44,10.43-8.44	MURDER	FR.
GANZ, Gustav	193622	M	Ger.	7.11.99	Factory Manager,Civilian,Brno(Czech.)39-45	MURDER	CZECH.
GANZ, Tony	185507	M	Ger.	00	SS Hptsturmfhr.Chief,CC Ebensee(Aust.)44	MURDER	FR.U.S.
GANZEL, Hermann	285	M	Ger.		Official NCO,Gestapo,SS Div.Das Reich,Paris(Fr.)43-44	MISC.CRIMES	FR.
GANZKERN	149482	M	Ger.		SS Gruppenfhr.CC Hohenlychen,Ravensbrueck(Ger.)5.44	TORTURE	FR.
GAPPA, Anni	147760	F		22	Woman Guard,Waffen SS,Grusenberg(Ger.)	TORTURE	FR.
GARAY	174139	M	Ger.		Sgt.Stalag 6A,CC Hemer(Ger.)44	TORTURE	U.S.
GARBAS, Arthur	141476	M	Ger.		Pillage of Jewishs property(Fr.)	PILLAGE	FR.
GARBAUM	119417	M	Ger.		General Lt.Comd.18 Geb.Korps,20 Army,Finmark(Nor.)10.44	MURDER	NOR.
GARBE, Leo	305140	M	Ger.		Sgt.Turkestan Legion,1 Regt.of Turkestan,Volunteers,Albi,Tarn(Fr.)8.44	MURDER	FR.
GARBLER, Arthur	161197	M	Ger.		Foreman , Work Commando 27,Stalag 4,Boehlen near Leipzig(Ger.)4.44	TORTURE	U.K.
GARCIA	257562	M		15	Kl-Kapo,KL Mauthausen(Aust.)	TORTURE	FR.
GARDE, Ernest	161196	M			Director,Work Commando,Schamborn(Fr.)	TORTURE	FR.
GARDHUN	149504	M	Ger.	95	Civilian,Demmin(Ger.)	TORTURE	FR.
GARDNER	23810	M	Ger.		Oschafhr.SS,Struthof(Fr.)	MISC.CRIMES	FR.
GARDNER	149484	M	Ger.		CC Mauthausen(Aust.)	MISC.CRIMES	FR.
GAREIS	122483	M	Ger.		Engineer,Civilian,CC Rattiborhammer(Ger.)6.41	TORTURE	U.K.
GAREIS	160999	M	Ger.		Pvt.SS Div.Adolf Hitler,12 Regt.,Maastricht(Neth.)9.45	INTERR.	NETH.
GAREIS	191439	M	Ger.		Dr.,Leader,Abt.Ernaehrung und Landwirtschaft Amt des General-Gouver-neurs,Lwow,Krakow(Pol.)9.39-44	PILLAGE	POL.
GAREIS, Karl	255129	M	Ger.	19.10.96	Civilian,Gossengrun-Haberspirk(Czech.)9.39	MURDER	CZECH.
GAREIS, Maittin	260619	M		91	Lt.Gen.Army Inf.	WITNESS	U.S.
GARITTE	259664	M			Doctor,SS Unterscharfhr.Sipo VI,Brussels(Bel.)	INTERR.	BEL.
GARITZ, Heinrich	262142	M	Ger.		CC Mauthausen(Ger.)(L.O.D.N.A.O.D)	SUSPECTS	U.S.
GARLEB	195308	M	Ger.		Dr.,manager, CC Schandelah, Braunschweig (Ger.) 44 - 45	TORTURE	BEL.
GARLING, Hans	130324	M	Ger.	05	Capt.Army or Airforce,O.C.Coy.No.52852,Chateau de Parisis-Fontaine, Noailles(Fr.)8.44	MURDER	FR.
GARLING, Karl	183126	M			SS Sturmmann,4 SS Totenkopf Sturmbann, CC Nordhausen-Dora-Mittelbau, Osterode(Ger.)43-45	WITNESS	U.S.
GARLIPP, Artur	250803	M			Pvt.Camp Artern Nordhausen(Ger.)	MURDER	U.S.
GARLOFF, Adolf	145380	M			Civilian	MURDER	U.S.
GARN D Aurigny	7479	M	Ger.		Army	TORTURE	FR.
GARNATZKY	193052	M	Ger.		SS Uschafhr.Waffen SS,CC Buchenwald(Ger.)38-40	TORTURE	U.S.
GARNY see GARY	152190						
GARR	252490	M			Lt.Police "Trento",Carpane(It.)9.44	MURDER	U.K.
GARRALS, Gerhardt	145381	M			Civilian,Borkum(Ger.)8.44	MURDER	U.S.
GARSKY, Lothar	259940	M	Ger.	17.5.01	Informer,Gestapo Prague,Collaboration with Gestapo probably living in Berlin,Lidice(Bohemia/Czech.)42	MISC.CRIMES	CZECH.
GARTLICK, Richard or GAWLICK	39641	M	Ger.	10	Sgt.Unit F.P.L.30182,Cazaux(Fr.)8.44	MURDER	FR.
GARTMANN, Max Bruns	258692	M	Ger.		Capt.Land.Schtz.Polizei,Bad Salzdetfurth(Ger.)11.44	MURDER	U.S.
GARTNER	147953	M	Ger.	05	Factory "Vomag"Goerlitz(Ger.)	TORTURE	FR.
GARTNER	301685	M	Ger.		Bde.Chief.057243 Mongolian Unit Oberland,St.Nazaire en Royans(Fr.) 7.-8.44	MURDER	FR.
GARTNER, Hans	106945	M	Ger.		FA,Sign.Sect.(nachrichtendienst)466 Inf.Regt.,Doerigsen(Ger.)4.45	MURDER	U.S.
GARTNER, Hans	144758	M	Ger.	05	Civilian,CC Oranienburg,Sachsenhausen(Ger.)	MURDER	U.S.
GARTNER, Martin	177738	M			Guard,SS,CC Muhldorf Ampfing(Ger.)	MURDER	U.S.
GARTNER, Philip	152191	M	Ger.		Member,Employee,NSDAP,Tschausch 3,Bruex(Czech.)6.44	MURDER	U.K.
GARTNER, Werner	125031	M	Ger.		Capt.Army,Poitiers,Chateau(Fr.)8.44	MURDER	FR.
GARTNER, Willy	67593	M	Ger.		Interpreter,Custom-House,Damprichard(Fr.)7.44	MURDER	FR.
GARUDINGER see GLANDINGER	72295						
GARWERT, Henri	252864	M	Ger.	28.2.14	Pvt.13 Coy.558 Gren.Regt.,Bruay-en Artois(Fr.)9.44	MURDER	FR.
GARY or GARNY	152190				SS Mann,SS Pz.Div.Das Reich,Regt.Der Fuehrer,3 Coy.1 Bn.,Oradour/Glane (Fr.)6.44	MURDER	FR.
GASMANN	305852	M	Ger.		Pvt.1 Aufkl.Abt.3 Coy.2 Col.XV Div.Afrika Korps,St.Leger(Arlon)9.44	MISC.CRIMES	BEL.
GASNER	122616	M	Ger.	90	Lt.Work-Commando, KL Graz(Aust.)2.45	TORTURE	U.K.
GASPAR	149483	M			Overseer,Civilian,Plasseville(Fr.)	TORTURE	FR.
GASPAR	305141	M	Ger.		Major, Commanding Officer of the 117 Unit,1 Div.,Argos(Grc.)5.-7.44	MURDER	GRC.
GASPAR, Peter	250225	M	Ger.	02	377 Jaeger Regt.,Vinkt,Meigen vicinity(Bel.)	BRUTALITY	BEL.
GASPARD	12429	M	Ger.		Standort Kommand.Kommandantur,Pontivy Locmine(Fr.)7.44-8.44	MURDER	FR.
GASPART	252305	M	Ger.		Civilian,Ampen Kreis Soest(Ger.)6.44	MURDER	FR.
GASSAUER, Karl	252420	M	Ger.	01	Judge,State Service,Bruenn(Czech.)42-45	MURDER	CZECH.
GASSELLICH	171869	M	Ger.		Dr.,Gouverneur,P.Off.Adm.of Poland,Lwow(Pol.)41	MISC.CRIMES	POL.
GASSER	149507	M	Ger.		Member NSDAP,Bad Kreuznach(Ger.)	TORTURE	FR.
GASSL, Franz	191877	M	Ger.		SS Pvt.1 SS Pz.Regt.Stabs Coy.L.A.H.,Staumont,Ligneuville(Bel.)12.44	WITNESS	U.S.
GASSMUS, Herbert	250799	M			SS Rottenfhr.Camp Ellrich/Mackenrode,Nordhausen(Ger.)	MURDER	U.S.
GASSNER	1982	M	Ger.		SS Sturmscharfhr.S.D.Aussenkdo.SS	MISC.CRIMES	U.K.
GASSNER	23816	M	Ger.		Feldgend.,St.Brienc(Fr.)44	MURDER	FR.
GASSNER	120613	M	Ger.	92	Lt.Arb.Kommando,170,-G.W.,Graz(Aust.)2.45	TORTURE	U.K.
GASSNER	161318	M	Ger.		Lt.Army,Stalag XVII,Markt Pongau(Aust.) 4.45	TORTURE	U.S.
GASSNER, George	188221	M	Ger.		Civilian,Muchenstrum or Muckensturm(Ger.)7.-8.44	WITNESS	U.S.
GASSNER, Johann	14275	M	Ger.	78	Civilian,Palling(Ger.)	MURDER	FR.
GASSNER, Joseph	23904	M	Ger.	21.3.06	Cpl.Nazi,SS,Carcassonne(Fr.)44	MURDER	U.S.
GAST	135171	M	Ger.		Polizei-Chef,Gendarmerie Chef,Aschaffenburg(Ger.)44	MURDER	U.S.

GAS-GEE

NAME	C.R.FILE NUMBER	SEX	NATIO-NALITY	DATE OF BIRTH	RANK OCCUPATION UNIT PLACE AND DATE OF CRIME	REASON WANTED	WANTED BY
GAST	167611	M	Ger.		Propaganda Ministerium (Ger.) 43	MURDER	U.S.
GAST, Adolf	183125	M			Pvt.,SS Totenkopf Sturmbann, C.C.Nordhausen-Dora Mittelbau-Osterode (Ger.) 43-45	WITNESS	U.S.
GAST, Hans	23817	M	Ger.		C.C. Natzweiler-Struthof (Fr.)	MURDER	FR.
GASTEIGER, Georg	187828	M	Ger.		Kriegsgef.Arb.Kdo.,C.C. Regensburg (Ger.) 41-45	TORTURE	U.S.
GASTGEB, Sigismund	250223	M			Cpl.,C.C. Ellrich, Nordhausen (Ger.)	MURDER	U.S.
GATERWALD	12627	M	Ger.		Pvt.,110 or 111 Pz.Gren.Rgt.,3 Group,Gourdon (Fr.) 6.44	MURDER	FR.
GATH	251575	M	Ger.		Sgt., 3 Heeres Cpl.-school, 338 Div., La Bresse (Fr.) 9.-11.44	MURDER	FR.
GATH, Helmut	106946	M			Lt., Sonder-Kdo.,Langenbach,Hohenlichte (Ger.) 3.45	MURDER	U.S.
GATTERMAIR, Ullrich	250208	M			Flyer, Camp Ellrich, Nordhausen (Ger.)	MURDER	U.S.
GATTERMANN	250798	M			Pvt., Camp Ellrich, Nordhausen (Ger.)	MURDER	U.S.
GATTERMAYER	177737	M			Hptscharfhr.,SS, C.C. Muhldorf,Ampfing (Ger.)	MURDER	U.S.
GATTERSLEBEN, Hugo	161195	M	Ger.	90 - 95	Col., Airforce, Herdla (Nor.) 7.44	WITNESS	NOR.
GATTHE, Fritz	261069	M			Member, German Mission,detailed at Schneider's Works, Le Creusot (Fr.) 2.44	INTERR.	FR.
GATTI, Giorgio or GHATTI	251552	M	Ger.		Dr. of law, believed to be of Ger.counter espionage-corps, Mesola and Ariano Polesing (It.) 12.44	TORTURE	U.K.
GATTNING	185501	M	Ger.		Lt.Stalag 18 A,Cmdt. Spittel (Aust.) 10.43	MURDER	U.S.
GATZ	192516	M	Ger.		Lt.Col., Inf.Rgt.357, 6 Coy (Nor.)	MURDER	NOR.
GAU	167622	M	Ger.		Prof.,Dr.,official,chief of office for special operations Einsatzstab Rosenberg, Berlin (Ger.) 40-44	PILLAGE	FR.
GAUBE, Karl	253660	M	Ger.	27. 4.13	Scharfhr., SS and Gestapo,Ceskalipa (Czech.) 39-45	MISC.CRIMES	CZECH.
GAUCH	186490	M		22	Usturmfhr., SS, 12 SS-Pz.Div."H.J.", near Caen (Fr.)	TORTURE	CAN.
GAUDEK	250780	M			Oscharfhr..SS, Camp Ellrich, Nordhausen (Ger.)	MURDER	U.S.
GAUDERER, Ludwiga	193621	F	Ger.		Civilian, Nurse, C.C. Lidice (Czech.) 42-44	WITNESS	CZECH.
GAUDICH	23820	M			Grpe.Espagn,Coy Brandenburg,Font St.Esprit (Fr.)	MURDER	FR.
GAUDIS	171650	M	Ger.		Dr.,leader, Ernaehrungs-and Landwirtschaft,Warsaw (Pol.) 9.39-44	MISC.CRIMES	POL.
GAUERKE	24836	M			Capt.,Army,337 Landes-Schz.Bn,2 Coy, Molofcus,Kradsc-Kralove (Czech.) 43,2.45	TORTURE	U.K.
GAUFER, Emil	161232	M	Ger.	00	Official, SD, Ingelfingen (Ger.)	TORTURE	FR.
GAUGER	252107	M			Oberwachtmstr., Pol.-officer,driver,Schupo,Stuetzpunkt Groningen, Westerbork (Neth.,Ger.) 9.-12.44	MURDER	NETH.
GAULK	132536	M	Ger.		Lt., Comm.Ortscmdr.,3 Btty de D.C.A. 649,Ville-le-Marclet (Fr.)8.44	MURDER	FR.
GAULLERT	156822	M	Ger.	10	Lt.,Army, 6 Para-Arty-Rgt.,1 Btty,Xanten (Ger.) 3.45	MURDER	CAN.
GAUOH	250766	M			Chief in Charge Equipment, Monsheim (Ger.)	BRUTALITY	FR.
GAUPP, Robert	132286	M	Ger.		Dr.,Lt.Col.,SS, SD Espionage Service University, Freiburg-Br. (Ger.)	MURDER	U.S.
GAURADT	152189	M	Ger.		Dir.,Convict-prison, Diez (Ger.)	MISC.CRIMES	FR.
GAURAUD MORIS, Violette	23822	F			Paris (Fr.)	MISC.CRIMES	FR.
GAUSE	260620	M		94	Lt.Col.	WITNESS	U.S.
GAUTER, Friedrich	177736	M			Labor Camp, C.C. Muhldorf,Ampfing (Ger.)	MURDER	U.S.
GAUTHIER, Wolfram alias WEINKOFF	251479	M	Ger.		Sturmbannfhr.,SS, SD, d'Avignon, Arpavon and Sahune (Fr.) 6.44	MISC.CRIMES	FR.
GAUZ	129632	M	Ger.		Lageraeltester, SS, C.C. Mauthausen (Aust.) 41-45	MURDER	U.S.
GAWENDA, Piotr	188251	M		05	Hptscharfhr.,Member, SS, Gestapo, Sasnowiec (Pol.) 8.43	MURDER	POL.
GAWICKE	23837	M	Ger.	15	Oscharfhr., Gestapo, Locmine (Fr.) 44	TORTURE	U.S.
GAWLICK, Richard see GARTLICK	39641						
GAWLITTA	250797	M			Pvt.,Camp Ellrich, Nordhausen (Ger.)	MURDER	U.S.
GAYDAN, August	132287	M	Ger.		Gestapo	MURDER	U.S.
GAYN	161551	M			Member, Volkssturm, Lichtenberg (Ger.)	MURDER	U.S.
GAZAU	23828	M	Ger.		Cpl.,Feldgend. (Fr.)	MURDER	FR.
GAZEN, Richard	250226	M			Pvt.,10 Coy, 377 Jaeger-Rgt.,Vinct,Meigem et environs (Bel.)	BRUTALITY	BEL.
GEBAUER	287	M			Sgt.,Troops occupying Prison Camp Caen (Fr.) 6.44	MURDER	FR.
GEBAUER	106947	M			Lt.,Army,Hq, 66 Corps,Orodour	MURDER	U.S.
GEBAUER	253663	M			Chief, Sipo IV E, Brussels (Bel.)	MISC.CRIMES	BEL.
GEBAUER	305853	M			Pvt.,1 Aufkl.Abt., 3 Coy, 2 Col.,XV Div. Afrika Corps, St.Leger Distr.Arlon (Bel.) 9.44	MISC.CRIMES	BEL.
GEBAUER, Alfred	133788	M			Pvt.,SS, C.C. Buchenwald (Ger.) 43-45	MURDER	U.S.
GEBAUER, Alfred	183116	M			SS-Mann., 4 SS Totenkopf-Sturmbann, C.C. Dora,Nordhausen,Monowitz (Ger.,Pol.)	MURDER	U.S.
GEBAUER, Josef	183114	M			SS-Pvt.,guard,4 SS Totenkopf Stuba,C.C. Dora,Nordhausen,Monowitz (Ger.,Pol.) 43-45	MURDER	U.S.
GEBAUER, Wilhelm	254491	M	Ger.	7.10.07	Osturmfhr.,SS, Gestapo, Pilsen (Czech.) 39-43	MURDER	CZECH.
GEBE	161713	M	Ger.		Co.Dir.,C.C. Freiberg (Ger.) 10.43-4.45	TORTURE	U.K.
GEBERL, Richard	193620	M			C.C. Dachau, (Ger.) 8.44	MURDER	U.S.
GEBERZAHN, Jakob	259803	M	Ger.		Pvt.,Army, 112 Coy, Dienststelle Nr.39837 E,Midsland (Terschelling) (Noord-Holland-Neth.) 8.44	MURDER	NETH.
GEBHARD	127355	M	Ger.		Camp-officer, C.C. Buch (Ger.) 5.44	MURDER	U.S.
GEBHARD	252418	M	Ger.		Hptscharfhr.,SS, Auschwitz-Birkenau (Pol.)	MISC.CRIMES	YUGO.
GEBHARD	255380	M	Ger.		Sturmbannfhr., C.C. Buchenwald (Ger.)	MURDER	U.S.
GEBHARD, Werner	252865	M	Ger.	16.10.25	Pvt., 13 Coy, 558 Rgt.,Bruay en Artois (Fr.) 9.44	MURDER	FR.
GEBHARDT	106948	M		92	SS-officer, Schonau (Ger.) 9.44	MURDER	U.S.
GEBHARDT or GIBHARDT	179726	M		10	Pvt., 397 Landes-Schz.Bn, 5 Coy, C.C. Gubin Stalag XX A(Pol.) 6.42	MURDER	U.K.
GEBHARDT	250796	M			Rottenfhr.,SS, Camp Ellrich Nordhausen (Ger.)	MURDER	U.S.
GEBHARDT, Fritz	176737	M			Arb.Cdo.,C.C. Muhldorf,Ampfing (Ger.) 6.44-4.45	MURDER	U.S.
GEBHARDT, Max	152188	M	Ger.		NSDAP-Member,C.C.Brux,Tschausch III Sud	TORTURE	U.K.
GEBHARDT, Max	161712	M	Ger.	00	Sturmbannfhr., SS-Standarte 'Thuringia',C.C. Buchenwald (Ger.) 42-45	WITNESS	U.S.
GEBHARDT, Wolfgang	254103	M	Ger.	19. 3.24	Rottenfhr., Waffen-SS, 12 SS-Pz.Div. "H.J.", Lublin (Pol.) 42-43	MISC.CRIMES	POL.
GEBRWIRTH	161407	M	Ger.		Civilian, Plettenberg (Ger.)	MURDER	U.S.
GECKER	156828	M	Ger.	15	Sgt., Waffen-SS, The Abbaye (Fr.)	INTERR.	CAN.
GECZY	252866	M			SS-Sturmann,SD,Toulouse (Fr.) 11.42-8.44	MISC.CRIMES	FR.
GEDLICK	161247	M			N.C.O.,Stalag 9 B, Bad Orb (Ger.) 44	MURDER	U.S.
GEDUSCH, Hermann	251028	M	Ger.		Capt., 377 Jaeger-Rgt.,Vinkt,Meigem (Bel.) 5.40	MURDER	BEL.
GEENT	145983	M	Ger.		Kommissar, Gestapo, Dessau (Ger.)	TORTURE	FR.
GEERSDORF	152187	M	Ger.		Engineer, Civilian,Boehlen (Ger.) 2.-4.45	TORTURE	U.K.

GEE-GEI

NAME	C.R.FILE NUMBER	SEX	NATIO-NALITY	DATE OF BIRTH	RANK OCCUPATION UNIT PLACE AND DATE OF CRIME	REASON WANTED	WANTED BY
GEESE, Josef	183115	M	Ger.		Pvt.,4 SS Totenkopf-Sturmbann,C.C.Dora,Nordhausen,Osterode(Ger.)43-45	MURDER	U.S.
GEESE, Karl	145384	M	Ger.		Sturmschfhr.,SS,Estouve(Fr.)	MURDER	FR.
GEESINK, Joseph	252122	M	Ger.	12. 2.01	Sgt.,Field-Police,Breda,Raamsdonksveer(Neth.) 8.44	MURDER	NETH.
GEEST	905142	M	Ger.		Sgt.,Feldgend.,Truppe 925,Troyes and Region(Fr.) 10.43-8.44	MURDER	FR.
GEEWE see PAUL, Friedrich	152200						
GEFKEN, Hermann	261376	M	Ger.		N.C.O.,Army,1 Coy.,377 Jaeg.Regt.,Vinkt,Meigem et Environs(Bel.) 5.40	WITNESS	BEL.
GEFREICHART	306300	M	Ger.		SS detachment of Adolf Hitler Unit L.51585 Bruessels, Rousseloy (Oise)(Fr.) 8.44	MURDER	FR.
GEGEL, Max	176736	M	Ger.		SS-Osturmbannfhr.,SS,C.C.Flossenburg(Ger.) 44-45	MURDER	CZECH.
GECINAT	62344	M	Ger.		Publ.Official,Reichs-Land-Organisation	MISC.CRIMES	UNWCC.
GECILATH	171649	M	Ger.		Leiter Ernaehrung und Landwirtschaftamt des Reichsstatthalters, Wartheland(Pol.) 9.39-44	MISC.CRIMES	POL.
GEGLER	258163	M	Ger.		Cpl.,2 Coy,Signal Troops,Bolnes(Neth.) 5.45	INTERR.	NETH.
GEGOSCH	146881	M	Ger.		Pvt.,SS Panz.Div."Das Reich",2 Coy.,Tulle(Fr.) 44	MURDER	FR.
GEGUSCH	253666	M	Ger.		crim.assist.,Sipo IV P,Bruessels(Bel.)	INTERR.	BEL.
GEHDER, Gerhardt	167394	M	Ger.		Cmdt.Verwaltungstruppe,Angers(Fr.) 40-41	PILLAGE	FR.
GEHEIDCES	253661	M	Ger.		Interpreter,Sipo V B,Bruessels(Bel.)	INTERR.	BEL.
GEHLERT, Oskar	171661	M	Ger.		Pvt.,9 Res.Gren.Regt.,Last Unit 4-181 5 M.G.Schuetze 1,1 Coy. Magny D'Anigon(Fr.) 9.44	MURDER	FR.
GEHLNER	12628	M			Pvt.,110 or 111 Panz.Gren.Regt.2 Coy.,Albine(Fr.) 6.44	MURDER	FR.
GEHNEING, Max	173452	M			2 Btty.,Inf.Regt.469,198 Inf.Div.,Le Tholy(Fr.) -11.44	PILLAGE	FR.
GEIR, Wilhelm	161404	M	Ger.	09	Oberzahlmeister(Civ.Teacher),Army.(Russ.) 44	MURDER	U.K.
GEHREIS	288	M			Dr.,Publ.Official,Landrat,Poznan(Pol.) 10.39-41	MISC.CRIMES	POL.
GEHRENDE	167993	M	Ger.		Col.,Stalag 6 C,C.C.Wittmarchen(Ger.) 43-44	MISC.CRIMES	FR.
GEHREY	250795	M			Pvt.,Camp Ellrich,Nordhausen(Ger.)	MURDER	U.S.
G.HRHARDT	250808	M			Pvt.,Camp Ellrich,Nordhausen(Ger.)	MURDER	U.S.
GEHRIG	72309	M			Sgt.,Waffen-SS,C.C.Sachsenhausen(Ger.) 9.41	MURDER	U.S.
GEHRIG	139145	M	Ger.		Amtsrat,Civilian,Abt.Music,Referat Heereswesen (Ger.) 38-40	WITNESS	U.S.
GEHRIG, Anton	256615	M	Ger.		Capt.,Army,near Bergen(Nor.) 5.45	MURDER	NOR.
GEHRING	139806	M			Lt.,Waffen-SS,C.C.Dora(Ger.) 4.45	MURDER	U.S.
GEHRING	186010	M	Ger.		W.O.,SS Panz.Gren.Regt.,Meyet de Montagne(Fr.) 6.44	TORTURE	FR.
GEHRING	306375	M	Ger.		SS-Staff-Sgt.,C.C.Dora-Nordhausen(Ger.) 40-45	MURDER	BEL.
GEHRING, Albin	250807	M			Cpl.,Camp Ellrich,Nordhausen(Ger.)	MURDER	U.S.
GEHRKE or GERKE	62345	M			Osturmbannfhr.,SS,Head of State Serv.Pol.Gestapo Protectorate, Moravia(Czech.)	TORTURE	UNWCC.
GEHRKE	132288	M			SS-Standartenfhr.,Gestapo,Prag(Czech.) 39-45	MURDER	CZECH.
GEHRKE, Erna	144772	F	Ger.		Guard,SS,C.C.Holleischen(Czech.)	TORTURE	FR.
GEHRKE, Ernst	253010	M	Ger.	22. 1.92	Inspector,Police,Lidice(Czech.) 6.42	MURDER	CZECH.
GEHRKE, Friedrich	161711	M	Ger.	02	Kriminalsekretaer,Sturmschfhr.,Sipo,SS,Bruessels(Bel.)	MURDER	BEL.
GEHRKE, Friedrich	250806	M			Cpl.,Camp Ellrich,Nordhausen(Ger.)	MURDER	U.S.
GEHRKE, Friedrich	901258	M	Ger.		Kriminalobersekretaer,Abt.IVA,SD(Sachsen),Bruessels(Bel.) 6.40-9.44	MURDER	BEL.
GEHRKE, Fritz	124776	M	Ger.	02	Sturmschfhr.and Krim.-Sekretaer,SS,Kom.16 z.b.V.,Ellenz(Ger.)	MURDER	U.S.
GEHRMANN	133341	M	Ger.		Pvt.,Army,Stalag,C.C.Hammelberg(Ger.)	MURDER	U.S.
GEHRMANN	192927	M	Ger.		SS-Schfhr.,C.C.Falstad(Nor.) 41-44	WITNESS	NOR.
GEHRMANN	250805	M			Pvt.,C.C.Harzungen,Nordhausen(Ger.)	MURDER	U.S.
GEHRMANN, Heinz	144267	M		10	Hptsturmfhr.,SS,Lublin(Pol.) 42-43	FR.	
GEHRMANN, Leonard	194105	M	Ger.	10	Maat,Guard,Navy Art.,C.C.Lueneburg-Wilhelmshaven(Ger.) 4.45	MURDER	U.K.
GEHRT, Louis see GERTH	188219						
GEHRT, Werner	161787	M	Ger.		Sailor,Navy,Goedereede and Overflakkee(Neth.)	MURDER	NETH.
GEHRUM	161355	M			SS-Sturmfhr.,KL.Struthof-Natzweiler(Fr.)	MURDER	FR.
GEHRUM, Julius or GERUM	147796	M	Ger.	14. 2.89	Osturmfhr.,SS,Gestapo Chief Strasbourg,C.C.Struthof-Natzweiler(Fr.) 9.-11.44	MURDER	FR.
GEHT	129796	M	Ger.		Capt.,Waffen-SS,Blaschow(Pol.) 44	MURDER	U.S.
GEIBEL, Werner	192408	M	Ger.		Dr.,Member Army,Ft.Zinna,Torgau(Ger.) 45	WITNESS	U.S.
GEIBERT, Oskar	250813	M			SS-Uschfhr.,C.C.Bodungen,Nordhausen(Ger.)	MURDER	U.S.
GEICH	23859	M		22. 6.19	SS-Sturmfhr.,SS Greney,Troyes-Bucheres(Fr.) 44	MURDER	FR.
GEIER	250767	M	Ger.		Capt.,98 Bn.,157 Res.Inf.Div.,L'Ain(Fr.) 3.-4.44	MISC.CRIMES	FR.
GEIER	252110	M	Ger.		Sgt.,25 Festungsstamm,Plumeliau(Fr.)	MURDER	FR.
GEIER, Alois	12629	M			Pvt.,Panz.Gren.Regt.110 or 111,2 Coy.,Albine(Fr.) 6.44	MURDER	FR.
GEIGENSCHEIDER	189065	M	Ger.		Hptschfhr.,SS,Political Dept.,C.C.Dachau(Ger.)	MURDER	BEL.
GEIGER	289	M			Police,Zugwachtmeister,C.C.Falstad(Nor.) 42	TORTURE	NOR.
GEIGER	23903	M			SS-Sturmfhr.,Passy Chatilon-Megeve(Fr.) 44	MURDER	FR.
GEIGER	124256	M			Oschfhr.,SS,1 Panz.Div.,Panz.Regt.1,9 Coy.,Malmedy(Bel.) 12.44	MURDER	U.S.
GEIGER	147952	M			Lt.,19 Police-Regt.,3 Coy.,Ugines(Fr.) 6.44	MURDER	FR.
GEIGER	173160	M	Ger.		Wachtmeister,C.C.Schirmeck,Rottenfels,Gaggenau(Fr.-Ger.) 9.44	INTERR.	U.K.
GEIGER	173443	M	Ger.		Uschfhr.,Gestapo,Le Mans(Fr.) 12.43-1.44	MURDER	FR.
GEIGER	185509	M	Ger.		SS-Osturmfhr.,Doctor,C.C.Ebensee,Mauthausen(Aust.) 44	MURDER	FR.
GEIGER	188841	M	Ger.		Sonderfhr.,Feldkdo.560,Besancon(Fr.) 2.44	PILLAGE	FR.
GEIGER	255128	M	Ger.		Lt.,Velke Mezirici(Czech.) 5.45	MURDER	CZECH.
GEIGER, Andreas	250804	M			SS-Sturmmann,C.C.Bodungen,Nordhausen(Ger.)	MURDER	U.S.
GEIGER, August	259727	M	Ger.	10	Oschfhr.,Gestapo,Area Angers,Maine and Loire(Fr.) 42,44	MISC.CRIMES	FR.
GEIGER, Hans	189979	M	Ger.		Maj.,Army Ober-Kdo.,Pozarevac(Yugo.) 41-43	MURDER	YUGO.
GEIGER, Joseph	185950	M	Ger.	04	SS-Usturmfhr.,Member NSDAP,SS Police-Regt.19,Chief of 3 Coy., Cmdt.of Cluces,Megeve(Fr.) 6.44	MISC.CRIMES	FR.
GEIGES	251020	M	Ger.	15	Officer,Art.Witternheim(Fr.) 1.45	PILLAGE	FR.
GEIGOLAND, Hugo	190525	M			W.O.,SS,Gestapo,Douai(Fr.) 3.44	MURDER	FR.
GEIGGLATH, H.	252118	M			Member SD,Meppe(Neth.) 12.44	TORTURE	NETH.
GEIKE	305854	M			Pvt.,1 Aufkl.Abt.,3 Coy.,2 Col.,XV Div.Africa Corps,St.Leger(Arlon)(Bel.) 9.44	MISC.CRIMES	BEL.
GEIKLER, Otto	106950	M			Civilian	MURDER	U.S.
GEILEN	257551	M	Ger.		SS-Usturmfhr.,C.C.Neuengamme(Ger.)	TORTURE	BEL.
GEILENBERG, Edmund	261142	M	Ger.		Plenipotentiary for special task,Armaments Ministry	WITNESS	U.S.
GEILENBERG, Philipp	167392	M	Ger.		Lt.,Army,Remoncourt(Fr.) 6.-7.40	PILLAGE	FR.

GEI-GEL

NAME	C.R.FILE NUMBER	SEX	NATIO-NALITY	DATE OF BIRTH	RANK OCCUPATION UNIT PLACE AND DATE OF CRIME	REASON WANTED	WANTED BY
GEILING (or GEILLING)	290	M	Ger.		Lager Sgt., Warder of Prison, Caen (Fr.) 6.44	MURDER	FR.
GEIPEL, Josef	163436	M	Ger.	15	Army, Molde (Nor.) 10.40	MURDER	NOR.
GEIPHAN	134718	M	Ger.		Brigadefhr., Major General (Ger.) 44	MISC.CRIMES	U.S.
GEIS, Josef	161739	M			Civilian, Bad Neustadt (Ger.) 9.44	WITNESS	U.S.
GEISBERG, Johann	147951	M			Sgt., Waffen SS, C.C. Dachau (Ger.)	TORTURE	FR.
GEISE	124775	M	Ger.		Camp Commandant, SA Standarte, C.C.Neusustrum (Ger.)	MURDER	U.S.
GEISE, Hermann	125161	M			Lt.Col., Army Stalag II B, Budon Hammerstein (Ger.) 12.44	TORTURE	U.S.
GEISEL	123980	M	Ger.		Polizeimeister, Orpo., Regierungssekr., Alsfeld (Ger.) 2.45	MURDER	U.S.
GEISEL, Heinrich	147948	M	Ger.	14.10.93	Sturmfhr., Waffen SS, C.C.Buchenwald (Ger.)	TORTURE	FR.
GEISEL, Heinrich	306746	M	Ger.		Civilian, Alsfeld (Ger.) 2.45	MURDER	U.S.
GEISELER, Elfrieda	262246	F	Ger.	5.10. ?	Secretary, Gestapo, Rennes (Fr.) 43-44	SUSPECT	FR.
GEISEN	256820	M	Ger.		Major, SS, C.C. Nordhausen (Ger.)	MURDER	U.S.
GEISENHOFER	167623	M	Ger.		Civ. Servant,Ostgebietsministerium, Rosenberg Einsatzstab, Dijon (Fr.) 40-44	PILLAGE	FR.,
GEISER	190399	M			Policeman, Police, Wiesbaden (Ger.) 43-45	TORTURE,MURDER	U.S.
GEISER	250814	M			SS Hptschfr., Camp Ellrich, Nordhausen (Ger.)	MURDER	U.S.
GEISHAUSER, Engelbert	176739	M			Sturmbannfhr., SS, C.C. Muehldorf,Ampfing (Ger.) 6.44-5.45	MURDER	U.S.
GEISLER	10066	M			Major, Army, Hesepe, 3.45	MURDER	U.K.
GEISLEP	252099	M			Capt., O.C. of Ger., Norcia (It.)	MURDER	U.K.
GEISLER	252108	M	Ger.		Lt.,Member, SS, Schutzpolizei,Luxembourg (Lux.)40-44	MISC.CRIMES	LUX.
GAISLER	259503	M			Cpl.,Mil., Office Staff,9 SS Pz.Div."Hohenstaufen",Beekbergen (Neth.) 9.44	WITNESS	NETH.
GEISLER (or MARTY), Georges	147723	M			Nantes (Fr.) 1.41	MISC.CRIMES	FR.
GEISLER (or GEISSLER), Hans	132289	M	Ger.	15	Scharfhr., SS, SD, Issel (Ger.) 1.45	MURDER	U.S.
GEISLER, Max	12630	M	Ger.		Pvt., 110 or 111 Pz.Gren.Rgt. 2 Coy., Albine (Fr.) 6.44	MURDER	FR.
GEISON	130648	M			Sturmbannfhr., SS, C.C. Mittelbau Dora, Nordhausen (Ger.)	MURDER	U.S.
GEISS, August	194972	M	Ger.		Civilian, Willerwald (Fr.)	PILLAGE	FR.
GEISS, Erika	147832	F	Ger.		Maidenfuehrerin, RAD, Schopfheim (Ger.)	TORTURE	FR.
GEISSEN	161740	M	Ger.	05	SS Sturmbannfhr., C.C. Ohrdruf (Ger.) 39-45	WITNESS	FR.
GEISSENDORFER, Fr.	192926	M			Schupo, C.C. Falstad, Trondheim (Nor.) 6.-8.42	MURDER	NOR.
GEISSER	192925	M			Schupo, C.C. Falstad, nr. Drontheim (Nor.) 9.42	MURDER	NOR.
GEISSER	254507	M			SS-Mann, SD, Toulouse (Fr.) 11.42-8.44	MURDER	FR.
GEISSER, Emil	144439	M	Ger.		Policeman, Police, Wiesbaden (Ger.) 2.45	MURDER	U.S.
GEISSLER	291	M	Ger.		Capt., Gestapo (Fr.) 43	MURDER	FR.
GEISSLER	129636	M			5 Fallschirmjaeger Rgt.,Jemappes,Quaregnon,Ghlin (Bel.) 9.44	MURDER	BEL.
GEISSLER	129797	M		05	Chief of Political Section, Waffen SS, Lussault (Fr.) 8.44	MURDER	U.S.
GEISSLER (see GEISLER), Hans	132289						
GEISSLER	139150	M			Agent, Gestapo, Hohenpitschen, Gleiwitz (Ger.) 9.39	WITNESS	U.S.
GEISSLER	144770	M	Ger.		Capt., SS, Muenchen (Ger.) 8.-9.44	MURDER	U.S.
GEISSLER	161381	M			SS,SD, Hptsturmfhr., Caen (Fr.)	MURDER	U.S.
GEISSLER	176738	M			SS Usturmfhr., C.C. Muehldorf, Ampfing (Ger.) 6.44-4.45	MURDER	U.S.
GEISSLER	186419	M	Ger.		Sgt., Air Force, C.C. Gusen (Ger.) 6.44	TORTURE	U.S.
GEISSLER	251567	M	Ger.		Specialiste photographe, Gestapo, Limoges (Fr.) 40-44	INTERR.	FR.
GEISSLER	251565	M	Ger.		Pvt., Unit 59 949, Langon (Fr.)	MURDER	FR.
GEISSLER, Dietmar	163450	M			Hptscharfhr., SD, Huismes (Fr.) 8.44	MURDER	FR.
GEISSLER, Gerhard	250810	M			Pvt., Camp Ellrich, Nordhausen (Ger.)	MURDER	U.S.
GEISSWINKLER	121221	M			Cpl., SS, Aude, Carassonne (Fr.)	MISC.CRIMES	FR.
GEIST	151775	F			Civilian, Hamburg (Ger.) 38	WITNESS	U.S.
GEIST	173161	M	Ger.		Staff at C.C.,Rotenfels,Gaggenau, Schirmeck (Ger.,Fr.) 6.44	INTERR.	U.K.
GEIST	190464	M	Ger.		Assessor, Beelitz Stiftung,NSDAP, Beelitz (Ger.) 40-45	MURDER	CZECH.
GEIST	259102	M	Ger.		SS Oschfhr., C.C. Dachau (Ger.) 2.43-45	MISC.CRIMES	YUGO.
GEIST, Alfred	23848	M			Pvt., II Res.Geb.Jaeg. Regt. 98	MISC.CRIMES	FR.
GEIST, Konrad	252141	M	Ger.	15	Sgt., Fieldpolice (Bel.)	INTERR.	BEL.
GEISTER, M.	147332	M			Lt., II Pz. Div. (Fr.) 44	MURDER	FR.
GEISTHEIMER	147827	M			Capt., Abwehr, Bathom (Ger.)	TORTURE	FR.
GEISTHOZ	12631	M	Ger.		Pvt., 110 or 111 Pz.Gren.Rgt. 2 Coy., Albine (Fr.) 6.44	MURDER	FR.
GEISTLAUBER, Johann	12632	M	Ger.		Pvt., 110 or 111 Pz.Gren.Rgt. 2 Coy., Albine (Fr.) 6.44	MURDER	FR.
GEISTNER, Heismund	257357	M	Ger.		Oschfhr., Guard, SS, Slave Labour Camp, Osen (Nor.) 6.42-3.43	MISC.CRIMES	YUGO.
GEITELER (or GEITLER)	292	M	Ger.		Capt., Chief of SD, Clermont-Ferrand (Fr.) 2.44-7.44	MURDER	FR.
GEITER	252139	F			Headwardress, Guard, Zuchthaus Anrath (Neth.) 1.42-3.44	BRUTALITY	NETH.
GEITH, Eduard	255130	M	Ger.	23. 9.99	Crim.Secretary, Gestapo, Munich (Ger.)	INTERR.	U.K.
GEITHER, Hans	192924	M	Ger.		Schupo, C.C. Falstad, Trondheim (Nor.) 10.42	MURDER	NOR.
GEITLER (see GEITELER)	292						
GEITZLER	23849	M			Chief of SD (Fr.)	MURDER	FR.
GELB	62346	M	Ger.		Deputy Chief of Staff (Neth.),Rosenbergs "Looting Office" (Ostgebiet Ministerium), (Neth.)	PILLAGE	U.N.W.C.C.
GELBERS, Ludwig	259661	M			Member, Lt., Gestapo at Lure or Luxeuil,Saulnot,Hte.Saone (Fr.)	INTERR.	FR.
GELBERT	146880	M	Ger.		Cpl., SS Pz.Div. "Das Reich", Miremon (Fr.) 44	MURDER	FR.
GELBECT, Oskar	256821	M			SS-Sgt., 5 Coy., Klein-Bodungen, C.C. Nordhausen (Ger.)	MURDER	U.S.
GELBHAAR, Irmgard	147829	F		10. 6.22	Woman-Guard, Waffen SS, C.C. Buchenwald (Ger.) 44	MISC.CRIMES	U.S.
GALBING, Josef	161239	M			Civilian, Ginnheim near Frankfurt-M. (Ger.) 11.44	MURDER	U.S.
GELBRICH, Magda	134846	F	Ger.	17	Secretary to Chief of Gestapo, Bensheim (Ger.)	WITNESS	U.S.
GELDMACHER	137068	M	Ger.	2.11.05	Policeman, Army, Gendarmerie Reserve Unit, Ruhen (Ger.) 4.44	MURDER	U.S.
GELDNER, Albrecht	183111	M		18. 9.93	Uschfhr., 4 SS Totenkopfsturmbann, C.C.Dora,Nordhausen, Auschwitz (Ger., Pol.) 43-45	MURDER	U.S.
GELECH	23851	M			Scharfhr., Army, 1 Bn. SS "Der Fuehrer" (Fr.) 44	MURDER	FR.
GELECH	23852	M		17	Sgt., Army, Condour-Oradour (Fr.) 44	MURDER	FR.
GELECH	23861	M			Scharfhr., SS Pz.Div. "Das Reich" (Fr.) 44	MISC.CRIMES	FR.
GELECH	185130	M	Ger.		Gondom (Fr.) 5.44	MURDER	FR.
GELERT, Herbert	194999	M	Ger.		Pvt., Army, Wuerttemberg (Ger.)	MURDER	FR.
GELFERT, Willi	195540	M	Ger.		Sturmmann, I Pz. Coy., Ligneuville (Bel.) 12.44	MURDER	U.S.
GELKE	260134	M			Cpl., 7 Pioneer-Rgt. d. Res.,Grenoble,Massif du Vercors, Drome et Isere (Fr.) 7.-8.44	SUSPECT	FR.
GELL, Karl	250812	M			Pvt., Camp Harzungen, Nordhausen (Ger.)	MURDER	U.S.

NAME	C.R.FILE NUMBER	SEX	NATIO-NALITY	DATE OF BIRTH	RANK OCCUPATION UNIT PLACE AND DATE OF CRIME	REASON WANTED	WANTED BY
GELLER	62180	M	Ger.		Oberkriegsverwaltungsrat, Mil., C C.Conseiller superieur militaire, Inspecteur des Prisons de Liege (Bel.)	MURDER	BEL.
GELLER (or GELLERT)	261728	M	Ger.	05	Inspector, SD, Kalisz (Pol.)	MURDER	POL.
GELLER, Franz	126322	M	Ger.		Civilian, Bedburdyck (Ger.)	TORTURE	U.S.
GELLER, Peter	147828	M		85	Graach (Ger.) 7.44	TORTURE	FR.
GELLERICH, Richard	174141	M	Ger.		Sgt., Stalag 6 A, Conc.Camp, Hemer (Ger.) 11.42-4.45	TORTURE	U.S.
GELLERT	166377	M			Sgt., Geh.Feldpolizei, Recoaro or Valdagno (It.) 1.45	MURDER	U.S.
GELLERT	166994	M			Sgt., Fieldpolice, Major, Special-mil.-Police	WITNESS	U.S.
GELLERT (see GELLER)	261728						
GELLINCK, Richard	129639	M	Ger.		Arb.Kdo. Officer, Conc.Camp, Magdeburg (Ger.) 44	TORTURE	BEL.
GELLING	161354	M	Ger.		Inspector, City-Official, Frankfurt (Ger.) 43-44	TORTURE	U.S.
GELSTER	183110	M			Uschfhr., 4.SS-Totenkopf-Sturmbann, Conc.Camp Dora, Osterode, Nordhausen (Ger.) 43-45	MURDER	U.S.
GEMAHL	183106	M			SS-Pvt., IV.SS-Totenkopf-Sturmbann, Conc.Camp, Mittelbau Dora, Nordhausen (Ger.) 43-45	WITNESS	U.S.
GEMECKER	174129	M			Chief of Guard, Stalag 6 A, Conc.Camp, Hemer (Ger.) 41-45	TORTURE	U.S.
GEMEINER (or GMEINER)	173162	M			Osturmfhr., SS, Gestapo, Conc.Camp, Gaggonau (Ger.) 6.44	MURDER	U.K.
GEMMHART	128862	M			Capt., 383.Landschutz-Bn., Stalag IV D, C.C., Falkenberg (Ger.) 6.44-4.45	TORTURE	U.K.
GEMER	250789	M			Cmdt., Army, Arandjelovac (Yugo.) 41	MURDER	YUGO.
GEMIND, Karl	62347	M	Ger.		Reichsofficial, High Economic Official (Yugo.)	MISC.CRIMES	UNWCC
GEMMECKE	300592	M			Cmdt., "Westerbork"-Camp, Amsterdam (Neth.) 10.44	MURDER	NETH.
GEMMIG	257967	M			Officer-Commanding, Spec.Sabotage Service, 150.Pz.Bde., Meuse-Bridge-Antwerp (Bel.) 12.44	MISC.CRIMES	U.S.
GEMNICKE	189994	M			Osturmfhr., SS, Gestapo, RSHA, Drontheim (Nor.) 43-44	TORTURE	NOR.
GEMPENISKI	161242	M	Ger.		Ger.Navy-Corps, St.Marine (Fr.) 6.44	MURDER	U.S.
GEMSBICK	189457	M			Sgt., Army, Vlissingen (Neth.) 9.44	MURDER	NETH.
GENARI	251568	M			Uschfhr., SS, 3.Coy., 1.Bn., SS-Div."Das Reich", Oradour sur Glane (Fr.) 6.44	INTERR.	FR.
GENAU, Hans	252304	M	Ger.		Employee, Custom-house, Chaum (Fr.) 6.44	MISC.CRIMES	FR.
GENDORF (or GINDORF, Carl)	252303	M	Ger.		Employee, Custom-house, Chaum (Fr.) 6.44	MISC.CRIMES	FR.
GENERICH	163451	M	Ger.		Capt., SA, Army, Braunschweig (Ger.) 4.45	TORTURE	FR.
GENESS	147825	M			Civilian, C.C., Kalwinken (Ger.)	TORTURE	FR.
GENEWEIN	188286	M	Ger.		Obermatrose, Kuestenueberwachungsstelle, Wiener-Neustadt (Aust.) 43-45	MISC.CRIMES	U.S.
GENGE	23858	M		16	France	TORTURE	FR.
GENGLER, Nikolaus	162937	M	Ger.	14.7.94	Dr., Catholic-Priest, Sommerhausen (Ger.) 3.45	WITNESS	U.S.
GENSCHEL	141959	M	Ger.		Schfhr., SS, Guard, Waldlager V and VI, near Ampfing (Ger.) 44-45	TORTURE	U.S.
GENSERT, Valentin	193196	M	Ger.		Sgt., Army, Akervika (Nor.) 42	MURDER	NOR.
GENSHEIMER	163452	M	Ger.		Capt., S.R.A.Gestapo, Stalag 6 C (Ger.)	MISC.CRIMES	FR.
GENSIOR	9660	M	Ger.		Usturmfhr., SS-Bauleiterfhr., Oranienburg (Ger.) 44	MURDER	CZECH.
GENSMER, Arno	186418	M	Ger.		Osturmfhr., SD, Pilsen (Czech.) 39-45	MURDER	CZECH.
GENT	161298	M	Ger.		Civilian, Pattensen (Ger.) 3.45	TORTURE	U.S.
GENTSCH (or GEUSC or GEUSE)	293	M			Lt., Army, 98.Rgt. of Mountain Troops II.Bn.,10.Coy., Massif du Vercors (Fr.) 9.44	MURDER	FR.
GENTSCH	185510	M	Ger.	07-10	Osturmfhr., SS-Police-Rgt.13, 1.Bn., Bleiburg (Aust.) 10.44	MURDER	U.S.
GENTSCH	252483	M	Ger.		Lt., 10.Coy., 2.Bn., 98.Rgt., (Fr.)	MISC.CRIMES	FR.
GENTSCHER	257360	M	Ger.		Oschfhr., SS, Slave Labour Camp, Osen (Nor.) 6.42-3.43	MISC.CRIMES	YUGO.
GENTZKE	261229	M	Ger.		Dr., Deputy, Mil.-Verwaltungsoberrat, Brussels (Bel.) 40-44	SUSPECT	BEL.
GENUNEL, Jakob	177729	M			Conc.Camp, Muehldorf, Ampfing (Ger.) 6.44-4.45	MURDER	U.S.
GENZ	147824	M	Ger.	28.8.19	Turkestanische Legion, St.Gaudens (Fr.)	TORTURE	FR.
GENZEL, Rudolph	132291	M			Instructor, Volkssturm, C.C., Gardelegen (Ger.)	MURDER	U.S.
GENZLE, Karl	145988	M	Ger.		Instructor, Volkssturm, 1.Volkssturm-Bn., Gardelegen (Ger.) 4.45	MURDER	U.S.
GEORG	147831	M	Ger.		Guard, Conc.Camp, Hersbrueck (Ger.)	MISC.CRIMES	FR.
GEORGE	253018	M	Ger.		Oschfhr., SD, Toulouse (Fr.) 11.42-8.44	MURDER	FR.
GEORGE, Gerda	259335	F			Lives at Grossorner, Ger., Mansfeld (Ger.) 3.44	WITNESS	U.S.
GEORGES	23876	M			Major, Gestapo, Carcassone (Fr.) 44	MISC.CRIMES	FR.
GEORGES	23877	M			Paris (Fr.) 44	TORTURE	FR.
GEORGES	260133	M	Ger.		Hilfs-Kapo, C.C., Dachau (Ger.) 42-44	BRUTALITY	FR.
GEORGES, Edmund	307105	M	Ger.	18.7.04	Member, SD, Aussenstelle Maastricht, Various Places, Limburg (Neth.) 40-44	MURDER	NETH.
GEORGESOLIER, Max	177585	M			Capt., Army, Raocourt (Fr.) 42	TORTURE	FR.
GEORGI	174960	M		09	Chief, Customhouse, Badlán near Thoiry (Fr.) 4.44	MURDER	FR.
GEORGI	250811	M			Pvt., Con.Camp Dora, Nordhausen (Ger.)	MURDER	U.S
GEORGI, Hans	307106	M	Ger.		Col., Deputy to Gen.Lt. Rossum, Kommandeur of P.O.W. in region X, Luebeck (Ger.) 4.44-5.44	MURDER	FR.
GEPART, Willi	171647	M	Ger.		Leader, Pol.Gen.Gouvern., Treuhandaussenstelle, Sosnowice, Chrzanow (Pol.) 9.39-44	MISC.CRIMES	POL.
GEPPERT	294	M	Ger.		Trustee, Konin (Pol.) 11.39	MURDER	POL.
GEPPHARDT,	295	M	Ger.		Dr., Physician, Prof.at a Ger. University,7.42-43	TORTURE	POL.
GEPPREID	163453	M	Ger.		Medical-Cmdt., Stalag I A, Stalbach (Ger.)	MURDER	FR.
GERARD	147820	M	Ger.		Lt., Gestapo, Chalons-sur-Marne (Fr.)	MISC.CRIMES	FR.
GERARD, Albert (or GIRARD)	261056	M	Ger.		Gend., Gendarmerie, Chateaulin (Fr.) 5.44	TORTURE	FR.
GERARD, Eduard	185511	M	Ger.		Osturmfhr., SS-Leibstandarte "Adolf Hitler", 1.Panz.Gren.Div., Stavelot (Bel.) 12.44	MURDER	BEL.
GERAT, Franz	251545	M	Ger.	02	Pvt., 1502-3 Flak-Abt.I, Strijpen (Bel.)	INTERR.	BEL.
GERBACHER	259368	M	Ger.		Director, Office of Travail of Muenster (Ger.) 40-44	PILLAGE	FR.
GERBADING	161305	M			Member, SA, Hohnebostel (Ger.) 5.44	TORTURE	U.S.
GERBEL, Heinrich	140838	M			Lt., Army, near Mittenwald (Ger.) 6.44	BRUTALITY	U.S.
GERBER	139142	M			Civilian, Stalag IX C, C.C., Berga (Ger.) 2.45-4.45	MURDER	U.S.
GERBER	147726	M	Ger.	12	Cmdt., Waffen-SS, Neuhaus - Schiensnitz (Ger.) 43	TORTURE	FR.
GERBER	167391	M			Richardmesnil (Fr.) 8.44-9.44	WITNESS	FR.
GERBER	260091	M	Ger.		Kapo, Conc.Camp, Dachau (Ger.) 42-44	TORTURE	FR.

GER-GER

NAME	C.R.FILE NUMBER	SEX	NATIO-NALITY	DATE OF BIRTH	RANK OCCUPATION UNIT PLACE AND DATE OF CRIME	REASON WANTED	WANTED BY
GERBER, Gerhard	129631	M			Osturmfhr.,SS,C.C.Mauthausen (Aust.) 41-45	MURDER	U.S.
GERBER, Heinrich	161494	M	Ger.	20	Pvt.,Waffen SS,Totenkopf Sturmbann,C.C.Buchenwald Weimar (Ger.)	MURDER	U.S.
GERBER, Jacob	306376	M	Ger.		SS-Sgt.,C.C.Buchenwald (Ger.) 5.38 and 10.43	MURDER	BEL.
GERBER, Willi	161315	M	Ger.	26	Civilian,Russelsheim Hessen (Ger.) 8.44	MURDER	U.S.
GERBERS (or GERDES)	300082	M	Ger.	00	Coyfhr.,Volkssturm,C.C.Brockzetel (Ger.) 45	MURDER	NETH.
GERBICH	129630	M			Uschfhr.,SS,Driver of Gas Druck at Camp Mauthausen (Aust.) 41-45	MURDER	U.S.
GERBIG	147772	M	Ger.	95	Cmdt.,C.C.Altenburg (Ger.) 42-44	MURDER	FR.
GERBIG	307107	M	Ger.		Hptsturmfhr.,leader of SD Kommando Gerbig,Almelo (Neth.) 9.44-2.45	MURDER	NETH.
GERBIG, Heinz	141477	M	Ger.		Capt.,Army,Mouleydier (Fr.) 6.44	TORTURE	FR.
GERBING	121258	M	Ger.	13	Schfhr.,SD, (Fr.)	MURDER	FR.
GERBING, Wilhelm	188689	M	Ger.		SS-Schfhr.,SS,C.C.Drancy (Fr.) 6.43	MURDER	FR.
GERBITZ, Wilhelm	250217	M			Pvt.,C.C.Harzungen,Nordhausen (Ger.)	MURDER	U.S.
GERBL, Martin	12633	M	Ger.		Pvt.,110 or 111 Pz.Gren.Rgt.2 Coy,Albine (Fr.) 0.44	MURDER	FR.
GERDES (see GERBERS)	300082						
GERDES	171953	M	Ger.		Civ.Member of district president,Langerich (Ger.) 8.44	TORTURE	U.S.
GERDES	253000	M			Lt.,Alarm Einheit 35 a-Bn.Heller,Mussy Seine (Fr.)	MISC.CRIMES	FR.
GERDES, Bruno	149511	M	Ger.		SS,firme burmeister,Pontoise (Fr.) 41-44	PILLAGE	FR.
GERDUNG, H.	133348	M			Rottfhr.,Waffen SS,Nachr.Schule d.Waffen SS,Leitmeritz (Czech.)	MISC.CRIMES	U.S.
GERECKE, Friedrich	257311	M	Ger.	8. 1.95	Crim.-police,chief-secr.,Gestapo,Prague,Bohemia (Czech.) 42-45	MISC.CRIMES	CZECH.
GEREKE, Wilma	171675	F	Ger.	22.10.26	SS-Hilfe,C.C.Natzweiler (Fr.) 42-44	MURDER	FR.
GERES	72292	M			Major,5 Para.Div.Hy.Werfer Bn.,Budesheim (Ger.) 3.45	MURDER	U.S.
GERETEHALMI-CZEYDNER, Ferenc	127356	M			General,SS, (Hung.)	MISC.CRIMES	IT.,U.S.
GERG	254112	M	Ger.		Adj.,Fieldpolice,Bourgoin,Salagnon (Fr.) 2.44	MURDER	FR.
GERGEL	193051	M	Ger.		Oschfhr.,Waffen SS,C.C.Buchenwald (Ger.) 42-45	TORTURE	U.S.
GERHAMMER, Franz	12634	M	Ger.		Pvt.,110 or 111 Pz.Gren.Rgt.2 Coy,Albine (Fr.) 6.44	MURDER	FR.
GERHARD	23845	M			Pvt.,Army,Albine (Fr.) 6.44	MURDER	FR.
GERHARD (see GERHARDT, Heinz)	190526						
GERHARD, August	134844	M		05	Policeman,Daun (Ger.) 12.44	MURDER	U.S.
GERHARDS, Peter	134847	M	Ger.		Civilian, (Ger.)	TORTURE	U.S.
GERHARDT	252146	M			Doctor,C.C.Ravensbrueck (Ger.)	TORTURE	BEL.
GERHARDT, Heinz	12635	M	Ger.		Pvt.,110 or 111 Pz.Gren.Rgt.2 Coy,Albine (Fr.) 6.44	MURDER	FR.
GERHARDT, Heinz (or GERHARD)	190526	M	Ger.		Pvt.,11 Pz.Div.2 Coy 2 AA-A 7,Bergerac Albine (Fr.) 7.-8.44	MURDER	FR.
GERHARDT, Jakob	258420	M			SS-Mann, Guard,SS,C.C.Ohrdruf (Ger.) 12.44-4.45	MURDER	U.S.
GERHARDT, Michael	161317	M			Officer,SS	MURDER	U.S.
GERHART	296	M			Commandant,Oflag 2 D, 40	TORTURE	FR.
GERHARZ	195536	M	Ger.		Sturmmann,1 Pz.Div.Leibst.Adolf Hitler,Ligneuville (Bel.) 12.44	MURDER	U.S.
GERHAUSER	129638	M	Ger.		Guard,C.C.Kaisheim (Ger.)	TORTURE	BEL.
GERHEIM	147736	M	Ger.		Guard,C.C.Diez (Fr.)	TORTURE	FR.
GERHLAV (or GERHLAU)	254783	M			Capt.,Parachute Coy,Urvillers (Fr.) 8.44	TORTURE	FR.
GERHOLD, Eugen	250218	M			Flyer,C.C.Ellrich,Nordhausen (Ger.)	MURDER	U.S.
GERICH	147735	M	Ger.		Wiesbaden (Ger.)	TORTURE	FR.
GERICH, Franc	173434	M	Ger.		Guard,SS Pol.Rgt.,C.C.Zemun,Belgrad,Sajmiste (Yugo.) 4.43	MURDER	YUGO.
GERICKE, Hermann ?	191864	M	Ger.	05	Pvt.,2 Luftwaffe Bau Bn.132 III,Bar du Foss (Nor.) 45	MURDER	NOR.
GERIEZ	255987	M	Ger.		Cmdt.,C.C.Mauthausen (Aust.) 4.45	INTERR.	FR.
GERIGK	167624	M			Dr.,Civ.Servant,Ostgebietsministerium Rosenberg,Zentralamt Einsatzstab Berlin, (Ger.) 40-44	PILLAGE	FR.
GERIKE	258687	M	Ger.		Kreisleiter,Landratsamt Helmstedt (Ger.) 6. or 7.44	MURDER	U.S.
GERIS	193619	M	Ger.	01	Major,105 parachute Div.F.P.Nr.L 60292 A Hy.Werfer Bn.5,Buedesheim (Ger.) 3.45	MURDER	U.S.
GERK, Georg	306080	M	Ger.		SS-Oschfhr.,C.C.Alderney and Kortemark (Channel B) (Fr.) 42-45	MURDER	CZECH.
GERKE (see GEHRKE)	62435						
GERKE	106952	M	Ger.	05	Sgt.,Waffen SS,Ellens (Ger.)	MURDER	U.S.
GERKE	141299	M		05	SS,Gestapo, Sturmschfhr.,Koblenz (Ger.)	MURDER	
GERKE	145389	M	Ger.		Osturmbannfhr.,SS, (Czech.) 44	MURDER	U.S.
GERKE	301409	M			Kapo,Kommando Stephankirchen,Posenheim (Ger.) 44-45	MISC.CRIMES	FR.
GERKE, Ernst	140834	M	Ger.	09	Lt.Col.,SS Gestapo,Dr.,Prague (Czech.) 42-45	MISC.CRIMES	U.S.
GERKE, Kurt	147734	M	Ger.			TORTURE	FR.
GERKEN	251547	M			Guard,Kapo,C.C.Gusen (Aust.)	TORTURE	BEL.
GERKEN, Arno	23886	M		15	Feldgendarm 307 de Pontivy (Fr.) 44	TORTURE	FR.
GERKEN, August	251029	M		93-95	Capt.,377 Jg.Rgt.,Vinkt,Meigem (Bel.) 5.40	TORTURE	BEL.
GERKENS	106949	M	Ger.	92	Cpl.,Army,Prison,Electro technical affairs,C.C.Hamburg-Altona (Ger.) 7.-11.44	TORTURE	U.S.
GERKER	127357	M			Hangman-Executioner,C.C.Sachsenhausen (Ger.)	MURDER	U.S.
GERKIN, Heinrich	129661	M			Cpl.,34 Festungsmaschinengewehrbn.,Aachen (Ger.) 9.44	MURDER	U.S.
GERL, Joseph	132658	M	Ger.		Feldgendarm,Feldgend.Truppe 624,Avallon (Fr.) 11.43	MURDER	FR.
GERLACH	23867	M	Ger.		Capt.,Gren.Rgt.361,Brianson (Fr.)	MURDER	FR.
GERLACH	143489	M			Schfhr.,SS,Oswiecim (Pol.) 6.40-1.45	MURDER	POL.
GERLACH	144774	M	Ger.	10	Hptsturmfhr.,SS,C.C.Sachsenhausen (Ger.)	MURDER	U.K.
GERLACH	147729	M			Sgt.,Air Force,Strassburg (Fr.) 44	MURDER	FR.
GERLACH	191872	M			Capt.,Rgt.361, 90 Inf.Div.,Lus La Croix Haute (Fr.) 7.44	MURDER	FR.
GERLACH	250219	M			Pvt.,C.C.Dora,Nordhausen (Ger.)	MURDER	U.S.
GERLACH	253001	M	Ger.		Lt.,Bn."Heller",Alarm Einheit 35 A,St.Martin (Fr.) 8.44	MISC.CRIMES	FR.
GERLACH	305407	M	Ger.		Lt.,Deputy to Kapitaen Lt.Gerdes,Precy,St.Martin,Aube,Lassicourt (Fr.) 8.44	MURDER	FR.
GERLACH, Eduard	195112	M	Ger.		Official,Prop.Reich Level (Lux.)	MISC.CRIMES	LUX.
GERLACH, Ernest	147733	M	Ger.		Niederzier (Ger.)	TORTURE	FR.
GERLACH, Gerhardt	193489	M	Ger.	09	Hauptwachtmeister,10 Coy 3 Bn.7 Schutzpol.Rgt.,Umbukta Drontheim (Nor.) 4.-5.44	TORTURE	NOR.
GERLACH, Lucie	147731	F		21	Woman Guard,Waffen SS,C.C.Wattenstedt (Ger.)	TORTURE	FR.
GERLAND	62348	M	Ger.		SS Major General,SS Gauleiter of Kurhessen	TORTURE	U.N.W.C.C.
GERLANDT, Heinrich (see also GERNANDT)	301081	M	Ger.	5.12.07	Legations Counsellor,Gaupropagandaleiter,German Legation Copenhagen (Den.) 44-45	MURDER	DEN.
GERLARD	260090	M	Ger.		Guard,Neckarelz Kdo.,Dachau (Ger.) 42-44	MURDER	FR.
GERLE	152199	M	Ger.		Lt.,Member,Army,RAD,Rgt.4-300,NSDAP,Grand Quevilly (Fr.) 4.44	MURDER	FR.
GERLF, Arno	186417	M	Ger.		W.Officer,Army,Vonkalite Detachment,Mebros (Grc.) 2.44	PILLAGE	GRC.

GER-GES

NAME	C.R.FILE NUMBER	SEX	NATIO-NALITY	DATE OF BIRTH	RANK OCCUPATION UNIT PLACE AND DATE OF CRIME	REASON WANTED	WANTED BY
ERLICH, Gerhard	253013	M	Ger.	25.10.13	Sgt., Ger.rural police, Vavrovice (Czech.) 1.45	MURDER	CZECH.
ERLING	177730	M			Civ., Org.Todt, C.C. Muehldorf,Ampfing (Ger.) 1.44-4.45	MURDER	U.S.
ERLING, Joseph	144776	M			Rheurdt (Ger.) 2.45	TORTURE	U.S.
ERLINGER	173444	M	Ger.		SS Oscharfhr., Waffen SS, C.C. Neckarelz (Ger.)	TORTURE	U.S.,FR.
ERLINGER	255266	M	Ger.		SS Oscharfhr., Neckargerrach (Ger.)	TORTURE	FR.
ERLITSKI, Kurt	166397	M			Police, Merano (It.) 4.45	MURDER	U.S.
ERLOFF, Helmut	59659	M	Ger.	94	Dr.,Generalmajor, Bde.Fhr., SS-police, technical academy		U.N.W.C.C.
ERLS, Hermann	185514	M		22. 2.07	Usturmfhr., crim.assist., S.D., Gestapo, Praha (Czech.) 39-45	MURDER	CZECH.
ERMAN	24835	M	Ger.	26. 4.19	Guard, Pvt., Army, 559.Rgt. 1.Coy., Ger., 2.45	MURDER	U.K.
ERMAN	192407	M	Ger.		Sgt., 4.Coy. Gross-Gerau, Cmdo. 2029 B, Burstadt-Worms (Ger.) 2.-3.45	TORTURE	BEL.
ERMANN, Fritz	132294	M	Ger.	20	SS Usturmfhr., S.D., Issel (Ger.) 1.45	MURDER	U.S.
ERMER, Walter	139149	M	Ger.		Group-leader, Member, NSDAP, S.A., Rohrberg (Ger.)	TORTURE	U.S.
ERMI	147289	M			Lt.,Bersaglieri C.C. Treviglio (It.)	WITNESS	U.K.
ERNANDT, Heinrich see GERLANDT	301081						
ERNHARDT	125700	M	Ger.		Lt., Gendarmerie, Bourg-Lastic (Fr.) 7.44	MURDER	FR.
ERNOTH	300084	M			Sturmscharfhr., B.D.S. The Hague, Silbertanne-Action at Groningen Nov.43, Groningen, Drente (Neth.) 43-45	MURDER	NETH.
EROSA	195130	M	Ger.		Leader, Ruestungslieferungsamt, R. 'erdam (Neth.) 40-45	PILLAGE	NETH.
EROWCHE or GEROWITZ	188165	M			Sgt., Guard, C.C. Stalag XVII B Krems (Aust.) 12.43	MURDER	U.S.
ERRES, Hans	146879	M			SS Panz.Div. "Das Reich" 19.Coy, Moissac (Fr.) 44	MURDER	FR.
ERRY, Edwald	123962	M		05	Civ. in a camp, C.C.Reichenbach, Wittinghausen (Ger.) 12.42-5.44	TORTURE	U.K.
ERSBACH	72290	M			Rottfhr., Waffen SS, C.C. Struthof-Natzweiler (Fr.) 42-44	MURDER	FR.
ERSBACH, Werner	174790	M			Leader, Gestapo, Dordogne (Fr.)	TORTURE	U.K.
see BIRKENFELD, Willy							
GERSPACHER	251569	M	Ger.		Agent, Gestapo, Limoges (Fr.)	INTERR.	FR.
GERSPACHER, Willy	140028	M	Ger.		Member, Gestapo, Perigueux (Fr.) 6.-7.44	MURDER	FR.
GERSPRACHER, G.	192923	M	Ger.		Schupo, C.C. Falstad nr.Drontheim (Nor.) 6.-8.42	MURDER	NOR.
GERST	141478				Osturmfhr., SS, Gestapo, Folking (Fr.) 9.44	MURDER	FR.
GERST	177584	M	Ger.	15	Osturmfhr., officer, SS police, Saarbruecken (Ger.)	MURDER	FR.
GERST, Adolf	31976	M	Ger.		Dr.,Landgerichtsrat, public official, Opava (Czech.) 2.40	MURDER	CZECH.
GERSTEIN, Kurt	34893	M	Ger.		Dr.	MURDER	U.S.
GERSTEMEIER, Wilhelm	298	M		17. 1.08	SS Hptscharfhr., C.C. Maidanek, 40-4.44	MURDER	POL.
GERSTEMEIER, Willi	161527	M		11	SS Hptscharfhr., C.C. Lublin (Pol.) 42-43	MISC.CRIMES	U.S.
GERSTEN	188252	M			Interpreter (Russian) Gestapo, Bruenn (Czech.) 39-45	WITNESS	CZECH.
GERSTENBERG	141860	M		20	Pvt. 590. Lds.Schtz.Bn. Stalag VII A, Waldenburg (Ger.) 1.45	TORTURE	U.K.
GERSTENBRANDT, Johann	250220	M			Cpl., C.C. Ellrich Nordhausen (Ger.)	MURDER	U.S.
GERSTER	251573	M			Capt., Fla.Kat.Abt. 276, 18.Panz.Div., Posterholt, Effeld (Neth.) 10.-11.44	INTERR.	NETH.
GERSTHOFER	305711	M	Ger.		Sturmbannfhr., SS, C.C. Dachau (Ger.) 9.44-5.45	MURDER	YUGO.
GERSTL, Leopold	250201	M	Ger.		Oscharfhr., C.C. Harzungen, Nordhausen (Ger.)	MURDER	U.S.
GERSTMAYR, Michael Otto	258414	M	Ger.	05	SS Hptsturmfhr., Waffen SS, C.C. Ohrdruf (Ger.) 12.44-4.45	MURDER	U.S.
GERSTMEYR	199050	M	Ger.		SS Hptsturmfhr., C.C. Buchenwald (Ger.) 42-45	TORTURE	U.S.
GERSTOFER	259177	M	Ger.		SS Sturmbannfhr.,,C.C. Dachau (Ger.) 9.44-45	MISC.CRIMES	YUGO.
GERT see GRUETNER	138271						
GERTH	185498	M			Polizei-Dir., Polizei, Luxembourg (LUX.)	TORTURE	LUX.
GERTH	194971	M			Officer, Army, Vaux le Penil (Fr.) 8.44	WITNESS	FR.
GERTH, Heinz	250768	M			Lt., Freiwillige Stamm-Div., L'Ain (Fr.) 7.44	MISC.CRIMES	FR.
GERTH or GEHRT, Louis	188219	M		00	Civ., Farm owner, Damerkow (Ger.) betw. 4.44 and 2.45	TORTURE	U.S.
GERTIG, Karl	161217	M		08	Civ.,C.C. Buchenwald (Ger.)	WITNESS	U.S.
GERTINGER, Joseph	12696	M			Pvt., 110. or 111.Panz.Gren.Rgt. 2.Coy., Albine (Fr.) 6.44	MURDER	FR.
GERTZ, Alfred	161324	M			SS, C.C. Flossenburg (Ger.)	TORTURE	U.S.
GERTZ, Friedrich	251030	M	Ger.		Cpl., 377. Jaeger-Rgt., Vinkt, Meigem (Bel.) 5.40	MURDER	BEL.
GERULAT	251021	M			Lt., BN.Ukrainiens 58290, Hameau du "Logis", Commune de Dompierre (Fr.) 6.44	MISC.CRIMES	FR.
GERUM, Julius see GEHRUM	147796						
GERVKE, Herman	167390	M			Adjutant chief, Art.Div. 197, Vercheny la Plaine (Fr.)	MURDER	FR.
GESAIG	23866	M			Lt., Army, 11.Panz. Div., Albine (Fr.) 8.44	MURDER	FR.
GESAIG	12637	M	Ger.		Lt., 110.or 111.Panz.Gren.Rgt., Gourdon (Fr.) 6.44	MURDER	FR.
GESBERG	23868	M			Madjank (Pol.) 43		
GESCHKA	19347	M			SS Uscharfhr., C.C. Flossenburg (Ger.)	TORTURE	U.S.
GESCHKE	187616	M	Ger.		Dr., SS Sturmfhr., R.Dir.Wke XXI	MURDER	U.N.W.C.C.
GESCHKE	301559	M			SS Standartenfhr., C.C. Mauthausen (Aust.) 40-45	MURDER	BEL.
GESCHKE, Hans	299	M	Ger.		SS Standartenfhr., Prag (Czech.) 9.41-7.42	MURDER	CZECH.
GESCHKE, Hermann	253019	M	Ger.	13. 2.17	Pvt., 13.Coy. 558.Gren.Rgt., Bruay (Fr.) 9.44	MURDER	FR.
GESCHWANDER	23869	M			Chembery (Fr.) 44	MURDER	FR.
GESCHWANDTNER	144499	M	Ger.		Col., Army, St.Jean-de-Maurienne (Fr.) 44	PILLAGE	FR.
GESCHWINDE, Herbert	261834	M	Ger.		Civ.,Firm Friedrich Flick, Rombacher Huettenwerke, Ger., Fr.	MISC.CRIMES	U.S.
GESELICK	253662	M	Ger.		SS Usturmfhr., SIPO, Abt. III D, Brussels (Bel.)	INTERR.	BEL.
GESELL	145390	M			Civ., Shoemaker, Neuss (Ger.)	WITNESS	U.S.
GESSEL, Alfred	192922	M	Ger.		Schupo, C.C. Falstad, Trondheim (Nor.) 6.-8.42	MURDER	NOR.
GESSINK see JESSINCK	167219						
GESSLER or GEUSEN	191873	M			Capt., Army, F.P.No. 159196 or 39196, Billy (Fr.) 8.44	INCENDIARISM	FR.
GESSLER, Adolf	185515	M	Ger.	08	Foreman, Factory Kabel- und Metallwerke Neumeyer, Nuernberg (Ger.)40-45	TORTURE	U.S.
GESSNER	306081	M			SS Uscharfhr., Alderney, C.C. (Channel Is) and Kortemark C.C. 42-45	MURDER	CZECH.
GESSNER, Erich	147797	M	Ger.	1. 7.08	Feldgend., Vitry le Francois (Fr.) 6.43	TORTURE	FR.
GESSNER, Willi	262205	M	Ger.	19. 6.18	SS Hptscharfhr., 51.SS Armoured-Bde., Bréviandes, Bucheres,Ste.Savine, Rivière de Corps, Troyes (Fr.) 8.44	BRUTALITY	FR.
GETADDER, Felix	147798	M	Ger.		Employee, C.C. Dora-Mittelbau Nordhausen (Ger.)	MURDER	FR.
GETENBERG	161215	M	Ger.		Pvt., Army, Stalag VIII A Waldenburg (Ger.) 1.45	MURDER	U.K.
GETERMANN	147801	M	Ger.		Crim.assist., Gestapo, Marseille (Fr.)	MURDER	FR.
GETET	195170	M		85	Civ. in Oflag C.C. Biberach (Ger.) 41-42	MURDER	U.S.
GETLE, Josef	177751	M			Civ. Muehldorf,Ampfing (Ger.) 6.44-4.45	MURDER	U.S.
GESZTESI	189940	M			Agent, Police, Novi Sad (Yugo.)	MURDER	YUGO.

GET-GIE

NAME	C.R.FILE NUMBER	SEX	NATIO- NALITY	DATE OF BIRTH	RANK OCCUPATION UNIT PLACE AND DATE OF CRIME	REASON WANTED	WANTED BY
GETHAT, Franz	132660	M	Ger.		Specialist artifice, Art., Velmanya (Fr.) 8.44	MURDER	FR.
GETNER	124961	M	Ger.		Wachtmstr., Police, C.C. Bremen-Farge (Ger.) 6.43	MURDER	U.K.
GETT	31562	M	Ger.		Hptsturmfhr., SS, C.C.Cmdt.,C.C.Cracow (Pol.) 40	MURDER	U.S.
GETTLER	183107	M	Ger.		Member, SD and SS, C.C. Pilsen (Czech.) 39-45	MURDER	CZECH.
GETTLER, Wilhelm	23871	M		9. 5.08	Capt.,932 Rgt., 1 Btty. Geryville (Fr.) 43	MISC.CRIMES	FR.
GETTMANN, Walter	137765	M	Ger.		Army, Fuerth (Ger.)	WITNESS	U.S.
GETTMANN, Walter	251550	M		08	Pvt., 102 Pz.Rgt.,9 Pz.Div., Breitenbach (Ger.) 9.44	INTERR.	U.S.
GETZ	147800	M	Ger.		Stalag XVII A (Ger.)	MURDER	FR.
GETZINGER, Arthur see JETZINGER	148437						
GETZLER, Kurt	252302	M	Ger.		Lt., Army, Cerisay (Fr.) 8.44	MURDER	FR.
GEUBIG, Franz	250202	M			Sgt., C.C. Ellrich, Nordhausen (Ger.)	MURDER	U.S.
GEUSC or GEUSE see GENTSCH	293						
GEUSEN	23836	M			Army, St.Germain des Fosses (Fr.) 44	MISC.CRIMES	FR.
GEUSEN see GESSLER	191873						
GEVIT	144767	M	Ger.		Major,Gen.,Ger.Airforce,Com IV,GAF Fleet 6, Runishment Bn, Ostrog (Sov.Un.) 9.43	MURDER	U.S.
GEWEKEN, Georges	252135	M	Ger.		Lt., P.W.-Camp Peronne (Fr.)	PILLAGE	FR.
GEWICKE	23837	M	Ger.		SS-Sgt., Gestapo, SD, secretary, Locmine (Fr.) 44	TORTURE	FR.
GEWIESSE, Karl	192169	M	Ger.		Bauleiter, Org.Todt,Firma Otto Menzel of Bittburg Alle sur Semois (Bel.) 5.-6.40	PILLAGE	BEL.
GEWSHEIMER	149559	M			Capt., Army, Stalag 60 (Ger.)	PILLAGE	FR.
GEYER	147721	M	Ger.		Capt., Gebirgsjaeger-Bn	MURDER	FR.
GEYSR	252121	M	Ger.		Col., commander of Stg VI C, Bathorn (Ger.) 1.,6.,7.42	MURDER	FR.
GEYER, Friedrich	255379	M	Ger.	29. 5.95	Schuetze, SS, Nordhausen (Ger.)	MURDER	U.S.
GEYER, Fritz	133349	M			Civilian, Lager Langenzenn, Nuernberg (Ger.) 43-4.45	TORTURE	U.S.
GEYER, Haribert	195131	M			Military-judge, Stalag XVIII B and D, C.C. (Aust.) after 41	WITNESS	U.K.
GEYER, Paul	261360	M	Ger.	20	Pvt.,1 Bn, Ger.Paratroop Rgt.,1 Div.,stationed in Calvi, Nr.22261,San-Benedetto near Montebuono (It.) 4.44	WITNESS	U.S.
GFOLLER	306118	M	Ger.		N.C.O., RSD Abt.VI S, Copenhagen (Dan.) 1.44	PILLAGE	DEN.
GHATTI see GATTI, Giorgio	251552						
GHEETS, Friedel	305855	M	Ger.		Cpl.,377 Inf.Rgt. under Capt.Lohmann, Vinct-Meigem (Bel.) 5.40	MURDER	BEL.
GHIGLIONI, Louis	147724	M			SS-Mann, Waffen-SS	MISC.CRIMES	FR.
GIBBE, Herbert	162036	M	Ger.	00	Sonderfhr., Art.Volkssturm, KUNKENAU near Marienwerder (Ger.) 45	TORTURE	U.K.
GIBHARDT see GEBHARDT	179726						
GIBSEN	147725	M		00	Waffen-SS, 45	TORTURE	FR.
GICKELTTER	256921	M			Obergauleiter, Org.Todt, Muehldorf (Ger.)	MURDER	U.S.
GIEBER	120610	M	Ger.		Civilian, C.C. Himmelfahrt Fundgrube Freiberg-Sa.(Ger.) 10.43-4.45	TORTURE	U.K.
GIEBEL	254102	M	Ger.		Cpl., Lantilly (Fr.) 5.44	MISC.CRIMES	FR.
GIECHE, Bodo	23874	M	Ger.	10. 9.96	Col.,Airforce, Kampfgeschwader 100, Carcassone (Fr.) 44	MURDER	FR.
GIEDLER, Harry	253020	M	Ger.	12. 7.25	Pvt., 13 Coy, 558 Gren.Rgt., Bruay en Artois (Fr.) 9.44	MURDER	FR.
GIEGEL, Johann	171660	M			Pvt.,9 Res.Gren.Rgt.,last Unit 6-R.G.R.765, Melder Coy, Magny d'Avignon (Fr.) 9.44	MURDER	FR.
GIEHRKE	171646	M	Ger.		SS-Sturmmann, guard, C.C. Sachsenhausen, Oranienburg (Ger.)39-4.45	MURDER	POL.
GIELKE	253667	M	Ger.		Crim.secr. Sipo Abt. IV A, Brussels (Bel.)	INTERR.	BEL.
GIENIESSE, Michel	147773	M			Member, Gestapo, Hamburg (Ger.)	MISC.CRIMES	FR.
GIENKE, Wilhelm	256937	M	Ger.	20. 9.91	Osturmfhr.,C.C. Sachsenhausen (Ger.)	MURDER	U.S.
GIEREND, Erwin	185949	M	Ger.		Sgt., Cmdtr. Loscwaye, Cognac (Fr.) 40-44	MURDER	FR.
GIERKE	161216	M		95	Platzmeister, C.C. Aschendorfer Moor (Ger.) 40-41	TORTURE	U.S.
GIERKE, August	147774	M	Ger.	92	Chief of factory-camp "Hoescha", Dortmund (Ger.)	MURDER	FR.
GIERLICH, Johann	250222	M			Pvt., C.C. Ellrich, Nordhausen (Ger.)	MURDER	U.S.
GIERMANN	147776	M		95	Fregatten-Kapitaen, Navy (Sem Def.Cdo.) Brest (Fr.)	MISC.CRIMES	FR.
GIERNIAK, Johann	132177	M	Ger.		Pvt., German Navy U 852,Atlantic Ocean,South o-Freetown, 3.44	WITNESS	U.K.
GIERNOLDEN, Ernst	305145	M	Ger.		Pvt.,guard, Kdo.760, Eupweiller (Ger.) 10.44	MURDER	FR.
GIERSH	167559	M		00	Commanding officer, Abwehr Btty 215 (Crimea,Sov.Un.) 45	MURDER	U.S.
GIERSZEWSKI	261357	M	Ger.		Lt.,2 Coy, 1 Ost-Bn 654, Nievre (Fr.) 6.44	MURDER	FR.
GIES, Otto	171645	M	Ger.		Warder or Kapo, C.C. Sachsenhausen, Oranienburg (Ger.) 39-4.45	MURDER	POL.
GIES, Robert	134285	M		02	Dr., Osturmbannfhr., SS, Berlin (Ger.)	MISC.CRIMES	CZECH.
GIESA, Helmut	253016	M	Ger.		Uscharfhr.,SS, C.C. Auschwitz-Birkenau (Pol.)	MURDER	YUGO.
GIESCHEL, Alwin	250221	M			Rottenfhr., SS, C.C. Harzungen, Nordhausen (Ger.)	MURDER	U.S.
GIESE	67596	M	Ger.		Major, Army Korps Nachr.Abt.431, General Kdo. 86, Dax (Fr.) 6.44	MURDER	FR.
GIESE	147795	M	Ger.		Dr., C.C. Ravensbrueck (Ger.) 5.44	TORTURE	FR.
GIESE	161302	M	Ger.		Rottenfhr., Waffen-SS, Totenkopf, C.C. Berga-Elster (Ger.) 4.45	MURDER	U.S.
GIESE	187826	M	Ger.		SS-Rottenfhr., guard, C.C. Mecklenburg, Ravensbrueck (Ger.) 42-45	TORTURE	U.S.
GIESE	191865	M	Ger.		Sgt., 184 P.O.W. Work-Bn, Bassis Tunnel (Nor.)	WITNESS	NOR.
GIESE, Anneliese	147794	F	Ger.	12.11.21	Woman-guard, W-SS, C.C. Buchenwald (Ger.)	MISC.CRIMES	FR.
GIESE, Artnur	132298	M	Ger.	27.10.87	Col., Army, asst.commander, Inf.Rgt.64, Oflag 13 B, Hammelburg (Ger.) 3-45	MURDER	U.S.
GIESE, Ernst	251543	M			SS-Sturmmann, C.C. Neuengamme (Ger.)	INTERR.	BEL.
GIESE, Kurt	261358	M	Ger.	15. 5.22	Cpl., SS-Art., 3 Bn, 12 Rgt., Tourouvre (Fr.) 8.44	MURDER	FR.
GIESE, Otto	305595	M	Ger.		Blockleiter, SA-Mann, SA, at or nr.Luebeck-Siems (Ger.) 8.44	MURDER	U.S.
GIESECK	255986	M			N.C.O., C.C. Mauthausen (Aust.)	TORTURE	FR.
GIESECKE, Gerhardt	195111	M			Dr.,Physician,health official, Economic Administration, C.C. Flossenburg, Erlangen (Ger.)	WITNESS	U.S.
GIESEL, Joachim	250214	M			Flyer, C.C. Ellrich, Nordhausen (Ger.)	MURDER	U.S.
GIESELMAN, Karl Friedrich Alois	305596	M	Ger.		Member, personal, C.C. at or nr.Flossenburg,Hersbruck,Wolkenburg, Ganacker and Leitmeritz (Ger.and Czech.) 1.42-5.45	MURDER	U.S.
GIESELMANN, Bernhard	161235	M	Ger.		Amtsleiter and Stadtkommissar,NSDAP, Public official, Przemysl-Lublin (Pol.) 41-44	MURDER	U.S.
GIESEN	187851	M			Lt., Feldgendarmerie, Arlon (Fr.) 8.44	MURDER	BEL.
GIESEN	252142	M	Ger.		Lt., Fieldpolice (Bel.)	INTERR.	BEL.
GIESEWETTER, Guillaume	147806		Ger.		Guard, C.C. Barmen (Ger.)	TORTURE	FR.

GIE-GLA

NAME	C.R.FILE NUMBER	SEX	NATIO-NALITY	DATE OF BIRTH	RANK OCCUPATION UNIT PLACE AND DATE OF CRIME	REASON WANTED	WANTED BY
GIESINGER	173164	M	Ger.		Staff,C.C.Schirmeck,Rotenfels,Gaggenau (Fr.-Ger.) 6.44	INTERR.	U.K.
GIESLER,Hermann	177732	M	Ger.		Hauptgauleiter,Org.Todt,C.C.Muhldorf,Ampfing (Ger.) 6.44-4.45	MURDER	U.S.
GIESLER,Paul	62349	M	Ger.		Obergruppenfhr.,Gauleiter,SA,NSDAP,Minister of interior, Muenchen (Ger.)	MISC.CRIMES	UNWCC
GIESS,Robert	132299	M	Ger.		Dr.,Col.,SS,Chief,S.D.,Prag (Czech.) 39-45	MURDER	CZECH.
GIESSELMAN	147805				Camp-Cmdt.,Waffen-SS,Dortmund (Ger.)	TORTURE	FR.
GIESSLER	161406	M			Hptsturmfhr.,SS,C.C.Caen (Fr.) 6.44	MURDER	U.S.
GIT	139807	M		10	Usturmfhr.,SS,Crakow (Pol.) 6.42	MURDER	POL.
GIT,Aman	147804			05	Lt.,Waffen-SS,Krakau (Pol.)	MURDER	FR.
GIETLER	145392	M			Oschfhr.,SS,Gestapo,Hoerde (Ger.)	MURDER	U.S.
GIFFELS	177733	M			Uschfhr.,SS,C.C.Muhldorf,Ampfing (Ger.) 6.44-4.45	MURDER	U.S.
GIGLE (or NAPOLEON)	163449				Buergermeister,Public official,C.C.Enzberg (Ger.)	TORTURE	FR.
GIHOFFER	144271	M		10	Col.,Army	MISC.CRIMES	FR.
GILBERT,Heinrich (or GOTZ)	193047	M	Ger.		Agent,SS,Gestapo,C.C.Buchenwald (Ger.) 42-45	TORTURE	U.S.
GILBRICH	145393	M			Lt.,SS,Gestapo,Hoerde (Ger.)	MURDER	U.S.
GILDEMEISTER,	161213	M	Ger.	83	Prof.Dr.,Civ.,SS,Robert-Koch-Institut,Berlin,C.C.Buchenwald(Ger.)43	MURDER	U.S.
GILG	185518	M	Ger.		SS-Mann,SS-Leibst."Adolf Hitler",Aufklaerungs-Abteilung, Renardmont,Stavelot (Bel.) 12.44	MURDER	BEL.
GILLARD	251570	M	Ger.		Gendarmerie,Mertzwiller (Fr.)1.-2.45	PILLAGE	FR.
GILLARDO,Jean (Alias: Besati GERARD)	259369	M	Ger.	30. 3.08	Policeman,S.D. of Nice,Colmars (Fr.) 1.44	INTERR.	FR.
GILLE	62184				Dr.,Major,NSDAP (Ger.)	MISC.CRIMES	U.S.
GILLE,Herbert	261138			97	SS-Obergruppenfhr.,Waffen-SS	WITNESS	U.S.
GILLERMANN	301506	M	Ger.		Rapportfhr.,C.C.Mauthausen (Aust.) 40-45	MURDER	BEL.
GILLES	1238	M	Ger.		Capt.,Internment Camp official,C.C.St.Denis (Fr.)	MISC.CRIMES	FR.
GILLET,Josef	250211	M			Cpl.,C.C.Ellrich,Nordhausen (Ger.)	MURDER	U.S.
GILOTOVITZ	161208	M			Capt.,Stalag III,South Camp near Sagan (Ger.) 42-44	TORTURE	U.S.
GILRATH	256900	M	Ger.		Employee,C.C.Heizungs-Lueftung FW 2,Nordhausen (Ger.)	MURDER	U.S.
GIMBEL	300467	M			Uschfhr.,(Commune de Moussey) and Etival,Le Harcholet(Fr.)10.44	MURDER	U.K.
GIMBEL,Heinrich	145394	M		4. 6.98	Civilian,Giessen (Ger.) 3.45	MURDER	U.S.
GIMLICH,Louis	147803	M			Block-leader,C.C.Buchenwald (Ger.) 2.45	TORTURE	FR.
GIMMLER,Hans	147818	M			Agent,S.D.,La Chapelle en Sernal (Fr.) 8.44	MURDER	FR.
GIMMY,Eugene	171144	M			Civilian,Merange (Ger.) 8.44	WITNESS	UNWCC
GINAL,Josef	177734	M			C.C.Muhldorf,Ampfing (Ger.) 6.44-4.45	MURDER	U.S.
GINBENTRIT	253026	M	Ger.		Pvt.,XI Pz.Div.,Lautrec (Fr.) 8.44	MURDER	FR.
GINDORF (see GENDORF,Carl)	252303						
GINKELFEL	186415	M	Ger.		Sect. for the Persecut. of jews,Athens (Grc.)	MURDER	GRC.
GINSCHEL	254508	M		20	Cpl.,Inf.1-714,Stalag XX A,Thorn (Ger.) 1.-3.45	INTERR.	U.K.
GINSCHEL,August	193633	M	Ger.		Guard,C.C.Flossenburg (Ger.) 5.44-4.45	TORTURE	BEL.
GINTER	176717	M			SS-Sturmmann,C.C.Muhldorf,Ampfing (Ger.) 6.44-4.45	MURDER	U.S.
GINTERS,Otto	125459	M	Ger.	86	Arb.Kdo.,(Work Camp 409-49),C.C.Leipzig (Ger.)	TORTURE	U.K.
GINTNER,Engelbert	193507	M	Ger.	28. 6.06	Ortsgruppenleiter,NSV,NSDAP,Habakladrau (Czech.)38-45	MISC.CRIMES	CZECH.
GINTSCHEL,Rudolf	194969	M	Ger.	09	Hptschfhr.,SS,S.D.,Kolin (Czech.) 39-45	MURDER	CZECH.
GINTSCHEL,Willi	256728	M	Ger.	19. 5.14	Employee,C.C.Nordhausen (Ger.)	MURDER	U.S.
GINZEL	147817	M	Ger.		Civilian,Michelstadt (Ger.)	TORTURE	FR.
GIPSEN	147833			03	Adjutant,Army,Nancy (Fr.)	TORTURE	FR.
GIRARD,Albert (see GERARD)	261056						
GIRKE	106954	M	Ger.		Regierungsrat,Chief,Gestapo (Ger.) 2.44	MURDER	U.S.
GIRKE	189066	M	Ger.		SS-Sturmbannfhr.,Gestapo-Chief,Darmstadt (Ger.) 44	MISC.CRIMES	POL.
GIRKE,Fritz	132300	M	Ger.	13	Sturmbannfhr.,Allg.SS,	MURDER	U.S.
GIRNDT	147815				Prof.,C.C.Ravensbrueck,Hohenlychen (Ger.) 44	TORTURE	FR.
GIRULLIS	251553	M	Ger.		Rottfhr.,SS,C.C.Neuengamme (Ger.) 40-44	TORTURE	BEL.
GISELE	173286	M	Ger.		Wachtmeister,Polizei,C.C.Gaggenau-Baden (Ger.) 44	WITNESS	U.K.
GISEVIUS	130185	M	Ger.		Pvt.,Stalag III A,Luckenwalde (Ger.) 3.44	MISC.CRIMES	U.K.
GISSON,Charles	147745	M			Pvt.,LVF,Niort (Fr.) 43	MISC.CRIMES	FR.
GISZ,Emil	134845	M			Civilian,Erfurt (Ger.) 44	TORTURE	U.S.
GITLER	261009	M			Rottfhr.,SS,C.C.Vaihingen (Ger.) 8.44-4.45	MURDER	U.S.
GITSCH	147810			95	C.C.Ravensbrueck (Ger.)	TORTURE	FR.
GITTER	167389	M			Cpl.,Feldgendarmerie,Montigny en Vescoul (Fr.) 7.44	MURDER	FR.
GITZEL,Arthur	139143	M	Ger.		Guard,SS,German Prison Camp,Volary (Czech.) 41-45	MURDER	U.S.
GITZEN,Nikolaus	250209	M			Pvt.,C.C.Ellrich,Nordhausen (Ger.)	MURDER	U.S.
GIULUES,Juli	131170	M	Ger.		Head of a Cement-work,Schwanebeck (Ger.) 44	TORTURE	BEL.
GLAEFKE	186008	M	Ger.		Capt.,Army,Kaserne der Artillerie,Perigueux (Fr.) 8.44	MURDER	FR.
GLAESCHER	124485	M			Lt.Col.,Oflag IV c,C.C.Colditz (Ger.)	MISC.CRIMES	U.K.
GLAESER	176720	M			Org.Todt,C.C.Muhldorf,Ampfing (Ger.) 6.44-4.45	MURDER	U.S.
GLAITSCHIS	173445	M	Ger.		Guard,Waffen-SS,C.C.Neckarelz (Ger.)	TORTURE	FR.-U.S.
GLAMKOWSKI (or GLARNKOWSKI, Zigmund)	176718	M			Sturmmann,SS,C.C.Muhldorf,Ampfing (Ger.) 6.44-4.45	MURDER	U.S.
GLAMMER (or PLAMMER)	161207	M	Ger.		Major-General,Army,Stalag II D,Stargard (Ger.) 7.44-2.45	TORTURE	U.K.
GLANDINGER,Franz (or GAHUDINGER)	72295	M	Ger.		Cpl.,Guard,Waffen-SS,C.C.Lublin (Pol.) 43	TORTURE	U.S.
GLANDSTATTER	195128	M	Ger.	12	Capt.,Police,Poggio Mirteto (Ital.)5.44	MURDER	U.K.
GLANSBERG	301		Ger.		Dr.,Prof.Med.-Lag.,C.C.Oswiecim (Pol.) 6.40-43	MURDER	POL.
GLARNKOWSKI,Zigmund (see GLAMKOWSKI)	176718						
GLAS,Konrad	32164	M	Ger.	6. 2.00	Oberbereichsleiter,Kreisleiter,NSDAP,Kolmar (Fr.) 40-44	MISC.CRIMES	U.S.
GLASCZ,Willy (see GLASER)	161396						
GLASER	36616	M	Ger.		Sgt.,Guard,Army,Stalag IV F,C.C.Stuzengrun (Ger.) 4.45	TORTURE	U.K.
GLASER	147078	M	Ger.		Dr.,Hptsturmfhr.,SS,Bled (Yugo.) 43	MURDER	YUGO.
GLASER	187822	M	Ger.		Obersturmfhr.,SS,C.C.Neckarelz (Ger.)	MURDER	U.S.
GLASER,Adam	250208	M			Sturmmann,SS,C.C.Ellrich,Nordhausen (Ger.)	MURDER	U.S.
GLASER,Helmut.	253012	M	Ger.		Major,Fliegerhorst,Landsberg (Ger.)	MURDER	FR.
GLASER,Philipp	147812	M	Ger.		Major,Waffen-SS,C.C.Hinzert (Ger.)	TORTURE	FR.
GLASER,Willy (or GLASCZ)	161396				Kapo,C.C.Platting (Ger.)	MURDER	U.S.

GLA-GME

NAME	C.R.FILE NUMBER	SEX	NATIO-NALITY	DATE OF BIRTH	RANK OCCUPATION UNIT PLACE AND DATE OF CRIME	REASON WANTED	WANTED BY
GLASEWAID, Peter	257316	M	Ger.	08	Gestapo, Tabor (Czech.) 3.39-45	MISC.CRIMES	CZECH.
GLASNER	250207	M			Uscharfhr., SS, C.C.Dora, Nordhausen (Ger.)	MURDER	U.S.
GLASS	147811	M	Ger.		Pvt., Waffen-SS	MISC.CRIMES	FR.
GLASS	167388	M	Ger.	6.2.00	Kreisleiter, N.S.D.A.P., Sintzenheim (Fr.) 1.45	PILLAGE	FR.
GLASS	256567	M	Ger.		Sturmbannfhr., SA, Plant manager, Przemysl (Pol.) 41-44	MURDER	POL.
GLASS	259690	M	Ger.		SS-Oscharfhr., Gestapo, Area of Angers Maine and Loire (Fr.) 42-44	MISC.CRIMES	FR.
GLASS, Josef	176721	M	Ger.		Labour camp, Muehldorf-Ampfing (Ger.) 6.44-4.45	MURDER	U.S.
GLASS, Josef	192040	M	Ger.	16.12.06	Pvt., Army, Inf., (Fr.)	MURDER	FR.
GLASS, Joseph	141364	M	Ger.		Pvt., Inf., (Fr.) 5.-6.40	MURDER	FR.
GLASS, Karl	161842	M	Ger.	07	Blockelder, Block 19, C.C.Mauthausen-Gusen (Aust.) 41-45	MURDER	U.S.
GLASS, Rudolf	161212	M	Ger.	95	Civilian C.C. Buchenwald (Ger.)	SUSPECT	U.S.
GIATENSHOF, Heinrich	191839	M	Ger.		C.C.Dachau (Ger.)	MURDER	U.S.
GLATT	143491	M	Ger.		Army, SS-Pz.Gren.Div."Hohenstaufen", 19 Regt., Arnheim (Neth.) 8.44	MURDER	U.K.
GLATT	302	M	Ger.		Hptsturmfhr., Gestapo, Alesund (Nor.) 40-41	TORTURE	NOR.
GLATT, Walther	252143	M	Ger.		N.C.O., Feldpolizei, (Bel.)	INTERR.	BEL.
GIATTENSHOF, Heinrich	250786	M	Ger.		SS-Hptsturmfhr., C.C.Dachau (Ger.) 42	MURDER	YUGO.
GIATTER, Rudolf	161211	M	Ger.	26.9.10	Pvt., Waffen-SS, Allg.SS, Guard-Coy., Mauthausen, Auschwitz (Aust., Pol.) 12.39-5.45	TORTURE	U.S., POL
GLATZ	256725	M	Ger.		SS-Sgt., med.attendant, Camp Ellrich, Nordhausen (Ger.)	MURDER	U.S.
GIATZEDER	257973	M	Ger.		Military, Sipo, Amsterdam (Neth.) 10-44	SUSPECT	NETH.
GIATZER	133345	M	Ger.		Hptsturmfhr., chief-leader, Waffen-SS, C.C.Ohrdruf (Ger.) 44-45	MURDER	U.S.
GIATZER	261199	M	Ger.		Pvt., 5-I N.Regt., 211,139 Arbeitsbereich Liane, Alleur-Lez-Liege (Bel.) 9.44	MURDER	BEL.
GLAUBER	124592	M	Ger.		Civilian, Camp Birkenau (Pol.)	TORTURE	BEL.
GIAUBERG	147813	M	Ger.	95	Doctor, C.C.Auschwitz (Pol.)	TORTURE	FR.
GIAUBERG or GLAUERBERG or GIAUBERK	148764	M	Ger.	85	Professor of Gynaecology practised artificial insemination in Block 10, C.C.Auschwitz (Pol.) 40-45	MURDER	FR.
GIAUDEVICH or GLAUDICH	161411	M		00	Capt., Army, Stalag Luft III C.Sagan (Ger.) 4.44	MURDER	U.S.
GLAUER	252136	M	Ger.		Oscharfhr., SS, Edo.Budi, C.C.Auschwitz (Pol.)	BRUTALITY	FR.
GLAUERBERG see GLAUBERG	148764						
GIAUKER or GIAUKNE	261055	M	Ger.	about 15	Sgt.,8 Coy., Div."Brandenburg", spec.unit, Var Vaucluse Bouche du Rhone (Fr.) 43-44	MISC.CRIMES	FR.
GIAUNER, Heinz	161388	M	Ger.	25	Kriegsgef.Arb.Bn. 188, Erwik (Nor.)	MURDER	NOR.
GLAVE, Wilhelm or GLAWE	173453	M	Ger.		Feldgendarm, Gendarmerie, Locmine (Fr.) 7.-8.44	MURDER	FR.
GLEFFERT, Henkel	300709	M	Ger.		Member, Gestapo, chauffeur, automobile service, Lyon (Fr.) 11.43-8.44	MISC.CRIMES	FR.
GLEISBERG	176722	M	Ger.		Carpenter, Org.Todt, C.C.Miehldorf-Ampfing (Ger.) 6.44-4.45	MURDER	U.S.
GLEISBERG	185517	M	Ger.		SS-Mann,1 SS-Pz.Div."Adolf Hitler",1 SS-Recon.Bn., Partondruy, Stavelot (Bel.) 12.44	MURDER	U.S.
GLEISCHAMM	171659	M	Ger.		Pvt., Army, Feldpostnr. 22942, Vasles, La Tricherie (Fr.) 8.44	MURDER	FR.
GLEISNER	260064	M	Ger.		Capt.,157 Res.Div.Bayern, Massif of Vercors Isere and Drome (Fr.) 7.-8.44	SUSPECT	FR.
GIEISS	161210	M	Ger.		Sgt., Airforce, Dulag Luft 5, Wetzlar, Moosberg (Ger.) 3.-4.45	TORTURE	U.S.
GLEIXNER, August	189243	M	Ger.	18.8.16	Crim.asst., SD, SS, Gestapo, Mlada Boleslav (Czech.) 40-45	MURDER	CZECH.
GLEMBIN, Herbert	186414	M	Ger.		Lt., Army, Rethymnon (Grc.) 44	MURDER	GRC.
GLICH, Bertel	250213	M	Ger.		Cpl., Camp Ellrich, Nordhausen (Ger.)	MISC.CRIMES	U.S.
GLICKS, Richard	303	M	Ger.		Gruppenfhr., SS, head of C.C.Oranienburg and C.C.Ravensbrueck (Ger.) 41-44	MURDER	POL.
GLIER, Grete	188253	F	Ger.	24.9.08	Employee, Gestapo, Bruenn (Czech.) 39-45	WITNESS	CZECH.
GLIGORIJEVIC, Branislav	195761	M	Ger.		Referent (Reporter), Special Police, Belgrad (Yugo.)	MISC.CRIMES	YUGO.
GLIMMINGAD, Emil	147744	M	Ger.	06	Clerk, D.A.F.	TORTURE	FR.
GLIMWITZ	161209	M	Ger.		Sgt., Stalag III Luft, near Sagan (Ger.) 42-43	TORTURE	U.S.
GLITE	72313	M	Ger.		Lt., Army, 2-714 Coy., 1 Bn., Hildesheim (Ger.) 3.45	TORTURE	U.K.
GLITZ	12698	M			Lt., Army, Chateauvillain (Fr.) 8.44	MURDER	FR.
GLOBER	147743	M	Ger.		Doctor, C.C.	TORTURE	FR.
GIOBOTSCHEK	252317	M	Ger.	05 - 10	Pvt., Army, Trieben (Aust.)	TORTURE	U.K.
GLOCKER	255122	M			Pvt., Auw.-Pruem (Ger.) 12.44	WITNESS	U.S.
GLOCKMAN, Luki	251548	M	Ger.		Guard or Kapo, C.C.Gusen (Ger.)	TORTURE	BEL.
GLOCKNER	252127	M	Ger.		Political instructor, Sgt., Waffen-SS, Izon la Bruisse-Sederon (Fr.) 2.44	MISC.CRIMES	FR.
GIODONEC	147756	M			Gruppenfhr., Waffen-SS, C.C.Boheme-Moravie (Pol.)	TORTURE	FR.
GLOECKNER	252487	M	Ger.		Scharfhr., Waffen-SS, SS-Waffenschuls, Vercoiran (Fr.) 3.44	MURDER	FR.
GLONTZ or GIUNZ	174986	M			Rottenfhr., SS, Schoerzingen (Ger.)	MISC.CRIMES	FR.
GIOS	148149	M	Ger.	15	SS-Uscharfhr., SS-Totenkopf-Div., C.C.Natzweiler (Fr.) 7.43-4.44	MURDER	FR.
GLOSKIE (I)	250215	M			Sturmmann, SS, C.C.Mackenrode, Nordhausen (Ger.)	MURDER	U.S.
GLOSKIE (II)	250216	M			Sturmmann, SS, C.C.Mackenrode, Nordhausen (Ger.)	MURDER	U.S.
GLOSS, Karl	192517	M		15.6.03	Oberwachtmeister, Strafgefangenenlager Nord, Finmark (Nor.) 6.42	MISC.CRIMES	NOR., YUGO.
GLOTMANN	252104	M	Ger.		Official, Custom, Saint Beat, Chaum (Fr.) 6.44	MURDER	FR.
GLOWKNER	141282	M	Ger.		Sgt., guard, Army, Pont Saint Esprit (Fr.)	MURDER	FR.
GLUCKER, Max	148148	M	Ger.	05	Civilian, Nuernberg (Ger.)	MISC.CRIMES	FR.
GIUCKNER	119418	M	Ger.		Major, Army, Comd.2 Geb.Jaeger-Regt., Finmark (Nor.) 44	MURDER	NOR.
GIUECK	307112	M			Lt., Airforce, Hoog-Soeren (Lager "Mia"), Apeldoorn, Woeste, Hoeve (Neth.) 10.-12.44 and 4.45	MURDER	NETH.
GLUECK, Georg	132301	M	Ger.		Sgt., SS-Sicherheitskdo.IIb, Thekina, Tiraspol (Rum., Sov.Un., Ger.) 41	WITNESS	U.S.
GIUECKS	72310	M			Obergruppenfhr., Waffen-SS, z.b.V.Totenkopfverband, C.C.Sachsenhausen (Ger.) 9.41	MURDER	U.S.
GLUECKS	174138	M			SS, C.C.Auschwitz, Oswiecim (Pol.)	TORTURE	U.S.
GLUECKS, Richard	260993	M	Ger.		Member, SS, C.C.Vaihingen a.d.Enz (Ger.) 8.44-4.45	MURDER	U.S.
GIUENERT	192406	M	Ger.		Kapo, C.C.-Block 6, C.C.Flossenburg (Ger.) 5.44-4.45	SUSPECT	BEL., U.S.
GIUNZ see GLONTZ	174986						
GIUSCHKE	250193	M			SS-Rottenfhr., Camp Nixei, Nordhausen (Ger.)	MURDER	U.S.
GIUTTIL, Joseph	12639	M	Ger.		Pvt., 110 or 111 Pz.Gren.Regt., 2 Coy., Albine (Fr.) 6.44	MURDER	FR.
GMEINER see GEMEINER	173162						
GMEINER	195110	M	Ger.		Civilian, Wirtschaftsministerium, Luxembourg Grand Duchy (Lux.)	PILLAGE	LUX.

GNA-GOE

NAME	C.R.FILE NUMBER	SEX	NATIO-NALITY	DATE OF BIRTH	RANK OCCUPATION UNIT PLACE AND DATE OF CRIME	REASON WANTED	WANTED BY
GNAUCK, Willy	255127	M	Ger.	26.3.03	Employee, Gestapo, Most (Czech.) 39-45	MISC.CRIMES	CZECH.
GNAUT, Paul	306837	M	Ger.	6.12.07	Hptwachtmeister, Sipo or S.D. at District Trondheim, Vollan, Trondheim (Nor.) 3.45	TORTURE	NOR.
GNEIDING, Alfred	144284	M	Ger.	20.2.15	Lt., SS 49.Panz.Gren.Bde., Montmirail (Fr.)	MURDER	FR.
GNEIST	306	M	Ger.		SS-Hptscharfhr., Gestapo Official, C.C.Falstad (Nor.) 42	TORTURE	NOR.
GNIEBSCH	185519	M	Ger.		Capt., Polizei, Flur Wohlsborn (Ger.) 44	MURDER	U.S.
GNUG	251569	M	Ger.		Oschfhr., SS Div. "Das Reich", Oradour sur Glane (Fr.) 10.6.44	MURDER	FR.
GNUG (or KNUG)	260869	M	Ger.		Oschfhr., Waffen-SS, Div."Das Reich", SS-Regt. "Der Fuehrer", I.Bn., 3.Coy., Oradour sur Glane (Fr.) 10.6.44	MURDER	FR.
GOBATZ, Henri	144601	M	Ger.	10 - 15	Interpreter, Feldgendarmerie, Laval (Fr.)	MURDER	FR.
GOBL	253021	M	Ger.		SS-Mann, S.D.-Gestapo, Toulouse (Fr.) 11.42-8.44	MURDER	FR.
GOBLER, Erich	306377	M	Ger.	27.1.98	SS-Uschfhr., C.C. Buchenwald (Ger.) betw. 5.38 and 10.43	MURDER	BEL.
GOBNER, Anton	146877	M	Ger.		Rottenfhr., SS-Panz.Div."Das Reich", 13.Coy., Moisaac (Fr.) 44	MURDER	FR.
GOBRICH	147784	M	Ger.		Dr., Kassel (Ger.)	MURDER	FR.
GOCHE	166257	M	Ger.		Reichs-Official, Occupied Territories (Bel., Fr.) 40-45	TORTURE	U.S.
GOCHT	183292	M			Hptsturmfhr., SS-Fuehrungsstab, C.C.Dora-Nordhausen (Ger.), Plaszow (Pol.) 43-45	WITNESS	U.S.
GOCKE	189977	M		96	SS-Osturmbannfhr., Camp Cmdt., C.C. Geta, Kovno (Lith.) 40-44	MURDER	YUGO.
GOCKE, Ruth	147783	F		4.8.23	Guard, Waffen-SS, C.C. Buchenwald (Ger.) 44	MISC.CRIMES	FR.
GOCKEGIE (or KOKOKRI)	252105	M	Ger.		Chief-W.O., 64.Coy. Scharfschuetzen-Ausb.Regt., Mugron (Fr.) 44	MURDER	FR.
GOCKEL	124843	M	Ger.		Sgt., SS-Pol.Regt.20, Stalag IV F, Chemnitz (Ger.) 10.43-3.45	MISC.CRIMES	U.K.
GODDEL	250192	M			Pvt., Camp Dora, Nordhausen (Ger.)	MURDER	U.S.
GODEKE, Rudolph	250777	M	Ger.		Cmdt., Osturmfhr., 9.SS-Div., I.Werwolf-Tr. 9 "Hohenstaufen", Molliens (Fr.) 26.8.44	PILLAGE	FR.
GODFRIED	260063	M	Ger.		Gendarm, Div.Oberland, Massif du Vercors, Isere and Drome (Fr.) 20.7.-5.8.44	SUSPECT	FR.
GODINA	261963		Ger.		Interpreter, various places Slovenia (Yugo.) 41-45	MISC.CRIMES	YUGO.
GODSCHALK	307113	M	Ger.		Member of S.D., Almelo (Neth.) 9.44-2.45	MURDER	NETH.
GODT, Fritz	252106	M	Ger.		Official, Custom-Office, Saint Beat, Chaum (Fr.) 3.6.44	MISC.CRIMES	FR.
GOEB, Martin	192518	M	Ger.	11.3.00	Sgt., Ministry of Justice, Strafgefangenenlager "Nord", Finmark (Nor.) 4.45	TORTURE	CZECH.
GOEBBEL	124593		Ger.		Civilian, C.C.Birkenau (Pol.)	TORTURE	BEL.
GOEBBEL, Hermann (or GOEBEL or GOEPPEL)	195508	M		08	Member, Gestapo, Salzburg (Aust.)	MURDER	U.S.
GOEBBELS (or GOEBEL)	147718	M		95	Dr., Block 10, C.C. Auschwitz (Pol.) 40-45	TORTURE	FR.
GOEBBELS	147782	M			Germany.	MISC.CRIMES	FR.
GOEBBELS, Willi	12640	M	Ger.		Pvt., 110. or 111. Panz.Gren.Regt.,2.Coy., Albine (Fr.) 29.6.44	MURDER	FR.
GOEBEL	31974	M			Dr., Landgerichtsrat, Public Official, Opava (Czech.) 21.2.40	MURDER	CZECH.
GOEBEL	39657				Cmdt., Army, Borkum (Ger.)	MURDER	U.S.
GOEBEL (see GOEBBELS)	147718						
GOEBEL	256761	M	Ger.		Employee, Armaturen B II-A, C.C.Nordhausen (Ger.)	MURDER	U.S.
GOEBEL	257866	M			Lt., 150.Panzer Bde., Meuse Bridge-Antwerp (Bel.) 12.44	MISC.CRIMES	U.S.
GOEBEL	258450	M	Ger.		Deputy-Chief, Medical Service at C.C.Auschwitz (Pol.) 42-45	TORTURE	POL.
GOEBEL	301897	M	Ger.		Osturmfhr., 6.SS Geb.Art.Regt., 6.Div.Nord, 20.Army, Finmark (Nor.) 10.11.44	MURDER	NOR.
GOEBEL	307114				Blockfhr., Kommando C.C. Buchenwald, Ohrdruf (Ger.) 44-45	MURDER	FR.
GOEBEL, Georg	194229	M	Ger.		SS-Sturmfhr., 12.SS Panz.Div."Hitler Jugend", 26.SS Panz.Gren.Regt., 9.Coy., Caen (Fr.) 6.-7.44	TORTURE	CAN.
GOEBEL, Hermann (see GOEBBEL)	195508						
GOEBEL, Johann Nikolaus	186412	M	Ger.	9.3.05	Pvt., Frontier-Pol., Boulade-Wiltz, Luxembourg (Lux.) 28.8.43	MURDER	LUX.
GOEBEL, Willy	165545	M	Ger.		Gestapo, C.C. Essen (Ger.)	TORTURE	BEL.
GOEBELL, Kurt	145397	M			Fregatten-Capt., Navy, Borkum (Ger.) 4.8.44	MURDER	U.S.
GOEBELS, Walter	147785	M			Rogasen (Ger.)	TORTURE	FR.
GOEBERT, Walter Leonhard	259802	M	Ger.		Member, SS, Hertogenbosch, Raamsdonkveer (Neth.) 3.44	PILLAGE	NETH.
GOEBL	161204				Capt., Army, 3.Coy., Kriegsgef.Arb.Bn.182, Buvir near Megarden (Nor.)	MURDER	NOR.
GOEBLER	723000			95	S.A. Roermond (Neth.) 10.44-1.45	TORTURE	U.S.
GOEDE, Hans	144599			05	Usturmfhr., S.D., Gap (Fr.) 9.-10.43	MURDER	FR.
GOEDICKE	195129			90	Capt., Stammlager XX A, Stab, Bromberg (Pol.) 5.44	WITNESS	U.K.
GOEDRICH	174962	M			Uschfhr., SS Div."Totenkopf", C.C.Sandweier (Ger.)	MISC.CRIMES	FR.
GÖRGELEIN	261359		Ger.		Lt., Inspector, Armament-Commando, Nancy (Fr.) 14.9.44	PILLAGE	FR.
GOEGER, Henry	67590	M	Ger.		W.O.-Chief, Feldgendarmerie, Maubeuge (Nord) (Fr.) 19.8.44	MURDER	FR.
GORGEY	162046	M	Ger.		Stalag 2 B, Hammerstein (Ger.) 44-45	TORTURE	U.S.
GOEGGERLE	250778	M	Ger.		SS-Usturmfhr., Gestapo, Section 5, Menil la Tour, Boucq-Trondes (Fr.) 15. 18.8.44	MISC.CRIMES	FR.
GOELLE (or KOEHLE)	141479	M	Ger.		Col., Legion Tartare, Bn."Wolga", Saugues (Fr.) 11.6.44	MURDER	FR.
GOELLER, Horst	192519	M	Ger.	8.2.17	Capt., Guard, Ministry of Justice, Strafgefangenenlager "Nord", Finmark (Nor.)	WITNESS	NOR.
GOELLER, Karl	183291	M			SS-Mann, 4.SS Totenkopf-Sturmbann, C.C.Dora-Nordhausen, Auschwitz (Ger., Pol.) 43-45	WITNESS	U.S.
GOELLES, Willy	181820	M	Ger.	17	Cpl., Abwehr, Luckenwalde (Ger.)	TORTURE	U.S.
GOELLING	257865	M			Lt., 150.Panzer Bde. 12.44	MISC.CRIMES	U.S.
GOELLNER	1383	M	Ger.		Capt., 20. SS-Pol.Regt.	MISC.CRIMES	U.K.
GOEPEL	307	M	Ger.	09	Chief-W.O., 9.SS Div."Das Reich", Regt."Der Fuehrer", Barthes Monthastrue, Bouzet, Tarn, Vienasses (Fr.) 7.44	MURDER	FR.
GOEPELS	148181	M	Ger.	15	Guard, C.C. Nordhausen (Ger.)	TORTURE	FR.
GOEPPEL	162037	M			Master, Pol., Eppstein (Ger.) 29.12.44	MURDER	U.S.
GOEPPEL, Anton	192520	M	Ger.	21.1.07	Oberwachtmeister, Ministry of Justice, Strafgefangenenlager "Nord", Finmark (Nor.) 42-45	MISC.CRIMES	NOR., YUGO.
GOEPPEL, Hermann (see GOEBBEL)	195508						
GOEPPEL, Karl	187405	M	Ger.	3.3.66	Master, Pol., Eppstein (Ger.) 29.12.44	TORTURE	U.S.
GOEPPERT	260957	M			SS-Rottenfhr., C.C. Vaihingen (Ger.) 8.44-4.45	MURDER	U.S.
GOEPPERT, Friedrich	144595	M	Ger.		Engineer, Civ., Carcassonne (Fr.) 8.44	TORTURE	FR.
GOEPSEL	148182	M	Ger.		Chief-W.O., Gestapo, Vesoul (Fr.) 11.43	MURDER	FR.
GOERIG	67592	M	Ger.		Army, Unit S.P. 15 201, Chenebier (Fr.) 27.9.44	MURDER	FR.
GOERING	148147	M	Ger.		Dr., Prof., C.C.Hohenlychen (Ger.)	TORTURE	FR.

GOE - GOL

NAME	C.R.FILE NUMBER	SEX	NATIO-NALITY	DATE OF BIRTH	RANK	OCCUPATION UNIT PLACE AND DATE OF CRIME	REASON WANTED	WANTED BY
GOERING, Herbert	260405	M	Ger.	9.12.89		Ch.Adm., Board "Weser" Flugzeugbau G.m.b.H.,Bremen (Ger.)	MISC.CRIMES	U.S.
GOERING, Werner	901196	M	Ger.			Member Hitler-Jugend, Huchenfeld (Ger.) 3.45	MURDER	U.K.
GOERKE	251564	M	Ger.			SS Mann, 3.Coy. 1.Bn. SS-Div. "Das Reich", Oradour sur Glane (Fr.)6.44	MURDER	FR.
GOERKE	253669	M	Ger.			Apl.crim.assist., SIPO Abt. IV D, Brussels (Bel.)	INTERR.	BEL.
GOERKE	307116	M	Ger.			Member S.D., Almelo (Neth.) 9.44-2.45	MURDER	NETH.
GOERKEN, Martin	186409	M				Lageraeltester SS, C.C. Mauthausen (Aust.)	TORTURE	U.S.
GOERLITZ	189455	M	Ger.			Pvt., Army, Vlissingen (Neth.) 9.44	MURDER	NETH.
GOERRES	162049	M	Ger.		03	Member Gestapo, Brussels (Bel.)	WITNESS	BEL.
GOERSCH, Hermann	148176	M	Ger.			C.C. Luebben, Stalag III B (Ger.)	PILLAGE	FR.
GOERTLEN	125743	M	Ger.			Stalag XX B C.C. Rosenberg (Ger.) 1.43-2.44	MISC.CRIMES	U.S.
GOERTZ	161205	M		about 10		Lt., Army, C.O. Sturmbn. AOK I, 3.Coy. Courcelles s.Nied (Fr.) 11.44	INTERR.	U.S.
GOERWIG	120566	M				Lt.,Untersturmfuehrer, SS, C.O.Dienststelle,Odessa (Sov.Un.)	MURDER	U.S.
GOEFZ	167619	M	Ger.			Capt., Army; Brueckstab Bruns, Riga (Latv.) 12.41	MURDER	U.N.W.C.C.
GOESCHLER	256762	M	Ger.			SS-Mann, Nordhausen (Ger.)	MURDER	U.S.
GOESLING, Julius	251031	M	Ger.	about 98		Dr., 377.Jaeger-Rgt., Vinkt-Meigem (Bel.) 5.40	MURDER	BEL.
GOETH	147755	M			07	Capt., Waffen SS, Krakau (Pol.)	MURDER	FR.
GOETH	183289	M				SS Hptsturmfhr., SS-Fuehrungsstab, C.C.Dora-Nordhausen, Plaszow (Pol.) 43-45	WITNESS	U.S.
GOETHERMANN	173439	M	Ger.			Dr., Hptsturmfhr., Waffen-SS, Oswiecim-Birkenau (Pol.) 39-45	MURDER	CZECH.
GOETSCH, Werner	161410	M	Ger.			Hptsturmfhr., SS, Ger.	MURDER	U.K.
GOETTERMANN	10167	M	Ger.		94	Capt., Army	MURDER	U.S.
GOETERT	176723	M				Polier, Org.Todt, C.C. Muehldorf-Ampfing (Ger.) 6.44-4.45	MURDER	U.S.
GOETZLER	171644	M	Ger.			Secretary of State, Generalgouvernement, Pol., 9.39-44	MURDER	POL.,U.N.W.C.C.
GOETZ	106958	M	Ger.			M-Sgt., Waffen SS, C.C. Thekla (Ger.)	MURDER	U.S.
GOETZ (or GOETZE)	173433	M				Oberwachtmeister, Police, C.C. Oslo (Nor.) 11.41-9.43	TORTURE	NOR.
GOETZ	257864	M				Sgt., 150.Panz.Bde., Operation Grief, 12.44	MISC.CRIMES	U.S.
GOETZ	261856	M				Hptscharfhr., SS, Vaihingen (Ger.) 8.44-4.45	SUSPECT	U.S.
GOETZ, Arthur	174786	M	Ger.		20	Cpl., Army, Bronzolo (It.) 9.43	WITNESS	U.K.
GOETZ, Carl	260876	M	Ger.	12. 6.85		Ch.AR. Dresdner Bank, Berlin (Ger.)	MISC.CRIMES	U.S.
GOETZ, Eduard	252876	M	Ger.			SS Uscharfhr., Lidice (Czech.) 42	MURDER	CZECH.
GOETZ, Erhard	90754	M	Ger.			NSDAP Obergemeinschaftsleiter, Oberbaldingen (Ger.)	MURDER	U.N.W.C.C.
GOETZ, Joseph	300086	M	Ger.			Member, Gestapo Paris (Fr.) 41-44	TORTURE	FR.
GOETZ, Karl	252123	M	Ger.			Guard, Prison, Camp Lahde-Weser (Ger.)	INTERR.	BEL.
GOETZ, Rudolf	251557	M	Ger.	24. 7.09		Police-master, Police, Ebenberg Caryhthie (Aust.) 11.44	INTERR.	U.S.
GOETZE	147790	M	Ger.			Geschwaderarzt, C.C. Ravensbrueck (Ger.) 5.44	TORTURE	FR.
GOETZE	174963	M				SS Oscharfhr., Teilenthal (Ger.)	MISC.CRIMES	FR.
GOETZE	193509	M				SS Oscharfhr., Leipzig (Ger.) 4.45	MURDER	POL.
GOETZE	306082	M	Ger.			SS Hptscharfhr., C.C.Alderney (Channel Is.), Kortemark (Fr.) 42-45	MURDER	CZECH.
GOETZE, Paul Franz	260924	M	Ger.	13.11.03		SS Sturmmann (Pvt.) SS Totenkopf-guard C.C. Auschwitz (Pol.) 42-44	BRUTALITY	POL.
GOETZE, Rudolf	188304	M	Ger.		06	SS Hptsturmfhr., Waffen SS, Kamp Krs.St. Goar (Ger.) 12.44	MURDER	U.S.
GOETZERIED	189244	M	Ger.		00	Civ., Kaisheim (Ger.) 39-45	TORTURE	CZECH.
GOETZMANN, Henri	147752	M	Ger.		09	Employee, Railway 43-44	MISC.CRIMES	FR.
GOEVERT	106961	M	Ger.			Cpl., Milit.prison, C.C. Graudenz (Pol.) 7.44	MURDER	U.K.
GOFERT	144592	M				Chauffeur, S.D., Lyon (Fr.)	TORTURE	FR.
GOGALA	199049	M	Ger.			Gestapo C.C. Buchenwald (Ger.) 42-45	TORTURE	U.S.
GOGL	145398	M				Uscharfhr., SS Totenkopf, C.C. Mauthausen (Aust.) 41-45	MURDER	U.S.
GOGOL	309	M	Ger.			SS Hptscharfhr., C.C. Falstad (Nor.) 42	TORTURE	NOR.
GOGOL, Joseph Gottlieb	258572	M	Ger.	8. 7.95		Civ., chief of camp, Blumenthal (Ger.) 4.45	MISC.CRIMES	POL.
GOGOLIN	185788	M	Ger.			Capt., 3.Sich.Rgt. 16, Bel. 44	MURDER	BEL.
COHLING	146876	M	Ger.			Usturmfhr., SS Panz.Div."Das Reich", Fr. south-west, 44	MURDER	FR.
GOHNOL	187825	M				SS Mann, Guard, 4.SS Totenkopf-Stuba, C.C.Dora-Nordhausen (Ger.) 9.43-4.45	WITNESS	U.S.
GOHRBAND	147789	M	Ger.			Generalstabsarzt, Police, C.C. Ravensbrueck (Ger.) 5.44	TORTURE	FR.
GOIKE, Fred	12641	M				Lt., Feldgendarmerie 577 of Romorantin, Orcay (Fr.) 43-44	MURDER	FR.
GOKE	136298	M	Ger.			Sgt., Feldgendarmerie de Verdun, Stenay (Fr.) 8.44	MURDER	FR.
GOLCHACH see GOLDCHACK	167387	M						
GOLD	259022	M	Ger.			SS Oscharfhr., S.D. Gestapo, Toulouse (Fr.) 11.42-8.44	MURDER	FR.
GOLD, Franz	31921	M	Ger.			Lt., Army, Bergues (Fr.)	MURDER	U.N.W.C.C.
GOLDBERG, Emil	163447	M	Ger.			Uscharfhr., SS Gestapo, Saone et Loire (Fr.) 43-44	MURDER	FR.
GOLDBERG, Karl	250784	M				Cpl., Camp Ellrich, Nordhausen (Ger.)	MURDER	U.S.
GOLDCHACK or GOLCHACH	167387	M	Ger.			Lt., 100.Alpine Bn. 2.Coy., Montgirod (Fr.) 3.and 8.44	MURDER	FR.
GOLDER	300593	M	Ger.			Member, Hptscharfhr., S.D., Amsterdam (Neth.) 10.44	MURDER	NETH.
GOLDERMANN, August	306378	M	Ger.	5.11.03		SS-Mann, C.C. Buchenwald (Ger.) 5.38 and 10.43	MURDER	BEL.
GOLDEWEY, Friedrich	129665	M	Ger.			Pvt., 34.Festungsmaschinengew.Bn., Aachen (Ger.) 9.44	MURDER	U.S.
GOLDHAMMER, N.	259015	M	Ger.		95	Lt., Orts-Cmdt., Army, Valjevo (Yugo.) 10.41	MURDER	YUGO.
GOLDHART, Rudolf	306596	M	Ger.			Pvt., Gendarmerie of Lannion (Cotes du Nord) (Fr.) 6.44	TORTURE	FR.
GOLDMANN	161906	M				Sgt., Army, Oflag 64 Schubin (Pol.) 12.44	MISC.CRIMES	U.S.
GOLDMANN	185525	M				Dr., Medic.officer, Flak-Einh. 3.Corps Gen.Cdo.III Flak-Corps, Malmedy (Bel.) 12.44	WITNESS	U.S.
GOLDMANN	251571	M	Ger.			Sgt., Security Bn. 194 Digne (Basses-Alpes), Taliard (Fr.) 8.44	MURDER	FR.
GOLDMANN, Karl	254095	M	Ger.			Dr.,SS-Sonderfhr.,SS-Waffenschule,Chaumont,Brussels (Bel.) 41-44	MISC.CRIMES	NETH.
GOLDNER	140867	M				Lt., Fallschirmjaeg.Rgt., Xanten (Ger.) 3.45	MURDER	CAN.
GOLDSCHMIDT	174970	M	Ger.			Civ., Jeserig (Ger.) 40	TORTURE	FR.
GOLDSCHMIDT, Heinrich	173446	M	Ger.			SS Osturmfhr., Guard, Waffen SS, Berlin (Ger.) 8.43	MURDER	FR.
GOLDSTEIN, Nelly	136296	F	Ger.		24	Overseer, SS, C.C. Bergen-Belsen (Ger.)	MURDER	FR.
GOLITZ, Fritz	144569	M				Chef du bloc 58, C.C. Buchenwald (Ger.)	MURDER	FR.
GOLKE, Otto or GOLTKA	252147	M	Ger.			Supervisor, C.C. Sachsenhausen (Ger.)	MISC.CRIMES	BEL.
GOLL, Bruno	257807	M	Ger.	21.12.09		Employee, Golnowbau, C.C. Nordhausen (Ger.)	MURDER	U.S.
GOLLA	148179	M				C.C.Hohenlychen, Ravensbruck (Ger.) 5.44	TORTURE	FR.
GOLLA	255267	M	Ger.			N.C.O., 2.Bn. of Renfort, 10.SS Pz.Div.Frundsberg, Louveciennes, Marly (Fr.) 8.44	MISC.CRIMES	FR.
GOLLASCH	36682	F	Ger.			Rapportfuehrerin, C.C. staff, Belsen (Ger.)	TORTURE	POL.
GOLLATZ	250809	M				Cpl., Camp Ellrich, Nordhausen (Ger.)	MURDER	U.S.
GOLLE, Bruno	148174	M			02	Kapo, Arb.Cdo. C.C. Dora-Nordhausen (Ger.) 44-45	MURDER	FR.

GOL-GOT

NAME	C.R.FILE NUMBER	SEX	NATIO-NALITY	DATE OF BIRTH	RANK OCCUPATION UNIT PLACE AND DATE OF CRIME	REASON WANTED	WANTED BY
GOLLER	252998	M	Ger.		Chief,Hospital,Rheimbach (Ger.) 40-45	BRUTALITY	FR.
GOLLER, Karl	250785	M			Pvt.,C.C.Auschwitz,Nordhausen (Pol.,Ger.)	MURDER	U.S.
GOLLER, Wilhelm	12642	M	Ger.		Pvt.,110 or 111 Pz.Gren.Rgt.2 Coy,Albine (Fr.) 6.44	MURDER	FR.
GOLLMANN	132303	M	Ger.	22	Crim.Asst.,Gestapo,Berlin (Ger.)	MISC.CRIMES	U.S.
GOLOB	147077	M	Ger.		Gestapo,St.Vid (Nor.) 43	MURDER	YUGO.
GOLOMBECK	161521	M	Ger.		Hpttruppfhr.,Org.Todt,C.C.Ampfing (Ger.)	MURDER	U.S.
GOLTKA (see GOLKE)	252147						
GOLTZ	127358	M			Osturmfhr.,SS 1 Pz.Gren.Div.,Renardmont-Stavelot (Bel.) 12.44	MURDER	U.S.
GOLTZ, Josef	162048	M			Sturmbannfhr.,SS Gestapo,Police attache at the German Embassy,Bratislava (Czech.)	MURDER	CZECH.
GOLTZINGER, J.A.	132302	M	Ger.		Civilian	TORTURE	U.S.
GOLTZSCH	307115	M	Ger.		Major-General,Commander of 606 Inf.Div.,Roermond Neth. 12.44-1.45	MURDER	NETH.
GOLZ	124257	M			Osturmfhr.,1 Pz.Div.SS,1 Pz.Rgt.C 0 Headquarters Comp.,Malmedy (Bel.) 12.44	MURDER	U.S.
GOLZ	174136	M			Camp Doctor,Stalag VI A,C.C.Hemer (Ger.) 41-45	TORTURE	U.S.
GOMBARTH	119421	M			Major,20 Army 8 Geb.Div.Staff,Finmark (Nor.)	MURDER	NOR.
GOMERSKI, Hubert	134914			11	Civilian,C.C.Hartheim (Aust.) 40-44	MURDER	U.S.
GOMMEL	29876	M			Lt.,Oflag 5 B (Ger.) 10.41	MURDER	U.K.
GONDESSEN	188693	M			Sgt.,Ile d' Oleron (Fr.) 4.45	TORTURE	FR.
GONSCH	261751	M			Sgt.,Gend.,Romilly sur Seine (Fr.) 6.44	TORTURE	FR.
GONSCHOREK, Helmut	161243	M	Ger.	17	Cpl.,SS Leibst.Adolf Hitler,Feld Ers.Bn.1,Rosbach (Ger.) 3.45	WITNESS	U.S.
GONSCHOPEK, Kurt	251580	M	Ger.		Master,Probably Pol.,Waffen-Schule III,near Arnheim (Neth.)	MURDER	NETH.
GONTIER-LEROUX,Jaques (see GPASSLER, Jules)	144453						
GONZOPECK,Jakob (or KONZOPECK,Jakob)	300469	M	Ger.	94	Party-Member,NSDAP,NSKK,NSV,A.R.P.,Gross Gerau (Ger.) 8.44	BRUTALITY	U.K.
GOOCHER	162046	M	Ger.		Capt.,Stalag 2 B,Hammerstein (Ger.) 44-45	TORTURE	U.S.
GOODE	261054	M	Ger.		Lt.,Coy Anti Terroriste Streif Korps Sued,Var-Vaucluse Bouche Du Rhone (Fr.) 44	MISC.CRIMES	FR.
GOODGSFLE	305146	M	Ger.		W.O.,Sgt.,Div."Koehler",H.Q.Chalandri Attika,Rovies,Euboea (Grc.)3.44	MISC.CRIMES	GRC.
GOOSCL (or GOSCH)	161310	M		85-86	Foreman,Civilian,Zschornewitz Mine near Bitterfeld (Ger.) 2.45	MURDER	U.K.
GOPFERT	126726	M			SD,Gestapo Agent,Paris (Fr.) 42	TORTURE	FR.
GOPON	31585	M			Sgt.,Kripo Stalag III,Sagan (Ger.) 3.44	MURDER	U.K.
GOPPERT	188694	M			Agent,Gestapo,C.C.Drancy (Fr.)	MURDER	FR.
GORAJ, Erich	256899	M	Ger.	1.12.10	Employee,Block 5,C.C.Ellrich,Nordhausen (Ger.)	MURDER	U.S.
GORARDY,Novak Elemer	259059	M			Acting-Feldmarschall,Crimes against Peace.War Crimes and Crimes against Humanity	WITNESS	U.S.
GORDAN, Jordan	106960	M	Ger.		Gauleiter,NSDAP,Gardelegen (Ger.)	MURDER	U.S.
GORDON, Karl	195109	M	Ger.	16	Interpreter,SS Court Martial to FGCM,Graz (Aust.) 2.45	WITNESS	U.K.
GORELLO (or HORLLO)	187824	M			Master,Arbeitskdo.,Firm of Heinrich Butzer,Aspfjord (Nor.)	TORTURE	NOR.
GORENS,Johannes (or GOSENS)	161312	M	Ger.		Civilian,Schlik Community of Wachtendunk (Ger.) 4.42	MURDER	U.S.
GORETZKI,Ewald	250779	M			Flyer,Camp Ellrich,Nordhausen (Ger.)	MURDER	U.S.
GORGAS	161522	M	Ger.		Reportfhr.,Rottfhr.,C.C.Muhldorf Ampfing (Ger.)	MURDER	U.S.
GORGELS,Josef	250212	M			Flyer,C.C.Ellrich,Nordhausen (Ger.)	MURDER	U.S.
GORGENS	306682	M	Ger.		Pvt.,331 Pion.Bn.,331 Inf.Div.,Mijnheerenland (Neth.) 5.45	PILLAGE	NETH.
GORGER	167386	M	Ger.		Lt.,Army,Richardmesnil M-Melle (Fr.) 8.-9.44	WITNESS	FR.
GORGES	147331	M	Ger.		Pvt.,11 Pz.Div.,3 Gruppe Kampfgr."Wilde", 44	MURDER	FR.
GORGES	306083	M	Ger.		Uschfhr.,SS,C.C.Hamburg Neuengamme (Ger.) 45	MURDER	CZECH.
GORGES, Walter	193159	M	Ger.	8.4.19	Ex Convict,Reichsjustizministerium,Feldstraflager,Finmark (Nor.) 42-45	WITNESS	NOR.
GORGOS,Otto	252320	M	Ger.	14	Sgt.,Flieger Ortskommandantur,Creil (Fr.) 8.44	MURDER	FR.
GORKE	310	M	Ger.		SS-Uschfhr.,C.C.Stutthof (Ger.) 9.39-41	MURDER	POL.
GORL	163448	M	Ger.		Member,Gestapo,Revin (Fr.) 6.44	MURDER	FR.
GORLACH, Paula	171143	F	Ger.		Civilian,Lang-Gons (Ger.)	WITNESS	U.N.W.C.C.
GORLICH	144291	M			Cmdt.,Army,Flakeinheit Boncourt et Noailles (Fr.) 8.44	MURDER	FR.
GOPNI	191866	M	Ger.		Cpl.,Army,C.C.Gossen (Nor.) 42-45	TORTURE	NOR.
GORNIAK, Rudolf	252132	M	Ger.	5. 5.89	Forester,Gestapo informer,Bystrice (Czech.) 39-45	INTERR.	CZECH.
GORNIK	125159	M		10	SS-Sturmbannfhr.,	MURDER	U.S.
GORRIS	137019	M	Ger.		Capt.,2 Pz.Div.Hqrs.,Sessenheim (Fr.) 1.45	MURDER	U.S.
GORSKI	306707	M			Head Horseman,Heer,Friesen Farm,Stein Kaspendorf,Dtsch.Eylau (Ger.) 4.41	BRUTALITY	U.K.
GORTZ	167385	M	Ger.		Pvt.,Army 486 I.Rgt.,C.C.Sidlinghausen (Ger.)	TORTURE	FR.
GORZELITZ,Karl	192170	M	Ger.		Zimmerpolier,Org.Todt,Firma Otto Menzel of Bittburg,Alle sur Semois (Bel.) 5.-6.40	PILLAGE	BEL.
GOSBERG	130186	M	Ger.		Hptsturmfhr.,Feldgendarmerie,C.C.Lublin (Pol.)	MURDER	YUGO.
GOSCH (see GOOSCH)	161310						
GOSCH	29874	F	Ger.		Doctor, (Ger.) 5.44	MISC.CRIMES	U.K.
GOSCH, Walter	143271	M			Member,Kommandantur,Lure (Fr.)	TORTURE	FR.
GOSENS, Johannes (see GOPENS)	161312						
GOSKI, Anni	161839	F	Ger.		Civilian,Plettenberg (Ger.) 10.43	TORTURE	U.S.
GOSLING	173249	M	Ger.	05	Sgt.,Guard,Torgau Prison (Ger.) 42	WITNESS	U.K.
GOSS	123983	M	Ger.	2.12.05	Osturmfhr.,SS,SD,Wallrabenstein (Ger.) 3.45	MURDER	U.S.
GOSS	143272	M			Army,Neuville (Fr.)	MURDER	FR.
GOSS, Julius	148177	M			Betriebsobmann,Civilian,Munich (Ger.)	TORTURE	FR.
GOSSEL, Georg	129625	M			Civilian in Camp Mauthausen (Aust.) 41-45	MURDER	U.S.
GOSSL, Franz	145399	M	Ger.	04	Civilian,Giessen (Ger.) 3.45	WITNESS	U.S.
GOTCHY	173454	M			Lt.,Army,Lanchatre (Fr.) 7.44	MURDER	FR.
GOTH	195108	M	Ger.		Hptschfhr.,SS,Lublin (Pol.) 40-44	MURDER	POL.
GOTH	250210	M			Hptsturmfhr.,SS,C.C.Plaszow,Nordhausen (Ger.)	MURDER	U.S.
GOTH, Gottlieb	257361	M	Ger.		SS-Sturmfhr.,SS slave labour camp,Beisfjord near Narvik (Nor.) 6.-11.42	MISC.CRIMES	YUGO.
GOTH, Karl	167384	M	Ger.		Adj.,Feldgendarmerie,Luneville Maixe (Fr.) 8.44	MURDER	FR.
GOTH, Otto	193048	M	Ger.		SS-Hptschfhr.,Waffen SS,C.C.Buchenwald (Ger.) 42-45	TORTURE	U.S.
GOTHRY,Robert (or ROBERT)	144784	M	Ger.		Oschfhr.,Gestapo,Clermont-Ferrand (Fr.) 45	MISC.CRIMES	FR.
GRABNER (see GRAUNER)	173440						

GOT - GRA

NAME	C.R.FILE NUMBER	SEX	NATIO-NALITY	DATE OF BIRTH	RANK OCCUPATION UNIT PLACE AND DATE OF CRIME	REASON WANTED	WANTED BY
GOTHELUCKEN see SPIES	305856						
GOTHRY, Robert	144784	M	Ger.		Oberscharfhr., Official, SS Gestapo, Clermont et Vichy (Fr.)	MISC.CRIMES	FR.
GOTLIB	147741	M		05	Room-Elder, C.C. Block II, Radisgau (Czech.)	TORTURE	FR.
GOTSCHALK	193158	M	Ger.		Capt., 2.Coy., Kgf. Bau-Arb.-Bn. 190 (Nor.) 43-45	MURDER	NOR.
GOTT	133339	M			Hauptsturmfhr., W.-SS, C.C. Cracow (Pol.)	MURDER	U.S.
GOTT	148178	M			Prison, Vichy (Fr.)	MISC.CRIMES	FR.
GOTTBERG	62988	M	Ger.		General-Commissar, Acting Commissioner Public Off. (Sov.Un.)	TORTURE	U.N.W.C.C.
GOTTELT, Else	195083	F	Ger.	22	Employee, Member, Gestapo, Kolin (Czech.) 39-45	MURDER	CZECH.
GOTHOLD, Michael	127359	M	Ger.		Hauptscharfhr., Weimar, Buchenwald (Ger.)	TORTURE	U.S.
GOTTINGER	1384	M	Ger.		Assistent, Naval Supply	MISC.CRIMES	U.K.
GOTTKE-HASKAMP, Heinz	72302	M			Cpl., SS Totenkopf, 6. SS Mtn. Div.	TORTURE	U.S.
GOTTLEIB	1385	M			Pvt., 903 Festungs Bat.- Army	MISC.CRIMES	U.K.
GOTTLIEB	147957	M	Ger.		Major, W.-SS, Hohenlychen (Ger.) 5.44	TORTURE	FR.
GOTTLIEB, Grundel	252114	M	Ger.		Pvt., K.Pl. Schuetzen Bn. 13, Juvisy (Fr.) 8.44	MISC.CRIMES	FR.
GOTTLIEB, Oskar	176724	M			Civilian, Arb.Kdo., Muehldorf,Ampfing (Ger.) 6.44-4.45	MURDER	U.S.
GOTLOB	144438	L			Dr., Kriegsgerichtsrat, Kriegsgericht, Rennes (Fr.)	MURDER	FR.
GOTLOB	187623	M			SS-Rottfhr., 4th Totenkopf Sturmbann (Nordhausen) (Ger.)	TORTURE	U.S.
GOTTRON	147950	M	Ger.		Professor, Oberfeldarzt, Hohenlychen (Ger.) 5.44	TORTURE	FR.
GOTTSCHALG or GOTSCHALK	250197	M			SS-Rottfhr., Camp Dora Nordhausen (Ger.)	MURDER	U.S.
GOTTSCHALK, Kuno	144780	M	Ger.	95	Gend.-Meister, Dueren (Ger.) 6.41	WITNESS	U.S.
GOTTSCHALK, Rudi	162045	M	Ger.	03	Civ., Buchenwald (Ger.) 43	WITNESS	U.S.
GOTTSCHALL, Eduard	250198	M			N.C.O., Camp Ellrich Nordhausen (Ger.)	MURDER	U.S.
GOTTSCHALL, Ludwig	12643	M	Ger.		Pvt., Pz.Gren.Rgt. 110. or 111. 2. Coy., Albine (Fr.) 29.6.44	MURDER	FR.
GOTTSCHIED	191946	F			Women Guard, Matron, Poitiers (Fr.) 6.44	MURDER	U.S.
GOTTSCHLICH or GOTTSCHLICK	161395	M	Ger.		Capt., Ger.Intelligence Corps, 280.Div. Stabsoffi. ,Stavanger (Nor.) 42	WITNESS	U.K.
GOTTSCHLING or GOTTSCHLINK	9661	M	Ger.		Sturmbannfhr., SS-Chef der Gestapo, (Czech.) 38 -44	TORTURE	CZECH.
GOTTSCHLING, Heinrich	181569	M	Ger.	05	Hauptsturmfr., Criminalrat, SD Gestapo, Prag, Kladno, Tabor (Czech.) 42-45	MURDER	CZECH.
GOTTSMANN	144436	M			Commissar, S R A Zollgrenzschutz, Saint-Jean-de-Luz (Fr.)	MISC.CRIMES	FR.
GOTTSMANN	147754	M		00	Lt.Col. 35. SD-Kdo., Rennes (Fr.) 44	MISC.CRIMES	FR.
GOTTWALD	162043	M	Ger.		Camp Guard, Untermassfeld (Ger.) 41-45	MURDER	U.S.
GOTTWALD	250204	M			Untersharfhr., SS C.C. Harzungen, Nordhausen (Ger.)	MURDER	U.S.
GOTTWALD, Edgar	255131	M	Ger.	24.12.99	Civilian, Prag (Czech.) 4.45	PILLAGE	CZECH.
GOTTWALD, Herbert	255982	M	Ger.	21. 8.07	Crim.Asst., Gestapo, Opava (Czech.) 39-45	MISC.CRIMES	CZECH.
GOTZ	132905	M	Ger.	12	SS-Hauptsturmfhr., Berlin (Ger.)	MISC.CRIMES	U.S.
GOTZ	173251	M	Ger.	08	Dr., Interrogator, Gestapo SS, Neailles (Fr.) 8.44	MURDER	U.K.
GOTZ	186408	M	Ger.		Civilian, Erding (Ger.) 12.44	WITNESS	U.S.
GOTZ, Armin	196725	M			Arb.Lager, Muehldorf, Ampfing (Ger.) 6.44-4.45	MURDER	U.S.
GOTZ, Ernst	252873	M	Ger.	12. 1.21	Pvt., 13.Coy., 558 Gren.Rgt., Bruay en Artois (Fr.) 9.44	MURDER	FR.
GOTZ, Heinrich see GILBERT	179047						
GOTZ, Karl	142306	M	Ger.	19	Hauptscharfhr., Gestapo N.C.O., Winterkasten (Ger.) 18.3.45	MURDER	U.S.
GOTZE, Georg	250203	M			Sturmmann, SS, Camp Harzungen, Nordhausen (Ger.)	MURDER	U.S.
GOTZHABER, Edith	300732	F	Ger.		Employee, Mickl & Co, Klagenfurth St. Peter Karlsweg 3 Auschwitz-Birkenau (Pol.) 39-45	MURDER	CZECH.
GOTZMAN	176766	M			Polier, Org.Todt, Muehldorf, Ampfing (Ger.) 6.44-4.45	MURDER	U.S.
GOUBAND, Walter	144433	M		15	Lt., Gestapo Chambery (Fr.)	MISC.CRIMES	FR.
GOUBEAUD, Walter	176581	M	Ger.	10	Adjudant-Chef, Fegiaz (Fr.)	MISC.CRIMES	FR.
GOUG or GOUNS	147751				Hemsen (Ger.)	TORTURE	FR.
GOUREZ see De VALERA or FELLMANN	188717						
GOURNONJE	254093	M			Lt., Bunker-Complex, Mistrai et West-Kapelle (Neth.) 28.9.44	TORTURE	NETH.
GOUTCHOUCH	147750	M			Chief, W.-SS, Waiblingen (Ger.)	TORTURE	FR.
GOY	311				Lt., Gestapo, Locmine (Fr.) 43-44	TORTURE	FR.,U.S.
GOY	165890	M	Ger.		SS-Untersturmfhr., La Rochelle (Fr.) 40-44	MISC.CRIMES	U.S.
GOY	188839	M	Ger.		Lt., Army, Morbihan (Fr.)	WITNESS	FR.
GOYMANN, Kurt	195537	M	Ger.		Sgt., W.O., SS-Div "Das Reich", Valence D'Agen (Fr.) 6.44	MURDER	FR.
GOYS, Kurt	161706	M	Ger.		Lt., Gestapo, Locmine (Fr.) 5.-8.44	TORTURE	FR.
GRAAB, Max	252101	M		09	Hitlerjugend-Scharfhr., Member SS and SA, Luxembourg (Lux.) 40-44	MISC.CRIMES	LUX.
GRAAF	147771				W.-SS, C.C. Ravensbrueck (Ger.)	TORTURE	FR.
GRAB	135172	M	Ger.		Police-Chief, Gend., Schweinfurt (Ger.)	MURDER	U.S.
GRABAUM	1306	M			Capt., 18 Mountain Police	MISC.CRIMES	U.K.
GRABE	167383	M	Ger.		Cpl., Feldgend., Montigny en Vesoul (Fr.) 16.7.44	MURDER	FR.
GRABEDUNKEL	197738	M	Ger.		SS-Chef-Adjutant, SS-Div."Das Reich", SS-Rgt. "Deutschland" Miremont (Fr.)	MURDER	FR.
GRABEL	119422	M	Ger.		Capt., Comd. 1-6 W.-SS Geb. Art. Regt., Geb.Div.Nord 20.Army 10.44	MURDER	NOR.
GRABENSBERGER	193156	M	Ger.		Dr., Officer Landesschuetzen Bn. 809 C.C. Orsa (Ger.)	MISC.CRIMES	NOR.
GRABER, Filip	250205	M			SS-Rottenfuehrer, C.C. Ellrich Nordhausen (Ger.)	MURDER	U.S.
GRABER	250206	M			Pvt., C.C. Mackenrode Nordhausen (Ger.)	MURDER	U.S.
GRABES	147770	M	Ger.	95	Informant, Gestapo, Eintrachts-Huette (Ger.) 42-45	MISC.CRIMES	FR.
GRABINGER or GRANBINGER	252318	M	Ger.	95	Colonel-Cmdt., Infantry Platz, Cuneo Province of Cuneo-It.) 12.12.43	MURDER	U.K.
GRABNER or GRABNER	313	M			Gestapo Official, C.C. Oswiecim,C.C. Birkenau (Ger.Pol.) 39-45	MURDER	YUGO.
GRABNER	173440	M			Lagerfhr., Untersturmfhr., Gestapo, Camp Oswiecim Birkenau (Pol.)	MURDER	CZECH.,POL.
GRABNER	306598	M			Superintendent, C.C. Ravensbrueck (Ger.) 42-45	MURDER	FR.
GRABNER, Hans	250187	M			N.C.O., Camp Ellrich Nordhausen (Ger.)	MURDER	U.S.
GRABNER, Max	145400	M		08	Untersturmfhr., SS, Chief of Political Dept. at C.C. Auschwitz Pol.) 43-44	TORTURE	FR.,U.S.
GRABNER, Najnar see KAHN,Norb.	254642						
GRABOL	187821	M			Meister, Arbeitskdo., Firm of Heinrich Butzer, Aspfjord (Nor.)	TORTURE	NOR.
GRABOWSKI	144292	M			Colonel, Feldkommandantur, Charleville (Fr.)	MURDER	FR.
GRABORSKI	144426	M			Sgt., Army Flak, Villamur (Fr.)	MURDER	FR.
GRABOW	148160	M			Guard, Salzhof (Ger.) 11.43	MURDER	U.S.
GRABOW	187820	M			SS-Hauptscharfhr., 4th SS Totenkopf Sturmbann Dora Nordhausen (Ger.) 9.43-4.45	WITNESS	U.S.
GRABOWSKI	314	M	Ger.		Colonel, Ardennes (Fr.) 6.44	MURDER	FR.

GRA-GRA

NAME	C.R.FILE NUMBER	SEX	NATIO- NALITY	DATE OF BIRTH	RANK OCCUPATION UNIT PLACE AND DATE OF CRIME	REASON WANTED	WANTED BY
GRABOWSKI	187404	M	Ger.	17	Lt.,150 SS Pz.Gren.Bde.,Honsfeld(Bel.) 12.44	MURDER	U.S.
GRABOWSKI see RAKOSKI	259222	M					
GRABS	162660	M	Ger.	10	Civilian,KL.Buchenwald (Ger.)	MURDER	U.S.
GRABS, Alfred	148161	M		19. 6.11	Member Feldgend.,Vitry Le Francois(Fr.) 6.43	TORTURE	FR.
GRABNER see GRABNER	313						
GRACH, Hans Ernst	124594	M	Ger.		Civilian,Camp Zeltingen(Ger.)	TORTURE	BEL.
GRADE	181570	M	Ger.		Hptsturmfhr.,Krim.Kommissar,SD,Kripo,Prag(Czech.) 40-45	MURDER	CZECH.
GRADE, Herbert	148162	M		10	Public Official Siemens A.G.,Berlin(Ger.) 15.5.43	MISC.CRIMES	FR.
GRADER	144295	M			Major,Army,Inf.,St.Die-Gerardmer(Fr.)	PILLAGE	FR.
GRADL, Heinrich	162039	M	Ger.		Group Leader,NSDAP,Gross-Hesselnlome(Ger.) 19.7.44	MURDER	U.K.,U.S.
GRADWITZ	162661	M			SS-Ogruppenfhr.,al.Buchenwald(Ger.)	MURDER	U.S.
GRADWITZ	193046	M			Professor,C.C.Buchenwald(Ger.) 42-45	MURDER	U.S.
GRAEBER	256763	M	Ger.		Cpl.,C.C.Dora,Nordhausen(Ger.)	MURDER	U.S.
GRAEBER, Karl	167382	M			Lt.,Army,St.Hilaire de Ville Franche(Fr.) 16.8.44	MURDER	FR.
GRAEBER, Werner	129640	M	Ger.	05	Hptschfhr.,SD,Kriminal-Oberassist.,Bonnet Arlon(Bel.) 1.9.44	MURDER	BEL.
GRAEBNER	254096	M			Army,19 SS Police-Regt.,Ferlach(Aust.) 44-45	MURDER	YUGO.
GRAEF	106962	M	Ger.		Sgt.,Believed to Hive at Markranstedt,Leipzig(Ger.) 11.43-44	TORTURE	U.K.
GRAEFE	148163	M			Agent,Gestapo,Foix(Fr.)	MISC.CRIMES	FR.
GRAEFE	252486	M	Ger.		Institut for Anatomie,Strasbourg(Fr.) 40-44	MURDER	FR.
GRAEFE, Alfred	146724	M		94	T-Sgt.,SS,Flossenburg(Ger.)	TORTURE	U.S.
GRAEFE, Karl	305148	M	Ger.		SS-Uschfhr.,SD,Grenzkommissariat,Foix and Ariege(Fr.) 11.42-8.44	MURDER	FR.
GRAEFF	148164	M			Doctor,C.C.Hohenlychen-Ravensbrueck(Ger.) 16.-18.5.44	MURDER	FR.
GRAEFF, Friedrich	162999	M	Ger.		Cpl.,Inf.Div.Landesschuetz.Bn.789,Sinzig(Ger.)20.12.41	WITNESS	U.S.
GRAEFF, Walter	162658	M	Ger.	05	Dr.,SS-Osturmfhr.,KL.Buchenwald(Ger.) 42	MURDER	U.S.
GRAEFFE	256923	M			Civilian,Genthin(Ger.) 12.44	MISC.CRIMES	U.S.
GRAEHAN or GREHAN	161223	M	Ger.		Col.,Army,355 Regt.,214 Inf.Div.,Egersund,Rogaland(Nor.) 41-43	MURDER	NOR.
GRAEHLING	161340	M			Railroadworker,Civilian,Mondorf and Bergheim(Ger.) 4.or.8.44	MURDER	U.S.
GRAESER, Fritz	259055	M	Ger.	88	Lt.-Gen.,Crimes Against Peace,War Crimes and Crimes Against Humanity	WITNESS	U.S.
GRAESSIE, August	261089	M	Ger.	98	Police-inspector,Foreign Labor Camp,Schoenblick(Ger.) 42-43	MISC.CRIMES	POL.
GRAETHER, Herrmann	252992	M			Employee,Gestapo,Breclav(Czech.) 39-45	TORTURE	CZECH.
GRAETZ, Heinz	188303	M	Ger.	14	Civilian,C.C.Nuernberg(Ger.)	WITNESS	CZECH.
GRAF	62389	M	Ger.		SS-Ogruppenfhr.,SS High Offic.of Commissariat for German Racialism.	MISC.CRIMES	UNWCC.
GRAF	12644	M	Ger.		Offizier,Puget-Theniers(Fr.) 3.5.44	MURDER	FR.
GRAF	140636	M			Lt.,Army,902 Pz.Gren.Regt.,Wardin(Bel.) 19.12.44	MURDER	U.S.
GRAF	148154	M		15	Unterlagerfhr.,C.C.Esslingen(Ger.)	MISC.CRIMES	FR.
GRAF	179753	M			Major,1 Flak Regt.,Div."Goering",Cavriglia(Ital.) 11.7.44	MURDER	U.K.
GRAF	193045	M			Dr.,SS-Official,Waffen-SS,C.C.Buchenwald(Ger.) 42-45	TORTURE	U.S.
GRAF	254094	M	Ger.		SS-Usturmfhr.,Sipo at Arnheim,Hengelo(Neth.) 30.4.45	INTERR.	NETH.
GRAF, Fritz	250188	M	Ger.		SS-Rottfhr.,Camp Harzungen,Nordhausen(Ger.)	MURDER	U.S.
GRAF, Georg	162935	M	Ger.	26. 1.01	SS-Osturmfhr.,Crim.Secretary,SS,Sipo-Gestapo Liege,Jalhay,Surister (Bel.-Ger.)	MISC.CRIMES	BEL.
GRAF, Hans	161409	M	Ger.		Mechanist,NSDAP,SS	TORTURE	U.S.
GRAF, Reinhold	174965	M		30. 4.02	Osturmfhr.,SS Kriegsgericht (Pol.)	MURDER	FR.
GRAF, Wilhelm	174964	M			Lagerfhr.,Maschinenfabrik,Weil(Ger.)	MURDER	FR.
GRAF, Willi	106964	M	Ger.		Pvt.,Army,1082 Sicherungs-Bn.,Sellerich(Ger.) 4.1.45	WITNESS	U.S.
GRAFE	147717	M			Oberfeldarzt,Army,C.C.Ravensbrueck(Ger.) 16.-18.5.44	TORTURE	FR.
GRAFE	188898	M	Ger.		Member Feldgend.,Bar le Duc(Fr.) 20.-23.8.44	MURDER	FR.
GRAFE, Fritz	147781	M			Guard,C.C.Kemna(Ger.)	TORTURE	FR.
GRAFE, Willy, or GRAFF	163446	M		9.12.11	Freiwillig. I-Ost Btty 447,Plouvien(Fr.) 8.44	TORTURE	FR.
GRAFEL, Ludwig	192405	M			C.C.Flossenburg(Ger.) 44-45	SUSPECT	U.S.
GRAFENBERGER	147780	M			Lt.,Army,C.C.Ravensbrueck(Ger.) 16.-18.5.44	TORTURE	FR.
GRAFF see KRAFF	67058						
GRAFF	144299	M			Civilian,Foreman,Aurigny(Fr.)	TORTURE	FR.
GRAFF	147716	M			Chief,Gestapo,Innsbruck(Ger.) 44	TORTURE	FR.
GRAFF	147762	M	Ger.	10	Waffen-SS,C.C.(Manager of Tailor Work-Shop),Ravensbrueck(Ger.) 43-44	TORTURE	FR.
GRAFF	147779				C.C.Drancy(Fr.) 42-44	MURDER	FR.
GRAFF see GRAFE, Willy	163446						
GRAFF	192404	M	Ger.		Prison Guard,C.C.Aachen(Ger.) 5.43-10.43	TORTURE	BEL.
GRAFF	255985	M	Ger.		Guard,C.C.Flossenburg(Ger.)	TORTURE	FR.
GRAFF	259613	M	Ger.		SS-Schfhr.,SS,Colmar Haut Rhin(Fr.) 12.44,1.45	PILLAGE	FR.
GRAFF	301000	M	Ger.		Gend.-Inspector,Gend.at Maurach,Pertisau-Maurach(Aust.) 13.7.44	MURDER	FR.
GRAFF	305797	M	Ger.		Lt.,Camp-Cmdt.(Oflag VI-C),Osnabrueck-Ewersheide(Ger.) 42-43	MURDER	YUGO.
GRAFF, Edouard	256924	M	Ger.		SD,Foix(Fr.) 11.42-8.44	MISC.CRIMES	FR.
GRAFF, Georg	192409	M	Ger.		Cmdt.,Gestapo,Verviers Liege(Bel.) 43	MURDER	BEL.
GRAFF, Hans	137632	M		18	Schfhr.,SS,Struthof(Fr.)	TORTURE	U.K.
GRAFF, Heinz	255265	M	Ger.		Navy,Heusden(Neth.) 11.44	PILLAGE	NETH.
GRAFF, Paul	144300	M			Civilian,St.Germain et Romainville(Fr.)	MURDER	FR.
GRAFF, Wilhelm	147778	M		10	Esslingen(Ger.)	TORTURE	FR.
GRAFFE	144901	M			Lt.,Army,St.Hilaire de Ville Franche(Fr.)	MURDER	FR.
GRAFFE, Alphonse	193917	M	Ger.		Lt.,Feldgend.,Ecoyeux Chateau Gaillard & Les Environs(Fr.) 15.,16.8.44	MURDER	FR.
GRAG	133344	M	Ger.	13	Major,SS"Das Reich",2 Coy.,II Recon.Bn.,St.Vith(Bel.) 1.45	MURDER	U.S.
GRAGABER	192921	M			Oschfhr.,SS,Falstad Willan(Nor.) 8.-12.42	MURDER	NOR.
GRAGERT, Wilhelm	305149	M	Ger.	7. 5.11	Kriminalassist.,Kongsvinger(Nor.) 11.41-4.45	MISC.CRIMES	NOR.
GRAGGOBER, Hans	162159	M	Ger.	03	Civilian,Oberwolz(Aust.)	TORTURE	U.S.
GRAGNER, Benedict	192909	M		07	Member NSDAP,Salzburg(Aust.) 6.44	TORTURE	U.S.
GRAHN, Gerard	148138	M	Ger.		Zugwachtmeister,Police,SS,Bobruisk(Russ.) 42	MURDER	FR.
GRAHN, Paul	191867	M	Ger.		Zugwachtmeister der Schupo,7 Pol.Regt.,3 Pol.Bn.,10 Coy.,Junkerdal (Nor.) 10.44	TORTURE	NOR.
GRAIL	315	M	Ger.		Lt.,98 Regt.Mountain Troops,9 Coy.,2 Btty.22.-31.8.44	MURDER	FR.
GRALKA, Martha	148142	F		23. 8.09	Guard,KL.Buchenwald(Ger.) 44	MISC.CRIMES	FR.
GRAM	301863	M	Ger.		Osturmfhr.,Cmdt.of Camp KLA 11-2,Berlin. 8.8.43	MURDER	FR.
GRAMAT	148143	M			Cmdt.,KL.Natzweiler(Fr.) 26.12.43	MURDER	FR.
GRAMBOW, Robert	254104	M	Ger.		Capt.,Stalag IIIB,3 Coy.,348 Regt.,Maerkisch-Buchholz(Ger.) 2.45	TORTURE	FR.
GRAMBOW, Wolf	171643	M	Ger.		SS-Sturmmann,SS,C.C.Oranienburg-Sachsenhausen(Ger.)	MURDER	POL.
GRAMMAR	145401	M			Hptschfhr.,SS,C.C.Auschwitz(Pol.) 43-44	MURDER	U.S.

GRA - GRE

NAME	C.R.FILE NUMBER	SEX	NATIONALITY	DATE OF BIRTH	RANK OCCUPATION UNIT PLACE AND DATE OF CRIME	REASON WANTED	WANTED BY
GRAMMINGER	258575	M	Ger.		Pvt.,Guard,Army,Oflag VII A,Murnau (Ger.) 3.45	MURDER	POL.
GRAMSS, Alfred	171642	M	Ger.		Leader,Ernaehrung und Landwirtschaft,Amt des Gouverneurs, Warsaw (Pol.),9.39-44	MURDER	POL.
GRAMT, Bruno	149350	M	Ger.		C.C.Oberscardorf (Ger.)	TORTURE	FR.
GRANBINGER (see GRABINGER)	252318						
GRANDCHAMPS	144309	M			Pvt.,Coy.Brandenburg,Pont St.Esprit (Fr.)	MURDER	FR.
GRANDE	124484	M		03 or 07	Major,Flakkampftruppe,C.O.Batt. 1e Group Grande,Rheims (Fr.) 7.44	MURDER	U.S.
GRANDE, Josef	188254	M	Ger.		Deer-keeper,Gestapo,Brno (Czech.) 39-45	WITNESS	CZECH.
GRANDERAT	192163	M	Ger.		Pvt.,Fliegerkorps,Rintent (Fr.) 3.41	PILLAGE	FR.
GRANDKE, Helmut	125461	M	Ger.		Cpl.,C.C.Brand-Erbledorf,Freiburg (Ger.) 8.44	TORTURE	U.K.
GRANDOW, Kristian	194966	M	Ger.	23 or 24	Stalag III A,Kommand.296,Zermutzel (Ger.) 9.44	MURDER	FR.
GRANDZ	188837	M	Ger.	10	Lt.,Army,Montclus (Fr.) 6.44	PILLAGE	FR.
GRANEFUL, Fide	171641	M	Ger.		Warder er Kapo,C.C.Oranienburg,Sachsenhausen (Ger.) 39-4.45	MURDER	POL.
GRANET	149512	M	Ger.		Prison-Director,C.C.Chalons sur Marne (Fr.) 3.44	MURDER	FR.
GRANIK, Hermann	250191	M			Sturmmann,SS,C.C.Harzungen,Nordhausen (Ger.)	MURDER	U.S.
GRANJEAN	144556	M			Dr.,Guard,Pz.Gren.Div.Brandenburg,Pont St.Esprit (Fr.)	MURDER	FR.
GRANMANN	162663	M	Ger.		Lt.,Army,Wirges (Ger.) 3.45	PILLAGE	FR.
GRANZMULER	144555	M			SS-Gruppenfhr.,SS,(Fr.)	MISC.CRIMES	FR.
GRAP,E	67594	M	Ger.		Cmdt.(Rittmeister),SS-Leibst."Adolf Hitler",11 SS-Regt. "Deutschland",Nouan le Fuzelier (Fr.) 8.44	MURDER	FR.
GRAPENTHIN, Oskar	193157	M	Ger.	10	Pvt.,4 Coy.,P.O.W. Labour Bn.188,Fjell (Nor.) 5.44	MURDER	NOR.
GRAPKE, Richard	252996	M	Ger.		Lt.,Feldpol.Tr.533,Troyes (Fr.) 43-44	MISC.CRIMES	FR.
GRAPS	124208	M	Ger.		Pol.-Hptwachtmeister,Prison C.C.Fuehlsbuettel,Hamburg (Ger.)	TORTURE	NOR.
GRASHORN	149324	M			Civilian,C.C.Spitzwald (Pol.) 41	MURDER	FR.
GRASS	149322	M	Ger.		Member,NSDAP,Bad Kreuznach (Ger.)	TORTURE	FR.
GRASS	149323	M			Dr.,C.C.Hohenlychen (Ger.) 5.44	TORTURE	FR.
GRASS	252871	M			SS-Sturmmann,Member,S.D.,Toulouse (Fr.) 11.42-8.44	MISC.CRIMES	FR.
GRASS, Walter	188695	M	Ger.		Sgt.,Inf.Regt.28,116 BEL,Sombrun (Fr.)	MURDER	FR.
GRASSANO	254342	M			Lt.,Commd.2-16 Brandenburg 6 Regt.	INTERR.	U.S.
GRASSE, Mathias	187819	M		14. 1.96	Guard,4 SS-Totenkopf-Sturmbann,C.C.Dora Nordhausen (Ger.) 43-45	WITNESS	U.S.
GRASSE, Peter, dit le Tueur gen.:der Toeter	185948	M			Kapo,C.C.Stephanskirchen (Ger.)	MURDER	FR.
GRASSENSTEINER	161233	F	Ger.		Civilian,Recklinghausen (Ger.)	WITNESS	U.S.
GRASSHOFF, Karl	161322	M	Ger.		Army,Jubar,Magdeburg (Ger.) 4.45	MURDER	U.S.
GRASSIE, Stefan	260938	M	Ger.	17. 2.05	Oschfhr.,SS-Totenkopf,Guard,C.C.Auschwitz,Dachau (Pol.-Ger.) 41-45	BRUTALITY	POL.
GRASSLER, Jules (or GONTIER-LEREUX,Jaques)	144453	M		20	Gestapo,Nice (Fr.)	TORTURE	FR.
GRASSMANN	124747	M	Ger.		Administrator,SA-Standarte,Neususturm (Ger.)	MURDER	U.S.
GRASSMANN	256922	M			Labour-Supervisor,Civ.Muhldorf (Ger.)	MURDER	U.S.
GRASSMEL	253678	M	Ger.		Major,Div."Hermann Goering",Regt.Kdo.,4 Parachute-Rgt., (Regt.Grassmel),Helchteren (Bel.) 9.44	INTERR.	BEL.
GRASSY, Mathias	250194	M			Pvt.,C.C.Harzungen,Nordhausen (Ger.)	MURDER	U.S.
GRASTH, Joseph	254105	M	Ger.	5.10.22	Pvt.,Aube (Fr.) 8.44	PILLAGE	FR.
GRATH, Paul	134915	M			Civ.,C.C.Hartheim (Aust.) 40-44	MURDER	U.S.
GRATOPF, Hans	161339	M	Ger.	03	Pvt.,Krg.Gef.Arb.Bn.188,II Coy.,Asane-Hjortland near Bergen(Nor)42-43	MURDER	NOR.
GRATZ, Willi	250195	M			N.C.O.,C.C.Ellrich,Nordhausen (Ger.)	MURDER	U.S.
GRAU	316	M	Ger.		Camp Guard,Sgt.,Major,Army,Stalag VIII C,Kunau (Ger.)	TORTURE	POL.
GRAU	129624	M			Lt.,SS,C.C.Mauthausen (Aust.) 41-45	MURDER	U.S.
GRAU	301866	M			Chief,Capt.,1e Liaison-Staff Tarbes (Fr.) 6.44	MURDER	FR.
GRAUECKER, Hans	252997	M	Ger.		Cpl.,Interpreter,Gestapo,Prison,Troyes (Fr.) 43-44	MISC.CRIMES	FR.
GRAUBERT, Paul	255268	M	Ger.		N.C.O.,Fieldpolice,Annys Bois (Fr.) 7.-8.44	MISC.CRIMES	FR.
GRAUDERT	173455	M	Ger.		Major,469 Inf.Regt.,198 Inf.Div.,Le Tholy (Fr.) 11.44	PILLAGE	FR.
GRAUEL	176954	M	Ger.		Gestapo,C.C.Hannover (Ger.)	MURDER	U.S.
GRAUER	132661	M	Ger.		Cmdt.,Army,Oberkommando,Gerardmer (Fr.) 9.-11.44	MISC.CRIMES	FR.
GRAUER, Karl	262289	M	Ger.		Officer,Gerardmer and le Tholy (Fr.) 11.44	MISC.CRIMES	FR.
GRAUER, Robert Karl	259735	M	Ger.	24. 8.12	Major,Generalstabs-Offizier,198 Inf.Div.,Gerardmer,le Tholy, Voages (Fr.) 9.-11.44	INCENDIARISM	FR.
GRAUER, Wilhelm	301134	M	Ger.		Guard,Dorendorf Prison (Ger.) 10.7.43	BRUTALITY	FR.
GRAUERT	144551	M		10	Major,Army,198 Inf.Div.,Gerardmer, le Tholy (Fr.)	PILLAGE	FR.
GRAUL	149320	M			SS-Uschfhr.,C.C.Auschwitz (Ger.)	MISC.CRIMES	FR.
GRAUL, Erich	178275	M	Ger.	10	Inspector,Railway,Leipzig (Ger.)	MURDER	U.K.
GRAULS (or GRUEL or GROLL)	133787	M			SS-Oschfhr.,C.C.Buchenwald (Ger.)	TORTURE	U.S.
GRAUMANN, Rudolf	252870	M	Ger.	28. 1.25	Pvt.,558 Gren.Regt.,Bruay en Artas (Fr.) 1.9.44	MURDER	FR.
GRAUNCKE	123984	M	Ger.		Osturmfhr.,SS Gestapo,(Pol.) 1.40	MURDER	POL.
GRAUNE	161320	M	Ger.		Civ.,Badisheim near Friedburg (Ger.) 6.44	TORTURE	U.S.
GRAUNER (Alias:GRAENER)	173440	M	Ger.		Lagerfhr.,Gestapo,C.C.Oswiecim,Birkenau (Pol.)	MURDER	CZECH,POL, YUGO,FR,BEL,
GRAUPNER	144550	M			Cmdt.,C.C.,Bayet et St.Loup (Fr.)	TORTURE	FR.
GRAUSE	194237	M	Ger.	17	SS-Lt.,12 SS-Pz.Div."Hitler Jugend",26 SS-Pz.Gren.Regt.,1 Bn. (Ordonnanz-Offizier),near Caen (Fr.) 6.6.-8.7.44	TORTURE	CAN.
GRAUTER	301001	M	Ger.		Member of Staff,C.C.Struthof,Natzweiler (Fr.) 42-44	MURDER	FR.
GRAUTS	149319	M			Dr.,SS-San.-Obergruppenfhr.,C.C.Belves	MURDER	FR.
GRAV	145402	M			SS-Oberstumfhr.	MURDER	U.S.
GRAVE	177735	M			Sturmmann,SS,C.C.Muhldorf,Ampfing (Ger.)	MURDER	U.S.
GRAVER, Remmer	161362	M			Ortsgruppenleiter,NSDAP,Woltorf (Ger.) 44	MURDER	U.S.
GRAVITZ	133343	M	Ger.		Dr.,Director of the German,Civ. Red Cross (Ger.)	WITNESS	U.S.
GRAVITZ	149318	M			San.-Obergruppenfhr.,SS,C.C.Hohenlychen (Ger.)	TORTURE	FR.
GRAWITZ, Ernst Robert	62390	M	Ger.	00	SS-Obergruppenfhr.,SS,C.C.Buchenwald (Ger.) 43	MURDER	U.S.
GRAY	187818	M			SS-Hptsturmfhr.,C.C.Gross Rosen (Ger.) 4.43	MURDER	U.K.BEL.
GRAZIA	252872	M	Ger.		Sturmmann,Member,S.D.,Toulouse (Fr.) 11.42-8.44	MISC.CRIMES	FR.
GREB	72304	M	Ger.		Pvt.,Guard,Waffen-SS,C.C.Hinzert (Ger.) 43	TORTURE	U.S.
GREB	106906	M			Civ.owner of firm "Greb & Co.",Muehlheim (Ger.) 25.2.45	MURDER	U.S.
GREEE, August	161382	M			Civilian,C.C.Lauenforde (Ger.)	TORTURE	U.S.
GREBER	72305	M	Ger.	00	Foreman Prison Guard,Waffen-SS,C.C.Wittlich (Ger.) 41-42	TORTURE	U.S.
GREBES, Hubert Dick	301670	M	Ger.		Osturmfhr.,SS,Verdenne,Marenne et Marche en Famenne (Bel.) 6.9.44	MURDER	BEL.
GREDING	250196	M			Pvt.,C.C.Ellrich,Nordhausen (Ger.)	MURDER	U.S.

GRE-GRE

NAME	C.R.FILE NUMBER	SEX	NATIONALITY	DATE OF BIRTH	RANK OCCUPATION UNIT PLACE AND DATE OF CRIME	REASON WANTED	WANTED BY
GREK, Hermann	10067	M			Landwache, Friesack (Ger.) 6.44	MURDER	U.S.
GREEN, Willi	256616	M		26. 9.02	Employee, Bereitstellungslager I, C.C.Nordhausen (Ger.)	MURDER	U.S.
GREENWALD	123981	M		15	Cpl., Stalag Luft 4, C.C.Wittenberg (Ger.) 7.44-3.45	TORTURE	U.S.
GREEVE	262206	M	Ger.		Lt., Unit L.50.656 A, Steene (Fr.) 5.-7.44	INTERR.	FR.
GREEVEN	257226	M	Ger.		Capt., Army, Oflag VII A, Murnau (Ger.)	BRUTALITY	POL.
GREFFELMEIER	305798	M			Capt., Camp Cmdt., Abwehr, Oflag VI C, Osnabrueck-Ewersheide (Ger.) 41-44	MURDER	YUGO.
GREGER, Felix	146874	M	Ger.		Sturmmann, SS Panz.Div. "Das Reich", Moissac (Fr.) 44	MURDER	FR.
GREGOR	161397	M			Oberfaehnrich, Army, C.C. vicinity Gardelegen (Ger.) 4.45	MURDER	U.S.
GREGOR	254341	M	Ger.		Member of Gestapo-S.D., Toulouse (Fr.) 11.42-8.44	INTERR.	FR.
GREGOR, Vendelin	252116	M		00	Ortsgruppenleiter, NSDAP, Cermna Polni (Czech.)	TORTURE	CZECH.
GREGORCEWSKI, Erich (or GREGORZWESKI)	193155	M	Ger.	1. 1.02	Sgt.-Guard, Reichsjustizministerium, Feldstraflager, Waffen-SS, Finmark (Nor.) 42-45	MISC.CRIMES	NOR., YUGO.
GREGORY, Paul	161841	M	Ger.		Employee, Civ., Plattenberg (Ger.)	TORTURE	U.S.
GREGORZWESKI, Erich (see GREGORCEWSKI)	193155						
GREHAN (see GRAEHAN)	161223						
GREIBERG	173447	M	Ger.		Chief, Arbeitskommando, C.C.Brie (Fr.)	MURDER	FR.
GREIF, Edithe(nee KNISCH)	193510	F	Ger.	28. 6.13	Agent, Gestapo, Uhersky Brod (Czech.) 39-45	MISC.CRIMES	CZECH.
GREIF, Franz	176734	M		17	SS-Uschfhr., SS, Waldlager, C.C.Muehldorf-Ampfing (Ger.) 6.44-4.45	MURDER	U.S.
GREIF, Hans	193511	M	Ger.	19.11.07	Member of NSDAP, Uhersky Brod (Czech.) 39-45	MISC.CRIMES	CZECH.
GREIFELT	62186	M	Ger.	90	SS-Bdefhr., H.Q., Berlin (Ger.) 41	MURDER	SOV.UN.
GREIFELT, Ulrich	62380	M			Pvt., SS Official of Commiss.f.Germ.Racialism	MISC.CRIMES	UNWCC
GREIFENBERGER	305892	M			SS-Sturmbannfhr., att.Befehlshaber Sipo, Leading capacity, C.C. Oswiecim-Birkenau (Pol.) 39-45	MURDER	CZECH.
GREIFENEDER	252319	M		20	SS-Hptscharfhr., SS, Graz (Aust.) 4.45	MISC.CRIMES	U.K.
GREIFENSTEIN	149533	M			Dr., Prof., Stabsarzt, C.C.Hohenlychen (Ger.) 5.44	TORTURE	FR.
GREIFENSTEIN, Karl	258424	M			SS-Mann, Guard, SS, C.C.Ohrdruf (Ger.) 12.44-4.45	MURDER	U.S.
GREIFF	189025	M		00	Cpl., 559. L.Coy. on the march from Stalag VIII B to the west (Czech.)45	TORTURE	U.K.
GREIFF	306599	M	Ger.		Section IV S.D., Lyons and surroundings (Fr.) 11.43-8.44	MURDER	FR.
GREIFF, Max	174974	M	Ger.		SS	MURDER	FR.
GREIGER	133337	M			Hptsturmfhr., Waffen-SS, C.C. Flossenburg (Ger.)	MURDER	U.S.
GREIGER, Karl	161241	M	Ger.	24. 7.05	Cpl.(Interpreter), Army, Krg.Gef.Arb.Bn.24, Augsburg (Ger.) 40-4.45	MURDER	U.S.
GREIK, Nikolaus	187816	M		21. 4.96	SS-Uschfhr., 4.Totenkopf-Sturmbann, C.C.Dora-Nordhausen (Ger.) 43-45	WITNESS	U.S.
GREIL	250199	M			Flyer, Camp Ellrich, Nordhausen (Ger.)	MURDER	U.S.
GREIL, Anton	144547	M	Ger.		Lt., 11.Res.Geb.Jaeger Regt.198, Vercors (Fr.)	TORTURE	FR.
GREIM (see GRIEM)	306155						
GREIM, Wilhelm	250180	M			Pvt., Camp Ellrich, Nordhausen (Ger.)	MURDER	U.S.
GREIN, Fritz	171677	M		19.10.12	SS-Rottenfhr., SS, C.C. Natzweiler (Fr.) 43-44	MURDER	FR.
GREINER	10068	M			Army, Stalag 9, (Ger.)	TORTURE	CAN.,U.K.,YUGO
GREINER	193638	M	Ger.		Capt., Abwehr, Stalag IX C Hauptlager, C.C.Bad Sulza (Ger.) 8.42	MURDER	YUGO.CAN.
GREINER, Artur	250181	M			Pvt., Camp Ellrich, Nordhausen (Ger.)	MURDER	U.S.
GREINER, Heinrich	193044	M	Ger.		SS-Tdenkopfverband, C.C.Buchenwald (Ger.) 42-45	TORTURE	U.S.
GREINER, Heinz	261137	M		95	Gen.Major, Army.	WITNESS	U.S.
GREISEL	149543	M		05	Civilian, Junker-Werke, Schoensbeck (Ger.)	TORTURE	FR.
GREISHAMER	252115	M	Ger.		Dr., Chief foreign personnel, Siemens-Schuckert, Nuernberg (Ger.) 40-45	MURDER	FR.
GREISS	162655	M	Ger.	80	Member of Gestapo, Leipzig (Ger.)	MISC.CRIMES	FR.
GREISS, Gunther	189625	M			SS-Osturmfhr., C.C. Blinzyn (Pol.) 40	MISC.CRIMES	U.K.
GREK	183288	M			SS-Uschfhr., 4.Totenkopf-Sturmbann, C.C.Dora, Nordhausen (Ger.) 43-45	WITNESS	U.S.
GRELL, Alvin	306747	M			Civilian, near Wittmar (Ger.) 28.9.44	BRUTALITY	U.S.
GRELLACK	144545	M			SS-Rottenfhr., SS, Struthof (Fr.) 2.8.43	MURDER	FR.
GREMANN (or GERMAN)	161405	M	Ger.		Guard, Army, Oflag XIII B, Security Camp Hammelburg (Ger.) 23.3.45	MURDER	U.S.
GREMSBERGER, Franz	250189	M			Pvt., C.C.Bodungen, Nordhausen (Ger.)	MURDER	U.S.
GRENER	167381	M			Lt., Funkeinsatztr., Thiel sur Acolin, Montbegny, Chapeau (Fr.) 5.9.44	MURDER	FR.
GRENNIKLOH, Werner	256729	M	Ger.	31. 5.16	Employee, C.C. Nordhausen (Ger.)	MURDER	U.S.
GRENSWEIG	161225	M			Cpl., Army, Arb.Kdo., Tauermoos (Aust.)	TORTURE	U.K.
GRENTSCH	149544	M			Lt., 98.Regt.Chass.Alp., 2.Bn., 10.Coy., Chamberry (Fr.)	MURDER	FR.
GRENZER	119423	M	Ger.		Major, Cmdt. Unit under 36.Geb.Corps, 20.Army, Finmark (Nor.) 44	MURDER	NOR.
GREPS, Herta (or KRIEBBS)	135167	F	Ger.		Civ.Woman-Guard, C.C.Helmbrechts (Ger.)	MURDER	U.S.
GRESCHAG, Martin	171658	M			Pvt., 9.Gren.Res.Regt. Last Unit 4-181 1 Coy, Magny d'Anigon (Fr.) 18.9.44	MURDER	FR.
GRESCHNER, Paul	149509	M	Ger.		Pvt., SS, C.C. Hinzert (Ger.)	TORTURE	FR.
GRESLLA, Willi	130650	M			Civilian, C.C.Dora, Nordhausen (Ger.)	MURDER	U.S.
GRESS	129798	M	Ger		Staffelfhr., NSKK, Gross-Gerau (Ger.) 29.8.44	MURDER	U.S.
GRESS	250182	M			SS-Sturmann, Camp Wieda, Nordhausen (Ger.)	MURDER	U.S.
GRESSE, Martyn	161226	M	Ger.		Sgt., SS 16.Inf.Div., Camp Denouatre (Jandl), Maille (Fr.) 25.8.44	MURDER	FR.
GRESSE, Rudolf	188255	M	Ger.	7. 5.06	Crim.secretary, Gestapo, Brno (Czech.) 39-45	MURDER	CZECH.
GRESSEL	149510	M			Lagerfhr., Gestapo, C.C. Platte.	MISC.CRIMES	FR.
GRESSEL	251566	M		95	Overseer, C.C. Flossenburg (Ger.)	INTERR.	FR.
GRESSER	149535	M			Civilian, Chief of Quarry.	TORTURE	FR.
GREST	252129	M			Lt.Gen., Army, Fort Zinna, Torgau-Elbe (Ger.) 43-45	MISC.CRIMES	U.S.
GRETHER	252111	M	Ger.	10	Specialist Leader (Lt.) H.Q., 65.Div. Ponzano Magra-La Spezia (It.) 9.43	INTERR.	U.K.
GRETSCHKE, K.	250184	M			Pvt., Camp Ellrich, Nordhausen (Ger.)	MURDER	U.S.
GREUACK	174135	M	Ger.		SS-Rottenfhr., SS, C.C. Natzweiler (Fr.) 43-44	MURDER	U.K.
GREUBERT	163445	M	Ger.		Pvt., 10.Panz.Div.SS - 36.Regt., Revin (Fr.) 6.44	MURDER	FR.
GREUEL, Gustav	121223	M		93	Lt., C.C.Buchenwald (Ger.)	MURDER	FR.
GREUGER	250769	M	Ger.		Lt., 2606 Turkestan Bn., L'Ain (Fr.) 7.-8.44	MISC.CRIMES	FR.
GREUIL	119424	M	Ger.		Hptsturmfhr., Cmdt.3-6 SS Geb.Art.Regt.6, Geb.Div. Nord, 20.Army Finmark (Nor.) 10.44	MURDER	NOR.
GREUL, Anton	171681	M	Ger.		Crim.secretary, Gestapo, Brno (Ger.) 4.40	TORTURE	NOR.,UNWCC
GREUL, Walter	305632	M	Ger.	22. 9.12	Cpl., Kongsberg (Nor.) 8.11.42	MURDER	NOR.
GREULICH, Elfriede	149537	F		83	Camp Chief, Rheinmetall-Borsig, Hundsfeld-Breslau (Ger.) 10.42-1.45	TORTURE	FR.
GREULING, Eugen	188256	M	Ger.	00	Wachtmeister, Polizei, Eddersheim (Ger.) 42-45	TORTURE	POL.
GREVE	253025	M	Ger.		Sturmfhr., SS-Unit 120-95 A., Wormhoudt (Fr.) 14.5.44	WITNESS	FR.

GRE - GRI

NAME	C.R.FILE NUMBER	SEX	NATIONALITY	DATE OF BIRTH	RANK, OCCUPATION, UNIT, PLACE AND DATE OF CRIME	REASON WANTED	WANTED BY
GREVE (see NAVE)	196246						
GREVE	261913	M	Ger.		Assistant of Dr. Winterberg, SS, Leeuwarden Several places in Province of Friesland (Neth.) 11.42	MISC.CRIMES	NETH.
GREVE, Ernst	193153	M	Ger.	02	Sgt.,Guard, Reichsministerium,Feldstraflager,Finnmark (Nor.) 3.45	TORTURE	NOR. YUGO.
GREWE, Hans	189246	M	Ger.		Member, Gestapo, 8.41 Stanislawow (Pol.) 8.41-10.42	MURDER	POL.
GREZI	252214	M	Ger.		Cmdt. of women's Camp, SS - C.C. Auschwitz-Birkenau (Pol.) 42-45	MURDER	YUGO.
GRIBNITZ	255132	M			Cpl., Camp Harzungen, Nordhausen (Ger.)	MURDER	U.S.
GRIEBEL	194235	M	Ger.	20	SS-Sturmfhr., 12.SS-Panz.Div. "Hitler Jugend", 26.SS Panz.Gren.Rgt. Caen (Fr.) 6.-7.44	TORTURE	FR.
GRIEBEL, Julius	176735	M	Ger.		SS-Rottenfhr. 3.SS Totenkopf Brigarde, C.C. Weida (Ger.)	MURDER	U.S.
GRIEBEL, Siegfried	252993	M	Ger.	5.12.98	Employee, Gestapo, Breclav (Czech.) 39 - 45	MURDER	U.S. CZECH.
GRIEGER, Friedrich	300087	M	Ger.		Bunkerwart at Brunswick,(Ger.) 3.45	MURDER	CZECH.
GRIEGOLEIDIS	144537	M			Lt. Army, F.P. 42072 D, Polota (Sov.Un.)	MURDER	SOV.UN.
GRIEM	195127	M	Ger.		Hauptscharfhr. SD, Einsatz Kdo., St. Die (Fr.)44	MURDER	U.K.
GRIEM (or GREIM)	306155	M	Ger.		Attached KDO. Of Dr. Ernst, St. Die (Fr.) 9.44	MURDER	U.K.
GRIEPHAN	144539	M			17.SS-Div. 39.Brigarde, Blindee de Gren.,Montmirail (Fr.)	MURDER	FR.
GRIER	253677	M	Ger.		Oberarzt, Div. "Hermann Goering" 4.Rgt., Helchteren et Hechtel (Bel.) 9.44	PILLAGE	BEL.
GRIER, Gustav	171657	M	Ger.		Pvt. 9.Res.Gren.Rgt. Last Unit 4-Gew.Schuetzen Coy. Magny D'Anigon (Fr.) 18.9.44	MURDER	FR.
GRIES	190241	M	Ger.		Gestapo, H.Q. Koeln (Ger.) 43-45	MURDER	U.K.
GRIESBACH, Gerhard	167626	M	Ger.		Pvt., SS-Panz.Gren.Div. "Das Reich",St.Lya (Fr.) 12.6.44	MURDER	FR.
GRIESBERGER, Jan	252991	M	Ger.	15. 3.11	Gestapo, Breclav (Czech.) 39-45	TORTURE	CZECH.
GRIESE	250791	M	Ger.	86	Colonel, 14.Pol.Rgt., Ogulin (Yugo.)	MISC.CRIMES	YUGO.
GRIESENGER, Wilhelm	257974	M		11	Gauleiter, NSDAP, Muehldorf (Ger.)	MURDER	U.S.
GRIESER (or ROBERTS)	161227	M			Sgt.,Stalag III West Lager, Sagan (Ger.)	TORTURE	U.S.
GRIESHABER	250171	M			Camp Rossla, Nordhausen (Ger.)	MURDER	U.S.
GRIESHAMMER	186404	M		97	Pvt., 62.Landesschuetzen Bn., 1.Cie. C.C. Berga (Ger.) 2.or 3.45	MURDER	U.S.
GRIESINGER, Ludwig	194035	M	Ger.	4. 1.97	Official, Gestapo, Cheb (Yugo.) 39-45	MURDER	CZECH.
GRIETZSCH	147739	M			Gallenstift-Innsbruck (Aust.) 43	PILLAGE	FR.
GRIEZE	250790	M	Ger.		Colonel, 14.Pol.Rgt., Potok (Yugo.) 10.43	MISC.CRIMES	YUGO.
GRIFFEL, Erhard	126547	M	Ger.		Pvt., 92.Inf. Div. Anti-Tank Bn., Kreopelin (Ger.) 6.or 7.44	WITNESS	U.S.
GRIGAR, Adolf	188257	M	Ger.	17.6. 02	Employee, Gestapo, Brno (Czech.) 39-45	MURDER	CZECH.
GRIGAR, Franziska	188392	F	Ger.		Clerk, Gestapo, Brno (Czech.) 39-45	WITNESS	CZECH.
GRIGAR, Julius	255383	M	Ger.	90	Deputy, District Chief, NSDAP, Mikulov (Czech.)	MURDER	CZECH.
GRIGO, Fritz	193692	M	Ger.		Oberscharfhr., SA, Arnheim (Neth.)	PILLAGE	NETH.
GRIGO, Hedi	193693	F	Ger.		Civilian, Arnheim, (Neth.) 11.und 12.44	WITNESS	NETH.
GRIGOLEIT	194034	M	Ger.		Prison, Kaisheim (Ger.) 38-45	MURDER	CZECH.
GRILK (A),N	252419	M	Ger.		Capt., Fieldpolice, Bjelovar (Yugo.) 19.10.43	MURDER	YUGO.
GRILL	186403	M	Ger.		Hauptscharfhr., SS, C.C. Mauthausen,Gusen (Aust.)	TORTURE	U.S.
GRILL	157472	M	Ger.	00	SS, Merlebach,(Fr.)	TORTURE	FR.
GRILL	301561	M	Ger.		Sgt., Camp Guard at Gusen C.C.,where he worked in post office, Mauthausen (Aust.) 40-45	MURDER	BEL.
GRILLE	254340	M			Cpl., 7.- 3.Brandenburg.Rgt.	INTERR.	U.S.
GRILLO, Michel	161228	M			Member, Gestapo Charlons sur Marne, Dun les Places (Fr.)	MURDER	FR.
GRIMM	39643	M	Ger.		Capt., Infantrie Feldpost Nr. 33 632, Bernayan Champagne (Fr.) 3.-9.41	MISC.CRIMES	FR.
GRIMM (see GUIMM)	134892						
GRIMM	137630	M			Obersturmfhr. SS-OC-Kommando at Husum on the Danish Border, Husum (Ger.)	TORTURE	U.K.
GRIMM	144757	M	Ger.	06	Obersturmfhr. SS, C.C. Neuengamme, (Ger.)	TORTURE	FR. U.K.
GRIMM	157471	M	Ger.	03	Soldat, C.C. Stalag II C, Torgelow (Ger.) 43	TORTURE	FR.
GRIMM	169482	M	Ger.		Paymaster Army, Gotha (Ger.) 2.44	TORTURE	U.S.
GRIMM	184208	M			Camp Official, C.C. Dora Nordhausen, Plaszo (Ger.) 9.43 - 4.45	WITNESS	U.S.
GRIMM	195360	M	Ger.		SS - Obersturmfhr. C.C. Sachsenhausen (Ger.)	MURDER	BEL.
GRIMM	251026	M	Ger.		Untersturmfhr., Kriminalkommissar, SD, Hengelo (Neth.)	WITNESS	NETH.
GRIMM	252323	M	Ger.		SS - Hauptscharfhr.,Gestapo, Allarmont (Fr.) 15.9.44	MURDER	FR.
GRIMM	300088	M	Ger.		Kommando-Nord, Headquarters at Assen "Silbertanne" action at Groningen, Drente (Neth.) 43-45	MURDER	NETH.
GRIMM, August	306600	M	Ger.		Sturmfhr., SS, C.C. Neuengamme (Ger.) 2.40 - 4.45	MURDER	FR.
GRIMM, Hans	319720	M	Ger.		Dr., Oberlandgerichtsrat, Public Official, Litomerice (Czech.) 2.40	MURDER	CZECH.
GRIMM, Hans	190552	M	Ger.	05	SS-Sturmfhr., Asst. to the prison governor, C.C. Hambourg, Neuengamme (Ger.) 43	MURDER	U.S. YUGO.
GRIMM, Heinz	177589	M	Ger.		Sturmscharfhr., Secret. SD, Gestapo, Saerbruecken (Ger.)	PILLAGE	FR.
GRIMM, Philipp	161361	M	Ger.	09	Obersturmfhr., Waffen SS, Totenkopf-Sturmbann, C.C. Buchenwald, Dora-Nordhausen (Ger.) 41 - 42	MURDER	U.S.
GRIMM, Rudolf	306379	M	Ger.	12.10.05	SS-Mann, C.C. Buchenwald (Ger.) 5.38-10.43	MURDER	BEL.
GRIMM, Wilhelm	62391	M	Ger.		Reichsleiter, NSDAP	MURDER	UNWCC
GRIMM, Willy	185944	M	Ger.		Pvt., Army Feldpost Nr. 57 572, Besumenil-Vosges(Fr.) 9.und 10.44	PILLAGE	FR.
GRIMME	252311	M	Ger.		Staff - Sgt. Legion Turkestan, Carmaux (Fr.) 7.44	PILLAGE	FR.
GRIMMER	144528	M	Ger.		Agent, SD, Annecy (Fr.) 12.43	TORTURE	FR.
GRIMMER, Walter	250177	M			N.C.O. Camp Ellrich, Nordhausen (Ger.)	MURDER	U.S.
GRIMSBERG	12645	M	Ger.		Overseer, Berger, steel-industry Factory, Remscheid (Ger.) 5.44	MURDER	FR.
GRIN	121224	M	Ger.		Cpl., Legion Scandinave SS, Feldpost Nr. 20 821 D Montferrier (Fr.)7.44	PILLAGE	FR.
GRIN	199918	M	Ger.	09 - 10	Lagerfhr. C.C. Flossenburg (Ger.)	MURDER	FR.
GRINBAUM	157561	M			Chief of Bloc, C.C. Birkenau (Pol.)	TORTURE	FR.
GRINGEL	255123	M	Ger.		Lt. or Sturmfhr., Army or SS, Beusden (Neth.) 11.44	INTERR.	NETH.
GRINKE, Gottfried	199004	M	Ger.		Guard, C.C. Buchenwald (Ger.) 42 - 45	TORTURE	U.S.
GRISBERGER	133336	M			Hauptscharfhr., Waffen SS, C.C. Flossenburg (Ger.)	TORTURE	U.S.
GRISCOT	174134	M			Physician, Stalag VI A, C.C. Section III, Homberg-Hemer (Ger.)41-45	TORTURE	U.S.
GRISHAMMER	149545	M			Civilian - Direktor, Siemenswerke, Nuernberg (Ger.)	MISC.CRIMES	FR.
GRISSWINKLER	144527	M	Ger.		Agent SD, Carassonne (Fr.)	TORTURE	FR.
GRITCH	188896	M	Ger.		SD, Official, near Lyon (Fr.)	MURDER	FR.

GRI-GRO

NAME	C.R.FILE NUMBER	SEX	NATIO-NALITY	DATE OF BIRTH	RANK OCCUPATION UNIT PLACE AND DATE OF CRIME	REASON WANTED	WANTED BY
GRITZEN, Willem	127360	M			Member, NSDAP, Bohnheim (er.)	TORTURE	U.S.
GRITZKA	144762	M			Chief-leader, C.C. Hallendorf (Ger.) 40-45	MURDER	U.S.
GRITZNER	250178	M			SS-Pvt., Camp Osterhagen-Ellrich, Nordhausen (Ger.)	MURDER	U.S.
GRNA, Franz	253008	M	Ger.	4. 1.88	Civilian, Tobacconist, Knezdub-Moravia (Czech.) 39-45	MISC.CRIMES	CZECH.
GROB	149546	M			Civilian, Melun (Fr.) 8.44	MURDER	FR.
GROB, Paul	146873	M	Ger.		SS-Mann, SS-Pz.Div."Das Reich",13 Coy, Moissac (Fr.) 44	MURDER	FR.
GROBAREK, Karl	171656	M	Ger.		Pvt.,Gew.Schuetze, 9 Res.Gren.Rgt., last Unit 4-1 B 1, Magny D'Avignon (Fr.) 9.44;	MURDER	FR.
GROBB	192065	M	Ger.	12	Pvt.,Arbeits-Kdo.52, Stalag XX B, C.C. Meichterswalde (Ger.) 22.9.43	MURDER	U.K.
GROBBE	305857	M	Ger.		Pvt.,1 Aufkl.Abt., 3 Coy, 2 Col.,XV Div. Afrika Korps, St.Leger Distr.Arlon (Bel.) 5.9.44	MISC.CRIMES	BEL.
GROBE	141480	M	Ger.		Attenbach in Wissental (Ger.)	TORTURE	FR.
GROCH, Agnes	149547	F			Civilian, Wuestensack Krs.Fulda (Ger.)	MISC.CRIMES	FR.
GROEGER	174969	M	Ger.	25.12.44	Lt., Army, (It.) 25.12.44	MURDER	U.S.
GROEMIG or GROEMING	195634	M	Ger.		Major, Schupo, Duesseldorf (Ger.)	INTERR.	U.K.
GROENER	62187	M			Camp-officer (Capt.), C.C. Stalag VI B or VI G (Ger.)	TORTURE	FR.
GROENHEIM, Guenther	161240	M			Sgt., 29 Flak-Rgt., between Hausen and Ginnheim (Ger.) 9.44	MURDER	U.S.
GROENWALD	12646	M	Ger.		Obermatrose, 4 Btty. Navy Art.,Quiberon (Fr.) summer 44	MURDER	FR.
GROENWALDT, Karl	306748	M	Ger.		Kreisamtsleiter, nr.Pingelshagen (Ger.) 21.6.44	MURDER	U.S.
GROER, Herta	188390	F	Ger.	16	Clerk, Gestapo, Brno (Czech.) 39-45	WITNESS	CZECH.
GROESCHER, Jakob	260939	M	Ger.	12. 2.11	Kapo, C.C. Auschwitz (Pol.) 40-45	MURDER	POL.
GROESCHL, Adolf	252133	M	Ger.	08	Civilian, Lives Reservelaz, Linz A, Budejovice (Czech.)	INTERR.	CZECH.
GROESSL	176727	M			Civilian, Org.Todt, C.C. Mahldorf, Ampfing (Ger.) 6.44-4.45	MURDER	U.S.
GROETZ	149352	M			Col., Stalag 369 Kobierzyn (Pol.)	MISC.CRIMES	FR.
GROETZ	149550	M		00	Member, SS, Gestapo, Strusenheim (Ger.)	MISC.CRIMES	FR.
GROETZINGER, Alois	306702	M	Ger.		Native of Strasbourg, Masnil-St.Blaise (Bel.) 5.-6.9.44	MURDER	BEL.
GROS	144523	M			Capt.,SS-Div."Das Reich", III Bn,,Justinclas,Marsoules (Fr.)	TORTURE	FR.
GROH	149549	M	Ger.		Oberarbeitsarzt, C.C. Hohenlychen, Ravensbrueck (Ger.)16.-18.5.44	TORTURE	FR.
GROH, Rudolf	252133	M	Ger.		Civilian, Mayor of Svedlar-Slovakia (Czech.)	MURDER	CZECH.
GROHE	305869	M	Ger.		Chief, Military administration,Brussels,Pessoux(Cinney), (Bel.) 27.8. and 9.44	MURDER	BEL.
GROHE, Ludwig	195107	M	Ger.		Civilian (Lux.)	MISC.CRIMES	LUX.
GROHMAN	305152	M	Ger.		Capt. or Naval commander, Liaison officer, SS, Calavrita,Mega,Apileon,Aghia Lavra (Grc.) 13.12.43	MURDER	GRC.
GROHMANN	193154	M	Ger.		Sgt., Schupo, C.C. Falstad (Nor.) 41-45	MURDER	NOR.
GROHMANN	193637	M	Ger.		Dr.,Reichskommissar Leiter, Festigung Deutschen Volkstums, Lidice (Czech.) 42-44	MISC.CRIMES	CZECH.
GROHSKLES, Gottfried or GROHSKLOS	162798	M	Ger.		Arbeitskommando Adolf Mine, Foreman C.C. Merkstein (Ger.) 6.44	MURDER	U.S.
GROHSSCHMIED, Stefan	252878	M	Ger.	12. 8.93	Dr.,Deputy-chief, Executive of District Mikulov, Raksice (Czech.) 38-45	MURDER	CZECH.
GROHT	161528	M	Ger.	12	Hptscharfhr.,SS, C.C. Lublin (Pol.) 42-43	TORTURE	U.S.
GROIS, Alois	192920	M	Ger.		Policeman, C.C.Falstad near Drontheim (Nor.) 6.-8.42	MURDER	NOR.
GROLL see GRAULS	133787						
GROLL	255377	M			Sgt.,SS, Buchenwald (Ger.)	MURDER	U.S.
GROLNEN, Hermann	191829	M	Ger.		Head, Gestapo, Paris (Fr.) 42	TORTURE	B.K.
GROM	146872	M	Ger.		Interpreter, SD, Annecy (Fr.) 44	MURDER	FR.
GRONAU	1387	M			Asst.,Naval-Supply	MURDER	U.K.
GRONAU	193490	M	Ger.		Cpl.,1 Kriegsgefangenen Bn 41,Nerlandsdal Kristiansund (Nor.) 41-45	TORTURE	NOR.
GRONEMANN	190396	M	Ger.		Dr.,physician-public health official, State health administration, Wiesbaden (Ger.) 43-45	MURDER	U.S.
GRONEN, Peter	161245	M	Ger.		Civilian, owner of textile factory, Rhein-Wollwerke, Monschau near Aachen (Ger.) 29.7. to 9.44	TORTURE	U.S.
GRONER or GROSSER	250179	M			Pvt.,Camp Harzungen, Nordhausen (Ger.)	MURDER	U.S.
GRONHORST, Heinrich	149235	M			Police-chief, Remscheidl (Ger.)	TORTURE	FR.
GRONIG, Hermann	250190	M			Flyer, Camp Ellrich, Nordhausen (Ger.)	MURDER	U.S.
GRONING, Hartwig	62173	M	Ger.	16. 9.26	Pvt., Ger.Army, Courlandon (Fr.) 22.8.44	MURDER	FR.
GROOSWANDT, Hans	192103	M	Ger.	10.12.08	Employee, Gestapo, Jicin (Czech.) 43-44	TORTURE	CZECH.
GROOTZ, Frederic	261352	M	Ger.		Gendarme, Drusenheim (Fr.)	BRUTALITY	FR.
GROPEL, Jakob	188391	M	Ger.	13	Crim.employee, Gestapo, Brno (Czech.) 39-45	TORTURE	CZECH.
GROS	149241	M			Agent, Gestapo, Foix (Fr.)	TORTURE	FR.
GROS	252137	M	Ger.		SS-Hptscharfhr.,Sipo, Groningen, Camp Westerbork (Neth.) 9.-12.44	MURDER	NETH.
GROSAM, William	67854	M			Pvt., Army, 396 Landes-Schz.Bn,2 Coy,C.C. Auschwitz, Dresden (Pol.,Ger.) 28.7.44	TORTURE	U.K.
GROSCH	145404	M			Civilian, C.C. Ottmannshausen (Ger.) 8.44	MURDER	U.S.
GROSCH	252877	M	Ger.		SS-Sturmfhr., Construction eng., Prague (Czech.) 40-45	INTERR.	CZECH.
GROSCH	255376	M			Scharfhr., C.C. Buchenwald, Weimar (Ger.) 8.44	MURDER	U.S.
GROSCH, K.	145404	M			Civilian, Ottmanshausen Czech.) 7.-8.44	MURDER	U.S.
GROSCH, Wolfgang	161489	M		07	Sturmbannfhr., Waffen-SS,Section I Staff, C.C. Buchenwald,Ohrdruf (Ger.) 41-45	WITNESS	U.S.
GROSHAM (or IKOSHAM)	106955	M	Ger.		Guard, Kdo.1261, C.C. Auschwitz, Dresden (Pol.,Ger.) 27.7.44	TORTURE	U.K.
GROSHAM	144519	M			Lt., Army, Boismont (Fr.)	MURDER	FR.
GROSJEAN	144518	M			Agent, Milice and Gestapo, Autun (Fr.)	MURDER	FR.
GROSKE	144517	M				PILLAGE	FR.
GROSKOPH (F), Herbert	251032	M	Ger.		Lt.,10 Coy,377 Jaeger-Rgt.	MURDER	BEL.
GROSKOPP	67597	M			Lt., Army, Aide de Camp d'General Elster, Dax (Fr.) 13.6.44	MURDER	FR.
GROSNIEDEN	149300	M			Gendarm, Gendarmerie, Langgonst (Ger.)	MURDER	FR.
GROSS	12463	M	Ger.		Dr., Hauptverbindungsstab Nr.588,Oradour by Glane (Fr.) 10.6.44	MURDER	POL.
GROSS	36683	M	Ger.		Rottenfhr., SS, C.C. Belsen (Ger.)	TORTURE	POL.
GROSS	123988	M		03	Capt., Stalag 3 B, Fuerstenberg-Oder (Ger.) 2.2.45	MISC.CRIMES	U.S.
GROSS	141430	M			Lt.,Army, 95 Rgt. Security 5,P.12 Coy,St.Flour (Fr.) 24.-26.8.44	MISC.CRIMES	FR.
GROSS	144515	M			Dr., Medicin Col.,Army, Hauptverbindungsstab 588,Clermont-Ferrand (Fr.) 12.4.44 and 6.-8.45	MURDER	FR.
GROSS	144516	M			Capt., Army, Pau (Fr.)	MURDER	FR.
GROSS	149301	M			Osturmbannfhr.,SS,C.C.Hohenlychen, Ravensbrueck (Ger.)16.-18.5.44	TORTURE	FR.
GROSS	149302	M			Sturmbannfhr., SS, Berlin (Ger.)	TORTURE	FR.
GROSS	149309	M	Ger.	07	Arb.Kdo.,chief d'Equipe,Vienna (Aust.)	MISC.CRIMES	FR.
GROSS	168519	F	Ger.	12	SS-Lagerfuehrerin, C.C. Bunzlau, Dora-Nordhausen (Ger.)	MURDER	UNWCC.
GROSS	173436	M	Ger.		Lt.,Army, Macva, Sabac (Yugo.) 41	MURDER	YUGO.

GRO - GRO

NAME	C.R.FILE NUMBER	SEX	NATIO NALITY	DATE OF BIRTH	RANK OCCUPATION UNIT PLACE AND DATE OF CRIME	REASON WANTED	WANTED BY
GROSS	188220	M	Ger.		Osturmbannfhr.,SS,Konstanz (Ger.) 24.6.44	MURDER	U.S.
GROSS	195126	M	Ger.		Hptschfhr.,Leibstandarte Adolf Hitler Div.,1.Coy.,Wormhoudt (Fr.,Bel.) Border 27.5.40	MURDER	U.K.
GROSS	250107	M			Rottfhr.,SS,Camp Mackenrode,Nordhausen (Ger.)	MURDER	U.S.
GROSS	250774	M			W.O.,Reg.Def.Bn.,Camp,Friedrichstal (Ger.) 6.44	WITNESS	U.S.
GROSS	250792	M	Ger.		N.C.O.,German Army,Nuernberg (Ger.) 41-45	MISC.CRIMES	YUGO.
GROSS	252119	M	Ger.		Usturmfhr.,SS,Unit SS Dienststelle F.P. 23474 E,Aigues Rives (Fr.)2.-3.44	PILLAGE	FR.
GROSS	253672	M		07	Standertenfhr.,SS,C.C. Dora,Nordhausen (Ger.)	BRUTALITY	FR.
GROSS	254506	M	Ger.		Dir.,the labour exchange,Kragujevav (Yugo.) 43	MISC.CRIMES	YUGO.
GROSS	258032	M			Guard,C.C.,Mauthausen (Aust.) 39-45	MURDER	FR.
GROSS	300089	M	Ger.		Member of staff,C.C.,Mauthsusen (Aust.) 11.42-5.45	MURDER	FR.
GROSS	301562	M	Ger.		R.A.D.Fhr.,Sgt.,SS,Camp,Guard at Gusen,C.C.Mauthausen (Aust.)40-45	MURDER	BEL.
GROSS	305153	M	Ger.		Standertenfhr.,SS,C.C.,Dora,Buchenwald (Ger.) 43-4.45	MURDER	FR.
GROSS	306261	M	Ger.		Oberwachtmeister,Gendarmerie Post at Viktring Carinthia (Aust.) 2.45	MURDER	U.K.
GROSS	306968	M	Ger.		Employee,C.C.,Vught, (Neth.) 43-44	MURDER	NETH.
GROSS, Gerard	161206	M	Ger.10 - 14		Officer,Gestapo,F.F.No. 05104 B or 85104 B,Cotes du Nord Uzel,(Fr.) 14.6.44	TORTURE	FR.
GROSS, Helmuth	144513	M	Ger.		Sturmbannfhr.,SS,Major,Dienststelle 34356,Vienne (Fr.)	TORTURE	FR.
GROSS, Helmuth	190529	M	Ger.		Capt.,950.Rgt. Indian Infantry,81.Div.,La Roche Posay (Fr.)27.-29.8.44	MURDER	FR.
GROSS, Herbert	252321	M		14	Sgt.,z.b.V. Kommando 31,Valasske,Mezirici (Czech.) 2.-5.45	MURDER	CZECH.
GROSS, Jean	1388	M			Pvt.,Army,194.Gren.Rgt.,2.Fl.,6.Sec.	MURDER	U.K.
GROSS, Johann	72307	M	Ger.		Pvt.,Fallschirmjaeger Bn.,Roermond (Neth.) 11.44-1.45	TORTURE	U.S.
GROSS, Josef	67599	M		24. 4.21	Sturmfhr.,SS,Struthof (Fr.)	WITNESS	FR.
GROSS, Karl	89591	M			Doctor,Sturmbannfhr.,SS,(Ger.)	TORTURE	U.N.W.C.C.
GROSS, Karl	149249	M			Civilian,Geisweid(Ger.)	MISC.CRIMES	FR.
GROSS, Karl	305154	M	Ger.		Foreman,Cement works,Kommando 1040 Stalag IX A,Geisweid (Ger.) 40-45	MISC.CRIMES	FR.
GROSS, Kurt	251960	M		16	Doctor,Sturmbannfhr.,SS,Radolfzell (Ger.) 20.7.44	MURDER	U.S.
GROSS, Oscar	163444	M	Ger.		Cpl.,SS,Detachement de Russes Blancs,Revin (Fr.) 6.44	MURDER	FR.
GROSS, Otto	126490	M		05	Chief inspector,(Oberwachtmeister,Gendarmerie,C.C.German Reserve at Colmar-Berg,Biertringen (Lux.) 7.44	TORTURE	U.S.
GROSS, Walter	62389	M	Ger.		Hauptdienstleiter,NSDAP,Head Racial office	MISC.CRIMES	U.N.W.C.C.
GROSS, Walter	251578	M	Ger.		Sgt.,Techn.Btty.,Nr.5.,3.Coy.,St.Macaire (Fr.) 24.8.44	MURDER	FR.
GROSS, Walter	257942	M	Ger.		Uschfhr.,SD,Foix (Fr.) 11.42	MISC.CRIMES	FR.
GROSS, Walter	300091	M	Ger.		Schfhr.,SS,SD at St.Girons,Ariege (Fr.) 11.42-8.44	MURDER	FR.
GROSS, Wilhelm	132312	M	Ger.		Civilian,	TORTURE	U.S.
GROSS, Wilhelm	174785	M	Ger.15 - 21		Cpl.,Army,Bronzolo (It.) 9.43	WITNESS	U.K.
GROSSCHUPP, Elie	31920	M	Ger.		Sgt.,Army,Nantes (Fr.) 7.44	TORTURE	U.N.W.C.C.
GROSSE	145405	M			Civilian,Ottmanshausen (Ger.) 8.44	MURDER	U.S.
GROSSE, Alfred	177740	M	Ger.		Hptschfhr.,Waffen SS,C.C.,Ohrdruf (Ger.)	MURDER	U.S.
GROSSE, Arthur (or HATJE)	195305	M			Chief,Kapo,Schandelah,Braunschweig (Ger.) 44-45	MURDER	BEL.
GROSSE, Ferdinand	305549	M	Ger.		Member,C.C.,Staff,Hannover,Ahlem,Stocken (Ger.) 44-45	MURDER	U.K.
GROSSE, Heinz	193006	M	Ger.		Kapo,Buchenwald (Ger.)	SUSPECT	U.S.
GROSSE, Karl	171639	M	Ger.		Warder of Kapo,C.C.,Oranienburg,Sachsenhausen (Ger.) 39-4.45	MURDER	POL.
GROSSE, Karl	187686	M	Ger.		Doctor,Dept.of Finance Bohemia-Moravia, office of Reichsprotector (Czech.)	TORTURE	U.N.W.C.C.
GROSSE, Kurt	144777	M	Ger.		Civilian,Stammham (Ger.) 45	TORTURE	U.S.
GROSSER	139803	M		05	Cpl.,Waffen SS,Arbeitskommando A 6,Buchenwald (Ger.)	MURDER	U.S.
GROSSER (see GRONER)	250179						
GROSSER, Ernst	132313	M	Ger.14. 2.95		Lt.Col.,Stalag 3444Lamsdorf (Ger.) 3.45	MISC.CRIMES	U.S.
GROSSER, Hans	306380	M	Ger.		Cpl.,SS,C.C.,Buchenwald (Ger.) 16.5.38-9.10.43	MURDER	BEL.
GROSSERT, Oswald	195304	M	Ger.20.11.03		Sturmschfhr.,SS,Secretaer,Gestapo,Niederdorfelden,Hanau,Hainmuehle near Marburg (Ger.) 42	MURDER	POL.
GROSSHARTLAG, Anton	250776	M	Ger.		Cafetier,Altenmelle (Ger.) 3.45	BRUTALITY	FR.
GROSSHENNIG	149250	M			Civilian,Paris (Fr.)	PILLAGE	FR.
GROSSKETTLER	144763	M			Oberstabsintendant,Army OKW,Subsection IV P.W.Affairs	MISC.CRIMES	U.S.
GROSSKOPF	319	M	Ger.		Sturmbannfhr.,SS,leader,SIPO, 40	MURDER	POL.
GROSSKOPF, Hans	12430	M	Ger.		Pvt.,Army,Panz.Gren.Rgt.110 or 111,Albine (Fr.) 29.6.44	MURDER	FR.
GROSSLE, Tilo	257818	M	Ger.		Oschfhr.,SS,SD,Foix (Fr.) 11.42-8.44	MURDER	FR.
GROSSMAN	149251	M			Civilian,D.W.M. Luebeck-Schlutup	TORTURE	FR.
GROSSMANN	161523	M	Ger.		Sgt.,6-5 Marine Art.Abt.,Torreilles (Fr.) 20.8.44	MURDER	FR.
GROSSMANN	171680	M	Ger.		Usturmfhr.,SS,Gestapo, (Nor.) 4.40	TORTURE	NOR.
GROSSMANN	250168	M	Ger.		Pvt.,Camp Ellrich,Nordhausen (Ger.)	MURDER	U.S.
GROSSMANN	251581	M	Ger.		Hauptwachtmeister,Schupo,3.Coy.,near Arnheim (Neth.) 3.45	MURDER	NETH.
GROSSMANN	300529	M	Ger.		Lt.,German Garrison,Milna,Island of Brac (Yugo.) 1.-3.44	MISC.CRIMES	YUGO.
GROSSMANN	305858	M	Ger.		Pvt.,1.Aufkl.Abt.,3.Coy.,2.Col.,XV.Div.,Afrika Korps,St.Leger (Arlon) 5.9.44	MISC.CRIMES	BEL.
GROSSMANN, Hermann	161223	M	Ger.	01	Osturmfhr.,SS Totenkopf Sturmbann,Bochum,Wernigerode (Ger.)42-45	TORTURE	U.S.
GROSSMANN, Hermann (Der Spiess)	255263	M	Ger.		Sgt-Major,(W.O.1) Army,Heusden (Neth.) 11.44	MISC.CRIMES	NETH.
GROSSMANN, Willy (alias: ABENDSCHOEN, Willy)	257315	M	Ger.27. 8.05		(Czech.)		
GROSSTE	256095	M	Ger.		Oschfhr.,SS,SD,St.Girons (Fr.) 11.42-8.44	MURDER	FR.
GROSZ	261353	F	Ger.		Capt.,Rgt.z.b.V. Col.Wolff Bn.Grosz,Environs de Maulson, Navarreux (Fr.) 6.-8.44	MURDER	FR.
GROSZER	252313	M	Ger.		Uschfhr.,SS,C.C.,Auschwitz (Pol.)	MURDER	FR.
GROSZERODE, Herman	300090	M	Ger.		Guard Kdo.,Mastholte-Westf.,(Ger.) 42-45	TORTURE	BEL.
GROTE	139938	M		10	Osturmfhr.,Waffen SS,Ohrdruf (Ger.) 12.44-4.45	MURDER	U.S.
GROTELUESCHEN, Adolf	251561	M	Ger.		Sgt.,377.Jaeger Rgt.,Vinkt-Meigem (Bel.) 25.-31.5.40	MISC.CRIMES	BEL.
GROTEWOLD, Heinz	144782	M	Ger. 4. 9.21		Uschfhr.,SS,Army Aufkl.Abt.mot.6,Lingen (Ger.)	TORTURE	FR.
GROTH	12654	M	Ger.		Oschfhr.,SS,Gestapo H.Q.,Bergen (Nor.) 41	TORTURE	NOR.
GROTH	163440	M	Ger.	13	Hptschfhr.,SS,Buchenwald (Ger.) 39-45	WITNESS	U.S.
GROTH, Ferdinand	250169	M	Ger.		Uschfhr.,SS,Camp Dora,Nordhausen (Ger.)	MURDER	U.S.
GROTH, Otto	195105	M	Ger.		Doctor,Member,SS,(Lux.)	MISC.CRIMES	LUX.
GROTHE	166256	M	Ger.		Chief,SD,R.S.H.A.,C.C.,Sachsenhausen (Ger.) 42	MISC.CRIMES	U.S.

NAME	C.R.FILE NUMBER	SEX	NATIO-NALITY	DATE OF BIRTH	RANK OCCUPATION UNIT PLACE AND DATE OF CRIME	REASON WANTED	WANTED BY
GROTHE	191628	M	Ger.		Prof. Dr., Ostgebietsministerium Rosenberg, Einsatzstab, Paris (Fr.) 40-44	PILLAGE	FR.
GROTHE, Heinrich	250170	M			Pvt., Camp Ellrich, Nordhausen (Ger.)	MURDER	U.S.
GROTHE, Hindrik	163441	M	Ger.	10	SS Osturmfhr., C.C.Ohrdruf, Buchenwald (Ger.) 39-45	WITNESS	U.S.
GROTHE, T.	1389	M	Ger.		Pvt., Army, 194.Inf.Rgt.	MURDER	U.K.
GROTHE, Walter	257654	M	Ger.	95	Major, Abwehr-Nebenstelle, Bergen (Nor.)	WITNESS	NOR.
GROTHE, Wilhelm	195920	M	Ger.		Civ., Berlin-Reinickendorf (Ger.) 21.6.44	MURDER	U.S.
GROTHEER, Hans	171655	M	Ger.		Pvt., 9.Res.Gren.Rgt., Last Unit 3-181, Gew.Schtz. 1.Coy., Magny d'Anigon (Fr.) 18.9.44	MURDER	FR.
GROTHER, Jonny	305156	M	Ger.		Sgt., Culembourg (Neth.) 10.11.44	MISC.CRIMES	NETH.
GROTHOF	305984	M	Ger.		Capt.Abwehroffiz.,attached to Oflag X-A in Itzehoe, then Oflag X-C, Luebeck, Itzehoe nr.Hamburg, Luebeck 39-41, 42-45	MURDER	POL.
GROTHUSMANN, Joseph	252488	M	Ger.	90	Capt., Army, Artillery - Stalag XX A Hannover (Ger.)	INTERR.	U.K.
GROTZINGER, Georg	255133	M			Pvt., Camp Ellrich, Nordhausen (Ger.)	MURDER	U.S.
GROUPMAN, Gabriel	173448	M	Ger.		SS Rottfhr., Kuechenleiter, Waffen SS, C.C. Thekla nr.Leipzig (Ger.) 18.4.45	MURDER	FR.
GROUSE or KRAUSS	125463	M	Ger.		Ortsgruppenleiter NSDAP, Hieflau (Aust.) 3.45	MURDER	U.S.
GROUZE	141313	M	Ger.		Lt., Army, Stalag XVIII A C.C. Gummern, Villach (Aust.) 44	MURDER	U.K.
GROVANNI	48622	M	Ger.	16	Lt., 12.Coy., 29.Gren.Rgt. It.	WITNESS	U.K.
GROVZ	149252	M			Cmdt., Commandantur of St.Flour, Coren (Fr.) 24.8.44	MURDER	FR.
GROWER H.D.F.B.	146187	M	Ger.		Sgt., Munitions-Depot, Unit L 37419 E, Bousu (Bel.) 44	INCENDIARISM	BEL.
GROYER	169442	M			SS, Voeght (Neth.)	MURDER	FR.
GRUBBE	192172	M	Ger.		Member Geheime Feldpolizei, Brussels (Bel.)	MISC.CRIMES	BEL.
GRUBE	124203	M	Ger.		Hauptwachtmeister, Dreibergen Prison, Buetzow (Ger.)	TORTURE	NOR.
GRUBE	125699	M	Ger.		Lt., Army, La Rochelle (Fr.) 44-45	TORTURE	FR.
GRUBE	191945	M	Ger.		Major, Stalag Luft VI C.C. Hegdeburg (Ger.) 27.4.44, 27.5.44	MURDER	U.S.
GRUBE	251025	M	Ger.		S.A., C.C.Buchenwald (Ger.)	BRUTALITY	FR.
GRUBE	305414	M	Ger.		Engineer, S.A.Leipzig, C.C. Buchenwald (Ger.) 42-45	MURDER	FR.
GRUBECK	261219	M	Ger.		Lt., 5-I N.Rgt.211, 139.Arbeits-Bereich Liane, Alleur-Lez-Liege (Bel.) 4.9.44	MURDER	BEL.
GRUBEL, Gottfried	907118	M	Ger.		Foreman, C.C. Auschwitz (Pol.) 43-45	BRUTALITY	POL.
GRUBER	119425	M	Ger.		Major, Army, 550.Nachr.Rgt. 20. Army, Finnmark (Nor.) 44	MURDER	NOR.
GRUBER	133353	M			Oscharfhr., Waffen SS, C.C. Flossenburg (Ger.)	MURDER	U.S.
GRUBER	179449	M	Ger.		Cpl., Reichs-military-court, Dax (Fr.) 13.6.44	MURDER	FR.
GRUBER	185945	F	Ger.		Woman-guard, C.C. Flossenburg (Ger.) 42-45	MURDER	FR.
GRUBER	252312	M	Ger.		SS Hptscharfhr., C.C. Auschwitz - Birkenau (Pol.)	MISC.CRIMES	FR.
GRUBER	252315	M	Ger.		Capt., Airforce, 63.Rgt. 3.Bn. 14.Coy., Chateauneuf d'Isere (Fr.) 15.-31.8.44	BRUTALITY	FR.
GRUBER	253004	M	Ger.		Head, police-station Leutershausen (Ger.) 43-45	BRUTALITY	POL.
GRUBER	259668	M	Ger.		Crim.secretary, SIPO IV E, Brussels (Bel.)	INTERR.	BEL.
GRUBER	260124	M	Ger.		Paymaster, 1.Artillery-Rgt. d.Res., Massif du Vercors, Isere and Drôme (Fr.) 20.7.-5.8.44	SUSPECT	FR.
GRUBER	260612	M	Ger.		Major, Formation Pferdetrossabtlg., Dunes des Plages-Nievre (Fr.)6.44	MURDER	FR.
GRUBER	901980	M			Oslo (Nor.) from may 42	MURDER	NOR.
GRUBER, Alois	258211	M		25. 9.86	Former mayor, state service, Martinszell (Ger.) 18.7.44	MURDER	U.S.
GRUBER, Franz	120629	M	Ger.		Cpl., Army, Stalag 17 B C.C. Flaxberg-Tulln (Ger.) 12.43-44	MISC.CRIMES	U.K.
GRUBER, Hans	144781	M		27. 1.26	Sturmmann, SS, Lingen (Ger.)	MURDER	FR.
GRUBER, Karl	186400	M		98	Leader NSDAP, Prague (Czech.)	MISC.CRIMES	CZECH.
GRUBER, Norbert	252308	M		1. 6.94	NSDAP, Amstetten (Aust.) 20.3.45	INTERR.	U.S.
GRUBER, Otto	195088	M	Ger.	21.12.94	SS Usturmfhr., Commander of SS, Kraslite (Czech.) 38-45	MISC.CRIMES	CZECH.
GRUBER, Peter	67598	M	Ger.		Cpl., Army, Dax (Fr.)	MURDER	FR.
GRUBERS	136322	M			2.SS Pz.Div."Das Reich", Venarque, Le Vernet (Fr.) 44	MURDER	FR.
GRUBERT	187769	M			Master, Arbeitskommando, Firm of Heinrich Butzer, Aspfjord (Nor.)	TORTURE	NOR.
GRUBL, Ewald	141481	M		19. 4.24	Chenebier-Etobon (Fr.) 27.9.44	MURDER	FR.
GRUBLER	149253	M			Civ., Meulun (Fr.)	MURDER	FR.
GRUDENAGE	148172	M	Ger.		Agent, Gestapo, Friedrichshafen (Ger.)	MISC.CRIMES	FR.
GRUDEWILLE	190008 A	M	Ger.		Dr., Col., Gendarmerie Gau Wartheland (Ger.)	MURDER	POL.
GEUDMAN	161710	M			Lt., 1.Bn.Sicherungs-Rgt. 74, Bde. Jesser, Clavieres (Fr.) 10.6.44	MURDER	FR.
GRUEB	1990	M	Ger.		Hptscharfhr., S.D., Aussenomdo.,SS	MISC.CRIMES	U.K.
GRUEBEL, Gottfried	300093	M	Ger.		Working Parties outside C.C. Auschwitz (Pol.) 8.43-7.44	BRUTALITY	POL.
GRUEBER	194033	M	Ger.		Major, Stalag Luft IV C.C. Grosstychow (Ger.) 16.6.44	MURDER	U.S.
GRUEBER, Karl	135173	M	Ger.	15.11.88	Sgt., police, Karlsruhe (Ger.) 31.3.45	WITNESS	U.S.
GRUEBER, Michael	250788	M	Ger.		Pvt., Army, Belgrade (Yugo.) 3.10.41-25.12.41	MURDER	YUGO.
GRUEKE	72908	M	Ger.		Guard, SS, C.C. Klingelpuetz (Ger.) 1..2.45	TORTURE	U.S.
GRUEL see GRAULS	135787						
GRUELICH, Hermann	261096	M	Ger.		People's councillor, people's court, extraordinary senate	SUSPECT	U.S.
GRUEN	301316	M	Ger.		Member Gestapo at Nove Mesto n.Vahom, C.C. Oswiecim-Birkenau (Pol.) 39-45	MURDER	CZECH.
GRUENAECK, Gottfried	183909	M	Ger.	19. 5.99	Civ., Foreman C.C. Martinswerk, Bergheim-Erft (Ger.) 43-45	TORTURE	U.S.
GRUENBERG, Georg	229807	M	Ger.	06	SS Osturmfhr., Waffen SS, C.C. Dachau (Ger.) 45	MURDER	U.S.
GRUENBERG, Georg	259017	M	Ger.		SS Oscharfhr., C.C. Auschwitz-Birkenau (Pol.) 11.42	MURDER	YUGO.
GRUENBERG, Olive see GRUNEWALD	193900 A						
GRUENDMANN, Fritz	193690	M	Ger.		Uscharfhr., S.D., Aussendienststelle der SIPO, Leeuwarden, Dokkum (Neth.) 13.4.44-14.4.45	MURDER	NETH.
GRUENER	12655	M	Ger.		Capt., Army, Finnmark (Nor.) 11.44	MISC.CRIMES	NOR.
GRUENER	171638	M	Ger.		SS Sturmmann, C.C. Oranienburg, Sachsenhausen (Ger.) 39-4.45	MURDER	POL.
GRUENERT	161248	M	Ger.	26	Uscharfhr., Waffen SS, 12.Panz.Div. Hitler-Jugend, Kislang, Cristot, Malmedy (Hung.,Fr.,Bel.) 16.6.44-15.12.44 3.45	MURDER	U.S.
GRUENEWALD	323	M	Ger.		Civ., C.C. Dachau (Ger.) 10.43, 9.44	MISC.CRIMES	U.K.
GRUENEWALD	12393	M	Ger.		Major, SS Deputy commander C.C. Dachau (Ger.) 38-44	TORTURE	CZECH.
GRUENEWALD	85085	M	Ger.		SS Hptsturmfhr., C.C. Vught (Neth.) 43-44	MURDER	BEL. NETH.
GRUENEWALD	140888	M	Ger.	97	Cpl., Army, Bilthoven (Neth.) 2.45	MURDER	NETH.
GRUENEWALD	171637	M	Ger.		SS Sturmbannfhr., Camp-cmdt., C.C.Oranienburg, Sachsenhausen (Ger.) 39-4.45	MURDER	POL.
GRUENEWALD see GRUNEWALD	252117						
GRUENHEIT, Karl	256727	M	Ger.	2. 1.91	Employee, 2.Bn. nacrr-Buesske, C.C. Nordhausen (Ger.)	MURDER	U.S.

GRU - GRU

NAME	C.R.FILE NUMBER	SEX	NATIO-NALITY	DATE OF BIRTH	RANK OCCUPATION UNIT PLACE AND DATE OF CRIME	REASON WANTED	WANTED BY
GRUENING	305859	M	Ger.		Cpl., 1.Aufkl.Abt., 3.Coy., 2.Col., XV.Div. Afrika-Korps, St.Leger (Arlon) (Bel.) 5.9.44	MISC.CRIMES	BEL.
GRUENLAUB, Robert	192463	M	Ger.	90	Cpl., Kgf.Arb.Bau-Bn.186 (Nor.) 40-42	MISC.CRIMES	NOR.
GRUENN	141063	M		04	Schfhr., SS, C.C., Pawiak (Pol.) 42-43	TORTURE	U.K.
GRUENUSS, Werner	133350	M			Lt., Chiefleader, Waffen-SS, C.C., Ohrdruf (Ger.) 44-45	MURDER	U.S.
GRUENWALD	1532	M	Ger.	05	Sturmbannfhr., SS, Lagerfuehrer, Sachsenhausen (Ger.)	MURDER	U.S.
GRUENWEDEL, Alfred	300602	M			Lt., Navy, Hopseidet-Finnmark (Nor.) 6.5.45	MURDER	NOR.
GRUENZNER, Hermann	259011	M	Ger.	11.2.96	Civilian, Budisov (Czech.) 45	MURDER	CZECH.
GRUENZWALD	259213	M	Ger.		Sturmbannfhr., SS, Dachau (Ger.) 42-45	MURDER	YUGO.
GRUETHHUSEN, Heinrich	250189	M		21.3.07	Flyer, Conc.Camp Ellrich, Nordhausen (Ger.)	MURDER	U.S.
GRUETNER, (or GERT)	138271	M	Ger.		SS-Adjutant, Gestapo, Lyon (Fr.)	MURDER	FR.
GRUETZENBACH, Josef	186399	M	Ger.	9.1.04	Civilian, Factory-Manager, Brno (Czech.) 39-45	PILLAGE	CZECH.
GRUFFER, Otto (or GRUFER)	140055	M	Ger.		Sgt., Army, Dienststelle No.4366 A - FP, Coudes (Fr.) 7.44	MURDER	FR.
GRUHN	256726	M	Ger.		Employee, Hauptlager L.III, C.C., Nordhausen (Ger.)	MURDER	U.S.
GRULL	255124	M			Flyer, Conc.Camp Ellrich, Nordhausen (Ger.)	MURDER	U.S.
GRUM	192402	M			Osturmfhr., SS, C.C., Flossenburg (Ger.) 44-45	SUSPECT	U.S.
GRUM	252416	M	Ger.		Col., Gestapo, Choisy (Fr.) 1.12.43	PILLAGE	FR.
GRUMPELT, Gerhard	306262	M	Ger.		Lt. (Ing.), Navy, Cuxhaven (Ger.) 6.,7.5.45	MISC.CRIMES	U.K.
GRUMS, Alfred Heinr. Franz	251556	M	Ger.	11.2.98	Osturmfhr., SS, Police-Presid., Kaiserslautern (Ger.) 6.11.44	MURDER	U.S.
GRUN	162673	M	Ger.		Cpl., Pvt., 263. D.J.Cmdo.343, Abwehr, Landerneau (Fr.) 6.44-8.44	MURDER	FR.
GRUN, Bruno (or KROEN and GRUNE)	300280	M	Ger.		N.C.O., Secret Fieldpolice, Utrecht (Neth.) 3.45-4.45	MISC.CRIMES	NETH.
GRUN, Erich	321	M	Ger.		Dr., Hptschfhr., SS, Conc.Camp-Doctor, C.C., Maidanek (Pol.) 40-4.44	MURDER	BEL., FR.
GRUN, Ernest	149256	M		15	Cmdo.Ordonanz, Conc.Camp, Wilhelmshaven (Ger.) 44-45	MURDER	FR.
GRUN, Paul	252867	M		3.8.15	Pvt., 13.Coy., 558.Gren.Rgt., Bruay en Artois (Fr.) 1.9.44	MURDER	FR.
GRUNAR	10069	M			Capt., Army, Stalag 4, Leipzig (Ger.) 10.43-11.43, 9.44-4.45	TORTURE	U.K.
GRUNBERG, Kurt	149257	M	Ger.	29.7.02	Feldgend., Vitry le Francois (Fr.)	TORTURE	FR.
GRUNBERG, Olive (see GRUNWALD)	193900						
GRUNBICHLER	252310	M	Ger.		Col., C.C., Royallieu (Compiegne) (Fr.) 41-44	MURDER	FR.
GRUND (see GRUNT)	148171						
GRUND	161408	M			Labour-Camp, C.C., Prazymiechi (Pol.) 41-44	TORTURE	U.S.
GRUND	162924	M			Oschfhr., SS, Friedrichshafen (Ger.) 43-44	TORTURE	FR.
GRUND	166992	M		14	Hptsturmfhr., 4.SS-Panz.Corps "Gille", Woods between Sur and Aka (Hung.) 7.3.45	MURDER	U.S.
GRUND	187202	M	Ger.	21	Usturmfhr., 12.SS-Panz.Div."Hitler-Jugend", Normandie (Fr.) 6.44-7.44	MISC.CRIMES	CAN.
GRUND	187562	M	Ger.	20	Usturmfhr., 12.SS-Pz.Div."Hitler-Jugend", 12.SS-Pz.Recce., Caen (Fr.) 6.44-7.44	TORTURE	CAN.
GRUND	187768	M	Ger.		Member, NSDAP, Stalag X III D, Woernitz-Ansbach (Ger.)	TORTURE	BEL.
GRUND, Christian	162941	M		4.4.28	Auto-upholsterer, Civilian, Sommerhausen (Ger.) 18.3.45	WITNESS	U.S.
GRUND, Franz	12464	M			N.C.O., 110.or 111.Pz.Gren.Rgt., Pvt., Albine (Fr.) 29.6.44	MURDER	FR.
GRUND, Gustav (or GRUNT)	130651	M		99	Oschfhr., SS, C.C. Mittelbau Dora (Ger.)	MURDER	U.S.
GRUND, Jakob	162942	M	Ger.	5.6.92	Grave-digger, Civilian, Sommerhausen (Ger.) 18.3.45	WITNESS	U.S.
GRUND, Paul	31971	M	Ger.		Dr.,Landgerichtsrat, Public Official, Prague (Czech.) 39-45	MURDER	CZECH.
GRUNDLER, Josef	255125	M			Sgt., Conc.Camp Ellrich, Nordhausen (Ger.)	MURDER	U.S.
GRUNDMAN	179728	M			Major, Fallschirmjaeger-Rgt.10, Castello (It.) 5.8.44	MURDER	U.K.
GRUNDMAN, Wilhelm	139148	M	Ger.	7.8.89	Civilian, Forsthaus Barenthal (Ger.) 4.45	MISC.CRIMES	U.S.
GRUNDMANN	1391	M			Major, 11.parachut-Regt.	MURDER	U.K.
GRUNDMANN, Friedrich	305158	M			Uschfhr., SS, SD, Akkerwoude and Leeuwarden (Neth.) 14.2.45	MISC.CRIMES	NETH.
GRUNDT, Wenzel	255126	M			Cpl., Conc.Camp Ellrich, Nordhausen (Ger.)	MURDER	U.S.
GRUNE, Bruno (see GRUN and KROEN)	300280						
GRUNEFELD	149260	M		10	Osturmfhr., SS-Totenkopf-Div., (Fin.)	TORTURE	FR.
GRUNER (or GRUNNER)	195087	M	Ger.		Med.Lt., a la prison, Fresnes (Fr.) 13., 15.4.42	WITNESS	FR.
GRUNER, Gerhard	171654	M	Ger.		Gruppenfhr., SS, 9.Res.Gren.Rgt., 1.Coy., Last Unit 2- Magny d'Anigon (Fr.) 18.9.44	MURDER	FR.
GRUNERVAID	176728	M			Hptschfhr., SS, Muehldorf, Ampfing (Ger.) 6.44-4.45	MURDER	U.S.
GRUNEWALD	322	M	Ger.		Major, Army, C.C. Vught, Mauthausen (Neth., Aust.) 43-44	TORTURE	NETH.
GRUNEWALD	12431	M	Ger.		Sipo, Clermont-Ferrand (Fr.)	TORTURE	FR.
GRUNEWALD	85083	M	Ger.		Leader of Camp, C.C., Dachau (Ger.) 43	MURDER	BEL.
GRUNEWALD	145407	M	Ger.		Hptsturmfhr., SS, Dachau (Ger.) 39	TORTURE	U.S.
GRUNEWALD	195303	M	Ger.		Major, SS, Sachsenhausen (Ger.)	MURDER	BEL.
GRUNEWALD	195572	M	Ger.		Official, Railway, Zdolbunow (Pol.) 42-43	TORTURE	POL.
GRUNEWALD	251542	M	Ger.		Deputy Cmdt., SS-Leader, C.C., Mauthausen (Aust.)	TORTURE	BEL.
GRUNEWALD (or GRUENEWALD)	252117	M	Ger.		Capt., Army, Oldenzaal (Neth.) 4.45	MISC.CRIMES	NETH.
GRUNEWALD, Martin	124118	M	Ger.		Member, Gestapo, Clermont-Ferrand (Fr.)	TORTURE	FR.
GRUNEWALD, Otto	188989	M	Ger.	12.12.87	Former Policeman, Chief of workcamps, Pfaffenwald nr.Hersfeld (Ger.) 44-45	MURDER	POL.
GRUNFELDER, Franz	185523	M	Ger.		Wachtmeister, Guard, Pris., C.C., Ebrach (Ger.) 39-45	MURDER	CZECH.
GRUNINGER	149261	M			Pvt., Army.	MISC.CRIMES	FR.
GRUNN	256098	M			Physician, Doctor, C.C., Flossenburg (Ger.)	MURDER	FR.
GRUNN	305159	M	Ger.		Dr., Camp-medical-officer, C.C., Flossenburg (Ger.) 42-45	MURDER	FR.
GRUNNER (see GRUNER)	195087						
GRUNOR, Walter	259296	M		06	Gestapo, Innsbruck (Aust.) 20.4.45	BRUTALITY	U.S.
GRUNOV	133334 A	M			Hptsturmfhr., SS	MURDER	U.S.
GRUNY	133351	M			Chief, Gestapo, C.C., Tarnoff (Ger.)	MURDER	U.S.
GRUNSTHEL	149262	M	Ger.		Chief, Civilian, Usine, Augsburg (Ger.)	TORTURE	FR.
GRUNT	324	M	Ger.		SS-Gestapo, Leszno (Pol.) 9.39-1.42	MURDER	POL.
GRUNT (see GRUND, Gustav)	130651						
GRUNT (or GRUND)	148171	M			Doctor, Police, Eisenberg (Ger.)	TORTURE	FR.
GRUNT, Emil	29872	M	Ger.		Pvt., C.C., Pomrensdorf (Ger.)	MISC.CRIMES	U.K.
GRUNTER, Otto	161352	M			Lt., Army	MISC.CRIMES	U.S.
GRUNTHER	149263	M		00	Uschfhr., SS	TORTURE	FR.
GRUNWALD	141482	M	Ger.		SS-Mann, Seine (Fr.) 40-45	MISC.CRIMES	FR.
GRUNWALD	142490	M	Ger.		Rottfhr., 1.SS-Pz.Div.,2.Pz.Gren.Rgt., 3.Bn., 12.Coy., Stavelot, Malmedy (Bel.) 22., 23.12.44	MURDER	U.S.

NAME	C.R.FILE NUMBER	SEX	NATIO-NALITY	DATE OF BIRTH	RANK OCCUPATION UNIT PLACE AND DATE OF CRIME	REASON WANTED	WANTED BY
GRUNWALD	171679	M	Ger.		SS-Sturmscharfhr.,SS-Gestapo Section IV 2B, (Nor.) 4.40	TORTURE	NOR.,UNWCC.
GRUNWALD	255989	M	Ger.		Chief,SS,C.C.Mauthausen (Aust.)	MURDER	FR.
GRUNWALD, Hans-Dietrich	189068	M	Ger.	14.12.98	General-Major,Commander of Uniformed Police in General Government Krakau (Pol.) 43-44	MURDER	POL.
GRUNWALD, Olive (or GRUNBERG)	193900	M	Ger.		Kommandofhr.,Stalag IX C. Kdo. 1114,Bad Sulza (Ger.)	MURDER	FR.
GRUNWALDER, Frantz	195086	M	Ger.		Sec.Chief,Gestapo,Savigny en Septaine (Fr.) 7. and 8.44	MURDER	FR.
GRUNWALDER, Frantz	257912	M	Ger.		Member of SD,Caen (Fr.) 42	SUSPECT	FR.
GRUNWALL	251560	M	Ger.		Lt.,377 Jg.Rgt.,Vinkt-Meigem (Bel.)	MISC.CRIMES	BEL.
GRUSCHWITZ, Paul (or STRUCHWITZ)	252324	M	Ger.		Werkfhr.,Roubaix (Fr.) 11.41-7.42	INTERR.	FR.
GRUSENDORF, Paul	252994	M	Ger.	94	Waiter,Civ.Firm.Oberndorf (Ger.)	BRUTALITY	FR.
GRUSS	256782	M			Civilian,Nordhausen (Ger.)	MURDER	U.S.
GRUSSING, Anton,Wilhelm	145408	M			Oltmannsfehn,Stapelmoor (Ger.) 20.11.43	MURDER	U.S.
GRUSSING, Fritz	145409	M	Ger.		Civilian,Oltmannsfehn (Ger.)	MURDER	U.S.
GRUTER, Heinrich	162923	M	Ger.	92	SS-Untersturmfhr.,Waffen-SS,Wachtbn.,C.C.Buchenwald (Ger.) 40-41	MISC.CRIMES	U.S.
GRUTINGEN	141410	M	Ger.		Cmdt.,Frontleitstelle Gare du Nord,Paris (Fr.) 20.8.44	MURDER	FR.
GRUTZKE	144501	M			Schuetze,Army,Pont de Niepps (Fr.) 4.9.44	TORTURE	FR.
GRUWALD	185524	M		25	Rottenfhr.,2 Rgt.,1 SS-Pz.Gren.Div. "Adolf Hitler" 3 Bn.,Malmedy (Bel.) 17.12.44	MURDER	U.S.
GRUZ, Paul	251559	M	Ger.		Sgt.,377 Jg.Rgt.,Vinkt-Meigem (Bel.)	MISC.CRIMES	BEL.
GRYCHYNECK	193491	M	Ger.		Master,O.T.,C.C.Moerary (Nor.) 44	MURDER	NOR.
GRYMATZ	305415	M	Ger.	28. 5.11	46 Rgt.,13 Coy.,558 Gren.Rgt.,Bruay en Artois,Pas de Calais (Fr.) 1.9.44	MURDER	FR.
GRYMATZ	252868	M	Ger.	28. 5.11	558 Gren.Rgt., 13 Coy., Pvt., Bruay en Artois (Fr.) 1.9.44	MURDER	FR.
GRZEGORCZYK, Robert	300094	M	Ger.		SS-Mann,Chief of Workshops,C.C.Gross Rosen (Ger.) 1.42-11.44	BRUTALITY	POL.
GRZELA, Willy	256783	M			Employee,C.C.Dora,Nordhausen (Ger.)	MURDER	U.S.
GRZIMEK, Josef	146726	M		05	Sgt.,SS,C.C.Flossenburg (Ger.)	TORTURE	U.S.
GRZYBINSKI, Max	250817	M		12.11.21	Flyer,C.C.Harzungen,Nordhausen (Ger.)	MURDER	U.S.
GRZYMEK	133352	M			Camp-Leader,Waffen-SS,C.C.Szebene (Pol.)	MURDER	U.S.
GRZYNSKI	250816	M			Pvt.,C.Ellrich,Nordhausen (Ger.)	MURDER	U.S.
GSCHWANDTER, Gustav	250818	M			Schuetze,Camp Bodungen,Nordhausen (Ger.)	MURDER	U.S.
GSTETTER, Wittmar	257593	M	Ger.		Crim.Asst.,SS-Oberscharfhr.,Feld-Polizei,Foix (Fr.) 12.42-44	INTERR.	FR.
GUATEMPER, Matyas	192401	M	Ger.	10. 2.99	Member,SD,Vetrni,Cecky,Krumlov (Czech.) 39-45	SUSPECT	CZECH.
GUBENMOS see GUGENMOS	136321						
GUBERSKY	259643	M	Ger.		Pvt.,Einheit "Lang",F.P. 22636 B,Obermorschwihr Ht.-Rhin (Fr.) 12.12.44	MURDER	FR.
GUBNER	250186	M			SS-Oberscharfhr., Camp Dora,Nordhausen (Ger.)	MURDER	U.S.
GUCKENBERGER	129800	M			Lt.,SD,Hanau (Ger.) 3.45	MURDER	U.S.
GUCKER (or GUECKER or GUECKEK)	62132	M		14 - 15	Oberscharfhr., 12 SS-Pz.Div."Hitler-Jugend" Feldgendarmerie Coy., Abbaye Ardenne (Fr.) 6.6.-8.7.44	TORTURE	U.K.,CAN.
GUDACKER (or GUTHACKER)	133789	M			Doctor,SS-Unterscharfhr.,Dr.Path.Inst.Jena,C.C.Buchenwald (Ger.)	TORTURE	U.S.
GUDAT	185521	M	Ger.		Obersturmfhr.,SS-Leibstandarte "Adolf Hitler", 1 Pz.Gren.Div., Stavelot (Bel.) 19.12.43	MURDER	BEL.
GUDE	260128	M	Ger.		Pvt.,SS-Slave Labour Camp,Botn near Rognan (Nor.) 8.42-3.43, 4.43-45	BRUTALITY	YUGO.
GUDEMANN	25214	M	Ger.		Member,NSDAP, in charge Belgian work parties, Loerrach, Dreilaender- eck (Ger.)	INTERR.	BEL.
GUDER	183308	M			Sturmmann,4 SS-Totenkopfsturmbann,C.C.Nordhausen,Dora Mittelbau Rosen,Aslan (Ger.)	WITNESS	U.S.
GUDERIAN	253024	M	Ger.		Lt., Pz.Div.,Unit 36-185,Lautrec (Fr.) 5.8.44	MISC.CRIMES	FR.
GUDERLEY	147330	M	Ger.		Lt.,11 Pz.Div.,36,185 or 37, 187 Coy., (Fr.) 44	MURDER	FR.
GUDERMANN, Hans	149232	M	Ger.		Civilian,Chemnitz (Ger.)	TORTURE	FR.
GUDEWILLE, Walter	325	M	Ger.		Dr., Polizei-Obersturmfhr., Wartheland (Pol.)	MURDER	POL.
GUECKASS (or GYGAS)	257225	M	Ger.		Capt.,Army,Oflag VII A,Murnau (Ger.)	SUSPECT	POL.
GUECKER (see GUCKER)	62132						
GUECKER (or GUCKER)	62132						
GUEDE, Gerard	193919	M	Ger.		Commander,Army,Angers (Fr.)	PILLAGE	FR.
GUHREN	195302	M	Ger.		Lt.Col.,SS.C.C.Ravensbrueck-Sachsenhausen (Ger.) 38-42	MURDER	BEL.
GUELDENZOH	191328	M	Ger.		Pvt.,Eis.Art.Btty. 717, F.P. 22380,Varsenare,St.Andries-le-Bruges (Bel.) 4.9.44	MURDER	BEL.
GUELICH	162601	M	Ger.	12	Unterscharfhr.,Waffen-SS,C.C.Ohrdruf (Ger.) 39-45	WITNESS	U.S.
GUEMA	144497	M		00	Civilian,C.C.Baumsnheim (Ger.)	MURDER	FR.
GUENTER, Friedrich	250172	M		15. 4.00	SS-Rottenfhr.,Camp Osterhagen-Ellrich,Nordhausen (Ger.)	MURDER	U.S.
GUENTHEL	161316	M		15	Sgt., SD,Toulouse,Agen,Cahors,Foix,Tarbes (Fr.) 6.-8.44	MURDER	U.S.
GUENTHER	129801	M		23 - 24	Pvt.,Army,Inf.Kampfgruppe Grande, near Reims (Fr.) 23-25.7.44	MURDER	U.S.
GUENTHER	140881	M	Ger.	05	Sgt.,Fliegerkorps 208,Hobsten (Ger.) 15.3.45	MURDER	CAN..
GUENTHER	141862	M	Ger.		Doctor,Stabsarzt,335 Rgt.,Army,214 Div.,Sletteb (Nor.) 12.42	TORTURE	U.K.
GUENTHER	145410	M	Ger.		Kapo,Vught (Neth.) 44	TORTURE	BEL.
GUENTHER	149233	M			Civilian,Neuengamme (Ger.)	TORTURE	FR.
GUENTHER	149234	M			SS-Sturmbannfhr., SS (Czech.)	MURDER	FR.
GUENTHER	173442	M	Ger.		Hauptsturmfhr.,Waffen-SS,C.C.Theresienstadt (Ger.) 44-45	TORTURE	NETH.
GUENTHER	190712	M	Ger.		N.C.O.,Eis.Art.Btty. 717,F.P. 22380,St.Andries,Varsenare,Bruegge (Bel.) 4.9.44	MURDER	BEL.
GUENTHER	192171	M	Ger.		SS-Officer,SS-Gestapo (Bel.)	MISC.CRIMES	BEL.
GUENTHER	194031	M	Ger.	25	SS-Obersturmfhr.,Lt.Col.,SS-Rassen Siedlungsamt,C.C.Prag,Teresin (Czech.) 39-45	TORTURE	CZECH.
GUENTHER	252198	M	Ger.		Doctor,Director,Penitentiary,Anrath (Ger.) 1.42-3.44	BRUTALITY	NETH.
GUENTHER	257811	M	Ger.		School-Teacher,Ramersdorf (Ger.) 44	WITNESS	U.S.
GUENTHER	301412	M	Ger.		SS-Major,Employee,Reichssicherheitshauptamt,C.C.German (Ger.)	MURDER	FR.
GUENTHER, Ernst	193005	M	Ger.		Lt.,Army,C.C.Buchenwald (Ger.) 42-45	TORTURE	U.S.
GUENTHER, Hinze	252874	M	Ger.		SS-Schuetze,C.C.Auschwitz-Birkenau (Pol.) 10.42	MISC.CRIMES	YUGO.
GUENTHER, Richard	148225	M	Ger.		C.C.Vienna (Aust.) Doctor	TORTURE	FR.
GUENTHER, Rolf	195104	M	Ger.		Police-Chief,Grand-Duchy (Lux.) Dr.	MURDER	LUX.
GUENTHER, T.	171636	M	Ger.		Doctor,High Official,Public Official,General Government Poland 39-4	MISC.CRIMES	POL.
GUENZEL	193008	M	Ger.		Cpl.,Waffen-SS,C.C.Buchenwald (Ger.) 42-45	TORTURE	U.S.
GUENZEL	254510	M			Lt.,2-3 Brandenburg Rgt.,	INTERR.	U.S.
GUENZEL, Wilhelm	250173			3. 8.28	SS-Rottenfhr.,Camp Harzungen,Nordhausen (Ger.)	MURDER	U.S.

GUE - GUN

NAME	C.R.FILE NUMBER	SEX	NATIO-NALITY	DATE OF BIRTH	RANK OCCUPATION UNIT PLACE AND DATE OF CRIME	REASON WANTED	WANTED BY
GUERFURTH	252098	M	Ger.		Lt., 12.SS-Art.Regt., F.P. 57666 A, Tourouvres (Fr.) 44	INTERR.	FR.
GUERGELEIN	261189	M	Ger.		Member, Staff of C.C. Ravensbrueck (Ger.)	SUSPECT	BEL.
GUERHING	149570				Paris (Fr.) 43-45	MISC.CRIMES	FR.
GUERLINGER, Walter	252316	M	Ger.		Lt., Railway (Mil.) Tonneins (Fr.) 8.44	MISC.CRIMES	FR.
GUERNOLDEN, Hans or Ernst	138325	M	Ger.		Pvt., Army,C.C.Eupweiler (Ger.) 44	MURDER	FR.
GUERTL, Gustav	301317	M	Ger.		Member, Gestapo at Trencin, C.C.Oswiecim-Birkenau (Pol.) 39-45	MURDER	CZECH.
GUERTLER, Paul	183311	M			Unterscharfhr., 4.SS-Totenkopf-Sturmbann, C.C. Mittelbau Nordhausen (Ger.) 43-45	WITNESS	U.S.
GUERTNER	258161		Ger.		Capt., Police, Kragujevac, Crasac, Gruza (Yugo.) 42-44	INTERR.	YUGO.
GUERTNER, Wilhelm	326	M	Ger.		Dr., Public Official, Reichsminister der Justiz, 1939	MISC.CRIMES	POL.
GUESCHL	193920	M	Ger.		Sicherungs-Regt. 95, 8.Bn., 13.Coy., Tulle (Fr.)	MURDER	FR.
GUESSELFELD	125039	M	Ger.		Lt., C.C. Tarmstedt, Bremen (Ger.) 5.42	MISC.CRIMES	U.K.
GUETE, Wilhelm	256784	M	Ger.	7. 3.16	Block 15, C.C. Dora, Nordhausen (Ger.)	MURDER	U.S.
GUETEMANN	222342	M	Ger.	20	Lt., 1.SS Panz.Div., Leibstandarte "Adolf Hitler", 8.44	MURDER	U.S.
GJETHOFF	174131	M	Ger.		Gerichtsoffizier, Stalag VI.A, C.C. Hemer (Ger.) 4.44	TORTURE	FR.
GUETLER, Hans	257368	M	Ger.		Crim.Secr., 4.Department of Gestapo, Dortmund, Iserlohn (Ger.) 4.45	INTERR.	YUGO.
GUETMANN	167630	M	Ger.		Prof.Dr., Civ., Ostgebietsministerium, Einsatzstab Rosenberg, Berlin (Ger.) 40 - 44	PILLAGE	FR.
GUETTINGER, Fritz	185522	M	Ger.	95	Mechanic, Kabel- und Metallwerke Neumeyer, Nuernberg (Ger.) 40-45	TORTURE	U.S.
GUETZLAFF	222541	M	Ger.		Guard, SS, C.C. Gusen (Aust.)	TORTURE	U.S.
GUGENBERGER, Hans	176729	M			Org.Todt, C.C. Muehldorf-Ampfing (Ger.) 6.44- 4.45	MURDER	U.S.
GUGEN'OS or GUGENMOS	136321	M			Pvt., 11.Panz.Div., 2.Coy., 2.A.A.-A.7, Bergerac, Albine (Fr.) 3.44- 8.44	MURDER	FR.
GUGGENBERGER	161360	M	Ger.	10	Chief, S.D., Hanau (Ger.) 2.45	MURDER	U.S.
GUGLER, Christian	162600	M	Ger.	03	C.C. Oranienburg (Ger.)	MURDER	U.K.
GUIER	124124	M	Ger.		Custom-official, Zollgrenzschutz, Creach-Maout (Fr.) 8.44	MURDER	FR.
GUIGKLE (see WEBER)	196909						
GUILLENER	157554	M		CO	Chief of Astrawerk, Chemnitz (Ger.) 45	TORTURE	FR.
GUIEN (see GUIM)	162599						
GUILLMAN	157552	M			Civilian,	MISC.CRIMES	FR.
GUILLNER	162598	M	Ger.		Cpl., Army, Morlaix (Fr.) 44	MURDER	FR.
GUILMANN	157549	M			Capt., Stalag 6 A and 6 D (Ger.)	TORTURE	FR.
GUIM, Kurt or GUIEN or GUIRN	162599	M	Ger.		Rottenfhr., SS-Div. "Das Reich", Houyet Dinant (Bel.)	PILLAGE	BEL.
GUIMM or GRIMM	134892	M			Lt., Cpl., W-SS, Camp Command.Hann.Stocker Camp, Gardelegen (Ger.) 4.45	MURDER	U.S.
GUING Lings	253023	M	Ger.		Pvt., 11.Panz.Div., Unit: 36-185, Lautrec (Fr.) 8.44	MISC.CRIMES	FR.
GUINSETT	149586	M			Dr., Member, NSDAP, Strasbourg (Fr.)	LOOTING	FR.
GUIRARD	251023	M	Ger.		Capt., 10.Coy., 7.Bn., Res.Pion., Meylan (Fr.) 6.44	INTERR.	FR.
GUIRN, Kurt (see GUIM)	162599						
GUISE	157548		Ger.		SS, C.C. Buchenwald (Ger.)	TORTURE	FR.
GUIZET	188835	M	Ger.		Capt., Standort-Kommandantur, La Machine (Fr.) 11.40	TORTURE	FR.
GULAREK	305860	M	Ger.		Pvt., 1.Aufklaerungsabteilung, 3.Coy., 2.Col., 15.Div. Africa corps St. Leger (Arlon) 9.44	MISC.CRIMES	BEL.
GULBERG, Clemens	174132	M	Ger.		Sgt., Stalag 6 A, C.C. Hemer (Ger.) 11.42- 4.45	TORTURE	U.S.
GULDE	149259	M			Civ., Niklasdorf (Ger.)	MISC.CRIMES	FR.
GULDE	173441	M	Ger.		Crim.Secr., Untersturmfhr., W-SS, Stapoleitstelle, Bruenn, Oswiecim-Birkenau (Czech., Pol.) 39-45	MURDER	CZECH.
GULDE, Hans	188419	M	Ger.		Employee, Gestapo, Brno (Czech.) 39-40	TORTURE	CZECH.
GULDEN	129666	M	Ger.		Lt., 183.Volksgren.Div., 330.Volksgren.Regt., 5.Coy., Linnich (Ger.) 16.1.45	MISC.CRIMES	U.S.
GULICH	260613	M	Ger.	15	Lt., Waffen - SS, Buchenwald (Ger.) 40-44	BRUTALITY	FR.
GULLE	192942	M	Ger.		Sgt., Schupo, C.C. Felstad near Drontheim (Nor.) 8.42-12.44	MURDER	NOR.
GUMBEL	1392	M			Capt., Panz.Jg.Abt., 10.Army,	MISC.CRIMES	U.K.
GUMBEL, Joachim	179757	M	Ger.	09	Capt., 590.Panz.Jaeg.Abtlg., Caviglia (It.) 8.44	MURDER	U.K.
GUMM, Hans	147076	M	Ger.		Obersturmfhr., Kreisleiter, SS, NSDAP, Dravograd (Yugo.) 43	MURDER	YUGO.
GUMMELT, Guenther	250185	M		5. 8.21	Flyer, Camp Ellrich, Nordhausen (Ger.)	MURDER	U.S.
GUNDEFACH	135166	M	Ger.	02	Secretary, Gestapo, Ruppertshutten, Wuerzburg (Ger.) 9.44	MURDER	U.S.
GUNDEL	193009	M	Ger.		Sgt., W-SS, C.C. Buchenwald (Ger.) 42-45	TORTURE	U.S.
GUNDER	261750	M	Ger.	95	Cmdt., Gend., St. Quentin (Fr.) 4.44	MURDER	FR.
GUNDER	167629	M	Ger.	19	W.O., SS-Div., "Das Reich", Oradour sur Glane (Fr.) 6.44	MURDER	FR.
GUNDER	250770	M	Ger.		Lt., Military Tribunal, St.Quentin-Aisne (Fr.) 4.44	INTERR.	FR.
GUNDLECH	176730	M			Leader, Org.Todt, C.C. Muehldorf-Ampfing (Ger.) 6.44- 4.45	MURDER	US.
GURDNACH	149568	M	Ger.		Civ.	TORTURE	FR.
GUNGER	149567	M			Cpl., Army, Tourlaville, St.Lo, Cherbourg (Fr.)	MURDER	FR.
GUNNEL, Kurt	306969	M	Ger.		Pvt., Probably serving in Section I, Semur-en-Auxois, Cote d'Or (Fr.) 8.44	MURDER	FR.
GUNST	161348	M	Ger.	95	Standartenfhr., SS, C.C. Lublin (Pol.) 40	MURDER	U.S.
GUNSTAN	36615	M			Manager, Civ., Gasworks Leipzig (Ger.)	TORTURE	U.K.
GUNTA, Paul	162041	M	Ger.		Policeman, Police, Hovestadt (Ger.) 41	MURDER	U.K.
CUNIER	173157	M	Ger.	10	Cpl., 397. Land.Schtz.Bn., Guard W.K. 128 at Stalag 20 B, Rahmel Sagorech (Ger.) 1.42	TORTURE	U.K.
GUNTER	162596	M	Ger.		Pvt., Army, C.C. 49, Klissau (Pol.) 6.41	TORTURE	U.K.
GUNTER	173158	M	Ger.		Sgt., C.C. Schirmeck-Rotenfels, Gaggenau (Fr., Ger.) 44	MURDER	U.K.
GUNTERMANN (see GUTEMANN)	1696						
GUNTHEL	149563	M			Scharfhr., SS, Toulouse (Fr.)	MISC.CRIMES	FR.
GUNTHEL	149564	M			Civ., Melun (Fr.) 8.44	MURDER	FR.
GUNTHER	162593	M	Ger.	98	Lt., Army, C.C. Buchenwald (Ger.) 39-45	WITNESS	U.S.
GUNTHER	146869	M	Ger.		Cpl., Dienststelle F.P. 4366 A, Courdes (Fr.) 44	MURDER	FR.
GUNTHER	157543	M			Civ., Bourget - Triage (Fr.) 8.44	MURDER	FR.
GUNTHER	157544	M			Sgt., Feldgendarmerie Staffel 1005, Monza (It.)	MURDER	FR.
GUNTHEP	161840	M			Kapo, C.C. Gusen (Aust.) 41-45	MURDER	U.S.
GUNTHER	162595	M			Lt., 74.Regt., Sicherungs-Bn., Clavières (Fr.) 44	MURDER	FR.
GUNTHER	257817	M	Ger.		Lt., Clairmares (Fr.) 9.44	INTERR.	FR.
GUNTHER	261749	M	Ger.		Cpl., Unit Art. H.D.V. 199/2235 N.D.F.Nr.F.P.27046 C, Lorgies (Fr.) 9.44	MURDER	FR.
GUNTHER, Anton	162594	M		09	Employee, Hauptscharfhr., Gestapo, Stavanger (Nor.) 11.42	MURDER	U.K.
GUNTHER, Felix	176731	M			SS-Mann, SS, C.C. Muehldorf-Ampfing (Ger.) 6.44- 4.45	MURDER	U.S.

NAME	C.R.FILE NUMBER	SEX	NATIO-NALITY	DATE OF BIRTH	RANK OCCUPATION UNIT PLACE AND DATE OF CRIME	REASON WANTED	WANTED BY
GUNTHER, Hans	140899	M		18	Lt.Verbindungsstab 331,Bolnes(Neth.)8.5.45	MURDER	NETH.
GUNTHER, Karl	139147	M	Ger.		Farmer,Civilian,	TORTURE	U.S.
GUNTHER, Paul	145411	M		23. 8.05	Uschafhr.NSDAP,Waffen SS,31 Coy.in Ebensee,Mauthausen(Aust.)5.44-5.45	MURDER	U.S.
GUNTHER, T.	191181	M	Ger.		Dr.,Official,Amt General Gouverneurs,High official,Abtlg.Treuhandverwaltung(Pol.)9.39-42	PILLAGE	POL.
GUNTHER, Ulrich	161356	M			Civilian,Chenebier Etabon(Fr.)27.9.44	MURDER	FR.
GUNTHER, Willy	250772	M	Ger.		Cmdt.Detention Barracks,Neuengamme(Ger.)	TORTURE	FR.
GUNTHER, Willy	305161	M	Ger.		Blockfhr.CC Neuengamme(Ger.)	MURDER	FR.
GUNTNER, Otto	260127	M	Ger.		Pvt.Navy,Sore(Landes/Fr.)23.-24.7.44	BRUTALITY	FR.
GURTSCHEMNUCHER	149557	M			Corporal-Chef,Army,Chateauroux(Fr.)	TORTURE	FR.
GUNTZ, Guenter	149556	M		26. 6.19	Lt.Waffen SS,Troyes,Bucheres,Crenay(Fr.)20.8.44	MURDER	FR.
GUNZEL, Herbert	253673	M	Ger.		Oschafhr.SS Gestapo,Troyes,Fandreville(Fr.)43-44	MISC.CRIMES	FR.
GUNZEL, Fritz	149224	M	Ger.		Dr.,Hptsturmfhr.S.D.Waffen SS,SS-Kriegsverwaltungsrat,Paris(Fr.)	PILLAGE	FR.
GUNZEL	306602	M	Ger.		Capt.5 Coy.586 Land.Schtz.,Rosenig,Silesia,17.12.43	MISC.CRIMES	FR.
GUPOSCHER, Willy	149555	M			Officer,Gestapo,Perigneuse(Fr.)	MURDER	FR.
GURA	306603	M			Sgt.,St.Andre le Gaz,Accueil,St.Marcellel(Fr.)8.7.44-26.7.44	MURDER	FR.
GURLICH	260092	M	Ger.		Lt.and Commander,Unity of D.C.A.,Noailles(Gers/Fr.)11.-13.8.44	INCENDIARISM	FR.
GUROW	176732	M			Civilian,Organisation Todt,CC Muhldorf,Ampfing(Ger.)6.44-4.45	MURDER	U.S.
GURSFI or GURSKY	67853	M	Ger.	95	Civilian,CC Himmelfahrt,Fundgrube Freiberg(Ger.)10.43-11.45	TORTURE	U.K.
GURSNER, Wilhelm	327	M	Ger.		Hptscharfhr.,Hazebrouck(Fr.)1.9.44	MURDER	FR.
GURTIS	191827	M	Ger.	19	Cpl.559 Land.Schtz.Bn.5 Coy.(Czech.)3.45	TORTURE	U.K.
GUSCHE, Fritz	250175	M		8. 2.04	SS Rottfhr.Camp Harzungen Nordhausen(Ger.)	MURDER	U.S.
GUSCHTAV	128859	M	Ger.		Pvt.Stalag VB,CC Allmendingen(Ger.)6.3.44	MISC.CRIMES	U.K.
GUSE	258388	M		21	Osturmfhr.Regimental Adjudant of SS Panz.Regt.37(Fr.)10.44	WITNESS	U.S.
GUSE, Guenther	259056	M	Ger.		Admiral,Crimes against Peace War Crimes and Crimes against Humanity	WITNESS	U.S.
GUSE, Karl	149553	M			Capt,Waffen SS,17 Panz.Gren.Div.,Montmirail(Fr.)	MURDER	FR.
GUSKE	120569	M	Ger.		Secretary,Geheime Feld Polizei,Glebockie(Pol.)8.-9.41	MURDER	U.S.
GUSS see GUIST, Erich	161308						
GUSSEFELDT or GUSSFELDT	140878	M	Ger.	09	Lt.Lager,Interpreter Marlag,KL Marlag,Milag(Ger.)5.42	MURDER	U.S.
GUSSNER, Wilhelm	192162	M	Ger.	02	Feldgendarm,Feldgendarmerie Cassel,Hazebrouck(Fr.)30.8.44	MURDER	FR.
GUST	133791	M	Ger.		SS Oschafhr.	MURDER	U.S.
GUST	162678	M	Ger.		Lagerfhr.SS Osturmfhr.KL Buchenwald(Ger.)9.44	TORTURE	U.K.U.S.
GUST,Erich or GUSS	161308	M	Ger.	09	Lt.Waffen SS,Totenkopf,CC Weimar,Buchenwald(Ger.)42-44	MURDER	U.S.
GUST, Johann	195105	M	Ger.	10	Pvt.Land.Schtz.Bn.,Oppeln-Haven(Ger.)20.11.42	MURDER	U.K.
GUSTA	250775	M	Ger.		Foreman,CC Buchenwald(Ger.)	BRUTALITY	FR.
GUSTAFFSON	149552	M		13	S.A.Officer,CC Neumuenster Stalag 10B,7.44	TORTURE	FR.
GUSTAFSON	222540	M	Ger.		Pvt.Army,Schleswig(Ger.)	MURDER	U.S.
GUSTAVE	173450	M			Kapo,Camp-official,CC Dora-Buchenwald(Ger.)	MURDER	FR.
GUSTEL	162040	M		09	Osturmfhr.,Buchenwald(Ger.)43-45	MURDER	POL.
GUSTELL	133792	M	Ger.		SS Scharfhr.CC Buchenwald(Ger.)	TORTURE	U.S.
GUT	121226	M			Capt.SS,St.Gingolph(Fr.)7.44	MURDER	FR.
GUTCHIE	174985	M			Capt.Stalag II B,Kommandantur,Kommando 1534,Gambin(Ger.)8.43	MURDER	U.S.
GUTEKUNST, Emil	252488	M	Ger.		SS Hptsturmfhr./Dr.S.D.Kdo."Bickler",Autum 1944	MURDER	U.K.
GUTEKUNST, Otto	195082	M	Ger.	2. 7.78	Dr.,Director,Hospital,Winnental(Ger.)40-45	MURDER	U.S.
GUTENBERGER, Karl	187687	M	Ger.	05	SS Ob.Gruppenfhr.Lt.General,Inspector of Kripo,Sipo and S.D.Commander of all PWS Wehrkr.VI,SS,Duesseldorf,Koeln and Ruhr(Ger.)43-45	TORTURE	UNWCC T
GUTENGUST	259685	M	Ger.	15	SS Uschafhr.Gestapo,Area of Angers(Fr.)42-44	MISC.CRIMES	FR.
GUTEMANN or GUNTERMANN	1696	M		17	Ob.Sturmfhr.SS Leibstandarte Adolf Hitler,Les Hogues(Fr.)25.8.44	MURDER	U.S.
GUTENHOENER, Wiut	301686	M	Ger.		05/243 Mongolian Unit"Oberland",St.Nazaire en Royans(Fr.)7.-8.44	MURDER	FR.
GUTENKUNST, Ludwig	250176	M			SS Sturmmann,Camp KL Bodungen,Nordhausen(Ger.)	MURDER	U.S.
GUTERMANN	149243	M		97	Civilian,Lyon(Fr.)	PILLAGE	FR.
GUTERMANN	259230	M			Agent,Gestapo of Poitiers,Antenne of Rochelle,Police-Inspector at Mannheim,Area Poitiers(Fr.)40-44	MISC.CRIMES	FR.
GUTH	133342	M		10	Uschafhr.Waffen SS,CC Hohenrheim near Plattling(Ger.)2.-5.45	MURDER	U.S.
GUTH	195085	M			SS Hptsturmfhr.SS Police,19 Regt.2 Coy.,Douvaine(Fr.)19.7.44	MURDER	FR.
GUTH, Fridolin	157474	M			19 Regt.of Police 2 Coy.,Ugines(Fr.)5.6.44	MURDER	FR.
GUTHACKER see Dr.GUDACKER	133789						
GUTHACKER	193010	M	Ger.		Lt.Waffen SS,CC Buchenwald(Ger.)42-45	TORTURE	U.S.
GUTHE	190711	M			Pvt.Eis.Art.Btty.717,Feldpost No.22380,St.Andries,Varsenare,Lez Bruges (Bel.)4.9.44	MURDER	BEL.
GUTHEIL, Rudolf	252100	M	Ger.	10. 7.02	Major,Strassen-Steinfurt,Luxembourg(Lux.)40-44	MISC.CRIMES	LUX.
GUTHER, Gronostay	252869	M	Ger.	19. 1.25	Pvt.13 Coy.558 Gren.Regt.,Bruayen Artois(Fr.)1.9.44	MURDER	FR.
GUTHMANN, Hugo	173159	M	Ger.		Lageraeltester,CC Natzweiler(Fr.)42-43	WITNESS	U.K.
GUTLER	251562	M		21	Lt.Commander,German Army,Sazussola(It.)18.10.44	INTERR.	U.K.
GUTMAN, Adam	138327	M			Policeman,Geheime Feldpolizei,Lille,Montigny-en-Gohelle(Fr.)14.3.44	MURDER	FR.
GUTMAN, Oskar	124258	M			1 SS Panz.Div.1 SS Panz.Regt.,Malmedy(Bel.)17.12.44	MURDER	U.S.
GUTMANN	250773	M			(F.G.P.)Gestapo,Lille(Fr.)40-44	MISC.CRIMES	FR.
GUTMANN	167630	M	Ger.,		Prof.Dr.,Member Ostgebietsministerium Rosenberg Einsatzstab Pre-History Section,Berlin(Ger.)40-44	PILLAGE	FR.
GUTMANN, Joseph	12465	M	Ger.		Pvt.110 or 111 Panz.Gren.Regt.3,Albine(Fr.)29.6.44	MURDER	FR.
GUTMANN, Josef	253674	M	Ger.		Gestapo Prison,Troyes(Fr.)43-44	INTERR.	FR.
GUTNACKER	255375	M			Lt.CC Buchenwald(Ger.)	MURDER	U.S.
GUTOUSKY or GUTOWSKI	162669	M	Ger.		Feldgendarmerie-Morlaix,St.Pol de Leon(Fr.)44	TORTURE	FR.
GUTSCHE	139805	M	Ger.		Capt.Camp-Supervisor,Stalag II B,Hammerstein(Ger.)8.43-2.45	MISC.CRIMES	U.S.
GUTSCHE	195124	M	Ger.		SS Scharfhr.S.D.Sonder and Wirtschaftskommando Beeck,Gorssel-Beeck (Neth.)23.-24.9.44	TORTURE	NETH.
GUTSCHKE	250815	M			Pvt.Camp Ellrich,Nordhausen(Ger.)	MURDER	U.S.
GUTSCHOW	188418	M	Ger.		Inspektor,Gestapo,Brno(Czech.)39-45	MURDER	CZECH.
GUTSELL	253027	M	Ger.		Agent Gestapo in the Avenue Foch,Paris(Fr.)12.8.44	MURDER	FR.
GUTSELL, Fritz	161307	M	Ger.	14	Sgt.SS Totenkopf,CC Buchenwald,Weimar(Ger.)39-42	TORTURE	U.S.
GUTTERER, Leopold	258955	M	Ger.	02	Bde.General,SS,Civ.Occ.1942 State Sec'y.of the Propaganda Ministry 4.44 chairman of the Board of Directors UFA film Coy.	SUSPECT	U.S.

GUT - HAB

NAME	C.R.FILE NUMBER	SEX	NATIO-NALITY	DATE OF BIRTH	RANK OCCUPATION UNIT PLACE AND DATE OF CRIME	REASON WANTED	WANTED BY
GUTTERNIGG	176733	M			SS-Rottfhr.,SS,C.C.Muhldorf,Ampfing (Ger.) 6.44-4.45	MURDER	U.S.
GUTTING	132178	M	Ger.		Civilian,I.G.Farben Industrie,Heidebreck (Ger.)	MISC.CRIMES	U.K.
GUTZAHR,Karl	124125	M	Ger.		Pvt.,Army,Creach-Maout (Fr.) 7.8.44	MURDER	FR.
GUTZEIT	149247	M	Ger.		Doctor,C.C.Hohenlychen,Ravensbrueck (Ger.)	MURDER	FR.
GUTZEIT,Gustav	252126	M	Ger.		Lived in Presbytery,Mouterre-Silly (Fr.) 25.6.40	INTERR.	FR.
GUYER	124487	M	Ger.		Capt.,Oflag IX A-Z,C.C.-officer,near Rotenburg (Hess.Nassau)(Ger.)45	TORTURE	U.K.
GUZ	328	M	Ger.		SS-Oschfhr.,C.C.Struthof (Ger.) 9.39-4.41	MURDER	POL.
GUZNER,Heinrich	127086	M	Ger.		Hptsturmfhr.,SS Pz.Div."Das Reich",Croix-Falgarde (Ger.)	MURDER	FR.
GYGANOWSKI	12468	M	Ger.		Oschfhr.,110 or 111 Pz.Gren.Rgt.,Gourdon (Fr.) 29.6.44	MURDER	FR.
GYGAS (see GUECKASS)	257225						
GYLEK	187973	M	Ger.		Fregatten Kapitaen,Marine,Stalag VIII B,Teschin (Ger.) 12.42-5.43	WITNESS	U.K.
HAA	253695	M			Foreman,Civilian,Siegburg (Ger.) 9.7.41	INTERR.	FR.
HAABICHT	72595	M			Culture-Chef,Public official,Longuion (Fr.) 43	MURDER	FR.
HAAG,Gunter	197804	M	Ger.		Adj.,Resenlieu (Fr.) 29.7.44	MISC.CRIMES	FR.
HAACK,Hans	252156	M		3. 3.07	Pvt.,Camp Ellrich,Nordhausen (Ger.)	MURDER	U.S.
HAACKE	252157	M			Flyer,Camp Ellrich,Nordhausen (Ger.)	MURDER	U.S.
HAAG	162450	M		95	Commandant,Jail,Camp official Citadelle C.C.Liege (Bel.)	MURDER	BEL.
HAAG (or HAG)	167797	M			Prison Warder,C.C.Ebersta (Ger.)	TORTURE	BEL.
HAAG,Hans	260093	M			Usturmfhr.,SS slave labour camp Botn near Rognan (Nor.) 4.43	BRUTALITY	YUGO.
HAAGE,Hans	165924	M	Ger.	09	SS-Sturmschfhr.,C.C.Bolzano (It.)	MURDER	U.S.
HAAGEN	72596	M			C.C.Strassburg (Fr.)	MISC.CRIMES	FR.
HAAGEN	255984	M	Ger.	00-05	Air-force,stationed at "Dekiek",Riel (Neth.) 22.4.44	MURDER	NETH.
HAAGEN	256750	M	Ger.	00-05	Cpl.,Military,Air-force,Alphen,Riel (Neth.) 22.4.42	SUSPECT	NETH.
HAAGEN,Eugen	258546	M	Ger.	96	Oberarzt,Air-force,Natzweiler (Ger.) 40-45	BRUTALITY	U.S.
HAAK	139792	M	Ger.		Capt.,Stalag X B,Sandbostel (Ger.) 1.-5.45	TORTURE	U.S.
HAAK	163092	M	Ger.		Member,SS,1 Coy 10 Pz.Div.,Revin (Fr.) 6.44	MURDER	FR.
HAAKNEUS (see ETLINGER)	233						
HAAKS,Willy	254938	M	Ger.		Pvt.,377 Jg.Rgt.,Vinkt (Bel.)	MURDER	BEL.
HAAN	24976	M	Ger.		Capt.,Army,246 Volksgren.Div. G 2 Section	TORTURE	U.S.
HAAN	174007	M	Ger.		Asst.to Capt.,Stalag VI A,C.C.Hemer (Ger.) 41-44	TORTURE	U.S.
HAAN (see HAHN)	260235						
HAAN,Albert	250823	M	Ger.		Sgt.,Oldenzaal (Neth.) 1.4.45	PILLAGE	NETH.
HAAR	138312	M	Ger.		SS-Sgt.,Gestapo,Lyon (Fr.) 6.-8.44	MURDER	FR.
HAARDT	250824	M	Ger.		Capt.,Army,Oldenzaal (Neth.) 1.4.45	INTERR.	NETH.
HAARSCHEIDT,Paul	252329	M		30.12.14	Flyer,Camp Ellrich,Nordhausen (Ger.)	MURDER	U.S.
HAAS	31970	M	Ger.		Landgerichtsrat,Opava (Czech.) 21.2.40	MURDER	CZECH.
HAAS	105916	M		12	Interpreter,C.C.Moosburg (Ger.)	WITNESS	U.S.
HAAS	115026	M	Ger.		Gestapo,Gaggenau (Ger.) 6.44	MURDER	U.K.
HAAS	121064	M	Ger.		Sgt.,Gestapo de Belfort and Army,Banvillars (Fr.) 10.10.44	MURDER	FR.
HAAS	124259	M			Uschfhr.,SS Pz.Rgt.1, 1 Pz.Div.,Penal Unit 1 Pl.9 Coy,Malmedy (Bel.) 17.12.44	MURDER	U.S.
HAAS	132706	M	Ger.		Col.,Pioneer Bn.28,Cray (Fr.) 41-42	RAPE	FR.
HAAS	141859	M	Ger.		Cpl.,326 field Replacement Bn.,Moosburg (Ger.)	WITNESS	U.K.
HAAS	162444	M	Ger.	95	SS,C.C.Buchenwald (Ger.)	TORTURE	U.S.
HAAS	162463	M	Ger.		Lt.Col.,Air-force,Art.,Barrou (Fr.) 27.8.44	PILLAGE	FR.
HAAS	163105	M	Ger.		Gestapo de Dijon,Dun les Places (Fr.) 27.-28.6.44	MURDER	FR.
HAAS	173567	M	Ger.		Kreiskommandant,Jasika Krusevac (Yugo.)	PILLAGE	YUGO.
HAAS	186004	M	Ger.	11	Lt.,Capt.,99 Geb.Jg.Bn.1 Coy Briancon,commanded Mongol-troops,La Batie,des Vigneaux (Fr.) 4.7.44-11.8.44	MURDER	FR.
HAAS	186598	M	Ger.		Civilian,Montgauthier,Dinant (Bel.) 20.9.43	MURDER	BEL.
HAAS	186599	M			Uschfhr.,4 SS Totenkopfsturmbann,SS Camp Fahrbereitschaft Nordhausen (Ger.) 43-45	WITNESS	U.S.
HAAS	189648	M	Ger.		Lt.Col.,Commandant,Art.L 54512,Barrou (Fr.)	PILLAGE	FR.
HAAS	190553	M	Ger.	95	SS-Major,Camp Commandant,Belsen-Bergen (Ger.) 40-44	MURDER	YUGO.
HAAS	222564	M	Ger.		SS-Hptschfhr.,3 SS Totenkopf Div.10 SS Begleit Coy M.G.Coy	TORTURE	U.S.
HAAS	250230	M	Ger.		Lt.,1 Coy 99 Bn.159 Res.Inf.Div. (Fr.) 10.and 21.7.44	MISC.CRIMES	FR.
HAAS	260361	M	Ger.		SS,C.C.Hinzert (Ger.) 42-45	INTERR.	FR.
HAAS	261190	M	Ger.		Pvt.,139 Arbeitsbereich Liane,5 Inf.Rgt.211,Alleur-lez-Liege (Bel.) 4.9.44	MURDER	BEL.
HAAS,Adolf	139791	M			Officer,Waffen SS,Wewellsburg (Ger.)	TORTURE	U.S.
HAAS,Alfred	72597	M			Sgt.,Waffen SS,C.C.Struthof (Ger.)	MURDER	FR.
HAAS,Anton	133666	M			Pvt.,Army,Kresti (Russ.)	WITNESS	U.S.
HAAS,Francois	1088	M	Ger.		Sgt.,Army,Feldgendarmerie,St.Dizier (Fr.)	WITNESS	FR.
HAAS,Georg (Juraj)	261971	M	Ger.	30. 3.08	Farmer,Prievidza,Handlova,Tuzina,Pravno,Nitrianske (Czech.) 8.44-4.45	MURDER	CZECH.
HAAS,Joseph	194785	M	Ger.		Guard,Kdo.375 Stalag VI G,Mechernich-Eifel (Ger.) 18.4.44	MURDER	FR.
HAAS,Karl	177512	M	Ger.		Feldgendarm,Feldgendarmerie,Roubaix (Fr.) 24.8.44	MURDER	FR.
HAAS,Karl	196086	M	Ger.		Usturmfhr.,Gestapo,H.Q.,Fredrikstad (Nor.)	TORTURE	NOR.
HAAS,Leopold	173206	M	Ger.	22. 1.00	Member,NSV,C.C.Kislau (Ger.) 41-45	TORTURE	U.S.
HAAS,Manfred	257855	M	Ger.		SS-Capt.,150 Pz.Bde.,Meuse Bridge-Antwerp (Bel.) 12.44	MISC.CRIMES	U.S.
HAAS,Mathias	186600	M			Pvt.,4 SS Totenkopfsturmbann,Camp Guard,Nordhausen (Ger.) 43-45	WITNESS	U.S.
HAAS,Walter	186602	M			Pvt.,4 SS Totenkopfsturmbann,Camp Guard,Nordhausen (Ger.) 43-45	WITNESS	U.S.
HAASE	145329	M	Ger.	00	Sturmfhr.,SS,Chief Camp Leader of Hirzenhain (Ger.) 25.-26.3.45	MURDER	U.S.
HAASE	173631	M			Foreman,Polier,Org.Todt,C.C.Muhldorf Ampfing (Ger.) 6.44-4.45	MURDER	U.S.
HAASE	254550	M	Ger.		SS-Uschfhr.,C.C.Buchenwald (Ger.) 42-45	BRUTALITY	FR.
HAASE	254790	M	Ger.		Lt.,377 Jg.Rgt.,Vinkt,Meigem (Bel.) 25.-31.5.40	MISC.CRIMES	BEL.
HAASE,Hermann	188599	M	Ger.	2. 8.09	Police secretary,Gestapo,Brno (Czech.) 39-45	MURDER	CZECH.
HAASE,Pol.	253697	M	Ger.		Lt.,Gend.Troop,de L'Aube (Fr.) 43-44	INTERR.	FR.
HAASE,Ulrich	196634	M	Ger.		Osturmfhr.,SS Div."Das Reich" Pz.Rgt.2,Tulle (Fr.) 9.6.44	WITNESS	FR.
HAASE,Wilhelm	250835	M	Ger.		Guard,Prison,Hagen (Ger.)	BRUTALITY	BEL.
HAASHAGEN	257970	M			Sgt.,150 Pz.Bde.,Meuse Bridge-Antwerp (Bel.) 12.44	MISC.CRIMES	U.S.
HAASS,Friedrich	251054	M	Ger.	06	SS-Sturmschfhr.,SS,Westerbork (Neth.)	INTERR.	NETH.
HABACHT	72602	M			Sgt.,SS Pz.Div."Der Fuehrer" 1 Bn.,Departm.Lot (Fr.) 44	TORTURE	FR.
HABACHT	127107	M	Ger.		Schfhr.,SS Pz.Div."Das Reich" (Fr.)	MURDER	FR.
HABASICK,Jonny or Johanny or Thonny	251173	M	Ger.		10 Coy 377 Jg.Rgt.,Vinkt Meigem (Bel.) 25.-31.5.40	MURDER	BEL.

HAB-HAD

NAME	C.R.FILE NUMBER	SEX	NATIO-NALITY	DATE OF BIRTH	RANK OCCUPATION UNIT PLACE AND DATE OF CRIME	REASON WANTED	WANTED BY
HABATCHT	192211	M	Ger.		SS-Hptschfhr.,SS Div."Das Reich",Regt."Der Fuehrer",I Bn., Frayssinet Le Gelat(Fr.) 21.5.44	MURDER	FR.
HABECKER or HANECKER	182572	M		90 - 95	Criminal-Commissar,Gestapo,R.S.H.A.,C.C.Mauthausen(Aust.)	MURDER	U.S.
HABECKER, Walter	125151	M	Ger.	95	Gestapo,Berlin(Ger.)	TORTURE	U.S.
HABEL	78910	M			Dr.,District-Arzt,Civilian,Frohnleiten a.d.Mur(Aust.) 4.3.45	TORTURE	U.S.
HABELAND	139793	M	Ger.		Sgt.,Stalag XB,Sandbostel(Ger.) 1.-5.45	TORTURE	U.S.
HABELSREITER, Otto	192971	M	Ger.		SS-Uschfhr.,SS,C.C.Buchenwald(Ger.) 42-45	TORTURE	U.S.
HABENBICHLER	146868	M	Ger.		Pvt.,SS-Div."Das Reich",1 Panz.Regt.,2 Coy.,Tulle(Fr.) 44	MURDER	FR.
HABEL	138219	M	Ger.		Lt.,15 Police-Regt.,St.Genis Laval(Fr.) 20.8.44	MURDER	FR.
HABERNER	329	M	Ger.		SS-Hptschfhr.,SD Police,Lille(Fr.) 28.4.44	MURDER	FR.
HABENER, Otto	194857	M	Ger.		Civilian,Wettelrode(Ger.)	TORTURE	U.S.
HABENICHT	162447	M	Ger.		Custom-Official,Zollgrenzschutz,Fillanges(Fr.) 14.-15.3.44,18.6.44	MURDER	FR.
HABENICHT	196693	M	Ger.		SS-Mann,SS Mauthausen(Ger.)	TORTURE	BEL.
HABERBOCK or HABERDOCH	260094	M			Gend.,Div."Oberland"Unity Russia-Germany,Massif of Vercors(Fr.)7.-8.44	SUSPECT	FR.
HABERER, Paul	259052	M			Pvt.,Camp Ellrich,Nordhausen(Ger.)	MURDER	U.S.
HABERFELLNER, J.	192786	M	Ger.		Schupo,C.C.Falstad,Stalag,Falstad(Nor.) 41-45	MURDER	NOR.
HABERL, Gottfried	900002	M			Member Landwacht at Maurach during 1944,Pertisau-Maurach(Aust.) 13.7.44	MURDER	FR.
HABERLACH	197807	M	Ger.		Capt.,Kreiskommandantur,Cherbourg(Fr.) 23.6.44	MISC.CRIMES	FR.
HABERLAND	254552	M	Ger.		Major,Pleucadeuc & Saint Marcol(Fr.) 18.-28.6.44	MISC.CRIMES	FR.
HABERLAND	258989	M		18	Sgt.,Signal-Bn.,559 Volks-Gren.Div.,Monthille(Fr.) 11.44	WITNESS	U.S.
HABERLAND	305417	M	Ger.		Usturmfhr.,2 SS Pz.Div.H.Q.,La Roche,Wibrin(Bel.) 1.45	MURDER	BEL.
HABERLE, Ernst	125152	M			Civilian (Pol.)	MURDER	U.S.
HABERLE, Karl	162445	M	Ger.		SS-Schfhr.,Gestapo,Dun les Places Chalons-Saone(Fr.)26.-28.6.44,43-44	MURDER	FR.
HABERLEIN	142914	M	Ger.		Work-Supervisor and Guard,Civilian,C.C.Erbach(Ger.) 9.44	TORTURE	U.S.
HABERMANN	161647	M	Ger.	07	Pvt.,Luftwaffe,Luftgau,C.C.	MURDER	NOR.
HABERMANN, Harald	188598	M	Ger.		Kriminalsekretaer,Gestapo,Brno and Opava(Czech.) 39-45	MURDER	CZECH.
HABERMAS	254802	M	Ger.		Major,Cmdt.,Finistere-Brest(Fr.) 9.9.44	MURDER	FR.
HABERSTROH	147088	M	Ger.		Osturmfhr.,Chief,SS,Gestapo,Fredrikstad(Nor.) 41	TORTURE	NOR.
HABERSTROH see SEIBEL, Lothar	182066						
HABERSTUMPF, Wilhelm	253053	M			Cpl.,Camp Ellrich,Nordhausen(Ger.)	MURDER	U.S.
HABERZET see HEDERZET	156718						
HABESZOTTEL, Kurt	173690				Work-Camp Mühldorf and Ampfing(Ger.) 6.44-4.45	MURDER	U.S.
HABIANITSCH, Klara	901662	F	Ger.		nr.Mostar. 9.44	MURDER	YUGO.
HABIERA, Josef	160905	M			CC.,Vicinity of Gardelegen(Ger.) 5.-14.4.45	MURDER	U.S.
HABNER, Hendrick	330	M		07	Sgt.,Air Force(Civ.Occ.Manufacturer),Cazaux(Fr.) 22.8.44	MURDER	FR.
HACH, L.	24978	M		05	Sturmbannfhr.,SS,Kriegsgefangenenlager 20,Bremen(Ger.)	TORTURE	U.S.
HACHMANN, Gertrude	194562	F	Ger.	11.11.12	Civilian,Oberkail(Ger.) 15.8.44	TORTURE	U.S.
HACHMEIER, Ernst	305659	M	Ger.		SA-Mann,NSDAP,,Lusbeck-Siems(Ger.) 6.8.44	MURDER	U.S.
HACHMIDA see ASCHMITAT	124997						
HACK	130654	M			SS Planing Staff,Mittelbau Dora(Ger.)	MURDER	U.S.
HACK or HAK	259096	M	Ger.		Lt.,Garrison Cmdt.at Touzj(Yugo.) 43	MISC.CRIMES	YUGO.
HACK	259054	M			SS-Osturmfhr.,Camp Dora,Nordhausen(Ger.)	MURDER	U.S.
HACK, August	154982	M	Ger.		Troop Leader O.T.,C.C. Saal on the Danube(Ger.) 1.12.44-22.4.45	MURDER	U.S.
HACK, Rudolf	162455	M	Ger.		Member NSDAP,Leipzig(Ger.) 44	TORTURE	U.S.
HACK, Willi	139794	M	Ger.	19	Lt.,Guard,Waffen-SS,C.C.Berga(Ger.) 4.45	TORTURE	U.S.
HACKBART, Kaete	142463	F	Ger.		Civilian, C.C.Hadamar(Ger.) 6.44-3.45	WITNESS	U.S.
HACKE	119426	M	Ger.		Major,Ic Aufkl.,20 Army Staff,Finmark(Nor.) 44	MURDER	NOR.
HACKE, Stephan or HACKEN	162446	M	Ger.		Member of Kdo.343,269 Inf.Div.,Landerneau(Fr.) 15.6.44,29.8.44	MURDER	FR.
HACKEL	10	M	Ger.		Army,Lt. (Fr.) 8.44	MURDER	FR.
HACKEL	125479	M	Ger.		Lt.,997 Inf.Regt.,19 Bn.(Fr.) 7.44	MURDER	U.K.,FR.
HACKEN see HACKE Stephan	162446						
HACKENBERG	254355	M		15	4 Coy.,515 L.S.-Bn.,Jawordzno(Pol.) 12.43	MURDER	U.K.
HACKENLOB	259055	M			Pvt.,Camp Dora,Nordhausen(Ger.)	MURDER	U.S.
HACKENSTEIN-HARTENSTEIN	154245	M	Ger.		SS-Sturmbannfhr.,C.C.Oswiecim(Pol.) 40-45	MURDER	POL.
HACKER	9681	M	Ger.		Oschfhr.,Waffen-SS,C.C.Natzweiler(Fr.) 42	MURDER	CZECH.
HACKER	143407	M	Ger.		Sgt.,Stalag IV,Bankau Fallingbostel(Ger.) 2.-3.45	MISC.CRIMES	U.K.
HACKER	258003	M			Lt.,Paratrooper(Ex.Bn.600)BD i.c.Engr.,150 Pz.Bde.,Meuse Bridge-Antwerp (Bel.) 12.44	MISC.CRIMES	
HACKER	261191	M	Ger.		Cpl.,139 Arbeitsbereich Liane 5 Inf.Regt.211,Alleur lez Liege(Bel.) 9.44	MURDER	BEL.
HACKER	305861	M	Ger.		Pvt.,1 Aufkl.Abt.,3 Coy.,2 Col.,XV Div.Africa Corps,St.Leger(Arlon) 9.44	MISC.CRIMES	BEL.
HACKER, Alois	62253	M			Inf.Div.243,Cpl.	MURDER	U.S.
HACKER, Fritz	160906	M			Prisoner,Civilian,C.C.,Wieda,Gardelegen(Ger.) 5.-14.4.45	MURDER	U.S.
HACKER, Herbert	24942	M	Ger.		SS-Sgt.,SS,C.C.Struthof-Natzweiler(Fr.)	MURDER	FR.
HACKER, Johann	31963	M	Ger.		Dr.,Landgerichtsrat,Public.Offis.,Litomerice(Czech.) 21.2.40	MURDER	CZECH.
HACKER, Max	192023	M	Ger.		Civilian,Burg a.d.Wupper(Ger.) 5.11.44	MURDER	FR.
HACKERS	192970	M	Ger.		Sgt.,SS,C.C.Buchenwald(Ger.) 42-45	TORTURE	U.S.
HACKETAHL	254518	M	Ger.		Medicin,C.C.Hinzert(Ger.)	INTERR.	FR.
HACKMANN	194888	M	Ger.		SS-Hptsturmfhr.,C.C.Lublin(Pol.) 40-42	MURDER	POL.
HACKMANN	254551	M	Ger.		SS-Osturmfhr.,C.C.Buchenwald(Ger.)	MISC.CRIMES	FR.
HACKMANN see MACKMANN	901580						
HACKMANN, Hermann	162453	M		13	SS-Hptschfhr.,C.C. Buchenwald, Lublin, Oranienburg(Ger.,Pol.)	TORTURE	U.S.
HACKMANN aliase JOHNNY	192969	M	Ger.		Capt.,SS,C.C.Buchenwald(Ger.) 38-39	TORTURE	U.S.
HACKNER	163104	M	Ger.		36 Panz.Regt.,10 Panz.Div.Frundsberg,Waffen-SS,Revin(Fr.) 6.44	MURDER	FR.
HADAMOVSKY, Eugen	187688	M	Ger.		Reichsleiter,Volksaufklaerungs-u.Propaganda-Ministerium	TORTURE	UNWCC.
HADEMANN, Heinrich	156721	M		94	Gestapo-Secretary,Cannes(Fr.)	MISC.CRIMES	FR.

HAD - HAG

NAME	C.R.FILE NUMBER	SEX	NATIONALITY	DATE OF BIRTH	RANK, OCCUPATION, UNIT, PLACE AND DATE OF CRIME	REASON WANTED	WANTED BY
HADER	306604	M	Ger.		N.C.O., Feldgendarmerie Chateaubriant (Loire-Inf.)St.Julien de Mouvantes,Juigne-les-Moutiers,Soudan,Le Teillais (Fr.) 21.7.44	MURDER	FR.
HADERS	167190	M	Ger.		Civ., Ersatz Stab Rosenberg, Paris (Fr.) 40-44	PILLAGE	FR.
HADERZET	162448	M	Ger.		Capt., Army, Amilly (Fr.) 20.8.44	MURDER	FR.
HADL, Ludwig	161993	M			Pvt., Army, Leipzig (Ger.)	TORTURE	U.S.
HADLEK	192968	M	Ger.		Usturmfhr., SS, C.C. Buchenwald (Ger.) 42-45	TORTURE	U.S.
HAEBER	127078	M	Ger.		Hptsturmfhr., 2.SS Pz.Div. "Das Reich"	MURDER	FR.
HAEBERLIN, Bernhard	193223	M	Ger.	28. 5.09	Dr.,Exconvict (convict physician),Reichsjustizministerium,Feldstraflager, C.C.Finnmark (Nor.) 3.45	WITNESS	NOR.
HAEBNER, Fritz	125633	M	Ger.	11	Member of Gestapo, Lille (Fr.)	MURDER	FR.
HAECK	256730	M	Ger.		Usturmfhr., SS, C.C. Harzungen, Nordhausen (Ger.)	MURDER	U.S.
HAECKEL	10081	M	Ger.		General, Kommando Lyon, St. Die (Fr.) 11.44	MISC.CRIMES	FR.
HAEFFNER	305862	M	Ger.		Pvt.,1.Aufkl.Abt.3.Coy.2.Col.XV Div.Afrika Korps,St.Leger,Arlon (Fr.) 5.9.44	MISC.CRIMES	BEL.
HAEGELE, Eugen	173629	M		95	Camp leader,Civ.firm Karl Kurtz,Hessental,Work Camp,C.C.Hessental (Ger.) 43-45	TORTURE	U.S.
HAEGER	252150	M		06	Capt., Fort Vincennes (Fr.) 20.8.44	MISC.CRIMES	FR.
HAEHNEL	126548	M	Ger.		Capt., Camp Werkschutzleiter, C.C. Hagen (Ger.) 43-45	MURDER	U.S.
HAEHNEL, Alfred	253707	M	Ger.	13. 2.02	Head of Gestapo, Litomerice (Czech.) 39-45	MURDER	CZECH.
HAEHNEL, Fritz	194904	M	Ger.	1. 3.02	Direktor, occupied territories, Luxemburg (Lux.)	PILLAGE	LUX.
HAEHNELDT (see HAENELDT)	194923						
HAEHR, Paul	305053	M	Ger.	2. 1.02	Gend., Feldgendarmerie at Alkmaar,Hugowaard,Wieringermeerdijk,Heer, (Neth.) 9.-12.44	MISC.CRIMES	NETH.
HAELCHE (or HELDTKE)	258711	M	Ger.		Doctor of Law,Oberkriegsgerichtsrat,Kriegsgericht Navy,Oslo(Nor.) 10.10.41	MURDER	NOR.
HAEMMERLE (or HAEMERLE), Albert	331	M	Ger.		Sgt., C.C.Birkenau,Oswiecim (Pol.) 39-45	MURDER	BEL.FR.POL.YU
HAENCHEN	197805	M	Ger.		Lt., Formation 05686, Neuvy (Fr.) 8.44	MISC.CRIMES	FR.
HAENDLEE	192967	M	Ger.		Sgt., SS, C.C. Buchenwald (Ger.) 38-42	TORTURE	U.S.
HAENDLER (see HAUSNER)	339						
HAENDLER, Werner	142913	M	Ger.		Sgt., Waffen SS,Totenkopfstandarte, C.C. Buchenwald (Ger.)	TORTURE	U.S.
HAENEL	9663	M	Ger.		Bdefhr.,Official of Reich,Sicherheitshauptamt, 40-44	MURDER	U.N.W.C.C.
HAENEL, Heinz	171258	M	Ger.	22	SS, Stumont (Bel.) 17.12.44	MURDER	U.S.
HAENELT	142921	M	Ger.	10	Lt., Adjutant, Waffen SS, C.C. Lublin (Pol.) 42	MURDER	U.S.
HAENELT (or HAEHNELDT)	194923	M	Ger.		Osturmfhr., SS, C.C. Lublin (Pol.) 40-44	MURDER	POL.
HAENELT	305051	M	Ger.		Sgt.,Major Army, F.P.No. 12406, Athen (Grc.) 10.43	PILLAGE	GRC.
HAENERT	186605	M			Hptschfhr., 4.SSTotenkopfsturmbann,SS Fahrbereitschaft, C.C. Nordhausen (Ger.) 43-45	WITNESS	U.S.
HAENICKE, Siegfried	21368	M	Ger.		General der Inf.,Commander of Wehrkreis Gov.Gen.,Gen.Gouvernement (Pol.)	TORTURE	U.N.W.C.C.
HAENISCH (or JEANISCH)	133667	M			SS Scharfhr., Charge of Bldg.Detail in Laveberg, Buchenwald (Ger.)	TORTURE	U.S.
HAENS, Vilroc	253972	M	Ger.		Pvt., Gend., Romorantin No.577, F.P.No.22501,Orcay (Fr.) 8.8.44	TORTURE	FR.
HAENTSCH, Fritz	261192	M	Ger.	01	Lt.-Cmdt., POW.54 Fara, Sabina (It.) School-teacher	SUSPECT	U.K.
HAERDT J	196631	M	Ger.		Medecin, Strasbourg (Fr.) 40-44	TORTURE	FR.
HAERINGER, Karl	252171	M	Ger.		Cpl., C.C.Ellrich, Nordhausen (Ger.)	MURDER	U.S.
HAERLEIN, Otto	185454	M	Ger.	05	Foreman, Work-Kdo, Factory, Nuernberg (Ger.) 40-45	TORTURE	U.S.
HAERTEL	154384	M			Usturmfhr., SS, C.C.Warsaw (Pol.)	TORTURE	U.S.
HAERTENIG, Fritz	197721	M	Ger.	9.12.20	Usturmfhr., SS, Reichsausbildungslager, Upice (Czech.) 5.45	MURDER	CZECH.
HAERTL, Karl	193419	M	Ger.	10. 7.89	Loc.Groupleader, Member,NSDAP,NSV,NSLB,Langendoerflas (Czech.)38-45	MISC.CRIMES	CZECH.
HAESER	256731	M	Ger.		C.C.Dora, Nordhausen (Ger.)	MURDER	U.S.
HAESIKER, August	145304	M			Oberfeldmstr.,RAD, Borkum (Ger.) 4.8.44	MURDER	U.S.
HAETZEL	332	M	Ger.	07	SA Osturmfhr., Camp leader, C.C.Mauthausen (Aust.) 41-42	TORTURE	NETH.
HAEUSER (see HAUSER),Georg	142460						
HAEUSLER, Richard	305052	M	Ger.		Deputy Chief,Dienstst.d.Reichskommissars f.Festigung d.Deutschtums, Marburg, Lower Styria (Yugo.) 41-42	PILLAGE	YUGO.
HAEVERNICK (or HERVIK)	256850	M	Ger.	95	Major, Abwehrnebenstelle, Bergen (Nor.) 40-41	WITNESS	NOR.
HAFEBURG (see HOFFERBURG)	152799						
HAFENRICHTER, Anton	255106	M	Ger.	13.11.01	Civ., Gossengrun, Haberspirk (Czech.) 9.39	MURDER	CZECH.
HAFER	190554	M			Lt., Ortskommandant at Cacak,Mrchjevicki,Bresnicki,Mosjinsacki (Yugo.) 43	MURDER	YUGO.
HAFER, W.	173615	M	Ger.		Dr., Admin. occupied territories (Fr.) 40-44	PILLAGE	FR.
HAFERBURG (see HOFFERBURG)	152799						
HAFERMANN	194784	M	Ger.		Civilian, St. Rambert (Fr.) 2.44	MISC.CRIMES	FR.
HAFFENBERG	154375	M			Policeman, Police, Wailrode (Ger.) 7.44	TORTURE	U.S.
HAFFENET	24979	M	Ger.		Former Civ., SS, Alsdorf (Ger.)	TORTURE	U.S.
HAFFENRICHTER, Wilibald	255105	M	Ger.		Civilian, Gossengrun, Haberspirk (Czech.) 9.39	MURDER	CZECH.
HAFFNER	194606	M			Col., Inf.Div. 36, Lepanges (Fr.) 9.44	PILLAGE	FR.
HAFFNER, George	142919	M			Guard, Mines C.C., Erkenschwick (Ger.)	TORTURE	U.S.
HAFFNER, Josef, Harry	261093	M	Ger.	5.00	Dr.,Sen.Public Prosecutor, President, People's Court, Court of Appeal, Hamm (Ger.)	SUSPECT	U.S.
HAFFNER, Matthias	251047	M	Ger.	6. 7.21	from Sgt. reduced to Pvt., Army, F.P.No.35130 E,Leersum (Neth.)9.44	WITNESS	NETH.
HAFNER	133668	M			SS Uschfhr., C.C. Buchenwald (Ger.)	TORTURE	U.S.
HAFNER	142917	M	Ger.		Lt., SS-Gestapo, C.C. Oedenburg (Hung.) 10.-11.44	MURDER	U.S.
HAFNER, Josef	194561	M	Ger.		Member, 2.SS Pz.Gren.Ausb.and Ers.Bn.12, Berneau (Bel.)	MURDER	BEL.
HAFNER, Pietro	306263	M	Ger.		Member,Gendarmerie Bressanone,Brixen (It.) 1.10.44	MURDER	U.K.
HAFRANKE, Raimund	188597	M	Ger.	15.10.06	Kriminalangestellter, Gestapo, Brno (Czech.) 39-45	MURDER	CZECH.
HAFT	188978	M	Ger.		Capt., Army, St.Martin du Mont (Fr.)	MISC.CRIMES	FR.
HAG (see HAAG)	167797						
HAG	197806	M	Ger.		Cpl., Lantilly (Fr.) 25.5.44	MURDER	FR.
HAGAR	333	M	Ger.		SS Usturmfhr., C.C. Boten (Nor.) 3.42-43	MURDER	YUGO.
HAGAR	161109	M	Ger.		Sgt., Army, Stalag Luft, on the march from Grosstychow to Fallingbostel (Ger.) 2.45-3.45	TORTURE	U.K.
HAGE	105918	F	Ger.		Gestapo, Investigator	TORTURE	U.S.
HAGE	300888	M	Ger.		Capt. and Adjutant, Oflag VI - B, Doessel nr.Warburg (Ger.) 39-45	MURDER	POL.
HAGE, Heinz	305418	M	Ger.		2.Ausb.Coy.,Pz.Gren.Ers.and Ausb.Bn.215 or 213,Bourcy nr.Bastogne (Lux.) 20.12.44	MURDER	BEL.
HAGEDORN, Kurt	168110	M			Pvt., Army, Slettego near Egersund, Stavanger (Nor.)	MURDER	U.K.

HAG-HAI

NAME	C.R.FILE NUMBER	SEX	NATIO-NALITY	DATE OF BIRTH	RANK OCCUPATION UNIT PLACE AND DATE OF CRIME	REASON WANTED	WANTED BY
HAGELMEISTER, Richard	334	M	Ger.		Army-Lager, KL. Oswiecim Birkenau (Pol.) 40	MURDER	FR.
HAGEL	185963	M	Ger.		Major, Geb.Art. Ers.Regt. 7, Detachment No.79 Mountain Art. Albertville (Fr.)	MURDER	FR.
HAGELWEISS, Hans Dietrich	259684	M	Ger.	12.11.10	Engineer, Civ. Dtsch. Lufthansa, Prague-Ruzyne (Czech.) 43	MURDER	CZECH.
HAGEMANN, Mina	250830	F	Ger.		Female Overseer, C.C. Lahde-Weser (Ger.)	INTERR.	BEL.
HAGEMANN, Toni	222538	M	Ger.	10	Pvt., Nachr.Regt. 506, 6th Coy., Bad Wildungen (Ger.) 45	MISC.CRIMES	U.S.
HAGEMEIER	173628	M			Uschfhr., C.C. Muhldorf (Ger.) 6.44-4.45	MURDER	U.S.
HAGEMEIER	253973	M	Ger.		SS-Sturmschfhr., SD, Toulouse (Fr.) 11.42-8.44	MISC.CRIMES	FR.
HAGEMES, Hermann	193222	M	Ger.	26.2.07	Ex Convict, Reichsjustizministerium, Feldstraflager Nord C.C. Finnmark (Nor.) 3.45	WITNESS	NOR.
HAGEMEYER, Johann	191622	M	Ger.		Prof., Director, Literatur Einsatzstab Rosenberg, Berlin (Ger.)40-44	PILLAGE	FR.
HAGEMIER	135542	M	Ger.		Civilian, Arbeitskdo. 101 Massbach (Ger.) 9.2.-12.12.44	TORTURE	U.K.
HAGEN	39802	M	Ger.		SS-Kanonier, Div. SS Feldpost No. 48963 B, St.-Sulpice, Montmisson Chateau (Fr.) 8.44	MURDER	FR.
HAGEN	196629	M	Ger.		Capt., Leader, Police SS, Bouscat, Bordeaux(Fr.) 10.41	MURDER	FR.
HAGEN	254519	M	Ger.		Major, 79. Res. Geb.Art.Abt., Feldpost No. 36121, Clery (Fr.) 5.44	MURDER	FR.
HAGEN	260614	M	Ger.		Lt., Coy. anti terrorist "Siegfried", Ampus (Fr.) 7.44	MURDER	FR.
HAGEN	306971	M	Ger.		SS-Mann, C.C. Auschwitz (Pol.) 41	MURDER	POL.
HAGEN, Hugo	256751	M	Ger.		Camp Senior Rottleberode, Nordhausen (Ger.)	MURDER	U.S.
HAGEN, Hermann	132034	M			Miscellaneous	MISC.CRIMES	U.S.
HAGENAECKER, Heinrich	305162	M			Cpl., O.K., Nebenstelle Hal-Leerbeek (Bel.) 44	MURDER	BEL.
HAGENBART	305550	M	Ger.	00	Capt., Member, SD Commanding Schlanderser Police, Borco Prov.of Trento (It.) 12.44	MURDER	U.K.
HAGENBUSCH	146866	M	Ger.		Upterscharfhr., SS-Panz.Div. "Das Reich", "Deutschland"-Regt., 3.Bn.	MURDER	FR.
HAGENBUCK	72565	M			Adjutant-Chief, W.-SS Div. "Das Reich" and "Der Fuehrer" Liège (Bel.)	TORTURE	FR.
HAGENBUSCH, Eberhard	142456	M	Ger.	22	Lt., 2. Army (AA) Art. 503nd Bde. 10th Batt. Hilden (Ger.) 4.45	WITNESS	U.S.
HAGENER	150311	M			Lt., Army, La Baffe (Fr.)	MURDER	FR.
HAGENMAIER, Erich	154376	M	Ger.	99	Police-Director, (Brigadefhr. SA) Police SA, Ulm (Ger.) 40-45	MURDER	U.S.
HAGER	186606	M			Pvt., 4. SS Totenkopfsturmbann, Camp Guard, Nordhausen (Ger.) 43-45	WITNESS	U.S.
HAGESTET, Karl Heinz	185665	M	Ger.		Unterscharfhr., 9th SS Pion.Coy. Leibst. Adolf Hitler, Malmedy (Bel.) 17.12.44	MURDER	U.S.
HAGETORN	62251	M			Stabsscharfhr., 12. SS Pz.Div. "H.J.",	MISC.CRIMES	CAN.
HAGG, Kornelius	252325	M		30.9.17	Sgt., Camp Ellrich; Nordhausen (Ger.)	MURDER	U.S.
HAGMAYER	258160		Ger.		Lt., German Army, Brzane (Yugo.) 8.41	MURDER	YUGO.
HAGMEIER, Frederich	142999	M	Ger.	17.12.93	Groupleader, Mayor, Civilian, NSDAP, Aufhausen (Ger.) 7.44	TORTURE	U.S.
HAGN, Georg	194560	M	Ger.	98	SS-Pol.-Fuehrer, SS Polizei, Nyrany (Czech.) 39-45	TORTURE	CZECH.
HAGN, Kaethe	194559	F	Ger.	07	Civilian, Nyrany (Czech.) 39-45	TORTURE	CZECH.
HAGUENER	167380	M	Ger.		Lt., Army, Richardmesnil, Metz (Fr.) 9.44	WITNESS	FR.
HAHM	179755	M	Ger.		Capt., Hermann Goering Div. Tank Regt., Bucuie (It.)9.7.44	MURDER	U.K.
HAHMANN, Hans see HAHRMANN	193221						
HAHMANN, Kurt	31954	M	Ger.		Sgt., Feldgend. 577. Romorantin (Fr.) 17.8.44	MURDER	FR.
HAHNS see HAHN	29868						
HAHN	10082	M	Ger.		N.C.O., 13.Coy. of 950. Indian-Regt., Ruffec (Fr.) 8.44	MURDER	FR.
HAHN	29867	M	Ger.		Capt., Army, Officer Commanding, Lorient Orleans (Fr.) 8.44	MURDER	U.K.
HAHN or HAHNS	29868	M			Cmdt., Stalag 3C, Sagan (Ger.) 1.44-2.45	MURDER	U.K.
HAHN	132543	M		95	Sturmbannfhr., SS, KL. Hallein (Aust.)	TORTURE	FR.
HAHN	134851	M			Cpl., Guard, 4. SS Bau-Bde. C.C. From Ehrlich to and at Gardelegen (Ger.) 4.-14.4.45	MURDER	U.S.
HAHN	141428	M	Ger.		Col., Commandantur, Menton (Fr.) 29.8.44	MURDER	FR.
HAHN	165925	M	Ger.	89	Lt.Col., Schlunder Pol. Regt., Camp Molon (It.) 2.45	MURDER	U.S.
HAHN	167191	M	Ger.		Lt., Pz.Jaeg. Abt. 227, 227 Inf.Div., Roxville (Fr.) 40-44	PILLAGE	FR.
HAHN	173568	M	Ger.		Official, Gestapo, Belgrade (Yugo.) 17.8.41	MURDER	YUGO.
HAHN	173579	M	Ger.		Capt, 1010 Pz.Regt., 2.Bn., 5. Coy., Chilleurs Aux Bois (Fr.) 8.44	MURDER	U.K.
HAHN	174239	M	Ger.		Lt. General, Hauptverbindungsstab 90, Lyon (Fr.) 9.11.43	MURDER	FR.
HAHN	185664	M			Adjutant, Feldgend., Baume Cornillame (Fr.)	MURDER	FR.
HAHN	186005	M			Pvt., Army, St. Andre Legaz (Fr.) 8.7.44	MURDER	FR.
HAHN	186607	M	Ger.		Rottenfhr., 4. SS Totenkopfsturmbann Camp Guard, Nordhausen (Ger.) 43-45	WITNESS	U.S.
HAHN	187938	M			N.C.O., 950th Indian Regt., 13. Coy., Ruffec (Fr.)	MURDER	FR.
HAHN	192024	M	Ger.		Colonel-Chief, Kommandantur, Menton (Fr.) 29.8.44	MURDER	FR.
HAHN	195215	M	Ger.		Cpl., SD Sonder-und Wirtschaftskomm., Beeck, Gorssel (Neth.) 9.44	MURDER	NETH.
HAHN	197809	M	Ger.		Dr., Sturmbannfhr., Councaller of State, Warschau (Pol.) 43-45	MURDER	POL.
HAHN	251612	M	Ger.		Hilfspolizei-Beamter, Interpreter "U-B" Abt.-Sipo, Bruessels (Bel.)40-45	INTERR.	BEL.
HAHN or HAAN	260235	M	Ger.		Sgt., Army, Domicile Fieflingen, Thuringia Oldenzaal, (Overijsel Neth.) 45	PILLAGE	NETH.
HAHN, Alfred	197810	M	Ger.		Blockman, Block 2, C.C. Flossenburg (Ger.)	MURDER	FR.
HAHN, Frits	250646	M	Ger.		SS-Hptsturmfhr., Gestapo, Lille (Fr.)	MISC.CRIMES	FR.
HAHN, Hans	256772	M		06	Scharfhr., or Unterscharfhr., SS, Muehldorf (Ger.)	MURDER	U.S.
HAHN, Ludwig	196626	M	Ger.		Dr., Cmdt., Gestapo and SD, Police, Warschau (Pol.)	INTERR.	POL.
HAHN, Paul Gerhard	301092	M	Ger.		Usturmfhr., Vorden (Neth.) 10.44	MURDER	U.K.
HAHNEL, Albert	252390	M			Flyer, Camp Ellrich, Nordhausen (Ger.)	MURDER	U.S.
HAHNEL, Heinz	195765	M	Ger.		SS-Unterscharfhr., SS 2nd Pz.Gren.Regt., Stevmont, Ligneuville (Bel.) 12.44	MURDER	U.S.
HAHNENKAMM, Josef	193899	M	Ger.	20.4.08	Blockleader, NSDAP, (Czech.)	MISC.CRIMES	CZECH.
HAHNER	72576	M	Ger.		Lt., Army, Foret Colettes (Fr.) 44	MURDER	FR.
HAHNER	169094	M			Lt., 19. Sich. Regt. 192, Loureux Bodemond (Fr.) 28.7.44	PILLAGE	FR.
HAHNLEIN, Hugo	160904	M			Guard, Civilian, C.C. Untermassfeld (Ger.) 41-45	MURDER	U.S.
HAHNRATHS, Heinrich	335	M	Ger.		Civilian KL. Alsdorf (Ger.) 42-44	MISC.CRIMES	U.S.
HAHNS or HAHN	178914	M	Ger.	97	Capt., Stalag VIII C, Sagan (Ger.) 2.45	TORTURE	U.K.
HAHRMANN, Hans or HAHMANN	193221	M	Ger.		Sgt., 2nd Leichte Flak Abt. 623, Malm near Levanger (Nor.) 9.44	WITNESS	NOR.
HAIDER, Friedrich	10083	M	Ger.		Pvt., Pz.Gren.Regt. 110 2nd Coy., Albine (Fr.) 29.6.44	MURDER	FR.
HAIDES	150307	M			Guard, C.C. Lustboekel (Ger.) 42	MURDER	FR.
HAIEN, Josef	192787	M	Ger.		Schupo, Stalag C.C. Falstad Drontheim (Nor.) 41-45	MURDER	NOR.
HAIETZ or HEITZ	167379	M	Ger.		Lt., Wolga Tartare Legion, Ruines (Fr.) 10.6.44	MURDER	FR.

-143-

HAI-HAM

NAME	C.R.FILE NUMBER	SEX	NATIO- NALITY	DATE OF BIRTH	RANK OCCUPATION UNIT PLACE AND DATE OF CRIME	REASON WANTED	WANTED BY
HAIGIS	162454	M	Ger.	96	Blockwalter, NSDAP, member of the Polit.Staff, Koenig near Erbach (Ger.) 10.12.44	MURDER	U.K.
HAIMANN	255577	M			Uscharfhr.,C.C. Buchenwald (Ger.)	MURDER	U.S.
HAIMERL, Max	252331	M			Pvt., Camp Ellrich, Nordhausen (Ger.)	MURDER	U.S.
HAIN, Franz	256885	M	Ger.		Zugwachtmeister,7 Coy,322 Bn,5 Schuetz.Rgt., Ljubljana, Cetje, Kranj (Yugo.) 42-43	MISC.CRIMES	YUGO.
HAIN, Friedrich	301318	M	Ger.		Member, Gestapo at Trencin, C.C. Oswiecim-Birkenau (Pol.) 39-45	MURDER	CZECH.
HAINBACH	301319	M	Ger.		Member, Gestapo at Trencin, C.C. Oswiecim-Birkenau (Pol.) 39-45	MURDER	CZECH.
HAINDL, Anton	253692	M	Ger.	29.12.02	Gendarm, Gendarmerie, Vsetin (Czech.) 39-45	MURDER	CZECH.
HAINDL, Rudolf	197719	M	Ger.	12	Scharfhr., SS, C.C. Terezin (Czech.)	TORTURE	CZECH.
HAINHORST	192965	M	Ger.		Sturmfhr.,SS, C.C. Buchenwald (Ger.) 42-45	TORTURE	U.S.
HAINOWSKI, Theofil	253051	M			Pvt.,Camp Ellrich, Nordhausen (Ger.)	MURDER	U.S.
HAINS, Thoms	167378	M	Ger.		Pvt.,Airforce, Troissereux Oise (Fr.) 15.,16.,18.8.44	MURDER	FR.
HAIPEL	188711	M			SS, Karlovy Vary (Czech.) 1.4.45	WITNESS	U.S.
HAISELE	72580	M			Lt.,Army, Ukraine (Sov.Un.)	MURDER	FR.
HAISER, Wilhelm	194783	M	Ger.		Intendant, Luftpark E.M.,Cambrai (Fr.) 40-41	PILLAGE	FR.
HAISMANN	301320	M	Ger.		Member, Gestapo at Trencin, C.C. Oswiecim-Birkenau (Pol.) 39-45	MURDER	CZECH.
HAIT	256090	M	Ger.		SS-Mann, SS-Bn, Meerveld, Utrecht (Neth.) 11.44	MURDER	NETH.
HAITMAN	185292	M	Ger.		N.C.O.,SS Police, Kapandriti,Athens (Grc.) 7.44	MURDER	GRC.
HAITSCHI, Georg	252167	M	Ger.		Rottenfhr.,SS, Camp Bodungen, Nordhausen (Ger.)	MURDER	U.S.
HAJDBA	167192	M	Ger.		W.O.,Georgian Bn, 1 Coy,Tuile-Correze (Fr.) 6.4.44	MISC.CRIMES	FR.
HAJDUK, Karl	251033	M	Ger.	7. 8.20	Confidential Agent, Gestapo, Breclav (Czech.) 39-45	MURDER	CZECH.
HAJEK, Jaroslav Vojtech	196936	M		97	Lt., Gendarmerie, Kolin (Czech.) 39-45	MISC.CRIMES	CZECH.
HAJEK, Josef	258091	M	Ger.	11. 6.91	Informer, SD-Gestapo, Horazdovice (Czech.) 42-45	MISC.CRIMES	CZECH.
HAJEK, Otto	194605	M	Ger.	88	Employee, SD, Kolin (Czech.) 39-45	SUSPECT	CZECH.
HAJOK, Ernst	24953	M			Sgt.,Fallschirmjaeger, Roermond (Neth.) 11.44-1.45	TORTURE	U.S.
HAK see HACK	253036						
HAK, Josef	132315	M	Ger.		N.C.O., Gendarmerie, Aachen (Ger.) 42-45	TORTURE	U.S.
HALAMA	130389	M			Uscharfhr.,W-SS,Div. Totenkopf, Mauthausen (Aust.) 41-45	MURDER	U.S.
HALAND, Otto	161979	M	Ger.		Sgt.,SS-Div.Hitlerjugend, Gollheim (Ger.) 15.9.44	MURDER	U.S.
HALBACH or HAIDACH	72544	M			Sgt., D.C.A.,Villemur (Fr.)	MURDER	FR.
HALBE	1698	M			Lt., Army,326 Div. 15-752 Rgt., Caumont (Fr.) 44	MURDER	U.K.
HALBIERS	252177	M			Pvt.,Camp Ellrich, Nordhausen (Ger.)	MURDER	U.S.
HALBLEIS	253853	M	Ger.	95	Uscharfhr.,SS,C.C. Auschwitz-Birkenau (Pol.) 42-45	MURDER	YUGO.
HALBSGUT	174171	M			Civilian, Org.Todt, C.C. Muhldorf,Ampfing (Ger.) 6.44-4.45	MURDER	U.S.
HALBURN	134739	M			Member of crew, Ger.Navy,Pointe de Mouaterlin.(Fr.) 30.6.44	MURDER	U.S.
HALCHE	305633	M	Ger.		Dr.,Oberkriegsgerichtsrat,President of Ger.Court Martial Obermarinekriegsgericht at Oslo (Nor.) 10.10.41	MURDER	NOR.
HAIDACH see HALBACH	72544						
HALDER, Franz	336	M	Ger.		Lt.Gen.,Army group, 1.9.39-30.10.39	MURDER	POL.
HALEINDORF	173601	M	Ger.		Sgt.,Camp Poitiers (Fr.) 40-8.44	MURDER	FR.
HALFAR, Marie-Monika	251034	F	Ger.		Agent, Gestapo of Prague and Benesov, Zbraslav (Czech.) 39-45	MISC.CRIMES	CZECH.
HALIBAUER, Heinrich	31962	M	Ger.		Landgerichtsrat, Public-official, Litomerice (Czech.) 21.2.40	MURDER	CZECH.
HALL, Karl	24980	M	Ger.		Civilian, formerly senior worker at Anna Mine,Alsdorf (Ger.)	MISC.CRIMES	U.S.
HALL, Karl see MIHALICEK, Karel	261119						
HALLA, Ferdinand	196624	M	Ger.		Oscharfhr.,SD Kdo. "Wenger", Baccarat, Etival (Fr.) 44	MURDER	U.K.
HALLA, Ludwig	31961	M	Ger.		Landgerichtsrat, public official, Litomerice (Czech.) 21.2.40	MURDER	CZECH.
HALLACKER	186633	M	Ger.		W.O.,Army, Unit 40539, Dep. Cotes du Nord (Fr.)	PILLAGE	FR.
HALLE or HOLLE	190339	M		10.10	Civilian, Farmer (Ger.)	MURDER	U.S.
HALLEMERS	189634	M	Ger.		Feldgendarmerie, L'Absie (Fr.) 24.8.44	WITNESS	FR.
HALLER	130387	M	Ger.	07	Officer, SA, C.C. Kahla (Ger.)	MISC.CRIMES	BEL.
HALLER	301414	M	Ger.		SS-Lt.Col.,chief of police Bromberg, C.C.	MURDER	FR.
HALLER, Max	260106	M			Kapo, C.C. Dachau (Ger.) 42-44	TORTURE	FR.
HALLINGER, Georg	174172	M			Work camp, C.C. Muhldorf,Ampfing (Ger.) 6.44-4.45	MURDER	U.S.
HALLITAU, Alfred	140778	M			Cpl.,Heimat-Wach-Bn 445, C.C. Bergen near Rosenheim (Ger.) 43-44	MURDER	U.S.
HALLMANN, Robert	259684	M	Ger.	18. 9.99	Lt., Gestapo, Area of Angers (Maine and Loire-Fr.) 42-44	TORTURE	FR.
HAILMANN, Rudolf	260943	M	Ger.	3. 3.08	Pvt.,SS-guard, C.C. Auschwitz (Pol.) 44-45	BRUTALITY	POL.
HALLOWE, Franz	142998	M	Ger.	05	Guard, 2 Pz.Gren.and Ausb.Bn, Stalag XVII B,Gneixendorf (Ger.) 10.41-4.42	MURDER	U.S.
HALMANN	192964	M	Ger.		Cpl.,SS, C.C. Buchenwald (Ger.) 42-45	TORTURE	U.S
HALSTENBERGER	189635	M	Ger.		Pvt.,Army, Welferding (Fr.) 6.1.44	MURDER	FR.
HALTMEIER, Wenzel	252178	M			Pvt., C.C.Rossla-Nordhausen (Ger.)	MURDER	U.S.
HALUPKA	11563	M			Sgt.,Inf.Rgt.858, Caen (Fr.) 44	MURDER	U.K.
HAM	29866	M			Capt.,Stalag 8 C (Ger.) 8.2.45	TORTURE	U.K.
HAMACHEK, Joseph	128863	M	Ger.		Civilian in Camp, foreman in stone Quarry,Mittletangenau(Ger.)3.11.41	MURDER	U.K.
HAMACHER	24941	M	Ger.		Sgt., SS, C.C. Struthof (Fr.)	TORTURE	FR.
HAMACHER	125079		Ger.		Civilian, 12.44	MURDER	U.K.,U.S.
HAMACHER	134713	M		15	Driver, Gestapo in Duesseldorf, Neuss (Ger.) 23.or 24.12.44	MURDER	U.K.,U.S.
HAMACHER, Bertram	252176	M		8. 2.09	Pvt., C.C. Ellrich-Nordhausen (Ger.)	MURDER	U.S.
HAMAKER	162836	M			Cpl.,Army,Kriegsgef.Arb.Bn 185, Aspefjord (Nor.)	TORTURE	NOR.
HAMAN, Max	193220	M		99	Civ.Serv.,Reichsjustizministerium, Feldstraflager, C.C. Finmark (Nor.) 42-45	MISC.CRIMES	NOR.
HAMANN, Ewald	252179	M			Flyer, C.C. Ellrich-Nordhausen (Ger.)	MURDER	U.S.
HAMARICHE	72545	M			Miscellaneous, Perigueux (Fr.)	TORTURE	FR.
HAMATCHEK, Josef	187984	M	Ger.	05	Foreman, Civilian, Stalag VIII B, Mittletangenau (Ger.) 7.42	TORTURE	U.K.
HAMBECK	162835	M	Ger.		Col.,Rgt.991,Div.277, Chapelle A Die (Bel.) 3.9.44	MURDER	BEL.
HAMBERLAND, Jr.	174173	M	Ger.		Civilian, Iserbrook (Ger.) 20.6.44	TORTURE	U.S.
HAMBRECHT	140029	M	Ger.		Chief, Gestapo, St.Crepin,De Richmont,Cantillac (Fr.)26.,27.3.-8.44	MURDER	FR.
HAMBROCK, Theodor	253974	M	Ger.	22. 1.23	Pvt.,13 Coy, 558 Gren.Rgt., Bruay en Artois (Fr.) 1.9.44	MURDER	FR.
HAMBRUST	132710	M	Ger.		Guard, C.C. Schirmeck, Freconrupt,Broque (Fr.) 7.3.44	MURDER	FR.
HAMBUSCH	254527	M	Ger.		Mayor, Ferlach (Aust.) 44-45	MURDER	YUGO.
HAMECHEN	301563	M	Ger.		Crim.commissar, C.C. Mauthausen (Aust.) 40-45	MURDER	BEL.
HAMEISTER, Werner	132179	M	Ger.		San.-Pvt., Ger.Navy U 852, Atlantic Ocean,South of Freetown .,13.3.44	WITNESS	U.K.
HAMEL, Hermann Georg Wilhelm	305164	M	Ger.		SS-Oscharfhr.,Gefaengnis-Oberwachtmstr., C.C. Grini (Nor.) 1.-5.45	MISC.CRIMES	NOR.

NAME	C.R.FILE NUMBER	SEX	NATIO-NALITY	DATE OF BIRTH	RANK OCCUPATION UNIT PLACE AND DATE OF CRIME	REASON WANTED	WANTED BY
HAMERL	167180	M	Ger.		Major, 950.Inf. Rgt., Ruffec (Fr.) 18.-21.8.44	MURDER	FR.
HAMERSCHT	72552	M			Chief of post, S.D., Perigueux (Fr.)	MURDER	FR.
HAMHANDS see SCHMIDT	129891						
HAMICH	191618	M	Ger.		Sgt., Feldgendarmerie, Briey (Fr.) 28.8.44	TORTURE	FR.
HAMIL	187971	M	Ger.	15	Guard, Pvt., Stalag IV F, C.C. Chemnitz (Ger.) 1.43	TORTURE	U.K.
HAMIL or HAMMEL	306584	M	Ger.		Pvt., A-K R. 124 Reichenbach nr.Jacobthal (Ger.) 9.44-4.45	BRUTALITY	U.K.
HAMM	130061	M	Ger.		Sgt., C.C. Galatas (Grc.) 12.6.41	MURDER	U.K.
HAMM	261198	M	Ger.		Pvt., 5-I Rgt.211, 139.Arbeitsbereich Liane, Alleur,Lez,Liege (Bel.) 9.44	MURDER	BEL.
HAMM	305893	M	Ger.		SS Oscharfhr., Head of the Zlin Aussenstelle, S.D.,Leitabschnitt Prague, Oswiecim C.C.Birkenau (Pol.) 9.42 - 45	MURDER	CZECH.
HAMM, Jakob	195373	M			Kapo, C.C. Braunschweig-Schandelah (Ger.)	TORTURE	BEL.
HAMMACHER, Friedrich	174298	M		8. 2.92	Civ., C.C. Struthof (Fr.)	MURDER	U.N.W.C.C.
HAMMAN	140870	M		circa 85	Kreisfuehrer NSDAP, Capt., Elten (Ger.) 16.9.44	MURDER	CAN.
HAMMAN or HARMANN, Georges	142416	M	Ger.		Sgt., Gestapo, Cannes (Fr.) 43	PILLAGE	FR.
HAMMEL see HAMIL	306584						
HAMMEMULLER	130159	M	Ger.	03	Sgt., Police Hamburg, Brussels (Bel.) 26.5.44-4.6.44	TORTURE	U.K.
HAMMER	36684	M	Ger.		Uscharfhr., C.C. Staff Belsen (Ger.)	TORTURE	POL.
HAMMER	152473	M	Ger.		SS Sturmscharfhr., Gestapo, S.D., Trondes, Boucq, Menil la Tour (Fr.) 15.8.44	MURDER	FR.
HAMMER	196621	M	Ger.		Capt., Sicherungs-Rgt. C.18, St.Marcel (Fr.)	MISC.CRIMES	FR.
HAMMER	250231	M	Ger.		Guard, C.C. Monsheim (Ger.) 44-45	BRUTALITY	FR.
HAMMER	252180	M	Ger.		Pvt., C.C. Dora - Nordhausen (Ger.)	MURDER	U.S.
HAMMER	253970	M	Ger.		Dr., Chief, Gestapo, Nis (Yugo.)	MURDER	YUGO.
HAMMER	254543	M	Ger.		Sturmscharfhr., Gestapo, 398.SS Div. Cmdt. 3.Bn. N.C.O.-school, La Bresse (Fr.)	MURDER	FR.
HAMMER	256774	M			Member, S.A., Gratkorn (Aust.) 2.45	MURDER	U.S.
HAMMER	257969	M	Ger.		SS Guard, Sgt., SS slave labour camp, Beisfjord nr/Narvik (Nor.) 6.-11.42	BRUTALITY	YUGO.
HAMMER	260148	M	Ger.		Lt., 157. Res.Div. Bavaria, Massif du Vercors, Isere et Drome (Fr.) 20.7.-5.8.44	SUSPECT	FR.
HAMMER, Albert	135177	M	Ger.	03	Obersekretaer, Kripo, Ruppertshutten (Ger.) 12.9.44	MURDER	U.S.
HAMMER, Eleonore	132570	F	Ger.	13. 1.24	Interpreter, Gestapo, Barcus (Fr.) 23.6.43	MURDER	FR.
HAMMER, Franz	175519	M	Ger.	00	Official, Abwehr - Werwolf, Schweiningen (Ger.)	MURDER	U.N.W.C.C.
HAMMER, Karl	252181	M			Flyer, C.C. Nordhausen - Ellrich (Ger.)	MURDER	U.S.
HAMMER, Max	190555	M			Lt., 893.Inf.Rgt., Sibenik, Zablac (Yugo.) 5.-6.44	MURDER	YUGO.
HAMMER, Otto	67851	M	Ger.		Subcontroller, Stalag XI B, Civ. H.G.Wenke,Brunswick, C.C. Fallingbostel (Ger.)	TORTURE	U.K.
HAMMER, Walter	187679	M	Ger.		Raidelbach (Ger.) 4.44	TORTURE	U.K.
HAMMER, Willy	255271	M	Ger.	1. 8.04	Employee, Crim.police, Prag (Czech.) 39-42	MISC.CRIMES	CZECH.
HAMMER, Willy	306382	M	Ger.	22. 8.92	SS Uscharfhr., C.C. Buchenwald (Ger.) betw.16.5.38 and 9.10.43	MURDER	BEL.
HAMMERER, Max	195767	M	Ger.		SS Rottfhr., 1.Panz.Div., C.C. Stoumont, Ligneuville (Bel.)17.,19.12.44	MURDER	U.S.
HAMMERICH, Georg	188709	M	Ger.	17. 6.93	Secretary, police, Lauf-Pegnitz (Ger.) 11.4.45	SUSPECT	POL.
HAMMERSCHMIDT	254520	M	Ger.		Sgt., Dienststelle Nr.67140, Enschede (Neth.) 1.4.45	WITNESS	NETH.
HAMMERSCHMIDT, Heinz	1120	M	Ger.		Lt., Army, 130.Panz.Lehr-Rgt. 5.Bn.	WITNESS	U.S.
HAMMERSCHMIDT, Hilmar	259093	M	Ger.		Col., XI. Jaeger-Rgt. (Yugo.) 44-45	MISC.CRIMES	YUGO.
HAMMES	162467	M	Ger.	97	SS-Mann, C.C. Buchenwald (Ger.)	TORTURE	U.S.
HAMMETMER	162466	M	Ger.		Cpl., 263.Inf.Div., Landerneau (Fr.) 44	MURDER	FR.
HAMMETMER see SMITH	167985						
HAMMON	72558	M			Lt.Col., German Gerichtshof, Villars s.Escor (Fr.)	MURDER	FR.
HAMON	72559	M			Major, Army, Chanas (Fr.)	TORTURE	FR.
HAMONT	147329	M	Ger.		Col., 11.Panz.Div., Fr. 44	MURDER	FR.
HAMPE, W.M.	72560				Pointe de Dieppe (Fr.)	TORTURE	FR.
HAMPEL	174174	M			Baufuehrer, leader, Org.Todt, C.C. Muehldorf, Ampfing (Ger.) 6.44-4.45	MURDER	U.S.
HAMPEL	255107	M	Ger.	95	Crim.Inspector, Gestapo, Breslau (Ger.)	INTERR.	U.K.
HAMPEL	261342	M	Ger.		Airforce L.52 511, Pau,Soumonton, Narp, Lescar (Fr.) 7.-8.44	MURDER	FR.
HAMPELS, Willi	194297	M	Ger.	20	Cpl., Gemischte Flak Abt. 515, 4 Btty., Rjukan (Nor.) 1.45	MURDER	U.K.
HAMPROTTER	72561	M			Adjutant-chief, Flak-Rgt. Art., Villemur (Fr.) 44	MURDER	FR.
HAMREL	186479	M			Cmdt., 950. R.J.H., Dep.Prov. Charente et Vienne (Fr.) 8.44	TORTURE	FR.
HAMSCHE	940	M	Ger.		SS Rottfhr., C.C. Maidanek (Pol.) 40, 4.44	MURDER	POL.
HAMSLER, Zeno	338	M	Ger.		SS officer, Fort Musson (Fr.) 3.8.44	MURDER	FR.
HANACHER	167808	M	Ger.		Dr., Trust-Leader Unterabt. Treuhandwesen, Lublin (Pol.) 9.39-44	PILLAGE	POL.
HANAK, Wenzel	252421	M	Ger.	13. 9.98	Pvt., C.C. Nordhausen (Ger.)	MURDER	U.S.
HANAUER, Johann	188595	M	Ger.	5.12.98	Prison-guard, Gestapo, C.C. Brno (Czech.) 39-45	TORTURE	CZECH.
HANAY	72562	M			Dr. jur., Oberkriegsgerichtsrat, Ger.Gerichtshof, Lyon (Fr.)	MURDER	FR.
HANCK, Erwin	142916	M			Sturmmann, Waffen SS, 2.SS Panz.Div."Das Reich", Tulle (Fr.) 5.44	WITNESS	U.S.
HANCKE, Louis	199219	M	Ger.	01	Sgt., C.C. Finnmark (Nor.) 42-45	MISC.CRIMES	NOR.
HAND, Alfred	252326	M	Ger.	9. 5.95	SS Uscharfhr., C.C. Nordhausen (Ger.)	MURDER	U.S.
HANDELER	300711	M	Ger.		Hptscharfhr., C.C. Auschwitz-Birkenau (Pol.) from 40	MISC.CRIMES	FR.
HANDL, Alfred Peter	257097	M			Pvt., Hermann Goering Parachute-Rgt., Rouen (Fr.) 6.44	BRUTALITY	U.S.
HANDLER	72584	M			Hptscharfhr., Waffen SS, C.C. Buchenwald (Fr.)	TORTURE	FR.
HANDLER	147328	M			Lt., 15.Panz.Rgt., 11.Panz.Div.,South-west Fr., 44	MURDER	FR.
HANDLER	173589	M			SS Osturmfhr., C.C. Auschwitz, Birkenau (Pol.)	MURDER	CZECH.POL. BEL.
HANDLER	906605	M			Sgt.,Interpreter, Feldgendarmerie Chateaubriant Loire-Interieur, Les Moutiers, Soudan le Teillais, St.Julien de Mouvantes, Juigne(Fr.) 21.7.44	MURDER	FR.
HANDLY	236859	M			Lt.Col., Army Strassbourg,Barkenbruegge (Ger.) 44-45	INTERR.	YUGO.
HANDRICH	142470	M			Public official, Buergermeister, Ettesberg (Ger.)	MURDER	U.S.
HANDSCHICK	186609	M			Rottfhr., 4.SS Totenkopf-Stuba, Fahrbereitschaft, C.C.Nordhausen (Ger.) 43-45	WITNESS	U.S.
HANDT, Alfred	186610	M		9. 5.95	Uscharfhr., 4.SS Totenkopf-Stuba, C.C. Nordhausen (Ger.) 43-45	WITNESS	U.S.
HANDTKE, Wilhelm	186611	M	Ger.		Hptscharfhr., Crim.secretary, SS, Kripo, Montgauthier-Dinant (Bel.)9.43	MURDER	BEL.
HANDTKE, Willy	192419	M	Ger.		Staff Sgt., S.D., Cerfontaine, Senzeille,Charleroi (Bel.) 2.-4.44	TORTURE	BEL.
HANDWERK, Karol	1699	M	Ger.		Sgt., 148. I.Rgt., Amiens (Fr.) 26.8.44	MURDER	U.K.
HANDWERKER	305863	M	Ger.		Pvt.,1.Aufkl.Abt.9.Coy.2.Col.XV.Div.Afrika-Corps,St.Leger (Arlon)5.9.44	MISC.CRIMES	BEL.

HAN-HAN

NAME	C.R.FILE NUMBER	SEX	NATIO-NALITY	DATE OF BIRTH	RANK OCCUPATION UNIT PLACE AND DATE IF CRIME	REASON WANTED	WANTED BY
HANEBERG, Gerd	123985	M	Ger.	25. 2.15	Lt.,Inf.Div.353, (Pol.) 1.40	MISC.CRIMES	POL.
HANECKER (see HABECKER)	182572						
HANECKER (see RABECKER)	193314						
HANEGGER, Anna	185532	F	Ger.		Civilian,C.C.,Zwilling (Ger.) 4.45	MURDER	U.S.
HANEL	252327	M			Pvt.,C.C.,Nordhausen (Ger.)	MURDER	U.S.
HANERT	157787	M			Civilian,C.C.,Ottmanshausen (Ger.) 8.44	MURDER	U.S.
HANESSE	31918	M	Ger.		Army,Pvt.,Parachutiste,Abbeville (Fr.) 31.8.44	MURDER	FR.
HANFELD, Wilhelm	252328	M	Ger.		Pvt.,C.C.,Nordhausen (Ger.)	MURDER	U.S.
HANGEL	165918	M			Sturmbannfhr.,SS,Lodz (Pol.) 40-45	PILLAGE	U.S.
HANGEL	259229	M			Capt.,Guard-Coy.,P.O.W. of Stalag VI D,Bn.17,Dortmund (Ger.) 3.45	MURDER	FR.
HANGELAR	24954	M			Interpreter,Gestapo,C.C.,Cologne,Klingelpuetz, 1.-2.45	TORTURE	U.S.
HANHER	301415	M	Ger.		Lt.,member,19.Sich.Rgt.,192 SD,Montlucon,Chappes,Louroux,Hodement Allier (Fr.) 28.7.44	MURDER	FR.
HANIEL, Karl	260205	M	Ger.	12. 2.77	Doctor,Ch.Ar.,Gutehoffnungshuette, Aktien-Verband,Bergbau und Huettenbetrieb,Nuernberg (Ger.)	MISC.CRIMES	U.S.
HANIG	124774	M		15	Osturmfhr.,SS,SD,C.C.,Niederkruchten 9.44-10.44	PILLAGE	U.S.
HANIG	141368	M			Lt.,Army,Serzy (Fr.) 28.8.44	MURDER	FR.
HANIG	162472	M		15	Osturmfhr.,SS,SD,Bruessels (Bel.)	MISC.CRIMES	BEL.
HANIG	174175	M	Ger.		Lt.,Army,Sekzy (Fr.) 28.8.44	MURDER	U.S.
HANISCH	157749	M	Ger.	00	Sgt.,Landesschuetzen Bn.439,1.Coy.,Bayreuth (Ger.) 11.4.45	MISC.CRIMES	U.K.
HANISCH	192005	M	Ger.		Sgt.,Army,C.C.,Gossen (Nor.)	TORTURE	NOR.
HANISCH, Alfred	125149	M	Ger.		Civilian,C.C.,Grueneberg (Ger.)	RAPE	U.S.
HANISCH, Wilhelm	190198	M	Ger.	23. 4.16	Crim.Asst.,Gestapo,Brno (Czech.) 39-45	TORTURE	CZECH.
HANK, Leander	258972	M	Ger.	20. 8.01	Sturmbannfhr.,SS,NSDAP, 11.9.38	INTERR.	U.S.
HANKE	62256	M	Ger.	05	Sgt.,SS,Kommando at Bad Gandersheim Prison,Clausthal,Zellerfeld (Ger.) 6.4.45	MURDER	U.S.
HANKE	72537	M		14	Lt.,Army,	TORTURE	FR.
HANKE	114570	F			Supervisor of women,Works-Command in C.C.,Muhldorf,Ampfing (Ger.) 6.44-4.45	MURDER	U.S.
HANKE	165919	M	Ger.		Gauleiter,NSDAP,Breslau (Ger.) 2.-5.45	MISC.CRIMES	FR.,U.S.
HANKE	186612	M	Ger.		Civilian,Montgauthier,(Dinant) (Bel.) 20.9.43	MURDER	BEL.
HANKE	253975	M	Ger.	12	Pvt.,guard,2.Coy.,747 Landesschuetzen Bn.,Stalag VIII A, Karlsbad,Maierhofen (Ger.) 25.-27.8.45	INTERR.	FR.
HANKE	257764	M	Ger.		Capt.,German Army,Unit No.25827,Zajecar (Yugo.) 41-44	MURDER	YUGO.
HANKE, Alfred	188594	M	Ger.	3. 7.10	Crim.Asst.,Gestapo,Brno (Czech.) 39-45	MURDER	CZECH.
HANKE, Otto Karl Dietrich	259811	M	Ger.	20	Director,Cinema at Heerlen,Valkenburg,Limburg (Neth.) 22.4.44	BRUTALITY	NETH.
HANKEL, Franz	196617	M	Ger.		Doctor,Mayor,Ahrweiler (Ger.) 5.-6.44	MISC.CRIMES	POL.
HANKEN, Joseph	145303	M			Civilian,Borkum (Ger.) 4.8.44	MURDER	U.S.
HANKEWIECZ	142084	M			Capt.,Army,Abwehr official Stalag XVII A,C.C., Kaisersteinbruch (Aust.) 5.43	TORTURE	U.S.
HANKO	186613	M		95	Major,710.Inf.Rgt.,Narvik (Nor.) 11.43	MURDER	NOR.
HANKO, Johann	186614	M			4.SS Totenkopfsturmbann,Nordhausen (Ger.) 43-45	WITNESS	U.S.
HANLEIN	134883	M			SS,C.C.,Ohrdruf (Ger.) 44-45	MURDER	U.S.
HANN (see HAHNS)	178314						
HANN, Eugen	135543	M	Ger.		Member,Gestapo,NSDAP,Heusteu near Bad Neustadt (Ger.) 5.8.41	TORTURE	U.K.
HANN, Fritz Heinz	72539	M			Army,Cleder (Fr.) 44	MURDER	FR.
HANN, Martin	252168	M			Pvt.,C.C.,Ellrich,Nordhausen (Ger.)	MURDER	U.S.
HANNA, Paul	114573	M		07	Interpreter,Kommandantur,Sanilhac (Fr.) 21.4.44	WITNESS	FR.
HANNAPPEL, Gustav	258172	M	Ger.	17. 7.94	Ausbildungstab D-Abwehr,Bruxelles (Bel.) 10.42-9.44	SUSPECT	BEL.
HANNEMAN	124372	M	Ger.	10	Sgt.,Air-force,Muhldorf (Ger.) 17.4.45	WITNESS	U.S.
HANNEMAN	307125	M			N.C.O.,Einheit F.P.No.55975,L.G.P.A. Unna Wf.,Laren, 4.11.44-22.2.45	PILLAGE	NETH.
HANNEMAN, Walter	129139	M	Ger.		Sgt.,Dulag-Luft,C.C.,Oberursel	TORTURE	U.K.
HANNEMANN	29865	M	Ger.		Sgt.,C.C.,Verona,Frankfurt (It.,Ger.) 6.-7.44	TORTURE	U.K.
HANNER	167376	M	Ger.		Lt.,Feldgendarmerie,La Rochemillay (Fr.) 11.8.44	PILLAGE	FR.
HANNICH	72534	M			Cpt.,Army,Semussac (Fr.)	MURDER	FR.
HANNIMAN, Walter	259034	M			A Dulag Luft Hospital, (Ger.) 43-4.45	BRUTALITY	U.S.
HANNING, Martin	301125	M	Ger.		Cmdt.,1.Bn.,Royan,Semoussac,Charente,Inferieure, 28.9.44	MURDER	FR.
HANNOT, Marius (or HANOT alias:WOHLER)	251046	M	Ger.		Member,SD,Meppel (Neth.) 18.12.44	TORTURE	NETH.
HANON	108998	M	Ger.		Sgt.,Stalag IV B,Muehlberg (Ger.) 8.-9.43	TORTURE	U.K.
HANOSCH (see ANUSCH)	196157						
HANOT, Marius (see HANNOT)	251046						
HANOVER	139670	M			Oschfhr.,SS,C.C.,Buchenwald (Ger.)	TORTURE	U.S.
HANRATHS, Peter	194296	M	Ger.	21	Cpl.,Gemischte Flak Abt 515,4.Btty.,Rjukan (Nor.) 1.45	MURDER	U.K.
HANREICH, Otto	31960	M	Ger.		Doctor,Oberlandgerichtsrat,Public official,Litomerice (Czech.)21.2.40	MURDER	CZECH.
HANRIKS (or HANRIKSON)	29864	M			Officer Commanding,Army 1010 (mot.) Rgt.,7.Coy.,2.Bn., Lorient,Orleans (Fr.) 13.-15.8.44	MURDER	U.K.
HANS	72543	M			Army,Dax (Fr.)	WITNESS	FR.
HANS	72474	M	Ger.		Capt.,Gestapo,Chartres (Fr.)	MURDER	FR.
HANS	72581				(Officer ?) C.C.,Drancy (Fr.)	MISC.CRIMES	FR.
HANS	129779	M	Ger.		Capt.,Waffen SS, Krim.Rat,Sommershausen (Ger.)	MURDER	U.S.
HANS	135176	M	Ger.		Kriminalrat,Kripo,Ruppertshutten (Ger.) 12.9.44	MURDER	U.S.
HANS	142471	M	Ger.		Uschfhr.,SS,Pankofen,Plattling (Ger.)	MURDER	U.S.
HANS	146697	M		10	Agent,Gestapo,SS,member,C.C.,Bilgoraj (Pol.) 8.1.43	MURDER	POL.
HANS	185533	M			Pvt.,Army,Sokara,(Crete) (Grc.)	MURDER	GRC.
HANS	185534	M			Sgt.,Army,Voutes (Crete) (Grc.) 12.3.44	MURDER	GRC.
HANS	194558	M	Ger.	15	Guard,C.C.,Neuengamme (Ger.) 44	MURDER	BEL.
HANS	258228	M			Doctor,Employee,C.C.,Neuengamme (Ger.)	TORTURE	BEL.
HANS, Alexander	252169	M		11. 4.01	Pvt.,C.C.,Ellrich,Nordhausen (Ger.)	MURDER	U.S.
HANS, Cornelius	72542	M			Army,F.P.No. 27817 c,Tourch (Fr.)	MURDER	FR.
HANS, Hans ?	141314	M	Ger.		Pvt.,Army,Arb.Kdo.178,Stalag XI A,C.C.,Halberstadt (Ger.)	TORTURE	U.K.

HAN-HAR

NAME	C.R.FILE NUMBER	SEX	NATIONALITY	DATE OF BIRTH	RANK OCCUPATION UNIT PLACE AND DATE OF CRIME	REASON WANTED	WANTED BY
HANS, Karl	148556	M	Ger.	07	SS-Hptsturmfhr.,Ers. und Ausb.-Regt.,SS-Flak "Freimann" Muenchen (Ger.) 7.44	MURDER	U.S.
HANSCH, Walter	186616	M	Ger.	13	Osturmfhr.,SS,C.C.Sachsenhausen (Ger.) 44	MURDER	POL.
HANSCHAK	196616	M	Ger.		Pvt.,393 Landesschuetzen-Bn.,Bensen (Czech.) 45	WITNESS	U.K.
HANSCHMANN	192962	M	Ger.		Sgt.,SS,C.C.Buchenwald (Ger.) 42-45	TORTURE	U.S.
HANSEK (see von HAUSER)	253850						
HANSEL, Karl	133335	M			Oschfhr.,Chief-Cook,Waffen-SS,C.C.Flossenburg (Ger.)	TORTURE	U.S.
HANSEMANN	10013		Ger.		Osturmfhr.,SS,Gestapo,Mlada (Czech.) 39-45	TORTURE	CZECH.
HANSEN	342	M	Ger.	10	Uschfhr.,SS,C.C.Grini (Nor.) 3.43	TORTURE	NOR.
HANSEN	9818	M			Police,Administration Police,Buss (Ger.)	MISC.CRIMES	UNWCC
HANSEN	72476	M			Cpl.,Waffen-SS,C.C.Buchenwald (Ger.)	MURDER	FR.
HANSEN	135184	M	Ger.		Kommissar,Gestapo,Hqs.Koeln (Ger.) 41-45	MURDER	U.S.
HANSEN	154378	M			Major,Adjutant of Remount-school,C.C.Vicinity of Gardelegen (Ger.)4.45	MURDER	U.S.
HANSEN (see HAUSEN)	162887						
HANSEN	254792	M	Ger.		Pvt.,3 Bn.,4 Coy.,225 Jaeg.-Regt.,Vinkt (Bel.)	MISC.CRIMES	BEL.
HANSEN	258004	M			Sgt.,150 Pz.Bde.,Meuse Bridge,Antwerp (Bel.) 12.44	MISC.CRIMES	U.S.
HANSEN	301096	M	Ger.		Asst.,to Crim.Secr.,Kesselmodel,Reichssicherheitsdienst Abt.IV 2 a Shellhuset,Copenhagen (Den.) 9.44	MISC.CRIMES	DEN.
HANSEN, Christian	259063	M	Ger.	85	Lt.General,Wanted as Witness,possibly,Defendant,Crimes Against Peace, war Crimes and Crimes Against Humanity	WITNESS	U.S.
HANSEN, Ede	252170	M			Pvt.,C.C.Ellrich,Nordhausen (Ger.)	MURDER	U.S.
HANSER, Stefan	305167	M	Ger.		Usturmfhr.,and Gendarmeriemeister,SS,Ebenberg.Drau,Carinthia (Aust)44	MURDER	U.S.
HANSJACOB, Marg.	142920	F			Civilian,C.C.Weiden (Ger.)	WITNESS	U.S.
HANSLER, Hans	261752	M	Ger.		Telephonist,Gestapo of Amiens,Gentelles (Fr.) 6.-8.44	MURDER	FR.
HANSLER, Teno	39806	M			Oschfhr., Waffen-SS	MURDER	FR.
HANSLICK, Paul	127363	M	Ger.	09	Cpl.,Army,Ld.Schtz.Probably,349 Bn.,Arbeitskommando, C.C.Blechhammer (Ger.) 29.7.44	MURDER	U.S.U.K.
HANSMANN	152475	M	Ger.		Capt.,111 Kampfgeschwader,Villaudric (Fr.) 20.8.44	MURDER	FR.
HANSMANN	187204	M	Ger.	17	Osturmfhr.,SS,12 SS-Pz.Div."Hitler Jugend",near Caen (Fr.)6.6.-8.7.44	MISC.CRIMES	CAN.
HANSNER, Martin	108829	M	Ger.	11	Pvt.,Feldgendarmerie,Lockeren (Ger.) 42	TORTURE	U.K.BEL.
HANSORGL, Max	250822	M			Hptsturmfhr.,SS,Graz (Aust.) 4.45	INTERR.	U.K.
HANTKE-HALMI, Oskar	253717	M	Ger.	31.8.87	Dr.,Civ.,attorney at Law,Bratislava (Czech.) 42	MISC.CRIMES	CZECH.
HANTON	121061	M	Ger.		Head of Volkssturm,Group Wasserhalfingen (Ger.)	MURDER	BEL.
HANTSCH	130391	M			Osturmfhr.,SS,C.C.Mauthausen (Aust.) 41-45	MURDER	U.S.
HANUSSA	135190	M			Lt.,19 SS-Pol.-Regt.,C.C.Oberkrain near Vigaun and Agen (Yugo.Fr.) 5.41-3.-10.44	MURDER	U.S.
HANVERLAND	188979	M			Capt.,Cmdt.,Ost-Bat. (Bat.-mongol.804-806) Tournon (Fr.) 6.7.44	MURDER	FR.
HAOTSCHILD	252149	M	Ger.		Inspector,C.C.Auschwitz (Pol.)	INTERR.	FR.
HAPPE, LLD	174176	M		95	Staatsanwalt,Member,Occupied Terr.,NSDAP,Prag (Czech.) 44-45	TORTURE	CZECH.
HAPPT (or HAPPTEST)	72480	M			Guard,Chief,Administration,Penitentiary,Ulm (Ger.)	MURDER	FR.
HARBAUM	173590	M	Ger.		Hptsturmfhr.,SS,W.V.H.A.,Oswiecim,Birkenau,Buchenwald (Pol.)	MURDER	CZECH.BEL.
HARBAUM	196585	M	Ger.		Capt.,C.C.Mauthausen (Ger.)	TORTURE	BEL.
HARBECKER	165920	M	Ger.		Criminal-Commissar,Gestapo,R.S.H.A.,C.C.Sachsenhausen (Ger.) 42	MURDER	U.S.
HARBEUTHER, Max	149515	M	Ger.		Sonderfhr.,SS,Stalag 369,C.C.Kobierzyn (Pol.) 6.8.44	TORTURE	FR. UNWCC
HAREY (or HENRY)	138345	M			Lt.,SS,Gestapo,Lyon (Fr.)	MURDER	FR.
HARCHMANN	188980	M	Ger.		Prison Interpreter,C.C.Avignon,St.Anne (Fr.) 40-44	TORTURE	FR.
HARDEGEN (or HARDIGEN)	174236	M			Lt.,7 Res.-Regt.,Gebirgs-Artillerie 79,Tours et Albert-Ville (Fr.) 23.6.44	MURDER	FR.
HARDEGEN	137610		Ger.	00	Kriminal-Kommissar,SS,Gestapo,Tilburg (Neth.) 9.7.44	MURDER	U.K.
HARDEMANN, Walter	301126	M	Ger.		Economist,employed at Weserhutte works,Stalag VI K,Weserhutte, Bad Oyenhausen (Ger.) 41-45	MISC.CRIMES	FR.
HARDER	119428	M	Ger.		Lt.Col.,Army,4 A 20.Army Staff,Finmerk (Nor.) 44	MURDER	NOR.
HARDER	119429	M	Ger.		Army,Armee-Pfarrer 7,4 A,20 Army Staff (Nor.) 44	MURDER	NOR.
HARDER	142949	M			Mayor,Civ.Aufhausen (Ger.) 7.7.44	WITNESS	U.S.
HARDICK	192961	M	Ger.		Lt.,SS,C.C.Buchenwald (Ger.) 42-45	MURDER	U.S.
HARDIG (or HARTIG, Willie)	188159	M	Ger.		Cpl.,Bruchsal (Ger.) 2.-3.2.45	PILLAGE	U.S.
HARDIGEN	344	M	Ger.		Army,Lt.,Mountain-Div.,Gresy sur Isere (Fr.) 9.8.44	MURDER	FR.
HARDIGEN (see HARDEGEN)	174236						
HARDIGGEN (or HARDINGEN)	174237	M			Lt.,Africa-Corps,Naves (Fr.) 10.6.44	MURDER	FR.
HARDKOFF	161164	M			Major,Army,Stettin (Ger.) 7.10.44	TORTURE	U.S.
HARDT, J.	24939	M	Ger.		Rottfhr.,SS,C.C.Struthof,Natzweiler (Fr.) 42-44	MURDER	FR.
HARDT, Theodor	193218	M	Ger.	12.11.13	Reichsjustizministerium,Feldstraflager,C.C.Finmark (Nor.) 3.45	WITNESS	NOR.
HARDT, Wilhelm	193217	M	Ger.	12.7.23	Reichsjustizministerium,Feldstraflager,C.C.Finmark (Nor.) 3.45	WITNESS	NOR.
HARDVIGEN	72485	M			Lt.,Army,Formation No.077927,Chambert le Vieux (Fr.) 44	MURDER	FR.
HARDWICH	250836	M	Ger.		Guard,Prison,C.C.Esterwegen (Ger.)	BRUTALITY	BEL.
HARE	141928	M			Capt.,Work-Kdo.,C.C.Leizen (Aust.) 12.4.44-13.4.45	MISC.CRIMES	U.K.
HARIERS, Hans	196448	M	Ger.		Capt.,Gestapo,S.D.,Den Haag (Neth.)	INTERR.	NETH.
HARILD	345		Ger.		Capt.,Kanea (Grc.)	MURDER	U.K.
HARILL, Fritz	188981	M			Army,18 Bn.,Busset (Fr.) 7.8.44	MURDER	FR.
HARING	39807	M	Ger.		Berufs-Offizier,Custom-house,Custom-officer,Damprichard (Fr.)16.7.44	MURDER	FR.
HARING	306585	M	Ger.		Member,S.D. or Gestapo,Oslo,Trandum near Oslo (Nor.) 19.1.43	MURDER	U.K.
HARING (or HIRYING, Wilhelm)	171969	M		29.3.90	Civilian,Dauelsen (Ger.) 10.43	TORTURE	U.S.
HARING, Maks	346	M	Ger.	27.8.10	Oschfhr.,SS,C.C.Maidanek (Pol.) 40-4.44	MURDER	POL.
HARKANGER	36614	M	Ger.		Sgt.,Army,Commando 535,Lager-Command,Milowitz,coal Mine, 515 Bn.,2 Coy.,Milowitz,Sud.Land (Czech.) 20.1.-10.2.45	MURDER	U.K.
HARKERS	305864	M	Ger.		Pvt.,1 Aufkl.-Abt.,3 Coy.,2 Column,XV Div.Africa-Corps, St.Leger (Arlon) 5.9.44	MISC.CRIMES	BEL.
HARLASS, Johann	189222	M	Ger.	14.11.84	Treasurer,NSDAP,Marianske,Usovice (Czech.) 39-45	MISC.CRIMES	CZECH.
HARLOS	185540	M			Dr.,Staatsanwalt,Sondergericht,Luxembourg,Gr.Duche (Lux.) 42-44	MURDER	LUX.
HARLOSS, Willy	254549	M	Ger.		Pvt.,St.Michielsgestel (Neth.) 9.44	PILLAGE	NETH.
HARM	158630	M	Ger.	95	Justiz-secr.,Justiz-Ministerium,Emsland (Ger.) 44	MURDER	U.S.
HARM, Ernst	252172	M	Ger.	20.9.09	Rottfhr.,C.C.Harzungen,Nordhausen (Ger.)	MURDER	U.S.

HAR - HAR

NAME	C.R.FILE NUMBER	SEX	NATIO-NALITY	DATE OF BIRTH	RANK OCCUPATION UNIT PLACE AND DATE OF CRIME	REASON WANTED	WANTED BY
HARMANN, Georges (see HAMMAN)	142416						
HARMS	72512	M			Lt., Army Unit Schoepplein, St. Eirons-Rimond (Fr.)	MURDER	FR.
HARMS	124018	M	Ger.		Sturmbannfhr., des SS Fuersorgekommandos, Woltwiesche, Schmedenstedt (Ger.) 24.8.44	MURDER	U.S.
HARMS	188708	M		95	SS-Brigadefuehrer, Vilach (Ger.) 12.44 - 1.45	SUSPECT	U.S.
HARMS	301321	M	Ger.		Member, Gestapo at Trenoin, C.C. Oswiecim-Birkenau (Pol., رر-45	MURDER	CZECH.
HARMS, Adolf	254793	M			Pvt., 377.Jaeger-Rgt., 10.Coy. Vinct (Bel.)	MISC.CRIMES	BEL.
HARMS, Ewald (or PRIEBE, Walter)	260820	M		07	Sturmbannfhr., SS, Muenstedt (Ger.) 24.8.44	MURDER	U.S.
HARMS, Carl	151660	M		10	SS-Untersturmfhr., Gestapo, Moselle (Fr.) 11.44	MURDER	FR.
HARMS, Karl	177511	M	Ger.		Untersturmfhr., SS, Saarbruecken (Ger.)	MURDER	FR.
HARMS, Willy	254794	M	Ger.		Cpl., 377.Jaeger-Rgt., 12.Coy. Vinkt (Bel.)	MISC.CRIMES	BEL.
HARNETZ	158628	M			Guard, SS, C.C.,Neubrenn (Ger.) 43-45	TORTURE	FR.
HARNI - SCHEEGER	142293	M		05	Gestapo, Duesseldorf, Hilden (Ger.) 38	TORTURE	U.S.
HARNICH	251603	M	Ger.		Obersturmfhr., SS,Bruessel (Bel.)	INTERR.	BEL.
HARNISCH, Gustav	72514	M			Zugwachtmeister, Schupo, Annecy (Fr.)	MURDER	FR.
HARNISCH, Stanislaus	31940	M			Dr., Landgerichtsrat, Ministry of justice, Cheb (Czech.)21.2.40	MURDER	CZECH.
HAROLD	29863	M	Ger.		Capt., Army, Canea,Crete (Gre.)	MISC.CRIMES	U.K.
HAROLT, Albert	255393	M		18. 5.05	Rottenfhr. C.C. Harzungen-Nordhausen (Ger.)	MURDER	U.S.
HARPST	131706	M	Ger.		Admiral, President, Navy,Level Public official, Berlin-Torgau (Ger.) 40-45	MURDER	FR.
HARRE, Friedrich	306247	M	Ger.	20. 6.04	Pvt. Air-Force, Lyngdal (Nor.) 19.5.43	MURDER	NOR.
HARRENBAUER, Heinrich	193925	M		87	Civilian, Wehrden, (Ger.)	WITNESS	U.S.
HARRESER	251621	M		11	Pvt., Field-Police-troop 532. Nave, (It.) 1.8.44	INTERR.	U.K.
HARRIG	174177	M			Organisation Todt, C.C. Muehldorf,Ampfing (Ger.) 6.44 - 4.45	MURDER	U.S.
HARRIUS	100840	M	Ger.		Officer, Army, Standortcommandant, Draveil (Fr.) 26.8.44	MISC.CRIMES	FR.
HARRS	158631	M	Ger.		Pvt. Waffen SS, 1.Panz.-Div. "Adolf Hitler" 1.Rcn.Bn. Parfondruy, Stavelot (Bel.)	MURDER	U.S. BEL.
HARRUS	178936	M			Army, O.C., Dravell, (Fr.) 8.44	TORTURE	FR.
HARSCHEIDT, Paul	255394	M			Flyer, C.C. Rottleberode, Ellrich-Nordhausen (Ger.)	MURDER	U.S.
HARSTER	21366	M	Ger.		SS - Brigadefhr.,General-Major (Neth.)	TORTURE	UNWCC.
HARSTER, Wilhelm	165922	M	Ger.		SS - Brigadefhr.,, Rom (It.) 43	MURDER	U.S.
HART	132709	M	Ger.		Baufuehrer, Organisation Todt, Ile d'Aurigny (Fr.) 43-44	TORTURE	FR.
HART	254523	M	Ger.		SS - Uschfhr., Gestapo, Paris (Fr.) 41-44	TORTURE	FR.
HART, Friedrich	140902	M	Ger.		Verbindungsstab 331, Bolnes (Neth.) 8.5.45	MURDER	NETH.
HARTEL	141858	M	Ger.		N.C.O., Hospital, Cosel (Ger.) 44 - 45	TORTURE	U.K.
HARTEL	173638	M			SS - Mann, C.C., Muehldorf and Ampfing (Ger.)	MURDER	U.S.
HARTEL	262150	M			Capt, Horsching (Aust.) 3.4.45 L.O.D.N.A.O.D.	SUSPECT	U.S.
HARTELL	194782	M			Capt., Landesschuetzen-Bn.396, 5.Coy. Ottendorf,Okrilla (Ger.) 12.45	MURDER	FR.
HARTEN	194295	M	Ger.		Pvt. K.G.F. Arb.-Bn. 41, 1. Coy. Aalesund (Nor.) 8.5.44	MURDER	NOR.
HARTENFELD	256810	M			Major, 109.Div. 919.Rgt. 2.Bn. St. Martin (Fr.) 14.4.44	MURDER	U.S.
HARTENFELS, Erwin	72518	M			Official, Gestapo, Chambery,Challes les Eaux, Arbin (Fr.) 6.44	MURDER	FR.
HARTINS, Fritz	179756	M	Ger.	20	Lt., Div. "Hermann Goering ", Bucine (It.) 9.7.44	MURDER	IT.
HARTENS, Fritz	196019	M	Ger.		Hauptscharfhr., SD, Zwolle (Neth.) 9.44 - 4.45	MURDER	NETH.
HARTENSTEIN	72528	M			C.C., Struthof, (Fr.)	MISC.CRIMES	FR.
HARTENSTEIN	300530	M	Ger.		Sturmbannfhr., SS, C.C. Auschwitz (Pol.) 9.42	MISC.CRIMES	YUGO.
HARTENSTEIN, Fritz	173591	M	Ger.		Cmdt., SS-Sturmbannfhr., C.C.,Waffen SS, Oswiecim-Birkenau (Pol.)39-45	MURDER	CZECH, FR. YUGO.
HARTER	173176	M	Ger.		Staff at C.C., Schirmeck, Rotenfels, Gaggenau (Fr. Ger.) 6.44	INTERR.	U.K.
HARTERICH, Leo	154379	M	Ger.	85	Lt., Civilian Burgomeister, SA, Ebertshausen (Ger.) 10.41 - 4.45	TORTURE	U.K. AUST.
HARTGENSTEIN	31917	M	Ger.	97	SS-Obersturmfhr., C.C., Struthof (Fr.)	MURDER	UNWCC.
HARTH, Bernhard	162842	M	Ger.		Reichsbahnoberassistent, Bertrix,Neufchateau (Bel.) 4.3.44	MURDER	BEL.
HARTH, Friedrich	188349	M	Ger.	03	Kriminaloberassistent, Gestapo, Brno (Czech.) 39-45	MURDER	CZECH.
HARTHAHN	251611	M	Ger.		Hauptscharfhr., SS, (Bel.) 40 - 42	INTERR.	BEL.
HARTI, Bernhard	167833	M	Ger.		Oberassistent, Reichsbahn, Nertrix (Bel.) 4.3.44	MURDER	BEL.
HARTIER	133332	M	Ger.	17	SS - Mann, SS	MURDER	U.S.
HARTIG	143003	M			SA	MURDER	U.S.
HARTIG	161165	M			Army, 397.Landesschuetzen Bn.,4.Coy. H.Q. Grossenhain,Groditz(Ger.)45	WITNESS	U.S.
HARTIG, Willie (see HARDIG)	188159						
HARTING	251610	M	Ger.		Untersturmfhr.,SS,Polizeisekretaer, (Bel.) 40 - 42	TORTURE	BEL.
HARTING	257796	M	Ger.		Civilian, Volkswagenwerk Fallersleben,Sochaux (Fr.) 40 - 44	INTERR.	FR.
HARTINGER, J	173569	M	Ger.		Official, Zentral Abteilung Kultur, C.C. Maribor (Yugo.)	MURDER	YUGO.
HARTISCH	196447	M	Ger.		C.C., Struthof - Natzweiler, (Fr.) 40 - 45	MISC.CRIMES	FR.
HARTJENSTEIN	37788	M	Ger.		Sturmbannfhr., SS, C.C. Natzweiler (Fr.) 2.9.44	MURDER	U.K. BEL.
HARTL	123508	M			SS - Unterscharfhr.	MURDER	U.S.
HARTL	154212	M			Uscharfhr., SS, C.C. Mauthausen (Aust.) 41 - 45	MURDER	U.S.
HARTL, Karl	253976	M	Ger.	19. 4.25	Pvt., 558.Gren. Rgt. 13.Coy. Bruayen Artois (Fr.) 1.9.44	MURDER	FR.
HARTLER	133328	M			Untersturmfhr., Waffen SS, C.C. Flossenburg (Ger.)	TORTURE	U.S.
HARTLIEB, Karl	257797	M	Ger.	24. 4.96	Gestapo Chief - Secr., Marova-Ostrava (Czech.) 29.8.44	MISC.CRIMES	U.S.
HARTLIEB, Martin	188698	M	Ger.	91	Civilian, Dachsbach Krs.Neustadt (Ger.) 43 - 45	SUSPECT	POL.
HARTMAN	137087	M			Capt., Stalag XX B, Cmdt., C.C. Marienburg (Pol.) 12.43 - 1.44	MISC.CRIMES	U.K.
HARTMAN, Richard	105919	M			Pvt., Army, 1082 Sichrungs-Bn., Sellerich (Ger.) 4.1.45	WITNESS	U.S.
HARTMANN	347	M	Ger.		Uscharfhr.,Interpreter, SS-Div. "Das Reich" Buzet (Fr.) 7.-8.44	MURDER	FR.
HARTMANN	1424	M	Ger.		Kreisleiter, NSDAP, Cleve bei Kranenburg (Ger.) 44	MURDER	U.K. U.S.
HARTMANN	12432	M	Ger.		Lt., 11. Panz.-Div. Courdon (Fr.) 29.6.44	MURDER	FR.
HARTMANN	24931	M			Pvt., Army, Fallschirmjaeger-Bn. Roermond (Neth.) 11.44-1.45	TORTURE	U.S.
HARTMANN	29862	M	Ger.		Steiger, Public official, Salzgitter (Ger.) 12.44	TORTURE	U.K.
HARTMANN	37800	M		06	SS-Lt.Colonel, Oberreg.Rat, SD, Gestapo and Sipo (Lux.) 9.42	MURDER	U.S.
HARTMANN	72525	M			Capt., Kommandantur, St. Flour, (Fr.)	MURDER	FR.
HARTMANN	72587	M			Laneuvelotte (Fr.)	MURDER	FR.
HARTMANN	121060	M	Ger.		Customs secretary, Zollgrenzschutz, St. Gingolph Fr.) 7.44	MURDER	FR.
HARTMANN	141563	M	Ger.		Guard, C.C., Jauer (Ger.)	TORTURE	FR.
HARTMANN	143002	M			Capt., 1.Panz.Coy., 7.Panz.rec.repl.and training Bn. Freilassing(Ger.)	WITNESS	U.S.
HARTMANN	151654	M			Capt., Army, Chenebelier-Etolon (Fr.) 6.44 and 9.44	MURDER	FR.
HARTMANN	156732	M			Major, Idriza - Sebesch (Sov.Un. Latv.) 43 - 44	MURDER	U.S.
HARTMANN	158627	M	Ger.	05	Criminal - secretary, Sipo, Stavanger (Nor.)	MURDER	U.K.

NAME	C.R.FILE NUMBER	SEX	NATIO-NALITY	DATE OF BIRTH	RANK OCCUPATION UNIT PLACE AND DATE OF CRIME	REASON WANTED	WANTED BY
HARTMANN	158629	M	Ger.		Justizoberwachtmeister,Justizministerium,Emsland(Ger.) 44	MURDER	U.S.
HARTMANN	161591	M	Ger.		SS-Usturmfhr.,C.C.Flossenburg,Wuestegiersdorf(Ger.)	MURDER	U.K.
HARTMANN	173175	M			Organisation Todt,C.C.Muhldorf-Ampfing(Ger.) 6.44-4.45	MISC.CRIMES	U.S.
HARTMANN	178277	M	Ger.	00	Overseer,Work-Kdo.,Stalag XIB,Ohlendorf(Ger.) 1.45	MURDER	U.K.
HARTMANN	192004	M			Hptschfhr.,SS Panz.-Regt.,Legnieuville Stoumont(Bel.)	WITNESS	U.S.
HARTMANN	192420	M	Ger.		Capt.,Gestapo,Air Field,Senzeille,Charleroi,Cerfontaine(Bel.) 2.-4.44	TORTURE	BEL.
HARTMANN	192960	M	Ger.		SS-Uschfhr.,SS,C.C.Buchenwald(Ger.)	TORTURE	U.S.
HARTMANN	193216	M	Ger.		Pionier-Sgt.,Army	TORTURE	NOR.
HARTMANN	194781	M	Ger.		Col.,Army,Ascq(Fr.) 1.-2.4.44	MURDER	FR.
HARTMANN	250229	M	Ger.		Guard,C.C.Monsheim(Ger.) 44-45	BRUTALITY	FR.
HARTMANN	254943	M	Ger.	03	Capt.,15 Germ.Police Regt.,Cescantino(Ital.) 8.9.44	INTERR.	U.K.
HARTMANN	256089	M	Ger.		Senior of the room block 15, C.C.Mauthausen(Ger.)	INTERR.	FR.
HARTMANN or Peterle	259683	F	Ger.	18	Typist,Gestapo,Angers,Maine and Loire(Fr.) 42-44	MISC.CRIMES	FR.
HARTMANN	260149	M	Ger.		Gend.,Div.Oberland,Unit Russia,German,Massif du Vercors,Isere et Drome, (Fr.) 20.7.-5.8.44	SUSPECT	FR.
HARTMANN	262248	M	Ger.		Lt.,3 Coy.,19 Inf.Regt.,106 Bde.,Div.armoured"Feldherrnhalle", Jngersheim(Fr.) 11.44-1.45	PILLAGE	FR.
HARTMANN	306983	M	Ger.		771 Bn.Inf.Landesschuetzen Einheit No.15468,Chateau de Foret and Ferme Labaye(Bel.) 6.9.44	MURDER	BEL.
HARTMANN, Albert	191614	M	Ger.		Oschfhr.,Waffen-SS,C.C.Struthof-Natzweiler(Fr.) 40-44	MURDER	FR.
HARTMANN, Alfred	259227	M			Director,Kdo.737-3 of Stalag XIA,Salzwedel(Ger.) 1.6.44	MURDER	FR.
HARTMANN, Alois	72522	M			Ministerialrat,Gestapo,Paris(Fr.)	TORTURE	NOR.
HARTMANN, Erich	251044	M			Civilian,Tiddische(Ger.) 30.5.44	WITNESS	U.S.
HARTMANN, Ernst	194350	M	Ger.		Cpl.,Army,Veigy Fonceney(Fr.) 6.10.43	TORTURE	FR.
HARTMANN, Friedrich	255395	M		9. 8.09	Cpl.,C.C.Rottleberode-Nordhausen(Ger.)	MURDER	U.S.
HARTMANN, Fritz	256748	M	Ger.	6. 5.04	Employee, Bn IL, "Lenge",Camp Nordhausen (Ger.)	MURDER	U.S.
HARTMANN, Georg	196657	M	Ger.		Pvt.,F.P.No.22640 H,Barbezieux(Fr.) 27.-28.8.44	WITNESS	FR.
HARTMANN, Heinz	131282	M			Block-Aeltester,KL.,Guard. 44	MURDER	U.S.
HARTMANN, Heinz	132180	M	Ger.		Obersteuermann,Ger.Navy,Atlantic Ocean South of Freetown.13.3.44	WITNESS	U.K.
HARTMANN, Hugo	167975	M	Ger.		W.O.,Army,Montigny(Fr.) 9.44	WITNESS	FR.
HARTMANN, Josef	251622	M	Ger.	19. 8.95	Capt.,Schupo,State Service,Breclav(Czech.) 24.1.45	MURDER	CZECH.
HARTMANN, Josef	256749	M	Ger.	98	Oberwachtmeister,Civ.Musician-Police,Lidice(Czech.) 22.6.42	MURDER	CZECH.
HARTMANN, Karl	192099	M	Ger.	95	Lt.,Gend.,Gestapo,SD,Litomysl(Czech.) 39-45	MURDER	CZECH.
HARTMANN, Kurt	251596	M	Ger.		Capt.,Army,Haute-Saone(Fr.)	MURDER	FR.
HARTMANN, Moritz	258139	M	Ger.		Guard,C.C.Esterwegen(Ger.) 44	SUSPECT	BEL.
HARTMANN, Nikolaus	192418	M	Ger.		Civilian,Dillingen(Ger.) 11.5.44	SUSPECT	U.S.
HARTMANN, Otto	256889	M		17. 2.07	Employee,C.C.Sachsenhausen(Ger.)	MURDER	U.S.
HARTMANN, Paul	158632	M			Civilian,Daasdorf,Guthmannshausen(Ger.) 7.-8.44	MURDER	U.S.
HARTMANN, Robert	173632	M	Ger.	01	Councillor of the District Court,Occupied Territories,Prague Bohemia Moravia (Czech.) 41-45	MURDER	CZECH.
HARTMANN, Wilhelm	142946	M			Waffen-SS,C.C.Flossenburg(Ger.)	TORTURE	U.S.
HARTMANN, Willy	185290	M	Ger.		Town Major of Fourne,Army,Fourne(Grc.) 10.2.44	MURDER	GRC.
HARTMAR or ROUTZIERO	185289	M	Ger.		Chief,Gestapo,Heraklion(Grc.) 7.44	MURDER	GRC.
HARTMUND or HARTWICK	252332	M	Ger.		C.C.Esterwegen(Ger.)	BRUTALITY	BEL.
HARTRAM	125741	M	Ger.	03	Capt.,18 Volksgren.Div.293,1 Regt.,Malmedy(Bel.) 12.44	MURDER	U.S.
HARTRICH, Leo	29861	M	Ger.		KL.Stalag XIIIC (Ger.) 42-44	TORTURE	U.K.
HARTSCHLAGE, Franz	194603	M	Ger.		Blockfuehrer,C.C. Bl.18,Mauthausen(Aust.) 45	MURDER	FR.
HARTSTANG	306384	M	Ger.		SS-Mann,SS,C.C.Buchenwald(Ger.) 16.5.38-9.10.43	MURDER	BEL.
HARTSTEIN, Eduard,see HARTSTENN	105920						
HARTSTEME, Eduard,see HARTSTENN	105920						
HARTSTENN, Eduard or HARTSTEIN or HARTSTEME	105920	M	Ger.		Physician, Kiew Institute,Kiew (Sov.Un.) 6.41-3.42	MURDER	U.S.
HARTSTER, Wilhelm	188158	M			Gruppenfhr.,SD,Bozen(Ital.) 19.3.45	MURDER	U.S.
HARTUNG	133327	M			Rottfhr.,Waffen-SS,C.C. Flossenburg(Ger.)	TORTURE	U.S.
HARTUNG	133331A	M			SS-Osturmbannfhr.,SS.	MURDER	U.S.
HARTUNG	135183	M	Ger.		Kommissar,Gestapo,Aussendienst,Koeln(Ger.)	MURDER	U.S.
HARTUNG	260150	M	Ger.		Capt.,Chief Gestapo of Grenoble,Massif du Vercors Isere et Drome (Fr.) 20.7.-5.8.44	SUSPECT	FR.
HARTUNG, August	171257	M	Ger.		Civilian, Grosswangen(Ger.)	WITNESS	U.S.
HARTUNG, Franz	189711	M	Ger.		Civilian,Essen-West,Mecklenbecksweg(Ger.) 13.12.44	MURDER	U.K.
HARTUNG, Hans	11549	M	Ger.	10	SS-Osturmfhr.,Crim.-Secretary,SS,Sipo,Bergen,Grenoble(Nor.,Fr.).41-44	MURDER	NOR.,FR.
HARTUNG, Kurt	165929	M			Civilian,Grocer,Bucha(Ger.) 7.7.44	TORTURE	U.S.
HARTWEGE	105921	M			Civilian,Physician Kiew Institute, Kiew(Russ.) 41-42	MURDER	U.S.
HARTWICH	173592	M	Ger.		SS-Oschfhr.,Waffen-SS,C.C.Oswiecim-Birkenau(Pol.) 39-45	MURDER	CZECH.
HARTWICK see HARTMUND	252332						
HARTWIG	185291	M	Ger.	95	Sturmschfhr.,SS,Tunis(Tunesia)	TORTURE	U.K.
HARTWIG	306084	M	Ger.		SS-Uschfhr. at Alderney C.C.(Channel) and Kortemark C.C., Alderney (Channel),Kortemark. 42-45	MURDER	CZECH.
HARTWIG, Artur	146705			8. 5.03	SS-Rottfhr.,C.C.Mauthausen,Ebensee(Aust.) 14.5.44-7.5.45	MURDER	U.S.
HARTWIG, Erich	255396				Uschfhr.,C.C.Wolfleben-Nordhausen(Ger.)	MURDER	U.S.
HARTWIG, Ludwig	255115	M	Ger.	03	Oberwachtmeister,Schupo,Prag-Kobylisy(Czech.) 41	MURDER	CZECH.
HARTWIK	139801			15	Uschfhr.,Waffen-SS,C.C.Aswic(Pol.) 7.43	PILLAGE	U.S.
HARTZ	348	M	Ger.		Bde.-Fhr.,SS,Toulon(Fr.) 10.-13.8.44	MURDER	FR.
HARTZ	167374	M	Ger.		Lt.,Army,Rehaupaul(Fr.) 9.9.44	MURDER	FR.
HARTZ	258963	M			Lt.-Gen.,Army.	WITNESS	U.S.
HARTZ, Bernhard	191779	M			Civ.-Servant,Reichsbahn,Bertrix(Bel.) 4.3.44	MURDER	BEL.
HARTZ, Bernhard	254795	M			Pvt.,Gren.Div."Hitler-Jugend",Hellenvillers(Fr.) 9.7.44	MURDER	FR.
HARTZINGER	192369	M	Ger.		C.C.Rollwald(Ger.) 44-45	MURDER	BEL.
HARWARDT	72531	M			St.Girond(Fr.)	MURDER	FR.
HARZ	253696	M	Ger.	00	Sgt.,Field-Police,Vielle-sous-les-Cotes(Fr.) 4.44	TORTURE	FR.
HAS	132705	M	Ger.		Army,Sgt.,Ouistery(Fr.)	MURDER	FR.
HAS	167973	M	Ger.		Sgt.,Parachute Regt.,Navilly Sermesse(Fr.) 9.-23.8.44	MURDER	FR.
HAS	256792	M	Ger.		Chief,SD,Calvados(Fr.) 42	INTERR.	FR.

HAS - HAS

NAME	C.R.FILE NUMBER	SEX	NATIO- NALITY	DATE OF BIRTH	RANK OCCUPATION UNIT PLACE AND DATE OF CRIME	REASON WANTED	WANTED BY
HASCHE	255398	M			Pvt., CC Rottleberode-Nordhausen (Ger.)	MURDER	U.S.
HASE	131286	M			SS Oschfhr, Commander District Krakau (Pol.) 13.9.43	MURDER	U.S.
HASE	173177	M	Ger.		Usturmfhr, SD Psson 6.-9.44	INTERR.	U.K.
HASE, Gerhard	192140	M	Ger.		Sgt., Secret Field Police, Brussels (Bel.)	TORTURE	BEL.
HASELBACH, Kurt	349	M			Cpl., Army, 6.43	MURDER	FR.
HASELBERG (or HASSELBERG)	194602	M	Ger.	10	Sturmbannfhr., Gestapo, SD Einsatz-Kdo.III, Sipo, Lublin (Pol.) 99	SUSPECT	POL.
HASEBRINK	142951	M	Ger.		Civilian, executive of "4 years plan", Cologne (Ger.) 39-45	WITNESS	U.S.
HASELBRUNNER	255400	M			Rottfhr, CC Dora, Nordhausen (Ger.)	MURDER	U.S.
HASELMANN	10085	M	Ger.		Adjutant, SS Div. "Der Fuehrer", Oradour (Fr.) 10.6.44	MURDER	FR.
HASELOFF, Kurt	21364	M	Ger.		General-Major, Sipo (Pol.) 39-45	TORTURE	U.K.
HASELMANN, W.	173697	M	Ger.	09	Lt., 132 Flak Untergruppe, Bad Duerrenberg (Ger.) 29.5.44	TORTURE	U.S.
HASENREIN	173205	M	Ger.		Polizeirat, Gestapo at Baden Baden, Karlsruhe; Police at CC Gaggenau (Ger.) -44	MURDER	U.K.
HASENBUSCH	189780	M	Ger.		Kriegsinspektor, Army, Feldzeug Bn.28, Krasne (Russia) 19.3.43	MURDER	U.K.
HASENKOPF, Karl	261904	M	Ger.	15.6.08	Customs Guard, Informer, Gestapo, Velka near Velicka (Czech.)40.44	SUSPECT	CZECH.
HASENODER	194331	M	Ger.		Pvt., K.G.F. Bau-Arb. Bn.206, 2 Coy, Mesjoen (Nor.) 7.44-5.45	MURDER	NOR.
HASENOHRL, Max	173636	M			Labour Camp Command, Muhldorf, Ampfing (Ger.) 6.44-4.45	MURDER	U.S.
HASENSTEIN, Leopold or Ludwig	165926	M	Ger.	about 11	Osturmfhr, or Oschfhr, SS, CC Bolzano (It.)	MURDER	U.S.
HASER	130660	M			SS Hptsturmfhr, CC Dora, Mittelbau, Nordhausen (Ger.)	MURDER	U.S.
HASEWEND	146700	M	Ger.		Hptschfhr, SS Totenkopf Div, CC Mauthausen (Aust.) 41-45	MURDER	U.S.
HASFER	142923	M	Ger.		Sturmfhr, W-SS, Totenkopf Div, CC Riga (Lettl.) 41-43	MURDER	U.S.
HASHAGEN, Hinrich	173635	M	Ger.	14.2.06	Civilian, Farmer in the vicinity of Bremen St.Magnus (Ger.) 4.45	MURDER	U.S.
HASKELE	253056	M			Uschfhr., SS, CC Auschwitz (Pol.)	MURDER	FR.
HASKENHOF, Heinrich	162843	M	Ger.		Civilian, Hoerste near Halle (Ger.) 41	MURDER	YUGO.
HASL	194601	M	Ger.		Pvt., Feld-Gend., Ploermel (Fr.) 18.6.44	TORTURE	FR.
HASLEBECK	305170	M	Ger.		Hptwachtmstr, Administrative Official, Strafgefangenen Lager Nord, Northern Norway 43-45	INTERR.	CZECH.
HASLER, Martin	140891	M	Ger.		N.C.O., Verbindungsstab 331, Bolnes (Neth.) 8.5.45	MURDER	NETH.
HASLI	167194	M	Ger.		Major, Pz.Jg.Abt.227, Royville (Fr.) 40-41	PILLAGE	FR.
HASLIN	163093	M	Ger.		SS-Mann, 10 SS Pz.Rgt.96, Revin (Fr.) 12. and 13.6.44	MURDER	FR.
HASLINGER	141857	M	Ger.	00	Pvt., 196 Sicherungs Rgt., 9 Coy, Bois de Guron, Deux-Sevres (Fr.) Rom (It.) 7.7.44	MURDER	U.K.
HASPEL	185461	M	Ger.	00	Civilian, Factory Foreman, CC Nuernberg (Ger.) 40-45	TORTURE	U.S.
HASS	1394	M	Ger.		Cpl., Army	MURDER	U.K.
HASS	12433	M	Ger.		Capt., Army, Africa Corps, Fontelnistiane (Fr.) 29.8.44	MURDER	FR.
HASS	72493	M			Adj.Chief, Army, Cerisan (Fr.)	MURDER	FR.
HASS	72505	M			Chef, Zollverwaltung, Rives sous Thonon (Fr.)	MURDER	FR.
HASS	135185	M	Ger.		SS-Mann, CC Hinzert, Wittlich (Ger.) 10.-41, 9.42, 2.43, 8.43	TORTURE	U.S.
HASS	169733	M	Ger.		Oschfhr, W-SS, CC Natzweiler (Fr.) 42-44	MURDER	FR.
HASS	173566	M	Ger.		Interpreter, Gestapo, Jasiko (Yugo.)	MURDER	YUGO.
HASS	173567	M	Ger.		Dr., Kreiskommandant, Kreiskommandantur, Jasika (Yugo.)	PILLAGE	YUGO.
HASS	259968	M	Ger.	95	Sturmbannfhr, SS, CC Auschwitz-Birkenau (Pol.) 42-45	MISC.CRIMES	YUGO.
HASS	256799	M			Deputy Leader, Propaganda NSDAP, Genthin (Ger.) 12.44	BRUTALITY	U.S.
HASS, Adolph	300531	M	Ger.	95	SS Sturmbannfhr, Cmdt, CC Bergen-Belsen, Auschwitz(Pol.,Ger.)42-45	MISC.CRIMES	YUGO.
HASS, Francois	124643	M	Ger.		Dr.,Lt., Army, Prisoner-Hospital, Heppenheim (Ger.) 9.44-5.45	TORTURE	U.S.
HASS, Heinrich	174240	M	Ger.		Sgt., Feld-Gend., St.Dizier (Fr.) -44	MURDER	FR.
HASS, Heinz	256799	M	Ger.	4.8.13	A.E.B. 17, CC Nordhausen (Ger.)	MURDER	U.S.
HASS, Mihailo	105917	M			Sgt., Army, 34 Fortress Machine Gun Bn., Aachen (Ger.) 13.9.44	MURDER	U.S.
HASS, R.	251055	M	Ger.		Interpreter, Ortskdtr., Kragujevac (Yugo.) 21.10.41	MURDER	YUGO.
HASS, Wilhelm	173602	M	Ger.		Kreisamtsleiter NSDAP, Wertheim (Ger.) -44	TORTURE	FR.
HASSE	186617	M	Ger.		Camp Leader, CC Bobingen (Ger.) 17.10.44	MURDER	POL.
HASSE	350	M	Ger.		SS-Mann, Warder in CC., Rajsko, Auschwitz (Pol.) 6.40-43	MURDER	POL.
HASSE	134852	F	Ger.	about 14	SS-Woman-Guard, CC Auschwitz-Birkenau (Pol.) 39-45	MURDER	U.N.W.C.C.
HASSE	185663	M	Ger.		Supervisor, CC Ravensbrueck (Ger.)	TORTURE	BEL.
HASSE (or HASSET)	196655	M	Ger.	95	Major, Police, Commander of Bn., Warschau (Pol.) 39-40	MISC.CRIMES	POL.
HASSE	306064	M	Ger.		Sgt., Abwehr at Stalag XII-D at Trier (Ger.) 41-43	MISC.CRIMES	YUGO.
HASSE, Eric	194600	M	Ger.	11	Head, Gestapo, Savigny en Septaine - Bourges (Fr.) 7.-8.44	MURDER	FR.
HASSE, Erich	256722	M	Ger.		Head, SD, Caen (Fr.) 42	INTERR.	FR.
HASSE, Hermann	105923	M	Ger.		War Camp, Chief of Prisoners, CC Oberkassel - Duesseldorf (Ger.) 20.12.43	TORTURE	U.S.
HASSE, Wilhelm	258962	M	Ger.	95	Lt.General, Army	WITNESS	U.S.
HASSEL	258171	M	Ger.		Usturmfhr, W-SS, Amsterdam (Neth.) 7.2.45	SUSPECT	NETH.
HASSELBACH	105924	M			Civilian, Surgeon	WITNESS	U.S.
HASSELBACH, Ernst (or HASSELBUCH)	192199	M	Ger.	12.2.05	Member Gestapo (Bel.)	TORTURE	BEL.
HASSELBERG (see HASELBERG)	194602						
HASSELBERG, Alfred	192366	M	Ger.		Dr., SS Sturmbannfhr, SS Schnell-Richter, Lublin (Pol.)	MURDER	POL.
HASSELBRUCK	186618	M	Ger.	10	Osturmbannfhr, SS, Gross-Rosen (Ger.)	TORTURE	U.K.
HASSELBUCH, Ernst (see HASSELBACH)	192139						
HASSELS	105925	M	Ger.	05	NCO in kitchen, Army prison, CC Hamburg-Altona (Ger.) 7.-11.44	TORTURE	U.S.
HASSER	257370	M			Sturmfhr, SS, Slave Labour Camp, Korgen (Nor.) 6.42-end of 43	MURDER	YUGO.
HASSET (see HASSE)	196655						
HASSLACHER, Jacob	195213	M	Ger.	83	Civilian, Manager, Timber Mill Owner, Sachsenberg near Spittal (Aust.) 1.-5.43	TORTURE	U.K.
HASSLER	352	M			Usturmfhr, SS, Perpignan (Fr.) 40-44	TORTURE	FR.
HASSLER	151652	M	Ger.		Etat-Major (Reg.Rat), Police Air Force, Me-Kampfgeschwader, Villandale, Villaudric (Fr.) 20.8.44		
HASSLER, Albert	124260	M			Pvt., 1 SS Pz.Div., 12 Parachute Inf. (2-Bv.), 12 Coy, Malmedy (Bel.) 17.12.44	MURDER	FR.
HASSLER, Georg	186619	M	Ger.		Manager of Harbour, Civilian, Regensburg (Ger.) 41-45	MURDER	U.S.
HASSMANN	193215	M	Ger.	95	Hilfswachtmeister, Reichsjustizministerium, Feldstraflager, CC Finmark (Nor.) 42-45	MURDER	U.S.
HASSMULLER, Rudolf	36685	M	Ger.	89	Forester, CC Oberessfeld (Ger.)	MISC.CRIMES	NOR.
HAST	167372	M			Sgt., Etat Major, stationed at Crest, La Rochette (Fr.) 3.8.44	TORTURE	U.K.
						MURDER	FR.

HAS-HAU

NAME	C.R.FILE NUMBER	SEX	NATIO- NALITY	DATE OF BIRTH	RANK OCCUPATION UNIT PLACE AND DATE OF CRIME	REASON WANTED	WANTED BY
HAST	168099	M			Adjutant,member of General staff,Kommandantur,Crest-Drome (Fr.)7.-8.44	MURDER	FR.
HASTREITER	31916	M	Ger.		Cpl.,Army,Cap de Nac,Montferrier (Fr.)	MURDER	FR.
HASTVOGEL	125464	M	Ger.		Guard,C.C.,Lebenhan (Ger.) 7.4.42	TORTURE	U.K.
HATHMANN	147324	M	Ger.		11.Panz.Div.,37-387 Coy.,Kampfgr."Wilde",South-West France	MURDER	FR.
HATJE	142466	M	Ger.		Chief,Kapo,C.C.,Schandelah,Braunschweig (Ger.) 44 - 45	MURDER	BEL.
HATJE (see GROSSE, Arthur)	195305						
HATLA	167807	M	Ger.		Osturmfhr.,SS,C.C.,Sachsenhausen (Ger.) (camp-doctor) 39 - 4. 45	MURDER	POL.
HATLALBUCH	191433	M	Ger.		Osturmfhr.,SS,C.C.,Sachsenhausen (Ger.)	MURDER	POL.
HATLAPA, Hans	129140	M	Ger.	17	Lt.,Dulag-Luft,Oberursel (Ger.)	TORTURE	U.K.
HATTFY	105926	M			Oberkriegsgerichtsrat,public official, (Bel.)	MURDER	U.S.
HATTLER	185536	M			Usturmfhr.,SS,doctor,C.C.,Flossenburg (Ger.)	MURDER	U.S.
HATTMAN, Friedrich	142952	M	Ger.		Civilian,Michelfeld (Ger.) 25.4.44	MURDER	U.S.
HATWIGER, Walter	253038	M	Ger.	20. 6.05	Member,Gestapo,Moravska,Ostrava (Czech.) 42-45	MURDER	CZECH.
HATZENDORFF	353	M	Ger.		W.C.O.,Air-force,Rodez (Fr.) 8.44	MURDER	FR.
HAU	195212	M	Ger.		Sgt.,SD Einsatz Kdo.z.b.V. 6,Saales St.Die (Fr.) 44	MURDER	U.K.
HAU, Georges	151656	M			Member,Gestapo,De'Angers (Fr.) 42-44	MURDER	FR.
HAUBELSHAFER	10086	M	Ger.		Pvt.,Panz.Gren.Rgt.,Albine (Fr.) 29.6.44	MURDER	FR.
HAUBER, Karl	259195	M	Ger.		Usturmfhr.,SS Div."Prinz Eugen",Niksic district Montenegro (Yugo.) 5.-6.43	MISC.CRIMES	YUGO.
HAUBER, Wilhelm	354	M	Ger.		Public official,Reichsamtsleiter,Berlin (Ger.) 9.39-43	MISC.CRIMES	POL.
HAUBER, Wilhelm	194748	M	Ger.		Sturmfhr.,Allg.SS,Abschnitt 42,Gnessenau (Pol.) 39-42	MISC.CRIMES	POL.
HAUBERT(alias:NERO)	130982	M	Ger.		O.C.,Mauthausen (Aust.) 4.44	MURDER	U.S.
HAUBITZ	255397	M			Pvt.,C.C.,Rottleberode,Nordhausen (Ger.)	MURDER	U.S.
HAUBITZ, Paul	139199	M	Ger.	07	Pvt.,Army,Kutno (Pol.)	MURDER	U.S.
HAUBT	190340	F	Ger.		Employee,Kripo,Wiesbaden (Ger.) 43-45	TORTURE	U.S.
HAUCH (or STRAUCH)	147323	M	Ger.		Lt.,11.Pz.Div.Kampfgruppe "Wilde",(Fr.) 44	MURDER	FR.
HAUCK	355	M			Capt.,Air-force,77.Flyer staff,Seguret and Vaison Violes (Fr.) 10.6.44-1.8.44	MURDER	FR.
HAUCK	72502	M			Lt.,Army,Cherenvilliers (Fr.)	MURDER	FR.
HAUCK	125695	M	Ger.		Lt.,SS Pz.Div.Hitler-Jugend,12.Pz.E.Abt.,1. 2. or 3.Coy.,Ascq (Fr.) 1.4.44	MURDER	FR.
HAUCK	136263	M			Gebirgsjaeger Div.,157.Flak Btty.598,Annecyet,Oyonnax (Fr.)2.-4.44	MURDER	FR.
HAUCK	167371	M			Civilian,Tyez (Fr.) 9.7.44	MURDER	FR.
HAUCK	186494	M	Ger.	19	Osturmfhr.,12.SS Pz.Div.Hitler-Jugend,near Caen (Fr.) 6.6.-8.7.44	TORTURE	CAN.
HAUCK	189350	F	Ger.		Feldgendarmerie,Bar le Duc (Fr.) 20.-23.8.44	MURDER	FR.
HAUCK	192959	M	Ger.		Agent,Gestapo,Stalag VII Z,C.C.,Laufen,Tittmoning (Ger.) 10.42-1.45	TORTURE	U.S.
HAUCK	250246	M	Ger.		Capt.,151.Inf.Res.Div.,98.Bn.,3.Coy.,Departm.l'Ain (Fr.)10.-21.7.44	MISC.CRIMES	FR.
HAUCK, Alfred	255999	M			Cpl.,C.C.,Ellrich,Nordhausen (Ger.)	MURDER	U.S.
HAUCK, Wilhelm	255403	M			Flyer,C.C.,Ellrich,Nordhausen (Ger.)	MURDER	U.S.
HAUDEL, Ernst	196708	M	Ger.	97	Civilian builder,building firm Walter Haudel in Blasewitz,Dresden (Ger.) 44-45	WITNESS	U.K.
HAUDENREISSER, Karl-Hans	195406	M	Ger.	02	Usturmfhr.,SS,Krim.Inspector,Gestapo Employee,Kolin (Ger.) 39-45	MURDER	CZECH.
HAUDISSEN	254786	M			Lt.Col.,377.Jg.Rgt.,Vinkt,Meigem (Bel.) 25.-31.5.40	MISC.CRIMES	BEL.
HAUENSTEIN (or HAUSENSTEIN) Ernst	194599	M	Ger.	10	Oschfhr.,SS Rgt."Germania",SIPO,Einsatz Kdo.,Radzyn,Biala,Lublin (Pol.)	TORTURE	POL.
HAUENSTEIN	305894	M	Ger.		In charge of food supplies,C.C.,Neugraben,Tiefstak (Ger.) 44-5.2.45	BRUTALITY	CZECH.
HAUENSTEIN, Heinrich	252153	M		15. 7.00	Hptschfhr.,SS,C.C.,Harzungen,Nordhausen (Ger.)	MURDER	U.S.
HAUER	18141	M	Ger.		Usturmfhr.,SS Pz.Div.Hitler-Jugend,1.Bn.,3.Coy.,Caen (Fr.)4.44-7.44	MURDER	FR.
HAUER	142048	M	Ger.		Lt.,Army,Stalag 17,Kaisersteinbruch (Aust.) 5.43	TORTURE	U.S.
HAUER, Anton	253715	M	Ger.		Pvt.,Army,Villmar (Ger.) 17.6.-15.8.44	MURDER	U.S.
HAUER, Joseph	167805	M	Ger.		Oberregierungsrat,leader,Abt.Forsten,Amt des Gouverneurs,Radom(Pol.) 9.39-44	PILLAGE	POL.
HAUER, Karl	162442	M	Ger.	25. 9.96	Civilian,Mechanic,Lampertsham (Ger.) 13.6.44	WITNESS	U.S.
HAUER, Kurt	161992	M			Pvt.,Army,Leipzig (Ger.)	TORTURE	U.S.
HAUER, Trenkle	192958	M	Ger.		Uschfhr.,SS,C.C.,Buchenwald (Ger.) 42-45	MURDER	U.S.
HAUF	196664	M	Ger.		W.O.Chief,Div."Das Reich",3.Pz.Gren.Rgt. SS "Deutschland" 3.Bn., Marsoulas,Mazieres,Betchat,Justiniac (Fr.) 10.6.-26.6.44	MISC.CRIMES	FR.
HAUF, Ferdinand	192210	M	Ger.		Sgt.,Army,C.C.,Soissons (Fr.) 15.8.44	WITNESS	FR.
HAUFE, Walter	255983	M			Foreman,Wilhelmshaven (Ger.)	TORTURE	FR.
HAUFE, Walter	305171	M	Ger.		Member,staff of C.C.,Neckargerach,Neckarelz (Baden) (Ger.) 42-45	MURDER	FR.
HAUFE, Walter	305172	M	Ger.		Member,Kommando Wilhelmshaven,C.C.,Neuengamme(Ger.) 42-45	MURDER	FR.
HAUFF	255404	M			Pvt.,C.C.,Ellrich,Nordhausen (Ger.)	MURDER	U.S.
HAUFF, Andreas	193214	M	Ger.	02	Civ.,Hauptwachtmeister,Feldstraflager,Strafgefang.Lager Nord,C.C., Finnmark(Nor.) 10.44	MISC.CRIMES	NOR.
HAUG	173283	M	Ger.	97	Officer,SS,member,Gestapo,SD,Noailles (Fr.) 9.8.44	MURDER	U.K.
HAUG	185662	M	Ger.		Employee,Gestapo,Saarbruecken (Ger.)	PILLAGE	FR.
HAUG	254796	M	Ger.		Capt.,1.-98.Geb.Rgt.,Le Chablais (Fr.) 21.5.44	MISC.CRIMES	FR.
HAUG	258170	M	Ger.		Sonderfhr.,Waffen SS,Kragujevac (Yugo.) 17.10.41	PILLAGE	YUGO.
HAUG, Karl	305785	M	Ger.		Hptschfhr.,SS,security police,(B.d.S.)Paris,Noailles,Oise (Fr.) 1.8.44	MURDER	U.K.
HAUG, Max	261354	M	Ger.		Sgt.,3.Watch Coy. of prison Francais during Campaign of Poland Unit Inf.(Commander von Manteuffel) Graudenz (Pol.) 43-44	BRUTALITY	FR.
HAUK	186560	M	Ger.	97	Member,Gestapo,Noailles (Fr.) 9.8.44	MURDER	U.K.
HAUK	192957	M	Ger.		Uschfhr.,SS,C.C.,Buchenwald (Ger.) 42-45	TORTURE	U.S.
HAUKE	194598	M	Ger.		Cpl.,Army,Bais (Fr.)	WITNESS	FR.
HAUKE	261174	M	Ger.		Member,staff of C.C.,Ravensbrueck (Ger.)	SUSPECT	BEL.
HAUKOHL	256755	M	Ger.		Chief of Sub-Sec.,Mittelwork Nordhausen (Ger.)	MURDER	U.S.
HAULLER	192026	M	Ger.	19	SS-Mann,19.Rgt.SS Polizei 3.Coy.,St.JEOIRE,Chatillon,s-CLUSES' TANINGES Balme (Fr.)	MURDER	FR.
HAUMAER	307127	M			Lagerfhr.,C.C.,Auschwitz,Birkenau (Pol.) 40	MURDER	FR.
HAUMANN (see HAUSMANN)	157747						
HAUMAYER	256754	M	Ger.		Sgt.,SS,Postenf.4 F.Me.Haberman Coy.,Nordhausen (Ger.)	MURDER	U.S.
HAUMAYER	300472	M	Ger.		Pvt.,attached to 01512 K Marine Inf.,partly composed of Waffen SS, Trebeurden,Plemeur-Bodou,Pierros-Guirec (Fr.) 6.-7.44	MISC.CRIMES	FR.
HAUMER	196663	M	Ger.		Aspirant,Ost Bn.615,Lantilly (Fr.) 25.5.44	MISC.CRIMES	FR.
HAUMEYER	255391	M			Uschfhr.,C.C.,Ellrich,Nordhausen (Ger.)	MURDER	U.S.
HAUN	250247	M	Ger.		Sonderfhr.,Interpreter,Kommandantur,Bourg (Fr.) 10.-21.7.44	MISC.CRIMES	FR.

HAU-HAU

NAME	C.R.FILE NUMBER	SEX	NATIONALITY	DATE OF BIRTH	RANK OCCUPATION UNIT PLACE AND DATE OF CRIME	REASON WANTED	WANTED BY
HAUNER, Engelhardt	255992	M		23. 6.97	Pvt., C.C. Ellrich, Nordhausen (Ger.)	MURDER	U.S.
HAUNOLD, Carl	196662	M	Ger., Aust.	05	Lt., Military security Police, F.P.No. 02039 Departm. Turin (It.) 12.43	WITNESS	U.K.
HAUPE, Walter	255520	M	Ger.		Clerk, Civilian, Neckargerach (Ger.)	MURDER	FR.
HAUPMANN	173633	M			Labour-camp, Muehldorf, Ampfing (Ger.) 6.44- 4.45	MURDER	U.S.
HAUPRICH, Otto	196932	M	Ger.	15	Major, SS, Benesov (Czech.)	MURDER	CZECH.
HAUPT	31914	M	Ger.		Sturmf., SA, C.C. Struthof (Fr.) 42-44	MURDER	FR.
HAUPT	136262	M	Ger.		Feldgendarm, Feldgendarmerie, Stenay (Fr.) 44	MURDER	FR.
HAUPT	146698	M	Ger.		Lt.Col., Army, Ludwigsburg (Ger.) 8.44	MISC.CRIMES	U.S.
HAUPT	192365	M	Ger.		Unterscharfhr., SS, C.C. Flossenburg (Ger.) 44-45	MURDER	U.S.
HAUPT	193672	M	Ger.		Sonderfhr., Army, Kressendorf (Ger.) 4.43	WITNESS	U.K.
HAUPT	255110	M	Ger.		Unterscharfhr., SS, Member, S.D. and Gestapo, Toulouse (Fr.) 11.42- 8.44	MISC.CRIMES	FR.
HAUPT	255388	M			Hauptscharfhr., C.C. Ellrich, Nordhausen (Ger.)	MURDER	U.S.
HAUPT	261045	M	Ger.		SS-Mann, 106.Panz.Gren.Regt. "Frundsberg", Boyelles (Fr.) 9.44	MURDER	FR.
HAUPT, Erika	135181	F	Ger.		Guard, Helmbrechts (Ger.) 7.44- 4.45	WITNESS	U.S.
HAUPT, Otto	306683	M			331.Pioneer-Bn., 331.Inf.Div., Mijnheerenland (Neth.) 5.45	PILLAGE	NETH.
HAUPTMANN	138236	M	Ger.	09	Unterscharfhr., SS, Gestapo, Mussidan (Fr.) 2.44	MURDER	FR.
HAUPTMANN	194557	M	Ger.	20	Guard, Block 21, CC. Flossenburg (Ger.) 45	MURDER	BEL.
HAUPTMANN	72521	M			Gen.-Kontrolleur, Public official	MURDER	FR.
HAUPTMANN	151657	M			Member, NSDAP, Brux (Czech.)	TORTURE	U.K.
HAUPTMANN	185448	M	Ger.		Dr., Obersturmfhr., SS, Farge, Nickelswalde (Ger.) 4.45	MURDER	BEL.
HAUPTMANN	254536	M	Ger.		Chief Police, C.C. Buchenwald (Ger.)	INTERR.	FR.
HAUPTMANN, Heinrich	162451	M		00	Civilian, C.C. Buchenwald (Ger.)	WITNESS	U.S.
HAUPTMANN, Wilhelm	139193	M	Ger.	95	Civ., 2.Kdo., C.C. Halle (Ger.) 4.45	TORTURE	U.S.
HAUPTMEYER	158626	M			Guard, SS, Poitier (Fr.) 3.44	TORTURE	U.S.
HAUPTON, Paul Emil	178315	M	Ger.	20	Sgt., Stalag 4-B, C.C. Muehlberg/Elbe, (Ger.) 6.44	MURDER	U.K.
HAUPTS, Leo	188699	M	Ger.	23. 9.11	Pvt., Army, Aachen (Ger.) 8.44	WITNESS	U.S.
HAURAN	256804	M	Ger.		Chief of Sub-Sec., Mittelbau, Nordhausen (Ger.)	MURDER	U.S.
HAURICKS or HAURICKSON	173558	M	Ger.		2.Bn., 1010.Panz.Regt., 7.Coy., Chilleurs aux Bois (Fr.) 8.44	MURDER	U.K.
HAUS	18203	M			Lt., Army, Charmes (Fr.)	MURDER	FR.
HAUS	120526	M	Ger.		SS-Col., Chef d.Personals d.Org.Beelitz,(Pol., It.)	TORTURE	FR.,BEL.
HAUS, Friedrich	188283	M			SS-Officer, C.C. (Ger.) 40-45	MISC.CRIMES	CZECH.,UNWCC.
HAUSBERG, Walter	261088	M	Ger.	28. 4.09	Oberscharfhr., SS, Camp-leader, C.C. Lublin, Cracow (Pol.) 41-44	MURDER	POL.
HAUSBLAS, Karl	24944	M	Ger.	14. 5.17	Army, Annemay (Fr.) 8.44	MURDER	FR.
HAUSCHEN (see HAUSCHMANN)	72594						
HAUSCHILD	142947	M	Ger.	95	Oberinspektor, Police, C.C. Auschwitz (Pol.) 10.42	MURDER	U.S.
HAUSCHILDEN	185537	M	Ger.	19	Untersturmfhr., SS, Prague (Czech.) 5.45	MURDER	CZECH.
HAUSCHMANN	162452	M	Ger.	99	Oberscharfhr., SS-Wach-Bn., C.C. Buchenwald (Ger.) 45	TORTURE	U.S.
HAUSCHMANN or HAUSCHEN	72594	M		40	Beauvais (Fr.)	MURDER	FR.
HAUSDORF, Georg	196661	M	Ger.		SS-Oberscharfhr., S.D. Dienststelle Zwolle, Kampen (Neth.) 10.44	MURDER	NETH.
HAUSE	255389	M			Pvt., C.C. Ellrich, Nordhausen (Ger.)	MURDER	U.S.
HAUSELMAN	10087	M	Ger.		Officer, Army, Mas de Breteuil (Fr.) 8.44	MURDER	FR.
HAUSEN or HANSEN	357	M			Officer, Army, Villenes (Fr.) 8.44	MURDER	FR.
HAUSEN	158625	M			General, SS "Das Reich", (Fr.) 40	MURDER	U.S.
HAUSEN or HAMERN	162887	M	Ger.		Sgt., Professional - prison guard, St. Gilles, Brussels (Bel.)	TORTURE	BEL.
HAUSENSTEIN (see HAUENSTEIN) Ernst	194599						
HAUSER	148170	M			Civ., Ailingen (Ger.) 7.44	MURDER	FR.
HAUSER	254607	M	Ger.		Lt., 2.Bn., 18.Fallschirmjg.Regt., "Hermann Goering", Amersfoort (Neth.) 5.45	MURDER	NETH.
HAUSER, Adam	255990	M		5. 9.98	SS-Mann, C.C. Dora - Nordhausen (Ger.)	MURDER	U.S.
HAUSER, Fritz	301198	M	Ger.		Group-leader, Pforzheim, Huchenfeld (Ger.) 3.45	MURDER	U.K.
HAUSER, Georg	162439	M	Ger.	19. 5.94	Hauptscharfhr., SS, C.C. Malk (Ger.)	TORTURE	U.S.
HAUSER, Georg or HAEUSER	142460	M		14	Capt., SS Einsatzgruppe Engerau, Minsk (Sov.Un.)	MURDER	U.S.
HAUSER, Hans	142465	M	Ger.		Crim.Secr., Cripo., C.C. Hennigsdorf (Ger.)	TORTURE	U.K.
HAUSER, Helmuth or Helmut	185447	M		07	SS probably Res., Friedrichshafen (Ger.) 7.44	MURDER	U.S.
HAUSER, Hermann	72589	M		14. 8.09	Capt., Army, 74.B.H.K., 9.G.F.B., Caen, Nantes (Fr.)	MURDER	FR.
HAUSER, Johann	186620	M		82	Miner, Adolf-Mine, Arb.-Kdo., Merkstein (Ger.) 6.44	WITNESS	U.S.
HAUSER, Karl	190197	M	Ger.	4. 8.12	Crim.Secr., Gestapo, Bruenn (Czech.) 39-45	MURDER	CZECH.
HAUSER, Wolfgang	305056	M	Ger.		Major General, Commander 41.Div., District of Strumica, Djevdjelija (Yugo.) 11.44	MISC.CRIMES	YUGO.
HAUSERMANN, Oscar	301827	M	Ger.		Luftfahrtministerium Berlin, C.C. Dachau, Auschwitz (Ger.,Pol.) 42-43	TORTURE	BEL.
HAUSHAHN	256712	M	Ger.		Employee, C.C. Nordhausen (Ger.)	MURDER	U.S.
HAUSHAHN, Wilhelm	154383	M		95	Gruppenfhr., 1.Volkssturm-Bn., 3.Coy., C.C. Vicinity of Gardelegen (Ger.) 4.45	MURDER	U.S.
HAUSHOFFER, Karl	21363	M	Ger.		Public official, lecturer propagandist	MISC.CRIMES	U.N.W.C.C.
HAUSKRECHT, Gustav	251594	M	Ger.	13. 6.13	Civ., Gestapo, Bratislava (Czech.) 39-45	MURDER	CZECH.
HAUSKRECHT, Karol	250819	M	Ger.	7. 7.09	Dr., Civ., Member of Gestapo, Bratislava (Czech.) 39-45	MURDER	CZECH.
HAUSLEIN	194556	M	Ger.		Guard, C.C. Donauwoerth, Kaisheim (Ger.) 44-45	TORTURE	CZECH.
HAUSLER, Teno	39806	M			Oberscharfhr., SS Div., F.P. No. 48963 B, Chateau-Gontier (Fr.) 44	MURDER	FR.
HAUSMACHER	189785	F	Ger.		S.D., C.C. Vught (Neth.) 6.44	MURDER	NETH.
HAUSMAN or HAUSSMAN	141962	M		02	SS-Oberscharfhr., Guard, Camp M-1, Mettenheim, Ampfing, Muehldorf (Ger.) 44-45	MURDER	U.S.
HAUSMANN	194555	M	Ger.	94	Stabsarzt, Dulag 377, Gerolstein (Ger.) 44-45	TORTURE	U.S.
HAUSMANN or HAUMANN	157747	M	Ger.	02	Cpl., Army, Sternberg (Czech.) 10.41	TORTURE	U.K.
HAUSMANN	185446	M	Ger.		Pvt., W-SS, Pz.Div."Adolf Hitler", 1.SS-Recon.Bn. probably Parfondruy, Stavelot (Bel.) 12.44	MURDER	U.S.,BEL.
HAUSMANN, Arthur	167370	M	Ger.	17	Cpl., Navy, C.C. Walchum (Ger.)	TORTURE	FR.
HAUSMANN, H.	257180	M	Ger.	01	Dr., Hauptsturmfuehrer, Pressburg prison at Bratislava Theben - Neudorf (Aust.) 4.45	WITNESS	U.S.
HAUSMANN, Richard	186622	M	Ger.	00	Pvt., 4.SS-Totenkopf-Sturmbann, C.C. Nordhausen (Ger.)	WITNESS	U.S.
HAUSMYFEL	119430	M	Ger.		Major, 163.Inf.Div., 20.Army, Finmark (Nor.) 44	MURDER	NOR.
HAUSNER or HAENDLER	339	M			SS-Oberscharf., C.C. Birkenau-Oswiecim, Rajsko (Pol.)	MURDER	POL.,BEL., U.N.W.C.C.

HAU-HEC

NAME	C.R.FILE NUMBER	SEX	NATIO-NALITY	DATE OF BIRTH	RANK OCCUPATION UNIT PLACE AND DATE OF CRIME	REASON WANTED	WANTED BY
HAUS	131281	M			Major,Army Oberkommando,O.K.W.(Kriegsgefangenenwesen)	MISC.CRIMES	U.S.
HAUSSMANN	191613	F	Ger.		Dr.,Civ.Servant,Ostgebietsministerium Einsatzstab Rosenberg(Fr.) 40-44	PILLAGE	FR.
HAUSSER	9682	M	Ger.		Gruppenfhr.,Inspect.der SS Verfuegungstr.,Berlin(Ger.) 38-44	MISC.CRIMES	CZECH.
HAUSSER, Paul	259419	M	Ger.	80	Oberstgruppenfhr.	WITNESS	U.S.
HAUSSER, Rene	154255	M		22.6.88		MISC.CRIMES	FR.
HAUSSMAN, Eugen	139797	M	Ger.	15	Sgt.,Camp-Leader,Waffen-SS,C.C.Muhldorf(Ger.) 44-45	MURDER	U.S.
HAUSMAN see HAUSMAN	141962						
HAUSER, Adam	255578	M	Ger.	5.9.98	SS-Mann,C.C.Nordhausen(Ger.)	MURDER	U.S.
HAUTEFAGE	151658	M	Ger.		Capt.,SS Panz.Gren.Regt.3"Deutschland",Div."Das Reich",Bazens(Fr.) 17.6.44	MURDER	FR.
HAUTER	186478	M	Ger.		Lt.,950 Regt.Inf.H.Col.Hindoué,Charente and Vienne(Fr.) 8.44	TORTURE	FR.
HAUTMAN, Eric	198931	M	Ger.		Policeman,Geheime Feldpolizei,Montigny-en-Gohelle(Fr.) 14.3.44	MURDER	FR.
HAUTMANN or HAUTMEYER	253044	M	Ger.		Lagerfhr.,C.C.Neuengamme(Ger.) 40	MURDER	BEL.
HAUZ, Herralt	261820	M	Ger.	08	SS-Hptschfhr.,SD Besancon,Belfort(Fr.) 7.9.44	MURDER	FR.
HAUZEMANN	173559	M	Ger.		Gend.,Gendarmerie Chateaudun,Logron(Fr.) 9.8.44	TORTURE	FR.
HAVELKA, Ferdinand	253714	M	Ger.	23.10.10	Employee,Gestapo,Litomerice(Czech.) 39-44	MURDER	CZECH.
HAVERCAMP	173634	M	Ger.		Lt.,Head Paymaster Stalag VIA,Hemer(Ger.) 44	TORTURE	U.S.
HAVERKAMP	151655	M	Ger.		Fliegerhorstkommandantur,Major,Villandrie(Fr.) 20.8.44	MURDER	FR.
HAVERLAND	132582	M			Major,104 Gren.Regt.Kommandantur,Crest(Fr.) 2.8.44	MURDER	FR.
HAVERLAND	260151	M	Ger.		Major,Omdt.,19 Gren.-Regt.,Massif du Vercors,Isere et Drome(Fr.) 20.7.-5.8.44	SUSPECT	FR.
HAVKE, Willi	301127	M	Ger.		Dienststelle L.01-159 Amtskasse L.3.32-179 L.G.K.Belgium and Northern France,stationed at La Pommereuil,La-Pommereuil Nord(Fr.) 21.8.44	MISC.CRIMES	FR.
HAVLAT, Erwin	194597	M	Ger.	08	SS-Hptschfhr.,SD,Kolin(Czech.) 39-45	MURDER	CZECH.
HAVRANEK nee KOSMAN,Marie or Maru	193421	F	Ger.	2.5.13	Agent,Gestapo,Uhersky Brod(Czech.) 39-45	MURDER	CZECH.
HAVRANEK, Vladimir	193420	M	Ger.	2.4.97	Agent,Member of SS,Gestapo,Uhersky Brod(Czech.) 39-45	MISC.CRIMES	CZECH.
HAVRE, Willi	196658	M	Ger.		Amtskasse,L 332179 L.G.K.Belgien,Pommereuil(Fr.) 21.8.44	WITNESS	FR.
HAWELKA	190536	M	Ger.		Sgt.,Gestapo.Trondes,Boucq,menil-la Tour(Fr.) 15.-18.8.44	MURDER	FR.
HAY	130655	M			Member SS Planing Staff,C.C.Mittelbau Dora,Nordhausen(Ger.)	MURDER	U.S.
HAYDEN, Josef	157748	M	Ger.		Major,Lageroffizier,Dulag Luft,Stalag VIIA,Enroute from Dulag Luft Wetzlar to Moosberg(Ger.) 25.3.-12.4.45	WITNESS	U.S.
HAYMAER	259226	M			Camp-Leader,C.C.Auschwitz(Pol.)	MURDER	FR.
HAYRHOFER	301687	M	Ger.		Brig.,Chef Du Train,05-243"Oberland"Mongolian Unit,St.Nazaire en Royans (Fr.) 20.7.-5.8.44	MURDER	FR.
HAZBACH	154381	M	Ger.		Chief,Kripo,Hemer(Ger.) 4.44	TORTURE	U.S.
HAZELBECK	252963	M	Ger.		Farmer,Moosfuhrt(Ger.)	TORTURE	FR.
HAZENFEUTER	196880	M	Ger.		Pvt.,C.C.Struthof-Natzweiler(Fr.) 40-44	MISC.CRIMES	FR.
HAZER	130659	M			Member of SS Planning Staff,SS C.C.Mittelbau Dora(Ger.)	MURDER	U.S.
HEBALD	161961	M	Ger.	92	Sgt.,Army,near Bitterfeld(Ger.) 2.45	MURDER	U.K.
HEBBEN	358	M	Ger.		Obertruppfhr.,RAD,Organisation Todt,Cherbourg(Fr.) 7.-16.5.44	MURDER	FR.
HEBEISEN, Martin	167221	M	Ger.		Cpl.,9 Gren.Res.Regt.,1 Coy.,Magni D'Avignon(Fr.) 18.9.44	MURDER	FR.
HEBEL	254544	M	Ger.		Uschfhr.,Gestapo,Limoges(Fr.)	INTERR.	FR.
HEBEL, Ferdinand	190191	M	Ger.		Pvt.,Army,714 Bn.,Labitsch(Ger.) 24.9.41	TORTURE	U.K.
HEBLE, Elisabeth	189052	F	Ger.	31.8.20	Clerk,Gestapo,Brno(Czech.) 39-45	WITNESS	CZECH.
HEBENSTREIT	193493	M	Ger.		SS-Sturmmann,SS C.C.Leipzig(Ger.)	MURDER	POL.
HEBER or UDET or UBER	100521	M	Ger.	95	Employee,Stalag Air III C.C.Sagan(Ger.) 24.-25.3.44	MURDER	U.K.
HEBER	119431	M	Ger.		Major,Army,137-2 Geb.Div.,20 Army,1 Geb.Jaeg.Regt.44	MURDER	NOR.
HEBER	125472	M	Ger.		Stabsintendant,Stalag IVA,Koenigswartha(Ger.) 2.10.44-9.3.45	MISC.CRIMES	U.K.
HEBER	130390	M	Ger.		Osturmfhr.,SS,C.C.Mauthausen(Aust.) 41-45	MURDER	U.S.
HEBER, Christa	161966	F	Ger.	23	SS,Buchenwald(Ger.) 39-45	WITNESS	U.S.
HEBER, Kaete	105927	F	Ger.		Assist.Camp-Leader,Civilian,C.C.Schenefeld(Ger.)	TORTURE	POL.,U.S.
HEBERLEIN	119432	M	Ger.		Lt.-Gen.,Army,Omdt.d.rueckw.Armeegebietes,20 Army 44	MURDER	NOR.
HEBERLING	190988	M	Ger.		Crim.-Secretary,Police,Wiesbaden(Ger.) 43-45	TORTURE	U.S.
HEBERSTREIT	105928	M	Ger.		SS CC.Thekla near Leipzig(Ger.)	MURDER	U.S.
HEBRUCHT	306607	M	Ger.		Lt.,Feldgend. of St.Nazaire en Royans Drome(Fr.) 20.7.-5.8.44	MURDER	FR.
HEBSTREIT, Kurt	190196	M	Ger.	24.5.11	Kriminalangestellter,Gestapo,Bruenn(Czech.) 39-45	MURDER	CZECH.
HEZER, Willy	189951	M	Ger.		Pvt.,Army,Le Bourget Triage(Fr.) 24.8.44	MURDER	FR.
HECHT	161173	M	Ger.		Cpl.,16 Inf.Div.SS,C.C.Maille(Fr.) 28.3.44	MURDER	FR.
HECHT	167368	M	Ger.		Lt.,1 Coy.,Ost-Bn.615,Avallon Hameau les Granges(Fr.) 18.8.44	MURDER	FR.
HECHT	168800	M	Ger.		SS-Rapportfuehrer,C.C.Druette(Ger.)	MURDER	UNWCC.
HECHT	190556	M	Ger.		Sgt.-Maj.,Feld-Kommandantur,Kragujevac(Yugo.) 21.10.41	MURDER	YUGO.
HECHT, Artur	255525	M	Ger.	23.9.15	Pvt.,C.C.Ellrich-Nordhausen(Ger.)	MURDER	U.S.
HECHT, Rudolf	31939	M	Ger.		Oberlandgerichtsrat,Public Official,Litomerice(Czech.) 21.2.40	MURDER	CZECH.
HECHTENBERGER	305865	M	Ger.		Pvt.,1 Aufkl.Abt.,3 Coy.,2 Col.,XV Div.,Africa Corps, St.Leger(Arlon) 5.9.44	MISC.CRIMES	BEL.
HECK	161172	M			Lt.-Col.,Air Force,Flak-Regt."Hermann Goering"(Ger.) 29.4.45	SUSPECT	U.S.
HECK see HECKZ, Rudolf	165927						
HECK	258776	M	Ger.	16	M-Sgt.,Darmstadt(Ger.) 4.-7.44	BRUTALITY	U.S.
HECK	258877	M	Ger.		Inspector,Custom-house,Loudres la region(Fr.) 1.-8.44	MURDER	FR.
HECK, Elisabeth	258088	F	Ger.	23.9.22	Civilian,Cechtice(Czech.) 8.5.45	MURDER	CZECH.
HECK, Heinrich	127964	M	Ger.		Civilian,Enkenbach(Ger.) 12.43-3.45	INTERR.	U.S.
HECK, Heinrich	193213	M	Ger.	97	Hilfswachtmeister,Reichsjustizministerium,Feldstraflager,C.C.Finmark (Nor.)	MISC.CRIMES	NOR.
HECK, Heinrich	257988	M	Ger.	14.10.14	Sgt.,392 Inf.Div.,Kriz Polje-Jezerane(Yugo.) 44	WITNESS	YUGO.
HECKBAU	130658	M			Civilian,C.C.Dora Mittelbau,Nordhausen(Ger.)	MURDER	U.S.
HECKBERG	179643	M		00	Civilian Foreman,O.T.,Muehldorf(Ger.) 6.44-4.45	MURDER	U.S.
HECKE, Hans	154254	M			Hptsturmfhr.,SS,Vaihingen near Stuttgart(Ger.)	TORTURE	FR.
HECKEL	21361	M			Dr.,Official Evacuation,Head School-Administration,Morgvia(Czech.)	MISC.CRIMES	UNWCC.
HECKENDORF	192138	M	Ger.	96	Officer,Geheime Feldpolizei,Liege(Bel.)	TORTURE	BEL.

HEC-HEI

NAME	C.R.FILE NUMBER	SEX	NATIO-NALITY	DATE OF BIRTH	RANK OCCUPATION UNIT PLACE AND DATE OF CRIME	REASON WANTED	WANTED BY
HECKENHOLT, (or HOCKENHOLT, HOCKELCHOC)	301405	M	Ger.		Constructor, of the Execution Chambers at Belzec C.C. Poland	MURDER	FR.
HECKER	232370	M	Ger.		Official, S.D. Osnabrueck, (Ger.)	PILLAGE	U.S.
HECKER	251604	M	Ger.		SS-Usturmfhr., Gestapo, Bruessel (Bel.)	MURDER	BEL.
HECKER	254643	M	Ger.		Opl., Field-Police, Vendome, (Fr.) 8.44	MURDER	FR.
HECKER	255523	M	Ger.		Pvt., C.C. Dora, Nordhausen (Ger.)	MURDER	U.S.
HECKER, Hans	43016	M	Ger.		SS-Lt., SS Stab, Abschnitt 42, Gniezno (Pol.)9.39-1.42	MURDER	POL.
HECKER, Hans	306385	M	Ger.	29.7.10	SS Sgt., C.C.Buchenwald (Ger.)	MURDER	BEL.
HECKERT	257812	M		12	Lt., Army, Zajecar, (Yug.)41-44	MISC. CRIMES	YUG.
HECKL, Oskar	167184	M	Ger.		Civ., Treuhaender, Firm Oros, Krakau (Pol.)9.39- end 44	PILLAGE	POL.
HECKMANN	173603	M	Ger.		Gauhauptstellenleiter N.S.D.A.P. Strassbourg (Fr.) 44	TORTURE	FR.
HECKMANN	254629	M	Ger.		Kreisleiter in Thann, Gnewenheim (Fr.)10.44	MURDER	FR.
HECKMANN	255524	M	Ger.		Hptschfhr., C.C.Ellrich Nordhausen (Ger.)	MURDER	U.S.
HECKNER	251625	M	Ger.		SS-Usturmfhr., Sipo, Bruessel (Bel.)	INTERR.	BEL.
HECKZ, Rudolf (or HECK)	165927	M			SS-Uschfhr., Vienne (Aust.) 44-45	TORTURE	U.S.
HECTOR (see MARTIN, Hector)	188645						
HEDDERICH, Heinrich	123997	M	Ger.		Criminalsekretaer, Gestapo Criminal Assistant near Saarburg (Ger.)44	MURDER	U.S.
HEDDERICH, Otto	253705	M	Ger.		Cpt., Commandant of parachutistes, Erquy (Fr.) 8.44	INTERR.	FR.
HEDELMEYER, Roman	173604	M	Ger.		Civ., Calfactor, C.C. Buchenwald (Ger.)42-45	MURDER	FR.
HEDEMANN, Heinrich	142474	M	Ger.	90	Secretary, Gestapo Cannes (Fr.)43-44	PILLAGE	FR.
HEDEMANN, Hicke	168807	M	Ger.	79	Local Group Leader, NSDAP.,Westerende (Ger.)	MISC. CRIMES	U.N.W.C.C.
HEDEMEYER	173642	M	Ger.		Civ., Stalag VIA, Labour Front, Hemer (Ger.)41-4.45	TORTURE	U.S.
HEDENKAMP, August	161962	M	Ger.	13	Opl., SS, Ohrdruf, Buchenwald (Ger.)	WITNESS	U.S.
HEDERER	119433	M	Ger.		Lt., Col.,Kdt.des Enackw.Armes Geb.525,44	MURDER	NOR.
HEDRICH	156717	M			Yonne (Fr.)	MURDER	FR.
HEDERICH	161967	M	Ger.		General Army, Dun Les Places (Fr.)26.-28.6.44	MURDER	FR.
HEDERICH, Wilhelm	250248	M	Ger.	80	General Lt., Lain, (Fr.)7.44	MISC. CRIMES	FR.
HEDERZET (or HABERZET)	156718	M			Cpt., Army Amilly (Fr.)	MURDER	FR.
HEDICK	137022	M	Ger.		Osturmbannfhr., SS, 150.Pz.Bde., Malmedy Liege Stavelot(Bel.)12.-1.45	MISC. CRIMES	U.S.
HEIMANN, Helmut	373	M			Adjutant-Chief, Army, Kassel (Ger.)	MURDER	FR.
HEDRICH, Max	196395	M	Ger.	95	Civilian, Poppenhausen (Ger.) 5.42	MURDER	POL.
HEDTKE	174831	M			Pay-master, Paratroops Rgt.2.Bn.2.Div.Plouzane (Fr.)44	MURDER	FR.
HEDWIG	124731	M			SS-Uschfhr., 1.SS Aufklaerungs-Bn. Renardmont-Stavelot (Bel.)12.44	MURDER	BEL.
HEDWIG	305057	M		05	Oberstabsschfhr., SS Prison Camp Vrasselt-Emmerich Wijnbergen (Neth.) 10.44-3.45	BRUTALITY	NETH.
HEEGER, Gustav	306386	M	Ger.	16.12.21	SS Pvt., C.C. Buchenwald (Ger.)	MURDER	BEL.
HEEN	301633	M			Hilfsverwalter, Erbach near Amberg (Ger.) up to 45	MURDER	CZECH.
HEENE	162438	M	Ger.		Civ., Praunheim,(Ger.)	MURDER	U.S.
HEER, Wilhelm (or WILLE, Wilhelm)	142442	M	Ger.	8.9.94	Local Group Leader, Truppfhr., NSDAP.SA. Hausen and Ginnheim (Ger.) 21.11.44	MURDER	U.S.
HEER	192956	M	Ger.		SS-Uschfhr., C.C. Buchenwald (Ger.)	TORTURE	U.S.
HEER, Hermann	156720	M	Ger.		Pvt., Unit L 20368 - Army, Baudrigues (Fr.) 19.8.44	MURDER	FR.
HEERDE, E.	133363	M	Ger.	76	Civilian	MURDER	U.S.
HEERDE, Ewald	133330	M	Ger.	24.11.89	Rottfhr., W-SS C.C. Flossenburg (Ger.)	MURDER	U.S.
HEERDEGEN	129782	M			Civ., Detain in C.C. Weimar Buchenwald (Ger.)	CRUELTY	U.S.
HEERE, Rudi	259603	M	Ger.		SS-Schfhr., Aussendienststelle SD.of Tarbes, Htes.-Pyre Nees (Fr.) 11.1942-8.1944	MISC. CRIMES	FR.
HEERE, Rudolf	255113	M	Ger.		Uschfhr., SS Gestapo, Toulouse (Fr.) 11.42-8.44	MISC. CRIMES	FR.
HEERKLOSS	173641	M	Ger.		Stalag VI A Hemer, (Ger.)41-45	TORTURE	U.S.
HEERMANN, Kaethe	193176	F	Ger.		Helferin, German Navy Girl, Wilhelmshaven (Ger.)10.44	WITNESS	CAN.
HEERSEN	137025	M	Ger.		Civ., Farmer, Stretum(Ger.) 1.45	WITNESS	U.S.
HEERWALD, Willy	24682	M	Ger.		Dr., Ministerial Director, SS Brigadefhr., W-SS Chancery	MISC. CRIMES	U.S.
HEESCH	196934	M	Ger.		Sgt., Gestapo Lyon, Plateau des Glieres (Fr.)3.-4.44	MISC. CRIMES	FR.
HEESE, Karl	255522	M		26.10.11	Pvt., C.C.Ellrich-Nordhausen (Ger.)	MURDER	U.S.
HEETTIG, Max	258138	M	Ger.		Cpt., W-SS Commander of C.C. Natzweiler, Alsace (Fr.)	SUSPECT	BEL.
HEFFEL	167367	M	Ger.		Pvt., Army Stalag XII A Limbourg (Ger.)	TORTURE	FR.
HEFFELS, Gerhard	361	M	Ger.		Civ., Anna-Mine, Labour Camp Alsdorf (Ger.)42-44	TORTURE	U.S.
HEFFNER	173640	M	Ger.	00	SS-Uschfhr., Guard in the C.C. Buchenwald (Ger.)40-45	MURDER	POL.
HEFFNER, Therese	151646	F	Ger.		Employee, Gestapo Sekretaer, Bretagne,Anjon,Poiteu (Angers (Fr.) 42-44	MURDER	FR.
HEFNER	194780	M	Ger.		Sgt., 7.Rgt.Artillerie Reserve, Albertville (Fr.)44	MURDER	FR.
HEFNER	306304	M	Ger.		Oberwachtmeister, 79.D.A.M. Les Glieres Blanches, Albertville Savoie (Fr.) 6.44	MURDER	FR.
HEGEMANN	124844		Ger.	00	Pol.Lt., Chief of Police, Nentershausen (Ger.)9.44	MURDER	U.S.
HEGEMANN	186689	M	Ger.	10	Uschfhr., SS-Nachrichtenzug, Worinhoudt (Fr.)5.40	MURDER	U.K.
HEGEMANN	188284	M	Ger.		Officer, Arbeitsgemeinschaft fuer erbbedingte Leiden (Ger.)	MISC. CRIMES	CZECH.
HEGENBARTH, Johann	196396	M	Ger.	06	Cpt., SS security corps, Carpane (It.) 9.44	MURDER	U.K.
HEGER	138212	M			Member and SS Cpt., Gestapo, Lyon (Fr.)44	MURDER	FR.
HEGER	300959	M	Ger.		Interpreter, Gestapo Office, Zlin, Hrabuyka near Moravska Ostrau (Czech.)3.44	MURDER	CZECH.
HEGER, Benno	9700	M	Ger.		Dr., Staatsanwalt Public Official, Cheb (Csech.)40	MURDER	CZECH.
HEGEL	305058	M	Russ.		SS Rottfhr., 84.Landsturm-Netherlandes Rgt., Rhenen, Vreewijk (Neth.) 2.45	MURDER	NETH.
HEGER, Hans	127366	M			Civilian, Enkenbach (Ger.)12.43-3.45	TORTURE	U.S.
HEGEWALD	120614	M	Ger.		Sgt., Army 2.Coy.394 Dresden C.C. Kdo.1169, Gorbitz-Dresden (Ger.) 10.43-4.45	TORTURE	U.K.
HEGHOLZ, Anne-Marie	262259	F	Ger.		Secretary, Gestapo, Rennes (Fr.) 43-44	SUSPECT	FR.
HEGLER, Willi	262258	M	Ger.	26.11.--	SS-Uschfhr., Gestapo, Rennes (Fr.)43-44	MISC. CRIMES	FR.
HEHENBERGER, Heinrich	255526	M		20.10.00	Pvt., C.C. Ellrich-Nordhausen (Ger.)	MURDER	U.S.
HEHRFELD, Fritz	10088	M	Ger.		Pvt., Army, Albine (Fr.) 44	MURDER	FR.
HEHRMANNSTRAUT (see EHRMANNSTRAUT)	9650						
HEICHER, Herbert	192002	M	Ger.		Sgt., Army 10.Coy.,3.Bn.,7.Police Rgt., Junkerdal (Nor.)10.44	TORTURE	NOR.
HEICKE	260228	M			Waffenmeister, Gerardmer (Fr.)5.44	WITNESS	U.S.
HEICKEL, Adolf	255387	M			Pvt., C.C. Ellrich-Nordhausen (Ger.)	MURDER	U.S.
HEIDAMMER	36687	M	Ger.		SS-Man, C.C. Bergen-Belsen (Ger.)	TORTURE	CZECH.
HEIDBRECHER	120611	M	Ger.		Dr., Civ. C.C. Bremen-Farge (Ger.)43	MISC. CRIMES	U.S.

HEI-HEI

NAME	C.R.FILE NUMBER	SEX	NATIO-NALITY	DATE OF BIRTH	RANK OCCUPATION UNIT PLACE AND DATE OF CRIME	REASON WANTED	WANTED BY
HEIDE, Herbert	256766	M	Ger.		Unterscharfhr., SD,Pontivy (Fr.) 44	MISC.CRIMES	FR.
HEIDECKE	161954	M	Ger.		Civilian,Punschau (Ger.)	WITNESS	U.S.
HEIDECKE	306608	M	Ger.		N.C.O.,Feldgendarmerie,Chateaubriant,Loire,Inferieure,St.Julien de Mouvantes,Juigne les Moutiers,Soudan le Taillais (Fr.) 21.7.44	MURDER	FR.
HEIDEL	165149	M	Ger.		Doctor,SS-Obersturmfhr.,SS,C.C.Stutthof (Pol.) 3.40	MURDER	U.S.
HEIDELBERG	137766	M			Capt.,29 Pz.Gren.Div.	WITNESS	U.S.
HEIDEMANN	124595	M	Ger.		Rottenfhr.,SS,C.C.Belsen (Ger.) 40	MURDER	BEL.
HEIDEMANN	130381	M			Kapo.,C.C.Mauthausen (Aust.) 41-45	MURDER	U.S.
HEIDEMANN, Heinz	306011	M	Ger.		SS-Member,Staff at Bergen-Belsen (Ger.) 42-45	MURDER	U.K.
HEIDEMANN, Wolfgang	105929	M			Pvt.,Army,85 Fuesilier Bn.,Hassefelde (Ger.)	MURDER	U.S.
HEIDEN	196397	M			C.C.Dachau (Ger.) 40	MURDER	POL.
HEIDENHEIM, Will	132076	M	Ger.		Engineer,SS,SD, joined NSDAP, C.C.Lippstadt (Ger.) 44-45	TORTURE	U.S.
HEIDER	362	M			Sgt.,Warder of Prison,C.C.Caen (Fr.) 6.44	MURDER	FR.
HEIDER	130380	M			Hauptscharfhr. SS-Div.Totenkopf,C.C.Mauthausen (Aust.) 41-45	MURDER	U.S.
HEIDER	173173	M			Untersturmfhr.,SS,C.C.Natzweiler (Fr.) 43-44	MURDER	U.K.
HEIDER	261961	M			Interpreter,various places in Slovenia (Yugo.) 41-45	MISC.CRIMES	YUGO.
HEIDER, Hans	256088	M			Chief Police,C.C.Mauthausen (Aust.)	MURDER	FR.
HEIDER, Karl	24937	M			SS-Lt.,SS,C.C.Struthof (Fr.)	MISC.CRIMES	FR.
HEIDER, Karl	173174	M	Ger.		M 1 Lager,C.C.Muehldorf-Ampfing (Ger.) 6.44-4.45	MURDER	U.S.
HEIDER, Willy	127368	M	Ger.	95	Oberscharfhr.,Waffen-SS,Totenkopfsturmbann,Gelsenkirchen-Horst (Ger.)	TORTURE	U.S.
HEIDER, Willy	132319	M	Ger.		SS-C.C.Erfurt (Ger.) 44	TORTURE	U.S.
HEIDEREICH	156728	M	Ger.		Campleader,C.C.Oranienburg,Sachsenhausen (Ger.)	MURDER	U.K.
HEIDERMANN	36688	M	Ger.		SS-Pvt.,Camp Staff Belsen (Ger.)	MURDER	CZECH.
HEIDKAEMPER, Otto	260610	M	Ger.	01	Major-General,Army,	WITNESS	U.S.
HEIDKAMP	24982	M	Ger.		SS-Lt.,Gestapo,Quirnbach,Helferskirchen (Ger.) 16.-17.3.45	MURDER	U.S.
HEIDKAMP, Kurt Nick-Name: SCARFACE	29860	M	Ger.	00	Mine Overseer, Capt.,Stalag VIII B,Bemsburg E 727 (Ger.) 42-7.44	MURDER	U.K.
HEIDKAMP	254630	M			Capt.,Torgau (Ger.) 43-45	MURDER	U.S.
HEIDL	255576	M			Doctor,C.C.Buchenwald (Ger.)	MURDER	U.S.
HEIDL, Anton	187383	M	Ger.		Treasurer,NSDAP,Landek (Czech.) 39-45	MISC.CRIMES	CZECH.
HEIDL, Otto	161952	M	Ger.	09	Obersturmfhr.,SS,C.C.Stutthof (Pol.) Buchenwald (Ger.)	WITNESS	U.S.
HEIDMANN, Helmut	192209	M	Ger.		Adjutant-Chief,Feldgendarmerie,Kassel,Hazebrouck (Fr.) 30.8.44	MURDER	FR.
HEIDRECHER	305551	M	Ger.	97	Doctor,Medical Officer,C.C.Farge-Bremen (Ger.) 1.43-4.45	MURDER	U.K.
HEIDRICH	12394	M			Major,SS Deputy Commander,C.C.Oranienburg (Ger.) 39-44	TORTURE	CZECH.
HEIDRICH	67852	M			Lt.,Army 714,Landesschuetzen Bn.,2 Coy.,C.C.Halberstadt (Ger.)8.4.45	TORTURE	U.K.
HEIDRICH (S)	137608	M		90	Foreman,Iron Mines,Stalag II B,C.C.Ohlendorf (Ger.) 12.43-3.44	MURDER	U.K.
HEIDRICH	139786	M		95	Plant-Manager,Arb.Kol.Georgenschacht,Waffen-SS,	MURDER	U.S.
HEIDRICH	195369	M	Ger.		Commandant,C.C.Sachsenhausen (Ger.)	MURDER	BEL.
HEIDRICH, Fritz	146865	M	Ger.		Rottenfhr.,Pz.Div."Das Reich",Tonneins (Fr.) 44	MURDER	FR.
HEIDRICH, Paul	189026	M	Ger.	97 - 98	Lt.-General,Airforce Paratroops, near Cassino (It.) 44	MURDER	U.K.
HEIDTMANN	142977	F	Ger.		Civilian,Homburg (Ger.) 10.44-3.45	TORTURE	U.S.
HEIDTMANN, Carl	142978	M	Ger.		Civilian,Homburg (Ger.) 26.10.44-2.3.45	MISC.CRIMES	U.S.
HEIER	189713	M	Ger.	90	Capt.,Army,Essen-West (Ger.) 13.12.44	MURDER	U.K.
HEIER	250837	M	Ger.		Guard (Bel.)	BRUTALITY	BEL.
HEIER, Eric	141836	M	Ger.	87	Capt.,Landesschuetzen Bn. 471,Essen (Ger.) 13.12.44	MURDER	U.K.
HEIGEL	161951	M	Ger.	90	Hauptscharfhr.,SS-Section I,Guard-House,C.C.Buchenwald (Ger.) 41-42	WITNESS	U.S.
HEIGL	189353	M	Ger.		Gendarm,Feldgendarmerie,Bar-le-Duc (Fr.) 20-23.8.44	MURDER	FR.
HEIJERMANN, Eberhard	254512	M	Ger.	20	Lt.,18 Pz.Div.Heeresflakart. Abt. 176, Posterholt-Effeld (Neth.) 10.-11.44	INTERR.	NETH.
HEIKE	258169	M	Ger.		Ortskommandant,Ortskommandantur Pozarecac (Yugo.) 12.9.41	INTERR.	YUGO.
HEIL (or HYLE)	135544	M	Ger.		Capt.,Abwehr Officer,Oflag IX,A-H and IX A-L,C.C.Spangenburg (Ger.) 42	TORTURE	U.K.
HEIL, Karl	256767	M	Ger.		SS-Cpl.,C.C.Harzungen, Nordhausen (Ger.)	MURDER	U.S.
HEIL, Rolf	301199	M	Ger.		Leader,Hitler-Jugend,Huchenfeld,Dillweissenstein (Ger.) 18.3.45	MURDER	U.K.
HEILAND, Helmut	161953	M	Ger.		Capt.,Army,Gren.Rgt.,984,Aulnois (Bel.) 3.9.44	MURDER	BEL.
HEILBAVER, Julius	194596	M	Ger.		Judge responsible,Justizministerium,Belle-Isle (Fr.)	MISC.CRIMES	FR.
HEILIGENSTAEDT, Barbara	167200	F	Ger.		Civilian,Einsatzstab Rosenberg,(Fr.) 40-44	PILLAGE	FR.
HEILIGER	188700	M	Ger.	95	Kreisleiter,Landrat,Gemeindetag NSDAP,Mayen (Ger.) 9.44	SUSPECT	U.S
HEILING	132021	M	Ger.		Hauptleiter,	TORTURE	U.S.
HEILING	133329	M	Ger.		Civilian,	TORTURE	U.S.
HEILINGER, Franz	193212	M	Ger.	24. 3.97	Hauptsturmfhr.,Camp-Leader,Waffen-SS,C.C.Flossenburg (Ger.) Civ.Servant,Hauptwachtmeister,Reichsjustizministerium,Strafgefangenenlager Nord,Finmark (Nor.) 42-45	MISC.CRIMES	NOR.,YUGO.
HEILLVOMS	174243	M	Ger.	20. 4.09	Inf.Rgt.,469,198 I.D.,Le Tholy (Fr.),13.2.44	PILLAGE	FR.
HEILMANN	363	M	Ger.	14	SS-Unterscharfhr.,C.C.Grini (Nor.) 42	TORTURE	NOR.
HEILMANN	256768	M	Ger.		Kriminalpolizei,Ingershein (Fr.) 9.1.44	MISC.CRIMES	FR.
HEILMANN, Erich	141934	M	Ger.		Civilian,Saege-Werke & Venser,Stockheim (Ger.) 1.43	TORTURE	U.K.
HEILMEIER, F.	142966	M	Ger.	20	Driver for Kreisleiter,NSDAP,Attenshein (Ger.) 13.6.44	MURDER	U.S.
HEIM	196399	M	Ger.		Lt.,C.C.Struthof-Natzweiler (Fr.) 40-44	TORTURE	FR.
HEIM, Albert	305174	M	Ger.		Major,Army, near Wollmatingen Krs.Konstanz (Ger.) 20.7.44	MURDER	U.S.
HEIM, Friedrich	165928	M	Ger.	24. 4.05	Civilian,Engineer,Ubach, (Ger.) 21.7.44	PILLAGE	U.S.
HEIM, Karl	140840	M	Ger.	1.10.15	Col.Standartenfhr.,SS,State-Official (Yugo.)	MURDER	U.S.
HEIMAN	151647	M	Ger.		Lt.,Army,La Cannette (Fr.) 15.6.44	MURDER	FR.
HEIMAN, Karl	253967	M	Ger.		SS-Obersturmfhr.,SS,C.C.Auschwitz-Birkenau (Pol.)1.43	MISC.CRIMES	YUGO.
HEIMANN	62258	M	Ger.		Administr.Officer,Stalag VI B or VI G,(Ger.) 44-45	TORTURE	U.S.
HEIMANN	186798	M	Ger.		SS-Obersturmfhr.,C.C.Ravensbrueck (Ger.) 42-45	MURDER	U.S.
HEIMANN	194595	M	Ger.		Pvt.,Feldgendarmerie,Ploermel (Fr.) 18.6.44	TORTURE	FR.
HEIMANN	256769	M	Ger.		Elektro.Kraftfahrer,C.C.Nordhausen (Ger.)	MURDER	U.S.
HEIMANN	259546	M			Doctor,Physician,Auerbach (Ger.)	INTERR.	U.S.
HEIMANN, Heinz	190557	M	Ger.		N.C.O.,C.C.Banjica (Yugo.)	MURDER	YUGO.
HEIMANN, Paul	134705	M	Ger.		Hauptsturmfhr.,SS,Nantes (Fr.) 42	MISC.CRIMES	U.S.
HEIMANN, Willi	189678	M	Ger.	02	Chief of Gendarmerie,Hochfelden (Ger.)	MURDER	FR.
HEIMANN, William	189636	M	Ger.		Lt.,Army-Unit 30976,Beziers la Cannette,Ferrals-les-Montagnes (Fr.) 7.6.-15.6.44	MURDER	FR.
HEIMANNSBERG	190336	M	Ger.		President,Police,Wiesbaden (Ger.) 43-45	TORTURE	U.S.
HEIMBERGER	196398	M	Ger.		C.C.Struthof-Natzweiler (Fr.) 40-44	TORTURE	FR.

HEI-HEI

NAME	C.R.FILE NUMBER	SEX	NATIO-NALITY	DATE OF BIRTH	RANK OCCUPATION UNIT PLACE AND DATE OF CRIME	REASON WANTED	WANTED BY
HEIMBRECHT	260232	M	Ger.		Sgt., 217.Gren.Bn.d.Res. (a Gap), Massif du Vercors (Fr.) 20.7.-5.8.44	SUSPECT	FR.
HEIMBUCH, Franz	177232	M	Ger.		SS Uscharfhr., Mittelbourg (Ger.)	MURDER	U.S.
HEIMBURGER	175451	M	Ger.	08	Official, Pvt., 4.Ersatz Bn.600, Abwehr-Cmdo.120, Salzwedel (Ger.)	MURDER	U.N.W.C.C.
HEIMDUK, Hem.	130385	M	Ger.		Farmer, Westenbrocken-Westf. (Ger.) 42	TORTURE	BEL.
HEIMEL	158618	M	Ger.	05	Scharfhr., Enschede (Neth.)	MURDER	U.K.
HEIMELER	158618	M	Ger.	05	Scharfhr., SS, Entschede (Neth.)	MURDER	U.K.
HEIMEN	364	M	Ger.		Pvt., Army, Baudrigues (Fr.) 19.8.44	MURDER	FR.
HEIMERL, Karl	255111	M	Ger.	11. 2.06	Member, Gestapo, Zlin (Czech.) 39-45	TORTURE	CZECH.
HEIMERSEN	301745	M	Ger.		OSF, Doctor, C.C. Auschwitz (Pol.) 40-45	MURDER	FR.
HEIMES, Wilhelm	24983				Interpreter, Pvt., Volksgren.Rgt. 316 2.Coy. Dulag 377,Gerolstein (Ger.) 1.45	TORTURE	U.S.
HEIMESATH	194594	M	Ger.		Usturmfhr., chief, SS, Gestapo, Loubens Foix (Fr.)	MURDER	FR.
HEIMPEL	119758	M	Ger.		Major, Cmdt. Stalag 3 D C.C. Berlin (Ger.)	MISC.CRIMES	U.K.
HEIMREICH	188698	M	Ger.		Capt., SS Police-Rgt. 19, St.Joire, Chatillon s.Cluse, Taninges Bolme (Fr.) 11.6.-20.7.44	TORTURE	FR.
HEIMS see HEINEN	158617						
HEIMS, Fritz	172749	M	Ger.	96	Agent, Member NSDAP, S.D., Oldenburg (Ger.)	MURDER	U.N.W.C.C.
HEIMS, Otto	142982	M	Ger.		Labor-supervisor, C.C. Linden (Ger.) 42-45	MURDER	U.S.
HEIN	142449	M	Ger.		Sturmscharfhr., SS, C.C. Lublin (Pol.)	MURDER	FR.
HEIN	256634	M	Ger.		Feldgend., Feldgend.Trupp 307, Pontivy (Fr.) 44	TORTURE	FR.
HEIN, Adolf see HEYN	250828						
HEIN, Ernst	253704	M	Ger.		Lt., Fieldpolice, Trupp 634, Aube (Fr.) 44	INTERR.	FR.
HEIN, Gustav	186799	M			Rottfhr., Guard, 4.SS Totenkopf-Stuba C.C. Nordhausen (Ger.) 43-45	WITNESS	U.S.
HEIN, Hermann	187669	M		92	SS Blockfhr., C.C. Oranienburg (Ger.)	MURDER	U.K.
HEIN, Mathias	193211	M	Ger.	04	Hauptwachtmeister, Reichsjustizministerium, Feldstraflager, C.C. Finmark (Nor.) 9.3.45	MISC.CRIMES	NOR.
HEINCKEL	301744	M	Ger.		C.C. Auschwitz (Pol.) 40	MURDER	FR.
HEINDE	255518	M	Ger.		Capt., Unit 48805 C, Lefaux (Fr.) 23.6.44	MURDER	FR.
HEINDEL	194390	M	Ger.		Pvt., Army, Stalag Akervika (Nor.) 42	MURDER	NOR.
HEINDL	253708	M	Ger.		SS Oscharfhr., Terezin (Czech.) 43-44	MURDER	CZECH.
HEINDL, F.	132485	M	Ger.		Farm labourer, Member NSDAP, Pietmannsdorf (Aust.)	TORTURE	U.K.
HEINDL, Hermann	10089	M	Ger.		Pvt., Panz.Gren.Rgt. III NCO, Albine (Fr.) 44	MURDER	FR.
HEINDRICH	151649	M	Ger.		N.C.O., Feldgendarmerie, Trignac (Fr.) 11.8.45	MURDER	FR.
HEINDRICH	195368	M	Ger.		Capt. (Hptsturmfhr.) SS, C.C. Sachsenhausen (Ger.)	MURDER	BEL.
HEINDRICK	174246	M		19	SS Scharfhr., S.D., Gestapo, Locmine (Fr.)	TORTURE	FR.
HEINDT, Rudey or Rudolph	177231	M	Ger.		SS Scharfhr., C.C. Theresienstadt (Czech.) 44-45	MURDER	U.S.
HEINE	68637	M			Director, Manager of the mine, Jawischwitz (Pol.)	MURDER	U.S.
HEINE	130378	M			Scharfhr., SS Div.Totenkopf C.C. Mauthausen (Aust.) 41-45	MURDER	BEL. U.S.
HEINE	253687	M	Ger.		Medical-assist.,SS, C.C. Auschwitz-Birkenau (Pol.) 42-45	MURDER	YUGO.
HEINE	254066	M	Ger.		Cpl., Brauderion, Leudaul (Fr.) 30.4.44	TORTURE	FR.
HEINE, Frank	251048	M	Ger.		Member S.D., Meppel (Neth.) 18.12.44	TORTURE	NETH.
HEINE, Franz	190537	M	Ger.		SS Usturmfhr. Gestapo, Douai (Fr.) 6.3.44	MURDER	FR.
HEINE, Franz	254545	M	Ger.		Lt., Unit F.P. 15177 A, Chabons (Fr.) 1.8.44	INTERR.	FR.
HEINE, Hans	174205	M		15. 1.00	Amtsgerichtsrat, occupied territories Boheme, Prague (Czech.) 42-45	MURDER	CZECH.
HEINE, Werner	253964	M	Ger.	23.10.09	Pvt., 13.Coy. 558 Gren.Rgt., Bruay en Artois (Fr.) 1.9.44	MISC.CRIMES	FR.
HEINECKE	142955	M	Ger.		Scharfhr., SS Totenkopf Standarte.Waffen SS, C.C. Berga (Ger.)	MURDER	U.S.
HEINECKE	222537	M	Ger.	11	Hptsturmfhr., S.D. official, Aussenstelle, C.C. Bordeaux, Zweibruecken, Sarrebourg (Fr.)	MISC.CRIMES	U.S.
HEINEKE	365		Ger.		Civ. in C.C. (Landowner), Wybranow (Pol.) 22.10.39	TORTURE	POL.
HEINEKE	192955	M	Ger.		SS Hptscharfhr., C.C. Buchenwald (Ger.) 42-45	TORTURE	U.S.
HEINELT	366	M	Ger.		Major, Inf.Rgt. 221, Rollainville (Fr.) 9.9.44	MURDER	FR.
HEINELT, Paul	190195	M	Ger.		Guard, Gestapo, C.C. Brno (Czech.) 39-45	TORTURE	CZECH.
HEINEMANN	137767	M			Capt., 29. Panz.Gren.Rgt.	WITNESS	U.S.
HEINEMANN	139790	M	Ger.		Capt., Stalag X B, Sandbostel (Ger.) 1.5.45	MISC.CRIMES	U.S.
HEINEMANN	190341	F	Ger.		Civ., Wiesbaden (Ger.) 43-45	WITNESS	U.S.
HEINEMANN	194281	M	Ger.		SS Scharfhr., S.D. Cmdo., Gorsel, Arnheim (Neth.)	MURDER	NETH.
HEINEMANN	306157	M	Ger.		Usturmfhr., Aussenstelle Zutphen, Vorden (Neth.) 10.44	MURDER	U.K.
HEINEMANN	307129	M	Ger.		Attached to the staff at C.C. Ravensbrueck (Ger.) 39-45	MURDER	U.K.
HEINEMANN, Heinrich	145908	M			Civ., Borkum (Ger.) 4.8.44	MURDER	U.S.
HEINEMANN, Ludwig	186376	M	Ger.	10	Usturmfhr., S.D., Vorden (Neth.)	MURDER	U.K.
HEINEN	151648	M			Pvt., Landesschuetzen-Bn. 399, Pankendorf (Pol.)	MURDER	U.K.
HEINEN or HEIMS	158617	M		00	Pvt., 209.Coy. Landesschuetzen, Pankendorf nr.Marienwerder (Ger.) 9.44	MURDER	U.K.
HEINEN, Johann	194554	M	Ger.	1. 8.79	Civ. Farmer, Seinsfeld (Ger.)	PILLAGE	U.S.
HEINERT, Georg	161958	M	Ger.		SS Mann, SS-Rgt. "Der Fuehrer", Houyet-Dinant (Bel.) 4.9.44	PILLAGE	BEL.
HEINES	195210	M	Ger.		Org.Todt, Assen (Neth.) 12.44	MURDER	NETH.
HEINICKE	194593	M	Ger.		Pvt., Feldgendarmerie Ploermel (Fr.) 18.6.44	TORTURE	FR.
HEININGER, Franz	305059	M	Ger.		Civ., Niedernhausen (Ger.) 10.44	BRUTALITY	U.S.
HEINISCH	125474	M	Ger.		Cpl., Working-Cmdo. 1326, C.C. Dresden (Ger.) 45	MURDER	U.K.
HEINISCH, Albert	195967	M	Ger.	18.10.19	Clerk, SS Usturmfhr., Gestapo, Sumperk (Czech.) 39-45	MISC.CRIMES	CZECH.
HEINKE	173743	M	Ger.		SS Hptscharfhr., S.D., Metz (Fr.)	MURDER	U.N.W.C.C.
HEINKELMANN	197723	M	Ger.		SS Hptscharfhr., C.C. Buchenwald (Ger.)	TORTURE	U.S.
HEINKEL	255519	M	Ger.		Capt., Unit 14217 C, Cheisy au Bac (Fr.) 40	PILLAGE	FR.
HEINL, Hans	187012	M	Ger.	14. 3.05	Dr., chief, Gestapo, S.D., Prague (Czech.) 39-45	MURDER	CZECH.
HEINLEIN, Alfred	252165	M	Ger.	24.10.04	Rottfhr., SS, C.C. Harzungen-Nordhausen (Ger.)	MURDER	U.S.
HEINLEY	161171	M	Ger.		Managing-director, Kriegsgefangene-Arbeitskommando, stone quarry, Lauban-Goerlitz (Ger.)	TORTURE	U.K.
HEINMAN	367		Ger.		Police office, Grenoble (Fr.) 11.43	MURDER	FR.
HEINRICH	24959	M			Gutsverwalter, Guard, SS, C.C. Lublin-Hinzert (Pol.,Ger.) 42-43	TORTURE	U.S.
HEINRICH	121058	M	Ger.		SS Uscharfhr., C.C. Buchenwald (Ger.)	TORTURE	FR. U.S.
HEINRICH	131285	M			Administrator, C.C.officer, Krekau (Pol.) 43	MURDER	U.S.
HEINRICH	133408	M	Ger.		Major, Stalag Luft VI, C.C. Heydekrug (Ger.) 7.44	TORTURE	U.K.
HEINRICH	141439	M	Ger.	02	Kriegsgerichtsrat, Feldkommandantur 529, Bordeaux, Souges (Fr.)	MURDER	FR.

NAME	C.R.FILE NUMBER	SEX	NATIO-NALITY	DATE OF BIRTH	RANK OCCUPATION UNIT PLACE AND DATE OF CRIME	REASON WANTED	WANTED BY
HEINRICH	142453	M			Dr., Sturmbannfhr., Chief of P.W.Affairs	WITNESS	U.S.
HEINRICH	173605	M		04	Officer, SD, Poitiers (Fr.) 24.,25.8.44	MURDER	FR.
HEINRICH	187014	M			Oschfhr., SS-Fuehrungshpt.Amt, Conc.Camp Dora-Mittelbau,Nordhausen (Ger.) 43-45	WITNESS	U.S.
HEINRICH	194886	M	Ger.		Osturmfhr., SS, Conc.Camp, Lublin (Pol.) 40-43	MURDER	POL.
HEINRICH	196400	M	Ger.		Cpl., Waffen-SS, Sederon (Fr.) 22.2.44	MISC.CRIMES	FR.
HEINRICH	254553	M	Ger.		Staff-Sgt., Fieldpolice Bourjon 924, La Folatiere (Fr.) 11.6.44	MURDER	FR.
HEINRICH	254554	M	Ger.		Pvt., 3.Coy., 1.Bn. Div."Das Reich", "Der Fuehrer", Oradour sur Glane (Fr.) 10.6.44	INTERR.	FR.
HEINRICH (or NAPOLEON)	254644	M	Ger.		Sturmschfhr., C.C., Hinzert (Ger.)	BRUTALITY	FR.
HEINRICH (see NAPOLEON)	300474						
HEINRICH, Albert	127369	M			Civilian, Enkenbach (Ger.) 12.43-3.45	TORTURE	U.S.
HEINRICH, Alwin	252164	M		27. 6.14	Pvt., C.C. Harzungen, Nordhausen (Ger.)	MURDER	U.S.
HEINRICH, Emil	253965	M		9. 3.25	Pvt., 13.Coy., 558.Gren.Rgt., Bruay en Artois (Fr.) 1.9.44	MISC.CRIMES	FR.
HEINRICH, Erich or Henri	261355	M		10	Uschfhr., Waffen-SS, 0.2836 D, Libourne, Castillon, Dordogne (Fr.) 9.43-11.43	MURDER	FR.
HEINRICH, Gerhard (or HENDRICH)	133671	M	Ger.	13. 2.22	Uschfhr., Waffen-SS,Totenk.Standarte,C.C., Buchenwald (Ger.)	MURDER	U.S.
HEINRICH, Hans-Joachim	132037	M	Ger.	.14	Hptsturmfhr., SS, SD, Issel (Ger.) 20.1.45	MURDER	U.S.
HEINRICH, Herbert	262329	M	Ger.	28	Wanted as a perpetrator in the alleged beating and also for the Murder of one of the Airmen caused by the beating,Velke-Heraltice, Ger., 8.44 L.O.D.N.A.O.D.	SUSPECT	U.S.
HEINRICH, Hermann	186377	M	Ger.	94	Hauptwachtmeister, Gend., Civilian, Luxembourg (Lux.)	MISC.CRIMES	LUX.
HEINRICH, Kurt	306387	M	Ger.		SS-Scharf.,CC. Buchenwald (Ger.) 1.58-10.43	MURDER	BEL.
HEINRICH, Kurt Erich	261044	M	Ger.	10	Sgt., Div."Brandenburg", Unit Special, 8.Coy., Var, Vaucluse, Prov. Bouche du Rhone (Fr.) 43-44	MISC.CRIMES	FR.
HEINRICH, Ludwig	196402	M	Ger.	06	Bakermaster, Intendancy 814, Bonnleres (Fr.)	PILLAGE	FR.
HEINRICH, Paul	193210	M	Ger.	00	Hptwachtmstr., Reichsjustizministerium, Feldstraflager, Strafgef. Lager Nord, Finmark (Nor.) 4.45	MISC.CRIMES	NOR.
HEINRICH, Richard	173639	M			Servant, Org.Todt, Conc.Camp, Muehldorf (Ger.) 6.44-4.45	MURDER	U.S.
HEINRICH-SOHN	186644	M	Ger.		Schfhr., SS, Conc.Camp, Drancy (Fr.)	MURDER	FR.
HEINRICHS	306972	M	Ger.		Lt., 1.Coy., 64.Police-Bn., Sabac, Serbia (Yugo.) 7.41-9.41	MURDER	YUGO.
HEINRICHS, Fritz	196085	M	Ger.		Oschfhr., Gestapo H.Q., Fredriketad (Nor.)	TORTURE	NOR.
HEINRICHS, Fritz	258773	M	Ger.		Erkrath (Ger.) 4.11.44	WITNESS	U.S.
HEINS	138294	M	Ger.		Member, NSDAP, Cdo. 715 F., Mine Elisabethenglueck,Dorchholz (Ger.)	TORTURE	FR.
HEINS	254787	M	Ger.		Lt., 377.Jaeger-Rgt., 10.Coy., Vinkt and Meigem (Bel.) 5.40	MISC.CRIMES	BEL.
HEINS, Conrad	188699	M	Ger.		Cpl., Army, Kerviherne Merleuevez (Fr.) 28.4.45	MURDER	FR.
HEINSLADEN, J.	10090	M	Ger.		Pvt., Panz.Gren.Rgt. III N.C.O., Albins (Fr.) 29.6.44	MURDER	FR.
HEINSLER, Ernest (see MAX)	192001						
HEINSOHN (see HEINSON)	146864						
HEINSON	226100	M	Ger.		Official, SD, Blois (Fr.) 44	TORTURE	FR.
HEINSON, Ludwig Heinrich Alexander (or HEINSOHN)	146864	M	Ger.	00	Capt., Gestapo, Chambery (Fr.) 44	MURDER	FR.
HEINSOTH, Franz	255402	M			Dr., Physician-Doctor, C.C.Dora, Nordhausen (Ger.)	MURDER	U.S.
HEINTEL	253966	M	Ger.		Civilian-admin.(G.z.A.) SD, Gestapo, Toulouse (Fr.) 11.42-10.44	MISC.CRIMES	FR.
HEINTGES, Anton	132520	M	Ger.		Civilian, Conc.Camp, Duisburg (Ger.)	TORTURE	U.S.
HEINTZ,	167185	M	Ger.		Commiss.Verwalter, Firm Spolem, Lodz (Pol.) 9.39-44	PILLAGE	POL.
HEINTZ, Adolph	173557	M	Ger.		Pvt., 487.Inf.Rgt., Oignies and Courrieres (Fr.) 28.5.40	MURDER	FR.
HEINTZ, Max	259225	M	Ger.		Hptsturmfhr., SS, Cdo.of Poitiers Area (Fr.) 41-44	MISC.CRIMES	FR.
HEINTZIEGER, Josef (or JOEP)	187016	M	Ger.		Member, Geh.Feldpolizei, Courtrai (Bel.)	TORTURE	BEL.
HEINTZMANN	161170	M			Sgt., Army, Sturmbn.A.O.K.1, 1.Coy., Courcelles sur Nied (Fr.)15.11.44	MURDER	U.S.
HEINZ	154362	M			Dr., Dienststellenleiter, SD, Caen (Fr.) 6.6.44	MURDER	U.S.
HEINZ	158617	M	Ger.	00	Pvt.,,Lds.Schtz.Bn., 209.Coy., Pankendorf (Ger.) 11.9.44	MURDER	U.K.
HEINZ	195769	M	Ger.		Capt., Gend., Conc.Camp, Sigmaringen (Ger.)	MURDER	FR.
HEINZ	251037	M	Ger.		Cpl., Navy, Beernem (Bel.) 5.,6.9.44	MURDER	BEL.
HEINZ	254597	M	Ger.		SS-Mann, C.C., Buchenwald (Ger.)	INTERR.	FR.
HEINZ	300475	M	Ger.		Lt., Braudrion and Laudraul (Morbihan) (Fr.) 30.4.44	MURDER	FR.
HEINZ	305419	M	Ger.		SS-Mann, C.C., Buchenwald (Ger.) 42-45	MURDER	FR.
HEINZ, F.W.	129777	M	Ger.	00	Mil.(C.I.C.) Officer, Altengrabow, Stalag 11 A (Ger.)	MISC.CRIMES	U.S.
HEINZ, Jacob	252163		Ger. or Hung.	6. 8.98	Schuetze, C.C., Nordhausen (Ger.)	MURDER	U.S.
HEINZ, Jann	300572	M	Ger.		N.C.O., 10.Coy., 377.Inf.Rgt., Vinkt-Meigem (Bel.) 5.40	MISC.CRIMES	BEL.
HEINZ, Paula	132819	F	Ger.		Public-Official, Civilian, Troppau (Czech.) 10.44	WITNESS	U.K.
HEINZ, Renate	134706	F			Civilian, Paris (Fr.) 42	WITNESS	U.S.
HEINZ, Siegle	254524	M	Ger.		Blacy (Fr.) 28.8.44	MURDER	FR.
HEINZ, Walter	253856	M	Ger.		Pvt., 11.Panz.Div., Lautrec (Fr.) 5.8.44	MURDER	FR.
HEINZ, Wilhelm	142963	M	Ger.	1. 4.14	Sgt., Lds.Schtz.E.Bn.24, Augsburg (Ger.) 44-4.45	MURDER	U.S.
HEINZE	29859	M	Ger.		N.C.O., Stalag, Marburg, Heydekrug, Swinemuende (Ger.) 42 and 44	MURDER	U.K.
HEINZE, Kurt	194553	M	Ger.		Civilian, Lidice (Czech.) 42-44	INTERR.	CZECH.
HEINZE, U.	167201	F	Ger.		Member,Einsatzstab Rosenberg,Admin.Staff (Fr.) 40-44	PILLAGE	FR.
HEINZEL	306609	M	Ger.		Senior W.O., Montferrier (Herault) 24.,25.8.44	MURDER	FR.
HEINZEL, Alfred	252426	M	Ger.	21. 4.03	C.C. Harzungen, Nordhausen)Ger.)	MURDER	U.S.
HEINZELER	167202	M			Interpreter, Reichs-Mil.Court, Faquet Morbihan (Fr.) 6.44-8.44	MURDER	FR.
HEINZELMANN, Kurt	192000	M	Ger.	04	Guard, Organ.Todt, Conc.Camp, Camiers (Fr.) 41-44	TORTURE	FR.
HEINZELMANN, Kurt	194591	M	Ger.		Conc.Camp, Condette (Fr.) 43	MURDER	FR.
HEINZER (or HENSEN or HINZEL)	130365	M	Ger.		Cpl., Army, Pion.Bn.717, St.Andries near Narsenaro Bruges (Bel.)4.9.44	MISC.CRIMES	BEL.
HEINZHAUSEN	306483	M	Ger.		Usturmfhr., SS, Staff Malines, C.C. 7.42-9.44	MURDER	BEL.
HEINZMANN, Fritz	189506	M	Ger.		Pvt., Army, Clever (Fr.) 8.8.44	MURDER	FR.
HEIPT, Max	161956	M			Sgt., Army, Montelimar (Fr.) 21.7.44	TORTURE	FR.
HEIR	194779	M	Ger.		Civilian, St.Rambert (Fr.) 2.44	MISC.CRIMES	FR.
HEIR, Wilhelm (or HERR)	123807	M	Ger.		Capt., Army, Lds.Schtz.Bn.877, Liezen (Aust.) 44-45	TORTURE	U.K.
HEIRING	121057	M			Etat Major, Commandait un etat Major de L'infanterie a la ferme Glassow, Sidi-Bou-Hadi D (Tunisie) 5.43	MURDER	FR.
HEIRMAN	369	M	Ger.		Osturmfhr., SS, C.C., Boten (Nor.) 3.42-43	MURDER	YUGO.
HEIRUNG, Adolf	187017	M			Sturmmann, 4.SS-Totenkopf-Stuba., C.C.Mittelbau Dora, Nordhausen (Ger.) 43-45	WITNESS	U.S.

HEI-HEL

NAME	C.R.FILE NUMBER	SEX	NATIO-NALITY	DATE OF BIRTH	RANK OCCUPATION UNIT PLACE AND DATE OF CRIME	REASON WANTED	WANTED BY
HEISE	10091		Ger.		Oberschuetze,Panz.Gren.Regt.111,Gomdon,29.6.44	MURDER	FR.
HEISER	187018	M	Ger.		Pvt.4 SS Totenkopfsturmbann,CC Dora-Nordhausen(Ger.)43-45	WITNESS	U.S.
HEISER	301688	M	Ger.		Bde.Chief,05/249 Mongolian"Oberland",St.Nazaire en Royans(Fr.) 20.7.-5.8.44	MURDER	FR.
HEISIFE, Hermann	188348	M	Ger.	00	Leader,S.A.,Volkssturm,Harzburg(Ger.)13.-17.1.45	MURDER	U.S.
HEISON	194349	M	Ger.		Capt.Gestapo of Chambery,Feissons s/Isere(Fr.)17.2.44	INCENDIARISM	FR.
HEISS, Friedrich	195770	M	Ger.		SS Standartenfhr.Editor,SS daily"Volk und Reich",Prague(Czech.)39-45	MISC.CRIMES	CZECH.
HEISS, Walter	300476	M	Ger.		Pvt.Attached to 01512K Navy Inf.partly composed of Waffen SS, Trebeurden,Plemeur-Bodou,Perros-Guirec(Fr.)6.-7.44	MURDER	FR.
HEISSE, Helmuth	197816	M	Ger.	18	Lt.C.O.Am.Depot,Drasice near Jicin(Czech.)39-45	MURDER	CZECH.
HEISSE, Karl	134856	M	Ger.		Civilian,Oberroblingen(Ger.)	TORTURE	U.S.
HEISSING	196372	M	Ger.		Capt.Schutzpolizei,near Arnheim(Neth.)3-45	MURDER	NETH.
HEISSMANN	260177	M	Ger.		Sgt.Group of Mountains Artillery d.Reserve No.79,Massif du Vercors (Fr.)20.7.-5.8.44	SUSPECT	FR.
HEISSMAYER	136264	M	Ger.		Professeur,Civilian,CC Neuengamme(Ger.)	MURDER	FR.
HEISSMEYER	121056	M	Ger.		Civilian,Neuengamme(Ger.)	TORTURE	BEL.
HEISSMEYER	137643	M	Ger.	05	DoctorC.C.Neuengamme(Ger.)	MURDER	U.K.
HEISSMEYER, Aug.	21358	M	Ger.	11.1.97	Obergruppenfhr.Official SS Polizeifhr.Berlin(Ger.)3.45	MISC.CRIMES	UNWCC
HEISSNER	151651	M			Hptsturmfhr.Gestapo SS,Besancon(Fr.)40-45	MURDER	FR.
HEISTER, Arnold	126329	M			Civilian,Bedburdyck(Ger.)	TORTURE	U.S.
HEISTERKAMP	161957	M			Ob.Sturmfhr.SS,Lorient(Fr.)44	MURDER	FR.
HEITKAMP	197724	M	Ger.	08	N.C.O.SS Gestapo,Koblenz,Neuenshr(Ger.)	MURDER	POL.
HEITKAMP, Hans	105930	M	Ger.		Sgt.SS Gestapo,Quirnbach(Ger.)20.3.45	MURDER	U.S.
HEITKAMP, Willi	127986	M	Ger.		NSDAP, Duisburg(Ger.)44	TORTURE	U.K.
HEITKE	196373	M	Ger.		Adjudant-Chef,Waffen SS,Sederon(Fr.)22.2.44	INTERR.	FR.
HEITLMEYER, Grosse	192788	M	Ger.		Interpreter,Schupo,CC Falstad(Nor.)41-45	MURDER	NOR.
HEITMANN, Heinrich	261472	M	Ger.		SS Rottfhr.Member S.D.,Ax-les-Thermes(Fr.)11.42-8.44	MURDER	FR.
HEITZ see HAIETZ	167379						
HEITZ, Rudolf(Rudolph)	166603	M	Ger.		Policeman,Army District Commandantur of St.Die,Gerardmer(Fr.)27.5.44	MURDER	U.S.
HEITZINGER	305866	M	Ger.		Pvt.1 Aufkl.Abt.3 Coy.2 Col.XV Div.Afrika Korps,St.-Leger(Arlon) 5.9.44	MISC.CRIMES	BEL.
HEITZMAN, Eric or Erwin	188707	M	Ger.		Sgt.Army,Courcelles(Fr.)15.11.44	WITNESS	U.S.
HEITZMANN	305867	M	Ger.		Pvt.1 Aufkl.Abt.2 Col.3 Coy.XV Div.Afrika Korps,St.-Leger(Arlon) 5.9.44	MISC.CRIMES	BEL.
HEIZE, Gertrude	306014	F	Ger.		Member,SS Staff at Bergen-Belsen CC(Ger.)42-45	MURDER	U.K.
HEKKERT	302020	M	Ger.		Secretary to Lager Cmdt.Klann,Arbeits Zuchtlager Merl-Huels,10.44	TORTURE	NETH.
HELBIG	127370	M	Ger.		Sgt.CC Buch(Ger.)5.44	MURDER	U.S.
HELBIG	133687	M			SS Scharfhr.CC Buchenwald)Ger.)	MURDER	U.S.
HELBIG	142932	M	Ger.	05	Lt.6 Coy.379 Land.Schtz.Bn.near Cruz(Czech.)8.5.45	MURDER	U.S.
HELBIG	252154	M			Oschafhr.SS CC Dora-Nordhausen(Ger.)	MURDER	U.S.
HELBIG	252155	M			Pvt.CC Ellrich-Nordhausen(Ger.)	MURDER	U.S.
HELBIG	257696	M	Ger.		Capt.F.P.No.18147E,Henrichemont(Fr.)9.40-3.41	PILLAGE	FR.
HELBIG	305420	M	Ger.		Stubafhr.SS CC Buchenwald Crematorium(Ger.)42-45	MURDER	FR.
HELBIG, Hermann	139788	M	Ger.	00	Cpl.Waffen SS,Arbeitskdo.A-6,Buchenwald(Ger.)	MURDER	U.S.
HELBIG, Werner	301128	M			Chief Adjutant,1 Bn.Royan,Semoussac,Charente,Inferieure(Fr.)28.9.44	MURDER	FR.
HELBLING	130377	M			Dr.,Officer,CC Mauthausen(Aust.)41	MURDER	U.S.
HELBRIG	257697	M	Ger.		SS Scharfhr.CC Nordhausen(Ger.)	MURDER	U.S.
HELBRIGEL	254525	M	Ger.		Lt.Col.Place Commander of Bourg,Tasseron(Fr.)24.6.44	INTERR.	FR.
HELD	370	M	Ger.		Ob.Lt.Lager,CC Tripoli,20.6.41	TORTURE	U.K.
HELD	124262	M			Uschafhr.1 SS Panzer Div.1 SS Panzer Regt.9 Coy.Engineers,Malmedy (Bel.)17.12.44	MURDER	U.S.
HELD	252158	M			Cpl.CC Harzungen-Nordhausen(Ger.)	MURDER	U.S.
HELD, Emil	132035	M	Ger.		Gestapo,Arbeits Erziehungslager Rudesberg(Ger.)	TORTURE	U.S.
HELD, Emil	251624	M	Ger.	12	Hptscharfhr.SS P.W.Camp,Oberndorf(Ger.)	MURDER	FR.
HELD, Erich	186239	M	Ger.		CC Blockaeltester,CC Gross Rosen(Ger.)40-43	TORTURE	U.S.
HELD, Erich	193209	M	Ger.	10	Official,Bauleiter,Org.Todt,Treudenes(Nor.)42-43	MISC.CRIMES	NOR.
HELD, Hans	62260	M	Ger.		Cell-Leader,NSDAP,37-45 in Fa.I.G.Farben,Dermagen,Zons(Ger.)	MURDER	U.S.
HELDMAKER	142503				Stalag,Pvt.	LOOTING	U.S.
HELDMANN, Constantin	57795	M	Ger.		Waffen-Grenadier Bde.SS 1st Officer	MISC.CRIMES	U.K.
HELDT	190558	M			Lt.264 Div.892 Gren.Regt.Island,Croatia(Yugo.)5.10.43-12.43	MURDER	YUGO.
HELDTKE see HAELCHE Dr.	258711						
HELENBROICK	105931	M			Gestapo,Bensheim(Ger.)2.45	MURDER	U.S.
HELENE	120594	F		20	P.P.F.Member Brest(Fr.)	MURDER	FR.
HELFER	136265	M			Lt.Legion Turkestan,Kampfgruppe Schuepplein,Rimont(Fr.)21.8.44	MURDER	FR.
HELFER	167366	M	Ger.		Capt.15 Afrika Korps Div.Vancourt,Xousse(Fr.)9.-10.44	LOOTING	FR.
HELFER	259179	M	Ger.		SS Untersturmfhr.German Army 1 Bn.14 Mountain Jg.Regt.Kosovska Mitrovica(Yugo.)12.42	MISC.CRIMES	YUGO.
HELFMANN see PFITSCH	185018						
HELHUND	31538	M	Ger.		Capt.Army,Etat Major,Lochmine(Fr.)7.44-3.8.44	MURDER	FR.
HELKES	167196	M	Ger.		Cpl.CC Asst.to Chief Warder of Prison,St.Lo(Fr.)6.-7.6.44	MURDER	FR.
HELL, Claus	196353	M	Ger.		Adjudant-Chef,250 Inf.Regt.Ardennes(Fr.)22.2.44	MISC.CRIMES	FR.
HELL, George	252159	M			Schuetze,CC Ellrich-Nordhausen(Ger.)	MURDER	U.S.
HELLA	253059	F			Woman-Guard,CC Auschwitz(Pol.)	MISC.CRIMES	FR.
HELLBRUECK, Otto	259826	M	Ger.	29.9.98	Master of Gend.Luxembourg(Lux.)	MISC.CRIMES	LUX.
HELLDORF	187019	M			Col.Army,Channel(Fin.)	TORTURE	U.K.
HELLE	119435	M	Ger.		Major,20 Army,Rovaniemi(Fin.)44	MURDER	NOR.
HELLE, Paul	256093	M	Ger.		SS Officer Commander,Commandt.of writing Chamber,Meerveld(Neth.)11.44	MURDER	NETH.
HELLEMANN	191999	M	Ger.		Lt.Gebirgs Jaeger Regt.85,Lus La Croixhaute(Fr.)10.7.44	MURDER	FR.
HELLEN	301322	M	Ger.		Member Gestapo at Trencin,CC Oswiecim-Birkenau(Pol.)39-45	MURDER	CZECH.
HELLENBROICH	162443	M	Ger.		Stubafhr.Official,SS Gestapo,Bensheim(Ger.)2.-3.45	MURDER	U.S.

NAME	C.R.FILE NUMBER	SEX	NATIO-NALITY	DATE OF BIRTH	RANK OCCUPATION UNIT PLACE AND DATE OF CRIME	REASON WANTED	WANTED BY
HELLENBROICH, Heinz	133359	M	Ger.	06	Major, Allg.-SS-Gestapo, Winterkasten-Reichelsheim (Ger.) 3.45	MURDER	U.S.
HELLENSCHMIDT	132714	M	Ger.		Capt., Oflag II D, Gross Born, Wietzendorf (Ger.) 45	MISC.CRIMES	FR.
HELLENTHAL	371	M	Ger.		SS-Rottenfhr., 2 SSPz.Div.3.Regt. SS Pz.Gren. (Fr.) 5.44	MURDER	FR.
HELLENTHAL	177510	M	Ger.		Sturmscharfhr., Secretaer, SD, Gestapo, Saarbruecken (Ger.)	MISC.CRIMES	FR.
HELLER	108597	M	Ger.		Obersturmfhr., SD Chief of Sonderkommando, Lyon, Region Lyonnaise (Fr.)	MISC.CRIMES	FR.
HELLER	130364		Ger.		Oberscharfhr., SS, C.C. Dachau (Ger.)	MURDER	BEL.
HELLER	154358	M	Ger.	15	Cpl., Army C.C. Tripoli (N.Afrika) 5.41-1.42	TORTURE	U.K.
HELLER	157752	M			Cpl., Adolf Hitler Div. SS 12.Regt. Stabs Coy., Maastricht to Arnheim (Neth.)	MURDER	NETH.
HELLER or KELLER	161169	M	Ger.		Sgt., W.-SS, Commander of Out-Camp, C.C. Schlossberg Dachau (Ger.)4.45	WITNESS	U.S.
HELLER	162654	M	Ger.		Hauptfeldw., Army, Seyssel (Fr.) 7.44	MURDER	FR.
HELLER	167365	M	Ger.		Sgt., Army, C.C. Sonnenberg near Kuestrin (Ger.)	TORTURE	FR.
HELLER	174204	M			SS Unterscharfhr., C.C. Muhldorf, Ampfing (Ger.)	MURDER	U.S.
HELLER	261964	M	Ger.		Administration-leader, SS, Abt.I and II Sipo, Belgrade, Valjevo (Yugo.) 8.42-9.44	SUSPECT	YUGO.
HELLER, Alfred	193919	M	Ger.		Member, Gestapo, Lanskroun (Czech.)	TORTURE	CZECH.
HELLER, Christian	260711	M			Block-leader, Capo, C.C. Hallein (Austr.)	MURDER	U.S.
HELLER, Franz	167222	M			Gruppenfhr., 9.Regt. Res. Gren. Magny d' Avignon (Fr.) 18.9.44	MURDER	FR.
HELLER, Walter	181562	M	Ger.	14.11.00	Chamberlain of the Town Prague, Public Official, Prague (Czech.)39-45	LOOTING	CZECH.
HELLIERDS	141315	M	Ger.		Major, Army, Kundorf (Pol.) 41	MISC.CRIMES	U.K.
HELLINGER	254645	M	Ger.		Capt., Unit 56300, Loc-Envol (Fr.) 8.44	INTERR.	FR.
HELLMAN	187559	M	Ger.	10	Pvt., 635 Landesschuetz.Bn. Muehlhausen (Ger.) 4.43	TORTURE	U.K.
HELLMAN, Erich	188364	M	Ger.		Civilian, Timber Mill Owner, Stockheim (Ger.) 43	TORTURE	FR.
HELLMANN	174203	M	Ger.		Civilian, Org.Todt, C.C. Muhldorf, Ampfing (Ger.) 6.44-4.45	MURDER	U.S.
HELLMANN	195893	M	Ger.		SS-Obersturmfhr., C.C. Hamburg, Neuengamme (Ger.) 40-44	MURDER	BEL.
HELLMANN, Alois	372	M	Ger.		SS-Untersturmfhr., C.C. Boten (Nor.) 3.42-43	MURDER	YUGO.
HELLMERICH see HELMRICH	140848						
HELLMOLD, Wilhelm	187020	M	Ger.		Police-Official, C.C. Bleckhammer, Lendringsen (Ger.) 45	MURDER	POL.
HELLMUTH, Otto	21357	M	Ger.	96	Dr., SA Gruppenfhr., Gauleiter,of Mainfranken NSDAP, Neustadt a-S. Schweinfurt 2.45	TORTURE	U.S.
HELLMUTH, Willi	240100	M	Ger.		Official, Gestapo, Tauber, Bischofsheim (Ger.) 44	MURDER	U.N.W.C.C.
HELLWIG	133357	M			Oberscharfhr., W.-SS, C.C. Flossenburg (Ger.)	TORTURE	U.S.
HELLWIG see HERMAN	149770						
HELLWIG	158623	M			Obersecretary, Gestapo, Innsbruck (Austr.)	MURDER	U.S.
HELLWIG or HELWIJ	161991		Ger.		Unterfhr., Stalag IX B, Bad Orb (Ger.) 44	MURDER	U.S.
HELLWIG, Hermann	162435	M		11	Pvt., 3 Kgfg. Arb.Bn. 180, Lista (Nor.) 4.17	MURDER	NOR.
HELM	166604	M	Ger.		General-Attorney, Ministry of Justice, (Ger.) 43	WITNESS	U.S.
HELM	173571	M	Ger.		Oberst-Standartenfhr., Gestapo SS, Belgrad (Yugo.) 10.41-43	MURDER	YUGO.
HELM	189637	M	Ger.		Inspector, Central Ersatzteillager 206, Paris (Fr.) 8.44	MURDER	FR.
HELM, Andreas	146691	M		10	Unterscharfhr., SS, C.C. Schleissheim near Munich (Ger.) 44	MURDER	U.S.
HELM, Richard	256331	M			Army, Kessel (Neth.) 11.44	MURDER	NETH.
HELMANN	125637	M	Ger.		Sous Officier, Army, NSDAP, Bourg-Lastic (Fr.) 7.44	MURDER	FR.
HELMAR	161187	M			Lt., Army Oflag VII B, Eichstaett (Ger.) 14.4.45	MURDER	U.K.
HELMEN	124121		Ger.		Untersturmfhr., Goetz von Berlichingen SS-Div.17, Segre-Renaze (Fr.) 7.44-8.44	MURDER	FR.
HELMER	254109	M	Ger.		Office-Chief, Factory Camp Schomberg (Ger.) 44-45	BRUTALITY	FR.
HELMER, Kurt	187670	M	Ger.		SS-Rottenfhr., C.C. Oranienburg,Sachsenhausen (Ger.)	MURDER	FR.
HELMERS	39808	M	Ger.		Adjutant, SS-17.Pz.Div.C.v.B. Adjutant Sturm Geschuetz Abt. 17 Pz. Jg. Abt. 17 , Maine et Loire Mayenne (Fr.) 44	MURDER	FR.
HELMERS, Peter	196956	M	Ger.		Sgt., C.C. Royallieu-Compiègne (Fr.) 41-44	MURDER	FR.
HELMREICH	194778	M	Ger.		Capt., 19.Regt. SS Police, Montelimar (Fr.) 9.12.43	MURDER	FR.
HELMRICH or HELMERICH	140848	M	Ger.	95	Capt., Renegade		
HELMSCHRON	254538	M	Ger.		Lt., 2.Pz.Div. 119.Art.Regt., Coufouleux (Fr.) 8.44	INTERR.	FR.
HELMSDORF, Baron	193576	M	Ger.	00	Civilian, Helmsdorf (Ger.) 15.9.44	MURDER	U.S.
HELMUT or HELMUTH	261821	M	Ger.		Member, Gestapo, Caen (Fr.) 40-45	MURDER	FR.
HELMUTH	185661	M	Ger.		Chief of block, C.C. Ebensee, Mauthausen (Austr.) 11.12.44	TORTURE	FR.
HELVIG, Karl	161960	M	Ger.		Guard, Schoerzingen (Ger.)	MURDER	U.S.
HELWES, Hans	194552	M	Ger.		C.C. Dachau, Bremen (Ger.)	MURDER	FR.
HELWIG	174202	M	Ger.	10	Pvt., 4.Coy. Landesschuetzen Bn. 515, Prague (Czech.) 3.45	MURDER	U.S.
HELWIG, Christian	306750	M	Ger.		Civilian, Nr.Nexterhausen (Ger.) 27.9.44	MURDER	U.K.
HELWIG, Otfried	189036	M	Ger.		SS-Sturmbannfhr., Allg.-SS, near Arolsen (Ger.) 3.45	MURDER	U.K.
HELWIJ see HELLWIG	161991						
HELWING	256603		Ger.		Obersturmbannfhr., Gestapo, Volkswagen-Werk, Sochaux (Fr.) 40-44	INTERR.	FR.
HELZE, Karl	134859	M	Ger.		Ortsbauernfhr., Public Official,	TORTURE	U.S.
HEMD	133688	M			SS-Scharfhr., C.C. Buchenwald (Ger.)	TORTURE	U.S.
HEMEL or HYME	132716	M	Ger.		Cdt., Detachement de douaniers de Vernet les Bains, Velmany (Fr.) 8.44	MURDER	FR.
HEMELT, Hans	190560	M	Ger.		Col., Army, Sibenik-Zablac (Yugo.) 6.44	MURDER	YUGO.
HEMERLING	24984		Ger.		Dr., Oberarzt, Inf.Div.340, 2.Sanit.Coy. 24.1.43	TORTURE	U.S.
HEMERLING	301746	M	Ger.		Head of Block 5, C.C. Auschwitz (Pol.) 40-45	MURDER	FR.
HEMINGHAUSEN	254060	M	Ger.		Lt., Saint-Briac (Fr.) 6.44	INTERR.	FR.
HEMLEYN or HENLEYN	302023	M	Ger.		Guard at Untermassfeld Prison (Ger.) 40-45	MURDER	BEL.
HEMMER	124123		Ger.		Oberleutnant, Gend. Thionville (Fr.) 44	MURDER	FR.
HEMMERICH	192207	M	Ger.		Major, 9.SS-Pz.Div. Hohenstaufen 4 Ers. Bn., Neuville-Les-Bois (Fr.) 8.44	MURDER	FR.
HEMMERICH	301747	M	Ger.		SS-Sgt., SS-Head of men's Labour Service, C.C. Auschwitz (Pol.) 40-45	MURDER	FR.
HEMMERS	194551	M	Ger.		Cpl., Pi. Bn. 23, (Engineer Unit), Oberkail, Bitburg (Ger.) 8.44	MURDER	U.S.
HEMMING BASSEWITZ-BEHR	301564	M	Ger.		Graf, SS-Obertgruppenfhr., Cmdts, in Chief of C.C. 's in Northern (Ger.), C.C. Neuengamme (Ger.) 40-45	MURDER	BEL.
HEMOLD	174201	M			SS-Wachmann, Muhldorf, Ampfing (Ger.) 6.44-4.45	MURDER	U.S.
HEMP or KEMP	173608	M	Ger.		Kreisleiter-Leader, NSDAP, Emmendingen (Ger.) 44	TORTURE	FR.

HEM-HEN

NAME	C.R.FILE NUMBER	SEX	NATIO-NALITY	DATE OF BIRTH	RANK OCCUPATION UNIT PLACE AND DATE OF CRIME	REASON WANTED	WANTED BY
HEMPEAL	161168	M	Ger.		Cpl.,Army,Stalag 8B,Lamsdorf (Ger.) 42	TORTURE	U.K.
HEMPEL	196299	M	Ger.		Lt.,28.R.I.,3.Coy.,116.Bn.,Tilhouse (Fr.) 19.6.44	MURDER	FR.
HEMPEL, Albert	139198	M			Guard,Stalag IX C,Work commando 625,Volkssturm,Berga (Ger.) 2.-4.45	MURDER	U.S.
HEMPEN, Johann	185915	M			Rottfhr.,4.SS Totenkopfsturmbann, Dora,Nordhausen,Ostcrode, Dachau (Ger.)	WITNESS	U.S.
HEMPF, Willy	259921	M	Ger.	24.9.14	Oschfhr.,SS,employee,Gestapo,Ceske,Budejovice (Czech.) 40-45	MISC.CRIMES	CZECH.
HEMPLEMANN	260170	M			Pvt.,SS,slave labour camp,Botn near Rognan (Nor.)8.42-3.43,4.43-5.5.45	BRUTALITY	YUGO.
HEMSTED	305176	M			Unterkommandant,Gruene Polizei,Dokkum,Akkerwoude, Leeuwarden (Neth.) 14.2.45	MISC.CRIMES	NETH.
HENCKEL	119436	M	Ger.		Oberstabsarzt,AB 20.Army staff,Finmark (Nor.) 44	MURDER	NOR.
HENCKEL	187640	M	Ger.		Cpl.,Feldgendarmerie,Goudriaan (Neth.) 22.5.44	MURDER	U.K.
HENCKEL, Bruno	259857	M	Ger.		Oschfhr.,SS,Sainte Savine (Fr.) 25.8.44	INTFHR.	FR.
HENCKELMANN	194550	M	Ger.		Civilian,Homberg (Ger.) 10.44	MURDER	U.S.
HENDE, Walter	10092	M	Ger.		Pvt.,Army,Panz.Gren.Rgt.111,Albine (Fr.) 29.6.44	MURDER	FR.
HENDEL	123998	M			Uschfhr.,Waffen SS Leibstandarte Adolf Hitler,1.Panz.Div., 2.Panz.Gren.Rgt.,Malmedy (Bel.) 17.12.44	MURDER	U.S.
HENDERICK, Andre	250844	M	Ger.		C.C.,Neuengamme (Ger.)	TORTURE	BEL.
HENDLER	128864	M	Ger.		Col.,Stalag IV A,C.C.,Hohenstein (Ger.)	TORTURE	U.K.
HENDLER	133689	M			Schfhr.,SS,C.C.,Buchenwald (Ger.)	TORTURE	U.S.
HENDRICH	374	M	Ger.		Oschfhr.,SS,Gestapo,Locmine (Fr.) 7.-8.44	MURDER	FR.
HENDRICH (see HEINRICH)	139671						
HENDRICH	188140				Feldgendarm,Feldgendarmerie,Jalhay,Surister,Verviers (Bel.) 3.10.43	MURDER	BEL.
HENDRIK	306973	F	Ger.		Wardress SS,political department,C.C.,Auschwitz (Pol.) 41-45	TORTURE	POL.
HENDRIKS	187470	M	Ger.	05	Lt.,Inf.Rgt.,Breskens (Neth.) 4.9.44	MURDER	NETH.
HENDRIKSON	254788	M	Ger.		Sgt.,10.Coy.,377.Jaeger Rgt.,Vinkt (Bel.)	MISC.CRIMES	BEL.
HENE	192952	M	Ger.		Oschfhr.,SS,C.C.,Buchenwald (Ger.)	TORTURE	U.S.
HENEKE, Arthur	24960	M			Major,Schupo,Muelheim (Ger.) 28.2.45	MURDER	U.S.
HENEMAN	133686	M			Member,SS,C.C,Buchenwald (Ger.)	TORTURE	U.S.
HENERLING, Ernst	167821	M	Ger.		Pvt.,9.Rgt.Res.Gren.,1.Coy.,Magny D'Avignon (Fr.) 18.9.44	MURDER	FR.
HENGST	258548	M	Ger.		Doctor,Physician,Hohenlychen (Ger.) 40-45	BRUTALITY	U.S.
HENGSTMANN	301898	M	Ger.		Sturmbannfhr.,Comd.SS Flak Abt.Nord 6.SS Geb.Div.Nord 20.Army Finmark (Nor.) 10.-11.44	MURDER	NOR.
HENICKE	137030	M		90	Obergruppenfhr.,SS,Weimar (Ger.)	MURDER	U.S.
HENING, Eugen	261973	M	Ger.	11.6.18	Merchant,Civ.Occup.,Bratislava (Czech.) 4.-9.42	MURDER	CZECH.
HENKE	167197	M	Ger.		Doctor,Army,Georgian Bn.,Tulle Correze (Fr.) 6.4.44	MISC.CRIMES	FR.
HENKE	256887	M	Ger.		Pvt.,7.Coy.,322 Bn.,5.Schuetz Rgt.,Ljubljana (Yugo.) 42-43	MISC.CRIMES	YUGO.
HENKE, Andor	21356	M			NSDAP,Head political,foreign office	MURDER	U.N.W.C.C.
HENKE, Fritz	154246	M	Ger.		Civilian,Olekszyn (Pol.) 12.39	PILLAGE	U.S.,POL.
HENKE, Karl	157751	M	Ger.	95	Civilian,Sachsenhausen,Oranienburg (Ger.)	MURDER	U.K.
HENKE, Walter	194589	M	Ger.	10	Agent,Gestapo,Savigny en Septaine Bourges (Fr.) 7.-8.44	MURDER	FR.
HENKEL	130168	M	Ger.		Lt.,Stalag III A,Luckenwalde (Ger.)	MURDER	U.K.
HENKEL	147322	M	Ger.		Lt.,15.Pz.Rgt.,11.Pz.Div.,(Fr.) 44	MURDER	FR.
HENKEL	154356	M	Ger.		Major,Smela (Sov.Un.) 10.41-11.42	MURDER	U.K.
HENKEL	190342	M	Ger.		Doctor,State health office,Wiesbaden (Ger.) 43-45	TORTURE	U.S.
HENKEL	258699	M			Uschfhr.,Staines near Lenden (Ger.) 1.45	MURDER	U.S.
HENKEL, Hugo	260192	M	Ger.	21.1.81	Ch.Ar.e.,Matthes u.Weber A.G.,Mem.Ar.Di.,Bank Adv.Henkel, Duisburg,Berlin (Ger.)	MISC.CRIMES	U.S.
HENKEL, Walter	124122	M	Ger.		Pvt.,Army,N.C.C.,Creach-Maout en Pleubin (Fr.) 7.8.44	MURDER	FR.
HENKEL, Willi	306974	M	Ger.		Kapo,C.C.,Auschwitz (Pol.) 41-45	TORTURE	POL.
HENKEL, William	130376	M	Ger.		Hptschfhr.,SS,Mauthausen (Aust.) 1.9.43	MURDER	U.S.
HENKEN	179477	M	Ger.		Customs official,Fillinges (Fr.) 15.9.44	MURDER	FR.
HENLEIN, Konrad	173594	M	Ger.		Reichsstatthalter,occupied territ.Boheme,Oswiecin,Birkenau (Pol.)	MURDER	CZECH.
HENLEYN (see HEMLEYN)	302023						
HENN	162412	M			Army,2-351 German Coy.,Schuetzen near Vienna (Aust.) 20.3.45	MURDER	U.S.
HENN	177509	M	Ger.		Osturmfhr.,SS,Saarbruecken (Ger.)	MISC.CRIMES	FR.
HENN	185969	M	Ger.		Capt.,Rgt.71,Caserne Lappalne Carcassonne,Villebazy(Fr.)17.7.44	PILLAGE	FR.
HENN, Adolph	169732	M	Ger.	06	Rottfhr., SS,Struthof,Natzweiler (Fr.)	MURDER	FR.
HENN, Albert	123986	M	Ger.	00	Police officer,Punderich (Ger.) 7.44	TORTURE	U.S.
HENN, Hubert	24985	M	.		Group-leader,NSDAP	MISC CRIMES	U.S.
HENN, Wilhelm	196358	M	Ger.		Standartenfhr.,SS,Luxemburg (Lux.) 40-45	PILLAGE	LUX.
HENNBRUCK(or HENNEBRUCK)	136300	M	Ger.		28.Rgt.Inf.Oberst.Meilhan,Tilhouse,Sombraun (Fr.).	MURDER	FR.
HENNCH, Kurt	188701	M	Ger.	01	Civilian,Nuernberg (Ger.) 34-45	WITNESS	CZECH.
HENNE	1078	M	Ger.		Lt.,Army,Feldgendarmerie,Chalencey,Auberive,Flagey,Langers (Fr.)43-44	TORTURE	FR.
HENNE	137024	M	Ger.		Civilian	MURDER	U.S.
HENNEBERGER	142980	M	Ger.		Driver,Kraftfahrpark,Pechbrunn (Ger.) 15.4.45	WITNESS	U.S.
HENNEBERG	167364	M	Ger.		Stalag II C,Commando 2298,Greifswald (Ger.)	TORTURE	FR.
HENNESBERG	174200	M			Uschfhr.,SS,Muhldorf,Ampfing (Ger.)	MURDER	U.S.
HENNTBERG	192206	M			Guard,Stalag II,Stettin (Ger.)	TORTURE	FR.
HENNESBERG	196357	M			Lt.,Gross-Rosen (Ger.)	TORTURE	BEL.
HENNEBERG	305896	M			Hptsturmfhr.,SS,head of the Mor.Ostrava Aussenstelle,of the Sicher- heitsdienst Leitabschnitt,Prague,Oswiecim,Birkenau (Pol.) 39-45	MURDER	CZECH.
HENNEBRUCK (see HENNBRUCK)	136300						
HENNECKE	62252	M		21	Lt.,SS,1.SS Pz.Div.,1.Rgt.,1.Coy.,Malmedy (Bel.)	MURDER	U.S.
HENNECKE	173920	M	Ger.	05	Public Prosecutor,Justice Ministry,Prag (Czech.) 44-45	TORTURE	CZECH.
HENNEICK	252234	M	Ger.		C.C.,Dachau,(Ger.)	TORTURE	BEL.
HENNEMAN	154357	M			Doctor,Stalag X B,Sandbostel (Ger.) 8.43	MURDER	U.S.
HENNER, Hermann	161100	M	Ger.	20.4.09	Interpreter,Kommandantur,Morlaiy (Fr.) 7.-8.44	TORTURE	FR.
HENNERICIE	306684	M			Pvt.,331.Pi.Bn.,331.Inf.Div.,Mijn Heerenland (Neth.) 5.45	PILLAGE	NETH.
HENNERMANN	185660	M	Ger.		Chief of Camp,Regierungsrat,Oflag,Civilian,C.C.,Ebrach (Ger.) 44-45	MURDER	CZECH.
HENNICH (see HENNIG)	192996						
HENNIG	146769	M	Ger.	90	pvt.,Army,Stalag IV A,5.Coy.,Landesschuetzen Bn.396,near Dresden (Ger.) 3.45	WITNESS	CAN.
HENNIG	152469	M	Ger.	10	Oschfhr.,Gestapo,SS,Vichy (Fr.) 44	MISC.CRIMES	FR.

NAME	C.R.FILE NUMBER	SEX	NATIO-NALITY	DATE OF BIRTH	RANK OCCUPATION UNIT PLACE AND DATE OF CRIME	REASON WANTED	WANTED BY
HENNIG	162406	M	Ger.	11	SS-Uschfhr.,C.C.Buchenwald (Ger.)	WITNESS	U.S.
HENNIG (or HENRICH)	192906	M	Ger.	00	Cpl.,Ldsch.Bn.396,Stalag 4 A Hohnstein b.Dresden (Ger.) 3.45	WITNESS	CAN.
HENNIG	196359	M	Ger.		Navy, Montceaux les Mines (Fr.)	MISC.CRIMES	FR.
HENNIG	301260	M	Ger.		Crim.-Secr., Abt.IV D,SD, Brussels (Bel.) 6.40-9.44	MURDER	BEL.
HENNIG, Paul	105952	M		97	Druggist,Civilian,Kloster-Mansfeld(Ger.) 2.11.44	WITNESS	U.S.
HENNIG, Wilhelm	1484	M	Ger.		Civilian, Eberswalde (Ger.) 9.44	TORTURE	U.S.
HENNIGER, Fritz	254548	M	Ger.		Pvt.,St.Michielsgestel(Neth.) 9.44	PILLAGE	NETH.
HENNICKS	195366	M			Kapo,C.C.Schandelah,Braunschweig (Ger.) 44-45	TORTURE	BEL.
HENNING	165150	M		07	SS,Kiew,Lemberg,Zwiakel (Pol.,Russ.) 41-42	MURDER	U.S.
HENNING	256006	M	Ger.		SS-Hptschfhr., Doctor in charge Abt.III a Sipo, Bruessel (Bel.) 40-44	MURDER	BEL.
HENNING	257914	M			150 Pz.Bde., Meuse Bridge-Antwerp (Bel.) 12.44	INTERR.	U.S.
HENNING, Bruno	253688	M	Ger.	17.4.12	Chief-Asst.,Police,Gestapo-Chief of labour camps,Hradisko,Mirosov,Prag (Czech.) 42-45	MURDER	CZECH.
HENNING, Fritz	142981	M			Electrician,Civilian,C.C.	TORTURE	U.S.
HENNING, Paul	162648	M	Ger.		SS-Usturmfhr., Gestapo, Chalous-Saone (Fr.)	MURDER	FR.
HENNING, Wilhelm	142965	M	Ger.		School-master, Civilian, Eberswalde (Ger.) 9.44	MURDER	U.S.
HENNINGS	142454	M			Major,SS,Chief of PW Affair,Dr.	WITNESS	U.S.
HENNINGS	202024	M	Ger.		SS-Mann, labour camp Schandelah ne. Brunswick (Ger.) 1.5.44-30.4.45	MURDER	U.K.
HENNINGSEN	306085	M	Ger.		SS-Hptschfhr.,C.C.Hamburg-Neuengamm (Ger.) 45	MURDER	CZECH.
HENRICH, Willy	302025	M	Ger.		Director, of Ste'Haas & Sohn at Sinna, Hessen-Nassau, Ste.Marie-aux-Mines (Fr.) 42-44	PILLAGE	FR.
HENRICI, Emil	167820	M	Ger.		Sgt.,Gruppenfhr.,9 Rgt.Res.Gren.1 Coy,Magny d'Avignon (Fr.) 18.9.44	MURDER	FR.
HENRY (see HARBY)	138345						
HENSCH	119437	M			Col.,20 Army,Cmd.of a Kampfgruppe,Finmark (Nor.) 10.44	MURDER	NOR.
HENSCHEL	142024	M	Ger.	23	Pvt.,12 SS Pz.Div.Hitler Jugend and Feldgendarmerie,Abbaye Ardenne near Caen (Fr.) 6.6.-8.7.44	TORTURE	CAN.
HENSCHEL	156833	M	Ger.	24	Pvt.,SS,Inf.,The Abbaye (Fr.)	INTERR.	CAN.
HENSCHEL	190710	M	Ger.		N.C.O.,Army,St.Andries,Varsenare-les-Bruges (Bel.) 4.9.44	MURDER	BEL.
HENSCHEL	194256	M	Ger.	03	Civilian,Sangershausen,Wallhausen (Ger.) 2.11.44	TORTURE	U.S.
HENSCHEL	194918	M	Ger.		SS-Oschfhr.,SS,C.C.Lublin (Pol.) 40-44	MURDER	POL.
HENSCHEL	250829	M			SS-Oschfhr.,C.C.Flossenburg (Ger.)	INTERR.	BEL.
HENSCHEL, Albert	256605	M		17	Sgt.,C.C.Muehldorf-Dachau (Ger.)	MURDER	U.S.
HENSCHEL, Kurt	197725	M	Ger.		Kreisamtsleiter,NSDAP,Schwalheim (Ger.) 11.and 1.12.44	MURDER	U.S.
HENSCHEL, Richard	142954	M	Ger.	26.8.10	Sgt.,SS-Totenkopf-Standarte,Buchenwald (Ger.) 42	TORTURE	U.S.
HENSCHEL S, Rudolf	167363	M	Ger.		Civilian, Le Glantiers (Fr.) 13.7.44	WITNESS	FR.
HENSCHKE, Hans	108680	M		22.5.08	Oberregierungsrat,Osturmbannfhr.,SD,Gestapo, SS-Dienst,Duesseldorf-Kiel (Ger.) 45	MISC.CRIMES	U.S.
HENSE	261476	M	Ger.		SS-Mann,Dirlewanger Rde.,Warsaw and other (Pol.) 40-44	MURDER	POL.
HENSEL	137664	M	Ger.		Chief,Engineer,Civilian,Auschwitz,Weimar (Pol.,Ger.) 2.44	TORTURE	U.K.
HENSELER	138306	M	Ger.		SS-Sgt.,SS-Gestapo,Lyon (Fr.) 6.-8.44	MURDER	FR.
HENSELER, Fritz	250834	M	Ger.		N.C.O.,field-police (Bel.)	INTERR.	BEL.
HENSELFF, Hildegard	179602	F	Ger.	18	Employee,Sipo,Bruessel (Bel.)	WITNESS	BEL.
HENSEN (see HEINZEN)	190365						
HENSEN	142964	M			Capt.,SD,Sipo,Kiew (Russ.) 15.3.42	MURDER	U.S.
HENSHEIM, Paul	121564	M	Ger.		Stalag 6,Atzenbach (Ger.)	TORTURE	FR.
HENSOLD, Karl	142446	M	Ger.		Schfhr.,SA,Pleinfeld (Ger.)	TORTURE	U.S.
HENTCHELL	188636	M	Ger.		N.C.O.,Army,Port Vendre (Fr.) 19.8.44	INCENDIARISM	FR.
HENTGEN	194910	M	Ger.		Policeman, Hptwachtmeister, Police, Differange (Lux.)	TORTURE	LUX.
HENTSCHEL	188216	M	Ger.	90	Official,Polizeirat,Hoehere SS,Polizeifhr.,Sosnowiec-Auschwitz (Pol.)44	MURDER	POL.
HENTSCHEL, Max	185973	M		11.6.92	Oschfhr.,4 SS Totenkopfsturmbann,Guard,C.C.Dora,Nordhausen Osterode (Ger.) 43-45	WITNESS	U.S.
HENTSCHEL, Rudolf	258535	M	Ger.		Civilian,Capo,C.C.Dachau (Ger.) 40-41	BRUTALITY	POL.
HENTZ	250245	M			Gendarm,field-police,Plouaret,Loguivy,Plougras (Fr.) 21.6.44	MURDER	FR.
HENTZ, Ernst	258390	M			Customs officer,Ponte Tresa (It.) 21.3.45	MURDER	U.S.
HENTZ, Martin	162437	M	Ger.		5 Coy Ldsch.Bn.,Stalag 6 G or 6 B Bonn (Ger.) 44-45	TORTURE	U.S.
HENTZE, Ernst	139196	M			Untergruppenfhr.,SS, 21.3.45	MURDER	U.S.
HENTZSCHEL, Erich	142953	M	Ger.	26.8.10	Sgt.,Waffen SS,SS Totenkopf-Standarte,C.C.Buchenwald (Ger.)	TORTURE	U.S.
HENYSEL	125471	M	Ger.		Schfhr.,SS,C.C.Sachsenhausen,Cranienburg (Ger.) 42,39-4.45	MURDER	U.K.,POL.
HENZE	252187	M	Ger.		Employee, Abt.IV Sipo, Bruessel (Bel.)	INTERR.	BEL.
HENZE	306793	M			Member,St.Quentin Gestapo,Vraignes en Vermandois Somme (Fr.) 29.8.44	MURDER	FR.
HENZEL, Walter	261822	M	Ger.	05	Usturmfrr.,SD,Besancon,Rioz (Haute Saone) (Fr.) 24.7.44	MURDER	FR.
HENZMANN, Willy	254789	M			Pvt.,377 Jg.Rgt.,Vinkt (Bel.)	MISC.CRIMES	BEL.
HEP, Ursel (or HESS)	301689	F	Ger.		O5-243 Mongolian "Oberland" Unit,St.Nazaire en Royans (Fr.)20.7.-5.8.44	MURDER	FR.
HEPFINGER, Georg	10093	M	Ger.		Pvt.,Army,Pz.Gren.Rgt.111,Albine (Fr.) 29.6.44	MURDER	FR.
HEPPE	250243	M	Ger.		SS-Hptsturmfhr.,SS,C.C.Neuengamme (Ger.)	TORTURE	FR.
HEPPNER	125638	M	Ger.		Lt.,Geb.Jg.Coy 18 Bn.,Eboulet (Fr.) 30.9.44-2.10.44	MURDER	FR.
HERAID (or HEFALD)	125465	M	Ger.		Sgt.,Stalag XIII C,Hammelburg (Ger.)	TORTURE	U.K.
HERALD (see HERAID)	125465						
HERAR (or HESER)	306394	M	Ger.		Kommissar,Lt.,Member of Gestapo,C.C.Dora,Nordhausen (Ger.) 40-45	MURDER	BEL.
HERBACH	256606				Employee,C.C.Nordhausen.	MURDER	U.S.
HERBER, Leonhard	195776	M			Civilian,Haslabronn (Ger.) 40-45	MISC.CRIMES	POL.
HERBERG	194777	M	Ger.		Head,SS Schutz Corps,Org.Todt,Habere-Lullin (Fr.) 25.12.43	MURDER	FR.
HERBERGER, G.	192790	M			Sohupo,C.C.Falstad Stalag (Nor.) 41-45	MURDER	NOR.
HERBERLEIN	301634	M			Werkmeister,Ebrach or Amberg (Ger.) 45	MURDER	CZECH.
HERBERT	31911	M	Ger.		Adj.-chief,Army,Det.of 12 Feldgendarmerie parach.,Abbeville (Fr.)31.8.44	MURDER	FR.
HERBERT	130375				Capo,C.C.Mauthausen (Aust.) 41-45	MURDER	U.S.
HERBERT	162403	M	Ger.	10	Pvt.,Arb.Coy 88,714 Ldsch.Bn.4 Coy,Gubin (Pol.) 30.6.42	MURDER	U.K.
HERBERT (or ERBERT)	165929	M			Sgt.,Special Military Police	MURDER	U.S.
HERBERT	166378	M		18	Geh.Feldpolizei,Rsocaro or Valdagno (It.) 1.45	MURDER	U.S.
HERBERT	167203	M	Ger.		Civilian,Dr.,Einsatzstab Rosenberg,Costume Expert,Berlin (Ger.) 40-41	PILLAGE	FR.
HERBERT	173919	M			Oberpolier,Org.Todt,C.C.Muhldorf Ampfing (Ger.) 6.44-4.45	MURDER	U.S.

HER-HER

NAME	C.R.FILE NUMBER	SEX	NATIO-NALITY	DATE OF BIRTH	RANK OCCUPATION UNIT PLACE AND DATE OF CRIME	REASON WANTED	WANTED BY
HERBERT	196360	M	Ger.	00	Capt., O.C.811 Heeres-Verpflegungs-Lager "Victoria" Castellucchio (It.) 12.8.43	INTERR.	U.K.
HERBERT	255270	M	Ger.		Sgt., 1 Coy, 6 SS Abt. Nachschub (Bel.)	PILLAGE	BEL.
HERBERT	256091	M			Overseer, C.C. Mauthausen (Aust.)	MURDER	FR.
HERBERT	260171	M	Ger.		Sgt., Russia-Germany Div.Oberland, Massif du Vercars (Isere et Drome Fr.) 20.7. to 5.8.44	SUSPECT	FR.
HERBERT, Arthur	39604	M	Ger.	15	Hptscharfhr., SS Police Rgt.Todt, Annemasse (Fr.) 14.12.43	PILLAGE	FR.
HERBERT, Heinrich	300900	M	Ger.		Weike Heraltice (Czech.) 7.8.44	BRUTALITY	CZECH.
HERBET	154365	M			Capt.,SS, Warsan (Pol.)	TORTURE	U.S.
HERBINGER	257681	M	Ger.		Scharfhr., Campleader Rossla, Nordhausen (Ger.)	MURDER	U.S.
HERBNER, Ludwig	197728	M	Ger.		Groupleader, NSDAP, Gudensberg (Ger.)	TORTURE	POL.
HERBOLD, Jacobina	142703	F	Ger.	80	Civilian, C.C. Hadamar (Ger.) 6.44-3.45	WITNESS	U.S.
HERBRANDT	250838	M	Ger.		Lt.,6 Coy, Unit 1018 (Bel.)	MISC.CRIMES	BEL.
HERES or HERST	141565	M	Ger.	14	SS-Hptsturmfhr. Hoechst (Ger.)	TORTURE	FR.
HERBST	24947	M			Manager, Salt Mine, Public official,Sandershausen (Ger.) 42	MURDER	U.K.
HERBST	24986	M			Capt., Gendarmerie, District Pol.leader,Fehrbellin (Ger.)10.43-5.45	MURDER	U.S.
HERBST	146863	M			Hptsturmfhr.,SS, Pz.Div. "Das Reich" (South-West-Fr.) 44	MURDER	FR.
HERBST	251052	M		94	Major, Police Commander of Perugia Province, SS or SD,Norcia (It.)5.44	INTERR.	U.K.
HERBST, H.	306202		Ger.		Member of Staff, C.C. Lodz (Pol.) 41-44	MURDER	CZECH.
HERBST, Hans	24962	M	Ger.		Uscharfhr.,SS, Gestapo, C.C. Klingelpuetz (Ger.) 1.,2.45	TORTURE	U.S.
HERBST, Hermann	137031	M			Civilian, Pullach (Ger.) 19.7.44	WITNESS	U.S.
HERBST, Else	165147	F	Ger.		Civilian, Wittmar (Ger.)	WITNESS	U.S.
HERBST, Wilhelm	127372	M			Civilian	TORTURE	U.S.
HERBUTT, Eugen	305061	M	Ger.		Pvt., Athen (Grc.) 10.43	PILLAGE	GRC.
HERCHEL, Karl	10094	M	Ger.		Pvt.,Army,Pz.Gren.Rgt.111, Albine (Fr.) 29.6.44	MURDER	FR.
HERCIAL	189211	M	Ger.		Sgt.,Army, Le Bourget (Fr.) about 44	WITNESS	FR.
HERDE see HERDER	162089						
HERDE, Josef	306389	M	Ger.	4. 9.09	Pvt.,SS, C.C. Buchenwald (Ger.) 16.5.38"9.10.43	MURDER	BEL.
HERDEF	194355	M	Ger.		Custom official, Grenzpolizei, Semaphore,le Creach Maout (Fr.)	MURDER	FR.
HERDER or HERDE	162089	M			Rottenfhr.,SS, C.C. Flossenburg (Ger.)	MURDER	U.S.
HERDRAM	162653	M	Ger.		Engineer, C.C. Wuppertal (Ger.) 2.44	MURDER	FR.
HERDRICH	196352	M	Ger.		Cpl.,Fallschirm-Pion.Bn 8, St.Amand-Mont-Rond (Fr.) 8.6.44	MURDER	FR.
HERENTRY	250235	M	Ger.		Rottenfhr.,SS, 1 SS Pz.Rgt.,6 Coy, Malmedy (Bel.) 17.12.44	MURDER	U.S.
HERGET	142972	M	Ger.		Civilian, Budisheim (Ger.) 6.45	MURDER	U.S.
HERGETH, Emil	195775	M	Ger.		Pionier, 1 SS Pz.Div., Stoument Ligneuville (Bel.)17.-19.12.44	MURDER	U.S.
HERGERT	133355	M			Osturmfhr.,W.O.,Waffen-SS, CC. Flossenburg (Ger.)	TORTURE	U.S.
HERGERT, Karl	167804	M	Ger.		Oscharfhr.,SS, C.C. Sachsenhausen,Oranienburg (Ger.) 39-4.45	MURDER	POL.
HERGERT, Pius	137777	M			Civilian, Solingen (Ger.) 5.11.44	MURDER	U.S.
HERICK	125639	M	Ger.		Capt., Geh.Feldpol.,Lille (Fr.)	MURDER	FR.
HERING	124263	M			Usturmfhr.,SS Pz.Rgt.1,1 SS Pz.Div.,9 Coy (engineers) Malmedy (Bel.) 17.12.44	MURDER	U.S.
HERING	162672	M	Ger.		Lt.,Feldgendarmerie,Formation 58520 C,St.Gerand,le Puy(Fr.) 10.43	MISC.CRIMES	FR.
HERING	167803	M	Ger.		Oscharfhr.,SS, C.C. Sachsenhausen,Oranienburg (Ger.)	MURDER	POL.
HERING	171974	M	Ger.		Blockleiter, SS, C.C. Oranienburg (Ger.) 39	MURDER	U.S.
HERING, Bruno	161102	M	Ger.		Civilian, Daasdorf and Guttmannshausen (Ger.) 7.,8.44	WITNESS	U.S.
HERING, Max	306390	M	Ger.		Sgt.,SS, C.C. Buchenwald (Ger.) 16.5.38-9.10.43	MURDER	BEL.
HERINGHAUS, Erich	300478	M	Ger.		Capt.,Lageroffizier, Deputy to the Abwehroffizier, Member of NSDAP, Yugo.officer's POW-Camp, Oflag 65, Strassburg, Barckenbruegge, Alexisdorf, (Ger.) 44-45	BRUTALITY	YUGO.
HERITSCH	257371	M	Ger.		Guard, Sgt., SS, slave Labour Camp,Beisfjord near Narvik (Nor.) 6.to 11.42	BRUTALITY	YUGO.
HERK	126739	M	Ger.		Officer, Kriegsgefangenen-Arbeits-Kdo.	TORTURE	FR.
HERK	188634	M	Ger.		Civilian, Dir.,Cement-factory, Oberkassel near Bonn (Ger.) 40-44	TORTURE	FR.
HERKE, Helmar see BECKER	170076						
HERKEL	167186	M	Ger.		Civilian, Treuhaender, Polish printing houses,Warschau(Pol.)9.39-44	PILLAGE	POL.
HERKENRATH, Simo	125147				Civilian, Efferen (Ger.) 2.10.44	MISC.CRIMES	U.S.
HERKLOTZ	174209	M			Polier,Org. Todt,C.C. Muhldorf,Ampfing (Ger.) 6.44-4.45	MURDER	U.S.
HERKLOTZ	259504	M	Ger.		Cpl.,9 SS Div."Hohenstaufen" (Pz.Div.) office Staff Beekbergen (Gelderland-Neth.) 10.or 11.9.44	WITNESS	NETH.
HERL	257682	M	Ger.		Capt., SD, Region Depontivy (Fr.) 44	MISC.CRIMES	FR.
HERL, Peter	186978	M	Ger.	09	Civilian, factory manager, Brno (Czech.) 39-45	PILLAGE	CZECH.
HERLEMANN	300574	M	Ger.		Probably serving in 377 Inf.Rgt.,Vinkt-Meigem (Bel.)25.-31.5.40	MISC.CRIMES	BEL.
HERMAN	375				SS-Oberfhr.,Regierungspraesident, public official,Danzig (Pol.)9.39-42	MURDER	POL.
HERMAN or HERRMANN	12395	M			Dr.,chief of Gestapo, Brno (Czech.) 39-44	TORTURE	CZECH.
HERMAN	105933	M			Sgt.,SS, C.C. Frondenberg (Ger.) 12.44	TORTURE	U.S.
HERMAN or HELLWIG	149770	M			Pvt., Grenzwacht 12, 2.45	MURDER	NOR.
HERMAN	186241	M	Ger.		Pvt.,guard, Army, Vasiliki (Creta-Grc.) 43-45	MURDER	GRC.
HERMAN	186481	M	Ger.		C.C. Rosenheim,Stephanskirchen,Bavaria (Ger.)	TORTURE	FR.
HERMAN	192128	M	Ger.		Arbeitsfhr.,SS, C.C. Breendonck (Bel.) since 41	MURDER	BEL.
HERMAN	195365	M	Ger.		Policeman, C.C. Mauthausen (Aust.) 11.5.42-10.5.45	MURDER	BEL.
HERMAN	258168	M	Ger.		Lawyer, Military, Amsterdam (Neth.) 7.2.45	SUSPECT	NETH.
HERMAN	305868	M	Ger.		Pvt.,6 Coy,16 Hubner Rgt.,Kinrooi, Limburg (Bel.) 9.44	MURDER	BEL.
HERMAN, Guenther	190194	M	Ger.		Criminalrat, Gestapo, Brno (Czech.) 39-45	MURDER	CZECH.
HERMAN, Helmut	145305	M	Ger.		Hptscharfhr.,1 Pz.Div.,Leibstandarte "Adolf Hitler",Malmedy(Bel.) 44	MURDER	U.S.
HERMAN, Karl	146686	M	Ger.		District treasurer, C.C.Bensov Vicinity of Gardelegen (Czech.,Ger.) 7.5.45-9.-14.4.45	MURDER	CZECH.,U.S.
HERMAN, Otto	194586	M	Ger.		Sgt.,Gendarmerie,326 Pol.Div.,Bucqueliers (Fr.) 44	TORTURE	FR.
HERMAN, Philip	189395	M	Ger.		Wachtmstr., Police, C.C. Tromsoya (Nor.) 18.6.42	TORTURE	NOR.
HERMANN	377	M	Ger.		Capt.,Waffen-SS, Valences d'Agen (Fr.) 13.6.44	MURDER	FR.
HERMANN	1398	M	Ger.		Pvt.,Army	MURDER	U.K.
HERMANN	24987	M	Ger.		Col.,Dulag 377, PWC., Gerolstein (Ger.) 27.1.45	MURDER	U.S.

NAME	C.R.FILE NUMBER	SEX	NATIO- NALITY	DATE OF BIRTH	RANK	OCCUPATION	UNIT	PLACE AND DATE OF CRIME	REASON WANTED	WANTED BY
HERMANN	125466	M	Ger.			Civilian,Dueren-Rolsdorf(Ger.) 6.-7.44			MURDER	U.K.,U.S.
HERMANN	129671	M	Ger.		Lt.,183 Volksgren.Div.,330 Volksgren.Regt.,7 Coy.(Ger.) 16.1.45				MISC.CRIMES	U.S.
HERMANN	133356	M		12	Lt.,Staff-Officer,W.O.,Waffen-SS,2 Pi.Ausb.Bn.,Passau(Ger.) 4.45				MURDER	U.S.
HERMANN	137088	M	Ger.		Sgt.,Oflag VIIC,C.C.Laufen(Ger.) 10.11.40				MURDER	U.K.
HERMANN	142971	M	Ger.		Sgt.,1 Panz.Coy.,Freilassing(Ger.) 16.4.45				WITNESS	U.S.
HERMANN	146862	M	Ger.		SS-Mann,SS-Panz.-Div."Das Reich", 2 Coy..(South-West Fr.) 44				MURDER	FR.
HERMANN	149520	M			Sgt.,SS,Schoerzingen(Ger.)				MISC.CRIMES	FR.
HERMANN	142466	M			Officer,Public Official,Guard,Lyon-Perrache(Fr.) 6.5.44				WITNESS	FR.
HERMANN	161969	M	Ger.		Interpreter,Feldgend.,St.Gerand Le Puy(Fr.) 6.-15.10.43				PILLAGE	FR.
HERMANN	162404	M			Civilian Doctor,Nyons(Fr.)				MURDER	FR.
HERMANN	167179	M			W.O.,Army Train,Acolin(Fr.) 15.-16.8.44				MURDER	UNWCC.
HERMANN	169798	M	Ger.		Sgt.,Gendarmerie, Chalencey,Auberive,Flagey,Coiffey(Fr.) 43-44				MURDER	FR.
HERMANN	177508	M	Ger.		Hptschfhr.,SD,Gestapo,Saarbruecken(Ger.)				MISC.CRIMES	FR.
HERMANN	186003	M	Ger.		Senior W.O.,99 Gebirgsjaeger Bn.,1 Coy.Briancon,La Batie des Vigneaux (Fr.) 4.7.44				MURDER	FR.
HERMANN	186480	M	Ger.		Guard,C.C.Kradischko-Flossenburg(Ger.)				TORTURE	FR.
HERMANN	188155	M	Ger.		SA-Mann, Overseer,Work Camp Schutzen am Gebirge(Aust.) 12.2.45				MURDER	U.S.
HERMANN	194294	M	Ger.		Cpl.,Kgf.Arb.Bn.184,Vassno(Nor.)				TORTURE	NOR.
HERMANN	194549	M	Ger.		Guard,C.C.Neuengamme(Ger.) 1940-45				TORTURE	BEL.
HERMANN	194587	M	Ger.		Senior-W.O.,Kraftfahr-Coy.,Pornichet St.Marguerite(Fr.)				PILLAGE	FR.
HERMANN	194588	M	Ger.		Sgt.,Army,F.P.No.14653D.TR.Victor,Nice(Fr.) 7.7.44				MURDER	FR.
HERMANN	250827	M	Ger.		16 Hubner Regt.,6 Coy.,Kinrooi(Bel.)				MURDER	BEL.
HERMANN	254532	M	Ger.		Kapo,C.C.Buchenwald(Ger.) 44-45				INTERR.	FR.
HERMANN	255973	M	Ger.		Chief of bloc 3 C.C.Mauthausen(Aust.)				MURDER	FR.
HERMANN	260397	M	Ger.		Headmaster,Slave Labour-Camp,Todt Organisation,working with Firm of Rolinger, Botn near Rognan(Nor.) 8.42-45				MURDER	YUGO.
HERMANN	261057	M	Ger.		Gend.-Interpreter,Gend.No.585200,La Balisse St.Gerand Le Puy(Fr.)43-44				MURDER	FR.
HERMANN	301416	M	Ger.		Kapo,Kdo.Stephankirchen,Nr.Rosenheim(Ger.) 44-45				MISC.CRIMES	FR.
HERMANN	301748	M	Ger.		Head Chemist,Army,C.C.Auschwitz(Pol.) 40-45				MURDER	FR.
HERMANN, Andreas	185972	M			SS-Mann,4 SS Totenkopfsturmbann,C.C.-Guard,Dora,Nordhausen,Osterode (Ger.) 43-45				WITNESS	U.S.
HERMANN, Eduard	305665	M	Ger.		Col.,Cmdt. of Dulag 377,Gerolstein(Ger.) 19.12.44-5.2.45				MISC.CRIMES	U.S.
HERMANN, Fritz	130392	M	Ger.		Guard,C.C.Halberstadt(Ger.) 44				TORTURE	BEL.
HERMANN, Fritz or Heinz	253686	M	Ger.		Shoemannfacture,Civilian,Stuttgart(Ger.) 44				INTERR.	FR.
HERMANN, Hans	152467	M	Ger.		SS-Sturmbannfhr.,Gestapo,SS,Foix(Fr.) 29.6.45				MURDER	FR.
HERMANN, Hans	256825	M	Ger.		Lt.,Valognes(Fr.) 6.6.44				MURDER	U.S.
HERMANN, Heinz	1067	M	Ger.		Sonderfuehrer,Army-Feldgend.,Epernay(Fr.)				TORTURE	FR.
HERMANN, Hetterich	188713	M	Ger.	1.11.88	Sgt.,Police,Lauf-Pegnitz(Ger.) 11.4.45				SUSPECT	POL.
HERMANN, Josef	193204	M	Ger.	5.12.02	Sgt.,Justizministerium,Feldstraflager Nord,Finmark(Nor.) 42-45				MISC.CRIMES	NOR.
HERMANN, Karl	173595	M	Ger.		Head, Staatspolizeistelle,C.C. Bruenn,Oswiecim-Birkenau (Czech.,Pol.) 39-45				MURDER	CZECH.
HERMANN, Konrad	196710	M	Ger.	11.9.96	Civilian-Inspector of slaughter-house,NSDAP,Kripo(Lux.)				MURDER	LUX.
HERMANN, Otto	145906	M	Ger.		Uschfhr.,Waffen-SS,1 SS Pz.Div.Leibstand.A.H.,Malmedy(Bel.) 44				MURDER	U.S.
HERMANN, Paul	193209	M	Ger.	03	Kgf.Arb.Bn.186 (Nor.) 40-45				MISC.CRIMES	NOR.
HERMANNS	186688	M	Ger.	09	Oschfhr.,SS-Nachrichtenzug,Wormhoudt(Fr.) 5.40				MURDER	U.K.
HERMANS	196709	M	Ger.		Guard,C.C.,Mauthausen(Aust.)				TORTURE	BEL.
HERMANS, Rene	9664	M			Civilian,Breendonck(Bel.) 40-44				TORTURE	BEL.
HERMANZ, Wilhelm	186240	M	Ger.		Lt.,Gestapo,Fourne-Creta(Grc.) 10.2.44				MURDER	GRC.
HERMELING	194776	M	Ger.		Civilian, St.Rambert(Fr.) 2.44				MURDER	FR.
HERMES	376	M	Ger.		SS-Osturmfhr.,C.C.Maidanek(Pol.) 40-4.44				MURDER	POL.
HERMES, Hubert	185451	M	Ger.		Pionier-Bn.669 Bn.,,1 Coy.of P.O.A.,Feldpost 29986,Werbomont, Villers-Ste-Gertrude,Ferrieres,Burnontige(Bel.) 9.44				MURDER	BEL.
HERMES, Wilhelm	192364	M	Ger.		C.C.Rosbach(Ger.)				MURDER	U.S.
HERMOUTH	152468	M	Ger.	21	N.C.O.,Marine Inf.,St.Pabo(Fr.) 7.8.44				MURDER	FR.
HERMS	105935	M	Ger.		SS-Sturmfhr.,Headquarters located at Brunswick,Ger., Schmedenstedt,Minstedt(Ger.)				MURDER	U.S.
HERNING	162647	M	Ger.		Gestapo,Dun les Places(Fr.) 26.-28.6.44				MURDER	FR.
HERNS	185658	M	Ger.		Oberkapo,C.C.Melk,Mauthausen(Aust.) 44				MURDER	FR.
HEROLD	52724	M	Ger.	95	Major,Sipo,Poitiers,Bois de Guron(Fr.) 7.7.44				MURDER	U.K.
HEROLD	161167	M	Ger.	00	Cpl.,German Army,Stalag 13C,Hammelburg(Ger.) 44-45				TORTURE	U.K.
HEROLD, Adam	250820	M	Ger.		Cmdt.,C.C.Moerchs near Frankenthal(Ger.)				MISC.CRIMES	FR.
HEROLD, Erich	167819	M	Ger.		Pvt.,9 Gren.Regt.,1 Coy.,Magny d'Anigon(Fr.) 18.9.44				MURDER	FR.
HEROLD, Walter	306391	M	Ger.	10.9.23	SS-Mann,SS,C.C.Buchenwald(Ger.) 16.5.38-9.10.43				MURDER	BEL.
HERON	6152	M		00	Lt.,Army,Art.,Morras(Ger.) 2.45				TORTURE	U.K.
HERPST	141935	M	Ger.		Guard,C.C.Koenigshofen(Ger.)				TORTURE	U.K.
HERPSTER	167178	M	Ger.		Senior W.O.,Army,Pont l'Abbe Plobaznalec(Fr.) 6.-8.44				MURDER	FR.
HERR see HEIR	123807									
HERR	258879	M	Ger.		SS-Block-Chief,SS-Guard,Ohrdruf(Ger.) 44 - 45				SUSPECT	FR.
HERR, Eugen	250833	M	Ger.		Member NSDAP,Loerrach(Ger.)				TORTURE	BEL.
HERR, Gibbe	36612	M	Ger.		Farmer,Civilian,Kuivkenpo(Ger.) 4.40				TORTURE	U.K.
HERR, Hugo	142956	M	Ger.	28.1.85	Sgt.,Guard,SS-Totenkopf-Stand.,Waffen-SS,C.C.Weimar(Ger.)				TORTURE	U.S.
HERR, Wilhelm	301793	M	Ger.	90	Capt.,Landesschuetz.Bn.877-3,Camp 180 G-W,Liezen(Aust.) 44-45				BRUTALITY	U.K.
HERREN or HERRN	96686	M	Ger.	00	Lt.,4-610 Landesschuetzen,between Marienburg and Hannover(Ger.) 25.1.-18.4.45				MISC.CRIMES	U.K.
HERRICK	261917	M	Ger.		377 Jaeger-Regt.,Vinkt,Meigem,Flandres East Orientale(Bel.) 25.-31.5.40				MURDER	BEL.
HERRICKA, Karl	142976	M		18	Room-Elder,C.C.Mauthausen(Aust.) 41-45				MURDER	U.S.
HERRIGER, Alfred	161104	M	Ger.		Civilian,Representant at France Continent.Oil Gesellschaft, Saint Gaudens(Fr.) 16.6.44				MISC.CRIMES	FR.

NAME	C.R.FILE NUMBER	SEX	NATIO- NALITY	DATE OF BIRTH	RANK	OCCUPATION	UNIT	PLACE AND DATE OF CRIME	REASON WANTED	WANTED BY
HERRIN	105936	M	Ger.		Lt., Army, C.C. Morass, Danzig (Ger.Pol.)				TORTURE	U.K.
HERRING	135545	M	Ger.		Lt., Army, Landesschuetzen-Bn.610, Brunswick (Ger.) 24.1.-24.3.45				TORTURE	U.K.
HERRING	142481	M	Ger.	05	SS Oscharfhr., C.C. Sachsenhausen, Oranienburg (Ger.)				TORTURE	U.K.
HERRING	193202	M	Ger.		Cpl., Pion., C.C. Bonnes (Nor.) 44-45				TORTURE	NOR.
HERRING, Waldorf	142983	M	Ger.		Stalag Luft 4, Kiefheide (Ger.) 2.-5.45				TORTURE	U.S.
HERRLICH, Joseph see ELIERCH	15736ª									
HERRLITZ	194901	M	Ger.		Lt.Col., Schupo, Luxembourg (Lux.)				MISC.CRIMES	LUX.
HERRMAN	121054	M	Ger.		Major, Landesschuetzen-Bn. 439, 2.Coy., C.C.Sagan-Stalag VIII C (Ger.) 9.-12.44				TORTURE	U.K.
HERRMANN see HERMAN	12395									
HERRMANN	121055	M	Ger.		SS Uscharfhr., Waffen SS, Carcossonne (Fr.)				MISC.CRIMES	FR.
HERRMANN	127077	M	Ger.		Osturmfhr., 2.SS Div. "Das Reich"				MURDER	FR.
HERRMANN	146861	M	Ger.		Hptsturmfhr., SS Panz.Div."Das Reich", Engineer-Coy., Valence d'Agen (Fr.) 44				MURDER	FR.
HERRMANN	147319	M	Ger.		Pvt., 11.Panz.Div. (Fr.) 44				MURDER	FR.
HERRMANN	191609	M	Ger.		Lt., Waffen SS Div."Das Reich" 1.Coy., St.Sixte (Fr.) 23.6.44				MURDER	FR.
HERRMANN	192028	M	Ger.		Officer, Army, Lyon, Perrache (Fr.)				MURDER	FR.
HERRMANN	254942	M	Ger.		Pvt., Fieldpolice, Vendome (Fr.) 9.8.44				MURDER	FR.
HERRMANN, Anton	253709	M	Ger.		Pvt., C.C. Freising (Ger.)				MISC.CRIMES	FR.
HERRMANN, Artur	259937	M	Ger.	about 01	Cpl., Bohemia and Moravia (Czech.) 44-45				WITNESS	CZECH.
HERRMANN, Fritz	259224	M	Ger.		Member, Gestapo, Poitiers Area (Fr.)				MISC.CRIMES	FR.
HERRMANN, Hermann	132324	M			SS Member, Gestapo, C.C. Brno (Czech.) 39-45				MURDER	CZECH.
HERRMANN, Johann	174210	M			Member SS, C.C. Muehldorf-Ampfing (Ger.) 6.44-4.45				MURDER	U.S.
HERRMANN, Richard	142979	M	Ger.	20. 8.02	SS Mann, Guard, SS Totenkopf-Standarte, Waffen SS, C.C. Weimar (Ger.)				TORTURE	U.S.
HERRN see HERREN	36686									
HERMETH, Friedrich or Fritz	134853	M		97	SS-Mann, Lagerfuehrer, Allg. SS, Rathsberg (Ger.)				TORTURE	U.S.
HERSBERG, Walther	257717	M		91	Baufuehrer, C.C. Dachau, Muehldorf-Area (Ger.)				MURDER	U.S.
HERSCH	125040	M	Ger.		Capt., Stalag IV A, Hohenstein (Ger.) 1.44				MISC.CRIMES	U.K.
HERSCHBACH	300774	M			Sgt., 1.Aufkl.Abt., 3.Coy. 2.Col. XV.Div. Afrika-Corps, St.Leger (Arlon) 5.9.44				MISC.CRIMES	BEL.
HERSCHBIEGEL	171975	M			Chief, Gestapo, Fouligny, Marange (Fr.) 9.8.44				MURDER	U.S.
HERSCHE	254593	M			Osturmfhr., Urbes (Fr.) 24.9.44, 4.-5.10.44				MURDER	FR.
HERSCHELMANN, Karl	185452	M		21. 4.02	Usturmfhr., Crim.secret., S.D. Gestapo, Praha, Lidice (Czech.)				MURDER	CZECH.
HERSCHELMANN, Karl	187021				Uscharfhr., S.D. C.C. Dora-Mittelbau, Nordhausen (Ger.) 43-45				WITNESS	U.S.
HERSCHLFIN, Alois	189676	M	Ger.	12. 3.03	Agent, Gestapo, Rombas (Fr.)				TORTURE	FR.
HERSCHLEIN, Willy	188965	M	Ger.		Crim.Inspector, Police, Rombas (Fr.)				TORTURE	FR.
HERSCHNEK, Helmuth	260546	M	Ger.	23.10.21	Uscharfhr., Waffen SS, Totenkopf, C.C. Auschwitz (Pol.) 41-45				BRUTALITY	POL.
HIRSEELD	136261	M	Ger.		Pvt., 11.Panz.Div. 2.Coy. 2.AA-A 7, Bergerac, Albine (Fr.) 7.8.44-3.44				MURDER	FR.
HERST see HERBS	141565									
HERTEL	9665	M	Ger.		N.C.O. Army, C.C. Breendonck (Bel.) -2.3.44				TORTURE	BEL.
HERTEL	133672	M			SS Uscharfhr., C.C. Buchenwald (Ger.)				TORTURE	U.S.
HERTEL	187042	M			Oscharfhr., 4.SS Totenkopf-Stuba., C.C. Dora-Mittelbau Nordhausen (Ger.) 43-45				TORTURE	U.S.
HERTEL	193288	M	Ger.		Guard, Landesschuetzen-Bn. C.C.Lamsdorf Stalag VIII B3 (Ger.) 29.12.41				MURDER	U.K.
HERTEL	257010	M	Ger.		Dr., Leader, SS, police court, Amsterdam (Neth.) 7.2.44				SUSPECT	NETH.
HERTEL, Alfred	98782	M	Ger.	about 15	Scharfhr., Waffen SS, Breendonck (Bel.)				MISC.CRIMES	BEL.
HERTEL, Franz	191431	M	Ger.		Director, Grundstuecksgesellschaft fuer Reichsgau, Danzig				PILLAGE	POL.
HERTEL, Irma	250232	F	Ger.		Woman-guard, SS, C.C. Geislingen (Ger.) 40-45				MURDER	POL.
HERTEL, Oskar	306993	M	Ger.	5. 1.09	SS-Mann, C.C. Buchenwald (Ger.) betw.16.5.38 and 9.10.43				MURDER	BEL.
HERTKLE	198328	M	Ger.		Capt., Geheime Feldpolizei, Lille, Montigny-en-Gohelle (Fr.) 14.3.44				MURDER	FR.
HERTER	161109	M			SS Mann, Waffen SS 1.Panz.Div. "Adolf Hitler", 1.SS Ers.Bn., Parfondruy, Stavelot (Bel.) 18.-22.12.44				MURDER	U.S.
HERTER, Wilhelm Gustav	258440	M	Ger.		Leader, Botanische Anstalten, Cracow (Pol.) Doctor				MISC.CRIMES	POL.
HERTHAUSER, Adolph	10096	M	Ger.		Pvt., Army, Panz.Gren.Rgt. 111, Albine (Fr.) 29.644				MURDER	FR.
HERTI	301749	M	Ger.		Pvt., Cmdt., Revin-Ardennes (Bel.) 13.-14.6.44				MURDER	FR.
HERTIG	255521	M	Ger.		Capt., 23.Div., Servanches (Fr.) 17.3.44				INTERR.	FR.
HERTIND	154243	M	Ger.		Etat Major, Army, Locmine (Fr.)				MURDER	FR.
HERTKORN, Theresia	250293	F	Ger.		Woman-guard, SS, C.C. Geislingen, Ludwigsburg (Ger.) 40-45				MURDER	POL.
HERTL	162651	M	Ger.		Pvt., 10. SS Panz.Div., 86.Panz.Rgt., Revin (Fr.) 12.-13.6.44				MURDER	FR.
HERTLEIN	137471	M			Lt.Col., 19.SS Polizei Rgt., 2.Bn. near Vigaun? (Yugo.) 5.41-3.44				MURDER	U.S.
HERTRICH, Robert Anton	133354	M	Ger.		Chief-gendarm, Gendarmerie, Bergoberbach (Ger.) 16.3.45				WITNESS	U.S.
HERTSCH, Walter	98849	M	Ger.	05	Sgt., Gestapo, Briey (Fr.)				MISC.CRIMES	FR.
HERTSCH	254797	M	Ger.		Cpl., Gestapo, 338.Div.Heeres-Unteroffizierschule, La Bresse (Fr.) 9.,11.44				MURDER	FR.
HIRTSCHEK, Francois	254058	M	Ger.	6. 7.25	Pvt., 13.Coy., 558.Gren.Rgt., Bruay en Artois (Fr.) 1.9.44				MURDER	FR.
HERTWIG	154364	M		10	Pvt., Army, Stalag VIII A betw.Goerlitz-Mellingen (Fr.) 2.45				TORTURE	U.K.
HERTY, Jacob	187096	M			Oscharfhr., 4.SS Totenkopf-Stuba, C.C. Dora-Nordhausen (Ger.)				TORTURE	U.S.
HERTZ, Erich	173281	M		02	Baufuehrer, Arbeits-Cmdo., C.C. Schlablau (Ger.) mid Nov.41				TORTURE	U.K.
HERTZ, Max	378	M			Feldgendarm, Feldgendarmerie, Prison, Gravenfort, 5.-7.41				TORTURE	FR.
HERTZEL	162407	M		00	Capt., Member, Army, NSDAP, C.C. Stalag IV B, 31.12.43				TORTURE	U.K.
HERTZNER, Fritz see HERZNER, Rudolf	257372									
HERTZOG	121053	M	Ger.		C.C. Ravensbrueck (Ger.) 42-45				MURDER	FR.
HERTZOG	255974	M	Ger.		Judge, military tribunal, Poitiers (Fr.) 6., 7.44				INTERR.	FR.
HERVIK see HAEVERNICK	256850									
HERWIG	173560	M		08	SS Uscharfhr., official, Gestapo, Waffen SS, Le Mans (Fr.)12.43-1.44				MURDER	FR.
HERZ	161105	M			Civ., Director of electric plant, near Gardelegen (Ger.) 10.-14.4.45				WITNESS	U.S.
HERZ, Adolf	142447	M		13	SS Oscharfhr., Waffen SS, Lublin (Pol.) 42-45				MURDER	FR.
HERZA	260853	M			SS Oscharfhr., Cmdt., C.C. Unterriexinger (Ger.) 12.44-3.45				MURDER	U.S.
HERZAN	254945	M			Dr. med., Physician, Hohenstein (Ger.)				TORTURE	U.S.
HERZBERG	142480	M			Haupttruppfuehrer, Org. Todt, C.C. Ampfing (Ger.)				MURDER	U.S.
HERZBERGER	190193	M	Ger.		Criminalrat, Gestapo, Brno (Czech.) 39-41				MURDER	CZECH.

NAME	C.R.FILE NUMBER	SEX	NATIO-NALITY	DATE OF BIRTH	RANK OCCUPATION UNIT PLACE AND DATE OF CRIME	REASON WANTED	WANTED BY
HERZENBURG	146860	M	Ger.		SS-Pz.Div."Das Reich", Rgt."Teutschland", Venerque le Vernet (Fr.) 44	MURDER	FR.
HERZIG	147317	M	Ger.		Lt., 11.Pz.Div.,Kampfgruppe "Wilde",Coy."Probst" (Fr.) 44	MURDER	FR.
HERZIG	196711	M	Ger.		Hptsturmfhr., Div."Das Reich",Pz.Rgt.2,1.Coy.,Tulle (Fr.) 9.6.44	WITNESS	FR.
HERZIG, Sepp	127100	M	Ger.		Osturmfhr., 2.Pz.Div."Das Reich", Canssades (Fr.)	MURDER	FR.
HERZNER	305063	M	Ger.		Uschfhr., SS, Slave Labour Camp, Osen (Nor.) 6.42-3.43	TORTURE	YUGO.
HERZNER, Rudolf (or HERTZNER, Fritz)	257372	M	Ger.		Sturmfhr., SS, Slave Labour Camp, Beisfjord near Narwik (Nor.) 6.42-11.42	MISC.CRIMES	YUGO.
HERZOG	379	M	Ger.		Dr., Public Prosecutor, Public Official, Prague (Czech.) 9.41-7.42	MURDER	CZECH.
HERZOG	133673	M			Kapo, Civilian, C.C., Buchenwald (Ger.)	TORTURE	U.S.
HERZOG	135221	M			SS Area of Strassenhaus, 1.45	MURDER	U.K., U.S.
HERZOG	251040	M	Ger.		Capt.,Coy.Leader, Div."Hermann Goering", 4.Parachute-Rgt., 1.Bn.,1.Coy., Helchteren, Hechtel (Bel.) 5., 11.9.44	TORTURE	BEL.
HERZOG	253706	M	Ger.		Adjudant, Calais (Fr.) 4.9.44	MURDER	FR.
HERZOG	255975	M	Ger.		Customs-Office, Lancrans (Fr.) 22.7.41	MURDER	FR.
HERZOG	258226	M	Ger.		Employee, C.C., Belsen (Ger.)	MURDER	BEL.
HERZOG	260167	M	Ger.		Master, O.T., working with the firm of Rolinger at Rognau, Slave Labour Camp, Botn near Rognau (Nor.) 8.42-3.43 and 4.43-5.45	MURDER	YUGO.
HERZOG, Franz	190550	M			N.C.O., C.C., Banfica (Yugo.) 41-45	MURDER	YUGO.
HERZOG, Friedrich	306975	M	Ger.		SS-Mann, C.C., Auschwitz (Pol.) 42-45	BRUTALITY	POL.
HERZOG, Heinrich	170554	M	Ger.	11	Oschfhr., SS, SD, Unit Koblenz, Strazzenhaus-Neuwied (Ger.)	MURDER	U.K.
HERZOG, Kate	194775	F	Ger.		C.C., Ravensbrueck (Ger.)	TORTURE	FR.
HERZOG, Pius	167818	M	Ger.		Pvt., 9.Res.Gren.Rgt.,1.Coy., Magny D'Avignon (Fr.) 18.9.44	MURDER	FR.
HERZOG, Rolf	192363	M	Ger.		Civilian, Justiz-Ministerium, Brussels (Bel.) 40-44	MURDER	BEL.
HERZUM	167177	M	Ger.		Stalag IV F, Hartmannsdorf (Ger.) 44	MURDER	FR.
HESCH, Rudolf	147075	M	Ger.		Member, Gestapo, St.Vid (Yugo.) 43	MURDER	YUGO.
HESCHE	380	M	Ger.		Osturmfhr., SS, C.C., Korgen (Nor.) 6.42-43	MURDER	YUGO.
HESCHL	253689	M	Ger.		Dr., Deputy Chief, SS medical-service, C.C.,Auschwitz-Birkenau (Pol.) 42-45	MISC.CRIMES	YUGO.
HESER (see HERAR)	306394	M	Ger.		Pvt., 1.Aufkl.Abt., 3.Coy., 2.Column, XV.Div. of the Afrika-Korps, Saint-Leger (Arlon) (Bel.) 5.9.44	MISC.CRIMES	BEL.
HESKEL (see HESS)	133674						
HESLER	139800	M		00	Lt., Waffen-SS, C.C., Auschwitz (Pol.) /.43	MURDER	U.S.
HESMER, Julius	256826	M		15	Zugwachtmstr., 7.Coy., 322.Bn., 5.Schuetz.Res., Ljubljana, Cetjeani Krany (Yugo.) 42, 43	MISC.CRIMES	YUGO.
HESPER (or HESTER)	149272	M			Lt., Police, Riga (Latv.)	MURDER	FR.
HESS	1999	M	Ger.		Asst., Naval-Supply	MURDER	U.K.
HESS	39809	M	Ger.		Dr., Sturmmann, SS, 7.Pz.Gren.Div."G.v.B.", Sturmgeschuetz-Abt.17 or Panz.Jaeg.Abt.17, Segre-Renaze (Fr.)	MURDER	FR.
HESS	124373	M			Lt., Army, SS, 12.Pz.Div., 25.SS-Rgt., 3.Bn., 6.Coy., Krinkelt-Rocherath, 17.12.44	MURDER	U.S.
HESS	125475	M	Ger.		Sgt., Conc.Camp, (Ger.) 8.40	TORTURE	U.K.
HESS (or HESKEL)	133674	M			Hptschfhr., SS, Conc.Camp, Buchenwald (Ger.)	TORTURE	U.S.
HESS	134000	M			Dr., Public-Official,Oberlandrat, Jihlava Iglau (Czech.)	MURDER	CZECH.
HESS	142969	M			Guard, Army, Stalag 9 B (Ger.) 7.43-8.43	TORTURE	U.S.
HESS	162932	M		15	Lt., Airforce, Flak-Rgt.46, Dorsten (Ger.) 15.10.44	TORTURE	U.S.
HESS	187098	M			Uschfhr., 4.SS-Totenkopf-Stuba., C.C.Dora, Nordhausen (Ger.) 43-45	TORTURE	U.S.
HESS	188966	M			Agent, Gestapo of Melun, Fontainebleau (Fr.) 24.8.43	TORTURE	FR.
HESS	190192	M	Ger.		Police-Inspector, Gestapo, Admin.Section, Brno (Czech.) 39-45	MURDER	CZECH.
HESS	193201	M			6.Coy., Inf.Rgt.357 (Nor.) 41	WITNESS	NOR.
HESS, Friedrich Wilhelm	197729	M			SS-Pvt., C.C., Buchenwald (Ger.)	TORTURE	U.S.
HESS, Fritz	24965	M			SS-Sgt., 20.Estonina SS-Freiw.Div.	TORTURE	U.S.
HESS, Hans	140896	M	Ger.		Funkmeister, Verbindungsstab 331, 2.Coy., Boines (Neth.) 8.5.45	MURDER	NETH.
HESS, Hermann	186474	M	Ger.		Gend., Feldgend., Trupp 626, Peronne Licourt (Fr.) 24.8.44	MURDER	FR.
HESS, Josef	174208	M	Ger.		SS-Guard, C.C., Muehldorf-Ampfing (Ger.) 6.44-4.45	MURDER	U.S.
HESS, Josef	253045	M	Ger.		Rottfhr., SS, 1.Coy., 1.SS-Pz.Rgt., 1.SS-Pz.Div., L.SS "A.Hitler", Malmedy (Bel.) 17.12.44	MURDER	U.S.
HESS, Josef	256570	M	Ger.		Hptfeldw., Airforce, Abergement De Varey (Fr.) 25.7.44	MURDER	FR.
HESS, Joseph	259963	M	Ger.		Schfhr., SS, Judge, Member, Gestapo, Poitiers Area (Fr.) 40-44	MISC.CRIMES	FR.
HESS, Philipp	257237	M	Ger.	22.1.94	Merchant, Civilian, Crim., Luxembourg (Lux.) 40-44	SUSPECT	LUX.
HESS, Ursel (see HEP)	301689						
HESS, Walter	174242	M	Ger.	18	Sgt., Army, Inf.Rgt.87, Mailloy le Camp (Fr.) 23.4.44	MURDER	U.S.
HESS, Wilhelm	174245	M	Ger.		Gend., Feldgend., Lochine (Fr.) 7.44-8.44	MURDER	FR.
HESSE	381	M	Ger.		Public-Official, Stellvertreter des Regierungspraesidenten (Warthe-land) (Pol.) 9.39-1.42	MURDER	POL.
HESSE	24946	M			Sgt., C.C., Weimar (Ger.) 40	TORTURE	U.K.
HESSE (or HESSER, ESSE)	62261	M			Capt., Army, 12.V.G.Div., 27.Fues.Rgt.,3.Coy., Petite Langville (Bel.) 1.45	MISC.CRIMES	U.S.
HESSE	179479	M	Ger.	85	Oschfhr., SS, C.C., Buchenwald (Ger.)	WITNESS	U.S.
HESSE	189621	M	Ger.		Oschfhr., Geh.Feldpolizei, SD, Area Lyonnaise (Fr.)	MISC.CRIMES	FR.
HESSE	253043	F	Ger.		Oberaufseherin, C.C., Oranienburg (Ger.)	TORTURE	BEL.
HESSE	254349	M	Ger.		Hptsturmfhr., SS, Chief,Abt.III Crim.cases,Staff-Coy.,Landsturm, Tiel (Neth.) 3.45-4.45	PILLAGE	NETH.
HESSE	301173	M	Ger.		Hptsturmfhr., Staff-Coy.,Landst.Nederland-Rgt.,Head of Section III, Provost-Marshal (penal Cases) Gelderland-Utrecht (Neth.) 45	PILLAGE	NETH.
HESSE, Alfred	174983	M	Ger.	14.4.02	Cpl., Prison, C.C., Vannes (Fr.) 42-44	TORTURE	FR.
HESSE, August	129775	M	Ger.	10	Ortsbauernfhr., Member, NSDAP, Rittergut Tuengeda nr.Gotha (Ger.)8.5.45	TORTURE	U.S.
HESSE, Fritz	140851	M	Ger.	6.12.98	Dr., Journalist, Public-Official, Foreign-Office	WITNESS	U.K.
HESSE, Karl Hans	257314	M	Ger.	24.1.14	Chief-Asst., Gestapo, Tabor Bohemia (Czech.) 40-45	MISC.CRIMES	CZECH.
HESSE, Kurt	127373	M	Ger.		Gren.(Pvt.), Inf.Rgt.815, 8.Coy., C.C., Buchenwald (Ger.) 8.44	MURDER	U.S.
HESSE, Walter	24966	M			Pvt., Army, Chabrehez (Bel.) 11.2.45	MURDER	U.S.
HESSEL	189456	M	Ger.		Lt., Ordnungspolizei, Enschede (Neth.) 9.44-3.45	MURDER	NETH.
HESSELMANN	57760	M			Oberst, Camp Army, C.C., Koenigsstein-Elbe (Ger.)	WITNESS	FR.
HESSELSCHMIDT	130366	M	Ger.		Oberfeldw., Army, Chievers (Bel.) 2.9.44	PILLAGE	BEL.
HESSER (see HESSE)	62261						
HESSERER, Joseph	10095	M	Ger.		Pvt., Army, Albine (Fr.) 29.6.44	MURDER	FR.

HES-HEY

NAME	C.R.FILE NUMBER	SEX	NATIO-NALITY	DATE OF BIRTH	RANK OCCUPATION UNIT PLACE AND DATE OF CRIME	REASON WANTED	WANTED BY
HESSHAUS, Mathias	173288	M	Ger.		Oschfhr.,SS,C.C.Halbau (Ger.)	MURDER	POL.
HESSLER	382	M	Ger.		Hptschfhr.,SS,Arbeitsdienstfuehrer,C.C.Oswiecim,Birkenau, Rajsko (Pol.)6.40 - 43	MURDER	POL.BEL.
HESSLER	125145	M	Ger.	27. 3.98	Camp-Commander (SA-Osturmfhr.,C.C.Auschwitz (Pol.) 42-45	MURDER	U.S.
HESSLER	130656	M			Osturmfhr.,SS,C.C.Dora Mittelbau (Ger.)	MURDER	U.S.
HESSLER	173596	M	Ger.	95	Osturmfhr.,Waffen-SS,C.C.Oswiecim,Birkenau (Pol.) 39-45	MURDER	POL.CZECH. BEL.YUGO.
HESSLING, Georg	305015	M	Ger.		Charge of children in Velpke Clinic (Ger.) 5.-12.44	MURDER	U.K.
HESSMAN	156513	M	Ger.		Usturmfhr.,2 SS-Pz.Div."Das Reich",Tulle	MURDER	U.S.
HESTER (see HESPER)	149272						
HET (see HOT)	29801						
HETKAMPF	174984	M	Ger.	15	Sgt.,Stalag XIII D,Kommando 1600,C.C.Nuernberg (Ger.) 44	TORTURE	U.S.
HETT	119438	M	Ger.		Major,Army,20 Geb.Div.,3 Jg.Bn.,8 Coy.,Finmark (Nor.) 44	MURDER	NOR.
HETT,William	10097	M	Ger.		Pvt.,Army,Pz.Gren.Regt.111,Albine (Fr.) 29.6.44	MURDER	FR.
HETTERMANN (see FLEISCHMANN, Walter)	254784						
HETTICH,Karl	306395	M	Ger.	12. 7.11	Sgt.,SS,C.C.Buchenwald (Ger.) 16.5.38-9.10.43	MURDER	BEL.
HETTIG	197740	M	Ger.		Sgt.,SS,C.C.Buchenwald (Ger.)	TORTURE	BEL.
HETTINGER, Rolf	196583	M	Ger.		Capt.,16 Coy.,2 Regt. of Brandenburg-Div.,Communanza (Ital.)15.3.44	MISC.CRIMES	U.S.
HETTLER	300776	M	Ger.		Pvt.,1 Aufkl.Abt.,3 Coy.,2 Col.,XV Div.Afrika Corps,St.Leger(Arlon)44	MISC.CRIMES	BEL.
HETZE, Horst	302026	M	Ger.		Reichsbahninspektor,employed in the Fernmeldemeisterei office at Amersfoort (Neth.) 10.44-5.45	PILLAGE	NETH.
HETZEL	174211	M			Civilian,Org.Todt,C.C.Muehldorf,Ampfing (Ger.) 6.44-4.45	MURDER	U.S.
HETZER	158616	M	Ger.		Civilian,Werdau (Ger.) 25.11.43	MISC.CRIMES	U.K.
HEUBAUM,Max	130373	M	Ger.	05	Cpl.,SS,NSDAP,31 Coy.Ebensee,C.C.Mauthausen(Aust.) 14.5.44-7.5.45	MURDER	U.S.
HEUBECK	173609	M	Ger.		Usturmfhr.,SS,C.C.Natzweiler,Struthof (Fr.) 40-44	MURDER	FR.
HEUBECK	258153	M	Ger.		Usturmfhr.,1 SS-Regt."Adolf Hitler",1.Coy.,Wanne near Stavelot(Bel.) 19.-21.12.44	MURDER	BEL.
HEUBECKER	196770	M			Lt.,Usturmfhr.,SS,1 Coy.,Ligneuville,Stoumont (Bel.) 17.-19.12.44	MURDER	U.S.
HEUBERGER (or NEUBERGER)	104881	M	Ger.	90 - 95	Osturmfhr.,or Major or Sturmbannfhr.,SS-Commander (Uffz.Training-School),Lyon (Fr.) 15.-20.8.44	MURDER	U.S.
HEUBERGER (or SCHNEEBERGER)	250244	M	Ger.		Capt.,157 Res.Inf.Div.,2 Coy.,98 Bn.,1'Ain (Fr.)10.-21.7.44	MISC.CRIMES	FR.
HEUDRICH	24993	M	Ger.		Capt.,SS,C.C.Struthof (Fr.) 42-44	TORTURE	FR.
HEUE	186491	M	Ger.	20	Osturmfhr.,SS,12 SS-Pz.Div."Hitler Jugend",near Caen (Fr.) 6.-7.44	TORTURE	CAN.
HEUER	11550	M	Ger.		Luftschutz-Offizier,Pol.,Luftschutz, 44	MISC.CRIMES	NOR.
HEUER	136260	M	Ger.		Adjudant-Chef,Feldgendarmerie,Stenay (Fr.) 5.8.44	MURDER	FR.
HEUER	162410	M	Ger.		Sgt.,Gebirgs-Corps,Alpine 5772,Vouvray,Corbonod (Fr.)Graz(Aust.)10.7.44	MURDER	FR.
HEUER	196712	M	Ger.	01	Usturmfhr.,S.D.,Maison-Lafitte (Fr.) 15.12.41-10.6.44	MISC.CRIMES	FR.
HEUER	306184	M	Ger.		Capt.,Prison Graudenz (Pol.)	MISC.CRIMES	BEL.
HEUER, August	188702	M		13	Uschfhr.,Waffen-SS, Camp Krs.St.Goar (Ger.) 29.12.44	MURDER	U.S.
HEUER, Heinz	306976	M	Ger.		Uschfhr.,SS,Political Department,C.C.Auschwitz (Pol.) 41-45	MURDER	POL.
HEUERICH, Hermann	191608	M	Ger.		Hptschfhr.,SS,C.C.Struthof,Natzweiler (Fr.)	MURDER	FR.
HEUERMANN	193200	M	Ger.		Cpl.,Kgf.Arb.Bn.190,C.C.Karasjok (Nor.) 8.43	TORTURE	NOR.
HEUFREL	255968	M	Ger.		Paymaster,Unit 38585,Army,Tuffe (Fr.) 8.8.44	WITNESS	FR.
HEUIRL	188967	M	Ger.		Civ.,Servant,Reichsbahn,Le Bourget (Fr.) 25.8.44	WITNESS	FR.
HEUKE, Siegfried	185657	M	Ger.		Hptwachtmeister,Pol.,Palleben (Ger.) 10. or 11.44	MURDER	U.S.
HEUKENSVELD	11547	M	Ger.		Pvt.,SS,Gestapo,C.C.Breda (Neth.) 42	TORTURE	NETH.
HEULL	255385	M			Civilian,Frein-Landstall (Aust.) 8.44	MURDER	U.S.
HEUMANN, Hans	195209	M	Ger.		Dr.,Direktor,Omnia Treuhand-Gesellschaft,Amsterdam,Administration Netherland (Neth.) 40-45	PILLAGE	NETH.
HEURITSCH	167802	M	Ger.		Leader,Wirtschaftsamt,Krakau (Pol.) 9.39-44	PILLAGE	POL.
HEUSCHEL	133675	M			Oschfhr.,SS,C.C.Buchenwald (Ger.)	TORTURE	U.S.
HEUSCHEL, Albert	139796	M	Ger.	15 - 30	Sgt.,Waffen-SS,Mittergars-Lager,Muhldorf (Ger.) 44-45	TORTURE	U.S.
HEUSCHEL, Paul	24967	M	Ger.		Zugwachtmeister,Pol.,official,Koblenz (Ger.)	WITNESS	U.S.
HEUSEL	39647	M	Ger.		Oberzahlmeister,Pol.,Tuffe (Fr.) 8.8.44	INTERR.	FR.
HEUSEL,Emil	254534	M	Ger.		Hptsturmfhr.,SS,S.D.Strasbourg,Beulotte,St.Laurent (Fr.)9.-10.44	MURDER	FR.
HEUSELER (or KEUSELER)	192129	M	Ger.		Capt.,Batteriechef,Dienststelle F.P.33146 B,Voesse,Alle sur Semois (Bel.) 4.9.44	PILLAGE	BEL.
HEUSER	105938	M	Ger.	93	Sgt.,Major,Prison Guard,Rheinbach bei Bonn (Ger.)	WITNESS	U.S.
HEUSER	127076	M	Ger.		Guard,C.C.Crefeld-Linn (Ger.) 28.3.45	MURDER	FR.
HEUSER	261974	M	Ger.		Dr.,leader,Gestapo,Police official,Benska,Bystrica and district (Czech.) 8.44-4.45	MURDER	CZECH.
HEUSER,Karl	130652	M			SS,C.C.Dora Mittelbau,(Ger.)	MURDER	U.S.
HEUSK	177233	M	Ger.		Kriminal-Kommissar,Gestapo,Koblenz (Ger.) 2.45	MURDER	U.S.
HEUTGES, Huber	186475	M	Ger.		Civilian,Pen-Autravu (Fr.)	MURDER	FR.
HEUTLER, Hans	175929	M	Ger.		Dienststelle F.P.No. N.R.L. L.9591 L.P.,Repel,Gironcourt sur Vraine, Poussay (Fr.) 8.-9.44	WITNESS	FR.
HEUTSCHEL,Albert (or HEUTSCHL)	139796	M	Ger.	15 - 30	Sgt.,W-SS,Mittergars-Lager,Muhldorf (Ger.) 44-45	TORTURE	U.S.
HEUTZ	139789	M		97	Cpl.,W-SS,Arbeitskdo.A-6	TORTURE	U.S.
HEUWES	162440	M	Ger.		Pvt.,Ldsschtz.-Bn.789,C.C.Sinzig (Ger.) 20.12.41	WITNESS	U.S.
HEVER	253047	M	Ger.		Sgt.,Unit "Alpine",Orbagnoux (Fr.) 10.7.44	INTERR.	FR.
HEVER,Karl	250826	M	Ger.		Guard,C.C.Lahde-Weser (Ger.)	INTERR.	BEL.
HEWEL	73675	M	Ger.		Bde.-Fuehrer,SS,	MISC.CRIMES	U.S.
HEX	162409	M	Ger.		Pvt.,Standort-Wach-Coy.,La Rochelle (Fr.) 11.2.45	MURDER	FR.
HEXE (see PETRI)	250424						
HEXEL	161968	M	Ger.	18	Cpl.,Guard,SS,Bn.,C.C.Buchenwald (Ger.)	WITNESS	U.S.
HEY	253060	M			Sturmmann,SS,C.C.Dora,Nordhausen (Ger.)	MURDER	U.S.
HEYDE	120527	M		00	Standartenfhr.,C.C. (Ger.)	MURDER	FR.
HEYDEL	167176	M	Ger.		Fieldpolice,Moulins,Larochemillay (Fr.)	MISC.CRIMES	FR.
HEYDEL	190709	M	Ger.		Pvt.,Eis.Art.Btty.717,Feldpost 22380,St.Andries,Varsenare,les Bruges (Bel.) 4.9.44	MURDER	BEL.
HEYDEN, Wilhelm	31561	M	Ger.		Lt.,Army,2 Regt.,Locmine (Fr.)	MURDER	FR.
HEYDRICH	383	M	Ger.		Cmdt.,Hptsturmfhr.,SS,C.C.Oranienburg (Ger.) 9.39-1.42	TORTURE	POL.
HEYDRICH	250242	M	Ger.		Col.Cmdt.,Commandantur,Bourg,l'Aim(Fr.)10.-21.7.44	MISC.CRIMES	FR.
HEYE	162650	M	Ger.		Adjutant,SS,86 Pz.Regt.,10 Pz.Div.,Revin (Fr.) 12.-13.6.44	MURDER	FR.
HEYE	193199	M	Ger.	05	Major,Army,Fjell (Nor.)5.44	INTERR.	NOR.
HEYE,Clemens	140868	M		94	Col.,21 Fortress Sigs Staff,Elten (Ger.) 16.9.44	MURDER	CAN.

HEY-HIL

NAME	C.R.FILE NUMBER	SEX	NATIO- NALITY	DATE OF BIRTH	RANK OCCUPATION UNIT PLACE AND DATE OF CRIME	REASON WANTED	WANTED BY
HEYERS, Berthold	334	M	Ger.		Capt.,SD.Official,Caen (Fr.) 6.44	MURDER	FR.
HEYER	254059	M	Ger.		Agent,SD.Toulouse (Fr.) 11.42-8.44	MISC.CRIMES	FR.
HEYERMANN, Herbert	167181	M	Ger.		Pvt.,Army,Plombieres (Fr.) 18.7.44	MURDER	FR.
HEYKING	137769	M			Capt.,29 Pz.Gren.Rgt.,15 Pz.Gren.Div.,3 Bn.,	WITNESS	U.S.
HEYL	188968	M	Ger.		Feldgendarmerie,Bar-le-Duc,(Fr.) 8.44	TORTURE	FR.
HEYLIGER	252188	M	Ger.		Interpreter,Sipo Abt. IV A,Brussels (Bel.)	INTERR.	BEL.
HEYMANN	98920	M	Ger.		Capt.,SS,Gestapo,Grenoble and the environs (Fr.) 43	MISC.CRIMES	FR.
HEYMANN	253700	M	Ger.		Sturmscharfhr.,Gestapo,Vieville sous les Cotes (Fr.) 4.44	TORTURE	FR.
HEYMANN, Hans	139200	M			Doctor,Civilian .	MISC.CRIMES	U.S.
HEYMANN, Hans	136242	M	Ger.		C.C.Direktor,Arb.Kdo.,C.C.	MURDER	GRC.
HEYMANS	165531	M	Ger.		Major,Army,Honville (Bel.) 12.44	MURDER	BEL.
HEYN, Adolf (or HEIN, Adolf)	250328	M	Ger.		Guard,Prison,Steinbergen (Ger.)	INTERR.	BEL.
HEYN, M.	301233	M	Ger.		Head of political Department,Brussels (Bel.) 40-44	MURDER	BEL.
HEYNE	173610	M	Ger.		Pvt.,4-635 Stalag IX,Bad Sulza (Ger.) 1.9.44	MURDER	FR.
HEYNE, Florus	152476	M	Ger.	01	Direktor,Camp Dromka,Leipzig (Ger.) 43-45	TORTURE	FR.
HEYNE, Werner	252136	M		29. 4.08	Pvt.,C.C.Ellrich-Nordhausen (Ger.)	MURDER	U.S.
HEYNEMEYER	196713	M	Ger.		Obersturmfhr.,SD. and Gestapo,Krakau (Pol.) 40-43	MISC.CRIMES	POL.
HEYNZ, Bernhard	256573	M	Ger.		Unterfhr.,SD. Calvadon,Caen (Fr.) 42	WITNESS	FR.
HEYSSMEYER, August	9683	M	Ger.		SS-Obergruppenfhr.,SS Fuehrer des Hauptamtes,Berlin (Ger.) 39-44	MURDER	CZECH.
HEZEL	250251	M	Ger.		Cmlt.,Feldpolizei,Kragujerav,Arandjelovac (Yugo.) 41	MURDER	YUGO.
HIBEL	251049	M	Ger.		Inspector,Devisen-Schutzkdo.,Amsterdam (Neth.) 12.42	PILLAGE	NETH.
HIBITZ	197730	M	Ger.		SS-Cpl.,SS,C.C.Buchenwald (Ger.)	TORTURE	U.S.
HICHTER	161970	M	Ger.		Lt.,Vercheny (Fr.) 44	MISC.CRIMES	FR.
HICKEL	257765	M			Agent,Lt.,3 Brandenburg Rgt.,	MISC.CRIMES	U.S.
HICKER, August	254061	M		9. 7.19	Pvt.,558 Gren.Rgt., 13 Coy.,Bruay en Artois (Fr.) 1.9.44	MURDER	FR.
HICKL, Rudolf	188971	M	Ger.		SS,18 Bn.,Busset (Fr.) 7.8.44	MURDER	FR.
HICKMANN	137768	M			Lt., 15 Pz.Gren.Rgt., 29 Pz.Gren.Div.,	WITNESS	U.S.
HIDDING,B.P.	189051	M			Civilian,Bain Clair (Neth.) 7.7.44	WITNESS	U.S.
HIEBL	39810	M	Ger.		SS-Schuetze,SS,17 Pz.Gren.Div.,"G.v.B.",Pz.Gren.Jg.Abt.,17 Maine-et-Loire,Mayenne (Fr.) 30.7.44 - 8.44	MURDER	FR.
HIEBSCH, Oscar	255581	M	Ger.	24. 7.03	Agent,Gestapo,Cesce Budejovice (Czech.) 39-45	TORTURE	CZECH.
HIEDMANN	39811	M	Ger.		Officer, chief of the German troops quartered in the Boarding-School for girls at Dax 48624 (Fr.) 13.6.44	MURDER	FR.
HIEGE, Ferdinand	211353	M	Ger.		Obersturmfhr.,High official of Commissariat for German Racialism.	TORTURE	UNWCC.
HIEMANN	253712	M	Ger.		Capt.,C.C.Flamersheim (Ger.)	TORTURE	U.S.
HIENTZ	146859	M	Ger.		Sturmmann,SS-Pz.Div.,"Das Reich",13 Coy.,Moissac (Fr.) 44	MURDER	FR.
HIEROMYMYS	119439	M	Ger.		Capt.,SS-Geb.Div. Nord,20 Army,4-6 Geb.Art.Rgt., 44	MURDER	NOR.
HIERONYMUS	251602	M			SS-Unterscharfhr.,SS,C.C.Dora-Nordhausen (Ger.)	MURDER	U.S.
HIERONYMUS, Hans	146696	M	Ger.	97	Gemeinschaftsleiter,NSDAP,Daensbach (Ger.) 43-45	MISC.CRIMES	U.S.
HIERCEMANN	134002	M			Doctor,Public-Official,Justice Regierungsrat,Prag (Czech.) 39-45	MURDER	CZECH.
HIERTHES, Heino	161973	M	Ger.	95	Col.,SS-Buchenwald (Ger.) 39	WITNESS	U.S.
HIENER	253035	M			Lt.,Garrison Commander,Nereziace on the island of Brac (Yugo.) 44	PILLAGE	YUGO.
HIKADO, Josef	195364	M	Ger.	17.12.11	Employee,Gestapo Official,Velky Ujezd,Prestavlky,Zarkov (Czech.) 4.45	MURDER	CZECH.
HILBACH (see HILBICH)	253710	M					
HILBACKER, Peter	177235	M			Town Construction Foreman,Krispl (Aust.) 44	WITNESS	U.S.
HILBERT	62263	M		23	SS-Cpl.,1 SS-Pz.Div., 1 Rgt., 1 Coy., Malmedy (Bel.)	MURDER	U.S.
HILBERS	140865	M			Capt.,C.O., 3 Coy., 17 Parachute Rgt., Xanten (Ger.) 8.3.45	MURDER	CAN.
HILBICH (or HILBACH)	253710	M	Ger.		Commandant,Army,Feldpolizei,Bajina-Basta (Yugo.) 15.11.43	MURDER	YUGO.
HILBIG	305065	M	Ger.		Lt.,Army,Brandenburg Rgt., Mayor of Levadia (Grc.) 9.12.43	MURDER	GRC.
HILBING	305181	M	Ger.		Capt.,Engineer,Naval Base of Salonike,Katirli,Kalamaria-Sal (Grc.) 10.9.44	MURDER	GRC.
HILBINGER, Egon	173611	M	Ger.	02	Civilian,C.C.Neckarelz (Ger.) 45	TORTURE	FR.
HILBRAND	194585	M			Pvt.,Feldgendarmerie,Ploermel (Fr.) 18.6.44	TORTURE	FR.
HILBURG, Edmund	105939	M	Ger.	06	Gestapo,H.Q.Ahlen,C.C.Seelhorst (Ger.) 6.4.45	MURDER	U.S.
HILBURG, Egon	132325	M	Ger.		SS-Oberscharfhr.,	TORTURE	U.S.
HILD, Fritz	133676	M			SS-Unterscharfhr.,C.C.Buchenwald (Ger.)	TORTURE	U.S.
HILDBRAND	141566	M	Ger.		Commandant, SS,Langeac,Pinols,Auvers (Fr.) 6.44	TORTURE	FR.
HILDE	24989	M			Capt.,SS-Div.,"Adolf Hitler",Odet (Bel.) 4.9.44	MURDER	U.S.
HILDEBRAND	387	M	Ger.		SS-Polizei,, Danzig (Pol.) 9.39 - 43	MURDER	POL.
HILDEBRAND	142988	M	Ger.		Cpl.,Waffen-SS,2 Pz.Gren.Rgt.,3 Bn., 12.Coy., 1 SS-Pz.Div.,Stavelot- Malmedy (Bel.) 23.12.44	MURDER	U.S.
HILDEBRAND	189345	M	Ger.		Commandant, SS,Langeac,Pinols (Fr.) 10.-16.6.44	MURDER	FR.
HILDEBRAND	190708	M	Ger.		Pvt.,Eis.Art.Btty. 717,F.P. 22980,St.Andries,Varsenare-lez-Bruges (Bel.) 4.9.44	MURDER	BEL.
HILDEBRAND	254940	M	Ger.	10	Officer,School of scholar,Dijon,Nievre (Fr.) 26.-28.4.41	MISC.CRIMES	FR.
HILDEBRAND, Friedrich	193296	M	Ger.		Police-Guard, Police CC,Frankfurt-Main,Preumgesheim (Ger.) 10.44	TORTURE	U.K.
HILDEBRAND, Herman	259920	M	Ger.		Criminal-Employee,Gestapo of Bruenn,Leakovec,Moravia (Czech.)12.4.45	MURDER	CZECH.
HILDEBRAND, Karl	386	M	Ger.	1. 2.02	SS-Unterscharfhr.,C.C.Maidanek (Pol.) 40-4.44	MURDER	POL.
HILDEBRANDT	251589	M			SS-Untersturmfhr.,C.C.Dora-Nordhausen (Ger.)	MURDER	U.S.
HILDEBRANDT	253031	M	Ger.		Attached to dept. Travel and Deportation (Bel.)	MISC.CRIMES	BEL.
HILDEBRANDT, Bruno	142986	M	Ger.		Gemeinschaftslager,Weferlingen (Ger.)	TORTURE	U.S.
HILDEBRANDT, F.	118810	M	Ger.		Gauleiter and Obergruppenfhr.,SS, Mecklenburg(Ger.)	TORTURE	UNWCC.
HILDEBRANDT, Friedrich	118810	M	Ger.		Gauleiter,NSDAP,Pingelshagen (Ger.) 21.6.44	MURDER	U.S.
HILDEBRANDT, Gerhard	262260	M	Ger.	27. 3.	SS-Oberscharfhr.,Gestapo,Rennes (Fr.) 43-44	MISC.CRIMES	FR.
HILDEBRANDT, Hans	253679	M	Ger.	12	Chief,Gestapo,Alencon (Fr.) 40-44	MISC.CRIMES	FR.
HILDEBRANDT, Karl	24870	M	Ger.		Pvt.,Paratrooper,Roermond (Neth.) 11.44-1.45	TORTURE	U.S.
HILDEBRANDT, Richard	21313	M	Ger.		Doctor,Pvt.,SS-Police Gren.Head of SS,	MURDER	UNWCC.
HILDEBRANDT, Walter	254354	M	Ger.	86	Farmer,Hasselfeld (Ger.) 3. or 4.45	MURDER	UNWCC.
HILDEBRANT	185704	M	Ger.		Hauptwachtmeister, Oflag,C.C.Ebrach (Ger.)	MURDER	FR.
HILDEBRECHT	162844	M	Ger.		Chief,Feldgendarmerie,Vielsalm (Bel.) 44	PILLAGE	BEL.
HILDEMANN, Fritz	305786	M	Ger.		Oberscharfhr.,SS,Truckdriver,Noailles,Oise (Fr.) 9.8.44	MURDER	U.K.
HILER, Adolf	255117	M	Ger.		Cpl.,377 Jg.Rgt.,Vinkt (Bel.)	MISC.CRIMES	BEL.
HILGEMANN, Ludwig	254062	M	Ger.	26. 6.10	Pvt.,13 Coy., 558 Gren.Rgt., Bruay en Artois (Fr.) 1.9.44	MURDER	FR.

NAME	C.R.FILE NUMBER	SEX	NATIO- NALITY	DATE OF BIRTH	RANK OCCUPATION UNIT PLACE AND DATE OF CRIME	REASON WANTED	WANTED BY
HILGENFELDT, Erich	21348	M	Ger.		SS-Gruppenfhr.,NSDAP,Dept.for Public Welfare	TORTURE	UNWCC.
HILGENSTCHLER, Gottlieb	161975	M	Ger.		Uschfhr.,SS,Gestapo,Saone et Loire(Fr.) 43-44	MURDER	FR.
HILGENSTCHLER, Gustave	161974	M			Uschfhr.,SS,Gestapo,Dun les Places	MURDER	FR.
HILGER	135182	M	Ger.		Konsul,Public Official,Councillor Ger. 43	TORTURE	U.S.
HILGER or HILKER, Heinrich	173172			05	Gestapo Strassburg,Moussey(Fr.) 7.-9.44	MURDER	U.K.
HILGERS, Alex	187011	M			Civilian,C.C.Merkstein,Adolf Mine(Ger.) 6.44	MURDER	U.S.
HILGERT	39812	M	Ger.		SS-Rottfhr.,SS-Div.Feldpost No.48963B,Portmisson,Chateau Gontier, St.Sulpice,Laval(Fr.) 6.8.44	MURDER	FR.
HILKER, August	305422	M	Ger.	19	83 Regt.,13 Coy.,558 Gren.Regt.,Bruay-en-Artois,Pas-de-Calais (Fr.) 1.9.44	MURDER	FR.
HILKER, Heinrich see HILGER	173172						
HILL, George	135175	M	Ger.	15	Sgt.,Wehrmacht,Rupperschutten(Ger.) 12.9.44	WITNESS	U.S.
HILL, Sis	169796	M		1.12.20	Uschfhr.,Waffen-SS,C.C.Natzweiler(Fr.) 43-44	MURDER	FR.
HILLE	188703	M	Ger.		Bde.-Fhr.,SS,Wiesbaden,Coblenz,Metz(Ger.,Fr.) 44	SUSPECT	U.S.
HILLE	192136	M	Ger.		Sgt.,Geheime Feldpolizei,Bruessels(Bel.)	WITNESS	BEL.
HILLE	306086	M	Ger.		Hptschfhr.,SS,C.C.Hamburg-Neuengamme(Ger.) -45	MURDER	CZECH.
HILLE, Kurt	251590	M			Cpl.,C.C.Ellrich-Nordhausen(Ger.)	MURDER	U.S.
HILLE, Louis	138919	M	Ger.	20. 3.86	Ortsgruppenleiter NSDAP,Gladebeek(Ger.)	MURDER	UNWCC.
HILLE, Raimond	251591	M		28.12.96	Uschfhr.,SS,C.C.Harzungen-Nordhausen(Ger.)	MURDER	U.S.
HILLE, Susanne	186671	F	Ger.	23	SS,Vuterluss(Ger.)	TORTURE	U.K.
HILLE, Walter	988	M	Ger.		Orpo,Police,Mbj.-Gen.,Wartheland(Pol.) 6.40-43	MURDER	POL.
HILLEBRAND, Hans	257535	M	Ger.		Sonderfhr.,Abwehr Northern,Tromsoe(Nor.) 11.44	WITNESS	NOR.
HILLEBRAND, Wilhelm	195472	M	Ger.	90	Agent,Gestapo,SD,Issel-Ehrang(Ger.)	WITNESS	U.S.
HILLEBRANDT	161972	M	Ger.	10	Uschfhr.,SS-Wirtschaftsverwaltungshauptamt,Ohrdruf,Buchenwald(Ger.) 39-45	MISC.CRIMES	U.S.
HILLEBRANDT, Hermann	190291	M	Ger.		Guard,Gestapo,Brno(Czech.) 39-45	TORTURE	CZECH.
HILLEN	251614	M			Major,C.C.Dora-Nordhausen(Ger.)	MURDER	U.S.
HILLENBRAND, Peter	10098	M	Ger.		Pvt.,Army,Pz.Gren.Regt.111,Albine(Fr.) 29.6.44	MURDER	FR.
HILLER	185453	M	Ger.		Pvt.,Waffen-SS,1 Pz.Div."A.Hitler",1 SS-Pz.Recon.Bn.,Parfondruy Stavelot(Bel.) 18.-22.12.44	MURDER	U.S.
HILLER	188370	M			Kriminalkommissar,Stapostelle,Frankfurt-M.(Ger.) 5.43	MISC.CRIMES	U.K.
HILLER	197731	M			SS-Mann,SS II Zug,I Gruppe,Stavelot(Bel.) 19.-20.12.44	MURDER	BEL.
HILLER	259680	M			Sgt.,Milit.Garrison Moulin des Ponts,Villemotier(Fr.) 19.8.44	INTERR.	FR.
HILLER	302027	M			Uschfhr.,Member SS,SD,Zwolle(Neth.) 1.-3.45	TORTURE	NETH.
HILLER, Karl	195208	M			Member SD,Sonder-u.Wirtsch.Kdo.,Beeck,Gorssel(Neth.) 23.-24.9.44	MURDER	NETH.
HILLER, Theo	194900	M			Studienrat,Occupied Territories (Lux.)	MISC.CRIMES	LUX.
HILLERMANN, H.	146770	M			Administration Official,C.C.Esterwegan(Ger.) 39-45	TORTURE	NETH.
HILLET	137034	M	Ger.		Lt.,192 Pz.Gren.,9-10 Coy.,CO.,Sessenheim(Fr.) 1.45	MURDER	U.S.
HILLIBRANDT	259825	M			Capt.,Recearo Terme(Ital.) 10.1.45	INTERR.	U.S.
HILLIG or HILLISCH	257536	M		96	Truppfhr.,O.T.,C.C.Muehldorf(Ger.)	MURDER	U.S.
HILLIG, Fritz	262257	M	Ger.	30. 8.19	SS-Hptsturmfhr.,51 SS armoured Bde.,Breviandes,Bucheres,St.Savine, La Riviera de Corps,Troyes(Fr.) 22.-25.8.44	BRUTALITY	FR.
HILLIG, Horst	191998	M			Uschfhr.,1 Pz.Regt.,Ligneuville Stoumont(Bel.) 17.-19.12.44	MURDER	U.S.
HILLIG, Karl	188161	M	Ger.		Chief Paymaster,Army,Bruchsal(Ger.) 2.-3.2.45	MURDER	U.S.
HILLING, Karl or HILLINGER	255269	M	Ger.		Paymaster,Bruchsal(Ger.) 2.-3.2.45	MURDER	U.S.
HILLISCH	142479	M	Ger.		Truppfhr.,SA.Ampfing(Ger.)	MURDER	U.S.
HILLISCH see HILLIG	257536						
HILLMER	146858	M	Ger.		Pvt.,SS-Pz.Div."Das Reich",2 Coy.,Tulle(Fr.) 44	MURDER	FR.
HILLSMAN	259064	M			Dulag Luft Hospital,Suspect was first aid man at the Hospital, Dulag Luft(Ger.) 43-45	BRUTALITY	U.S.
HILLZATT	157750	M	Ger.		Cpl.,Wehrmacht Arb.-Kdo.10620-G.W.,Klagenfurt(Aust.) 23.11.43	TORTURE	U.K.
HILMER	185705	M	Ger.		Osturmfhr.,SS,Gambsheim(Fr.)	MURDER	FR.
HILMER	250899	M			Pvt.,Pepingen(Bel.) 2.-9.44	WITNESS	BEL.
HILPRIT, Siegfried	171968	M	Ger.		Usturmfhr.,Allg.SS,C.C.Mauthausen(Aust.)	MISC.CRIMES	U.S.
HILPERT	167204	M	Ger.		Hptsturmfhr.,SS,Subordinate Officer Deportation Trains from France to Germany,Royallieu(Fr.) 41-44	MURDER	FR.
HILPERT	185970	M	Ger.		Cpl.,Army,Regensburg(Ger.) 41-45	TORTURE	U.S.
HILPERT	305870	M	Ger.		Feldgend.,Avenue Plantin Moretus,Antwerpen(Bel.) 22.10.42	MURDER	BEL.
HILPERT, Karl	258961	M	Ger.	88	Lt.-Gen.	WITNESS	U.S.
HILPERT, Werner	161971	M	Ger.	95	Civilian,Buchenwald(Ger.) 38-45, Dr.	MISC.CRIMES	U.S.
HILPRECHT	306978	M	Ger.		Working at the Aussenstelle des Reichsministers fuer Bewaffnung und Munition,Krs.Groningen,Frieslend,Drente,Meppel(Neth.) 9.44	PILLAGE	NETH.
HILSEMAN	194774	M	Ger.		Lt.-Col.,Army,Ambuis(Fr.) 31.8.44	MURDER	FR.
HILT, Karl	262151	M	Ger.	19. 6.18	SS-Oschfhr.,Chief,8 Coy.,51 SS Armoured Platoon,Chasers Platoon K.N. Number 2,Breviandes,Bucheres,Ste Savine,La Riviera de Corps,Troyes (Fr.) 22.-25.8.44	BRUTALITY	FR.
HILTNER	186679	M			Pvt.,Army,Arb.-Kdo.,Regensburg(Ger.) 41-45	TORTURE	U.S.
HILTSCHER, Wilhelm	193910	M	Ger.	12.10.87	Police Official,Dvur Kralove(Czech.)	MISC.CRIMES	CZECH.
HILZ	132717	M	Ger.		Capt.,Standortkommandantur,Gerarömer(Fr.) 9.-11.44	MISC.CRIMES	FR.
HIMES	190343	M			Civilian,Merdendorf(Ger.) 44	TORTURE	U.S.
HIMMEL	306119	M	Ger.		Sturmfhr.SS.Serving with BSD,Abt.VI S,Copenhagen(Den.) 1.44	PILLAGE	DEN.
HIMMELMANN see NIMMELINE	301697						
HIMMELSBACH, Peter	258991	M			Guard,C.C.Ohrdruf(Ger.) 12.44-4.45	MURDER	U.S.
HIMMER	194773	F	Ger.		Guard,C.C.Ravensbrueck(Ger.)	TORTURE	FR.
HIMMLER	62264	M	Ger.		SS,KL,Buchenwald(Ger.)	MISC.CRIMES	U.S.
HIMMLER	167205	M	Ger.		Capt.,deputy Chief,Public Official Gestapo,Lyon-Rhone(Fr.) 42-43	MURDER	FR.
HIMMLER	251598	M			Pvt.,C.C.Dora-Nordhausen(Ger.)	MURDER	U.S.
HIMMLER, Heinrich	260971	M	Ger.		Member SS,C.C.Vaihingen(Ger.) 13.8.44-7.4.45	MURDER	U.S.
HIMMLICH	142974	M	Ger.		Sgt.,SS-Totenkopf-Div.,Waffen-SS,C.C.Riga(Latv.) 41-43	MURDER	U.S.
HIMMER, William	142985	M	Ger.		Civilian,C.C.Frankenberg(Ger.) 20.3.45	MURDER	U.S.
HIMPERLICH, Karl	162402	M	Ger.	21	Uschfhr.,1 SS Panz.Div.,Feldgend.,Weissenbach(Aust.) 12.4.45	MURDER	U.S.
HIMPKAMP, Bruno	142990	M			Civilian (Russ.)	WITNESS	U.S.
HIMPINGER	257537	M	Ger.		Gendarm,Gend.,Ingersheim(Fr.) 9.1.44	MISC.CRIMES	FR.
HINCKE see HINKE	256092						

HIN-HIR

NAME	C.R.FILE NUMBER	SEX	NATIO-NALITY	DATE OF BIRTH	RANK OCCUPATION UNIT PLACE AND DATE OF CRIME	REASON WANTED	WANTED BY
HINDORF, Oskar	154374	M			Policeman, Police, Wallrode (Ger.) 7.44	TORTURE	U.S.
HINDRICHS, Helen	174213	F			Interpreter and clerk, Working-camp C.C. Muhldorf-Ampfing (Ger.) 6.44-4.45	MURDER	U.S.
HING or RING	136284	M			Cpl.,11 Pz.Div.	MURDER	FR.
HINGHOLZ, Johann	187285	M	Ger.		Sturmscharfhr.,Crimsecr.,SS, Gestapo, Brno (Czech.) 39-45	MURDER	CZECH.
HINGST	259364	M	Ger.		Uscharfhr.,active Member of Gestapo,Poitiers Area (Fr.) 40-44	MISC.CRIMES	FR.
HINIHORTH, Wiastans	167817	M	Ger.		Pvt.,9 Res.Gren.Rgt.,2 Coy, M.G.-Schtz.,Magny d'Anigon (Fr.)18.9.44	MURDER	FR.
HINK see HINKE	256092						
HINKE or HINCKE or HINK	256092	M	Ger.		Osturmfhr.,SS,Comm.of the writeroom,probably Meerveld (Neth.)11.44	MURDER	NETH.
HINKEL, Erich	133358	M		09	Sgt., Waffen-SS, Gestapo, Winterkasten (Ger.) 18.3.45	MURDER	U.S.
HINKEL, Hans	167800	M	Ger.		Sondertreuhaender, administration of Poland (Wartheland-Pol.)9.39-44	PILLAGE	POL.
HINKEL, Paul	10099	M	Ger.		N.C.O., Pz.Gren.Rgt.110, Albine (Fr.) 29.6.44	MURDER	FR.
HINKELMANN	146683				Oscharfhr.,SS,/Dora-Gardelegen (Ger.) 4.-14.4.45	MURDER	U.S.
HINKELMANN	9686	M	Ger.		Hptscharfhr.,SS, C.C. Buchenwald (Ger.) 39-42	TORTURE	U.S.,CZECH.
HINKELMANN	186672				Hptscharfhr., SS, Natzweiler (Fr.) 5.41	TORTURE	U.S.
HINKELMANN, Eduard	143021	M	Ger.		Hptscharfhr.,Waffen-SS,Totenkopf Standarte,C.C. Buchenwald(Ger.)39-41	TORTURE	U.S.
HINKELMANN, Erich	161977	M	Ger.	06	Sgt.,SS Totenkopf,Buchenwald (Ger.) 39-41	TORTURE	U.S.
HINKELMANN, Karl	31937	M	Ger.		Dr.,Oberlandgerichts-Dir.,Public official,Opava (Czech.) 21.2.40	MURDER	CZECH.
HINNEMANN	10100	M	Ger.		Sgt.,3 Gruppe,110 or 111 Pz.Ren.Rgt.,Gourdon(Fr.) 29.6.44	MURDER	FR.
HINRICHE	24975	M	Ger.		Scharfhr., SS, C.C. Natzweiler-Struthof (Fr.) 42-43	MURDER	FR.
HINRICHS	255118	M	Ger.		Lt.,377 Jg.Rgt., Unit F.P.30305 D, Vinkt (Bel.)	MISC.CRIMES	BEL.
HINRICHSEN	306979	F	Ger.		Guard, SS, C.C. Auschwitz (Pol.)	BRUTALITY	POL.
HINRINCKS, Karl	194584	M	Ger.		Civilian, merchant, Machine of agriculture,Augustfehn(Ger.)18.7.44	MURDER	U.K.
HINS or HINZ	256574	M	Ger.		Employee, SD, Region de Pontivy (Fr.) 44	MISC.CRIMES	FR.
HINSCH, Karlheinz	306394	M	Ger.	31. 1.25	Pvt.,SS, C.C. Buchenwald (Ger.) between 16.5.38 and 9.10.43	MURDER	BEL.
HINSEN	119440	M	Ger.		Dr.,Oberstabsarzt, 20 Army 4 B,169 Inf.Div., Finmark(Nor.)	MURDER	NOR.
HINSER	128846	M	Ger.		Arbeits-Kdo.771, Niesse (Ger.) 6.44-2.45	TORTURE	U.K.
HINSTORFF	301890	M	Ger.		Dr.,Landgerichtsrat, Litomerice (Czech.) 21.2.40	BRUTALITY	CZECH.
HINTEIBEIN	125736	M	Ger.		Sgt.,Gr.751,8 Coy,326 Inf.Div., Boulogne (Fr.) 5.44	MURDER	U.K.
HINTEREGGER, Gerhardt	254307	M	Ger.		Dir.,Fa.Hinteregger, Paris (Fr.) 41-44	PILLAGE	FR.
HINTEREGGER, Robert	254627	M	Ger.		Dir.,Fa.Hinteregger, Paris (Fr.) 41-44	PILLAGE	FR.
HINTERREGER nee BRUNNER Francesca	305066	F			Civilian, Fa.Hinterreger, Muenich, Paris, (Fr.) 41-8.44	PILLAGE	FR.
HINTERREGER, Richard	305067	M	Ger.		Civilian,Fa.Hinterreger, Muenich, Paris (Fr.) 41-8.44	PILLAGE	FR.
HINTERMEIER	149328	M	Ger.	05	Osturmbannfhr.,SS, C.C. Dachau (Ger.) 44-45	MURDER	FR.
HINTRINGER, Karl	195426	M	Ger.		Crim.secr., Gestapo, Moravska,Ostrova,Vsetin (Czech.) 39-45	MISC.CRIMES	CZECH.
HINTZ	254063	M	Ger.		Gendarm, Gend.Romorantin 577,Orcay (Fr.) 8.8.44	MISC.CRIMES	FR.
HINTZ, Helmuth	306794	M	Ger.		Cpl.,7 Coy of Rutzko Bn 896 R.I.,Kermessenetin,Kervignac,Morbihan (Fr.) 20.8.44	MURDER	FR.
HINTZ, Johann	192791	M	Ger.		Schupo, C.C. Stalag Trondheim,Falstad (Nor.) 41-45	TORTURE	NOR.
HINTZE	190551				Sgt.,SS, Gestapo, C.C. Banfica,Belgrad (Yugo.) 41-45	MURDER	YUGO.
HINTZELMANN	126745	M	Ger.	90	Fuehrer der Org.Todt, C.C. Camiers (Fr.) 43-44	TORTURE	FR.
HINZ	39814				Uscharfhr.,SS,17 Pz.Gren.Div. "G.v.B.",Sturm-Gesch.Abt.17 or Pz.Jg.Abt.17, Segre-Renaze (Fr.) 30.7.44,6.8.44	MURDER	FR.
HINZ	165532	M	Ger.		Lt., Army, Lutrebois (Bel.) 31.12.44	WITNESS	BEL.
HINZ see HINS	256574						
HINZ, Bruno	251599	M			Rottenfhr.,SS, C.C. Ellrich-Nordhausen (Ger.)	MURDER	U.S.
HINZ, Karl	132708	M	Ger.		Chore-master, foreman, Org.Todt,C.C.Ls.Auvigny (Fr.) 43-44	TORTURE	FR.
HINZ, Paul	262199	M	Ger.	2.10.?	Uscharfhr.,SS, Gestapo, Rennes (Fr.) 43-44	INTERR.	FR.
HINZE	24971	M	Ger.	07	SS-Sgt.,Schutz-Pol., Muelheim (Ger.) 28.2.95	MURDER	U.S.
HINZE, Kurt	260972	M	Ger.		Hptsturmfhr.,SS, Castel Franco Emilia(Modena) (It.) 14.-18.1244	MURDER	U.S.
HINZE, Walter	190190	M	Ger.		Member, employee, Gestapo, Brno (Czech.) 39-45	MURDER	CZECH.
HINZEL see HEINZEN	130365						
HINZEN, Heinz	254556	M	Ger.	16. 2.16	Capt.,SS or SD, Strassburg,Beulotte,St.Laurent (Fr.)	MISC.CRIMES	FR.
HINZMANN	254064	M	Ger.		Revier-Oberwachtmstr., SD, Toulouse (Fr.) 11.42-8.44	MISC.CRIMES	FR.
HINZMANN, Alfred	185455	M	Ger.		Osturmfhr.,SS, SS-Pz.Gren.Div.,Leibstandarte "A.H.",Stavelot(Bel.) 19.-20.12.44	MURDER	BEL.
HIPFEL	257533			21	Pvt.,SS, Muehldorf Area (Ger.)	MURDER	U.S.
HIPFINGER, Herbert	253690	M	Ger.		Employee, Gestapo, Tesin (Czech.) 39-45	MURDER	CZECH.
HIPMER	186590	M	Ger.		Lt., Waffen-SS, Athen (Grc.)	TORTURE	GRC.
HIPP	190344	M			C.C. Dachau (Ger.)	MURDER	U.S.
HIPP, Wilhelm	259362	M	Ger.		Scharfhr.,active member of Poitiers-Gestapo,Poitiers Area (Fr.)40-44	MISC.CRIMES	FR.
HIPPKE	195834	M	Ger.		Gen.,Oberstabsarzt,Professor, Airforce,C.C.Dachau,Auschwitz (Ger.,Pol.) 26.2.43	MURDER	BEL.
HIPPLER	190543	M	Ger.		Sgt., Feldgendarmerie, Stenay (Fr.) 40-5.8.44	MURDER	FR.
HIPPLER	250843	M	Ger.		Lt., 5 Bn. Flak Rgt.5, Celles (Bel.)	MURDER	BEL.
HIPPLER, Erich	257534	M	Ger.		Cpl., Navy, Hopseidet (Nor.) 6.5.45	MURDER	NOR.
HIPPLER, Fritz	98293	M		09	Ministerial Dirigent, Reichs-Propaganda-Ministerium, head of the Film Div.	MISC.CRIMES	UNWCC.
HIPPO	252189	M	Ger.		Crim.secr., Sipo, Abt.IV E, Brussel (Bel.)	INTERR.	BEL.
HIRDT	196556	M	Ger.		Oscharfhr.,SS, C.C. Struthof-Natzweiler (Fr.) 40-44	TORTURE	FR.
HIRH, Auguste	196555	M	Ger.		Osturmfhr.,SS, Dir.of Institut of Anatomie,Medicin-Facultaet, Strassburg (Fr.) 40-44	MURDER	FR.
HIRLE, Karl	192362	M	Ger.	11. 4.20	Army, C.C. Zinna, Torgau (Ger.) 45	WITNESS	U.S.
HIRLEMANN, Otto	255119	M	Ger.		Cpl., 12 Coy, 377 Jg.Rgt., Vinkt-Meigem (Bel.) 25.-31.5.40	MISC.CRIMES	BEL.
HIRN, Andreas	165148	M	Ger.		Civilian, baker, coffee master,Rothenberg a.d.Pegnitz (Ger.)20.2.45	TORTURE	U.S.
HIRNER, Ludwig	1079	M	Ger.		W.O.chief, Feldgendarmerie,Army, Langres (Fr.) 43-44	MURDER	FR.
HIRNKOTT, Heinrich	132726	M		11	Lagerkapo, Camp Dora (Ger.)	MURDER	FR.
HIRNTSCHIRSCH, Felix	31936	M	Ger.		Landgerichts-Dir.,Public official, Litomerice (Czech.) 21.2.40	MURDER	CZECH.
HIRSCH	11238	M	Ger.		Uscharfhr.,Reichsfuehrer SS, SS Div.16.Strettoia (It.) 15.9.44	MURDER	FR.
HIRSCH	24935	M	Ger.	13	Lt.,Paratroopen, Roermond (Neth.) 9.44,18.1.45	TORTURE	U.S.,NETH.
HIRSCH	147074	M	Ger.		Abteilungsfuehrer, Kamnik (Yugo.) 43	MURDER	YUGO.
HIRSCH	167175	M	Ger.		Oberjaeger, Bachivillers (Fr.) 29.8.44	INTERR.	FR.
HIRSCH	191886	F	Ger.		Civilian, Luschkau near Waldau (Pol.) 24.4.44	MURDER	U.K.

NAME	C.R.FILE NUMBER	SEX	NATIO- NALITY	DATE OF BIRTH	RANK OCCUPATION UNIT PLACE AND DATE OF CRIME	REASON WANTED	WANTED BY
HIRSCH	253048	M	Ger.		Lt., Pay-Master, Feldpost No. 30815 or 37503 E, Saint Aubin Les Elbeuf (Fr.) 24.8.44	MISC.CRIMES	FR.
HIRSCH	254065	M	Ger.	19	Lt., 1.Coy. 515 Inf.Regt., Mielin (Fr.) 21.10.44	MISC.CRIMES	FR.
HIRSCH	301566	M			SS-Sgt., stationed C.C. Mauthausen (Austr.) 40-45	MURDER	BEL.
HIRSCH, Erich	186477	M	Ger.		Feldgend., Feldgend. Truppe 626, Peronne-Lequort (Fr.) 24.8.44	MURDER	FR.
HIRSCH, Heinrich	302028	M	Ger.		Reichsbahn Official, employed in the Fernmeldemeisteret office at Amersfoort (Neth.) 10.44-5.45	PILLAGE	NETH.
HIRSCH, Karl	190189	M	Ger.		Member, Gestapo, Brno (Czech.) 39-45	TORTURE	CZECH.
HIRSCH, Rudolf	130372	M			Mauthausen (Austr.) 41-45	MURDER	U.S.
HIRSCHANN	190544	M	Ger.		Cpl., Feldgend., Stenay (Fr.) 40-5.8.44	MURDER	FR.
HIRSCHBERG	167207	M	Ger.		Civilian, Private secretary, Ersatzstab Rosenberg, Paris (Fr.) 40-44	PILLAGE	FR.
HIRSCHELMANN, Karl	251601	M			Usturmfhr., SD, SS, C.C. Nordhausen (Ger.)	MURDER	U.S.
HIRSCHFELD	251600	M			Flyer, C.C. Wolfleben-Nordhausen (Ger.)	MURDER	U.S.
HIRSCHFELD, Helmut	39579	M		15.12.25	Pvt., 14.Fallschirm. Jaeger Regt., 4.Coy., Montmarin,Commone De Giury (Fr.) 8.44	MURDER	FR.
HIRSCHFELD, Willy or HIRSCH- FELT	167831	M	Ger.		Cmdt., Feldgen. Zepperen,St. Trond, Limbourg (Bel.) 24.12.43	MURDER	BEL.
HIRSCHFIELD	154371	M			Major, C.C. Gardelegen (Ger.) 4.45	MURDER	U.S.
HIRSCHHAEUSER, Heinrich	167816	M	Ger.		Cpl. Gruppenfhr., 9.Res.Gren.Regt.1.Coy.Unit 41151 Magny d' Anigon (Fr.) 18.9.44	MURDER	FR.
HIRSCHINGER	301201	M	Ger.		Member, NSDAP, Huchenfeld (Ger.) 17.3.45	MURDER	U.K.
HIRSCHLMEIER	171970	M			Civilian, C.C. Nordhausen (Ger.) 43-44	TORTURE	U.S.
HIRSCHMANN	136259	M	Ger.		Adjutant, Feldgend., Stenay (Fr.) 44	MURDER	FR.
HIRSCHMANN, Adolf	141316	M	Ger.		Pvt., 368 Coy., Landesschuetzen Bn., Bodenbach (Czech.)	MURDER	U.K.
HIRSCHNER	253685	M	Ger.		Political-Chief, SS,C.C. Auschwitz-Birkenau (Pol.) 42-45	MURDER	YUGO.
HIRSH	390	M			Police-Director, Police, Krakow (Pol.) 9.39-1.42	MURDER	POL.
HIRSH	169018	M	Ger.	15	SS-Unterscharfhr., C.C. Sachsenhausen, Riga (Ger.,Latv.)	MURDER	U.N.W.C.C.
HIRSSKORN, Julius	193285	M	Ger.	97	Pvt., Guard, Landesschuetzen Bn., Stalag VIII B, Lamsdorf (Ger.) 41	MURDER	U.K.
HIRT	254623	M	Ger.		SS-Sturmmann, C.C. Buchenwald (Ger.)	INTERR.	FR.
HIRT, Adolf	189702	M	Ger.		Crim.-Secretary, Police, (Lux.)	MURDER	LUX.
HIRT, August	174234	M		98	SS-Hauptsturmfhr., Dr., Camp Official-Medecin, Sachsenhausen,Dachau, Struthof, Strasbourg (Ger.,Fr.)	MURDER	U.S.,BEL.,UNWCC
HIRT, Edward	189050	M	Ger.27.11.14		Crim.-Employes, Gestapo, Brno (Czech.) 39-45	MURDER	CZECH.
HIRT, M.	167815	M			Pvt., 9. Res. Gren. Regt., Magny d' Anignon (Fr.) 9.44	MURDER	FR.
HIRT, Robert	305760	M	Ger.17. 9.18		Zugwachtmeister, Schutzpolizei, Lifjell nr. Notoddem (Nor.) 11.44	MURDER	NOR.
HIRTES	254624	M	Ger.		Pvt., 2.Coy. Messner of Bn. Heptin, Le Clion s-Mer (Fr.) 9.44	TORTURE	FR.
HIRTES, Richard	139678	M			Civilian, C.C. Buchenwald (Ger.)	TORTURE	U.S.
HIRTH, August	6150	M	Ger.		Professor d' Anatomie, Allg. SS, Strasbourg (Fr.) 44	MURDER	FR.
HIRYING,see Wilhelm HARING	171969						
HIRZEL	300777	M	Ger.		Cpl., I.Aufkl.Abt.3.and 2. Column XV Div. of the Afrika Korps Saint Leger (Arlon),(Bel.) 5.9.44	MISC.CRIMES	BEL.
HISSINGER	161978	M	Ger.		Lt., Army, Amilly (Fr.) 10.44	MURDER	FR.
HISS see HUESS	191990						
HITLER, Adolf	1	M	Ger.	89	Reichsfuehrer,	MURDER	POL.,CZECH.,FR.
HITSCHFELD, Albin	188547	M	Ger.		Member, Gestapo, Brno (Czech.) 39-45	WITNESS	CZECH.
HITTICH	9687	M			Hauptsturmfhr., SS, C.C., Buchenwald, Natzweiler (Ger.,Fr.) 39-45	MURDER	CZECH.
HITZ, Johann	174233	M	Ger.30.10.96		Cpl., SS Bau-Coy. Treppin bei Berlin, Neustadt-Aisch (Ger.) 42-45	TORTURE	U.S.
HITZEGRAD, Ernst	132327	M			SS-Gruppenfhr., Chief of Ger.Police in Protectorate, Prague (Czech.)45	MURDER	CZECH.
HITZELBERGER	391	M	Ger.		Cpl., Airforce, Rodez (Fr.) 44	MURDER	FR.
HITZER, Georg	306752	M	Ger.		German Civilian, Raunheim (Ger.) 1.45	BRUTALITY	U.S.
HITZIG	254352	M	Ger.		Sgt., SD, Jagodina (Yugo.) 15.2.44	MISC.CRIMES	YUGO.
HITZLER, Eugen	261949	M	Ger.		Crim.-Secretary, Gestapo, Various places in Slovenia (Yugo.)41-45	MISC.CRIMES	YUGO.
HITZLLINGLER	261044	M	Ger.		Former, Supplies Chief, Metal-works Plant, C.C., Spechinger (Ger.)	PILLAGE	FR.
HIWITZ	197732	M	Ger.		SS-Scharfhr., Buchenwald (Ger.)	TORTURE	U.S.
HIZE	167209	M	Ger.		Adjutant-Chief, Georgian Bn. 1.Coy., Tulle, Coreze (Fr.) 6.4.44	MISC.CRIMES	FR.
HLACKEPT	300690	M	Ger.		Dr., Public Prosecutor, Oberstaatsanwaltschaft, Ministry of State Department of Justice, Prague, Rohemia, Moravia (Czech.) 21.240	MISC.CRIMES	CZECH.
HLAWACEK	257375	M	Ger.		SS-Guard, Sgt., SS-slave labour-camp, Beisfjord near Narwik (Nor.)42	BRUTALITY	YUGO.
HLAWATSCH, Leopoldine	259032	F	Ger. 4.11.20		Secretary, Gestapo, Olomouc-Moravia (Czech.) 42	MISC.CRIMES	CZECH.
HLAWISKA	301381	M			Crim.-Secretary, Oslo (Nor.) 5.42	MURDER	NOR.
HLOCKO	196557	M	Ger.		Asst.Chief, Customs Office, St. Beat Chaum (Fr.) 6.44	TORTURE	FR.
HNIDA, Erich	186593	M	Ger.3. 7.03		Employee, Factory, Brno (Czech.) 39-45	PILLAGE	CZECH.
HOACHIMSEN or JOACHIMSEN	252190	M	Ger.		Crim.-Asst., Sipo, Abt. IV E, Bruessel (Bel.)	INTERR.	BEL.
HOBBE	133679	M			SS-Unterscharfhr., C.C. Buchenwald (Ger.)	TORTURE	U.S.
HOBBE, Erich	161990	M	Ger.		Pvt., SS Div. "Das Reich ", Altenkirchen (Ger.) 13.9.44	MURDER	U.S.
HOBE	157754	M			SS-Mann, 1.SS Pz.Div. "Adolf Hitler", Parfondroy, Stavelot (Bel.)44	MURDER	U.S.,BEL.
HOBOHM, Joachim	147316	M	Ger.		Capt., II. Pz.Div. (Fr.) 44	MURDER	FR.
HOCEVAK or HOCEVAR or HOCEVER	135547	M	Ger.	95	Dr., Civilian D Kdo. 180, C.C. Liezen (Austr.) 44-45	TORTURE	U.K.
HOCH	166611	M	Ger.		Civ. Reichskommissar of Ukraine, (Sov.Un.) 41-44	TORTURE	U.S.
HOCH	189392	M	Ger.		SS Hauptscharfhr., Dachau (Ger.)	MURDER	BEL.
HOCH, Adolf	191995	M			SS Rottenfhr., 1.SS Pz.Regt., Stabs Coy., Ligneuville, Stoumont (Bel.) 12.44	WITNESS	U.S.
HOCH, Anton	192719	M	Ger.	16	Police Sgt., Prague (Czech.) 42	MURDER	CZECH.
HOCH, Kurt	133680	M	Ger. 5. 3.11		SS-Unterscharfhr., C.C. Buchenwald (Ger.)	TORTURE	U.S.
HOCH, Martin	193198	M	Ger.	05	Cpl., Kgf. Arb. Bn. 186 (Nor.) 40-45	MISC.CRIMES	NOR.
HOCHE	254804	M	Ger.		Secretary, Custom-house, St. Gervais (Fr.) 8.44	INTERR.	FR.
HOCHBAUM, Friedrich	260667	M		94		WITNESS	U.S.
HOCHGREWE, Alfred	11565	M	Ger.		Sgt., Inf. Regt. 744, 44	MURDER	U.K.
HOCHHAUS	261238	M			Pvt., C.C. Mackenrode, Nordhausen (Ger.)	MURDER	U.S.
HOCHLAND see MOCHLAND	259203						
HOCHMANN	150910	M	Ger.		Adjutant, SS, CC. Lublin (Pol.) 42-44	MURDER	FR.
HOCHMANN	257759	M	Ger.	01	Employee,C.C. Muhldorf-Dachau (Ger.)	MURDER	U.S.
HOCHMANN, Anton	190188	M	Ger.10. 4.10		Chief Crim.Asst. Gestapo, Brno (Czech.) 39-45	MURDER	CZECH.
HOCHMUTH, Wenzl	174212	M	Ger.		Servant, Civ. Arbeitsverteilung, Groglitz (Ger.) 6.44-4.45	TORTURE	U.S.
HOCHREITER, Ernst	252427	M			Pvt., C.C. Ellrich-Nordhausen (Ger.)	MURDER	U.S.

HOC-HOE

NAME	C.R.FILE NUMBER	SEX	NATIONALITY	DATE OF BIRTH	RANK OCCUPATION UNIT PLACE AND DATE OF CRIME	REASON WANTED	WANTED BY
HOCHSCHUJA (or HOCHULTZE or HOCHSCHULDER)	192951	M	Ger.		Rapportfhr., SS, C.C. Buchenwald (Ger.) 42-45	TORTURE	U.S.
HOCHSTEINER	196084	M	Ger.		Kreisleiter, NSDAP (Yugo.) 5.42	MURDER	YUGO.
HOCHSTETTER, Johann	195774	M	Ger.		Member, Waffen-SS, Bratislava (Czech.) 39-45	MURDER	CZECH.
HOCK	170543	M	Ger.		Capt., Army, Oflag 6 C, C.C. Osnabrueck (Ger.) 41-42	MURDER	YUGO.
HOCK	196945	M	Ger.		C.C.Struthof-Natzweiler (Fr.) 40-44	TORTURE	FR.
HOCKARTH, Paul	145326	M	Ger.		Pvt., Army, I.Coy. 621.Landesschuetzen-Bn., Berga,Elsta (Ger.) 45	BRUTALITY	U.S.
HOCKE, Josef	192720	M		86	Leader, NSDAP, Praha (Czech.)	MISC.CRIMES	CZECH.
HOCKELCHOC (see HECKENHOLT)	301405						
HOCKENHOLT (see HECKENHOLT)	301405						
HOCKENMAIER	306795	M	Ger.	7.12.06	SS-Mann, Telephonist, S.D. Vichy (Fr.) 10.43-9.44	MURDER	FR.
HOCKHAUF, Helmut	105942	M	Ger.		Lt., probably Air Force. Parachute Replacement Center, 3.Coy., Eistedt, Gardelegen (Ger.) 4.45	MURDER	U.S.
HODBOD, Wilhelm	256160	M			Flyer, C.C.Ellrich-Nordhausen (Ger.)	MURDER	U.S.
HODINa LL.D.Frantisek	186594	M		77	Leader, NSDAP, Praha (Czech.)	MISC.CRIMES	CZECH.
HODITCHKE	250821	M	Ger.	06 or 07	Sgt. Chief, 1.Coy. Landesschuetzen-Bn. 690, Gironde, Saucats (Fr.) 7.43	INTERR.	FR.
HODL, Hubert	301005	M	Ger.		Deputy to Fiers, Hubert (Chief Forest Guard), Pertisau-Maurach (Aust.) 13.7.44	MISC.CRIMES	FR.
HODLATZ	173613	M	Ger.		Sgt. 3.Coy.Landesschuetzen Bn.276, Bassin de Briey (Fr.)	MURDER	FR.
HOEBER, Erich	142996	M	Ger.	20. 4.10	Sgt., S3 Totenkopf-Standarte, Waffen-SS, C.C.Buchenwald (Ger.)	TORTURE	U.S.
HOECH	196553	M	Ger.		Institute for Anatomy, Strassburg (Fr.) 40-44	TORTURE	FR.
HOECKER	194889	M	Ger.		SS-Osturmfhr., SS, C.C. Lublin (Pol.) 40-44	MURDER	POL.
HOAD, Johanden	162415	M		8. 2.28	E.A.Bn. 11, Graz, Wenzelsdorf (Aust.) 2.45	WITNESS	U.S.
HOEDEL, Hans	193492	M	Ger.	7. 9.78	Blockleiter, NSDAP, Uhersky Brod (Czech.) 39-45	TORTURE	CZECH.
HOEFELS, Jacob	132328	M	Ger.		Member, S.A., Duisburg (Ger.)	TORTURE	U.S.
HOEFER, Johann	188704	M	Ger.	24.11.95	Member, Gestapo, Dachsbach Krs.Neustadt (Ger.) 43	TORTURE	POL.
HOEFERT	125470	M	Ger.	22	Lt., 150.Panz.Bde., Parschute Hunter Regt. z.b.V., 2.Bn., Meuse Bridge-Antwerp (Bel.) 12.44	MISC.CRIMES	U.S.
HOEFFERT	259663	M	Ger.		Gendarm, Gendarmerie, Thum, Haut-Rhin (Fr.) 10.44	BRUTALITY	FR.
HOEFFLE (or HOEFLE) Josef or Hermann	142979	M	Ger.	98	Hoeherer SS- u.Pol.fhr., Gen.Lt.d.Polizei, Wehrkreis XI, Viennesburg (Ger.) and occupied countries 40-45	WITNESS	U.S.
HOEFFNER	190569	M			Capt., Verbindungsoffizier d.Transp.Chef b.deutschen General in Zagreb, Ljubljana, Zagreb (Yugo.) 4.41-5.43	MURDER	YUGO.
HOEFFNER, Emil	193181	M	Ger.		Criminal-asst., Staatspolizei, Trandum (Ger.) 19.1.43	MURDER	NOR.
HOEFLE	1702	M			General, SS. 44	MURDER	U.K.
HOEFLE, Josef or Hermann (see HOEFFLE)	142979						
HOEFLMAYER, Hans	139203	M			Civilian.	MISC.CRIMES	U.S.
HOEFNER	300960	M	Ger.		SS-Oschfhr., official of S.D. Leitabschnitt Prague, Oswiecim-Birkenau (Pol.) 39-45	MURDER	CZECH.
HOEGELOW	306087	M	Ger.		SS-Hptscharfhr., Cmdt. of the SS Guard, Alderney C.C. (Channel Is) (Fr.) 42-45	MURDER	CZECH.
HOEGER	39569	M	Ger.		Capt., Air Force, C.O. of a Coy. Flugzeugfuehrerschule, Prenzlau (Ger.) 7.44	MURDER	SOV.UN.
HODER, Heinrich	251586	M			Pvt., C.C. Ellrich-Nordhausen (Ger.)	MURDER	U.S.
HOEGNL	190335	M	Ger.		Kapo, C.C. Dachau (Ger.)	MURDER	U.S.
HOEH	259812	M	Ger.		Staff-Intendant, Army, Kommando "Raumboot", Breda,Noord-Brabant(Neth.)44	INTERR.	NETH.
HOEHLE	119441	M	Ger.		Capt., Cmd.III, Gren.Regt.378, 169.Inf.Div., 20. Army, Finmark (Nor.) 10.44	MURDER	NOR.
HOEHLE, Heinrich	142995	M	Ger.	19. 4.11	Sgt., SS Totenkopf-Standarte, Waffen-SS, C.C.Buchenwald (Ger.)	TORTURE	U.S.
HOEHMAN, Gottlieb	186595	M	Ger.	7. 1.07	Chief, S.D., Gestapo, Prague (Czech.) 39-45	MURDER	CZECH.
HOEHMANN, Erich	189541	M		4. 3.10	Crim.secretary, Pol., Flebour, Lipperscheiderdelt (Lux.) 6.9.44	MISC.CRIMES	LUX.
HOEHN, Walter (see IOHN, Walter)	261912						
HOEHNE	173595	M	Ger.	10	Chief Judge, occupied territories Boehmen, Prague (Czech.) 39-45	TORTURE	CZECH.
HOEHNEL, Herbert	189347	M	Ger.		Sgt. W.O.Sen., Inf.Btty. 116, 28. R.I., Meilhan, Lannemezan (Fr.) 7.44	MISC.CRIMES	FR.
HOEHNER, Karl	251592	M		5. 2.03	Cpl., C.C. Harzungen-Nordhausen (Ger.)	MURDER	U.S.
HOEHNECHEIDT	166609	M	Ger.		SS-Sturmbannfhr., SS, Athen (Gre.) 42	MURDER	U.S.
HOEHNSCHEIDT, Karl	185460	M		07	SS-Osturmbannfhr., SS, S.D., Chief of the Security Service (S.D.-Dienststelle), Prague (Czech.) 39-44	MURDER	CZECH.
HOEHR, Karl	193192	M	Ger.	05	Sgt., Guard, Ministry of Justice, Feldstraflager, Finmark (Nor.) 3.43	MISC.CRIMES	NOR.
HOEIZL	179601	M	Ger.		Capt., Army, 3.Coy., 395.Landesschuetzen Bn. Stalag IV B, Muehlberg (Ger.) 44-45	MURDER	U.S.
HOEKER	150586	M	Ger.		Member, Gestapo, C.C. Fredrikstad (Nor.) 41	TORTURE	NOR.
HOEID (see NOEID)	195955						
HOELER	301750	M	Ger.		SS-Uschfhr., C.C. Auschwitz (Pol.) 40	MURDER	FR.
HOELGE	191994	M	Ger.		Capt., Army, Sarthe Change (Fr.)	WITNESS	FR.
HOELGER, Karl	260370	M	Ger.	2. 7.02	SS-Guard, SS, C.C. Natzweiler (Fr.)	MURDER	FR.
HOELLINGER, Louis	192031	M	Ger.		Pvt., SS Panz.Div."Das Reich", Oradour sur Glane (Fr.) 10.6.44	MURDER	FR.
HOELLENSPERGER, Hans	124261	M			Physician, SS, Army, Malmedy (Bel.) 17.12.44	MURDER	U.S.
HOELLMANN, Bernhard	189540	M		17. 4.82	Civ., Hunting rights in the Consthum region (Lux.) 12.8.44	MURDER	LUX.
HOELSCHER	173584	M	Ger.		SS-Hptscharfhr., Gestapo, SS, Stavanger (Nor.) 3.42	TORTURE	NOR.
HOELTER	254529	M			13. SS Pol.Regt., Ferlach (Aust.) 44-45	MURDER	YUGO.
HOELZ, Johannes	206668	M		06	Crimes against peace. War crimes and crimes against humanity.	WITNESS	U.S.
HOELZEL, Otto	125042	M	Ger.		Arbeitskommando 1178, Dresden, Heinsberg (Ger.)	MISC.CRIMES	U.K.
HOELZEL, Rudolf	251043	M	Ger.	12. 7.05	Estate manager, Civ., Dymokury (Czech.)	PILLAGE	CZECH.
HOELZER	191603	M	Ger.		I. Ostgeoietsministerium, Einsatzstab Rosenberg, Berlin (Ger.)	PILLAGE	FR.
HOELZITZER, Otto	142445	M			.... olitz (Ger.) 44	TORTURE	FR.
HOELZL, Siegfried	166393	M		02 or 03	... uptamt (H.Q.), Trente (Italy)	MURDER	U.S., IT.
HOEMANN	161179	M	Ger.		...ber, Gestapo, Innsbruck (Aust.) 18.4.45	MURDER	U.S.
HOEMANN, Erich	194899	M	Ger.	4. 5.10	Crim.secretary, Territ.Occup., Luxembourg (Lux.)	MURDER	LUX.
HOEMER, Alfred	305071	M			Civilian, Niedernhausen (Ger.) 10.44	BRUTALITY	U.S.
HOENER, Bruno	149329	M	Ger.	95	SS-Hptscharfhr., C.C. Ravensbrueck (Ger.)	TORTURE	FR.
HOENICKE	261058	M	Ger.	05	W.O., 8.Coy., Div."Brandenburg", Special Unit, Var-Vaucluse, Bouche du Rhone (Fr.) 43-44	MISC.CRIMES	FR.

HOE - HOF

NAME	C.R.FILE NUMBER	SEX	NATIO-NALITY	DATE OF BIRTH	RANK OCCUPATION UNIT PLACE AND DATE OF CRIME	REASON WANTED	WANTED BY
HOENIG, Alexander	190561	M	Ger.	20. 9.22	Member, Gestapo, Dantica, Belgrade (Yugo.) 41	MURDER	YUGO.
HOENIG, Egon	129798	M	Ger.		Waffen SS, Tender of Block 4 at Bolke Kaserne, Nordhausen (Ger.)4.45	MURDER	U.S.
HOENIG, Ernst Wolfgang	194566	M	Ger.	3. 2.04	Member, Gestapo, Klatovy (Czech.) 39-45	TORTURE	CZECH.
HOENIG, Heinz	193189	M	Ger.	2.12.18	Ex Convict, Reichsjustizministerium, Feldstraflager Finmark (Nor.)3.45	WITNESS	NOR.
HOENIG, Walter	11243	M	Ger.		Sgt., Army, Gestapo, Sizun (Fr.) 6.7.44	MURDER	FR.
HOENIGER, Klaus (aliases:KOPACKA Stanislav)	98539	M	Ger.	24. 4.97	Regierungskommisser, Gestapo, C.C.Boleslav (Czech.) 39-45	MURDER	CZECH.
HOENSCH, Joachim	188969	M	Ger.		Chief Paymaster, Army, Dury-les-Amiens (Fr.) 44	WITNESS	FR.
HOENSCHFIDT	305897	M	Ger.		SS-Osturmbannfhr., head of the Leitabschnitt SD, Prague, C.C.Oswiecim-Birkenau (Pol.) 39-45	MURDER	CZECH.
HOEPEL, Hans	258377	M	Ger.	10. 9.17	Karlovy Vary (Czech.) 40-45	BRUTALITY	CZECH.
HOEPELE, Joseph	260372	M	Ger.	9. 5.02	SS-Guard, SS, C.C.Natzweiler (Fr.)	MURDER	FR.
HOEPNER, Meta	194545	F	Ger.		Civilian, Lidice (Czech.) 42-43	WITNESS	CZECH.
HOEPKEN, Hans	181140	M		13	Crim.Asst., Member, Gestapo, SD, SS, Benesov, Brno, Praha (Czech.) 39-45	MURDER	CZECH.
HEPNER	21318	M			Leader, Public official, Dpt.of Food and Agriculture (Pol.)	TORTURE	U.N.W.C.C.
HEPPEL	120572	M			Secretary, Geheime Feldpolizei, Drissa (Russ.) 43	MURDER	U.S.
HOEPPNER	128847	M			Sgt., Stalag IV C, C.C.Mannesmann (Ger.) 12.44	MURDER	SOV.UN.
HOEPPNER	193188	M		05	Sgt., Guard, Reichsjustizministerium Feldstraflager Waffen SS, Finmark (Nor.) 42-45	MISC.CRIMES	NOR., YUGO.
HOERBING	196574	M			Oberwachtmeister, Schupo Stuetzpunkt, Groningen Camp Westerbork(Neth.) 9.44	MURDER	NETH.
HOERIG	152801	M			Der Beauftragte fuer den Vierjahresplan, (Pol.) 39-45	SUSPECT	U.S.
HOERLE	186596	M			SS Art.training and replacement Rgt., Prague (Czech.)	MURDER	CZECH.
HOERMANN	195773	M	Ger.		Kreisleiter, NSDAP, Ehingen (Ger.)	MURDER	FR.
HOERNLEIN	21317	M	Ger.		Major General, Army, Div.Grossdeutschland	MURDER	U.N.W.C.C.
HOERNSCHWEIGER, Hans	24974	M			Cpl., Army, Habrebez (Bel.) 11.2.45	MURDER	U.S.
HOERR, Otto	191993	M	Ger.	80	Farmer, Civilian, Frauenriedhausen (Ger.) 40-45	TORTURE	POL.
HOES	256947	M			Major, Mittelbau-chief of Off.DI,SS, Nordhausen (Ger.)	MURDER	U.S.
HOES, Otto	256901	M			Uschfhr., Command staff, SS, Harzungen, Nordhausen (Ger.)	MURDER	U.S.
HOESEN, Henricius	251588	M			Pvt., C.C.Ellrich, Nordhausen (Ger.)	MURDER	U.S.
HOESER	256946	M			Osturmfhr., Camp Dora, Nordhausen (Ger.)	MURDER	U.S.
HOESLER, Franz	173015	M		07	Lt., SS, C.C.Auschwitz (Pol.) 40-45	MURDER	U.S.
HOESS	195639	M	Ger.		N.C.O., Air Force, Oswiecim (Pol.) 40	MURDER	FR., YUGO., POL.
HOESSELBAPTH (or HOSSELBARTH or HOLBACH)	83843	M	Ger.	2. 4.07	Hptsturmfhr., Sipo, SD, RSHA.Amt VI, Athens (Grc.) 7.44	MURDER	U.S.
HOESSLER	192721	M			Lt., SS, C.C.Neckarelz (Ger.) 45	TORTURE	U.S.
HOESSLIN, Wilhelm	173573	M			Major General, Gebirgs-Div.188, Slovenia (Yugo.)	MURDER	YUGO.
HOESZ	143016	M	Ger.	04	Lt.Col., SS, C.C.Auschwitz (Pol.) 40-45	MURDER	U.S.
HOET	163656	M	Ger.		Chef de Chantier, Civilian, Beaulieu (Fr.)	WITNESS	FR.
HOETTIG (see RETTIG)	128943						
HOETTIG	197733	M			SS-Schfhr., SS, C.C.Buchenwald (Ger.)	MURDER	U.S.
HOETZEL	190562	M			Lt., Commandant, Feldgendarmerie, Kragujevac (Yugo.) 21.10.41	MURDER	YUGO.
HOEVELER, Johann	134850	M	Ger.		Civilian, Efferen (Ger.) 2.10.44	WITNESS	U.S.
HOF	173614	M			Kreisleiter, NSDAP, Holsheim (Fr.)	TORTURE	FR.
HOF, Johann	125041	M	Ger.		Civilian, Ruoishau (Ger.) 7.44	TORTURE	U.K.
HOFACKER	185462	M			SS-Mann,1 Pz.Div."Adolf Hitler",1 SS Recon.Bn.2 Zug, Stavelot, Parfondruy (Bel.) 18.-22.12.44	MURDER	BEL., U.S.
HOFBAUER	132466	M			SS-Oschfhr.,	MURDER	U.S.
HOFBAUER	133332	M	Ger.	17	Sturmmann, Waffen SS, C.C.Hohenrhein near Plattling (Ger.) 2.5.45	MURDER	U.S.
HOFBAUER, Franz	305182	M			Hpttruppfhr., RAD, Neigh Bourhood of Schutzen am Gebirge Krs.Eisenstadt (Aust.) 13.and 14.2.45	MURDER	U.S.
HOFELER	261173	M	Ger.		Pvt.,5-I N.Rgt.211,139 Arbeitsbereich Liane, Alleur-lez-Liege (Bel.) 4.9.44	MURDER	BEL.
HOFELNER, Johann	251053	M		25. 4.04	Ortsgruppenleiter, NSDAP, SA, Gestapo, Praporiste District Kayne (Czech.)	MISC.CRIMES	CZECH.
HOFINBFPG, Arthur	162854	M		24. 2.99	Chief, Doctor, Inf.Rgt.517, Bn.Staff III, Virelles les Chimay (Bel.)	PILLAGE	BEL.
HOFER	124773	M		18	Usturmfhr., Crim.Commissar, SS, Gestapo, Kom.16 z.b.V., Bruessel (Bel.)44	MURDER	U.S.
HOFER	166610	M			Chief of Operational Zone (Aust.) 39-45	TORTURE	U.S.
HOFER	252191	M			SS-Uschfhr., Sipo Abt.IV E, Bruessel (Bel.)	INTERR.	BEL.
HOFER, Franz	190187	M	Ger.		Crim.Oberasst., Gestapo, Brno (Czech.) 39-45	TORTURE	CZECH.
HOFER, Hans	131284	M			Uschfhr., SS, Buna-Auschwitz (Pol.)	MURDER	U.S.
HOFER, Josef	132463	M		02	Ortsgr.NSDAP, Wellbach (Aust.) 15.4.45	MURDER	U.S.
HOFFP, Olaf	253061	M		6. 9.19	Civilian, Railroad-employee, Bergedorf (Ger.) 6.11.44	TORTURE	U.S.
HOFER, Oskar	174787	M		00	Pvt., Army, Bronzolo (It.) 9.43	WITNESS	U.K.
HOFER, Paul	174232	M		10. 1.01	Cpl., Official, C.C.Vannes (Fr.) 42-44	TORTURE	FR.
HOFER, Peter	162428	M		05	SS-Hptsturmfhr., Waffen SS, Sect.V.Medical, C.C.Buchenwald (Ger.) 43-44	TORTURE	U.S.
HOFER, Waldemar Arthur "Willy"	143323	M	Ger.	03	SS-Osturmbannfhr., C.C.Buchenwald (Ger.)	MURDER	U.S.
HOFERICHIER	196564	M	Ger.		Osturmfhr., Camp Royallieu (Fr.) 41-44	MISC.CRIMES	FR.
HOFF	11566	M	Ger.		Lt., Army	MISC.CRIMES	U.K.
HOFF	105943	M	Ger.		Lt., 990 Inf.Rgt.4 Coy (Fr.) 6.6.44	MURDER	U.K.
HOFF	132074	M		12	Oschfhr., SS, SD, Hoidal, Falstad (Nor.) 20.1.45	MURDER	U.S.
HOFF, Friedrich	192794	M			Oberwachtmeister, Schupo, Stalag, C.C.Falstad (Nor.) 41-45	MURDER	NOR.
HOFF, Johann	250236	M	Ger.		Adj., Gestapo, Geh.Feldpolizei, Lille (Fr.) 40-44	MURDER	FR.
HOFFE	254946	M	Ger.		Employee, Hospital, Hohenstein (Ger.)	TORTURE	U.S.
HOFFEBERT, Fritz	186476	M	Ger.		Cpl., Arbeitskdo.2522 Stalag XIII D, C.C.Nordlingen (Ger.) 3.7.43	MURDER	FR.
HOFFELDER	301837	M			Capt., Police, Wissembourg (Bas-Rhin) (Fr.) 10.12.44	MURDER	FR.
HOFFEMEYER	185962	M			SS-Usturmfhr., SD of Moutiers, Bourg St.Maurice (Fr.) 8.44	MURDER	FR.
HOFFER (see AUFER)	189576						
HOFFER	196563	M	Ger.		W.O., Ison-la Bruisse, Sederon (Fr.) 22.2.44	TORTURE	FR.
HOFFER	300480	M	Ger.		Lt., Commanding 19056 Btty.A stationed at Camp Laurent at La Seyne sur Mer, (Fr.) 7.8.44	MISC.CRIMES	FR.
HOFFERBURG, Rudolf (or HAFEBURG, HAFERBURG)	152799	M			Civilian, Billroda (Ger.) 7.10.44	TORTURE	U.S.
HOFFIG, Adolph	261819	M	Ger.		Insp., Gestapo Amiens, Gentelles (Fr.) 6.-8.44	MURDER	FR.

NAME	C.R.FILE NUMBER	SEX	NATIONALITY	DATE OF BIRTH	RANK, OCCUPATION, UNIT, PLACE AND DATE OF CRIME	REASON WANTED	WANTED BY
HOFFMAN	393	M	Ger.		Polizei Direktor,Radom,Lublin, (Pol.) 9.39-1.42	MURDER	POL.
HOFFMAN	394	M	Ger.		Capt.,SS Div."Das Reich¦ 7.-8.44	MURDER	FR.
HOFFMAN	395	M	Ger.		Capt.,Lagerkommandant,Waffen SS,Auschwitz (Pol.) 43	MURDER	POL.,BEL.
HOFFMAN	24930	M	Ger.		Sgt.,SS,C.C.,Lublin (Pol.) 43	TORTURE	U.S.
HOFFMAN	35142	M			Hptsturmfhr.,SS,Neckarels (Ger.) 44	MURDER	U.S.
HOFFMAN	36689	M		95	Sgt.,guard or Interpreter,C.C.54,Latrina (It.) 6.44	MURDER	U.K.,U.S.
HOFFMAN	105944	M	Ger.		Lt. or Capt.,Inf.Rgt.998,4.Bn, (Fr.) 6.6.44	MURDER	U.K.
HOFFMAN	125142	M			SS,C.C.,Schlesiersee (Ger.)	TORTURE	U.S.
HOFFMAN	125476	M	Ger.		Pvt.,Arbeitskdo.,C.C.,Camp No.427,Uhyst (Ger.) 11.-20.3.	TORTURE	U.K.
HOFFMAN	126937	M	Ger.		Rottfhr.,SS men of this guard supplied,Buchenwald (Ger.) 44-45	TORTURE	U.S.
HOFFMAN	129773	M			Major,Army,Munich (Ger.) 3.45	MISC.CRIMES	U.S.
HOFFMAN	194901	M	Ger.	22	Lt.,Waffen SS,St.Vith (Bel.) 1.45	MURDER	U.S.
HOFFMAN ("Jew Killer")	140843	M			Capt.,SS,Wehrbezirkskommando,Linz-Donau (Aust.)	MISC.CRIMES	U.S.
HOFFMAN	141856	M	Ger.		Lt.,Sicherheitspolizei,Rom (Fr.) 7.7.44	WITNESS	U.K.
HOFFMAN	142464	M	Ger.	17	Uschfhr.,Army SS	MURDER	U.K.
HOFFMAN	142933	M	Ger.	95	Capt.,Camp commander,Army,Ilag 7,Laufen (Ger.) 6.-8.44	TORTURE	U.S.
HOFFMAN	142934	M			Sgt.,18.V.G. Div.,293 Gr.Rgt.,2.Bn.,6.Coy.,Bleialf (Ger.) 20.12.44	MURDER	U.S.
HOFFMAN	142936	M			Commanding-officer,German Navy corps,St.Marine (Fr.) 30.6.44	MURDER	FR.
HOFFMAN	146186	M			Sgt.,Prison,Charleroi (Bel.) 44	TORTURE	BEL.
HOFFMAN	154369	M			Uschfhr.,SS,4.Baubde.,(Formerly SS Div.Totenkopf) C.C.,Ellrich, Gardelegen (Ger.) 5.-14.4.45	MURDER	U.S.
HOFFMAN	161108	M	Ger.		Guard,C.C.,Vicinity Arizo (It.)	MURDER	U.S.
HOFFMAN	162425	M	Ger.	15	Oschfhr.,Sect.IV Admin.,SS,Buchenwald (Ger.) 42-43	WITNESS	U.S.
HOFFMAN	173598	M	Ger.		Osturmfhr.,SS,Cmdt.,Waffen SS,C.C.,Oswiecim,Birkenau (Pol.) 39-45	MURDER	CZECH.,POL.,BEL.
HOFFMAN	185458	M	Ger.		Rottfhr.,SS,Panz.Gren.Div.,Leibstandarte "Adolf Hitler", Stavelot (Bel.) 19.-20.12.44	MURDER	BEL.
HOFFMAN	194989	M	Ger.		Capt.,3.Coy.,988 Inf.Rgt. 7.44	MISC.CRIMES	U.K.
HOFFMAN	196562	M	Ger.		Osturmfhr.,Paris (Fr.) 7.44	TORTURE	FR.
HOFFMAN	253040	M	Ger.		Guard,SS or Gestapo,C.C.,Bremen-Farge (Ger.)	TORTURE	U.K.
HOFFMAN	254526	M	Ger.		Lt.,D.C.A. 08C72 and 51983,Maizieres,la Grande,Paroisse (Fr.) 8.44	PILLAGE	FR.
HOFFMAN (or HOFMANN)	301202	M	Ger.		Ogruppenfhr.,chief of police,SS area "South West"-Alsace, Vosges area, (Fr.) 44	MURDER	U.K.
HOFFMAN	306417	M	Ger.		Sonderfhr.,Camp 82 P.G. Laterina (It.) 3.-6.44	MURDER	U.K.
HOFFMAN, Albert	140780	M			Sgt.,Army,Mittenwald (Ger.) 6.44	TORTURE	U.S.
HOFFMAN, Alfred	142938	M	Ger.		Gardener,Civilian,Ginnheim (Ger.) 11.44	WITNESS	U.S.
HOFFMAN, Ed.	142937	M			Cabinet-maker,Civilian,Ginnheim (Ger.) 11.44	WITNESS	U.S.
HOFFMAN, Ernst	905184	M	Ger.		Kapo,C.C.,Neuengamme (Ger.)	MISC.CRIMES	FR.
HOFFMAN, Franz	195470	M			Member of police,Kreisleiter,NSDAP,Buttstadt (Ger.) 29.7.44	MISC.CRIMES	U.S.
HOFFMAN, Fritz	29854	M	Ger.		Sgt.,Army, (Ger.)	TORTURE	U.K.
HOFFMAN, Fritz	142940	M	Ger. 10 -	15	Guard,C.C.,Buchenwald (Ger.)	MURDER	U.S.
HOFFMAN (or HOFFMANN) Fritz	190398	M			Commander,C.C.,Dachau (Ger.)	MURDER	U.S.
HOFMAN, Heinrich	142912	M	Ger.	90	Professor,Reichsphotographer,Civilian	PILLAGE	U.S.
HOFFMAN, Reinhold	194546	M	Ger.		Guard,C.C.,Flossenburg (Ger.) 44-4.45	TORTURE	BEL.
HOFFMAN, Rudolf	24951	M	Ger.		Pvt.,Army,130.Pz.Lehr Rgt.,2.Coy.,	MISC.CRIMES	U.S.
HOFFMAN, Steiner	99815	M	Ger.			TORTURE	U.K.
HOFMAN, Walter	154270	M			Doctor,Civilian,C.C.,Lauenforde (Ger.)	TORTURE	U.K.
HOFMAN, Willi	129771	M	Ger.		Member,Gestapo,Giessen (Ger.) 26.-27.3.45	MURDER	U.S.
HOFFMANN	396	M	Ger.		Lt.,SD,Rotterdam (Neth.) 43	MURDER	NETH.
HOFFMANN	11567	M	Ger.		Capt.,Army,Inf.Rgt.988,Western Front, 44	MURDER	U.K.
HOFFMANN	24992	M	Ger.		Capt.,SS,Div."Das Reich",Rgt. "Der Fuehrer",Bozet (Fr.) 7.7.44	TORTURE	FR.
HOFFMANN	39603	M	Ger.		Lt.,Feldgendarmerie de Quimper (Fr.) 29.7.-8.8.44	TORTURE	FR.
HOFFMANN,	124644	M			Rottfhr.,SS,Guenterngrube,Oswiecim (Pol.) 1.44	MURDER	U.S.
HOFFMANN	124952	M	Ger.		General,Stalag Luft III, Sagan (Ger.) 25.3.44	MISC.CRIMES	U.K.
HOFFMANN	125143	M		05	Lt.,SIPO,Vierrers (Fr.) 3.-7.7.44	MURDER	U.S.
HOFFMANN	130971	M			SS,C.C.,Mauthausen (Aust.) 41-45	MURDER	U.S.
HOFFMANN	132050	M	Ger.	22	Osturmfhr.,SS "Das Reich",2.Reconnaissance Bn.,St.Vith (Bel.) 1.45	MURDER	U.S.
HOFFMANN	132051	M			Sgt.,Army,4.SS Baubde.,Gardelegen (Ger.)	MURDER	U.S.
HOFFMANN	132586	M	Ger.		Senats Praesident,Mil.Tribunal,Berlin,Torgau (Ger.) 5.40-45	MURDER	FR.
HOFFMANN	137098	M	Ger.		Crim.Secretary,SIPO,Poppentin (Ger.) 7.-8.44	WITNESS	U.S.
HOFFMANN	137650	M	Ger.	07	Guard,Oschfhr.,C.C.,Auschwitz (Pol.)	TORTURE	U.K.
HOFFMANN	138254	M	Ger.		Adjutant,14.Coy.,SS formation walker,Gembsheim (Ger.) 9.12.45	MURDER	FR.
HOFFMANN	141855	M			Sgt.,Army,interpreter,C.C. Laterina (It.) 17.6.44	MURDER	U.S.
HOFFMANN	142412	M	Ger.	90	Hptsturmfhr.,SS,C.C.,Lublin (Pol.)	MURDER	FR.
HOFFMANN	142418	M			Capt.,Army,Freney D'Oisans (Fr.)	MURDER	FR.
HOFFMANN	142468	M			Arbeitslager,C.C.,Elwerath,Mienhagen (Bel.) 11.8.44	MURDER	BEL.
HOFFMANN	142942	M	Ger.		Lt.,SS Totenkopf Standarte,Waffen SS C.C.,Buhenwald (Ger.)	TORTURE	U.S.
HOFFMANN	146857	M	Ger.		Adjutant,Oschfhr.,SS,police Rgt.19,4.Coy.,Annecy (Fr.) 44	MURDER	FR.
HOFFMANN	148187	M			Pvt.,Army,2.Pz.Div.,Kampfgruppe Wilde,(South West Fr.) 44	MURDER	FR.
HOFFMANN	149521	M			Sgt.,SS,C.C.,Natzweiler (Fr.)	MURDER	FR.
HOFFMANN	161107	M			Member,NSDAP,Civilian,Weimar,Daasdorf,Guttmannshausen (Ger.) 7.-8.44	MURDER	U.S.
HOFFMANN	162424	M	Ger.	98	Capt.,Guard,Army,Section III,guard Bn., Buchenwald (Ger.)	TORTURE	U.S.
HOFFMANN	162427	M	Ger.		Capt.,Ortskommandant,Ortskommandantur,St.Marie,Osmonville (Fr.)27.8.44	WITNESS	FR.
HOFFMANN	163097	M	Ger.		Pvt.,Army,C.C.,Chaudion (Fr.) 17.1.41	MURDER	FR.
HOFFMANN	165146	M	Ger.	05	Osturmbannfhr.,SS,Kiew (Sov.Un.) 41-42	MURDER	U.S.
HOFFMANN	179053	M	Ger.	97	Osturmfhr.,SS,head,Gestapo,Eberlin (Ger.)	MURDER	U.S.
HOFFMANN	174229	M	Ger.		Pvt.,Fallschirmjaeger Bn.5,4.Coy.,	MURDER	U.N.W.C.C.
HOFFMANN	174981	M	Ger.		Capt.,Inf.Rgt.469,198.Inf.Div.,Le Tholy (Fr.) 13.11.44	PILLAGE	FR.
HOFFMANN	177592	M	Ger.		Rapportfhr.,C.C.,Neuengamme (Ger.)	TORTURE	FR.
HOFFMANN	177599	M	Ger.		Osturmfhr.,SD,Gestapo,Sarrebruck (Ger.)	MISC.CRIMES	FR.
HOFFMANN	187864	M	Ger.		Capt.,C.C.,Mienhagen (Ger.) 11.4.44	MURDER	BEL.
HOFFMANN	188655	M	Ger.		Adjutant chief,Kriegslazarett,Ch.Romeuf au Puy (Fr.) 17.8.44	TORTURE	FR.
HOFFMANN	188556	M	Ger.		Sgt.,SS Einheit Walker,Gembsheim (Fr.) 12.44-9.1.45	MURDER	FR.
HOFFMANN	188657	M	Ger.		Fallschirmjaeger Rgt.5,4.Coy.,St.Laurent de Cuves (Fr.) 3.7.44	MURDER	FR.

HOF-HOF

NAME	C.R.FILE NUMBER	SEX	NATIO-NALITY	DATE OF BIRTH	RANK OCCUPATION UNIT PLACE AND DATE OF CRIME	REASON WANTED	WANTED BY
HOFFMANN	188970	M	Ger.		Sgt., Army, Paris (Fr.) 19.8.44	MURDER	FR.
HOFFMANN	190067	M	Ger.		Pol.Director, Police, Lublin (Pol.) 11.41	MURDER	POL.
HOFFMANN	192130	M	Ger.		Interpreter, Geh.Feldpolizei, Brussels (Bel.)	MISC.CRIMES	BEL.
HOFFMANN	192772	M			Standartenfhr., SS-Fuehrungsstab, Hauptamt, Conc.Camp Dora-Mittelbau, Nordhausen (Ger.) 43-45	TORTURE	U.S.
HOFFMANN	192948	M	Ger.	10 - 15	Usturmfhr., SS, Conc.Camp, Buchenwald (Ger.) 42-45	MURDER	U.S.
HOFFMANN	194354	M	Ger.		Cpl., Stalag IX C, Conc.Camp, Bad Sulza (Ger.) 9.40	MURDER	FR.
HOFFMANN	194547	M	Ger.		Civilian, (Ger.)	MURDER	U.S.
HOFFMANN	194750	M	Ger.		Director, Police, Radom (Pol.) 9.39-1.42	MURDER	POL.
HOFFMANN	196420	M	Ger.		Lt.Col., C.C., Rosen (Ger.)	TORTURE	BEL.
HOFFMANN	196559	M	Ger.		Blockfhr., C.C., Neuengamme (Ger.)	TORTURE	BEL.
HOFFMANN	196560	M	Ger.		Cpl., C.C., Dachau (Ger.)	TORTURE	BEL.
HOFFMANN	240101	M	Ger.	08	Usturmfhr., SD, Official, Sipo, Rotterdam (Neth.) 43	MURDER	UNWCC
HOFFMANN	250237	M	Ger.		Kapo, C.C., Neuengamme (Ger.) 45	BRUTALITY	FR.
HOFFMANN	250832	M	Ger.		Judge, of Court Material of Arlon, Feldgend., (Bel.)	INTERR.	BEL.
HOFFMANN	252161	M			Cpl., C.C., Harzungen-Nordhausen (Ger.)	MURDER	U.S.
HOFFMANN	253034	M	Ger.		Capt., Garrison-Commander at Nerezisce, Milna on the Island of Brac (Yugo.) 16.1.44	PILLAGE	YUGO.
HOFFMANN	254540	M	Ger.		Lt.,DC.a.F.D. 51983, Origny-le-Sec (Fr.) 22.,23.8.44	PILLAGE	FR.
HOFFMANN	254798	F	Ger.		Agent, Gestapo, Limoges (Fr.) 40-45	INTERR.	FR.
HOFFMANN	254801	M	Ger.		Capt., Kreiskommandant of Cherbourg F.P.No.03597, Bretteville (Fr.) 22.8.41	WITNESS	FR.
HOFFMANN	255120	M	Ger.		Capt., 377.Jaeg.Rgt. F.P.No.30084, Vinkt (Bel.)	MISC.CRIMES	BEL.
HOFFMANN	255582	M	Ger.		Capt., SS, C.C., Neckargerach (Ger.)	MURDER	FR.
HOFFMANN	255982	M	Ger.		Bn.Doctor (Physician) Army, Hedel (Neth.) 11.44	PILLAGE	NETH.
HOFFMANN	257601	M	Ger.		Dr., Bn.-Doctor, Heusden (Neth.) 5.11.44	SUSPECT	NETH.
HOFFMANN	257602	M	Ger.		Landrat und Kreisleiter, Weimar, Ottmannshausen (Ger.) 8.44	MURDER	U.S.
HOFFMANN	257775	M	Ger.		Dr., Oberstabsarzt, Mil., Amsterdam (Neth.) 23.10.44	MURDER	NETH.
HOFFMANN	300481	F	Ger.	23	Attached to Gestapo at Limoges, Hte.Vienne, Creuse, Correze, Dordogne, Indre (Fr.) 40-44	MURDER	FR.
HOFFMANN	300779	M	Ger.		Pvt., 1.Aufkl.Abt., 3.Coy., 2.Column, XV.Div. of the Afrika-Korps, Saint-Leger (Arlon) 5.9.44	MISC.CRIMES	BEL.
HOFFMANN	301135	M	Ger.		Osturmfhr., Gestapo, Paris (Fr.) 7.44	MISC.CRIMES	FR.
HOFFMANN	301261	M	Ger.		Employee, Abt.Lage-und Taetigkeitsbericht, SD, Brussels (Bel.) 6.40-9.44	MURDER	BEL.
HOFFMANN	301630	M	Ger.		Uschfhr., SS, 10.Coy., Renardmont and Stavelot (Bel.) 19.,20.12.44	MURDER	BEL.
HOFFMANN	301657	M	Ger.		Aide, Feldgend. Langres, Coiffy le Haut (Fr.) 9.43,11.43,1.44,8.44	MURDER	CZECH.
HOFFMANN	302030	M	Ger.		Member of the SD, Limburg (Neth.) 9.43-10.44	MURDER	NLTH.
HOFFMANN	305553	M	Ger.		Guard, SS or Gestapo at Bremen-Farge, C.C., (Ger.) 1.43-4.45	MURDER	U.K.
HOFFMANN	306586	M	Ger.		Hptschfhr., SS, SD, Stavanger (Nor.) 11.42	MURDER	U.K.
HOFFMANN, Adolph	67046	M			Pvt., SS, Conc.Camp, Struthof (Fr.)	MISC.CRIMES	FR.
HOFFMANN, Adolph	125032	M	Ger.		Photographer, Civilian (Fr.) 40-44	PILLAGE	FR.
HOFFMANN, Albert	21375	M	Ger.		Gruppenfhr., SS, Westfalia (Ger.)	TORTURE	UNWCC
HOFFMANN, Alfred	142941	M	Ger.	23. 7.04	Uschfhr., SS-Totenkopf-Standarte, C.C., Buchenwald (Ger.)	TORTURE	U.S.
HOFFMANN, Anni nee JUNG	253851	F	Ger.		Secr., Gestapo, Koblenz-Altwied (Ger.)	SUSPECT	U.S.
HOFFMANN, Baldwin	252162	M	Ger.		Pvt., C.C. Ellrich-Nordhausen (Ger.)	MURDER	U.S.
HOFFMANN, Bruno	306397	M	Ger.	22. 2.24	SS-Sgt., C.C., Buchenwald (Ger.) 5.38-10.43	MURDER	BEL.
HOFFMANN, Charlotte	173997	F	Ger.	15. 4.25	Police, Conc.Camp, Langenzenn (Ger.) 43-45	WITNESS	U.S.
HOFFMANN, Edmund	196561	M	Ger.	30. 1.10	SS-Guard, C.C., Struthof-Natzweiler (Fr.) 40-44	TORTURE	FR.
HOFFMANN, Emil	306017	M	Ger.		Member, C.C.Staff, Neuengamme (Ger.) 42-45	TORTURE	U.K.
HOFFMANN, Erich	145241	M		95	Oberlagerfhr., Organ.Todt, Ziegenhals Blechhammer (Ger.) 41-45	MURDER	FR.
HOFFMANN, Ernest	192770	M	Ger.		Room-Leader, C.C., Neckarelz (Ger.)	TORTURE	U.S.
HOFFMANN, Ernst	132033	M		17	Lt., Army, Hammelburg (Ger.) 44-45	MURDER	U.S.
HOFFMANN, Franz	133681	M			Uschfhr., SS, Conc.Camp, Buchenwald (Ger.)	MURDER	U.S.
HOFFMANN, Franz	145909	M	Ger.		Hptsturmfhr., SS, Bavaria (Ger.) 41-42	TORTURE	U.S.
HOFFMANN, Franz	167174	M			Pvt., Aviation, Troissereux (Fr.) 44	MURDER	FR.
HOFFMANN, Franz	261438	M	Ger.	05 - 15	Hptsturmfhr., Waffen-SS, C.C., Auschwitz (Pol.) 41-44	MURDER	POL.
HOFFMANN, Franz	306398	M	Ger.		SS-Lt., C.C.Dora, Nordhausen (Ger.) 40-45	MURDER	BEL.
HOFFMANN, Fritz	130986	M	Ger.		Employee, Conc.Camp, Kahla (Ger.) 44-45	MURDER	BEL.
HOFFMANN, Fritz (see HOFFMANN)	190338						
HOFFMANN, Fritz (see HOFMANN)	250845						
HOFFMANN, Fritz	252174	M			Sgt., C.C. Ellrich-Nordhausen (Ger.)	MURDER	U.S.
HOFFMANN, Georg	195425	M	Ger.	13	Scharfhr., SS, Gestapo-Employee, Kolin (Czech.)	MURDER	CZECH.
HOFFMANN, Gerhard	194583	M	Ger.	10	Kommandeur, Sipo, Oschfhr., SS, Lublin, Radzyn (Pol.) 40-44	TORTURE	POL.
HOFFMANN, Gustav	191504	M	Ger.	21	Agent, Gestapo, Bande (Lux.)	MURDER	BEL.
HOFFMANN, Hans	196421	M	Ger.	25. 4.04	Strumbannfhr., SS, Schupo, Prague (Czech.) 39-45	MISC.CRIMES	CZECH.
HOFFMANN, Herbert	149330	M	Ger.		Civilian, Lourche (Fr.)	PILLAGE	FR.
HOFFMANN, Herbert	167210	M	Ger.		Uschfhr., SD, Carcassonne, Camurac (Fr.) 30.11.43	MURDER	FR.
HOFFMANN, Hermann	252182	M			Pvt., C.C. Ellrich-Nordhausen (Ger.)	MURDER	U.S.
HOFFMANN, Hugo	132032	M	Ger.		Oschfhr., SS-Warden at Dachau, C.C., (Ger.) 44-45	MURDER	U.S.
HOFFMANN, Johann	127105	M	Ger.		Foreman, C.C., Buchenwald (Ger.) 42-45	TORTURE	FR.
HOFFMANN, Johann	196552	M	Ger.		Informer, Gestapo, Prague (Czech.)	MISC.CRIMES	CZECH.
HOFFMANN, Josef	252183	M			Oschfhr., C.C. Ellrich-Nordhausen (Ger.)	MURDER	U.S.
HOFFMANN, Josef	306840	M	Ger.	6. 1.02	Staff-Surgeon, SS-Pol.Bn.7-2 SD, Vollan - Trondheim district - (Nor.) 44-45	MURDER	NOR.
HOFFMANN, Karl	62103	M	Ger.		Lt., Feldgend., Louroux Deboublé (Fr.) 15.6.44	MURDER	FR.
HOFFMANN, Karl	132330	M	Ger.	05	Hptwachtmstr., Schupo, C.C., Amberg (Ger.) 43	TORTURE	U.S.
HOFFMANN, Karl	142414	M	Ger.	07	Oschfhr., SS, C.C., Lublin (Pol.)	MURDER	FR.
HOFFMANN, Karl	146856	M	Ger.		Lt., Feldgend., Gannat (Fr.) 18.7.44	MURDER	FR.
HOFFMANN, Karl	193197	M	Ger.	05	Oberwachtm.,guard,Reichsjustiz-Ministerium,Feldstraflager, Waffen-SS. Finmark (Nor.) 42-45	MISC.CRIMES	NOR., YUGO.
HOFFMANN, Karl	251609	M	Ger.	6.11.05	C.C., Ardennes Chaudion (Fr.) 17.1.41	MURDER	FR.
HOFFMANN, Karl	252184	M	Ger.	11. 6.02	Pvt., C.C. Ellrich-Nordhausen (Ger.)	MURDER	U.S.
HOFFMANN	305424	M	Ger.		Head of Detachment, Sonderkmdo.Gestapo, 2.SS-Pz.Div., H.Q., La Roche, Wibrin, 10.1.-12.1.45	MURDER	BEL.

HOF-HOF

NAME	C.R.FILE NUMBER	SEX	NATIO-NALITY	DATE OF BIRTH	RANK OCCUPATION UNIT PLACE AND DATE OF CRIME	REASON WANTED	WANTED BY
HOFFMANN, Karl	254941	M	Ger.		9 Coy.,SS-Pol.Rgt.,Totenkopf 28,Habere,Lullin (Fr.) 25.12.43	MURDER	FR.
HOFFMANN, Marga	149331	F	Ger.	15	SS-Aufseherin,C.C.Ravensbrueck (Ger.)	MISC.CRIMES	FR.
HOFFMANN, Oskar	12398	M	Ger.		Doctor,Liaison-Official,Reichswirtschaftskammer,Maehren,Brno (Czech)	TORTURE	UNWCC.,CZECH.
HOFFMANN, Otto	21774	M	Ger.		Lt.,General,Waffen-SS,SR,Policeleader,W.K.R.,Chief of SS Office Race Settlement.	TORTURE	UNWCC.
HOFFMANN, Otto	139784	M	Ger.	05	Pvt.,Guard,Waffen-SS,Arbeitslager 101,Buchenwald,Magdeburg (Ger.) 44-45	TORTURE	U.S.
HOFFMANN, Otto	195216	M	Ger.	80	Obergruppenfhr.,NSDAP,Higher Police,SS,Vosges Alsace (Fr.) 44	MURDER	U.K.
HOFFMANN, Otto	259361	M	Ger.		Obersturmfhr.,Member of Gestapo,Poitiers area (Fr.) 40-45	MISC.CRIMES	FR.
HOFFMANN, Paul	151689	M	Ger.	8. 3.13	Paratroop Rgt.,St.Laurent de Cuves,(Fr.) 3.7.44	MURDER	FR.
HOFFMANN, Paul	194387	M	Ger.	05	Guard,C.C.Lublin (Pol.) 42-44	MURDER	POL.
HOFFMANN, Reinhold	167814	M	Ger.		Pvt., 9 Regt.,Res.Gren. 1 Coy., Magny D'Avignon (Fr.) 18.9.44	MURDER	FR.
HOFFMANN, Renate	251620	F	Ger.		Employee,Sipo,Abt. IV A,Brussels (Bel.) 40-45	INTERR.	BEL.
HOFFMANN, Rudolf	122587	M	Ger.		Member,Gestapo de Chambery,Challes les Eaux et Arbin (Fr.)	MURDER	FR.
HOFFMANN, Rudolf	194909	M	Ger.	11. 1.94	Officer,Police,Petange (Lux.)	PILLAGE	LUX.
HOFFMANN, Werner	62265	M	Ger.		Sgt.,Army, 18 V.G.Div.,293 Rgt., 6 Coy., 2 Bn.,Bleialf (Ger.)12.44	MURDER	U.S.
HOFFMANN, Wilhelm	133692	M			SS-Unterscharfhr.,C.C.Buchenwald (Ger.)	TORTURE	U.S.
HOFFMANN, Willy	132712	M	Ger.		Surveillant de Chantier,O.T.,Ile D'Auvigny (Fr.)	TORTURE	FR.
HOFFMANN, Willy	154239	M	Ger.	28. 2.93	SS-Unterscharfhr.,C.C.Hinzert (Ger.)	TORTURE	FR.
HOFFMAYER	11239	M	Ger.		Adjutant,Police,Ugine (Fr.) 44	MURDER	FR.
HOFFMAYER, Johann	251584	M		5.12.97	SS-Rottenfhr.,SS,C.C.Ellrich-Nordhausen (Ger.)	MURDER	U.S.
HOFFMEIER	139787	M		05	Plant-Manager,Arb.Kdo. Georgenschacht,Waffen-SS.	MURDER	U.S.
HOFFMEIER	166605	M	Ger.		SS-Obersturmbannfhr.,SS (Pol.) 40	MURDER	U.S.
HOFFMEINE	173280	M	Ger.	98	Camp Officer,Oflag 2,C.C.Salonika (Grc.) 41	TORTURE	U.K.
HOFFMEISTER	194596	M	Ger.		Lt.Col.,Abwehr,Athenes (Grc.) 42-44	MISC.CRIMES	U.K.
HOFFNER	260169	M	Ger.		SS-Mann,SS, (Nor.) 8.42-3.43, 4.43-5.45	BRUTALITY	YUGO.
HOFFSCHILE	132715	M	Ger.		Camp Leader,C.C.Buchenwald (Ger.)	TORTURE	FR.
HOFFSOMMER	149271	M			Cpl.,Stalag 6 C.	PILLAGE	FR.
HOFFSOMMER	256094	M	Ger.		Naval Lt.,Cmdt of the personnal,Werkendam (Neth.) 4.45	MURDER	NETH.
HOFHEINZ, Walter	24938	M	Ger.		SS-Unterscharfhr.,SS,C.C.Struthof (Fr.) 42-44	MURDER	FR.
HOFINGER	259647	M	Ger.		Lt.Col.,Staff of Air-Fleet 3,Paris Seine (Fr.) 24.6.42	INTERR.	FR.
HOFLE, Herrmann	21373	M	Ger.		General Lt., Police,SS,W.K.R. XI 44	MURDER	UNWCC.
HOFLER	300772	M	Ger.		Unterscharfhr.,Chief of House Painting Section,Birkenau Kommando C.C.Auschwitz-Birkenau (Pol.) 40	MURDER	FR.
HOFMAN	130367	M	Ger.		Leader,Volkssturm,C.C.Kaisheim (Ger.)	TORTURE	BEL.
HOFMAN	162587	M		10	SS-Obersturmfhr.,SS,C.C.Buchenwald (Ger.) 43-44	TORTURE	U.S.
HOFMAN	171973	M			Ortsgruppenleiter,NSDAP,Freiensee (Ger.) 11.9.44	MURDER	U.S.
HOFMAN	174470	M		00	Capt.,Army,Caen,Abbaye,Ardenne (Fr.)	WITNESS	CAN.
HOFMAN	256827	M	Ger.	96	Capt.,Laufen,Tittmoning (Ger.) 44.-45	MISC.CRIMES	U.S.
HOFMAN, Helmut	134858	M	Ger.		Civilian (Ger.)	TORTURE	U.S.
HOFMANN	397	M	Ger.		Hauptsturmfhr.,Army,Waffen-SS,Caen (Fr.) 6.44	MURDER	FR.
HOFMANN	1080	M			Gendarm,Army,Feldgendarmerie,Langres-Flagoy (Fr.)	TORTURE	FR.
HOFMANN	132052	M	Ger.		Doctor,Medical General,Army,Oflag 13 B,C.C.Hammelburg (Ger.)1.10.44	MURDER	U.S.
HOFMANN	133931	M			Obersturmbannfhr.,Waffen-SS,C.C.Flossenburg (Ger.)	MURDER	U.S.
HOFMANN	133333	M		12	N.C.O.,SS.	MURDER	U.S.
HOFMANN	146702	M	Ger.		P.O.,Proffessor,Member ministry education (Ger.)	MISC.CRIMES	U.S.
HOFMANN	149523	M			Sturmfhr.,S.A.,Schoerzingen (Ger.)	MISC.CRIMES	FR.
HOFMANN	162598	M	Ger.	05	SS-Unterscharfhr.,SS,C.C.Buchenwald (Ger.) 42-45	TORTURE	U.S.
HOFMANN	173623	M	Ger.		Obergruppenfhr.,General,SS,Police,Stuttgart (Ger.) 44	TORTURE	FR.
HOFMANN	188415	M	Ger.		Coy.Commander, Lt., SS-Div.,"Das Reich",near St.Vith (Bel.) 12.44	MURDER	U.S.
HOFMANN	189391	M	Ger.		Kreisleiter,NSDAP,Weimar (Ger.)	MURDER	U.S.
HOFMANN	251098	M	Ger.	5.10.02	Oberscharfhr.,S.A.,Vodnany (Czech.)	MURDER	CZECH.
HOFMANN	251618	M	Ger.		Police Employee,Sipo Abt. IV D,Brussels (Bel.) 40-45	INTERR.	BEL.
HOFMANN	254625	M	Ger.		Obersturmfhr.,SS Coy., Anville (Fr.) 23.3.-5.7.43	PILLAGE	FR.
HOFMANN	254799	M	Ger.		Sgt.,Gend.Trupp 533,Le Chablais (Fr.) 19-21.5.44	MISC.CRIMES	FR.
HOFMANN	254805	M	Ger.		Unterscharfhr.,Gestapo,Paris (Fr.) 41-44	TORTURE	FR.
HOFMANN	260168	M	Ger.		Lt.,7 Army Regt.d.Res.,Massif du Vercors,Isère and Drôme (Fr.) 44	SUSPECT	FR.
HOFMANN	300714	M	Ger.		Unterscharfhr.,SS,Secret Field Police,Hotel Bratford,Paris (Fr.) 41-44	MISC.CRIMES	FR.
HOFMANN (see HOFFMAN)	301202						
HOFMANN, Adam	261610	M	Ger.		Farmer,Civilian,Poppenhausen Krs.Tauberheim (Ger.) 44	MURDER	POL.
HOFMANN, Arno	11240	M	Ger.		Pvt.,Army,Pz.Gren.Rgt.,111,Albine (Fr.) 29.6.44	MURDER	FR.
HOFMANN, Franz	398	M			Lt.,Lagerfhr.,Waffen-SS,C.C.Dachau (Ger.) 40-43	MURDER	FR.
HOFMANN, Franz	7867	M			H.J.Oberstfhr.,Public Official,Weimar (Ger.)	MURDER	FR.
HOFMANN, Friedrich	105947	M	Ger.	90	Ortsgruppenleiter,NSDAP, Freiensee (Ger.) 5.-6.44	MURDER	U.S.
HOFMANN (or HOFFMANN Fritz)	250845	M	Ger.		SS-Obersturmfhr.,SS,C.C.Dachau (Ger.) 42	MURDER	YUGO.
HOFMANN, Gustave	165567	M	Ger.	1. 3.21	Staff Pvt., Gestapo,Special Detachment "Standgericht" Bande (Lux.) 24.-25.12.44	MURDER	BEL.
HOFMANN, Henri	194582	M	Ger.		Pvt.,Assist. Custom-House,Veigy Foncenay (Fr.) 6.10.43	TORTURE	FR.
HOFMANN, Kurt	186670	M	Ger.	10. 3.04	Doctor,Oberstaatsanwalt,Justizministerium, (Lux.) 8.40-12.41	MURDER	LUX.
HOFMANN, Michael	173574	M	Ger.		Pvt.,Guard,C.C.Stargard (Yugo.) 27.2.43	MURDER	YUGO.
HOFMANN, Paul	141961	M			Camp Leader,D.A.F.,Zella-Mehlis (Ger.) 42-45	TORTURE	U.S.
HOFMANN, Rudolf (Rudi)	142459	M			Proffessor,SD,Chambery (Fr.)	MURDER	FR.
HOFMANN, Walter	167813	M	Ger.		Pvt.,Army, 9 Res.Gren.Rgt., 1 Coy., Magny D'Avignon (Fr.) 18.9.44	MURDER	FR.
HOFMAYER	130370	M			SS,C.C.Mauthausen (Aust.) 41-45	MURDER	U.S.
HOFMEISTER	167164	M	Ger.		Obermeister,Kreiskommandantur de Lunsville,Vitrimont (Fr.)16.10.40	WITNESS	FR.
HOFMEYER	194772	M	Ger.		Pvt.,Gebirgs-Jaeger Rgt.,100,Col du Petit,St.Bernard (Fr.) 27.-28.8.44	MURDER	FR.
HOFNER	301752	M	Ger.		SS-Sgt.,Rapport Fuehrer,C.C.Auschwitz (Pol.) 40	MURDER	FR.
HOFRIETER	130657	M			SS,C.C.Dora Mittelbau,Nordhausen (Ger.)	MURDER	U.S.
HOFS, Erich	194580	M	Ger.		Assist.,Custom-House,Veigy Foncenex (Fr.) 6.10.43	TORTURE	FR.
HOFSCHULTE, Herman-Josef	121050	M	Ger.	4. 4.08	SS-Oberscharfhr.,SS-Totenkopfsturmbann,Command Staff,Buchenwald(Ger)	MURDER	FR., U.S.

HOF - HOL

NAME	C.R.FILE NUMBER	SEX	NATIONALITY	DATE OF BIRTH	RANK OCCUPATION UNIT PLACE AND DATE OF CRIME	REASON WANTED	WANTED BY
HOFSTEDTER	301099	M	Ger.		Criminal-secr.,served with the R.S.D.,Abteilung V,Copenhagen (Den.) 8.43	INTERR.	DEN.
HOFT	162421	M	Ger.		Army,Gren.Ers.Bn.346,Aulnois (Bel.)	WITNESS	BEL.
HOGE	193182	M	Ger.		Cpl.,Kgf.Arb.Bn.190,Karasjok (Nor.) 8.43	MURDER	NOR.
HOGENKOPF	162414	M	Ger.		Head,Standartenfhr.,Gestapo,SS,Berlin (Ger.-Czech.) 39-45	MURDER	CZECH.
HOGER,Josef	306399	M	Ger.	25. 2.20	Cpl.,SS,C.C.Buchenwald (Ger.) 16.5.38-9.10.43	MURDER	BEL.
HOG-EYES (see JUNKER,Carl)	137781						
HOGLMEIER,Josef	196653	M	Ger.	11.11.04	Employee,techn.Civ.firm,Army.	TORTURE	FR.
HOHAUZ	306203		Ger.		Member of Staff,small fortress,C.C.Theresienstadt (Czech.) 1.10.38	MURDER	CZECH.
HOHEISEL	254356	M	Ger.		Lt.Col.,Army,Bonn (Ger.) 43-45	WITNESS	U.S.
HOHEISEL,Ermgard	135180	F	Ger.		Guard,Civ.,C.C.Helmbrechts (Ger.)	TORTURE	U.S.
HOHENAUER	258708	M			Commander of Hannover Eastern District police,Bad Salzdetfurth(Ger)44	MURDER	U.S.
HOHENBERG,Arthur	162854	M	Ger.	24. 2.99	Chief,Physician,Inf.Regt.517,Bn.Stab IV,Heinaut,Virelles les Chimay (Bel.) 5.-6.40	PILLAGE	BEL.
HOHENDALL	152803	M			Feldwebel,Army,Stalag Luft III C,Sagan (Ger.) 9.4.44	MURDER	U.S.
HOHENSCHEID	194895	M	Ger.		Osturmfhr.,SS,Athens (Gre.) 43-44	MISC.CRIMES	U.K.
HOHENSTEIN	132075				N.C.O.,Guard,4 SS-Baubrigade,SS-Div.Totenkopf,Ellrich,Gardelegen (Ger.) 4.-14.4.45	MURDER	U.S.
HOHLE,Ali	190570	M		06	Dr.,Hptsturmfhr.,SS,C.C.Neuengamme (Ger.) 43	MURDER	YUGO.
HOHLER,Heinrich	196654	M	Ger.		C.C.Struthof,Natzweiler (Fr.) 40-44	TORTURE	FR.
HOHLER	399	M	Ger.		Kriminal-Ober-Asst.,Gestapo,Oslo (Nor.) 41	TORTURE	NOR.
HOHLER,Karl	257822	M	Ger.	12 or 13	Krimn.-Asst.,Oschfhr.,SS,S.D.,Referat E,Abt.IV,Oslo (Nor.) 40-44	INTERR.	NOR.
HOHLOCH,Gottlob	134854	M	Ger.		Secr.,Kripo,Huppertshuetten (Ger.) 12.9.44	MURDER	U.S.
HOHLS,Hermann	146685	M	Ger.	90	C.O.,Volkssturm,Gardelegen (Ger.) 9.-14.4.45	MURDER	U.S.
HOHMANN	143010	M			Civilian,Ginnheim bei Frankfurt (Ger.) 11.44	WITNESS	U.S.
HOHN	251587	M			Cpl.,C.C.Ellrich,Nordhausen (Ger.)	MURDER	U.S.
HOHN	252428	M	Ger.		Usturmfhr.,SS,C.C.Oranienburg (Ger.)	MURDER	BEL.
HOHN,George	135179	M			Guard,SS,Helmbrechts (Ger.) 7.44-13.4.45	TORTURE	U.S.
HOHN,Heiner	255580	M	Ger.	15	Stabsamtsleiter,state service,Krakow (Pol.) 44	MISC.CRIMES	POL.
HOHN,Moritz	130388	M	Ger.		Dr.,Prison,Siegburg (Ger.) 2.-8.42	INTERR.	U.S.LUX. BEL.
HOHN,Walter (or HOEHN,Walter)	261912	M	Ger.		Capt.,Army,Sued und West Leder-Im-Export,Fa.Walter Hoohn,Meiningen Waalwijk and Heusden (Neth.) 5.43-10.44	PILLAGE	NETH.
HOHNE	154251	M		05	Uschfhr.,SS,W-SS,C.C.Sachsenhausen (Ger.)	MURDER	U.K.
HOHNE	196566	M			Cpl.,C.C.Neuengamme (Ger.)	TORTURE	BEL.
HOHNE,Reinhardt	132713	M	Ger.		Fermier,Civ.,Schlabach (Ger.) 12.42	MURDER	FR.
HOHNE,Siegfried	306400	M	Ger.	16.10.21	Cpl.,SS,C.C.Buchenwald (Ger.) 16.5.38-9.10.43	MURDER	BEL.
HOHNNANOS,Otto	260371	M	Ger.		Oberwachtmeister,SS,Penitentiary,Nord-Norway (Nor.) 6.42-5.45	MURDER	YUGO.
HOHREN	251607	M	Ger.		Krimn.Obersekr.,Sipo,Bruessel (Bel.)	INTERR.	BEL.
HOINS	255112	M	Ger.		Lt.,Army,Wassennaar near the Haag (Neth.) 17.11.44.	WITNESS	NETH.
HOIS,Otto	251593	M			Sturmmann,SS,C.C.Harzungen,Nordhausen (Ger.)	MURDER	U.S.
HOIZ,Karl	257895	M			Asst.,Gauleiter,NSDAP,150 Pz.Bie.,Meuse Bridge,Antwerp (Bel.) 12.44	MISC.CRIMES	U.S.
HOIZAMMER	11241	M	Ger.		M.F.V.,Medecin Chef,St.Monehould (Fr.) 29.8.44	MURDER	FR.
HOJCI	301323	M	Ger.		Member of the Gestapo at Trencin,C.C.Oswiecim,Birkenau (Pol.)39-45	MURDER	CZECH.
HOKSEMA,Reinhardt	145307	M			Civilian,Borkum (Ger.) 4.8.44	MURDER	U.S.
HOLAND,Ernst	163658	M	Ger.		Chief,Civ.,Firm "Katch",Hildburghausen (Ger.)	MURDER	FR.
HOLB	9688	M	Ger.		Hptsturmfhr.,SS,Comnd.Camp,Oranienburg (Ger.) 39-44	MURDER	CZECH.
HOLBACH (see HOESSELBARTH)	83843						
HOLBACH (see BOLBACH)	138281						
HOLCZAK,Franz	31935		Ger.		Landgerichtsdirektor,Ministry of Justice,Opava (Czech.) 21.2.40	MURDER	CZECH.
HOLD,Theresia	300901	F	Ger.		Head,Cafe Pfandler,Pertisau-Maurach (Aust.Tyrol) 13.7.44	MURDER	FR.
HOLDAMPF,Georg	192766	M			4 SS-Totenkopfsturmbann,C.C.Nordhausen,Dora Mittelbau (Ger.) 43-45	WITNESS	U.S.
HOLDEFEHR	300780	M	Ger.		Pvt.,1 Aufkl.-Abtl.,3 Coy,,2 Column,XV Div. of the Afrika Corps. St.Leger (Arlon) 5.9.44	MISC.CRIMES	BEL.
HOLDERER (or HOLZRI)	189505	M			Lager-Commandant of Prison for P.O.W. and Civ.,Freiburg-Breisgau (Ger.) 44	MURDER	FR.
HOLDERLEIN,Otto	185118	M	Ger.		Chef d'Atelier,Civ.,SS,C.C.Dachau (Ger.)	MURDER	FR.
HOLDORF,Herbert	252884	M		15. 3.13	Pvt.,C.C.Ellrich,Nordhausen (Ger.)	MURDER	U.S.
HOLDT,Max	162589	M	Ger.		Lt.,Inspector of Arms and Munition-works,Arbeitslager C.C.Regensburg (Ger.) 27.4.45	TORTURE	U.S.
HOLENIA	11551	M	Ger.		Usturmfhr.,SS,Gestapo,Bergen (Nor.) 41	TORTURE	NOR.
HOLERICHTER,Helmuth	194567	M	Ger.		Navy, 18 S.S.T.A.,Schiffsstamm-Abteilung,Montceau, Les Mines (Fr.) 22.7.44	MURDER	FR.
HOLFELD,Erich	105949	M			Sonder-Kommando at Suttrop,Civ.,Langenbacktel,Hohenlichte (Ger.) 22.3.45	MURDER	U.S.
HOLIK,Ferdinand	261890	M	Ger.	18. 1.91	Member,SA,Jablonov District Velke Mezirici (Czech.) 44	SUSPECT	CZECH.
HOLINAICHER,Josef	173996	M			Guard,SS,C.C.Muhldorf,Ampfing (Ger.) 6.44-4.45	MURDER	U.S.
HOLLACHER	188414	M		18	Cpl.,Army,Wehrkreis XII,Wiesbaden,Hullenberg (Ger.) 21.9.44	MURDER	U.S.
HOLLACK	192793	M	Ger.		Capt.,SS,S.D.,Stalag,C.C.Falstad (Nor.) 41-44	MURDER	NOR.
HOLLACK	253702	M	Ger.		Chief,Gestapo,Wilhelmshaven (Ger.) 10.7.44	INTERR.	FR.
HOLLAK	302032	M	Ger.		Sturmbannfhr.,SS,Falstad slave labour camp (Nor.) 42-43	MURDER	YUGO.
HOLLAND,Fritz or Hans	188365	M		14	Crim.secr.,Stapo-Leistelle,Frankfurt-Main (Ger.) 43	TORTURE	U.K.
HOLLAND,Rudolph Hans	105950	M		12	Employed at Polte Minitions factory,Magdeburg (Ger.) 44-45	MISC.CRIMES	U.S.
HOLLAENDER,Alfred	186669	M	Ger.	8. 1.12	Member,Gestapo,Luxembourg (Lux.)	MURDER	LUX.
HOLLANDS	306980	M	Ger.		Navy,attached to the Army,Leenwarden (Neth.) 27.10.44	MURDER	NETH.
HOLLAUF,Hubert	173998	M			Arbeitslager,C.C.Muhldorf,Ampfing (Ger.) 6.44-4.45	MURDER	U.S.
HOLLBORN	126550		Ger.		Leiter,Gestapo,Officer,C.C.Hagen (Ger.) 40-45	MURDER	U.S.
HOLLE	132711	M	Ger.		Lt.,Military Prison,Wien,Vienne (Aust.) 43-44	TORTURE	FR.
HOLLE	161176	M			Civ.,Daasdorf,Guthmannshausen (Ger.) 7.-8.44	INTERR.	U.S.

NAME	C.R.FILE NUMBER	SEX	NATIO-NALITY	DATE OF BIRTH	RANK	OCCUPATION UNIT PLACE AND DATE OF CRIME	REASON WANTED	WANTED BY
HOLLE	167799	M	Ger.			Wirtschaftsamt Lwow-Galizia(Pol.) 9.39-44	PILLAGE	POL.
HOLLE see HALLE	190339							
HOLLEI	125735	M	Ger.			SS-Uschfhr.,SS,C.C.Flossenburg(Ger.) 44-45	MURDER	U.S.
HOLLENDER, Willi	122588	M	Ger.			Prt.,Army,F.P.Nr.56067D,Semaphore de Greach Maout,Pleubian(Fr.) 5.8.44	MURDER	FR.
HOLLENHORST	39816	M	Ger.			SS-Rottfhr.,SS-Div.F.P.Nr.48963B,St.-Sulpice,Fortmusson Chateau Gontier(Fr.) 2.-6.8.44	MURDER	FR.
HOLLER	163251	M	Ger.			Senior-W.O.,Army,Revin,Ardennes(Fr.) 13.-14.4.44	MURDER	FR.
HOLLER	192361	M	Ger.			Krim.-Assist.,Gestapo,Brno(Czech.) 39-40	MURDER	CZECH.
HOLLER	193190	M				Cpl.,6 Coy.,Inf.Regt.357,Nordreisa(Nor.) 41	MURDER	NOR.
HOLLER	306088	M	Ger.			SS-Uschfhr.,C.C.Hamburg-Neuengamme(Ger.) -45	MURDER	CZECH.
HOLLER, Hans	260819	M	Ger.	15		Osturmfhr.,SS,Mienstedt(Ger.) 24.8.44	MURDER	U.S.
HOLLER, Jakobine Mina	192523	F	Ger.	19.6.23		Civilian,Schussbach(Ger.) 14.3.45	TORTURE	U.K.
HOLLER, M.	196582	M	Ger.			Schollach(Ger.)	MURDER	U.S.
HOLLER, Roli	250252	M	Ger.			Staff-Sgt.,6 Coy.,II Bn.,893 Inf.Regt.,264 Inf.Div.,Primosten(Yugo.)7.44	MURDER	YUGO.
HOLLERT	140095		Ger.			SS-Hptsturmfhr.,Gestapo de Lyon,Perigeux(Fr.) 6.-7.44	MURDER	FR.
HOLLERT, Fritz	189622	M	Ger.			Member SD,Lyon(Fr.)	MISC.CRIMES	FR.
HOLLIDT, Karl	258960	M	Ger.	91		Col.-Gen.	WITNESS	U.S.
HOLLMAN, George	143022	M				Agent,Gestapo,Bielefeld(Ger.) 41-45	MURDER	U.S.
HOLLMANN	254800	M	Ger.			Cpl.,Gend.,Vendome(Fr.) 9.8.44	MURDER	FR.
HOLLMANN	305188	M	Ger.			Capt.,Brandenburg-Regt.,Dienststelle Feldpost-Nr.36302,Mil.-Cmdt.at Livadia,Arachova,Livadia(Grc.) 8.-9.10.43, 5.11.and 10.12.43	INTERR.	GRC.
HOLLMANN, Alois	252885	M				Uschfhr.,SS,C.C.Harzungen-Nordhausen(Ger.)	MURDER	U.S.
HOLLMANN, Emil	254628	M	Ger.			Sgt.,Sipo,Raon l'Etappe(Fr.) 4.9.44	MURDER	FR.
HOLLMANN, Hans	901417	M	Ger.			W.O.,Waffen-SS,15-727 Pont St.Esprit Gard.from 28.2.44-25.8.45,Carsan (Fr.) 6.3.44	MURDER	FR.
HOLLSTEIN, D.	132080					Chief Doctor,Stalag VIF,KL.Munster(Ger.)	MURDER	U.S.
HOLM	253057	M	Ger.			Schfhr.,SS,Apeldoorn(Neth.) 2.10.44	MURDER	U.S.
HOLM	254806	M	Ger.	06		Schfhr.,SS,Gestapo,Paris(Fr.) 41-44	TORTURE	FR.
HOLM, Erich	192360	M	Ger.			Kriminal-Assist.,Oschfhr.,Gestapo,SS,Antwerpen(Bel.) 42-43	Murder	BEL.
HOLM, Erich	302033	M	Ger.			Oschfhr.,SS,SD,Apeldoorn,Woeste Hoeve(Neth.) 44,7.4.45	MURDER	NETH.
HOLM, Fritz	189249	M	Ger.			Leader,Occupied Territories,Poznan(Pol.) 39-43	PILLAGE	POL.
HOLM, Otto	306160	M	Ger.			Oschfhr.,St.Die(Fr.) 9.44	MURDER	U.K.
HOLMAN	162856	M	Ger.			SS Adolf Hitler,Odet(Bel.) 4.9.44	MURDER	BEL.
HOLMANN	151691	M				Brandenburg-Div.Member,Pont St.Esprit(Fr.) 44	MURDER	FR.
HOLMANN, Hans	196567	M	Ger.			W.O.,Waffen-SS,Sederon-Jzen Le Bruisse(Fr.) 22.2.44	MISC.CRIMES	FR.
HOLMANN, Hans	161175	M	Ger.			Waffen-SS,Pont St.Esprit(Fr.)	MURDER	FR.
HOLMANN, Hans	188972	M	Ger.			W.O.,Waffen-SS,Carsan(Fr.) 6.3.44	MURDER	FR.
HOLMEIER or HOLMEIN	300696	M	Ger.			Panzer-Grenadier,SS,Gembloux(Bel.) 4.9.44	MURDER	BEL.
HOLSCHUHER, Heinrich	262128	M	Ger.	15.6.13		Mason,Civ.Occup.,NSDAP,SA,RAD,Muenchen(Ger.) (L.o.D.N.A.o.D.)	SUSPECT	U.S.
HOLSCHUMACHER	39817	M	Ger.			SS-Sturmfhr.,Div.SS,Feldpost-Nr.48963B,St.Sulpice,Fortmusson,Chateau Gontier(Fr.)	MURDER	FR.
HOLSER, Emile	196568	F	Ger.			Agent,Gestapo,Curgies(Fr.) 6.44	MISC.CRIMES	FR.
HOLST or HOLSTE, Hans	29798	M	Ger.			Lt.,Army,Faquet(Fr.) 20.6.-9.8.44	MURDER	FR.
HOLST	127106	M	Ger.			Prt.,Panz.Div.Staff 11,2 Coy.,2 AA 7A,Albine(Fr.) 12.8.44	MURDER	FR.
HOLST, Paul	257823	M	Ger.			Wachtmeister,SS-Pol.,Oslo(Nor.) 45	MURDER	NOR.
HOLSTE	191287	M	Ger.			Prt.,Eis.Art.Bn.717,St.Andries Varsenare Les Bruges(Bel.)	MURDER	BEL.
HOLSTE, Hans see Holst	29798							
HOLSTEIN	161178	M	Ger.	90		Sgt.,Army,Inf.,C.C.Fresnes,Paris(Fr.) 42-44	TORTURE	U.K.
HOLSTEIN	161969	M	Ger.			Medicin Chief Stalag VIE,KL.Muenster(Ger.)	MISC.CRIMES	FR.
HOLSTEIN	257776	M	Ger.			Engineer,Daimler-Benz A.G.,Sochaux(Fr.) 11.44	PILLAGE	FR.
HOLSTEIN	305189	M	Ger.			SS-Sgt.,SS,Ludwigshafen,Constanz(Ger.) 28.4.45	MURDER	NETH.
HOLTERMANN	167212	M	Ger.			Civilian"Einsatz Rosenberg" 40-44	PILLAGE	FR.,UNWCC.
HOLTMANN	132078					Capt.,Stalag VIF,KL.Muenster(Ger.) 42-45	MURDER	U.S.
HOLTZ	9689	M	Ger.			SS-Hptsturmfhr.,Gestapo Kommissar,Prag(Czech.) 39-44	TORTURE	CZECH.
HOLTZ	257760					Employee,C.C.Dora-Nordhausen(Ger.)	BRUTALITY	FR.
HOLTZ, Hans	253703	M	Ger.			Lt.,25 Cycle Regt.,Le Saint(Fr.) 10.7.44	INTERR.	FR.
HOLTZ, Kurt	161177	M	Ger.	10		Military Service SS,Poznan(Pol.) 39-43	MURDER	POL.
HOLTZ, Walter	131289	M	Ger.	06		SS N.C.O.,Arnstadt-Thuer.(Ger.)	MURDER	U.S.
HOLTZEIMER	39818	M	Ger.			C.C.Schonmoor-Elbing(Ger.) 7.41	MURDER	U.K.
HOLUFKA	258990	M				Guard,SS,KL.Hohenrheim near Plattling(Ger.) 2.-5.45	MURDER	U.S.
HOLVEC, Karl	253049	M	Ger.			Capt.,Admin Bureau,Balaives-Ardennes(Fr.) 30.8.44	MISC.CRIMES	FR.
HOLZ	29800		Ger.			Army,N.C.O.	MURDER	FR.
HOLZ	75916		Ger.			Assist.Gauleiter,SS,Nuernberg Oflag 13B(Ger.) 1.10.44-45	TORTURE	U.S.
HOLZ	147313	M	Ger.			11 Pz.Div.,Prt.,South West France	MURDER	FR.
HOLZ	191992	M	Ger.			Lt.,Army,Pontivy(Fr.) 3.8.44	MURDER	FR.
HOLZ	192219	M	Ger.			Lt.,Army,Ruffauden Meiraud(Fr.)	PILLAGE	FR.
HOLZ	196570	M	Ger.			Capt.,25 Festungsstamm,Plumeliau(Fr.)	MURDER	FR.
HOLZ (al."Buby")	254947	M	Ger.			Lt.,377 Jaeg.Regt.,1 Inf.Bn.,Vinkt and Meigem(Bel.) 25.-31.5.40	MISC.CRIMES	BEL.
HOLZ	256881	M	Ger.			Schfhr.,SS Weida,Nordhausen(Ger.)	MURDER	U.S.
HOLZ	261781	M	Ger.			Lt.,Art.H.D.V.199-2235 N.D.F.No.270460,Lorgies(Fr.) 3.9.44	MURDER	FR.
HOLZ, Hans	192137	M	Ger.			Sgt.,Geheime Feldpolizei,Brussel(Bel.)	TORTURE	BEL.
HOLZ, Josef	256944	M	Ger.	8.4.05		Employee at C.C.Nordhausen(Ger.)	MURDER	U.S.
HOLZ, Karl	21377	M	Ger.			Gruppenfhr.,Gauleiter,SA,NSDAP	TORTURE	UNWCC.
HOLZ, Karl	143008	M	Ger.			Civilian (Ger.)	TORTURE	U.S.
HOLZ, Wilhelm	126938	M	Ger.			Civilian,Niederheimbach(Ger.) 9.43	TORTURE	U.S.
HOLZAMMER	187935	M				Medicin-Chief,Miscellaneous,M.F.U.,St.Mene Hould(Fr.)	MURDER	FR.

HOL-HOP

NAME	C.R.FILE NUMBER	SEX	NATIO-NALITY	DATE OF BIRTH	RANK OCCUPATION UNIT PLACE AND DATE OF CRIME	REASON WANTED	WANTED BY
HOLZAPFEL	143012	M	Ger.		Pvt.Guard,Air Force,CC Thekla/Leipzig,Buchenwald(Ger.)	MURDER	U.S.
HOLZAPFEL	174292	M			Capt.Abwehr Off.Stalag 55 VD,Aulendorf(Ger.)8.42	MURDER	YUGO.
HOLZAPFEL	196569	M			Interpreter,Gendarmerie-Field,Hennebont(Fr.)	TORTURE	FR.
HOLZDORFER, Philipp	173999	M			Member,SS CC Muhldorf-Ampfing(Ger.)6.44-4.45	MURDER	U.S.
HOLZENTHAL, Georg	167220	M	Ger.		Pvt.F.P.No.37199 B,Plombieres Vosges(Fr.)18.7.44	MURDER	FR.
HOLZER	12434	M	Ger.		Hpttruppenfhr.Organisation Todt(S.K.)Tinteniac(Fr.)3.8.44	MURDER	FR.
HOLZER	250238	M	Ger.		Gestapo,Lille(Fr.)40-44	MURDER	FR.
HOLZER, Corbinan	132391	M	Ger.	5.12.06	Civil Policeman,Police N.C.O.Muhldorf(Ger.)Spring 43	TORTURE	U.S.
HOLZER, Franz	196572	M	Ger.		Cpl.Kdo.1502-Stg.XII B,Buebingen(Ger.)28.4.41	TORTURE	FR.
HOLZER, Georg	253716	M	Ger.		Policeman,State Service,Pravetin(Czech.)23.3.45	MURDER	CZECH.
HOLZER, Hedwig	190186	F	Ger.	18.9.17	Clerk Gestapo,Bruenn(Czech.)39-45	TORTURE	CZECH.
HOLZER, Walter	401	M	Ger.		Adjudant,Gestapo,Valenciennes(Fr.)43-44,1.9.44	MURDER	FR.
HOLZHAI, Max	252886	M			Pvt.CC Ellrich-Nordhausen(Ger.)	MURDER	U.S.
HOLZHAUER, Gerhard	154368	M	Ger.	17 - 20	Hptgefolgschaftsfhr.Hitler Jugend,CC Gardelingen(Ger.)8.-14.4.45	MURDER	U.S.
HOLZHAUSER	174000	F	Ger.		Civilian,House-wife,Bad Durrenberg(Ger.)29.5.44	TORTURE	U.S.
HOLZHEIMER	135189	M	Ger.		C.O.Gendarmerie,Kreis Chief,Hassfurt(Ger.)44	MURDER	U.S.
HOLZHEIMER	162631	M	Ger.	90	Civilian,Forester,Arb.Kdo.35,Stalag XX B,Schonmoor(Ger.)6.41	TORTURE	U.K.
HOLZHEUER, Robert	255114	M	Ger.	3.12.12	Gestapo,Zlin(Czech.)40-45	INTERR.	CZECH.
HOLZINGER	186665	M	Ger.		SS Art.Ausb.u.Ers.Regt.Prag(Czech.)5.5.45	MURDER	CZECH.
HOLZINGER	301567	M			On the staff at CC Mauthausen(Aust.)40-45	MURDER	BEL.
HOLZINGER, Erwin	163651	M	Ger.		Pvt.9 Res.Gren.Regt.1 Coy.Gew.Schuetze,Magny D'Anigon(Fr.)18.9.44	MURDER	FR.
HOLZLOHNER, E.	195832	M	Ger.		Dr.,Professor of Phsiology,Medical-School,CC Dachau,Auschwitz(Ger.)42-26.2.43	MURDER	BEL.
HOLZMANN	39819	M	Ger.		Substitute for Custom House Officer,at St.Hyppolyte,Soulce,Ger.(Fr.)	MURDER	FR.
HOLZMANN	125141	M			District Commissar,Schupo,Barbrastz,Alexandrewska(Ukraine)(Russ.)40	MURDER	U.S.
HOLZMANN, Jack	11242	M	Ger.		Pvt.Army,Panz.Gren.Regt.111,Albine(Fr.)29.6.44	MURDER	FR.
HOLZNER, Ludwig	250234	M	Ger.		Police Bn.72,Warschau and Czestochowa(Pol.)39-40	MISC.CRIMES	POL.
HOLZRI see HOLDERER	189505						
HOLZSCHNEIDER	167188	M	Ger.	98	Sturmscharfhr.S.D.Gestapo,Bergen(Nor.)4.40	TORTURE	NOR.
HOLZSCHWAN	143013	M	Ger.	15	Pvt.Guard,Waffen SS Totenkopf,CC Buchenwald(Ger.)	MURDER	U.S.
HOMAN	192069	M		12	Pvt.714 Land.Schtz.Bn.Danzig(Free State)	TORTURE	POL.
HOMANN	105951	M			Lt.Col.Sonderkdo.et Suttrop,CC Langenback(Ger.)22.3.45	MURDER	U.S.
HOMANN, Karl	194908	M	Ger.	15.11.00	Orts-Group-Leader,NSDAP,(Lux.)	TORTURE	LUX.
HOMMA, Adolf	145854	M	Ger.		Obergrenadier,SS Das Reich,Panzer Div.13 Comn.,Moissac(Fr.)44	MURDER	FR.
HOMMES	350072	M			Uschafhr.SS,Rhenen,Vreewijk(Neth.)2.45	MURDER	NETH.
HOMMES, Peter	301568	M			Gendarm,Gendarmerie,Sohan,Pepinster,Theux,5.-6.9.44	MURDER	BEL.
HOMMRICH, Ludwig	254517	M	Ger.		Oschafhr.Army,Landsturm Regt.83,Tiel(Neth.)3.-4.45	PILLAGE	NETH.
HOMOLKA, Alex	253041	M			Civilian,Member,S.A.Gestapo,Zdirec(Czech.)39-45	WITNESS	CZECH.
HOMPL, Wilhelm	190568	M			Sgt.Kreiskommandantur,Kragujevac(Yugo.)21.10.41	MURDER	YUGO.
HONEQUE	194771	M	Ger.		Lt.Luftpark,Cambrai(Fr.)40-41	PILLAGE	FR.
HONIG	39820	M	Ger.	93	Officer,Einsatz Officer,KL Schoenabeck-Elbe(Ger.)3.45	TORTURE	U.K.
HONIG, Walter	162430	M	Ger.	10	Chief Cmdt.Gestapo,2 Fallschirm-Div.,Quimperch(Fr.)44	TORTURE	FR.
HONIGSSCHMIED, Victor	31934	M			Dr.,Landgerichtsdirektor,Public Official,Cheb(Czech.)21.2.40	MURDER	CZECH.
HONNDORF, Willy	146853	M	Ger.		Rottfhr.SS Panzer Div.Das Reich,13.Coy., Moissac (Fr.) 44	MURDER	FR.
HOFFINGE, P.H.	151662	M	Ger.		NSDAP,Oberpolier Firm:Hochtief Essen,KL Bruex-Sudetenland(Czech.)2.6.44	TORTURE	U.K.
HONOLD, Ferdinand	1401	M	Ger.		Pvt.Festungs Bn.N.C.O.	MURDER	U.K.
HOMTJES	305899	M			Hptscharfhr.CC Oranienburg(Ger.)39-45	MURDER	CZECH.
HOOCK	174231	M	Ger.		Zugwachtmeister,19 Police Regt.6 Coy.,Aurillac(Fr.)13.-15.6.44	MURDER	FR.
HOOF, August	192765	M	Ger.		Member NSDAP,Stalag XIII D,CC Ansbach,Woernitz(Ger.)	TORTURE	BEL.
HOOF, Georg	251816	M	Ger.	25.4.06	Gestapo,Hradec Kralove(Czech.)39-45	MURDER	CZECH.
HOOFNAGEL	39821	M	Ger.		Pvt.KL Lickenau(Ger.)3.44	MISC.CRIMES	U.K.
HOOGEVKEN, Albert	199179	M	Ger.	10	Pvt.Army,212 Det.18 Searchlight-Btty.Wilhelmshaven)Ger.)15.10.44	WITNESS	CAN.
HOOK	186002	M			Zugwachtmeister,19 Regt.Pol.Aurillac(Fr.)	MURDER	FR.
HOOK	196573	M	Ger.		Uschafhr.CC Struthof-Natzweiler(Fr.)40-44	BRUTALITY	FR.
HOOKER, Harry or HOOLAM or Eric v.BRANDENBURG or Jimmy Le BOUQUEN	11244	M	Ger.		C.O.Waffen SS,Div.Brandenburg,Cannes,Nice(Fr.)7.44-8.44	MURDER	FR.
HOORN, Gustav	31933	M	Ger.		Dr.,Landgerichtsrat,Publ.off.,Opava(Czech.)21.2.40	TORTURE	CZECH.
HOOS	162622	M	Ger.	90	Hptscharfhr.CC Waffen SS,Buchenwald(Ger.)	TORTURE	U.S.
HOOS	173171	M		20	SS Uschafhr.CC Natzweiler,Gaggensau(Fr.Ger.)44	MURDER	U.F.
HOOVER	197735	M	Ger.		SS Hpschafhr.CC Buchenwald(Ger.)	MURDER	U.S.
HOP Along (Nickname)	39822	M	Ger.		Officer,KL Graudenz(Pol.)	TORTURE	U.K.
HOPF, Karl	254626	M	Ger.		Civilian,Roesrath(Ger.)15.2.45	MURDER	FR.
HOPFE	306685	M	Ger.		Pvt.331 Pioneer Bn.331 Infantry Div.,Mijn Heeren Land(Neth.)5.45	PILLAGE	NETH.
HOPFENSITZ	143020	M			Sgt.Sipo and S.D.,Toulouse,Agen,Cahors,Foix,Pau,Tarbes(Fr.)6.-8.44	MURDER	U.S.
HOPFEUER, Theodor	258210	M			Dr.,Commander,Ordensburg Sonthofen,Martinszell(Ger.)18.7.44	MURDER	U.S.
HOPFLINGER	192212	M	Ger.		Cpl.Army,No.63194,Vineuil(Fr.)	WITNESS	FR.
HOPNER	147312	M	Ger.		Sgt.11 Panzer Div.(Fr.)44	MURDER	FR.
HOPNER	151664	M	Ger.		Major,NSDAP Member,Mittweida-Sa.,Muenchen(Ger.)3.45	TORTURE	U.K.
HOPNER	253681	M	Ger.		W.O.Panz.Div.Unit 36185,Lautrec(Fr.)5.8.44	MURDER	FR.
HOPNER	305190	M	Ger.		Member,Geheime Feldpolizei,20,Rue de Terremonde,Lille(Fr.)40-44	MURDER	FR.
HOPP	253694	M	Ger.		Lt.Sicherheits Regt.199,Fandreville,Ligueres (Fr.)44	MISC.CRIMES	FR.
HOPP, Friedrich	252335	M	Ger.		Lt.,St.Huibrechts-Lille(Fr.)	WITNESS	BEL.

NAME	C.R.FILE NUMBER	SEX	NATIO-NALITY	DATE OF BIRTH	RANK	OCCUPATION	UNIT	PLACE AND DATE OF CRIME	REASON WANTED	WANTED BY
HOPP, Ronaldo	167213	M	Ger.		Capt., SS Div. "Das Reich", St. Lys (Fr.) 12.6.44				MURDER	FR.
HOPPE see POPPE	141420									
HOPPE	163119	M	Ger.		Civilian, Stalag IV F, C.C., Hartmannsdorf (Ger.) 44				MURDER	FR.
HOPPE	167173	M	Ger.		Adjutant, Feldgend., Montigny En Vesoul, (Fr.) 16.7.44				MURDER	FR.
HOPPE, Adolf	149513	M	Ger.		Gestapo, Fontainebleau-Melun (Fr.) 3.8.44				TORTURE	FR.
HOPPE, Heinrich	254541	M	Ger.		Pvt., 338 Div. Cdt.Bn.3, La Bresse (Fr.) 9.-11.44				MISC.CRIMES	FR.
HOPPE, Helmuth	195400	M	Ger.		Chief of III Sec. of SD, Bratislava (Czech.) 39-45				TORTURE	CZECH.
HOPPE, Helmuth	257824	M	Ger.	06 or 04	Hptsturmfhr., SD, Stavanger (Nor.) 41-43				WITNESS	NOR.
HOPPE, Herman	127375	M	Ger.		Pvt., Army: A.A.Art.2.Army (A.A.) 10.Battr.503 Bde. Hilden-Hassel (Ger.) 16.4.45				MURDER	U.S.
HOPPE, Otto	142997	M	Ger.	10	Sgt., SS-Totenkopfstandarte W.-SS, C.C., Buchenwald (Ger.)				TORTURE	U.S.
HOPPE, Reinhold	146852	M	Ger.		Unterscharfhr., SS "Das Reich" Pz.Div., (Fr.) 44				MURDER	FR.
HOPPE, Werner	251041	M	Ger.	20. 7.20	Civilian, Cepcin, Turcsko (Slovakia,Czech.) 44				MURDER	CZECH.
HOPPENSTOCK	192764	M			SS-Pvt., Guard, 4.SS Totenkopfsturmbann, C.C. Nordhausen Mittelbau (Ger.) 43-45				MURDER	U.S.
HOPFER	192070	M	Ger.	86	SS-Gruppenfhr., Anatomy Institute Danzig (Free State)				TORTURE	POL.
HOPFERT	196498	M	Ger.		Cpl., Unit 59949, Langon (Fr.) 16.6.44				MURDER	FR.
HOPFNER	143011	M	Ger.		Cpl., SS 2.Pz.Gren.Regt.3.Bn.12.Coy., Stavelot,Malmedy (Bel.)23.12.44				MURDER	U.S.
HORAK, Rudolf	190972	M	Ger.	98	Door-Keeper, Gestapo, Brno (Czech.) 39-45				WITNESS	CZECH.
HORBACH	252425	M			Pvt. C.C. Dora Nordhausen (Ger.)				MURDER	U.S.
HORBANJUK, Nikofor	251595	M	Ger.	13. 3.91	Agent, SD, Prag (Czech.) 39-45				MURDER	CZECH.
HORBASCHEK, Josef	190367	M	Ger.	2. 1.12	Crim.-Commissary Obersturmfhr., Gestapo, SD, Praha (Czech.) 39-45				MISC.CRIMES	CZECH.
HORBOL, Anton	192762	M			Guard, SS-Pvt., 4.SS-Totenkopfsturmbann, C.C. Nordhausen Dora, Mittelbau (Ger.) 43-45				MURDER	U.S.
HORCHER, Christians	254515	M	Ger.		Cpl., Montjean and Mesnil-en-Vallee (Fr.) 10.-26.10.40				INTERR.	FR.
HORCICZKA	196575	M	Ger.		Guard or Kapo, C.C. Gusen (Austr.)				TORTURE	BEL.
HOREDT	127109	M	Ger.		"Das Reich", SS Div. 2, Venerque-Le-Vernet (Fr.)				MURDER	FR.
HOREIS	306981	M			Lt., Meppel (Neth.) 9.44				PILLAGE	NETH.
HORELS, Willy	139201	M			Army, Bentwisch (Ger.) 7.43				WITNESS	U.S.
HOREMANS, Gustaaf	306982	M	Ger.	30.11.98	Member, Interpreter, Sicherheitsdienst Leeuwarden, 9.44-4.45 served Interpreter, Leeuwarden (Neth.) 20.3.45				BRUTALITY	NETH.
HOREN, Josef	105946	M			Cpl., Army, 34. fortress maschine gun Bn., Aachen (Ger.) 13.9.44				MURDER	U.S.
HORENSKI, Edmund	252424	M			Sgt., C.C. Ellrich-Nordhausen (Ger.)				MURDER	U.S.
HORER	252429	M			Uscharfhr., SS, C.C. Rottleberode-Nordhausen (Ger.)				MURDER	U.S.
HORHDAN, Ernst	174769	M			Lt.Col., Kgf.Arb.Bn.184, C.C. Drag-Area (Nor.)				MURDER	NOR.
HORKEL, Josef	199904	M	Ger.	16.12.85	SS-Member, Head of Research work, (Czech.)				MISC.CRIMES	CZECH.
HORLE, Heinrich	137778	M	Ger.		Prison Warden, Civilian, KL. Diez-Lahn (Ger.) 43-45				TORTURE	U.S.
HORLITZ	251666	M	Ger.		SS-Uscharfhr., Sipo, Bruessel (Bel.)				INTERR.	BEL.
HORMAN	300489	M	Ger.		Chief, H.Q. Military Training Centre in Belgrade, Bela Crkva (Yugo.) Summer 43				MURDER	YUGO.
HORMANN	305898	M	Ger.		Obersturmfhr., C.C. Oranienburg (Ger.) 39-45				MURDER	CZECH.
HORN	402	M	Ger.		Chief of Forced Labour Office, Tulle (Fr.) 4.44				MISC.CRIMES	FR.
HORN	39823	M			SS-Schuetze, SS 17.Pz.Gren.Div. "G.V.B.", Sturm Gesch.Abt. 17 or Pz.Jaeg.Abt. 17, Segre, Renaze (Fr.) 6.8.44-30.7.44				MURDER	FR.
HORN	11552	M	Ger.		Capt., Ortskommandantur , Kirkenes (Nor.)				TORTURE	NOR.
HORN	125468	M	Ger.		Hauptscharfhr., SS, C.C. Sachsenhausen, Oranienburg (Ger.) 42				MURDER	U.K., POL.
HORN	165542	M	Ger.		Gestapo, Wibryck-Anvers (Bel.) 3.2.44				TORTURE	BEL.
HORN	177168	M	Ger.	11	Sgt., Abwehr Official Fst 215, 45				MURDER	YUGO.
HORN	254572	M			Surgeon, C.C. Buchenwald (Ger.) 44-45				MURDER	FR.
HORN	257966	M			Lt., 150.Pz.Div.Bde., Meuse-Bridge, Antwerp (Bel.) 12.44				MISC.CRIMES	U.S.
HORN, Fritz	24991	M			Civil. Internee, Civ.Int. SS Informer for the SS, C.C. Sachsen- hausen (Ger.) 9.41-5.43				MURDER	U.S.
HORN, Fritz	162081	M	Ger.	2. 6.06	Civilian, NSDAP Erbach, Konic (Ger.)				MURDER	U.K.
HORN, Gustav	254353	M	Ger.		SS-Uscharfhr., W.-SS, C.C. Auschwitz-Birkenau (Po.,Ger.) 10.42				MISC.CRIMES	YUGO.
HORN, Hans	167187	M	Ger.	3.10.13	Civilian, trustee, Firm Jutrzenko, Krakow (Pol.) 9.39-44				PILLAGE	POL.,UNWCC
HORN, Hans	191991	M		02	Cpl., 190.P.O.W. Working Bn. C.C. Russanes (Nor.) 11.44-5.45				MURDER	NOR.
HORN, Josef	255116	M	Ger.	1. 9.06	Employee, State service Gestapo, Kolin (Czech.) 39-45				MISC.CRIMES	CZECH.
HORN, Theodore	252148	M	Ger.		Lt., Balaives (Fr.) 30.8.44				MISC.CRIMES	FR.
HORN, Ursula	143014	F	Ger.		Civilian Camp on the Rhine (Ger.)				WITNESS	U.S.
HORN, Walter	149333	M	Ger.		Civilian, Physician, Wernick (Ger.)				MURDER	FR.
HORNBACH	143007	M	Ger.		SS-Pvt., 2.Pz.Gren.Regt. 3.Bn.12.Coy., Malmedy (Bel.) 17.12.44				MURDER	U.S.
HORNBOSTEL	403	M			SS Lt. 9.39-1.42				MURDER	POL.
HORNBURG, Emile	39824	M	Ger.		SS, II Cie. Charmes (Vosges) (Fr.) 5.9.44				MURDER	FR.
HORNE	162845	M			Cpl. P.O.W. Work Bn. 190, Botex (Nor.)				TORTURE	NOR.
HORNE, Kurt	24973	M			Cpl. SS II.SS Mtn.Regt.				MURDER	U.S.
HORNER, Rudolf	31931	M	Ger.		Dr., Senats-Praesident, Public Official, Litomerice (Czech.) 21.2.40				MURDER	CZECH.
HORNFELL	151690	M	Ger.		Capt., Reichsarbeitsdienst, Purpau (Fr.)44				WITNESS	FR.
HORNIG, Oswin	133683	M			SS-Cpl., C.C. Buchenwald (Ger.)				TORTURE	U.S.
HORNISCH, Franz	190371	M	Ger.	20. 1.15	Agent, Gestapo, Brno (Czech.) 39-45				MURDER	CZECH.
HORNISFEGGER	250239	M	Ger.		Dr., Gestapo, Lille (Fr.) 40-44				MURDER	FR.
HOHNN	302604	M			Major, Slot Moermond at Renesse (Neth.) 10.12.44				MURDER	NETH.
HORNS, Wilhelm	252422	M			Pvt., C.C. Ellrich-Nordhausen (Ger.)				MURDER	U.S.
HORNUNG	136258	M	Ger.		Feldgendarm, Feldgend. Stenay (Fr.) 44				MURDER	FR.
HORNUNG	167170	M	Ger.		Lt., Army, Herschweiler (Fr.) 11.44				MISC.CRIMES	FR.
HORNUNG, Emil	162846	M	Ger.		Feldgend. Vielsalm (Bel.) 40-44				PILLAGE	BEL.
HORNY, Walther	404	M		20	Wachtmeister, Police, C.C. Grini (Nor.) 9.41				TORTURE	NOR.
HORCLLO see GORELLO	187824									
HORR, Eugene	259360	M	Ger.		Unterscharfhr., activ Member of Poitiers-Gestapo, Poitiers (Fr.)				MISC.CRIMES	FR.
HORSCHER, Johann	195401	M	Ger.	20	Employee, Gestapo, Kolin (Czech.) 39-45				MURDER	CZECH.

HOR-HOY

NAME	C.R.FILE NUMBER	SEX	NATIO-NALITY	DATE OF BIRTH	RANK OCCUPATION UNIT PLACE AND DATE OF CRIME	REASON WANTED	WANTED BY
HORSELJAN	129768	M			Civilian, C.C. Buchenwald (Ger.)	BRUTALITY	U.S.
HORST	1402		Ger.		Naval Supply.	MURDER	U.K.
HORST	163095	M	Ger.		Chief, Railway, Simard, Navilly, Sermesse (Fr.) 8.44	MURDER	FR.
HORST	191753	M			Cpl., SS Div. "Das Reich", St.Lys (Fr.)	MURDER	FR.
HORST, Joseph	12435	M	Ger.		Pvt., 110. or 111. Panz.Gren.Regt. 2.Coy., Albine (Fr.) 29.6.44	MURDER	FR.
HORSTKOCLE, Henritz	406	M	Ger.		Sgt., Army, Paratroop Coy., Saint Segal (Fr.) 23.7.44	MURDER	FR.
HORSTKOOTE (see NORSTKOOTE)	194505						
HORSTMANN	62266	M	Ger.		Lt.Col., 38.Regt. SS Div. "Goetz von Berlichingen", C.C. Montmartin-en-Craignes (Fr.) 17.6.44	MURDER	U.S.
HORSTMANN	121048	M	Ger.		Col. SS Formation, Rou Marson (Fr.) 13.8.44	WITNESS	FR.
HORSTMANN	124962	M	Ger.	10	Dr., Public Official, Belsen (Ger.)	MURDER	U.K.
HORSTMANN	173599	M	Ger.		Dr., SS-Hptsturmfhr., Waffen-SS, C.C. Oswiecim-Birkenau (Pol.) 39-45	MURDER	CZECH.
HORSTMANN	251605	M	Ger.		Sipo, Brussels (Bel.)	INTERR.	BEL.
HORSTMANN	300781	M	Ger.		Pvt., 1.Aufkl.Abt., 3.Coy., 2.Col., XV. Div. of the Afrika Korps, Saint-Leger (Arlon) (Bel.) 5.9.44	MISC.CRIMES	BEL.
HORTEL	137089	M			Sgt., Stalag XIII D, Nuremberg (Ger.) 45	MURDER	SOV.UN.
HORTH	162434	M		17	Cmdt., Panz. Gren.Div., Condorgen (Fr.) 19.3.44	MURDER	FR.
HORTSMANN	185177	M	Ger.		SS-Osturmfhr., SS, S.D., C.C. Sachsenhausen (Ger.)	TORTURE	FR.
HORTZ, Hans	257761	M	Ger.		10. Flottille, Quilly Gomarch (Fr.) 3.7.44	MURDER	FR.
HORWATH, Stefan	192761				4. SS Totenkopf-Sturmbann, C.C. Dora, Nordhausen(Ger.) 43-45	MURDER	U.S.
HOSCH, Kurt	306401	M		5. 3.11.	SS-Scharfhr., SS, C.C. Buchenwald (Ger.) betw.5.38 and 10.43	MURDER	BEL.
HOSE	124772	M		98	Crim.secretary, Sipo, Geh.Feldpol., C.C.Erlenz (Ger.)	TORTURE	U.S.
HOSEL	302035	M			Head of C.C.Ganacker (sub-camp of Flossenburg), Ganacker (Ger.) 45	MURDER	BEL.
HOSEL	305191	M			Lt., SS-Pol., Geb.Regt., 18.Div., Vrastamites near Livadia, Beotia (Grc.) 8.44	MISC.CRIMES	GRC.
HOSELR	169811	M	Ger.		Chief, C.C. Oswiecim (Pol.) 44	TORTURE	POL.
HOSKE	252173	M			Pvt., C.C. Herzungen, Nordhausen (Ger.)	MURDER	U.S.
HOSKES, Jean	251613	M	Ger.	21. 1.25	Pvt., 558. Gren.Regt., 13.Coy., Bruay-en-Artois (Fr.) 1.9.44	MURDER	FR.
HOSNAEL	196578	M	Ger.		Cpl., Kerlize-Naizin (Fr.) 11.7.44	INTERR.	FR.
HOSS	156729	M	Ger.	05	Camp-Cmdt., C.C. Sachsenhausen (Ger.)	TORTURE	U.K.
HOSS	190566	M			Major, 892. Gren.Regt., 264. Div., Sucuraj-Muc (Yugo.) 10.43-12.43	MURDER	YUGO.
HOSS	196577	M			C.C. Ravensbrueck (Ger.)	TORTURE	BEL.
HOSS, Rudolf	253855	M		95	Osturmfhr., SS, C.C.Auschritz-Birkenau (Pol.) 42-45	MURDER	YUGO.
HOSS, Rudolf	196579	M			Osturmbannfhr., SS, C.C. Mauthausen (Aust.)	TORTURE	BEL.
HOSSARE	192759	M	Ger.		Lt.Col., SS, C.C. Ravensbrueck (Ger.) 44-45	MURDER	U.S.
HOSSELBARTH (see HOESSELBARTH)	83843						
HOSSFELD, Hans	166613	M	Ger.		Lt., Army, 3.Brandenburg Regt. 44	WITNESS	U.S.
HOSSLER	173621	M			Osturmfhr., SS, Buchenwald (Ger.)	MURDER	FR.
HOSSLER	177596	M			Sturmscharfhr., Secretary, S.D.-Gestapo, Saarbruecken (Ger.)	PILLAGE	FR.
HOSSLER, Franz	146688	M	Ger.		Osturmfhr., SS, C.C. Birkenau (Pol.) 43-44	TORTURE	U.S.
HOST, Emil	251608	M	Ger.		Game-keeper, Alsheim near Worms (Ger.) 14.5.43	MURDER	FR.
HOSTEN, Heinrich	146695	M	Ger.		Osturmfhr., SS, C.C. Auschwitz (Pol.) 43-44	MURDER	U.S.
HOSTERBACH	174001	M	Ger.		Capt., Stalag VI A, C.C. Hemer (Ger.) 41-42	TORTURE	U.S.
HOSWALD, Emile	167165	M			Civilian, Montigny (Fr.) 9.44	WITNESS	FR.
HOT (or HET)	29801	M			Col., Army, Paquet (Fr.) 6.44-8.44	MURDER	FR.
HOTH	253978	M			SS-Sturmbannfhr., Chief S.D., Toulouse (Fr.) 10.43-3.44	INTERR.	FR.
HOTH	254069	M			Sturmbannfhr., SS-Gestapo, Nancy, Boucq-Trondes (Fr.) 8.44	MURDER	FR.
HOTH	305425	M			SS-Sturmbannfhr., W.O., Head of the S.D. Nancy, Pau, South-West-France, especially Toulouse, Hte.-Garonne, Gers, Tarn (Fr.) 42-8.44	MURDER	FR.
HOTHARN	185656	M			Civilian, Palleben (Ger.) 10. or 11.44	WITNESS	U.S.
HOTHORN, Alfred	253682	M	Ger.	15	Inspector, S.D. Rouen, Alencon (Fr.) 40-44	MISC.CRIMES	FR.
HOTREITT	174228	M			Capt., Afrika Korps, Naves (Fr.) 10.6.44	MURDER	FR.
HOTREITT	194770	M	Ger.		Lt., Feldgendarmerie, Villargerel, Aigueblance (Fr.) 3.-4.44	MURDER	FR.
HOTTINGER	196580	M	Ger.	01	Lt., Pol., Carpane (It.) 9.44	WITNESS	U.K.
HOTTNER, Johann	252881	M		1. 1.01	SS-Rottenfhr., SS, C.C.Herzungen, Nordhausen (Ger.)	MURDER	U.S.
HOTZ	141409	M	Ger.		Capt., Frontleitstelle, Paris (Fr.) 20.8.44	MURDER	FR.
HOTZE, Hermann	143005	M	Ger.	92	Major, Army, Landesschuetzen Bn.24, C.C. Augsburg, Muehlberg Stalag 4 B (Ger.) 44-45	MURDER	POL., U.S.
HOUBEN	174230	M			Sgt., Dienststelle Houssay, Repel, Giron Court (Fr.) 8.44-9.44	WITNESS	FR.
HOUBEN, Johann (or HUBEN)	192758	M	Ger.		Miner, Arbeitskdo. "Adolf Mine", C.C. Merkstein (Ger.) 2.44	TORTURE	U.S.
HOUBER (aliases:HOUBIER)	254542	M	Ger.		Oschfhr., Gestapo, Anrath near Krefeld (Ger.)	INTERR.	NETH.
HOUBIN	196581	M	Ger.		Shiftmaster, Artificial Silk Factory, Anrath near Krefeld (Ger.) 1.42-44	TORTURE	NETH.
HOUIPP	179604	M			W.O., Army.	TORTURE	FR.
HOULT	188973	M			Capt., Gestapo of St.Etienne, Tournon (Fr.) 6.7.44	MURDER	FR.
HOUNGEN	141567	M	Ger.		Cpl., Gestapo, Chenebier, Etobon (Fr.) 27.9.44	MURDER	FR.
HOUSMAN	259066	M		11	Lt.,A Dulag Luft Hospital (Ger.) 43-4-45	BRUTALITY	U.S.
HOUSSE	39825	M			Cpl., Army, 28. Div. E., Noailles (Fr.) 3.4.44	MURDER	FR.
HOUSSELL	250240	M			Major, Department L'Ain (Fr.) 7.44	MISC.CRIMES	FR.
HOVEL, Werner	105957	M			Pol.Inspector, Gestapo, Headquarters Ahlem (Ger.) 6.4.45	MURDER	U.S.
HOVEN	9690	M			SS-Hptsturmfhr., SS, Buchenwald (Ger.) 38-44	MURDER	CZECH.
HOVEN, Waldemar	121047	M	Ger.		Dr., Capt., C.C. Buchenwald (Ger.)	TORTURE	FR.
HOVER	250841	M			16. Huebner Regt. 6.Coy., Kinrooi (Bel.)	MURDER	BEL.
HOVER	250842	M			Physician, C.C. Gusen-Mauthausen (Aust.)	INTERR.	BEL.
HOWAK	163096	M			S.D., Chappes (Fr.) 28.7.44	MISC.CRIMES	FR.
HOWEN	162457	M	Ger.	09	Dr., SS-Hptsturmfhr., SS, C.C. Buchenwald (Ger.) 40-43	MURDER	POL.
HOWT	252879	M			Sgt., C.C. Ellrich-Nordhausen (Ger.)	MURDER	U.S.
HOYA, Emil	105958	M	Ger.		Asseln (Ger.) 25.3.45	MISC.CRIMES	U.S.
HOYEN	195374	M	Ger.		Major, Leader of the telephone administration, Army, occupied territories, Antwerpen (Bel.) 6.44	MURDER	BEL.
HOYER	162922	M	Ger.		SS-Mann, 10.SS Panz.Div."Frundsberg", 36.Panz.Regt., Revin (Fr.) 6.44	MURDER	FR.

HOY-HUE

NAME	C.R.FILE NUMBER	SEX	NATIO-NALITY	DATE OF BIRTH	RANK, OCCUPATION, UNIT, PLACE AND DATE OF CRIME	REASON WANTED	WANTED BY
HOYER (or NOYER)	252563	M	Ger.		SS or Gestapo,C.C.Bremen-Farge (Ger.)	TORTURE	U.K.
HOYER	255970	M	Ger.		Sgt.,Hospital of Oflag IV B,Koenigstein (Ger.) 8.40	MURDER	FR.
HOYER	300766	M	Ger.		Dr.,Senatspraesident,Oberlandesgericht,Litomerice, Leitmeritz (Czech.) 21.2.40	MURDER	CZECH.
HOYER,Josef	31929	M	Ger.		Landgerichts-Direktor,Publ.office,Cheb (Czech.) 21.2.40	MURDER	CZECH.
HOZEL	194298	M	Ger.		Major,Army,Akerviku (Nor.) 42	MURDER	NOR.
HOZZA	253683	M	Ger.		Cmdt.,2 Bn.,347 Regt.,392 "Blue Div.",Lokve (Yugo.)4.4.45	INTERR.	YUGO.
HRONEK,Hubert	31928	M	Ger.		Dr.,Oberlandgerichtsrat,Public official,Prag (Czech.) 21.2.40	MURDER	CZECH.
HRONY,Joseph	31212	M	Ger.		Dr.,Landgerichtsdirektor,Public official,Bruenn (Czech.) 21.2.40	MURDER	BEL.
HREY	130369				Guard,C.C.Mauthausen (Aust.) 41-45	MURDER	U.S.
HRUBOBKA,Arthur	254401	M	Ger.	26. 8.04	Informer,Gestapo,Pilsen (Czech.) 42-45	MURDER	CZECH.
HUALA,Otto	251096	M	Ger.	14.11.10	Employee,Gestapo,Breclav (Czech.) 39-45	MURDER	CZECH.
HUBA	257008	M	Ger.		Sgt.,Army,Kreis-Kdtr.,Kragujevac,Orasag,Oruza (Yugo.) 42-44	INTERR.	YUGO.
HUBIC	173575	M	Ger.		Major,Governor,C.C.Meljank,Maribor (Yugo.) 4.41-44	MURDER	YUGO.
HUE	199799	M	Ger.		Lt.General,Army (Russ.) 43-44	MISC.CRIMES	U.S.
HUE,Friedrich	255981	M	Ger.		Pion.,Army,Pioneer-group,Heusden (Neth.) 5.11.44	PILLAGE	NETH.
HUEKI	193324	M			Uschfhr.,W-SS,C.C.Flossenburg (Ger.)	TORTURE	U.S.
HUBEN,Johann (see HOUBEN)	192758						
HUBER	407	M			Pvt.,Army,Baudrigues (Fr.) 19.8.44	MURDER	FR.
HUBER (see HUBERT)	12399						
HUBER	162395	M		08	Truppfuehrer-Lt.,SA,Eshing,Neufahrn,Vicinity,Freising (Ger.) 44-45	MURDER	U.S.
HUBER	162921	M			President,Miscell (Tribunal spec.),Strasbourg (Fr.) 16.2.43	MURDER	FR.
HUBER	171972	M		07	Truppfhr.,SA,Furholzen (Ger.) 31.7.44	MURDER	U.S.
HUBER	179592	M			Interpreter,Feldgendarmerie of la Palisse (Allier), St.Gerand le Puy (Fr.) 15.10.43	PILLAGE	FR.
HUBER	260172	M	Ger.		Pol.-Insp.,Pol.Munich,Dachau (Ger.) 42-44	BRUTALITY	FR.
HUBER	301382	M			Oslo (Nor.) 5.42	TORTURE	NOR.
HUBER	301635	M			Oberwachtmeister,Kbrach near Amberg (Ger.) 45	MURDER	CZECH.
HUBER	306686	M			Pvt.,331.Pionier-Bn.,331.Infantry-Div.,Mijnheerenlands (Neth.) 5.45	PILLAGE	NETH.
HUBER,Augustin	197737	M	Ger.	1. 4.04	SS-Sgt.,Teacher (Czech.)	MISC.CRIMES	CZECH.
HUBER,Elisabeth (nee VON LOWENBACH)	262202	F	Ger.	6. 9. ?	Secr.,Gestapo,Rennes (Fr.) 43-44	SUSPECT	FR.
HUBER,Erich	125479	M	Ger.	20	Cpl.,Army,Working-Kommando,Rei 95 F,Merseburg-Halle (Ger.) 9.12.43	MURDER	U.K.
HUBER,Fritz	250840	M	Ger.		Member,NSDAP,Loerrach-Dreilaendereck (Ger.)	INTERR.	BEL.
HUBER,Georg	162857	M	Ger.		Oschfhr.,SS,Venloo (Neth.)	TORTURE	BEL.
HUBER,Georg	171971	M	Ger.	24. 4.94	Physician,Civ.,C.C.Buchenwald,Seffenberg (Ger.) 7.4.40-3.3.45	WITNESS	U.S.
HUBER,George	137032	M			Civ.,	MURDER	U.S.
HUBER,Josef	142926	M	Ger.		Mayor,Ortsbauernfhr.,Truppfhr.,Civ.,NSDAP,SA	TORTURE	U.S.
HUBER,Josef	174005	M			Oschfhr.,SS,C.C.Muhldorf,Ampfing (Ger.)	MURDER	U.S.
HUBER,Josef	193186	M	Ger.	15. 2.02	Sgt.,Guard,Reichsjustiz-Ministerium,Feldstraflager,Waffen-SS, Finmark (Nor.) 42-45	MISC.CRIMES	NOR.YUGO.
HUBER,Karl	162398	M	Ger.	09	Civ.,C.C.Buchenwald	WITNESS	U.S.
HUBER,Karl Joseph	142083	M	Ger.	89	Agent,Gestapo,Neckarsulm (Ger.) 21.3.45	MURDER	U.S.
HUBER,Ludwig	12436	M			Pvt.,110 or 111 Pz.Gren.Regt.,2 Coy,Albine (Fr.) 29.6.44	MURDER	FR.
HUBER,Margarete (or VILLECHNER)	136393	F	Ger.		Civ.,Altenkirchen (Ger.)	WITNESS	U.S.
HUBER,Rudo?	137776	M			Civ.	WITNESS	U.S.
HUBER,Willi	408	M			Oschfhr.,SS,Pol.-Regt.Org.Todt,Payzac (Fr.) 16.2.44	MURDER	FR.
HUBERT (or HUBER,Brothers)	12399	M	Ger.		Blockfhr.,Charge of Czech.-Coy.,C.C.Dachau (Ger.) 39	TORTURE	CZECH.
HUBERT	62268			00 or 05	2 J.C. of Kraftfahrpark,Bukow (Pol.) 1.43-44	TORTURE	U.S.
HUBERT	254343	M	Ger.		Scharfhr.,Gestapo,Limoges (Fr.)	INTERR.	FR.
HUBERT	257603	M	Ger.		Chief of Section,Mittelwerk,Nordhausen (Ger.)	MURDER	U.S.
HUBERT,Eric	6153	M	Ger.		Cpl.,Army,Halle (Ger.) 8.12.43	MURDER	U.K.
HUBERT,Willi (or Willi HUBERT)	186661	M	Ger.	95	Sturmbannfhr.,SS,Art.Ausb.und Ers.Regt.,Prague (Czech.) 5.5.45	MURDER	CZECH.
HUBLER	29803		Ger.		Lt.,Army,Kerlars la Roche Maurice (Fr.) 7.44	MURDER	FR.
HUBNER	62269	M	Ger.		SA or Green-police,Parachut.,Roermond (Neth.) 1.-2.45	TORTURE	NETH.U.S.
HUBNER	121045	M			Sgt.,SS,C.C.Buchenwald (Ger.) 41-45	TORTURE	FR.BEL.
HUBNER	132727	M			President, Tribunal de Guerre Allemand de Besancon, Besancon (Fr.) 18.9.43	MURDER	FR.
HUBNER	173619	M	Ger.		Scharfhr.,SS,C.C.Buchenwald (Ger.) 42-45	TORTURE	U.S.
HUBNER	305426	M	Ger.		Betriebsfuehrer,Work-manager at Schorzingen, Schorzingen-Wuerttemberg (Ger.) 44-45	MISC.CRIMES	FR.
HUBNER,Heinrich Hendrick	39594	M	Ger.		Cpl.,Army,Cazaux (Fr.) 22.8.44	MURDER	FR.
HUBNER,Karl	254521	M			Agent,Gestapo,Limoges (Fr.)	INTERR.	FR.
HUBNER,Otto	166607	M		05	Sturmbannfhr.,SS,Major,S.D.,Theresienstadt (Czech.) 43	WITNESS	U.S.
HUBRACH,Walter	261397	M			Onturmfhr.,SS,Arco (Ital.) 8.2.45	MURDER	U.S.
HUBRICH	305900	M	Ger.		Member,SS,C.C.Dachau (Ger.) 3.-4.45	MURDER	CZECH.
HUBSCH,Marcel	151692	M	Ger.		Gestapo,S-Officer,Brive (Fr.) 44	TORTURE	FR.
HUCHTHAUSEN	192756	M	Ger.		Guard,4 SS-Totenkopf-Sturmbann,C.C.Dora Mittelbau,Nordhausen, (Ger.) 43-45	MURDER	U.S.
HUCK,Franz (or MUCK)	136257	M	Ger.		Wachtmeister,Gend.,Clermont-Ferrand,la Bourboule (Fr.) 27.4.44	MURDER	FR.
HUDETZ,Georg	192755	M			Guard, 4 SS-Totenkopf-Sturmbann,Conc.Camp Nordhausen,Dora Mittelbau, Nordhausen (Ger.) 43-45	MURDER	U.S.
HUDLER,Emil	260422	M	Ger.	20. 7.12	Locksmith,Civ.Firm,Suche Vrbne,Bohemia (Czech.) 41-43	MURDER	CZECH.
HUDLER,Josef	257310	M	Ger.	8. 8.13	Interpreter,Gestapo,Tabor,Bohemia (Czech.) 15.4.39-8.5.45	MISC.CRIMES	CZECH.
HUBER	84928	M			Dr.,Sturmbannfhr.,Regierungsrat,SS,Head of Gestapo, Salzburg (Aust.)	MISC.CRIMES	UNWCC
						MURDER	CZECH.
HUEBL,Heinrich	190370	M	Ger.	8. 1.89	Employee,Gestapo,Bruenn (Czech.) 39-45	MURDER	U.S.
HUEBLER,Albert	259486	M	Ger.	19.10.98	Gend.master,Gendarmerie,Wolfisheim,Alsace (Fr.) 14.8.44	TORTURE	U.S.
HUEBNER (HUBNER)	133684	M			Scharfhr.,SS,C.C.Buchenwald (Ger.		

HUE-HUL

NAME	C.R.FILE NUMBER	SEX	NATIO- NALITY	DATE OF BIRTH	RANK OCCUPATION UNIT PLACE AND DATE OF CRIME	REASON WANTED	WANTED BY
HUEBNER	166608	M	Ger.		SS-Standartenfhr.,Col.,SS,head of Volksdeutsche Mittelstelle (Pol.) 40-45	PILLAGE	U.S.
HUEBNER	253713	M			Freising (Ger.) 8.44	WITNESS	U.S.
HUEBNER, Bruno	178074	M	Ger.	11	Pvt.,Nachschub Coy,Munic-Rheden (Neth.) 12.44-1.45	MURDER	NETH.
HUEBNER, Georg	250825	M	Ger.	9.10.25	Pvt.,1 Coy Pion.Bn.331, 53 Rgt.,Nieuw Beyerland (Neth.) 7.5.45	MURDER	NETH.
HUEBNER, Oscar	254350	M	Ger.		SS-Uschfhr.,83 Landsturm Rgt.Nederland,Tiel (Neth.) 3.-4.45	PILLAGE	NETH.
HUEBNER, Otto	166607	M	Ger.	05	Sturmbannfhr.,SD,Theresienstadt (Czech.) 43	WITNESS	U.S.
HUEBNER, Otto	262284	M	Ger.	4.12.?	SS-Osturmfhr.,Gestapo,Rennes (Fr.) 43-44	MISC.CRIMES	FR.
HUEBNER, Walter	139785	M	Ger.		Waffen SS,C.C.Dora,Nordhausen (Ger.) 23.2.45	MURDER	U.S.
HUEBSCH	126551	M			Officer,SS,Hagen (Ger.) 4.45	MURDER	U.S.
HUEBSCHER, August	142930	M	Ger.	5.3.09	Cpl.,SS Totenkopf Standarte,Waffen SS,C.C.Buchenwald (Ger.)	MISC.CRIMES	U.S.
HUECK	255971	M	Ger.		General,SS,C.C.Mauthausen (Aust.)	MURDER	FR.
HUEHN	141931	M	Ger.		Col.,Air Force,Dulag Luft,Brandenburg (Ger.) 5.43	WITNESS	U.K.
HUEHN, Erhard	142929	M	Ger.	15.9.12	Cpl.,SS Totenkopf Standarte,2 Totenkopf Coy,Waffen SS,C.C.Buchenwald (Ger.)	TORTURE	U.S.
HUEHN, Gerhard	255575	M			Uschfhr.,C.C.Buchenwald (Ger.)	MURDER	U.S.
HUEHNEFMANN, Rudolf	260615	M			Lt.General,Army	WITNESS	U.S.
HUEHNLEIN	185939	M	Ger.		C.C.Oberwalter,C.C.Ebrach (Ger.) 39-45	MISC.CRIMES	CZECH.
HUELF	142925	M	Ger.		Major,Councillor,SD,Sipo (Sov.Un.) 15.4.43	MURDER	U.S.
HUELF, Wilhelm Heinrich	257599	M	Ger.	1.9.07	Osturmbannfhr.,Sipo,Sochaux (Fr.) 43, 40-44	BRUTALITY	FR.,POL.
HUELIG	301136	M	Ger.		Commandant,C.C.Struthof-Natzweiler (Fr.) 42-44	MURDER	FR.
HUELLE	167215	M	Ger.		Dr.,Civilian,Member,Finanzstab Rosenberg, 40-44	PILLAGE	FR.,UNWCC
HUELLER, Klemens	251024	M	Ger.	29.6.99	Worker,Civilian,Poustevna (Czech.) 4.43	MURDER	CZECH.
HUELZER, Engelbert	134885	M	Ger.		Civilian,Efferen (Ger.) 2.10.44	WITNESS	U.S.
HUENDGEN, Martin	24992	M	Ger.		Auxiliary Policeman,Merzach (Ger.)	TORTURE	U.S.
HUENEFELD (see HUENFELD)	192946						
HUENEKE, Friedrich	154361	M			Schutzhaeftling,Oberlahnstein near Boppard (Ger.) 1.-10.1.45	MURDER	U.S.
HUENFMOERDER	142452	M			Major,Dr.,Army,Oberkommando PW Affairs	WITNESS	U.S.
HUENENFELD	256541	M	Ger.		Lt.,SS Command staff Harzungen,C.C.Nordhausen (Ger.)	MURDER	U.S.
HUENFELD, Willi (alias HUENE- FELD)	192946	M	Ger.		SS-Osturmfhr.,C.C.Buchenwald (Ger.) 42-43	TORTURE	U.S.
HUEPFEL, Nikolaus	174002	M			SS-Mann,SS,C.C.Muhldorf Ampfing (Ger.) 6.44-4.45	MURDER	U.S.
HUERS, Otto	137036	M			Kraftfahr Ers.Ausb.Abt.6, 1 Coy,Bielefeld (Pol.,Sov.Un.)	WITNESS	U.S.
HUESCHEN, Hubert	192685	M	Ger.		Civilian,Werkstein (Ger.) 43	WITNESS	U.S.
HUESENBUSCH, Franz	134884	M	Ger.		Obergruppenfhr.,SA,Herten Scherlbeck (Ger.)	MISC.CRIMES	U.S.
HUESER	174003	M	Ger.		Capt.,Stalag VI A,C.C.Hemer (Ger.)	TORTURE	U.S.
HUESER	195205	M			Sgt.,SS Leibstandarte "Adolf Hitler" 3 Coy,Wormhoudt (Fr.,Bel.) 5.40	MURDER	U.K
HUESSEL, Theodor	306983	M			Oschfhr.,SS,C.C.Auschwitz (Pol.) 42-44	MURDER	POL.
HUESS (or HISS)	291990	M	Ger.		Major,Kommandantur,Gerardmer (Fr.) 27.-29.5.44	MURDER	U.S
HUETTEL, Willi	154367	M	Ger.	15	Lt.,2 Feer.Muester Art.Rgt.981,Holsor-Vaagso (Nor.) 6.-7.12.44	TORTURE	NOR.
HUETTEFMANN	300782	M	Ger.		Pvt.,1 Aufkl.Abt.3 Coy,2 Col., XV Div. of the Afrika Corps,Saint Leger (Arlon) 5.9.44	MISC.CRIMES	BEL.
HUETTIG, Hans	142945	M	Ger.		Capt.,SS Totenkopf Standarte,Waffen SS,C.C.Buchenwald (Ger.)	TORTURE	U.S.
HUETTIG, Hans	192490	M	Ger.		SS-Sturmbannfhr.,SS Wacht-Bn.VI (Nor.) 41-43	MISC.CRIMES	NOR.
HUETTIG, Hans	195433	M	Ger.		SS-Osturmfhr.,C.C.Sachsenhausen (Ger.) 40-45	MURDER	BEL.
HUETTIG, Max	192977	M	Ger.		Lt.,SS,C.C.Natzweiler,Buchenwald (Fr.,Ger.) 42-45	TORTURE	U.S.
HUFTTL, Leopold	192684	M	Ger.		Leader,NSDAP,Velke,Rledsebe (Czech.) 39-45	MISC.CRIMES	CZECH
HUF, Ludwig	301100	M	Ger.		Usturmfhr.,Crim.-Oberasst.,served with the R.S.D.Abt.VI-S,Copenhagen (Den.) 43-1.44	MISC.CRIMES	DEN.
HUFENDIEK	178316	M	Ger.		Osturmfhr.,12 SS Pz.Div. "Hitler Jugend", 25 SS Pz.Gren.Rgt.,Abbaye Ardenne (Fr.) 6.6.-8.7.44	TORTURE	CAN.
HUFER	256542	M	Ger.		Employee,Askaniahalle 13,Nordhausen (Ger.)	MURDER	U.S.
HUFSCHMIDT	133323	M			Obersturmfhr.,Waffen SS,C.C.Flossenburg (Ger.)	TORTURE	U.S.
HUG	261477	M	Ger.		SS-Sgt.,Dirlewanger Bde.,Police,District Sluck (Pol.) 40-44	MURDER	POL
HUG,G.	179603	M	Ger.		Scharfhr.,SS,C.C.Mauthausen,Buchenwald (Ger.)	MURDER	U S.
HUG, Julius	255104	M	Ger.	12	Crim.-Asst.,Gestapo,Danzig (Pol.)	MURDER	U.K.
HUG, Paul	255972	M	Ger.		Chief of the Hospital C.C.Flossenburg (Ger.)	INTERR.	FR.
HUG, Wilhelm	188974	M	Ger.		Civilian,Wasserbauverw.and Forstwirtschaft fuer Elsass and Herzogtum Baden,Still (Fr.) 22.10.44	MURDER	FR.
HUGEL, Johann	260518	M	Ger.	9.1.05	SS-Guard,C.C.Natzweiler (Fr.)	MURDER	FR
HUGELMANN	21320	M	Ger.		Deputy-chief,Einsatzstab Rosenberg, (Fr.) 40-44	PILLAGE	FR.
HUGL, Hans	190337	M	Ger.		Civilian,Wiesbaden (Ger.) 43-45	WITNESS	U.S.
HUGO	142462	M	Ger.		Member,Gestapo,Bielefeld (Ger.)	TORTURE	BEL
HUGO	254344	M	Ger.		Scharfhr.,Agent,Gestapo,Limoges (Fr.)	INTERR.	FR.
HUGO	300534	M	Ger.	15	Chief of Room III Block XXVII,C.C.Dachau (Ger.) 44-45	MISC.CRIMES	YUGO.
HUGO, Wolf	179593	M	Ger.		SS-Cpl.,SS, St.Sulpice s-Risle (Fr.) 10.6.44	MURDER	FR.
HUHN	409	M	Ger.		SS-Hptsturmfhr.,Arnheim (Neth.) 12.42	MURDER	NETH.
HUHNE	137035	M	Ger.		Col.,155 Pz.Art.Coy,Sessenheim (Fr.) 1.45	MURDER	U.S.
HUHNFFELD	252887	M			Osturmfhr.,SS,C.C.Harzungen,Nordhausen (Ger.)	MURDER	U.S.
HUHNEMORDER	36653	M	Ger.		Capt.,Air Force Inspection Stalag Luft III,Sagan (Ger.) 3.44	WITNESS	U.K.
HUHNERBEIN	192358	M	Ger.	00	Major,Prison,C.C.Ft.Zinna,Torgau (Ger.) 45	MURDER	U S.
HUHNOLD, Klaus	140892	M	Ger.		Cpl.,Verbindungsstab 331,Bolnes (Neth.) 8.5.45	MURDER	NETH.
HUHR, Hermann	252888	M	Ger.	1.5.97	Flyer,Air Force,C.C.Ellrich,Nordhausen (Ger.)	MURDER	U.S
HUINING, Jan	189049	M	Ger.		Civilian,Beinflair (Neth.) 7.7.44	WITNESS	U.S.
HUISKEN, Menno	305073	M	Ger.	1.9.93	Member,NSDAP,SD,"Holland Action" Commission,Apeldoorn (Neth.) 43	INTERR.	NETH.
HUKFER	259648	M	Ger.		W.O.,Railway at Agen,Aude,Herault,Gard (Fr.) 8.44	MISC.CRIMES	FR.
HULENBRUCH, Erich	142927	M	Ger.		Ortsgruppen-Propagandaamtsleiter,Camp-leader,NSDAP,Camp Blue 155 (Ger.)	TORTURE	U S
HULL, Johann	126552	M	Ger.		Civilian,Arbeitskdo.,C.C.Alsdorf (Ger.) 42-44	TORTURE	U.S.
HULL, Karl	254345	M	Ger.		Sgt.,Dancourt (Fr.) 22.7.44	WITNESS	FR.
HULLE	302037	M	Ger.		SS-Wachtmeister,SS,Falstad slave labour camp (Nor.) 42 and 43	MURDER	YUGO.
HULLEN, Christian Joseph	192491	M	Ger.		Worker-game warder,Civilian,Liessen-Bad Godesberg (Ger.) 23.11.43	MISC.CRIMES	POL.
HULLERT, Otto	253979	M	Ger.		Feldgendarm,Feldgendarmerie Romorantin Nr.577,F.P.Nr.22501,Orcay (Fr.) 8.8.44	MURDER	FR.

NAME	C.R.FILE NUMBER	SEX	NATIO-NALITY	DATE OF BIRTH	RANK OCCUPATION UNIT PLACE AND DATE OF CRIME	REASON WANTED	WANTED BY
HULLINGER	140036	M	Ger.		Chief,Gestapo,Perigueux(Fr.) 6.-8.44	MURDER	FR.
HULLMANNS, Hans	257235	M	Ger.		SS-Hptschfhr.,Abt.III,Sipo and SD,Anvers(Bel.) 40-45	BRUTALITY	BEL.
HULTICK	197739	M	Ger.		SS,C.C.Buchenwald(Ger.) 42-45	MURDER	U.S.
HULSER, Heinrich	139195	M	Ger.		Oschfhr.SS,Werwelskirchen(Ger.)	TORTURE	U.S.
HULSMANN, Erich	190969	M	Ger.	27.1.08	Crim.-Secretary,Gestapo,Brno(Czech.) 39-45	MURDER	CZECH.
HULPE	167167	M	Ger.		Lt.,Army,Nepvant(Fr.) 2.9.44	WITNESS	FR.
HULMA	301324	M	Ger.		Member of the Gestapo at Nove Mesto n.Vahom,C.C.Oswiecim-Birkenau (Pol.) 39-45	MURDER	CZECH.
HUMBERT	167842	M	Ger.	10	Osturmfhr.,SD,C.C.Breendonck(Bel.) 2.-3.9.44	MURDER	BEL.
HUMBRECHT	410	M	Ger.		Gestapo-Official,Perigueux(Fr.) 6.44	MURDER	FR.
HUMEL	11875	M	Ger.		Pvt.,Panz.Gren.Regt.111,Albine(Fr.) 29.6.44	MURDER	FR.
HUMER, Conrad	185116	M			Jouanier,Zollgrenzschutz,Taningos(Fr.) 17.6.44	MURDER	FR.
HUMICHEL, Emile	251815	M	Ger.	28.4.06	Agent,SD,Hte.Garonne,Toulouse(Fr.) 11.42-8.44	MURDER	FR.
HUMM, Martin	142959	M	Ger.	15.10.05	Kapo,Civilian,C.C.Flossenburg(Ger.)	MURDER	U.S.
HOMMEL, Rudolf	260927	M		95	Police Sgt.,Police,Ahrweiler(Ger.) 41-45	BRUTALITY	POL.
HUMMEL	196565	M			1 Pl.,3 Pz.Pl.,1 SS Panz.Div.,Leibstand.Adolf Hitler,Lignouville and Stoumont(Bel.)	MURDER	U.S.
HUMMEL, Hubert	167798	M	Ger.		Stellvertr.Gouverneur,Generalgouvernement,Warsaw(Pol.) 9.39-44	PILLAGE	POL.,UNWCC.
HUMMEL, Jan	190368	M	Ger.	9.4.03	Employee,Gestapo,Brno(Czech.) 39-45	MURDER	CZECH
HUMMEL, Johann	162091	M			SS,C.C.Flossenburg(Ger.)	TORTURE	U.S.
HUMMEL, Kurt	252429	M			C.C.Ellrich-Nordhausen(Ger.)	MURDER	U.S.
HUMMERICK, Albert	105960	M	Ger.		Pvt.,Army,62 Volksgren.Div.,190 V.G.Regt.,Neuhammer(Ger.) 27.11.44	MURDER	U.S.
HUMMRICH	190565	M			SS-Hptsturmfhr.,Stabschef d.Umsiedlg.Verwaltg.b.Chef der Zivilverwaltg. Untersteiermark,C.C.Sued-Steiermark,Ljubljana-Maribor(Yugo.)4.41-44	MURDER	YUGO.
HUMPEL, August	142961	M	Ger.		Civilian,Hemer(Ger.) 43	TORTURE	U.S.
HUMPEL, Karl	142962	M	Ger.		Civilian,Hemer(Ger.) 43	TORTURE	U.S.
HUMPLIK, Hans	253711	M	Ger.	8.6.08	SS-Sturmbannfhr.,Kromeriz(Czech.) 39-45	MURDER	CZECH.
HUNCK, Johann	185940	M	Ger.	3.9.98	Civilian,Factory Employee,Brno(Czech.) 39-45	PILLAGE	CZECH.
HUNDECKER	254346	M	Ger.		Sgt.,Cotes du Nord(Fr.) 15.7.44	INTERR.	FR.
HUNDGEN, Heinrich	306772	M			German Civilian,Miel(Ger.) 7.10.44	BRUTALITY	U.S.
HUNDRICH	250227	M	Ger.		Gestapo,Lille(Fr.) 40-44	MURDER	FR.
HUNDT	125663	M	Ger.		Sgt.,Section Speciale de Gendarmerie,Boarg Lastic(Fr.) 7.44	MURDER	FR.
HUNDT, Gotthilf	261731	M	Ger.		Guard,C.C.Greditz	MURDER	FR.
HUNDT, Wilhelm	167811	M	Ger.		Pvt.,9 Gren.Res.Regt.,1 Coy.,Magny D'Anigon(Fr.) 18.9.44	MURDER	FR.
HUNECK	259050	M	Ger.		C.C.Mauthausen(Aust.)	MURDER	BEL.
HUNECKE, Paul	253693	M	Ger.		Doctor,Official,State Service,Prag(Czech.) 6.42	MISC.CRIMES	CZECH.
HUNEWELD	193685	M			SS-Oschfhr.,C.C.Buchenwald(Ger.)	TORTURE	U.S.
HUNFELD	162400	M	Ger.	10	SS-Hptsturmfhr.,SS,C.C.Buchenwald(Ger.)	TORTURE	U.S.
HUNFELD, Willi	255574	M			Osturmfhr.,C.C.Buchenwald(Ger.)	MURDER	U.S.
HUNGER	112465	M	Ger.		Oschfhr.,Army,Panz.Gren.Regt.111,Gourdon(Fr.) 29.6.44	MURDER	FR.
HUNGER	124846		Ger.		Arb.-Kdo.Working Camp 688,Chemnitz(Ger.) 10.43-14.3.45	TORTURE	U.K.
HUNGER, Karl	192792	M	Ger.		Schupo,C.C.Falstad Stalag,Falstad(Nor.) 41-45	TORTURE	NOR.
HUNLICH	261782	M	Ger.		Feldkommandantur 602,Lt.,Saint Quentin(Fr.) 7.4.44	INTERR.	FR.
HUNNEL	301234	M	Ger.		Militaerverwaltungsoberrat,Bruessels(Bel.) 40-44	MURDER	BEL.
HUNNING	1404	M			Army,305 Div.,578 Gren.	MISC.CRIMES	U.K.
HUNSER	141878	M			Guard,Stalag,714 or 724 Coy,Brahnau(Pol.) 19.9.42	MURDER	U.K.
HUNSINGER, Georg	255579	M	Ger.	24.3.96	SS-Mann,C.C.Nordhausen(Ger.)	MURDER	U.S.
HUNTER	192681	M		05	Guard,714 Landesschuetzen Bn.,Stalag XXI,Brahnau(Pol.) 19.9.42	MURDER	U.K.
HUNZE	305799	M	Ger.		Capt.,Camp-Cmdt.Oflag VI-C,Osnabrueck-Ewersheide(Ger.) 41-45	MURDER	YUGO.
HUNZE, Hermann	156790	M	Ger.		SA-Member,Gronau(Ger.)	MISC.CRIMES	U.S.
HUNZELMAN	142475	M			Sgt.,Army,Oflag Altburgund. 6.-7.44	TORTURE	U.S.
HUPL	142472	M			Civilian,Ettenberg(Ger.) 1.8.44	MURDER	U.S.
HUPENKOTTEN	166606	M		05	Sturmbannfhr.,SS.(Pol.) 39	TORTURE	U.S.
HUPER	142958	M				WITNESS	U.S.
HUPFAUER, H. see REIBCHAUER	165152						
HUPFAUER, Theo	21919		Ger.		DAF	TORTURE	UNWCC.
HUPFER, Hans	142944	M		13	Sgt.,SS-Totenkopf-Stand.,Waffen-SS,C.C.Buchenwald(Ger.) 41-42	MURDER	U.S.
HUPPER	301569	M			Col.,stationed at Mauthausen C.C.,Mauthausen(Aust.) 40-45	MURDER	BEL.
HUPPERT, Greta	188705	F		17	Civilian,Wehrden-Saar(Ger.) 8.44	SUSPECT	U.S.
HURMALS	119445	M			Major,Army,7 Geb.Div.,20 Army,1 B. 44	MURDER	NOR.
HURTH, Heinrich	170989	M		07	Obgfr.,Stabs-Coy,Wolgn,Tartaren Bn.627,Quaregnon Jemappes-Ghlin (Bel.) 2.-3.9.44	MURDER	BEL.
HURZLMEIER, Johann	140841	M	Ger.		Ortsgruppenleiter NSDAP,Civilian-Farmer,C.C.Illbach(Ger.)	BRUTALITY	U.S.
HUSAR, Willi	241946	M	Ger.		Waffen-SS,Various Places in Slovenia(Yugo.) 41-4	MISC.CRIMES	YUGO.
HUSE	301753	M	Ger.		Capt.,Feldgend.of Clermont Ferrand (Group 689),Venarey Les Laumes (Fr.) 9.44	MURDER	FR.
HUSER	21321	M	Ger.		SS-Gruppenfhr.,Polizei,SS,B.F.W.K.R.XVII	MURDER	CZECH.
HUSING	193185	M	Ger.		Sgt.,6 Coy.,Inf.Regt.357,Nordreisa(Nor.) 8.41	WITNESS	NOR.
HUSKA	240102	M	Ger.		Agent,Gestapo,Zwolle(Neth.) 45	MURDER	UNWCC.
HUSKES, Johannes	305427	M	Ger.	21.1.25	80 Regt.,13 Coy.,558 Gren.Regt.,Bruay-en-Artois,Pas-de-Calais(Fr.) 44	MURDER	FR.
HUSMANN	253063	M			SS-Sturmmann,C.C.Mackenrode-Nordhausen(Ger.)	MURDER	U.S.
HUSS	253064	M			Flyer,C.C.Ellrich-Nordhausen(Ger.)	MURDER	U.S.
HUSSAREK, Paul	301878	M	Ger.		Dr.,Chief,C.C.Dachau Press Office,Dachau and Auschwitz(Ger.,Pol.) 3.42 and 26.2.43	TORTURE	BEL.
HUSSENDORFER, Robert	167166	M			Cpl.,Army,Remoncourt(Fr.) 6.7.40	PILLAGE	FR.
HUSSMANN, Eugen	259019	M		05-15	SS-Oschfhr.,SS,Mühldorf Area(Ger.)	MURDER	U.S.
HUSSMANN-ZAEHLE, Karl Hans	261172	M	Ger.	27.9.09	SS-Osturmbannfhr.,SS,(Bel.)	WITNESS	BEL.
HUSSNER	261789				Cpl.,Art.H.D.V.199-2295 N.D.F.No.F.P.27.0460,Lorgies(Fr.) 3.9.44	MURDER	FR.

HUS - ILG

NAME	C.R. FILE NUMBER	SEX	NATIO-NALITY	DATE OF BIRTH	RANK OCCUPATION UNIT PLACE AND DATE OF CRIME	REASON WANTED	WANTED BY
HUSTADT	300783	M	Ger.		Pvt., 1.Aufkl.Abt.3.Coy.2.Column XV. Div. of the Afrika Korps Saint, L'eger, (Arlon), (Fr.) 5.9.44	MISC. CRIMES	BEL.
HUSTEK (see ERBER)	306984						
HUSTERT	188661	M			SS-Major, Charmes (Fr.) 5.9.44	MURDER	FR.
HUSTETT	252151	M	Ger.		Sgt., Fort de Vincennes (Fr.) 20.8.44	TORTURE	FR.
HUSTON	142943	M	Ger.		Officer, Stalag XI A, near Magdeburg (Ger.) 4.45	MURDER	U.S.
HUTEN	158624	M	Ger.		Officer, W-SS, Div.1.SS Panz.Div.Adolf Hitler, 1 Rcn.Bn. Stavelot, (Bel.) 18.-22.12.44	MURDER	U.S.
HUTFLES, Mathias	253858	M	Ger.		SS-man, 4.SS.T.Stuba., C.C. Auschwitz-Birkenau (Pol.) 10.42	MURDER	YUG.
HUTHMANN, Karl-Heinz	142960	M	Ger.	25	Sturmmann, W-SS, Leibstand. Adolf Hitler, 1.SS Div. Rosbach (Ger.) 4.3.1945	WITNESS	U.S.
HUTLER, Josef	258601	M	Ger.	98	Member, Land.Schuetzen Police, Bad Salzdetfurth (Ger.) 4.11.44	MURDER	U.S.
HUTT	173170	M	Ger.		Staff at C.C. Schirmeck,Rotenfels,Gaggenau (Fr.Ger.) 44	INTERR.	U.K.
HUTTEMAN	253058	M	Ger.		Manager, Civ.firm, Apeldoorn (Neth.) 2.10.44	MURDER	U.S.
HUTTEMANN	67034	M	Ger.		Pvt., SS Div., St.Sulpice, Furtmusson,Chateau Gontier (Fr.)6.8.44	MURDER	FR.
HUTTER	141411	M	Ger.		Sgt., Feldgend., Dreux (Fr.)	WITNESS	FR.
HUTTER, Vinzenz	142701	M		7. 6.96	Civilian, Palling (Ger.) 22.9.44	MURDER	U.S.
HUTTICH	133334	M			Hptsturmfhr., W-SS C.C. Flossenburg (Ger.)	MURDER	U.S.
HUTTICH	133340	M		17	Hitler Jugend, Bannfhr.,	MURDER	U.S
HUTTIG	29806	M		95	Hptsturmfhr., SS, Struthof-Natzweiler (Fr.)	MURDER	FR.
HUTTIG	121044	M	Ger.		SS-Major, C.C. Buchenwald (Ger.)	TORTURE	FR.
HUTTIG, Max	254522	M	Ger.	95	Osturmfhr., C.C. Buchenwald (Ger.)	MURDER	FR.
HUTTL, Friedrich	140027	M			Landgerichtsrat Justisminist.,Public Official, Cheb (Czech.)21.2.40	MURDER	BEL.
HUTTMANN	152471	M			Lt., 111. Kampfgeschwader, Villaudric (Fr.) 20.8.44	MURDER	FR.
HUTTMANN, Hans	253037	M	Ger.	2.12.25	Pvt., 13.Coy.558.Gren.Rgt. Bruay en Artois (Fr.) 1.9.44	MURDER	FR.
HUTTNER	174004	M			SS-Uschfhr., C.C. Muhldorf, Ampfing (Ger.) 6.44-4.45	MISC.CRIMES	U.S.
HUTZ	31564	M	Ger.		Lt., Etat Major, Munitions Verwaltung, Bannalec (Fr.)4.8. u. 6.8.44	MURDER	FR.
HUTZLER, Adam	149334	M	Ger.		Krim.Secretaer, Police C.C. Dachau, (Ger.)	MURDER	U.S.
HUWE	252883	M			Krim.Obersecretaer, Crim.Police, C.C. Dora Nordhausen (Ger.)	MURDER	U.S.
HUX	152472	M	Ger.		Chief, Hattejelsdal (Ger.) 19.8.45	MURDER	FR.
HUX	257883	M			Lt., 150.Panzer Brigade, Meuss-Bridge Antwerp, (Bel.)12.44	MISC. CRIMES	U.S.
HUZMANN, Erich	255109	M	Ger.		Ob.Wachtmeister d.Res. Gestapo, Toulouse (Fr.) 11.42-8.44	MISC. CRIMES	FR.
HYAR, Willi	194897	M	Ger.		Stadt Inspector, Terr.Occupied, Grevenmacher, (Lux.)	MISC. CRIMES	LUX.
HYBNER (see HUEBNER)	133684	M					
HYLAND	133409	M	Ger.		Sgt , Stalag Luft IV, Bankau (Ger.) 2.-3.45	MISC. CRIMES	U.K.
HYLE	67035	M	Ger.		Cpt., Oflag IX.A.Z. Rockensuess (Ger.) 29.3.45	MURDER	U.K.
HYLE (see HEIL)	135544						
HYMEL (see HEMEL)	132716						
HYNAIS	300535	M	Ger.		SS-Hptsturmfhr., S.D.Fiume, (It.) 10.3.45	MISC. CRIMES	YUG.
HYNAS	253969	M	Ger.		SS-Hptsturmfhr., S.D. SS-Police, Fiume (It.) 10.3.45	MURDER	YUG.
HYNE, Anna, Maria	139795	F	Ger.		Woman Guard, W-SS Arbeitslager 701 (Buchenwald) Magdeburg (Ger.)44-45	TORTURE	U.S.
HYNEK, Willi	252882	M			SS-Rottfhr., C.C. Ellrich Nordhausen (Ger.)	MURDER	U.S.
HYSER	142013	M	Ger.	22	Obermaat, Navy, Fort Prinshendrik near Ooltgensplaat (Neth.)12.6.45	MURDER	NETH.
IAKETZKO, Ursule	259357	F	Ger.		Typist, Gestapo of Poitiers (Fr.)	SUSPECT	FR.
IANKOVITCH	305193	M	Ger.		Attached, C.C. Dora and C.C. Buchenwald (Fr.) 43-2.4.45	MISC. CRIMES	FR.
IAPS,August	124847	M	Ger.	95	Civilian, Nentershausen (Ger.) 20.9.44	WITNESS	U.S.
IBACH, Friedrich	135192	M	Ger.		Major, Army, (Milit.Dist.13 Nuernberg) C.C. Ruppertsbuch (Ger.)23.4.45	WITNESS	U.S.
IBALI	102983	M			SS NCO., Thekla (Ger.) 18.4.45	MURDER	U.S. POL.
IBIRKIOT	154390	M			Cpt., Hptsturmfhr., SS, Muenich-Ries (Ger.)	MISC. CRIMES	U.S.
ICKS, Arthur, Maximilian	194124	M	Ger.	13. 7.04	Civilian, Gouda, (Neth.)31.12.44	MURDER	NETH.
IDE, Heinrich	191989	M	Ger.		Ortsgruppenleiter NSDAP., Bochum (Ger.)	MURDER	U.S.
IDEN	191429	M	Ger.		Dr., High Official, Ostdeutschelandbewirtschaftungsgesellschaft m.b.H. Hpt.Geschaeftsstelle fuer Gau Wartheland, Posnan (Pol.)9.39-44	PILLAGE	POL.
IEGER	306773	M	Ger.		Stabsfhr., Dorheim, (Ger.) 7.44	BRUTALITY	U.S.
IEHLE (or JEHLE)	132624	M	Ger.		Vice Praesident of Military Administration in France Intendant of Majestic Hotel Paris, Gerardmer, (Fr.) 11.44	PILLAGE	FR.
IEKOVITCH	167216	M	Ger.		Lt., Army, Lizant Ol'vray, St. Gaudent (Fr.) 28.8.44	MURDER	FR.
IEMKE	128979	M	Ger.		Kor.Kapitain, 262. Naval Rgt. Brest Peninsula (Fr.) 1.-9.9.44	MISC. CRIMES	U.S.
IESSER	125683	M	Ger.		General Cmdt., Army 66. ème Corps d'Army	MISC.CRIMES	FR.
IFFLAND, Rolf	306589	M	Ger.		Guard Ld.Schuetz., Bn. 622, Vacha Kr.Eisenach (Ger.) 4.43-4.45	MURDER	U.K.
IGASCHAP, Ladislaus	174018	M	Ger.		SS-Mann, C.C. Muhldorf Ampfing (Ger.) 6.44-4.45	MISC. CRIMES	U.S.
IGEL	179747	M	Ger.	19	Lt., 61. Flak Ausb. Abt. Montemignaio (It.) 29.7.44	MURDER	U.S.
IGEL, Hans	191985	M	Ger.		Oberwachtmeister Pol.Rgt.7 Pol.Bn.3 Camp 10 O.C.Junkerdal (Nor.)10.44	TORTURE	NOR.
IGNATZ	102982	M	Ger.		Lt., Dulag, Klosterwald (Ger.)	TORTURE	U.K.
IGNATZ, Andreas	169731	M			SS-Sturmmann, C.C. Struthof Natzweiler (Fr.)	MURDER	FR.
IHAMPEL	141568	M	Ger.		Cmdt., Festung Metz (Fr.)	TORTURE	FR.
IHRES	131724	M			Chief, Customs, Velmanya Pareignan (Fr.) 1.8.44	MURDER	FR.
IHL, Josephine	134860	F	Ger.		Civ., Efferen- (Ger.)	TORTURE	U.S.
IHLE	1068	M	Ger.		Lt., Army Feldgend., Epernay (Fr.)	MURDER	FR.
IHLE, Hans	162473	M	Ger.		SS-Unchfhr., W-SS, C.C. Sect.1, Motor Pool, Buchenwald (Ger.)	WITNESS	U.S.
IHNE, Fritz	250261	M	Ger.		Kapo, C.C. Halle 16, Neuengamme (Ger.)	TORTURE	FR.
IHNEN	261141	M			Civ., Occup.,Crimes against peace.War Crimes and Crimes against humanity	WITNESS	U.R.
IHNER	250255	M			Lt., 28. Gr.Rgt., 116 Bn. 1.Coy., Bordes (Fr.)13.8.44	INTERR.	FR.
IHRENBURGH(see IHRENBURG)	137602						
IKARIUS	305901	M	Ger.		Hptschfhr., C.C. Oranienburg (Ger.) 11.39-45	MURDER	CZECH.
IKOSHAM (see GROSHAM)	106955						
ILBERT	167845	M	Ger.		Lt., Army, Chateau D'etoile (Fr.) 9.7.44	MURDER	FR.
ILDEBRANDT	258927	M	Ger.		Guard, Prison, Frankfurt Preungesheim (Ger.) 42-44	BRUTALITY	FR.
ILGEN, Fritz, Otto	305787	M	Ger.	8.10.10	Osturmfhr., SS, NSDAP., Gestapo Paris, Noailles, Oise (Fr.) 9.8.44	MURDER	U.K.

NAME	C.R.FILE NUMBER	SEX	NATIONALITY	DATE OF BIRTH	RANK OCCUPATION UNIT PLACE AND DATE OF CRIME	REASON WANTED	WANTED BY
HIADKY	146851	M	Ger.		SS Pz.Div."Das Reich", Rgt."Deutschland", 3 Bn., Venerque le Vernet (Fr.) 44	MURDER	FR.
ILLAUER	198952	M			Sgt., SS, Gestapo, Lyon (Fr.)	MURDER	FR.
ILLER	306985	M	Ger.		F.C.O., Member of Secret Field Police (taken from the 6 Parachuter-Div) Velp and Arnhem (Neth.) 1.45	BRUTALITY	NETH.
ILLGENS	411	M			Sgt., Army, Comblanchien (Fr.) 21.-22.8.44	MURDER	FR.
ILIERS	196378	M	Ger.		Dr., member of Org.Contr., Compiegne-Royailleu (Fr.) 41-44	INTERR.	FR.
ILING, Josef	192677	M	Ger.	95	Leading member NSDAP, Praha (Czech.)	MISC.CRIMES	CZECH.
ILING, Paul	10012	M	Ger.		Ofhr, SS,Chef des Aufbaustabes des SS Abschnittes, 39-44	TORTURE	CZECH.
ILLMER	173578	M	Ger.		Sturmbannfhr, W-SS,Staatspolizeistelle,CC Auschwitz-Birkenau(Pol.)42	MURDER	CZECH.
ILLNER, Joseph	31214	M	Ger.		Dr.,Oberlandesgerichtsrat,Public Official,Litomerice(Czech.)21.2.40	MURDER	BEL.
IBARGUE	188977	M	Ger.	20	Cpl., Army, Montclus (Fr.)	PILLAGE	FR.
I'GIT, Joseph	174982	M			Dienststelle, Gironcourt sur Vraine, Poussay Repel(Fr.) 24.8.44-1.9.44	WITNESS	FR.
IMHOFF	251056	M			Uschfhr, SS, CC Wieda, Nordhausen (Ger.)	MURDER	U.S.
IMKE, Karl	306986	M	Ger.		Member SS, Zakopane (Pol.) 41-45	BRUTALITY	POL.
IMMENDORF, Martin	257572	M	Ger.	26. 3.99	Employee, CC Dora, Block 107, Nordhausen (Ger.)	MURDER	U.S.
IMER, Elisabeth	130662	F	Ger.		SS, CC Dora, Mittelbau, Nordhausen (Ger.)	MURDER	U.S.
IMERLE	189784	M	Ger.		Dr., SS Hptsturmfhr, CC Vught (Neth.) 6.6.44	MURDER	NETH.
IMTING, Valentin	142085	M			Civilian, Camp Leader, CC, 9.43-44	TORTURE	U.S.
INDERHOLZ, Josef	193494	M	Ger.	3. 8.89	Informer, Gestapo, Trebon (Czech.) 39-45	MURDER	CZECH.
IN DER STROTH, Heinrich	192845	M	Ger.	05	Sgt., Ministry of Justice, Feldstraflager Nord, CC Finmark (Nor.) 41-45	MISC.CRIMES	NOR.
INDRA, Franz	9691	M	Ger.		Dr., Reg.Rat., Ministry of Labour, Publ.Off.,Prague (Czech.) 42-44	TORTURE	CZECH.
INDRAK	257573	M	Ger.		Employee CC, Sub.Sec.Mittelwerk, Nordhausen(Ger.)	MURDER	U.S.
INGALL (see ENGELS)	142440						
INGEBRAND	133325	M	Ger.		Kreisleiter NSDAP, Schweinfurt (Ger.) 44	MURDER	U.S.
INGELHARD, Bill	259033	M	Ger.		Dulag Luft Hospital, A Dulag Luft (Ger.) 43-4.45	BRUTALITY	U.S.
INGENSIEP	190564	M			Major, Army, Staff, Pozarevac (Yugo.) 41-45	MURDER	YUGO.
INGERLE, Mrs.	192674	F	Ger.		Member NSDAP, Pilsen (Czech.) 39-45	MISC.CRIMES	CZECH.
INGERLE, Miss (minore)	192675	F	Ger.		Member NSDAP, Pilsen (Czech.) 39-45	MISC.CRIMES	CZECH.
INGERLE, Miss (Major)	192676	F	Ger.		Member NSDAP, Pilsen (Czech.) 39-45	MISC.CRIMES	CZECH.
INGIS	125719	M	Ger.		CC Traun (Aust.) 1.1.44	MURDER	U.S.
INGLE (see ENGELS)	142440						
INGLESKIRCHER, Johann	67706	M	Ger.		Cpl., Kdo.Fuehrer E 209 Bobrek, Schonburg (Ger.) 8.-10.41	MURDER	U.K.
INNPRETTER	250263	M	Ger.		Gestapo, Lille (Fr.) 40-44	MURDER	FR.
INTEMANN, Didrych	171962	M	Ger.	21.11.03	Civilian, Davelsen (Ger.)	TORTURE	
INTERMANN, Wilhelm	189718	M			Civ., 6 Sebaldbruck Str., Bremen, Dauelsen (Ger.) 10.43	TORTURE	U.K.
IODKUN	126725	M	Ger.		Agent, Gestapo, Paris (Fr.) 42	TORTURE	FR.
IOFEL	257574	M			W-SS, Muhldorf Area (Ger.)	MURDER	U.S.
IRBER	174017				Org.Todt., CC Muhldorf Arpfing (Ger.) 6.44-4.45	MISC.CRIMES	U.S.
IRIE (or IRLE), Artur	260452	M	Ger.	14.10.99	Lt., Chief of Squadron, Court, Sarzyna (Pol.) 39	MURDER	POL.
IRION	250259	M	Ger.		Agent, Gestapo, Offenburg (Ger.) 11.44	MURDER	FR.
IRQOU	250262	M	Ger.		Cpl., Air Force, Entzheim (Fr.) 42-44	TORTURE	FR.
IRLBECK	250265	M			Pvt., CC Dora, Nordhausen (Ger.)	MURDER	U.S.
IRLE, Artur (see IRIE)	260452						
IRMER	251058	M	Ger.	19. 8.23	Pvt., Army,2 Coy,443 Jg.Rgt.,Belgrad(Yugo.) 3.10-25.12.41	MURDER	YUGO.
IRMER, Karl	257575	M	Ger.	1918 -21	Usturmfhr, SS, Automotive-Techn.Training School,Wien, Frein a.d.Muerr (Aust.) 23.8.44	MURDER	U.S.
IRMLER	145245	M	Ger.		Uschfhr, 1 ss Pz.Div., 2 Pz.Gren.Rgt., 3 Bn., 12 Coy., Stavelot, Malmedy (Bel.) 22-23.12.44	MURDER	U.S.
IRMLER, Joseph	31215	M	Ger.		Landgerichtsrat, Public Official, Cheb (Czech.) 21.2.40	MURDER	BEL.
IRPGANG	250267	M			Pvt., CC Ellrich, Nordhausen (Ger.)	MURDER	U.S.
IRRGANG, Xaver	167849	M	Ger.		Pvt., 9 Gren.Res.Rgt.,1 Coy, Magny D'Anigon(Fr.) 18.9.44	MURDER	FR.
ISACK, Arnold	250266	M			Flyer, CC Ellrich, Nordhausen (G er.)	MURDER	U.S.
ISBACH, Bernhard Wilhelm	167162	M	Ger.	4. 5.14	Adjut.Chief, Army, 19 Rgt.SS Police, 2 Coy, St.Gingolph, Douvaine (Fr.) 19.7., 27.7.44	MURDER	FR.
ISCHEBECK, Erich(Walter)	305196	M	Ger.		Member SD and the Commission "Holland Action", engaged in recruiting workers for the "Arbeitseinsatz" in Germany, Apeldoorn (Neth.)17.2.43	INTERR.	NETH.
ISCHEBECK, Wilhelm	162815	M	Ger.	21. 1.03	Civilian, Montigny (Fr.) 40 - 44	TORTURE	FR.
ISENHOOD	126895	M	Ger.		Cpl., Lds.Schtz.Bn.439, CC Falkenau (Ger.) 9.3.45	TORTURE	U.K.
ISENMANN, Otto Friedrich	257805	M	Ger.	5. 5.91	Capt., Gend. (Police), Wolfisheim near Strasbourg (Fr.)14.-15.8.44	MURDER	U.S.
ISENSEE, Albert	143182	M	Ger.		Civilian	MURDER	U.S.
ISER, Peter	250258	M	Ger.	22. 4.06	Gren., 13 Coy, 558 Gren.Rgt., Bruay en Artois (Fr.) 1.9.44	MURDER	FR.
ISERMAGEN	250254	M	Ger.		Capt., Comdt. 7 Coy, 376 Jg.Rgt., Vinkt (Bel.)	MURDER	BEL.
ISERMANN, Ivan	250257	M	Ger.	28. 6.25	Pvt., 13 Coy, 558 Gren.Rgt., Bruay en Artois (Fr.) 1.9.44	MURDER	FR.
ISING	250256	M	Ger.		Pvt., Pepingen (Bel.)	WITNESS	BEL.
ISKRA, Mathous	145357	M			CC Mauthausen (Aust.) 41-45	MURDER	U.S.
ISMER	124848	M		87	Lt.Col., Kraftfahrers.Abt.9, Hersfeld (Ger.) 7.-8.44	MURDER	U.S.
ISOKOST	301325	M	Ger.		Member of Gestapo at Trencin,CC Auschwitz-Birkena.(Pol.)39-45	MURDER	CZECH.
ISRAEL	67707	M			Uschfhr, SS Pz.Gren.Div."G.v.B.", Sturmgesch.Abt.17, Lerge-Renaze (Fr.) 6.8.44, 30.7.44	MURDER	FR.
ISTEL, August	187680	M	Ger.	00	Civilian, Mayor, Eutingen (Ger.) 29.7.44	MURDER	U.K.
ISTELFORST	173168	M			Gestapo, CC Gaggenau, Schirmeck (Ger. Fr.)	MURDER	U.K.
ISING	250847	M			Pvt., CC Ellrich-Nordhausen (Ger.)	MURDER	U.S.
ISSLEIB, Werner	145204	M	Ger.	10	Uschfhr, W-SS,Totenkopf Standarte, 2 Totenk.Coy, Buchenwald(Ger.)	MISC.CRIMES	U.S.
ISTHERNER, Max (see ISTHORNER)	250260						
ISTHORNER, Max (or ISTHERNER, Max)	250260	M	Ger.	12	Pvt., Army or Air Force, Gambin (Pol.) 28.8.43	INTERR.	U.S.
ISTOK, Timotheus	306416	M	Ger.		Col., Cmdr. Gend., Slovakia (Czech.) 40 - 45	BRUTALITY	CZECH.
ISTSCHUK	174016	M	Ger.		Officer, Stalag VI A, CC Hemer (Ger.) 41-45	TORTURE	U.S.
ITERBECK, Gerard	132022	M	Ger.	15	Member SD Issel (Ger.) 20.1.45	MURDER	U.N.W.C.C.

ITT - JAE

NAME	C.R.FILE NUMBER	SEX	NATIO-NALITY	DATE OF BIRTH	RANK OCCUPATION UNIT PLACE AND DATE OF CRIME	REASON WANTED	WANTED BY
ITTAMEIER, Ernst or ITTERMEIER	253671	M	Ger.		Farmer, Mayor and Kreisleiter, Wassertrudingen (Ger.) 3.45	INTERR.	U.S.
ITTNER	305430	M	Ger.		Lt., Bordes, Htes.Pyrenees (Fr.) 13.8.44	MURDER	FR.
ITZE	193184	M	Ger.		Cpl., Kgf.Arbeits-Bn. 190, Storjord (Nor.) 8.43	MURDER	NOR.
IUFFER	191352	M	Ger.		Pvt., 2-188.Kgf.Arb.Bn., Lekanger, Ervik (Nor.) 10.42	INTERR.	NOR.
IVAN	192908	M	Ger.		Kapo, C.C. Flossenburg (Ger.)	MURDER	U.S.
IVAN	186473	M	Ger.		Lt., Gren.Rgt. 950, Vienne Charente (Fr.) 8.44	TORTURE	FR.
IVERSEN	190519	M			Capt., Feldkommandantur, nr.Les Parres, St.Germain, Liard (Fr.) 25.7.44	MURDER	FR.
IVIANONTANWITCH LACOMEYER	149767	M			Interpreter, Sonderfuehrer, SS, C.C. Stavern (Nor.) 5.44	MURDER	NOR.
IWERKOL	257490	M			Usturmfhr., C.C. Nordhausen (Ger.)	MURDER	U.S.
IZENHOFER, Kurt	161981	M			Baufuehrer,Org.Todt, Firm Rollinger, Botn (Nor.)	MURDER	NOR.
JAAN, Willy or JAN	253065	M	Ger.		Guard, S.D., C.C. Lahde-Weser (Ger.)	MISC.CRIMES	BEL.
JABLONOWSKI, Arthur	193183	M		17.6.20	Ex convict, Reichsjustizministerium, Feldstraflager, Finmark (Nor.)3.45	WITNESS	NOR.
JABST, Willy see JOBST, Willy	192548						
JACK	251088	M	Ger.		SS Rottfhr., Buchenwald (Ger.)	INTERR.	FR.
JACKEL	139782	M	Ger.	95	Hptsturmfhr., Waffen SS,Arbeitslager 101 (Buchenwald),Magdeburg (Ger.) 44-45	TORTURE	U.S.
JACKEL, Hermann	167834	M	Ger.		Capt., Army, Orck (Bel.) 1.9.44	MURDER	BEL.
JACKEL, Jakob	250861	M			C.C. Harzungen, Nordhausen (Ger.)	MURDER	U.S.
JACKENHAFER or JOGVENHOFER	259738	M	Ger.		Lt., Unit 22 942 B stat.at St.Michel Clouq, La Chapelle,Montreuil, Deux Sevres Vienne (Fr.) 25.8.44-28.8.44	MURDER	FR.
JACKERT	251647	M	Ger.		Pvt., 3.Coy. 2.Zug 1.Aufkl.Rgt. 15.Div.Afrika-Corps, St.Leger (Bel.) 5.9.44	MURDER	BEL.
JACKES	167161	M	Ger.		Adjutant, Army, I.Coy. 729.Bn., Champenoux (Fr.) 1.9.44	MURDER	FR.
JACKLE, Georg	906755	M	Ger.		German Civ., Bremen (Ger.) 24.2.45	BRUTALITY	U.S.
JACKOWSKY, Andre	256069	M			Secretary, Block XXX, XV C.C. Mauthausen (Aust.)	INTERR.	FR.
JACKS	125081	M			Dr. Civ., Weissenbach, St.Galleon (Aust.) 20.8.44	MISC.CRIMES	U.K.
JACKSCH	250280	M			SS Rottfhr., C.C. Dora - Nordhausen (Ger.)	MURDER	U.S.
JACKWES	194457	M	Ger.	4.23	Lt., 9.Panz.Div. 102. Panz.Rgt., Fuerth (Ger.) 13.9.44	MURDER	U.S.
JACKY or RAUE	132720	M	Ger.	10.1.09	Lt., Gestapo, Lalinde (Fr.)	PILLAGE	FR.
JACMIN	251644	M			16. Huebner-Rgt., 6.Coy., Kinrooi (Bel.) 9.44	INTERR.	BEL.
JACOB	67711	M	Ger.		Pit manager, C.C., Ger.	TORTURE	U.K.
JACOB	130664	M	Ger.		Chief engineer, Civ.in Camp Dora-Mittelbau - Nordhausen (Ger.)	MURDER	U.S.
JACOB	149335	M	Ger.		SC Oscharfhr., C.C. Dachau (Ger.)	MURDER	FR.
JACOB	151285	M	Ger.		Sgt.Major, C.C. Zeitz Stalag 4 F (Ger.) 13.4.45	MURDER	U.K.
JACOB	161987	M		06	SIPO-Agent, Brussels (Bel.)	MURDER	BEL.
JACOB	174013	M	Ger.		Assist., C.C. Hemer Stalag VI A (Ger.) 41-45	TORTURE	U.S.
JACOB	190520	M			Lt., Army,Plantier,Crapoum sur Arzon,Chomelix (Fr.) 20.7.44-20.8.44	MURDER	FR.
JACOB	261784	M	Ger.		Kapo, C.C. Dora - Nordhausen (Ger.)	MURDER	U.S.
JACOB	301190	M	Ger.		Lt.,Quevillon, Seine-Interieure, Chateau de la Riviere,Bourdet (Fr.) 12.40 and Jan.41	PILLAGE	FR.
JACOB	301755	M	Ger.		Kapo, C.C. Auschwitz (Pol.) 40-45	MURDER	FR.
JACOB, Karl	251646	M	Ger.		Owner firm "Steingaesser", Miltenberg (Ger.) 43-45	MISC.CRIMES	POL.
JACOB, Karl Heinz	258891	M	Ger.		Lt., Legion Tartare, Hte.Loire,Crapoume sur Arzon, St.Paulien (Fr.) 19.8.44	INTERR.	FR.
JACOB, Wilhelm	150905	M	Ger.	00	Bloc-leader, C.C. Sachsenhausen, Oranienburg (Ger.)	TORTURE	J.K.
JACOBI	162839	M	Ger.	10	Osturmfhr., S.S., C.C. Erzingen (Ger.) 4-5.45	MURDER	FR.
JACOBIE	189070	M	Ger.		Sgt.,C.C. Hammerstein Stalag 2 B, (Ger.) 27.12.43	MURDER	U.S.
JACOBS	174015	M	Ger.		Dr.,Physician, Arzt, C.C. Hemer Stalag VI A (Ger.) 41-45	TORTURE	U.S.
JACOBS	194768	M	Ger.		General, Forstmeister, Reichsforstamt, Iburg (Ger.) 30.5.44	TORTURE	FR.
JACOBS	255527	M	Ger.	26	Lt., Army, Heusden (Neth.) 11.44	PILLAGE	NETH.
JACOBS	305198	M	Ger.		Lt., 749.Rgt., Calavrita, Mega, Apileon, Agtlialavra (Gr.) 13.12.43	MISC.CRIMES	GRC.
JACOBS, Annie	144422	F	Ger.		Member SS, C.C. Duderstadt (Ger.)	MISC.CRIMES	U.S.
JACOBS, Friedrich	143167	M	Ger.		Sgt., City police, Stendal (Ger.) 41-45	TORTURE	U.S.
JACOBS, Fritz	132020	M			Foreign laborer, C.C.	TORTURE	U.S.
JACOBS, Max or JAKOBS	192307	M	Ger.		Guard, C.C. Flossenburg (Ger.) 44 - 45	MURDER	U.S. BEL.
JACOPS, Wilhelm	306402	M	Ger.		SS Staff Sgt., C.C. Buchenwald (Ger.) betw. 16.5.38 and 9.10.43	MURDER	BEL.
JACOBSE	194358	M	Ger.		Usturmfhr., SS Div."Das Reich", Rgt. "Deutschland", Miremont (Fr.) 2.6.44	MURDER	FR.
JACOBSEN	250853	M	Ger.		SS Osturmfhr., Gestapo, District of Limoges (Fr.) 40-45	INTERR.	FR.
JACOBSEN	251074	M	Ger.		Oberfhr., Cmdt.instruction Cernay, Urbes (Fr.) 24.9.44, 4., 5.10.44	MURDER	FR.
JACOBSE	300074	M	Ger.		N.C.O., 1.Aufkl.Abt. 3.Coy. 2.Col. XV.Div. Afrika-Corps, St.Leger (Arlon) 5.9.44	MISC.CRIMES	BEL.
JACOBSEN - JAKOBSSEN	149771	M			Sgt., Bautruppen, Lossett (Nor.) 43	MURDER	NOR.
JACOBSEN, Gustav	306020	M			Member, C.C. staff Neuengamme (Ger.) 39-45	TORTURE	U.K.
JACOBY	251690	M	Ger.		Capt., Pioneer-Coy. 4-21, Acheux en Amienois (Fr.) 17.8.44	TORTURE	FR.
JACOBY, Jacob	151291	M	Ger.		SS Aide Major ? Div."Das Reich" Rgt. "Deutschland", Aiguillon (Fr.) 17.6.44	MURDER	FR.
JACQUES	165949	M	Ger.		Hptsturmfhr., S.D., Aussendienststelle, La Prade, Baradoux-Mende (Fr.) 44	MURDER	FR.
JACQUES	251635	M	Ger.	15	Mine-controller SS, C.C. Auschwitz (Pol.)	BRUTALITY	FR.
JADKE, Richard	157225	M			Member, Volkssturm, Gardelegen (Ger.) 10.-14.4.45	WITNESS	U.S.
JADRNICER, Karl	31216	M	Ger.		Landgerichtsdirektor, Public official, Prag (Czech.) 21.2.40	MURDER	BEL.
JAECKEL	162477	M	Ger.	93	Official, C.C. Buchenwald (Ger.)	WITNESS	U.S.
JAECKL see JAUCKEL, Hermann	162840						
JAECKTEL	252194	M	Ger.		SS Ogruppenfhr., Police and SS, Baranowicze (Pol.) 43	MISC.CRIMES	POL.
JAEGER	137636	M	Ger.	10	Rottfhr., SS, C.C. Neuengamme (Ger.)	TORTURE	U.K.
JAEGER	139660	M		12	Pvt., Army, Leipzig, Salzburg (Ger.,Aust.) 4.45	WITNESS	U.S.
JAEGER	196321	M			Zugwachtmeister, probably 8.Coy. Schupo, nr.Arnheim (Neth.) 3.45	MURDER	NETH.
JAEGER	251080	M	Ger.		Dr., SS Osturmfhr., C.C. Neuengamme (Ger.)	MURDER	BEL.
JAEGER	257376	M	Ger.		SS guard, Sgt., SS slave labour camp, Beisfjord-Narvik (Nor.) 6.-11.42	BRUTALITY	YUG.
JAEGER	251698	M	Ger.		SS Standartenfhr., SIPO, Rowne (Pol.) 39-45	MURDER	POL.
JAEGER	251648	M	Ger.		Pvt., Pepingen (Bel.) 2.-9.44	WITNESS	BEL.
JAEGER	252195	M	Ger.		Leader, Labour front, Heidenheim (Ger.) 41-45	MURDER	POL.
JAEGER, Erich	196340	M	Ger.	10	Pvt., Compiegne-Royallieu (Fr.) 41-44	MURDER	FR.
JAEGER, Ernst	252192	M	Ger.		SS Rottfhr., Gestapo, L'Aube (Fr.) 43-44	INTERR.	FR.
JAEGER, Georg	162070	M	Ger.		Leader NSDAP, Erbach, Konig (Ger.) 21.11.44	MURDER	U.K.
JAEGER, Johanna	261427	F	Ger.	13.8.08	Civ. Interpreter, SS and C.C. Auschwitz (Pol.) 42-45	BRUTALITY	
JAEGER, Philipp	906756	M	Ger.		German Civ., Dromersheim, Bingen (Ger.) 11. and 12.9.44	MURDER	U.S.
	130684	M			SS Osturmfhr., Lagerarzt, C.C. Neuengamme (Ger.) 43	MURDER	YUGO

JAE-JAK

NAME	C.R.FILE NUMBER	SEX	NATIO-NALITY	DATE OF BIRTH	RANK OCCUPATION UNIT PLACE AND DATE OF CRIME	REASON WANTED	WANTED BY
JAEGERS	139847	M			Oberscharfhr., SS, C.C. Waldlager 6 and M I, Muehldorf-Dachau (Ger.) 44-45	MURDER	U.S.
JAEHNCHEN, Rudolf	189839	M	Ger.		Rottenfhr., I.Div.SS Leibstandarte "Adolf Hitler" I. Regt., Renardmont,Stavelot (Bel.) 19.-20.12.44	MURDER	BEL.
JAEKEL, Josef	192673	M	Ger.	88	Leiter, Member, NSDAP, Prag (Czech.)	MISC.CRIMES	CZECH.
JAERL, Erika	157223	F	Ger.30.11.02		Nurse, Ger."Red Cross", Katzdorf,District Perg (Austr.) 25.4.45	MURDER	U.S.
JAENCHEN, Rudolf	251649	M	Ger.		Rottenfhr., I.SS Pz.Gren.Div. "Leibstand. Adolf Hitler" I. Regt. Renardmont Stavelot (Bel.) 19.-20.12.44	MURDER	BEL.
JAENECKE, Erwin	258981	M			Lt. General, Army,	INTERR.	U.S.
JAENICHEN, Fritz	192107	M	Ger.	04	Agent, SS-Gruppenfhr., Gestapo, SS, Boheme (Czech.)	MURDER	CZECH.
JAENICKE, Ernst or JEANICKE	261785	M	Ger.		Inspector, Gestapo of Amiens, Gentelles (Fr.) 6. and 8.44	MURDER	FR.
JAENIGGER or JAHNIGE	195396	M	Ger.	95	Sgt., Command Camp 2780, Langwied-Muenchen (Ger.) 2.42	TORTURE	U.K.
JAENISCH, Johann	146760	M	Ger.		SS-Totenkopf-Standarte, Unterscharfhr., KL.-Buchenwald (Ger.)	TORTURE	U.S.
JAENSCH	157224	M	Ger.		Capt., Army Ger.Art., Lansdorf (Ger.) 1.42	MURDER	SOV.UN.
JAENSCH	301101	M	Ger.		Crim.-Obersecretary, served with the R.S.D. Abt. IV-Ia, Copenhagen (Den.) 43	INTERR.	DEN.
JAESCHKE see LIECHKI	162925						
JAESCHLE	191988	M	Ger.		Pvt., Army 184.Kgf.Arb.Bn.C.C. Bassins-Tunnel (Nor.)	MURDER	NOR.
JAGER	1703	M	Ger.		Unterscharfhr., Rottenfhr., 3.SS Totenkopf Div. Dunkirk (Fr.)	MURDER	U.K.
JAGER	145337	M	Ger.		SS, Mauthausen (Austr.) 41	MURDER	U.S.
JAGER	167182	M	Ger.		Dr., Civilian Commiss. Verwalter, Commercial Bank, Krakau (Pol.)39-44	PILLAGE	POL.
JAGER	190945	M			Dr., C.C. Dachau (Ger.)	MURDER	U.S.
JAGER	191286	M	Ger.		Pvt., Eis.Art.Abt. 717, St. Andries Varsenare-Le-Bruges (Bel.)4.9.44	MURDER	BEL.
JAGER	250865	M		16	SS Obsturmfhr., C.C. Dora Nordhausen (Ger.)	MURDER	FR.
JAGER	258137	M	Ger.		Dr., SS Physician, C.C. Belsen (Ger.)	MURDER	BEL.
JAGER	301756	M	Ger.		SS Sgt., Builder, C.C. Auschwitz (Pol.) 40	MURDER	FR.
JAGER	305199	M	Ger.		SS-Obersturmfhr., C.C. Dora Camp and Buchenwald (Ger.) 43-4.45	MURDER	U.S.
JAGER, Albert	143169	M	Ger.		C.C. Weferlingen (Ger.)	TORTURE	U.S.
JAGER, Albert	192306	M	Ger.	03	SS-Rottenfhr., C.C. Rosbach (Ger.)	MURDER	U.S.
JAGER, Albrecht	250278	M		22.9.18	Pvt., C.C. Harzungen-Nordhausen (Ger.)	MURDER	U.S.
JAGER, Fritz	145347	M	Ger.		Factory Superintendent, SA, Freiheit (Ger.)	TORTURE	U.S.
JAGER, Hans	250855	M	Ger.		Lt., Russ.Ger.Unit,Caserne Turenne, Langres L'Ain (Fr.) 10.-21.7.44	MISC.CRIMES	FR.
JAGER, Hans	251082	M	Ger.		Lt., Russ.-Ger. Unit, Chaumont-Hte Marne (Fr.) 15.6.44	BRUTALITY	FR.
JAGER, Hans	305431	M	Ger.		Lt., Laferte sur Aube, Marac, Montigny-le-Roi, Nogent-en-Bassigay (Fr.) 15.6.44,27.8.44, 1.9.44	MURDER	FR.
JAGER, Theo	414	M	Ger.		Sgt., Army, Feldgend. Abbeville (Fr.) 31.8.44	MURDER	FR.
JAGER, Willi	191861	M	Ger.		SS-Obersturmfhr., SS,C.C. Kowno, Belsen (Sov.Un.,Ger.) 40-44	MURDER	YUGO.
JAGER, Willi	301039	M	Ger.		Dr., Obersturmfhr., C.C. Neuengamme (Ger.) 40	MURDER	BEL.
JAGSCHUTZ	174014	M	Ger.		SS-Oberscharfhr., C.C. Muhldorf, Ampfing (Ger.) 6.44-4.45	MISC.CRIMES	U.S.
JAHCH	130666	M	Ger.		Oberscharfhr., SS, C.C. Dora Mittelbau, Nordhausen (Ger.)	MURDER	U.S.
JAHER, Albert	143166	M	Ger.	03	Pvt., W.-SS Leibstand. "Adolf Hitler" I.Ers.Bn., Rosbach (Ger.)4.3.45	MURDER	U.S.
JAHLE, Ernst	133793	M	Ger.		SS-Unterscharfhr., C.C. Buchenwald (Ger.)	TORTURE	U.S.
JOHLITZ, Fritz	260224	M	Ger.	3.98	Head of Gau Labour Office, Essen (Ger.) 4.44	MISC.CRIMES	U.S.
JAHN	129677	M	Ger.		Civilian, Duesseldorf (Ger.) 10.11.44	TORTURE	U.S.
JAHN	132648	M	Ger.		Chief of Industrie-Hof Ravensbrueck, C.C. Ravensbrueck (Ger.)	MURDER	BEL.,FR.
JAHN	140901	M	Ger.		Oberwachtmeister, Verbindungs Abt. 331 Batt. Nachrichtentruppen Bohnes (Neth.) 8.5.45	MURDER	NETH.
JAHN	189164	M	Ger.		Colonel, Feldkommandentur, Le Creusot (Fr.)	MISC.CRIMES	FR.
JAHN	251075	M	Ger.		Lt., 3.Pz.Gren.Div. 29. Pz.Gren.Regt., Robert-Espagne,Couvognes, Beury, Hogneville (Fr.) 29.8.44	MISC.CRIMES	FR.
JAHN	251080	M	Ger.		Capt., 1. and 2. Bn., Sicherheits.Regt. 197, Estang (Fr.)	INTERR.	FR.
JAHN	256517	M	Ger.		Sgt., Feldgendarmerietrupp, Region De Pontivy (Fr.) 44	TORTURE	FR.
JAHN	306797	M	Ger.		Cpl., Feldgend. Vesoul, Montigny Les Vesoul -Hte Saone (Fr.) 17.7.44	MURDER	FR.
JAHN	306987	M	Ger.		Guard, Arbeitserziehungs-Camp, Lahde-Weser, Labour Camp (Ger.)5.43-45	MURDER	U.K.
JAHN	302043	M	Ger.10.1.06		Head Cook, SS, at Schendelah near Brunswick(Ger.)1.5.44-30.4.45	MURDER	U.K.
JAHN, Karl	259835	M	Ger.	92	Civilian Buyer, Ger.Address: Niederlehme, near Koenigswusterhausen C.C. Sachsenhausen in 1934, (Ger.) 41-43	INTERR.	NETH.
JAHN, Max	259919	M	Ger.		Crim.Secretary, Gestapo, Jicin, Bohemia (Czech.) 40-42	MISC.CRIMES	CZECH.
JAHN, Max Paul	305902	M	Ger.		Kommando-Fuehrer, C.C. Neugraben and Tiefstak (Ger.) 44-5.2.45	CRUELTY	CZECH.
JAHN, Otto	130147	M	Ger.		Civilian, C.C. Mauthausen (Austr.) 41-45	MURDER	U.S.
JAHN, Willy	259358	M	Ger.		Untersturmfhr., active Member of Poitiers-Gestapo, Poitiers,Area (Fr.)	MISC.CRIMES	FR.
JAHN, Guillaume,Willy	260676	M	Ger.	08 or 10	Lt., Unit 48,148A Div.Staff, Sabres Landes (Fr.) 23.8.44	BRUTALITY	FR.
JAHNE	250860	M	Ger.		Lt., Army, 443 Jaeg.Regt., Belgrad (Yugo.) 10.-12.41	MURDER	YUGO.
JAHNIGE see JAENIGGER	195396						
JAHNKE	127381	M	Ger.	03	SS-Rottenfhr., C.C. Oranienburg,Sachsenhausen (Ger.) 2.45	MURDER	U.S.
JAHNKE	183461	M			SS Pvt., Guard, SS Totenkopfsturmbann, C.C. Aslau-Rosen,Nordhausen Dora, Mittelbau 43-45	TORTURE	U.S.
JAHNKE, Otto	67708	M	Ger.	02	Scharfhr., Gestapo, C.C. Le Mans (Fr.) 29.12.-3.1.44	MURDER	FR.
JAHNKUT	259723	M	Ger.	10	Lt., 292. Inf.Div. of Bignolas (Var.), Bauduen (Fr.) 22.7.44	INTERR.	FR.
JAHNS	415	M	Ger.		Civilian, Landowner, Tulczyn (Pol.) 22.10.39	MURDER	POL.
JAHNS	146759	M	Ger.		Oflag VI A, Civilian Wlodlzimiens (Sov.Un.) 41	WITNESS	U.S.
JAHR, Willi	138300	M	Ger.		Baufuehrer, Punkewitz (Ger.)	MURDER	U.S.
JAICH	256496	M	Ger.		Lt., Unit 13178, Olonne sur Mer (Fr.) 24.8.44	BRUTALITY	FR.
JAITNER, Edmund	417	M	Ger.12.8.13		SS-Unterscharfhr., C.C. Maidanek (Pol.) 40-4.44	MURDER	BEL.
JAKOB	146850	M	Ger.		Pvt., SS "Das Reich" 2.Coy. Pz.Div., Tulle (Fr.) 44	MURDER	FR.
JAKOB	194767	M	Ger.		SS-Sgt., C.C. Ravensbrueck (Ger.)	MURDER	U.S.
JAKOB	250282	M			Cpl. C.C. Ellrich-Nordhausen (Ger.)	INTERR.	YUGO.
JAKOB	250851	M	Ger.		Lt., Army 13. SS Pol.Regt., Ferlach (Aust.) 44-45	MURDER	YUGO.
JAKOB	261423	M	Ger.		Capt., Unit Airforce L 52511, Pau, Sommoutou,Narp,Lescar (Fr.)8.44.	CRUELTY	CZECH.
JAKOB	305903	M	Ger.		Guard, Bamberg Prison (Ger.) 44-45	MURDER	FR.
JAKOB	306611	M	Ger.		SS-Sgt., Ravensbrueck (Ger.) 42-45	MURDER	U.S.
JAKOB, Hermann	144573	M	Ger.		Work-Supervisor, KL. Bamberg (Ger.) 3.45	TORTURE	U.S.
JAKOB, Richard	255528	M	Ger.		Employee, Gestapo, Opava (Czech.) 39-45	TORTURE	CZECH.
JAKOBI, Emil see JAKOBS	133794						
JAKOBI, Jakob	145342	M	Ger.	89-93	Oberscharfhr., SS Guard, Camp Reichenau (Austr.) 44-45	TORTURE	U.S.
JAKOBICKA, Ralf	250281	M			Pvt., C.C. Ellrich-Nordhausen (Ger.)	MURDER	U.S.

JAK-JAN

NAME	C.R.FILE NUMBER	SEX	NATIONALITY	DATE OF BIRTH	RANK, OCCUPATION, UNIT, PLACE AND DATE OF CRIME	REASON WANTED	WANTED BY
JAKOBS	192559	M	Ger.		Pvt., 822. M.Fl.A., Svelgane near Voss (Nor.) 5.5.45	MURDER	NOR.
JAKOBS	194924	M	Ger.		Dr. Leiter des Arbeitsamtes, occupied territories, Luxembourg (Lux.)	MISC.CRIMES	LUX.
JAKOBS	255530	M			Sgt., C.C. Buchenwald (Ger.)	MURDER	U.S.
JAKOBS	300553	M	Ger.	25	Lt. (formerly Oberfaehnrich), Pion.Group, Heusden (Neth.) 5.11.44	MURDER	NETH.
JAKOBS, Emil (or JAKOBI)	133794	M		18. 6.95	SS-Hptscharfhr., Kommandantur, C.C. Buchenwald (Ger.)	TORTURE	U.S.
JAKOBS, Horst	130668	M	Ger.		SS, C.C. Dora, Nordhausen (Ger.)	MURDER	U.S.
JAKOBS, Johann	194906	M	Ger.	25.11.00	Kreisleiter, NSDAP, Luxembourg (Lux.)	MISC.CRIMES	LUX.
JAKOBS, Mrx (see JACOBS, Max)	192307						
JAKOBS, Wilhelm	154986	M	Ger.	09	Pvt., Mar.Art., Svelgane (Nor.)	MURDER	NOR.
JAKOBSEN	192976	M			Sgt., SS, C.C. Buchenwald (Ger.) 42-45	TORTURE	U.S.
JAKOBSEN-JACOBSEN	149771	M			Sgt., Bautruppen, Lossett (Nor.) 43	MURDER	NOR.
JAKUB	192975	M	Ger.		Sgt., SS, C.C. Buchenwald (Ger.) 42-45	MURDER	U.S.
JAKUBECK, Johann	302045	M			Railway-Official, employed in the Fernmeldemeisterei Officeat Amersfoort (Neth.) 10.44-5.45	PILLAGE	NETH.
JAKUBIKI	154385	M			Oschfhr., SS, C.C.Alt Dora near Gardelegen (Ger.) 4.45	MURDER	U.S.
JAKUSCHER, Josef	143170	M			Pvt., 9.SS Panz.Div. "Hohenstaufen", 19.Panz.Gren.Regt., 10.Coy., Bastogne (Bel.) 45	MISC.CRIMES	U.S.
JAMBOR	250279	M			Uschfhr., C.C. Dora, Nordhausen (Ger.)	MURDER	U.S.
JAMKOWSKI, Franz	132028	M	Ger.		Civilian, Slave Worker C.C. Herne (Ger.)	TORTURE	U.S.
JAMMEL	258479	M			Blockfhr., SS-Sturmmann, SS, C.C. Ohrdruf (Ger.) 12.44-4.45	MURDER	U.S.
JAN	250854	M	Ger.		Agent, Gestapo, Prison Pierre Leree, Poitiers (Fr.) 2.44	MISC.CRIMES	FR.
JAN, Willy (see JAAN)	253065						
JANAK, Hans	143162	M	Ger.		Civilian, near Oberplan (Czech.) 4.45	MURDER	U.S.
JANCKE	167217	M	Ger.		Sgt., Army, Schnelle Abteilung 602, Ferte St. Aubin (Fr.) 8.44	MURDER	FR.
JANCKE, Jup	250852	M	Ger.		Stabsscharfhr., SS, Gouda-Utrecht (Neth.) 10.44	INTERR.	NETH.
JANDA	145340	M			Master at Quarry, C.C. Mauthausen (Aust.) 41-45	SUSPECT	U.S.
JANDA, Marie (nee HNILICA)	189388	F	Ger.	2. 4.06	Clerk, Gestapo, Brno (Czech.) 39-45	WITNESS	CZECH.
JANDEL, Otto	187406	M	Ger.	12. 5.01	Member, S.A., Brno Moravia (Czech.)	MISC.CRIMES	CZECH.
JANDER, Wilhelm	167183	M			Civilian, Treuhaender, Restaurant "Zum Kameraden", Poznan (Pol.) 9.39-44	PILLAGE	POL.
JANEKE	167218	M			S.D., Carcassone, Belcaire and Camurac (Fr.) 11.43	MURDER	FR.
JANEKE, Johann	147095	M			Agent, Gestapo, Montjardin (Fr.) 5.44	TORTURE	FR.
JANEN	251641	M			Lt., St.Huibrechts-Lille (Bel.) 16.9.44	INTERR.	BEL.
JANESCH, Josefina	261947	F	Ger.		Secretary, Gestapo, Bled (Yugo.) 4.41-5.45	SUSPECT	YUGO.
JANETZKO, Ursula	302041	F	Ger.		Typist, employed at Headquarters of the Gestapo, Poitiers, La Rochelle (Fr.) 40-45	MURDER	FR.
JANICKE, Friedrich	250287	M			Pvt., C.C. Osterode-Nordhausen (Ger.)	MURDER	U.S.
JANIK	250869	M			SS-Sturmmann, SS, C.C. Dora, Nordhausen (Ger.)	MURDER	U.S.
JANISCH (or JEANISCH)	133795	M			SS-Uschfhr., C.C. Buchenwald (Ger.)	BRUTALITY	U.S.
JANISCH	145350	M			Usturmfhr., SS, Auschwitz (Pol.) 43-44	TORTURE	U.S.
JANISCH	162476	M	Ger.	10	SS-Osturmfhr., -é Wirtschafts-Verwaltungs-Hauptamt, C.C.Ohrdruf (Ger.)	WITNESS	U.S.
JANISCH, Erich	250868	M		27. 9.05	Cpl., C.C.Harzungen-Nordhausen (Ger.)	MURDER	U.S.
JANISCH, Johann	146760	M			SS Totenkopf-Standarte, C.C.Buchenwald (Ger.)	TORTURE	U.S.
JANISSEN (or JANNESSENS)	251078	M	Ger.		Capt., 3.Div.101.Coy. SS, Puginier (Fr.) 19.8.44	INTERR.	FR.
JANISSI, Franz	195771	M	Ger.		Uschfhr., SS, S.D., Prag (Czech.) 44-45	MURDER	CZECH.
JANITSCHKE, Franz	143171	M	Ger.	90	Sgt., Waffen-SS, Totenkopf-Standarte, 2.Coy., C.C.Muhlhausen (Ger.)	TORTURE	U.S.
JANITZ	250864	M	Ger.		Pvt., C.C.Woffleben, Nordhausen (Ger.)	MURDER	U.S.
JANIZEG	192560	M	Ger.		Pvt., POW Working Bn. 190, Hattras (Nor.) 11.43	MURDER	NOR.
JANK	187403	M	Ger.		Lt., 11. Panz.Gren.Regt., Honsfeld (Bel.) 12.44	MURDER	U.S.
JANKA, Erich	9692	M	Ger.		Staatsanwalt, Dr.,(Public Prosecutor),County Court. 21.2.40	MURDER	CZECH.
JANKE	67709	M			Pvt., SS, 17.Panz.Gren.Div.6, Sturmgesch.Abt.17, Serge-Renaze (Fr.) 8.44	MURDER	FR.
JANKE (or YANKE)	250850	M		08	Kapt.Lt., Nevy, Gerardmer (Fr.)	INTERR.	U.S.
JANKO	192305	M	Ger.		SS Panz.Div."Adolf Hitler", Modave (Bel.) 7.9.44	WITNESS	U.S.
JANKOWSKI	157227	M	Ger.	18	Pvt., 365.Landesschuetzen Bn., 2.Coy. Seubersdorf (Ger.) 3.2.43	MURDER	U.K.
JANKOWSKY, Albert	144572	M	Ger.		SS Totenkopf-Verband, C.C.Buchenwald (Ger.)	MISC.CRIMES	U.S.
JANKU	250285	M			Lt., Div."Hermann Goering" 4.Parachute Hunter Regt., 2.Bn., 8.Coy., Helchteren and Hechtel (Bel.) 9.44	PILLAGE	BEL.
JARN, Heinz	251069	M	Ger.		Cpl., 10.Coy., 377. Hunter Regt., Vinkt-Meigem and environs (Bel.) 5.40	INTERR.	BEL.
JANNECKE	261755	M	Ger.		Cpl., Art.H.D.V.199-2235, N.D.F.No. of F.P.27046 C, Lorgies (Fr.) 3.9.44	MURDER	FR.
JANNER, Joachim	258014	M	Ger.	11. 3.26	Pvt., 150.Panz.Bde., Meuse Bridge-Antwerp (Bel.) 12.44	MISC.CRIMES	U.S.
JANNESSENS (see JANISSEN)	251078						
JANNICK	140037	M	Ger.		Pvt., Army, Cleder (Fr.) 8.8.44	MURDER	FR.
JANNIS, Willy (see YANNIS)	305200						
JANNSSEN, Jens	162475	M	Ger.	15	SS-Hptscharfhr., SS Comd.Staff, C.C. Eisenach (Ger.) 44-45	TORTURE	U.S.
JANOSCHEK, Jan	250283	M	Ger.	17. 2.02	Civilian, Breclav (Czech.) 39-45	INTERR.	CZECH.
JANOSIK, Johann (or JANOSSIK)	257333	M	Ger.		SS-Sturmfhr., SS-Slave Labour Camps, Beisfjord and Osen (Nor.) 6.42-3.43	MISC.CRIMES	YUGO.
JANOWITZ, A.	188369	M	Ger.		Buergermeister, Public Official, near Koenitz (Pol.) 41	MURDER	U.K.
JANOWITZ, Karl	251642	M	Ger.		C.C. Lahde-Weser-Steinbergen (Ger.)	MURDER	BEL.
JANOWSKY, Eduard	31217	M	Ger.		Landgerichtsdirektor, Public-Official, Litomerice (Czech.) 21.2.40	MURDER	BEL.
JANS	173576	M	Ger.		Major, Cmdt., Army, Pion.Bn. (Yugo.) 11.43-8.44	MURDER	YUGO.
JANS, Karl	251070	M			Pvt., 10.Coy., 377.Hunter Regt., Vinkt-Meigem and environs (Bel.) 5.40	INTERR.	BEL.
JANSEN	128999	M	Ger.	76	Gruppenfhr., S.A.Nachrichten, C.C.Aachen-Adelbert (Ger.) 41-44	MURDER	U.S.
JANSEN	140031	M	Ger.	28. 8.04	Lt., Army, Ligueil (Fr.)	MURDER	FR.
JANSEN	150304	M	Ger.	02	Uschfhr., SS, C.C.Sachsenhausen-Oranienburg (Ger.)	TORTURE	U.S.
JANSEN	157222	M			Guard, C.C. Voeght (Neth.)	MURDER	FR.
JANSEN (or LAUTZER)	192671	M	Ger.		SS-Uschfhr., SS, C.C.Ravensbrueck (Ger.)	MURDER	U.S.
JANSEN, August	251640	M	Ger.	03	Usturmfhr., Ers.Div. "Goetz von Berlichingen", SS, Chatellerault (Fr.)8.44	MURDER	FR.
JANSEN, Fritz	195336	M			Uschfhr., SS, C.C.Sachsenhausen-Oranienburg (Ger.)	MISC.CRIMES	U.K.
JANSEN, Gwer	162458	M			S.A.-Scharfhr., S.A., Windhausen (Ger.) 11.44	TORTURE	U.S.
JANSEN, John	418	M	Ger.	8. 3.20	SS-Uschfhr., C.C.Maidanek (Pol.) 40-4.44	MURDER	POL.
JANSEN, Martha	250295	F	Ger.		Chief, Gestapo, Wilhelmshaven (Ger.)	BRUTALITY	FR.
JANSER	146456	F			Helferin, SS-Guard, C.C.Erfurt (Ger.) 44	TORTURE	U.S.
	145352	M			Guard, SS, C.C. Reichenau (Aust.) 44-45	TORTURE	U.S.

JAN-JEK

NAME	C.R.FILE NUMBER	SEX	NATIO-NALITY	DATE OF BIRTH	RANK OCCUPATION UNIT PLACE AND DATE OF CRIME	REASON WANTED	WANTED BY
JANSOHN, Rudolf	250867	M		23.3.15	Cpl.CC Ellrich,Nordhausen(Ger.)	MURDER	U.S.
JANSON	251073	M	Ger.		SS Usturmfhr.Gestapo,Limoges Area(Fr.)40-44	INTERR.	FR.
JANSON, Fritz	145205	M	Ger.		Civilian	TORTURE	U.S.
JANSEN	167159	M	Ger.		Pvt.Army,Bachivillers(Fr.)	WITNESS	FR.
JANSSEN	192974	M	Ger.		Sgt.SS CC Buchenwald(Ger.)42-45	MURDER	U.S.
JANSSEN, Karl	129156	M	Ger.		Guard,N.C.O.KL Dachau(Ger.)42	TORTURE	BEL.
JANSSENS, Georg	251071	M	Ger.		12 Coy.377 Jaeger Regt.,Vinkt,Meigem,Environs(Bel.)25.-31.5.40	INTERR.	BEL.
JANSZEN, Johann	302047	M	Ger.	21.1.10	SS Hptscharfhr.S.D.Chauffeur to the S.D.at Arnhem,Apeldoorn(Neth.)44-45	MURDER	NETH.
JANTSCH, Erich	9693	M	Ger.		Dr.,Staatsanwalt,Public Official,Staatsanwaltschaft beim Landgericht Brno(Czech.)40-42	MURDER	CZECH.
JANTSCH, Stephanie	189387	F	Ger.		Clerk,Gestapo,Bruenn(Czech.)39-45	WITNESS	CZECH.
JANTUR, Heinz	186625	M	Ger.	8.9.09	Hptsturmfhr.Kriminalkommissar,S.D.Gestapo,SS,Praha(Czech.)39-45	MURDER	CZECH.
JANTURA	173563	M	Ger.		Criminal-Commissar,Gestapo,Staatspolizeileitstelle,CC Birkenau,Oswiecim(Pol.)39-45	MURDER	CZECH.
JANTZEN	419	M	Ger.	10	Police Zugwachtmeister,CC Grint(Nor.)5.42	TORTURE	NOR.
JANTZEN, Walter	39601	M	Ger.		Lt.Member S.D.Gestapo,S.D.d'Angers,Chief of Section 4.E.St.Sulpice,Fortmusson-Chauteau(Fr.)31.7.-6.8.44	MURDER	FR.
JANUS	251645	M	Ger.		4 Coy.16 Hubner Regt.Finrooi(Bel.)9.44	MURDER	BEL.
JANZEN, Heinrich	250268	M			Pvt.CC Bodungen-Nordhausen(Ger.)	MURDER	U.S.
JAPEL, Hans	261426	M	Ger.	95	Major,Unit of Cavalry,Bresles(Fr.)40	PILLAGE	FR.
JAPS	167156	M	Ger.		Cpl.Feldgendarmerie,Montigny en Vesoul(Fr.)16.7.44	MURDER	FR.
JAQUET	254357	M	Ger		Scharfhr.Gestapo,Toulouse(Fr.)11.42-8.44	MISC.CRIMES	FR.
JARATH	174012	M			SS Uschafhr.CC Muhldorf,Ampfing(Ger.)6.44-4.45	MISC.CRIMES	U.S.
JARISCH	251452	M	Ger.		Dr.Prof.,Dachau(Ger.)3.42	TORTURE	BEL.
JARITZ, Werner	125132	M	Ger.		Commander,SS,Helmbrecht,Velary(Czech.)	MURDER	U.S.
JARKE	420	M	Ger.		Police,Ob Lt.,Warczawa(Pol.)9.39-1.42	MURDER	UNWCC,POL.
JARMER, Ludwig	192942	M	Ger.	07	SS Rottfhr.Gestapo,Lanskroun(Czech.)38-45	TORTURE	CZECH.
JARMUTH	260840	M			Pvt.Block-Leader,SS and CC,Unterriexinger(Ger.)12.44-3.45	MURDER	U.S.
JAROLIN or JAROLIM	190346	M			Official,CC Dachau(Ger.)	MURDER	U.S.
JAROLY	185180	M	Ger.		Commandant,CC Dachau(Ger.)	WITNESS	FR.
JAROSCHKA	51218	M	Ger.		Dr.,Oberlandsgerichtsrat,Public Official,Litomerice(Czech.)21.2.40	MURDER	BEL.
JAROSIK, Franz	130150	M	Ger.		SS,NCO,Arrested 28th of May 45 by 7th CIC,Mauthausen(Aust.)41-45	MURDER	U.S.
JARROSCH	157228	M	Ger.		Stabsintendant,Wehrmacht,Rothenstedt(Ger.)16.4.45	MISC.CRIMES	U.K.
JAROST	305201	M	Ger.		Capt.Army,Lt Col.v.Sollen's Command,Culemborg(Neth.)10.11.44	MISC.CRIMES	NETH.
JAS, Anton see STRIZ	258098						
JASCHEK	190240	M	Ger.	10 or 11	Crim.Commissar,Gestapo,HQ.Cologne(Ger.)45-45	MURDER	U.K.
JASCHKE	72282	M			Capt.Weffen SS,CC Theresienstedt(Pol.)12.41	TORTURE	U.S.
JASINSKI	300785	M	Ger.		Pvt.1 Aufkl.Abt.3 Coy.2 Col.XV Div.of the Afrika Korps,Saint Leger(Arlon)5.9.44	MISC.CRIMES	BEL.
JASINSKY	190493	M			Pvt.Panzer Div.11,2 Coy.Bergerac,Albine(fr.)7.-8.44	MURDER	FR.
JASFULSKY	301326	M	Ger.		Member of the Gestapo at Trencin,CC Oswiecim-Birkenau(Pol.)39-45	MURDER	CZECH.
JASMIEWITZ	174011	M			SS Mann,CC Muhldorf,Ampfing(Ger.)6.44-4.45	MISC.CRIMES	U.S.
JASPER	257607	M	Ger.		Chief,Sub.Sec.Mittelwerk,Nordhausen(Ger.)	MURDER	U.S.
JASPERT, William	127113	M	Ger.		Untersturmfhr.-Lt.SS Panz.Div.Das Reich,Venerque-Le-Vernet(Fr.)	MURDER	FR.
JASSEY	250269	M			Pvt.CC Rottleberode-Nordhausen(Ger.)	MURDER	U.S.
JASSEN, Olaf	196335	M		25	Pvt.11 Coy.2 Panz.Gren.Regt.Leibst.Adolf Hitler,Malmedy(Bel.)23.12.44	SUSPECT	U.S.
JASMUTH	227329	M	Ger.		Crim.secretary,Gestapo,Ratibor(Czech.)10.44	TORTURE	U.S
JASSON	254507	M	Ger.		Coal-Mine Manager,Wasseralfingen-Wuertemberg(Ger.)44-45	MURDER	POL.
JAUCH, Hermann	240103	M	Ger.		SS Hptscharfhr.Sipo,S.D.Official,Dachau(Ger.)	MURDER	UNWCC
JAUCKEL, Hermann or JAECKEL	142840	M	Ger.		Civilian,CIE 24528D Munich,Orqu.Tournai(Bel.)1.9.44	MURDER	BEL.
JAUD, Johann	157264	M	Ger.	08	Obsturmfhr.Gestapo,SS,Innsbruck(Aust.)18.4.45	MURDER	U.S.
JAUD, Paul	251059	M	Ger.		Cpl.Gendarmerie(Bel.)	INTERR.	BEL.
JAUERNEC	192571	M	Ger.		Lt.POW working Bn.184,CC Drag Nordland(Nor.)4.45	TORTURE	NOR.
JAUREN	250857	M	Ger.		Inspector,Gestapo,Lille(Fr.)40-44	MISC.CRIMES	FR.
JAVITZ	146849	M	Ger		Rottfhr.SS Panz.Div.Das Reich,Villaudrie(Fr.)44	MURDER	FR.
JEAN "dit JEANNOT" see KRUPPOY	188745						
JEANICKE, Ernst see JAENICKE	261785						
JEANISCH see HAENISCH	133667						
JEANISCH see JANISCH	133795						
JEANNOT see DELCHIAPPO	150912						
JEBRAMEC or JEBRANCK	189451	M	Ger.		Sgt.Army,Vlissingen(Neth.)9.44	MURDER	NETH.
JECK	191368	M	Ger.		SS Hptsturmfhr.CC Falstad(Nor.)41-44	MURDER	NOR.
JECKEL, Edith	189386	F	Ger.		Clerk,Gestapo,Bruenn(Czech.)39-45	WITNESS	CZECH.
JECKEL, Herbert	1704	M	Ger.		Cpl.Army-Probeabtlg.2 Inf Regt.148,Amiens(Fr.)26.8.44	MURDER	U.K.
JECKEL, Wilhelm	167846	M	Ger.		Pvt.Army,9 Gren.Regt.Res.1 Coy.Magny D'Avignon(Fr.)18.9.44	MURDER	FR.
JECKELN, Friedrich	21322	M	Ger.		SS Obgruppenfhr.Gen.d.Police,Leader Ostland,Member Reichstag	TORTURE	UNWCC
JECKELN, Fritz	143165	M	Ger.	95	Lt.General,SS,Lublin(Pol.)40	MURDER	U.S.
JEDELE	11246	M	Ger.		Sgt.Army 110 Panz.Gren.Regt.Albine(Fr.)29.6.44	MURDER	FR.
JEDLITSCHKA, Ernst	194454	M	Ger.	23.2.06	Blockleiter,NSDAP,Prag-Rozdelov(Czech.)41-45	LOOTING	CZECH.
JEDWILL	149494	M	Ger.		SS Capt.Paris(Fr.)42	MURDER	FR.
JEEWE	146848	M	Ger.		Capt.SS and S.D.Annecy(Fr.)44	MURDER	FR.
JEGER	257559	M	Ger.		CC Muehldorf,Dachau(Ger.)	MURDER	U.S.
JEGER	306305	M	Ger.		Lt.Col.attached to garrison at St.Malo(Ille et Vilaine)(Fr.)6.-13.8.44	PILLAGE	FR.
JEGER, Otto	132029	M	Ger.		Civilian(Ger.)	MURDER	U.S.
JEHERS	422	M	Ger.		Cpl.Army POW Camp,CC Nozderney(Ger.)25.5.42	MURDER	POL.
JEGOST, Fritz	72289	M	Ger.		SS Hptscharfhr.CC Struthof-Natzweiler(Fr.)42-44	MURDER	YR.
JEHLE see IEHLE	132624						
JEHLE	157224	M	Ger.		President(General)Hoeres-Verwaltung,Saint Gaudens(Fr.)16.6.44	WITNESS	FR.
JEIP	306512	M	Ger.		NCO,Feldgendarmerie Chsteaubriant Loire-Inferieure,St.Julien de Mouvantes Juigne les Moutiers,Soudan,le Taillais(Fr)21.7.44	MURDER	FR.
JEFEL	157261	M	Ger.		Polizeileiter,General,SS und Police,Talsen(Kurland-Lat.)44	MURDER	U.S.
JEKOVITCH	167216	M	Ger.		Lt.Army O.C.Unit No.22446,Taize-Aize Lizant,St.Gaudent,Civray,St.Pierre d'Exideuil,Vienne Charente(Fr.)28.8.44	MURDER	FR.
JEKOWIC	260237	M	Ger.		Interpreter,SS,Belgrade(Yugo.)1.-9.44	MISC.CRIMES	YUGO.

JEL-JOA

NAME	C.R.FILE NUMBER	SEX	NATIO-NALITY	DATE OF BIRTH	RANK OCCUPATION UNIT PLACE AND DATE OF CRIME	REASON WANTED	WANTED BY
JELINEK, Richard	189072	M	Ger.	23. 2.98	Criminal-Employee,Gestapo, Brno (Czech.) 39-45	TORTURE	CZECH.
JELITO	133410	M	Ger.		Guard, Stalag 357, C.C. Thorn (Ger.) 7.44	MURDER	U.S.
JELKE, Rudolf	301496	M	Ger.	3. 6.10	SS-Sturmmann, C.C., Buchenwald (Ger.) 5.38 und 10.43	MURDER	BEL.
JELLINECK (or JUMBO,Wilhelm)	162474	M	Ger.	14	Civilian, C.C. Buchenwald (Ger.) 39 - 45	WITNESS	U.S.
JEMDAUDE, Felix	130152	M	Ger.		Interpreter, C.C., Chemnitz (Ger.) 43	TORTURE	BEL.
JEMESKY (see Bruno De MASQUIT)	189644						
JEMFORT	192678	M	Ger.		Capt.,Cief of Gestapo, Athen (Gre.)	LOOTING	GRC.
JENATSCHKE, Alfred	262201	M	Ger.	28.10.21	Uscharfhr., 51.SS-Armoured Bde., Artilleriedetachement, Bucheres, Breviandes, St. Savine, La Riviera de Corps,Troyes (Fr.) 8.44	BRUTALITY	FR.
JENQUER, Fredric	138349	M			SS-Adudant-Cief, Gestapo,SS, Lyon (Fr.)	MURDER	FR.
JENCZ	196348	M	Ger.		Sgt., SS, C.C.,Gusen (Ger.)	TORTURE	BEL.
JENDE, Kurt	194564	M	Ger.		Stalag II B, C.C. Aurith (Ger.) 12.4.44	MURDER	FR.
JENDERZOK	423	M	Ger.		Lt., Paratroop-Coy. Saint Segal, Menez-Bos,(Fr.) 29.7.44	MURDER	FR.
JENDRENKO	173616	M	Ger.		Civilian, Engineer, Bassin De Briey, Meurthe und Moselle (Fr.)	MURDER	FR.
JENEBERG, Max	11248	M	Ger.		Pvt., Army, 111. Panz.-Gren.Rgt.N.C.O.,Albine (Fr.) 29.6.44	MURDER	FR.
JENGE (see JENTSCH)	41342						
JENICEK	258167	M	Ger.		Signal Troops, 2.Coy. Bolnes (Neth.) 8.5.45	INTERR.	NETH.
JENKE	130170	M	Ger.		Sonderfhr., Stalag, Luckenwalde (Ger.)	MISC.CRIMES	U.K.
JENKENS (see JENDGES)	305074						
JENNEBERG, Max	187933	M			Pvt., 2.Panz.-Gren.Rgt., Albine (Fr.)	MURDER	FR.
JENNER, Nikolas (or JONNER)	173561	M	Ger.		SS - Mann, Waffen SS, C.C. Bergen,Belsen, Auschwitz (Ger.Pol.) 10.39 - 4.45	MURDER	UNWCC
JENNERWEIN (see BRÜCK,Victor)	134913						
JENNESSEN, Hans	256519	M	Ger.		Obersturmbannfhr., SD, Stavanger and Fromsoe (Nor.) 41-42	MURDER	NOR.
JENS	141891	M	Ger.		Lt., Artillery	MURDER	U.K.
JENS	173278	M	Ger.	05	Lt. C.C. Stalag VIII B, Lamsdorf (Ger.)	MURDER	U.K.
JENSEN	424	M	Ger.		SS - Sturmscharfhr., Sfax (Tunisie) 1.-8.43	MISC.CRIMES	FR.
JENSEN (alias JO)	12437	M	Ger.		Gestapo Chief, Cahors (Fr.)	MURDER	FR.
JENSEN	143163	M		17	Sturmscharfhr., Sipo and SD, Toulouse, Agen, Cahors, Foix, Tarbes, Pau, Montauban (Fr.) 6. - 8.44	MURDER	D.S.
JENSEN	148436	M	Ger.		Rottenfhr., SS, C.C. Neuengamme (Ger.)	MURDER	U.K.
JENSEN	191301	M			Pvt., Eisenbahn Art.Bn.717, St. Andries,Varsenare les Bruegge (Bel.)44	MURDER	BEL.
JENSEN	251061	M	Ger.		SS - Sturmmann, C.C.. Neuengamme (Ger.)	MURDER	BEL.
JENSEN	259485	M			Lumber dealer, Lengerich (Ger.) 8.44	BRUTALITY	D.S.
JENSEN	305434	M	Ger.		Sturmscharfhr., SS, Section IV, Gestapo, Toulouse,Gers,Tarn (Fr.) 11.42 - 8.44	MURDER	FR.
JENSEN, Henri	151286	M	Ger.		Sturmscharfhr., Gestapo, SS, Cahors (Fr.) 44	MURDER	FR.
JENTKES (see JENDGES)	305074						
JENTSCH	72283	M	Ger.		Sgt.,Crim.Secr., Gestapo, Waffen SS, C.C. Klingelputz (Ger.)	MISC.CRIMES	U.S.
JENTSCH (or JENGE)	141342	M	Ger.		Capt., Army, Lamsdorf (Ger.) 42	MURDER	U.K.
JENTSCH	190494	M			Hauptwachtmstr., Gestapo, Trondes Bousq Menil la Tour (Fr.)	MURDER	FR.
JENTSCH	192670	M			Uscharfhr., SS, C.C., Gusen (Ger.) 41 - 42	MURDER	U.S.
JENTSCH	256070	M	Ger.		Sgt., C.C. Mauthausen (Ger.)	INTERR.	FR.
JENTSON	301570	M	Ger.		SS - Sgt., Mauthausen C.C., Meuthsusen (Aust.) 40 - 45	MURDER	BEL.
JENTZEN, Walter	134707	M	Ger.		Uscharfhr., SS, Paris (Fr.) 42	TORTURE	U.S.
JEPSEN	250294	M			SS - Div. "Germania", Wilhelmshaven (Ger.)	TORTURE	FR.
JEPSEN	305202	M			Member, Kommando Wilhelmshaven, C.C. Neuengamme, Wilhelmshaven (Ger.) 42 - 45	MISC.CRIMES	FR.
JERNK	157263	M			Lt., C.C.4.Coy., Sturmbattalion AOK I,Courcelles sur Nied (Fr.) 11.44	MURDER	U.S.
JEREMIES, Otto	251631	M	Ger.	14. 1.10	Pvt., 13.Coy., 552.Gren.Rgt., Bruay en Artois (Fr.) 1.9.44	MURDER	FR.
JERGAS	139783	M	Ger.	96	Sgt., Waffen SS, Waldlager V, C.C. Mushldorf (Ger.) 44 - 45	MURDER	U.S.
JERMARK, Arseny	183456	M			Pvt., 4.Totenkopfsturmbann, SS, Nordhausen,Mittelbau Monowitz (Pol.Ger.) 43 - 45	WITNESS	U.S.
JERRE	256878	M	Ger.		Capt., O.C.,5.Coy.,322.Bn. 5.Schuetz.Pol.Rgt.Ljubljana,Cetje and Krany (Yugo) 42 - 43	MURDER	YUGO.
JERRIE, (or BYR or BYER or BEYER)	123418	M			Civilian, Foreman of Erecting Firm J.&S., Halle,Merseburg (Ger.) 10.44 - 4.45	TORTURE	U.K.
JESCH, Ralph	257884	M			150. Panz.Brigade, Maeuse-Bridge-Antwerp(Bel.) 12.44	MISC.CRIMES	U.S.
JESCHKE	137728	M			Chief, Police, Breslau (Ger.)	MURDER	CZECH.SCV.UN.
JESKE	162479	M	Ger.	14	Lt., Army, W.G. Ohrdruf (Ger.)	MURDER	U.S.
JESKE	195778	M	Ger.	05	Civilian, Kreislandwirt, Kiwerce (Pol.) 42	MURDER	POL.
JESSEN	250286	M	Ger.		Lt. 4.Fallschirm-Jaeg.Rgt.Div."Hermann Goering" Helsetorenland Hachtal (Bel.)9.44	PILLAGE	BEL.
JESSEN	251083	M	Ger.		Obersturmfhr., SS, Gestapo, Limoges (Fr.) 40 - 45	INTERR.	FR.
JESSER, Erwin	196309	M		8. 4.92	Dr., military Hospital, Amstetten (Aust.) 20.3.45	MISC.CRIMES	U.S.
JESUITER, Walter	259730	M	Ger.		Cpl., Unit F.N.G. 13 983 B.LGFr.Paris, Le Coudray (Fr.) 16.8.44	WITNESS	FR.
JETZINGER, Arthur (or GETZINGER)	148437	M	Ger.	18. 2.91	Crim.-chief, Police,Sipo, Kleinzerbst (Ger.) 7.44	MURDER	U.S.
JEUISCH	192973	M	Ger.		Sgt., C.C., Buchenwald (Ger.) 42 - 45	TORTURE	U.S.
JEWCZENKO	183454	M			Pvt., 4.SS-Totenkopfsturmbann,C.C. Nordhausen Dora Mittelbau(Ger.)43-45	WITNESS	U.S.
JEWDUSZENKO, Wasili	183453	M			Pvt., 4.SS-Totenkopfsturmbann, C.C. Nordhausen Dora Mittelbau, Bismarckhuette (Ger.) 43 - 45	WITNESS	U.S.
JEWE	426	M	Ger.		Gestapo,(Fr.) 43	MURDER	FR.
JEZUITER, Max	427	M	Ger.		Sturmbannfhr., SS, Gestapo, Police, Warschau, Krakow (Pol.) 40-43	MURDER	POL.
JEZZ	183451	M			Pvt., 4.SS-Totenkopfsturmbann, C.C. Dora-Nordhausen (Ger.) 43 - 45	WITNESS	U.S.
JILLY, Theodor	192669	M	Ger.	01	Member, NSDAP, Prag,(Czech.)	MISC.CRIMES	CZECH.
JIM La TRIGUE (see DIEDRICH)	150929						
JIRASSEK, Werner	195777	M	Ger.		Pionier, 1.SS-Div. Leibstandarte "Adolf Hitler" 3.Pionier Coy. Ligneuvil-Stoumont (Bel.) 12.44	MURDER	U.S.
JIRMANN, Fritz	301497	M	Ger.	11. 1.14	Sturmmann - SS, C.C. Buchenwald (Ger.) 5.38 und 10.43	MURDER	BEL.
JO (see JENSEN)	12437						
JOA	256486	M	Ger.		Lt., Henrichemont (Fr.) 9.40 - 3.44	PILLAGE	FR.
JOA, Hermann	192795	M	Ger.		Schupo, C.C., Stalag, Falstad-Drontheim (Nor.) 41-45	MURDER	NOR.

JOA - JON

NAME	C.R.FILE NUMBER	SEX	NATIO-NALITY	DATE OF BIRTH	RANK OCCUPATION UNIT PLACE AND DATE OF CRIME	REASON WANTED	WANTED BY
JOALI	177599	M	Ger.		C.C. Neu-Brenn (Ger.)	MURDER	FR.
JOB, Vojtech	258086	M	Ger.	28. 3.07	Informer, Gestapo, Roudnice (Czech.) 42	MISC.CRIMES	CZECH.
JOBST, Adam	192667	M	Ger.	00	Member, NSDAP, Prag (Czech.)	MISC.CRIMES	CZECH.
JOBST, Adolph	157262	M	Ger.		Guard, Prison Untermassfeld (Ger.) 41-45	MURDER	U.S.
JOBST, Willy or JABST	192548	M	Ger.	27	Officer, SS-Div."Adolf Hitler", Mean, Faulx-les-Tombes (Bel.) 9.44	MURDER	BEL.
JOCAAN, Jacob	177598	M	Ger.		Capt., 3.SS-Regt., "Deutschland", Aiguillon (Fr.) 6.44	WITNESS	FR.
JOCHIM, Kurt	251062	M			Cmdt., St.Huibrechts - Lille (Bel.) 9.44	INTERR.	BEL.
JOCHIMS	250270	M			Flyer, C.C. Ellrich, Nordhausen (Ger.)	MURDER	U.S.
JOACHIMSEN (see HOACHIMSEN)	252190						
JOCHIMSKI, Fritz	259650	M	Ger.		SS-Unterscharfhr., S.D. Aussendienststelle Tarbes (Fr.) 11.42- 8.44	INCENDIARISM	FR.
JOCHINTKE, Wilhelm	256485	M	Ger.	12	Lt., Police, State service, Lidice (Czech.) 6.42	MURDER	CZECH.
JOCKEL, Walter	251639	M	Ger.		Sturmbannfhr., St. Savoir (Fr.) 8.44	PILLAGE	FR.
JOCKENHOFER	189647	M	Ger.		Lt., Unit 8852 B, Hameau de Breville (Fr.) 45	LOOTING	FP.
JOCKENHOFER (see JACKENHAFER)	259738	M					
JODKUN	189356	M	Ger.		Agent, Gestapo, C.C. Drancy (Fr.)	MURDER	FR.
JOECKEL, Johanna or SOECKEL	192663	F	Ger.	27	C.C. Terezin (Czech.) 39-45	TORTURE	CZECH.
JOECKEL, Elisabeth (nee BAENFER)	192664	F	Ger.		C.C. Terezin (Czech.) 39-45	MURDER	CZECH.
JOECKELOVI, Heinrich or YOCKL	157497	M	Ger.	00	Hauptsturmfhr., SS, C.C. Theresienstadt (Czech.) 45	TORTURE	U.K.
JOECKEN, Heinrich	165916	M	Ger.	00	SS-Hauptsturmfhr., C.C. Theresienstadt (Czech.) 43	MURDER	U.S.
JOECKL, Walter	133322	M			Hauptsturmfhr., SS or S.D., C.C. Theresienstadt (Czech.)	MURDER	U.S.
JOEHREN	171966	M	Ger.		Member, Gestapo, Saarburg (Ger.) 44	MURDER	U.S.
JOEHREN, Karl	192662	M	Ger.		Member, Gestapo, Luxemburg (Lux.)	MURDER	LUX.
JOEKEN, Heinrich	126341	M	Ger.		Pvt., 192. Sicherungs-Regt., Mont Lucon (Fr.) 8.44	WITNESS	U.S.
JOEL	261425	M	Ger.	10	Sgt., C.C. Schirmeck, Moussey (Fr.) 10.44	PILLAGE	FR.
JOENG, Karl	251085	M		15	Sgt., St. Michielsgestel (Neth.) 9.44	PILLAGE	NETH.
JOEP	148435	M	Ger.		C.C. Vught (Neth.) 43-44	MURDER	BEL.
JOEP, Josef (see HEINTZIEGER)	187016						
JOEPSEL	301069	M	Ger.		Dr., Obersturmfhr., SS, C.C. Oranienburg (Ger.) 11.39- 45	MURDER	CZECH.
JOERES, Hermann	137042	M	Ger.		Member, NSKK, Luxemburg (Lux.) 9.44	PILLAGE	LUX.,U.S.
JOERG, Wilhelm	11249	M	Ger.		Lt., Heeres-Flak-Abtlg. 600, Blaye le Mines (Fr.) 8.44	MURDER	FR.
JOERSS, Wilhelm	137040	M	Ger.		Oberwachtmeister d.Res., Police, Poprentin (Ger.) 8.44	MURDER	U.S.
JOFAN	301758	M			Sgt., Builder, C.C. Auschwitz (Pol.) 40	MURDER	FR.
JOGLER	190565	M			Cpl., Ortskommandantur, Kragujevac (Yugo.) 10.41	MURDER	YUGO.
JOHAN	428	M	Ger.		Guard, C.C. Saarbruecken (Ger.) 1.44	TORTURE	FR.
JOHANN	250271	M			Pvt., C.C. Harzungen, Nordhausen (Ger.)	MURDER	U.S.
JOHANN, Fritz	122184	M	Ger.	07	Arb.Kdo., C.C. Peggua (Aust.) 8.41- 4.42	MURDER	U.K.
JOHANN, Karl	194921	M	Ger.	31. 3.04	Innkeeper, Civ., Occupied territories, Kylburg (Ger.) 43	MISC.CRIMES	LUX.
JOHANNA	305209	F	Ger.		Interpreter, German military command, Livadia, Gruppe Geheime Feld-Polizei 510, Dienststelle No. 47661 Distomon, Beotia, Kalemion, (Grc.) 6.44	MISC.CRIMES	GRC.
JOHANNES, Erich	148434	M	Ger.		Foreman, Meat-factory Eichorward & Co., Prisoner, M.G. Protective Custody, Koeln (Ger.) 42-45	MISC.CRIMES	U.S.
JOHANNES, Erwin Paul	258413	M	Ger.	23. 6.08	Ober-Kapo, C.C. Chrdruf (Ger.) 12.44 - 4.45	MURDER	U.S.
JOHANNESSON, Gustav	11250	M	Ger.		Agent, Gestapo, Cahors (Fr.) 6.44	MURDER	FR.
JOHANNSEN	192972	M	Ger.		Dr., Med.Section, C.C. Buchenwald (Ger.) 42-45	TORTURE	U.S
JOHANNSEN	251650	M			Sturmmann, 1.SS Panz.Div., Leibstandarte "Adolf Hitler", 1.Regt. Malmedy (Bel.) 12.44	MURDER	U.S.
JOHANNSEN, Helmut	258973	M	Ger.	28. 1.08	Dr., SS-Obersturmbannf., SS-No. 69470, NSDAP-No. 756620, 4.1944	INTERR.	U.S.
JOHANNSEN, Johann or JOHANSSEN	162886	M	Ger.		Feldgendarmerie, Vielsalm (Bel.) 40-44	PILLAGE	BEL.
JOHANNSEN, Peter	161985	M	Ger.		SS-Navy, Engineer, Hennebont, Vannes (Fr.) 44	MURDER	FR.
JOHANNSEN, Werner Emil	192562	M	Ger.	4. 8.04	Sgt., Reichsministerium of Justice, Strafgef.Lager Nord Finmark (Nor.) 6.42	MISC.CRIMES	NOR.
JOHANSEN	300034	M	Ger.		N.C.O., S.D., worked with Ruetting, Driebergen, Scheveningen (Neth.) 44	TORTURE	NETH.
JOHANSEN, Otto	174556	M	Ger.	03	Pvt., 337.Land.Schtz.Bn., 6.Coy., Stalag 8-B, C.C. Schoppinitz Moosburg (Ger.) 1.-4.45	TORTURE	U.K.
JOHANSON	125717	M	Ger.		Stalag 20-B, C.C. Rosenberg (Pol.) 1.43- 2.44	MISC.CRIMES	U.K.
JOHANSON, Otto	72287	M			Pvt., 6-337.Coy., H.Q., Bratz (Czech.) 4.45	TORTURE	U.K.
JOHANSSEN, Johann (see JOHANNSEN)	162886						
JOHIMSKI	141350	M	Ger.		Pvt., Stalag 8-B, Lamsdorf (Ger.) 6.41	TORTURE	U.K.
JOHN	67824	M	Ger.		Dr., Civ., Stalag, C.C. Gleina (Ger.) 3.45	TORTURE	U.K.
JOHN	257494	M	Ger.		Crim.Insp., SS-Obersturmf., Feldpolizei, Foix (Fr.) 12.42- 44	INTERR.	FR.
JOHN, Alfred	306120	M	Ger.		Crim.Insp., Gestapo, Leader of the Main Station of the Gestapo Elsinore, Snekkersten (Den.) 8.44	MURDER	DEN.
JOHN, Friedrich Wilhelm	62423	M	Ger.		Lt.Gen., Army, Dipl.Ing., Cmdg.Generalbez., (Latv.)	TORTURE	U.N.W.C.C.
JOHN, Johann	31219	M	Ger.		Senatspraesident, Public officiel, Prague (Czech.) 2.40	MURDER	U.S.,BEL.
JOHN, Leonhard	300035	M	Ger.	12. 8.00	SS-Untersturmf., Jewish of Labour Section, Cracow District Labour Camp Pleszow near Cracow (Pol.) 44	MURDER	POL.
"JOHNNY" (see HACKMANN)	192969						
JOHNSCHITS	430	M			SS, Fortmisson (Fr.) 8.44	MURDER	FR.
JOHNWEIS	251628	M			Pvt., SS, C.C. Auschwitz-Birkenau (Pol.) 43	MURDER	YUGO.
JOKAN, Michael	196307	M	Ger.		Cpl., Chief SS, 3.Pz.Div."G.v.Berlichingen", Dompierre du Mont (Fr.) 44	WITNESS	FR.
JOKISCH	132645	M	Ger.		SS-Oberscharfhr., C.C. Buchenwald (Ger.)	TORTURE	FR.
JOKOB, Gustav	257560	M	Ger.	4. 4.09	Employee, C.C. Nordhausen (Ger.)	MURDER	U.S.
JOKOR	162478	M	Ger.		Civ., Schliersee	WITNESS	U.S.
JOKSCH	301327	M	Ger.		Member, Gestapo, Nove Mesto n.Vahom, C.C.Oswiecim-Birkenau (Pol.) 39-45	MURDER	CZECH.
JOLK, Emil	259199	M	Ger.		SS-Untersturmf., C.C. Dachau (Ger.) 10.42- 45	MISC.CRIMES	YUGO.
JON	199846	M		95	Lt., W-SS, Cracow (Pol.) 6.42	MURDER	U.S.
JONACK, Gustav	9697	M	Ger.		Dr., Oberlandrat, Referent d.Justiz-Abt., Moravska (Czech.) 39 - 44	MISC.CRIMES	CZECH.
JONAS	132031	M	Ger.	07	Lt., Schupo, S.D., II B from Berlin, Thekina, Tiraspol (Ger.) 41	MURDER	U.S.
JONAS, Joep	259832	M	Ger.		Staff-Sgt., Gend.Wehrmachts-Kdtr., Utrecht (Neth.) 1.45	MURDER	NETH.
JONASCH, Johann	195403	M	Ger.	20	Scharfhr., SS, Employee, Gestapo, Kolin (Czech.) 39 - 45	MURDER	CZECH.

JON - JUN

NAME	C.R.FILE NUMBER	SEX	NATIONALITY	DATE OF BIRTH	RANK OCCUPATION UNIT PLACE AND DATE OF CRIME	REASON WANTED	WANTED BY
JONCKMANN	251064	M	Ger.		Cpl.,377 Jg.Rgt.,Vinkt (Bel.) 25.-31.5.40	INTERR.	BEL.
JONFRAL	258688	M	Ger.		Secretary,Helmstedt (Ger.) 6.or 7.44	WITNESS	U.S.
JONEN	133796	M			Pvt.,Army,Krestl (Sov.Un.)	WITNESS	U.S.
JONES, Charles	143164	M			Dr.,Civilian,Simmern (Ger.) 8.44	WITNESS	U.S.
JONG, Karl	251081	M	Ger.		Sgt.,Parachutist,St.Michielsgestel (Neth.) 9.-10.44	PILLAGE	NETH.
JONGER, Arthur	251637	M	Ger.		Uschfhr.,SS,Gestapo,St.Lo (Fr.) 44	TORTURE	FR.
JONISCHKIES, Herbert	192563	M	Ger.	15.12.12	Ex Convict,Reichsjustizministerium,Straflager Nord,Finmark (Nor.)	MISC.CRIMES	NOR.
JONK, Franz	252193	M	Ger.		Supervisor,Medicien,C.C.Dachau (Ger.) 3.44	BRUTALITY	BEL.
JONTER (see JENNER,Nikolas)	173561						
JOOP (T)	179768	M		95	Capt.,Army,Gubbio (It.) 22.6.44	MURDER	U.K.
JOOST	36690	M	Ger.		Cpl.,Army 515 L.S.Bn.,19.1.45-20.3.45	TORTURE	U.K.
JOOST, Christian	192461	M			Capo,C.C.Flossenburg (Ger.) 44-45	SUSPECT	U.S.,BEL.
JOOST, Hermann	121043	M	Ger.		Member,Grenzschutz of the dutch-belgian frontier,St.Jansteen Hulst Kemeseke-Paal (Bel.,Neth.)	WITNESS	BEL.
JOOSTEN, Emil	251079	M	Ger.		Sgt.,Dienststelle Nr.24827 L.G.P.Amsterdam or Bentheim,Uden (Neth.) 5.9.44	INTERR.	NETH.
JOPPEN	251084	M	Ger.		SS-Uschfhr.,Crim.Asst.,Gestapo,Limoges (Fr.) 40-44	INTERR.	FR.
JORAM	6154	M		15	Sgt.,Army,Inf.,Grossen Mulde (Ger.) 7.44	TORTURE	U.K.
JORDAN	139781	M	Ger.	97	Member,NSDAP,Hoof-Kassel (Ger.)	TORTURE	U.S.
JORDAN	145349	M	Ger.		Osturmfhr.,SS,Auschwitz (Pol.) 43-44	TORTURE	U.S.
JORDAN	194766	M	Ger.		Capt.,Feldgendarmerie,Grenoble,Malleval,Cognin les Gorges (Fr.) 1.44	MISC.CRIMES	FR.
JORDAN	221077	M	Ger.	00	Kreisleiter,NSDAP,Auerbach (Ger.) 6.44	MISC.CRIMES	U.S.
JORDAN	251076	M	Ger.		Capt.,Commander of Feldgendarmerie,Grenoble (Fr.) 14.8.44	MURDER	FR.
JORDAN	306614	M	Ger.		Member of a party searching for escaped POW nr.Stalag X B Sandbostel Neuengamme (Ger.) 24.4.45	MURDER	FR.
JORDAN, Heinrich	196306	M	Ger.		Zugwachtmeister,Arnheim (Neth.) 3.45	MURDER	NETH.
JORDAN, Peter	188352	M	Ger.		Civilian,Mulheim (Ger.) 22.2.44	TORTURE	U.S.
JORDAN, Rudolf	62468	M	Ger.		Pvt.,SS,Gauleitung Reichs-Govern of Braunschweig and Anhalt.Magdaburg (Ger.)	TORTURE	UNWCC
JORDEN	145354	M	Ger.		Gestapo,SS,Bilgoraj (Pol.) 8.1.43	MURDER	POL.
JORDEN, Peter	161989	M	Ger.		Kreisleiter,NSDAP,Mulheim (Ger.) 27.3.45	TORTURE	U.S.
JORION	130667	M	Ger.	95	Doctor,SS,C.C.Mittelbau,Dora,Nordhausen (Ger.)	MURDER	U.S.
JOREITZ, Robert	241065	M	Ger.	12	10 Coy 377 Jg.Rgt.,Vinkt,Meigem (Bel.) 25.-31.5.40	INTERR.	BEL.
JORES (or JORFS,see JORGS, Wilhelm)	258591						
JORG	251633	M	Ger.		Pvt.,100 Geb.Jg.Rgt.,Feissons (Fr.) 5.8.44	MURDER	FR.
JORGA, Willi	257561	M	Ger.	01	Civilian,foreman,Raidroadgang,Pegau (Ger.) 18.3.45	MURDER	U.S.
JORGS (JORES or JORFS,Wilhelm)	258591	M	Ger.		Oberwachtmeister,Police,Poppentin (Ger.) 7.or 8.44	SUSPECT	U.S.
JORNES, Wilhelm	183515	M			SS-Pvt.,4 SS Totenkopfsturmbann,Auschwitz,Nordhausen,Mittelbau,Dora (Pol.,Ger.) 43-45	WITNESS	U.S.
JORSS, Wilhelm	250858	M	Ger.		Sgt.d.Res.,Poppentin (Ger.) 7.-8.44	INTERR.	U.S.
JOSCHT, Karl	301498	M	Ger.	3. 7.15	SS-Uschfhr.,SS,C.C.Buchenwald (Ger.) 16.5.38 and 9.10.43	MURDER	BEL.
JOSE	131759	M	Ger.		Gestapo,Grenoble (Fr.)	MURDER	FR.
JOSEPH	250293	M	Ger.		Chief Kdo.,C.C.Ravensbrueck,Valbau (Ger.)	BRUTALITY	FR.
JOSSIGER, Otto	250272	M	Ger.		Pvt.,C.C.Ellrich,Nordhausen (Ger.)	MURDER	U.S.
JOST	102915	M	Ger.		Crim.Commissar,Gestapoamt,Ahlem (Ger.) 6.4.45	MURDER	U.S.
JOST	141421	M			Director,Bank von Frankreich,Paris (Fr.)	MISC.CRIMES	FR.
JOST	145343	M			Sturmbannfhr.,SS,Mauthausen (Aust.) 42	MURDER	U.S.
JOST	300485	M	Ger.		Soldier,Astene (Bel.) 5.9.44	MURDER	BEL.
JOST, Anton	188706	M	Ger.		Civilian,Wehrden (Ger.) 8.44	SUSPECT	U.S.
JOST, Heinrich	132039	M	Ger.	15	Usturmfhr.,SS,SD,Issel (Ger.) 20.1.45	MURDER	U.S.
JOST, Nikolaus	250278	M	Ger.		Cpl.,C.C.Ellrich,Nordhausen (Ger.)	MURDER	U.S.
JOST, Wilhelm	194920	M	Ger.		Mayor,Occ.territories,Diekirch (Ger.)	MISC.CRIMES	LUX.
JOSTEN	173564	M	Ger.		SS-Osturmbannfhr.,Cmdt.,C.C.Oswiecim-Birkenau (Pol.) 39-45	MURDER	CZECH.
JOSTEN	192660	M	Ger.		SS-Lt.,C.C.Auschwitz (Pol.) 43-44	MURDER	U.S.
JOSTIN	257606	M	Ger.		SS-Lt.,Camp-leader,Auschwitz (Pol.)	MURDER	U.S.
JOTZO, Emil	162837	M			Sgt.,Army,C.C.Chaudion (Fr.) 7.1.41	MURDER	FR.
JOUANOVIC, Mil	135276	M			Lt.,Jougoslavian Army,Hammelburg (Ger.) 44-45	TORTURE	U.S.
JOUP	258227	M	Ger.		Employee,C.C.Neuengamme (Ger.) 9.41	MISC.CRIMES	BEL.,FR.
JOURDAN, Wilhelm	301204	M	Ger.		Member,Hitler Jugend,Buchenfeld,Dillweissenstein (Ger.) 17.-18.3.45	MURDER	U.K.
JUBNER	131	M	Ger.		N.C.O.,Waffen SS,Birkenau,Auschwitz,Raisko (Pol.) 40-43	MURDER	POL.
JUCHELEK	192669	M	Ger.		Blockfhr.,SS,C.C.Gross Rosen (Ger.) 42	MURDER	U.S.
JUD, Cenel	193936	M	Ger.	19. 1.96	Zollenleiter,NSDAP (Ger.)	MISC.CRIMES	CZECH.
JUDEY	139780	M		95	Cpl.,Waffen SS,Arbeitskdo.A-6, (Ger.)	MURDER	FR.
JUFLICHER	251072	M	Ger.		SS-Oschfhr.,C.C.Buchenwald (Ger.)	BRUTALITY	FR.
JUENGER Heinrich or JUNGER	251630	M	Ger.		Pvt.,39 Volks Gren.Rgt.,Stavelot La Gleize (Bel.)	WITNESS	U.S.
JUERGELITT	261221	M	Ger.	17.10.12	Police-official, (Pol.) 40-45	MURDER	POL.
JUERGENS	300786	M	Ger.		Member,Staff of C.C.Ravensbrueck (Ger.)	SUSPECT	BEL.
					Soldier,Army under the command of the late Capt.Bakels,Nuland (Neth.) 9.-10 44	PILLAGE	NETH.
JUFTTNER, Hans	193940	M	Ger.		Oberstgruppenfhr.,Chief,SS Fuehrungshptamt.,Waffen SS,C.C.Buchenwald (Ger.)	TORTURE	U.S.
JUGEHARD	187671	M	Ger.		Engineer,Member,leader of the factory Glinda,Arbeitskdo.,NSDAP,C.C. (Ger.)	TORTURE	U.S.
JUGENLAND	194765	M	Ger.		SS-leader,C.C.Ravensbrueck (Ger.)	MURDER	FR.
JUGMANN, Leo	195404	M	Ger.		Civilian,Schwalbach (Ger.) 8.44	WITNESS	U.S.
JUHL, Hans	301102	M	Ger.		Crim.Obersecr.,leader,RSD Abt.IV 3 c in Helsing,Northeast coast of Sjaelland, 43	MISC.CRIMES	DEN.
JULIKA	194764		Ger.	28	Woman Guard,C.C.Ravensbrueck (Ger.) 11.44-3.45	TORTURE	FR.
JULIUS	189027	M	Ger.		Sturmbannfhr.,SD,Gestapo,Member of staff Lyon (Fr.) 43	TORTURE	U.K.
JULOWSKI, Josef	130133	M	Ger.	88	Civilian,Ruppertshuetten (Ger.) 12.9.44	WITNESS	U.S.
JUMB (see JELLINECK,Wilhelm)	162174						
JUNCKLAUS (see JUNGCLAUS)	128315						
JUNG	1405	M	Ger.		Pz.Gren.Rgt.1044,Army,	MISC.CRIMES	U.K.
JUNG	102879	M	Ger.		Pvt.,Army,1082 d Sicherungs Bn.,Sellerich (Ger.) 4.1.45	WITNESS	U.S.
JUNG	122716	M	Ger.		Lt.,Army,Pax (Fr.) 13.6.44	MURDER	FR.
JUNG	125718	M	Ger.	05	SS-Sturmbannfhr.,SD,C.C.Belgrade (Yugo.) 1.-10.3.44	MISC.CRIMES	U.K.
JUNG	130065	M	Ger.		Member,Planning SS staff,Mittelbau,Dora,Nordhausen (Ger.)	MURDER	U.S.

NAME	C.R.FILE NUMBER	SEX	NATIO- NALITY	DATE OF BIRTH	RANK	OCCUPATION	UNIT	PLACE AND DATE OF CRIME	REASON WANTED	WANTED BY
JUNG	137780	M	Ger.		Hptscharfhr., SS, C.C. Natzweiler (Fr.)				MURDER	U.S.
JUNG	141066	M	Ger.		Prof.of Anatomy, Anatomical Institute Strasbourg (Fr.) 42-44				TORTURE	U.K.
JUNG	141963	M	Ger.		O.T.master, SS-Waldlager V A VI guard,C.C.Ampfing,Muhldorf, Mettenheim (Ger.) 44-45				TORTURE	U.S.
JUNG	142086	M	Ger.	15	Lt.,SS, C.C. Dachau (Ger.) 40-45				MURDER	POL.
JUNG	146847	M	Ger.		Army, Capestang (Fr.) 44				MURDER	FR.
JUNG	147311	M	Ger.		Lt.,11 Pz.Div. (Fr.) 44				MURDER	FR.
JUNG	161986	M	Ger.		Lt.,SS, Dachau (Ger.)				TORTURE	FR.
JUNG	162838	M	Ger.		Inf.Bn 348, 4 Coy, Stalag 3 Goerlitz (Ger.) 8.6.44				MURDER	FR.
JUNG	167154	M	Ger.		Lt.,Army, Montigny (Fr.) 9.44				WITNESS	FR.
JUNG	173279	M	Ger.	05	Dr., Gestapo, Belgrad (Yugo.) 3.44				TORTURE	U.K.
JUNG	173577	M	Ger.		Dr., Gestapo, Belgrad (Yugo.) 17.8.41				MURDER	YUGO.
JUNG	177597	M	Ger.		Hptsturmfhr.,SS, Gestapo, SD, Sarrbruck (Ger.)				MISC.CRIMES	FR.
JUNG	190203	M	Ger.		Dr.,Camp-chief, C.C. Banjica (Yugo.) 41-45				MURDER	YUGO.
JUNG	190204	M	Ger.		Sgt., Kreiskommandantur, Kragujevac (Yugo.) 21.10.41				MURDER	YUGO.
JUNG	194919	M	Ger.		Landrat, occupied territories, Luxembourg (Lux.)				MISC.CRIMES	LUX.
JUNG	250863	M	Ger.		Lt.,SS, Vujnovic (Yugo.) 27.10.43				MISC.CRIMES	YUGO.
JUNG	259090	M	Ger.		Lt.,SS, Schutzhaftlagerfuehrer, C.C. Dachau (Ger.) 44-45				MISC.CRIMES	YUGO.
JUNG	301137	M	Ger.		Employee, office for registration of deaths, C.C. Struthof-Natzweiler (Fr.) 42-44				MURDER	FR.
JUNG or YUNG	301418	M	Ger.		W.O., 33 Pion XV Div. Afrika Korps, Vaucourtet Xousse (Meurthe et Moselle) (Fr.) 9.-10.44				PILLAGE	FR.
JUNG	305800	M	Ger.		Capt.,Abwehr officer,chief of parcels an Mail Section, Oflag VI-C,Osnabrueck-Ewersheide (Ger.) 41-45				MURDER	YUGO.
JUNG, Albrecht	102878	M	Ger.		Army, Ld.Schz.Bn 777, Sgt.Gravenech,Weilburg (Ger.) 26.3.45				TORTURE	U.S.
JUNG, Alfred	250274	M	Ger.		Pvt., C.C. Ellrich-Nordhausen (Ger.)				MURDER	U.S.
JUNG, Franz	162456	M	Ger.	05	Civilian, Ladung (Czech.) 14.4.45				MURDER	U.S.
JUNG, Fritz	129679	M	Ger.		Civilian, Paris (Fr.) 39-45				PILLAGE	U.S.
JUNG, Fritz	191597	M	Ger.		Officer, Ostgebiet Ministerium Rosenberg, Paris (Fr.) 40-44				PILLAGE	FR.
JUNG, Fritz	192657	M	Ger.	19. 4.14	Member, Gestapo, Luxembourg (Lux.) 40-44				MISC.CRIMES	LUX.
JUNG, Georges	102866	M	Ger.		Civilian, Muehlheim, Diedesheim (Ger.) 25.2.45				MURDER	U.S.
JUNG, Hans	130156	M	Ger.		Uscharfhr.,SS				MURDER	U.S.
JUNG, Hans	302049	M	Ger.		Guard, SS, C.C. Auschwitz (Pol.) 40-45				BRUTALITY	POL.
JUNG, Heinrich	130157	M	Ger.		Civilian, C.C. Sythen, Westphalia (Ger.) 41				MURDER	BEL.
JUNG, Herbert	240104	M	Ger.	04	Sturmbannfhr.,SS, official,Insp. of Prison Gestapo,Dr. at the Gestapo Prison at Belgrad and chief of Banjica Camps Ambulance, Belgrade (Yugo.) 5.44				MURDER	U.S.
JUNG, Jean	132019	M	Ger.		Civilian to be detained,Muhlheim-Main (Ger.) 22.2.45				MISC.CRIMES	U.S.
JUNG, Josef	250275	M	Ger.		Pvt., C.C. Ellrich-Nordhausen (Ger.)				MURDER	U.S.
JUNG, Karl	253657	M	Ger.	9. 6.11	Pvt., 558 Gren.Rgt., Bruayen,Artois (Fr.) 1.9.44				MURDER	FR.
JUNG, Krisztl	132017	F			SS-girl, C.C. Vicinity (Ger.) Summer 44				TORTURE	U.S.
JUNG, Martin	183507	M	Ger.		Pvt.,4 SS Totenkopf Sturmbann, SS-Camp-guard, C.C. Dora-Nordhausen, Osterval (Ger.) 43-45				WITNESS	U.S.
JUNG, Martin	250273	M			Cpl., C.C. Ellrich-Rossla,Nordhausen (Ger.)				MURDER	U.S.
JUNG, Peter	130661	M	Ger.		C.C. Mittelbau Dora-Nordhausen (Ger.)				MURDER	U.S.
JUNG, Rudolf	187697	M			Dr.,SS-Gruppenfhr., Labour Reich Level				TORTURE	UNWCC.
JUNG, Stefan	173169	M	Ger.		Member, SS, C.C. Muhldorf,Ampfing (Ger.) 6.44-4.45				MURDER	U.S.
JUNG, Walter	102914	M	Ger.		Sonder-Kdo., C.C. Warstein, Suttrop (Ger.) 20.-21.or 22.3.45				MURDER	U.S.
JUNG, Werner	192656	M	Ger.	20. 4.09	Major, Fallschirmschule 3, Pesse (Neth.) 4.45				MURDER	NETH.
JUNG, Wilhelm	185495	M	Ger.	90	Mayor, groupleader, Public official, NSDAP, Oberweier (Ger.) 29.7.44				MURDER	CAN.
JUNG, Wilhelm	192564	M	Ger.	95	Sgt., Kgf.Arbeits Bn 186 (Nor.) 40-45				MURDER	NOR.
JUNG, Wilhelm	261396	M	Ger.		Chief, Civ.Firm "Wilhelm Jung", Posen (Pol.) 42-43				MURDER	POL.
JUNGBLUTH, Fritz	255967	M	Ger.		Officer, Army, C.C. Mauthausen (Aust.)				MURDER	FR.
JUNGBLEITT or JUNGELUTT	1406	M	Ger.		N.C.O., Inf.Rgt.194 (Ger.)				MISC.CRIMES	U.K.
JUNGCLAUS, Richard or JUNGLAUS or JUNCKLAUS	128315	M	Ger.	17. 3.05	SS-Gruppenfhr. official, Gestapo, Brussels (Bel.) 44				MURDER	U.S.
JUNGE	250859	M	Ger.		Sgt., living of Berlin, Enschede (Neth.) 15.5.42-1.4.45				INTERR.	NATH.
JUNGE	258883	M	Ger.		Dr.,Major, Gestapo (Gestapo Prison),Belgrad (Yugo.) 41-45				BRUTALITY	CZECH.
JUNGE, Alex	174009	M	Ger.		Foreman-oberpolia, Org.Todt, C.C. Muhldorf,Ampfing (Ger.)6.44-4.45				MURDER	U.S.
JUNGE, Erich	174008	M	Ger.		Foreman, Org.Todt, C.C. Muhldorf,Ampfing (Ger.) 6.44-4.45				MISC.CRIMES	U.S.
JUNGE, Karl Heinz	259067	M			A Dulag Luft Hospital (Ger.) 43-4.45				BRUTALITY	U.S.
JUNGE, Richard Arthur	261901	M	Ger.	22. 2.01	Uscharfhr.,Blockfhr.,and deputy commander, SS, C.C. Rabstein (Czech.) 42-45				SUSPECT	CZECH.
JUNGE, Walter	192655	M			Kapo, SS, C.C. Mauthausen (Aust.)				MURDER	U.S.
JUNGE, Walter	196305	M	Ger.		Guard or Kapo, C.C. Gusen (Ger.) 40-42				TORTURE	BEL.
JUNGEN	183503	M			Rottenfhr,SS, 9 SS Totenkopf Sturmbann,Nordhausen-Dora-Mittelbau (Ger.) 43-45				WITNESS	U.S.
JUNGER alias DJFDUR	191595	M	Ger.		Member, Gestapo, SD, St.Lo (Fr.)				MURDER	FR.
JUNGER, Ella	139134	F			Civilian, Soemmerda (Ger.) 27.3.45				WITNESS	U.S.
JUNGER see JUENGER, Heinrich	251636									
JUNGFLEISCH, Rudolf	301499	M	Ger.		Rottenfhr.,SS, C.C. Buchenwald (Ger.) 16.5.38-9.10.43				MURDER	BEL.
JUNGHANS	72288	M	Ger.		Sgt., Waffen-SS, C.C. Struthof (Fr.)				MISC.CRIMES	FR.
JUNGHANS	141351	M	Ger.		Cpl.,Army, Rittel (Pol.)				TORTURE	U.K.
JUNGHANS	161984	M	Ger.		SS-Mann, Hennebout (Fr.) 44				MURDER	FR.
JUNGINGER	102867	M			Civilian, Gernsbach (Ger.) 8.8.44				MURDER	U.S.
JUNGINGER, H.	13212	M	Ger.	13	Concentration Camp				MURDER	U.S.
JUNGINGER, Hermann	132021	M	Ger.		Civilian, Geislingen (Ger.)				TORTURE	U.S.
JUNGKLAUS, Richard	62470	M	Ger.		Official officer, Gestapo (Bel.)				MURDER	UNWCC.
JUNCLAUS see JUNGCLAUS	128315									
JUNGLING	1407	M	Ger.		SD-Aussenkdo.				MISC.CRIMES	U.K.
JUNGNICK, Hugo	188207	M	Ger.		Scharfhr.,SS, Gestapo, Marianske,Lazne (Czech.) 39-45				TORTURE	CZECH.
JUNI	193939	M	Ger.		SS, C.C. Buchenwald (Ger.)				TORTURE	U.S.
JUNICKER (JUNINGER)	171967	M	Ger.	18-20	Groupleader, NSDAP, Gerusbach and Weissbach (Ger.) 9.8.44				MURDER	U.S.
JUNK	132027	M			SS, C.C. Gardelegen (Ger.)				MURDER	U.S.
JUNK	145346	M			Guard, SS, C.C. Ellrich, Gardelegen (Ger.) 4.-14.4.45				MISC.CRIMES	U.S.
JUNK	191594	M	Ger.		Pvt., Army, La Roche sur Yon (Fr.) 28.8.44				MISC.CRIMES	FR.

NAME	C.R.FILE NUMBER	SEX	NATIO-NALITY	DATE OF BIRTH	RANK, OCCUPATION, UNIT, PLACE AND DATE OF CRIME	REASON WANTED	WANTED BY
JUNK, Emile	132647	M	Ger.		Guard, Prison, Hundling (Moselle), Benning (Fr.) 11.1.44	MURDER	FR.
JUNKAR, Benone	124264	M	Ger		Lt., Army, Malmedy (Bel.) 17.12.44	MURDER	U.S.
JUNKER	67710	M	Ger.		Sgt., Conc.Camp,	MISC.CRIMES	U.K.
JUNKER (see YOUNGER)	67754						
JUNKER	124228	M			Hptsturmfhr., SS, 1.Panz.Div.,1.Rgt., Malmedy (Bel.)	MURDER	U.S.
JUNKER, Carl (or HOG-EYES)	137781	M	Ger.	08	Guard, Comrdo.1579, C C , Mehlgast Stalag 2 B (Ger.) 2.8.44	TORTURE	U.S.
JUNKER, Emile	194357	M	Ger.		W O , Army, La Tranche sur Mer (Fr.) 3.9.44	MURDER	FR.
JUNKER, Pol	251066	M	Ger.		10 Coy ,377 Jgd.Rgt., Vinkt, Meigem and District (Bel.) 25.5.-31.5.40	INTERR.	BEL.
JUNKMANN, Johann	251067	M	Ger.		Sgt , 377.Jgd.Rgt., Vinkt (Bel.)	MISC.CRIMES	BEL.
JUNKS	141964	M			O.T.-Meister, C C., Waldlager V und VI, Ampfing, Muehldorf, Mehenheim (Ger.) 44-45	TORTURE	U.S.
JUNKS, Albert	174010	M	Ger.		Leader, Organ.Todt, Muehldorf, Ampfing (Ger) 6.44-4.45	MISC.CRIMES	U.S.
JUNTERMANNS, Fritz	174562	M	Ger.		2.Bn.,469.Rgt.,198.I.D., Le Tholy (Fr.) 13.11.44	INCENDIARISM	FR.
JUNTZINGER	183295	M			SS-Mann, 4.SS-Totenkopf-Sturmbann, C.C Dora-Mittelbau, Nordhausen (Ger.) 43-45	WITNESS	U.S.
JUNY, Alfred	151287	M	Ger.		Custom-Official, Custom-frontier-guard, Lancrans (Fr.) 22.7.41	MURDER	FR.
JUP	250848	M	Ger.		Foreman, Wilhelmshaven (Ger.)	MURDER	FR
JURA	125687	M	Ger.		Sgt., SS-Pz.Div."Hitler-Jugend",1.Rgt., Ascq (Fr.) 1.4.44	MURDER	FR
JURAK, Anton	189384	M	Ger.	2. 2.00	Crim.Employee, Gestapo, Brno (Czech.) 39-45	MURDER	CZECH
JURASEK, Kurt	134879	M	Ger.		Sgt., SS	TORTURE	U.S.
JURD	188905	M	Ger.		Oschfhr.,SS-Pz.Div."Hitler-Jugend",1.,2.or 3.Coy.,12.Armoured case Reconnaissance, Ascq (Fr.) 1.4.44	MURDER	FR.
JURDA	37348	M			Head, Aussenpolit.Amt der NSDAP	MISC.CRIMES	U.S.
JUREK, George (see TREPCZYK)	140816						
JUREN	72284	M	Ger.		Sgt. and Block-leader, Waffen-SS, C.C., Sachsenhausen (Ger.)9.41-5.43	MURDER	U.S.
JURETSCHKE, Oswald	305904	M	Ger.	29. 8.27	Civilian, Velke Heraltice (Czech.) 7.8.44	BRUTALITY	CZECH.
JURGELEIN (Nickname: LE GRAND MAOUPA)	147550	M		95	Uschfhr., SS	TORTURE	FR.
JURGEN	259649	M	Ger.		Capt and Staffelfhr.,Feldwirtschaftskdo.3,Erkundungs-Staffel, Guebwiller and Issenheim - Haut-Rhin (Fr.) 18.1.45	PILLAGE	FR.
JURGHENS	306616	M	Ger.		Cpt., Hospital of La Pallice, La Rochelle (Fr.) 44-45	MISC.CRIMES	FR.
JURITSCH, Josef	301328	M	Ger.		Member, Gestapo, C.C., Trencin, Oswiecim-Birkenau (Pol.) 39-45	MURDER	CZECH
JURKIEWICZ	300786	M	Ger.		Pvt., 1.Aufkl.Abt , 3.Coy., 2 Column, XV.Div. of the Afrika-Korps, Saint-Leger (Arlon) (Bel.) 5.9.44	MISC.CRIMES	BEL.
JURKOWSKI, Robert	189383	M	Ger.		Prison-Warder, Gestapo, Brno (Czech.) 39-45	TORTURE	CZECH.
JURKOWSKY	192653	M	Ger.		SS-Sgt., C.C., Auschwitz (Pol.) 43-44	TORTURE	U.S.
JURKSCHARDT	72286	M	Ger.		Col., Inf.Rgt.127, Oxcourt (Fr.) 10.44	MISC.CRIMES	U.S.
JURSS	196302	M	Ger.		Cpl., Guard, C.C Royallieu, Compiegne (Fr.) 41-44	MURDER	FR.
JUSCHENKO	250277	M	Ger.		Sturmmann, C.C. Auschwitz, Nordhausen (Pol., Ger.)	MURDER	U.S
JUSEK, Hubert	121042	M	Ger.		Kapo -Chef de l'infirmerie, C.C., Laura-Thueringen (Ger.)	MURDER	FR.
JUSSUF	167163	M	Ger.		Sgt., Army, Oberkommando, Etat-Major stationed at Crest (Drome) La Rochelle (Fr.) 3.8.44	MURDER	FR
JUSSUFF	167847	M	Ger.		W.O , Kommandantur, Crest (Fr.) 7.44-8.44	WITNESS	FR.
JUST	193938	M	Ger.		Osturmfhr., SS, C.C., Buchenwald (Ger.)	TORTURE	U.S
JUST	300256	M	Ger.		Lt., Feldgend.,Truppe M 44,Romilly-sur-Seine,Troyes and Region (Fr.) 10.43-8.44	MURDER	FR.
JUST, Benno	161982	M			Cpl., SS Gestapo, Saone et Loire (Fr.) 44	MURDER	FR
JUST, Ernst	194541	M		19	Obermaat, II.-504 Marine Art.Abt., Fjell (Nor.) 43-44	TORTURE	NOR
JUSTUS, Rolf	136297	M	Ger.	00	Sgt., Prison of Baumettes, C.C., Marseille (Fr.) 6.44	MURDER	FR.
JUSZENKO	183298	M			SS-Mann, 4.SS-Totenkopf-Stuba.,C.C., Nordhausen,Dora,Auschwitz (Ger., Pol.) 43-45	WITNESS	U.S.
JUTTNER	130663	M	Ger.		SS-Conc.Camp, Dora-Mittelbau, Nordhausen (Ger.)	MURDER	U.S
JUTTNER	132646	M	Ger.		Major, German Court Martial, Besancon (Fr.) 18.9.43	MURDER	FR.
JUTTNER	145353	M			Ogruppenfhr., SS, Ludwigsburg (Ger.) 11.8.44	MISC.CRIMES	U.S.
JUTTNER	187863	M			Oberstgruppenfhr., Waffen-SS, Goerlitz (Ger.)	MURDER	BEL.
KAAS, Franz (or LE BOYEUR)	132571	M		3. 1.22	Member, Gestapo, Parcus (Fr.) 23.6.43	MURDER	FR.
KABAS, Othmar	189382	M	Ger.	28. 5.07	Employee, SS-Junkerschule, Gestapo, Bruenn (Czech.) 39-45	MURDER	CZECH.
KABATT, Emil	257326	M	Ger.		Sturmfhr., SS, Slava Labour Camp, Osen (Nor.) 6.42-3.43	MISC.CRIMES	YUGO
KABO	255548	M	Ger.		Major, 19.Rgt.,SS-Police, Charente (Fr.) 23.6.44	INTERR.	FR
KABO (see KOBATH)	258921						
KABOLA	252363	M	Ger		Usturmfhr., SS, C.C., Schomberg (Ger) 44-45	BRUTALITY	FR.
KABOT	167683	M	Ger.		Schfhr., SS, C.C. Korgen (Nor.) 42	MURDER	NOR
KABSCHAK, Margaret	145227	F	Ger.		SS-Aufseherin, C.C Ravensbrueck (Ger.)	MISC.CRIMES	U.S.
KABUS, Fred	433	M	Ger.		Guard, Feldgend., C.C Vesoul (Fr.) 43-44	MURDER	FR.
KACHA	131424	M	Ger		Sentinel, Stalag XIII C, Work-Cdo 1199 G, Hammelburg (Ger.)	BRUTALITY	BEL
KACHENIKE, Josef (or KACHINIKE or MACHENIKE)	434	M			N.C.O., 711.Div , 73.Inf Rgt., 13.Coy. (Fr.) 7 44	MURDER	U.K.
KACHSTADT	252235				Uschfhr., SS, C.C. Gusen (Ger.)	TORTURE	BEL.
KACZARCZYK, Hans Karl	262173	M	Ger.	23. 1.21	Uschfhr., SS, Technical-chief, Art.detachment of 51.SS-Armoured Bde., Breviandes, Bucheres, Ste Savine, La Riviere de Corps,Troyes(Fr.)8.44	BRUTALITY	FR.
KACZEROWSKI	167091	M	Ger.		Pvt., Army, Bachivillers (Fr.) 28.8.44	WITNESS	FR
KACZMAREK	194156	M	Ger.	95 - 00	Sgt., Army, Leipzig (Ger.) 11.3.45	MURDER	U.S.
KADA, Stepan	254962	M	Ger.	17. 7.90	Engineer, civilian, Zilina (Czech.) 44	BRUTALITY	CZECH.
KADACH, Gustav	29807	M	Ger.		Rottfhr., SS, Gestapo, Lous le Saulnier (Fr.) 9.44	MURDER	FR
KADELKA (or KADELKE)	145836	M	Ger.		Col., Camp Commander, Stalag XVIII G, C.C., Markt Pongau (Aust.)44-3.45	TORTURE	U.K., "
KADEN	253115	M			Pvt., Conc.Camp Ellrich, Nordhausen (Ger.)	MURDER	U.S.
KADEN, Paul	254839	M			Capt., Camp-W.O., C.C., Laterina (It.)	INTERR.	U.S.
KADING, Paul	252503	M			Pvt., C.C. Ellrich, Nordhausen (Ger.)	MURDER	U.S.
KADK	99648	M	Ger.		Sgt., Div. Parachutist, Carhai (Fr.)	MURDER	FR
KADLER, Max	183426	M	Ger.		Rottfhr., SS, 4.SS-Totenkopf-Stuba.,Mittelbau-Dora,Nordhausen (Ger.) 43-45	WITNESS	U.S.
KADNAR	435	M	Ger.		Oschfhr., SS, Fort Musson (Fr.) 3.8.44	MURDER	FR.
KADO	39648	M	Ger.		Sgt.,Parachutist-Div.,8.Rgt., Div.Kreta, Carhaı (Fr.) 8.u.9.6.44	MURDER	FR
KADUCK (see CADUK)	196013						
KADUCK	254583	M	Ger.		Oschfhr., SS, Conc.Camp, Auschwitz-Birkenau (Pol.) 42-45	MURDER	YUGO

KAD-KAI

NAME	C.R.FILE NUMBER	SEX	NATIONALITY	DATE OF BIRTH	RANK OCCUPATION UNIT PLACE AND DATE OF CRIME	REASON WANTED	WANTED BY
KADUCKS	260175	M	Ger.		Member,SS Camp Admin.,Dachau (Ger.) 42-44	MURDER	FR.
KADUK	122614	M	Ger.		Second in command of camp,SS,C.C.,Auschwitz (Pol.) 42-44	MURDER	FR.
KAILK	125173	M	Ger.	05	Rapportfhr.,C.C.Auschwitz (Pol.) 42-45	MURDER	U.S.
KADUK	139778	M		05	Sgt.,Waffen SS,C.C.Aswie (Pol.) 7.43	MURDER	U.S.
KADUK	145212	M			Uschfhr.,Blockfhr.,C.C.,Mauthausen (Aust.) 41-45	TORTURE	
KADIK	252232	M	Ger.		Cpl.,Fieldpolice Trupp 533,Le Chablais (Fr) 19.5.44	MISC.CRIMES	FR.
KADLK	300715	M	Ger.		Lt.,Feldgendarmerie,Argonnex,Hte.Savoie (Fr.) 18.12.43	MISC.CRIMES	FR.
KADUL, Oswald	153330	M	Ger.	26.8.06	SS,C.C.,Oswiecim (Pol.) 1.45	MURDER	U.S.,POL.
KADUPH	191453	M	Ger.		Uschfhr.,SS Div.Totenkopf,Mauthausen (Aust.)	MURDER	U.S.
BAEBE,Heinz (or KAEBER)	172477	M			Rottfhr.,SS,C.C.,Muhldorf,Ampfing (Ger.) 6.44-4.45	MURDER	U.S.
KAEBERNICK	126736	M	Ger.	02	Osturmfhr.,Gestapo,SC, (Fr.) 42	TORTURE	FR.
KAEBERNICK	188906	M	Ger.		Osturmfhr.,SS,Drancy (Fr.)	MURDER	FR.
KAEBI	251688	M	Ger.		Capt.,392.Inf.Blue Div.,Lika (Yugo.) 44-45	MISC.CRIMES	YUGO.
KAEFLR, Alois	301663	M	Ger.		Foreman,Mayreder & Keilist,near Mostar, 8.44	MURDER	YUGO.
KAECLER (or KOEGEL) Max	133320	M	Ger.	16.10.95	Osturmbannfhr.,Waffen SS,Camp commander,C.C.,Flossenburg (Ger.)5.44-4.45	MURDER	U.S
KAEGLER	145234	M	Ger.	80	Osturmbannfhr. Camp leader,Flossenburg (Ger.) 42	TORTURE	U.S.
KAEGLER	145236	M	Ger.	84	Doctor Med.,Osturmbannfhr.,Flossenburg (Ger.) 42	MISC.CRIMES	U.S.
KAEHIER, F.G.	124291	M	Ger.		Public official,Mayor,	MURDER	U.S.
KAEHLER	126555	M	Ger.		Mayor,Public official,Civilian to be detained,Kroepeln (Ger.) 6.-7.44	MURDER	U.S.
KAEHLER	130189	M	Ger.		Konteradmiral,Kriegsmarine,Oberkommando,Brest	MISC.CRIMES	U.K.
KAEHLNER, Hans	260617	M	Ger.	98	Bde.General,Army	WITNESS	U.S.
KAEHMEL	258800	M	Ger.		Employee,factory worker,C.C.,Nordhausen (Ger.)	MURDER	U.S.
KAEMPER	300787	M	Ger.		Pvt.,1.Aufkl.Abt.,3.Coy.,2.Column,XV.Div.,Afrika Korps,St.Leger (Arlon) 5.9.44	MISC.CRIMES	BEL
KAEMFER, Gustav Heinrich	190201	M	Ger.		Osturmfhr.,SS,C.C.,Banjica (Yugo.) 41-45	MURDER	YUGO.
KAEMPER, R.	190202	M	Ger.		Capt.,Kreiskommandantur,Bjelusa,Visoka,Seveine,Uzice (Yugo.) 42-43	MURDER	YUGO.
KAEMPFE	436	M	Ger.		Generallt.,Army,31.Inf.Div., 1.9.39-30.10.39	MURDER	POL.
KAEMPFE,(R.),(or KAEMPFER)	173726	M	Ger.		Capt.,Kreiskommandantur,Urice (Yugo.) 21.10.41 u. 43	MURDER	YUGO.
KAEMPFE, Helmut	145184	M	Ger.		Sturmbannfhr.,SS Div."Das Reich", Tulle (Fr.) 5.44	MURDER	U.S
KAEMPFLE	138309	M	Ger.		Lt.,SS,Member,Gestapo,Lyon (Fr.)	MURDER	FR.
KAEMFER	161506	M	Ger.	48	Hptschfhr.,Waffen SS,Buchenwald (Ger.)	WITNESS	U.S.
KAEMPFER (see KAEMPFE)	173726						
KAEMPFER, Gustav	140908	M	Ger.	17	Osturmfhr.,SS,C.C.,Breendonck (Bel.) 43-44	TORTURE	BEL.
KAENEL	179890	M	Ger.		Sturmschfhr.,SS,secretary,SD,Gestapo,Saarbruecken (Ger.)	PILLAGE	FR.
KAEMCES	174116	M	Ger.		Officer,Stalag VI A,Hemer (Ger.) 44-45	TORTURE	FR.
KAERMER	250325	M	Ger.	00	W.O.chief,Custom secretary,Sentenac d'oust (Fr.) 12.9.43	INTERR.	FP.
KAESER, Marie	133294	F	Ger.		Civilian,Munich (Ger.)	TORTURE	U.S
KAESER Max	194718	M	Ger.	10	Oschfhr.,SS,SD Einsatz Kdo.3,Padzyn,Lublin (Pol.) 39-43	SUSPECT	POL
KAESSLEP	127102	M	Ger.		Guard,Arbeitskommando,Erfurt (Ger.)	TORTURE	FR.
KA STLE	256854	M	Ger.		Oschfhr.,SS,Report leader,C.C.,Dora Nordhausen (Ger.)	MURDER	U.S.
KAESTNER	260696	M	Ger.		Doctor,Chief counselor,Labor Ministry	MISC.CRIMES	U.S.
KAISNYRA, Edith	157794	F	Ger.		Civilian,Proudy,Svatojanske (Czech.) 44	SUSPECT	U.K.,CZECH.
KAMIE	151325	M	Ger.	11	Gestapo,Angers,Anjou,Poitou (Fr.) 42-44	MURDER	FR.
KAFZ, J.	187469	M	Ger.	00	Pvt.,210.Inf.Rgt.,Breskens (Neth.)	MURDER	NETH
KAFEL, Gernard	437	M	Ger.		Lt.,Army,4.Coy.,226.Div.Riffle Batty.,Octeville (Fr.) 2.-3.9.44	MURDER	FR.
KAGEL	120849	M	Ger.		Major,Abwehr official,Stalag IV F,Chemnitz (Ger.) 11.43-4.45	TORTURE	U.S.,U.K.
KAHI	301571	F	Ger.		SS woman,C.C. Mauthausen (Aust.) 40-45	MURDER	BEL.
KAHL, Alfred	192385	M	Ger.		Pvt.,Army,Dienststelle 10748 N,Bayet (Fr.)	TORTURE	FR.
KAHL, Herbert	126556	M	Ger.		Oberfunkmeister,Panz.Art.102 Div.,1.Rgt.,Fuerth (Ger.) 9.44	MURDER	U.S.
KAHL, Rudolf	301501	M	Ger.	24.5.18	SS-Mann,C.C.,Buchenwald,(Ger.) 16.5.38-9.10.43	MURDER	BEL.
KAHLENBERG, Paul	257879	M			Pvt.,150.Pz.Bde.,Meusebridge,Antwerpen (Bel.) 12.44	INTERR.	U.S
KAHLERT, Paul	199059	M	Ger.		Lt.,SD,Gestapo,police secretary,Dresden (Ger.) 19.1.43	MURDER	NOR.
KAHLES, Michael	172471	M			Civilian,C.C. Muhldorf,Ampfing (Ger.) 6.44-4.45	MURDER	U.N.W.C.C.
KAHMAPP, Adolf	102980	M	Ger.			WITNESS	U.S.
KAHMANN, Adolf	126345	M	Ger.		Army,Warsleben (Ger.) 12.9.44	TORTURE	U.S.
KAHLER, Ilse	160836	F	Ger.		Civilian,Grossorne (Ger.) 3.44	MURDER	U.S.
KAH	133822	M	Ger.		Doctor,Civ.lawyer,C.C.,Hellendorf bei Braunschweig (Ger.)	WITNESS	U.S.
KAHN	158599	M	Ger.	07	Hptsturmfhr.,SS Div."Das Reich", "Der Fuehrer",3.Coy.,1.Bn.,Oradour (Fr.) 10.6.44	MURDER	FR.
KAHN	190200	M	Ger.	10	Leader,Klinkswerke,C.C. Neuengamme (Ger.) 43	MURDER	YUGO
KAHN	192192	M	Ger.		Arbeitsfhr.,Camp,Breendonck (Bel.) 4-5.44	MURDER	BEL.
KAHN	192384	M	Ger.		Hptsturmfhr.,SS Div."Das Reich",SS Rgt."Der Fuehrer",1.Bn.,3.Coy., Frayssinet le Celat (Fr.) 21.5.44-10.6.44	MURDER	FR.
KAHN	254988	M	Ger.		Capt.,3.Coy.,"Das Reich",St.Junien (Fr.)	MURDER	FR.
KAHN	254659	M	Ger.		Guard,C.C. Lohde-Weser,(Ger.)	INTERR.	BEL.
KAHR	125656	M	Ger.		Medecin chief,C.C Nordhausen,Dora (Ger.) 44-45	MURDER	FR.
KAHR, Karl	161499	M	Ger.	12	Lt.,Waffen SS Kdo.Amt.,H.Q. staff,C.C.,Buchenwald (Ger.) 44-45	WITNESS	U.S.
KAHR, Hermann	193801	M	Ger.		Sgt.,Feldgendarmerie,Tourcoins (Fr.) 2.9.44	MURDER	FR.
KAWEL	132967	M	Ger.		Osturmfhr.,Camp doctor,C.C.,Nordhausen (Ger.)	MURDER	U.S
KAI BEL	259180	M			Lt.,SS Div."Prinz Eugen",14.Mountain Rgt.hunter,1.Bn.,Kosovska, Mitrovica (Yugo.) 12.42	MISC.CRIMES	YUGO.
KAIBER, Albert	124232	M	Ger.		Civilian,Oberndorf (Pfalz) (Ger.)	MURDER	U.S.
KAIDUSCH, Erna	189380	F	Ger.		Clerk,Gestapo,Bruenn (Czech.) 39-45	WITNESS	CZECH.
KAIEFER, Dieter	186761	M			Capt.,Army,Nevers (Fr.) 43	PILLAGE	FR.
KAIGER, Werner	252246	M	Ger.		Pvt.,Fieldpolice,Vendome (Fr.) 9.8.44	MURDER	FR.
KAIMASI	173118	M			C.C. Schirmeck,Rotenfels,Gaggenau (Fr.,Ger.) 44	INTERR.	U.K.
KAIMLER, Leonhard	11251	M	Ger.		Pvt.,110.Panz.Gren.Rgt.,N.C.O. Albine (Fr.) 29.6.44	MURDER	UK.
KAINDL	250895	M	Ger.		Standartenfhr.,C.C. Neuengamme (Ger.)	INTERR.	BEL.
KAINDL	131454	M	Ger.		Osturmfhr.,SS,Mauthausen (Aust.) 41-45	MURDER	U.S.
KAIN, Karl	252502	M	Ger.	21.3.03	Rottfhr.,SS,C.C.,Harzungen,Nordhausen (Ger.)	MURDER	U.S.
KAIS, Hans (or KEIS)	145958	M	Ger.	30.11.98	Doctor,Civilian,Freising,Altenkirchen (Ger.) 13.6.44	MURDER	U.S.
KAISLR	1550	M	Ger.	15-17	Cschfhr.,SS Totenkopfstandarte,Sachsenhausen (Ger.) 39-45	MURDER	U.S.
KAISER	1705	M		16	Hptsturmfhr.,SS,12.SS Pz.Div."Hitler-Jugend",near Caen (Fr.) 6.6.-8.7.44	MURDER	U.K.
KAISLR	124770	M	Ger.		Sturmfhr.,Standarte SA,C.C. Neususturm (Ger.)	MURDER	U.S.
KAISER	128985	M	Ger.		Hptsturmfhr.,SS,C.C. Esterwegen (Ger.)	MURDER	U.S.
KAISER	132968	M	Ger.		Lt.,Flakbtty.,F.P.No. 23499,Esching (Ger.) 31.7.44	MURDER	U.S.

KAI-KAL

NAME	C.R.FILE NUMBER	SEX	NATIO-NALITY	DATE OF BIRTH	RANK OCCUPATION UNIT PLACE AND DATE OF CRIME	REASON WANTED	WANTED BY
KAISER	136233	M	Ger.		Pvt., 11 Pz.Div., Albine (Fr.)	MURDER	FR.
KAISER	139773	M	Ger.	10	Oberfeldmeister, RAD, near Plave (Brandenburg (Ger.) 8.44	MURDER	U.S.
KAISER	142401	M	Ger.		Oschfhr SS, CC Sachsenhausen, Oranienburg (Ger.) 39-45, 9.41-5.43	MURDER	POL., U.S.
KAISER	151326	M	Ger.		Civ., NSDAP, Engineer, Hoch u.Tiefbau(Essen), Brux (Czech.) 2.6.44	TORTURE	U.K.
KAISER	166068	M	Ger.		Civ., Chief of Personnel, Firm Paul Katch,Hildburghausen(Ger.)	MURDER	FR.
KAISER	172102	M	Ger.		Org.Todt, CC Muhldorf, Ampfing (Ger.) 6.4-4.45	MURDER	U.S.
KAISER	174667	M	Ger.		Major, Lds.Schtz.Bn.445,Oberndorf,Buechelheiden(Ger.) 22.11.44	WITNESS	U.N.W.C.C.
KAISER	188757	M			Capt., Gestapo, Tournon (Fr.) 6.7.44	MURDER	FR.
KAISER	190497	M			Pvt., 11 Pz.Div., 2 Coy, 2 AA-A 7, Bergerac and Albine (Fr.) 7-8.44	MURDER	FR.
KAISER	193967	M	Ger.		Pvt.,31 Lds.Schtz.Bn.,CC Schonwald(Ger.)	TORTURE	CAN.
KAISER	196208	M	Ger.		Custom-House-Officer, Custom-House, Chaum(Fr.) 3.6.44	MURDER	FR.
KAISER	251677	M	Ger.		SS Usturmfhr, BDS France, SD Komm.z.b.V."Fullmer",Cirey(Fr.) 8.44	TORTURE	U.K.
KAISER	251689	M	Ger.	06	Major, Army,392 Inf.Blue Div.,Lika(Yugo.) 44-45	MISC.CRIMES	YUGO.
KAISER	252505	M			SS Hptschfhr, CC Dora, Nordhausen (Ger.)	MURDER	U.S.
KAISER	254158	M	Ger.		Hptwachtmstr, SD, Arnheim (Neth.) 3.45	INTERR.	NETH.
KAISER	254593	M	Ger.	08	Hptsturmfhr,W-SS,12 SS Div.,26Pz.Gren.Rgt., Le Haut de Bosqn(Fr.) 11.6.44	INTERR.	U.K.
KAISER (see KAIZER)	254638						
KAISER	254980	M	Ger.		3 Lds.Schtz.Bn.,Rgt.565,Arbeitskomm.E 569,Schonwalde(Ger.) 4.1.44	BRUTALITY	CAN.
KAISER	258925	M	Ger.		Blockfuehrer SS "Kommando" Ohrdruf (Thueringen,Ger.) 44-45	MURDER	FR.
KAISER	261011	M			Oschfhr SS., CC Vaihingen(Ger.) 13.8.44-7.4.45	MURDER	U.S.
KAISER	300257	M	Ger.		Major,Army, near Oberndorf(Aust.)on or about 22.11.44	MURDER	U.S.
KAISER	300788	M	Ger.		Pvt.,1 Aufkl.Abt.,3 Coy,2 Col., XV Div.Africa Corps,Saint Léger(Arlon) 5.9.44	MISC.CRIMES	BEL.
KAISER, Adolf	259682	M	Ger.	97	Member Gestapo,Area of Angers,Maine and Loire(Fr.)42-44	MISC.CRIMES	FR.
KAISER, Albin	143177	M	Ger.		Guard,SS Totenk.,CC Buchenwald(Ger.) 42-45	MISC.CRIMES	U.S.
KAISER, Aloys	185991	M	Ger.		SS-Mann,SS Leibst."Adolf Hitler",1 Pz.Gren.Div.,Stavelot(Bel.) 19.-20.12.44	MURDER	BEL.
KAISER (or KAYSER),Cornelius	170552	M	Ger. or Lux.	03	Uschfhr,SS,SD, H.Qn.,Strassenhaus near Rengsdorf(Ger.) 23.12.44-14.2.45	WITNESS	U.S.,U.K.
KAISER, Dora	192032	F	Ger.		Civilian, Burg a.d.Wupper(Ger.) 5.11.44	MURDER	FR.
KAISER, Emile	196207	M	Ger.		Uschfhr,W-SS, St.Etienne(Fr.) 15-16.4.44	INTERR.	FR.
KAISER, Karl	145262	M	Ger.	16.9.19	Uschfhr,W-SS,SS Totenkopf Standarte,Leader of the Baracke,CC Buchenwald, Weimar (Ger.)	TORTURE	U.S.
KAISER, Artur	125710	M	Ger.		Lt.,13,916 Gren.Rgt.,352 Inf.Div.,Normandy(Fr.) 9.6.44	MURDER	U.S.
KAISER, Franz	167963	M	Ger.	10.4.95	Oschfhr.SS,CC Struthof,Natzweiler(Fr.)	MURDER	FR.,POL.
KAISER,Hermann	262170	M	Ger.		Oschfhr,Gestapo,Rennes(Fr.) 43-44	MISC.CRIMES	FR.
KAISER, Jakob	133296	M	Ger.	1910-15	Oschfhr,W-SS, CC Flossenburg, Ohrdruf(Ger.)	TORTURE	U.S.
KAISER, Karl	170551	M	Ger.	03	Oschfhr,SS,SD,Strassenhaus,Neuwied,Koblenz,Rengsdorf(Ger.)	MURDER	U.K.
KAISER, Karol	162567	M	Ger.		Civilian,Farmer,Bierstadt near Wiesbaden(Ger.) 41-43	TORTURE	POL.
KAISER, Kurt	142199	M	Ger.		Sturmschfhr.SS, Lublin(Pol.)	MURDER	FR.
KAISER, Marte	192033	F	Ger.		Civilian, Burg a.d.Wupper(Ger.) 5.11.44	MURDER	FR.
KAISER, Michael	300258	M	Ger.		Kreisfhr,Bezirksoberlt., Farmer, Gend., near Moerlach(Ger.)16-7.44	MISC.CRIMES	U.S.
KAISER, Oskar	167689	M	Ger.		Treuhaender,Firm Erste Krakauer Hutfabrik, J.A.Appenkraut Krakau (Pol.) 9.39-12.44	PILLAGE	POL.
KAISER Paul	174056	M			Rottfhr,SS, CC Gusen(Aust.)	MURDER	U.S.
KAISER, Walter	124771	M	Ger.	08	Sturmschfhr, SS, Crim.Secr.,Army Kdo.16 z.b.V.,Brussels(Bel.)9.44-3.45	MURDER	U.S., BEL.
KAISER, Wilhelm	257328	M	Ger.	08	Osturmfhr. SS; W.O. of Polizeichef Serbia; Unit commander of III Bn., V Police Rgt.,Kragujevac, Belgrad (Yugo.) 1.42-3.44	MISC.CRIMES	YUGO.
KAITEL	123972	M	Ger.		Army Officer	MURDER	U.S.
KAIZER (or KAISER)	254638	M	Ger.		Pvt.,Oldenzaal, Overijassel(Neth.) 1.4.45	WITNESS	NETH.
KAJNER	186281	M	Ger.		N.C.O.,Civilian,Servant, Police Administration of occupied Territories, Athen (Grc.)	TORTURE	GRC.
KAJUMI	438	M			N.C.O.,Jg.Rgt.738, 2 Bn.or Coy, Kolasin	MURDER	YUGO.
KAKES, Tomas	255172	M	Ger.	20.10.20	Glasscutter,Civilian,Budejovice(Czech.) 39	MURDER	CZECH.
KALABIS, Willy	145175	M	Ger.		Civilian	MURDER	U.S.
KALASCH	150676	M			Pvt.,Nachschub Bn., Les Haques(Fr.)	MURDER	FR.
KALB	301867	M			Gend.,Vichy,Clermont-Ferrand(Fr.) 7.44, 8.44	MURDER	FR.
KALBFUSS	196206	M	Ger.		Sgt.,2 Coy,Feldausbild.Bn.189,116 Inf.Rgt.,Clermont-Dessus(Fr.)-17.8.44	MURDER	FR.
KALBHEN	191592	M	Ger.		Ostgebietsministerium Official,Eins.Abt.Rosenberg,Le Havre(Fr.)40-44	PILLAGE	FR.
KALBHENN	145183	M	Ger.		Lt., Army, Loire-Inferieure (Fr.)	WITNESS	U.S.
KALBHENN, Ruth	191591	F	Ger.		Lt., Gestapo, Feldkommandantur, Nantes(Fr.)22.10.41-15.12.41	MURDER	FR.
KAIDOLF	194030	F	Ger.		Civilian, CC Cracow, Lublin, Plaszow (Pol.) 42-44	WITNESS	POL.
KALEMBACH,Albert(or Arthur)	261754	M	Ger.		Lt., St.Quentin (Fr.) 7.4.44	INTERR.	FR.
KALENDER	254841	M	Ger.	1918 or 20	Sgt., H.Q. Secret Field Police, Roccaro (It.)	INTERR.	U.S.
KALIGE (or KALIGA or GALLIGER)	161508	M	Ger.		Osturmfhr, SS Wirtschafts und Verwaltungs-Hauptamt, CC Buchenwald (Ger.)	WITNESS	U.S.
	254967	M		10	Guard, 559 Lds.Schtz.Bn., Domstadl (Ger.) 11.43	WITNESS	U.K.
KALINOWSKI, Friedrich	439	M	Ger.	6.9.98	Schfhr, W-SS, CC Maidanek (Pol.) 40-4.44	MURDER	POL.
KALINOWSKI, Willi Emil	260176	M	Ger.		SS-Mann, Slave-Labour-Camp. Botn near Bognan (Nor.) 8.42-5.45	BRUTALITY	YUGO.
KALISCHEWSKI, Rudolf	301502	M	Ger.		SS-Mann, CC Buchenwald (Ger.) 16.5.38-9.10.43	MURDER	BEL.
KALIVIN, Otto	158530	M	Ger.		Civilian, NSDAP, Gernrode - Harz (Ger.)	MURDER	U.K.
KALIWITSKY	11252	M			Major, Army, Hauptverbindungsstab Nr.588, Oradour(Fr.) 10.6.44	MURDER	FR.
KALK	301829	M	Ger.		Dr., Chief surgeon-major, Air Ministry Berlin, CC Dachau and Auschwitz (Ger., Pol.) 3.42-26.2.43	TORTURE	BEL.
KALKBRENNER	158532	M	Ger.	07	Pvt., 515 Lds.Schts.Ba., 4 Coy, Jung-Bunzlau (Czech.) 2.45	TORTURE	U.K.
KALKMANN, Karl Heinz	145246	M	Ger.		Rottfhr, 1 SS Pz.Div., 2 Pz.Gren.Rgt., 3 Bn., 12 Coy, Stavelot, Malmedy (Bel.) 22.-23.12.44	MURDER	U.S.
KALKNOW, Karl Heinz	181145	M	Ger.	25	SS-Rottfhr, SS Leibstand."Adolf Hitler", 2 Pz.Gren.Rgt., Malmedy (Bel.) 17.12.44	MURDER	U.S.
KALKOFF, Fritz	254823	M	Ger.	1890-95	Dr., Capt., Att. Fieldpolice near Bedonia (It.) 10.4.44	MURDER	U.K.
KALIX	1706	M	Ger.		Pvt., Army, Inf.Rgt.148, Amiens (Fr.) 25.-26.8.44	MURDER	U.K.

KAL-KAM

NAME	C.R.FILE NUMBER	SEX	NATIO-NALITY	DATE OF BIRTH	RANK OCCUPATION UNIT PLACE AND DATE OF CRIME	REASON WANTED	WANTED BY
KALLENBACH	145801	M			Capt.,C.O.Transient Camp Remount School,Gardelegen(Ger.) 10.-14.4.45	MURDER	U.S.
KALLENBACH, Eugen	167701	M	Ger.		Pvt.,Army,9 Gren.Res.Regt.,1 Coy.,Magny D'Anigon(Fr.) 18.9.44	MURDER	FR.
KALLER, Max	252504	M			Sturmmann, C.C.Mackenröde,Nordhausen(Ger.)	MURDER	U.S.
KALLHOF	252233	M	Ger.		Cadet, 9 Gestapo,3 Bn.,338 Div. Vosges(Fr.) 9.-11.4.44	MURDER	FR.
KALLWEIT, Fritz	158531	M		30	Hitler Youth, KL.Javenitz Gardelegen(Ger.)	MURDER	U.S.
KALMBACH	250876	M	Ger.		Farmer,Civilian,Egenhausen(Ger.) 18.3.43	MURDER	POL.
KALON	306687	M	Ger.		Pvt.,331 Pioneer Bn.,331 Inf.Div.,Mijnheerenland(Neth.) 5.45	PILLAGE	NETH.
KAISKI, Jean	254385	M			SS-Sgt.,SS Charleval(Fr.) 13.2.44	MURDER	FR.
KALSTEISS see KALTSEISS (Jos. or Sepp)	29808						
KALT	260174	M	Ger.		C.C.Location 25,Bleichenneg,Dachau(Ger.) 42-44	BRUTALITY	FR.
KALTENBERG	172472	M			Civilian,Org.Todt,C.C.Muhldorf-Ampfing(Ger.) 6.44-4.45	MISC.CRIMES	U.S.
KALTENBERGER	300961	M	Ger.		SS-Hptsturmfhr., Official of SD Prag,Oswiecim-Birkenau(Pol.) 39-45	MURDER	CZECH.
KALTENBRUNNER	301572	M			Dr.,C.C.Mauthausen(Aust.) 40-45	MURDER	BEL.
KALTENBRUNNER, Ernest	62472	M	Ger.		Pvt., SS,Head of the Gestapo	MURDER	UNWCC.
KALTENBRUNNER, Franz	257307	M	Ger.	8.08	Crim.-Secretary,Gestapo,Tabor-Boshima(Czech.) 2.-5.45	MISC.CRIMES	CZECH.
KALTENBRUNNER, Roland	145211	M	Ger.		Clerk,C.C.Mauthausen(Aust.) 41-45	TORTURE	U.S.
KALTOFEN, Hans Heinrich	194202	M	Ger.	25.4.09	SS-Hptsturmfhr., SS and Pol.Panz.Gren.Regt.1,Zbydnjow(Pol.)24.-25.6.44	MURDER	POL.
KALTSEISS (Joseph or Sepp) or Kalsteiss	29808	M	Ger.	10	Uschfhr., Kriminal-Assist.,Gestapo,SD,Clermont-Ferrand(Fr.) 43-44	MURDER	FR.
KALUS	62524	M	Ger.		Pvt.,Army,Halberstadt(Ger.)	TORTURE	U.S.
KALUS	161887	M			SS-Usturmfhr.,SS,Mannheim(Ger.)	MURDER	U.S.
KALVA	630	M	Ger.	95	Sgt.,Army,Inf.	TORTURE	CAN.
KALVEIT	252435	M			Ogfr.,C.C.Ellrich,Nordhausen(Ger.)	MURDER	U.S.
KALZ	133816	M			SS-Oschfhr., KL.Weimar and Buchenwald(Ger.)	MURDER	U.S.
KAM	251100	M	Ger.		SS-Kapo,C.C.Neuengamme(Ger.)	INTERR.	BEL.
KAMAKARIS, Nicolaus	134878	M			Civilian	WITNESS	U.S.
KAMANN	254986	M			Guard,Uschfhr.,C.C.Auschwitz(Pol.)	INTERR.	FR.
KAMAS, Joseph	167088	M			W.O.,Gend.Luneville,Maixe(Fr.) 16.8.44	MURDER	FR.
KAMAUR	301760	M	Ger.		Uschfhr.,Builder, C.C.Auschwitz(Pol.) from 40	MURDER	FR.
KAMBACH, Walter	161504	M	Ger.	09	SS-Hptsturmfhr., Waffen-SS, C.C.Buchenwald(Ger.)	WITNESS	U.S.
KAMEID, Ewald	137055	M			Steimke(Ger.) 22.2.45	TORTURE	U.S.
KAMEITH, Paul	158533	M			W.O.,Volkssturm Bn.,Gardelegen(Ger.) 10.-14.4.45	MURDER	U.S.
KAMENZ	145182	M	Ger.	95	Bank-Direktor Posen(Pol.) 42	MISC.CRIMES	U.S.
KAMERER or KAMER	157789	M			Lt.,Army,Etobon Chenebier(Fr.) 27.9.44	MURDER	FR.
KAMERICH or KAMMERICH	252436	M			Pvt.,C.C.Ellrich,Nordhausen(Ger.)	MURDER	U.S.
KAMHOLZ, Werner	161503	M	Ger.	07	Doctor,SS-Sturmoannfhr.,Waffen-SS,C.C.Buchenwald(Ger.)	MISC.CRIMES	U.S.
KAMIETH	167090	M	Ger.		Opl.,Gend.,Montigny en Vesoul(Fr.)	MURDER	FR.
KAMILLO	301503	M	Ger.		Employee, C.C.Buchenwald(Ger.) 16.5.38-9.10.43	MURDER	BEL.
KAMIN, Alfred	137470	M	Ger.	19.9.07	Kapo,KL.Flossenburg,Regensburg,Lebenau-Laufen. 3.-4.45	MURDER	U.S.
KAMINCHECK	257632	M	Ger.		Officer,14 Regt."Flak",2 or 11 Btty,Finistère(Fr.) 7.-8.44	MURDER	FR.
KAMINSKI or KAMINSKY, Alfons	259356	M	Ger.	18.8.01	Kapo, German Prisoner C.C.Auschwitz(Pol.) 41-45	MURDER	FR.
KAMINSKI, Ludwig	145813	M	Ger.		Civilian,Ermsleben(Ger.)	WITNESS	U.S.
KAMINSKY	189981	M	Ger.	16	SS-Schfhr.,SS-Totenkopf-Stand.,Brest Litowsk,Brzesc Bugiem(Pol.) 10.41	MURDER	POL.
KAMINSKY	255604	M	Ger.		Chief of Personnel, Berliner Paketfahrt Speditions-Lagerhaus,Berlin-Middelburg (Ger.) 10.43-17.6.44	INTERR.	NETH.
KAMINSKY see KAMINSKI	259356						
KAMINSKY, Kurt	251693	M	Ger.		N.C.O.,Army,Nereziace on the Island of Brac(Yugo.) 44	PILLAGE	YUGO.
KAMLAH, Willi	139821	M	Ger.	02	Pvt.,Geheime Feldpolizei,Gruppe 713	MURDER	U.S.
KAMLEI, Peter	185982	M	Ger.		Civilian,Wittenberg(Ger.) 8.44	MURDER	U.S.
KAMMBACH	194029	M	Ger.		Sgt.,SS,C.C.Buchenwald(Ger.) 42-45	TORTURE	U.S.
KAMMENADO or KAMMENDO	125709	M	Ger.		Sgt.,Stalag 183 C.C.Salonica(Grc.) 7.-8.41	TORTURE	U.K.
KAMMER	192881	M			Hauptwachtmeister,Schupo,C.C.Falstad near Drontheim(Nor.) 4.43-3.44	MURDER	NOR.
KAMMERER	301761	M	Ger.		Lt.,S.P.15201,Etobon,Chenebier(Hte.-Saone)(Fr.) 27.9.44	MURDER	FR.
KAMMERER, Alphonse	261756	M	Ger.		Driver,Gestapo Amiens,Gentelles(Fr.) 6.-8.44	MURDER	FR.
KAMMERER, Hans	131451	M	Ger.		C.C.,Senior Block 16,Mauthausen(Aust.)	MURDER	U.S.
KAMMERICH see KAMRICH	252436						
KAMMLER	39777	M	Ger.		Army,Oberstabsarzt,Dieburg(Ger.) 11.40-4.44	MISC.CRIMES	U.K.
KAMMLER	102979	M		06	Dr.Ing.,SS-Ogruppenfhr., KL.Warstein,Suttrop(Ger.)20.-21.or 22.3.45	MURDER	U.S.
KAMMLER	133825	M			SS-Bdefhr.,C.C.Buchenwald(Ger.)	TORTURE	U.S.
KAMMLER	161502	M	Ger.	00	SS-Gruppenfhr.,SS Wirtsch.-Verw.-Hauptamt,C.C.Buchenwald(Ger.)	WITNESS	U.S.
KAMMLER	187862	M			SS-Bdefhr.,C.C.Buchenwald(Ger.) 41-4.45	MURDER	BEL.,CZECH.
KAMMLER	251113	M	Ger.		Major-Gen.,Chief of works in C.C.Mauthausen(Aust.)	TORTURE	BEL.
KAMMLER, Hans	185999	M	Ger.	01	Dr.,SS-Ogruppenfhr.,W.V.H.A.,Camp Dora(Ger.) 40-45	MURDER	U.S.,FR.
KAMMRAD, Robert	132212	M			Civilian Dentist	MISC.CRIMES	U.S.
KAMOELZ, Werner	161501	M	Ger.	10	SS-Guard,Regt.C.C.Buchenwald(Ger.)	WITNESS	U.S.
KAMP	162559	M	Ger.	20	SS-Schfhr.,Enschede(Neth.)	MURDER	U.K.
KAMP	255598	M			Lagerfuehrer, C.C.Buchenwald(Ger.)	MURDER	U.S.
KAMPE	142090	M	Ger.	15	SS-Osturmfhr.,SS,C.C.Dachau(Ger.) 40-45	MURDER	POL.
KAMPE	191459	M	Ger.		SS-Usturmfhr.,SS,C.C.Sachsenhausen-Oranienburg(Ger.) 39-4.45	MURDER	POL.
KAMPE, Hans	161500	M	Ger.	10	Osturmfhr.,Kdo.-Amt,C.C.Buchenwald(Ger.) 39-45	MISC.CRIMES	U.S.,POL.,U.K.
KAMPE, Hermann	441	M	Ger.	15	Usturmfhr.,C.C.Dachau,Sachsenhausen(Ger.),9.41	SUSPECT	FR.
KAMPE, Rudolf	157790	M	Ger.	99	Bn.-Cmdt.,Volkssturm,C.C.Javenitz and Gardelegen(Ger.) 10.-14.4.45	MURDER	U.S.
KAMPER see KAMPFER	253722						
KAMPER, Gustav	140908	M		17	SS-Osturmfhr.,KL.Breendonck(Bel.)	TORTURE	BEL.
KAMPERT, Wilhelm	305438	M	Ger.	14.4.10	558 Gren.Regt.,13 Coy.,Brnay-en-Artois Pas-de-Calais(Fr.) 1.9.44	MURDER	FR.
KAMPF	146846	M	Ger.		Chief SD,Annecy(Fr.) 44	MURDER	FR.
KAMPF	194028	M	Ger.		SS-Usturmfhr.,SS,C.C.Buchenwald(Ger.) 42-45	TORTURE	U.S.
KAMPF, Joachim	251690	M		11	Capt.,SD,Police,Fiume(It.) 44-45	TORTURE	YUGO.
KAMPF, Wilhelm	189084	M	Ger.		Crim.-Assist.,Gestapo,Brno(Czech.) 39-45	MURDER	CZECH.
KAMPFER	193477	M	Ger.		Engineer,C.C.Buchenwald(Ger.) 42-45	MISC.CRIMES	U.S.
KAMPFER see KEMPFER	194024						
KAMPFER or KAMPER	253722	M	Ger.		SS-Osturmfhr.,Abt.5,Sipo,Bruessel(Bel.)	INTERR.	BEL.
KAMPFMUELLER	192092	M	Ger.		Employee,Gestapo,Klatovy(Czech.) 39-45	MURDER	CZECH.

KAM-KAR

NAME	C.R.FILE NUMBER	SEX	NATIO-NALITY	DATE OF BIRTH	RANK OCCUPATION UNIT PLACE AND DATE OF CRIME	REASON WANTED	WANTED BY
KAMPIN	124963	M	Ger.		Member, Gestapo, C.C. Bremen-Farge (Ger.) 6.43	TORTURE	U.K.
KAMPIN (or CAMPIAN)	305545	M	Ger.		Guard, SS or Gestapo, Staff at C.C.Bremen-Farge (Ger.) 1.43-4.43	MURDER	U.K.
KAMPMANN, Fritz	162640	M	Ger.		General-Superintendant, "Adolf Mine", C.C.Merkstein (Ger.) 42-44	MURDER	U.S.
KAMPRAT, Hans-Georg	253107	M	Ger.	1.10.25	Flyer, Air Force, C.C.Ellrich-Nordhausen (Ger.)	MURDER	U.S.
KAMPS	161509	M	Ger.	00	Uschfhr., Kommandoamt, C.C. Buchenwald (Ger.)	MISC.CRIMES	U.S.
KAMPS	251661	M	Ger.	00	Capt., Le Pirou (Fr.) 40-42	PILLAGE	FR.
KAMPS, Ted	254652	M	Ger.		Pvt., Parachute-Pioneer Bn. L 60191 A of the 6 Parade-Div., Mijnsheerenland, Oud Beierland (Neth.) 4.5.45	MURDER	NETH.
KAMRAT	162560	M	Ger.		Director, Erla-Werke, Arbeitslager, Johann Georgenstadt (Ger.) 42-45	TORTURE	FR.
KAMRICH	261686	M	Ger.		Official, Luxembourg (Lux.)	WITNESS	LUX.
KAMSTIESS	258166	M	Ger.		Cpl., 2.Coy. Signal Troops, Bolnes (Neth.) 8.5.45	INTERR.	NETH.
KAMJS, Iwan	183755	M			SS-Mann, 4.SS-Totenkopf-Sturmbann, C.C.Dora-Nordhausen, Auschwitz (Ger., Pol.) 43-45	WITNESS	U.S.
KANBLER, Adolf	302051	M	Ger.		SS-Wachtmeister, SS-Slave Labour Camp, Falstad (Nor.) 42 and 43	MURDER	YUGO.
KANC, Georg	179727	M	Ger.		Guard, SS Pol. Regt., Sajmiste, Zemun, Belgrad (Yugo.) 28.4.43	MURDER	YUGO.
KANCHESTER (or KANCHUSTER)	9668	M	Ger.		SS-Osturmfhr., C.C. Breedonck (Bel.) 12.42	TORTURE	BEL.
KANDERS	1707	M			Lt., 1049.Regt.12. Normandie (Fr.) 9.6.44	MURDER	U.K.
KANDZIORA	252362	M	Ger.		Cpl., Seclin (Fr.) 8.44	WITNESS	FR.
KANGROSS	191890	M			Inspector, Pol., Gravendorf (Aust.)	MURDER	U.S.
KANICKIE	173236	M		02	Sgt., 814. Landesschuetzen-Bn., Poznan (Pol.) 6.41	TORTURE	U.K.
KANIKIE	128850	M			Sgt., Camp Wickenham (Ger.) 5.-6.41	TORTURE	U.K.
KANISH	102978	M	Ger.		Pvt., Camp-Leader, Stalag IX C, C.C.Rentsmuehle. 12.41-12.42	TORTURE	U.K.
KANITZLER	185984	M	Ger.		Rapportfhr., SS, C.C.Dora, Nordhausen (Ger.)	MURDER	BEL.
KANNENGIESSER, Josef	193058	M		17.10.00	Ex-convict, Ministry of Justice, Feldstraflager, Finmark (Nor.) 42-45	WITNESS	NOR.
KANNSCHUSTER	131449	M	Ger.		SS-Osturmfhr., SS, C.C. Mauthausen (Aust.)	MURDER	U.S., FR.,U.K.
KANNSCHUSTER	193475	M	Ger.		SS-Hptsturmfhr., C.C. Buchenwald (Ger.) 42-45	MISC.CRIMES	U.S.
KANNSCHUSTER	250896	M	Ger.		SS-Osturmbannfhr., C.C. Dachau (Ger.)	INTERR.	BEL.
KANOSKA	251662	M	Ger.		Gestapo, Lille (Fr.) 40-44	MURDER	FR.
KANTEL	153328	M	Ger.		Rottenfhr., SS, C.C. Oswiecim (Pol.) 1.45	MURDER	POL.
KANTNER	162639	M	Ger.	18	Sgt., Guard, 610.Landesschuetzen-Bn., Stalag XX B, Altfelde (Ger.) 7.44	WITNESS	U.K.
KANTSCUSTER	142089	M	Ger.		Lt., SS, C.C. Dachau (Ger.)	MURDER	U.S.
KANUTSKI (or KARNTZKIE) Artbur	257631	M		25	SS-Guard, C.C. Mihldorf area (Ger.)	MURDER	U.S.
KANZ, Herbert	1708	M			Cpl., Army, 2.Jagd-Kom.245.Div., 935.Inf.Regt. (Fr.) 44	MURDER	U.K.
KANZLE	157791	M	Ger.		Cpl., 398.Landesschuetzen-Bn. C.C.Schoenberg near Beuthen (Ger.)17.5.44	MURDER	U.K.
KANZY	67814	M	Ger.		Dr., Civilian, C.C. Gleima (Ger.) 3.45	TORTURE	U.K.
KAFER, Otto	254584	M	Ger.		SS-Oschfhr., C.C. Auschwitz-Birkenau (Pol.) 1.42	MURDER	YUGO.
KAPERS	260173	M	Ger.		Sgt., 1.Geb.Jaeger Regt.d.Res., Massif du Vercors, Isere and Drome (Fr.) 7.-8.44	SUSPECT	FR.
KAPFENBERGER	255158	M	Ger.		Capt., 1.Coy. Pion.Bn.46, Budinci (Yugo.) 9.43	MURDER	YUGO.
KAPITAN, Franz	189085	M		14.11.01	Employee, Gestapo, Brno (Czech.) 39-45	MURDER	CZECH.
KAPITAN, Karl	162564	M	Ger.		W.O., Gestapo, Brive (Fr.) 44	MURDER	FR.
KAPITZA	39778	M			Officer, Army. 5.43	TORTURE	U.K.
KAPLAN (or KAPPLAN or KAPPLAAN)	24875	M	Ger.		Gestapo, C.C.Koeln-Klingelpuetz (Ger.) 45	TORTURE	U.S.
KAPLANEK	253106	M			Camp Rottleberode, Nordhausen (Ger.)	MURDER	U.S.
KAPMAYER	301762	M	Ger.		Rottenfhr., Member of the SS-Institute of Hygiene, C.C.Auschwitz (Pol.) 40-45	MURDER	FR.
KAPP	259204	M	Ger.	95	Chief of "Kapo", C.C. Dachau (Ger.) 42-44	MISC.CRIMES	YUGO.
KAPPE	131448	M			Dr., SS-Osturmfhr., Dentist, Mauthausen (Aust.) 41	MURDER	U.S.
KAPPE, Otto	102977	M	Ger.	97	Army, Hildesheim near Hannover (Ger.)	WITNESS	U.S.
KAPPE, Otto	151968	M	Ger.		Civilian, Aderstedt (Ger.) 12.9.44	WITNESS	U.S.
KAPPEL	253105	M			Gewehrfhr., Camp Dora, Nordhausen (Ger.)	MURDER	U.S.
KAPPER	186280	M	Ger.		Uschfhr., SS, C.C. Auschwitz (Pol.) 43-44	MURDER	U.S.
KAPPES, Ferdinand	172473	M			SS-Mann, SS, C.C.Muehldorf-Ampfing (Ger.) 6.44-4.45	MURDER	U.S.
KAPPES, Paul	187620	M	Ger.	29	Civilian, "Hitler Youth", Aachen (Ger.)9.8.44	TORTURE	U.S.
KAPPLAAN (see KAPLAN)	24875						
KAPPLI, Artur	149495	M	Ger.		Cpl., SS, C.C. Schoerzingen (Ger.)	MISC.CRIMES	FR.
KAPPUHN, Fritz	186279	M	Ger.		Civilian, Genthin (Ger.) 2.44	MURDER	U.K.
KAPREHITZKI, Hermann	193359	M	Ger.		Pvt., 3.Bau Pion.Bn., C.C. Narvik (Nor.) 9.43	WITNESS	NOR.
KAPS	143156	M	Ger.	15	T-Sgt., SS, C.C. Lublin (Pol.) 42-43	TORTURE	U.S.
KAPS	193474	M	Ger.		SS-Uschfhr., C.C.Buchenwald (Ger.) 42-45	MISC.CRIMES	U.S.
KAPS	301419	M	Ger.		Member of S.D. Mont Lucon, Chappes,Louroux, Hodement (Allier) (F..)7.44	MURDER	FR.
KAR	172475	M	Ger.	10 - 15	Civilian, C.C. Muehldorf-Ampfing (Ger.) 6.44-4.45	MURDER	U.S.
KARAS	126733	M	Ger.	00	Lt., Gestapo, Nancy (Fr.)	TORTURE	FR.
KARASCH	160855	M			General (Bde.-Leader), SS, Beneschau (Czech.) 4.45	MURDER	U.S.
KARASCH	254647	M	Ger.		SS-Oberfhr., SS Trainingfield, Benesow (Czech.) 42-45	MISC.CRIMES	CZECH.
KARATKIN	301329	M			Member, Gestapo at Trencin, C.C.Auschwitz-Birkenau (Pol.) 39-45	MURDER	CZECH.
KARAUS, Erich	145833	M			Rottenfhr., 1.SS Panz.Div., 6.SS Panz.Gren.Regt. 2, Paris (Fr.)	MURDER	U.S.
KARAUSE (see KRAUS)	125658						
KARBIENER, Nikolaus	183742	M	Ger.	97	SS-Mann, 31.SS Gren.Inf.Div. C.C.Dora, Nordhausen, Dachau (Ger.)	TORTURE	U.S.
KARBIENER, Wilhelm	253104	M			SS-Sturmmann, C.C.Bodungen, Nordhausen (Ger.)	MURDER	U.S.
KARBUS, Laurenz	256886	M	Ger.	1. 6.98	Hptsturmfhr., State Service, SS, Gestapo-Employee, Prague (Czech.)40-45	PILLAGE	CZECH.
KARBUS, Marie (nee MUSIL)	256890	F	Ger.	14. 9.11	Member, Gestapo, Prague (Czech.) 40-45	MURDER	CZECH.
KARCHENVSKI	186155	M			CC-Chief, C.C.Dora-Nordhausen (Ger.)	TORTURE	FR.
KARCHER, Wilhelm	62525	M	Ger.	95	Civ., NSKK, Member NSDAP, Gernsbach (Ger.) 6.44	MURDER	U.S.
KARELL, Ruppert	253118	M	Ger.	13. 5.97	Pvt., Camp Dora, Nordhausen (Ger.)	MURDER	U.S.
KARER, Karl	122615	M	Ger.		Pvt., Army, Husum (Ger.) 21.4.45	MURDER	SOV.UN.
KARG, Fritz	174110	M	Ger.	02	Civ. Production engineer, Fella-Works, Arbeitslager Feucht (Ger.) 40-45	TORTURE	U.S.
KARG, Hans	121546	M	Ger.		W.O.Sen., Feldgendarmerie No.624, Avallon (Fr.) 16.3.44	MURDER	FR.
KARG, Wilhelm	260002	M	Ger.	90	Hptsturmfhr., Crim.secretary, Gestapo, Pilsen, Bohemia (Czech.) 39-40	INTERR.	CZECH.
KARGER	183580	M			SS-Mann, 4.SS-Totenkopf-Sturmbann, C.C.Dora-Nordhausen (Ger.) 43-45	WITNESS	U.S.
KARGER	195488	M	Ger.		Osturmfhr., SS, C.C.Sachsenhausen (Ger.) 37-44	MURDER	BEL.
KARGER	250897	M	Ger.		SS-Osturmfhr., C.C.Neuengamme (Ger.)	INTERR.	BEL.
KARGER, Karl	253737	M	Ger.		Hptwachtmeister, Schutzpol-Jagdstaffel, Lidice (Czech.)10.5.42	MURDER	CZECH.

KAR-KAS

NAME	C.R.FILE NUMBER	SEX	NATIO-NALITY	DATE OF BIRTH	RANK OCCUPATION UNIT PLACE AND DATE OF CRIME	REASON WANTED	WANTED BY
KARGER, Otto	189086	M	Ger.	20. 5.13	Crim.Asst., Gestapo, Brno (Czech.) 39-45	MURDER	CZECH.
KARH	301040	M	Ger.		Guard, Labour Camp, Lahde-Weser (Ger.) 43-45	MURDER	BEL.
KARI	189396	M	Ger.		Zugwachtmeister, Police, C.C. Tromsoe (Nor.) 18.6.42	MISC.CRIMES	NOR.
KARK see " La Rouquine "	147548						
KARKHOFF or KHARKOFF	254646	M	Ger.	05	Lt., SD or Feldgend., Bardi (It.) 3.6.44	MURDER	U.K.
KARKOWSKI	305985	M			Colonel-Cmdt., of Camp Oflag VO-B, successor to Colonel Brinkort Doessel nr.Warburg (Ger.) till 45	MURDER	POL.
KARL	9699	M	Ger.		Dr., SS-Untersturmfhr., Gestapo-Chef-SS, Prerov (Czech.) 39-44	MURDER	CZECH.
KARL	62527	M	Ger.	07	SS-Cpl., SS-Medical, C.C. Hinzert (Ger.)	TORTURE	U.S.
KARL	131447	M	Ger.		Leader, Officer of Block 19, C.C. Mauthausen (Austr.) 41-45	MURDER	U.S.
KARL	137092	M	Ger.		Pvt., Arbeits-Kdo., E 10, KL. Jacobswalde (Ger.) 7.40	TORTURE	U.K.
KARL	147041	M			Agent, Gestapo, Joerde, Dortmund (Ger.)	MURDER	U.S.
KARL	167956	M	Ger.		Member, Dr.,Einsatzstab Rosenberg (Fr.) 40-44	PILLAGE	FR.
KARL	195487	M	Ger.		Kapo, C.C. Mauthausen (Austr.) 11.5.42-10.5.45	MURDER	BEL.
KARL, Alexander(Nickn.:"Spitz")	262172	M	Ger.	25. 9.	Hschfhr., Gestapo, Rennes (Fr.) 43-44	MISC.CRIMES	FR.
KARL, Andreas	167702	M	Ger.		Pvt., Army, 9.Regt.Reserve Gend.I.Coy., Magny d' Anigon (Fr.) 18.9.44	MURDER	FR.
KARL, Anton	141317	M	Ger.	95		WITNESS	U.K.
KARL, Antony	257453	M	Ger.		Sgt., Feldgend., Zajecar (Yugo.) 41-44	MURDER	YUGO.
KARL, Michael	145804	M	Ger.	18. 9.09	Civilian, Country-Farmer-leader-Employee, Kreis Freising,Altenkirchen (Ger.) 13.6.44	MURDER	U.S.
KARL, Paul	162638	M	Ger.		Chief, Feldgend., Manlay (Fr.) 29.7.44	PILLAGE	FR.
KARLE	62528	M	Ger.		Cpl., Inf.Div. 110, 255. Regt. 8.Coy. 2.Bn., Rzhew (Sov.Un.) 6.42	MURDER	U.S.
KARLER, Karl	195629	M	Ger.		Pvt., I. Pz.Coy., Ligneuville (Bel.) 17.-19.12.44	INTERR.	U.S.
KARLES	39649	M	Ger.		Pvt., Inf. Ers., Bernay, Champagne (Fr.) 9.41	WITNESS	U.N.W.C.C.
KARLITSCHEK	250318	M			SS-Unterscharfhr., C.C. Buchenwald (Ger.)	INTERR.	FR.
KARLS	139756	M	Ger.		Stabsintendant, Stalag X-B, C.C. Sandbostel (Ger.) 1.-5.45	TORTURE	U.S.
KARLSBERGER, Hans	305441	M	Ger.		Umsiedlungs-Commissar at Jesenice, Slovenia (Yugo.) 11.41-3.43	INTERR.	YUGO.
KARLSBERGER, Milica	305442	F	Ger.		Wife, Jesenice, Slovenia (Yugo.) 11.41-3.43	PILLAGE	YUGO.
KARLSRATH see KARLSTAD	162245						
KARLSTADT or KARLSRATH	162245	M	Ger.		Officer, SS-Totenkopfverband, Stockem (Bel.) 3.9.44	MURDER	BEL.
KARLSTAEDTER, Leopold	178961	M	Ger.		Guard, Prison, Ebrach (Ger.)	MURDER	CZECH.
KARLTMEYER	138238	M	Ger.		Oberfeldwebel, Army, St.Martin, Nigelle-Chartres (Fr.) 8.-14.12.43	MURDER	FR.
KARMANN, Simon	24876	M	Ger.		Pvt., Fallschirmjaeger Regt., Roermond (Neth.) 11.44-1.45	TORTURE	U.S.
KARMAZIN, Franz	254573	M	Ger.	1. 9.01	Civilian, Engineer, employee, Bratislava (Czech.) 39 - 45	MURDER	CZECH.
KARNA	130099	M	Ger.		Foreman, Arbeitskdo., 107 GW, Graz (Austr.) 10.44-3.45	TORTURE	U.K.
KARNATZ	172476	M			SS-Scharfhr., C.C. Muehldorf, Ampfing (Ger.) 6.44-4.45	MURDER	U.S.
KARNER, Franz	250892	M			Pvt., Furth (Ger.) 23.9.44	MURDER	FR.
KARNEZKIE, Arthur see KANUTSKI	257631						
KARNO	151330	M	Ger.		Lt., SA, Leoben (Austr.) 7.44	TORTURE	U.K.
KAROCO, Otto	443	M	Ger.		Pvt., Gestapo, Member, Valenciennes (Fr.) 43-44	MURDER	FR.
KAROL	195486	M	Ger.		Kapo, C.C. Mauthausen (Aust.) 11.5-42 - 10.5.45	MURDER	BEL.
KAROVA	254658	F	Ger.		SS-Woman, C.C. Ravensbrueck (Ger.)	BRUTALITY	FR.
KAROW, Hans	183579	M			SS-Man, 4.SS Totenkopf-Stuba, Nordhausen-Dora-Mittelbau (Ger.) 43-45	WITNESS	U.S.
KARPER	302052	M	Ger.		Member, of the Sicherheitsdienst, Almelo District (Neth.) 9.44-2.45	MURDER	NETH.
KARPINKE	188529	M		00	Lt., Gestapo, Brussels (Bel.) 8.41	TORTURE	U.K.
KARR, August	195077	M	Ger.		SS-Untersturmfhr., Raeumungs-Aktion der Army, Arnhem (Neth.) 1.-2.44	PILLAGE	NETH.
KARR, Georges	260121	M	Ger.		Block-Chief, C.C. Dachau (Ger.) 42.44	BRUTALITY	FR.
KARRENBAUER, Reinhold	189600	M	Ger.	10.12.04	Civilian, Werden-Saar (Ger.) 7.8.44	WITNESS	U.S.
KARRER	29777	M	Ger.		Major, Geb.Armee Korps 19, Fismark (Nor.) 11.44	MURDER	NOR.
KARRHER, F.	173722	M	Ger.		Kreisleiter,Hauptgemeinschaftsleiter, NSDAP, Karlsruhe (Ger.) 44	TORTURE	FR.
KARS	166066	M			SD Mont Lucon, Chappes (Fr.) 28.7.44	TORTURE	FR.
KARS	255599	M			Unterscharfhr., C.C. Buchenwald (Ger.)	MURDER	U.S.
KARSCH	174664	M	Ger.	27. 8.07	Cpl., Army, Vannes (Fr.) 42-44	TORTURE	FR.
KARST	253116	M			SS-Rottenfhr., Camp Wieda, Nordhausen (Ger.)	MURDER	U.S.
KARST, Ludwig	157793	M	Ger.	07	Cpl., Army, Remount School, Gardelegen (Ger.) 10.-14.4.45	MURDER	U.S.
KARSTEN see CARSTEN	302053						
KARTE, Karl	120631	M	Ger.		Army, C.C. St. Leonhard (Austr.)	BRUTALITY	U.K.
KARTLE	146844	M	Ger.		Pvt., SS-Pz.Div. "Das Reich", Tulle (Fr.) 44	MURDER	FR.
KARTSCH see KARTZCH	39804						
KARTZCH or KARTSCH	39804	M	Ger.		Adjutant, Army, N.C.O. Unite SP 15201, Chenebier (Fr.) 27.9.44	MURDER	FR.
KARUS	24877	M	Ger.		Sgt., Guard, SS, C.C. Lublin,Hinzert (Pol.,Ger.) 42-43	TORTURE	U.S.
KARUTZ, Gertrud	257233	F	Ger.	02 - 03	Typist, Abt. I, Sipo and SD-Anvers (Bel.) 40-45	SUSPECT	BEL.
KASANICKY, Johann	255277	M	Ger.	17. 9.08	Cmdt., C.C. Birkenau (Pol.) 39-45	MURDER	CZECH.
KASAR	172474	M	Ger.		SS-Pvt., C.C. Muehldorf, Ampfing (Ger.) 6.44-4.45	MURDER	U.S.
KASBERG, Herbert	252508	M			Pvt., C.C. Ellrich Nordhausen (Ger.)	MURDER	U.S.
KASCHE	39779	M	Ger.		Lt., (Oberlt.) Army, 1010. Mot. Gren.Regt. 6.Coy. 2.Bn. Loriet Orlenais (Fr.) 13.,14.8.44	MURDER	U.K.
KASCHE	155630	M	Ger.	95	Justice Secret. Justizministerium, Emsland (Ger.) 44	MURDER	U.S.
KASCHE	173700	M	Ger.		Lt., 1010. Pz.Regt.2.Bn., Chilleurs Aux Bois (Fr.) 13.,15.8.44	MURDER	U.K.
KASCHINSKI, Franz	252507	M			Rottenfhr., C.C. Ilfeld-Rottleberode, Nordhausen (Ger.)	MURDER	U.S.
KASCHKE, Julia	189601	F	Ger.		Teletypistin, Gestapo, Brno (Czech.) 39-45	WITNESS	CZECH.
KASCHUH, Heinz	127987	M	Ger.		Sgt., C.C. Auschwitz (Pol.)	MURDER	U.K.
KASE, Max	131446	M	Ger.		Leader, Officer of Block 15, C.C. Mauthausen (Austr.)	MURDER	U.S.
KASEBERG	9698	M	Ger.		SS, C.C. Natzweiler (Ger.) 14.3.42-4.8.42	TORTURE	CZECH.
KASEBERG	136234	M	Ger.		Sgt., Feldgend. Stenay (Fr.) 40-44,15.8.44	MURDER	FR.
KASER, Michael	137790	M	Ger.		Member, Gestapo, Wittlebacher (Ger.)	TORTURE	U.S.
KASIX, Johann	258085	M	Ger.	16. 6.26	Agent, Gestapo, Olomouc (Czech.) 41-44	MISC.CRIMES	CZECH.
KASOVA or KATSOVA, Greta	301330	F	Ger.		Member of the Gestapo at Nove Mesto-n - Vahom, C.C. Oswiecim-Birkenau (Pol.) 39-45	MURDER	CZECH.
KASPAR	124641	M			Pvt., Gunther Grube, SS, C.C. Auschwitz Oswiecim (Pol.) 1.44	MURDER	U.S.
KASPAR, Fritz	138195	M	Ger.		Polizier de la, Landwacht Pol. Ampen et Ostoennen (Ger.) 8.6.44	MURDER	FR.
KASPAR, Hubert	252509	M		19. 9.06	Pvt., C.C. Ellrich Nordhausen (Ger.)	MURDER	U.S.
KASPAR, Josef	189089	M	Ger.	23. 1.11	Crim.Asst., Gestapo, Brno (Czech.) 39-45	MURDER	CZECH.

KAS - KAT

NAME	C.R.FILE NUMBER	SEX	NATIO-NALITY	DATE OF BIRTH	RANK OCCUPATION UNIT. PLACE AND DATE OF CRIME	REASON WANTED	WANTED BY
KASPAR, Rapp	136237	M	Ger.		SS, C.C. Uckermark, Ravensbrueck (Ger.) 1.45	MURDER	FR.
KASPARD	122613	M	Ger.		SS-Gestapo de Chambery, Challes Les Eaux Et Arvin (Fr.)	MURDER	FR.
KASPARD	136236	M	Ger.		SS-Pvt., Chambery (Fr.)	MISC.CRIMES	FR.
KASPER, Johannes	195076	M	Ger.	15. 4.03	Civilian, Amsterdam, (Neth.)	MURDER	NETH.
KASPER	1408				Schfhr., SD.-Aussenkdo.,	MISC.CRIMES	U.K.
KASPER, Franz	255169	M	Ger.	19.10.96	Obergruppenfhr., S.A.,Railroad, Kromeriz (Czech.) 44-45	MISC.CRIMES	CZECH.
KASPER, Josef	254560	M	Ger.	19. 3.93	Factory Ingeneer, Civilian, Gestapo Agent, K.Dvur (Czech.) 44	MISC.CRIMES	CZECH.
KASPER, Rudolf	12401	M	Ger.		Head of the Verbindungsstelle German Staatsministry zu den Gewerkschaften 42-44	MURDER	CZECH.
KASPER, Rudolf	132070	M	Ger.		Civ., Protector Official of the Staatsministry in Prague Bohemia and Moravia (Czech.) 40-44	TORTURE	CZECH.
KASPERT	39776	M	Ger.		Lt., Army Caserne au College Condrillon a Dax (Fr.) 13.6.44	MURDER	FR.
KASPRIWIAK, Helene (nee SZYMANSKI)	261753	F	Ger.		Douai, (Fr.) 40-44	MURDER	FR.
KASSBERG (or KASZBERG)	301174	M	Ger.		Sgt., Major 54.Landst., Neth., SS, Bennekom, Ede (Neth.)25.3.-1.4.45	MURDER	NTH.
KASSECKERT	254372	M	Ger.		Hptschfhr., S.T.Mann, SD., Toulouse (Fr.) 11.42-10.44	MISC.CRIMES	FR.
KASSEN	194716	M	Ger.		Officer, Feldkommandantur 117, Rouen (Fr.) 43-44	WITNESS	FR.
KASSLER	124499	M	Ger.		Schfhr., SS., C.C. Sachsenhausen Oranienburg (Ger.) 42	MURDER	U.K.
KASSLER	138262	M	Ger.		Lt., SS Gestapo Section I Administration, Lyon (Fr,)	PILLAGE	FR.
KASSLER	139177	M			Baker, Civilian, Schollach (Ger.)	MURDER	U.S.
KASSLER	191464	M	Ger.		SS-Sgt., C.C. Sachsenhausen-Oranienburg (Ger.) 39-4.45	MURDER	POL.
KASSLER	300716	M	Ger.		Osturmfhr., SS-SD., Section I Administration Attignat,Ain (Fr.)15.6.44	MISC.CRIMES	FR.
KASSLER, Kastial	133820				SS-Oschfhr., C.C. Weimar Buchenwald (Ger.)	TORTURE	U.S.
KASSNER, Erich	133819	M	Ger.	05	Cpl., Geheime Feldpolizei, Gruppe 713	MURDER	U.S.
KASSNER, Karl	252510	M		30.10.14	Cpl., C.C. Harzungen Nordhausen (Ger.)	MURDER	U.S.
KASSOVIC, Jan	300038	M			Dr., Head, of the office of the Slovak Minister of the Interior, (Slov.)40-45	TORTURE	CZECH.
KASTEL	162566	M	Ger.		Camp official, Col., Army Stalag V A, Ludwigsburg (Ger.) 45	MISC.CRIMES	U.K.
KASTELLIOU	186565	M	Ger.		Cpl., Army, Kastelliou, (Gre.) 6.-7.43	MURDER	GRC.
KASTEN (or KASTNER)	102975	M	Ger.	17	Civ., Gebiets Kommissar, C.C.Kowel (Sov.Un.).5.6.-9.42	MURDER	SOV.UN.
KASTEN	131461	M	Ger.		5.Fallschirmjaeger Rgt., (Nachrichtenzug), Quaregnon (Bel.) 44	MURDER	BEL.
KASTEN	251683	M	Ger.		Sgt., Fieldpolice, (Bel.)	INTERR.	BEL.
KASTEN, Billy	174665	M	Ger.	19.5.97	Cpl., Army, Vannes (Fr.) 42-44	TORTURE	FR.
KASTENBERGER	11254	M	Ger.		Pvt., 110. Pz.Gren.Rgt., 2. Coy., Albine (Fr.) 44	MURDER	FR.
KASTENING, Wilhelm (alias "BOUDIN BLANC")	194715	M	Ger.	20	Cpl., Army, Rouen (Fr.) 41	TORTURE	FR.
KASTENS	300789	M	Ger.		Pvt., 1.Aufkl.Abt.3.Coy.,2.Column.XV.Div.of the Afrika Korps Saint L'eger, (Arlon) 5.9.44	MISC.CRIMES	BEL.
KASTL, Josef	31222	M	Ger.		Landgerichtsdirektor, Public official, Litomerice (Czech.) 21.2.40	MURDER	BEL.
KASTLE	252340	M			SS-Hptschfhr., C.C. Nordhausen (Ger.)	MURDER	U.S.
KASTNER (see KASTEN)	102975						
KASTNER	251110	M	Ger.		SS-Oschfhr., Official of Amt I or II of W.V.H.A., Zentrale Bauinspektion, Mauthausen (Aust.)	INTERR.	BEL.
KASTNER	252434	M			Pvt., C.C. Dora Nordhausen (Ger.)	MURDER	U.S.
KASTNER, Andreas	252433	M		7.11.06	Flyer, C.C. Ellrich Nordhausen (Ger.)	MURDER	U.S.
KASTNER, Kurt	187135	M			Civ., Miner, Arbeitskdo., Adolf Mine, Merkstein (Ger.) 43	WITNESS	U.S.
KASTNER, Ludwig	187134	M			Employee, Arbeitskdo., C.C. Merkstein (Adolf Mine),(Ger.) 11.44	WITNESS	U.S.
KASTNER, Max	134873	M			Civ., C.C. Ampfing (Ger.)	TORTURE	U.S.
KASTNER, Rudolf	186566	M	Ger.		Employee, Gestapo, Budejovice (Czech.) 39-45	MURDER	CZECH.
KASULKE, Anna	189088	F	Ger.		Clerk, Gestapo, Brno., (Czech.) 39-45	WITNESS	CZECH.
KASZ, Joseph, Daniel	167228	M			SS-Oschfhr., Hungarian SS, Kampfgruppe Ney, between Sur and Aka (Hung.) 7.3.45	MURDER	U.S.
KASZBERG (see KASSBERG)	301174						
KATCHER	250874	M	Ger.		Rottfhr., 1.SS Pz.Div.L.A.H. Malmedy (Bel.) 17.12.44	MURDER	U.S.
KATEE, Petrus Antonis Hermanius	300260		Ger.		Member, Former of the W-SS, of camp fire service and the camp Police C.C. Mauthausen (Aust.) 43-45	MISC.CRIMES	NTH.
KATERZNISKY, Miletislav	173672	M	Ger.		Prisoner No. 8516, C.C. Oswiecim (Pol.) 39-45	MURDER	CZECH.
KATHEK	189745	M	Ger.		Col., Germ.Flak Btty., Gondin (Ger.) 1.44	TORTURE	U.S.
KATHER, Erich	301504	M	Ger.	7. 1.92	SS-Schfhr., C.C. Buchenwald (Ger.) between 16.5.38 and 9.10.43	MURDER	BEL.
KATHREIN, Max (or KATREIN alias SCHNEIDER)	191782	M	Ger.	18	Official, Gestapo, Orleans (Fr.) 10.6.44	MURDER	FR.
KATSCHMAK, Karl	254373	M			SS-Sturmschfhr., Gestapo, Toulouse (Fr.) 11.42-8.44	MISC.CRIMES	FR.
KATSCHMARECK	191371	M		circa 00	Pvt., Air Force, Bau Bn., 132 III, Bardenfoss (Nor.)	MURDER	NOR.
KATSOVA (see KASOVA), Greta	301330						
KATTERLE	250898	M	Ger.		SS-Obersturmfhr., C.C. Neuengamme (Ger.) 40-44	MURDER	BEL.
KATTLER	130675	M			C.C. Mittelbau Dora Nordhausen (Ger.)	MURDER	U.S.
KATTWINKEL, Karl	252432	M			Cpl., C.C. Ellrich Nordhausen (Ger.)	MURDER	U.S.
KATZ	128989	M	Ger.	90	Lt., Col., Police Wiesbaden (Ger.) 3.2.45	MURDER	U.S.
KATZ	132540	M	Ger.		SD, Marseille (Fr.) 43-44	MISC.CRIMES	FR.
KATZ	191372	M	Ger.		Pvt., 184. Kgf., Arb.Bn., Bassis Tunnel (Nor.)	MURDER	NOR
KATZ	193358	M	Ger.		Lt., 505. Marine Art.Abt., Karihola and Kristiansund (Nor.) 43-45	TORTURE	NOR.
KATZ, Adolf	258974	M	Ger.	9. 3.99	SS-Brigadefhr., NSDAP.	INTERR.	U.S.
KATZ, Friedrich	306757	M	Ger.		German Policeman, Wiesbaden (Ger.) 2.2.45	BRUTALITY	U.S.
KATZ, Sandor	257630	M		06	ZellenaeltesterC.C. Muehldorf area, (Ger.)	MURDER	U.S.
KATZEMICH, Arthur	196204	M	Ger.	02	Usturmfhr., SD., Maison-Laffitte (Fr.) 15.12.41-10.6.44	TORTURE	FR.
KATZENBERGER	162562	M	Ger.		Policeman, Untermassfeld (Ger.) 41-45	MURDER	U.S.
KATZENELLENBOGEN	133818	M			Dr., C.C. Buchenwald (ger.)	TORTURE	U.S.
KATZMANN	445	M	Ger.		SS-Oberfhr., Police Leader, Radom (Pol.) 39-43	MURDER	POL.
KATZMANN, Emil	167503	M	Ger.	08	SS-Standartenfhr., SD, (Pol.) 43-45	MISC.CRIMES	U.S.
KATZMANN, Friedrich	145652	M	Ger.	00	Brigadefhr., Brig.General SS Chief of Police Radom (Pol.) 40-43	MURDER	U.S.
KATZMANN, Fritz	62474	M	Ger.		Regierungs-Comm., Germanisation of occup.territories officials	MISC.CRIMES	U.N.W.C.C.
	185992	M	Ger.	6. 5.06	General Major, SS Oberfhr., SS-and Policefhr., Distr.Radom and Lwow (Pol.) 39-40	MURDER	POL.
KATZMARECK	187133	M	Ger.		Civ., Factory Owner, Bad Durrenberg (Ger.) 43	TORTURE	U.K.
KATZMASKI	146843	M	Ger.		Soldier, SS Das Reich, 2. Comp., Panzer Div., Tulle (Fr.) 44	MURDER	FR.
KATZMUELLER, Willy (see KITZMULLER)	167082						

KAU-KEH

NAME	C.R.FILE NUMBER	SEX	NATIO-NALITY	DATE OF BIRTH	RANK OCCUPATION UNIT PLACE AND DATE OF CRIME	REASON WANTED	WANTED BY
KAU	62530	M	Ger.	01 - 05	Chief Construction Commander,O.T.,Constr.Works,Public-Official Bedburg (Ger.)	TORTURE	U.S.
KAUBE, Frantz	174669	M			Lt.,Alpinjg.,No.15,Narnhec (Fr.) 7.44	WITNESS	FR.
KAUDER, Bruno	129142	M	Ger.		Lt.,Dulag Luft,Navy,Frankfurt-Main,Obermursel (Ger.)5.43	TORTURE	U.K.
KAUF	141937	M	Ger.	15	Sgt.,Member,4 Coy.,427 Ober-Silesia Bn., NSDAP,Brausch,Konitz (Ger.) 20.1.45-4.45	MISC.CRIMES	U.K.
KAUF, Franz	195512	M	Ger.	11. 2.02	SS-Sgt.,Employee,SD.,Gestapo,Kolin (Czech.) 39-45	MURDER	CZECH.
KAUFER, Karl	172479	M	Ger.		Civilian,West Essen (Ger.) 1.45	MURDER	U.S.
KAUFFENBACH	24878	M	Ger.		Official,Gestapo,C.C.Klingelpuetz 1.-2.45	TORTURE	U.S.
KAUFFLER, S.D.G.	131445	M	Ger.		SS-Unterscharfhr.,SS,Mauthausen (Aust.) 41-45	MURDER	U.S.
KAUFFMANN, Karl	62475	M	Ger.		SS-Lt.General,Gauleiter and Statthalter,Hamburg,Sea-Shipping (Ger.)	TORTURE	UNWCC.
KAUFFMANN, Ludwig (or KAUFMANN)	187861	M			Pvt.,Gendarmerie,Zepperen,Limbourg (Bel.) 24.12.43	MURDER	BEL.
KAUFHOLT	252431	M			Pvt.,C.C.Mackenrode,Nordhausen (Ger.)	MURDER	U.S.
KAUFMAN	254840	M		06	Lt.,Paymaster,755 Rgt.,334 Inf.Div.,	INTERR.	U.S.
KAUFMAN, Moritz	132213	M	Ger.	95	Capt.,Stabsintendant,Army,Oflag III B,Hammelburg (Ger.) 44-45	MURDER	U.S.
KAUFMANN	12402	M			Capt.,SS Kommissar der Gestapo, Prag (Czech.) 39-44	TORTURE	CZECH.
KAUFMANN	124265	M	Ger.		Untersturmfhr.,SS-Pz.Div.1,SS-Pz.Rgt.1,2 Coy.,Malmedy (Bel.)17.12.44	MURDER	U.S.
KAUFMANN	130672	M			C.C.Dora Mittelbau,Nordhausen (Ger.)	MURDER	U.S.
KAUFMANN	183904	M			SS-Unterscharfhr.,4 SS-Totenkopf-Sturmbann,C.C.Dora Mittelbau Nordhausen (Ger.) 43-45	WITNESS	U.S.
KAUFMANN	187912	M			Crim.Commissar,SS,Gestapo,Prag (Czech.) 39-44	TORTURE	CZECH.
KAUFMANN	250311	M	Ger.		Doctor,Air-Force,C.C.Auschwitz (Pol.) 42-43	BRUTALITY	U.K.
KAUFMANN, Erhard	261811	M	Ger.		Staff Sgt.,Feldgendarmerie,Romilly sur Seine (Fr.) 10.6.44	MISC.CRIMES	FR.
KAUFMANN	194097	M	Ger.	30.10.08	Hauptwachtmeister,Sgt.,SS,Police,The Hague,Apeldoorn (Neth.)42-3.45	MISC.CRIMES	NETH.
KAUFMANN, Helmuth	251105	M	Ger.	21	Untersturmfhr.,Malmedy (Bel.) 17.12.44	MURDER	U.S.
KAUFMANN, Karl	126561	M	Ger.		Lt.,SS-Schupo-Officer,Saarbruecken (Ger.) 1.-2.45	MURDER	U.S.
KAUFMANN, Ludwig	167227	M	Ger.		Subordinate to Commandant,Feldgendarmerie,St.Trond (Bel.) 24.12.43	MURDER	BEL.
KAUFMANN, Ludwig (see KAUFFMANN)	187861						
KAUFMANN, Walter	301505	M	Ger.		SS-Oberscharfhr.,(No.10895),SS-Sgt.,SS,C.C.Buchenwald (Ger.)5.38-43	MURDER	BEL.
KAUFPANN, Leopold	131443	M	Ger.		Guard,C.C.Mauthausen (Aust.) 41-45	MURDER	U.S.
KAUL	11561	M			SS-Gruppenfhr.,hoehere SS and Pol.Fuehrer bei d.Reichsstatth. Wehrkr. 5,Wuerttemberg-Baden (Ger.) 41-42	MURDER	POL.
KAUL	177542	M	Ger.		Obersturmfhr.,SD.,Gestapo,Saarbruecken (Ger.)	MISC.CRIMES	UNWCC.
KAUL	188106	M			Major,General,SS,Police,Elsass (Fr.)	MURDER	POL.
KAULBACH	306688	M	Ger.		Pvt.,331 Pion.Bn.,331 Inf.Div.,Mijnheerenland (Neth.) 5.45	PILLAGE	NETH.
KAULIN	146708	M			T.Sgt.,SS,C.C.Flossenburg (Ger.)	MURDER	U.S.
KAULMANN, Heinz	145797	M		23	SS-Unterscharfhr.,Schleissheim (Ger.) 6.-9.44	MURDER	U.S.
KAUMANN	192035	M	Ger.		Col.,Army,Manebos en Lanester (Fr.) 9.8.44	MURDER	FR.
KAUMBACH	132214	M			Sgt.,Sicherungsrgt.,192,Mont Lucon (Fr.) 13.8.44	MURDER	U.S.
KAUMBACH	166392	M		09	Staff Sgt.,Police,H.Q.,Recoaro (It.) 1.45	INTERR.	U.S.
KAUNT	151333	M	Ger.		Doctor Med.,Civilian,Mosbach (Ger.)	MURDER	FR.
KAUPERT, Willy	192191	M	Ger.		Sgt.,Feldkommandantur,Feldgendarmerie,Malines,Antwerp (Bel.) 42	TORTURE	BEL.
KAUSSMANN	103340	M	Ger.		Leader,Gestapo,Leipzig (Ger.)	MISC.CRIMES	U.S.
KAUSZ	259092	M	Ger.		SS-Oberscharfhr.,SS,C.C.Dachau (Ger.) 2.43-45	MISC.CRIMES	YUGO.
KAUTHEN, Roger	255547	M	Ger.		Kapo,C.C.Neckargerach (Ger.) 5.44-6.44	BRUTALITY	FR.
KAUTZ	253721	M	Ger.		Employee,Abt.IV E,Sipo,Brussels (Bel.)	INTERR.	BEL.
KAUTZ, Wilhelm	134868	M	Ger.		Civilian,Efferen (Ger.) 2.10.44	WITNESS	U.S.
KAVAN, Karl	254655	M	Ger.	22.10.94	Ortsbauernfuehrer,Farmer,Civilian,NSDAP,Vranovska,Ves (Czech.) 38	INTERR.	CZECH.
KAVERMANN, Arthur	193061	M	Ger.	2.11.03	Ex Convict,Reichsjustizministerium,Feldstraflager,C.C.Finmark (Nor.)	WITNESS	NOR.
KAWAN, Alois	302054	M	Ger.		Custom-House-Officer,Operational Kommando,Lourdes,Custom-House 44	MURDER	FR.
KAWENZ	162565	M	Ger.		N.C.O.,Arbeitskommando E 232,C.C.Lauban (Ger.)	TORTURE	U.K.
KAYSER	194027	M	Ger.		Rottenfhr.,SS,C.C.Buchenwald (Ger.) 42-45	TORTURE	U.S.
KAYSER	234294	M	Ger.	88	Inspector,SD.,Gestapo,Sipo,Krefeld (Ger.) 1.45	MISC.CRIMES	U.S.
KAYSER, Cornelius (see KAISER)	170552						
KAYSER, Karl	192382	M	Ger.	05	SS-Hauptscharfhr.,SS,Rengsdorf (Ger.) 12.44	MURDER	U.S.
KAYSER, Walter	194714	M	Ger.		Sgt.,Kommandantur,Fornichet St.Marguerite (Fr.)	PILLAGE	FR.
KAZEN, Kristian	250320	M	Ger.		Pvt.,377 Jg.Rgt.,10 Coy.,Vinkt-Meigem (Bel.) 25.3.-5.40	MISC.CRIMES	BEL.
KAZIMIR	195075	M	Ger.		Camp-Leader,Employee,Hecker-Werke,Kriegs-Production,Heidenau (Ger.) 11. 2.45	MURDER	NETH.
KAZMIRZAK	188756	M	Ger.		Pvt.,Stalag VI J,C.C.Wickrath (Ger.) 14.10.42	MURDER	FR.
KEBEL, Johann	254596	M	Ger.		Employee,Gestapo,Jagodina (Yugo.) 15.2.44	INTERR.	YUGO.
KEBLERMANN (or KERBLERMAN)	252221	M			Capt.,Morbihan (Fr.) 18.6.44	MISC.CRIMES	FR.
KEBPERSKI	165386	M	Ger.		Sgt.,SS,Revin (Fr.) 6.44	MURDER	FR.
KEBSCH, Erich	186118	M			SS-Pvt.,4 SS-Totenkopf-Sturmbann,C.C.Dora Mittelbau,Nordhausen (Ger.) 43-45	WITNESS	U.S.
KECHLO	252430	M			Oberscharfhr.,C.C.Dora,Nordhausen (Ger.)	MURDER	U.S.
KECK	165385	M	Ger.		Sarrebourg (Fr.) 10.44	PILLAGE	FR.
KECK, Mathias	167086	M	Ger.		Cpl.,Feldgendarmerie,Montigny,Vesoul (Fr.) 16.7.44	MURDER	FR.
KEDOR, Johann	250321	M	Ger.		Major,377 Jg.Rgt., 2 Bn., F.P. 30305 A,Vinkt (Bel.) 25.-31.5.40	MISC.CRIMES	BEL.
KEEBITZ	194026	M	Ger.		SS,C.C.Buchenwald (Ger.) 42-45	TORTURE	U.S.
KEEK, Karl	164701	M	Ger.		SS-Sturmbannfhr., 10 SS-Pz.Div."Frundsberg"	MURDER	UNWCC.
KEEL	67036	M	Ger.		Cpl.,Command at Fort 14,714 Bn., C.C.Thorn,Lichnau (Pol.) 7.43-44	MURDER	U.K.
KEEN	133817	M			SS-Unterscharfhr.,C.C.Buchenwald (Ger.)	TORTURE	U.S.
KEEN	141319	M	Ger.		Capt.,Army,Drauskawitz (Ger.) 45	MURDER	U.K.
KEER, Martin	251099	M	Ger.		Kapo,C.C.Neuengamme (Ger.)	INTERR.	BEL.
KEERVER, Josef	162251	M	Ger.		Butcher,Kriegsgefangenenarbeitskommando,Adolf Mine,C.C.Merkstein 44	TORTURE	U.S.
KEET, Kornelius	134867	M	Ger.		Civilian,Efferen (Ger.) 2.10.44	WITNESS	U.S.
KEGEL	446				SS-Obersturmfhr.,Chief of C.C.Maidanek (Pol.) 40-4.44	MURDER	FR.,U.K.,POL.
KEGEL, Hugo	301506	M	Ger.	26.10.93	SS-Oberscharfhr.,SS-Sgt.,SS,C.C.Buchenwald (Ger.) 16.5.38-9.10.43	MURDER	BEL.
KEGELMANN	252211	M	Ger.		Lt.,F.P. L 50909,Romilly s-Seine (Fr.) 8.44	PILLAGE	FR.
KEGLER	167085	M	Ger.		Oberlagerfhr.,Metallwerke,Enzefeld (Aust.)	TORTURE	FR.
KEGLER	188911	M	Ger.		Lt.Col.SS-Totenkpf.Verband,C.C.Flossenburg (Ger.) 44	MURDER	U.S.
KEHE, Adolf	252896	M			Rottenfhr.,SS,C.C.Bodungen,Nordhausen (Ger.)	MURDER	U.S.
KEHINADE, Oskar	141876	M	Ger.	06	Sgt.,Stalag,Saloniki (Gre.) 7.41	MURDER	U.K.
KEHL, Augustin	254814	M	Ger.	30.10.04	Civilian,Hotel-Keeper,Liberec (Czech.) 39-43	MURDER	CZECH.
KEHL, Hugo	259166	M	Ger.		Member,SS,C.C.Dachau (Ger.) 9.42-45	MISC.CRIMES	YUGO.
KEHL, Wilhelm	174991	M	Ger.	06	SS-Rottenfhr.,SS-Totenkpf.Sturmbn.,C.C.Auschwitz (Pol.)	MURDER	U.S.

KEH-KEL

NAME	C.R.FILE NUMBER	SEX	NATIO-NALITY	DATE OF BIRTH	RANK OCCUPATION UNIT PLACE AND DATE OF CRIME	REASON WANTED	WANTED BY
KEHLE, Hans Max	192882	M	Ger.		Schupo,CC Falstad near Drontheim(Nor.)7.-8.42	MURDER	NOR.
KEHLENBOCH	150677	M	Ger.		Cpl.Army,Tours(Fr.)	MURDER	FR.
KEHLER or FOHLER	62531	M			Lt.CO of 4 Coy.923 Fortress Bn.Sicily(It.)12.6.43	TORTURE	U.S.
KEHLERT	172194	M			SS Rottfhr.Waffen SS,CC Muhldorf,Ampfing(Ger.)6.44-4.45	MURDER	U.S.
KEHR, Christian	305637	M	Ger.	26.10.05	Capt.Member,of the Standgericht,Summary Court Martial,Oslo(Nor.)2.-3.45	MURDER	NOR.
KEHR-FUCKEL, Albin	172894	M	Ger.		Civilian,Steinbach(Ger.)2.44	MURDER	U.S.
KEHREIN, Elizabeth	137468	F	Ger.		Employee,Gestapo,Koblenz(Ger.)43-44	TORTURE	U.S.
KEHREN	197132	M	Ger.		NCO,Camp Supply Leader,Stalag VI A,CC Hemer(Ger.)43-45	TORTURE	U.S.
KEHRER	306089	M	Ger.		SS Oschafhr.at Alderney,CC(Channel Is)CC Kortemark,42-45	MURDER	CZECH.
KEHRL, Hans see KERRL, Dr.	62478						
KEHRWALD, Karl	254578	M	Ger.		Cpl.Kommandofhr.Stalag 344,Maehr.-Aussee(Ger.)30.5.44	MURDER	U.K.
KEIDEL	157504	M	Ger.		Deputy General,Pub.Off.Mines Office,Attorney(Ger.)43	MISC.CRIMES	U.S.
KEIDEL	302055	M	Ger.		Orderly to Sgt.Boehm,Rotterdam(Neth.)15.1.45	PILLAGE	NETH.
KEIFFER	173238	M		05	Stubafhr.SS Gestapo,Noalles(Fr.)9.8.44	MURDER	U.K.
KEIL	11255	M	Ger.		Dr.,General,Gestapo,Nice(Fr.)29.2.44-15.8.44	MURDER	FR.
KEIL	135210	M	Ger.		Capt.Hauptmann der SS,1 Panz.Div.Lutrebois(Bel.)3.-10.1.45	MURDER	U.S.
KEIL	257518	M			Lt.Col.709 Div.919 Regt.St.Martin(Fr.)14.4.44	MURDER	U.S.
KEIL, Ewald	186123	M			SS Rottfhr.SS Guard,4 SS Totenkopf Stuba,CC Nordhausen Dora,Auschwitz (Pol.)43-45	MURDER	U.S.
KEIL, Theo	187131	M	Ger.		Reichsleiter NSDAP,Praha(Czech.)	MISC.CRIMES	CZECH.
KEILER	252895	M			Oschafhr.SS CC Nordhausen(Ger.)	MURDER	U.S.
KEILHAVER, Erwin	189744	M	Ger.		Civilian,Ratischovas(Ger.)1.1.45	WITNESS	U.S.
KEILING, Karl	305666	M	Ger.		Member of CC Personnel,CC Flossenburg,Hersbruck,Wolkenburg,Ganacker, Leitmeritz(Ger.and CSR)1.1.42-8.5.45	MISC.CRIMES	U.S.
KEILLERIN	250319	M	Ger.		Adjutant Chief,Fieldpolice de Bourgoin,Salagnon(Fr.)15.2.44	MISC.CRIMES	FR.
KEIM, Ewald	301765	M	Ger.		Rottfhr.CC Auschwitz(Pol.)40	MURDER	FR.
KEIM, George	306590	M	Ger.		Policeman,Jugesheim near Frankfurt(Ger.)6.1.45	BRUTALITY	U.K.
KEINDEL	1531	M	Ger.		SS Stubafhr.KL Sachsenhausen(Ger.)	MURDER	U.S.
KEINDEL	31645	M	Ger.	95	Lt.SS Command,CC Berlin,Sachsenhausen(Ger.)5.43	MURDER	U.S.
KEINDEL	208056	M	Ger.		Cmdt.Major,Stalag Luft III,Oranienburg,Sagan(Ger.)3.44	MURDER	U.K.
KEINDL	194025	M	Ger.		Major,SS CC Buchenwald(Ger.)42-45	TORTURE	U.S.
KEINERT, Georg	306783	M	Ger.		Grenadier,SS No.05452C,Houyet,Dinant(Bel.)4.9.44	PILLAGE	BEL.
KEIP, Jakob	193252	M	Ger.		Civilian,Koeln,Volkhoven(Ger.)18.-25.2.45	MURDER	CAN.
KEIPER, Ludwig Hermann	251525	M	Ger.	23.4.94	Lt.Gen.Army(Yugo.)12.43-8.44	MURDER	YUGO.
KEIS, Hans see KAIS, Dr.	145958						
KEISER	173671	M	Ger.		CC Inspector,Gestapoleitstelle,CC Brno(Czech.)(Pol.)39-45	MURDER	CZECH.
KEISS	141318	M	Ger.		Dr.,Stabsarzt,Stalag VII A,Moosburg(Ger.)2.45	TORTURE	U.K.
KEISS	260123	M	Ger.		High Master,Chief-Supervisor,CC Dachau(Ger.)42-44	BRUTALITY	FR.
KEITLER	147308	M	Ger.		Pvt.11 Panzer Div.Kampfgruppe"Wilde"(Fr.)44	MURDER	FR.
KEIZER	62532	M	Ger.		SS Pvt.Waffen SS,CC Amersfoort(Neth.)11.42	MURDER	U.S.
KEJRER, Alfred	167700	M	Ger.		Dr.,High Official,Amt des Generalgouverneurs Treuhandverwaltung(Pol.) 9.39-44	MISC.CRIMES	POL.
KELBER, Lld.	179940	M	Ger.		SS Hptsturmfhr.S.D.stellvertr.Leiter of Dienststelle,Praha(Czech.)39-45	MURDER	CZECH.
KELCH, Paul	252984	M			Pvt.CC Dora,Nordhausen(Ger.)	MURDER	U.S.
KELDER	252497	M			Rottfhr.CC Rottleberode,Nordhausen(Ger.)	MURDER	U.S.
KELESCH	254567	M	Ger.		SS or Gestapo,CC Bremen(Ger.)	TORTURE	U.K.
KELL	259418	M	Ger.		Hptscharfhr.SS CC Dachau(Ger.)	MURDER	YUGO.
KELLER	448	M	Ger.		Police-Major,Warschau(Pol.)9.39-1.42	MURDER	POL.
KELLER	12403	M	Ger.		Dr.,Regierungsrat,Oberlandsratamt,Moravska-Ostrava(Czech.)39-44	TORTURE	CZECH.
KELLER	12439	M	Ger.		SS Sgt.SS Panz.Div.Das Reich,NCO,Oradom(Fr.)10.6.44	MURDER	FR.
KELLER	67038	M	Ger.		Lt.SS Das Reich,St.Credin de Richemont,Cantillac(Fr.)26.-27.3.44	MURDER	FR.
KELLER	124116	M	Ger.		Bahnhofskommandantur Officer,Reichsbahn,St.Germain,Billy(Fr.)8.41-8.44	MURDER	FR.
KELLER	126562	M	Ger.		SS Mann,KL Hagen(Ger.)40-45	MURDER	U.S.
KELLER	135202	M	Ger.		SA Sturmfhr.KL Regensburg,KL Weichenfeld(Ger.)Chief of Camp in Ober-Franken Region,1.-3.45,40-3.45	TORTURE	U.S.
KELLER	145834	M	Ger.	07	SS Gestapo Member KL Bilgoraj(Pol.)8.1.43	MURDER	POL.
KELLER see HELLER	161169						
KELLER	172193	M			SS Scharfhr.CC Waffen SS,Muhldorf,Ampfing(Ger.)6.44-4.45	MURDER	U.S.
KELLER	173085	M	Ger.		Lt.Gestapo,Morlaix(Fr.)44	MURDER	FR.
KELLER	173728	M	Ger.		Wachtmeister,Police,Savag(Yugo.)41	MURDER	YUGO.
KELLER	173729	M	Ger.		CC Commandant,Maribor(Yugo.)4.41-44	MURDER	YUGO.
KELLER	179891	M	Ger.		Vertrauensmann,Gestapo,Saarbruecken(Ger.)	PILLAGE	FR.
KELLER	186115	M	Ger.		Lt.Marine,Crete(Grc.)	MURDER	GRC.
KELLER	188755	M	Ger.		SS Osturmfhr.Lt.Gestapo,SS,Beaumont(Fr.)20.12.43	MURDER	FR.
KELLER	189379	M	Ger.		Policeman,Police Eilenstedt(Ger.)41-45	MURDER	U.S.
KELLER	193357	M	Ger.		Capt.Army,Molde(Nor.)9.42	WITNESS	NOR.
KELLER	196202	M	Ger.		Member Gestapo,Grenoble(Fr.)	MISC.CRIMES	FR.
KELLER	254368	M	Ger.		Lt.Inf.Unit,Ecueille(Fr.)30.-31.8.44	PILLAGE	FR.
KELLER	255275	M	Ger.		Capt.Stalag XII A,Limburg(Ger.)	MURDER	U.S.
KELLER	257327	M	Ger.		Foreman,Organisation Todt Schutz Kommando,Slave Labour Camps,Erlandet Oeusand Trola(Nor.)6.42-45	MURDER	YUGO.
KELLER	259642	M	Ger.		Lt.Navy 09909,Wimereux(Pas de Calais-Fr.)40-44	INCENDIARISM	FR.
KELLER	259653	M	Ger.		Chief of railway station,Batignolles,Paris(Seine-Fr.)18.-19.8.44	INTERR.	FR.
KELLER	260119	M	Ger.		SS Mann,Slave Labour Camp,Botn near Rognan(Nor.)8.42-3.43,4.43-8.45	BRUTALITY	YUGO.
KELLER	260120	M	Ger.		Agent,Gestapo of Grenoble,Massif du Vercors(Drome and Isere,Fr.) 20.7.-5.8.44	SUSPECT	FR.
KELLER	260122	M	Ger.		Lt.Chief of Tchornowik-camp,Dachau(Ger.)42-44	TORTURE	FR.
KELLER	261812	M	Ger.	10	Hptwachtmeister,Gend.S.D.of Vichy,Clerval(Fr.)28.8.44	MURDER	FR.
KELLER	301765	M	Ger.		Uschafhr.Blockfhr.CC Auschwitz(Pol.)40	MURDER	FR.
KELLER	301893	M	Ger.		Osturmfhr.at Limoges(Fr.)2.4.44	MURDER	FR.
KELLER	305445	M	Ger.		Lt.Inf.Unit,Ecueille,Indre(Fr.)30.-31.8.44	PILLAGE	FR.
KELLER, Alfred	254641	M	Ger.	13.1.04	Agent Gestapo,Prag(Czech.)	MISC.CRIMES	CZECH.
KELLER, Erich	254595	M	Ger.	10	Army,S.D.at Ortskommand.,Valjevo(Yugo.)22.10.41	MURDER	YUGO.
KELLER, Ernst	121547	M	Ger.		Hptscharfhr.S.D.,SS,Herault(Fr.)	MISC.CRIMES	FR.

KEL-KEP

NAME	C.R.FILE NUMBER	SEX	NATIO-NALITY	DATE OF BIRTH	RANK OCCUPATION UNIT PLACE AND DATE OF CRIME	REASON WANTED	WANTED BY
KELLER, Filip	186119	M			SS Rottfhr., Guard,4.SS Totenkopf-Stuba CC.Nordhausen-Dora (Ger.)43-45	MURDER	U.S.
KELLER, Georges	189119	M			Lt., Army, St.Germain, d'Esteuil Hameau de Liard (Fr.) 25.7.44	MURDER	FR.
KELLER, Hans	186116	M	Ger.		Overseer for fortifications, Apokorowov (Grc.) 5.44	TORTURE	GRC.
KELLER, Helmuth	252498	M		16. 9.17	Sgt., C.C. Ellrich, Nordhausen (Ger.)	MURDER	U.S.
KELLER, Josef	24883	M	Ger.		Pol.Hauptwachtmeister, Polizei Koblenz (Ger.)	TORTURE	U.S.
KELLER, Karl	262171	M	Ger.		Lt. (probably), Gestapo, St.Pol de Leon (Fr.) 5.8.44	TORTURE	FR.
KELLER, Max	167682	M	Ger.		Osturmbannfhr., SS, S.D., Gestapo, Oslo (Nor.) 4.40	TORTURE	NOR.
KELLER, Walter	139754	M	Ger.		Leutnant, Waffen SS Totenkopf-Div.	MURDER	U.S.
KELLERMAN	189378	M			SS Mann, C.C. Mauthausen, Cursen (Aust.) 25.7.44	MURDER	U.S.
KELLERMANN	255177	M	Ger.		Employee, Abt. 4 A SIPO, Brussels (Bel.) 40-44	INTERR.	BEL.
KELLERMANN	300790	M	Ger.		Pvt., 1.Aufkl.Abt. 3.Coy. 2.Col. XV.Div.Afrika-Corps, St.Leger (Arlon) 5.9.44	MISC.CRIMES	BEL.
KELLERMANN, Heinz	145202	M			Lt., Airforce, 29.Flak-Rgt., Hausen, Ginnheim (Ger.) 9.44	WITNESS	U.S.
KELLERS	255178	M	Ger.		Employee, SIPO, Abt. IV, Brussels (Bel.) 40-44	INTERR.	BEL.
KELLERS, Paul	161650	M	Ger.		Pvt., Airforce Luftgau, C.C. Eggemoen, Honefoss, Buskeruch (Nor.)	MURDER	NOR.
KELLISH	121964	M	Ger.		Member SS or Gestapo, Bremen-Farge (Ger.) 6.43	TORTURE	U.K.
KELLNER	122481	M	Ger.		Sgt., Arbeitskommando, C.C. Doebeln (Ger.) 29.10.44	TORTURE	U.K.
KELLNER	252499	M			Rottfhr., C.C. Osterhagen, Nordhausen (Ger.)	MURDER	U.S.
KELLNER, Franz	186117	M	Ger.	97	Party leader NSDAP, Praha (Czech.)	MISC.CRIMES	CZECH.
KELLNER, Otto	192883	M	Ger.		Schupo, C.C. Falstad nr.Drontheim (Nor.) 8.42	MURDER	NOR.
KELLNER, Walter	193062	M	Ger.	15	Ex convict, Reichsjustizministerium, Feldstraflager, Finmark (Nor.)4.45	WITNESS	NOR.
KELLNER, Werner	172478	M	Ger.		SS Guard, C.C. Osterhagen (Ger.)	TORTURE	U.S.
KELM	124639	M	Ger.	15	Uscharfhr., SS, C.C. Birkenau, Oswiecim (Pol.) 8.43-1.44	MURDER	U.S.
KELM, Ewald	254589	M	Ger.		SS Rottfhr., Staff of command, C.C. Auschwitz-Birkenau (Pol.) 10.42	MURDER	YUGO.
KELS, Waldemar	162252	M	Ger.	98	Oscharfhr., Waffen SS, Administration, C.C. Buchenwald (Ger.) 43-45	MISC.CRIMES	U.S.
KELSLERT, Albert	172195	M			Civ., C.C. Muehldorf.Ampfing (Ger.) 6.44-4.45	MURDER	U.S.
KELTERBORN	122612	M	Ger.		Sgt., Stalag 122, Compiegne-Oise (Fr.)	BRUTALITY	FR.
KELZ	121548	M	Ger.		SS Uscharfhr., Waffen SS C.C. Buchenwald (Ger.)	TORTURE	FR.
KELZ	193816	M			SS Oscharfhr., C.C. Weimar-Buchenwald (Ger.)	MURDER	U.S.
KELZ, Georges	306618	M	Ger.		Staff-Sgt., Gendarmerie Lannion, Cotes du Nord, 12.6.44	TORTURE	FR.
KEMA	162990	M			Sgt., Bau-Pion.Bn. (K) 2, Army, Setsaa (Nor.)	TORTURE	NOR.
KEMEDER	193356	M	Ger.		Sgt., 2.Coy. PW work-Bn.206, Mosjeen (Nor..Fin.Ger.) 7.44-5.45	MURDER	NOR.
KEMETER, Josef	189090	M	Ger.	18. 2.06	Crim.secret., Gestapo, Brno (Czech.) 39-45	MURDER	CZECH.
KEMETER, Kurt	256735	M	Ger.	3. 3.19	Employee, C.C. Dora-Nordhausen (Ger.)	MURDER	U.S.
KEMF	251526	M	Ger.		Capt., Gestapo, Nuernberg (Ger.) 41-45	MISC.CRIMES	YUGO.
KEMF, Jakob	189977	M	Ger.	10.10.05	Civ., Klein-Zerbst (Ger.) 7.7.44	MURDER	U.S.
KEMINADA	161262	M	Ger.		Sgt., Saloniki (Grc.) 6.-8.41	MURDER	U.K.
KEMINY, Anton	142221	M		93	Kripo Germany	TORTURE	U.S.
KEMKE	254661	M			Guard, C.C. Lahde-Weser (Ger.)	INTERR.	BEL.
KEMLER	260190	M	Ger.		Lt., Unit 13 907 A, Massif du Vercors, Isere et Drome (Fr.) 20.7.-8.44	SUSPECT	FR.
KEMMAPD	449	M	Ger.		Sgt., Army, C.C. Salonika (Grc.) 41	TORTURE	U.K.
KEMMER, Ferdinand	256736	M	Ger.	24.12.05	Employee, C.C. Dora - Nordhausen (Ger.)	MURDER	U.S.
KEMMKE	257858	M			150.Panz.Bde., Meuse-Bridge Antwerp (Bel.) 12.44	MISC.CRIMES	U.S.
KEMNITZ see CHEMNITZ, Arno	122070						
KEMNITZ	145842	M	Ger.		Stabsscharfhr., 3.SS Bau-Bde., C.C. Wieda-Gardelegen (Ger.) 4.-14.4.45	MURDER	U.S.
KEMP	9669	M	Ger.		Medical-Corps, C.C. Breendonck (Bel.) 40-3.9.44	MURDER	U.K. BEL.
KEMP see HEMP	173608	M	Ger.		Kreisleiter NSDAP, Emmendingen (Ger.) 44	TORTURE	FR.
KEMPE	162602	M	Ger.	15	Hptscharfhr., Waffen SS, Sect.I, C.C. Buchenwald (Ger.)	WITNESS	U.S.
KEMPE	185089	M	Ger.		SS Uscharfhr., S.D., C.C. Dachau (Ger.)	TORTURE	FR.
KEMPE	186154	M	Ger.		SS Uscharfhr., C.C. Leonberg (Ger.)	TORTURE	U.S.
KEMPE	193063	M	Ger.		Capt., Kgf.Arb.Bn. 184, C.C. Basis Tunnel (Nor.) 4.44	MURDER	NOR.
KEMPE	305905	M	Ger.		SS Oberfhr., commander of the SS Nachrichtenschule at Litomerice (Czech.) 1.10.38-44	MURDER	CZECH.
KEMPER, Bernhard	189743	M	Ger.	17. 2.12	Kreisfachredner, Ortsgruppenleiter NSDAP, Prague (Czech.) 43-45	PILLAGE	CZECH.
KEMPER, Bernhard	301671	M	Ger.		Monceau sur Sambre (Bel.) 2.-3.9.44	PILLAGE	BEL.
KEMPER, Julius	135209	M	Ger.		Civ. Farmer	MURDER	U.S.
KEMPER, Paul	253860	M	Ger.		Proprietor-Director, Civ., Frankfurt a.M. (Ger.)	MISC.CRIMES	FR.
KEMPERS	186120	M			SS Uscharfhr., 4.SS Totenkopf-Stuba, C.C. Dora-Mittelbau-Nordhausen (Ger.) 43-45	WITNESS	U.S.
KEMPF, Jakob	145795	M	Ger.	05	Member, Crim.police, Klein-Zerbst (Ger.) 7.7.45	MURDER	U.S.
KEMPFE, Helmut	184305	M	Ger.	31. 7.09	Osturmbannfhr., 2.Bn. Rgt."Der Fuehrer" SS "Das Reich", Tulle (Fr.)	TORTURE	FR.
KEMPFER	9670	M	Ger.		Oberlt., Army, Breendonck (Bel.) 42-44	TORTURE	U.K. BEL.
KEMPFER or KAMPFER	194024	M	Ger.		Sgt. SS (Hptscharfhr.), C.C. Buchenwald (Ger.) 42-45	TORTURE	U.S.
KEMPH	157799	M	Ger.		Capt., Army, C.C. Hammelburg Oflag XIII B (Ger.) 23.3.45	MURDER	U.S.
KEMPI	252951	M	Ger.		Cpl., C.C. Muehlberg (Ger.)	MURDER	U.S.
KEMPIN, Hanne	257181	M	Ger.		Hptsturmfhr., Waffen SS, 1.Coy. 1.Bn. Rgt."Der Fuehrer",Foret de Nieppe (Fr.) 10.5.40	SUSPECT	U.K.
KEMPINSKI, Robert	145959	M	Ger.		Oscharfhr., SS, Wloclawek (Pol.) winter 44	MURDER	POL.
KEMPRATH, Hans Georg	252500	M	Ger.	21.10.25	Flyer, C.C. Ellrich, Nordhausen (Ger.)	MURDER	U.S.
KENDEL	256855	M	Ger.		Head of Sub-sec. C.C. Nordhausen (Ger.)	MURDER	U.S.
KENEN or KLEIN	134872	M			Member of Crew, German Navy, Gast de Marine nr.Bernodet, Porte de Mousterlin, 30.6.44	MURDER	U.S.
KENN	43510	M	Ger.		SS Uscharfhr., Waffen SS, C.C. Buchenwald (Ger.) 42-45	TORTURE	FR.
KENN, Rudolf	141966	M	Ger.	9.10.14	Osturmfhr., SS Totenkopf-Standarte, Member of the commander staff, C.C. Buchenwald (Ger.)	TORTURE	U.S.
KENNECKE, Willi	252501	M	Ger.	6. 1.05	SS Rottfhr., C.C. Harzungen-Nordhausen (Ger.)	MURDER	U.S.
KENNELBACH alias:dit "Arthur"	179892	M	Ger.		Agent, Gestapo, Err (Fr.) 5.-9.43	PILLAGE	FR.
KENNETH, Pitchford	132209	M	Ger.	07	Ogruppenfhr., SS, Gestapo, Polizeileiter, Modlin (Pol.) 22.1.44	TORTURE	U.K.
KENNITZER	127384	M	Ger.	19	Standartenfhr. (Col.), SS, C.C. Buchenwald-Weimar (Ger.)	MURDER	U.S.
KENNITZER	193815	M			SS Uscharfhr., C.C. Buchenwald (Ger.)	TORTURE	U.S.
KENT	189620	M			Col., Feldgendarmerie, Grenoble (Fr.) 25.2.44	MURDER	FR.
KENZIAN, Gerhard	145173	M	Ger.		SS Rottfhr., SS Panz.Gren.Rgt., Stavelot, Malmedy (Bel.) 23.12.44	MURDER	U.S.
KEPELLER	146841	M	Ger.		SS Panz.Div. "Das Reich" 1.Panz.Rgt., Tulle (Fr.) 44	MURDER	FR.
KEPER, Eric or KEPFER	162253	M	Ger.		263.Inf.Div., Kommando de Landerneau, Bretagne-Finisters (Fr.) 44	MURDER	FR.
KEPER, Heinrich	167955	M	Ger.		Abwehr-Kommando 343, Landerneau (Fr.) 15.6.44-29.8.44	MURDER	FR.
KEPFER see KEPER, Eric	162253						

KEP - KES

NAME	C.R.FILE NUMBER	SEX	NATIO-NALITY	DATE OF BIRTH	RANK OCCUPATION UNIT PLACE AND DATE OF CRIME	REASON WANTED	WANTED BY
KEPKA, Karel	258081	M	Ger.		District-leader, Fascist Organisation "Vlajka" Gestapo Pribram (Czech.) 39 - 45	MISC.CRIMES	CZECH.
KEPKE	450	M	Ger.	14	Guard, C.C. Unterbuchsbau (Ger.) 9.-10.39	MURDER	POL.
KEPP	194023	M	Ger.		SS, C.C. Buchenwald (Ger.) 42 - 45	TORTURE	U.S.
KEPPEL	306758	M	Ger.		Chief, Gestapo, Giessen (Ger.) 3.45	MURDER	U.S.
KEPPEL, Friedrich	194022	M	Ger.	22.11.08	Pvt., Army, Gestapo, Griessen (Ger.) 3.45	MURDER	U.S.
KEPPLER	240106	M	Ger.	82	Secr., Obergrup., SS, Ministry for foreign affairs, Berlin (Ger.)	MISC.CRIMES	U.S.
KEPPLER	62533	M	Ger.		Capt., parachuter, under the command of Major Matthaeas, Roermond (Neth.) 11.44- 1.45	TORTURE	U.S.,NETH.
KEPPLER	191465	M	Ger.		President, Reichsministerium des Auswaertigen, Berlin (Ger.) 9.39- 44	PILLAGE	POL.
KEPPLER, Wilhelm	260878	M	Ger.	17.12.82	Reichs-Commissioner for the Ostmark, State Sec. for Special Assign's in Foreign-Office.	MISC.CRIMES	U.S.
KEPPLINGER	62534	M	Ger.		SS-Major, 17.SS Pz.Bde., St.Aubin, Duperron (Fr.) 6.44	MURDER	U.S.
KEPPNER	533	M	Ger.		Capt., parachuter, Roermond (Neth.)	TORTURE	U.S.
KEPPNER, Anton	145812	M	Ger.		Director of repair shop, Civ., Schwerte (Ger.)	TORTURE	U.S.
KERBACH	139758	M	Ger.		Capt., Stalag X-B, C.C. Sandbostel (Ger.) 1.- 5.45	TORTURE	U.S.
KERBER	251695	M	Ger.		Sgt., Army, Belgrad (Yugo.) 10.-12.41	MURDER	YUGO.
KERBER, Otto	157800	M			C.C. Gardelegen (Ger.) 4.45	MURDER	U.S.
KERBLEMAN (see KEBLERMANN)	252221						
KERBOTH, Otto	262239	M	Ger.		SS-Oberscharfhr., Gestapo, Rennes (Fr.) 43-44	MISC.CRIMES	FR.
KERCHAF	125082	M	Ger.		Cpl., Army, Groupe (Pol.) 2.42	TORTURE	U.K.
KERCHINICK	251665	M	Ger.		Lt., 157.Res.Inf.Div., 5.Coy., 99.Bn., l'Ain (Fr.) 7.44	MURDER	FR.
KERCHNER or KIRCHNER	174670	M			Chief, Gestapo, Grenoble (Fr.) 11.42- 9.43	MURDER	FR.
KIRCHOFF	100430	M	Ger.		N.C.O., Army, Groupe (Pol.) 2.42	TORTURE	U.K.
KERGER, Franz	11256	M			Pvt., Army, 11.Pz.Gren.Regt., Albine (Fr.) 6.44	MURDER	FR.
KERGER, Willi	167703	M	Ger.		Pvt., Army, 9.Gren.Res.Regt., Magny d'Anigon (Fr.) 9.44	MURDER	FR.
KERICHMANN	251664	M		05	Capt., Le Pirou (Fr.) 40-42	PILLAGE	FR.
KERLER, Karl	254831	M			Blockleiter, NSDAP,	INTERR.	FR.
KERN	11562	M	Ger.		Member of a government board, office of Reichsstatthalter Karlsruhe (Ger.) 41-42	MURDER	POL.
KERN	124266	M			Scharfhr., 1.Pz.Div., 1.Pz.Regt., C.C. Penal Unit of 9.Coy. (Engineers), Malmedy (Bel.) 12.44	MURDER	U.S.
KERN	141384	M	Ger.		Zugwachtmeister, Polizei-Wache, Koeln, 2.Coy., Lieu (Fr.)	MURDER	FR.
KERN	146840	M	Ger.		Scharfhr., SS Pz.Div."Das Reich", Valence d'Agen (Fr.) 44	MURDER	FR.
KERN	173696	M	Ger.		Zugwachtmeister, Police-Coy.,"Stollberg", (Fr.)	MURDER	FR.
KERN	251108	M	Ger.		Guard or Kapo, C.C. Gusen (Ger.)	INTERR.	BEL.
KERN	257859	M			Pvt., 150.Panz.Bde., Meuse-Bridge, Antwerp (Bel.) 12.44	MISC.CRIMES	U.S.
KERN	259093	M			Coy.-Commander, SS-Obersturmfhr., SS-Div."Prinz Eugen" Niksic district Montenegro (Yugo.) 6.43	MISC.CRIMES	YUGO.
KERN	259820	M	Ger.		Capt., Receare Terme (It.) 1.45	INTERR.	U.S.
KERN	301006	M	Ger.		Member of the Maurach Landwacht, Pertisau-Maurach (Aust.) 7.44	MURDER	FR.
KERN	306591	M	Ger.		Member, S.D. or Gestapo, Oslo, Trandum (Nor.) 1.43	MURDER	U.K.
KERN, Adam	193064	M	Ger.		Sgt., Gestapo, S.D., RSHA, Berlin, Trendum (Ger.,Nor.) 1.43	MURDER	NOR.
KERN, Conradt	149517	M	Ger.	00	Public official,	MURDER	FR.
KERN, Franz	252496	M		24. 2.14	Sgt., C.C. Ellrich, Nordhausen (Ger.)	MURDER	U.S.
KERN, Karl	62535	M	Ger.		Works for firm "Casimir Kast", Civ., Gernsbach (Ger.) 6.44	MURDER	U.S.
KERN, Lothar	261748	M	Ger.	11.12.20	Guard, SS, C.C. Natzweiler (Fr.)	MURDER	FR.
KERN, M.	301848	F	Ger.		Stabsleiterin, Gaufrauenschaftsleitung Strassburg (Fr.) 44	BRUTALITY	FR.
KERNDORF, Heinrich	137057	M			Ortsgruppenfhr., Kreisbauernfhr., NSDAP, Barleben (Ger.)	WITNESS	U.S.
KERNER, Adolf	189091	M	Ger.	21. 2.05	Crim.Employee, Gestapo, Brno (Czech.) 39-45	MURDER	CZECH.
KERNER, Frans	189742	M	Ger.	27. 8.02	Crim.Employee, Gestapo, Brno (Czech.) 39-45	MISC.CRIMES	CZECH.
KERNSTECK	11257	M	Ger.		N.C.O., Army, Pz.Gren.Regt., No.111, Albine (Fr.) 6.44	MURDER	FR.
KEHRL, Hans	452	M			Public official, Member of Reichs-Government, 5.42	MURDER	CZECH.
KEHRL, Hans or KEHRL	62478	M	Ger.		Dr., Siemens-Schuckert, Berlin (Ger.)	TORTURE	U.N.W.C.C.
KERSCH	126952	M	Ger.		Officer, 2.SS-Pz.Div. "Das Reich", La Croix - Falgarde (Fr.)	MURDER	FR.
KERSCHBAUMER	11258	M	Ger.		Pvt., Army, Panz.Gren.Regt.111, Albine (Fr.) 6.44	MURDER	FR.
KERSCHBAUMER, Johann	137792	M	Ger.		Civ., Liezen (Aust.)	WITNESS	U.S.
KERSCHENSTEINER	50297	M	Ger.	84	Reichsinsp., Labour under Sauckel, Koenigsberg (Ger.)	MISC.CRIMES	U.N.W.C.C.
KERSCHER	301507	M	Ger.		SS-Unterscharfhr., C.C. Buchenwald (Ger.) 5.38-10.43	MURDER	BEL.
KERSTEIN, Gunter	300040	M			Red-cross-man, Of Geppingen, Drente (Neth.) 43-45	MURDER	NTH.
KERSTEN	125661	M	Ger.		Lt., parachuter-pioneer, Bn., Decize, Montaron Vandenesse (Fr.) 7.44	MURDER	FR.
KERSTEN	173713	M	Ger.		SS-Fuehrer, Alsace (Fr.) 44	TORTURE	FR.
KERSTIEN	191369	M			N.C.O., 190.Kriegsgef.Bn., Org.Todt, Russanes (Nor.) 11.44- 5.45	MURDER	NOR.
KERSTING	196201	M			Lt., Navy, 18.S.T.A.-Section, Montceau les Mines (Fr.) 7.44	MISC.CRIMES	FR.
KERSTING, Fritz	252495	M	Ger.		SS-Unterscharfhr., C.C. Harsungen, Nordhausen (Ger.)	MURDER	U.S.
KERTEL	62536	M	Ger.	17	Cpl., W-SS, C.C. Hinzert (Ger.)	TORTURE	U.S.
KERTEL	131729	M	Ger.		Commissar, Zollgrensschuetze, Vilmanya (Fr.) 8.44	MURDER	FR.
KERTEN	72536	M	Ger.		SS-Unterocharfhr., W-SS, C.C. Hinzert (Ger.)	MURDER	FR.
KERTL, Hugo	139814	M	Ger.		SS-Unterscharfhr., C.C. Buchenwald (Ger.)	BRUTALITY	U.S.
KERZ	102973	M	Ger.		Lt., Gestapo, Prag (Czech.)	MURDER	U.K.
KESPERSKI	301766	M			Sgt., Order of Condt. of Ardennes, Revin (Bel.) 6.44	MURDER	FR.
KESSAL	39780	M	Ger.		Cpl., Army, 12.42	MISC.CRIMES	U.K.
KESSEK	194021	M	Ger.		Pvt., SS, C.C. Buchenwald (Ger.) 42-45	TORTURE	U.S.
KESSEL	122480	M		93	Sgt., Arb.Kdo. 502, Stalag 4-A, C.C. Burghammer (Ger.) 7.43	TORTURE	U.K.
KESSEL (Black Mamba)	193671	M		03	Landessch.Bn. 325, (Ger.) 6.43	TORTURE	U.K.
KESSEL	139760	M		05	Cpl., SS, Arb.Kdo. A-6, C.C. (Ger.)	MURDER	U.S.
KESSEL	254990	M	Ger.		Guard, Prison Siegburg (Ger.) 11.44	TORTURE	FR.
KESSEL	300262	M			Warder, Sieburg Fortress nr.Bonn, 41-45	MISC.CRIMES	FR.
KESSEL, Walter	145846	M			Blockaeltester, Kapo, C.C. Hohenrheim near Plattling (Ger.) 2.-5.45	MURDER	US.
KESSELERG	306090	M			Vorarbeiter, C.C. Lublin (Pol.) 42	MURDER	CZECH.
KESSELER, Kaspar	187129	M	Ger.	00	Sgt., 2-10.Navy Kuesten-Art.-Abt., Den Burg (Neth.) 4.45	TORTURE	NETH.
KESSELMODEL	301103	M	Ger.		Crim.Secr., served with R.S.D. Abt.4-2-a., Kopenhagen (Den.) 9.44	TORTURE	DEN.
KESSELRATH	191469	M	Ger.		5.parachuter-Regt., Nachrichtenzug, Quareinom (Bel.) 44	MURDER	BEL.

NAME	C.R.FILE NUMBER	SEX	NATIO-NALITY	DATE OF BIRTH	RANK OCCUPATION UNIT PLACE AND DATE OF CRIME	REASON WANTED	WANTED BY
KESSLER	62493	M	Ger.		Civilian, Landwacht, Bad Koesen (Ger.) 11.44	MURDER	U.S.
KESSLER	150585	M	Ger.		Gestapo-Employee, CC Frederikstad (Nor.) 44	TORTURE	NOR.
KESSLER	191825	M	Ger.	86?	Sgt., 372 Lds.Schtz.Bn., CC Stalag IV-A, Burghammer(Ger.) 9.43	TORTURE	U.K.
KESSLER	252494	M			Rottfhr, CC Mackenrode, Nordhausen (Ger.)	MURDER	U.S.
KESSLER	305906	M	Ger.		Uschfhr, CC Oranienburg (Ger.) 11.39-45	MURDER	CZECH.
KESSLER, Helmut	256840	M	Ger.		Hptfeldwebel, Air Force, Abergement de Varey(Fr.) 25.7.44	MURDER	FR.
KESSLER, Joseph	167705	M	Ger.		Pvt., Army, 9 Gren.Res.Rgt.,1 Coy, Magny d'Avigon(Fr.)	MURDER	FR.
KESSLER, Magnus	126454	M	Ger.		Civilian, spy for the Gestapo	MURDER	U.S.
KESSLER, Philipp	62466	M	Ger.		Siemens-Schuckert	TORTURE	U.N.W.C.C.
KESTAL, Josef	139775	M	Ger.		Uschfhr, W-SS, CC Buchenwald (Ger.) 3.5.45	MURDER	U.S.
KESTEL, Josef	301508	M	Ger.	29.10.04	Oschfhr, SS, CC Buchenwald (Ger.) 16.5.38-9.10.43	MURDER	BEL.
KESTEN, Dicker	196200	M	Ger.		Sturmbannfhr, 2 Bn, 2 SS-Pz.Rgt."Das Reich", Tulle(Fr.) 9.6.44	INTERR.	FR.
KESTER, Max	125660	M	Ger.		Adjutant, Gestapo, Baccarat (Fr.) 8.-10.44	MURDER	FR.
KESTERMANN	261948	M	Ger.		Oschfhr. SS, Belgrad and Valjevo (Yugo.)	SUSPECT	YUGO.
KESTING (see KESTRING)	174778						
KESTING	254846	M			Capt., Com.Abwehr TP 373, 2 Brandenb.Rgt.3	INTERR.	U.S.
KESTING, Alex	62494	M	Ger.	00	Kapo, CC Gandersheim (Ger.) 6.4.45	MURDER	U.S.
KESTLE	139762	M	Ger.	05	Hptschfhr, W-SS, CC Nordhausen (Ger.) 43-45	TORTURE	U.S.
KESTLER	130669	M	Ger.		Hptsturmfhr, SS, CC Dora Mittelbau, Nordhausen(Ger.)	MURDER	U.S.
KESTNER	196897	M	Ger.		SS-Sgt., CC Metz-Moselle (Fr.) 40-44	INTERR.	FP.
KESTRING (or KESTING)	174778	M	Ger.	95	Capt, 2 Bn. Brandenburg Div.3, Communanza (It.) 2.5.44	WITNESS	U.K.
KETCHEDI (or KITCHEDI)	167084	M	Ger.		SS Bn. Instruction No.18, Tiers (Fr.) 25.8.44	PILLAGE	FR.
KETHOF	453	M			SS Standartenfhr,Chief of Staff in General Government 39	MURDER	POL.
KETKING, Bruno	137786	M			Major, commanding 29 Pz.Gren.Div.,15 Pz.Gren.Rgt., 3 Bn.	WITNESS	U.S.
KETT, Bruno	306024	M	Ger.		Dr., member of staff at CC Neuengamme (Ger.) 6.40-5.45	MURDER	U.K.
KETT, Franz	145190	M	Ger.	06	Rottfhr, SS Leibstandarte "Adolf Hitler",Rossbach(Ger.) 4.3.45	MURDER	U.S.
KETTEL, Max	194020	M	Ger.		Uschfhr, SS, CC Buchenwald (Ger.) 42-45	TORTURE	U.S.
KETTELBEIL, Richard	121552	M	Ger.		Civilian, CC Untermassfeld (Ger.)	TORTURE	BEL.
KETTELBORN, Fritz	196896	M	Ger.	14	Sgt., CC Royallieu (Fr.) 41-44	INTERR.	FR.
KETTENBEIL	150667	M	Ger.	08	Rottfhr, SS, CC Neuengamme (Ger.)	TORTURE	U.K.
KETTENBEIL, Richard	902058	M	Ger.		at Untermassfeld Prison (Ger.) 40-45	MURDER	BEL.
KETTERER	123962	M	Ger.	24	Lt., Inf.Rgt., Longueil (Fr.) 24.6.44	MURDER	U.S.
KETTERER	145213	M	Ger.	10.10.00	Osturmfhr, SS, CC Gross-Rosen, Mauthausen (Aust.) 41-45	WITNESS	U.S.
KETTLE	150656	M	Ger.		Major, Air Force, Bosquet D'Orb (Fr.) 17.8.44	MURDER	FR.
KETTLER	104157	M	Ger.		Col.,Head of Cypher Section,OKW, 12.43-4.45	MISC.CRIMES	U.S.
KETTLER, Kurt	129687	M	Ger.		Civilian, Camp Dora, Nordhausen (Ger.)	MURDER	U.S.
KETTNER	196835	M	Ger.		Lt., Unit 01512 K, Trebeurden (Fr.)	MISC.CRIMES	FR.
KETZER	252493	M			CC Rottleberode, Nordhausen (Ger.)	MURDER	U.S
KETZLER	252492	M			Rottfhr. SS, CC Osterhagen (Ger., Nordhausen (Ger.)	MURDER	U.S.
KEUCHEL	50917	M	Ger.		Officer, Army, Kreiskommandantur, Chateaubriant (Fr.) 41	MURDER	FR.
KEUCHEN	172073	M			SS-Sturmann, CC Mühldorf, Ampfing (Ger.) 6.44-4.45	MURDER	U.S.
KEUFER, Wilhelm	192189	M	Ger.		Member of Org.Todt, Soissons (Fr.) 40-41	TORTURE	BEL.
KEUHS	150668	M	Ger.	07	Uschfhr, SS, CC Neuengamme and Drustte (Ger.)	TORTURE	U.K.
KEUL, Joseph	186760	M	Ger.		Sgt., Army, Ussel (Fr.) 8.10.44	MURDER	FR.
KEULER	194009	M	Ger.		Sgt., 47 Inf.Rgt., Sevenum (Neth.) 20.9.44	WITNESS	NETH.
KEULING, Otto	161260	M			Civilian, Bad Neustadt (Ger.) 29.9.44	WITNESS	U.S.
KEUN	194019	M	Ger.		Sgt. SS, CC Buchenwald (Ger.) 42-45	TORTURE	U.S.
KEUNEKE	254660	M	Ger.		Guard, CC Lahde-Weser (Ger.)	INTERR.	BEL.
KEUSELER (see HEUSELER)	192129						
KEUTTGEN, Hermann	162858	M	Ger.		Chief K.G.F. Arb.Kdo., CC Aachen (Ger.)	TORTURE	BEL.
KEVERITSCH	257860	M			Lt., 150 Pz.Bde., Meuse Bridge, Antwerpen (Bel.) 12.44	MISC.CRIMES	U.S.
KEWIKER	127385	M	Ger.	about 95	SS, CC Leau (Ger.) 14.4.45	MURDER	U.S.
KEZ, Jacob	254565	M	Ger.		Foreman, Waldenmaier Plant, Heidenheim (Ger.) 41-45	BRUTALITY	POL.
KHARKOFF (see KARKHOFF)	254646						
KHARR	185988	M	Ger.		Dr.,Osturmfhr, SS, CC Dora, Nordhausen (Ger.)	MURDER	BEL.
KHIL (see KIEL)	456						
KHOL, Joseph (Sepp)	174683	M			Interpreter, Army, St.Barthelemy de Cun (Fr.) 27.-30.7.44	TORTURE	FR.
KHOLAS	168108	M	Ger.	02	Army, 610 Lds.Schtz.Bn., Pvt., Elding	TORTURE	U.K.
KHOLAS, Bruno	67039	M	Ger.		Pvt., Army, 610 Coy, Schonmoor, Elbing (Ger.)	TORTURE	U.K.
KHORN	150655	M	Ger.		Capt., Army, Montbartier (Fr.) 24.8.44	MURDER	FR.
KHULMANN	67040	M	Ger.		Capt., 16 Div. Flak, Army, Wasquehal (Fr.) 7.-8.10.42	MURDER	FR.
KHUNDT	145808	F			Civilian, Borkum (Ger.) 4.8.44	MURDER	U.S.
KHUNT	6120	M	Ger.		Lt., SS "Das Reich", Rgt. "Der Fuehrer", Buzet sur Tara (Fr.) 7.7.44	MURDER	FR.
KHUNT	167953	M	Ger.		Osturmfhr, SS Div."Das Reich",Rgt."Der Fuehrer", 7.-8.44	MURDER	FR.
KHUNT	191590	M	Ger.		Osturmfhr, SS Div."Das Reich",Rgt."Der Fuehrer",6.-8.44	MURDER	FR.
KICHERER, Karl	256888	M	Ger.	96	Capt., Schutzpolizei, Lidice (Czech.) 10.6.42	MURDER	CZECH.
KICK	149305	M	Ger.		Crim.Commissary Sipo, Chief CC Dachau (Ger.) 41-45	TORTURE	FR.,YUGO.
KICKDUSCH, Hans	301767	M	Ger.		SS-Mann, CC Auschwitz (Pol.) from 40	MURDER	FR.
KICKINGER, Ferdinand	189741	M	Ger.		Criminal Secretary, Gestapo, Brno, Prerov (Czech.)	MISC.CRIMES	CZECH.
KICKISH, Adolf	141936	M	Ger.		Foreman, Stalag IV-C, Tschausch (Czech.) 5.8.44	WITNESS	U.K.
KIDERLEN	172101	M	Ger.		Civilian, General-Manager, Org.Todt, Firm Bruno Hoffmann, Mühldorf, Ampfing (Ger.) 6.44-4.45	MURDER	U.S.
KIELE	259652	M	Ger.		Guard, Coy of Guards at Wolfratshausen -L 425 -, Buckendorf(Ger.)30.8.42	MURDER	U.S.
"KID" (see Held)	106327						
KIECH	254971	M	Ger.		Member German Police, Avians les Bains (Fr.) 16.1.44	INTERR.	FR.
KIEHMANN	136238	M	Ger.		Feld-Gend., Stenay (Fr.) 5.8.44	MURDER	FR.
KIEFER	152527	M	Ger.	1905-07	Sturmbannfhr, SS, Paris (Fr.)	WITNESS	U.K.
KIEFER	191453	M	Ger.		Hptsturmfhr, SS, CC Boten (Ger.) 3.42-43	MURDER	NOR, YUGO.
KIEFER	191929	M	Ger.	95	Sturmbannfhr, Gestapo, SS Hauptamt, Noailles (Fr.) 9.8.44	MURDER	U.K.
KIEFER	250894	M		05	Lt., Chief Gestapo, Fouligny (Fr.)	MURDER	U.S.
KIEFER, Bernhard	260854	M			Pvt., Army, Elversberg (Ger.) 17.-19.7.44	WITNESS	U.S.
KIEFER, J.	31702	M	Ger.		Cpl., Guard, CC Official, Auschwitz (Pol.) 6.41-1.45	MURDER	POL.
KIEFER, Karl	251684	M	Ger.		Civ., District, Lorrach (Ger.)	TORTURE	BEL.
KIEFER, Ludwig	131405	M	Ger.		SS Uschfhr, Mauthausen (Aust.) 41-45	MURDER	U.S.
KIEFER, Max	258549	M	Ger.	89	Osturmbannfhr, SS, W.V.H.A. (Ger.) 40-45	BRUTALITY	U.S.
KIEFERT	257391	M	Ger.		Sturmschfhr, SS, Slave Labour Camp, Beisfjord near Narvik (Nor.)6-11.42	BRUTALITY	YUGO.

KIE - KIL

NAME	C.R.FILE NUMBER	SEX	NATIO- NALITY	DATE OF BIRTH	RANK	OCCUPATION	UNIT	PLACE AND DATE OF CRIME	REASON WANTED	WANTED BY
KIEFFER	12440	M	Ger.		Sgt.chief, SS Div.Der Fuehrer, 2 Coy, Oradon (Fr.) 10.6.44				MURDER	FR.
KIEFFER	24859	M	Ger.	07	Osturmfhr.,SS Abwehr, Faulquemont (Fr.) 8.44				MURDER	U.S.
KIEFFER	305446	M	Ger.		Member, Gestapo, Paris (Fr.) 12.8.44				MURDER	FR.
KIEFFER, Willy	254815	M	Ger.		Employee, Gestapo, Ledec (Czech.) 39-45				MURDER	CZECH.
KIEFNER, Josef	254568	M	Ger.	15.5.01	Scharfhr.,SS, Stod (Czech.) 13.-15.4.45				MURDER	CZECH.
KIEGEL	455	M	Ger.		Cmdt., C.C. Ravensbrueck (Ger.) 41-42				TORTURE	POL.
KIEGEL see KOGEL	188896									
KIEHL, Willy	257633	M	Ger.		Agent, Sgt.,SD, D'Evian (Fr.) 16.1.44				INTERR.	FR.
KIEHN or KUHNE	165248	M			Civilian, Lelm (Ger.) 5.44				TORTURE	U.S.
KIEIN or KLEIN	259479	M			Major, Illesheim (Ger.) 1.12.43				MURDER	U.S.
KIEK	141967	M	Ger.	95	Crim.secr., Police, Dachau (Ger.) 40-42				WITNESS	U.S.
KIEKBUSCH, Alfred	145229	M	Ger.		Osturmfhr., SS				MISC.CRIMES	U.S.
KIEKHAFFER, Rudolf alias Jeanle BRAZ	191902	M	Ger.	11	SD, Bois de Melannay (Fr.) 10.7.44				MURDER	FR.
KIEL or KHIL	456	M		09	Uscharfhr., Waffen-SS, C.C. Grini (Nor.) 42				MISC.CRIMES	NOR.
KIEL	252902	M			Usturmfhr.,SS, C.C. Harzungen-Nordhausen (Ger.)				MURDER	U.S.
KIEL	301175	M	Ger.		Member, NSDAP, head of O.T., Bennekom, Ede (Neth.) 25.3.-1.4.45				MURDER	NETH.
KIEL, Friedrich	141873	M	Ger.		Sgt., Fliegerhorst Cmdtr. A 208-XI, Hobsten (Ger.) 5.43				WITNESS	U.K.
KIELERMANN see KILLERMANN	131403									
KIELFER, Huni	41702	M	Ger.		Cpl., C.C. Oswiecim (Pol.)				MURDER	POL.
KIELINGER, Paul	301064	M	Ger.		Arbeitsfuehrer, Reichsarbeitsdienst, Marianske,Lazne,Bohemia (Czech.) 42-44				INTERR	CZECH.
KIELT	257330	M	Ger.		Sturmfhr.,SS, slave Labour camp, Beisfjord near Narvik(Nor.)6.-11.42				BRUTALITY	YUGO.
KIEN	189073	M	Ger.		Member, Schupo, Stanislawow (Pol.) 8.41-1.10.42				MURDER	POL.
KIEN, Alfred or KLEIN	457	M	Ger.		Guard, Lager official, C.C. Auschwitz,Rajsko (Pol.) 6.40-43				MURDER	POL.,BEL.,YUGO.
KIENAST, Thomas	252899	M			Pvt., C.C. Dora-Nordhausen (Ger.)				MURDER	U.S.
KIENBAUM, Heinrich	252900	M			Pvt., C.C. Ellrich-Nordhausen (Ger.)				MURDER	U.S.
KIENE, Wilhelm	252901	M			Cpl., C.C. Ellrich-Nordhausen (Ger.)				MURDER	U.S.
KIENER	187860	M	Ger.		Hptsturmfhr.,SS, C.C. Buchenwald (Ger.) 41-4.45				MURDER	BEL.,CZECH.
KIENER	251109	M	Ger.		Hptsturmfhr.,SS, C.C. Mauthausen (Aust.)				INTERR.	BEL.
KIENS	251685	M	Ger.		Lt.Gen., Liege (Bel.) 9.11.42				MURDER	BEL.
KIENZIE	192884	M	Ger.		Schupo, C.C. Falstad near Drontheim (Nor.) 8.42				MURDER	NOR.
KIEP, Otto	1409	M			Pvt., Inf.Rgt.194, Army				MISC.CRIMES	U.K.
KIEPER, Herbert	262240	M	Ger.	26.11.?	Uscharfhr.,SS, Gestapo, Rennes (Fr.) 43-44				MISC.CRIMES	FR.
KIEPPEL, Jacob	186743	M	Ger.		Obertruppfuehrer, SA, Bayonne (Fr.)				TORTURE	FR.
KIERSAMER or KIRSAMER	133299	M			Hptsturmfhr.,Waffen-SS, C.C. Flossenburg (Ger.)				TORTURE	U.S.
KIES	131404	M	Ger.		SS, C.C. Mauthausen (Aust.) 41-45				MURDER	U.S.
KIES, Friedmar	195633	M			Sturmmann, 1 Pz.Div. L.A.H., 3 Pio.Coy, Ligneuville (Bel.)17.-19.12.44				MURDER	U.S.
KIESBECK	145180	M			Civilian, guard, Bamberg (Ger.) 3.45				TORTURE	U.S.
KIESCH	139759	M		23	SS-Mann, Waffen-SS, C.C. Dora (Ger.) 44				MURDER	U.S.
KIESEL	139087	M			Dr., chief, Civil.admin., Belgrade (Yugo.) 41-45				MURDER	YUGO.
KIESEL	190211	M			Oberfeldkommandantur, Ljubljana (Yugo.) 41-44				MURDER	YUGO.
KIESEL, Friedrich	252903	M			Sturmmann, SS, C.C. Ellrich, Dora, Nordhausen (Ger.)				MURDER	U.S.
KIESEL, Johan or KIESSEL	29810	M	Ger.		Pvt., Flak-Rgt. Zug I, Gresmc (Fr.) 26.3.44				MURDER	FR.
KIESEL, Otto	1409	M	Ger.		Pvt.,Army				MISC.CRIMES	U.K.
KIESENWETTER	251107	M			Osturmfhr.,SS, C.C. Gusen (Aust.)				INTERR.	BEL.
KIESEROW	31701	M	Ger.		Cpl., C.C. Oswiecim (Pol.) 46-1.45				MURDER	POL.
KIESEWETTER	255959	M	Ger.		Dr., physician, C.C. Mauthausen (Aust.)				TORTURE	FR.
KIESIEL see CISSEL, Josef	10063									
KIESSLING	252212	M	Ger.		Inf., 658 Bn, 2 Coy, Sennecey les Macon (Fr.) 20.7.44				INTERR.	FR.
KIESSLING, Josef	189739	M	Ger.	4.5.01	Employee, Gestapo, Brno (Czech.) 39-45				MISC.CRIMES	CZECH.
KIESSELBACH	301800	M	Ger.		Member, SD Dinant, Cerfontaine,Senzeilles (Bel.) 44				TORTURE	BEL.
KIESSELBACH	192381	M	Ger.		Member, SD,Charleroi, Dinant,Cerfontaines,Senzeille(Bel.)2.-4.44				MURDER	BEL.
KIESSLIN see KISSLING	259641									
KIESSLING	193722	M	Ger.		Sgt.,Reichsjustizministerium,Strafgefangenenlager Nord Finmark (Nor.) 12.43				MISC.CRIMES	NOR.
KIETZEROV	254691	M	Ger.		W.O.,Sicherungsrgt.618, St.Marcel (Fr.) 13.9.44				WITNESS	FR.
KIEV, Alfred	173669	M	Ger.		SS-Sturmbann, C.C. Oswiecim (Pol.) 39-45				MURDER	CZECH.
KIEVEN, Hermann or RIEVEN	251094	M	Ger.		Pvt., Army, Avelgem (Bel.) 6.9.44				WITNESS	BEL.
KIEVIST, Jan	145839	M			Civilian, Postman, Borkum (Ger.) 4.8.44				MURDER	U.S.
KIGAULEITER	251654	M	Ger.		Org.Todt, Rosny-Bois (Fr.) 20.8.44				INTERR.	FR.
KIHM, Alois	147307	M	Ger.		Sonderfhr., Feldkommandantur 515, Granville (Fr.) 44				MURDER	FR.
KIKHAFER, Rudolf	458	M	Ger.		Lt., Army, St.Brieuc (Fr.) 8.44				TORTURE	FR.
KILAT, Ernst	185990	M	Ger.		SS Leibstandarte A.H., 1 Pz.Gren.Div., Stavelot (Bel.) 19.12.44				MURDER	BEL.
KILB	252511	M			Rottenfhr., C.C. Osterhagen, Nordhausen (Ger.)				MURDER	U.S.
KILB, Heinz Friedrich	143186	M	Ger.		Oscharfhr., SD, Alsace (Fr.)				MURDER	FR.,U.S.
KILIAN	186130	M	Ger.		Hauptwachtmstr., C.C. Ebrach (Ger.) 39-45				MURDER	CZECH.
KILIAN	192980	M	Ger.	17	SS-Sturmmann, Rosbach (Ger.)				MURDER	U.S.
KILIAN	193355	M	Ger.		Cpl.,2 Coy,PW work Bn 206,12 SS Pz.Div.H.J., Mosjoen (Nor.Fin.Ger.) 7.44-5.45				MURDER	NOR.
KILIAN, George	145189	M	Ger.		Rottenfhr., Waffen-SS, Leibstandarte A.H., Rosbach (Ger.) 4.3.45				MURDER	U.S.
KILIAN, Karl	102933	M	Ger.		Civilian, NSDAP, Muelheim, Dietesheim (Ger.) 25.2.45				MURDER	U.S.
KILIBAY see ZOLBRAT-KOILIBAY	39625									
KILL	141386	M	Ger.		Capt.,Frontleitstelle Paris (Fr.) 20.8.44				MURDER	FR.
KILLAT	167713	M	Ger.		Sgt., Interpreter, Indian Inf.Rgt.950, 7.44				MURDER	FR.
KILLEIT	172100	M			Oscharfhr.,SS,Waffen-SS, C.C. Muhldorf,Ampfing (Ger.) 6.44-4.45				SUSPECT	U.S.
KILLEMAN or KILLMANN	145214	M			Oscharfhr., SS, Mauthausen (Aust.) 41-45				SUSPECT	U.S.
KILLER, Joseph	140787	M	Ger.		Sgt., Army, Mittenwald (Ger.) 6.44				TORTURE	U.S.
KILLER, The	137580	M	Ger.		Civilian, C.C. Stalag IV D, Zschornewitz (Ger.) 6.4.45				MURDER	U.K.
KILLERMANN, Michael or KIELERMANN or KUHLEMANN	131403	M	Ger.	90 - 00	Oscharfhr.,SS-Totenkopf-Verband,C.C. Gusen (Ger.) 25.7.-8.8.44				MURDER	U.S.,BEL.
KILLERMANN	255960	M			Cmdt., C.C. Mauthausen (Aust.)				TORTURE	FR.
KILLIAN	173712	M			Executioner,camp and factory-employing,C.C.Dora(Ger.)43-4.45				MURDER	FR.
KILLIAN	188728	M			Sturmann, Gestapo, SD, Montech,Montauban(Fr.) 27.7.44				MURDER	FR.
KILLIAN	188729	M			SS-Police, 3 Coy,19 Rgt.,Taninges,Balme,Chatillon(Fr.)6.-7.44				TORTURE	FR.
KILLIAN	250322	M	Ger.		Capt.,377 Jaeger-Rgt., (Bel.) 25.-31.5.40				INTERR.	BEL.

KIL - KIR

NAME	C.R.FILE NUMBER	SEX	NATIO-NALITY	DATE OF BIRTH	RANK OCCUPATION UNIT PLACE AND DATE OF CRIME	REASON WANTED	WANTED BY
KILLIAN, Johann	305907	M	Ger.		Civilian, Velke, Heraltice (Czech.) 7.8.44	BRUTALITY	CZECH.
KILLIAN, Joseph	188727	M	Ger.		SS-Mann, Argeles Gazost (Fr.) 43	MURDER	FR.
KILLINGER	459	M	Ger.		Major, Cmdt., C.C. Dulag Luft (Ger.) 5.43	MURDER	U.K.
KILLINGER	12404	M	Ger.		Capt., SS, C.C. Sachsenhausen, Oranienburg (Ger.) 39-44	TORTURE	CZECH.BEL.
KILLINGER	173668	M	Ger.		Official, Staatspolizei-Leitstelle, Prague, Oswiecim, Birkenau(Czech.Pol.) 39-45	MURDER	CZECH.
KILLINGER, Karl	259114	M			Flyer, C.C. Ellrich, Nordhausen (Ger.)	MURDER	U.S.
KILLMANN (see KILLEMAN)	145214						
KILLMEIER	257304	M	Ger.		Capt., Pol., Krs. Rastatt, Bernbach (Ger.) 9.8.44	MURDER	U.S.
KILMANN (or KUHLMANN or KULMANN)	139771	M	Ger.		Uschfhr., Waffen-SS, C.C. Waldlager V und VI, Muhldorf (Ger.) 44-45	MURDER	U.S.
KILNE	123145	M	Ger.		Chief-Sonderfhr., Stalag 317, Markt Pongau (Aust.) 6.44-45	MISC.CRIMES	U.K.
KILSER	301768	M	Ger.		Member, Gestapo, Rumanien-Kdo., Vichy (Fr.) 10.43-9.44	MURDER	FR.
KILZ (see RILZ, Hans)	253285						
KIMMEL, Hans	186124	M	Ger.	19.9.89	SS-Oschfhr., 4 SS-Totenkopf-Stuba. C.C. Dora Mittelbau, Nordhausen(Ger)45	WITNESS	U.S.
KIMMEL, Walter	62496	M	Ger.		SS-Mann, C.C. Hamburg (Ger.)	MURDER	POL.CZECH.
KIMNITZ	132215	M	Ger.		Stabsscharfhr., SS, C.C. Gerdelegen (Ger.)	MURDER	U.S.
KIN (or DIN)	166401	M	Ger.		Usturmfhr., SS, Hauptamt, Rocaro (Ital.) 1.45	MURDER	U.S.
KINAS	460	M	Ger.		Sgt., Jg.-Regt.738, 2 Bn.or Coy., 118 Jg.Div., 7.43-1.44	MURDER	YUGO.
KINAS	147545	F		00 or 05	Woman-Guard, C.C. Wattenstedt (Ger.)	TORTURE	U.S.
KINDA	193721	M	Ger.		Pvt., Kgf.Arb.Bn.190, Berghomes (Nor.) 44-45	TORTURE	NOR.
KINDELER	253862	M	Ger.		Lt., Pekzugfhr., Div."Herm.Goering', 4 Regt. Paratrooper;., Hechteren et Hechtel (Bel.) 5. and 11.9.44	MISC.CRIMES	BEL.
KINDER, Franz	172884	M		91	Pvt., Stalag XX B, C.C. Schablau (Ger.) 22.4.42	WITNESS	U.K.
KINDER, Hans	189092	M		11	Crim.Asst., Gestapo, S.D., Mlada Boleslav (Czech.) 43-45	MURDER	CZECH.
KINDER, Johannes	195506	M		4.3.00	Employee, Gestapo, Kolin (Czech.) 39-45	MURDER	CZECH.
KINDERMANN	150665	M		12	Sgt., Signal-Corps, Tank-Corps, Grafenwoehr (Ger.) 2.11-1.12.44	MISC.CRIMES	U.S.
KINDERMANN	257629	M			Pvt., SS, C.C. Muhldorf Area (Ger.)	MURDER	U.S.
KINDEHVATER	156248	M		12	Member, SS, C.C. Buchenwald, Weimar (Ger.)	TORTURE	U.S.
KINDERVATER	305908	M	Ger.		Osturmfhr., C.C. Oranienburg (Ger.) 11.39-45	MURDER	CZECH.
KINDERVATER, Waldemar	145257	M			Scharfhr., SS, leader bf barracks, Totenkopf-Standarte, C.C. Buchenwald(Ger)	BRUTALITY	U.S.
KINDGEN, Otto	192379	M			Civilian, Rosbach (Ger.)	MURDER	U.S.
KINDL	145243	M	Ger.		Oschfhr., SS, J-SS-Totenkopf-Standarte, C.C. Buchenwald, Lublin(Pol.Ger.)	TORTURE	U.S.
KINDL	196796	M	Ger.		Sgt., Sipo, Groningen, Westerbork Camp (Neth.) 9.-12.44	TORTURE	NETH.
KINDLE	193670	M		98	Dr. (not medical), Civ., Perlmoser Cement Fabrik, Werndorf (Aust) 41-42	TORTURE	U.K.
KINDLER	167083	M	Ger.		Lt., Feldgendarmerie de Nancy, Nattexey (Fr.) 30.6.45	MURDER	FR.
KINDLER, Werner	145249	M	Ger.		Uschfhr., SS, 1 SS-Pz.Div., 2 Pz.Gr.Regt., 3 Bn., 12 Coy., Stavelot, Malmedy (Bel.) 22.-23.12.44	MURDER	U.S.
KINDT, Eduard	191368	M	Ger.		Oberwachtmeister, 7 Pol.Regt., 3 Pol.-Bn., Junkerdan (Nor.)	TORTURE	NOR.
KINE	131727	M	Ger.		Cpl., Zollgrenzschutz, Velmanya (Fr.) 1.8.44	MURDER	FR.
KINENHOF, Erich (or KINENHOM)	11259	M	Ger.		N.C.O., Army, Pz.Gren.Regt.111, 2 Coy., Albins (Fr.) 29.6.44	MURDER	FR.
KINEST, Thomas	186125	M			Guard, 4 Totenkopf-Sturmbann, C.C. Dora Mittelbau, Nordhausen(Ger)43-45	INTERR.	U.S.
KING	124492	M	Ger.		Cpl., Stalag XX B, C.C. Marienburg (Pol.) 4.44	MISC.CRIMES	U.K.
KINIPP	461	M	Ger.		Sgt., Chief, Navy, Marine-Flak, Poglas de Lampezelleg (Fr.) 4.44	MURDER	FR.
KINKEL	150657	M	Ger.		Agent, Gestapo, Bourg Madame (Fr.) 43-44	TORTURE	FR.
KINKEL, Ludwig	121556	M	Ger.		Civ., Obermeister Usine, Neurod (Ger.)	TORTURE	FR.
KINNBERGER, Ludwig	252892	M			Sgt., C.C. Ellrich, Nordhausen (Ger.)	MURDER	U.S.
KINNIG, Hans	145199	M			Blockleiter, C.C. Mauthausen, Gusen (Aust.) 41-45	MURDER	U.S.
KINSKY, Rudolf	254824	M	Ger.	13.6.98	Former, Civ. owner, Moravsky, Krumlov (Czech.) 38-45	INTERR.	CZECH.
KINTLER, W.	300044	M			Worker, Works manager of the "d Amstel", Waalwijk, Heusden, 43-10.44	PILLAGE	NETH.
KINTHUP, Albert	252891	M			Flyer, C.C. Ellrich, Nordhausen (Ger.)	MURDER	U.S.
KINTZ	194713	M	Ger.		Member, Volkssturm, Weimbohla (Ger.) 5.45	MURDER	FR.
KINYSENHAUS	172189	M			Scharfhr., Waffen-SS, C.C. Muhldorf, Ampfing (Ger.) 6.44-4.45	MURDER	U.S.
KINZA	186551	M	Ger.	10	Pvt., 610 Ldsschtz.-Bn., Stalag XX B, C.C. Marienberg (Ger.) 6.43	TORTURE	U.K.
KINZEL	104258	M	Ger.		Pol.-Inspector, Gestapo, Breslau (Ger.) 3.44	MURDER	U.K.
KINZEL, Erich	189738	M			Angestellter, Gestapo, Bruenn (Czech.)	MISC.CRIMES	CZECH.
KINZEL, Franz	192188	M	Ger.	29.12.87	Member, Gestapo (Bel.)	TORTURE	BEL.
KINZIG, Franz	179801	M	Ger.	20	Uschfhr., SS-Totenkopf-Verband, C.C. Gusen (Aust.)	MURDER	U.S.
KINZINGER	252889	M			Rottfhr., SS, C.C. Ellrich, Nordhausen (Ger.)	MURDER	U.S.
KIOTZBACH	300791	M			Sgt., 1 Aufkl.-Abtl., 3 Coy, 2 Column, XV Div. Afrika Korps, St.Leger (Arlon) 5.9.44	MISC.CRIMES	BEL.
KIOWSKY, Fritz	305909	M	Ger.		Chauffeur, Gestapo at Zlin-CSR, Habuvka near Moravska, Ostrava(Czech.)44	MURDER	CZECH.
KIPERT	251678	M	Ger.		Usturmfhr., S.D., Kdo.z.b.V, 7 "Pullmer", Cirey (Fr.) 8.44	TORTURE	U.K.
KIPING, Hans	11260	M	Ger.		Maat, 4 Marine-Art.-Bn., 6 Coy., Quiberon (Fr.) 44	MURDER	FR.
KIPINSKI, Phil	251004	M			Guard, C.C. Gusen (Aust.)	TORTURE	BEL.
KIPKE	172191	M			Civ., Org.Todt, C.C. Muhldorf, Ampfing (Ger.) 6.44-4.45	MURDER	U.S.
KIPP	260690				Dr.Prof., Major d.Res., Army	WITNESS	U.S.
KIPP, Otto	126929	M	Ger.	05	Kapo, Political P.W., C.C. Buchenwald (Ger.) 43	WITNESS	U.S.
KIPF, Wilhelm	252893	M			Pvt., C.C. Ellrich, Nordhausen (Ger.)	MURDER	U.S.
KIPF, Wilhelm	300045	M	Ger.		Farmer, Schefe Krs. Soest (Ger.) 42-44	MISC.CRIMES	POL.
KIPPE	261052	M			Oschfhr., SS, C.C. Vaihingen (Ger.) 13.8.44-7.4.45	MURDER	U.S.
KIPPENAU	24911	M	Ger.		Oschfhr., SS, C.C. Struthof (Fr.) 42-44	TORTURE	FR.
KIPPER, Ewald	259732	M	Ger.		Cpl., Unit SS 20607 K, Maintenance Coy. for Vehicles, St.Pierre du Palais, Charente Maritime (Fr.) 29.1.44	WITNESS	FR.
KIPPER, Franz	24869	M	Ger.	05	Pvt., Army, 361 Coy., Bauerwitz (Ger.) 12.43	MURDER	U.K.
KIPPERT	172099	M			Z.V.L., Org.Todt, C.C. Muhldorf, Ampfing (Ger.) 6.44-4.45	MURDER	U.S.
KIPPFMUELLER, Ludwig	192187	M	Ger.	15.11.07	Member, Gestapo (Bel.)	TORTURE	BEL.
KIRBERGER, Leopold	258975	M	Ger.	18.4.92	Dr., Sturmbannfhr., SS, NSDAP, 1.9.42	INTERR.	U.S.
KIRCH	139192	M	Ger.		Hpt. Wachtmeister, SS, Kamp (Ger.)	MURDER	U.S.
KIRCH, Heinrich	172187	M			Baufhr., Civ., Org.Todt, Muhldorf, Ampfing (Ger.) 6.44-4.45	MURDER	U.S.
KIRCH	179583	M	Ger.	90	Major, Dulag Luft, Oberursel, Frankfurt-Main (Ger.) 5.43	TORTURE	U.K.
KIRCH, Georges	196795	M	Ger.		Officer, Customhouse, Moraine (Fr.) 30.12.43	MISC.CRIMES	FR.
KIRCH, Heinrich	172187	M			Baufhr., Civ., Org.Todt, C.C. Muhldorf, Ampfing, (Ger.) 6.44-4.45	MURDER	FR.
KIRCH, Kurt	255961	M	Ger.		Kapo, C.C. Flossenburg (Ger.)	MISC.CRIMES	FR.
KIRCHBAUMER	254171	M	Ge.		Gestapo, Ferlach (Aust.) 44-45	INTERR.	YUGO.
KIRCHBERG, Bruno	179742	M	Ger.	15	Major, Org.Todt, Partins (Ital.) 13.4.44	MURDER	U.K.

KIR - KIS

NAME	C.R.FILE NUMBER	SEX	NATIO-NALITY	DATE OF BIRTH	RANK OCCUPATION UNIT PLACE AND DATE OF CRIME	REASON WANTED	WANTED BY
KIRCHDORFER	192675	M	Ger.		Hptsturmfhr.,SS,C.C.,Woippy (Fr.)	TORTURE	FR.
KIRCHDORFER, Friedrich	187217	M	Ger.	28. 4.09	Hptsturmfhr.,SS,Gestapo,Metz,Woippy (Fr.) 6.-7.44	TORTURE	CAN.,BEL.,FR
KIRCHDORFNER	138201	M	Ger.	95	Osturmfhr.,SS,C.C.,Woippy (Fr.) 44	TORTURE	FR.
KIRCHENLR, Hans	167961	M	Ger.		C.C.,Natzweiler (Fr.) 42-44	MURDER	FR.,BEL.
KIRCHENWAGER(see KIRCHSCHWAGER)	250302						
KIRCHER	174672	M			Adjutant,Feldgendarmerie,Valence (Fr.)	MISC.CRIMES	FR.
KIRCHERT	301331	M	Ger.		Member of the Gestapo at Trencin,C.C.,Oswiecim,Birkenau (Pol.) 39-45	MURDER	CZECH.
KIRCHERT, Werner	112972	M	Ger.		Osturmbannfhr.,SS,C.C.,Buchenwald (Ger.)	MURDER	U.S.
KIRCHESSNER, Franz	306993	M	Ger.		Rottfhr.,SS,C.C.,in charge of prisoners kitchen,Auschwitz (Pol.)41-45	BRUTALITY	POL.
KIRCHHOEFEL, Albert	258576	M	Ger.	15.11.07	Pvt.,guard,State service,Army,Gren.Ers.Bn.62,Landshut-Bavaria, Murnau,Oflag VII A (Ger.) 1.3.45	MURDER	POL.
KIRCHHOF	1410	M	Ger.		Capt.,Rgt.1044,Army,Frankfurt-Oder,(Ger.)	MISC.CRIMES	U.K.
KIRCHHOF	250499	M	Ger.	10	Mil.,Gebirgsjaeger,Haarlem (Neth.) 27.2.45	TORTURE	NETH.
KIRCHHOF, Fritz	252890	M			Pvt.,C.C.,Ellrich,Nordhausen (Ger.)	MURDER	U.S.
KIRCHHOFER, Anton	257790	M	Ger.	19	Zugwachtmeister,7.Coy.,322.Bn.,5.Schutz Rgt.,Slovenia,Ljubljana (Yugo.) 42-43	MISC.CRIMES	YUGO.
KIRCHHOFFER	170540	M	Ger.	10	Osturmfhr.,Army,C.C.,Woippy near Metz (Fr.) 6.-7.44	TORTURE	CAN.
KIRCHMAIER (or KRICHMAIER)	172192	M			Civilian,Org.Todt,C.C.,Muhldorf,Ampfing (Ger.) 6.44-4.45	MURDER	U.S.
KIRCHMANN, Karl	186132	M	Ger.		Lageraeltester,C.C.,Gross-Rosen (Ger.) 40-43	TORTURE	U.S.
KIRCHNI	174673	M	Ger.		Inf.Rgt.469,2.Bn.,Ind.Div.198,Le Tholy (Fr.) 13.11.44	PILLAGE	FR.
KIRCHNER	62112	M	Ger.		Osturmfhr.,SS,12.SS Pz.Div."Hitler Jugend",St.Sulpice (Fr.) 6.44	MURDER	U.S.,CAN.
KIRCHNER	131467	M	Ger.		Hptschfhr.,9.Pz.Gren.Div."Totenkopf",C.C.,Mauthausen (Aust.) 41-45	MURDER	U.S.
KIRCHNER	150669	M	Ger.	05	Hptschfhr.,SS,C.C.,Lieberose (Ger.)	TORTURE	U.K.
KIRCHNER	173087	M	Ger.		Civilian,Execution Comissioner,Mannheim (Ger.) 1.45	MURDER	U.S.
KIRCHNER	173121	M			Doctor,Sturmbannfhr.,SS,C.C.,Buchenwald (Ger.)	MURDER	U.S.
KIRCHNER (see KIRCHNER)	174670						
KIRCHNER	185985	M	Ger.		Pvt.,Waffen SS,1.Pz.Div."Adolf Hitler",1.SS Recon.Bn.,Parfondruy,Stavelot 18.-22.12.44	MURDER	U.S.
KIRCHNER	194017	M	Ger.		Pvt.,SS, 2.Gruppe,2.Zug,Stavelot (Bel.) 19.-20.12.44	MURDER	BEL.
KIRCHNER (or KIRSCHNER)	261813	M	Ger.		Lt.,participated in massacre of 2 civilians and execution of 15 hostages,St.Pol de Leon,Morlaix (Fr.)	MURDER	FR.
KIRCHNER	301262	M	Ger.		Employee,Abt.IV C,SD,Brussels (Bel.) 6.40-9.44	MURDER	BEL.
KIRCHNER	301573	M	Ger.		SS doctor,Sturmbannfhr.,SS,C.C.,Mauthausen (Aust.) 40-45	MURDER	BEL.
KIRCHNER, Hans	254587	M	Ger.		Oschfhr.,SS,Auschwitz,Birkenau (Pol.) 1.43	MURDER	YUGO.
KIRCHNER, Otto	254371	M	Ger.	21. 7.24	Pvt.,13.Coy.,558.Gren.Rgt.,Bruay en Artois (Fr.) 1.9.44	MURDER	FR.
KIRCHNER	254374	M		2. 2.20	Pvt.,13.Coy.,558.Gren.Rgt.,Bruay en Artois (Fr.) 1.9.44	MURDER	FR.
KIRCHNER, Heinrich	241367	M			Feldkriegsasst.,Feldkommandantur 529,Bordeaux,Souges (Fr.)	MURDER	FR.
KIRCHNER, Albert	305440	M	Ger.	10	Lt.,Gebirgsjaeger,Commander of a Army Coy.,Haarlem (Neth.)6.12.44-4.45	TORTURE	NETH.
KIRCHSCHWAGER (or KIRCHENWAGER)	250302	M	Ger.		Uschfhr.,SS,1.Pz.Div.Leibstandarte "Adolf Hitler",2.Pz.Gren.Rgt., 9.Coy.,Malmedy (Bel.) 17.12.44	INTERR.	U.S.
KIRCHLOF	102971	M	Ger.		Pvt.,SS,C.C.,Thekla near Leipzig (Ger.)	MURDER	U.S.
KIEJALM	185987	M	Ger.		Lt.,Pion.Bn.669,1.Coy.,Villers,St.Gertrude,Werbomont,Ferrieres, Burmontige (Bel.) 9.44	MURDER	BEL.
KIAKBERGER	253123	M			Pvt.,C.C.,Rottleberode,Nordhausen (Ger.)	MURDER	U.S.
KIPKS	254564	M	Ger.		Sgt.,Army,Villmar, (Ger.) 17.6.-15.8.44	MURDER	U.S.
KIRESE	164130	M	Ger.		Lt.,Air-force,Rydelstedt (Ger.) 7.4.45	MURDER	U.K.
KIRST	254654	M	Ger.		Sgt.,Air-force,stationed in Huize de Breul,Zeist Prov.of Utrecht Langbroek,(Neth.) 6.44	MURDER	NETH.
KIRI	172188	M			Hptschfhr.,Waffen SS,C.C.,Muhldorf,Ampfing (Ger.) 6.44-4.45	MURDER	U.S.
KIRBL, Arno	160665	M	Ger.		Village blacksmith,Civilian,Punschrau (Ger.)	TORTURE	U.S.
KIRSAMPP (see KIERSAMPP)	133299						
KIRSCH	462	M	Ger.		Sgt.,Army,Breedonok (Bel.)	MURDER	BEL.
KIRSCH, Victor (or FISCH)	139767	M	Ger.	00	Oschfhr.,Waffen SS,Camp leader,C.C.,Camp Mittergars,Muhldorf (Ger.)44-45	TORTURE	U.S.
KIRSCH	142202	M	Ger.	05	Hptsturmfhr.,SS,Lublin (Pol.)	TORTURE	FR.
KIRSCH	186126	M			Rottfhr.,SS,guard,4.Totenkopfsturmbann,C.C.,Mittelbau,Dora, Nordhausen (Ger.) 43-45	MURDER	U.S.
KIRSCH	193720	M	Ger.		Lt.,Kgf.Arb.Bn. 184, 230.Div.,Engen (Nor.) 6.-7.44	MURDER	NOR.
KIRSCH	252247	M	Ger.		Cpl.,Fieldpolice (Fr.) Vendom, 9.8.44	MURDER	FR.
KIRSCH	254957	M	Ger.		Lt.,SS,Prag (Czech.)	MURDER	CZECH.
KIRSCH	255176	M	Ger.		Osturmfhr.,Abt.VC,Bruessel,Prag (Bel.) 40-44, 5.5.45	MURDER	BEL.,CZECH.
KIRSCH, Angèle	195463	F	Ger.	14. 4.84	Civilian,Luxembourg (Lux.) 40-45	TORTURE	LUX.
KIRSCH, Emmi	196113	F	Ger.	22	Official,C.C.,Ravensbrueck (Ger.)	TORTURE	FR.
KIRSCH, Hans	193702	M	Ger.	3. 1.02	Sgt.,Oberwachtmeister,Reichsjustizministerium,Strafgefangenenlager Nord,Finmark (Nor.) 4.45	MISC.CRIMES	NOR.,YUGO.
KIRSCHNEK, Erwin	189737	M	Ger.	15.12.07	Employee,Gestapo,Brno (Czech.) 39-45	MISC.CRIMES	CZECH.
KIRSCHNER	463	M	Ger.		Oschfhr.,SS,C.C.,Oswiecim Ragske (Pol.) 6.40-43	MURDER	POL.,BEL.
KIRSCHNER	162106	M	Ger.		Lt.,Army,St.Pol de Leon-Morlaix (Fr.) 44	MURDER	FR.
KIRSCHNER	172190	M			Civilian,Org.Todt,C.C.,Muhldorf,Ampfing (Ger.) 6.44-4.45	MURDER	U.S.
KIRSCHNER	173102	M	Ger.		C.C.,Schirmeck,Rotenfels,Gaggenau (Ger.,Fr.) 44	MURDER	U.K.
KIRSCHNER	250881	M	Ger.	17	Capt.,Police,Warschau (Pol.) 39-40	MISC.CRIMES	POL.
KIRSCHNER	253122	M			Oschfhr.,SS,C.C.,Dora,Nordhausen (Ger.)	MURDER	U.S.
KIRSCHNER (see KIRCHNER)	261813						
KIRSCHNER, Kurt	143157	M	Ger.	12	Hptschfhr.,SS,C.C.,Lublin (Pol.) 4.42	MURDER	U.S.
KIRSCHOFF	67041	M	Ger.		Cpl.,C.C.,Gruppe No.143, (Ger.)	TORTURE	U.K.
KIRSCHOFF	187128	M	Ger.	00	Cpl.,714 Landesschuetzen Bn.,Stalag XX a,C.C.,Thorn (Pol.) 1.42	TORTURE	U.K.
KIRSCHSTEIN, Herbert	120565	M	Ger.		Uschfhr.,SS,Semi-Military,Odessa (Sov.Un.) 41-42	MURDER	U.S.
KIRSCHT, Louise	124598	F	Ger.	95	Civilian,C.C.,Oberemmel,Flussbach (Ger.)	TORTURE	BEL.
KIRSLING, Anton	258419	M	Ger.		Kapo,4.Coy.,Gren.Rgt.5,148,between Neufohatel,Rouen (Fr.)	WITNESS	U.S.
KIRSTEN	174671	M			Lt.,Fallschirmjaeger Rgt.,2.Bn.,2.Div.,F.P.No.39714, Plouzane (Fr.) 44	MURDER	FR.
KIRSTER, Paul	194099	M	Ger.		Guard,Stalag IV A,Bahnmeisterei,Riesa Nr.460, (Ger.) 24.3.44-45	MURDER	NETH.,U.S.
KIRSTHALER	131402	M	Ger.		5.Fallschirmjaeger Rgt.,Nachrichtenzug,Quaragnon,Jamappes,Ghlin (Bel.) 2.-5.9.44	MURDER	BEL.
KITTNITZ (see KITNITZ)	124491						
KISCH	191466	M	Ger.		Uschfhr.,SS,C.C.,Mauthausen (Aust.) 41-43	MURDER	U.S.
KISCH (see KIRSCH) Viktor	139767						

NAME	C.R.FILE NUMBER	SEX	NATIO-NALITY	DATE OF BIRTH	RANK	OCCUPATION	UNIT	PLACE AND DATE OF CRIME	REASON WANTED	WANTED BY
KISCH	139768	M	Ger.	95	Sgt., Waffen SS, C.C. Mittergars-Lager,Muehldorf (Ger.) 44-45				TORTURE	U.S.
KISCH, Friedrich	250299	M		14. 3.97	Member, NSDAP, Amstetten (Aust.) 20.3.45				INTERR.	U.S.
KISCHINSKY (see WISCHINSKY)	180641									
KISKI, Erich	305910	M	Ger.	05 - 10	Member, Organisation Todt, Velke, Heraltice (Czech.) 7.8.44				BRUTALITY	CZECH.
KISMANN	165384	M	Ger.		Lt., Army, C.C., Chatillon-Leyment (Fr.) 9.6.44				TORTURE	FR.
KISMANN	179893	M	Ger.		Cmdt, C.C., Gevrieux,Laynent (Fr.) 11.6.44				MURDER	FR.
KISOLOJOV	301332	M	Ger.		Member of the Gestapo at Nove Mesto n-Vakom, C.C., Oswiecim-Birkenau (Pol.) 39 - 45				MURDER	CZECH.
KISS	131465	M	Ger.		Rottenfhr., SS, C.C. Mauthausen (Aust.) 41 - 45				MURDER	U.S.
KISSEL, Wilhelm	192378	M	Ger.		SS-Unterscharfhr., C.C., Flossenburg (Ger.) 44.- 45				MURDER	U.S.
KISSELBACH	254834	M	Ger.		SS - Medicin, Strasbourg (Fr.) 40 - 44				MURDER	FR.
KISSER, Hermann	173091	M	Ger.		Volkssturmmann, 1.Volkst.Bn.,C.C., Gardelegen (Ger.) 4.45				INTERR.	U.S.
KISSLING	72498	M	Ger.		Oberjaeger, Army, Fallschirm-Jaeger Bn., St. Segal (Fr.) 44				MURDER	U.K.
KISSLING (or KIESSLIN or KUSLING)	259641	M	Ger.	95	Sgt., Brignoles (Var), Bauduen (Fr.) 22.7.44				MURDER	FR.
KISSNER	261613	M	Ger.		Capt., Gestapo L'Yonne, (Fr.)				BRUTALITY	FR.
KISSNER, Hilmar	167962	M	Ger.	22.12.23	SS - Helfer, C.C., Natzweiler ( ) 42 - 44				MURDER	FR.
KISTLER	104353	M	Ger.		Cpl., Oflag VII C-H, Laufen (Ger 21.1.41				MURDER	U.K.
KITCHE, Adalbert	162864	M	Ger.		N.C.O., SS Unit 12611 C, La Cala..e (Bel.) 6.9.44				MURDER	BEL.
KITCHEDI (see KETCHEDI)	167084									
KITH	301769	M	Ger.		Dr., C.C., Birkenau-Auschwitz (Pol.) 44 - 45				MURDER	FR.
KITLER	123313	M	Ger.	01	Civilian, C.C. B.E.4,Bitterfeld (Ger.) 6.44 - 4.45				MURDER	U.K.
KITNITZ (or KIRTNETZ)	124491	M	Ger.		Sgt., Army, Blechhammer (Ger.) 44				TORTURE	U.K.
KITT	464	M	Ger.		Phisician, C.C., Oswiecim (Pol.) 6.40 - 43				MURDER	POL. BEL.
KITT	145960	M	Ger.		Dr.,SS-Hauptsturmfhr., C.C., Auschwitz (Pol.) 43 - 44				MURDER	U.S.
KITT	177537	M	Ger.		Official, C.C., Neuengamme (Ger.)				MURDER	FR.
KITT	301574	M	Ger.		SS - Jscharfhr., C.C. Mauthausen (Aust.) 40 - 45				MURDER	BEL.
KITTEL	146838	M	Ger.		Soldier, SS-Panz.Div. " Das Reich " 2.Coy, Tulle (Fr.) 44				MURDER	FR.
KITTEL	162610	M	Ger.		Major,General, Army Stalag XX A, C.C. Falkenburg (Pol.) 6.43				MISC.CRIMES	U.K.
KITTEL	252219	M	Ger.		Lt., Pleucadeuc, St. Marcel (Fr.) 6.44				MISC.CRIMES	FR.
KITTEL, Gerhard	150670	M			Civilian, Jena (Ger.)				TORTURE	FR.
KITTLER	395650	M	Ger.		Kommandeur, SA, C.C., Przekoran (Pol.) 41				MURDER	SOV.UN.
KITIMUELLER	253121	M			SS, C.C., Rottleberode, Nordhausen (Ger.)				MURDER	U.S.
KITZ	125672	M	Ger.		W.O.Sen., Gestapo, Hambrecht, Perlgueux (Fr.) 8.44				MURDER	FR.
KITZIG, Arthur	254598	M	Ger.		SS - Schuetze, C.C., Auschwitz-Birkenau (Pol.) 10.42				MURDER	YUGO.
KITZINGER (see KRITZINGER)	62416									
KITZINGER	62538	M	Ger.		Obersturmfhr., SS, 3.Coy.SS-Panz.-Bn.Raide (Fr.) 6.44				MURDER	U.S.
KITZINGER, Paul	167226	M	Ger.		Pay-Master, Staff III Bn. Jaeger Rgt.517, Virelles Leza Chimay (Bel.)40				PILLAGE	BEL.
KITZMANN	306994	M	Ger.		SS - Guard, C.C., Auschwitz (Pol.) 42 - 45				TORTURE	POL.
KITZMULLER, Willy (or KATZMULLER)	167082	M	Ger.		Pvt., Air-Force, Troissereux (Fr.) 8.44				MURDER	FR.
KIZZEL	130187	M	Ger.		Cpl., Stalag 383, Hohenfels (Ger.) 10.42 - 4.43				TORTURE	U.K.
KLAAR	126963	M	Ger.		Unterstumfhr., SS-Panz.Div. "Das Reich" (Fr.) 44				MURDER	FR.
KLAARE (see KLARR)	261902									
KLAAZE (see KLARR)	261902									
KLABBER, Johannes	191300	M	Ger.		Pvt., Army, St.Andries, Bruegge, Varsenare (Bel.) 4.9.44				MURDER	BEL.
KLADDE	250323	M	Ger.		Cpl., 377.Jaeger Rgt., 12.Coy. Vinkt, Meigem (Bel.) 5.40				BRUTALITY	BEL.
KLADNIK, Rajko	139185	M			Civilian, Gellneukirchen (Aust.) 44 - 45				WITNESS	U.S.
KLAEHR (or LECLAIR)	133812	M			Hauptscharfhr., SS-Assistant to Gestapo Secretary C.C.Weimar-Buchenwald (Ger.) 44 - 45				BRUTALITY	FR.
KLAEHR	257018	M	Ger.		Cpl., 2.Nachrichten Coy.,Army, Bolnes (Neth.) 8.5.45				INTERR.	NETH.
KLAEMPFERT	138359	M	Ger.		Adjudant, Gestapo, SS, Lyon (Fr.)				MURDER	FR.
KLAFFL	262363	M	Ger.		Artill.Fahnenjunkerschule,VII.Inspection, Nepomuk (Czech.) 26.4.45				SUSPECT	CZECH.
KLAGE	127099	M	Ger.		Lt., 2.SS-Panz.Div. "Das Reich" (Fr.)				MURDER	FR.
KLAHR, Erwin	112611	M	Ger.		Member, Gestapo, Cahors (Fr.) 25.6.44				MURDER	FR.
KLAIBER	465	M	Ger.		Sgt., Army, C.C. Caen (Fr.) 6.44				MURDER	FR.
KLAITENHOF	10015	M	Ger.		Hauptsturmfhr., SS, C.C. Dachau (Ger.) 38 - 44				MURDER	CZECH.
KLAMM	466	M	Ger.		Obersturmbannfhr., Waffen SS, Kosciany (Pol.) 9.-11.39				MURDER	POL.
KLAMMER, Friedrich	256660	M			Civilian, Gratkorn (Aust.) 2.45				WITNESS	U.S.
KLAMMER, Nina	256659	F			Civilian, Gratkorn (Aust.) 2.45				WITNESS	U.S.
KLAMPFER, Franz	253119	M			Pvt., C.C. Ellrich, Nordhausen (Ger.)				MURDER	U.S.
KLAMROTH	306995	M	Ger.	7. 8.99	Major, Commanding III.Bn.377.Inf.Rgt. Vinkt,Eastern,Flanders (Bel.)5.40				MURDER	BEL.
KLAMT, Ottokar	301509	M	Ger.		Oberscharfhr., SS, C.C. Buchenwald (Ger.) 3.38 - 10.43				MURDER	BEL.
KLAN	149518	M	Ger.	07	Cmdt., SA, Marl (Fr.)				MISC.CRIMES	FR.
KLANCKE, F.	300897	M	Ger.		Saddler, Louvain (Bel.) 5.40				MISC.CRIMES	BEL.
KLANOWSKI, K.	254122	M			Zugwachtmstr. Araheim (Neth.) 3.45				MURDER	NETH.
KLANT	190210	M			Sgt., SD, Gestapo,C.C., Banjica (Yugo.) 41 - 43				MURDER	YUGO.
KLAPETZ, Max	172200	M			Unterscharfhr.,Member of M-I SS Lager, C.C. Muehldorf-Ampfing (Ger.) 6.44 - 4.45				MURDER	U.S.
KLAPPENBACH	256839	M			Lt., SD, Region De Pontivy (Fr.) 44				MISC.CRIMES	FR.
KLAPPER	191367	M			Col., Army, C.C. Gossen (Nor.) 42 - 45				MURDER	NOR.
KLAPPER, Fritz	191366	M	Ger.	05 - 15	Navy, Kriegsmarinewerft, Bergen, Marte in Maasfjord (Nor.) 10.42				MURDER	NOR.
KLAPRODT, Theodor	254651	M	Ger.		Ortsgruppenleiter, Civilian, Langenhagen (Ger.) 3.43				MISC.CRIMES	NTH.
KLAPROTH	257035	M			Guard, Camp of Schomberg, (Ger.) 44 - 45				SUSPECT	FR.
KLAR	39774	M	Ger.		Lt., Army,Landesschuetzen Bn. 398, Stalag VIII B.C.C. Schomberg (Ger.)				MURDER	U.K.
KLAR	129686	M	Ger.		Rottenfhr., SS, C.C. Dora-Nordhausen(Ger.)				MURDER	U.S.
KLAR	137646	M	Ger.	15	Oberscharfhr.,SS, C.C. Auschwitz (Pol.)				MURDER	U.K.
KLAR	157801	M	Ger.	26	Untersturmfhr., SS-Panz.Div. "Das Reich" 3.Coy. 1.Bn.Oradour-Glane (Fr.)MURDER 10.6.44					FR.
KLAR	254970	M	Ger.		Lt., 3.Coy. SS-Panz.Div. "Das Reich",Saint-Junien (Fr.) 10.6.44				MURDER	FR.
KLARENBACH	253120	M			Cpl., C.C. Ellrich, Nordhausen (Ger.)				MURDER	U.S.
KLARENBACH, Heinrich	31703	M	Ger.		Settler, Olekozyn (Pol.) 12.39				INCENDIARISM	POL.
KLASS	255155	M	Ger.		Obersturmfhr., Sipo, Bruessel (Bel.) 40 - 45				MURDER	BEL.
KLASS, Heinrich	172202	M	Ger.		Guard, C.C. Osterhagen (Ger.)				TORTURE	U.S.
KLASSEN	146709	M			Oberscharfhr., C.C., Flossenburg (Ger.)				MURDER	U.S.
KLATTE (see von KLATTE,Hermann)	194581									

KLA-KLE

NAME	C.R.FILE NUMBER	SEX	NATIO-NALITY	DATE OF BIRTH	RANK OCCUPATION UNIT PLACE AND DATE OF CRIME	REASON WANTED	WANTED BY
KLATTENHOF	259423	M	Ger.		Standartenfhr., SS, C.C., Dachau (Ger.) 42-45	MURDER	YUGO.
KLATZ, Johann	29774	M	Ger.		Dr., Landgerichtsrat, Public-Official, Cheb (Czech.) 21.2.40	MURDER	BEL.
KLAU (or KLAV)	135548	M	Ger.		Capt., Security Officer,Oflag VII B,Conc.Camp,Eichstatt (Ger.)2.44-5.44	MISC.CRIMES	U.K.
KLAU	187199	M			Lt.Col., Stalag VI A, Conc.Camp, Hemer (Ger.) 41-45	MURDER	U.S.
KLAUBERG	173667	M	Ger.		Dr., Medical-Official, Conc.Camp, Oswiecim,Birkenau (Pol.) 39-45	MURDER	CZECH.
KLAUCKE, F.	251093	M			Pvt., Louvain (Bel.) 5.40	WITNESS	BEL.
KLAUCKE, Hans	252898	M			Pvt., Conc.Camp Ellrich, Nordhausen (Ger.)	MURDER	U.S.
KLAUG, Eric	151328	M	Ger.		Cpl., Army,1-337.Bn. Kdo.Fuehrer, C.C., (Ger.) 13.4.45	TORTURE	U.K.
KLAUKE, Erich	260736	M		13	Hptschfhr., SS, Eppstein-Taunus (Ger.) 10.44	MURDER	U.S.
KLAUS	1709	M	Ger.		Major, Conc.Camp, San-Vittare (It.)	TORTURE	U.K.
KLAUS	39772	M	Ger.		Pvt., Army, Marburg, Heydekrug, Swinemuende (Ger.) 1.42, 2.u.3.44	MURDER	U.K.
KLAUS	39773	M	Ger.		Sgt., Conc.Camp, Stalag XI B, Ohlandorf (Ger.)	TORTURE	U.K.
KLAUS	111144	M	Ger.		Major, Conc.Camp, San.Vittorio Prison, Milan (It.)	MURDER	U.K.
KLAUS	131377	M	Ger.		Uschfhr., SS-Panz.Gren.Div."Totenkopf", C.C.,Mauthausen (Aust.) 41-45	MURDER	U.S
KLAUS	131431	M	Ger.		Rottfhr., SS, Conc.Camp, Mauthausen (Aust.) 41-45	MURDER	U.S.
KLAUS	173082	M	Ger.		Usturmfhr., SS, Mannheim (Ger.) 1.45	MURDER	U.S.
KLAUS	190636	M	Ger.		Asst.Director, Volkssturm, Iba Bebra, (Ger)	MURDER	U.S.
KLAUS	196112	M	Ger.		Oberwachtmstr., 7.Art.Frs Rgt.,Albertville (Fr.)	MURDER	FR.
KLAUS	306091	M	Ger.		SS-Mann, C.C., Alderney Channel Is and Kortemark, 42-45	MURDER	CZECH.
KLAUS	306996	F	Ger.		SS-Guard, C.C., Auschwitz (Pol.) 42-45	TORTURE	POL.
KLAUS, Gustav	306025	M	Ger.		In charge of children in Velpke Clinic, Velpke (Ger.) 5.44-12.44	MURDER	U.K.
KLAUS, Hilda	139763	F	Ger.		Woman-Guard, Waffen-SS, Arbeitslager 101 (Buchenwald) C.C.Magdeburg.45	TORTURE	U.S.
KLAUS, Kurt	162247	M	Ger.		Overseer, Kriegsgef.Arb.Kmdo.,C.C. Adolf-Mine,Merkstein (Ger.)42-45	TORTURE	U.S.
KLAUS, Paul	186133	M	Ger.	95	Capt., Art.Ausbildung, C-O Battery, Prague (Czech.) 5.5.45	MURDER	CZECH.
KLAUSA, Emanuel	252897	M			Pvt., Conc.Camp Ellrich, Nordhausen (Ger.)	MURDER	U.S.
KLAUSE	179746	M			Sgt., 590.Panz.Jaeg.Abt., Ponte Buggianese (It.) 7.44-8.44	MURDER	U.K.
KLAUSEN	122611	M	Ger.		Rapportfhr., Conc.Camp, Auschwitz (Pol.) 42 - 43 -44	MURDER	FR.
KLAUSEN	157802	M			Usturmfhr., SS, Conc.Camp, Auschwitz (Pol.)	MURDER	U.S.
KLAUSEN	173666	M	Ger.		Oschfhr., SS, C.C., Oswiecim, Birkenau (Pol.) 39-45	MURDER	CZECH.
KLAUSER, Richard	172203	M	Ger.		Civilian, Grosswaugen (Ger.)	WITNESS	U.S.
KLAUSMANN, Josef	252196	M			Pvt., C.C. Ellrich, Nordhausen (Ger.)	MURDER	U.S.
KLAUSNITZER	256822	M			Sanitaeter, Military, Amsterdam (Neth.) 23.10.44	MURDER	NETH.
KLAUSNITZER, Richard	192377	M	Ger.	89	Gend.Meister, Gend., Littitz (Czech.) 45	MURDER	U.S.
KLAUSS	251087	M	Ger.		Major, Huy (Bel.)	INTERR.	BEL.
KLAUSS	252366	M			Pvt., C.C., Dora, Nordhausen (Ger.)	MURDER	U.S.
KLAUSSE	1081	M	Ger.		Chief, Feldgend., Langres (Fr.)	TORTURE	FR.
KLAUTZ, Eric (see KLOTZ)	123870						
KLAV (see KLAU)	135548						
KLAVACEK, Rudolf	305788	M	Ger.		Pvt., Arb.Kdo.253-1, Trieben (Aust.) 2.45	BRUTALITY	U.K.
KLAVON, Emil (see KLAWON)	193354						
KLAWATCHEK	160677	M		90	Leader, Abwehr FAT (CIC) 318, Witebsk (Sov.Un.) 7.43-8.43	MURDER	U.S.
KLAWITER, Arnold	252202	M			Cpl., C.C.Ellrich, Nordhausen (Ger.)	MURDER	U.S.
KLAWON (or KLAVON or KLAWAN, Emil)	193354	M	Ger.		Pvt., 1.Kgf.Arb.Bn.41, 1.Coy.,Kristiansund Nerlandsdal (Nor.) 41-45	TORTURE	NOR.
KLEBAUER	190502	M			Sgt., 11.Pz.Div.,2.Coy., 2 AA - A 7,nr.Bergerac and Albine (Fr.)7.-8.44	MURDER	FR.
KLEBE	467	M			Sgt., Conc.Camp, Caen (Fr.) 6.44	MURDER	FR.
KLEBE, August	189074	M			Gend.Meister, Police, Hergarten (Ger.) 7.44-8.44	MURDER	U.S.
KLEBECK	306092	M			Osturmfhr.,SS,Deputy-Camp-Cmdt.,C.C. Alderney, 42-45	MURDER	CZECH.
KLEBEK	468	M			Sgt., 125.Pz.Rgt.,E.Bn.,1.Coy. (Fr.?) 6.44	MURDER	U.K.
KLEBER	191805	M			Osturmfhr., SS, Conc.Camp, Sachsenhausen (Ger.) 39-4.43	MURDER	POL.
KLEBER	255602	M			Sgt., Parachutist, Kessel (Limburg) (Neth.) 7.11.44	SUSPECT	NETH.
KLEBER	256891	M		24	Sgt., Mil.Paratroops, (Neth.) 7.11.45	WITNESS	NETH.
KLEBER, Else	187618	F	Ger.		Civilian, Plzen (Czech.) 39-45	MISC.CRIMES	CZECH.
KLEBER, Johann	186753	M			Sgt., Army, Ussel (Fr.) 8.10.44	MURDER	FR.
KLEBERT	252240	M	Ger.		Capt., SS, Percy (Fr.) 1.8.44	MISC.CRIMES	FR.
KLEBIN	186135	M			Lt., Police, Chania (Grc.) 2.44	MURDER	GRC.
KLECANEK (see KLETSCHANEK, Anton)	254816						
KLEE	189397	M			Wachtmeister, Police, C.C., Tromsoya (Nor.) 18.6.42	TORTURE	NOR.
KLEE, Erwin	252201	M			Rottfhr., SS, C.C., Harzungen, Nordhausen (Ger.)	MURDER	U.S.
KLEEBERGER	185479	M			Osturmfhr., SS, 1.Coy.,6.SS-Abt., N.K.Nachschub,Dolembreux (Bel.)5.9.44	MURDER	BEL.
KLEEBOLTE, Bernard	132068	M	Ger.		Rottfhr., SS, SD, Allgem.SS, Lippstadt (Ger.) 44-45	TORTURE	U.S.
KLEEMAN	178312	M	Ger.	93	Capt.,368.Lds.Schtz.Bn., Stalag IV C, Br. Bodenbach (Czech.) 7.44	MURDER	CZECH.
KLEEMAN	250312	M	Ger.		Oschfhr., SS, Swientochlowice (Pol.) 43-44	MURDER	U.K.
KLEEMANN	39155	M	Ger.		zPvt.,10.Stalag IX C, Conc.Camp, Nordhausen (Ger.)	TORTURE	U.K.
KLEEMANN	173730	M	Ger.		Army-Chief, "Straflager" at the Boz mines (Yugo.) 42	TORTURE	YUGO.
KLEEMANN	306799	M			N.C.O., Feldgend.,Cdt.Bad Oeynhausen,Montigny Les Vesoul-Hte.Saone (Fr.) 16.7.44	MURDER	FR.
KLEEMANN, Erich	254634	M	Ger.	4.11.07	Z.b.V.Kommando 31, Valasske Mezirici (Czech.) 2.-5.45	TORTURE	CZECH.
KLEES, Filip	258447	M			SS-Mann, Guard, SS, C.C., Ohrdruf (Ger.) 12.44-4.45	MURDER	U.S.
KLEESZ, Karl	255538	M	Ger.	23. 4.97	SS-Mann, C.C., Nordhausen (Ger.)	MURDER	U.S.
KLEFFEL	11262	M			Col., Army, Chaumont (Fr.) 24.8.44	MURDER	FR.
KLEFFEL, Phillipp	259587	M		87	General	WITNESS	U.S.
KLEFFNER, Franz	195074	M	Ger.		Osturmfhr., SS-Totenkopf-Div., Le Paradis (Fr.) 27.5.40	WITNESS	U.K.
KLEFFNER, Fritz	129144	M	Ger.	95	Lt., Dulag Luft, Oberursel (Ger.)	TORTURE	U.K.
KLEHR, Josef	157805	M			Oschfhr., SS, Conc.Camp, Auschwitz (Pol.)	MURDER	U.S., FR.
KLEIBAUER	122610	M	Ger.		SS Gestapo, Challes les Eaux and Arvin (Fr.) 8.1.44	MURDER	FR.
KLEIBAVER (see KLEINBAUER, Henri)	132566						
KLEIBERGER, Alfons	11263	M	Ger.		Pvt., Army, Pz.Gren.Rgt.111, Albine (Fr.) 29.6.44	MURDER	FR.
KLEIBL, Franz	195635	M	Ger.		Agent, Gestapo, Vozice (Czech.) 39-45	MURDER	CZECH.
KLEIBL, Wilhelm	251680	M	Ger.		Special-Fhr., Section I-e, Krs.Kommandantur,Kragujevac (Yugo.)	INTERR.	YUGO.
KLEICH (see KNECHT, Clara)	52675						
KLEIMEIER, Karl	145252	M	Ger.		Civilian, Head of Police-Works at Stadtwerke, Bielefeld (Ger.) 11.43	TORTURE	U.S.

KLE-KLE

NAME	C.R.FILE NUMBER	SEX	NATIO-NALITY	DATE OF BIRTH	RANK OCCUPATION UNIT PLACE AND DATE OF CRIME	REASON WANTED	WANTED BY
KLEIMHEIM, Willy	174674	M	Ger.		469 I.Regt.,2 Bn.,198 I.Div.,Le Tholy(Fr.) 13.11.44	INCENDIARISM	FR.
KLEIN see KIEN, Alfred	457						
KLEIN	29812	M	Ger.		Chief Custom Inspector,Langon(Fr.) 3.8.41	MURDER	FR.
KLEIN	62421	M	Ger.		SS-Oberfuehrer,Police	TORTURE	UNWCC.
KLEIN	12441	M	Ger.		Lt.,Army,Armenian Legion,Col de La Tourette(Fr.) 28.5.44	MURDER	FR.
KLEIN	24879	M	Ger.		Dr.,Oberfeldarzt,Stalag VI G(Ger.)	TORTURE	U.S.
KLEIN	24886	M	Ger.		Lt.,Army,5 Para Art.Regt.,Quirnbach Helferskirchen(Ger.)16.-17.3.45	MURDER	U.S.
KLEIN	24887	M	Ger.		SS-Osturmfhr.,C.C.,Hinzert(Ger.) 43	TORTURE	U.S.
KLEIN	39775	M	Ger.		Cpl.,Army,C.C.Heydekrug Swinemuende(Ger.) 44	MURDER	U.K.
KLEIN	124233	M	Ger.		Oberstabsarzt,Army,Stalag 3B,Fuerstenberg(Ger.)	MURDER	U.S.
KLEIN	124599	M	Ger.		Doctor,C.C.Auschwitz-Birkenau(Pol.)	MURDER	BEL.
KLEIN	126563	M	Ger.		Wachtmeister,Police,Kroepelin(Ger.) 6.or 7.44	MURDER	U.S.
KLEIN see KENEN	134872						
KLEIN	145207	M	Ger.		German Marine Corps,St.Marine(Fr.) 30.6.44	MURDER	U.S.
KLEIN	145247	M	Ger.		Uschfhr.,1 SS Panz.Div.,2 Panz.Gren.Regt.,3 Bn.,12 Coy., Stavelott Malmedy(Bel.) 22.-23.12.44	MURDER	U.S.
KLEIN	145837	M	Ger.		Dr.,Civilian,C.C.Markt Pangau(Ger.)	MISC.CRIMES	U.S.
KLEIN	145961	M	Ger.		Dr., SS-Osturmfhr., C.C. Auschwitz (Pol.) 43 - 44	MURDER	U.S.
KLEIN	147905	M	Ger.	17	Lt.,11 Panz.Div. (Fr.) 44	MURDER	FR.
KLEIN	150669	M	Ger.		Lt.,Legion Azerbaijanian,Parade(Fr.) 27.5.44	MURDER	FR.
KLEIN	157804	F	Ger.		Gestapo de Sarrebruck,Folking(Fr.) 11.44	MURDER	FR.
KLEIN	164708	M	Ger.		SS-Mann,10 Panz.Div.Frundsberg,36 Panz.Regt.,Bevin(Fr.)12.-13.6.44	MURDER	FR.
KLEIN	173665	M	Ger.		Dr.,SS-Hptsturmfhr.,C.C. Oswiecim-Birkenau(Pol.) 39-45	MURDER	CZECH.
KLEIN	177535	F			Employee,Gestapo,Saarbruecken(Ger.)	MURDER	FR.
KLEIN	178311	M	Ger.	15	Sonderfuehrer,Stalag XVIIIC,Markt Pongau(Ger.) 6.44	TORTURE	CAN.,U.K.
KLEIN	186276	M			SS-Mann,Guard,4 SS-Totenkopfsturmbann,C.C.Dora,Nordhausen(Ger.), Auschwitz(Pol.) 43-45	WITNESS	U.S.
KLEIN	186763	M	Ger.		3 Navy Inf.Regt.,2 Coy.,Quevin(Fr.)	MURDER	FR.
KLEIN	191365	M	Ger.		Cpl.,184 Kgf.Arb.Bn.,Bassis Tunnel(Nor.)	WITNESS	NOR.
KLEIN	194711	M	Ger.		Member Gestapo,Nice(Fr.) 1.4.44	MISC.CRIMES	FR.
KLEIN	251671	M	Ger.		Member Gestapo,Lille(Fr.) 40-44	MURDER	FR.
KLEIN	252214	F	Ger.		Agent Gestapo,Limoges(Fr.) 40-45	INTERR.	FR.
KLEIN	252215	M	Ger.		Capt.,338 Div.Field-Div.-Police,La Bresse(Fr.) 9.-11.44	MURDER	FR.
KLEIN	252216	M			Rottenfhr.,C.C.Rottleberode(Ger.)	MURDER	U.S.
KLEIN	252217	M			Hptsturmfhr.,C.C.Dora,Nordhausen(Ge..)	MURDER	U.S.
KLEIN	253980	M	Ger.		Member SS,C.C.Auschwitz-Birkenau(Pol.) 42-45	MURDER	YUGO.
KLEIN	255156	M	Ger.		SS-Rottfhr.,Sipo Abt. Ia,Bruessel(Bel.) 40-44	INTERR.	BEL.
KLEIN	257017	M	Ger.		Capt.,Army,Kragujevac,Gresag and Gruza(Yugo.) 42-44	MURDER	YUGO.
KLEIN	257819	M	Ger.		Lt.,Military,Nuland(Neth.) 9.-1⁰.44	SUSPECT	NETH.
KLEIN	258136		Ger.		Medicial Officer,Dr.,C.C.Natzweiler(Fr.)	MURDER	BEL.
KLEIN	259145	M	Ger.	15	Lt.,Coy.-Cmdt.,Div."Hermann Goering",Fuzine(Yugo.) 43	MURDER	YUGO.
KLEIN see KIEIN	259479						
KLEIN	259606	M	Ger.		Sgt.,Afrika Div.999,15 Pz.Gren.Div.,Section Ic,Semur-Auxois(Fr.)25.8.44	MURDER	FR.
KLEIN	300488	F	Ger.		Wife of Stockenberger at the Gestapo at Limoges, Hte.Vienne,Creuse, Correze,Dordogne,Indre(Fr.) 40-45	MURDER	FR.
KLEIN	301104	M	Ger.		Wachtmeister in Froslev C.C. (Russ.and Pol.) -45	MISC.CRIMES	DEN.
KLEIN	305911	M	Ger.		SS-Hptsturmfhr.,Att.Befehlshaber in a Leading Capacity, C.C. Oswiecim-Birkenau(Pol.) 39 - 45	MURDER	CZECH.
KLEIN	306440	M	Ger.		SS-Staff-Sgt.,C.C.Oranienburg(Ger.) 39-45	MURDER	CZECH.
KLEIN, Alfred	469	M	Ger.		C.C.Oswiecim-Birkenau(Pol.)	MURDER	FR.,YUGO.
KLEIN, Alois	24885	M	Ger.		Polizeimeister,Police Official,Koblenz(Ger.)	TORTURE	U.S.
KLEIN, Alphonse	102969	M	Ger.	14	SA,C.C.Hadamar,Lemberg(Pol.) 1.6.44 and 29.3.45	MURDER	U.S.
KLEIN, Claus	225027	M	Ger.	15	SS-Oberfhr.,Army,Gestapo,SS,Lyon,Strassburg(Fr.)	MURDER	FR.
KLEIN, Emil	179941	M	Ger.		SS-Oberfhr.,Cmdt.of SS-Pioneer-School,C.C.Hradistko(Czech.) 42-45	MURDER	CZECH.
KLEIN, Ernst	25484	M	Ger.		Member,Einsatz-Kdo.Ernst,BDS-Strasbourg,Wolfisheim(Fr.) 14.-15.8.44	MURDER	U.S.
KLEIN, Ferdinand	262138	M	Ger.		Wanted for the Murder of three American Prisoners of War,Illesheim(Ger.)	SUSPECT	U.S.
KLEIN, Fritz	187663	M	Ger.	14. 4.84	Civilian, Camp Kreis St.Goar(Ger.) 29.12.44	MURDER	U.S.
KLEIN, Fritz	257772	M	Ger.	30. 8.08	Employee,Camp Dora,Nordhausen(Ger.)	MURDER	U.S.
KLEIN, Fritz	300536	M	Ger.		Dr.,Medical Officer,SS-Mann,C.C.Auschwitz(Pol.) 42-45	MISC.CRIMES	YUGO.
KLEIN, Georg	259568	M	Ger.		SS-Hptschfhr.,Sipo(Security-Police),Brussels (Bel.) 40-44	SUSPECT	BEL.
KLEIN, Gerhard	252218	M			Pvt.,C.C.Ellrich,Nordhausen(Ger.)	MURDER	U.S.
KLEIN, Gottfried	186764	M	Ger.		Sgt.,Member,Army,SA,NSDAP,Cognac(Fr.) 40-45	MURDER	FR.
KLEIN, Gunther	131428	M	Ger.		SS-Sgt.,C.C.Mauthausen(Aust.) 41-45	MURDER	U.S.
KLEIN, Hans	161490	M	Ger.		Stalag XIIA,Limburg(Ger.) 12.44	WITNESS	U.S.
KLEIN, Hein	195073	M	Ger.		SD Alsace Kdo.z.b.V.6,Saales, St.Die(Fr.) 9.44	MURDER	U.K.
KLEIN, Heinrich	145845	M		10	Dr.,Assist.Surgeon,Air Corps Medical Dpt.(Hos.),Neupukov-Rerik(Ger.) 16.-17.3.44	MURDER	U.S.
KLEIN, Heinrich	259644	M	Ger.		SS-Rottfhr.,Gestapo,area Angers,Maine and Loire(Fr.) 42-44	MISC.CRIMES	FR.
KLEIN, Herbert	254369	M	Ger.	24. 2.25	Pvt.,15 Coy.,558 Gren.Regt.,Bruay en Artois(Fr.) 1.9.44	MURDER	FR.
KLEIN, Jakob	257770	M	Ger.	4.10.07	Camp Dora,Block 27,Nordhausen(Ger.)	MURDER	U.S.
KLEIN, Josef	251098	M	Ger.		9 SS-Pz.Gren.Regt."Das Reich",Mormont(Bel.) 5.9.44	MURDER	BEL.
KLEIN, Josef	252219	M	Ger.		Pvt.,C.C.Harzungen,Nordhausen(Ger.)	MURDER	U.S.
KLEIN, Josef	262241	M	Ger.	14. 4.	SS-Uschfhr.,Gestapo,Rennes(Fr.) 43-44	MISC.CRIMES	FR.
KLEIN, Klaus see Barbier	57						
KLEIN, Kristif	257771	M	Ger.	29.10.02	Employee,Factory Worker,Camp Nordhausen(Ger.)	MURDER	U.S.
KLEIN, Kurt	139186	M	Ger.		Civilian,Kami(Ger.)	MURDER	U.S.
KLEIN, Otto	167953	M	Ger.		Dr., member, Einsatzstab Rosenberg (Fr.) 40 - 44	PILLAGE	FR.
KLEIN, Peter	187662	M	Ger.		Civilian,Dachsbach(Ger.) 43-45	TORTURE	POL.
KLEIN, Richard	255534	M	Ger.		SS-Pionier,F.P.Nr.28955 (Fr.) 17.8.44	INTERR.	FR.
KLEIN, Wilhelm	174675	M	Ger.	2.11.05	Interpreter,Army,Vannes(Fr.) 42-45	TORTURE	FR.
KLEIN, Wilhelm	252220	M			Pvt.,C.C.Ellrich,Nordhausen(Ger.)	MURDER	U.S.
KLEIN-MEYER	167081	M			Cpl.,Army,Montigny(Fr.) 9.44	MURDER	FR.
KLEINBACH see KLEINBERG	195072						

KLE-KLE

NAME	C.R.FILE NUMBER	SEX	NATIO-NALITY	DATE OF BIRTH	RANK OCCUPATION UNIT PLACE AND DATE OF CRIME	REASON WANTED	WANTED BY
KLEINBAUER, Henri (or KLEIBAVER)	132566	M	Ger.		Sgt., SD, Gestapo, Chambery (Fr.)	TORTURE	FR.
KLEE BETTEL	252222	M	Ger.		Pvt., Lagerfhr., Cavalry Unit 272 Coy, Gambin (Pol.) 28.8.43	MURDER	U.S.
KLEINBERG	193353	M	Ger.		Pvt., Army, C.C.Akervika (Nor.) 42	MURDER	NOR.
KLEINBERG (or KLEINBACH)	195072	M	Ger.		Cpl., Army Stalag XI, Altengrabow (Ger.) 7.44	PILLAGE	U.K.
KLEINBERG	192969	M	Ger.		Officer, Stalag II A, C.C.Altengrabow (Ger.) 4.8.44	TORTURE	U.K.
KLEINBERGER	252206	M			Pvt., C.C.Ellrich, Nordhausen (Ger.)	MURDER	U.S.
KLEINDIENST, Alfred	256843	M		11.93	Dr., Oberkirchenrat, Protestant Minister in charge of Polish Protestamt Church, Lodz and other (Pol.) 39-45	INTERR.	POL.
KLEINDIENST, Karl	254590	M	Ger.		SS-Rottfhr., SS, C.C.Auschwitz-Birkenau (Pol.) 42	MISC.CRIMES	YUGO.
KLEINE	2/866	M	Ger.		Lt., Army, F.P.Nr.48349, Manthelan, Dolus Lesoc, Loches (Fr.) 20.-22.8.44	MURDER	FR.
KLEINE	132821	M	Ger.		Lt., Para Rgt.8,	WITNESS	U.K.
KLEINE	172205	M			SS-Uschfhr., SS, C.C.Muhldorf-Ampfing (Ger.) 6.44-4.45	MURDER	U.S.
KLEINE	192186	M	Ger.		Pvt., Geh.Feldpolizei, Group 648, Liege (Bel.)	MISC.CRIMES	BEL.
KLEINE	261217	M	Ger.		Pvt.,139 Arbeitsbereich Liane5.Inf.Rgt.211,Alleur-lez-Liege (Bel.) 4.9.44	MURDER	BEL.
KLEINE, Albert	196785	M	Ger.		Maat, Navy, Trebeurden (Fr.)	INTERR.	FR.
KLEINE, Fritz	11264	M			Pvt., Army, Pz.Gren.Rgt.111, Albine (Fr.) 29.6.44	MURDER	FR.
KLEINE FIRAM	157806	M	Ger.	00	Zugfhr., C.C.Emsland (Ger.) 44	MURDER	U.S.
KLEINEMASS	300792	M	Ger.		Pvt.,1 Aufkl.Abt.3 Coy 2 Col.XV Div.of the Afrika Corps,Saint Leger (Arlon) 5.9.44	MISC.CRIMES	BEL.
KLEINEMBROISCH	174676	M	Ger.		469 R.I 2 Bn.,198 Inf.Div.,Le Tholy (Fr.) 13.11.44	PILLAGE	FR.
KLEINERT	172206	M			SS-Oschfhr., SS, C.C.Muhldorf-Ampfing (Ger.) 6.44-4.45	MURDER	U.S.
KLEINERT	300267	M	Ger.		Lt., Inf.attached to the staff of the "Kohler" Div.H.Q.Chatandri Ahika, Povies, 21.3.44	PILLAGE	GRC.
KLEINERT, Willi	147807	M			Member, Hitler Jugend, C.C.near Gardelegen (Ger.) 10.-14.4.45	MURDER	U.S.
KLEINHANS	252207	M			SS-Rottfhr., C.C.Vieda, Nordhausen (Ger.)	MURDER	U.S.
KLEINHANS, Ernst	470	M	Ger.		Pvt., Army, Baudrignes (Fr.) 19.8.44	MURDER	FR.
KLEINHENN	24889	M	Ger.	10	SS-Schfhr., Waffen SS, C.C.Hinzert (Ger.)	TORTURE	U.S.
KLEINILBECK, Gustav	258695	M	Ger.		Kreisleiter, Erkrath (Ger.) 3.11.44	INTERR.	U.S.
KLEINKNECHT	251672	M	Ger.		Officer, T.A., Dijon L' Ain (Fr.) 10.-21.7.44	MURDER	FR.
KLEINHO, Heinz	300047	M	Ger.		Lt., Commandant of Com.(Dienststelle L.G.P.A.Amsterdam u.Bentheim, Noordwijk,27.and 28.9.44	TORTURE	NETH.
KLEINPAUL	165541	M	Ger.		Gestapo, Brussels (Bel.)	TORTURE	BEL.
KLEINPLAUPEN	254991	M	Ger.		Chief-Guard, C.C.Ravensbrueck (Ger.)	INTERR.	FR.
KLEINSCHMID	142198	M	Ger.	09	SS-Osturmfhr., C.C.Lublin (Pol.)	MURDER	FR.
KLEINSCHMIDT	125676	M	Ger.	00	Lt., Feldgendarmerie de Creil (Fr.) 8.44	MURDER	FR.
KLEINSCHMIDT	157808	M	Ger.	16	Pvt.,1-717 Ldsch.Bn.,C.C.Kielau Stalag 20 B KO 517 (Ger.) 7.4.44	MURDER	U.K.
KLEINSCHMIDT, Kurt	191462	M	Ger.		Dr., Manager, Deutsche Umsiedlungs Treuhand Ges., Berlin (Ger.) 9.39-44	PILLAGE	POL.
KLEIS	250885	M	Ger.		Schuetze, Pepingen (Bel.) 2.-9.44	INTERR.	BEL.
KLEISER, Karl	139176	M			Mayor, Public-official, Schollach (Ger.)	MURDER	U.S.
KLEISSING, Erwin	167080	M	Ger.		Adj.-chief, Feldgendarmerie, Luneville, Maixe (Fr.) 16.and 17.8.44	MURDER	FR.
KLEIST, Jack	138235	M	Ger.	10	Gruppenfhr., SS, Gestapo, Mussidan (Fr.) 2.44	MURDER	FR.
KLEIST, Joachim	29813	M		08	SS-Sturmschfhr., Crim.-Asst., Kommissariat De Dresde (Saxe)Perigueux(Fr.) Dresden (Ger.)6.-7.8.44	MURDER	FR.
KLEIST, Joachim	252204	M	Ger.		SS-Oschfhr., Gestapo, Limoges (Fr.) 40-44	MISC.CRIMES	FR.
KLEM	1710				SS-Major, Milan (It.)	TORTURE	U.K.
KLEM	131427	M	Ger.	15	SS-Uschfhr., C.C.Mauthausen (Aust.) 41-45	MURDER	U.S.
KLEM	193719	M	Ger.		General-Major, General staff Arbeitsstab, Drag (Nor.) 11.44	TORTURE	NOR.
KLEM	251673	M	Ger.		SS-Capt., Colonne S.P.58498 A, Ey, Moutiers (Fr.) 23.7.44	MURDER	FR.
KLEM	252242	M	Ger.		SS-Capt., Bujaleuf (Fr.) 24.7.44	PILLAGE	FR.
KLEMAN	251691	M	Ger.		Deputy chief of Police, SD, Fiume (Yugo.) 44-45	TORTURE	YUGO.
KLEMENT	167950	M	Ger.		Member, Dr., Einsatz Rosenberg, Ostgebietsministerium (Fr.) 40-44	PILLAGE	FR.
KLEMENT	190209	M	Ger.		Sgt., Army, Kadinjaca (Yugo.) 29.11.41	MURDER	YUGO.
KLEMENT, Edgar	306026	M			Member, C.C.Neuengamme (Ger.) 39-45	TORTURE	U.K.
KLEMENT, Karel	189375	M	Ger.	5. 4.10	Chief-Warder, Gestapo, C.C.Brno (Czech.) 39-45	TORTURE	CZECH.
KLEMENT, Ottomar	29776	M	Ger.		Landgerichtsrat, Public-official, Cheb (Czech.) 21.2.40	MURDER	BEL.
KLEMENT, Rudolf	189752	M	Ger.	16. 3.14	Police-asst., Gestapo, Bruenn (Czech.) 39-45	MISC.CRIMES	CZECH.
KLEMENZ, Otto	260123	M	Ger.	23.10.84	Manager, "Skoda-Factory", Bruenn, Moravia (Czech.) 42	MISC.CRIMES	CZECH.
KLEMEYER	190714	M	Ger.		Officer, Eisenbahn Art.Btty.717, F.P.Nr.22380, St.Andries, Varsenare-lez-Bruges (Bel.) 4.9.44	MURDER	BEL.
KLEMKE	253754	M			Rottfhr., SS, C.C.Nixei, Nordhausen (Ger.)	MURDER	U.S.
KLEMM	250310	M	Ger.	11-16	Sgt., Major, SD, Milan (It.) 10.8.44	INTERR.	U.K.
KLEMM	254982	F	Ger.		Overseer, C.C.Ravensbrueck (Ger.)	TORTURE	FR.
KLEMM	306997	M	Ger.		Sgt., H.Q.of Bn.II-98,1 Res.Rgt.of Gebirgsjg., Massif du Vercors, Isere Drome (Fr.) 20.7.-5.8.44	MURDER	FR.
KLEMM, Franz	186230	M			4 SS Totenkopf-Sturmbann, C.C.Dora Mittelbau, Nordhausen (Ger.) 43-45	WITNESS	U.S.
KLEMM, Herbert	62479	M	Ger.		Pvt., SA, Sec.of Minist.of Justiz	TORTURE	UNWCC
KLEMM, Karl	194016	M	Ger.	28. 1.01	Sturmfhr., Member , SA, NSDAP, Upice-Trutnov (Czech.) 38-45	MISC.CRIMES	CZECH.
KLEMM, Willy	257454	M	Ger.		Interpreter, SD, Caen (Fr.) 42	INTERR.	FR.
KLEMPT, Josef	253112	M	Ger.	23. 7.15	Cpl., C.C.Ellrich, Nordhausen (Ger.)	MURDER	U.S.
KLENDA	186232	M	Ger.		SS-Oschfhr., Pysely (Czech.) 6.5.45	TORTURE	CZECH.
KLENER	173670	M	Ger.		SS-Hptsturmfhr., official in office grouppe D' of the Reichsfhr.SS, Oswiecim-Birkenau (Pol.) 39-45	MURDER	CZECH.
KLENK, Karl	139774	M	Ger.	13. 2.01	Pvt., Army, Heilbronn (Ger.) 21.5.45	WITNESS	U.S.
KLENKE	256487	M	Ger.		Criminalrat, Ingersheim (Fr.) 9.1.44	MISC.CRIMES	FR.
KLEPFLEISCH,Walter (see KLOP-FLEISCH)	162393						
KLEPPE	160678			05	Leader, Abwehr FAT CIC Det.318,Witebsk (Sov.Un.) 7.-8.43	MURDER	U.S.
KLEPPER	257462	M	Ger.		Capt., Sochaux (Fr.) 9.-11.44	PILLAGE	FR.
KLEPSKI	254985	M	Ger.		Veterinary Surgeon, Quimper (Fr.)	MURDER	FR.
KLER	471	M	Ger.		SS-Mann, C.C.Oswiecim-Birkenau (Pol.) 39-45	TORTURE	POL.,FR.,BEL.
KLERBERGER	121566	M	Ger.		SS-Osturmfhr., command of a Unit which was stationed, Esneux (Bel.) 9.44	MURDER	BEL.
KLERCH	253111	M	Ger.		SS-Uschfhr., C.C.Artern, Nordhausen (Ger.)	MURDER	U.S.
KLERMANN	173663	M	Ger.		SS-Oschfhr., C.C.Oswiecim (Pol.) 39-45	MURDER	CZECH.
KLERNER	143154	M			SS-Uschfhr., C.C.Mauthausen (Aust.) 41-45	MURDER	U.S.

KLE-KLO

NAME	C.R.FILE NUMBER	SEX	NATIO- NALITY	DATE OF BIRTH	RANK OCCUPATION UNIT PLACE AND DATE OF CRIME	REASON WANTED	WANTED BY
KLEROURER	185871	M	Ger.		Lt., Department for Communism, Byron-Athens (Grc.) 3.44	PILLAGE	GRC.
KLESE	149497	M	Ger.		Hptscharfhr., SS-Div."Totenkopf", C.C. Sandweier (Ger.)	MISC.CRIMES	FR.
KLESS, Hans	125673	M	Ger.		Capt., Army, Chamalieres (Fr.) 29.8.44	MURDER	FR.
KLESS, Karl	253110	M		24.10.95	Pvt., C.C. Nordhausen (Ger.)	MURDER	U.S.
KLESSING	167079	M	Ger.		W.O.Sen., Feldgendarmerie, Mattexey (Fr.) 30.4.45	MURDER	FR.
KLESTIL, Gustav	255539	M	Ger.	21. 9.98	Agent, Abwehr, Prague (Czech.) 39-45	TORTURE	CZECH.
KLETSCHANEK, Anton (or KLECANEK)	254816	M	Ger.		Agent, S.D., Prague (Czech.) 39-45	MURDER	CZECH.
KLETSOCK	150673	M	Ger. or Rum.		Guard, S.D., C.C. Lahde-Weser (Ger.)	TORTURE	BEL.
KLETT	133811	M			Scharfhr., SS, C.C.Weimar-Buchenwald (Ger.)	BRUTALITY	U.S.
KLETTKE, Walter	300048	M		21.10.13	Sgt., Army, Berlin (Ger.) 24.3.44	MURDER	U.K.
KLEVER	301105	M	Ger.		Crim.asst., German Passport Control Office, Copenhagen, Helsingor and Wisborg (Den.) 6.44	TORTURE	DEN.
KLEWER	261814	M	Ger.		Lt., Cmdt. 2.Coy., Volga Tartar Legion, Bde. "Jesser", Le Puy, Yssin- geaux, Cayres, Castares and other places (Fr.) 40-45	MURDER	FR.
KLEYENSTENDER	258924	M	Ger.		Cpl., Custom-House, Member of the "Aktionskommando", Lourdes de la Region (Fr.) 1.-8.44	MURDER	FR.
KLEYER	106672	M	Ger.		Guard, Cpl., Stalag Luft Landesschuetzen Coy.4-6, C.C.Sagan (Ger.)3.44	WITNESS	U.K.
KLEYN, G.	302060	M			Pvt., Rotterdam (Neth.) 1.45	PILLAGE	NETH.
KLIBER, Guido	185870	M	Ger.	98	Leading member, NSDAP, Prague (Czech.)	MISC.CRIMES	CZECH.
KLICPERA, Odo	189374	M	Ger.	18. 6.05	Crim.employee, Gestapo, Brno (Czech.) 39-45	MURDER	CZECH.
KLIEBINGAT, Kurt	252229	M	Ger.		4.Coy., Pol.Waffen-Schule, Apeldoorn (Neth.) 3.45	MURDER	NETH.
KLIEGER, Franz	185685	M	Ger.		Civilian, Steimker-Berg (Ger.) 29.6.44	WITNESS	U.S.
KLIEM, Friedrich Wilhelm	306027	M	Ger.		SS-Hptsturmfhr., Cmdt., C.C.Neugraben-Tiefstak. 44-45	MURDER	U.K.
KLIER, Karl-Heinz (or KOENIG)	254581	M	Ger.		SS-Usturmfhr., S.D., Section C - Chief of Sect. III A, Prague (Czech.) 39-45	MURDER	CZECH.
KLIER, Walter	10014	M	Ger.		Dr., Public Prosecutor, Ministry of Justice, Litomerice (Czech.) 40	MURDER	CZECH.
KLIER, Wenzel	29775	M	Ger.		Landgerichtsdirektor, Public Official, Cheb (Czech.) 21.2.40	MURDER	BEL.
KLIMA	260129	M	Ger.		Hptwachtmeister, SS, Strafgefangenenlager North-Norway (Nor.) 6.42-45	MURDER	YUGO.
KLIMACHEWSKI	39782	M			Uschfhr., SS, 17. Panz.Gren.Div. "Goetz von Berlichingen", Segre- Ronaze (Fr.) 8.44	MURDER	FR.
KLIMBURG	255157	M	Ger.		Sturmfhr., Sipo, Abt. III A, Brussels (Bel.) 40-44	INTERR.	BEL.
KLIMENSCHEK	173092	M			Pvt., Sturm-Bn. A.O.K.I, 1.Coy., Courcelles Nied (Fr.) 4.44	MURDER	U.S.
KLIMESCH, Konrad	167686	M	Ger.		Civ., Treuhaender, Firm: "Bracia Grossmann", Krakow (Pol.) 9.39-12.44	MISC.CRIMES	POL.
KLIMOWITZ, Johann	300049	M			Blockfhr., 2.Labour Camp, Salzgitter (Ger.) 42-43	MISC.CRIMES	POL.
KLIMSER	131426	M	Ger.	19	Osturmfhr., SS, Mauthausen (Aust.) 41-45	MURDER	U.S.
KLIMSOM	1711	M		18 - 20	Scharfhr., SS, Milan (Italy)	TORTURE	U.K.
KLIMZSA	162250	M	Ger.	12	Dr., Osturmfhr., SS Standarte "Thueringen", C.C.Buchenwald (Ger.) 39	MISC.CRIMES	U.S.
KLINBERG, Hans (see KLINGENBERG)	193718						
KLINE	126564	M	Ger.		Dr., 257. Field Hospital, Budesheim (Ger.) 12.44-2.45	TORTURE	U.S.
KLINEBEETLE, Hans	126456	M	Ger.		Guard, Stalag II B, Kommando 1534, C.C.Gambin-Hammerstein (Ger.) 8.43	MURDER	U.S.
KLING	179475	M	Ger.		SS-Mann, 1. Panzer Div. "Adolf Hitler", 1.Reconstruction Bn., Stavelot (Bel.) 44	MURDER	U.S.
KLING, Georges	122609	M		06	Chief of Camp Bronneck I, Member of Org.Todt, Boulogne sur Mer (Fr.) 44	TORTURE	FR.
KLING, Gerard	187198	M			Usturmfhr., S.D., Gent (Bel.) 12.42	TORTURE	BEL.
KLING, Hans	146837	M	Ger.		Osturmfhr., SS Panz.Gren.Div."Das Reich", 1.Panzer Regt., Caussade (Fr.) 44	MURDER	FR.
KLINGBEIL (or KLINGBIELL)	173717	M	Ger.		Official, Gestapo, S.D., Hertogenbosch, Tilburg (Neth.) 7.44	MURDER	U.K.
KLINGBEIL, Karl	137601	M		10	Hptsturmfhr., Sicherheitsdienst of Gestapo, Tilburg (Neth.) 7.44	MURDER	U.K.
KLINGBELL (see KLINGBEIL)	173717						
KLINGBELL, Paul	102967	M	Ger.		Sonderkommando, C.C.Suttrop, Langenbach, Hohenlichte (Ger.) 3.45	MURDER	U.S.
KLINGE, Hans	36691	M	Ger.		Quartermaster, Portland Cement Works, Stalag XI A, Nienburg-Saale (Ger.) 26.8.44	TORTURE	U.K.
KLINGE, Herbert	256845	M	Ger.		Sgt., Navy, Hopseidel-Finmark (Nor.) 5.45	MURDER	NOR.
KLINGE, Karl Hans Hermann	306841	M	Ger.		Crim.asst., Sipo, S.D., Gestapo H.Q., Oslo (Nor.) 10.44-5.45	MURDER	NOR.
KLINGEL	179584	M	Ger.		Engineer, Arbeitskommando 121, Gams (Aust.) 4.-10.44	MISC.CRIMES	U.K.
KLINGELHOEFER	124230	M			Hptsturmfhr., SS 1.Regt., 1.Panz.Div., Malmedy (Bel.) 12.44	MURDER	U.S.
KLINGENBERG	306093	M	Ger.		SS-Sturmmann, SS, C.C.Alderney (Channel Is) and C.C.Kortemark. 42-45	MURDER	CZECH.
KLINGENBERG, Hans (or KLINBERG)	193718	M	Ger.	05	Oberwachtmeister, Ministry of Justice, Strafgefangenen-Lager "Nord", Finmark (Nor.) 10.44	MISC.CRIMES	NOR.
KLINGENBERG, Hubert	253109	M		8. 9.98	Uschfhr., C.C.Hoblstedt-Ellrich, Nordhausen (Ger.)	MURDER	U.S.
KLINGER	152528	M			Sgt., Pol., Waldau-Oberlausitz (Ger.)	MURDER	U.K.
KLINGER	261976	M	Ger.		Member, Gestapo, Osturmfhr., SS, Banska-Bystrica (Czech.) 8.44-4.45	MURDER	CZECH.
KLINGER, Otto	255540	M	Ger.	8.10.85	Civilian, Podbrezova (Czech.) 40-45	MISC.CRIMES	CZECH.
KLINGKVIEL	257886	M	Ger.		Lt., 150.Panzer Bde., Meuse-Bridge Antwerp (Bel.) 12.44	MISC.CRIMES	U.S.
KLINGHAMER, Eduard (or KLINKHAMMER)	261122	M	Ger.	14.10.01	Informant, Gestapo, Moravska-Ostrava (Czech.) 44	MISC.CRIMES	CZECH.
KLINKHAMMER, Andreas	302061	M	Ger.		Railway Official, Fernmeldemeisterei Office, Amersfoort (Neth.)betw. 10.44 and 5.45	PILLAGE	NETH.
KLINKHAMMER, Eduard (see KLINGHAMER)	261122						
KLINKMUELLER	172207	M			Civ.Organisation Todt, C.C.Muhldorf-Ampfing (Ger.) 6.44-4.45	MURDER	U.S.
KLINKSIECK (or KLINKSIEK)	189248	M	Ger.		Leader, Occupied Territories, Poznan (Pol.) 39-43	PILLAGE	POL.
KLINOFF, Eugen	195525	M	Ger.	05	Cpl., S.D., Employee, Gestapo, Kolin (Czech.) 39-45	MURDER	CZECH.
KLIPER	254382	M	Ger.		Cmdt., 197.Div.Alpine, Vercheny La Plaine (Fr.) 7.44	INTERR.	FR.
KLIPAR	306998	M	Ger.		Major, 157. Bav.Reserve-Div.Massif du Vercors,Isere-Drome (Fr.) 7.-8.44	MURDER	FR.
KLIPPEL, Heinrich	185690	M	Ger.	15. 4.92	Bezirkslt., Gendarmerie, Luxembourg (Lux.)	MURDER	LUX.
KLOCK	27782A	M	Ger.		Major, Finmark (Nor.)	MURDER	NOR.
KLOCKMANN, Ernst	260942	M	Ger.	5. 2.14	SS-Rottenfhr., Guard, C.C.Auschwitz (Pol.) 44-45	BRUTALITY	POL.
KLOCKMANN, Friederich	31589	M	Ger.		N.C.O., Guard, Arbeitskommando POW Camp Lamstedt (Ger.) 2.-9.43	MURDER	SOV.UN.
KLOEBE, Josef	11265	M	Ger.		Pvt., Army, Panz.Gren.Regt.111, Albine (Fr.) 6.44	MURDER	FR.
KLOEPFEL	173732	M	Ger.		Capt., Freiskommandantur, Krusevac (Yugo.) 4.41-44	MURDER	YUGO.
KLOEPFEL	300799	M	Ger.		Sgt., 1.Aufkl.Abt.,3.Coy.,2.Col.XV.Div.Afrika Korps,St.Leger (Arlon)9.44	MISC.CRIMES	BEL.
KLOESS, Michael	186273	M			SS-Mann, 4.SS Totenkopf-Sturmbann, C.C.Dora,Nordhausen (Ger.) 43-45	WITNESS	U.S.

KLO-KLU

NAME	C.R.FILE NUMBER	SEX	NATIO- NALITY	DATE OF BIRTH	RANK OCCUPATION UNIT	PLACE AND DATE OF CRIME	REASON WANTED	WANTED BY
KLOETERS	167699	M	Ger.		Polit.Leiter, Generalgovernment, Treuhandstelle, Radom (Pol.)9.39-44		PILLAGE	POL.
KLOETZER, Helmut	305769	M	Ger.	6. 1.10	Sturmscharfhr., Crim. Secret. Head of Aussendienst, Hoeyanger, Soga (Nor.) 1.-2.45		MURDER	NOR.
KLOFANDA, Emil	169343	M	Ger.	90	Lt. Colonel, Czech. Army, Pisek (Czech.)		MISC.CRIMES	CZECH.
KLOFANDA, Harry	194014	M	Ger.25. 6.18		Member, H.J. SS, Pisilk (Czech.) 38-45		MISC.CRIMES	CZECH.
KLOFANDOVA, Elsika	194013	F	Ger.29.11.92		Member, NSDAP, Pisek (Czech.) 38-45		MISC.CRIMES	CZECH.
KLOIBER	195484	M	Ger.		Director, Arb.Kdo. C.C. Braunschweig, Schandelah (Ger.) 44-45		TORTURE	BEL.
KLOIBER, Hans	162696	M	Ger.		Civilian, Muenchen (Ger.)		WITNESS	U.S.
KLOLER	261051	M	Ger.		Major, Patrol-Corps Sued Frankreich, Vaucluse-Var-Bouche Prov. Du Rhone-Gard-Basses-Alpes (Fr.) 44		MISC.CRIMES	FR.
KLONE, Ernst	258923	M	Ger.		Lt., Unit 12061, Haumont (Fr.) 24.6.44		WITNESS	Fr.
KLONNE, Ernst Moritz	102949	M			Capt., Sonder-Kdo., C.C. Stuthof (Ger.) 20.-21.or22.3.45		MURDER	U.S.
KLOOCK	300794	M	Ger.		Pvt., I.Aufkl.Abt. 3.Coy.2.Columm XV Div of the Afrika-Korps Saint Leger (Arlon) 5.9.44		MISC.CRIMES	BEL.
KLOPEL	167078	M	Ger.		Member, Feldgend. de Moulins, Larochemillay (Fr.) 11.8.44		PILLAGE	FR.
KLOPF, Hugo	252200	M		22. 9.98	Cpl., C.C. Ellrich-Nordhausen (Ger.)		MURDER	U.S.
KLOPFER	472	M	Ger.		Pvt., Army, Baudrigues (Fr.) 19.8.44		MURDER	FR.
KLOPFER	102937	M	Ger.		Factory-Director, Stalag 09, C.C. Nordhausen (Ger.) 5.42-6.43		TORTURE	U.K.
KLOPFER, Gerhard	60570	M	Ger.18. 2.05		Dr., SS-Gruppenfhr., Minist.Director, Public Law Questions		MISC.CRIMES	U.N.W.C.C.
KLOPFLEISCH, Walter or KLEPF- LEISCH	162393	M	Ger.		Sturmfhr., SA, Niedertreba (Ger.) 7.44		MURDER	U.S.
KLOPMANN	260396	M	Ger.		Lt., Chief of political section, Chief of Lublin-Camp,Dachau (Ger.) 42-44		MURDER	FR.
KLOPPERT, Oswald	240107	M	Ger.	20	Agent, Pvt., Abwehr Off. Nachr.Regt. 50, 6.Coy. Bad Wildungen (Ger.)45		MISC.CRIMES	U.S.
KLOPPMANN	473	M			Hauptsturmfhr., SS, C.C. Maidanek (Pol.) 40-4.44		MURDER	POL.,FR.,BEL.
KLOPPMANN, Otto	145263	M	Ger.	08	Hauptscharfhr., SS, C.C. Lublin (Pol.) 40-44		MURDER	POL.
KLOPSCH	11269	M	Ger.		Sgt., Hafenueberwach., Calais (Fr.) 4.9.44		TORTURE	FR.
KLOSCHEK	29814	M	Ger.		Sonderfhr., Army, Georgien-Legion, Castres (Fr.) 6.44		MURDER	FR.
KLOSE	10016	M	Ger.		Oberlandrat, Public Official Departm of Justice, Brno (Czech.) 39-45		TORTURE	CZECH.
KLOSE, Georg	145248	M	Ger.		Rottenfhr., 1.SS-Pz.Div., 2.Pz.Gren.Regt. 3.Bn.12.Coy., Stavelot Malmedy (Bel.) 22.-23.12.44		MURDER	U.S.
KLOSE, Gerhard	167960	M	Ger.12. 6.20		Unterscharfhr., SS, C.C. Natzweiler (Fr.) 42-44		MURDER	FR.
KLOSE, Walter	106760	M	Ger.		Police Inspector, Crim.Asst., Gestapo, Breslau (Ger.) 3.44		MURDER	U.K.
KLOSKA, Paul	252199	M		1. 2.14	Pvt., C.C. Ellrich, Nordhausen (Ger.)		MURDER	U.S.
KLOSOWSKI, Addi	192376	M	Ger.		C.C. Flossenburg (Ger.) 44-45		MURDER	U.S.
KLOSS, Michael	252198	M			Pvt., C.C. Bismarck, Nordhausen (Ger.)		MURDER	U.S.
KLOSS, Reinhold, Max	133810	M	Ger.		Unterscharfhr., or Sturmmann, SS, C.C. Weimar, Buchenwald (Ger.)40-43		BRUTALITY	U.S.
KLOSSINGER, Heinrich	132048	M	Ger.	14	Civilian, C.C. Vicinity of Nammering (Ger.) 19.-25.4.45		WITNESS	U.S.
KLOSTER	250899	M	Ger.		SS-Rottenfhr., C.C. Neuengamme (Ger.)		INTERR.	BEL.
KLOSTERMAYER, Adolf	251694	M	Ger.		Farmer, Civilian, Arpka near Hannover (Ger.) 8.9.41		INTERR.	YUGO.
KLOSTERMEIER	60603	M	Ger.	15	SS-Unterscharfhr., SD,SS, Scheveningen (Neth.)		TORTURE	U.S.
KLOT or KLUT	192373	M	Ger.	95	Lt. Colonel, C.C. Zinna, Torgau (Ger.) 45		MURDER	U.S.
KLOTERS, Josef	193717	M	Ger.		Sgt. 7.Army Kuesten Art. Regt. 972, 7. Bn., (Nor.)		MURDER	NOR.
KLOTH	177678	M			Haupttruppfhr., NSKK, Transportstaffel N 8, Brest Fort de Keranroux (Fr.) 41-42		TORTURE	FR.
KLOTZ	139755	M	Ger.		Stabsintendant, Stalag X-B, C.C. Sandbostel (Ger.) 1.-5.45		TORTURE	U.S.
KLOTZ	196199	M	Ger.		Cpl., Oberwachtmeister, Ger. Police Camp, C. Westerbork (Neth.)9.44		MURDER	NETH.
KLOTZ, Eric or KLAUTZ	123870	M	Ger.		Lt., Army Center of Instruction, Signes (Fr.) 18.7.44		MURDER	FR.
KLOTZ, Horst	252197	M	Ger.		SS-Sturmmann, C.C. Ellrich Nordhausen (Ger.)		MURDER	U.S.
KLOTZ, Josef	140786	M	Ger.		Civilian, C.C. Mittenwald (Ger.) 6.44		TORTURE	U.S.
KLOTZ, Konrad	254582	M	Ger.		Official, Civilian, Ministry of Agriculture, Hradec Kralove (Czech.)45		INTERR.	CZECH.
KLOTZ, Maria	250901	F	Ger.		Woman SS Guard, C.C., Geislingen (Ger.) 40-45		MURDER	POL.
KLOTZBACH, Hans	10151	M	Ger.		Camp leader, Stalag IX C Kdo.137, Unterbriezbach (Ger.)8.40-45		TORTURE	U.K.
KLOTZER, Walter	300491	M	Ger.		Pvt. 01512 K Navy Inf. Partly Composed of W.-SS, Trebeurden,Pleumeur- Bodou, Perros-Gutrec (Fr.) 6.,7.44		MURDER	FR.
KLOW	185687	M	Ger.		Police-Man, Police, Agis Galiwi (Grc.)		TORTURE	GRC.
KLOWAL, Hiltrude	252203	F	Ger.		Agent, Gestapo, Limoges (Fr.)40-44		INTERR.	FR.
KLOZE	139777	M			Oberscharfhr., W.-SS, C.C. Aswic (Pol.) 7.43		MURDER	U.S.
KLUBERG, Johannes	185863	M	Ger.		Warrant Officer, Army, Fieldgrn. Amar (Crete) (Grc.)9.44		MURDER	GRC.
KLUCH, Paul	250890	M	Ger.		Sgt., Army, Passontia (Pr.) 44		MURDER	POL.
KLUCZKA, Eduard	145806	M		10	SS-Unterscharfhr., W.-SS, Schleissheim near Munich (Ger.) 7.,8.,9.44		MURDER	U.S.
KLUEHE	302063	M	Ger.		Member, Sicherheitsdienst, Steenwijk Diever (Neth.) 10.4.45		MURDER	NETH.
KLUENGER, Hermann	179720	M	Ger.	12	SS-Sturmscharfhr., Crim.-Commissar, SD, Gestapo, Prague (Czech.)		MURDER	CZECH.
KLUENNER, Karl	300906	M	Ger.		Untersturmfhr., Flushing Niddelburg (Neth.) 19.9.44,9.10.44		MURDER	NETH.
KLUENTER, Johann	189075	M	Ger.		Crim.-Secretary, Police, Hergarten (Ger.) 7.-8.44		WITNESS	U.S.
KLUESS	172209	M	Ger.		Civilian, Org.Todt, C.C. Muehldorf, Ampfing (Ger.) 6.44-4.45		MURDER	U.S.
KLUETE	259834	M	Ger.		Chief-Pay-Master, Army, Commando Raumbot, Breda Nordbrabant (Neth.)44		PILLAGE	NETH.
KLUETING	257009	M	Ger.		Crim.Secretary, Military, Amsterdam (Neth.) 7.2.45		SUSPECT	NETH.
KLUETSCH, Peter	24860	M			Army, Stalag VI G, Duisdorf (Ger.) 15.2.,17.2.45		TORTURE	U.S.
KLUFFLER	29815	M	Ger.		Lt., Army, Georgian Legion, Castres (Fr.) 6.44		TORTURE	FR.
KLUG see CLOUK	125413							
KLUG or KLUTH	162248	M	Ger.		Commanding Officer, Prison Zenna, C.C. Torgau (Ger.) 44		TORTURE	U.S.
KLUG	190713	M	Ger.		Sgt., Eisenbahn Art. Battr. 717, Feldpost No.22380, St. Andries, Varsenare les Brugee (Bel.) 4.9.44		MURDER	BEL.
KLUG	252440	M			Sgt., C.C. Harzungen Nordhausen (Ger.)		MURDER	U.S.
KLUG, Joseph	129685	M	Ger.		Kgf. Arbeitskdo., Krakau (Pol.) 42-43		MURDER	U.S.
KLUGE	131425	M	Ger.		SS Oberscharfhr., (Sgt.,) SS, C.C. Mauthausen (Austr.) 41-45		MURDER	U.S.
KLUGE	139169	M	Ger.		Sonderfhr., SS, C.C. Stalag 7 A, Moosburg (Ger.) 8.44-5.45		TORTURE	FR.
KLUGE	146836	M	Ger.		Obersturmfhr., SS Pz.Div."Das Reich", South West (Fr.) 44		MURDER	FR.
KLUGE	251006	M	Ger.		SS-Oberscharfhr., C.C. Gusen (Ger.)		TORTURE	BEL.
KLUGE	261469	M	Ger.		Colonel, armament command, Nancy (Fr.) 14.9.44		INCENDIARISM	Fr.
KLUGE, Helmut	12442	M	Ger.		Lt., 18. Div.Feldgend., Bergues (Fr.) 16.11.43		MURDER	FR.
KLUGE, Herbert	102946	M	Ger.		Pvt., Sonderkdo., C.C. Warstein, Suttrop (Ger.) 3.45		MURDER	U.S.
KLUGEL	255166	M	Ger.		St.Mann, Civilian SD Admin., Toulouse (Fr.) 11.42-8.44		MURDER	FR.
KLUGER	102947	M	Ger.		SS-Fuehrer SS Stalag 7. C.C. Moosburg (Ger.)		WITNESS	U.K.
KLUGER	162360	M	Ger.	95	Sonderfhr., Army, Stalag VII A, Moosberg (Ger.)		MISC.CRIMES	U.K.
KLUGER, Konrad	193716	M	Ger.19. 2.01		Oberwachtmeister, Reichsjustizministerium,Strafgefangenenlager Nord Finmark (Nor.)		MISC.CRIMES	NOR.
KLUGHARDT, Karl	306553	M	Ger. 1.10.09		SS-Staff-Sgt., Crim.Secretary, Sicherheitspolizei SD, Oslo (Nor.) 8.43-4.45		MURDER	NOR.

KLU-KNE

NAME	C.R.FILE NUMBER	SEX	NATIO- NALITY	DATE OF BIRTH	RANK OCCUPATION UNIT PLACE AND DATE OF CRIME	REASON WANTED	WANTED BY
KLUM	301333	M	Ger.		Member,Gestapo,Trencin,C.C.Oswiecim-Birkenau (Pol.) 39-45	MURDER	CZECH.
KLUMP	179585	M			Major,Air-Force,Sagan (Ger.) 2.45	TORTURE	U.K.
KLUMPE, Erich	186498	M	Ger.	13	Lt.,Army,Renesse,Schouwen (Neth.) 12.44	MURDER	NETH.
KLUMPIT	188751	M	Ger.		Feldgendarm,Feldgendarmerie,Bar de Luc (Fr.) 20.-23.8.44	MURDER	FR.
KLUMPP, Isidor	172204	M	Ger.		Gernsbach,Weissenbach (Ger.) 9.8.44	MURDER	U.S.
KLUNERT	192374	M	Ger.		C.C.Flossenburg,(Ger.) 44-45	MURDER	U.S.
KLUNK, Johann	251007	M	Ger.		Guard or Kapo,C.C.Gusen (Ger.)	TORTURE	BEL.
KLUNKER	145242	M			Col.,Stalag VII A,Mooseburg (Ger.) 9.-12.43	MURDER	U.S.
KLUPFEL	135203	M	Ger.		Kreis-Chief,Gendarmerie,Mittenberg (Ger.) 44	MURDER	U.S.
KLUPSCH, Adolf	190668	M	Ger.		Pvt.,Army,St.Andries les Bruges,Varsenare (Bel.) 4.9.44	MURDER	BEL.
KLUSE, Bernhard	193715	M	Ger.	05	Sgt.,Reichsjustizministerium,Strafgefangenenlager,Nord,Finmark (Nor.)	MISC.CRIMES	NOR.
KLUSMANN (see KROSSMANN)	133798						
KLUSSNER, Hermann	167077	M	Ger.	10	Scharfhr.,SS,Woippy (Fr.) 44	TORTURE	FR.
KLUT	475	M	Ger.		SS-Scharfhr.,Prison-Camp-Official,C.C.Stutthof (Pol.)9.39-4.41	MURDER	POL.
KLUT (see KLOT)	192373						
KLUTE, Wilhelm	173716	M	Ger.		Major,Military-Prison,Graudenz (Pol.) 7.44	MURDER	U.K.
KLUTGEN	254379	M	Ger.	29. 8.10	Pvt.,558 Gren.Rgt.,13 Coy.,Bruay en Artois (Fr.) 1.9.44	MISC.CRIMES	FR.
KLUTH (see KLUG)	67821	M	Ger.		S.A.Member,C.C.Kranenburg (Ger.) 17.9.44	WITNESS	U.K.,U.S.
	162248						
KLUTH	165249	M	Ger.	94	Lt.Col.,Prison Camp,Army,Torgau (Ger.)	TORTURE	U.S.
KLUTIG	11266	M	Ger.		Pvt.,Army,Pz.Gren.Rgt.110 or 111,2 Coy.,Albine (Fr.) 29.6.44	MURDER	FR.
KLUTING	300492	M	Ger.		Police-Official,(Colleague of Siemon),probably stationed in Rotterdam 11.42	BRUTALITY	NETH.
KLUVERS, Arnold	255606	M	Ger.	05	Navy,Heusden (Neth.) 11.44	SUSPECT	NETH.
KLUVKEN, Werner	255000	M			Lt.,O.T.,Noria(It.) 5.44	INTERR.	U.K.
KLYELEIN	185481	M	Ger.	90	Oberlagerfuehrer,Chief,Arb.Kdo.,Nuernberg (Ger.) 40-45	TORTURE	U.S.
KLYSZCZ, Leo	145208	M	Ger.	20. 2.95	Cpl.,Army,Ld.Sch.Ers.Bn.24,3 Coy.,Augsburg (Ger.) 40-4.45	MURDER	U.S.
KMUTTLER	130676	M	Ger.		SS-Oberscharfhr.,SS,C.C.Dora,Nordhausen (Ger.)	MURDER	U.S.
KNAACK, W.	128851	M	Ger.		Tiefbauunternehmer,Member,NSDAP,Kriegsgefangenen Arb.Kdo.771, C.C.Niesse (Ger.) 6.44-2.45	MISC.CRIMES	U.K.
KNAB (or KNAPP)	476	M		05	Doctor,Chief,Gestapo,Lyon (Fr.) 40-42	MURDER	FR.
KNAB	132579	M	Ger.		SS,Lt.Col.SD.,Plateau de Glieres (Fr.) 3.-4.44	MURDER	FR.
KNAB	257779	M	Ger.	05	Major,SD,Head of Abt.4,Oslo,(Nor.) 40-42	TORTURE	NOR.
KNABE	10070	M			Capt.,C.C.Molsdorf (Ger.) 43	TORTURE	U.K.
KNABE	173709	M	Ger.		Kreisleiter,NSDAP,Pforzheim (Ger.)	TORTURE	FR.
KNABE	254811	M	Ger.	86	Capt.,Army Art.,Stalag IX C,Bad Sulza (Ger.) 43-45	TORTURE	U.K.
KNABE, A.	167949	F	Ger.		Member,Einsatzstab Rosenberg (Fr.) 40-44	PILLAGE	FR.
KNABEL	31533	M	Ger.		SS-Hauptsturmfhr.,,SS-Pz.Gren.Rgt.,4 Coy.,F.P.16566 E,St.Nicolas Des Biefs (Fr.) 22.7.-17.8.44	MURDER	FR.
KNABEL	132217	M	Ger.		Untersturmfhr.,SS,Sd.,Issel (Ger.) 20.1.45	MURDER	U.S.
KNABEL, Alois	477	M	Ger.		SS-Hauptsturmfhr.,Waffen-SS,4 Coy.,Pz.Gren.Bn.,St.Yan,27.8.44-4.9.44	MURDER	FR.
KNABEL, Oscar	139180	M	Ger.		Manufactorer,C.C.Volary (Czech.) 44-45	WITNESS	U.S.
KNABELBURGIR	67043	M	Ger.		C.C.Ostrow (Ger.)	MURDER	U.K.
KNACKFUSS	4780	M	Ger.		Col.,Army,Channels Islands (U.K.) 9.42-2.43	MISC.CRIMES	U.K.
KNACKE, Adolf	252441	M	Ger.	03	SS-Sturmmann,C.C.Harzungen,Nordhausen (Ger.)	MURDER	U.S.
KNACKFUSS	187195	M	Ger.	95	Col,Army, Jersey, Channel Island 42-43	TORTURE	U.K.
KNAK	139764	M	Ger.	95	Member,NSDAP,Famburg (Ger.)	TORTURE	U.S.
KNALLMAYER, Alexander	260420	M	Ger.	90	Member,Gestapo,Pelhrimov-Bohemia (Czech.) 39-45	MISC.CRIMES	CZECH.
KNANA	301334	M	Ger.		Member,Gestapo,Nove Mesto n-Vahom,C.C.Oswiecim-Birkenau (Pol.)39-45	MURDER	CZECH.
KNAP, Karlo	190208	M	Ger.		Member,Gestapo,C.C.Banjica (Yugo.)	MURDER	YUGO.
KNAPEL	302064	M	Ger.		Member,Staff of the Prison,Diez-Lahn (Ger.) 40-45	MURDER	BEL.
KNAPP (see KNAB, Dr.)	476						
KNAPP	131423	M	Ger.		Hauptwachtmeister,Schutzpolizei,Ziegenhain (Ger.) 43-44	TORTURE	BEL.
KNAPP	194710	M	Ger.		Doctor,Stalag 27002,C.C.Kaprun (Aust.) 40-41	TORTURE	FR.
KNAPP, Gustav	252442	M		05	Flyer,C.C.Ellrich,Nordhausen (Ger.)	MURDER	U.S.
KNAPP, Robert	301860	M	Ger.		Ogruppenfhr.SS-Chief,Absch.XXXVII,Sudetenl.,CC Oswiecim (Pol.) 39-45	MURDER	CZECH.
KNAPP (see KUAPP)	29755						
KNAPP, Viktor	258976	M	Ger.	10. 1.97	SS-Oberfhr.,SS,SD,NSDAP, 20.4.42	INTERR.	U.S.
KNAPPE	192885	M	Ger.		SS-Sgt.,SS,C.C.Falstad (Nor.) 43	WITNESS	NOR.
KNAPPE	194200	M	Ger.		Lt.,Adjutant,Army,F.P. L 63512,Horst (Neth.) 19.10.44	WITNESS	NETH.
KNAPPE	252355	M			SS-Unterscharfr.,C.C.Osterhagen,Nordhausen (Ger.)	MURDER	U.S.
KNAPPE, Fritz	191364	M	Ger.		Sgt., 7 Pol.Rgt., 3 Pol.Bn., 10 Coy.,Junkerdal (Nor.) 10.44	MURDER	NOR.
KNAPPER	124849	M	Ger.		Cpl.,Stalag III D,C.C.Bitterfeld (Ger.) 5.-11.44	TORTURE	U.K.
KNAPPICH, Hans	124267	M	Ger.		SS-Hauptscharfhr.,1 SS-Pz.Div., 1 SS-Pz.Rgt., 2 Cot.,Malmedy (Bel.)	MURDER	U.S.
KNAPPMOELLER	252443	M			Pvt.,C.C.Ellrich,Nordhausen (Ger.)	MURDER	U.S.
KNARE	24871	M			Civilian,Customs-Agent,Wyler (Neth.) 9.44	MURDER	U.S.
KNARR	185861	M	Ger.		Capt.,Chief of Department for Communism,Athens,Saloniki (Grc.)43-44	MURDER	GRC.
KNAST, Hans	257332	M			Sgt.,Inf.Repl.Bn.29, 3 Coy., 1 Plat.,129 Pz.Gren.Rgt.,Giovannie Paolo, (It.) 13.10.43	MURDER	U.S.
KNAUER	130041	M	Ger.		Capt., Inf.Rgt.959 2 Bn.,Westen of France 4.44	MURDER	U.K.
KNAUER	193947	M	Ger.		Capt.,Army,Eloise (Fr.)	MURDER	FR.
KNAUF, Walter	145241	M	Ger.	16. 8.14	SS-Oberscharfhr.,Waffen-SS,Totenkopf-Sturmbann,Buchenwald-Weimar (Ger.)	TORTURE	U.S.
KNAUP	194709	M			Feldgendarm,Feldgendarmerie,Bar le Duc.,(Fr.) 27.11.43	MURDER	FR.
KNAUPP, Franz	254983	M	Ger.	10	Cpl.,Fieldpolice,Vie Ville sous les Cotes (Fr.) 4.44	TORTURE	FR.
KNAUS, Fritz	173733	M	Ger.		Doctor,Lord-Mayor,Public-Official,Landrat Gau Steiermark,Maribor (Yugo.) 4.41-44	MURDER	YUGO.
KNAUSEDER, Rudolf	187194	M	Ger.		Member,Gestapo,Liege (Bel.) 8.44	MURDER	BEL.
KNAUSS	185480	M	Ger.		SS-Pvt.,Waffen-SS,1 Pz.Div."A.H.",1.SS Recon Bn.Stavelot,Parfondruy (Bel.) 18.-22.12.44	MURDER	U.S.
KNAUSS	189751	M	Ger.		Civilian,Alsfeld (Ger.) 22.2.45	MURDER	U.S.
KNAUSS	194012	M	Ger.		SS-Sturmmann,SS II Zug,1 Gruppe,Stavelot (Bel.) 19.-20.12.44	MURDER	BEL.
KNAUTS	151966	M	Ger.		Civilian, Ingnieur en Chef of plant,Wegelin & Hubner Merseburgerstr. 153 Halle (Ger.)		U.S.
KNEBEL, Karl	254838	M	Ger.	10	Untersturmfhr.,SS,near Strassennaus (Ger.)	MURDER	U.K.
KNEBL, Anton	244579	M	Ger.	09	Sturmmann,Army,Buchenwald (Ger.)	MURDER	U.S.

KNE - KNO

NAME	C.R.FILE NUMBER	SEX	NATIO-NALITY	DATE OF BIRTH	RANK OCCUPATION UNIT PLACE AND DATE OF CRIME	REASON WANTED	WANTED BY
KNECHT or KLEICH, Clara	52675	F		14	Interpreter, Gestapo, Lussault, Fouraine (Fr.) 4.8.44	MURDER	U.S.
KNECHT	174677	M	Ger.		Standartenfhr., SS, Freiburg-Breisgau (Ger.)	PILLAGE	FR.
KNECHT, Christian	189372	M		13. 1.90	Crim.employee, Gestapo, Brno (Czech.) 39-45	MURDER	CZECH.
KNECHT, Max	173662	M	Ger.		SS Hptscharfhr., SS Staatspolizei-Leitstelle, C.C.Brno, Auschwitz, Birkenau (Czech.,Pol.) 39-45	MURDER	CZECH.
KNEER, Hans	146711	M			Civ. Kapo, C.C. Flossenburg (Ger.)	TORTURE	U.S.
KNEFFEL, Georg	252354	M		30..1.15	Cpl., C.C. Ellrich, Nordhausen (Ger.)	MURDER	U.S.
KNEGENDORF, Heinrich	252353	M			Pvt., C.C. Ellrich, Nordhausen (Ger.)	MURDER	U.S.
KNEHEL	185086	M	Ger.		Guard, C.C. Sachsenhausen (Ger.)	TORTURE	FR.
KNEISEL	152530	M	Ger.		Cpl., 1.Rgt. Tartare, Le Puy (Fr.) 28.6.44	MURDER	FR.
KNEISKE	252341	M			SS Rottfhr., C.C. Mackenrode, Nordhausen (Ger.)	MURDER	U.S.
KNEISS, Karl	172075	M			SS Uscharfhr., Guard at M-1 Lager, Muehldorf,Ampfing (Ger.) 6.44-4.45	MURDER	U.S.
KNEISSEL, Paul	127387	M	Ger.		Guard, C.C. Weimar-Buchenwald (Ger.)	TORTURE	U.S.
KNEISSL, Michael	219104	M	Ger.	30.11.91	SS Hptsturmfhr., Commander of AA Wachbn., Brno (Czech.) 41-44	MURDER	CZECH.
KNETTINGER	198290	M	Ger.		Lt.Col., Army, 157.Gren.Rgt., Fr. 8.44	MURDER	FR.
KNEZEL, Paul	121575	M	Ger.		Civ., Medicin chef chirurgie, C.C. Sassfeld (Ger.)	MURDER	FR.
KNELL, Adolf	145963	M	Ger.		Civ., Bingen (Ger.) 8.44	TORTURE	U.S.
KNELLS, Erich	67044	M	Ger.		Guard, C.C. Schoensee Stalag 20 A (Ger.)	MURDER	U.K.
KNELS, Erich	132183	M	Ger.	03	Guard, Volkssturm (Hilfswache), Schoensee nr.Thorn (Pol.) 5.3.44	WITNESS	U.K.
KNEREK, Ernst	257769	M	Ger.	6. 1.15	Bloc Senior, Bloc No.10, Nordhausen (Ger.)	MURDER	U.S.
KNEZEVIC	260001	M			SS Rottfhr., SS-guard at the transport of prisoners from Zittau to Flossenburg, Plana nr.Marianske Lazne-Bohemia (Czech.) 15.4.45	MURDER	CZECH.
KNIE, Robert	193351	M	Ger.		Gruppenfhr., Org. Todt, Firm of Stuag, Nordland Morsvy,Tommenes (Nor.)	TORTURE	NOR.
KNIEP, Friedrich	195071	M	Ger.	31. 7.93	Sturmfhr., S.A., Epe Vreden (Ger.) 10.44-2.45	TORTURE	NETH.
KNIEPER, Katherina	189371	F	Ger.		Prison warder, Gestapo, C.C. Brno (Czech.) 39-45	TORTURE	CZECH.
KNIEPP see KNIPP	102951						
KNIES	152531	M	Ger.	about 08	Justizoberwachtmeister, S.A., C.C. Emsland (Ger.) 44	MURDER	U.S.
KNIEST	300050	M			Member of the Sonderkommando "Feldmeier", Groningen, Drente (Neth.) 43-45	MURDER	NETH.
KNIP, Richard	162359	M			Lt., Army, Rgt. Stabs-Coy. 27, Bod (Nor.)	MURDER	NOR.
KNIPP or KNIEPP	102951	M			Lt., Army, 49.Div. 3.Coy. fusileer, Fr. 6.6.44	MURDER	U.K.
KNIPPEL	1712	M			Lt.Col., Army, Inf.Rgt. 987, Fr..44	MURDER	U.K.
KNIPPEL	256896	M			Hptsturmfhr., SS, C.C. Dora - Nordhausen (Ger.)	MURDER	U.S.
KNIPPELBERGER, Adolf	255414	M		07	Crim.secretary, Gestapo, Brno (Czech.) 2.4.45	INTERR.	U.K.
KNIPPERT	172208	M			Foreman, Org.Todt, C.C. Muehldorf,Ampfing (Ger.) 6.44-4.45	MURDER	U.S.
KNIPPING, Franz	187199	M	Ger.	22.10.99	SS Uscharfhr., C.C. Dora-Nordhausen (Ger.)	MURDER	U.S.
KNIPSCH	256856	M	Ger.		Civ., Ottmannschlausen (Ger.) 8.44	MURDER	U.S.
KNISPEL, Berthold	257506	M			Obertruppfhr., SS, Muehldorf Area (Ger.)	MURDER	U.S.
KNIT, Ewald	145195	M	Ger.		Civ., Flettenberg (Ger.) 4.44	MISC.CRIMES	U.S.
KNITBERGER, Josef	11267	M	Ger.		Pvt., Army, Panz.Gren.Rgt. 111, Albine (Fr.) 29.6.44	MURDER	FR.
KNITTEL	60804	M	Ger.	27.11.14	SS Sturmbannfhr.,Waffen-SS, 1.Panz. (Recon.)Ers.Bn., Ulm (Ger.) 45	MURDER	U.S.
KNITTEL	179894	M	Ger.		Secretary, Hptscharfhr., Gestapo, S.D., Saarbruecken (Ger.)	PILLAGE	FR.
KNITTEL	189840	M	Ger.		SS Sturmbannfhr., 1. SS Aufkl.Bn., Renardmont,Stavelot (Bel.) 19.12.44	MURDER	BEL.
KNITTEL	254597	M			Uscharfhr., Waffen SS, C.C. Auschwitz-Birkenau (Pol.) 11.42	MURDER	YUGO.
KNITTEL, Gustav	60804	M	Ger.	14	Sturmbannfhr., Waffen SS, Panz.Gren.Div. Leibstandarte "Adolf Hitler", Ardennes-Offensive (Ger.) 12.44-1.45	MURDER	U.S.
KNITTLER	1544	M	Ger.		SS Hptscharfhr., C.C. Sachsenhausen (Ger.)	MURDER	U.S.
KNITTLER, Ernst	126990	M	Ger.	10	Oscharfhr., S.D., C.C. Dora-Nordhausen (Ger.) 40-45	MISC.CRIMES	FR.
KNOBLAUCH	29779	M	Ger.		Col., Army, Geb.Jg.Rgt. 218, 7.Geb.Div., Finmark (Nor.) 11.44	MURDER	NOR.
KNOBLAUCH	185683	M	Ger.		Oscharfhr., SS - Leibstandarte "Adolf Hitler", 1.Panz.Gren.Div., Stavelot (Bel.) 19.,20.12.44	MURDER	BEL.
KNOBLAUCH	195070	M	Ger.		Officer Adjutant, SS Totenkopf Div., Adj.to Gen.Eicke, Le Paradis (Fr.) 27.5.40	MURDER	U.K.
KNOBLAUCH	252225	M	Ger.		SS Oscharfhr., C.C. Buchenwald (Ger.)	INTERR.	FR.
KNOBLICH	129685	M	Ger.		Lt., 390.Inf.Rgt.	MURDER	U.S.
KNOBLICH, August	301771	M	Ger.	28. 8.04	SS Uscharfhr., Struthof (Fr.)	MURDER	FR.
KNOBLICK	9671	F	Ger.		SS overseer, C.C. Maidanek (Pol.) 40-44	TORTURE	BEL.
KNOBLICK, Ferdinand	479	M	Ger.	4.10.16	SS Oscharfhr., C.C. Maidanek (Pol.) 40-4.44	MURDER	POL. BEL.
KNORLOCH, Ludwig	252344	M			SS Rottfhr., C.C. Bodungen, Nordhausen (Ger.)	MURDER	U.S.
KNOBLOCK, Rudi	179895	M	Ger.		Hptscharfhr., 2.SS Pz.Gren.Rgt. L "Adolf Hitler", 10.Coy. 3.Bn., Malmedy (Bel.)	MURDER	U.S.
KNOCHE	167698	M			Director, Siedlungsgesellschaft, Warsaw (Pol.) 9.39-44	MISC.CRIMES	POL.
KNOCHE	194708	M	Ger.		Pvt., Feldgendarmerie, Ploermel (Fr.) 18.6.44	TORTURE	FR.
KNOCHE	254376	M	Ger.		SS Scharfhr., Gestapo, S.D., Toulouse (Fr.) 11.42-8.44	MISC.CRIMES	FR.
KNOCHEN	62480	M	Ger.		Scharfhr., SS, Fr.	TORTURE	U.N.W.C.C.
KNOCHEN	195069	M	Ger.		SIPO, Befehlshaber, France, Vosges (Fr.) 8.44	MURDER	U.K.
KNOCHEN	252243	M	Ger.		Osturmfhr., Gestapo, Paris (Fr.) 41	MISC.CRIMES	FR.
KNOCHEN, Helmuth	134702	M	Ger.		Dr., SS Standartenfhr., Gestapo, S.D., Paris, Nantes, Le Mans, Tours (Fr.) 42	MISC.CRIMES	U.K. U.S. FR.
KNOCHENBRUCH, Karl alias KUCHENBRUCH	124766	M	Ger.		Civ., internee at C.C. Sachsenhausen (Ger.)	MURDER	U.S.
KNOCHK, Heinrich	164709	M	Ger.		Pvt., Nachrichten-Coy. 34304, Lamanon (Fr.) 10.6.44	WITNESS	FR.
KNOCKE	259013	M		16	Baker, Bremen, Parchim (Ger.) 19.-20.3.45	MURDER	U.S.
KNOCKEL	251008	M	Ger.		SS Oscharfhr., C.C. Gusen (Aust.)	TORTURE	BEL.
KNOCKEN	132592	M	Ger.		Chief, Gestapoamt, Paris (Fr.)	MURDER	FR.
KNOCKER	149498	M	Ger.		SS Guard, C.C. Schoerzingen (Ger.)	MISC.CRIMES	FR.
KNODLER, Eugene	162357	M	Ger.	10	SS Hptscharfhr., Gestapo, Chalons-Saone (Fr.) 26.-28.6.44	MURDER	FR.
KNODT, Hermann	167688	M	Ger.		Kommissarischer Verwalter "Fahrzeugbau G.m.b.H.", Warsaw (Pol.) 9.39-12.44	MISC.CRIMES	POL.
KNOECHEL, Gustav	185859	M	Ger.	98	Leading Member NSDAP, Praha (Czech.)	MISC.CRIMES	CZECH.
KNOECHEL, Karl	11268	M	Ger.		Pvt., Army, Panz.Gren.Rgt. 111, Albine (Fr.) 29.644	MURDER	FR.
KNOEDLER Oscar	258922	M	Ger.		Secretary, custom house, Member "Aktionskommando" Lourdes custom house, Lourdes (Fr.) 1.-8.44	MURDER	FR.
KNOEDLER, Pius	252345	M		18. 5.00	Cpl., C.C. Ellrich, Nordhausen (Ger.)	MURDER	U.S.
KNOEGLER, Matyas	253865	M	Ger.	23.10.13	Employee, Gestapo, Breclav (Czech.)	SUSPECT	CZECH.
KNOFFE	480	M	Ger.		SS Bde.Fuehrer, Generalmajor der Polizei, Poznan (Pol.) 10.39-43	MURDER	POL.
KNOGGE	146835	M	Ger.		SS Mann, SS Panz.Div. "Das Reich", Tulle (Fr.) 44	MURDER	FR.

KNO-KOC

NAME	C.R.FILE NUMBER	SEX	NATIO-NALITY	DATE OF BIRTH	RANK OCCUPATION UNIT PLACE AND DATE OF CRIME	REASON WANTED	WANTED BY
KNOLL	11554	M	Ger.		Dr.,Capt.Army,44	MISC.CRIMES	NOR.
KNOLL	132588	M	Ger.		Lt.Army,Hochfelden(Fr.)19.7.41	PILLAGE	FR.
KNOLL, Fritz	173125	M	Ger.		Kapo,CC Natzweiler(Fr.)42-43	MURDER	U.K.
KNOLL, Hans	167704	M	Ger.		Pvt.Army 9 Res.Gren.Regt.1 Coy.Magny d'Avignon(Fr.)18.9.44	MURDER	FR.
KNOLL, Johann	192886	M	Ger.		Schupo,CC Falstad(Nor.)42	MURDER	NOR.
KNOLLE, Ernst	173152	M	Ger.	98	Civilian,Lauenau(Ger.)11.44	WITNESS	U.S.
KNOOP see KNOP, Erwin	195068						
KNOP	250889	M	Ger.		Hptsturmfhr.CC Neuengamme(Ger.)	INTERR.	BEL.
KNOP, Albert or KNOPF	160898	M	Ger.		Policeman,Police,Ermsleben(Ger.)11.4.45	MURDER	U.S.
KNOP, Erwin or KNOPP or KNOOP	195068	M	Ger.		Osturmfhr.S.D.Sonderkdo.Knopp, Umerhof (Neth.) 5.- 6.4.45	MURDER	NETH.
KNOP, Hermann	195637	M	Ger.		Guard,Pvt.CC Stalag IX C,Sulza(Ger.)	MURDER	CZECH.
KNOPF, Albert see KNOP	160898						
KNOPKE, Joseph	140782	M	Ger.	24.8.85	Civilian,Chief,CC Leipzig(Ger.)	TORTURE	U.S.
KNOPP see KNOP, Erwin	195068						
KNOPP, August	261941	M	Ger.		Sturmscharfhr.SS,Belgrad and Valjevo(Yugo.)15.8.42-10.9.44	SUSPECT	YUGO.
KNOPP, Erwin see KNOP, KNOOP	195068						
KNOPS	121580	M	Ger.		Adjutant,Arbeits Kdo."Hard",CC Dortmund(Ger.)	MISC.CRIMES	BEL.
KNORP, Karl	133809	M	Ger.	19.2.23	SS Scharfhr.CC Weimar-Buchenwald(Ger.)	TORTURE	U.S.
KNORR	179896	M	Ger.		Employee,Gestapo,Saarbruecken(Ger.)	PILLAGE	FR.
KNORR	185858	M	Ger.		Warrant Officer,Abwehr,Department of Sabotage and Counter Sabotage,Athens(Grc.)	TORTURE	GRC.
KNORR	189076	M	Ger.		SS Untersturmfhr.Gestapo,Groningen,Westerbork(Neth.)12.40-3.45	MURDER	NETH.
KNORR	240108	M	Ger.	20	SS Rottfhr.S.D.Office,Sipo,Scheveningen(Neth.)	TORTURE	U.S.
KNORR	252343	M			SS Hptscharfhr.CC Nixei,Nordhausen(Ger.)	MURDER	U.S.
KNORR	260728	M	Ger.		SS Uscharfhr.CC Buchenwald(Ger.)40-44	BRUTALITY	FR.
KNORR, Bernard	195459	M	Ger.		Luxembourg,Wormeldange(Lux.)	PILLAGE	LUX.
KNORR, Frieda	193948	F	Ger.		Employee,Kriegsgefangenen-Arbeits-Kdo.Elsterberg(Ger.)	TORTURE	FR.
KNORR, Gerhard	252342	M			Pvt.CC Ellrich,Nordhausen(Ger.)	MURDER	U.S.
KNORR, Otto	253113	M		07	Flyer,Airforce,CC Ellrich,Nordhausen(Ger.)	MURDER	U.S.
KNORRE	254161	M	Ger.		Lt.Army,SS,Gouda-Utrecht(Neth.)10.44	TORTURE	NETH.
KNORRE, Richard	185857	M	Ger.	00	Leading Member NSDAP,Praha(Czech.)	MISC.CRIMES	CZECH.
KNORREK, Hellmuth	192887	M	Ger.		Schupo,CC Falstad(Nor.)10.42	MURDER	NOR.
KNOSP	194396	M	Ger.		Sgt.CC FT Zinna,Torgau(Ger.)2.-4.45	MURDER	U.S.
KNOSPE, Lothar	301510	M	Ger.		SS Uscharfhr.No.319260,CC Buchenwald(Ger.)16.5.38-9.10.43	MURDER	BEL.
KNOSPE, Otto	301264	M	Ger.		Crim.secretary,Abt.IV A.S.D.,Brussels(Bel.)6.40-9.44	MURDER	BEL.
KNOTH	191363	M	Ger.	00	Pvt.2 Luftwaffen Bau Bn.132-111,Bardufoss(Nor.)45	MURDER	NOR.
KNOTT, Meta	187661	F	Ger.	06	Office Employee,Prison,Nuernberg(Ger.)34-45	WITNESS	CZECH.
KNUBEN, Rudolf	188750	M	Ger.		Feldgendarm,Feldgendarmerie,Brive(Fr.)6.-7.44	TORTURE	FR.
KNUDTSEN, Karl	250880	M	Ger.	93	SS Hptscharfhr.SS Police,Lublin(Pol.)	MISC.CRIMES	POL.
KNUEPPEL	252298	M			Lt.CC Dora,Nordhausen(Ger.)	MURDER	U.S.
KNUEPPEL, Max	187192	M			SS Uscharfhr.4 SS Totenkopf Sturmbann,Camp Dora,Osterode,Nordhausen (Ger.)43-45	INTERR.	U.S.
KNUEPPER, Heinz	67822	M	Ger.		Cpl.Camp Commander,CC Stalag 4 D,Bitterfeld(Ger.)5.-8.44	MURDER	U.K.
KNUG or GNUG	260869	M			SS Oscharfhr.Waffen SS,Div.Das Reich,SS Regt.Der Fuehrer,1 Bn.3 Coy. Oradour sur Glane(Fr.)10.6.44	MURDER	FR.
KNUGER	188111	M			Untersturmfhr.SS,Gestapo,Lillehammer(Nor.)	TORTURE	NOR.
KNUPFER, H.	1713	M	Ger.		Lt.5 Bn.Inf.Regt.935-245 Div.(Fr.)44	MURDER	U.K.
KNUPPE, Eugene	52671	M	Ger.		Capt.Army,Feldkommandantur No.916,C.O.of Comm.at Argentan,Argentansees(Fr.)7.6.44	MURDER	U.S.
KNUPPEL	162609	M	Ger.		Lt.Gestapo,Hennebont Lorient Vannas(Fr.)43-44	MURDER	FR.
KNUPPER	152532	M	Ger.	15	Cpl.355 Land.Schtz.Bn.,Bitterfeld(Ger.)	TORTURE	U.K.
KNUPPERT, Hubert	165708	M	Ger.		SS Scharfhr.Gestapo,Chalons-Saone Dun Les Places(Fr.)26.-27.and 28.6.44	MURDER	FR.
KNUTH, Gerhardt	172201	M			SS Sturmmann,CC Muhldorf,Ampfing(Ger.)6.44-4.45	MURDER	U.S.
KNUTT	240108	M	Ger.	20	SS Rottfhr.S.D.Office,Sipo,Scheveningen(Neth.)	TORTURE	U.S.
KNUZ	251655	M	Ger.		Col.Gestapo,Paris(Fr.)41-44	TORTURE	FR.
KNY	190206	M	Ger.		Major,Kreiskommandant,Kreiskommandantur,Krusevac(Yugo.)43	MURDER	YUGO.
KOACHER	151958	M	Ger.		Adjutant,S.D.Aussendienststelle de Mende(Lozens)Badaroux(Fr.)29.5.45	MURDER	FR.
KOANSKY	133808	M	Ger.		SS Oscharfhr.CC Weimar-Buchenwald(Ger.)	TORTURE	U.S.
KOB, Fritz	300051	M	Ger.		Major,2 Bn.of the 1 Regt.Turkestan Volunteers,Le Garric Tarn.17.8.44	MURDER	FR.
KOBAN, August or KOPAN	260431	M	Ger.	3.2.14	Living at Moerfelden,Tannenstr.6.,Mielec by Krakow(Pol.)42-44	MURDER	POL.
KOBAN, Rudolf	192371	M	Ger.		Civilian,CC Plaisance(Fr.)8.40	MURDER	FR.
KOBATH or KABO	258921	M	Ger.		SS Major,19 Regt.der SS Police,Limoges,Confolens(Fr.)23.6.44	INCENDIARISM	FR.
KOBEE von HOFMAN	174679	M	Ger.		Lt.Army,7 Art.Res.Regt.Geb Art.Regt.79,Tours Albertville(Fr.)8.-25.6.44	MURDER	FR.
KOBER	192888	M	Ger.		Wachtmeister,Schupo,CC Falstad(Nor.)2.-3.42	MURDER	NOR.
KOBER	257820	M	Ger.		Hptwachtmeister,SS Pol.Regt.7,Trondheim(Nor.)	INTERR.	NOR.
KOBER, Walter	31704	M	Ger.		Civilian,Settler,Olekczyn(Pol.)12.39	INCENDIARISM	POL.
KOBER, Wilhelm	189485	M			Olekszyn(Pol.)12.39	INCENDIARISM	POL.
KOBER, Willy	261050	M	Ger.	06	Osturmfhr.S.D.Var(Fr.)10.43-8.44	MISC.CRIMES	FR.
KOBERLE	254377	M	Ger.		Capt.515 Inf.Regt.Miellin(Fr.)21.10.44	PILLAGE	FR.
KOBES	251097	M	Ger.		Kapo,CC Neuengamme(Ger.)	INTERR.	BEL.
KOBINGER	167073	M	Ger.		Senior W.O.Gendarmerie,Montigny en Vesoul(Fr.)16.7.44	MURDER	FR.
KOBITSCH	126566	M	Ger.		Major,Army Kampfgruppe Hauer,sec.Commandant N.C.O.School Heidelberg SE.of Ockten(Ger.)25.2.45	MURDER	U.S.
KOBLER, Paul	135198	M	Ger.		Camp Guard,CC Helmbrechts(Ger.)7.44-13.4.45	WITNESS	U.S.
KOBLOFSKY, Josef	192370	M	Ger.	19.5.01	Ortsgruppenfhr.NSDAP,Frenstadt(Czech.)42-45	MISC.CRIMES	CZECH.
KOBUS	254378	M	Ger.		Member,Gestapo S.D.Toulouse(Fr.)11.42	MISC.CRIMES	FR.
KOCH	483	M	Ger.		SS Standartenfhr.Lagerfhr.CC Maidanek(Pol.)40-4.44	MURDER	POL.FR.
KOCH	485	M	Ger.		Major,Army CC Caen(Fr.)	MURDER	U.K.
KOCH	486	M	Ger.		Dr.,Chief Gestapo District Warszawa(Pol.)40	MURDER	POL.
KOCH	24892	M			S.D.CC Terezin(Pol.)12.41	TORTURE	U.S.
KOCH	60203	M	Ger.		Director of Airplane Factory,Armament and War Production,Heinkel,Oranienburg,Berlin(Ger.)18.4.44	MURDER	FR.

NAME	C.R.FILE NUMBER	SEX	NATIO- NALITY	DATE OF BIRTH	RANK OCCUPATION UNIT PLACE AND DATE OF CRIME	REASON WANTED	WANTED BY
KOCH	102944	M	Ger.		Capt., Army (Bel.) 20.12.44	MURDER	U.S.
KOCH	125083	M	Ger.		Dr., Officer, Stalag-Doctor, CC Sandbostel (Ger.)30.6.41-2.7.41	MURDER	U.K.
KOCH	126950	M	Ger.	10	N.C.O., 9 Staatspolizeileitstelle, Karlsruhe Durath (Ger.)	MURDER	FR.
KOCH	128992	M	Ger.		Civilian, Teacher, Gr.Gerau(Ger.) 29.8.44	MURDER	U.S.
KOCH	143185	M			Civilian, near Winkelheid (Ger.) 4.45	TORTURE	U.S.
KOCH	147304	M	Ger.		11 Pz.Div. (Fr.) 44	MURDER	FR.
KOCH	152871	M	Ger.		Cpl., Army, 368 Lds.Schtz.Bn.,Stalag IV A.K.,Bodenbach(Czech.)8.7.42	MURDER	U.K.
KOCH	161515	M	Ger.		Oschfhr, Gestapo, SD, CC Buchenwald (Ger.)	WITNESS	U.S.
KOCH	162268	M	Ger.		Uschfhr, SS Leibstandarte "Adolf Hitler", Bierwart (Bel.) 5.9.44	PILLAGE	BEL.
KOCH	166071	M	Ger.		Major Gestapo, Army, Oberkommando, Mantua (Fr.) 12.-16.7.44	TORTURE	FR.
KOCH	169488	M	Ger.	07	Pvt., Army, Lds.Schtz.Bn.298, 2 Coy, CC Ohringen (Ger.) 3.41	MURDER	U.K.
KOCH	172598	M			Schacht Meister, Org.Todt, CC Muhldorf, Ampfing (Ger.) 6.44-4.45	MURDER	U.S.
KOCH	174768	M			Pvt.,`Kriegsgefangenenbau Arbeits-Bn.184, CC Aspfjord(Nor.)	TORTURE	NOR.
KOCH	185143	M			Lt., SS Police, Org.Todt, 9 Coy, Annemasse (Fr.) 29.1.44	WITNESS	FR.
KOCH	185144	M	Ger.	95	Lagerkapo, SS, CC Dachau (Ger.)	TORTURE	FR.
KOCH	187569	M	Ger.		Lt., 65 Inf.Div. Rgt.1,47, Cisa-Pass, Genova, Spezia (It.) 3.10.43	WITNESS	U.K.
KOCH	187704	M			Dr., Norway	PILLAGE	U.N.W.C.C.
KOCH	189498	M			Lt., Luftnachrichten Ausbildungs Rgt.302, Nogent en Bassigny (Fr.) 13.9.44	INCENDIARISM	FR.
KOCH	189604			07	Crim.Asst. Police, Uschfhr. SS, Colmar (Fr.) 21.1.45	TORTURE	U.S.
KOCH	190207	M	Ger.		Member of Gestapo, CC Banjica (Yugo.) 40-45	MURDER	YUGO.
KOCH	190667	M	Ger.		Pvt., Eis.Btty 717, St.Andries, Verserarles, Bruges (Bel.) 4.9.44	MURDER	BEL.
KOCH	193360	M	Ger.		Pvt., 2 Coy, Lds.Schtz.Bn.309, Smalaasen (Nor.) 6.2.45	MURDER	NOR.
KOCH	252396	M	Ger.		Lt., 3 or 10 Parachute Div., Environs d'Ussel (Fr.) 7.4.44	PILLAGE	FR.
KOCH	255174	M	Ger.		Interpreter, Abt.IV p, Brussels (Bel.) 40-44	INTERR.	BEL.
KOCH	255605	M			Commander Bn., Army, Hedel (Neth.) 11.44	SUSPECT	NETH.
KOCH	256917	M	Ger.		Commander,-Bn., Army, Heusden (Neth.) 5.11.44	SUSPECT	NETH.
KOCH	259307	M			Lt. Camp Thekla near Leipzig (Ger.) 18.4.45	MURDER	U.S.
KOCH	259605	M	Ger.		Chief Pay Master, Unit H.U.V. 282, Paris, Railway Station of Batignolles - Seine (Fr.) 18.-19.8.44	MURDER	FR.
KOCH	260689	M	Ger.		Engineer, Fa."Anschutz", Buchenwald (Ger.) 40-44	MURDER	FR.
KOCH	262456	M	Ger.	about 05-15	SS Schfhr, Command.Leader, CC Radom (Pol.) 40-45	MURDER	POL.
KOCH	301177	M	Ger.		Dr, Officer SD at the Hague (Neth.) 20.5.44	MISC.CRIMES	NETH.
KOCH	306620	M	Ger.		SS Sturmfhr att. staff of Capt.Bogenrieder cmdg. det.school of Parachutists at La Courtine SP 49-029 L, Aubusson(Creuse) Fr. 8.-9.1.44, 19.-20.2.44, 23.3.44, 27.3.44	MURDER	FR.
KOCH, Adam	254662	M	Ger.		Guard, CC Steinbergen (Ger.)	INTERR.	BEL.
KOCH, Albert	195430	M	Ger.		Policeman, Group-Leader NSDAP, Gruenmacher (Lux.)	MISC.CRIMES	LUX.
KOCH, Albert	254984	M	Ger.		Sturmscharfhr, Gestapo, L'Aube (Fr.) 43-44	INTERR.	FR.
KOCH, Anita	162394	F			Civilian, CC Buchenwald (Ger.)	MURDER	U.S.
KOCH, Anton	252296	M			Uschfhr, SS, CC Harzungen, Nordhausen (Ger.)	MURDER	U.S.
KOCH, Daniel	167709	M	Ger.		Zugfhr, Army, 9 Res.Gren.Rgt., 1 Coy, Magny d'Anigon(Fr.) 18.9.44	MURDER	FR.
KOCH, Erich	487	M	Ger.		Reichskommissar, Gauleiter, Public Official, Bialystock(Pol.Russia) 6.40-45	MURDER	U.S.,POL.
KOCH, Ernst	189336	M	Ger.	24.3.--	Criminal Commissary, Gestapo, Brno (Czech.) 39-45	TORTURE	CZECH.
KOCH, Friedhelm	191418	M	Ger.	8.8.19	Pvt., 627 Wolga-Tartars Legion, Stabs Coy, 2.-3.9.44	MURDER	U.S.
KOCH, Friedrich	134710	M	Ger.	11.8.96	Civilian,Director,Administration Office Messerschmidt Works(Ger.)153-45	WITNESS	U.S.
KOCH, Fritz or Friedrich	301041	M	Ger.		Schupo,Guard, Labour Camp,Lahde-Weser (Ger.) 43-45	MURDER	BEL.
KOCH, Gerhard	301511	M	Ger.	21.11.20	SS-Mann, SS, CC Buchenwald (Ger.) 16.5.38-9.10.43	MURDER	BEL.
KOCH, Gunter	145253	M	Ger.	23	Rottfhr, SS Leibstandarte"Adolf Hitler", Feld-Ers.Bn.1, Rosbach (Ger.) 4.3.45	WITNESS	U.S.
KOCH, Hans	124268	M	Ger.		Usturmfhr, 1 SS Pz.Gren.Rgt., 2 Coy, Malmedy(Bel.) 17.12.44	MURDER	U.S.
KOCH, Hans	252297	M			Uschfhr, SS, CC Dora, Nordhausen (Ger.)	MURDER	U.S.
KOCH, Heinz	255173	M	Ger.	1903 or 04	Oberwachtmstr,Schupo,Prag-Kobylisy (Czech.)	MURDER	CZECH.
KOCH, Helmuth	251112	M	Ger.		Usturmfhr, 12 SS Pz.Div., Malmedy (Bel.) 17.12.44	MURDER	U.S.
KOCH, Herbert	102945	M	Ger.	10	Civilian, Policeman, CC Ellerstedt, 41-45	SUSPECT	U.S.,POL.
KOCH, Herbert	250314	M	Ger.	15	Oschfhr, SS, 4 Coy, 5 Signal - Depot Bn.	INTERR.	U.S.
KOCH, Hermann	489	M	Ger.	95	SS Osturmfhr, CC Grini (Nor.) 6.41-6.42	MISC.CRIMES	NOR.
KOCH, Ilse	161517	F		05	Civilian, CC Buchenwald (Ger.)	WITNESS	U.S.
KOCH, Jacob	195458	M			Police-Master, Bau-Polizei, Neukirchen (Ger.)	WITNESS	U.S.
KOCH, Johann	174680	M	Ger.	27.7.04	Cpl., CC Vannes, Morbihan, Bretagne (Fr.) 42-44	TORTURE	FR.
KOCH, Josef (alias KUCHAR)	253983	M	Ger.	21or23.7.08	Employee, Gestapo, Vsetin (Czech.) 39-45	MURDER	CZECH.
KOCH, K.A.	490	M	Ger.		SS Standartenfhr, Camp Cmdt., Buchenwald (Ger.)	MURDER	POL.
KOCH, Karl	143178	M	Ger.	94	SS-Standartenfhr, CC Lublin (Pol.) 40-45	MURDER	U.S.
KOCH, Karl	145256	M	Ger.		Standartenfhr, SS Totenkopf-Verband, Cmdt. of Camp, Buchenwald - Weimar (Ger.)	TORTURE	U.S.
KOCH, Karl	259545	M	Ger.		Director, Savings-Bank, Lengerich (Ger.) 8.44	WITNESS	U.S.
KOCH, Karl	301421	M			SF., CC Dachau (Ger.)	MURDER	FR.
KOCH, Leonard	24909	M	Ger.		Uschfhr, SS, CC Struthof (Fr.)	MISC.CRIMES	FR.
KOCH, Louis	148155	M			CC Mauthausen (Aust.)	MISC.CRIMES	FR.
KOCH, Ludwig	60240	M		95	Standartenfhr, SS, CC Buchenwald (Ger.)	MURDER	FR.
KOCH (see KOCK,Ludwig)	133807						
KOCH, Ludwig	259645	M	Ger.	about 18	SS Rottfhr, Gestapo, Area Angers, Maine and Loire (Fr.) 42-44	MISC.CRIMES	FR.
KOCH, Maria	171954	F			Civilian Marange near Fouligny (Fr.) 9.8.44	WITNESS	U.S.
KOCH, Martin	254068	M	Ger.		SS Blockfhr, CC Auschwitz-Birkenau (Pol.) 42-45	MISC.CRIMES	U.S.
KOCH, Orilo	194100	M	Ger.		Osturmfhr, SS, Dussen (Neth.) 30.10.44	MISC.CRIMES	YUGO.
KOCH, Otto	133298	M			Kreispropagandaleiter, Osturmbannfhr SA	PILLAGE	NETH.
KOCH, Otto	145226	M	Ger.		Uschfhr, Allg.SS, Weimar (Ger.)	TORTURE	U.S.
KOCH, Otto	189746	M	Ger.	04	Warden, Gestapo, Brno (Czech.) 39-45	MISC.CRIMES	U.S.
KOCH, Otto	254979	M	Ger.	29.5.92	Sturmfhr, SA, Mornshausen (Ger.) 10.12.44	MISC.CRIMES	CZECH.
KOCH, Paul	259526	M			Asst.Mayor, No.19 Hauptstrasse, Grossorner(Ger.), Mansfeld(Ger.)15 3.44	INTERR.	U.K.
KOCH, Pauwel	162722	M	Ger.		Civ.,Foreman "Fours a Chaux"Adolphe Willekens,Oker-Harz(Ger)12.44-4.45	WITNESS	U.S.
KOCH, Rudolf	11571	M	Ger.		Major-General, Army, Erpach	TORTURE	BEL.
KOCH, Rudolf	193712	M	Ger.	about 03	Pvt., KGF.Arb.Bn.186, Norway 40-45	MURDER	U.K.
KOCH, Victor	139769	M	Ger.	25	SS-Mann, Waldlager V, W-SS,Mittergars-Lager, CC Muhldorf(Ger.)44-45	MISC.CRIMES	NOR.
KOCH, Walter	254586	M	Ger.		SS Usturmfhr, Garnisonstab SS, Auschwitz-Birkenau(Pol.) 11.42	MURDER	U.S.
						MURDER	YUGO.

NAME	C.R.FILE NUMBER	SEX	NATIO-NALITY	DATE OF BIRTH	RANK OCCUPATION UNIT PLACE AND DATE OF CRIME	REASON WANTED	WANTED BY
KOCH, Werner	191384	M			SS-Oberscharfhr., 1.SS-Pz.Regt., 7.Coy., Stoumont, Ligneuville (Bel.)	MURDER	U.S.
KOCH, Willi	193713	M	Ger.	05	Sgt., Straf-Leger, Reichsjustizministerium, Finmark (Nor.) 42-45	MISC.CRIMES	NOR.
KOCH, Willy	166072	M	Ger.	23. 7.13	1.Ost Freiwillig.Bn. 447, Plouvien (Fr.) 8.44	TORTURE	FR.
KOCH, Wolfhard	129145	M	Ger.	07	Lt., Dulag-Luft, Oberursel (Ger.)	TORTURE	U.K.
KOCHAN	141570	M	Ger.		Civilian, Paris, C.C. Austerlitz (Fr.) 42 - 44	TORTURE	FR.
KOCHANN	491	M			Camp-Officer, C.C. Birkenau (Pol.)	MURDER	FR.
KOCHELL	254968	M	Ger.		Inspector, Roubaix (Fr.) 8.41	INTERR.	FR.
KOCHER, Hugo	301512	M		17. 3.19	SS-Pottenfhr., C.C. Buchenwald (Ger.) 5.38-10.43	MURDER	BEL.
KOCHERSCHEIDT	257887	M			Lt., 150.Panz.Bde., Meuse-Bridge, Antwerp (Bel.) 12.44	MISC.CRIMES	U.S.
KOCHEPT, Otto	252346	M		13. 8.17	Sgt., C.C. Ellrich, Nordhausen (Ger.)	MURDER	U.S.
KOCH-KNOPF, Franz	188749	M	Ger.		Feldgendarm, Feldgendarmerie, Bar le Duc (Fr.) 8.44	MURDER	FR.
KOCHLIN or LOCHLIN, Max	301209	M	Ger.		Obersturmfhr., Hon.Col., H.J., Huchenfeld (Ger.) 3.45	MURDER	U.K.
KOCHLING	9672	M			Doctor, Army, Breedonck (Bel.) 40-44	TORTURE	BEL.
KOCHLING, Fritz	191362	M	Ger.		Oberwachtmeister, 10.Coy., 3.Pol.Bn., 7.Pol.Regt., Junkerdal (Nor.) 44	TORTURE	NOR.
KOCHS	208072	M		98	Lt. 731.Gren.Regt., 3.Bn., Stalag 8-B, Cosel (Ger.) 6.-12.40	MURDER	U.K.
KOCHS	132671	M			Sgt., Standort-Kdtr., Gerardmer (Fr.) 9.-11.44	WITNESS	FR.
KOCHSTEIN, Berthold	124367	M			Unterscharfhr., W-SS, Leibst."A.Hitler", 1.Ers.Bn., Rosbach (Ger.) 3.45	MURDER	U.S.
KOCHY	139101	M			Gen.Major, Airforce, Lyseford (Nor.)	MURDER	U.K.
KOCK	167968	M			Sgt., Feldgendarmerie, Auberive Flagey, Coiffey Chalency (Fr.) 43-44	MURDER	FR.
KOCK	257519	M			Oberzahlmeister, 919. Regt., 2.Bn., near St.Martin (Fr.) 4.45	WITNESS	U.S.
KOCK	260727	M	Ger.		Chief, Stalag 325, Stryj (Pol.) 7.-9.42	MURDER	FR.
KOCK, Elfriede (nee LOTZE)	251686	F	Ger.		SS-Overseer, C.C. Oswiecim, Ravensbrueck, Duderstadt (Pol.,Ger.) 40-45	TORTURE	POL.
KOCK, Ewald	252299	M		11. 9.25	Pvt., C.C. Ellrich, Nordhausen (Ger.)	MURDER	U.S.
KOCK or KOCH, Ludwig	139517	M			SS-Oberscharfhr., C.C. Buchenwald (Ger.)	BRUTALITY	U.S.
KOCK, Otto	24869	M			Foreman, Borsig-Werke, Blechhammer (Ger.) 1.44	TORTURE	U.K.
KOCUR	251015	M	Ger.		SS-Oberscharfhr., C.C. Gusen (Ger.)	TORTURE	BEL.
KODEHUS	124269	M	Ger.		Unterscharfhr., 1.SS-Pz.Gren.Regt., Headquarters-Coy., Malmedy (Bel.) 12.44	MURDER	U.S.
KODIDEC, Karl	161876	M	Ger.		SS-Unterscharfhr., 16.Inf.Div., Maille (Fr.) 8.44	MURDER	FR.
KODRA	300795	M	Ger.		Pvt., 1.Aufklaerungsabteilung, 3.Coy., 2.Col., 15.Div. of the Africa corps, St. Leger (Arlon) 9.44	MISC.CRIMES	BEL.
KOEBE	102943	M		87	Major, Oflag, C.C. Hamburg-Altona (Ger.) 7.-11.44	TORTURE	U.S.
KOEBE, Walter	24912	M			SS, C.C. Struthof (Fr.)	MISC.CRIMES	FR.
KOEBELE	29780	M			Dr., Col., Inf.Div. 169, Finmark (Nor.) 11.44	MURDER	NOR.
KOEBELE, Fritz	193711	M		08	Regierungsbaumeister, Org.Todt, Oslo (Nor.) 42-43	MISC.CRIMES	NOR.
KOEBERLEIN, Friedrich	258547	M		85	SS-Standartenfhr., W.V.H.A., (Ger.) 40-45	BRUTALITY	U.S.
KOEBES	131421	M	Ger.		N.C.O., C.C.Neuengamme (Ger.)	TORTURE	BEL.
KOEBL	127191	M			Pvt., Army, C.C. Obertraubling (Ger.) 1.45	MURDER	U.S.
KOEBLER, Peter	254163	M		05	Guard, factory, Hoechst (Ger.) 8.44	MURDER	POL.
KOEBLINGER	135207	M	Ger.		Lt.Col. 19.SS-Pol-Regt., Vigaun, Oberkrain, Toulouse, Compiegne, Tulle (Yugo., Fr.) 5.41- 3.44, 3.44- 10.44	MURDER	U.S.
KOEBRISCH, Kurt	161518	M	Ger.	96	Hauptsturmfhr., W-SS, Kdo.-Amt, C.C. Buchenwald (Ger.) 41	WITNESS	U.S.
KOECHEL, Willi	250303	M	Ger.		Pvt., 11.Pz.Gr.Coy., 2.Pz.Gr.Regt., Malmedy (Bel.) 12.44	INTERR.	U.S.
KOECK	239099	M	Ger.		SS-Div."Hitler Jugend", Tongres (Bel.) 11.45	MURDER	BEL.
KOECUBSHKE	188748	M	Ger.		Reichsbahn, Le Bourget, Triage (Fr.) 8.44	WITNESS	FR.
KOEF	189725	M			Pvt., 4.Coy., Landessch.Bn. 143, C.C. Widenau (Ger.) 2.45	MURDER	U.K.
KOEFFLER	191413	M	Ger.		SS-Unterscharfhr., Mauthausen (Aust.) 41-45	MURDER	U.S.
KOEGEL (Brother of KOEGEL, Max)	132184	M	Ger.		Dr., SS-Sturmbannfhr., C.C. Flossenburg (Ger.) 44-45	SUSPECT	US.
KOEGEL	250887	M			SS-Hauptsturmfhr., C.C. Mauthausen (Aust.)	INTERR.	BEL.
KOEGEL, Johann	252947	M		20.10.19	Pvt., C.C. Ellrich, Nordhausen (Ger.)	MURDER	U.S.
KOEGEL, Max (see KAEGLER)	133320						
KOEGL	250907	M	Ger.		SS-Obersturmbannfhr., C.C. Ravensbrueck (Ger.)	INTERR.	BEL.
KOEHL	260140	M	Ger.		Insp., S.D., Charlesville, Ardennes (Fr.) 7.44	TORTURE	FR.
KOEHLE (see GOELLE)	141479	M					
KOEHLER	1413	M	Ger.		SS-Hauptsturmfhr., S.D. Aussen-Kdo.,	MISC.CRIMES	U.K.
KOEHLER	172096	M			Org.Todt, C.C. Muhldorf - Ampfing (Ger.) 6.44- 4.45	MURDER	U.S.
KOEHLER	257756	M	Ger.		Employee, Chief of Sub-Sec. Mittelbau, Nordhausen (Ger.)	MURDER	U.S.
KOEHLER	261268	M	Ger.		Gend. of the Bde., Oberhergheim (Fr.) 7.41	BRUTALITY	FR.
KOEHLER, Ernst	150666	M			Lt., Signal-corps, Grafenwoehr (Ger.) 11.-12.44	MISC.CRIMES	U.S.
KOEHLER, Friedel	240109	M			Official, Sturmfuehrer, Pol.Secr., Gestapo, Sec.II, Darmstadt Bensheim (Ger.) 9.44	TORTURE	U.S.
KOEHLER, Friedrich	129146	M	Ger.	05	Lt., Dulag-Luft, Oberursel (Ger.)	TORTURE	U.K.
KOEHLER, Friedrich	29773	M	Ger.		Oberlandgerichtsrat, Public official, Litomerice (Czech.) 2.40	MURDER	BEL.
KOEHLER, Gerhard	191361	M		05	Cpl. 190.Kriegsgef.Arb.Bn., 2.Coy., C.C. Russanes (Nor.) 11.44- 5.45	MISC.CRIMES	NOR.
KOEHLER, Gilbert	252348	M		25	Pvt., C.C. Ellrich, Nordhausen (Ger.)	MURDER	U.S.
KOEHLER, Hermann	255175	M	Ger.		Referendar, Abt. IV D Sipo, Bruessel (Bel.) 40-44	INTERR.	BEL.
KOEHLER, K.	254160	M	Ger.		Zugwachtmeister, near Arnheim (Neth.) 3.45	MURDER	NETH.
KOEHLER, Karl	254849	M	Ger.	22. 5.01	Sgt., Z.b.V. Kdo. 31, Velaseka Mezirici (Czech.) 2.-5.45	MURDER	CZECH.
KOEHLER, Otto	258882	M		9.10.02	Hauptwachtmeister, Schupo, Luxemburg (Lux.)	SUSPECT	LUX.
KOEHLER, Rudolf	149179	M	Ger.	10	SS-Hauptscharfhr., C.C. Lublin (Pol.) 42-43	TORTURE	POL.
KOEHLER, Sigmund	251111	M			Sturmmann, 3.Pz.Pi.Coy., 1.Pz.Regt., 1.SS-Pz.Div., Leibstandarte "Adolf Hitler", Malmedy (Bel.) 12.44	MURDER	U.S.
KOEHLER, Willi	258083	M	Ger.	03	SS-Hauptscharfhr., State service, Gestapo, Val, Mezirici (Czech.) 44-45	MURDER	CZECH.
KOEHLING	193710	M	Ger.	05	Baurat, Org.Todt, Narvik (Nor.) 42-43	MISC.CRIMES	NOR.
KOEHN, Bernhard	6103	M			Feldgendarm, 518.Feldgendarmerie, St. Herblein (Fr.) 6.-7.44	MURDER	FR.
KOEHN, Joachim	131419	M	Ger.	31. 5.19	Cpl., Stabs-Coy.1, Wolga-Tataren Legion Bn. 627, Quaregnon Jemappes (Bel.) 44	MURDER	BEL.
KOEHN, Richard	254165	M	Ger.	6. 8.05	Official, Fieldpolice, 5.Coy., 34.Div., Tiel (Neth.) 3.-4.45	PILLAGE	NETH.
KOEHNE	194154	F	Ger.		Dr., Physician, Civ., C.C. Lidice Puschkau (Czech.) 42-44	INTERR.	CZECH.
KOEHNE, Walter	252349	M		6.11.18	Cpl., C.C. Ellrich, Nordhausen (Ger.)	MURDER	U.S.
KOEHNEN	127393	M	Ger.		Obersturmfhr., Lt., SS, Gestapo, C.C. Buchenwald (Ger.)	TORTURE	U.S.
KOEHNKE, Paul	187184	M	Ger.		SS-Oberscharfhr., S.D., Montgau, Thisr (Bel.) 9.43	MURDER	BEL.
KOEHNLE	142197	M	Ger.	95	SS-Untersturmfhr., Lublin (Pol.)	MURDER	FR.

KOE-KOE

NAME	C.R.FILE NUMBER	SEX	NATIO-NALITY	DATE OF BIRTH	RANK OCCUPATION UNIT PLACE AND DATE OF CRIME	REASON WANTED	WANTED BY
KOELBL	253756	M			Sturmmann, SS, C.C. Dora, Nordhausen (Ger.)	MURDER	U.S.
KOELBLINGER	147303	M	Ger.		Lt.Col., 19.SS- and Police-Rgt.,St.Pierre D'Albigny (Fr.)	MURDER	FR.,UNWCC
KOELEL	256640	M	Ger.		SS-Mann, Legal Sec.Camp Dora, Nordhausen (Ger.)	MURDER	U.S.
KOELLEGAM	186752	M			Oschfhr., SS-Pol.Rgt.Todt,9.Coy., Annemasse (Fr.) Bernex, Haute-Savoie 12.43 - 1.44	WITNESS	FR.
KOELLENSPERGER	125721	M	Ger.		Arzt, 3.Fallschirmjaeger-Div.,8.Rgt., Malmedy Arnheim (Bel., Neth.)9.44	MURDER	U.S.
KOELLER	185091	M	Ger.		Vizille (Fr.)	MURDER	FR.
KOELLER	240055	M		89	Interpreter, SD, Gestapo, Bergen (Nor.)	TORTURE	U.S.
KOELLER, Otto	195638	M			Commissar-Official, Mizocz (Pol.) 14.10.42	MURDER	POL.
KOELLING, Gustav	131414	M		09 - 10	Crim.Secr., Sturmschfhr., SD, SS, Officer, Feldgend., Arlon (Bel.) 25.8.44	MURDER	BEL.
KOELLNER, Fritz	185850	M	Ger.	04	Leader, NSDAP, Prague (Czech.)	MISC.CRIMES	CZECH.
KOELNER	173123	M	Ger.		Guard, Conc.Camp, Gaggenau, Schirmeck, Rothenfels (Ger., Fr.) 44	INTERR.	U.K.
KOELPLINGER	138220	M	Ger.		Lt Col., 15.Rgt., Police, St.Genis Laval (Fr.) 20.8.44	MURDER	FR.
KOELZER, Franz	145172	M	Ger.	18. 3.15	Pvt., Airforce, Fliegerhorst-Coy.E.222-VII, Bozen-Tirol, Neckarsulm (Ger.) 21.3.45	MURDER	U.S.
KOELZOW, Hans	255536	M	Ger.		Sturmbannfhr., Waffen-SS, SD, Inowrodaw (Pol.) 39	MISC.CRIMES	POL.
KOENECKE, Fritz	260225	M	Ger.		Dr., Ch.Vorstand and Manager - Mem.AR, Ges.A.G. Continental-Gummi, Reichs-Kredit-Werke A.G., Berlin, Hannover (Ger.)	MISC.CRIMES	U.S.
KOENECKE, Herbert	253759	M			Uschfhr., SS, C.C. Harzungen, Nordhausen (Ger.)	MURDER	U.S.
KOENEN	145209	M	Ger.		Marine-Korps, St.Marine (Fr.) 30.6.44	MURDER	U.S.
KOENIG	492	M	Ger.		Hptsturmfhr., SS, Limoges (Fr.) 8.6.44	MURDER	FR.
KOENIG	12405	M	Ger.		Osturmfhr., Waffen-SS, Conc.Camp, Buchenwald (Ger.) 39-44	TORTURE	CZECH.
KOENIG	31706	M	Ger.		Dr., Physician, Conc.Camp, Oswiecim (Pol.) 6.41-1.45	MURDER	POL.
KOENIG	64513	M			Oschfhr., 4.SS-Totenkopf-Stuba.,C.C.Dora,Nordhausen (Ger.) 43-45	WITNESS	U.S.
KOENIG	124600	M	Ger.		Dr., SS-Mann, Physician, Conc.Camp, Birkenau-Auschwitz (Pol.) 42-45	MURDER	BEL.
KOENIG	127104	M	Ger.	10	Hptschfhr., SS, Conc.Camp Dora (Ger.)	MURDER	FR.
KOENIG	127394	M	Ger.	19 - 20	Oschfhr., SS, Conc.Camp, Weimar, Buchenwald (Ger.)	TORTURE	U.S.
KOENIG	133321	M			Member, Waffen-SS, C.C., Flossenburg (Ger.)	MURDER	U.S.
KOENIG	133325 A	M	Ger.		Kreisleiter, NSDAP	MURDER	U.S.
KOENIG	137056	M	Ger.		Capt., 395.Lds.Schtz.Bn., Stalag IV B, C.C., Muehlburg (Ger.) 44-45	MURDER	U.S.
KOENIG	141938	M	Ger.	10	Rottfhr., SA, Works-Control-Officer at Arb.Kdo.,Tschausch,Bruex (Czech.) 5.8.44	MISC.CRIMES	U.K.
KOENIG	161874	M	Ger.	00	Capt., Cdt. Stalag IV B, C.C., between Muehlberg and Jacobsthal (Ger.) 9.43-10.43	TORTURE	U.K.
KOENIG	161885	M	Ger.		Capt., Kommandantur (Army) Laveissiere (Fr.) 44	MURDER	FR.
KOENIG	166119	M	Ger.		Cmdt., C.C. (Ex-Stalag V C) Pforzheim (Ger.)	MURDER	FR.
KOENIG	178310	M	Ger.	20	Osturmfhr.,12.SS-Pz.Div.H.J., 25.SS-Pz.Gren.Rgt.,Abbaye,Ardenne nr. Caen (Fr.) 6.6.44-2.7.44	TORTURE	CAN
KOENIG	178761	M	Ger.	03	Pvt., Army, A-K.538,Stalag IX C, C.C.,Rentsmuehle (Ger.) 12.41-12.42	TORTURE	U.K.
KOENIG	187189	M			Hptschfhr., 4.SS-Totenkopf-Stuba.,C.C.Dora,Nordhausen (Ger.) 43-45	TORTURE	U.S.
KOENIG	188899	M			Capt., Army, Laveissiere (Fr.) 44	MURDER	FR.
KOENIG	195456	M	Ger.		Gauamtsleiter, NSDAP, Luxembourg (Lux.) 40-45	MISC.CRIMES	LUX.
KOENIG	252205	M	Ger.		Gend., Fieldpolice, Chaumont (Fr.) 24.8.44	MISC.CRIMES	FR.
KOENIG	253977	M	Ger.		Member, SS, Auschwitz-Birkenau (Pol.) 42-45	MURDER	YUGO.
KOENIG	254989	M	Ger.		Major and Cmdt., Straf-Coy., Kragujevac (Yugo.) 19.-21.10.41	MURDER	YUGO.
KOENIG	301774	M	Ger.		Uschfhr., SS, Dr.-Selection, C.C., Auschwitz (Pol.) 40-45	MURDER	FR.
KOENIG	305806	M	Ger.		Major, Deputy Cmdt., Oflag VI C,Osnabrueck-Ewersheide (Ger.) 43-45	MURDER	YUGO.
KOENIG, Alexander	257891	M	Ger.		Cpl., 150.Panz.Bde., Meuse-Bridge-Antwerp 12.44	MISC.CRIMES	U.S.
KOENIG, Franz	254362	M	Ger.		Chief, Undertaker Organ.Todt, Tour-Laville (Fr.) 43	TORTURE	FR.
KOENIG, Fritz	301573	M	Ger.		Hptsturmfhr., SS, C.C., Buchenwald (Ger.) betw.5.38 and 10.43	MURDER	BEL.
KOENIG, Georg	142195	M	Ger.	10	Hptschfhr., Waffen-SS-Totenkopf.Stuba.,C.C.,Weimar-Buchenwald (Ger.)	MURDER	FR.,U.S.
KOENIG, Gottswind	172095	M	Ger.		Civilian, Connected with M-1 Camp,Muehldorf,Ampfing (Ger.) 6.44-4.45	MURDER	U.S.
KOENIG, Hans	256623	M	Ger.		SS-Sgt., Conc.Camp Dora, Nordhausen (Ger.)	MURDER	U.S.
KOENIG, Heinrich	259135	M			Police-Official, Laufen (Aust.) 44	BRUTALITY	U.S.
KOENIG, Johann	253755	M			Rottfhr., SS, C.C. Nixei, Nordhausen (Ger.)	MURDER	U.S.
KOENIG (see KLIER,Karl-Heinz)	254581						
KOENIG, Kurt	131417	M	Ger.	3. 1.25	Pvt., Airforce, Jaeger-Rgt.35,Quaregnon,Jemappes ,Ghlin (Bel.)3.9.44	MURDER	BEL.
KOENIG, Paul	24910	M			Sturmmann, SS, Conc.Camp, Struthof (Fr.)	MISC.CRIMES	FR.
KOENIG, Paul (or KOND , Karl)	133806	M			Hptschfhr., SS, C.C., Weimar-Buchenwald (Ger.)	MURDER	U.S.
KOENIG, Rudolph	129684	M	Ger.		Hptschfhr., SS, C.C., Dora, Nordhausen (Ger.)	MURDER	U.S.
KOENIG, Werner	167695	M	Ger.		Director, Grundstuecks-Gesellschaft, Danzig (Ger.)	MISC.CRIMES	POL.
KOENIG, Wilhelm	172094	M			SS Connected with Gendorf Camp, Muehldorf, Ampfing (Ger.) 6.44-4.45	MURDER	U.S.
KOENIG, Willy	156514	M	Ger.		Sgt., L.G.P.A.Brussels, Gruppe Verwaltung, Biache,St.Vaast (Fr.)24.8.44	WITNESS	FR.
KOENIGE	189028	M	Ger.	05	Cpl., 714.Lds.Schtz.Bn., Rippin (Ger.) 41	TORTURE	U.K.
KOENIGER	189766	M	Ger.		Member of Staff C.C., Army Staffs, Banjica (Serbia)	MURDER	YUGO.
KOENIGS	167697	M	Ger.		High-Official, Reichsverkehrs-Ministerium (Pol.) 9.39-44	MISC.CRIMES	POL.
KOENIGS, Hermann	187188	M	Ger.		Guard, Arb.Kmdo., C.C., (Adolf-Mine) Merkshein (Ger.) 8.42-10.44	TORTURE	U.S.
KOENIGSBERGER	253091	M			Flyer, C.C.Ellrich, Nordhausen (Ger.)	MURDER	U.S.
KOENIGSEDER, Ernst	306070	M	Ger.		Sgt.,12.SS-Pz.Div."Hitler-Jugend" Panz.Jaeg.Abt.,Waremme, 20.8.44	PILLAGE	BEL.
KOENIGSHOFEN	189748	M	Ger.		Pvt., 1.Coy. Ausb.Ers.Abt.116, Marburg (Ger.)	WITNESS	U.S.
KOENIGSHORF	252237	M			Capt., Cdt.-Unit D.C.A.No. 45964, Sottevast (Fr.) 6.44	PILLAGE	FR.
KOENING, Paul	145235	M	Ger.	84	Office-Worker, Civilian, C.C., Flossenburg (Ger.) 42	MISC.CRIMES	U.S.
KOENKE, Paul	301514	M	Ger.		Crim.Asst. at Montgauthier (Dinant) (Bel.) 20.9.43	MURDER	BEL.
KOENNECKE	150675	M	Ger.		Group-leader, NSDAP, Elwerath Menzelen nr.Celle (Ger.)	MURDER	BEL.
KOENNER	128853	M			Capt., Arb.Kmdo.501, Duenaburg (Esth.)	MISC.CRIMES	U.K.
KOENNOR	178279	M	Ger.	95	Capt., Army, Stalag IV D, Merseburg, Leipzig (Ger.) 1.44-4.45	MISC.CRIMES	U.K.
KOEPEL, Max	123408	M	Ger.		Schfhr., SS, Conc.Camp, Drancy (Fr.) 43-44	TORTURE	FR.
KOEPF, Margareth	250297	F	Ger.		Woman-SS-Guard, C.C. Geislingen (Ger.) 40-45	INTERR.	POL.
KOEPF, Richard	67056	M	Ger.		Gestapo, Dax (Fr.) 13.6.44	MURDER	FR.
KOEPFLER	259403	M	Ger.		Director, ex.Landkommissariat Colmar, Munster Haut-Rhin (Fr.) 40-43	PILLAGE	FR.
KOEPKE, Walter	196806	M	Ger.		Jailkeeper, Civilian, Grevesmuehlen (Ger.) 6.44	WITNESS	U.S.
KOEPP, Ewald	260517	M	Ger.		SS-Guard, C.C., Natzweiler (Fr.)	MURDER	FR.
KOEPP, Hermann (see KOPP)	172092						
KOEPPCKE, Hermann	24861	M	Ger.		SS-Mann, Kriegsgef.Lager 20, Bremen (Ger.)	TORTURE	U.S.

KOE-KOH

NAME	C.R.FILE NUMBER	SEX	NATIO- NALITY	DATE OF BIRTH	RANK OCCUPATION UNIT PLACE AND DATE OF CRIME	REASON WANTED	WANTED BY
KOEPPEL	162266	M	Ger.	07	Member,Civ.,Gestapo,Giessen (Ger.) 27.3.45	MURDER	U.S.
KOEPPEL	195482	M	Ger.	01	Kommissar,Gestapo,Metz,Autin le Tiche Metz (Fr.) 20.8.44	MURDER	U.S.
KOEPPEN	167948	F	Ger.		Dr.,Einsatz-Stab Rosenberg,Berlin (Ger.) 40-44	PILLAGE	FR.
KOEPPEN	179740	M			Capt.,870 Inf.Regt.,356 Div.,Vecchiazzano (Ital.) 7.11.44	MURDER	U.K.
KOEPPEN	215768	M	Ger.		Master,NSDAP,C.C.Papenburg (Ger.) 45	TORTURE	U.S.
KOEPPKE (or KOPKE)	1275				Public-official, head of the Chesnoy Farming Enterprise	TORTURE	U.S.
KOEPPL,Max (see KOPPEL)	254366						
KOEPSEZ	167076	M	Ger.		Adjutant,Feldgend.,Montigny en Vesoul (Fr.) 16.7.44	MURDER	FR.
KOERFER,Hubert	254574	M	Ger.		President,Ind. u.Handelskammer,State service,Inowroclaw (Pol.)39-45	PILLAGE	POL.
KOERFER,Josef	187190	M	Ger.		Civ.,owner of butcher shop,Merkstein (Ger.) 43-44	TORTURE	U.S.
KOERLINGS,Arnold	157109	M			Arbeits-Kdo.,(Mine),C.C.Eschweiler,Bruchweiden,Martandorf(Ger.)42-44	MISC.CRIMES	U.S.
KOERNER	11548	M	Ger.		Hauptabteilungsleiter,Reichspostministerium (police-official) 44	INCENDIARISM	NETH.
KOERNER	137784	M			Col.,Commanding,15 Pz.Gren.Regt.,29 Pz.Gren.Div.	WITNESS	U.S.
KOERNER	188530	M			Driver,16 Pz.Art.Regt.,Salerno (Ital.) 9.43	MISC.CRIMES	U.K.
KOERNER	191449	M			SS-Bde.Fuehrer,leader,SS,Poland Governor General (Pol.)	PILLAGE	POL.
KOERNER	191450	M			Staatssekr.,Stellvertr.des Leiters der Dienststelle des Beauftragt. f.d.Vierjahresplan,General-Government,Krakau (Pol.)	PILLAGE	POL.
KOERNER	253743	M			Rottfhr.,SS,C.C.Mackenrode,Nordhausen (Ger.)	MURDER	U.S.
KOERNER	256641	M	Ger.		Employee,C.C.Harzungen,Nordhausen (Ger.)	MURDER	U.S.
KOERNER,Hans	252437	M	Ger.	24. 9.16	Scharfhr.,SS,C.C.Nordhausen (Ger.)	MURDER	U.S.
KOERNER,Karl	189750	M	Ger.	18. 3.05	Crim.-Employee,Gestapo,Bruenn (Czech.) 39-45	MISC.CRIMES	CZECH.
KOEPPER	156550	M	Ger.		Leiter,DAF,Kleve (Ger.)	PILLAGE	U.S.
KOERSCHNER	252439	M			Oschfhr.,SS,C.C.Dora,Nordhausen (Ger.)	MURDER	U.S.
KOERTGE,Albert	174685	M	Ger.		6 Coy.,Ldsschtz.-Bn.400,Gross-Orner,Hettstedt (Ger.) 9.44	WITNESS	U.S.
KOESSLING	195480	M	Ger.	10	Gestapo of Thionville,Audun le Tiche (Fr.)	MURDER	U.S.
KOESTER	161514	M	Ger.	00	Osturmfhr.,Wirtschafts-Verwaltgs-Hauptamt,C.C.Ohrdruf, Buchenwald (Ger.)	WITNESS	U.S.
KOESTER	257014	M	Ger.		Lt.,Military,2 Nachr.-Coy.,Bolnes (Neth.) 8.5.45	INTERR.	NETH.
KOESTER,Wilhelm	132072	M	Ger.		Reichsprotecter,Ing.official of the Staatsministerium,Prague, Moravia,Bohemia (Czech.) 40-44	TORTURE	CZECH.
KOESTERS	300962	M	Ger.		Hptschfhr.,SS,official of S.D. Leitabschnitt,Prague,Oswiecim, Birkenau (Pol.)' 39-45	MURDER	CZECH.
KOETZLE	254174	M	Ger.	05	Lt.,Army,Fallschirmjg.-Regt.,Tiel (Neth.) 45	PILLAGE	NETH.
KOEVER,Ernst Heinz	254952	M	Ger.	28. 1.15	Butcher,Civ.,Javoricko (Czech.) 5.5.45	MURDER	CZECH.
KOFFEN,Elfi	166064	F			Interpreter,Gestapo,Dun les Places (Fr.) 26.-28.6.44	MURDER	FR.
KOFFLER,Giuseppe,Josef	174779	M	Ger.	06	Sgt.,Brandenburg-Div.,16 Coy.,2 Regt.,Communanza (Ital.) 15.3.44	WITNESS	U.K.
KOFFMANE	102942	M			Uschfhr.,SS,19 Panzer-Grenadier-Regt.,9 SS-Panzer-Division, 10 Coy.,Arnheim (Neth.)	MURDER	U.S.
KOFFMANN	192416	M			Lt.,Munitions-Lager,Bayet (Fr.)	TORTURE	FR.
KOFLER	131412	M	Ger.		Uschfhr.,SS,C.C.Mauthausen (Aust.) 41-45	TORTURE	U.S.
KOFLERAUS	143155	M			Uschfhr.,SS,Blockfuehrer,C.C.Mauthausen (Aust.) 41-45	MURDER	U.S.
KOFNIG	189765	M	Ger.		Major,Cmdt.,Straf-Coy.,Meckovac (Yugo.)	MURDER	YUGO.
KOGE	10163	M	Ger.	90	Osturmbannfhr.,SS,C.C.Staff,Flossenburg (Ger.) 29.3.44	MISC.CRIMES	U.K.U.S.
KOGEL	121602	M	Ger.		Hptsturmfhr.,SS,C.C.Ravensbrueck(Ger.) 43	MURDER	FR.
KOGEL	131411	M	Ger.	21	Usturmfhr.,SS,C.C.Mauthausen (Aust.) 41-45	MURDER	U.S.
KOGEL,Max	152872	M			Osturmbannfhr.,SS,C.C.Flossenburg (Ger.)	MURDER	U.S.
KOGEL (or KOEGEL or KIEGEL)	188896	M			Cmdt.,C.C.Ravensbrueck (Ger.) 41,42-45	MURDER	FR.POL.
KOGEO	187183	M	Ger.		Sturmbannfhr.,SS,C.C.Ravensbrueck,Mecklenburg (Ger.) 41-44	MURDER	U.S.
KOGGE	167967	M	Ger.		Adjutant,Gendarmerie,Coiffy,Auberive,Chalen,Cey,Flagey(Fr.) 43-44	MURDER	FR.
KOGLER	182577	M	Ger.		Lt.,SA-Ldsschtz.-Bn.27,P.C.W.Camp,Chodau (Cz.)	MURDER	U.S.
KOGON,Eugene	126692	M	Ger.		N.C.O.,Party secretary,C.C.Buchenwald (Ger.)	TORTURE	FR.
KOHAUPT	167947	M	Ger.		Director,Red Cross,Hanau (Ger.) 8.1.43	TORTURE	FR.
KOHL	139752	M	Ger.		Policeman,City Police Force,Aken (Ger.) 30.5.44	TORTURE	U.S.
KOHL (or KOHN)	187187	M	Ger.		Lt.,Stalag VI A,C.C.Hemer (Ger.) 41-45	TORTURE	U.S.
KOHL	196805	M	Ger.		Capt.,SS,Royallien (Fr.) 41-44	INTERR.	FR.
KOHL	250315	M			Sturmscharfhr.,Gestapo (Fr.) 40-45	INTERR.	FR.
KOHL	259604	M	Ger.		Chief,Station-Batignolles,Paris,Seine (Fr.) 18.-19.8.44	INTERR.	FR.
KOHL,Hans	132047	M		17	Rottfhr.,SS,C.C.Plattling (Ger.) 2.-5.45	MURDER	U.S.
KOHL (or KOHLS,Hermann)	250316	M	Ger.		Pvt.,Probablement 377, Jaeg.-Regt.,Vinkt Meigem (Bel.) 25.-31.5.40	BRUTALITY	BEL.
KOHL,Oskar	193709	M	Ger.	10	Pvt.,Krgf.Arb.Bn.186 (Nor.)	MURDER	NOR.
KOHI,Wolfgang	305913	M	Ger.		Sturmbannfhr.,SS,Head of the Brno-Aussenstelle of the S.D. Leitabschn. Prague,Oswiecim,Birkenau (Pol.) 39-45	MURDER	CZECH.
KOHLA,Fritz	306051	M	Ger.		Member,Crim.Police Dessau,Bernburg (Ger.) 7.7.44	MURDER	U.S.
KOHLAAS	165392	M	Ger.		Gendarm,Jendarmerie,Wihr en Plaine (Fr.) 30.7.44	MURDER	FR.
KOHLAASE,Gabriel	131410	M	Ger.	9. 1.04	Rottfhr.,SS,C.C.Mauthausen (Aust) 14.5.44-7.5.45	MURDER	U.S.
KOHLBERG	254127	M	Ger.		Sturmscharfhr.,Gestapo,Limoges (Fr.) 40-45	INTERR.	FR.
KOHLE	167946	M	Ger.		Capt.,SS, 7.8.44	TORTURE	FR.
KOHLE	173086	M	Ger.		Capt.,Stalag IX B,C.C.Badorf (Ger.) 45	TORTURE	U.S.
KOHLEN,Rudolf	1412	M	Ger.		Pvt.,Army,274 Hqu.Coy.(Eng.Pl.)	MISC.CRIMES	U.K.
KOHLENBACH	196957	M	Ger.		Capt.,Ldsschtz.-Bn.4-438,Velka,Krase (Czech.) 16.2.45	MURDER	U.K.
KOHLENDORF	260153	M	Ger.		Capt.,157 Res.Div."Bavaria",Massif du Vercors,Isère et Drôme (Fr.) 20.7.-5.8.44	SUSPECT	FR.
KOHLER	493	M	Ger.		SS,Fort Musson (Fr.) 3.8.44	MURDER	FR.
KOHLER	1174	M	Ger.		Interpreter,Public official	MISC.CRIMES	U.S.
KOHLER	1714	M			Lt.,Commanding officer,4 Coy.,923 Pz.Bn.,Sicily (Ital.) 12.7.43	TORTURE	U.K.
KOHLER (see KEHLER)	62531						
KOHLER	67049	M	Ger.		Hptschfhr.,SS-Div.,St.Sulpice,Fortmusson,Chateau,Gontier(Fr.)6.8.44	MURDER	FR.
KOHLER	67050	M	Ger.		Pvt.,SS,17 SS-Panzer-Gren.Div."Goetz von Berlichingen",Sturmge- schuetz-Abtl.17 or Pz.Jg. Abt.17,Segre,Renaze (Fr.) 7.-8.44	MURDER	FR.
KOHLER	102941	M	Ger.		Policeman,Pol.,Kisdritz (Ger.) 25.5.45	MURDER	U.S.
KOHLER	124270	M	Ger.		Uschfhr.,SS,1 SS-Pz.Gren.Regt.,C.O. 9 Coy.(Engineers),SS o.C. of SS-Unterfuehrer-Schule,Malmedy,Ljubana (Bel.Yugo.) 17.12.44	MURDER	U.S.
KOHLER	126793	M	Ger.		Officer,Chief,Abwehr (Gestapo),Oflag XVII A.C.C.(Ger.)	MISC.CRIMES	FR.
KOHLER	192665	M	Ger.		Adjudant,German Tribunal of war,Besançon (Fr.) 18.9.43	MURDER	FR.

KOH - KOL

NAME	C.R FILE NUMBER	SEX	NATIONALITY	DATE OF BIRTH	RANK OCCUPATION UNIT PLACE AND DATE OF CRIME	REASON WANTED	WANTED BY
KOHLER	132669	M			Capt.,Abwehr official,C.C.Edelbach Oflag XVII A,Edelbach (Aust.)	MURDER	FR.
KOHLER	136235	M	Ger.		SS,C.C.Uckermark near Ravensbrueck (Ger.) 44-5.45	MURDER	FR.
KOHLER	145823	M			SS-Usturmfhr.,SS,Gestapo,Hoerde (Ger.)	MURDER	U.S.
KOHLER	162570	M	Ger.		Adj.or Aspirant,10 Inf.Rgt.2 Coy,St.Georges De Didonne (Fr.) 10.44	MURDER	FR.
KOHLER	186751	M	Ger.		Lt.,C.C.Flossenburg (Ger.)	MISC.CRIMES	FR.
KOHLER	187186	M	Ger.		Civilian,Stalag VI A C.C.Hemer (Ger.) 41-45	TORTURE	U.S.
KOHLER (or KOLHER)	196804	M	Ger.		Major,13 Flak Div.Btty.70-XIII,Commune de Galanterie en Brix (Fr.)4.45	WITNESS	FR.
KOHLER	254381	M		2.12.15	Sgt.,Courchamps (Fr.) 29.8.44	MURDER	FR.
KOHLER	255153	M	Ger.		Employee,Abt.IV A,Bruessel (Bel.) 40-44	INTERR.	BEL.
KOHLER	301422	M	Ger.		SS-Pvt.,C.C.Ravensbrueck (Ger.) 42-45	MURDER	FR.,BEL.
KOHLER,Edith	191385	F	Ger.	24. 2.14	Civilian,Grocery Store Clerk,Schwalbach (Ger.) 8.44	TORTURE	U.S.
KOHLER,Franz	192184	M	Ger.		SS-Guard,C.C.Uckermark (Ger.) 45	MURDER	BEL.
KOHLER,Heinz	301517	M	Ger.	5. 2.21	SS-Pvt.,C.C.Buchenwald (Ger.) 16.5.38-9.10.43	MURDER	BEL.
KOHLER,Magdalena	139179	F	Ger.		Guard,German prison Camps Aufseherin,C.C.,SS,Volary (Czech.) 41-45	MURDER	U.S.
KOHLER,Max	137043	M	Ger.		Policeman,Police,Dept.of Muldorf (Ger.) 15.4.45	MURDER	U.S.
KOHLER,Rudi	143179	M	Ger.	10	SS-Hptschfhr.,Rapportfhr.,C.C.Lublin (Pol.) 42-43	TORTURE	U.S.
KOHLER,Rudolf	301518	M	Ger.		SS-Hptschfhr.,SS,C.C.Buchenwald (Ger.) 16.5.38-9.10.43	MURDER	BEL.
KOHLER,W.	305712	M	Ger.	2.12.15	Soldier,Serving in Courchamps (Fr.) 28.8.44	MISC.CRIMES	FR.
KOHLER,Walter	131409	M	Ger.	11. 4.07	SS-Officer,Dentist,SS,C.C.Mauthausen (Aust.) 41-45	MURDER	U.S.
KOHLEPOSS	29781	M	Ger.		Major,Felders.Bn.148 20 Army,Finmark (Nor.) 11.44	MURDER	NOR.
KOHLERT	145250	M	Ger.		Osturmfhr.,1 SS Pz.Div.2 Pz.Gr.Rgt.3 Bn.11 Coy,Stavelot Malmedy (Bel.) 22.-23.12.44	MURDER	U.S.
KOHLE-SCHMIDT	250883		Ger.	90	Farmer,Civilian,Poppenhausen (Ger.) 11.5.42	MURDER	POL.
KOHLHAUSSEN	306565	M	Ger.		Director,German National Museum,(Pol.) 3.40	PILLAGE	POL.
KOHLMEIER,Adolf	141383	M	Ger.		Sgt.,Chief overseer of prison of Douai (Fr.) 8.44	TORTURE	FR.
KOHLRAUSCH,Robert	258978	M	Ger.	9. 3.04	SS-Sturmbannfhr.,SS, 10.9.39	INTERR.	U.S.
KOHLS (see KOHL,Hermann)	250316						
KOHLSTADT	174109	M	Ger.	00	Amtsgerichtsrat,Member,occ.territories Boheme,NSDAP,Budejovice,Prag (Czech.) 40-45	MURDER	CZECH.
KOHLSTEDT,Franz	196102	M	Ger.	93	Dieren (Neth.) 41	MISC.CRIMES	NETH.
KOHN (see KOHL)	187187						
KOHN	257509	M	Ger.		Employee,Volkswagenwerk Peugeot,Sochaux (Fr.) 9.-11.44	PILLAGE	FR.
KOHN,Norbert (alias GRABNER, Najnar)	254642	M		1. 7.08	Informer,Gestapo official,Prag (Czech.)	MISC.CRIMES	CZECH.
KOHN,Richard	254173	M	Ger.	6. 8.05	Gendarm,5 Coy 34 Div.Feldgendarmerie,Tiel (Neth.) 45	PILLAGE	NETH.
KOHN,Werner	301772	M	Ger.		Sgt.,of the Rutz K.O.(Wege) Bn.of 896 Th.R.I.,Kermassenet in Kervignac (Morbihan) (Fr.) 20.8.44	MURDER	FR.
KOHNEN	250870	M	Ger.		Pvt.,Pepingen (Bel.) 2.-9.44	INTERR.	BEL.
KOHNEN,Gerhard	302068	M	Ger.		Reichsbahn official,employed in the Fernmeldemeisterei office,Amersfoort (Neth.) 4.10.44-5.45	PILLAGE	NETH.
KOHNKE	167075	M	Ger.		Pvt.,Army,Bachivillers (Fr.) 20.8.44	WITNESS	FR.
KOHNKE	261815	M	Ger.		Lt.,Unit Art.H.D.V.199-2235,N.D.F.N.,F.P.Nr.27046 C,Lorgies (Fr.)9.44	MURDER	FR.
KOHNZ	258844	M	Ger.	10	Lt.,207 Jg.Rgt. 11 Coy,Zota-Wola (Pol.) 11.9.44	MURDER	POL.
KOHR	151336	M	Ger.		SS-Schfhr.,SS Div. "Das Reich" Rgt. "Deutschland",Aiguillon (Fr.)17.7.44	MURDER	FR.
KOHRING,Alfred	301519	M	Ger.	6.10.11	SS-Hptschfhr.,SS,C.C.Buchenwald (Ger.) 16.5.38-9.10.43	MURDER	BEL.
KOHRMANN	193708	M	Ger.		Capt.,2 leichte Flak Abt.823,Malm (Nor.) 9.44	MURDER	NOR.
KOHROODE	300796	M	Ger.		Pvt.,1 Aufkl.Abt.3 Coy 2 Col.XV Div.of the Afrika Corps,Saint Leger (Arlon) 5.9.44	MISC.CRIMES	BEL.
KOHSR,Gerhard	262186	M	Ger.	24.12.19	SS-Oschfhr.,51 SS Armoured Bde.,Breviandes,Bucheres,Ste.Savine,Troyes, Riviere De Corps (Fr.) 22.-25.8.44	BRUTALITY	FR.
KOISS	251096	M	Ger.		SS,C.C.Neuengamme (Ger.)	INTERR.	BEL.
KOJ,Johann	254821	M	Ger.	17. 5.04	Z.b.V.Kommando 31,Valasske,Weliricil (Czech.)	TORTURE	CZECH.
KOKAIL	67051	M	Ger.		Col.,C.C.Stalag XX A,Graudenz (Pol.) 43-44	TORTURE	U.K.
KOKERT	301007	M	Ger.		Farmer,Civilian,Merwitz nr.Oschatz,Saxony (Ger.) 5.9.40	MISC.CRIMES	FR.
KOKESCH	131408	M	Ger.		SS-Officer,C.C.Mauthausen (Aust.) 41-45	MURDER	U.S.
KOKOKRIE (see GOCKEGIE)	252105						
KOKOSINSKY	301881	M	Ger.		Warder or Kapo,C.C.Sachsenhausen,Oranienburg (Ger.) 39-4.45	MURDER	POL.
KOLARZ,Franz	255159	M	Ger.	24. 3.91	Blockleader,Civilian-worker,NSDAP,St.Mesto (Czech.) 39-45	MISC.CRIMES	CZECH.
KOLASSE,Alfred	135195	M	Ger.		Civilian,Kapo,C.C.Lehanau Laufen,Flossenburg,Regensburg (Ger.)3.-4.45	TORTURE	U.S.
KOLB	420	M	Ger.		5 Fallschirmjg.Rgt.	MURDER	BEL.
KOLB	10151	M	Ger.		Cpl.,Army,C.C K Kdo.137,622 Ldsch.Bn.,C.C.Unterbreizbach (Ger.) 1.42	TORTURE	U.K.
KOLB	31359	M		95	Hptsturmfhr.,SS,C.C.Sachsenhausen (Ger.) 43	MURDER	U.S.
KOLB	122494	M	Ger.		Lt.,Commanding officer,Bn.2 Fusilier Regt.272-2 (Fr.) 44	MURDER	U.K.
KOLB	132057	M	Ger.		President,House of German Art.	MISC.CRIMES	U.S.
KOLB	132069	M	Ger.		Officer,SS-Sgt.,SS,C.C.Flossenburg (Ger.)	MURDER	U.S.
KOLB	137785	M	Ger.		Lt.,6 Coy 15 Pz.Gren.Rgt.,29 Pz.Gren.Div.	WITNESS	U.S.
KOLB	207639	M	Ger.		Ldsch.Bn.622,C.C.Unterbreizbach,Stalag IX C (Ger.) 1.42	MISC.CRIMES	U.K.
KOLB	301008	M	Ger.		Sturmbannfhr.,C.C.Oranienburg,Sachsenhausen (Ger.) 42-45	MURDER	FR.
KOLB,August Gustav	195337	M	Ger.	95-00	Capt.,SS,C.C.Oranienburg,Sachsenhausen (Ger.)	MISC.CRIMES	U.K.
KOLB,Josef	306759	M	Ger.		German Civilian,Solln-Munich (Ger.) 19.7.44	BRUTALITY	U.S.
KOLB,Max	250884	M	Ger.	24. 3.01	Mechanist,Civilian,Dachau (Ger.) 41	TORTURE	POL.
KOLB,Wilhelm	252350	M			Pvt.,C.C.Ellrich,Nordhausen (Ger.)	MURDER	U.S.
KOLBE	148156	M	Ger.	00	Employee,DAF,42-45	MISC.CRIMES	FR.
KOLBELS	137638	M	Ger.		N.C.O.,Kapo,C.C.Neuengamme (Ger.)	TORTURE	FR.
KOLBENTOT	124768	M	Ger.		Sturmfhr.,SA Standarte Emsland,C.C.Neusustrum (Ger.)	MURDER	U.S.
KOLBERG,Hans	162396	M	Ger.		Adj.chief,Member,Army,Gestapo,Brive et Region (Fr.) 44	MURDER	FR.
KOLBINGER,Michel	11271	M	Ger.		Pvt.,Pz.Gren.Rgt.111,Albine (Fr.) 29.6.44	MURDER	FR.
KOLCK	29782	M	Ger.		Probatl.Transp.Officer,Major,Gebirgsarmee Korps 19 Staff 20 Army, Finmark (Nor.) 11.44	MURDER	NOR.
KOLECZKO,Jan	145186	M		12	Civilian	WITNESS	U.S.
KOLECZKO,Joseph	251102	M	Ger.		Guard or Kapo,C.C.Gusen (Ger.)	INTERR.	BEL.

KOL-KON

NAME	C.R.FILE NUMBER	SEX	NATIO- NALITY	DATE OF BIRTH	RANK OCCUPATION UNIT PLACE AND DATE OF CRIME	REASON WANTED	WANTED BY
KOLENDOWITZ, Guenther	187182	M		4. 3.29	Civ., C.C. Merkstein (Ger.) 44	WITNESS	U.S.
KOLENSKI	192889	M	Ger.		Oberwachtmeister, Schupo, C.C. Falstad (Nor.) 41-42	TORTURE	NOR.
KOLESNIKOW, Grigorji	157108	M	Ger.		Mine, Arbeitskommando, C.C. Martandorf nr.Eschweiler, Bruchweiden (Ger.) 42-44	TORTURE	U.S.
KOLETZKI	252352	F	Ger.		Civ., Fallersleben (Ger.) 8.44	WITNESS	U.S.
KOLF, Wilhelm	252350	M	Ger.		Pvt., C.C. Ellrich, Nordhausen (Ger.)	MURDER	U.S.
KOLH	300494	M	Ger.		Oscharfhr., Section for the repression of partisans at Gestapo Limoges, Hte.Vienne, Creuse, Correze, Dordogne (Fr.) 40-44	MURDER	FR.
KOLHEPP	261166	M	Ger.		Pvt., 211.N.Rgt., 139.Arbeits-Bereich Liane, Alleur-Lez-Liege (Bel.) 4.9.44	MURDER	BEL.
KOLHER see KOHLER	196804						
KOLHER	306419	M	Ger.		Civ.official, Worthlah Iron Ore Mine nr.Salzgitter (Ger.) 24.12.43-4.45	BRUTALITY	U.K.
KOLTCH	257461	M	Ger.		Chief, Gestapo, Uzice (Yugo.) 2.12.42	BRUTALITY	YUGO.
KOLKE	301575	M	Ger.		SS Scharfhr., C.C. Mauthausen (Aust.) 12.42	MURDER	BEL.
KOLKER, Heinrich	300495	M	Ger.		Pvt., Astene (Bel.) 5.9.44	MURDER	BEL.
KOLL or DUMBERT, Carol	185851	M	Ger.		W.O., Town Mayor of Pokarowo (Territ) (Grc.) 2.44	PILLAGE	GRC.
KOLL	192089	M	Ger.	05	Dr., Civ. Anatomy institute, Danzig (Pol.)	TORTURE	POL.
KOLL	192090	F	Ger.		Dr.Med.,Civ., Anatomy institute, Danzig (Pol.)	TORTURE	POL.
KOLL	254125	M	Ger.		Hptsturmfhr., SS Pol.Rgt. Todt, 10.Coy. 3.Bn., Bernex (Fr.) 17.12.43	MURDER	FR.
KOLL, Bruno	186151	M	Ger.		Foreman, C.C. Dora-Nordhausen (Ger.)	MURDER	F.L.
KOLL, Hans	132218	M	Ger.		Pvt., 1.Coy. 78.Volksgr.Rgt., Stalag 28275 Euskirchen (Ger.) 5.-10.44	BRUTALITY	U.S.
KOLLACHNY	124271	M	Ger.		Usturmfhr., H.Q. Coy., 1.SS Panz.Rgt., 1. SS Panz.Div., Malmedy (Bel.) 17.12.44	MURDER	U.S.
KOLLACK, Karl	191422	M	Ger.		N.C.O., C.C. Siegburg (Ger.) 3.-8.42	MURDER	BEL.
KOLLATSHNY	189841	M	Ger.		Osturmfhr., 1.SS Rec.Bn., Renard Mont, Stavelot (Bel.) 19.12.44	MURDER	BEL.
KOLLBACK	260843	M	Ger.		Oberwachtmeister, Brushl (Ger.) 17.1.45	BRUTALITY	U.S.
KOLLEBAR see KOLLEBEY	162265						
KOLLEBEY or KOLLEBAR	162265	M	Ger.	90	Capt., Army, Commander of B.A.B.21, 518.Inf.Coy., Blechhammer, Moosberg (Ger.) 9.43-4.45	TORTURE	U.K.
KOLLENBACK	192219	M	Ger.		Stabsintendant, C.C. Gardelegen (Ger.)	MURDER	U.S.
KOLLER	137604	M	Ger.		Foreman, Ohlendorf Iron Mine, C.C. Ohlendorf (Ger.) Stalag XI B	MISC.CRIMES	U.K.
KOLLER	161513	M	Ger.	05	Civ. C.C.Buchenwald (Ger.)	WITNESS	U.S.
KOLLER	186750	M	Ger.		SS Rottfhr., C.C. Flossenburg (Ger.)	TORTURE	FR.
KOLLER	254248	M			Lt., Pmr Brandenburg Rgt.	MISC.CRIMES	U.S.
KOLLER	901265	M	Ger.		Crim.secretary, Abt. IV A S.D., Brussels (Bel.) 6.40-9.44	MURDER	BEL.
KOLLER	301773	M	Ger.		Uscharfhr., Member of the SS Institute of hygiene, C.C. Auschwitz (Pol.) 40-45	MURDER	FR.
KOLLER, Alfred	906435	M	Ger.		Roloven, on or about 26.11.44	BRUTALITY	U.S.
KOLLER, Hugo	254575	M		21. 3.80	Civ., Bratislava (Czech.) 44	MURDER	CZECH.
KOLLER, Maximilian	31220	M	Ger.		Landgerichtspraesident, Public official, Brno (Czech.) 21.2.40	MURDER	BEL.
KOLLER, Victor	300268	M	Ger.		S.D.-Mann at Hertogenbosch, Hague, Scheveningen (Neth.) 12.1.44, 22.3.44	MURDER	NETH.
KOLLES, Hubert or KOLLOS	254966	M		05	Civ., Maehrisch Truebau(Czech.) 10.44	BRUTALITY	U.K.
KOLLES, Nikolaus	194159	M	Ger.	20. 8.98	Truppfuehrer, S.A. Civ. Farmer, Sinfsfeld (Ger.) 15.8.44	MISC.CRIMES	U.S.
KOLLIBAR	67052	M	Ger.		Capt., Army, Nieder-Oels (Ger.)	MISC.CRIMES	U.K. U.S.
KOLLIBAR or COLLIBAY	167074	M			Councillor, Customs and Excise , St.Gingolph (Fr.)	PILLAGE	FR.
KOLIMANN	253757	M			Pvt., C.C. Ellrich, Nordhausen (Ger.)	MURDER	U.S.
KOLIMER	161512	M	Ger.	00	SS Commandant, Osturmfhr., C.C. Nordhausen (Ger.)	WITNESS	U.S.
KOLINER, Gustav	145191	M	Ger.	91	Civ., Meister der Schutzpolizei	TORTURE	U.S.
KOLLOS see KOLLES, Hubert	254966						
KOLLOS, Hubert	306030	M	Ger.		Saw mill owner, Maehrisch Truebau (Czech.) 10.44	MISC.CRIMES	U.K.
KOLLWITZ, Willi Rudolf	187180	M	Ger.	20.10.98	SS Oscharfhr., Blockfuehrer, C.C. Nordhausen -Dora-Mittelbau (Ger.) 43-45	TORTURE	U.S.
KOLM	253758	M			Pvt., C.C. Ellrich, Nordhausen (Ger.)	MURDER	U.S.
KOLM	258539	M	.		Arbeitsdienstfuehrer, SS Uscharfhr., Ohrdruf (Ger.) 12.44-4.45	MURDER	U.S. FR.
KOLMORGEN	254588	M	Ger.		S.A., Gadebusch (Ger.)	MURDER	U.S.
KOLODZUPKI,Mieczystau see KOTODZIEJSKI, Muczystar	162569						
KOLONIE see LAMBERG	252258						
KOLOUGH, Eugen	31221	M	Ger.		Dr., Landgerichtsdirector, Public official, Litomerice (Czech.)21.2.40	MURDER	BEL.
KOLRER, Horst	179708	M	Ger.	09	Capt., Army, Inf.Rgt. 487, Dignies, Courieres (Fr.) 28.5.40	MURDER	FR.
KOLSCH	151963	M			Dr., Legationsrat, German Foreign office	MISC.CRIMES	U.S.
KOLWATSCH	905450	M	Ger.		SS Hptsturmfhr., H.Q. 2.SS Panz.Div., La Roche Wibrin (Bel.) 1.45	MURDER	BEL.
KOLZ	133816	M			Oscharfhr., SS, C.C. Weimar,Buchenwald (Ger.)	MURDER	U.S.
KOLZAUZER, Arnold alias: dit Arnold	196803	M	Ger.		Scharfhr., chief SS, St.Etienne (Fr.)	TORTURE	FR.
KOLZERT	905609	M	Ger.		N.C.O. Cartridge factory, Chateau de Vincennes, Seine (Fr.) 19.8.44	MURDER	FR.
KOMES, Hans	259690	M	Ger.		SS Uscharfhr., Gestapo, Area Angers, Maine and Loire (Fr.) 42.44	MISC.CRIMES	FR.
KOMINSKIE, Jupp	190638	M	Ger.		Civ., Wiesbaden (Ger.) 43-45	WITNESS	U.S.
KOMOR	133805	M	Ger.		Oscharfhr., SS, C.C. Weimar,Buchenwald (Ger.)	TORTURE	U.S.
KOMPENHAUS	256906	M	Ger.		SS Hptsturmfhr., Stadtkommandant des Senats, Paris (Fr.) 22.8.44	MURDER	FR.
KONACHIE, Herman	179083	M	Ger.		Arbeitskommando, C.C. Rippen (Pol.) 41	TORTURE	U.K.
KONECNY, Rudolf	254978	M	Ger.	12	SS Hptscharfhr., Gestapo, Kolin (Czech.) 39-45	MURDER	CZECH.
KONETUNG, Guenther	250909	M	Ger.	16	Lt., Marine Bord Flak Coy., Bogliasco (It.) 12.12.44	INTERR.	U.K.
KONGEL	186152	M			SS Guard, C.C. Neubrenn (Ger.)	TORTURE	FR.
KONIECZYN	261003	M			SS Rottfhr., C.C. Vaihingen (Ger.) 13.8.44-17.4.45	MURDER	U.S.
KONIG	123140	M	Ger.		Capt. Cmdt., Muehlberg Stalag IV B, 11.43	MURDER	U.K.
KONIG	179734	M	Ger.		Warder, Gestapo, C.C. Belgrad (Yugo.) 7.8.41	MURDER	YUGO.
KONIG	190637	M	Ger.		Chief NSDAP, Bohmte (Ger.) 15.2.45	MURDER	U.S.
KONIG	252226	M	Ger.		Sgt., C.C. Buchenwald (Ger.) 42-45	MURDER	FR.
KONIG	254833	M	Ger.		Sgt., Interpreter, Fieldpolice, Morlaix, Plongasnon (Fr.)	MURDER	FR.
KONIG nicknamed "Monty"	906593	M	Ger.	about 17	Pvt., controller at railway yard of Messrs.Reuschling mining engineers, Brux (Czech.) 5.8.44	MURDER	U.K.
KONIG, Fritz	145800	M	Ger.	89	Civ., 1.Coy. Volkssturm-Bn. Gardelegen (Ger.) 9.-14.4.45	MURDER	U.S.

KON-KOP

NAME	C.R.FILE NUMBER	SEX	NATIO-NALITY	DATE OF BIRTH	RANK OCCUPATION UNIT PLACE AND DATE OF CRIME	REASON WANTED	WANTED BY
KONIG, Gerhard	143188	M	Ger.	90	Scharfhr., SS, C.C.Gross-Beeren (Ger.) 43	TORTURE	U.S.
KONIG, Hans	129683	M	Ger.		Officer, C.C. Dora-Nordhausen (Ger.)	MURDER	U.S.
KONIG, Heinz	64502	M	Ger.		SS-Mann, SS-Div., St.Sulpice, Mont-Messon, Chateau Gontier (Fr.) 8.44	MURDER	FR.
KONIG, Karl (see KOENIG Paul)	133806						
KONIG, Ludwig	140789	M	Ger.	24. 8.00	Member, NSDAP, C.C.Ludwigshafen (Ger.) 1.45	TORTURE	U.S.
KONIG, Willy	151337	M	Ger.		Pvt., Landesschuetzen-Bn. 349-18, Bische-St.Waast (Bel:, Fr.) 8.42	MURDER	FR.
KONIGBAUM, Wilhelm	137772	M	Ger.		Member, SS, Gestapo (Ger.)	TORTURE	U.S.
KONIGSDORF	102940	M		13	Group-leader, NSDAP, C.C.Wichrath-Burgsdorf (Ger.)	MURDER	U.S.
KONIGSDORF, Ernst	132055	M		18. 6.22	Group-leader, NSDAP, Teacher, Public School.	MURDER	U.S.
KONING	192183	M			Sgt., Geh.Feldpolizei, Antwerp (Bel.) 44.	TORTURE	BEL.
KONI OR	250301	M			Pvt., 2.Panz.Gren.Regt., 2.Panz.Gren.Coy.SS, Malmedy (Bel.) 12.44	INTERR.	U.S.
KONITSCH, Franz	192460	M		13. 5.26	SS-Mann, SS Panz.Gren.Ausb.u.Ers.Bn.4, 2.Coy, 7.Group, Yves-Gomezee (Bel.) 3.9.44	MURDER	BEL.
KONITZ	189754	M	Ger.		Agent, Abwehr, Prague (Czech.) 38-39	MISC.CRIMES	CZECH.
KONITZER	250886	M	Ger.		SS-Osturmfhr., C.C. Neuengamme (Ger.) 40-44	INTERR.	BEL.
KONNECKE	187857	M	Ger.		Ortsgruppenleiter, NSDAP, C.C. Menhagen (Ger.)	MURDER	BEL.
KONOLZER, Franz	162859	M			Capt., Army, 4.Coy., Kgf.Arb.Bn.190, Bergholner, Botn (Nor.) 44-45	TORTURE	NOR.
KONRAD	29783	M	Ger.		Major, Cmi.Felders.Bn.48, 20.Army, Finmark (Nor.) 11.44	MURDER	NOR.
KONRAD	67055	M			Army, Tempelburg, Bromberg, Graudenz, Danzig (Pol.) 9.-11.44	TORTURE	U.K.
KONRAD	124601	F	Ger.		Woman-Guard, C.C.Allendorf near Ziegenhain (Ger.)	TORTURE	BEL.
KONRAD	148157	M		05	Public Official.	TORTURE	FR.
KONRAD	189767	M			Lt., Army, Sibenik, Zablac (Serbia) 5.-6.44	MURDER	YUGO.
KONRAD	193077	M			Sgt., POW Working Bn.190, Karasjok (Nor.) 43-45	TORTURE	NOR.
KONRAD	259308				Camp Manager, Camp Thekla near Leipzig (Ger.) 4.45	MURDER	U.S.
KONRAD	259388				Agent, Gestapo, Antenne-Angouleme, Poitiers Area (Fr.) 40-45	MISC.CRIMES	FR.
KONRAD, Franz	257106	M			Osturmfhr., Waffen-SS, Lodz, Warsaw (Pol.) 39-43	MISC.CRIMES	POL.
KONRAD, Horst	187179	M	Ger.	28	Hitler Jugend, C.C.Maientsl near Tempelburg (Pol.) 9.-10.44	TORTURE	U.K.
KONRAD, Jacob	137788	M	Ger.		Civ., Guard over foreign workers.	TORTURE	U.S.
KONRAD, Joseph	172093	M			SS-Wachmann, Camp Gendorf, Muhldorf-Ampfing (Ger.) 6.44-4.45	MURDER	U.S.
KONRAD, Paul	193078	M			Capt., 3.Coy., POW Working Bn.204, C.C. Skibotn (Nor.)	MURDER	NOR.
KONRADT (see CONRAD)	188015						
KONRADY	102939	M		00	Sgt., Oflag C.C.Altona-Hamburg (Ger.) 7.-11.44	TORTURE	U.S.
KONST, August	253090	M			Pvt., C.C. Ellrich, Nordhausen (Ger.)	MURDER	U.S.
KONSTANTIN	253089	M			C.C. Rossla, Nordhausen (Ger.)	MURDER	U.S.
KONTER	29817	M	Ger.		W.O., Army, Transport Coy. No.40-601, La Burthe, St.Leger de Balson, St.Symphonien (Fr.) 8.44	MURDER	FR.
KONTER	189497	M	Ger.		Sgt., Transport Coy., C.C. St.Symphorien (Fr.) 8.44	MURDER	FR.
KONUG, Heinz	494	M	Ger.		Officer, SS, Fort-Musson (Fr.) 8.44	MURDER	FR.
KONZALLA, Paul	301521	M	Ger.	18. 7.09	SS-Mann, SS, C.C.Buchenwald (Ger.) betw.5.38 and 10.43	MURDER	BEL.
KONZELMANN, Alfred	191407	M		12. 7.94	Uschfhr., SS, C.C. Mauthausen (Aust.) 5.44-3.45	MURDER	U.S.
KONZOREK, Jakob (see GONZORECK)	300469						
KOOP	254959	M	Ger.		Capt., Roubaix (Fr.) 2.41	WITNESS	FR.
KOOTHAYE	121614	M	Ger.		Blockfhr., C.C. Neuengamme-Hamburg (Ger.) 42	MURDER	BEL.
KOOWEL, Heinrich	150662	M			Civ. Wachtmeister-Landjaeger, C.C.Recklinghausen (Ger.) 12.43	TORTURE	U.S.
KOPACKA, Stanislav (or HOENIGER, Klaus)	98539	M		97	Regierungskommissar, Gestapo, C.C. Boleslau (Czech.) 39-45	MURDER	CZECH.
KOPAN, August (see KOBAN)	260431						
KOPEL	29761		Ger.		Asst., Custom-House, St.Michel near Mauriennes (Fr.) 3.44	MURDER	FR.
KOPELCHEK	195454	M	Ger.		Pvt., Working Camp Steinach-Trieben (Aust.) 2.45	INTERR.	U.K.
KOPETSCHKE, Edgar	305555	M	Ger.		Head of the Constr.Supervising Department, Bohlers Factory, Kapfenberg, Marien-Mertzoul (Aust.) 10.43-5.45	BRUTALITY	U.K.
KOPEZYNSKI	253093	M			Pvt., C.C.Osterhagen, Nordhausen (Ger.)	MURDER	U.S.
KOPF	137665	M	Ger.		Pvt., Army, Grosse Krosse, Widenau, Freiwaldau (Czech.) 2.45	MURDER	U.K.
KOPF	128854	M	Ger.		Capt., Cmit. Stalag VI J, Gerrisheim, Duesseldorf (Ger.) 5.44-5.45	TORTURE	U.K.
KOPF	173660	M	Ger.		Dr., Member of a Government Board, C.C. Oswiecim (Pol.) 39-45	MURDER	CZECH.
KOPF, Franz	253092	M			Flyer, C.C.Ellrich, Nordhausen (Ger.)	MURDER	U.S.
KOPFNER	300269	M			Hptsturmfhr., SS Stab, 11.SS Panz.Gren.Regt.No.7, Destomon Beotia (Grc.) 6.44	MURDER	GRC.
KOPFSTEIN, Ferdinand	254951	M	Ger.	20. 2.03	Agent, Gestapo, Trebou (Czech.) 42-45	MISC.CRIMES	CZECH.
KOPKA	188895				Guard, C.C. Ravensbrueck (Ger.) 42-45	MURDER	FR.
KOPKA	260706	M	Ger.		Sgt., Fieldpolice, Enghien les Bains, Domont (Fr.) 8.44	WITNESS	FR.
KOPKE (or KOEPPKE)	1275	M		12	Public Official, Head of the Chesnoy Farming Enterprise.	TORTURE	U.S.
KOPKE (or KOPPKE)	126352	M	Ger.	95	Civ.Foreman, Farming Enterprise Chesnoy-Boncourt (Bel.) 9.42-45	TORTURE	U.S.
KOPKO	125175	M	Ger.	11	Osturmfhr., SS-Gestapo, Berlin (Ger.)	TORTURE	U.S.
KOPLER	495	M	Ger.		Sturmbannfhr., SS Feldkommandantur 528, Missidon (Fr.) 11.44	TORTURE	FR.
KOPLING	102938	M	Ger.		Major, Army, C.C. Suttrop, Warstein (Ger.) 3.45	MURDER	U.S.
KOPP	162264	M	Ger.		263.Inf.Div. Kommando de Landerneau (Fr.) 44	MURDER	FR.
KOPP	177536	M			Lt., SS-Formation L.54275, Jouy-Josas (Fr.) 8.44	MURDER	FR.
KOPP	253742	M			Pvt., C.C.Dora, Nordhausen (Ger.)	MURDER	U.S.
KOPP	255154	M	Ger.		Sturmscharfhr., SS, Sipo, Brussels (Bel.) 40-44	MURDER	BEL.
KOPP, Hermann (or KOEPP)	172092	M			Civ.Foreman, Org.Todt, C.C.Muhldorf-Ampfing (Ger.) 6.44-4.45	MURDER	U.S.
KOPPE	496	M	Ger.		Obergruppenfhr., SS-Gestapo, Wartheland (Pol.) 11.43	MURDER	POL.
KOPPE, Kurt	254997	M	Ger.	07	Lt., Army, 92.Inf.Div., 192.Signal Unit 1.Coy., Farnese (It.) 6.44	INTERR.	U.K.
KOPPE, Richard	195066	M	Ger.		Farmer, Bosewig (Ger.) 9.43	MURDER	NETH.
KOPPE, Wilhelm	301522	M	Ger.	22. 2.92	Scharfhr., SS, C.C.Buchenwald (Ger.) betw.5.38 and 10.43	MURDER	BEL.
KOPPEL (or KOZLING)	187706	M	Ger.		Obergruppenfhr., SS-Polizei, .	MURDER	UNWCC
KOPPEL, Max (or KOEPPL)	162742				Gestapo, Audun Le Tiche (Fr.) 3.44	MURDER	U.S.
KOPPELMAIER, Georg	254366	M	Ger.		SS-Scharfhr., St.Jean de Maurienne (Fr.) 3.44	INTERR.	FR.
	145260	M	Ger.		Hptsturmfhr., Waffen-SS, "Totenkopf"-Sturmbann, C.C.Weimar-Buchenwald (Ger.)	TORTURE	U.S.
KOPPEN	174681	M	Ger.		Pvt., 2.Bn., Parachute Hunter Regt., Plouzane (Fr.) 44	MURDER	FR.
KOPPEN, Alfred	162058	M	Ger.		Member, Gestapo, Saone et Loire (Fr.) 43-44	MURDER	FR.

NAME	C.R.FILE NUMBER	SEX	NATIO-NALITY	DATE OF BIRTH	RANK OCCUPATION UNIT PLACE AND DATE OF CRIME	REASON WANTED	WANTED BY
KOPPENBERG, Heinrich	260209	M	Ger.	14. 3.80	Chief Vorstand,Dr., Junkers Flugzeug-u.Motorenwerke A.G., Later Owner of Argus (Aircraft Factory),Dessau(Ger.)	MISC.CRIMES	U.S.
KOPPENHOEFER	10018	M	Ger.		Usturmfhr.,SS,Vertreter der Gestapo,Brno(Czech.) 39-44	MURDER	CZECH.
KOPPENHOFEN	132054	M			SS-Usturmfhr.,Gestapo,Deputy Cmdt.,Brno,Brunn(Czech.) 39-45	TORTURE	CZECH.
KOPPER	259687	M	Ger.		Major,Aufklaerungsgruppe 123F,Paris(Fr.) 24.6.42	INTERR.	FR.
KOPPKE see KOPKE	126352						
KOPPS, Arthur Hans	300270		Ger.		N.C.O.,95 Security Regt.,4 Bn.,Naucelles,Cantal,Aurillac.20.7.44	MURDER	FR.
KOPPS, Willi	254380	M	Ger.		Cpl.,11 Pz.Div.,Lantrec(Fr.) 5.8.44	MISC.CRIMES	FR.
KOPSCH	259833	M	Ger.		Chief-pay-master,Army,Kdo."Raumboot",Breda,Noord-Brabant(Neth.) 9.44	PILLAGE	NETH.
KORAUB	121616	F	Ger.		Woman-Guard,C.C.Ravensbrueck(Ger.)	MURDER	FR.
KORB	62498	M	Ger.		Sturmbannfhr.(Werkschutzleiter),Waffen-SS,C.C.Bohlen(Ger.) 7.-11.44	MURDER	U.S.
KORBARK	185848	M	Ger.		Lt.,Police,Kalithea Sfageia(Grc.)	MURDER	GRC.
KORBEL, Hans	306032	M	Ger.		Dr.,Member of Staff of Baby Clinic,Wolfsburg and Ruehen(Ger.)	MURDER	U.K.
KORBEL, Otto	102936	M	Ger.		SS-Sturm-Bn.AOKI,4 Coy.,Courcellesinied(Fr.) 14.11.44	MURDER	U.S.
KORCZANY	258070	M	Ger.		Ing.,Member Gestapo,Bratislava(Czech.) 45	MURDER	CZECH.
KORDECKY nee SEIDEL, Claire	306441	F	Ger.		Amsterdam-Zuid(Neth.) 6.43	INTERR.	CZECH.
KORDEK	189619	M	Ger.		Lt.,Feldgend.,Vittel(Fr.) 17.8.44	TORTURE	FR.
KORDERS, Hans or FISCHER,Willy	307097	M	Ger.		Member of Feldgend.,Dordrecht(Neth.) 11.-12.44,1.-2.45	MURDER	NETH.
KORDES, Johann	145192	M	Ger.		Civilian. 9.40	TORTURE	U.S.
KORDRESKI	256129	M	Ger.		Chief,Room 6 Block 2,Flossenburg(Ger.)	INTERR.	FR.
KORES, Josef	257687	M	Ger.	6. 5.89	Dr.,Manager of Firm,Civilian,Prag(Czech.)	PILLAGE	CZECH.
KOHELL, Robert or Rupert	185816	M	Ger.or Hung.		SS-Mann,SS-Totenkopf-Sturmbann,C.C.Mittelbau Dora,Nordhausen(Ger.)43-45	WITNESS	U.S.
KORF	150659	M			Sgt.,Army,Brunswick(Ger.) 8.3.45	MURDER	U.S.
KORF, Karl	193079	M	Ger.		Sgt.-Guard,Reichsjustizministerium,Feldstraflager,Finmark(Nor.) 42-45	MISC.CRIMES	NOR.
KORF, Walter	179898	M	Ger.		SS-Uschfhr.,SS-Pion.Coy.Ad.Hitler,Malmedy(Bel.) 1.12.44	MURDER	U.S.
KORF, Willy (KORFF)	29760	M	Ger.		Chief,Gestapo,Melun(Fr.) 27.4.44	MURDER	FR.
KORFF, Ernst	195524	M	Ger.	4. 3.90	Lt.,Kriminal-Inspektor, SS,Kripo,Kolin(Czech.) 39-45	MURDER	CZECH.,YUGO.
KORFF, Willy see KORF, Willy	29760						
KORFF, Willy see SCHRIEDMANN	177571						
KORGER	151332	M	Ger.		Civilian,Stalag XXB,C.C.Elbing(Pol.)	MISC.CRIMES	U.K.
KORGER, Karl	25410	M	Ger.		Polizeimeister,Schupo,Prag(Czech.) 42	MURDER	CZECH.
KORGL	138228	M	Ger.		Osturmbannfhr.,C.C.Flossenburg(Ger.) 43	MURDER	FR.,BEL.
KORLIN, Gunter	129682	M	Ger.	15	Civilian,C.C.Dora,Nordhausen(Ger.)	MURDER	U.S.
KORMANN	497	M	Ger.		W.O.,Army,Brive(Fr.) 20.6.44	PILLAGE	FR.
KORMANN	179897	M	Ger.		Lt.,C.C.Ravensbrueck(Ger.)	TORTURE	FR.
KORMER, Jacob	173088	M	Ger.	21. 9.94	Meister,Gend.,Brumath(Fr.)	PILLAGE	FR.
KORMES, Andreas	173701	M	Ger.		Pvt.,Army,Ischpelt,Tarchamps(Lux.) 10.1.45	MURDER	LUX.
KORN	11272	M	Ger.		SS-Stand.-Fhr.,Munster(Fr.) 7.9.44	MURDER	FR.
KORN	189159	M	Ger.		Capt.,Gestapo of Montaubois,Montech(Fr.)	MURDER	FR.
KORN	232155	M	Ger.		Sgt.,Sicherheitspolizei Groningen,Westerbork(Neth.) 9.-12.44	MURDER	NETH.
KORN	254961	M	Ger.		Pvt.,100 Regt.Alpine Troops,Feissons (Fr.) 5.8.44	INTERR.	FR.
KOHN, Heinz	301523	M	Ger.		SS-Oechfhr.SS,C.C.Buchenwald(Ger.) 16.5.38-9.10.43	MURDER	BEL.
KORNALEWICZ, Werner	162740	M		15	Civilian,Hamelin(Ger.) 2.45	TORTURE	U.S.
KORNBERGER, Kurt	300947	M	Ger.		Leader,Punishment Coy.,Untersteiermark,O.C."Villa Maternitsch" Rogaska Slatina, Cilli(Celje)(Yugo.) 12.2.45	MURDER	YUGO.
KORNBLUM	259631	M	Ger.		Capt.,Guard-Coy.,E 34 of POW Tilsit,Breitenstein(Ger.) 21.10.43	MURDER	FR.
KORNDORFER	259094	M	Ger.		Cmdt.,German Police for Croatia,Zagreb(Yugo.) 8.-9.9.43	MISC.CRIMES	YUGO.
KORNEL-KESSEL	191903	M	Ger.		Civilian,Tain L'Hermitage(Fr.) 24.8.44	PILLAGE	FR.
KORNELIS see CORNELIS	196010						
KORNER	150661	M	Ger.	05	Usturmfuehrer,SS,C.C.Oranienburg-Sachsenhausen(Ger.)	MURDER	U.K.
KORNER, Michael	305789	M	Ger.		Uschfhr.,Lagerfuehrer at C.C.Sachsenhausen(Ger.)1.40-4.45	MURDER	U.K.
KORNEHREICH	11273	M	Ger.		Capt.,Army-Cmdt.1a Garnison, Ile D'Aurigny(Island) 43	TORTURE	FR.
KOHNFROEST	252438	M			Pvt.,C.C.Nordhausen(Ger.)	MURDER	U.S.
KOROSINEKY	167696	M	Ger.		Official,Warder or Kapo,C.C.Sachsenhausen-Oranienburg(Ger.) 39-4.45	MURDER	POL.
KORPI	193361	M	Ger.		Pvt.,P.O.W.Working-Bn.41,C.C.Nerlandsdal-Kristiansund(Nor.) 41-45	TORTURE	NOR.
KORPIUM	193362	M	Ger.		Pvt.,P.O.W.Working-Bn.41,C.C.Nerlandsdal-Kristiansund(Nor.) 41-45	TORTURE	NOR.
KORRIES	254836	M			Oberzahlmeister,C.C.de Royallieu,Compiegne(Fr.) 41-44	MISC.CRIMES	FR.
KORSACZENKO, Paul	185817	M			Pvt.,4 SS Totenkopf-Sturmbann,C.C.Mittelbau Dora,Nordhausen(Ger.)40-45	WITNESS	U.S.
KORSCHER	301524	M			SS-Rottfhr.,SS,C.C.Buchenwald(Ger.) 16.5.38-9.10.43	MURDER	BEL.
KORSHENRICH	187858	M			SS-Hptsturmfhr.,Wirtschafts- und Verwaltungshauptamt, C.C.Buchenwald(Ger.) 41-45	MURDER	BEL.
KORSITZKY	131406	M	Ger.	13	Scharfhr.,SS-Panz.Gren.Div."Das Reich",C.C.Mauthausen(Aust.) 41-45	MURDER	U.S.
KORSS	136241	M	Ger.		Air Force,SS,Asserans(Fr.) 19.8.44	MURDER	FR.
KORSS	254359	M	Ger.		SS-Sturmfhr.,Air Force,Valleiry(Fr.) 16.8.44	TORTURE	FR.
KORT, Hans	252223	M	Ger.	94	Sgt.,Orts-Coy.,Bn.Nr.311859,Vitry(Fr.) 20.7.44	TORTURE	FR.
KORTA	1414	M	Ger.		Capt.,Army,334 Eng.Bn.	MURDER	U.K.
KORTEN	306800	M	Ger.		SS-Uschfhr.prob.of Abt.I Gestapo Vichy(Fr.) 10.43-9.44	MURDER	FR.
KORTER, Philipp	102935	M		08	Pvt.,Army,C.C.Warstein (Ger.) 20.-21.or 22.3.45	MURDER	U.S.
KORTING	133804	M			Oschfhr.,SS,C.C.Weimar-Buchenwald(Ger.)	TORTURE	U.S.
KORTS (KAVIS) Hans-Joachim	152507	M			Ortsgruppenleiter NSDAP,SS,C.C. Estedt and Gardelegen(Ger.)10.-14.4.45	WITNESS	U.S.
KORTUM	498	M	Ger.		Feldgend.,Feldgendarmerie-Army,Abbeville(Fr.) 31.8.44	MURDER	FR.
KORTZ or KURZ	530	M	Ger.	00	SS-Hptschfhr.C.C.,Hauptwachtmeister Police,Ulven,Grini(Nor.) 43	MURDER	NOR.
KORVARD see KORWARD,Willy	162397						
KORWARD, Willy or KORVARD	162397	M	Ger.		SS-Pvt.,16 Inf.Div.,Maille(Fr.) 25.8.44	MURDER	FR.
KORZEWA	193089	M	Ger.	00	Sgt.,Guard,Reichsjustizministerium,Feldstraflager,C.C.,Finmark (Nor.) 45	MISC.CRIMES	NOR.
KORZI, Stephan	167072	M	Ger.		Pvt.,Army,Paris(Fr.) 44	WITNESS	FR.

KOS - KOV

NAME	C.R.FILE NUMBER	SEX	NATIO-NALITY	DATE OF BIRTH	RANK OCCUPATION UNIT PLACE AND DATE OF CRIME	REASON WANTED	WANTED BY
KOS, Anton	162061	M		21. 3.10	1 SS Freiwilligen Bat.447, Plouvien (Fr.) 44	TORTURE	FR.
KOSAK, Hans	172090	M			Connected with M 1 Lager, Muhldorf,Ampfing (Ger.) 6.44-4.45	MURDER	U.S.
KOSCHE	152508	M	Ger.	10	Civilian, C.C. Bohlen (Ger.) 4.44-5.45	TORTURE	U.K.
KOSCHEL	192459	M		95	Sgt., SD, Gestapo, Brieg (Ger.) 39-45	SUSPECT	CZECH.
KOSCHINSKI	131416	M			Commanding officer, C.C. Mauthausen (Aust.) 41-45	MURDER	U.S.
KOSCHORKE, Helmut	189755	M	Ger.	11. 8.05	Regierungsrat, Gestapo, Territories Occupied official, Brno (Czech.) 39-45	MISC.CRIMES	CZECH.
KOSCHUB, Emil	173659	M	Ger.		Senior Sgt., Major, C.C. Oswiecim-Birkenau (Pol.) 39-45	MURDER	CZECH.
KOSFELD	185682	M	Ger.		Rottenfhr.,SS, Leibstandarte Adolf Hitler,Renardmont-Stavelot (Bel.) 19.12.44	MURDER	BEL.
KOSKA, Willi	137046	M			12 SS Pz.Div. H.J., probably Hq.Co.Ren.Bn,St.Sulpice sur Risle (Fr.) 10.6.44	MURDER	FR.
KOSLIN, Walter	185094	M	Ger.		Guard, C.C. Papenburg (Ger.)	TORTURE	FR.
KOSLOWSKI, Franz	142222	M	Ger.	24. 1.83	Policeman, Gestapo, (Ger.)	MURDER	U.S.
KOSLOWSKI, Otto	192458	M	Ger.		Kriminalrat, Gestapo, Bruenn (Czech.) 39-45	SUSPECT	CZECH.,U.K.
KOSMANN	195481	M	Ger.		Kapo, C.C. Braunschweig,Schandelah (Ger.) 44-45	TORTURE	BEL.
KOSMECKI	192890	M	Ger.		Schupo, C.C. Falstad, Dronthem (Nor.) 11.42	MURDER	NOR.
KOSNICK, Erwin	140898	M	Ger.		Verbindungsstab 331, 2 Coy, Bolnes (Neth.) 8.5.45	MURDER	NETH.
KOSNOPEL, Konrad	185546	M	Ger.		Employee, Gestapo, Budmjovice (Czech.)	MURDER	CZECH.
KOSRZEWA	260363	M	Ger.		Oberwachtmstr.,SS,Penitentiary Nord-Nor. 6.42-45	MURDER	YUGO.
KOSSAR	132486	M	Ger.-Aust.		Civilian, Dr., Kindberg (Aust.) 10.43-4.44	MISC.CRIMES	U.K.
KOSSAK, Rudolf	305915	M			Hptsturmfhr.,SS, head of the Hradec Kralove, Aussenstelle of the Sicherungsdienst Leitabschnitt Prague,Oswiecim-Biekenau(Pol.)39-41	MURDER	CZECH.
KOSSITZKY	131415	M	Ger.		Hptsturmfhr.,SS, Mauthausen (Aust.) 41-45	MURDER	U.S.
KOST	187178	M	Ger.		Dir.,Arbeits-Kdo. (Coal Mine)C.C.Homberg,Rocheide Stalag VI(Ger.)41-45	TORTURE	U.S.
KOSTAL, Bohumil-Gottlieb	192457	M	Ger.-Czech.?		Employee, driver, Gestapo, Bruenn (Czech.) 39-45	WITNESS	CZECH.
KOSTE	147301	M	Ger.		Lt., 15 Pz.Rgt., 11 Pz.Div. (Fr.) 44	MURDER	FR.
KOSTEINIK, Alois	185841	M			4 SS Totenkopf Sturmbann,C.C.Mittelbau Dora-Nordhausen(Ger.) 43-45	WITNESS	U.S.
KOSTEN, Heinrich	24894	M			Pvt., Fallschirm-Jg.Rgt.,Roermond (Neth.) 11.44-1.45	TORTURE	U.S.
KOSTER	186749	M	Ger.		Col.,Flak-Bde, Saintes (Fr.) 44	WITNESS	FR.
KOSTERS, Hans	256880	M			Sgt., Airforce, Abergement de Varey (Fr.) 25.7.44	MURDER	FR.
KOSTHEYE	196802	M			Capt., Fallschirm Bn 8 SPL 50633 Blg PA Paris,St.Amand Montrond (Fr.) 8.6.44	INTERR.	FR.
KOSTIAL	499	M	Ger.		Oberscharfhr.,SS, C.C. Maidaner (Pol.) 40-4.44	MURDER	POL.,BEL.,FR.
KOSTIAL	121543	M	Ger.		Uscharfhr.,SS, C.C. Buchenwald (Ger.)	TORTURE	FR.
KOSTIAL, Ernst	145261	M	Ger.		Oscharfhr., Waffen-SS, Totenkopf Standarte,C.C. Buchenwald,Weimar(Gar.)TORTURE		U.S.
KOSTIDE, Heinrich	306225	M			Administrative Insp.,nr.Bramher, 2.11.44	BRUTALITY	U.K.
KOSTJAL, Ernst	143181	M	Ger.	14	Oscharfhr.,SS, C.C. Lublin (Pol.) 42-43	TORTURE	POL.
KOSTRAKIEWITSCH	28720	M	Ger.		Landgerichtsrat, Public official, Opava (Czech.) 21.2.40	MURDER	BEL.
KOTAS, Alois	254822	M	Ger.	9. 2.96	Blocleader,Civilian Informer, NSDAP, Gestapo,Slananice(Czech.)39-45	MISC.CRIMES	CZECH.
KOTAS, Alois	254825	M	Ger.	28. 8.27	SS and H.J. Div., Brno-Slapanice (Czech.) 39-45	MISC.CRIMES	CZECH.
KOTAS, Hedwig nee TRIZNA	254656	F	Ger.		Blocleader, NSDAP, Slapanice (Czech.) 39-45	INTERR.	CZECH.
KOTER, Wolfgang	255278	M	Ger.	4.10.11	Employee, Gestapo, Olomouc (Czech.) 43-45	MURDER	CZECH.
KOTH	138307	M	Ger.		Sgt.,SS, Gestapo, Lyon (Fr.) 6.-8.44	MURDER	FR.
KOTH	252339	M			Uscharfhr., SS, C.C.Sangershausen-Nordhausen (Ger.)	MURDER	U.S.
KOTHE see ROTHE	165569						
KOTHER, Paul	162739	M	Ger.	02	Osturmfhr.,SS,chief of Baubetriebs-Dienststelle,C.C.Chrdruf(Ger.)	WITNESS	U.S.
KOTHMULLER	149268	M	Ger.		Col., Stalag VI C,Dithmarschen (Ger.) 18.9.44	MISC.CRIMES	FR.
KODOTZIEJSKI,Muczystav or KOLODZUPKI, Mieczystav	162569	M		22	Civilian,political prisoner,Rottleberode,Gardelegen(Ger.)5.-14.4.45	WITNESS	U.S.
KOTSCHI	146545	M	Ger.		Oscharfhr.,SS, Gestapo, Prag (Czech.)	TORTURE	CZECH.
KOTTAS, Eric	191904	M	Ger.		Aspirant, Army, St.Hilaire,St.Mesmen (Fr.) 19.-25.8.44	MURDER	FR.
KOTTER	141571	M	Ger.		Lt.,Army, 9 Pz.Div.,5 Coy,2 Bn, Sarras and Andance (Fr.) 13.6.44	MURDER	FR.
KOTTER	187176	M	Ger.		Civilian, Stalag VI A, Hemer (Ger.) 41-45	TORTURE	U.S.
KOTTER	189231	M	Ger.		Lt., 9 Pz.Div.,20 Bn, Andance (Fr.) 13.6.44	MURDER	FR.
KOTTER, Hans	257611	M	Ger.		Oscharfhr.,SD,Foix (Fr.) 11.42-8.44	MISC.CRIMES	FR.
KOTTERMANN	194006	M	Ger.		SS-Schuetze, II Zug, II Gruppe, Stavelot (Bel.) 19-20.12.44	MURDER	BEL.
KOTTERMANN	185684	M	Ger.		Pvt., I SS Pz.Div."Hitlerjugend" Parfondruy,Stavelot(Bel.)18.-22.12.44	MURDER	U.S.
KOTTHAUS, Fritz	139183	M	Ger.		Hauptfhr.,SA,SS,NSDAP, (Ger.)	MURDER	U.S.
KOTTMANN	192456	M	Ger.		Col.,SS, Kaltenherberg,Elsenborn (Ger.,Bel.) 10.9.44	MURDER	BEL.
KOTTNER	301335	M	Ger.		Member, Gestapo Trencin, C.C. Oswiecim-Birkenau (Pol.) 39-45	MURDER	CZECH.
KOTTRÉ	254361	M	Ger.		Oscharfhr.,SS, SD, Toulouse, (Fr.) 11.42-8.44	MISC.CRIMES	FR.
KOTZIAN, Albert	62500	M	Ger.	27	Pvt.,Army,Volks-Gren.Rgt.,5 Coy,77 IR,26 VGD, 1 Km Southwest of Givry (Bel.) 6.1.45	MISC.CRIMES	U.S.
KOTZMACHER	131780	M	Ger.		Hptsturmfhr.,SS	TORTURE	U.S.
KOTZMACHER	132466	M	Ger.		Oscharfhr.,SS,in the Vicinity,Neunkirchen (Ger.) 3.45	MURDER	U.S.
KOTZNER	111083	M	Ger.		Lt.,Army,Lebenhan (Ger.) 7.4.42	TORTURE	U.K.
KOTZYBIK	185842	M			Oscharfhr.SS Totenkopf Sturmbann, C.C.Mittelbau-Dora-Nordhausen, Auschwitz (Ger.,Pol.) 43-45	WITNESS	U.S.
KOUACK	500	M	Ger.		Staff officer, Army,Clermont,Ferrant (Fr.) 9.6.44	MURDER	FR.
KOUCH	261392	M	Ger.		Cpt.,Bn Spielberg, Rgt.z.b.V. Col.Wolff, environs of Mauleon-Navarreux (Fr.) 6.and 8.44	MURDER	FR.
KOUDELKA, Vladimir	261118	M	Ger.	29. 9.21	Member, Informant,NSDAP Vlajka,Gestapo,Prag and Neratovice,(Czech.)44	MISC.CRIMES	CZECH.
KOUM or KOUNN	29759	M			Lt.,Army,le Faouet (Fr.) 26.6.44,3.8.44	MURDER	FR.
KOUPTIS or KYPTIS or SCHMIDT, Wladimir	254835	M	Ger.		SS-NCO, Gestapo, Paris (Fr.) 7.44	MISC.CRIMES	FR.
KOURM, Youp	257648	M	Ger.		Ammunition Store keeper, Navy,10 Flottille, Guilligomarch(Fr.)3.6.44	MURDER	FR.
KOURT, Frank	254360	M	Ger.		Feldgendarm, Gendarmerie, Allarmont (Fr.) 18.8.44	MISC.CRIMES	FR.
KOURTCHIVER, Henri	150658	M	Ger.		Member, Gestapo, Folking (Fr.) 11.44	MURDER	FR.
KOUTNY, Josef	254953	M	Ger.	8. 1.04	Sgt., Gendarmerie, Jaworiko (Czech.) 5.5.45	MURDER	CZECH.
KOUZIELLA	29757	M	Ger.		Lt., Army, le Faouet (Fr.)26.6.44,2.8.44	MURDER	FR.
KOVALEV, Walter	135197	M	Ger.		SS-guard, C.C. Helmbrechten (Ger.) 7.44,13.4.45	TORTURE	U.S.

KOV-KRA

NAME	C.R.FILE NUMBER	SEX	NATIO-NALITY	DATE OF BIRTH	RANK OCCUPATION UNIT PLACE AND DATE OF CRIME	REASON WANTED	WANTED BY
KOVALEVSKY	11274	M	Ger.		Pvt., Chief of Coy.Disciplin.OT Stalag 10.Coy. Sonder Abt. des Strafarbeits-Kommandos, Army, C.C. Hannover-Wolfringhausen (Ger.) 40 - 2.41	TORTURE	FR.
KOVANDA, Julius	253727	M	Ger.		Merchant, Civilian, Prag (Czech.) 39 - 45	MISC.CRIMES	CZECH.
KOVATSCH	125176	M	Ger.		Kripo, C.C. Helmbrechts-Gruenberg (Ger.)	MURDER	U.S.
KOWACHT	150654	M	Ger.	10	Hauptsturmfhr., SS-Panz.-Div. "Das Reich" Tulle (Fr.) 9.6.44	MURDER	FR.
KOWACHT (or TOWACHT)	173735	M	Ger.		Lt., Air-Force,Commandentur, Maintenon (Fr.) 4.40	PILLAGE	FR.
KOWAL	131295	M	Ger.		Unterscharfhr., SS, C.C. Jawischowitz (Pol.) 43 - 44	MURDER	U.S.
KOWAL, Hans	193065	M	Ger.	7. 3.20	Ex-Convict, Reichsjustiz-Ministerium,Feldstraflager,Finmark (Nor.) 8.45	WITNESS	NOR.
KOWALD, Joseph	135200	M	Ger.		Civilian, Prison Guard, C.C., Regensburg (Ger.) 4.45	TORTURE	U.S.
KOWALSCHEK, Paul	129689	M	Ger.		Civilian, C.C. Bund - Auschwitz (Pol.)	MURDER	U.S.
KOWALSKI	189077	M	Ger.		Cmdt., Gestapo of Stanislawow (Pol.) 8.41 - 10.42	MURDER	POL.
KOWALSKI, Albert	252338	M	Ger.		Sgt., C.C. Ellrich, Nordhausen (Ger.)	MURDER	U.S.
KOWARSCHIK, Eduard	31223	M	Ger.		Dr., Oberlandgerichtsrat, Public Official Litomerice (Czech.) 21.2.40	MURDER	BEL.
KOWSCHYRIN, Paul	172084	M	Ger.		Pvt., Arb.Kommando 1015,Stalag IX,C.C.Bischofferode(Ger.) 16.3.43	TORTURE	U.K.
KOX, Georges	196800	M		19	Sgt., Caserne Vandamine, Lille (Fr.) 28.4.44	INTERR.	FR.
KOZIKOWSKI, Josef	252337	M			Pvt., C.C. Ellrich, Nordhausen (Ger.)	MURDER	U.S.
KOZLING (see KOPPEL)	162742						
KOZLIANIC, Joseph	11275	M	Ger.		Pvt., Army, 2.Coy.110.Panz.-Gren.Rgt.III, Albine (Fr.) 29.6.44	MURDER	FR.
KOZLOWSKI	253981	M			C.C., Ellrich, Nordhausen (Ger.)	MURDER	U.S.
KOZOUREK, Hans	179932	M	Ger.	3. 4.08	SS-Sturmmann, SD, Gestapo, Benesov (Czech.) 39 - 43	MURDER	CZECH.
KPAS, Josef	302525	M	Ger.	17.11.14	Uscharfhr., SS, C.C. Buchenwald (Ger.) 5.38 - 10.43	MURDER	BEL.
KRAACK	190666	M	Ger.		Pvt., Eisenbahn-Btty.717,St.Andries,Varsena les Bruges (Bel.)4.9.44	MURDER	BEL.
KRAAL	174102	M		05	Pvt.,Landesschuetzen Bn.398, C.C.Altstadt (Czech.) 23.9.44	WITNESS	U.K.
KRAATZ	128836	M		95 - 05	Capt., Air-Crafttender,Ger.Merchant Navy,Danzig-Luebeck (Ger.)3.45	TORTURE	U.K.
KRAATZ	253866	M	Ger.		Untersturmfhr., SS,Sipo, Bruessel (Bel.) 40 - 44	MURDER	BEL.
KRABBE, Ralf,Frantz	167069	M			Sgt., SD, St.Nectaire (Fr.) 1.11.43	MISC.CRIMES	FR.
KRABBE, Rolf	62104	M	Ger.	18	Hauptscharfhr., SD de Vichy Abt. IV 3a, Clermont,Ferrand (Fr.) 7.44	MURDER	FR.
KRABEL	174827	M	Ger.		Chief, Art.Ers.Rgt.7, Tours-Albertville (Fr.) 6.44	MURDER	FR.
KRABER	193066	M			Lt., 3.Fahrrad-Coy. C.C., Bones-Salangsdalen (Nor.)	TORTURE	NOR.
KRABITZA, Josef	251527	M	Ger.		Police, Maribor (Yugo.) 44	MURDER	YUGO.
KRACHT	121624	M			Lt.,Stalag,Luft VII, C.C. Bankau (Ger.) 12.44	TORTURE	U.K.
KRACHT, Rudolf	152515	M			Ortsgruppenleiter,NSDAP,CO.OF CC.5 Volkssturm Bn. Vicinity of Estedt und Gardelegen (Ger.) 4.45	MURDER	U.S.
KRACKER	196799	M	Ger.		Foreman, Rijke Artificial Silk Factory, Anrath (Ger.) 1.42 - 3.44	WITNESS	NETH.
KRAEH	29784	M	Nor.		Major, Army, Werk Btty.206,Finmark (Nor.) 11.44	MURDER	NOR.
KRAELE	163279	M	Ger.	85 - 90	Colonel, Reichskriegsgericht, Berlin (Ger.) 43 - 10.44	MISC.CRIMES	U.K.
KRAELL	131707	M	Ger.		Oberstaatsanwalt, Kriegsgericht, Berlin and Torgau (Ger.) 40-5.45	MURDER	FR.
KRAEMER	102952	M	Ger.		Cmdt., SS-Panz.-Div. "Hitler Jugend", Hellenthal (Ger.) 18.12.44	MURDER	U.S.
KRAEMER (or CREMER)	150664	M	Ger.	07	Dr., Kreisleiter, NSDAP, C.C., Hameln (Ger.) 4.4.45	MURDER	U.K.
KRAEMER	191448	M	Ger.		Dr., Official,Geschaeftsfuehrer, Ostdeutsche Revision-und Treuhandgesellschaft, Krakau (Pol.) 9.39 - 44	PILLAGE	POL.
KRAEMER	194707	M	Ger.		Kreisleiter, NSDAP, Neustadt a.d.Aisch (Ger.) 40 - 45	SUSPECT	POL.
KRAEMER	250873	M			Brigardefhr., 6.SS-Panz.Army, Malmedy (Bel.)	MURDER	U.S.
KRAEMER	300054	M	Ger.		On Staff, C.C. Mauthausen (Aust.)1942-5.45	MURDER	FR.
KRAEMER	307001	M	Ger.		Member of the Staff, C.C. Ravensbrueck (Ger.) 40 - 45	BRUTALITY	BEL.
KRAEMER, Franz	260533	M	Ger.	15. 6.25	SS - Guard, C.C. Natzweiler (Fr.)	MURDER	FR.
KRAEMER, Fritz	136242	M	Ger.		Lt., Feldgendarmerie, Oberseebach (Fr.) 7.44	MURDER	FR.
KRAEMER, Gustav	262309	M	Ger.		Lt., 7.Panz.Reconnaissance Coy.Sillersdorf(Ger.)16.4.45 L.O.D.N.A.C.D.	WITNESS	U.S.
KRAEMER, Kurt	253073	M		19.10.05	Flyer, C.C. Ellrich, Nordhausen (Ger.)	MURDER	U.S.
KRAEMER, Walter	131292	M	Ger.		Pvt., Guard, SS, C.C. Monowitz (Pol.)	MURDER	U.S.
KRAENERT	193067	M			Cpl., 2.Bau-Pionier Bn. (K.),Namsos, Akervika (Nor.) 10.42	MURDER	NOR.
KRAENZLEIN, Fritz	254591	M			Wassertrudingen (Ger.) 1.3.45	WITNESS	U.S.
KRAETSCHMANN, Heinz	131378	M	Ger.		Pvt., Fallschirm-Jaeger Bn. (Ers.) Quaregnon,Jemappes ,Galin (Bel.)	MURDER	BEL.
KRAETZ	250308	M			Col., 234.Jg.Rgt., Vinkt Meigem (Bel.) 25.-31.5.40	INTERR.	BEL.
KRAETZ, Josef	254562	M	Ger.	24. 2.08	Employee, Gestapo, Vsetin (Czech.) 39 - 45	MISC.CRIMES	CZECH.
KRAETZER	39566	M	Ger.		N.C.O., SD,N.S.C.O.,C.C., near Haslack Vulkanlager (Ger.)12.44-2.45	MURDER	SOV.UN.
KRAETZER	196793	M			C.C., Struthof - Natzweiler (Fr.) 40 - 44	MISC.CRIMES	FR.
KRAETZER	307002	M	Ger.		Obersturmfhr., SS, C.C., Auschwitz (Pol.) 44	MURDER	POL.
KRAETZLI, Franz	10020	M	Ger.		Dr., Erster Staatsanwalt, Public Official, Opava (Czech.) 21.2.40	MURDER	CZECH.
KRAFCZYCK	251656	M	Ger.		Chief, Transport, Wismar (Ger.) 32 - 43	INTERR.	FR.
KRAFF (or GRAFF)	67058	M			Public Official, Organisation Todt, Ile D'Aurigny (U.K.)	TORTURE	FR.
KRAFFT	24895	M	Ger.		Lt.,Col., Oberkommando des Wehrmacht, Sektions Chef(Segeletz (Ger.).44	MURDER	U.S.
KRAFFT	185686	M			SS - Mann, C.C. Ravensbrueck (Ger.) 4.42 - 4.45	MURDER	BEL.
KRAFFT, Otto	501	M	Ger.	09	Oberscharfhr., C.C. Maidaneck (Pol.) 40 - 4.44	MURDER	BEL. POL.
KRAFT	502	M	Ger.		Cpl., Army, 118.Jaeger Div., 738.Rgt.,2.Btty. 7.43 - 1.44	MURDER	YUGO.
KRAFT	12443	M	Ger.		Organisation Todt Cherbourg, Aldernay (U.K.) 7.43	MURDER	FR.
KRAFT	24913	M	Ger.		Oberscharfhr.,SS, C.C. Natzweiler,Strutthof (Fr.) 42 - 44	MISC.CRIMES	FR.
KRAFT	31536	M	Ger.		Lt., Army, 89.Inf.Div.,1055.SS-Rgt. 1.Bn.	MISC.CRIMES	U.S.
KRAFT	103546	M	Ger.		Major, Stalag XIII, Hammelburg (Ger.) 7.44,9.44 und 12.44	TORTURE	U.K.
KRAFT	132066	M	Ger.		Sturmmann, SS, Hohenrheim near Platting (Ger.)	MURDER	U.S.
KRAFT	151967	M			Lt.Col., Oberkommando der Wehrmacht	MISC.CRIMES	U.S.
KRAFT	163456	M	Ger.		Feldgendarmerie, Vielsalm (Bel.) 40 - 44	LOOTING	BEL.
KRAFT	172088	M			Oberscharfhr., SS, C.C. Muehldorf,Ampfing (Ger.) 6.44 - 4.45	MURDER	U.S.
KRAFT	173749	M	Ger.		Hauptsturmfhr., SS, Wirtschaftsgruppe C, Polizei (Yugo.) 42 - 44	MURDER	YUGO.
KRAFT (or KRAUSS)	188747	M			SS, Beaurepaire (Fr.)	MURDER	FR.
KRAFT	253066	M			Cpl., C.C. Ellrich, Nordhausen (Ger.)	MURDER	U.S.
KRAFT	257329	M	Ger.	15	SS - Guard, slave labour camp, Beisfjord near Narvik (Nor.)6.-11.42	BRUTALITY	YUGO.
KRAFT, Bruno	102965	M	Ger.		Crim.-Asst.,SS-Uscharfhr.,Kripo Abtlg. IV Bruessel Kdo.16 z.b.V., Gestapo Koblenz, Ellens (Ger.)	MURDER	U.S. BEL.
KRAFT, Christian	187175	M	Ger.	22. 5.12	Civilian, C.C. Regensburg-Ober-Traubling (Ger.) 42 - 45	WITNESS	U.S.
KRAFT, Georg	253067	M	Ger.		Sturmmann, C.C. Bodungen, Nordhausen (Ger.)	MURDER	U.S.
KRAFT, Hermann	166069	M	Ger.		Major, Abwehr, Stalag 317, Markt Pongau (Ger.)	TORTURE	FR.

KRA-KRA

NAME	C.R.FILE NUMBER	SEX	NATIO-NALITY	DATE OF BIRTH	RANK OCCUPATION UNIT PLACE AND DATE OF CRIME	REASON WANTED	WANTED BY
KRAFT, Hermann	301085	M	Ger.	27.10.07	Pionier, Venduvre, Aube (Fr.) 29.,30.8.44	PILLAGE	FR.
KRAFT, Karel	301266	M	Ger.		Crim.Asst. Abt. IV A, SD, Brussels (Bel.) 6.40-9.44	MURDER	BEL.
KRAFT, Wilhelm	67059	M	Ger.		Pvt., 610.Bn.3.Coy.Dcnziger Kaserne,Elbing, Kdo. 605, Kraksu(Czech.) 11.,12.43	MISC.CRIMES	U.K.
KRAFT, Wilhelm	191387	M	Ger.	3.12.90	Ortsgruppenleiter, NSDAP, Luxembourg-City (Lux.)	MISC.CRIMES	LUX.
KRAFT, Wilhelm	306784	M	Ger.		Pvt., Inf.Nachr.Ers.Coy.112, Sars-La-Bruyere Hainaut (Bel.) 3.,4.9.44	TORTURE	BEL.
KRAHAN	141874	M	Ger.		Colonel, Sletteb (Nor.) 12.42	WITNESS	U.K.
KRAHE, Erich	187174	M	Ger.		Civilian, Camp Ellrich Nordhausen (Ger.)	MURDER	U.S.
KRAHE, Gertrude	134863	F	Ger.		Civilian, Efferen (Ger.)2.10.44	WITNESS	U.S.
KRAHL	167711	M	Ger.		Cpl., General Staff Kommandantur, Crest (Fr.) 7.8.44	MURDER	FR.
KRAHL	193949	M	Ger.		Cpl., Army, Staff, La Rochelle (Fr.)	MURDER	FR.
KRAICZKI	253070	M			Crim.Secretary, Gestapo, C.C. Dora Nordhausen (Ger.)	MURDER	U.S.
KRAIGER, Anna	255171	F	Ger.		Civilian, wife of Gestapo-man, Zlin (Czech.)	WITNESS	CZECH.
KRAIKENBAUM	24863	M	Ger.		Lt.Colonel, Gen. Repl.Bn., Thorn (Pol.) 4.-5.9.44	TORTURE	POL.
KRAINER	189768	M	Ger.		Dr., Expert, at Ger. Legation Zagreb, Sued-Steyermark Laibach Serbia) 41-44	MURDER	YUGO.
KRAINZ, Johann	167708	M	Ger.		Pvt., Army 9.Regt. Res. I. Coy., Magny d' Avignon(Fr.) 18.9.44	MURDER	FR.
KRAIPPE see KREIPPES	300278						
KRAJASCHUTZ	253069	M			Cpl., C.C. Ellrich Nordhausen (Ger.)	MURDER	U.S.
KRAJEWSKY	24896	M	Ger.		Guard, C.C. Hinzert (Ger.) 43	TORTURE	U.S.
KRAL, Georg	255161	M	Ger.	12. 2.19	Informent, SD, Roudnice (Czech.) 42	MISC.CRIMES	CZECH.
KRAL, Hubert (Robert)	305916	M	Ger.	21. 3.92	Farmer, Velke, Heraltice (Czech.) 7.8.44	BRUTALITY	CZECH.
KRAL, Miroslav	255170	M	Ger.	7. 8.14	Confident, Gestapo, SD, Roudnice (Czech.) 42	MURDER	CZECH.
KRALICEK, Anna	192454	F	Ger.	26. 7.14	Clerk, Gestapo, Bruenn (Czech.) 39-45	WITNESS	CZECH.
KRALKA	123139	M	Ger.		Lt., Stalag Official, Employed as censor-at Stalag Luft III Sagan 5.43-1.45	MURDER	POL.
KRALL, Otto	253075	M			Pvt., C.C. Dora Nordhausen (Ger.)	MURDER	U.S.
KRAM	172089	M			Civilian, Org.Todt, C.C. Muehldorf, Ampfing (Ger.)6.44-4.45	MURDER	U.S.
KRAMEL, Josef	253074	M		01	Rottenfhr., C.C. Wolffleben Nordhausen (Ger.)	MURDER	U.S.
KRAMER	1715				SS-Obersturmbannfhr., SS, Strasbourg, Dachau (Ger.)	TORTURE	U.K.
KRAMER	12406	M	Ger.		Lt., CC.Conc.Camp Natzweiler (Fr.) 16.9.42-4.8.42	TORTURE	U.K.,CZECH.
KRAMER	29786	M	Ger.		Capt., Finmark (Nor.)	MURDER	NOR.
KRAMER	125179	M	Ger.		Officier, Gestapo, Schluechtern (Ger.) 20.3.45	MURDER	U.S.
KRAMER	126567	M	Ger.		SS-Hauptsturmfhr., SS, C.C., Natzweiler	MURDER	U.S.
KRAMER	128837	M	Ger.		Pvt., Arbeitskdo. 7902, Stalag V-B C.C. Allmendingen (Ger.)6.3.44	TORTURE	U.K.
KRAMER	131379	M	Ger.		SS-Hauptsturmfhr., (Capt.) C.C. Mauthausen (Austr.) 41-45	MURDER	U.S.
KRAMER	134009	M	Ger.	05	SS-Hauptsturmfhr., C.C. Auschwitz-Birkenau (Pol.) 40-45	MURDER	U.S.
KRAMER	148158	M	Ger.		SS-Unterscharfhr., C.C. Scharziagen (Ger.)	MISC.CRIMES	FR.
KRAMER	169490	M	Ger.	00	Dr., Stabsarzt, Army, Laufen (Ger.) 1.43-7.44	TORTURE	U.K.
KRAMER or KRAMMER	173658		Ger.		SS-Capt., C.C. Brzezink, Birkenau (Pol.)	MURDER	CZECH.,POL.
KRAMER	174775	M	Ger.		Sgt., Kgf. Arb.Bn 2-189 C.C., Fjell (Nor.) 5.44	MURDER	NOR.
KRAMER	194668	M	Ger.		Leiter, Org.Todt, Pornichet (Fr.)	PILLAGE	FR.
KRAMER	256893	M	Ger.		SS-Guard, C.C. Dora, Nordhausen (Ger.)	INTERR.	FR.
KRAMER	300274				Guard, Employing-men, SS serving Dora Camp and Factory C.C. Buchenwald 43- 4.45	MURDER	FR.
KRAMER	301775	M	Ger.		Member, Roumanian Kdo., Gestapo, Vichy (Fr.) 10.,3-9.44	MURDER	FR.
KRAMER	305917	M	Ger.		Oberscharfhr., C.C. Oranienburg (Ger.) 11.39-45	MURDER	CZECH.
KRAMER	305667	F	Ger.		Civilian, Amstetten (Austr.) 20.3.45	MISC.CRIMES	U.S.
KRAMER, B.F.	251103	M	Ger.		Leader, 6.SS Pz.Army, Malmedy (Bel.) 17.12.44	MURDER	U.S.
KRAMER, Frederck or Fritz	305556	M	Ger.		Lt., SS-Untersturmfhr., Gend., Nr. Oberseebach 28.7.44	MURDER	U.K.
KRAMER, Friedrich	172087	M	Ger.		Connected with M-I Lager, Muehldorf, Ampfing (Ger.) 6.44-4.45	MURDER	U.S.
KRAMER, Fritz or KREMER	164134	M	Ger.	16	Pvt., 3-188. Arb.Bn., Between Le Kauger Ervik (Nor.) 10.42	MURDER	NOR.
KRAMER, Fritz or Friedrich	192453	M	Ger.	23.10.01	Lt. Army, Oberseebach (Ger.)	MURDER	CAN.
KRAMER, Josef	190635	M	Ger.		Civilian,Criminalrat, Police, Wiesbaden (Ger.) 43-45	TORTURE	U.S.
KRAMER, Josef	306033	M	Ger.		Kreisleiter, Hameln (Ger.) 4.4.45	MURDER	U.K.
KRAMER, Joseph	24874	M	Ger.	15	Commandant, SS-Hauptsturmfhr., C.C. Struthof (Fr.) 41-42	TORTURE	FR.
KRAMER, Max	254363	M	Ger.		Chief of public security, C.C. Auschwitz-Birkenau (Pol.) 42-45	MISC.CRIMES	YUGO.
KRAMER, Oscar	260155	M	Ger.		Pvt., Army,Luneviller (Meurthe et Mosella)(Fr.)	PILLAGE	FR.
KRAMER, Rupert	254948	M	Ger.		Pvt., Straelen (Ger.) 11.44	MURDER	U.S.
KRAMER, Wilhelm	300055	M	Ger.		Shepherd, Lochtum ar. Vienenburg (Ger.) 19.5.44	MURDER	U.S.
KRAMHOELLER	300948	M	Ger.		Chief, Gestapo, Cilli (Celje)(Yugo.) 12.2.45	MURDER	YUGO.
KRAMKE	172086	M	Ger.		Civilian, Grossnangen (Ger.) 9.44	WITNESS	U.S.
KRAMMER	1415	M	Ger.		Asst., Navy, Naval Supply.	MISC.CRIMES	U.K.
KRAMMER	148159	M	Ger.		Commandant, C.C., Bergen-Belsen (Ger.)	MURDER	FR.
KRAMMER see KRAMER	173658						
KRAMMER	257653		Ger.		Major, SS, Chabris (Fr.) 15.8.44	MURDER	FR.
KRAMMER	254892	M	Ger.		Camp-leader, C.C. Lindenbluete (Ger.) 1.45	BRUTALITY	FR.
KRAMMER, Fritz	12445	M	Ger.		Sgt., Feldgend. 577, Romorantin (Fr.) 7.,8.44	TORTURE	FR.
KRAMMER, Max	261837	M	Ger.		Member, Gestapo, Caen (Fr.)	MURDER	FR.
KRAMPER	178075	M	Ger.		Sturmfhr., SA, C.C. Recklinghausen (Ger.)	TORTURE	U.K.
KRAMUSCHKE	195065	M	Ger.		SS-Rottenfhr., SD, Sonder und Wirtschaftskdo. Beeck, Grossel-Beck (Neth.) 23.9.44	WITNESS	NETH.
KRAN	257504				Employee, O.T., Muhldorf (Ger.)	INTERR.	U.S.
KRANCH or KRANSCH	257015	M	Ger.		Cpl., 2. Nachr.Coy., Bolxes (Neth.)8.5.45	INTERR.	NETH.
KRANCHELER, Michael	253072	M		10. 5.07	Flyer, C.C. Ellrich Nordhausen (Ger.)	MURDER	U.S.
KRANEBITTER, Fritz	188295	M			Dr., Official, Police, Bolzano (It.) 19.3.45	MURDER	U.S.
KRANEFELD	165549	M	Ger.		Kgf.Arb.Kdo. Chief, Deilmen works, C.C. Wernigerode (Ger.) 44	TORTURE	U.K.,BEL.
KRANEFUSS, Fritz	260212	M	Ger.	19.10.00	Mem., Braunkohle-Benzin A.G., Berlin (Ger.)	MISC.CRIMES	U.S.
KRANEK see BRANEK	137058						
KRANEM	252227				Lt., O.C.D.C.A. 51510, Aube (Fr.) 8.44	PILLAGE	FR.
KRANENBROECKER	306094	M	Ger.		SS-U'Scharfhr., SS, at Alderney C.C. (Channel Is)and Kortemark 42-45	MURDER	CZECH.
KRANICH, Hugo	253071	M		11. 5.02	Rottenfhr., C.C. Dora-Ellrich, Nordhausen (Ger.)	MURDER	U.S.
KRANICHSFELD	253077	M			Pvt., C.C. Rossla, Nordhausen (Ger.)	MURDER	U.S.
KRANIXFELD	252228	M	Ger.		Guard, SS, C.C. Buchenwald (Ger.)	INTERR.	FR.
KRANKEMANN	31708	M	Ger.		Cpl., Army, C.C. Oswiecim (Pol.)	MURDER	POL.
KRANKSCHUK	152516	M	Ger.	05	Cpl., Army, 585. Landesschuetzen Bn., Koels near Breslau (ger.)12.43	TORTURE	U.K.

KRA-KRA

NAME	C.R.FILE NUMBER	SEX	NATIO-NALITY	DATE OF BIRTH	RANK OCCUPATION UNIT PLACE AND DATE OF CRIME	REASON WANTED	WANTED BY
KRANS	300797	M	Ger.		Pvt.,1.Aufkl.Abt.,3.Coy.,2.Column,XV.Div.,Afrika Korps,Saint Leger (Arlon) 5.9.44	MISC.CRIMES	BEL.
KRANSCH (see KRANCH)	257015						
KRANZ	504	M	Ger.		Usturmfhr.,SS,C.C.,Boten (Nor.) 3.42-43	MURDER	YUGO.
KRANZ	187568	M	Ger.	83	Sgt.,Brandenburg Div.,C.C.,Oflag IV C,Colditz (Ger.)	TORTURE	U.K.
KRANZ	190506	M			Lt.,Art.Rgt.,Ile D'Oleron (Fr.) 44-17.4.45	TORTURE	FR.
KRANZ, Arthur	152517	M	Ger.	04	4.Coy.,Volkssturm Bn.,Vicinity of Gardelegen (Ger.) 10.-14.4.45	MURDER	U.S.
KRANZ, Erich	128994	M	Ger.	03 - 05	Inspector,Civilian,C.C.,2 B Kommando,Vile Gelow (Ger.) 9.5.44	MURDER	U.S.
KRANZ, Fritz	253082	M			Pvt.,C.C.,Ellrich,Nordhausen (Ger.)	MURDER	U.S.
KRANZ, Gustav	251088	M	Ger.		Feldgendarmerie, (Bel.)	INTERR.	BEL.
KRANZ, Karl	261047	M	Ger.		Staff Sgt.,Gend.,Sables D'Olonne,Benet (Fr.) 25.8.44	MURDER	FR.
KRAPATEN	301776	M	Ger.		Rottfhr.,Blockfhr.,C.C.,Auschwitz (Pol.) 40	MURDER	FR.
KRAPE, Kurt	186748	M			Lt.Col.,950 Inf.Rgt.,Charente,Maritime,Vienne (Fr.) 8.44	TORTURE	FR.
KRAPF	1090	M			Capt.,Army,46.Inf.Rgt.,2.Bn.	MURDER	U.K.
KRAPF	256625	M	Ger.		Sgt.,SS,C.C.,Harzungen,Nordhausen (Ger.)	MURDER	U.S.
KRAPFEL, Michel	254987	M	Ger.	23. 8.92	Gendarm,Gendarmerie,Sierentz,Stetten (Fr.) 23.1.44	MURDER	FR.
KRAPP	505	M	Ger.		Commandant,Army,62.Volksgren.Div.,190.Volksgren.Rgt.,1.Bn., Habscheid,Poitiers, (Ger.,Fr.) 19.or 20.12.44, 8.44	MURDER	U.S.,FR.
KRAPP	256622	M	Ger.		SS-Mann,Bloc leader,Boelke-Kaserne,C.C.,Nordhausen (Ger.)	MURDER	U.S.
KRAPPE	11276	M	Ger.		Col.,Army,Rueffec (Fr.),21.8.44	MURDER	FR.
KRAPPE	186747	M	Ger.		Col.,Army,Vienne (Fr.)	MURDER	FR.
KRAPPE	301245	M	Ger.		Rottfhr.,SS,1.Pz.Aufkl.Abt.12,Ascq (Nord) (Fr.) 1.-2.4.44	MURDER	FR.
KRASCHANSKY, Sebastian	125180	M	Ger.		Guard,SS,C.C.,Helmbrechts,Volary (Czech.)	MURDER	U.S.
KRASCHKEINSKY, Selwastel	135196	M	Ger.		Guard,SS,C.C.,Helmbrechts (Ger.) 7.44-13.4.45	TORTURE	U.S.
KRASERT	167064	M			Capt.,14.Rgt.Parachutiste,Div.53,Adolf Hitler,Villey,St.Etienne (Fr.) 4.9.44	MURDER	FR.
KRASMANN, Walter	173736	M	Ger.		Lt.,487.Inf.Rgt.,Dignies,Courrieres (Fr.) 28.5.40	MURDER	FR.
KRASS	256907	M	Ger.		Lt.,Henrichemont (Fr.) 9.40-3.41	PILLAGE	FR.
KRASS	258782	M			Brigadefhr.,Steines near Lenden (Ger.) 1.45	INTERR.	U.S.
KRAST, Emil	254956	M	Ger.	18. 4.98	Agent,Gestapo,NSDAP,Civilian,Kresice (Czech.) 40-45	INTERR.	CZECH.
KRAST, Emil jun.	254954	M	Ger.	6. 2.21	Officer,SS,Prag (Czech.) 45	MURDER	CZECH.
KRASZ, Karol	258078	M		28.12.99	Civilian,Several places in Slovakia (Czech.) 44	MURDER	CZECH.
KRATH, Peter	240111	M	Ger.	20	Pvt.,Abwehr Nachr.Rgt.506,6.Coy.,Abwehr official,Bad Wildungen (Ger.)45	MISC.CRIMES	U.S.
KRATOCHWILL, Johann	186272	M			Guard,4.SS Totenkopfsturmbann,C.C.,Nordhausen,Dora,Osterode (Ger.)43-45	INTERR.	U.S.
KRATOCHWILL	11277	M	Ger.		Lt.Col.,Army,Chaumont (Fr.) 24.8.44	MURDER	FR.
KRATZ	122524	M	Ger.		Col.,Gestapo,Metz (Fr.) 10.-11.43	TORTURE	U.K.
KRATZ	167223	M	Ger.		Chief of Prison,C.C.,Eberstad (Ger.) 3.44	TORTURE	BEL.
KRATZ	253081	M	Ger.		Cpl.,C.C.,Ellrich,Bischofer,Nordhausen (Ger.)	MURDER	U.S.
KRATZ	301838	M	Ger.		Pvt.,Neighbourhood of Guise (Aisne) (Fr.) 8.44	MURDER	FR.
KRATZ, Adolf	194152	M	Ger.	95	Sgt.,SA,Annerod (Ger.)	MURDER	U.S.
KRATZORN	11278	M			Pvt.,Army,Pz.Gren.Rgt.111,Goudon (Fr.) 29.6.44	MURDER	FR.
KRATZENSTEIN, Karl	164047	M	Ger.		Adjutant,chief,Feldgendarmerie,Montauben (Fr.) 19.8.44-26.7.44	MURDER	U.K.
KRATZER	196762	M	Ger.		Sgt.,Armourer,Izon la Bruisse,Sederon (Fr.) 22.2.44	TORTURE	FR.
KRATZER	301526	M	Ger.		Usturmfhr.,SS,C.C.,Buchenwald (Ger.) 16.5.38-9.10.43	MURDER	BEL.
KRATZER, Anton	259398	M	Ger.		Pvt.,1.Landesschuetzen Bn.540,Sapogne,Ardennes (Fr.) 4.11.42	MURDER	FR.
KRATZLER	135204	M	Ger.		Kreis chief,Gendarmerie,Gerolzhofen (Ger.) 44	MURDER	U.S.
KRAUCHNER, Adolf	141875	M	Ger.	05	Oberarzt,Lazarett,Lamsdorf,Teschen (Ger.) 41-42	TORTURE	U.K.
KRAUER	301010	M			Member of staff C.C.,Struthof,Natzweiler (Fr.) 42-44	MURDER	FR.
KRAUMPFL	169491	M	Ger.	85	Capt.,Army,C.C.,Laufen (Ger.) 11.42-3.43	TORTURE	U.K.
KRAUNESIGIESSER	254358	M	Ger.		Inspector,Gestapo,Charleville,Etalle (Fr.) 6.7.44	MURDER	FR.
KRAUPATZ,Alfred	254637	M	Ger.		Skomlin (Pol.) 30.8.44	MISC.CRIMES	POL.
KRAUS	1416	M	Ger.		N.C.O.,Asst.,Naval Supply.	MISC.CRIMES	U.K.
KRAUS	11556	M	Ger.		Lt.,Air-force,Flak Rgt.,Ortskommandant,Berlevag (Nor.) 44	TORTURE	NOR.
KRAUS	29787	M	Ger.		Major,Army,Gebirgs Div.7,Rgt.82,Finmark (Nor.) 11.44	MURDER	NOR.
KRAUS	29788	M	Ger.		Capt.,Inf.Rgt.324,163.Inf.Div.,Finmark (Nor.) 11.44	MURDER	NOR.
KRAUS	124638	M	Ger.		Cpl.,SD,C.C.,Vulkanlager,Schirmeck (Ger.,Fr.) 16.12.44-1.2.45	MURDER	U.S.
KRAUS (or KARAUSE)	125658	M	Ger.		Lt.,Fallschirmpionier Ers.Bn.,S.P. No. 49925 A,Montaron, Vandenasse (Fr.) 11.7.44	MURDER	FR.
KRAUS	199776	M			Hptsturmfhr.,Waffen SS,Counsel,General Government, (Pol.) 40-44	MISC.CRIMES	U.S.
KRAUS	188113	M			Lt.,Ortskommandantur,Berlevac (Nor.)	MURDER	NOR.
KRAUS	189769	M	Ger.		Doctor,Gestapo,C.C.,Banjica (Yugo.)	MURDER	YUGO.
KRAUS	190665	M	Ger.		Pvt.,Eisenbahn Art.Btty.717,St.Andries,Varsenaye-Gez-Bruges (Bel.) 4.9.45	MURDER	BEL.
KRAUS	192891	M	Ger.		Schupo,C.C.,Falstad,Drontheim (Nor.) 8.-9.42	TORTURE	NOR.
KRAUS	254648	M	Ger.	11	Lt.,F.P.No. 44011 D,Varallo (It.) 18.6.44	MURDER	U.K.
KRAUS	256321	M	Ger.	21	SS Sturmmann,Waffen SS Att.to SS Btty.,Meerveld (Neth.) 11.44	MURDER	NETH.
KRAUS	261642	M	Ger.		Camp-leader,C.C.,Haslach (Ger.)	BRUTALITY	FR.
KRAUS	301777	M	Ger.		Doctor specialist,for injection of formol,C.C.,Auschwitz (Pol.)40-45	MURDER	FR.
KRAUS, Albert	102964	M	Ger.		Civilian,Camp,Hildesheim (Ger.)	MISC.CRIMES	U.S.
KRAUS, Alfred	260412	M	Ger.	22. 6.00	Sgt.,German rural-police,Zalhostice,Bohemia (Czech.) 2.1.44	MURDER	CZECH.
KRAUS, Franz-Xaver	173657	M	Ger.		Sturmbannfhr.,SS,C.C.,Oswiecim,Birkenau (Pol.) 11.44-2.45	MURDER	CZECH.,POL.
KRAUS, Hans	254364	M	Ger.		Sturmbannfhr.,Waffen SS,State service,Cracow (Pol.) 43-44	MISC.CRIMES	POL.
KRAUS, Heinrich	259629	M	Ger.	10	Lt.,guard,Camp Candau des Angles,Avignon,Vaucluse (Fr.) 15.8.44 (Civ.Occ.: Probable. member of corps Ensign at Koblenz)	MURDER	FR.
KRAUS, Heinz	186270	M	Ger.		Oschfhr.,SS,Pysely (Czech.) 6.5.45	TORTURE	CZECH.
KRAUS, Jacob	240112	M	Ger.	14	Pvt.,Nachr.Rgt.506,6.Coy.,Abwehr official,Bad Wildungen (Ger.)42-45	MISC.CRIMES	U.S.
KRAUS, Josef	255162	M	Ger.	23. 7.93	Civilian,Gossengrun,Haberspirk (Czech.) 9.39	MURDER	CZECH.
KRAUS, Karl	145840	M	Ger.		Civilian,factory owner,Neustadt (Ger.)	MURDER	U.S.
KRAUS, Karl	257718	M	Ger.		Employee,C.C.,Dora-Nordhausen (Ger.)	MURDER	U.S.
KRAUS, Mathias	163713	M	Ger.		SS-Mann,La Calamine (Bel.)	MURDER	BEL.
KRAUS, Moritz	301636	M	Ger.		Ebrach near Amberg (Ger.) 45	MURDER	CZECH.
KRAUS, Oskar	302072	M	Ger.		Reichsbahn official,employed in the Fernmeldemeisterei office at Amersfoort (Neth.) 10.44-5.45	PILLAGE	NETH.
KRAUS, Willi	125181	M	Ger.		Police,C.C.,Grueneberg,Helmbrecht (Ger.)	MURDER	U.S.
KRAUSE	1417	M	Ger.		Lt.,Army,1.Coy.,590 A.Bn.,	MURDER	U.K.

KRA-KRA

NAME	C.R.FILE NUMBER	SEX	NATIO-NALITY	DATE OF BIRTH	RANK OCCUPATION UNIT PLACE AND DATE OF CRIME	REASON WANTED	WANTED BY
KRAUSE	24914	M	Ger.	05	Secretary, Gestapo, C.C. Prague (Czech.) 3.39	TORTURE	U.S.
KRAUSE	40541	M	Ger.		Lt.Col., C.C. Kalcar (Italy) 11.44	TORTURE	U.K.
KRAUSE (see KUEHNE, Karl Otto)	186703						
KRAUSE	102963	M	Ger.		Crim.secretary, Gestapo, C.C. Cuxhaven (Ger.) 3.45	MURDER	U.S.
KRAUSE	103644	M	Ger.		Hptsturmfhr., SS, Kopenhagen (Den.) 40	MISC.CRIMES	DEN.
KRAUSE	122608	M	Ger.		Sturmbannfhr., SS, C.C. Auschwitz (Pol.) 42-44	MURDER	FR.
KRAUSE	125182	M	Ger.		Civilian, C.C. Schlesiersee (Ger.)	MURDER	U.S.
KRAUSE	135206	M			Lt., SS, 19.Pol.Regt., 2.Bn., C.C. near Vigaun (Yugo.), Tulle (Fr.) 5.41-10.44	MURDER	U.S.
KRAUSE	137633	M		97	Osturmfhr., SS. (Lith.)	MURDER	U.K.
KRAUSE	143175	M			Agent, Gestapo, Werkschutzleiter, Werkhoerde, Huettenverein, Hoerde (Ger.)	TORTURE	U.S.
KRAUSE	143187	M	Ger.		Osturmfhr., SS Totenkopf-Div., Riga (Latv.), Auschwitz (Pol.) 7.41-43	MURDER	U.S.
KRAUSE	149562	M			Osturmfhr., SS, Cmdt. of Ghetto, Riga (Latv.) 41	MURDER	FR.
KRAUSE	162568	M			Civilian, Gardelegen (Ger.) 4.45	WITNESS	U.S.
KRAUSE	165234	M		95	Dr., Capt., Army, Dossel (Ger.) 45	WITNESS	POL.
KRAUSE	179743	M		15	Lt., 590. Panz.Jaeger Abt., Fucecchio-Marshes (Italy) 7.-8.44	MURDER	U.K.
KRAUSE	190401	F	Ger.		Employee, Kripo, Wiesbaden (Ger.) 43-45	TORTURE	U.S.
KRAUSE	190632	M	Ger.		Crim.-commissar, Gestapo, Brno (Czech.) 39-45	MURDER	CZECH.
KRAUSE	250307	M	Ger.	11	Lt., 2 I-c. S.D., Gestapo for Lombardia Legion, Milan (Italy) 8.44	INTERR.	U.K.
KRAUSE	250905	M	Ger.		Pvt., Seclin (Fr.) 8.44	MURDER	FR.
KRAUSE	252364	M	Ger.		W.O., C.C. Brauderich (Fr.) 30.4.44	TORTURE	FR.
KRAUSE	253083	M			Lt., C.C.Dora-Nordhausen (Ger.)	MURDER	U.S.
KRAUSE	257719	M	Ger.		SS-Sgt., C.C. Mackenrode, Nordhausen (Ger.)	MURDER	U.S.
KRAUSE	259402	M	Ger.		Capt. or Cmdt., SS No.57403 Coy. A.E. and D. Olendon (Fr.) 13.7.44	WITNESS	FR.
KRAUSE	260734			19	Member SS, Eppstein-Taunus (Ger.) 10.44	MURDER	U.S.
KRAUSE	261478	M	Ger.		SS-Sgt., Dirlewanger-Bde., Warsaw and other places (Pol.) 40-44	MURDER	POL.
KRAUSE	300499	M	Ger.		W.O.,Sen., Braudrion, Laudraul (Morbihan) (Fr.) 30.4.44	MURDER	FR.
KRAUSE	300798	M	Ger.		Pvt.,1 Aufkl.Abt.3 Coy.,2 Column,XV Div.of the Africa Corps, Saint Lager(Arlon) 5.9.44	MISC.CRIMES	BEL.
KRAUSE	307003	M	Ger.		Oschfhr.,SS,C.C.Auschwitz(Pol.) 42-45	BRUTALITY	POL.
KRAUSE, Albert	187173	M			Uschfhr.,SS Totenkopf-Sturmbann 4,C.C.Dora Mittelbau,Nordhausen(Ger.) 43-45	TORTURE	U.S.
KRAUSE, Alfred	192892	M	Ger.		Schupo, C.C.Falstad-Dronthein(Nor.) 11.42	TORTURE	NOR.
KRAUSE, Antoin	167063	M		15. 7.89	SS,Hagondange(Fr.) 20.11.43	MURDER	FR.
KRAUSE, Arnost	192452	M		4. 6.04	Sgt.,SS,Zellenleiter NSDAP,Bohemia(Czech.)	SUSPECT	CZECH.
KRAUSE, Clemens	262185	M	Ger.		Member Gestapo, Rennes(Fr.) 43-44	SUSPECT	FR.
KRAUSE, Friedrich	193802	M	Ger.	10	Senior-W.O.,Schnelle Abt.602,Chambord(Fr.) 21.,22.8.44	MURDER	FR.
KRAUSE, Helga	151350	F	Ger.		Secretary,Police,Wiesbaden(Ger.) 2.2.45	MURDER	U.S.
KRAUSE, Herbert	254604	M	Ger.	19. 3.14	Pvt.,13 Coy.,558 Gren.Regt.,Bruayen-Artois(Fr.) 9.44	MURDER	FR.
KRAUSE, Herbert	187257	M			SS-Guard, SS-Mann,4 SS Totenkopf-Stuba,C.C.Dora-Mittelbau,Nordhausen (Ger.) 43-45	MURDER	U.S.
KRAUSE, Horst	191383	M			SS-Usturmfhr.,1 SS Pz.-Regt.,Leibstand.A.H.,Ligneuville,Stoumont (Bel.) 17.-19.12.44	WITNESS	U.S.
KRAUSE, Karl	129690	M	Ger.		Civilian, C.C.Dora,Nordhausen(Ger.)	MURDER	U.S.
KRAUSE, Waldemar	261910	M	Ger.		Lt., Leuze(Bel.) -7.44	MURDER	BEL.
KRAUSE, Wilhelm	1064	M	Ger.		Cmdt.,Army,Feldgend.,Vitry le Francois(Fr.)	TORTURE	FR.
KRAUSE, Willibald	259510	M	Ger.	00	Hauptmannschaftsfuehrer,Gend.-Police,Wolfisheim(Fr.) 14.-15.8.44	SUSPECT	U.S.
KRAUSEN, Arnold	134866	M	Ger.		Civilian,Efferen(Ger.) 2.10.44	WITNESS	U.S.
KRAUSER or KRAUTZER	254569	M	Ger.	95	Member SS Marine Pol.,C.C.Bremen Farge(Ger.)	TORTURE	U.K.
KRAUSER, Albert	253080	M			SS-Uschfhr.,C.C.Mackenrode-Osterode,Nordhausen(Ger.)	MURDER	U.S.
KRAUSER, Johann	145811	M	Ger.		Civilian Farmer,Winkelheid(Ger.)	TORTURE	U.S.
KRAUSKOPF, Edmond	143174	M	Ger.		Ortsgruppenleiter NSDAP,Ruehen,Brechdorf,Passau,Obnsbeck,Bergfeld (Aust.-Ger.)	MISC.CRIMES	U.S.
KRAUSMANN	124981	M	Ger.		Sgt.,C.C.Paris,Prison of Fresnes, Paris,Fresnes(Fr.) 44	TORTURE	FR.
KRAUSS see GROUSE	125463						
KRAUSS	139761	M			Uschfhr.,Guard,Waffen-SS,C.C.Nordhausen(Ger.) 2.45	MURDER	U.S.
KRAUSS	142205	M			Sous Officer,C.C.Flossenburg(Ger.)	MURDER	U.S.
KRAUSS	163712	M	Ger.		Member,Feldgend.,Jalhay Surister(Bel.)	PILLAGE	BEL.
KRAUSS	167066	M	Ger.		Lt.,Army,Placay Buyon(Fr.) 8.-9.44	WITNESS	FR.
KRAUSS	173679	M			Sturmbannfhr.,SS,C.C. Oswiecim-Birkenau(Pol.)	MURDER	CZECH.
KRAUSS see KRAFT	188747						
KRAUSS	257657	M	Ger.		Capt., 338 Div.Cdt.Coy.Pion.,La Bresse(Fr.)	TORTURE	FR.
KRAUSS	260157	M			Gend.,Div.Oberland,Unit.Russ.Ger.,Massif du Vercors Isere et Drome (Fr.) 20.7.-5.8.44	SUSPECT	FR.
KRAUSS	301527	M	Ger.		Uschfhr.,SS,C.C.Dora,Nordhausen(Ger.) 40-45	MURDER	BEL.
KRAUSS	301778	M	Ger.		Doctor, C.C.Auschwitz-Birkenau(Pol.) 40-45	MURDER	FR.
KRAUSS	307004	M	Ger.		Pvt.,Kriegsgericht Utrecht(Neth.) 7.7.44	BRUTALITY	NETH.
KRAUSS, Alfred	189618	M	Ger.	08	Cpl.,Wachtruppe,Chaumont en Vexin(Fr.) 12.8.44	MURDER	FR.
KRAUSS, Bernhard	256879	M	Ger.		Agent,Gestapo,Abbeville(Fr.) 31.8.44	MURDER	FR.
KRAUSS, Franz see EISENBURG	259350						
KRAUSS, Freddy	260156	M	Ger.		C.C.Dachau(Ger.) 42-44	BRUTALITY	FR.
KRAUSS, Joseph or Jupp	257674	M	Ger.		Kapo,C.C.Neuengamme(Ger.)	BRUTALITY	FR.
KRAUSS, Karl	196761	M	Ger.		Lagerfuehrer C.C.Schirmeck(Fr.) 40-44	BRUTALITY	FR.
KRAUSS, Otto	253068	M	Ger.	28. 8.11	Pvt.,C.C.Ellrich,Nordhausen(Ger.)	MURDER	U.S.
KRAUSS, Paul	256132	M	Ger.		Unit 59660B,Louargat(Fr.) 30.1.44	INTERR.	FR.
KRAUSS, Richard	121542	M	Ger.		Oschfhr.,Member SD,Gestapo,Chatel Guyon Clermont-Ferrand(Fr.) 16.8.44	MURDER	FR.
KRAUSS, Willie	261853	M	Ger.		Inspector,Gestapo-Amiens,Gerntelles(Fr.) 6.-8.44	MURDER	FR.
KRAUSS, Willy Bernard	166070	M	Ger.		Uschfhr., Agent Gestapo,SD,Abbeville(Fr.)	MURDER	FR.
KRAUSSEN, Anton	186746	M	Ger.		Feldgend.,Feldgendarmerie Truppe 626,Peronne,Licourt(Fr.) 24.8.44	MURDER	FR.
KRAUT	127403	M	Ger.		Sgt.,SS Trooper,C.C.Ostheim(Ger.)	TORTURE	POL.,U.S.
KRAUT	300799	M	Ger.		Pvt.,1 Aufkl.Abt.,3 Coy.,2 Column,XV Div.of the Africa Corps, Saint L'eger(Arlon) 5.9.44	MISC.CRIMES	BEL.
KRAUT, Hans	187968	M	Ger.		SS-Mann,SD,Gestapo,SS,Trieste(Ital.) 10.44-1.45	TORTURE	U.K.
KRAUTHACKER, Josef	253984	M			C.C.Artern,Nordhausen(Ger.)	MURDER	U.S.
KRAUTHEIM	128996	M	Ger.		Capt.,Kraftfahrpark,KL.Wuerzburg(Ger.) 1.-3.45	TORTURE	U.S.

KRA-KRE

NAME	C.R.FILE NUMBER	SEX	NATIO-NALITY	DATE OF BIRTH	RANK OCCUPATION UNIT PLACE AND DATE OF CRIME	REASON WANTED	WANTED BY
KRAUTKRAEMER, Adam I	186271	M	Ger.	24.12.98	Civilian,Owner of a Factory,Arbeitskommando,Budenheim(Ger.)40-44	TORTURE	U.S.
KRAUTZ, Wilhelm	192893	M	Ger.		Schupo,CC Falstad,Drontheim(Nor.)8.42	MURDER	NOR.
KRAUTZER see KRAUSER	254569						
KRAUZ, Hans	187157	M	Ger.	95	Pvt.4 Coy.Landesschuetzen Bn.515,Jedibab(Czech.)28.2.45	TORTURE	U.K.
KRAUZER	301779	M	Ger.		Dm.,Stubafhr.Selection-CC Auschwitz(Pol.)40	MURDER	FR.
KRAVER	196760	M	Ger.		CC Struthof-Natzweiler(Fr.)40-44	WITNESS	FR.
KRAWATT, Herbert	142037	M	Ger.	15 or 16	Sgt.German Airforce,Uffz,Lehr Kdo.Fliegerhorst,T.C.27,Hopsten(Ger.) 21.3.45	SUSPECT	U.K.U.S.
KRAZERT	306801	M	Ger.		Capt.C.O.Unit nr.Villey,St.Etienne M&M(Fr.)4.9.44	MURDER	FR.
KRAZILIUS see CRISELLIOS	188532						
KREB	135199	M	Ger.		SS Scharfhr.)Sgt.)CC Wittlich,Hinzert(Ger.)41,42,43	TORTURE	U.S.
KREBA, Josef	140784	M			Farmer,Civilian,Krefeld(Ger.)9.42	MURDER	U.S.
KREBBERS, Karl	259821	M	Ger.	9.10.82	Ortsgruppenleiter,Civilian,NSDAP,Freisleitung at Einhoven,S.D., Oirscnot(North Brabant Neth.)43	SUSPECT	NETH.
KREBER	172196	M			SS Uschafhr.Waffen SS,CC Muhldorf,Ampfing(Ger.)6.44-4.45	MURDER	U.S.
KREBS	122607	M			SS Sonderfhr.CC Compiegne(Fr.)	TORTURE	FR.
KREBS	146768	M	Ger.	00	Sgt.Guard,396 Landesschuetzen Bn.Stalag IVA,5 Coy.Dresden(Ger.)3.45	WITNESS	CAN.
KREBS	172084	M	Ger.		Civilian,Grosswangen(Ger.)9.44	TORTURE	U.S.
KREBS	193471	M	Ger.		SS Uschafhr.CC Buchenwald(Ger.)42-45	MISC.CRIMES	U.S.
KREBS	193677	M	Ger.		Lt.Army,Sulmona(It.)30.9.45	MURDER	U.K.
KREBS	253735	M			Cpl.CC Ellrich,Nordhausen(Ger.)	MURDER	U.S.
KREBS, Adolf	251086	M	Ger.		Landwacht,Dist.Lorrach-Dreilaendereck(Ger.)	INTERR.	BEL.
KREBS, Dietrich	253723	M	Ger.		Lagerfhr.CC Sossenheim(Ger.)	BRUTALITY	FR.
KREBS, Ernst	250331	M	Ger.		Member,Nazi-Party,Lorrach-Dreilaendereck(Ger.)	INTERR.	BEL.
KREBS, Gerhard	257401	M	Ger.		SS Usturmfhr.SS-Slave Labour Camp,Osen(Nor.)6.42-3.43	MISC.CRIMES	YUGO.
KREBS, Hans	258987	M	Ger.	98	General,Crimes against peace,War Crimes and Crimes against Humanity	INTERR.	U.S.
KREBS, Hermann	145174	M			Civilian	TORTURE	U.S.
KREBS, Herta	139178	F	Ger.		SS Guard,German Prison,CC Volary(Czech.)	MURDER	CZECH.U.S.
KREBS, Kurt	261488	M	Ger.	08	SS Hptsturmfhr.Gestapo,Montpellier,Mende(Lozere-Fr.)43-44	SUSPECT	FR.
KREBS, Valentin	302074	M	Ger.	13. 2.09	SS Mann,CC Auschwitz(Pol.)9.44-1.45	BRUTALITY	POL.
KREBSACH	141389	M	Ger.		Medecin,SS CC Mauthausen(Aust.)	MURDER	FR.
KREBSBACH, Edward	131382	M	Ger.		Dr.,SS Usturmfhr.CC Mauthausen(Aust.)41-45	MURDER	U.S.
KREBSER	139802	F			CC Weimar-Buchenwald,Dr.(Ger.)42-43	TORTURE	U.S.
KRECHEL, Johann	250306	M	Ger.	2. 1.99	Ortsgruppenleiter,Civilian,NSDAP,Reinsfeld(Ger.)26.12.45	MURDER	U.S.
KREDER, Paul	147299	M	Ger.		Cpl.11 Panzer Div.(Fr.)44	MURDER	FR.
KREEN, Hans or KRIEN	162630	M	Ger.	17	Inspector,Arbeits Kdo.430,Stalag XX B,Bonin(Ger.)23.6.44	MURDER	U.K.
KREFFT, A.	145228	M	Ger.		Sonderfhr.Nantes(Fr.)	WITNESS	U.S.
KREGERSMAN	300057	M	Ger.		Civilian,Signed receipt for leather requisitions from "de Kroon" and taken away by Walter Hohn,Waalwijk and Heusden,43-44	PILLAGE	NETH.
KREHNKE, Hans	507	M	Ger.		SS Osturmbannfhr.Lt.SS,Schupo,Poznan(Pol.)9.39-1.42	MURDER	POL.
KREIBACH	253734	M			Flyer,CC Ellrich,Nordhausen(Ger.)	MURDER	U.S.
KREICZFI	257721	M	Ger.		Criminal secretary,CC Nordhausen(Ger.)	MURDER	U.S.
KREIENBROCK	252208	M			SS Rottfhr.CC Osterhagen,Nordhausen(Ger.)	MURDER	U.S.
KREIFT	252244	M	Ger.		Lt.Gestapo,Paris(Fr.)40-44	TORTURE	FR.
KREIGER	152509	M			SS Scharfhr.SS Signal-Corps,Durnhart(Ger.)26.4.45	MURDER	U.S.
KREIGSKORTE, Werner	24897	M	Ger.		SS Oschafhr.SS Panz.Gren.Div.Das Reich,SS MTN Div.SS Totenkopf	TORTURE	U.S.
KREIMER	134869	M			Guard,SS CC 8 Ohrdruf(Ger.)12.44-4.45	MURDER	U.S.
KREIMER	255550	M	Ger.		Cpl.2 Bn.SS,10 Div.Frundsberg,Remfort Louveciennes-Harly(Fr.)19.-23.8.44	INTERR	FR.
KREIMER, Otto	169489	M	Ger.	07	Pvt.4 Coy.622L.S.Bn.Stalag IX C,Ilmenau(Ger.)6.43	TORTURE	U.K.
KREIN	508	M	Ger.		Stabsfrontfhr.Public Official Organisation Todt,Cherbourg(Fr.)7.-16.5.44	MURDER	FR.
KREIN, Heinz	67825	M	Ger.		Civilian ,Farm Inspector,Deutsch Eylau(Ger.)21.6.44	MURDER	U.K.
KREINDL, Gustav	132829	M	Ger.		SS Uschafhr.CC Mauthausen(Aust.)41-45	MURDER	U.S.
KREINGS	127103	M	Ger.		Doctor,CC Dumeberg,Geestacht(Ger.)	MURDER	FR.
KREIPE	139757	M	Ger.		Oberzahlmeister,Stalag X B,CC Sandbostel(Ger.)1.-5.45	TORTURE	U.S.
KREIPE or KRAIPPE	300278	M	Ger.		Military Commander of the Fortress,West Kissamos Crete,28.-29.8.44	MISC.CRIMES	GRC.
KREIS, Alf.	141573	M	Ger.		Civilian(Fr.)42-43,44	INCENDIARISM	FR.
KREISCHE	133315	M		21	Usturmfhr.Waffen SS,2 Pion.Ausb.Bn.,Passau(Ger.)4.45	MURDER	U.S.
KREISCHE, Walter	506	M	Ger.	93	SS Oschafhr.CC Maidanek(Pol.)40-4.44	MURDER	POL.BEL.
KREISEL, Rudolf	261489	M	Ger.		Lt.Finance-Office and Administration Officer Laterina Camp, Laterina(It.)6.44	SUSPECT	U.S.
KREISER, Adalbert	254847	M			Lt.Finance and Admin.Officer,CC Laterina(It.)	MISC.CRIMES	U.S.
KREISHEIM	139184	M			Pvt.Army CC Guard,Stalag IX C,Kdo.625,Berga(Ger.)	MURDER	U.S.
KREISSER	306926	M	Ger.		Gend.Hauptwachtmeister Ortsgruppenfhr. Golldorf District of Ptuj.4.41-44	MURDER	YUGO.
KREISSL, Anton	194005	M	Ger.	14. 2.95	Dr.,Buergermeister,SS Standartenfhr.Gauhptleiter,Public Official SS, NSDAP,Member of the Reichstag,Podmokly(Czech.)38-45	TORTURE	CZECH.
KREISSNER	173750	M	Ger.		Ortsgruppenfhr.Hptwachtmeister,NSDAP,Gendarmerie,Golldorf(Yugo.)4.41-44	MURDER	YUGO.
KREITENHOF	10021	M	Ger.		SS Hptsturmfhr.CC Dachau(Ger.)39	MURDER	CZECH.
KREITENHOF	189341	M	Ger.		SS Mann,CC Dachau(Ger.)	TORTURE	BEL.
KREITLER, Max	194010	M	Ger.		Cook,Flak Abt.His Comm.was Capt.Sperlbaum,Helden(Neth.)23.10.44	WITNESS	NETH.
KREITLOW	186269	M			SS Uschafhr.CC Mauthausen(Aust.)	TORTURE	
KREITZ see BARBIER	57						
KREITZ	193363	M	Ger.		Cpl.3 Kgf.Arb.Bn.206,Verdalsoera(Nor.)1.-4.45	TORTURE	NOR.
KREITZ	225927	M	Ger.	15	SS Hptscharfhr.-Official,Gestapo,SS,Lyon,Strassburg(Fr.)	MURDER	FR.
KREITZ, Karl	172199	M			SS Uschafhr.Waffen SS,CC Muhldorf,Ampfing(Ger.)6.44-4.45	MURDER	U.S.
KREJA	252209				Oberschuetze,CC Mackenrode,Nordhausen(Ger.)	MURDER	U.S.
KREJOZI, Theo-	167707	M	Ger.		Pvt.Army,9 Regt.Reserve,1 Coy.Magny d'Anigon(Fr.)18.9.44	MURDER	FR.
KREKE	300279		Ger.		Local Commandant,of the Organisation Todt,Rhenen,17.11.44-17.4.45	PILLAGE	NETH.
KREKELER, Theo	301423	M	Ger.		Commandant d'Intendance,FPN.59-250,La Roche sur Yon(Fr.)28.8.44	PILLAGE	FR.
KREKER	167693	M	Ger.		Dr.,Leader,Ernaehrung 5 and Landwirtschafts-Amt,Warschau(Pol.)9.39-44	MISC.CRIMES	POL.
KRELL, Hans	254981				SS Oschafhr.Asst.Gestapo,Troyes,C'Aube(Fr.)43-44	MISC.CRIMES	FR.
KRELLE	252210	M			Schuetze,CC Rottleberode,Nordhausen(Ger.)	MURDER	U.S.
KRELLER, Jean	257515	M	Ger.		Krim.Ob.Asst.Hptscharfhr.Feldpolizei,Foix(Fr.)42-44	INTERR	FR.
KRELLMANN	257720	M	Ger.		SS Scharfhr.Medical Attendent in charge CC Nordhausen(Ger.)	MURDER	U.S.

KRE - KRE

NAME	C.R.FILE NUMBER	SEX	NATIO- NALITY	DATE OF BIRTH	RANK OCCUPATION UNIT PLACE AND DATE OF CRIME	REASON WANTED	WANTED BY
KRELIMANN	306095	M	Ger.		SS-Oberscharfhr., Alderney C.C. (Channel I S) and Kortemark C.C. 42-45	MURDER	CZECH.
KREM, Andreas	172197	M			Member, W-SS, C.C. Mühldorf, Ampfing (Ger.) 6.44- 4.45	MURDER	U.S.
KREMA, Otto	194149	M	Ger.		2.SS Panzer-Gren.-Ausb.und Ers.Bn. 12, Berneau (Bel.) 44	MURDER	BEL.
KREMER	131980	M	Ger.		Cpl., Army, Gievenbeck (Ger.) 3.45	MURDER	BEL.
KREMER, Adolf	131381	M	Ger.		Civ., Siegburg (Ger.) 3.-8.42	MURDER	BEL.
KREMER, Franz	187664	M	Ger.	18. 8.92	Scharfhr., SA, Aachen (Ger.) 8.44	TORTURE	U.S.
KREMER, Fritz (see KRAMER)	164134						
KREMER, Willy	121631	M	Ger.		N.C.O., 986. Feldgendarmeristrupp, St.Illide (Fr.) 3.44	INCENDIARISM	FR.
KREMMEL	179934	M			Sturmscharfhr., S.D., Secr., Gestapo, Saarbruecken (Ger.)	PILLAGE	FR.
KREMMET, Georges	254973	M	Ger.	17. 8.93	SS-Sturmfhr., Chief of Gestapo, Sare (Fr.)	INTERR.	FR.
KREMP, Paul	179935	M	Ger.		Unterscharfhr., S.D., Secr., Gestapo, Saarbruecken (Ger.)	PILLAGE	FR.
KREMSER, Karl	179936	M	Ger.		Obersturmfhr., SS 14 1.Pz.Regt., Leibst."A.Hitler", Malmedy (Bel.) 44	MURDER	FR.
KRENDT, Ewald	187706	M	Ger.		Pvt., 9.Regt., Res., 1.Coy., Magny d'Anigon (Fr.) 9.44	MURDER	FR.
KRENN, Max	259928	M	Ger.		Crim.Secr., Gestapo, Leskoc near Brno, Moravia (Czech.) 4.45	MURDER	CZECH.
KRENNER	196790	M	Ger.		Pvt., C.C. Struthof-Natzweiler (Fr.) 40-45	MISC.CRIMES	FR.
KRENNITZ-MULLER	189229	M	Ger.		SS Pol.-Regt. 19, 3.Coy., St. Jeore Chattillon, Luces, Taninges (Fr.) 6.-7.44	TORTURE	FR.
KRENZ	176843	M	Ger.		Group-leader, NSDAP, Muggelherin (Ger.) 3.45	TORTURE	U.S.
KRENZKI, Kurt	62415	M	Ger.		Lt.Gen., Inf., Military Cmdt., Saloniki (Grc.)	TORTURE	U.N.W.C.C.
KREPS	103725	M	Ger.		Capt., Gestapo, Err (Fr.) 5.-9.43	PILLAGE	FR.
KREPS	132590	M			SS-Obersturmbannfhr., Sousse (Tunisie)	TORTURE	FR.
KRESBACH, Edward or Eduard	131384	M		95	SS-Sturmbannfhr., Physician, C.C. Mauthausen (Aust.) 41-45	SUSPECT	YUGO.
KRESEL	257402	M	Ger.		SS-Guard, Slave labour camp, Beisfjord near Narvik (Nor.) 6.-11.42	BRUTALITY	YUGO.
KRESS	145166	M		17	Agent, NSDAP, S.D., Attenkirchen, Sillertshausen (Ger.) 6.44	MURDER	U.S.
KRESS	167943	M	Ger.		Stabsfhr., Einsatzstab Rosenberg, (Fr.) 40-44	PILLAGE	FR.
KRESS, Heinrich	250305	M	Ger.	28. 8.93	W.O., 4046.Volkssturm-Bn., Dirmstein (Ger.) 2.45	MURDER	U.S.
KRESSBACH	179937	M			Cmdt., Dr., Official, C.C. Mauthausen (Aust.)	MURDER	FR.
KRESSE	161256	M			Lt., Army, Sturm-Bn. AOK, 1.Coy., Courcelles sur Nied (Fr.) 15.11.44	WITNESS	U.S.
KRESTCHNER	188746	M	Ger.		Member, Feldgendarmerie, Bar-le-Duc (Fr.) 20.,21. and 28.8.44	MURDER	FR.
KRESTCHNER	306621	M	Ger.		N.C.O., 5 Coy. 100 Bn., Gebirgsjaeger, Vilette (Savoie) (Fr.) 9.6.44	MURDER	FR.
KRESTOSCHWIL	11279	M	Ger.		Pvt., Army, Pz.Gren.Regt.111, Albine (Fr.) 29.6.44	MURDER	FR.
KRETA	67060	M	Ger.		Major, Army, Artl., C.C. Heydebreck (Ger.) 8.44	TORTURE	U.K.
KRETEK, Emil	252356	M		28. 1.09	SS-Uscharfhr., C.C. Nordhausen (Ger.)	MURDER	U.S.
KRETER, Karl	187136	M	Ger.		Civilian, Ladenburg (Ger.)	TORTURE	U.S.
KRETSCHAMER	173714	M	Ger.		Sgt., warder in C.C. Hemburg (Ger.) 41-42	TORTURE	BEL.
KRETSCHAR	510	M			Officer, Gestapo, C.C. Pilla (Ger.) 9.-12.39	TORTURE	POL.
KRETSCHMAR	127404	M			SS-Osturmfhr., Gestapo, C.C. Buchenwald (Ger.)	TORTURE	U.S.
KRETSCHMAR	131988	M	Ger.		Sgt., C.C. Neuengamme (Ger.) 41-42	TORTURE	BEL.
KRETSCHMAR	162054	M	Ger.		Foreman, Adolf-Mine, Merkstein (Ger.) 42-44	TORTURE	U.S.
KRETSCHMAR,Hans	252357	M			Pvt., C.C. Ellrich, Nordhausen (Ger.)	MURDER	U.S.
KRETSCHMAR, Karl	187155	M	Ger.	01	SS-Mann, guard, 4 SS-Totenkopf-Sturmbann, C.C. Dora-Mittelbau, Nordhausen (Ger.) 43-45	TORTURE	U.S.
KRETSCHMAR, Werner	306622	M	Ger.		Officer commanding, 5 Coy., St. Viand (Loire-Inferieure), Le Moulin Neuf (Fr.) 12.9.44	MURDER	FR.
KRETSCHMER,Emil	254559	M	Ger.	9. 2.99	Employee an country estate, civilian, Pardubice (Czech.) 39-45	MISC.CRIMES	CZECH.
KRETSCHMER,Karl	252358	M	Ger.	11. 4.01	Pvt., C.C. Nordhausen (Ger.)	MURDER	U.S.
KRETSCHMER,Wilhelm	258080	M	Ger.	29. 5.97	Member, State Service, Abwehrstelle, Prag (Czeh.) 39-45	MURDER	CZECH.
KRETTEK,Emil	187154	M	Ger.	28. 1.09	SS-Uscharfhr., 4 SS-Totenkopf-Sturmbann, C.C. Dora-Mittelbau, Nordhausen (Ger.) 43-45	TORTURE	U.S.
KRETZER	131760	M	Ger.		Oberwachtmeister, C.C. Schirmeck (Fr.) 40-44	MISC.CRIMES	FR.
KRETZER	161880	M	Ger.		Civilian, Schouweise (Ger.)	WITNESS	U.K.
KRETZER	185092	M	Ger.		Sgt., guard, C.C. Schirmeck (Fr.)	MURDER	FR.
KRETZER	301781	M	Ger.		Osturmfhr., Transportfhr., C.C. Auschwitz (Pol.) from 1940	MURDER	FR.
KREUER	251675	M	Ger.		Lt., 2606 Ers.Bn. Turkestan, Massif du Vercors (Fr.) 7.-8.44	MURDER	FR.
KREUGER	305668	M	Ger.		Capt., Dulag 377, Gerolstein, between 1912.44 and 5.2.45	MISC.CRIMES	U.S.
KREUGER,Hans-Joachim	141872	M	Ger.	4. 3.25	Pvt., Fallsch.Jaeger-Regt.16, II Coy., 3 Bn.	WITNESS	U.S.
KREUSCHNER,Peter	261942	M	Ger.		Interpreter, SS, Belgrad and Valjevo (Yugo.) 8.42-9.44	SUSPECT	YUGO.
KREUSER	24898	M	Ger.	05	Sgt., Army, C.C. Rheinbach (Ger.)	TORTURE	U.S.
KREUTLER	29789	M			Bde.-Gen., Army, Finmark (Nor.)	MURDER	NOR.
KREUTZ	179938	M			Sturmscharfhr., SD, secretary, Gestapo, Sarrebruck (Ger.)	PILLAGE	FR.
KREUTZ,Albert	306420	M	Ger.		SS-Uscharfhr., SD, Ulven near Bergen (Nor.) about 7.43	MURDER	U.K.
KREUTZ,Louis	259399	M	Ger.		Hptscharfhr., Gestapo of Poitiers (Fr.) 40-45	MISC.CRIMES	FR.
KREUTZEN,Max	130328	M	Ger.		Cpl., Airforce, Westertimke and Zex (Ger.) 1945	MURDER	U.K.
KREUTZER or KREUZER	191905	M	Ger.		Osturmfhr., SS, Prasvalle Moutiers en Beauce Villebon (Fr.) 6.44-8.44	MURDER	FR.
KREUTZER	252359	M			SS-Hptscharfhr., C.C. Dora, Nordhausen (Ger.)	MURDER	U.S.
KREUTZINGER	29790	M	Ger.		SS-Hptsturmfhr., SS-Geb.Jg.Regt.12, Finmark (Nor.) 11.44	MURDER	NOR.
KREUZ,Alfred	255406	M	Ger.		Usturmfhr., SS, Both (Nor.) 41-43	MURDER	YUGO.
KREUZ, Christian	173228	M		12	Pvt., 4 Coy., 515 Landesschtz.-Bn., Prag (Czech.) 3.45	MURDER	U.K.
KREUZ, Ferdinand	254570	M	Ger.		Manager of restaurant, C.C. Moravska-Ostrava (Czech.) 1945	INTERR.	CZECH.
KREUZ, Jan	254963	M	Ger.		Executioner, civilian, Prag (Czech.) 43-45	MURDER	CZECH.
KREUZ,Johann or KRIZ	254964	M	Ger.	18. 6.93	Stone-cutter, civilian, Prag (Czech.) 39-45	MURDER	CZECH.
KREUZ,Wilhelm	253738	M	Ger.	13. 8.15	Member, Gestapo, Hradec Kralove (Czech.) 39-45	MURDER	CZECH.
KREUZ,Wilhelm	127405	M	Ger.		Guard, C.C. Buchenwald (Ger.)	TORTURE	U.S.
KREUZER	162052	M	Ger.	05	Pvt., Army, Walberberg (Ger.) 1941	MURDER	POL.
KREUZER	136244	M	Ger.		Cpl., C.C. Marseille (Fr.)	MURDER	FR.
KREUZER	138297	M	Ger.		SS-Usturmfhr., chief of Aussenkdo., Chartres (Fr.) 1942	MURDER	FR.
KREUZER	139172	M	Ger.		Standartenfhr., N.S.K.K.	WITNESS	U.S.
KREUZER	189225	M	Ger.		Usturmfhr., SS Hauptamt, Martin de Nigelle, Chartres (Fr.) 8.-14.12.43	MURDER	FR.
KREUZER see KREUTZER	191905						
KREUZER, Peter	252360	M		14.12.09	Flyer, C.C. Ellrich, Nordhausen (Ger.)	MURDER	U.S.
KREUZER,Renate	124602	F	Ger.		C.C. Hannover-Limmer (Ger.)	TORTURE	BEL.
KREUZER,Richard	138210	M	Ger.		C.C. Woippy (Fr.)	TORTURE	FR.

NAME	C.R.FILE NUMBER	SEX	NATIO-NALITY	DATE OF BIRTH	RANK OCCUPATION UNIT PLACE AND DATE OF CRIME	REASON WANTED	WANTED BY
KREUZINGER	62542	M	Ger.	09	Pvt.,Army,Paratrooper under command of Major Matthaeas, Roermond(Neth) 26.11.44-18.1.45	TORTURE	U.S.
KREUZNACKER	152510	M	Ger.		Lt.,Army,Oflag VII-C, CC Laufen(Ger.) 10.11.40	MURDER	U.K.
KREUZTHALER	306204		Ger.		Member SS,Kochendorf, Dachau(Ger.) 3.4.45	MURDER	CZECH.
KREY, Hans	167687	M	Ger.		Dr., Civilian, Firma "Fabryka Jedwakiv",Gmurowski,Poznan(Pol.) 9.39-12.44	MISC.CRIMES	POL.
KREYSING, Hans	258989	M	Ger.	90	General,crimes against peace,war crimes and crimes against humanity	WITNESS	U.S.
KRIBPE, Franz	240113	M	Ger.	07	Official,SD,Head of Abteilung IV,Vichy(Fr.) 44	MISC.CRIMES	U.S.
KRIBITZ, Gustav	250313	M			Cpl.,3 Brandenbg.Rgt. (Ger.)	INTFR.	U.S.
KRICHELDORF, Gerhard	172192				Member Hitler Jugend, CC Gardelegen(Ger.) 10.-14.4.45	MURDER	U.S.
KRICHMAIER (see KIRCHMAIER)							
KRICHTEL	255165	M	Ger.		Scharfhr, SD, Toulouse (Fr.) 11.42-6.8.44	MURDER	FR.
KRICK, Karl	132517	M	Ger.	07	Cpl., Army,Nachr.Coy,Heikstal Radio Station (Ger.) 12.9.44	TORTURE	U.S.
KRICKBERGER	253076				SS Schfhr, CC Rottleberode, Nordhausen (Ger.)	MURDER	U.S.
KRICKELS	194150	M	Ger.		Officer, 2 SS Pz.Gren.Ausb.Ers.Bn.12,Berneau(Bel.) 5.9.44	MURDER	BEL.
KRICKS, Willi	151351	M		17	Pvt.,Army,Oflag 64, CC Schubin(Pol.)19.12.44	PILLAGE	U.S.
KRIDEE	24864	M	Ger.		Col.,Army,CC Stalag VI, Duisdorf(Ger.)	TORTURE	U.S.
KRIEBES(see GREPS)	135767						
KRIECHBAUM, Franz Xaver	240114	M	Ger.		Crim.Secr.,Gestapo,Regensburg, Poland 45	MURDER	U.N.W.C.C.
KRIEG, Hermann	142206	M			Civilian, Gernsbach(Ger.)	MURDER	FR.
KRIEG, Karl (see KRIKE)	173752						
KRIEG, Nicholas	172082	M	Ger.		Leader of Landwacht Group,Gernsbach,Weissenbach(Ger.)9.8.44	MURDER	U.S.
KRIEG, Peter	102962				Sgt., CC Warstein and Suttrop(Ger.)20.-21.or 22.3.45	MURDER	U.S.
KRIEGEL, Georges	165383	M	Ger.	23.12.94	SS, Hagondange (Fr.) 20.11.43	MURDER	FR.
KRIEGELSTEIN	139801	M			SS Oschfhr, CC Weimar, Buchenwald (Ger.)	TORTURE	U.S.
KRIEGELSTEINER, Josef	254977	M	Ger.		Commissioner, Rassenpolitik,Cheb (Czech.)39-45	MURDER	CZECH.
KRIEGER (see KRIGER)	126457						
KRIEGER	145185	M	Ger.		Kit.Asst.,Gestapo, CC Breslau(Ger.)	TORTURE	U.S.
KRIEGER	189078	M	Ger.	88	Commander,Gestapo, Stanislawow(Pol.) 8.41-1.10.42	MURDER	POL.
KRIEGER	255537	M	Ger.		Capt.,Hallainville(Fr.) 10.44	PILLAGE	FR.
KRIEGER, Adolf	255541	M	Ger	03	Oberwachtmstr, Member firing squad.,Prag-Kobylisy(Czech.) 42	MURDER	CZECH.
KRIEGER, August	187153	M			SS-Mann, 4 SS Totenk.Sturmbann, CC Dora,Mittelbau,Nordhausen(Ger.) 43-45	MURDER	U.S.
KRIEGER, Bruno	178965	M		12	Osturmfhr, Crim.Comm., SD, Gestapo, Praha,Tabor(Czech.)42-44	MURDER	CZECH.
KRIEGER, Eberhard (see KRUEGER)	261650						
KRIEGER, Friedrich Wilhelm	260677	M			Crimes against peace,war crimes and crimes against humanity	WITNESS	U.S.
KRIEGER, Hans Walter	261121	M	Ger.	22.2.10	Dr.,SS Hptsturmfhr,Crim.Comm.,Gestapo,Prag(Czech.) 42-45	MISC.CRIMES	CZECH.
KRIEGER, Ludwig	258425	M			Guard, SS, CC Ohrdruf(Ger.) 12.44-4.45	MURDER	U.S.
KRIEGER, Maximilian	261641	M	Ger.		Proxy, Northwest France 40-45	BRUTALITY	FR.
KRIEGER, Peter	189770	M			Deputy Cmdt., CC Banjica (Yugo.)	MURDER	YUGO.
KRIEGER, Richard	162271	M	Ger.	84	Dr., SS Sturmbannfhr,W-SS, CC Dachau,Buchenwald(Ger.) 43-44	WITNESS	U.S.
KRIEGER, Richard	301138	M			Doctor, Medical Officer, CC Struthof-Natzweiler(Fr.) 42-44	MURDER	FR.
KRIEGERMEIER, Fritz	189079	M	Ger.		Member Gestapo,Stanislawow(Pol.) 8.41-1.10.42	MURDER	POL.
KRIEN, Hans (see KREEN)	162630						
KRIEPP	511	M	Ger.		O.C., Army,Fussilier Bn.,3 Coy, Vernon(Fr.) 21.8.44	MURDER	U.K.
KRIES, Hermann	152512	M	Ger.	90	Civilian,Foreman on Railway, CC Bitterfeld(Ger.)10.43-4.45	TORTURE	U.K.
KRIESE, Edmund	259151	M	Ger.		Rottfhr, SS, CC Dachau(Ger.) 9.42	MISC.CRIMES	YUGO.
KRIESER, Helmut	512	M	Ger.		Dr., Legal Official in justice Department,Prag(Czech.)27.9.41-3.7.42	MURDER	CZECH.
KRIEWALD, Herbert	193075	M	Ger.	7.10.05	Hptwachtmstr,Guard,Ministry of Justice,Feldstraflager,W-SS, Finmark(Nor.) 42-45	MISC.CRIMES	NOR, YUGO.
KRIGER, Werner	126457	M	Ger.		Orpo(Feld-Gend.), Verdonce(Fr.) 10.8.44	MURDER	U.S.
KRIJOM	191452	M	Ger.		Hptschfhr, SS, Crim.Secr., Gestapo, Norway 4.40	TORTURE	NOR.
KRIKE,Karl (or KRIEG)	173752	M	Ger.		Prison, Vannes (Fr.) 44	MURDER	FR.
KRIMKOVSKI	250872	M	Ger.		Pvt., Pepingen (Bel.) 2.-9.44	INTERR.	BEL.
KRIMM, Heintz	177601	M	Ger.		SS Sturmschfhr, Gestapo, Saarbruecken(Ger.)	MURDER	U.K.
KRIMMEL	196788	M	Ger.		Cpl., Overseer, CC Compiegne (Fr.) 41-44	INTERR.	FR.
KRINER, Rudolf	195523	M	Ger.	12	Employee, SS-Sgt., Gestapo, SD, Kolin (Czech.) 39-45	MURDER	CZECH.
KRINGEL	254897	M			Insp., H.Q.Brandenburg Div.	INTERR.	U.S.
KRINGS, Hans	240115	M	Ger.	15	Official, Nachr.Rgt.506 Abwehr, 6 Coy, Bad Wildungen(Ger.)40-45	MISC.CRIMES	U.N.W.C.C.
KRINNER, Josef	151320	M	Ger.	25.11.81	Civilian, Town-priest of Seyboldsdorf,Nilsbiburg(Ger.)28.4.45	WITNESS	U.S.
KRIPHER, Hans	141871	M	Ger.	07	Cpl., Inf.Div. 355,214, CC Slettab, Hellelland, Stavanger(Nor.)20.11.42	WITNESS	U.K.
KRIPPNER	121693	F	Ger.		SS Overseer, CC Ravensbrueck (Ger.) 42-45	MURDER	FR.
KRIPPNER	306629	M	Ger.		Sgt., Interpreter with the Feld-Gend.Chateaubriant(Loire-Inf'erieure), St.Julien de Mouvantes Soudan Juigne-les-Moutiers le Teillais (Loire-Inferieure) France 21.7.44	MURDER	FR.
KRIPPS, Michael	167510	M	Ger.	1907-17	Wachtmstr,Pol.Rgt.Schlanders,2 Bn.,8Coy,Campomelon(It.)	MURDER	U.S.
KRIPS, Karl Heinz	192451	M	Ger.		Army Prisoner, FT Zinna(Ger.) 45	MURDER	U.S.
KRISCH	253867	M	Ger.		Auxiliary Police Official, Dep.III A Sipo,Brussels(Bel.) 40-44	INTERR.	BEL.
KRISCHER	24899	M			SS Doctor, CC Hinzert(Ger.) 43	TORTURE	U.S.
KRISMER	162355	M			Dir., PoW-Arbeits-Kdo.; Mines Siemens,Nuernberg(Ger.)	TORTURE	FR.
KRISPONEIT, Lothar	261048	M			Engineer at Patins firm, Berlin, Besancon (Fr.)31.8.44	PILLAGE	FR.
KRIST	146988	M	Ger.		Hptsturmfhr, SS Police, 19 Rgt., Alex (Fr.) 44	MURDER	FR.
KRIST, Engbert	302076	M	Ger.		Member of Sonderkdo.Feldmeier,Apeldoorn,Arnhem(Neth.)16.1.43, 19.7.44, 28.10.44, 6.7.44	MURDER	NETH.
KRIST, Franz	257107	M	Ger.	25.1.08	Guard, Prison, Bruenn (Czech.) 39-45	TORTURE	CZECH.
KRISTANDT	195453	M	Ger.		Reg.Rat, occupied territories, Luxemburg 40-45	PILLAGE	LUX.
KRISTEL, Johann	11280	M	Ger.		Pvt., 110 or 111 Pz.Gren.Rgt., Albine (Fr.) 29.6.44	MURDER	FR.
KRISTIAN	259401	M	Ger.		Chief of Civilian Budget, Registrar of Camp,Auschwitz(Pol.)	BRUTALITY	FR.
KRISTL, Franz	301065	M	Ger.		SS-Mann,CC Oranienburg(Ger.) 11.39-45	MURDER	CZECH.
KRISTIAN	28843	M	Ger.		Dr., Oberlandgerichtsrat,Public Official,Litomevice(Czech.)21.2.40	MURDER	BEL.
KRISTOF, Paul	306096	M	Ger.		SS-Mann, Alderney CC(Channel Is), Kortemark CC 42-45	MURDER	CZECH.
	173751				Pvt., Mmtr,70 Rgt.,d'artillerie de reserve, Tours,Albertville(Fr.) 8. and 23.6.44		
KRISTUKAT	167942	M	Ger.		Kreiskommandant, Kreiskommandantur,Chateaubriant(Fr.)28.10.41-15.12.41	MURDER	FR.
KRITTER	186745	M	Ger.		Lt., 950 R.I.H., Charente et Vienne (Fr.) 8.44	TORTURE	FR.
KRITZINGER (or KITZINGER)	62416	M	Ger.		Officer, Army, MilitaryComdr.Ukraine (Russia)	MURDER	U.N.W.C.C.

KRI - KRO

NAME	C.R.FILE NUMBER	SEX	NATIO-NALITY	DATE OF BIRTH	RANK OCCUPATION UNIT PLACE AND DATE OF CRIME	REASON WANTED	WANTED BY
KRITZINGER	251663	M	Ger.	10	Guard, PW Camp Laterina (It.)	MURDER	U.K.
KRITZSCH	257722	M	Ger.		SS-Capt.,Camp-leader,Ellrich,Nordhausen (Ger.)	MURDER	U.S.
KRIVAN, Alois	186268	M	Ger.		Cpl.,Army,Floria (Grc.) 9.44	MURDER	GRC.
KRIWAISKI, Martin	187150	M			SS-Pvt.,Guard,4 SS Totenkopf Sturmbann,C.C.Dora Mittelbau,Nordhausen (Ger.) 43-45	TORTURE	U.S.
KRIZ,Johann (see KREUZ)	254964						
KRIZ	257791	M	Ger.		Aid Man 37 Rgt.Station,St.Eny (Fr.)	MURDER	U.S.
KRMASCHEK, Rudolf	254580	M	Ger.	7.4.85	Town official,local Government of Gestapo,Frydek (Czech.) 39-45	MURDER	CZECH.
KRNHN, Josef	133800	M	Ger.		SS-Uschfhr.,	TORTURE	U.S.
KRNBATH, Valentin	254159	M			Member,Landwache,Ferlach (Aust.) 44-45	MURDER	YUGO.
KROCH, Clement	302077	M			SS-Mann,serving in Section IV Gestapo Poitiers,La Rochelle (Fr.)40-44	MURDER	FR.
KROCK, Clement	259400	M			SS-Major,Sturmbannfhr.,Gestapo,Poitiers Area (Fr.) 40-44	MISC.CRIMES	FR.
KROECHEL	11281	M	Ger.		Pvt.,110 or 111 Pz.Gren.Rgt.,Albine (Fr.) 29.6.44	MURDER	FR.
KROEGEL	253079	M			C.C.Rottleberode,Nordhausen (Ger.)	MURDER	U.S.
KROEGER	102934	M	Ger.		Capt.,C.C.Dulag Luft,Klosterwald (Ger.)	TORTURE	U.K.
KROEGER, Walter	179927	M	Ger.		Member,Gestapo,Pardubice (Czech.) 39-45	TORTURE	CZECH.
KROEK, Albert	187149	M	Ger.		Arzt,Stalag VI A,C.C.Hemer (Ger.) 40-45	MURDER	U.S.
KROELING, Wilhelm	260411	M	Ger.	02	Member,Gestapo,Pelhrimov (Czech.) 39-45	MISC.CRIMES	CZECH.
KROELLING, Ignac	250304	M			SS-Mann,Konopiste (Czech.) 19.4.45	INTERR.	U.S.
KROEMER	301782	M	Ger.		Hststurmfhr.,Dr.Garrison staff,C.C.Auschwitz (Pol.) 40	MURDER	FR.
KROEMER, Charlotte	189753	F	Ger.		Clerk,Gestapo,Brno (Czech.) 39-45	WITNESS	CZECH.
KROEN, Bruno (or GRUN or GRUNE)	300280		Ger.		N.C.O. of the secret Fieldpolice,Utrecht (Neth.) 3.3.45-5.4.45	MISC.CRIMES	NETH.
KROENER	254958	M	Ger.	90	Osturmfhr.,C.C.Auschwitz-Birkenau (Pol.) 40	MURDER	FR.
KROENERT	191284	M			Pvt.,Eisenbahn Art.Btty.717,St.Andries Varsenare les Bruges (Bel.)9.44	MURDER	BEL.
KRUENPPING	126955	M	Ger.		Officer,chief of labour camp,Gestapo,Anrath (Ger.) 41-45	MURDER	FR.
KROEPEL, Franz	253101	M		11.6.11	Flyer,C.C.Ellrich,Nordhausen (Ger.)	MURDER	U.S.
KROEPLIN, Joachim	62543	M			Pvt.,Paratrooper,Roermond (Neth.) 11.44-1.45	TORTURE	U.S.
KROESSER, Rudolf	190664	M	Ger.		Crim.-employee,Gestapo,Brno (Czech.) 39-45	MURDER	CZECH.
KROESSMANN	162392	M			Pvt.,7-4 Ldsch.Bn.,Stalag XX A,Borowke (Pol.) 15.12.41	MURDER	U.K.
KROG	254594	M	Ger.		SA,Gadebusch (Ger.)	MURDER	U.S.
KROGER, Aloys	172080	M			Civilian,Railway-man,Railway,Lengerich (Ger.) 24.8.44	TORTURE	U.S.
KROGER, Paul	162788	M	Ger.		SS-Sturmbannfhr.,Waffen SS,Sec.Guard,C.C.Buchenwald (Ger.) 40	WITNESS	U.S.
KROH	174823	M			Col.,20 Div.Parachutist,Finistere (Fr.) 44	MURDER	FR.
KROH, Fritz	260522	M		22.8.11	SS-Guard,C.C.Natzweiler (Fr.)	MURDER	FR.
KROHF	196787	M			Sgt.,treasurer,Jzon la Bruisse (Fr.) 22.2.44	MISC.CRIMES	FR.
KROHN	191285	M			Pvt.,Eisenbahn Art.Abt.717,St.Andries Varsenare les Bruges,(Bel.)4.9.44	MURDER	BEL.
KROHN (or KROHNE)	261025	M		05	Senior W.O.,8 Coy Brandenburg Div.,spec.unit,Bouche du Rhone,Var Vaucluse (Fr.) 43-44	MISC.CRIMES	FR.
KROHN, Alfred	174824	M			Pvt.,Fallschirmjg.Rgt. 2 Bn.,Plouzane (Fr.) 44	MURDER	FR.
KROHN, Bruno	162791	M		07	Pvt.,Ldsch.Bn.398, 5 Coy Arbeitskdo.E 132,Stalag VIII B,Gogolin (Ger.) 7.42	MURDER	U.K.
KROHN, Josef (or KRON)	162789	M	Ger.	10	Untersturmfhr.,Waffen SS,C.C.Buchenwald (Ger.) 42-45	TORTURE	U.S.
KROHNE	196786	M	Ger.		W.O.,Section-Instruction,Jzon la Bruisse Sederen (Fr.) 22.2.44	MISC.CRIMES	FR.
KROHNE (see KROHN)	261025						
KROHNE	306231	M	Ger.		Aide,Waffen SS,Vercoiran (Drome) (Fr.) 9.3.44	MURDER	FR.
KROL (or KRUEL)	132799	M			SS-Oschfhr.,C.C.Weimar,Buchenwald (Ger.)	MURDER	U.S.
KROL	255600	M			Hptschfhr.,C.C.Buchenwald (Ger.)	MURDER	U.S.
KROLIKOVSKI, Walter	145807	M			Korvetten Kapitaen,Navy,Borkum (Ger.) 4.8.44	MURDER	U.S.
KROLL, Nicolas	131385	M	Ger.		SS-Guard,SS,C.C.Dachau (Ger.) 42	TORTURE	BEL.
KROLL	193080	M	Ger.		Sgt.,Kgf.Arb.Bn.190,Mattras (Nor.)	MURDER	NOR.
KROLL	253078	M			Pvt.,C.C.Ellrich,Nordhausen (Ger.)	MURDER	U.S.
KROLL, Rudolf	195452	M	Ger.		Obergrupenfhr.,SS Totenkopfverband (Ger.)	MURDER	U.S.
KROLL, Rudolf	258537	M	Ger.		Sturmbannfhr.,SS,Ohrdruf (Ger.) 12.4.-4.45	MURDER	U.S.
KROLL, Rupp	254830	M			Of Service Ferroviaire S.P.15577,Amberieu (Fr.) 8.6.44	INTERR.	FR.
KROLLMANN	253084	M			Pvt.,C.C.Ellrich,Nordhausen (Ger.)	MURDER	U.S.
KROLLPFEIFER, Felix	62544	M	Ger.		Civilian,C.C.Buchenwald (Ger.)	WITNESS	U.S.
KROLN, Rudolf	127406	M	Ger.		Cpl.,SS Totenkopf Sturmbann,C.C.Buchenwald,Ohrdruf (Ger.)	MURDER	U.S.
KROLOFF, Alois	195451	M	Ger.		Guard,Stalag,C.C.Wolfstein (Ger.)	MURDER	U.S.
KRON	167941	M	Ger.		Lt.,Pz.Unit 789 Dept.mot.Inf.,Chateau de Dammarie en Puisaye (Fr.) 3.10.40	PILLAGE	FR.
KRON, Josef (see KROHN)	162789						
KRONAPPEL (see FRONAPFEL)	277						
KRONARD	179582	M	Ger.	20	Schfhr.,SS,Enschede (Neth.)	MURDER	U.K.
KRONARD, Johannes (or KROMARDT, Johannes)	195063	M	Ger.	19.8.19	Rottfhr.,SD,Sonder and Wirtschaftskdo.,Beeck,Gorssel Beek (Neth.) 24.9.44	MURDER	NETH.
KRONAUER	39651	M	Ger.		Hptwachtmeister,Police,F.P.Nr.59436,Chanceaux Dolusle Sec (Fr.) 27.7.44	MURDER	FR.
KRONBERG, August	306226	M	Ger.		German Civilian,Member,SA,Wattenscheid (Ger.) 11.9.44	BRUTALITY	U.K.
KRONCKE, Ernst	254992	M	Ger.		Vorarbeiter,Wilhelmshaven (Ger.)	TORTURE	FR.
KRONCKE, Ludi	167062	M	Ger.	22.7.06	Sturmschfhr.,SD,Gestapo,Vichy (Fr.) 44	MISC.CRIMES	FR.
KRONE	250336	M	Ger.		Osturmfhr.,Urbes (Fr.) 24.9.44-5.10.44	MURDER	FR.
KRONE	253103	M			C.C.Rottleberode,Nordhausen (Ger.)	MURDER	U.S.
KRONE, Heinrich	1874	M	Ger.	2.4.00	SS-Sturmbannfhr.,C.C.Buchenwald (Ger.) 39-45	MISC.CRIMES	CZECH.,U.S.
KRONE, Joseph	255601	M			Uschfhr.,C.C.Buchenwald (Ger.)	MURDER	U.S.
KRONE, Wilhelm	174825	M	Ger.	13	Oberfeldmeister,RAD 6-352,Schuetzen (Aust.) 13.2. and 3.45	MURDER	U.S.
KRONEN, Kurt	140890	M			2 Coy Verbindungsabt.331 Bn.,Bolnes (Neth.) 8.5.45	MURDER	NETH.
KRONENBURGER	62545	M	Ger.	95	SS-Uschfhr.,C.C.Hinzert (Ger.)	TORTURE	U.S.
KRONER, Hugo	145201	M			Lt.,German Air Force,29 Flak Rgt.,Hausen,Ginheim,Suburbs of Frankfurt (Ger.) 9.44	WITNESS	U.S.
KRONERS, Karl (or KROPLA)	62521	M	Ger.		Civilian,Coal-miner,Castrop-Rauxel (Ger.) 25.3.45	TORTURE	U.S.
KRONHOLZ, Robert	306271	M	Ger.		Director General of "Schenker" A.D. Belgrade and Austrian Consul General in Belgrade (Serbia) 4.41-10.44	MURDER	YUGO.
KRONING, Walter	191374	M	Ger.		Rev Oberwachtmeister,10 Coy 3 Pol.Bn.VII Pol.Rgt.,Junkerdal (Nor.)10.44	MURDER	NOR.
KRONMUELLER, Reinhold	253102	M		9.11.05	Pvt.,C.C.Ellrich,Nordhausen (Ger.)	MURDER	U.S.

KRO-KRU

NAME	C.R.FILE NUMBER	SEX	NATIO-NALITY	DATE OF BIRTH	RANK OCCUPATION UNIT PLACE AND DATE OF CRIME	REASON WANTED	WANTED BY
KROMN	254850	M	Ger.		Adjudant, Army SS Station, Cavaillon, Vercoiran (Fr.) 9.3.44	MURDER	FR.
KROON, Adolf	250326	M	Ger.		Probabl. 10.Coy., 377.Jaeger-Rgt., Vinkt, Meigem (Bel.) 25.-31.5.40	INTERR.	BEL.
KROOG	306265	M	Ger.	about 15	Fuehrer, Hitler-Jugend, Gadebusch (Ger.) 10.9.44	MURDER	U.K.
KROON, H.B.	149558	M			Public official, Osnabrueck (Ger.)	TORTURE	FR.
KROPF	253100	M			Arbeitseinsatzfuehrer, Camp Harzungen, Nordhausen (Ger.)	MURDER	U.S.
KROPLA see KROMERS	62521						
KROPLIN, Joachim	151491	M	Ger.		Parachutist, Roermond (Neth.) 11.44-1.45	MISC.CRIMES	U.S.
KROPP	132518	M	Ger.		SS Uscharfhr., C.C. Dora-Mittelbau Nordhausen (Ger.)	MURDER	U.S.
KROPP	179928	M	Ger.		Civ.	PILLAGE	FR.
KROPP	253099	M			SS Mann, C.C. Nordhausen (Ger.)	MURDER	U.S.
KROPP, Heinrich	253094	M			Flyer, Camp Ellrich, Nordhausen (Ger.)	MURDER	U.S.
KROPP, Werner	187707	M	Ger.		S.A. Bde.Fuehrer, Labour Fronts Central Organ.Office	TORTURE	U.N.W.C.C.
KROPP, Wilhelm	193081	M	Ger.	00	Oberwachtmeister, Sgt., Reichsjustizministerium Feldstraflager, Finmark (Nor.) 4.45	MISC.CRIMES	NOR. YUGO.
KROSCHE	253861	M	Ger.		Paymaster, Lt., 2.Bn. 4.Rgt.Parachutist Grassmel Div. Hermann Goering, Helchteren, Hechtel (Bel.) 5. and 11.9.44	MISC.CRIMES	BEL.
KROSMAN	177540	M	Ger.		Member Gestapo, Chateau de Porteau, Poitiers (Fr.) 28.8.44	MURDER	FR.
KROSS	196245	M	Ger.		Lt., Kommandantur, St.Flour (Fr.) 14.6.44	MURDER	FR.
KROSS	194665	M	Ger.		Official, Capt., Org. Todt, Pornichet (Fr.)	PILLAGE	FR.
KROSSMANN see GROSSMAN	188570						
KROSSMANN or KLUSMANN	133798	M			SS Oscharfhr., C.C. Weimar, Buchenwald (Ger.)	TORTURE	U.S.
KROST, Franz	253095	M		12.7.98	Cpl., Camp Harzungen, Nordhausen (Ger.)	MURDER	U.S.
KROUG	29758	M	Ger.		N.C.O., Army Cmdt., Parjols (Fr.) 27.7.44	MURDER	FR.
KROUTIL, Herbert	23842	M			Oberlandgerichtsrat, Public official, Litomerice (Czech.) 21.2.40	MURDER	BEL.
KROUYZE	254828	M	Ger.		Oberlt., Unit F.F. 02244, Parentis en Born (Fr.) 25.7.44	INTERR.	FP.
KROPALLEC	254603	M	Ger.		Sgt., Unit Pion.Festungs P. 1.Coy. 4 21, Acheux en Amiencia (Fr.) 8.44	MURDER	FR.
KRSTEV	194341	M			Sgt., Police, Pirot (Yugo.)	TORTURE	YUGO.
FRUBER	192449	M			SS Oscharfhr., C.C. Flossenburg (Ger.) 44-45	SUSPECT	U.S.
KRUCHEL	132053	M	Ger.	92	Ortsgruppenleiter NSDAP, Sambansdorf (Ger.) 1.1.45	TORTURE	U.S.
KRUCHT	255276	M	Ger.		Factory "Glaswerke Ruhr", Karnapp-Essen (Ger.) 44	MURDER	BEL.
KRUCHTEN	194664	M	Ger.		Cpl., Feldgendarmerie, Ploermel (Fr.) 18.6.44	TORTURE	FR.
KRUCK	254671	M	Ger.		Employee, SIPC V B, Brussels (Bel.) 40-45	INTERR.	BEL.
KRUCKENBERGER, Ferdinand	260996	M	Ger.	10.12.22	SS-Mann, SS Totenkopf-guard, C.C. Auschwitz (Pol.) 43-45	BRUTALITY	POL.
KRUCKI	131387	M	Ger.		C.C. Mauthausen (Aust.) 41-45	MISC.CRIMES	U.S.
KRUCFI	251013	M			Guard or Kapo, C.C. Gusen.(Aust.)	TORTURE	BEL.
KRUDWIG, Hans (Heinz)	145847	M			Camp senior, C.C. Plattling, Hohenrhein (Ger.)	MURDER	U.S.
KRUEBEL, Rudolf	253096	M			Legionaer, Camp Harzungen, Nordhausen (Ger.)	MURDER	U.S.
KRUEDER	172985	M	Ger.		Civ., Dirmstein (Ger.) 21.2.45	WITNESS	U.K.
KRUEG	257403	M	Ger.		SS Guard, SS slave labour camp, Beisfjord nr.Narvik (Nor.) 6.-11.42	BRUTALITY	YUGO.
KRUEGEL, Gerhard	262181	M	Ger.	26.7.?	Uscharfhr., Gestapo, Rennes (Fr.) 43-44	MISC.CRIMES	FR.
KRUEGER	24915	M			Capt., Camp Cmdt. at Dulag 377, Gerolstein (Ger.) 1.45	MURDER	U.S.
KRUEGER	29791	M			Major, Pion. 20. Army Staff, Finmark (Nor.) 11.44	MURDER	NOR.
KRUEGER	102956	M	Ger.	23	Sturmbannfhr., SS 6. Mountain-Div. C.C. Mauthausen (Aust.) 41-45	MURDER	U.S.
KRUEGER	11556	M	Ger.		SS Usturmfhr., Army, Camp Cmdt., Lillehammer (Nor.) 40	TORTURE	NOR.
KRUEGER	131386	M	Ger.		SS Sturmbannfhr., C.C. Mauthausen (Aust.)	MURDER	U.S.
KRUEGER	132519	M	Ger.		SS Ogruppenfhr., Gestapo, SS and state-police, Pol. 39-44	MISC.CRIMES	U.S.
KRUEGER	134905	M	Ger.		SS Ogruppenfhr. (Gen.), Pol. 39-41	TORTURE	U.S.
KRUEGER	145264	M	Ger.		Sturmbannfhr., Waffen SS, C.C. Sachsenhausen (Ger.)	MISC.CRIMES	U.S.
KRUEGER	145890	M	Ger.		SS Sturmbannfhr., C.C. Mauthausen (Aust.)	MURDER	U.S.
KRUEGER	149215	M	Ger.		SS Oscharfhr., C.C. Schorzingen (Ger.)	TORTURE	FR.
KRUEGER	151969	M			W.O., Army, Stalag 7 A (Ger.) summer 43	TORTURE	U.S.
KRUEGER	173738	M	Ger.		Head, Gestapo, Chalons-Saone (Fr.) 7.44	MURDER	FR.
KRUEGER	186765	M	Ger.		Chief, customs and excise, Megeve (Fr.) 18.6.44	PILLAGE	FR.
KRUEGER	188112	M			SS Ogruppenfhr., 20.Army	MURDER	NOR.
KRUEGER	188534	M	Ger.		Major, Luftgau III, Berlin (Ger.) 8.44	MURDER	U.K.
KRUEGER see SCHMIDT	188999						
KRUEGER	194168	M	Ger.	95	Capt., Army, Dulag 377, Gerolstein (Ger.) 19.12.44-5.2.45	MISC.CRIMES	U.S.
KRUEGER	255407	M	Ger.		Major, 3.Bn. Gross-Deutschland Rgt., Pancevo (Yugo.) 4.41	MURDER	YUGO.
KRUEGER	300800	M	Ger.		Pvt., 1.Aufkl. Abt. 3.Coy. 2.Col. XV.Div. Afrika-Corps, St.Leger (Arlon) 5.9.44	MISC.CRIMES	BEL.
KRUEGER	306935	M	Ger.		Dr., Struthof C.C. Natzweiler (Fr.) 42-44	MURDER	FR.
KRUEGER, Andreas	191892	M	Ger.	97	Civ. Printer, Dillingen (Ger.) 11.5.44	WITNESS	U.S.
KRUEGER, Eberhard or KRIEGER	261905	M	Ger.		SS Standartenfhr., C.C. Fradiako (Czech.) 45	SUSPECT	CZECH.
KRUEGER, Emil	193082	M	Ger.	03	Oberwachtmeister, Sgt., Guard, Reichsjustizministerium, Feldstraflager, Waffen SS, Finmark (Nor.) 45	MIS.CRIMES	NOR.
KRUEGER, Franz	195479	M	Ger.		Capt., Army, Forges (Bel.) 29.5.40	PILLAGE	BEL.
KRUEGER, Franz	253098	M			Rottfhr., Camp Ellrich - Nixei, Nordhausen (Ger.)	MURDER	U.S.
KRUEGER, Friedrich	187708	M			SS Gruppenfhr., Pol.	TORTURE	U.N.W.C.C.
KRUEGER, Heinrich	250327	M	Ger.		Dr., 377.Jaeger-Rgt., Vinkt, Meigem (Bel.) 25.-31.5.40	INTERR.	BEL.
KRUEGER, Heinz	256912	M	Ger.-Aust.		Zugwachtmeister, 7.Coy. 322.Bn. 5.Schuetz.Rgt., Ljubljana Cetje, Kranj (Yugo.) 42-43	MISC.CRIMES	YUGO.
KRUEGER, Herbert	125723	M	Ger.	27	Pvt., II Gr. 959, nr.Caen (Fr.) about 16.8.44	MURDER	U.K.
KRUEGER, Jakob	258423	M			Guard, SS, C.C. Ohrdruf (Ger.) 12.44-4.45	MURDER	U.S.
KRUEGER, Kurt	255164	M	Ger.	31.3.13	Member Gestapo, Zlin (Czech.) 39-45	MISC.CRIMES	CZECH.
KRUEGER, Max	257757	M	Ger.	about 10	Usturmfhr., S.D., Lillehammer (Nor.) 40-45	TORTURE	NOR.
KRUEGER, Richard	259085	M	Ger.	4.11.91	Dr., Oberfeldarzt d.Res., Standartenfhr., S.S., NSDAP	INTERR.	U.S.
KRUEGER, Werner	259896	M			Second officer, Ger.Submarine, Atlantic Ocean, Route betw. Cardiff and New York, 23.2.43	WITNESS	NETH.
KRUEGER, Wilhelm	143173	M	Ger.	95	Police-chief of station on Ad.Hitler square, Leslau (Pol.) 41-42	TORTURE	U.S.
KRUEL see KROL	133799						
KRUEMMEL, Hans	31709	M			Cpl., Army, C.C. Oswiecim (Pol.) 6.41-1.45	MURDER	POL.
KRUEMMER	142458	M			Dr., Capt. Army-Oberomdo. VI PW affairs	WITNESS	U.S.
KRUESEMANN, Peter	260729	M	Ger.		SS Hptscharfhr., S.D., Amsterdam (Neth.) 7.42	WITNESS	NETH.

KRU-KRU

NAME	C.R.FILE NUMBER	SEX	NATIO-NALITY	DATE OF BIRTH	RANK OCCUPATION UNIT PLACE AND DATE OF CRIME	REASON WANTED	WANTED BY
KRUESSEL	300801	M	Ger.		Pvt., 1.Aufkl.Abt., 3.Coy., 2.Column, XV.Div. of the Afrika-Korps, Saint Leger (Arlon) 5.9.44	MISC.CRIMES	BEL.
KRUETER	193457	M	Ger.		Usturmfhr., SS, C.C., Buchenwald (Ger.) 42-45	TORTURE	U.S.
KRUEZTHALER	126568	M	Ger.		SS-Officer, Hutten (Ger.) 4.45	MURDER	U.S.
KRUFKE	255603	M	Ger.	05	Officer, Den Haag (Neth.) 16.8.42	INTERR.	NETH.
KRUG	300501	M	Ger.		Dr., Colleague of General-Commissar, Amsterdam (Neth.) 7.2.45	MURDER	NETH.
KRUG, Franz	162356	M	Ger.		Foreman, Working-Camp,Adolf-Mine, Merkstein (Ger.) 42-44	MURDER	U.S.
KRUG, Hans	194663	M	Ger.		Doctor, C.C., Neuengamme (Ger.)	MURDER	FR.
KRUG, Joseph	12446	M	Ger.		N.C.O., 110.Pz.Gren.Rgt., Albine (Fr.)	MURDER	FR.
KRUGAR	67061	M	Ger.		Major, Army, Conc.Camp, Swinemuende, Memel (Ger.)	MURDER	U.K.
KRUGE	24872	M	Ger.	85	Sturmbannfhr., SS, C.C., Struthof (Fr.)	TORTURE	FR.
KRUGE	24900	M	Ger.		Guard and Hangman, Gestapo, Klingelpuetz Cologne (Ger.) 1.3.45	MURDER	U.S.
KRUGE, Herbert	199364	M	Ger.		Cpl., 505.Marine-Art.Abt.,Karihola-Kristiansund (Nor.) 43-45	TORTURE	NOR.
KRUGE, Karl	123014	M	Ger.		Lt., Feldgend., Sur le Chateau (Fr.) 29.8.44	MURDER	FR.
KRUGEL, Georges	256133	M	Ger.		C.C. (Krematorium) Mauthausen (Aust.)	MURDER	FR.
KRUGER	513	M	Ger.		Lt., Gestapo, Montbeliard (Fr.)	MURDER	FR.
KRUGER	62417	M	Ger.		SS-Pol.-Ogruppenfhr., SS-Gen.Major	TORTURE	UNWCC
KRUGER	123015	M	Ger.		Usturmfhr., Freikorps Daenemark, Legion Slandinave SS, Montferrier (Fr.) 8.7.44	PILLAGE	FR.
KRUGER	124234	M	Ger.		Oberstabsarzt, Army, Stalag 3 B, C.C., Fuerstenberg-Oder (Ger.)	MISC.CRIMES	U.S.
KRUGER	124235	M	Ger.	07	Oberlagerfhr., C.C., Torgau (Ger.) 3.42	MISC.CRIMES	U.S.
KRUGER	126984	M	Ger.		Schfhr., SS-Pz.Div."Das Reich" (Fr.) 44	MURDER	FR.
KRUGER	139770	M	Ger.		Sturmmann, Waffen-SS, C.C.Waldlager V u.VI,Muehldorf (Ger.)6.44-5.45	TORTURE	U.S.
KRUGER	143159	M	Ger.		Hptschfhr., SS, C.C., Mauthausen (Aust.) 41-45	MURDER	U.S.
KRUGER	145240	F	Ger.		Civilian, Vienenburg (Ger.) 44	WITNESS	U.S.
KRUGER	146984	M	Ger.		SS-Lt., SS-Scandinavian-Legion, Montferrier (Fr.)	PILLAGE	FR.
KRUGER	146985	M	Ger.		Schfhr., SS-Pz.Div."Das Reich", Valence D'Agen	MURDER	FR.
KRUGER	146986	M	Ger.		Sturmbannfhr., SS-Pz.Div."Das Reich", Montauban (Fr.) 44	MURDER	FR.
KRUGER	146987	M	Ger.		Oberstgruppenfhr., SS-Pz.Div."Das Reich", (Fr.) South-West, 44	MURDER	FR.
KRUGER	165388	M	Ger.		Usturmfhr., SS, Gestapo, Dun les Plages (Fr.)	MURDER	FR.
KRUGER	187709	M	Ger.		Obergruppenfhr., SS Pol.	TORTURE	UNWCC
KRUGER	189617	M			Reg.Rat, Custom-frontier-guard,Feissons sur Isere (Fr.) 5.8.44	MURDER	FR.
KRUGER	192448	M			Lt., Munitions-Lager, Bayet (Fr.)	TORTURE	FR.
KRUGER	194004	M	Ger.		Rottfhr., SS, 2.Zug, 3.Gruppe, Stavelot (Bel.) 19.,20.12.44	MURDER	BEL.
KRUGER	196757	M	Ger.		Staff-Sgt., SS E M.12.Rgt.Art. Cuirasse F.P.No.57666 A,Tourouvres (Fr.) 13.8.44	MURDER	FR.
KRUGER	196759	M	Ger.		Capt., Formation Bode, St.Pierre D'Eyrand (Fr.) 19.6.44	MURDER	FR.
KRUGER	250332	M	Ger.		Pvt., Unit F.P.No.59949, Langon (Fr.) 16.6.44	INTERR.	FR.
KRUGER	251014	M		18. 5. 12	Official, Office I or II of W.V.H.A., C.C.,Mauthausen (Aust.)	TORTURE	BEL.
KRUGER	253097	M			Uschfhr., Camp Harzungen, Nordhausen (Ger.)	MURDER	U.S.
KRUGER	301139	M	Ger.		Oschfhr., SS E.M. 12.Armoured Art.Rgt.,F.P.No.57-666 A, Tourouvres, Orne (Fr.) 13.8.44	MURDER	FR.
KRUGER	301528	M	Ger.	18.5.12	Civ.Employee, Official in Amt I or II of W.V.H.A., Zentrale Bauin-spektion, C.C. Mauthausen (Aust.) 40-45	MURDER	BEL.
KRUGER	306624	M	Ger.		Councillor, PC of Customs Chambery, Megeve (Hte.Savoie) 18.6.44	PILLAGE	FR.
KRUGER, Bernhard	185093	M	Ger.	04	Sturmbannfhr., SS, SD, Sachsenhausen C.C. (Ger.) 42-45	MURDER	FR.
KRUGER, Ernst	301528	M	Ger.	18. 1.87	Schfhr., SS, C.C., Buchenwald (Ger.) between 16.5.38 and 9.10.43	MURDER	BEL.
KRUGER, Erwin	254375	M		11	Inspector, SD-Gestapo, Alencon (Fr.) 6.44-8.44	MISC.CRIMES	FR.
KRUGER, Friedrich Wilhelm	145796	M	Ger.	92	Obergruppenfhr., SS-Police, Krakow, Warszawa (Pol.) 42-43	MURDER	U.S.
KRUGER, Hans	262198	M	Ger.		Osturmfhr., SS and Gestapo, Section IV,Rennes (Fr.) 43-44	MURDER	FR.
KRUGER, Heinrich Wilhelm	514	M			Obergruppenfhr., Hoehere-SS,	MURDER	POL.
KRUGER, Heinz	261320	M	Ger.	21. 5.22	Cpl., 3.Bn.,12.Rgt.,SS-Art.,Tourouvre (Fr.) 13.8.44	MURDER	FR.
KRUGER, Helmut	301529	M	Ger.		Oschfhr., SS, (No.43525) C.C., Buchenwald (Ger.) betw.5.38 and 10.43	MURDER	BEL.
KRUGER, Kurt	255413	M	Ger.	13. 3.13	Crim.Secr., Gestapo, Zlin (Czech.)	INTERR.	U.K.
KRUGER, Max	152874	M	Ger.		Hptsturmfhr., SS, Conc.Camp, Stuthof - Danzig (Ger.)	MURDER	U.K.
KRUGER, Richard	261321	M	Ger.	13. 2.20	Cpl., SS-Art.,3.Bn.,12.Rgt., Tourouvre (Fr.) 13.8.44	MURDER	FR.
KRUGER, Wilhelm	301530	M	Ger.	9. 1.01	SS-Mann, Conc.Camp, Buchenwald (Ger.) betw.16.5.38 and 9.10.43	MURDER	BEL.
KRUGGER	196514	M	Ger.		Guard, C.C., Struthof-Natzweiler (Fr.) 40-44	INTERR.	FR.
KRUGNER, Karl	152184	M	Ger.		Eisleben (Ger.) 41-45	TORTURE	U.S.
KRUK	250875	M	Ger.	05	Store-Keeper, Civilian, Stoebnitz (Ger.) 40-45	MISC.CRIMES	POL.
KRUK	260841	M			Rottfhr., Chief of the Kitchen, SS and C.C., Unterriexingen (Ger.) 12.44-3.45	MURDER	U.S.
KRUL	160634	M	Ger.	06	Lt., Abwehr FAT 317, Talsen Kuridan (Latv.) 44-45	MURDER	U.S.
KRULA, Karl	186631	M	Ger.		Officer, Pion.Bn.669,1.Coy., Ferrieres,Burnontige,Villers-Ste-Ger-trude,Werbomont (Bel.) 9.44	MURDER	BEL.
KRULI	515	M	Ger.		SS-Sgt., Lyon (Fr.) 7.44-8.44	MURDER	FR.
KRULL (or ZETSER)	194003	M	Ger.	01	Asst., Conc.Camp, Malines (Bel.) 42-44	TORTURE	BEL.
KRULL, Alfred	185095	M	Ger.		Foreman, Conc.Camp, Dachau (Ger.)	TORTURE	FR.
KRULL, Otto	102955	M	Ger.		Civilian, Aderstadt (Ger.) 11. or 12.9.45	MURDER	U.S.
KRULL, Otto	253108	M			Pvt., Camp Ellrich, Nordhausen (Ger.)	MURDER	U.S.
KRUMBACH, Harry (Joseph)	259936	M			Dr., Investigator,Interpreter, Member, Geh.Feldpolizei (IC - AO), Reccare Terms (It.) 10.1.45	MURDER	U.S.
KRUMES, Adam	258407	M			Guard, SS, C.C., Ohrdruf (Ger.) 12.44-4.45	MURDER	U.S.
KRUMEY	194221	M	Ger.		SS-Lt., Leader, Umwanderer-Zentrale, Lidice (Czech.) 42	MISC.CRIMES	CZECH.
KRUMM	29792	M	Ger.		Major, Geb.Rgt.137,2.Div., Finmark (Nor.) 11.44	MURDER	NOR.
KRUMMACHER	260670	M			Col., Army	WITNESS	U.S.
KRUMMT	11282	M	Ger.		Capt., 110.Pz.Gren.Rgt.111, Gourdon (Fr.) 29.6.44	MURDER	FR.
KRUMPEL	194661	M	Ger.		Gend., Feldgend., Ploermel (Fr.) 18.6.44	TORTURE	FR.
KRUMPSCHMIED, Max	253744	M		6. 2.10	Pvt., C.C. Ellrich, Nordhausen (Ger.)	MURDER	U.S.
KRUND, Roudy	167061	M	Ger.		Pvt., Army, Jussarupt (Fr.) 21.10.44	WITNESS	FR.
KRUPANEK	301783	M	Ger.		SS-Mann, Blockfhr., C.C. Auschwitz (Pol.) 40	MURDER	FR.
KRUPATZ	185815	M			Uschfhr., SS, 4.SS-Totenkopf-Stuba., C.C., Dora-Mittelbau, Plaszow, Nordhausen (Ger.) 9.43-4.45	WITNESS	U.S.
KRUPE	190507	M			Col., Inf.Rgt.950, Laroche Possy (Fr.) 27.-29.8.44	MURDER	FR.
KRUPICKA	255163	M	Ger.		Interpreter, SD, Toulouse (Fr.) 11.42-8.44	MURDER	FR.

KRU-KUC

NAME	C.R.FILE NUMBER	SEX	NATIO- NALITY	DATE OF BIRTH	RANK OCCUPATION UNIT PLACE AND DATE OF CRIME	REASON WANTED	WANTED BY
KRUPKA	173720	M	Ger.		Officer,Gestapo official,Staatspolizeistelle,C.C.Prague, Oswiecim,Birkenau (Czech.Pol.) 39-45	MURDER	CZECH.
KRUPKA	193365	M	Ger.		Sgt.,Kgf.Arb.Bn.41,Nerlandsdal,Kristiansund (Nor.) 41-45	WITNESS	NOR.
KRUPKE,Heinz	145848	M	Ger.	10	Hptsturmfhr.,SS (Czech.) 41-42	MISC.CRIMES	U.S.
KRUPMANN	301690	M	Ger.		05-243 Mongolian "Oberland" Unit,St.Nazaire en Royans(Fr.) 7.-8.44	MURDER	FR.
KRUPOK	190508	M			Member,SS,Detachment,Busset (Fr.) 7.8.44	MURDER	FR.
KRUPP	24901	M	Ger.		Agent,Gestapo,C.C.Klingelpuetz (Ger.) 45	TORTURE	U.S.
KRUPP	257505	M			Master,Org.Todt,C.C.Mühldorf (Ger.)	MURDER	U.S.
KRUPP,Johann	193083	M	Ger.	03	Pvt.,Kgf.Arb.Bn.186 (Nor.) 40-45	MISC.CRIMES	NOR.
KRUPP,Paul	217766	M	Ger.	07	Osturmfhr.,Employee,S.D.,Sipo,Tilburg (Ger.) 43	MURDER	U.S.
KRUPPA,Paul	193084	M	Ger.	03	Pvt.,Kgf.Arb.Bn.186 (Nor.) 40-45	MISC.CRIMES	NOR.
KRUPPA,Paul	253746	M			Pvt.,C.C.Dora,Nordhausen (Ger.)	MURDER	U.S.
KRUPPKE	173719	M	Ger.		Kriminalrat,Head of Dept.II B,Staatspolizeistelle,C.C.Prague, Oswiecim,Birkenau (Czech.Pol.) 39-45	MURDER	CZECH.
KRUPPOK,Joachim (or Jean dit Jeannot)	188745	M			Oschfhr.,SS,18 Bn.SS,Busset (Fr.) 7.8.44	MURDER	FR.
KRUPTFALMER	138233	M	Ger.		Dr.,Civ.,Member of Peinetive-Party,Bourg-Lastic (Fr.) 15.7.44	MURDER	FR.
KRUSC	186632	M	Ger.		Pvt.,1 Pz.Div."Adolf Hitler",1 Rec.Bn.,Parfonduy,Stavelot (Bel.)12.44	MURDER	U.S.
KRUSCHE,Alfred	39652	M	Ger.		Lt.,Feldgend.,Maubeuge (Fr.) 19.8.44	MURDER	FR.
KRUSCHE,Max	24908	M	Ger.		Uschfhr.,SS,C.C.Struthof (Fr.)	MISC.CRIMES	FR.
KRUSE	516	M	Ger.		Sgt.,Army,118 Jaeg.Div.,(Yugo.)	MURDER	YUGO.
KRUSE	193959	M	Ger.		Pvt.,SS,Stavelot (Bel.)	MURDER	BEL.
KRUSE	254072	M	Ger.		Crim.Cmdt.,Abt.IV A,Sipo,Bruessel (Bel.) 40-45	INTERR.	BEL.
KRUSE,Gerhard	143172	M	Ger.		Sturmbannfhr.,SS,C.C.Mulhouse (Fr.) 2.45	TORTURE	U.S.
KRUSEMEYER,Bernhard	259849	M	Ger.	1. 5.07	Rottfhr.,SS,2 Group,1 Zug,Probably stationed at Bergeyk, Noord Brabant (Neth.) 11.9.44	MURDER	NETH.
KRUST	165387	M	Ger.		Sgt.,Army,Revin (Fr.) 13.-14.6.44	MURDER	FR.
KRUSTE	259116	M	Ger.		Sturmfhr.,SS,Coy.Commander,SS-Div."Prinz Eugen",Niksic district Montenegro (Yugo.) 5.-6.43	MISC.CRIMES	YUGO.
KRUSZKOESKI	256801	M		2.11.02	Employee,Block No.11,C.C.Dora,Nordhausen (Ger.)	MURDER	U.S.
KRUTCHECK	305715	M	Ger.		Dr.,Member of the Staff,C.C.Auschwitz,Birkenau (Pol.) 40	MURDER	FR.
KRUTH,Stephan	517	M	Ger.	27. 4.17	Rottfhr.,SS,C.C.Maidanek (Pol.) 40-4.44	MURDER	BEL.POL.
KRUTTI,Franz	253745	M			Pvt.,C.C.Bodungen,Nordhausen (Ger.)	MURDER	U.S.
KRUTZ	167059	M	Ger.		Civ.,Durn (Ger.)	MISC.CRIMES	FR.
KRUTZEL	167058	M	Ger.		Sgt.,General Staff,Kommandantur,Station Crest,La Rochette(Fr.)7.-8.44	MURDER	FR.
KRYCHAN,Kurt	254602	M	Ger.	16.10.25	Pvt.,13 Coy,558 Gren.Regt.,Bruay en Artois (Fr.) 1.9.44	MURDER	FR.
KRZYWON,Walter	259929	M	Ger.	8. 4.12	Confidential-Agent,Gestapo,Stritez district Cesky Tesin,Moravie (Czech.) 39-45	MISC.CRIMES	CZECH.
KRZYZANOFSKI,Sigmund	62522	M	Ger.		N.C.O.,Pol.Army and German Prisoner of War	WITNESS	U.S.
KUAPP (or KNAPP)	29755	M	Ger.		Lt.,Army,Faquet (Fr.) 6.-8.44	MURDER	FR.
KUBA	250906	M	Ger.		Inspector,C.C.Ravensbrueck (Ger.)	INTERR.	BEL.
KUBALE	67062	M	Ger.		Capt.,Army,1010 mot.Regt.,3 Bn.,Chilleurs aux Bois (Fr.)6.+8.44	MURDER	U.K.
KUBALIK,Maria	259926	F	Ger.		Informer,Collaboration with Gestapo,Pilsen,Bohemia (Czech.) 40-41	SUSPECT	CZECH.
KUBAT,Herbert	301531	M	Ger.		Rottfhr.,SS (No.292513),Pvt.,SS,C.C.Buchenwald (Ger.)16.5.38-9.10.43	MURDER	BEL.
KUBAT,Karl	193085	M	Ger.	30.10.04	Oberwachtmeister,Sgt.,Reichsjustizministerium,Feldstraf- Lager,Waffen-SS,Finmark (Nor.) 5.45	MISC.CRIMES	NOR.
KUBE	179929	F	Ger.		Aufseherin,C.C.Uckermark near Ravensbrueck (Ger.) 1.45	TORTURE	FR,BEL.
KUBIAK	124368	M	Ger.		Oschfhr.,SS-Pz.Div."Hitler Jugend",25 SS-Regt.,6 Coy.,2 Bn., Krinkelt-Rocherath (Bel.) 17.12.44	MURDER	U.S.
KUBIC (see KUBITZ,Otto)	2110						
KUBICK,Anton	128838	M	Ger.		N.C.O.,Guard,Camp 7005 (Ger.) 4.42	TORTURE	U.K.
KUBIS	191283	M	Ger.		Pvt.,Eis.Art.Abt.717,St.Andries,Varsenare,Les Bruges (Bel.) 4.9.44	MURDER	BEL.
KUBIS	253749	M	Ger.		Uschfhr.,SS,C.C.Dora,Nordhausen (Ger.)	MURDER	U.S.
KUBISCH	301831	M	Ger.		N.C.O.,1 Coy.,Bayreuth Det.Ldsschtz.Bn.439,Bayreuth (Ger.) 11.4.45		BEL.
KUBITS (see KUBITZ,Otto)	2110						
KUBITZ,Otto (or KURITZ,KUPITZ KUBITS,KUBIC)	2110	M	Ger.	22	Uschfhr.,W-SS,Totenkopf-Stand.,leader of the Barracks, C.C.Buchenwald (Ger.) 39-45	MURDER	U.S.
KUBITZKA,Otto	28841	M	Ger.		Dr.,Landgerichtsrat,Public official,Opava (Czech.) 21.2.40	MURDER	BEL.
KUEKE	257502	M	Ger.		Civ.,Police,Genthin (Ger.) 12.44	WITNESS	U.S.
KUBLER (or KUEBLER)	132063	M			Hptschfhr.,SS,C.C.Flossenburg (Ger.)	MISC.CRIMES	U.S.FR.
KUBLER	149218	M			Ortsgruppenleiter,NSDAP,Fellbacht (Ger.)	MURDER	FR.
KUBLER	186766	F			Wardress,C.C.Flossenburg (Ger.) 42-45	MURDER	FR.
KUBLER (see BUBELER)	192272						
KUBLER	195527	M	Ger.		Major-General,118 Jaeg.Div., 43-44	MURDER	YUGO.
KUBLER,Hans	146712	M			Oschfhr.,SS,C.C.Flossenburg (Ger.) 40-45	MURDER	BEL.U.S.FR.
KUBLER,Johann	145232	M	Ger.		Rottfhr.,SS-Totenkopf	MISC.CRIMES	U.S.
KUBLER,Karl	132063	M	Ger.		Hptschfhr.,SS,C.C.Flossenburg (Ger.)	TORTURE	U.S.
KUBSCHNER	259404	M			Oschfhr.,SS,Auschwitz (Pol.)	MURDER	FR.
KUBUSCH,Theodor	162364	M	Ger.	02	Pvt.,Army,Tank-Div.,Neuruppin,Friesack (Ger.) 8.-9.44	WITNESS	U.S.
KUBZ,Karl	165390	M	Ger.		10 Pz.Div.,Revin (Fr.) 6.44	MURDER	FR.
KUCHAR	251658	M	Ger.		Lt.,3 Coy.,A.O.K.I.,C.C.Lachat Tours,Moulin de la Chaise Clion(Fr.)	MURDER	FR.
KUCHAR	255545	M			Lt.,Sturm-Bn.,A.O.K.I.,3 Coy.,near Concielles (Fr.) 15.11.44	MURDER	U.S.
KUCHAR (see KOCH,Josef)	253983						
KUCHARSKI	29793	M	Ger.		Col.,20 Army,Comd.Geb.Art.Regt.82-7 Geb.Div.,Bez.Finmark (Nor.) 11.44	MURDER	NOR.
KUCHENBACKER	62419	M	Ger.		Dr.,leader,Bureau Landregulation,Public official,General-Gouv.(Pol.)	MURDER	UNWCC
KUCHENBECKER,Walter	251692	M	Ger.	16	Lt.,2 Coy.,Pion.369 Bn."Devil Div.",Island of Slano (Yugo.) 44	PILLAGE	YUGO.
KUCHENBRUCH,Karl (see KNOCHENBRUCH)	124766						
KUCHER	179930	M			Adjudant,Feldgendarmerie de Valence,Baunne,Cornillane (Fr.)	MURDER	FR.
KUCHERER	185814	M		95	Capt.,20 Pol.Regt.,2 Bn.,Prague (Czech.) 7.-8.42	MURDER	CZECH.
KUCHLER	123993	M	Ger.		N.C.O.,Prison Guard,Civ.,C.C.Diez (Ger.) 1.1.43-29.3.45	MISC.CRIMES	U.S.
KUCHLER	251659	M	Ger.		Sgt.,Luftnachr.Regt.302,2 Coy.,Brethenay (Fr.) 4.9.44	MURDER	FR.
KUCHLER,Rudolf	257309	M	Ger.	25. 6.13	Crim.Asst.,Gestapo,Tabor,Bohemia (Czech.) 11.40-5.45	MISC.CRIMES	CZECH.
KUCHMANN	167940	M	Ger.		Gestapo,Puivert (Fr.) 14.4.44	MURDER	FR.
KUCHS,Karl	252230	M	Ger.		SS-Pol.Regt.Todt,N.28,9 Coy.,Habere-Lullin (Fr.) 25.12.43	INTERR.	FR.
KUCK	174689	F	Ger.	05	Woman-warder,SS,C.C.Birkenau,Auschwitz (Pol.42-45	TORTURE	POL.

KUC - KUE

NAME	C.R.FILE NUMBER	SEX	NATIO-NALITY	DATE OF BIRTH	RANK OCCUPATION UNIT PLACE AND DATE OF CRIME	REASON WANTED	WANTED BY
KUCKE	187468	M	Ger.		Sgt.,210 Inf.Rgt. Breskens (Neth.) 4.9.44	MISC.CRIMES	NETH.
KUCKUCK	302081	M	Ger.		Crim.Commissar (member,SD) district Almelo (Nsth.) 9.44-2.45	MURDER	NETH.
KUCZERA see KUZERA	253736						
KUCZYNSKI, Friedrich	188412	M	Ger.	4.9.14	Oberassessor,Prof.,Hoehere SS and Pol.-Fuehrer Sosnowice, C.C. Sosnowice-Auschwitz (Pol.) 40-44	MURDER	POL.
KUDDOCK	519	M	Ger.		W.O.,Pz.Div.12, Ascq (Fr.) 1.4.44	MURDER	FR.
KUDRAS	102954	M	Ger.		Pvt.,Medical Corps Stalag VIII B, C.C. Lamsdorf (Ger.) 2.41	WITNESS	U.K.
KUDRCE, Wilhelm	169435	M			Cpl., Kriegsgef.Arb.Bn 185,Aspfjord (Nor.)	TORTURE	NOR.
KUEBASAK, Johann	172091	M			Connected with M 1 Lager,C.C. Muhldorf-Ampfing (Ger.) 6.44-4.45	MURDER	U.S.
KUEBERLING, Walter	167730	M	Ger.	24.12.09	Sgt.-Major, 517 Jaeger-Rgt., Virelles,Chimay (Bel.) 4.-6.40	PILLAGE	BEL.
KUEBLER see KUBLER	132063						
KUEBLER	137051	M	Ger.	11	Hptscharfhr.,SS, C.C Flossenburg (Ger.) 42	TORTURE	UNWCC.
KUEBLER, Jos.	260671	M			Lt.Gen.,Army	WITNESS	U.S.
KUEBLER, Karl or Oskar	193086	M	Ger.	05	Pvt., 4 Coy, POW-Labour Bn 188, Fjell (Nor.) 5.44	MURDER	NOR.
KUEBLER, Ludwig	259075	M	Ger.	89	Lt.Gen.,	MISC.CRIMES	U.S.
KUECHENMEISTER	258005				Pvt.,150 Pz.Bde, Meuse Bridge-Antwerp (Bel.) 12.44	MISC.CRIMES	U.S.
KUECHLER	253750	M			Pvt., C.C. Ellrich-Nordhausen (Ger.)	MURDER	U.S.
KUECHLER, Georg	518	M	Ger.		Gen.,3 Army,Ostpreussen (Ger.) 9.,10.39	MURDER	POL.
KUECHLER, Oskar	167692	M	Ger.		Leader,Abt.Forster,Amt des Gouverneurs,Warschau (Pol.)9.39-44	MISC.CRIMES	POL.
KUEBEL, Stefan	253747	M			Flyer, C.C. Ellrich-Nordhausen (Ger.)	MURDER	U.S.
KUEHBLER	189793	M	Ger.	15	Pvt.,Arb.Kdo.2780,Stalag VII A,Langwied,Muenchen (Ger.) 20.2.42	TORTURE	U.K.
KUEHL, Horst Wilhelm Johann	173739	M	Ger.		Lt.,50 Gren.Rgt.,8 Bn.4 Res.Coy, 2.9.44	MURDER	FR.
KUEHL	254557	M			Osturmfhr.,SS, Army,Krakow-Plassow (Pol.) 2.4.44	TORTURE	YUGO.
KUEHLE, Elisabeth	258069	F	Ger.	11.11.19	Civilian, Student, Benescov (Czech.) 7.5.45	WITNESS	CZECH.
KUEHLER	185813	M			Osturmfhr,SS,Fahndungshauptamt,Fuehrungsstab, C.C. Mittelbau, Dora-Nordhausen, Plaszow (Ger.) 43-45	WITNESS	U.S.
KUEHLWEIM	102953	M	Ger.		Gen.,Army, 406 Inf.Div., Sellrich (Ger.) 4.1.45	MURDER	U.S.
KUEHLWEIN, Anton	253731	M		6.6.04	Rottenfuehrer, C.C. Harzungen-Nordhausen (Ger.)	MURDER	U.S.
KUEN	124272	M	Ger.		Usturmfhr.,SS, Pz.Div.I, SS Pz.Rgt.I,9 Coy (engineers) Malmedy (Bel.) 17.12.44	MURDER	U.S.
KUEHN	149297	M	Ger.	95	SA, Radebeul near Dresden (Ger.)	TORTURE	FR.
KUEHN	151774	M			Gestapo official, Hamburg (Ger.) 38	MURDER	U.S.
KUEHN	174542	M	Ger.	95	Capt.,4 Coy,427 Ld.Schz.Bn,Bautzen Area (Ger.) 3.45	MURDER	U.K.
KUEHN	175752	M	Ger.	98	Crim.secr., SD, Celle (Ger.) 45	TORTURE	UNWCC.
KUEHN	179931	M	Ger.		Platoon leader, SS Div. Leibstandarte A.H, Malmedy (Bel.) 17.12.44	MURDER	U.S.
KUEHN	189771	M	Ger.		Legationsrat, Ger.Embassy in Zagreb, Ljubljana (Serb.) 4.41-5.43-44	MURDER	YUGO.
KUEHN	256642	M	Ger.		Cpl., C.C.Harzungen-Nordhausen (Ger.)	MURDER	U.S.
KUEHN	301336	M	Ger.		Member, Gestapo Trencin, C.C. Oswiecim-Birkenau (Pol.) 39-45	MURDER	CZECH.
KUEHN, Erich	300058	M	Ger.		NCO, belonging to an Inf.Unit,Soesterberg, 30.-31.3.45	PILLAGE	NETH.
KUEHN, Ferdinand	189757	M	Ger.		Crim-employee, Gestapo, brno (Czech.) 39-45	MISC.CRIMES	CZECH.
KUEHN, Hermann	194660	M	Ger.	9.8.05	Hptsturmfhr.,SS, Gestapo, SD, Dortmund,Essen,Koeln,Lukow(Ger.)39	SUSPECT	POL.
KUEHN, Karl	145203	M	Ger.		Sgt.,Army,Lds.Schz.Ers.Bn 24, Augsburg (Ger.) 44-4.45	MURDER	U.S.
KUEHN, Ludvik	253739	M	Ger.		Usturmfhr.,SS, Lidice (Czech.) 10.6.42	MURDER	CZECH.
KUEHN, Max	253729	M			Pvt., C.C. Harzungen-Nordhausen (Ger.)	MURDER	U.S.
KUEHN, Walter	253730	M			Flyer, C.C. Ellrich-Nordhausen (Ger.)	MURDER	U.S.
KUEHNE	179741	M	Ger.		Capt., 1 Fallschirm Pion.Bn, Castello (It.) 5.8.44	MURDER	U.K.
KUEHNE, Heinrich	254650	M	Ger.		Guard, C.C. Lahde-Weser (Ger.)	INTERR.	BEL.
KUEHNE, Karl Otto or KRAUSE	186703	M		95	Capt., Festungs-Nachrichtenstab P1 21, Elten (Ger.) 16.9.44	MURDER	U.K.
KUEHNE, Otto	139765	M	Ger.	10	Unterfeldmstr.,Zugfhr.,RAD,Army,1 Rgt.,Div."Schlagater" Rosche (Ger.) 18.3.45	MURDER	U.S.
KUEHNE, Philippe	258781	M	Ger.	00	Kreishauptmann,Offenbacha.M.,Rumpenheim,Breitenstr.1,Radzyn(Pol.)40-41	MURDER	POL.
KUEHNE, Theodor	140869	M	Ger.	92	Festungs-Nachrichten-Stab P.l 21,Elten (Ger.) 16.9.44	MURDER	CAN.
KUEHNE, Viktor	186109	M	Ger.	94	SS-Pvt.-guard, 4 SS Totenkopf Stuba,C.C.Dora-Nordhausen,Buchenwald (Ger.) 43-45	WITNESS	U.S.
KUEHNEMANN	124495	M	Ger.		Lt.Col., Marine Flakabt.810,2 Btty,Walcheren(Neth.) 10.44	MURDER	U.S.
KUEHNER	257012	M	Ger.		Major, Army, Kragujevac,Orasac,Gruza (Yugo.) 42-44	MURDER	YUGO.
KUEHNER, Heinz	253732	M			Pvt., C.C. Ellrich-Nordhausen (Ger.)	MURDER	U.S.
KUEHNERT, Herbert	252234	M	Ger.		Agent, Military SD, Arnheim (Neth.) 5.44	WITNESS	NETH.
KUEHNERT, Johannes	193958	M	Ger.	89	Member, NSDAP and SS, Zlin (Czech.)	MISC.CRIMES	CZECH.
KUEHNHOLD	120575	M	Ger.		Major, Army, (Sov.Un.)	TORTURE	U.S.
KUEHNLE, Richard	174103	M	Ger.		Groupleader, NSDAP, Neckar Westheim Landkrs.Heilbronn(Ger.)4.-12.12.44	MURDER	U.S.
KUELTER, Egon	135208	M	Ger.		Gestapo chief, SS, Koeln (Ger.) 41-45	MURDER	U.S.
KUEMME	29795	M	Ger.		Capt.,Army, Rgt.82,Geb.Div.7, Finmark (Nor.) 11.44	MURDER	NOR.
KUEMMEL	132468	M	Ger.	12	Scharfhr.,SS,camp Staff, C.C. Neuengamme (Ger.)	MURDER	U.K.
KUEMMEL	137049	M	Ger.		Col.,21 Pz.Div.H.W.,Sessenheim (Fr.) 1.45	MURDER	U.S.
KUEMMEL, Hans Joachim	161250	M	Ger.	26	Cpl.,Army, Sturm Bn AOK I, 1 Coy, Courselles sur Nied (Fr.)15.11.44	WITNESS	U.S.
KUEMMEL, Paul	258980	M	Ger.	13.4.11	Sturmbannfhr.,Ss, NSDAP, 9.11.43	INTERR.	U.S.
KUEMPF, Josef or KUNZ	301804	M	Ger.		Chief of Gestapo Paris,Herschbach b. Selters(Ger.) 17.10.44	MURDER	BEL.
KUENNEMANN	62519	M	Ger.		Lt.,Army, 2 Btty,Mar.FlakAbt.810,Walcheren (Neth.) 10.44	MURDER	U.S.
KUENNEMANN, Robert	261002	M	Ger.	18.5.01	Fireman, Railroad, Walle,(Ger.) Summer 44	SUSPECT	U.S.
KUENZEL, Ferdinand	260410	M	Ger.	99	Member, Gestapo, Pelhrimov (Czech.) 39-45	MISC.CRIMES	CZECH.
KUENZIG	186261	M			Uscharfhr.,SS, C.C. Mauthausen-Gusen (Aust.) 7.43 or 44	MURDER	U.S.
KUEPPER, Franziska	134865	F	Ger.		Civilian, Efferen (Ger.) 2.10.44	WITNESS	U.S.
KUEPPER, Peter	134864	M	Ger.		Civilian, Efferen (Ger.) 2.10.44	WITNESS	U.S.
KUEPPERS	253760	M			Sturmmann, C.C. Rottleberode-Nordhausen (Ger.)	MURDER	U.S.
KUEPPERS, Edmund	188476	M	Ger.		Civilian, C.C. Zeulenroda (Ger.) 40-45	MURDER	CZECH.
KUERHNE, Johann	250377	M	Ger.	00	Farmer, Civilian, Poppenhausen (Ger.) 11.5.42	MURDER	POL.
KUERSCHNER	142012	M	Ger.	06	Hptscharfhr., 12 SS Pz.Div. Hitlerjugend,Feldgendarmerie Abbaye, Ardenne (Fr.) 6.6.-8.7.44	TORTURE	CAN.
KUERSCHNER, Edmund	145810	M	Ger.		Civilian, Schweina (Ger.) 7.44	MURDER	U.S.
KUERSCHNER, Kurt	195477	M	Ger.		Cpl.-guard, PW Camp Stammlager 9 C, Bad Sulza (Ger.) 44-45	MURDER	CZECH.
KUERT, Hermann	251667	M	Ger.		Guard, C.C. Neuengamme (Ger.) 44	TORTURE	FR.

KUE-KUH

NAME	C.R.FILE NUMBER	SEX	NATIO-NALITY	DATE OF BIRTH	RANK OCCUPATION UNIT PLACE AND DATE OF CRIME	REASON WANTED	WANTED BY
KUERTEL	261077	M	Ger.		Former chief personnel, Messerschmidt Plants-C.C. Leonberg, Augsburg-Leonberg (Ger.)	MISC.CRIMES	FR.
KUERZEL, Johann	253086	M		5. 6.20	Pvt., Camp Ellrich, Nordhausen (Ger.)	MURDER	U.S.
KUES	1418	M	Ger.		Grenadier, Inf.Regt.,194	MURDER	U.K.
KUESGEN	24865	M	Ger.		Police Force, Rheinbach (Ger.) 28.1.45	TORTURE	U.S.
KUESGEN, Wilhelm	250882	M	Ger.		Policeman, Broichweiden (Ger.) 5.42	MURDER	POL.
KUESSNER, Guenther	191373	M	Ger.	20	Pvt., Verst.Kg.Arb.Bn.188 2.Coy., Assame near Bergen (Nor.) 42-43	TORTURE	NOR.
KUESTER, Gerhard	257758	M	Ger.	21	Pvt., A.Horst Coy. Luftwaffe, Lista (Nor.)8.44	MURDER	NOR.
KUESTER, Paul	186112	M			Pvt., 4.SS Totenkopf Sturmbann, Mittelbau Nordhausen, Dora (Ger.)	MURDER	U.S.
KUESTERS	167690	M	Ger.		Dr., Oberregierungsrat, Leiter der Abt.Wirtschaft Amt des General-gouverneurs, Radom (Pol.) 39-44	MISC.CRIMES	POL.
KUETGENS, Felix	138339	M	Ger.		Dr., Civilian, Paris, Larthe (Fr.) 40-44	MISC.CRIMES	FR.
KUETHE	533	M	Ger.		Hauptsturmfhr., Gestapo, Wolvenkoch (Neth.) 2.41	TORTURE	NETH.
KUFER, Rudolf	257305	M	Ger.		Major, Blofeld (Ger.) 5.44	SUSPECT	U.S.
KUFFAHL	196125	M	Ger.		Chauffeur, SD, Chateau, Gaillard, Saintes (Fr.)	MURDER	FR.
KUFFMEIER	187146	M	Ger.		Admiral, Navy, Channel Islands	TORTURE	U.K.
KUFFNER, Otto	252231	M	Ger.		Cpl., Fieldpolice, Vendome (Fr.)9.8.44	INTERR.	FR.
KUFN or KUEN	145523	M	Ger.		Colonel, Stalag 17-B, Krems (Austr.) 8.43-4.45	MURDER	U.S.
KUGE, Fritz	253748	M			Pvt., C.C. Ellrich, Nordhausen (Ger.)	MURDER	U.S.
KUGEL	122605	M	Ger.		Custom-House, Semaphore De Greach Maout, Pleubian (Fr.) 5.8.44	MURDER	FR.
KUGEL	145168	M	Ger.		SS-Untersturmfhr., SS-Leibstandarte "Adolf Hitler", Mosbach (Ger.)3.45	MURDER	U.S.
KUGELMANN	193087	M	Ger.		Sgt., Schupo, C.C., Falstad (Nor.) 41-45	MURDER	NOR.
KUGLER	29771	M	Ger.		Lt.Colonel, Inf.Regt.329, (Nor.) 11.44	MURDER	NOR.
KUGLER see KULGER	62482						
KUGLER	123409	M	Ger.		Cpl., Army, Creachmaout (Fr.) 5.-7.8.44	MURDER	FR.
KUGLER	176675	M			Capt., 190. Inf.Regt. 1.Bn., Winterspelt (Ger.) 20.12.44	MURDER	U.S.
KUH	179474	M	Ger.		Lt., Army, Kandum (Lat.) 44-45	MURDER	U.S.
KUHL	151964	M	Ger.		Civilian, Hadamar (Ger.) 6.44-3.45	WITNESS	U.S.
KUHL	167057	M	Ger.		Feldgend. Moulins, Larochemillay (Fr.)	PILLAGE	FR.
KUHL	188174	M	Ger.		Inspector, Flieger Korps, Zilly-Heiketal (Ger.) 15.9.44	MURDER	U.S.
KUHL	254374	M	Ger.		Agent SD, Le Teil (Fr.) 21.244	INTERR.	FR.
KUHL	260152	M	Ger.		Capt., Navy, Cantellen S.I (Fr.) 26.8.44	INCENDIARISM	FR.
KUHL, Edwald	150680	M	Ger.	03	Civilian, Hadamar (Ger.)	WITNESS	U.S.
KUHL, Richard	256643	M	Ger.		Employee, Camp, Nordhausen (Ger.)	MURDER	U.S.
KUHLE	161881	M	Ger.		Capt., Stalag IX-B C.C., Badorf (Ger.)	TORTURE	U.S.
KUHLE, Friedrich	139171	M	Ger.		Blocleader, C.C. Sorginsen (Ger.)	TORTURE	U.S.
KUHLEMANN see KILLERMANN, Michael	131403						
KUHLER	1419	M	Ger.		Grenadier, Army, Inf.Regt.194 2Pl. 6.Sec.	MURDER	U.K.
KUHLER, Emil	259051	M	Ger.	11. 6.12	SS-Sturmbannfhr., NSDAP, SS	INTERR.	U.S.
KUHLER, Heinz	145835	M	Ger.		SS-Obersturmfhr., Chief of Food Supply, C.C. Auschwitz (Pol.) 43-44	TORTURE	U.S.
KUHLMAN	152186	M	Ger.	17	Cpl., 355 Landesschuetzen Bn., Bitterfeld (Ger.) 11.43-4.45	TORTURE	U.K.
KUHLMANN	129691	M	Ger.		Civilian, Dora C.C. Nordhausen (Ger.)	MURDER	U.S.
KUHLMANN see KILMANN	139771						
KUHLMANN	195640	M	Ger.		Sgt., W.-SS, Zdolbunow (Pol.) 13.10.42	MURDER	POL.
KUHLMANN	29794	M	Ger.		Dr., Capt., Inf.Regt.379-169.Div. 20.Army, Finmark (Nor.)11.44	MURDER	NOR.
KUHLMANN	306035	M	Ger.		Member of Staff of Baby Clinic, Wolfsburg and Ruehen (Ger.)	MURDER	U.K.
KUHLMANN	306697	M	Ger.		SS-U'Sturmfhr., at Alderney C.C. (Channel I S)and Kortemark C.C.42-45	MURDER	CZECH.
KUHLMANN, Heinrich	133319	M			Schuetze, W.-SS, C.C. Flossenburg (Ger.)	TORTURE	U.S.
KUHM, Peter	24906	M	Ger.		SS-Rottenfhr., W.-SS, C.C. Struthof (Fr.)	TORTURE	FR.
KUHN	124496	M	Ger.		O.-Stabs-Arzt, Lagerarzt Doctor Offizier i.c.Stalag IV-A,Holmstein Stalag IV-A (Ger.) 10.44	TORTURE	U.K.
KUHN	124497	M	Ger.	15-17	SS-Hauptscharfhr., Rapportfhr., C.C. Dachau, Ravensbrueck (Ger.)5.44-2.45	MURDER	POL.,U.K.,FR.
KUHN	131460	M	Ger.		SS-Unterscharfhr.,(Sgt.,) SS-Pz.Div."Totenkopf", C.C. Mauthausen (Austr.) 41-45	MURDER	U.S.
KUHN	132667	M	Ger.		Sgt., Army, du general Schiel,Martimre Et Nayemont (Fr.) 11.44	INCENDIARISM	FR.
KUHN see KUFN	145233						
KUHN	145827	M			SS-Unterscharfhr., SS-Totenkopf Div. C.C. Mauthausen (Austr.) 41-45	MURDER	U.S.
KUHN	167056	M	Ger.		Capt., 2.Coy.615 Bn., Avallon (Fr.) 18.8.44	MURDER	FR.
KUHN	173755	M	Ger.		Lt., 198 Inf.Div.,469Inf.Regt.2.Bn. 7.Coy., Le Tholy (Fr.) 13.11.44	PILLAGE	FR.
KUHN	188923	M			Cpl., Army, Gerardmer (Fr.) 9.10.-11.44	MISC.CRIMES	FR.
KUHN	193088	M	Ger.		Major, Bau-Pi.-Bn.(K.) 2, Nemsos, Akervika (Nor.) 10.42	MURDER	NOR.
KUHN	193803	M	Ger.		Agent (Chef), Gestapo, Wittenberg (Ger.) 27.3.45	TORTURE	FR.
KUHN	194659	M	Ger.		Civilian-Employee, Schirgiswald (Ger.) 8.5.45	MURDER	FR.
KUHN	254817	M	Ger.		Pvt., Unit 32009, Pas-de-Calais (Fr.) 22.5.40	MURDER	FR.
KUHN	254972	M			Scharfhr, Gestapo Lyon, Plateau des Glieres (Fr.) 22.3.-5.4.44	BRUTALITY	FR.
KUHN	306943	M	Ger.		Gestapo official employed in Ger. Information Service, Nice (Fr.)9.43	TORTURE	FR.
KUHN, Erich	254955	M	Ger.	91	Civilian, Prag (Czech.) 42	MURDER	CZECH.
KUHN, Ernst	149267	M	Ger.		Doctor, Civilian, Jena (Ger.)	MURDER	U.S.
KUHN, Franz	253728	M		11. 1.05	Rottenfhr., C.C. Rottleberode-Ellrich, Nordhausen (Ger.)	MURDER	U.S.
KUHN, Friedrich	254845	M	Ger.	27. 3.12	Untstffhr., SS,SD,Sipo, Prag (Czech.) 39-45	MISC.CRIMES	CZECH.
KUHN, Fritz	178072	M	Ger.		Pvt., Air Force, Muenchen, Rheden (Ger.,Neth.)	MURDER	NETH.
KUHN, Hildegard	161257	F	Ger.		Civilian, Daasdorf, Guthmannshausen (Ger.) 7.8.44	WITNESS	U.S.
KUHN, Josef	193957 A	M	Ger.	6.11.04	Secretary, Gestapo, Hradec, Kolove (Czech.)	TORTURE	CZECH.
KUHN, Josef	260833	M		87	City Police, Resides at Oberstr. 8, Ehrang, Schweich (Ger.) 15.1.45 L.O.D.N.A.O.D.	WITNESS	U.S.
KUHN or KULM, Karl	300281		Ger.		Dr., Cief and Cmdt., from Stabsvet. and Coy. of a Military Unit Stationed in the annex of the Sivitanidios School "Nea Sphaghia-Athens (Grc.) 2.5.44	MURDER	GRC.
KUHN, Leopold	189340	M	Ger.		SS-Obersturmfhr., Manager, SS-Arb.-Kdo., Parschnitz (Czech.) 39-42	TORTURE	POL.
KUHN, Milena	254843	F	Ger.	28.12.23	Typist, Gestapo Skrivany (Czech.) 39-45	MISC.CRIMES	CZECH.
KUHN, Rudolf	145819	M	Ger.	09	Capt., Remount-School, Gardelegen (Ger.) 10.-14.4.45	MURDER	U.S.

KUH - KUN

NAME	C.R.FILE NUMBER	SEX	NATIO-NALITY	DATE OF BIRTH	RANK OCCUPATION UNIT PLACE AND DATE OF CRIME	REASON WANTED	WANTED BY
KUHN, Wilhelm Friedrich August	254976	M		8.12.96	Feldgendarm,Fieldpolice 625,Fresnes au Mont (Fr.) 22.8.44	MURDER	FR.
KUHNE	1420	M	Ger.		Fallschirmjaeger Div.4.,Rgt.11,Army	MURDER	U.K.
KUHNE (see KIEHN)	165248						
KUHNE	167965	M	Ger.		Pvt.,Feldgendarmerie,Langes,Auberive,Flagey,Coiffey,Chalencey (Fr.) 43-44	MURDER	FR.
KUHNE	195450	M	Ger.		Doctor,Oberfinanzpraesident,occupied territories,Luxembourg (Lux.) 40-45	MISC.CRIMES	LUX.
KUHNE	254148	M	Ger.		Capt.,engineer,Unit F.P. L 06459,Romilly sur Seine (Fr.) 8.44	PILLAGE	FR.
KUHNE, Helmut	102957	M			Lt.,Army Funk Coy.,signal Bn.900,F.P.No.67695 B	WITNESS	U.S.
KUHNE, Richard	62520	M		97	Kapo,Police,Verfuegungspolizei,Clausthal,Zellerfeld,Braunlage (Ger.) 6.4.45	MURDER	U.S.
KUHNE, Richard	128839	M	Ger.		Major,Arbeitskommando 251,C.C.,Mitteltan-Genau,Trautenau (Ger.)3.11.41	MURDER	U.K.
KUHNER, Albert	196758	M	Ger.		Sgt.,SS,Gestapo,St.Etienne,et La Region (Fr.) 40-45	INTERR.	FR.
KUHNER, Erwin	250330	M		95	Major,1.Bn.,377.Jaeger Rgt., (Bel.)	INTERR.	BEL.
KUHNER, Kurt	131457	M	Ger.	21	Sgt.,2.Pz.Gren.Div."Das Reich",Marche en Famenne (Bel.) 6.9.44	TORTURE	BEL.
KUHNERT, Erich	132222	M	Ger.		Civilian,C.C.,Gardelegen (Ger.)	MURDER	U.S.
KUHNOW (see CUNO)	152021						
KUHR	137048	M	Ger.		Police Capt.,Defence Police,Waren,Foppentin (Ger.) 7.or 8.44	MURDER	U.S.
KUHRT	521	M	Ger.		Capt.,Army,Noisy-le Roy (Fr.) 3.8.44	MURDER	FR.
KUINTEL, Jean	167054	M	Ger.		Official,guard,C.C.,Schirmeck (Fr.) 40-45	MURDER	FR.
KUIPER	305621	M	Ger. or Dut.		Member of the Sicherheitsdienst at Amsterdam (Neth.) 24.10.44	MURDER	NETH.
KUISSIG	141388	M			Uschfhr.,SS,C.C.,Gusen (Aust.)	TORTURE	FR.
KUKALA	162736	M			Osturmfhr.,SS,member,Gestapo,Manager,head-office,Berlin (Ger.)39-45	MURDER	CZECH.
KUELEMAPNI	67064	M	Ger.		Capt.,Oflag 6 B,C.C.,Warburg (Ger.) 12.42	TORTURE	U.K.
KUKUK, Emil	302082	M			Reichsbahn official,employed in the Fernmeldemeisterei office at Amersfoort (Neth.) 4.10.44-5.4.45	PILLAGE	NETH.
KUKUK, Fedinand	139189	M	Ger.		Local chief of construction,civilian,Oeynhausen (Ger.) 9.43	MURDER	U.S.
KUKUSCHKA (see KUKUTSCHKA)	253763						
KUKUTSCHKA, Johann (or KUKUSCHKA)	253763	M			Pvt.,C.C.,Ellrich,Nordhausen (Ger.)	MURDER	U.S.
KULAYE	187144	M			Capt.,Army,Montgauthier (Bel.) 20.9.43	MURDER	BEL.
KULCHEWSKI	67065	M	Ger.		Uschfhr.,SS,17.Pz.Gren.Div. "Goetz v. Berlichingen",Sturmgesch. Abt.17,Segre Renaze (Fr.) 30.7.44-6.8.44	MURDER	FR.
KULECZKA, Marian	306703	M	Ger.		Pvt.,Polish subject,Termonde (Bel.) 4.9.44	MURDER	BEL.
KULEN, Paul	102958	M	Ger.		Guard,Army,C.C.,Boergermoor (Ger.)	TORTURE	U.S.
KULETTA, Otto	186108	M	Ger.		Oschfhr.,4.SS Totenkopfsturmbann,C.C.,Nordhausen,Dora,Mittelbau (Ger.) 43-45	WITNESS	U.S.
KULGER (or KUGLER)	62482	M	Ger.		Capt.,Army,62.Volksgren.Div.,190.Volks Rgt.,1.Bn.,Habscheid (Ger.) 19.or 20.12.44	MURDER	U.S.
KULGER (or RUGELHORN)	141369	M			Cpl.,SS "Der Fuehrer",Theil sur Vannes (Fr.) 18.8.44	MURDER	FR.
KULI	145805	M			Lt.,Rgt."Von Einem",3.Prov.Coy.,near Gardelegen,Edstedt (Ger.) 10.-14.4.45	MURDER	U.S.
KULICH	133823	M			Schfhr.,SS,C.C.,Weimar,Buchenwald (Ger.)	TORTURE	U.S.
KULIDIEB, Kolisc	131459	M			C.C.,Mauthausen (Aust.) 41-45	MURDER	U.S.
KULISCH, Alfred	301532	M	Ger.		Uschfhr.,SS,C.C.,Buchenwald (Ger.) 16.5.38-9.10.43	MURDER	BEL.
KULISEK, Josefa	254844	F	Ger.	3.5.02	Informer,Gestapo,Skrivany (Czech.) 39-45	INTERR.	CZECH.
KULITZSCHER	258878	M	Ger.		Regierungsrat,Chief-commander,member of the "Actions-Kommando" of Lourdes (Fr.) 1.-8.44	MURDER	FR.
KULKE	193804	M			Officer,Inf.Lostihuel (Fr.) 21.7.44	MURDER	FR.
KULLE	173754	M			Sgt.,Army	PILLAGE	FR.
KULLER	132666	M	Ger.		Velmanya (Fr.)	MURDER	FR.
KULLINAT, August	188744	M	Ger.		Guard,Stalag 1 b,C.C. (Ger.) 1.45	MURDER	FR.
KULLMANN	256644	M	Ger.		Employee,Labor Asgnt.,Dora Nordhausen ,C.C., (Ger.)	MURDER	U.S.
KULLMANN, Charles	254809	M	Ger.		Gendarm,Muttersholtz (Fr.) 4.7.44	MURDER	FR.
KULM, Karl (see KUHN)	300281						
KULMANN	522	M	Ger.		Sgt.,Police,SIPO,Div."Bremer",Brive la Gaillarde (Fr.) 3.4.44	PILLAGE	FR.
KULMANN	523	M	Ger.		Gendarme,Police,Obernai (Fr.) 20.7.44	MURDER	FR.
KULMANN (see KILMANN)	139771						
KULMANN	189616	M	Ger.		Sgt.,Central Ersatzteillager 206,Paris (Fr.) 21.8.44	MURDER	FR.
KULMANN, Wilfred	252052	M	Ger.		Shoemaker,Civilian,Holzhausen,Tosbusch (Ger.)	WITNESS	U.S.
KULMAYER, Adolf	132664	M	Ger.		Stabsfeldwebel,German prison at Douai (Fr.) 6.3.44	MURDER	FR.
KULMER, Herbert	145962	M			Member,police-force,Dist.1,Weimar,Ottmanshausen (Ger.) 8.44	MURDER	U.S.
KULMEY, Ernst	253764	M		29.7.05	Rottfhr.,C.C.,Harzungen,Nordhausen (Ger.)	MURDER	U.S.
KULMS, Emma	149265	F	Ger.	17	Civilian,C.C.,Grueneberg (Ger.)	MISC.CRIMES	FR.
KULTZER, Egon (see KULZER)	101805						
KULZER, Egon (or KULTZER)	101805	M		27.6.06	Doctor,Sturmbannfhr.,SS,Oberregierungsrat,Gestapo,O.C.,Cologne,Opava,Troppau (Ger.,Czech.) 40-45	MURDER	U.K.,CZECH.,U.S
KUMALO	67066	M	Ger.		Mine overseer,Stalag VIII B,C.C.,Sardinia (It.) 4.-10.43, 7.44	MURDER	U.K.
KUMAN	301337	M	Ger.		Member, of the Gestapo at Trencin,C.C.,Oswiecim,Birkenau (Pol.)39-45	MURDER	CZECH.
KUMBARCKE (or KUMBARTZKE)	257011	M	Ger.		Lt.,German Army,Tank Div.,Jagodina (Yugo.) 10.4.41	INTERR.	YUGO.
KUMBIER	1717	M	Ger.		Uschfhr.,Reichsfhr.,SS,16.Gren.Rgt.25,Rotz, 44	MURDER	U.K.
KUMBLER	62483	M	Ger.		Uschfhr.,SS,12.SS Pz.Div."Hitler-Jugend"	MISC.CRIMES	CAN.
KUMINSKY	161261	M			Prison C.C.,Papa (Hung.) 9.45	TORTURE	U.S.
KUMM	524	M	Ger.	1.10.09	Oschfhr.,SS,Bdefhr.,7.Gebirge Div."Prinz Eugen", 23.5.44	MURDER	YUGO.
KUMM	196082	M			Bdefhr., 1.Pz.Div.SS Leibstandarte "Adolf Hitler",Stavelot (Bel.)	MURDER	BEL.
KUMMEL	1422	M			Inspector,Naval Supply,	MISC.CRIMES	U.K.
KUMMEL	251095	M	Ger.		Uschfhr.,SS,C.C.,Neuengamme (Ger.)	INTERR.	BEL.
KUMMEL	251669	M	Ger.		Kommandofhr.,C.C.,Neuengamme (Ger.) 44	MURDER	FR.
KUMMEL	256134	M	Ger.		Oschfhr.,SS,C.C.,Dora,Nordhausen (Ger.)	INTERR.	FR.
KUMMEL, Karl	131455	M	Ger.		N.C.O.,Org.Todt,Alten Essen (Ger.) 43-44	TORTURE	BEL.
KUMMEL, Otto	129692	M	Ger.	74	Doctor,Civilian,Occ.General Director,State Museums of Russia	PILLAGE	U.S.
KUMMER	29796	M	Ger.		Col.,Armee Oberkommando 20,Finmark (Nor.) 11.44	MURDER	NOR.
KUMMER	153325	M			Hptsturmfhr.,SS,F.P.No. 25341 Vercoiran (Fr.) 9.4.44	MURDER	FR.
KUMMERFELD	139772	M			Policeman,Police,C.C.,Ronnenberg (Ger.)	WITNESS	U.S.
KUMPA, Joseph	62174	M	Ger.		N.C.O.,Army,Nancy (Fr.) 19.8.44	MURDER	FR.
KUMSCH (see KUNSCH)	133411						
KUN, Hugo	260147	M	Ger.		Guard,SS,slave labour camp,Botn near Rognan (Nor.) 8.42-3.43,3.43-45	BRUTALITY	YUGO.
KUNO, Karl	252049	M	Ger.		Osturmfhr.,SS,SD,Ceske (Czech.)	MURDER	CZECH.

KUN-KUP

NAME	C.R.FILE NUMBER	SEX	NATIO-NALITY	DATE OF BIRTH	RANK OCCUPATION UNIT PLACE AND DATE OF CRIME	REASON WANTED	WANTED BY
FUNACEK see EGENER, Franz	260719						
FUNDE	131291	M	Ger.		Officer,FL Administrator Krakau(Pol.)	MURDER	U.S.
FUNDISCH, Felix	253724	M			Tiddische(Ger.)30.5.44	WITNESS	U.S.
FUNDT, Ernst	525	M	Ger.	15. 4.97	Governor,Major,Public Official of district Radom,Krakau(Pol.)42-45	MURDER	POL.
FUNE, Joseph	194658			05	Sgt.Army,Rouen(Fr.)41	TORTURE	FR.
FUNEMUND	259626	M	Ger.		Gendarm,Gendarmerie,Tham(Haut-Rhin)(Fr.)19.-22.and 29.10.44	BRUTALITY	FR.
FUNER, Fritz jr.	167514				Waffen SS,Panzer Unit,Son of Kreisleiter Kuner CR No.167513,Ubach(Ger.) 21.7.44	MURDER	U.S.
FUNER, Fritz	167513	M	Ger.		Kreisleiter,NSDAP,Ubach(Ger.)21.7.44	MURDER	U.S.
FUNERT	173721	M			Crim.secretary,Head of Transport Dept.,Police,CC Prag,Auschwitz,Birkenau(Czech.Pol.)39-45	MURDER	CZECH.
FUNERT, Kurt	186627	M	Ger.		Civilian,Seimke-Berg(Ger.)24.6.44	MURDER	U.S.
FUNETKA, Antonin	254640	M	Ger.		Custom secretary,Customs Official ML,Boleslav (Czech.)39-45	MURDER	CZECH.
FUNICKE	254067	M			SS Osturmfhr.Doctor,CC Auschwitz-Birkenau,Pol.)7.44	MISC.CRIMES	YUGO.
KUNIG	254595	M			Rapportfhr.CC Dora-Nordhausen(Ger.)	INTERR.	FR.
FUNISCH, August Franz	145820	M	Ger.	91	Civilian,Giessen(Ger.)26.-27.3.45	WITNESS	U.S.
FUNKESSITZ	155591	M			Member,Gestapo,Dun les Flages(Fr.)26.-28.6.44	MURDER	FR.
FUNKOWSKI	253762	M			Pvt.CC Ellrich No.dhausen(Ger.)	MURDER	U.S.
FUNNE, Otto	262200	M			SS Uschafhr.Gestapo,Rennes(Fr.)43-44	MISC.CRIMES	FR.
FUNNER, Egon	254600	M	Ger.		Sgt.Trouper cantonnees a Chateauroux Garrison Villdien(Fr.)15.8.44	INTERR.	FR.
FUNRERT	167053	M	Ger.		Cpl.Feldgendarmerie,Montigny en Vescul(Fr.)16.7.44	MURDER	FR.
FUNO see CUNO	305879						
KUNSCH or FUMSCH	133411	M		10	Sgt.CC Mellingen-Zeigenheim(Ger.)	TORTURE	U.F.
FUNSCH, Bernard	190353	M		20	720 Landesschuetzen bn.CC Rodleben(Ger.)11.6.44	TORTURE	U.F.
FUNSCHNER	250296	M			SS Hptsturmfhr.Army SS,Ronopiste(Czech.)	MURDER	U.S.
FUNST, Josef	253761	M			Sturmmann,CC Bodungen,Nordhausen(Ger.)	MURDER	U.S.
FUNSTDIER	259625	M	Ger.		Sonderfhr.Pion.Coy.at Biesheim-Quartiermeister L à IV A.K.Colmar Haut-Rhin(Fr.)12.44	PILLAGE	FR.
FUNSTLER, Karl	133316	M		12. 1.01	Ob.Stubafhr.Waffen SS,CC Flossenburg(Ger.)38-45	TORTURE	U.S.
FUNSTMANN	133317	M	Ger.		Staff-Leader,Waffen SS,Oflag XIIIB,Hammelburg,Nuernberg(Ger.)1.10.44-45	TORTURE	U.S.
FUNT	10024	M	Ger.		Uschafhr.CC Weimar-Buchenwald(Ger.)39-44	MURDER	CZECH.
FUNT	173706	M			Lt.Commandantur,Sete(Fr.)12.8.44	MURDER	FR.
FUNTJE, Fritz	250329	M			377 Jaeger Regt.Vinkt,Meigem Area(Bel.)25.-31.5.40	INTERR.	BEL.
FUNTNER, Leopold	254599	M	Ger.		Sturmscharfhr.S.D.,Toulouse(Fr.)42-44	MISC.CRIMES	FR.
KUNTSCHIK, Walter	192447	M		7. 7.06	Leader NSDAP,Frenstat(Czech.)	SUSPECT	CZECH.
FUNTTZE	260184	M			Osturmfhr.SS,Belgrad(YUGO.)1.-9.44	MISC.CRIMES	YUGO.
FUNTZ	167938	M			Dr.Einsatzstab Rosenberg(Fr.)40-44	PILLAGE	FR.
FUNTZ	196797	M			Sonderfhr.CC Royallieu,Compiegne(Fr.)	SUSPECT	FR.
FUNTZ	254993	M			Lt.Feldpolizei Trupp 694,Marseille Langom(Fr.)6.44	PILLAGE	FR.
FUNTZ, Edwin	167691	M			Leader,Unter Abt.Treuhandverwaltg.Amt des Gouverneurs,Luwow(Galizia-Pol.)39-44	MISC.CRIMES	POL.
KUNTZ, Hans	165951	M	Ger.		Chief,Feldgendarmerie,Gestapo,Arlon(Bel.)25.8.44	MURDER	BEL.
KUNTZE	526	M	Ger.	16	SS Uschafhr.CC Grini(Nor.)10.44	MURDER	NOR.
KUNTZE	254813	M			Lt.Fieldpolice,Fresnes-au-Mont(Fr.)22.8.44	MURDER	FR.
FUNTZE	258077	M		09	SS Osturmfhr.Pol.Official,State Service,Special Police,Bystrice P.H. (Czech.)44-45	MURDER	CZECH.
KUNTZEL, Leo	195061	M	Ger.	96	Civilian-Servant,Labour Office Arnheim(Neth.)43-44	MISC.CRIMES	NETH.
FUNTZEN, Heinz	250328	M			Pvt.377 Jaeger Regt.Vinkt,Meigem(Bel.)25.-31.5.40	INTERR.	BEL.
KUNTZMANN	188743	M			Capt.Geb.Jaeger Bn.,Petit Coeur(Fr.)12.8.44	PILLAGE	FR.
FUNZ	29799	M			Col.26 Gren.Div.Inf.Div.169	MURDER	U.S.
KUNZ	135205	M	Ger.		Freis Chief,Gendarmerie,Karlstadt(Ger.)44	MURDER	U.S.
KUNZ	137054	M	Ger.		Capt.21 Panz.Div.220 Engr.Bn.Sessenheim(Fr.)1.45	MURDER	FR.
KUNZ	145178	M	Ger.		Civilian,Buergermeister,Eching(Ger.)13.7.44	WITNESS	U.S.
FUNZ	149217				Bde.Kommandeur,Army	PILLAGE	FR.
FUNZ	173237			24	Pvt.Guard,Prison CC Torgau(Ger.)42	TORTURE	U.K.
FUNZ	191282				Pvt.Eis.Art.Bn.717,St.Andries Varsenare Les Bruges(Bel.)4.9.44	MURDER	BEL.
FUNZ	252245	M	Ger.		SS Uschafhr.Gestapo,Paris(Fr.)41-44	TORTURE	FR.
FUNZ, Edith	193174	F	Ger.		Helferin,German Navy Girl,Wilhelmshaven(Ger.)15.10.44	WITNESS	CAN.
FUNZ, Heinrich	206761	M	Ger.		German Civilian,nr.Bingen(Ger.)12.9.44	MURDER	U.S.
KUNZ, Horst	145228	M		18.10.02	SS Stubafhr.Dir.in office of SS Pol.Leader(Grc.)43-44	MURDER	U.S.
KUNZ, Josef	301804	M			Chief,Paris Gestapo,Herschbach b.Selters(Ger.)17.10.44	MURDER	BEL.
FUNZ, Karl	123410	M	Ger.	05	Agent,Gestapo,Arles sur Fesch(Fr.)29.6.44	MURDER	FR.
FUNZ, Otto	254558			4. 2.04	Commander,CC Moencheberg,Fassel(Ger.)43-44	MISC.CRIMES	POL.
FUNZ, Wilhelm	166694	M	Ger.	10	Sgt.Scharfhr.SS,Theresienstadt(Czech.)43	MURDER	U.S.
FUNZE	124236	M	Ger.		Stubafhr.Reichssicherheits-Hauptamt,Segeletz(Ger.)24.5.44	MISC.CRIMES	U.S.
FUNZE	125724	M	Ger.		Civilian,Bingen(Ger.)11.44	MURDER	U.F.
FUNZE	161258	M	Ger.		Osturmfhr.SS Reichssicherheits-Hauptamt,Berlin near Steglitz(Ger.)	MURDER	U.S.
FUNZE	170542	M	Ger.		Capt.Army,Oflag VI C,CC Osnabrueck(Ger.)44	MURDER	YUGO.
FUNZE	250335	M			Lt.119 Art.Regt.11 Panzer Div.Coufouleux(Fr.)9.8.44	INTERR.	FR.
FUNZE	301868				Col.Tarbes(Fr.)10.6.44	MURDER	FR.
KUNZE, hans	131456	M		00	Sturmscharfhr.Sipo,S.D.Crim.secretary,Arlon(Bel.)25.8.44	MURDER	BEL.
FUNZE, Herbert	500283	M			Lt.Army,nr.Wollmatingen Kr.Konstanz(Ger.)20.7.44	MURDER	U.S.
FUNZE, Johannes	163457	M			Sturmscharfhr.Crim.secretary,Gestapo,SS,Jalhay-Surister(Bel.)22.-23.10.43	MURDER	BEL.
FUNZEL	137050	M	Ger.		Capt.21 Panzer Div.Hqrs.,Sessenheim(Fr.)1.45	MURDER	U.S.
FUNZEL	194395	M	Ger.		SS Staff Sgt.CC Gusen(Aust.)25.7.44	MURDER	U.S.
FUNZEL	251676			16	Lt.Supply Coy.Castellucho(It.)12.8.43	INTERR.	U.K.
FUNZEN, Hans	135201	M			Leader,SS Food-Leader,CC Erfurt(Ger.)44	TORTURE	U.S.
FUNZER	173227	M		10	Staff Sgt.Guard,397 Land.Schtz.Bn.Stalag XXB,CC Freystadt,Bitterfeld (Ger.)1.-4.45	TORTURE	U.F.
FUPZIG, August	132594				Secretary,Kommandantur,Chauny(Fr.)	MURDER	FR.
FUTZLER	167097				Civilian,Moulins-Metz(Fr.)	PILLAGE	FR.
FUNZMANT	251668				Capt.100 Bn.157 Res.Inf.Div.L'Ain(Fr.)10.-21.7.44	MURDER	FR.
KUPESSER, Fritz	24907				SS Rottfhr.CC Struthof(Fr.)42-44	MISC.CRIMES	U.S.
FUPFER	132231				SS Uschafhr.Occ.SS	MURDER	U.S.
FUPFER	145818				SS Uschafhr.4 SS Baubde.formerly SS Totenkopf Div.Asst.to Camp Cmdt. CC Ellrich-Gardelegen(Ger.)4.-14.4.45	MURDER	U.S.
FUPFER	254812	M	Ger.		Adjudant,157 Inf.Div.Mountains Plateau des Glieres(Fr.)22.3.-5.4.44	TORTURE	FR.

KUP-KUR

NAME	C.R.FILE NUMBER	SEX	NATIO-NALITY	DATE OF BIRTH	RANK OCCUPATION UNIT PLACE AND DATE OF CRIME	REASON WANTED	WANTED BY
KUPFER, Alfred	189339	M			Hptwachtmeister, Police, Poppenhausen, Rodach, Heldburg (Ger.) 5.42	MURDER	POL.
KUPFER, Georg	145225	M	Ger.		SS-Hptscharfhr., Waffen-SS, C.C. Buchenwald (Ger.)	MISC.CRIMES	U.S.
KUPFER, Hans	193455	M	Ger.		SS-Hptscharfhr., C.C. Buchenwald (Ger.) 42-45	TORTURE	U.S.
KUPFER, Ludwig	193254	M	Ger.	30. 6.89	Official, Ruestungs-Kriegsproduktions-Ministerium, Uherski-Brod (Czech.) 39-45	MURDER	CZECH.
KUPITZ see KUBITZ, Otto	2110						
KUPITZ	173702	M	Ger.	14	Official, Gestapo, Uscharfhr., SS, Abt. IV 3a, Clermont-Ferrand, Vichy Puy de Dome (Fr.)	WITNESS	FR.
KUPKE	254994	M	Ger.		Pvt., Fieldpolice troop 694, Marseille Lancon (Fr.) 6.44	PILLAGE	FR.
KUPPELHUBER, Robert	193255	M	Ger.	21. 4.04	S.A.-Truppfhr., (Czech.)	MISC.CRIMES	CZECH.
KUPPENBENDER	150660	M			Dr., public official, Jena (Ger.)	TORTURE	U.S.
KUPPER	136247	M	Ger.		Cmdt., Army, La Ferte sur Aube (Fr.) 15.4.44	MURDER	FR.
KUPPER	192446	M	Ger.		Official, Dr., prison, C.C. Aachen (Ger.) 1943	TORTURE	BEL.
KUPSCH	132587	M	Ger.		Judge, Col., German Military Court, Berlin and Torgau (Ger.)5.40-45	MURDER	FR.
KUPSCK	260154	M	Ger.		Lt., 7 Res.Artl.Regt., Massif du Vercors Isere et Drome (Fr.) 7.-8.44	SUSPECT	FR.
KURBIS, Lothar	251106	M	Ger.		Lt., 6 Coy., 16 Hübner-Regt., Kinrooi (Bel.) 9.44	INTERR.	BEL.
KURCHBAUM, A.	132487	M	Ger.-Aust.		Guesthousekeeper, civilian, Wagendorf near Liebnitz (Aust.) 25.2.44	TORTURE	U.S.
KURCHER, Hans	142204	M	Ger.		Guard, C.C. Flossenburg Floeha (Ger.)	MISC.CRIMES	FR.
KURCIN	147109	M	Ger.		Member, Gestapo, St. Vid (Nor.) 1943	MURDER	YUGO.
KURCK or KURT	250904	M			Foreman, C.C. Buchenwald (Ger.)	BRUTALITY	FR.
KURCZAWA (KURCZWA) see KURZAWA	254950						
KURDYS, Johann	253753	M		20.12.17	Pvt., C.C. Ellrich, Nordhausen (Ger.)	MURDER	U.S.
KURITZ see KUBITZ, Otto	2110						
KURITZ	137475	M			SS-Uscharfhr., C.C. Buchenwald Weimar (Ger.)	MURDER	U.S.
KURK	146983	M	Ger.		Lt., Army, Feldpost-Nr.10261 A, Capestang (Fr.) 1944	MISC.CRIMES	FR.
KURMANN	193805	M	Ger.		Estate agent, "Rittergut" Zermutzel (Ger.) 30.9.44	WITNESS	FR.
KURNER	139174	M			Kreisleiter, N.S.D.A.P., Schollach (Ger.)	MURDER	U.S.
KURNER	139175	M			Civilian, (K. is the son of the Kreisleiter Kurner), Schollach (Ger.)	MURDER	U.S.
KUROV	260674	M	Ger.		Sgt., Army, 3 Coy., Graudenz (Pol.) 7.44	MURDER	FR.
KURPANLAK	124640	M		15	Uscharfhr., SS, C.C. Birkenau, Oswiecim (Pol.) 8.43-1.44	MURDER	U.S.
KURSAMER	186759	M	Ger.		Hptsturmfhr., SS, C.C. Flossenburg (Ger.)	TORTURE	FR.
KURSAVE	258079	M	Ger.		SS-Uscharfhr., Special Police, Val Mezirici (Czech.) 44-45	MURDER	CZECH.
KURSAWA	300284	M	Ger.		Osturmfhr., Agent, Police-secretary, SD. Troyes and Berlin, from the "Rennes-Gestapo", Troyes and region (Fr.) 3.10.43-22.8.44	MURDER	FR.
KURSCHNER	187647	M	Ger.	87	Cpl., Arb.Kdo., Stalag IX C, Vacha (Ger.)	MURDER	U.K.
KURSCHNER	302083	M	Ger.		Oscharfhr., deputy to heads of political bureau, C.C. Auschwitz-Birkenau (Pol.) from 1940	MURDER	FR.
KURSCHNER, Edmund	102960	M	Ger.		(Landwachtpostenfhr.), Army, Inf., Schweina (Ger.) 2.44-20.7.44	MURDER	U.S.
KURSCHNER, Kurt	134871	M			SS, C.C. Ohrdruf (Ger.) 10.44-4.45	MURDER	U.S.
KURSCHNER, Richard	191906	M			Cpl., Army, Massiac (Fr.) 7.8.44	MISC.CRIMES	FR.
KURSNER	173753	M			Paymaster, Verbindungsstab, Valence (Fr.)	MISC.CRIMES	FR.
KURSSA	254070	M	Ger.		Employee, Sipo, IV D, Bruessel (Bel.) 40-45	INTERR.	BEL.
KURST	161492	M	Ger.		Sgt., C.C. Morlaix (Fr.) 1944	MURDER	FR.
KURT	137667	M	Ger.		Sgt., 369 Landesschuetzen-Bn., Engledorf (Ger.) 12.12.43	TORTURE	U.K.
KURT	173740	M	Ger.		Rottenfhr., SS, C.C. Buchenwald (Ger.) 42-45	MURDER	FR.
KURT	193951	F	Ger.		Officer, C.C. Ravensbrueck (Ger.)	TORTURE	FR.
KURT	193952	M	Ger.		Lt., C.C. Ravensbrueck (Ger.)	TORTURE	FR.
KURT see KURCK	250904						
KURT	254975	M	Ger.		Pvt., Unit 59949, Langon (Fr.) 16.6.44	MURDER	FR.
KURT	306421	M	Ger.	about 05	Control senior, N.C.O., administration of working commando East-Leipzig-Area (Ger.) about 12.12.43	BRUTALITY	U.K.
KURT, Franz	151334	M	Ger.		Customs official, Zollgrenzschutz, Lancrans (Fr.) 22.7.41	MURDER	FR.
KURTEN	167052	M	Ger.		Pvt., 21 Pz.Div., 125 Escadron, 8 Coy., Reherrey (Fr.) 7.10.44	MURDER	FR.
KURTEN, Kurt	149298	M	Ger.		SS-Standartenfhr., Muenchen (Ger.)	MURDER	FR.
KURTH	39653	M			Argenton (Fr.) 9.6.44	MURDER	FR.
KURTH	307005	M	Ger.		Female medical officer, C.C. Ravensbrueck (Ger.) 40-45	BRUTALITY	BEL.
KURTH, Wolf or COURTH	250334	M	Ger.		377 Jaeger-Regt., Vinkt, Meigem Area (Bel.) 25.-31.5.40	INTERR.	BEL.
KURTZ	528	M		12	Police-asst., (Zugwachtmeister), Police, C.C. Grini (Nor.) 1942	MURDER	NOR.
KURTZ	125043	M	Ger.		Capt., Stalag IV A, Hohnstein (Ger.) 1.44	MISC.CRIMES	U.K.
KURTZ	178308	M	Ger.	15	Pvt., Landesschuetzen-Bn., Arbeits-Kdo.176, C.C. Kolando (Pol.)12.41	MURDER	U.K.
KURTZ	253740	M			Civilian, Gambin, Kreis Stolp (Ger.) 4.7.44	MISC.CRIMES	U.S.
KURTZ	257647	M	Ger.		Engineer, Daimler-Benz-A.G., Sochaux (Fr.) 9.-11.44	PILLAGE	FR.
KURTZ	259627	M	Ger.		Capt., 125 Escadron, 21 Pz.-Div., Recherrey Meurthe and Moselle (Fr.) 10. and 11.44	PILLAGE	FR.
KURTZ, Anton	300285	M	Ger.		Cpl., Vontes Crete (Grc.) 12.8.44	MISC.CRIMES	GRC.
KURTZAHN, Willy	167050	M	Ger.		Lt., Army, 240 Regt., D.C.U.S., Salieu Cote d'Or (Fr.) 6.9.44	MURDER	FR.
KURTZWEG	31944	M	Ger.		Pvt., N.C.O., Army, 2 Regt., Locmine (Fr.) 1944	MURDER	FR.
KURTZWEI	260099	M	Ger.		Block-chief, C.C. Dachau (Ger.) 42-44	SUSPECT	FR.
KURZ see KORTZ	530						
KURZ	129693	M	Ger.		Uscharfhr., SS, C.C. Dora, Nordhausen (Ger.)	MURDER	U.S.
KURZ	137053	M	Ger.		Capt., 125 Pz.-Gren.Regt., 111 Bn., 9-10 Coy.C.O., Sessheim (Fr.)1.45	MURDER	U.S.
KURZ	143160	M			SS-Osturmfhr., station doctor, C.C. Mauthausen (Aust.) 41-45	MURDER	U.S.
KURZ	189760	M	Ger.	00	Factory Boss, civilian, Frieben (Aust.) 5.5.45	TORTURE	U.S.
KURZ, Alois	529	M		17	SS-Usturmfhr., C.C. Maidanek (Pol.) 40-4.44	MURDER	POL.
KURZ, Walter	253752	M			Pvt., C.C. Ellrich, Nordhausen (Ger.)	MURDER	U.S.
KURZ, Wilhelm	253085	M			Flyer, Camp Ellrich, Nordhausen (Ger.)	MURDER	U.S.
KURZ, Willy	167966	M	Ger.		Sgt., Feldgendarmerie, Auberive, Flagy, Coiffy, Challencey (Fr.)	MURDER	FR.
KURZAWA or KURCZAWA (KURCZWA), Alexander	254950	M	Ger.		Milker, civilian, Wolfsburg (Ger.) 29.6.44	TORTURE	U.S.
KURZER	186260	M	Ger.		SS-Hptscharfhr., C.C. Gross-Rosen (Ger.) 1941	MURDER	U.S.
KURZINGER	253087	M			Pvt., Camp Ellrich, Nordhausen (Ger.)	MURDER	U.S.
KURZINGER, Franz	11283	M	Ger.		Pvt., Pz.Gren.Regt.110 or 111, 2 Coy., Albine (Fr.) 29.6.44	MURDER	FR.
KURZIK	252256	M	Ger.		Cpl., chief, Fort de Ceclin (Fr.) 29.-30.8.44	INTERR.	FR.
KURZKE, Alfred	129694	M	Ger.		SS-Osturmfhr., C.C. Dora-Mittelbau, Nordhausen (Ger.)	MURDER	U.S.
KURZNER	146982	M			Scharfhr., SS-Pz.Div. "Das Reich", Valence D'Agen (Fr.) 1944	MURDER	FR.
KURZWEIL, Toni	191891	M	Ger.		Civilian, Lorkenhoe (Ger.)	MURDER	U.S.

KUS-LAB

NAME	C.R.FILE NUMBER	SEX	NATIONALITY	DATE OF BIRTH	RANK OCCUPATION UNIT PLACE AND DATE OF CRIME	REASON WANTED	WANTED BY
KUSCH	194222	M	Ger.		Capt.,Army,Geh.Feldpolizei,Liege (Bel.) 5.41	TORTURE	BEL.
KUSCHEL	142010	M	Ger.		SS-Usturmfhr.,Gestapo,Belgrade (Yugo.) 16.2.44,3.3.44	TORTURE	YUGO.
KUSCHEP	254601	M	Ger.		Rottfhr.,SD,Toulouse (Fr.) 11.42-8.44	MURDER	FR.
KUSCHKA	254818	M	Ger.		Insp.,Marine,Hennebout (Fr.)	MURDER	FR.
KUSCHNIK	178307	M	Ger.		Pvt.,394 Inf.Rgt.,Laband near Gleiwitz (Ger.) 23.10.44	MURDER	U.K.
KUSCHOW	134715	M			SS-Bdefhr.,Nuernberg (Ger.) 44	MURDER	U.S.
KUSCHY	260675	M	Ger.		Chief of Camp Buchenwald (Ger.) 40-44	MURDER	FR.
KUSDAS	532	M			Capt.,Boulon (Fr.) 14.7.44,10.-13.8.44	MURDER	FR.
KUSEL	126752	M	Ger.		Sonderfhr.,Oflag IV C,Koenigstein (Ger.)	MISC.CRIMES	FP.
KUSELMECKI	192894	M			Wachtmeister,Schupo,C.C.Falstad (Nor.) 41-44	WITNESS	NOR.
KUSIN	300060		Ger.		Member of the staff,Mauthausen (Aust.) 42-45	MURDER	FR.
KUSIENS,Wilhelm	151959	M	Ger.		Police-chief,Police Weiden (Ger.) 41-45	TORTURE	U.S.
KUSKI	259387	M			Camp-chief,Auschwitz (Pol.)	BRUTALITY	FR.
KUSLING (see KISSLING)	259641						
KUSWIERZ	138356	M			SS-Adj.,Gestapo,SS,Lyon (Fr.) 6.-8.44	MURDER	FR.
KUSMIREK	1421				Cpl.,Army,194 Gren.Rgt.	MISC.CRIMES	U.K.
KUSOLITSCH,Joseph	302084	M	Ger.		Insp.,Lourdes Custom-House (operational Kommando),Lourdes,Htes-Pyrenees (Fr.) 1.-8.44	MURDER	FR.
KUSS	124273	M	Ger.		Pvt.,SS Pz.Rgt.I,SS Pz.Div.I,9 Coy,Malmedy (Bel.) 17.12.44	MURDER	U.S.
KUSS	137093	M	Ger.		Doctor,Arbeitskdo.7006,C.C.Adelebsen (Ger.)	TORTURE	U.K.
KUSS	187646	M	Ger.	94	Doctor,Arbeitskdo.,C.C.Stalag XI B,Bramburg (Ger.) 43-45	TORTURE	U.K.
KUSS	192445	M	Ger.		SS-Hptschfhr.,C.C.Flossenburg (Ger.) 44-45	SUSPECT	U.S.
KUSS	253863	M			SS-Oschfhr.,Zavist (Czech.)	MURDER	CZECH.
KUSS	256136	M			Commander,C.C.Flossenburg (Ger.)	BRUTALITY	FR.
KUSS,Leo	147072	M			Kreisleiter,Osturmfhr.,NSDAP,SS,Kranj (Yugo.)	MURDER	YUGO.
KUSSE,Gustav	250879	M	Ger.	79	Farmer,Civilian,Poppenhausen (Ger.) 11.5.42	MURDER	POL.
KUSSER,Armand	167048	M	Ger.		Feldgendarm,Feldgendarmerie,Luneville-Maixe (Fr.) 16.-17.8.44	MURDER	FR.
KUSSIER	149269	M			Adj.,Stalag VI C,	MURDER	FR.
KUSSMER	254157	M	Ger.		Arbeitsfhr.,SD,C.C.St.Michielsgestel (Neth.) 8.-9.44	PILLAGE	NETH.
KUSTCHER	186758	M	Ger.		Lt.,950 R.I.H.,Charente et Vienne (Fr.) 8.44	TORTURE	FR.
KUSTER	138253	M	Ger.		SS-Sturmbannfhr.,SS,Gambsheim (Fr.) 12.44	MURDER	FR.
KUSTER	193806	M	Ger.		Lt.,Kommandantur,Rochelongue pres d'Agde (Fr.) 18.3.43	WITNESS	FR.
KUSTER,Hans	142148	M	Ger.		Army,Kgf.Arb.Bn.188, 3 Coy,Herdla,Bratholmen,Fure (Nor.)	MURDER	U.K.
KUSTERS	167690	M	Ger.		Governor General,Ober-Reg.Rat,Dr.,Radom (Pol.) 9.39-44	PILLAGE	POL.
KUTCHERA (see KUZERA)	253736						
KUTGENS	167729	M	Ger.		Dr.,Director,Civilian,Kunstschutz,Aix La Chapelle (Fr.) 9.41-44	PILLAGE	BEL.
KUTH	253982	M	Ger.		Lt.,Coy Fuehrer,2 Bn.6 Coy Div."Hermann Goering" 4 Rgt.Fallschirmjg.Rgt.,Helchteren and Hechtel (Neth.) 5.and 11.9.44	PILLAGE	BEL.
KUTNABEL	260101	M	Ger.		Capt.,Unit 13907 A,Massif du Vercors,Isère and Drôme (Fr.) 20.7.-5.8.44	SUSPECT	FR.
KUTSCH	534	M	Ger.		SS-Sturmfhr.,C.C.Mauthausen (Ger.) 41-42	TORTURE	NETH.
KUTSCHBACH,Wilhelm	251652	M	Ger.		Lt.,Toulon (Fr.) 19.7.44	WITNESS	FR.
KUTSCHER	195060	M	Ger.		SS-Uschfhr.,SD,Sonder u.Wirtschaftskdo.Beeck,Gorssel-Beck (Neth.) 23.-24.9.44	MURDER	NETH.
KUTSCHER,Christian	102961	M	Ger.		Civilian,Luisenhohen (Ger.) 4.-5.12.44	WITNESS	U.S.
KUTSCHER,Richard	145838	M			Civilian,Borkum (Ger.) 4.8.44	MURDER	U.S.
KUTSCHEPA,Franz	147071	M	Ger.		Doc.territeries chief,Administration,Slovenia (Yugo.) 42	MURDER	YUGO.
KUTSCHERA,Richard	123037	M	Ger.		C.C.XVII A	TORTURE	BEL.
KUTSCHERAUER,Johann	189759	M	Ger.		Clerk,Gestapo,Brno (Czech.) 39-45	MISC.CRIMES	CZECH.
KUTSCHMANN,Walter	257516	M			Oschfhr.,chief of Grenz-Commissariat,SD,Foix (Fr.) 11.42	MURDER	FR.
KUTSCHNER	306594	M	Ger.	83-85	Cpl.,Guard A-K 191,Vacha Thuringia,Stalag IV C (Ger.) 30.11.44	MURDER	U.K.
KUTTEP	127985	M	Ger.		Officer,Kommissar,Gestapo,C.C.Brauweller (Ger.) 24.11.44	MURDER	U.K.
KUTTER	137469	M			Kommissar,Gestapo,SS Aussendienst,Koeln (Ger.)	MURDER	U.S.
KUITER,Willi	31710	M			Settler,Gniezno Olekszyn (Pol.) 12.39	INCENDIARISM	POL.
KUTTNAR	189796	M		05	Sgt.,Arbeitskdo.,Benghazi (Nord-Afrika) 41	TORTURE	U.K.
KUTTNER,Bernard	128840	M			Civilian,Village of Stettin (Ger.)	MISC.CRIMES	U.K.
KUTTRUFF,Frederich	187141	M	Ger.	25	Army,Lorch (Ger.) 11.4.45	MURDER	U.S.
KUTZ	256137	M	Ger.		Commander,C.C.Flossenburg (Ger.)	TORTURE	FR.
KUTZNEP	165389	M		00	Civilian	TORTURE	FR.
KUTZNEP,Helmut Otto	261095	M	Ger.	8.93	Dr.,Ministerial-Dirigent,Ministry of Justice,Sub-Dept.B.Dept.IV	SUSPECT	U.S.
KUYPER	152505	M			Capt.,Stalag XVIII D,C.C.Peggau (Aust.)	TORTURE	U.K.
KUZ,Erwin	254649	M	Ger.	25. 9.00	Factory manager,Civilian,Chrast (Czech.) 39-45	PILLAGE	CZECH.
KUZ,Robert	133797	M			SS-Uschfhr.,C.C.Weimar,Buchenwald (Ger.)	BRUTALITY	U.S.
KUZERA (or KUCZERA or KUTCHERA)	253736	M			Rottfhr.,C.C.Vackenrode,Nordhauser (Ger.)	MURDER	U.S.
KUZNINAKI,Stefan	145176	M			Civilian,Lauf (Ger.) 44	WITNESS	U.S.
KVAPIL,Hermann	254639	M	Ger.	16. 3.07	Gaustellenleiter,NSV School,Vysoke-Jilemnice (Czech.) 4.5.45	MURDER	CZECH.
KVASNITSCHKA	186114	M	Ger.		Member,SS,SD,Gestapo,Pilsen (Czech.) 39-45	MURDER	CZECH.
KWATELBAUM	134870	M	Ger.		SS,Erfurt (Ger.) 44	TORTURE	U.S.
KWICH,Leopold	253733	M		24.12.18	Cpl.,C.C.Ellrich,Nordhausen (Ger.)	MURDER	U.S.
KWINT	131290	M	Ger.		Sturmmann,SS,C.C.Jawischowitz near Auschwitz (Pol.) 44	MURDER	U.S.
KWITCHINSKY	121537	M			Cpl.,Interpreter,Feldgendarmerie Trupp 986,St.Illide (Fr.) 15.3.44	PILLAGE	FR.
KY	254657	M			Pvt.,Army,Andel Babylonienbrock-Genderen (Neth.) 5.45	MURDER	NETH.
KYNAST	187645	M			Lt.,Feldgendarmerie,Goudriaan (Neth.) 22.5.44	MURDER	U.K.
KYNAST,Erwin	132225	M	Ger.	09	Civilian, member of SS,C.C.Osterode (Ger.) 42-45	TORTURE	U.S.
KYNZL,Albert	306066	M	Ger.		N.C.O.,Director,Gestapo Prison Karmen at Dubrovnik (Yugo.) 44	MURDER	YUGO.
KYPTIS (see KOUPTIS)	254835						
LAAS,Alfred	254622	M	Ger.	00	SS-Usturmfhr.,Konopiste (Czech.) 45	PILLAGE	CZECH.
LAASER,Gertrud	257491	F			Org.Todt,Vuhldorf (Ger.)	INTERR.	U.S.
LABBERT	255555	M	Ger.		Lt.,125 Bo.Gren.Rgt.,	PILLAGE	FR.
LABBERTH	254609	M	Ger.		Lt.,125 Gren.Rgt.,Hablainville (Fr.) 10.44	PILLAGE	FR.
LABDAWSKI,Rudolf	260519	M	Ger.	12. 2.19	SS-Guard,C.C.Natzweiler (Fr.)	MURDER	FR.
LABINON,Charles	257492	M			Chief of S.I.,Chinay,St.Remy (Bel.) 22.4.44	MURDER	U.S.
LABOUDIE	186701	M		78	Works manager,Civilian,Saw Mills,Beuthen (Ger.) 3.43	MURDER	U.K.
LABRECH	157107	M			N.C.O.,3 SS Baubde.,C.C.Osterhagen,Gardelegen (Ger.) 5.-14.4.45	MURDER	U.S.

LAB - LAM

NAME	C.R.FILE NUMBER	SEX	NATIONALITY	DATE OF BIRTH	RANK OCCUPATION UNIT PLACE AND DATE OF CRIME	REASON WANTED	WANTED BY
LABS	129696	M	Ger.		Capt., Army, 330 Inf.Rgt., 183 Volksgren.Div., Linnich(Ger.)16.1.45	MISC.CRIMES	U.S.
LARCH (or LARSCH, LARSCHL)	12574	M	Ger.		Sgt.,110 or 111 Pz.Gren.Rgt.,Gourdon(Fr.) 29.6.44	MURDER	FR.
L'CACE, Heinz	140053	M	Ger.		Lt.,Army,Puiseaux(Fr.) 10.8.44	MURDER	FR.
LACCOURT	255013	M	Ger.		Official, Auxiliary Police, Abt.III B, Sipo. Brussels(Bel.)40-45	INTER.	BEL.
LACH, Kurt	179828	M		13	Hptsturmfhr, Crim.Comm, SD,Gestapo,Lidice,Lezaky(Czech.)6.42	MURDER	CZECH.
LACHEMEYER	196823	M			Lt.,100 Geb.Bn.,2 Coy,St.Germain d'Joux (Fr.) 7.-8.44	INTERR.	FR.
LACHEMEYER, Wilhelm	259734	M			Lt.,157 Inf.Div.(Reserve),Area L'Ain(Fr.) 7.44	MISC.CRIMES	FR.
LACHERUND, S.F.Z.	156103	M			Inf.Off.,Army, Oberkommando 18, Siwerkaia(Russia) 42-44	MURDER	U.S.
LACHETER	1425	M	Ger.		Hptsturmfhr, SS Pol.Rgt.18	MURDER	U.K.
LACHFELD	160995	M			Pvt.,Army, Leipzig(Ger.)	TORTURE	U.S.
LACHMANN	536	M	Ger.		SS Oschfhr. (Guard), CC Auschwitz-Birkenau (Pol.) 39-45	MURDER	CZECH.,U.S.,BEL., POL.
LACHMANN	146002	M			Mayor, Civilian, Berchtesgaden (Ger.)	MURDER	U.S.
LACHMANN	150696	M			Civilian, Ruesselsheim (Ger.) 25.8.44	MURDER	U.S.
LACHMANN	260673	M			Major,crimes against peace,war crimes and crimes against humanity	WITNESS	U.S.
LACHMUND	162354	M		05	Leader, Army, Ober-Kdo., Schapki (Latvia) 42-44	MURDER	U.S.
LACHMUND	196822	M	Ger.		Adjutant, W-SS, Izon la Bruisse - Sederon (Fr.) 22.2.44	INTERR.	FR.
LACHNER, Franz	187140	M	Ger.	5.1.91	Civilian, Regensburg (Ger.) 9.44	TORTURE	CZECH., U.S.
LICHNER, Franz	260368	M			Oberwachtmstr,SS,Penitentiary,Northern Norway, 6.42-5.45	MURDER	YUGO.
LACIFER, Heinrich	189615	M	Ger.		Cpl., Kampfgeschwader 55, Chartres (Fr.) 1.3.41	MURDER	FR.
LA CIGOYNE(see STORCH,Wilfried)	1526						
L'CKNER (see LACKNER)	188921	M					
LACKMANN	173741	M	Ger.		Capt., Azerbaidjan Bn.,Chennes,St.Donat(Fr.) 15.6.44	MURDER	FR.
LACKMANN	301785	M	Ger.		Uschfhr, Political Bureau, CC Auschwitz(Pol.) 40-45	MURDER	FR.
LACKOUD (or ACKOUD)	151961	M	Ger.		Adjutant, Army,8 Coy of Brandenburg,Pont-St-Esprit(Fr.) 44	MURDER	FR.
LACKNER	67577	M	Ger.		Rottfhr, 17 SS Pz.Gren.Div."G.v.B.",Segre-Renaze(Fr.) 6.8.44- 30.7.40	MURDER	FR.
LACKNER (or LACKENER)	188921	M			Sgt.,Army,Chambery Biollay(Fr.) 8.1.44	MURDER	FR.
LADE	67561	M	Ger.		Unit S.P. 15201,Chenebier (Fr.) 27.9.44	MURDER	FR.
LADE	167011	M	Ger.		Capt.,Parachute Abt., Commercy (Fr.) 24.8.44	WITNESS	FR.
LADEGAST, Karl	261836	M	Ger.		Telephone-caller, Gestapo,Amiens, Gentelles(Fr.) 6.-8.44	MURDER	FR.
LA DICK	195059	M	Ger.		Capt., 2 Coy, 877 Lds.Schtz.Bn., Veitsch(Aust.) 9.10.42	TORTURE	U.K.
LADWIG	191377	M	Ger.		Sgt.,Army,Kgf.Arb.Bn.202,3 Coy,Lonsdal(Nor.)	WITNESS	NOR.
LAEB	256562	M	Ger.		Chief of Sub-Section, Mittelwerk CC Nordhausen(Ger.)	MURDER	U.S.
LAEBEL	305918	M	Ger.		SS Sturmbanfhr,SD,Leitabschnitt Dept.,Prague,Auschwitz-Birkenau(Pol.) 39-45	MURDER	CZECH.
LAEDEMPIPT, Heinz	253135	M	Ger.	30.8.20	Cpl., z.b.V. Kdo.31,Valasske Mezirici(Czech.) 2.-5.45	MURDER	CZECH.
LAEDLE, Paul	261094	M	Ger.	11.92	Judge, peoples court, Germany	SUSPECT	U.S.
LAERBUSCH, Hans	300292	M	Ger.		Cpl., L 05258, LGPA Wien, Herklion Crete (Grc.) 10.44	MISC.CRIMES	GRC.
LAFEUPE (see FAFERRE)	155419	M					
LAFFAREZ	257485	M	Ger.		Dr., Employee, Volkswagenwerk, Sochaux(Fr.) 41-44	BRUTALITY	FR.
LAFONTAINE	192743	M		about 12	Leader, Org.Todt,Hauptbauleitung Oslo (Nor.) 42-43	MISC.CRIMES	NOR.
LA FOUINE (or FRANK)	171697	M	Ger.		Sgt., Gestapo, Briey(Fr.) 28.8.44	TORTURE	FR.
LAGNUS	130594	M	Ger.		CC Mauthausen (Aust.) 41-45	MURDER	U.S.
LAGOMEYER (see IVIANONTANWITCH)	149767						
LAHGE	193367	M	Ger.		Pvt.,Kriegsgef.Arb.Bn.41,Nerlandsdal,Kristiansund(Nor.) 41-45	TORTURE	NOR.
LAHLEN	252450	M			Oschfhr, SS Dienstst. F.P.23474 E, Aigues Rives(Fr.) 2.-3.44	PILLAGE	FR.
LAHM	162872	M	Ger.		Doctor, Stalag IV F, Hartmannsdorf(Ger.) 44	MURDER	FR.
LAHN	251119	M			Lt.Col., Hohenstein(Ger.)	SUSPECT	U.S.
LAHRER	302086	M	Ger.		Warder, Diez-Lahn Prison (Ger.) 40-45	MURDER	BEL.
LAHOUSEN, Erwin	261248	M			Lt.General, Army	WITNESS	U.S.
LAHR, Anton	195449	M	Ger.	25.11.08	Occupied Territories, Luxembourg, Junglinster (Lux.) 40-45	MISC.CRIMES	LUX.
LAJUSZ	253780	M	Ger.		Sturmbannfhr, SD, Hengelo (Neth.) 30.4.43	MURDER	NETH.
LAIKE	187927	M			Pvt., 110 Pz.Gren.Rgt., Gourdon (Fr.)	MURDER	FR.
LADER	186148	M	Ger.		Capt, Army, Periqueux (Fr.) 10.8.44	MURDER	FR.
LAINZ	142193	M			Penitentiary, Ziegenhain (Ger.)	TORTURE	FR.
LAIS (LEIST or LEYS)	9601	M	Ger.		Guard, Lt., CC Breendonck (Bel.) 41-42	TORTURE	BEL.
LAIS, Wilhelm	39655	M	Ger.		N.C.O., Army, Feldpost Nr.21309 E, Mouterre Solly(Fr.) 27.6.40	MISC.CRIMES	FR.
LAISS, Ernst	140909	M	Ger.	03	Usturmfhr. SS, CC Breendonek (Bel.) 41-42	TORTURE	BEL.
LALKE	12572	M	Ger.		Pvt.,Army,110 or 111 Pz.Gren.Rgt.,3 Gruppe,Gourdon(Fr.) 29.6.44	MURDER	FR.
LALHEN	301140	M	Ger.		Oschfhr, SS, Aiguesvives, Gard (Fr.) 2.3.44	PILLAGE	FR.
LILLEFSACK	191376	M	Ger.		Sgt.,184 Kgf.Arb.Bn.,Bassia Tunnel(Nor.)	WITNESS	NOR.
LAMARTIN (see LAMMERDING)	1718						
LAMARTINE	62102	M		00	General, Army, Tulle (Fr.) 9.6.44	MURDER	FR.
LAMATSCH	161418	M			Uschfhr, SS, CC Buchenwald (Ger.) 40-42	TORTURE	U.S.
LAMATSCH	250358	M			Rottfhr, CC Dora, Nordhausen (Ger.)	MURDER	U.S.
LAMBACHER	151957	M	Ger.	1907-10	Schfhr, SS, Paris (Fr.)	BRUTALITY	U.K.
LAMBERG (or KOLONIE)	252258	F			Civilian, Berlin (Ger.) 21.6.44	WITNESS	U.S.
LAMBERT, Ludwig	251703	M		31.8.02	Civilian, Thanham (Ger.) 16.4.45	WITNESS	U.S.
LAMBRECHT	185133	M			Sgt., Army, Condom (Fr.) 5.44	MURDER	FR.
LAMBRECHT	252448	M	Ger.		Lt., Army, Monte Morlo (It.)	INTERR.	U.K.
LAMBRIGTS	253778	M	Ger.		Official, Sipo, Hengelo (Neth.) 30.4.43	INTERR.	NETH.
LAMERIC	67566	M	Ger.		Pvt., Army, Germany 10.43	TORTURE	U.K.
LAMFERMANN, Wilhelm	134806	M			Leader,Ostarbeiterlager, Zwekekal(Ger.)	MISC.CRIMES	U.S.
LAMGE, Hermann	72279	M			Usturmfhr. W-SS, CC Struthof Natzweiler (Fr.) 42-44	MISC.CRIMES	FR.
LAMICH	194657	M	Ger.		Adj., Feld-Gend., Glandee (Fr.) 12.9.42	MURDER	FR.
LAMM	130603	M			Uschfhr, SS, CC Mauthausen (Aust.) 41-45	MURDER	FR.
LAMM, Karl	252369	M	Ger.	18.11.07	Hptschfhr, Official, SD, Army, Middelburg, Zeeland,Tilburg(Neth.)10.44	MURDER	U.S.
LAMMER, Kaiden	192895	M	Ger.		Schupo, CC Falstad (Nor.) 11.42	MURDER	NETH.
LAMMERDING,Heinz(or LAMARTIN)	1718	M	Ger.		Bde.Fhr, Div.Commander,SS Pz.Div."Das Reich",Normandy,South France	MURDER	NOR.
LAMMERS	124765	M		10	Gestapo, SD, Wassenberg (Ger.) 12.44	MURDER	U.K.,U.S.,FR.
LUMERS, Willi	253777			10	Usturmfhr, SS, Effeld(Ger.) 1.11.44	MURDER	U.S.
LAMMERSDORF, Heiny	194103	M	Ger.		Obermaat Marine Art., Guard CC Lueneburg,Wilhelmshaven(Ger.)7-10.4.45	MURDER	NETH.
LAMES, Matthias	260852	M		00	Civ.,Schweich(Ger.)15.1.45; resides at Ehrang(Ger.)	MURDER	U.K.
LAMTIAGER, Hans (or LAUNTIAGER)	192010	M	Ger.		SS Pz.Div., Feldpost Nr.37446 C, Port St.Foix la Fleix(Fr.)	WITNESS	U.S.
						MURDER	FR.

LAM-LAN

NAME	C.R.FILE NUMBER	SEX	NATIO-NALITY	DATE OF BIRTH	RANK OCCUPATION UNIT PLACE AND DATE OF CRIME	REASON WANTED	WANTED BY
LAMOTTE, Karl	53873	M	Ger.	95	Hptsturmfhr.,SS,C.C.Breendonck(Bel.) 40-9.44	TORTURE	BEL.
LAMP	250359	M			Uschfhr.,C.C.Rottleberode,Nordhausen(Ger.)	MURDER	U.S.
LAMPE	540	M	Ger.		Oschfhr.,SS,C.C.Korgen(Nor.) 6.42-43	MURDER	YUGO.
LAMPE see CAMPE	199894						
LAMPE	261090	M	Ger.		Lt.,1 Coy.,1 Bn.,933 Gren.Regt.,244 Inf.Div.,Auriol(Fr.) 10.6.44	MURDER	FR.
LAMPE, Andreas	167718	M	Ger.		Geschaeftsleiter Civilian,Kattowitz(Pol.) 9.39-44	MISC.CRIMES	POL.
LAMPE, Georg	305919	M	Ger.		Hptsturmfhr.SS,SD Leitabschnitt Prag,Oswiecim-Birkenau(Pol.) 39-45	MURDER	CZECH.
LAMPE, Joachim	191745	M	Ger.		Co.Chief,F.J.Lehr-Regt.,Coegnies Chaussee(Bel.) 3.9.44	MURDER	BEL.
LAMPE, Walter	195522	M	Ger.		Employee,SS-Sgt.,Gestapo,SD,Kolin(Czech.) 45	MURDER	CZECH.
LAMPERT, Henni	190406	F	Ger.		Civilian,Wiesbaden(Ger.) 43-45	WITNESS	BEL.
LAMPERT, Wilma	190405	F	Ger.		Civilian,Wiesbaden(Ger.)	WITNESS	U.S.
LAMPRECHT	199040	M	Ger.	85	Wachtmeister,SD,Gross-Beeren(Ger.) 43	MURDER	U.S.
LAMPRECHT	189789	M	Ger.		SD,C.C.Vught(Neth.) 6.6.44	MURDER	NETH.
LAMPRECHT	192897	M	Ger.		Unterwachtmeister,Schupo,C.C.Falstad(Nor.) 42	TORTURE	NOR.
LAMPRECHT	250360	M			Uschfhr.,C.C.Osterhagen,Nordhausen(Ger.)	MURDER	U.S.
LAMPRECHT, Gerhard	192741	M	Ger.	31.10.11	Ex convict,Feldstraflager Nord,Reichsjustizministerium,C.C.Finmark (Nor.)	WITNESS	NOR.
LAMPS, Fritz	253875	M	Ger.		SS-Mann,Corneilles(Fr.) 29.8.44	INTERR.	FR.
LANSCHULTZ	126995	M	Ger.		SS Panz.Div."Das Reich" 44	MURDER	FR.
LANARDT	122962	M	Ger.		Capt.,Lager,Upper-Silesia,Bayrouth(Ger.) 22.1.,29.4.45	TORTURE	U.K.
LANAU	91711	M	Ger.		Cpl.,Army,C.C.Oswiecim(Pol.)	MURDER	POL.
LANBERGER	146949	M	Ger.		Usturmfhr.,SS Panz.Div."Das Reich",Regt."Deutschland" 3 Bn., Venerque Le Vernet(Fr.) 44	MURDER	FR.
LANDAU, Felix	301338	M	Ger.		Member of the Gestapo at Trencin,C.C.Oswiecim-Birkenau(Pol.) 39-45	MURDER	CZECH.
LANDER	124989	M	Ger.		Capt.,Gestapo,SD-Agent,Poitiers Chateau de Porteau(Fr.) 23.8.44	MURDER	FR.
LANDER, R.	301577	M	Ger.		Sgt.of the German Red Cross B 710,Termonde(Bel.) 4.9.44	MURDER	BEL.
LANDES	258785	M	Ger.		Lt.,Army,Ile de Seine(Fr.) 4.8.44	INCENDIARISM	FR.
LANDFRIED	256708	M	Ger.		Interpreter,Feldpolizei,Ariege(Fr.) 12.42-8.44	INTERR.	FR.
LANDFRIED, Friedrich Walter	542	M	Ger.		Dr.,Public Official,Staatssekretaer Reichswirtschaftsministerium, Sturmbannfhr.SS.(Pol.)	MISC.CRIMES	POL.
LANDFRIED, Walter	191982	M			SS-Rottfhr.,1 SS Panz.Regt.,Staff Coy.,Leibstand."Adolf Hitler", Ligneuville and Stoumont(Bel.) 17.-19.12.44	WITNESS	U.S.
LANDGRABE see LAUBGREVE	137553						
LANDGRAF	53890	M	Ger.		Sturmbannfhr.,Oberregierungsrat,SS,Gestapo,Muenster(Ger.)	MISC.CRIMES	UNWCC.
LANDGEN, Paul see LANGEN	46066						
LANDGREVE see LAUBGREVE	137553						
LANDHAUSER	259876	M	Ger.		Cmdt.,C.C.for British Prisoners,Vittel(Fr.) 6.40	PILLAGE	FR.
LANDKAMMER, Franz	262422	M	Ger.	8.6.07	Informer,Gestapo,Lomnice n.L.(Czech.) 39-45	SUSPECT	CZECH.
LANDLEITER	193454	M	Ger.		Oschfhr.,SS,C.C.Buchenwald(Ger.) 38-42	MURDER	U.S.
LANDMANN	12573	M	Ger.		Cpl.,Army,110 or 111 Panz.Gren.Regt.,3 Gruppe,Gourdon(Fr.) 29.6.44	MURDER	FR.
LANDMANN, Werner	305920	M	Ger.		Dr.,Hptsturmfhr.,SS,SD Leitabschnitt Prag,C.C.Oswiecim-Birkenau (Pol.) 39-45	MURDER	CZECH.
LANDNER	255286	M	Ger.		Sgt.,3 Coy.,15 Regt.G.R.,Clermont,Ferrand,Saint-Avit(Fr.) 9.6.44	INTERR.	FR.
LANDROCH	146004	M	Ger.		Civilian Mayor of Berchtesgaden(Ger.)	MISC.CRIMES	U.S.
LANDSCHUKE, Reinhard	67571	M	Ger.	18.3.26	SS,11 Coy.,Charmes(Fr.) 5.9.44	MURDER	FR.
LANDSCHULZE	167012	M	Ger.		Pvt.,Army,Bachvillers(Fr.) 29.8.44	WITNESS	FR.
LANDSDORFER	187066	M			Oschfhr.,C.C.Fahrbereitschaft,Dora,Nordhausen(Ger.) 43-45	TORTURE	U.S.
LANDSHOFF	125185	M	Ger.	95	Hptsturmfhr.and Crim.-Com.,SS,Koenigsberg(Ger.) 41-45	MISC.CRIMES	U.S.
LANDSKRON	191306	M	Ger.		Kis.Art.Btty 717,St.Aneres,Varsenare Les Bauges(Bel.) 4.9.44	MURDER	BEL.
LANDTALER	156101	M	Ger.		SS-Mann,1 SS Panz.Div.(Adolf Hitler),1 SS Rec.Bn.,Parfondruy,Stavelot (Bel.) 18.-22.12.44	MURDER	BEL.
LANDWEHR	139041	M	Ger.		Cpl.,Kraftfahrpark,Pechbrunn(Ger.) 15.4.45	MURDER	U.S.
LANDWEHR	250908	M	Ger.	11	Capt.,Army,Village Potok(Yugo.) 10.43	INTERR.	YUGO.
LANKA	255551	M			SS-Rottfhr.,C.C.Buchenwald(Ger.)	MURDER	U.S.
LANG	29772	M	Ger.		Hptsturmfhr.,SS,Finmark(Nor.) 11.44	MURDER	NOR.
LANG	62486	M	Ger.		Uschfhr.,SS,Guard,C.C.Hinzert(Ger.)	TORTURE	U.S.
LANG	136224	M			Capt.,Sicherungstruppen,St.Flour(Fr.)	MURDER	FR.
LANG	141969	M	Ger.		SS-Rottfhr.,Waldlager V & VI,Guard,C.C. near Ampfing(Ger.) 44-45	TORTURE	U.S.
LANG or LANGER	162254	M	Ger.	06	Cpl.,Army,Landesschuetzen-Bn.997,C.C.Stalag XXB,Schlablau(Ger.) 11.41 & 4.42	TORTURE	U.K.
LANG	162871	M	Ger.		Chirurgien,Kdo.Stalag IVF,C.C.Hartmannsdorf(Ger.) 44	MURDER	FR.
LANG	175705	M	Ger.		Assist.,Stalag VIA,Stemmer(Ger.) 41-45	TORTURE	U.S.
LANG	192390	M	Ger.		C.C.Rollwald(Ger.) 44-45	MURDER	BEL.
LANG	194752	M	Ger.		Chief,Oflag E.,C.C.Neubrandenburg(Ger.)	TORTURE	POL.
LANG	194656	M	Ger.		Sgt.-Guard,Prison,C.C.Kaisheim near Donauwoerth(Ger.) 39-45	SUSPECT	CZECH.
LANG	250909	M	Ger.		Lt.,Garrison Cmdt.,Army,Vrbovsko(Yugo.) 11.-12.11.44	PILLAGE	YUGO.
LANG	253779	M			Doctor,Hohenstein(Ger.)	MURDER	U.S.
LANG	260118	M	Ger.		Officer of (Ordonanz) Order,157 Res.Div.Bayern,Massif Du Vercors (Fr.) 20.7.-5.8.44	SUSPECT	FR.
LANG	261197	M	Ger.		Member of Staff of C.C.Ravensbrueck(Ger.)	SUSPECT	BEL.
LANG	261496	M	Ger.		Lt.,Bn.Spielberg,Regt.z.b.V.Col.Wolff,near Maulson-Navarreux(Fr.)	MURDER	FR.
LANG	300287	M	Ger.		Oberwachtmeister,Strafgefangenenlager Nord,Northern(Nor.) 43-45	BRUTALITY	CZECH.
LANG (II)	306442	M	Ger.		Erbach near Amberg(Ger.) 45	MURDER	CZECH.
LANG or LING	301637	M	Ger.		Erbach near Amberg(Ger.) -45	MURDER	CZECH.
LANG, Bruno	10901	M			Staatsanwalt,Public Official Ministry of Justice,Amtsgerichtsrat, Cheb(Czech.) 40	MURDER	CZECH.
LANG, Edward	300288		Ger.		Sgt.of the Feldgend.,District of Zajecar (Serbia) 41-44	MURDER	YUGO.
LANG, Franz	165563	M	Ger.	05	Cmdt.,Capt.,Feldgend.,Gestapo"Standgericht",Bande(Bel.) 24.-25.12.44	MURDER	BEL.
LANG, Franz	254853	M	Ger.		Sgt.,Feldgend.,Marche and Environs(Bel.) 40-45	INTERR.	BEL.
LANG, Franz	258010	M	Ger.		150 Pz.Bde.,Meuse Bridge-Antwerp(Bel.) 12.44	MISC.CRIMES	U.S.
LANG, Friedel	257234	F	Ger.	23	Typist,Abt.IVB,Sipo and SD-Anvers(Bel.) 40-45	SUSPECT	BEL.
LANG, Fritz	160394	M		19	Richter,Public Official,Ministry of Justice,Leipzig(Ger.) 10.44	MURDER	U.S.
LANG, Fritz	255593	M	Ger.		Sturmfhr.,SS Acting Orts-Cmdt.,Delft(Neth.) 10.44	MURDER	NETH.
LANG, Georg	194220	M	Ger.		Lt.,Army,Darmstadt(Ger.)	MURDER	U.S.
LANG, Gottlieb	194828	M	Ger.		Camp-Leader,Arb.-Kdo.,Civilian.	TORTURE	U.S.
LANG, Heinrich	194653	M	Ger.		Feldgend.,Feldgendarmerie,Ploermel(Fr.)	TORTURE	FR.
LANG, Hermann	140789	M	G.		Chief,Civilian,KL.Muhldorf(Ger.)	MURDER	U.S.

LAN-LAN

NAME	C.R.FILE NUMBER	SEX	NATIO-NALITY	DATE OF BIRTH	RANK OCCUPATION UNIT PLACE AND DATE OF CRIME	REASON WANTED	WANTED BY
LANG, Johann	261090	M	Ger.		Civ., Subject is at present Living at Mittel-Muehle Post Reuth Erbendorf, Regensburg (Ger.) 43	MURDER	POL.
LANG, Ludwig	256744	M			Rottfhr., Camp Muehldorf area, (Ger.)	MURDER	U.S.
LANG, Mathias	187067	M			SS-Pvt., 4.SS Totenkopf Sturmbann, C.C. Nordhausen Dora, (Ger.) 43-45	TORTURE	U.S.
LANG, Mathias	254615	M	Ger.		Pvt., SS C.C. Auschwitz Birkenau (Pol.)12.42	MURDER	YUGO.
LANG, Oskar	251123	M			Pvt., C.C. Ellrich Rottleben Nordhausen (Ger.)	MURDER	U.S.
LANG, William	171950	M	Ger.		Civ., Langgons (Ger.)	MURDER	U.S.
LANGANKE, Paul	130615	M	Ger.	27. 8.25	Navy Kriegsmarine, Jemappes (Bel.) 3.9.44	TORTURE	BEL.
LANGBEIN	256532	M			Lt., Army Officer of Abwehr at Oflag 65, Strassburg, Barkenbruegge (Ger.) 44-45	MISC.CRIMES	YUG.
LANGBEIN, Willi	227797	M	Ger.		Pvt., Abwehr Nachr.Rgt., 506, Stuttgart (Ger.) 44	MISC.CRIMES	U.S.
LANGE	544	M	Ger.		SS-Oberfhr., Lods (Pol.) 9.39-1.42	MURDER	POL.
LANGE	545	M	Ger.		SS-Usturmfhr., Camp Guard, C.C.Oswiecim and Majako (Pol.)	MURDER	POL
LANGE	546	M	Ger.		Army Major, 749. Jaeg.Rgt. (Grc.)12.43	MURDER	GRC.
LANGE	122370	M	Ger.		Cpl., Stalag XI A, C.C. Aschersleben (Ger.) 6.44	TORTURE	U.K.
LANGE	125682	M	Ger.		Lt., Police Gend., Bourg-Lastic (Fr.) 9.-15.7.44	MURDER	FR.
LANGE	126996	M	Ger.		Uschfhr., SS., C.C. Buchenwald (Ger.)	TORTURE	FR.
LANGE	128841	M	Ger.		Amtmann, Civ., in C.C. Stalag IV D., Falkenberg (Ger.) 6.44-4.45	MISC.CRIMES	U.K.
LANGE	133412	M	Ger.		Sonderfhr., C.C. Lamsdorf, (Ger.) 12.41-3.44	TORTURE	U.K.
LANGE	134799	M	Ger.		Kommissar, Gestapo RSH., Koeln, (Ger.)	MURDER	U.S.
LANGE	137599	M	Ger.		Cpt., German Army, Tirana,(Yugo.) 1.44	MISC.CRIMES	U.K.
LANGE	139691	M		10	Uschfhr., W-SS Waldlager V and VI, Muhldorf (Ger.) 44-45	MURDER	U.S.
LANGE	142577	M	Ger.		Cpt., Freiw.Stamm Rgt. 2, La Parade (Fr.) 27.5.44	MURDER	FR.
LANGE	146950	M	Ger.		Officer, SS Pz.Div. Das Reich, 1.Pz.Rgt.2.Coy. (Tulle, (Fr.) 44	MURDER	FR.
LANGE	148231	M	Ger.		C.C. Kaltenkirchen Springkirsch (Ger.)	MURDER	FR.
LANGE	165165	M	Ger.		Dr., Leader, Gestapo, (Latv.) 41-44	MURDER	U.S.
LANGE	167717	M	Ger.		Dr., Leader, Public Official, Radom (Pol.)	MISC.CRIMES	POL.
LANGE	169453	M	Ger.	90	Director, Railway, Falkenburg (Ger.) 10 43-3.45	TORTURE	U.K.
LANGE	185131	M	Ger.		Cpt., Pz.Rgt., L 1000, St. Setiers (Fr.) 27.7.44	TORTURE	FR.
LANGE	185132	M	Ger.		Cpl., Army, Castets, (Fr.)	MURDER	FR.
LANGE	188918	M			Cpt., Freiwillig.Stammrgt., Baradoux (Fr.)	MURDER	FR.
LANGE	193956 A	M	Ger.		Sturmbannfhr., Waffen-Schule, Hraditska Prague (Czech.)	MURDER	CZECH.
LANGE	196211	M	Ger.		Inspector Coy.-Leader, Railway, Langon (Fr.) 16.6.44	MURDER	FR.
LANGE	196882	M	Ger.		Cmdt., Army Artillerie, Ciral (Fr.) 8.8.44	INTER.	FR.
LANGE	251124	M	Ger.		SS-Rottfhr., Neuengamme (Ger.) 44	MURDER	FR.
LANGE	251705	M	Ger.		Usturmfhr., SS C.C. Mauthausen (Aust.)	TORTURE	BEL.
LANGE	252516	M	Ger.		W.O. Chief, C.C. Krammer, Lindenbluete (Ger.) 1.45	ILLTREATMENT	FR.
LANGE	253130	M	Ger.		Lt., Troupes russes of Chaumont, Vauxbons Voisines (Fr.) 30.6.44	MURDER	FR.
LANGE	254136	M	Ger.		Lt., Russo-German Unit Stationed at Chaumont, La'Ferste Sur Aube (Fr.) 15.6.44	MURDER	FR.
LANGE (or LANGEN)	254397	M	Ger.		Cpt., 377. Jaeger Rgt. Reg. B. Vinkt and Meigem (Bel.) 25.-31.5.40	MISC.CRIMES	BEL.
LANGE	258012	M			Lt., 150. Pz.Brigade, Meuse Bridge Antwerp (Bel.) 12.44	MISC.CRIMES	U.S.
LANGE, Christe	167836	F	Ger.		Einsatzstab Rosenberg, Paris (Fr) 40-44	PILLAGE	FR.
LANGE, Elfriede	134811	F	Ger.		Women-Guard, C.C. Helmbrechts (Ger.) 7.44-13.4.45	MURDER	U.S.
LANGE, Elfrieda	139162	F	Ger.		Guard, SS-German Prison Camp, Votary, (Czech.)41-45	MURDER	U.S.
LANGE, Fritz	256531	M	Ger.	13. 1.17	Staff Sgt., SS, Genthin (Ger.) 12.44	BRUTALITY	U.S.
LANGE, Gustav	140790	M	Ger.		Uschfhr., SS Totenkopf C.C. Ravensbrueck and Buchenwald (Ger.)44-45	TORTURE	U.S.
LANGE, Gustav	190642	M	Ger.	08	Prison Warder, Gestapo, Brno., (Czech.) 39-45	MURDER	CZECH.
LANGE, Hans, Ulrich	10302	M			Dr., Staatsanwalt, Public Official, Opava (Czech.) 40	MURDER	CZECH.
LANGE, Hermann	261474	M	Ger.	circa 10	Cpl., Camp of Castets (Landes) 2.42	MURDER	FR.
LANGE, Julius	187987	M	Ger.	85	Guard, Stalag XX Landwache, C.C. Briesenfeld (Ger.) 5.42	MURDER	U.K.
LANGE, Kurt	139689	M		15	SS-Officer, W-SS	MURDER	U.S.
LANGE, Otto, Wilhelm	195494	M	Ger.	3. 9.84	Major, SS, Kokorin, Czech.) 38-45	MISC.CRIMES	CZECH.
LANGE, Oscar	140857	M	Ger.	10	Sonderfhr., SS-Chief Recruter for British Free Corps	WITNESS	U.K.
LANGE, Traugott	251125	M			Pvt., C.C. Ellrich Nordhausen (Ger.)	MURDER	U.S.
LANGE, Wilhelm	187064	M			SS-Pvt., Guard, 4.SS Totenkopfsturmbann, C.C. Nordhausen-Dora (Ger.) 43-45	TORTURE	U.S.
LANGE, Willi	254398	M	Ger.		Cpl., 10.Coy. 377 Jaeger Rgt. Vinkt Meigem (Bel.) 25.-31.5.40	MISC.CRIMES	BEL.
LANGELOH, Wilhelm (or BAUER, Felix)	256530	M	Ger.	16.11 91	Waiter, Civ., Appen (Ger.) 7.44	MURDER	U.S.
LANGEMAIER	547	M	Ger.		Army Medical Abteilungskommandeur, Einville (Fr.) 8.-9.44	MURDER	FR.
LANGEN, (or LANGDEN, Paul)	46066	M		07	Lt., SS Head of Gestapo at Tours, Lussault Tourine (Fr.) 4.8.44	MURDER	U.S.
LANGEN (see LANGE)	254397						
LANGEN, Paul	151960	M		16. 4.07	Gestapo and SS, Chef, Lt., Angers Tours (Fr.)	MURDER	FR.
LANGENBACH (see ALTMANN)	136223						
LANGENBACH, Fritz	187063	M			4.SS Totenkopfsturmbann, C.C. Nordhausen Dora Mittelbau (Ger.) 43-45	TORTURE	U.S.
LANGENBAHN, Johann	193807	M	Ger.		Faulquemont (Fr.)	PILLAGE	FR.
LANGENECK	251127	M			Pvt., C.C. Mackenrode Nordhausen (Ger.)	MURDER	U.S.
LANGENFELD	548	M			Chief Supervisor, C.C. Ravensbrueck (Ger.) 41-44	MURDER	POL.
LANGENFELD, Hugo	191381	M	Ger.	5. 4.17	Civilian, Office Clerk, Schwalbach (Ger.) 8.44	WITNESS	U.S.
LANGENS, Nikolaus	252367	M	Ger.	15. 7.10	Tailor, Luxemburg (Lux.)	INTERR.	LUX.
LANGER	39660	M			Army Cpl., Borkum, (Ger.)	MURDER	U.S.
LANGER	132228	M	Ger.	09	Pvt., W-SS, C.C. Hohenreim-Plattling (Ger.) 2.-5.45	MURDER	U.S.
LANGER	141970	M	Ger.	10	SS Uschfhr., C.C. Guard, C.C. Muehldorf (Ger.) 45	MURDER	U.S.
LANGER	146005	M	Ger.	23	Pvt., Army, Borkum (Ger.) 4.8.44	MURDER	U.S.
LANGER (see LANG)	162254						
LANGER	250368	M			Rottfhr., C.C. Mackenrode Nordhausen (Ger.)	MURDER	U.S.
LANGER	253138	M	Ger.		Cpt., Morez (Fr.) 8.44	MISC.CRIMES	FR.
LANGER	254138	M	Ger.		Cpt., 338.Div.La Bresse (Fr.) 11.44	PILLAGE	FR.
LANGER	255594	M			Pvt., C.C. Mackenrode Nordhausen (Ger.)	MURDER	U.S.
LANGER	259045	M			Schachtmeister, Todt Org., Mushldorf area	MURDER	U.S.
LANGER	262212	F			Dr., Gestapo, Rennes (Fr.) 43-44	MISC.CRIMES	FR.
LANGER, Alice	190643	F	Ger.	21	Clerk, Gestapo, Brno., (Czech.) 39-45	WITNESS	CZECH.
LANGER, Berthold	260496	M	Ger.	2. 7.15	SS-Guard, C.C. Natzweiler (Fr.)	MURDER	FR.
LANGER, Eberhard	194655	M	Ger.		Sgt., Grenspolizei, Veigy, Foncenex (Fr.) 6.10.43	TORTURE	FR.
LANGER, Erich	194654	M	Ger.	05	SS-Sgt., Sipo, SS Chelm, Radzyn, Radom (Pol.) 40-44	SUSPECT	POL.
LANGER, Erich (or Wilhelm)	306762	M	Ger.		German Civilian, Borkum Island, (Ger.) 4.8.44	MURDER	U.S.

LAN-LAS

NAME	C.R.FILE NUMBER	SEX	NATIO-NALITY	DATE OF BIRTH	RANK	OCCUPATION	UNIT	PLACE AND DATE OF CRIME	REASON WANTED	WANTED BY
LANGER, Kurt see LANGNER, Franz	137554									
LANGER, Kurt	146733	M			SS Standartenfhr., C.C. Flossenburg (Ger.)				TORTURE	U.S.
LANGER, Otto	133291	M	Ger.	91	Osturmfhr., Waffen SS, 2.Pion.Ausb.Bl., Passau (Ger.) 4.45				MURDER	U.S.
LANGER, Paul	255284	M		about 22	Capt., 755. Rgt., 334. Inf.Div.				MISC.CRIMES	U.S.
LANGER, Rodolphe	196824	M	Ger.		SS Mann, Gestapo, St.Etienne, La Region (Fr.)				MISC.CRIMES	FR.
LANGERMANN, Armand	173680	M	Ger.		SS Hptsturmfhr., C.C. Oswiecim, Birkenau (Pol.) 39-45				MURDER	CZECH.
LANGES	122377	M	Ger.		Uscharfhr., SS, Aude (Fr.)				TORTURE	FR.
LANGEFLDT	254404	M			Cmdt., Oflag V C, Wurzach (Ger.) 20.8.41				MURDER	FR.
LANGHAMMER, Frantisek	189080	M	Ger.		Pvt., S.D. Agent, Gestapo-Informer, Trebon (Czech.) 39-45				MURDER	CZECH.
LANGHAMMER, Richard	195521	M	Ger.	13.3.09	SS Sgt., Employee, S.D., Gestapo, Kolin (Czech.) 39-45				MURDER	CZECH.
LANGHANS	190645	M	Ger.		Crim.secretary, chief, Gestapo, Brno (Czech.) 39-45				MURDER	CZECH.
LANGHARD, Richard	139168	M	Ger.		Policeman, Police Wollendorf (Ger.) 23.10.43				WITNESS	U.S.
LANGHAUS	67564	M	Ger.		Dr., SS Hptsturmfhr., SS-Div."Das Reich" 1.Bn., Trebons, Pouzat, Bagneres, de Big (Fr.) 11.6.44				MURDER	FR.
LANGHAUS, E.	127071	M	Ger.		Hptsturmfhr.2.SS Panz.Div."Das Reich", Venerque, Le Vernet (Fr.)				MURDER	FR.
LANGHOLZ, Ernest	67567	M	Ger.		Sgt. (Adj.Chef), Feldgendarmerie, Maubeuge (Fr.) 19.8.44				MURDER	FR.
LANGHOLZ, Hans-Peter	253877	M	Ger.		Civ., St.Python (Fr.) 2.9.44				MURDER	FR.
LANGHOSER, August	192896	M	Ger.		Schupo, C.C. Falstad (Nor.) 10.42				TORTURE	NOR.
LANGWAIER	150628	M			Capt., Army, 29.Panz.Gren.Div.				WITNESS	U.S.
LANGNER	254405	M			Civ. Reichsbahnrat, Epernay (Fr.) 1.44				INTERR.	FR.
LANGNER, Eric	253765	M	Ger.	06	SS Usturmfhr., Gestapo, Paris (Fr.) 41-44				TORTURE	FR.
LANGNER, Frantz	253985	M	Ger.		Civ., Urbes (Fr.) 24.9.44-5.10.44				MURDER	FR.
LANGNER, Franz or LANGER, Kurt	137554	M	Ger.		Uscharfhr., SS, C.C. Weimar, Buchenwald (Ger.)				TORTURE	U.S.
LANGNER, Frantz	254141	M	Ger.	28.12.97	Usturmfhr., SS, S.D. Strassbourg, Beulotte, St.Laurent (Fr.) 16.9.44				MURDER	FR.
LA.GRABE, Paul	150639	M	Ger.		Scharfhr., Waffen SS Totenkopf-Standarte, C.C. Weimar, Buchenwald (Ger.) Oranienburg(Ger.) 41				TORTURE	U.S.
LANGRANGE	196504	M	Ger.		Lt. Unit 01512 K, Trebeurden (Fr.)				MURDER	FR.
LANGROCK	300291	M	Ger.		Col., commanding 670. Artillery-Rgt., Tripolis (Afr.) 3.44				MISC.CRIMES	GRC.
LANGRUN	253872	M	Ger.		W.O. chief, C.C. Hinzert (Ger.)				MURDER	FR.
LANIA	120632	M	Ger.		Pvt., Army, Ger.Coy. Military 867, St.Leonhard (Aust.)				MISC.CRIMES	U.K.
LANY see BLANK	151754									
LANKES, Martin	176933	M	Ger.	11.11.93	Civ. Carpenter, Krakau (Pol.) 42-43				TORTURE	U.S. POL.
LANKNER	130618	M	Ger.		5.Parachutist - Rgt. Nachrichtenzug, Quarsgnon, Jemappes, Chin (Bel.) 2.-3.9.44				TORTURE	BEL.
LANN	91622	M			Dr., Col. Arzt, 20.Army I V b staff, Nor., 10.-11.44				MURDER	NOR.
LANNERT	67565	M			Capt., 2.Coy. 439.Bn.Lardesschustzen, Blechhammer-Silesia(Ger.)6.-12.44				TORTURE	U.K.
LANNIAGER see LAMMAGER, Hans	192010	M								
LANSBERG	136222	M	Ger.		Interpreter, 28.Inf.Rgt. 116.Bn., Meilhan Lannemezan (Fr.) 7.44				MURDER	FR.
LANSCH	167013	M	Ger.		SS Sturmfhr., C.C. Braunschweig (Ger.) 6.-9.44				TORTURE	FR.
LANSTRAS, Albert	124274	M	Ger.		SS Panz.Div. 1, SS Panz.Rgt. 1, 9.Coy. (Engineers), Malmedy (Bel.)12.44				MURDER	U.S.
LANZER	187117	M	Ger.		Head physician, Stalag VI A Civ. C.C. Hemer (Ger.) 44				TORTURE	U.S.
LANZIUS	259157	M	Ger.		SS Osturmfhr., C.C. Dachau (Ger.) 9.42-45				MISC.CRIMES	YUGO.
LAP	148290	M	Ger.		Agent, Gestapo, Luebeck (Ger.)				MISC.CRIMES	FR.
LAPACH	147298	M	Ger.		Sgt., 11.Panz.Div.SS, 2.Grp., Kampfgr."Wilde", Fr., 44				MURDER	FR.
LAPANSKI	251128	M	Ger.		Workmaster, Factory Rigtersbeek, Enschede (Neth.) 15.5.42-1.4.45				INCENDIARISM	NETH.
LA PANTHERE see BRANDT, Ursula	177743									
LAPIERRE, Maurice	173705	M	Ger.	21.9.93	Civ., C.C. Thekla nr.Leipzig (Ger.) 18.4.45				MURDER	FR.
LAPOUYADE	306900	M			French Member, Gestapo, Perigueux (Fr.) 6.-8.44				MURDER	FR.
LAPP	162390	M		85	Lt.Col., Army, Hadamar (Ger.) 11.43				MURDER	U.K.
LAPPAS	190390	M	Ger.		Crim.Secret., Police, Wiesbaden (Ger.) 43-45				TORTURE	U.S.
LAPZCH (see LABZCH or LABSCHL)	12574									
LARBEER, Kurt	102930	M			Prison-Capt., Stalag 12 A, C.C. Limburg (Ger.) 21.9.40 - 3.45				MURDER	U.S.
LARBICH	259046	M			SS Oscharfhr., Army (Waffen-SS ?), Muehldorf Area (Ger.)				MURDER	U.S.
LARBIG, Paul	255010	M	Ger.	15.7.01	Head, post office, Pardubice (Czech.) 42-45				MISC.CRIMES	CZECH.
LARESCH or LARISCH, Johanna	257689	F		1.3.08	Clerk, S.D. Gestapo, Praha (Czech.) 40-45				INTERR.	CZECH.
LARISCH, Anton	141574	M	Ger.	10	Lt. Army, C.C. Sagan Stalag VIII C (Ger.) 2.45				MISC.CRIMES	U.K. FR.
LARISCH	258577	M	Ger.		Official, State service, Army, Murnau Oflag VII A (Ger.)				BRUTALITY	POL.
LARISCH see LARESCH, Johanna	257689									
LARKMUNDT or LARTMUND	261068	M		about 10	Senior W.O., Div. Brandenburg Unit Special, 8.Coy., Var, Vaucluse, Bouche du Rhone (Fr.) 43-44				MISC.CRIMES	FR.
LARNOOL or ARNOOL	301132	M	Ger.		Chief of police, Arnstadt (Ger.) 43-45				MISC.CRIMES	FR.
"LA ROUQUINE" alias KARK	147548	F		10	SS overseer, C.C. Neuengamme, Wattenstedt (Ger.) 45				TORTURE	U.S.
LARRISCH	67563	M	Ger.		Capt., Lagerfuehrer Stalag 8 c Sagan (Ger.) 11.44-2.45				PILLAGE	U.K.
LARSCH	195642	M	Ger.		Lt. Gendarmerie, Voorburg (Neth.) 14.2.45				MURDER	NETH.
LARSEI	124764	M	Ger.		Lt.Col., 1.Sturm-Bn., Laufen (Ger.) 12.44				MURDER	U.S.
LARSEN	142579	M			Agent, Gestapo, Stalag Markt Pongau (Aust.) 10.44				MURDER	U.S.
LARSEN, Gustav	147297	M			Pvt., 11.Panz.Div., Kampfgruppe "Wilde", Fr., 44				MURDER	FR.
LARSEN, Gustave	258915	M	Ger.		Cpl. Chief, Army, 110.March-Bn. 2.Coy. XI Panz.Div., Montreal (Fr.)7.44				MURDER	FR.
LARSEN, Otto	199693	M		05	Sturmfhr., SS, Gestapo, nr.Oberndorf, area Salzburg (Aust.) 22.11.44				MURDER	U.S.
LARTMUND see LARKMUNDT	261068									
LASAAK	174064	M	Ger.	90	SS Standartenfhr., Police Director, Giessen (Ger.) 9.10.44				TORTURE	U.S.
LASCH	124237	M	Ger.	98	Stalag officer				MISC.CRIMES	U.S.
LASCH	199688	M	Ger.		Dr., Governor, General-Government, C.C., Pol., 42				MISC.CRIMES	U.S.
LASCH, Karl	62370	M	Ger.		Dr., District-chief, Public official, Galicia (Pol.)				MURDER	U.N.W.C.C.
LASCH, Karl	300062	M	Ger.		Member, Geheime Feldpolizei, Utrecht (Neth.) 1.45				TORTURE	NETH.
LASCHNIKA	259694	M	Ger.		Lt., Unit F.P. 07382, Villequiers (Fr.) 7.40-6.41				INCENDIARISM	FR.
LASER	257298	M	Ger.		Lt.Col., Police, Poppentin (Ger.) 7.or 8.44				MURDER	U.S.
LASKAWSKI	252251	M	Ger.		16.Huebner-Rgt. 6.Coy., Kinroci (Bel.) 9.44				MURDER	BEL.
LASKI	36641	M	Ger.		Pvt., Army, 2-515 Bn., Redoubi (Czech.)				MURDER	U.K.
LASKIN	187061	M			Wachtmeister, SS Scharfhr., 4.SS Totenkopf-Stuba, C.C. Nordhausen-Dora (Ger.) 43-45				TORTURE	U.S.

LAS - LAU

NAME	C.R.FILE NUMBER	SEX	NATIO-NALITY	DATE OF BIRTH	RANK OCCUPATION UNIT PLACE AND DATE OF CRIME	REASON WANTED	WANTED BY
LASKOWSKI	551	M	Ger.		Uscharfbr., SS, C.C. Stutthof (Ger.) 9.39 - 4.41	MURDER	POL.
LASMANN	196821	M	Ger.		Agent, Gestapo, Corenc, (Fr.) 12.4.44	INTERR.	FR.
LASOGGA	300802	M	Ger.		Prt., 1.Aufkl.Abt.3.Coy. 2.Column, XV Div. of the Afrika Korps, Saint Leger (Arlon) (Bel.) 5.9.44	MISC.CRIMES	BEL.
LASZKY, Josef	306205	M	Ger.		Prt., Garage-manager, SS, C.C., Large Fortress, Theresienstadt (Czech.) 1.10.38 - 44	MURDER	CZECH.
LATERMANN	254140	M	Ger.		Officer, Erquedes (Fr.) 1. - 2.41	INTERR.	FR.
LATHMANN	253770	M	Ger.		Lt.Col., 1.Bn.3, 338.Div., School-N.C.O., Labrosse (Fr.) 9.-11.44	MISC.CRIMES	FR.
LATIF	186285	M	Turk.		Crete (Gra.)	MURDER	GRC.
LATSCH, Kurt	262213	M	Ger.	19.11	Oberscharfhr., Gestapo, Rennes (Fr.) 43 - 44	MISC.CRIMES	FR.
LATSCHAK, Adam	127411	M	Ger.		Civilian in C.C., Enkenbach (Ger.) 12.43 - 3.45	TORTURE	U.S.
LATTE, Karl	124365	M	Ger.		Reichsminister, Minister im Ger.Government, Dietz (Ger.) 1.43-3.45	TORTURE	U.S.
LATTMANN,	254077	M	Ger.		Dr., Member, Torgau Mil. Court, Halle (Ger.) 2.44	MURDER	FR.
LATWEIN, Peter	139046	M	Ger.		Foreman, Civilian Factory, Plettenberg (Ger.) 4.44	TORTURE	U.S.
LATZER, Hans	12575	M	Ger.		Prt.SS Army, 110.or 111.Panz.Gren.Rgt. 2.Coy.,Albine (Fr.) 29.6.44	MURDER	FR.
LAU	257645	M	Ger.		Oberscharfhr., C.C., Dora-Nordhausen (Ger.)	BRUTALITY	FR.
LAUB	300803	M	Ger.		Prt., 1.Aufkl.Abt. 3.Coy., 2.Column, XV.Div. of the Afrika Korps, Saint Leger (Arlon) (Bel.) 5.9.44	MISC.CRIMES	BEL.
LAUBENDER	301786	M	Ger.		Member, Roumanian Kommando, Gestapo, Vichy (Fr.) 10.43 - 9.44	MURDER	FR.
LAUBER	67562	M	Ger.		Capt., C.C., Lindberg-Hannover (Ger.) 7.-12.44	TORTURE	U.K.
LAUBER (see LAUBERT)	253766						
LAUBER, Hans	300064	M	Ger.		Chief, Ophthalmic Clinic of the University (Cracow (Pol.)	MISC.CRIMES	POL.
LAUBERGER	252451	M	Ger.		Lt., SS-Div.30.Pz.Gren.Rgt. SS "Deutschland", Masoulas, Mazieres, Betchat, Justiniac (Fr.) 6.44 und 26.3.45	MURDER	FR.
LAUBERT (or LAUBER)	253766	M	Ger.		Uscharfhr., 3.Coy., Das Reich", Oradour sur Glane (Fr.)10.6.44	INTERR.	FR.
LAUBERT	300804	M	Ger.		Prt., 1.Aufkl.Abt. 3.Coy. 2.Column XV.Div. of the Afrika Korps, Saint Leger (Arlon) (Bel.) 5.9.44	MISC.CRIMES	BEL.
LAUBGREVE (or LANDGREVE or LANDGRABE)	137553	M	Ger.		Sgt., SS, C.C., Buchenwald, Weimar (Ger.)	TORTURE	U.S.
LAUBMANN, August	260409	M	Ger.	92	Member, Gestapo, Pelhrimov (Czech.) 39 - 45	MISC.CRIMES	CZECH.
LAUCHTER	196110	F	Ger.		Aufseherin, C.C. Ravensbrueck (Ger.)	TORTURE	FR.
LAUDE	102729	M	Ger.		Oberscharfhr., SS, C.C., Cuxhaven (Ger.) 3.45	MURDER	U.S.
LAUDE, Erwin	254076	M	Ger.		Cpl., 4.Coy. 24.Rgt. "Utersen" 1.Bn., Neuves-Maisons(Fr.) 31.8.44	MURDER	FR.
LAUDEL	250352	M	Ger.		Sgt. C.C., Ellrich, Nordhausen (Ger.)	MURDER	U.S.
LAUDEN	125760	M	Ger.		Custom-Secretary, Custom House, Comine (Fr.) 43 - 44	MISC.CRIMES	FR.
LAUDEN (see LAUSEN)	253143						
LAUDORF	250910	M	Ger.		Deputy Head, SS of Gestapo, Maribor (Yugo.) 44	MURDER	YUGO.
LAUEN	189037	M	Ger.	00 - 04	Sturmbannfhr., Major, Cmdt. of Area North of Vicenza, Former Coy. Cmdt.of SA - Standarte "Feldherrnhalle" Shio (It.)	MURDER	U.K.
LAUENROTH	120086	M	Ger.		Dr.,Leader, Gestapo, Saarbruecken (Ger.)	MISC.CRIMES	U.S.
LAUENROTH, G.	255004	M	Ger.		Sturmmann, SS Div. Blinde " Das Reich ", Amay (Bel.) 9.44	INTERR.	BEL.
LAUER	10303	M	Ger.		Sturmbannfhr., SS,C.C. Oranienburg (Ger.) 39 - 44	TORTURE	CZECH.
LAUER	31573	M	Ger.		Lt., Waffen SS, C.C., Sachsenhausen (Ger.) 9.41	MURDER	U.S.
LAUER	31601	M	Ger.		Army, Gebirgsarmeekorps 19, 20.Armee, Finmark (Nor.) 10.-11.44	MURDER	NOR.
LAUER, Stevan (Stefan)	156091	M	Ger.		Sgt., Army, Morlaix (Fr.) 44	MURDER	FR.
LAUER	162383	M	Ger.		Prt., SS, C.C. Mauthausen (Aust.) 8.-9.44	WITNESS	U.S.
LAUF, Theodor	252383	M	Ger.	1. 3.93	SS-Oberfuehrer, Plenipotentiary for Cooperatives, Prag (Czech.)39-45	PILLAGE	CZECH.
LAUFE	173678	M	Ger.		Lt., SS, C.C., Oswiecim, Birkenau (Pol.) 39 - 45	MURDER	CZECH.
LAUFEL	180044	M	Ger.		Interpreter, Gestapo, Saarbruecken (Ger.)	PILLAGE	FR.
LAUFENBERG	192388	M	Ger.		Civilian, Siegburg-Bautzen (Ger.) 9.44	TORTURE	BEL.
LAUFENBERG	192389	M	Ger.		Guard, C.C., Aachen (Ger.) 45	TORTURE	BEL.
LAUFER	148227	M	Ger.		NSKK	PILLAGE	FR.
LAUFER, Gustav	250351	M	Ger.		Prt., C.C., Ellrich, Nordhausen (Ger.)	MURDER	U.S.
LAUFKA, Emil	195519	M	Ger.	18. 5.10	Sgt., Employee, SS, SD, Gestapo, Kolin (Czech.) 39 - 45	MURDER	CZECH.
LAUKENS	250350	M	Ger.		Prt., C.C., Ellrich, Nordhausen (Ger.)	MURDER	U.S.
LAUKERT	195058	M	Ger.		Rottenfhr., SD, Sonder-und Wirtschafts-Kdo.Beeck,Gorssel(Neth.)9.44	MURDER	NETH.
LAUKO	254616	M	Ger.		Sturmmann, Member, SD, Toulouse (Fr.) 11.42 - 8.44	MISC.CRIMES	FR.
LAUKORST	158254	M	Ger.		Prt., Army, Chenebier Etobon (Fr.) 27.9.44	MURDER	FR.
LAUMANN	260664	M	Ger.		Infirmier, Buchenwald (Ger.) 40 - 44	MURDER	FR.
LAUNE	138288	M	Ger.		Lt. Heeres Verwaltung , Armainvilliers (Fr.) 25.7.44	MURDER	FR.
LAUNER, Kurt	195057	M	Ger.	10. 9.06	Obersturmbannfhr., SS-Totenkopf-Div. Le Paradis (Fr.) 27.5.40	MURDER	U.K. U.S.
LAUNERT, Oskar	167726	M	Ger.		Cpl., 9.Rgt.Res.Gren., 1.Coy. Magny d'Avignom (Fr.) 18.9.44	MURDER	FR.
LANNIAGER, Hans(see LAMMTAGER)	192010						
LAUPHEIM, Esely	128842		Ger.		Cpl.,Arbeitskommando 7902,Kommandofhr.,Stalag V B,Allmendingen(Ger.)44	TORTURE	U.K.
LAUREK	151962	M	Ger.		Scharfhr., SS-Div. "Das Reich" Reg.8, Aiguillon (Fr.) 6.44	MURDER	FR.
LAUREL, Johann	187058	M			Prt., 4.SS-Totenkopfsturmbann, C.C. Dora-Mittelbau,Nordhausen (Ger.) 43 - 45	TORTURE	U.S.
LAURENCE	260117	M	Ger.		Lt., Div.Oberland Sov.Un.,Ger. Massif du Vercors (Fr.) 7.-8.44	SUSPECT	FR.
LAURENZEN	552	M	Ger.		Lager-Waerter C.C., Ravensbrueck (Ger.)	MURDER	POL.
LAURENZEN	130619	M	Ger.		Unterscharfhr., SS, C.C., Neuengamme (Ger.)	TORTURE	BEL.
LAURHORST, Ernst	174684	M			Civilian, Brioude (Fr.) 4.44	WITNESS	FR.
LAURITZ, Karl	300949	M			Member of SD, Fiume, Susak and Trieste (Yugo.It.) 3.2.44	MURDER	YUGO.
LAURITZEN, Carl	68910	M	Ger.		Prt., Army 34, Fortress machine Gun Bn.,Aachen (Ger.) 13.9.44	MURDER	U.S.
LAUSBERG	250349	M	Ger.		C.C. Rottleberode, Nordhausen (Ger.)	MURDER	U.S.
LAUSEN (or LAUDEN)	253143	M	Ger.		Lt., Brigade"Jesser", Tortebesse (Fr.) 22.8.44	MISC.CRIMES	FR.
LAUSTER, Adolf	167725	M	Ger.		Prt., 9.Rgt.Res.Gren., 1.Coy., Magny d'Avignon (Fr.) 18.9.44	MURDER	FR.
LAUTEMANN	142015	M	Ger.		Cpl.,Army, Kriegsgef.Res.Laz., Heppenheim (Ger.)	TORTURE	U.S.
LAUTENBACK, Walter	193453	M	Ger.		Uscharfhr.,SS, C.C., Buchenwald (Ger) 42 - 43	TORTURE	U.S.
LAUTENSCHIRMER	102927	M	Ger.		Civilian, C.C., Berga (Ger.)	MISC.CRIMES	U.S.
LAUTENSCHLAGER	257727	M	Ger.		Capt., Army, Strassburg (Ger.) 44 - 45	INTERR.	YUGO.
LAUTENSCHLAGER	306185	M	Ger.		Hauptscharfhr., C.C., Kahla (Ger.) 40 - 45	MURDER	BEL.
LAUTERBACH	130620	M	Ger.		5.Fallschirm-Jaeger Rgt.,Nachrichtenzug,Quaregnon,Jemappes,Chlin (Bel.) 9.44	MURDER	BEL.

LAU-LEH

NAME	C.R.FILE NUMBER	SEX	NATIO-NALITY	DATE OF BIRTH	RANK OCCUPATION UNIT PLACE AND DATE OF CRIME	REASON WANTED	WANTED BY
LAUTERBACH, Peter	192387	M	Ger.		Conc.Camp, Flossenburg (Ger.) 44-45	MURDER	U.S.
LAUTZER	553	M	Ger.		Usturmfhr., SS, Chatellerault (Fr.) 25.8.44	MURDER	FR.
LAUTZER (see JANSEN)	251640						
LAUZER, Walter	12577	M	Ger.		Pvt.,110.or 111.Pz.Gren.Rgt.2.Coy., Albine (Fr.) 29.6.44	MURDER	FR.
LAVERLIK	252252	M	Ger.		6.Coy., 16.Hubner-Rgt., Kinrooi (Bel.) 9.44	MURDER	BEL.
LAWRENZ	255018	M	Ger.		Osturmfhr., SS, Abt.IV Sipo, Brussels (Bel.) 40-45	MURDER	BEL.
LAX	250348	M	Ger.		Pvt., C.C. Ellrich, Nordhausen (Ger.)	MURDER	U.S.
LAYE	62169	M	Ger.		Major, Schnellabtlg. 602, F.P.No.27690 A, Loroux,Bottereau et Bergrolles (Fr.) 16.8.44	MURDER	FR.
LAZ	190617	M			Sgt., Army, Ile D'Oleron (Fr.) 44-4.45	TORTURE	FR.
LAZAR	129698	M	Ger.		SS, Conc.Camp, Dora, Nordhausen (Ger.)	MURDER	U.S.
LAZARI, Gerhard	254664	M	Ger.	27. 5.03	Manager, Bruenn (Czech.) 5.45	PILLAGE	CZECH.
LAZARUS	137090	M	Ger.		Pvt., Arb.Kmdo., Guard, Zempelburg (Pol.) 8.41-3.42	MISC.CRIMES	U.K.
LAZARUS, Maria	194219	F	Ger.	00	Civilian, Seinsfeld (Ger.) 15.8.44	WITNESS	U.S.
LAZI, Michael	250353	M			Pvt., C.C. Dora, Nordhausen (Ger.)	MURDER	U.S.
LAZSKY, Josef	193955	M	Ger.	00	SS-Bewerber, Volkssturm, SS, Conc.Camp, Terezin (Ger., Czech.)	TORTURE	CZECH.
LE BAGNARD	189060				Oberwachtmstr., SS Arb.Kmdo., Guard, C.C.,Harzenwinkel,Gusterloh (Ger.)	MURDER	BEL.
LEBEMANN, Ernst	254399	M	Ger.		Pvt., 10.Coy.,377.Jaeger-Rgt., Vinkt (Bel.) 25.-31.5.40	MISC.CRIMES	BEL.
LEBENCKI, Otto	162365	M	Ger.		Policeman- Police - Ruedesheim (Ger.)	TORTURE	U.S.
LEBER, Alphonse	253769	M	Ger.		Schfhr., Gestapo, Limoges (Fr.) 40-45	INTERR.	FR.
LEBER, Johann	173113	M	Ger.		SS-Lt., Gestapo, Conc.Camp, Schirmeck, Rotenfels (Fr.)	TORTURE	U.K.
LEBERICH, Josef	250354	M			Pvt., Conc.Camp Ellrich, Nordhausen (Ger.)	MURDER	U.S.
LEBHRINCK	190357	M	Ger.		Lt.Col., Army, Fontana Di Liri (It.) 12.12.43	INTERR.	U.K.
LEBING, Erich	306422	M	Ger.		SS-Sgt., Villa Hooge, Boekel, Enschede (Neth.) 21.11.44	MURDER	U.K.
LEBKNECHNER	189338	M	Ger.		Dr., Sturmbannfhr., SS, Crim.Counsellor, Gestapo, C.C.,Dachau (Ger.) 40-45	MURDER	BEL.
LEBOR	253986	M	Ger.		Schfhr., Gestapo, Limoges (Fr.)	INTERR.	FR.
LE BOUQUIEN, Jimmy (see HOOKER, Harry)	11244						
LE BOXEUR (see KAAS)	132571						
LE BOXEUR	138202	M	Ger.		Schfhr., SS, Conc.Camp, Woippy (Fr.) 44	TORTURE	FR.
LE BOXEUR (see PELSER)	254689						
LE BRAZ, Jean (see KIEKHAFFER)	191902						
LEBRECHT, Walter	193954	M	Ger.	18.11.91	Ortsgruppen-Leiter, NSDAP, Dobratice (Czech.) 17.1.45	MURDER	CZECH.
LEBRENZ, Hans	179770	M	Ger.	17	26.Panz.Div., Fucecchio Marshes (It.) 23.8.44	MURDER	U.K.
LE BRIN	125191	M	Ger.		Interpreter, Custom-frontier-guard, Creach' - Maout (Fr.) 7.8.44	SUSPECT	FR.
LE CANADIEN (see HENCK WERSBASCH)	138329						
LECHENS, Otto	171951	M	Ger.		SR-Man, Lang Gons (Ger.)	MURDER	U.S.
LECHERNER	252512	M	Ger.		Gend., Feldgend., Sables D'Olonne, Benet (Fr.) 25.8.44	INTERR.	FR.
LECHLEDER	253987	M	Ger.		Chief, Cmdo., Dietz-Lahn (Ger.)	INTERR.	FR.
LECHMATE, Paul	134810	M	Ger.		Guard, Conc.Camp, Helmbrechts (Ger.) 7.44-4.45	WITNESS	U.S.
LECHNER, Leo	258702	M	Ger.		Oschfhr., Waffen-SS, 2.Bn.,38.SS-Rgt., "Goetz v.Berlichingen-Div."Kennat (Ger.) 20.10.44	WITNESS	U.S.
LECHNITZKY, Alexander	301208	M	Ger.		Member,Gestapo,Banska Bystrica,Distr.-Czech,Kremnicka (Czech.)20.11.44	MURDER	U.K.
LECKER, Konrad (or LEIKER)	301340	M	Ger.		Member,Gestapo at Trencin,C.C., Oswiecim-Birkenau (Pol.) 39-45	MURDER	CZECH.
LECKLEDER	307131	M	Ger.		Labour-Inspector, Prison, Diez-Lahn (Ger.) 40-45	MURDER	BEL.
LECKMANN	253129	M	Ger.		Capt., Etat-Major, Valence (Fr.)	INTERR.	FR.
LECLAIR	122409	M	Ger.		Hptschfhr., SS, Conc.Camp, Buchenwald (Ger.) 42-45	MURDER	U.S., FR.
LECLAIR (see KLAEHR)	133812						
LECLAIRE	161422	M	Ger.	12	Agent, Gestapo, Conc.Camp, Buchenwald 42-43	TORTURE	U.S.
LECLAIRE, Hubert	155713	M	Ger.		Sturmschfhr., SS-Totenk., Waffen-SS, Comm.Staff, Gestapo, Dep.II, Member, NSDAP, SD, Kripo, C.C., Buchenwald,Weimar (Ger.) 40-45	TORTURE	U.S.
LEDEBUR, Franz	194102	M	Ger.	15	Pvt., Guard, Marine-Art., Conc.Camp, Lueneburg,Wilhelmshaven (Ger.)4.45	MURDER	U.K.
LEDER, Hermann	166708	M	Ger.		Civilian, Lochtum (Ger.) 24.2 or 3.3.45	MURDER	U.S.
LEDERER, Hans	193953	M	Ger.	14.12.12	Hptschfhr., SS, C.C. Terezin (Czech.)	TORTURE	CZECH.
LEDERER, Heinrich	187116	M	Ger.		Conc.Camp, Regensburg (Ger.) 11.42	TORTURE	U.S.
LEDERER, Josef	250355	M		29. 6.97	Pvt., Conc.Camp, Ellrich, Nordhausen (Ger.)	MURDER	U.S.
LEDNOR	301339	M	Ger.		Member, Gestapo at Nove Mesto n-Vahom, C.C.,Oswiecim-Birkenau (Pol.) 39-45	MURDER	CZECH.
LEEB	145991	M			Uschfhr., SS, C.C., Mauthausen (Aust.) 41-45	WITNESS	U.S.
LEEBER	128975	M	Ger.		Capt., Gestapo, Paris (Fr.)	TORTURE	FR.
LEEMANN, Heinz	254400	M	Ger.		Cpl., 10.Coy.,377.Jaeger-Rgt., Vinkt (Bel.) 25.-31.5.40	MISC.CRIMES	BEL.
LEEMANS	261196	M	Ger.		Member, Staff of C.C., Ravensbrueck (Ger.)	SUSPECT	BEL.
LEEMANS, Otto	165952	M	Ger.		Gestapo, Conc.Camp, Charleroi (Bel.) 44	TORTURE	BEL.
LEEPS (see LEIPS)	132233						
LEEST	257634	M			Member, SA, Gratkorn (Aust.) 2.45	MURDER	U.S.
LEETZ	306627	M	Ger.		SS-Sgt., C.C., Neuengamme (Ger.) 2.40-4.45	MURDER	FR.
LEFELER	142576	M		07	Sgt. or Cpl., Oflag 64, C.C. Schubin (Pol.) 19.12.44	MISC.CRIMES	U.S.
LEFEVRE	186147	F	Ger.		Aufseherin, Guard, Conc.Camp, Koenigsberg-Oder (Ger.)	TORTURE	FR.
LEGAT, Walter	262187	M	Ger.	20. 7. ?	Oschfhr., SS, Gestapo, Rennes (Fr.) 43-44	MISC.CRIMES	FR.
LEGRAIS, Alain	195446	M	Ger.		Dr., Physician, Civ. in Conc.Camp, Flossenburg (Ger.)	WITNESS	U.S.
LEGG	196210	M	Ger.		Meister, Gend., Ordnungspol., Westerbork (Neth.) 9.-12.44	MURDER	NETH.
LEGLER	192386	M	Ger.		Major, 9.SS-Pz.Div."Hohenstaufen", Neuville les Bois (Fr.)	WITNESS	FR.
LEGNER, Josef	190651	M	Ger.	21. 2.03	Employee, Gestapo, Brno (Czech.) 39-45	MURDER	CZECH.
LE GRAND MAOUPA (see JURGELEIN)	147550						
LE GROM, Jakob	257636	M			Guard, SS, Conc.Camp, Muehldorf Area (Ger.)	INTERR.	U.S.
LEHERT	67569	M	Ger.		Pvt.,17.SS-Pz.Gren.Div."G.v.B.",Sturmgesch.Abt.u.Pz.Jg.Abt.17, Segre-Renaze (Fr.) 7.44-8.44	MISC.CRIMES	FR.
LEHL	161423	M	Ger.	16	SS-Sgt., Conc.Camp, Buchenwald (Ger.) 44	TORTURE	U.S.
LEHMAN	72281	M	Ger.	85	Capt., Army, Stalag IX C, C.C. Muehlhausen (Ger.) 1.8.43	MURDER	U.K.
LEHMAN	124275	M	Ger.		Uschfhr.,SS-Pz.Rgt.1,SS-Pz.Div.1, H.Q.Coy., Malmedy (Bel.) 17.12.44	MURDER	U.S.
LEHMAN	150640	M	Ger.		Inspector, Civilian, C.C., Auschwitz and Birkenau (Pol.) 10.42	MURDER	U.S.
LEHMAN	180308	M	Ger.		Uschfhr., Leibstand.SS Adolf Hitler,Aufkl.Abt.,Renardmont,Stavelot,44	MURDER	BEL.
LEHMAN	254075	M	Ger.		Oschfhr., Conc.Camp, Buchenwald (Ger.)	INTERR.	FR.

LEH-LEI

NAME	C.R.FILE NUMBER	SEX	NATIO- NALITY	DATE OF BIRTH	RANK OCCUPATION UNIT PLACE AND DATE OF CRIME	REASON WANTED	WANTED BY
LEHMAN	305453	M	Ger.		Oschfhr.,SS,Member of SS "Klosterwerk",Commander Blankenburg- Harz,C.C.Buchenwald (Ger.) 42-45	MURDER	FR.
LEHMANN	6155	M			Capt.,Zweilager IX C,Muehlhausen (Fr.) 6.-8.44	TORTURE	U.K.
LEHMANN	31621	M	Ger.		Sturmbannfhr.,SS,Comd.3,SS-Geb.Jg.Regt.12-6,Geb.Div.Nord(Nor)10.-11.44	TORTURE	NOR.
LEHMANN	124476	M	Ger.		Cpl.,SS,C.C.Sachsenhausen,Oranienburg (Ger.) 42	TORTURE	U.K.
LEHMANN	124850	M	Ger.	98	Capt.,Stalag IX C,Bad Sulza (Ger.)	TORTURE	U.S.
LEHMANN	125044	M	Ger.		Oberfw.,Camp	MISC.CRIMES	U.K.
LEHMANN	139048	M	Ger.	10	Sturmbannfhr.,S.D.Sipo,Toulouse and other Towns(Fr.) 6.8.44	MURDER	U.S.
LEHMANN	140927	F	Ger.	19	Woman-guard,C.C.Ravensbrueck (Ger.) 42-44	TORTURE	U.K.
LEHMANN	141360	M	Ger.		Pvt.,Army,114 Ldsschtz.Bn.,Warsch near Kulm (Pol.)	TORTURE	U.K.
LEHMANN	146728	M	Ger.		Legal Departement Armed Forces (Ger.) 41-42	INTERR.	U.S.
LEHMANN	156089	M	Ger.		Lt.,Army,Ansbach (Ger.) 15.4.45	MURDER	U.S.
LEHMANN	173120	F	Ger.		C.C.Schirmeck,Rotenfels,Gaggenau (Fr.Ger.) 44	INTERR.	U.K.
LEHMANN	179237	M	Ger.	99	Civ.,C.C.Lahde-Weser (Ger.)	MURDER	BEL.
LEHMANN	186696	M	Ger.	95	Sturmscharfhr.,SS,Leibstand."Adolf Hitler",Wormhoudt (Fr.) 5.40	MURDER	U.K.
LEHMANN	191215	M	Ger.		Cpl.,Member of Camp Guard,C.C.Sachsenhausen,Oranienburg (Ger.)	MURDER	U.K.
LEHMANN	252517	M	Ger.		Professor Medicine,University,Strassburg (Fr.) 40-44	MURDER	FR.
LEHMANN	254389	M	Ger.		Sgt.,Member,Gestapo,S.D.,Toulouse (Fr.) 11.42	MISC.CRIMES	FR.
LEHMANN	301043	M	Ger.		Guard,Labour Camp,Lahde-Weser (Ger.) 43-45	MURDER	BEL.
LEHMANN,Albert	254494	M	Ger.	06	Pvt.,Probably 192 Signal-Bn.,Inf.Div.92,Farnese (Ital.) 6.6.44	INTERR.	U.K.
LEHMANN,Andre	254387	M	Ger.		W.O.,Gestapo,Toulouse (Fr.) 11.42-8.44	MISC.CRIMES	FR.
LEHMANN,Anton	190649	M	Ger.		Crim.Secr.,Gestapo,Bruenn (Czech.) 39-45	MURDER	CZECH.
LEHMANN,Bruno	187056	M			Oschfhr.,4 SS-Totenk.-Sturmbann,C.C.Dora,Nordhausen (Ger.)	TORTURE	U.S.
LEHMANN,Franz	131299	M	Ger.		Blockaeltester,Guard,C.C.Jawischowitz,Auschwitz (Pol.) 44	MURDER	U.S.
LEHMANN,Friedrich	250356	M			Pvt.,C.C.Ellrich,Nordhausen (Ger.)	MURDER	U.S.
LEHMANN,Fritz	145987	M	Ger.		Civ.,in Charge of P.W.Camp (Ger.)	TORTURE	U.S.
LEHMANN,Johannes	252379	M	Ger.		Crim.Secr.,C.C.Lahde-Weser (Ger.)	MISC.CRIMES	BEL.
LEHMANN,Johannes	254854	M	Ger.	28.12.02	Employee,Gestapo,Litomerice (Czech.) 39-45	MURDER	CZECH.
LEHMANN,Joseph	142192	M		75	Civ.,Locten (Fr.)	TORTURE	FR.
LEHMANN,Kurt	301805	M	Ger.		SS-Mann,1 SS-Pz.Div."Leibstand.Adolf Hitler",Region of Stavelot (Bel.)19.-20.12.44	MURDER	BEL.
LEHMANN,Otto	162558	M	Ger.		Staff-Sgt.,Feldgendarmerie,Roye (Fr.) 2.5.44	WITNESS	FR.
LEHMANN,Otto	192179	M	Ger.		Member,Geh.Feld-Pol.,Charleroi (Bel.)	MURDER	BEL.
LEHMANN,Rudolf	250357	M			Pvt.,C.C.Ellrich,Nordhausen (Ger.)	MURDER	U.S.
LEHMANN,Rudolf	252250	M	Ger.		Standartenfhr.,1 SS-Pz.Regt.,1 SS-Corps,Malmedy (Bel.) 17.12.44	MURDER	U.S.
LEHMANN,Walter (or Andre)	305454	M	Ger.		Scharfhr.,S.D.,Section IV,Gestapo,Toulouse,Ht.Garonne, Gers and Tarn,South-West (Fr.) 11.42-19.8.44	MURDER	FR.
LEHMANN,Willy	300293	M	Ger.		Kapo,Common Law Prisoner,C.C.Flossenburg (Ger.) 42-45	MURDER	FR.
LEHMANN-KALTOFEN,Charlotte, Elfriede	188413	F	Ger.	21	Guard,SS,Schoenefeld,Leipzig (Ger.) 44-45	TORTURE	POL.
LEHMEIER,Josef	262336	M		22. 3.01	Wanted for the Murder of an American Flyer,Sillersdorf (Ger.)16.4.45 L.O.D.N.A.O.D.	WITNESS	U.S.
LEHMUELLER	554	M	Ger.		Army,Feldwebel,Caen (Fr.) 6.44	MURDER	FR.
LEHMUELLER	152823	M		05	Civilian,Caen (Fr.) 6.6.44	MURDER	U.S.
LEHNARD	257637	M			Meister,O.T.,Muehldorf (Ger.)	MURDER	U.S.
LEHNARD	259822	M	Ger.		Cpl.,2 Coy.,Nachr.Truppen,Zuid Holland,Bolnes municihality Ridderkerk, (Neth.) 8.5.45	SUSPECT	NETH.
LEHNAU	142102	M	Ger.	92	Scharfhr.,SS-Totenk.Stand.,W-SS,C.C.Buchenwald,Weimar (Ger.)	TORTURE	U.S.
LEHNE,Walter	179829	M	Ger.	92	Chief,Gestapo,Pardubice (Czech.) 40-45	MURDER	CZECH.
LEHNECKE,Louis	132230	M	Ger.		Civ.,C.C. near Ruehen (Ger.)	TORTURE	U.S.
LEHNER	31574	M		15	Commissar,Gestapo,Prag (Czech.) 3.39	TORTURE	U.S.
LEHNER	173114	M	Ger.		C.C.Gaggenau,Schirmeck,Rotenfels (Ger.Fr.) 44	MURDER	U.K.
LEHNER,Alois	190650	M	Ger.		Crim.Comm.Gestapo,Bruenn (Czech.) 39-45	MURDER	CZECH.
LEHNER,Christian	186288	M	Ger.		N.C.O.,Army,Anogeia,Crete (Grc.)	MURDER	GRC.
LEHNER,Franz	178756	M	Ger.	05	Pvt.,878 Ldsschtz.Bn.,1 Coy,C.C.Leonard (Aust.) 2.44	MURDER	U.K.
LEHNER,Fritz	139164	M	Ger.		Civilian,C.C.Nuernberg (Ger.)	MISC.CRIMES	U.S.
LEHNERT,Fritz	187115	M	Ger.		Member,NSDAP,C.C. Stalag XIII D,Woernitz,Ansbach (Ger.)	TORTURE	BEL.
LEHNERT,Johann	305922	M	Ger.	27. 2.02	Soldier in Res.,Velke,Heraltice (Czech.) 7.8.44	BRUTALITY	CZECH.
LEHNERT,Paul	142095	M	Ger.		Oschfhr.,W-SS,Totenk.Stand.,C.C.Buchenwald (Ger.)	MURDER	U.S.
LEHNHARD	257002	M	Ger.		2.Nachr.Coy.,Bolnes (Neth.) 5.45	INTERR.	NETH.
LEHNHARTZ	250361	M			Pvt.,C.C.Ellrich,Nordhausen,Mackenrode (Ger.)	MURDER	U.S.
LEHNHOFF	196825	M	Ger.		Sgt.,Sipo,C.C.Westerbork (Neth.)	INTERR.	NETH.
LEHNIG-EMDEN,Wolfgang	192938	M	Ger.	23.11.25	Lt.,3 Pz.Div.,29 Pz.Gren.Regt.,3 Coy.,1 Platoon,San Giovannie, Paolo near Caiazzo (Ital.) 13.10.43	MURDER	U.S.
LEHNKERING,Karl Heinz	195444	M	Ger.	11. 5.11	Chief,SS,Luxembourg (Lux.) 40-45	MISC.CRIMES	LUX.
LEHR,Hans	124851	M	Ger.	93	Capt.,Stalag IX C,Bad Sulza (Ger.)	TORTURE	U.K.
LEHR,Hans	128977	M	Ger.		NSDAP,Friedrichsfeld (Ger.) 25.4.45	TORTURE	U.S.
LEHRBASS	306910	F	Ger.		Farmer's-wife,Gut Freydeck (Ger.) 2.7.45	MURDER	U.K.
LEHRHOLD	122402	M	Ger.		Cpl.,Army,Creach'-Maout(Fr.) 7.8.44	MURDER	FR.
LEHRMAN,Hugo	166710	M	Ger.	96	Civilian,Wackerleben (Ger.)	MURDER	U.S.
LEHRMANN	187637	M	Ger.		Pvt.,Feldgendarmerie,Goudriaan (Neth.) 22.5.44	MURDER	U.K.
LEHSE,Otto	185956	M	Ger.		Member,NSDAP,Bayonne (Fr.) 40-45	MISC.CRIMES	FR.
LEHUMANN	185136	M	Ger.		Lt.,Army,Hennebont (Fr.) 6.8.44	MURDER	FR.
LEHWALD	126569	M	Ger.		Major,Arbeits-Kdo.,Werkschutzleister,Hagen (Ger.) 41-45	MURDER	U.S.
LEIA	29753	M	Ger.		Soldier,Feldgendarmerie,Parachute N.C.O.,Abbeville (Fr.) 31.8.44	MURDER	FR.
LEIB,Otto	250367	M			Pvt.,C.C.Ellrich,Nordhausen (Ger.)	MURDER	U.S.
LEIBER,Gottfried	173116	M	Ger.		C.C.Staff,Niederbuehl (Ger.) 44	MURDER	U.K.
LEIBER,Max	190653	M	Ger.		Pol.Secr.,Gestapo,Bruenn (Czech.) 39-45	MURDER	CZECH.
LEIBHOLT	219367	M	Ger.	95	Hptwachtmann,NSDAP,C.C.Papenburg (Ger.) 4.45	TORTURE	U.S.
LEIBICH	259068	M	Ger.		Lt.,A Dulag Luft,Hospital (Ger.)43-4-45	BRUTALITY	U.S.
LEIBNITZ,Otto	257692	M			Oberpolier,O.T.,Muehldorf (Ger.)	WITNESS	U.S.
LEIBRANDT	62373	M	Ger.		Dr.,Reichsamtsleiter,NSDAP,Rosenberg's Looting off."ERR" (Osten)	PILLAGE	UNWCC
LEIBRECHT	252378	M	Ger.	02	Capt.,O.C.Supply Coy.,Castellucchio (Ital.) 12.8.43	INTERR.	U.K.
LEIBSCHEDER	250366	M			Pvt.,C.C.Rottleberode,Nordhausen (Ger.)	MURDER	U.S.
LEICHEL,Egon	255290	M	Ger.		SS,Eyne (Bel.) 4.-6.9.44	INTERR.	BEL.
LEICHER	167934	M	Ger.		Lt.,s Sicherungs-Regt.,10 Coy.C.C.,Torce en Charnie(Fr.)6.-7.8.44	MURDER	FR.

LEI-LEM

NAME	C.R.FILE NUMBER	SEX	NATIO-NALITY	DATE OF BIRTH	RANK OCCUPATION UNIT PLACE AND DATE OF CRIME	REASON WANTED	WANTED BY
LEICHER, Karl	194218	M	Ger.	27. 9.98	Sturmfhr.,SA, Koprivnice (Czech.) 39-45	MISC.CRIMES	CZECH.
LEICHNER	195055	M	Ger.		Leader, Ruestungslieferungsamt,Amsterdam (Neth.) 40-45	PILLAGE	NETH.
LEICHNER, Horst	67560	M	Ger.	27	SS-Pvt.,Hitlerjugend, C.C. Maiental nr.Zempelburg, Graudenz, Bromberg (Ger.) 18.11.44	TORTURE	U.K.
LEICHSENRING	162368	M	Ger.		Osturmfhr.,19 Pz.Gren.Rgt.,SS-Div.Hohenstaufen,Palmerskirchen(Ger.) 12.44	MURDER	U.S.
LEICHT	255554	M	Ger.		Cpl.,2 Bn"De Renfort",10 SS Pz.Div.Frundsberg,Louveciennes, Marly (Fr.) 19.-23.8.44	INTERR.	FR.
LEICHT, Lillian	135549	M	Ger.		Farmer,Civ.Abt.Kino 7006,C.C.Alsleben (Ger.)	MURDER	U.K.
LEICKE, Max	124276	M	Ger.		Usturmfhr.,SS Pz.Gren.Rgt.2,1 Pz.Div.,9 Coy,Malmedy(Bel.) 17.12.44	MURDER	U.S.
LEIDEL	193452	M	Ger.		Rottenfhr.,SS, C.C. Buchenwald (Ger.) 42-45	MISC.CRIMES	U.S.
LEIDENTOPF	193451	M	Ger.		Sturmbannfhr.,SS, C.C. Buchenwald (Ger.) 42-45	TORTURE	U.S.
LEIDREITER	156086	M	Ger.		Osturmfhr.,1 SS Pz.Div.(Adolf Hitler)Parfondruy,Stavelot(Bel.)12.44	MURDER	U.S.
LEIDRER	252518	M	Ger.		Sgt., Waffen-SS, Cavaillon,Vercoiran (Fr.) 9.3.44	MURDER	FR.
LEIDZMANN, Waldemar	186290	M	Ger.		Employee,Gestapo,Budejovice (Czech.) 39-45	MURDER	CZECH.
LEIFELOTS	123136	M	Ger.		Cpl.,Army-Lager,C.C. Spremberg (Ger.) 2.2.45	BRUTALITY	U.K.
LEIFHEIT, Theodor	250365	M		30. 6.17	Pvt., C.C. Ellrich-Nordhausen (Ger.)	MURDER	U.S.
LEIFNER	261213	M	Ger.		Pvt., 139 Arbeitsbereich Liane,5-Inf.Rgt.211,Alleur-lez-Liege (Bel.) 4.9.44	MURDER	BEL.
LEIKAM	141869	M	Ger.		Lt.,355 Art.Rgt.,12 Coy,214 Div., Sletteb (Nor.) 12.42	WITNESS	U.K.
LEIKER, Konrad see LECKER	301340						
LEIMANN	192739	M	Ger.		Sgt.,Kf.Arb.Bn 190, Krasjok (Nor.)	TORTURE	NOR.
LEIMER	305923	M	Ger.		Crim.secr.,(in charge of"questioning"prisoners) Prison small fortress, Therisienstadt (Czech.) 1.10.38-44	MURDER	CZECH.
LEIMITZ	194394	M	Ger.		Pvt.,C.C.Zinna, Torgau (Ger.)2.-4.45	MURDER	U.S.
LEINKUEHLER, Willi	192738	M	Ger.	21. 4.18	Reichsjustiz-Min.Strafgef.Lg.Nord,C.C.Finmark(Nor.) 4.45	MISC.CRIMES	NOR.
LEINER, Joseph	167933	M	Ger.	19	W.O.,SS Div."Das Reich",1 Bn,1 Coy, Oradour s.Glane(Fr.)10.6.44	MURDER	FR.
LEINGANG	134803	M	Ger.		Kreischef,Gendarmerie, Gmunden (Ger.) 44	MURDER	U.S.
LEINHOS	258011	M			Pvt.,150 Pz.Bde, Meuse Bridge-Antwerp (Bel.)12.44	MISC.CRIMES	U.S.
LEINHOS, Paul	255279	M			Pvt.,C.C.Ellrich-Nordhausen (Ger.)	MURDER	U.S.
LEINWATHER	145990	M			Usturmfhr.,SS,C.C. Mauthausen (Aust.)41-45	MISC.CRIMES	U.S.
LEINWEBER, Hermann	253137	M	Ger.	19.10.16	Turner, Civilian, Skrivany (Czech.) 39-45	MISC.CRIMES	CZECH.
LEIPE	156081	M	Ger.		Guard, Gestapo, Vienna (Aust.) 10.44	MURDER	U.S.
LEIPOLD	130623	M	Ger.		Usturmfhr.,SS,C.C. Mauthausen (Aust.) 41-45	MURDER	U.S.
LEIPOLD	195445	M	Ger.		Osturmfhr.,SS, C.C. Lublin (Pol.) 40-43	MURDER	POL.
LEIPOLD	251702	M	Ger.	26	Usturmfhr.,SD,chief of section III-C,Koblenz,Rengsdorf(Ger.)12.44-45	WITNESS	U.S.
LEIPS alias LEEPS	132233	M	Ger.		Mil.guard,311 Arb.Kdo., Dettmannsdorf (Ger.) 1.12.44	TORTURE	U.S.
LEISEMANN, Wilhelm	174144	M	Ger.	22	Civilian, Lauenau (Ger.) 11.44	WITNESS	U.S.
LEISER, Fritz or LEIZER	174687	M	Ger.		Commanding-officer,1 Hpt.Kol.Transportstaffel 65,NSKK, Brest-Fort Meranoux (Fr.) 41-44	TORTURE	FR.
LEISING	555	M			Oscharfhr.,SS, C.C. Stutthof (Pol.) 4.41	MURDER	POL.
LEISKAU	192736	M	Ger.		Cpl.,SS,SD,C.C.Trondheim,Falstad,Vollan (Nor.) 41-45	MURDER	NOR.
LEISS, Robert	187045	M			Hptscharfhr.,4 Totenkopf Stuba,C.C.Mittelbau Dora-Nordhausen(Ger.) 43-45	TORTURE	U.S.
LEISSNER, Heinz	255151	M	Ger.	6. 9.16	Reg.Insp.,State Service, Pelhrimor (Czech.) 39-45	MURDER	CZECH.
LEIST	556	M	Ger.		Lt.,Police, Breendonck (Bel.) 40-41	TORTURE	BEL.
LEIST	557	M	Ger.		Oberfhr.,SS,Public official, deputy governor,Warszawa(Pol.)9.39-1.42	MURDER	POL.
LEISTEN, Martin	150641	M	Ger.		Civilian,C.C. Bielefeld (Ger.) 9.44	WITNESS	U.S.
LEISTER	31712	M	Ger.		Cpl.,Waffen-SS,C.C.Oswiecim (Pol.) 6.40-1.45	MURDER	POL.
LEISTER, Georges	257685	M	Ger.		Pvt., Navy,10 Flotille, Guilligomarch (Fr.) 3.7.44	MURDER	FR.
LEISTER, Peter	173743	M	Ger.	00	Kapo, C.C. Neckarelz (Ger.) 45	BRUTALITY	FR.,U.S.
LEISTNER	178305	M	Ger.	09	Pvt., Stalag IV F,Obersturztgren (Ger.) 11.43	MURDER	U.K.
LEIT	257683	M			Employee, C.C. Dachau,Muhldorf Area (Ger.)	WITNESS	U.S.
LEITERS, Jakob	161421	M	Ger.		Civilian, Huber-Inn (Ger.)	WITNESS	U.S.
LEITHOFF, Emil	160392	M	Ger.	10	Lt.,SS,Command Staff, C.C. Buchenwald (Ger.) 44	TORTURE	U.S.
LEITHOLD, Edgar	127412	M	Ger.	26	Pvt.,SS,1.Pz.Gren.Div.engineer platoon,H.Q.Coy, Renardmont, Stavelot (Bel.) 19.12.44	MURDER	U.S.
LEITINGER	160391	M	Ger.	20	Cpl.,SS, C.C. Buchenwald (Ger.)	TORTURE	U.S.
LEITINGER	193450	M	Ger.		Rottenfhr.,SS, C.C. Buchenwald (Ger.) 42-45	MISC.CRIMES	U.S.
LEITMER or LEITNER	132628	M	Ger.	07	Sgt.,SS, SD, Grenoble (Fr.)	MISC.CRIMES	FR.
LEITMEYER, Mathias	185955	M	Ger.		Sgt.,Feldgend. Truppe 626, Peronne,Licourt (Fr.) 24.8.44	MURDER	FR.
LEITMER see LEITMER	132628						
LEITNER	150643	F			C.C. Mauthausen (Aust.) Spring 45	MISC.CRIMES	U.S.
LEITNER	307006	M	Ger.		Scharfhr.,SS, Gestapo Grenoble,Massif du Vercors,Isere,Drome (Fr.) 20.7.-5.8.44	MURDER	FR.
LEITNER, Georg	190654	M	Ger.		Employee, Gestapo, Brno (Czech.) 39-45	MURDER	CZECH.
LEIST see LAIS	9601						
LEITNER, Wilhelm	162367	M	Ger.		W.O.,Feldgendarmerie d'Auch,l'Isle Jourdain (Fr.) 12.6.44	MURDER	FR.
LEITREITER	124722	M	Ger.		Osturmfhr.,SS Leibstandarte A.H.,1 Div.,3 Rgt.,Renardmont(Bel.)12.44	MURDER	U.S.,BEL.
LEITZ	132550	M	Ger.		Oscharfhr.,SS,C.C. Neuengamme (Ger.)	MURDER	FR.
LEITZ	255280	M			Rottenfuehrer,Mackenrode-Nordhausen (Ger.)	MURDER	U.S.
LEIZER, Fritz see LEISER	174687						
LEITZNER, Johann	261977	M	Ger.		Member, NSDAP,Freiw.Schutzstaffel,Bratislava (Czech.)4.42-4.45	MURDER	CZECH.
LEKEBUSCH	250911	M	Ger.		Capt., 14 Pol.Rgt., Tuk (Yugo.) 27.10.43	INTERR.	YUGO.
LEKER, Konrad	259927	M		10	Oscharfhr.,SS, Gestapo, Trentin (Czech.) 11.44-2.4.45	MURDER	CZECH.
LEKREMEIER	253146	M	Ger.		Lt.,Unit Alpine, Orbagnoux (Fr.) 10.7.44	INTERR.	FR.
LELL, Max	146734	M			Kapo, Civilian,C.C. Flossenburg (Ger.) 40-45	MURDER	U.S.,BEL.
LELLIG, Peter	257684	M	Ger.		Mar.Obermaat, U-Boot 318,992, northern Hopseidet-Finmark(Nor.)6.5.45	MURDER	NOR.
LELLING	252253	M	Ger.		SS-Stand.Fuehrer,Dr.,C.C. Neuengamme (Ger.)	BRUTALITY	BEL.
LEILINGER	252449	M	Ger.	11	Osturmfhr.,SS, Graz (Aust.) 4.45	INTERR.	U.K.
LEM	150645	M			Lt.Col.,Army,27 Fuesilier-Rgt.,Einigen (Bel.) 18.12.44	MISC.CRIMES	U.S.
LEMANN, Willy	256322	M	Ger.		Kapo, C.C. Flossenburg (Ger.)	MURDER	FR.
LEMBEEK	130624	M	Ger.		Civilian, Kaisheim (Ger.)	MURDER	BEL.
LEMBERG, Fritz	558	M			Oberwachtmstr.,Pol.-Revier,C.C.Oswiecim-Birkenau(Pol.) 40	MURDER	POL.
LEMBERGER, Franz	250362	M			Uscharfhr.,C.C.Ellrich-Nordhausen (Ger.)	MURDER	U.S.
LEMBINSKY, Casimir	252937	M	Ger.	98	Master,Schutzpol.,C.Troop,34 Bn,Gren.Div.Landsturm,Tiel (Neth.)	PILLAGE	NETH.
LEMEKE or LEMEQUE	259688	M			Marine of Rochefort,Charente Maritime Tonnay-Charente(Fr.)24.8.44	MURDER	FR.
LEMER or LEMMER	257665	M			Magaziner, O.T., Muhldorf Area (Ger.)	INTERR.	U.S.

LEM-LEO

NAME	C.R.FILE NUMBER	SEX	NATIO- NALITY	DATE OF BIRTH	RANK OCCUPATION UNIT PLACE AND DATE OF CRIME	REASON WANTED	WANTED BY
LEMKE	560	M	Ger.		N.C.O.,SS Pz.Div."Das Reich",Rgt."Der Fuehrer",Buzet (Fr.)7.7.44	MURDER	FR.
LEMKE	196764	M	Ger.		Aufseher,NSDAP,C.C.,Flossenburg (Ger.)	MISC.CRIMES	FR.
LEMKE	300805	M	Ger.		Pvt.,1.Aufkl.Abt.,3.Coy.,2.Column,XV.Div.,Afrika Korps,Saint- Leger (Arlon) 5.9.44	MISC.CRIMES	BEL.
LEMKE, Frieda	152877	F	Ger.		Employee,Gestapo,Angers (Fr.) 42-44	MURDER	FR.
LEMKE, Gerhard (see LUNKE)	192182						
LEMKE, Karl	150646	M			Civilian,Schladen,Buchladen (Ger.) 28.9.44	TORTURE	U.S.
LEMKI	261495	M	Ger.		Sturmbannfhr.,SS,Dirlewanger Bde.,Sluck (Pol.) 40-44	MURDER	POL.
LEMM	300806	M	Ger.		N.C.O.,1.Aufkl.Abt.,3.Coy.,2.Column,XV.Div.,Afrika Korps,Saint- Leger (Arlon) 5.9.44	MISC.CRIMES	BEL.
LEMME, Walter	139165	M	Ger.		Civilian,C.C., (Ger.)	MISC.CRIMES	U.S.
LEMMER	155712	M			Guard,SS,C.C.,Wieda near Gardelegen (Ger.)4.45	MURDER	U.S.
LEMMER (see LEMER)	257665						
LEMOUS, Frantz	186287	M	Ger.		Sailor,Marine,Chania,Crete (Grc.)	MURDER	GRC.
LEMP, Karl	174686	M	Ger.	30. 5.25	Pvt.,Army,Morlaix,St.Pol de Leon (Fr.) 7.-8.44	TORTURE	FR.
LEMPER, Adolf	250343	M	Ger.	7. 1.05	Cpl.,C.C.,Ellrich,Nordhausen (Ger.)	MURDER	U.S.
LEMPKE	561	M	Ger.		Lt.,Army,Magny,Darrignon (Fr.) 18.9.44	MURDER	FR.
LEMPOWITZ, Rudolf	254614	M	Ger.		Pvt.,SS,Auschwitz,Birkenau (Pol.) 1.43	MURDER	YUGO.
LENAERTZ	132234	M	Ger.		Stalag,Capt.,	MURDER	U.S.
LENAHN, Dietrich	254396	M	Ger.	23.11.08	Pvt.,Aude (Fr.) 29.-30.8.44	PILLAGE	FR.
LENAUER	251706	M	Ger.		Doctor,Hptsturmfhr.,SS,C.C.,Mauthausen (Aust.)	MURDER	BEL.
LENCK, Karl	254074	M	Ger.		Sturmschfhr.,Gestapo, (Fr.)	INTERR.	FR.
LENDEL, Johann	250915	M		19. 06	Pvt.,C.C.,Harzungen,Nordhausen (Ger.)	MURDER	U.S.
LENDNER	150647	M	Ger.		Osturmfhr.,SS,C.C.,Auschwitz,Birkenau (Pol.) 10.42	MURDER	U.S.
LENDOWSKI	185954	M	Ger.		Sgt.,Navy Inf.2.Coy.,Queven (Fr.)	MURDER	FR.
LE NEGUS (see NEWE)	189643						
LENERT	562	M	Ger.		Sgt.,Army,Inf.Rgt.,Merville (Fr.) 9.6.44	MURDER	U.K.
LENG	141969	M			Rottfhr.,SS,Waldlager V & VI,Guard,near Ampfing (Ger.)	TORTURE	U.S.
LENGAEUP, Franz	179771	M		95	Capt.,Police,Quota (It.) 7.44	MURDER	U.K.
LENGEMANN	300807	M	Ger.		Pvt.,1.Aufkl.Abt.,3.Coy.,2.Column,XV.Div.,Afrika Korps,Saint Léger (Arlon) 5.9.44	MISC.CRIMES	BEL.
LENGER, Alfred	255150	M	Ger.	30. 7.07	Informer,NSDAP,SA,Gestapo,Blansko. (Czech.) 40-42	PILLAGE	CZECH.
LENGER, Vinzenz	301533	M	Ger.		Uschfhr.,SS,C.C.,Buchenwald (Ger.) 16.5.38-9.10.43	MURDER	BEL.
LENGNEY	150648	M			Capt.,Army, C.O. of Arb.Kdo.,Stalag 3B,C.C.,Fuerstenberg-Oder,(Ger.) 43-44	MURDER	U.S.
LENHARDT, Walter	12578	M	Ger.		Pvt.,110. or 111.Pz.Gren.Rgt.,2.Coy.,Albine (Fr.) 29.6.44	MURDER	FR.
LENHARDT, Willi	152878	M	Ger.		Interpreter,Feldgendarmerie,Creil (Fr.)	TORTURE	FR.
LENHOF	179823	M	Ger.		Vertrauensmann,Gestapo,Sarrebruck (Ger.)	PILLAGE	FR.
LENINGER, Henri	256323	M	Ger.		Kapo,C.C.,Mauthausen (Ger.)	BRUTALITY	FR.
LENIEN	301534	M	Ger.		Crim.Asst.,Montgauthier,(Dinant) (Bel.) 20.9.43	MURDER	BEL.
LENK	124277	M	Ger.		Uschfhr.,1.SS Pz.Div.,1.Pz.Rgt.,9.Coy. engineer,Malmedy (Bel.)17.12.44	MURDER	U.S.
LENK	152876	M	Ger.		Pvt.,Gestapo,Brive (Fr.) 44	MURDER	FR.
LENK	255012	M		99	Bdefhr.,SS, (Ger.)	INTERR.	FR.
LENK, Georg	260402	M	Ger.	12.12.88	Ch.Ar.,Auto Union A.G.,A.G.Saechsische Werke,Chemnitz,Dresden(Ger.)	MISC.CRIMES	U.S.
LENK, Johann	174063	M			Guard,Arbeitslager,Graylitz (Ger.) 42-45	TORTURE	U.S.
LENK, Johann	255011	M	Ger.	22. 6.04	Metalworker,Civilian,Rotava (Czech.) 40-45	TORTURE	CZECH.
LENNAKERS, Anna	134881	F	Ger.		Civilian,Efferen (Ger.)	WITNESS	U.S.
LEN'ART	186556	M	Ger.		Capt.,Army,Stalag 711 A,Eger,Heydebreck (Ger.) 22.1.45	MURDER	U.K.
LENNE, Herald	162868	M	Ger.		Adjutant,Army,Revin (Fr.) 19.-14.6.44	MURDER	FR.
LENNIER	189614	M	Ger.		Major,Zentral Ersatzteillager 206,Paris (fr.) 21.8.44	MURDER	FR.
LENS, Ernst	253776	M	Ger.	05	Pvt.,Army,Ysselstein (Neth.) 4.45	MURDER	NETH.
LENSANDT, Leonhard	192898	M	Ger.		Schupo,C.C.,Falstad (Nor.) 7.42	MURDER	NOR.
LENSCH	253988	M	Ger.		Oschfhr.,3.Coy.,Bn."Des Reich","Der Fuehrer",Oradono-Glane (Fr.)	MURDER	FR.
LENSET, Willi	262183	M	Ger.	2. 8.14	Lt.,9.Coy.,Anti Aircraft Detachment,51.SS Armoure Bde.,Breviandes, Bucheres,St.Savine,La Riviere de Corps Troyes (Aube) (Fr.)22.-25.8.44	MURDER	FR.
LENSSEN	255562	M			Pvt.,C.C.,Dora,Nordhausen (Ger.)	MURDER	U.S.
LENTES	257987	M			Lt.,150.Pz.Bde.Meuse-Bridge,Antwerpen (Bel.) 12.44	MISC.CRIMES	U.S.
LENTSCH, Stefan	250913	M	Ger.		Flyer,C.C.,Ellrich,Nordhausen (Ger.)	MURDER	U.S.
LENZ	31620	M	Ger.		Major,20.Army,19.Geb.Korps Staff,Finmark (Nor.) 10.-11.44	MURDER	NOR.
LENZ	142587	M	Ger.		Blockleiter,Camp,C.C.,Vught (Neth.) 43-44	TORTURE	BEL.
LENZ	167016	M	Ger.		Interpreter,Fallschirm,F.P.No. 27817 C,Tourc'h (Fr.) 44	MURDER	FR.
LENZ	173699	M	Ger.		Sonderfhr.,C.C.,Berlin (Ger.) 8.8.43	MURDER	FR.
LENZ	253144	M	Ger.		President,Mil.Courts,Finistere (Fr.)	MURDER	FR.
LENZ, Alois	250918	M		97	Pvt.,C.C.,Harzungen,Nordhausen (Ger.)	MURDER	U.S.
LENZ, Hildegard	306037	F	Ger.		Member,SS of staff at Sasel C.C.,(Ger.) 10.44-4.45	TORTURE	U.K.
LENZ, Karl	139077	M	Ger.		Civilian,Ermsleben (Ger.) 42	MURDER	U.S.
LENZ, Karl	145986	M			SS Pz.Div."Das Reich",Oschfhr.,Oradour sur Glane (Fr.)	MURDER	FR.
LENZ, Michael	253771	M	Ger.	86	Civilian,Budesheim (Ger.) 10.44	WITNESS	U.S.
LENZ, Richard	252513	M	Ger.	8. 7.12	SS-Mann,Skrivany (Czech.) 39-45	INTERR.	CZECH.
LENZ, Rudolf	100427	M	Ger.		Army,SS Pz.Gren.Div.Hohenstaufen,Arnheim (Neth.) 44	MURDER	U.K.
LENZ, Rudolf	187044	M			Pvt.,guard,4.SS Totenkopf Sturmbann,C.C.,Nordhausen,Mittelbau, Dora, (Ger.) 43-45	TORTURE	U.S.
LENZ, Theodor	250919	M		24. 4.01	Flyer,C.C.,Harzungen,Nordhausen (Ger.)	MURDER	U.S.
LENZEN	301769	M	Ger.		Crim.employee,Abt. IV D,SD,Brussels (Bel.) 6.40-9.44	MURDER	BEL.
LENZEN, Heinrich	187112	M	Ger.		Oschfhr.,SS,Montgauthier (Bel.) 20.9.43	MURDER	BEL.
LENZER	141870	M		85	Capt.,Stalag XX B,Lager Cmdt.,Willerberg,Marienburg (Ger.) 43-44	TORTURE	U.K.
LENZIAN, Emil	254621	M	Ger.		Uschfhr.,SS,Geisenheim (Ger.) 12.44-4.45	MISC.CRIMES	POL.
LENZMANN	142588	M	Ger.		C.C.,Schandelah,Braunschweig (Ger.) 44-45	TORTURE	BEL.
LEONARD	257404	M	Ger.		Usturmfhr.,SS,slave labour camp,Osen (Nor.) 6.42-3.43	MISC.CRIMES	YUGO.
LEONARD, Henrich	301341	M	Ger.		Member,Gestapo,Trencin,Oswiecim,Birkenau,C.C.,(Pol.) 39-45	MURDER	CZECH.
LEONARDI	250920	M			Pvt.,C.C.,Dora,Nordhausen (Ger.)	MURDER	U.S.
LEONHARD	160386	M	Ger.		Pvt.,Army,Leipzig (Ger.)	TORTURE	U.S.
LEONHARD, John	258446	M	Ger.	12. 8.00	Usturmfhr.,SS,Lagerfhr.,C.C.,Plaszow near Cracow (Pol.) 43	MURDER	POL.
LEONHARD, Otto	257955	M	Ger.		Member,SA,Army,Serbia (Yugo.)	WITNESS	YUGO.
LEONHARDI	255418	M			Pvt.,C.C.,Dora,Nordhausen (Ger.)	MURDER	U.S.

NAME	C.R.FILE NUMBER	SEX	NATIO-NALITY	DATE OF BIRTH	RANK OCCUPATION UNIT PLACE AND DATE OF CRIME	REASON WANTED	WANTED BY
LEONHARDT	180312	M	Ger.		W.-SS, I.Pz.Div. "Adolf Hitler" I.Ers.Bn.2.Zug, Parfondruy, Stavelot (Bel.) 18.-22.12.44	MURDER	U.S.
LEONHARDT	193952	M	Ger.		SS-Schuetze, SS, Stavelot (Bel.)	MURDER	BEL.
LEONHARDT	253989	M	Ger.		Oberscharfhr., Gestapo, Limoges (Fr.)	INTERR.	FR.
LEONHARDT	254403	M	Ger.		Cpl.Chief, Lentilly (Fr.) 25.5.44	MURDER	FR.
LEONHARDT, Felix	161425	M	Ger.	14	Oberinspector, Luftwaffe, C.C. Buchenwald (Ger.)	TORTURE	U.S.
LEONHARDT, Fritz	259196	M	Ger.		SS-Unterscharfhr., C.C. Dachau (Ger.) 10.42-45	MISC.CRIMES	YUGO.
LEONHARDY	254366	M	Ger.		Sturmmann, Member, SD,Gestapo, Toulouse (Fr.) 11.42-8.44	MISC.CRIMES	FR.
LEONNECKER	167018	M	Ger.		Adjutant-Chief, Feldgend., Pontarlier (Fr.) 5.44	MURDER	FR.
LEOPOLD	129135	M	Ger.	90	Pvt., Landesschuetzen Bn.379, K.L. 22 A Bruex (Czech.) 2.45-9.3.45	MURDER	U.K.
LEOPOLD	179785	M	Ger.		Manager, Arbeitskdo. C.C. Stalag III-B, Trattendorf (Ger.) 1.9.43-1.7.44	MURDER	U.S.
LEOPOLD	189730	M	Ger.		Pvt., Landesschuetz.Bn.379, Stalag IV, Bruex (Czech.) 9.3.45	MURDER	U.K.
LEOPOLD, Max	257405	M	Ger.		SS-Truppenfhr., SS, Erlandet, Oeusand, Trola (Nor.) 6.42-45	MURDER	YUGO.
LEOPOLD, Rudolf	195493	M	Ger.		Engineer, Arb.-Kdo., C.C. Lahde-Weser (Ger.)	TORTURE	BEL.
LEOPOLDT, Alfons	301044	M	Ger.		Foreman, at Polensky & Zoellner's, Labour Camp, Lahde-Weser (Ger.)43-45	MURDER	BEL.
LEPA, Karl	152827	M	Ger.	91	Mayor, Public Official, Gardelegen (Ger.) 10.-14.8.45	MURDER	U.S.
LEPIEN, Walter	255019	M	Ger.	5. 6.10	Crim.Oberasst., Abt.IV D Sipo, Gestapo, Brussels (Bel.)	INTERR.	BEL.
LEPPICH	146947	M	Ger.		SS-Pz.Div. "Das Reich", Regt."Deutschland" 3.Bn., Venerque le Vernet (Fr.) 44	MURDER	FR.
LE PRUSSIEN	150930	M	Ger.	95	SS-Cpl., C.C. Buchenwald (Ger.)	MURDER	FR.
LEPSCHI, Johann	192391	M	Ger.	24.10.24	SS-man, SS, Vetrni Cesky Krumlov (Czech.) 39-45	MISC.CRIMES	CZECH.
LERCH	151323	M	Ger.		Unterscharfhr., SS-Gestapo, Folkling (Fr.) 11.44	MURDER	FR.
LERCH	167019	M	Ger.		Member, Feldgend., Larochemillay (Fr.) 11.8.44	PILLAGE	FR.
LERCH	253124	M	Ger.		Untersturmfhr., B.D.S. SD,Kdo. z.B.V. "Pullmer" Cirey (Fr.) 44	TORTURE	U.K.
LERCH, Kurt	262282	M	Ger.		SS-Oscharfhr., Gestapo, Rennes (Fr.) 43-44	MISC.CRIMES	FR.
LERCH, Tony	179820	M	Ger.		Untersturmfhr., Crim.Obersecretary, SD, Gestapo, Sarrebruck (Ger.)	PILLAGE	FR.
LERCHE "SPATZ"	195786	M	Ger.	10	SS-Oberscharfhr., Brigadefhr., SS,HJ, SS Standarte "Kurt Eggers" Arnheim (Neth.)	MURDER	NETH.
LERCHER	300909	M	Ger.		Kreisfhr., Driver to Dorfmeister, Cilli (Celje) Slovenia (Yugo.)12.2.45	MURDER	YUGO.
LERHOLD	193809	M	Ger.		Cpl.,Army, Semaphore de Creache-Maout (Fr.) 5.8.44	MURDER	FR.
LERICK	253145	M	Ger.		Lt., Grand-Bourg (Fr.) 23.7.44	INTERR.	FR.
LERINGER	259646	M	Ger.		SS-Mann,Gestapo, Area, Angers (Maine and Loire Fr.) 42-44	MISC.CRIMES	FR.
LERMER, Franz	142580	M	Ger.		Oberscharfhr., SS-Totenkopf Div. KL. Buchenwald (Ger.) 39-45	MURDER	U.S.
LES, Willi	255008	M		97	Kapo, Camp Dora (Fr.)	INTERR.	FR.
LESCH, Anton	255152	M	Ger.	05	Oberwachtmeister, Schutzpolizei, Prague-Kobylisy (Czech.) 41	MURDER	CZECH.
LESAK, Emil	192940	M	Ger.	28. 5.19	Newspaper-Reporter, C.C. Flossenburg (Ger.) 44-45	WITNESS	U.S.
LESCH	188741	M	Ger.		Lt., 28. Regt.Gren.46Bn.2.Coy., Puydarrieux (Fr.) 27.6.44	MURDER	FR.
LESCH, Elwir	255417	M		18.12.10	Pvt., C.C. Ellrich,Nordhausen (Ger.)	MURDER	U.S.
LESCH, Georg	189219	M	Ger.	17. 7.11	Lt., 3.Coy.116.Bn.28.Inf.Regt., Tilhouse, Meilhan,Lagnemezan (Fr.) 29.6.44-7.44	MURDER	FR.
LESCHE	300963	M	Ger.		SS-Oberscharfhr., Official of SD Leitabschnitt, Prague,Oswiecim-Birkenau (Pol.) 39-45	MURDER	CZECH.
LESCHE, F.	31713	M	Ger.		Settler, Olekszin (Pol.)	LOOTING	POL.
LESCHE, K.	31714	M	Ger.		Settler, Olekszin (Pol.) 12.39	LOOTING	POL.
LESCHKE	250342	M			Pvt., C.C. Wolffleben-Rottleb,Nordhausen (Ger.)	MURDER	U.S.
LESCHKE	255419	M			Pvt., C.C. Ellrich,Nordhausen (Ger.)	MURDER	U.S.
LESCHKOWSKI, Josef	250340	M		14. 6.00	Pvt., C.C. Ellrich, Nordhausen (Ger.)	MURDER	U.S.
LESCHNER, Martin	190655	M			Kapo, Dachau (Ger.)	MURDER	U.S.
LESHIK	151346	M	Ger.		Civ., Sosnowitz Mine, C.C. Sosnowitz (Pol.)	MURDER	U.K.
LESK, Karl	255007	M	Ger.	19. 6.97	Hauptwachtmeister, Weaver, SS, Prdhradni, Lhota (Czech.) 11.12.44-2.1.45	MURDER	CZECH.
LESMEISTER	137557	M			Feldwebel, Army, 340.Feld Ers.Bn.3.Coy.	MURDER	U.S.
LESOK, Leonard	195518	M	Ger.		SS-Sgt., Employee, Gestapo, SD, Kolin (Czech.) 39-45	MURDER	CZECH.
LESSING	564	M			SS-Untersturmfhr., SS Gren.Regt."Deutschland", Aussonne (Fr.)1.5.44	MURDER	FR.
LESSMANN, Arthur	165162	M	Ger.		Farmer, Burgdorf (Ger.) 28.9.44	MURDER	U.S.
LETOW, LETOV see LETTOW	132235						
LETTENBIECHER	186488	M		21	Unterscharfhr., 12.SS Pz.Div.H.J., Caen (Fr.) 6.6.-8.7.44	TORTURE	CAN.
LE TUEUR see COERTS	185349						
LETTOW or LETOW, LETOV	132235	M	Ger.		SS-Sturmfhr., Gestapo, Brno (Czech.) 39-45	MURDER	CZECH.
LETZ	142589	M	Ger.	05	Oberscharfhr., SS, Neuengamme (Ger.)	TORTURE	U.K.
LETZ, Friedrich	141068	M	Ger.		Dr., Civ., Doctor at C.C. Natzweiler (Fr.)	MURDER	U.K.
LETZ, Fritz	252519	M	Ger.		Medecin, Strasbourg (Fr.) 40-44	MURDER	FR.
LETZ, Rudolf	80512	M	Ger.		Director, Public-Offic. Justizministerium,	MISC.CRIMES	U.N.W.C.C.
LEUDEKE, Rudolf	300576	M	Ger.		Pvt., Army 377 Inf.Regt., Vinckt-Meigem (Bel.) 25.-31.5.40	MISC.CRIMES	BEL.
LEUDEP	124278	M	Ger.		Engineers, SS Pz.Div.Pz.Regt., 9.Camp Malmedy (Bel.) 17.12.44	MURDER	U.S.
LEUETTWITZ, Smila or VON LUETT-WITZ	260654	M	Ger.		General, Army,	WITNESS	U.S.
LEUFFEN, Franz	258873	M		23. 7.17	Civilian, Luxembourg (Grand Duchy)	MISC.CRIMES	LUX.
LFUSCHKE	306689	M	Ger.		Pvt., 331.Pio.Bn.,331.Inf.Div., Mijnheerenland (Neth.) 5.45	PILLAGE	NETH.
LEUSSO	124279	M	Ger.		Pvt., 1.SS Pz.Div., 1.SS Pz.Regt., 9.Camp (Engineers) Malmedy (Bel.) 17.12.44	MURDER	U.S.
LEUTE	254663	M	Ger.		SS-Obersturmfhr., SS, Auschwitz-Birkenau (Pol.)12.42	MISC.CRIMES	YUGO.
LEUTE, Albert	72317	M			Pvt., SS, C.C. Struthof (Fr.) 42-44	MISC.CRIMES	FR.
LEUTERITZ, Kurt	250339	M		17. 4.07	Pvt., C.C. Ellrich, Nordhausen (Ger.)	MURDER	U.S.
LEUTERK	191909	M	Ger.		Major, Army, Art. Gosnay (Fr.) 1.and2.9.44	MURDER	FR.
LEUTHNER	256683	M	Ger.		Adjutant-Chief, Volkswagenwerk, Sochaux (Fr.) 40-44	MISC.CRIMES	FR.
LEUXEFELD	255020	M	Ger.		Hauptsturmfhr., Sipo Abt. III D, SS, Brussels (Bel.)	INTERR.	BEL.
LEVAN, Viktor	250338	M			Flyer, C.C. Ellrich, Nordhausen (Ger.)	MURDER	U.S.
LEVEN, Ernst	250344	M		5. 6.97	Col. C.C. Ellrich, Nordhausen (Ger.)	MURDER	U.S.
LEVERKANN, Karl	139687	M	Ger.		Crim.-Inspector, Gestapo-SS, Lemberg (Pol.) 40-44	MISC.CRIMES	U.S.
LEVINSKI	257666	M			Employee, Railway, Ussel (Fr.) 10.6.44	SUSPECT	FR.
LE VISEUR	139692	M			Lt.Colonel, Oflag 64 C.C. Schubin (Pol.)	TORTURE	U.S.
LEVRENEC	62488	M	Ger.	18	Lt., Inf.Div.110.Regt.225 8.Coy., Rzhew (Sov.Un.) 6.42-1.43	MURDER	U.S.

LEW-LIE

NAME	C.R.FILE NUMBER	SEX	NATIO-NALITY	DATE OF BIRTH	RANK OCCUPATION UNIT PLACE AND DATE OF CRIME	REASON WANTED	WANTED BY
LEWANDOWSKI, Thea	141397	F			Warden,CC Uckermark near Ravensbrueck(Ger.)42-45	MURDER	FR.BEL.
LEWANDOWSYY	67576	M	Ger.		Pvt.SS Div.Fp.48963B,St.Sulpice,Fortmusson,Chateau,Gontier(Fr.)6.8.44	MURDER	FR.
LEWE or EWE	137558	M			Dr.,Hptscharfhr.SS,KL Weimar-Buchenwald(Ger.)	MURDER	U.S.
LEWE, Victor	161424	M	Ger.	13	Dr.,Untersturmfhr.SS,CC Buchenwald(Ger.)42	TORTURE	U.S.
LEWEKE, Gustav	150042	M			Civilian,KL Bielefeld(Ger.)	WITNESS	U.S.
LEWENTZ, Josef	187617	M	Ger.	05	Ortsgruppenleiter,NSDAP,Camp St.Goar(Ger.)29.12.44	MURDER	U.S.
LEWERENTZ, Bruno	195517	M	Ger.	12	SS Sgt.Employee,Gestapo,S.D.Kolin(Czech.)39-45	MURDER	CZECH.
LEWERING, Leopold	148226	M	Ger.		SS,Calais,Arras,Bethunes,Bergk Plage,St.Pol,Beriement,Boulongne s-Mer,St.Omer(Fr.)43	TORTURE	FR.
LEWERING, Leopold	185134	M	Ger.		SS Chief of Personnel,SS CC Sachsenhausen(Ger.)	MURDER	FR.
LEWERFUS	72275	M	Ger.		Groupleader NSDAP,Roermond(Neth.)44	TORTURE	U.S.
LEWIN	192150	M	Ger.		SS Mann,CC Breendonck(Bel.)	MURDER	BEL.
LEWING, Franz	145988	M	Ger.	20. 2.18	M-Sgt.Asst.Doctor,Medical Academy,German Air Corps,Wuerzburg,between Neubukow and Rerck(Ger.)16.-17.3.44	WITNESS	U.S.
LEWINSKY	187043	F	Ger.		Dr.Member,Gestapo,SS,S.D.,Pilsen(Czech.)39-45	MURDER	CZECH.
LEWOHL, Karl	190652	M	Ger.		Crim.Employee,Gestapo,Bruenn(Czech.)39-45	MURDER	CZECH.
LEWONIG	300808	M	Ger.		N.C.O.1 Aufkl.Abt.3 Coy.2 Column XV Div.of the Afrika Korps,Saint Leger,Arlon,5.9.44	MISC.CRIMES	BEL.
LEX	156080	M			Asst.of camp commander.CC Parzymiechi(Pol.)41-44	MURDER	U.S.
LEX, Jean	162867	M	Ger.	19. 1.99	Civilian,Moselle(Fr.)	PILLAGE	FR.
LEXEN, Wilhelm	257667	M			SS Pvt.Dachau-Muehldorf(Ger.)	WITNESS	U.S.
LEY or DE LAYE or DE MAYE	156087	M	Ger.		Major,Commandant Schnelle Abt.No.602,Felpost 27690A and 23855A,Begrolles,Loraux,Botteraux(Fr.)44	MURDER	FR.
LEY, Kurt	240003	M	Ger.	20	Pvt.Abwehr-Nachr.Regt.506,6 Coy.Bad Wildungen(Ger.)45	MISC.CRIMES	U.S.
LEYA	125685	M	Ger.		Lt.648 Feldgendarmerie Trupp,Loc Maria Berien(Fr.)3.-4.44	MURDER	FR.
LEYA, Bruno	565	M	Ger.		Lt.Army,Feldgendarmerie,Troop 648,CC Huelgaet(Fr.)7.44	TORTURE	FR.
LEYE, Robert	193810	M	Ger.	95	Major,Schnelle Abt.602,Chambord(Fr.)21.-22.8.44	MURDER	FR.
LEYENDECKER	300809	M	Ger.		Pvt.1 Aufkl.Abt.3 Coy.2 Column, XV Div.of the Afrika Korps,Saint Leger Arlon,5.9.44	MISC.CRIMES	BEL.
LEYGENS, Johann	307135	M	Ger.		Reichsbahn Official,Fernmeldemeisterei Office at Amersfoort(Neth.) 4.10.44-5.45	MURDER	NETH.
LEYKE	124280	M	Ger.		Usturmfhr.1 SS Pz.Div.1 SS Pz.Regt.19 Coy.(Engineers)Malmedy(Bel.) 17.12.44	MURDER	U.S.
LEYMANN	252520	M	Ger.	09	Pvt.Sicherungs Regt.618,St.Marcel(Fr.)13.9.44	INTERR.	FR.
LEYMANN	253768	M	Ger.		Organisation Todt,Rosny-Bois(Fr.)20.8.44	MISC.CRIMES	FR.
LEYS see LAIS	9601						
LEYSER, Ernst Ludwig	21346	M	Ger.		Obergruppenfhr.S.A.Commissioner Gen.of Shitomir,Gauleiter Deputy for Westmark,NSDAP(Fr.)	TORTURE	UNWCC
LHOSE	253134	M	Ger.		Col.CC Compiegne(Fr.)41-44	MURDER	FR.
LIBAN, Trudi	134805	F			SS Guard,CC Vicinity of Erfurt(Ger.)44	MISC.CRIMES	U.S.
LIBIG	257672	M	Ger.		Camp,Chief of Sub.Sec.Mittelwerk,Nordhausen(Ger.)	MURDER	U.S.
LIBORSKI	156082	M	Ger.		Ob.Lt.SS 16 Div.Inf.Camp Mouaire,Maille(Fr.)25.8.44	MURDER	FR.
LICHKERN or LICHKEIM	167020	M	Ger.		Lt.Grenzpolizei,Montigny,Fr.)9.44	MURDER	FR.
LICHNOK	306306	M	Ger.		Lt.attached to garrison,St.Malo(Ille-et Vilaine)(Fr.)6.-12.8.44	PILLAGE	FR.
LICHSL	173698	M	Ger.		Pvt.Thiers(Fr.)25.8.44	PILLAGE	FR.
LICHT	12255	M	Ger.		Lt.Representing chief et civil adm.Lorraine	MISC.CRIMES	U.K.
LICHTBLAU	142093	M	Ger.		N.C.O.Army,Stalag 18,Kaisersteinbruch(Aust.)5.43	TORTURE	U.S.
LICHTENBERG	192737	M	Ger.	09	Sgt.Airforce,Land.Schtz.127-17,Lista(Nor.)	WITNESS	NOR.
LICHTENBERG, Hans	307007	M	Ger.	5.12.10	Sub.Director of the firm "M.van Damm en Zonen",Textiel-Fabriken,Enschede (Neth.)41-45	PILLAGE	NETH.
LICHTENECKER, Heinrich	139163	M	Ger.		Member,Farmer,Owner Cafe,Mayor,NSDAP,Volary(Czech.)45	WITNESS	U.S.
LICHTENTHALER	141576	M			Kreishptamtsleiter,NSDAP,Bischwiller(Fr.)12.45	MURDER	FR.
LICHTENWALTER, Wilhelm	250345	M		6. 3.22	Flyer,CC Ellrich,Nordhausen(Ger.)	MURDER	U.S.
LICKEFELT, Fritz	155711	M			Mayor,Public official Civilian KL Darlingerode(Ger.)44	WITNESS	U.S.
LICKLEDER	179821	M	Ger.		Osturmfhr.Kriminalrat,S.D.Gestapo,Sarrebruck(Ger.)	PILLAGE	FR.
LIEB	29770	M	Ger.		Capt.Army,Montferrier(Fr.)26.6.44-25.8.44	MURDER	FR.
LIEB	255592	M	Ger.		Capt.Legion Azerbaidjan,Aveyron(Fr.)8.44	MISC.CRIMES	FR.
LIEBE, Arthur	21344	M	Ger.		SS W.u.V.H.A.Osturmfhr.	TORTURE	UNWCC FR.
LIEBEGOTT	191830	M	Ger.		Capt.Army,Paris(Fr.)41	TORTURE	U.K.
LIEBEL	196458	M	Ger.		Usturmfhr.SS Div.Das Reich,3 SS Pz.Gren.Regt.Deutschland,Marsoulas(Fr.)	MURDER	FR.
LIEBEL	260116	M		05 or 10	CC Dachau(Ger.)42-44	BRUTALITY	FR.
LIEBELAU	192181	M	Ger.		Member Gestapo(Bel.)	TORTURE	BEL.
LIEBEN	191908	M			Lt.Army,St.Hilaire,St.Mesnin(Fr.)19.-25.8.44	MURDER	FR.
LIEBEN	194652	M	Ger.		Lt.Army,St.Laurent des Eaux(Fr.)18.-19.8.44	MURDER	FR.
LIEBENAU, Otto	253990	M	Ger.	10	Lt.Russ.Germ.Unit,Chaumont,La Ferte sur Aube(Fr.)15.6.44	MURDER	FR.
LIEBENER	167716	M	Ger.		Dr.,Public Official,Ostdeutsche Landbewirtschaftungsgesellschaft-Hauptgeschaeftsstelle,Posen(Pol.)9.39-44	MISC.CRIMES	POL.
LIEBENHENSCHEL, Arthur	31715	M	Ger.		SS Ostubafhr.SS Zentralamt of CC Auschwitz,Birkenau,Warschau(Pol.)40-40	TORTURE	U.S.BEL.POL.
LIEBENHOF, Emmy	173115	F	Ger.		CC Schirmeck,Rotenfels,Gaggenau(Fr.Ger.)40-45	MURDER	U.F.
LIEBENOF, Fred	165953	M	Ger.		Agent,Gestapo,Charleroi(Bel.)44	TORTURE	BEL.
LIEBENOW	10305	M			Ministerialdirektor,Public official,Prague(Czech.)39-44	TORTURE	CZECH.
LIEBER	177555	M	Ger.		SS Lt.SS Unit 154275,Jouy en Josas(Fr.)	MURDER	FR.
LIEBER	254605	M	Ger.		SS Sturmscharfhr.Member,SS,S.D.,Toulouse(Fr.)11.42-8.44	MISC.CRIMES	FR.
LIEBERENZ	254606	M	Ger.		Director,in Firmen Hippelt-Lieberenz,Margival(Fr.)43	TORTURE	FR.
LIEBERGOTH	301426	M	Ger.		President,Military,Tribunal of Dax(Landes)Councillor to the Court(Fr.) 13. 6.44	MURDER	FR.
LIEBERHANSCHL	124115	M	Ger.		Osturmfhr.SS,Auschwitz(Pol.)42-44	MURDER	FR.
LIEBERMANN	260722	M		97	SS Hptsturmfhr.CC Hallein(Aust.)	MURDER	U.S.
LIEBERSBACKAS	127414	M	Ger.		SS Leibstandarte Adolf Hitler, N.C.O.	MURDER	U.S.
LIEBESKIND	196775	M	Ger.		Sonderfhr.CC Royallieu,Compiegne(Fr.)41-44	MISC.CRIMES	FR.
LIEBETRUD, Karl	172077	M	Ger.		Civilian,Grosswangen(Ger.)9.44	WITNESS	U.S.
LIEBGOTT, Adalbert	195516	M	Ger.	95	Employee,Gestapo,Kolin(Czech.)39-45	MURDER	CZECH.
LIEBGOTT, Johann	195515	M	Ger.	03	Employee,Gestapo,Kolin(Czech.)39-45	MURDER	CZECH.
LIEBHARDT, Richard	257671	M		1. 2.11	Sonderfhr.Abwehr,Oslo-Bergen-Tromsoe(Nor.)	WITNESS	NOR.

NAME	C.R.FILE NUMBER	SEX	NATIO-NALITY	DATE OF BIRTH	RANK	OCCUPATION	UNIT	PLACE AND DATE OF CRIME	REASON WANTED	WANTED BY
LIEBIG	186485	M	Ger.	21	Usturmfhr.,12 SS Pz.Div.H.J.,Caen(Fr.) 6.6.-8.7.44				TORTURE	CAN.
LIEBKE, Hans	192395	M	Ger.		C.C.Flossenburg(Ger.) 44-45				MURDER	U.S.
LIEBL, Georg	255145	M	Ger.		Pvt.,1 Coy.,Pion.Bn.4',Budinci(Yugo.) 9.43				MISC.CRIMES	YUGO.
LIEBLER, Ludwig	195443	M	Ger.		Chief Occupied Territories,Luxembourg(Lux.) 40-45				MISC.CRIMES	LUX.
LIEBLICH see LIEBLING	192546									
LIEBLING	156090	M	Ger.	05	Scharfhr.,SS,Enschede(Neth.)				MURDER	U.K.
LIEBLING aliases LIEBLICH	192546	M	Ger.		Lt.,4 Para-Coy.,116 Pz.Div.,Rabczes-Herstal(Bel.)				MURDER	BEL.
LIEBRICH, Richard	187108	M			Sub-Foreman,Arb.Kdo.C.C.Adolf Mine,Merkstein(Ger.) 8.42-10.44				WITNESS	U.S.
LIEBSCH, Anna	255292	F	Ger.	24. 3.03	Employee,Gestapo,Praha(Czech.) 39-45				MISC.CRIMES	CZECH.
LIEBSCH, Fritz	255597	M	Ger.		Official,Gestapo,Opava(Czech.) 39-45				MISC.CRIMES	CZECH.
LIEBSCH, Maria	195514	F	Ger.	12	Employee,Gestapo,Kolin(Czech.) 39-45				MURDER	CZECH.
LIECHKI or JAESCHKE	162925	M	Ger.		Capt.,Feldgend.,St.Gerand-Le Puy(Fr.) 6.10.43-44				PILLAGE	FR.
LIEDECKE, Ewald	167715	M	Ger.		Official,Landesplaner,Raumordnung und Ost Kolonisation Landesplaner, Danzig(Pol.) 9.39-44				MISC.CRIMES	POL.
LIEDEICK	254613	M	Ger.		Pvt.,XI Panz.Div.Unite 36-185,Lautrec(Fr.) 5.8.44				MURDER	FR.
LIEDKE, Paul	189406	M		21. 3.95	Crim.-Secretary,Gestapo,Reichssicherheits-Hauptamt,Trondheim(Nor.) 44				TORTURE	NOR.
LIEDO or LUTH, Elisabeth	306098	F	Ger.		Member SS,of the staff at Sasel C.C.,Sasel(Ger.) 10.44-4.45				TORTURE	U.K.
LIEDOLF, Hugo	173136	M	Ger.		Gestapo,area Vosges(Fr.)				TORTURE	U.K.
LIEDTKE	196774				Pvt.,Guard,C.C.Royallieu,Compiegne(Fr.) 41-44				MISC.CRIMES	FR.
LIEDTKE, Karl	240004	M	Ger.	10	Sturmfhr.,Crim.-Com.,Gestapo,SS,Danzig				MISC.CRIMES	U.S.
LIEDTKE, Welbech	259152	M	Ger.		Rottfhr.,SS,C.C.Dachau(Ger.) 12.42-45				MISC.CRIMES	YUGO.
LIEDTKEMEIER aliases LUTKEMEIER	251701	M	Ger.		Osturmfhr.,SS,C.C.Neuengamme(Ger.)				BRUTALITY	BEL.
LIEFELING, Hermann	259374	M	Ger.		Sgt.,Feldgend.,Douai-Arras(Fr.) 40-41				TORTURE	FR.
LIEGL, Lorenz	133292	M	Ger.		Surveyor of Highway Repairs,Civilian,Moosinning(Ger.) 20.7.44				MURDER	U.S.
LIEHNER, Willi	167724	M	Ger.		Pvt.,9 Regt.Gren.,1 Coy.,Magny D'Anigon(Fr.) 18.9.44				MURDER	FR.
LIEMANN	260110	M	Ger.		Gend.,Div."Oberland",Unity Russ.-Ger.,Massif du Vercors,Isère et Drôme (Fr.) 20.7.-5.8.44				SUSPECT	FR.
LIEN, Robert see COMBIER, KLEBER	62250									
LIENBATH	126991	M	Ger.		Paymaster,SS Pz.Div."Das Reich",Regt."Deutschland",3 Bn., Venerque Le Vernet(Fr.) 44				MURDER	FR.
LIENHARDT	254395	M	Ger.	17	Lt.,15 Police Regt.,Hqu.Venelli,Under Col.Buch,Crescentino(Ital.) 8.9.44				INTERR.	U.K.
LIENHART, Franz	306052	M	Ger.		Civilian,Strassgang(Aust.) 4.3.45				MURDER	U.S.
LIENHART, Markus Max Karl	306053	M	Ger.		Pvt.,Strassgang(Aust.) 4.3.45				MURDER	U.S.
LIENKE, Gerhard or LEMKE	192182	M	Ger.	06	Osturmfhr.,SS,Gestapo,Police-Insp.,Bruessels(Bel.)				MURDER	BEL.
LIENOL, Victor	262238	M	Ger.	23. 7.17	Usturmfhr.,Admin.-Officer,SS,51 SS Armoured-Bde.,Breviandes,Bucheres, Ste Savine,La Riviere de Corps,Troyes-Aube(Fr.) 22.-25.8.44				BRUTALITY	FR.
LIER	124281	M	Ger.		Uschfhr.,1 SS Pz.Div.,1 SS-Pz.-Regt.,9 Coy.(Engineers),Malmedy(Bel.) 17.12.44				MURDER	U.S.
LIER	195054	M	Ger.	15	Lt.,Army,Bressanone(Ital.) 10.10.44				MURDER	U.K.
LIERMANN	193955	M	Ger.		Interpreter,Feldgend.,St.Bressan(Fr.)				TORTURE	FR.
LIERMANN, Willi	300508	M	Ger.		Cpl.,278 Inf.Div.,Guard of T.c.W.on Hospital Train (Ital.-Ger.), between Lucca and Lamsdorf(Ital.,Ger.) 9.43				BRUTALITY	U.K.
LIERS	307008	F	Ger.		SS-Guard,SS,C.C.Auschwitz(Pol.) 42-45				TORTURE	POL.
LIEBSCH, Arthur	190387	M	Ger.		Crim.-Inspector,Police,Wiesbaden(Ger.) 43-45				TORTURE	U.S.
LIESCHE, Gustav	191907	M	Ger.		Civilian,Lorient(Fr.)				MURDER	FR.
LIESE	141968	M			Lt.,Stalag 8 C,Goerlitz(Ger.) 3.-8.40				TORTURE	U.S.
LIESE, Willy	189212	M	Ger.		Civilian,Toulon(Fr.) 25.8.44				MURDER	FR.
LIESEBACH	169111	M	Ger.		Capt.,3 Coy.,67 Inf.Bn.,Manlay(Fr.) 29.7.44				MISC.CRIMES	FR.
LIESS	188924	M	Ger.		Guard,Stalag VI J,Wickrath(Ger.) 14.10.42				MURDER	FR.
LIETZ	191799	M	Ger.		Instructor,Hilfspolizei Saarbruecken,C.C.Mauthausen(Aust.)10.-20.4.44				MURDER	FR.
LIETZERODT, Walter	196773	M	Ger.		Sgt.,SS,Secin Crime Repress.Unit.,Gestapo,Lyon(Fr.)				MURDER	FR.
LIEZ	567	M	Ger.		Crim.-Secretary,Gestapo,Alesund(Nor.) 42				MISC.CRIMES	NOR.
LIGMANOWSKI, Teophil	257406	M		24. 4.11	3 Coy.,129 Pz.Gren.Regt.,San Giovanni e Paolo near Caiazzo(Ital.)13.10.43				WITNESS	U.S.
LIGNER	192394	M	Ger.		Lt.,Stab of the 19 Army,Pont de Vaux(Fr.) 1.9.44				WITNESS	FR.
LIKI	568	M	Ger.		Sturmbannfhr.,SS,(Pol.) 40-44				MURDER	FR.,POL.
LIKNEKE, William	158239	M	Ger.		Coy.-Cmdt.,Volkssturm,C.C.Gardelegen(Ger.) 10.-14.4.45				MURDER	U.S.
LIKOFF, Wilhelm	102923	M			Civilian male Nurser,KL.Hadamar(Ger.) 1.6.44-29.3.45				MURDER	U.S.
LILENTHAL, Marie-Louise	300298	F	Ger.		Typist-Interpreter,SD,Troyes & Region(Fr.) 3.10.43-22.8.44				MURDER	FR.
LILIOT, Gubrot	259731	M	Ger.		Pvt.,F.P.L 50831 LGPA,Paris, St.Pierre de Semilly-Manche(Fr.) 9.42				WITNESS	FR.
LILKAR	6114	M	Ger.		Sgt.,Army Pz.Jaeger Ers.-Bn.,14 Coy.,Ecole en Bauges(Fr.) 44				MURDER	FR.
LILL, Andreas	126509	M	Ger.		Obgfr.,Feldgend.,Vendome(Fr.) 10.8.44				MURDER	U.S.
LILL, Gertrude nee DEMEL	255016	F	Ger.	30. 9.10	Civilian,Trebic(Czech.) 39-45				MURDER	CZECH.
LILL, Karl	255144	M	Ger.	17. 7.09	Civilian,Gossengrun,Haberspirk(Czech.) 9.39				MURDER	CZECH.
LILL, Leopold	255015	M	Ger.	10.12.12	Clerk,Civilian,Trebic(Czech.) 39-45				MURDER	CZECH.
LILLER, Adolf	167723	M	Ger.		Gruppenfhr.,Gren.Regt.9,1 Coy.,Magny D'Anigon(Fr.) 18.9.44				MURDER	FR.
LILLICH	160989	M	Ger.	05	Physician,Civilian,C.C.Buchenwald(Ger.)				TORTURE	U.S.
LIMBECK	67568	M	Ger.		SS-Mann,17 Pz.Gren.Div."G.V.B.",Pz.Jaeg.Abt.17,Segre-Renaze(Fr.) 30.7.-6.8.44				MURDER	FR.
LIMBER	150651	M			Lt.,Army,15 Pz.Gren.Regt.				WITNESS	U.S.
LIMBERGER, Gisela	173704	F	Ger.		Secretary,Occupied countries,Personnel Secretary of Goering,40-44				PILLAGE	FR.
LIMBURG	12580	M	Ger.		Pvt.,Army,110 or 111 Panz.Gren.Regt.,2 Coy.,Albine(Fr.)				MURDER	FR.
LIMBURG, Willi	307009	M	Ger.		Guard at Botn C.C.,near Rognan(Nor.) 8.42				MURDER	YUGO.
LIMLAUF, Hans Jean Robert	301193	M	Ger.		Oberkapo of Altenhammer Kdo.,C.C.Flossenburg(Ger.) 42-45				MURDER	FR.
LIMMAR	189792	M	Ger.	19	Pvt.,C.C.Stalag 4B(Ger.) 5.8.44				MURDER	U.K.
LIMMEL	189772	M	Ger.		Capt.,Kreis-Cmdt.,Kreiskommandantur,Ljubic(Yugo.) 42				TORTURE	YUGO.
LIMMER, Max	12581	M	Ger.		Pvt.,Army,110 or 111 Panz.Gren.Regt.,2 Coy.,Albine(Fr.) 29.6.44				MURDER	FR.
LIMPACK, Josef	187104	M	Ger.		Oschfhr.,SS,Montgauthier(Bel.) 20.9.43				MURDER	BEL.
LINBURG	147070	M	Ger.		Pvt.,Army,Boten-Camp,Rognan(Nor.) 43				MURDER	YUGO.
LINCKE see LINKE	187114									
LINCKLER	173715	M	Ger.		Cpl.,P.O.W.Camp,Tripolis(Tripolitaine) 20.6.41-10.8.41				TORTURE	U.K.
LIND,Heinrich	161420	M	Ger.	14	Bannfhr.,Hitler-Jugend,Giessen(Ger.) 11.9.44				MURDER	U.S.
LINDAU	186297	M	Ger.		Manager,Arb.-Kdo.,Sulzach(Ger.)				TORTURE	U.S.
LINDAUER, Franz	124282	M	Ger.		SS-Mann,1 SS Pz.-Div.,1 SS Pz.-Regt.,2 Coy.,Malmedy(Bel.) 17.12.44				MURDER	U.S.
LINDE	137559	M	Ger.	07	Feldpol.-Kommissar,Geh.Feldpol.Gruppe 713.				TORTURE	U.S.
LINDE, Richard	262469	M	Ger.		SS-Mann,Manager,Civ.Firm of "Auto-Union",Stettin(Pol.) 41-45				MURDER	POL.

NAME	C.R.FILE NUMBER	SEX	NATIO-NALITY	DATE OF BIRTH	RANK OCCUPATION UNIT PLACE AND DATE OF CRIME	REASON WANTED	WANTED BY
LINDEGGER	300810	M	Ger.		Pvt.,1 Aufkl.Abt.,3 Coy, 2 Col.,XV Div.Afrika Korps St.Leger Distr.Arlon (Bel.) 5.9.44	MISC.CRIMES	BEL.
LINDEKE, Fritz	158240	M			Member, Hitlerjugend,Gardelegen (Ger.) 10.-14.4.45	MURDER	U.S.
LINDEMAN	569	M	Ger.		Sonderfhr.,Army, Propaganda-Abt., Caen (Fr.) 6.44	MURDER	FR.
LINDEMANN	36692	M	Ger.		Cpl.,Army, Lazarettzug,Lucca,Lamsdorf (Ger.) 30.9.43	MISC.CRIMES	U.K.
LINDEMANN	102922	M			Capt.,Stalag Luft 4"Advere" officers of camp,Kief-Hyde(Ger.)8.44-3.45	TORTURE	U.S.
LINDEMANN	151347	M	Ger.		Capt.,Stalag Luft 4, I-C Abwehr-Staff Luftwaffe,Gross Tychow(Ger.)7.44	PILLAGE	U.K.
LINDEMANN	156084	M			Oberregierungsrat,Police, C.C.Emsland Moor,Papenburg(Ger.) 44	MURDER	U.S.
LINDEMANN	254607	M	Ger.		Interpreter, member,SD, Toulouse (Fr.) 11.42-8.44	MISC.CRIMES	FR.
LINDEMANN	261809	M	Ger.		Cpl.,Art.H.D.V.199-2235 H.D.F.Nr. of F.P.27046 C,Lorgies(Fr.)3.9.44	MURDER	FR.
LINDEMANN, Werner Guenther	186697	M	Ger.	15	Rottenfhr.,2 SS Pz.Div. "Das Reich",Wormhoudt (Fr.) 5.40	MURDER	U.K.
LINDEMAYER	160390	M	Ger.		Capt., Police, Unter-Haid (Ger.) 12.44	MURDER	U.S.
LINDEN	191207	M	Ger.	90	Ministerial-Dirigent, Reichs-Ministry of Interienz,Berlin(Ger.)	MISC.CRIMES	UNWCC.
LINDEN, Hans	262233	M	Ger.	23. 3.20	Uscharfhr.,Platoon 3,51 SS Armoured Bde,Dreviandes,Bucheres, St.Savine,la Riviere de Corps(Troyes) (Fr.) 22.-25.8.44	BRUTALITY	FR.
LINDEN, Herbert	161886	M	Ger.		Standartenfhr.,SS,Reichs Comm.for Hospital and Nursing homes, SS Gouv.official (Pol.,Sov.Un.)	MURDER	U.S.
LINDEN, Wilhelm	167727	M	Ger.		Secretary,Custom office,Bayonne (Fr.) 22.8.44	MURDER	FR.
LINDENAU	162370	M	Ger.	05	SS-Usturmfhr., SS-Pz.Gren., Condorcet (Fr.) 19.3.44	MURDER	FR.
LINDENAU	306098	M	Ger.		Scharf.,SS, guard,commander,Alderney,C.C.(Channel Is.) and Kortemark (Fr.) 42-45	MURDER	CZECH.
LINDENBERG	257986	M			Lt.,150 Pz.Bde,Meuse Bridge-Antwerp.(Bel.) 12.44	MISC.CRIMES	U.S.
LINDENER	262328	M	Ger.		Sgt.,Army,Wulfingerode(Ger.) 7.44, L.O.D.N.A.O.D.	SUSPECT	U.S.
LINDER	12582	M	Ger.		Pvt.,Army,110 or 111 Pz.Grn.Rgt.,2 Coy,Albine (Fr.) 29.6.44	MURDER	FR.
LINDER	162371	M	Ger.	93	Pvt.,Army, 361 Lds.Schz.Bn Ostfeld Stalag IV A,Ostfeld (Ger.) 6.43	MURDER	U.K.
LINDER or LINDNER	193194	M	Ger.		Pvt., Army, C.C. Akervika (Nor.) 42	MURDER	NOR.
LINDER, Alfred	192899	M	Ger.		Schupo, C.C. Falstad (Nor.) 7.42	MURDER	NOR.
LINDER, Berthel	253140	M	Ger.		Kapo, Cdo.178, C.C. Auschwitz (Pol.)	BRUTALITY	FR.
LINDER, Karl	70660	M	Ger.		Gauleiter, NSDAP, Deputy, Hessen-Nassau (Ger.)	MISC.CRIMES	UNWCC.
LINDERMANN	196772	M	Ger.		Chief, C.C. factories Arnstadt (Ger.)	MISC.CRIMES	FR.
LINDERMANN, Hans	254668	M	Ger.		Crim.secr.,SD, Toulouse (Fr.) 11.42-8.44	MISC.CRIMES	FR.
LINDGENS	126571	M	Ger.		Civilian,Arbeits-Kdo, Hagen (Ger.) 40-45	MURDER	U.S.
LINDHART or LINEHART	125481	M	Ger.		SS, Strassgang-Graz (Aust.) 3.45	MURDER	U.K.
LINDHOLM, Fritz	122437	M	Ger.		Oscharfhr.,SA,Duisburg,Venloo (Ger.,Neth.)	TORTURE	BEL.
LINDHORST	178766	M	Ger.		Lt.,4 Coy, 714 Lds.Schz.Bn, Gresse (Ger.) 20.3.45	MURDER	U.K.
LINDHORST	253141	M	Ger.		Oberzahlmeister, Fort de Vincennes (Fr.) 20.7.44	MISC.CRIMES	FR.
LINDIG	162926	M	Ger.		Oberstabsarzt, C.C. Stalag IV Hartmannsdorf (Ger.) 44	MURDER	FR.
LINDNER	127415	M	Ger.		Hptsturmfhr.,SS, Gestapo, C.C. Weimar-Buchenwald (Ger.)	TORTURE	U.S.
LINDNER	156100	M			Cpl., Arbeits-Kdo.531,Stalag IV A, Ostfeld (Ger.) 6.43	MURDER	U.K.
LINDNER	185138	M	Ger.		Cpl.,Army, Hennebont (Fr.) 6.8.44	MURDER	FR.
LINDNER	188411	M	Ger.	95	Sturmbannfhr.,SS, Hoehere SS and Pol.Fhr.,C.C.Sosnowice(Pol.)	MURDER	POL.
LINDNER see LINDER	193194						
LINDNER	259208	M			Sturmbannfhr.,SS, camp-insp. (Fr.)	BRUTALITY	FR.
LINDNER	300811	M	Ger.		Pvt.,1 Aufkl.Abt.,3 Coy, 2 Col.,XV Div. Afrika Korps, St.Leger,Distr.Arlon (Bel.) 5.9.44	MISC.CRIMES	BEL.
LINDNER, Charles	194651	M	Ger.		Cpl.,Grenzpol.,Veigy,Foncenex (Fr.) 6.10.43	TORTURE	FR.
LINDNER, E.	167685	M	Ger.		Civilian, Treuhaender [Firm.H.Lichtig, Kraków (Pol.) 9.39-12.44	MISC.CRIMES	POL.
LINDNER, Friedrich	29688	M	Ger.		Oberlandesgerichtsrat, Public official, Litomerice (Czech.) 40	MURDER	CZECH.
LINDNER, Johann	187079	M			Uscharfhr.,4 SS Totenkopf Stuba,C.C.Nordhausen-Dora Mittelbau (Ger.) 43-45	TORTURE	U.S.
LINDNER, Max	142091	M	Ger.	92	SS-Mann, Waffen-SS,Totenkopf-Standarte,C.C.Buchenwald(Ger.)	TORTURE	U.S.
LINDOW, Kurt	142575	M	Ger.	04	Sturmbannfhr.,SS and Gestapo	MISC.CRIMES	U.S.
LINDT, Heinrich	166712	M	Ger.	10 - 11	Oberbannfhr., Hitlerjugend, Giessen (Ger.)	MURDER	U.S.
LINDTNER	31619	M	Ger.		Major,20 Army Comd.M.G.Bn 14,210 Inf.Div. (Nor.) 10.,11.44	MURDER	NOR.
LINECK	257673	M	Ger.		Hilfspol.Cmdtr.at Bor, Zajecar (Yugo.) 41-44	MURDER	YUGO.
LINEHART see LINDHART	125481						
LINFKE, Alfred	192735	M	Ger.	05	Hauptwachtmeister,Reichsjustizministerium,Strafgefangenenlager Nord Finmark (Nor.) 6.42-45	MISC.CRIMES	NOR.
LING	192900	M	Ger.		Lt.,SS, C.C. Falstad (Nor.) 40	MURDER	NOR.
LING	301342	M	Ger.		Member, Gestapo,Trencin, C.C.Oswiecim-Birkenau (Pol.) 39-45	MURDER	CZECH.
LING see LANG	301637						
LINGE nee SCHWAB	173703	F	Ger.		Interpreter, Gestapo, le Mans (Fr.) 20.12.43-7.1.44	WITNESS	FR.
LINGENFELDER, Karl	167021	M	Ger.		Array (Fr.) 5.41	INCENDIARISM.	FR.
LINGENHELD, Karl	187069	M	Ger.	15.11.89	Oscharfhr.,4 SS Totenkopf Stuba.C.C.Nordhausen-Dora,Mittelbau (Ger.) 43-45	TORTURE	U.S.
LINGL, Barthol.	192901	M	Ger.		Schupo, C.C. Falstad (Nor.) 9.42	MURDER	NOR.
LINGMANN see LINKMANN	253142						
LINHARD, Heinrich	255282	M			Osturmfhr., C.C.Latterina (It.)	MISC.CRIMES	U.S.
LINHART, Mathilde	190658	F	Ger.	7. 4.08	Clerk, Gestapo, Bruenn (Czech.) 39-45	WITNESS	CZECH.
LINHUBER or LINOBER	142092	M	Ger.		Cpl.,SS Waldlager V and VI,C.C.Muhldorf (Ger.) 44-45	TORTURE	U.S.
LINK	132627	M			Member, SD, Gestapo, Perigueux (Fr.)	TORTURE	FR.
LINK	137560	M			Hptscharfhr.,SS,C.C.Weimar-Buchenwald (Ger.)	MURDER	U.S.
LINK, Josef (Rudolf)	187080	M	Ger.		Member,Crim.Employee,SD,SS,Gestapo, Pilsen (Czech.) 39-45	MURDER	CZECH.
LINK, Karl	142094	M	Ger.	05	Member, NSDAP, DAF, Neckarsulm (Ger.) 21.3.45	MURDER	U.S.
LINK, Powel	132189	M	Ger.		C.C. of PW-Lager	TORTURE	U.K.
LINK, Vinsent	174368	M	Ger.	15	Pvt., 92 Inf.Div.,192 Signal, Farnese (It.) 6.6.44	INTERR.	U.K.
LINKE	31571	M	Ger.		Employee,A.S.W. Plant,Boehlen (Ger.) 4.44-5.44	TORTURE	U.K.
LINKE	128843	M	Ger.		Lds.Schz.Bn515,Kompt.4,C.C.3 Km from Tunglau-Bunz(Czech.) 2.45	MURDER	U.K.
LINKE or LINCKE	187114	M	Ger.	22	Capt.,18 Army-Corps-Fuehrer Reserve, Mittenwald (Ger.) 6.44	TORTURE	U.S.
LINKE	259375	M			Policeman, Police of the Camp Auschwitz (Pol.)	BRUTALITY	FR.
LINKE, Helene nee JURASEK	190659	F	Ger.	22. 4.15	Clerk, Gestapo, Bruenn (Czech.) 39-45	WITNESS	CZECH.
LINKERT	177550	M	Ger.		Pvt.,Rottenfhr.,Gestapo,SD,Lyon,Montluc (Fr.)	TORTURE	FR.
LINKLER	252384	M	Ger.	06 - 16	Cpl.,guard,Army,working camp,Fieldpost 12545,Tripolis(Afr.)5.41-1.42	MISC.CRIMES	U.K.

LIN - LIS

NAME	C.R.FILE NUMBER	SEX	NATIO- NALITY	DATE OF BIRTH	RANK OCCUPATION UNIT PLACE AND DATE OF CRIME	REASON WANTED	WANTED BY
LINKMANN (or LINGMANN)	253142	M	Ger.		Custom-official,Custom-office of Annemasse,Machilly-Loisin,Brens Fr. 26.4.44	TORTURE	FR.
LINN	46060	M	Ger.	18	SS-Commander,Hptsturmfhr.,SD,Bois de Guron,Romm (Fr.) 7.7.44	MURDER	U.K.,FR.
LINN	119227	M	Ger.	09	SS-Capt.,Gestapo,SD,Poitiers,Chateau-Porteau (Fr.) 23.,24.8.44	MURDER	FR.
LINN	125187	M	Ger.	19	Hptsturmfhr.,Sipo,Vierriers (Fr.) 3.-7.7.44	MURDER	U.S.
LINN	141359	M	Ger.		Cpl.,Army,Hochkirch (Ger.) 28.2.45-8.5.45	MURDER	U.K.
LINN	158257	M	Ger.		Commander ,Gestapo,Poitiers (Fr.) 12.6.44.	MURDER	FR.
LINN	174547	M	Ger.	00	Cpl.,427 Ldsch.Bn.4 Coy,Bautzen (Ger.) 3.45	MURDER	U.K.
LINN,Walter	259415	M	Ger.		Uschfhr.,Member,SS,Gestapo,Poitiers Area (Fr.) 40-44	MISC.CRIMES	FR.
LINN,Wilhelm	139167	M	Ger.		Chief,Police,Wollendorf (Ger.) 23.10.44	WITNESS	U.S.
LINNE	300813	M	Ger.		N.C.O.,1 Aufkl.Abt.3 Coy 2 Col.XV Div.of the Afrika Corps,Saint Léger Arlon (Bel.) 5.9.44	MISC.CRIMES	BEL.
LINNE,Ernst	188169	M	Ger.		Sgt.,Art.Rgt.237 7 Bn.,Marzano,Canfanaro (It.) 3.45	WITNESS	U.K.
LINNER,Rudolf	195513	M	Ger.	17. 6.12	SS-Sgt.,Employee,SD,Gestapo,Kolin (Czech.) 39-45	TORTURE	CZECH.
LINNEWEBER,Hermann	12583	M	Ger.		Pvt.,Army,110 or 111 Pz.Gren.Rgt. 2 Coy,Albine (Fr.) 29.6.44	MURDER	FR.
LINNBER (see LINHUBER)	142092						
LINOFF	253992	M	Ger.		Lt.,Colonne Caucasienne,St.Amand le Petit (Fr.) 6.4.44	MURDER	FR.
LINRMANN	194650	M	Ger.		Secr.,Grenzpolizei,Veigy Foncenex (Fr.) 12.43	TORTURE	FR.
LINSEN	156098	M	Ger.		Adj.,Morlaix (Fr.) 44	MURDER	FR.
LINSMEYER	189773	M	Ger.	11	SS-Hptschfhr.,Dentist,SS,C.C.Belsen (Ger.) 40-44	MURDER	YUGO.
LINTERND	154328	M	Ger.		Officier,Fabriksdirector,Gestapo,C.C.Mauthausen (Ger.)	TORTURE	FR.
LINTZ,Wolfgang	253091	M	Ger.	13.12.14	Lt.,Fallschirmjg.Lehrrgt.,St.Remy aux Bois (Fr.,Bel.) 5.and 7.9.44	MISC.CRIMES	FR.,BEL.
LIOFFER,Giuseppe (or Joseph)	174780	M	Ger.		Sgt.,Brandenburg 16 Coy,Communanza (It.) 2.5.44	WITNESS	U.K.
LIOFFER,Joseph (see Giuseppe)	174780						
LIOTKE (see LUWKE,Joseph)	29768						
LIPF	31618	M	Ger.		Dr.,Oberstabsarzt,Army	MURDER	IRAN
LIPFERT	135550	M	Ger.		Sgt.,Arb.Kdo.,Army,Massbach (Ger.) 9.2. - 12.12.44	TORTURE	U.K.,U.S.
LIPHARDT	570	M			Police,Sipo,Kommandeur,Radom (Pol.) 39-43	MURDER	POL.
LIPINSKI,Ernst	131298	M			Capo,Verfuegungspolizei or Kasernierte Polizei,Gusen (Aust.)	MURDER	U.S.
LIPINSKY,Emil	306851	M	Ger.		Warder-Capo,C.C.Gusen (Aust.) 40-44	MURDER	POL.
LIPP,Otto	572	M			Gestapo,Valenciennes (Fr.) 1.9.44	MURDER	FR.
LIPP,Paul	173745	M	Ger.	07	Capo,Camp official,C.C.Neckarelz-Mosbach (Ger.) 2.45	MURDER	U.S.,FR.
LIPP,Walter	251115	M	Ger.		Lt.,Russian-German Unit,stationed at Chaumont,La Fertel sur Aube (Fr.) 15.6.44	MURDER	FR.
LIPP,Werner	252376	M	Ger.		6 Coy 16 Hubner Rgt.,Kinrooi (Bel.) 9.44	MURDER	BEL.
LIPPE-HENSCHEL	174062	M			SS-Osturmfhr.,C.C.Mauthausen (Aust.) 43	MURDER	U.S.
LIPPEL	251126	M	Ger.		Official,Ministery of Material Supplies,Rotterdam (Neth.)	INTERR.	NETH.
LIPPELT,Willy	254667	M	Ger.	29.10.03	Rottfhr.,Gestapo IV Section,Region d'Angers,Saint Julien (Fr.)21.7.44	MURDER	FR.
LIPPE/EIER	195442	M	Ger.		Occ.territories,Luxembourg (Lux.) 40 - 44	PILLAGE	LUX.
LIPPER	301734	M	Ger.		Capt.,Senior-officer,Camp 102 Aquila (It.) 8.12.43	MURDER	U.K.
LIPPERLEIM	146943	M	Ger.		Officier,SS Pz.Div."Das Reich" 1 Pz.Rgt. 2 Coy,Tulle (Fr.) 44	MURDER	FR.
LIPPERT	122443	M	Ger.		Major,Kreiskommandantur,Arlon (Bel.) 25.8.44	MURDER	BEL.
LIPPERT	124224	M	Ger.		Oberwachtmeister,Schupo,Dreibergen Prison C.C.Bustzow (Ger.)	MURDER	NOR.
LIPPERT	136230	M			Pvt.,II Pz.Div.,2 Coy 2 AA-A 7,Albine (Fr.) 12.3.44	MURDER	FR.
LIPPERT	186708	M	Ger.	93	Sgt.,622 Ldsch.Bn.,Massbach near Wacha (Ger.) 11.12.44	MURDER	U.K.
LIPPERT	252371	M	Ger.		Cmdt.,84 Rgt.,Bennekom (Neth.) 3.-4.45	MURDER	NETH.
LIPPERT	260183	M	Ger.		Aspirant,german unit stationed of depot-guard at Rena,Lent Ain (Fr.) 28.8.44	MISC.CRIMES	FR.
LIPPERT	301638	M	Ger.		Werkmeister,Ebrach nr.Amberg (Ger.) 45	MURDER	CZECH.
LIPPERT,Heinz	146942	M	Ger.		Rottfhr.,SS Pz.Div."Das Reich" 13 Coy,Moissac (Fr.) 44	MURDER	FR.
LIPPERT,Johann	12584	M	Ger.		Pvt.,Army,11 Pz.Div. 2 Coy 2 AA-A 7,near Bergerac Albine (Fr.)7.,8.44	MURDER	FR.
LIPPERT,Julius	130625	M	Ger.		Dr.,Mayor,Public-official,Arlon (Bel.) 25.8.44	MURDER	BEL.
LIPPITSCH	251697	M	Ger.		Pvt.,Army,Pepingen (Bel.) 2.44-9.45	WITNESS	BEL.
LIPPMAN	160387	M	Ger.		Sgt.,Army,Steinbruck (Ger.) 2.44	MURDER	U.S.
LIPPMANN	126997	M	Ger.		Lt.,Commandant,C.C.Landsberg (Ger.)	TORTURE	U.S.
LIPPMANN,Hans	195441	M	Ger.		Luxembourg (Lux.) 40 - 44	MISC.CRIMES	LUX.
LIPPMANN,Hellmuth	180309	M	Ger.		Bannfhr.,Hitler Jugend,Steinkerberg (Ger.) 29.6.44	MURDER	U.S.
LIPPOLD,Otto	187068	M			SS-Pvt.,Guard,4 SS Totenkopf Sturmbann,C.C.Dora Mittelbau,Nordhausen (Ger.) 43-45	TORTURE	U.S.
LIPPS	173117	M	Ger.		Sgt.,Police,C.C.Schirmeck,Rotenfels,Gaggenau (Fr.,Ger.)	MURDER	U.K.
LIPPUSCH,Franz	301667	M	Ger.		Worker's asst.,nr.Mostar, 44	MURDER	YUGO.
LIPPUSCH,Margarete	301665	F	Ger.		Wife of a worker's asst.,nr.Mostar, 44	MURDER	YUGO.
LISA	193956	F	Ger.	00	Nurse,C.C.Ravensbrueck (Ger.)	MURDER	FR.
LISBERG,Franz	186298	M	Ger.		SS-Blockaeltester,SS,C.C.Mauthausen,Gusen (Aust.)	MURDER	U.S.
LISCHEVSKI	192734	M	Ger.		Pvt.,Kgf.Arb.Bn.190,Bergholnes (Nor.) 44-45	TORTURE	NOR.
LISCHKA	132739	M			Leiter,Gestapo,H.Q.,Paris (Fr.)	MURDER	FR.
LISCHKA,Joseph	10073	M			Sgt.,Army,Hesepe Air-Field (Ger.) 23.3.45	MURDER	U.S.
LISCHKA,Kurt (alias:LISCHKDA)	119268	M	Ger.	16. 8.09	Osturmbannfhr.,official,SS,Gestapo,H.Q.,Berlin (Ger.) 39-45	MURDER	CZECH.
LISCHKE	142016	M	Ger.		Police-Insp.,Member of Gestapo,Stalag Luft 3,Berlin (Ger.) 3.44 and 39-45	MURDER	U.K.
LISCHKE	162372	M	Ger.		Crim.Commissar,Gestapo,Berlin (Ger.) 4.45	MURDER	CZECH.
LISIEWITZ,Hilde	173691	F	Ger.		SS-woman,C.C.Bergen-Belsen (Ger.) 1.10.39-30.4.45	MURDER	UNWCC
LISKA	250912	M	Ger.		Lt.,Kragujevac (Yugo.) 21.10.41	MURDER	YUGO.
LISKA,Peter	186294	M	Ger.		Sgt.,Army,Hesepe (Ger.) 3.45	MURDER	U.K.
LISKA,Walter Hans	142194	M		11.12.99	Sturmbannfhr.,SS,Gestapo,Cracow,Lublin (Pol.) 39-41	MURDER	FR.
LISKE	160388	M	Ger.	14	Civilian,C.C.Buchenwald (Ger.)	TORTURE	U.S.
LISKOWSKY,Alois	187094	M			SS-Rottfhr.,Camp Guard,4 SS Totenkopf Sturmbann,C.C.Dora Mittelbau,Nordhausen (Ger.) 43-45	TORTURE	U.S.
LISS,Winfried	174061	M	Ger.	10. 3.08	Oberstaatsanwalt,Occ.territories Boheme,Prag (Czech.) 42-45	MURDER	CZECH.
LUSSEK	174060	M		87	Foreman,Arbeitslager,C.C.Feucht (Ger.) 40-45	TORTURE	U.S.
LIST	133950	M			SS-Hptsturmfhr.,C.C.Alderney (Fr.) 43-1.44	TORTURE	U.K.
LIST	139160	M	Ger.		Osturmfhr.,SS,C.C.Neuengamme (Ger.) 41-42	TORTURE	BEL.
LIST	191568	M	Ger.		Capt.,SS "West-Bde.",Commandant,C.C.Sachsenhausen (Ger.) 39-4.45	MURDER	POL.
LIST	301691	M	Ger.		Bde.05-243 Mongolian "Oberland" Unit,St.Nazaire en Royans (Fr.) 20.7.-5.8.44	MURDER	FR.

LIS - LOE

NAME	C.R.FILE NUMBER	SEX	NATIONALITY	DATE OF BIRTH	RANK OCCUPATION UNIT PLACE AND DATE OF CRIME	REASON WANTED	WANTED BY
LIST, Hedwig	252445	F	Ger.		Oberstudienraetin, Luxembourg	LOOTING	LUX.
LIST, Helmuth	255283	M			755 Rgt. 334 Inf.Div.	SUSPECT	U.S.
LISY, Fritz	122448	M	Ger.	10	Pvt., SD, Chambery, Challes les eaux Arbin (Fr.)	MISC.CRIMES	FR.
LISZT, Franz	574	M	Ger.		SS Officer, Amsterdam (Neth.)	MISC.CRIMES	NETH.
LITSCHKO, Johann	187095	M			Guard, 4 SS Totenkopf Sturmbann, CC Dora,Mittelbau,Nordhausen(Ger.) 43-45	TORTURE	U.S.
LITTAU	300299	M			Uschfhr. belonging to the 1 SS Unterfuehrerschule,Velperweg, Arnhem, Gameren (Neth.) 15.9.44	MURDER	NETH.
LITTERER	257407	M	Ger.		Guard, SS, Slave Labour Camp,Beifsjord near Narvik(Nor.)6-11.42	BRUTALITY	YUGO.
LITTMANN	1428	M	Ger.		Capt., Army, Air Force, Jg.Rgt.40	MURDER	U.K.
LITTMANN, Fritz	174059	M	Ger.	23. 7.04	Amtsgerichtsrat, occupied territories Boheme, Prag (Czech.)42-43	TORTURE	CZECH.
LITVIN	301343	M	Ger.		Member of Gestapo at Trencin, CC Auschwitz-Birkenau(Pol.)39-45	MURDER	CZECH.
LITWA	140866	M			Capt., 3 Coy, 17 Para Rgt., Xanten(Ger.)	MURDER	CAN.
LITZ	194649	M	Ger.		Head, Gestapo, Pornichet (Fr.)	PILLAGE	FR.
LITZ	258916	M	Ger.		Capt., Air Force, No.L 05207, Fliegerhorstkommandantur 40,XIII, Grenade s-Adour et Cere (Fr.) 13.6.-21.8.44	MURDER	FR.
LITZ	307010	M	Ger.		Sgt., commandant of an army detachment,Leeuwarden(Neth.)27.10.44	MURDER	NETH.
LITZ, Hans	307011	M	Ger.		Pvt., Semur en Auxois, Cote d'Or (Fr.) 25.8.44	MURDER	FR.
LITZENBERG	187093	M			Rottfhr, 4 SS Totenkopf-Sturmbann,CC Dora,Nordhausen(Ger.)44-45	TORTURE	U.S.
LITZMANN	145985	M			Hptsturmfhr,SS,Gestapo,Hoerde(Ger.)	MURDER	U.S.
LITZMANN, Karl S.	21343	M			SS Ogruppenfhr, deputy Gauleiter for Westmark, (Fr.) commissioner gener. of Shitomir and Esthonia	TORTURE	U.N.W.C.C.
LIVIA, Bronislava (see MAURER,Bronislava)	195632						
LIZT	195162	M	Ger.		Kampfkommandant,Arb.Klo., CC Boeswig (Ger.) 9.43	TORTURE	NETH.
LOBACH, Heinrich	260827	M	Ger.		Uschfhr, SS, Muenstedt (Ger.) 24.8.44	MURDER	U.S.
LOBAUER, Hilde (or LOBHAUER)	173690	F	Ger.		Woman Kapo, CC Auschwitz, Bergen-Belsen(Pol.,Ger.)1.10.39-30.4.45	MURDER	U.N.W.C.C.
LOBECK	575	M	Ger.		Army, Lt., Oflag 2-D, CC Grossborn(Ger.) 40	TORTURE	FR.
LOBEL	252249	M	Ger.		Uschfhr, SS, CC Mauthausen(Aust.)	TORTURE	BEL.
LOBEL, Werner	192902	M	Ger.		Schupo, CC Falstad (Nor.) 11.42	TORTURE	NOR.
LOBER (or LORBEER, LOHRBEER)	255289	M	Ger.		Capt.,Stalag XII-A,Limburg(Ger.)	MURDER	U.S.
LOBERSTERTER, Otto	12585	M	Ger.		Pvt., Army, 110 or 111 Pz.Gren.Rgt., 2 Coy, Albine(Fr.) 29.6.44	MURDER	FR.
LOBHAUER,Hilde(see LOBAUER)	173690						
LOBIUS	173685	M	Ger.		Cmdt., CC Maribor(Yugo.) 4.41-44	MURDER	YUGO.
LOBODEFF	146941	M	Ger.		Hptsturmfhr, SS Pz.Div."Das Reich",Mongiscard(Fr.) 44	MURDER	FR.
LOBSANG	31617	M	Ger.		Col., 20 Army, Finmark(Nor.) 10.-11.44	MURDER	NOR.
LOBSTEIN	173746	M	Ger.		Kreishauptstellenleiter NSDAP,Strasbourg(Fr.) 44	TORTURE	FR.
LOCATELLI	253878	M	Ger.		Col., 88 Inf.Rgt.,Santo Pietro Di-Tenda(Fr.)19.-31.8.43	TORTURE	FR.
LOCAY	187856	M	Ger.		Physician, CC Solingen (Ger.)	TORTURE	BEL.
LOCH	142097	M	Ger.		Rottfhr, SS, Waldlager 5 and 6, CC Muhldorf(Ger.) 44-45	TORTURE	U.S.
LOHRGE (or LORGA)	174133	M	Ger.		Uschfhr, SS Totenkopf Div., Przemysk (Pol.)	MURDER	POL.
LOCHBUEHLER, Heinz	256818	M		22. 2.25	Pvt., Army, Viernmein (Fr.) 5.9.44	BRUTALITY	U.S.
LOCHELDER	1429	M	Ger.		Doctor (Officer), Naval Supply	MISC.CRIMES	U.K.
LOCHER	190660	M	Ger.		Crim.Asst.Gestapo,Bruenn(Czech.) 39-45	MURDER	CZECH.
LOCHLIN (see KOCHLIN,Max)	301209						
LOCHMULLER	156079	M	Ger.		Hptsturmfhr.,SS, 16 Inf.Div.,Maille (Fr.); Cmdt. Camp Nouatre (Fr.) 25.8.44	MURDER	FR.
LOCHNER	257919	M			SS Usturmfhr, 150 Pz.Bde., Meuse Bridge, Antwerpen(Bel.)12.44	MISC.CRIMES	U.S.
LOCHNER (brother)	257920				150 Pz.Bde.,Bie.Stab Scherff,Meuse Bridge, Antwerpen(Bel.)12.44	MISC.CRIMES	U.S.
LOCHTE, Robert	145992	M	Ger.		Civilian NSDAP, SA-member, Machinist	TORTURE	U.S.
LOCHTMANN	261153	M	Ger.		Member Staff of CC, Ravensbrueck(Ger.)	SUSPECT	BEL.
LOCK	257701	M			SS Rottfhr, CC, Muhldorf, Dachau (Ger.)	MURDER	U.S.
LOCK, Artur	254666	M	Ger.		SS-Mann, Auschwitz-Birkenau(Pol.) 12.42	MISC.CRIMES	YUGO.
LOCKE	133289	M			Oschfhr, W-SS, CC Ellrich, Gardelegen(Ger.) 4.-14.4.45	MURDER	U.S.
LOCKER	62506	M	Ger.		Kreisobmann NSDAP, DAF, Erdorf(Ger.) 17.8.44	MURDER	U.S.
LOCKNER	254073	M	Ger.		Agent,Gestapo, Limoges (Fr.)	INTERR.	FR.
LOCS, Georg	188738	M	Ger.	12. 5.05	Driver, Chartres (Fr.) 16.2.41	TORTURE	FR.
LOCUS	260165	M	Ger.		Osturmfhr, SS, Slave Labour Camp,Botn near Rognan(Nor.) 8.42-3.43, 4.43-5.45	BRUTALITY	YUGO.
LODE	67559	M	Ger.		Lt., 1010 motorised Rgt., Pithiviers, Orleans, Chilleurs aux Bois Loriet (Fr.) 6.7.44, 13.-15.8.44	MURDER	FR.,U.K.
LODE	173707	M	Ger.		Lt., 1010 Motor.Rgt., Chateau de Chamerolles, Chilleurs aux Bois(Fr.)	MURDER	U.K.
LODZ	67557	M	Ger.		Res.Hospital(Civilian),Obermassfeld(Ger.)1.-5.45	TORTURE	U.K.
LODZ, Willy	193811	M	Ger.	01	Chief of Kdo., CC Dachau (Ger.)	MURDER	FR.
LOE, Karl	301702	M	Ger.		Factory Manager, Vacha near Eisenach (Ger.) 4.43-4.45	MURDER	U.K.
LOEB	173675	M	Ger.		Gestapoleitstelle, CC Auschwitz-Birkenau(Pol.) 39-45	MURDER	CZECH.
LOEB	12657	M			SS-Sgt., Gestapo, Bergen (Nor.) 41	TORTURE	NOR .
LOEB	145999	M	Ger.		Kapo, CC Hohenrheim near Plattling(Ger.) 2.-5.45	MURDER	U.S.
LOEB, F.	255596	M	Ger.		Managing partner of the Utrechtsche Machinale Stoelen Meubelfabrik, Utrecht (Neth.) 44-45	PILLAGE	NETH.
LOEBEL	146791	M			SS Hptschfhr, CC Flossenburg (Ger.)	MURDER	U.S.
LOEBEL	162375	M	Ger.		SS Usturmfhr, Chief of Prison,Gestapo , SS,Bratislava(Czech.)44	MURDER	CZECH.
LOEBEL	306852	M	Ger.		SS Uschfhr, Official in Amt I or II of WVHA, Zentrale Bauinspektion, Mauthausen and Gusen (Aust.) 40 - 44	MURDER	POL.
LOEBITZ (or LOEVITZ), Fritz	137669	M	Ger.	17	Pvt.,Army,714 Lds.Schtz., Stalag XX-A, CC Luschkau(Pol.) 24.4.44	MURDER	U.K.
LOEBLICH	576	M			Osturmfhr. SS, Gestapo, Perpignan (Fr.) 25.3.43, 8.-12.43	MURDER	FR.
LOECHNER	12586	M	Ger.		Capt., Army, Marsch Bn., Dusigny(Fr.) 23.8.44	MURDER	FR.
LOEDDENBUSCH	102920	M	Ger.		Arbeitskommando, CC Wulfen (Ger.) 25.3.45	MURDER	U.S.
LOEDEMANDY	301344	M	Ger.		Member of Gestapo at Nove Mesto near Vahom, CC Auschwitz-Birkenau(Pol) 39-45	MURDER	CZECH.
LOEFFL, Joseph	12532	M	Ger.		Pvt., 110 Pz.Gran.Rgt., 2 Coy, Albine(Fr.) 29.6.44	MURDER	FR.

LOE-LOH

NAME	C.R.FILE NUMBER	SEX	NATIO-NALITY	DATE OF BIRTH	RANK OCCUPATION UNIT PLACE AND DATE OF CRIME	REASON WANTED	WANTED BY
LOEFFLE	300691	M	Ger.		Obergruppenfhr., successor to General Berger (C-in-C all SS Units) SS, Slovakia (Czech.) 44	MISC.CRIMES	CZECH.
LOEFFLER	257918	M			Sgt., 150.Panz.Bde. Meuse-Bridge Antwerp (Bel.) 12.44	MISC.CRIMES	U.S.
LOEFFLER, Karl	190661	M	Ger.	20. 1.05	Crim.secretary, Gestapo, Bruenn (Czech.) 39-45	MURDER	CZECH.
LOEH	162927	M	Ger.		Sgt., Army, Revin (Fr.) 13.-14.6.44	MURDER	FR.
LOEHNER, Albert	257930	M			SS Usturmfhr., 150.Panz.Bde., Meuse-Bridge Antwerp (Bel.) 12.44	MISC.CRIMES	U.S.
LOEHNER, Josef or LOHNER	257929	M			Usturmfhr., 150. Panz.Bde., Meuse-Bridge Antwerp (Bel.) 12.44	MISC.CRIMES	U.S.
LOEHNERT, Alfred	189337	M			Dr., Physician, Arb.Kdo., Parschnitz (Czech.) 39-42	TORTURE	POL.
LOEHNERT, Anton	260951	M		05	Usturmfhr., SS, living at Backmang (Wttbg.),Stuttgartstr. 132, Lwow and other (Pol.) 41-43	MURDER	POL.
LOEHNERT, Anton	262417	M	Ger.	17. 6.06	Osturmfhr., SS, Lemberg (Pol.) 41-43	MURDER	POL.
LOEHR	62507	M	Ger.		Oberzahlmeister, Stalag 6 C Muenster-Westf. (Ger.)	TORTURE	U.S.
LOEHR	166647	M	Ger.	85	Gen., Army, Yugo. 41-44	MURDER	U.S.
LOEHR, Alexander	259583	M	Ger.	85	Gen.	WITNESS	U.S.
LOEHRER, Margaretha	134891	F	Ger.		Civ., Efferen (Ger.)	WITNESS	U.S.
LOELGEN	259309	M			SS Sturmbannfhr., Thekla nr.Leipzig (Ger.) 18.4.45	MURDER	U.S.
LOENHOLD, Karl	196832	M	Ger.		SS Sturmbannfhr., Gestapo, Prag (Czech.) 43	MISC.CRIMES	CZECH.
LOENIG	125188	M	Ger.	95	Capt., Army, officer commanding I, C.C. Trottendal (Ger.) 5.43-5.44	MISC.CRIMES	U.S.
LOENER	260109	M	Ger.		Sgt., 217.Res.Gren.Bn., Massif du Vercors, Isere and Drôme (Fr.) 20.7.-5.8.44	SUSPECT	FR.
LOENER, Jean	29767	M	Ger.		Secretary, Interpreter, customs office, St.Michel de Maurienne (Fr.) 9.3.44	MURDER	FR.
LOENSCH or LOESCH	301693	M	Ger.		05-243 Mongolian "Oberland" Unit, St.Nazaire en Royans (Fr.)20.7.-5.8.44	MURDER	FR.
LOERCH, Albert	306764	M	Ger.		Ger.Civ., Solln, Munich (Ger.) 19.7.44	BRUTALITY	U.S.
LOERNER, Hans	258550	M	Ger.	93	SS Oberfhr., SS W.V.H.A., Ger., 40-45	BRUTALITY	U.S.
LOESCH	124656	M	Ger.		C.C. Heppenheim (Ger.) 9.44-5.45	TORTURE	U.S.
LOESCH	251116	M	Ger.		Cpl., Airforce, Entzheim (Fr.) 42-44	TORTURE	FR.
LOESCH see LOENSCH	301693						
LOESCH, Franz	146790	M			SS, C.C. Flossenburg (Ger.)	TORTURE	U.S.
LOESCHE, Herman	251707	M	Ger.	08	Civ., Gross-Rosen (Pol.) 41-45	MURDER	POL.
LOESCHICK	196890	M			Sgt. Oberwachtmeister, Schupo, Stuetzpunkt Groningen Camp Westerbork (Neth.) 9.44	MURDER	NETH.
LOESCHNER, Otto	255006	M	Ger.	6. 7.95	Lt., Gestapo and Abwehratelle, Prag (Czech.) 42	MURDER	CZECH.
LOESCHNIGG, Fritz	195491	M	Ger.	16	Hptsturmfhr., SS Panz.Div. Leibstandarte, Munich (Ger.) 8.-9.44	MISC.CRIMES	U.S.
LOESEL	12593	M	Ger.		N.C.O., Army, 110.or 111.Panz.Gren.Rgt. 2.Coy., Albine (Fr.) 29.6.44	MURDER	FR.
LOESENBECK	577	M	Ger.		Major or Cmdt., Army, Clermont-Ferrand (Fr.) 1.2.44-15.7.44	MURDER	FR.
LOESER, Fritz Johann Friedr.	151341	M	Ger.	93	Landrat, Public official, Langenselbold (Ger.) 12.12.44	MURDER	U.S.
LOESER, Fritz	253772	M	Ger.		Civ., Hanau (Ger.) 10.44	MISC.CRIMES	U.S.
LOESNER, Erich	187101	M	Ger.		SS Uscharfhr., Crim.Assessor, S.D., Montgauthier (Dinant),Cerfontaine, Senzeiller, Charleroi (Bel.) 2.-4.44	MURDER	BEL.
LOESSENHOP	146795	M	Ger.		Lt., Oflag XI A, Wlodlzimierоz (Sov.Un.) 41	INTERR.	U.S.
LOEVITZ, Fritz see LOEBITZ	137669						
LOEW	255147	M			Pvt., 2.Coy. Lt.M.G. Sturmbn. A.O.K., Courcelles (Fr.) 15.11.44	MURDER	U.S.
LOEW, Hans	255589	M	Ger.	00	Cook, Pioneer-group, Heusden (Neth.) 5.11.44	MISC.CRIMES	NETH.
LOEWE	193152	M	Ger.		SS Scharfhr., Waffen-SS, C.C. Buchenwald (Ger.) 42-45	TORTURE	U.S.
LOEWE, Paul	192695	M	Ger.	30.11.11	Reichsjustizministerium, Strafgefangenenlager Nord, Finmark (Nor.)	MISC.CRIMES	NOR.
LOEWI	67558	M	Ger.		Cpl., Army, Klein Zimmern, Dieburg (Ger.)11.40 -4.41	MISC.CRIMES	U.K.
LOEWL	146729	M	Ger.		SS Hptscharfhr., C.C. Flossenburg (Ger.)	TORTURE	U.S.
LOFFLER	301270	M	Ger.		Crim.secretary, Abt. IV C, S.D., Brussels (Bel.) 6.40-9.44	MURDER	BEL.
LOFFLER	306628	M	Ger.		Sgt., Head of Grp. 9.Coy. SS Verfuegungstruppe 52.R.S.T.S.S. SS Rgt."Deutschland", Div. "Das Reich", Miremont, Hte.Garonne (Fr.)6.44	MURDER	FR.
LOFFLER	301692	M	Ger.		05-243 Mongolian "Oberland" Unit, St.Nazaire en Royans (Fr.) 20.7.-5.8.44	MURDER	FR.
LOFFLER, Christian	75292	M	Ger.		Kreisamtsleiter N.S.D.A.P., N.S.K.O.V., Noerdlingen (Ger.)	WITNESS	BUL.
LOFHRMANN, Julius	261390	M	Ger.		SS Guard, C.C. Auschwitz (Pol.) 42-45	MURDER	POL.
LOGAUER	126358	M	Ger.		Ortsgruppenleiter (Deputy Kreisleiter) NSDAP, Dueren-Rolsdorf (Ger.)	MURDER	U.S.
LOGE, Paul	578	M	Ger.		Adjutant-Chef, Army, Feldgendarmerie, Darracq (Fr.) 13.6.44	TORTURE	FR.
LOGES, Hans Werner	1719	M	Ger.	13. 3.24?	Lt., 13.Parachutiste-Rgt. 8.Bn., Normandy (Fr.) 25.1.44	MURDER	U.K. U.S.
LOHAS, Friedrich	162380	M	Ger.		Staff physician, Land.Schuetz.Bn. Stalag VI C, C.C. Flamersheim (Ger.) 21.3.45	MURDER	U.S.
LOHERT, Walter	167922	M	Ger.		Zugfuehrer, 9.Res.Gren.Rgt. 1.Coy., Magny d'Avignon (Fr.) 18.9.44	MURDER	FR.
LOHFINK	128981	M	Ger.		Camp Civ., C.C. Weimar, Buchenwald (Ger.)	TORTURE	U.S.
LOHLEHNER	259873	M	Ger.		Sgt., Feldgendarmerie, Vendome (Fr.) 9.8.44	MURDER	FR.
LOHMAN	142591	M	Ger.		SS Rottfhr., 2.Panz.Gren.Rgt. 3.Bn., Stavelot, Malmedy (Bel.) 12.44	MURDER	U.S.
LOHMANN	146796	M	Ger.		SS Uscharfhr., C.C. Flossenburg (Ger.)	MURDER	U.S.
LOHMANN, Franz	254391	M	Ger.		Capt., 377. Jaeger-Rgt., Vinkt (Bel.) 25.-31.5.40	MISC.CRIMES	BEL.
LOHMANN, Fritz	256819	M	Ger.		Employee, C.C. Nordhausen (Ger.)	MURDER	U.S.
LOHMANN, Wilhelm	134404	M	Ger.	89	Civ., Cemetery caretaker, Camp Lintfort (Ger.) 10.-11.44	WITNESS	U.S.
LOHMAYER, Bruno	187357	M			SS Scharfhr., 4.SS Totenkopf-Stuba, C.C. Dora-Mittelbau-Nordhausen (Ger.) 43-45	MURDER	U.S.
LOHMAYER, Heinrich	187083	M	Ger.	4. 1.91	Guard, 4.SS Totenkopf-Stuba, C.C.Dora-Mittelbau-Nordhausen (Ger.)43-45	TORTURE	U.S.
LOHMER, Josef	121763	M	Ger.	29	Student, Civ., Bad Godesberg (Ger.) 1.-2.45	TORTURE	U.S.
LOHN, Peter	251698	M	Ger.		Pol.chief, Police, Ahrweiler (Ger.) 5.-6.44	MISC.CRIMES	POL.
LOHNER, Josef see LOEHNER	257929						
LOHNES, Wilhelm	189597	M			Assistent, Sigefroi (Lux.) 31.8.-1.9.44	INCENDIARISM	LUX.
LOHR	130172	M	Ger.		Officer, S.A., Luetzen (Ger.) 43	TORTURE	U.K.
LOHR	166695	M	Ger.		Gen., Grc. 43	MURDER	U.S.
LOHR, Alexander	21342	M	Ger.		Gen.Oberst, Army	MISC.CRIMES	U.N.W.C.C.
LOHR, Hermann	130034	M	Ger.		Stalag XI B, Fallingbostel (Ger.) 27.6.44	MURDER	U.K.
LOHRBEER see LOBER	255289						
LOHANS or SCHAUSS	177534	M	Ger.	07	Guard chief, Camp official, C.C. betw. Kassel and Lofelden (Ger.)	MURDER	FR.
LOHRMANN, Robert	305028	M	Ger.		Proprietor of a tinned food factory, Luebeck (Ger.) 41-5.45	MISC.CRIMES	POL.
LOHSE	139049	M	Ger.	10	Hptsturmfhr., Crim.Commis., S.D. SIPO, Toulouse and other towns (Fr.) 6.8.44	MURDER	U.S.
LOHSE	142581	M	Ger.		Dr.,Gestapo, Cannes (Fr.) 44	PILLAGE	FR.

LOH - LOR

NAME	C.R.FILE NUMBER	SEX	NATIO-NALITY	DATE OF BIRTH	RANK OCCUPATION UNIT PLACE AND DATE OF CRIME	REASON WANTED	WANTED BY
LOHSE	187356	M			Rottenfhr., 4.SS Totenkopf-Sturmbann, C.C.Dora,Nordhausen (Ger.)43-45	MURDER	U.S.
LOHSE	193151	M	Ger.		Sgt., WaffenSS, C.C. Buchenwald (Ger.) 42-45	TORTURE	U.S.
LOHSE	256602	M	Ger.		Interpreter Civ., St.Jean de Maurienne (Fr.) 22.8.44	MURDER	FR.
LOHSE, Bruno	21341	M	Ger.		Dr., Chief-asst. of Rosenbergs Looting-Office.	PILLAGE	UNWCC
LOHSE, Rudolph (or CLAUDIUS)	259491	M		12. 2.04	Oberfhr., Allg.SS, Wolfisheim (Fr.) 8.44	MURDER	FR.
LOHSE, Wieland	167714	M	Ger.		Leader, Abt.Ernaehrung und Wirtschaft, Amt des Gouverneurs, Warschau (Pol.) 9.39-44	MISC.CRIMES	POL.
LOISCH, Karl	162471	M		98	Crim.secretary, Gestapo, Giessen (Ger.)	MURDER	U.S.
LOJDA, Josef	190662	M	Ger.	20. 3.08	Prison Guard, Gestapo, C.C. Bruenn (Czech.) 39-45	MURDER	CZECH.
LOKORKIR	146732	M			Dr., Civilian, C.C. Flossenburg (Ger.)	WITNESS	U.S.
LOLGINGER (see LUGINGER)	139038						
LOLLING, Benno	21339	M	Ger.	95 or 12	Dr., SS-Osturmbannfhr., SS-Hauptamt, Wehrwirtschaftshauptamt, SS-Doctor, Chief of the Office D.III, C.C. Dachau, Mauthausen, Belsen, Kowno (Ger.,Aust., Latv.) 38-45	MURDER	U.K.,U.S.,BEL., YUGO.,POL.,NETH.
LOMAUER (or LONAUER)	174058	M			Dr., C.C. Hartheim (Aust.)	MURDER	U.S.
LOMMATSCH	251708	M	Ger.		Pvt., Pepingen (Bel.) 2.44-9.44	PILLAGE	BEL.
LOMMATZSCH, Erhard	170652	M	Ger.		Prof. Civ.Public Official, Einsatzstab Rosenberg, Berlin (Ger.) 40-44	PILLAGE	FR.
LOMMER	193150	M	Ger.		Waffen-SS, C.C. Buchenwald (Ger.) 42-45	TORTURE	U.S.
LOMMES	140884	M		00	Cpl., Fliegerhorstkommandantur 208, Hobsten (Ger.) 15.3.45	MURDER	CAN., U.S.
LONAUER (see LOMAUER, Dr.)	174058						
LONAUER	301579	M	Ger.		Dr., SS-Hptsturmfhr., stationed at C.C.Mauthausen (Aust.) 40-45	MURDER	BEL.
LONG	141578	M			Sgt., Army, Sarras and Andance (Fr.) 13.6.44	MURDER	FR.
LONGE, Erich	261883	M	Ger.		Sturmbannfhr., SS Engineer Bn., Hradistko (Czech.) 45	SUSPECT	CZECH.
LONGIN	252385	M	Ger.		General, Air Force, Prague (Czech.)	INTERR.	CZECH.
LONGIN	259162	M	Ger.		Lt., Army, "Oak Leaf"-Div., 3. and 4. Bn., Cara (Yugo.) 1.44	MISC.CRIMES	YUGO.
LONGUSCH, Otto	256601	M	Ger.	9. 1.07	Employee, C.C. Nordhausen (Ger.)	MURDER	U.S.
LONTSCHAP, Adalbert	189775	M	Ger.		Cmdt., Feldkommandantur, Pozaverac (Yugo.) 42-43	MURDER	YUGO.
LOOCK, Friedrich Wilhelm Paul	305029	M	Ger.		Zellenleiter, Sandkamp. 43-45	MISC.CRIMES	POL.
LOOFT	301271	M	Ger.		Crim.secretary, S.D. Abt. IV D, Brussels (Bel.) 6.40-9.44	MURDER	BEL.
LOOHS	253879	M	Ger.		Cpl., Chief, Seclin (Fr.) 8.44	MURDER	FR.
LOOMES, Hermann	254608	M	Ger.	00	Sgt., Hopsten (Ger.) 3.45	MURDER	U.S.
LOONEY	124762	M		95	Capt., Stalag 3 B, Fuerstenberg-Oder (Ger.)	TORTURE	U.S.
LOOS	195440	M	Ger.		Dr.Feldpol.-Direct.Geh.Feldpolizei-Gruppe, Averoff Prison, Athen (Grc.) 43-44	MISC.CRIMES	U.S.
LOOS(or LOOSE)	186146	M			SS-Expectant, SS Panz.Gren.Regt., 4.Coy., Mayet de Montagne (Fr.) 6.44	TORTURE	FR.
LOOSE	253868	M	Ger.		Lt., Formation No.31308 B, Le Touquet (Fr.) 43-44	PILLAGE	FR.
LOOSE, Guenther	254665	M	Ger.		Hptsturmfhr., SS, Toulouse (Fr.) 11.42-8.44	MISC.CRIMES	FR.
LOPERTZ	189214	M	Ger.		SS-Sturmscharfhr., C.C. Drancy (Fr.)	MURDER	FR.
LOQAY	142586	M	Ger.		Camp-Doctor, CC Kaisergarten, Solingen (Ger.) 44-45	TORTURE	BEL.
LOQUI (or COQUI or COCUIN)	31345	M			Col., 66. Army Corps, Bourg-Lastie (Fr.) 16.7.44	MURDER	FR.
LORBEER (see LOBER)	255289						
LORBER	300901		Ger.		Member, Gestapo, Hagen (Ger.) 3.4.45	MURDER	U.K.
LORCH	258917	M	Ger.		Sgt., Army, 255.Landesschuetzen Bn., 4.Coy., Neu-Dessau, Friedeberg near Driesen (Ger.) 16.3.44	MURDER	FR.
LORD	252370	M	Ger.		Pvt., Army, Oldenzaal (Neth.) 1.4.45	PILLAGE	NETH.
LORE (or LORENZ)	124472	M	Ger.		Lt., Camp-Cmdt., C.C.Sachsenhausen-Oranienburg (Ger.) 40-42	MURDER	U.K., BEL., POL.,CZECH.
LORE	130628	M	Ger.		Guard, Prison Siegburg (Ger.) 45	TORTURE	BEL.
LOREI	193369	M	Ger.		Baurat, Air Force, C.C. Orlandet, Uthe... (Nor.) 9.41-42	WITNESS	NOR.
LOREN, Friedrich	258135	M		01	SS-Officer, Chief of Administration (Foundation Beelitz), Member, NSDAP (Ger.)	INTERR.	BEL.
LORENS, Franz	186302	M	Ger.		Cpl., Army, Heraklion, Crete (Grc.) 43	MURDER	GRC.
LORENT, Friedrich	134917	M	Ger.	04	Osturmfhr., SS, C.C. Hartheim (Aust.) 40-44	MURDER	U.S.
LORENT, Friedrich (or LORENZ)	189776	M	Ger.		SS-Officer, SS, C.C.Belsen and Kowno (Ger.,Latv.) 40-44	MURDER	YUGO.,CZECH.
LORENT, Friedrich	191204	M	Ger.	02	SS-Officer Head, SS, Beelitz-Stiftung, C.C. (It., Pol.)	MURDER	UNWCC
LORENTSEN, Anton Toni	142574	M	Ger.	4. 2.11	Civilian, Ebensee (Aust.) 44-45	WITNESS	U.S.
LORENTZ	130629	M	Ger.		Guard, C.C. Mauthausen (Aust.) 41-45	MURDER	U.S., FR.
LORENTZ	174688				C.C.Struthof-Natzweiler (Fr.)	MURDER	FR.
LORENTZ	187086	M	Ger.		Uschfhr., 4.SS Totenkopf-Sturmbann, C.C.Dora, Nordhausen (Ger.) 43-45	MURDER	U.S.
LORENTZ, Erich	305030	M	Ger.	24. 7.11	Officer, of the Coy. 1.Bn., 62.Regt."Todt", SS Polizeitruppen of the Krimnalpolizei, (Almelo) (Neth.) 5.43	MURDER	NETH.
LORENTZEN	158253	M		05	Uschfhr., SS, C.C.Hamburg-Neuengamme (Ger.)	MURDER	U.K.
LORENTZEN	162377	M		90	Col., Cmdt., Stalag XX B, Willenburg (Ger.) 1.-3.45	TORTURE	U.K.
LORENZ	29689	M			Dr.Oberlandesgerichtsrat, Publ.Official, Prague (Czech.) 21.2.40	MURDER	CZECH.
LORENZ	31572	M			SS-Sgt., Waffen-SS, C.C.Struthof (Fr.)	MISC.CRIMES	FR.
LORENZ	120550	M			Obergruppenfhr., SS C.O.Umsiedlungskdo., Odessa(Sov.Un.) 40-42	MURDER	U.S.,POL.
LORENZ	130630	M	Ger.		Civilian, C.C. Mauthausen (Aust.) 41-45	MURDER	U.S.
LORENZ	137561	M		03	Cpl., Geh.Feldpolizei, Gruppe 713, Kresti (Sov.Un.)	MURDER	U.S.
LORENZ	141358	M			Col., Stalag IV C, Saalhans, Bruex (Czech.) 44-45	MURDER	U.K.
LORENZ	142096	M		20	Camp-Sen., Waldlager 5 and 6, C.C. Muhldorf (Ger.) 44-45	TORTURE	U.S.
LORENZ	153381	M			Employee, Civ., Dresden (Ger.)	MISC.CRIMES	U.K.
LORENZ (see LORE)	124472						
LORENZ	173747	M	Ger.		Dr., Deutsche Arbeitsfront. 44	TORTURE	FR.
LORENZ	195644	M	Ger.	95	Bde.-Leader, Waffen-SS, C.C.Sachsenhausen (Ger.) 9.11.40	MURDER	POL.
LORENZ	195645	M	Ger.		Official, Government, Chlupanin (Pol.) 43	MURDER	POL.
LORENZ	251704	M	Ger.		Hptsturmfhr., C.C. Dachau (Ger.) 39	TORTURE	BEL.
LORENZ	255285	M	Ger.	90	Builder, Cossebaude near Dresden (Ger.) 44-45	BRUTALITY	U.K.
LORENZ	255591	M	Ger.		Pvt., Mauthausen (Aust.)	BRUTALITY	FR.
LORENZ	256599	M	Ger.		Oschfhr., SS, Med. Camp Dora, Nordhausen (Ger.)	MURDER	U.S.
LORENZ	300964	M	Ger.		Cmdt., C.C.Stettin-Poelitz (Ger.) 44	MURDER	CZECH.
LORENZ, Dietz	132565	M			Lt., Army. (Fr.)	MURDER	FR.
LORENZ, Erwin	261124	M	Ger.		Dr.Minister.-Dirig., Ministry of Food and Agriculture.	SUSPECT	U.S.
LORENZ, Friedrich	188475	M			SS-Officer, C.C. Berlin (Ger.) 40-45	MURDER	CZECH.
LORENZ, Friedrich (see LORENT)	189776						

LOR-LOW

NAME	C.R. FILE NUMBER	SEX	NATIO-NALITY	DATE OF BIRTH	RANK OCCUPATION UNIT PLACE AND DATE OF CRIME	REASON WANTED	WANTED BY
LORENZ, Kurt	262177	M	Ger.	9.10.22	Oschfhr., 3.Coy. Platoon 3. 51.SS Armoured Brigade, Breviandes Bucheres, Sts Savine, La Riviere De Corps Troyes (Fr.) 22.-25.8.44	BRUTALITY	FR.
LORENZ, Viktor	258946	M	Ger.		Assist. to Otto Dietrich, Reichspresse Chief Propaganda Ministry editor "German Newspaper" Ungarn war reporter	WITNESS	U.S.
LORENZ, Werner ("LORE")	11868	M	Ger.	95	Osturmfhr., SS Cmdt., C.C. Oranienburg (Ger.) 39-45	MURDER	CZECH. FR. U.K. POL.
LORENZ, Werner	21338	M	Ger.		Police General High Official of the Commissariat for German Racialism	MISC.CRIMES	U.N.W.C.C.
LORENZEN	72277	M	Ger.	95	Groupleader, NSDAP., Officer SA. Cmdt., Roermond (Neth.) 9.44-10.44	MURDER	U.S. NETH.
LORENZEN	162378	M	Ger.		Staff Sgt., Gestapo Army, Lorient, Auray (Fr.) 44	MURDER	FR.
LORENZEN	255005	M	Ger.		Uschfhr., SS C.C. Neuengamme (Ger.)	TORTURE	BEL.
LORENZEN	257931	M			Major, 150. Brigade, Meuse-Bridge Antwerp (Bel.) 12.44	MISC.CRIMES	U.S.
LORENZEN	261808	M	Ger.		Cpl., Gend., Romilly sur Seine (Fr.) 10.6.44	MISC.CRIMES	FR.
LORENZEN, Fritz	189083	M	Ger.		Crim.,Secr., SD,SS, Gestapo, Mlada Boleslav (Czech.) 45	MURDER	CZECH.
LORER, Hugo	256877	M	Ger.		Officer, Army, Village of Misaca, (Yug.) 3.43	INTERR.	YUG.
LORET	196831	M			Sgt., 2. Coy. 100.Bn. de Chasseurs de Montagne, Masseit du Vercors St. Germain de Joux (Fr.) 18.7.44	INTERR.	FR.
LOREY	259231	M	Ger.		Member of Gestapo, area Poitiers (Fr.)	MISC.CRIMES	FR.
LOREZ, Friedrich	300684	M	Ger.	01	Officer, Head of Administration Member, SS-Beelitz Stiftung and its ancillary institutions NSDAP., worked in close contact with Reichsschatzmeister Schwartz, (Ger.) 40	MISC.CRIMES	BEL.
LORGA (see LOHRGE)	174133						
LORIIS	140791	M			Oberfhr., SS, Donau, C.C. Linz (Aust.)	MISC.CRIMES	U.S.
LORITZ	579	M	Ger.		SS-Obergruppenfhr., Camp Cmdt., C.C. Dachau (Ger.) 9-39-1-42	MURDER	POL.
LORMAN	142585	M	Ger.		Major, Brussels (Bel.) 2.9.44	LOOTING	BEL.
LORNER	145431	M	Ger.		SS-Brigadefhr., SS Wirtschafts u. Verwaltungshauptamt	MISC.CRIMES	U.N.W.C.C.
LORS (see LORZ)	253993						
LORSBACHER	174057	M	Ger.		Assistant to Opt., Stalag 6 A, C.C. Hemer (Ger.) 41-45	TORTURE	U.S.
LORTEN, Addy	256600	M	Ger.		Matrose, Navy, Boulogne (Fr.) 7.42	MURDER	FR.
LORZ (or LORS)	253993	M	Ger.		Customs Officer, Tain (Fr.) 11.6.43	INTERR.	FR.
LOEZ, Valentin	301347	M	Ger.		Customs Official at Thonon St. Gingolph Hte- Savoie (Fr.) 23.7.44	MURDER	FR.
LOSACK, Oscar	151339	M			Guard, Civ., C.C. Leipzig - Celle (Ger.)	TORTURE	U.S.
LOSACKER, Josef	160385	M	Ger.	12	Lt., SS Wirtschafts Verwaltungs Hauptamt, C.C. Ohrdruf (Ger.)	TORTURE	U.S.
LOSACKER, Ludwig	21337	M	Ger.		Dr., Governor, Public Official of District Cracow (Pol.) 6.11.43	MURDER	U.N.W.C.C.
LOSCH, Karl	124655	M	Ger.	98	Inspector, Gestapo C.C. Giessen (Ger.) 26.-27.3.45	MURDER	U.S.
LOSCHMID	187099	M	Ger.		Major, Camp official, Kapo, C.C. Beech, (Ger.)	TORTURE	BEL.
LOSCHET (or LOSCHING)	195491	M	Ger.		Gestapo, Audin Le Tiche, Thionville (Fr.) 20.8.44	MURDER	U.S.
LOSCHING	255966	M	Ger.		Pvt., SS Bn., Meerveld, (Neth.) 11.44	MURDER	NETH.
LOSEN	255557	M			Camp Capo, C.C. Mauthausen, (Aust.)	INTERR.	FR.
LOSEN (or von LOSEN)	151340	M		10	Capo, C.C. Mauthausen (Aust.) 41-45	MURDER	U.S.
LOSENKI, Herbert	195646	M	Ger.		SS-Man, 1.SS Pz.Div. Leibstandarte Adolf Hitler 3. Pi.Coy. Ligneuville (Bel.), 19.12.44	MURDER	U.S.
LOSER	136231	M	Ger.		Lt., Army, Chermont Pouguilhe (Gers), (Fr.) 8.6.44	MURDER	FR.
LOSER, Fritz	134802	M			Landrat Official, Hanau (Ger.) 2.42-3.45	TORTURE	U.S.
LOSERT	300814	M	Ger.		Emi., 1.Aufkl.Abt. 3.Coy. 2. Column.XV. Div. of the Afrika Korps Saint L'eger, (Arlon) (Bel.) 5.9.44	MISC.CRIMES	BEL.
LOSMANN	179824	M	Ger.		SS-Guard, C.C. Auschwitz (Pol.) 8.43	MURDER	BEL.
LOSSE	189216	M	Ger.		3. Coy, 19.Rgt. SS Hohenstaufen Div., St. Jeoire, Chatillon Clauses, Taninges, Balle (Fr.) 11.6.44-20.7.44	TORTURE	FR.
LOSSE, Josef	190663	M	Ger.		Polizeirat, Gestapo, Bruenn, (Czech.) 39-45	TORTURE	CZECH.
LOSSET	67573	M	Ger.		SS-Man, SS Div. Fp. 48963 B, Château Contier St.Sulpice Moutmussop (Fr.) 6.8.44	MURDER	FR.
LOSSOW	142570	M			Col., Armee Oberkdo.,	MISC.CRIMES	U.S.
LOTA-DORNER	151348	M	Ger.		"SS-Sturmmann", Pz. Gren.Rgt. 3 Deutschland,Das Reich 2.Bn. Aiguillon (Fr.) 17.6.44	MURDER	FR.
LOTBIT	165166	M	Ger.	15	SS-Usturmfhr., SS Lemberg, Kiew, Zwiakel (Sov.Un., Pol.) 41-42	MURDER	U.S.
LOTHMANN	253127	M	Ger.	07	Sgt., 1.Coy., 192. Signal Unit, 92. Inf.Div., Parnese (It.) 6.6.44	INTERR.	U.K.
LOTHRINGER, Stefan	189777	M	Ger.		Member, Army Staff. C.C. Banjica (Yug.)	MURDER	YUG.
LOTI, Pietro	189887	M			Commissioner, Ital. Police, Koter, (Yug.)	MURDER	YUG.
LOTSCHER	252386	M	Ger.	00-05	Lt., Feldgendarmerie, Monte Penna area Bedonia (It.) 10.4.44	INTERR.	U.K.
LOTTA	157106	M	Ger.	00	Civ., Petrol Factory C.C. Brux (Czech.) 8.55-5.45	TORTURE	U.K.
LOTTAWA, Fritz (see SLOTAWA)	138322						
LOTTENBURG, Erick	254137	M	Ger.		Platsbetriebsfhr., Civ., Gettersee, (Ger.) 7.43	TORTURE	NETH.
LOTTMANN	170653	M	Ger.		Cpt., Army Dortmund (Ger.) 12.43	MURDER	FR.
LOTTMANN	259580	M	Ger.		Cpt., Commander, 9.Coy., 3.Bn. SS Pol.Rgt.Todt in Aix les Bains Bernex, Hte. Savoie (Fr.) 17.12.43	MISC.CRIMES	FR.
LOTTMANN, Hans	39583	M	Ger.		Cpt., SS Pol. Todt No. 28, Annemasse (Fr.) 11.-12.43	MURDER	FR.
LOTTNE	31616	M	Ger.		20. Army IVb 18. Geb. Korps Finnmark (Nor.) 10.-11.44	MURDER	NOR.
LOTUED - HARIEGG (see LOTVET - HARIEGG)	39584						
LOTTS	128528	M	Ger.		Works Manager, Civilian, Exinberch, Vache, Stalag 9 c (Ger.) 12.44-5.45	TORTURE	U.K.
LOTZ	173684	M	Ger.		Civ., Servant Zentral Abt. Kultur C.C. Maribor (Yug.) 4.41-44	MURDER	YUG.
LOTZ, Fritz	255017	M	Ger.		Farmer, Civ., Budesheim (Ger.) 10.44	MISC.CRIMES	U.S.
LOTZ, Georg	160384	M	Ger.	08	Pvt., Airforce C.C. Ohrdruf (Ger.)	TORTURE	U.S.
LOTZE	189407	M	Ger.		Major, Army 722. Inf.Rgt. 1. St.Bn., Overhalla (Nor.) 9.9.42	MURDER	NOR.
LOUSQ	138304	M	Ger.		Sgt., C.C. La Rochelle (Fr.) 45	BRUTALITY	FR.
LOUBREY	67556	M	Ger.		Cpt., Army Stalag XII C.C. Sagan, (Ger.)	TORTURE	U.K.
LOUZ (see LUUZ)	6117						
LOUZ	146939	M	Ger.		Panzerjaeger Ersats 7.Bn., Hautes Alpes (Fr.)	MURDER	FR.
LOUZER	141357	M	Ger.		Cpt., Stalag XVIII C, Gummen, Villach, (Aust.) 1.-3.44	MURDER	U.K.
LOVITZ	305924	M	Ger.		Oberfhr., C.C. Oranienburg (Ger.) 11.39-45	MURDER	CZECH.
LOVITZ, Fritz	67555	M	Ger.	17	Pvt., Ld.Schts.Bn.,714 Stalag XX A , Luschkaun, Waldau (Pol.)	MURDER	U.K.
LOWAK, Erich	173674	M	Ger.		SS-Oschfhr., Gestapoleitstelle C.C. Brno,Auschwitz Birkenau (Pol. Czech), 42	MURDER	CZECH.
LOWE	254401	M	Ger.		Lt., Pleucadec St.Marcel (Fr.) 18.-28.6.44	MISC.CRIMES	FR.

LOW - LUD

NAME	C.R.FILE NUMBER	SEX	NATIO-NALITY	DATE OF BIRTH	RANK OCCUPATION UNIT PLACE AND DATE OF CRIME	REASON WANTED	WANTED BY
LOWEN, Heinrich	301535	M	Ger.	24. 3.13	Oschfhr., SS (No.22375) C.C., Buchenwald (Ger.) betw.5.38 and 10.43	MURDER	BEL.
LOWENBERG	128982	M	Ger.	17	Warden, N.C.O., C.C., Aachen (Ger.)	TORTURE	U.S.
LOWENDAY, Friedrich	31718	M	Ger.	15. 2.13	SS Conc.Camp, Oswiecim (Pol.) 6.40-1.45	MURDER	POL.
LOWERING	156083	M	Ger.		Zugfhr., Techn.Hilfe, C.C.Emsland, Papenburg (Ger.) 44	MURDER	U.S.
LOWIN	252248	M	Ger.		Dr., Sturmbannfhr., SS, Conc.Camp, Mauthausen (Aust.)	MURDER	BEL.
LOWITSCH	129700	M	Ger.		Guard, SS, 4.Bau-Bde., C.C., Ellrich (Ger.) 4.4.45	MURDER	U.S.
LOX	256326	M	Ger.		Sturmbannfhr., Muehldorf (Ger.)	WITNESS	U.S.
LOY	167022	M	Ger.		Chief, Peasants of that region, Haha (Ger.) 45	MURDER	FR.
LOY	167024	M	Ger.		Mayor, Stalag XIII D Gunzenhausen, Haha nr.Nuremberg (Ger.) 45	MURDER	FR.
LOYET-HARDEGG (see LOYVET-HARDEGG)	39584						
LOYS	167023	M	Ger.		Hptschfhr., Conc.Camp, SS, Natzweiler (Fr.) 42-44	MURDER	FR.
LOYVET-HARDEGG (or LOYET-HARDEGG, LOTUED-HARDEGG)	39584	M	Ger.	06	Lt.Col. C.O.,7.Parachute-Div.,21.Rgt., Carhaix - Alsace (Fr.) 8..9.6.44-2.45	MURDER	U.S., FR.
LUA	185141	M	Ger.		Pvt., Army, Hennebont (Fr.) 6.8.44	MURDER	FR.
LUBBE, Fritz	122463	M	Ger.		Officer, Arb.Kmdo., C.C., Jena (Ger.)	TORTURE	BEL.
LUBBE, Mathias	301536	M	Ger.		SS-Schfhr., (No.148765) C.C., Buchenwald (Ger.) betw.5.38 and 10.43	MURDER	BEL.
LUBBEN	254392	M	Ger.		Cpl., 10.Coy.,377.Jaeger-Rgt., Vinkt (Bel.) 25.-31.5.40	MISC.CRIMES	BEL.
LUBBERS, Joseph	195178	M	Ger.		Pvt., "Brandenburg-Rgt.", 3.Coy.,II.Bn., Montel Paro (It.) 21.3.44	MURDER	U.K.
LUBIN, Harris	251117	M	Ger.		Member, Gestapo, Lilli (Fr.) 40-44	MURDER	FR.
LUBINA, Arthur	254619	M	Ger.		SS-Mann, 2.SS T.Stuba., Auschwitz-Birkenau (Pol.) 10.42	MURDER	YUGO.
LUBITZ	301787	M	Ger.		Uschfhr., Builder, C.C. Auschwitz (Pol.) 40	MURDER	FR.
LUBLIG (see LUNBLIG)	254618						
LUBLIG (or LUMBLIG)	305718	M	Ger.		Usturmfhr., Gestapo, Alencon and throughout Orne-Department (Fr.) 6.44-8.44	MURDER	FR.
LUBLING	165630	M	Ger.		4.Coy.Chars Parach, Capt., H.Goering Dienststelle, Raboset, Les Herstal (Bel.) 5.9.44	MURDER	BEL.
LUBNOWL	132814	M	Ger.		Camp-Capt.	MURDER	U.K.
LUBZYK	160380	M	Ger.	15	Cpl., Station Complement, C.C., Buchenwald (Ger.) 42-45	TORTURE	U.S.
LUCANEK	194216	M	Ger.	90	Hptsturmfhr., SS, Camp 377, Gerolstein (Ger.) 12.44-2.45	TORTURE	U.S.
LUCAS	10154	M			Capt., Camp-Cmdt., C.C. Stalag 21 D, Posen (Pol.)	MURDER	U.K.
LUCAS	156085	M	Ger.	00	Capt., Wehrm.Landschutz-Bn.,226.Coy.,Khundorf (Pol.) 12.5.42	MURDER	U.K.
LUCAS, Erich	259389	M	Ger.		Schfhr., Gestapo, Poitiers Area (Fr.) 40-45	MISC.CRIMES	FR.
LUCAS, Friedrich	29690	M	Ger.		Landgerichts-Direktor,Ministry of Justice,Litomerice (Czech.) 21.2.40	MURDER	CZECH.
LUCAS, Leo	150632	M	Ger.		Conc.Camp, Ickern (Ger.)	MURDER	U.S.
LUCASSEN	179773	M	Ger.	05	Capt., Parachute-Rgt.1, Padulivo (It.) 10.,11.7.44	MURDER	U.K.
LUCHERT	256327	M	Ger.		Baufhr., O.T., Muehldorf (Ger.)	WITNESS	U.S.
LUCHMANN, Waldemar	187162	M	Ger.		Gestapo-Employee, Budejovice (Czech.) 39-45	MURDER	CZECH.
LUCHS	151349	M	Ger.		N.C.O., Army, Guard-Comm.Hahn & Co., Danzig (Ger.) 6.42	TORTURE	U.K.
LUCHS	255146	M	Ger.	98	Crim.Secr., Gestapo, (Ger.)	INTERR.	U.K.
LUCHTEMAYER	257661	M	Ger.		Sturmfhr., SS, C.C. Dora, Nordhausen (Ger.)	MURDER	FR.
LUCHTERHAND, Otto	262082	M	Ger.	85	Former Director of a Plant in Neustadt (Ger.)	BRUTALITY	FR.
LUCI	195714	M	Ger.		Col., Gestapo, Susak (Yugo.) 3.41	MURDER	YUGO.
LUCK	67813	M	Ger.		Cpl., Army, Stalag 20 B, Marienburg,Neubrandenburg,Mecklenburg (Ger.)	TORTURE	U.K.
LUCK	124283	M	Ger.		Lt.,SS-Pz.Div.1,12.Parachute-Inf.Rgt.,12.Coy., Malmedy (Bel.)17.12.44	MURDER	U.S.
LUCK	173230	M	Ger.	00	Cpl., Stalag XX B, C.C., Danzig (Ger.)	TORTURE	U.K.
LUCK, Hans	142572	M	Ger.	95	Civilian, C.C. Hadamar (Ger.) 6.44-3.45	WITNESS	U.S.
LUCK, Kurt	583	M	Ger.		SS-Bde.Fhr., Lublin (Pol.) 9.39-43	MURDER	POL.
LUCKE	151342	M			Guard, C.C., Civilian, Leipzig - Celle (Ger.)	TORTURE	U.S.
LUCKE (see LUECKE)	152824						
LUCKE	174563	M	Ger.		Pvt., Stalag VI, C.C., Hemer (Ger.) 15.10.41	TORTURE	U.S.
LUCKENHEIM, Kurt	257708	M	Ger.		Sgt., Feldgend., Zajecar (Yugo.) 41-44	MURDER	YUGO.
LUCKERT, Walter	130632	M	Ger.		Dr., Hptschfhr., SS, C.C., Dentist, Mauthausen (Aust.) 41-45	MURDER	U.S.
LUCKHARDT	261107	M	Ger.		Crim.investigation officer, Gestapo, Wiesbaden (Ger.) 44-45	MURDER	U.S.
LUCKNER	156093	M	Ger.		Pvt., Luftnachr.Coy.21, Marseille (Fr.)	MURDER	FR.
LUCYNSKI	124966	M	Ger.		Wachtmeister,C.C., Bremen-Farge (Ger.) 6.43	MURDER	U.K.
LUDDECKE	251118	M			Schfhr., SS, C.C., Dora	MURDER	FR.
LUDDECKE, Werner	251121	M			Oschfhr., SS, C.C., Buchenwald (Ger.)	MURDER	U.S.
LUDDECKE, Bernhard	132239	M	Ger.		Civilian, Billroda (Ger.) 45	TORTURE	U.S.
LUDEKE, Rudolf	254393	M	Ger.		Pvt., 377.Jaeger-Rgt., Vinkt (Bel.) 25.-31.5.40	MISC.CRIMES	BEL.
LUDEMANN, Heinrich	256325	M	Ger.		Cultivator, Westerrecht (Ger.) 6.2.44	MURDER	FR.
LUDEWIG	156095	M	Ger.		Capt., Stalag 357, Fallingbostel (Ger.) 10.4.45	TORTURE	U.K.
LUDEWIK	257662	M	Ger.		Major, Army, Commune of Blazevo (Yugo.) 42	MURDER	YUGO.
LUDICKE, Fritz	186550	M	Ger.		Pvt., Kriegsgef.Arb.Bn.187,2.Coy., Potthus Korgen (Nor.)	MURDER	NOR.
LUDINA, Alfred	301788	M	Ger.		SS-Mann, C.C., Auschwitz (Pol.) 40	MURDER	FR.
LUDOLF	253874	M	Ger.		Hptsturmfhr., SS, Loihl-Pass (Ger.) 7.-9.43	MURDER	FR.
LUDOLF, Julius	174115	M	Ger.	26. 3.91	SS-Clerk, C.C., Melk (Aust.) 1.45	MURDER	U.S.
LUDOLPH	130634	M	Ger.		Osturmfhr.,SS, Conc.Camp, Mauthausen (Aust.) 41-45	MURDER	U.S.
LUDOLPH	141416	M	Ger.		Osturmfhr., SS, C.C., Melk (Aust.)	TORTURE	FR.
LUDOLPHI	1521	M	Ger.		Lt., Army, Guise (Aisne) (Fr.) 44	MURDER	FR.
LUDOLPHY	12534	M	Ger.		Lt.,799.Georgians Inf.Bn.,2.Coy., Grand-Bourg - St. Pierre de Fursac (Fr.) 1.44	MURDER	FR.
LUDOLPHY	254857	M	Ger.		Lt., Unit Georgiens, Noyales (Fr.) 10.8.44	PILLAGE	FR.
LUDORF	300510	M	Ger.		Capt., Waffen-SS, Head, La Bollene, Vaucluse (Fr.) 28.2.44	MURDER	FR.
LUDOVIGY, Guenther	255003	M	Ger.	28. 4.26	Member, Waffen-SS (Pol.) 39-45	INTERR.	LUX
LUDTKE	301272	M	Ger.		Osturmfhr., SS, Leiter, Personalausgaben Reisekosten-Abt.SD II A 1, Police-Inspector, Brussels (Bel.) 6.40-9.44	MURDER	BEL.
LUDVIK, Annamarie	252514	F	Ger.	2. 6.00	Agent, Police, Gestapo, Konciny (Czech.) 42-45	INTERR.	CZECH.
LUDWICK (or LUDWICKZMY)	72280	M	Ger.	14	Annonay (Fr.) 4.8.44	MURDER	FR.
LUDWIG	6122	M	Ger.		SS-Div."Das Reich" Rgt. "Der Fuehrer", Buzet s-Tara (Fr.) 7.7.44	MURDER	FR.
LUDWIG	122465	M	Ger.		Civilian, C.C., Buchenwald (Ger.) 45	MURDER	FR.
LUDWIG	128983	M	Ger.	10	Uschfhr.,SS, Admin.Sect.IV, C.C. Weimar-Buchenwald (Ger.) 39-43	TORTURE	U.S.

LUD-LUK

NAME	C.R.FILE NUMBER	SEX	NATIO- NALITY	DATE OF BIRTH	RANK OCCUPATION UNIT PLACE AND DATE OF CRIME	REASON WANTED	WANTED BY
LUDWIG	130635	M	Ger.		Leader,Block I,C.C.Mauthausen(Aust.) 41-45	MURDER	U.S.
LUDWIG	150633	M	Ger.		Dr.,Interpreter,Army,29 Pz.Gren.Div.	WITNESS	U.S.
LUDWIG	152822	M			Civ.,C.C.Gardelegen (Ger.)	MURDER	U.S.
LUDWIG	156096	M	Ger.	00	Member,SS,C.C.Wetzlar,Nuernberg (Ger.) 28.2.-4.3.45	TORTURE	U.S.
LUDWIG	162388	M	Ger.		Engineer,SS,Navy,Hennebout-Vannes (Fr.) 44	MURDER	FR.
LUDWIG	167684	M	Ger.		Dr.,Kommissarischer Verwalter,Adminstr.,Pszczyna (Pol.)9.39-12.44	MISC.CRIMES	POL.
LUDWIG	173673	M	Ger.		Prefect,Occupied territories,Boheme,Ceske,Oswiecim,Budejovic,Birkenau (Pol.Czech.) 39-45	MURDER	CZECH.
LUDWIG	188399	M	Ger.	05	Capt.,Official of the Sonderbeauftragter des Reichsfuehrers-SS,C.C.Auschwitz,Sosnowice (Pol.)	MURDER	POL.
LUDWIG	191572	M	Ger.		SS-Mann,SS-Div."Das Reich",Regt."Der Fuehrer" (Fr.) 6.-8.44	MURDER	FR.
LUDWIG	193957	M	Ger.		Pvt.,5 Coy.,396 Ldsschtz.Bn.,Stalag IV A,C.C.Altendorf,Okrilla(Ger.)	MURDER	FR.
LUDWIG	253131	M	Ger.		Director,C.C.Auschwitz (Pol.)	MURDER	FR.
LUDWIG	255014	M	Ger.		Crim.Secr.,Abt.IV C,Bruessel (Bel.) 40-45	INTERR.	BEL.
LUDWIG	305717	M			In Command of Auschwitz-Kdo.,C.C.Auschwitz,Birkenau (Pol.) 40	MURDER	FR.
LUDWIG,Conrad	301537	M	Ger.	1. 1.08	Pvt.,SS (No.263698) C.C.Buchenwald (Ger.) 16.5.38-9.10.43	MURDER	BEL.
LUDWIG,Erich	161417	M	Ger.	00	Cpl.,Waffen-SS,C.C.Buchenwald (Ger.) 42-45	MURDER	U.S.
LUDWIG,Ernst	160382	M	Ger.	17	Uschfhr.,SS,Pz.Div."Das Reich",Altenkirchen (Ger.) 13.9.44	MURDER	U.S.
LUDWIG,Franc Josef	10306	M	Ger.	03	Oberstaatsanwalt,Justizminist.Landgericht,Prag (Czech.) 43-45	MURDER	CZECH.
LUDWIG,Roth	255552	M	Ger.		Uschfhr.,SS,Buchenwald (Ger.)	MURDER	U.S.
LUDWING,Karl	261810	M	Ger.		Member,Gestapo,Caen,near Calvados (Fr.) 40-44	MURDER	FR.
LUE	156094	M	Ger.		Dr.,Physician,Civ.,C.C.Gerolstein (Ger.) 12.43	TORTURE	U.S.
LUEBBE,Mathias	582	M	Ger.	23. 4.13	Hptschfhr.,SS,C.C.Maidanek (Pol.) 40-4.44	MURDER	BEL.,POL.
LUEBBEN,Ewald	257739	M	Ger.		Lt.,Navy,Hopseidet in Finmark,Northern (Nor.) 6.5.45	MURDER	NOR.
LUEBECK (or NUEBECK)	130631	M	Ger.		Chief,SS,C.C.Neu-Kamerum,Halberstadt (Ger.) 44	TORTURE	BEL.
LUEBECK	186695	M	Ger.	15 or 17	Osturmfhr.,SS,C.C.Zwieberge near Halberstadt (Ger.)	MURDER	U.K.
LUEBER	36611	M	Ger.		Sgt.,Wach-Bn.565,Grulich (Czech.) 3.-4.45	TORTURE	U.K.
LUECKE	190456	M	Ger.		Dr.,Assessor,C.C. (Ger.) 40-45	MURDER	CZECH.
LUECK,Siegfried	180306	M	Ger.		Sgt.,Fallschirm-Div.,near Caen (Fr.)	MURDER	U.S.
LUECKE	102918	M	Ger.	95	Officer,Gestapo,Seelhorst (Ger.) 6.4.45	MURDER	U.S.
LUECKE (or LUCKE)	152824	M	Ger.		Sgt.,Hospital,Feldlazarett Tangerhuette (Ger.)	MISC.CRIMES	U.K.
LUECKE	183303	M			Uschfhr.,SS,4 SS-Totenk.Sturmbann,Mittelbau,Nordhausen (Ger.) 43-45	WITNESS	U.S.
LUECKE,Arthur	187161	M	Ger.		Member,Gestapo,Liege (Bel.) 43-45	MURDER	BEL.
LUECKE,Fritz	139039	M	Ger.	05	Oschfhr.,SS,official,C.C.Gross-Beeren (Ger.) 43	MURDER	U.S.
LUECKEN,Ditrich	256771	M	Ger.		Sgt.,Feldgendarmerie,Zajecar (Yugo.) 41-44	MURDER	YUGO.
LUEDMAN,Heinrich	132240	M	Ger.		Scharfhr.,SA,NSDAP	TORTURE	U.S.
LUEDERS	183302	M			Sturmmann,Guard,SS,4 SS-Totenk.Sturmbann,C.C.Dora,Nordhausen,Rosen,Aslau (Ger.) 43-45	WITNESS	U.S.
LUEDI,Albert	252374	M	Ger.		Member,NSDAP,Dreilaendereck,Loerrach (Ger.)	INTERR.	BEL.
LUEDIKE	196829	M	Ger.		Lt.,Usturmfhr.,Sicherheitspolizei Groningen,C.C.Westerborg(Neth.)12.44	INTERR.	NETH.
LUEDTKE	124760	M	Ger.	90	Landesgerichts-Praesident,Reichsjustiz-Ministerium(Lux.) 9.42	MURDER	U.S.
LUEDTKE,Walter	186304	M	Ger.	86	Dr.,Senatspraesident,.Justiz-Minist.,Oberlandgericht (Lux.)8.9.40-44	MURDER	LUX.
LUEG	254856	M	Ger.		Hptwachtmeister,Siegburg (Ger.) 45	INTERR.	FR.
LUEG,Ludwig	173718	M	Ger.		Warder,C.C.,Strafgef.-Lager,Rheinische Zellwolle A.G.,Siegburg(Ger)42	TORTURE	BEL.
LUEGER	141879	M	Ger.		Col.,Cmdt.,Stalag VIII B,C.C.Lamsdorf (Ger.) 42	TORTURE	U.K.
LUGGMUND	257001	M	Ger.		Sgt.,German-Army,Bobovo (Yugo.)10.41	PILLAGE	YUGO.
LUEHH	250346	M			Flyer,C.C.Ellrich,Nordhausen (Ger.)	MURDER	U.S.
LUEHRS	127417	M	Ger.		Osturmfhr.,SS,Army,Buchenwald (Ger.) 8.44	MURDER	U.S.
LUEHRS	222507	M	Ger.		Cmdt.,C.C.Thekenberge (Ger.) 44	MURDER	U.S.
LUENEBURG,Fritz	260501	M	Ger.	29. 7.25	Guard,SS,C.C.Natzweiler (Fr.)	MURDER	FR.
LUERMANN	31615	M	Ger.		Dr.,Oberarzt,20 Army,IV b Staff	MURDER	NOR.
LUETERS,Rudolph	260666	M		83	Crimes against peace, War crimes and crimes against humanity	WITNESS	U.S.
LUETGEMEIER	161530	M	Ger.	15	Hptsturmfhr.,SS,C.C.Wuestegiersdorf (Ger.)	MURDER	U.K.
LUETGENS	138355	M	Ger.		Adjudant-chief,SS,Gestapo,Lyon (Fr.)	MURDER	FR.
LUETGENS	146940	M	Ger.		Sgt.,SS,Sicherheitsdienst,Annecy (Fr.) 44	MURDER	FR.
LUETH	145164	M	Ger.		Dr.,Civ.,Administrator (Fr.Neth.CSR) 39-45	MISC.CRIMES	U.S.
LUETH,Johann	124205	M	Ger.		Kammerverwalter,official,officer,Dreibergen Prison,C.C.Buetzow(Ger.)	TORTURE	NOR.
LUETICH,Ernst (Alias:"THE JEW")	72278	M	Ger.	22	Lt.,Waffen-SS,Kriegsgef.-Lager 20,Bremen (Ger.)	TORTURE	U.S.
LUETKE-MUELLER	162632	M	Ger.	95	Capt.,Oflag,Berlin (Ger.) 4.43-5.44	TORTURE	U.K.
LUETKEMEIER,Franz	139043	M	Ger.		Cpl.,Kraftfahrpark Wuerzburg,Pechbrunn (Ger.) 15.4.45	MURDER	U.S.
LUETKEMEIER,Moritz	301068	M	Ger.		Osturmfhr.,SS,C.C.Hamburg,Neuengamme (Ger.) 45	MURDER	CZECH.
LUETKENHUS	301178	M	Ger.		Krim.Kommissar,Osturmfhr.,SS,Kampen (Aust.) 10.44	MURDER	NETH.
LUETEP,Arthur Emil Robert	300304	M	Ger.	25. 4.95	Ortsgruppenleiter,Verwalter,NSDAP in Apeldoorn "Head of the Commission",Holland-Action,over various Jewish businesses,Apeldoorn (Neth.) 5.40-45	INTERR.	NETH.
LUETTGENHUS	196828	M	Ger.		Osturmfhr.,Krim.Kommissar,Gestapo,S.D.,Zwolle (Neth.) 9.44-4.45	INTERR.	NETH.
LUETKE,Walter	305035	M	Ger.		Leader,Member,Arbeitsamt,Parteigericht,Swiecie (Pol.) 39-1.45	MISC.CRIMES	POL.
LUFT	158256	M	Ger.		Lt.,SS,Tarascon (Fr.) 14.9.43	MURDER	FR.
LUGAR (or LUGER)	128827	M	Ger.		Lt.,Stalag VIII B,Lamsdorf (Ger.) 18.7.43	TORTURE	U.K.
LUGER	156092	M	Ger.		Procureur General aupres tribunal special,Strasbourg (Fr.) 44	MURDER	FR.
LUGER,Josef	300302	M	Ger.		Lt.,Turkestan Legion,Albin,Tarn (Fr.) 18.8.44	MISC.CRIMES	FR.
LUGER,Ludwig	162928	M	Ger.		Staatsanwalt,Procureur,Strasbourg (Fr.) 40-43	MURDER	FR.
LUGG,Ludwig	139161	M	Ger.	10.11.93	Guard,C.C.Siegburg (Ger.) 3.-8.42	TORTURE	BEL.
LUGINGER,Johann (or LOLGINGER)	139038	M	Ger.		Civilian (Pol.) 39-40	MURDER	U.S.
LUH	254669	M	Ger.		Oberwachtmeister,S.D.,Toulouse (Fr.)11.42-8.44	MISC.CRIMES	FR.
LUHE	139690	M	Ger.		Col.,Cmdt.Stalag X B,C.C.Sandbostel (Ger., 1.-5.45	TORTURE	U.S.
LUHE,Wilhelm	146009	M		90	Civilian,Osterwieck (Ger.) 7.44	TORTURE	U.S.
LUHM (see LUM)	251700						
LUHRAN,Emanuel	62508	M	Ger.	95 or 99	Pvt.,Army,2 Btty.Mar.Flak-Abt.810,Walcheren (Neth.) 10.44	WITNESS	U.S.
LUICK,Ottmar	192725	M	Ger.	12. 6.00	Reichsjustiz-Ministerium,Strafgefangenen-Lager Norol,Finmark (Nor.) 4.45	MISC.CRIMES	NOR.
LUISTER	261010				Rottfhr.,SS,C.C.Vaihingen (Ger.) 13.8.44-7.4.45	MURDER	U.S.
LUK	139159	M	Ger.		Hpt.-Wachtmeister,Pol.,C.C.Siegburg (Ger.) 7.44	TORTURE	U.S.

LUK - LUT

NAME	C.R.FILE NUMBER	SEX	NATIO- NALITY	DATE OF BIRTH	RANK OCCUPATION UNIT PLACE AND DATE OF CRIME	REASON WANTED	WANTED BY
LUKAR	146944	M	Ger.		Panzerjaeger Ersatzbn.Sgt.Gap(Fr.)	MURDER	FR.
LUKAS	122474	M	Ger.		Medecin,SS CC Hospital,Ravensbrueck(Ger.)	TORTURE	FR.
LUKAS	146014	M	Ger.		Dr.,Osturmfhr.SS,Auschwitz(Pol.)43-44	MURDER	U.S.
LUKAS or LUKUS	189218	M	Ger.		Dr.,SS Osturmfhr.CC Ravensbrueck(Ger.)42-45	MURDER	FR.BEL.
LUKAS, Alois	254620	M	Ger.	10. 6.96	SS Sturmfhr.Chief,Guard,SS,Gestapo,Crim.Pol.Sumperk(Czech.)31.3.45	MURDER	CZECH.
LUKAS, Friedrich	128029	M	Ger.		Col.Airforce,Jaeger Regt.	MURDER	U.S.
LUKAS, Friedrich	189234	M	Ger.		Landgerichtsdirector,Occup.Ternt.Litomerice(Czech.)	MISC.CRIMES	CZECH.
LUKAS, Karl	257660	M	Ger.	17. 4.10	Block No.7,Dora,Nordhausen(Ger.)	MURDER	U.S.
LUFASCHIK, Leo	167720	M	Ger.		Pvt.6-9 Regt.Res.Grenadier,1 Coy.Magny d'Anigon(Fr.)18.9.44	MURDER	FR.
LUKASIK	301789	M	Ger.		Uschafhr.Blockfhr.CC Auschwitz(Pol.)40	MURDER	FR.
LUKINGER	306919	M	Ger.		Employee,St.Germain des Fosses(Allier)Billy(Allier)(Fr.)8.44-26.8.44	PILLAGE	FR.
LUKOWSKY, Alois	187411	M	Ger.	19. 6.05	SS Schuetze,Camp Guard,4 SS Totenkopf Stuba,CC Nordhausen-Dora(Ger.)	TORTURE	U.S.
LUKSH, Leo	254617	M	Ger.		Pvt.Panzer Div.Unit 36-185,Lautrec(Fr.)5.8.44	MURDER	FR.
LUKUS see LUKAS, Dr.	189218						
LULAY	305034		Ger.	05	SS Officer,Commandant Prison Camp,Vrasselt,Emmerich,Wignbergen(Neth.) 10.44-3.45	TORTURE	NETH.
LULEY	1430	M	Ger.	10	Capt.1 Para.Div.Padulivo(It.)22.6.44	MURDER	U.K.
LULKET, Alfred	251120	M	Ger.		Interpreter,Feldgendarmerie of Plouaret,Loquivy-Plougras,Fredrez(Fr.) 3.2.44-21.6.44	MURDER	FR.
LULKIE, Willie	255553	M	Ger.		Commander,Boat 25 Anland Waterweg Police,Ijselmeer(Neth.)11.44	MURDER	U.S.
LULLIES	253133	M	Ger.		Professor,Strasbourg(Fr.)40-44	MURDER	FR.
LULTGEAMEYER see LUTTGENMEYER	133290						
LUM or LUHM	251700	M	Ger.		SS Sturmmann,1 SS Panz.Regt.2 Coy.Malmedy(Bel.)17.12.44	MURDER	U.S.
LUMBLIG see LUBLIG	305718						
LUMPE, Alexander	250369	M			Flyer,CC Ellrich,Nordhausen(Ger.)	MURDER	U.S.
LUMBLIG or LUBLIG	254618			16	Lt.Chief,Usturmfhr.S.D.,Alencon(Fr.)40-44	MISC.CRIMES	FR.
LUMD, Theo	300511	M	Ger.		Cpl.01.512 K.Marine Inf.of Waffen SS,Cotes-du-Nord(Fr.)6.-7.44	MURDER	FR.
LUNENSCHLOSS	139037	M	Ger.		Betriebsleiter,SS Totenkopf,Riga(Lat.)43	MURDER	U.S.
LUNG	256928	M	Ger.		O.T.,Muhldorf(Ger.)	WITNESS	U.S.
LUNGWITZ	141361	M	Ger.	07	Lagerfhr.Organisation Todt,St.Heller(Jersey)42-44	TORTURE	U.K.
LUNKENHEIMER	160383	M	Ger.	05	Cpl.SS Wirtschafts-Verw.Hauptamt,CC Ohrdruf(Ger.)	TORTURE	U.S.
LUNNOW, Arthur	152826	M			Kreisobmann,D.A.F.Poppentin(Ger.)7.-8.44	MURDER	U.S.
LUNOW	192726	M			Pvt.Bau Pi.Bn.429,2 Coy.	MURDER	NOR.
LUMSDORF, Willy	185142	M	Ger.		Medecin,SS CC Sachsenhausen(Ger.)	MURDER	FR.
LUNTZ, Oskar	150534	M	Ger.		Pvt.Army(Ger.)11.44-1.45	MISC.CRIMES	U.S.
LUMY	260115	M	Ger.		Major,157 Bavarian Div.d.Res.Massif du Vercors,Isere and Drôme(Fr.) 20.7.-5.8.44	SUSPECT	FR.
LUPPE, Ludwig	252257	M			QMS,Major,German Paratrooper Regt.	MURDER	U.S.
LUPPERMAN ("Jew Killer")	140792	M			Capt.Wehrbezirkskommando SS CC Linz-Donau(Aust.)	MURDER	U.S.
LUPPERT, Paul	192396	M	Ger.		Asst.Capo,CC Flossenburg(Ger.)5.44-4.45	MURDER	U.S.BEL.
LURCH, Selmar	192727	M	Ger.	80	Lt.Col.Kommandeur,Kgf.Arb.Bn.186(Nor.)	MISC.CRIMES	NOR.
LURKER, Otto	173683	M	Ger.		Standartenfhr.Gestapo,SS CC Maribor(Yugo.)41-45	MURDER	YUGO.
LURS	125686	M	Ger.		Lt.Fallschirm Pio.Ers.Bn.S.F.N.49925,Montaron,Vandenesse(Fr.)10.-11.7.44	MURDER	FR.
LURZ, Wilhelm	255149	M	Ger.	05	Oberwachtmeister,Schutzpolizei,Prague-Kobylisy(Czech.)41	MURDER	CZECH.
LUST	67572	M			SS Kanonier,SS Div.Fp.48963B,Chateau-Contien,St.Sulpice,Montmusson (Fr.)6.8.44	MURDER	FR.
LUST see LUTZ	255559						
LUST, Fritz	195177	M	Ger.		Uschafhr.SS Leibstandarte Adolf Hitler,Wermbrandt(Bel.)27.5.44	WITNESS	U.K.
LUSWICZAK, Josef	256770	M		12. 3.09	Factory worker,Camp Dora,Nordhausen(Ger.)	MURDER	U.S.
LUTCHEIMEIRER	177533	M	Ger.		Camp Official,CC Neuengamme(Ger.)	MURDER	UNWCC
LUTFER	31941	M	Ger.		Stabsfeldwebel,Police,Feldgendarmerie,Gestapo,Josselin(Fr.)44	MURDER	FR.
LUTGEMEIER, Albert	122477	M	Ger.		Osturmfhr.SS CC Neuengamme(Ger.)42	MURDER	BEL.
LUTH	301538	M	Ger.		SS Uschafhr.CC Buchenwald(Ger.)16.5.38-9.10.43	MURDER	BEL.
LUTH see LIEDO, Elisabeth	306098						
LUTHER	120616	M	Ger.		Cpl.Arbeitskommando,Land.Schtz.Bn.396,Stalag IV A,CC.Groditz(Ger.) 11.44-4.45	TORTURE	U.K.
LUTHER, Martin	134906	M	Ger.	95	Standartenfhr.S.A.(Pol.)39-43	WITNESS	U.S.
LUTHER, Stephan	254858	M	Ger.		Factory-Manager,Civilian,Lutin(Czech.)42-45	PILLAGE	CZECH.
LUTHERDT, Albin	12535	M	Ger.		Pvt.110 or 111 Panz.Gren.Regt.2 Coy.,Albine(Fr.)29.6.44	MURDER	FR.
LUTJENS, Alfred	29769	M	Ger.		Hptsturmfhr.SS,Lons-de-Saulnier(Fr.)9.44	MURDER	FR.
LUTKE	253139	M	Ger.		Uschafhr.Plateau des Glieres(Fr.)22.3.-5.4.44	MISC.CRIMES	FR.
LUTKEMEIER see LIEDTKEMEIER	251701						
LUTKEMEYER	252255	M	Ger.		CC Neuengamme(Ger.)	MURDER	BEL.
LUTSCHER	130698	M	Ger.		Uschafhr.SS Totenkopf,CC Mauthausen(Aust.)41-45	MURDER	U.S.
LUTT, Peter	31510	M	Ger.		Pvt.Army,2 Regt.F.N.O.,Loomine(Fr.)	MURDER	FR.
LUTTGEMEINER, Moritz	189778	M		16	SS Osturmfhr.CC Neuengamme(Ger.)11.42-11.43	MURDER	YUGO.
LUTTGENMEYER or LULTGEA- MEYER	133290	M			SS Osturmfhr.CC Neuengamme,Hannover,Gardslegen(Ger.)44-45	MURDER	U.S.
LUTZEE, Ernst	188380	M	Ger.		Pvt.Heeres Kuest.Art.Abt.1240 Bn.,Ostduinkerke(Bel.)8.9.44	MURDER	BEL.
LUTZ	130639	M			Kapo,CC Mauthausen(Aust.)41-45	MURDER	U.S.
LUTZ	132556		Ger.		Kapo,CC Neuengamme(Ger.)	TORTURE	FR.
LUTZ	173748	M	Ger.		Hptscharfhr.SS,CC Neckarelz(Ger.)	TORTURE	U.S.
LUTZ	252377	M	Ger.		SS Oschafhr.Flossenburg(Ger.)43-45	MURDER	BEL.
LUTZ	253870	M	Ger.		W.O.,Feldgendarmerie of Bourgoin,Salagnon(Fr.)15.2.44	MURDER	FR.
LUTZ	254402	M	Ger.		Lt.1/98 Gebirgs Regt.,Le Chablais(Fr.)19.-21.5.44	MISC.CRIMES	FR.
LUTZ	254855	M	Ger.		Lt.Airforce,77 Combat-Unit,Seguret,Vaison(Fr.)10.6.44	MURDER	FR.
LUTZ or LUST	255559	M	Ger.		Lt.,Neckargerach(Ger.)	WITNESS	FR.
LUTZ	255560	M	Ger.		Sgt.Chief,of mining,Neckargerach(Ger.)	BRUTALITY	FR.
LUTZ	260105	M	Ger.		Camp Guard,CC Dachau(Ger.)43-44	MURDER	FR.
LUTZ	305458	M	Ger.		On staff of CC Buchenwald(Ger.)42-45	MURDER	FR.
LUTZ, Friedrich	260530	M	Ger.	14.10.98	SS Guard,CC Natzweiler(Fr.)	MURDER	U.S.
LUTZ, Karl	250347	M	Ger.	04	Rottenfhr.SS,CC Harzungen,Nordhausen(Ger.)	PILLAGE	U.S.
LUTZE	253871	M	Ger.		Lt.,Vittel(Fr.)		FR.

NAME	C.R.FILE NUMBER	SEX	NATIO-NALITY	DATE OF BIRTH	RANK OCCUPATION UNIT PLACE AND DATE OF CRIME	REASON WANTED	WANTED BY
LUTZE	301639		Ger.		Erbrach near Amberg (Ger.) 45	MURDER	CZECH.
LUTZE, Alfred	306457	M	Ger.		Scharfhr.,C.C.,SS, Buchenwald (Ger.) 5.38 - 10.43	MURDER	BEL.
LUTZE, Eberhard	306566	M	Ger.		Dr., Konservator,Later Director, Stadt.Art.Collection Nuernberg, Cracow (Pol.) 10.39 - 3.40	PILLAGE	POL.
LUTZMANN, Johann	301348	M	Ger.		Pvt., Servise of the Gast at Loguivy de la Mer, nr.Paim-Pol Cotes-du-Nord (Fr.) 14.2.45	PILLAGE	FR.
LUTZWEILLER, Gustav	142115	M			Guard, C.C., Mauthausen (Aust.)	TORTURE	FR.
LUUZ (or LOUZ)	6117	M	Ger.		Pvt., Pz.-Jaeger-Ers.7.Btty.14.Coy.,Bauges (Fr.) 44	MURDER	FR.
LUWKE, Joseph (or LIOTKE)	29768	M	Ger.		Hauptscharfhr.,Gestapo, Lyon,Grenoble,Lons le Saunier (Fr.) 9.44	MURDER	FR.
LUX	189408	M			Guard, Prison C.C.,Tromsoya (Nor.) 18.6.42	TORTURE	NOR.
LUX, Paul,Gert	138204	M	Ger.		Employee, a la Mairie Daimler-Benz a Colmar,Reichshof (Pol.) 40 - 41	MURDER	POL.
LUX, Peter	191375	M	Ger.		Oberwachtmeister,10 Coy, 3 Pol.Btn., 7 Pol.Rgt.,Junkerdal(Nor.)10.44	MURDER	NOR.
LUY, Peter	195439	M	Ger.	31. 1.84	Administration of OCC. Territoris,Luxenburg (Lux.) 45	LOOTING	LUX.
LUZECA, Emil	192728	M	Ger.		Pvt., Army (Nor.)	MISC.CRIMES	NOR.
LWJYROFF	252452	M	Ger.or Russ.		Lt., 190 Legion Armenienne, Chanac (Fr.) 16.8.44	PILLAGE	FR.
LYDORF, Kurt	195438	M	Ger.	20. 7.20	Occupied Territories,Luxenburg (Lux.) 45	LOOTING	LUX.
LYKLEMA (see NYKLEMA)	307190						
LYNEN	179826	M	Ger.		SS-Mann, Waffen SS, Panz.-Div. "Adolf Hitler" Parfondruy-Stavelot (Bel.) 12.44	MURDER	U.S.
LYTGEMAYER	132473	M	Ger.		Obersturmbannfhr., C.C. Neuengamme,Hannover (Ger.)	TORTURE	U.K.

AAR - BUT

NAME	C.R.FILE NUMBER	SEX	NATIO-NALITY	DATE OF BIRTH	ALL AVAILABLE INFORMATION AS TO THE RANK, OCCUPATION (CIVIL, PARTY OR MILITARY), PARTICULARS OF CRIME AND PHYSICAL DESCRIPTION - IF KNOWN.	WANTED BY
AARON, H.E.	259488	M			S-Sgt. Wanted as witness at Wolfsberg (Ger.) on June 29, 44.	U.S.
ACHTERT	259017	M		96	Sgt. Murder at Parchim (Ger.) on March 45.	U.S.
ADAM	196300	M	Ger.		Guard or Kapo. Responsible for tortures and massacres of Belgian prisoners at Gusen-camp.	BEL.
AERENS	250024	M	Ger.		Ill-treatment of Belgian civilians in the Hagen jail.	BEL.
ALBRECHT, Wilhelm	250608	M			Pvt. (Perpetrator). Murder and atrocities at Nordhausen, Camp Ellrich.	U.S.
AMBORN	163437	M			Murder of a Jewish woman. The authors of the crime are two brothers, sons of Cristopher Amborn, of Monsheim.	FR.
ANDELMANN, Rudi	257188	M	Ger.		Murder, Givenville (Fr.) betw. June 44 and May 45.	U.S.
ANDES, Heinrich	196161	M	Ger.	25. 3.03	Wanted as a war criminal. Pillage of Luxembourg properties.	LUX.
APPE	259011	M			Headmaster, Daimler-Benz-Werke. Wanted for the hanging and beating of Polish PW's, at the Daimler-Benz, Mannheim, American Zone of Germany, on Sept.44	U.S.
ARIESS	195888	M	Ger.		Wanted for alleged atrocities committed in Struthof C.C. at Natzweiler.	FR.
ARMBRUSTER	195887	M	Ger.		Employee. Wanted for alleged atrocities committed at Shirmeck C.C. 40-44	FR.
BACH	135134	M	Ger.		Kriminalrat, Gestapo, Hqs, Koeln. Suspect.	U.S.
BACHMANN	257585	M	Ger.		Member of garrison. Bachmann and Caminsky were members of the garrison of the Island of Sein. On the 4th of August 1944, at 20.30, acting on the orders of the Lt. Landes, of Lorient, they fired explosive charges, and blew up the two light-houses and power stations of the island. This was accomplished without reference to any war necessity.	FR.
BAEG, Yvonne	250073	F	Ger.		Interpreter at Abteilung IV A Sipo, Brussels. Suspect.	BEL.
BAHNSAMER, Karl	250060	M			Wanted for the beating with a rifle of Damaso M. Galindo, an American prisoner of war, at a prison camp in Kreis Stolp, in what is now Poland, on 15.Nov.44	U.S.
BALDAMUS, Willibald	250064	M	Ger.		Subject is responsible for shooting of 11 Slovak nationals in Nov.44 at Cepcin and Turcek in Slovakia (Suspect).	CZECH.
BALTHASAR, Edouard	258863	M	Ger.	9. 2.09	Wanted as a war criminal. Denunciations of Luxembourg subjects. Grand-Duchy Luxembourg. 40-45	LUX.
BARDIX	250043	M			Murder and atrocities at Nordhausen, Camp Rottleberode. (Perpetrator.)	U.S.
BARDOK	250044	M			Murder and atrocities at Nordhausen, Camp Dora. (Perpetrator.)	U.S.
BARON	196131	M			Kapo. Wanted for the torture of inmates of Dachau Concentration Camp, Germany in 1944. Subject, one of the camp's capos, worked in the camp hospital, where he cruelly beat the sick patients.	POL.
BARTHEL, Otto	259420	M			Wanted as a witness to the alleged murder of 2 or 3 American airmen in the vicinity of Mansfeld, March 44.	U.S.
BARTOSZYNSKI, Josef	168598	M			Pvt., Army, 1.Coy, M.G.Schutz. 4, 9.Gfen.Ers.Regt. last Unit: 8.Gren.Ers.Regt.9 Date of crime: 18.9.44. Town of crime: Magny-Danigon. Murder.	FR.
BAST, Rudolf	196130	M		21. 4.80	Dr. Lawyer. Wanted for the assult which resulted in great bodily harm to 12-15 American airmen by a mob of German citizens between 16.30 and 18.00 hrs. on 20 March 1945 on the market square of Amstetten, Austria in the Russian Zone of Austria. Last known residence: Marcus Orr, Salzburg. (Suspect)	U.S.
BECKER, Adam	259318	M			Wanted for participation in the murder of an American airman and the believed murder of three other airmen. Area of Bechtheim (Ger.) betw.Sept. and Dec.44	U.S.
BECKER, Emil (Nickname: Grand Mmile)	252260	M	Ger.		Suspected of having killed Mr. Gauthier, at Erquy (Cotes du Nord) on June 23, 1944.	FR.
BERG	259750	M	Ger.		Wanted for the murder of 2 young people at Rives in June, 1944.	FR.
BERKNER	253570	M	Ger.		Author of slaughters, arson, pillaging and deportations, committed in Chateau-villain on 24. of August 1944.	FR.
BEUTNER, Max	262139	M	Ger.	24. 2.09	Wanted for the murder of countless number of American soldiers in the Malmedy-area of Belgium.	U.S.
BIERMANN-RATJEN, Ernest	259285	M			Wanted as a witness to the murder of an unknown American airman. Martin Camp (Fr.)	U.S.
BILDGEN, Reinhard Jacques	258862	M	Ger.	10. 8.15	Denunciations of Luxembourg subjects. Grand-Duchy Luxembourg, 40-45.	LUX.
BOEHM, Franz	251986	M	Ger.	18. 7.09	Subject is responsible for destruction of a factory at Rosice, Czechoslovakia, in May 1945 before the end of the war. He is living at Zwickau, Leipzigerstr.46, III, with Family Kolbe, Russian Zone.	CZECH.
BODIACHER, Stephen	261229	M			Murder and atrocities at Buchenwald C.C.	U.S.
BOSEL, Friedrich	259299	M			Town Mayor. Lives at No.36 Hoheleiterstrasse, Leimbach (Ger.) Russian Zone. Wanted as witness to the alleged murder of 2 or 3 American airmen at Mansfeld area on March 44.	U.S.
BRANDSTEDT, Eberhard	196174	M	Ger.		SS-Sturmfhr. Looting of Luxembourg properties.	LUX.
BRAUN, Otto	255262	M	Ger.		Police-clerk. Wanted for alleged mistreatment, torture and deportation of prisoners. Subject was an employee of Gestapo in Opava and in this capacity is alleged to have committed the above mentioned crimes and even caused the death of many Czech. political prisoners. (Suspect)	CZECH.
BRAUNER	259548	M	Ger.		Dr. Wanted as witness. Murder of an American airman; believed to be Sidney L. Neuson, at Wolfsburg (Ger.) on June 29, 44.	U.S.
BREDOW, Alexis	261212	M	Ger.		Murder. Execution of 20 hostages, at Gosselies, on August 24, 1944.	BEL.
BRUGGER	257183	M	Ger.		Sgt. Wanted for the alleged murder of eleven unknown American PW's. Hoefle (FNU) General gave the order to shoot them, on or about April 1945. The killing occured about 2 km from at Theben-Neudorf (Aust.). Witness.	U.S.
BRUMBERGER	195857	M	Ger.		Employee at C.C.Struthof-Natzweiler. Atrocities committed at C.C.Struthof-Natz-weiler.	FR.
BUERGIN, Christian	254289	M	Ger.		Frontier-guard. Member of the Nazi-Party. Suspected of having ill-treated Belgian-workers. District of Lorrach-Dreilaendereck.	BEL.
BUGAJ, Nikita	259470	M			Witness lives at Mainz-Kastel (Ger.) (DP Camp). Wanted as a witness to the murder of an American airman after he was wounded at Burg (Ger.) on February 45.	U.S.
BURBACH, Gustav	259751	M	Ger.		Murder of P.o.W. Guibert at Stalag XII D.	FR.
BURGHARD, Karl (see STRAKA, Engelbert)	251349	M	Ger.	9. 9.21	Suspect.	CZECH.
BURGHARDT, Gustav	261086	M	Ger.		Mistreatment of French Slave Labourers at Sossenheim (Ger.) from 43 to 45.	FR.
BUSCH	254269	M	Ger.		Murders, plunder and arson in the village of "La Trouche" from October 6 to October 9, 1944. His father was a director of the opera in Berlin. His brother is a great musician.	FR.
BUTTENS, Ferdinand	196176	M			Wanted as a witness for the murder of an unknown American airman, by beating to death at Berlin-Reinickendorf-West, on or about 21 June 1944. Witness was the informant in this case. Home address: Berlin-Reinickendorf-West, Eichborrdarw92	U.S.

THE CENTRAL REGISTRY OF WAR CRIMINALS AND SECURITY SUSPECTS

CONSOLIDATED WANTED LIST — PART 1
(M – Z)

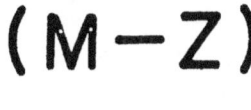

GERMANS ONLY

NOTE: ALL PREVIOUS CROWCASS WANTED LISTS SHOULD BE DESTROYED

CROWCASS
ALLIED CONTROL AUTHORITY
APO 742,
U.S. ARMY

TELEPHONE: BERLIN (TEMPELHOF) 5336, 5775
TELEPRINTER: BERLIN / STATION DHBP.

MARCH 1947

INDEX.

	PAGE.
FRONTISPIECE.	(i)
CONCERNING THE UNITED NATIONS WAR CRIMES COMMISSION.	(ii)
NAMES COMMENCING WITH LETTER - M	1
N	34
O	42
P	44
Q	66
R	66
S	91
T	150
U	169
V	172
W	184
X	214
Y	214
Z	215
NAMES ESPECIALLY LISTED UNDER DIFFERENT HEADINGS (M-Z)	224
APPENDIX - 'A': TABLE SHOWING TOTAL NUMBERS OF PERSONS LISTED IN CONSOLIDATED WANTED LIST, PART I (GERMANS), AS WANTED BY EACH OF THE ALLIED NATIONS.	230
APPENDIX - 'B': PERSONS LISTED AS WANTED IN CONSOLIDATED WANTED LIST, PART I (GERMANS) AND NOW EITHER DETAINED OR NO LONGER WANTED.	231

ABBREVIATIONS OF COUNTRIES.

UNITED STATES OF AMERICA	U.S.	GREECE	GRC.
GREAT BRITAIN (UNITED KINGDOM)	U.K.	ITALY	IT.
		FINLAND	FIN.
FRANCE	FR.	HUNGARY	HUNG.
SOVIET UNION (RUSSIA)	SOV.UN.	AUSTRIA	AUST.
BELGIUM	BEL.	CANADA	CAN.
HOLLAND (NETHERLANDS)	NETH.	AUSTRALIA	AUSTL.
POLAND	POL.	NEW ZEALAND	N.Z.
DENMARK	DEN.	SOUTH AFRICA	S.A.
NORWAY	NOR.	UKRAINE	UKR.
CZECHOSLOVAKIA	CZECH.	SLOVENIA	SLOV.
LUXEMBOURG	LUX.	ROUMANIA	RUM.
YUGOSLAVIA	YUGO.	LATVIA	LATV.
		GERMANY	GER.

GENERAL ABBREVIATIONS.

ARMY RANKS.		ARMY FORMATIONS.		GENERAL TERMS.	
PRIVATE	PVT.	SECTION	SEC.	MILITARY	MIL.
CORPORAL	CPL.	COMPANY	COY.	DIRECTOR	DIR.
SERGEANT	SGT.	BATALLION	BN.	COMMANDANT	CMDT.
NON COMMISSIONED OFFICER.	NCO.	REGIMENT	REGT.	OFFICER COMMANDING	O.C.
WARRANT OFFICER	W.O.			GENDARME	GEND.
OFFICER CANDIDATE	O/CAND.			CONCENTRATION CAMP	C.C.
LIEUTENANT	LT.			ASSISTANT	ASST.
CAPTAIN	CAPT.			SABOTAGE UNIT	SAB.
COLONEL	COL.				
GENERAL	GEN.				

SPECIAL ABBREVIATION.

L.O.D.N.A.O.D. - Locate only - do not arrest or detain.

NOTE. German Party Ranks are too numerous to list and any abbreviations used in this Publication should be easily recognisable.

CONSOLIDATED WANTED LIST (PART I - GERMANS)

IT IS IMPORTANT THAT YOU READ THIS !

1. This List is the first part of the Consolidation of the names of all persons in CROWCASS Records who are wanted in connection with War Crimes and includes all Wanted Reports received up to 31 Jan.1947 plus a few additional names not published in previous lists.

2. This list contains the names of all persons stated to be of German nationality who according to the information passed to CROWCASS are still wanted by the Allied Nations in connection with War Crimes. Persons who are stated to be of nationality other than German will be listed in the second part of this Consolidated List, which is in course of preparation and will be distributed shortly. All persons of UNKNOWN name will also be included in the second part.

3. This list also includes the names of all persons stated to be of German nationality who have been listed in the United Nations War Crimes Commission Lists Nos. 1 - 50 who, so far as CROWCASS is aware, are still wanted.

4. It is considered probable that some of the persons listed have been detained, some tried, some sentenced and others may be no longer wanted. If that is so, CROWCASS has not been informed and the various Allied Authorities who can supply such information are requested to do so immediately in order that CROWCASS Records may be adjusted. It is also possible that some Wanted Reports went astray during the move of CROWCASS from Paris to Berlin and the names are therefore not included in this list. If such is the case new Wanted Reports should be submitted immediately and the names will be published in a supplementary List.

5. Names of persons known to be detained, and where the Wanting Authority has been informed accordingly, are not included in this list.

6. It is hoped that by now all authorities receiving a copy of this List will also have received and read the pamphlet entitled "What is CROWCASS?" in order that a better understanding may be reached concerning the functions of this organization and the service given to and required from all using agencies.

7. All recipients of this List are reminded of the following requirements as previously set out in the frontispieces of CROWCASS Wanted Lists:

   (i) If any person listed should be located and detained the CROWCASS Detention Report (to be invariably submitted in respect of all Detainees) should be completed showing Reason for Arrest as "CROWCASS Consolidated Wanted List (Part i) CR.NO. ..." or "Possibly CROWCASS Consolidated Wanted List (Part i) CR.NO. ...". If a Wanted Person is located only and not detained as full a description as possible of the person located should be set out in letter form and forwarded to CROWCASS including the reason for non-detention.

   (ii) In the event of CROWCASS thus receiving information of a match or possible match between a Wanted Person and a Detained or located Person the wanting nation is immediately informed, even although the Detainee may be held in the custody of that nation. In some cases where the persons name has not been listed by the UNWCC and where extradition is applied for considerable delay may be unavoidable. (See page (ii)). If and when the extradition of a CROWCASS Wanted Personality has taken place CROWCASS should be informed immediately.

   (iii) If a Detaining Authority receives instructions to Release or Transfer any Detainee who is possibly or definitely a CROWCASS Wanted Personality a check should first be made with that Authority's War Crimes Group HQ. and a copy of the communication endorsed to CROWCASS.

   (iv) The information given in this list about each person is all that is contained on the Wanted Reports filed with CROWCASS The descriptions given are not summaries.

8. It is particulary requested that the War Crimes HQ.'s of all the Allied Nations endeavour to make special arrangements to have this List distributed to all Detaining Authorities, Prisoner of War Information Bureaus (or the equivalent) and all other HQ.'s or Formations which may be albe to assist in locating the persons listed.

9. No doubt the Inter-Allied National policy as regards the probable duration of the Investigation of War Crimes will depend to quite a considerable extent upon the number of Alleged War Criminals "still at large" in the sense of not being in the custody of the nation who wants them. To help to reduce this period of duration and the enormous expenditure and man power involved all Allied Nations are again requested to exploit every means within their power to reduce this List as quickly as possible.

10. Pages 224 to 229 of Volume M-Z include the names of persons (also M-Z), especially listed under different headings owing to a lack of detailed information suitable for listing under the normal headings.

11. At Appendix "A" will be found a table showing the total number of persons included in this List who are wanted by each of the Allied Nations.

12. At Appendix "B" will be found a list of persons (herein listed as wanted) regarding whom Detention Reports have been received since the preparation of this List for publication was commenced.

13. CROWCASS has a teleprinter station in its office. It is "Station DHPB - Berlin". Using agencies are requested to make use of it as it greatly speeds up replies to requests for information.

14. CROWCASS holds large stocks of Blank Wanted and Detention Reports and they can be had on application by TPM, Signal or letter.

15. Whilst every effort has been made to eliminate error from this List there may still be left a few discrepancies which although unavoidable are regretted.

CONCERNING THE UNITED NATIONS WAR CRIMES COMMISSION.

The following is quoted from Section X of Information Paper No. 1 issued by the Reference Division of the United Nations Information Organisation, London:

INTER-ALLIED DECLARATION OF DECEMBER 17, 1942

On December 17, 1942, a Declaration was made simultaneously in London, Moscow, and Washington in connection with reports that the German authorities were engaged in exterminating the Jewish people in Europe. In this Declaration, the Governments of Belgium, Czechoslovakia, Greece, Luxembourg, the Netherlands, Norway, Poland, the United States of America, the United Kingdom, the Soviet Union and Yugoslavia and the French National Committee reaffirmed their solemn resolution that those responsible should not escape retribution and their intention to press on with the necessary practical measures to that end.

There was some delay in setting up the United Nations War Crimes Commission, but it was eventually brought into being by a meeting of Government representatives at the British Foreign Office on October 20, 1943.

COMPOSITION OF THE COMMISSION

The Commission consists of seventeen members: the representatives of the Governments of Australia, Belgium, Canada, China, Czechoslovakia, Denmark, France, Greece, India, Luxembourg, the Netherlands, New Zealand, Norway, Poland, the United Kingdom, the United States of America and Yugoslavia. The representatives are all distinguished lawyers or diplomats.

If a representative is unable to act, or for some other special reason, he may be replaced.

The Commission may hear experts.

The first Chairman was the United Kingdom representative, Sir Cecil Hurst, Vice-President of the Permanent Court of International Justice, formerly legal Adviser to the Foreign Office. After his resignation on account of illhealth, he was replaced by the Right Hon. Lord Wright, Lord of Appeal in Ordinary, who represents Australia on the Commission. Lord Wright has been Chairman since January 31, 1945.

TERMS OF REFERENCE OF THE COMMISSION

The Commission has limited functions. It is primarily a fact-finding body, though it has also advisory functions.

Its terms of reference were defined in the Lord Chancellor's statement of October 7, 1942. Its purpose, he said is to investigate war crimes committed against nationals of the United Nations, recording the testimony available, and to report from time to time to the Governments of those nations cases in which such crimes appear to have been committed, naming and identifying wherever possible the persons responsible.

After its creation, it was entrusted with advisory functions, namely to make recommendations to the Governments on the methods to be adopted to ensure the surrender or capture of the persons wanted for trial as war criminals and on the tribunals by which they should be tried.

HOW THE COMMISSION OPERATES

The United Nations War Crimes Commission prepares lists of war criminals on the basis of evidence submitted by National War Crimes Offices which have been set up to detect, investigate and record evidence of war crimes committed against the citizens or subjects of their own countries.

The lists are furnished to the apprehending authorities - at present the military authorities - in order that the persons accused of crimes against people or property may be sent back to the country against which they have offended. This was the procedure contemplated in the Moscow Declaration on Atrocities by President Roosevelt, Mr. Winston Churchill and Marshal Stalin which was issued on November 1, 1943 and by the Foreign Secretaries of their three countries, who had been attending the Moscow Conference of October 16 to 30.

After referring to the atrocities, massacres and mass executions which were being perpetrated by the Hitlerite forces, the Declaration said:

"The United Kingdom, the United States and the Soviet Union ....

"... speaking in the interests of the thirty-two United Nations ... solemnly declare and give full warning of their declaration as follows: At the time of the granting of any armistice to any Government which may be set up in Germany, those German officers and men and members of the Nazi Party who have been responsible for or who have taken a consenting part in the above atrocities, massacres and executions will be sent back to the countries in which their abominable deeds were done in order that they many be judged and punished according to the laws of these liberated countries and of the Free Governments which will be erected therein. Lists will be compiled in all possible detail from all these countries ..."

Offences against members of the Allied armed forces will be dealt with summarily by military courts, in accordance with international custom.

The following is a Statement issued by UNWCC especially for incorporation in this Consolidated Wanted List:

"All Allied Authorities concerned are reminded that in order to secure extradition they should submit to the United Nations War Crimes Commission in London dossiers with charges concerning the offences committed by persons wanted. The United Nations War Crimes Commission in accordance with its terms of reference decides whether there appears to be either prima facie evidence sufficient to justify the handing over for trial of individuals accused of War Crimes or else sufficient ground to consider the wanted persons as suspects or material witnesses"

MAA-MAE

NAME	C.R.FILE NUMBER	SEX	NATIO-NALITY	DATE OF BIRTH	RANK OCCUPATION UNIT PLACE AND DATE OF CRIME	REASON WANTED	WANTED BY
MAACK, Paul	193762	M	Ger.		Betriebs-Asst., Staatspolizei (administration) Dept. II, Trandum (Nor.) 43	MURDER	NOR.
MAAG	141579	M	Ger.		SS (Fr.) 40-45	MISC.CRIMES	FR.
MAAG	251147	M	Ger.	00	Usturmfhr., Gestapo-SS, Paris (Fr.) 41-44	INTERR.	FR.
MAAG, Wilhelm	260547	M	Ger.	4.12.92	District Farm Leader, Reihen (Ger.) 40-45	BRUTALITY	POL.
MAAR, Josef	183693	M			SS-Rottenfhr., Guard, 4.SS Totenkopf-Sturmbann, C.C. Dora, Nordhausen, Monowitz (Ger., Pol.)	TORTURE	U.S.
MAAS	183702	M			SS-Mann, Guard, 4. Totenkopf-Sturmbann, C.C. Dora, Nordhausen (Ger.) 43-45	WITNESS	U.S.
MAAS	253255	M			Uscharfhr., C.C. Dora, Nordhausen (Ger.)	MURDER	U.S.
MAAS	306099	M	Ger.		Uscharfhr., SS, C.C. Hamburg-Neuengamme (Ger.) 45	MURDER	CZECH.
MAAS, Joseph	135534	M	Ger.		Civilian, Effern (Ger.) 10.44	BRUTALITY	U.S.
MAASS	188452	M	Ger.		Hptsturmfhr., SS Leibstandarte "Adolf Hitler", Nachschubkommando, Bautzen (Ger.) 1.44	MURDER	U.K.
MAASS	301849	M	Ger.		Gauamtsleiter, Amt fuer Rassenpolitik, Strassburg (Fr.) 44	BRUTALITY	FR.
MAASS, Herbert	132241	M	Ger.	16. 5.93	Lt.Col., 50. Inf.Regt., Staff-Officer, Stalag 7 A Moosberg (Ger.) 10.44	MURDER	U.S.
MAASSE, Willi	254457	M	Ger.	2.11.14	Rayon-Inspector, 44.Kraftfahr-Staffel, 20.Pol.Regt., Lidice (Czech.)6.42	MURDER	CZECH.
MAAT (or TER MAAT)	305036				Camp-Leader, Hospital Camp at Vrasselt, Punishment Camp at Rees, Vrasselt, Emmerich, Wijnbergen (Neth.) 10.44-3.45	MISC.CRIMES	NETH.
MAATZ, Ernst	194440	M	Ger.		Schupo, C.C. Falstad (Nor.) 41-44	MURDER	NOR.
MACH	173803	M	Ger.		Osturmfhr., SS-Gestapo, Maribor (Yugo.) 4.41-44	MURDER	YUGO.
MACH	173804	M	Ger.		Major, Army, Cmdt. of 4. Don Regt., Croatia (Yugo.) 11.43-8.44	MURDER	YUGO.
MACHATCHEK	306125	M	Ger.		Scharfhr. of the Kommando of Angers Gestapo, Allarmont, Vosges, St-Die, (Fr.) 9.44	MURDER	FR.
MACHE	584	M	Ger.		Osturmfhr., SS Gren.Regt. "Deutschland", 16.Coy., Aussone (Fr.) 5.44	MURDER	FR.
MACHEINER, Christine	190377	F	Ger.		Clerk, Gestapo, Brno (Czech.)39-45	WITNESS	CZECH.
MACHENIKE (see KACHENIKE)Josef	434						
MACHER, Peter	189093			17	Crim.Commissar, Gestapo, Tomazow, Mazowiki (Pol.) 6.42	MURDER	U.K.
MACHEWSKI	256687	M	Ger.		Stabsarzt, German Military Hospital, Trondheim (Nor.)	BRUTALITY	NOR.
MACHHEIM	157025	M	Ger.		Rottenfhr., 1.SS Panzer Div., 2.Regt., 3.Bn., 12.Coy., Stavelot-Malmedy (Bel.) 12.44	MURDER	U.S.
MACHIAK (or MALCHIA)	132467	M	Ger.		N.C.O., SS, Neunkirchen (Ger.)	MURDER	U.S.
MACHINSON (or MACKENSON)	67818	M			Capt., Army, O.C. 1-714 Coy. H.Q. Kulmsee Westpr. 1.-2.45	MURDER	U.K.
MACHISON (see MACKASEN)	104843						
MACHNER	257582	M	Ger.		Lt., Geh.Feldpolizei, Benet, Niort (Fr.) 3.44	TORTURE	FR.
MACHOLD, Ernst	253256				Pvt., C.C. Ellrich, Nordhausen (Ger.)	MURDER	U.S.
MACHON	300816	M	Ger.		Pvt., 3.Coy., 2.Bn., 15.Africa-Div. 1.Aufkl.Abt., St. Leger (Bel.) 9.44	MURDER	BEL.
MACHULE	173802	M	Ger.		Dr. Gestapo-Official, Maribor (Yugo.) 4.41-44	MURDER	YUGO.
MACIEVSKY, Kumibert	301069	M	Ger.		Oberarbeitsarzt, Reichsarbeitsdienst, Marianske, Lazne, Bohemia (Czech.) 42-44	INTERR.	CZECH.
MACK	1720	M			Lt., Feldgendarmerie-Cmdt.	TORTURE	U.K.
MACK	183695	M			Sturmmann, Camp-Guard, 4.SS Totenkopf-Sturmbann, C.C. Dora, Nordhausen, Auschwitz (Ger., Pol.) 43-45	WITNESS	U.S.
MACK	196017	M	Ger.		SS-Usturmfhr., Sipo, C.C. Westerbork (Neth.) 9.-12.44	MURDER	NETH.
MACK	254460	M	Ger.		Lt., Feldgendarmerie, Acheux en Amienois (Fr.) 8.44	TORTURE	FR.
MACK, Albert	170066	M	Ger.	21	Lt., SS-H.Q., 4.Coy., Vipetero (Italy) 7.44	WITNESS	U.S.
MACK, Edward	251132	M	Ger.		Usturmfhr., SS, N.C.O.-School, Radolfzell (Ger.) 7.44	SUSPECT	U.S.
MACK, Willy	253262	M	Ger.		Hptscharfhr., S.D., Zeist (Neth.)	MURDER	NETH.
MACKASEN (or MACHISON)	104843	M	Ger.		Capt., Army, 714.Inf.Bn., Stettin to Brandenburg (Ger.) 2.-3.45	MURDER	U.S.
MACKE	121209	M	Ger.		Lt., I.SS. Div."Adolf Hitler", Coulonges (Fr.) 6.44	MURDER	FR.
MACKEL, Hans	254459	M	Ger.		SS-Oschfhr., S.D., Toulouse (Fr.)	MISC.CRIMES	FR.
MACKENSEN, Adolf	126573	M	Ger.	26. 5.86	Pvt., Air Force, Seesen (Ger.) 6.44	MURDER	U.S.
MACKENSON	39847	M			Capt., Cmdt. at Fort XVII Krs.Kulm, 1.Coy., 714.Landesschuetzen-Bn., Marienburg, Thorn, Lichnau, Krs.Kulm (Ger.,Pol.) 7.43-4.45	TORTURE	U.S.
MACKENSON (see MACHINSON)	67818						
MACKENSON, Edgar	140847	M			Lt., 3.Bn.Fallschirm-Jaeger-Regt.16, 11.Coy., Calcar (Ger.) 3.45	MURDER	CAN., U.K.
MACKERT, Alice	152110	F			Agent, Gestapo, Nice (Fr.)	TORTURE	FR.
MACKMANN (or HACKMANN)	301580	M	Ger.		SS-Lt., stationed at C.C. Mauthausen (Austria) 40-45	MURDER	BEL.
MACKS	257583	M			Member of S.A., Gratkorn (Austria) 2.45	MURDER	U.S.
MADALINSKI, Edmund	145979	M	Ger.		Sturmfhr., SS, Gestapo, Wloclawek (Pol.) 44	MURDER	POL.
MADDENACH	178755	M	Ger.		Civ., Factory-Engineer, Firm of Bohler of Kapfenburg, Marien-Martzahl (Austria) 9.43-3.45	TORTURE	U.K.
MADEL, Maria (see MANDEL)	587						
MADENACH, Hans	305557	M	Ger.	95 or 00	Techn.Engineer, Bohlers Factory, Marien-Martzpul (Austria) 10.43-4.45	MISC.CRIMES	U.K.
MADER	585	M	Ger.		Pvt., Guard, Army, C.C. Caen (Fr.) 6.44	MURDER	FR.
MADER	21335	M	Ger.		Deputy Chief of Staff Rosenberg, Looting Office (Bel.)	LOOTING	UNWCC
MADER, Franz	306458	M	Ger.		Oschfhr., SS, C.C. Buchenwald (Ger.) betw.5.38 and 10.43	MURDER	BEL.
MADER, Tony	188948	M	Ger.	06	Sgt., Feldgendarmerie, Bar le Duc (Fr.) 8.44	MURDER	FR.
MADERA (see BAUMANN)	250620						
MADLEINER	31613	M	Ger.		Capt., Jaeger-Regt.218, 7.Geb.Div., Finmark (Nor.) 10.-11.44	MURDER	NOR.
MADLENER, Anton (or MADLENES)	192269	M	Ger.	04	Army, Zinna-Torgau (Ger.) 45	WITNESS	U.S.
MADNER	194613	M	Ger.		Guard, Stalag 18-14 L, Lankewitz (Pol.) 5.42	MURDER	FR.
MADZ	251146	M	Ger.		Lt., Unit S.P. Nr.5824, Les Autels, St.-Bazile (Fr.)	INTERR.	FR.
MAECHE (or MAEKE)	188014			19	Sgt., Guard., 396.Landesschuetzen-Bn., 5.Coy., Stalag IV A, near Dresden (Ger.) 3.45	WITNESS	CAN.
MAECHETTI, Gottfried	190376	M	Ger.		Employee, Gestapo (Driver), Brno (Czech.) 39-45	WITNESS	CZECH.
MAECK	72610	M	Ger.		Major, Army, St.Die (Fr.)	MURDER	FR.
MAEHLICH	173797	M	Ger.		Pol.Director, Pol., Karloux-Vary, Oswiecim-Birkenau (Czech., Pol.) 39-45	MURDER	CZECH.
MAEHLOP, Johan Diderich	305037	M	Ger.	9. 3.06	Crim.secretary, Sicherheitsdienst Groningen and Drente (Neth.) 43-45	MURDER	NETH.
MAIER	257584	M	Ger.		Employee (Factory worker) C.C. Nordhausen (Ger.)	MURDER	U.S.
MAEKE (see MAECHE)	188014						

MAE - MAI

NAME	C.R.FILE NUMBER	SEX	NATIO-NALITY	DATE OF BIRTH	RANK OCCUPATION UNIT PLACE AND DATE OF CRIME	REASON WANTED	WANTED BY
MAEKENSEN	24833	M	Ger.		Capt.,Landesschuetzen-Bn.714,Stalag XXA,Magdeburg(Ger.) 2.-3.45	MURDER	U.K.
MAENDL, Emile	259390	M	Ger.		Rottfhr.,Gestapo of Poitiers, Poitiers Area(Fr.) 40-45	MISC.CRIMES	FR.
MAENNER	307012	M	Ger.		Baurat,Foreign Branch of Ministry of Supply, Kreis Groningen, Friesland and Drente, Meppel(Neth.) 9.44	PILLAGE	NETH.
MAENNER	307013	M	Ger.		Member of the Sicherheitsdienst,Apeldoorn District(Neth.)9.44-4.45	MURDER	NETH.
MAENNEN	194614	M	Ger.		Lt.,Gren.Ers.Regt.28,2 Bn.,Loubeas(Fr.) 5.44	MURDER	FR.
MAERKEL, Walter	156849	M	Ger.	13	Oschfhr.,C.C.Lublin(Pol.) 40-44	TORTURE	U.S.
MAERTENS	166991	M	Ger.		Sgt.,Army,Arco(Ital.)	MURDER	U.S.
MAERTENS	170067	M		00	Sgt.,H.Q.-Government Porte Olivette,Trente(Ital.) 2.45	SUSPECT	U.S.
MAERTIN, Paul	260497	M	Ger.	23.11.14	Civ.Farmer,Neusarbem Distr.Czarakow(Pol.) 39	MURDER	POL.
MAERTZ, Hermann	255057	M	Ger.	07	Civilian, Gossengrun(Czech.) 9.39	INTERR.	CZECH.
MAERTZ, Paul	38870	M			Informer for SS,Civ.Int.C.C.Sachsenhausen(Ger.) 9.41-5.43	MURDER	U.S.
MAERZ, Georges	189016	M		15	Capt.,Volunteer Regt.1,Labrespy(Fr.)	SUSPECT	FR.
MAERZ, Resl	199680	F	Ger.		Woman-Guard,Waffen-SS,Arbeitslager 101(Buchenwald),Magdeburg(Ger.)44-45	TORTURE	U.S.
MAES	163225	M	Ger.	02	Interpreter,SS, Trie Le Chateau(Fr.) 8.44	MURDER	FR.
MAESCHKE	132776	M	Ger.		Pvt.,Flak-Regt.13,13 Btty.,Quaygnon-Jemappes-Chlin(Bel.) 9.44	MURDER	BEL.
MAESER	161942	M	Ger.	14	SS-Uschfhr.,Command Staff,C.C. Buchenwald(Ger.)	WITNESS	U.S.
MAESGEN, Johann	140063	M	Ger.		Pvt.,Camp Stalag VIG,Duisdorf(Ger.) 2.45	TORTURE	U.S.
MAESSEN, Hans	132822	M	Ger.	14	Lt.,O.K.H.,Bingen(Ger.) 11.44	WITNESS	U.K.
MAETZ	127424	M	Ger.		Capt.,Military Prison Guards,Tegel(Ger.) 11.43-5.44	TORTURE	U.S.
MAEYR	257486		Ger.		Factory Worker,C.C.Nordhausen(Ger.)	MURDER	U.S.
MAEZAMA	306320		Ger.		Employee, St.Germain des Fosses (Allier),Billy(Allier)(Fr.) 8.44	PILLAGE	FR.
MAGALOFF, Georges	168012	M	Ger.	31.5.20	Officer, Sicherheits-Police,Marseille(Fr.) 4.44	PILLAGE	FR.
MAGER	255477	M	Ger.	15	Cmdt.,Fallschirm Jaeger Regt.,Alphen en Riel(Neth.) 7.-10.44	MURDER	NETH.
MAGER, Kurt	170070	M	Ger.		Kreisleiter Civilian,NSDAP-Assist.,Reifenhausen(Ger.) 8.44	TORTURE	U.S.
MAGERS, Otto or Horst	300306		Ger.		Manager,Governor of the Copais Coy.of the region of Thebe, Vrastamites,Domvraina,Hostia,Thisvy,Thebes. 41-44	MISC.CRIMES	GRC.
MAGIN, Johann	253220	M			Pvt., C.C.Ellrich, Nordhausen(Ger.)	MURDER	U.S.
MAGNER	306459	M	Ger.		SS-Staff-Sgt., Laundry,SS, C.C.Dachau(Ger.) from 43	MURDER	BEL.
MAGNET, Mathias	62510	M			Police Man.Gend.,Weiden(Ger.)	TORTURE	U.S.
MAGNUS	132765	M			Guard, SS, C.C. Mauthausen (Aust.) 41-45	MURDER	U.S.
MAGRE see MAYRE	254895						
MAGUNIA, Waldemar	55577	M	Ger.		NSDAP, Gen.-Kommissar,Kiew(Russ.)	MURDER	UNWCC.
MAHAT, Alex	185706	M	Ger.		Wachtmeister, Gestapo, Police, St.Nikolas(Grc.)	MURDER	GRC.
MAHER	301640	M	Ger.		Werkmeister, Ebrach nr.Amberg(Ger.) -45	MURDER	CZECH.
MAHKOTA, Anton	186621	M	Ger.	03	Miner,Arb.-Kdo.Adolf Mine,Merkstein(Ger.) 43	WITNESS	U.S.
MAHLER	252542	M	Ger.		Lt.,1 Inf.Bn.,977 Jaeger-Regt.,Vinkt and Meigem(Bel.) 5.40	MISC.CRIMES	BEL.
MAHLING, Friedrich	256284	M	Ger.	03	Hptwachtmeister,Prag-Kobylisy(Czech.)	MURDER	CZECH.
MAHLOW	194615	M	Ger.		Cpl.,Army,F.P.No.18132D,Beauvoir s-Mer(Fr.) 9.41	MURDER	FR.
MAHLOW see MALOW	305720						
MAHNE, Robert	257487	M	Ger.		Cpl.,Air Force-AAA,Vierheim(Ger.) 9.44	BRUTALITY	U.S.
MAHR, Ferdinand	301054	M	Ger.		Dr.,Senior Medical Officer of Ger.Military Hospital Diest,Bel., St.Joseph Hospital Diest(Bel.) 4.44	BRUTALITY	CAN.
MAHRING, Willy	300308		Ger.		Crim.-Assist.,Kongsvinger. 11.41-4.45	TORTURE	NOR.
MAHRZAHN	255053	M	Ger.		Usturmfhr.,SS Paratroops, Perriers(Fr.) 6.44	INTERR.	U.S.
MAI or MAIER	38899	M			Capt.,Army,127 Gren.Regt.,Xocourt(Fr.) 10.44	MISC.CRIMES	U.S.
MAI, Ernst	38897	M			Betriebsfhr.,Anna I Bergbau,Alsdorf(Ger.)	TORTURE	U.S.
MAI, Ernst see MAY	257488						
MAI, Karl	187773	M	Ger.	00	Civilian,Wehrden-Saar(Ger.) 8.44	TORTURE	U.S.
MAI, Mathias	137644	M	Ger.	07	Kapo, Hospital Kapo,Neuengamme(Ger.)	MURDER	U.K.
MAIBACH	194215	M			SS,C.C.,Buchenwald(Ger.) 42-45	TORTURE	U.S.
MAICK see MAREK	174698						
MAIDANSKI, Artur	253219	M			Uschfhr.,SS,C.C.Bodungen, Nordhausen(Ger.)	MURDER	U.S.
MAIER	36694	M	Ger.		Sgt.,Army,Camp-Cmdt.,Arbeits-Kdo.713,Stalag VIIIB,Kazimierz(Pol.)1.44	MISC.CRIMES	U.K.
MAIER see MAI	38899						
MAIER	58992	M			Hptsturmfhr.,12 SS Pz.Div.Hitler-Jugend	WITNESS	CAN.
MAIER	62720	M		15	Hptsturmfhr.,12 SS Pz.Div.Hitler-Jugend,Unit Quartiermeister, formerly O.C.5 Coy.,near Caen(Fr.) 6.-7.44	MURDER	CAN.
MAIER	132785	M			Fallschirm Jaeger Regt.5,Nachrichtenzug,Quaygnon-Jemappes-Chlin(Bel.) 9.44	MURDER	BEL.
MAIER see MAYER	133281						
MAIER	142557	M	Ger.	07	Oschfhr.,SS,KL.Sachsenhausen,Oranienburg(Ger.)	TORTURE	U.K.
MAIER	142558	M	Ger.	10	Dr.,SS, KL.Sachsenhausen,Oranienburg(Ger.)	TORTURE	U.K.
MAIER	148237	M	Ger.		Guard,SS,Calais,Arras,Bethune,Berk,Plage,St.Pol,Berlement,Boulogne, S-Mer,St.Omer. 43	TORTURE	FR.
MAIER	157023	M	Ger.		Kreisleiter NSDAP, Ulm(Ger.) 40-45	MURDER	U.S.
MAIER	157024	M	Ger.		Lt.-Col.,Gestapo, Brive(Fr.) 44	MURDER	FR.
MAIER	163115	M	Ger.	13	Lt.,Air Force,46 Flak Regt.,Dorsten(Ger.) 10.44	TORTURE	U.S.
MAIER	256504	M			Front-Fhr., O.T.	MURDER	U.S.
MAIER	259040	M			Sozialbetreuer O.T., Mühldorf Area(Ger.)	MURDER	U.S.
MAIER	301013	M	Ger.		Warden, Camp III,C.C. Oranienburg-Sachsenhausen(Ger.) 42-45	MURDER	FR.
MAIER or MEYER	307144	M			Landkommissar,Bourtzwiller-Haut-Rhin(Fr.) 6.40	INCENDIARISM	FR.
MAIER, Alfred	305459	M	Ger.		Stabs-Gren.Regt.694,Bourey nr.Bastogne(Lux.) 12.44	MURDER	BEL.
MAIER, Erhard	253218	M			Rottfhr.,C.C.Dora,Wieda,Nordhausen(Ger.)	MURDER	U.S.
MAIER, Ernest	259427	M	Ger.	15.7.14	Kreisleiter,Altkirch-Ht.Rhin(Fr.) 9.44	BRUTALITY	FR.
MAIER, Franz	257340	M	Ger.	7.3.98	Commissar,Field Police,Belgrade(Yugo.) 41	MISC.CRIMES	YUGO.
MAIER, Friedrich	305098	M	Ger.	12.5.01	Sgt.Sicherheits-Coy.of the XXV Festungsstamm,Pontivy,Morbihan.4.-8.44	TORTURE	FR.
MAIER, Josef	253227	M			Flyer,C.C.Ellrich, Nordhausen(Ger.)	MURDER	U.S.
MAIER, Karl	140793	M	Ger.	9.9.03	Member NSDAP,Electrician,KL.Ludwigshafen(Ger.) 1.45	TORTURE	U.S.
MAIER, Karl	253216	M			Pvt.,C.C.Ellrich, Nordhausen(Ger.)	MURDER	U.S.
MAIER, Leonhard see MAYER	142561						
MAIER, R.	38874	M	Ger.		SS-Schfhr.,SS,C.C.Struthof(Fr.)	MISC.CRIMES	FR.
MAIER, Walter	254672	M	Ger.		N.C.O.,St.Michel sur Orge(Fr.) 8.44	MURDER	FR.
MAIER, Willi	186441	M	Ger.		Civilian, Manager, Regensburg(Ger.) 41-45	MURDER	U.S.

NAME	C.R.FILE NUMBER	SEX	NATIO-NALITY	DATE OF BIRTH	RANK OCCUPATION UNIT PLACE AND DATE OF CRIME	REASON WANTED	WANTED BY
MAIERL	146766	M			Osturmfhr., SS, C.C. Flossenburg (Ger.)	TORTURE	U.S.
MAIGLER, R.	38875	M	Ger.		SS-Mann, C.C. Struthof (Fr.)	MISC.CRIMES	FR.
MAILER	132693	M	Ger.	95	Capt., aviation, C.C. Vienne (Aust.) 43-44	BRUTALITY	FR.
MAILER, Josef	156846	M	Ger.		Forrest warden, Allg.SS, Kruenn (Ger.) 7.44	TORTURE	U.S.
MAINBERG	161941	M	Ger.	85	Uscharfhr., SS, C.C. Buchenwald (Ger.)	WITNESS	U.S.
MAINER	157022	M	Ger.		W.O.-Chief,19 Rgt.,SS-Pol. Todt,4 Coy,Cran (Fr.) 6.44	MURDER	FR.
MAINHAUSEN	253553	M			Hptschfhr.C.C. Dora, Nordhausen (Ger.)	MURDER	U.S.
MAINHEAD	142030	M	Ger.		Scharfhr., Waffen-SS, Fontana-Liri (It.)12.43	MURDER	U.K.
MAINNER	185195	M	Ger.		Oscharfhr., C.C. Sachsenhausen (Ger.)	MURDER	FR.
MAINS, Helmuth	261379	M	Ger.		Lt.,Cdt of Unit II 614 Dienststelle F.P.Nr.46002, Villepinte (Fr.)8.44	MURDER	FR.
MAINSCHEIN, Paul	256502	M	Ger.		Uscharfr., SS,Med attendet Camp Rossla, Nordhausen (Ger.)	MURDER	U.S.
MAINZ, Elli	134812	F	Ger.		Woman-guard, C.C. Helmbrechts (Ger.) 7.44-4.45	WITNESS	U.S.
MAINZER	256023	M	Ger.		Uscharfhr., SS, Muhldorf (Ger.)	WITNESS	U.S.
MAINZER, Maria	135277	F	Ger.		Civilian, Efferen (Ger.) 10.44	WITNESS	U.S.
MAIR see MAYER	133281						
MAIR see MEYER	253928						
MAIS	139676	M.		05	Plant manager, W-SS, Arbeits-Kdo.A-6	MURDER	U.S.
MAISCHEIN, Paul	253556	M			Rottenfhr.,C.C.Osterode,Rottleberode,Nordhausen (Ger.)	MURDER	U.S.
MAISHIRN	301273	M	Ger.		Crim.asst. Abt.IV E, SD, Bruessel (Bel.) 6.40-9.44	MURDER	BEL.
MAITA or META	192077	M	Ger.		N.C.O., 65 Inf.Rgt.,Kerasson (Grc.) 8.44	TORTURE	GRC.
MAITSCH	173189	M			Staff at C.C. Natzweiler (Fr.) 44	INTERR.	U.K.
MAIWALD	123404	M	Ger.		Cpl., Gestapo Chambrey, Challes les Eaux et Albine (Fr.)	MURDER	FR.
MAIWALD	161940	M	Ger.	90	Usturmfhr., SS, Command Staff, C.C. Buchenwald (ger.) 45	WITNESS	U.S.
MAIWALD	195195	M			Sturmbannfhr.,Cdt.of Bn.19 Rgt., SS Pol.9, Station of Annecy, Valliery (Fr.) 6.44	MURDER	FR.
MAIWALD, Albert	250380	M	Ger.	16	Cpl., Zittau (Ger.) 3.45	MURDER	U.S.
MAIX	253552	M			Oscharfhr., C.C. Dora, Nordhausen (Ger.)	MURDER	U.S.
MAJEK	261807	M	Ger.		Cpl., Art.H.D.V.199-2255 N.D.F.,F.P.Nr.27046 C,Lorgies (Fr.) 9.44	MURDER	FR.
MAJER	145976	M		17. 2.13	Sturmmann, W-SS, Schleissheim near Munich (Ger.) 6.-9.44	MURDER	U.S.
MAJEWSKI, Erich	161939	M	Ger.	08	Dental-Techn., Civilian, C.C. Buchenwald (Ger.)	WITNESS	U.S.
MAJOR	163587	M	Ger.		Capt., Ost-Bn 654, Dun les Plages (Fr.)	MURDER	FR.
MAJOR	186143	M	Ger.		Capt., Army, Arlewf (Fr.) 8.45	MURDER	FR.
MAJOR	253156	M			C.C. Rossla, Nordhausen (Ger.)	MURDER	U.S.
MAJOR, Otto	29691	M			Dr., Vice-president, Public-official, Cheb (Czech.) 2.40	MURDER	CZECH.
MAKAWSKI, Edmund	168039	M			Pvt., Army, 9 Res.Gren.Rgt., 1 Coy, M.G.Schuetze 2, Magny-D'Anigon (Fr.) 9.44	MURDER	FR.
MAKENSEN	29766	M	Ger.		Col., Army, Perigueux (Fr.) 6.-7.44	MURDER	FR.
MAKLO, Kurt	31507	M	Ger.		Cpl., Gestapo, Feldgendarmerie, Josselin (Fr.) 44	MURDER	FR.
MAKRUTZKI, Wilhelm	253923	M	Ger.	10. 5.09	Employee, Gestapo, Litomerice (Czech.) 39-45	MISC.CRIMES	CZECH.
MAKS	259148	M	Ger.	00	Kapo, C.C. Dachau (Ger.) 44-45	MURDER	YUGO.
MAKS see MAX	62514						
MALAIKA	306308	M	Ger.		Gendarmerie-officer,attached to garrison St.Malo(Ille et Viloime) (Fr.) 8.44	PILLAGE	FR.
MALAJEW	39585	M			Pvt., Army, Pouldreuzic (Fr.) 8.44	RAPE	FR.
MALARZ	1479	M	Ger.	13	Cpl., W-SS, C.C. Dzialdowo (Pol.) 41	TORTURE	POL.,U.S.
MALAT	2692	M	Ger.		Public-official,Prag (Czech.) 40	MURDER	CZECH.
MALBIN, Josef	253157	M		27. 3.01	C.C. Harzungen, Nordhausen (Ger.)	MURDER	U.S.
MALCHIA see MACHIAK	132467						
MALDERLE	161937	M	Ger.	90	Oscharfhr., SS, guard-Rgt.,2 Coy, C.C. Buchenwald (Ger.) 40-42	WITNESS	U.S.
MALDET, Otto	146938	M			Rottenfhr.,SS-Pz.Div."Das Reich", Pz.Gren.Rgt.3 "Deutschland", Miremont (Fr.) 44	MURDER	FR.
MALESKI	141356	M	Ger.		Pvt., Army, Bautzen (Ger.) 3.45	MURDER	U.K.
MALETZI	189018	M			Oscharfhr., SS, Adjutant of SD at Annecy, St.Jeoire,Chatillon, Taninges et Balme,S-Cluses (Fr.) 6.-7.44	TORTURE	FR.
MALEY	31612	M	Ger.		Capt.,Army, Gren.Rgt.378, 169 Inf.Rgt. (Nor.)	MURDER	NOR.
MALICHEK	146172	M			Col.,Camp-commander, Stalag,Sagan (Ger.)	TORTURE	U.S.
MALICK, Mathilde	307145	F	Ger.		Guard, C.C. Auschwitz (Pol.) 40-45	BRUTALITY	POL.
MALIE, Heinz	306690	M	Ger.		Sgt., 331 Pion.Bn, 331 Inf.Div., Mijnheerenland (Neth.) 5.45	PILLAGE	NETH.
MALINA, Otto	138313	M	Ger.		N.C.O.Sgt.,Chief Member,Oscharfhr.,SS, Gestapo, Lyon (Fr.)	MURDER	FR.
MALINA, Rudolf see ANGERBAUER, Friedrich	196158						
MALINGER, Mathias	153368	M		31. 8.04	Pvt., C.C. Ellrich, Nordhausen (Ger.)	MURDER	U.S.
MALINITZ	254037	M	Ger.		Crim.secr., Sipo, Bruessel (Bel.) 40-45	INTERR.	BEL.
MALINOWSKI, Herblec	174692	M	Ger.	24.10.18	Cpl., 394 Landes-Schz.Bn, 3 Coy, Luckenwalde Kdo 726 B (Ger.) 1.44	MURDER	FR.
MALINSKI	257495	M	Ger.		C.C. Dora, Nordhausen (Ger.)	MURDER	U.S.
MALITTE	253159	M			Pvt., C.C. Dora, Nordhausen (Ger.)	MURDER	U.S.
MALITZ	163224	M	Ger.		Stalag VI C, C.C. (Ger.)	MISC.CRIMES	FR.
MALKE, Hellmuth	194128	M	Ger.	14	Sturmscharfhr., SS, Lanskroun (Czech.) 38-45	TORTURE	CZECH.
MALKOVSKY, Adolf or ZWEIN	305965	M	Ger.		Uscharfhr., C.C. Oranienburg (Ger.) 11.39-45	MURDER	CZECH.
MALL, Hermann Karl	253884	M	Ger.	1. 5.07	Employee, Gestapo, Vsetin (Czech.) 39-45	MURDER	CZECH.
MALLEHNER	261377	M			Osturmfhr., SS, Bologna (It.) 6.44	MURDER	U.S.
MALLINGER	195696	M	Ger.	05	Sgt., SS-Wirtschafts-Verwaltungs-Hauptamt, Muenchen (Ger.) 8.-9.44	WITNESS	U.S.
MALLMANN	194210	M	Ger.		Uscharfhr., SS, C.C. Buchenwald (Ger.) 42-45	MURDER	U.S.
MALLOTH, Anton	194130	M	Ger.	13. 2.12	Scharfhr.,SS Police, C.C. Terezin (Czech.) 40-45	MURDER	U.S.
MALLY	166902	M			Lt., Army, Plachy-Bruyon (Fr.) 8.-9.44	MURDER	FR.
MALMANN	161936	M	Ger.	22	Uscharfhr., SS, Command Staff, C.C. Buchenwald (Ger.)	WITNESS	U.S.
MALMANN, Anton	306460	M	Ger.	1.11.21	SS-Mann, C.C. Buchenwald (Ger.) 5.38-10.43	MURDER	BEL.
MALMENDIER	189409	M			Lt., Army, Overhalla (Nor.) 42	MURDER	NOR.
MALNOR	259846	M	Ger.		Deputy-Chief, green Police at Hague, Wassenaar,Zuid-Holland (Neth.)44	SUSPECT	NETH.
MALOW or MAHLOW	305720	M	Ger.		N.C.O.,Unit Nr.18132 D,stationed at Beauvoir-sur-Mer(Vendee), (Fr.) 9.41	MURDER	FR.
MALTE	191405	M		90	Lt., Festungs-Pionier-Stab 4, Fure (Nor.) 42-43	MISC.CRIMES	NOR.
MALTER, Richard	173901	M	Ger.	2. 6.92	Inspector, Deutscher Gemeindetag, Fuerth (Ger.) 4.45	WITNESS	U.S.
MALTER, Wilhelmine nee GUTH	254467	F	Ger.	21. 4.00	Civilian, Burbach-Saarbruecken (Ger.) 8.44	MISC.CRIMES	U.S.

MAL - MAN

-4-

NAME	C.R.FILE NUMBER	SEX	NATIO-NALITY	DATE OF BIRTH	RANK OCCUPATION UNIT PLACE AND DATE OF CRIME	REASON WANTED	WANTED BY
MALTERLE	194172	M	Ger.		Uschfar.,Guard,SS,2 Coy.,C.C.Buchenwald (Ger.) 42-45	BRUTALITY	U.S.
MALTZ,Fritz	260826	M		08	Director,G.F.F.,Recoaro Terme (Ital.) 1.45	WITNESS	U.S.
MALTZAHN,Hans Karl	305721	M	Ger.		Capt.,Commanding,285 Bn.,(Russian Cyclist),at Larmor Plage, Morbihan (Fr.) 8.44	MURDER	FR.
MALTZAIN (see MALTZHAN)	168073						
MALTZAN,Otto	142533	M	Ger.		Civ.,C.C.Hadamar (Ger.) 6.44-3.45	WITNESS	U.S.
MALTZHAN (or MATZAIM or MALTZAIN or MATZAIN)	168073	M	Ger.		Officer,Army,Roujan (Fr.)	PILLAGE	FR.
MALTZER,Kurt	300311	M			General-Lt.,Commandant of Rome,the Ardeatine Caves,Rome, 3.44	MURDER	U.K.
MAMBOORN (see MAMLHORN,Herbert)	147292						
MAMINGER	161935	M	Ger.	14	Oschfhr.,SS,Com.Staff.,C.C.Buchenwald (Ger.) 39-45	WITNESS	U.S.
MAMLHORN (or MAMBOORN,Herbert)	147292	M	Ger.		Sgt.,11.Pz.Div. (Fr.) 44	MURDER	FR.
MAMMENGA,Gustav	306709	M	Ger.		German Civ.,Borkum,Island (Ger.) 4.44	MURDER	U.S.
MAMSCH	104844	M	Ger.		Kriminal-Kommissar,Gestapo,C.C.Cuxhaven (Ger.) 3.45	MURDER	U.S.
MAND	188844	M	Ger.		Pvt.,Army,Rethouille (Fr.) 8.1.42	RAPE	FR.
MANDEL	254769	M	Ger.		Cmdt.,SS,C.C.Auschwitz,Birkenau (Ger.) 42-45	MURDER	YUGO.
MANDEL,Maria,(or MANDL or MADEL)	587	F			Chief,Woman Supervisor,C.C.Muhldorf,Auschwitz,Ravensbrueck (Pol.-Ger.) 39-45	MURDER	U.S.-FR.-CZECH.-POL.BEL.
MANDEL,Richard	191499	M	Ger.		Kapo,C.C.Sachsenhausen,Oranienburg (Ger.) 39-4.45	MURDER	POL.
MANDISSEN	300577	M	Ger.		Lt.,Army,377 Inf.Regt.,Vinkt-Meigem (Bel.) 5.40	MISC.CRIMES	Bel.
MANDL	125190	F	Ger.		SS,C.C.Auschwitz (Pol.)	MURDER	U.S.
MANDL	189020	F			Female Warder,C.C.Ravensbrueck (Ger.)	MURDER	FR.-POL.-BEL.-CZECH.
MANDL (see MAYRE)	254895						
MANDL,Erich	168040	M	Ger.		Pvt.,Army,Reserve 9 Regt.Grenadier,1 Coy.,M.G.Schuetze 2, Magny D'Anigon (Fr.) 9.44	MURDER	FR.
MANDL (see MANDEL,Maria)	587						
MANDSON	194616	M	Ger.		Head,Gestapo,Douvaine (Fr.) 7.44	MURDER	FR.
MANDT	301694	M	Ger.		05-243 Mongolian,Oberland Unit,St.Nazaire en Royans (Fr.) 7.-8.44	MURDER	FR.
MANFELD	186144	F	Ger.		Fimale Overseer,C.C.Koenigsberg (Ger.)	TORTURE	FR.
MANGELDORF,Gustav	189095	M	Ger.		Mayor,Police Chief,Bindfelde (Ger.) 4.45	MURDER	U.S.
MANGELDORFF	62511	M	Ger.		Col., Cmdt. of Stalag 9 A,Ziegenhain (Ger.) 1.-3.45	TORTURE	U.S.
MANGOLD,Kaspar	301808	M	Ger.		SS-Mann,SS-Pz.Div.1,Leibstandarte "Adolf Hitler", Region of Stavelot (Bel.) 12.44	MURDER	BEL.
MANGOLD	31502	M	Ger.		Lt.,Organ.Todt,2 Lt.,Lyon,St.Die (Fr.)	MURDER	FR.
MANHARD	194489	M	Ger.		Techn.Secr.,Gestapo,Bruenn (Czech.) 39-45	TORTURE	CZECH.
MANHARDT	253160	M			C.C.Rottleberode, Nordhausen (Ger.)	MURDER	U.S.
MANHART,Hans	132764	M		29. 5.04	Uschfar.,SS,C.C.Mauthausen (Aust.) 5.44-5.45	MURDER	U.S.
MANHGIM	12571	M			Pvt.,144 Pol.19,Dienststelle,Ugine (Fr.) 44	MURDER	FR.
MANIERA,Oskar	257341	M	Ger.		SS-Mann,SS,Serbo-Croat,Interpreter at Gestapo at Dortmund, Iserlohn (Ger.) 4.45	TORTURE	YUGO.
MANIG	251156	M	Ger.		Usturmfhr.,SS,Gestapo,Paris (Fr.) 41-44	INTERR.	FR.
MANIGER	141974	M	Ger.		Guard,SS,Waldlager V and VI,Ampfing,Muhldorf,Mettenheim (Ger.)44-45	TORTURE	U.S.
MANIKER	194171	M	Ger.		Scharfhr.,SS,C.C.Buchenwald (Ger.)	BRUTALITY	U.S.
MANINGER,Wilhelm	306462	M	Ger.	23. 3.11	Scharfhr.,SS,(No.108745),C.C.Buchenwald (Ger.) 5.38-10.43	MURDER	BEL.
MANJOKE	132154	M	Ger.		Scharfhr.,Waffen-SS,C.C.Dora Nordhausen (Ger.)	MURDER	U.S.
MANJOKS,Hans	253250	M			Hptschfhr.,C.C.Niedersachswerfen,Nordhausen (Ger.)	MURDER	U.S.
MANN	1431	M	Ger.		Major,Army,18 SS-Motor-Pol.	MISC.CRIMES	U.K.
MANN	166901	M		92	Medical Officer,Army,C.C.Limburg,Stalag 12 A,Limburg (Ger.) 40	MISC.CRIMES	FR.
MANN	251138	M	Ger.		Sgt.,Feldgendarmerie 924,La Folatiere (Fr.) 6.44	MURDER	FR.
MANN	307147	M	Ger.		Member,Staff of C.C.Auschwitz,Birkenau (Pol.) 40	MURDER	FR.
MANN,Franz	160710	M	Ger.		Kdos.706,754,756,Klingen (Ger.)	TORTURE	FR.
MANN,Herbert	307148	M	Ger.		Head,Kriminal-Polizei,Kiel,Oflag X C Luebeck (Ger.) 4.-5.44	MURDER	FR.
MANN,Louise	142532	F	Ger.		Civ.,C.C.Hadamar (Ger.) 6.44-3.45	WITNESS	U.S.
MANN,Max	253254	M			Cpl.,C.C.Ellrich,Nordhausen (Ger.)	MURDER	U.S.
MANN,Walter	191496	M	Ger.		Oberlandforstmeister,Abtl.-Leiter,Hauptabteilung,Forstamt des General-gouverneurs (Pol.) 39-44	PILLAGE	POL.
MANNEL,Kurt	262176	M	Ger.	26.11. ?	Usturmfhr.,Gestapo,Rennes (Fr.) 43-44	MURDER	FR.
MANNER,Ludwig	305040	M	Ger.	13	SS-Oschfhr.,Kriminalangestellter,Leiter der Abtl.II-C,Sicherheits-dienst,Sicherheitspol.Anvers,Antwerpen (Bel.) 6.40-9.44	MURDER	BEL.
MANNHEIM,Wilhelm	162226	M	Ger.		Foreman, Kriegsgefangenen-Arbeitskommando,Adolf Mine,Merkstein (Ger.) 42-44	TORTURE	U.S.
MANNHOFER	132242	M			SS-Mann,SS,C.C.Flossenburg (Ger.)	TORTURE	U.S.
MANNIG	256286	M			Rottfhr.,C.C.Wieda,Nordhausen (Ger.)	MURDER	U.S.
MANNS	251136	M			W.O.,Fieldpolice,Salagnon (Fr.) 2.44	MURDER	FR.
MANNS,Heinz	257989	M			Lt.,150 Pz.Brig.,Meuse Bridge,Antwerp (Bel.) 12.44	MISC.CRIMES	U.S.
MANNSCH,Angela	253925	F	Ger.		Cmdt.,C.C.Ravensbrueck (Ger.)	INTERR.	FR.
MANNUEL,Erich	262175	M		4. 4.21	Lt.,1 Group,51 SS-Armoured Brigade,Bucheres,Breviandes,St.Sevine, La Riviere de Corps,Troyes (Aube).(Fr.) 8.44	BRUTALITY	FR.
MANS	124464	M	Ger.	17	Capt.,Oc of "Einheit Mans",Pz.Bde.150,Ardenne (Fr.) 12.44	MISC.CRIMES	U.S.
MANS	191404	M			Sturmann,1 SS-Panzer-Div.Leibst."Adolf Hitler",Ligneuville,Stoumont (Bel.) 12.44	SUSPECT	U.S.
MANSEL	62512	M	Ger.		Pvt.,Fallschirmjaeger,Former Employment,Plumber,Roermond(Neth.)44-45	MISC.CRIMES	NETH.
MANSHOLD,Karl (see MENDSON)	158933						
MANSTEIN,Erich	588	M			General,Army,9.-10.39	MURDER	POL.
MANTEUFEL,Karl	253251	M			Cpl.,C.C.Ellrich,Nordhausen(Ger.)	MURDER	U.S.
MANZ,Erwin	195123	M	Ger.	8. 8.11	Member,SA,Luxembourg (Lux.)	MISC.CRIMES	LUX.
MANZ,Heinrich	136225	M	Ger.	15	Osturmfhr.,SS,Queret (Fr.)	MURDER	FR.
MANZEL (see MENZEL)	173220				Fallschirmjg.-Regt.5,Nachr.-Zug,Quaregnon,Jemappes(Bel.) 9.44	MURDER	BEL.
MANZIK,Johann	254893	M	Ger.		SS-Mann,SS,C.C.Auschwitz,Birkenau (Pol.-Ger.) 11.42	MURDER	YUGO.
MANZKE	257997	M			Lt.,150 Pz.Bde.,Meuse Bridge,Antwerp (Bel.) 12.44	MISC.CRIMES	U.S.

NAME	C.R.FILE NUMBER	SEX	NATIO-NALITY	DATE OF BIRTH	RANK OCCUPATION UNIT PLACE AND DATE OF CRIME	REASON WANTED	WANTED BY
MARA (or MARX)	137476	M			Uschfhr., SS, Conc.Camp, Weimar-Buchenwald (Ger.)	BRUTALITY	U.S.
MARANSKI	256026	M	Ger.		Schuetze, SS, Muehldorf (Ger.)	WITNESS	U.S.
MARBACH	254466	M			Major, Bonn (Ger.) 43-45	WITNESS	U.S.
MARBACH	258693	M	Ger.		Major, Commander, Lds.Schtz.Bn.785, Darmstadt (Ger.) 7.44	BRUTALITY	U.S.
MARBURGER, Karl	127426	M	Ger.		Civilian, Conc.Camp, Enkenbach (Ger.) 12.43-3.45	TORTURE	U.S.
MARC	173816	M	Ger.		Arbeitsstatistik, Camp Factory employing, Buchenwald, Camp Dora (Ger.) 43-4.45	MURDER	FR.
MARCHAL, Andre	122155	M	Ger.		Civilian Camp	MURDER	U.S.
MARCHE, Armand	123130	M	Ger.	05	Pvt., Army, Stalag III D, C.C., Teltow b.Berlin (Ger.) 3.43	MURDER	U.K.
MARCHI, Arturo	160711	M			Gestapo de Chalons-Saone (Fr.)	MURDER	FR.
MARCKSTALLER, Adolph	12536	M	Ger.		Firm Leinhart at Saarbruecken, Sarrable (Fr.) 44	MURDER	FR.
MARCZEWSKI, Felix	257990	M	Ger.	00	Russian Laborer, Hilden (Ger.) 4.45	WITNESS	U.S.
MAREK (or MAICK)	174698	M	Ger.		Brest (Fr.) 43-44	WITNESS	FR.
MAREK, Gerhard	301345	M	Ger.		Member, Gestapo at Trencin, C.C., Oswiecim-Birkenau (Pol.) 39-45	MURDER	CZECH.
MAREK, Paul (see MEREK)	156880						
MARFS, Marto	257522	M		27. 9.14	Employee, Block 18, Camp Dora, Nordhausen (Ger.)	MURDER	U.S.
MARESCH, Josef (or MARESH)	54751	M	Ger.		Civilian, Prison Warden, Gestapo, Brno (Czech.) 39-45	MURDER	CZECH.
MARGES, Charlotte	261375	F	Ger.	5. 4.04	Overseer, SS-Guard, C.C., Auschwitz (Pol.) 41-44	BRUTALITY	POL.
MARIA	253804	F	Ger.		Woman-Guard, Conc.Camp, Auschwitz (Ger.)	BRUTALITY	FR.
MARIANNE	300914	M	Ger.		Employing-man, attached to Camp Dora and Factory from CC B, Buchenwald, (Ger.) 43-4.45	MISC.CRIMES	FR.
MARIC, Damljan	156854	M			Civilian, Gallneukirchen (Aust.)	WITNESS	U.S.
MARIEN, Gertrudi	142531	F	Ger.	23.10.02	Civilian, C.C., Hadamar (Ger.) 6.44-3.45	WITNESS	U.S.
MARIEN, Hans	257520	M	Ger.	14. 7.13	Employee, P.o.W.Camp Narova and Ostrava (Czech.) 8.44	MURDER	U.S.
MARIN	138203	M	Ger.	10	Member of Staff, Conc.Camp, Woippy (Fr.) 44	TORTURE	FR., BEL.
MARINOWITZ	126923	M	Ger.		Oschfhr., SD, C.C., Neustadt (Ger.)	TORTURE	FR.
MARINOWITZ	177529	M	Ger.		Oschfhr., SS, Conc.Camp, Ravensbrueck (Ger.)	TORTURE	FR.
MARIO	590	M	Ger.		Airforce, Interpreter, Brennilis (Fr.) 4.44	LOOTING	FR.
MARISCHEK (see MAZILECK)	39843	M					
MARISCHLER, Franz	190375	M	Ger.	7. 6.10	Agent, Gestapo, Civilian, Brno (Czech.) 36-45	MURDER	CZECH.
MARK (see MARKS)	194223						
MARK, Gustave	12537	M	Ger.		Pvt., Pz.Gren.Rgt.110 or 111, 2.Coy., Albine (Fr.) 6.44	MURDER	FR.
MARK, Heinz	301704	M	Ger.		Tailor, Civilian, Juegesheim (Ger.) 1.45	BRUTALITY	U.K.
MARK, Hermann Joseph	301705	M	Ger.		Tailor, Juegesheim (Ger.) 1.45	BRUTALITY	U.K.
MARK, Karl	161938	M	Ger.		Osturmfhr., SS, Command Staff, Conc.Camp, Buchenwald (Ger.) 41	WITNESS	U.S.
MARK, Paul	255878	M			Schfhr., SS, Conc.Camp, Buchenwald (Ger.)	MURDER	U.S.
MARKASSCHAFER	174699	M			Hauptverbindungsstab, Lt., Valence Drome (Fr.)	MISC.CRIMES	FR.
MARKER, Peter	255880	M			Sgt., Conc.Camp, Buchenwald (Ger.)	MURDER	U.S.
MARKERT	173815	M	Ger.		Lt., Army, Unit 30463 D, Blaye (Fr.) 6.44	TORTURE	FR.
MARKERT	253253	M			Oschfhr., Conc.Camp Mackenrode, Nordhausen (Ger.)	MURDER	U.S.
MARKERT, Hans	253252	M		17. 7.11	Pvt., Conc.Camp Ellrich, Nordhausen (Ger.)	MURDER	U.S.
MARKHART, Willy	259749	M	Ger.	14	Uschfhr., Gestapo, Area Angers, Maine and Loire (Fr.) 42-44	MISC.CRIMES	FR.
MARKL	174700	M	Ger.		Cpl., 7.Art.Rgt., Tours, Albertville (Fr.) 6.44	MURDER	FR.
MARKL, Englbert	12538	M	Ger.		Pvt., Army, 110.or 111.Panz.Gren.Rgt., 2.Coy., Albine (Fr.) 6.44	MURDER	FR.
MARKLE (see MERKLE)	162073						
MARKOFF, Rudolf	307149	M			Uschfhr., 2.Bn.Landsturm Niederlande, Apeldoorn, Hoog-Soeren, Lager "Mia", (Neth.) 44	MURDER	NETH.
MARKOVSKY	178078	M			Pvt., Kriegsgefangenen-Arbeits-Bn.183, Dunderlang (Nor.)	MURDER	NOR.
MARKS	10155	M			Stabsfw., 635.Lds.Schtz.Bn., Niederorschel (Ger.) 1.43	TORTURE	U.K.
MARKS	146765	M			Dr., Conc.Camp, Civ., Flossenburg (Ger.)	WITNESS	U.S.
MARKS (or MARK)	194223	M	Ger.	07	Uschfhr., SS, Conc.Camp, Buchenwald (Ger.) 42-45	MISC.CRIMES	U.S.
MARKS, Lyndhart	156850	M	Ger.		Officer, Local-Police, Graz (Aust.) 45	MURDER	U.S.
MARKS, Paul	141978	M	Ger.	98	Oschfhr., Waffen-SS Totenkopf-Standarte, Member of Commander-Staff, Conc.Camp, Buchenwald (Ger.)	BRUTALITY	U.S.
MARKSCHEFFEL, Walter	250373	M	Ger.		Pvt., Ortskommandantur, Hengelo (Neth.)	PILLAGE	NETH.
MARKUAD (see MARQUARD)	196018	M					
MARKUS	190257	M			Dr., Chief, Police, Sibenik Zablac, Fiume (Yugo., It.) 5.44-6.44	MURDER	YUGO.
MARKUS, Georg	253930	M	Ger.	4.12.15	Dr.Ing., SS, SD, Gestapo, Pragus (Czech.) 39-45	MISC.CRIMES	CZECH.
MARKUS, Hermann	194488	M	Ger.		Clerk, Gestapo, Brno (Czech.) 39	MURDER	CZECH.
MARL, Hilde	139053	F	Ger.		Civilian, Plettenberg, Lettmecke (Ger.) 4.45	TORTURE	U.S.
MARMON, Franz	100206	M	Ger.	11. 6.08	SS-Gestapo, Hanau, Marburg, Niederdorfelden (Ger.) 42, 44-45	MURDER	POL., U.S.
MAROCK, Albert	254764	M	Ger.	90	Cpt., Schutzpolizei, Prague-Kobylisy (Czech.) 41	MURDER	CZECH.
MAROHR	1432	M	Ger.		Lt., Army, Pion.Bn.331	MISC.CRIMES	U.K.
MARON, Otto	157019	M			Oschfhr., 1.SS-Panz.Div."Adolf Hitler", 2.Pz.Gr.Rgt., 3.Bn., Malmedy, 44	MURDER	U.S.
MARON	160713	M	Ger.		Cpl., 263.Div.Kommando de Landerneau, Finistere (Fr.) 44	MURDER	FR.
MARQUARD (or MARKUARD)	196018	M	Ger.		Hptsturmfhr., SS, Enghien (Fr.) 8.44	WITNESS	FR.
MARQUARDT	170068	M	Ger.	95	Lt.Col., Army (Pol.) 39-45	SUSPECT	U.S.
MARQUARDT	196781	M	Ger.		Lt., Osturmfhr., Conc.Camp, Neuengamme (Ger.)	BRUTALITY	BEL.
MARQUART	306691	M	Ger.		Pvt., 331.Pion.Bn., 331.Inf.Div., Mijnheerenland (Neth.) 5.45	PILLAGE	NETH.
MARQUARTH, Werner	262174	M	Ger.	31. 7.20	Uschfhr., Cmdt., Platoon 4, 51.SS Armoured Bde., Breviandes, Bucheres, Ste Savine, La Riviere de Corps (Troyes) (Fr.) 8.44	BRUTALITY	FR.
MARRENBACH	160708	M	Ger.		Capt., 77.Inf.Rgt., Oflag VI D, Muenster (Ger.)	TORTURE	FR.
MARRENBACH, Fritz	21333	M	Ger.		Bde.Fhr., SA, DAF, NSDAP	MISC.CRIMES	UNWCC
MARRZAK	256027	M	Ger.		SS-Schuetze, Muehldorf (Ger.)	WITNESS	U.S.
MARSALEK	301582	M	Ger.		Secr.No.2 at C.C. Mauthausen (Aust.) 40-45	MURDER	BEL.
MARSAU, Willi	253224	M			Pvt., Conc.Camp Ellrich, Nordhausen (Ger.)	MURDER	U.S.
MARSCH	173217	M	Ger.	05	Pvt., 4.Coy., 515.Landschutz-Bn., Prague (Czech.) 3.45	MURDER	U.K.
MARSCH, Friedrich	29693	M	Ger.		Dr., Landgerichtsdirektor, Public Official, Cheb (Czech.) 40	MURDER	CZECH.
MARSCH, Gunther	194498	M	Ger.		Leader, Abt.Liegenschafts-Hauptverwaltung, Amt des Gouverneurs,Warsaw	PILLAGE	POL.
MARSCHA, Josef	194487	M	Ger.	2. 9.07	Blockleiter, NSDAP, Dep. Bohemia (Czech.)	MISC.CRIMES	CZECH.
MARSCHAAL	12539	M	Ger.		Commandant, Army, Chef des Verbindungstabes 735,Grenoble (Fr.) 11.43	MISC.CRIMES	FR.
MARSCHAL	160705	M	Ger.	90	Justizoberwachtmeister, Police, SA, C.C., Emsland (Ger.) 44	MURDER	U.S.

MAR - MAR

NAME	C.R.FILE NUMBER	SEX	NATIO-NALITY	DATE OF BIRTH	RANK OCCUPATION UNIT PLACE AND DATE OF CRIME	REASON WANTED	WANTED BY
MARSCHAL	189209	F			Female Guard, C.C. Ravensbrueck (Ger.) 42-45	MURDER	FR.
MARSCHAIK, Hans	172465	M	Ger.	02 or 03	Capt., POW Working Commando 188, C.C. Bergem district (Nor.) 42-43	MURDER	NOR.
MARSCHALL	1722	M			Lt., S.D.	MURDER	U.K.
MARSCHALL	145966	M			Oschfhr., SS, Vicinity of Munich (Ger.) 7.44	MURDER	U.S.
MARSCHALL	187926	M			Cmdt., Major, Verbindungsstab, Grenoble (Fr.)	MISC.CRIMES	FR.
MARSCHALL, Elisabeth	132636	F	Ger.		Oberschwester, C.C. Ravensbrueck (Ger.)	MURDER	FR.
MARSCHALL, Georg	195651	M	Ger.		Official, Mzocz (Pol.) 10.42	MURDER	POL.
MARSCHALL, Wilhelm	258948	M	Ger.		Admiral of the fleet.	WITNESS	U.S.
MARSCHALLEK, Johann (see MEINBERGER,Johann)	138034						
MARSCHLER	398466	M	Ger.		Capt., 10. mot.Regt. I.Bn., Chilleurs au Bois (Fr.) 8.44	MURDER	U.K.
MARSHAL	208047	M	Ger.		Member, Gestapo, S.D., Usturmfhr., Stalag Luft III, Sagan (Ger.) 3.44	MURDER	U.K.
MARSKE	142556	M		95	Luftschutzleiter, Air Force, C.C.Sachsenhausen-Oranienburg (Ger.)	TORTURE	U.K.
MARSKE	307150	M	Ger.		Cpl., F.P.No.L.55,975, Laren, 11.44-2.45	PILLAGE	NETH.
MARSZALEK, Irmgard	126360	F	Ger.		Civilian. (Ger.)	MISC.CRIMES	U.S.
MARTELLO, Romano	307282	M	Ger.		Member, Ital.Fascist Black Bde., near Caselle Fressana Prov.Verona (Italy) 1.45	MURDER	U.K.
MARTELOCK-MICHELFEIT, Hildegarde	195200	F	Ger.	22	Member, Gestapo, Kolin (Czech.) 39-43	MURDER	CZECH.
MARTEN	139055	M	Ger.	10	Sturmscharfhr., S.D., Sipo, Toulouse and other towns (Fr.) 11.42-8.44	MURDER	U.S.
MARTEN	300817	M	Ger.		Pvt., I.Aufkl.Abt., 3.Coy, 2.Col., XV. Div.of the Afrika Korps, Saint Leger (Arlon) (Bel.) 9.44	MISC.CRIMES	BEL.
MARTENS	166900	M	Ger.		Capt., Army, Athienville (Fr.) 9.44	TORTURE	FR.
MARTENS	250559	M	Ger.		Major, Airforce Field Clothing Office, Enschede (Neth.) 42-45	PILLAGE	NETH.
MARTENS	260104	M	Ger.		Sgt., Feldgendarmerie of Luneville (Meurthe and Moselle) (Fr.) 40-45	PILLAGE	FR.
MARTENS	307014	M	Ger.		Member, Sicherheitsdienst, Apeldoorn district (Neth.) 9.44-4.45	MURDER	NETH.
MARTENS	307151	M	Ger.	15	Uschfhr., SS, Apeldoorn, Hoog-Soeren (Lager "Ma") (Neth.) 10.-12.44	MURDER	NETH.
MARTENS, Fritz	196019	M	Ger.		Hptschfhr., S.D., Zwolle (Neth.) 9.44-4.45	INTER.	NETH.
MARTH	31611	M	Ger.		Major, Army Transport-Verbind.Stab, Finmark (Nor.) 10. - 11.44	MURDER	NOR.
MARTHES	104845	M	Ger.	85	Capt., Army, Guard-Coy., Hamburg-Altona (Ger.) 7-11.44	TORTURE	U.S.
MARTIN	591	M			Polizei-Unterwachtmeister, C.C. Boten (Nor.) 3.42-43	MURDER	YUGO.,NOR.,UNWCC
MARTIN	1007	M		10.10.06	Staatsanwalt, Public official, Prague (Czech.) 40-42	MURDER	CZECH.
MARTIN	38891	M	Ger.		SS-Osturmbannfhr., SS, C.C. Hinzert (Ger.) 42-43	TORTURE	U.S., FR.
MARTIN	124238	M	Ger.		Supervisor of Optical Factory, C.C. Dietz (Ger.) 1.43-3.45	MISC.CRIMES	U.S.
MARTIN	128831	M	Ger.		Guard, Lager Enstalstumach, Gullensgraben (Austria) 12.42	MURDER	U.K.
MARTIN	130071	M	Ger.		Pvt.,(Guard), C.C. Hindenburg (Ger.) 5.42	TORTURE	U.K.
MARTIN	140051	M	Ger.		Pvt., Army, Working Party E 608 C.C.Herschfelde,Oppeln (Ger.) 7.43	MURDER	U.K.
MARTIN (see SCHUTZ)	157015						
MARTIN	157017	M			Pvt., Stalag Luft III C, Sagan (Ger.) 4.44	MURDER	U.S.
MARTIN	160712	M	Ger.		Lt., SS, Plomvien (Fr.) 44	MURDER	FR.
MARTIN (see TROEGER)	189677						
MARTIN	193850	M	Ger.		Capt., 1.Coy.Kriegsgef.Arb.Bn.190 (Nor.) 45	MURDER	NOR.
MARTIN	251135	M	Ger.		Lt., 1-98.Gebirgs-Regt., Le Chablais (Fr.)	MURDER	FR.
MARTIN	252533	M	Ger.	06	Lt., Milan (Italy) 8.44	INTER.	U.K.
MARTIN	300615	M	Ger.		Meister, "Optisches Werk Ernst Leitz" Wetzlar (Dietz Fortress an der Lahn near Frankfurt-Main) (Ger.) 42-45	MURDER	FR.
MARTIN	301850	M	Ger.		Hptsturmfhr., SS, Chief of Camp at Thekla near Leipzig (Ger.) 4.45	MURDER	FR.
MARTIN	305462	M	Ger.		Lt., Gebirgsjaeger Bn. 1-98, Le Chablais, Maxilly-sur-Leman (Fr.) 5.44	MURDER	FR.
MARTIN	305722	M	Ger.		Uschfhr., in charge of the Pisce Culture at Armeaza near Auschwitz, C.C.Auschwitz-Birkenau (Pol.) 40	MURDER	FR.
MARTIN, Albert	12328	M	Ger.		Pvt., 1-427.Landesschuetzen-Bn. Stalag Hirschfelde (Ger.) 7.44	MURDER	U.K.
MARTIN, Erich	142566	M	Ger.	05	Oberreviermeister, C.C. Lahde-Weser (Ger.) 43-45	TORTURE	BEL.
MARTIN, Erich	161933	M	Ger.	95 or 00	Master, Civ. Prison warder and optician, Diez-Lahn (Ger.) 43-45	TORTURE	U.S.
MARTIN, Erich	161934	M	Ger.	06	Hptscharfhr., SS, command staff, C.C. Buchenwald (Ger.) 41-45	WITNESS	U.S.
MARTIN, Hans	259223	M			Pvt., C.C. Ellrich, Nordhausen (Ger.)	MURDER	U.S.
MARTIN, Hector	188645	M		28.5.08	Uscharfhr.,SS,Gestapo,SD.,Paris,Clermond,Ferrand,Pinols,Auvers,7.44	MURDER	FR.
MARTIN, Josef	306463	M	Ger.	23. 3.22	SS-Mann, SS, C.C. Buchenwald (Ger.) betw.5.38 and 10.43	MURDER	BEL.
MARTIN, Karl	137477	M	Ger.		SS-Uschfhr., C.C. Weimar-Buchenwald (Ger.)	BRUTALITY	U.S.
MARTIN, Karl	255478	M		29. 7.04	Rottenfhr., C.C. Harzungen, Nordhausen.(Ger.)	INTER.	U.S.
MARTIN, Karl	259747	M	Ger.	15. 8.05	Sturmscharfhr., Gestapo, area of Angers, Maine and Loire (Fr.) 42-44	MISC.CRIMES	FR.
MARTIN, Louis	259806	M			Uschfhr., C.C. Auschwitz.(Pol.)	MISC.CRIMES	FR.
MARTIN, Max	307015	M	Ger.	12. 1.91	Oberwachtmeister, Arbeitserziehungslager Lahde-Weser (Ger.) betw.5.43-4.45	MURDER	U.K.
MARTIN, Moritz August Maurice (or MUELLER)	240132	M		15	Sturmbannfhr., SS, S.D. Leader Abt.IV, Marseille, Berlin (Fr.,Ger.)44	PILLAGE	U.S.
MARTIN, Neume	21332	M		93	SS-Obergruppenfhr., C.C. Flossenburg (Ger.)	TORTURE	U.S.
MARTIN, Schall	39849	M	Ger.		SS-Rottenfhr., Guard, C.C.Struthof-Natzweiler (Fr.)	TORTURE	FR.
MARTIN, Willi	178302	M	Ger.		SS-Mann, 12.SS Panz.Div. "Hitler Jugend" 25.SS Panz.Gren.Regt.,15.Coy., Abbaye-Ardenne near Caen (Fr.) 6.-7.44	TORTURE	CAN.
MARTINETTO, Bruno	254773	M	Ger.		Agent,S.D., Toulouse (Fr.) 11.42-8.44	MISC.CRIMES	FR.
MARTINI	305463	M	Ger.	95 or 00	Revierhauptwachtmeister, Gruene Polizei, Lahde near Hannover (Ger.)45	MISC.CRIMES	NETH.
MARTINI, Giulie	259933	M	Ger.		Major, Adjutant in POW Camp of Ghedi, Rescare Terme (Italy). Home address Scheuern near Nassau-Lahn, Brueckenstr.37, Germany.	MURDER	U.S.
MARTSCHIK, Franz	194486	M	Ger.	31.10.06	Guard-Chief, Gestapo, Brno (Czech.) 39-45	MURDER	CZECH.
MARTTEN, Heinz	126361	M	Ger.	27. 6.29	Civilian, farm labourer, Moers (Ger.) 2.45	MISC.CRIMES	U.S.
MARTUNEL, Karl	156852	M			Driver, C.C. Flossenburg (Ger.)	WITNESS	U.S.
MARTUNG	131758	M	Ger.	10	Hptsturmfhr., SS, Grenoble (Fr.) 7.44	MISC.CRIMES	FR.
MARTY (see GEISLER)	147723						
MARU; Marie nee KOSMAN (see HAVRANEK)	193421						
MARWEDEL, August	253935	M	Ger.	16. 6.84	Capt., Schupo 20 Bn., (DAVA), Lidice (Czech.) 6.42	MURDER	CZECH.
MARWEID	192505	M	Ger.		Uschfhr., SS, C.C. Flossenburg (Ger.) 44-45	MURDER	U.S.
MARX	592	M			Oschfhr., SS, Alesund (Nor.)	TORTURE	NOR.
MARX (see MARA)	137476						
MARX	170069	M	Ger.		SS (Ger.) 43	SUSPECT	U.S.

MAR-MAT

NAME	C.R.FILE NUMBER	SEX	NATIO-NALITY	DATE OF BIRTH	RANK OCCUPATION UNIT PLACE AND DATE OF CRIME	REASON WANTED	WANTED BY
MARX	190613	M	Ger.		Lt., Tuerkestan Legion, Rimont (Fr.) 8.44	MURDER	FR.
MARX	256293	M			Uschfhr., C.C. Buchenwald (Ger.)	MURDER	U.S.
MARX (or MAX)	301790	M	Ger.		Attached Cossack Cavalry Unit, Etobon, Chenebier, Hte Saone (Fr.) 9.44	MURDER	FR.
MARX, Bernhard	196819	M	Ger.	20. 6.89	Gend. Wachtmeister, Police (Daua),Seinsfeld,Oberkall (Ger.) 8.44	MISC.CRIMES	U.S.
MARX, Fritz	194445	M	Ger.		SS Oschfhr., SD;, Neuwarden, Gent (Neth.)	MURDER	NETH.
MARX, Georges	307016	M	Ger.		Capt., commanding the 4 Bn. of the "Turkestan" Legion, Boulogne sur Gesse, Hte.-Garonne (Fr.) 8.44	MURDER	FR.
MARX, Heinz	253268	M	Ger.	14. 1.23	Pvt., 1 Flak.Ers.Abt. 19 2457a, Strijpen (Bel.) 9.44	MURDER	BEL.
MARX, Hugo,Robert,Hermann	254456	M	Ger.	03	Lt., Elstener Moor (Ger.) 11.44	MISC.CRIMES	U.S.
MARX, Johann	157014	M	Ger.	1o.11.02	Pvt.,1038 Landesschuetzen Bn.,Stalag Luft I,C.C.Barth (Ger.) 3.45	MURDER	U.K.
MARX, Josef	253222	M		29. 7.96	Pvt., C.C. Harzungen, Nordhausen (Ger.)	MURDER	U.S.
MARX, Paul	145982	M	Ger.		Labor leader, NSDAP, near Gardelegen (Ger.) 4.45	MURDER	U.S.
MARX, Peter	132156	M	Ger.		Civilian, C.C. Nordhausen Camp Dora (Ger.)	MURDER	U.S.
MARX, Philip	121307	M	Ger.		Foreman,Neurode (Ger.)	BRUTALITY	FR.
MARXEN	255877	M			Hptsturmfhr., SS, C.C. Buchenwald (Ger.)	MURDER	U.S.
MARZ	256292	M			Rottfhr., C.C. Buchenwald (Ger.)	MURDER	U.S.
MARZ, Emil	193849	M	Ger.	95	Sgt., POW Working Bn. 186 (Nor.) 42	MISC.CRIMES	NOR.
MARZ, Richard	132763	M			SS, C.C. Mauthausen (Aust.) 41-45	MURDER	U.S.
MARZAHN	142541	M			Major, Army, Oberkdo.	MISC.CRIMES	U.S.
MARZINSKI, Erich	183857	M		10.12.93	Guard, 4 SS Totenkopfsturmbann,C.C.Dora-Mittelbau,Nordhausen (Ger.) 43-45	WITNESS	U.S.
MARZOTKO, Gerhard	255479	M		4. 4.12	Pvt., C.C. Harzungen, Nordhausen (Ger.)	MURDER	U.S.
MASCHATSCHEK, Paul	307153	M	Ger.	08	Schfhr., SS, Gestapo, Angers, Maine-et-Loire,Sarthe-et-Mayenne (Fr.) 42-8.44	MURDER	FR.
MASCHE	38889	M	Ger.		Hptsturmfhr., Waffen SS, C.C.Klingelpuetz (Ger.) winter 44-45	TORTURE	U.S.
MASCHKE	104846	M	Ger.		Sgt., Army, 71.Engr.Constr.Bn. (Ger.)	MISC.CRIMES	U.S.
MASCHTSCHEK, Paul	259695	M		08	SS Schfhr.,Gestapo,Guard of forest,Area of Angers,Maine,Loire (Fr.) 42-44	MISC.CRIMES	FR.
MASCKE	593	M	Ger.		Gestapo, Capt., Dr., St. Brieuc (Fr.) 8.44	TORTURE	FR.
MASCUS, Hellmuth	254891	M	Ger.	30. 3.91	Police Inspector, Ordnungs-Pol.,Salzburg (Yugo.) 4.41-2.42	MISC.CRIMES	YUGO.
MASER	306464	M	Ger.		SS-man, C.C. Buchenwald (Ger.) 5.38-10.43	MURDER	BEL.
MASERSKI	137474	M			SS Oschfhr.,C.C.Weimar, Buchenwald (Ger.)	BRUTALITY	U.S.
MASHOFF, Karl	156858	M	Ger.		Civilian, Bolingen (Ger.) 11.44	MURDER	U.S.,CAN.
MASIN, Siegfried	194485	M	Ger.		Employee, Gestapo, Bruenn (Czech.) 39-45	MURDER	CZECH.
MASKE	174365	M			Col.,Commander, Air-Force, Bau-Bn., (Nor.)	MURDER	NOR.
MASKOW	300818	M	Ger.		Pvt.,1.Aufkl.Abt.3 Coy.2 Ool.XV Div.Afrika Korps,St.Leger,Arlon 9.44	MISC.CRIMES	BEL.
MASLEK	141977	M	Ger.	22	Rottfhr.,Waffen SS Totenkopf Stand.,C.C.Buchenwald (Ger.)	BRUTALITY	U.S.
MASLIENDER, Heinrich	192123	M	Ger.	06	Member, Gestapo (Bel.)	TORTURE	BEL.
MASLO	183909	M			Pvt., Kg F. Arb. Bn. 184 3 Coy., Kraakmoen (Nor.)	WITNESS	NOR.
MASS	127427	M	Ger.		Osturmbannfhr., C.C. Buchenwald (Ger.) 5.44	MURDER	U.S.
MASS, Paul	142571	M	Ger.	09	Staff-Schfhr.,C.C.Neuengamme (Ger.)	TORTURE	U.K.
MASSALSKY	144411	M			Lt., Army, 2 Rgt.Feldpost Nr. L.62 546 A, Locmine (Fr.)	MURDER	FR.
MASSAR	124606	M	Ger.		SS-man, C.C. Ravensbrueck (Ger.)	TORTURE	BEL.
MASSART	307017	M	Ger.		Member of Staff, C.C. Ravensbrueck (Ger.) 40-45	BRUTALITY	BEL.
MASSBAENDER	132772	M	Ger.	06	SD, Official, SS Hptsturmfhr., Bruessel (Bel.)	INTERR.	U.S.
MASSEN, Peter	186442	M	Ger.		Sturmschfhr.; Crim.Secretary, SD, Police,Montgauthier,Dinant (Bel.)43	MURDER	BEL.
MASSMANN	256287	M			Rottfhr., C.C. Mackenrode, Nordhausen (Ger.)	MURDER	U.S.
MASSOUW	62168	M			Capt., Army,Schnell-Abt.602 FP.27690A,Larove-Bottereau,Bergrol.(Fr.) 8.44	MURDER	FR.
MASSUI	142116	M			Agent, Gestapo, Paris (Fr.)	LOOTING	FR.
MASSYN, Hans	188020	M	Ger.		Cpl. Chief, SS Army 16 Inf.Div.,Maille Mantua (Fr.)	MURDER	FR.
MASTEROUBEU	142117	M			Ingelheim (Ger.)	TORTURE	FR.
MASUR	38890	M	Ger.		Foreman Prison Guard, Waffen SS, C.C. Wittlich (Ger.)	TORTURE	U.S.
MASUR, Willi	193847	M	Ger.	05	Sgt.,Reichsjustizministerium,Strafgefangenenlager, C.C. Finmark (Nor.) 42-45	MISC.CRIMES	NOR.,YUGO.
MATASEVSKI	260164	M	Ger.		Guard SS, Slave Labour Camp,Botn nr.Rognan (Nor.)8.42-3.43,4.43-45	MURDER	YUGO.
MATAUSCH, Emil	260007	M	Ger.	6. 9.25	SS-man,Member of SS in Usti is believed to be at Wehrlingen nr. Augsburg,Gasthof Seitz 36,Schwaben (Ger.),Cesky Bukov (Czech.)9.43	MURDER	CZECH.
MATCHATSHEK	157013	M	Ger.		Cpl., Gestapo, Anju, Pointon (Fr.)	MURDER	FR.
MATEHJKOVA	301146	M	Ger.		Member Gestapo, Trencin, Oswiecim-Birkenau (Pol.) 39-45	MURDER	CZECH.
MATENAERS, Johann	126362	M	Ger.		Night-watchman (Civ.), Arb.Kdo. NCO, Edelstahlwerke (Ger.) 44-45	TORTURE	U.S.
MATERNA, Friedrich	21314	M	Ger.		General, Army Inf., 43	TORTURE	U.N.W.C.C.
MATERNE	254035	M			Employee, Sipo, Brussels (Bel.) 40-45	INTERR.	BEL.
MATESIUS	594	M			SS Oschfhr., C.C. Stutthof (Ger.) 9.39-4.41	MURDER	POL.
MATH, Otto	147291	M			11 Pz. Div. (Fr.) 44	MURDER	FR.
MATHAU	141396	M	Ger.		Lt.,Luftlandesschts.Rgt.5 Coy.,Le Bousquet (Fr.)	MISC.CRIMES	U.K.
MATHE, Fritz	1433	M			Army, Fortress-Bn. 903	MURDER	U.S.
MATHEA	260998	M	Ger.		Rottfhr., SS, C.C. Vaihingen a.d.Enz (Ger.) 8.44-4.45	MURDER	NETH.
MATHEAUS	38888	M			Major, Army, Paratroop, Roermond (Neth.) 11.44-1.45	MURDER	U.K.
MATHES	192913	M	Ger.	06	Pvt.,Guard Camp 3,367 or 365 Ldschtz.Bn.Stal.IVG,Gaschwitz (Ger.)43	TORTURE	NETH.
MATHES	307154	M			Col. of Unit to which Lt.Smiths-Porten belonged,Zoelen (Neth.)1o.44	TORTURE	U.S.
MATHES, ADOLPH	188214	M	Ger.		Osturmfhr., SS Konstans (Ger.) 6.44	MURDER	U.N.W.C.C.
MATHES, Hubert	130721	M			S.D. Abschnitt Sipo. Agent Aachen (Ger.)	MURDER	U.S.
MATHES (see MATTHES), Max	170071						
MATHES, Rudolf	135280	M	Ger.		Werkmeister Civ. Factory Manager Wetzendorf (Ger.)	TORTURE	U.S.
MATHESIUS	126477	M	Ger.		Osturmfhr., SS Wachtkommando Salza and Ellrich (Ger.)	TORTURE	FR.
MATHEUS	121187	M	Ger.		Luftwaffe 2.Div.3.D.Landesschuets.Rgt.Lt. Mont Jardin (Fr.) 5.44	MURDER	U.S.
MATHEY, Willi	142540	M			N.S.D.A.P. Ortsgruppe Hausen,Gimmheim, (Ger.) 11.44	MURDER	POL.
MATHIA	253924	M			Guard, C.C. Moenchenberg, Kassel (Ger.) 43	TORTURE	U.S.
MATHIAS	161932	M			Oschfhr.,Security Guard C.C. Buchenwald Ohrdruf (Ger.) 45	WITNESS	FR.
MATHIAS	251831	M			Lt., Pleucadeux, St. Marcel (Fr.) 6.44	MURDER	U.S.
MATHIAS, Erich	156845	M		02	Farmer, Civilian, Gardelegen (Ger.) 4.45	MURDER	NOR.
MATHIESEN	193846	M			Hptsturmfhr., S.D. Trondheim, (Nor.) 41-45	MURDER	U.S.
MATHIS	194175	M	Ger.		Cpt. C.C. Buchenwald Ohrdruf (Ger.) 42-45	TORTURE	FR.
MATHIS	306631	M	Ger.		Kapo, C.C. Neuengamme (Ger.) 2.40-4.45	MURDER	FR.

MAT-MAU

NAME	C.R.FILE NUMBER	SEX	NATIO-NALITY	DATE OF BIRTH	RANK OCCUPATION UNIT PLACE AND DATE OF CRIME	REASON WANTED	WANTED BY
MATHIS, Martin	141886	M	Ger.	03	Farmer,Civilian,Nielub(Ger.) 6.-7.44	INTERR.	U.K.
MATHLENER	132783	M	Ger.		Fallschirmjaeger Regt.5,Nachricht.Zug,Quaregnon-Jemappes(Bel.) 9.44	MURDER	BEL.
MATHOL, Karl	192264	M	Ger.		C.C. Flossenburg(Ger.) 44-45	MURDER	U.S.
MATHUSCHA, Joseph	257342	M	Ger.		SS-Guard,SS-slave labour camp,Beisfjord near Narvik(Nor.) 6.-11.42	BRUTALITY	YUGO.
MATHWIG, Herta,nee HARTMANN	259682	F	Ger.	25.8.03	Employee,Gestapo,Litomerice(Czech.) 39-45	MURDER	CZECH.
MATHYS	132782	M	Ger.		Kapo,Camp Neuengamme(Ger.)	TORTURE	BEL.
MATIE	260988	M			SS-Rottfhr.,C.C.Vaihingen(Ger.) 8.44-4.45	MURDER	U.S.
MATIEU	162224	M			Civilian-Foreman,Kriegsgef.Arb.-Kdo.Adolf Mine,KL.Merkstein(Ger.) 42-44	TORTURE	U.S.
MATIJAS, Michael	173801	M			Guard,SS Police Regt.,C.C.Bajmiste,Zemun,Belgrad(Yugo.) 4.43	MURDER	YUGO.
MATINSKI	132157	M	Ger.		Civilian,C.C.Dora,Nordhausen(Ger.)	MURDER	U.S.
MATIS	596	M	Ger.		SA-Sturmfhr.,Assist.-Cmdt.C.C. Stutthof(Ger.) 9.39-4.41	MURDER	POL.
MATIS, Martin	99845	M	Ger.		Civilian Farmer,Rittergut Niederlub-Briesen(Ger.) 6.44	MURDER	U.K.
MATISKUK, Wilhelm	193845	M	Ger.	05	Sgt.,Reichsjustizministerium,Strafgefangenenlager,C.C.Finmark(Nor.) 6.42-45	MISC.CRIMES	NOR.,YUGO.
MATL, Mathias	194484	M	Ger.	18.1.15	Crim.-Employee,Gestapo,Brno(Czech.) 39-45	MURDER	CZECH.
MATLAMANN	163471	M			Technical-Inspector,Civilian,Marialwe,Florennes(Bel.)	MURDER	BEL.
MATLOK	255887	M			N.C.O.,2 Bn.Renfort.10 SS Pz.Div.Frundsberg,Louveciennes,Marly(Fr.) 8.44	WITNESS	FR.
MATCHES	31610	M	Ger.		Major,Gebirgsdiv.7	MURDER	NOR.
MATOI, Hans	192263	M	Ger.		Kapo,C.C. Flossenburg(Ger.) 5.44-4.45	MURDER	U.S.,BEL.
MATSCHUCK, Wilhelm	254670	M	Ger.		Sgt.,St.Sarvise(Fr.) 8.44	TORTURE	FR.
MATSCHINER, Hans	12540	M	Ger.		Pvt.,Army 110 or 111,Pz.Gren.Regt.,2 Coy.,Albine(Fr.) 6.44	MURDER	FR.
MATSCHULAT	173898	M	Ger.		Civilian,Iserbrock near Osdorf(Ger.) 6.44	TORTURE	U.S.
MATSZKE	134826	M	Ger.		Kriminalrat,Gestapo,SS,Koeln(Ger.)	MURDER	U.S.
MATT	260896	M	Ger.		Col.,Commanding Officer of Order Police,Kassel,(Ger.) 43-45	MURDER	U.S.
MATT, Zepp	254774	M	Ger.		Sgt.,Chateau Roux Garrison,Villedieu(Fr.) 8.44	MURDER	FR.
MATTAUS or MATTAUX	185214	M	Ger.		Lt.,Luftwaffen Feld-Div.,Inf.Regt.,Villebazy(Fr.) 7.44	PILLAGE	FR.
MATTEIS, Ludwig	127428	M	Ger.		Civilian,C.C.Enkenbach(Ger.) 12.43-3.45	TORTURE	U.S.
MATTERMYCH	260999				SS-Uschfhr.,SS,C.C.,Vaihingen a.d.Enz(Ger.) 8.44-4.45	MURDER	U.S.
MATTERN	160706		Ger.	00	Employee, Gestapo	WITNESS	BEL.
MATTES	160703	M	Ger.		SS-Mann,Pz.Div."Adolf Hitler"SS Zugaufstellung,2 Zug,Parfondruy,Stavelot(Bel.) 12.44	MURDER	U.S.
MATTES	257523	M	Ger.		Kapo,Camp Dora,Nordhausen(Ger.)	MURDER	FR.
MATTES	300319		Ger.		Assist.,Osturmfhr.,Employing,SS Jaeger attached "Dora" and Factory from C.C.Buchenwald. 43-45	MURDER	FR.
MATTES, Willy	256680	M	Ger.		Interpreter,SD,Foix(Fr.) 11.42	MURDER	FR.
MATTHEI, Ernst	256288	M	Ger.		Pvt.,Nordhausen(Ger.)	MURDER	U.S.
MATTHEIS	257299	M	Ger.	12	SS-Mann,Waffen-SS,Regimental Aid-Station,Regt.37,Div."Goetz von Berlichingen", near St.Eny(Fr.) 7.44	INTERR.	U.S.
MATTHEIS	257975	M	Ger.	12	Sturmmann,SS Div."Goetz von Berlichingen", St.Eny(Fr.)	WITNESS	U.S.
MATTHES	31610	M	Ger.		Major,20 Army M.G.Bn.13-7 Geb.Div.(Nor.) 10.-11.44	MURDER	NOR.
MATTHES	188225	M			Ortsgruppenleiter,SS Special-Coy.,NSDAP,Behefeld-Erzgeb.(Ger.) 4.45	MURDER	U.S.
MATTHES or MATHES, Max	170071	M	Ger.		Ubach(Ger.) 7.44	SUSPECT	U.S.
MATTHES, Max	306775	M	Ger.		nr. Schollach(Ger.) 7.44	MURDER	U.S.
MATTHES, Rudolf	135280	M	Ger.		Civ.in a Factory,KL.Etzendorf(Ger.)	TORTURE	U.S.
MATTHESIUS	104847	M	Ger.		Osturmfhr.,SS,C.C. Wanzleben(Ger.) 4.45	MURDER	U.S.
MATHEUS, Johann	595	M	Ger.		Sturmschfhr.,SS Lager-Fhr.,Beisfjord(Nor.) 3.42-43	MURDER	YUGO.
MATTHEY	162225	M	Ger.		Civilian,Praunheim(Ger.)	MURDER	U.S.
MATTHEY, Ewald	261324	M	Ger.		SS-Guard,SS C.C. Auschwitz(Pol.) 44-45	BRUTALITY	POL.
MATTHIAC	185215	M	Ger.		Admiral,Navy,Landaul(Fr.) 4.44	MURDER	FR.
MATTHIAS	260987		Ger.		SS-Rottfhr.,C.C. Vaihingen(Ger.) 8.44-4.45	MURDER	U.S.
MATTIAT, Friedrich	259586	M	Ger.	9.8.09	Crimes Against and Crimes Against Humanity	WITNESS	U.S.
MATTHIE, Friedrich	193844	M	Ger.	2.9.01	Sgt.,Reichsjustizministerium,Strafgefangenlager C.C.Finmark(Nor.) 6.42-5.45	MISC.CRIMES	YUGO.,NOR.
MATTHIES, Brunhilde	254468	F	Ger.	10	House-Wife,Civilian,Saarbruecken-Burbach(Ger.) 8.44	WITNESS	U.S.
MATTHIESSEN	300320		Ger.		Oberwachtmeister,Strafgefangenlager Nord-Norway,Northern(Nor.) 43-45	MISC.CRIMES	CZECH.
MATTHIS	161931	M	Ger.	10	Capt.,Army,Versuchsstab Kessler,C.C.Ohrdruf,Buchenwald(Ger.)	WITNESS	U.S.
MATTHUS	307156	M			Lt.,Blot-Moermond(Neth.) 12.44	MURDER	NETH.
MATTHUS	250989	M		16	Hptsturmfhr.,SS,Gorinshem(Neth.) 10.44	INTERR.	NETH.
MATTHYS	254029	M	Ger.		Section Leader,Sipo,Bruessels(Bel.) 40-45	INTERR.	BEL.
MATTISKEN	12658	M			Hptsturmfhr.,Sipo and SD.44	MISC.CRIMES	NOR.
MATUSCHEK, Herbert	256285	M	Ger.		Crim.-Assist.,Gestapo,Opava(Czech.) 39-45	TORTURE	CZECH.
MATYYS	301583	M	Ger.		Capo Revier,C.C. Neuengamme(Ger.) 40-45	MURDER	BEL.
MATZ	185709	M	Ger.		Usturmfhr.,5 SS Totenkopf-Regt.,Plock(Pol.) 2.-9.41	MURDER	POL.
MATZ	259043	M	Ger.		SS-Mann,Muhldorf Area(Ger.)	MURDER	U.S.
MATZ, Josef	195650	M	Ger.	16.2.97	Leader,Manager of a Firm,NSDAP,Havlickuv Brod(Czech.) 38-45	TORTURE	CZECH.
MATZ, Karl	305925	M			Prison-Guard,Theresienstadt,Small Fortress(Czech.) 10.38-44	MURDER	CZECH.
MATZAIN see MALTZAHN	168079						
MATZAK, Sophia	156855	F			Civilian,Hermansdorf(Aust.)	WITNESS	U.S.
MATZALM see MALTZAHN	168079						
MATZE, Philipps	255888	M	Ger.		Sentry Kdo.456 A Stalag XII D,Langenlonsheim(Ger.) 3.42	MURDER	FR.
MATZEIT	256289	M			C.C.Dora,Nordhausen(Ger.)	MURDER	U.S.
MATZKE, Willy	196020	M			Hptsturmfhr.,2 Pz.Regt."Das Reich",Tulle(Fr.) 6.44	WITNESS	FR.
MATZUCA	256290	M			Cpl.,C.C.Ellrich,Nordhausen(Ger.)	MURDER	U.S.
MAUBACH	301275	M			Geschz.Angestellter,Abt.IVD,SD,Bruessels(Bel.) 6.40-9.44	MURDER	BEL.
MAUCHENHEIM or Gustav Frhr.v.BECHTOLSTEIN	260611	M			Maj.-Gen.,Army	WITNESS	U.S.
MAUDANZ, Hermann	254890	M	Ger.	22.11.07	H.Q.Milit.,Bela Crkva(Yugo.) 43	MURDER	YUGO.
MAUE	124759	M	Ger.		Sturmfhr.,SA-Stand.,KL.Neususturm(Ger.)	MURDER	U.S.
MAUEHRER	157011	M	Ger.		Ortsgruppenleiter NSDAP,Bergheim-Mondorf(Fr.and Ger.) 4.and 8.44	MURDER	U.S.
MAUER	191409	M	Ger.	02	Capt.,Army,Stalag 330 C.C.Olga(Nor.) 3.45	MURDER	NOR.
MAUER	193843	M	Ger.		Capt.,Abwehr,Stalag 330,Camp Olga(Nor.)	MURDER	NOR.
MAUER	254887	M	Ger.		Pvt.,C.C.Dora,Nordhausen(Ger.)	MURDER	U.S.
MAUER, Hans	189096	M	Ger.		Member Gestapo,Stanislawow(Pol.) 8.41-10.42	WITNESS	POL.
MAUER, Willy	189097	M	Ger.		Member Gestapo,Stanislawow(Pol.) 8.41-10.42	MURDER	POL.

MAU-MAY

NAME	C.R.FILE NUMBER	SEX	NATIO-NALITY	DATE OF BIRTH	RANK OCCUPATION UNIT PLACE AND DATE OF CRIME	REASON WANTED	WANTED BY
MAUERHOFF, Ehwardt	260107	M	Ger.		Lt., Unit 58.512, Luneville, Meurthe and Moselle (Fr.) 14.3.44	INCENDIARISM	FR.
MAUERSBERGER	254886	M		15. 5.16	Flyer, C.C. Ellrich, Nordhausen (Ger.)	MURDER	U.S.
MAUESBERGER	301809	M	Ger.		SS-Mann, 1.SS-Panz.Div. Leibstandarte "Adolf Hitler", Region of Stavelot (Bel.) 19.-20.12.44	MURDER	BEL.
MAUL, Georg	141981	M	Ger.	95	SS-Mann, Waffen SS, Totenkopf-Standarte,C.C. Muehlhausen, Junkers-Works (Ger.)	MISC.CRIMES	U.S.
MAUL, Otto	182100	M	Ger.		Oberscharfhr., Manager, SD, Prague (Czech.) 39 - 45	TORTURE	CZECH.
MAURACH	167000	M	Ger.	90	Capt., Army, (Serb.)	TORTURE	U.S.
MAUREK	192122	M			Interpreter, Geheime-Feldpolizei, Liege (Bel.)	MISC.CRIMES	BEL.
MAURER	1723	M			Obersturmfhr., SS-Feldgendarmerie,10.SS-Panz.Div.,Lisieux(Fr.)15.1.44	MISC.CRIMES	U.K.
MAURER	124239	M	Ger.	93	Capt., Army, C.C. Poitiers (Fr.)	TORTURE	FR.
MAURER	151363	M			N.C.O., SS, "Das Reich", "Der Fuehrer", Oradour s.Glane (Fr.)10.6.44	MURDER	FR.
MAURER	157010	M			Capt., Army, 31286 H.U.V. Rgt. "Lisieux", Cabrespuies(Fr.) 8.8.44	MURDER	FR.
MAURER	186444	M	Ger.	16 - 22	Lt., Army - Infantry, Konig-Odenwald (Ger.) 21.11.44	MURDER	U.K.
MAURER	252532	M	Ger.	95	Ober-Inspector, 15.Police-Rgt., Crescentino (It.) 8.9.44	INTERR.	U.K.
MAURER	253554	M	Ger.	17	Hauptsturmfhr., SS, Graz (Aust.) 4.45	INTERR.	U.K.
MAURER	306632	M	Ger.		Director of the works Maurer Sohn, Muenich (Fr.) 41 - 45	MISC.CRIMES	FR.
MAURER, Anton	195358	M	Ger.	10. 1.00	Member, SA, Moravske-Budejovice (Czech.) 39 - 45	MISC.CRIMES	CZECH.
MAURER, August	183225	M	Ger.	5. 7.96	Sturmbannfhr., SD, Praha (Czech.) 39 - 45	MURDER	CZECH.
MAURER, Bronislava (or LIVIA, Bronislava)	195632	M	Ger.	18.11.21	Switchboard Operator, Cililian, Prag (Czech.) 39 - 45	MISC.CRIMES	CZECH.
MAURER, Emil	189208	M	Ger.		Cpl., Panz.-Div. "Das Reich", 3.Coy.,1.Bn., Cradour sur Glane (Fr.)6.44	MURDER	FR.
MAURER, Ernst	256546	M	Ger.	20. 6.15	Hauptscharfhr., SS-Guard, Coy.Cmdt., Bystrice near Benesoy (Czech.) 44	MURDER	CZECH.
MAURER, Fritz	301851	M	Ger.		Feldgendarm, Feldgendarmerie at St. Jean d'Angely, Ternant, (Charente-Maritime) (Fr.) 31.7.44	MURDER	FR.
MAURER, Gebhard	254885	M		07	Major, C.C. Dora Nordhausen (Ger.) 40 - 45	MURDER	U.S.
MAURER, Gerhard	12409	M	Ger.		Obersturmfhr., SS-Member of G.H.Q. Berlin, Oranienburg (Ger.) 39 - 44	MISC.CRIMES	BEL. CZECH.
MAURER, Gerhard	31719	M	Ger.		Obersturmbannfhr., SS, Head of Amt II, Dept. "D" Br.H.Q.SS, Berlin (Ger.) 6.40 - 1.45	MURDER	BEL. CZECH. POL.
MAURER, Gerhard	193726	M	Ger.		Standartenfhr., SS, C,C, Buchenwald (Ger.) 42 - 45	TORTURE	U.S.
MAURER, Hermann	194174	M	Ger.		Uscharfhr., SS, C.C. Buchenwald-Ohrdruf (Ger.)	TORTURE	U.S.
MAURER, Josef	240007	M			Oberscharfhr., SS, Sipo, SD, Turin (It.) 45	MURDER	U.S.
MAURER, Michael	260503	M		2. 7.08	Guard, SS, C.C. Natzweiler (Fr.)	MURDER	FR.
MAURER, Otto	168041	M			San.-Cpl., Army, 9.Rgt. Gren.Sanit.1.Coy., Magny-Anigon (Fr.) 18.9.44	MURDER	FR.
MAURER, Raimond	172469	M	Ger.	29. 1.09	Civilian, Laborer, C.C. Flossenburg (Ger.)	TORTURE	U.S.
MAURER, Rubard	163069	M		09	Rttfhr., C.C. Natzweiler-Struthof (Fr.)	MURDER	FR.
MAURER, Sohn	192356	M	Ger.		Chief, P.O.W. working Kdo. 2463, Stalag VII A, Muenchen (Ger.) 41-45	MURDER	FR.
MAURICE	240132	M	Ger.	15	Sturmbannfhr., SS, SD, Berlin, Marseille (Ger.Fr.)	PILLAGE	U.S.
MAURICE (see MORITZ)	138344	M					
MAURITZ	254230	M	Ger.		Employee, Sipo, Brussels (Bel.) 40 - 45	INTERR.	BEL.
MAURRER	196021	M	Ger.		Custom-official, Chaum (Fr.) 3.6.44	MURDER	FR.
MAUS	257998	M			Usturmfhr., 150 Pz.-Brig., Meuse-Bridge-Antwerpen (Bel.) 12.44	MISC.CRIMES	U.S.
MAUS, Jacob	186445	M	Ger.		Sturmscharfhr., SD, Ghent (Bel.) 42 - 43	TORTURE	BEL.
MAUSER	29764	M			Gestapo-Befehlshaber, Cannes (Fr.)	MURDER	FR.
MAUSER	126455	M			Lt., Army, La Tremblade (Fr.)	PILLAGE	FR.
MAUSER, Joseph (or MOSER)	142553	M		06	Gestapo-Chief, Cannes (Fr.) 14.7.44 - 16.8.44	MURDER	FR.
MAUSER	186581	M			Schutzhaftlagerfhr., SS, C.C. Dora Nordhausen (Ger.)	TORTURE	BEL.
MAUSER, Josef	261089	M			Uscharfhr., C.C., Natzweiler (Fr.)	BRUTALITY	FR.
MAUSER, Karl (or MOSER)	191941	M	Ger.		Major, Police, Gerardmer (Fr.) 27.5.44	WITNESS	U.S.
MAUSERSAUL	141354	M			Capt., Stalag 3 D-401, Berlin (Ger.) 4.42	TORTURE	U.K.
MAUSS (see MAUTZ)	121351						
MAUSSER	188845	M	Ger.		Member, Feldgendarmerie, Bar le Duc (Fr.) 20. - 23.8.44	MURDER	FR.
MAUSTRUM, Willy	1724	M			Pvt., Army-Picnier-Corps, Hercuvilette (Fr.) 6.6.44	MURDER	U.K.
MAUTH	254036	M	Ger.		Foreman, Fisher Plant, Frankenburg (Ger.)	MISC.CRIMES	FR.
MAUTNER	132158	M	Ger.		Cpl., C.C. Dora-Nordhausen (Ger.)	MURDER	U.S.
MAUTNER, Karl (or KORSITZKY)	254252	M	Ger.	27.10.97	Ortsgruppenleiter, NSDAP, Hilovec (Czech.) 42 - 45	MISC.CRIMES	CZECH.
MAUTZ (or MAUSS)	121351	M			Gestapo, Belfort, Banvillars (Fr.)	MURDER	FR.
MAUTZIG	161365	M	Ger.		Lt., Kommandantur, Millau - Rodez (Fr.) 6.8.44	WITNESS	FR.
MAUTZKE	196022	M			Cpl., C.C., Compiegne (Fr.) 41 - 44	MURDER	FR.
MAUVALD	142552	M	Ger.		Hauptscharfhr., SS, Gestapo, Chambery (Fr.)	WITNESS	FR.
MAUZIK, Johann	301791	M	Ger.		SS - Mann, C.C. Auschwitz (Pol.) 40	MURDER	POL.
MAWRENZ, Nieter	168042	M			Pvt., Army, 9.Rgt.Res.Gren., 1.Coy. MG-Schuetze,Magny d'Anigon(Fr.)44	MURDER	FR.
MAX (or MAKS)	62514	M	Ger.		Arbeitsdienstfhr., SS, RAD, C.C. Amersfoort(Neth.) 11.42	TORTURE	U.S.
MAX	132159	M	Ger.		Sturmfhr., Waffen SS, C.C. Dora-Nordhausen(Ger.)	MURDER	U.S.
MAX	141395	M	Ger.		Block-chief, SS, C.C. Heinkelwerke bei Wien (Aust.)	TORTURE	FR.
MAX	174862	M	Ger.		Obermeister, Arbeitskommando, Wansleben-See, Buchenwald (Ger.) 43-45	TORTURE	FR.
MAX (see HEINSLER, Ernest)	192001	M	Ger.		Feldgendarm, Feldgendarmerie, Gerardmer (Fr.) 27.5.44	MURDER	FR.
MAX	194618	M	Ger.		Adjudant, Inf.Rgt. 636, Pont Lorois en Belz (Fr.) 20.8.44	PILLAGE	FR.
MAX	196023	M	Ger.		Member, Gestapo, Grenoble (Fr.)	MURDER	FR.
MAX	240008	M		07	Subordinate official, Economic Section Gestapo, Prague (Czech.)39	TORTURE	U.S.
MAX (see MARX)	301790						
MAX	306606	M	Ger.		Foreman, C.C. Dora and factory, Nordhausen (Ger.) 40 - 45	MURDER	BEL. FR.
MAX, Peter	256649	M	Ger.		Employee, C.C. Dora-Nordhausen (Ger.)	MURDER	U.S.
MAX, Victoria	139682	F	Ger.		Woman - Guard, Waffen SS, Arbeitslager 101, C.C. Buchenwald (Ger.)	TORTURE	U.S.
MAX, Viktor	184147	M	Ger.	03	Kriminalangestellter, SD, Gestapo, Praha (Czech.) 39 - 45	MURDER	CZECH.
MAXAMER, Karl	254884	M			Pvt., C.C., Dora-Nordhausen (Ger.)	MURDER	U.S.
MAXEINER, Wilhelm	301210	M	Ger.		Member, Volkssturm in Dillstein nr.Pforzheim, Huchenfeld,Dillweissenstein (Ger.) 17. - 18.3.45	MURDER	U.K.
MAXIAME	256329	M	Ger.		Interpreter, SD, St. Girons (Fr.) 11.42 - 8.44	MISC.CRIMES	FR.
MAY	597	M	Ger.		Oberscharfhr., Prisoner Kitchener, C.C. Dachau (Ger.)	MURDER	FR.
MAY	12410	M	Ger.		Sturmfhr., Gestapo Kommissar, Tabor-Bohemia (Czech.) 39 - 45	TORTURE	CZECH.
MAY	38885	M	Ger.		Pvt., Army Paratroops, Roermond (Neth.) 43	TORTURE	U.S.
MAY	141982	M	Ger.		Factory-Guard, Waffen SS, Totenkopf Commando Martha C.C. Muehlhausen (Ger.)	BRUTALITY	U.S.
MAY	142550	M	Ger.		Truppfhr., SA, Ampfing (Ger.)	MURDER	U.S.
MAY	190259	M	Ger.		Generalmajor-Befehlshaber, Ordnungspolizei, Pozauerac (Yugo.) 41-43	MURDER	YUGO.
MAY	194173	M	Ger.		Uscharfhr., SS, C.C. Buchenwald (Ger.) 42 - 45	MURDER	U.S.

MAY-MAY

NAME	C.R.FILE NUMBER	SEX	NATIO- NALITY	DATE OF BIRTH	RANK OCCUPATION UNIT PLACE AND DATE OF CRIME	REASON WANTED	WANTED BY
MAY (or MAI), Ernst	257488	M		04	Truppfhr.,Obermeister, Org.Todt, C.C. Muehldorf (Ger.)	MURDER	U.S.
MAY, Reinhold	126491	M	Ger.		SS-Panz.Div. Leibstandarte "Adolf Hitler" Rgt.,I	MURDER	U.S.
MAY, Wilhelm	257343	M		7.12.12	Pvt. Army-Inf. 3 Coy. 129.Pz.Gren.Rgt.,San Giovanni e Paolo (It.)10.43	WITNESS	U.S.
MAYBAUM	256547	M	Ger.		Employee, Military Sipo, Amsterdam (Neth.) 10.44	SUSPECT	NETH.
MAYENBURG, Wolfgang	254766	M	Ger.	15. 5.00	Civilian, Teplige-Sandy (Czech.) 11.39	TORTURE	CZECH.
MAYER (see BARBIER)	57						
MAYER	5980	M	Ger.		SS-Obersturmfhr. Guard C.C.Oswiecim,Rajsko (Pol.)6.40-43	MURDER	POL.
MAYER	12542	M			Pvt. 110.Panz.Gren.Rgt.1.Gruppe, Gourdon (Fr.) 6.44	MURDER	FR.
MAYER	38869	M			Pvt. Army Landessch.Bn. " H " 5.Coy. 2.45	TORTURE	U.S.
MAYER	104877	M			Dr. Lt. Institut, Kiew (Sov.Un.) 41/42	MURDER	U.S.
MAYER	125061	M			Navy-Pvt. LCFL. MV. Portland 41	MURDER	U.K.
MAYER	132634	M	Ger.		Lt. Cuisery (Fr.) 8.44	MURDER	FR.
MAYER	132761	M	Ger.		SS-Oberscharfhr. C.C.Mauthausen (Aust.) 41-45	MURDER	U.S.
MAYER	132762	M			Prisoner C.C. Medical Dept., Mauthausen (Aust.) 41-45	MURDER	U.S.
MAYER	132781	M	Ger.		Oberwachtmstr. C.C. Kaicheim, (Ger.)	TORTURE	BEL.
MAYER (or MEIER, MAIER, MAIR, MEYER)	133281	M		09	SS-Uscharfhr. SS Div. "Das Reich" 3.or 4.Coy.2.Reconnaissance Bn. near St.Vith (Bel.) 12.44 - 1.45	SUSPECT	U.S.
MAYER	146936	M	Ger.		Lt. Army, Capestang (Fr.) 44	MISC.CRIMES	FR.
MAYER	157009	M		15	C.C. Rawa-Ruska (Pol.)	TORTURE	FR.
MAYER	160707	M	Ger.		Pvt. Army, Stalag VI G,Flamersheim (Ger.) 2.45	TORTURE	U.K. U.S.
MAYER	166899	M			Lt. Parachutist, Nalilly Sermesse (Fr.) 8.44	WITNESS	FR.
MAYER	168056	M			SS-Oberscharfhr., Guard C.C. Sachsenhausen,Oranienburg (Ger.) 45	MURDER	POL.
MAYER, (alias MEYER)	173794	M			Obersturmfhr. SS C.C. Oswiecim, Birkenau (Pol.) 39-45	MURDER	CZECH.POL.BEL
MAYER	179814	M			Lt. Fallschirmjaeger-Einheit, Cuisery (Fr.)	MURDER	FR.
MAYER	185711	M			Officer, 5.SS-Totenkopf Rgt., Plock (Pol.) 3.41	MURDER	POL.
MAYER	188846	M			Sgt. 804. Bau Bn. , Tournon (Fr.)	TORTURE	FR.
MAYER	189029	M			Oberwachtmstr., Gestapo, Member of Staff at Lyons (Fr.) 43	TORTURE	FR.
MAYER	191942	M	Ger.		Cpl. SD. Landerneau (Fr.)	TORTURE	FR.
MAYER	193297	M			Sonderfhr.,Interpreter, Army, C.C. Stalag VIII.B. Lamsdorf (Ger.)7.43	TORTURE	U.K.
MAYER (see MEYER)	194182	M	Ger.				
MAYER	225027	M			Hauptscharfhr. Gestapo, SS Official, Lyon, Strasbourg (Fr.)	MURDER	FR.
MAYER (or MEYER)	250386	M			Capt. 98.Bn. 157 Inf.Div. 4.Coy. L'Ain (Fr.) 7.44	MISC.CRIMES	FR.
MAYER	251827	M		15	SS - Unterscharfhr. C.C.,Buchenwald (Ger.)	MISC.CRIMES	FR.
MAYER (see MOUIE.)	251899	M	Ger.				
MAYER (see MEYER)	253549	M					
MAYER	254214	M	Ger.		Cpl. 118.Alpenjaeger Div. 738 Rgt., Bosnia and Herzegovina(Yugo.)43-44	MISC.CRIMES	YUGO.
MAYER (see MEYER)	254455	M	Ger.				
MAYER	254894	M			Chief, Organisation Todt, Toulouse (Fr.) 11.42 - 8.44	MISC.CRIMES	FR.
MAYER	256548	M			Sturmscharfhr. ,Waffen SS, Muehldorf (Ger.)	MURDER	U.S.
MAYER	261000	M	Ger.		Commander, Major Garrison, Urbino (It.) 6.44	MURDER	U.S.
MAYER	261001	M	Ger.		SS - Rottenfhr. C.C. Vaihingen a.d.Enz (Ger.) 8.44 - 4.45	MURDER	U.S.
MAYER	261851	M			Cpl.,Chief of C.C. Arrest Baracke Stalag XVIII C. ,Markt Pongau, Salzburg (Aust.) 8.44	MURDER	FR.
MAYER (or MEYER)	301857	M	Ger.		Obersturmfhr. SS C.C. Oswiecim-Birkenau (Pol.) 39-45	MURDER	CZECH.
MAYER (see MEYER)	305466						
MAYER	305724	M	Ger.		Capt.Commanding Unit 59-034,Chatelaudren, Cotes-du-Nord (Fr.) 8.44	MURDER	FR.
MAYER	306729	M	Ger.		Sgt., 118.Alpen-Jaeger Div., 738.Rgt. Brac, Tronova (Yugo.)1.44	MURDER	YUGO.
MAYER, Albert	254883	M			Pvt. C.C. Nixei - Nordhausen (Ger.)	MURDER	U.S.
MAYER, Alfred	168043	M	Ger.		Staatssekretaer, Reichsministerium f.d.besetzten Ostgebiete (Pol.) 44	PILLAGE	POL.
MAYER, Alois	38884	M			SS - Scharfhr.,C.C. Lublin (Pol.) 43	TORTURE	POL.
MAYER, Arthur	12541	M			Interpreter, Gestapo , Sizun (Fr.) 7.44	TORTURE	FR.
MAYER, August	139054	M			Foreman, Civilian Factory, Ansal (Ger.) 4.44	TORTURE	U.S.
MAYER, Bello	160709	M			Cpl. 263.D.I. Kommando de Landerneau, Finistere (Fr.) 44	MURDER	FR.
MAYER, Friedrich	182099	M	Ger.		Sturmbannfhr., Regierungsrat, SD, Gestapo, Prague (Czech.) 43-44	PILLAGE	CZECH.
MAYER, Gustav	256291	M			Pvt. C.C. Buchenwald, (Ger.)	MURDER	U.S.
MAYER, Hermann	194483	M	Ger.		Police-Inspector, Gestapo, Bruenn (Czech.) 39-45	MURDER	CZECH.
MAYER, Jakob (see MEIER)	195631						
MAYER, Johann, Leonhard	140795	M	Ger.	4. 1.99	Manufacturer, Ciwilian, Konig, (Ger.)	MURDER	U.S.
MAYER, Josef	256651	M			Sgt. SS-Postenfhr.,Cdo.2 F.MA.Bormann, Nordhausen (Ger.)	MURDER	U.S.
MAYER, Karl	194206	M	Ger.		Butcher, C.C. Flossenburg (Ger.) 5.44 - 4.45	TORTURE	BEL.
MAYER, Kurt	254777	M	Ger.		Sgt.,Feldpolice, La Courtine,Busseau-Greuse (Fr.) 2.44	MURDER	FR.
MAYER, Leonhard (or MAIER)	142561	M	Ger.	4. 1.99	Civilian, Konig and Zell,(Ger.) 11.44	MURDER	U.S.
MAYER, Ludwig	184143	M		30. 7.17	Rottenfhr. 4.SS Totenkopfsturmbann C.C. Dora Nordhausen (Ger.)43-45	WITNESS	U.S.
MAYER, Ludwig	256650	M	Ger.	19. 2.94	Forester, Civilian, Pardubice (Czech.) 6.46	MURDER	CZECH.
MAYER, Martin	145976	M		17. 2.13	Sturmmann, Waffen SS, Schleissheim near Munich (Ger.) 44	MURDER	U.S.
MAYER, Otto	251829	M	Ger.		Pvt.,377.Jaeger Rgt. Vinkt-Meigem (Bel.) 5.40	MISC.CRIMES	BEL.
MAYER, Paul	128969	M			Cpl. Prisoner, Guard C.C. Wuerzburg (Ger.) 1.-5.45	TORTURE	U.S.
MAYER, Paul (or MEIER)	156847	M			Unterscharfhr. Waffen SS, Saal on the Danube (Ger.) 12.44-4.45	MURDER	U.S.
MAYER, Peter	125430	M			Pvt. Army, 110.or 111.Panz.Gren.Rgt. 2.Coy.Albine (Fr.) 6.44	MURDER	FR.
MAYER, Robert	259392	M	Ger.		SS-Untersturmfhr. Gestapo of Poitiers, Chief of Antenne of Niort Poitiers Area (Fr.)	MISC.CRIMES	FR.
MAYER, Theo	161929	M	Ger.	10	Pvt. C.C. Buchenwald SS , (Ger.)	WITNESS	U.S.
MAYER, Walter	104849	M	Ger.		Oberfaehnrich, Army (Ger.)	MURDER	U.S.
MAYER, Wilhelm	148711	M	Ger.	17. 4.19	Member, Wachgesellschaft Niedersachsen, Lahde-Weser (Ger.) 43-45	TORTURE	BEL.
MAYER, Wilhelm	192262	M		22. 5.25	Ciwilian, Falkenau (Czech.) 10.44	WITNESS	U.S.
MAYERBERGER	160714	M			Capt., Ostlegion Langogne (Fr.) 6.-7.44	PILLAGE	FR.
MAYERHOF, Karl	185485	M	Ger.		SS C.C. Mauthausen (Aust.) 45	MURDER	FR.
MAYERHOFER, Charles	132760	M			C.C. Mauthausen, (Aust.) 41-45	MURDER	FR.
MAYERHOFER, Josef	193842	M	Ger.	00	P.O.W. working Bn. 186 (Nor.) 40-45	MISC.CRIMES	U.S.
MAYERHOFER, Rudolf	196833	M		21. 3.95	Shoemaker , Member NSDAP, Mastetten (Aust.) 3.45	MISC.CRIMES	NOR.
MAYERHOFER, Vincenc	194482	M	Ger.		Crim.Obersecr., Gestapo ,Brno (Czech.) 39-45	MURDER	CZECH.
MAYERICH	301584	M	Ger.		SS-Gruppenfhr. C.C. Mauthausen (Aust.) 40-45	MURDER	BEL.
MAYER ° Lehr (see MEYER)	611						

MAY-MEI

NAME	C.R.FILE NUMBER	SEX	NATIO- NALITY	DATE OF BIRTH	RANK OCCUPATION. UNIT PLACE AND DATE OF CRIME	REASON WANTED	WANTED BY
MAYERS	39844	M	Ger.		Lager Zippendorf (Ger.) 2.44	MISC.CRIMES	U.K.
MAYES (see MOLOTAU)	174861	M	Ger.		Chief,Arb.Kdo.,C.C.Wansleben-See (Ger.) 43-45	TORTURE	FR.
MAYES	305464	M	Ger.		Betriebsfhr.,Arb.Kdo.,C.C.Buchenwald (Ger.) 42-45	MURDER	FR.
MAYGUT, Sylvester	255879	M			Civilian,C.C.Buchenwald (Ger.)	MURDER	U.S.
MAYHOFFER	194609	M	Ger.		SS-O'Sturmfhr.,SS-Div."Das Reich",SS Rgt."Der Fuehrer" Fontanilles (Fr.) 21.5.44	TORTURE	FR.
MAYOR	305725	M	Ger.		Hauptsturmfhr.,C.C.Auschwitz-Birkenau (Pol.) 40	MURDER	FR.
MAYR (see MAYRE)	254895						
MAYR, Hans	306040	M	Ger.		Member of Staff of Baby Clinic,Wolfsburg,Ruehen (Ger.)	MURDER	U.K.
MAYRE (or MACRE or MAYR or MANDL)	254895	M	Ger.		Interpreter,S.D.Toulouse (Fr.) 11.42-8.44	MISC.CRIMES	FR.
MAYRINGER	255056	M			Flyer,C.C.Ellrich-Nordhausen (Ger.)	MURDER	U.S.
MAYWALD	160704	M			Sgt.,C.C. Parzymiecki (Pol.) 41-44	MURDER	U.S.
MAYWALD, Franz	254765	M	Ger.	4.12.11	Head,Gestapo,Most (Czech.) 39-45	TORTURE	CZECH.
MAZAN, Anton	185881	M			Pvt.,Slovake Army,Slovakia (Czech.) 44-45	MURDER	CZECH.
MAZAN, Paul	183672	M			SS-Guard,4 SS-Totenkopf-Stuba.,C.C.Dora Mittelbau,Nordhausen (Ger.) 43-45	WITNESS	U.S.
MAZANETZ, Wilhelm	260721	M	Ger.	23. 3.05	Member,Firing Guard,Prague,Kobylisy (Czech.) 6.42	MURDER	CZECH.
MAZANOWSKI	255054	M			N.C.O.,C.C.Ellrich-Nordhausen (Ger.)	MURDER	U.S.
MAZANOWSKI, Bruno	253221	M			U'Scharfhr.,C.C.Harzungen,Nordhausen (Ger.)	MURDER	U.S.
MAZILECK (see also MARISCHEK)	306266	M	Ger.		Lt.Col.,Cmdt. of Stalag VIII C,Sagan (Ger.) 8.1.45	MURDER	U.K.
MAZUM, Wilhelm	21331	M			Obergruppenfhr.,SS General Lt. der Polizei, W.K.R. II	TORTURE	UNWCC
MAZUR	301641	M	Ger.		Oberwachtmeister,Ebrach near Amberg (Ger.) 45	MURDER	CZECH.
MEARKINS (or NIERCKENS)	137594	M	Ger.	19 - 21	Sgt.,20 Army Korps, 2 Coy.,Heydebreck (Ger.) 40-43	TORTURE	U.K.
MEBIS	251155	M	Ger.	00	Cpl.,3 Coy.,Techn.Bn. 5,St.Nazaire (Fr.) 24.8.44	MISC.CRIMES	FR.
MECHELKE	254469	M	Ger.		Capt.,Div.H.Goering,4 Parachute Rgt.,2 Bn.,5 Coy.,Helchteren (Bel.) 5.-11.9.44	PILLAGE	BEL.
MECHLING	148710	M			Capt.,Army,	MISC.CRIMES	U.S.
MECIAR, Stanislav	305042	M	Ger.		Doctor, Secretary of the Slovakian School Association,Slovakia (Czech.) 40-45	INTERR.	CZECH.
MECKE	31720	M	Ger.		SS-Hauptsturmfhr.,Administr.Manager of Crematorium,Oswiecim (Pol.) 6.40-1.45	MURDER	POL.
MECKE, Richard	194178	M	Ger.		Guard,C.C.Buchenwald (Ger.) 42-45	MURDER	U.S.
MECKEL	158942	M	Ger.		Pvt.,SS-Pz.Div."Adolf Hitler",2 Zug,1 Ron.Bn., Parfondruy,Stavelot (Bel.) 18.-22.12.44	MURDER	U.S.
MECKEL, Otto	10308	M	Ger.		U'Sturmfhr.,SS-Kommissar der Gestapo,Prague (Czech.)39-44	TORTURE	CZECH.
MECKENDORF	253938	M	Ger.		U'Scharfhr.,C.C.Auschwitz (Pol.)	MURDER	FR.
MECKEL (see MICHL)	253551						
MECKLEINBURG	163589	M		85	Major,Army,Douzy (Fr.)	WITNESS	FR.
MECKLENBURG, Hilde	135281	F			Civilian,Gelsenkirchen (Ger.)	MISC.CRIMES	U.S.
MEDEK, Franz	254261	M	Ger.	18. 8.97	Agent,Gestapo,Hradec,Kralove (Czech.) 39-45	MURDER	CZECH.
MEDER	195095	M	Ger.		SS-U'Sturmfhr.,SS Div. Leibstandarte "Adolf Hitler" 3 Coy., Wormhoudt (Fr.,Bel) 27.5.40	MURDER	U.K.
MEDER	195122	M	Ger.	15	Capt.,Army,14 Pz.Korps,Fontana Liri (It.) 43	WITNESS	U.K.
MEDING, Heinrich (or MEDINA)	193841	M	Ger.	07	Sgt.,Reichsjustizministerium,Strafgefangenenlager,C.C.Finmark (Nor.) 40-9.3.45	MISC.CRIMES	NOR.
MEEDER	39842	M	Ger.		Lt.,Stalag XII C,Hammelberg (Ger.) 7.44	MISC.CRIMES	U.K.
MEERKAMP	168015	M	Ger.		Civilian,Ostgebietsministerium,Einsatzstab Rosenberg,Paris (Fr.) 44	PILLAGE	FR.
MEERWARTH, Robert	142114	M			S.D.	MURDER	FR.
MEES, Peter	305043	M			N.C.O., serving in 4836 Unit of the L.G.P.A. Luftwaffe,Vosselare Flandre orientale,43	MURDER	BEL.
MEESE, Wilhelm	173896	M		21	Member, Landwacht,Lauenau (Ger.) 11.44	WITNESS	U.S.
MEESER	39841	M	Ger.		Sgt.,Inf.Rgt.,515,3 Coy.,Auschwitz (Pol.) 21.1.-5.2.45	MISC.CRIMES	U.K.
MEGER, Edmund	168043	M	Ger.		Pvt.,Army, 9 Gren.Rgt., 1 Coy., Melder,Magny D'Avignon (Fr.)18.9.44	MURDER	FR.
MEHAM, Wilhelm	145973	M	Ger.		Civilian,Manager,Ottmannsfehn,Stapelmoor (Ger.) 43	MURDER	U.S.
MEHL	1434	M	Ger.		Lt.,Army, 26 Pz.-Rgt.,	MISC.CRIMES	U.K.
MEHL	178299	M			Crim.Commissar,Gestapo,Saarbruecken (Ger.)	PILLAGE	FR.
MEHL	300820	M			Pvt.,1 Aufkl.Abt. 3 Coy., 2 Col., XV Div., Afrika Korps,St.Leger Arlon (Fr.) 5.9.44	MISC.CRIMES	BEL.
MEHL, Ernst	255248	M			Pvt.,C.C.Ellrich-Nordhausen (Ger.)	MURDER	U.S.
MEHL, Heinz	307158	M	Ger.		SS-O'Scharhr., 13 SS-Pz.Handzar Div.,Srem,Bosnia (Yugo.) 9.44	MURDER	YUGO.
MEHL, Phillipp, Jacob	157006	M	Ger.	16. 2.03	O'Sturmfhr.,Crim.Commissar,SS-Kripo,St.Avold-Marange (Fr.)9.8.44	MURDER	U.S.
MEHLBER	255055	M			Pvt., 2 Coy.,Sturmbn. AOK-I,MG,Cooroelles (Fr.) 15.11.44	MURDER	U.S.
MEHLER, Heinz	191223	M	Ger.		SS-Mann,SS,Magny D'Avignon (Fr.)	MURDER	FR.
MEHLHORN, Herbert	600	M	Ger.	24. 3.03	Doctor,Oberfhr.,Regierungsdirector,SS-Gau Wartheland,Hauptamt Poznan,Kulmhof (Pol.) 9.39-42	MURDER	POL.
MEHLHOSE (or MEHLHOS)	158937	M			SS-Scharfhr.,SS,Caen (Fr.)	MURDER	U.S.
MEHLITZ, Kurt, Erich	305044	M	Ger.	10. 4.99	O'Wachtmeister,Police,Berlin (Ger.) 24.3.44	MURDER	U.K.
MEHLKOFF, Hubert	192261	M	Ger.		Block-Senior,C.C.Flossenburg (Ger.) 44-45	MURDER	U.S.
MEHNERT	192355	M	Ger.		Pvt.,Army,Dienststelle 10748 N,Bayet (Fr.)	TORTURE	FR.
MEHNERT	251832	M			O'Scharfhr.,Gestapo,Limoges (Fr.)	INTERR.	FR.
MEHNERT, Walter	253265	M	Ger.	20	Cpl.,5-VII,Luftwaffenverw.,Merano (It.) 29.4.45	WITNESS	U.K.
MEHR (or MOEHR or MOEHER)	190374	M	Ger.		Cmdt.,Prison,Augsburg (Ger.) 27.2.45	TORTURE	U.S.
MEIBERG	10309	M	Ger.		Gestapo Kommissar,Pragus (Ger.) 39-44	TORTURE	CZECH.
MEIBERG	173793	M	Ger.		Gestapo,Staatspolizeileitstelle,C.C.Oswiecim-Birkenau (Pol.) 39-45	MURDER	CZECH.
MEIBERT	104850	M	Ger.		Sgt.,SS-Sturm Bn., AOK,Courcelles-Sur-Nied (Fr.) 15.11.44	MURDER	U.S.
MEIDLIGER, Martin	255249	M			Pvt.,C.C.Dora,Nordhausen (Ger.)	MURDER	U.S.
MEIER	38883	M	Ger.		Civ.Employee,Forstschutz Polizei,Segeletz 24.5.44	MURDER	U.S.
MEIER	38896	M	Ger.		Employee,Waffen-SS,employed Butzbach,Caucasus (Sov.Un.)	MURDER	U.S.
MEIER	39863	M	Ger.		1010 Motorized Rgt., 1 Bn.,Lt. Chillburs aux Bois,Loiret Orleanais (Fr.) 13 or 15.8.44	MURDER	U.K.
MEIER	104851	M			Abwehr,Stalag 8 B,Lansdorf (Ger.) 2.41	TORTURE	U.K.
MEIER	124240	M			Civilian Forest Inspector,Segeletz (Ger.)	MURDER	U.S.
MEIER (see MAYER)	133281						
MEIER	141412	M	Ger.	99	Gestapo,Mussida,Dordogne (Fr.) 2.44	MURDER	FR.
MEIER	146935	M	Ger.		Pvt.,SS-Pz.Div."Das Reich" (Fr.) 44	MURDER	FR.
MEIER	152159	M	Ger.		Sturmscharfhr.,SS,Muehldorf,Poing (Ger.) 21.4.45	MURDER	U.S.

MEI-MEI

NAME	C.R.FILE NUMBER	SEX	NATIO-NALITY	DATE OF BIRTH	RANK OCCUPATION UNIT PLACE AND DATE OF CRIME	REASON WANTED	WANTED BY
MEIER (see MEYER)	162227						
MEIER	173813	M	Ger.		Osturmbannfhr.,SS,C.C.,Struthof (Fr.)	MURDER	FR.
MEIER	173899	M	Ger.	91	Camp official,foreman,C.C.,Fella Works,Feucht (Ger.) 40-45	TORTURE	U.S.
MEIER (or MEYER)	174294	M	Ger.		Lt.,Oflag 55 VD,Aulendorf (Ger.) 8.42	MURDER	YUGO.
MEIER	178900	M	Ger.	10 - 15	Sgt.,814.Landesschuetzen,Stalag VIII C,Sagan, Bad Orb (Ger.) 2.-3.45	TORTURE	U.K.
MEIER (see MEYER)	187974						
MEIER	187989	M	Ger.	16	Cpl.,Stalag 344,C.C.,Ottmuth (Ger.)	MURDER	U.K.
MEIER (or MEYER)	193827	M	Ger.		Sonderfhr.,181.P.O.W. Labour Bn.,3.Coy.,More Og Romsdal (Nor.)26.12.44	MURDER	NOR.
MEIER	194176	M	Ger.		Cpl.,SS,C.C.,Kuehlhaus Weimar,Buchenwald (Ger.) 42-45	TORTURE	U.S.
MEIER	194177	M	Ger.		Mann,SS,C.C.,Buchenwald (Ger.) 42-45	TORTURE	U.S.
MEIER	196072	M	Ger.		Oberwachtmeister,Schupo,Stuetzpunkt Groningen,Westerbork (Neth.)9.44	MURDER	NETH.
MEIER (see MEYER)	229576						
MEIER (see MEYER)	253928						
MEIER	255250	M			Oschfhr.,Gestapo,C.C.,Dora,Nordhausen (Ger.)	MURDER	U.S.
MEIER	257618	M	Ger.		Chief,SD,Caen (Fr.) 42	INTERR.	FR.
MEIER (see MEYER)	259393						
MEIER	300721	M	Ger.		Lt.,Commander,Company,Plateau des Clieres,Haute-Savoie,(Fr.) 22.3.44-5.4.44	PILLAGE	FR.
MEIER	300821	M	Ger.		Pvt.,1.Aufkl.Abt.,3.Coy.,2.Column,XV.Div.,Afrika Korps,St.Leger,(Arlon) 5.9.44	MISC.CRIMES	BEL.
MEIER	301874	M	Ger.		Sturmbannfhr.,Kintz Kommando,Sicherheitspolizei,(Second in command after Muhler) Marseille (Fr.) 15.6.44	MURDER	FR.
MEIER	306937	M	Ger.		Osturmbannfhr.,SS Chief of Gestapo at Limoges (Fr.) 3.-4.44	MURDER	FR.
MEIER, August	252538	M	Ger.		Osturmbannfhr.,Gestapo,Limoges (Fr.) 40-45	INTERR.	FR.
MEIER, Bernhard	254454	M	Ger.		Hptsturmfhr.,SS,12.SS Panz.Div.,Panz.Spaeh Coy.,St.Sulpice sur Risle,Eure (Fr.) 6.6.44	WITNESS	U.S.
MEIER, Emil (or MEYER)	173188	M	Ger.		Rottfhr.,SS,C.C.,Natzweiler (Fr.) 44	MURDER	U.K.
MEIER, Fritz	156863	M	Ger.		Ortsgruppenleiter,NSDAP,Bostel,(Ger.)	MURDER	U.S.
MEIER, Fritz	260520	M	Ger.	21.9.00	SS,Guard,Natzweiler (Fr.)	MURDER	FR.
MEIER, Georg	12544	M			Pvt.,Army,110.or 111.Panz.Gren.Rgt.,2.Coy.,Albine (Fr.) 29.6.44	MURDER	FR.
MEIER, Georg	260735	M			Army,104.Flak Rgt.,Dortmund,Brackel (Ger.)	SUSPECT	U.S.
MEIER, Gerhard	307159	M	Ger.		Uschfhr.,SS,13.SS "Handzar" Div.,Srem,Bosnia (Yugo.) 3.-9.44	MURDER	YUGO.
MEIER, Hans	251144	M	Ger.		Director,Paris (Fr.) 41-44	PILLAGE	FR.
MEIER, Hans	257652	M	Ger.		Sgt.,German Army,Hopseidet in Finmark,Northern (Nor.) 6.5.45	MURDER	NOR.
MEIER, Heinrich	195196	M	Ger.	22.10.08	Member,Gestapo,Sturmschfhr.,SS,Employee,Kolin (Czech.) 39-45	TORTURE	CZECH.
MEIER, Heinrich	260521	M	Ger.	28.5.13	SS Guard,Natzweiler (Fr.)	MURDER	FR.
MEIER, Herbert	156874	M	Ger.	27	Sgt.,188.Kriegs Gefangenen Arbeits Bn.,2.Coy.,Ervik (Nor.) 42-43	MURDER	NOR.
MEIER, Jakob (or MAYER)	195631	M	Ger.		Farm-Owner,Civilian,Haslabroenn,(Ger.) 40-45	TORTURE	POL.
MEIER, Johannes	189590	M	Ger.	08	Lagerfhr.,Adjutant,Arbeitskommando,C.C.,Breme (Ger.) 21.10.44	MURDER	FR.
MEIER, Otto Paul	137478	M		10	Rottfhr.,SS,C.C.,Weimar,Buchenwald (Ger.)	MURDER	U.S.
MEIER, Paul (see MAYER)	156847						
MEIER, Peppi	195630	M	Ger.		Schfhr.,1.SS Panz.Div.L.A.H.,3.Pi.Coy.,Ligneuville (Bel.) 17.-19.12.44	MURDER	U.S.
MEIER, Rudolf (see MEYER,Rudolf)	142646						
MEIER, Theo	142039	M	Ger.	21	Sgt.,Air-Force, Fliegerhorstkdtr. 208,Hopsten (Ger.) 21.3.45	MURDER	U.S.,U.K.
MEIERDRESS, Erwin	300322	M	Ger.		Hptsturmfhr.,SS,Head of the Meierdress Unit,Troyes,Region,Dienville,Aube 9.10.43-22.8.44	MURDER	FR.
MEIERHOFFER	256089	M	Ger.		O.T.,Mühldorf (Ger.)	WITNESS	U.S.
MEIERL, Georg	192260	M	Ger.		Capt.,SS,C.C.,Flossenburg (Ger.) 44-45	MURDER	U.S.
MEIGEL	156876	M		00	Lt.,Army,Flottil.Stamm Rgt.,11.Bn.,Eisden (Bel.) 8.44	MISC.CRIMES	U.S.
MEIHOFFER	146934	M	Ger.		Osturmfhr.,SS Panz.Div.,"Das Reich",Valence D'agen,(Fr.)	MURDER	FR.
METHOFFER	168016	M	Ger.	16	Lt.,SS Div."Das Reich",Staff officer,Oradours-Glane (Fr.) 10.6.44	MURDER	FR.
MEIJER (see MEYER)	300323	M	Ger.				
MEIJER	300324	M	Ger.		Accomplice of Dr.Richard Winterberg also accused,Leeuwarden, 11.42	PILLAGE	NETH.
MEILE, Julius	260166	M	Ger.		Mann,SS,Slave Labour Camp,Botn near Rognan,(Nor.) 8.42-3.43,3.43-45	MURDER	YUGO.
MEILER	251139	M	Ger.		Concerned in execution fort de Seclin (Fr.)	INTERR.	FR.
MEIMANN, Heinz	255251	M			Rottfhr.,C.C.,Artern,Nordhausen (Ger.)	MURDER	U.S.
MAINBERG	166273	M	Ger.		Obergruppenfhr.,SS,Staatsrat, (Fr.,Neth.,Czech.) 39-45	WITNESS	U.S.
MEINBERGER,Johann(alias: MARSCHALLEK)	138034	M	Ger.		Truppfhr.,SA,Sprengkommando,Recklinghausen (Ger.)	TORTURE	U.S.
MEINBURG, Berthold	305045	M	Ger.		Policeman,Police,Brunswick,(Ger.) 3.45	MURDER	CZECH.
MEINDEL	601	M	Ger.		Osturmfhr.,Gestapo,Perpignan (Fr.) 12.42-4.43	MURDER	FR.
MEINDEL (or MEINDL)	127429	M			Son of Maj.General Meindl,Eugen, Staryarussa (Sov.Un.)	WITNESS	U.S.
MEINDL, Albert	255476	M	Ger.		Lt.,Member,S.T.Mann,Abt.I.SD,Toulouse (Fr.) 11.42	MISC.CRIMES	FR.
MEINDL, Eugen	153295	M	Ger.	92	Major General,Parachute Korps II,Staryarussa (Sov.Un.)	MURDER	U.S.
MEINDLE, Franz	156864	M	Ger.		Night-Watchman,Civilian,Volary (Czech.) 41-45	WITNESS	U.S.
MEINDT, Peter	255243	M	Ger.		Pvt.,C.C.,Ellrich,Nordhausen (Ger.)	MURDER	U.S.
MEINECKE	187036	M	Ger.		Commandant,Army,Flachybuyon (Fr.) 8.-9.44	WITNESS	FR.
MEINECKE	260663	M	Ger.		Charge of some Werwolf,Buchenwald (Ger.) 40-44	MISC.CRIMES	FR.
MEINECKE, Fritz	255706	M		6.8.05	Rottfhr.,C.C.,Harzungen,Nordhausen (Ger.)	MURDER	U.S.
MEINEL	251898	M	Ger.		Oschfhr.,Gestapo,Limoges (Fr.)	MISC.CRIMES	FR.
MEINEL	260413	M	Ger.	18 - 20	Lt.,Commandant,German Air-force Garrison,Former,Uvaly (Czech.)8.5.45	MURDER	CZECH.
MEINER, Julius	260163	M	Ger.		Pvt.,SS Slave Labour Camp,Botn near Rognan (Nor.) 8.42-3.43,3.43-45	MURDER	YUGO.
MEINHARD, Juergen	306467	M	Ger.	10.12.19	Pvt.,SS,C.C.,Buchenwald (Ger.) 16.5.38-9.10.43	MURDER	BEL.
MEINHARDT	305046	M	Ger.		Purchaser,of factory "de Amsel",Waalwijk,Heusden, 5.43-10.44	PILLAGE	NETH.
MEINHARDT, Karl	252522	M	Ger.		Oschfhr.,SS,C.C.,Oranienburg,Sachsenhausen (Ger.)	INTERR.	BEL.
MEINHARDT, Tich	168044	M	Ger.		Pvt.,Army,9.Res.Gren.Rgt.,1.Coy.,Coy.Schreiber,Magny D'Anigon (Fr.) 18.9.44	MURDER	FR.
MEINHOLD	189846	M	Ger.		Capt.,Eis.Art.Abt.717,Feldpost 22380,St.Andries,Varsenare,Bruges (Bel.) 4.9.44	MURDER	BEL.
MEINHOLT, Conradt	162066	M			SS Adolf Hitler Div.,12.Rgt.,Stabsccy.,Arnhem (Neth.)	MURDER	U.S.
MEINICKE, Bernhard	168055	M	Ger.		High official,Abt.Treuhandverwaltung,Amt des Generalgouverneurs (Pol.) 39-44	PILLAGE	POL.
MEINKE	124375	M	Ger.		Germ.,NSDAP,Kreisleiter,Erdorf (Ger.) 17.8.44	MURDER	U.S.
MEINLSCHMIDT, Hans	255058	M	Ger.	7.10.09	Civilian,Gossengruen (Czech.) 9.39	INTERR.	CZECH.
MEINLSCHMIEDT, Rudolf	253555	M	Ger.	10.11.09	Guard,C.C.,Pustkow,Kraslice,(Czech.) 38-42	MURDER	CZECH.
MEINOTE, Rudi	250385	M	Ger.		Cpl.,Air-force,Entzheim (Fr.) 42-44	TORTURE	FR.
MEINTZ, Karl	141580	M		23.3.15	Civilian,Chenebier,Etobon,(Fr.) 27.9.44	MURDER	FR.

MEI-MEL

NAME	C.R.FILE NUMBER	SEX	NATIO- NALITY	DATE OF BIRTH	RANK OCCUPATION UNIT PLACE AND DATE OF CRIME	REASON WANTED	WANTED BY
MEINTZER, Willy	168045	M	Ger.		Pvt., 9.Res.Gren.Regt., 1.Coy., Magny d'Anigon (Fr.) 9.44	MURDER	FR.
MEINZ, Joachim	142559	M	Ger.	11.11.19	Member, Signal corps, Interpreter's-Coy., Grafenwoehr (Ger.) 12.44	MISC.CRIMES	U.S.
MEINZER	131308	M	Ger.		Officer, Stabsintendant, Stalag XX-B, Marienburg (Ger.) 2.-3.45	TORTURE	U.S.
MEINZER, Wilhelm	186181	M	Ger.		Lt., Panz.Pionier 669.Bn., 1.Coy., P.O.A., Ferrriers, Villers St. Gertrude, Werbomont, Burnontige (Bel.) 9.44	MURDER	BEL.
MEINZHAUSEN	195357	M	Ger.		Lt., SS, C.C. Malines (Bel.) 42-44	TORTURE	BEL.
MEIRDRESS, Erwin	253926	M	Ger.		Chief, Gestapo, Lachaise (Fr.) 7.44	MISC.CRIMES	FR.
MEISCH	174691	M	Ger.		Pvt., 2.Bn., 469.Regt., 198.Inf.Div., Le Tholy (Fr.) 11.44	PILLAGE	FR.
MEISEL, Hubert	127430	M	Ger.		Head Guard, C.C. Stolwerk (Ger.) 1.43	TORTURE	U.S.
MEISEL, Willy	307160	M	Ger.		Asst., Registrar, Operational Commando attached to the Lourdes Custom-house, Lourdes, Htes.Pyrenees and District (Fr.) 1.-8.44	MURDER	FR.
MEISENBACHER, Emil	39861	M	Ger.		Rottenf., SS, C.C. Struthof (Fr.)	MURDER	FR.
MEISENHALTER	146933	M	Ger.		Obersturmf., SS Panz.Div. "Das Reich", South West France, 44	MURDER	FR.
MEISER	142104	M	Ger.	00	SS-Scharf., C.C. Muehldorf, Ampfing (Ger.) 44-45	TORTURE	U.S.
MEISHEN, Wilhelm	146025	M	Ger.		Mine-worker, Civ., Duisburg (Ger.)	TORTURE	U.S.
MEISINGER	146024	M	Ger.	00	S.D., Sipo., Warschau (Pol.) 40-44	MURDER	U.S.
MEISNER	261070	M	Ger.		Lt.Col., Patrol-corps, Sued-Frankreich, Vaucluse - Bouche du Rhone - Var - Gard - Basses Alpes (Fr.) 44	MISC.CRIMES	FR.
MEISNER, Fritz	186447	M	Ger.	10	Shop-keeper, Land.Schtz.Bn. 398 Coy., Troblowitz (Ger.) 9.40	TORTURE	U.K.
MEISSEL	39864	M	Ger.		Cpl., Army, C.C. Torgau, Berlin (Ger.) 42-4.44	MURDER	U.K.
MEISSEN	199840	M	Ger.		Pvt., Kgf.Arb.Bn.184, C.C. Kobbelvik (Nor.) 6.44	MURDER	NOR.
MEISSEN, Kurt	186448	M	Ger.	24	Pvt., Land.Schtz.Bn., 4.Panz.Div., Merseburg (Ger.) 11.44	MURDER	U.K.
MEISSENBACHER, Emil	301141	M	Ger.		Rottenf., Guard of C.C. Struthof-Natzweiler (Fr.) 42-44	MURDER	FR.
MEISSLER	141581	M	Ger.		Lt., Army, Adjudant, Albertville (Fr.) 8.44	MURDER	FR.
MEISSNER	167034	M	Ger.	15	Lt., 14.Fallschirmjaeger-Regt. (mot.) Richardmenil (Fr.) 9.44	MURDER	FR.
MEISSNER	602	M	Ger.		Sgt., Army, Feldgendarmerie, Gray (Aust.) 8.44	MURDER	FR.
MEISSNER	168092	M			Lt., Army, Staff-Officer, Formation No., 077927 P.C. Dienststelle Albertville (Fr.) 8.44	MURDER	FR.
MEISSNER	173800	M	Ger.		Official, Gestapo, (Yugo.) 42-44	MURDER	YUGO.
MEISSNER	185482	M			Civ., Palleben (Ger.) 11.44	WITNESS	U.S.
MEISSNER	255715	M			SS-Rottenf., C.C. Mackenrode, Nordhausen (Ger.)	MURDER	U.S.
MEISSNER	257993	M			Capt., 150. Panz.Bde., Meuse-Bridge, Antwerp (Bel.) 12.44	MISC.CRIMES	U.S.
MEISSNER, August	252537	M	Ger.		Lt.General, Pres.Mil.Court Torgau, Halle (Ger.) 2.44	MURDER	FR.
MEISSNER, Karl	257612	M	Ger.	11. 8.08	Lt. or Capt., Schupo, Commander of a firing squad, Kobilisy and Lidice (Czech.) 6.42	MURDER	CZECH.
MEISTER	132759	M			Civilian, C.C. Mauthausen (Aust.) 41-45	MURDER	U.S.
MEISTER	135551	M	Ger.		Cpl., Army, Torgau (Ger.) 7.-11.42	MURDER	U.K.
MEISTER	193809	M	Ger.		Lt., Army, C.C. Drag (Nor.) 44	TORTURE	NOR.
MEISTER, Franz	195657	M	Ger.	8.10.14	Interpreter, Member, SS-Standarte 107, NSDAP, Tvorihraz (Czech.)39-45	MISC.CRIMES	CZECH.
MEISTER, Hubert	146029	M	Ger.	85	Capt., Staleg 317, Pongau (Aust.) 3.-5.45	TORTURE	U.S.
MEISTER, Paul	62516	M	Ger.		Master, Civilian, Schornivitch, Gadawitsch, 2.45	MURDER	U.K.
MEISTRIK, Fritz	259922	M	Ger.	20. 3.98	Employee, Gestapo, Litomerice (Czech.) 39-45	MISC.CRIMES	CZECH.
MEISZNER	191305	M	Ger.		Pvt., Eis.Art.Bn. 717, St.Andries, Varsenare-Bruges (Bel.) 9.44	MURDER	BEL.
MEITERT, Johann	194481	M	Ger.		Pvt., Guard, 4.SS Totenkopf-Sturmbann, C.C. Nordhausen - Dora - Mittelbau, Bismarckhuette, Nordhausen (Ger.) 43-45	MURDER	U.S.
MEITTINGER	141582	M	Ger.		Adjudant, Chief, Pionier-Schule, Abt. 6, Cosne (Fr.) 7.44	MURDER	FR.
MEITZNER	255705	M			Pvt., C.C. Ellrich, Nordhausen (Ger.)	MURDER	U.S.
MEIXNER, Konrad	254768	M	Ger.	19. 2.04	Civilian, Pisek (Czech.) 40	PILLAGE	CZECH.
MEIXNER, Marie nee Huenig	254767	F	Ger.	25. 3.08	Civilian, Pisek (Czech.) 40	PILLAGE	CZECH.
MEIZER	36609	M	Ger.		Sgt., Army, (Ger.) 45	TORTURE	U.K.
MEJER	168056	M			SS-Oberscharf., Guard, C.C. Sachsenhausen, Oranienburg (Ger.)	MURDER	POL.
MEJSTRIK, Wilhelm	194133	M	Ger.	6. 1.28	Member, Hitler Jugend, Susice (Czech.) 4.45	MURDER	CZECH.
MEKISKA, Karel	259999	M	Ger.	15. 9.95	Manufacturer, Informer, Gestapo, Pardubice, Litovel, Bohemia (Czech.) 40-45	INTERR.	CZECH.
MEKUSCH, Emilie	305927	F	Ger.		SS-Notdienstverpflichtete, guarding female prisoners, Theresienstadt Prison (Czech.) 10.38-44	MURDER	CZECH.
MELATO, Alfred	128973	M	Ger.	05	Haupteinsatzleiter, NSDAP-member	MURDER	U.S.
MELBACH, Hans	127431	M	Ger.		SS-Obersturmf., Lt., C.C.-Weimar-Buchenwald (Ger.)	TORTURE	U.S.
MELBERT, Hermann	194439	M	Ger.		Schupo, C.C. Falstad (Nor.) 41-44	MURDER	NOR.
MELCER or MELTSER	187881	M			SS-Hauptsturmf., C.C. Maidanek (Pol.)	MURDER	BEL.
MELCHER	604	M	Ger.		Lt., Army, Mende (Fr.) 44	MURDER	FR.
MELCHER, Marie	189226	F	Ger.	15. 4.03	Kanzleiangestellte, Gestapo, Prague (Czech.). 39-45	WITNESS	CZECH.
MELCHERS, Johann Gerhard	307161	M	Ger.	22. 7.77	Caretaker of a house, NSDAP at Meertensdijk (Neth.) 5.44	BRUTALITY	NETH.
MELCHIOR II., Johann	162229	M	Ger.	29. 1.06	Carpenter, SS, Gross Linden (Ger.) 9.44	MURDER	U.S.
MELDE, Wilhelm	252536	M	Ger.		Leader, Kdo. of culture, 56 I.St., 3.Bn., Babow (Ger.) 43-45	BRUTALITY	FR.
MELDER	140057	M	Ger.		Cpl., Army, Coudes (Fr.) 7.44	MURDER	FR.
MELDER	146932	M	Ger.		Cpl., Dienststelle Ep. and 4.366 A, Coudes (Fr.) 44	MURDER	FR.
MELHER, Heinz	168046	M	Ger.		Pvt., Army, 9.Res.Gren.Regt., 1.Coy., M.G.Schuetze 4, Magny d'Anigon (Fr.) 9.44	MURDER	FR.
MELHERS	173799	M	Ger.		SS-Sturmf., C.C. Sajmiste, Zemun (Yugo.) 4.43	MURDER	YUGO.
MELHOFFER	185216	M	Ger.		Lt., Army, Condom (Fr.) 5.44	MURDER	FR.
MELLE or VON MELLE	257007	M	Ger.		Standartenf., SS-Leibstand."Adolf Hitler" Einsatzgruppe Sipo, S.D. Houffalize (Bel.) 12.44	INTERR.	BEL.
MELLE, Heinrich	255716	M			Pvt., C.C. Harzungen, Nordhausen (Ger.)	MURDER	U.S.
MELLE, Lenente	1725	M			Milan (It.)	MISC.CRIMES	U.K.
MELLER, Kurt	260986	M			SS-Oberscharf., C.C. Vaihingen (Ger.) 8.44-4.45	MURDER	U.S.
MELLIG	255718	M			Flyer, C.C. Ellrich, Nordhausen (Ger.)	MURDER	U.S.
MELLIWA, Rudolf	29694	M	Ger.		President, Public official, Litomerice (Czech.) 40	MURDER	CZECH.
MELLO	251897	M	Ger.		Agent, Gestapo, Limoges (Fr.)	INTERR.	FR.
MELLOCH	168047	M	Ger.		Sgt., Kreiskommandantur, Chateau Briant (Fr.) 9.44	MURDER	FR.
MELNYK	191495	M	Ger.		SS-Sturmmann, Bde., C.C. Sachsenhausen (Ger.) 30-4.45	MURDER	POL.
MELPERT	185486	M	Ger.		Dr., Reichsaerztekammer, Public health, Lyon (Fr.)	SUSPECT	FR.
MELTSCH, Johann	254453	M	Ger.	25. 3.91	Agent, Gestapo, Koprivnice (Czech.) 39-45	MISC.CRIMES	CZECH.
MELTSER (see MELCER)	187881						

MEL-MER

NAME	C.R.FILE NUMBER	SEX	NATIO-NALITY	DATE OF BIRTH	RANK OCCUPATION UNIT PLACE AND DATE OF CRIME	REASON WANTED	WANTED BY
MELTZ	132161	M	Ger.		Sgt.Waffen SS,CC Nordhausen-Dora(Ger.)	MURDER	U.S.
MELZ, Heinrich	132162	M	Ger.	14. 5.95	1st Lt.Waffen SS,4 SS Totenkopf Stuba.CC Nordhausen-Dora,Mittelbau(Ger.)	MURDER	U.S.
MELZER	156848	M	Ger.	95	SS Osturmfhr.Hptsturmfhr.CC Lublin(Pol.)40-44	TORTURE	U.K.
MELZER	251834	M	Ger.		Scherfhr.Gestapo,Limoges(Fr.)	INTERR	FR.
MELZER	300517	M	Ger.		Scherfhr.Gestapo Limoges,Hte.Vienne,Gironde(Fr.)40-44	MURDER	FR.
MELZER, Franz	38877	M	Ger.	15. 5.14	SS Oscharfhr.CC Natzweiler Struthof(Fr.)42-44	MURDER	FR.
MELZER, Heinrich	306468	M	Ger.		SS Pvt.(No.341672),CC Buchenwald(Ger.)5.38-10.43	MURDER	BEL.
MELZER, Horst	255719	M			Pvt.CC Ellrich,Nordhausen(Ger.)	MURDER	U.S.
MEMDSON,Karl or MANSHOLD	158933	M		95	2nd Lt.Army,Annemasse(Fr.)	TORTURE	FR.
MEMEL	123405	M	Ger.		Cpl.Army,CC Ratibor Stalag VIIIB(Ger.)41-42	TORTURE	U.K.
MEMPEL, Siegfried	306633	M	Ger.		Adjutant of 2 Coy.7 Bn.Navy Artillery No.689,3 Regt.Trp.of Lorient Pocket.,Bourg of Queven(Morbihan) 18.8.44	PILLAGE	FR.
MENCEL or MENTZEL	99871	M	Ger.		Civilian(Czech.)9.45	MISC.CRIMES	U.K.
MENCKL see MENZEL	173220						
MENDE	134899	M	Ger.	-	Civilian,Amtsleiter D.A.F.,Berlin(Ger.)39-40	MISC.CRIMES	U.S.
MENDE	306207	M	Ger.		Member of Staff,Small Fortress CC Theresienstadt(Czech.)10.38-44	MURDER	CZECH.
MENDE, Heinrich	259668	M	Ger.		SS Uschafhr.Gestapo,Area Angers,Maine and Loire(Fr.)42-44	MISC.CRIMES	FR.
MENDE, Herbert	194135	M	Ger.	2. 1.19	SS Oschafhr.Oberwachtmeister,SS Police,CC Terezin(Czech.)44-45	MURDER	CZECH.
MENDE, Hilde	194134	F	Ger.	6.11.22	SS Guard(notdienstverpflichtet)CC Terezin(Czech.)44-45	TORTURE	CZECH.
MENDRINA, Eduard	262204	M	Ger.		SS Oschafhr.Gestapo,Rennes(Fr.)43-44	MURDER	FR.
MENE	133285	M			Uschafhr.Waffen SS,CC Theresienstadt(Czech.)	MURDER	U.S.
MENEL	167033	M	Ger.		Sonderfhr.Gestapo CC Leipzig(Ger.)43	MISC.CRIMES	FR.
MENG	31609	M	Ger.		Col.Army Inf.Div.163 Regt.307,Finmark(Nor.)10.-11.44	MURDER	NOR.
MENGDEN	606	M	Ger.		Sgt.Army,Bizerta(Tunisia)42-4.43	MURDER	FR.
MENGE, Inge or MENKE	137652	F	Ger.		Luftwaffenhelferin,Auxiliary service of German Airforce,Halten(Ger.)44-45	WITNESS	U.K.
MENGE, Josef	183673	M			SS Rottenfhr.4 SS Totenkopf Stuba,CC Dora Mittelbau,Nordhausen,Osterode (Ger.)43-45	WITNESS	U.S.
MENGE, Karl or Heinrich	104875	M	Ger.	99 or 00	SS Untersturmfhr.SS Gendarmerie,Kreisfhr.,Runzhausen/Gladenbach,Krs Biedenkopf(Ger.)12.44	MURDER	U.S.
MENGEL, Georg	148712	M			Member,SS Erschiessungskdo..Utrecht(Neth.)	MURDER	U.S.
MENGELE see MENGLER	124607						
MENGELE	306469		Ger.		SS Capt.Lagerarzt,CC Nordhausen,Camp Dora(Ger.)40-45	MURDER	BEL.
MENGELE, Joseph	119405	M	Ger.	11	SS Hptsturmfhr.Chief Physician,Dr.,CC Auschwitz-Birkenau(Pol.)43-44	SUSPECTS	U.S.POL.CZECH.YUGO.
MENGELE, Peter	62517	M	Ger.		Officer,Doctor,CC Auschwitz,Belsen(Pol.Ger.)43-45	MURDER	U.K.
MENGER, Werner	255717	M		8.12.13	Pvt.CC Harzungen,Nordhausen(Ger.)	MURDER	U.S.
MENGES	141414	M	Ger.		Uschafhr.28 Inf.Regt.116 Bn.1 Coy.Maubeurquet(Fr.)7.44	MURDER	FR.
MENGES	189206	M			Uschafhr.1 Coy.116 Bn.28 Regt.,Sombrun(Fr.)7.44	MURDER	FR.
MENGES, Ludwig	259624	M	Ger.		Uschafhr.Aussendienststelle S.D.of Tarbes,Htes Pyrenees(Fr.)11.42-8.44	MISC.CRIMES	FR.
MENGLER or MENGELE	124607	M	Ger.		Doctor ,CC Birkenau(Ger.)	MURDER	BEL.
MENKE	254031	M			Crim.Secretary,Sipo,Brussels(Bel.)40-45	INTERR.	BEL.
MENKE, Inge see MENGE	137652						
MENKEL	183674	M			SS Sturmmann,4 SS Totenkopf Sturmbann,Guard CC Dora-Nordhausen-Mittel-bau(Ger.)	TORTURE	U.S.
MENNE, Anton	255897	M			Pvt.CC Blankenburg,Nordhausen(Ger.)	MURDER	BEL.
MENNE, Karl	148264	M	Ger.		SS Gardien,Calais,Arras,Bethune,Berck Plage,St.Pol,Berlemont,Boulogne,Stomer(Fr.)43	TORTURE	FR.
MENNE, Karl	185217	M	Ger.		Guard,CC Sachsenhausen(Ger.)	TORTURE	FR.
MENNENGA, Jahn-Uden	607	M	Ger.	1. 1.16	SS Oscharfhr.CC Maidanek(Pol.)40-4.44	MURDER	POL.
MENNER	156873	M			Capt.Oflag 64,Schubin(Ger.)12.44	MISC.CRIMES	U.S.
MENRATH, Christian	124377	M	Ger.	20. 7.91	Capt.Marsch Bn.59,Volksturm,Bergisch-Gladbach(Ger.)	MURDER	U.S.
MENSCHIK	195173	M		90	Lt.Col.Schutzpolizei,Marte Graffa(It.)9.44	WITNESS	U.K.
MENSEL see MENZEL	173220						
MENSENKAMP, Wilhelm	146020	M	Ger.		Gendarmerie	TORTURE	U.S.
MENTZ, Henry	185715	M		09	SS Interrogator,16 Section,Department for Communism.,Athens(Grc.)	TORTURE	GRC.
MENTZEL	12545	M			Untersturmfhr.Police,Sipo,SS,Gesancon(Fr.)6.44	MURDER	FR.
MENTZEL	39869	M	Ger.		Oberstabsarzt,Army,Oberlangendorf Stalag VIIIB(Ger.)2.45	MISC.CRIMES	U.K.
MENTZEL see MENCEL	39871						
MENZE	253270	M	Ger.		Guard,CC Lahde/Weser(Ger.)	INTERR.	BEL.
MENZEL	132779	M	Ger.		Fallschirmjaeger Regt.5,Nachrichtenzug,Quaregnon,Temappes,Gulin(Bel.)9.44	MURDER	BEL.
MENZEL or MENSEL or MANZEL or MENCKL	173220	M	Ger.	10	N.C.O.Probably 185 Land.Schtz.Bn.439 Land.Schtz.Bn.CC Blechhammer Moosburg(Ger.)1.-4.45	TORTURE	U.K.
MENZEL or MEUZEL	192121	M	Ger.		Officer,Geheime Feldpolizei,Liege(Bel.)	TORTURE	BEL.
MENZEL, Alfons (Franz)	254264	M	Ger	95 or 00	Sgt.Army,Airforce,Munitionsnachschubeinheit 12/VII,Ebnet(Ger.)2.45	MURDER	U.S.
MENZEL, Herbert	189675	M	Ger.	15. 4.96	Untersturmfhr.S.D.,Praha(Czech.)39-44	MURDER	CZECH.
MENZEL, Kurt	306470	M	Ger.		SS Pvt.No.170669,CC Buchenwald(Ger.)5.38-10.43	MURDER	BEL.
MENZEN	185487	M	Ger.		Ob.secretary,Gestapo,Saarbruecken(Ger.)	PILLAGE	FR.
MENZNER, Christian	133284	M	Ger.	95	Capt.Oflag IIIB,Hammelburg(Ger.)44-45	MURDER	U.S.
MENZNER, Josef	255740	M		8. 3.19	Flyer,Airforce,Ellrich,Nordhausen(Ger.)	MURDER	U.S.
MEPHISTO (Swen)	1533	M	Ger.		SS Oschahr.CC Sachsenhausen(Ger.)	MURDER	U.S.
MERBACH	137479	M			SS Oschafhr.CC Weimar,Buchenwald(Ger.)	BRUTALITY	U.S.
MERKER, Georg	158940	M	Ger.	00	Civilian,Kasel(Ger.)	TORTURE	U.K.
MERCKLE	104853	M			Doctor,Civilian-Presumable,Gernsbach(Ger.)8.44	MURDER	U.S.
MERCKLE	174663	M			Officer,Reichsbahndirektor,Railway,Valence(Fr.)	MISC.CRIMES	FR.
MERCKMANN	194619	M	Ger.		Capt.5 Coy.Land.Schtz.Bn.680,Siedenburg(Ger.)4.42	MURDER	FR.
MERDSCHE, Fritz	195172	M			Hptsturmfhr.S.D.,Wiesbaden(Ger.)44-45	SUSPECTS	U.S.
MEREIEN, Johann	260864	M		97	Civilian,Resides at Ehrang,(Ger.),L.O.D.N.A'.O.D.,Schweich(Ger.)1.45	WITNESS	U.S.
MEREK	12330	M	Ger.		POW-Hausmeister,working Party E608 of P.O.W.,CC Stalaga XXIb,6.44	MURDER	U.K.
MEREK	123406	M	Ger.	-	Civilian,Stalag VIIIB CC Hirschfeld(Ger.)7.44	MURDER	U.K.

MER-MES

NAME	C.R.FILE NUMBER	SEX	NATIO-NALITY	DATE OF BIRTH	RANK	OCCUPATION	UNIT	PLACE AND DATE OF CRIME	REASON WANTED	WANTED BY
MEREK, Paul (or MAREK)	156880	M	Ger.	05		Foreman, Asst.Guard, Civilian, Hirschfelde (Ger.) 7.44			MURDER	U.K.
MERFEISS, Karl	900822	M	Ger.		Sgt., 377 Inf.Rgt., serving under Capt.Lohmann, Vinct-Meigem (Bel.) 5.40				MURDER	BEL.
MERFEIT, Emil Anton	254259	M	Ger.	27. 8.05		Prison-Guard, Civilian, Hradec Kralove (Czech.) 39-45			TORTURE	CZECH.
MERFELS, Karl	251830	M	Ger.		Sgt., 377 Jaeger-Rgt., Vinct (Bel.) 5.40				MURDER	BEL.
MERGEN	141887	M			Capt., Stalag XX B, CC Willenberg - Marienburg (Ger.) 41-44				WITNESS	U.K.
MERGENZ, Matilde	134821	F			SS Overseer, CC Erfurt (Ger.) 44				TORTURE	U.S.
MERHLEIN	251835	M	Ger.	01	Rottenfhr. Agent, Gestapo, Limoges (Fr.) 40-44				INTERR.	FR.
MERIE	257994	M			O-Cand., 150 Pz.Bde., Meuse Bridge, Antwerpen (Bel.) 12.44				MISC.CRIMES	U.S.
MERING	185716	M			Lt. Police, Athen (Grc.)				MURDER	GRC.
MERK	253939	M			President, Military Courts, Finistere (Fr.)				MURDER	FR.
MERK	301852	M			Gauamt fuer Landvolk, Strassburg (Fr.) 44				BRUTALITY	FR.
MERK, Friedrich	135282	M		10	Civilian, Administration, Stewart of Estate, Machtildshausen (Ger.) 40-45				BRUTALITY	POL.
MERKEL	156860	M	Ger.		Capt., 111 Kampfgeschwader 100, Villaudric (Fr.) 8.44				MURDER	FR.
MERKEL	161928	M	Ger.		SS Hptschfhr, Command Staff, CC Buchenwald (Ger.) 42				WITNESS	U.S.
MERKEL, Gustav	192259	M	Ger.		CC Gelsenkirchen (Ger.) 43-45				TORTURE	BEL.
MERKEL, Rudolph	172468	M		12. 4.28	Civilian, Gernsbach, Weissenbach (Ger.) 8.44				MURDER	U.S.
MERKER	132758	M			Uschfhr, SS Totenkopf, CC Mauthausen (Aust.) 41-45				MURDER	U.S.
MERKER	178297	M			Director, Stalag VIII B, CC Bensburg (Ger.) 4.43-5.45				TORTURE	U.K.
MERKER, Fritz	177528	M		22. 1.93	Group-Leader, NSDAP, Boulay (Fr.) 8.-11.44				MISC.CRIMES	FR.
MERKER, Jacob	3°°76	M			SS Uschfhr, CC, W-SS, Struthof (Fr.)				MISC.CRIMES	FR.
MERKER, Peter	141979	M	Ger.	22. 2.90	Oschfhr, W-SS, Totenkopf, Leader of the Outside-Work-Troop Gustloff, Weimar (Ger.)				TORTURE	U.S.
MERKERT	256667	M	Ger.		SS Sgt., Camp Mackenrode, Nordhausen (Ger.)				MURDER	U.S.
MERKL	196025	M	Ger.		Owachtmstr., Schupo, Stuetzpunkt Groningen, Westerbork (Neth.) 9.44				MURDER	NETH.
MERKL	251140	M	Ger.		Major, Army, Plain-Faing (Fr.) 10.-11.44				PILLAGE	FR.
MERKLE (or MARKLE)	162073	M	Ger.		Mayor, Public Official, Dirmstein (Ger.) 2.45				MURDER	U.K.
MERKLE	256669	M			Lt., Camp Wieda, Nordhausen (Ger.)				MURDER	U.S.
MERKLE, Fritz	158935	M	Ger.		Army Gren. Ers.Bn.111, Aulhois (Bel.) 9.44				MURDER	BEL.
MERKLE, Kurt	132163	M	Ger.		Cpl., W-SS, CC Dora, Mittelbau, Nordhausen (Ger.)				MURDER	U.S.
MERKLE, Kurt	156875	M			Usturmfhr, 3 SS Bau-Bie., Gardelegen (Ger.) 4.45				MURDER	U.S.
MERKLER	1726	M			Oschfhr SS, Dachau (Ger.)				MISC.CRIMES	U.K.
MERKS	307164	M	Ger.		Member of Sonderkommando Feldmeier, Apeldoorn, Arnhem, Wageningen (Neth.) 10.43, 7.44, 10.44				MURDER	NETH.
MERKWITZ	255891	M			Lt, CC Harzungen, Nordhausen (Ger.)				MURDER	U.S.
MERRICK	124126	M	Ger.	15	SS Lagerfuehrer, CC Liexen (Ger.) 2.44, 45				TORTURE	U.K.
MERRIDGER, Alois	254461	M	Ger.		SS-Mann, CC Auschwitz-Birkenau (Pol.) 10.42				MURDER	YUGO.
MERS	141583	M	Ger.		Lagerfuehrer, CC Oberlansgstein (Ger.)				PILLAGE	FR.
MERSCH	251836	M	Ger.		Agent, Gestapo, Poitiers, Pierre-Leves (Fr.) 2.44				TORTURE	FR.
MERSCHAOTH	188847	M			Chief Gend. of Mertzwiller, Nietesheim (Fr.) 6.45				PILLAGE	FR.
MERSCHROTH, Karl	194620	M		90	Meister, Schupo, Mietesheim (Fr.) 1.-4.45				PILLAGE	FR.
MERSMAYER	174869	M			Lt., Leader, Army, SD, Valence (Fr.) 40-41				TORTURE	FR.
MERTEN	194324	M			Interpreter, Feld-Gend., Leschatelets (Fr.) 2.45				WITNESS	FR.
MERTENS, Helmut	12546	M	Ger.		Pvt., Army, 110 or 111 Pz.Rgt., 2 Coy, Albine (Fr.) 6.44				MURDER	FR.
MERTENS, Willi	158940				Innkeeper, Civilian, Camp Gardelegen (Ger.) 4.45				MURDER	U.S.
MERTHENS	307019	M	Ger.		Uschfhr, SS, CC Auschwitz (Pol.) 44				BRUTALITY	POL.
MERTHER, Hans	187211	M			Civilian, CC Windischenschenbach (Ger.) 41				MISC.CRIMES	POL.
MERTINAT	255892	M			Pvt., CC Rottleberode, Nordhausen (Ger.)				MURDER	U.S.
MERTSCHING	261979	M			Major, Army, Bologna (It.) 6.44				WITNESS	U.S.
MERTZ, Hans	256084	M	Ger.		Uschfhr, Muhldorf (Ger.)				WITNESS	U.S.
MERTZER	146931	M	Ger.		Schfhr, SS Pz.Div."Das Reich", Bn.of Valence D'Agen (Fr.)				MURDER	FR.
MERWA, Tadeusz	253260	M		18. 8.21	Worker, Civilian, Tiddische (Ger.) 5.44				WITNESS	U.S.
MERX, Josef	163473	M	Ger.		Civilian, CC Aachen (Ger.)				TORTURE	BEL.
MERXMUELLER, Jakob	156882	M			Civilian, Farmer				TORTURE	U.S.
MERZ, Helmut	104854	M			SS Hptsturmfhr,Public Prosecutor, SS Court, CC Vaugenbach, Hohenlichte (Ger.) 3.45				MURDER	U.S.
MERZ, Otto	250375	M	Ger.		Gestapo, Lille (Fr.) 40-44				MURDER	FR.
MERZ, Toni	185951	M	Ger.		Lt., 2 Bn., Inf.Rgt.1037, 64 Div., 6 Coy, Vron (Fr.) 8.44				MURDER	FR.
MERZ, Willi	156865	M	Ger.		Office Clerk, Civilian, Pullach (Ger.) 7.44				MURDER	U.S.
MERZEFI, Georg	183676	M.			Pvt., 4 SS Totenkopf-Sturmbann, Guard CC Nordhausen, Dora, Monowitz (Ger. and Pol.)				TORTURE	U.S.
MERZIG (or HERZIG)	185965	M	Ger.		Lt., 11 Pz.Div., Kampfgruppe "Wilde", Roc (Fr.) 41-45				MURDER	FR.
MESAROSCH, Josef	190364	M	Ger.		Rottenfhr, SS Driver of Gestapo, Zajecar (Yugo.) 42				MURDER	YUGO.
MESCHEDE, Anton	137595	M	Ger.		Pvt., Medical Orderly 2,156 P.G.R., Elst (Neth.) 10.44				WITNESS	U.K.
MESCKO, Frantz	168048	M			Pvt., Army, 9 Res.Gren.Rgt., 1 Coy, Magny D'Anigon (Fr.) 9.44				MURDER	FR.
MESER	194209	M	Ger.		SS Uschfhr, CC Buchenwald (Ger.) 42-45				MISC.CRIMES	U.S.
MESER, Heinrich	104855	M			Civilian, NSDAP				BRUTALITY	U.S.
MESIKEN, Kurt	306423	M	Ger.	Age 20	Pvt. - Guard, Formerly 4 Tank Div. - Arb.Kdo. ME 40 E (Stalag IV D), Merseburg (Ger.) 11.44				MURDER	U.K.
MESSAK	254892	M	Ger.		Section Leader, SD, Toulouse (Fr.) 11.42-8.44				MISC.CRIMES	FR.
MESSENER	31607	M	Ger.		Major General, Army, Finmark (Nor.)				MURDER	NOR.
MESSERSCHMIDT	140876	M	Ger.		Civilian, Farmer, Sharpau (Russia)				WITNESS	U.K.
MESSERSCHMIDT	193898	M	Ger.	06 or 96	Inspector, Straflager, Justizministerium, CC Finmark (Nor.)				MISC.CRIMES	NOR, YUGO.
MESSERSCHMIDT	253264	M			Member, Guard, SD, Meppel (Neth.) 12.44				TORTURE	NETH.
MESSERSCHMIDT	306594	M			Member SD, Meppel (Neth.) 12.44				TORTURE	NETH.
MESSING, Otto	179786	M			Civilian, 5.45				MURDER	U.S.
MESSMER, Hans	12547	M	Ger.		Pvt., Army, 110 or 111 Pz.Gren.Rgt., 2 Coy, Albine (Fr.) 6.44				MURDER	FR.
MESSNER	152323	M	Ger.		Lt., 21 Pz.Div. Hqrs., Sessheim (Fr.) 1.45				MURDER	U.S.
MESSNER	188397	M	Ger.	15	Official, Sonderbeauftragter des Reichsfuehrers SS, Sosnowiec - Auschwitz (Pol.) 40-44				MURDER	POL.
MESSNER, Josef	260512	M	Ger.		SS - Guard, CC Natzweiler (Fr.)				MURDER	FR.

MES-MEY

NAME	C.R.FILE NUMBER	SEX	NATIO- NALITY	DATE OF BIRTH	RANK OCCUPATION UNIT PLACE AND DATE OF CRIME	REASON WANTED	WANTED BY
MESSOW, Kurt	256668	M		5. 5.14	Factory-worker, Employee C.C. Nordhausen (Ger.)	MURDER	U.S.
MEST, Josef	168049	M	Ger.		Interpreter, attached to fortress, Lesneven (Fr.) 8.44	MURDER	FR.
MESTING	261372	M	Ger.		Capt.,command Abwehr TP 373, attached 2 Brandenburg Rgt.3, San Vittoria (South of Ancona nr.Aso River) (It.) 3.44	WITNESS	U.S.
MESZ, Marga	134822	F			SS Aufseherin, C.C. Erfurt (Ger.) summer 44	TORTURE	U.S.
META see MAITA	192077						
METAL, Pavel	194480	M		28. 6.08	Guard, Gestapo, Brno (Czech.)	MURDER	CZECH.
METELSKI, Leon	138035	M	Ger.	24. 5.08	SS Mann, C.C. Liebenau, Lahde (Ger.)	MURDER	U.S.
METH	179214	M	Ger.		Staff C.C. Gaggenau, Rotenfels, Schirmeck (Ger.,Fr.)	MURDER	U.K.
METH, Max	256666	M	Ger.	21. 7.99	Factory-worker C.C. Nordhausen (Ger.)	MURDER	U.S.
METHE	1435	M	Ger.		Assistant, Naval supply	MISC.CRIMES	U.K.
METHFESSEL	180496	M	Ger.		Lt., Div. "Hermann Goering", It., 7.44	MURDER	U.K.
METHUEN, Josef	158939	M	Ger.		Capt., Army	TORTURE	U.K.
METISKA, Johann	255252	M			Pvt., C.C. Ellrich, Nordhausen (Ger.)	MURDER	U.S.
METSLER see METZLER	132757						
METT	608	M	Ger.		Capt., Airforce, Violes (Fr.) 8.44	MURDER	FR.
METT	254257	M	Ger.		Capt., Airforce, 77.Kampfgeschwader, Seguret (Fr.) 6.44	BRUTALITY	FR.
METTE	31606	M	Ger.		SS Hptsturmfhr., 20.Army Reinhard Heydrich Rgt. SS Geb.Div.Nord (Nor.) 10.-11.44	MURDER	NOR.
METTE or MUETTER	187213	M			Civ., C.C. Merkstein (Adolf Mine) (Ger.) 8.42-10.44	WITNESS	U.S.
METTE, Erich	141976	M		23	Uscharfhr., SS Totenkopf-Div., Kissenbruck (Ger.) 6.or 7.44	MURDER	U.S.
METTERNICH	900823	M	Ger.		Pvt., 1.Aufkl.Abt. 3.Coy., 2.Col. XV.Div. Afrika-Corps, St. Leger (Arlon) 9.44	MISC.CRIMES	BEL.
METTERNICH, Graf Wolff	191721	M	Ger.		Director, Professor, sciences and education, organisation for protection works of art, Bonn (Ger.) 41-9.44	PILLAGE	BEL.
METTGER	29762	M	Ger.		Col., Feldgendarmerie, Bains nr.Privas (Fr.) 6.44	MURDER	FR.
METTIN	191943	M	Ger.		Officer, Army, Change-Sarthe (Fr.)	WITNESS	FR.
METZ	10188	M	Ger.		Cpl., Gestapo, C.C. Oflag VII B-Bavaria (Ger.) 2.44	WITNESS	U.K.
METZ	104856	M	Ger.	about 93	Sgt. German army, Schwarzhammer, Totten, Wunsiedel, Berga (Ger.) 12.44-4.45	TORTURE	U.S.
METZ	123994	M	Ger.	95	Sgt., 1.Coy. Ld.Schtz.Bn.621, C.C. Berka (Ger.) 45	MURDER	U.S.
METZ	186694	M	Ger.	08	Osturmfhr., SS Nachrichtenzug, Wormhoudt (Fr.) 5.40	MURDER	U.K.
METZ	196071	M	Ger.		Guard, C.C. Royallieu, Compiegne (Fr.) 41-44	MURDER	FR.
METZ, Alfons	130160	M	Ger.	14	Cpl., Army, Oflag VII B Eichstaett (Ger.) 2.44	MURDER	U.K.
METZ, Alfred	255893	M			Pvt., C.C. Ellrich, Nordhausen (Ger.)	MURDER	U.S.
METZ, Christian	124652	M	Ger.		Capt., Army, C.C. Heppenheim (Ger.) 9.44-5.45	TORTURE	U.S.
METZ, Erwin	139683	M	Ger.	95	Cpl., Camp-cmdt., Army, C.C. Berka (Ger.) 4.45	MURDER	U.S.
METZ, Willi	255361	M	Ger.	about 89	Major, Stalag XII A Limburg (Ger.)	WITNESS	U.S.
METZ, Willy or Wilhelm	185719	M	Ger.	98	Sgt., 1.Coy. 621.Landesschuetzen-Bn., Bad Orb, Berka (Ger.) 3.45	MURDER	U.S.
METZE	132164	M	Ger.		Uscharfhr., SS, probably 3.Bau-Bde.,from Wieda to Gardelegen (Ger.)4.45	MURDER	U.S.
METZGER	257686	M			School-teacher, Damersdorf (Ger.) spring 44	MURDER	U.S.
METZGER	901835	M			N.C.O., prison Tournai (Bel.) 42	TORTURE	BEL.
METZGER, August	126948	M			Civ. Lageraeltester, C.C. Buchenwald (Ger.)	MURDER	FR.
METZGER, Karl	141415	M			Public official, Reichsbahn	MURDER	FR.
METZGER, Wilhelm	194498	M	Ger.		Schupo, C.C. Falstad (Nor.) 41-44	MURDER	NOR.
METZKER	194621	M		95	Interpreter, prison Rouen (Fr.) 41	TORTURE	FR.
METZLER or METSLER	132757	M			C.C. Mauthausen (Aust.) 41-45	MURDER	U.S.
METZLER, Gerhard	166896	M			Sgt., 2.Div. Parachut., St.Lo (Fr.) 44	MURDER	FR.
METZNER	142560	M			Civ., Kunsebeck (Ger.) 9.45	MURDER	U.S.
METZNER, Rudolf	191492	M			Leiter, stellvertretender Reichsstatthalter,Gau Oberschlesien (Pol.) 9.39-44	PILLAGE	POL.
MEUER	194451	M	Ger.		Pvt., 3.Coy. 184.Kgf.Arb.Bn. C.C. Moersry (Nor.) 44	MURDER	NOR.
MEUER	257995	M			150. Panzer-Bde., Meuse Bridge Antwerp (Bel.) 12.44	MISC.CRIMES	U.S.
MEUGART or NEUGART	256085	M	Ger.		O.T., Muehldorf Area (Ger.)	WITNESS	U.S.
MEUILER	257690	M			Employee, Factory-worker, C.C. Nordhausen (Ger.)	MURDER	U.S.
MEULLER, Adam	158934	M	Ger.		Pionier-Bn.,Bridge, Speicher (Ger.) 6.44	MISC.CRIMES	U.S.
MEULMANN	194981	M	Ger.		Capt., Army, Appengendon, Zijedijk (Neth.) 2.44	MURDER	NETH.
MEURER	57754	M	Ger.		Col., SS, Oflag XIII B, C.C. Hammelburg (Ger.)	MURDER	U.S.
MEURER, Anni	190378	F	Ger.		Civ., Wiesbaden (Ger.) 43-45	MISC.CRIMES	U.S.
MEURER, Friedrich	260504	M	Ger.	21. 8.13	SS Guard, C.C. Natzweiler (Fr.)	MURDER	FR.
MEURER, Karl	142543	M	Ger.	11	Civ., C.C. Hadamar (Ger.) 6.44-3.45	WITNESS	U.S.
MEURS, Peter	156867	M			Red-cross-man, Civ., Lintfort (Ger.) 10.-11.44	MURDER	U.S.
MEUSEL	141429	M			Adjutant, 1.Coy. 116.Bn. 28.I.R., Tarbes (Fr.) 7.44	MURDER	FR.
MEUSER	126364	M	Ger.	98	Member, SS, S.D., Opladen (Ger.)	MISC.CRIMES	U.S.
MEUSER	257713	M			Crim.assist., Hptscharfhr., Fieldpolice, Foix (Fr.) 12.42-8.44	INTERR.	FR.
MEUZEL see MENZEL	192121						
MEWERT, Heinrich	253271	M			Guard, C.C. Lahde-Weser (Ger.)	INTERR.	BEL.
MEXIS	12548	M	Ger.		Lt.Col.(Etat-Major) Army, Cmdt.of Josselin 2.Rgt. F.N.P.L. 62 546 A, Locmine (Fr.) 44	MURDER	FR.
MEYENBERG, Walter	189677	M	Ger.	11.12.16	SS Oscharfhr., Crim.assist., S.D. Gestapo, Praha (Czech.) 40-44	MURDER	CZECH.
MEYER	609	M	Ger.		Deputy command., C.C. Ravensbrueck (Ger.) 41-44	MURDER	POL.
MEYER or MAYER-LEHR	611	M	Ger.		Doctor,Stubaf.,Gestapo SS, Cracow (Pol.) 9.39-end 43	MURDER	POL.
MEYER see MONCK	622						
MEYER	1496	M	Ger.		Naval supply	MISC.CRIMES	U.K.
MEYER	31605	M	Ger.		Corps-veterinaer, Oberstabsveterinaer, 20.Army, 163.Inf.Div.,Finmark (Nor.) 10.-11.44	MURDER	LUX.,NOR.
MEYER	38866	M	Ger.	18.12.95	Osturmfhr., SS, C.C. Struthof (Fr.)	MISC.CRIMES	FR.
MEYER	38868	M	Ger.		Inspector, Gestapo, Public official foreign, Klingelpuetz Cologne (Ger.) 1. and 2.45	TORTURE	U.S.
MEYER	39836	M	Ger.		Capt., Army, Dax (Fr.) 6.44	MURDER	FR.

MEY-MEY

NAME	C.R.FILE NUMBER	SEX	NATIO-NALITY	DATE OF BIRTH	RANK OCCUPATION UNIT PLACE AND DATE OF CRIME	REASON WANTED	WANTED BY
MEYER	39870	M	Ger.		C.C. Lamsdorf (Ger.) 2.41	TORTURE	U.K.
MEYER	121181	M	Ger.		Lt., Gestapo, Ferryville (Tun.) 1.43	TORTURE	FR.
MEYER	121182	M	Ger.		Special Officer, SS	PILLAGE	FR.
MEYER	124378	M			SS, 12 Pz. Div. Hitler Jugend, Krinkelt-Rochrath (Bel.) 12.44	MURDER	U.S.
MEYER	12659	M	Ger.		Scharfhr., Gestapo, Christiansand (Nor.) 43	TORTURE	NOR.
MEYER	127127	M	Ger.		Officer, SS Div. "Das Reich" 2.SS Pz.Div.,Croix-Foldgarde (Fr.)	MURDER	FR.
MEYER	130049	M	Ger.		Pvt., Stalag VI G, Berg-Neustadt (Ger.) 2.45	TORTURE	U.K.
MEYER	132165	M	Ger.		Waffen SS, C.C. Dora, Nordhausen (Ger.)	MURDER	U.S.
MEYER (see MAYER)	133281			09			
MEYER	134825	M	Ger.		Lt., Army, Oflag 13 B, Hammelburg (Ger.) 3.45	MURDER	U.S.
MEYER (or MYER)	141355	M			Navy, Farge Bremen (Ger.)	TORTURE	U.K.
MEYER	141885	M		17	Cpl. Army, Stalag XXI D (Ger.) 8.44	MURDER	U.K.
MEYER	141972	M	Ger.		Col., Commandant,Permanent Court Master, Ansbach (Ger.) 4.45	MURDER	U.S.
MEYER	146958	M	Ger.		Officer, SS Pz. Div. "Das Reich", La Croix-Falgarde (Fr.) 44	MURDER	FR.
MEYER	146959	M	Ger.		Hptsturmfhr., SS Pz. Div. "Das Reich" (Fr.) 44	MURDER	FR.
MEYER (see MEIER)	152159						
MEYER	156869	M			Scharfhr., Waffen SS, C.C. Aschendorfer Moos (Ger.)	TORTURE	U.S.
MEYER	156870	M			Capt., Army, Stalag 18 A, C.C. Spittal (Aust.) 10.43	WITNESS	U.S.
MEYER	156871	M	Ger.	00	Sgt., Guard, Prison Verona (It.) 3.44-8.44	TORTURE	U.K.
MEYER	157005	M	Ger.		Major, Oflag, XI A, C.C. Altengrade (Ger.) 4.45	MURDER	U.S.
MEYER (or MYER)	161924	M	Ger.		Cpl., Stalag IX B, Bad Orb (Ger.) 44	MURDER	U.S.
MEYER	163286	F	Ger.		Civilian, Stadtinspektor, near Werl (Ger.) 45	WITNESS	U.K.
MEYER	163474	M			Feldgendarmerie, Vielsalm (Bel.) 44-44	LOOTING	BEL.
MEYER	163591	M	Ger.		Major,Landesschuetzen Bn.740, C.C.Bodendorf (Ger.)	MURDER	FR.
MEYER (or TEYER)	163592	M			Lt., 19 Sicherungs Rgt. 192, Chappes (Fr.)	TORTURE	FR.
MEYER	163594	M	Ger.		SS-Mann, 36.Rgt., 1o.Pz. Div., Revin (Fr.)	MURDER	FR.
MEYER	166894	M	Ger.		Adjutant Chief, Gendarmerie, Montigny en Vesoul (Fr.) 7.44	MURDER	FR.
MEYER	166895	M	Ger.		Capt., Army, Plomion (Fr.) 8.44	MURDER	FR.
MEYER	168005	M	Ger.		Feldgendarmerie, Vielsalm (Bel.) 44	PILLAGE	BEL.
MEYER (see MAYER)	173794						
MEYER (see MEIER)	174294						
MEYER	174661	M			Sgt., Fallschirmjaeger Rgt. 2.Div., Plouzane (Fr.) 44	MURDER	FR.
MEYER	174662	M			Lt., 7.Res. Art. Rgt., Tours at Albertville (Fr.) 6.44	MURDER	FR.
MEYER (or MEIER)	185720	M	Ger.	00	Staatsanwalt,Member,occupied territories,NSDAP, Prague (Czech.)42-45	MISC.CRIMES	CZECH.
MEYER	187974	M	Ger.	16	Cpl.,Guard,Stalag 344-4-427.Ld.Sch.Bn.,Ottmuth near Gogolin (Pol.)	TORTURE	U.K.
MEYER	188396	M	Ger.		SS Uscharfhr., SS Div. "Das Reich", near St.Vith (Ger.)	MURDER	U.S.
MEYER	188848	M			Cpl., Army, Tournon (Fr.) 7.44	MURDER	FR.
MEYER	190600	M			Capt., Art.Rgt., Hte d'Oleron (Fr.) 44-4.45	TORTURE	FR.
MEYER	191798	M	Ger.		Feldgendarmerie, Vialsalm (Bel.) 44	PILLAGE	BEL.
MEYER (see MEIER)	193837						
MEYER	194180	M	Ger.		SS-Mann, C.C. Buchenwald (Ger.) 44-45	MISC.CRIMES	U.S.
MEYER	194181	M	Ger.		Capt., SS, C.C. Buchenwald, Struthoff (Ger.) 42-45	MISC.CRIMES	U.S.
MEYER (or MAYER)	194182	M	Ger.		Civilian, Brebach (Ger.)	MURDER	U.S.
MEYER	194622	M	Ger.		Sgt., Feldgendarmerie, Ploermel (Fr.) 6.44	TORTURE	FR.
MEYER	196070	M	Ger.		Sgt., Stalag VI C, Bathorn (Ger.) 1.,6.,7.42	MURDER	FR.
MEYER (or MEIER)	229576	M	Ger.	80	Crim.Secretary, Kripo, Hamburg (Ger.) 42	TORTURE	U.S.
MEYER	250376	M			Capt., Colonne Russia-German,Langres Barracks,L'Ain (Fr.) 7.44	MURDER	FR.
MEYER (see MAYER)	250386						
MEYER (or MAYER)	252549	M			Capt., Russia-German-Unit,La Fertesur Aube (Fr.) 6.44	MURDER	FR.
MEYER	252551	M	Ger.		Lt., 1-98 Ch asseurs de Montagne, Le Chablais (Fr.) 5.44	MISC.CRIMES	FR.
MEYER (or MEIER or MAIR)	253928	M	Ger.		Lt., 1.Coy. 956 Gren.Rgt., Monte Murlo (It.)	MURDER	U.K.
MEYER (or MAYER)	254455	M	Ger.		Col., Cmdt. Div."Hitler Jugend",F.P.No.59 900,Sovet (Bel.) 9.44	BRUTALITY	BEL.
MEYER (or MYER or MUYER)	254465	M	Ger.		Police-Man, SS or Gestapo or Police, C.C.Bremen-Farge (Ger.)	INTERR.	U.K.
MEYER	254681	M	Ger.		Uschfhr., SS, C.C. Auschwitz-Birkenau (Pol.) 42-45	MURDER	YUGO.
MEYER	255882	M	Ger.		SS, C.C. Mauthausen (Aust.)	INTERR.	FR.
MEYER	256648	M	Ger.		Lt., Formation Bode, St.Pierre D'Eyraud (Fr.) 6.-7.44	MURDER	FR.
MEYER	257608	M	Ger.		Gendarm, Feldgendarmerie Trupp No.307, Pontivy (Fr.) 44	TORTURE	FR.
MEYER (or MEIER)	259393	M	Ger.		Sgt., Feldgendarmerie of Roanne ,Loire (Fr.) 40-44	WITNESS	FR.
MEYER	260141	M	Ger.		Capt., Command of Cavaillon, Vaucluse (Fr.) 11.43	INTERR.	FR.
MEYER (or MEIJER)	300323	M	Ger.		Local Kommandant of the Organisation Todt, Rhenen, 12.44	PILLAGE	NETH.
MEYER	301585	M	Ger.		SS Sturmfhr., stationed at C.C. Mauthausen (Aust.) 40-45	MURDER	BEL.
MEYER (see MAYER)	301857						
MEYER (or MAYER)	305466	M		99	Capt., La Ferte sur Aube, Marac,Montigny-le-Roi,Nogent-en-Dassigny (Fr.) 6.44,8.44,9.44	MURDER, ILL-TREATMENT	FR.
MEYER (see MAIER)	307144						
MEYER, A.	253269	M	Ger.		16. Hubner Rgt., 6. Coy., Kinrodi (Bel.) 9.44	MURDER	BEL.
MEYER, Alfred	21316	M.	Ger.		Gauleiter of Westphalia-North,NSDAP,Rosenberg Adm. (Ger.)	MURDER	U.N.W.C.C.
MEYER-BARTHOLD	38895	M	Ger.		Lt.Col., Army,Rgt.Inf.Div.89,Hqu.1055,Rgt. Gr.	MISC.CRIMES	U.S.
MEYER, Bernhard	130048	M	Ger.		Pvt., C.C., Fliegerhorst Rheine (Ger.) 3.45	MISC.CRIMES	U.K.
MEYER, Charles	163593	M	Ger.		Member, Gestapo, Revin (Fr.)	MURDER	FR.
MEYER, Conrad	21315	M			Commissar for Ger.Racial,Official Commissariat	MISC.CRIMES	U.N.W.C.C.
MEYER, Emil (see MEIER)	173188						
MEYER, Emil	193836	M	Ger.	10	Pvt., Army, 4.Coy.PW Labour Bn. 188, Fjellsotra (Nor.) 5.44	MURDER	NOR.
MEYER, Erich	251141	M	Ger.		Lt., NS-Fuehrungs-Officer, Guewenheim (Fr.) 10.44	MURDER	FR.
MEYER, Eyrol	252524	M	Ger.		16. Hubner Rgt., 6. Coy., Kinrodi (Bel.) 9.44	MISC.CRIMES	BEL.
MEYER, Frantz	254673	M	Ger.		Member, Gestapo , Alencon (Fr.) 40-44	MURDER	FR.
MEYER, Franz	29695	M	Ger.		Dr., Landgerichtsrat, Public Official, Cheb (Czech.) 40	MURDER	CZECH.
MEYER, Franz or Hans (or MEYERS, MYER, MUYER, MUYES)	124967	M	Ger.		Wachtmeister, SS or Gestapo or Police, Bremen-Farge (Ger.) 6.43	MISC.CRIMES	U.K.
MEYER, Franz	305047	M	Ger.	20.11.97	Member,Executor-Partner,NSDAP,Goering Werke,Factory at Mesum i. Westphalia, Enschede (Ger.) 7.41, 9.43	PILLAGE	NETH.
MEYER, Franz	305558	M	Ger.		Guard, possibly Deputy, Camp Commandant,C.C.Bremen-Farge (Ger.) 1.43-4.45	MURDER	U.K.
MEYER, Friedrich	145974			94	SA Truppfhr., Farmer, Arzen (Ger.) 44	TORTURE	U.S.
MEYER, Fritz	173900	M			Sgt., Army, Stalag 6 A, Hemer (Ger.) 44	TORTURE	U.S.
MEYER, Fritz	174703	M			Col., Oberkommando, Annecy (Fr.) 6.44	MURDER	FR.
MEYER, Fritz	252540	M	Ger.		Col., Cmdt. North Zone, Le Chablais (Fr.) 5.44	MISC.CRIMES	FR.

MEY-MIC

NAME	C.R.FILE NUMBER	SEX	NATIO- NALITY	DATE OF BIRTH	RANK OCCUPATION UNIT PLACE AND DATE OF CRIME	REASON WANTED	WANTED BY
MEYER, Georg	301142	M	Ger.		Doctor, Medical-Officer, C.C., Struthof-Natzweiler (Fr.) 42-44	MURDER	FR.
MEYER, Georges	252550	M	Ger.		Hptschfhr., SS, Gestapo, Annecy, La Chablais (Fr.) 5.44	MISC.CRIMES	FR.
MEYER, Gerhard	254450	M	Ger.		Pvt., F.P.Nr.01140 C - Army - Fontvieille (Fr.) 8.44	INTERR.	FR.
MEYER, Hans	174702	M	Ger.	99	Oschfhr., Allgem.SS, Neustadt a.d.Aisch, Mittelfranken (Ger.)	MURDER	U.S.
MEYER, Heinrich	194325	M	Ger.		SD, Chateau Gaillard et Saintes (Fr.) 8.44	MURDER	FR.
MEYER, Heinrich	254260	M	Ger.	23. 6.12	Member, Gestapo, Hradec Kralove (Czech.) 39-45	MURDER	CZECH.
MEYER, Heinrich	262148	M	Ger.		Civilian, Walle (Ger.) 44	SUSPECT	U.S.
MEYER, Herbert	191402	M	Ger.		Pvt., 2-188 Kgf.Arb.Bn., Botw.Lekanger and Ervik (Nor.) 10.42	MURDER	NOR.
MEYER, Hermann	260417	M	Ger.	02	Member, Gestapo, Pelhrimov, Bohemia (Czech.) 39-45	MISC.CRIMES	CZECH.
MEYER, Hermann	300326	M	Ger.		Hptschfhr., SS formerly served with the Aussendienststelle of the Sipo and the SD in Rotterdam, previously in Himmlers body guard, Rotterdam (Neth.) 9.44-10.44	MURDER	NETH.
MEYER, Josef	195195	M	Ger.	10	Member, Employee, Gestapo, Kolin (Czech.) 39-45	MURDER	CZECH.
MEYER, Josef (or BARBE)	254684	M	Ger.		Schfhr., SS, Gestapo, Limoges (Fr.)	INTERR.	FR.
MEYER, Josef	255894	M	Ger.		Pvt., C.C. Ellrich, Nordhausen (Ger.)	MURDER	U.S.
MEYER, Joseph	191801	M	Ger.	10	Uschfhr., SS, Dordogne (Fr.) 3.44	MURDER	FR.
MEYER, Karl Emil	146175	M		89	Informant, Gestapo, Neustadt (Ger.) 42	TORTURE	U.S.
MEYER, Kurt	62518	M	Ger.		Bde.Fhr., 12.SS-Panz.Div. "Hitler-Jugend",23.Pz.Gren.Rgt.	MISC.CRIMES	UNWCC,CAN.
MEYER, Kurt	123995	M	Ger.		Standartenfhr., 12.SS-Panz.Div. "Hitler-Jugend", Krinkelt-Rocherath ,44	MURDER	U.S.
MEYER, Kurt	134819	M	Ger.		Member, Gestapo, Koeln (Ger.)	MURDER	U.S.
MEYER, Leonhard (see MAYER)	142561						
MEYER, Marcel	251151	M	Ger.		Guard, Civilian, C.C., Hinzert (Ger.)	BRUTALITY	FR.
MEYER, Max	161927	M	Ger.	02	Uschfhr., SS-Wirtschafts-Verwaltungshauptamt, Amtsgruppe C, Conc. Camp,Buchenwald (Ger.)	WITNESS	U.S.
MEYER, Max (or MEIER)	162227	M	Ger.		Foreman, Civilian, Conc.Camp, Adolf Mine, Merkstein (Ger.) 42-44	TORTURE	U.S.
MEYER, Paul	128972	M	Ger.		Florian Geyer SS-Div., SS-Veterinary-Res.Abt., Lublin (Pol.) 10.43	MURDER	U.S.
MEYER, Rudolf (or MEIER)	142546	M			Civilian, Landjaegermeister, Halchter (Ger.) 9.44	MURDER	U.S.
MEYER, Traugott	166275	M	Ger.		Hptsturmfhr., SS, Conc.Camp, Struthof (Fr.) 3.40	MURDER	U.S.
MEYER, Walter	139673	M	Ger.		Chief-Secr., Gestapo, SS, Lemberg (Pol.) 40-44	MISC.CRIMES	U.S.
MEYER, Werner	146960	M	Ger.		Gren., SS-Panz.Div."Das Reich", Moissac (Fr.) 44	MURDER	FR.
MEYER, Wilhelm	142103	M	Ger.	17	SS-Guard, Muehldorf-Ampfing (Ger.) 45	TORTURE	U.S.
MEYER, Wilhelm	307020	M	Ger.	21. 2.22	Guard, Arbeitserziehungslager, Lahde-Weser, Labour Camp (Ger.) 5-43-4.45	MURDER	U.K.
MEYER, Willi	163590	M			Kapo, SS, Marickule No.7266	MURDER	FR.
MEYER, Xaver	254896	M	Ger.		Ambulance-man, Helkoffen (Ger.) 40-45	BRUTALITY	FR.
MEYERHUBER (see MEYERSHUBER)	120529						
MEYER ZUR KNOLLE	307167	M	Ger.		W.O., to Major Hornn, Slot Moermond at Renesse (Neth.) 12.44	MURDER	NETH.
MEYERS, Franz or Hans (see MAYER)	124967						
MEYERS-GERHARDS, Klaas	306710	M	Ger.		Ger. Civilian, Borkum Island (Ger.) 8.44	MURDER	U.S.
MEYERSHUBER (or MEYERHUBER)	120529	M	Ger.		Lt., Police, Chief of M-T Park Hartheim-Linz-Donau (Aust.) 40, 43-45	MURDER	BEL.
MEYN, Kurt	161926	M	Ger.	16.10.23	Rottfhr., Waffen-SS, 1.SS-Pz.Div. (L.A.H.), Feldgend.Coy., Weissenbach (Aust.) 4.45	MURDER	U.S.
MEYN, Marta	306042	F	Ger.		Member, SS of the staff at Sasel C.C., Sasel (Ger.) 10.44-4.45	TORTURE	U.K.
MEYR, Hans	190379	M	Ger.		Conc.Camp, Dachau (Ger.)	MURDER	U.S.
MEZZLER (or NEZZLER)	161925	M	Ger.		Hitler-Youth-Agent, Stalag IX B, Conc.Camp, Bad Orb (Ger.) 44	MURDER	U.S.
MIA (Sister)	62489	F	Ger.		Nurse, Conc.Camp, Heppenheim (Ger.)	TORTURE	U.S.
MIAMOUSNOSKI	256633	M	Ger.		Pvt., Beny-Boccage (Fr.) 7.44	INTERR.	FR.
MIBACH, Arthur	613	M	Ger.		Sgt., Army, Candresse (Fr.) 6.44	MISC.CRIMES	FR.
MIBOLENSKI	196069	M	Ger.		Lt., Feldgend., Chief, Gestapo, Roanne (Fr.)	TORTURE	FR.
MICEL	145972	M			Uschfhr., SS, 3.Bau-Bde., Conc.Camp, Osterhagen-Gardelegen (Ger.)	MURDER	U.S.
MICEZERA (see MIEZERA)	255244						
MICHAEL	121198	M	Ger.		Lt., Army, 11.Coy., Karlas-Laroche (Fr.) 7.44	MURDER	FR.
MICHAEL	127433	M	Ger.	17	Hptschfhr., SS, Conc.Camp, Buchenwald-Weimar (Ger.)	MISC.CRIMES	U.S.
MICHAEL	145975	M			Driver, Gestapo, Hoerde (Ger.)	MURDER	U.S.
MICHAEL	166893	M	Ger.	00	Hptsturmfhr., SS, SD, Chamalieres (Fr.) 6.43	PILLAGE	FR.
MICHAEL	250377	M	Ger.		Chief, Conc.Camp, Mauthausen (Aust.) 44-45	BRUTALITY	FR.
MICHAEL	300327	M	Ger.		Deputy Camp-leader, C.C., Neuengamme (Ger.)	MURDER	FR.
MICHAEL, Bruno	121180	M	Ger.		Oschfhr., SS, Conc.Camp, Buchenwald (Ger.)	TORTURE	FR.
MICHAEL, Gotthold Manfred	137480	M	Ger.	12	Hptschfhr., SS, Conc.Camp, Weimar-Buchenwald (Ger.) 38-42	TORTURE	U.S.
MICHAEL, Herbert	306471	M	Ger.	24. 5.19	SS-Mann, C.C., Buchenwald (Ger.) 5.38-10.43	MURDER	BEL.
MICHAEL, Manfred	306472	M	Ger.		Schfhr., SS, C.C., Buchenwald (Ger.) 5.38-10.42	MURDER	BEL.
MICHAEL, Leonhard	170074	M	Ger.	1. 6.99	Lt., Army, La Roche Maurice (Fr.) 41-45	MURDER	FR.
MICHAELIS	173791	M	Ger.		Crim.Commissar, Staatspolizeileitstelle, Prague, Oswiecim, Birkenau (Czech.) 39-45	MURDER	CZECH.
MICHAELIS	190380	M	Ger.		Conc.Camp, Dachau (Ger.)	MURDER	U.S.
MICHAELIS	253215	M	Ger.		Polit.Leiter or Leader from SD, C.C., Dachau (Ger.) 42	MISC.CRIMES	YUGO.
MICHAELIS, Hannes	305467	M	Ger.		Lt., 3.Coy., Pz.Aufkl.Abt.II, Fraiture Prov.Liege (Bel.) 9.44	MURDER	BEL.
MICHAELIS, Hans	258992	M			Rear-Admiral, Crimes against peace, Crimes against Humanity	WITNESS	U.S.
MICHARLSON, Walter	256613	M	Ger.		Chief, SD, Chipay and St.Reny (Bel.) 4.44	MURDER	U.S.
MICHAELZIEG	614	M	Ger.		Zugwachtmeister, SS, Conc.Camp, Boten (Nor.) 3.42-43	MURDER	YUGO., NOR.
MICHAEN	194179	M	Ger.	02	Pvt., Airforce, Conc.Camp, Buchenwald, Thekla (Ger.) 45	MURDER	U.S.
MICHAIL	192354	M	Ger.		Lt., Army, La Roche Maurice (Fr.)	MURDER	FR.
MICHAL, Stephanie	194479	F	Ger.	31. 5.09	Clerk, Gestapo, Brno (Czech.) 39-45	MURDER	CZECH.
MICHALIS, Hannes	127434	M	Ger.		Lt., Army, 2.Panz.Div., 3.Coy., Fraiture (Bel.)	MURDER	U.S.
MICHAILSKY	31604	M	Ger.		Capt., III.Inf.Rgt. 310-162 Inf.Div., Finnmark (Nor.) 10.44-11.44	MURDER	UNWCC, NOR.
MICHALOWSKI (or MICHACOWSKI)	196068	M	Ger.		Officer, Army, Eyrieu (Fr.) 3.44-6.44	MURDER	FR.
MICHALSKI, Alex (or BUCHALSKI)	261992	M	Ger.	18. 7.08	SS-Mann, Waffen-SS Gren.Div.No.36 Dirlewanger-Bde., Warsaw and other (Pol.) 40-44	MURDER	POL.
MICHALSKI, Josef	306473	M	Ger.		Schfhr., SS, C.C., Buchenwald (Ger.) 5.38-10.43	MURDER	BEL.
MICHEIKE	127435	M	Ger.		Pvt., Conc.Camp, Ger.Mil.Prison, Bush, Berlin Area (Ger.) 5.44	MURDER	U.S.
MICHEL	12549	M	Ger.		Pvt., Army, Panz.Gren.Rgt.111, 110, Gourdon (Fr.) 6.44	MURDER	FR.
MICHEL	124608	M	Ger.		Oschfhr., SS, Continental-Werke, Conc.Camp, Hannover-Linden (Ger.)	MURDER	BEL.
MICHEL	146957	M	Ger.		Dr., Civilian, Director, Office of Placement, Beziers (Fr.) 44	MISC.CRIMES	FR.

MIC-MIK

NAME	C.R.FILE NUMBER	SEX	NATIO-NALITY	DATE OF BIRTH	RANK OCCUPATION UNIT PLACE AND DATE OF CRIME	REASON WANTED	WANTED BY
MICHEL see MICHELE,MISCHELE MISCHELER	194136						
MICHEL	195171	M	Ger.		SS-Hptsturmfhr.,C.C.Lublin(Pol.) 40-44	MURDER	POL.
MICHEL	252534	M	Ger.		Kapo,Chief of Bloc 31,C.C. Buchenwald(Ger.)	BRUTALITY	FR.
MICHEL	255883	M	Ger.		Shoemaker,Kapo,C.C. Mauthausen(Aust.)	BRUTALITY	FR.
MICHEL	258044	M	Ger.		Guard-Sgt.,C.C. Neckargerach(Ger.) 40-45	BRUTALITY	FR.
MICHEL	306474				SS-Sturmfhr.,SS,C.C.Buchenwald(Ger.) 5.38-10.43	MURDER	BEL.
MICHEL, Erich	140064	M	Ger.	15	Senior W.O.,Luftnachrichten-Schule 4 Coy.,Luftwaffe,Lyon(Fr.) 8.44	MURDER	FR.
MICHEL, Hans	256140	M	Ger.		Farmer,Civilian,Essfeld(Ger.) 43	MISC.CRIMES	POL.
MICHEL-BERGER, Stefan	255902	M			Pvt.,C.C. Nordhausen(Ger.)	MURDER	U.S.
MICHELE	194336	F			Kapo,C.C.Ravensbrueck(Ger.)	TORTURE	FR.
MICHELE, Hans Paul or MICHEL, MISCHELE, MISCHELER	194136	M	Ger.	10	Civilian-Teacher,SS,Wallrabenstein(Ger.) 3.45	MURDER	U.S.
MICHELER	67819	M	Ger.	02	Cpl.,Army-Stalag IVC,C.C.Lueptitz(Ger.) 3.45	MURDER	U.K.
MICHELFEIT, Franz	194459	M		9.10.85	Guard,Gestapo,C.C.Brno(Czech.) 39-45	MURDER	CZECH.
MICHELFEIT, Jan	192257	M		02	Member SS,NSDAP, Bedri-Havlicku Brod(Czech.)	MISC.CRIMES	CZECH.
MICHELFEIT, Josef	195194	M		10	Member Employee,Gestapo,Kolin(Czech.) 39-45	MURDER	CZECH.
MICHELS	1437	M	Ger.		Pvt.,Army,2 Pl.4 Sec.194 Gr.	MISC.CRIMES	U.K.
MICHELS	133283	M			Uschfhr.,C.C.Flossenburg(Ger.)	TORTURE	U.S.
MICHELS	192536	M	Ger.		SS-Scharfhr.,SS,C.C.Flossenburg(Ger.) 44-45	MURDER	U.S.
MICHELS	256612	M	Ger.		Cpl.,Mackenrods C.C.Nordhausen(Ger.)	MURDER	U.S.
MICHELS	301014	M			Member of staff C.C.Struthof-Natzweiler(Fr.) 42-44	MURDER	FR.
MICHELS	257996	M			Lt.,150 Pz.Bde.,Meuse Bridge-Antwerp.(Bel.) 12.44	MISC.CRIMES	U.S.
MICHELS, Heinz Josef	307168	M	Ger.		Kriminalsekretaer,Nordhausen(Ger.) 4.45	MURDER	POL.
MICHELSBERGER, Stefan	183679	M			SS-Mann,SS Totenkopf-Sturmbann,C.C.Monowitz(Pol.),Dora-Mittelbau, Nordhausen(Ger.) 43-45	WITNESS	U.S.
MICHELSEN	142816	M		04	Schfhr.,Waffen-SS,C.C.Stutthof(Pol.) 44	TORTURE	U.S.
MICHERS, Franz	194437	M	Ger.		Schupo,C.C.Falstad(Nor.) 41-44	MURDER	NOR.
MICHEWC	305801	M	Ger.		Capt.,Abwehr at Oflag VI-C,Osnabrueck-Ewersheide(Ger.) 41-45	MURDER	YUGO.
MICHELS	132166	M			Rottfhr.,SS,probably 3 SS Bau-Bde.,C.C., Wieda b.Gardelegen, Dora-Nordhausen(Ger.) 4.45	MURDER	U.S.
MICHL or MECKL or MUCKEL Johanna	253551	M	Ger.	93	Gen.(Commanding above),Military,392 Inf.Blue Div.,Lika(Yugo.) 44-45	INTERR.	YUGO.
MICHL, Dozorce	306272		Ger.		Member of the Gestapo at Trencin,C.C.Oswiecim-Birkenau(Pol.) 39-45	MURDER	CZECH.
MICHLAN	152324	M		99	Pvt.,Guard,Air Force,C.C.Leipzig,Thekla,Buchenwald(Ger.)	MURDER	U.S.
MICHLER, Karl	186440	M		82	Chief NSDAP, Praha(Czech.)	MISC.CRIMES	CZECH.
MICHNA	194450	M	Ger.		Sonderfhr.,2 Coy.,Arb.-Bn.206,Kavesmenes Mosjaen,Rovanimie(Nor.) 45	MURDER	NOR.
MICK, Adolf	10310	M	Ger.		Dr.,Staatsanwalt,Public Official,Staatsanwaltschaft beim Landgericht Brno(Czech.) 40-42	MURDER	CZECH.
MICKENHEIM see MICKELHEIM	194187						
MICKEY see BOULKEY, Ferdinand	136176						
MICKUFASCH	12550				Col.,Army,Cmdt.Camp de Secteur Post 31904 A.G.,Valdalon(Fr.) 6.44	MURDER	FR.
MICKNITZ, Gottfried	193835	M	Ger.	95	Sonderfhr.(Z.) Kgf.Arb.Bn.186,Narwik(Nor.) 42-43	MISC.CRIMES	NOR.
MICURA	255908	M			Pvt.,C.C. Wolfleben,Nordhausen(Ger.)	MURDER	U.S.
MIDDELSDORF, Gustav	168057	M	Ger.		High-Official,Amt des General-Gouverneurs,Abt.Treuhandverwaltung (Pol.) 9.39-12.45	PILLAGE	POL.
MIEBACH, Hermann	162223	M	Ger.		Army,6 Coy.,Landesschuetzen-Bn.,Stalag VIG or VIB,Bonn(Ger.) 44-45	TORTURE	U.S.
MIEDIK	199894	M	Ger.		Sgt.,Kgf.Arb.Bn.190,Karasjok(Nor.) 8.43	TORTURE	NOR.
MIEHE	158944	M			Uschfhr.,SS,Magdeburg(Ger.) 10.44-5.45	TORTURE	U.S.
MIEIKE, Johannes	142569	M			Cpl.,Army-Nachschub-Bn.612 K.Supply Coy.,Les Hoegues(Fr.) 5.45	WITNESS	U.S.
MIELEC, Oskar	151961	M			Member,worked for Gestapo,Tarnow(Pol.)	TORTURE	U.K.
MIELKE	173899	M	Ger.		Sgt.,Anti-Air Craft,Unit L.12804,Gleuel(Ger.) 11.44	TORTURE	U.S.
MIELKE	254897	M			Capt.,Army,Miribel(Fr.) 8.44	INTERR.	FR.
MIELKE, Fritz	151964	M	Ger.	12. 5.19	Sgt.,Army,St.Privat D'Allier(Fr.) 44	MURDER	FR.
MIELLER	260142	M	Ger.		Lt.,Gestapo of Grenoble,Massif Du Vercors,Isere and Drome(Fr.) 7.-8.44	SUSPECT	FR.
MIELLERS, Fritz	196067	M	Ger.		Sturmfhr., Gestapo,SS,Grenoble(Fr.)	MURDER	FR.
MIEROV	301587	M			SS-Sturmfhr.,stationed at C.C.Mauthausen(Aust.) 40-45	MURDER	BEL.
MIERUCH, Ernst	189680				SS-Uschfhr.,4 SS Totenkopf-Sturmbann,C.C.Dora-Mittelbau,Nordhausen(Ger.) 43-45	WITNESS	U.S.
MIERZYNSKI, Leon	262209	M	Ger.	22.10. 7	SS-Rottfhr.,Gestapo,Rennes(Fr.) 43-44	MISC.CRIMES	FR.
MIESBACH, Al.	184158	M	Ger.		Dr.,SD and Gestapo,SS,Pilzen(Czech.) 39-45	MURDER	CZECH.
MIESBACH, Albrecht	254256	M	Ger.		Dr.,Civilian-Director of Shoe Plant Bata, Zlin(Czech.) 40-45	PILLAGE	CZECH.
MIESCHER, X.	39862	M	Ger.		Schfhr.,SS,C.C.Struthof-Natzweiler(Fr.) 40-44	MURDER	FR.
MIESEN see NIESEN	139057						
MIETH	300928		Ger.		Lt.,Feldgend.,Loguivi,Plougras,Cotes du Nord. 6.44	MURDER	FR.
MIETH, Arthur	252552	M	Ger.		Nurse,Cmdt.Bn.9,N.C.O.SCHOOL,398 Div.,La Bresso(Fr.) 9.-11.44	MISC.CRIMES	FR.
MIETKE	256086	M			Foreman, O.T.,Mieshldorf Area(Ger.)	WITNESS	U.S.
MIETROU or MIETROW	255242	M			Pvt.,C.C.Dora,Nordhausen(Ger.)	MURDER	U.S.
MIETSCHKE	185483		Ger.		Sturmschfhr.,Sekretaer,SD,Gestapo,Sarrebruck(Ger.)	PILLAGE	FR.
MIEZERA or MICEZERA	255244	M			Pvt.,C.C. Mackenrode,Nordhausen(Ger.)	MURDER	U.S.
MIGLER	139381	M			C.C.Auschwitz(Pol.)	MURDER	U.S.
MIHA	139674	M			Uschfhr.,Waffen-SS,Arbeitslager 101 (Buchenwald) C.C. Magdeburg (Ger.) 44-45	TORTURE	U.S.
MIHAJLOVIC, Milorad	152327	M			Civilian, Gallneukirchen(Aust.) 44-45	WITNESS	U.S.
MIHALICEK, Karel (aliases Karl HALL)	261119	M	Ger.	8. 4.13	Member,Informant,Nazi Organisation,Gestapo,Vlajka,Prag (Czech.)39-45	MISC.CRIMES	CZECH.
MIKA, Emanuel	253883	M	Ger.	25. 2.08	Employee,Gestapo,Litomerice(Czech.) 39-45	MURDER	CZECH.
MIKA, Jan	194460	M	Ger.		Kriminalkommissar,Gestapo,C.C.Brno(Czech.) 39-45	MURDER	CZECH.
MIKELHEIM	137481	M			SS-Mann,C.C.Weimar-Buchenwald(Ger.)	TORTURE	U.S.
MIKELHEIM or MICKENHEIM	194187	M	Ger.		Guard,Kapo,SS Prisoner Foreman,C.C.Buchenwald(Ger.) 42-45	MURDER	U.S.
MIKEMANN	121199	M	Ger.		Parachutist,Feldgend.,Abbeville(Fr.) 8.44	MURDER	FR.

MIK-MIR

NAME	C.R. FILE NUMBER	SEX	NATIO-NALITY	DATE OF BIRTH	RANK OCCUPATION UNIT PLACE AND DATE OF CRIME	REASON WANTED	WANTED BY
MIKKA	250378	M	Ger.		Capt.,2606 Ers.Bn.,Turkestan Macon ,(L'Ain)Massif du Vercors (Fr.) 7.-8.44	MURDER	FR.
MIKLEJEWSK,Edmund	131305	M	Ger.		Kapo,C.C.Auschwitz,Jawischowitz (Pol.) 43-44	MURDER	U.S.
MIKOLLASCHEK	196817	M	Ger.		Pvt.,1 Pz.Div.,1 Pz.Regt.,2 Coy.,Stoumont La Gliese (Bel.) 12.44	MURDER	U.S.
MIKOR	158946	M	Ger.		Doctor,civilian,C.C.Berghausen (Aust.) 12.4?	TORTURE	U.K.
MIKOWSKI	255241	M			Pvt.,C.C.Rottleberode,Nordhausen (Ger.)	MURDER	U.S.
MIKULA,Hans	195193	M	Ger.	11. 2.10	Member,Gestapo,SS-Scharfhr.,employee,Kolin (Czech.) 39-45	MURDER	CZECH.
MIKULA,Rudolf	10311	M			Public prosecutor,Litomerice (Czech.) 40	MURDER	CZECH.
MIKULIEZ	194186	M			SS-Hptscharfhr.,C.C.Buchenwald (Ger.) 42-45	MURDER	U.S.
MILAN	306273	M	Ger.		Member of the Gestapo at Nove Mesto n-Vahom,C.C.Oswiecim-Birkenau (Pol.) 39-45	MURDER	CZECH.
MILANKA	307021	F	Ger.		SS-chief overseer,SS,C.C.Auschwitz (Pol.) 40-44	MURDER	POL.
MILANOVITSCH,Adam	173897	M	Ger.-Rum.	22	Uscharfhr.,SS,between Wien and Mauthausen (Aust.) 1.-4.45	MURDER	U.S.
MILANZ	194335	M			Rapportfhr.,C.C.Dachau (Ger.)	MURDER	FR.
MIBRADT,Udo	136616	M		10	Lawyer,Dr.,civilian,Poznan (Pol.) 39-44	MISC.CRIMES	U.S.,POL.
MILCH	142568	M			Lt.Gen.,C.C.Schandelah-Braunschweig (Ger.)	MURDER	BEL.
MILCH	194185	M			Officer,C.C.,SS,Buchenwald (Ger.) 42-45	MURDER	U.S.
MILDBENSKI	174582	M			Cmdt.,Major,Feldgendarmerie,Gestapo,Roanne (Fr.) 44	TORTURE	FR.
MILDE	253927	M			Lt.,1 Coy.,Gren.Regt.956,Monte Murlo (It.)	INTERR.	U.K.
MILDEN	1439	M			Pvt.,Army,2 Pl.,4 Sec.,194 Gr.	MISC.CRIMES	U.K.
MILDER	260850		Ger.	02	SS-Col.,security police,Fulda-Werra (Ger.) 43-45	MURDER	U.S.
MILDNER	142551	M			Standartenfhr.,SS,SD,Gestapo,Dr.	MISC.CRIMES	U.S.
MILDNER	142555			07	SS-Hptscharfhr.,C.C.Sachsenhausen,Oranienburg (Ger.)	TORTURE	U.K.
MILENZ	142809	M			Rottenfhr.,Waffen-SS,C.C.Stutthof (Pol.)44	TORTURE	
MILES	185722	M	Ger.		Lt.,Army,Voutes (Grc.) 3.44	MURDER	GRC.
MILEWSKI	98881	M			SS-officer,C.C.Gusen (Aust.)	TORTURE	U.S.
MILEWSKI,Johann	168050	M	Ger.		Pvt.,Army,9 Res.Regt.,1 Coy.,Gew.Schuetze,Magny d'Anigon (Fr.) 9.44	MURDER	FR.
MILHAN	139679	M			Capt.,Stalag X B,C.C.Sandbostel (Ger.) 1.-5.45	TORTURE	U.S.
MILICEWITSCH,Tichomir	255240	M			Legionar,C.C.Harzungen (Ger.)	MURDER	U.S.
MILIS	169495	M	Ger.	00	Capt.,Army,Stalag IV C,(Czech.) 12.44	TORTURE	U.K.
MILIUS	123996	M			SS-Osturmbannfhr.,12 Pz.Div."Hitler-Jugend",25 SS-Regt., Krinkelt-Rocherath (Bel.) 12.44	MURDER	U.K.,CAN.,U.S.
MILJOUANOVICE	135276	M	Ger.		Lt.,Serbian Army,Oflag III B,C.C.Hammelburg (Ger.) 44-45	BRUTALITY	U.S.
MILLER	38880	M	Ger.		Capt.,C.C.Lublin (Pol.) 43-44	MURDER	U.S.
MILLER	104858	M	Ger.		Civilian,C.C.Goerlitz (Ger.) 1.-2.45	MURDER	U.S.
MILLER	133282	M	Ger.		SS,C.C.Auschwitz (Pol.)	MURDER	U.S.
MILLER	135283	M			SS-Usturmfhr.,Mannheim (Ger.)	MURDER	U.S.
MILLER	190381	M			Chief,Volkssturm,IBA mine near Bebra-Kassel (Ger.)	MURDER	U.S.
MILLER see MOLLER or MULIER	191182						
MILLER or MUELLER	194449	M	Ger.		Major,2 Coy.,P.W.work-Bn.206,Rovanimie Mostoen Kvemenes (Nor.) 44-45	MURDER	NOR.
MILLER	196065	M	Ger.		SS-Sturmscharfhr.,C.C.Struthof-Natzweiler (Fr.) 40-44	MURDER	FR.
MILLER see MUELLER	229924						
MILLER	300930		Ger.		Lt.,Voutes,Crete. 8.44	MISC.CRIMES	FR.
MILLER	305081	M	Ger.		Military Governor,Fortress of Crete,Mayor of Heraklion (Crete) (Grc.) 9.43-5.44	MISC.CRIMES	GRC.
MILLER,Georg	256610	M		24. 7.02	Factory-worker,employee,Camp Nordhausen (Ger.)	MURDER	U.S.
MILLER,J.	300331		Ger.		Warrant-officer,Calavrita,Mega,Apileon,Hagia-Lavra (Grc.) 12.43	MURDER	GRC.
MILLER,Max or VON MILLER	252526	M	Ger.		Major,Army,Ordingen (Bel.) 5.40	PILLAGE	BEL.
MILLER,Wilhelm	305048	M			Head customs official,Luz St.Sauveur,Htes.-Pyrenees. 8.44	PILLAGE	FR.
MILLER,Xaver or MUELLER	132637	M	Ger.	05	SS-Sturmscharfhr.,C.C.Schirmeck (Ger.)	TORTURE	FR.
MILLING	173219	M		about 00	Capt.,398 Landesschtz.Bn.,Altstadt,Stalag IV C (Czech.) 9.44	TORTURE	U.K.
MILY	255239	M			Pvt.,C.C.Mackenrode,Nordhausen (Ger.)	MURDER	U.S.
MILZ	190597	M			Standort-Offizier,Standort-Kmdtr.and Gerardmer (Fr.) 9.-11.44	MISC.CRIMES	FR.
MILZ,Johannes	191401	M	Ger.	94	Lt.,190 Kgf.Arb.Bn.,2 Coy.,C.C.Russanes (Nor.) 11.44-5.45	MURDER	NOR.
MILZON	256609				Cpl.,C.C.Nordhausen (Ger.)	MURDER	U.S.
MILZOW,Kurt	255238	M		1. 7.10	Cpl.,C.C.Harzungen,Nordhausen (Ger.)	MURDER	U.S.
MINASSACK	253934	M	Ger.	06	Guard,prison,Moulins (Fr.)	TORTURE	FR.
MINB,Jacob or MIND or MINSZ	123407	M			Pvt.,Army,Creach-Maout (Fr.) 8.44	MURDER	FR.
MINCKE	141370	M			Adjutant,SS "Der Fuehrer",Theil sur Vanne (Fr.) 8.44	WITNESS	FR.
MINDER see BINDER	256808						
MINK	254032	M	Ger.		Employee,Sipo,Bruessel (Bel.)	INTERR.	BEL.
MINK (Junior)	307170	M			Member,Sonderkdo.Feldmeier,Apeldoorn,Arnheim,Wageningen (Neth.) 10.43 and 7.44 and 10.44	MURDER	NETH.
MINK (Senior)	307171	M			Member,Sonderkdo.Feldmeier,Apeldoorn,Arnheim,Wageningen (Neth.) 10.43 and 7.44 and 10.44	MURDER	NETH.
MINKMAR,Dorothea	195192	F	Ger.	12	Employee,Gestapo,Kolin (Czech.) 45	MURDER	CZECH.
MINKOS,Herbert	306475	M	Ger.		SS-Scharfhr.,C.C.Buchenwald (Ger.) between 5.38 and 10.43	MURDER	BEL.
MINNER	139685	M			Capt.,Oflag 64,Schubin (Pol.) 6.43-1.45	TORTURE	U.S.
MINSINGER aliases:POSCHINGER or BORNEMANN	190092				Lt.Col.,Stalag VIII B	MURDER	U.K.
MINSZ see MINB	123407						
MINUTE	146956	M	Ger.		Osturmfhr.,SS-Pz.Div."Das Reich",Villaudric (Fr.) 44	MURDER	FR.
MINUTH	188884	M			Hptsturmfhr.,9 Pz.Div.,1 Pz.Gren.Regt.II,Mayenne (Fr.)	WITNESS	FR.
MIRX	104860	M			SS-Usturmfhr.,SS-Troop-Headquarters,between Schmedenstedt and Munstedt (Ger.) 8.44	MURDER	U.S.
MIOTHE,Franz	158947	M			Pvt.,Army,Gren.Ers.Bn.398,Stamm-Coy.,Aulnois (Bel.) 9.44	MURDER	BEL.
MIRBACH	255481	M			C.C.Rottleberode,Nordhausen (Ger.)	MURDER	U.S.
MIRBAUER,Karl	256283	M	Ger.	11.10.05	Gestapo,Prag (Czech.) 42	MURDER	CZECH.
MIRBETH,Hans	252548	M	Ger.		SS-Scharfhr.,C.C.Buchenwald (Ger.)	MISC.CRIMES	FR.
MIROFF	256141	M	Ger.		SS-Usturmfhr.,C.C.Mauthausen (Aust.)	INTERR.	FR.
MIROR	152325	M	Ger.		Major,Army,Stalag Luft 4,Kiefheide (Ger.) 2.45	MISC.CRIMES	U.S.

MIR-MOE

NAME	C.R.FILE NUMBER	SEX	NATIO-NALITY	DATE OF BIRTH	RANK OCCUPATION UNIT PLACE AND DATE OF CRIME	REASON WANTED	WANTED BY
MIRSCH, Eduard	254458	M	Ger.	7. 9.14	Employee,Gestapo,Vsetin (Czech.) 39-45	MURDER	CZECH.
MIRZBERGER	260967	M	Ger.		Employee,Civilian,Coal Firm Jean Bohl,Nuernberg (Ger.)	BRUTALITY	POL.
MISBACH	152326	M	Ger.		Capt.,Feldkommandantur,Sanilhac (Fr.) 21.4.44	MURDER	FR.
MISCH	186487	M	Ger.		Oschfhr.,12.SS Panz.Div."Hitler Jugend",Caen (Fr.) 6.6.-8.7.44	TORTURE	CAN.
MISCH, Erhard	255482	M			Pvt.,C.C.,Ellrich,Nordhausen (Ger.)	MURDER	U.S.
MISCHELE (see MICHEL,MICHELE, MISCHELER)	194136	M					
MISCHELER(see MISCHELE,MICHEL, MICHELE)	194136						
MISCHINGER, Josef	257308	M	Ger.	31.10.06	Criminal Asst.,Gestapo,Tabor,Bohemia (Czech.) 1.7.40-5.45	MISC.CRIMES	CZECH.
MISCHKA, Rudi (see MISCHKER)	138319	M					
MISCHKE	259257	M	Ger.		S-Sgt.,Air-force,Hamburg (Ger.)	MURDER	U.S.
MISCHKE, Alfred	258551	M	Ger.	08	Doctor,Sturmbannfhr.,SS,W.V.H.A., (Ger.) 40-45	BRUTALITY	U.S.
MISCHKE, Georg	183681	M	Ger.	15. 8.08	Usturmfhr.,SS,Kriminalobersekretaer,SD,Gestapo,Prague (Czech.)39-45	MURDER	CZECH.
MISCHKER, Rudi (or MISCHKA)	138319	M			Sgt.,SS,Gestapo,Unterabt.,IV D,Bellecour,Lyon (Fr.)	MURDER	FR.
MISCHLER	255483	M			C.C.,Rottleberode,Nordhausen (Ger.)	MURDER	U.S.
MISCHORA, Paul	162221	M	Ger.		Policeman,Adolf Mine,C.C.,Merkstein (Ger.) 42-44	TORTURE	U.S.
MISKA	250390	M	Ger.		Army,Stalag IV B,Muehlberg (Ger.) 1.45	INTERR.	U.S.
MISKA	261850	M	Ger.		Kapo,C.C.,Dora Nordhausen (Ger.)	MURDER	U.S.
MISOPH, Hermann	162220	M			Civilian,Walsum (Ger.) 9.44	TORTURE	U.K.
MISSAUER, Alois	194478	M	Ger.	4. 1.07	Ortsgruppenleiter,NSDAP,SA,Schoenwald (Czech.) 38-45	PILLAGE	CZECH.
MISSUWEIT, Erwin	193833	M	Ger.	00	Oberwachtmeister,Straflager,Justizministerium,Finmark (Nor.) 1.45	MISC.CRIMES	NOR.,YUGO.
MITCHE	196063	M	Ger.		Lt.,Army,Cheingy (Fr.) 6.6.44	WITNESS	FR.
MITISKA, Margarita	262307	F			Lives at Freilassing,(Ger.) Sillersdorf (Ger.) 16.4.45 L.O.D.N.A.O.D.	WITNESS	U.S.
MITJE, Nicolas	62491	M	Ger.	00	Kapo,C.C.,Bad Gandersheim,(Ger.) 6.4.45	MURDER	U.S.
MITSCHKE, "Bruno(alias:BRAUER)	183224	M	Ger.	7. 8.10	Kriminalassistent,SS,SD,Gestapo,Benescv (Czech.) 39-45	MURDER	CZECH.
MITSCHKE, Paul	255486	M		2. 3.01	Pvt.,SS,C.C.,Harzungen,Nordhausen (Ger.)	MURDER	U.S.
MITSCHLER	253932	M	Ger.		Oberinspektor,C.C.,Auschwitz (Pol.)	INTERR.	FR.
MITTAG, Walter	255484	M			Pvt.,C.C.,Ellrich,Nordhausen (Ger.)	MURDER	U.S.
MITTELBORG	146955	M			Uschfhr.,SS Panz.Div."Das Reich",La Croix,Falgarde (Fr.) 44	MURDER	FR.
MITTELHUBER	300934	M			"Lt.,Police Dienststelle No.12085,Vrastamites near Livadia Bedia,8.1.44	MISC.CRIMES	GRC.
MITTELMANN	185721	M			Guard,Werkschutzltr.,Arbeitskommando,C.C.,Frankfurt-Main (Ger.) 42	TORTURE	U.S.
MITTELMAYER	185220	M			Osturmfhr.,SD,Moutiers,Bourg,Seez,Montgeraud (Fr.) 8.44	MURDER	FR.
MITTELMAYER	194340	M	Ger.		Lt.,7.Art.Rgt.,Albertville (Fr.)	MURDER	FR.
MITTELSTENSCHEID, Hans Fr.	301179	M	Ger.		Fachberater,Provincial labour exchange,Middelburg 9.10.44	MISC.CRIMES	NETH.
MITTERLEHNER, Ferdinand	121177	M	Ger.		N.C.O.,Army,F.P.21535 K,Louvetot (Fr.) 28.8.44	INCENDIARISM	FR.
MITTERMAYER	121176	M	Ger.		Lt.,7 alpine-Art.Rgt.,Tour Smisea,St.Paul sur Leere(Fr.)15.6.44	MURDER	FR.
MITTERMAYER	136228	M	Ger.		Lt.,7.Rgt.Art.Res.,La Bathie (Fr.) 28.-29.6.44, 23.8.44	MURDER	FR.
MITTERMAYER, Johann	306476	M	Ger.	8. 4.09	Mann,SS,C.C.,Buchenwald (Ger.) 16.5.38-9.10.43	MURDER	BEL.
MITTEROCHER	255245	M			Flyer,C.C.,Ellrich,Nordhausen (Ger.)	MURDER	U.S.
MITTERWILSER, Martin	255246	M	Ger.		Pvt.,C.C.,Ellrich,Nordhausen (Ger.)	MURDER	U.S.
MITTINGS	104861	M			Usturmbannfhr.,SS,6.Mountain Div.Nord Waffen SS, 4.-18.1.45	MURDER	U.S.
MITTLEBERGER, Franz	255485	M		13. 1.05	Flyer,C.C.,Harzungen,Nordhausen (Ger.)	MURDER	U.S.
MITZ, Franz (or PAUCO,Josef Dr.)	261884	M	Ger.	26. 2.14	Agent,SD;Civilian Editor in Chief,Bratislava (Czech.)39-45	SUSPECT	CZECH.
MITZNER, Gerhard	307173	M	Ger.	15- 18	Uschfhr.,SS,2.Bn.,Landsturm Niederlands,Apeldoorn,Woeste,Hoog Soeren (Neth.) 10.-12.44, 7.4.45	MURDER	NETH.
MIVLAVIRT	186180	M	Ger.		Pvt.,3.Sich.Rgt.16, (Bel.) prob.44	MURDER	BEL.
MIXA	174693	M			Lt.,2.Bn.,Fallschirmjaeger Rgt.,2.Div.,Plouzane (Fr.) 44	MISC.CRIMES	FR.
MIXA, Frank	158943	M			Civilian,Daasdorf,Gutmannshausen (Ger.) 7.-8.44	MURDER	U.S.
MIZER	62492	M	Ger.		Sgt.,Army,Landesschuetzen Bn.515,3.Coy.,Troppau (Czech.) 1.-2.45	TORTURE	U.K.
MLEKUSCH, Emilie	194138	F		1. 2.09	Guard,Notdienstverpflichtet,C.C.,Terezin (Czech.) 44-45	TORTURE	CZECH.
MNICH	29696	M			Doctor,Landgerichtsdirector,Public official,Brno,(Czech.) 40	MURDER	CZECH.
MOBINS, Werner	194436	M	Ger.		Schupo,C.C.,Falstad (Nor.) 41-44	MURDER	NOR.
MOBIUS	138938	M	Ger.		Civilian Prof.,Archaeologie,Paris (Fr.) 44	PILLAGE	FR.
MOBIUS	196062	M	Ger.		Capt.,C.C.,Compiegne (Fr.) 41 - 44	MURDER	FR.
MOBUS	306477	M	Ger.		Schfhr.,SS,C.C.,Buchenwald (Ger.) 16.5.38-9.10.43	MURDER	BEL.
MOCHLAND (or HOCHLAND)	259203	M	Ger.		Oschfhr.,SS Div."Prinz Eugen",Niksic district Montenegro (Yugo.)5.-6.43	MISC.CRIMES	YUGO.
MOCK	156879	M	Ger.	11	Gestapo,Angers (Fr.) 42-44	MURDER	FR.
MOCK, Stephan	262180	M	Ger.	3.12.15	Hptschfhr.,51.SS Armoured Bde.,3.Bn.,chief of Technical Group Breviandes,Bucheres Ste Savine,La Riviere de Corps (Troyes) (Fr.) 8.44	BRUTALITY	FR.
MOCKEL	616	M	Ger.		Lt.,Army,Feldschule Art.,Autun (Fr.) 7.44	INCENDIARISM	FR.
MOCKEL	258001	M			Lt.,150.Pz.Bde.,Meusebridge Antwerpen (Bel.) 12.44	MISC.CRIMES	U.S.
MOCKEL, Herbert	617	M	Ger.	4.12.14	Hptschfhr.,SS,C.C.,Maidanek (Pol.) 40-4.44	MURDER	POL.,BEL.
MOCKEL, Siegfried (see MOKEL)	166889						
MOCZEGEBA	185221	M			Guard,SS C.C.,Sachsenhausen (Ger.)	TORTURE	FR.
MOCZEGEBA	301015	M	Ger.		Warden,C.C.,Oranienburg,Natzweiler (Ger.) 42-45	MURDER	FR.
MODEL	192120	M	Ger.		Marschall,Army staffs,Prov.Liege (Bel.) 9.44	PILLAGE	BEL.
MODEL, Hans	132167	M	Ger.		Civilian,C.C.,Nordhausen-Dora (Ger.)	MURDER	U.S.
MODERHACK, Otto	305726	M	Ger.		N.C.O.,"Turkestan" Legion,Carmaux,Tarn., 18.-2.1.7.44	MURDER	FR.
MODES, Artur	147354	M			Pvt.,11.Pz.Div.Kampfgr."Wilde", (Fr.) 44	MURDER	FR.
MODINGER, Heinz	146954	M	Ger.		Cpl.,Army,Courcival (Fr.) 40	MURDER	FR.
MODL	136924	M			Sgt.,19.SS Pol.Rgt.,2.Bn.,5.Coy.,Oberkrain,Toulouse,Agen,Compiègne, Tulle, (Yugo.)(Fr.) 5.41-3.44,3.44-10.44	MURDER	U.S.
MODL, Franz	194477	M	Ger.		Kriminalasst.,Gestapo,Brno,(Czech.) 39-45	MURDER	CZECH.
MOIR, Jan	254255	M	Ger.	18.11.01	Mann,SA,Javoricko (Czech.) 11.44	MURDER	CZECH.
MODROW	189445	M	Ger.		Praesident,Major,Kriegsgericht,Army,Delft (Neth.) 10.10.45	MURDER	NETH.
MOECKEL	194137	M	Ger.		Sgt.,SS,C.C.,Buchenwald (Ger.) 42-45	MURDER	U.S.
MOECKEL	251840	M	Ger.		Lt.,Gendarmerie,(Fr.) 28.6.44	PILLAGE	FR.
MOECKEL, Alexander	163476	M	Ger.		Major,Btty.,Stab III,I.R. 517,Virelles Chimay (Bel.) 5.6.40	PILLAGE	BEL.
MOECKEL, Herbert	157004	M	Ger.	14	Hptschfhr.,SS,Work detail leader,C.C.,Lublin (Pol.) 42-43	MISC.CRIMES	U.S.
MOEDEL, Johann	257687	M	Ger.	4. 8.12	Employee,Factory worker,C.C.,Nordhausen (Ger.)	MURDER	U.S.

MOE-MOH

NAME	C.R.FILE NUMBER	SEX	NATIO-NALITY	DATE OF BIRTH	RANK OCCUPATION UNIT PLACE AND DATE OF CRIME	REASON WANTED	WANTED BY
MOEHER (see MEHR)	190374						
MOEHLEM	166891	M	Ger.	95	Wachtmeister, Guard, C.C. Schirmeck (Fr.)	MURDER	FR.
MOEHLMANN, Arie	254250	M	Ger.		Osturmfhr., SS, C.C.Auschwitz-Birkenau (Pol.) 43	MURDER	YUGO.
MOEHLMEYER, Wilhelm	307174	M	Ger.		Railway-official, Fernmeldemeisterei, Office at Amersfoort (Neth.) betw.10.44-5.45	PILLAGE	NETH.
MOEHMICHEN, Karl	301143	M	Ger.		Dr., Med.Off. at C.C. Struthof-Natzweiler (Fr.) 42-44	MURDER	FR.
MOEHR (see MEHR)	190374						
MOEHRES, Otto	257688	M	Ger.	8. 7.92	Employee, C.C. Nordhausen (Ger.)	MURDER	U.S.
MOEHRING	68945	M	Ger.	98	Major, Abwehr.	WITNESS	BEL.
MOEHRING	252530	M	Ger.		Pvt., Army, Pepingen (Bel.) 2.-9.44	LOOTING	BEL.
MOEL, Harry (or MUHL)	255736	M	Ger.	10	Pvt., Army, Heusden-Noord-Brabant (Neth.) 11.44	PILLAGE	NETH.
MOELDERS	125084	M	Ger.		Civilian. (Ger.)	MURDER	U.K.
MOELLER	38861	M	Ger.	15	Cpl., Army, Berlin (Ger.) 5.43	MURDER	U.S.
MOELLER	142569	M	Ger.		SS-Uschfhr., C.C. Neuengamme (Ger.)	WITNESS	U.K.
MOELLER	156859	M	Ger.	07	Sgt., Waffen-SS, Leibstandarte "Adolf Hitler", Feld-Ers.Bn. I, Rosbash (Ger.) 3.45	WITNESS	U.S.
MOELLER	168488	M	Ger.		Criminal-secretary, Kripo-Leitstelle, Stettin (Ger.)	MURDER	U.S.
MOELLER	173192	M	Ger.		Staff, C.C. Schirmeck, Rotenfels, Gaggenau (Fr., Ger.) 9.44	MURDER	U.K.
MOELLER	187207	M	Ger.	16	Osturmfhr., 12.Panz.Div. "Hitler-Jugend", near Caen (Fr.) 6.-7.44	MISC.CRIMES	CAN.
MOELLER	190262	M	Ger.		Cmdt., Feldgendarmerie, Pozaverac (Yugo.) 4.43-10.44	MURDER	YUGO.
MOELLER	195093	M	Ger.		Hptsturmfhr., SS, S.D. Einsatzkommando "Wenger", C.C. Baccarat Etival (Fr.) 9.44	MURDER	FR.
MOELLER	252523	M	Ger.		Pvt., Army, Pepingen (Bel.) 2.-9.44	LOOTING	BEL.
MOELLER	253550	M	Ger.		SS-Osturmbannfhr., S.D.-Cmdt., Susak (Yugo.) 2.44	INTERR.	YUGO.
MOELLER	300898	M	Ger.		Pvt., Pepingen (Bel.) 2-9.44	PILLAGE	BEL.
MOELLER	306067	M	Ger.		Osturmbannfhr., S.D.-Cmdt. at Fiume. Susak (Yugo.) 2.44	INTERR.	YUGO.
MOELLER, Friedrich	255909	M	Ger.	7.12.02	Pvt., C.C. Ellrich, Nordhausen (Ger.)	MURDER	U.S.
MOELLER, Fritz	261938	M	Ger.		Hptsturmfhr., SS, Belgrad and Valjevo (Yugo.) 8.42-9.44	SUSPECT	YUGO.
MOELLER, G.	300824	M	Ger.		Pvt., 1.Aufkl.Abt., 3.Coy., 2.Col., XV. Div. of the Afrika Korps, Saint-Leger (Arlon) (Bel.) 9.44	MISC.CRIMES	BEL.
MOELLER, Hermann Heinrich Friedrich	306067	M	Ger.	29. 4.98	SS-Osturmbannfhr., Oberst der Polizei, Befehlshaber der Ordnungs-polizei, Belgrad (Yugo.) 4.43-10.44	MURDER	YUGO.
MOELLER, Horst	196818	M			Pvt., 1.SS Panz.Div., 1.Panz.Regt., 2.Coy., Stoumont, La Gliese (Bel.) 12.44	MURDER	U.S.
MOELLER, Kurt	1548	M	Ger.		SS-Oschfhr., Waffen-SS, Radom, Lublin, Oranienburg,Vaihingen(Pol.,Ger.) 40-45	MURDER	U.S.
MOELLER, Otto	194191	M	Ger.		Uschfhr., SS, C.C. Buchenwald (Ger.) 42-45	MISC.CRIMES	U.S.
MOELLER, Reinhard	305674	M	Ger.		Civilian, near Aachen. 11.44	MURDER	U.S.
MOELLERS, Alfred	194579	M	Ger.		Civ. Auditor, Territ.occupation, Prague (Czech.) 39	MURDER	CZECH.
MOELTER	194334	M	Ger.	10	Interpreter, Adjutant, Professor, Prisons Dept.III, Fresnes (Fr.).4.42	MURDER	FR.
MOENICH (or MOENIGH)	12552	M	Ger.		Capt., Feldgendarmerie-Trupp B 687 mot., Le Vigeant, Lussac, Charroux (Fr.) 8.44	MURDER	FR.
MOENNICH, Willy	196499	M	Ger.		Hptscharfhr., Crim.secretary, S.D., Zwolle (Neth.) 9.44-4.45	INTERR.	NETH.
MOENNING, Arnold	254451	M	Ger.		Chief Culture, Bulsen (Fr.) 42-43	TORTURE	FR.
MOERDER	255911	M			Pvt., C.C. Nordhausen (Ger.)	MURDER	U.S.
MOERDER	256632	M	Ger.		SS-Sturmfhr., Bloc-leader, Boelke-Kaserne, Nordhausen (Ger.)	MURDER	U.S.
MOERHING	301588	M	Ger.		Capt., Adjutant to Lippert at Arlen (Bel.) 8.-9.44	MURDER	BEL.
MOERIXBAUER, Joseph	168058	M	Ger.		Dr., Leader, Abt.Treuhandverwaltung, Amt des Generalgouverneurs, Krakau (Pol.) 9.39-44	PILLAGE	POL.
MOERL, Ernst	185925	M	Ger.		Agent, Gestapo, Prague (Czech.)	MISC.CRIMES	CZECH.
MOERLER	31602	M	Ger.		Capt., Army, 169.Inf.Div. III.Gren.Regt. (Nor.) 11.44	MURDER	NOR.
MOERLING	121175	M	Ger.		Capt., Adjunct of Major Lippert, Kreiskommandant at Arlon (Bel.) 8.44	MURDER	BEL.
MOERS	250379	M	Ger.		Kapo, C.C. Neuengamme (Ger.) 44	TORTURE	FR.
MOES, Ernst	194148	M	Ger.	98	Hptsturmfhr., SS, Reichssicherh.-Hauptamt Berlin, Terezin (Ger.,Czech.)	MURDER	CZECH.
MOESER	136229	M	Ger.	00	Osturmfhr., SS, C.C. Dora, Nordhausen (Ger.)	MURDER	FR.
MOESKES	196061	M	Ger.		Pvt., C.C. Compiegne (Fr.) 41-44	MURDER	FR.
MOESLE	12555	M	Ger.		N.C.O., Army, Panz.Gren.Regt. 110, 111, 2.Coy., Albine (Fr.) 6.44	MURDER	FR.
MOESS	173831	M	Ger.		Hptsturmfhr., SS, Inspector of all Jewish Camps.44-45	TORTURE	NETH.
MOESSLACHER	193040	M	Ger.		Lt., Gendarmerie, Viktring (Austria) 2.45	MURDER	U.K.
MOESSNER, Emile	254898	M		11	Inspector, S.D., Alençon (Fr.) 40-44	MURDER	FR.
MOESTL	140886	M		80 or 85	Sgt., 208. Fliegerhorst, Hobsten (Ger.) 3.45	MURDER	CAN.
MOEWIUS	156994	M	Ger.		Civilian, Dortmund-Asseln (Ger.)	MURDER	U.S.
MOEZKO, Werner	31508	M	Ger.		Pvt., Gestapo, Feldgendarmerie, Josselin (Fr.) 44	MURDER	FR.
MOHAUPT (see MOHRHAUPT)	258002						
MOHAUPT, Anna	194476	F	Ger.		Employee, Gestapo, Brno (Czech.) 39-45	MURDER	CZECH.
MOHAUPT, Kurt	128970	M	Ger.	04	Specialist-officer, SS, Lussault (Fr.)8.44	MURDER	U.S.
MOHIS, Michael	301642	M	Ger.		Cpl., Slovakia. 40-45	BRUTALITY	CZECH.
MOHL (or MOLL)	618	M	Ger.		SS-Oschfhr., Guard, C.C. Oswiecim, Rajsko (Pol.) 6.40-12.43	MURDER	POL., BEL.
MOHL	139681	M	Ger.		Hptscharfhr., Waffen-SS, C.C. Gleiwitz (Pol.) 18.1.45	MURDER	U.S.
MOHL (see MOLL)Adolf,Adelbert	46092						
MOHL, Johann (see MOLL)	142534						
MOHL, Otto	157002	M	Ger.	10	SS-Hptscharfhr., C.C. Auschwitz (Pol.) 40-45	MURDER	U.S.
MOHLENBECK	305674	M	Ger.		Purchaser, Factory "de Kroon", Waalwijk and Heusden (Neth.)43-10.44	PILLAGE	NETH.
MOHLKY	254452	M			Sgt., S.D., Toulouse (Fr.) 11.42-8.44	INTERR.	FR.
MOHLMEYER, Wilhelm	142549	M	Ger.	06	S.A.-Truppfhr.	MISC.CRIMES	U.S.
MOHN	166890	M			Secretary, SS, Busset (Fr.) 8.44	MURDER	FR.
MOHNKE, Wilhelm	1728	M	Ger.		SS-Standartenfhr., 12.SS-Panz.Div."Hitler Jugend", Army, Caen (Fr.)44	MISC.CRIMES	CAN., U.K.,U.S.
MOHR	1440	M	Ger.		Pvt., Army, 1.Pion.Regt., 3.Sect., 194.Gr.	MISC.CRIMES	U.K.
MOHR	104862	M	Ger.	10	Usturmfhr., S.D. or Kripo or Gestapo, C.C. Stalag-Luft III (Ger.) 3.44	MURDER	U.K.
MOHR	116305	M	Ger.	00	Lt., Army, Bronzolo (Italy) 9.43	WITNESS	U.K.
MOHR	121174	M	Ger.		Capt., Army, Glux, Chalon sur Saone (Fr.) 5.-6.44	MURDER	FR.
MOHR	188947	M	Ger.		Inspector, Engineer, Ruestungsinspektion, Aussenstelle, Belfort (Fr.) 10.-11.44	PILLAGE	FR.
MOHR	191822	M		10	Officer, Usturmfhr., Gestapo, S.D., Kripo. 3.44	MURDER	U.K.

MOH-MOO

NAME	C.R.FILE NUMBER	SEX	NATIO-NALITY	DATE OF BIRTH	RANK OCCUPATION UNIT PLACE AND DATE OF CRIME	REASON WANTED	WANTED BY
MOHR	192119	M	Ger.		Member, Geheime Feldpolice, Bruessels (Bel.)	TORTURE	BEL.
MOHR	193832	M	Ger.		Pvt. Kgf.Arb.Bn.190, Hattras (Nor.) 11.43	MURDER	NOR.
MOHR	194333	M	Ger.		Feldgendarm, Feldgendarmerie, Feldpost 43.800 Tourcoing (Fr.) 9.44	WITNESS	FR.
MOHR, Christian	305673	M	Ger.		Scharfhr. SS,Leitmeritz,Flossenburg,Hersbruck,Wolkenburg,Ganacker (Ger.Czech.) 1.42 - 5.45	MURDER	U.S.
MOHR, Ernst	134815	M	Ger.	00	Civilian, Building, Contractor, Oberbettingen (Ger.)	MISC.CRIMES	U.S.
MOHR, Erwin	255247	M	Ger.		Cpl. C.C. Ellrich, Nordhausen (Ger.)	MURDER	U.S.
MOHR, Eugen	301882	M	Ger.		Leader, Abt.Wirtschft.Amt des Reichsstatthalters,Danzig (Pol.) 9.39-44	PILLAGE	POL.
MOHR, Franz	125193	M	Ger.		Civilian, Volks-Sturm,Strenz-Nauendorf (Ger.) 4.45	MURDER	U.S.
MOHR, Heinrich	252539	M	Ger.		Pvt. 377.Jg.Rgt., F.P. 34.430, Vinkt (Bel.) 5.40	MISC.CRIMES	BEL.
MOHR, Karl	122620	M	Ger.		Cpl. Pz.-Corps 5.40	MURDER	U.K.
MOHR, Karl	192351	M	Ger.		Sturmfhr. SA, Niederohmen (Ger.)	TORTURE	U.S.
MOHRA, Georg	137483	M			SS-Rottfhr. C.C. Buchenwald,Weimar (Ger.)	CRUELTY	U.S.
MOHRHAUPT (or MOHAUPT)	258002	M			Sgt. 150.Pz.Bge. Meuse Bridge Antwerp.(Bel.) 12.44	MISC.CRIMES	U.S.
MOHRING	619	M			Sgt. Army, Greville Hague (Fr.) 5.44	WITNESS	FR.
MOHRING, Walter, Rudolph	195899	M	Ger.	06	Kriegsverwaltungsoberrat, Landrat, Arlon (Bel.)	MURDER	BEL.
MOHRSTADT, Ludwig	194190	M	Ger.		Scharfhr. SS C.C. Buchenwald, (Ger.) 42-45	MISC.CRIMES	U.S.
MOJZES, Eva	259149	F	Ger.		Civilian, Varazdin (Yugo.)	SUSPECT	YUGO.
MOKEL, Siegfried (or MOCKEL)	166889	M	Ger.		Capt. Army, 7.Rgt. Pionier, Vercors, St. Barthelemy (Fr.) 7.44	MURDER	FR.
MOKRAUS, (or MOKRUS)	124609	M	Ger.		Dr. Uscharfhr. C.C., Birkenau (Ger.)	TORTURE	BEL.
MOKSEMBURG	185924	M			Master, Army, Firm of Heinrich Butzer, Aspfjord (Nor.)	TORTURE	NOR.
MOLIK	305050	M	Ger.	24. 5.08	N.C.O. Feldgen. Truppe no 307 Distr.of Pontivy Morbihan (Fr.) 4.-8.44	MURDER	FR.
MOLINARI	163221	M			Sturmbannfhr.,10.SS-Pz.-Div., 36 Rgt.,Revin (Fr.)6.44	MURDER	FR.
MOLITOR	258000	M			Lt. 150. Pz. Bge. Meuse Bridge Antwerp (Bel.)12.44	MISC. CRIMES	U.S.
MOLITOR	261366	M	Ger.		Pay-Master, Air-Force L. 52.511 Pau, Sou Monton,Narp,Lescar (Fr.) 8.44	MURDER	FR.
MOLITORIS, Hans, Albert	257999	M			SS - Usturmfhr., 150.Pz.-Bge., Meuse Bridge Antwerp.(Bel.) 12.44	MISC.CRIMES	U.S.
MOLKENTIN, Oskar	39587	M	Ger.		Cpl. Army Standort-Kdtr.,Chateau-Gontier (Fr.) 7.-8.44	WITNESS	FR.
MOLL	194189	M	Ger.		Scharfhr. SS, C.C. Buchenwald (Ger.)	MISC.CRIMES	U.S.
MOLL	306859	M	Ger.		SS-Sgt., Commandant of crematorium C.C. Auschwitz (Pol.) 40 - 45	MURDER	FR.
MOLL	307175	M	Ger.		Surgeon, Member, 1.Bn. 24.Rgt. of Fallschirmjaeger Huebner Roermond (Neth.) 12.44-1.45	MURDER	NETH.
MOLL (see MOHL)	618						
MOLL (or MOHL) Adolf, Adelbert	46092	M	Ger.	02	N.C.O., SS, Member Gestapo at Tours, Lussault,Touraine (Fr.)8.44	MURDER	U.S.
MOLL, Fritz	179891	M	Ger.	17. 7.05	Major, Gendarmerie, Bleiburg (Aust.) 10.44	WITNESS	U.S.
MOLL, Johann (alias MOHL)	142534	M			SS-Rottfhr. SS-Totenkopfverband	WITNESS	U.S.
MOLLER	125530	M	Ger.		Pvt. Army, Pz.Gren.Rgt. 110,111 3.Group, Gourdon (Fr.) 6.44	MURDER	FR.
MOLLER	121172	M	Ger.		Uscharfhr. SS, Carcassonne (Fr.)	MISC.CRIMES	FR.
MOLLER	124500	M	Ger.		SS-Uscharfhr. C.C., Staff, Sachsenhausen,Oranienburg (Ger.) 42	MURDER	U.K.
MOLLER	157000	M	Ger.		Capt. Army, Dueren (Ger.)	TORTURE	U.K.
MOLLER	166888	M	Ger.		Capt. C.C. Stalag VI C S.R.A.	TORTURE	FR.
MOLLER	185222	M	Ger.		Hauptsturmfhr. SS-Totenkopf Coy.C.C. Sachsenhausen (Ger.)	MURDER	FR.
MOLLER (see MILLER or MULLER)	191182	M	Ger.		Cpl.Guard, SS C.C. Sachsenhausen,Oranienburg (Ger.) 39-45	MURDER	POL.
MOLLER	300116	M	Ger.		Hauptsturmfhr. Head, 2-44 Totenkopf Coy.,Sachsenhausen(Ger.)42-45		
MOLLER	259199	M			Unterscharfhr., SS, Muhldorf Area. (Ger.)	MURDER	U.S.
MOLLER, Franz	156868	M	Ger.		Oberwachtmstr. Schupo, Frankfurt (Ger.) 43-44	TORTURE	U.S.
MOLLER, Heinrich	173055	M	Ger.	93	Capt. 2.Coy.,71.Pionier Bau Bn.,Chartres,Dueren,Obermanbach (Ger.)7.44	TORTURE	U.K.
MOLLER, Heinrich (see MULLER)	156985						
MOLLER, Johann	185723	M	Ger.		SS-Interrogater, 17.Departement, Kokkinia-Athen (Gre.)	MURDER	GRC.
MOLLIN - Happel, Carl	142554	M	Ger.	05. to.07	Kreishauptstellenltr. NSDAP, Ruesselsheim-Main (Ger.) 1.44	MURDER	U.S.
MOLOTOW (see MAYES)	174861						
MOLTEN	173191	M	Ger.		Staff at C.C. Schirmeck, Gaggenau, Rotenfels (Ger.Fr.) 44	MURDER	U.K.
MOLTER, Leo	620	M			Capt. Pionier Corps., 716 Distr.eng.Bn. 1.Coy.Herouvillette (Fr.)6.44	MURDER	U.K.
MOLTOFF	621	M	Ger.		Guard, C.C. Saarbruecken (Ger.) 1.44	TORTURE	FR.
MOLTZ	259394	M	Ger.		Cmdt. and Chief, C.C., Crematorium, Auschwitz (Pol.)	BRUTALITY	FR.
MOLTZEN (or TOLTZEN)	163220	M			Lt. Sicherungsrgt. 19-192, 8.Coy. St.Plaisir (Fr.) 8.44	MURDER	FR.
MOMKA	126475	M	Ger.		Standartenfhr.,SS-Pz.-Div.Leibstandarte "Adolf Hitler" Malmedy (Bel.)44	MURDER	U.S.
MOMPERT, Albert	135284	M			Civilian, Bierhingen (Lux.) 7.44	WITNESS	U.S.
MONCK (or MEYER)	622	M			Hauptsturmfhr., 1.SS-Pz.Div. "Hitler Jugend" 25.Rgt.,Plomion(Fr.)8.44	MURDER	FR.
MONCKEN, Jonny	252543	M	Ger.		Pvt. Rgt.B-377.Jaeger Rgt.1.Coy., Vinkt (Bel.) 5.40	MISC.CRIMES	BEL.
MONDEN	166276	M	Ger.		Civilian, Manager, "Hermann Goering Werk "(Fr.Czech.Neth.) 39-45	WITNESS	U.S.
MONDO, Delt	132489	M	Aust.		Buergermeister, Public official, St.Gallen,Wiessenbach (Aust.)8.44	MISC.CRIMES	U.K.
MONDORF	257039	M	Ger.		Architect, Specher's Fabrik,Wiesbaden ,Alzin-Moselle (Fr.) 5.46	PILLAGE	FR.
MONDSCHER, Franz	262130	M		19.10.12	Farmer, Civ.-Farm,Muenchen (Ger.) LODNAOD	SUSPECT	U.S.
MONERWEG	124654	M			C.C. , Heppenheim (Ger.) 9.44-5.45	TORTURE	U.S.
MONIKA	306478	M			Supervisor C.C.,Uckermarok (Ger.) 40-45	MURDER	BEL.
MONK (see MUENK)	128923						
MONKOS, Franz	194475	M	Ger.	28. 2.93	Uscharfhr. 4.SS-Totenkopfsturmbann C.C. Dora Mittelbau ,Nordhausen (Ger.) 43 - 45	WITNESS	U.S.
MONNIG	191821	M	Ger.	10	Guard, Cpl. Army, Arbeitskommando Stalag IV D,Eisleben (Ger.) 3.45	MURDER	U.K.
MONREAL, Erich (or MONREAAL)	259795	M	Ger.		Sgt., Gren.Kommando attached to Ortskommandantur, Breda (Neth.) 8. - 9. 45	MURDER	NETH.
MONTALBERT de	623				Colonel, Army, Rodez (Fr.)	MURDER	FR.
MONTER	196060	M			Major, Parachute School, Chaveroone, Ussel (Fr.) 12.43	MURDER	FR.
MOOR	38879	M			Hangman, C.C. Klingelpuetz - Koeln (Ger.) 1.-9.45	TORTURE	U.S.
MOOR	186580	M			SS - Mann, Leibstandarte SS " Adolf Hitler " Stavelot-Renardmont (Bel.)	MURDER	BEL.
MOOR, Alex	127436	M	Ger.	10	Guard, C.C.Dessau (Ger.) 4.45	MURDER	U.S.
MOOR, Franz	127437	M	Ger.	10	Guard, C.C. ,Dessau (Ger.) 4.45	MURDER	U.S.
MOOR, Peter	121171	M	Ger.		Rheinhausen (Ger.)	TORTURE	BEL.
MOORLING	254470	M	Ger.		Lt., Army, Beernem (Bel.) 9.44	INTERR.	BEL.
MOOSE	173789	M	Ger.		Gestapo, Staats Pol. Leitstelle,C.C.Brno,Oswiecim,Birkenau (Pol.,Czech.) 39-45	MURDER	CZECH.
MOOSER, Andreas	260505	M	Ger.	25.11.09	Guard, SS, C.C. Natzweiler (Fr.)	MURDER	FR.
MOOTZES, Fritz	251158	M	Ger.		SS-Unit K.G.II.,S.P. 09 III , Aux Essarts (Fr.) 8.44	SUSPECT	FR.

MOR-MOU

NAME	C.R.FILE NUMBER	SEX	NATIO-NALITY	DATE OF BIRTH	RANK	OCCUPATION UNIT PLACE AND DATE OF CRIME	REASON WANTED	WANTED BY
MORANDELL, Rudolf	306326	M	Ger.			Pvt., 8.Coy. Schlanders Police-Rgt.,stat. at Roncegno, 3.45	MURDER	U.K.
MORATH	141379	M	Ger.			Chief, customs and excise, Paris (Fr.)	WITNESS	FR.
MORATH, Robert	177349	M	Ger.	89	Sea-cmdt., Fregatt.Capt.Navy, Bergen (Nor.) 7.43		MISC.CRIMES	NOR.
MORAWETZ, Josef	255910	M				Pvt., C.C. Ellrich, Nordhausen (Ger.)	MURDER	U.S.
MORAWIETZ	251142	M				Pvt., Army, Fr.	INTERR.	FR.
MORAWITZ, August	254033	M	Ger.			Police-official, SIPO, Brussels (Bel.)	INTERR.	BEL.
MORDER	172467	M	Ger.			Civ., Blockleiter, C.C. Vicinity of Nordhausen (Ger.) 43-44	TORTURE	U.S.
MOREK	307176	M	Ger.			Wachtmeister, SS, Falstad slave labour camp, (Nor.) 42-43	MURDER	YUGO.
MOREL, Siegfried	254778	M	Ger.			Capt. or Lt., Coy. Mongols, Gresse Boissard (Fr.) 7.44	INTERR.	FR.
MORELL, Theodor	133288	M	Ger.			Doctor, Civ., Ger.	WITNESS	U.S.
MOREN	196783	M				Guard or Kapo, C.C. Gusen (Ger.)	BRUTALITY	BEL.
MORGEN	156996	M	Ger.	08		Capt.,Doctor, SS, S.D., C.C. Lublin (Pol.)	MURDER	U.S.
MORGEN	260985	M				SS Rottfhr., C.C. Vaihingen (Ger.) 8.44-4.45	MURDER	U.S.
MORGENROT, Emile	194332	M		12		Cpl., Schnelle Abt. 602, F.P.No. 27690 A, Chambord (Fr.) 8.44	MURDER	FR.
MORGENROTH, Alfred	145977	M	Ger.	00		Cpl., Stalag 317 C.C. Markt Pongau (Aust.) 3.-5.45	TORTURE	U.S.
MORGENSTEIN, Frank	180498	M	Ger.	about 15	Lt., 721.Jaeger-Rgt., Sanseboloro (It.) 8.44		MURDER	U.K.
MORGENSTERN, Ewald	121170	M	Ger.			Lt., 24.Panz.Rgt., Hainaut (Bel.) 9.44	MURDER	BEL.
MORGENSTERN, Fritz	124852	M	Ger.			Cpl., Landesschuetzen-Coy. 398, C.C. Chemnitz (Ger.) 10.43-3.45	TORTURE	U.K.
MORITZ alias MAURICE	138844	M				Lt., Gestapo SS, Lyon (Fr.)	MURDER	FR.
MORITZ	251159	M				Major, Gestapo, Paris (Fr.)	MISC.CRIMES	FR.
MORITZ	257710	M				Usturmfhr., S.D., Tromsoe-Northern (Nor.) 43-44	TORTURE	NOR.
MORITZ, August or MORITZ alias MUELLER,MARTIN,MAURICE	240132	M	Ger.	15	SS Sturmbannfhr., Cmdt., S.D. official, Marseille, Berlin (Fr.,Ger.)		PILLAGE	U.S.
MORITZ, Cuno	168051	M	Ger.			Pvt., Army, 9.Res.Gren.Rgt., 1.Coy. Sanitaeter, Magny d'Anigon (Fr.)9.44	MURDER	FR.
MORITZ, Joseph	156881	M		07		Cpl., Gestapo, Angers (Fr.) 42-44	MURDER	FR.
MORITZ, Lothar	259141	M				SS-guard, Muehldorf Area (Ger.)	MURDER	U.S.
MORK	194435	M	Ger.			Wachtmeister, Schupo, C.C. Falstad (Nor.) 41-44	MURDER	NOR.
MORK	257911	M				Pvt., 7.Coy. 1322.Bn. 5.Schtz.Rgt., Ljubljana (Yugo.) 42-43	MURDER	YUGO.
MORKES	254676	M				Police-Capt., Police, Aachen (Ger.) 7.44	INTERR.	U.S.
MORKUS, Franz	195355	M	Ger.	27.11.17	Member, SS, occupied territories legal official, Moravske,Budejovice (Czech.) 39-45		INTERR.	CZECH.
MORLE	189594	M	Ger.			Major, Zentral-Ersatzteillager 206, Paris (Fr.)	MURDER	FR.
MORLON or MORLEF	166887	M	Ger.			Sgt., Adjudant, Fallschirmjaeger 14, Richardmenil (Fr.)	MURDER	FR.
MORO GAVINO see GARINO	145470							
MORR, Johannes Otto	260919	M	Ger.	25. 5.06	SS Uscharfhr., Warsaw (Pol.) 40-44		MURDER	POL.
MORRELL	104869	M				Doctor	WITNESS	U.S.
MORREN, Mathias	255360	M	Ger.			Pvt., Army, Eyne (Bel.) 9.44	INTERR.	BEL.
MORSCH, Jakob	194188	M	Ger.	91		Hauptwachtmeister, Gendarmerie, Dudweiler (Ger.) 7.44	WITNESS	U.S.
MORSER, Franz or MORSE	194139	M	Ger.	17. 2.07	Civ., Machinist, Lidice (Czech.) 42-43		WITNESS	CZECH.
MORTAK	166886	M	Ger.			Feldgendarmerie, Larochemilly (Fr.)	PILLAGE	FR.
MORTEIMANS	254038	M				Section-leader, Sipo, Brussels (Bel.)	INTERR.	BEL.
MORTFELD	196059	M				Lt., 18.Schiffs-Stm.Abt., Navy, Replacement-Section,Montceau-les-Mines (Fr.) 7.44	TORTURE	FR.
MORTITZ see MORITZ, August	240132							
MORTSHEIM	124241	M	Ger.			Uscharfhr., 1.SS Panz.Gren.Div. 12.Coy., Malmedy (Bel.) 12.44	MURDER	U.S.
MORY, Theofil	258009	M				Cpl., 150. Panz.Bde., Meuse Bridge Antwerp.(Bel.)12.44	MISC.CRIMES	U.S.
MOSALLE	624	M				Feldgendarm, Feldgendarmerie, Army, Longwy (Fr.) 8.-9.42	TORTURE	FR.
MOSCHNER	185880	M	Ger.			Pvt., Navy, Ostende (Bel.)	MURDER	BEL.
MOSE, Heinrich	190348	M	Ger.	00		Cpl., Feldgendarmerie, Dortrecht (Neth.) 10.44	TORTURE	CAN.
MOSEL	1222	M	Ger.			Capt., Airforce, 3.Luftfl.Nachr.Rgt. 4, Ramnicusurat (Rum.)	MURDER	U.S.
MOSENHEWER	254679	M	Ger.			Oscharfhr., NSKK, Landratsamt, Helmstedt (Ger.) 6. or 7.44	WITNESS	U.S.
MOSENTHIN	192357	M				Usturmfhr.SS,Lt. Feldgendarmerie, St.Pourcain,Siculen (Fr.)	MURDER	FR.
MOSER	123127	M	Ger.			N.C.O., Lager, C.C. Tanzeldorf (Aust.) 3.42	MURDER	U.K.
MOSER	185172	M	Ger.			Sgt., Feldgendarmerie Trupp 533, St.Jorioz (Fr.) 6.44	MURDER	FR.
MOSER	192256	M				C.C. Flossenburg (Ger.) 44-45	MURDER	U.S.
MOSER, Alois	256087	M				SS Oscharfhr., Muehldorf (Ger.)	WITNESS	U.S.
MOSER, Hans	161923	M		05		SS Osturmfhr., H.Q. Staff, C.C. Buchenwald (Ger.) 44-45	WITNESS	U.S.
MOSER, Hans	256871	M		07		SS Major, chief of office, C.C. Dora-Mittelbau Nordhausen (Ger.)40-45	MURDER	U.S.
MOSER, Hans Joseph see MAUSER	142553							
MOSER, Ignace	257709	M	Ger.			Lt., German airforce, Abercement de Varey (Fr.) 7.44	MURDER	FR.
MOSER, Joseph	12554	M				N.C.O., Army, Panz.Gren.Rgt.110, 111 2.Coy.,Gourdon (Fr.) 6.44	MURDER	FR.
MOSER, Josef	132969	M				SS Oscharfhr., C.C. Dora-Mittelbau Nordhausen (Ger.)	MURDER	U.S.
MOSER, Josef	145980	M				Civ. Ortsgruppenleiter NSDAP, Ger.	MURDER	U.S.
MOSER, Karl see MAUSER	191941							
MOSER, Leonhard	306314	M				Pvt., 8.Coy. Schlanders Police, Rgt. Roncegno (It.) 3.45	MURDER	U.K.
MOSER, Willi	187714	M				General, Administration of occupied territories Art., Nor.	TORTURE	UNWCC
MOSES	164987	M		00		Agent, SIPO, Brussels (Bel.)	MURDER	BEL.
MOSKOPFF	307022	M	Ger.			Chief of Ersatzcmdo. at Brussels, Huy-Wavre (Bel.) 8.44	MURDER	BEL.
MOSLER, Arthur	260511	M	Ger.	13. 1.98	SS-guard, C.C. Natzweiler (Fr.)		MURDER	FR.
MOSLER, Pavel	194474	M	Ger.	20. 7.09	Crim.assist., Gestapo, C.C. Brno (Czech.) 39-45		MURDER	CZECH.
MOSSAL	196058	M	Ger.	05		Sgt., Feldgendarmerie Nancy, Pierre-Percine Treves (Fr.) 6.44	TORTURE	FR.
MOSSER	168017	M	Ger.			Sgt., Interpreter, Airforce, Aviation camp, Arles-Chanoine (Fr.) 8.44	PILLAGE	FR.
MOSSLER	192970	M				SS Osturmfhr., C.C. Dora-Mittelbau Nordhausen (Ger.)	MURDER	U.S.
MOTIK, Hanna	194479	F	Ger.	29. 1.05	Guard, Gestapo, C.C. Brno (Czech.) 39-45		MURDER	CZECH.
MOTNECKE or WOTNECKE	141584	M				Lt. Col., SS, Langeac, Auvers, Pinols (Fr.) 6.44	MURDER	FR.
MOTT, Georg	145981	M		00		SS Osturmfhr., C.C. Reichenau near Innsbruck (Aust.) 42-44	MURDER	U.S.
MOTTET	125764	M				Guard, C.C. Flossenburg (Ger.) 44-45	MURDER	U.K.
MOTYCZKA, Heinrich	259263	M	Ger.	14. 7.89	Liquidation-administrat. of a jewish business, Amsterdam (Neth.) 7.43		MISC.CRIMES	NETH.
MOTZ	626	M	Ger.			Cpl., SS-Div. "Das Reich" Rgt."Der Fuehrer", Buzet (Fr.) 7.-8.44	MURDER	FR.
MOTZ	190382	M	Ger.			Policeman, Police, Wiesbaden (Ger.) 43-45	TORTURE	U.S.
MOTZER	251143	M	Ger.			Lt., Army, Maasbracht (Neth.) 12.44	SUSPECT	NETH.
MOUGET	627	M	Ger.			SS Rottfhr., 2.SS Panz.Div. 3.Rgt. SS Panz.Gren., Fr. 5.44	MURDER	FR.
MOUIER or MAYER	251839	M	Ger.			Cpl., Army, Fort de Romainville (Fr.) 8.44	MURDER	FR.

MOU-MUE

NAME	C.R.FILE NUMBER	SEX	NATIO-NALITY	DATE OF BIRTH	RANK OCCUPATION UNIT PLACE AND DATE OF CRIME	REASON WANTED	WANTED BY
MOUNOLD	188949	M	Ger.		Specialist Officer,540 Feldkommandantur,Besancon(Fr.)2.44	PILLAGE	FR.
MOUT, Karl	131304	M	Ger.		Crim.Ob.secretary,Orpo,CC Jawischowitz near Auschwitz(Pol.)44	MURDER	U.S.
MOUTI	188950	M	Ger.		Legal Official,CC St.Anne,Avignon(Fr.)40-44	TORTURE	FR.
MOVOKOWSKI	156995	M			Detachement of SS,St.Yorre,Busset(Fr.)	MURDER	FR.
MOWES	185484	M	Ger.		Inspector,Overseer,CC Ravensbrueck(Ger.)	MURDER	BEL.
MOYT	36638	M	Ger.		Major,Army,Soegel(Ger.)4.45	MISC.CRIMES	CAN.
MOYZES, Friedrich	193891	M		23. 4.01	Oberwachtmeister,Strafgef.Lager,Justizministerium,CC Finmark(Nor.)42-45	MISC.CRIMES	NOR.
MOZER	132971	M			SS Uschafhr.CC Mittelbau Dora Nordhausen(Ger.)	MURDER	U.S.
MRAZEK	301672	M	Ger.		Major,Sohan Pepinster Theux(Bel.)9.44	MURDER	BEL.
MROS, Paul	194192	M	Ger.		SS Uschafhr.CC Buchenwald(Ger.)42-45	TORTURE	U.S.
MRUGOSKY, Max	194208	M	Ger.		Physican,SS Oberfhr.Chief of Hygiene Institute,CC Buchenwald(Ger.)	TORTURE	U.S.
MUCH, Hans	161922	M	Ger.	22	SS Rottenfhr.CC Buchenwald(Ger.)42-45	WITNESS	U.S.
MUCHA, Friedrich	255707	M			Pvt.CC Ellrich,Nordhausen(Ger.)	MURDER	U.S.
MUCHER or MUCHA	301695	M	Ger.		05/243"Oberland"Unit(Mongolian),St.Nazaire en Royans(Fr.)7.-8.44	MURDER	FR.
MUCHITSCH	259095	M	Ger.		SS Osturmfhr.Adjudantfhr.SS Div.Prinz Eugen,Niksic district Montenegro (Yugo.)5.-6.43	MISC.CRIMES	YUGO.
MUCK	132756	M			SS Uschafhr.SS Totenkopf,CC Mauthausen(Aust.)41-45	MURDER	U.S.
MUCK see HUCK	188659						
MUCK, Frantz or HUCK	136257	M	Ger.		Gendarmerie Meister,La Bourboulemont Dore(Fr.)6.44	MURDER	FR.
MUCK, Marcel	166885	M	Ger.		Feldgendarm,Feldgendarmerie,Luneville-Maixe(Fr.)8.44	MURDER	FR.
MUCKE, Alfred	132755	M	Ger.	00	Dr.,SS Hptscharfhr.CC Mauthausen(Aust.)41	MURDER	U.S.
MUCKEL see MICHL	253551						
MUCKHARDT	194448	M			Oberstabsarzt,Inf.Div.250,P.O.W.Work Bn.181,Drag(Nor.)	MURDER	NOR.
MUDHA	151429	M	Ger.		Sgt.Stalag VIIIB,CC Sosnowitz(Pol.)4.43	TORTURE	U.K.
MUECK	1441	M	Ger.		SS Untersturmfhr.36 SS Panz.Gr.1 Coy.,	MISC.CRIMES	U.K.
MUECKE	162219	M	Ger.	15	Lt.955/214 Inf.Div.,Helleland near Stavanger(Nor.)11.42	MURDER	U.K.
MUEDDER, Gerhard	185727	M	Ger.	7.10.00	Civilian,Abwehr Official,Brno(Czech.)39-45	PILLAGE	CZECH.
MUEHLEN	107541	M	Ger.	94	Oberstlt.Abwehr Official,Bordeaux(Fr.)42	MISC.CRIMES	FR.
MUEHLPFORT, Willi	256759	M	Ger.	19. 6.94	Employee,Camp Dora Nordhausen(Ger.)	MURDER	U.S.
MUEHLPFORTE	139678	M			Justizoberinspector,Reichskriegsgericht,Leipzig(Ger.)	MURDER	U.S.
MUEHLRADT	104864	M	Ger.		Pvt.Kraftfahrpark,Wuerzburg(Ger.)8.44	WITNESS	U.S.
MUELLAN	306860	M	Ger.	10	Head-Overseer,SS,CC Auschwitz(Pol.)40-45	MURDER	FR.
MUELLENHOLZ, Heinrich	161921	M	Ger.	26.11.12	SS Uschafhr.Command Staff,SS Totenkopf,CC Buchenwald(Ger.)	TORTURE	U.S.
MUELLER	628	M	Ger.		Dr.,Polizeivizepraesident,Police,Gdynia(Pol.)42	MURDER	POL.
MUELLER	629	M	Ger.		Generalquartiermeister,Army,Feldzug gegen Polen,9.39	MISC.CRIMES	POL.
MUELLER	635	M	Ger.		Capt.Army Feldkommandantur 755,Le Mans(Fr.)40-44	PILLAGE	FR.
MUELLER	1443	M	Ger.		Lt.Army,26 Pz.Gr.2 Coy.	MISC.CRIMES	U.K.
MUELLER	10074	M			Pvt.21 Army Group,CC Stalag 20A(Ger.)11.44	MURDER	U.S.U.K.
MUELLER	10312	M	Ger.		Sturmfhr.SS Commissar der Gestapo,Tabor,39-44 -	TORTURE	CZECH.
MUELLER	31402	M	Ger.		Capt.Army,99/7 Geb.Div.Geb.Pz.Jaeg.Abt.,Finmark(Nor.)44	MURDER	NOR.
MUELLER	31403	M	Ger.		Capt.Army,91/6 Geb.Div.Geb.Pi.Bn.,Bezirk Finmark(Nor.)44	MURDER	NOR.
MUELLER	31404	M	Ger.		Oberstrichter,Army,General's Staffel,20 Army,Bezirk Finmark(Nor.)	TORTURE	NOR.
MUELLER	36695	M	Ger.		Cpl.Army-Stalag III G,K.D.30/434,Grossteinberg(Ger.)10.43	TORTURE	U.K.
MUELLER	38862	M	Ger.	10	Sgt.Feldgendarmerie,Bruggen(Ger.)2.45	MURDER	U.S.
MUELLER	38863	M	Ger.	95 or 00	Lt.Col.GAF.Signal Regt.C.O.of GAF 205 Nachr.Regt.12 Nachtjagd Corps, (Ger.)44	TORTURE	U.S.
MUELLER	38864	M	Ger.		Kommissar,Gestapo,CC Prague(Czech.)3.39	TORTURE	U.S.
MUELLER	39867	M	Ger.		Sgt.(Stabsfeldwebel),KL Kulm-Littemburg(Ger.)	TORTURE	U.K.
MUELLER	62400	M	Ger.		Lt.Army,Fallschirmjaeger,Roermond(Neth.)11.44-1.45	TORTURE	U.S.
MUELLER	62401	M	Ger.	95	SS Uschafhr.CC Hinzert(Ger.)	TORTURE	U.S.
MUELLER	90847	M	Ger.	15	SS Hptscharfhr.CC Buchenwald,Waffen SS(Ger.)44	TORTURE	U.S.
MUELLER	104868	M	Ger.		Dr.,Civilian,Kiew Institute(Physician)Kiew(Russ.)41-42	MURDER	U.S.
MUELLER	123180	M	Ger.		Pvt.Cpl.Comp.No.427,CC Uhyst(Ger.)	TORTURE	U.K.
MUELLER	125085	M	Ger.		Pvt.Guard,CC Bautzen(Ger.)1.45-5.45	MISC.CRIMES	U.K.
MUELLER	127498	M	Ger.		SS Oschafhr.Guard,CC Buchenwald(Ger.)	TORTURE	U.S.
MUELLER	128832	M	Ger.		Pvt.Interpreter,Coy.Kassel,CC Grimmenthal,Obermassfeld(Ger.)8.43	TORTURE	U.K.
MUELLER	131303	M	Ger.		SS Rottenfhr.CC Monowitz(Pol.)	MURDER	U.S.
MUELLER	131307	M	Ger.		SS Oschafhr.Work Camp,Krakau(Pol.)42-32	MURDER	U.S.
MUELLER	132250	M	Ger.		SS Major,Gestapo,C.O.Sicherh.Commando 11B,Thekina,Tiraspol(Rum.Russ.)41	MURDER	U.S.
MUELLER	132254	M	Ger.		SS Untersturmfhr.Gestapo,CC Tabor(Czech.)39-45	MURDER	CZECH.
MUELLER	132257	M	Ger.		SS,Erfurt(Ger.)44	TORTURE	U.S.
MUELLER	132258	M	Ger.	21	Rottenfhr.Waffen SS,CC Hohenrheim-Plattling(Ger.)2.-5.45	MURDER	U.S.
MUELLER	132640	M	Ger.		Guard,CC Schirmeck(Fr.)3.44	MURDER	FR.
MUELLER	132777	M	Ger.		Fallschirmjaeger Regt.5,Nachrichtenzug,Quaregnon Jemappes Ghlin(Bel.) 2.39-44	TORTURE MURDER	BEL.
MUELLER	134817	M	Ger.	03	SS Gruppenfhr.CC Buchenwald(Ger.)	MURDER	U.S.
MUELLER	134907	M	Ger.	00	SS Obergruppenfhr.(Pol.)	TORTURE	U.S.
MUELLER	137670	M	Ger.		Civilian,Naundorf(Ger.)3-45	TORTURE	U.K.
MUELLER	139885	M	Ger.		Lt.Col.Army OKW(Ger.)	MURDER	U.K.
MUELLER	139888	M	Ger.		SS Obersturmfhr.Waffen SS(Ger.)	MURDER	U.K.
MUELLER	141971	M	Ger.		Major,Commandant St.Gilles Prison,Bruessel(Bel.)7.-9.44	TORTURE	U.S.
MUELLER	152157A	M	Ger.	19 - 23	SS Uschafhr.CC Neuengamme(Ger.)	TORTURE	U.K.
MUELLER	152158	M	Ger.		Criminal secretary,Gruppenfhr.Gestapo and SS, Berlin(Ger.)39-45	MURDER	U.S.
MUELLER	152161	M	Ger.	95	Civilian,Airplane Factory Construction CC,Muehldorf,Ampfing(Ger.) 44-45	TORTURE	U.S.
MUELLER	154822	M	Ger.		Capt.Luftwaffe CC, Stalag Luft IV, Kiefheide(Ger.)6.44	TORTURE	U.S.
MUELLER	156991	M	Ger.		Guard,Army 414 Bn.,Ludwigslust(Ger.)	MURDER	U.K.
MUELLER	163477	M			Master, Firm of Heinrich Butzer,Organisation Todt, Aspfjord(Nor.)	TORTURE	NOR.
MUELLER	163478	M	Ger.		Lt.Gestapo,Mons(Bel.)9.44	TORTURE	BEL.

MUE - MUE

NAME	C.R.FILE NUMBER	SEX	NATIO-NALITY	DATE OF BIRTH	RANK OCCUPATION UNIT PLACE AND DATE OF CRIME	REASON WANTED	WANTED BY
MUELLER	168019	M	Ger.		Dr., Civilian, Ostgebietsministerium Einsatzstab Rosenberg, St.Germain (Fr.) 40-44	PILLAGE	FR.
MUELLER	168059	M	Ger.		Leader, Abt.Wirtschaftsamt des Generalgouverneurs, Lublin (Pol.)39-44	PILLAGE	POL.
MUELLER	169493	M	Ger.	85	Col., Army, C.C. Laufen (Ger.) 11.42-3.43	TORTURE	U.K.
MUELLER	173784	M	Ger.		Cpl., C.C. Tripolis (Africa) 6.41-8.41	TORTURE	U.K.
MUELLER	173786	M	Ger.		Hptsturmfhr., C.C. Oswiecim-Birkenau (Pol.) 39-45	MURDER	CZECH.,POL.,BEL.
MUELLER	173787	M	Ger.		SS-Gruppenfhr., Lt.Gen., SS, Gestapo, Polizei, C.C. Oswiecim-Birkenau (Pol.) 39-45	MURDER	CZECH.,BEL.
MUELLER	173788	M	Ger.		Reg.Vizepraesident, Public official, C.C. Oswiecim-Birkenau, Karlovy Vary (Pol.,Czech.) 39-45	MURDER	CZECH.
MUELLER	173811	M	Ger.		SS-Gruppenfhr., SS, Gestapo, Chief of Amt IV. 44	TORTURE	FR.,BEL.,CZECH.
MUELLER	173830	M	Ger.		SS-Gruppenfhr., SS. 44-45	TORTURE	NETH.
MUELLER	174170	M	Ger.	11	Oschfhr., Allg.SS, C.C. Krakau, Plaszow (Pol.) 42-43	MURDER	U.S.
MUELLER	178298	M	Ger.	05	714.Landesschuetzen-Bn., Ludwigslust (Ger.)	MURDER	U.K.
MUELLER	178754	M	Ger.	05	Capt. 398.Landesschuetzen-Bn. at Gross-Strehlitz in 1942, Gogolin (Ger.) 7.42	MURDER	U.K.
MUELLER	180495	M	Ger.	18	Pvt., Engineer, 2.Coy., Pion.Bn.334, Eng.Bn., Le Vigne near Caselle di Agna (Italy) 8.44	MURDER	U.K.
MUELLER	185734	M	Ger.		Osturmfhr., SS. Art.Training and Replacement Regt., Prague (Czech.)5.45	MURDER	CZECH.
MUELLER	185728	M	Ger.	05	Osturmfhr., SS, Prague (Czech.) 5.45	MURDER	CZECH.
MUELLER	187967	M	Ger.	13	Interpreter, Feldwebel, SS-Gebirgs-Div., Triest (Italy)	TORTURE	U.K.
MUELLER	189202	M			Osturmfhr., SS. Formation Tannenberg, 5.and 6.Bn., Champs le Duc (Fr.) 9.44	PILLAGE	FR.
MUELLER	189763	M	Ger.		Major, Kreiskommandantur, Zajecar (Yugo.) 43	MURDER	YUGO.
MUELLER	190626	M			Cpl., Heeres-Verwaltung Regt. Keuten, Chateau, d'Armain-Villiers and Gretz (Fr.) 7.44	MURDER	FR.
MUELLER	191585	M	Ger.		Official, Ostgebietsministerium, Einsatzstab Rosenberg (Fr.)40-44	PILLAGE	FR.
MUELLER	192252	M			Dr., C.C. Flossenburg (Ger.) 44-45	MURDER	U.S.
MUELLER	194212	M	Ger.		SS-Gruppenfhr., C.C. Buchenwald (Ger.) 42-45	TORTURE	U.S.
MUELLER (see MILLER)	194449						
MUELLER	194472	M			Hptscharfhr., 4.SS Totenkopf-Sturmbann, C.C.Nordhausen, Plaszow (Ger., Pol.) 43-45	MURDER	U.S.
MUELLER	194992	M	Ger.		Hptsturmfhr., SS, C.C. Auschwitz, Rajsko (Pol.) 43-5.44	TORTURE	BEL., POL.
MUELLER	195101	M	Ger.		S.D., C.C. Natzweiler (Fr.) 9.44	MURDER	U.K.
MUELLER	195103	M	Ger.		Leader, Organisation Todt, Assen (Neth.) 12.44	MURDER	NETH.
MUELLER (Nickname: Polizeimueller)	195169	M	Ger.		Civilian, Luxemburg (Lux.)	PILLAGE	LUX.
MUELLER	195652	M	Ger.		Regierungsbaurat, Government-official, Rowno (Pol.) 42	MURDER	POL.
MUELLER	196052	M	Ger.		Oberwachtmeister, Sipo, C.C. Westerbork (Neth.) 9.-12.44	MURDER	NETH.
MUELLER	196780	M	Ger.		Lt., C.C. Neuengamme (Ger.)	TORTURE	BEL.
MUELLER	221521	M	Ger.	95	Uschfhr., Waffen-SS, C.C. Hinzert (Ger.) 45	TORTURE	U.S.
MUELLER (or MILLER)	229924	M	Ger.	90	Major, Crim.Commissar, S.D., Sipo, Moravski (Czech.)	TORTURE	U.S.
MUELLER	250384	M	Ger.		Capt., Army, 13.SS Polizei-Regt., Ferlach (Aust.) 44-45	INTERR.	YUGO.
MUELLER	253213	M	Ger.	01	Guard, P.W.Camp Fallingbostel (Ger.) 41	BRUTALITY	YUGO.
MUELLER	253267	M	Ger.		Guard, C.C. Labde-Weser (Ger.)	INTERR.	BEL.
MUELLER	253549	M	Ger.		Oschfhr., SS, Fiume (Italy) 44-45	INTERR.	YUGO.
MUELLER	253929	M	Ger.		Lt., Army, 1.Coy. Gren.Regt.956, Monte Mirlo (Italy)	INTERR.	U.K.
MUELLER	254034	M	Ger.		Criminal secretary, Sipo, Brussels (Bel.)	INTERR.	BEL.
MUELLER	254253	M	Ger.		Inspector of schools at Cracow (Pol.)	INTERR.	POL.
MUELLER	254674	M	Ger.		Capt., 12. Paratroop Regt., Fresshluneberg (Ger.) 11.44	MURDER	U.S.
MUELLER	254677	M	Ger.		Interpreter, SS, S.D., Polizei-Stadion, Fiume (Italy) 3.45	INTERR.	YUGO.
MUELLER	254770	M	Ger.		Dr., Member of SS, C.C.Auschwitz-Birkenau (Pol.) 42-45	MURDER	YUGO.
MUELLER	254780	M	Ger.		Lt., S.D., Toulouse (Fr.) 11.42-8.44	MISC.CRIMES	FR.
MUELLER	255875	M			Col., SS, C.C. Buchenwald (Ger.)	MURDER	U.S.
MUELLER	256745	M	Ger.		Employee, factory worker, C.C. Nordhausen (Ger.)	MURDER	U.S.
MUELLER	256746	M	Čer.	91	Major-Gen., Polizei, Kassel, Ersrode (Ger.) 8.44-45	MURDER	U.S.
MUELLER	256869	M			T-Sgt., Ers.Art.Bttr. 717, Saint-Andre (Bel.) 9.44	MURDER	BEL.
MUELLER	257344	M	Ger.		Uschfhr., SS - Slave Labour Camp, Osen (Nor.) 6.42-3.43	MISC.CRIMES	YUGO.
MUELLER	258465	M	Ger.		Foreman, Railway-station, Warsaw (Pol.) 40-45	MISC.CRIMES	POL.
MUELLER	258918	M	Ger.		Sgt., Army, Renescure (Fr.) 9.44	WITNESS	FR.
MUELLER	261034	M	Ger.		Uschfhr., SS-Guard, Osen (Nor.)	MURDER	YUGO.
MUELLER	300940		Ger.		Member of C.C. Neckarelz and C.C. Neckargerach (Ger.) 42-45	MURDER	FR.
MUELLER	300730	M	Ger.		Hptsturmfhr., 13. SS Polizei-Regt., Ferlash (Austria) 4.44-5.45	MURDER	YUGO.
MUELLER	301215	M	Ger.		Cpl., Staff of Camp E 3, Stalag 344, on the march Blechhammer O.S.-Moosburg (Bayern) (Pol.,Ger.) 1.-3.45	BRUTALITY	U.K.
MUELLER	301696	M	Ger.		SS-Lt., Officer Commanding, 5. and 6. Btty., SS-Formation "Tannenberg", Lyons and surroundings (Fr.) 11.43-8.44	MURDER	FR.
MUELLER	301735	M	Ger.	20	Pvt., Guard, Stalag III A with Working Party at Wolfshagen, Wolfshagen, Perleberg (Ger.) 8.44	MURDER	U.K.
MUELLER	305081	M	Ger.		Military Governor, Mayor. Governor of the Fortress of Crete. Mayor of Heraklion (Crete), Crete (Greece) 9.43-5.44	MISC.CRIMES	GRC.
MUELLER	305082	M	Ger.		SS-Cmdt., stationed at Deesburg. Lulay's Superior, Vrasselt, Emmerich, Wijnbergen (Neth.) 10.44-3.45	INTERR.	NETH.
MUELLER	305930	M	Ger.		Guard, Wachtmeister, Prison Bamberg (Ger.) 44-45	BRUTALITY	CZECH.
MUELLER	305931	M	Ger.		Administrator, Prison Ebrash near Amberg (Ger.) 45	MURDER	CZECH.
MUELLER	305932	M	Ger.		SS-Obergruppenfhr., Amtschef of Department IV of the Reichssicherheits-Hauptamt Berlin. Hrabuvka near Moravska Ostrava (Czech.) 3.44	MURDER	CZECH.
MUELLER	306208		Ger.		Member of Staff, Small Fortress, C.C. Theresienstadt (Czech.) 10.38-44.	MURDER	CZECH.
MUELLER	252545	M	Ger.		N.C.O., 2.Coy., 438.Bn., Schmargersdorf (Ger.) 9.44	MURDER	FR.

MUE-MUE

NAME	C.R.FILE NUMBER	SEX	NATIONALITY	DATE OF BIRTH	RANK OCCUPATION UNIT PLACE AND DATE OF CRIME	REASON WANTED	WANTED BY
MUELLER	306228	M	Ger.		Dr., Staff-Sgt., SS, Fiume, Susak (It., Yugo.) 44-45	MURDER	YUGO.
MUELLER	306951	M	Ger.		Dr., Police-Praesident, Gdynia (Pol.) 42	MURDER	POL.
MUELLER, Albrecht	193828	M			Major, Kgf.-Arb.Bn.206, C.C., Koemeues (Nor.) 12.44-1.45	MURDER	NOR.
MUELLER, Alfons	175724	M			Rottfhr., SS, 4.SS-Totenkopf-Sturmbann, Conc.Camp, Mittelbau Dora, Nordhausen (Ger.)	WITNESS	U.S.
MUELLER, Alfred (or MULLER)	174367	M	Ger.	24	Parachutiste-Guard, Utrecht (Neth.) 10.44	WITNESS	CAN.
MUELLER, Andres	190383	M	Ger.		Civilian, Wiesbaden (Ger.) 43-45	WITNESS	U.S.
MUELLER, Bartel	255709	M			Pvt., C.C., Klein Bodungen, Nordhausen (Ger.)	MURDER	U.S.
MUELLER, Dietrich	255708	M			Pvt., C.C., Ellrich, Nordhausen (Ger.)	MURDER	U.S.
MUELLER, E.	300825	M	Ger.		Pvt., 1.Aufkl.Abt., 3.Coy., 2.Column, XV.Div. of the Afrika Korps, Saint Leger (Arlon) 9.44	MISC.CRIMES	BEL.
MUELLER, Edward	256911	M	Ger.	19.12.10	Employee, C.C., Factory-worker, Nordhausen (Ger.)	MURDER	U.S.
MUELLER, Erich	194578	M	Ger.	30.8.02	Dr., Sturmbannfhr., Asst., SD, Sipo, Lublin, Warschau (Pol.) 41-43	MURDER	POL.
MUELLER, Erich	254678	M	Ger.		Otruppfhr., NSKK, Helmstedt (Ger.) 6.44 or 7.44	WITNESS	U.S.
MUELLER, Ernst	306711	M	Ger.		Master of Gend., Altenburg (Ger.) 8.44	MURDER	U.S.
MUELLER, Felix	255051			04	Zugwachtmeister, Schupo, Member, Executions Firing Squad, Prague (Czech.) 5.42-6.42	INTERR.	CZECH.
MUELLER, Fr.	258015	M			150.Pz.Bde., Meuse-Bridge-Antwerp (Bel.) 12.44	MISC.CRIMES	U.S.
MUELLER, Franz	152156	M	Ger.	00	Miner, Civilian, Neutershausen (Ger.)	MURDER	U.S.
MUELLER, Franz	168082	M	Ger.	15	Crim.Clerk, Gestapo, Uschfhr., SD, Prague (Czech.) 45	MURDER	CZECH.
MUELLER, Franz	179832	M	Ger.		Wachtmeister, Guard, Prison, Conc.Camp, Ebrach (Ger.) 39-45	MURDER	CZECH.
MUELLER, Franz	252528	M	Ger.		Member, SD, Meppel (Neth.) 12.44	TORTURE	NETH.
MUELLER, Franz	259004	M	Ger.	5.9.94	SS-Standartenfhr., SS-No.: 277157, NSDAP-No.: 1679774	INTERR.	U.S.
MUELLER, Fritz	138284	M	Ger.		Lt., SS, Gestapo, Lyon (Fr.)	MURDER	FR.
MUELLER, Fritz	161920	M	Ger.		SS, Conc.Camp, Buchenwald (Ger.)	WITNESS	U.S.
MUELLER, Fritz	165956	M	Ger.	00	Uschfhr., SS, Conc.Camp, Buchenwald (Ger.) 5.44-4.45	TORTURE	U.S.
MUELLER, Fritz Guenther	307023	M	Ger.	10	Hptsturmfhr., SS, Chief of the V b.Department of the SD, Liaison Officer between the Gestapo and H.Q. of the Military Commandant for South-East with H.Q. of the II Armoured Corps, SD (Gestapo) in Belgrade, NSDAP, SA, Belgrade and Serbia (Yugo.) 41-10.44	MURDER	YUGO.
MUELLER, Georg	194471	M			Rottfhr., Guard, 4.SS-Totenkopf-Sturmbann, Conc.Camp, Dora Mittelbau, Monowitz, Nordhausen (Ger., Pol.) 43-45	MURDER	U.S.
MUELLER, Georg	257795	M	Ger.	06	Hptsturmfhr., SD, Tromsoe (Nor.) 42-45	TORTURE	NOR.
MUELLER, Gerhard	193827	M	Ger.		Oberwachtmstr., Justizministerium, Strafgefangenenlager, Conc.Camp	MISC.CRIMES	NOR., YUGO.
MUELLER, Gerhard	250383	M	Ger.	24.6.07	Acting Reg.Commander, 83.Rgt.Landsturm, Tiel (Neth.) 3.45-4.45	PILLAGE	NETH.
MUELLER, Gerhard	255905	M	Ger.	28.11.06	Pvt., C.C., Ellrich, Nordhausen (Ger.)	MURDER	U.S.
MUELLER, Gert	254463	M	Ger.	20	Sturmfhr., SS, Conc.Camp, Auschwitz, Birkenau (Pol.) 42-45	MISC.CRIMES	YUGO.
MUELLER, Guenther	190384	M	Ger.		Civilian, Beckendorf (Ger.) 10.44	WITNESS	U.S.
MUELLER, Guenther	250393	M	Ger.		Pvt., Holzhausen-Tosbusch (Ger.) 9.44	WITNESS	U.S.
MUELLER, Hans	137484	M			Dr., Uschfhr., SS, Conc.Camp, Buchenwald (Ger.)	TORTURE	U.S.
MUELLER, Hans	193826	M	Ger.	98	Oberwachtmstr., Reichsjustizministerium, Strafgefangenenlager, Conc.Camp, Finnmark, (Nor.)6.42-4.45	MURDER	YUGO., NOR.
MUELLER, Heinrich (Herman)	132252	M	Ger.		Police-leader, Schupo, Ruhen (Ger.) 44	MURDER	U.S.
MUELLER, Heinrich	160702	M	Ger.	28.4.00	Gruppenfhr., SS, RSHA (Den.) 43	MISC.CRIMES	U.S.
MUELLER, Heinrich	260970	M			Member, SS, C.C. Vaihingen (Ger.) 8.44-4.45	MURDER	U.S.
MUELLER, Hermann	187210	M	Ger.		Civilian, Conc.Camp, Ellrich (Ger.) 44-45	MURDER	BEL.
MUELLER, Hermann	256870	M	Ger.	18.5.07	Employee, Goma Deu, C.C., Nordhausen (Ger.)	MURDER	U.S.
MUELLER, Horst	152153	M	Ger.		Arbeitskmdo., Conc.Camp, Osterode (Ger.) 2.45	MURDER	BEL.
MUELLER, Irmgard	185921	F	Ger.	22.8.02	Stenographer, Conc.Camp, Bayreuth Lauban (Ger.) 42-45	WITNESS	U.S.
MUELLER, Johann	255907	M		30.3.03	Pvt., SS, C.C. Harzungen, Nordhausen (Ger.)	MURDER	U.S.
MUELLER, Johannes Hermann	260963	M	Ger.	30.7.95	Sturmbannfhr., SS, Crim.investigation officer, State-Service-Police, (RSHA) Sipo and SD, Warschau and Lublin (Pol.) 40-43	MURDER	POL.
MUELLER, Josef	141585	M	Ger.		Chief, Werkschutz, Wetzlar (Ger.)	TORTURE	FR.
MUELLER, Josef	185729	M	Ger.	2.9.01	Employee, Arbeitskommando, Brno (Czech.) 39-45	PILLAGE	CZECH.
MUELLER, Josef	194469	M	Ger.	6.6.91	Ortsgr.Amtsleiter, NSDAP, Hals (Czech.) 38-45	MISC.CRIMES	CZECH.
MUELLER, Joseph	306043	M	Ger.		Member, SS, C.C. Neugraben-Tiefstak 44-45	MURDER	U.K.
MUELLER, Julius	252525	M	Ger.	19.4.95	Pvt., L.Pl.Coy.528, Wervick (Bel.) 9.44	MURDER	BEL.
MUELLER, Karl	137545	M			Hptschfhr., SS, Conc.Camp, Weimar, Buchenwald (Ger.)	TORTURE	U.S.
MUELLER, Karl	154825	M	Ger.	12	Lt., Art.Rgt.981, Haler (Nor.) 12.44	MURDER	NOR.
MUELLER, Karl	173895	M	Ger.		Overseer at a Farm, Civilian, Osterweddingen (Ger.) 11.42	MURDER	POL.
MUELLER, Karl	185730	M	Ger.		Civilian 4.45	MURDER	U.S.
MUELLER, Karl	193825	M	Ger.	97	Kgf.Arb.Bn.186 (Nor.) 42-45	MISC.CRIMES	NOR.
MUELLER, Karl	258016	M	Ger.		O-Cand, 150.Pz.Bde., Meuse-Bridge-Antwerp (Bel.) 12.44	MISC.CRIMES	U.S.
MUELLER, Karl	258588	M	Ger.	27.2.18	Former porcelain worker, Civilian, Blechhammer near Pullenried, (Ger.) 4.45	MURDER	U.S.
MUELLER, Konrad	262313	M	Ger.	04	Member, Organ.Todt, L.O.D.N.A.O.D., Velke-Heraltice (Czech.) 8.44	SUSPECT	U.S.
MUELLER, Konrad	305929	M	Ger.	95 - 05	Driver, Labour Dept. he transported Russian P.o.W.'s Daily to their work, Velke Heraltice (Czech.) 8.44	TORTURE	CZECH.
MUELLER, Kurt	154819	M	Ger.	00	Oschfhr., SS, Conc.Camp, Flossenburg (Ger.) 40-45	TORTURE	POL.
MUELLER, Kurt	185488	M		27	Schuetze, 2.SS-Panz.Gren.Rgt."A.Hitler", 3.Bn., 12.Pz.Gren.Coy., Malmedy (Bel.) 12.44	MURDER	U.S.
MUELLER, Marie	195168	F	Ger.	4.7.17	Civilian, Kylburg (Ger.) 43	MISC.CRIMES	LUX.
MUELLER, Martin Maurice (see MORITZ)	240132						
MUELLER, Matthaeus	162230	M	Ger.	9.3.90	Farmer, Civilian, Sommerhausen (Ger.) 3.45	WITNESS	U.S.
MUELLER, Max Willi	145983	M	Ger.	27.3.04	Police-Asst., Ordnungspolizei-Verwaltung, C.C., Dachau (Ger.) 44-45	WITNESS	U.S.
MUELLER, Michael	255869	M			Pvt., C.C., Bodungen, Nordhausen (Ger.)	MURDER	U.S.
MUELLER, Michael (or MORITZ)	261978	M	Ger.	20	Commander, Jail., Banska-Bystrica (Czech.) 8.44-4.45	MURDER	CZECH.
MUELLER, Moritz (or MORITZ)	240132	M	Ger.	15	Sturmbannfhr., Cmdt., SD Official, Marseille, Berlin (Fr.,Ger.)	PILLAGE	U.S.
MUELLER, Otto (see MULLER)	132261						
MUELLER, Otto	132262	M	Ger.		Mayor, Civilian, Stalag 12 D, Winningen (Ger.) 11.44	MURDER	POL.
MUELLER, Otto	134814	M	Ger.	10	Army, Oberbettingen near Hildesheim (Ger.) 9.44-3.45	TORTURE	U.S.
MUELLER, Otto	255050	M	Ger.	1.7.14	Member, Gestapo, Breclav (Czech.) 4.45	INTERR.	CZECH.
MUELLER, Otto	255900	M	Ger.	10.1.25	Flyer, C.C. Ellrich, Nordhausen (Ger.)	MURDER	U.S.

MUE-MUH

NAME	C.R.FILE NUMBER	SEX	NATIONALITY	DATE OF BIRTH	RANK OCCUPATION UNIT PLACE AND DATE OF CRIME	REASON WANTED	WANTED BY
MUELLER, Otto	306045	M	Ger.		Major,Chief of Police at Luneburg, 2.-9.4.45	MURDER	U.K.
MUELLER, P.	300826	M	Ger.		Pvt.,1.Aufkl.Abt.,3.Coy.,2.Column,XV.Div.,Afrika Korps,Saint Leger (Arlon) 5.9.44	MISC.CRIMES	BEL.
MUELLER, Paul	254248	M			Osturmfhr.,SS,C.C.,Auschwitz,Birkenau (Ger.) 42	MURDER	YUGO.
MUELLER, Paul	259096	M			Schachtfhr.,O.T.,Mühldorf Area (Ger.)	MURDER	U.S.
MUELLER, Peter	142034	M	Ger.	05	Policeman,Police,Org.Todt,St.Helier,Island Jersey,Channel , 43	TORTURE	U.F.,SCV.UN.
MUELLER, Philipp	173832	M	Ger.		K.D.F. Stadt, 43-44	TORTURE	BEL.
MUELLER, Robert	193824	M	Ger.		Pvt.,Kgf.Arb.Bn. 190,Starnes (Nor.) 7.44	MURDER	NOR.
MUELLER, Robert	255901	M		14. 9.00	Pvt.,C.C.,Harzungen,Nordhausen (Ger.)	MURDER	U.S.
MUELLER, Robert	262181	M	Ger.	8.11.	Oschfhr.,Gestapo,Rennes (Fr.) 43-44	MISC.CRIMES	FR.
MUELLER, Robert Karl August Ernst	307024	M	Ger.	2. 8.08	Functionary,NSDAP,of the Administration Police at Lahde -Weser, Labour Camp (Ger.) 5.43-4.45	MURDER	U.K.
MUELLER, Rudolf	195354	M	Ger.	14	Employee,Police,Napajedla (Czech.) 14.10.44	MURDER	U.S.
MUELLER, Rudolf	300341	M	Ger.		Major and Kreiskommandant,District of Zajecar (Serbia) 8.43-10.44	MURDER	YUGO.
MUELLER, Siegfried	62402	M	Ger.		Sturmbannfhr., Army,12.SS Panz.Div.,Hitler-Jugend,	MISC.CRIMES	CAN.
MUELLER, Siegfried	260851	M	Ger.	16	Lt.,Adjutant,SS,Kassel (Ger.) 43	MURDER	U.S.
MUELLER, Simon	256897	M	Ger.	19. 9.08	Uschfhr.,Head labor Ellrich B 12,Nordhausen (Ger.).	MURDER	U.S.
MUELLER, Theo	155424	M		10	Troop leader,Org.Todt,Saal on the Danube (Ger.) 1.12.44-22.4.45	MURDER	U.S.
MUELLER, Walter	36637	M	Ger.		Glass-worker,Glass-factory of Holsher,Civilian,Mienburg (Ger.)42-43	MISC.CRIMES	SOV.UN.
MUELLER, Walter (or MULLER)	195582	M	Ger.		Guard,Parachutist,C.C.,Dordrecht (Neth.) 15.10.44	WITNESS	CAN.
MUELLER, Werner	190625	M			Pvt.,11.Panz.Div.,2.Coy.,2.A.A.A. 7,Bergerac,Albine (Fr.) 7.-8.44	MURDER	FR.
MUELLER, Werner	188395	M	Ger.	6. 6.11	Interpreter,Reichssicherheitshauptamt,Mauthausen (Aust.) 1.45	WITNESS	U.S.
MUELLER, Wilhelm	630	M	Ger.		Lt.,Navy,Gouesnou,(Fr.) 7.44	MURDER	FR.
MUELLER, Wilhelm	194993	M	Ger.		Pvt.,11.Pz.Gren.Rgt.,Albine (Fr.) 29.6.44	MURDER	FR.
MUELLER, Wilhelm	256143	M			Section of Politik,SS,C.C.,Mauthausen (Aust.)	INTERR.	FR.
MUELLER, Wilhelm Walter	306535	M	Ger.	17. 7.07	Capt.,Sicherheitspolizei at Baarm,Prov.Noord-Holland (Neth.)25.4.45	MURDER	NETH.
MUELLER, Willi	252521	M	Ger.	00	Pvt.,Landesschuetzen Bn.,No.unknown,Daun (Ger.) 23.12.44	WITNESS	U.S.
MUELLER, Willi	192255	M	Ger.	18	Pvt.,77.Volksgren.Rgt.,1.Wach Coy.,Stalag 28275,Euskirchen,(Ger.) 3.-10.44	TORTURE	U.S.
MUELLER, Willy	193823	M	Ger.	04	Kriegsgefg.Arb.Bn.186,(Nor.) 40-45	MISC.CRIMES	NOR.
MUELLER, Xavier (or MILLER)	132637	M	Ger.	05	Sturmschfhr.,SS,C.C.,Schirmeck (Fr.) 7.3.44	TORTURE	FR.
MUELLER, Xaver (see MILLER)	132637						
MUELLER, Forait	124853	M	Ger.		Capt.,C.C.,Dietz (Ger.)	TORTURE	U.S.
MUELLHAUSEN	1442	M	Ger.		Lt.,Gebirgsjaeger Div.98,12.Coy.,	MISC.CRIMES	U.K.
MUELLING	178296	M	Ger.	95	Capt.,368 Coy.,Landesschuetzen Bn.,Kdo.162 A,Stalag IV c,Bodenbach (Ger.) 7.44	MURDER	U.K.
MUENCH	139677	M		00	Officer,Waffen SS,Arbeitskommando A-6	TORTURE	U.S.
MUENCH	194994	M	Ger.		Pvt.111 Pz.Gren.Rgt.,Albine (Fr.) 29.6.44	MURDER	FR.
MUENCH	258445	M	Ger.		Usturmfhr.,Medical Service at C.C.,Auschwitz (Pol.) 40-45	TORTURE	POL.
MUENCH	900520	M	Ger.		Possibly SS,Etival com.de Moussey (Fr.) 10.44	MURDER	FR.
MUENCH, Heinrich	104869	M	Ger.		Ortsgruppenleiter,NSDAP,Mayor,Public official,Geilshausen Harbach (Ger.) 3.-9.44	MURDER	U.S.
MUENCH, Otto	193878	M	Ger.	05	Pvt.,Kriegs-Arb.-Bn.186,(Nor.)	MURDER	NOR.
MUENCHEN	195100	M	Ger.	88	Usturmfhr.,SS,SD Einsatz Kommando Wenger,F.F.No.030069 CC,Baccarat, Etival,(Fr.) 8.44	MURDER	NETH.
MUENCHENBURGER	154824	M	Ger.	13	Cpl.,515.Landesschuetzen Bn.,Regensburg (Ger.) 2.45-20.4.45	MURDER	U.K.
MUENK, Peter	128923	M		22	Cpl.,Army,C.C.,Vilegelow (Ger.) 9.5.44	MURDER	U.S.
MUENSTER	190290	M	Ger.		Capt.,Kreiskommandantur,Uzice (Yugo.) 7.41	MURDER	YUGO.
MUENSTER	301845	M	Ger.		Capt.,Kreiskommandantur,Uzice (Yugo.) 7.41	MURDER	YUGO.
MUENTZ	257984	M			Lt.,150.Pz.Bde., Meusebridge Antwerpen 12.44	MISC.CRIMES	U.S.
MUENZEL, Turis	161919	M	Ger.	99	Doctor,Capt.,Command staff,Army,C.C.,Buchenwald (Ger.) 44	WITNESS	U.S.
MUENZL, Anna	135285	F	Ger.		Civilian,Efferen (Ger.) 2.10.44	WITNESS	U.S.
MUER, Rudolf	132754	M			Uschfhr.,SS,C.C.,Mauthausen (Aust.) 41-45	MURDER	U.S.
MUESCH	259997	M	Ger.		Uschfhr.,SS,guard at the transport of prisoners from Zittau to Flossenburg, Plana,Bohemia (Czech.) 15.4.45	MURDER	CZECH.
MUESCHEN	185731	M	Ger.	00	Staatsanwalt,Member,Ministry of Justice,NSDAP,Prague (Czech.)	MURDER	CZECH.
MUETTER (see METTER)	187213						
MUETTER	188448	M		00	Interpreter,Gestapo,Dijon (Fr.) 6.44	INTERR.	FR.
MUEYES, Hans (see MEYER)	124967						
MUGORWSKY	127190	M	Ger.		Chef Supreme,Service de Santes SS,C.C.,Buchenwald (Ger.)	MURDER	FR.
MUHE, Charles	194577	M	Ger.		Sgt.,Chief of poste,Custom-house Veigy,Foncenex (Fr.) 6.10.43-4.12.43	TORTURE	FR.
MUHE, Hans	250981	M		96	Major,Army,Geradmer (Fr.) 29.5.44	WITNESS	U.S.
MUHER	253266	M	Ger.		Lt.Col., Field-police,Monte Penna (It.)	INTERR.	U.K.
MUHL	190628	M			Lt.,Art.Rgt.,Ile D' Olfron (Fr.) 44-17.4.45	TORTURE	
MUHL, Harry (see MOEL)	255736						
MUHL, Robert	631	M	Ger.	28.10.12	Chief of Org.Todt,Feldgendarm,Feldgendarmerie,N.S.D.A.P. C.C.,Hazebrouck (Fr.) 1.9.44	MURDER	POL.
MUHLAU	186138	M	Ger.		Agent,Gestapo,C.C.,Dora (Ger.)	TORTURE	FR.
MUHLE, Karl	193830	M	Ger.	06	Oberwachtmeister,Strafgefangenen Lager,Justizministerium, Finmark (Nor.) 9.3.45	MISC.CRIMES	NOR.,YUGO.
MUHLER	191586	M	Ger.		Sturmbannfhr.,SD,Kommandeur,Marseille (Fr.) 15.6.44	MURDER	FR.
MUHLER, Alvin	154827	M			Civilian,Steimke,(Ger.) 22.2.45	TORTURE	U.S.

NAME	C.R.FILE NUMBER	SEX	NATIO-NALITY	DATE OF BIRTH	RANK	OCCUPATION	UNIT	PLACE AND DATE OF CRIME	REASON WANTED	WANTED BY
MUHLHAUFFER	146953	M	Ger.		SS Panz.Div. "Das Reich" Regt."Deutschland", 3.Bn., Venerque, Le Vernet (Fr.) 44				MURDER	FR.
MUHLHAUSEN	632	M	Ger.		Pol.Cmdt. of Transit Camp Pila (Ger.) 9.-12.39				TORTURE	POL.
MUHLHAUSER	251180 A	M	Ger.		SS-Uschfhr., Gestapo, Paris (Fr.)				INTERR.	FR.
MUHLHAUSLER	305727	M	Ger.		SS-Uschfhr., Geheime Feldpolizei, Hotel Bratford, Paris. Member of Sonderkommando IV-A-2, 11 rue des Saussaies, Paris (Fr.) 41-44				TORTURE	FR.
MUHLHOLZER, Friedrich	140794	M	Ger.	21.12.03	Member of NSDAP, Locksmith. Ludwigshafen (Ger.) 1.45				TORTURE	U.S.
MUHLICH	186505	M	Ger.		Lt., Kommandantur, Saintes (Fr.) 8.44				WITNESS	FR.
MUHLING	156993	M	Ger.		Physician, Arbeitskommando 728, C.C. Groditz (Ger.)				MURDER	U.S.
MUHLMEISTER, Karl	160698	M	Ger.		Civilian.				TORTURE	U.S.
MUHS, Hans	187771	M	Ger.	00	Lt., Polizei, Oberfhr., SS, Aachen (Ger.) 8.44				MURDER	U.S.
MUHSAM	142544	M	Ger.	15	SS-Uschfhr., near Ampfing (Ger.) 44-45				TORTURE	U.S.
MUIS, Walter	252531	M	Ger.		10.Coy., 377.Jaeger-Regt., Vinkt-Meigem (Bel.) 5.40				MISC.CRIMES	BEL.
MULENZ	156992	M	Ger.		SS-Guard, C.C. Varsovie (Pol.)				TORTURE	FR.
MULHEIM	131309	M	Ger.	90 or 95	Capt., Stalag VII A, Mooseberg (Ger.) 9.44-4.45				TORTURE	U.S.
MULHOFF	255362	M			Dr., Glaswerk-Ruhr, Kernapp-Essen (Ger.) 44				BRUTALITY	BEL.
MULKA	254251	M	Ger.	95	Osturmfhr., SS, C.C.Auschwitz-Birkenau (Pol.)				MURDER	YUGO.
MULLAK	194447	M	Ger.		Pvt., POW Work Bn.41, Kristiansund, Nerlandsdal (Nor.) 41-45				TORTURE	NOR.
MULLE, Karl	141973	M	Ger.		O.T.-Master, Organisation Todt (airplane factory construction), Mettenheim, Ampfing-Mühldorf (Ger.) 44-45				TORTURE	U.S.
MULLEMANN	256747	M	Ger.		Kapo, C.C. Nordhausen (Ger.)				TORTURE	FR.
MULLEN	124987	M	Ger.		Officer, Gestapo, S.D.de Bordeaux, Poitiers (Fr.) 8.44				MURDER	FR.
MULLER	633	M	Ger.		SS-Osturmfhr., Crim.asst., S.D., St.Brieuc (Fr.) 8.44				TORTURE	FR.
MULLER	634	M	Ger.		Pol.Cmdt., Polizei, Toulouse (Fr.) 4.44				MURDER	FR.
MULLER	635	M	Ger.		Capt., Army, Feldkommandantur 755, Le Mans (Fr.)				PILLAGE	FR.
MULLER	636	M	Ger.		Chief of Gestapo, St.Brieuc (Fr.) 7.44				MURDER	FR.
MULLER	637	M			Chief of Gestapo, Warsaw (Pol.) 41				MURDER	POL.
MULLER	638	M	Ger.		SS-Hptsturmfhr., C.C. Oswiecim, Rajsko (Pol.) 6.40-43				MURDER	POL.
MULLER	639	M	Ger.		Lt., Polizei, Gestapo, C.C.Breedonck (Bel.) 40-44				MURDER	BEL.
MULLER	1258	M	Ger.		Cmdt., Kommandantur, Maille-Tours (Fr.)				WITNESS	FR.
MULLER	1445	M	Ger.		Naval Supply.				MISC.CRIMES	U.K.
MULLER	31511	M	Ger.		Lt., Army, Gestapo, Lyon, St.Die (Fr.)11.44				MURDER	FR.
MULLER	36695	M	Ger.	95	Cpl., Army, K.D.30-434 Stalag III G, Gross-Steinberg (Ger.) 10.43				TORTURE	U.K.
MULLER	38865	M	Ger.		SS-Osturmfhr., Waffen-SS, C.C. Lublin (Pol.)				TORTURE	U.S.
MULLER	39588	M	Ger.		Lt., Army, Carhaix (Fr.) 6.44				MISC.CRIMES	FR.
MULLER	39590	M	Ger.		Interpreter, Public official, F.P.No.43661 A, Coudes (Fr.) 7.44				MURDER	FR.
MULLER	69158	M	Ger.		Capt., Stalag III D, Berlin (Ger.) 4.43				TORTURE	U.K.
MULLER	104872	M	Ger.						WITNESS	U.S.
MULLER	120617	M	Ger.		Capt., Army, C.C. Stalag 4 A Bremen (Ger.) 43-45				WITNESS	U.K.
MULLER	121159	M	Ger.		Capt., Army, C.C. Stalag 122 Compiegne (Oise) (Fr.)				MISC.CRIMES	FR.
MULLER	123126	M	Ger.	19	Pvt., Stalag C.C. Wolfshagen (Ger.) 7.-8.43				MURDER	U.K.
MULLER	124093	M	Ger.	90	Capt., C.C. Chemnitz (Ger.) 2.45				MURDER	U.K.
MULLER	124986	M	Ger.	05	S.D.official, Gestapo-S.D.de Bordeaux, Poitiers (Fr.) 8.44				MURDER	FR.
MULLER	125046	M	Ger.		Capt., linguist speaks English, Dutch, French, Ital.and Czech. 6-396 L-S Coy., C.C. Hainsberg, Dresden (Ger.) 11.44				MISC.CRIMES	U.K.
MULLER	125194	M	Ger.		SS-Uschfhr., SS-Ilag XVIII, Spittal-Drav-Kaernten (Aust.)44-45				MISC.CRIMES	U.S.
MULLER	126758	M	Ger.		Interpreter, Army, Sect.Postale 43661, Coudesk (Fr.) 7.44				MURDER	FR.
MULLER	126867	M	Ger.		Asst., Gestapo.				U.S.	
MULLER	127120	M	Ger.		SS-Uschfhr., SS, C.C.Dora, Nordhausen (Ger.)				TORTURE	FR.
MULLER	127122	M	Ger.		SS-Uschfhr., C.C. Buchenwald, Ohrdruf (Ger.)				MURDER	FR.
MULLER	127131	M	Ger.		Officer, SS Div."Das Reich", 2.Panz.Div., La Craise Felgarde (Fr.)				MURDER	FR.
MULLER	128833	M	Ger.	90	Capt., Arbeitskommando, C.C.Chemnitz (Ger.) 2.45				MURDER	U.K.
MULLER	130161	M	Ger.	95	Capt., Army, Brussels (Bel.) 5.44				TORTURE	U.K.
MULLER	132256	M	Ger.		Oschfhr., Waffen-SS, C.C. Flossenburg (Ger.)				TORTURE	U.S.
MULLER	132640	M	Ger.		Guard, Camp Prison, C.C.Schirmeck (Fr.)				MURDER	FR.
MULLER	134820	M	Ger.		SS-Scharfhr., Wittlich, Hinzert (Ger.)				TORTURE	U.S.
MULLER	134823	M	Ger.		Kreischief, Gendarmerie, Alzenau (Ger.) 44				MURDER	U.S.
MULLER	136216	M	Ger.		Pvt., II.Panzer Div. 2.Coy., Albine (Fr.) 3.44				MURDER	FR.
MULLER	136217	M	Ger.		Lt., Sicherungstruppen, St.Flour (Fr.) 6.44				MURDER	FR.
MULLER	136218	M	Ger.		Pvt., Feldgendarmerie, 10.Panzer Div. - 36. Panzer Regt., Revin-Stenay (Fr.) 40-44				MURDER	FR.
MULLER	136219	M	Ger.		Sgt., Feldgendarmerie de Mezières, Stenay-Revin (Fr.) 40-44				MURDER	FR.
MULLER	136612	M	Ger.		Civ., Prison Guard, C.C. Bamberg (Ger.) 44				TORTURE	U.S.
MULLER	137091	M	Ger.		Lt., Stalag XX B, C.C. Marienburg (Pol.) 12.41				TORTURE	U.K.
MULLER	138249	M	Ger.		SS-Usturmfhr., SS Formation "Tannenberg", 5.and 6.Btty., Champ le Duc (Fr.) 9.44				MISC.CRIMES	FR.
MULLER	138250	M	Ger.		Lt., 27. Inf.Regt., 12.Coy, Faymont (Fr.) 10.44				MURDER	FR.
MULLER	138287	M	Ger.		Cpl., Heeres-Verwaltung, Armainvilliers (Fr.) 7.44				MURDER	FR.
MULLER	146967	M	Ger.		S.D.-Section IV, Annecy (Fr.) 44				MURDER	FR.
MULLER	146969	M	Ger.		Officer, SS Panz.Div."Das Reich", La Croix-Lagarde (Fr.) 44				MURDER	FR.
MULLER	146970	M	Ger.		Pvt., SS Panzer Div."Das Reich", Tulle (Fr.) 44				MURDER	FR.
MULLER	147352	M	Ger.		11. Panzer Div. (Fr.) 44				MURDER	FR.
MULLER	148189	M	Ger.		Cook, C.C. Stassfurt (Ger.) 40-44				MURDER	FR.
MULLER	151430	M	Ger.		Sgt., Army, Stalag XX B, C.C. Elbing (Ger.) 8.42				TORTURE	U.K.
MULLER	154833	M			Oschfhr., SS, C.C. Dora and Gardelegen (Ger.) 4.45				MURDER	U.S.
MULLER	155425	M	Ger.	06	SS-Rottenfhr., C.C. Pawiak near Warsaw (Pol.) 42-43				TORTURE	POL.
MULLER	155426	M	Ger.		Lt., Feldgendarmerie Group 689, Venarey - Les Laumes (Fr.) 9.44				MURDER	FR.
MULLER	155428	M	Ger.		Capt., Landesschuetzen Bn., Villaudric (Fr.) 8.44				MURDER	FR.
MULLER	156988	M	Ger.		Oberwachtmeister, Guard, C.C. Sarrebruck (Ger.)				MURDER	FR.
MULLER	156989	M	Ger.		Capt., 157. Inf.Div., Saillans (Fr.)				PILLAGE	FR.
MULLER	158950	M	Ger.	02	Sgt., Army, Stalag XX B Guard W.K.229, Neudorf (Ger.) 42				MURDER	U.K.
MULLER	158951	M	Ger.		Guard, SS, C.C. Nerbrenn (Ger.) 43-44				TORTURE	FR.
MULLER	160699	M	Ger.		Sgt., Army, Sturm-Bn. A.O.K.I, Courcelles (Fr.) 11.44				WITNESS	U.S.
MULLER	167025	M	Ger.		Parachutist.				MURDER	FR.

MUL-MUL

NAME	C.R.FILE NUMBER	SEX	NATIO-NALITY	DATE OF BIRTH	RANK OCCUPATION UNIT PLACE AND DATE OF CRIME	REASON WANTED	WANTED BY
MULLER	167026	M	Ger.		Major, 276.Art.Rgt. Lourdes, Moy s.Aisne (Fr.) 9.44	PILLAGE	FR.
MULLER	167027	M	Ger.		Adjutant chief, Feldgendarmerie, Larochemillay (Fr.) 8.44	PILLAGE	FR.
MULLER	167028	M	Ger.		Civ. Infirmier, Olbernhau, Gruenthal (Ger.) 4.45	MURDER	FR.
MULLER	167030	M	Ger.		Rehaupaul (Fr.) 9.44	MURDER	FR.
MULLER	167031	M	Ger.		Lt., S.D. Toulouse, Corcieux (Fr.) 9. and 11.44	PILLAGE	FR.
MULLER	168002	M	Ger.		Sgt., Feldgendarmerie de Langes, Auberive,Flagey,Coiffey,Chalencey (Fr.) 43-44	MURDER	FR.
MULLER	168003	M	Ger.		Capt., Army, Fontaine Notre Dame (Fr.) 8.44	MURDER	FR.
MULLER	168018	M	Ger.		Commander, Gestapo, Marseille (Fr.) 42-43	MURDER	FR.
MULLER	168052	F	Ger.		Interpreter, S.D., St.Lo (Fr.) 9.44	MURDER	FR.
MULLER	168053	M	Ger.	about 85	General, O.C. force of occupation, Channel Islands (U.K.) 2.43	MISC.CRIMES	U.K.
MULLER	170073	M	Ger.		Officer, S.S., C.C., Ger., 43	SUSPECT	U.S.
MULLER	173190	M	Ger.	about 98	Lt., 397.Ld.Schtz.Bn., 610.Ld.Schtz.Bn., Stalag XX B, Freystadt - Bitterfeld (Ger.) 1.-4.45	TORTURE	U.K.
MULLER	173268	M	Ger.	90	Officer, S..., Stalag IV F, Chemnitz (Ger.) 10.43-3.45	TORTURE	U.K.
MULLER	173806	M	Ger.		Official, officer, Abwehr, S.D., Poitiers (Fr.)	MURDER	FR.
MULLER	173809	M	Ger.		Policeman, Police, Frecomrupt, La Broique (Fr.) 3.44	MURDER	FR.
MULLER see MUELLER, Alfred	174367						
MULLER	174695	M	Ger.		Capt., C.C. Withmarchen Stalag VI C (Ger.) 44	PILLAGE	FR.
MULLER	174696	M			Capt., Army, S.D., Cavaillon, Arpavon (Fr.) 3.43-6.44	MURDER	FR.
MULLER	175619	M	Ger.		Member NSDAP, Muggelheim (Ger.) 3.45	TORTURE	U.S.
MULLER	178760	M	Ger.	21	Pvt., 714.Ld.Schtz.Bn., Fedelhausen (Pol.) 2.44	MURDER	U.K.
MULLER	185171	M	Ger.		Lt., SS, C.C. Dachau (Ger.)	TORTURE	FR.
MULLER	185490	M	Ger.		Lt., Parachute-unit, Roermond (Neth.)	MURDER	NETH.
MULLER	185732	M	Ger.		Major-Gen., Army, Crete (Grc.) 9.44	MURDER	GRC.
MULLER	185733	M	Ger.		General, Army, Heraklion (Grc.) 9.43	MURDER	GRC.
MULLER	186139	M	Ger.		Lt., Army, Perigueux (Fr.) 8.44	MURDER	FR.
MULLER	186504	M	Ger.		Cmdt., Commandantur, Saintes (Fr.) 44	WITNESS	FR.
MULLER	186584	M	Ger.		SS-Mann, Leibstandarte Adolf Hitler, Aufklaerungsabt., Renardmont, Stavelot (Bel.) 12.44	MURDER	BEL.
MULLER	187682	M	Ger.		Sgt., Feldgendarmerie, Goudriaan (Neth.)	MURDER	U.K.
MULLER	187809	M	Ger.		Civ., Kreis- or local-farmer-leader, Bingen (Ger.) 44	MURDER	U.S.
MULLER	188379	M	Ger.		Lt., Dienststelle, F.P.No. 60692, St.Andries,Varsenare,Bruegge (Bel.) 9.44	MURDER	BEL.
MULLER	188951	M	Ger.		Pvt., Army, Le Bourget, Triage (Fr.) 8.44	MURDER	FR.
MULLER	189038	M	Ger.	00	Civ. engineer, Arbeitskommando 1170, in charge of Copper Mine at Schmiedeberg (Ger.) 3.45	MURDER	U.K.
MULLER	189055	M	Ger.		Gruppenfhr., SS, Gestapo Munich, C.C. Dachau (Ger.) 40-45	TORTURE	BEL.
MULLER	189199	M			SS-guard, Camp Neubrenn-Saar (Ger.)	TORTURE	FR.
MULLER	189201	M	Ger.		Lt., 21.Inf.Rgt., Faymont (Fr.) 10.44	MURDER	FR.
MULLER	189592	M	Ger.		Osturmfhr., S.D., Lyon (Fr.)	MISC.CRIMES	FR.
MULLER	190291	M	Ger.		Officer, Ogruppenfhr., SS, Gestapo, C.C. Banjica (Yugo.) 41-44	MURDER	YUGO.
MULLER	190385	M			C.C. Dachau (Ger.)	MURDER	U.S.
MULLER see MOLLER or MILLER	191182						
MULLER	191303	M	Ger.		Eis.Art.Bn. 717, St.Andries, Varsenare, Bruegge (Bel.) 9.44	MURDER	BEL.
MULLER	191940	M	Ger.		Chief, S.D., Bois de Malannay (Fr.) 7.44	MURDER	FR.
MULLER	192116	M	Ger.		Lt.Gen., Army, Chaudfontaine (Bel.) 9.44	PILLAGE	BEL.
MULLER	192254	M	Ger.		Pvt., 116. Panz.Div., Schwere Werfer-Abt., 1.Bn., Rabozee Herstal (Bel.) 9.44	MURDER	BEL.
MULLER	193829	M	Ger.		Member, Zugwachtmeister S.D., Schupo, Falstad, Trondheim (Nor.) 41-45	MURDER	NOR.
MULLER	194147	M	Ger.		Capt., Commissar, SS, S.D., Gestapo, Drogen (Ger.) 5. or 6.44	MURDER	U.S.
MULLER	194227	M	Ger.	23	Usturmfhr., 12.SS Panz.Div., 26.SS Panz.Rgt., Caen (Fr.)	TORTURE	CAN.
MULLER	194345	M	Ger.		Capt., Flak-Unit, Chateau-Gaillard (Fr.) 8.44	PILLAGE	FR.
MULLER	194461	M	Ger.		Lt., 10.Flugmelde-Era.Rgt. 57, La Bazoche-Goust (Fr.) 8.44	PILLAGE	FR.
MULLER	194574	M	Ger.		Officer, Interpreter, Gestapo H.Q., Bourges, Savigny-en-Septaine (Fr.) 7.-8.44	MURDER	FR.
MULLER	195102	M		about 08	Cpl., Army, Stalag E III, Moosburg (Ger.) 1.-3.45	TORTURE	U.K.
MULLER see MUELLER, Walter	195582						
MULLER	195738	M	Ger.		Cpl., C.C. Breendonck (Bel.)	TORTURE	BEL.
MULLER	196053	M	Ger.		Lt., Army, Langon, Villefranche s.Cher (Fr.) 8.44	MURDER	FR.
MULLER	196054	M	Ger.	00	Capt., C.C. Royallieu (Fr.) 41-44	MURDER	FR.
MULLER	196055	M	Ger.		Sturmbannfhr., 44.SS-Div., Mouen (Fr.) 6.44	WITNESS	FR.
MULLER	196056	M	Ger.		Member of staff, C.C. Struthof-Natzweiler (Fr.) 40-44	MURDER	FR.
MULLER	196057	M	Ger.		Gend., Gendarmerie, Herpf (Ger.) 44	MURDER	FR.
MULLER	240088	M	Ger.		SS Osturmbannfhr., Member, Gestapo, Krakau (Pol.)	MISC.CRIMES	U.S.
MULLER	250370	M	Ger.		Osturmfhr., Fort Quelulou (Fr.)	TORTURE	FR.
MULLER	250387	M	Ger.		Lt., C.C. Neuengamme (Ger.) 42-45	TORTURE	FR.
MULLER	250916	M	Ger.		Lt., Ausb.Bn. d.Res. 15, Hossegor (Fr.) 8.44	MISC.CRIMES	FR.
MULLER	251841	M	Ger.		Sgt., Fort de Romainville (Fr.) 8.44	INTER.	FR.
MULLER	251842	M	Ger.		SS Uscharfhr., C.C. Hinzert (Ger.)	INTER.	FR.
MULLER	251843	M	Ger.		Capt., Army, Grignols (Fr.) 6.44	INTER.	FR.
MULLER	253933	M	Ger.		Major, S.D., d'Avignon, Sahune et Arpavon (Fr.) 6.44	MISC.CRIMES	FR.
MULLER	254254	M	Ger.		Civ., Polleben (Ger.)	WITNESS	U.S.
MULLER	254462	M	Ger.		Capt., Stalag 4 A, Ger.	MURDER	U.S.
MULLER	258920	M	Ger.		Rapportfuehrer SS, Former, Blockfuehrer Lublin and Auschwitz, Ohrdruf (Ger.) 44-45	MURDER	
MULLER	260098	M	Ger.		Lt., Unit 58 512, Luneville, Meurthe and Moselle (Fr.) 3.44	INCENDIARISM	FR.
MULLER	260669	M	Ger.		Member, Fieldpolice, Enghien, Les Bains-Domont (Fr.) 8.44	WITNESS	FR.
MULLER	260965	M			SS Oscharfhr., C.C. Vaihingen (Ger.) 8.44-4.45	MURDER	U.S.
MULLER	261067	M	Ger.		Dr., Major, Feldkommandantur of Tours, Maille (Fr.) 8.44	MURDER	FR.
MULLER	261848	M	Ger.		Kapo, C.C. Dora, Nordhausen (Ger.)	MURDER	FR.
MULLER	261849	M	Ger.		Sgt., Fieldgend., Romnilly s.Seine (Fr.) 6.44	MISC.CRIMES	FR.

MUL-MUL

NAME	C.R.FILE NUMBER	SEX	NATIO- NALITY	DATE OF BIRTH	RANK OCCUPATION UNIT PLACE AND DATE OF CRIME	REASON WANTED	WANTED BY
MULLER see WEIDEN see WEIDENMULLER	262156	M					
MULLER	300521	M	Ger.		SS-Cpl.,C.C.Hinzert,Treves (Ger.) 42-45	MURDER	FR.
MULLER,Nick Name "The Hangman"	300522	M	Ger.		Kapo,C.C.Schomberg (Ger.) 44-45	MURDER	FR.
MULLER	300827	M	Ger.		Lt.Col.,Angleur, 40	MISC.CRIMES	BEL.
MULLER	301276	M	Ger.		Crim.Secretary,Abt.IV D,SD,Brussels (Bel.) 40-44	MURDER	BEL.
MULLER	301277	M	Ger.		Crim.Secretary,Abt.IV A,SD,Brussels (Bel.) 40-44	MURDER	BEL.
MULLER	301589	M	Ger.		SS-Lt.,C.C.Mauthausen (Aust.) 40-43	MURDER	BEL.
MULLER	301590	M	Ger.		SS-Gruppenfhr.,C.C.Mauthausen (Aust.) 40-45	MURDER	BEL.
MULLER	301653	M	Ger.		Chief aide,Feldgendarmerie Moulins,Laroche-Millay (Fr.) 44	PILLAGE	CZECH.
MULLER	301853	M	Ger.		Unterscharfhr.,C.C.Dora and factory,C.C.Buchenwald,Nordhausen (Ger.) 43-45	MURDER	FR.
MULLER	305080	M	Ger.		Green Police,Groningen,Drente, (Neth.) 43-45	MISC.CRIMES	NETH.
MULLER	305559	M	Ger.		Kreisleiter,Jena,Muehlhausen,Frankfurt-Main (Ger.) 45	MURDER	U.K.
MULLER	306274	M	Ger.		Member of the Gestapo at Trencin,Oswiecim-Birkenau (Pol.) 39-45	MURDER	CZECH.
MULLER	306480	M	Ger.		4 Coy.,771 Bn.,Landesschuetzen Einheit 15468, Chateau de Foret, Ferme,Labeye,Territory of Foret, Prov. of Liege (Bel.) 44	MURDER	BEL.
MULLER	306634	M	Ger.		Capt.,A.A.Bn.,Saintes,Chateau Guillard, Comme Juicg,Charente (Fr.) 44	MURDER	FR.
MULLER	306861	M	Ger.		Lt.,SD,Toulouse,Gorcieux-Vosges (Fr.) 44	MISC.CRIMES	FR.
MULLER	306862	M	Ger.		Adjutant-Chief under order of commandant of Ardennes,Revin (Bel.) 44	MURDER	FR.
MULLER	306863	M	Ger.		Pvt.,under order of commandant of Ardennes,Revin (Bel.) 44	MURDER	FR.
MULLER	306991	M	Ger.		Capt.,commanding the Kampfgruppe Kaiser,Massif du Vercors Isere,Drome (Fr.) 44	MURDER	FR.
MULLER, Adam	256360	M	Ger.		Foreman, O.T.,Muehldorf (Ger.)	WITNESS	U.S.
MULLER, Adolf	165553	M	Ger.		Guard, C.C.Kahla, (Ger.)	TORTURE	BEL.
MULLER, Al.	12556	M	Ger.		Pvt.,Pz.Rgt.,110 or 111, 2 Coy. Gren.Rgt.,Albine (Fr.) 44	MURDER	FR.
MULLER, Albert	192117	M		15	Member,Geh.Feldpol.,Brussels (Bel.)	TORTURE	BEL.
MULLER, Andre	256024	M	Ger.		Flossenburg (Ger.)	WITNESS	FR.
MULLER, Annie	301951	F			Member,Staff,C.C.Ravensbruck (Ger.) 40-45	BRUTALITY	BEL.
MULLER, Armand	139593	M	Ger.		Pvt.,SS-Div "Das Reich",Flamrens (Fr.) 44	MURDER	FR.
MULLER, August	300342	M	Ger.		SS-Member,SS-Div.,"Adolf Hitler",Marle,Aisne (Fr.) 44	PILLAGE	FR.
MULLER, Auguste	156987	F	Ger.	19	SS-Officer,Marle (Fr.)	PILLAGE	FR.
MULLER, Christian	104873	M	Ger.	00	Policeman,Police,Schweina (Ger.) 45	WITNESS	U.S.
MULLER, Christian	132752	M			SS-Scharfhr.,C.C.Mauthausen (Aust.) 41-45	MURDER	U.S.
MULLER, Conrad	121161	M	Ger.	05	SS-Sgt.,Gestapo de Chambery,Challes les Eaux et Arbin (Fr.)	MURDER	FR.
MULLER, Emil	132751	M			SS-Oberscharfhr.,SS-Totenkopf,C.C.Mauthausen (Aust.)41-45	MURDER	U.S.
MULLER, Erich	259372	M	Ger.		N.C.O.,Kdo.737-3 of Stalag XI A,Salzwedel.(Ger.)!42	MURDER	FR.
MULLER, Ernst	168111	M	Ger.		Camp Kapo,Schandelah,Braunschweig (Ger.)	TORTURE	BEL.
MULLER, Ernst	194142	M	Ger.	16. 1.18	Capt.,C.C.Terezin (Czech.) 39-45	TORTURE	CZECH.
MULLER, Ernst	254781	M	Ger.		W.O.,Garrison Chatesuroux,Villedieu (Fr.) 44	INTERR.	FR.
MULLER, Ernst	255912	M			Pvt.,C.C.Ellrich,Nordhausen (Ger.)	MURDER	U.S.
MULLER, Eugen	255903	M			Sgt.,C.C.Ellrich,Nordhausen (Ger.)	MURDER	U.S.
MULLER, Ewald	307177	M	Ger.	8. 1.15	SS-Mann,SS-Totenkopf,C.C.Auschwitz (Pol.) 43-45	BRUTALITY	POL.
MULLER, Felix	255904	M		5. 1.10	Pvt.,C.C.Ellrich,Nordhausen (Ger.)	MURDER	U.S.
MULLER, Filipp	130856	M	Ger.		Civilian,C.C.K.D.F.Stadt (Ger.) 43-44	TORTURE	BEL.
MULLER, Frantz	12558	M	Ger.		Pvt.,Pz.Gren.Rgt.,110 or 111, 2 Coy.,Albine (Fr.) 44	MURDER	FR.
MULLER, Frantz	156986	M	Ger.		Sgt.,Dolmetscher, 2 Div.,Parachutist SS-Gestapo,Quimper Sizun (Fr.)	MURDER	FR.
MULLER, Franz	12559	M	Ger.		Agent-Interpreter,Gestapo,Sizun (Fr.) 44	MURDER	FR.
MULLER, Franz	132259	M	Ger.		Hauptwachtmeister,Police,Civilian, Prison Guard,Amberg,Embrach (Ger.)	TORUTRE	U.S.
MULLER, Franz	132767	M	Ger.	21 - 22|	Prison-Guard,Mainz (Ger.) 43-45	MURDER	BEL.
MULLER, Franz	165559	M	Ger.		Pvt.,4 Coy.,Chars Parach,H.Goering Dienststelle L X,Raboset le Herstal (Bel.) 44	MURDER	BEL.
MULLER, Franz	173808	M	Ger.		Sgt.,SS-Guard at the Piennes Mine Camps,Briey (Fr.) 40-44	MURDER	FR.
MULLER, Franz	191400	M	Ger.		Civilian,Nentershausen(Ger.) 44	SUSPECT	U.S.
MULLER, Friedrich	254770	M	Ger.		SS-Sgt.,Scharfhr.,Standortfuehrung E I 145 Zug I,Allarmont (Fr.) 44	TORTURE	FR.
MULLER, Fritz	12560	M	Ger.		Cpl.,Pvt.,Pz.Gren.Rgt., 110 or 111, 2 Coy.,Albine(Fr.) 44	MURDER	FR.
MULLER, Fritz	121160	M	Ger.		C.C.Duisburg (Ger.)	MURDER	BEL.
MULLER, Fritz	127128	M	Ger.		SS-Sturmbannfhr.,Mayor,2 SS Pz.Div. "Das Reich",Venerque-le-Vernet (Fr.)	MURDER	FR.
MULLER, Fritz	146952	M	Ger.		SS-Sturmbannfhr.,SS-Pz.Div."Das Reich" Rgt.,"Deutschland" 3 Bn. Venerque-le-Vernet (Fr.) 44	MURDER	FR.
MULLER, Fritz	155429	M	Ger.		Cpl.,1 SS-Pz.Div.,2 Pz.Gren.Rgt., 3 Bn. 12 Coy.,Stavelot Malmedy 44 (Bel.)	MURDER	U.S.
MULLER, Fritz	192253	M	Ger.		Oberinspector,Feldgericht der Luftwaffe,Brussels (Bel.) 41-44	MURDER	BEL.
MULLER, Fritz	252527	M	Ger.		Labour-Administrator,Dreilaendereck,Loerrach (Ger.)	INTERR.	BEL.
MULLER, Georg	132260	M	Ger.	91	Lt.,Paymaster,Army,C.C.Oflag III B,Hammelburg (Ger.) 44-45	MURDER	U.S.
MULLER, Georg	255710	M			Rottenfhr.,C.C.Monowitz,Nordhausen (Ger.)	MURDER	U.S.
MULLER, Georg	301810	M	Ger.		SS-Mann,1 SS Pz.Div. Leibstandarte,Stavelot (Bel.) 44	MURDER	BEL.
MULLER, Georges	194575	M	Ger.		Kapo,C.C.Mauthausen (Aust.)	TORTURE	FR.
MULLER, Gerard	121162	M			Capt.,SS-Pz.Div."Adolf Hitler" Astrofer Bn.,Coulonges (Fr.) 44	MURDER	FR.
MULLER, Gerard	156746	M	Ger.		Capt.,SS-Div."Adolf Hitler",Hellen,Villiers (Fr.) 44	MURDER	U.K.
MULLER, Gerhard	251149	M	Ger.	24. 6.07	83 Rgt.,Landsturm,2 Command, Tiel (Neth.) 45	SUSPECT	NETH.
MULLER, Gertrude	254899	M	Ger.	21	Secretary,Gestapo,Alencon (Fr.) 40-44	MURDER	FR.
MULLER, Hans	130855	M			Chief,O.T.,Hinzgen (Ger.) 43	TORTURE	BEL.
MULLER, Hans	139684	M	Ger.		Waffen-SS,C.C.Dora,Nordhausen (Ger.) 44	MURDER	U.S.
MULLER, Hans	250371	M	Ger.		Cpl.,Army,Lechelle (Fr.) 44	MURDER	FR.
MULLER, Hans	300343	M	Ger.		Oberwachtmeister,Strafgefangenenlager Norway,Northern (Nor.) 43-45	MISC.CRIMES	CZECH.

MUL - MUL

NAME	C.R.FILE NUMBER	SEX	NATIO-NALITY	DATE OF BIRTH	RANK OCCUPATION UNIT PLACE AND DATE OF CRIME	REASON WANTED	WANTED BY
MULLER, Hans	300523	M	Ger.		Osturmfhr., SS Belgian Div.83 Coy, Fort de Queuleu Metz (Fr.) 3.44	MURDER	FR.
MULLER, Hans	306636	M	Ger.		Chief, W.O., Gestapo Digne Prads et la Javie Mezel (Basses-Alpes) 7.44	MURDER	FR.
MULLER, Hans-Joachim	30313	M	Ger.		Dr., Staatsanwalt, Public-official, Litomerice (Czech.) 40	MURDER	CZECH.
MULLER, Heinrich	134816	M	Ger.	00	Chief, Obergruppenfhr., Gestapo, RSHA, SS, Berlin (Ger.)	MURDER	U.S.
MULLER, Heinrich (or MOLLER)	156985	M			SS-Mann, SS Pz.Gren.Rgt., Condorcet (Fr.)	MURDER	FR.
MULLER, Heinrich	160700	M			Kreisabschnittsleiter, Mayor, NSDAP, Civilian, Daasdorf, Guthmannshausen (Ger.) 7.-8.44	MURDER	U.S.
MULLER, Heinrich	187715	M	Ger.		Lt.General, Gestapo, Reichssicherheitshauptamt	MURDER	U.N.W.C.C.
MULLER, Heinrich	188383	M	Ger.		Chef, SD, Gestapo of RSHA, Goerlitz (Ger.) 3.-5.44	MURDER	BEL.
MULLER, Heinrich	255906	M		19. 9.07	Sgt., C.C.Ellrich, Nordhausen (Ger.)	MURDER	U.S.
MULLER, Heinz Walter	185735	M	Ger.	30.11.10	Schfhr., SA, C.C.Herbertow (Pol.) 44	TORTURE	U.S.
MULLER, Hermann	172464	M	Ger.	31. 8.85	Mayor, Public-official, Dauelsen (Ger.) 10.43	TORTURE	U.S.
MULLER, Hermann	190047	M			Mayor, Public-official, Dauelsen (Ger.) 10.43	TORTURE	U.K.
MULLER, Hermann	250392	M			W.O.-Chief, Gestapo, Lille (Fr.) 40-44	MURDER	FR.
MULLER, Herms	190386	M	Ger.		Civilian, Leeheim (Ger.) 7.-8.44	MURDER	U.S.
MULLER, Horst	191304	M	Ger.		Cpl., Army, St.Andries, Varsenare, Bruegge (Bel.) 9.44	MURDER	BEL.
MULLER, Hugo	126924	M	Ger.		Usturmfhr., 2 SS Pz.Div."Das Reich" (Fr.) 44	MURDER	FR.
MULLER, Hugo	146951	M	Ger.		Usturmfhr., SS Pz.Div."Das Reich" 1 Pz.Rgt., Caussade (Fr.) 44	MURDER	FR.
MULLER, Johann	12561	M	Ger.		Pvt., Pz.Gren.Rgt.2 Coy, Albine (Fr.) 6.44	MURDER	FR.
MULLER, Johann (Karl)	259137	M			Uschfhr., SS, Muhldorf Area (Ger.)	MURDER	U.S.
MULLER, Johannes	142109	M	Ger.	90	Osturmbannfhr., SS, C.C.Lublin (Pol.) 42-44	TORTURE	FR.
MULLER, Josef	194140	M	Ger.	22. 2.94	Major, Army, Pisek (Czech.) 38-45	MISC.CRIMES	CZECH.
MULLER, Karl	132750	M			C.C.Mauthausen (Aust.) 41-45	MURDER	U.S.
MULLER, Karl	146001	M			Blockschreiber, C.C.Mauthausen (Aust.) 41-45	WITNESS	U.S.
MULLER, Karl	155427	M	Ger.	20	Sgt., Army, Vivonne (Fr.) 8.44	TORTURE	FR.
MULLER, Karl	158953	M	Ger.		Capt., Army, Parachutist, Uzes (Fr.) 8.44	MURDER	FR.
MULLER, Karl	160701	M	Ger.		Engineer, Civilian, C.C.Untermassfeld (Ger.) 41-45	MURDER	U.S.
MULLER, Karl	189203	M			Capt., Fallschirmjaeger, Uzes (Fr.)	MURDER	FR.
MULLER, Karl	253257	M	Ger.		Sgt., Major, SS, Mil.Garrison, Norcia (It.) 5.44	WITNESS	U.K.
MULLER, Karl	301952	M	Ger.		Director, Badische Bank Karlsruhe Mot.Trsp.Haut-Rhin, Mulhausen (Fr.) 44	PILLAGE	FR.
MULLER, Konrad	167017	M		10	Cpl., SD, St.Jean de Maurienne (Fr.) 9.43	PILLAGE	FR.
MULLER, Kurt	251150	M	Ger.	4. 5.90	Cook, SS, C.C.Buchenwald-Neustadtfurt (Ger.)	BRUTALITY	FR.
MULLER, Leo	190627	M	Ger.		Adj.-chef, Feldgendarmerie, Stenay (Fr.) 40-44	MURDER	FR.
MULLER, Leo	251133	M	Ger.		Staff-Sgt., Gestapo of Verdun, Muzeray (Fr.) 7.44	MURDER	FR.
MULLER, Leo	252547	M	Ger.		Sgt., Field-police, Verdun, Savannes (Fr.) 8.44	TORTURE	FR.
MULLER, Ludwig	305676	M	Ger.		Civilian, Nr.Lang-Goms, 3.45	MURDER	U.S.
MULLER, Lukas	255898	M			Pvt., C.C.Klein Bodungen, Nordhausen (Ger.)	MURDER	U.S.
MULLER, Max	254900	M	Ger.		Customs-official, Customs, Arzon (Fr.)	TORTURE	FR.
MULLER, Max	142113	M		15	SS, C.C.Lublin (Pol.) 42-45	MURDER	FR.
MULLER, Nicolaus	255890	M			Pvt., C.C.Rossla, Nordhausen (Ger.)	MURDER	U.S.
MULLER, Otto (or MUELLER)	132261	M	Ger.		Civilian, Landwacht, Ruhen (Ger.) 44	TORTURE	U.S.
MULLER, Otto	306481	M	Ger.		SS-Sgt., SS, C.C.Buchenwald (Ger.) 5.38 and 10.43	MURDER	BEL.
MULLER, Otto	141984	M	Ger.	6.12.10	Hptschfhr., SS Totenkopf Standarte, C.C.Weimar Buchenwald (Ger.) 42-45	MURDER	U.S.
MULLER, Paul	194344	M	Ger.		SS-Cpl., C.C.Flossenburg (Ger.)	TORTURE	FR.
MULLER, Paul	259339	M			SS-Pvt., SS, Muhldorf Area (Ger.)	MURDER	U.S.
MULLER, Paul	259373	M	Ger.		Uschfhr., Gestapo of Poitiers antenne of Niort, Poitiers Area (Fr.) 40-44	MISC.CRIMES	FR.
MULLER, Paul	134830	M		13	Civilian, C.C.Buchenwald (Ger.)	MURDER	U.S.
MULLER, Robert	154831	M	Ger.		Kreisamtsleiter, NSDAP	MURDER	U.S.
MULLER, Robert	258876	M	Ger.		Verw.Oberinsp., Subdirector Prison Frankfurt-Preungesheim (Ger.) 42-44	TORTURE	FR.
MULLER, Rudolf	259703	M	Ger.		Civilian, Stuttgart W.Reinsburgstr.Nr.120, Saintes Marie aux Mines Haut-Rhin (Fr.) 40-44	PILLAGE	FR.
MULLER, Simon	255896	M			Capt., C.C.Ellrich-Wieda, Nordhausen (Ger.)	MURDER	U.S.
MULLER, Walter	262182	M	Ger.	11. 5. ?	Capt., 3 Bn.51 SS Armoured Bde., Bucheres, Breviandes, Ste.Savine, La Riviere de Corps Troyes (Fr.) 8.44	MURDER	FR.
MULLER, Werner	12562	M	Ger.		Pvt., Army, Pz.Gren.Rgt.110 or 111 2 Coy, Albine (Fr.) 6.44	MURDER	FR.
MULLER, Wilhelm	640	M	Ger.		Director, Lt., of Mine, SS, Bazaille (Fr.) 12.43 and 9.44	TORTURE	FR.
MULLER, Wilhelm	132749	M	Ger.		Uschfhr., SS Div.Totenkopf, C.C.Mauthausen (Aust.) 41-45	MURDER	U.S.
MULLER, Wilhelm	135286	M			Civilian, Foreman, Mine, C.C. (Ger.)	TORTURE	FR.
MULLER, Wilhelm	152152	M			Civilian worker, SA, Rail yards at Muenster, Westbevern (Ger.) 9.44	MURDER	U.S.
MULLER, Wilhelm	185919	M	Ger.	79	Leading Member, NSDAP, Praha (Czech.)	MISC.CRIMES	CZECH.
MULLER, Wilhelm	194193	M	Ger.	16. 1.83	Civilian, Miner, Hostenbach (Ger.) 10.44	TORTURE	U.S.
MULLER, Willem	146000	M			SS Totenkopf, C.C.Mauthausen (Aust.)	MURDER	U.S.
MULLER, Willi	190571	M	Ger.	03	Hptschfhr., Member, SS, Gestapo, Negotin and Zajegar (Yugo.) 41-43	TORTURE	YUGO.
MULLER, Willi	258886	M	Ger.		SS-Capt., Gestapo, Paris (Fr.) 4.44	PILLAGE	FR.
MULLER, Willy	252544	M			Warder, Kdo.86 A Stalag 3 B, Coschen (Ger.) 8.42	MURDER	FR.
MULLER-ALTENAU	170158	M	Ger.	90	SS-Gruppenfhr., chief, SS-Bodenamt Gau Administr., Reichenberg (Czech.) 39-45	PILLAGE	U.S.
MULLER-BRAND, Hermann	163222	M	Ger.		Col., Army, service of intendance, Angers (Fr.) 40-42	PILLAGE	FR.
MULLER FAURE, Heinz	104871	M	Ger.	17	Sonderfhr."Z", Interrogation Detachment, Moosburg (Ger.)	MURDER	YUGO.
MULLER-HACCIUS, Otto	173798	M	Ger.		Dr., SS-Oberfhr., (Yugo.) 4.41-44	MURDER	YUGO.
MULLER, John	126368	M	Ger.		SS-Standartenfhr., SS at one time commanded Reich musical Pln., Eastern (Pol.) 41	MURDER	U.S.
MULLER-BULENKAMPF, Hans	121201	M	Ger.		SS-Schfhr., Gestapo of Lons-le-Saunier (Fr.) 9.44	MURDER	FR.
MULLERS, Heinrich	255711	M			Flyer, C.C.Ellrich, Nordhausen (Ger.)	TORTURE	U.S.
MULLERSCHON	133287	M			Oschfhr., Waffen SS, C.C.Flossenburg (Ger.)	MURDER	FR.
MULLET	250388	M	Ger.		Gestapo, Lille (Fr.) 40-44	MISC.CRIMES	U.K.
MULLER-WESTIG	125047	M	Ger.		Lt., Jg.Rgt.35 3 Coy, area Bray-Dune (Fr.) 9.43	TORTURE	U.S.
MULLHAUPT	133286	M			Krim.Kommissar, Kripo, C.C.Flossenburg (Ger.)	MURDER	U.S.
MULLHEIM	138037	M		00	Capt., Commander at Stalag 7 A, C.C.Moosburg (Ger.) 2.45	WITNESS	FR.
MULLIG (or MURLIG)	121158	M	Ger.		Lt., Sicherungsbn.11-638, Saintes (Fr.) 8.44	MURDER	NETH.
MULLING, Friedrich	194442	M	Ger.		SS-Hptschfhr., Aussendienststelle d.Sipo and SD, Leeuwarden, Gent (Neth.) 9.44-4.45	MURDER	NETH.

MUL-MUS

NAME	C.R.FILE NUMBER	SEX	NATIO-NALITY	DATE OF BIRTH	RANK OCCUPATION UNIT PLACE AND DATE OF CRIME	REASON WANTED	WANTED BY
MULLNER	1082	M	Ger.		Sgt., Army, Feld-Gend., Langres (Fr.)	TORTURE	FR.
MULLNER	168004	M	Ger.		Sgt., Feld-Gend. de Langres, Auberive Flagey Coiffey Chalencey (Fr.) 43-44	MURDER	FR.
MULLNER, Max	124094	M	Ger.		Camp Cmdt., CC, Army, I Coy, 877 Lds.Schtz.Bn., Nicklasdorf (Aust.) 9.44-3.45	TORTURE	U.K.
MULLNER	124095	M	Ger.		Cpl., Camp 255 G.W. Germany 10.44-4.45	TORTURE	U.K.
MULTERER, Karl	127125	M	Ger.	10	Rottenfhr, SA, Camp Dora, Nordhausen (Ger.)	MURDER	FR.
MUMM, Frederich	38878	M	Ger.		Lt., Commander of a submarine, Atlantic 9.42	MISC.CRIMES	U.S.
MUMMENTEI	192251	M			SS Osturmbannfhr, CC Flossenburg (Ger.) 44-45	MURDER	U.S.
MUMMENTHEY	196782	M	Ger.		Major, CC Mauthausen (Aust.)	TORTURE	BEL.
MUMMENTHEY, Karl	188385	M	Ger.	06	Osturmbannfhr, Verwaltungshauptamt, CC Buchenwald (Ger.) 40-45	MURDER	BEL.
MUNCH	641	M	Ger.		Hptschfhr, SS, CC Falstad and Drontheim (Nor.) 40-44	TORTURE	NOR.
MUNCH	154829	M	Ger.		Capt, Army, Cabrespines (Fr.) 4.43	MURDER	FR.
MUNCH	194995	M	Ger.		N.C.O., 111 Pz.Gren.Rgt., Albine (Fr.) 6.44	MURDER	FR.
MUNCH, Alois	255047	M	Ger.		Oberwachtmstr, SD, Toulouse (Fr.) 11.42-8.44	MISC.CRIMES	FR.
MUNCH, Hans	307178	M	Ger.		CC Auschwitz and Mauthausen (Pol. and Aust.) 40-45	MURDER	FR.
MUNCHER	154890	M			Civilian, Schladen - Buchladen (Ger.) 9.44	MURDER	U.S.
MUNCHMEYER	185953	M	Ger.		Capt., Medical Chief, Army, Honfleur (Fr.) 8.44	WITNESS	FR.
MUNDEL, Hermann	255712	M		29. 8.98	Cpl., CC Ellrich, Nordhausen (Ger.)	MURDER	U.S.
MUNDELEIN, Hans	136630	M			Civilian, Rothenburg (Ger.) 3.45	WITNESS	U.S.
MUNDER	642	M	Ger.		Capt, Army, Chaveroche (Fr.) 11.43	MURDER	FR.
MUNDER, August	255052	M	Ger.	94	Head, Field Police, Erquelinnes (Bel.) 6.44	INTER.	BEL.
MUNDES	120562	M	Ger.	00 - 05	Wachtmeister, Schutzpolizei, Aken (Ger.) 7.44	MURDER	U.S.
MUNDINGER	255713	M			Sturmschfhr., Camp Dora, Nordhausen (Ger.)	MURDER	U.S.
MUNDL, Rupert	12563	M	Ger.		Pvt, 110 or 111 Pz.Gren.Rgt., 2 Coy, Albine (Fr.) 6.44	MURDER	FR.
MUNDT, Friedrich	257656	M	Ger.	22.12.14	Employee, CC Block 108 Dora, Nordhausen (Ger.)	MURDER	U.S.
MUNDT, Jindrich	194144	M	Ger.	24. 2.00	Civilian, Ratibor (Ger.) 39-45	TORTURE	CZECH.
MUNIER, Henri	643	M	Ger.		Agent, Gestapo, Hazebrouck (Fr.) 9.44	MURDER	FR.
MUNK (see MUENK)	128929						
MUNKER, Bert.	255737	M	Ger.	30 years	Army, Pion. Group, Heusden,Nord Brabant (Neth.) 11.44	PILLAGE	NETH.
MUNS	158952	M	Ger.		Sgt., 16 Inf.Div., Maille (Fr.) 8.44	MURDER	FR.
MUNSCH, Georg	174697	M	Ger.		Sgt., Army, CC Buchenwald, Wansleben am See (Ger.) 45	TORTURE	FR.
MUNSEL, Georg	180497	M	Ger.	14	Major, Army, Hermann Goering Div., Patrina (It.) 4.44	MURDER	U.K.
MUNSTERMANN	136221	M	Ger.		2 SS Pz.Div. "Das Reich"., Rgt."Deutschland", Venerque le Vernet (Fr.) 44	MURDER	FR.
MUNT, Johannes	194867	M	Ger.		Criminal Commissary, Sipo, Scheveningen, Gorssel, The Hague (Neth.) 9.44-3.45	MURDER	NETH.
MUNTGER	154828	M			Doctor, Gestapo, Bretagne, Anjou, Poitou (Fr.)	MURDER	FR.
MUNTSCH	195098	M	Ger.		SS Usturmfhr., SD Einsatzkommando Wenger, Pexonne (Fr.) 44	MURDER	U.K.
MUNZ, Erich	301811	M			SS-Mann, 1 SS Pz.Div. Leibstandarte "Adolf Hitler", Region of Stavelot (Bel.) 12.44	MURDER	BEL.
MUNZ, Karl	254262	M	Ger.	98	Owner of "Schlosskaffee", Civilian, Oberndorf (Ger.)	MISC.CRIMES	FR.
MUNZER	255714	M	Ger.		Pvt., CC Dora, Nordhausen (Ger.)	MURDER	U.S.
MUNZIG, Franz	305933	M	Ger.		Prison-Guard, Prison, Small Fortress, Theresienstadt (Czech.)10.38-44	MURDER	CZECH.
MUNZNER	136220	M	Ger.		Pay-Master, Army, Flexicourt, Ville le Marelet (Fr.) 44	WITNESS	FR.
MURER, Blasius	190050	M			Civilian, Leading Party, Arbeits-Kdo., CC Bodendorf, St.Georgen, Murau (Aust.) 12.44	TORTURE	U.K.
MURER, Jean	194329	M	Ger.		Crim.Secr., Sgt., Grenzpolizei, Veigy Foncenex (Fr.) 10.43	TORTURE	FR.
MURGORWSKY	173805	M	Ger.		Dr., Gen., Physician, SS, CC Buchenwald (Ger.) 42-45	MURDER	FR.
MURIC	644	M	Ger.		Pvt., Air Force, Baudrigues (Fr.) 8.44	WITNESS	FR.
MURLIG (see MULLIG)	121158						
MURMAN	256805	M	Ger.	95	Plant Manager, Plant 2, Warsaw, Treblinka, Fonitatowo (Pol.)41-45	MURDER	POL.
MURMANN	189053	M			Crim.Insp., Gestapo, Muenchen, CC Dachau (Ger.) 40-45	TORTURE	BEL.
MURR	134824	M	Ger.		Gend. - Kreis-Chief, Police, Eberau (Ger.) 44	MURDER	U.S.
MURR, Jean	306909	M	Ger.		Customs Secretary, Veigy, Foncenex (Hte-Savoice) (Fr.) 10.43	TORTURE	FR.
MURR, Wilhelm	253880	M			SS Ogruppenfhr, Gauleiter, Reichsstatthalter	TORTURE	FR.
MURRA, Wilhelm	154826	M			Civilian, Lauf (Ger.)	WITNESS	U.S.
MUROCH, Ernst	255738	M			Schfhr, Camp Dora, Nordhausen (Ger.)	MURDER	U.S.
MURZYNSKI	183686	M			SS-Sturmmann, Guard, 4 Totenkopf Sturmann, Camp Dora Mittelbau, Nordhausen (Ger.) 43-45	WITNESS	U.S.
MUS	104876	M	Ger.		Policeman, Master of Police, Aachen (Ger.) 8.44	BRUTALITY	U.S.
MUSAL	120558	M			Capt, Army, 18 Geb.Jg.Rgt., Veldes (Yugo.)	MURDER	U.S.
MUSAL, Georg	257324	M	Ger.	about 16	Crim. Secretary, Gestapo, Tabor (Czech.) 2.-5.45	MISC.CRIMES	CZECH.
MUSCHACK, Willi	260506	M	Ger.	24. 3.02	Guard, SS, CC Natzweiler (Fr.)	MURDER	FR.
MUSCHAL	168020	M	Ger.		Official, Ostgebietsministerium, Einsatzstab Rosenberg, Rouen (Fr.) 40-44	PILLAGE	FR.
MUSCHIK	152328	M			Uschfhr, SS, CC Mauthausen (Aust.) 41-45	MURDER	U.S.
MUSCHINSKY	173187	M	Ger.		Staff at CC Schirmeck - Rotenfels - Gaggenau (Fr. - Ger.)Autumn 44	MURDER	U.K.
MUSCHKE, Erich	124650	M	Ger.	24	Civilian (Student) Beltershain (Ger.) 12.44	MURDER	U.S.
MUSCHKL	168020	M	Ger.		Official, Ostgebietsministerium, Einsatzstab Rosenberg, Chief, Rouen (Fr.) 40-44	PILLAGE	U.N.W.C.C., FR.
MUSCHNA	160697	M	Ger.		Teacher, Civilian, Vicinity of Gardelegen (Ger.) 4.45	MURDER	U.S.
MUSCHULUS	142562	M	Ger.	03	Major or Lt.Col., Signal Corps Interpreters Coy, Gravenwoehr (Ger.) 11.-12.44	MISC.CRIMES	U.S.
MUSELER	132748	M	Ger.		Gestapo-Agent, CC Mauthausen (Aust.) 41-45	MURDER	U.S.
MUSFELD	183685	M	Ger.	19	Osturmfhr, Leader, 12 SS Pz.Div."Hitler Jugend", 12 SS Pz. Recce Unit, near Caen (Fr.) 6.-7.44	TORTURE	CAN.
MUSIKANT, Gottlieb	132747	M	Ger.		SS Schfhr, CC Mauthausen (Aust.) 41-45	MURDER	U.S.
MUSIL	300828	M	Ger.		Pvt., 1 Aufkl.Abt., 3 Coy, 2 Col., XV Div. of the Africa Corps, Saint Leger (Arlon) 9.44	MISC.CRIMES	BEL.
MUSKUSS	142567	M	Ger.		Gestapo Chief, CC Kaisergarten near Solingen (Ger.) 44-45	TORTURE	BEL.
MUSKAY (or MUSZKAY or MUSZSKAY)	134011	M			Sturmbannfhr, SS, Gestapo-Officer, Brno (Czech.) 39-44	MURDER	CZECH.
MUSSBERGER	127123	M	Ger.	00	Lt., Schutzpolizei, Schirmeck (Fr.) 43-44	MURDER	FR.
MUSSEIHAHN	258406	M			Employee, Group-Leader, CC Ohrdruf (Ger.) 12.44-4.45	MURDER	U.S.

MUS - NAG

- 34 -

NAME	C.R.FILE NUMBER	SEX	NATIO-NALITY	DATE OF BIRTH	RANK OCCUPATION UNIT PLACE AND DATE OF CRIME	REASON WANTED	WANTED BY
MUSSELMANN	300829	M	Ger.		Pvt., 1.Aufklaerungs-Abtlg., 3.Coy., 2.Col., 15.Div. of the Africa corps, Saint Leger (Arlon) 9.44	MISC.CRIMES	BEL.
MUSSFELD, Erich	187896	M			SS-Oberscharf., SS, C.C. Maidanek (Pol.) 40-45	TORTURE	BEL,POL,FR.
MUSSIG, Konrad	135552	M	Ger.		Farmer, Civilian, Arb.Kdo. 7006, Alsleben (Ger.)	MISC.CRIMES	U.K.
MUSTERT	39838	M		23	Lt., SS, Charmes (Fr.) 9.44	MURDER	FR.
MUSZHOFF	191902	M	Ger.		Pvt., Eis.Art.Bn. 717, St.Andries, Varsenare, Les Bruges (Bel.) 9.44	MURDER	BEL.
MUSZKAY (see MUSKAY)	134011						
MUTH	154834	M			Pvt., SS, C.C. Warsan (Pol.)	MURDER	U.S.
MUTH, Fritz	305083	M	Ger.		Probably one of the persons in the Air Raid Shelter at No.7, Schoenleinstr., Berlin (Ger.) 3.44	MURDER	U.K.
MUTS	254782	M			Sgt., Member, S.D., Gestapo, Toulouse (Fr.) 11.42-44	MISC.CRIMES	U.S.
MUTSCHLER	646	M			Gendarme, Police, Obernai (Fr.)	MURDER	FR.
MUTTER	158949	M	Ger.		Interpreter, Gestapo, Dijon (Fr.) 7.44	TORTURE	U.K.
MUTTER, Franz	255739	M		99	Pvt., C.C. Harzungen, Nordhausen (Ger.)	MURDER	U.S.
MUTTERER	196050	M			C.C. Struthof - Natzweiler (Fr.) 40-44	MURDER	FR.
MUTUR, Steven J.B.	189048	M			Civilian, Bainflair (Neth.) 7.44	WITNESS	U.S.
MUTZECK, Rudolf	306054	M	Ger.		Civilian, Giessen (Ger.) 12.44	MURDER	U.S.
MUYER (see MEYER)	254465						
MUYER, Franz or Hans (see MEYER)	124967						
MUYES, Franz or Hans (see MEYER)	124967						
MUZAWSKI, Vincentz	141883	M			Pvt., 266. Art.Regt., 9.Tp., (Fr.) 6.44	WITNESS	U.S.
MUZERHAFER, Martin	12565	M	Ger.		Pvt., 110. or 111.Panz.Gren.Regt., 2.Coy., Albine (Fr.) 6.44	MURDER	FR.
MYC, Johann	260962	M	Ger.		Farmer, Civilian, Eschenau (Ger.)	MISC.CRIMES	POL.
MYER	39865	M	Ger.		Pvt., Army, Bindorf-factory, C.C. Zenzig (Ger.) 4.44	BRUTALITY	U.K.
MYER	39866	M	Ger.		Sgt., Army, Military prison St.Leonardo-Verona (It.) C.C. Struthof (Fr.) Verona (It.) 4.44	BRUTALITY	FR.
MYER (see MEYER)	141355						
MYER	156983	M	Ger.		Arb.Kdo. 340, C.C. Aschersleben, Gross-Schierstedt (Ger.)	TORTURE	U.K.
MYER (see MEYER)	161924						
MYER	195166	M	Ger.	92	Civilian, Sangerhausen, Wallhausen (Ger.) 11.44	TORTURE	U.S.
MYER (see MEYER)	254465						
MYER, August	118522	M	Ger.		Civilian, C.C. Dulag 4 F, Lossnitz (Ger.) 2.-4.45	TORTURE	U.K.
MYER, Franz or Hans (see MEYER)	124967						
MYERS	156866	M	Ger.		Bannf., Hitler Jugend, Niederschlesien (Ger.) 10.42	TORTURE	U.K.
MYNY	300344		Ger.		Member, Sicherheitsdienst at Heerenveen, Luinjeberd (Neth.) 4.45	MURDER	NETH.
MYRES	121149	M	Ger.		Cpl., Army, in charge Fort Grolman, Stalag 21-D, Posen (Pol.) 9.42	MURDER	U.K.
NABEL	192558	M			C.C. Flossenburg (Ger.) 44-45	SUSPECT	U.S.
NABER	647	M			Capt., Army, Rodez (Fr.) 8.44	MURDER	FR.
NACHSEL, Paul	167101	M			Zoll-Beamter, Zollgrenzschutz, Annemasse (Fr.) 7.44	TORTURE	FR.
NACHTIGAL	173859	M	Ger.		Capt., Valence/Compiegne (Fr.) 41-44	MISC.CRIMES	FR.
NACHTINGALL	192017	M	Ger.		Adjutant-Chief, Army, Kerviherne-en-Merlevenez (Fr.) 4.45	MURDER	FR.
NACHTINGALL	306637	M	Ger.		N.C.O., Feldgendarmerie Chateaubriant (Loire) St.Julien de Mouvantes, Soudan, Juigne les Moutiers (Fr.) 7.44	MURDER	FR.
NACKE	189632	M	Ger.		Lt.General, Inf.Div. 264 (Yugo.)	TORTURE	YUGO.
NACKE	195143	M	Ger.		Reichsbahnrat, Deutsche Reichsbahn bei den Niederlaendischen Eisenbahnen (Ger.)	MISC.CRIMES	NETH.
NACKENSTURM, Willy	136291	M	Ger.		Chef de culture, Feldgendarmerie, Stenay (Fr.) 40-44	MURDER	FR.
NADLER, Karl	259441	M	Ger.		Jailor, C.C. Esterwegen (Papenburg) (Ger.)	BRUTALITY	BEL.
NADLER, Rudolf	199275	M	Ger.	30. 4.23	SS-Unterscharf., Boehmen (Czech.)	MISC.CRIMES	CZECH.
NARDELE	300830	M	Ger.		Pvt., 1.Aufklaerungs-Abtlg., 3.Coy., 2.Col., 15.Div. of the Africa corps, Saint Leger (Arlon) 9.44	MISC.CRIMES	BEL.
NAEGEL, Maurice	132629	M	Ger.		Kapo, C.C. Dora (Ger.)	TORTURE	FR.
NAEGELE	648	M	Ger.		Capt., Army, Clermont-Ferrand (Fr.) 7.44	MURDER	FR.
NAEGELE	186715	M	Ger.		Gestapo, Strasbourg Vosges area (Fr.) 9.44	WITNESS	U.K.
NAEGELE, Hans	138224	M	Ger.		Adjudant, Cmdt., C.C. Niederbuehl (Ger.)	TORTURE	FR.
NAEGELS	128964	M	Ger.		Untersturmf., Lt., 3.SS Panz.Regt., Eng.-Coy., (Sov.Un.)	MURDER	U.S.
NAENLEIN, Oswald	121020	M			Capt., Army, C.C. Untermassfeld (Ger.)	BRUTALITY	BEL.
NAETHER, Oswald	306483	M	Ger.	24.11.91	SS-Scharf., C.C. Buchenwald (Ger.) 5.38-10.43	MURDER	BEL.
NAGEGAST (see NAGERGAST)	305084						
NAGEL	104879	M			Major, Civilian, Bad Kossen (Ger.) 11.44	MURDER	U.S.
NAGEL	167102	M	Ger.		Field-Police-Moulins, La Rochemill Ay (Fr.) 8.44	PILLAGE	FR.
NAGEL	185492	M	Ger.		Kapo, Camp official, C.C. Mauthausen (Aust.)	MURDER	FR.
NAGEL	194236	M	Ger.	22	SS-Lt., 26.SS Panz.Gren.Regt., 12.SS Panz.Div., Hitler Jugend Caen (Fr.) 7.44	TORTURE	CAN.
NAGEL	194514	M		00	Stabsscharf., S.D., Gestapo, Nice (Fr.) 8.44	MURDER	FR.
NAGEL	251809	M	Ger.		Crim.Secr., Staatspolizeileitstelle, Karlsruhe (Ger.) 40-43	MURDER	POL.
NAGEL	255753	M			Unterscharf., C.C. Ellrich, Nordhausen (Ger.)	MURDER	U.S.
NAGEL	256999	M	Ger.		Cpl., 2.Signal-Coy., Bolnes (Neth.) 5.45	INTERR.	NETH.
NAGEL	257724	M			SS-Scharf., Camp Ellrich, Nordhausen (Ger.)	MURDER	U.S.
NAGEL	259035	M			Pvt., SS, Muehldorf area (Ger.)	MURDER	U.S.
NAGEL	301953	M	Ger.		Lagerfhr., Labour Camp Lidellschule, Karlsruhe (Ger.) 4.45	MURDER	NETH.
NAGEL, Anton	183281	M			Sturmmann, 4.SS-Totenkopf-Stuba., C.C. Auschwitz, Dora, Nordhausen (Pol., Ger.) 43-45	WITNESS	U.S.
NAGEL, Friedrich Hermann	255700	M	Ger.	1. 1.18	SS-Pvt., Junker der Panzer-Gren.-Schule, Neveklov-Benesov (Czech.) 45	MURDER	CZECH.
NAGEL, Hans	306275	M			Member of the Gestapo at Trencin, C.C. Oswiecim-Birkenau (Pol.) 39-45	MURDER	CZECH.
NAGEL, Maurice	174457	M	Ger.		Kapo, C.C. Dora - Buchenwald (Ger.) 43-4.45	MURDER	FR.
NAGEL, Peter	138209	M			C.C. Fresnes (Fr.) 44	TORTURE	FR.
NAGEL, W.	167103	M			Capt., Stalag 6-C, Bathorn (Ger.)	BRUTALITY	FR.
NAGELE	1446	M			Grenadier, Army, 903.Fortress Bn.	MISC.CRIMES	U.K.
NAGELER, Viktor	257646	M	Ger.	14. 3.03	Member, Gestapo, Bratislava (Czech.) 44	MURDER	CZECH.
NAGELSCHMIDT	251814	M	Ger.		SS-Unterscharf., S.D., Toulouse (Fr.) 11.42-8.44	MISC.CRIMES	FR.
NAGENGAST, Baptist	136629	M	Ger.		Pvt., Prison-guard, Bamberg (Ger.) 3.45	TORTURE	U.S.

NAG-NEH

NAME	C.R.FILE NUMBER	SEX	NATIO-NALITY	DATE OF BIRTH	RANK OCCUPATION UNIT PLACE AND DATE OF CRIME	REASON WANTED	WANTED BY
NAGERGAST or NAGEGAST	305084	M	.		Lt.,Crete (Grc.) 9.43	MISC.CRIMES	GRC.
NAGLER	132630	M	Ger.		Usturmfhr.,Gestapo,Gerardmer (Fr.) 9.-11.44	MISC.CRIMES	FR.
NAGLER	138320	M			SS-member,Gestapo,Lyon (Fr.)	MURDER	FR.
NAGLY	256076	M	Ger.		Pvt.,SS,Miehldorf (Ger.)	WITNESS	U.S.
NAHRGANG,Paul,Karl,Heinrich	185912	M	Ger.	15.10.00	Hptwachtmeister,Police,Offenbach (Ger.) 2.45	MURDER	U.S.
NAISSE	185119	M			Oberkapo,SS,C.C.Dachau (Ger.)	MURDER	FR.
NAJHAN	306276	M	Ger.		Member of the Gestapo at Trencin,C.C.Oswiecim-Birkenau (Pol.) 39-45	MURDER	CZECH.
NAMENDORF,Fritz	251810	M	Ger.		Usturmfhr.,SS,Sainte Savire (Fr.) 8.44	MISC.CRIMES	FR.
NANNKHE	195962	M			Cpl.,Army,Martaize (Fr.) 8.44	MURDER	FR.
NANNT	255752	M			Rottenfhr.,C.C.Osterhagen,Nordhausen (Ger.)	MURDER	U.S.
NAPELEON	188441	M			SS,C.C.Karlovy-Vary (Czech.) 4.45	MURDER	U.S.
NAPIWOTZKY,Hildegard	178962	F	Ger.	11.12.15	Employee,Gestapo,Prag (Czech.) 39-45	WITNESS	CZECH.
NAPOLEON see GIGLE	163449						
NAPOLEON see HEINRICH	254644						
"NAPOLEON" (Nick-name) (or HEINRICH)	300474	M			SS-Usturmfhr.,SS,C.C.Hinzert,Treves (Ger.) 42-45	MURDER	FR.
NAPPENER	12566	M	Ger.		Lt.,Feldpostnr.10105 A,Houeilles (Fr.) 8.44	MURDER	FR.
NARATH,Rudolf	184217	M	Ger.	16.12.10	Councellor,Countrycourt,leader,Hitler-Jugend,Prag (Czech.) 41-45	MURDER	CZECH.
NARORAHT,Walter	167104	M	Ger.		Civilian,Leffinckroueke (Fr.) 44	MURDER	FR.
NARRER	146965	M	Ger.		Sturmbannfhr.,SS-Pz.Div."Das Reich",Villaudrie (Fr.) 44	MURDER	FR.
NASAR	132265	M		21	SS,C.C.Hohenheim Plattling (Ger.) 2.-5.45	MURDER	U.S.
NASDANOV	189964	M			Agent,Police,Pirot (Yugo.)	MISC.CRIMES	YUGO.
NASSAU,Philippe	162682	M	Ger.		Sgt.,Gestapo,Sceaux-Buisne (Fr.) 7.44	MURDER	FR.
NASSAULT,Philip	125627	M	Ger.		Sgt.,Kraftfahrpark,526 Div.,Cormes (Fr.) 7.44	MURDER	FR.
NATCZYNSKI	190258	M	Ger.		Sgt.,Feldgendarmerie,Pozaverse (Serb.) 41-42 and 43	MURDER	YUGO.
NATEBOSH,Emil	250406	M	Ger.		Member,Gestapo,Geheime Feldpolizei,Lille (Fr.) 40-44	MURDER	FR.
NATER	188843	M	Ger.	.	Lt.Col.,C.C.Souges (Fr.) 1.-4.44	MURDER	FR.
NATHUSIUS,Hans	3156	M	Ger.		Sturmbannfhr.,SS,Magdeburg (Ger.) 44-45	MISC.CRIMES	U.S.
NATUSCHIK	250404	M	Ger.		Guard,C.C.Monsheim (Ger.)	BRUTALITY	FR.
NAU	167774	M	Ger.		Oscharfhr.,SS-Div."Das Reich",Monthezat de Querzy (Fr.) 5.44	MURDER	FR.
NAU,Hermann	250405	M	Ger.		Cdo.-leader,Neuengamme (Ger.) 44	BRUTALITY	FR.
NAUDE,Horst	10315	M	Ger.		Ministerialrat,public official,Maehren Bruenn (Czech.) 39-44	TORTURE	CZECH.
NAUHEIM,Paul	125626	M	Ger.	15	Gestapo,SD,Nord (Fr.)	MISC.CRIMES	FR.
NAUJOCKS	104880	M	Ger.		Pvt.,Army,Ochsenfort (Ger.) 8.44	WITNESS	U.S.
NAUJOK,Albert	255751	M		24.4.10	Staff-Sgt.,C.C.Ellrich,Nordhausen (Ger.)	MURDER	U.S.
NAUJOKS	166988	M		08	Lt.,Police,HQ.Orpo,Campomolon (It.) 2.45	MURDER	U.K.
NAUJOKS	194512	M	Ger.		Cpl.,Feldgendarmerie,Ploermel (Fr.) 6.44	TORTURE	FR.
NAUJOKS,Hermann	194859	M		11	Lt.,8 Coy.,Police-Bn.2,Roncegno Tonenza (It.) 3.45	MURDER	U.K.
NAUJOX,Alfred	155513	M	Ger.		Sturmbannfhr.,SS,(Ger.)	MURDER	U.K.
NAUKE,Kurt	184218	M	Ger.	05	Member,N.S.D.A.P.,public prosecutor,occupied territory, Prag (Czech.) 40-44	MURDER	CZECH.
NAUMANN	187717	M	Ger.			TORTURE	UNWCC.
NAUMANN	192733	M	Ger.		Physician,SS-Uscharfhr.,C.C.Buchenwald (Ger.) 42-45	TORTURE	U.S.
NAUMANN	251179	M	Ger.		Lt.,84 Regt.,13 Coy.,Rhenen (Neth.)	PILLAGE	NETH.
NAUMANN	254097	M	Ger.		SS-Brigade-Fhr.,Befehlshaber der Sicherheitspolizei,Elzendorp (Neth.) 8.44	MURDER	NETH.
NAUMANN	255701	M	Ger.		SD,(working just under Gen.Rauter),Gemert (Neth.) 8.44	MURDER	NETH.
NAUMANN,Erhard	306484	M	Ger.		SS-Pvt.,SS,C.C.Buchenwald (Ger.) between 5.38 and 10.43	MURDER	BEL.
NAUMANN,Heinrich	161265	M	Ger.	10	Usturmfhr.,Waffen-SS,command staff,C.C.Buchenwald (Ger.)	WITNESS	U.S.
NAUMANN,Karl	62451	M	Ger.		Geschaeftsfuehrender Leiter,head of Department of Wood and Agriculture	MURDER	POL.,UNWCC.
NAUMANN,Reinhard	250397	M	Ger.		Pvt.,C.C.Hamer (Ger.) 3.45	WITNESS	U.S.
NAUMANN,Robert	255919	M	Ger.	11.6.18	Supervisor,Panenske Brezany (Czech.) 40-42	TORTURE	CZECH.
NAUMANN,Rudolf	29698	M	Ger.		Oberlandesgerichtsrat,Amtsgerichtsdirektor,Ministry of Justiz, Litomerice (Czech.) 40	MURDER	CZECH.
NAUMENKO,Charlampi	255750			10.2.08	C.C.Harzungen,Nordhausen (Ger.)	MURDER	U.S.
NAUS,Otto	12567	M	Ger.		Sgt.,Army,110 or 111 Pz.Gren.Regt.,2 Coy.,Albine (Fr.) 6.44	MURDER	FR.
NAVE or GREVE or REESE	196246	M	Ger.		Rottenfhr.,C.C.Neuengamme (Ger.) 37-44	TORTURE	BEL.
NAWROTH	255749				C.C.Dora,Nordhausen (Ger.)	MURDER	U.S.
NAWROTH	256077	M	Ger.		Pvt.,SS,Miehldorf (Ger.)	WITNESS	U.S.
NAYMAN	146964	M	Ger.		Officer,SS-Pz.Div."Das Reich",La Croix-Falgarde (Fr.) 44	MURDER	FR.
NEAU	155485	M	Ger.		Civilian,C.C.Laimitz (Ger.) 40-41	MURDER	U.S.
NEBAUER	174161	M	Ger.		Oscharfhr.,SS,official,Gestapo,Le Mans (Fr.) 12.43-1.44	MURDER	FR.
NEBEL	162195	M	Ger.	90	Capt.,Army,command staff,Buchenwald (Ger.)	WITNESS	U.S.
NEBEL	255744	M			SS-Sgt.,Nordhausen (Ger.)	MURDER	U.S.
NEBEL,Wilhelm	255913	M			Cpl.,C.C.Buchenwald (Ger.)	MURDER	U.S.
NEBELUNG,Guenther	261112	M	Ger.	3.96	Senats-President,People's Court	SUSPECT	U.S.
NEBEST,Wilhelm	119404	M	Ger.	1.4.15	Blockfuehrer,Waffen-SS,C.C.Oswiecim (Pol.) 6.40-1.45	MURDER	POL.
NECKMANN	196915	M			Laterina Camp,Laterina (It.)	WITNESS	U.S.
NEDBOLA	257531	M			Sgt.,Waffen-SS,Dental clinic Dora,Nordhausen (Ger.)	MURDER	U.S.
NEDOMA	300348	M	Ger.		Officer,commanding HQ.Truppe 670,Artl.Regt.,Tripolis, 3.44	MISC.CRIMES	GRC.
NEDOMA,Margarete	199280	F	Ger.		Clerk,Gestapo,Bruenn (Czech.) 39-45	MURDER	CZECH.
NEDWET,Max or NEDWET	49809	M	Ger.	90	SS-Osturmbannfhr.,Gestapo,chief of administration,civilian,Dr. Innsbruck,Koeslin,Stettin,Kassel (Ger.) 9.44	MISC.CRIMES	POL.,U.S.
NEDWET,Max or NEDWED	49809						
NEEB	260041	M	Ger.		Capt.,157 Bavarian Div.d.Res.,Massif du Vercors Isere and Drome (Fr.) 7.-8.44	SUSPECT	FR.
NEEF	126978				Officer,C.C.Dora,Nordhausen (Ger.)	TORTURE	FR.
NEEF	174156	M	Ger.		Engineer,factory employing men from C.C.Dora-Buchenwald (Ger.) 43-4.45	MURDER	FR.
NEFF,Walter or NEFFE or NEEFKE	190314	M	Ger.		Kapo,C.C.Dachau (Ger.) 40-45	MURDER	YUGO.,U.S.
NEGER	257346	M	Ger.		SS-Sturmscharfhr.,guard,SS,slave labour camp,Beisfjord near Narvik (Nor.) 6.-11.42	BRUTALITY	YUGO.
NEGRINER	174162	M	Ger.		SS-Mann,official,Gestapo,Le Mans (Fr.) 12.43-1.44	MURDER	FR.
NEGUS see REINHARDT	186787						
NEHER,Mase	251811	M	Ger.		Bauernfhr.,Hemilly (Fr.) 9.44	PILLAGE	FR.
NEHLS	173858	M	Ger.		Lt.,469 Inf.Regt.,198 Inf.Div.,2 Bn.,5 Coy.,Le Tholy (Fr.) 11.44	MISC.CRIMES	FR.
NEHLS	255746	M			Sgt.,C.C.Ellrich,Nordhausen (Ger.)	MURDER	U.S.

NEH-NEU   -36-

NAME	C.R.FILE NUMBER	SEX	NATIO-NALITY	DATE OF BIRTH	RANK OCCUPATION UNIT PLACE AND DATE OF CRIME	REASON WANTED	WANTED BY
NEHLS, Karl	255745	M		7. 2.97	Uschfhr., C.C. Wolffleben, Nordhausen (Ger.)	MURDER	U.S.
NEHMER	121013	M	Ger.		Pvt., Army, Cresch-Maut (Fr.) 8.44	MURDER	FR.
NEHRING	141586	F	Ger.		Civilian. (Fr.) 42-44	PILLAGE	FR.
NEHSNER, J.	12568	M	Ger.		Pvt., 2.Coy. Panz.Gren.Regt. 110, Albine (Fr.) 6.44	MURDER	FR.
NEIBOECK, Hermann	252553	M	Ger.	02	Chief of Staff, Kreisleiter of Kaplitz (Ger.) 12.44	MURDER	U.S.
NEIDENIK, Franz	306055	M	Ger.		Lt., Strassgang (Aust.) 3.45	MURDER	U.S.
NEIDER, Peter	255914	M		3. 9.98	SS-Mann, C.C. Nordhausen (Ger.)	MURDER	U.S.
NEIDHARD	162681	M	Ger.		Judge, Ministry of Justice, Strasbourg (Fr.) 2.43	MURDER	FR.
NEIDHARD, Werner	251819	M		15. 2.12	Sgt., Driver, z.b.V.Kommando 31, Valasske, Mezirici (Czech.) 5.45	MURDER	CZECH.
NEIDHOLT, Fritz	167792	M		90	Lt.Gen., 369. Inf.Div., Zagnjezde and Udora (Yugo.) 7.44	MURDER	YUGO., U.S.
NEIMANN	174155	M	Ger.		Cpl., Work Camp, Briey (Fr.)	MURDER	FR.
NEIS, Aloys	187867	M		07	Civilian, Wehrden-Saar (Ger.) 8.44	TORTURE	U.S.
NEISSEL	173913	M	Ger.		Wachtmeister, Polizei, C.C.Gaggenau (Ger.)	MURDER	U.K.
NEISSER, Marie nee SCHINDLER	251826	F	Ger.	18. 9.93	Teacher, Kindergarten, Member of NSDAP, NSV, Bystrice (Czech.) 39-45	BRUTALITY	CZECH.
NEITZ	121012	M	Ger.		Pvt., C.C. Olur-Halbstadt (Ger.) 8.44	TORTURE	U.K.
NEITZEL, Karl	196798	M	Ger.		Wachtmeister, Polizeistation, Ahrweiler (Ger.) 5.-6.44	BRUTALITY	POL.
NEIBOCK, Hermann	142537	M	Ger.	07	S.A.-Sturmbannfhr. near Kaplitz (Ger.)	WITNESS	U.S.
NEIBOECK	161266	M	Ger.		Member of NSDAP, Chief of Staff to Kreisleiter, Unterhaid (Ger.) 12.44	MURDER	U.S.
NELGES, Ferdinand	141838	M	Ger.	20	Cpl. 6.Landesschuetzen-Bn. 471, Essen (Ger.) 12.44	MURDER	U.K.
NELIS (see STOEVER)	920						
NELLE	151514	M	Ger.		Uschfhr., SS Div. "Das Reich", Oradour s.Glane (Fr.) 6.44	MURDER	FR.
NELLER	301643	M	Ger.		Secretary, Ebrach near Amberg (Ger.)	MURDER	CZECH.
NELLESSEN	173912	M	Ger.		Officer, Stalag VI A, Hemer (Ger.) 41-45	TORTURE	U.S.
NELLISEN	162680	M	Ger.		Stalag-leader, Stalag VI C (Ger.)	TORTURE	FR.
NELTE	183279	M			Rottenfhr., 4.SS-Totenkopf-Sturmbann, C.C.Dora, Nordhausen (Ger.) 43-45	WITNESS	U.S.
NEITZHOEFFER, Peter	67015	M			Sgt., C.C. Struthof (Fr.)	MISC.CRIMES	FR.
NEMEC, Johann	258076	M	Ger.	7. 5.87	Informer, Gestapo, C.C.Budejovice (Czech.) 43-45	MURDER	CZECH.
NEMETH, Imre	139056	M			Lt., Hung.-SS-Div. 26, Ujvidek (Hung.)	MURDER	U.S.
NEMETSCHKE	255747	M	Ger.		Cpl., C.C.Ellrich, Nordhausen (Ger.)	MURDER	U.S.
NEMETZ, Adolf	29697	M	Ger.	96	Dr., Councellor (Landgerichtsrat), Prague and Hradec Kralove (Czech.)40	MURDER	CZECH.
NEMLEIN	191997	M			Cmdt., C.C. Gossen (Nor.) 42-45	MURDER	NOR.
NEMMER, Josef	140798	M	Ger.		Sturmfhr., S.A., Ranshofen (Aust.)	TORTURE	U.S.
NENBERG	196875	M	Ger.		Sgt., C.C. Auschwitz (Pol.) 40	MURDER	FR.
NENKE	136290	M			Adjutant Chief (Oberfeldw.), Feldgendarmerie, Stenay (Fr.) 40-44	MURDER	FR.
NENOKIL (see VALENTIN)	162834						
NERGE (or NERGI)	190398	M	Ger.		Wachtmeister, Polizei, Wiesbaden (Ger.) 43-45	TORTURE	U.S.
NERICH	262242	M	Ger.		SS-Hptsturmfhr., Gestapo, Rouen (Fr.) 41-44	MURDER	FR.
NERMANN	136325	M	Ger.		Chief, Gendarmerie, Ochsenfurt (Ger.) 44	MURDER	U.S.
NESCHKE	145969	M	Ger.		Cpl., Army, vicinity of Munich (Ger.) 7.44	MURDER	U.S.
NESTLER	10156	M	Ger.		Cpl., Army, Stalag 4 F (Ger.) 6.44	MURDER	U.K.
NESTLER, Helmut	193279	M	Ger.		Prison Guard, Gestapo, Brno (Czech.) 39-45	MURDER	CZECH.
NESTLER, Helmuth	251170	M		23	Sturmmann, SS, Malmedy (Bel.) 12.44	MURDER	U.S.
NESTLER, Richard	188454	M		14	Cpl., Landesschuetzen, C.C. Muhlbach (Ger.) 44	MURDER	U.K.
NESTMANN, Richard	157997	M	Ger.		SS and Gestapo, Hennebont (Fr.) 8.44	MURDER	FR.
NESZBACH, Otto	137546	M			Uschfhr., SS, C.C.Weimar-Buchenwald (Ger.)	TORTURE	U.S.
NET	259197	M	Ger.		Crim.secretary, Member Gestapo Berlin, C.C.Dachau (Ger.) 44-45	MISC.CRIMES	YUGO.
NETSCHER	196876	M		04	Sgt., SS, Gestapo, Vichy (Fr.)	MURDER	FR.
NETTER	162679	M	Ger.		Capt., Cmdt., Gestapo, Neuville s.Ain (Fr.) 7.44	TORTURE	FR.
NETZE	256509	M	Ger.		Oschfhr., SS, C.C.Nordhausen (Ger.)	MURDER	U.S.
NETZGOLD, Hugo	256079	M	Ger.		Magaziner, SS, Mühldorf (Ger.)	WITNESS	U.S.
NETZWICKI	301954	M	Ger.		Rottenfhr., SS, Staffel-Sanitaeter, C.C.Auschwitz (Pol.) 42-45	MURDER	POL.
NEU, Eugene	171952	M			Civilian, Merange, Fourligny (Fr.) 8.44	WITNESS	U.S.
NEU, Gerhard	251820	M	Ger.	15. 9.05	Cpl., z.b.V.Kommando 31, Valasske, Mezirici (Czech.) 5.45	MURDER	CZECH.
NEUBACHER (or NEUMACHER)	307182	M			Member, S.D., Apeldoorn, Hoog-Soeren (Lager "Mia") (Neth.) 10.44-4.45	MURDER	NETH.
NEUBACHER, Fritz	307183	M	Ger.	4. 7.05	SS-Sturmscharfhr., SS, Criminal secretary, Sicherheitspolizei, Sicherheitsdienst, Kommando Gerbig, Kriminalpolizei, Almelo (Neth.) 9.44-2.45	MURDER	NETH.
NEUBACHER, Hermann	305471	M	Ger.		Special-Commissioner for South-East Europe, Foreign Office, Belgrad, Serbia (Yugo.) 43-44	MISC.CRIMES	YUGO.
NEUBAUER	651	M			SS-Oschfhr., C.C.Stutthof (Pol.) 9.39-4.41	MURDER	POL.
NEUBAUER	72721	M			S.D., C.C. Theresienstadt (Pol.) 12.41	TORTURE	U.S.
NEUBAUER	188442	M			SS, C.C. Karlovy-Vary (Czech.) 4.45	MURDER	U.S.
NEUBAUER	188952	M	Ger.		Feldgendarmerie, Bar-le-Duc (Fr.) 8.44	MURDER	FR.
NEUBAUER	251187	M	Ger.		Uschfhr., SS "Das Reich", "Der Fuehrer", 3.Coy., 1.Bn., Oradour (Fr.)	INTERR.	FR.
NEUBAUER	251188	M	Ger.		Dr., Kreisgerichtsrat, Dienststelle F.P.No.24576 (Russia) 1.44	MURDER	FR.
NEUBAUER	255748	M			Sturmscharfhr., C.C.Dora, Nordhausen (Ger.)	MURDER	U.S.
NEUBAUER, Adalbert	193660	M	Ger.	21.12.10	SS-Sgt., Pol.Guard, C.C. Terezin (Czech.) 40-45	MURDER	CZECH.
NEUBAUER, Antonin	257323	M	Ger.	16. 9.13	Crim.asst., Gestapo, Tabor (Czech.) 11.40-5.45	MISC.CRIMES	CZECH.
NEUBAUER, August	180505	M	Ger.	13	Member, SS, S.D., Gestapo, Benesov (Czech.) 6.44	MURDER	CZECH.
NEUBAUER, Ernst	259696	M	Ger.	12	SS-Oscharfhr., Gestapo, Area of Angers, Maine-Loire (Fr.) 42-44	MISC.CRIMES	FR.
NEUBAUER, Leopold	255924	M		28. 5.95	Pvt., C.C.Ellrich, Nordhausen (Ger.)	MURDER	U.S.
NEUBAUER, Otto	193987	M	Ger.	21. 3.12	Member, S.A., NSDAP, Rural Pol., Moravske, Budejovice (Czech.) 39-45	MISC.CRIMES	CZECH.
NEUBAUER, Raimund	193586	M	Ger.	15	Crim.asst., Polizei, Gestapo, Moravia, Napajedla (Czech.) 40-45	MURDER	U.S.
NEUBAUR, Bruno	195145	M	Ger.	18	Army, Stalag XVIII B, U.C. Pottenbrun (Aust.) 44-45	TORTURE	U.K.
NEUBER	306485	M	Ger.		SS-Mann, SS, C.C.Buchenwald (Ger.) betw. 5.38 and 10.43	MURDER	BEL.
NEUBER, Karl	306436	M	Ger.		Member, Gestapo, Hanau (Ger.) 2.45	MURDER	U.S.
NEUBERG	192730	M	Ger.		SS-Uschfhr., C.C. Buchenwald (Ger.) 42-45	MURDER	U.S.
NEUBERGER (see HEUBERGER)	104881						
NEUBERGER, Michael	193331	M	Ger.		Guard, 4.SS Totenkopf-Sturmbann, C.C.Dora, Nordhausen (Ger.) 43-45	MURDER	U.S.
NEUBERT	652	M	Ger.		Cpl., Warder of Prison, C.C. Caen (Fr.) 6.44	MURDER	FR.
NEUBERT	39591	M	Ger.		Capt., SS, Polizei, Organisation Todt, Alby and Gruffy (Hte Savoire)	MURDER	FR.
NEUBERT	128965	M	Ger.		Official, Gestapo, Hanau (Ger.) 3.45	MURDER	U.S.
NEUBERT	188317	M	Ger.		Buergermeister, Hartbau (Ger.) 3.45	WITNESS	U.K.

NAME	C.R.FILE NUMBER	SEX	NATIO- NALITY	DATE OF BIRTH	RANK OCCUPATION UNIT PLACE AND DATE OF CRIME	REASON WANTED	WANTED BY
NEUBERT	301955	M	Ger.		Uschfhr, SS, CC Auschwitz (Pol.) 42-45	MURDER	POL.
NEUBERT, Gerhard	255920	M		12.6.09	Uschfhr, SS, CC Monowitz, Nordhausen (Ger.)	MURDER	U.S.
NEUBURT	192333	M			Usturmfhr, SS, Camp Dora, Nordhausen (Ger.)	MURDER	U.S.
NEUDECK, Annie	261170	F	Ger.		Member of Staff of CC, Ravensbrueck (Ger.)	SUSPECT	BEL.
NEUDECK, Ruth	142112	F	Ger.		Guard, CC Ravensbrueck (Ger.)	TORTURE	FR.
NEUDORF	130174	M	Ger.		Civilian, Fischbeck (Ger.) 6.44	MURDER	U.S.
NEUEBURGER	141587	M	Ger.		Factory Canteen Manager, Kassel (Ger.)	TORTURE	FR.
NEUGART (see MEUGART)	256085						
NEUGEBAUER	167752	M	Ger.		Sgt., Feld-Gend., Auberive Flagey, Goiffy, Chalencey (Fr.) 43-44	MURDER	FR.
NEUGEBAUER (or NEWGEBAUER)	251615	M	Ger.		Lt., Air Force, Unit 34.305, Berre L'Etang, Bouches du Rhone (Fr.)8.44	MURDER	FR.
NEUGEBAUER, Emanuel	255918	M	Ger.	8.11.93	Employee, Gestapo, Opava (Czech.) 39-45	TORTURE	CZECH.
NEUGEBAUER, Paul	151521	M		05	Civ.Vormann, CC Gross Rosen (Aust.) 41-45	MURDER	U.S.
NEUHAUS	188842	M			Stabsarzt, Army, Durcy-les-Amiens (Fr.) 44	WITNESS	FR.
NEUHAUS	251824	M	Ger.	15	Capt. or Major, Adj., 65 Div. H.Q., Ponzano Magra (It.) 9.43	INTERR.	U.K.
NEUHAUS, Hans	153294	M		17	SS Hptsturmfhr., Heym	MURDER	U.S.
NEUHAUSEN	187719	M			Pvt., Army Administration	PILLAGE	U.N.W.C.C.
NEUHEUSEN	62455	M	Ger.		SS Ogruppenfhr, Chief of Military Administration "South East"	MISC.CRIMES	U.N.W.C.C.
NEUHOF	905729	M			Rottfhr, Kdo.Fuehrer, CC Auschwitz-Birkenau (Pol.) from 40	MURDER	FR.
NEUHOFF	135559	M	Ger.		Capt., Army, Goerlitz (Ger.) 2.-3.45	MISC.CRIMES	U.K.
NEUHOFF, Heinz	192753	M	Ger.		Schupo CC Falstad (Nor.) 41-44	MURDER	NOR.
NEUHOP	251823	M			Rottfhr., CC Auschwitz (Pol.)	BRUTALITY	FR.
NEUHOSS	259216	M	Ger.		Rottfhr, Gestapo, Area of Poitiers (Fr.) 40-45	MISC.CRIMES	FR.
NEUJOCKS, Guenther	151516	M			Lt., Fallschirmjaeger Rgt.5, 4 Coy, St.Laurent de Cavis (Fr.) 7.44	MURDER	FR.
NEUKAM	301644	M	Ger.		Hptwachtmstr, Ebrach near Amberg (Ger.) -45	MURDER	CZECH.
NEUKATER, Gunther	104884	M	Ger.		Sgt., 85 Inf.Rgt, 2 Inf.Rgt., 85 Fuss.Bn., 1 Coy, Hasselfelde (Ger.)	MURDER	U.S.
NEUKE	900699	M			Public Prosecutor, Oberstaatsanwaltschaft, Ministry of State, Department of Justice, Prague, Bohemia and Moravia (Czech.) 2.40	MISC.CRIMES	CZECH.
NEUKIRCHERER	125195	M	Ger.		Top Foreman, CC Gruseneberg (Ger.)	TORTURE	U.S.
NEULANN, Arthur	139671	M		02	Hptsturmfhr, Werkschutzleiter, W-SS, CC, Germany	MURDER	U.S.
NEULINGER	199458	M	Ger.		Sgt., 28 Inf.Rgt., 116 Bn., 2 Coy, Meilhan-Lannemezan (Fr.) 7.44	MURDER	FR.
NEULIST	190049	M		26	Pvt., Lds.Schtz.Bn.102 or 107, Oflag XII B, CC Hadamar (Ger.) 11.43	TORTURE	U.K.
NEULITZ	157998	M		27	107 Lds.Schtz.Bn..., Pvt., Hadamar (Ger.)	MURDER	U.K.
NEUMACHER (see NEUBACHER)	907182						
NEUMAIER, Heinrich Wilh.	199602	M		14.9.94	T.-Sgt., Army, 439 Inf.Rgt., 56 Lds.Schtz.Coy, Ryglice (Pol.) 11.39	PILLAGE	POL.
NEUMAN	654	M			Lt., CC Auschwitz-Birkenau (Pol.) 40	MURDER	FR.
NEUMAN	10075	M			Prod.-Chief for Herm.Wegenes Stone Works, Hannover, CC Bramberg (Ger.) 1.44-2.45.	MISC.CRIMES	U.K.
NEUMAN	187990	M		05	Pvt., Stalag XX A, near Briessenfeld (Ger.) 5.42	MURDER	U.K.
NEUMAN, Alexander	174086	M	Ger.		Oberfhr, SS Sturmbann, CC Auschwitz (Pol.) 39-45	MURDER	CZECH.,POL., YUGO.,FR.,U.K.
NEUMANN	12660	M	Ger.		SS Osturmfhr, Gestapo H.Q., Bergen (Nor.) 41	TORTURE	NOR.
NEUMANN	12661	M	Ger.		SS Osturmfhr, Oslo, (Nor.) 43	TORTURE	NOR.
NEUMANN	62407	M	Ger.	20	SS Uschfhr, CC Hinzert (Ger.)	MURDER	U.S.
NEUMANN	104882	M	Ger.		Interpreter, Stg.VIII B, Lamsdorf (Ger.) 2.41	WITNESS	U.K.
NEUMANN	104883	M	Ger.		Dr., Physician, Institute Kiew (Russia) 41-42	MURDER	U.S.
NEUMANN	121005	M	Ger.		Milit. Berater, Army, Montvilliers (Fr.) 9.44	WITNESS	FR.
NEUMANN	132332	M			Camp Dora, Nordhausen (Ger.)	MURDER	U.S.
NEUMANN	132585	M	Ger.		General, Senats-Praesident, Kriegsgericht, Berlin, Torgau (Ger.) 5.40-45	MURDER	FR., U.K.
NEUMANN	137094	M	Ger.		Civilian, Arbeits-Kdo. 7006, CC Adelebsen (Ger.)	TORTURE	U.K.
NEUMANN	139457	M	Ger.		N.C.O., SS Pz.Div. "Das Reich"	MURDER	FR.
NEUMANN	139672	M	Ger.		Capt., Stalag X B, CC Sandbostel (Ger.) 1.-5.45	TORTURE	U.S.
NEUMANN	140799	M			SS Sturmann, CC Frankfurt (Main) 3.45	MURDER	U.S.
NEUMANN	146969	M			Uschfhr, SS Pz.Div. "Das Reich", Montauban (Fr.) 44	MURDER	FR.
NEUMANN	155491	M			Justiz-Oberwachtmeister, Police, CC Ensland (Ger.) 44	MURDER	U.S.
NEUMANN	162646	M			Cmdt., Army, 36 Div., Lepanges (Fr.) 9.44	PILLAGE	FR.
NEUMANN	169866	M			Army, PoW-Camp 190, 4 Work.Bn., Berholnes (Nor.)	MURDER	NOR.
NEUMANN	165704	M	Ger.	17	SS Usturmfhr, Lemberg, Kiew, Zwiakel (Pol., Russia) 41-42	MURDER	U.S.
NEUMANN	174167	M	Ger.		Adviser, Kommandantur, Montvilliers (Fr.) 9.44	WITNESS	FR.
NEUMANN	186987	M	Ger.		Unterwachtmeister, Feld-Gend., CC Beverloo (Bel.) 10.43	TORTURE	BEL.
NEUMANN	192720	M	Ger.		SS Obersturmfhr, Prof. Dr., CC Buchenwald (Ger.) 42-45	MURDER	U.S.
NEUMANN	199002	M	Ger.		Pvt., Kgf. Arb.Bn.190, Bergholnes (Nor.) 7.44-5.45	TORTURE	NOR.
NEUMANN	199601	M	Ger.		Pvt., Army, CC Neuengamme (Ger.) 42	MURDER	BEL.
NEUMANN	195989	M	Ger.		Doctor, SS Hptsturmfhr, CC Sachsenhausen (Ger.)	MURDER	BEL.
NEUMANN	195961	M	Ger.		Hptwachtmstr., CC Westerbork (Neth.) 9-12.44	MURDER	NETH.
NEUMANN	196916	M			SS Sturmbannfhr.	MISC.CRIMES	U.S.
NEUMANN	196918	M			Lt., Cmdt., 7.3, Brandenbg. Rgt.	MISC.CRIMES	U.S.
NEUMANN	251180	M	Ger.		Pvt., Field-Police, Vendome (Fr.)	INTERR.	FR.
NEUMANN	256508	M	Ger.		Oschfhr, SS, CC Nordhausen (Ger.)	MURDER	U.S.
NEUMANN	256552	M	Ger.		Employee, Camp Dora, Nordhausen (Ger.)	BRUTALITY	FR.
NEUMANN	257726	M	Ger.		SS-Mann, Transportation Section, CC Nordhausen (Ger.)	MURDER	U.S.
NEUMANN	261847	M	Ger.		Cpl., Field-Gend., Romilly sur Seine (Fr.) 6.40	MISC.CRIMES	FR.
NEUMANN	900351	M	Ger.		Employee, Camp Dora and Factory from CC Buchenwald, Nordhausen and Buchenwald (Ger.) 43-4.45	MURDER	FR.
NEUMANN	301145	M	Ger.		Commanding the 36 Inf.Div., Lepanges, Vosges (Fr.) 9.44	PILLAGE	FR.
NEUMANN	301743	M	Ger.	about 09	SS Agent, Manager of Stone Quarry at Bramburg, where PoW from A-K 7006, Stalag XI-B, were employed by quarrying firm of Herman Wegerner of Hannover, Bramburg near Adelebsen (Hannover) Germany 43-44	BRUTALITY	U.K.
NEUMANN	301956	M	Ger.	about 95	Commander of Kuestenverteidigung at Bloemendaal, Texel(Neth.)4.45	MURDER	NETH.
NEUMANN	906100	M	Ger.		SS, Sturmmann, CC in Charge of Police Dogs, Alderney CC (Channel Is) and Kortemark CC (Czech.) 42-45	MURDER	CZECH.
NEUMANN, Albert	199001	M			Sgt., Kgf.Arb.Bn.188,II, Fjell (Nor.) 43	TORTURE	NOR.
NEUMANN, Alexander	655	M	Ger.		Camp-Warder, CC Auschwitz-Birkenau (Pol.) 40	MURDER	FR.
NEUMANN, Erich	191340	M		95	Major, K.G.F. Arbeits Bn.202, Lonsdal, Krokelva, Bjornelva (Nor.)	MURDER	NOR.
NEUMANN, Ernst	262261	M	Ger.	28.4.23	Hptsturmfhr, 5 SS Armoured Bde, Breviandes, Bucheres, St.Savine, La Riviere de Corps, Troyes (Aube) (Fr.) 8.44	BRUTALITY	FR.
NEUMANN, Frans	250402	M			Foreman, Camp Dora, Nordhausen (Ger.)	BRUTALITY	FR.

NAME	C.R.FILE NUMBER	SEX	NATIO-NALITY	DATE OF BIRTH	RANK OCCUPATION UNIT PLACE AND DATE OF CRIME	REASON WANTED	WANTED BY
NEUMANN, Franz	300352	M	Ger.		Employee, attached to Dora Camp and Factory from C.C. Buchenwald (Ger.) 43-45	MURDER	FR.
NEUMANN, Fritz	195159	M	Ger.	19.10.03	Untersturmfhr., SS, Member, Employee, Gestapo, Kolin (Czech.) 39-45	TORTURE	CZECH.
NEUMANN, Gerhart	255472	M	Ger.	05	Oberwachtmeister-Schupo, Schutzpolizei, SA-Sturmfhr., SA-Sturm, NSDAP, Prague, Kobylisk (Czech.) 41	MURDER	CZECH.
NEUMANN, Hans Hendrik	62456	M	Ger.		Head of NSDAP, Reichskommissar (Nor.)	MURDER	U.N.W.C.C.
NEUMANN, Josef	193332	M	Ger.		Sturmmann, 4.SS-Totenkopf-Sturmbann, C.C. Mittelbau - Dora, Nordhausen, Auschwitz (Ger., Pol.) 43-45	INTERR.	U.S.
NEUMANN, Margit	301957	F	Ger.		Asst. of Prof. Dr. Clauberg, C.C. Auschwitz (Pol.) 43-44	BRUTALITY	POL.
NEUMANN, Maria (see SCHWESTER MARIE)	305085	F	Ger.		Nurse, Hospital Camp, Member, NSDAP, Vrasselt, Emmerich, Wijnbergen (Neth.) 10.44- 3.45	TORTURE	NETH.
NEUMANN, Max	250400	M	Ger.		Officer, Gestapo, Lille (Fr.) 40-44	MURDER	FR.
NEUMANN, Otto	151518	M	Ger.		Lt.-Gen., Gren.Staffel (Ger.) 41-42	WITNESS	U.S.
NEUMANN, Richard	255922	M			Pvt., C.C. Ellrich, Nordhausen (Ger.)	MURDER	U.S.
NEUMANN, Richard	255923	M			Sgt., C.C. Osterh.-Rottleber, Nordhausen (Ger.)	MURDER	U.S.
NEUMANN, Fred (Siegfried)	6569	M			SS-Standartenfhr., (Ger.)	MURDER	CZECH.
NEUMANN, Siegfried	137547	M			Hauptscharfhr., SS, C.C. Weimar-Buchenwald (Ger.)	MURDER	U.S.
NEUMANN, Willy	251174	M	Ger.		Sgt., 377.Jg.Regt., 12.Coy., Vinkt-Meigem (Bel.) 5.40	MURDER	BEL.
NEUMARKER	251168	M			General-Director, Heinkel-Aircraft Industry, C.C. Oranienburg (Ger.)	INTERR.	BEL.
NEUMEIER	305086	M	Ger.		Head of Sicherheitspolizei, Sicherheitspolizei at Utrecht Hoogland near Amersfoort (Neth.) 9.44	MURDER	NETH.
NEULEIER, Otto	12570	M			Pvt., 110. or 111.Panz.Gren.Regt., 2.Coy., Albine (Fr.) 6.44	MURDER	FR.
NEUMENN, Erna	252561	F	Ger.	07	Civil - Labour, Siemens-factory, C.C. Ravensbrueck (Ger.)	BRUTALITY	FR.
NEUMEYER,	194860	M	Ger.		Police-Director, Police, Luxembourg (Lux.)	TORTURE	LUX.
NEUMULLER	146961	M	Ger.		Untersturmfhr., SS, Panz.Div. "Das Reich", Montauban (Fr.) 44	MURDER	FR.
NEUNER, Joseph	256505	M		10	Hauptscharfhr., SS	MURDER	U.S.
NEUNOBLE	124637	M		95	Farmer, Civilian, Beltershain (Ger.) 12.44	MURDER	U.S.
NEUNZIG, Hans	121002	M	Ger.		Cpl., Feldgendarmerie, Arlou (Bel.) 8.44	MURDER	U.K.
NEUFAUER, Emil	132190	M	Ger.		15.Army, 326. Div., 752.Gren.Regt., 2 B, 6.Coy., Caumont (Fr.) 7.44	WITNESS	U.K.
NEUFERT, Rudolph	12502	M	Ger.		Pvt., Pz.Gren.Regt.110 or 111, 2.Coy., Albine (Fr.) 6.44	MURDER	FR.
NEURAUTHER	305205	M	Ger.		Crim.Employee, Gestapo, Hagen (Ger.) 4.45	MURDER	U.K.
NEUFEUTHER	67718	M	Ger.	90	Lt., Arb.Kdo., Benghazi (North-Africa) 41-44	TORTURE	U.K.
NEURICHT, Guenther	255921	M			Pvt., C.C. Ellrich, Nordhausen (Ger.)	MURDER	U.S.
NEUSCHUB	126981	M	Ger.		Unterscharfhr., SS, C.C. Buchenwald (Ger.)	TORTURE	FR.
NEUSCHWANGER	195959	M			Zugwachtmeister, Shirmeck (Fr.)	TORTURE	FR.
NEUSIELD, Joseph	12503	M	Ger.		Pvt., 110. or 111.Panz.Gren.Regt., 2.Coy., Albine (Fr.) 6.44	MURDER	FR.
NEUSSBERGER	195958	M			Lt., Camp de Shirmeck (Fr.) 40-44	TORTURE	FR.
NEUSTADT, Oswald	169497	M	Ger.	01	Sgt., Land.Schtz.Bn.298, 2.Coy., Ohringen (Ger.) 3.41	INTERR.	U.K.
NEUSUS, Hans	167105	M	Ger?	15	Sgt., 159.Inf.Div., Regt.1210, Cernay (Fr.) 45	MURDER	FR.
NEUWIRTH	174087	M			Gestapoleitstelle, C.C. Brno, Auschwitz, Birkenau (Pol.,Czech.) 39-45	MURDER	CZECH.
NEUWIRTH	251822	M	Ger.		Cpl., 1.Regt. Caucasien Volunteers, Cambounes (Fr.) 7.44	TORTURE	FR.
NEUWIRTH, Franz	193948	M		98	Untersturmfhr., 4.SS-Totenkopfsturmbann, Mittelbau Nordhausen (Ger.)	MISC.CRIMES	U.S.
NEWE, Eric Theodore or LE NEGUS	189643	M	Ger.	17. 7.99	Member, Driver, Gestapo, Digne (Fr.) 6.-8.44	TORTURE	FR.
NEWGEBAUER (see NEUGEBAUER)	251615						
NEWIS	151520	M			Civilian, Schladen and Buchladen (Ger.) 9.44	TORTURE	U.S.
NEWMAN, Walter	124096	M	Ger.		Ortsgruppenleiter, NSDAP, Arb.Kdo. 234, Neundorf - Pirna (Ger.) 4.45	MISC.CRIMES	U.K.
NEY	251185	M	Ger.		Capt., Cmdt., Sicherheitsbereich, Overijse, Green-Police, Hengelo (Neth.) 4.43	INTERR.	NETH.
NEY, Margarete	135287	F		16	Civilian, Biertringen (Lux.) 7.44	WITNESS	U.S.
NEY, W.	307184	M			Capt., Cmdt., Ordnungspolizei, Sicherungsbereich Overijssel (Neth.) 43	MURDER	NETH.
NEYE, Adolf	305678	M			Member of C.C.personnel, Leitmeritz near Flossenburg, Hersbrueck, Wolkenburg, Genacker (Czech., Ger.) 1.42-5.45	MURDER	U.S.
NEYER	300694	M	Ger.		Public-Prosecutor, Oberstaatsanwaltschaft, Ministry of State Department of Justice, Prague, Bohemia and Moravia (Czech.) 2.40	MISC.CRIMES	CZECH.
NEZZLER (see MEZZLER)	161925						
NHOFFER, Franz	251190	M	Ger.		Employee, Gestapo, Limoges (Fr.)	INTERR.	FR.
NICHER	193816	F	Ger.		Guard, C.C. Ravensbrueck (Ger.)	TORTURE	FR.
NICHMANN	305207	M	Ger.		Dr., Medical Officer, attached to C.C. Neckarelz and Neckargerach (Ger.) 42-45	TORTURE	FR.
NICHOY	257019	M	Ger.		Lt., 5.Pol.Regt., 392.Bn., Orasac Gruza, Kragujevac (Yugo.) 42-44	MURDER	YUGO.
NICHUSEN	10488	M	Ger.		Crim.Secr., Gestapo, Cuxhaven (Ger.) 3.45	MURDER	U.S.
NICKE, Paul	140871	M	Ger.	04	Zollsekretaer, Civilian, Elten (Ger.) 9.44	WITNESS	CAN.
NICKEL	193043	M	Ger.		Lt., 3.Coy., Bau-Pionier-Bn. 428, (Nor.)	MURDER	NOR.
NICKEL	251189	M	Ger.		Hauptscharfhr., SS, Gestapo, Annecy Post, La Chablas (Fr.) 5.44	MISC.CRIMES	FR.
NICKEL	900409	M	Ger.		Lt., 1/98. Mountain-Bn., Le Chablais (Fr.) 5.44	MISC.CRIMES	FR.
NICKEL, Franz	193947	M		96	Unterscharfhr., 4.SS-Totenkopfsturmbann, C.C. Nordhausen, Auschwitz (Ger., Pol.)	MISC.CRIMES	U.S.
NICKEL, Hans	251616	M	Ger.		SS-Oberscharfhr., S.D., Toulouse (Fr.) 11.42- 8.44	MISC.CRIMES	FR.
NICKEL, W.E.	195147	M	Ger.	28. 5.92	Agent, Gestapo, Avereest (Neth.)	MISC.CRIMES	NETH.
NICKELS, Jany	251189	M	Ger.		Engaged in treatment of sick, C.C. Buchenwald (Ger.)	BRUTALITY	FR.
NICKENIG, Phil.	192754	M			Sgt., Schupo, C.C. Falstad (Nor.) 41-44	MURDER	NOR.
NICKERL VON RAGENFELD, Olga Maria (nee KENDIK)	190054	F	Ger.	29.12.82	Member, S.D., Gestapo, Pisek (Czech.) 37-45	MISC.CRIMES	CZECH.
NICKERMANN	185910		Ger.		Dr., C.C. Neckarelz (Ger.)	MURDER	U.S.
NICKL	252555	M			Hauptscharfhr., O.C. Abt. II.C. I Sipo, SS, Bruessel (Bel.)	MISC.CRIMES	BEL.
NICKLOCHECK	24892	M			Capt., C.C. Haydebreck (Ger.) 2.42- 1.45	MISC.CRIMES	U.K.
NICKMANN	185909	M	Ger.		Dr., C.C. Neckarelz (Ger.)	MURDER	U.S.
NICKOLSHAUSER	196751	M	Ger.		Sturmfhr., 3.Panz.Gren.Regt., SS, Mazeres - Marsoulas (Fr.) 6.44	INTERR.	FR.
NICOLAI or NICOLA	121126	M	Ger.	15	Unterscharfhr., S.D. Vichy Abt. 4 2 A, Bourg Lastig (Fr.) 7.44	MURDER	FR.
NICOLAI or FREDDY	188388	M	Ger.		Feldgendarm, Feldgendarmerie, Jalhay - Surister Verviers (Bel.) 10.43	MISC.CRIMES	BEL.
NICOLAI, Bob	261950	M	Ger.		Member, NSDAP, H.J., (Bel.) 40-44	MISC.CRIMES	BEL.
NICOLAIEFF, Alex (see NICOLAYE)	250401	M	Ger. Russ.				
NICOLAUS	1447	M	Ger.		Lt., Inf.Regt. 194.	MISC.CRIMES	U.K.

NAME	C.R.FILE NUMBER	SEX	NATIO-NALITY	DATE OF BIRTH	RANK OCCUPATION UNIT PLACE AND DATE OF CRIME	REASON WANTED	WANTED BY
NICOLAYE, Alex (or NICOLAIEFF)	250401	M	Ger., Russ.		Capt., Colonne Russo-Allemande, Chaumont, Caserne Fuch, l'Ain (Fr.) 7.44	MISC.CRIMES	FR.
NICOLE	196441	M	Ger.		Lt., Gebirgs-Jaeger, 157.Div., Plateau des Glieres (Fr.) 3.44-4.44	INTERR.	FR.
NICOLETT, Albert	151508	M			Oberwachtmstr.der Polizei, Bressanone (It.)	MURDER	U.S., U.K.
NICOLSHAUSER	126977	M	Ger.		Usturmfhr., SS-Panz.Div."Das Reich", Venerque le Vernet (Fr.) 44	MURDER	FR.
NICOT, Paul	104886	M			Wachtmstr., worked for the Special-Cmdo. at Suttrof, Arnsberg-Lippstedt (Ger.) 3.45	MURDER	U.S.
NIDEL, Kurt	194510	M	Ger.	01	Under-Chief, Gestapo, Bourget, Savigny-en-Septaine (Fr.) 7.44-8.44	MURDER	FR.
NIDESWETTER	301591	M	Ger.		Dr., Osturmfhr., SS, stationed at C.C. Mauthausen (Aust.) 40-45	MURDER	BEL.
NIDSKI	657	M	Ger.		Oberwachtmstr., Police, C.C. Falstad (Nor.) 40-43	TORTURE	NOR.
NIEB	188962	M	Ger.		Uschfhr., SS, C.C., Flossenburg (Ger.)	MURDER	FR.
NIEBAN	250403	M	Ger.		Commissar, Head of Department (Abt.IV N) Maribor (Yugo.) 44	MURDER	YUGO.
NIEBEL	658	M	Ger.	10	Unterfhr., Waffen-SS, Conc.Camp, Grini (Nor.) 42	MISC.CRIMES	NOR.
NIEBELING	300527	M	Ger.	08	Hptfw., Senior N.C.O., Hospital compound Stalag XI - B, Fallingbostel (Ger.) 10.44-4.45	BRUTALITY	U.K.
NIEBLING	67717	M	Ger.		Sgt., Stalag XI B, Conc.Camp, Fallingbostel, Leipzig Stalag (Ger.) 44	TORTURE	U.K.
NIEBUHR	12504	M	Ger.		Sgt., 110.or 111.Pz.Gren.Rgt.,Stellv.Zugfhr.,3.Zug, Gourdan (Fr.) 6.44	MURDER	FR.
NIEBURG, Wilhelm	130162	M	Ger.	07	N.C.O., Inf.Rgt.744, Inf.Div.711, Chateau-Granges,Dives-sur-Mer, 6.44	MURDER	U.K.
NIEDBALLA	255702	M			Uschfhr., C.C. Dora, Nordhausen (Ger.)	MURDER	U.S.
NIEDER	185494	M	Ger.		Hptschfhr., SS, Secr., Gestapo, Saarbruecken (Ger.)	PILLAGE	FR.
NIEDERMAIER, Michel	12505	M			Pvt.,110.or 111.Pz.Gren.Rgt.,2.Coy., Albine (Fr.) 6.44	MURDER	U.K.
NIEDERMAYER	129761	M			Sgt., Waffen-SS, Conc.Camp, Mauthausen (Aust.).41-45	MURDER	U.S.
NIEDERMEIER	256078	M	Ger.		Pvt., SS, Muehldorf (Ger.)	WITNESS	U.S.
NIEDERMEYER	1729	M			Schfhr., SS,. Dachau (Ger.)	MISC.CRIMES	U.K.
NIEDERWANGER	141353	M	Ger.		Agent, Abwehr (Sabotage Unit) Innsbruck (Aust.)	MISC.CRIMES	U.K.
NIEDERWIPPER, Hubert	255925	M			Flyer, C.C. Ellrich, Nordhausen (Ger.)	MURDER	U.S.
NIEDNER	104887	M	Ger.	11	Osturmbannfhr., 6.Waffen-SS Mountain-Div., 1.45	MURDER	U.S.
NIEGERMAN	155642	M			Capt., Stalag III C, C.C., Kuestrin (Ger.) 1.45	TORTURE	U.S.
NIEGSCH	196877	M			Cmdt., Yves (Fr.) 9.44	INCENDIARISM	FR.
NIEHAUS	196755	M	Ger.		Capt., SD Cmdo. "Wenger", Baccarat and Etival (Fr.) 44	WITNESS	U.K.
NIEHENKE, Paul	194507	M	Ger.	07	Sturmschfhr., SS Gestapo, Crim.Secr., Stelle Bromberg,Radzyn,Lublin (Pol.) 43-44	TORTURE	POL.
NIEHOFF, Heinrich	660	M	Ger.		Gen., Oberfeldkdt., Army, Lille (Fr.) 7.42	MISC.CRIMES	FR., U.K., U.S.
NIEHOFF, Heinz	301854	M	Ger.		Member, SS, Tank-Gren.,12.A.u.E.Bn. or SS 7.Stamm-Tank A.u.E.12, Anhee (Bel.) 9.44	TORTURE	BEL.
NIELAND	72145	M	Ger.	02	Ortsgr.Leiter, NSDAP, Roermond (Neth.) 9.44-11.44	MISC.CRIMES	U.S.
NIELAS	661	M	Ger.		Capt., Army	WITNESS	FR.
NIELAS (see NIKLAS)	122717						
NIEMAND, Albert	173914	M	Ger.		Construction-worker, Firm: Josef Klug, Krakau (Pol.) 7.43	MISC.CRIMES	U.S.
NIEMANN	186011	M			Oberfhr., Chief, SS and Sipo, Rhein-Westmark (Ger.) 44-45	MISC.CRIMES	U.S.
NIEMANN, Bernard	162676	M	Ger.		Major, 10.Panz.Div.,36.Panz.Rgt., Revin)Fr.) 6.44	MURDER	FR.
NIEMANN, Johannes	174771	M	Ger.	85	Leader, Organ.Todt, Matre-Maasfjord (Nor.) 42	WITNESS	NOR.
NIEMETZ, August	29699	M	Ger.		Landgerichtsrat, Ministry of Justice, Public Official,Litomerice (Czech.) 40	MURDER	CZECH.
NIEMEYER	155490	M	Ger.	96	Cpl., Lds.Schtz.Bn.610, Conc.Camp, Marienburg (Ger.) 6.44	MURDER	U.K.
NIEMEYER	305730	M	Ger.		Rottfhr., Transportfhr., "Gute Hoffnung"-Cmdo.,C.C. Auschwitz-Birkenau (Pol.) 40	MURDER	FR.
NIEMIEZ, Paul	196752	M		15.7.84	Merchant, Civilian, Amstetten (Aust.) 3.45	MISC.CRIMES	U.S.
NIEMIJER	256362	M	Ger.		Cpl., Navy, Werkendam (Neth.) 4.45	MURDER	NETH.
NIENAU, Richard	189057	M	Ger.	2.2.06	Crim.Asst. Gestapo, SD, SS, Mlada Boleslav (Czech.) 39-45	MURDER	CZECH.
NIENDORFE, Hans	306253	M	Ger.	12.1.00	Oschfhr., Chief, Sipo, Mosjoeen (Nor.) 5.42-12.43	TORTURE	NOR.
NIER, Max	255917	M	Ger.	30.11.95	Informer, Gestapo, Kraslice (Czech.) 43-45	MISC.CRIMES	CZECH.
NIERATSCHLER, Hugo	193950	M	Ger.	09	Ortsgr.Leiter, NSDAP, Employee,Gestapo,Opavan Karbory Nary (Czech.)	TORTURE	CZECH.
NIERCKENS (see MEARKINS)	137594						
NIERENHOTHER, Karl	140797	M	Ger.		Ortsgr.Leiter,NSDAP, Member by Civ.-Farmer, Fritztar (Ger.)	TORTURE	U.S.
NIERING, Richard	255926	M		20.6.03	Rottfhr., C.C. Harzungen, Nordhausen (Ger.)	MURDER	U.S.
NIERS, Nicolas	151509	M	Ger.		Civilian, Simmern (Ger.) 8.44	WITNESS	U.S.
NIERZWICKI, Hans	196878	M	Ger.		Uschfhr., SS, Conc.Camp, Auschwitz (Pol.) 12.42	MURDER	FR.
NIES	133278	M	Ger.		Oschfhr., Waffen-SS Totenkopf-Stuba., Flossenburg (Ger.) 44	MURDER	U.S., FR.
NIESCH	194508	M			Senior N.O.,12.Coy.,Fieldres,Bn.114,Montesquieu de Lautogais (Fr.)8.44	PILLAGE	FR.
NIESEN	139057	M	Ger.		Oberstabsarzt, Stalag 6 G, Siegburg (Ger.) 10.44	TORTURE	U.S.
NIESL	196438	M	Ger.		Sgt., Gebirgsjaeger Div.157, Plateau des Glieres (Fr.) 3.44-4.44	MISC.CRIMES	FR.
NIESNER, Oscar	151510	M	Ger.		Rottfhr., 1.SS-Pz.Div., 2.Pz.Gren.Rgt., Stavelot-Malmedy (Bel.) 12.44	MURDER	U.S.
NIESSLER, Wilhelm	193278	M	Ger.		Crim.Secr., Gestapo, Brusnn (Czech.) 39-45	MURDER	CZECH.
NIESSNER	192159	M	Ger.		Sgt., Geh.Feldpolizei, Gent (Bel.)	TORTURE	BEL.
NIESSNER, Oskar	261084	M	Ger.	11.7.23	Sgt., SS, Waffen-SS L.A.H.,Div."Das Reich" (Fr.) 42-44	MURDER	FR.
NIETCHE	104890	M	Ger.	04	Member, SS-Mann, Volkssturm, Stalag IX C, Rentsmuhle (Ger.) 12.41-12.42	TORTURE	U.K.
NIETMANN, Georg	195146	M	Ger.		Director of the Omnia Treuhand-Ges. (Holland) 40-45	PILLAGE	NETH.
NIETNER	251178	M	Ger.		Lt., 95.Security-Rgt.-SS, St.Germain,Chameyrat (Fr.) 7.44	MURDER	FR.
NIETNER	251817	M	Ger.		Lt., 19.Rgt., SS-Police, Panirignes (Fr.) 7.44	MISC.CRIMES	FR.
NIETOSKTAEK, Walter	155487	M			Sturmbn. A.O.K.1, Courselles sur Nied (Fr.) 11.44	INTERR.	U.S.
NIETSCH	141069	M	Ger.		Oschfhr., Waffen-SS, C.C., Natzweiler, Struthof (Fr.) 6.43	TORTURE	U.K.
NIETSCH	261171	M	Ger.		Pvt.,5.Ln.Rgt.211,139.Arb.Ber.Liane, Alleur-Lez-Liege (Bel.) 9.44	MURDER	BEL.
NIETSCHE	662	M			Gestapo, Maastricht (Neth.) 3.44-4.44	TORTURE	NETH.
NIETSCHE	155489	M	Ger.	10	Lt., SD, Helden (Neth.) 8.45	MURDER	NETH.
NIETSCHE	306425	M	Ger.	04	Abt.Fhr., Works-manager, SA-quarry,Volkssturm-SS,Rentzmuehle (Ger.)42	BRUTALITY	U.K.
NIETSCHKE	192752	M	Ger.		Sgt., Schupo, C.C. Falstad (Nor.) 41-44	TORTURE	NOR.
NIETSCHKE	251184	M	Ger.		Capt., Army, 13.SS-Police-Rgt., Ferlach (Aust.) 44-45	MURDER	YUGO.
NIETSCHMANN	193370	M	Ger.		Dr., Stabsarzt, Airforce, Uthaug Orlandet (Nor.) 9.41-9.42	WITNESS	NOR.
NIETSCHE	306426	M	Ger.	95	Lt., Camp-Cmdt.,348.Btty.Landschutz, Klausberg, 7.40-1.45	BRUTALITY	U.K.
NISTURA	260062	M	Ger.		Sturmfhr., SS, Belgrad (Yugo.) 1.44-9.44	MISC.CRIMES	YUGO.
NIETZ	167106	M	Ger.		Pvt., Army, Bachivillers (Fr.)	WITNESS	FR.
NIETZINGER	251825	M	Ger.		Pvt., 100.Alpine-Rgt., Feisson sur Isere (Fr.) 8.44	MURDER	FR.
NIEUWENHUIZEN	307185	M	Ger.		Member of the Sipo Almelo District (Neth.) 9.44-2.45	TORTURE	NETH.
NIEWEG	257898	M	Ger.		Sgt., 150.Panz.Bde., Meuse-Bridge-Antwerp (Bel.) 12.44	MISC.CRIMES	U.S.
NIEZCHLAG	258217	M	Ger.		Lt.Col., 17.SS-Div., 37.Rgt., Merzig (Ger.)	MURDER	U.S.

NIE-NOL

NAME	C.R.FILE NUMBER	SEX	NATIO-NALITY	DATE OF BIRTH	RANK OCCUPATION UNIT PLACE AND DATE OF CRIME	REASON WANTED	WANTED BY
NIEZOLDI	39592	M	Ger.		Col.,Army,Verbindg.Stab,Ecole en Beauges (Fr.) 1.5.44	MURDER	FR.
NIEZURAWSKI,(or NIEZYRAWSKI)	193014	M	Ger.	05	Werkfhr.,Guard,Reichsjustizministerium,Feldstraflager,SS,C.C., Finmark (Nor.) 42-45	MISC.CRIMES	NOR.
NIGGL, Franz	307186	M	Ger.		Reichsbahn official,Fermeldemeisterei,office at Amersfoort,(Neth.) 4.10.44-5.45	PILLAGE	NETH.
NIKLANS	136327	M	Ger.		Chief,Gendarmerie,Hamelburg (Ger.) 44	MURDER	U.S.
NIKLAS (or NIKLAS)	122717	M	Ger.		Major,Feldkommandantur,Dax (Fr.) 13.6.44	MURDER	FR.
NIKLAS, Wilhelm	301216	M	Ger.		Krs.Stabfhr.,Buchenfeld,Dillweissenstein (Ger.) 17.-18.3.45	MURDER	U.K.
NIKLOJER	10157	M	Ger.	95	Capt.,Army,Heydebreck (Ger.) 42-45	MISC.CRIMES	U.K.
NIKLOWITZ, Heinrich	196756	M	Ger.	16.5.97	Luxembourg (Grand-Duchy)	MISC.CRIMES	LUX.
NIKOLAI	162215	M	Ger.	13	Hptschfhr.,SS,C.C.,Buchenwald (Ger.) 44-45	WITNESS	U.S.
NIKOLAUS	256559	M			Chief of Sub.Sec.,Mittelwerk,C.C.,Nordhausen (Ger.)	MURDER	U.S.
NIKOLAUS, Klaus	190243	M	Ger.		Gestapo, H.Q.,Koeln (Ger.) 43-45	MURDER	U.K.
NIKOTIN, Josef	255930	M		17.9.26	Flyer,C.C.,Ellrich,Nordhausen (Ger.)	MURDER	U.S.
NILL, Karl	133277	M			Oschfhr.,Waffen SS,Prisoner Hospital,Flossenburg (Ger.)	MURDER	U.S.
NILSSON, Hermann	251175	M	Ger.		377.Jg.Rgt.,10.Coy.,Vinkt,Meigem (Bel.) 25.-31.5.40	MURDER	BEL.
NIMENLINE (or HIMMELMANN)	301697	M	Ger.		Senior,N.C.O.,or officer,05-243 Mongolian "Oberland" Unit, St.Nazaire en Royans (Fr.) 20.7.-5.8.44	MURDER	FR.
NIMITZ	67716	M	Ger.		Cpl.,Interpreter,Landesschuetzen Bn.439,1.Coy.,Bayreuth (Ger.) 11.4.45	MURDER	U.K.
NIMMOCHECK	151511	M	Ger.		Civilian,C.C.,Brux (Czech.) 2.6.44	TORTURE	U.K.
NINHAUS	196874	M			Uschfhr.,C.C.,Auschwitz (Pol.) 40	MURDER	FR.
NINIRCHUER	104889	M	Ger.		Major,Gestapo,Obergruppenfhr.,SS,Konstanz (Ger.) 20.7.44	MURDER	U.S.
NINK	252558	M	Ger.		Lt.,Div.Hermann Goering,4.Rgt.,Fallschirmjaeger,(Rgt.Grassmel) Helchtern and Hechtel (Bel.) 5.-11.44	MISC.CRIMES	BEL.
NIOF	195956	M	Ger.		General,Commandantur,Breslau (Ger.) 45	MURDER	FR.
NIPPGEN	129760	M			Hptschfhr.,Waffen SS,Div.Totenkopf,scull and crossbones organisation C.C.,Mauthausen (Aust.) 41-45	MURDER	U.S.
NIPPKE	252560	M	Ger.		Doctor,General,Oberstabsarzt,Professor,Medic.,C.C.,Dachau (Bel.)3.42	TORTURE	BEL.
NIPPL, Jan or Johann	189056	M	Ger.	1.3.99	Agent,SD,National Estate and Forestery Administration,Trebon (Czech.) 39-45	MURDER	CZECH.
NIPPLER	136289	M			Cpl.,Feldgendarmerie de Verdun,Stenay (Fr.) 5.8.44	MURDER	FR.
NIRK, Herta	193276	F	Ger.		Clerk,Gestapo,Bruenn,(Czech.) 39-45	MURDER	CZECH.
NISSEN,Diederich	251176	M	Ger.		Pvt.377.Jaeger Rgt.,10.Coy.,Vinkt,Meigem (Bel.) 25.-30.5.40	MURDER	BEL.
NISSOFFEN	190610	M			Commandant,German Army,Hameau de Liard (Fr.) 25.7.44	MURDER	FR.
NISZL	307187	M	Ger.		Lt.,Command of A.VI Btty.,F.P.No.L 55975 L.G.P.A. Una WF.,Laren (Neth.) 4.11.44-22.2.45	PILLAGE	NETH.
NITCHE, Kurt	146979	M	Ger.		Cpl.,SS Panz.Div."Das Reich",La Croix-Falgarde (Fr.) 44	MURDER	FR.
NITCHEFF	142538	M			Lt.General,Freiw.Stamm Div.,La Parade,Badaroux (Fr.) 27.-29.5.44	MURDER	FR.
NITCHZE	155511	M	Ger.	95	Lt.,O.Cmdt.,Landesschuetzen Bn.348,N.51,C.C. Klausberg (Ger.) 2.43	TORTURE	U.K.
NITSCH	258703	M			Hptsturmfhr.,SS,2.Bn.,38.SS Rgt.,"Goetz von Berlichingen" Div., Kemnat (Ger.) 20.10.44	WITNESS	U.S.
NITSCH, Robert	30186	M	Ger.	9.9.99	Oschfhr.,C.C.,Natzweiler (Fr.) 26.8.44	MURDER	U.S.
NITSCHE	104891	M			Oschfhr.,SS,NSDAP,Maastricht,(Neth.) 7.2.44	MISC.CRIMES	U.S.
NITSCHE	188472	M	Ger.		Doctor,Civilian,Professor,Chief medical,C.C.,Beelitz (Ger.)	MISC.CRIMES	CZECH.
NITSCHE, Richard	251186	M	Ger.		Rottfhr.,SS,C.C.,Buchenwald (Ger.)	INTERR.	FR.
NITSKKE	184224	M			Officer,Heeres Kuesten Art.,Crete (Grc.) 5.44	MURDER	GRC.
NITTEL, Jony	194509	M	Ger.	04	Agent,Gestapo,Bourges,Savigny en Septaine (Fr.) 7.-8.44	MURDER	FR.
NITZ, Emil	252557	M	Ger.		Prison,Guard,Lageraeltester,Wilhelmshaven,(Ger.) 27.7.44	BRUTALITY	FR.
NITZSCHE	174168	M	Ger.		General,Army,Oberkommando,Tarbes,Toulouse (Fr.) 10.6.44	MURDER	FR.
NITZWETZKI,	257897	M			Pvt.,150.Panz.Bde.,Meusebridge Antwerpen (Bel.) 12.44	MISC.CRIMES	U.S.
NOACK	104892	M	Ger.	95	Major,Chief of R.A.L.,Harbach or Ettingshausen (Ger.) 9.44	MURDER	U.S.
NOACK, Johann	255929	M			Cpl.,C.C.,Ellrich,Nordhausen (Ger.)	MURDER	U.S.
NOACK, Otto	260040	M	Ger.		Gendarm,Unit,Russia-Germany,Div."Oberland",Massif du Vercors,Isere and Drome (Fr.) 24.7.-5.8.44	SUSPECT	FR.
NOACK, Werner	167773	M			Expert,Einsatzstab Rosenberg, Dr., (Fr.) 40-44	PILLAGE	FR.
NOBAUER	307189	M	Ger.		Oschfhr.,SS C.C.,Auschwitz (Pol.) 41-45	BRUTALITY	POL.
NOBERHEIT	165957	M	Ger.		Adjutant,Civilian prison,Charleroi (Bel.) 44	TORTURE	BEL.
NOCHEM, Paul	250395	M	Ger.		Member,Gestapo,Lille (Fr.) 40-44	MURDER	FR.
NOCHLER, Otto	255928	M		26.2.05	Pvt.,C.C.,Harzungen,Nordhausen (Ger.)	MURDER	U.S.
NOCHTER	251172	M			1.SS Pz.Rgt.,1.Coy.,Malmedy (Bel.) 17.12.44	MURDER	U.S.
NOE, Adolf	192709	M	Ger.		Civilian,C.C.,Buchenwald (Ger.) 42-45	TORTURE	U.S.
NOE, Max	251193	M	Ger.		Sgt.,Field-police,Grenoble,Rives (Fr.) 21.7.44	INTERR.	FR.
NOEDING	261335	M			Capt.,Chief,Kreiskommandantur,Vire (Fr.) 8.7.44	INTERR.	FR.
NOELD (er HOELD)	195955	M	Ger.		Lt.,Parachute unit of la Courtine camp,Correze (Fr.) 9.3.44	WITNESS	FR.
NOELL	62458	M	Ger.		Osturmfhr.,SS,high official of commissanat for German racialism	MISC.CRIMES	U.N.W.C.C.
NOELL	151544	M			Capt.,Army,29.Panz.Gren.Div.,15.Rgt.,	WITNESS	U.S.
NOELL	195687	M	Ger.		Lt.,Volksturm	MISC.CRIMES	U.S.
NOELL, Werner	187720	M	Ger.		Osturmfhr.,SS,commissariat for German radicalism,(Ger.) 40-45	MISC.CRIMES	U.N.W.C.C.
NOELLE	174089	M			Regierungsrat,Osturmbannfhr.,SS,Gestapoleitstelle,Brnon, Auschwitz,Birkenau (Czech.,Pol.) 39-45	MURDER	CZECH.
NOELLE, Friedrich	151523	M		98	Civilian,Lomitz (Ger.) 23.9.45	TORTURE	U.S.
NOELLE, Wilhelm	192550	M	Ger.	26.1.04	Regierungsrat,Gestapo,government concellor,Bruenn,(Czech.) 39-45	SUSPECT	CZECH.
NOEMEIER, Rudolf	12507	M	Ger.		Pvt.,Army,110.or 11.Panz.Gren.Rgt., 2.Coy.,Albine (Fr.) 29.6.44	MURDER	FR.
NOEPPEL, Martin Karl	251818	M	Ger.	28.5.08	Uschfhr.,Gestapo,Bourg Lastic (Fr.) 9.7.44	MISC.CRIMES	FR.
NOESER	155494	M	Ger.		Vorarbeiter,Arbeitskommando 22,Boehlen Stalag 4G (Ger.) 10.-15.4.45	TORTURE	U.K.
NOGLIK, Ernst	62410	M	Ger.		Cpl.,Kapo,C.C.,Gandersheim (Ger.) 6.4.45	MURDER	U.S.
NOHL	142536	M	Ger.		Doctor,Gestapo,(Gestapo service recuparation des Oeuvres d'Art) (Service Central a Paris-Section 6 ou 1) Cannes (Fr.)	PILLAGE	FR.
NOHR, Kurt	262262	M		30.9.15	Osturmfhr.,SS,51.SS Armoured Bde.,Breviandes,Bucheres,St.Savine, La Riviere de Corps (Aube) 22.-25.8.44	BRUTALITY	FR.
NOHRING, Otto	251813	M		06	Inspector,SD,Alencon (Fr.) 40-44	INTERR.	FR.
NOJER	163867	M			Interpreter,Army 184,Work Bn.,P.O.W.,Kroken (Nor.)	TORTURE	NOR.
NOLDE, Oskar	57818	M	Ger.	95	Local group leader,NSDAP,Angerburg (Ger.) 11.44	MISC.CRIMES	U.S.
NOLL	174293	M			Lt.,Lager officer,Oflag 55 VD,Anlendorf (Ger.) 8.42	MURDER	YUGO.
NOLL, Karl Heinrich	195375	M	Ger.		Farmer,Civilian,Medenbach near Wiesbaden (Ger.) 3.40-4.45	TORTURE	POL.
NOLLE	255697	M	Ger.		Osturmbannfhr.,SS,chief of Gestapo,Brne (Czech.)	INTERR.	U.K.

NAME	C.R.FILE NUMBER	SEX	NATIO-NALITY	DATE OF BIRTH	RANK OCCUPATION UNIT PLACE AND DATE OF CRIME	REASON WANTED	WANTED BY
NOLLENBERGER, Hans	12506	M	Ger.		Pvt., Army, 110 or 111 Pz.Gren.Rgt., 2 Coy, Albine (Fr.) 6.44	MURDER	FR.
NOLLER, Karl	252554	M	Ger.		Crim. Employee, Sec.IV B, Sipo, Brussels (Bel.) 40-45	INTERR.	BEL.
NOLTE	62411	M	Ger.		Staff-Sgt., Stalag 344, CC Lamsdorf (Ger.)	MURDER	U.K.
NOLTE	145970	M			SS Oschfhr., Gestapo, Hoerde (Ger.)	MURDER	U.S.
NOLTE, Horst	185915	M	Ger.	4. 3.09	Civilian, Innkeeper, CC Lauban (Ger.) 42-45	WITNESS	U.S.
NOLTE, Karl	195957	M			Uschfhr., SS, Gestapo, Massif du Vercors (Fr.) 20.7.-5.8.44	MURDER	FR.
NOLTE, Paul	125576	M			SA Gruppenfhr., Weissenborn near Luederode (Ger.) 5.-6.44	MISC.CRIMES	U.S.
NOLTE, Peter	192732	M			SS-Mann, CC Buchenwald (Ger.) 42-45	TORTURE	U.S.
NOLTE, Wilhelm	306692	M	Ger.		Pvt., 391 Pion.Bn., 391 Inf.Div., Mijnheerenland (Neth.) 5.45	PILLAGE	NETH.
NOMENSEN	196778	M			Osturmfhr., CC Neuengamme (Ger.)	TORTURE	BEL.
NONALT	67726	M	Ger.		Col., Army, Inf., Chenebier (Fr.)	MURDER	FR.
NONNAST, Walter	192021	M	Ger.		Pvt., Navy, Werftpolizei, La Baule, St.Nazaire, Chantier de Penhoet (Fr.) 41-44	MURDER	FR.
NONNE	104893	M		05	Gestapo H.Q., Wuelfel-Ahlen (Ger.)64.45	MURDER	U.S.
NONNENBACHER	167107	M			Member Frontier Police Montigny (Fr.) 9.44	WITNESS	FR.
NOPENEKI (or NOPPENHEY) (alias NOPENHEIM)	195388	M	Ger.		Camp Chief, CC Malines (Bel.) 43	TORTURE	BEL.
NORD, Felix	251177	M	Ger.	01	Col., 25 Flak Div., 197 Flak Rgt. H.Q., Selvaggio-Giaveno (It.)20.5.44	MURDER	U.K.
NORDAN, Willy	194506	M	Ger.		SS Oschfhr, SD Einsatz-Kdo. 3 Sipo, Radom, Radzyn, Lublin (Pol.) 39-44	TORTURE	POL.
NORDEN	133280	M	Ger.	95	Dr.,civilian,German Red Cross,outer camp III.5 III,Thueringen(Ger.)	TORTURE	U.S.
NORDHANN	188961	M			Feld-Gend., Bar le Duc (Fr.) 8.44	MURDER	FR.
NORDHEIM	146978	M	Ger.		Cpl., 7 Pz.Jg.Ers.Bn. Cap Savoie (Fr.)	MURDER	FR.
NORDMANN	67714	M	Ger.		Cpl., Inf.Rgt.714, on Staff of Stalag XX A, Thorn (Pol.) 8.40	TORTURE	U.K.
NORDMANN	186501	M	Ger.		Sgt., 1 Bn. Pz.Gren.Rgt.200, Lauslebourg (Fr.) 6.-7.44	MURDER	FR.
NORDMANN	301698	M	Ger.		Feld-Gend. of Bar le Duc, Comble en Barrois (Meuse) France 20.-21.8.44, 23.8.44	MURDER	FR.
NORDSTERN	121141	M	Ger.	10	Capt., Air Force, Lds.Schtz.Rgt., 2 Bn., 5 Coy, Montjardin (Fr.) 23.5.44	TORTURE	FR.
NORICK	167772	M	Ger.		Lt., Festung, Lesneven (Fr.) 7.8.44	MURDER	FR.
NORKOFF	67713	M	Ger.		Major, Stalag VIII-B, CC Lamsdorf (Ger.)	TORTURE	U.K.
NORMANN	301217	M	Ger.		Sgt., Guard at Camp 13, Stalag XX A, Thorn (Pol.) 27.10.40	BRUTALITY	U.K.
NORMANN	167791	M	Ger.		Leader, Ministry of Food and Economics (Pol.), 9.39-44	PILLAGE	POL.
NORMANN	173916	M			Officer, Stalag VI-A, Hemer (Ger.) 41-45	TORTURE	U.S.
NORMANN, Ernst	140911	M	Ger.		Uschfhr, SS, CC Breendonck (Bel.) 42	MURDER	BEL.
NORMANN, Hans	255696	M			Section-Leader (technical) CC Dora, Nordhausen (Ger.)	MURDER	U.S.
NORMANN, Willy	151525	M			Pvt., Army, Olde (Ger.) 45	TORTURE	U.S.
NOROSCHAT (or NORUSCHAT)	669	M			Commander, Army, Dax (Fr.)	MURDER	FR.
NORR	166714	M	Ger.		Official, SS, Ministry of Justice (Ger.)	MURDER	U.S.
NORSTKOOTE (or HORSTKOOTE)	194505	M	Ger.		Adjutant, Luftgau 53-474, St.Segal (Fr.) 22.7.44	TORTURE	FR.
NORTHERMANN, Magdalene	192731	F	Ger.		Guard, SS, CC Buchenwald, Ravensbrueck (Ger.) 42-45	TORTURE	U.S.
NORTLER	196919	M	Ger.		Cpl. - Chief, Army - SS, Vercoiran (Fr.) 9.3.44	MURDER	FR.
NORTMANN, Alphonso	138315	M			Rottfhr, SS and Gestapo, Lyon (Fr.) 6.-8.44	MURDER	FR.
NORUSCHAT (or NOROSCHAT)	669	M	Ger.		Commander, Army, Dax (Fr.)	MURDER	FR.
NOSKE, Kuno	255927	M		18. 2.16	Pvt., CC Ellrich, Nordhausen (Ger.)	MURDER	U.S.
NOSKO	186012	M	Ger.		SS-Mann, W-SS, Leibstandarte "Adolf Hitler", II Zug, 1 Gruppe, Parfondruy, Stavelot (Bel.) 18.-22.12.44	MURDER	U.S., BEL.
NOSSCHETSKA	193971	M	Ger.		Capt., PoW-Working Bn.206, Mosjeen (Nor.) 2.45	MISC.CRIMES	NOR.
NOSSEK, Anton	255916	M		11. 7.04	CC Mackenrode, Nordhausen (Ger.)	MURDER	U.S.
NOSTITZ	10316	M			Osturmfhr., SS, CC Oranienburg (Ger.) 39-44	MURDER	BEL., CZECH.
NOTHAFT, Gregor	173905	M		18. 4.93	Civilian - Construction-Engineer, Crew Foreman, Firm of Josef Klug, Krakau (Pol.) 43	TORTURE	POL.
NOTHAGEL	174084	M	Ger.		Lt., Army, Doncols (Lux.) 19.12.44	MURDER	LUX.
NOTHALF	1448	M	Ger.		Lt.,Geb.Div.,5 Mtn.Div.,2 Fl.D.Repl.Depot, Army, (It.) 7.9.44	MURDER	U.K.
NOTHELFER, Anton	199604	M	Ger.	11.11.02	Gend.Meister, Gend. Oberkail, Budapest, Binsfeld (Hung.) 15.8.44	TORTURE	U.S.
NOTHEN, Karl	192729	M		16. 6.89	Otruppfhr, SA, Ginnheim (Ger.)	MURDER	U.S.
NOTHHARDT	145971	M			Army, Ludwigsburg (Ger.) 11.8.44	MISC.CRIMES	U.S.
NOTHWANG, Heidi	259637	F	Ger.		Employee, Gestapo, Angers, Maine and Loire (Fr.) 42-44	MISC.CRIMES	FR.
NOTTEBOHM	260731	M	Ger.		Senior W.O., Unit 48, I. 48 A, Div.Stab, Sabres (Fr.) 8.44	BRUTALITY	FR.
NOTTEL	250998	M		16	Bricklayer, German Army, Gerardmer (Fr.) 29.5.44	WITNESS	U.S.
NOTTHOFF, Heinrich	12508	M	Ger.		Pvt., Army, 110 or 111 Pz.Gren.Rgt., 2 Coy, Albine (Fr.) 29.6.44	MURDER	FR.
NOTWANG	151524	M	Ger.		Gestapo Agent, Bretagne, Anjou, Poitou (Fr.)	MURDER	FR.
NOUACK, Paul (or NOVAK, or OMA)	188455	M	Ger.	11	Chief, CC Neuengamme, Wilhelmshaven (Ger.) 42-45	MURDER	U.K., FR.
NOUHOLD (or NOUNOLD)	262269	M	Ger.		Sonderfuehrer, Feldkommandantur, Besancon (Fr.) 11.2.44	MISC.CRIMES	FR.
NOUMOURCHAKOFF	251194	M			Aspirant, 784 Bn. Turkestans, Clairac, Marmande, Aiguillon (Fr.) 14.-21.8.44	MISC.CRIMES	FR.
NOUNOLD (see NOUHOLD)	262263	M					
NOVACK, Paul	155499	M			Army, Wilhelmshaven (Ger.) End of Febr. ?	MURDER	U.K.
NOVAK	39563	M	Ger.		Officer, SD, Stalag 327, CC Taroslau (Pol.) 41	MURDER	SOV.UN.
NOVAK (or NOUACK), Paul or OMA	188855						
NOVAK	251169	M	Ger.		Lt.Col., CC Prenzlau (Ger.)	INTERR.	BEL.
NOVAK	255699	M	Ger.	about 20	Lt., IX Coy of 369 Rgt. "Devis-Division", Slano (near Dubrovnik) (Yugo.) 5.44	INTERR.	YUGO.
NOVAKOWSKI	190609	M			Member SS, Busset (Fr.) 7.8.44	MURDER	FR.
NOVARO (see ALVARO, A.)	72298						
NOVERMANN, Paul	258789	M	Ger.		Erkrath (Ger.) 4.11.44	WITNESS	U.S.
NOVOTNY (see SCHAFFELHOFER, Josef)	181288						
NOVOTNY, Ludwig	255474	M	Ger.	21. 6.97	Group-Leader NSDAP, SS Osturmfhr, Civilian, Kromeriz (Czech.) 44-45	MISC.CRIMES	CZECH.
NOVOTNY, Rudolf	255473	M	Ger.	29. 3.20	Shop-Asst., Civilian, C.Budejovice (Czech.) 39	MURDER	CZECH.
NOVROCKY, Adolf	192112	M	Ger.	08	Member NSDAP, Police Employee, Zadovice (Czech.) 39-42	TORTURE	CZECH.
NOWACK	192751	M	Ger.		Lt., Schupo, CC Falstad (Nor.) 41-44	MISC.CRIMES	NOR.
NOWACKE	252556	M	Ger.		SS Hptsturmfhr, Abt.III-B Sipo, Brussels (Bel.) 40-45	INTERR.	BEL.
NOWAK, Walter Gottlieb Heinrich	300722	M	Ger.		Member of Gestapo, Lyon, Sub-Section IV f, Oyonna, Ain, Attignat, Lyon surroundings (Fr.) 11.43-8.44	MURDER	FR.
NOWACKI	10317	M	Ger.	about 10	SS Oschfhr, Oranienburg,Sachsenhausen (Ger.)39-44	TORTURE	CZECH.;U.K.
NOWACKY	191488	M	Ger.		SS Oschfhr (Pol.) 39-4.45	MURDER	POL.
NOWACZEK, Emil	29700	M	Ger.		Landgerichtsrat, Public Official, Cheb (Czech.) 40	MURDER	CZECH.
NOWAK	162645	M	Ger.		Civilian, Oflag VI-B, Doessel (Ger.) 45	WITNESS	POL.
NOWAK	195563	M	Ger.		Sgt., Gend., Ostrog (Pol.) 10.42	MURDER	POL.

NAME	C.R. FILE NUMBER	SEX	NATIO-NALITY	DATE OF BIRTH	RANK OCCUPATION UNIT PLACE AND DATE OF CRIME	REASON WANTED	WANTED BY
NOWAK	251521	M	Ger.		1. Sec., 10. Coy., Rgt., "Das Reich" Limoges (Fr.) 40-45	MISC.CRIMES	FR.
NOWAK, Hans	133279	M			Hptschfhr., W-SS, C.C. Flossenburg (Ger.)	TORTURE	U.S.
NOWAK, Johann	258075	M	Ger.	16.7.06	Informer, Clerk, Gestapo Civ., Kyjov (Cze.) 39-42	MURDER	CZE.
NOWAK, Walter	251191	M	Ger.		Hptschfhr., Gestapo SS., Le Chablais (Fr.) 5.44	MISC.CRIMES	FR.
NOWAK, Walter	260568	M	Ger.		SS-Schfhr., Gestapo Lyon Isere et Drome Massif du Vercors (Fr.) 7.44-8.44	MISC.CRIMES	FR.
NOWAKY, Hans	256560	M	Ger.	30.6.06	Employee Block.5.C.C. Dora Nordhausen (Ger.)	MURDER	U.S.
NOWAKY	191214	M			Oschfhr., Guard SS., C.C.Sachsenhausen-Oranienburg (Ger.)42	MURDER	U.K.
NOWISKI	146719	M			SS-Oschfhr., C.C.Flossenburg (Ger.)	MURDER	U.S.
NOWITZ (or NOWITS)	251167	M	Ger.		Member, SD., Meppel (Neth.) 12.44	TORTURE	NETH.
NOWITZKI, Franz	193013	M	Ger.	24.9.21	Reichsjustizministerium, Feldstraflager, C.C.Finmark (Nor.)	WITNESS	NOR.
NOWOCZYN, Max	193281	M	Ger.	17.8.93	SS Oschfhr., 4.SS Totkpf., Sturmbann Nordhausen-Anschwitz (Ger.Pol.) 1943-1945	MURDER	U.S.
NOYER (see HOYER)	252563	M					
NUBER, Michael	258444	M			SS-man., Guard, C.C. Ohrdruf (Ger.) 12.44-4.45	MURDER	U.S.
NUCKLIES	255703	M			Pvt., C.C. Ellrich, Nordhausen (Ger.)	MURDER	U.S.
NUEBECK, (see LUEBECK)	130631						
NUERGE	104694	M	Ger.		Cpl., Army 15.V.G. 293.Rgt.,2.Bn., Bleialf (Ger.) 44	MURDER	U.S.
NUESSEL, Margot	180504	F	Ger.	18	Secretary, Gestapo, Praha (Cze.) 39-45	WITNESS	CZE.
NUSSLE	300831	M			Pvt., 1.Aufkl.,Abt.3.Coy.,2.Column XV.Div.of the Afrika Korps Saint Leger (Arlon)(Fr.) 5.9.44	MISC.CRIMES	BEL.
NUESSLEIN, Franz	10318	M	Ger.	12.10.09	Dr.,Attorney-General, Public Prosecutor, Brno.,-Prag (Cze.)40-45	MURDER	CZE.
NUESSLEIN, Theodor	167790	M			Executor, Forest Office,Government Abtlg.,Forsten,Lublin(Pol.)9.39-44	PILLAGE	POL.
NULTZ	124127	M	Ger.		Sgt., Camp Lamsdorf, (Ger.) 44	MURDER	U.K.
NUEMI	301959	M			Uschfhr., SS Political Department C.C.Auschwitz (Pol.)41-45	MURDER	POL.
NURNBERG, Paul	166389	M		10	SS Cpt., Hptwachtmeister, SS Pol., Subordinate Kdo.,Fundres(It.)6.44	MURDER	U.S.
NURNBERG, Peter	255704	M			Pvt., C.C.Ellrich, Nordhausen (Ger.)	MURDER	U.S.
NURNBERGER, Hans	195954	M	Ger.		Unit 01512, Trebeurden, Bretagne (Fr.)	TORTURE	FR.
NURTHAM	136613	M			SS-Cpt., C.C.Limburg (Ger.)10.44	TORTURE	U.S.
NUSS, Erika	157999	F	Ger.		Gestapo, Chaloris sur Saone (Fr.) 43-44	MURDER	FR.
NUSSBAUM	174055	M	Ger.	3.11.93	Crim.Director, Kripo Head,C.C.Brno-Oswiecim,Birkenau (Czech.Pol.)39-45	MURDER	CZE.
NUSSE	167771	M			Member, Einsatzstab Rosenberg Administrative Staff (Fr.)40-44	PILLAGE	FR.
NUSSI	260732	M			Cpl., Stalag 325, Stryj (Pol.) 9.42	MURDER	FR.
NUSSER, Johann	193333	M			SS-Pvt., 4.SS Totkpf.Sturmbann., Nordhausen, Dora Mittelbau Anschwitz (Ger.Pol.) 43-45	MURDER	POL.
NUSSGEN	256361	M			Officer, Army, Quemper-Quessanes (Fr.) 9.44	INTERR.	FR.
NUTTGENS, Leo	196779	M	Ger.	00	Usturmfhr Gestapo-Chief Barcelonnette (Fr.)	MISC.CRIMES	FR.
NUTZEL, Andrea	185917	M	Ger.		Civilian, Stalag XIII D,CC Woernitz-Ansbach (Ger.)	TORTURE	BEL.
NUTZHORN	174065	M			Dr., Sturmbannfhr.,Polizeipraesident SS-Pol.,Oswiecim Birkenau (Pol.) 1939-1945	MURDER	CZE.
NUYTTEN, Remy	134527	M	Ger.		Civilian,Camp Lintfort(Ger.) 11.44	WITNESS	U.S.
NYKLEMA (or LYKLEMA)	307190	M	Ger.		Member, Sonderkdo., "Feldmeier,"Apeldoorn, Arnheim, Wageningen (Neth.) 16.10.43, 7.44, 10.44	MURDER	NETH.
NZISSER	251512	M	Ger.		S.D.Mann, Gestapo, Toulouse (Fr.)11.42-5.44	MURDER	FR.
OALICHS, Leo	161	M	Ger.		Pol.,Wachtmstr.,Hoffnungsthal (Ger.)	MURDER	U.S.
OBERG	301963	M	Ger.		Lt., 13.907 A Detachment, Massif du Vercors,Isere (Fr.) 7.-8.44	MURDER	FR.
OBERBERTHUR	193795	M	Ger.	04	Major, Luftpark, Cambrai (Fr.) 40-41	PILLAGE	FR.
OBBERTS	129717	M			Ward at the Camp, Strafgef.Lager Rh.Zellwelle A.G.Siegburg (Ger.) 42	MURDER	BEL.
OBERHAUS	256072	M	Ger.		Dr., Stalag II B, Jessenitz (Ger.) 43-44	INTERR.	FR.
OBER, Willy	250407	M	Ger.		Oschfhr., Gestapo, Limoges (Fr.) 40-44	MISC.CRIMES	FR.
OBERACKER	250406	M	Ger.		Hptschfhr., Gestapo, Limoges (Fr.) 40-44	MISC.CRIMES	FR.
OBERBATZEN	36607	M			L-Cpl., Stalag Camp B 715 9.44	TORTURE	U.K.
OBER-BERGER	162513	M	Ger.		Pvt., 10.Ps.Div.36.Ps.Rgt.SS, Revin (Fr.) 6.44	MURDER	FR.
OBERBUSCH (or OBERBOERSCH)	301964	F	Ger.		Stabshelferin, Secr., to Dr.Schuhmacher Presidant of Kriegsgericht Utrecht (Neth.)7.44	BRUTALITY	NETH.
OBERGLOCK	162512	M	Ger.		Pvt., 10.Ps.Div.36.Ps.Rgt.SS Revin (Fr.) 6.44	MURDER	FR.
OBERHANUSER	140923	M	Ger.		Dr., SS, C.C.Ravensbrueck (Ger.)	TORTURE	U.K.
OBERHAFER, Bert.	12509	M	Ger.		Pvt., Army 110.or 111.Ps.Gren.Rgt.2.Coy., Albine (Fr.) 6.44	MURDER	FR.
OBERHALIS	185478	F	Ger.		Doctoresse C.C.Ravensbrueck (Ger.)	TORTURE	FR.
OBERHAUSER	666	F			Civilian, Doctor, C.C. Ravensbrueck (Ger.) 41-44	MURDER	POL.
OBERHAUSER	106426	M	Ger.		Doctor, W-SS C.C. Auschwitz (Pol.)	MURDER	DEN.
OBERHAUSER, Kurt	183277	M	Ger.	27.5.03	Crim.Secr., Usturmfhr., Gestapo SD., Praha (Cze.)39-45	MURDER	CZE.
OBERHEIM	155505	M			Civ., Kuussbeck (Ger.)	MURDER	U.S.
OBERHOFF, Johann	255233	M			Pvt., C.C. Ellrich, Nordhausen (Ger.)	MURDER	U.S.
OBERHUBER, Ferdinand	251808	M	Ger.	11.6.01	Accounting clerk textile factory N.Styak (Cze.)5.45	PILLAGE	CZE.
OBERKIRSCH, Markus	258405	M			SS-Pvt., Guard, C.C.Ohrdruf (Ger.) 12.44-4.45	MURDER	U.S.
OBERKNOL	144395	F	Ger.		Female overseer C.C. Vught (Neth.) 43-44	MURDER	BEL.
OBERLAND	196446	M	Ger.		Major, Army, Valence (Fr.) 40-44	INTERR.	FR.
OBERLANDER	157991	M	Ger.		Sgt., Gestapo, Vannes, Aurey,Lorient (Fr.) 44	MURDER	FR.
OBERLEIN, August	261969	M	Ger.	5.2.04	Blockleiter, NSDAP, Zilina, Turany and Vahom (Cze.)8.44-4.45	MURDER	CZE.
OBERLIES, Friedrich (Franz)	257190	M	Ger.	15	Sgt., Airforce, Freiburg i.Br. (Ger.) 12.44	MURDER	U.S.
OBERLINDOBER, Hans	251807	M	Ger.		Obergruppenfhr., State Service S.A.Auschwitz Majdanek (Pol.)39-45	MISC.CRIMES	POL.
OBERMAIER	251223	M	Ger.		Sgt., Field Pol.,924 Bourjon La Polartierre (Fr.)6.45	MURDER	FR.
OBERMAIER, Josef	255085	M			Pvt., C.C. Bodungen, Nordhausen (Ger.)	MURDER	U.S.
OBERMAJER, Harry	194516	M	Ger.	19.3.13	Member, Gestapo, Klatovy (Cze.)39-45	TORTURE	CZE.
OBERMANN, DIESLER	155515	M	Ger.		Inf., Rgt., 35. Talmont (Fr.) 8.44	MURDER	FR.
OBERMANN	136332	M			Lt., 19.SS Pol.Rgt., Vignau,Oberkrain, between Toulouse,Compigne Tulle (Fr.) 5.41-3.44-10.44	MURDER	U.S.
OBERMANN (or ORRMANN)	138255	M			SS Sgt., Gestapo, Lyon (Fr.)	MURDER	FR.
OBERMANN	251203	M			SS-Sgt.,Sect.IV Pol.Crime Repre.,Counterspionage Gestapo, Lyon (Fr.)	MISC.CRIMES	FR.
OBERMANN	251232	M	Ger.		Lt., 191. Gren.Rgt., Drano (Ger.) 4.45	MURDER	FR.
OBERMANN, Henri	250409	M	Ger.		Adjutant Chief G.S.D. of Bordeaux and Bayonne Estang,Gers.(Fr.) 7.44	MURDER	FR.
OBERMAYER	12329	M	Ger.		Lt., Army, Amspildungs Kp., 208, Hovere (Fr.) 7.44	MURDER	U.K.
OBERMAYER	31406	M	Ger.		Cpt., 14-210.Inf.Div.Army (Nor.) 44	MURDER	NOR.

OBE-OFF

NAME	C.R.FILE NUMBER	SEX	NATIO-NALITY	DATE OF BIRTH	RANK OCCUPATION UNIT PLACE AND DATE OF CRIME	REASON WANTED	WANTED BY
OBERMAYER	129718	M			Major, Waffen SS, C.C. Mauthausen (Aust.) 41-45	MURDER	U.S.
OBERMAYER	148660	M			SS Sturmbannfhr., C.C. Mauthausen (Aust.) 41-45	MURDER	U.S.
OBERMAYER, Ludwig	262131	M	Ger.		Farmer, Civ.farm, Muenchen (Ger.) (L.o.D.N.A.o.D.)	SUSPECT	U.S.
OBERMEYER	301350	M	Ger.		SS Hptsturmfhr., C.C. Belzec (Pol.)	MURDER	POL.
OBERMULLER	62459	M	Ger.		Col., High Econdmic Official (Yugo.)	MISC.CRIMES	U.N.W.C.C.
OBERNAUER	15504	M	Ger.		Stalag.Oberst., Stargardt (Ger.)	TORTURE	U.K.
OBERREICHT, Otto	173860	M	Ger.	16. 3.12	Cpl., Army, Loc.Brevallaine, La Chapelle de Balanant, St. Pol de Leon (Fr.) 7.-8.44	TORTURE	FR.
OBERSCHMIDT	305935	M	Ger.		Osturmfhr., C.C. Oranienburg (Ger.) 39-45	MURDER	CZECH.
"OBERSLHESIEN, Jellilte Neisse"	144492	M			Sgt., Stalag XVII B, Guard, C.C. Gneixendorf (Aust.) 25.7.44	MURDER	U.S.
OBERST	136301	M	Ger.		Pvt., Army, St. Flour (Fr.) 14.6.44	MURDER	FR.
OBERST	255064	M			Pvt., Rottfhr., C.C. Nixei, Nordhausen (Ger.)	MURDER	U.S.
OBERSTELLER, Fritz	251212	M	Ger.		Prison-Warder, C.C. Lahde (Ger.)	BRUTALITY	BEL.
OBERSTFELDER	669	M	Ger.		Major General, Army, 28.Inf.Div., 9.-10.39	MURDER	POL.
OERTTEL	167108	M		10	Sgt., Army, Guise (Fr.)	MURDER	FR.
OBLADEN, Hans	240009	M		15	Pvt., Nachr.Rgt. 506, 6.Coy., Bad Wildungen (Ger.) 45	MISC.CRIMES	U.S.
OBLER, Walter	667	M			Obervorarbeiter, C.C.Breendonck (Bel.) 40-41	TORTURE	BEL.
OBLISS, Juf	148657	M			Kapo,C.C. Mieste, Gardelegen (Ger.) 4.45	MURDER	U.S.
OBOLIN	174764	M			Interpreter, Kriegsgef.Arbeits-Bn.184, C.C. Aspfjord (Nor.)	TORTURE	NOR.
OBRADOWITSCH	300832	M	Ger.		Pvt.,1.Aufkl.Abt. 3 Coy. 2 Column XV Div. of the Afrika Korps, Lt. Leger, Arlon (Fr.) 5.9.44	MISC. CRIMES	BEL.
OBRECHT	12512	M	Ger.		General, Army of Lyon Kommando DC, Fraize (Fr.) 11.44	TORTURE	FR.
OBRLIK, Gustav	184229	M	Ger.	05	Reichsleiter, NSDAP, Praha (Czech.)	MISC.CRIMES	CZECH.
OBST	256075	M	Ger.		Schuetze, SS, Muehldorf (Ger.)	WITNESS	U.S.
OCHERNAL	153202	M	Ger.		Col., PW Camp XI A, Altengrade (Ger.) 17.4.45	MURDER	U.S.
OCHLER (or OCKLER), Herbert	258144	M	Ger.		SS Uschfhr., Cmdt., Waffen SS, C.C. Schoerzingen (Fr.)	MURDER	BEL.
OCHLERT (see OHLER)	141070						
OCHME, Rudolf	12513	M	Ger.		Pvt., Army 110 or 111 Pz.Gren.Rgt. 2.Coy., Albine (Fr.) 29.6.44	MURDER	FR.
OCHS, Christian	161913	M	Ger.	88	Sgt., Command Staff, Army, C.C. Buchenwald (Ger.)	WITNESS	U.S.
OCHSE	1449	M			Col., SS Police Rgt., 20.Bn.	MURDER	U.K.
OCHSE	21463	M			Sgt., Army, 2.Co., 72 Bau Pion.Bn., 3.45	MISC. CRIMES	U.S.
OCHSENFELD	260966	M			SS-Mann, C.C. Vaihingen (Ger.) 8.44-4.45	MURDER	U.S.
OCHTERBACK	104895	M			Oberstürmfhr., SS, Cuxhaven (Ger.) 45	MURDER	U.S.
OCHTRUP, Werner	12514	M	Ger.		Pvt., Army, 110 or 111 Pz.Gren.Rgt. 2.Coy, Albine (Fr.) 29.6.44	MURDER	FR.
OCKLER (see OCHLER, Herbert)	258144						
OCTTERER, Max	151498	M	Ger.		Section personnel and responsible for Mess, Gestapo of Angers, Bretagne, Anjou, Poitou.(Fr.)	MURDER	FR.
ODEHNAL, Johann	29701	M	Ger.		Landgerichtsrat, Public Official, Brno (Czech.) 40	MURDER	CZECH.
ODEHNAL, Willy	192551	M	Ger.	16. 6.15	Crim.Asst., Gestapo, Brno (Czech.) 39-45	SUSPECT	CZECH.
ODENBREIT (or ODENBRETT)	240010	M	Ger.	05	Pvt., Wehrwirtschaftsstelle VI, Welfare Officer, Bad Wildungen(Ger.)45	MISC.CRIMES	U.S.
ODENDAHL, Otto	135289	M			C.C. Gelsenkirchen (Ger.)	MISC.CRIMES	U.S.
ODOY, Fritz	251214	M		24	1.SS Div., 1.SS Pz.Rgt., 1.Coy., Malmedy (Bel.) 17.12.44	MURDER	U.S.
ODREAN, Friedrich	193812	M	Ger.		Cpl., Army, F.P.No. 21.750 D, Pontoux sur L'Adour (Fr.) 16.6.40	RAPE	FR.
OEBECKE	124923	M	Ger.		Uschfhr., SS Landesschuetzen Coy., 4-6 C.C.Silesia,Stalag Luft III Sagan (Ger.) 25.3.44	WITNESS	U.K.
OEBEN (alias Mr.JEAN), Hans	125625	M		10	Cashier, SD, Nord (Fr.)	MISC.CRIMES	FR.
OEBERLE (see HEBERLE), Frantz	121059						
OEBERLE (or HEBERLE), Karl	174154	M	Ger.		Member, SD, Chalons s.Saone,Montbeliard,Vaudoncourt (Fr.)8.44	MURDER	FR.
OEHLER	24999	M	Ger.	15	Rottfhr., SS, C.C. Struthof (Fr.)	TORTURE	FR.
OEHLER, Herbert	251204	M	Ger.	05	SS Uschfhr., Prison-Administrator, Schorzingen (Ger.)	BRUTALITY	FR.
OEHLSCHLAEGER	301965	M	Ger.		Blockfhr., SS, C.C. Auschwitz (Pol.) 44-45	MURDER	POL.
OELCKE	155506	M			Supervisor, C.C., K.d.F., Gardelegen (Ger.) 4.45	MURDER	U.S.
OELS	188471	M	Ger.		Oschfhr., SS, Berlin (Ger.) 40-45	MURDER	CZECH.
OELSE	193323	M	Ger.		Uschfhr.,SS, 4 Totenkopfsturmbann,C.C.Mittelbau Dora,Nordhausen (Ger.), Auschwitz (Pol.) 43-45	MURDER	U.S.
OELSNER	259638	M	Ger.		Member, Gestapo, Area of Angers,Maine and Loire (Fr.) 42-44	MISC.CRIMES	FR.
OENNING	300833	M			Pvt.,1.Aufkl.Abt. 3.Coy. 2.Col.XV Div. of the Afrika Korps, St.Leger, Arlon (Fr.) 5.9.44	MISC. CRIMES	BEL.
OER	256522	M		10	Arbeitseinsatzleiter, C.C. Muehldorf (Ger.)	MURDER	U.S.
OERKE	670	M	Ger.		Oschfhr., Gestapo, Alesund (Nor.) 42	TORTURE	NOR.
OERKLE	185962	M		9. 4.19	Kapo, C.C. Stephanskirchen (Ger.)	TORTURE	FR.
OERMANN, Walter	306486	M			Uschfhr., SS, C.C. Buchenwald (Ger.) 5.38-10.43	MURDER	BEL.
OERTTEL	196873	M	Ger.		Sgt., 860 Rgt., 348 D.I., Guise (Fr.) 8.44	MURDER	FR.
OESCHEY, Rudolf	261111	M	Ger.	5.03	Gauhauptstellenleiter,President,NSDAP,County Court Justice	SUSPECT	U.S.
OESER	128834	M	Ger.		Sgt., Feldgendarmerie, St.Peter Port (Guernesey) 10.3.42	TORTURE	U.K.
OESER	174069	M	Ger.		Sgt., Army, Guernesey (Br.)	TORTURE	U.K.
OESER, Gerhard, Willi	260941	M	Ger.		Leader of the General Administration, Food, Supply, Civ.Merchant,Civ. Administration-Detachment I, Lublin (Pol.) 40	MISC. CRIMES	POL.
OESS	254449	M	Ger.		SD-Mann, Uschfhr., Gestapo, Toulouse (Fr.) 11.42-8.44	MISC. CRIMES	FR.
OESS, Fritz	259599	M	Ger.		Schfhr., Aussendienststelle SD of Tarbes,Htes-Pyrenees (Fr.)11.42, 8.44	MISC.CRIMES	FR.
OESTERICH	67703	M	Ger.		Sgt., Army, C.C.Graudenz,Berlin,Torgau,Wormditt (Pol.,Ger.) 7.44	MURDER	U.K.
OESTERREICHER, Wilhelm	104896	M	Ger.	91	Standartenfhr.,SA, Police Dir.(retired 1942),Goeppingen (Ger.)	TORTURE	U.S.
OETH (see UTH)	72072						
OEVER, Arie Ten	307191	M			Member, Landwacht Almelo (Neth.) 9.44-2.45	TORTURE	NETH.
OFERNAM	191396	M			Director of Censorship, Dr., SD, Official,La Bourboule,le Montdore (Fr.) 27.4.44	MURDER	FR.
OFFENBAUER, Grete	192554	F	Ger.		Clerk, Gestapo, Brno (Czech.) 39-45	WITNESS	CZECH.
OFFENBLACH, Kurt	151499	M	Ger.		Uschfhr.,Employee,Civ.Hoch-Tiefbau Essen, Brux (Czech.) 2.6.44	TORTURE	U.K.
OFFERDINGER (or OFFTERDINGER), Otto	261914	M	Ger.	20 or 22	Sgt., presumably belonging to an Anti-Aircraft-Btty.,S'Heerenhoek (Neth.) 8.9.44	MURDER	NETH.
OFFERGELD, Erwin	12515	M	Ger.		Pvt., Army,110 or 111 Pz.Gren.Rgt.2.Coy, Albine (Fr.) 29.6.44	MURDER	FR.
OFFERMAN	259069	M			Capt., A Dulag Luft Hospital (Ger.) 43-4.45	BRUTALITY	U.S.
OFFERMAN, Heinrich	193324	M	Ger.	27. 7.97	Uschfhr.,4.SS Totenkopfsturmbann, C.C.Dora Mittelbau,Nordhausen (Ger.) 43-45	MURDER	U.S.
OFFERMANN	104897	M	Ger.		Civ.,Physician,Civ.Institut physician, Kiew (Sov.Un.) 41-42	MURDER	U.S.
OFFERMANN	136302	M	Ger.		Lt., Army, La Ferte sur Aube (Fr.) 15.4.44	MURDER	FR.

OFF-OLL

NAME	C.R.FILE NUMBER	SEX	NATIO- NALITY	DATE OF BIRTH	RANK OCCUPATION UNIT	PLACE AND DATE OF CRIME	REASON WANTED	WANTED BY
OFFMANN	191820	M			Adj.,Army,Billy (Fr.) 7.43-8.44		PILLAGE	FR.
OFFMANN	250411	M	Ger.		Capt.,Cdr.of.Pioneer-Parc,stationed at Romans,Peyrius (Fr.) 6.44		INTERR.	FR.
OFFMANN,Emil	39593	M	Ger.		Pvt.,SS,Army,Civilian,Bernay en Champagne (Fr.) 9.41		WITNESS	FR.
OFFMANN,Gerald	250410	M	Ger.		Officer,Truppendienststelle L 35079,Ferrieres en Bale (Fr.) 24.8.44		INTERR.	FR.
OFFMEYER	185962	M			Usturmfhr.,SD of Moutiers,Bourg St.Maurice (Fr.) 8.44		MURDER	FR.
OFFNER	190293	M	Ger.		A.D.C.to Stoetzelat,Poxaverac-Serbia (Yugo.) 41-43		MURDER	YUGO.
OFFTERDINGER,Otto (see OFFERDINGER)	261914							
OFTERRINGEN	196872	M			Executioner,C.C.Birkenau,Auschwitz (Pol.) 40-45		MURDER	FR.
OGASCHAK	256074	M	Ger.		Waffen SS,Mushldorf (Ger.)		WITNESS	U.S.
OHCTERBERG (see ORTERBERG, Wilhelm)	195390							
OHL	167779	M	Ger.		Director,Treuhandstelle fuer ehemals Poln.Sparkassen,Wartheland (Pol.) 9.39-44		PILLAGE	POL.
OHL	251199	M		83	Doctor,Kdo.1366,Stalag II B,K.O.F.Palersleben (Ger.) 29.2.44		MURDER	FR.
OHL,Rene	671	M		11	SS-Oberscharfhr.,SS,Gestapo,Limoges (Fr.)		TORTURE	FR.
OHL,Rene	672	M			Interpreter,Paysac (Fr.) 16.2.44		MURDER	FR.
OHL,Willi	300910	M			Dr.,Member of Staff of.Baby Clinic,Wolfsburg Ruehen		MURDER	U.K.
OHLANDT	251200	M	Ger.		Kdo.-Fuehrer,277 Stalag X,C,Anstedt ueber Twistringen Krs.Solingen (Ger.) 20.3.45		MURDER	FR.
OHLEMACHER,Willi	260502	M		7. 7.05	SS-Guard,SS,C.C.Natzweiler (Fr.)		MURDER	FR.
OHLENBUSCH	196319	M	Ger.		Head of Propaganda,Department of Gen.Gov.,(Pol.) 39-45		MISC.CRIMES	POL.
OHLENDORF	1450	M			Cpl.,Army 194 Gr.2.Pl.7 Coy		MISC.CRIMES	U.K.
OHLENDORF	133257	M	Ger.		SS-Oberfuehrer,Waffen SS,Einsatzgruppe D,Sicherheitskdo.II b,Thekima,Timaspol (Rum.) 41		MURDER	U.S.
OHLENS	261805	M	Ger.		Chief,Kommando 1004 G.W. a Pitten 3 Coy 393 Bn.,Pitten (Aust.) 2.5.43		MURDER	FR.
OHLER (or OCHLERT)	141070	M			SS-Rottfhr.,SS,C.C.Natzweiler (Fr.) 6.43		TORTURE	U.K.
OHLINGER,Josef	132631	M	Ger.		Cpl.,1 Coy of 873 Bn.Territorial,Leogang (Aust.)		MURDER	FR.
OHLMANN	190459	M			Eisenb.Art.Bn.717,St.Andries,Varsenare,les Bruges (Bel.) 4.9.44		MURDER	BEL.
OHLMANN	255229	M			C.C.Rottleberode,Nordhausen (Ger.)		MURDER	U.S.
OHLMER	260730	M	Ger.	02	Sgt.,Chief,Army,Block Graudeas,Thorn,Kempten (Pol.,Ger.) 1.45		MURDER	FR.
OHLSEN	24995	M			(Dr.,Capt.,Army,394 Inf.Div.Staff, 6. - 7. 44		MISC.CRIMES	U.S.
OHLSON	300834	M	Ger.		Pvt.,1 Aufkl.Abt.3 Coy 2 Col.XV Div.of the Afrika Korps,Saint Leger (Arlon) 5.9.44		MISC.CRIMES	BEL.
OHM	1483	M			Police,Eberswalde (Ger.)		MISC.CRIMES	U.K.
OHM	151543	M	Ger.		Air Raid Warden,Eberswalde (Ger.) 9.44		MURDER	U.S.
OHM (or UHM)	251207	M	Ger.		Pvt.,1 Unterfuehrerschule,Arnheim,Kerkwijk (Neth.) 9.44		MURDER	NETH.
OHM,Ludwig	193999	M			Member,SA,C.C.Gudensberg (Ger.) 41-45		TORTURE	POL.
OHMANN,Erwin	174075	M			Crim.-official,Gestapoleitstelle,Prag,Oswiecim,Birkenau,(Czech.,Pol.) 39-45		MURDER	CZECH.
OHNESORGE	1451	M			Cpl.,Army 194 Gr.,		MISC.CRIMES	U.K.
OHNMAIS,Karl	132520	M		00	Officer,Arbeitskdo.Stalag 317 (XVIII C),C.C.Markt Pongau Gollnig Labor Camp,(Aust.) 23.1.45-4.5.45.		MURDER	U.S.
OHRFANDL	261251	M	Ger.		Pvt.,2 Col.3 Coy 1 Aufkl.Abt.XV Div.Afrika Corps,St.Leger Distr.Arlon (Bel.) 5.9.44		MISC.CRIMES	BEL.
OHRMANN,Friedrich	251196	M	Ger.	03	Pvt.,Guard,Stalag XX A P.W.,Rabenhurst (Pol.) 19.11.41		MURDER	U.K.
OHRNER	142123	M		10	SS-Oschfhr.,SS,C.C.Lublin (Pol.)		MURDER	FR.
OHRT,Hans	305679	M	Ger.		Civilian,ar.Lubeck-Siems (Ger.) 6.8.44		MURDER	U.S.
OIDE-BOERHUIS	255232	M			Capt.,C.C.Buchenwald (Ger.)		MURDER	U.S.
OISSER	151500	M			SS-Uschfhr.,SS,Camp leader in K.A.Bn.11,Gras Wenzelsdorf (Aust.) 2.45		WITNESS	U.S.
OKORN,Hans	129720	M	Ger.		Pvt.,5 Fallschirm-Rgt.,Guarassem,Jemappes,Ghiin (Bel.) 1.44		MURDER	BEL.
OLAFF	256523	M	Ger.	19	Capt.,Army,Bourseul (Fr.) 31.10.43-23.11.43		MURDER	FR.
OLAFF	305089	M	Ger.	19	Capt.,Unit of Russians and Germans stationed at Bourseul at Matignon Cotes-du-Nord, (Fr.) 43 and 44		MISC.CRIMES	FR.
OLASCH	162814	M		95	Oschfhr.,SD,C.C.Ersingen (Ger.)		TORTURE	FR.
OLBECK	302088	M	Ger.		Member,SD,Apeldoorn Hoog-Soeren (Neth.) 10.-12.44-7.4.45		MURDER	NETH.
OLBERS	260023	M			Lt.,Detachment L.B.907,A,Massif du Vercors,Isere et Drome (Fr.)7.-8.44		SUSPECT	FR.
OLBERTS	174068	M			C.C.Warder,C.C.Siegburg (Ger.) 3.-8.42		TORTURE	BEL.
OLBRICH	192244	M			SS-Usturmfhr.,SS Div."Das Reich" Rgt."Der Fuehrer" 1 Bn.,Frayssinet Le Gelat (Fr.) 21.5.44		MURDER	FR.
OLBRICH	306640	M	Ger.		Lt.,1 Bn."Der Fuehrer"Rgt.,Div."Das Reich",Frayssinet-le-Gelat (Fr.) 21.5.44		MURDER	FR.
OLDAG	31407	M			Capt.,Army 163 Inf.Div.Pz.Jg.Abt., (Nor.) 44		MURDER	NOR.
OLDENBURHUIS	156749	M	Ger.	87	SS-Hptsturmfhr.,SS,C.C.Outercamp S III Buchenwald Thueringen (Ger.) 42-45		TORTURE	U.S.
OLDENBURG (or OLDENBORGHUIS)	161917	M	Ger.	95	SS-Hptsturmfhr.,SS,Bruttig,Treis (Ger.) 44		MURDER	U.S.
OLDENBURG	196318	M			Sgt.,3 Brandenburg Rgt.,		MISC.CRIMES	U.S.
OLDENBURG	261049	M			Capt.,adjoint to Major Becker,Amiens (Fr.) 20.5.-25.6.40		INCENDIARISM	FR.
OLDENDORF,Frans	255237	M			Flyer,C.C.Ellrich,Nordhausen (Ger.)		MURDER	U.S.
OLDRES,Jose (aliase:ROSSI)	251208	M		22	Interpreter,Gestapo,Arlon (Bel.)		INTERR.	BEL.
OLDIDORNIS,Gerrit Johann	133254	M		21. 3.95	Hptsturmfhr.,Waffen SS,Ohrdruf (Ger.) 44-45		MURDER	U.S.
OLDOFREDY	185550	M	Ger.		Leader,NSDAP,Praha (Czech.)		MISC.CRIMES	CZECH.
OLDORF	300685	M			Kdo.Kapo,Prasifix-Kdo.,C.C.Dachau (Ger.) 43-45		MISC.CRIMES	BEL.
OLDORFF,Friedrick	262340	M			Gend.Capt.,Wanted as a witness to the shooting of an unarmed American Soldier,L.O.D.N.A.O.D.,Appen (Ger.) 18.1.44 or 18.6.44		WITNESS	U.S.
OLDRIZ	129877	M	Ger.	87	Head warden,Prison Aachen,Adelbert prison (Ger.) 41-44		TORTURE	U.S.
OLECHNOWITSCH,Oswald	192552	M		3.11.04	Civ.empl.,driver,Gestapo,Brno (Czech.) 39-45		SUSPECT	CZECH.
OLEP	251806	M	Ger.		Employee,Sipo Abt.IV-C,Bruessel (Bel.)		INTERR.	BEL.
OLESCH,Paul	24998	M	Ger.		SS-Sturmbannfhr.,SS,C.C.Struthof (Fr.) 42-44		TORTURE	FR.
OLESCHKERG,Kurt	179769	M		15	Sgt.,26 Pz.Div.,Mareshes Fucecchio (It.) 23.8.44		MURDER	U.K.
OLHENDORF,Otto	11870	M			Bdefhr.,SD, 40-44		TORTURE	U.K.
OLIROG	196871	M			Feldgendarmerie D 9.666 At Caveassone,Belcaire (Fr.) 25.11.43		MISC.CRIMES	FR.
OLIVER	196326	M		10	Interpreter,Geheime Feldpolisei H.Q.		MISC.CRIMES	U.S.
OLIVERO (see ZEITLER)	166381							
OLIVIERO (see ZEITLER,Fritz)	166381							
OLLIG	251209	M	Ger.		Station master,Bobigny (Fr.) 19.8.44		INTERR.	FR.
OLLROG	157995	M	Ger.		Feldgendarmerie D 966,Belcaire (Fr.) 29.11.43		TORTURE	FR.

OLM-ORT

NAME	C.R.FILE NUMBER	SEX	NATIO-NALITY	DATE OF BIRTH	RANK	OCCUPATION	UNIT	PLACE AND DATE OF CRIME	REASON WANTED	WANTED BY
OLMA	192556	M	Ger.		Major, Air Force, Senzeille, Charleroi (Bel.) 2.-4.44				TORTURE	BEL.
OLOFFS	191341	M	Ger.		Major, Army, CC Gossen (Nor.) 42-45				MURDER	NOR.
OLSCHER, Alfred	260194	M	Ger.	8. 9.87	Mem.Vorst. Reichs-Kredit-Gesellschaft, Dep.Ch.Honor Court of the German Economy, Berlin (Ger.)				MISC.CRIMES	U.S.
OLSCHEWSKI, Hans	300911	M	Ger.		SS, Member of Staff at CC.Stocken and Ahlem 44 and 45				MURDER	U.K.
OLSCHEWSKI, Willi	305680	M	Ger.		Kapo, CC, near Flossenburg, Hersbruck, Wolkenburg, Ganacker, Leitmeritz (Ger. and Czech.) between 1.1.42-8.5.45				MURDER	U.S.
OLSE	255236	M			Capt, CC Auschwitz, Nordhausen (Ger.)				MURDER	U.S.
OMA (see NOUACK, Paul or NOVAK)	188455	M	Ger.	11	Chief, CC Wilhelmshaven (Ger.)				MURDER	U.K.
OMANN, Paul	192717	M	Ger.		Rottfhr, SS, CC Buchenwald (Ger.) 42-45				TORTURE	U.S.
ONDERKA, Anton	180506	M	Ger.	23. 7.89	Hptsturmfhr, SS, SD, Praha (Czech.) 39-45				MURDER	CZECH.
ONKEN	192243	M	Ger.		Oschfhr, 9 SS Pz.Div.Hohenstaufen, Neuville les Bois (Fr.)				MURDER	FR.
ONKEN, Reinhard	252564	M			SS-Mann, 12 SS Pz.Div. Panz.Sp., St.Sulpice (Fr.) 6.6.44				WITNESS	U.S.
ONNEN, August	164192	M	Ger.	26.11.93	Major, Inf.Rgt.Wiese, Eydelstedt (Ger.) 7.4.45				MURDER	U.K.
ONNEN, Kurt	167758	M	Ger.		Uschfhr, SS, CC Natzweiler (Fr.) 43-44				MURDER	FR.
OPAL	148659	M			Male-Nurse, Special Reservation, CC Mauthausen (Aust.) 41-45				MURDER	U.S.
OPDERBECK, Paul	29703	M	Ger.		Dr.,Landgerichtsrat, Public Official, Brno, (Czech.) 40				MURDER	CZECH.
OPELMANN	141985	M	Ger.		SS-Guard, CC near Ampfing (Ger.) 44-45				MURDER	U.S.
OPELT (or OPPEL)	161912	M		10	SS Usturmfhr, Security Main Office, CC Ohrdruf, Buchenwald (Ger.)				WITNESS	U.S.
OPELT (see OPPELT, Fritz)	46103									
OPFER	167761	M	Ger.		Prof., Civilian, Member of Einsatzstab Rosenberg, Administrative Staff 40-44				PILLAGE	FR.
OPHOVES	143024	F	Ger.		Civilian, CC Jauer (Ger.) 42-45				TORTURE	U.S.,FR.,CZECH.
OPITZ	121202	M	Ger.		SS-Officer, W-SS, Ressons, Le Long (Fr.) 1.9.44				MURDER	FR.
OPITZ	251197	M	Ger.	about 05	Civilian, SS-Chief of Tailor-Workshops, CC Ravensbrueck (Ger.)				INTERR.	FR.
OPITZ, Theodor	259096	M	Ger.		Oschfhr, SS, CC Dachau (Ger.) 42-45				MISC.CRIMES	YUGO.
OPLAENDER	10319	M	Ger.		SS Oberfhr., Chief of Security Service, O.C.Abschn.39(Czech.)39-44				TORTURE	CZECH.
OPLAENDER	174074	M	Ger.		Befehlhaber, Sipo, CC Auschwitz-Birkenau (Pol.) 39-45				MURDER	CZECH.
OPLAENDER, Paul	133253	M	Ger.		SS-Oberfhr, SS and SD., Prague (Czech.) 39-45				MURDER	CZECH.
OPLAENDER, Walther	109672	M	Ger.	27. 2.06	Osturmfhr, W-SS, Personalhauptamt, Leader of Oberabschnitt, Bohemia - Moravia (Czech.) 45				TORTURE	U.S.
OPPEL (see OPELT)	161912									
OPPEL	195949	M	Ger.	20	Lt., Sommieres (Fr.) 27.7.44				SUSPECT	FR.
OPPEL	306621	M	Ger.		Pvt., 5 Coy, 100 Bn. Gebirgsjg., Vilette (Savoie) Fr. 9.6.44				MURDER	FR.
OPPEL, Franz	174073	M			Gestapoleitstelle, Brno, Auschwitz, Birkenau (Czech., Pol.) 39-45				MURDER	CZECH.
OPPELMANN	151501	M	Ger.		Gestapo, CC Commandant, Breslau (Ger.)				TORTURE	U.S.
OPPELT	194000	M	Ger.		Usturmfhr, SS, CC Buchenwald (Ger.) 42-45				TORTURE	U.S.
OPPELT, Fritz (or OPELT)	46103	M		06	SD Einsatz KKo. z.b.V. 6, Gestapo, SS, La Grande Fosse Lussault Touraine (Fr.) 4.8.-5.10.44				MURDER	U.K., U.S.
OPPENHEIM, Leo	185491	M			Stalag VII, Internee CC Laufen - Operndorf (Ger.) 3. or 4.1.45				WITNESS	U.S.
OPPERBECK, Josef	258540	M	Ger.	00	Sturmbannfhr, SS, W.V.H.A. (Ger.) 40-45				BRUTALITY	U.S.
OPPERMANN	126791	M			Capt., Army, Inf., Louvres (Fr.) 27.8.43				MURDER	FR.
OPPERMANN	132082	M			Hptschfhr, SS, CC Flossenburg (Ger.)				TORTURE	U.S.
OPPERMANN	191884	M			Camp Doctor, Oflag 79, CC Brunswick (Ger.) 44-45				TORTURE	U.K.
OPPERMANN, Ewald	62462	M	Ger.		NSFK-Ogruppenfhr, General-Commissioner of the Ukraine (Russia)				MURDER	U.N.W.C.C.
OPPERMANN, Heinrich	255063	M		27. 7.97	Uschfhr, CC Nordhausen (Ger.)				MURDER	U.S.
OPPERMANN, Heinz	104898	M	Ger.	1921-22	Lt., Army, 18 V.G.Div., 293 Rgt., Bleialf (Ger.) 20.12.44				MURDER	U.S.
OPPERMANN, Karl	172456	M	Ger.		Policeman, Vienenburg (Ger.) 5.44				MURDER	U.S.
OPPERMANN, Matthias	257558	M		22	SS, CC Muhldorf (Ger.)				MURDER	U.S.
OPPERMANN, Walter	306487	M	Ger.	2.12.14	SS Schfhr., CC Buchenwald (Ger.) between 16.5.38 and 9.10.43				MURDER	BEL.
OPTIER, Jacob	255062	M			Pvt., Army, Nuland (Neth.) 9.44				PILLAGE	NETH.
ORDALMANN, Hermann	259433	M	Ger.		Cpl., Kampfgr. 38 Rgt., 17 SS Div., Caen (Fr.) 15.7.44				WITNESS	U.S.
ORDONANZ	192242	M	Ger.		G.E.F.R., Kommandantur, Etat Major of Crest (Droeme), La Rochette (Fr.) 3.8.44				WITNESS	FR.
OREI	256524	M			Oschfhr. pro CC Leader, Nordhausen (Ger.)				MURDER	U.S.
ORENDI	123039	M		18	Camp Doctor, Oberjunker SS, CC Ravensbrueck (Ger.)				MURDER	FR., BEL.
ORGIS, Otti	250417	M	Ger.		Secretary, Agent Gestapo, Kirchbaumer, Ferlach (Aust.) 44-45				WITNESS	YUGO.
ORHODIE (see ORMODIE)	120618									
ORLICH, Rudolf	122719	M			SS Uschfhr, Guard Camp Struthof (Fr.)				MURDER	FR.
ORLICH, Willi	24997	M	Ger.		U-Schfhr, W-SS, CC Struthof (Fr.)				TORTURE	FR.
ORLIEB	1452	M	Ger.		Lt.Col., Inf.Rgt.754, 334 Inf.Div.				MISC.CRIMES	U.K.
ORLOSWOSKI, Hans (alias ORLOWSKI, Heinz)	126513	M	Ger.		Orpo, Feld-Gend., Vendome (Fr.) 10.8.44				MURDER	U.S.
ORLOWSKI	196092	M	Ger.	13	Landrat, Kreisleiter NSDAP, Jarocin, Poznan (Pol.) 39-45				MURDER	POL.
ORLOWSKI, Otto	251805	M	Ger.	07	Foreman, Factory-Civilian, Vyskov (Czech.) 42-45				MURDER	CZECH.
ORLOWSKI, Heinz	250418	M	Ger.		Sgt., Field-Police, Vendome (Fr.) 9.8.44				MURDER	FR.
ORLAMUENDER, Ewald	251201	M	Ger.	16. 8.00	SD, Adamov (Czech.) 44-45				INTERR.	CZECH.
ORMELCH	251804	M	Ger.		Lt., Paymaster, Div. "Hermann Goering, 4 Rgt.Paratroopers.,1 Bn., Helchteren (Bel.) 5.-11.9.44				MISC.CRIMES	BEL.
ORMINSKI, Marian	194517	M	Ger.	26	Civilian, Chateau Regnault and Levrezy (Fr.)				WITNESS	FR.
ORMODIE (or ORHODIE)	120618	M	Ger.		Lt., Army, 2,515 Bn.Lds.Schtz.-Stalag VIII-B, Niwka near Bensburg (Ger.) 12.4.43				TORTURE	U.K.
ORNEMANN (see OBERMANN)	138255									
OREST	138921	M			Adj., Chief SS, Gestapo, Lyon (Fr.)				MURDER	FR.
ORNIT	255235	M			Pvt., CC Dora, Nordhausen (Ger.)				MURDER	U.S.
ORNOLZ	188958	M	Ger.		Sgt., Army, Dury les Amiens (Fr.) 44				WITNESS	FR.
ORSTADT, Hans	193513	M	Ger.		Sturmschfhr, SD, Moussey (Fr.) 44				MURDER	FR.
ORTEL	195842	M			Capt., Russian Bn.35518 D, Tresbeurden (Fr.)				PILLAGE	FR.
ORTELT, Anton	255066	M	Ger.	30. 5.95	Oschfhr SA, Member SD, Kromeris (Czech.) 43-45				MISC.CRIMES	CZECH.
ORTERBERG (or OHTERBERG),Wilhelm	195390	M	Ger.	6. 5.08	Osturmfhr, SS, Gestapo, Niederdorfelden, Hanau-Heinmuehle near Marburg (Ger.) 42				MURDER	POL.
ORTH, Christoph	255067	M		18. 9.01	Rottfhr, CC Harzungen, Nordhausen (Ger.)				MURDER	U.S.
ORTH, Philipp	124246	M			1 SS Pz.Div., 2 SS Gren.Rgt., 12 Coy, Malmedy (Bel.) 17.12.44				MURDER	U.S.
ORTMANN, Erich	251218	M	Ger.		Lt., 377 Jg.Rgt., 9 Coy, Vinkt Meigem (Bel.) 25.-31.5.40				INTERR.	BEL.
ORTLEPP, Udo Alfred	260944	M	Ger.	9. 5.92	Gend.-Insp., State Service, Gend. Commander of Police, Warsaw and other Towns (Pol.) 39-44				MURDER	POL.

ORT-OTT

NAME	C.R.FILE NUMBER	SEX	NATIO-NALITY	DATE OF BIRTH	RANK OCCUPATION UNIT PLACE AND DATE OF CRIME	REASON WANTED	WANTED BY
ORTMANN	196312	M	Ger.		Dr.med.,Osturmfhr.,C.C.Neuengamme (Ger.)	TORTURE	BEL.
ORTMANN	300580	M	Ger.		Lt.,Army,9 Coy.,Prob.192 Inf.Regt.,Vinkt-Meigen (Bel.) 5.40	MISC.CRIMES	BEL.
ORTNER	167110	M	Ger.		Feldgendarmerie de Moulins,Laroche-Millay (Fr.) 11.8.44	PILLAGE	FR.
ORTNER,Josef	192557	M	Ger.		Scharfhr.,SS,C.C.Flossenburg (Ger.)44-45	SUSPECT	U.S.
ORTSMANNS	126577	M	Ger.		Civilian,Lichtenbusch,Langfeld, Aachen (Ger.) 9.8.44	MISC.CRIMES	U.S.
ORTSTADT,Hans	169478	M	Ger.		Kriminalsekretaer,Gestapo,Strasbourg (Fr.) 9.-11.44	TORTURE	U.K.
OSCAR	193813	M	Ger.		Kapo,C.C.Dachau (Ger.)	MURDER	FR.
OSCHING	123042	M	Ger.		Pvt.,Army,Semaphore,-Creach-Maout (Fr.) 5.-7.8.44	MURDER	FR.
OSCHMAN,Karl	161918	M	Ger.		Civilian,Steinbach (Ger.) 2.44	WITNESS	U.S.
OSFOLK	196870	M	Ger.		Member,Gestapo,Vichy (Fr.) 43-44	MURDER	FR.
OSKOPP	302089	M	Ger.		Member,S.D.,Apeldoorn,Hoog-Soeren (Neth.)10.-12.44, 7.4.45	MURDER	NETH.
OSNABRUECK,Max	167778	M	Ger.		Guard,C.C.Sachsenhausen,Oranienburg (Ger.) 39-4.45	MURDER	POL.
OSSA	185551	N			Miner,Arbeitskommando,Adolf-Mine,Merkstein (Ger.) 8.42-10.44	TORTURE	
OSSEIMAN	251206	M	Ger.		Oberarzt,Army,1 Div.,1 Para-Regt.,II Bn.,Benevento (Ital.)43	PILLAGE	U.K.
OSSENKOPF	151505	M			Civilian,Pattensen (Ger.) 12.3.45	TORTURE	U.S.
OSSIG	257351	M	Ger.		Guard,Hptwachtmeister,SS,Slave labour camp,Beisfjord near Narvik (Nor.)6.-11.42	BRUTALITY	YUGO.
OSSINER	151504	M			Inspector,Gestapo,"Comite" de Paix, Sociale Bureau,9 Boulevard Foch Angers,Anjou,Poitou,Bretagne (Fr.)	MURDER	FR.
OSSMANN	158130	M		15	Official,SS,Praha (Czech.)	MURDER	U.S.
OSSMANN,Franz	255234	M		30. 8.98	Pvt.,SS,C.C.Dora,Nordhausen (ger.)	MURDER	U.S.
OSTREICHER	155497	M	Ger.		Capt.,Landesschuetzen-Bn.891,C.C.Feldbach (Aust.)	TORTURE	U.K.
OSSTRA	193814	M	Ger.		Feldgendarm,Feldgendarmerie,Tourcoing (Fr.) 2.9.44	WITNESS	FR.
OST,Viktor	1075	M			Adjutant,Feldgendarmerie,Chaumont (Fr.)	TORTURE	FR.
OSTENDORF	255068	M	Ger.		Lt.,Velke,Mezirici (Czech.) 7.5.45	INTERR.	CZECH.
OSTENLAND	188957	M			Lt.,74 R.S.M. Flak-Regt.,Stab,Chaudes Aigues (Fr.)20.6.44	MURDER	FR.
OSTERDORF	258218	M	Ger.		Col.,SS,17 SS-Div.,Regt.37,Merzig (Ger.)	MURDER	U.S.
OSTERINGER,Rudolf	676	M	Ger.		Guard,C.C.Auschwitz,Birkenau (Pol.) 39-45	MURDER	CZECH.FR.BEL.YUGO.POL.
OSTERLAND	157993	M			Lt.,74 Sicher.Regt.,1 Bn.,2 Coy.,Army,Clauvieres (Fr.).10.-11.6.44	MURDER	FR.
OSTERLE	256520	M			Oschfhr.,SS	MURDER	U.S.
OSTERLEICH	124098	M	Ger.		Civ.,Information from engl.speaking german.In this man's presence cummings N.Z.E.F.Stated to the camp Cmdt. that he was the Member of the british free corps and he was toremain in battle dress, as he was to Act. as a Spy in camp 107-G.W.,Graz (Aust.)	MISC.CRIMES	U.K.
OSTERLOH,Dietrich	251219	M	Ger.		Pvt.,377 Jaeg.Regt.,Vinkt,Meigen (Bel.) 25.-31.5.40	INTERR.	BEL.
OSTERMANN	31408	M	Ger.		Lt.Col.,Army,82-7deb.Div.,Geb.Art.Regt.,Finmark (Nor.)44	MURDER	NOR.
OSTERMANN	126484	M			Uschfhr.,SS-Leibst.Adolf Hitler/1 Bn.,1 SS-Pz.Regt.,Headquarters Compa. Malmedy (Bel.)17.12.44	MURDER	U.S.
OSTERMANN	136333	M	Ger.		Civ.,High School Principal,C.C.Oberbeitingen, near Hildesheim(Ger.)44	TORTURE	U.S.
OSTERMANN	300541	M	Ger.		Lt.,German Garrison,Milna,Island of Brac (Yugo.)1.-3.44	MISC.CRIMES	YUGO.
OSTERMAN,Antoine	136626	M	Ger.	90	Capt.,C.C.Muhldorf,Ampfing,Area Mettenheim (Ger.) 44-45	MURDER	U.S.
OSTERMEIER,Johannes	123045	M	Ger.		Pvt.,Creach,Maout (Fr.) 5.-7.8.44	MISC.CRIMES	FR.
OSTERREICH (see OESTERICH)	67703						
OSTERREICH	255231	M			Pvt.,C.C.Ellrich,Nordhausen (Ger.)	MURDER	U.S.
OSTERRICH	141895	M	Ger.		General,Cmdt.,Stalag,Wehrkreis XX,Marienberg (Ger.) 40	MURDER	U.K.
OSTERRIEDER,Georg	148661	M			Civilian,Schotten,Nassau (Ger.)	TORTURE	U.S.
OSTERTAG	126939	M	Ger.	95	Usturmfhr.,SS,C.C.Schirmeck (Fr.) 43-44	MISC.CRIMES	FR.
OSTERTAG,Julius	141588	M		18.11.04	Landeskommissar,Bischwiller (Fr.)	MURDER	FR.
OSTERWALD	147351	M	Ger.		Oschfhr.,11 Pz.Div.Kampfgruppe "Wilde",3 Gruppe,(South-west Fr.)44	MURDER	FR.
OSTREICHER (see OESTERICH)	67703						
OSTREICHER	167111	M	Ger.		Officer,paratrooper,-Regt.14,Div."Ad.Hitler",Villy St.Etienne(Fr.)9.44	MURDER	FR.
OSTRINGER	255230	M			Cpl.,C.C.Dora,Nordhausen (Ger.)	MURDER	U.S.
OSWALD	123046	M			N.C.O.,Interpreter,Freekorps,Legion Scandinave SS,Montferrier(Fr.)7.44	PILLAGE	FR.
OSWALD	136328	M			Lt.,Army,Paulusbrunn (Czech.) 23.4.45	MURDER	U.S.
OSWALD	174166	M			Feldgendarm,Gendarmerie,Cormainville,Chateauceun,Logron(Fr.)9.-17.8.44	MISC.CRIMES	FR.
OSWALD	255061	M			Pvt.,C.C.Osterhagen,Nordhausen (Ger.)	MURDER	U.S.
OSWALD,Johann	258443	M			SS-Mann,Guard,SS,C.C.Ohrdruf (Ger.)12.44-4.45	MURDER	U.S.
OSTWALD,Wilhelm	136331	M			Guard,Pol.,C.C.Hanau (Ger.) 2.42-3.45	MISC.CRIMES	U.S.
OSWALT,Josef	305681	M	Ger.		Member,C.C.Flossenburg,Hersbruck,Wolkenburg,Ganacker,Leitmeritz (Ger.-Czech.) 1.1.42-8.5.45	MURDER	U.S.
OSWISKA,Anton	301357	M	Ger.		Kapo,Kdo. at Stephankirchen near Rosenheim (Ger.) 44-45	MISC.CRIMES	FR.
OTA (see ODA,Kanashu)	186905						
OTE,Willy	251220	M	Ger.		Pvt.,377 Jaeg.Regt.,10 Coy.,Vinkt (Bel.) 25.-31.5.40	INTERR.	BEL.
OTHMER	251803	M	Ger.		Obfhr.,Coy.Officer,Div."Hermann Goering",4 Regt.,parachuter 1.Bn.,2 Coy.,Helchteren (Bel.) 5.-11.9.44	MISC.CRIMES	BEL.
OTKEN	177530	M			Cmdt.,Official,C.C.Aulnat (Fr.)	TORTURE	FR.
OTOP	147350	M	Ger.		Capt.,11 Pz.Div.,(South-West Fr.) 44	MURDER	FR.
OTREMBA	54501	M			Capt.,19 SS-Pol.Regt.,3 Bn.,Sussac,Pompadour (Fr.)7.-8.44	INTERR.	FR.
OTT	677	M			Cpl.,Stalag IV C.C.C. 43	MURDER	CZECH.
OTT	12411	M			Osturmbannfhr.,SS,Podebrady (Czech.) 39-44	TORTURE	CZECH.
OTT	21642	M			Pvt.,Army,12 Volksgrenadier-Div.,27 Fuss.Regt.,3 Coy.,Petit Langville (Bel.) 1.45	WITNESS	U.S.
OTT	124202	M			Oberwachtmeister,Schupo,C.C.Buetzow (Ger.)	TORTURE	NOR.
OTT	135290	M			Obersturmfhr.,SS,Podebrady,Bohemia (Czech.) 39-44	MURDER	CZECH.
OTT	144490	M	Ger.		SS-Mann,SS-Waldlager V and VI,C.C.Muhldorf,Ampfing (Ger.) 44-45	TORTURE	U.S.
OTT	251210	M	Ger.		Capt.,Fort de Vincennes (Fr.) 20.8.44	INTERR.	FR.
OTT	251216	M	Ger.		Guard,Prison,C.C.Lahde-Weser (Ger.)	INTERR.	BEL.
OTT	256563	M			Pvt.,SS,C.C.Muhldorf Area (Ger.)	MURDER	U.S.
OTT	305095	M	Ger.		Lt.,Ordnungs-Pol.,Groningen,Drente (Ger.) 43-45	MURDER	NETH.
OTT,Hans	195841	M		27.10.03	Lt.Pol.Off.,Gendarmerie,C.C.Groningen,Westerbork (Neth.) 9.-12.44	MURDER	NETH.
OTT,Heinrich	24996	M		09	Army,Annonay (Fr.) 4.8.44	MURDER	FR.
OTT,Hermann	167112	M	Ger.		Pvt.,Army,Billy sur Mangrennes (Fr.) 31.7.44	WITNESS	FR.
OTT,Johann	29704	M			Dr.,Landgerichtsrat,Public official,Cheb (Czech.) 40	MURDER	CZECH.
OTT,Rudolph	155501	M			Lt.,Army,Morlaix,St.Pol de Leon (Fr.) 44	MURDER	FR.
OTTA	167770	M	Ger.		Einsatzstab,Paris (Fr.) 40-44	PILLAGE	FR.

NAME	C.R.FILE NUMBER	SEX	NATIO-NALITY	DATE OF BIRTH	RANK OCCUPATION UNIT PLACE AND DATE OF CRIME	REASON WANTED	WANTED BY
OTTE	193326	M	Ger.		Hptschfhr.,SS,4.SS Totenkopf Sturmbann,C.C.,Mittelbau Dora, Nordhausen,Auschwitz (Ger.,Pol.) 43-45	MURDER	U.S.
OTTE	300835	M	Ger.		Pvt.,1.Aufkl.Abt.,3.Coy.,2.Column,XV,Div.,Afrika Korps,St.Leger, (Arlon) 5.9.44	MISC.CRIMES	BEL.
OTTE, Carl	62463	M			Administration of the Occupied Nor. (Nor.)	MISC.CRIMES	U.N.W.C.C.
OTTE, Karl	187722	M	Ger.		High official,Economic Administration, (Nor.)	PILLAGE	U.N.W.C.C.
OTTEINHEIM, Hugo	251222	M			Oschfhr.,Gestapo,Limoges (Fr.)	INTERR.	FR.
OTTEN, Berta Maria	133255	F	Ger.	15. 1.01	Nurse,Kriegslazarett,Berg Oberbach (Ger.) 16.3.45	WITNESS	U.S.
OTTENBACHER	126374	M			Generallt.,C.C. of Special Action against underground Army in Southern-France,Mont-Lucon (Fr.) 13.8.44	MURDER	U.S.
OTTENDORFER, Fritz	160434	M		05	Ortsbauernfhr.,Ortsbauernschaft,Member of SA,NSDAP,Strobnitz (Aust.)44	TORTURE	U.S.
OTTENHEIMER	305486	M	Ger.		S.D.Mannstationed in Amsterdam (Neth.) 20.4.45	MISC.CRIMES	NETH.
OTTER	141425	M	Ger.		Cpl.,28.Pi.,116.Bn.,1.Coy.,Tarbes (Fr.) 16.7.44	MURDER	FR.
OTTER	189108	M			Pvt.,1.Coy.,116.Inf.Bn.,28.Rgt.,Sombrun (Fr.) 15.-27.7.44	MURDER	FR.
OTTER-BACHER	62464	M	Ger.		Commandeur,Army,Deputy Mil.Commander North France(North France)	TORTURE	U.N.W.C.C.
OTTERER, Max	259669	M	Ger.		Uschfhr.,SS,Gestapo Area Angers,Maine,Loire (Fr.) 42-44	MISC.CRIMES	FR.
OTTES	141589	M			Stalag IX B,Rodan (Fr.) 7.43	TORTURE	FR.
OTTINGER	148658	M			Hptsturmfhr.,SS,Gestapo,Hoerde (Ger.)	MURDER	U.S.
OTTINGER, Ludwig	193328	M	Ger.		Sturmmann,4.SS Totenkopf Sturmbann,C.C.,Dora-Mittelbau,Nordhausen (Ger.)	MURDER	U.S.
OTTMAN	262304	M			Doctor,Physician,L.O.D.N.A.C.D.,Kaufbeuren (Ger.) 29-45	MURDER	U.S.
OTTMANN	155502	M	Ger.	99	Hptschfhr.,Gestapo,Vichy (Fr.) 44	TORTURE	FR.
OTTMANN	157994	M	Ger.	98	Hptschfhr.,SS,Gestapo,Hameau des Rosches (Fr.) 5.3.44	MURDER	FR.
OTTMANN, Ludwig	192553	M	Ger.		Crim.Employee,Gestapo,Brno (Czech.) 39-45	SUSPECT	CZECH.
OTTMANN, Matthias	136334	M	Ger.	90	Director,Civilian,Kinderheim,Burgkirchen (Ger.) 44-45	MURDER	U.S.
OTTMAR	255069	M		11.11.05	Pvt.,C.C.,Nordhausen,Harzungen (Ger.)	MURDER	U.S.
OTTO	678	M	Ger.		Doctor,Reichskommissar,Public official,Warsaw (Pol.) 9.39-1.42	MURDER	POL.
OTTO	679	M	Ger.		Generallt.,Army,13.Motor Div.,(Ger.) 1.9.30-10.39	MURDER	POL.
OTTO	680	M	Ger.		Lt.,Army,9C.Motor Inf.Div.,1.Bn.,Savoy (Fr.) 22.-31.8.44	MURDER	FR.
OTTO	128025	M			Col.,Flak Rgt.12,	MURDER	U.S.
OTTO	137095	M	Ger.		Pvt.,Arbeitskommando E 10,C.C.,Jacobswalde (Ger.) 7.40	TORTURE	U.K.
OTTO	144393	M	Ger.		Officer,Abwehr,Paris (Fr.) 40-45	TORTURE	FR.
OTTO	152162	M	Ger.		Capt.,Kriegsmarine,St.Marine (Fr.) 30.6.44	MURDER	U.S.
OTTO	155498	M	Ger.		Major,Oberstabsarzt,C.C.,Torgau Stalag 4 D,(Ger.) 4.44-4.45	MURDER	U.K.
OTTO	161915	M	Ger.		Criminalrat,Reichsicherheitshauptamt,Kripo,C.C.,Buchenwald (Ger.)43-45	WITNESS	U.S.
OTTO	165711	M	Ger.		Osturmfhr.,SS,C.C.,Struthof (Pol.) 3.40	MURDER	U.S.
OTTO	167769	M	Ger.	43	Capt.,Sich.Rgt.,Paris (Fr.)	TORTURE	FR.
OTTO	173263	M	Ger.	12	Usturmfhr.,SS,Gestapo,SD,Interrogator,Noailies (Fr.) 9.8.44	MURDER	U.K.
OTTO	174152	M	Ger.		Osturmfhr.,SS,C.C.,Struthof (Fr.)	MURDER	FR.
OTTO	184227	M		89	Major,621.Landesschuetzen Bn.,C.C.,Berga (Ger.) 4.45	MURDER	U.S.
OTTO	185476	M		10	Uschfhr.,SD de Grenoble,Seyssinet (Fr.) 22.7.44	MURDER	FR.
OTTO	185477	M			Oschfhr.,2.SS Panz.Gren.Rgt."A.-H.",10.Coy.,3.Bn., Malmedy (Bel.)17.12.44	MURDER	U.S.
OTTO	189410	M			Hptschfhr.,SS,Gestapo,R.S.H.A.,SS attached,Trondheim (Nor.) 41	TORTURE	NOR.
OTTO	192746	M	Ger.		Lt.,SS,C.C.,Falstad (Nor.) 41-44	TORTURE	NOR.
OTTO	196313	M	Ger.		Lt.,C.C.,Dachau (Ger.) 10.44	TORTURE	BEL.
OTTO	250412	M	Ger.		Lageraeltester,C.C.,Buchenwald (Ger.)	INTERR.	FR.
OTTO	250413	M			Lt.,Cmdt.,6.Div.Paratroopers.17.Rgt.,Almkerk,Nieuwaal (Neth.) 14.-15.1.45	WITNESS	NETH.
OTTO	251221	M	Ger.		Lt.,Unit 35350 B,St.Remy Aux Bois (Fr.) 5.-7.9.44	MISC.CRIMES	FR.
OTTO	301070	M	Ger.		Osturmfhr.,SS,Chief of the political department of C.C.,Oranienburg (Ger.) 11.39-45	MURDER	CZECH.
OTTO	301839	M	Ger.		Interpreter,Feldgendarmerie,Pontarlier (Doubs) (Fr.) 5.44	MURDER	FR.
OTTO	301966	M	Ger.		Kapo,C.C.,Auschwitz (Pol.) 44	MURDER	POL.
OTTO, Armin	257956	M			Pvt.,150.Pz.Bde.,Meusebridge,Antwerpen (Bel.) 12.44	MISC.CRIMES	U.S.
OTTO, Bruno	196314	M	Ger.		Guard or Kapo,C.C.,Gusen (Aust.)	TORTURE	BEL.
OTTO, Erwin	192555	M	Ger.	19. 2.10	Head warden,Gestapo,Brno (Czech.) 39-45	SUSPECT	CZECH.
OTTO, Fritz	302090	M	Ger.		Kriminalsekretaer,Nordhausen (Ger.) 4.45	MURDER	POL.
OTTO, Fritz Johannes	137564	M			Oschfhr.,SS,C.C.,Weimar,Buchenwald (Ger.)	MURDER	U.S.
OTTO, Gisela	185549	F	Ger.	5.12.03	District leader of NSDAP women,Marcanske Lazne (Czech.) 39-45	MISC.CRIMES	CZECH.
OTTO, Johan	139058	M		19	Pvt.,Guard,Eno.248,Offel (Ger.) 41	MURDER	U.S.
OTTO, Johannes	193012	M	Ger.	16.11.06	Guard,Reichsjustizministerium,Prisoner Camp,C.C.,Finmark (Nor.) 9.3.45	MISC.CRIMES	NOR.
OTTO, Karl	196930	M	Ger.		Civilian,C.C.,Lintfort (Ger.) 10.-11.44	WITNESS	U.S.
OTTO, Karl	139739	M	Ger.		Lt.Col.,Army,Military Barracks,C.C.,Neckarsulm (Ger.) 3.45	MURDER	U.S.
OTTO, Ottomar	173294	M	Ger.	96	Sturmbannfhr.,SS,chief,Gestapo,C.C.,Langenzenn (Ger.) 43-45	MURDER	U.S.
OTTO, Wolfgang	161916	M	Ger.	11	Oschfhr.,SS,C.C.,Buchenwald (Ger.)	WITNESS	U.S.
OUGER, Anneliese	256073	F	Ger.		Guard,C.C.,Flossenburg (Ger.) 42-45	MURDER	FR.
OUTZ	192745	M	Ger.		Sanitaeter,Schupo,C.C.,Falstad (Nor.) 41-44	MISC.CRIMES	NOR.
OVENKAMPF	173215	M		15	Pvt.,610.Landesschuetzen Bn.,Stalag 20 B,C.C.,Haibstadt (Pol.)3.-11.41	TORTURE	U.K.
OVER, Helmut	240011	M	Ger.	18	Pvt.,Nachrichten Rgt.506,6.Coy.,Bad Wildungen (Ger.) 45	MISC.CRIMES	U.S.
OVERBACK, Johannes	256564	M	Ger.		Col.,Erasrode (Ger.) 27.9.44	MURDER	U.S.
OVERDECK	132083	M			N.C.O.,Sgt.,SS,C.C.,Flossenburg (Ger.)	TORTURE	U.S.
OVERDICK	250414	M			Major,Cmdt.,De Pace Vittel (Fr.) 6.40-44	PILLAGE	FR.
OVERDICK, Heinrich	306712	M	Ger.		German Civilian,near Bingen (Ger.) 12.9.44	BRUTALITY	U.S.
OVERHAGEN, Willy	262927	M	Ger.		7.Panz.Reconnaissance Coy.,L.O.D.N.A.O.D.,Sillersdorf (Ger.) 4.45	WITNESS	U.S.
OVERLACK (or OVERLOCK)	172457	M		99	Civilian,Baden-Baden,Gernsbach (Ger.) 9.8.44	MURDER	U.S.
OVERLOCK (see OVERLACK)	172457						
OX, Fred	31501	M	Ger.		Feldwebel,Feldgendarmerie 577,Romorantin (Fr.)	MURDER	FR.
PAAK	126478	M			Hptschfhr.,SS,C.C.,guard,Weimar,Buchenwald (Ger.)	TORTURE	U.S.
PAAPE (or VON PAAPE, or PAPER) Wilhelm	162687	M	Ger.		Geheime Feldpolizei,Bruessels (Bel.)	TORTURE	BEL.
PAAR, Karl	305211	M	Ger.		Chief,Secretary,Geheime Feldpolisei Gruppe 510,Gestapo of Livadia, Distomon,Kalamion,Aracbora,Vrastamites (Grc.) 43-44	MURDER	GRC.
PAARMAN, Walter	121482	M	Ger.	05	Inspector,Gestapo de Lille,Valenciennes,Maubeuge (Fr.) 29.12.43	MURDER	FR.
PABSTDORF	124757	M	Ger.	10	Uschfhr.,SS,Crim.Asst.,Kripo Lublin (Pol.)	MURDER	U.S.
PACH, Ferdinand Fritz	305096	M	Ger.		Lt.,Chief,Gestapo,Heraklion Grete,Svtia-Grete, 5.44	MURDER	GRC.
PACHELT	121491	M	Ger.		Sgt.,Army,Landesschuetzen Bn.439,2.Coy.,C.C.,Stalag VIII c, Freiwaldau (Ger.) 9.-12.44	TORTURE	U.K.

PAC-PAN

NAME	C.R.FILE NUMBER	SEX	NATIO-NALITY	DATE OF BIRTH	RANK	OCCUPATION UNIT	PLACE AND DATE OF CRIME	REASON WANTED	WANTED BY
PACHEN, Hermann	905682	M	Ger.			Member of C.C. personnel, C.C. Flossenburg, Hersbruck, Wolkenburg, Gramacker, Leitmeritz, betw. 1.1.42 and 8.5.45		MURDER	U.S.
PACHER, Hans	198323	M				SS-Scharfhr., Gestapo, Lyon (Fr.) 6.-8.44		MURDER	FR.
PACHERRA, Max	906488	M	Ger.			SS Uscharfhr., C.C.Buchenwald (Ger.) betw.16.5.38 and 9.10.43		MURDER	BEL.
PACHOLIK, R.	254904	M	Ger.			Dr., Lab.assist., C.C. Dachau.(Ger.) 3.42		INTERR.	BEL.
PACHUR	141432	M	Ger.	.03		Kriegsgerichtsrat, Feldkommandantur 529, Bordeaux, Souges (Fr.)		MURDER	FR.
PACKE, Richard	129759	M	Ger.			Ward at the camp, Strafgef.Lager Rhein.Zellwolle A.G., Siegburg (Ger.) 9.-8.42		MURDER	BEL.
PACKERT	253542	M	Ger.			Employee, SIPO, Brussels (Bel.) 40-44		INTERR.	BEL.
PACKHEISSER, Max	255617	M				Flyer, C.C. Ellrich, Nordhausen (Ger.)		MURDER	U.S.
PADE, Willi	192934	M	Ger.	.12		C.C. Flossenburg (Ger.) 44-45		MURDER	U.S.
PADOCK	252578	M	Ger.			Sgt., Army, Op den Koem, Oldenzaal (Neth.) 1.4.45		PILLAGE	NETH.
PADUCH, Karl	180501	M	Ger.	14. 9.00		SS.Hptsturmfhr., C.C. Hradistko (Czech.) 42-45		MURDER	CZECH.
PAELICKE, Arnoldt	185981	M	Ger.			Adjutant-chief, 3.Inf.Rgt. Navy 2.Coy., Queven (Fr.)		MURDER	FR.
PAEPE, Rudolf	255199	M	Ger.			Pvt. 377.Jaeger-Rgt. 10.Coy., Vinkt-Meigem (Bel.) 25.-31.5.40		MISC.CRIMES	BEL.
PAERSCH, Fritz	199082	M	Ger.			Head, Bureau of banks insurance, Gen.Government, Pol.		MISC.CRIMES	POL.
PAETEL	193596	M	Ger.			Civ., Lezaki (Czech.) 42		MISC.CRIMES	CZECH.
PAETOW, Fritz	159197	M				Sturmfhr., Camp-cmdt., S.A., Labour-camp, Bautorf (Ger.)		TORTURE	U.S.
PAETOW, Fritz	151545	M				Cmdt., C.C. Kunsebeck (Ger.) 26.3.45		MURDER	U.S.
PAETZ	174165	M	Ger.	.00		Official, SS Mann, Gestapo, prison of vert galant, Le Mans (Fr.) 29.12.43-7.1.44		MURDER	FR.
PAETZ	900727	M.	Ger.			Member of a Cmdo at St.Die (Fr.) 9.44		MURDER	U.K.
PAETZELT, Paul	199961	M		.05		Crim.secretary, SS-Sturmscharfhr., Gestapo, Lanskron (Czech.) 38-45		TORTURE	CZECH.
PAFSLER or PAHSLER	146975	M	Ger.			Lt., Army phil.Panz.Div., South-west, Le Roc, Lot (Fr.) 28.6.44		MURDER	FR.
PAGEK	257484	M	Ger.			Employee, C.C. Dora-Nordhausen (Ger.)		MURDER	U.S.
PAGEL	132347	M				Civ., C.C. Dora-Nordhausen (Ger.)		MURDER	U.S.
PAGEL, Thomas see POGEL	136306								
PAGELS, August	151599	M	Ger.			Civ., C.C.Ra (Stahlwerk) Hannover (Ger.) 42-45		MURDER	U.S.
PAHL	12516	M	Ger.			Pvt., Army, Panz.Gren.Rgt. 110 or 111.Rgt., Gourdon (Fr.) 29.6.44		MURDER	FR.
PAHL	257477	M	Ger.			Oscharfhr., S.D., Kirkenes (Nor.)		WITNESS	NOR.
PAHL, Robert	259294	M	Ger.			SS.Mann, Muehldorf Area (Ger.)		MURDER	U.S.
PAHNKE	195153	M	Ger.			SS Osturmfhr., 1.SS Unterfuehrerschule Arnheim, Rossum-Alemand, Kerkwijk (Neth.)		MURDER	NETH.
PAHSLER see PAFSLER	146975								
PAIBEL	126375	M	Ger.			Hptscharfhr., Guard, SS, Magdeburg, Buchenwald (Ger.) 44-45		TORTURE	U.S.
PAIM	187557	M	Ger.			SS Osturmfhr., 12.SS Panz.Div., Cafn (Fr.)		TORTURE	CAN.
PAINE	166627	M	Ger.			Farmer, Civ., Wackersleben (Ger.) 7.44		TORTURE	U.S.
PAINOR	260021	M	Ger.			Gendarm, Russ.Ger.Division Oberland, Massif du Versors, Isere et Drome (Fr.) 20.7.-5.8.44		SUSPECT	FR.
PAK, Ferdinand Fritz	186246	M	Ger.			Lt., Gestapo, Toplou-Sitea (Grc.)		MURDER	GRC.
PAL, Naudor	189107	M				Dr., Police-chief, Kolozsvar (Hung.) 5.44		MISC.CRIMES	FR.
PALAND, Wilhelm	166626	M	Ger.			Civ. probably farmer, Reiffenhausen (Ger.) 8.44		TORTURE	U.S.
PALES, Karl	255871	M	Ger.			Pvt. Army, most probably Pioneer-group, Group Heudsen (Neth.) 11.44		PILLAGE	NETH.
PALES, Rudolf	261968	M	Ger.	4. 7.22		Gajdel, Prievidza (Czech.), Joiner, 9.44		MURDER	CZECH.
PALFNER, Gerhardt	161901	M	Ger.	11		Usturmfhr., SS, C.C. Buchenwald (Ger.)		WITNESS	U.S.
PALIG	108891	M	Ger.			Hptscharfhr., Waffen SS, C.C. Auschwitz (Pol.)		TORTURE	U.S.
PALIMER	136904	M	Ger.			Sgt., Feldgendarmerie, Parachutist 6.Div., Domart, Ville le Marolet (Fr.) 8.44		MURDER	FR.
PALIS, Gustav	149067	M	Ger.	86		Sgt. Major, Volkssturm, I.Coy., Gardelegen (Ger.) 9.4.45-14.4.45		MURDER	U.S.
PALISCH	173289	M	Ger.			SS, Hptscharfhr., C.C. Auschwitz (Pol.)		MURDER	POL.
PALITISCH	174083	M				Oberfhr. S.D., C.C. Oswiecim-Birkenau (Pol.) 39-45		MURDER	CZECH.POL. FR.YUGO.BEL.
PALITSCH	118113	M	Ger.			Hptscharfhr., SS, C.C.Auschwitz (Pol.) 40-45		MURDER	POL.U.K.,U.S.
PALITSCH	190055	M	Ger.			SS Oscharfhr., C.C. Oswiecim (POL.) 4.42-4.44		MURDER	YUGO.
PALITSCH	196407	M	Ger.			Hptsturmfhr., C.C. Neuengamme (Ger.)		TORTURE	BEL.
PALITSCH	300542	M	Ger.			Recording-officer, SS, Arbeitsdienstfuehrer, C.C.Auschwitz, Birkenau (Pol.) 42-45		MISC.CRIMES	YUGO.
PALK, Frank	682	M	Ger.			Gestapo, Lyon (Fr.) 27.7.44		MURDER	U.S.
PALKZ	153196	M		.14		Oscharfhr., Waffen SS, C.C. Auschwitz (Pol.)		MURDER	U.S.
PALL	255618	M				Pvt., C.C. Dora-Nordhausen (Ger.)		MURDER	U.S.
PALLAND, Fritz	255619	M				Uscharfhr., C.C. Ellrich, Nordhausen (Ger.)		MURDER	U.S.
PALLANOL, Georg	255726	M				SS.Mann, C.C. Harzungen, Nordhausen (Ger.)		MURDER	U.S.
PALLEEF	185552	M	Ger.			Civ., Member of S.D., Montgauthier (Dinant) (Bel.) 20.9.43		MURDER	BEL.
PALM, Guenther	187208	M	Ger.			Osturmfhr., 12. SS "Hitler-Jugend", 12.SS Panz.Div., 12.SS Panz.Recce Unit, Caen (Fr.) 6.6.-8.7.44		TORTURE	CAN.
PALM	257651		Ger.			Employee, Factory-worker, C.C. Nordhausen (Ger.)		MURDER	U.S.
PALM, Liesel	135291	F	Ger.			Civ., Effern (Ger.) 2.10.44		WITNESS	U.S.
PALMANN	173868	M	Ger.			Lt., Feldgendarmerie, St Pol de Leon, Morlaix (Fr.) 7.-8.44		MURDER	FR.
PALMIE	250425	M	Ger.			SS Uscharfhr., C.C. Buchenwald (Ger.)		MISC.CRIMES	FR.
PALUK	260686	M	Ger.			SS, Buchenwald (Ger.) 40-44		BRUTALITY	FR.
PAMAN, Albert	157541	M		05		Uscharfhr., SS, C.C. Weimar-Buchenwald (Ger.)		TORTURE	U.S.
PAMER	136939	M	Ger.			Uscharfhr., SS, Hinzert, Wittlich (Ger.) 41-43		WITNESS	U.S.
PAMMER, Anton	38845	M	Ger.	31. 9.09		Oscharfhr., Guard, SS, C.C. Hinzert, Buchenwald (Ger.) 42-45		TORTURE	U.S.
PAMMINGER	257022	M.	Ger.	about 19		Oscharfhr., Waffen SS, SS-N.C.O.-school, Radolfzell (Ger.) 20.7.44		MURDER	FR.
PAMP, Walter	251229	M	Ger.			Kapo, C.C. Neuengamme (Ger.) 44		TORTURE	FR.
PAMPERL	142072	M	Ger.			Col., Army, Artillery, Cmdt. of Stalag 17, C.C. Kaisersteinbruch (Aust.) 44-45		TORTURE	U.S.,U.K.
PAMPUS	137542	M				Oscharfhr., SS, C.C. Weimar-Buchenwald (Ger.)		TORTURE	U.S.
PANAROWSKI	185109	M	Ger.			SS-chief, C.C. Sachsenhausen,Oranienburg (Ger.)		TORTURE	FR.
PANBERG	193973	M	Ger.			Major-Gen. 230. Inf.Div., Nor.		MURDER	NOR.
PANCZYK, Vincenz	196869	M	Ger.	19. 7.20		SS-Mann, Waffen SS, Guard-Coy., C.C. Auschwitz (Pol.) 40-45		MURDER	FR.,POL.
PANDEL	132084	M	Ger.			Civ., Bad Duerrenberg (Ger.) 29.5.44		TORTURE	U.S.
PANEK	901592	M	Ger.			Secretary, C.C. Mauthausen, (Aust.) 40-45		MURDER	BEL.
PANENKA, Karl	10320	M	Ger.			Dr., Public prosecutor, Ministre of justice, Cheb (Czech.) 40		MURDER	CZECH.
PANGERT, Kurt	905214	M	Ger.			N.C.O., Infant. at Breskens and commandant by F.Lt. Hendriks, F.P. No. 02744 or 37214 B, Breskens (Neth.) 4.9.44		MURDER	NETH.
PANITZ, W.	190921	M				C.C. Dachau (Ger.)		MURDER	U.S.
PANK, Johann	255727	M				SS Mann, C.C. Ellrich, Nordhausen (Ger.)		MURDER	U.S.
PANKE, Paul	155694	M				Civ., C.C. Gardelegen (Ger.) 4.45		MURDER	U.S.

PAN-PAT

NAME	C.R.FILE NUMBER	SEX	NATIO-NALITY	DATE OF BIRTH	RANK OCCUPATION UNIT PLACE AND DATE OF CRIME	REASON WANTED	WANTED BY
PANNECK	191339	M			Sturmmann, Leibst."A.Hitler" 1.SS-Panz.Regt., Ligneuville (Fr.) 12.44	WITNESS	U.S.
PANNITZ	250426	M	Ger.		Commander, C.C. Dachau (Ger.) 42	MURDER	YUGO.
PANNKUCH, Gerhardt	161894	M			Lt., SS-Div. "Adolf Hitler", 12.Regt., Arnheim (Neth.) 9.44	MURDER	NETH.
PANNY	108892	M	Ger.	97	Cpl., Army, 890.Landessch.Coy., C.C. Mistelbach (Ger.) 7.44-4.45	TORTURE	U.K.
PANTCHAU	193796	M	Ger.	16	Cashier, Civ.firm, Glanzstoff-works, Elserberg (Ger.) 12.40	BRUTALITY	FR.
PANTEL, Heinz	254090	M	Ger.		Unterscharfhr., SS, Gouda, Utrecht (Neth.) 10.44	MURDER	NETH.
PANTKE	39679	M	Ger.		Sgt., 398.Land.Schtz.Bn., 5.Coy., Schomberg (Ger.) 44	MURDER	U.K.
PANTLI or PAUTLI, Franz	256125	M	Ger.		SS-Mann, C.C. Muehldorf (Ger.)	WITNESS	U.S.
PANWITZ	189908	M			Sgt., Kgf. 3.Coy., Arb.Bn. 184, Kraakmoen (Nor.)	WITNESS	NOR.
PANY, Ignace	185104	M			Sgt., Army, St.Gerand (Fr.) 10.43	WITNESS	FR.
PANZEGRO	121483	M	Ger.	25	N.C.O., SS, C.C. Yaworzno (Ger.)	MURDER	FR.
PANZER	38847	M	Ger.		Dr., Gestapo, Prison Klingelpuetz (Ger.) 44-45	TORTURE	U.S.
PANZER	166972	M	Ger.		Lt., Kauk.Bn., Pont L'Abbe, St.Pol de Leon (Fr.) 6.-8.44	MURDER	FR.
PANZER, Anton	196609	M	Ger.		Member, Gestapo, (Czech.)	MISC.CRIMES	CZECH.
PANZERGRO	306642	M	Ger.		W.O., SS-Camp, Blechammer, Jaworzno Camp, Silesia, 43-45	MURDER	FR.
PANZL, Siegfried	255864	M	Ger.	7.10.95	Civilian, Podbrezova (Czech.) 40-45	INTERR.	CZECH.
PAOL, Willy	125632	M	Ger.		Guard, Prison of Pierre Leves, C.C. Poitiers (Fr.) 40-44	MURDER	FR.
PAOLI	306643	M	Ger.		Col., Cmdt., C.C. Neuengamme (Ger.) 2.40-4.45	MURDER	FR.
PAPALA	195840	M	Ger.		Custom-official, Zollgrenzschutz St.Beat, Chaum (Fr.) 6.44	MURDER	FR.
PAPE	12517	M			Pvt., Pz.Gren.Regt. 111.or 110. Regt., 2.Coy., Albine (Fr.) 6.44	MURDER	FR.
PAPE	139668	F			Guard, W-SS, Arbeitslager.101, C.C. Buchenwald, Magdeburg (Ger.) 44-45	TORTURE	U.S.
PAPE	162686	M	Ger.		Lt., Army, 3. Landesschuetzen-Bn. 444 or 9. Art.Regt. 295 Sunndalsoera (Nor.) 45	TORTURE	NOR.
PAPEN, Wilhelm (see PAAPE)	162687						
PAPENHAGEN	900836	M	Ger.		Pvt., 1. Aufklaerungsabteilung, 3.Coy., 2.Col., 15. Div. of the Africa corps, St. Leger (Arlon) 9.44	MISC.CRIMES	BEL.
PAPERTZ	133265	M			Sgt., W-SS, C.C. Flossenburg (Ger.)	TORTURE	U.S.
PAPKE or PAPKI or PAPKA	124968	M			Wachtmeister, Gestapo, C.C. Bremen-Farge (Ger.) 6.43	MURDER	U.K.
PAPLICEK	143028	M			Hauptscharfhr., C.C. Flossenburg (Ger.)	MURDER	U.S.
PAPE	157986	M	Ger.		Capt., W-SS, Gestapo, Bratislava (Czech.) 42-44	MURDER	CZECH.
PAPPENMEYER, Fritz	153194	M			Civilian, Fattensen (Ger.) 3.45	TORTURE	U.S.
PAPPLEL or POPPEL, Max	255728	M			Pvt., C.C. Ellrich, Nordhausen (Ger.)	MURDER	U.S.
PAPRICHARK	143027	M			Unterscharfhr., SS, C.C. Flossenburg (Ger.)	MURDER	U.S.
PAPROTNY	256124	M	Ger.		SS-Mann, C.C. Mushldorf (Ger.)	WITNESS	U.S.
PAPSYNSKE, Alex	193178	M	Ger.		Cpl., Scheinwerfer-Abtlg., Wilhelmshaven (Ger.) 10.44	WITNESS	CAN.
PAQUET, Vinzens	141380	M	Ger.		Lt., Luftnachr.Coy. 8, Villemoustaussou (Fr.) 8.44	PILLAGE	FR.
PARAI	34419	M	Ger.		Major, Nebelwerf-Abtlg., Finmark (Nor.)	TORTURE	NOR.
PARAKENINGS, Max	259165	M	Ger.		SS-Sturmmann, C.C. Dachau (Ger.) 12.42-45	MISC.CRIMES	YUGO.
PARASINI	131914	M			Pvt., SS, C.C. Jawischowitz (Pol.) 44	MURDER	U.S.
PARCHI or PORCHI	901596	M	Ger.		Col., operating in Monceau sur Sambre (Bel.) with German troops 9.44	PILLAGE	BEL.
PARCHMANN	191484	M	Ger.		Reichsforstmeister, Reichsforstamt (Pol.) 9.39-44	LOOTING	POL.
PARCK, Werner	137540	M	Ger.		Unterscharfhr., SS, C.C. Weimar-Buchenwald (Ger.)	TORTURE	U.S.
PARDON	153193	M	Ger.	10.	Sgt., Totenkopf-Standarte, W-SS, C.C. Buchenwald (Ger.)	TORTURE	U.S.
PARDUHN, Karl	153192	M	Ger.	21. 9.87	Sturmscharfhr., SS-Totenkopf-Standarte, 5.Coy., C.C.Buchenwald (Ger.)	TORTURE	U.S.
PARK, Werner	137540	M	Ger.		SS-Unterscharfhr., C.C. Weimar-Buchenwald (Ger.)	TORTURE	U.S.
PARKAS	129736	M			Rottenfhr., W-SS, C.C. Mauthausen (Aust.) 41-45	MURDER	U.S.
PARKE	10158	M	Ger.	95 - 00	Sgt., Army, Working-Party K 593, 398.Bn., 5.Coy., Beuthen-Schoemberg (Ger.) 3.43	MURDER	U.K.
PARKE, Erich	153191				Member, Hitler Jugend, C.C. Gardelegen (Ger.) 4.45	MURDER	U.S.
PARKER	192504	M	Ger.		Employee, Gestapo, Brno (Czech.) 39-45	WITNESS	CZECH.
PARKS, Paul	306489	M	Ger.	12. 2.07	Pvt., SS, C.C. Buchenwald (Ger.) 5.38-10.43	MURDER	BEL.
PARMANN	121489	M	Ger.		Sturmfhr., SS, Landrecies (Fr.) 1.44	MISC.CRIMES	FR.
PARNAWALD (see BARNEWALD)	133760						
PARNOW, Greta	139669	F	Ger.	19	Guard, Arbeitslager 101, W-SS, C.C. Magdeburg (Ger.) 44-45	TORTURE	U.S.
PARRISIUS, Felix	261102	M	Ger.	24. 3.85	Attorney General, Peoples Court,	SUSPECT	U.S.
PARSCH, Kurt	255182	M			Cpl., C.C. Ellrich, Nordhausen (Ger.)	MURDER	U.S.
PARTA, Wladislawa	153189	F			Civilian, Lauf (Ger.)	WITNESS	U.S.
PARTENHEIMER, Frida	192606	F	Ger.		Oberwachtmeisterin, Schupo, S.D., Trondheim (Nor.) 41-45	MURDER	NOR.
PASCH	135211	M	Ger.		Guard, C.C. Oppien near Krefeld (Ger.)	TORTURE	FR.
PASCH, Paul	126479	M	Ger.		Member, NSDAP, Kreis Kempen (Ger.)	TORTURE	U.S.
PASCHEN	153188	M	Ger.	95	Lt.Col., W-SS, C.C.Flossenburg (Ger.) 40-45	TORTURE	U.S., POL.
PASCHEN, Ernst	306490	M	Ger.	10. 1.22	Pvt., SS, C.C. Buchenwald (Ger.) 5.38-10.43	MURDER	BEL.
PASCHER	161907	M	Ger.		Unterscharfhr., C.C. Buchenwald (Ger.)	WITNESS	U.S.
PASCHEK, Albert	254915	M	Ger.	21. 2.10	Kommandantur, Niergnies, Cambrai (Fr.) 8.44	TORTURE	FR.
PASCHKE	139722	M			Betriebsleiter, Glanzstoffwerke, Koeln (Ger.) 40	MURDER	U.S.
PASCHOTTA, Josef	251230	M	Ger.		Cmdt., Lt., Huybergen (Neth.)	PILLAGE	NETH.
PASENAU, Paul	192607	M	Ger.	01	Sgt., Guard, Reichsjustizministerium, Strafgef.Lg.Nord C.C. - Nord, Finmark (Nor.) 42-45	MISC.CRIMES	NOR., YUGO.
PASMAN	306911	M	Ger.		Prison-warder, Almelo (Neth.) 3.45	MURDER	U.K.
PASQUALI	190294	M	Ger.		Major, Kommandantur, Kraljevo (Yugo.) 43	MURDER	YUGO.
PASSAVANT	167789	M	Ger.		Capt., Army, Chateaufoux (Fr.) 9.44	MURDER	FR.
PASSEK, Rudolf	259998	M			Wachtmeister, Schupo, 6.Coy., 209.Bn., Believed to live in Hassfurth am Main, U.S.-Zone, Germany, Praha and Kobylisy Bohemia (Czech.) 42	MURDER	CZECH.
PASSELT (see PASSET)	155532						
PASSENT	305802	M	Ger.		Capt., Camp Command Oflag VI-C, Osnabrueck-Ewersheide (Ger.) 43-45	MURDER	YUGO.
PASSET or PASSELT	155532	M			Member, Volkssturm, C.C. Gardelegen (Ger.) 4.45	MURDER	U.S.
PASSLAK, Karl	255184	M		12. 9.99	Pvt., C.C. Harzungen, Nordhausen (Ger.)	MURDER	U.S.
PASSMANN	191849	M			Sgt., F.P. 59156 or 39196, Billy (Fr.)	INCENDIARISM	FR.
PAST	261960	M	Ger.		SS-Obersturmfhr., S.D., various places in Slovenia (Yugo.) 41-45	MISC.CRIMES	YUGO.
PASZEK	119402	M	Ger.		Cpl., Army, C.C. Oswiecim (Pol.) 6.40-1.45	MURDER	POL.
PATACK	198326	M	Ger.		Policeman, Geheime Feldpolizei, Montigny en Gohelle (Fr.) 9.44	MURDER	FR.
PATCH	254755	M	Ger.		Officer, Custom-house, Machilly Loisin (Fr.) 4.44	TORTURE	FR.
PATCH, Arthur	124100	M		85	Pvt., Stalag 4-G, 4.Coy., Inf., Ammelshain near Leipzig (Ger.) 44-45	MISC.CRIMES	U.K.
PATGEN, Robert	260828	M	Ger.		Pvt., Army, Elversberg (Ger.) 7.44	WITNESS	U.S.
PATIG, Herbert	10321	M	Ger.		Dr., Staatsanwalt, Ministry of Justice, Cheb (Czech.) 40	MURDER	CZECH.

PAT-PAW

NAME	C.R.FILE NUMBER	SEX	NATIO-NALITY	DATE OF BIRTH	RANK OCCUPATION UNIT PLACE AND DATE OF CRIME	REASON WANTED	WANTED BY
PATIG, Karl	305936	M	Ger.		Dr.,SS Hptsturmfhr.,Head of the Plzen Aussenstelle of the SD.Leitab-schnitt,Prague,Oswiecim,CC Birkenau(Pol.)39-45	MURDER	CZECH.
PATIK, Raimund	192495	M	Ger.	13.7.99	Employee,Gestapo,Brno(Czech.)39-45	SUSPECT	CZECH.
PATRON, Johann	306491	M	Ger.	12.12.91	SS Scharf., CC Buchenwald (Ger.) 16.5.38 - 9.10.43	MURDER	BEL.
PATSCH	192505	M	Ger.		Employee,Gestapo,Brno(Czech.)39-45	SUSPECT	CZECH.
PATSCH	192608	M	Ger.	05	Ob.Wachtmeist.Sgt.Reichsjustizministerium-Feldstrafl.CC Nord,Finmark (Nor.)6.42-45	MISC.CRIMES	NOR. YUGO.
PATT, Theodore	144397	M			Policeman,Police Koeln(Ger.)3.3.45	WITNESS	U.S.
PATTI, Leo	139062	M			Civilian	MURDER	U.S.
PATZ	39678	M	Ger.		Pvt.(SS Kanonier)SS Div.Chateau Gontier,F.P.No.48963B,St.Sulpice Mt.Musson(Fr.)6.8.44	MURDER	FR.
PATZAK, Julius	174082	M	Ger.		Gestapo,Leitstelle,CC Brno,Oswiecim-Birkenau (Pol.) 39-45	MURDER	CZECH.
PATZAK, Ludmila	192496	F	Ger.	16.1.10.	Clerk,Gestapo,Brno(Czech.)39-45	WITNESS	CZECH.
PATZELT, Antonin	193962	M	Ger.	13.2.06	Hptwachtmeister,Gendarmerie,Dolni-Cerekev(Czech.)9.4.45	MURDER	CZECH.
PATZELT, Julius	253538	M	Ger.		Civilian,Clerk,Prag(Czech.)42	MURDER	CZECH.
PATZELT, Robert	190295	M	Ger.		Inspector,Reichsbahn,Laibach,Zagreb,Sued-Steiermark(Yugo.)4.41,5.43-44	MURDER	YUGO.
PATZHOLD, Alfred	306492	M	Ger.		Scharfhr.,SS,(No.236277)CC Buchenwald(Ger.)16.5.38 - 9.10.43	MURDER	BEL.
PATZOLD, Alfred	162064	M	Ger.		Sgt.Camp,Hustad Bud(Nor.)3.9.43	MURDER	NOR.
PATZOLD, Herbert	38894	M	Ger.		Oschafhr.Army SS Totenkopf,Pz.Jg.Abt.1006	TORTURE	U.S.
PATZOLO, Francois	151527	M		02	Sgt.(SS Stabsfeldwebel)Director of mines,Knutange(Fr.)4.9.44	TORTURE	FR.
PAUCKNEL, Alois	261605	M	Ger.	23.4.06	Member,Gestapo of Mulhouse,domicile Lambrecht(Bavaria)(Fr.)	BRUTALITY	FR.
PAUCO, Josef alias Franz Mitz	261884	M	Ger.	26.2.14.	Dr.,Agent,City Editor Chief,S.D.Bratislava(Czech.)38-45	SUSPECT	CZECH.
PAUKER	257957	M			Lt.Member of Freese's Det.150 Pz.Bde.Meuse Bridge Antwerp,12.44	MISC.CRIMES	U.S.
PAUL	31410	M	Ger.		Lt.Col.Army Pi.Regt.550,Finmark(Nor.)44	MURDER	NOR.
PAUL	155711	M	Ger.		Lt.Army,10 Coy.Unit 57515C,Cleder(Fr.)8.8.44	MURDER	FR.
PAUL	185027	M	Ger.		N.C.O.Army,8 Bde.Foye(Crete)(Grc.)8.44	MURDER	GRC.
PAUL	185028	M	Ger.		Cpl.Army,Kissamou(Grc.)9.44	MURDER	GRC.
PAUL	253225	M	Ger.		Hptscharfhr.SS Sipo,Abt.III B,Bruessel(Bel.)40-44	INTERR.	BEL.
PAUL	254120	M	Ger.		Lt.Police,5 Coy.Amsterdam(Neth.)19.3.45	MURDER	NETH.
PAUL	254750	M	Ger.		SS Kapo, CC Neuengamme(Ger.)	MURDER	BEL.
PAUL	257653	M	Ger.		SS or S.D.,Saarbruecken(Ger.)7.-8.44	MISC.CRIMES	U.S.
PAUL, Christian	255183	M			Sturmmann,CC Bodungen/Nordhausen(Ger.)	MURDER	U.S.
PAUL, Egbert	196408	M	Ger.	7.4.08	Dr.,Chief of District,Civil Service,Hodonin(Czech.)41-45	SUSPECT	CZECH.
PAUL, Ewald	192497	M	Ger.	13.4.06	Warder,Gestapo,Prison,Brno(Czech.)39-45	SUSPECT	CZECH.
PAUL, Friedrich or POHL or GEEWE	153200	M	Ger.		Lt.Gestapo,Varzay(Fr.)20.1.44	TORTURE	FR.
PAUL, Fritz	132653	M	Ger.	6.1.00	Oschafhr.SS Gestapo,Perigueux(Fr.)1.3.44	TORTURE	FR.
PAUL, Georg	255185	M		10.12.01	Schuetze,CC Harzungen/Nordhausen(Ger.)	MURDER	U.S.
PAUL, Karl	141590	M	Ger.		Adjudant-Chief,Feldgendarmerie,Beaune(Fr.)42	TORTURE	FR.
PAUL, Oscar	126578	M	Ger.		Civilian,CC Hagen(Ger.)40-45	MURDER	U.S.
PAUL, Otto	193372	M	Ger.	95	Oberstabsarzt,710 Div.CC Botn(Nor.)	MURDER	NOR.
PAUL, Walter	305684	M	Ger.		Kapo of the Potato Peelers,nr.CC Flossenburg,Hersbruck,Wolkenburg,Genacker,Leitmeritz(Ger.C.S.R.)1.1.42-8.5.45	MURDER	U.S.
PAUL, Willi	123946	M	Ger.	03	N.C.O.Army,Member of Guard Det.of Prison,Portiers(Fr.)11.43	TORTURE	U.S.
PAULCZYNSKI, Josef	196409	M		17.6.95	17 Pionier Regt.Amstetten(Aust.)20.3.45	SUSPECT	U.S.
PAULE, Gustav	253273	M	Ger.	93	Guard,Prison Camp,Oberndorf(Ger.)	TORTURE	FR.
PAULENTZ or PAULINTZ	153199	M	Ger.		Doctor,Arbeitskdo.476,CC Wewelsfeth(Ger.)	TORTURE	FR.
PAULMANN, Hermann	256028	M	Ger.		Pvt.Inf.Div."Treue Ist Ehre"Unite Saxome,Dampierre(Fr.)3.-4.41	PILLAGE	FR.
PAULI	121488	M	Ger.		SS Stubafhr.CC Neuengamme(Ger.)	TORTURE	FR.BEL.
PAULI	126480	M	Ger.		Stubafhr.(Major)SS Div.Totenkopf	MURDER	U.S.
PAULI	194838	M	Ger.	08	Lt.Adjutant,114 Jaeger Div.3 Bn.741,Comachio,Pavalo(It.)9.44-1.45	MURDER	U.K.
PAULI	305216	M	Ger.		SS Gruppenfhr.CC Buchenwald(Ger.)43-4.45	MURDER	FR.
PAULI, Georg	140801	M	Ger.		Ortsgruppenamtsleiter,NSDAP,Civilian Farmer,Annerod(Ger.)	TORTURE	U.S.
PAULI, Max	190296	M	Ger.	06	SS Stubafhr.CC Neuengamme(Ger.)43	MURDER	YUGO.
PAULIK, Rudolf	255355	M	Ger.	11.1.15	Employee,S.D.,Klatovy(Czech.)40-42	TORTURE	CZECH.
PAULINTZ see PAULENTZ	153199						
PAULMANN, Werner K.	261336	M	Ger.		Stubafhr.Waffen SS,CC Auschwitz,Majdanek,Treblinka,Gr.Rosen(Pol.)40-45	MURDER	POL.
PAULOKAT, Karl	192651	M	Ger.	99	Member Landwacht,Schlossberg,Petershausen(Ger.)25.10.43	MURDER	BEL.
PAULSEN	167795	M	Ger.	08	Crim.secretary,Sturmscharfhr.Gestapo,SS,Brussels(Bel.)44	MURDER	BEL.
PAULSEN	250427	M	Ger.		Lt.Army,443 Jaeger Regt.,Belgrad(Yugo.)3.10.41-25.12.41	MURDER	YUGO.
PAULSEN	306101	M	Ger.		Rottfhr.Blockfhr.,Alderney(Channel 15)CC Kortemark,42-45	MURDER	CZECH.
PAULSEN	306567	M	Ger.		Prof.Dr.,SS Lt.Kommando Paulsen for the Sicherstellung von Kulturge schichtlichen Denkmaeler in Polen,Cracow(Pol.)10.39	PILLAGE	POL.
PAULSEN, Paul or PAULSEN, Karsten or PAULSEN, Fritz	161896	M	Ger.	11	SS Scharfhr.SS Pz.Div.Das Reich,A Coy.Inst.Abt.2,Altenkirchen Krs.Kusel (Ger.)9.44	MURDER	U.S.
PAULSEN, Wilhelm	158073	M	Ger.	08	SS Oschafr,Krim.Asst.SS Sipo,Brussels(Bel.)	MURDER	BEL.
PAULUS	153187	M	Ger.		Capt.Army,Hermann Goering Div.Parachute-Unit,Mentana(It.)27.10.43	MURDER	U.K.
PAULUS	186137	M	Ger.		Pvt.Army,La Roche Posay(Fr.)28.8.44	MURDER	FR.
PAULUS	186769	M	Ger.		Sgt.Chief,Army,La Vienne(Fr.)	MURDER	FR.
PAULUS	305217	M			Interpreter second-in-command,Geheime Feldpolizei Group 510,Dienststelle 47661,Geheime Feld Blitzer of Livadia,Vrastamites nr.Livadia Beotia (Grc.)8.1.44	MURDER	GRC.
PAULUS, Friedrich	255195	M	Ger.	90	Generalfeldmarschall,Army,Vinkt,Meigem(Bel.)25.-31.5.40	MURDER	BEL.
PAULY	683	M			SS Osturmbannfhr.CC Stutthof(Ger.)9.39 - 42	MURDER	POL.
PAULY	255304	M	Ger.	19	Medical Surgeon Capt.21 Regt.7 parachute Div. Elsass (Fr.)	MURDER	U.S.
PAULY	256127	M	Ger.	02	SS Gruppenfhr.CC Dora/Nordhausen(Ger.)	TORTURE	FR.
PAULY, Karl	260865	M			Resides at House No.38,Igel,Ger.French Zone,LODNACO,Schweich(Ger.)1.45	WITNESS	U.S.
PAULZEN	132795	M			5 paratrooper-Regt.Nachrichtenzug,Quaregnon-Jemappes,Ghlin(Bel.)9.44	MURDER	BEL.
PAUMGARTNER	189650	M	Ger.		Osturmfhr.Adjutant,SS Totenkopfverband,CC Flossenburg(Ger.)44	MURDER	FR.
TAUR	195566	M	Ger.		Lt.Gendarmerie,Mizocz(Pol.)14.10.42	MURDER	POL.
PAUSEN	196600	M	Ger.		Unit F.P.50510,Plougras(Fr.)6.6.44	MURDER	FR.
PAUTLI see PANTLI, Franz	256125						
PAVLOWSKI	145974	M			Pvt.SS Pz.Div.Das Reich,Tulle(Fr.)44	MURDER	FR.
PAVOSBERCH	188954	M			1st Class Agent of Train,Railway,Le Bourget-Triage(Fr.)24.8.44	WITNESS	FR.
PAWALOWSKI, Stephan	254108	M			Pvt.Army,Maasbracht(Neth.)29.12.44	MURDER	NETH.

PAW-PEL

NAME	C.R.FILE NUMBER	SEX	NATIO-NALITY	DATE OF BIRTH	RANK	OCCUPATION UNIT PLACE AND DATE OF CRIME	REASON WANTED	WANTED BY
PAWEL	131177	M	Ger.			Lt., Army, Herschbach-Selters (Ger.)	TORTURE	BEL.
PAWLESKI, Alex	21488	M		21	Pvt., Army, Rzhev (Sov.Un.) 6.42-1.43		MURDER	U.S.
PAWLICZEK	133263	M			Uschfhr., SS, Conc.Camp, Flossenburg (Ger.)		TORTURE	U.S.
PAWLIK, Franz	186554	M	Ger.		Manager, Saw-mill, Oppeln (Ger.) 1.45-5.45		WITNESS	U.K.
PAWLINSKY	161906	M	Ger.	00	Uschfhr., SS, Conc.Camp (Canteen) Buchenwald (Ger.) 44-45		WITNESS	U.S.
PAWLOWSKI	132650	M	Ger.		Pvt., 3.Coy.305, Stalag III A, Cdo.796, O.C.Schlalach-Brandenburg (Ger.) 7.41		MURDER	FR.
PAWON	196601	M	Ger.		Lt., Unit F.P. 59662, Plounevez-Moedec (Fr.) 6.8.44		MURDER	FR.
PAYER, Arthur	185578	M	Ger.	3. 7.99	LL.D., Sturmbannfhr.,SS,Counsellor of the Government,SD,Cripo, Prague (Czech.) 39-45		PILLAGE	CZECH.
PAZOFSKY, Vojtech	192498	M	Ger.	20.12.10	Crim.Asst., Gestapo, Brno (Czech.) 39-45		SUSPECT	CZECH.
PAZZA	1065	M			Pvt., Army, Feldgend., Vitry le Francois (Fr.)		MISC.CRIMES	FR.
PAZZIJI	194496	M	Ger.		Cdo.Fhr., Kriegsgef.Cdo.27002, Kaprun nr.Zell am See (Aust.)10.40-41		TORTURE	FR.
PEAHL	188346	M	Ger.	10 - 15	Sgt.,Volksgren.Rgt.103,Tailor,Civilian, Mons (Bel.) 3.9.44		WITNESS	U.S.
PEBESS, Fritz	132085	M	Ger.		Landwacht, Civilian, Ruhen (Ger.) 44		MURDER	U.S.
PECH	193966	M	Ger.		Oschfhr., SS, Conc.Camp, Buchenwald (Ger.) 42-45		MURDER	U.S.
PECHACEK, Jan	259995	M	Ger.	23.10.04	Dr., Founder of the Nazi-Organization "Vlajka", Gestapo and SD, Prague, Dachau and Buchenwald (Czech., Ger.) 39-45		SUSPECT	CZECH.
PECHACHEK	305099	M	Ger.		For many years resident in Waalwijk and Heusden, 5.43 and 10.44		PILLAGE	NETH.
PECHMANN	185026	M	Ger.		Civilian, Gentin (Ger.) 2.44		MURDER	U.K.
PECHTEL, Anton	252570	M	Ger.	30. 3.03	Caretaker, Civilian,House, Kamenicky Senov (Czech.) 39-45		MISC.CRIMES	CZECH.
PECHTLER	255026	M	Ger.		Gend., Fieldpolice, Choumont Chateauvillain (Fr.) 24.8.44		BRUTALITY	FR.
PECKE	251231	M	Ger.		Pvt., Airforce, Entzheim (Fr.) 42-44		TORTURE	FR.
PECKERT	166970	M	Ger.		W.O., Fieldgend., Montigny or Vesoul (Fr.) 16.7.44		MURDER	FR.
PECKMANN, Heinz	194504	M	Ger.	08	Crim.Asst., Usturmfhr., SS, Gestapo Koeln, Lwow-Radzyn (Pol.) 40-42		TORTURE	POL.
PECKRUN	192601	M	Ger.	02	Sgt., Strafgefl.-Nord, Guard, Finmark (Nor.) 1.45		MISC.CRIMES	NOR.
PEDERS	39677	M	Ger.		Rottfhr., SS, 17.Pz.Gren.Div."G.v.B.",Sturmgeschuetz-Abt.17 or Panzer-Jaeger-Abt.17, Segre-Renaze (Fr.) 7.44-8.44		MURDER	FR.
PEDERSEN, Werner	254147	M		7. 3.27	1.SS-Div., 1.Panz.Rgt., 1.Coy., Malmedy (Bel.) 17.12.44		MURDER	U.S.
PEDOE	38843	M			Employee, Civilian, Railway, Conc.Camp, Bitterfeld (Ger.) 10.43-4.45		TORTURE	U.K.
PEDROTTI	39676	M			Uschfhr., SS, 17.Panz.Gren.Div."G.v.B.", Sturmgeschuetz-Abt.17 or Panzer-Jaeger-Abt.17, Segre-Renaze (Fr.) 7.44-8.44		MURDER	FR.
PEECK, Alfred	133262	M	Ger.	10	Crim.Secr., Gestapo, Ahlem (Ger.)		MURDER	U.S.
PEEMOLLER, Otto	187672	M	Ger.		Officer, Gestapo (Ger.)		MURDER	U.S.
PEER, Franz	256107	M	Ger.		Kapo, Conc.Camp, Flossenburg (Ger.)		TORTURE	FR.
PEESZ, Hans	192750	M	Ger.		Schupo, Conc.Camp, Falstad nr.Drontheim (Nor.) 41-44		TORTURE	NOR.
PEETERS, Erich	255196	M	Ger.		Cpl., 377.Jaeger-Rgt., 12.Coy., Vinkt (Bel.) 25.5.-31.5.40		MURDER	BEL.
PEETERS, Henri	253226	M	Ger.		Interpreter, Sipo, Abt.IV C, Brussels (Bel.) 40-44		INTERR.	BEL.
PEETZ	122732	M	Ger.		Usturmfhr., SS, Inspector, Conc.Camp, Wanzleben (Ger.) 5.44-4.45		MURDER	U.S.
PEETZ	139721	M		10	SS-Officer, Arb.-Cdo.A-6, Conc.Camp		TORTURE	U.S.
PEEZ	257650	M			Labour-Supervisor, O.T., Muehldorf Area (Ger.)		MURDER	U.S.
PEGGAU	300898	M	Ger.		Pvt., 1.Aufkl.Abt.,3.Coy., 2.Column, XV.Div. of the Afrika-Korps, Saint Leger (Arlon) 5.9.44		MISC.CRIMES	BEL.
PEGLOW	174164	M	Ger.	03	Official, Gestapo, Oschfhr., SS,Prison of Vert Galant,Le Mans(Fr.)43-44		MURDER	FR.
PEGLOW, Kurt	126749	M	Ger.		N.C.O., Chauffeur, Gestapo, Cournon D'Auvergne (Fr.) 28.1.44		MURDER	FR.
PEHAM	194854	M	Ger.		Commissary, Geh.Feldpolizei, Aueroff-Athenes (Grc.) 43-44		MISC.CRIMES	U.K.
PEHSI, Peter	251225	M	Ger.		Sgt., Conc.Camp, D'Hinzert (Fr.)		MISC.CRIMES	FR.
PEICHERT, Erich	300899	M	Ger.		Pvt., 377.Inf.Rgt. serving under Capt.Lohmann, Vinkt-Meigem (Bel.) 5.40-31.5.40		MISC.CRIMES	BEL.
PEICHL, Alvis	259154	M	Ger.		Rottfhr., SS, Conc.Camp, Dachau (Ger.)		MISC.CRIMES	YUGO.
PEICHL, Ernest	142078	M	Ger.	10. 7.07	Police-Lt., 2.Pol.Rgt., Minsk, Thorn, Grodno (Sov.Un., Pol.) 44-45		MURDER	U.S., POL.
PEIFFERT, Erich	255198	M	Ger.		Pvt., 377.Jaeger-Rgt., Vinkt-Meigem (Bel.) 5.40		MISC.CRIMES	BEL.
PEIKERT	254752	M	Ger.		Pvt., Gestapo, Rottfhr., Toulouse (Fr.) 11.42-44		MURDER	FR.
PEIKERT, Helmuth	252565	M	Ger.	10. 2.11	Civ. Manager, Chamber of Commerce, Prague (Czech.) 42-45		PILLAGE	CZECH.
PEIKERT, Konrad	188363	M	Ger.	14	Usturmfhr., SS, Gestapo, Sosnowiec (Pol.) 42-43		MURDER	POL.
PEILL	257649	M	Ger.		Employee, Factory-worker, C.C., Nordhausen (Ger.)		MURDER	U.S.
PEIN	191850	M			Lt., Feldgend., Pontivy (Fr.)		MURDER	FR.
PEINE	126376	M	Ger.	95	Crim.Secr., Gestapo, Wuppertal (Ger.)		MISC.CRIMES	U.S.
PEINE	166627	M	Ger.		Farmer, Civilian, Wakersleben (Ger.) 7.44		TORTURE	U.S.
PEIPER	68855	M	Ger.		C.O. of Battle Group Pieper (Kampfgruppe) (Bel.) 20.12.44		MURDER	U.S.
PEIPER	257928	M			Osturmbannfhr., SS, 150.Pz.-Bde., 12.44		MISC.CRIMES	U.S.
PEIPER, Joachim	133959	M		15	Osturmbannfhr., 1.Pz.-Div., Malmedy (Bel.)		MURDER	U.S.
PEISE	31412	M	Ger.		Lt.Col., Army, 379.-169.Gren.Rgt., Finmark (Nor.) 44		MURDER	NOR.
PEKABER	194492	M	Ger.		Pvt., Feldgend., Ploermel (Fr.) 18.6.44		TORTURE	FR.
PEKO (or PEKR)	306277	M	Ger.		Member,Gestapo at Trencin,C.C.Oswiecim-Birkenau (Pol.) 39-45		MURDER	CZECH.
PEKKIES, Michael	137543	M	Ger.		Uschfhr., SS, Conc.Camp, Weimar-Buchenwald (Ger.)		TORTURE	U.S.
PELGNER	21487	M	Ger.		Pvt., Army, 12.Volks-Gren-Rgt., Petit-Langville-(Bel.) 10.1.45		MURDER	U.S.
PELICHTSTEIN (see PELISHTEN)	259097							
PELIEGER, Emile	121476	M	Ger.		Agent, Gestapo del Chamberu, Challes les Eaux et Arbin (Fr.)		MURDER	FR.
PELIKAN, Alois	192499	M	Ger.	10. 1.05	Head, Gestapo, Warden, Prison, Brno (Czech.) 39-45		SUSPECT	CZECH.
PELIMAN	254753	M			Pvt., Rottfhr.,C.C., Auschwitz-Birkenau (Pol.)		MURDER	FR.
PELISHTEN (or PELICHTSTEIN)	259097	M	Ger.		Osturmfhr., SS, 1.Geb.Jaeg.Rgt., SS-Div."Prinz Eugen",Niksic(Yugo.)43		MISC.CRIMES	YUGO.
PELLENGAHR	190042	M	Ger.	83	Gen., Div. operating at Tretton (Nor.) 40		MURDER	U.K.
PELLENS, Siegfried	12518	M	Ger.		Pvt., 110.or 111.Pz.Gren.Rgt.,2.Coy., Albine (Fr.) 29.6.44		MURDER	FR.
PELLER	193261	M	Ger.		Pvt.,Guard,4.SS-Totenk.Sturmbann,C.C.Dora-Mittelbau,Nordhausen (Ger.)45		MURDER	U.S.
PELLMAN	1542	M	Ger.	15	Hptschfhr., SS, Conc.Camp, Sachsenhausen (Ger.) 9.41-5.43		MURDER	U.S.
PELLMANN, Friedrich Heinrich	195941	M	Ger.	1. 8.91	Member, NSDAP, Barneveld (Neth.)		TORTURE	NETH.
PELSER (LE BOXEUR)	254689	M	Ger.		Kapo, Conc.Camp, Mauthausen (Aust.)		BRUTALITY	BEL.
PELUEGER, Justus	257657	M	Ger.	96	Major, O.C., Gend., Alsace (Fr.) 44		MURDER	U.S.
PELZ, Hermann	167777	M	Ger.		Trustee,Public-Official, "Gaststaette Bauhuette",Poznan (Pol.) 9.39-44		PILLAGE	POL.
PELZ, Otto	129749	M	Ger.		Pvt.,5.Fallschirmjaeg.-Rgt.,Quaregnon,Jemappes-Ghlin (Bel.) 2.,3.9.44		MURDER	BEL.
PELZ, Otto	131313	M	Ger.		Kapo, Pol., Conc.Camp, Jawischowitz (Pol.) 44		MURDER	U.S.
PELZER	196404	M	Ger.		Col., Royallieu Compiegne (Fr.) 41-44		INTERR.	FR.
PELZER, Gerath	684	M	Ger.		Civilian, Camp-mine "Anna III", Alsdorf (Ger.) 42-44		TORTURE	U.S.
PELZER, Josef	129725	M			Conc.Camp, Mauthausen (Aust.)		MURDER	U.S.
PELZER, Otto	129726	M			Conc.Camp, Mauthausen (Aust.) 41-45		MURDER	U.S.

PEL-PET

NAME	C.R.FILE NUMBER	SEX	NATIO-NALITY	DATE OF BIRTH	RANK OCCUPATION UNIT PLACE AND DATE OF CRIME	REASON WANTED	WANTED BY
PELZL	685	M	Ger.		Major,Police,Gendarmerie,Cracow (Pol.) 9.39-1.42	MURDER	POL.
PEZLAEUSCHEN	122734	M	Ger.		Civilian,Kiew-Institute,Kiew (Sov.Un.) 6.41-3.42	MURDER	U.S.
PEMSEL	31413	M	Ger.		Generalmajor,Army,Comd.6.Geb.Div.20 Army,Finmark (Nor.) 10.-11.44	MURDER	NOR.
PENDEL	185585	M	Ger.		SS-Oschfhr.,C.C.Gusen,Mauthausen (Aust.) 12.44	MURDER	FR.
PENDFLE	301830	M	Ger.		Col.u.Reg.Rat,Luftfahrtministerium Berlin,C.C.Dachau,Auschwitz (Ger.,Pol.) 3.42-26.2.43	TORTURE	BEL.
PENEDER (or SEPP)	70978	M	Ger.	20	Pvt.,Abwehr Nachr.Rgt.506,Angers,Wiesbaden (Fr.,Ger.) 44	MISC.CRIMES	U.S.
PENGLER,Henrich	167754	M	Ger.	11. 4.20	Rottfhr.,SS,C.C.Natzweiler (Fr.) 42-44	MURDER	FR.
PENIAS,Gertrude	192503	F	Ger.	17. 3.19	Clerk,Gestapo,Brno (Czech.) 39-45	WITNESS	CZECH.
PENKA,Karl	252566	M	Ger.	6. 9.00	SS-Oschfhr.,State Service,Labour office head,Kromeriz (Czech.)39-45	INTERR.	CZECH.
PENKER,Josef	261101	M	Ger.	.00	Pvt.,Schupo,Lidice (Czech.) 6.42	SUSPECT	CZECH.
PENKWITT,Walter	306704	M	Ger.		Engineer,Constance,Unit Nr.26-039 E,Att.Soissons Prison (Fr.) 15.8.44	MURDER	FR.
PENNDORF	185584	M	Ger.		Secretary,Hptschfhr.,Gestapo,SD,Sarrebruck (Ger.)	PILLAGE	FR.
PENNE,Hermann	174146	M	Ger.		SS and Polizeifhr.,SS Wirtschaftsgruppe-Hoehere SS,SD,Chef der Bau-leitung (Yugo.) 42-44	MURDER	YUGO.
PENNERS	254121	M	Ger.		Pvt.,Pepingen (Bel.) 2.-9.44	WITNESS	BEL.
PENNEWITZ,Kurt	119401	M	Ger.		Cpl.,Army,C.C.Oswiecim (Pol.)	MURDER	POL.
PENNIKAMP,Willi	153185	M	Ger.		Guard,Mines,C.C.Erkenschwick (Ger.)	TORTURE	U.S.
PENS	253283	M	Ger.		Capt.,St.Denis le Gast (Fr.) 8.7.44	MURDER	FR.
PENSA	132654	M	Ger.		Lt.,Feldgendarmerie Commander,Gerardmer (Fr.) 10.44	MISC.CRIMES	FR.
PENSENTHEIMER (see PESENTHEIMER)	686						
PENSKWITT,Walter	192248	M	Ger.		Pvt.,Army,Soissons (Fr.) 15.8.44	WITNESS	FR.
PENZ,Karl	257638	M	Ger.	20. 2.99	Employee,Block 13 Camp Dora,Nordhausen (Ger.)	MURDER	U.S.
PENZENSTADLER,Josef	255186	M			Pvt.,C.C.Ellrich,Nordhausen (Ger.)	MURDER	U.S.
PENZIEN,Franz	306714	M	Ger.		Nr.,Pingelshagen (Ger.) 21.6.44	MURDER	U.S.
PEPE (see BERGET)	176371						
PEPELINSKI	193964	M	Ger.		SS-Uschfhr.,C.C.Buchenwald (Ger.) 42-45	TORTURE	U.S.
PEPETZ,Henry	257922	M			150 Pz.Bde.,Meuse Bridge-Antwerp (Bel.) 12.44	MISC.CRIMES	U.S.
PEPLINSKI	185648	M	Ger.		SS-Pvt.,SS Pz.Div.Adolf Hitler,Stavelot Parfondruy (Bel.) 18.-22.12.44	MURDER	BEL.,U.S.
PEPPLER	255024	M	Ger.		Pvt.,SS-Rgt."Das Reich" 3 Coy. 1 Bn., Oradour sur Glane (Fr.) 44	MISC.CRIMES	FR.
PEPSCHEL	196868	M	Ger.		Pvt.,C.C.Auschwitz (Pol.)	MURDER	FR.
PERATHONER	179610	F	Ger.	14	Overseer,Gestapo,Vichy Allier (Fr.) 44	MISC.CRIMES	FR.
PFRBEL,Elizabeth	196405	F	Ger.	16.11.97	NSDAP,Amstetten (Aust.) 3.45	MISC.CRIMES	U.S.
PERBETLUTZER	136305	M	Ger.		SS-Mann,2 SS Pz.Div."Das Reich" Rgt.Deutschland 3 Bn.,Nernequs le Vernet (Fr.)	MURDER	FR.
PERCHON	161903	M	Ger.	15	SS-Oschfhr.,Command Staff,C.C.Buchenwald (Ger.) 42	WITNESS	U.S.
PERCIARE,Kl.	140802	M	Ger.		SS-Commander,C.C.Linz-Donau (Aust.)	MISC.CRIMES	U.S.
PFRGER	255298	M			Pvt.,C.C.Dora,Nordhausen (Ger.)	MURDER	U.S.
PERIZONIUS	194855	M	Ger.		Dr., official, Propaganda, Luxembourg Grande Duchy (Lux.)	MISC.CRIMES	LUX.
PERKERT,Ernst	255356	M	Ger.	24.11.09	Member,SD,Gestapo,Prag Kobylisy (Czech.) 9.41	MURDER	CZECH.
PERLE,Fritz	12595	M	Ger.		N.C.O.,Pz.Gren.Rgt.110 or 111 2 Coy,Albine (Fr.) 29.6.44	MURDER	FR.
PERM	173871	M	Ger.		Gendarm,Gendarmerie,Morhange (Fr.) 41	PILLAGE	FR.
PERMENTIER,Alex (aliases: PER-MENTER)	258864	M	Ger.	7.11.08	Tinsmith-inductor,Luxembourg Grand Duchy (Lux.) 45	MISC.CRIMES	LUX.
PERNER	129727	M			SS-Rottfhr.,C.C.Mauthausen (Aust.) 41-45	MURDER	U.S.
PERREMANS	301961	M	Ger.		Member,SD Apeldoorn District (Neth.) 9.44-4.45	MURDER	NETH.
PERSCHAM,Hans (see PERSCHON)	139063						
PERSCHEL	173872	M	Ger.	22	Arbeitsdienstfhr.,Official,SS,C.C.Auschwitz-Birkenau (Pol.) 42-45	MURDER	POL.
PERSCHKE	192247	M	Ger.		Pvt.,Air Force,Rinxent (Fr.) 31.3.41	MISC.CRIMES	FR.
PERSCHON,Hans (or PERSCHAM)	139063	M	Ger.	14	SS-Oschfhr.,SS,SD,C.C.Lublin (Pol.) 42-43	MURDER	U.S.,POL.
PERSIN	126487	M		21	SS-Uschfhr.,SS,1 SS Pz.Div.1 SS Pz.Rgt.1 Pl.9 Coy (Engineer),Malmedy (Bel.) 17.12.44	MURDER	U.S.
PERSKE	147346	M	Ger.		Cpl.,11 Pz.Div.Kampfgr."Wilde" Coy "Probst" (Fr.) 44	MURDER	FR.
PERSTENJUK,Otto	306279	M	Ger.		Member,Gestapo at Trencin,C.C.Oswiecim-Birkenau (Pol.) 39-45	MURDER	CZECH.
PERSTERER,Franz	124756	M		05	SS-Osturmbannfhr.,Oberreg.Rat,SS Kommando 16 z.b.V.,C.C.Bruessels (Bel.) 12.44-3.45	MURDER	U.S.
PEPTHES,Joachim	306493	M	Ger.	15. 3.99	SS-Cpl.,SS,C.C.Buchenwald (Ger.) 16.5.38 and 9.10.43	MURDER	BEL.
PERZ	188955	M	Ger.		Feldgendarmerie,Bar-le-Duc Meuse (Fr.) 8.44	MURDER	FR.
PESCH,Josef	187866	M	Ger.	9. 3.99	Civilian,Aachen (Ger.) 9.8.44	TORTURE	U.S.
PESCHEL	39675	M	Ger.		Major,Army,Bankow by Krewsberg (Ger.) 27.12.44	MURDER	U.K.
PESCHEL	301218	M	Ger.		Member,Gestapo Banska Bystrica-District,Kremnicka (Czech.) 20.11.44	MURDER	U.K.
PESCHEL,A.	156844	M	Ger.	95	Major,Air Force (Abwehr) Stalag Luft VII,near Breslau (Ger.)12.44,2.45	MURDER	CAN.,U.K.
PESCHEL,Alfred Erich	193262	M	Ger.	5.11.06	Guard,Pvt.,4 SS Totenkopf-Sturmbann,C.C.Dora-Mittelbau,Nordhausen (Ger.) 43-45	MURDER	U.S.
PESCHKA,Ernst	185024	M	Ger.	00	Ing.,Reichsleiter,NSDAP,Praha (Czech.)	MISC.CRIMES	CZECH.
PESCHKE,Elizabeth	254128	F	Ger.		SS.Woman-Guard,SS,Geislingen (Ger.) 40-45	MISC.CRIMES	POL.
PESCHKE,Heinrich	255299	M			Uschfhr.,Camp.Ellrich,Nordhausen (Ger.)	MURDER	U.S.
PESCHKE,Marta	166971	F	Ger.	90	Civ,Farmer,C.C.Neusachsen (Ger.) 16.1.45	TORTURE	FR.
PESCHKE,Otto	126579	M	Ger.		Pvt.,1 Bn.Pz.Div.IX,102 Pz.Art.Rgt.,Fuerth near Neukirchen (Ger.)9.44	MURDER	U.S.
PESCHKO,Martin	262264	M	Ger.	4.-7.21	Uschfhr.,10 Coy 51 SS Armoured Bde.,Breviandes,Bucheres,Ste.Savine, La Riviere De.Corps (Troyes) (Fr.) 22.-25.8.44	BRUTALITY	FR.
PESCHKO,Wolfgang	1278	M	Ger.		Cpl.,F.P.Nr.18651 en 1944.Nr.01411 D,Lelude (Fr.)6.43,7.44	PILLAGE	FR.
PESENTHEIMER (or PENSENTHEIMER)	686	M	Ger.		SS-Oschfhr.,Gestapo,Locmine (Fr.) 7.-8.44	MURDER	FR.
PESOLD,Jakob	257613	M		19. 6.07	Employee,Police,Camp Dora,Nordhausen (Ger.)	MURDER	U.S.
PESSINGER	153184	M	Ger.		Col.,Cmdt.,Oflag 77,C.C.Debling (Pol.)	MURDER	U.S.
PEST,Erich	256113	M	Ger.		Foreman,Org.Todt,Muhldorf (Ger.)	INTERR.	U.S.
PETAS	185023	M	Ger.		Pvt.,Army,Chania-Crete (Grc.) 9.44	MURDER	GRC.
PETENHAUSEN	131176	M	Ger.		SS-Mann,Guard,SS,C.C.Gneisenau (Ger.) 40-45	TORTURE	BEL.
PETER	687	M	Ger.		Officer,Air Force,Blangy s.Bresles (Fr.) 8.44	MURDER	FR.
PETER	122736	M	Ger.		Capt.,Commanding officer at Camp Wenisza (Sov.Un.) 41	MURDER	U.S.
PETER	124969	M	Ger.		Head,chief-i.balley,Gestapo,C.C.Bremen-Farge (Ger.) 15.-18.6.43	MURDER	U.K.
PETER	141401	M	Ger.		Chief of Block 1,C.C.Mauthausen (Aust.)	MURDER	FR.
PETER	153182	M	Ger.		Lt.,9 SS Pz.Div."Hohenstaufen",Nimes (Fr.) 2.3.44	MISC.CRIMES	FR.
PETER	162809	M	Ger.	03-05	Kreisleiter,NSDAP,Weissenburg Hunspach (Fr.) 10.12.44-26.11.44	MURDER	FR.
PETER	173179	M	Ger.		Staff at C.C.Natzweiler (Fr.) 44	INTERR.	U.K.

PET-PET

NAME	C.R.FILE NUMBER	SEX	NATIO-NALITY	DATE OF BIRTH	RANK OCCUPATION UNIT PLACE AND DATE OF CRIME	REASON WANTED	WANTED BY
PETER	174163	M	Ger.		Guard, Official, Prison, Chalons-sur-Saone (Fr.) 5.44-6.44	MURDER	FR.
PETER	185583	M	Ger.		Hptschfhr., Secretary, SD, Gestapo, Sarrebruck (Ger.)	PILLAGE	FR.
PETER	193817	M	Ger.		SS, C.C. Ravensbrueck (Ger.)	TORTURE	FR.
PETER	194495	M	Ger.	04	Agent, Gestapo, Bourges Savigny en Septaine (Fr.) 7.-8.44	MURDER	FR.
PETER	255202	M	Ger.		Uschfhr., SS, Guewenheim (Fr.) 4.10.44	MURDER	FR.
PETER	257349	M	Ger.		SS-Guard, SS-Slave Labour Camp,Beifsjord near Narvik (Nor.)6.-11.42	BRUTALITY	YUGO.
PETER	259217	M			Kapo, Chief of Block, SS, Auschwitz (Pol.)	MURDER	FR.
PETER	259434	M			Camp Manager, C.C. Thekla near Leipzig (Ger.) 18.4.45	MURDER	U.S.
PETER (or WERTH,SCHAEFER)	306123	M	Ger.		SS Sturmfhr., served with RS.D.Abt.VI-5,Copenhagen (Den.) 1.44	PILLAGE	DEN.
PETER, Adam	258435	M			SS-Mann, Guard, C.C. Ohrdruf (Ger.) 12.44-4.45	MURDER,BRUTALITY	U.S.
PETER, Erwin	261087	M	Ger.	20-22	SS Uschfhr., SS-Murder of French Nationals,Guewenheim (Ger.)	MURDER	FR.
PETER, Hans	186692	M	Ger.	22	Uschfhr., SS Leibstandarte Adolf Hitler,Nachrichtenzug, Wormhoudt (Fr.) 5.40	MURDER	U.K.
PETER, Jakob	258392	M			SS-Mann,SS-Guard,Waffen SS,C.C.Ohrdruf (Ger.) 12.44-4.45	MURDER,BRUTALITY	U.S.
PETER, Johann	153183	M			Civilian, Leppin (Ger.)	WITNESS	U.S.
PETER, Johann	193263	M			Guard, 4.SS Totenkopf-Sturmbann,Nordhausen,Dora Mittelbau (Ger.)	MURDER	U.S.
PETER, Josef	196698	M	Ger.		Oberwachtmeister,Schupo,2.Coy.134.Bn.(Lux.)	INTERR.	LUX.
PETER, Joseph	38835	M			SS Uschfhr., C.C. Struthof (Fr.)	MISC.CRIMES	FR.
PETER, Karl	253545	M	Ger.		Guard, PW Camp, Oberndorf (Ger.)	MISC.CRIMES	FR.
PETER, Leopold	192500	M	Ger.	15.11.91	Manager, Gestapo, Garage, Bruenn (Czech.) 39-45	WITNESS	CZECH.
PETER (see PETTER),Wilhelm	255201						
PETER, Willy	196867	M	Ger.	03 or 05	Kreisleiter, Wissembourg (Fr.) 9.43-2.44	MURDER	FR.
PETDIRICH, Michael	255626	M		4.10.98	Sgt., Camp Ellrich, Nordhausen (Ger.)	MURDER	U.S.
PETERKA, Marie	192501	F	Ger.	5. 3.23	Clerk, Gestapo, Bruenn (Czech.) 39-45	WITNESS	CZECH.
PETERKOCH	129728	M			C.C. aid to C.Med.Personnel, Mauthausen (Aust.) 41-45	MURDER	U.S.
PETERLE (see HARTMANN)	259683						
PETERMANN	174043	M	Ger.		Lt., Inf.Rgt.469, 2.Bn., Le Tholy (Fr.) 13.11.44	ARSON	FR.
PETERMANN, Erna	255300	F			Lagerfuehrerin,Camp Gross Werther,Nordhausen (Ger.)	MURDER	U.S.
PETERS	100607	M	Ger.		Major, Gebirgs Div.525 (Staff), Finnmark (Nor.) 44	MURDER	NOR.
PETERS	121473	M		10	Gestapo of Valencienne, Maubeuge (Fr.) 29.12.43	MURDER	FR.
PETERS	142125	M			General, Army, St.Die, Vosges (Fr.) 11.44	TORTURE	FR.
PETERS	153176	M		20	Pvt., Army, Graudenz to Waiden (Pol., Ger.) 45	TORTURE	U.K.,U.S.
PETERS	153178	M			Schladen, Buchladen (Ger.) 28.9.44	MURDER	U.S.
PETERS	153180	M			Pvt., Stalag X B, Sandbostel (Ger.) 8.43	MURDER	U.S.
PETERS	174149	M	Ger.		Member, Gestapo, Maubeuge, Valenciennes (Fr.) 29.12.43	MURDER	FR.
PETERS	190705	M	Ger.		Pvt., Eis.Bn.717,St. Andries,Varsenare-Lez-Bruges (Bel.) 4.9.44	MURDER	BEL.
PETERS	190706	M			Sgt., Army, St.Andries, Varsenare-Les-Bruges (Bel.) 4.9.44	MURDER	BEL.
PETERS	195940	M	Ger.		SS Sgt., Waffen SS, Sederon Izon la Bruisse (Fr.) 22.2.44	MURDER	FR.
PETERS	196599	F	Ger.		Wife of Foreman Civ.Stone Quarry, Rodendorf (Ger.) 10.44	WITNESS	FR.
PETERS	254156	M	Ger.	11	Lt.,H.Q.,137.Flak Rgt.,25.Flak Div.,Selvaggio-Giareno (It.) 20.5.44	INTERR.	U.K.
PETERS	255025	M	Ger.		Capt., Feldpost C.R.L.55 975, Dancourt (Fr.) 22.7.44	MURDER	FR.
PETERS	255729	M	Ger.		Oschfhr., Camp Wolffleben (Aust.), Nordhausen (Ger.)	MURDER	U.S.
PETERS	260034	M	Ger.		Bn.Commander,SS Wehrmachtsarbeitskdo.,Slave Labour Camp, Botn near Rognan (Nor.) 8.42-3.43, 4.43-45	MURDER	YUGO.
PETERS	260036	M	Ger.		Kapo, C.C. Dachau (Ger.) 42-44	MISC.CRIMES	FR.
PETERS	302093	M	Ger.		Major,Wachtkommandant, Zutphen, Laren (Neth.) 44-2.45	PILLAGE	NETH.
PETERS	306494	M	Ger.		SS-Mann, C.C. Buchenwald (Ger.) 5.38-10.43	MURDER	BEL.
PETERS, Albert	136337	M		96	Minister of Transportation, Public Official, Berlin (Ger.)	TORTURE	U.S.
PETERS, Amandis	167767	M			Kommando 343, Landerneau (Fr.) 6.-8.44	MURDER	FR.
PETERS, Georges or Willi	153181	M			Agent, Gestapo, Folkling (Fr.) 11.44	MURDER	FR.
PETERS, Hans	179144	M	Ger.		Army, Neumuenster (Ger.) 43 or 44	MURDER	U.K.
PETERS, Heinrich	240013	M	Ger.	10	Pvt., Abwehr Nachr.Rgt. 506, Paris (Fr.)	MISC.CRIMES	U.S.
PETERS, Heinrich	302094	M	Ger.		Commanding Officer,Lagerbewachungstr., Ravensbrueck C.C. (Ger.) 39-45	MURDER	U.K.
PETERS, Josef	153177	M			Uschfhr., Waffen SS, Totenkopf-Stand., C.C. Buchenwald (Ger.)	TORTURE	U.S.
PETERS, Karl	12519	M	Ger.		Pvt.,Army,110 or 111 Pz.Gren.Rgt. 2.Coy.,Albine (Fr.) 29.6.44	MURDER	FR.
PETERS, Max	137544	M			Uschfhr., SS, C.C. Weimar-Buchenwald (Ger.)	TORTURE	U.S.
PETERS, Otto	141988	M	Ger.	23	Sailor, Navy, Kissenbruck (Ger.) 6.or 7.44	MURDER	U.S.
PETERS, Richard	136338	M			SS, C.C. Erfurt (Ger.) 44	MISC.CRIMES	U.S.
PETERS, Rudolf	261337	M	Ger.	27. 7.03	Criminalsecretary, Gestapo, Strassburg (Fr.) 40-44	TORTURE	FR.
PETERSCHIK, Josef	253282	M	Ger.	6. 4.15	Jailer, Gestapo, Pilsen (Czech.) 41-44	MURDER	CZECH.
PETERSEIL	301593	M	Ger.		SS Sturmbannfhr., stationed C.C. Mauthausen (Aust.)40-45	MURDER	BEL.
PETERSEN	12663	M	Ger.		SS Hptsturmfhr., Gestapo, H.Q., Kristiansand (Nor.) 43	TORTURE	NOR.
PETERSEN	31415	M	Ger.		Hptsturmfhr., 6.SS Geb.Div.Nord, 6.SS Pion.Bn.,Beurk Finnmark (Nor.) 44	MURDER	NOR.
PETERSEN	31503	M			Capt., Army, 2.Rgt., L.62546 A, Locmine' (Fr.) 44	MURDER	FR.
PETERSEN	141402	M			General, Air Force 4.Feldkorps,125.Pz.Gren.Rgt., Carcassonne (Fr.)41-44	MURDER	FR.
PETERSEN	141892	M		98	Usturmfhr., Kriminalobersekr.,Sipo,SS, Sletteb (Nor.) 12.42	WITNESS	U.K.
PETERSEN	174095	M			Col., Pz.Gren.Rgt.125, Salonika (Grc.)	MURDER	YUGO.
PETERSEN	190297	M	Ger.		Kommandant,Osturmfhr.,SS Geb.Jaeger Rgt. "Prinz Eugen" Div., Sinj Drasnica (Yugo.) 11.43-4.44	MURDER	YUGO.
PETERSEN	255197	M			Lt., Cmdt. of Coy., 8.Coy.376 Jaeger Rgt.,Vinkt,Meigem (Bel.)5.40	MURDER	BEL.
PETERSEN	257290	M	Ger.		Col., Police, Poppentin (Ger.) 7.-8.44	MURDER	U.S.
PETERSEN, Heinz	301180	M	Ger.		Deserter, probably SS Oschfhr. or SS Usturmfhr.,Haarlem (Neth.)12.44	PILLAGE	NETH.
PETERSEN, Wilhelm	257965	M	Ger.		General, 125.Pz.Gren.Rgt.,Meuse Bridge, Anvers (Bel.) 41	MURDER	YUGO.
PETERSMANN, Heinrich	254151	M	Ger.		Civilian, Uden (Neth.) 5.9.44	INTERR.	NETH.
PETERSON	174081	M	Ger.		Gestapo-Leitstelle,C.C.Bruenn (Czech.)Oswięcim-Birkenau (Pol.)39-45	MURDER	CZECH.
PETERSON, Otto	12520	M	Ger.		Adjutant, Army, munitions-depot, Brienne le Chateau (Fr.)27.8.44	MURDER	FR.
PETERZANI	192161	M	Ger.	01	Member, Geheime Feldpolice, Brussels (Bel.)	TORTURE	BEL.
PETO	192747	M	Ger.		Staff-Sgt., SS, C.C. Falstad (Nor.) 41-42	TORTURE	NOR.
PETRAK	256103	M	Ger.		Oschfhr., SS, Muehldorf (Ger.)	WITNESS	U.S.
PETRASKAR, Heinz	167784	M	Ger.	28. 1.17	Coy.-Chief, III F.I.Lehr-Rgt., Goegnies Chaussee (Bel.) 3.9.44	MURDER	BEL.
PETRI	144482	M	Ger.	09	Hptsturmfhr., SS, C.C. Sachsenhausen (Ger.)	MURDER	U.S.
PETRI	153175	M			Official,Reichskommissar fuer die Festigung deutschen Volkstums, Berlin (Ger.)	MURDER	U.S.
PETRI (or PETRI)	162811	M	Ger.	14	Lt., Air Force, Douay (Fr.) 30.8.44	MURDER	FR.
PETRI	185020	M	Ger.		Officer, C.C. Kapo, Dachau (Ger.)	TORTURE	FR.

PET-PFE

NAME	C.R.FILE NUMBER	SEX	NATIONALITY	DATE OF BIRTH	RANK OCCUPATION UNIT PLACE AND DATE OF CRIME	REASON WANTED	WANTED BY
PETRI	195939	M	Ger.		SS-Untersturmfhr., Crim.Commissar, Gestapo SD, The Hague, Assen (Neth.) 40-45	MURDER	NETH.
PETRI or "HEXE"	250424	M	Ger.		Oberscharfhr., Camp Buchenwald (Ger.)	MISC.CRIMES	FR.
PETRI	253277	M	Ger.		Untersturmfhr., Army, Amersfoort-Zeist (Neth.) 9.44	WITNESS	NETH.
PETRI, Emil	132088	M	Ger.	10.12.92	Police-Master, German Police, Hanau (Ger.)	MISC.CRIMES	U.S.
PETRI, Siegfried	255730	M		6.1.25	Flyer, Camp Ellrich, Nordhausen (Ger.)	MURDER	U.S.
PETRI, Willi	119400	M	Ger.		Settler, Olekszyn (Pol.) 12.39	PILLAGE	POL.
PETRICH	126485	M			SS-Oberscharfhr., Guard, SS, C.C. Weimar Buchenwald (Ger.)	TORTURE	U.S.
PETRICH, Franz	194862	M	Ger.	27.2.93	Civilian, Luxembourg (Lux.)	TORTURE	LUX.
PETRIE	39674	M	Ger.		Lt. (Oberleutnant) Army, C.C. Verona (It.), Oberursel Frankfurt (Ger.) 6.-7.44	TORTURE	U.K.
PETRIE see PETRIK	139064						
PETRIE	194001	M	Ger.		SS, C.C., Buchenwald (ger.) 42-45	MURDER	U.S.
PETRIK,Heinz or PETRIE or PETRITZ	139064	M	Ger.	14	SS-Oberscharfhr., Work detail leader, SS C.C. Lublin (Pol.)	TORTURE	U.S.
PETRINACK, Karl	194494	M			Chief of Block, Kdo. D'Erhensee, C.C. Mauthausen (Austr.)	MURDER	FR.
PETRITZ see PETRIK	139064						
PETRITZIG	254916	M			Driver, Alencon (Fr.) 40-44	MURDER	FR.
PETROU, Vladimir	187397	M		30.6.96	Member, SD, Boleslav (Czech.) 39-45	MURDER	CZECH.
PETRUSCHKE	139869	M	Ger.		Wachtmeister, Schupo C.C. Berlin-Moabit (Ger.)	MURDER	U.K.
PETRY	129747	M	Ger.		5th paratrooper - Regt., Nachrichtenzug, Ghlin, Quaregnon Jemappes (Bel.) 2. - 3.9.44	MURDER	BEL.
PETRY see PETRI	162811						
PETSCHALL	190354	M			Pvt., 393th Landes Bn. St. IV C C.C. Bensen AK 22 (Ger.) 23.12.44	MURDER	U.K.
PETSCHAUER, Hermann	147068	M	Ger.		SS-Obersturmfhr., SS Political Kommissar, NSDAP Kreisleiter Litija (Yugo.) 43	MURDER	YUGO.
PETSCHELL, Martin	180489	M	Ger.	15	Sgt., 590 Pz.Jaeger Abt. Army, (It.) 7. - 8.44	MURDER	U.K.
PETSCYNSKI, Wasyl	193265	M			Guard, 4.SS-Totenkopf-Stuba, Dora C.C. Mittelbau, Auschwitz,Nordhausen (Pol.Ger.) 43-45	MURDER	U.S.
PETTER	191853	M	Ger.		Pvt., Kommando of Landerneau, Finistère (Fr.)	TORTURE	FR.
PETTER or PETER, Wilhelm	255201	M	Ger.		Production Chief, St. Hinteregger, Paris (Fr.) 41-44	PILLAGE	FR.
PETTINGER	255023	M			Scharfhr., Gestapo, Limoges (Fr.) 40-44	INTERR.	FR.
PETTREK	185582	M	Ger.		Guard, C.C. Ravensbrueck (Ger.) 44	TORTURE	FR.,BEL.
PETZ	129729	M			SS-Hauptscharfhr., SS Div. Totenkopf C.C. Mauthausen (Austr.) 41.-45	MURDER	U.S.
PETZDEUSCHEG	153429	M			SS-Hauptsturmfhr., SS Div. "Adolf Hitler" 12. Regt. Stabs Coy. Maastricht-Arnheim (Neth.) 43-44	MURDER	U.S.,NETH.
PETZEL	305937	M	Ger.		Unterscharfhr., C.C. Oranienburg (Ger.) 11.39-45	MURDER	CZECH.
PETZEL, Othmar	29705	M			President, Public Official, Opava (Czech.) 40	MURDER	CZECH.
PETZER	254910	M	Ger.		Major, Army Flak, Seguret and Vaison (Fr.)10.6.44	MURDER	FR.
PETZOLD, Fritz	174044	M	Ger.		SS Unterscharfr., 17.SS Div. "Goetz von Berlichingen" 1.Coy. Raids (Fr.) 6. - 7.44	MURDER	U.S.
PETZOLDT	259435	M			Crim.-Inspector, Camp Thekla near Leipzig (Ger.) 18.4.45	MURDER	U.S.
PETZOLDTE, Karl	300912	M	Ger.		Member, SS of the Staff at C.C. Sasel (Ger.) 10.44-4.45	TORTURE	U.K.
PEUCKERT, Rudolf	62194	M	Ger.		Staatsrat (Man-Power) Delegate in the East (Ger.)	MISC.CRIMES	BEL.,UNWCC.
PEULICH	137550	M	Ger.		SS Unterscharfr. C.C. Weimar, Buchenwald (Ger.)	TORTURE	U.S.
PEUSE, August	192502	M	Ger.		Crim.-Asst., Gestapo, Bruenn (Czech.) 39-45	SUSPECT	CZECH.
PEUTSCH, Willy	196403	M	Ger.		Cpl., Plougasnou (Fr.)	MURDER	FR.
PEZKY	190298	M	Ger.		Pvt., Army, Sucuraj (Croatia,Yugo.) 5.10.43	MURDER	YUGO.
PEZON	254756	M	Ger.		Sgt., Oberscharfhr., SS, SD, Toulouse (Fr.) 11.42 - 8.44	MISC.CRIMES	FR.
PFAADM, Joseph	12522	M	Ger.		Pvt., 110. Pz. Gren.Regt. 2. Coy., Albine (Fr.) 29.6.44	MURDER	FR.
PFAFF	195938	M	Ger.		Lt., Parachutist-school, Chaveroche de Ussel (Fr.) 18.12.43	MISC.CRIMES	FR.
PFAFF, Ernest	688	M			Army, Le Cap Ferrets (Fr.) 8.44	MURDER	FR.
PFAFF, Fritz	153173	M	Ger.	26.9.94	Hauptscharfhr., W.-SS Totenkopf Standarte C.C. Buchenwald (Ger.)	TORTURE	U.S.
PFAFF, Georg	255625	M		99	Pvt., Camp Dora Nordhausen (Ger.)	MURDER	U.S.
PFAFF, Hans	194497	M	Ger.	2511.11	Member, Gestapo, Klatovy (Czech.) 39-45	TORTURE	CZECH.
PFAFF, Jacob	167788	M			Cpl. Gruppenfhr., Army, 9th Res.Gren.Regt. 1.Coy., Magny d'Anigon (Fr.) 18.9.44	MURDER	FR.
PFAFFE	39673	M	Ger.		Capt., Stalag VIII B C.C. Schomberg (Ger.) 6.44	MURDER	U.K.
PFAHL	300840	M	Ger.		Pvt., 1.Aufkl.Abt.3rd Coy. 2nd Column XV Div. of the Afrika Korps Saint Léger (Arlon) 5.9.44	MISC.CRIMES	BEL.
PFAHLER, Josef	173906	M	Ger.		Police-Wachtmeister, Police, C.C. Gaggenau (ger.)	MURDER	U.K.
PFAIFORT	185019	M	Ger.		Officer, Espionage and counter espionage, section Abwehr, Athens (Grc.)	MISC.CRIMES	GRC.
PFALZER	124247	M			SS Oberscharfhr., 2nd Gren.Regt., SS Pz.Div. 12th Coy. Malmedy (Bel.) 17.12.44	MURDER	U.S.
PFALZER, Giovanni	306315	M	Ger.		Member, Gend. stationed at Bressanone (Brixen) Province of Bolzano Bressanone (It.) 1.10.44	MURDER	U.K.
PFALZGRAF, Erich	255624	M			Pvt., Camp Ellrich Nordhausen (Ger.)	MURDER	U.S.
PFANNENMULLER, Johann	132089	M			Wachtmeister, Guard, Schupo, C.C. Amberg (Ger.) 4.45	TORTURE	U.S.
PFANNENSTIEL	196814	M			Lt., Commd."Pi. Versuchs Bn." 3.Brandenberg Regt.,	MISC.CRIMES	U.S.
PFANNENSTIEL	301352	M	Ger.		Dr., SS Lt.Colonel, Professor, at Marburg University	MURDER	FR.
PFANNER	250423	M	Ger.		Lt., Schutzpolizei, Urbes (Fr.) 24.9.44-5.10.44	MURDER	FR.
PFANNER	256106	M	Ger.		Lt., Osturmfhr., Gestapo, Mihiel, Melle (Fr.) 9.9.44	MURDER	FR.
PFANNER, Heinz	255200	M	Ger.		Obersturmfhr., Gestapo, Section 4, Nancy (Fr.) 15.- 18.8.44	MISC.CRIMES	FR.
PFANNSTIEL	167766	M			Member of Bordeaux Staff, Ostgebietministerium Rosenberg Einsatz-Stab, Bordeaux (Fr.) 40-44	PILLAGE	FR.,UNWCC.
PFAU	260733	M	Ger.		Staff-Sgt., Field Pol., Enghienles Bains-Domont (Fr.) 8.44	WITNESS	FR.
PFAIL	195154	M		14	Pvt., Guard at AK22, 393 Lds.-Ba. C.C. Bensen St. IV C (Czech.)12.44	MURDER	U.K.
PFEIFER	1072	M			SS-Scharfhr., SD, Troyes, Reims (Fr.)	TORTURE	FR.
PFEIFER	192611	M			Sgt., Kfg. Bn. 41, 1.Coy. C.C. Rotelven (Nor.) 2.42	TORTURE	NOR.
PFEIFER	255622	M			Camp Rottleberode ,Nordhausen (Ger.)	MURDER	U.S.
PFEIFER, Erich	254914	M	Ger.	8.8.13	Gendarm, Gend. Ersteia (Fr.) 40-45	TORTURE	FR.
PFEIFER, Hans	126765	M	Ger.	08	SS-Oberscharfhr., Hausmeister, Gestapo, Troyes (Fr.)	TORTURE	FR.
PFEIDEN	254905	M			Lt., Unit Dienststelle 14 255, Aiguillan-Sur-Mer (Fr.) 9.6.44	INTERR.	FR.
PFEIDLERER	259607	M			SS-Hptschfhr., Gestapo Area of Angers, Maine and Loire (Fr.) 42-44	MISC.CRIMES	FR.
PFEIFER	690	M			SS-Unterscharfhr., C.C. Dachau (Ger.) 40-43	MURDER	BEL.,FR.
PFEIFER	195937	M			Master, Schupo, C.C. Westerbork (Neth.) 9. - 10.44	MURDER	NETH.
PFEIFER	196670	M			Lt., C.C. Struthof-Natzweiler (Fr.)40-44	BRUTALITY	FR.
PFEIFER	257658	M			SS-Scharfhr., Office, Dora Nordhausen (Ger.)	MURDER	U.S.
PFEIFER	300841	M	Ger.		Pvt. I Aufkl.Abt.3 Coy.2 Column XV Div. of the Afrika Korps Saint Léger (Arlon) (Bel.) 5.9.44	MISC.CRIMES	BEL.

NAME	C.R.FILE NUMBER	SEX	NATIO-NALITY	DATE OF BIRTH	RANK OCCUPATION UNIT PLACE AND DATE OF CRIME	REASON WANTED	WANTED BY
PFEIFER nee POLOCEK, Albine	180502	F	Ger.	21.11.17	Employee,Civ.,Occupied territory,Public official,Prag(Czech)39-45	PILLAGE	CZECH.
PFEIFER, Thea	254146	F	Ger.	2. 1.15	Field-Police (Bel.)	WITNESS	BEL.
PFEIFER, Wilhelm (or PFEIFFER)	122737	M	Ger.	16.10.09	Kreisleiter in Goslar,NSDAP,Vienenburg,Lochtum,Heiningen (Ger.)19.5.45	MURDER	U.S.
PFEIFFEN, Gerhard	167787	M	Ger.		Cpl.,Gruppenfhr.,Army,9 Res.Gren.Regt.,1 Coy.,Magny d' Anigon (Fr.) 18.9.44	MURDER	FR.
PFEIFFENBERGER, Herbert	255428	M			Cpl.,C.C.Ellrich,Nordhausen (Ger.)	MURDER	U.S.
PFEIFFER	689	M	Ger.		Gestapo,Mussy sur Seine (Fr.) 2.-4.8.44	PILLAGE	FR.
PFEIFFER	50768	M		16	Uschfhr.,SS,12 SS-Pz.Div."Hitler Jugend",Feldgendarmerie, C.C.Abbaye (Fr.) 44	TORTURE	CAN.FR.
PFEIFFER (see Pfeifer)	122737						
PFEIFFER	126486	M	Ger.		Sgt.,Prison Guard,Military Prison Camp.Tegel near Berlin (Ger.)43-44	TORTURE	U.S.
PFEIFFER	161847	M			Sturmbannfhr.,SS,12 SS-Panzer-Regt.,SS-Div."Adolf Hitler", Arnheim,Maastricht (Neth.) 43-44	WITNESS	U.S.
PFEIFFER	162810	M	Ger.		Lt.,Gestapo,Chalons-Saone,Dun les Plages (Fr.)27.-28.6.44	MURDER	FR.
PFEIFFER	167783	M	Ger.		Dr.,Leader,Lawyer,Amt des Gouverneurs f.District Galizia-Lwow, Abt.Ernaehrung und Landwirtschaft,Galizia-Lwow (Pol.)9.39-44	PILLAGE	POL.
PFEIFFER	174094	M	Ger.		Lt.Col.,Kommandant des 2 Regt.Rip. (Yugo.) 42-44	MURDER	YUGO.
PFEIFFER	191342	M	Ger.		Lt.,4 Coy.,Bau-Pi.Bn.427,at Sea (Nor.) 21.-22.4.45	MURDER	NOR.
PFEIFFER	194493	M	Ger.		Pol.-Asst.,Zollgrenzschutz,Foncenex,Veigy (Fr.)10.-12.43	TORTURE	FR.
PFEIFFER	255022	M	Ger.		Major,Air Force,Chateau d' Armain,Villiers (Fr.) 41-44	PILLAGE	FR.
PFEIFFER	259293	M			Pvt.,SS,Muhldorf Area (Ger.)	MURDER	U.S.
PFEIFFER	301711	M	Ger.	05	Mine-Manager,Freiburg,Saxony,Himmelfahrt,Fundgrube Mine (Ger.)43-44	BRUTALITY	U.K.
PFEIFFER	306802	M	Ger.		Cpl.,Feldgendarmerie,Montigny les Vesoul,Hte Saone (Fr.)16.7.44	MURDER	FR.
PFEIFFER, Albert	138226	M	Ger.		Cmdt.,C.C.Niederbuhl (Ger.) 44	MURDER	FR.U.K.
PFEIFFER, Alfred	132090	M	Ger.	03	Pvt.,1 Wach-Coy.,77 Volksgren.Regt.,C.C.Euskirchen (Ger.)3.-10.44	TORTURE	U.S.
PFEIFFER, Fritz	188305	M	Ger.		Civ.,Member,NSDAP,Dachsbach (Ger.) 43-45	TORTURE	POL.
PFEIFFER, Gerhardt	255429	M			Cpl.,C.C.Ellrich,Nordhausen (Ger.)	MURDER	U.S.
PFEIFFER, Hans	141893	M	Ger.		Pvt.,3-142 or 4-132,Stalag X B 6-395 Landesschtz.-Bn.,C.C. Muhlberg (Ger.) 28.8.41	MURDER	U.K.
PFEIFFER, Hans	258934	M			Hptsturmfhr.,SS,Personal Adjutant to the Fuehrer (43)	INTERR.	U.S.
PFEIFFER, Hans	261959	M	Ger.		Waffen-SS,Several places in Slovenia (Yugo.) 41-45	MISC.CRIMES	YUGO.
PFEIFFER, Ignaz	255357	M		17. 6.04	Employee,Gestapo,State Service,UH. Hradiste (Czech.) 39-45	MURDER	CZECH.
PFEIFFER, Jakob	192612	M		05	Kriegsgef.Arbeits-Bn.186,Strafgefangenen-Lager Nord,C.C. Finmark (Nor.)40-45	MISC.CRIMES	NOR.
PFEIFFER, Karl Heinrich	167783	M	Ger.	6.12.96	Dr.,Lawyer,Wirtschaftsamt,Berlin (Ger.) 9.39-44	PILLAGE	POL.
PFEIFFER, Karl	255430	M			Pvt.,Q.C.Bodungen,Nordhausen (Ger.)	MURDER	U.S.
PFEIFFER, Rudolf	255865	M	Ger.	27. 2.87	Sgt.,State Service,Army,SS,Heppenheim,Ueberlingen (Ger.) 41-45	BRUTALITY	POL.
PFEIFFER, Wilhelm	192613	M	Ger.	15. 4.10	Reichsjustizministerium,Feldstraflager Nord,C.C.Finmark(Nor.) 4.45	WITNESS	NOR.
PFEIFROTH, Josef	255431	M		29. 8.03	Flyer,C.C.Ellrich,Nordhausen (Ger.)	MURDER	U.S.
PFEIL, Alfred	126581	M	Ger.	95	Policeman,Coy.Commander,Police,Volkssturm-Coy.,Vienenburg (Ger.)5.44	MURDER	U.S.
PFENNIG	39672	M	Ger.		Rottfhr.,SS,17 SS-Pz.Gren.Div."Goetz von Berlichingen",Sturm-Geschuetz-Abt.17,Pz.Jg.Abtl.17,Segre Renaze (Fr.)6.8.44	MURDER	FR.
PFENNIG, Arthur Wilhelm	260481	M		28. 2.96	SS-Sturmmann,Waffen-SS,Guard,Totenkopf-Sturmbann,C.C. Auschwitz (Pol.) 44-45	BRUTALITY	POL.
PFERSICH, Emil	167767	M	Ger.	15. 3.07	Uschfhr.,SS,C.C.Natzweiler (Fr.) 42-44	MURDER	FR.
PFEUFER	155637	M			Volkssturm,Techn.Nothilfe,Gardelegen (Ger.) 4.45	MURDER	U.S.
PFIFRATER (or ACHAMER-PIFFRADER)	301594	M	Ger.		Dr.,Lt.,SS,stationed C.C.Mauthausen (Aust.) 40-45	MURDER	BEL.
PFIGGEL (see FINKEL)	155401						
PFINGST	192711	M	Ger.		Cpl.,SS,C.C.Buchenwald,Kalkum (Ger.) 42-45	TORTURE	U.S.
PFISTER	256105	M	Ger.		Pvt.,4 Coy.,Pz.Div.,St.Germain or Mons (Fr.) 21.6.44	MURDER	FR.
PFISTER, Albert	259219	M	Ger.		Agent,Gestapo of Poitiers,Antenne of Rochelle,Poitiers Area(Fr)40-45	MISC.CRIMES	FR.
PFISTERER	301736	M	Ger.	98	Pvt.,Landesschtz.-Bn.3-788,Kommandofuehrer of punishment Column, Steinach-Steiermark (Aust.) 12.43	MURDER	U.K.
PFITSCH, Erich (or HELFMANN)	185018	M	Ger.	12	Sturmschfhr.,Secr.,S.D.Crim.,Gestapo,Praha,Lidice (Czech.) 39-45	MURDER	CZECH.
PFITZINGER	253227	M	Ger.		Hilfspol.-Beamter,Abt.IV D,Sipo,Bruessel)Bel.) 40-45	INTERR.	BEL.
PFITZNER	153170	M	Ger.		Lt.,Army,Kampfgeschwader 100,Villaudric (Fr.) 20.8.44	MURDER	FR.
PFITZNER	167765	M	Ger.		Dr.,Kriegsverwaltungsrat,H.Q. of Supreme Military Command, Army,Oberkommando (Fr.) 40-44	PILLAGE	FR.
PFITZNER	259300	M			Pvt.,SS,Muhldorf Area (Ger.)	MURDER	U.S.
PFLAB	253824	M	Ger.		Lt.,Army,Finche Bray (Fr.) 5.4.45	SUSPECT	U.S.
PFLAUM	691	M			Lt.,General,Army,157 Geb.Div.(Res.),St.Pierre D' Albigny,Thones (Fr.) 23.3.,5.4.,19.4.44	MURDER	FR.
PFLAUM	121463	M			Dr.,C.C.Ravensbrueck (Ger.) 42-45	MURDER	FR.BEL.
PFLAUM	305731	M	Ger.		Oschfhr.,Arbeitseinsatz,C.C.Auschwitz,Birkenau (Pol.) 40	MURDER	FR.
PFLAUM, Karl	195936	M	Ger.		Lt.,Army,Trebeurden (Fr.)	MURDER	FR.
PFLAUMEN (see FLAUMEN)	144734						
PFLAUMER	301873	M	Ger.		Minister,of State, 4.41-1.42	MURDER	POL.
PFLAUN	136341	M	Ger.		Gendarm,Chief,Police,Marthirdenfeld (Ger.) 44	MURDER	U.S.
PFLEGER	166967	M	Ger.		Lt.,Army,Vercheny la Plaine (Fr.) 21.7.44	MURDER	FR.
PFLIEGER, Emile	144400	M	Ger.	10 or 11	Offizier,Photographe,S.D.,Chambery Officer,Bordeaux,Toulouse, Marseille,Hte.Savoie,Biollery,Chambery (Fr.) 44	TORTURE	FR.
PFLIFFER, Hans (or PIFFER, Hans)	193800	M	Ger.		Pvt.,Interpreter,Kommandantur,100 Jg.Regt.,Col du Petit, St.Bernard (Fr.) 27. or 28.8.44	MURDER	FR.
PFLUEGER	189273	M	Ger.		Regierungsrat,Gestapo,C.C.Dachau (Ger.) 40-45	MURDER	BEL.
PFLUEGER	196767	M	Ger.		Uschfhr.,1 SS-Pz.Regt.,1 Coy.,Ligneuville (Bel.) 12.44	WITNESS	U.S.
PFLUG	153169	M			Civ.,Ginnheim (Ger.) 11.44	WITNESS	U.S.
PFLUG, Gerhard	692	M	Ger.		Air Force,Paroy sur Saulx,Valhouzet (Fr.) 17.8.44	TORTURE	FR.
PFLUG, Kurt	255432	M			Sgt.,C.C.Ellrich,Nordhausen (Ger.)	MURDER	U.S.
PFLUG, Otto	254107	M	Ger.		Osturmfhr.,83 Landsturm-Regt.,Tiel (Neth.) 45	PILLAGE	NETH.
PFLUGBEIL, Kurt	258985	M	Ger.	90	Lt.General	WITNESS	U.S.
PFLUGER, Otto	305687	M	Ger.		Civilian,near Lang-Gors, 2.3.45	MURDER	U.S.
PFLUGLER, Joseph	153167	M	Ger.		Civilian,Eching (Ger.) 11.-13.7.44	WITNESS	U.S.
PFLUGMACHER	31416	M	Ger.		Capt.,Army,392-169 Inf.Div.,II Gren.Regt.,Finmark (Nor.) 44	MURDER	NOR.
PFLUNGER	195935	M			Lt. or Adjudant-Chief,Scharfschuetzen-Ausb.Coy.64 R.Mugron-Lahosse(Fr.) 8.-12.7.44	MURDER	FR.
PFORTE	257921	M			Lt.,150 Pz.Bde.,Meuse Bridge,Antwerp (Bel.)12.44	MISC.CRIMES	U.S.

PFO - PIE

NAME	C.R.FILE NUMBER	SEX	NATIO-NALITY	DATE OF BIRTH	RANK OCCUPATION UNIT PLACE AND DATE OF CRIME	REASON WANTED	WANTED BY
PFOSCH, Erich	305105	M	Ger.		Employed at Hemm,Westphalia,Kirchlengern Krs.Herford	TORTURE	NETH.
PFOSSER, Wenzel	255623	M			Rottenfhr.,Camp Dora,Nordhausen (Ger.)	MURDER	U.S.
PFOTENHAUER	137671	M	Ger.		Dr., Stalag IX C, C.C. Pothen (Ger.) 4.42	TORTURE	U.K.
PFRIMER, Gerhard	174093	M	Ger.		Dr.,Polizeibevollmaechtigter, Police (Yugo.) 4.41-44	MURDER	YUGO.
PFUHL	185883	M	Ger.	10	Lt.,commander of Pion.Troup, Heusden (Neth.) 5.,6.11.44	MURDER	NETH.
PFUHLSTEIN, Alexander	62196	M	Ger.		Brigadier Gen.,Army,Cmdr. of Brandeburg Div.,Brandenburg (Ger.)	TORTURE	UNWCC.
PFULLER	257023	M	Ger.		Lt.,Army, Belfort (Fr.) 7.44	MURDER	U.S.
PFUNDTNER	693	M			Praesident, Staatssekretaer, Innenministerium (Pol.) 39-42	MISC.CRIMES	POL.
PHARZHEIM, Otto	173870	M	Ger.		469 Inf.Rgt.,2 Bn,198 Inf.Div., Le Tholy (Fr.) 13.11.44	PILLAGE	FR.
PHATSWALD, Arthur	306324	M	Ger.		Sgt.,Mijnsheerenland Oud-Beverland (Neth.) 4.-5.5.45	MURDER	NETH.
PHENCH	137096	M	Ger.		Cpl.,Arb.Kdo.7012, Stalag XI B, C.C. Dinklar (Ger.)	MURDER	U.K.
PHESTEREN see FRESTICH	125454						
PHIFFER	67807	M	Ger.		Civilian, C.C. Himmelfahrt,Fundgrube Freiberg (Ger.) 43-4.45	MISC.CRIMES	U.K.
PHILIP, Peter	12523	M	Ger.		Pvt., Army,110 or 111 Pz,Gren.Rgt.,2 Coy, Albine (Fr.) 29.6.44	MURDER	FR.
PHILIPP	306496	M	Ger.		Sgt., SS, C.C. Buchenwald (Ger.) between 16.5.38 and 9.10.43	MURDER	BEL.
PHILIPP, Georges	168968	M	Ger.		Pvt., Stalag, Altmansdorf (Ger.) 21.8.41	MURDER	FR.
PHILIPP, Inn	190303	M	Ger.		Ensign 04678, Rechlin (Ger.) 21.6.44	MURDER	U.S.
PHILIPP, Viktor	255189	M	Ger.	85	Lt.,Gendarmerie officer, Muettersholtz Krs.Schlettstadt (Fr.)21.7.44	MURDER	U.S.
PHILIPP, Walter	161651	M	Ger.	08	Cpl., Airforce, Luftgau, C.C.Egeremoen,Hoenefosa,Buskernd (Nor.)	MURDER	NOR.
PHILIPPE	694	M	Ger.		Lt., Police, Gendarmerie, Obernai (r.) 20.7.44	MURDER	FR.
PHILIPPE	12524	M	Ger.		Officer, SS-Div. "Das Reich", Castel Maurou (Fr.) 27.6.44	MURDER	FR.
PHILIPPE	125394	M	Ger.		Sgt., SS, C.C. Sachsenhausen (Ger.)	MURDER	BEL.
PHILIPPE	300842	M	Ger.		Pvt., 1 Aufkl.Abt.,3 Coy, 2 Col.,XV Div. Afrika Korps, St.Leger Distr. Arlon (Bel.) 5.9.44	MISC.CRIMES	BEL.
PHILLIP	193820	M	Ger.		Lt., SS Div. "Das Reich", SS Rgt. "Deutschland", 9 Coy, Mixemont (Fr.) 2.6.44	MURDER	FR.
PHILLIPS	306102	M	Ger.		Sturmmann,SS, C.C. Alderney (Channel Is) and Kortemark 42-45	MURDER	CZECH.
PHLEGER, Arthur	166969	M	Ger.		Gendarm, Gendarmerie, Hangienbieten (Fr.) 14.8.44	MURDER	FR.
PHLEPS, Arthur	174092	M	Ger.		Lt.Gen.,Waffen-SS, Geb.Jg.Corps Kroatien, 41-44	MURDER	YUGO.
PHOENTIC see PRINISKI	257208						
PHUELSTEIN	165706	M	Ger.	95	Major, Gen., Army, (Serbia-Yugo.).44	TORTURE	U.S.
PIAKOWSKI	153164	M			Sturmbannfhr., Waffen-SS, C.C. Dachau (Ger.)	TORTURE	U.S.
PIAZZA	125645	M	Ger.		Medicin chief, C.C. Dora (Ger.)	MURDER	FR.
PICARD	253228	M	Ger.		Hilfspol.Beamter, Sipo Abt.III B, Bruessel (Bel.) 40-44	INTERR.	BEL.
PICHA, Maximilian	29706	M	Ger.		Amtsgerichtsrat, Ministry of Justice, Public official, Litomerice (Czech.) 40	MURDER	CZECH.
PICHL	147369	M	Ger.		Pvt.,11 Pz.Div.,2 Group, Kampfr. "Wilde"(South-West-Fr.) 44	MURDER	FR.
PICHER, Otto	190322	M	Ger.		Sgt.,Army, Lehrte, Braunschweig (Ger.)	MURDER	U.S.
PICHLER	695	M	Ger.		Lt.,Army, 98 Rgt. of Mountain Troops, 3 Coy, 1 or 2 Bn,22.-31.8.44	MURDER	YR.
PICHLER	132547	M	Ger.		Osturmfhr.,SS, C.C. Hollein (Ger.)	MURDER	FR.
PICHLER, Hans	302096	M	Ger.	16.11.01	Uscharfhr.,SS, U.C. Auschwitz (Pol.) 40-1.45	MURDER	POL.
PICHLER, Josef	199945	M	Ger.	21. 1.82	Local groupleader, NSDAP, Klanovice (Czech.)	TORTURE	CZECH.
PICHLER, Peter	252575	M	Ger.	09	Interpreter, Gestapo, Jagodina (Yugo.) 15.2.44	INTERR.	YUGO.
PICHOTKA, Fritz	173869	M	Ger.	25. 5.93	Cpl., Prison C.C. Vannes (Fr.) 42-44	TORTURE	FR.
PICHT	126582	M	Ger.		Major, Army, Kampfgruppe Picht, Steinbergen (Ger.)9. and 10.4.45	MURDER	U.S.
PICK, Alfred	258109	M	Ger.	8. 1.01	Uscharfhr.,SS, State Service, Police official, Val. Mezirici (Czech.) 44-45	MURDER	CZECH.
PICKARD	10076	M	Ger.	95	Capt., Luftwaffe, C.C. Stalag Luft 4 Kiepheide (Ger.) 18.7.44	TORTURE	U.K.
PICKARTZ	696	M	Ger.		Cpl., Army, Issy les Moulineaux (Fr.) 8.44	MURDER	FR.
PICKE, Hans	193267	M	Ger.	4. 6.96	Uscharfhr.,SS, 4 SS-Totenkopf Stuba., C.C. Nordhausen, Auschwitz (Ger.,Pol.) 43-45	MURDER	U.S.
PICKEL	31417	M	Ger.		Major, Army, 8 Geb.Div., Kampfgr. Kraeutler,Finmark (Nor.) 44	MURDER	NOR.
PICKEL	153162	M	Ger.		Lt., Parachute Unit "Hermann Goering" Div.,Mentana (It.) 27.10.43	MURDER	U.K.
PICKEL, Fritz	153161	M			Civilian, Rothenburg (Ger.) 3.45	WITNESS	U.S.
PICKELMANN	166966	M	Ger.		Sgt., Army, Petit Rederching (Fr.) 8.-9.40	PILLAGE	FR.
PICKERT	258781	M			SS-T.Sgt., C.C. Nordhausen (Ger.)	MURDER	U.S.
PICKERT, Franz	153160	M	Ger.		Sgt., Landes-Schz.Bn 349-18, Blache, St.Waast (Fr.) 24.-25.8.42	MURDER	FR.
PICKHARDT	108893	M	Ger.		Capt., C.C. Stalag Luft Kief-Heide, (Ger.) 8.44-3.45	MURDER	U.S.
PICTSCH, Erwin	255301	M			Pvt., Camp Ellrich, Nordhausen (Ger.)	MURDER	U.S.
PIDUN, Helmuth	254119	M			Hptscharfhr.,1 SS Pz.Rgt., 1 Coy, Malmedy (Bel.) 17.12.44	MISC.CRIMES	U.S.
PISCONKA	185016	M	Ger.	05	Amtsgerichtsrat, District Court Bohemia-Moravia, Prague (Czech.) 39-43	MURDER	CZECH.
PIEEHLER, Anton	262234	M	Ger.	2.12.19	Oscharfhr.,SS,5 Coy, 2 Platoon,51 SS Armoured Bde, Breviandes, Bucheres, St.Savine,La Riviere, De Corps (Troyes) (Fr.) 22.-25.8.44	BRUTALITY	FR.
PIEHLER, Karl Heinz	230454	M	Ger.		Cpl., Abwehr-Nachr.Rgt. 506, Abano (It.) 44	MISC.CRIMES	U.S.
PIEHTER	133950	M			Mil.Verw.Oberrat (Ger.)	WITNESS	U.S.
PIEIER	189441	M			Prison-guard, C.C. Tromsoy (Nor.)	TORTURE	NOR.
PIEL	195148	M	Ger.		Leader, Ruestungs-Lieferungsamt, The Hague (Neth.) 40-45	PILLAGE	NETH.
PIELEN	186136	F	Ger.		Cdo.-Fuehrerin, C.C. Koenigsberg-Neumark (Ger.)	MURDER	FR.
PIELTNER	1453	M			Sturmmann, SS, 16 SS Pz.Gren.	MURDER	U.K.
PIENLER, Herbert	196866	M	Ger.		Cpl., SS, Auschwitz (Pol.) 12.42	MURDER	FR.
PIEPENSTOCK	133261	M			Uscharfhr.,SS	MURDER	U.S.
PIEPER, Dr.	29707	M	Ger.		Dr., Landgerichtspraesident, public official, Prague (Czech.) 40	MURDER	CZECH.
PIEPER alias PEIPER	161895	M	Ger.		Dr.,Civilian, Langenbrand (Ger.) 44	MURDER	U.S.
PIEPER, Ferdinand	153159	M			Painter, Civilian	TORTURE	U.S.
PIEPERS, Heinrich	305106	M	Ger.		Crim.Asst., Uscharfhr.Gestapo, SS Staffel, Prague (Czech.) 39-45	MURDER	CZECH.
PIERKAMP	194865	M	Ger.		SS-Oberfhr., SD, Gestapo, Simferopol (Sov.Un.)	MISC.CRIMES	SOV.UN.
PIERZYNA	255302	M			Uscharfhr.,Camp Mackenrode, Nordhausen (Ger.)	MURDER	U.S.
PIESCH, Ernest	29708	M	Ger.		Dr., Landgerichtsrat, Public official, Opava (Czech.) 40	MURDER	CZECH.
PIESCHE, Richard	29709	M	Ger.		Senatspraesident, Public official, Litomerice (Czech.) 40	MURDER	CZECH.
PIESCHEL	184234	M			Arbeits-Kdo., C.C. Passau (Ger.) 43-45	TORTURE	U.S.
PIESTE	129730	M			Uscharfhr., SS, C.C. Mauthausen (Aust.) 41-45	MURDER	U.S.
PIESTON, Hermann	155523	M			Osturmfhr.,SS, C.C. Sachsenhausen, Oranienburg (Ger.)	TORTURE	U.K.
PIETRI	186164	M	Ger.		Kapo, Arbeits-Kdo., C.C. Leonberg, Stuttgart (Ger.)	TORTURE	FR.
PIETSCH	124610	M	Ger.		Uscharfhr., SS, C.C. Birkenau (Pol.)	MURDER	BEL.

PIE-PIT

NAME	C.R.FILE NUMBER	SEX	NATIO- NALITY	DATE OF BIRTH	RANK OCCUPATION UNIT PLACE AND DATE OF CRIME	REASON WANTED	WANTED BY
PIETSCH	300843	M	Ger.		Officier,1 Aufkl.Abt.3 Coy 2 Col.XV Div.Afrika Corps,Saint Leger (Arlon) 5.9.44	MISC.CRIMES	BEL.
PIETSCH,Georg	192609	M	Ger.	06	Oberwachtmeister,Reichsjustizministerium,Feldstraflager,C.C.Finmark (Nor.) 9.3.45	MURDER	NOR.,YUGO.
PIETSCH, Hans	195465	M	Ger.	05	Hptsturmfhr.,Flak Rgt.,Freimann Kaserne,Muenchen (Ger.) 8.-9.44	MURDER	U.S.
PIETSCHMANN,Erich	167782	M	Ger.		Deputy leader,Ernaehrungs and Landwirtschaftsministerium,Lwow (Gal., Pol.) 9.39-44	PILLAGE	POL.
PIETZ	38838	M	Ger.		SS-Osturmbannfhr.,C.C.Lublin (Pol.)	TORTURE	U.S.
PIETZSCHKE (see BIETZSCHKE)	162488						
PIEURER (or FUCHPER,Adolph)	262272	M		04	Lt.,1 Coy East Bn.654,Simard (Fr.) 2.-4.9.44	PILLAGE	FR.
PIEZONKA	173862	M	Ger.		Lt.,paratrooper- Rgt.2, 2 parachut.Div.,Depart.Finistere (Fr.) 44	MURDER	FR.
PIFFER,Hans (see PFLIFFER,Hans)	193800						
PIFFRADER	253274	M	Ger.		Standartenfhr., Sipo and Army,SS,Baranowicze (Pol.) 43	MISC.CRIMES	POL.
PIGULLA	136309	M			Pvt.,11 Pz.Div.2 Coy 2 AA-A 7,Bergerac,Albine (Fr.) 7.-8.44	MURDER	FR.
PILARCZYK	132345	M			N.C.O.,Member,SS,Krakau (Pol.) 11.42-2.43	MURDER	U.S.
PILARCZYK	255308	M			Pvt.,Camp Dora,Nordhausen (Ger.)	MURDER	U.S.
PILGAR,Victor	136602	M			Senior Medical Officer,Major,Stalag XVII B,C.C.Krems Gneixendorf (Aust.) 10.43-4.45	MURDER	U.S.
PILGER	185581	M	Ger.		Crim.Apst.,Oschfhr.,Gestapo,SD,Sarrebruck (Ger.)	PILLAGE	FR.
PILHLER (or PILHEF)	193946	M			Sipo,Dorgen (Ger.)	WITNESS	U.S.
PILITZS	147067	M			Chief,Gestapo,Radovljica (Yugo.) 43	MURDER	YUGO.
PILL,Theodor	260989	M	Ger.		SS-St.Mann,C.C.Vaihingen (Ger.) 13.8.44-7.4.45	MURDER	U.S.
PILLEN	193818	F	Ger.		SS-overseer,C.C.Ravensbrueck (Ger.)	TORTURE	FR.
PILLEPT	132652	M	Ger.		Sgt.,Prison militaire de Vienne (Aust.)	BRUTALITY	FR.
PILLINGS,Theo	162806	M			Civilian,Revin (Fr.) 6.44	MURDER	FR.
PILLION	254757	M	Ger.		Pvt.,13 Coy 558 Gren.Rgt.,Bruay en Artois (Fr.)	MURDER	FR.
PILNYMU,Friedrich	192507	M	Ger.	29.3.12	Doctor.,Gestapo,Bruenn (Czech.) 39-45	SUSPECT	CZECH.
PILS	195934	M			Manager,Spinning Hall,Anrath (Ger.) 1.42-3.44	TORTURE	NETH.
PILS,Joseph	153157	M			Agent,Gestapo,Angers (Fr.)	MURDER	FR.
PILZ	155522	M		11	Pvt.,Army,101 or 102 Rgt.or 69 Rgt.,C.C.Oflag IV C,Colditz (Ger.)9.43	TORTURE	U.K.
PILZ (see PRINZ)	187991						
PILZ	261803	M	Ger.		Supervisor,C.C.Dora,Nordhausen (Ger.)	MURDER	FR.
PILZ,Josef	195152	M	Ger.		SS-Hptschfhr.,SD Einsatz Kdo.,Saales and St.Die (Fr.)	MURDER	U.K.
PILZ,Josef or Fritz	259699	M	Ger.		SS-Uschfhr.,Gestapo,Area of Angers Maine and Loire (Fr.) 42-44	MISC.CRIMES	FR.
PILZ,Max	256647	M	Ger.		Ma.-Pvt.,Navy,Hopseidel,Finmark (Nor.) 6.5.45	MURDER	NOR.
PILZER	147368	M	Ger.		Cpl.,11 Pz.Div.,Kampfgr."Wilde",(Fr.) 44	MURDER	FR.
PIMMER,Johann	153155	M	Ger.		Doctor,Civilian,C.C.Volary (Czech.) 44-45	WITNESS	U.S.
PIMPEL,Rudolf	167786	M	Ger.		Pvt.,Army,9 Res.Gren.Rgt.1 Coy,Magny d'Anigon (Fr.) 18.9.44	MURDER	FR.
PINAERT	254912	M			Guard,Chief,Prison Siegburg (Ger.)	INTERR.	FR.
PINDUR,Johann	253541	M	Ger.	84	Town Major,Vsetin (Czech.) 39-45	MISC.CRIMES	CZECH.
PINGEL	132092	M			Lt.Col.,Deputy C.O.,Stalag VI F,C.C.Munster Stalag VI E (Ger.) 42-45	MURDER	U.S.
PINGEL	139665	M			Capt.,Stalag X B,C.C.Sandbostel (Ger.) 1.-5.45	TORTURE	U.S.
PINGEL,Ernst	254913	M	Ger.		Aeltester Block 3,Wilhelmshaven (Ger.)	MURDER	FR.
PINICPANCKE,Erich	144403	M			Pvt.,SS,Rheurdt (Ger.) 21.2.45	TORTURE	U.S.
PINK	149159	M	Ger.	10	SS-Rottfhr.,C.C.Hirzenhaiin (Ger.)	MURDER	U.S.
PINK,Franz	185554	M			Arbeitskdo.,C.C.Regensburg (Ger.) 41-45	TORTURE	U.S.
PINKARD (see SCHIMMEL)	155973						
PINKEPANK,Karl-Heinz	255309	M			Pvt.,Camp Ellrich,Nordhausen (Ger.)	MURDER	U.S.
PINKERNELL	62121	M	Ger.		SS-Hptsturmfhr.,12 SS Pz.Div.Hitler Jugend	WITNESS	U.S.,CAN.
PINKERT	196531	M			Capt.,3 Brandenburg Rgt.Commd.II,	MISC.CRIMES	U.S.
PINKES,Arthur	192610	M	Ger.	18.9.01	Sgt.,Reichsjustizministerium,Guard,Feldstraflager Nord,Finmark (Nor.) 6.42-45	MISC.CRIMES	YUGO.,NOR.
PINKOWSKI	149160	M	Ger.		SS,Zamose (Pol.)	MURDER	POL.
PINKUS	259218	M			SS-Chief of Block,SS,Auschwitz (Pol.)	BRUTALITY	FR.
PINN	300844	M	Ger.		Pvt.,1 Aufkl.Abt.3 Coy 2 Col.XV Div. of Afrika Corps,Saint Leger (Arlon) 5.9.44	MISC.CRIMES	BEL.
PINNENKAMPER,Adolf August	149070	M		16	Civilian,C.C.Gardelegen (Ger.) 5.4.45-14.4.45	MURDER	U.S.
PINSKER,Otto	153152	M	Ger.		Factory-Dir.,Civilian,C.C.Volary (Czech.) 44-45	WITNESS	U.S.
PINTRSEE	256115	M	Ger.		Pvt.,Muhldorf (Ger.)	INTERR.	U.S.
PINZLER,Karl	194096	M	Ger.		Funkmeister,Pz.Abt.,Gendringen (Neth.) 9.10.44	WITNESS	NETH.
PIOTROWSKI (or PITROWSKI)	193349	M			Capt.,1 Kgfg.Arb.Bn.41,Aalesund (Nor.) 8.5.44	TORTURE	NOR.
PIOTROWSKI,Ernst	255310	M		21.6.17	Cpl.,Camp Ellrich,Nordhausen (Ger.)	MURDER	U.S.
PIPKOLN	302097	M	Ger.		Sub.-Lt.,Kalamac,(Grc.) 2.44	MURDER	GRC.
PIRAZZI	133260	M			Major,Army,Hammelburg (Ger.) 44-45	MURDER	U.S.
PIRET	253190	M	Ger.		Employee,Abt.III D Sipo,Bruessels (Bel.)	INTERR.	BEL.
PIRKAMP (see BIERKAMP)	93	M					
PIRNY	50751	M	Ger.		Rottfhr.,SS,Gusen (Aust.)	MISC.CRIMES	BEL.
PIRZER,Matteus	255312	M		25.1.05	Flyer,Camp Ellrich,Nordhausen (Ger.)	MURDER	U.S.
PISAROV,Mitko	189961	M			Governeur,Administration of Occ.territories,Pirot (Yugo.)	TORTURE	YUGO.
PISCHKOWITZ	137551	M			SS-Sturmmann,C.C.Weimar,Buchenwald (Ger.)	TORTURE	U.S.
PISCHLER	185580	M			3 Coy Geb.Jg.Bn.,Region of the Maurienne (Fr.)	MURDER	FR.
PISKA,Erich	255311	M			Sgt.,C.C.Ellrich,Nordhausen (Ger.)	MURDER	U.S.
PISKALLA	300845	M	Ger.		Pvt.,1 Aufkl.Abt.3 Coy 2 Col.XV Div.of Afrika Corps,Saint Leger (Arlon) 5.9.44	MISC.CRIMES	BEL.
PISKE	252569	M	Ger.		Kreis-Cmdt.,Army,Radosin near Jagodina (Yugo.) 8.41	MURDER	YUGO.
PISSARD	196865	M			Ortsgruppenleiter,NSDAP,Wintzenheim (Ger.) 1.45	MISC.CRIMES	FR.
PISSARECK	189641	M			Douanier,Zollgrenzschutz,Feissons-Isere (Fr.) 5.8.44	MURDER	FR.
PISTER	184235	M	Ger.		N.C.O.,Gestapo,Heralion (Grc.)	MURDER	GRC.
PISTER	300846	M	Ger.		Pvt.,1 Aufkl.Abt.3 Coy 2 Col.XV Div.of Afrika Corps,Saint Leger (Arlon) 5.9.44	MISC.CRIMES	BEL.
PISTER,Herrmann	12413	M	Ger.	85	SS-Sturmfhr.,C.C.Buchenwald (Ger.)	MURDER	CZECH.
PISTOL	185882	M			SS-Guard,C.C.Neckarels (Ger.)	MURDER	U.S.
PISTOR	185106	M			SS Chef Arzt,SS,C.C.Sachsenhausen (Ger.)	TORTURE	FR.
PISTORIUS	188245	M	Ger.		N.C.O.,Army,Bruchsal (Ger.) 2.-3.2.45	MURDER	U.S.
PITCH	185649	M	Ger.	95	SS-Mann,C.C.Ravensbrueck (Ger.) 21.4.42-26.4.45	MISC.CRIMES	BEL.,FR.
PITKAU,Hugo	254758	M	Ger.	17.2.21	Pvt.,13 Coy 553 Gren.Rgt.,Bruay en Artois (Fr.) 1.9.44	MURDER	FR.

PIT-PLA

NAME	C.R.FILE NUMBER	SEX	NATIO-NALITY	DATE OF BIRTH	RANK OCCUPATION UNIT PLACE AND DATE OF CRIME	REASON WANTED	WANTED BY
PITLER, Michel	174070	M	Ger.		SS-Mann, SS Pz.Gren.Ausb.and Ers.Bn.12, Anhee (Fr.) 9.4.44	MURDER	BEL.
PITROCH, Alfons	179737	M	Ger.	20	Doctor, 9.Pz.Gren.Rgt., Fucecchio Marshes (It.) 23.8.44	MURDER	U.K.
PITRON, Max	306693	M	Ger.		Sgt., 331.Pion.Bn.,331 Inf.Div.,Mijnheerenland (Neth.) 5.45	PILLAGE	NETH.
PITROWSKI (see PIOTROWSKI)	193349						
PITSCH	166965	M	Ger.		Capt., Stalag VI C. (Ger.)	TORTURE	FR.
PITT	252571	M	Ger.	18	Lt., O.C.Army Group Signals Rgt. No.598, Ala (It.) 13.9.43	MURDER	U.K.
PITTELKOW	254124	M			Pvt., Pepingen (Bel.) 2.-9.44	INTERR.	BEL.
PITTERMANN, Georg	192508	M	Ger.		Crim.Asst., Gestapo, Brno (Czech.) 39-45	SUSPECT	CZECH.
PITTHAN, Heinrich	240013	M	Ger.	10	Pvt., Abwehr-Nachr.Rgt.506, Paris (Fr.)	MISC. CRIMES	U.S.
PITTNER, Marie	192510	F	Ger.	9. 9.97	Civ., Swichboard-Operator, Gestapo, Brno (Czech.) 39-45	WITNESS	CZECH.
PITTROH	141591	M	Ger.		Civ. Dr.med., Medecin at the firm V.D.M., Hedderheim (Ger.) 44	MURDER	FR.
PITULA, Josef	256116	M	Ger.		SS, Muehldorf (Ger.)	WITNESS,INTERR.	U.S.
PITZ	251226	M		12	Army (When civ.-tennis champion), Nordhausen,Gerardmer (Ger.,Fr.)5.44	WITNESS	U.S.
PITZ, August	132589	M	Ger.	28. 7.99	Civilian, mayor, public official, Sierck les Bains (Fr.)	MURDER	FR.
PITZ, Johann	257245	M	Ger.	05	SS-Staffelmann, Interpreter,Abtlg.IV,Sipo and SD, Anvers (Bel.)40-44	BRUTALITY	BEL.
PKEIFFER	166964	M	Ger.		Cpl., Feldkommandantur, Montigny en Vesoul (Fr.) 16.7.44	MURDER	FR.
PLAANT	301353	M	Ger.		SS-Mann, 19.Rgt. of Police, St.Gingolph Hte-Savoie (Fr.) 23.7.44	MURDER	FR.
PLAASMANN	126481	M	Ger.	94	Uschfhr., SS Totenkopf Div. Sturmbann, Gelfenberger Benzin A.G., Gelsenkirchen, Horst (Ger.)	TORTURE	U.S.
PLAATZ (or SPAATZ)	196610	M	Ger.		W.O., Cmdt., Field-Police, St. Laurent (Fr.) 40-44	WITNESS	FR.
PLACH, Mathias	153150	M	Ger.		SS-Guard, C.C. Volary (Czech.) 44	MURDER	U.S.
PLACK, Werner	140854	M	Ger.	20. 4.07	Public-Official	WITNESS	U.K.
PLACKE	301967	M	Ger.		Lagerfhr. in Gypsy Camp, Auschwitz (Pol.) 43-44	MURDER	POL.
PLADDE, Waldi	167776	M	Ger.		Treuhaender, Public Official, Rigaer Gaststaette, Poznan (Pol.) 39-44	PILLAGE	POL.
PLADETSKA, Frantz	147367	M	Ger.		11.Pz.Div., Kampfgruppe "Wilde" (Fr.) 44	MURDER	FR.
PLAGE	196864	M	Ger.		Hptsturmfhr., S.S., Auschwitz (Pol.) 40	MURDER	FR.
PLAGEMAN	255303	M	Ger.		N.C.O., Sturm-Bn., A.O.K. No.1,2.Coy. Lt.MG, near Courcelles sur Nied (Fr.) 15.11.44	MURDER	U.S.
PLAGGE	153149	M			Oschfhr.,Rapportfhr., Waffen SS, C.C.Birkenau (Pol.)	TORTURE	U.S.
PLAGGE, Wilhelm,Hugo,Ernst	195150	M	Ger.	30. 3.01	Member, Sipo, Arnheim (Neth.) 40-45	MISC.CRIMES	NETH.
PLAKET	195151	M	Ger.		Unterwachtmeister,Gestapo,Hq.Avenue Foch,Paris,Noailles (Fr.) 44	MURDER	U.K.
PLAKMER (see GLAMMER)	161207						
PLANK	129746	M	Ger.		C.C. Kaisheim (Ger.) 6.44	TORTURE	BEL.
PLANK	142074	M			SS-Hptschfhr., C.C. Dachau (Ger.)	MURDER	U.S.
PLANK (see BLANK)	151754						
PLANK	255863	M			SS-Mann, C.C. Buch-enwald (Ger.)	MURDER	U.S.
PLANK, Heinz, E.	262081	M	Ger.		Former Member of Gestapo, Paris (Fr.)	MISC.CRIMES	FR.
PLASCHE, Franz	256117	M	Ger.		Pvt., SS, Muhldorf (Ger.)	WITNESS	U.S.
PLASCHKA	36696	M	Ger.or Pol.		Pvt., Army, Landesschuetzen Bn. 875, 2.Coy.(Pol.) 17.2.45	MURDER	U.K.
PLASKE	121275	M	Ger.		SS Oschfhr., C.C. Ravensbrueck (Ger.) 42-45	TORTURE	FR.,BEL.
PLASKE	124101	M	Ger.		Pvt., Army 2.Coy. 515 Bn.,Freihafen near Koeniggraetz (Ger.)17.2.45	MURDER	U.K.
PLASS (or BLASS)	192160	M	Ger.		Sgt., Geheime Feldpolizei, Brussels (Bel.)	TORTURE	BEL.
PLASSMAN	153148	M	Ger.		Agent, Gestapo, Bielefeld (Ger.) 11.43	TORTURE	U.S.
PLATEN, Jacob	262129	M	Ger.		Murder of an American airman, Muenchen,Priel (Ger.) L.O.D.N.A.O.D.	SUSPECT	U.S.
PLATENIK, L.	699	M			Beauftragter d.Bankaufsichtstelle,Public-Official	MISC.CRIMES	ARG.,POL.
PLATH	174552	M	Ger.		Uschfhr., SS, C.C.Sachsenhausen,Flossenburg (Ger.)	WITNESS	U.K.
PLATH	196674	M	Ger.		Hauptwachtmeister, Police Waffen School III,Arnheim (Neth.)3.45	MURDER	NETH.
PLATH, Alfred	153147	M	Ger.		Volkssturm 3.Coy., C.C. Gardelegen (Ger.) 4.45	MURDER	U.S.
PLATHE	191343	M	Ger.		Commander, Capt., Festungspioniere, Kristiansand (Nor.) 45	MURDER	U.K.
PLATOWSKI	251233	M			Uschfhr., C.C. Neuengamme (Ger.)	BRUTALITY	FR.
PLATOWSKY	121277	M	Ger.		SS Usturmfhr., C.C. Neuengamme (Ger.) 42	MURDER	BEL.
PLATSA (see PLAZA), Max	129873						
PLATT, Max	143030	M			SS, C.C. Flossenburg (Ger.)	TORTURE	U.S.
PLATT, R.G.	125205	M	Ger.		Arb.-Kommando, C.C.Stollwerk (Factory) (Ger.) 1.43	TORTURE	U.S.
PLATTE	173908	M	Ger.		Lt., Army, C.C. Hemer (Ger.) Stalag 6A. 43 - 45	TORTURE	U.S.
PLATTE	300847	M	Ger.		Pvt.,1.Aufkl.Abt.,3.Coy.2.Column XV Div.of the Afrika Korps, St.Leger, Arlon (Fr.) 5.9.44	MISC.CRIMES	BEL.
PLATTEN	252572	M	Ger.	06	Capt., Air Force 734 Lt.Flak Bn., Ciacomo (It.) 3.1.44	INTERR.	U.K.
PLATTNER, Josef	142077	M	Ger.	05	SS-Sturmmann, Guard, Waffen SS,SS-Totenkopf-Stand.,C.C.Leipzig, Thekla (Ger.)	TORTURE	U.S.
PLATTNER, Karl	144401	M	Ger.		Civilian, C.C. Hadamar (Ger.) 6.44-3.45	WITNESS	U.S.
PLATZ	21464	M	Ger.		Lt.Col., Army, Paris (Fr.) 7.2.44	TORTURE	U.K.
PLATZ (or SPATZ)	136206	M	Ger.		Feldgendarmerie,Adjutant Chief, Macon Charolles Feillens (Fr.)	MURDER	FR.
PLATZ	188953	M	Ger.		Sgt., Feldgendarmerie, Arbigny (Fr.) 25.5.44	MURDER	FR.
PLATZ	195933	M	Ger.		Capt., Parachutist School, Ussel, Chaveroche (Fr.) 18.12.43	TORTURE	FR.
PLATZ	260026	M	Ger.		Sgt.,Div.Oberland,Unit Russian German, Massif du Vercors,Isere et Drome (Fr.) 7.-8.44	SUSPECT	FR.
PLATZ, Erick	196863	M			Pvt., 2.Coy. 223.Inf.Rgt., Yves (Fr.) 20.9.44	MISC.CRIMES	FR.
PLATZA	121279	M	Ger.		Osturmfhr., SS, C.C. Buchenwald (Ger.)	TORTURE	FR.
PLATZE	38843	M	Ger.	15	Dr.med., Hptsturmfhr., SS, C.C. Struthof (Fr.)	MISC.CRIMES	FR.
PLATZER	155635	M	Ger.		Foreman, Civ. Overseer, Automobile Plant, Mannheim (Ger.) 1.45	MURDER	U.S.
PLATZER	167781	M	Ger.		Dr., Manager,Ernaehrungs-and Landwirtschafts-Ministerium,Krakau (Pol.) 9.39-44	PILLAGE	POL.
PLAUEL (see BLAUEL)	133750						
PLAUEL	196673	M	Ger.		Blockfhr., C.C. Neuengamme (Ger.)	TORTURE	BEL.
PLAUL, Wolfgang	4878	M	Ger.	09	Osturmfhr., SS Totenkopf, C.C.Buchenwald (Ger.)	TORTURE	U.S.
PLAUMANN	253540	M	Ger.		Lt., Coy.Fhr.,3.Coy.1.Bn.4.Rgt. paratrooper. (Rgt. Grassmel) Div.Hermann Goering,Helchteren, Hechtel (Bel.) 9.44	MISC.CRIMES	BEL.
PLAWITZKI, Friedrich	255059	M		23. 6.15	Feldwebel, Camp Ellrich, Nordhausen (Ger.)	MURDER	U.S.
PLAZA	10322	M	Ger.		Osturmfhr., SS, C.C. Buchenwald (Ger.) 38-44	MURDER	CZECH.,U.S.
PLAZA	167755	M	Ger.		Hptsturmfhr., SS, C.C.Natzweiler (Fr.) 42-44	MURDER	FR.
PLAZA, Heinrich	300913	M	Ger.		Dr., on staff at Camp,Struthof-Natzweiler (Fr.) ab.7.or 8.44	MURDER	U.K.
PLAZA (or PLATSA or PLATT)Max	129873	M			Dr., Civ.-retain, C.C. Buchenwald (Ger.)	MURDER	U.S.
PLAZZA	132344	M			Osturmfhr., SS, C.C.Dora, Nordhausen (Ger.)	MURDER	U.S.
PLAZZA, Heinz	149062	M			Hptsturmfhr., SS, C.C.Auschwitz (Pol.) 43-44	MURDER	U.S.

PLE-POE

NAME	C.R.FILE NUMBER	SEX	NATIO-NALITY	DATE OF BIRTH	RANK OCCUPATION UNIT PLACE AND DATE OF CRIME	REASON WANTED	WANTED BY
PLECHINGER, Franz	254906	M	Ger.		Pvt.,F.P.II-178,Romilly (Fr.) 8.44	PILLAGE	FR.
PLECHINGER, Wilhelm	254907	M	Ger.		F.P.No.II-178,Romilly-Seine (Fr.) 8.44	PILLAGE	FR.
PLEIAS	174079	M	Ger.		Gestapo-Leitstelle,C.C.Bruenn,Oswiecim,Birkenau (Czech.Pol.) 39-45	MURDER	CZECH.
PLEIGER, Paul	165705	M	Ger.	29. 9.99	General-Manager,Staatsrat,Berlin(Ger.)	MISC.CRIMES	U.S.
PLEIL, Josef	254123	M	Ger.	30. 1.93	Ortsgruppenleiter,NSDAP,Kynspek (Czech.) 38-45	MISC.CRIMES	CZECH.
PLEISENER, Emil (or BLEISNER)	129872	M		13	Rottfhr.,Waffen-SS,Totenkopf-Verband,C.C.Weimar,Buchenwald(Ger)37-42	MURDER	U.S.
PLEISNER	254761	M	Ger.		Sgt.,Oschfhr.,SS,C.C.Gusen,Mauthausen (Ger.)	MURDER	BEL.
PLEISSNER, Emil	148473	M	Ger.	23. 5.13	Hptschfhr.,SS,Totenkopf,C.C.Buchenwald (Ger.) 42-45	MURDER	U.S.
PLEITZNER, Emil	306497	M	Ger.	23. 5.13	Sgt.,SS-Staff (No.132345),C.C.Buchenwald (Ger.) 16.5.38-9.10.43	MURDER	BEL.
PLENISS	193374	M	Ger.		Pvt.,1 Kgf.Arb.Bn.41,C.C.Nerlandsdal,Kristiansund (Nor.) 41-45	TORTURE	NOR.
PLENZLER	177348	M	Ger.		Pvt.,Arbeits-Kdo.2263,C.C.Eichenborn bei Bad Pyrmont(Ger.) 7.43	MURDER	YUGO.
PLERENSTOCK	133261	M			Uschfhr.,SS,C.C.Flossenburg (Ger.)	MURDER	U.S.
PLESCHER, Karl	132192	M	Ger.		Cpl.,Army,352 Inf.Div.,13-916 G.R. (Fr.) 9.6.44	WITNESS	U.S.
PLESSL, Eric	261730	M	Ger.	7. 7.19	Lt.,490 Armoured Artillery Bds.,Montmirail (Fr.)	MURDER	FR.
PLETZ	153146	M	Ger.		Sgt.,Major,Feldgendarmerie 958,Sisteron (Fr.) 6.6.44	WITNESS	FR.
PLEUEN, Karl	260364	M	Ger.		Oberwachtmeister,SS-Penitentiary (Nord-Norway) 6.42-45	MURDER	YUGO.
PLICHT, Hans (or BLIGHT)	137571	M	Ger.	12. 6.14	Uschafhr.,SS-Totenkopf-Sturmbann,leader of the Work Troop"Steinbruch" C.C.Buchenwald,Halle (Ger.) 42-45	MURDER	U.S.
PLICHT, Johann	161908	M	Ger.	12. 6.14	Uschfhr.,SS-Totenkopf,C.C.Buchenwald (Ger.)	TORTURE	U.S.
PLIESS	162690	M	Ger.		Usturmfhr.,Waffen-SS,Totenkopf-Standarte,Com.Staff,C.C.Buchenwald(Ger.)	TORTURE	U.S.
PLIHAL	300848	M	Ger.		Pvt.,1.Aufkl.-Abt.,3 Coy.,2 Column,XV Div. of the Afrika-Corps, St.Leger (Arlon) 5.9.44	MISC.CRIMES	BEL.
PLINKE, Melle	259220	F	Ger.		Typist,Gestapo of Poitiers Area (Fr.) 40-45	SUSPECT	FR.
PLISCHEK (or PLISEK, Friedrich)	260415		Ger.	12. 4.84	Member,S.D,Jicin,Kopidlno,Bohemia (Czech.) 40-5.45	MISC.CRIMES	CZECH.
PLISCHER	254759		Ger.		Sgt.,Oschfhr.,S.D.,Toulouse (Fr.) 11.42-8.44	MURDER	FR.
PLISEK, Friedrich (see PLISCHEK)	260415						
PLITZ	38840	M	Ger.		SS,C.C.Auschwitz (Pol.)	MURDER	U.S.
PLOCH	192749	M	Ger.		SS,C.C.Falstad,Trontheim (Nor.) 41-44	MURDER	NOR.
PLOCH, Hans	122542	M	Ger.	95	Civ.,Personnel manager Polte,Munitions factory,C.C.Magdeburg(Ger.) 45	TORTURE	U.S.
PLODECK, Oskar	196671	M	Ger.		Head-Chief,office of Trustees,Administration of Gen.Gouv.(Pol.)39-45	MISC.CRIMES	POL.
PLOENING	140889	M	Ger.		Verbindungsstab 331,2 Coy.,Bolnes (Neth.) 8.5.45	MURDER	NETH.
PLOENNIGS	258199	M	Ger.		Sgt.,2 Coy.,Signal Troops,Bolnes (Neth.) 8.5.45	INTERR.	NETH.
PLOESSER, Heinrich	254129	M	Ger.	20.12.03	Gardener,Civ.,St.Sauvier,Normandy (Fr.) 7.6.44	MURDER	U.S.
PLOETS (or PLOTZ VON KNEIS)	700	M	Ger.		Major,Army,Patras (Grc.) 12.43	MURDER	GREC.
PLOETZ	177526	M	Ger.		Sgt.,Army,Sisteron (Fr.)	MURDER	FR.
PLOETZ	254808	M	Ger.		Sgt.,Field-Police,Troop 533,Dannecy le Chablais (Fr.)	MISC.CRIMES	FR.
PLOGER	261802	M	Ger.		Pvt.,Fieldgend.,Romilly sur Seine (Fr.) 10.6.44	MISC.CRIMES	FR.
PLOGER, Fritz (or PLUEGER)	194857	M	Ger.	26. 9.04	Member,Grenzschutz-Polizei,(Lux.)	MURDER	LUX.
PLOHN, Wilhelm	185209	M	Ger.	09	Civ.,Factory-Employee,Bruenn (Czech.) 39-45	LOOTING	CZECH.
PLOI, Peter	167785	M	Ger.		Pvt.,Army, 9 Res.Gren.Regt.,1 Coy.,Magny d' Anigon (Fr.) 18.9.44	MURDER	FR.
PLONZKE	166959	M	Ger.		Kommandofuehrer, Arbeits-Kdo.,C.C.Lutau,Kdo.517,Lutau (Ger.) 23.2.45	MURDER	FR.
PLOOG	254909	M	Ger.		Lt.,338 Div.Pion.Unit 02010,La Bresse (Fr.) 9.-11.44	MURDER	FR.
PLOTHE	124970	M	Ger.		SS-Mann,SS or Gestapo,C.C.Bremen,Farge (Ger.) 6.43	MISC.CRIMES	U.K.
PLOTNER, Kurt	258411	M	Ger.	19.10.05	Sturmbannfhr.,SS,C.C.Dachau (Ger.)	SUSPECT	U.S.
PLOTZ	166963	M			Adjutant Chief,Army,Annecy (Fr.) 28.7.44	PILLAGE	FR.
PLOTZ, Ullrich	132094	M	Ger.		Dr.,SS,"Feme" (Ger.)	MURDER	U.S.
PLUDKY, Franz (or PRUDKY)	174077	M	Ger.		Gestapo-Leistelle,C.C.Bruenn,Oswiecim, Birkenau (Czech.Pol.) 39-45	MURDER	CZECH.
PLUEGER (see PLOGER, Fritz)	194857						
PLUEGER	254118		Ger.		Employee,Labour-office,Loerrach,Dreilaendereck (Ger.)	BRUTALITY	BEL.
PLUENNECKE	125069	M	Ger.		Capt.Lt.,Navy,Capt. of the MV "Portland" 1941	TORTURE	U.K.
PLUES, Viktor	262235	M	Ger.	19. 7.12	51 SS-Armoured-Bde.,Bacheres,Breviandes,St.Savine,la Riviere de Corps (Troyes) (Fr.) 22.-25.8.44	BRUTALITY	FR.
PLUM	194502	M	Ger.		Member,SS,Puettlingen (Ger.) 41-45	TORTURE	POL.
PLUM	261826		Ger.		Formerquarter master officer in Chalons sur Marne,Domicile:Biebrier- Str., Wiesbaden-Schierstein,Chalons sur Marne (Fr.) 41	BRUTALITY	FR.
PLUM, Heinrich	132096		Ger.		Civ.,C.C.Eschweiler (Ger.) 9.42-11.44	TORTURE	U.S.
PLUMECKE	132095	M		95	Gestapo,Ahlem (Ger.)	MURDER	SOV.UN.
PLUMER, Hans	179736	M	Ger.	18	Cpl.,S.-Uffz.,171 Sanit.Corps,Sanpola (Ital.) 14.7.44	MURDER	U.K.
PLUN	253191		Ger.		Employee,Abtl.,IV B,Sipo,Bruessel (Bel.)	INTERR.	BEL.
PLUNNECKE, Willi	138032	M			Civ.,Woltorf (Ger.) 8.44	WITNESS	U.S.
PLUSCHKE	152144	M	Ger.		Uschfhr.,SS,Pz.Gren.Regt.,Stavelot,Malmedy (Bel.)	MURDER	U.K.
PLUSKAT	192602	M	Ger.		Sonderfhr.,Army,2 Coy.Bau-Bn.429,C.C.Syria (Fin.) 43	WITNESS	NOR.
PLUSKOTA, Ferdinand	257348	M	Ger.		Hptsturmfhr.,SS,slave labour Camp,Osen (Nor.) 6.42-3.43	MISC.CRIMES	YUGO.
PLUSKOTA, Franz	257350	M	Ger.		Hptsturmfhr.,SS,slave labour camp,Beisfjord near Narvik (Nor.)6.-11.42	MISC.CRIMES	YUGO.
PLZAK, Gottlieb	195161	M	Ger.	15	SS-Mann,Member,Employee,SS,Gestapo,Kolin (Czech.) 39-45	MURDER	CZECH.
PLZER, Karl	258108	M	Ger.	2. 3.01	Agent,Gestapo,Liny (Czech.) 39-45	MURDER	CZECH.
PNIEWSKI, Jzdzislaw	170842	M			Civ.,C.C.Gardelegen (Ger.) 12.-14.4.45	MURDER	U.S.
POCHE	163281	M	Ger.	90	Sgt.,Army,Landesschtz.,C.C.Znin (Pol.) 25.8.40	TORTURE	U.K.
POCHE	178292	M	Ger.		Obersturmbannfhr.,SS,Reg.Rat,SS Stapostelle,Frankfurt-M(Ger.) 4.-9.43	MURDER	U.K.
POCHE	257669	M	Ger.		Reg.Rat,Osturmbannfhr.,Head of S.D. in Tromsoe in Tronthern(Nor)44-45	TORTURE	NOR.
POCHE	260022	M	Ger.		Major,Cartridge factory,Vincennes,Seine (Fr.) 19.8.44	MURDER	FR.
POCHE, Oswald	178292	M	Ger.	28. 1.08	Lt.Col.,SS-Gestapo,S.D.Hauptamt,Chief of Gestapo,Frankfurt a.M. (Ger.) 5.43	TORTURE	U.K.
POCHER, Joseph	128820	M	Ger.		Civilian,Farmer,Durnfeld (Kaernten),(Aust.) 8.41-12.42	TORTURE	U.K.
POCHER, Karl	185108	M	Ger.		Gardien,SS,C.C.Sachsenhausen (Ger.)	TORTURE	FR.
POCHE	196693	M	Ger.		C.C.Struthof,Natzweiler (Fr.) 40-44	TORTURE	FR.
PODOLSKI, Georg	161848	M	Ger.	02	Stalag,Tuttlingen (Ger.) 45	MURDER	U.S.
POEGEL, Werner	1214	M	Ger.		SS-Standartenfhr.,Standarte 108 (Prague)(Czech.) 39-45	MURDER	CZECH.
POEHLS	300965	M	Ger.		SS-Oschfhr.,official of S.D. Leitabschnitt,Prag,Oswiecim,Birkenau (Pol.) 39-45	MURDER	CZECH.
POENISCH	195149	M	Ger.		Capt.,Army,Groleus,Graber (Aust.) 12.42	MURDER	U.K.
POENITZSCH	166962	M	Ger.		Tyez,Hte.Savoie (Fr.) 9.7.44	MURDER	FR.
POENSGEN, Ernst	62197	M	Ger.		Director,public official,Vereinigte Stahlwerke	MURDER	UNWCC

POE - POL

NAME	C.R.FILE NUMBER	SEX	NATIO-NALITY	DATE OF BIRTH	RANK OCCUPATION UNIT PLACE AND DATE OF CRIME	REASON WANTED	WANTED BY
POEPPEL, Franz	12527	M	Ger.		Pvt., 2.Coy., 110.Panz.Gren.Regt., Albine (Fr.) 29.6.44	MURDER	FR.
POERTL, Karl	185208	M	Ger.	98	Volkssturm-Leiter, Officer, SA-Standarte, Public Prosecutor Occupied Territories, Prague, Ceske, Bude Jovice (Czech.) 39-45	MURDER	CZECH.
POESCHEL	193268	M	Ger.		Pvt., 4.SS-Totenkopf-Sturmbann, C.C. Mittelbau - Dora Nordhausen (Ger.) 43-45	MURDER	U.S.
POESCHER	301595	M	Ger.		Member, Gestapo, Linz, C.C. Mauthausen (Aust.) 40-45	MURDER	BEL.
POESCHL, Rudolf	305233	M	Ger.		Oberscharfhr., Sipo, Einsatz-Kdo. Albrecht, Akkerwoude, Leeuwarden (Neth.) 11.44- 2.45	PILLAGE	NETH.
POETHMANN, Paul	300414	M	Ger.		Administrator, Owner of firm Pothmann, artificial lace factory Wupperthal - Oberbarmen, Amsterdam (Neth.) 4.42- 8.44	PILLAGE	NETH.
POETISCH	254087	M	Ger.		Oberpfarrer, Navy, (Neth.)	WITNESS	NETH.
POETSCHKE (see POTSCHKE) Werner	133960						
POETZEL, Ernst	252577	M	Ger.	6. 8.03	Group-leader, NSDAP, Kdyne (Czech.) 38-45	MISC.CRIMES	CZECH.
POGADL, Adalbert	196689	M	Ger.		SS-Officer, Slovakia (Czech.) 44	MURDER	CZECH.
POGEL, Thomas or PAGEL	136306	M	Ger.		Porter, Civilian, Stanffersbuch (Ger.) 25.8.40	MURDER	FR.
POGGENWISCH, Hermann	257038	M	Ger.	14. 8.04	Architect, Alzin/Moselle (Fr.)	PILLAGE	FR.
POH	167794	F	Ger.	05	Interpreter and Translater, Gestapo, Bruessel (Bel.) 23.9.44	TORTURE	BEL.
POHFAL	192604	M	Ger.		Pvt., Army, (Nor.) 74.44	MURDER	NOR.
POHL	149065	M	Ger.	95	Gruppenfhr., SS, C.C. Auschwitz (Pol.) 40-44	PILLAGE	U.S.
POHL	38836	M	Ger.	98	General Lt., W-SS, Berlin (Ger.) 5.43	MURDER	U.S.
POHL	701	M	Ger.	09	Oberscharfhr., SS, C.C. Grini (Nor.) 4.43	MISC.CRIMES	NOR.
POHL (see PORETSCHKIN)	61161						
POHL	702	M			SS-Hauptscharfhr., Tunis (Tunisia) 12.42	TORTURE	FR.
POHL	703	M			Major, C.C. Saloniki (Grc.) 41	MURDER	U.K.,U.S.
POHL	1454	M	Ger.		Lt., R H Q. Sqd 36 Tk Regt.	MISC.CRIMES	U.K.
POHL	9607	M	Ger.		Major, Doctor in the Army, C.C. Breendonck (Bel.) 40-44	TORTURE	BEL.
POHL	58061	M			SS-Obergruppenf., C.C. Mauthausen (Aust.) 41-45	MURDER	U.S.
POHL	132649	M	Ger.		Lt.General, Army, C.C. Ravensbrueck (Ger.)	MURDER	FR.
POHL (see PAUL), Friedrich	132823	M	Ger.		Lt., Oberfeld-Kommandantur 670, Lille (Fr.)	WITNESS	U.K.
POHL (see POOL)	153200						
POHL	155524	M	Ger.		Pvt., Army, Hennebont (Fr.) 6.8.44	PILLAGE	FR.
POHL	185109	M	Ger.		S.D., Chateau Gaillard and Saintes (Fr.) 44	MURDER	FR.
POHL	193799	M	Ger.		Head of C.C. Ravensbrueck (Ger.)	TORTURE	BEL.
POHL	196688	M	Ger.		Capt., Army, Oflag 7-A, Murnau (Ger.)	BRUTALITY	POL.
POHL (see GEEWE)	258578	M	Ger.				
POHL	259417	M	Ger.		Lt., Engineer Unit F.P.No. 15 483-A, Beaupuy (Lotet - Garonne) (Fr.) 21.4.44	TORTURE	FR.
POHL, Andreas E.	306939	M	Ger.	20. 4.09	Factory supervisor, Civ., Labour Camp Budenheim (Ger.) 40-44	TORTURE	U.S.
POHL, Ernst	183282	M	Ger.		Dr., Landgerichtsrat, Public official, Litomerice (Czech.) 40	MURDER	CZECH.
POHL, Franz	29710	M	Ger.	13	Sgt., Cmdt., Conde, St.Lô (Fr.) 1.44	TORTURE	U.K.
POHL, Franz	191218	M	Ger.		Sgt., Army, Feldgendarmerie Truppe 648, C.C. Huelgoat (Fr.) 7.44	TORTURE	FR.
POHL, Gunther	704	M	Ger.	20	SS-Sturmmann, SS-Nachrichtenzug, Wormhoudt (Fr.) 5.40	MURDER	U.K.
POHL, Joseph	186691	M	Ger.		Pvt., Army, Baudrigues near Carcassone (Fr.) 19.8.44	MURDER	EST.,FR.
POHLE, Walter	705	M	Ger.		Untersturmfhr., W-SS, Totenkopf-Standarte, C.C. Buchenwald (Ger.) Chief of Gen.Staff. censure office 1938	TORTURE	U.S.
POHLER, Karl	162691	M	Ger.	15	Cpl., S.D. of Besancon (Doubs) belonged Equally to Abwehr, Rioz (Fr.)44	MISC.CRIMES	FR.
POHLMAN	261801	M	Ger.	95	Col., Festungs-Cmdt., Sables d'Olonne, Royan, Semussac (Fr.) 25.9.44	INTERR.	FR.
POHLMANN	173864	M			Flyer, Camp Ellrich, Nordhausen (Ger.)	MURDER	U.S.
POHLMANN, Fritz	256241	M	Ger.	15	Sgt., C.C. Auschwitz (Pol.)	MURDER	FR.
POHLS	254754	M	Ger.		Pol.-Lt., Police, Breendonck (Bel.) 40-44	MURDER	BEL.
POHRENSA or POLRENSD	706	M	Ger.		Pvt., 2.SS-Div., "Das Reich" 3.Bn., Venerque la Vernet (Fr.) 44	MURDER	FR.
POHTZ, Henryk	136307	M	Ger.		Member, Selbstschutz Organisation, Starogrod (Pol.) 39-45	BRUTALITY	POL.
POILINSKI	302098	M	Ger.		Unterscharfhr., SS, Blockleiter, C.C. Nordhausen (Ger.)	MURDER	U.S.
POINTNER, Johann	256813	M			Pvt., Army, Borkum (Ger.)	MURDER	U.S.
POINTNER, Werner	149164	M	Ger.	10. 8.10	Crim.Asst., Gestapo, Brno (Czech.) 39-45	SUSPECT	CZECH.
POKORNY, Maximilian	192509	M	Ger.		Dr., Landgerichtsdirektor, Public official, Prag, Bruenn (Czech.) 40	MURDER	CZECH.
POKORNY, Walther	29711	M	Ger.	20	Oberscharfhr., SS, Frein (Aust.) 23.8.44	MURDER	U.S.
POLACK	256815	M	Ger.		Capt., Zollgrenzschutz, Bayonne (Fr.) 22.8.44	MURDER	FR.
POLACZEK or POLATSCHEK	167764	M			Hauptscharfhr., SS, C.C. Birkenau (Pol.)	MURDER	U.S.
POLACZEK	124648	M	Ger.		Lt.Col., SS, Auschwitz (Pol.) 40	MURDER	FR.
POLAND	196862	M		97	Mine Insp. Civ., Stalag 13-B, (Ger.) 11.44	MURDER	U.S.
POLATSCHEK (see POLACZEK)	125199						
POLCHEN, Gerard	124648						
POLDER	162805	M	Ger.		Scharfhr., SS, 36.Panz.Regt., 9.Coy., Revin (Fr.) 12- 19.6.44	MURDER	FR.
POLDT, Willy	256812	M	Ger.		Sturmmann, S.D., Grenzkommissariat, Foix (Fr.) 11.42 - 8.44	MURDER	FR.
POLECK	1279	M			Lt., Army, Signes (Fr.)	MURDER	FR.
POLEITH	260708	M			Cdt., Army,	MISC.CRIMES	U.S.
POLENC, Erich	193798	M	Ger.		Lt., Feldgendarmerie, F.P.No., 34 844, Villargerel (Fr.) 5.5. - 3.6.44	MURDER	FR.
POLENZ, Friedrich	253543	M	Ger.	17. 8.04	School-master, Civ., Haj (Czech.) 44-45	MISC.CRIMES	CZECH.
POLENZ, Walter	252567	M	Ger.	17. 1.02	Bank-clerk, Civ., Opava (Czech.) 45	PILLAGE	CZECH.
POLEUSKE, Guenther	149162	M	Ger.		Hauptsturmfhr., SS, C.C. Auschwitz (Pol.)	TORTURE	U.S.
POLGER, Fritz	12525	M			Pvt., 110. or 111.Panz.Gren.Regt., 2.Coy., Albine (Fr.) 29.6.44	MURDER	FR.
POLHUS	252568	M	Ger.		Sgt., Army, Villmar (Ger.) 17.4. - 15.6.44	WITNESS	U.S.
POLICEK, Nikulas	162684	M			Pvt., Kgf.Arb.Bn.190, 4.Coy., Botn (Nor.)	TORTURE	NOR.
POLICH, Georg	305488	M	Ger.		Deputy-Commander, Werkschutz Skoda works, Dubnica near Vahom (Czech.) 44 - 45	MURDER	CZECH.
POLIFKA, Albert	149161	M	Ger.	00	Unterscharfhr., SS, W-SS, Schleissheim (Ger.)	MURDER	U.S.
POLINSKI	146971	M	Ger.		Rottenfhr., SS Panz.Div."Das Reich", Moissac (Fr.) 44	MURDER	FR.
POLITZ, Otto	139670	M	Ger.		Unterscharfhr., Guard, W-SS, C.C. Nordhausen (Ger.)	MURDER	U.S.
POLIZEIMUELLER (see MUELLER)	192605	M	Ger.	19.11.02	Sgt., Justizminist., Guard, Feldstrafl.C.C. Nord, (Nor.) 42-45	MISC.CRIMES	NOR.,YUGO.
POLKE, Erich	195169						
POLKEHN	29713	M	Ger.		Landgerichtsrat, Public official, Opava (Czech.) 40	MURDER	CZECH.
POLKEHN	155530	M			Pvt., Straf-Bn. 999, Aschendorfer Moor (Ger.) 40-41	WITNESS	U.S.

NAME	C.R.FILE NUMBER	SEX	NATIO-NALITY	DATE OF BIRTH	RANK OCCUPATION UNIT PLACE AND DATE OF CRIME	REASON WANTED	WANTED BY
POLL	707	M	Ger.		Adjutant, Gestapo, Valenciennes (Fr.) 43-44	MURDER	FR.
POLLACK	196860	M	Ger.		Lt., SS, Auschwitz (Pol.) 40	MURDER	FR.
POLLACK, Fritz	174148	M	Ger.		Chief of Block 57 at C.C. Buchenwald (Ger.) 42-45	MURDER	U.S.
POLLAK	255180	M			Flyer, Camp Ellrich, Nordhausen (Ger.)	MURDER	U.S.
POLLAK, Gerard	189642	M	Ger.		Interpreter, Kommandantur, Infantery, Plouguerneau (Fr.)	WITNESS	FR.
POLLAND, Georg	183274	M			Hptschfhr., 4.SS Totenkopfsturmbann, C.C.Nordhausen,Dora-Mittel-bau, Osterode (Ger.) 43-45	WITNESS	U.S.
POLLANDT, Emma	192544	F	Ger.	26. 9.21	Clerk, Gestapo, Brno (Czech.) 39-45	WITNESS	CZECH.
POLLARD, Fritz	256814	M			Sgt., Postenf. 5 Kom. 5 B.B.IV, Nordhausen (Ger.)	MURDER	U.S.
POLLATSCHEK	196859	M	Ger.		Lt., Head of all camps during construction, Auschwitz (Pol.)40	MURDER	FR.
POLLETER	128958	M			Capt., Stalag Luft 17 B, Army, Krems (Aust.) 11.,12.43	MURDER	U.S.
POLLEY	188946	M	Ger.		Navy, Tregomel, Pont de Letir, En St.Caradec (Fr.) 5.7.44	MURDER	FR.
POLLMAN	143029	M			SS Oschfhr., Army, C.C. Flossenburg (Ger.)	TORTURE	U.S.
POLLNER	166961	M	Ger.		Lt., Army, Billy sur Mangiennes (Fr.)	PILLAGE	FR.
POLLOCK	149163	M	Ger.		Usturmfhr., SS, C.C. Auschwitz (Pol.)	TORTURE	U.S.
POLLWITZ	255181	M			Cpl., Camp Ellrich, Nordhausen (Ger.)	MURDER	U.S.
POLNY	306280	M	Ger.		Member of Gestapo Trencin, Oswiecim-Birkenau (Pol.) 39-45	MURDER	CZECH.
POLONY	253192	M	Ger.		SS-Oschfhr., Employee, Abteilung VI, Sipo, Brussels (Bel.)	INTERR.	BEL.
POLOTZE, K.Wilhelm	306499	M	Ger.	1. 1.14	Sgt., (No.319787) SS, C.C. Buchenwald (Ger.) between 5.38 and 10.43	MURDER	BEL.
POLRENSD (see POHRENSA)	136307						
POLSDORF	190043	M		96	Prison-Chief-doctor, C.C. Graudenz (Pol.)	TORTURE	U.K.
POLT	129737	M			Uschfhr., Waffen SS Totenkopf, C.C. Mauthausen (Aust.) 41-45	MURDER	U.S.
POLT, Rudolf	196692	M	Ger.	08	Lt., Army, Security Police F.P.No.02039,Forno Caavanese (It.)	WITNESS	U.K.
POLT, Walter	253281	M	Ger.	19. 9.09	Member of SS, Gestapo-Agent, Praha (Czech.) 42-45	MISC.CRIMES	CZECH.
POLTE	250422	M	Ger.		Oschfhr., SS, Gestapo, Paris (Fr.) 41-44	TORTURE	FR.
POLTERSNICH	196683	M	Ger.		Camp-leader, C.C. Mauthausen (Aust.)	TORTURE	BEL.
POLUS, Karl	141990	M		11	Civilian, Warsleben (Ger.) 12.9.44	BRUTALITY	U.S.
POLZ, Max	708	M	Ger.	17. 8.11	Uschfhr., SS, C.C. Maidanek (Pol.) 40-4.44	MURDER	POL.,BEL.
POMME, Josef	254691	M			Pvt., St.Huibrechts-Lille (Bel.) 16.9.44	INTERR.	BEL.
POMMERANING	189276	M	Ger.		Sturmbannfhr., SS and Polizeirat Gestapo,C.C.Dachau (Ger.)	MURDER	BEL.
POMMERKLE	255869	M	Ger.		Chief, Block III, C.C. Mauthausen (Aust.)	BRUTALITY	FR.
POMMERN	186768	M			2.Coy.,3.Rgt. Inf. of Navy, Queven (Fr.)	MURDER	FR.
POMPESE (or POMPEUSE), Fritz	21484	M		85-90	Leader SA, Member NSDAP, Railway-Station, Gernsbach-Baden (Ger.)6.44	MURDER	U.S.
PONART (or PONATH)	133232	M			Oschfhr., SS, C.C. Flossenburg (Ger.)	TORTURE	U.S.
PONATH	254917	M	Ger.		Genie Coy., Verines (Fr.) 27.6.40	MURDER	FR.
PONGRATZ	193821	M	Ger.		Oschfhr., C.C. Dachau (Ger.)	MURDER	FR.
PONISCH, Helmuth	192102	M			SS Usturmfhr., 1.SS Pz.Rgt.,Leibstandarte "Adolf Hitler" Staff Coy. (Bel.) 12.44	WITNESS	U.S.
PONN	256120	M	Ger.		Sgt., Muhldorf (Ger.)	INTERR.	U.S.
PONNING, Bartholomeus	179459	M	Ger.		Oberwachtmeister, C.C. Ebrach Prison (Ger.) 39-45	MURDER	CZECH.
PONSCHIKOWSKI	192748	M	Ger.		SS-W.O., C.C. Falstad (Nor.) 41-44	MURDER	NOR.
POOL (or POHL)	155524	M	Ger.		Obergruppenfhr.(Lt.Gen.) SS (Pol.) 42	MURDER	U.S.
POPELKA	21490	M			Pvt., Army 12.SS Pz.Div. "Hitler Jugend"	WITNESS	CAN.,U.S.
POPITZ	139667	M			Dr., Civilian, Salzburg (Aust.) 4.45	MISC.CRIMES	U.S.
POPIU	151541	M			Guard, Hilfspolizei, German Prison-Camps, Volary (Czech.) 41-45	MURDER	U.S.
POPJELK	192071	M		10	Civilian, Arb.Kdo. Stalag VIII B, Beuthen (Ger.) 5.44	TORTURE	U.K.
POPOV, Georgi	189960	M			Executor, Administration of occupied territories, Pirot (Yugo.)	MISC.CRIMES	YUGO.
POPP	126489	M			Sgt., Guard, Military Prison, Berlin-Tegel (Ger.) 11.43-5.44	TORTURE	U.S.
POPP (see POPPE)	259539						
POPP	306103	M	Ger.		SS-Mann, Alderney,C.C.Channel Is. and Kortemark CC.,42-45	MURDER	CZECH.
POPP, Alfred	12526	M	Ger.		Pvt., Army 110 or 111 Pz.Gren.Rgt. 2.Coy., Albine (Fr.) 29.6.44	MURDER	FR.
POPP, August	132097	M	Ger.	21.11.92	Dr., Lt.Col.,Pz.Rgt.36 Stalag 7 A, Moosburg (Ger.) 10.44	TORTURE	U.S.
POPP, Franz.Josef	240014	M	Ger.	14. 1.86	Member NSDAP, Director Bayerische Motoren Werke AG, Muenchen(Ger.)	MISC.CRIMES	U.S.
POPPE (or HOPPE)	141420	M	Ger.		Sgt., 28.Inf.Rgt. 116 Bn., Tarbes (Fr.) 20.7.44	MISC.CRIMES	FR.
POPPE	151496	M			Lt., Oflag 64, Schubin (Ger.) 19.12.44	PILLAGE	U.S.
POPPE	189186	M			Sgt., 1.Coy.,116.Bn.,28.Inf.Rgt.,Sombrun (Fr.) 7.44	MURDER	FR.
POPPE (or POPP), Max	259539	M	Ger.		Officer of Police, Lengerich (Ger.) 8.44	WITNESS	U.S.
POPPEL (see PAPPLEL) Max	255728						
POPPENBERGER, Franz	192935	M		2. 4.95	C.C. Flossenberg (Ger.) 44-45	WITNESS	U.S.
POPPERDICK	254901	M			SS Osturmfhr., C.C. Dachau (Ger.) 3.42	INTERR.	BEL.
POPPERDICK	301812	M			Osturmbannfhr.,Grawitz's Office, C.C.Dachau,Auschwitz (Ger.,Pol.) 3.42-2.43	TORTURE	BEL.
POPPERL	255103	M			Pvt., Camp Wolffleben, Nordhausen (Ger.)	MURDER	U.S.
POPPINGHAUS	173911	M	Ger.		Capt., Stalag VI A, Army, Hemer (Ger.) 42-45	TORTURE	U.S.
POQUI	126583	M	Ger.		Civilian,Manager, Gouley Mine, C.C. Wuerselen (Ger) 41-45	TORTURE	U.S.
PORCHI (see PARCHI)	301596						
PORETSCHKIN (or POHL,POREMSKIN, POREMSKY)	61161	M	Ger.	15	Major,Oberregierungsrat,Official,Nachrichten Rgt.506,Abwehr, Prague (Czech.) 44	MISC.CRIMES	U.S.
PORGES	188945	M	Ger.		Feldgendarmerie, Bar le Duc, (Fr.) 8.44	MURDER	FR.
PORLASKI	36636	M	Ger.		Civilian, Sosnovice (Pol.) 1.44-1.45	MISC.CRIMES	U.K.
PORMANN	196690	M	Ger.		Hptschfhr., C.C.Struthof-Natzweiler (Fr.) 40-44	TORTURE	FR.
PORN, Heinrich	191888	M	Ger.	08	Civilian (mason), Dillingen (Ger.) 5.44	WITNESS	U.S.
PORSCHMANN	151497	M			Agent, Gestapo, Leipzig, Celle (Ger.) 42-45	TORTURE	U.S.
PORSTER, T.	171696	M	Ger.		SS Uschfhr., SS Commandantur, C.C.Struthof,Natzweiler (Fr.)	MURDER	FR.
PORTEN (or DELAGE)	141523	M	Ger.		Gestapo-Chief, Marseille (Fr.)	MURDER	FR.
PORTEN, Paul	192614	M	Ger.	16. 4.14	Feldstraflager,Reichsjustizministerium,C.C.Finnmark (Nor.)42-45	WITNESS	NOR.
PORTH	142073	M			Administrator, Waffen SS,Totenkopf-Sturmbann,C.C.Muelhausen, Martha (Ger.)	TORTURE	U.S.
PORTHD	192246	M	Ger.		Pvt., Army, Unit 26033 E, Soissons (Fr.) 15.8.44	WITNESS	FR.
PORTL, Karl	10323	M	Ger.		Dr., Staatsanwalt, Country Court, Prague (Czech.) 40-42	MURDER	CZECH.
PORTMANN	192245	M	Ger.	04	Lt., Gestapo, Landrecis (Fr.) 1.,2.,44	TORTURE	FR.
POSCHEL	251935	M			Pvt., C.C. Nordhausen (Ger.)	MURDER	U.S.
POSCHINGER, Albert	300735	M	Ger.		Member of the Landwache, Ferlach (Aust.) 4.44-5.45	MURDER	YUGO.
POSCHKE	256104	M	Ger.		Pvt., SS, St.Marie (Fr.) 7.44	MURDER	FR.

NAME	C.R. FILE NUMBER	SEX	NATIO-NALITY	DATE OF BIRTH	RANK OCCUPATION UNIT PLACE AND DATE OF CRIME	REASON WANTED	WANTED BY
POSCHL, Josef	262210	M	Ger.	15.3.21	Uschfhr., 51.SS, Armoured Brigade, Art.Detachment, Breviandes Bucheres, Ste Savine, La Riviere, de Corps,Troyes (Fr.) 8.44	BRUTALITY	FR.
POSCHL, Rudi	193566	M	Ger.		SS-Staff Sgt., SD. Sipo Leeuwarden (Neth.)9.44-4.45	MURDER	NETH.
POSCHNER, Johann	255045	M			Pvt., Camp Ellrich,Nordhausen (Ger.)	MURDER	U.S.
POSE, Frans	255426	M	Ger.		Civ., Landowner, Aldrewitz (Ger.)8.-9.41	INTERR.	YUG.
POSERT, Eduard	305234	M	Ger.		Member, Staff C.C. Neckargerach and Neckarels (Ger.)42-45	TORTURE	FR.
POSPICH, Fritz	306500	M	Ger.	23.7.15	SS-Cpl., C.C. Buchenwald (Ger.) 5.38-10.43	MURDER	BEL.
POSPISIL	306445	M	Ger.		Lt., Commander C.C. Ilowa- (Slov.) 40-45	BRUTALITY	CZECH.
POSSE, Hans, Ernst	240016	M	Ger.	96	Staatssecretary, Ministry of Economics, Berlin (Ger.)	MISC.CRIMES	U.S.
POSSECHEL	121281	M	Ger.		Major (Cmdt.) Stalag 122, Compiegne (Oise) (Fr.)	TORTURE	FR.
POSSELT	21469	M	Ger.		Pvt., Army, 12.Volks-Gren.Div.2.Fuss.Rgt.3.Coy.Petit Langville (Bel.)	WITNESS	U.S.
POSSINKE nee HEYN, Hildegard	186779	F	Ger.		Member Organ. Todt, Chatou (Fr.)8.44		
POST, Albert	134746	M	Ger.		Civilian, Budesheim (Ger.) 6.44	MISC.CRIMES	U.S.
POSTBICHEL	131699	M	Ger.		SS-Uschfhr., C.C. Vaihingen (Ger.)	MURDER	FR.
POTOK, Josef	256587	M	Ger.		Cpt., German Army, Zajecar (Yug.)41-44	MURDER	YUG.
POTSCHKE, Werner (or POETSCHKE)	133960	M		16	Sturmbannfhr., SS Pz.Div.Leibst."A.H.", Malmedy (Bel.)12.44	MURDER	U.S.
POTT, Erich	122733	M	Ger.	15	SS Oschfhr., Gestapo-Official, C.C. Berghausen near Gummersbach Koblenz (Ger.) 4.45	MURDER	U.S.
POTTHOF, Rudolf	151540	M	Ger.		Civilian, Nuernberg, (Ger.)	MISC.CRIMES	U.S.
POTTING,	255031	M	Ger.		Schfhr., Gestapo, Limoges (Fr.) 40-44	INTERR.	FR.
POTTINGER	155531	M	Ger.		Oberst, Com. Stalag VIII B, Lamsdorf (Ger.) 44	BRUTALITY	U.K.
POTTINGER	173182	M	Ger.		Staff C.C. Natzweiler Baden, (Ger.) 8.44	INTERR.	U.K.
POTZ, Willi	190319	M	Ger.		Civilian, Wiesbaden (Ger.)43-45	WITNESS	U.S.
POUL	136308	M	Ger.		Chief, C.C. (Siedelung) Hirschberg (Ger.)	BRUTALITY	FR.
POUTS, LImilios	185206	M	Ger.		N.C.O., Police, Vasihni, Elfa-Crete-Massafa, (Grc.)12.43	TORTURE	GRC.
POWILEIT	193269	M	Ger.		Guard Cpl., 4.SS Totenkopfsturmbann C.C Dora Nordhausen, Auschwitz (Ger.Pol.)43-45	MURDER	U.S.
POZEKEL	196691	M	Ger.		Lt.,Col., Compiegne (Fr.)41-44	MISC.CRIMES	FR.
POZIMSKI, Anton	138029	M	Ger.		Member, NSDAP, NSV., Pensberg (Ger.) 4.45	MURDER	U.S.
POZYTEK	193270	M	Ger.		Schfhr., 4.SS Totenkopfsturmbann C.C. Dora Mittelbau, Platzow, Nordhausen (Pol.Ger.) 43-45	MURDER	U.S.
PRACHT	173867	M			Stabsarzt, 2.Div.Parachut 2.Bn. Fallschirmjaeger Rgt. Plousane (Fr.) 44	MURDER	FR.
PRACHTEL	149167	M	Ger.		Dr., SS Obersturmfhr., C.C. Dachau (Ger.)	TORTURE	U.S.
PRADEL	12528	M	Ger.		Chief, SD, De Tarbes (Gestapo), Monceaux (Fr.) 7.44	MURDER	FR.
PRADER, Josef	260360	M	Ger.	22.2.10	Regierungsinspector, Bresice, Slovenia and Trborlje (Slov.)4.41-1.42	INTERR.	YUG.
PRAEGER, Paul	302100	M	Ger.		Representative for Region X of the Reichssicherheitshauptamt Luebeck, (Ger.) 20.4.-1.5.44	MURDER	FR.
PRAETZ	1455	M	Ger.		NCO., SD, Aussenkdo.,	MISC.CRIMES	U.K.
PRAG	174557	M	Ger.		Pvt., Army Land.Schts.Bn.398 or 395 5.Coy.Stalag VIII B. Working Com. B 132, Gogolin (Ger.) 7.42	MURDER	U.K.
PRAGER (or PRAGE)	153129	M			Lt., 29. Pz.Gren.Div.	INTERR.	U.S.
PRAGER	190299	M			Oberarbeitsfhr., RAD, Military Befehlshaber Suedost, Uzice (Yug.) 1942-1943	TORTURE	YUG.
PRAGER, Rudi	169519	M			Civilian, Borkum (Ger.) 44	MURDER	U.S.
PRAHL, Arthur	255046	M			Pvt., Camp Ellrich, Nordhausen (Ger.)	MURDER	U.S.
PRANG, Alfred	4351	M	Ger.	87	Ministerialdirector, Reichsverkehrsministerium Berlin, (Ger.)	MISC.CRIMES	U.S.
PRANG, Wilhelm	162214	M	Ger.		Civ., Teplitz (Ger.)8.44	WITNESS	U.S.
PRANGE, Paul	135295	M	Ger.		Carpenter, C.C. 4.45	MURDER	U.S.
PRANZ	15568	M			SS-Hptschfhr., W-SS, Magdeburg (Ger.) 10.44-4.45	TORTURE	U.S.
PRANZKAT	258198	M	Ger.		Commander, Feldgend., Jexdina (Yug.) 12.46	PILLAGE	YUG.
PRASCH	188453	M	Ger.	16	SS-Obersturmfhr., SD, Marzana-Canfanaro (It.)3.4 5	MURDER	U.K.
PRASCHITA, Stephan	29714	M	Ger.		Dr., Landgerichtsdirektor, Public Official, Oprava (Czech.)40	MURDER	CZECH.
PRASS, Hugo	256568	M	Ger.	27.7.03	Employee, Block 31. Dora C.C. Nordhausen (Ger.)	MURDER	U.S.
PRASSE	67806	M			Sgt., Army C.C. Himselfahrt Fundgrube (Ger.)10.43-4.45	MISC.CRIMES	U.K.
PRASSE, Arno	128817	M	Ger.	97	Sgt.,Landesschuetz.,C.C. Freiburg (Ger.)10.43-10.44	TORTURE	U.K.
PRASSER	147365	M	Ger.		Lt., 11.Pz.Div., (Fr.) 44	MURDER	FR.
PRAST	253229	M	Ger.		Hptsturmfhr., Army SS State Service, SD., Lodz (Pol.)39-40	MISC.CRIMES	POL.
PRATEURS	153128	M	Ger.		Ingenieur, Arb.Kdo.C.C. Siegen (Ger,)	TORTURE	FR.
PRATOBUS	141592	M	Ger.		Col., Oflag IX B, C.C. Arnswalde (Ger.)	TORTURE	FR.
PRATSCHER (or ROST Or ROTOT)	255424	M	Ger.		SS Pion., F.P.N. 28955, (Fr.) 8.44	MURDER	FR.
PRATTES, Johann	146990	M	Ger.		SS Stummann, "Das Reich", Montastruce (Fr.)	MURDER	FR.
PRATZ	255870	M	Ger.		Cpt., Unit 48805 O, Lefaux (Fr.) 6.44	WITNESS	FR.
PRAUN, Albert	262192	M	Ger.	94	Major General, 277.Inf.Div., F.P.No.25924, Capestang (Fr.)6.44	MURDER	FR.
PRAUS, Wenzel	251844	M	Ger.	99	Employee, Gestapo, Pardubice (Czech.)39-45	MURDER	CZECH.
PRAUSE	188228	M	Ger.		Pvt., Airforce, Maffles (Bel.)	PILLAGE	BEL.
PRAUSE	254996	M			Pvt., Camp Dora, Nordhausen (Ger.)	MURDER	U.S.
PRAUSE	259301	M			Schfhr., SS, Muhldorf Area (Ger.)	MURDER	U.S.
PRAUSE, L.	254692	M	Ger.		Pvt., L 26329 F.L.G.P.A. Maffles (Bel.)9.44	INTERR.	BEL.
PRAUSE, Max	253539	M	Ger.		Agent, Gestapo, Prison, Troyes (Fr.)43-44	INTERR.	FR.
PRAUSER, Karl	259990	M	Ger.		SS-Member,Guard, Ghetto, Theresienstadt, Bohemia (Czech.)39-45	TORTURE	CZECH.
PRAUSS, Arthur	61099	M	Ger.	93	SS Untersturmfhr., C.C. Breendonck (Bel.) 40-44	TORTURE	BEL.
PRAUTSCH	162688	M	Ger.	95	SD, Obersturmfhr., Gestapo, Innsbruck (Aust.)	TORTURE	U.S.
PRAUTTER	255873	M			Cpl., Camp Ellrich Nordhausen (Ger.)	MURDER	U.S.
PRAVEZ	255620	M			Oschfhr., Camp Dora Nordhausen (Ger.)	MURDER	U.S.
PRAVITT	57753	M			Major, Army, Koenigstein-Elbe (Ger.)	WITNESS	FR.
PRAWITT	121446	M	Ger.		Major Cmdt., Oflag IV C, C.C. Colditz (Ger.)	WITNESS	FR.
PRAWKOFF, Mary	153127	F	Ger.		Civilian, Hermansdorf (Aust.) 5.44	WITNESS	U.S.
PRCHAL, Otto	306645	M	Ger.		SS-Pvt., 1.Bn.Rgt."Der Fuehrer" Div."Das Reich" Fraysinet le Gelatlet (Fr.) 5.44	MURDER	FR.
PREBECZ, Alois	185204	M	Ger.	04	Leader, PublicProsecutor, Occupied Territories Bohemia Morvia Prague (Czech.) 41-45	MURDER	CZECH.
PRECHT, Elmar (or PRECHTER)	167756	M	Ger.	12	Obersturmfhr., SS Dr., C.C. Natzweiler (Ger.) 43-44	MURDER	FR.
PRECHTL, Johann	195393	M	Ger.		Chief Reichs Official Administrative Offce Skoda Works Dubnica Nad Vahom (Czech.) 39-45	PILLAGE	CZECH.

NAME	C.R.FILE NUMBER	SEX	NATIO-NALITY	DATE OF BIRTH	RANK OCCUPATION UNIT	PLACE AND DATE OF CRIME	REASON WANTED	WANTED BY
PRECKER, Otto	133259	M			Civilian,Krumm & Co.CC Remscheid(Ger.)		TORTURE	U.S.
PREFI	151538	M		9. 5.99	SS Osturmfhr.CC Treblinka(Pol.)41-43		MURDER	U.S.
PREHAUSER, Johann	254690	M	Ger.		Rottfhr.9 SS Pz.Gren.Regt.Das Reich,F.P.No.20092,Morment(Bel.)5.9.44		MURDER	BEL.
PREIBICH, Herbert	300728	M	Ger.		Engineer employed,CC Area of Sachsenhausen(Ger.)1.40-4.45		MURDER	U.K.
PREICE, Gustav	35604	M	Ger.		Pvt.Army,Sicherungs Regt.610,Litchfelde(Pol.)44-45		TORTURE	U.K.
PREIDT, Gerhard	193271	M	Ger.		Sturmmann/Pvt.4 SS Totenkopf Sturmbann, CC Dora Mittelbau, Nordhausen Osterode(Ger.)43-45		MURDER	U.S.
PREIER	172458	M			Civilian,Block Leader,CC Vicinity Nordhausen(Ger.)43-44		TORTURE	U.S.
PREIER	255874	M			Rottfhr.SS CC No.dhausen(Ger.)		MURDER	U.S.
PREIL, Gerhart	125629	M			Lt.S.D.Einsatz Kommando Wenger,F.P.No.03069,CC Baccarat-Etival(Fr.)44		MURDER	U.K.
PREINFELTER	136335	M		00	Capt.Army(Ger.)1.45		TORTURE	U.S.
PREIPER, Hilmar	173907	M		15	Pvt.610 Land.Schtz.Bn.CC Stalag XX B,Solainen(Ger.)		MURDER	U.K.
PREIS	141352	M			Kreisleiter,NSDAP,Innsbruck(Aust.)		WITNESS	U.K.
PREISNER	256589	M			Sturmfhr.Gestapo,Zajecar(Yugo.)41-44		MURDER	YUGO.
PREISS	710	M			Oschafhr.Prison Cell Leader,Waffen SS,CC Dachau(Ger.)40-43		MURDER	FR.
PREISS	1456	M			Lt.Pz.Gren.Regt.		MISC.CRIMES	U.K.
PREISS	189275	M			SS Rottfhr.CC Dachau(Ger.)		MURDER	BEL.
PREISS	255030	M			Lt.Col.1 Bn.338 Div.La Bresse(Fr.)11.44		MURDER	FR.
PREISS	300415				Member,Gestapo,Nancy,La Bresse(Vosges)(Fr.)9.-11.44		MISC.CRIMES	FR.
PREISS, Wilhelm	253544	M	Ger.		Lt.Schutz Pol.20 Regt.,Prag,Lidice(Czech.)10.6.42		MURDER	CZECH.
PREISSER	192514	F	Ger.		Employee Gestapo,Brno(Czech.)39-45		WITNESS	CZECH.
PREISSLER, Johan	306122	M	Ger.		SS Lt.served with R.S.D.Abt.VI-S,Copenhagen(Den.)1.44		PILLAGE	DEN.
PREISSNER	187556	M	Ger.		Lt.65 Inf.Div.Coy.Cmdr.,Cisa Pass(It.)3.10.43		MURDER	U.K.
PREISZ, Friedrich	257734	M	Ger.	00	Stubafhr.S.D.,Oslo(Nor.)40-44		TORTURE	NOR.
PRELL	21467	M	Ger.		Lt.Col.Assistant Commanding Officer,Stalag 6 B,Muenster(Ger.)		MISC.CRIMES	U.S.
PREMGELMANN	1549	M			SS Oschafhr.CC,Blockfhr.,Sachsenhausen(Ger.)9.41-5.43		MURDER	U.S.
PRENGELMANN	144405	M	Ger.		SS Uschafhr.CC Vught(Neth.)43-44		MURDER	BEL.
PRENNET	193272	M			Pvt.4 SS Totenkopf Stuba,CC Dora,Nordhausen(Ger.)43-45		MURDER	U.S.
PRENTYE, Leo	255872	M			Rottfhr.CC Blankenburg,Nordhausen(Ger.)		MURDER	U.S.
PREPIN, Johann	261133	M	Ger./Rum.	10. 9.16	Member,S.D.Staff-Coy.Bruessel(Bel.)		SUSPECT	BEL.
PRES or PRESS	193298	M	Ger.		Civ.Sew.Prison,Guard at Strafgefaengnis,Frankfurt/M.Preungesheim(Ger.)42-44		TORTURE	U.K.FR.
PRESCHERS	254918	M	Ger.		Officer,Berck-Plage(Fr.)8.-9.44		INTERR.	FR.
PRESS see PRES	193298							
PRESSI, Johann	196677	M		11. 7.87	Civilian,Amstetten(Aust.)20.3.45		MISC.CRIMES	U.S.
PRESSLAUER, Alfred	192545	M	Ger.		Crim.secretary,Gestapo,Brno(Czech.)39-45		SUSPECT	CZECH.
PRESSLER, Stefan	255188	M	Ger.	24. 7.98	Employee Gestapo,Breclav(Czech.)7.4.45		MISC.CRIMES	CZECH.
PRESTEN,Franz or PRESTIN	305094	M	Ger.		SS Osturmfhr.Osen Slave Labour Camp,Norway(Nor.)6.42-3.43		MISC.CRIMES	YUGO.
PRETORIUS	126961	M	Ger.	95	Col.Oflag II D,CC at Wietzendorf,Gross Born(Ger.)45		TORTURE	FR.
PRETORIUS	153125	M	Ger.		Major,19 Armenia-Legion,Chanac(Fr.)16.8.44		MURDER	FR.
PRETSCHNER, Arthur	125086	M	Ger.		Factory Owner,Normas Works,Pirna/Neundorf(Ger.)2.45		MISC.CRIMES	U.K.
PRETSCHUK, Johann	255731	M		22. 4.06	Pvt.Camp Ellrich,Nordhausen(Ger.)		MURDER	U.S.
PRETTER	257861				SS Uschafhr.150 Panz.Bde.,Meuse Bridge Antwerp,12.44		MISC.CRIMES	U.S.
PREUEL	192716	M	Ger.		SS Sgt.CC Buchenwald(Ger.)42-45		TORTURE	U.S.
PREUN	176612	M			Lt.O.C.2 D.C.A.-Group 102,Baisse(Fr.)16.6.44		MISC.CRIMES	FR.
PREUR	257732	M			SS Cpl.Block-Leader,Boelke-Kaserne,CC Nordhausen(Ger.)		MURDER	U.S.
PREUSLER see PREUSSLER	711							
PREUSS	124248	M			Osturmfhr.SS Panz.Gren.Regt.2 Bn.10 Coy.7 Panz.Div.Malmedy(Bel.)		MURDER	U.S.
PREUSS	129748	M	Ger.		5 paratrooper Regt.5,Nachrichtenzug,Quaregnon/Jemappes,Ghlin(Bel.)2.-3.9.44		MURDER	U.K.
PREUSS	185651	M	Ger.		SS Osturmfhr.SS Leibstand.Adolf Hitler 1 Pz.Gr.Div.10 Coy.Stavelot(Bel.)19.-20.12.44		MURDER	BEL.
PREUSS, Bernhard	255732	M			Rottfhr.Camp Ellrich/Dora,Nordhausen(Ger.)		MURDER	U.S.
PREUSS, Edouard	195950	M	Ger.		Navy-Section,18 S.T.A.Remplacement-Section,Montceau les Mines(Fr.)7.44		TORTURE	FR.
PREUSS, Paul	194095	M	Ger.	05	Pvt.Guard,Marine Art.CC Lueneburg,Wilhelmshaven(Ger.)7. - 10.4.45		MURDER	U.K.
PREUSS, Walter	1733	M			Sgt.Army		TORTURE	U.K.
PREUSSER, Paul	174071	M	Ger.		Pvt.Army,Ischpelt(Lux.)10.1.45		MURDER	LUX.
PREUSSIRE	257733	M			SS Chief of Labor Admin.Ellrich,Nordhausen(Ger.)		MURDER	U.S.
PREUSSLER or PREUSLER	711	M			Capt.Army 118 Jaeger Div.733 or 738 Regt.Montenegro(Yugo.)7.43-1.44		MURDER	YUGO.
PREUSSNER	255733	M			Uschafhr.Camp Ellrich,Nordhausen(Ger.)		MURDER	U.S.
PREUSSNER	255866	M			Judge,State Service,Dresden(Ger.)43-45		MURDER	CZECH.
PREYER	139061	M		17	Uschafhr.S.D.and Sipo,Toulouse,Agen,Montaubaun,Cahors,Foixe,Tarbes Pau.(Fr.)11.42-8.44		MURDER	FR.U.S.
PREYSS	137302	M	Ger.		Dr.,Stabsarzt,POW Camp Hospital,Cosel(Ger.)		WITNESS	SOV.UN. U.K.
PREZ	254117	M	Ger.		Sgt.Army,Inf.Baustab,Rosendaal(Neth.)5.8.44		MISC.CRIMES	NETH.
PREZIUS	161905	M	Ger.		Pvt.Land.Schtz.Bn.789,Sinzig,Kr.Ahrweiler(Ger.)12.41		WITNESS	U.S.
PRIBIL	305938	M			Crim.secretary,Gestapo,Hraburka nr.Moravska Ostrava(Czech.)29.3.44		MURDER	CZECH.
PRIBIX, Rudolf	141417	M	Ger.		Watchman,Block 8,Lazerett CC Mauthausen(Aust.)		MURDER	FR.
PRIBYL, Victor	192515	M	Ger.	20. 3.08	Crim.secretary,Gestapo,Brno(Czech.)39-45		SUSPECT	CZECH.
PRICHAL	188242	M			SS Hptsturmfhr.CC Wiener-Neustadt(Aust.)43-45		TORTURE	U.S.
PRIEBE, Walter see HARMS,Ewald	260820							
PRIEBSCH	195953	M	Ger.		Oberwachtmeister,Schupo,CC Westerhof(Neth.)9.44		MURDER	NETH.
PRIEGL	240017	M			Pvt.Abwehr Official		MISC.CRIMES	U.S.
PRIEGNITZ, Kurt	252573	M		12	Hptwachtmeister,Army Group Sign.Regt.No.598,Ala(It.)13.9.43		INTERR.	U.S.
PRIEN	123966	M			Capt.Oflag IV C,Colditz(Ger.)		MURDER	U.K.
PRIES	185652	M			SS Uschafhr.SS Leibstandarte Adolf Hitler,Renardmont-Stavelot(Bel.)12.44		MURDER	BEL.
PRIESTER	192715	M			SS Sgt.CC Buchenwald(Ger.)42-45		MURDER	U.S.
PRIETL	255734	M			Pvt.Camp Ellrich,Nordhausen(Ger.)		MURDER	U.S.
PRILLER	256122	M			O.T.,Muhldorf(Ger.)		WITNESS	U.S.
PRIMA	1481	M			Dr.,Capt.Army,medical,Hallein(Aust.)18.-20.2.44		MURDER	U.S.
PRIMA	173264	M		05	Cpl.Stalag XXI D,814 Land.Schtz.Bn.CC Poznan(Pol.)6.41		TORTURE	U.K.
PRIMAS	12529	M			Oschafhr.Army,110 or 111 Panz.Gren.Regt.2 Group,Gourdon(Fr.)29.6.44		MURDER	FR.
PRIMKE	132098	M		86	SS Rottfhr.CC Plattling(Ger.)2.45-5.45		MURDER	U.S.
PRIMN	144404	M			SS CC Mittergars,Muhldorf(Ger.)2.5.45		MURDER	U.S.
PRIMMEL, Otto	189241	M			Prison Warden,Prison Brno(Czech.)39-45		MURDER	CZECH.
PRINC, Alfons	139657	M	Ger.	00	Obertruppfhr.Civilian,Foreign Camp,CC Muhldorf(Ger.)44-45		TORTURE	U.S.

NAME	C.R.FILE NUMBER	SEX	NATIO-NALITY	DATE OF BIRTH	RANK OCCUPATION UNIT PLACE AND DATE OF CRIME	REASON WANTED	WANTED BY
PRINISKI, George or (Phonetic)	257208	M	Ger.		Capt., Army, Parchim (Ger.), 19 and 20.3.45	MURDER	U.S.
PRINSBACH	177527	M	Ger.		Sgt., Feldkommandantur St.Germain les Corbeil (Fr.) 23.8.44	MURDER	FR.
PRINZ	124379	M	Ger.		Policeman, Police, CC Oberdorfelder (Ger.) 2.42-9.45	MURDER	U.S.
PRINZ	151596	M			Civilian near Frankfurt (Main), Ginnheim (Ger.) 11.44	MURDER	U.S.
PRINZ	162689	M	Ger.		Osturmfhr, SS Totenkopfstandarte, Comm.Staff, CC Buchenwald (Ger.)	TORTURE	U.S.
PRINZ	179918	M			N.C.O., Stalag 6-A, CC Hemer (Ger.) 41 - 4.45	TORTURE	U.S.
PRINZ (or PILZ)	187991	M	Ger.	11	Pvt.,Guard,Saechs.Gren.Rgt., Oflag IV-C,Colditz(Ger.) 1.-3.9.44	MURDER	U.K.
PRINZ, Obscht	259221	M	Ger.		Officer, Army, F.P.No.32136,D, La Basses (Fr.) 1.-3.8.44	MURDER	FR.
PRINZ, Waltraut	193177	F	Ger.	22	Asst., German Navy Girl, Wilhelmshaven(Ger.) 15.10.44	WITNESS	CAN.
PRINZIK	301107	M			Crim.Asst. of Sipo, Kopenhagen (Den.), Autumn 43	INTERR.	DEN.
PRINZLER	300f 49	M	Ger.		Pvt., 1 Aufkl.Abt., 3 Coy, 2 Col, XV Div.Africa Corps, Saint Leger(Arlon) 5.9.44	MISC.CRIMES	BEL.
PRION	126936	M	Ger.		SS Usturmfhr, 2 SS Pz.Div."Das Reich", Valence D'Agen(Fr.) 44	MURDER	FR.
PRISCHMANN	178293	M	Ger.	95	Major, Stalag XVIII C, Markt Pongau (Ger.) 6.44	TORTURE	U.K.
PRISTENBURGER	190050	M	Ger.		Guard, SS, CC Gusen (Aust.) 8.8.44	MURDER	U.S.
PRITZ, Helmut	151535	M	Ger.		SA, Wiewiocki, Chelmo (Pol.) 10.39	MURDER	U.K.
PRIVASSEL	198218	M	Ger.		Lt., 19 Police Rgt., II Coy, St.Genis Laval (Fr.) 20.8.44	MISC.CRIMES	FR.
PROBS, Willy	255029	M	Ger.		F.P. No. L 06459, Romilly (Fr.) 8.44	PILLAGE	FR.
PROBST	12530	M	Ger.		Lt., Army, 110 or 111 Pz.Gren.Rgt., Gourdon (Fr.) 29.6.44	MURDER	FR.
PROBST	155640	M	Ger.		Lt., Army, Le Roc (Fr.) 6.44	MURDER	FR.
PROBST	261887	M	Ger.		Member, SS, Camp Malines (Bel.) 7.42-9.44	BRUTALITY	BEL.
PROBST	305236	M	Ger.		Lt.Col.,98,99,100 Bn.Geb.Jg.,157 Inf.Res.Div.,Ain Dep.(Fr.)10.-21.7.44	MURDER	FR.
PROBST, Alfred Gustav Carl	147092	M	Ger.	31.5.14 or 19	Lt.,11 Pz.Div. Kampfgr. "Wilde", 34.02 Coy.,South West France 44	MURDER	FR., U.N.W.C.C.
PROBST, Eugen	161646	M	Ger.	04	Pvt.,Air-Force,Luftgau 105,XI (later 133,III), Luft Bau Bn., CC Eggemoen, Hoenefoss (Nor.)	MURDER	NOR.
PROBST, Rheinhold	306501	M	Ger.		CC Nordhausen - Dora 40-45	MURDER	BEL.
PROCHASKA	301597	M	Ger.		Agent, Gestapo, CC Mauthausen (Aust.) 40-45	MURDER	BEL.
PROCHAZKA, Georg	195160	M	Ger.	95	Employee, Gestapo, Kolin (Czech.) 39-45	MURDER	CZECH.
PRODEHL	61015	M	Ger.	02	Capt., Abwehr Nachr.Rgt.506, Wiesbaden (Ger.)	MISC.CRIMES	U.S.
PROFFER, Karl	153119	M	Ger.		Army, Vic la Gardiole (Fr.) 19.8.44	PILLAGE	FR.
PROGER	129742	M	Ger.		Guard, CC Mauthausen (Aust.) 41-45	MURDER	U.S.
PROKOP, Ernst	121440	M	Ger.		Sgt., Army, F.P.56067 D, Crfach, Maout, Pleubian (Fr.) 7.8.44	MURDER	FR.
PROKOP, Ernst	196678	M	Ger.		Confidential man of Karmazin (Czech.)	WITNESS	CZECH.
PROKOP, Karl	255187	M	Ger.	20.11.11	Informer, Gestapo, Prag (Czech.) 39-45	MISC.CRIMES	CZECH.
PROKOP, Viktor	255735	M			Pvt., Camp Ellrich, Nordhausen (Ger.)	MURDER	U.S.
PROKOSCH	129741	M			Uschfhr, W-SS, Guard CC Mauthausen (Aust.) 41-45	MURDER	U.S.
PROKSCH, Franz	195319	M	Ger.	07	Member Gend., Blockleiter NSDAP, Moravske, Budejovice (Czech.)	MISC.CRIMES	CZECH.
PROKSCH, Willibald	182570	M	Ger.	20	Uschfhr, SS, CC Mauthausen (Aust.) 1.45	MURDER	U.S.
PROKSDE, Willibald	305090	M	Ger.		Arrestfuehrer, CC Mauthausen (Aust.) 11.42-5.45	MISC.CRIMES	FR.
PROLL	136936	M	Ger.		Kriminalrat, Gestapo, Koeln (Ger.)	MURDER	U.S.
PROMMERSBERGER, Josef	192599	M		13.12.01	Owachtmstr,Strafger.Lager Nord,Ministry of Justice,Finmark(Nor.)4.45	MISC.CRIMES	NOR, YUGO.
PRONATH, George	192506	M			Mayor, Guard, CC Flossenburg, Schwarzenfelt(Ger.) 44-45	SUSPECT	U.S.
PRONIK	713	M	Ger.		Pvt.,Army.Art.Btty L 49, 300 Brussels,Brebrieres(Fr.) 1.9.44	MURDER	FR.
PROPST	196611	M	Ger.		Lt.Col., Plateau des Glieres(Fr.) 22.3.-5.4.44	WITNESS	FR.
PROPST	251227	M	Ger.		Lt.Col., 1 Res.Inf.Div.L'Ain(Fr.) 21.7.44	MISC.CRIMES	FR.
PROSCHWATTA	1221	M	Ger.		Capt., 3 Luftfl.Nachr.Rgt.4, Air Force, Rammicusurat(Rum.) 43-44	TORTURE	U.S.
PROSE	62097	M	Ger.		Cpl., Army, 10 Coy, Feldpost Nr.57515 C, Cleder (Fr.) 8.8.44	MURDER	FR.
PROSHKO	194858	M	Ger.		Dr.,Capt.,Frontaufkl.Edo., CC Averoff,Athen(Grc.) 43-44	MISC.CRIMES	U.K.
PROSINGER	31419	M	Ger.		Lt.Col., 169 Inf.Div.Staff, 20 Army, Finmark(Nor.) 44	MURDER	NOR.
PROSKE, Oskar	192094	M	Ger.	2.5.16	SS Usturmfhr.,Member Gestapo, SD, Prague(Czech.)	MISC.CRIMES	CZECH.
PROSS	166958	M	Ger.		Cpl.,Feld-Gend.,Montigny en Vesoul (Fr.) 16.7.44	MURDER	FR.
PROSTE	257951	M			Lt.,150 Pz.Bde., Meuse Bridge, Antwerpen(Bel.) 12.44	MISC.CRIMES	U.S.
PROTT, Hubert	129740	M	Ger.	07	Sgt., W-SS, CC Mainz (Ger.) 43-45	MURDER	BEL.
PROTT, Leonard	192600	M	Ger.		Usturmfhr, SS Wacht-Bn.6, CC Osen Nordland(Nor.) 42-43	MURDER	YUGO.,NOR.
PROTTE	192713	M	Ger.		Hptschfhr, SS, CC Buchenwald (Ger.) 42-45	TORTURE	U.S.
PROTZ, Georg	255358	M	Ger.	15.10.89	Civilian, Gossengrun, Haberspirk (Czech.) 9.39	MURDER	CZECH.
PROTZE	253193	M	Ger.		Employee, Abtlg.VI, Sipo, Brussels (Bel.)	INTERR.	BEL.
PRUDKY,Franz(see PLUDKY,Franz)	174077						
PRUEDLICH, Ernst	302101	M	Ger.		Member NSDAP, Org.Todt, Heelsum, Osterbeek(Neth.) 2.-4.45	MURDER	NETH.
PRUEHSMANN	195952	M	Ger.	98	Cpl., Interpreter, CC Royalhen (Fr.) 41-44	WITNESS	FR.
PRUEM, Albert	38841	M	Ger.		Zugwachtmeister, Police, Koblenz (Ger.)	MURDER	U.S.
PRUESS, Fritz	196680	M	Ger.	10	SS Sturmbannfhr., Gestapo, Huellenberg-Neuried, Bez.Koblenz(Ger.)21.9.44	MURDER	U.S.
PRUESSE	12531	M	Ger.		Lt., Hafenueberwachungsstelle, Calais (Fr.) 4.9.44	TORTURE	FR.
PRUETZMANN, Hans Adolf	62199	M	Ger.		SS Ogruppenfhr, Gen.d.Police and W-SS, SS and Police Leader,Ukraine 41-44; Reichstag Member	MURDER	U.S.,UNWCC
PRUGER, F.	167775	M	Ger.		Treuhaender, Konditorei Kaffee H.Dzierza,Poznan(Pol.) 9.39-44	PILLAGE	POL.
PRUGER, Rudolf	306503	M	Ger.		SS Sgt., CC Buchenwald(Ger.)16. 5.38!-9.10.43	MURDER	BEL.
PRUGGER, Ortmann	254902	M	Ger.		Cpl., II Pz.Div., 36-185, Lautrec (Fr.) 5.8.44	MURDER	FR.
PRUHS	193944 A	M	Ger.	98	Osturmbannfhr,Gestapo,SS Official,Bad Neuenahr(Ger.)	MURDER	POL.
PRUM	146185	M	Ger.		Col.,SS Police, 19 Rgt., 4 Coy, Alex (Fr.) 44	MURDER	FR.
PRUM	166957	M	Ger.		Civilian, Kommand 85, Stalag 12 D, Velhen (Ger.)	TORTURE	FR.
PRUETZMANN	149122	M			Ogruppenfhr, SS	MISC.CRIMES	U.S.
PRUSCH	189709	M			Korv.Kap., Navy,Stalag X-B,Bremervoerde,Sandbostel(Ger.)6.41-1.43	TORTURE	U.K.
PRUSCHA, Zdenko	192511	M	Ger.	15.3.07	Member SS, Prostejov (Czech.)	SUSPECT	CZECH.
PRUSCHOWSKI	300850	M	Ger.		Pvt.,1Aufkl.Abt.,3 Coy,2 Col.,XV Div.Africa Corps,St.Leger(Arlon)5.9.44	MISC.CRIMES	BEL.
PRUSER, Wilhelm	255028	M	Ger.		Guard, Rouen (Fr.) 43-44	TORTURE	FR.
PRUSSAC	155639	M	Ger.	05	Foreman,Sugar Beet Factory,Arbeitslager CC Oberglogau(Ger.) 5.41	TORTURE	U.K.
PRUSSE, Teo	262225	M	Ger.		Civ.,Gend.,near Zapelde Distr.Hannover(Ger.)18.10.43 L.O.D.N.A.O.D.	SUSPECT	U.S.
PRUSSING, Erich	151534	M	Ger.	15	Pvt.,4 Coy,Lds.Schts.Bn.263,Poischendorf(Ger.) 19.5.44	MURDER	FR.
PRUSSMANN	195951	M	Ger.		Guard, Camp Compiegne (Fr.) 41-44	MISC.CRIMES	FR.
PRZBICIN, Josef	259701	M	Ger.	about 00	SS Schfhr, Gestapo, Area of Angers, Maine and Loire (Fr.) 42-44	MISC.CRIMES	FR.
PRZEGENOZA, Emil	193279	M	Ger.	20.12.02	SS-Mann, 4 SS Totenk.Stuba,CC Dora,Mittelbau,Nordhausen(Ger)43-45	MURDER	U.S.
PRZIBILLA, Reinhold	306504	M	Ger.	23.9.09	Uschfhr,SS,CC Buchenwald (Ger.) 16.5.38-9.10.43	MURDER	BEL.
PRZYBILSKI	256119	M	Ger.		Pvt., SS Muhldorf (Ger.)	WITNESS	U.S.
PSOTHA	129731	M			Rottfhr., W-SS, CC Mauthausen (Aust.) 41-45	MURDER	U.S.

NAME	C.R.FILE NUMBER	SEX	NATIO-NALITY	DATE OF BIRTH	RANK, OCCUPATION, UNIT, PLACE AND DATE OF CRIME	REASON WANTED	WANTED BY
PSOTKA	129732	M			Uschfhr., W-SS Totenkopf, CC Mauthausen (Aust.) 41-45	MURDER	U.S.
PSOTKA	255867	M	Ger.		Chief of the kitchen, CC Mauthausen (Aust.)	INTERR.	FR.
PSOTTA	254149	M	Ger.	03	Capt.,15 Pol.Rgt., H.Q.,Vercelli,Assentino(It.) 8.9.44	INTERR.	U.K.
PUCHER	192512	M	Ger.		Employee,Gestapo,Brno (Czech.) 39-45	SUSPECT	CZECH.
PUCHER, Friedrich	255359	M	Ger.	22. 5.96	Civilian,Barrister,Leader of NSDAP,Jaroslavice(Czech.) 39-45	MISC.CRIMES	CZECH.
PUCK	188180	M	Ger.		SS-Sturmfhr., CC Struthof,Schirmeck,Natzweiler (Fr.) 2.-3.9.44	MURDER	FR.
PUEHLER	185655	M	Ger.		SS-Mann,SS Leibst.Adolf Hitler,Renardmont Stavelot (Bel.) 19.12.44	MURDER	BEL.
PUEL	251228	M	Ger.		Commander,Gestapo,SD,Dijon (Fr.) 21.7.44	MISC.CRIMES	FR.
PUELLEN, Paul	196676	M	Ger.		Farmer,Civilian,Vettelhofen (Ger.) 44	MISC.CRIMES	POL.
PUERFER, Albert	261908	M	Ger.		Cpl., G.F.P.Gr.8,Gand-Bruges-Renaix et Courtrai (Bel.) 42-44	MURDER	BEL.
PUETZ	139067	M			Dr.,Major,Sipo,SD,Rowna,Pinsk,Kamenec,Podolsk,Staro,Konstantin (Sov.Un.) 12.41-12.43	MURDER	U.S.
PUETZ	167762	F	Ger.		Member of Administrative staff,Ostgebietsministerium,Einsatzstab Rosenberg (Fr.) 40-44	PILLAGE	FR., U.N.W.C.C.
PUETZ	173180	M	Ger.		Gestapo, CC Gaggenau (Ger.)	MURDER	U.K.
PUETZ	194501	M	Ger.	05	Leiter,Sturmbannfhr.,Gestapo,SS,Lublin,Posen(Pol.) 43-44	MURDER	POL.
PUETZ, Gunther	195316	M	Ger.	29. 6.13	Dr.,Major,RSHA,Commander of the SD,Rowno(Pol.) 11.41-13.7.42	MURDER	POL.
PUETZ, Wilhelm	185201	M	Ger.	28. 5.93	Factory Manager,Civilian,Brno(Czech.) 39-45	PILLAGE	CZECH.
PUGELSHEIM, Hans	146184	M	Ger.		Oberjunker, SS Pz.Div."Das Reich" 13 Coy,Moissac (Fr.) 44	MURDER	FR.
PUHL	157990	M	Ger.	95	Pvt.,714 Ldsch.Bn.,Waldau (Ger.) 24.4.44	INTERR.	U.K.
PUHL, Friedrich	135296	M	Ger.		Civilian, Efferen (Ger.) 2.10.44	WITNESS	U.S.
PUHZE, Edgar	193943	M	Ger.	21. 4.06	Uschfhr., SS, CC Terezin (Czech.)	TORTURE	CZECH.
PULFER, Martin	262132	M	Ger.	7.11.01	Beating and mistreatment of an American airman,Muenchen(Ger.) LODNAOD	TORTURE	U.S.
PULKRABEK, Jan	260015	M	Ger.	4. 2.90	Lt.Col.,Slovak Fascist Army,Presov,Czech.-Eastern-Front,Slovakia (Czech.) 41-45	MURDER	CZECH.
PULLEM	173909	M	Ger.	03	Stabsschfhr.,SS,CC Vienna and Mauthausen (Aust.) 1.-18.4.45	MURDER	U.S.
PULIMANN	196613	M	Ger.		Commander,Oflag X-B,Nienburg-Weser (Ger.) 6.10.42	WITNESS	FR.
PULLMER, Hartmut (or PULMER)	195681	M	Ger.	9.11.08	Lt.Col.,SD,Gestapo,Regensburg (Ger.) 5.45	MISC.CRIMES	U.S.
PULMER	179910	M	Ger.	08	Osturmbannfhr., SS, CC Langenzenn (Ger.) 43-45	MURDER	U.S.
PULMER	305237	M	Ger.	9.11.--	SS-Standartenfhr.,Head of the Gestapo Rennes,Troves and region (Fr.) 15.-22.8.44	MURDER	FR.
PULMER,Hartmut (see PULLMER)	195681						
PULOW	255190	M			Camp Dora, Nordhausen (Ger.)	MURDER	U.S.
PULS, Willi	31506	M	Ger.		Sgt., Army, F.P.Nr.50750, Bannalec (Fr.) 44	MURDER	FR.
PULSDORF	155525	M	Ger.	95	Chefarzt, Army, CC Graudenz (Pol.) 44	TORTURE	U.K.
PULVER	149072	M	Ger.		SS Schfhr., CC Gardelegen, Hannover (Ger.)	MURDER	U.S.
PUNKE, Willy	153110	M			Oschfhr., W-SS, CC Aschendorfer Moos (Ger.)	TORTURE	U.S.
PUNKER, Hermann	255191	M		19. 4.00	Rottfhr., Camp Harzungen, Nordhausen (Ger.)	MURDER	U.S.
PUNSCHAU	39664	M			Rottfhr.,Div.SS, F.P.Nr.48963-B,Chateau Gontier,St.Sulpice,Fortmusson (Fr.) 8.44	MURDER	FR.
PUNTIGAN, Adolf	255192	M			Cpl., Camp Ellrich, Nordhausen (Ger.)	MURDER	U.S.
PUNZENBRUNER	254903	M	Ger.		Dr.,Chemist-Lab.-Asst., CC Dachau (Ger.) 3.42	INTERR.	BEL.
PUR	167780	M	Ger.		Oschfhr., SS "West Bis.", CC Sachsenhausen (Ger.) 39-4.45	MURDER	POL.
PURASUHN, Daniel	254693	M	Ger.		Guard, CC Lahde-Weser (Ger.)	INTERR.	BEL.
PURETZ, Marta	902103	F	Ger.		Confidential Agent, Cracow and Hung., (Pol.,Hung.) 42	INTERR.	POL.
PURMA	305298	M	Ger.		Worker, factory former, CC Dora, Buchenwald (Ger.) 43-4.45	MISC.CRIMES	FR.
PURS	255621	M			Uschfhr., Camp Gross Rosen-Aslau,Nordhausen (Ger.)	MURDER	U.S.
PURUCKER, Reinhold	129733	M			Hptschfhr., W-SS Totenkopf, CC Mauthausen (Aust.) 41-45	MURDER	U.S.
PURUCKER, Martin	255199	M		31. 5.16	Sgt., Camp Ellrich, Nordhausen (Ger.)	MURDER	U.S.
PUSCHAU	147963	M	Ger.		Rottfhr.,SS,St.Sulpice,Fortmusson,Chateau,Gontier(Fr.)	MURDER	FR.
PUSCHMANN, Erich	151532	M			Civilian, Aachen (Ger.)	MURDER	U.S.
PUSCHNER, Friedrich	255194	M		26. 7.98	Cpl., Camp Ellrich, Nordhausen (Ger.)	MURDER	U.S.
PUSITZ	129734	M			Uschfhr., SS Totenkopf, CC Mauthausen (Aust.) 41-45	MURDER	U.S.
PUSKAREV	189959	M			Commandant,Police, Pirot (Yugo.)	TORTURE	YUGO.
PUSL	136303	M			Pvt., 11 Pz.Div. 2 Coy 2 AA-A 7,Albine (Fr.) 12.3.44	MURDER	FR.
PUSSTA	142042	M	Ger.	05	Hptschfhr., W-SS, Totenkopf-Sturmbann,CC Dora,Nordhausen (Ger.)	MURDER	U.S.
PUSTA	149071	M			Hptschfhr.,SS,CC Dora,Gardelegen (Ger.) 4.-14.4.45	MURDER	U.S.
PUSTA	186161	M	Ger.		Sgt., Army, CC Dora, Nordhausen (Ger.)	MURDER	U.S.
PUSTRAK, E.	39663	M			SS-Mann, SS Div.,F.P.Nr.48963 B,Chateau Contier,St.Sulpice,Montmusson (Fr.) 8.44	MURDER	FR.
PUTER, Martin	256118	M	Ger.		Pvt., SS, Muhldorf (Ger.)	INTERR.	U.S.
PUTERS	261132	M	Ger.		Lt.,234 Flyer Rgt.,Alleur near Liege (Bel.) 4.9.44	MURDER	BEL.
PUTKARADSE	256108	M	Ger.		Org.Todt, Muhldorf (Ger.)	WITNESS	U.S.
PUTSCHER	257952	M			Lt.,150 Pz.Bde.,Jagdv.,Meuse Bridge-Antwerp (Bel.) 12.44	MISC.CRIMES	U.S.
PUTSCHOEGEL	301699	M			Bde.-chief., 05-243 Mongolian "Oberland" Unit,St.Nazaire en Royans (Fr.) 20.7.-5.8.44	MURDER	FR.
PUTSH, Henrich	124109	M	Ger.		Pvt.,Stalag VIII-B,Lamsdorf (Ger.) 10.10.42-16.8.43	TORTURE	U.K.
PUTTCHER	1457	M			Cpl., Army, 2 Pl.2 Sec.194 Gr.	MISC.CRIMES	U.K.
PUTTER	193797	M	Ger.		Lt.,Sicherungs Rgt.194,Prade et La Favie (Fr.) 30.7.44	MURDER	FR.
PUTTKAMMER	167763	M	Ger.		Prof.,Dr.,Chief,Zentralamt,Einsatzstab Rosenberg,Berlin(Ger.) 40-44	PILLAGE	U.N.W.C.C., FR.
PUTTNER	38837	M	Ger.	08	Oschfhr., SS, CC Struthof (Fr.)	MISC.CRIMES	FR.
PUTZ	39662	M	Ger.		Osturmbannfhr., SS,CC Lublin (Pol.) 7.44	MURDER	FR., U.K.
PUTZ	153109	M	Ger.		Usturmfhr.,Gestapo,SS,CC Oedenburg (Hung.) 10.-11. 44	INTERR.	U.S.
PUTZ	179181	M	Ger.		Dr.,Chief,Gestapo,CC Gaggenau(Ger.) 25.11.44	MURDER	U.S.
PUTZ	185200	M	Ger.	98	Sturmbannfhr., SS,Rowno (Pol.) 41-42	MURDER	U.S.
PUTZ, Johann	255306	M			SS-Mann, CC Bodungen, Nordhausen (Ger.)	MURDER	U.S.
PUTZ, Karl	138292	M			Pvt., Stalag XIII-C,C.C.Bochum Werne (Ger.) 25.3.45	MURDER	U.S.
PUTZ, Peter	254749	M	Ger.		Pvt., Juvisy (Fr.) 24.8.44	MURDER	FR.
PUTZKE, Fritz	256760	M	Ger.		Employee, Block Senior, Camp Nordhausen (Ger.)	MURDER	U.S.
PUTZLER, Fritz	132341	M			Block-leader, CC Dora, Nordhausen (Ger.)	MURDER	U.S.
PUTZNER	155527	M			Officer,Gestapo, CC Kunsebeck (Ger.) 3.45	MURDER	U.S.
PYERS	193274	M	Ger.		Uschfhr., 4 SS Totenkopfverband, CC Mittelbau Dora,Nordhausen (Ger.) 43-45	MURDER	U.S.
PYRKALA, Joachim	255905	M			Oschfhr.,Camp Dora, Nordhausen (Ger.)	MURDER	U.S.

QUA-RAD

NAME	C.R.FILE NUMBER	SEX	NATIO- NALITY	DATE OF BIRTH	RANK OCCUPATION UNIT PLACE AND DATE OF CRIME	REASON WANTED	WANTED BY
QUACKERWACK, Walter	119398	M	Ger.		Uscharfhr.,Waffen SS, C.C. Oswiecim (Pol.) 6.40 - 1.45	MURDER	POL.
QUADT, Josef	165151	M	Ger.		Civilian	MURDER	U.S.
QUAISSER	256684	M	Ger.		Kriminalinspektor and Obersturmfhr.,Feldpolice, Foix (Fr.) 12.42-8.44	BRUTALITY	FR.
QUAKERNAK, Walter	300914	M	Ger.		Member, SS of Staff at C.C., Hanomag. Hannover (Ger.) 8.44-4.45	MURDER	J.K.
QUAL, Alfred (or QUELE)	173937	M	Ger.		Feldgendarmerie, Locmine (Fr.) 7.-8.44	MURDER	FR.
QUAMBUCH	258885	M	Ger.		Capt.-Cmdt., Flak of Hossejon F.P. 32 926, Voeuil (Fr.) 28.8.44	MURDER	FR.
QUANDT	256247	M			Pvt.C.C. Mackenrode, Nordhausen, (Ger.)	MURDER	U.S.
QUANT	193137	M			Zugwachtmeister, Guard, Police, C.C. Falstad (Nor.) 41-44	MURDER	NOR.
QUARTZ, Einhart	250433	M	Ger.		Capt., 338. Div. La Bresse (Fr.) 44	MISC.CRIMES	FR.
QUASSNY	173946	M	Ger.		Kreiskommandant, Kreiskommandantur, Sabac (Yugo.) 41	MURDER	YUGO.
QUAST (or QWAST)	180724	M	Ger.		Kreiskommandant, Kreiskommandantur, Charleroi (Bel.)	PILLAGE	BEL.
QUAST	261906	M	Ger.		Capt., Kreiscommander, Mons (Bel.) 24.8.44	INTERR.	BEL.
QUAST, Erwin	256246	M	Ger.		Flyer, C.C. Ellrich, Nordhausen (Ger.)	MURDER	U.S.
QUECK, Hans	250429	M	Ger.		Painter, C.C. Dachau (Ger.) 42	TORTURE	BEL.
QUECKE, Hans	260195	M	Ger.		Ministerial-Counsel, R.W.M. Crimes against peace, war crimes against humanity	MISC.CRIMES	U.S.
QUELE, Alfred (see QUAL)	173937						
QUELLE, Johann	250430	M			Pvt., 377. Jaeger-Rgt., Vinkt (Bel.) 5.40	MISC.CRIMES	BEL.
QUELLER, Kurt	250432	M	Ger.		Pvt., 377.Jaeger-Rgt. 1.Coy., Vinkt, Meigem (Bel.) 5.40	MISC.CRIMES	BEL.
QUENTIN	193017	M	Ger.		Sgt., Army-Engineering-Unit, C.C. Syria (Fin.)	MURDER	NOR.
QUERNER, Rudolf	21007	M	Ger.	18. 6.93	Oberpruppenfhr.-General,SS-Police,Abwehr Official, Wehrkreis XI Hannover-Braunschweig (Ger.) 40 - 45	SUSPECT	U.S.
QUERNHORST, Wilhelm	136342	M	Ger.		Civilian, Vicinity of Camp Lintfort (Ger.)10.-11.44	WITNESS	U.S.
QUEST	173099	M	Ger.		SS - Scharfhr., 121.Panz.-Div."Hitler Jugend" 2.SS-Panz.Gren.Rgt. Abbaye Ardennes nearCaen (Fr.)	TORTURE	CAN.
QUETCH	166989	M			Colonel, Kommandantur de Monthucon, Premillat (Fr.) 6.44	MURDER	FR.
QUINCQUERT,	260039	M	Ger.		Capt. Detachement Nr. 13 907 A, Massif du Vercors, Isere and Drome (Fr.) 7. - 8.44	SUSPECT	FR.
QUITT	256245	M			Pvt. Camp Dora, Nordhausen (Ger.)	BRUTALITY	U.S.
QURTZ	124242	M			Kreisleiter, Regional-Official, NSDAP, Alsfeld (Ger.) 2.45	MURDER	U.S.
QWAST (see QUASR)	180724						
RAAB	196944	M	Ger.		Lt., SS, C.C. Neuengamme (Ger.)	TORTURE	BEL.
RAAB, Johann	256111	M			Pvt.,Oberinspector-Rottenfhr.,O.T.,Muehldorf (Ger.)	INTERR.	U.S.
RAAB, Josef	251249	M	Ger.		Civilian, Vranovice (Czech.) 40	INTERR.	CZECH.
RAABE	39630	M	Ger.		Sgt., Standortkommandantur,F.P.42462,Chateau-Gontier (Fr.) 7.und8.44	MISC.CRIMES	FR.
RAABE	142081	M	Ger.	08	Civilian, SA, Szepetowka-Sdobbunow (Sov.Un.) 41 - 44	MISC.CRIMES	U.S.
RAABE	146182	M	Ger.		Unterscharfhr., SS-Panz.Div. " Das Reich ", Valence,Agen (Fr.) 44	MURDER	FR.
RAABE	150589	M	Ger.		Standort Kommandantur, Fortmusson Laval Chateau-Gonthier, St. Sulpice (Fr.)	MURDER	FR.
RAABE	165154	M	Ger.		Civilian, Manager, "Montanblock" Hermann Goering Works (Fr.Neth.Czech)	MISC.CRIMES	U.S.
RAABE	191575	M	Ger.		Cpl., SS Div."Das Reich", 1.Coy. of Pioneer or Pontoons, St. Sixte Lot-et-Garonne (Fr.) 23.6.44	MURDER	FR.
RAABE, Josef	257803	M	Ger.		Employee, C.C. Nordhausen (Ger.)	MURDER	U.S.
RAAF, Josef	260010	M	Ger.	27. 2.94	Major, Ger. Army, Lidice,Bohemia (Czech.) 42	MURDER	CZECH.
RAAF, Michael	122680	M		11	SS - Sturmscharfhr., Gestapo, Allgem.SS, Bensheim (Ger.) 2.45 und 3.45	MURDER	U.S.
RAASCH	139072	M	Ger.		Streifenfhr.,SS, Hutten (Ger.) 4.45	MURDER	U.S.
RABE	124611	F	Ger.		Lt.,Women Guard,C.C.Ravensbruck (Ger.)	TORTURE	BEL.
RABE	158223	M			Lt., 74.Safety, Rgt., 1.Coy., 1.Bn. Claivieres (Fr.) 1.44	MURDER	FR.
RABE	188822	M			Lt., Army, 14.Sicherungs Rgt. (mot.) 1.Coy. 1.Bn. Chaudes Aigues (Fr.) 20.6.44	MURDER	FR.
RABE	193437	M	Ger.		Sturmmann, 4.SS-Totenkopfsturmbann, C.C.Mittelbau,Dora,Nordhausen(Ger.)	MURDER	U.S.
RABE, Karl	141992	M	Ger.		SS-Uscharfhr.,Guard, Buchenwald-Weimar (Ger.)	TORTURE	U.S.
RABE, Oskar	137565	M	Ger.		SS-Uscharfhr., C.C. Weimar-Buchenwald (Ger.)	PILLAGE	U.S.
RABECKER (or HANECKER)	193314	M	Ger.	95	Crim.-Commissary, SD, R.S.H.A., C.C. Mauthausen (Aust.) 1.45	MURDER	U.S.
RABEL	255338	M			Capt. Camp Plaszow, Nordhausen (Ger.)	MURDER	U.S.
RABEL, Ewald	255326	M	Ger.	19. 8.02	Pvt., Camp Harzungen, Nordhausen (Ger.)	MURDER	U.S.
RABENHOFER, August	262302	M			Civ.,lives at:Freilassing (Ger.) Sillersdorf (Ger.)4.45,L.O.D.N.A.O.D.	WITNESS	U.S.
RABENSTEIN	140920	M		05	SS - Wardress, C.C. Ravensbrueck (Ger.)	MURDER	U.K.
RABING	147362	M			Colonel, 11.Panz.Div. South-West (Fr.) 44	MURDER	FR.
RABOLD	195917	M		08	Pvt., Feldgendarmerie of Nancy, Pierre-Percee (Fr.) 2.6.44	TORTURE	FR.
RABSCH, Max	193438	M	Ger.		Oberscharfhr., 4.SS-Totenkopfsturmbann C.C., Dora Mittelbau, Nordhausen, Osterode (Ger.) 43 - 45	MURDER	U.S.
RABSILBER	126497	M	Ger.		Sgt. C.C. Buch, Nordhausen (Ger.) 5.44	MURDER	U.S.
RABUS	196004	M			Capt., 100. Geb.Bn. 2.Cie. 157.Div. Inf.de Res. St.Germain de Tour (Fr.)	MURDER	FR.
RABUSKE	193018	M			Capt.,KGF. Arb.Bn.189, Army, Drag (Nor.) 44	MURDER	NOR.
.ACHERS	38851	M			Hauptscharfhr., SS, Berlin (Ger.) 9.41	MURDER	U.S.
RACH-WERNAU, Erich	152346	M			Civilian-Staatsschauspieler, Emsland (Ger.)	WITNESS	U.S.
RACK	206796	M	Ger.		Officer, Director,Arbeitskommando C.C., Erika Coal mins (Ger.) 41-44	TORTURE	U.K.
RACKASS, Bernhard	32340	M				MURDER	U.S.
RACKE, Albert	255340	M		30. 1.02	SS-Rottenfhr., C.C. Nordhausen (Ger.)	MURDER	U.S.
RACKEL, Erik	156048	M	Ger.	05 - 07	Agent, Gestapo, C.C. Sachsenhausen-Oranienburg (Ger.)	MURDER	U.K.
RACKERS	142079	M		09	Hauptscharfhr., SS-Totenkopf-Sturmbann, C.C.,Buchenwald (Ger.)	TORTURE	U.S.
RACKERS, Bernhard	255327	M			Sgt., Camp Monow, Gleiwitz,Nordhausen (Ger.)	MURDER	U.S.
RADATZ, Georger	251873	M	Ger.		Foreman, Navy, Wilhelmshaven (Ger.) 3.44	MURDER	FR.
RADAZEK, Hans	186649	M			Cpl., Army, Kpoussons (Grc.) 4.44	MURDER	GRC.
RADDATZ	314200	M			Major, 20.Army 55-6 Geb.Div. Panz.-Jaeger Abt. (Nor.) 44	MURDER	NOR.
RADDATZ	195556	M	Ger.		Col. SS and Sipo, Duesseldorf (Ger.)	INTERR.	U.K.
RADDATZ, Kurt	262306	M	Ger.	10	Home is: Schneidemuehl,Pol., Velke-Heratice (Czech.)8.44 L.O.D.N.A.O.D.	SUSPECT	U.S.
RADDATZ, Paul	135297	M		15	Pvt. Kommando Jatzkow (Ger.) 25.8.43	MURDER	U.S.
RADE	258133	M	Ger.		Guard, Waffen SS, C.C. Neuengamme (Ger.)	TORTURE	BEL.
RADE, Otto	193436	M		12. 9.92	C.C. Dora, Nordhausen, Auschwitz (Ger.Pol.)	MURDER	U.S.
RADECK	166991	M	Ger.		Lt., Feldgendarmerie of Vesoul, Montigny en Vesoul (Fr.)15.7.44	MURDER	FR.
RADEMACHER (or REIDMARKE or RADEMAKER)	67579	M	Ger.		Capt. Camp Abwehr Officier, Warburg (Ger.) 12.42	BRUTALITY	U.K.
RADEMACHER	139718	M	Ger.		Capt., C.C. Stalag X B, Sandbostel (Ger.) 1.5.45	MISC.CRIMES	U.S.
RADEMAKER (see RADEMACHE)	67579						

RAD-RAK

NAME	C.R.FILE NUMBER	SEX	NATIO-NALITY	DATE OF BIRTH	RANK OCCUPATION UNIT PLACE AND DATE OF CRIME	REASON WANTED	WANTED BY
RADEMACHER	252604	M	Ger.		Pvt., Pepingen (Ger.) 25.2.44-3.9.44	PILLAGE	BEL.
RADER see RAYDER	189705						
RADERMACHER	714	M	Ger.		Capt., Army, C.C. Oflag 6 B (Ger.) 13.12.41	MISC.CRIMES	U.K.
RADERMACHER, Karl	21456	M	Ger.		Flak 1-37, Balkan - Russia. 41-42	WITNESS	SOV.UN.
RADESTOK	158224	M	Ger.		Civ., Punschau (Ger.)	WITNESS	U.S.
RADFAHRN	1463	M			Capt., SS police Rgt. 20	MURDER	U.K.
RADHE	152065	M			Lt., 21.Panz.Div. H.Q., Sessenheim (Fr.) 1.45	MURDER	U.S.
RADISCHAT, Hans	167488	M	Ger.		Dr., High official, Abt.Treuhandverwaltung, Amt des General-Gouverneurs, Pol. 9.39- end of 44	PILLAGE	POL.
RADKE, Bruno	141594	M		21	Col., Chenebier, Etoboni (Fr.) 27.9.44	MURDER	FR.
RADKE, Jacob	132101	M			Arbeitskommando	TORTURE	U.S.
RADKE, Max	67578	M	Ger.		C.C. Weissmusser (Ger.) 12.43-12.2.45	MISC.CRIMES	U.K.
RADKE, Otto	38852	M		20	SS Uscharfhr., SS Div. "Das Reich", Kriegsgefang.Lager 20,Bremen(Ger.)	TORTURE	U.S.
RADKE, Siegfried	250440	M	Ger.		Pvt., Celais (Fr.) 8.-9.44	MURDER	FR.
RADL, Ernst	253523	M	Ger.	15	Lt., Army, 118.Inf.Div., Lowiste, Klagenfurt (Yugo.Ger.) 24.8.44	INTERR.	YUGO.
RADLIN	901023	M			Member of staff, C.C. Struthof-Natzweiler (Fr.) 42-44	MURDER	FR.
RADLOF	173955	M	Ger.		Rottfhr., SS, C.C. Buchenwald (Ger.) 42-45	MURDER	U.S.
RADLOF	253244	M	Ger.		W.O., Fieldpolice, Salagnon (Fr.) 15.2.94	INTERR.	FR.
RADLOFF, Emil	193433	M	Ger.	20. 1.94	SS-Mann, C.C. Dora-Nordhausen (Ger.) 43-45	MURDER	U.S.
RADLOFF, Heinrich	190324	M	Ger.		Crim.Obersecretaer, Gestapo, Wiesbaden (Ger.) 43-45	TORTURE	U.S.
RADMAN	10159	M		91	Civ., Factory-manager, C.C. Niederursel (Ger.) 3.1.43	TORTURE	U.K.
RADMULLER	121990	M	Ger.		Cpl., Army, F.P. 56 067, Creach-Maout (Fr.) 7.8.44	MURDER	FR.
RAINUZ, Walter	715	M			Pvt., Army, L 20368, Baudrigues (Fr.) 19.8.44	MURDER	FR.
RADOG	255939	M			Camp Rottleberode, Nordhausen (Ger.)	MURDER	U.S.
RADRE	126496	M	Ger.	20	Officer, SS Panz.Ers. und Ausb.Rgt. Sennelager, Friedrichsbrunn (Ger.) 15.4.45	MISC.CRIMES	U.S.
RADTKE, R. or RADTKER	193136	M	Ger.		Schupo, C.C. Falstad (Nor.) 41-44	MURDER	NOR.
RADTKE, Erich	193432	M	Ger.	5. 4.95	SS Mann, 4.SS Totenkopf-Stuba, C.C. Dora-Mittelbau Nordhausen (Ger.) 43-45	MURDER	U.S.
RADTKE, Goich	152058	M	Ger.		Guard, SS, C.C. Stalag X B Sandbostel (Ger.) 4.45	MURDER	U.S.
RADTKE, Karl	255042	M	Ger.	16. 6.00	Informer, Gestapo, Trest (Czech.) 45	INTERR.	CZECH.
RADTKER see RADTKE, R.	193136						
PADUSH, Friedrich	187025	M	Ger.	20. 3.06	Factory-employes, Civ., Brno (Czech.) 39-45	PILLAGE	CZECH.
RADZIEJ	31421	M	Ger.		Brigadier-General, Army, Finnmark (Nor.)	MURDER	NOR.
RAEBEL	258534	M		12. 6.06	Hptsturmfhr., SS-Fuehrungsstab, C.C. Dora - Nordhausen,Plazow (Ger.,Pol.) 41-45	MURDER	U.S.
RAEDEL	190300	M			Officer, Standortkommandantur, Pozaverac (Yugo.) 41-43	MURDER	YUGO.
RAEDER	1458	M	Ger.		Major, Army, SS Panz.Gren.	MURDER	U.K.
RAEDER	152067	M	Ger.		SS Osturmfhr., Waffen SS, C.C.,Kreis St.Goar (Ger.) 29.12.44	MURDER	U.S.
RAEDER	179739	M	Ger.		Sturmbannfhr. or Osturmfhr., SS, Army, 16.SS Recce Unit, Apuanian-alps (It.) 29.6.44	MURDER	U.K.
RAEDWITZ	194755	M	Ger.		Deputy commander, C.C. Ravensbrueck (Ger.) since 3.43	TORTURE	BEL.
RAETZEL, Heinrich or RAETSEL	193019	M	Ger.	05	Guard,Hilfswachtmeister, Overseer, Feldstraflager, Waffen SS,Reichsjustizministerium, C.C. Finnmark (Nor.) 3-45	MISC.CRIMES	NOR.,YUGO.
RAFALZIG	196008	M	Ger.		C.C. Struthof-Natzweiler (Fr.) 40-44	MURDER	FR.
RAFALZIG, Hans	906505	M	Ger.	29. 6.13	Scharfhr., (Nr.287201) SS, C.C. Buchenwald (Ger.) betw.16.5.38 - 9.10.43	MURDER	BEL.
RAFFENBERG, Heinz	177580	M	Ger.	07	Tortionnaire, C.C. Neubrenn nr.Saabruecken (Ger.)	TORTURE	FR.
RAFFLER, Otto	31505	M	Ger.		Pvt., Army, Perigueux (Fr.)	MURDER	FR.
RAFORTH, Lothe	196351	F			SS Guard, C.C. Erfurt (Ger.) 44	TORTURE	U.S.
RAGALLER, Klaus	255337	M			Camp Dora - Nordhausen (Ger.)	MURDER	U.S.
RAHAGEL	180738	M	Ger.		SS Usturmfhr.,Platoon-leader, 1.Panz.Rgt. Leibstandarte Adolf Hitler, 1.Platoon, 7.Coy., Malmedy (Bel.) 17.12.44	MURDER	U.S.
RAHM	144372	M	Ger.	98	Lt., Army, Kampfgruppe Sachs, 1.Coy.,Billingsbach (Ger.) 17.4.45	WITNESS	U.S.
RAHM, Karl	193982	M	Ger.	2. 4.07	SS Osturmfhr., C.C., Teregia (Czech.) 39-45	TORTURE	CZECH.
RAHN, Helmut	253205	M	Ger.	21	Lt., Army, Kistanje (Yugo.) 17.11.43	INTERR.	YUGO.
RAHN, Hermann	141991	M	Ger.		SS Mann, SS Totenkopf Guard, C.C. Buchenwald,Weimar,Auschwitz (Ger., Pol.)	BRUTALITY	U.S.
RAHN, Jakob	259436	M			Guard, Policeman, Bechtheim (Ger.) betw. 9. and 12.44	MURDER	U.S.
RAHNFELD	255336	M			Cpl., Camp Ellrich, Nordhausen (Ger.)	MURDER	U.S.
RAIE, Ruth	136350	F			SS Guard, C.C. Erfurt (Ger.) 44	TORTURE	U.S.
RAIMANN, Hans	300417	M	Ger.		337.Anti-Tank-Bn. St.Ag., Bourcy nr.Bastogne (Lux.) 20.12.44 et seq.	MISC.CRIMES	BEL.
RAIN see RHEIN	170541						
RAINER	129050	M			Dr., Col.Gen. (Oberleiter) SS, C.C. Mauthausen (Aust.) 41-45	MURDER	U.S.
RAINER	144471	M	Ger.		Pvt., Panz.Corps, Gravenwoehr (Ger.) 1.12.44	MISC.CRIMES	U.S.
RAINER	166665	M	Ger.		Public official, leader, chief of Civ.administration, Kaernten Krain (Aust.) 39-45	TORTURE	U.S.
RAINER, Fren	186380	M	Ger.		N.C.O., Army, Guard, Amariou (Grc.) 4.43	RAPE	GRC.
RAINER, Friedrich	147066	M	Ger.		Chief, Public official, Administrat. Temtones occupes, Slovenia (Yugo.) 39-45	MURDER	YUGO.
RAINER, Karl	262193	M	Ger.	25. 2.22	SS Osturmfhr., 8.Coy., 51.SS Armoured-Bde.,Breviandes, Bucheres, St.Savine, La Riviere de Corps (Troyes) (Fr.) 22.-25.8.44	BRUTALITY	FR.
RAINHART	186379	M	Ger.		Lt., Army, Athens (Grc.) 44	PILLAGE	GRC.
RAINTHALER, Hans (Johann)	148556	M	Ger.	07	SS Hptsturmfhr., SS Ers.und Ausb.Rgt. (Flak) Freimann, Muenchen (Ger.) 7.44	MURDER	U.S.
RAISER	146181	M	Ger.		Lt., Army, Coudes (Fr.) 44	MURDER	FR.
RAISNER, Rudolf	12467	M	Ger.		Sgt., Army, 110.or 1.1.Panz.Gren.Rgt. 2.Coy., Albine (Fr.) 29.6.44	MURDER	FR.
RAITHEL, Max	199135	M	Ger.		Schupo, C.C. Falstad (Nor.) 41-44	MURDER	NOR.
RAITZ	122681	M	Ger.		SS, C.C. Thekla (Ger.) 18.4.45	MURDER	U.S.
RAITZIG	255335	M			Cpl., Camp Dora - Nordhausen (Ger.)	MURDER	U.S.
RAKACH	196858	M			SS Mann, Auschwitz (Pol.)	MURDER	FR.
RAKAS or RAKERS	137566	M			Kommandofuehrer, SS, C.C. Weimar,Buchenwald (Ger.)	TORTURE	U.S.
RAKE	253293	F			Secretary of Hptsturmfhr., Thomson, Hengelo (Neth.) 11.44	WITNESS	NETH.
RAKERS see RAKAS	137566						
RAKERS	196857				Hptsturmfhr., SS, Auschwitz (Pol.) 40	MURDER	FR.
RAKOSKI or GRABOWSKI	259222	M	Ger.		Agent, Gestapo, Poitiers (Fr.) 40-44	SUSPECT	FR.
RAKRS	305939	M	Ger.		Hptscharfhr., C.C. Oranienburg (Ger.) 11.39-45	MURDER	CZECH.

RAL-RAT

NAME	C.R.FILE NUMBER	SEX	NATIO-NALITY	DATE OF BIRTH	RANK OCCUPATION UNIT PLACE AND DATE OF CRIME	REASON WANTED	WANTED BY
RALFS	300851	M	Ger.		N.C.O.,1 Aufkl.Abt.,3 Coy,2 Col., XV Div.Africa Corps,St.Léger(Arlon) 5.9.44	MISC.CRIMES	BEL.
RALFS, Guenter	161643	M	Ger.	95	Capt.,Army,HKA Rgt.977,37 Btty,Ramsy(Nor.)	WITNESS	NOR.
RALL, Gustav	258541	M	Ger.	83	SS Osturmbannfhr,WVHA, SS HA (Ger.) 40-45	BRUTALITY	U.S.
RAMBAUSKE,Ernst	162698	M			Kdo.3280,Gestapo,Liebtahl(Czech.) 7.42	MISC.CRIMES	FR.
RAMBOW, Alfred	259223	M	Ger.		Lt.Gend.,Sierentz-Rischeim(Fr.) 12.43-44	MISC.CRIMES	FR.
RAMBRECHT	305484	M	Ger.		SS-Osturmfhr,2 Coy,35 Rgt. Reichsf.Div.,Strettoia(It.) 7.44	MURDER	FR.
RAMCKE	21243	M	Ger.		Major-General,Army,Fortress,Brest(Fr.) 1.-9.9.44	MISC.CRIMES	U.S.
RAMDEHR	189185	M	Ger.		Crim.Asst.,Gestapo, Ravensbrueck(Ger.)	MURDER	BEL.
RAMDORFF	306506	M	Ger.		Employee, CC Ravensbrueck(Ger.) 40-45	MURDER	BEL.
RAMER, Ernst	190247	M	Ger.		Gestapo, HQ, Koeln (Ger.) 43-45	MURDER	U.K.
RAMHARTER, Josef	195970	M		3. 1.05	Amstetten (Aust.) 20.9.45	MISC.CRIMES	U.S.
RAMKE	67554	M	Ger.		Camp Dir., CC Dachsgrube (Ger.) 3.43-8.44	MURDER	U.K.
RAMKE	173924	M	Ger.		Gen. Col., 2 Parachut.Div.,Finistere (Fr.) 44	MURDER	FR.
RAML, William	123946 A	M		03	Cpl., Camp	TORTURE	U.S.
RAMMANN, Hans	252623	M	Ger.		Sgt., 10 Coy, 377 Jg.Rgt., Vinkt and Meigem(Bel.) 25-31.5.40	MISC.CRIMES	BEL.
RAMP, Bernhard	189412	M	Ger.		Zugwachtmeister, Tromsoey (Nor.) 18.6.42	TORTURE	NOR.
RAMPAS, Max	192541	M	Ger.	13	Employee, Gestapo, Brno (Czech.) 39-45	SUSPECT	CZECH.
RAMPF	148561	M	Ger.		SS Hptsturmfhr, near Munich (Ger.) 7.44	MURDER	U.S.
RAMPFEL, S.A.	122548	M	Ger.		Group-Leader NSDAP, Bruck and Murn(Aust.) 2.45	TORTURE	U.K.
RAMPRECHT	1459	M	Ger.		Osturmfhr, SS Div."Reichsfuehrer", 16 Pz.Rgt.,2 Coy,Strettoia(It.) 4.9.-5.9.44	MURDER	FR., U.K.
RAMSAU (or RAMSAUER,RAMSAUA)	190333	M	Ger.	about 15	Dr.,Osturmfhr,SS,CC Dachau(Ger.) 42	MURDER	YUGO.
RAMSK, Karl	252622	M	Ger.		377 Jg.Rgt., Vinkt and Meigem(Bel.) 25.-31.5.40	MISC.CRIMES	BEL.
RAMSAUA,(see RAMSAUER, RAMSAU)	190333						
RAMSTETTER, Arnulf	186856	M	Ger.		Lt.,Army,Hennebont (Fr.) 6.8.44	MURDER	FR.
RAN, Eugen	125214				Civ., CC Enkenbach, Foundry (Ger.) 12.43-3.45	TORTURE	U.S.
PANCARI	256112	M	Ger.		Pvt., SS, Muhldorf (Ger.)	WITNESS	U.S.
RANDORFF	132719		Ger.		Agent, Gestapo, Ravensbruecke (Ger.) 42-45	MURDER	FR., BEL.
RANEILMEIER	12466	M	Ger.		SS-Mann, 116 or 111 Pz.Gr.Rgt.,2 Coy,Albine(Fr.) 29.6.44	MURDER	FR.
RANFT, Waldemar	132193	M	Ger.		Lt. Engineer, Navy U-852, South of Freetown, Atlantic 13.3.44	WITNESS	U.K.
RANIG, Wali	136343	F	Ger.		Guard, CC Helmbrechts (Ger.) 7.44-13.4.45	TORTURE	U.S.
RANK, Alfred	251244	M	Ger.	about 01	Driver, SD, Alencon (Fr.) 40-44	PILLAGE	FR.
RANK, Hans	257191	M	Ger.	14	stationed at command, Camp No.1684 (Ger.) 7.44, 10.44	BRUTALITY	U.S.
RANK, Richard	257109	M	Ger.	89	Uschfhr, SS, CC Gross Rosen, Flossenburg (Ger.) 44	MURDER	POL.
RANKE	67811	M	Ger.		Sgt., Camp Commander, Limburg,Mühlburg,Gleina(Ger.) 9.44	MISC.CRIMES	U.K.
RANKE, Hermann	121208	M	Ger.	99	General, Platz Cmdt., Kommandantur, Brest (Fr.) 27.8.44	PILLAGE	FR.
RANS	177579	M	Ger.		Sgt., Field Command. 775, Le Mans (Fr.)	PILLAGE	FR.
RAPERT (see RAPPERT)	168100						
RAPFALZIG	192823	M	Ger.		SS Oschfhr, CC Buchenwald, Flossenburg (Ger.) 40-45	TORTURE	U.S.
RAPHAELSON, Paul	255742	M	Ger.		Kapo, Camp Wulkau, Schnarrtenreuth-Wulkau(Ger.) 42-45	MURDER	CZECH.
RAPP	174047	M	Ger.		Capt.,Stalag VI A, Hemer (Ger.) 41-45	TORTURE	U.S.
RAPP	189309	M	Ger.		SS Oschfhr, CC Dachau (Ger.)	MURDER	BEL.
RAPP	196651	M	Ger.		SS-Mann, Ravensbrueck (Ger.)	TORTURE	BEL.
RAPP	255334	M			Pvt., Camp Dora, Nordhausen (Ger.)	MURDER	U.S.
RAPP, Kaspar	189183	M			SS Guard, CC Uckermark near Ravensbrueck (Ger.) 42-45	MURDER	FR.,BEL.
RAPPEL (or ROEPPEL)	301700	M	Ger.		05,243 Mongolian"Oberland"Unit,St.Nazaire en Royans(Fr.)20.7.-5.8.44	MURDER	FR.
RAPPERT (or REPPER, RAPERT)	168100	M	Ger.		Capt.,Air Force,Stalag Luft 4,Kiefheide(Ger.) 7.44	TORTURE	U.S.
RAPPL	188821	M	Ger.		Pvt.,Army, Le Triage Bourget (Fr.) 24.8.44	MURDER	FR.
RAPPL	189308	M	Ger.		SS Uschfhr, CC Dachau (Ger.)	MURDER	BEL.
RARTHERT(see RATHERT,William)	132104						
RASCH, Jupp	196856	M	Ger.		Lt., F.P.15201, Etobon Chenebier (Fr.) 27.9.44	MURDER	FR.
RASCHDORF	255333	M			Arbeitseinsatz Camp Dora, Nordhausen (Ger.)	MURDER	U.S.
RASCHE	132103	M	Ger.	08	Crim.Secr., Gestapo, Ahlem (Ger.)	MURDER	SOV.UN.
RASCHE (or RASCHER)	137627	M	Ger.	15	Dr., Physician,Air Force, CC Dachau (Ger.)	MURDER	U.S.,FR.,U.K.
RASCHE	305241	M	Ger.		Comm.Officer, Unit of Vrastamites, SS Pol.Geb.Rgt.18,Police Haystrian Vrastamites near Livadia, Beotia (Grc.) 9.-12.8.44	PILLAGE	GRC.
RASCHER	122682	M		10	SS Hptsturmfhr	MURDER	U.S.
RASCHER (see RASCHE)	137627						
RASCHER,Nini (nee DIEHL)	301813	F	Ger.		Dr.Raschers Wife, CC Dachau and Auschwitz (Ger., Pol.) 26.2.43	TORTURE	BEL.
RASCHER, Siegmund	10324	M	Ger.		SS Usturmfhr, CC Dachau (Ger.) 39-44	TORTURE	CZECH.,U.S.,BEL.
RASCHKE	1734				Lt.Army, Rgt.Cdo., 9 Div.,29 Rgt.,1 Bn.,Aversa(It.) 19.9.43	MISC.CRIMES	U.K.
RASCHKE	305242	M	Ger.		SS Rottfhr, SD, Troyes Region (Fr.) 3.10.43-22.8.44	MURDER	FR.
RASECHKE	126911	M	Ger.		SD, Chatillon s-Cluses, St.Jeoire, Taninges(Fr.)11.6.-20.7.44	MISC.CRIMES	FR.
RASHOFFER	187554	M		15	Lt.,Army,65 Inf.Div.,Cisa (It.) 3.10.43	WITNESS	U.K.
RASKK (or RECKE)	125070	M	Ger.	00	Pvt., Army, 61b Coy,Inf.Stalag IX-B, 3.2.42	MURDER	U.K.
RASKE	174051	M	Ger.		Sgt., Stalag 6 A, CC Hemer (Ger.) 41-42	MISC.CRIMES	U.S.
RASKO, Fritz	131319	M			Guard, Arb.Kdo. Stalag II-B, CC Neuschwessin(Ger.) 6.44	MURDER	U.S.
RASMUS, Karl	302105	M	Ger.		Railway Official, Fernmeldemeisterei,Amersfoort(Neth.)4.10.44-5.45	PILLAGE	NETH.
RASONG	196855	M	Ger.		Member Gestapo and Rumanian Kdo., Vichy (Fr.) 43-44	MURDER	FR.
RASPUTNIAK, Emil	252605	M	Ger.		Guard, CC Lahde-Weser (Ger.)	BRUTALITY	BEL.
RASSI	12469	M	Ger.		Sturmfhr, SS, 19 Police Rgt. Todt, 1 Coy,Ugines,Cran(Fr.)15.6.44	MURDER	FR.
RASSINGER	255592	M	Ger.		CC Rottleberode,Osterode,Nordhausen(Ger.)	MURDER	U.S.
RASSNER	180735	M	Ger.		Vertrauensmann, Gestapo, Saarbruecken(Ger.)	LOOTING	FR.
RAST, Helmut	129047	M		20. 7.03	Rottfhr, SS, CC Mauthausen (Aust.) 14.5.44-7.5.45	MURDER	U.S.
RASTEL, Simon	196354	M	Ger.		Guard, CC Helmbrechts (Ger.) 7.44-13.4.45	MURDER	U.S.
RASTELLI, Georges	216479	M		3. 3.89	Group-Leader NSDAP, Mellendorf (Ger.) 39	MISC.CRIMES	U.S.
RASTIG, Otto	137591	M	Ger.		Civ., NSKK Representative, CC near Torgau (Ger.) 1.44	MISC.CRIMES	U.K.
RATGEN	259902	M	Ger.		Cmdt., Military, Customs Frontier Guard, Ouddorp (Neth.) 17.9.42	MURDER	NETH.
RATH	186788	M	Ger.		Rottfhr, SS, Guard at Prison, Mecklenburg (Ger.) 42-45	TORTURE	U.S.
RATH	193673	M	Ger.	24	Pvt.,Army, Ober-Kdo.324,Stalag IX-B, 218 Bn.,CC Felchen(Ger.) 6.42	TORTURE	U.K.
RATH	247950	M			Sgt.,150 Pz.Bde.,Meuse Bridge,Antwerpen(Bel.)12.44	MISC.CRIMES	U.S.
RATH, Guenther	192540	M	Ger.		Doctor, Prison, Straubing - Bay. (Ger.) 43-45	SUSPECT	CZECH.

RAT-RAU

NAME	C.R.FILE NUMBER	SEX	NATIO-NALITY	DATE OF BIRTH	RANK OCCUPATION UNIT PLACE AND DATE OF CRIME	REASON WANTED	WANTED BY
RATH, Hans	167486	M	Ger.		Aviation Camp at Chanoine, Arles (Fr.)8.44	MISC.CRIMES	POL.
RATH, Karl-Heinz	255344	M		5.9.16	Sgt., C.C. Nordhausen-Ellrich, (Ger.)	MURDER	U.S.
RATH, Oswald	305243	M	Ger.		Foreman, RAD, Schutzen am Gebirge Kr.Eisenstadt (Aust.) 2.45	MURDER	U.S.
RATHER (see RAUTHER) Wilhelm	144380						
RATHERT (see RAUTHER)	144380						
RATHERT, Fritz	152066	M	Ger.		Civilian, Erkeuschwick, (Ger.)	TORTURE	U.S.
RATHERT (RARTHERT) William	132104	M	Ger.	95	Chief, Stalag II B, Civ.,Manager of State Farm,Seefelde (Ger.)12.44	MURDER	U.S.
RATHKE	258146	M	Ger.		Employee, Dr., C.C.Dachau (Ger.)	TORTURE	BEL.
RATHMANN	193342	M	Ger.		SS-Oschfhr., C.C.Falstad Drontheim (Nor.)3.-4.44	TORTURE	NOR.
RATJEN	717	M	Ger.		Adjutant Chief, Army, Comblanchien (Fr.) 8.44	MURDER	FR.
RATJEN, Otto-Franz	252621	M	Ger.		Pvt., 377.Jaeger Rgt.,30054 A,B, Vinkt (Bel.)5.40	MISC.CRIMES	BEL.
RATKE	300097	M	Ger.		Major President of the Military Court during the Occ., Athen (Grc.) 43	MURDER	GRC.
RATKE, Siegfried	253311	M	Ger.	04	W.O., Inf. Navy. Calais, (Fr.) 9.44	MURDER	FR.
RATKO	300098	M	Ger.		Lt., Serving in Xanthi, (Grc.)3.44	TORTURE	GRC.
RATKOWSKI	253288	M	Ger.		Osturmfhr., C.C. Buchenwald (Ger.)	TORTURE	FR.
RATMANN	256308	M	Ger.		Baufhr., O.T., Muhldorf (Ger.)	WITNESS	U.S.
RATOMSKY	718	M	Ger.		SS-Sturmbannfhr., Chaidarion (Grc.)43-44	MURDER	GRC.
RATSCHEK, Ceeslaus	258601	M	Ger.		Opt., Abwehr, slave labour camp, Erlandst,Ocusand,Trola(Yugo.)6.42-45	MISC.CRIMES	NOR.
RATSKA, Johann	196854	M	Ger.		Pvt., C.C. Auschwitz (Pol.) 40	MURDER	FR.
RATSMANN	136607	M	Ger.	90	Bank Director, Public Official (Ger.) 42	MISC.CRIMES	U.S.
RATTAJ	255343	M			Rottfhr., Camp Nixei Nordhausen (Ger.)	MURDER	U.S.
RATTELSDORFER, Michael	255345	M		16.5.99	Opl., Camp Ellrich, Nordhausen (Ger.)	MURDER	U.S.
RATTMANN	719	M	Ger.		Oschfhr., Gestapo, Drontheim (Nor.) 43	TORTURE	NOR.
RATZ, Peter	306508	M	Ger.		SS-Sgt., C.C.Buchenwald (Ger.)5.38-10.43	MURDER	BEL.
RATZEE, Michael	251245	M	Ger.		Lt., Hermaville Aubigny, Artois (Fr.)5.40	INTERR.	FR.
RATZEI	188820	M	Ger.		Sgt., Feldgend., Louhans, (Fr.)10.43	TORTURE	FR.
RATZER	62202	M	Ger.		Leader, Public Official Instruction Department	TORTURE	U.N.W.C.C.
RATZKA, Johann	251239	M	Ger.		SS-man, C.C. Auschwitz Birkenau (Pol.) 12.42	MURDER	YUGO.
RATZKE	261338	M	Ger.		Opt., Rgt.Z.B.V.Col.,Wolff, Bn,Ratzke, Environ Mauleon-Navarreux (Fr.) 6.-8.44	MURDER	FR.
RATZKE	720	M	Ger.		Opt., Army, Magny Darrigon (Fr.) 9.44	MURDER	FR.
RATZMANN	167457	M	Ger.		Leader, Treuhandstelle, Posnan (Pol.)9.39-44	PILLAGE	POL.
RATZMANN	189255	M	Ger.	85	Bank Director, Bank Occupied Territories, Posnan (Pol.)40-41	PILLAGE	POL.
RAU	139716	M	Ger.		SS-Opl.	MURDER	U.S.
RAU	254425	M	Ger.		Gestapo SD, Sgt., Toulouse (Fr.) 11.42- 8.44	MISC.CRIMES	FR.
RAU	255342	M	Ger.		Uschfhr., C.C. Harzungen, Nordhausen (Ger.)	MURDER	U.S.
RAUBUCH	141399	M	Ger.	15	SS Osturmfhr., Chief, Mauthausen (Aust.)	TORTURE	FR.
RAUCA, Helmut	139075	M	Ger.		Hptschfhr., SS Cross and Skull Div.C.C.Dachau (Ger.)	TORTURE	FR.
RAUCH	67022	M	Ger.		Oberarzt, Army Unit B.F.15201, Chenebier (Fr.)27.9.44	MURDER	FR.
RAUCH	125211		Ger.		O.-Stabsarzt, Medical Officer at Ilag XVIII C.C. Spittal-Drau (Aust.) 1944-1945	MISC.CRIMES	U.S.
RAUCH	126584	M	Ger.		Schupo, Wachtmeister, Gend., Vicinity of Koenigshofen (Ger.)8.4.45	MURDER	U.S.
RAUCH (see ROORCH)	128948						
RAUCH	158225	M	Ger.		Sgt., Army C.C. Kobiersyn, (Pol.)6.8.44	MISC.CRIMES	FR.
RAUCH	192086	M	Ger.		Civ., Farmer, Martinschteten,pris.Schanfing (Ger.) 6.10.44	TORTURE	FR.
RAUCH	195969	M	Ger.		Pvt., SS 1.Pz.Div.,Leibstandarte Adolf Hitler, Ligneuville Stoumont (Bel.) 17.-19.12.44	MURDER	U.S.
RAUCH	259622	M			Lt., Air Force 9.Coy., 54.Rgt.,Plouganou, Finistere (Fr.) 4.-5.7.44	TORTURE	FR.
RAUCH, Gotthold (see ROSCHER)	128949						
RAUCH, Hermann	193424	M		8.9.93	SS Schfhr., 4.SS Totenkopfsturmbann, Nordhausen C.C.Dora Mittelbau Bismarckhuette, (Ger.) 43-45	MURDER	U.S.
RAUCH, Rudi	152362	M	Ger.		Major, Chenebier, Etobon (Fr.) 27.9.44	MURDER	FR.
RAUCHER, (see RAUHRER)	261841	M	Ger.				
RAUDER	193922	M			SS, C.C. Ravensbrueck (Ger.)	TORTURE	FR.
RAUEN (JACQUES see JACKY)	132720						
RAUER	10077	M			Sgt., Army, Bindhof-Schapen (Ger.) 3.45	MURDER	U.S.
RAUFELDER, Eugen	121396	M			Pvt., (Secretar), Army, Creach Maqut (Fr.)7.8.44	MURDER	FR.
RAUH	132339	M	Ger.		Lt., Inf.Rgt.330 8.Bn.,183 Volksgren.Div.,Linnich (Ger.)16.1.45	MISC.CRIMES	U.S.
RAUH, Johann	152068	M			Civilian, Graz (Aust.)	WITNESS	U.S.
RAUH, Max	258997	M	Ger.	17.11.09	Sturmbannfhr., SS,NSDAP, 9.11.41	INTERR.	U.S.
RAUH, Theo	196650	M	Ger.		Pvt., SS, Malmedy (Bel.)44	MURDER	U.S.
RAUHBUCH	129046	M			SS-Oschfhr., Totenkopf C.C.Mauthausen (Aust.)41-45	MURDER	U.S.
RAUHEN	121209	M	Ger.		Opl., Gestapo, Perigueux (Fr.)	MURDER	FR.
RAUHRER (or RAUCHER)	261841	M	Ger.	15	Lt., Div. Goets von Berlichingen Feldpost No.23201 E,Montreuil-Bellay (Fr.) 8.44	MURDER	FR.
RAUK, Alphonse	186185	M	Ger.		Kapo, C.C. Dachau (Ger.)	MURDER	FR.
RAULN.CH	256734	M	Ger.		Employee, C.C. Nordhausen (Ger.)	MURDER	U.S.
RAUM	141324	M	Ger.		Pvt., Army, Danzig (Ger.) 7.1.44	MURDER	U.K.
RAUM, Ernst	132105	M	Ger.	27.6.94	Lt.Col., Geb.Jaeger Rgt.98 Army Assist.Commander,Eichstett Oflag 7 B (Ger.) 1944	MURDER	U.S.
RAUMKENS	167136	M	Ger.		Opl., Feldgend., Montigny En Vesoul (Fr.)16.7.44	MURDER	FR.
RAUNDT (see RAUNT)	253351						
RAUNT	152344	M			Platoon leader, Volkssturm 1.Bn.C.C. Gardelegen (Ger.)4.45	MURDER	U.S.
RAUNT (or RAUNDT)	255341	M			C.C. Osterhagen, Nordhausen (Ger.)	MURDER	U.S.
RAUPACH, Rudolphe	188819	M	Ger.		Opt., Kreiskommandantur, Besancon,(Fr.)40-42	PILLAGE	FR.
RAUPERT (or RAYPERT)	162781	M	Ger.		Opt., Army, C.C. Stalag Luft IV Grosstychow (Ger.)	TORTURE	U.S.
RAUS	722	M	Ger.		Sgt., Fieldkommandantur 755 Army, Le Mans (Fr.)40-44	PILLAGE	FR.
RAUSCH	173921	M	Ger.		Sgt., Abwehr Stalag XIII C, Hammelburg (Ger.)40-44	MISC.CRIMES	FR.
RAUSCH	306509	M	Ger.		SS-Sgt., C.C. Buchenwald (Ger.)16.5.38-9.10.43	MURDER	BEL.
RAUSCH	306715	M	Ger.		Sect.Leader, Nounberg, near Altenburg (Ger.)30.8.44	MURDER	U.S.
RAUSCH, Alfred	255331	M			Pvt., C.C. Ellrich, Nordhausen (Ger.)	MURDER	U.S.
RAUSCH, Guenther	253310	M			Opt., Gestapo, Lille, (Fr.)40-44	MURDER	FR.
RAUSCH, Jos.	121397	M			Pvt., Army Fp.56067, Creach Maqut (Fr.) 5.8.44	MURDER	FR.
RAUSCH, Willy	169043	M	Ger.	28.3.15	W-SS C.C. Natzweiler (Fr.)42-44	MURDER	FR.
RAUSCHAL	188373	M			SS-Mann, C.C. Karlovy-Vary (Czech)14.4.45	WITNESS	U.S.
RAUSCHCPF, Josef	152071	M		00	Hptschfhr., Gestapo SS, Bydgoscss (Pol.)11.12.41-16.6.42	MURDER	U.S.
RAUSCHER	174975	M	Ger.		Uschfhr., SS Gestapo, Le Mans (Fr.) 29.12.43- 7.1.44	MURDER	FR.

RAU-RED

NAME	C.R.FILE NUMBER	SEX	NATIONALITY	DATE OF BIRTH	RANK	OCCUPATION	UNIT	PLACE AND DATE OF CRIME	REASON WANTED	WANTED BY
RAUSCHER	196002	M	Ger.		Sgt., Mot.Unit, Auray (Fr.)				WITNESS	FR.
RAUSCHER, Karl	250439	M	Ger.		Uschfhr., S.D., Toulouse (Fr.) 11.42-8.44				MISC.CRIMES	FR.
RAUSLOW	261135	M	Ger.		Member Staff of C.C. Ravensbrueck (Ger.)				SUSPECT	BEL.
RAUTENBERG	12470	M	Ger.		Sgt., Hafenueberwachungsstelle, Calais (Fr.) 4.9.44				TORTURE	FR.
RAUTENBERG	192821	M	Ger.		Sturmbannfhr. (Major), SS, C.C.Godesberg,Winzerstube,Buchenwald (Ger.) 42-45				TORTURE	U.S.
RAUTER	136608	M			97 SS-Gruppenfhr., SS. (Ger.) 42				MISC.CRIMES	U.S.
RAUTER	134896	M			Generalkommissar, Sipo. (Neth.) 43				MURDER	U.S.
RAUTER	252632	M			Employee, Sipo, Brussels (Bel.)				INTERR.	BEL.
RAUTER	252637	M			Civilian, Apeldoorn (Neth.) 2.10.44				MURDER	U.S.
RAUTER, Hans	723	M	Ger.		SS-Gruppenfhr., SS. (Neth.) 43					NETH.
RAUTFAB (or RAUTHASZ or RAUTFASZ or RAUTFAD)	121405	M	Ger.		Custom-official, Zollgrenzschutz, Semaphore de Gresch Maout, Pleubian (Fr.) 5.8.44				MURDER	FR.
RAUTHER, Wilhelm (or RATHER or RATHERT)	144380	M			97 Chief, Stalag II B, Civ., Hammerstein (Ger.)				MURDER	U.S.
RAUWENDA, Willem	302106	M	Ger.		Member, Sonderkommando Feldmeier, Apeldoorn, Arnheim, Wageningen (Neth.) 16.10.43-28.10.44				MURDER	NETH.
RAWOLLE, Fritz	255212	M		5. 6.06	Prt., Rottenfhr., Camp Barzungen, Nordhausen (Ger.)				MURDER	U.S.
RAY	256914		Ger.		Oschfhr., SS, Chief of Labour Asignment, C.C.Harzungen, Nordhausen (Ger.)				MURDER	U.S.
RAYDER (or NYDER)	156046	M	Ger.	00	Prt., 226.Landesschuetzen-Bn., Stalag XXI D - Arb.Kdo., Khundorf-Posen (Pol.) 12.5.42				MURDER	U.K.
RAYNA, Georgiewa	300100				Dentist at Munich, Altleimersck 8. Paris (Fr.) betw.41-8.44				PILLAGE	FR.
RAYNER	301598	M	Ger.		Gauleiter, C.C.Mauthausen (Aust.) 40-45				MURDER	BEL.
RAYPERT (see RAUPERT)	162781									
RAZARIENER	167137	M			Cmdt., Army, St.Julien-en-St.Albain (Fr.) 29.6.44				PILLAGE	FR.
RAZNY, Eduard	250438	M	Ger.		SS-Rottenfhr., S.D., Toulouse (Fr.) 11.42-8.44				MISC.CRIMES	FR.
REAY	188446	M	Ger.	09	Cpl., Army, Landesschuetzen-Bn.515, Stalag 538, Sosnowitz (Pol.) 43-45				TORTURE	U.K.
REBEL, Karl	167138	M	Ger.	27.10.92	Lt., Gendarmerie-Polizei, Wolfisheim,Hangenbieten (Fr.) 14.8.44				MURDER	FR.
REBENICH	724	M			Sgt., C.C. Caen (Fr.) 6.44				MURDER	FR.
REBER, Hans	305770	M	Ger.		Prt., Rjukan (Nor.) 14.12.43				MURDER	NOR.
REBER, Karl	260857	M	Ger.	01	Civilian, Farm Labourer, Michelfeld (Ger.) 25.4.44				MURDER	U.S.
REBESKY, Hubert	216899	M	Ger.		Secretary, Gestapo, Neuss (Ger.)				MURDER	U.S.
REBHAHN, Alfons	122685	M		25	Prt., Landesschuetzen-Bn. 1012. 31.8.44				MURDER	U.K.
REBHOLZ, Mathias	257471	M		20	SS-Mann, C.C. Muehldorf (Ger.)				MURDER	U.S.
REBL, Josef	187026	M	Ger.	97	SS-Osturmfhr., SS, C.C. Schwarzenfeld (Ger.) 39-45				TORTURE	U.S.
REBLE	257953	M			Capt., 150.Panzer-Bde., Meuse Bridge-Antwerp (Bel.) 12.44				MISC.CRIMES	U.S.
REBMANN	253195	M	Ger.		Cpl., Gendarmerie, Le Chablais (Fr.) 44				MISC.CRIMES	FR.
REBOHLE	180734	M	Ger.		SS-Sturmscharfhr., Chief-secretary, SS,S.D.,Gestapo, Sarrebruck (Fr.)				PILLAGE	FR.
REBS	167456	M	Ger.		Uschfhr., SS, C.C.Sachsenhausen (Ger.) 39-4.45				MURDER	POL.
REBSAMEN	167455	M	Ger.		Oberreg.Rat.,Abt.Wirtschaft, Amt des General-Gouverneurs, Radom (Pol.) 39-44				MISC.CRIMES	POL.
REBSTOCK, Hermann	173922	M	Ger.		W.O., Zollgrenzschutz, La Chaux, Neuve (Fr.) 17.3.44				MURDER	FR.
RECH	186186	M	Ger.		Civilian, Vergt de Biroa (Fr.) 5.44				PILLAGE	FR.
RECH (see RECK) Anton	256109									
RECHE, Gerhardt	12471	M	Ger.	2. 2.96	Prt., 111. or 110.Panz.Gren.Regt.,2.Coy., Albine (Fr.) 29.6.44				MURDER	FR.
RECH, Richard	195968	M			Mayor, Public Official, Ortsgruppenleiter, NSDAP, Breitenbach(Ger.)9.44				MURDER	U.S.
RECHENBERG	126498	M		15	SS-Uschfhr., SS Totenkopf-Standarte, C.C. Buchenwald (Ger.) 39-45				TORTURE	U.S.
RECHERT	136279	M			Prt., 11.Panz.Div., 2.Coy., 2 AA-A 7, Albine (Fr.) 12.3.44				MURDER	FR.
RECHSCHUTZ	258775	M	Ger.	98	S-Sgt., Darmstadt (Ger.)				INTERR.	U.S.
RECHSIEK, Erwin (or RECKSISK)	191573	M			269. Inf.Div., Finistere Bretagne (Fr.)				MURDER	FR.
RECHT	167485	M	Ger.	20	Sgt., SS-Div. "Das Reich", Oradour-Glane (Fr.) 10.6.44				MURDER	FR.
RECHT (or RETCH)	196001	M			Scharfhr., SS-Div. "Das Reich", Vergt de Biroa (Fr.) 21.5.44				MURDER	FR.
RECHTE (or RIETE)	39598	M			Capt., Feldpost-Nr.L.49458 L.G.P.A.Paris (Fr.) 8. or 9.6.44				MURDER	FR.
RECHTSSTEINER	193981	M	Ger.		Clerk, Gestapo, Brno (Czech.) 39-45				MURDER	CZECH.
RECK, Anton (or RECH)	256109	M	Ger.		Kapo, C.C. Flossenburg (Ger.)				MURDER	U.S.
RECKE (see RASKE)	125070									
RECKE	255778		Ger.		1.Regt., Turkestan, 2.Bn., Le Carrie (Fr.) 17.8.44				TORTURE	FR.
RECKER (or BECKER)	167139	M	Ger.		Sgt., Army, Unit of Transmission, Brioude (Fr.) 6.44				MURDER	FR.
RECKERT, Lorenz	135298	M	Ger.	00	Civ. Officer in charge of the Fire Service, Oekenheim (Ger.) 40-45				MISC.CRIMES	POL.
RECKEWEG	132106	M			Guard, SS, C.C. Gardelegen (Ger.)				MURDER	U.S.
RECKLEBEN	255641	M	Ger.		Civ., Chief of Culture, La Neuville (Fr.) 21.8.44				WITNESS	FR.
RECKLINGHAUSEN	163769	M	Ger.		W.O., Stalag VI B.				TORTURE	FR.
RECKMANN	194833	M	Ger.		Deputy Official, Admin.of occ.Territories, Gauleiter,NSDAP,Luxembourg (Lux.)				MURDER	LUX.
RECKMANN, Frederick	148540	M	Ger.	85 - 95	Civ.in charge of Kommando Camp, Halle (Ger.)				TORTURE	U.S.
RECKNAGEL	129149	M	Ger.	00	Sonderfhr., Air Force, Dulag-Luft, O.C.Ob erursel,Frankfurt-Main(Ger.)				TORTURE	U.K.
RECKSICK	144357		Ger.		Capt., OKW, Subsection VI P.W.Affairs.				WITNESS	U.S.
RECKSISK,Erwin (see RECHSISK)	191573									
RECKSISK, Heinz	192085	M	Ger.		Prt., S.D.Kommando, Landerneau (Fr.)				TORTURE	FR.
RECKZEH, Alfred	252600	M	Ger.	16. 2.02	Hilfsgendarm, Polizei, Tournai (Bel.)				BRUTALITY	BEL.
REDDERASEN, Heinrich	300915	M	Ger.		Member of Staff at C.C.Waldelust (Ger.) 8.44-4.45				MURDER	U.K.
REDDEWIER, Willi (or REDDEWIER or REDDEMEIER)	192539	M	Ger.		C.C.Flossenburg (Ger.) 44-45				SUSPECT	U.S.
REDDER, Egger	191717	M	Ger.		Chief-Official, Civil Administration (Fr.) 41-9.44				PILLAGE	BEL.
REDDERMEIER (see REDDEWIER)	192539									
REDDQUE, Frans	148661		Ger.		Watchman, Civ. Flottmann Factory, Herne (Ger.) 45				TORTURE	U.S.
REDEKE	167140				Sen.W.O., Army, Pont l'Abbe, Plobannalee (Fr.) 6.-8.44				MURDER	FR.
REDEL	252639	M		about 14	Agent, Gestapo, Rouen (Fr.) 43-44				TORTURE	FR.
REDEMUND	192084	M			Sen.W.O., Army, Pontivy (Fr.) 8.44				MURDER	FR.
REDHARD	726	M			Payer, C.C. Oswiecim (Pol.) 40				MURDER	POL.
REDIESS	137567	M			Member, SS, C.C.Weimar-Buchenwald (Ger.)				TORTURE	U.S.
REDIGER	728	M			Osturmbannfhr., SS, Deputy Cmdt., Stutthof (Ger.) 39-41				MURDER	POL.
REDIGER	136649	M			Capt., Schutzpolizei, 7.Coy. Arnheim (Neth.) 3.45				MURDER	NETH.
REDLI (or REDLICH)	729	M			Guard, Waffen-SS, C.C. Maidaneck (Pol.) 40-4.44				MURDER	POL., BEL.
REDLIN	199767				C.C. Struthof-Natzweil r (Fr.) 40-44				MURDER	FR.
REDLIN, Hugo	255215	M		11.11.13	Rottenfhr., Camp Ellrich, Nordhausen (Ger.)				MURDER	U.S.
REDLINGSHOFER, Hans	167528	M	Ger.		Sen.W.O., Feldgendarmerie, Haute Marne (Fr.) 43-44				MURDER	FR.
REDLINGSHOFER	1089		Ger.		Sen.W.O., Army, Feldgendarmerie, Langres (Fr.)				TORTURE	FR.
REDROCK (see RETSCHEK)	136282									
REDNER, Rudolf	167454	M	Ger.		Prt., SS, C.C.Sachsenhausen-Oranienburg (Ger.) 39-4.45				MURDER	POL.

NAME	C.R.FILE NUMBER	SEX	NATIO-NALITY	DATE OF BIRTH	RANK	OCCUPATION	UNIT	PLACE AND DATE OF CRIME	REASON WANTED	WANTED BY
REDSECK	188818	M	Ger.		Hauptsturmfhr., SS, SD, Lyon (Fr.)				MISC.CRIMES	FR.
REDSEK (see RETSCHEK)	136282									
REDSEK	125671	M	Ger.		Capt., Gestapo, Baccarat (Fr.) 8.-9.44				MURDER	FR.
REDWITZ	1736	M			Hauptsturmfhr., C.C., SS, Dachau (Ger.)				MURDER	U.K. U.S.BE. CZECH.YUGO.
REDWITZ	306446	M	Ger.		Lt., SS, C.C. Oranienburg (Ger.) 11.39 - 45				MURDER	CZECH.
REDZEK, Helmut	253289	M	Ger.		Capt., Det. Sicherheits Polizei, Raon L'Etape (Fr.) 4.9.44				MURDER	FR.
REESE	132107	M	Ger.		Untersturmfhr., SS, Gestapo, Crim.Assistent, Berlin (Ger.)				MISC.CRIMES	U.S.
REEGE	152335	M	Ger.		Dr., Stabsarzt, Army medical-corps, Ladenburg (Ger.) 3. - 9.43				BRUTALITY	U.K.
REED	67812	M	Ger.		Cmdt., Oflag VII B C.C. Eichstaedt (Ger.) 25.2.44				MURDER	U.K.
REEDER, Eggert	62203	M	Ger.		Generalleutnant, SS, Chief of military administration(Bel.)				MURDER	UNWCC BEL.
REEH, Hugo	195190	M	Ger.	11	Sgt., 515.Landesschuetzen-Bn. C.C. Sosnowitz (Pol.) 42-44				TORTURE	U.K.
REEMAKERS, Peter	12472	M	Ger.		Pvt., 110.or 111.Panz.-Gren.Rgt. 2.Coy. Albine (Fr.) 29.4.44				MURDER	FR.
REES	140879	M	Ger.	09	Dr.,Stabsarzt, Stalag, medical-corps, C.C. Waldenburg (Ger.) 3.-8.44				TORTURE	U.S. U.K.
REESE	122684	M	Ger.		Sgt., Army, 85.Inf.Div. Hasselfelde (Ger.) 18.4.45				MURDER	U.S.
REESE	132474	M	Ger.	11	Unterscharfhr., SS Kommando-Fhr. at C.C. Neuengamme (Ger.)				TORTURE	U.K.
REESE (see ROESE)	132551									
REESE (see NAVE or GREVE)	196246									
REESE, Heinrich	193020	M	Ger.	07	Guard, Reichsjustiz-Ministerium, Strafgefangenenlager,C.C. Finnmark (Nor.) 3.45				MURDER	NOR.
REETE (see RECHTE)	39598									
REETZ	136609	M	Ger.	95	Dr. Director Dept.of Trusteeship,Altreich, Berlin (Ger.) 42				MISC.CRIMES	U.S. POL.
REGELER (or ROEGLER, Hans)	251246	M	Ger.	16	Inspector, Interpreter, Gestapo, Alencon (Fr.) 40 - 44				INTERR.	FR.
REGELSBERGER, Josef	192538	M	Ger.	14. 3.99	Criminal-Assistent, Gestapo, Brno (Czech.) 39-45				SUSPECT	CZECH.
REGENHARDT	128940	M			Civilian, Foreman, C.C., Buchenwald (Ger.)				TORTURE	U.S.
REGENSBURGER, Max	255213	M		2. 6.05	Pvt., C.C. Harzungen-Nordhausen, Oranienburg (Ger.)				MURDER	U.S.
REGIN	190331	M			Crim.-Secretary, Police, Wiesbaden (Ger.) 43 - 45				MURDER	U.S.
REGNER, Andreas	254880	M	Ger.		Pvt., Pioneer-Bn. 46, 1.Coy. Budinci near Belgrade (Yugo.) 9.43				MISC.CRIMES	YUGO.
REGUTER, Horst	262194	M	Ger.	12. 2.20	Oberscharfhr.,Chief of the Platoon 3. 7.Coy.51.SS Armoured-Brig. Bucheres,Breviandes,St.Savine,La Riviere de Corps (Troyes)(Fr.) 8.44				BRUTALITY	FR.
REHBEIN, Gerhard	193980	M	Ger.	7. 7.12	Untersturmfhr., SS, C.C. Terezin (Czech.) 39-45				TORTURE	CZECH.
REHBERG	156043	M	Ger.		Lt., 608.mobile Bn. 3.Squn..Angers (Fr.) 8.44				MURDER	U.S.
REHBGLE, Fritz	141596	M	Ger.		Interpreter, Gestapo, Folkling (Fr.) 11.44				MURDER	FR.
REHBOCK, H.	167484	M	Ger.		Member, Einsatzstab Rosenberg, administrative staff (Fr.) 40-44				PILLAGE	FR.
REHDER - KNOSPEL	10326	M	Ger.		First, Staatsanwalt, Staatsanwaltschaft beim Landgericht,(Prag(Czech.) 39 - 45				MURDER	CZECH.
REHHORN	253314	M			Civilian, Duisburg (Ger.) 5.-14.3.45				MURDER	U.S.
REHM	194832	M	Ger.		Lt., Schupo, Luxembourg (Lux.)				MISC.CRIMES	LUX.
REHM	254424	M	Ger.		Sturmmann, SD, Gestapo, Toulouse (Fr.) 11.42 - 8.44				MISC.CRIMES	FR.
REHM	257565	M	Ger.		SD, Foix (Fr.) 11.42 - 10.44				MURDER	FR.
REHM, Eugen	129043	M	Ger.	04	Cpl., Feldgendarmerie, Feldpost-Nr. 31 562, Arlon (Bel.) 25.8.44				MURDER	BEL.
REHN	156047	M	Ger.	15	Untersturmfhr., SS, C.C. Sachsenhausen,Oranienburg(Ger.)				MURDER	U.K.
REHRENS (or BEHRENS)	260429	M	Ger.		Capt.,Cmdt., Schutzpolizei, 309 Btty. 221.SS-Div. Okolniki (Pol.)6.41				MURDER	POL.
REHRENS, H.F.	126253	M		02	C.C. Maschen (Ger.)				TORTURE	U.S.
REHRMANN	31422	M	Ger.		Capt., Army 67-2.Geb.Div.Nachr.Abt., Finnmark (Nor.) 44				MURDER	NOR.
REIBER, A.	300101	M	Ger.		Purchaser, Factory "de Amstel" Waalwijk,Heusden (Neth.) 5.43-10.44				PILLAGE	NETH.
REIBL	302107	M	Ger.		Dr., Verwalter, Textile Firm Spanjaard, Overijssel Province (Neth.)5.43				DEPORTATION	NETH.
REIBLE, Frans	301971	M	Ger.	28. 5.01	Dr., Member,Verwalter,Reichstag,NSDAP,NSV, Textilfabriken Enschede (Neth.) 41 - 45				DEPORTATION	NETH.
REIBRICH	126910	M	Ger.		Scharfhr., SS-Panz.-Div. "Das Reich" FPN 15807, Valence D'Agen (Fr.)44				MURDER	FR.
REICH	670190	M	Ger.		Pvt., SS - Div., St. Sulpiel Portmusson,Chateau-Gontier (Fr.) 8.44				MURDER	FR.
REICH	174976	M	Ger.	04	SS-Mann, Gestapo, SS, Le Mans (Fr.) 12.43 - 1.44				MURDER	FR.
REICH	193979	M	Ger.		Member, Police, Schwalheim (Ger.) 11.44				MURDER	U.S.
REICH	195189	M	Ger.		HR., secretary, Administration of Wehrmachts, Arnheim (Neth.) 1.-7.45				WITNESS	NETH.
REICH	255642	M			Sgt., C.C. Harzungen,Nordhausen (Ger.)				MURDER	U.S.
REICH	257473	M	Ger.		Kitchen - Harzungen, Nordhausen (Ger.)				MURDER	U.S.
REICH	260025	M	Ger.		Interpreter, Div.Oberland, Unit Sov.Ua.,Ger., Massif du Vercors, Isere - Dome (Fr.) 7.-8.44				SUSPECT	FR.
REICH	260037	M	Ger.		Guard, SS - Slave Labour Camp, Botn near Rognan (Nor.) 6.42 - 45				BRUTALITY	YUGO.
REICH, Adolf	193430	M			Rottenfhr., 4.SS-Totenkopfsturmbann,C.C. Dora Mittelbau,Nordhausen (Ger.) 43 - 45				MURDER	U.S.
REICH, Bernhard	132108	M			Kapo, C.C. Gardelegen (Ger.) 5. - 14.4.45				MURDER	U.S.
REICH, Eistor	67553	M	Ger.		Civilian, Graudenz (Pol.) 7.44				MURDER	U.K.
REICH, Oscar	189180	M			Agent, Gestapo C.C. Drancy (Fr.) 6.43				MURDER	FR.
REICH, Simon	260088	M	Ger.		Pvt., Gendarmerie, Wehrmachtskommandantur,Utrecht (Neth.) 1.45				MURDER	NETH.
REICHARDT, Heinz	255643	M	Ger.	23. 1.22	Rottenfhr., C.C. Harzungen,Nordhausen (Ger.)				MURDER	U.S.
REICHARDT, Paul	162703	M	Ger.		Obersturmfhr.,Waffen SS, Totenkopf-Standarte Com.Staff,C.C. Bad-Sulza (Ger.)				TORTURE	U.S.
REICHARDT, Wilhelm	251247	M	Ger.		Cpl., in Charge Mail KDO I,109 stalag XII A,Rheingoenheim (Ger.) 5.41				BRUTALITY	FR.
REICHARDT	12473	M			Sgt., SS-Div. "Der Fuehrer" 2.Coy. 10.6.44				MURDER	FR.
REICHAUSSEN	194646	M			Cmdt., Army, Belle Isle en Terre (Fr.) 44				MISC.CRIMES	FR.
REICHE	166663	M			Colonel, Army, Warschau (Pol.) 42				TORTURE	U.S.
REICHEL	258888	M			Member,(Sec.Chief) Aktions-Kommando of Custom-House,Lourdes(Fr.) 1.-8.44				MURDER	FR.
REICHEL, Robert	121389	M			Cpl., Army,2.Nachr.Bn., FP.12 356,Enghien (Bel.) 3.9.44				TORTURE	BEL.
REICHELT	193275	M			Oberscharfhr., SS-Rgt. "Das Reich" 2.Coy.,II Reconn.Bn St.Vith(Bel.)45				MURDER	U.S.
REICHELT	192724	M		07	Dr.Med.,Stabsarzt, Air-Force, C.C. Buchenwald (Ger.) 42-45				TORTURE	U.S.
REICHELT, Otto	192537	M		20. 6.12	Employee, Gestapo, Brno, (Czech.) 11.39 - 45				MISC.CRIMES	CZECH.
REICHENBACH	132398	M			Obersturmfhr., SS, C.C. Dora-Nordhausen (Ger.)				MURDER	U.S.
REICHENBACH	180732	M			Oberscharfhr., C.C. Mittelbau, Nordhausen (Ger.)				MURDER	U.S. BEL.
REICHENEICK	251874	M	Ger.		Sgt., Geh. Feldpolizei, Gand (Bel.) 43 - 44				TORTURE	BEL.

NAME	C.R.FILE NUMBER	SEX	NATIO-NALITY	DATE OF BIRTH	RANK	OCCUPATION	UNIT	PLACE AND DATE OF CRIME	REASON WANTED	WANTED BY
REICHERT	146179	M	Ger.		Pvt., Panz.Div."Das Reich", Tulle (Fr.) 44				MURDER	FR.
REICHERT	256909	M	Ger.		Magaziner, O.T., Muehldorf (Ger.)				WITNESS	U.S.
REICHERT	300852	M	Ger.		Pvt., 1.Aufkl.Abt. 3.Coy. 2.Col. XV. Div.Afrika-Corps, St.Leger (Arlon) 5.9.44				MISC.CRIMES	BEL.
REICHERT, Max	255654	M		4.11.99	Flyer, Camp Ellrich, Nordhausen (Ger.)				MURDER	U.S.
REICHERT, Otto or Johann	253519	M	Ger.	11	Cpl., on anti partisan duties, Polesine, Mesola, Ariano (It.) 12.44				INTERR.	U.K.
REICHERT, Tilde	262332	F			Office clerk, Member NSDAP, Kaufbeuren (Ger.) 29-45 L.O.D.N.A.C.D.				SUSPECT	U.S.
REICHERZ, Fritz	158297	M			Civ.Dr., Leader NSDAP, Speicher (Ger.) 6.44				TORTURE	U.S.
REICHL	306646	M			Cpl., 7.Coy. Sicherheits-Rgt. 200, Leboulin 26.6.44				MURDER	FR.
REICHL, Johann	144375	M	Ger.	31. 3.09	Sgt. (Wachtmeister), Chauffeur in Gendarmerie, Kaplitz (Czech.) 12.44				MURDER	U.S.
REICHLE, Hermann	113809	M	Ger.	17	SS.Osturmfhr., Grenoble (Fr.)				PILLAGE	FR.
REICHMANN	127118	M	Ger.		SS Uscharfhr., C.C. Neustadt nr.Coburg (Ger.)				TORTURE	FR.
REICHMANN	186159	M	Ger.		SS Guard, C.C. Ravensbrueck (Ger.)				MURDER	FR.
REICHMUT, Albert or TEICHMUT	261319	M	Ger.	21. 5.20	Cpl., 12.SS Art.Rgt. 3.Bn., Tourouvre (Fr.) 13.8.44				MURDER	FR.
REICHOLT	188360	M	Ger.		Oscharfhr., SS Div."Das Reich" 2.Reconnaiss.Bn. 2.Coy.,St.Vith (Bel.) 12.44				MURDER	U.S.
REICHTER, Johann	253528	M	Ger.	23	Cpl., Anti-partisan duties, Mesola, Ariano, Polesine (It.) 12.44				INTERR.	U.K.
REICHTERT	194645	M	Ger.		Interpreter, Feldgendarmerie, Gestapo, Vercoiran, Montelimar (Fr.) 9.3.44				MURDER	FR.
REICKEL, Robert	174979	M	Ger.		Cpl., Army, Petit Enghein (Bel.) 3.9.44				MURDER	BEL.
REIDEL, Hubert	261816	M	Ger.		Interpreter, Gestapo Amiens, Gentelles (Fr.) 6.-8.44				MURDER	FR.
REIDELBACH, Michael	135299	M	Ger.	05	Civ., C.C. Mechtildshausen (Ger.) 40-45				BRUTALITY	POL.
REIDMARKE see RADEMACHE	67579									
REIER	192104	M			Oscharfhr., 2.SS Panz.Gren.Rgt. 11.Coy., Ardennes (Bel.) 17.12.44				WITNESS	U.S.
REIF	161727	M			Sgt., Army, Prison, Leipzig. (Ger.)				SUSPECT	U.S.
REIF, Herbert	128941	M	Ger.	07	Lt.Col., Feldgendarmerie Abt. 521 3.Bn.				MURDER	U.S.
REIF, Josef	252593	M	Ger.	5. 7.94	Town mayor, Hora (Czech.) 39-45				PILLAGE	CZECH.
REIF, Otto	192536	M	Ger.		Prison warden, Gestapo, Brno (Czech.) 39-45				SUSPECT	CZECH.
REIFF, Heinrich	255652	M	Ger.		Pvt., C.C. Ellrich, Nordhausen (Ger.)				MURDER	U.S.
REIFFS see REISS	169452									
REIFGENS, Josef	256263	M			Flyer, C.C. Ellrich, Nordhausen (Ger.)				MURDER	U.S.
REIFGERSTE, Heinz	167141	M	Ger.		Lt., Army, 4.Coy., Parachute.7.Bn. 24.Rgt. Utersen, 429 425 E.Paris, Neuves Maisons, St Mard (Fr.) 25.6.44, 31.8.44, 4.9.44				MURDER	FR.
REIFLING	152931	M	Ger.		Foreman, Stalag IX C, C.C. Berga (Ger.)				MURDER	U.S.
REIFS	141323	M	Ger.		Sgt. Army, Zirkelschacht (Ger.) 44				MURDER	U.K.
REIG see RIEG	173952									
REIGEL, Georg	255653			29. 1.01	Pvt., C.C. Harzungen, Nordhausen (Ger.)				MURDER	U.S.
REIHER	255782	M			Staff surgeon, C.C. Buchenwald (Ger.)				MURDER	U.S.
REIHER, Herbert	255651	M			Capt.,Dr., C.C. Staff Physician, Ellrich, Nordhausen:(Ger.)				MURDER	U.S.
REIL	186635	M	Ger.		C.C. Gusen, Mauthausen (Aust.) 43-45				TORTURE	U.S.
REILE, Ernest	148543	M	Ger.	23.12.89	Carpenter, Civ., Hebsack Krs. Waiblingen (Ger.) 6.44				TORTURE	U.S.
REIM	261194	M	Ger.		Standartenfhr., Alleur nr.Liege (Bel.) 4.9.44				WITNESS	BEL.
REIMANN	126446	M	Ger.		N.C.O., C.C. Buch-Berlin (Ger.) 5.44				MURDER	U.S.
REIMANN	146720	M	Ger.		Sturmbannfhr., SS.Panz.Div. "Das Reich", South-west Fr., 44				MURDER	FR.
REIMANN, Egon	255650	M		16. 9.90	C.C. Ellrich, Nordhausen (Ger.)				MURDER	U.S.
REIMCHEN, Heinz alias Dickie Heinz	36635	M	Ger.		SS Mann, C.C. Oxerhof (Neth.) 5.-6.4.45				MURDER	NETH.
REIMECKE see REINECKE, Otto	10927									
REIMER	158228	M	Ger.		Major, Army, Dauville (Fr.) 25.7.44				MURDER	FR.
REIMER	193429	M			Osturmfhr., SS Fuehrungstab, C.C. Dora - Nordhausen (Ger.) 43-45				WITNESS	U.S.
REIMER	255645	M			Rottfhr., C.C. Osterhagen, Nordhausen (Ger.)				MURDER	U.S.
REIMER	901278	M	Ger.		SS Hptsturmfhr., Criminalrat, Leiter der Abt. V Verbrecherbekaempfung, S.D., Brussels (Bel.) 40- 9.44				MURDER	BEL.
REIMER, Gertrude	192559	F	Ger.	24. 9.18	Clerk, Gestapo, Brno (Czech.) 39-45				WITNESS	CZECH.
REIMER, Heinz	252624	M	Ger.		377. Jaeger.Rgt., F.P. 30905 B, Vinkt, Meigem (Bel.) 25.-31.5.40				MISC.CRIMES	BEL.
REIMERS	152943	M			SS Osturmfhr., C.C. Mauthausen (Aust.)				TORTURE	U.S.
REIMERS, Bruno	158226	M	Ger.		Officer, 269. D.I., Finistere (Fr.) 44				TORTURE	FR.
REIMERS, Guido or REINER	161720	M	Ger.	05	SS Osturmfhr., C.C. Buchenwald (Ger.) 42-44				WITNESS	U.S.
REIMERS, Werner	906510	M	Ger.	6. 4.20	Uscharfhr., SS, C.C. Buchenwald (Ger.) betw. 16.5.38 and 9.10.43				MURDER	BEL.
REIMOND, Adam	174046	M			Civ. Farmer, Eberbach (Ger.) 40-45				TORTURE	POL.
REIMOND	258600	M	Ger.		SS Rottfhr., SS slave labour camp, Osen (Nor.) 6.42-3.43				MISC.CRIMES	YUGO.
REIMOND, Adam	148551	M	Ger.	92	Bricklayer, Civ., Messbach (Ger.) 2.44-4.44				MISC.CRIMES	U.S.
REIN	110062	M	Ger.		SS.Hptsturmfhr., SS or Army, C.C.commander, Wanzleben (Ger.) 4.-5.45				MURDER	U.S.
REIN see RHEIN	170541									
REIN	192534	M	Ger.		Pvt., Army, Chatou (Fr.) 25.8.44				WITNESS	FR.
REIN	193428	M			Rottfhr., 4.SS Totenkopf-Stuba, C.C. Dora-Mittelbau-Nordhausen (Ger.) 43-45				MURDER	U.S.
REINART, Viktor	199178 A	M	Ger.		Civ., Farmer, Opmunden (Ger.)				TORTURE	U.S.
REINARTZ	253245	M	Ger.		Scharfhr., 95. SS police-Rgt., St. Germain, Chamayrat (Fr.)				PILLAGE	FR.
REINBERG	257872	M			Pvt., 150.Panz.Bde. Meuse-Bridge Antwerp (Bel.) 12.44				MISC.CRIMES	U.S.
REINBOLD, Erich	199023	M	Ger.	05	Oberinspektor, Feldstraflager Reichsjustizministerium, Waffen SS Finnmark (Nor.) 6.42-45				MISC.CRIMES	NOR. YUGO.
REINDT	193435	M			Uscharfhr., 4.SS Totenkopf-Stuba, C.C.Dora-Mittelbau-Nordhausen (Ger.) 43-45				MURDER	U.S.
REINECK, Willy	124694	M			N.C.O. Flakabteilung, Arsimont (Bel.) 7.42				TORTURE	BEL.
REINECKE	139276	M			Hptscharfhr., Waffen SS, C.C. Flossenburg (Ger.)				MURDER	U.S.
REINECKE	144358	M			Lt.Col., O.K.W. Subsection II PW Affairs				WITNESS	U.S.
REINECKE	253287	M	Ger.		Major, Verbindungsstab 998, Combovin (Fr.) 22.6.44				MURDER	FR.
REINECKE, August	306776	M			Mayor, Heiningen, Borssum (Ger.) 28.9.44				MURDER	U.S.
REINECKE, Karl	152091	M			Sgt., Police, City jail, Sov.Un.				MURDER	U.S.
REINECKE, Otto alias REIMECKE	10927	M	Ger.		Usturmbannfhr., Waffen SS, C.C. Dachau (Ger.) 39-44				TORTURE	CZECH.
REINELT	195911	M	Ger.		Cpl., Army, various towns (Fr.) 19.-24.8.44				WITNESS	FR.
REINEMANN	252633	M			Employee, SIPO, Abt. V D, Brussels (Bel.)				INTERR.	BEL.

NAME	C.R.FILE NUMBER	SEX	NATIONALITY	DATE OF BIRTH	RANK, OCCUPATION, UNIT, PLACE AND DATE OF CRIME	REASON WANTED	WANTED BY
REINEN, Fritz	255649	M			Oscharfhr., C.C. Dora-Nordhausen (Ger.)	MURDER	U.S.
REINER	260020	M	Ger.		Staff-Sgt.,SS (Stab) Slave Labour Camp,Botn near Rognan(Nor.) 8.42-5.45	MISC.CRIMES	YUGO.
REINER	261317	M	Ger.		Member, SS Totenkopf-Unit, Laterina (It.) 6.44	MURDER	U.S.,CZECH.
REINER	300894	M	Ger.		Commissioner, Zone of operations Adriatic Coast, Susak and Triest (Yugo..It.) 3.2.44	MURDER	YUGO.
REINER, August	260035	M	Ger.		Sturmfhr.,SS, Slave Labour Camp, Botn near Rognan (Nor.) 8.42 to 3.43 and 4.43-5.45	BRUTALITY	YUGO.
REINER, Guido see REIMERS	161720						
REINERBOTH	162695	M	Ger.		Pvt., SS,10 Pz.Div., 36 Pz.Rgt., Revin (Fr.) 6.44	MURDER	FR.
REINERS	129027	M			Uscharfhr.,SS Totenkopf,(Skull and Crossbonca Organization) C.C. Mauthausen (Aust.) 41-45	MURDER	U.S.
REINERS	137628	M	Ger.		Frontleader, C.C. Munster (Ger.)	TORTURE	U.K.
REINERS	25291	M	Ger.	18	Lt.,65 Div.H.Q., Ponzano-Magra (It.) 21.9.43	INTERR.	U.K.
REINERS	255780	M	Ger.		Gauleiter, NSDAP, Mauthausen (Aust.)	TORTURE	FR.
REINERT	193926	M	Ger.		Cpl., Army, La France sur Mer (Fr.)	MURDER	FR.
REINERT, Johann	193024	M	Ger.	8. 2.02	Sgt.,guard, Justizministerium,Feldstraflager,C.C.Finmark(Nor.)	MISC.CRIMES	NOR.,YUGO.
REINERTH, Hans	167489	M	Ger.		Dr.,chief, Einsatzstab Rosenberg,pre-history Section,Berlin(Ger.)40-44	PILLAGE	FR.
REINERTZ see REINITZ	734						
REINETTE	253294	M	Ger.		Lt.,10 Coy,3 Bn,SS-Pol.Rgt.Todt,Mt.Saxonnex (Fr.) 3.1.44	INTERR.	FR.
REINFELD, Herbert	255647	M		13. 5.09	Sgt., C.C. Ellrich-Nordhausen (Ger.)	MURDER	U.S.
REINGART, Victor	305489	M			Pvt.,Marine Inf. Partly composed of Waffen-SS,St.Anne-en-Tregastel, Trebeurden-Gross-er-Gollot (Fr.) 4.6.44-21.7.44	MISC.CRIMES	FR.
REINGRUBER	142023	M	Ger.	19	Uscharfhr.,SS, 12 SS-Pz.Div.(H.J.),Feldgendarmerie,Abbaye(Fr.)6.,7.44	TORTURE	CAN.
REINHALDT	193025	M	Ger.		Sgt.,SD, Schupo, Trondheim (Nor.) 41-45	MURDER	NOR.
REINHARD	147209	M			Lagerfuehrer, Boten-Camp, C.C. Rognan (Nor.) 43	MURDER	YUGO.
REINHARD	167464	M	Ger.		Regierungsrat,SS-Sturmbannfhr., Gestapo,SS,(Nor.) 4.40	TORTURE	NOR.
REINHARD	187553	M		15	Lt.,65 Inf.Div., Cisa (It.) 3.10.43	WITNESS	U.K.
REINHARD	193902	M	Ger.		Dmdt.,Army, Loire and Ampuis (Fr.) 28.-31.8.44	MURDER	FR.
REINHARD, Georges	156042	M	Ger.		Capt.,Feldkommandantur 754a Carcassonne,Boullens (Fr.) 19.8.44	MURDER	FR.
REINHARD, Hans	62204	M	Ger.		Gen.,Army,Inf.,Cmdr of Army Troops in the Neth.	MURDER	UNWCC.
REINHARD, Heinrich	191808	M	Ger.	95	Civilian, Seiwalbach (Ger.)	TORTURE	U.S.
REINHARDT	1460	M			Lt.,Inf.Rgt.578,5 Ccy	MISC.CRIMES	U.K.
REINHARDT	1737	M			Osturmfhr.,SS, SS-Bn, 37 Rgt.	MURDER	U.K.
REINHARDT	125761	M			SS-guard, 37 SS PGR "Goetz von Berlichingen	MURDER	U.S.
REINHARDT	129029	M	Ger.		5.Fallschirm-Rgt.,Quaregnon,Jemappes,Ghlin (Bel.) 2.-3.9.44	MURDER	BEL.
REINHARDT	152093	M			Dr., Legal Adviser, Army, 29 Pz.Gren.Div., H.Q.	WITNESS	U.S.
REINHARDT	173925	M	Ger.		Gen.,Fieldcmdt., Field-Cmdtr.518, Nantes,Saffre (Fr.) 40-44	MURDER	FR.
REINHARDT	252691	M	Ger.		Sgt.,Gestapo,336 Div.,Cdt.Bn, Cpl.-school, La Bresse (Fr.)9.-11.44	MURDER	FR.
REINHARDT	255214	M			Osturmfhr.,1 Bn,17 SS Pz.Gren.Div., Carentan (Fr.) 19.7.44	MURDER	U.S.
REINHARDT	260688	M	Ger.		Works-leader, Buchenwald (Ger.) 40-44	BRUTALITY	FR.
REINHARDT, Adolf alias NEGUS	186787	M	Ger.		Oberkapo, C.C. Neckarelz (Ger.) 10.44-2.45	TORTURE	U.S.
REINHARDT, Alvin	186794	M	Ger.	85	Miscellaneous, Riestedt (Ger.) 16.7.44	WITNESS	U.S.
REINHARDT, Curt	195910	M	Ger.		Asst.from Finance, Army, Fieldpost 03429, Selles-Cher (Fr.) 31.8.44	WITNESS	FR.
REINHARDT, Emil see SAHL	161655						
REINHARDT, Fritz	62205	M	Ger.		Public official, Berlin (Ger.and Fr.)	MISC.CRIMES	UNWCC.
REINHARDT, Georg	121210	M	Ger.		Fuehrungs-Offizier, Feldkommandantur 734, 19.8.44	MURDER	FR.
REINHARDT, Georg	199026	M	Ger.		Sgt.Army (Nor.) 45	MISC.CRIMES	NOR.
REINHARDT, Hans	257563	M	Ger.	1. 3.87	Col.Gen., State Service Army,Fuehrer-Reserve, 1.45	INTERR.	U.S.
REINHARDT, Helmut	156041	M	Ger.	10	Sturmbannfuehrer, SS,Gestapo H.Q. Oslo (Nor.) 1.43	MURDER	U.K.
REINHARDT, Karl	256498	M	Ger.	21. 1.11	Employee, C.C. Nordhausen (Ger.)	MURDER	U.S.
REINHARDT, Kurt	228482	M	Ger.		Capt., SD, Falstad (Nor.) 41-44	TORTURE	NOR.
REINHARDT, Nicolaus	300729	M	Ger.		Uscharfhr.,Blockfhr., Area of Sachsenhausen (Ger.) 1.40-4.45	MURDER	U.K.
REINHARDT, Otto	135300	M	Ger.		Fuehrer, SA, SS, C.C. Erfurt (Ger.) 44	TORTURE	U.S.
REINHARDT, Otto	172461	M	Ger.		Policeman, Police, Vienenburg (Ger.) 5.44	MURDER	U.S.
REINHARDT, Paul	132825	M	Ger.		Pvt., Army, Weissenborn (Ger.) 1.-2.44	WITNESS	U.K.
REINHARDT, Valentine	152342	M			Civilian,Political Prisoner (Ger.) 12.-14.4.45	MURDER	U.S.
REINHART, Albert	259620	M	Ger.		Groupleader, NSDAP, Riedsels (Bas-Rhin-Fr.) 1.and2.45	INTERR.	FR.
REINHART, Fritz	193903	M	Ger.		Chef expeditionnaire a l'usine Glanzstoff Elsterberg(Ger.) 12.40	TORTURE	FR.
REINHOLD	121211	M	Ger.		N.C.O.,Interpreter,Georgian Legion,Army, Castres (Fr.) 6.44	TORTURE	FR.
REINICKE	192827	M	Ger.		Oscharfhr.,SS, C.C. Buchenwald (Ger.)	TORTURE	U.S.
REINIGER, Elisabeth	186789	F	Ger.	91	Member, NSDAP,District office,Racial Affairs Subsection, Marianske,Lazne (Czech.) 39-45	MISC.CRIMES	CZECH.
REININGHAUS, Walter	67024	M	Ger.		Osturmfhr.,SS-Div.,St.Sulpice,Fortmusson,Chateau,Gontier(Fr.)2.-6.8.44	TORTURE	FR.
REINISCH, Peter	733	M	Ger.		Oscharfhr., SS Pol.Rgt.Todt, Payzac (Fr.) 16.2.44	MURDER	FR.
REINITZ or REIMERTZ	734	M	Ger.	10	SS-Oberwachtmstr.,Gestapo official, Bauleiter,C.C.Grini(Nor.) 42	TORTURE	NOR.
REINKE	109693	M	Ger.		Pvt.,guard, 4-717 Ld.Schz.Bn A-K 313,W.C.313 Stalag 20 B Osterwick (Ger.) 20.1.45	TORTURE	U.K.
REINKE	253313	M	Ger.	11	Capt., Schutzpol., Folno, Canavese (It.) 11.43	INTERR.	U.K.
REINKE, Alwin Otto Christian	251850	M	Ger.	28.12.99	City-employee, Ascheberg (Ger.) 21.5.44	MURDER	U.S.
REINKENSMEIER, Friedrich	152092	M	Ger.	20. 3.07	Scharfhr.,SA,Labour Camp guard, Heimathof (Ger.) 41-42	TORTURE	U.S.
REINMANN, Paul	255648	M			Pvt., C.C. Ellrich-Nordhausen (Ger.)	MURDER	U.S.
REINMILLER, Heinrich	306170	M	Ger.		Local-chief, Labor front, Bochum (Ger.) 24.3.45	MURDER	U.K.,U.S.
REINHOLD, Karl	29715	M	Ger.		Dr.,Amtsgerichtsdir., Ministry of Justice,Prague (Czech.) 40	TORTURE	CZECH.
REINRICH	124995	M	Ger.	03	Interpreter, officer, Gestapo, SD of Bordeaux, Poitiers (Fr.)24.8.44	MURDER	FR.
REINSCHILT see RUNSCHILL	195894						
REINSCHMIDT, Otto	255669	M		24. 6.04	Uscharfhr., C.C. Harzungen-Nordhausen (Ger.)	MURDER	U.S.
REINSCHMIDT, Otto	256696	M	Ger.	19. 9.08	Sgt.,SS Medical Attendant Harzungen-Nordhausen (Ger.)	MURDER	U.S.
REINTHALER, Franz	252585	M		7. 7.16	Hptsturmfhr.,SS Police, Lidice (Czech.) 10.6.42	MISC.CRIMES	CZECH.
REINTHLER	183648	M	Ger.		Lt.,20 Pol.Rgt.,2 Bn, 2 Coy, Prague (Czech.) 7.-8.42	MURDER	CZECH.
REINWALD	735	M	Ger.		Wachtmstr., Police, C.C. Falstad (Nor.) 41-42	TORTURE	NOR.

REI-REM

NAME	C.R.FILE NUMBER	SEX	NATIO-NALITY	DATE OF BIRTH	RANK OCCUPATION UNIT PLACE AND DATE OF CRIME	REASON WANTED	WANTED BY
REINZUCH	67017	M	Ger.		SS-Mann,SS Div.,St.Sulpice-Chateau Gontier Fortmusson (Fr.) 2.8. and 6.8.44	MURDER	FR.
REIP (or RIP)	260687	M	Ger.		Capt.,Cdt.Stalag 125,Stryj (Pol.) 7.-9.42	MURDER	FR.
REIPS,Willi	251248	M	Ger.		Pvt.,11 Pz.Div.,Lautrec (Fr.) 5.8.44	INTERR.	FR.
REIS	1461	M			Capt.,4 Paratrooper,Art.Rgt.	MISC.CRIMES	U.K.
REIS	255038	M			Sonderfhr.,Interpreter,Gestapo,SS,Belgrad (Yugo.) 16.2.44	TORTURE	YUGO.
REIS,Richard	173926	M		17. 9.02	Opl.,Prison Vannes (Fr.) 42-44	TORTURE	FR.
REISCH	300853	M	Ger.		Pvt.,1 Aufkl.Abt.3 Coy 2 Col.IV Div.of the Afrika Corps,Saint Leger (Bel.) 5.9.44	MISC.CRIMES	BEL.
REISCHAUER (alias HUPFAUER,R.)	165152	M	Ger.		Civilian, (Ger.) 43	MURDER	U.S.
REISEBURG,Walter	260823	M	Ger.	06	SS-Osturmfhr.,SS,Stapelburg (Ger.) 16.8.45	MURDER	U.S.
REISEN	189179	M			Oberschutzmeister,Goets v.Berlichingen Pz.Rgt.,Mussidan (Fr.) 13.6.44	PILLAGE	FR.
REISENER	736	M			Commandant,Army,Rodes (Fr.) 8.44	MURDER	FR.
REISENGER	253521	M	Ger.		Col.,347 Rgt. 392 Blue-Div.,Lokve (Yugo.) 4.4.45	INTERR.	YUGO.
REISER	123647		Ger.			MURDER	FR.
REISER	136280	M	Ger.		Lt.,Army,74 Rgt.de Securite motorise,Clavieres,St.Floret (Fr.) 10.-11.6.44	MISC.CRIMES	FR.
REISER	189178	M	Ger.		Lt.,Army,Commander of Detachment at Issoire,St.Floret (Fr.) 30.6.44	MISC.CRIMES	FR.
REISER	196853	M	Ger.		74 Police Rgt.mot.,Clavieres (Fr.) 11.6.44	MURDER	FR.
REISER	253246	M	Ger.		Capt.,Gestapo,Paris (Fr.) 41-44	INTERR.	FR.
REISER,Heinrich	257325	M	Ger.	00	Crim.-Rat,Gestapo,Tabor (Czech.) 17.3.39-10.40	MISC.CRIMES	CZECH.
REISIGE	195909	M	Ger.		Sonderfhr.,Nach.Bn.,C.C.Compiegne Royallieu (Fr.) 41-44	MURDER	FR.
REISING	21457	M			Capt.,Army,Commanding officer,	MISC.CRIMES	U.K.
REISING	141904	M	Ger.	92	196 Sicherungs Rgt. 9 Coy,Rom (Fr.) 7.7.45	MURDER	U.K.
REISINGER	193027	M			Capt.,3 Fahrrad Coy,C.C.Bones (Ger.)	MISC.CRIMES	NOR.
REISINGER	253522	M	Ger.		Col.,392 Inf.Blue-Div.,Lika (Yugo.) 44.-45	INTERR.	YUGO.
REISINGER,Leopold	193978	M			Crim.Commissar,Gestapo,Brno (Czech.)	MURDER	CZECH.
REISINGER,Rudolf	256499	M		2. 4.02	Czech.-Police-chief,Narava-Ostrava (Cze.n.) 29.8.47	BRUTALITY	U.S.
REISKE,Hans	194644	M			Adj.-chief,Parachute-Unit, St.Segal (Fr.) 22.7.44	TORTURE	FR.
REISKY	300966	M			SS-Usturmfhr.,official of SD Leitabschnitt,Prague,Oswiecim-Birkenau (Czech.Pol.) 39-45	MURDER	CZECH.
REISMANN	174761	M			Lt.,POW Working Bn.184,Kroken (Nor.)	MURDER	NOR.
REISMUELLER	252641	M			Oschfhr.,Gestapo,Limoges (Fr.)	INTERR.	FR.
REISMUELLER,Josef	305774	M			Uschfhr.,Sipo Aussendienststelle,Drammen (Nor.) 18.10.44-45	MURDER	NOR.
REISNER	182567	M			SS-Osturmfhr.,C.C.Mauthausen (Aust.) 1.45	MURDER	U.S.
REISNER,Michael	152095	M	Ger.		Ldsch.Coy 864,Emerding (Aust.) 15.4.44	MURDER	FR.
REISS (or REIFFS)	169452	M	Ger.	90	Sgt.,Army,400 Bn.Ldsch.,Stalag IV D,Eisleben (Ger.) 19.6.44	MURDER	U.K.
REISS,Albert	12474	M			Pvt.,Army,110 or 111 Pz.Gren.Rgt.2 Coy,Albine (Fr.) 26.9.44	MURDER	FR.
REISS,Fritz	195908	M			Lt.,Kommandantur,Tregastel,Trebeurden (Fr.)	TORTURE	FR.
REISSENWAHER,Herbert	167461	M			Pvt.,9 Ers.Rgt.Gren. 1 Coy,Magny d'Avignon (Fr.) 18.9.44	MURDER	FR.
REISSER	195188	M			Major,Army,	WITNESS	U.K.
REISSER	250436	M			Sturmmann,SD,Gestapo,Toulouse (Fr.) 11.42-8.44	MISC.CRIMES	FR.
REISSIG	161731	M		80	SS-Uschfhr.,SS,C.C.Buchenwald (Ger.) 42-45	WITNESS	U.S.
REISSMUELLER,Otto	256697	M	Ger.		Uschfhr.,SD,Drammen (Nor.)	MURDER	NOR.
REISSNER,Michael	306128	M			Guard at Kdo.C 1089-L belonging in 1943 and 1944 to Ldsch.Bn.4-864 at Ried,Canton inn upper Danube,Mattighofen,Emerding,Feldkirchen (Aust.) 15.4.45	MURDER	FR.
REISTER	255661	M			SS-Sturmmann,C.C.Bodungen,Nordhausen (Ger.)	MURDER	U.S.
REIT	260692	M			Capt.,157 bavarian Res.Div.,Massif du Vercors,Isere et Drome (Fr.) 20.7.-5.8.44	MISC.CRIMES	FR.
REIT,Erna	175874	F	Ger.		Clerk,SD official,Berlin (Ger.)	SUSPECT	U.S.
REITAU	183650	M			Col.,Military Court,Berlin,Torgau (Ger.)	MURDER	FR.
REITENER	129023	M	Ger.		Officer,Ortsgruppenleiter,SS,Hitler Jugend,Herschbach b.Selters (Ger.) 17.10.44	TORTURE	BEL.
REITER	122688	M			C.C.Buchenwald (Ger.)	MURDER	U.S.
REITER	196852	M	Ger.		Member,Gestapo,Rumanian Commando,Vichy (Fr.) 43-44	MURDER	FR.
REITER	252625	M	Ger.		Capt.,1 Inf.Bn.377 Jg.Rgt.,Vinkt and Meigem (Bel.) 25.-31.5.40	MISC.CRIMES	BEL.
REITER	255779	M	Ger.		Legal Advisor,Dr.,C.C.Mauthausen (Aust.)	MISC.CRIMES	FR.
REITER,Bruno	250435	M	Ger.		SS-Uschfhr.,SD,Gestapo,Toulouse (Fr.) 11.42-8.44	MISC.CRIMES	FR.
REITER,Marija	253526	F	Ger.		Civ.Interpreter,Kreiskommandantur,Kragujevac (Yugo.) 21.10.41	MURDER	YUGO.
REITH,Franjo	252642	M	Ger.		Col.,Chief of the Serbian-Police, Banat (Yugo.) 41-45	MISC.CRIMES	YUGO.
REJTHAR,Josef	258106	M		18. 5.06	Informer,teacher,Gestapo,Civilian,Prague (Czech.) 39-45	MURDER	CZECH.
REITHELE	134903	M		07	Oschfhr.,SS,	MURDER	U.S.
REITMEYER	167482	M	Ger.		Kreiskommandant,Kreiskommandantur of Arras,Viache St.Vaast (Fr.)24.8.44	MURDER	FR.
REITSCHEL,Ella	152332	F	Ger.		SS-Guard,Prison Camp Valary (Czech.) 41-45	MURDER	U.S.
REITZ	132112	M	Ger.		Crim.-Insp.,Gestapo,SD,Berlin (Ger.)	MISC.CRIMES	U.S.
REITZ	190269	M	Ger.		Capt.,Kreiskommandantur,Kratjevo (Yugo.) 43	MURDER	YUGO.
REITZ	193404	M			SS-Sturmmann,Leipzig-Theckla (Ger.)	MURDER	POL.
REITZ,Erich	261817	M	Ger.		Pvt.,F.P.Nr.47517,L.G.R.A. Paris,Nieppe (Fr.) 3.9.44	MURDER	FR.
REITZAM	253206	M	Ger.		Staff Sgt.,2 Bn.738 Rgt.118 Alpenjg.Div.,Jajce (Yugo.) 42,5.and 6.43	MURDER	YUGO.
REITZIG	190301	M			Member,C.C.official,Banjica (Yugo.) 41	MURDER	YUGO.
REKOPP	255655	M			Camp Osterhagen,Nordhausen (Ger.)	MURDER	U.S.
RELBEIN	136281	M			Pvt.,11 Pz.Div.2 Coy 2 AA-A 7,Albine (Fr.) 12.3.44	PILLAGE	FR.
RELLER	257564	M	Ger.		Beamter,Feldwirtschaftskdo.9,Sochaux (Fr.) 9.44-11.44	PILLAGE	FR.
RELS	190302	M			Officer,Org.Todt,Zagubica,Posavirac (Serbia) 41,42,45	MURDER	YUGO.
REMBACHER	253308	M	Ger.		Custom-official,Custom-office,100 Rgt.,Feissons sur Isere (Fr.)5.8.44	MURDER	FR.
REMELE,Josef (see REMMELE)	738						
REMMELE	190325	M			SS-Hptschfhr.,Roll-Call leader,C.C.Dachau (Ger.)	MURDER	U.S.
REMER	261818	M	Ger.		Member,Gestapo,Caen Departement Calvados (Fr.) 40-44	MURDER	FR.
REMERLE (see REMMELE,Josef)	738						
REMES	255043	M	Ger.		Camp-leader,factory of Glass-Ruhr,Karnapp-Essen (Ger.) 44	BRUTALITY	BEL.
REWETZ	737	M	Ger.		Oschfhr.,C.C.Dachau (Ger.) 40-43	MURDER	FR.
REMKE (or REMPKE,Wilhelm)	135555	M	Ger.	10	Civilian,foreman,C.C.Jaworzno (Pol.) 25.2.43	MURDER	U.K.

REM -RES

NAME	C.R.FILE NUMBER	SEX	NATIO- NALITY	DATE OF BIRTH	RANK OCCUPATION UNIT PLACE AND DATE OF CRIME	REASON WANTED	WANTED BY
REMLINGER	192723	M	Ger.		SS Guard duty,C.C.,Buchenwald,Braunsdorf,Flossenburg,Laura (Ger.) 42-45	TORTURE	U.S.
REMM	165964	M	Ger.		Officer,Feldgendarmerie,Charleroi (Bel.) 44	TORTURE	BEL.
REMME, Liesel	189306	F	Ger.	95	Civilian,Eilenstedt-Halle (Ger.) 41-45	MURDER	POL.
REMMELE, Josef (or REMERLE or REMELE)	738	M	Ger.	10	Hptschfhr.,SS,C.C.,Dachau (Ger.) 40-43	MURDER	U.S.,FR.,U.K.
REMMERT, Albert	167465	M	Ger.	15. 2.22	Ordonnans officer,III.F.J. Lehr Rgt.,Goegnies Chausse (Bel.) 9.9.44	MURDER	BEL.
REMMLER	257566	M	Ger.		Krim.Sekr.,State service Police,Ingersheim (Fr.) 9.1.44	MISC.CRIMES	FR.
REMP	262080	M	Ger.		Guard,Former SS,C.C.,Ueberlingen,Aufkirch (Ger.)	BRUTALITY	FR.
REMPE	21482	M	Ger.		Agent,Gestapo,Vaucrjno (Sov.Un.) 2.43	MURDER	U.K.
REMPEL, Hans	255660	M			C.C. Ellrich,Nordhausen (Ger.)	MURDER	U.S.
REMPKE (see REMKE) Wilhelm	135555						
REMPL	189305	M	Ger.		Member,Gestapo,C.C.,Dachau (Ger.) 40-45	MURDER	BEL.
RENAR, Johann	190268	M	Ger.		Member of staff,C.C.,Banjica (Yugo.) 41-45	MURDER	YUGO.
RENAT	251855	M	Ger.		Lt.,Coy.leader,4. Paratrooper - Rgt.,7.Coy.,2.Bn.,"Hermann Goering" Div.,Helchteren (Bel.) 5.-11. 9.44	INTERR.	BEL.
RENATH, Hans	260024	M	Ger.		Hauptwachtmeister,SS,Strafgefangenenlager(Nord-Nor.) 6.42-45	MURDER	YUGO.
RENDAT, Otto	193029	M	Ger.	05	Sgt. guard,Justizmin.,Feldstraflager,C.C.,Finmark (Nor.) 6.42-45	MISC.CRIMES	NOR.,YUGO.
RENDE	192826	M	Ger.		Uschfhr.,SS,C.C.,Buchenwald (Ger.) 42-45	MURDER	U.S.
RENDELN	121212	M			Lt.Col.,Army,Perigueux (Fr.) 44	MURDER	FR.
RENDOLF	121358	M	Jer.		Director de la Direction Politique,C.C.,Ravensbrueck (Ger.)	TORTURE	FR.,BEL.
RENDULIC, Lothar	739	M	Ger.	87	General Oberst,20.Army,(Croat.) 29. 5.44	MURDER	NOR.,YUGO.,U.S.
RENEFAHRT, Heinz	62206	M	Ger.		Regional official,public official,German racialism,regional official	MISC.CRIMES	U.N.W.C.C.
RENEKE, Gustav	195187	M	Ger.	05	Pvt.,Feldstraflager 398,P.O.W. Stalag 8,Krapitt (Ger.) 19.11.42	MURDER	U.K.
RENKE, Heinz	192532	M	Ger.		Pvt.,Flak Ers.Abt.51,Chaton,Seine and Oise (Fr.) 25.8.44	WITNESS	FR.
RENKEL, Walter	152353	M	Ger.		Wiewiocki,Chelmo (Pol.) 10.39	MURDER	U.K.
RENKEN	191810	M	Ger.		Douanier,Cousises (Fr.) 18.6.44	MURDER	FR.
RENNEN	300734	M	Ger.		Former chief,Sicherheitsdienst,Quderkerkaan de Ijsel,Gouda,Utrecht (Neth.) 18.or 19.10.44	MISC.CRIMES	NETH.
RENNER	132336	M			Uschfhr.,SS,C.C.,Dora,Nordhausen (Ger.)	MURDER	U.S.
RENNER	191394	M	Ger.		Cpl.,Panz.Div. "Das Reich",Oradour-Glane (Fr.) 10.6.44	MURDER	FR.
RENNER	191815	M	Ger.		Einsatzleiter,Org.Todt,Bjornelva,Krokel va Lonsdal,(Nor.)	WITNESS	NOR.
RENNER	192144	M	Ger.		Sgt.,Kreiskommandantur Malines,Feldgendarmerie,Feldkommandantur 520 Malines (Bel.)	TORTURE	BEL.
RENNER	253307	M	Ger.		Cpl.,SS Div. "Das Reich",3.Coy.,Saint-Junien (Fr.) 10.6.44	MURDER	FR.
RENNER	901108	M	Ger.		Crim.Asst.,served with the R.S.D.,Abt.IV 2,Copenhagen (Den.) 8.45	INTERR.	DEN.
RENNER, Ernst	148560	M	Ger.		Member,Waffen SS,Leibstandarte Adolf Hitler,Malmedy (Bel.) 44	MURDER	U.S.
RENNER, Fritz	252597	M	Ger.	16	523.Inf.Div.,R-A.A.,Wervick (Bel.) 4.9.44	WITNESS	BEL.
RENNER, Grete	192591	F	Ger.		Clerk,Gestapo,Brno (Czech.) 39-45	WITNESS	CZECH.
RENNER, Johann	196851	M	Ger.		Sturmfhr.,SS,C.C.,Auschwitz (Pol.) 40	MURDER	FR.
RENNER, Johann	251235	M	Ger.		SS-Mann,C.C.,Auschwitz,Birkenau (Pol.) 12.42	MURDER	YUGO.
RENNERT	152354	M	Ger.		Cpl.,SS Div. "Das Reich",Div."Fuehrer",Oradour sur Glane (Fr.) 10.6.44	MURDER	FR.
RENNHOFFER	67020	M	Ger.		Uschfhr.,SS,17.Pz.Gren.Div."Goetz v.Berlichingen" Sturmgesch.Abt.17 Segre Renaze (Fr.) 30.7.44-6.8.44	MURDER	FR.
RENNING, Bartolomaeus	901645	M	Ger.		Oberverwalter,Ebrach near Amberg (Ger.) 45	MURDER	CZECH.
RENNINGER, Anton	1462	M			Officer,SS,Bad Kissingen (Ger.)	MISC.CRIMES	U.K.
RENNO	120530	M		03	Doctor,officer,SS,C.C.,Auschwitz (Pol.)	MURDER	FR.
RENNO, Georg	134921	M	Ger.	07	Civilian,C.C.,Hartheim (Aust.) 40-44	MURDER	U.S.
RENOLD	741	M	Ger.		Pvt.,Army,Foucarville (Fr.) 5.-6.44	MURDER	FR.
RENOULD	31423	M	Ger.		Col.,Army,Finmark (Nor.) 44	MURDER	NOR.
RENSING	173929	M	Ger.		Pvt.,6.H.Q. Coy.,Landesschuetzen Bn.400,Hettstedt,Gros Orner (Ger.)	WITNESS	U.S.
RENSINGHOFF, Walter	113996	M	Ger.		Pvt.,Nachr.Rgt.506,Abwehr official,Bordeaux (Fr.) 44?	MISC.CRIMES	U.S.
RENTENAUER	156057	M	Ger.		Interpreter,Sarlat,Civilian,Le Roc (Fr.) 28.6.44	MURDER	FR.
RENTSCH	252606	M			Osturmbannfhr.,SS,C.C.,Lahde-Weser (Ger.)	MISC.CRIMES	BEL.
RENTSCHLER, Alfred	167529	M	Ger.	20	Rottfhr.,SS,C.C.,Struthof,Natzweiler (Fr.) 43-44	MURDER	FR.
RENZ	31424	M			Hptsturmfhr.,6-6 SS Geb.Div.Nord,SS Schtz.Bn.,Finmark (Nor.) 44	MURDER	NOR.
RENZ	193292	M	Ger.	10	Lt.,Nebeltruppenschule,Celle (Ger.) 3-9.4.45	MURDER	U.K.
RENZ, Hans	262083	M		2.10.00	Actually believed to be police Lt.,Mannheim,Ehingen (Ger.)	MURDER	FR.
REOFOLD	144386	M	Ger.		C.C.,Mühldorf (Ger.) 2.5.45	MURDER	U.S.
REPITZ, Josef	193422	M	Ger.		Pvt.,4.SS Totenkopfsturmbann,C.C. Dora Mittelbau,Nordhausen(Ger.)43-45	TORTURE	U.S.
REPKE	152349	M	Ger.	00	SA,Horse driver,Civilian,Emsland (Ger.) 44	MURDER	U.S.
REPKE	169045	M	Ger.		Adjutant,chief,Coiffy-Flagey (Fr.) 43-44	MURDER	FR.
REPKE, Walter	1084	M			Adjutant,chief,Feldgendarmerie,Langres,Rivières les Fosses (Fr.)	MURDER	FR.
REPP	136946	M	Ger.		Gendarmerie chief,Police,Mellerichstadt (Ger.) 44	MURDER	U.S.
REPP, Karl-Heinz or Georg	259621	M	Ger.		Oschfhr.,Gestapo,Area Angers,Maine,Loire (Fr.) 42-44	MISC.CRIMES	FR.
REPPER (see RAPPERT)	168100						
REPRICH, E.O.	167497	M	Ger.		Treuhaender,Civilian,GrandCafe Restaurant,Poznan (Pol.) 9.39-44	MISC.CRIMES	POL.
REPRO	301973	M	Ger.		Member,SS,SD,Leeuwarden (Neth.) 10.44	TORTURE	NETH.
REQUARD	190267	M	Ger.		Standartenfhr.,SD,Civil Servant,Foreign office,Ojubljana,Laibach Sued Steiermark (Yugo.) 4.41-5.43,44	MURDER	YUGO.
RESAG	255346	M	Ger.	20	Lt.,Pioneer group,Heusden (Neth.) 11.44	PILLAGE	NETH.
RESATZ, Josef	257567	M	Ger.		Krim.Oberasst.,Hptschfhr.,Feldpolizei,Foix (Fr.) 9.42-8.44	BRUTALITY	FR.
RESCH	128942	M			Pz.Gren.Ausb.Bn.,Gneixendorf near Krems (Aust.) 41-42	MURDER	U.S.
RESCH	300418	M			Hptsturmfhr.,SS,2.SS Tank Div.,H.Q.,La Roche,Wibrin (Bel.)10.-12.1.45	MISC.CRIMES	BEL.
RESCHE	255772	M			C.C.,Buchenwald (Ger.)	MURDER	U.S.
RESCHKE	12391	M	Ger.		Cpl.,148.Inf.Rgt.,2.Bn.,Amiens (Fr.) 26.8.44	MURDER	U.K.
RESCHKE	192825	M	Ger.		Kapo,C.C.,Gustloff side Camp,Buchenwald (Ger.) 42-45	TORTURE	U.S.
RESCHL, Leo	254879	M	Ger.	22. 6.04	Clerk,Civ.Firm,Krumlov (Czech.) 39-42	BRUTALITY	CZECH.
RESI	305940	M	Ger.		Staf
fhr.,SS,Lagerfhr.,C.C.,Neugraben,Tiefstak (Ger.) 44-5.2.45	BRUTALITY	CZECH.
RESKI	193905	M	Ger.		Lt.,26.Pioneer Coy.,Gazères (Fr.)	MURDER	FR.
RESS, Otto	259798	M	Ger.		Pay-master,Army,Kommando "Raumbot",Breda,Noord-Brabant (Neth.) 9.44	INTERR.	NETH.
RESSE, Johann	300917	M	Ger.		Member of staff at C.C.,Neuengamme (Ger.) 6.40-5.45	MURDER	U.K.

NAME	C.R.FILE NUMBER	SEX	NATIO-NALITY	DATE OF BIRTH	RANK, OCCUPATION, UNIT, PLACE AND DATE OF CRIME	REASON WANTED	WANTED BY
RESSEGUIER	742	M	Ger.		Capt., 2.Bn., 98.Rgt., Mont.Troops, 22.8.-31.8.44	MURDER	FR.
RESSEL, Gustav	144385	M			Capt., Police, Halchter (Ger.) 28.9.44	MURDER	FR.
RESSMANN, Erich	196598	M	Ger.	16.11.12	Agent, Gestapo, Prostejov (Czech.) 39-45	MURDER	CZECH.
RESSNER	305733	M	Ger.		W.O., Caucasian Rgt. of Volunteers, Fieldpost-No.12-700, Camboules, Tarn (Fr.) 28.7.44	MURDER	FR.
RESTLE	192041	M	Ger.		Pvt., Eis.Art.Bn.717,Fieldpost-No.22380, St.Andries Varsenare Les Bruges (Bel.) 4.9.44	MURDER	BEL.
RETCH (or RETSCH)	126913	M	Ger.		Schfhr., SS Pz.Div."Das Reich", Valeros D'Agen (Fr.) 44	MURDER	FR.
RETCH (see RECHT)	196001						
RETCHECK	12476	M	Ger.		Hptsturmfhr., Waffen-SS, Lussac, Chanoux Le Vigeant (Fr.) 3.-5.8.44	MURDER	FR.
RETSCHEK (or REDSEK, REDNECK, Capt.SCHMIDT)	136282	M	Ger.		Osturmbannfhr., SD, Marseille (Fr.) 43-44	BRUTALITY	FR.
RETSCHEK	162696	M			Hptsturmfhr., SS, Nord-Afric.-Region, Poitiers (Fr.) 8.44	MISC.CRIMES	FR.
RETSCHEK, Helmut (or DE MONTARGNE)	190576	M		99	Capt., Member, Gestapo, Pexonne, Le Harcholet and Moyenmoutier (Fr.) 44	MURDER	U.K.
RETSECK	167480	M	Ger.		Osturmbannfhr., SS, Gestapo, Toulouse (Fr.)	MURDER	FR.
RETE	167479	M	Ger.		Civilian, Einsatzstab Rosenberg, Paris (Fr.) 40-44	PILLAGE	FR.
RETTIG	128943	M			Rottfhr., SS, C.C. Weimar-Buchenwald (Ger.)	TORTURE	U.S.
RETTIG	255656	M			Rottfhr., Camp Nixei, Nordhausen (Ger.)	MURDER	U.S.
RETTIG, August	255657	M			Sgt., C.C. Ellrich, Nordhausen (Ger.)	MURDER	U.S.
RETTMANN	259112	M	Ger.		SS-Mann, C.C. Dachau (Ger.)	MISC.CRIMES	YUGO.
RETZ, Albert	300918	M			Member of Staff C.C. Neuengamme and else where (Ger.) 39-45	TORTURE	U.K.
RETZER, Ludwig	148541	M	Ger.	05	Sturmschfhr., SS, Guard, C.C., Reichenau nr.Innsbruck (Aust.) 44-45	TORTURE	U.S.
RETZKY	68756	M	Ger.		Col., 5.Parachute-Art.Rgt., near Quirnbach (Ger.) 20.3.45	MURDER	U.S.
RETZLAFF, Theodor	305688	M	Ger.		Member of C.C. personnel, nr.Flossenburg, Hersbrueck, Wolkenburg, Ganacker, Leitmeritz (Ger. and Czech.) 1.42-5.45	MURDER	U.S.
RETZLER	256940	M	Ger.	15	Lt., 322.Bn. 5.Schupo.Rgt., Ljubljana Cetje and Kranj (Yugo.) 42,43	MISC.CRIMES	YUGO.
RETZPACH	132546	M	Ger.	15	Osturmfhr., SS, C.C., Hallein (Aust.)	TORTURE	FR.
REUBER	174049	M	Ger.		Lt., Army, Stalag 6.A, Conc.Camp, Hemer (Ger.) 40-45	TORTURE	U.S.
REUCH	167487	M	Ger.		Interpreter, SS, 8.Bn., St.Nicolas Des Biefs (Fr.) 7.44-8.44	WITNESS	FR.
REUL (see ROHL)	156045						
REUL, Karl	139069	M			Foreman, Civilian, C.C., Krispl (Aust.)	TORTURE	U.S.
REUNIG, Erwin	250437	M	Ger.		Chief of Culture, Civilian, Bulson-Ardennes (Fr.) 42-43	TORTURE	FR.
REUPSCH	188817	M	Ger.		Uschfhr., SS, Conc.Camp, Flossenburg (Ger.)	MURDER	FR.
REUSINGER	743	M	Ger.		Police (Green-Police) Breda (Neth.) 3.42	TORTURE	NETH.
REUTEMANN, Max	259256	M		18	Sgt., Kochel (Ger.) 2.5.45	MURDER	U.S.
REUTER	744	M	Ger.		Lt., Army, Toulourenc (Fr.) 8.44	MURDER	FR.
REUTER	67552	M	Ger.		Oberhauer, C.C., E.72, Beuthen (Ger.) 10.43	TORTURE	U.K.
REUTER	129041	M			Uschfhr., SS, Skull and Crossbones Organization,Mauthausen (Aust.)41-45	MURDER	U.S.
REUTER	132213	M			Guard, SS, Conc.Camp, Gardelegen (Ger.)	MURDER	U.S.
REUTER	141325	M			Stalag VIII B, Army, Blechammer (Ger.) 10.42	MURDER	U.K.
REUTER	161716	M	Ger.		Uschfhr., SS, C.C., Buchenwald (Ger.)	WITNESS	U.S.
REUTER	186644	M	Ger.	00	LL.D., Oberstaatsanwalt, Admin.of occupied Territory,Prague (Czech.)44	MURDER	CZECH.
REUTER	187638	M	Ger.	93	Sgt., Stalag 1 G, Leipzig (Ger.)	TORTURE	U.K.
REUTER	192530	M	Ger.		Capt., 5.Coy., Lds.Schtz.Bn.216, Schaki (Lith.) 45	MISC.CRIMES	BEL.
REUTER	240092	M	Ger.		Ogruppenfhr., SS, SD Official, Gen. der Polizei, Gen.Kommissar	MURDER	U.S.
REUTER	258401	M	Ger.	08	Capt., Medical-Office, Hemevez (Fr.) 6.6.44	MURDER	U.S.
REUTER, Arthur	193030	M	Ger.	22.10.02	Sgt., Guard, Waffen-SS, Justiz-Ministerium,Feldstraflager,C.C., Finmark (Nor.) 6.42-45	MISC.CRIMES	NOR.
REUTER, Richard	192831	M	Ger.		Uschfhr., SS, C.C., Buchenwald (Ger.) 42-45	TORTURE	U.S.
REUTERMANN	173138	M	Ger.		Zugwachtmstr., C.C., Schirmeck, Rotenfels-Gaggenau (Ger.,Fr.)	MURDER	U.K.
REUTGEN	255658	M	Ger.		Pvt., Conc.Camp Dora, Nordhausen (Ger.)	MURDER	U.S.
REUTTER	10328	M	Ger.		Dr., Hptsturmfhr., SS, C.C., Sachsenhausen (Ger.) 39-44	TORTURE	CZECH.,BEL.
REUTTER	156059	M	Ger.		Lt., Army, Morlaix (Fr.) 44	TORTURE	FR.
REVALSKI, Michel	138027	M	Ger.		Guard, C.C., Erkenschwick (Ger.)	TORTURE	U.S.
REX	152356	M	Ger.		Sgt., Festungs-Div., 9.Div., St.Georges de Didonne (Fr.) 44	PILLAGE	FR.
REX	192130	M	Ger.		Pvt., Eis.Art.Bn.717, F.P.No.22380,St.Andries Varsenare Les Bruges (Fr.) 4.9.44	MURDER	BEL.
REX, W.	139717	M		95	Officer, Police, Bebra (Ger.)	TORTURE	U.S.
REX, Wilhelm	196647	M	Ger.		Police-Officer, Civilian, (Czech.) 39-45	MISC.CRIMES	CZECH.
REY, Alban	136283	M	Ger.		Dr., Sgt., Ortskommandantur de Sedan, Gaulier (Fr.) 44	MURDER	FR.
REYBERG	125048	M	Ger.		Sgt., Camp-Commander, C.C., Dirschau (Ger.) 24.1.45	MISC.CRIMES	U.K.
REYMYGE	253301	M	Ger.		Paymaster, Roubaix (Fr.) 1.2.8.41	WITNESS	FR.
REYNAUD	301601	M	Ger.		SS-Dr., stationed at C.C. Mauthausen (Aust.) 40-45	MURDER	BEL.
REYNAUDS	174050	M			Dr., Conc.Camp, Hartheim-Mauthausen (Aust.)	MURDER	U.S.
REYNEKE	156058	M	Ger.		Uschfhr., SS, Guard of Camp, Voecht (Neth.)	TORTURE	FR.
REYZEN	252616	M	Ger.		Lt., 10.Coy., 377.Jaeger-Rgt., Vinkt and Meigem (Bel.) 25.5.-31.5.40	INTERR.	BEL.
RHAM	253210	M	Ger.		Capt., 119.Art.Rgt., 11.Panz.Div., Coufouleux (Fr.) 9.8.44	INTERR.	FR.
RHEIN (or REIN or RAIN)	170541	M	Ger.		Lt.Col., Army, Oflag VI.C, C.C., Osnabrueck (Ger.) 41-42	MURDER	YUGO.
RHEIN, Emil	255659	M		20.1.17	Pvt., C.C. Ellrich, Nordhausen (Ger.)	MURDER	U.S.
RHEINBERG	122690	M	Ger.		Employee, I.G.Farben, SA-Official, Verdingen (Ger.)	WITNESS	U.S.
RHEINBERG	152363	M			SA-Official, Nierstand Stratum (Ger.) 1.45	MURDER	U.S.
RHEINCKE	137635	M	Ger.	10	Sturmmann, SS, C.C., Neuengamme (Ger.)	TORTURE	U.K.
RHEINHARDT	21458	M			Lt.Col.,Waffen-SS Div.G.v.B., 1.Bn., St.Eny (Fr.)	MURDER	U.S.
RHEINHART	189442	M	Ger.		Col., Army, Vlissingen (Neth.) 9.44	MURDER	NETH.
RHEINLAENDER, Alfred Joseph Paul	300419	M	Ger.	22.1.00	Director, N.V.Normina and C.V.Norma,Delft, Sohiedam (Neth.) 16.6.41-45	PILLAGE	NETH.
RHEINTHALER, Hans	195511	M	Ger.	14	Lt., Kampfgruppe "Dirnagel", 352.Volksgren.Div., Muenchen (Ger.)8.-9.44	MISC.CRIMES	U.S.
RHIESS, Sigmund	167530	M	Ger.		C.C., Struthof-Natzweiler (Fr.) 42-44	MURDER	FR.
RHITTERBUSCH, W.	62208	M	Ger.		Admin.of the Occ.Neth.territories Regionals officials	TORTURE	UNWCC
RHODE (see ROHDE, Dr.)	141072						
RHODE	144487	M			Capt., Abw.Geh.Fieldpol., Group727,C.C., Idriza,Sebeschamdnowo,Rschew,Russ.	MURDER	U.S.
RHODE	173931	M			Dr., C.C., Struthof-Natzweiler	MURDER	UNWCC
RHODE, Diana	122667	F	Ger.		Civilian, C.C. Boegermoor (Ger.)	TORTURE	U.S.
RHODE, Walter	122674	M	Ger.	01	Commander, C.C., Boegermoor (Ger.)	TORTURE	U.S.
RHODE, Werner	186646	M	Ger.	1.2.15	Staatsanwalt, Admin.of Occupied Territory,Prague (Czech.) 40-45	MURDER	CZECH.

NAME	C.R.FILE NUMBER	SEX	NATIO- NALITY	DATE OF BIRTH	RANK	OCCUPATION UNIT PLACE AND DATE OF CRIME	REASON WANTED	WANTED BY
RHODES, Joseph	162700	M	Ger.			Rottfhr.,SS,La Calamine (Bel.) 9.44	MURDER	BEL.
RHODS	260990	M				Osturmfhr.,SS,C.C.Vaihingen (Ger.) 13.8.44-7.4.45	MURDER	U.S.
RHONE	260991					Dr.,Standortarzt,SS,C.C.Vaihingen (Ger.) 13.8.44-7.4.45	MURDER	U.S.
RHUL, Werner	173234	M	Ger.	15		Member,SS,Gestapo,S.D. IV E or Security police H.Q.,Noailles (Fr)8.44	MURDER	U.K.
RHUR, Carl	67021	M	Ger.			Interpreter,Working camp for jews,Bizerte(Tunisie)11.42-5.43	TORTURE	FR.
RHURMAN	67758	M	Ger.			Cpl.(Lagerfuehrer),Arbeitskommando 7009 Stalag XI B,C.C.Falling- bostel (Ger.)	TORTURE	U.K.
RIBGOLS	141994	M	Ger.	21		Guard,SS,C.C.Waoslager V,VI,Muhldorf,Ampfing,Mettenheim (Ger.)44-45	TORTURE	U.S.
RICARD	126448	M	Ger.	94		Capt.,Army,Camp Abwehr-officer,Potsdam (Ger.)	TORTURE	U.S.
RICH, Michael	256719	M	Ger.	17. 5.99		Employee,C.C.Nordhausen (Ger.)	MURDER	U.S.
RICHARD	745					Gestapo,Dax (Fr.)	MISC.CRIMES	FR.
RICHARD	162699	M	Ger.	15		Examiner,Geheime Feldpol.,Bruessel (Bel.)	MISC.CRIMES	BEL.
RICHARD	188816	M	Ger.			Prison Feldgend.,C.C.Avignon (Fr.) 40-44	TORTURE	FR.
RICHARD	193427	M	Ger.			Osturmfhr.,SS-Fuehrungsstab,C.C.Dora,Nordhausen,Plaszow(Ger.Pol.)43-45	MURDER	U.S.
RICHARD	194643	M	Ger.			Physician,C.C.Neuengamme (Ger.)	MURDER	FR.
RICHARD	301355	M	Ger.			Warder and forturer at Kdo.,Kradischko,Flossenburg (Ger.) 42-45	MURDER	FR.
RICHARD,G.	746	M	Ger.	08 or 10		Sgt.,Air Force,Cazaux (Fr.) 22.8.44	MURDER	FR.
RICHARD, George	141905	M	Ger.			Cpl.,La Pitie Hospital,Paris (Fr.) 8.44	WITNESS	U.K.
RICHARD, Paul	6431	M	Ger.			Pvt.,Army,Bierwart (Bel.) 5.9.44	WITNESS	BEL.
RICHARDS, Karl	305803	M	Ger.			N.C.O.,Camp Command Oflag VI C,Osnabrueck,Ewersheide (Ger.) 41-45	MURDER	YUGO.
RICHARDT	121213	M	Ger.			Pvt.,Feldgendarmerie,Parachutiste,Abbeville (Fr.) 31.8.44	MURDER	FR.
RICHEART	173137	M	Ger.			Staff at C.C.Baden,Natzweiler (Ger.Fr.) 44	WITNESS	U.K.
RICHEK, "Deby-Daby"	173928	M	Ger.	21		Lager-Schuetze,C.C.Wausbelen-See (Ger.) 43-45	TORTURE	FR.
RICHELE, Hans	189304	M	Ger.			Osturmbannfhr.,SS,C.C.Dachau (Ger.) 43	MURDER	BEL.
RICHEY	256718					General Manager,Mittelwerk,Nordhausen (Ger.)	MURDER	U.S.
RICHMAN	156060					Policeman,Civ.,C.C.Gardelegen (Ger.) 10.44-45	MURDER	U.S.
RICHON, Heinz	192816	M	Ger.			Oschfhr.,SS,C.C.Buchenwald,Lublin (Ger.Pol.) 42-45	TORTURE	U.S.
RICHSIED, Imre	166662	M				Scharfhr.,SS,Hungarian SS-Kampfgruppe "Ney",between Sur and Aka (Hung.) 7.3.45	MURDER	U.S.
RICHTER	12475	M	Ger.			Cpl.,Army,950 Indian,13 Coy.,Ruffec (Fr.) 18.-21.8.44	MURDER	FR.
RICHTER (or RITCHER)	36697	M	Ger.	15		Pvt.,L 210 Coy.,Working Camp,Freudenthal (Ger.) 44	TORTURE	U.K.
RICHTER	39600	M	Ger.			Kommandeur,Army, Unit 304-631,Dordogne (Fr.) 31.3.-2.4.44	MURDER	FR.
RICHTER	45099	M	Ger.			Usturmfhr.,SS,C.C.Mauthausen (Aust.)	TORTURE	FR.
RICHTER	67757	M	Ger.			SS,Belgrad (Yugo.) 4.-9.42	TORTURE	U.K.
RICHTER	126914	M	Ger.			Scharfhr.,2 SS-Pz.Div. "Das Reich",Vergt de Biron (Fr.) 21.5.44	MURDER	UNWCC
RICHTER	136597	M	Ger.	90		Hptschfhr.,SS,C.C.Flossenburg (Ger.) 42	TORTURE	U.S.
RICHTER	138026	M	Ger.			Guard,att. at mines C.C.Erkenschwick (Ger.)	TORTURE	U.S.
RICHTER	141597	M	Ger.			Lt.,Police,Eichstatt (Ger.)	MURDER	FR.
RICHTER	146176	M	Ger.			Usturmfhr.,SS,Pz.Div."Das Reich",Montauban (Fr.) 44	MURDER	FR.
RICHTER	147065	M	Ger.			Scharfhr.,SS-Pz.Div. "Das Reich",Bn.,Valence d' Agen (Fr.) 44	MURDER	FR.
RICHTER	152338	M	Ger.			Justizoberwachtmeister,C.C.Emsland (Ger.) 44	MURDER	U.S.
RICHTER	156066	M	Ger.			Lt.,Feldpost-No.04249,Lussan(Fr.) 24.8.44	MURDER	FR.
RICHTER	162783	M	Ger.	10		Employee,SS-Mann,Gestapo,SS,Belgrad (Yugo.) 8.42	TORTURE	U.K.
RICHTER	166667	M	Ger.	97		Lt.Col.,Army (Pol.) 39-45	MISC.CRIMES	U.S.
RICHTER	167142	M				Lt.,Army,Puy de Dome (Fr.) 29.6.44	MURDER	FR.
RICHTER (No.II)	167451	M	Ger.			Warder,Civ.,C.C.Sachsenhausen,Oranienburg (Ger.) 39-4.45	MURDER	POL.
RICHTER (No. I)	167452	M	Ger.			Warder,Civ.,C.C.Sachsenhausen (Ger.) 39-4.45	MURDER	POL.
RICHTER	167453	M	Ger.			Leader,Civ.,Grundstuecksgesellschaft,Gdynia (Pol.) 9.39-4.45	MISC.CRIMES	POL.
RICHTER	167478	M	Ger.	17		Sgt.,SS-Div."Das Reich",1 Coy., 1 Section,Oradour-Glane (Fr.) 10.6.44	MURDER	FR.
RICHTER	173953	M	Ger.			Lt.General,Commander of E.M.-Div.,Thuir-Velmanya (Fr.) 1.8.44	MURDER	FR.
RICHTER	177272	M	Ger.			School-Teacher,Member,NSDAP,Mueggelheim (Ger.) 3.45	TORTURE	U.S.
RICHTER	186183	M	Ger.			Civilian,Vergt de Biron (Fr.) 5.44	MISC.CRIMES	FR.
RICHTER	188815	M	Ger.			Hptschfhr.,SS,C.C.Flossenburg (Ger.)	MURDER	FR.
RICHTER	189002	M				Lt.,Army,Lussan (Fr.) 24.8.44	MURDER	FR.
RICHTER	189303		Ger.			Foreman,Civ.,Arbeitskommando "Messerschmidt-Werke",C.C.Dachau(Ger.)45	TORTURE	BEL.
RICHTER	190266	M	Ger.			Gruppenfhr.,Inspector,Gestapo,S,D,C.C.Banjica (Yugo.) 40-45	MURDER	YUGO.
RICHTER	193313	M	Ger.			Oschfhr.,SS,C.C.Falstad,Drontheim (Nor.) 41-44	MURDER	NOR.
RICHTER	193927	M	Ger.			Employee,Stalag IX C,C.C.Bad Sulza (Ger.)	MURDER	FR.
RICHTER	196646	M	Ger.			Sgt.,SS,Vercoiran (Fr.) 9.3.44	MURDER	FR.
RICHTER	252630	M	Ger.			Lt.,Unit L 21228,Cormainville (Fr.)	TORTURE	FR.
RICHTER	252635	M	Ger.			Osturmfhr.,SS,Sipo,Abtl.III D,Bruessel (Bel.)	INTERR.	BEL.
RICHTER	252638	M	Ger.	06		Oschfhr.,SS,Gestapo,Prag,(Czech.) 44-45	MISC.CRIMES	CZECH.
RICHTER	253150		Ger.			Chief-paymaster,Stabsintendant,Feldbekleidungsamt der Luftwaffe I-XI, Enschede (Neth.) 2.42-4.45	PILLAGE	NETH.
RICHTER	253207	M	Ger.			Member,Military court,Torgau,Halle (Ger.) 4.2.44	INTERR.	FR.
RICHTER	253208	M	Ger.			Dr.,Kriegsverwaltungsrat,Kommand.713,Pion.Bn.Form.31308 A,Le Touquet, Paris (Fr.) 43-44	PILLAGE	FR.
RICHTER	255438	M				Uschfhr.,C.C.Dora,Nordhausen (Ger.)	MURDER	U.S.
RICHTER	255775	M	Ger.			Dr.,Physician,C.C.Mauthausen (Aust.) 40-45	INTERR.	FR.BEL.
RICHTER	261788	M	Ger.			Inspector,Gestapo,D' Amiens,Gentelles (Fr.) 7.-8.44	MURDER	FR.
RICHTER	305734	F	Ger.			Woman guard,C.C.Auschwitz,Birkenau (Pol.) 40	MURDER	U.S.
RICHTER, Alfons	186643	M	Ger.	29.12.02		Secr. of Mayor,Administ.of Occupied territory,Prague (Czech.)39-45	MURDER	CZECH.
RICHTER, Alfred	252617	M	Ger.			Lt.,377.Jaeg.Regt.,Vinkt (Bel.) 25.-31.5.40	MISC.CRIMES	BEL.
RICHTER, Christian	195906	M	Ger.	14		Agent,Member,S.D.,Maisons Laffite (Fr.) 15.12.41-10.6.44	TORTURE	FR.
RICHTER, Emil	306512	M	Ger.	1.10.88		Sgt.,SS,C.C.Buchenwald (Ger.) 16.5.38-9.10.42	MURDER	BEL.
RICHTER, Erhardt	261318	M	Ger.	15		Administrative-officer,paymaster,Dulag-132,Laterina (Ital.) 6.44	WITNESS	U.S.
RICHTER, Erich	300967		Ger.			Dr.,official of S.D.,Leitabschnitt,Prag,Oswiecim, Birkenau (Pol.)39-45	MURDER	CZECH.
RICHTER, Ernst	255743	M	Ger.	22.10.13		SS-Mann,S.D.,Prague (Czech.) 5.45	MURDER	CZECH.
RICHTER, Franz	186647	M	Ger.	25.-3.06		Member,Agent,Merchant,DAF,Gestapo,Uysokemyto (Czech.) 38-45	MURDER	CZECH.
RICHTER, Friedrich	196850	M	Ger.			Uschfhr.,SS,C.C.Auschwitz (Pol.) 40	MURDER	FR.
RICHTER, Friedrich	261163	M	Ger.	29. 9.11		Member,G.F.P. Group of 738,Mons (Bel.) 41-42	SUSPECT	BEL.
RICHTER, Georg	256638	M	Ger.	24. 2.12		Employee,C.C.Nordhausen (Ger.)	MURDER	U.S.
RICHTER, Gustav Helmuth	306716	M	Ger.			German Civilian,Bremen (Ger.) 24.2.45	BRUTALITY	U.S.
RICHTER, Harald	306513	M	Ger.			Sgt.,SS,C.C.Buchenwald (Ger.) 16.5.38-9.10.43	MURDER	BEL.

RIC-RIE

NAME	C.R.FILE NUMBER	SEX	NATIO-NALITY	DATE OF BIRTH	RANK OCCUPATION UNIT PLACE AND DATE OF CRIME	REASON WANTED	WANTED BY
RICHTER, Herbert	254423	M	Ger.		Hptscharfhr., S.D., Toulouse (Fr.) 42-43	INTERR.	FR.
RICHTER, Herbert	256699	M	Ger.	21.6.08	SS Hptscharfhr., S.D., Foix (Fr.) 11.42-8.44	MURDER	FR. CZECH.
RICHTER, Hermann	180729	M	Ger.		SS Uscharfhr., C.C. Mauthausen (Aust.)	TORTURE	FR.
RICHTER, Hugo	156062	M			Civ., Ellersleben, Mannstedt, Daasdorf, Guthmannshausen (Ger.)7.-8.44	MURDER	U.S.
RICHTER, Johann	252607	M	Ger.		Guard, C.C. Lahde-Weser (Ger.)	INTERR.	BEL.
RICHTER, Josef	193439	M	Ger.	16.1.07	Scharfhr. S.A., Czech.	MISC.CRIMES	CZECH.
RICHTER, Kurt Max Walter	194642	M	Ger.	20.11.08	Head, Gestapo, Jicin (Czech.) 39-45	SUSPECT	CZECH.
RICHTER, Kurt	901978	M	Ger.		Rotterdam, Leiden, Oegstgeest (Neth.) 5.11.42-9.9.44	TORTURE	NETH.
RICHTER, Otto	156069	M			Civ. Farmer, Daasdorf, Guthmannshausen (Ger.) 7.-8.44	MURDER	U.S.
RICHTER, Otto or RECHTER	158291	M	Ger.		Dr.,Verwaltungs-assist., police, Dinant-Ciney (Bel.) 9.44	MISC.CRIMES	BEL.
RICHTER, Rene	167143	M	Ger.		Pvt., 9.SS Div., Panz.Gren.Rgt. 21,Senonches La Saucelle (Fr.)	PILLAGE	FR.
RICHTER, Rudolf	261060	M	Ger.		Member, Gendarmerie, Chateaulin (Fr.) 20.5.44	MISC.CRIMES	FR.
RICHTER, Theodor	167450	M	Ger.		Leader, public official, Ernaehrung und Landwirtschaft, Lublin (Pol.) 9.39-end 44	MISC.CRIMES	POL.
RICHTER, Waldemar	192529	M	Ger.	22	Crim.assist., Gestapo, Bruenn (Czech.) 39-44	WITNESS	CZECH.
RICHTER, Walter	138351	M			SS Adjutant, SS, Gestapo, Lyon (Fr.)	MURDER	FR.
RICHTER, Waltraut	188447	F	Ger.	26	Civ. Berlin (Ger.) 8.44	WITNESS	U.K.
RICHTER, Werner	141322	M	Ger.		Guard, Army, Dt.Eylau, Rosenberg (Pol.) 8.44	MURDER	U.K.
RICHTER, Willy	300968	M	Ger.		Dr., SS Hptsturmfhr., official S.D. Leitabschnitt, Prag, C.C.Oswiecim-Birkenau (Pol.) 39-45	MURDER	CZECH.
RICHTER, Wolfgang	55966	M	Ger.	01	Leader NSDAP, Praha (Czech.)	MISC.CRIMES	CZECH.
RICK	251236	M	Ger.	10	SS Osturmfhr., C.C. Auschwitz-Birkenau (Pol.) 42-45	MURDER	YUGO.
RICK, Adolf	169042	M	Ger.	06	SS Uscharfhr., Waffen SS, C.C. Natzweiler (Fr.) 43-44	MURDER	FR.
RICK, Arnold	255499	M			Pvt., C.C. Ellrich, Nordhausen (Ger.)	MURDER	U.S.
RICKBUSCH, Hans	251240	M			SS-Mann, C.C. Auschwitz-Birkenau (Pol.) 10.42	MURDER	YUGO.
RICKE, Ferdinand	195185	M	Ger.		Uscharfhr., S.A., Dorsten (Ger.) 10.44-2.45	TORTURE	NETH.
RICKEN	148548	M			SS Hptscharfhr., C.C. Mauthausen (Aust.) 41-45	MURDER	U.S.
RICKENBERG	255440	M			Uscharfhr., C.C. Ellrich, Nordhausen (Ger.)	MURDER	U.S.
RICKERT	905246	M			SS Sturmbannfhr., Military-Cmdt., Stab 1 SS Panz.Gren.Rgt. 7 Livadia Distomon, Beotia, Kalamion (Grc.) 10.6.44-12.6.44	MURDER	GRC.
RICKERT, Adam	258430	M			SS-Mann, Guard, C.C. Ohrdruf (Ger.) 12.44-4.45	MURDER	U.S.
RICKFELDER	190629	M	Ger.		Oberwachtmeister, Adjudant, Gestapo, Trondes, Boucq, Menil, La Tour (Fr.) 15.-18.8.44	MURDER	FR.
RICKFELDER, Bernhard or RICKFORD	156067	M	Ger.		Civ. Gardener, Muenster (Ger.) 17.3.45	TORTURE	U.S.
RICKFORD see RICKFELDER	156067						
RICKHEY, George	132335	M			Director of camp, C.C. Dora-Mittelbau Nordhausen (Ger.)	MURDER	U.S.
RICKISCH or RIKISH	906708	M	Ger.		Civ. Foreman, Working party, Bruex (Czech.) 5.8.44	MURDER	U.K.
RICKLING	173929	M			Cpl., 2.Bn. Parachutiste-Rgt., Plouzane (Fr.) -44	MURDER	FR.
RICKMANN, Wilhelm Heinrich	300102	M	Ger.	8.1.00	Administrator, NSV, NSDAP, Enscheds (Neth.) betw.24.6.41 and 1.4.45	PILLAGE	NETH.
RICKWER	906281	M	Ger.		Member, Gestapo at Trencin, C.C. Oswiecim-Birkenau (Pol.) 39-45	MURDER	CZECH.
RIDEL	261855	M	Ger.		Inspector, Gestapo Amiens, Gentelles (Fr.) 6.8.44	MURDER	FR.
RIDLEY, Frantz	62098	M	Ger.		N.C.O., Army, Cleder (Fr.) 8.8.44	MURDER	FR.
RIEBEL, Karl	260489	M	Ger.	15.11.12	SS Sgt., Waffen SS, Guard, C.C.Auschwitz (Pol.) 43-45	BRUTALITY	POL.
RIEBELING	162697	M			S.D. of Montlugon, Chappes (Fr.) 7.44	MURDER	FR.
RIEBER, Heinrich	132114	M			Dr., Oberregierungsrat, state-ministry in Prague, Public official, Prague (Czech.) 42-45	MISC.CRIMES	CZECH.
RIEBLING, Karl	186184	M	Ger.		Capt., Army, Terrasson (Fr.) 2.half march 44	MURDER	FR.
RIECHERMANN	144391	M			Mayor of Volkerade, Public official, Wattenbuttel (Ger.)	TORTURE	U.S.
RIECK, Helmut	262161	M	Ger.	28.2.7	Oscharfhr., Gestapo, Rennes (Fr.) 43-44	MURDER	FR.
RIED	158293	M			Col., Army, Oflag VII B, C.C.Eichstaett (Ger.) 25.2.44	MURDER	U.K.
RIED	196849	M	Ger.		Member NSDAP, Lagerfuehrer factory, Busenbach (Ger.) 43-45	TORTURE	FR.
RIED, Walter	300969	M			SS Osturmfhr., official of S.D.,Leitabschn.Prag,Oswiecim-Birkenau (Pol.) 39-45	MURDER	CZECH.
RIEDEL	105108	M	Ger.		Polizei-Inspector, Gestapo official, Breslau (Ger.) 3.44	MURDER	U.K.
RIEDEL	126792	M	Ger.		Capt., Oflag XVII A, Edelbach (Aust.) 9.44	MISC.CRIMES	FR.
RIEDEL see FRIEDEL	173998						
RIEDEL	256635	M	Ger.		Factory-worker, C.C. Nordhausen (Ger.)	MURDER	U.S.
RIEDEL, Arthur see ROEDEL	10332						
RIEDEL, Eric see RIEDER	251241						
RIEDEL, Gerold	306514	M	Ger.	4.11.20	SS-Mann, C.C. Buchenwald (Ger.) betw.16.5.38 and 9.10.43	MURDER	BEL.
RIEDEL, Gustav	255441	M		7.6.97	Pvt., C.C. Harzungen, Nordhausen (Ger.)	MURDER	U.S.
RIEDEL, Heinz	126980	M			Doctor, Sturmfhr., S.D., C.C. Dachau (Ger.)	MURDER	U.S.
RIEDEL, Kurt	193031	M	Ger.	03	Oberwachtmeister, Sgt., Reichsjustizministerium, Feldstraflager C.C. Finmark (Nor.)	TORTURE	NOR.
RIEDEL, Richard	262308	M	Ger.	01	Home is: Dresden (Ger.) Russian-Zone, Velke-Beraltice (Czech.)7.8.44 L.C.D.N.A.O.D.	SUSPECT	U.S.
RIEDELE	129057	M			C.C. Mauthausen (Aust.) 41-45	MURDER	U.S.
RIEDER	141598	M			Cpl., Gestapo, Chenebier, Etobon (Fr.) 27.9.44	MURDER	FR.
RIEDER	180728	M			Hptscharfhr., Secretary, S.D.,Gestapo,Sarrebruck (Ger.)	PILLAGE	FR.
RIEDER	190265	M			Deputy chief, Konrad Einheit, Sibenik, Zablac (Yugo.) 5.-6.44	MURDER	YUGO.
RIEDER	252601	M		15	Member, Gend., Brussels (Bel.)	INTERR.	BEL.
RIEDER	261885	M			Non commissioned officer, Fieldgendarmerie,Arlon (Bel.) 2.44	TORTURE	BEL.
RIEDER, Anton	259748	M		01	Schfhr., Gestapo, Area of Angers,Maine, Loire (Fr.) 42-44	MISC.CRIMES	FR.
RIEDER, Eric or RIEDEL	251241	M		about 17	Inspector, S.D., Alencon (Fr.) 40-44	PILLAGE	FR.
RIEDERER, Max	187028	M		96	C.C. Fuehrer, C.C. Kaufhausen (Ger.)	TORTURE	U.S.
RIEDIGER	747	M	Ger.		Dr.,stellv.Regierungspraes.,public off.,Wartheland (Pol.) 9.39-1.42	MURDER	POL. U.N.W.C.C.
RIEDL	174052	M	Ger.		Paymaster, Stalag 6 A C.C. Hemer (Ger.) 41-45	TORTURE	U.S.
RIEDL	257871	M			SS Osturmfhr., 150.Panz.Bde. Meuse-Bridge-Antwerp (Bel.) 12.44	MISC.CRIMES	U.S.
RIEDL	305594	M	Ger.		Owachtmstr., Camp Sandvik b.Billefjord, 6.44	MISC.CRIMES	CZECH.
RIEDL, Edmund	195905	M	Ger.	15.9.96	Civ. Farmer, Vranovska, Okresznojmo (Czech.) 10.10.38	MISC.CRIMES	CZECH.
RIEDL, Emil	194429	M	Ger.	5.9.20	NSDAP, Vranovska, Znojmo (Czech.) 39-45	BRUTALITY	CZECH.
RIEDL, Karel	255211	M	Ger.	22.11.99	Civ., Trnava (Czech.) 44	MISC.CRIMES	CZECH.
RIEDL, Kurt	906515	M	Ger.		SS Sgt. (No. 198931), C.C. Buchenwald (Ger.) betw.16.5.38 and 9.10.43	MURDER	BEL.
RIEDLER	257024	M			Lt., Executive officer, Army, Stalag 4 b, Bau-und Arb.Bn. Muehlberg 40-45	MISC.CRIMES	POL.
RIEDLER	258599	M			SS-Guard, SS slave labour camp, Beisfjord nr.Narvik (Nor.) 6.-11.42	BRUTALITY	YUGO.
RIEDLER, J.	140893	M			Army, 2.Coy.,Verbindungsabt. 391.Batt., Bolnes (Neth.) 8.5.45	MURDER	NETH. POL.
RIEFERT, Elisabeth	195302	F	Ger.		Civ. Efferen (Ger.) 2.10.44	WITNESS	U.S.
RIEFFS	87755	M			Sgt., C.C. Stalag 40	MURDER	U.K.
RIEFL see RIEPL	256312						

NAME	C.R.FILE NUMBER	SEX	NATIO-NALITY	DATE OF BIRTH	RANK OCCUPATION UNIT	PLACE AND DATE OF CRIME	REASON WANTED	WANTED BY
RIEG or REIG	173952	M	Ger.		SS-Unt.Scharfhr., C.C. Neckarelz-Neckargerach (Ger.)		TORTURE	U.S.,FR.
RIEGE	256714				Sgt., SS,SD, Nordhausen (Ger.)		MURDER	U.S.
RIEGE, Johann	306516	M	Ger.	15.11.09	SS-Pvt., (No.46 413) SS, C.C. Buchenwald (Ger.)between 16.5.38-9.10.43		MURDER	BEL.
RIEGE, Paul	194757	M	Ger.	27. 4.88	SS-Major-General, Ordnungspolizei, 9.41		MURDER	POL.
RIEGEL	255442				Oberscharfhr., C.C. Dora, Nordhausen (Ger.)		MURDER	U.S.
RIEGEL	255451				Cpl. C.C., Wolffleben, Nordhausen (Ger.)		MURDER	U.S.
RIEGELE	257870	M			Freg.Capt., 150. Pz.Bde., Meuse Bridge-Antwerp (Bel.) 12.44		MISC.CRIMES	U.S.
RIEGER	1557		Ger.		Sgt.-Major, Army Res. Lazarett (Hospital) (Dentist) Heppenheim (Ger.)		TORTURE	U.S.
RIEGER	126757	M			Sgt., Inf., Coudes (Fr.) 7.44		MURDER	FR.,UNWCC
RIEGER	129879	M			Hauptscharfhr., W.-SS, Buchenwald-Weimar (Ger.)		MISC.CRIMES	U.S.
RIEGER	259797	M	Ger.		Lt., SD Dienststelle: The Hague, Nassaulaan, Wassenaar, Zuid-(Neth.) 3.11.44		SUSPECT	NETH.
RIEGER, Andreas	12455				Pvt., 110 or 111. Pz.Gren. Regt. 2.Coy., Albine (Fr.) 29.6.44		MURDER	FR.
RIEGER, Gustav	129058	M			Civilian-Lawyer, Mauthausen (Austr.) 41-45		MURDER	U.S.
RIEGER, Hans	124646		Ger.		Sgt., Kriegslazarett, Heppenheim (Ger.) 9.44-5.45		MISC.CRIMES	U.S.
RIEGER, Josef	260523	M	Ger.	29. 4.94	SS-Rottfhr., W.-SS, Guard Coy. Monowitz-Auschwitz (Pol.) 11.42-1.45		BRUTALITY	POL.
RIEGER, Julius	187657			95-15	Stabsfhr., SA, Dorheim (Ger.) 7.44		MURDER	U.S.
RIEGER, Karl	192830	M			SS-Scharfhr., Sgt., C.C. Buchenwald (Ger.) 42-45		TORTURE	U.S.
RIEGER, Willi	300103	M	Ger.		N.C.O., Gelonging to an armoured division, Seesterberg (Neth.) 30.-31.3.45		PILLAGE	NETH.
RIEGLER	70651	M			Unterscharfhr., SS, Mauthausen (Austr.) 41-45		TORTURE	U.S.
RIEGNER, Herbert	196848	M	Ger.		Sturmfhr., Auschwitz (Pol.) 40		MURDER	FR.
RIEGNER, Herbert	251237	M			SS-Sturmann, SS, Auschwitz (Pol.) 1.43		MURDER	YUGO.
RIEHBERG	195184	M			SS-Unterscharfhr., SS-Unterfuehrerschule, Arnheim, Rossum (Neth.) 24.9.44		MURDER	NETH.
RIEHLMANN	158232				Civilian, Punschau (Ger.)		MURDER	U.S.
RIEK, Gustav	253286	M		23. 5.00	Hptsturmfhr., Hinzert (Ger.)		INTERR.	FR.
RIEKENBURG, Wilhelm	180726	M	Ger.	29. 3.98	Cpl., Airforce Driving Centre Np. 5, Munster (Ger.) 21.5.45		MURDER	U.S.
RIEKER, Kurt Ernst	45325		Ger.		Informant Agent, Gestapo, Chrudim (Czech.) 36-45		MURDER	CZECH.
RIEKOETTER, Med. see RIETKOETTER	133267							
RIELLAERDS, Adolf Emiel	301974	M	Ger.	11.10.99	Chauffeur, SD, Apeldoorn District (Neth.)9.44-4.45		MURDER	NETH.
RIELSKI	12477	M			Pvt., 110.,111. Pz.Gren.Regt. I. Gruppe, Gourdon (Fr.) 29.6.44		MURDER	FR.
RIEMANN	192567	M	Ger.		Sturmbannfhr..9.SS Pz.Div..Neuville les Bois(Fr.)11.8.44		MURDER	FR.
RIEMANN	301840	M	Ger.		SD, Vichy (Fr.) 10.43-9.44		MURDER	FR.
RIEMANN, Friedrich Wilhelm	300104	M	Ger.		Crim.Asst., Member, Gestapo, Warsaw (Pol.) 1.-9.41		TORTURE	POL.
RIEMANN, Heinrich	255452			15. 6.22	Pvt., C.C. Ellrich, Nordhausen (Ger.)		MURDER	U.S.
RIEMER or RIEULER	129061	M			SS, C.C. Mauthausen (Aust.) 41-45		MURDER	U.S.
RIEMER, Fred	188361	M	Ger.		Cpl., Nachrichten Abt., Zilly Heiketal (Ger.) 15.9.44		MURDER	U.S.
RIEMER, Otto	156716	M			SS-Obersturmfhr., SS, Mauthausen (Austr.) 41-45		MURDER	U.S.
RIENGER, Herbert	300543	M			SS-man, SS, C.C. Auschwitz-Birkenau (Pol.) 1.43		MISC.CRIMES	YUGO.
RIEPEL	139052	M			Capt., Kraftfahrpark Wuerzburg, Pechbrunn (Ger.) 15.4.45		MURDER	U.S.
RIEPEN	186852	M			Lt., 200. Pz.Gren.Regt.l.Bn., Lansleboug (Fr.) 6.-7.44		TORTURE	FR.
RIEPEN, Margarethe	193440	F	Ger.		Agent, Gestapo, Prague, Drnovsky (Czech.) 1.44		MURDER	CZECH.
RIEPING, Hubert	124380	M			Oberscharfhr., (Schirrmeister Motor N.C.O.) W.-SS, Leibstand. (A.H.) Rosbach (Ger.) 4.3.45		WITNESS	U.S.
RIEPL or RIEFL	256312	M	Ger.		O.T., Muhldorf (Ger.)		WITNESS	U.S.
RIES	193977	M	Ger.		SS-Schuetze, SS, Stavelot (Bel.) 19.-20.12.44		MURDER	CZECH.,BEL.
RIES	258380	M	Ger.	08	Chief of Personnel Section Bds., Gestapo Bds., Prague (Czech.)42-45		MISC.CRIMES	CZECH.
RIES, Bernhard	190330	M	Ger.		Civilian, Wiesbaden (Ger.) 43-45		WITNESS	U.S.
RIES, Erwin	39599	M			Lt. of Feldpost, Army, Carlaies (Fr.) 8. or 9.6.44		MURDER	FR.
RIES, Franz	190329	M	Ger.		Civilian, Wiesbaden (Ger.) 43-45		WITNESS	U.S.
RIES, Jakob	190393	M	Ger.		Civilian, Wiesbaden (Ger.) 43-45		WITNESS	U.S.
RIES, Jakob	258393	M			Guard, SS, C.C. Ohrdruf (Ger.) 12.44-4.45		MURDER	U.S.
RIES, Karl	190328	M	Ger.		Civilian, Wiesbaden (Ger.) 43-45		WITNESS	U.S.
RIESBAUER	161725	M			Civilian (Ger.)		WITNESS	U.S.
RIESEBURG, Walter	144360	M	Ger.	02	SS Obersturmfhr., SS, Stapelburg (Ger.) 16.8.44		MURDER	U.S.
RIESEL	253243	M			Major, Pion.Bn., Le Touquet-Paris (Fr.) 43-44		PILLAGE	FR.
RIESEN	258111	M			Capt., State Service, Member Abwehrstelle, Prague (Czech.) 40		MURDER	CZECH.
RIESENECKER, Jean	250441	M	Ger.	7. 1.16	Pvt., 13.Coy., 558 Gren.Regt., Bruayen Artois (Fr.) 1.9.44		MISC.CRIMES	FR.
RIESENWETTER, Willibald	148558	M			Dr., SS, Mauthausen (Austr.) 41-45		MURDER	U.S.
RIESER, Willibald	255448	M			Flyer, C.C. Ellrich, Nordhausen (Ger.)		MURDER	U.S.
RIESKE, Wilhelm	121897	M			Civilian, Neurod (Ger.)		MISC.CRIMES	FR.
RIESKE, Wilhelm	196847	M			Foreman, Busenbach (Ger.) 43-45		TORTURE	FR.
RIESSICKE see VON RESECKE	193904							
RIETERS	251250	M	Ger.	14	Arbeitsdienstfhr., SS, Auschwitz-Birkenau (Pol.) 42-45		MURDER	YUGO.
RIETH, Johann	257318	M	Ger.	14	Crim.Asst., Gestapo, Tabor, (Bohemia ,Czech.) 6.9.39		MISC.CRIMES	CZECH.
RIETKOETTER or RIEKOETTER	133267	M	Ger.	11	Dr.,med.., Hauptsturmfhr., W.-SS, Camp S III, Thueringen (Ger.)		TORTURE	U.S.
RIETZ	255449	M			Unterscharfhr., Camp Nixie, Nordhausen (Ger.)		MURDER	U.S.
RIEULER see RIEMER	129061							
RIEVEN see KIEVEN, Hermann	251094							
RIFEL	1464				Lt., Pion.Bn. 334, 2.Coy.		MISC.CRIMES	U.K.
RIFFELMACHER, Karl	251851	M	Ger.		Wolfsburg (Ger.) 29.6.44		WITNESS	U.S.
RIFFLE	129060		Ger.		Civilian, Siegburg (Ger.)3.-8.42		MURER	BEL.
RIFLIN	38854	M			SS Hauptscharfhr., C.C. Struthof (Fr.)		MISC.CRIMES	FR.
RIGER, Otto	138299	M	Ger.		Pvt., Army, C.C. Deiselhorst (Ger.) 4.7.41		MURDER	FR.
RIGL, Albert	161723	M			Pvt., Gren.Engineer- and Fuessilier Bn., Leipzig (Ger.) 10.44		WITNESS	U.S.
RIGUSCH	255450				C.C. Ellrich, Nordhausen (Ger.)		MURDER	U.S.
RIHA, Johann	255437	M		23.11.05	Pvt., Sturmann, C.C. Harzungen, Nordhausen (Ger.)		MURDER	U.S.
RIHMER	255776	M	Ger.		Camp-leader, C.C. Mauthausen (Austr.) 23.3.44		MISC.CRIMES	FR.
RIJORT, Franic	152098	M			Civilian, Reistedt (Ger.) 7.-8.44		TORTURE	U.S.
RIKL, Anne	152364	F	Ger.		Layer-out, Civilian, Pullach (Ger.) 19.7.44		WITNESS	U.S.
RIKOFF see RECKOW	134097							
RILENTHAL, Marie-Louise	253701	F	Ger.		Dactylo, Interpreter, Gestapo, Troyes, Greney (Fr.) 43-44		MURDER	FR.
RILGER	186450	M			N.C.O., Police, 17.Section, Athens (Gre.)		MURDER	GRC.
RILZ, Hans er KILZ	253285	M			Sgt., Gend., Vendome (Fr.) 9.8.44		MURDER	FR.
RIMARSKI	251857	M			Lt., 4.Paratrooper.Regt., Div. Herm. Goering, Helchteren et Hechtel (Bel.) 5.-11.9.44		INTERR.	BEL.
RIMBACH	147361	M			Pvt., 11.Pz.Div., Kampfgr. "Wilde", South West-(Fr.) 44		MURDER	FR.

RIM-RIT

NAME	C.R.FILE NUMBER	SEX	NATIO- NALITY	DATE OF BIRTH	RANK OCCUPATION UNIT PLACE AND DATE OF CRIME	REASON WANTED	WANTED BY
RIMBACH, Emil	148547	M	Ger.	18. 2.13	Pvt.,Werkstatt-Coy.(mot) 123,Borkum (Ger.) 8.44	MURDER	U.S.
RIMER	749	M	Ger.		Untersturmfhr., Waffen SS,C.C., Roten (Nor.) 3.42 - 43	MURDER	YUGO.
RIMKUS, Hans	306282	M	Ger.		Member of the Gestapo at Trencin,C.C., Oswiecim-Birkenau(Pol.)39-45	MURDER	CZECH.
RIMLAEGER (seeREMLINGER)	109624						
RIMMLER	180725	M	Ger.		Cmdt., C.C./Ebensee,Mauthausen (Aust.) 5.44	MURDER	FR.
RIMRODT	67018	M			Pvt., SS - Div., St. Sulpice,Fort Musson Chateau Gontier (Fr.)8.44	MURDER	FR.
RINAST, Adolf	193425	M			SS-Mann,Guard,4.SS-Totenkopf-Stuba,C.C. Nordhausen,Dora Mittelbau, Osterode (Ger.) 43 - 45	WITNESS	U.S.
RINDEL, Willi	156073	M			Luftschutz, Kruden (Ger.)	TORTURE	U.S.
RINDER, Sebastian	255435	M			Uscharfhr.. C.C. Nordhausen (Ger.)	MURDER	U.S.
RINDFLEISCH	750	M	Ger.		Hptschfhr., SS,C.C., Majdanek (Pol.) 40-44	MURDER	UNWCC,FR. POL.BEL.
RINDFLEISCH	255433	M			Dr.,Lt., Ober sturmfhr., Camp Physician Dora,Nordhausen(Ger.)	MURDER	U.S.
RING	133268	M			Ustumfhr., Waffen SS, C.C., Flossenburg (Ger.)	TORTURE	U.S.
RING (or HING)	136284	M			Pvt., 11.Panz.-Div. 2.Cie. 2.A.A.G.A.Z.,Albine (Fr.) 12.3.44	MURDER	FR.
RING	190593	M			Pvt., 11.Panz.-Div.,2.Coy. Bergerac-Albine(Fr.) 7.-8.44	MURDER	FR.
RINGEISEN, Edmund	259814	M	Ger.	30.10.94	Director, Post-office,Muenster,Ht.Rhin (Fr.) 40 - 44	PILLAGE	FR.
RINGEL,Detlef	194831	M	Ger.		Landrat, Gemeindetag,Luxemburg (Lux.)	PILLAGE	LUX
RINGEL,Walter	250447	M	Ger.	21.11.88	Ob.-Landrat,Hradec Kralove (Czech.) 39 - 45	MISC.CRIMES	CZECH.
RINGER	124467	M			Lt.,SS, NSDAP, Maribor (Ger.) 10.44	MURDER	U.S.
RINGER	132804	M	Ger.		Cpt., Stalag 317 XVIII C, Markt Pongau (Aust.) 44 - 45	TORTURE	U.K.
RINGER, Franz,Josef	195091	M		28. 1.11	Wachtmeister,Employee,Gestapo,Kolin(Czech.) 39-45	MURDER	CZECH.
RINGHAND	196643				W.O., Feldgendarmerie, Hennebout (Fr.)	WITNESS	FR.
RINGLEHAN	156069	M			Civilian, Hunting Master of Jagdschloss Springe (Ger.) 26.11.44	MURDER	U.S.
RINGLER, Philippe	259251	M	Ger.		Rottenfhr., Gestapo of Poitiers Area,(Fr.) 40 - 45	MISC.CRIMES	FR.
RINGLING, Heinrich	255436	M		9.11.07	Cpl., C.C., Ellrich,Nordhausen(Ger.)	MURDER	U.S.
RINGMANN, Fritz	177577	M	Ger.		SS, C.C., Striegau, (Ger.) 31.1. - 15.5.44	TORTURE	FR.
RINK	166664	M			SS - Oberfhr.,- Colonel, Lodz (Pol.) 40 - 45	MISC.CRIMES	U.S.
RINK	190264	M			Hptsturmfhr. SS,Verwaltungefhr., C.C. Geta.Kovno(Yugo.)40-44	MURDER	YUGO.
RINK, Eugen	156072	M			Rottenfhr., SA, Technical Mechanic,Muehlberg (Ger.) 3.42	MURDER	U.S.
RINKE, Gustav	29717	M	Ger.		Dr.,Amtsgerichtsrat-Landgerichtsrat,Ministry of Justice,Public- Official,Opava (Czech.) 40	MURDER	CZECH.
RINKEN,Reinhold	12478	M	Ger.		Pvt.and N.C.O.,Army,110. and 111.Pz.-Gren.Rgt.,2.Coy.Albine(Fr.)29.6.44	MURDER	FR.
RINN	156070	M	Ger.		Civilian Physian,Stalag XII A, Limburg,Braunfels (Ger.) 3.45	WITNESS	U.S.
RINNARD	255434	M	Ger.		Pvt., C.C. Ellrich,Nordhausen(Ger.)	MURDER	U.S.
RINNE, Heinrich	193976	M	Ger.	25. 5.09	Hauptsturmfhr., SS, C.C., Trezin (Czech.) 39 - 45	TORTURE	CZECH.
RINNENTHALER,Hans	262310	M	Ger.		Civilian, Lives at Freilassing,Sillersdorf (Ger.) 16.4.45L.O.D.N.A.O.D.	WITNESS	U.S.
RIP (see REIP)	260687						
RIPKA	126586	M	Ger.		Flakalarmabteilung 503,10.Bn. Hilden (Ger.) 16.4.45	MURDER	U.S.
RIPKA, Wilhelm	29718	M			Vice President,Public official,Prague,Litomerica (Czech.) 40	MURDER	CZECH.
RIPKE	124972	M			Member, Gestapo,C.C., Bremen-Farge (Ger.) 6.43	TORTURE	U.K.
RIPP	255328	M	Ger.		Pvt., C.C. Harzungen,Nordhausen (Ger.)	MURDER	U.S.
RIPPEL	74109	M	Ger.		Capt., Abwehr-Official, Lilli (Fr.) 9.44	MURDER	U.S. U.K.
RIPPER, Franz	252587	M	Ger.	18. 1.14	Employee, Gestapo, Pardubice, (Czech.) 39 - 45	MISC.CRIMES	CZECH.
RIPPES	129059		Ger.		Member, Gestapo, C.C., Braunschweig,(Ger.) 44	TORTURE	BEL.
RIS	253529	M	Ger.		Pvt., Army,443.Rgt. Belgrad(Yugo.) 10.und 12.41	MURDER	YUGO.
RISBECK, Heinrich	156074	M	Ger.		SS - Schuetze,Guard, C.C., Volary (Czech.) 44 - 45	MURDER	U.S.
RISCH	136352	M			C.C. Hinzert (Ger.) 41 - 43	TORTURE	U.S.
RISCH	191816	M			Capt., K.G.Arbeits.Bn., 302,,3.Coy.,Lonsdal(Nor.)	MURDER	NOR.
RISCH, Walter	300919	M	Ger.		Member, SS of Staff at C.C., Sasel (Ger.) 10.44-4.45	TORTURE	U.K.
RISCHE, Oscar	306517	M	Ger.		Uscharfhr.,SS,C.C. Buchenwald (Ger.) 5.38 und 9.10.43	MURDER	BEL.
RISCHER	183656	M	Ger.		General, Reich-Military-Court,Berlin,Torgau (Ger.) 43 - 45	MURDER	U.S.
RISCHER, Heini	301086	M	Ger.	21.10.21	Pvt., Vendeuvre Aube (Fr.) 8.44	PILLAGE	FR.
RISCHEWSKI, Kurt	259252	M	Ger.		Rttfhr., SS, Gestapo, Poitiers, Area (Fr.) 40 - 45	MISC.CRIMES	FR.
RISKE	142132	M	Jer.	05	Oberscharfhr., SS. C.C., Lublin (Pol.) 42 - 44	MURDER	FR.
RISNEMANN	147360	M	Ger.		Oberscharfhr.,11.Pz.-Div.,3.Gruppe,Kampfgr."Wilden",South-West(Fr.)44	MURDER	FR.
RISOTER	256313	M			Hauptscharfhr., Muehldorf (Ger.)	WITNESS	U.S.
RISSE, Wolfgang	255329	M	Ger.		Pvt., C.C. Ellrich,Nordhausen (Ger.)	MURDER	U.S.
RISSLER	256314	M	Ger.		Hauptscharfhr., Muehldorf (Ger.)	WITNESS	U.S.
RISSMANN	156061	M			Manager, C.C. Glogau (Ger.) 42-45	TORTURE	U.S.
RIST	133269	M			Hauptscharfhr., Waffen SS, C.C.Flossenburg (Ger.)	TORTURE	U.S.
RIST, Fritz	162780	M	Ger.		Lt., Inf.Army, (Ger.)	MURDER	U.S.
RISTAD, Gustav	300105	M	Ger.		Police-Inspector, Prague (Czech.) 39-45	MISC.CRIMES	CZECH.
RISTAU, Oskar	193975	M	Ger.		Police-Oberinspector, SD, Gestapo, Prague (Czech.) 39 - 45	MURDER	CZECH.
RISTTER, Kurt	256720	M	Ger.		Sgt., Feldgendarmerie, Zajecar (Yugo.) 41 - 44	MURDER	YUGO.
RITCHER (See RICHTER)	36697						
RITCRAFF (or RITCROFF,von)	252595	M			Capt., SS, Hamburg (Ger.) 30.8.43	MURDER	U.S.
RITOVSKI	125087	M	Ger.		Cpl.,Stalag 317,XVIII O.,O.C., Salem Kae (Aust.) 3.45	TORTURE	U.K.
RITRICH, Max	191860	M	Ger.		Civilian, Dr., Ing., Didier-Werke A.G.Ofenbau,Belgrad(Yugo.)43-44	MISC.CRIMES	YUGO.
RITSCHER, Paul	255203	M		26. 9.04	Rttfhr., C.C., SS., Harzungen,Nordhausen(Ger.)	MURDER	U.S.
RITTAU	132595	M	Ger.		Staatsanwalt, Kriegsgericht, Torgau (Ger.) 5.40. - 45	MURDER	FR.
RITTER	132681	M	Ger.		Lt., SS, Gestapo, Ile de Djerba (Tun.) 13.2.43	RAPE	FR.
RITTER	138208	M	Ger.		Prison,Guard, C.C. Fresnes (Fr.) 44	TORTURE	FR.
RITTER	152339	M	Ger.	05	805.Land.Schuetzen Bn., Stalag XIII C.C., Ebertshausen(Ger.) 10.41-5.42	TORTURE	U.K., AUSTL.
RITTER	161724	M	Ger.	20	Uscharfhr., SS, Finance Office,C.C., Buchenwald (Ger.) 42	WITNESS	U.K.
RITTER	179776	M		05	Lt., 114.Jaeger Div., Gubbio (It.) 22.6.44	MURDER	U.K.
RITTER	189413	M	Ger.		Obersturmfhr., SS, SS-Att.To.Gestapo H.Q. Falstad-Drontheim(Nor.)41-44	MURDER	NOR.
RITTER	192569	M	Ger.		Employee, Gestapo, Brunn (Czech.) 39 - 45	SUSPECT	CZECH.
RITTER	196088	M	Ger.		C.C. Struthof-Natzweiler (Fr.) 40	TORTURE	FR.
RITTER	252579	M	Ger.		Lt., 8.Coy.,98.Bn.,157.Inf.Div. L'Ain (Fr.) 7.44	MURDER	FR.
RITTER, Felix	256713	M		05	Obersturmfhr., SD, Trondheim (Nor.) 43 - 44	MURDER	NOR.
RITTER, Horst	301432	M	Ger.	9. 8.22	Uscharfhr., SS,C.C. Buchenwald (Ger.) 5.38 - 10.43	MURDER	BEL.
RITTER, Walter	751	M			Lt., Army,98. Rgt.of Mountain-Troops,8.Coy.2.Btty.	MURDER	FR.
RITTER, Willi	12456	M	Ger.		Sgt., Gestapo, Sisun (Fr.) 6.7.44	MURDER	FR.
RITTERKAMP	196642	M	Ger.		Pay - Master, Tigy (Fr.) 20.8.44	WITNESS	FR.

RIT - ROD

NAME	C.R.FILE NUMBER	SEX	NATIO- NALITY	DATE OF BIRTH	RANK OCCUPATION UNIT PLACE AND DATE OF CRIME	REASON WANTED	WANTED BY
RITTERLING, Heinz	253284	M	Ger.		Sgt., Gend., Vendome (Fr.) 9.8.44	MURDER	FR.
RITTERS	305735	M			Fuehrer, labour-section, C.C.Auschwitz-Birkenau (Pol.) 40	MURDER	FR.
RITTMAN, Paul	255204	M		2. 3.13	Cpl.,C.C.Ellrich,Nordhausen (Ger.)	MURDER	U.S.
RITTMAYER	132680	M	Ger.	00	Capt.,Oflag XI D,Wetzendorf (Ger.)	TORTURE	FR.
RITTMUELLER	255205	M			SS,C.C.Rottleberode,Nordhausen (Ger.)	MURDER	U.S.
RITTZIR	252634	M	Ger.		Interpreter,Sipo,V.D.,Bruessels (Bel.)	INTERR.	BEL.
RITZ	136285	M	Ger.	22	SS-Usturmfhr.,SS,C.C.Dora, Ellrich (Ger.)	MURDER	FR.
RITZ	256715	M	Ger.		Leader,C.C.Ellrich,SS,Nordhausen (Ger.)	MURDER	U.S.
RITZ, Willy	162782	M			Ldsch.Bn.H 6 Coy,C.C.Stalag VI B or VI G, (Ger.) 44-45	TORTURE	U.S.
RITZEL, Michael	196641	M	Ger.		Lt.,SS, Auligny en Artois (Fr.) 22.5.40	WITNESS	FR.
RITZEN, Hans	126258	M	Ger.		SS-Uschfhr.,SS Totenkopf Sturmbann, Ravensbrueck,C.C.Buchenwald (Ger.)	TORTURE	U.K.
RITZHARD	252580	M			Sgt.,Gendarmerie of Macon,L'Ain (Fr.) 10.-21.7.44	MISC.CRIMES	FR.
RIVOLA	122691	M			777 Ldsch.Bn.,Gravenech and Weilburg (Ger.) 26.3.45	TORTURE	U.S.
RIX	752	M	Ger.		Sgt.,Army,Caen (Fr.) 6.44	MURDER	FR.
RIXEN,Heinrich	156068	M	Ger.		Pvt.,Army,Springe (Ger.) 26.11.44	MURDER	U.S.
RIXEN, Willy	122692	M			Pvt.,Stalag VI G, (Ger.) 17.-18.2.45	TORTURE	U.S.
RJASANTZEW (or DROBNY) Stepan	251856	M	Ger.		Agent, Gestapo, Roudnice-Kladno (Czech.) 41-42	INTERR.	CZECH.
ROBATSCH	300854	M	Ger.		Pvt.,1 Aufkl.Abt. 3 Coy 2 Col. XV Div. of the Afrika Corps,Saint Leger Arlon (Bel.) 5.9.44	MISC.CRIMES	BEL.
ROBENBURG	152090	M	Ger.		Rottfhr.,2 SS Pz.Gren.Rgt, 1 Pz.Div.,Stavelot-Malmedy (Bel.) 12.44	MURDER	U.S.
ROBERS, Josef	214020	M		05	Official,Pvt.,Abwehr,Nachr.Rgt.506,Bad Wildungen (Ger.) 45	MISC.CRIMES	U.S.
ROBERT	139074	M			Rottfhr.,SS,C.C.Gusen (Aust.) 41-45	MURDER	U.S.
ROBERT (see GOTHRY)	144784						
ROBERT,Heinrich	162705	M		16. 4.13	Volunteer, 1-Ost. Bn.447,Plouvien (Fr.) 44	TORTURE	FR.
ROBERTS (see GRIESER)	161227						
ROBERTS	194641	M	Ger.	12	Agent,Gestapo,Savigny en Septaine (Fr.) 7.-8.44	MURDER	FR.
ROBERTS, Willi (or ROBERTZ)	67580	M	Ger.	90-95	Sgt.,Army,Feldkdtr.916,Argentan-Sees (Fr.) 6.44	MURDER	U.S.
ROBH (or RUBH)	753	M	Ger.		Sgt., Bizerta (Tunisia) 12.42-4.43	MURDER	FR.
ROBIN	253291	M	Ger.		Sgt.,Orgay (Fr.) 8.8.44	MURDER	FR.
ROBIN	29648	M	Ger.		Sgt., Abwehr,Feldgendarmerie,Romorantin (Fr.) 17.8.44	MURDER	FR.
ROBOW	196087	M	Ger.		Sgt.,360 Rgt. 1 Bn. 4 Coy,St.Loup-Semousse (Fr.) 15.9.44	MURDER	FR.
ROBYN,Frans	252618	M	Ger.		377 Jg.Rgt. Unit 30305 B,Vinkt,Meigem (Bel.) 25.-31.5.40	MISC.CRIMES	BEL.
ROCH,Willy	194640	M	Ger.	04	Agent,Gestapo,Savigny en.Septaine (Fr.) 7.-8.44	MURDER	FR.
ROCHEL	192570	M	Ger.		Capo,C.C.Flossenburg (Ger.) 44-45	SUSPECT	U.S.
ROCHER	121886	M	Ger.		SS-Oschfhr.,SS,C.C.Buchenwald (Ger.) 42-45	TORTURE	FR.
ROCHER	250442	M	Ger.		Director, "Usine Rocher" Kdo.3462 Stalag VI C,Luestringen (Ger.)10.3.41	TORTURE	FR.
ROCHITA,Richard	1465	M	Ger.		Officer,Waffen SS	MISC.CRIMES	U.K.
ROCHLING, Hermann	62209	M	Ger.		Head of factories,public official	MISC.CRIMES	UNWCC
ROCHLITZ,Gustav	167481	M	Ger.		Civilian, Agent,Commandant of Kunstschutz, 40-44	PILLAGE	FR.
ROCK	12665	M	Ger.		SS-Mann,Employee,Gestapo H.Q.,Bergen (Nor.) 41	TORTURE	NOR.
ROCK, Raymond	167144	M	Ger.		Lt.,Army,Billy-Mangiennes (Fr.) 31.7.44	PILLAGE	FR.
ROCKEL,Klemens Johannes	305248	M	Ger.		Administrator, anti aircraft forces during the war,The Hague, Rijswijk (Neth.) 3.9.42, 43	PILLAGE	NETH.
ROCKEL-KROON	305395	F	Ger.	30. 7.11	Wife,The Hague,Rijswijk (Neth.) 3.9.42, 43	PILLAGE	NETH.
ROCKFORT	301815	M	Ger.		Foreman,Damag factory,Dessau (Ger.) 10.44-3.45	TORTURE	BEL.
ROCKSTROCK,Ernst	252619	M	Ger.		Sgt.,377 Jg.Rgt.,Vinkt,Meigem,(Bel.) 25.-31.5.40	MISC.CRIMES	BEL.
ROCKSTROH, Karl	187551	M	Ger.	05-15	Pvt.,2-354 Ldsch.Bn., Guard,Stalag XX Bn., Schardau (Ger.) 26.4.41	MURDER	U.K.
ROCKTESCHEL (or ROCKTEGEL)	754	M	Ger.		Capt.,Grenzpolizei,Annemasse (Fr.)	MURDER	FR.
RODACKER	12479	M			Kreisleiter,NSDAP,Fenstrange (Fr.) 40-44	MURDER	FR.
RODE	38855	M	Ger.	10	SS-Osturmfhr.,Med.,C.C.Auschwitz,Struthof (Pol.,Fr.) 42-43, 44	MISC.CRIMES	FR.
RODE	152078	M	Ger.		Lt., 21 Pz.Div.H.Q.,Sessenheim (Fr.) 1.45	MURDER	U.S.
RODE	173943	M	Ger.		Rottfhr.,SS,C.C.Oswiecim-Birkenau (Pol.) 39-45	MURDER	CZECH.
RODE	251251	M	Ger.	03	Member,SS,Birkenau (Pol.) 42-45	MURDER	YUGO.
RODE	255348	M	Ger.	15-20	Gendarm,Feldgendarmerie, Haarlem (Neth.) 11.8.42	MURDER	U.S.,NETH.
RODE	300106	M	Ger.		Lt.,Levadia (Grc.) 9.-12.9.43	MISC.CRIMES	GRC.
RODE,Karl (SVOBODA)	187658	M	Ger.	30. 5.88	Member,SS, Brno,Moravia (Czech.)	PILLAGE	CZECH.
RODECK	253302	M	Ger.		Capt.,Balaives (Fr.) 30.8.44	MISC.CRIMES	FR.
RODEL,Arthur (see ROEDEL)	10332						
RODEL,Werner	262167	M	Ger.	21.11.18	Hptschfhr.,,Cdt.,7 Coy Platoon 2, 51 SS Armoured Bde., Breviandes, Bucheres,Ste.Savine,La Riviere de Corps (Troyes). (Fr.) 25.8.44	BRUTALITY	FR.
RODENBERG,Carl Heinz	132118	M	Ger.		Dr.,SS-Gruppenfhr.,Gov't official 4 SS, Reichsinnenministerium (Ger.)	MURDER	U.S.
RODENBUSCH	252636	M	Ger.		Crim.Oberasst.,Sipo Abt.IV,B I, Bruessels (Bel.)	INTERR.	BEL.
RODENBUSCH,Josef	193423	M	Ger.		SS-Mann, Guard,4 SS Totenkopf Sturmbann,C.C.Dora-Mittelbau,Nordhausen Bismarkhuette (Ger.) 43-45	INTERR.	U.S.
RODENKO,Nicholai	258008	M			Farmer,Civilian,Reichertsdorf (Ger.) 8.or 9.44	WITNESS	U.S.
RODER (or ROHTER)	195904	M	Ger.		Adj.,Scharfschuetzen Ausb.Coy 64,Magron et Lahosse (Fr.) 8.-12.7.44	TORTURE	FR.
RODER	252581	M	Ger.		Cmdt.,Waffen SS,C.C.Neusengamme (Ger.)	MURDER	FR.
RODER	255347	M			Sturmschfhr.,C.C.Nordhausen (Ger.)	MURDER	U.S.
RODER	261789	M	Ger.		Cpl.,Feldgendarmerie,Romilly sur Seine (Fr.) 10.6.44	MISC.CRIMES	FR.
RODER,Heinz	38858	M	Ger.		SS-Hptschfhr.,Jg.Ers.Coy,Kraftf.Ers.Rgt.,	MISC.CRIMES	U.S.
RODER,Rudolf	301433	M	Ger.	7. 8.10	Scharfhr.,SS,C.C.Buchenwald (Ger.) 16.5.38-9.10.43	MURDER	BEL.
RODERBURG	137303	M	Ger.		Sgt.,C.C.Stalag VIII B, Gleiwits (Ger.) 3.40	MURDER	U.K.
RODERMANN, Hans	194830	M	Ger.	29. 9.01	Cash-leader,Social-insurance,Luxembourg (Lux.)	PILLAGE	LUX.
RODEWALD	253290	M	Ger.	08	SS-Usturmfhr.,Gestapo,Paris (Fr.) 41,42	TORTURE	FR.
RODIS, Simon	183660	M	Ger.		Official,Police,C.C.Blechhammer,Lendringsen (Ger.) 45	MURDER	POL.
RODL,Arthur (see ROEDEL)	128945						
RODL	306864	M	Ger.		SS-Lt.Col.,C.C.Auschwitz (Pol.) 43	MURDER	FR.
RODL,Arthur (see ROEDEL)	10332						
RODLOF	126915	M	Ger.		SS-Rottfhr.,SS,C.C.Buchenwald (Ger.)	TORTURE	FR.
RODLOF	195903	M	Ger.		Sgt.,Feldgendarmerie,Beaurepaire (Fr.) 5.8.44	MURDER	FR.
RODOLF	136286	M	Ger.		Lt.,Kommandantur,St.Flour (Fr.) 14.6.44	MURDER	FR.
RODOLPH	256752	M	Ger.		Lt.,German Air Force,Abergement de Varey (Fr.) 25.7.44	MURDER	FR.
RODT, Eberhardt	147069	M	Ger.	95	Major General,15 Pz.Gren.Div.,San Giebstino,Longwy Haut (It.,Fr.)	MURDER	U.K.,FR.

ROE - ROE

NAME	C.R.FILE NUMBER	SEX	NATIO-NALITY	DATE OF BIRTH	RANK OCCUPATION UNIT DATE AND PLACE OF CRIME	REASON WANTED	WANTED BY
ROEBICHT	152079	M	Ger.		Sgt.,Gestapo,Trondes-Boucq,Menil la Tour,(Fr.) 44	MURDER	FR.
ROECHER	141599	M	Ger.		Civilian,C.C.;Lustringen (Ger.) 10.3.41	MURDER	FR.
ROECK, Gustav	253781	M	Ger.	06	Head-foreman,Volkswagen Fabrik,Fallersleben (Ger.) 8.44	MURDER	U.S.
ROEDEL	124481	M			Pvt.,16.Waffen SS Panz.Div."Reichsfuehrer",3.Sekt.,2.Coy.,Res.Btty. Strettoia (It.) 15.9.44	MURDER	FR.
ROEDEL	193403	M	Ger.		Uschfhr.,4.SS Totenkopf-Sturmbann,C.C.,Nordhausen,Dora-Mittelbau(Ger.) 43-45	MURDER	U.S.
ROEDEL	301434	M	Ger.		Hptschfhr.,SS,Commandant,C.C.,Gross Rosen (Ger.) 40-43	MURDER	BEL.
ROEDEL,Arthur (or ROEDER,ROEDL, RODL,RODE,RUDEL,RIEDEL)	10332	M	Ger.	90 - 01	Standartenfhr., commander,SS,C.C.,Buchenwald,Natzweiler,Gross-Rosen (Ger.,Fr.) 38-45	MURDER	U.S.,FR.,CZECH. POL.,BEL.
ROEDEL, Arthur (or RODL)	128945	M			Schfhr.,SS,C.C.,Buchenwald (Ger.)	BRUTALITY	U.S.
ROEDEL, Max	152084	M	Ger.		SS-Mann,guard,C.C.,Volary (Czech.) 44-45	MURDER	U.S.
ROEDEL, Max	186796	M	Ger.		N.C.O.,Stalag XIII D,C.C.,Woernitz-Ansbach (Ger.)	TORTURE	BEL.
ROEDER	128821	M	Ger.		Capt.,Landesschuetzen Bn. 400,Halle (Ger.) 10.-12.8.44	TORTURE	U.K.
ROEDER	132679	M	Ger.		Chief,SD,Charleville,Fort-Mahon (Fr.)	MURDER	FR.
ROEDER	195902	M	Ger.		Chief,SD,St.Pol de Leon (Fr.)	WITNESS	FR.
ROEDER	253199	M			Sturmschfhr.,Camp Ellrich,Nordhausen (Ger.)	MURDER	U.S.
ROEDER	300855	M			Pvt.,1.Aufkl.Abt.,3.Coy.,2.Column,XV.Div.Afrika Korps,Saint Leger, (Arlon) 5.9.44	MISC.CRIMES	BEL.
ROEDER,Arthur (see ROEDEL)	10332						
ROEDER, Josef	152081	M	Ger.		Civilian,Wollendorf (Ger.) 29.10.43	WITNESS	U.S.
ROEDERER, Oskar	253200	M		12.12.05	Pvt.,Camp Ellrich,Nordhausen (Ger.)	MURDER	U.S.
ROEDIER	152085	M	Ger.		Lt.,Camp XI A,Altengrade(Ger.) 17.4.45	MURDER	U.S.
ROEDINGER	259632	M	Ger.	20	Employee,Gestapo,Angers,Maine,Loire (Fr.) 42-44	MISC.CRIMES	FR.
ROEDL	10331	M	Ger.		Osturmfhr.,SS,C.C.,Natzweiler (Fr.,Ger.) 42	TORTURE	CZECH.,BEL.
ROEDL, Arthur (see ROEDEL)	10332						
ROEGELEIN	300856	M	Ger.		Pvt.,1.Aufkl.Abt.,3.Coy.,2.Column,XV.Div.Afrika Korps,Saint Leger (Arlon) 5.9.44	MISC.CRIMES	BEL.
ROEGLER,Hans (see REGELER)	251246						
ROEHDEL	186793	M	Ger.	00	Osturmfhr., or Standartenfhr.,SS,Police,C.C.,Gross Rosen (Ger.)	TORTURE	U.K.
ROEHE	125712	M	Ger.	95	Capt.,Army,Flg.Horst Coy.,Rheine, 1.1.45	MURDER	U.K.
ROEHLER	305249	M	Ger.		Blockfhr.,SS,C.C.,Neuengamme (Ger.)	MURDER	FR.
ROEHLING	148562	F	Ger.		Woman guard,C.C.,Hirzenhein (Ger.) 3.45	MURDER	U.S.
ROEHM	301737	M	Ger.	95 - 05	Pvt.,guard,Stalag XX B,610.Landesschuetzen Bn.,Kalbuda near Danzig (Pol.) 13.1.44	MURDER	U.K.
ROEHMER	144356	M			Major,OKW Subsection II PW Affaires	WITNESS	U.S.
ROEHNERT, Hellmuth	62210	M	Ger.		General director,Public official	TORTURE	U.N.W.C.C.
ROEHR, Otto	256051	M	Ger.		Dr.,Org.Todt,Mahldorf (Ger.)	WITNESS	U.S.
ROEHRER, Ferdinand	193402	M	Ger.	19. 2.97	Rottfhr.,SS, (Czech.)	MISC.CRIMES	CZECH.
ROEHRICHT (or ROERICHT)	39605	M	Ger.		Capt.,Inf.4366,Bde.,Jesser,F.P.No.4366 A,Tortebesse (Fr.)22.8.44	MURDER	FR.
ROEHRKASSE, Karl Wilhelm August	301975	M		18. 1. ?	Guard,Arbeitserziehungslager,labour camp,Lahde-Weser,(Ger.)5.43-4.45	MURDER	U.K.
ROEHRLECH, Richard	122673	M	Ger.		SS-Mann,Aachen (Ger.) 9.8.44	MISC.CRIMES	U.S.
ROELER	252582	M	Ger.		Blockfhr.,SS,Neuengamme (Ger.)	MURDER	FR.
ROELLER, Leo (or SCHMIDT)	261490	M	Ger.	90	Chief,Crim.Police,Lodz (Pol.) 39-45	MURDER	POL.
ROELLICH, Johannes	181559	M	Ger.	10.11.02	Crim.Secretary,Sturmschfhr.,Gestapo,SD,SS,Prague (Czech.) 39-43	MURDER	CZECH.
ROEM, Hans (see VON ROEMEN,Hans)	128946						
ROEMER	124645	M	Ger.		Kriegsgefangenenlazarett,Heppenheim (Ger.) 9.44-5.45	TORTURE	U.S.
ROEMER	152082	M			Capt.,Army,27.Fusillier Rgt.,1.Bn.,12.Volksgren.Div.,Hingene (Bel.) 18.12.44	MISC.CRIMES	U.S.
ROEMER	253197	M			Uschfhr.,Camp Hohlstedt,Nordhausen (Ger.)	MURDER	U.S.
ROEMER, Hugo (or ROMER)	192574	M	Ger.	21. 9.97	Councillor,Gestapo,Brno (Czech.) 39-45	SUSPECT	CZECH.
ROEMER, Willi	306105	M	Ger.		Uschfhr.,SS,guard, commander,C.C., Alderney,Channel,Kortemark(Fr.)42-45	MURDER	CZECH.
ROEMHILDT	161735	M	Ger.		Cpl.,Army,Landesschuetzen Bn.789,Sinzig (Ger.) 20.12.41	WITNESS	U.S.
ROEMICH, Samuel	253196	M			Pvt.,Camp Kl.Bodungen,Nordhausen (Ger.)	MURDER	U.S.
ROEMMELE	12480	M	Ger.	28	Pvt.,Waffen SS,16.Pz.Div."Reichsfuehrer",3.Sect.,2.Coy., Strettoia (It.) 15.9.44	MURDER	FR.
ROENGEN, Agnes	195899	F	Ger.		Home address:Boenninghausen 126,Krs.Luebbecke	INTERR.	NETH.
ROENIER, Wilhelm	180739	M		10 - 15	Osturmfhr.,13.SS Pol.Rgt.,18.Bn.,Bleiheng (Aust.) 14.10.44	MURDER	U.S.
ROENS, Franz	193405	M	Ger.		Pvt.,4.SS Totenkopf-Sturmbann,C.C.,Nordhausen,Monowitz(Ger.,Pol.)43-45	MURDER	U.S.
ROENTGEN	161793	M	Ger.	05	Sturmfhr.,NSKK,C.C.,Ohrdruf,Buchenwald (Ger.)	WITNESS	U.S.
ROEPKE, Hans Werner	140856	M	Ger.		Hptsturmfhr.,SS,Com.British Freecorps	WITNESS	U.K.
ROEPFEL (see RAFFEL)	301700						
ROERICH	253303	M	Ger.		Capt.,Btty No.1210 or 1294(Georgiens) Boulazag (Fr.) 11.6.44	MURDER	FR.
ROERICHT	190589	M	Ger.		Oberwachtmstr.,Gestapo,Trondes,Boucq,Menila Tour,Nancy (Fr.)15.8.44	MURDER	FR.
ROERICHT, Kurt	193399	M	Ger.	28.11.87	Sgt.,4.SS Totenkopf-Sturmbann,C.C.,Nordhausen,Mittelbau,Dora, Auschwitz (Ger.,Pol.) 43-45	MURDER	U.S.
ROESCH	142128	M			Buehl (Ger.)	MURDER	FR.
ROESCH	253524	M			Pvt.,C.C.,Osterhagen,Nordhausen (Ger.)	MURDER	U.S.
ROESCH, Alvons	190394	M	Ger.		Civilian,Wiesbaden (Ger.) 43-45	WITNESS	U.S.
ROESCHMAN	122675	M	Ger.		Lt.,SS,Sturm Bn.,Courcelles sur Nied (Fr.) 15.11.44	WITNESS	U.S.
ROESE	21453	M	Ger.	15	Uschfhr.,SS,C.C.,Hamburg (Ger.) 8.44	MURDER	CZECH.
ROESE (or REESE)	192551	M	Ger.	05	Uschfhr.,SS,Blockfhr.,C.C.,Neuengamme (Ger.)	MURDER	FR.,YUGO.
ROESE, Heinrich	152086	M	Ger.		Policeman,Police,field,Ginnheim (Ger.) 11.44	WITNESS	U.S.
ROESEN, Ernst	186791	M	Ger.	15.10.94	Leader,NSDAP district office,Civilian,Mariansko,Lasno (Czech.)39-45	MISC.CRIMES	CZECH.
ROESLMANN	67025	M	Ger.		Capt.,Army,Dax (Fr.) 19.6.44	MURDER	FR.
ROESEN	193336	M			Oberassistenarzt,Navy,hospital,Drontheim (Nor.) 4.44	TORTURE	NOR.
ROESLER, Josef	186437	M			Kapo,SS,C.C.,Mauthausen (Aust.)	MURDER	U.S.
ROESLER, Josef	186438	M	Ger.	01	Chief,NSDAP,Praha (Czech.)	MISC.CRIMES	CZECH.
ROESLER, Wilhelm	194829	M	Ger.	28. 2.95	Mayor,public official,Luxembourg,Junglinster (Lux.)	PILLAGE	LUX.
ROESNER	21478	M	Ger.		Pvt.,12.SS Pz.Div. Hitler-Jugend	WITNESS	CAN.
ROESNER, Fritz	165157	M	Ger.		Air-force,Stabsbildabt.,F.P.No.35070B,Avignon (Fr.) 8.8.44	MURDER	FR.
ROESNER, Helmut	177162	M	Ger.		Pvt.,12.SS Pz.Div."Hitler-Jugend", near Caen (Fr.) 6.6.-7.7.44	TORTURE	CAN.
ROESSL	257763	M			Krim.Oberasst.,SS,Field police,Foix (Fr.) 42-44	INTERR.	FR.
ROESSLER	253532	M			Rottfhr.,C.C.,Mackenrode (Nixe),Nordhausen (Ger.)	MURDER	U.S.
ROESSLER, Franz	192819	M	Ger.		Oschfhr.,SS,C.C.,Buchenwald (Ger.) 42-45	MURDER	U.S.

ROE-ROJ

NAME	C.R.FILE NUMBER	SEX	NATIO-NALITY	DATE OF BIRTH	RANK OCCUPATION UNIT PLACE AND DATE OF CRIME	REASON WANTED	WANTED BY
ROESSLER, Julius	252588	M	Ger.	13. 3.04	Butcher, admin. of Jewish property, Jablonne n-O district Zamberk and Dol Cermina, district Lauskroun (Czech.) 39-45	MISC.CRIMES	CZECH.
ROESSNER	161730	M	Ger.	10	Osturmfhr, SS, Wirtschafts- und Verwaltungshauptamt, CCOhrdruf(Ger.)	WITNESS	U.S.
ROETGER	196640	M	Ger.		W.O., Sicherungs-Rgt.618,St.Marcel(Fr.) 13.9.44	WITNESS	FR.
ROETGERS	302114	M	Ger.		Member SD,Almelo district (Neth.) 9.44-2.45	PILLAGE	NETH.
ROETHKE	756	M	Ger.		SS Osturmfhr, CC Drancy,Pithiviers,Compiegne,Beaune,La Rolande(Fr.)43	MURDER	FR.
ROETTIG, Otto	12333	M	Ger.	22. 7.87	Lt.General,Inspec. General of POW-camps,Germany 25.3.44,8.2.44	MURDER	U.K.,UNWCC
ROETTKE (see ROTKE)	214025						
ROETZEL, Wilhelm	193426	M	Ger.	92	Sgt., 4 SS Totenkopf-Sturmbann,CC Nordhausen,Auschwitz, Mittelbau, Dora, Nordhausen (Ger., Pol.) 43-45	MURDER	U.S.
ROEWE	253537	M			Hptschfhr, CC Ellrich, Nordhausen (Ger.)	MURDER	U.S.
ROFETER	252608	M			Oschfhr, 2 Coy, SS Pz.Rgt.,Malmedy(Bel.) 17.12.44	MISC.CRIMES	U.S.
ROFLING	252583	M	Ger.		Member Gestapo,Lille (Fr.) 40-44	MISC.CRIMES	FR.
ROGALA, Helmut	156051	M	Ger.		Pvt., 76 Gren.Ers.Ausb.Bn., CC Stalag VI C (Ger.) 45	WITNESS	U.S.
ROGALL	193337	M	Ger.		Pvt., 1 Kriegs-Arb.Bn.41,Nerlandsdal,Kristiansund (Nor.) 41-45	TORTURE	NOR.
ROGALLA, Emil	67581	M	Ger.		Cpl., military prison, Graudenz (Pol.)	MISC.CRIMES	U.K.
ROGALLA, Paul	256915	M	Ger.		Foreman, O.T., Muhldorf (Ger.)	WITNESS	U.S.
ROGEL, Arthur	301603	M	Ger.		SS Osturmbannfhr, CC Gross-Rosen, Mauthausen (Aust.) 40-45	MURDER	BEL.
ROGENSTEIN	99606	M	Ger.		Capt.,German customs service,Ville la Grande,Hte. Savoie (Fr.)8.7.44	MURDER	FR.
ROGER	21479	M	Ger.		near Orleans (Fr.) 8.44	MURDER	U.S.
ROGER	301435	M	Ger.		Agent, Gestapo, CC Dora, Nordhausen (Ger.) 40-45	MURDER	BEL.
ROGERS	168846	M	Ger.		SS Oschfhr, Cmdt. of Crematorium,Auschwitz(Pol.)40-45	MURDER	FR.
ROGGE	12666	M			Dr., public official, responsible for plans of evacuation, Finmark (Nor.) 10.,11.44	TORTURE	NOR.
ROGGE	188108	M			Dr., Reichskommissar, Ministry of Navy	MURDER	NOR.
ROGGE	255447	M	Ger.		Sturmschfhr, CC Ellrich, Nordhausen (Ger.)	MURDER	U.S.
ROGGINDORF, Willy	167145	M	Ger.		Field-police-man, field-police, Luneville Maixe (Fr.) 16..17.8.44	MURDER	FR.
ROGGOL (see ROGOLL)	135556						
ROGHE	188819	M	Ger.		Brig., Army, Le Bourget Triage (Fr.) 24.8.44	WITNESS	FR.
ROGOLL (or ROGGOL)	135556	M	Ger.		Pvt., Army, Jaworsno (Pol.) 12.2.43	MURDER	U.K.
ROGY, Emmerich	259005	M	Ger.		Lt.General., crimes against peace. war crimes and crimes against humanity	WITNESS	U.S.
ROH	180744	M	Ger.		Employee, Schfhr, Gestapo, SD, Saarbruecken (Ger.)	PILLAGE	FR.
ROHDE	1466	M	Ger.		Insp., Naval supply	MISC.CRIMES	U.K.
ROHDE (or RHODE)	141072	M	Ger.		Dr., Capt., CC Natzweiler (Fr.) 1-2.9.44	MURDER	U.S., U.K.
ROHDE	148598	M	Ger.		Dr., SS Osturmfhr, CC Auschwitz (Pol.) 43-44	MURDER	U.S.
ROHDE	173949	M	Ger.		Usturmfhr, SS, CC Struthof (Fr.)	MURDER	FR.
ROHDE	199906	M	Ger.		Civilian, St.Rambert (Fr.)	SUBJECT	FR.
ROHDE	257869	M	Ger.		Cpl., 150 Pz.Bde.,Meuse Bridge, Antwerpen(Bel.) 12.44	MISC.CRIMES	U.S.
ROHDE, Gunter	192571	M	Ger.	22	Army prisoner at Ft.Zinna,Torgau (Ger.)45	WITNESS	U.S.
ROHDE, Ludwig	167477	M	Ger.		Civ.,member of adm.staff,Einsatzstab Rosenberg (Fr.) 40-44	PILLAGE	FR.
ROHDE, Walter	122674	M		01	Officer, Camp-leader of CC Boegermoor(Ger.)	TORTURE	U.S.
ROHDEWALD, August	214022	M	Ger.	4. 9.97	Member NSDAP; Director, Reichskreditges.A.G.,Berlin,Wien(Ger.Aust.)	INTER.	U.S.
ROHFF	252629	M	Ger.		Uschfhr, Gestapo, Limoges(Fr.)	MISC.CRIMES	FR.
ROHL	144962	M	Ger.	05	CC Muhldorf near Mittergars (Ger.) 12.44	MURDER	U.S.
ROHL(or REUL)	156045	M	Ger.	15	Schfhr, SS, Enschede (Neth.)	MURDER	U.K.
ROHL, Hans	193317	M	Ger.		CC Dachau (Ger.)	TORTURE	U.S.
ROHLE, Minna	252599	F	Ger.		Secretary, CC Lahde-Weser (Ger.)	INTER.	BEL.
ROHLENDER	190057	M	Ger.		Officer, Camp Cmdt., CC Galatas (Grc.) 12.6.41	MURDER	U.K.
ROHLIG	158229	M	Ger.		Member Gestapo,Army,Saone and Loire (Fr.) 43-44	MURDER	FR.
ROHLIG, Fritz	162692	M	Ger.		Pvt., Gestapo, Dun les Places (Fr.) 6.44	MURDER	FR.
ROHLING	132682	M	Ger.		Officer, Standortkommandantur, Gerardmer (Fr.) 9.-11.44	MISC.CRIMES	FR.
ROHLKE	156050	M	Ger.	1910 - 11	Uschfhr, SS, CC Sachsenhausen, Oranienburg(Ger.)	MURDER	U.K.
ROHMEIER, Erich	253198	M		30. 9.14	Sgt., Camp Ellrich, Nordhausen (Ger.)	MURDER	U.S.
ROHMER (or ROHNER)	10334	M	Ger.		Dr., public prosecutor, Prague (Czech.) from 40	MURDER	CZECH.
ROHNDE, Gustav	259181	M	Ger.		Rottfhr, SS, CC Dachau (Ger.)	MISC.CRIMES	YUGO.
ROHNER, Claus	12482	M	Ger.		Pvt., 110,111 Pz.Gren.Rgt., 2 Coy,Albine(Fr.) 29.6.44	MURDER	FR.
ROHNER (see ROHMER)	10334						
ROHNERT, Franz	193444	M	Ger.		Rottfhr, 4 SS Totenkopfsturmbann,CC Dora,Mittelbau,Nordhausen, Osterode (Ger.) 43-45	MURDER	U.S.
ROHR	74520	M	Ger.		Hptsturmfhr, W-SS,Totenkopfsturmbann,leader of camp Berga-Elster, CC Buchenwald (Ger.)	MURDER	U.S.
ROHR	137592	M			Lt., Stalag IV-D,Torgau (Ger.) 1.44	MISC.CRIMES	U.K.
ROHR	195965	M			CC Struthof - Natzweiler (Fr.)	MURDER	FR.
ROHR	259288	M			Usturmfhr, SS, Innsbruck (Aust.) 20.4.45	BRUTALITY	U.S.
ROHR	260681	M			Crimes against peace, war crimes and crimes against humanity	WITNESS	U.S.
ROHR	301899	M	Ger.		Capt.,comd.II Geb.Jg.Rgt.,139,8 Geb.Div.,20 Army,Finmark(Nor)10-11.44	MURDER	NOR.
ROHR, Hanns	141999	M	Ger.	10	Camp senior,labour camp,Waldlager V and VI, near Ampfing(Ger)44-45	TORTURE	U.S.
ROHRBACHER	196005	M	Ger.		CC Struthof,Natzweiler (Fr.) 40-44	MURDER	FR.
ROHRBACHER, Peter	260550	M	Ger.		Chief Police, Jasa Tomic, Banat (Yugo.) 42	MISC.CRIMES	YUGO.
ROHRER, Herbert	214024	M	Ger.	3.or 6.6.01	President,Osram GmbH, Berlin (Ger.)	MISC.CRIMES	U.S.
ROHRICHT, Kurt	255446	M		26.11.97	Schfhr, CC Nordhausen (Ger.)	MURDER	U.S.
ROHRING	128947	M			Schfhr, SS, CC Weimar - Buchenwald (Ger.)	MURDER	U.S.
ROHRLECH, Richard	126587	M			Schfhr, SS-Trooper, Aachen (Ger.) 9.8.44	TORTURE	U.S.
ROHRO	29647	M	Ger.		Lt., Army, Locmine (Fr.) 44	MURDER	FR.
ROHRS	190591	M			Cadet officer, Turkestan legion, Rimont (Fr.) 21.8.44	MURDER	FR.
ROHRS, Albert	193938	M	Ger.		Sgt., Kriegsgefangenen-Arbeits-Bn.,184,Drag (Nor.)	WITNESS	NOR.
ROHRSCHACH, Ernst	10935	M	Ger.		Camp senior, SS, CC Natzweiler (Fr.) 42	TORTURE	CZECH.
ROHTER (see ROTER)	195904						
ROIKO (see ROYKO)	24890						
ROISNEL, Francis	193916	M	Ger.		Civilian	WITNESS	U.S.
ROITSCH, Alfred (or ROITZSCH)	193092	M	Ger.	8. 2.02	Sgt., Guard, Ministry of Justice, Feldstraflager CC Finmark(Nor.) 6.42-45	MISC.CRIMES	NOR.,YUGO.
ROJCKE (or ROPKE)	192083	M	Ger.		Lt., Army, F.P.Nr. 03591 D. Plessis L'Eveque(Fr.) 21.8.44	WITNESS	FR.
ROJKO	124755	M	Ger. or Czech.		Sgt., CC Theresienstadt (Czech.) 12.41-3.45	TORTURE	U.S.
ROJKO, Stephan	193321	M	Ger.	15.12.10	Guard, Oschfhr, SS Police Service, CC Terezin (Czech.) 40-45	MURDER	CZECH.

ROJ-ROS

NAME	C.R.FILE NUMBER	SEX	NATIO-NALITY	DATE OF BIRTH	RANK OCCUPATION UNIT PLACE AND DATE OF CRIME	REASON WANTED	WANTED BY
ROJKO, Zilly	193319	F	Ger.	23.11.13	Warden, SS-Notdienstverpflichtete, C.C., Terezin (Czech.) 40-45	MISC.CRIMES	CZECH.
ROKINI	186439	M	Ger.		Lt., Abwehr, Athens (Grc.)	TORTURE	GRC.
ROKITA	306186	M	Ger.		Uschfhr., C.C., Kahla (Ger.) 40-45	MURDER	BEL.
ROLAND, Klara	152060	F	Ger.		Guard, Member, SS, C.C., Duderstadt (Ger.)	WITNESS	U.S.
ROLAND, Leni	152059	F	Ger.		Guard, Member, SS, C.C., Duderstadt (Ger.)	WITNESS	U.S.
ROLF	255777	M	Ger.		Store-keeper, C.C., Neckargerach, Neckarelz (Ger.)	INTERR.	FR.
ROLF	306785	M	Ger.		Pvt., SS, Feldpost-No.: 05452 B or C, Panz.Gren., or 15807 B, Houyot, Dinant (Bel.) 4.9.44	PILLAGE	BEL.
ROLF, Charlotte	193318	F	Ger.	10	Civilian, Oberkall, Krs. Wittlich (Ger.) 15.8.44	WITNESS	U.S.
ROLF, Rudolf	129032	M	Ger.		Civilian, Bielefeld (Ger.) 43	TORTURE	BEL.
ROLFF, Justus	167476	M	Ger.		Sgt., Director of Prison of Baumettes, C.C., Marseille (Fr.) 44	MURDER	FR.
ROLFS, Albert	261062	M	Ger.	07	Sturmschfhr., SD of Draguignan, Var (Fr.) 8.44	MURDER	FR.
ROLL	256052	M	Ger.		Schuetze, Muehldorf (Ger.)	WITNESS	U.S.
ROLL, Karl	141600	M	Ger.		Chief of Kitchen No.967, Florisdorf, Schwechat (Aust.) 43-44	TORTURE	FR.
ROLLE	757	M		10	Sgt., Lds.Schtz.Bn.398 or 348, Stalag VIII B, C.C., Klausberg (Pol.) 16.,17.12.41	MURDER	U.K.
ROLLE	255445	M			Pvt., C.C. Ellrich, Nordhausen (Ger.)	MURDER	U.S.
ROLLER	121878	M	Ger.		Capt., Army, Unit: F.P.No.: 13353 E, Chievres (Bel.)	INCENDIARISM	BEL.
ROLLER, Albert	305689	M	Ger.		Sturmschfhr., SS, C.C., Flossenburg, Hersburg, Wolkenburg, Ganacker, Leitmeritz (Ger. and Czech.) 1.42-5.45		U.S.
ROLLER, Fritz	186851	M	Ger.		Oberkapo, C.C., Flossenburg, Pomelsbrunn (Ger.)	MURDER	FR.
ROLLIN	195900	M	Ger.	94	Capt., Camp de Royallieu, Compiegne (Fr.) 41-44	MISC.CRIMES	FR.
ROLLINS	194698	M	Ger.		Col., Army, Plancher Bas (Fr.) 3.10.44	WITNESS	FR.
ROLLO	122549	M	Ger.		Sgt., Army, 5-398.Coy., C.C., Hindenburg (Ger.) 17.12.41	MURDER	U.K.
ROLLWAGE	1741	M			Cpl., Navy	MURDER	U.K.
ROLLWAGE, Fryderyk	12332	M	Ger.		Cpl., Army, 145.Inf.Rgt., 2.Bn., Amiens (Fr.) 21.8.44	MURDER	U.K.
ROLOFF	188811	M	Ger.		Cpl., Lds.Schtz.Bn.4, 4.Coy., Rue Troncke a-Lyon (Fr.) 24.8.44	MURDER	FR.
ROLSCHER	129039	M	Ger.		5.Parachute-Rgt., Quaregnon, Jemappes, Ghlin (Bel.) 2.,3.9.44	MURDER	BEL.
ROMAL	128824	M			Sgt., Army, Genoa-Mantova (It.) 2.43-11.43	TORTURE	U.K.
ROMALIN	183669	M			Rottfhr., SS, IV.SS-Totenkopf-Stuba., C.C., Mittelbau-Dora,Plaszow, Nordhausen (Ger.) 43-45	WITNESS	U.S.
ROMANN	183668	M			Sturmmann, IV.SS-Totenkopf-Stuba, C.C., Dora,Rosen Aslau,Nordhausen (Ger.) 43-45	WITNESS	U.S.
ROMANN, Hans	38850	M	Ger.		Uschfhr., SS, C.C., Struthof (Fr.)	TORTURE	FR.
ROMBACH	258195	M	Ger.		Chief of Admin., Deputy, Beauftragter, Reichscommissariat, Amsterdam (Neth.) 7.2.45	SUSPECT	NETH.
ROMEI, Rudolf	261100	M	Ger.	26.4.12	Chief-clerk, Factory "Ceskomoravke Strojirny", Prague (Czech.) 42	MISC.CRIMES	CZECH.
ROMEIKAT, Franz	260460	M	Ger.	7.10.04	Uschfhr., SS, Allgem.SS, Guard and Admin.,C.C.,Auschwitz (Pol.) 41-44	BRUTALITY	POL.
ROMER	1742	M			Uschfhr., SS, C.C., Dachau (Ger.)	TORTURE	U.K.
ROMER	259280	M			SS-Mann, Muehldorf Area (Ger.)	MURDER	U.S.
ROMER, Hugo (see ROEMER)	192574						
ROMER, Ida	300921	F	Ger.		Member, SS of Staff, C.C. Sasel (Ger.) 10.44-4.45	TORTURE	U.K.
ROMERMANN, Helgar	144362	F	Ger.		Civilian, C.C., Hadamar (Ger.) 6.44-3.45	WITNESS	U.S.
ROMETSCH	306106	M			SS-Mann, C.C. Alderney (Channel Is.) and C.C. Kortemark (Fr.) 42-45	MURDER	CZECH.
ROMMEL	129038	M			Rottfhr., SS, C.C., Mauthausen (Aust.) 41-42	MURDER	U.S.
ROMMEL	166668	M			Lt., Div."Brandenburg", 3.Brandenburg-Rgt., San Vittore (It.)	MURDER	U.S.
ROMMEL	186435	M	Ger.		Amtsgerichtsrat,Justizvollzugsanstalt, Ebrach (Ger.) 43	MURDER	CZECH.
ROMMEL	192145	M			Capt., Geh.Feldpolizei, Brussels (Bel.)	TORTURE	BEL.
ROMMEL, Erich	182576	M			Rottfhr., SS, C.C., Mauthausen (Aust.) 1.45	MURDER	U.S.
ROMMEL, Max	195183	M	Ger.		Director, Omnia-Treuhand-Ges., La Hague (Neth.)	PILLAGE	NETH.
ROMMICK	193033	M	Ger.		Capt., SS, SD, C.C. Falstadt (Nor.) 41-45	MURDER	NOR.
ROMPA (or ROMPER)	189707	M			Sgt., Guard, Stalag X B, Bremervoerde, Sandbostel (Ger.) 6.41-1.43	TORTURE	U.K.
ROMPER	125049	M			Sgt., Stalag X B, C.C., Sandbostel (Ger.) 4.41-6.41	TORTURE	U.K.
ROMPER (see ROMPA)	189707						
RONACHER, Emil	190365	M	Ger.		Oschfhr., SS, Gestapo, Negotin Zajecar (Yugo.) 41-43	TORTURE	YUGO.
RONEICH (or ROMESCH)	260143	M	Ger.		Gend.,Div.Oberland,Russ.Ger., Massif Du Vercors,Isere and Drome (Fr.) 7.44-8.44	SUSPECT	FR.
RONGE, Wilhelm	141601	M			Chenebier-Etobon (Fr.) 27.9.44	MURDER	FR.
RONKL	29719	M			Dr., Oberlandgerichtsrat, Ministry of Justice, Prague (Czech.) 40	TORTURE	CZECH.
RONOLD	251242	M			Agent du Service, Gestapo, Offenburg (Ger.) 11.44	INTERR.	FR.
RONS	255444	M			Pvt., C.C. Monowitz, Nordhausen (Ger.)	MURDER	U.S.
RONSEL	140887	M	Ger.		Capt., Army, Bilthaven (Neth.) 2.45	MURDER	NETH.
ROOKFORT	165552	M	Ger.		Civilian Guard, Dessau (Ger.) 10.43	TORTURE	BEL.
ROORCH, Gotthold (see ROSCHER)	128949						
ROORCH	255770	M			Rottfhr., C.C., Buchenwald (Ger.)	MURDER	U.S.
ROOS, Karl	255443	M		19.2.05	Flyer, C.C. Ellrich, Nordhausen (Ger.)	MURDER	U.S.
ROOST (or ROST)	192146	M	Ger.		Major, Geh.Feldpolizei, Liege (Bel.)	TORTURE	BEL.
ROOT, Karl-Heinz	251875	M	Ger.	05	Secretary, Buyer, (D.A.U.A.) Betonwerk, Lausbig (Ger.) 43-45	BRUTALITY	U.K.
ROPKE, N.	251872	M	Ger.		Farmer, Civilian, Member, SA, (Ger.) 43-45	TORTURE	POL.
ROPEL	256053	M			Uschfhr., SS, Muehldorf	WITNESS	U.S.
ROPEN, Otto	124243	M	Ger.	00	Forester, Stalag 2 A, C.C., Corshagen nr.Rostock (Ger.)	TORTURE	U.S.
ROPERS	162784	M	Ger.	85	Wachtmeister, C.C. Sasel (Ger.)	MURDER	U.K.
ROPKE (see ROJCKE)	192089						
ROPKE	255330	M			Pvt., C.C. Dora, Nordhausen (Ger.)	MURDER	U.S.
ROPMER	196639	M			Lt., Flyer-Rgt:91 III.Bn., Lamarolle - Sologne (Fr.) 17.8.44	WITNESS	FR.
ROPPERT, Friedrich	29720	M	Ger.		Dr., Landgerichtsrat, Public Official, Litomerice (Czech.) 40	MURDER	CZECH.
ROPPKE	179460	F	Ger.		Civilian, Helmstedt (Ger.) 9.44	TORTURE	U.S.
RORSCH	253306	M			Sgt., Monsheim (Fr.)	INTERR.	FR.
ROSALIE	251852	F		13	Guard, C.C. Ravensbruek (Ger.)	INTER.	FR.
ROSAK, Wilhelm	189670	M	Ger.	16.5.02	Lt., Gend., Havlickuv Brod (Czech.) 44-45	MURDER	CZECH.
ROSBACH, Franz	196658	M	Ger.	06	Pvt., Army, Kiskirchen (Ger.) 3.44	MISC.CRIMES	POL.
ROSCH	174142	M			SS, C.C. Auschwitz (Pol.)	TORTURE	U.S.
ROSCH, Anton	12489	M			Pvt.,110.,111.Gren.Rgt.,2.Coy., Albine (Fr.) 29.6.44	MURDER	FR.
ROSCH, Heinrich	132117	M	Ger.	10	Lt., SS and SD, Issel (Ger.) 20.1.45	MURDER	U.S.
ROSCH, Johann	133272	M	Ger.	90	Capt., Ger.Army, Oflag 13 B, Hammelburg (Ger.) 44-45	WITNESS	U.S.
ROSCH, Lothar	300423	M	Ger.		Staff II, 694.Gren.Rgt.2, Bourcy nr.Bastogne (Lux.) 12.44	MISC.CRIMES	BEL.

ROS-ROS

NAME	C.R.FILE NUMBER	SEX	NATIO-NALITY	DATE OF BIRTH	RANK OCCUPATION UNIT PLACE AND DATE OF CRIME	REASON WANTED	WANTED BY
ROSCHANEK, Rudolf	195090	M	Ger.	00	Member-Employee,Gestapo,Kolin(Czech.) 39-45	MURDER	CZECH.
ROSCHEK, Karl Albert	260438	M	Ger.	31.3.04	SS-Mann,Waffen-SS,Guard-Coy.,C.C.Auschwitz(Pol.) 7.43-1.45	BRUTALITY	POL.
ROSCHENTHALER, Franz	254881	M	Ger.	5.3.01	Civilian,Gossengrun-Haberspirk(Czech.) 9.99	MURDER	CZECH.
ROSCHER see ROORCH	128948						
ROSCHER, Gotthold	128949	M			SS-Scharfhr.,C.C.Buchenwald(Ger.) 42-45	MURDER	U.S.
or RAUCH or ROORCH							
ROSCHER, Helmut	141995	M	Ger.	24.11.17	Oschfhr.,Waffen-SS,Totenkopf-Verband,C.C.Buchenwald(Ger.)	MURDER	U.S.
ROSCHER, Karl	181561	M	Ger.	20	Oschfhr.,Guard,SS,Totenkopf-Stand.,C.C.Weimar-Buchenwald(Ger.) 39-45	MURDER	CZECH.
ROSCHE	199070				Schfhr.,SS-Div.Totenkopf,Riga(Latv.),Auschwitz(Pol.) 41-43	MURDER	U.S.
ROSCHMANN	301900	M	Ger.		Lt.-Col.,Ia,2 Geb.Div.,20 Army,Finmark. 10.-11.44	MURDER	NOR.
ROSCHMIEDER	147359	M	Ger.		Lt.,11 Pz.Div.,(South West Fr.) 44	MURDER	FR.
ROSCHS	306289	M	Ger.		Member of the Gestapo at Trencin,C.C.Oswiecim-Birkenau(Pol.) 39-45	MURDER	CZECH.
ROSE	148542	M			SS-Uschfhr.,Cmdt.,C.C.Ilfeld or Gardelegen(Ger.) 4.45	MURDER	U.S.
ROSE	152077	M			Cmdt.,SS,Koeln(Ger.) 10.44	MURDER	U.S.
ROSE	161792	M	Ger.	00	Oberstarzt,Air Corps,Gen.-Staff,C.C.Buchenwald(Ger.)	WITNESS	U.S.
ROSE	167466	M	Ger.		Sgt.,Indian Inf.,950 Regt.,Charente et Vienne(Fr.) 18.-21.8.44	MURDER	FR.
ROSE	257859	M	Ger.		Sgt.,Gend.,Vieville-Sous-Les-Cotes(Fr.)	TORTURE	FR.
ROSE	261886	M	Ger.		Major,Prison,Graudenz(Ger.)	BRUTALITY	BEL.
ROSE, Richard	256775	M	Ger.	26.1.21	C.C.Prison Dora,Nordhausen(Ger.)	MURDER	U.S.
ROSEMANN	193974	M	Ger.		Rottfhr.,SS,Stavelot(Bel.) 19.,20.12.44	MURDER	BEL.
ROSEMBERG, Adolf	253304	M	Ger.		Chief of Block 9, C.C.Auschwitz(Pol.)	TORTURE	FR.
ROSENAU	67582	M	Ger.		Lt.,Landesschietzen Bn.439,I Coy.,Bayreuth(Ger.) 11.4.45	MURDER	U.K.
ROSENBAUM	251871	M	Ger.	10	Usturmfhr.,SS,SD,Rabka(Pol.) 43	MISC.CRIMES	POL.
ROSENBAUM, Franz	195182	M	Ger.	16	Sturmschfhr.,SS,SD,Einsatz-Kdo.Wenger,Baccarat Enval(Fr.) 8.,9.44	MURDER	U.K.
ROSENBAYER	152075	M	Ger.		Pvt.,Gestapo,Brive(Fr.) 44	MURDER	FR.
ROSENBERG	152341	M			Platoon-Leader,Volkssturm,1 Bn.,Gardelegen(Ger.) 10.-14.4.45	MURDER	U.S.
ROSENBERG	173223	M	Ger.		Pvt.,Landesschuetzen Bn.,Stalag XXI D,Posen(Pol.) 15.4.45	MURDER	U.K.
ROSENBERG	174978	M	Ger.		Interpreter,Oflag IV B,C.C.Konigsten(Ger.) 19.1.45	MURDER	FR.
ROSENBERG	186849	M	Ger.		Officer,Air Force,Evreux(Fr.) 41-42	PILLAGE	FR.
ROSENBERGER, Hermann	253525	M			Pvt.,C.C.Kllrich,Nordhausen(Ger.)	MURDER	U.S.
ROSENBRUCK	125648	M	Ger.		Major,Farachute-Pioneer Ers.Bn.,S.F.Nr.49925A,Decize-Montaron-Vandenesse(Fr.) 10.,11.7.44	MURDER	FR.
ROSENBUSCH	162702	M	Ger.		SS-Osturmfhr.,Waffen-SS,Totenkopf-Stand.,Com.Staff C.C.Buchenwald(Ger.)	TORTURE	U.S.
ROSENDABLE	12484	M	Ger.		Military-court, Lille(Fr.) 1.44	TORTURE	FR.
ROSENDAEL, Georg see ROSENTHAL	129040						
ROSENDAHL, Hermann	125649	M	Ger.	13	Gestapo-Police,(Nord.-Fr.)	MISC.CRIMES	FR.
ROSENFEL or ROSENFELD	190356	M	Ger.	15	Capt.,Air Force,Corva(Ital.) 25.9.43	MURDER	U.K.
ROSENFELD	253297	M	Ger.		Inspector,Gestapo,Nord Lille(Fr.) 40-44	MURDER	FR.
ROSENGART	152079	M	Ger.		Lt.,Kampfgeschwader III,Villaudric(Fr.) 20.8.44	MURDER	FR.
ROSENGRANTZ	253298	M	Ger.		Lt.,157 Res.Inf.Div.,L'Ain(Fr.) 10.-21.7.44	MURDER	FR.
ROSENHAIN	161728	M			Pvt.,Army,C.C.Leipzig(Ger.)	SUSPECT	U.S.
ROSENHEUER, Karl	256863	M			Supervisor,Volkswagenwerk Fallersleben,Soehaux(Fr.) 40-44	SUSPECT	FR.
ROSENKRANS, Karl	253315	M	Ger.		Sgt.,377 Jaeger-Regt.,Vinkt and Meigem(Bel.) 25.-31.5.40	MURDER	BEL.
ROSENKRANZ, Heinrich	253534	M			Pvt.,C.C.Kllrich,Nordhausen(Ger.)	MURDER	U.S.
ROSENKRANZ, Karl	135905	M	Ger.		Civilian,Efferen(Fr.) 2.10.44	WITNESS	U.S.
ROSENKRANZ, Meija	306239	M			Ambulance Man (M.63834),Genderen,Babylonienbroek.18.4.45	MURDER	NETH.
ROSENKRANZ, Walter	162707	M	Ger.		Hptschfhr.,SS,Sipo,Revin(Fr.) 6.44	MURDER	FR.
ROSENMAYER	250443	M	Ger.		Officer,Chatou(Fr.) 27.8.44	MURDER	FR.
ROSEN-RUNGEN	192082	M	Ger.		Interpreter,Arb.-Kdo.,Province Finistere(Fr.)	TORTURE	FR.
ROSENSTOCK see ROSENTOCK	192575						
ROSENTHAL, Georg or ROSENDAEL	129040	M	Ger.		Civilian,Mont-sur-Marchienne(Bel.) 9.4.41	MURDER	BEL.
ROSENTOCK or ROSENSTOCK	192575	M	Ger.		Osturmfhr.,SS-Regt.,"Der Fuehrer",SS Div."Das Reich",1 Bn.,4 Coy., Gelat Frayssinet(Fr.) 21.5.44	MURDER	FR.
ROSENTOCK	255773	M			Cpl.,2 Ba.,10 SS Panzer-Div.Trundsberg,Marly-Louveciennes(Fr.)19-29.8.44	WITNESS	FR.
ROSENWEIG	260684	M			Sgt.,Field-Police,Enghien Les Bains-Domont(Fr.) 16.-16.8.44	WITNESS	FR.
ROSENWINKEL	12485	M			Pvt.,Army,110 or 111 Pz.Gren.Regt.,Gourdon(Fr.) 29.6.44	MURDER	FR.
ROSER	180740	M			SS-Man,SS-Leibstand."Adolf Hitler" Aufklaerungsabt.,Renardmont, Stavelot(Bel.) 19.12.44	MURDER	BEL.
ROSER	305253	M	Ger.		Capt.,W.O.,670 Art.Regt.,Tripolis. 3.44	MURDER	GRC.
ROSI, Karl	252612	M	Ger.		Sgt.,Unit.F.P.Nr.235116,La Bresse(Fr.) 9.-11.44	MISC.CRIMES	FR.
ROSIN	192087	M	Ger.		Civilian,Interpreter,Paix(Fr.) 22.8.44	MURDER	FR.
ROSIN, Albert	198024	M			Ortsgruppenorg.-Leiter NSDAP (Ger.)	MURDER	U.S.
ROSIN, Alfred	253533	M			Pvt.,C.C.Kllrich,Nordhausen(Ger.)	MURDER	U.S.
ROSING	152074	M	Ger.		Lagerfuehrer C.C.Guard,Muehlheim(Ger.) 12.2.44	TORTURE	FR.
ROSKAMP, Diet.	167475	M	Ger.		Dr.,Expert,Einsatzstab Rosenberg(Fr.) 40-44	PILLAGE	FR.
ROSKOPAL, Friedrich	29721	M	Ger.		Dr.,Landgerichtsrat,Public Official,Brno(Czech.) 40	MURDER	CZECH.
ROSKOTHEN, Ernst	31542	M	Ger.		Major,Gestapo,Paris(Fr.) 19.5.43	TORTURE	FR.
ROSLER	258887	M	Ger.		Capt.(Stabsintendant),Navy,Dienststelle of Bordeaux,Lignieres Sonneville(Fr.) 30.8.44	WITNESS	FR.
ROSLER, Frans	301436	M			Uschfhr.,Capt.,SS,C.C.Buchenwald(Ger.) 16.5.98-9.10.43	MURDER	BEL.
ROSLER, Hans	15808	M	Ger.	26.7.19	Cpl.,polish Interpreter,Army,Kriegsgefangenenbau Arb.-Bn.24, C.C.Augsburg(Ger.) 40-4.45	MURDER	U.S.
ROSLMEIER, Karl	258696	M	Ger.		machinist,Air Field Wieseck(Ger.) 3.or 4.44	WITNESS	U.S.
ROSNER	136347	M			SS-Hptsturmfhr.,19 SS Pol.-Regt.,C.C.Oberkrain,Agen,Tulle,Toulouse, Compiegne(Yugo.,Fr.) 5.41-3.44,9.-10.44	MURDER	U.S.
ROSNER	137589	M	Ger.		Official,SS,SD,Gestapo,Hertogenbosch,Tilburg(Neth.) 9.7.44	MURDER	U.K.
ROSNER	192694	M	Ger.		Uschfhr.,9 SS Panz.Div."Hohenstaufen",Neuville les Bois(Fr.)	MURDER	FR.
ROSOLI, Gustav	305941	M	Ger.		C.C.Guard,C.C.Neugraben and Tiefstak(Ger.) 44-5.2.45	BRUTALITY	CZECH.
ROSOW, Karl	251298	M	Ger.		SS-Mann,SS,Auschwitz-Birkenau(Pol.) 1.43	MURDER	YUGO.
ROSS	15026	M	Ger.		W.O.,Army,Morlaix(Fr.)	MURDER	FR.
ROSS, Amalie	161717	F	Ger.	10.7.02	Housewife,Civilian,Sommerhausen(Ger.) 18.9.45	WITNESS	U.S.
ROSSBACH, Helga	195181	F	Ger.		Secretary,Raeumungs-Aktion der Wehrmacht,Arnheim(Neth.) 1.-2.44	PILLAGE	NETH.
ROSSBERG	261164	M	Ger.		Capt.,Gosselies(Bel.) 24.8.44	MURDER	BEL.
ROSSFUEHRER	180741	M			Civilian,Palleben(Ger.) 10.or 11.44	WITNESS	U.S.
ROSSI see OLDERS, Jose	251208						

-85-

ROS - ROT

NAME	C.R.FILE NUMBER	SEX	NATIO- NALITY	DATE OF BIRTH	RANK OCCUPATION UNIT PLACE AND DATE OF CRIME	REASON WANTED	WANTED BY
ROSSKOFF	12486	M	Ger.		Pvt.,Army,110 or 111 Pz.Gren.Div.,2 Coy.,Albine (Fr.) 29.6.44	MURDER	FR.
ROSSLER	1468	M	Ger.		Pvt.,Army,2 Pl. 4 Sec.,194 Gr.	MURDER	U.K.
ROSSLER, Berth	301437	M	Ger.	18.10.09	Rottfhr.,SS,C.C.Buchenwald (Ger.) 16.5.38-9.10.43	MURDER	BEL.
ROSSLER, Gotthard	128950	M			Oschfhr.,SS,C.C.Buchenwald (Ger.)	TORTURE	U.S.
ROSSMAN	148649	M			Rottfhr.,SS-Div.Totenk.,4 SS-Baubde.,C.C.Gardelegen,Ellrich(Ger)4.45	MURDER	U.S.
ROSSMANECK, Otto	187027	M		05	Wachtmeister,Schupo,Velen (Ger.) 25.-26.3.45	MURDER	U.K.
ROSSMANN	129037	M			Uschfhr.,SS-Totenk.-Sturmbann,C.C.Mauthausen (Aust.) 41-45	MURDER	U.S.
ROSSMANN, Adam	193529	M	Ger.		SS-Mann,4 SS-Totenk.-Sturmbann,C.C.Dora Mittelbau,Nordhausen(Ger.) 43-45	MURDER	U.S.
ROSSMANN, Franz	253530	M		14. 2.03	Flyer,C.C.Ellrich,Nordhausen (Ger.)	MURDER	U.S.
ROSSMANNECK, Otto	144368	M	Ger.		Member of Hitler Jugend,Velen (Ger.)	MURDER	U.K.
ROSSMELL, Karl	193034	M	Ger.	00	Kgf.,Arb.Bn.186 (Nor.) 42-45	MISC.CRIMES	NOR.
ROSSOF, Karl	196845	M	Ger.		Sturmfhr.,SS,C.C.Auschwitz (Pol.) 40	MURDER	FR.
ROSSOIETER	144381	M	Ger.	85	Oschfhr.,SS,Waldlager V,C.C. Ampfing (Aust.)	TORTURE	U.S.
ROSSOW	1239	M	Ger.		Oberzahlmeister,C.C.Compiegne (Fr.)	MISC.CRIMES	U.S.FR.
ROSSOW	188810	M	Ger.		Member,Feldgendarmerie,Bar Le Duc (Fr.) 20.-23.8.44	MURDER	FR.
ROSSOW, Karl Friedrich W.	260439	M	Ger.	12. 1.07	Stoker,Rottfhr.,Waffen-SS,Guard and Administration service, Auschwitz (Pol.) 9.41-2.45	BRUTALITY	POL.
ROSST	128822	M	Ger.	10	Civilian,Betonwerk Laussig (Ger.) 10.43-1.45	MISC.CRIMES	U.K.
ROSSWEIN	67023	M	Ger.		Oberfunker,SS-Div."Das Reich", 1 Bn.,Trebons,Pouzat,Bagneres De Bigorre (Fr.) 44	MURDER	FR.
ROST	761	M	Ger.		Cadt.,Army,Detachment (Selbstschutz),Swiecie (Pol.)10.-17.9.39	MURDER	POL.
ROST	1469	M	Ger.		Capt.,Platzkommandant	MISC.CRIMES	U.K.
ROST	173141	M	Ger.		C.C.Rotenfels,Gaggenau (Ger.) 44	INTER.	U.K.
ROST	173947	M	Ger.		Hptschfhr.,SS,military court,C.C.Struthof (Fr.) 40-44	TORTURE	FR.
ROST (see ROOST)	180742	M	Ger.		Cpl.,Army,Semoussac (Fr.) 28.9.44	MURDER	FR.
ROST (see ROOST)	192146						
ROST (see FRATSCHER)	255424						
ROST, Nicolaus	136344	M	Ger.	94	Consulat-General,Public offic., foreign office,Ribbentrop (Ger.)43	TORTURE	U.S.
ROSTERG, August	260198	M	Ger.	20. 2.70	Ch.Vorstand,Wintershall A.G.,Berlin (Ger.)	MISC.CRIMES	U.S.
ROSTOCK, Max Fritz (or ROSTOSK)	252589	M	Ger.	12	Osturmfhr.,SS,Gestapo Head,Kladno,Lidice (Czech.) 40-42	MISC.CRIMES	CZECH.
ROSUMEK, Helmut	262168	M	Ger.		Crim.Commis.,Gestapo,Neustadt (Ger.) 1.41	MURDER	FR.
ROSZBERG	301976	M	Ger.		Capt. IV (W.T.),723 Gren.Regt.,Kriegsgericht Utrecht (Neth.) 7.7.44	BRUTALITY	NETH.
ROSZNOG	156052	M			Civilian,C.C.Gardelegen (Ger.) 10.44-45	WITNESS	U.S.
ROTACK	143031	M			Uschfhr.,SS,C.C.Flossenburg (Ger.)	MURDER	U.S.
ROTBAUER	253531	M			Pvt.,C.C.Dora,Nordhausen (Ger.)	MURDER	U.S.
ROTH	762	M	Ger.		Hptschfhr.,SS,C.C.Falstad (Nor.) 42	TORTURE	NOR.
ROTH	1558	M	Ger.		Sgt.,Gestapo,Heppenheim (Ger.)	MISC.CRIMES	U.S.
ROTH	12487	M	Ger.		S.D.,Sicherheitspolizei,Clermont-Ferrand (Fr.) 43-44	TORTURE	FR.
ROTH	129035	M	Ger.	13	Hptschfhr.,Kapo,SS,C.C.Mauthausen (Aust.) 41-45	MURDER	U.S.
ROTH	152080	M			Civilian,Budesheim (Ger.) 6.44	MURDER	U.S.
ROTH	152096	M			Lt.,Oflag 64,Schubin (Ger.) 19.12.44	MISC.CRIMES	U.S.
ROTH	165546	M			Chief,C.C.Essen (Ger.) 44-45	TORTURE	BEL.
ROTH	169041	M			Usturmfhr.,Waffen-SS,C.C.Natzweiler (Fr.) 42-44	MURDER	FR.
ROTH	191819	M			Lt.General,Air Force,Bardufoss (Nor.) 45	MURDER	NOR.
ROTH	191855	M			Leader,SS,C.C.Dachau (Ger.) 34-35	TORTURE	U.K.
ROTH	193929	M	Ger.		Custom-house,officer,Zollgrenzschutz,Semaphore of Breach-Maout (Fr.)	MURDER	FR.
ROTH	252613	M	Ger.		Cpl.,Gend. Troup 533,Annecy,La Chablais (Fr.) 19.-21.5.44	MISC.CRIMES	FR.
ROTH	252614	M	Ger.		Capt.,338 Div.,Labresse (Fr.) 9.-11.44	MISC.CRIMES	FR.
ROTH, Albin	126382	M	Ger.		Civ. to be located and if attitude is hostile,witness will be detained,otherwise not, Schweina (Ger.) 2.44	WITNESS	U.S.
ROTH, Andreas	252598	M	Ger.		Civ.,C.C.Lahde-Weser (Ger.)	MURDER	BEL.
ROTH, Anton	173942	M	Ger.		Gestapo,Staatspolizeistelle,Brno,Auschwitz Birkenau (Czech.-Pol.) 39-45	MURDER	CZECH.
ROTH, Emil	21452	M	Ger.		Sgt.,Kriegsgef.-Res.Lazarett,Heppenheim (Ger.)	MISC.CRIMES	U.S.
ROTH, Fritz	147061	M	Ger.		Oschfhr.,Pol.,19 Regt.,4 Coy.,Annecy (Fr.) 44	MURDER	FR.
ROTH, Georg Karl	144364	M	Ger.	30. 6.86	Carpenter,Gestapo,Duesseldorf (Ger.)	MURDER	U.S.
ROTH, Heinrich	128951	M	Ger.		Sgt.,Kraftfahrersatz-Ausb.-Abt.,Harsfeld near Fulda (Ger.)	MURDER	U.S.
ROTH, Johanna	174980	F	Ger.		Woman,SS,C.C.Bergen-Belsen (Ger.) 1.10.39-30.4.45	MURDER	UNWCC
ROTH, Johann	193322	M	Ger.		Guard,SS,4 SS-Totenk.-Sturmbann,C.C.Mittelbau Nordhausen (Ger.)	WITNESS	U.S.
ROTH, Karl	253535	M	Ger.	1. 2.01	Rottfhr.,C.C.Harzungen,Nordhausen (Ger.)	MURDER	U.S.
ROTH, Marie	186790	F	Ger.	1. 5.06	Kreiskinder-Gruppenleiterin,NSDAP,district office,Marianske, Lazne (Czech.) 39-45	MISC.CRIMES	CZECH.
ROTH, Martin	182575	M		12.12.14	Hptschfhr.,SS,C.C.Mauthausen (Aust.) 1.45	MURDER	U.S.
ROTH, Robert	251243	M	Ger.		Interpreter,Gestapo,Vichy (Fr.)	INTER.	FR.
ROTH, Vitus	256777	M			Employee,C.C.Nordhausen (Ger.)	MURDER	U.S.
ROTH, Wilhelm	132120	M	Ger.	30.11.84	Civ.,Farmer,Schweina near Meiningen (Ger.) 24.2.44	TORTURE	U.S.
ROTH, Wilhelm	195898	M	Ger.		Lt.,Verdun (Fr.)	TORTURE	FR.
ROTH, Willi	192528	M	Ger.		Pvt.,Army,Chatou (Fr.) 25.8.44	MURDER	FR.
ROTH, Willi	257862	M	Ger.		Lt.,150 Pz.Bie.,Meuse Bridge,Antwerp (Bel.) 12.44	MISC.CRIMES	BEL.
ROTH, Willy	252615	M	Ger.	25 _ 30	Lt.,Gend.,Savannes (Fr.) 31.8.44	MISC.CRIMES	FR.
ROTHAAR, Franz	193339	M	Ger.	94	Capt.,Abwehrstelle,Oslo (Nor.) 10.42	MURDER	U.K.
ROTHAAS, Theo (see ROTHHAAS)	140065						
ROTHACKER, Hans	306777	M	Ger.		Civ.,Gernsbach or Weissenbach (Ger.) 9.8.44	MURDER	U.S.
ROTHAR	193035	M	Ger.		Lt.,Army,Umschlagstab,Drag (Nor.) 44	TORTURE	NOR.
ROTHAUG, Oswald	261123	M	Ger.	5.97	Reichs-Prosecutor,Presidant,people's court,Special court,Nuernberg	SUSPECT	U.S.
ROTHAUESSLER	261645		Ger.		Brewer-master,Domicile Mannheim,Kafertholst-Str.164-166,Brewery.43-44	BRUTALITY	FR.
ROTHBERG	128953	M	Ger.	21	Capt.,(Inf.Regt.) Heeres Regt.,Aww (Ger.) 16.12.44	MURDER	U.S.
ROTHE (or KOTHE)	165569	M	Ger.		Sgt.,SS,Unit 12,622,Beauvechain (Bel.) 3.9.44	MURDER	BEL.
ROTHE	194828	M	Ger.		Revierfoerster,Civ.,Luxemburg (Lux.)	TORTURE	LUX.
ROTHE, Georg	135306	M	Ger.	01	Civilian,Birtungen (Lux.) 7.44	TORTURE	U.S.
ROTHE, Gothard	121648	M	Ger.		Orderly of Dr.Bonsch,Army,Nice (Fr.) 22.7.-7.8.44	WITNESS	FR.

ROT-RUB

NAME	C.R. FILE NUMBER	SEX	NATIO-NALITY	DATE OF BIRTH	RANK OCCUPATION UNIT PLACE AND DATE OF CRIME	REASON WANTED	WANTED BY
ROTHE, Hans	193036	M	Ger.	2. 7.07	Sgt., Guard Reichsjustizminist.,Feldstraflager W-SS C.C. Finnmark (Nor.) 6.42-45	MISC.CRIMES	NOR. YUG.
ROTHE, Walther	301110	M	Ger.		Engineer, Dr. Consular Official served in the German Consulate Copenhagen (Den.) 43	INTERR.	DEN.
ROTHEIGNER, Heinz	196637	M	Ger.	21. 2.06	Waiter, Tailor, Civ. C.C. Dachau Sachsenhausen, (Ger.) 39-45	WITNESS	CZECH.
ROTHEL, Otto	122670	M	Ger.		Civ., Pol.Sgt., Police Dept., Aderstedt (Ger.) 12.9.44	MURDER	U.S.
ROTHENBERGER	12488	M	Ger.		Sgt., Hafenueberwachungsstelle, Calais (Fr.) 4.9.44	TORTURE	FR.
ROTHENBUSCH, Adam	191818	M	Ger.		Wachtmeister, 7.Pol.Rgt. 7.Pol.Bn. 10.Coy., Junkerdal (Nor.)10.44	TORTURE	NOR.
ROTHENSTEIN	1470	M	Ger.		Army 305. Div. 274 Gr.H.Qu.Coy. (Eng.Bn.)	MISC.CRIMES	U.K.
ROTHFUCHS	165155	M	Ger.	05	Opt., Army, (Serb.) 44	TORTURE	U.S.
ROTHFUCHS, Hugo, August	161722	M	Ger.	12	Oberfhr. H.J., Langenlonsheim (Ger.) 4.12.44	SUSPECT	U.S.
ROTHFUSS	253247	M	Ger.		Adjutant, Gend., Salacnon (Fr.) 15.2.44	INTERR.	Fr.
ROTHHAAS, (or ROTHAAS, Theo)	140065	M	Ger.	02	Sgt., Gestapo Agent in Army, Ld.Schts.Bn.H, 6.Coy. Coeln-Ehrenfeld (Ger.) 11.44	MURDER	U.S.
ROTHMAR	193928	M	Ger.		Custom-house Officer, Zollgrenzschutz Semaphore Breach Maout (Fr.)	MURDER	FR.
ROTHMEIER, Franz	186792	M	Ger.		Employee, Gestapo, Budejovice (Czech.) 39-45	MURDER	CZECH.
ROTHMUELLER	21481	M	Ger.		Colonel Army Stalag 6 C.C. Muenster (Ger.)	TORTURE	U.S.
ROTKE, (alias ROETHKE, ROETTKE)	214025	M	Ger.	03	SS Lt.Col., SD, Abtl. IX B, Beaune la Rolande Drancy Pithivier Paris, Compiegne (Fr.) 44	MURDER	U.S.
ROTLICH, Hubert	152087	M	Ger.		Civilian, Chief air raid warder, Bad Oeynhausen (Ger.) 30.3.45	MURDER	U.S.
ROTMANN	73853	M			Ortsgruppenleiter N.S.D.A.P., near Graz Strassgang (Aust.) 44	MURDER	U.S.
ROTOT (see PRATSCHER)	255424						
ROTT, Ernst	152089	M	Ger.		Dr.med., Sturmbannfhr., S.A. Holzminden (Ger.)	TORTURE	U.S.
ROTTANDER	124971	M			Member Gestapo, C.C. Bremen-Farge (Ger.) 6.43	TORTURE	U.K.
ROTTAU	139071	M	Ger.	95	Sturmbannfhr., Polizeirat SS Pol.Praesidium Berlin, Grossbeeren (Ger.) 43	MISC.CRIMES	U.S.
ROTTENBURGER, Josef	252584	M	Ger.	06	Schfhr., SS, SD, Meldekopf 4, Borgo (It.) 20.12.44	MURDER	U.S.
ROTTENMANNER, Franz	193037	M	Ger.	5.10.05	Sgt., Guard Reichsjustizminist. Feldstraflager W-SS C.C. Finnmark (Nor.) 6.42-45	MISC.CRIMES	NOR.
ROTTER	186848	M	Ger.		Opt., Army Cdt.D'armes, A'provencieres Sur Fave (Fr.) 22.11.44	PILLAGE	FR.
ROTTER	173941	M	Ger.		Crim.Obersecretaer Staatspolizeistelle , Prague, Oswiecim, Birkenau (Czech.Pol.) 39-45	MURDER	CZECH.
ROTTER	193340	M	Ger.		Lt., P.O.W. working Bn. 184 C.C. Drag (Nor.)	TORTURE	NOR.
ROTTER, Karl	181558	M	Ger.	21. 6.90	SS Usturmfhr., Crim.Inspector, SS.Sd. Gestapo, Prag Benesov (Czech.) 39-45	MURDER	CZECH.
ROTTER, Karl	189302	M	Ger.	22. 4.93	Crim.Commissar SS, SD, Gestapo Mlada Boleslav, Chrudim, Varnsdorf (Czech.) 42-45	MURDER	CZECH.
ROTTGER	156054	M	Ger.	00	Pvt., Arbeitskdo., Stalag IV F, C.C. Falkenstein (Ger.) 1.45	TORTURE	U.K.
ROTTIEL	255040	M	Ger.	16	Col., Stalag XII A, Limburg (Ger.)	MURDER	U.S.
ROTTIG (see RETTIG)	128943						
ROTTIG, Otto	31907	M			Lt.General, Army	MURDER	U.K.
ROTTIG, Wilhelm	763	M	Ger.		SS-Oberfhr., SS Leibstandarte Adolf Hitler, 1.9.39-30.10.39	MURDER	U.N.W.C.C.,POL.
ROTTINGH	251858	M	Ger.		SS-Div.Das Reich, F.P.No. 20022, Amay (Bel.) 3.-4.9.44	INTERR.	BEL.
ROTTLOFF, Hermann	253305	M	Ger.		Kde.-Fuehrer, Kdo. 795 (Stalag V B) Hohenegelsen (Ger.) 43-44	MISC.CRIMES	FR.
ROTTOCK	190254	M	Ger.		Major Army, Radinjaca Sabac, (Yug.) 29.11.41	MURDER	YUG.
ROTWANGER	165554	M	Ger.		Lt., Army Forrieres (Bel.) 7.1.45	MURDER	BEL.
ROTWANGER	191714	M	Ger.		Lt., SS Luxembourg (Lux.) 7.1.45	MISC.CRIMES	BEL.
ROTWITZ	148559	M			SS-Usturmfhr., SS C.C. Gusen Mauthausen (Aust.) 41-45	MURDER	U.S.
ROUBAL, Ivan, Vladimir	261889	M	Ger.	4. 6.02	Dr., Member, informer, Physican Nazi Organisation Gestapo SD, Vlaika, Prag (Czech.) 40-45	SUSPECT	CZECH.
ROUCH	156071	M	Ger.	12	Cpl., Camp Guard C.C. 41 Leipzig (Ger.) 4.44	TORTURE	U.K.
ROUDI	186650	M	Ger.		Pvt., Army Crete (Gr.)	TORTURE	GRC.
ROUER	167474	M	Ger.		Paymaster, Army La Roche Yon (Fr.) 28.8.44	MISC.CRIMES	FR.
ROULI	194637	M	Ger.		Parachute Unit L.G. 53-474, St. Segal (Fr.) 22.7.44	TORTURE	FR.
ROUSLER	147060	M	Ger.		Chief, Gestapo, Beziers (Fr.) 44	MISC.CRIMES	FR.
ROUSSEAU, Max	167460	M	Ger.		Pvt., 9.Res.Ersatz Gren.Rgt. 1.Coy. Magny d'Anigon (Fr.) 18.9.44	MURDER	FR. UNWCC.
ROUSSEAU, Mme.	259250	F	Ger.		Typist, Gestapo Antenne, Poitiers area (Fr.)40 - 45	SUSPECT	FR.
ROUSSEL	147358	M	Ger.		SS Oschfhr., 11.Panz.Rgt. 1.Gruppe Kampfgruppe "Wilde" 44	MURDER	FR.
ROUTZIERO, Hartmann	185289	M	Ger.		Chief, Gestapo, Heraklion (Grc.) 7.44	MISC.CRIMES	GRC.
ROUVEL, Paul	193038	M	Ger.	00	Sgt., P.O.W. working Bn. 186 (Nor.) 40-45	MISC.CRIMES	NOR.
ROVE (see ROYE)	193515						
ROVEIDER	125714	M	Ger.		Civilian, Brakel near Lueneburg (Ger.) 21.1.45	TORTURE	U.S.
ROVEKAMP	136287	M	Ger.		Sgt., Feldgend., de Verdun, Stenay (Fr.) 5.8.44	MURDER	FR.
ROVENICH	167146	M	Ger.		Adjutant Chief, Feldgend., Montigny en Vesoul (Fr.) 16.7.44	MURDER	FR.
ROVER	191744	M	Ger.		Paymaster, Army Feldpost No. 59250, Vendee La Roche (Fr.) 28.8.44	PILLAGE	FR.
ROWALDT	253299	M	Ger.		Uschfhr., SS Neuengamme (Ger.) 44	MURDER	FR.
ROWELL	136594	M	Ger.	00	N.C.O., Airforce, Nagyszian (Hung.) 4.2.45	TORTURE	U.S.
ROWOLD	162706	M	Ger.		SS-Uschfhr., SS Wattenstedt (Ger.) 25.1.44	MURDER	FR.
ROWOLDT, Hans	195180	M	Ger.		Sgt., Gestapo, Strassburg (Fr.) 44	WITNESS	U.K.
ROY, Christa	188410	F			Civilian, Bollane (It.) 19.3.45	WITNESS	U.S.
ROYCE	67583	M	Ger.		Chief of Factory public official Stickstoffwerke, Koenigshuette (Ger.) 41-44	BRUTALITY	U.K.
ROYE (or ROVE)	251849	M	Ger.		Employee Sipo. Bruessels (Bel.)	INTERR.	BEL.
ROYE (or ROVE)	193515	M	Ger.		Dr., SS Standartenfhr., SS Franeker (Neth.) 3.45	MISC.CRIMES	NETH.
ROYKO (or ROIKO)	24830	M	Ger.	10	SS Hptschfhr., SS and SD, C.C. Theresienstadt (Czech.)	MURDER	U.S. U.K.
ROZEK, Maximilian	262420	M	Ger.	15. 4.09	Informer confident Gestapo and SD, Zlin (Czech.) 41-44	SUSPECT	CZECH.
ROZKO	145868	M	Ger.		SS-Oschfhr., SS C.C. Theresienstadt (Czech.)	MURDER	U.S.
ROZMANN	173944	M	Ger.		Oschfhr., SS Maribor (Yug.) 4.41-44	MURDER	YUG.
RUBACKE, Heinz	258194	M	Ger.		Major, German Army, Kragujevac, Orasac, Gruza (Yug.) 42-44	INTERR.	YUG.
RUBEL	31425	M			Major General, Army, Finmark (Nor.)	MURDER	NOR.
RUBH (see ROBH)	753						
RUBINSTEIN	166669	M			Civilian, (Pol.) 42	WITNESS	U.S.
RUBLER	764	M			Major General, Army O.C. 118.Jaeger Rgt. (Ger.) 7.43-1.44	MURDER	YUG.
RUBNER, Valentin	194827	M	Ger.		Pvt., 5.Coy. 2. Police Bn. Roncegno (It.) 2.45	MURDER	U.K.
RUBNICK, Alois	191817	M	Ger.		Pvt., Kgf. Arb.Bn. 2-158 between Lekanger and Ervik (Nor.)16.42	MURDER	NOR.
RUBOTTA	129054	M	Ger.		5. Fallschirmtrooper - Nachr.Zug Quaregnon, Jemappes Ghlin (Bel.) 9.44	MURDER	BEL.

RUB - RUE

NAME	C.R.FILE NUMBER	SEX	NATIONALITY	DATE OF BIRTH	RANK OCCUPATION UNIT PLACE AND DATE OF CRIME	REASON WANTED	WANTED BY
RUBSAM, Armand	38860	M	Ger.		Pvt., Army, Lignieres, La Doucelles (Fr.) 13.,14.6.44	MURDER	FR.
RUBSAMEN	174053	M	Ger.		Civ., Ger. 11.44	TORTURE	U.S.
RUBSAMEN, Paul	144373	M	Ger.	05	Pvt., Army, Nentershausen (Ger.) 27.9.44	MURDER	U.S.
RUBY, Hans	141602	M			Chenebier, Etobon (Fr.) 27.9.44	MURDER	FR.
RUCFTER, Richard	1743	M			Lt., Army, Corbeil, North-Paris (Fr.) 44	MURDER	U.K.
RUCK	765	M	Ger.		SS Osturmfhr., Physician, C.C Oswiecim (Pol.) 6.40 and 43	MURDER	POL.,BEL. CZECH.
RUCK, Else	252609	F	Ger.		SS-Guard, Geislingen (Ger.) 40-45	MISC.CRIMES	POL.
RUCK, Friedrich	252592	M		28. 5.97	Farmer and Smith, Civ., Budesheim (Ger.) 10.44	BRUTALITY	U.S.
RUCKEN	129052	M			Civ., C.C. Mauthausen (Aust.) 41-45	MURDER	U.S.
RUCKER	133270	M			Prisoner-chief of hospital, C.C. Flossenburg (Ger.)	TORTURE	U.S.
RUCKER, Max	167448	M	Ger.		Dr., Civ. comm.administrator, Firm Sila, Leder- und Riemenfabrik, Zywiec (Pol.) 9.39 to end 44	MISC.CRIMES	POL.
RUCKOLDT	255771	M			Rottfhr., C.C. Buchenwald (Ger.)	MURDER	U.S.
RUDA, Anton	191811	M	Ger.		SS Rottfhr., Toulouse (Fr.) 21.11.43	MURDER	FR.
RUDA, Herbert	253300	M	Ger.		W.O., Gestapo, Lille (Fr.) 40-44	MURDER	FR.
RUDECKE or RUDNICK	39607	M	Ger.		Lt., Bde.Fuehrer, Waffen SS (44181 A) F.Nr. 59436,Selondigny (Fr.) 27.7.44	MURDER	FR.
RUDEL, Arthur see ROIDEL	10332						
RUDELCFF	173934	M	Ger.		Major, 7.Pioneer-Rgt., Grenoble,Malleval,Cognin les Georges, St.Nizier de Moucharotte (Fr.) 15.-17.6.44, 7.-8.44	MISC.CRIMES	FR.
RUDELOFF	188808	M			Sgt., Feldgendarmerie, Beaurepaire (Fr.) 5.8.44	MURDER	FR.
RUDERER	12489	M	Ger.		Pvt., Army, 110.or 111.Panz.Gren.Rgt., Albane (Fr.) 29.6.44	MURDER	FR.
RUDERICH, Alfred	259249	M	Ger.		Uscharfhr., Gestapo, Area Poitiers (Fr.) 40-44	MISC.CRIMES	FR.
RUDI see STHAL, STAHL,Henri	198256						
RUDI	148535	M		11	SS Rottfhr., Waffen SS, Schleissheim nr.Muenchen (Ger.)	MURDER	U.S.
RUDI or WILHELM	190363	M			Official, Gestapo, Bukovo (Yugo.) 43	MURDER	YUGO.
RUDI	252259	M			Ober-Kapo, C.C. Auschwitz (Pol.)	INTERR.	FR.
RUDIGER, Fritz	255206	M		5. 2.20	Cpl., C.C. Ellrich, Nordhausen (Ger.)	MURDER	U.S.
RUDIGER, Kurt	261012	M	Ger.		Commander, Castelfranco Emilia - Modena (It.) 14.-18.12.44	MURDER	U.S.
RUDLOF or RUDOFF	253212	M	Ger.		Lt., 1.Coy. of transmission, 7.Res.Pion.Bn., Meylan (Fr.) 17.5.44	INTERR.	FR.
RUDNICK see RUDECKE	39607						
RUDOFF, Antoine	250444	M	Ger.		Gendarm, Gend.Romorantin No. 577, Orcay (Fr.) 8.8.44	MURDER	FR.
RUDOFF see RUDLOF	253212						
RUDOLF	16419	M			Police secretary, Gestapo Breslau, Hirschberg (Ger.) 3.44	MURDER	U.K.
RUDOLF	46110	M		20	Lt., Airforce, Parachutist-Sect., Luftgau Lager Paris 62546 Guegon, Paris (Fr.) 20.6.44	PILLAGE	FR.
RUDOLF	141903	M	Ger.	13	Oberarzt, Stalag VIII, C.C. Lamsdorf (Ger.) 40-41	MURDER	U.K.
RUDOLF	167147	M	Ger.		Adjutant, Feldgendarmerie, Luneville (Fr.) 1.8.44	MISC.CRIMES	FR.
RUDOLF	167148	M	Ger.		Adjutant, Feldgendarmerie de Luneville, Matlexey (Fr.) 30.6.44	MURDER	FR.
RUDOLF	191814	M			Interpreter, Kgf.Arb.Bn., Bjornelva (Nor.)	WITNESS	NOR.
RUDOLF	193300	M	Ger.	85	Civ., Prison-guard, C.C. Prison Preungesheim,Frankfurt-M.(Ger.)42-44	TORTURE	U.K. FR.
RUDOLF	258193	M	Ger.		Capt., German Army, Smolari nr.Strumica (Yugo.) 17.9.44	INTERR.	YUGO.
RUDOLF	260144	M	Ger.		Capt., Res.Div. "Bavaria", Massif du Vercors, Isere et Drome (Fr.) 20.7.-5.8.44	SUSPECT	FR.
RUDOLF	302115	M	Ger.		Osturmfhr., SS, Police, Karasjok, Northern (Nor.) 22.6.-10.42	MURDER	YUGO.
RUDOLF, Heinz	253596	M		5. 1.10	Pvt., C.C. Ellrich, Nordhausen (Ger.)	MURDER	U.S.
RUDOLF, Jan	251848	M		27. 5.02	Member, Jagd-Cdo., Gestapo, Litencice (Czech.) 22.4.45	SUSPECT	CZECH.
RUDOLF, Rudolf	260003	M		8. 9.92	Capt., Slovak-Gendarmerie, Zvolen, Banska, Bystrica, Zilina, Kremnica - Slovakia,(Czech.) 9.44-4.45	MISC.CRIMES	CZECH.
RUDOLFI	253151				Rottfhr., C.C.Rottleberode, Nordhausen (Ger.)	MURDER	U.S.
RUDOLPH	766	M	Ger.		SD, Guingamp (Fr.) 10.7.44	MURDER	FR.
RUDOLPH	29631	M	Ger.		Lt., German Army Staff, 2.Rgt., Locmine (Fr.) 44	MURDER	FR.
RUDOLPH	67584	M	Ger.		Assistentarzt, C.C. Lamsdorf Stalag VII B (Ger.) 2.41	MURDER	U.K.
RUDOLPH	195897	M	Ger.		Officer chief, Airforce 151, 8.,9.,10.Coy., Mainzac Charente (Fr.) 25.7.44	INTERR.	FR.
RUDOLPH	250445	M	Ger.		Agent, SD, Toulouse (Fr.) 11.42-8.44	MISC.CRIMES	FR.
RUDOLPH	256915	M	Ger.		Manager Mittelwerk Nordhausen (Ger.)	MURDER	U.S.
RUDOLPH, Hans	192818	M	Ger.		SS Hptscharfhr., C.C. Buchenwald (Ger.) 42-45	TORTURE	U.S.
RUDOLPH, Karl	195424	M	Ger.		Cpl., Airforce 16.Felddiv. Army and SS, Amsterdam (Neth.) 6.3.43	MURDER	NETH.
RUDOLPH, Kurt	259584	M		17. 3.08		MISC.CRIMES	U.S.
RUDOLPH, Walter	132334	M	Ger.	99	N.C.O., SS, Airforce, Heilsetal Radio-Stat. (Ger.) 12.12.44	TORTURE	U.S.
RUDOLPH, Wilhelm	167447	M	Ger.		Treuhaender, Administration, Gastaette L.Nowitzki, Poznan (Pol.) 9.39 to end 44	MISC.CRIMES	POL.
RUDOLPH, Wilhelm	193516	M	Ger.		SS Sturmscharfhr., SD, Leeuwarden (Neth.)	MISC.CRIMES	NETH.
RUDOLPHI	152358	M			Chief, Navy, occupied countries of Europe, Ger. 41-42	MISC.CRIMES	U.S.
RUDPRECHT, Willi	124630	M		10	Lt. and Osturmfhr., SS and SD, Paris (Fr.) 42-44	MURDER	U.S.
RUECKER, Alvin	194826	M	Ger.	14. 7.05	Civ. Strassenbaumeister, Luxemburg (Lux.)	MISC.CRIMES	LUX.
RUECKERT, Friedrich	148545	M	Ger.		SS Hptscharfhr., SS-hospital, Bad Aussee (Aust.) 40-45	MURDER	U.S.
RUECKHOLDT	128954				Civ., C.C. Weimar, Buchenwald (Ger.)	TORTURE	U.S.
RUECKNER, Fritz	131320	M			Bloc-senior, Guard, C.C. Jawischowitz (Pol.) 44	MURDER	U.S.
RUEDEL	252628	M	Ger.		Guard, Cdo. 260 Stalag IX B Bingenheim (Ger.) 20.11.43	BRUTALITY	FR.
RUEDL, Josef	214027	M	Ger.		SS Oscharfhr., Gestapo, SD, Turin (It.)	MURDER	U.S.
RUEFFRECK, Richard	253152	M	Ger.	19. 9.24	Pvt., C.C. Ellrich, Nordhausen (Ger.)	MURDER	U.S.
RUEGE	253153				Pvt., C.C. Harzungen, Nordhausen (Ger.)	MURDER	U.S.
RUEGER	252611	M			Pvt., Pepingen (Bel.) 2.44-3.9.44	WITNESS	BEL.
RUEGER	306694	M	Ger.		Pvt., 331.Pion.Div., 331.Inf.Div., Mijnheerenland (Neth.) 5.45	PILLAGE	NETH.
RUEGER	306923	M	Ger.		Abschnittsleiter, Kreisleiter NSDAP, Muehlhausen (Fr.) 44	BRUTALITY	FR.
RUEGER, Babtist	300123	M	Ger.	about 00	Employee, Hamm-Westphalia, Kirchlengern Krs.Herford (Ger.)	TORTURE	NETH.
RUELAND	193015	M	Ger.		Sgt., POW working Bn. 204 3.Coy, Nor. 44	MURDER	NOR.
RUEHLE, Erich	196006	M	Ger.	15	Commander 44 Stalag IV G Mugeln (Ger.) 15.11.44	MURDER	U.S.
RUEHLING	301901	M	Ger.		Capt., Ocmd. I.Gren.Rgt. 392, 169.Inf.Div. 20.Army, Finmark (Nor.) 10.-11.44	MURDER	NOR.
RUEHMKE	306947	M	Ger.		Major, Leader, Wirtschaftspruefer at Baarn (Neth.) 42-43	INTERR.	NETH.
RUESS	162701	M	Ger.		Osturmfhr., Waffen SS, Totenkopf-Standarte,Com.Staff, C.C. Buchenwald, Weimar (Ger.)	TORTURE	U.S.

NAME	C.R.FILE NUMBER	SEX	NATIO-NALITY	DATE OF BIRTH	RANK OCCUPATION UNIT	PLACE AND DATE OF CRIME	REASON WANTED	WANTED BY
RUEISBILDT, Herbert or RUISBILD or HUESZBILDTH	193016	M	Ger.	10. 2.05	Oberwachtmeister, SS, Reichsjustizministerium, Strafgefangenenlager, Finmark (Nor.) 6.42-45		MISC.CRIMES	NOR.,YUGO.
RUELE	1471	M	Ger.		Naval supply.		MISC.CRIMES	U.K.
RUEMKE see RUMKE	39597							
RUEMKORF, Othmar	259198	M	Ger.		SS-Unterscharfhr., SS, C.C., Dachau (Ger.) 41-45		MISC.CRIMES	YUGO.
RUEMMEL-EIN, Paul,Heinz,Heinrich	254882	M	Ger.		Civilian, Dobroviz (Czech.) 7.5.45		MURDER	CZECH.
RUEPPERT, Willi	139079	M	Ger.	10	Obersturmfhr., Technical Leader, SS, Guard Bn. C.C. Lublin (Pol.)42		TORTURE	U.S.
RUESCH	257915	M			Cpl., 150.Pz.Bde., Meuse Bridge, Antwerp (Bel.) 12.44		INTERR.	U.S.
RUESS	194224	M	Ger.		Sgt., Army, 3. punish ment Bn. C.C. Ft.Zinna, Torgau (Ger.) 45		MURDER	U.S.
RUESS, Wilhelm	132123	M			Obersturmfhr., SD and SS, Prague (Czech.) 43-45		MURDER	CZECH.
RUESTER	253202	M			Uschfhr., C.C. Rottleberode, Nordhausen (Ger.)		MURDER	U.S.
RUESZBILDTH, Herbert see RUEISBILDT	193016							
RUETER, Johann	302117	M	Ger.		Reichsbahn Official employed in the Fernmeldemeister Office, Amersfoort (Neth.) 4.10.44-5.45		PILLAGE	NETH.
RUETERS	301978	M	Ger.		Oschafhr., SS, Arbeitsdienstfhr., C.C. Auschwitz (Pol.) 41-45		MURDER	POL.
RUETING	302118	M	Ger.		Member, SD, Almelo District (Neth.) 9.44-2.45		TORTURE	NETH.
RUETT, Heinrich	260453	M	Ger.	4.11.90	SS-Rottfhr., W.-SS, Guard Coy. C.C. Auschwitz (Pol.) 6.44-1.45		BRUTALITY	POL.
RUETTING, Fritz	300126	M	Ger.		N.C.O., Sicherheitsdienst at the Hague Worked under Crim.Commissar Frank, Driebergen and Scheveningen (Neth.) 4-7.44		TORTURE	NETH.
RUETZ	173935	M			Major, 7. Art.-Group, St.Nizier de Moucherotte (Fr.) 15.-17.6.44		PILLAGE	FR.
RUETZ	193935				Army, Malleval Cognin les Georges (Fr.)		MISC.CRIMES	FR.
RUETZ, Willy	167459	M	Ger.		Pvt., 9. Gren.Ers.Regt. 1.Coy., Magny d'Anigon (Fr.) 18.9.44		MURDER	FR.
RUETZEL	302119	M	Ger.		Cpl., Member, VI Batt. Einheit F.P. L. 55 975 LGPA Una Wf. NSDAP Laren (Neth.) 4.11.44-22.2.45		PILLAGE	NETH.
RUF	173247	M	Ger.		Civilian, physician, Putlitz (Ger.)		WITNESS	U.K.
RUF, Johann	262169	M	Ger.	25. 6.14	Hschfhr., 51 SS Armoured Bde., Breviandes, Bucheres, Ste Savine, La Riviere de Corps, Troyes (Fr.) 22-25.8.44		BRUTALITY	FR.
RUF, Kreszentia	252610	F	Ger.	15. 4.19	SS-Guard, SS, Geislingen (Ger.) 40-45		MISC.CRIMES	POL.
RUF, Otto	10337	M	Ger.		Sturmfhr., Crim.Commissar, SA, Gestapo, Prag (Czech.) 39-45		TORTURE	CZECH.
RUFF, Heinrich	260510	M	Ger.		SS Uschfhr., Blocleader, SS Guard, C.C. Auschwitz (Pol.) 44-45		BRUTALITY	POL.
RUFF, Karl	136353	M	Ger.		Guard, C.C. Helmbrechts, Fr.44-13.4.45		MURDER	U.S.
RUFFENACH, Paul	259796	M	Ger.	19. 1.20	SS-Mann, SS, 1.Zug, 2. Group, Probably stationed at Bergeyk (Noord-Brabant, Neth.) 11.9.44		MURDER	NETH.
RUGE, Heinrich	300923	M	Ger.		Member of Staff, C.C. Neuengamme (Ger.) 6.40-5.45		MURDER	U.K.
RUGE, Karl	138242	M	Ger.		Chief, De Culture, Beaulieu (Fr.) 22.8.44		MURDER	FR.
RUGELHORN see KUGLERKORNE	141369							
RUGER	301279	M	Ger.		Crim. Oberasst., Abt. IV A, SD, Bruessels (Bel.) 6.40-9.44		MURDER	BEL.
RUGIERO, Robert	300124	M	Ger.		Sonderfhr., Chief, of counter Intelligence service of Heraklion Crete 42-43		MURDER	GRC.
RUGLER	767	M	Ger.	01	C.C. Caen (Fr.) 6.44		MURDER	FR.
RUH, Karl	253154	M		31. 5.12	Rottfhr., C.C. Harzungen (Ger.)		MURDER	U.S.
RUHE	259837	M	Ger.		Chief-Paymaster., Army, Commando Raumbot, Breda (Neth.) 9.44		PILLAGE	NETH.
RUHF, Jakob	152357	M	Ger.		Civilian (Ger.)		WITNESS	U.S.
RUHGOLA	122550	M	Ger.		Sgt., Oflag C.C. Graudenz (Ger.)		MURDER	U.K.
RUHL, J	141071	M	Ger.		Dr., Civilian, C.C. Natzweiler, Struthof (Fr.)		TORTURE	U.K.
RUHL	196007	M	Ger.		C.C. Struthof-Natzweiler (Fr.) 40-44		MURDER	FR.
RUHL, Helmutt	196695	M	Ger.		Medical Air Force, Special. Chemistry, Strasbourg (Fr.) 40-44		TORTURE	FR.
RUHL, Werner	305479	M	Ger.		Pvt., Marine Inf. partly composed of W.-SS, Trebeurden Groass- Ste- Anne-en- Tregastel (Fr.) 7.7.44-9.7.44		MISC.CRIMES	FR.
RUHL, Wilhelm	148652	M	Ger.		Prison Supervisor, Gestapo, Giessen (Ger.) 3.45		MURDER	U.S.
RUHLAND	195896	M	Ger.		Capt., Schiffsstammabt, SS TA., Montceau les Mines (Fr.) 22.7.44		MURDER	FR.
RUHLE	122551	M	Ger.		Director, of Salt-Mine, Sachsen-Weimar, Rhoen, Working Camp 137 Unterbreizbach (Ger.)		TORTURE	U.K.
RUHLE, Wilhelm	261087	M	Ger.		SS-Oschfhr., C.C. Bisingen (Ger.)		BRUTALITY	FR.
RUHLMANN	152361	M	Ger.	05	Member, Gestapo, Grenoble (Fr.) 43-44		TORTURE	FR.
RUHLMANN, Paul	147059	M	Ger.		Interpreter, Police of the Champagne, Capestang (Fr.) 44		MISC.CRIMES	FR.
RUHNKE	256055	M	Ger.		Sturmscharfhr., Muhldorf (Ger.)		WITNESS	U.S.
RUHSAM	258105	M	Ger.		Major, State Service, Police Officier, Val. Mezirici (Czech.)44-45		MURDER	CZECH.
RUISBILD,Herbert see RUEISBILDT	193016							
RUITERS, Hans	124612	M	Ger.		SS Sturmbannfhr., SS-Arb.Fhr., SS, C.C. Birkenau (Ger.)		MURDER	BEL.
RUKERT	12491				Pvt., Army 110. or 111 Pz.Gren.Regt. 2. Coy., Albine (Fr.)29.6.44		MURDER	FR.
RUMEN see RUMEN	253316							
RUMENOFF	252627	M	Ger.		Lt., Autonome of Turkestan, Clarvag (Fr.) 1.4.-21.8.44		MISC.CRIMES	FR.
RUMKE or RUEMKE	39597	M	Ger.		Cadet Officer, Pion. Schule Abt. 16 AZ 12, Thauvenay-Cosnes (Fr.) 25.6.44		MURDER	FR.
RUMME	141609	M	Ger.		Lt., Pion. Schule Abt. 4, Cosnes (Fr.) 6.7.44		MURDER	FR.
RUMMEL, Gerd	255041	M	Ger.		Crim.Asst., Gestapo, (Lux.) 3.-4.9.44		INTERR.	BEL.
RUMMELSBERGER	151773	M			Officier, Gestapo official, Hamburg (Ger.) 38		MURDER	U.S.
RUMEN or RUMEN	253316	M	Ger.		Col., 377 Jaeger-Regt., Winkt Meigem (Bel.)		MURDER	BEL.
RUMP	142011	M	Ger.	17	Lt., Kriegsmarine, Fort Prins Hendrik near Ooltgensplaat (Neth.) 12.6.45		MURDER	NETH.
RUMP, Max	195895	M	Ger.	98	SS-Hauptscharfhr., SD, Maison-Laffitte (Fr.)15.12.41-10.6.44		TORTURE	FR.
RUMPF, Fritz	122669	M	Ger.		Civilian.		MURDER	U.S.
RUMPEL, Fritz	162699	M	Ger.	04	Pvt., 1. Ost Bn. 447, Plouvien (Fr.) 44		TORTURE	FR.
RUMPF, Erich	180743	M	Ger.		SS-Obersturmfhr., SS 9. Pion.Coy. Leibstand."Adolf Hitler", Malmedy (Bel.) 17.12.44		MURDER	U.S.
RUMPF, Hermann	253155	M			Flyer, C.C. Ellrich, Nordhausen (Ger.)		MURDER	U.S.
RUMPF, Walter	252609	M	Ger.		Officer, Army, Bruessels (Bel.) 3.9.44		INTERR.	BEL.
RUNDE, Ernst Walter	260538	M	Ger.	12. 8.05	SS-Uschfr., W.-SS, Guard-Coy., C.C. Stutthof and Auschwitz (Ger.,Pol.) 11.41-9.44		BRUTALITY	POL.
RUNGE	125050	M	Ger.		Lt., Jaeger Regt. 35, 3. Coy., Bray-Dunes (Fr.) 9.43		MISC.CRIMES	U.K.
RUNGE	152948	M			Member, Volkssturm, Gardelegen (Ger.) 10.-14.4.45		MURDER	U.S.
RUNGE	258192	M	Ger.		Member, SD, Amsterdam (Neth.) 7.2.45		SUSPECT	NETH.
RUNGE, Helmut	262211	M	Ger.	2.3.22	Oschfhr., 51. SS Armoured Bde. 3.Coy. 4.Platoon, Breviandes, Bucheres, Ste Savine, La Riviere de Corps, Troyes (Fr.)22.-25.8.44		BRUTALITY	FR.

RUN - RYB

NAME	C.R.FILE NUMBER	SEX	NATIO-NALITY	DATE OF BIRTH	RANK OCCUPATION UNIT PLACE AND DATE OF CRIME	REASON WANTED	WANTED BY
RUNGEL	305256	M	Ger.		Police Capt.Military Commander,Livadia,Dienststelle No.12085 Vrastamites nr.Livadia Beotia(Grc.)8.1.44	MISC.CRIMES	GRC.
RUNKEL	188469	M	Ger.		Dr.,Civilian,Doctor,CC Berlin(Ger.)40-45	MURDER	CZECH
RUNKEL	253201	M			Lt.CC Ellrich,Nordhausen(Ger.)	MURDER	U.S.
RUNKEL, Albert	300924	M	Ger.		Member SS of Staff CC Neugraben-Tiefstak(Ger.)44-45	MURDER	U.K.
RUNKEWITZ	252626	M	Ger.		Sgt.Sicherungs-Bn.S.D.,Chalons-Saone,Nievre(Fr.)26.-28.6.44	MISC.CRIMES	FR.
RUNKI, Otto	257804	M	Ger.	18.9.99	Capo,Camp Dora,Nordhausen(Ger.)	MURDER	U.S.
RUNSCHILL or REINSCHILT	195894	M	Ger		Korvetten-Capt.Kriegsmarine-Arsenal,Landau(Fr.)	WITNESS	FR.
RUNTE, Hans Joach.	257916	M			Pvt.150 Panz.Bde.Meuse Brigie Antwerpen(Bel.)12.44	MISC.CRIMES	U.S.
RUNTSCHKE	261382	M	Ger		SS Sgt.magistrate Dirlewanger Bde.,Sluck(Pol.)40-44	MURDER	POL.
RUNZER, Willibald	260922	M	Ger.	18.5.13	SS Rottenfhr.(Pvt.)Waffen SS,Guard Coy. CC Auschwitz(Pol.)41-42	BRUTALITY	POL.
RUOFF, Katarina	144361	F	Ger.	90	Civilian,CC Hadamar(Ger.)6.44-3.45	WITNESS	U.S.
RUPERT see RUPPERT	124468						
RUPERT	129055	M	Ger.	00	SS.Osturmfhr.CC Dachau(Ger.)44-45	MURDER	BEL.
RUPERT	251252	M	Ger.	15	SS Raportfhr.CC Auschwitz(Pol.)42-45	MURDER	YUGO.
RUPERT, Elisabeth	260419	F	Ger.		SS Guard,SS Supervisor,CC Auschwitz(Pol.)40-45	BRUTALITY	POL.
RUPP	187552	M	Ger.	19	Opl.Guard at A-K 1174 sttd Stalag IV A 1944,Dresden(Ger.)10.44	MURDER	U.K.
RUPP	259742	M	Ger.		Officer,Unit SS 20.607 K Maintenance-Coy.for Vehicles,St.Pierre du Palais,Charente Maritime(Fr.)29.1.44	WITNESS	FR.
RUPP, Fritz	255741	M	Ger.		Crim.secretary,Gestapo,Opava-Moravia(Czech.)39-45	MISC.CRIMES	CZECH.
RUPP, Heinrich	191813	M	Ger.	10.9.00	Civilian,Miner,Schwalbach(Ger.)8.44	TORTURE	U.S.
RUPP, Josef	260539	M	Ger.	18.11.23	SS Pvt.Waffen SS,Guard-Coy.CC Auschwitz(Pol.)10.42-1.45	BRUTALITY	POL.
RUPPE	152359	M	Ger.		Capt.VI Bn.Guard,11 Coy.,Olde(Ger.)45	TORTURE	FR.
RUPPE, Robert	192055	M	Ger.		Sgt.Eis.Art.Bn.717,St.Andries Varsenare Les Bruges(Bel.)4.9.44	MURDER	BEL.
RUPPELMEIER	192822	M	Ger.		SS Hptscharfhr.CC Buchenwald(Ger.)42-45	MURDER	U.S.
RUPPENHAGEN, Otto	253296	M	Ger.		Staff Sgt.German Army,Gend.,Fonda(It.)9.-10.43	INTER.	YUGO.
RUPPERT	771	M	Ger.		Capt.Prison governor,Army,CC(Kasbah prison)Tunis,12.42-4.43	MURDER	FR.
RUPPERT	21454	M	Ger.	05	Commander,CC Dachau(Ger.)	MURDER	U.S.
RUPPERT or RUPERT	124468	M	Ger.	01	SS,CC Dachau(Ger.)12.43-4.44	MURDER	U.K.
RUPPERT	193341	M	Ger.		Sgt.P.O.W.working Bn.203,CC Aspfjord(Nor.)	TORTURE	NOR.
RUPPERT, Fritz	158236	M	Ger.	00	SS Rottenfhr.Gestapo,Chalon sur Saone(Fr.)43-44	MURDER	FR.
RUPPERT, Robert	162694	M	Ger.		96 Pz.Regt.9 Coy.,Revin(Fr.)6.44	MURDER	FR.
RUPPERT, Herbert	173996	M	Ger.		SS Sgt.Gestapo,Nantes(Fr.)	MURDER	FR.
RUPPERT, Werner	194636	M	Ger.	01	Head,Gestapo,Nantes(Fr.)	MISC.CRIMES	FR.
RUPPERT, Wilhelm	770	M	Ger.	24.2.05	SS Usturmfhr.CC Maidanek(Pol.)40-4.44	MURDER	POL.
RUPPERT, Willi	300125	M	Ger.		Unterlagerfhr.Labour Camp,Salzgitter(Ger.)43-5.44	MISC.CRIMES	POL.
RUPPERTS	305736	F	Ger.		Rapportfhr.CC Auschwitz-Birkenau(Pol.)40	MURDER	FR.
RUPPMANN	166666	M	Ger.		SS Stubafhr.Major,SS(Pol.)40	MURDER	U.S.
RUPPRECHT	257025	M	Ger.		Dr.,District Leader,State Service,Warsaw(Pol.)39-45	INTER.	POL.
RUPPRECHT, Georg	12492	M	Ger.		Pvt.Army,110 or 111 Panz.Gren.Regt.2 Coy.Albine(Fr.)29.6.44	MURDER	FR.
RUPPRECHT, Kilian	191812	M	Ger.	21.12.14	Member,S.D.Gestapo,Pisek(Czech.)39-45	MURDER	CZECH.
RUPPSAM, Walther	167472	M	Ger.		Adjutant,Feldgendarmerie,Quimperle(Fr.)20.6.44-9.8.44	MURDER	FR.
RUPRECHTER, P.	193134	M	Ger.		Schupo,CC Falstad(Nor.)41-44	MURDER	NOR.
RUSBAN, Walter	137574	M	Ger.		Sgt.Army,Querrier(Fr.)	MURDER	U.K.
RUSCH	124381	M	Ger.		Lt.Army,unknown Co stationed at Quiberville,Longueil(Fr.)24.6.44	WITNESS	U.S.
RUSCH	214028	M	Ger.		Pvt.Official,Abwehr Nachrichten Regt.506,Tirana(Albany)44	MISC.CRIMES	U.S.
RUSCH	255207	M			Pvt.CC Nixie,Nordhausen(Ger.)	MURDER	U.S.
RUSCHIL	193973	M	Ger		Crim.Ob.Asst.Gestapo,CC Bruenn(Czech.)39-45	MURDER	CZECH.
RUSICKA see RUZIKA, Emil	256054						
RUSKE, Kurt	173933	M	Ger.	4.3.01	Opl.Prison,CC Vannes(Fr.)42-44	TORTURE	UNWCC
RUSKE, Max	181556	M	Ger.	95	SS Lt.,Crim.Inspector,SS,S.D.,Gestapo,Usti-Labem,Prag(Czech.)39-45	MURDER	CZECH.
RUSS, Paul	251854	M	Ger.	5.3.92	Master,Gend.,Erstein(Fr.)40-45	TORTURE	FR.
RUSSEL, Hermann	255208	M	Ger.	1.5.04	Pvt.CC Ellrich,Nordhausen(Ger.)	MURDER	U.S.
RUSSY, Richard	193972	M	Ger.	9.9.97	Agent,Gestapo,Karlsbad(Czech.)39-45	MURDER	CZECH.
RUST	301977	F	Ger.		Overseer,SS,CC Auschwitz(Pol.)42-45	BRUTALITY	POL.
RUST	62301	M	Ger.		Dr.,Reichsminister,S.A.Obergruppenfhr.Reichsministerium for Scienne and Education.	MURDER	UNWCC
RUST, Bernhard	188990	M			Dr.,Reich-Official,Government,41-45	MURDER	BEL.CZECH.
RUST, Erich	152347	M			Coy.Fhr.Volkssturm,Gardelegen(Ger.)10.-14.4.45	MURDER	U.S.
RUSTER, Gustav	165560	M	Ger.		Civilian,Zugleitung Mons(Bel.)	MURDER	BEL.
RUSTER, Gustav	190326	M	Ger.		Railway-Inspector,Zugleitung Zug and Bahnhofwach-Abt.,Mons(Bel.)	MURDER	U.S.
RUSTEMEYER	184160	M	Ger.		Dr.,Member Gestapo,S.D.,Plzen(Czech.)39-45	MURDER	CZECH.
RUTCHMANN	167463	M	Ger.		SS Hptscharfhr.Gestapo,Section 4 IB(Nor.)4.40	TORTURE	NOR.
RUTGERS, Gundo	167445	M	Ger.		Comm.Administrator,Kattowice(Pol.)9.39-44	MISC.CRIMES	POL.
RUTH, Jean	253203	M	Ger.		Pvt.CC Ellrich-Nixei,Nordhausen(Ger.)	MURDER	U.S.
RUTH, Oscar	29722	M	Ger.		Landgerichtsdirector,Public,official,Cheb(Czech.)40	MURDER	CZECH.
RUTHE	147087	M	Ger.		SS Oschafhr.Fredrikstad(Nor.)41	TORTURE	NOR.
RUTHL	129051	M	Ger.		Officer,Commandant,CC Edelstahlwerks,Crefeld(Ger.)43	MURDER	BEL.
RUTKOWSKI, Antoni	255349	M		12.2.24	Legionaer,CC Harsungen,Nordhausen(Ger.)	MURDER	U.S.
RUTSCH, Gerhard	255350	M			Opl.CC Ellrich,Nordhausen(Ger.)	MURDER	U.S.
RUTSCHMANN, Oskar	255209	M			SS Rottfhr.CC Dora,Dental Clinic Dora,Nordhausen(Ger.)	MURDER	U.S.
RUTTEN, Gerhard	193400	M	Ger.		SS Mann,4 SS Totenkopf Stuba,CC Mittelbau-Dora,Nordhausen(Ger.)43-45	MURDER	U.S.
RUTTERS	196844	M	Ger.		Uschafhr.CC,Arbeitsfhr.,Auschwitz(Pol.)40	MURDER	FR.
RUTTINGER	262207	M	Ger.		Secretary,Gestapo,Rennes(Fr.)43-44	SUSPECT	FR.
RUTTREICH	255210	M			CC Ellrich,Nordhausen(Ger.)	MURDER	U.S.
RUYDELEKER	251253	M	Ger.		Lt.66 Art.Regt.Rehaupal(Fr.)9.44	PILLAGE	FR.
RUYDELEKI	306911	M	Ger.		Lt.5 and 6 Btty. of 66 Art.Regt.,Rehaupal(Vosges)Tendon(Vosges)(Fr.)9-9-44	MURDER	FR.
RUZICIC, Bernhard,Theodor Erich	260454	M	Ger.	1.3.07	SS Staff Scharfhr.Guard-Coy.Administration Service,CC Auschwitz(Pol.)12.40-1.45	BRUTALITY	POL.
RUZIKA or RUSICKA, Emil	256054	M	Ger.		SS Schuetze,Muhldorf(Ger.)	WITNESS	U.S.
RUZISCHKA	304498	M	Ger.		Scharfhr.-SS Sgt.,CC Buchenwald(Ger.)16.5.38-9.10.43	MURDER	BEL.
RYBKA	773	M	Ger.		SS Hptsturmfhr.SS Fallschirmjaeger Bn.500,23.5.44	MURDER	YUGO.
RYBOW	174055	M	Ger.		SS Member,Zdunska Wola-Lodz(Pol.)8.42-8.43	MURDER	POL.

NAME	C.R.FILE NUMBER	SEX	NATIO- NALITY	DATE OF BIRTH	RANK, OCCUPATION, UNIT, PLACE AND DATE OF CRIME	REASON WANTED	WANTED BY
RYBNICEK, Edeltraut	192527	F	Ger.		Clerk, Gestapo, Brno. (Czech.) 39-45	WITNESS	CZECH.
RYDER (see RAYDER)	156046						
RZIHA, Alfred	181557	M	Ger.	09	Member, Crim.employee, SD,Gestapo, Kolin, Benesov(Czech.) 39-45	MURDER	CZECH.
SAAKEL, Rudi	135307	M			Inf. "Gross-Deutschland" Div., Daun (Ger.) 23.12.45	MURDER	U.S.
SAALA	62178	M	Ger.		Agent, Gestapo, Seales (Fr.) 15.4.43	MURDER	FR.
SAALBACH, Franz	1472	M	Ger.		Cpl., Army, 194 Gr., 1 Coy	MISC.CRIMES	U.K.
SAALBERG	141614	M	Ger.		SS, Paris (Fr.) 40-45	MISC.CRIMES	FR.
SAALMANN	167321	M	Ger.		Capt. Pz.Jg.Abt.227, 227 Inf.Div.,Royuille (Fr.) 40-44	LOOTING	FR.
SAALMANN, Georg	39608	M	Ger.		Gestapo, SD Angers, Chorus-leader, Chateau Gontier (Fr.)4. or 5.8.44, lived at Laval 64, Rue Magenta (Fr.)	MURDER	FR.
SAALMANN, Georges	147056	M	Ger.		Agent, Sicherheitsdienst, Angers (Fr.) 44	MURDER	U.N.W.C.C.
SAALMUELLER, Fritz	305257	M	Ger.		Lt., Army, Wollmatingen near Konstanz (Ger.) on or about 20.7.44	MURDER	U.S.
SAALWACHTER	253918	M	Ger.		Chief of camp, Neuengamme (Ger.) 44	MURDER	FR.
SAALWAECHTER, Alfred	259007	M	Ger.		Admiral of the fleet, crimes against peace, war crimes and crimes against humanity	WITNESS	U.S.
SAAM, Friedrich	167899	M	Ger.		Pvt., 9 Res.Gren.Rgt., 1 Coy, Magny d'Anigon(Fr.) 18.9.44	MURDER	FR.
SAAR	257917	M	Ger.		Uschfhr, 150 Pz.Bde., Meuse Bridge, Antwerpen(Bel.) 12.44	MISC.CRIMES	U.S.
SAAT	142219	M	Ger.	00	Sgt., PoW working Bn.180, 3 Coy, CC Ellenes Lista(Nor.)	MURDER	NOR.
SAATHOFF	156016	M	Ger.		SS Uschfhr, CC Voeght (Neth.)	TORTURE	FR.
SAATMANN, Ewald	300970	M	Ger.		SS Osturmfhr, official of SD, Leitabschnitt Prague, CC Auschwitz-Birkenau (Pol.) 39-45	MURDER	CZECH.
SABEL	256373	M	Ger.		Oschfhr, SS, Muhldorf (Ger.)	WITNESS	U.S.
SABINSKY	156015	M		03	SS Doctor, CC Neuengamme (Ger.)	TORTURE	U.K.
SAELIAR	306865	M	Ger.		Member of Rumanian Command, Gestapo Vichy (Fr.) 10.43-9.44	MURDER	FR.
SABOTH	186823	M	Ger.		Cpl., Stalag-XIII D, CC Noerdlingen (Ger.) 3.7.43	MURDER	FR.
SABOTTKA	259910	M	Ger.		Sgt., Strijbeek (Neth.) 7.9.44	TORTURE	NETH.
SACH (or SACK), Friedrich	251365	M	Ger.	19. 7.91	Medical Major, 38 Bn., 28 Rgt.,189 Res.Div., hunter of foot, Trie s-Baise et Montaner (Fr.) 29.6.44, 10.7.44	MISC.CRIMES	FR.
SACHAR	301979	F	Ger.		Overseer, SS, knitting room, CC Auschwitz (Pol.) 42-45	BRUTALITY	POL.
SACHAROW	193870	M			Schfhr, 4-SS Totenkopf Sturmbann, CC Dora - Mittelbau, Nordhausen (Ger.) 43-45	INTERR.	U.S.
SACHE (see SACHER)	126925						
SACHEB	12494	M	Ger.		Lt., Pz.Gren.Rgt.110 or 111, Gourdon (Fr.) 29.6.44	MURDER	FR.
SACHER (or SACHE, SACHER)	126925	M	Ger.		Lt., 11 Pz.Div., 2 Coy, AAA 7, Bergerac and near Albine(Fr.)7.-8.44	MURDER	FR.
SACHER (see SACHEB)	126925						
SACHMEISTER (or SAGMEISTER)	189631	M	Ger.		Usturmfhr, 11 Pz.Gr.Ausb.Train.Bn., Gras (Aust.) 3.-4.45	MURDER	U.K.
SACHS	31558	M	Ger.		Osturmfhr, SS, prison guard, Lublin (Pol.) 43	MISC.CRIMES	U.S.
SACHS (see SAX), Johann	255684						
SACHSE	36649	M	Ger.		Cpl., 635 Lds.Schtz.Bn., 5 Coy	MISC.CRIMES	U.K.
SACHSE	159114	M	Ger.		SS Doctor, Chatillon Coligny (Fr.) 29.3. - 7.44	WITNESS	FR.
SACHSE, Max	156014	M	Ger.	92	Hptwachtmstr, Gestapo, Stavanger (Nor.) 11.42	MURDER	U.K.
SACHTLER, Gustav Heinr. Walter	251285	M	Ger.	28. 4.04	Civilian, highest ranking official, labour exchange office, Hradec, Kralove (Czech.) 39-45	INTERR.	CZECH.
SACK	180873	M	Ger.		Dr.med., CC Ebrach (Ger.)	MURDER	FR.
SACK (see SACH, Friedrich)	251365						
SACK, Helmuth	164002	M	Ger.		Cpl., Army, Brugge (Ger.) 9.45	WITNESS	U.S.
SACK, Kurt	774	M	Ger.		Major, Chief of German Police, CC Lublin (Pol.) 43-44	MURDER	FR.
SACK, Kurt	251262	M	Ger.		Medical officer, Camp Burg Erbach (Ger.)	MURDER	FR.
SACK, Paul	305690	M	Ger.		Civilian, near Luebeck-Siems (Ger.) about 6.8.44	MURDER	U.S.
SACK, Ursule	164001	F	Ger.		Civilian, Brugge (Ger.) 9.45	WITNESS	U.S.
SACKENHEIM, Jacob	261899	M	Ger.	05	Cpl., Interpreter, SD of Besancon(Doubs),Ricq(Fr.) 24.7.44	BRUTALITY	FR.
SACKMANN, Eddy	255689	M	Ger.		Civilian, chief of Block I and III, CC Mauthausen (Aust.)	INTERR.	FR.
SACKMANN, Max	132692	M	Ger.	29.11.19	Kapo, CC Dora, Nordhausen (Ger.)	RAPE	FR.
SACRECZEWSKY	188181	M	Ger.	19. 9.13	Member Gestapo, Luxemburg 40-45	MISC.CRIMES	LUX.
SADEK	306284	M	Ger.		Member Gestapo at Trencin, CC Auschwitz-Birkenau(Pol.) 39-45	MURDER	CZECH.
SADOWSKI, Alfred	255687	M	Ger.		Flyer, CC Ellrich, Nordhausen (Ger.)	MURDER	U.S.
SADOWSKI	39795	M	Ger.		Rottfhr, SS Pz.Gren.Div. "Goets von Berlichingen", Sturm- Geschuets- Abt.17, Pz.Jg.Abt.17, Segre-Renaze(Fr.)30.7.44,6.8.44	MURDER	FR.
SADOWKL	306695	M	Ger.		Pvt., 331 Pion.Bn., 331 Inf.Div., Mijnheerenland(Neth.) 5.45	PILLAGE	NETH.
SAEGER (or DAEGER)	302131	M	Ger.		Capt., member of the Standgericht, 1 Bn., 24 Reg. Parachutist Huebner 7 Div. General-Major Erdmann, Roermond(Neth.) 12.44-1.45	MURDER	NETH.
SAEKEL	142245	M	Ger.	11	Dr., SS-Sturmbannfhr, leader, Gestapo RSHF, Minsk (Russia)	TORTURE	U.S.
SAENDISCH	259111	M	Ger.		Usturmfhr, SS Div. "Prinz-Eugen", Niksic district Montenegro(Yugo.) 5. 6.43	MISC.CRIMES	YUGO.
SAENGER	259342	M			CC Osterhagen, Nordhausen (Ger.)	MURDER	U.S.
SAENGER, Kurt	251456	M	Ger.	1.10.95	Ortsleiter, NSDAP., Kynsperk (Czech.) 38-45	INTERR.	CZECH.
SAEVECKE	252697	M	Ger.	11	Capt., SD for Lombardia Region, Milano (It.) 10.8.44	MURDER	U.K.
SAFFA	187547	M	Ger.	10	Major, 65 Inf.Div., Rgt.147, between Genua, Cisa-Pass and Spezia(It.) 9.10.43	WITNESS	U.K.
SAFFE, Ernst	72055	M			Usturmfhr, 12 SS Geb.Jg.Rgt.	TORTURE	U.S.
SAFTIG	188333	M	Ger.	07	Sgt., Lds.Schtz.Bn. 775 or 777, 6 Coy, Waldrach(Ger.) 9.8.44	TORTURE	U.S., U.K.
SAGER	139707	M	Ger.		Lt.Col., Asst.Cmdt., Stalag II-B, CC Hammerstein(Ger.)8.43-2.45	TORTURE	U.S.
SAGGAU	252686	M	Ger.	90	Major, Cmdt., Landers Hutzer Bn.676, 19 Corps, Mesola(It.)17.12.44	TORTURE	U.K.
SAGLER	306649	M	Ger.		Pvt., Feld-Gend.Chateaubriant(Loire-Inf), St.Julien de Mouvantes Juigne les Moutiers Soudan (Fr.) 21.7.44	MURDER	FR.
SAGMEISTER (see SACHMEISTER)	189631						
SAHL, Alfred	121693	M	Ger.		Sgt., Infantry, Louvetot (Fr.) 28.8.44	PILLAGE	FR.
SAHL, Emil (or SUDEKUM, REINHARDT, FELTES)	161655	M	Ger.	05	Pvt., Guard, Army, Mosaic factory, Sinzig(Ger.) 19-20.12.41	TORTURE	U.S.
SAHLE, Franz	21477	M	Ger.	16. 6.98	Official, CC Westhausen (Ger.)	TORTURE	U.S.
SAHLMANN	253320	M	Ger.		Capt., Cmdt. of Bn., 11 Bn., 376 Jg.Rgt., Vinkt Meigen(Bel.)25-31.5.40	MURDER	BEL.
SAHM	156075	M	Ger.		Doctor, Georgian Bn., Tulle (Fr.) 6.4.44	MISC.CRIMES	FR.
SAHM, Willi	251297	M	Ger.		Gestapo, S.D.R.E.P.Z., Mussidan, Dordogne, (Fr.) 11.6.44	MURDER	FR.
SAIBER	186158	M	Ger.	15	Guard, SS, CC Rottenburg (Ger.)	TORTURE	FR.

SAI - SAN

NAME	C.R.FILE NUMBER	SEX	NATIO-NALITY	DATE OF BIRTH	RANK OCCUPATION UNIT PLACE AND DATE OF CRIME	REASON WANTED	WANTED BY
SAIKO, Rudolf	255720	M		26.12.23	Pvt.,C.C.Ellrich,Nordhausen (Ger.)	MURDER	U.S.
SAILA	300113	M			Head of camp,C.C.Mauthausen (Aust.) 11.42-5.45	MISC.CRIMES	FR.
SAILER (or SEILER)	188332	M	Ger.	03	Sgt.,Gendarmerie,nearTomaszow (Pol.) 7.-8.43	MURDER	POL.
SAILER	306650	M	Ger.		Feldgendarm,Feldgendarmerie,Chateau briant (Loire Inf.),St.Julien de Mouvantes,Soudan,Juigne les Moutiers,Le Teillais (Fr.) 21.7.44	MURDER	FR.
SAILFE	12495	M	Ger.		Sgt.,Army, 3 Bn.Inf. 4 Coy,Macon (Fr.) 8.6.44	MURDER	FR.
SAILLER	775	M	Ger.		Sgt.,Army,C.C.Caen (Fr.) 6.44	MURDER	FR.
SAINT-MOND	181003	M		95	SS-Oschfhr.,SS,C.C.Siemens-Schuckert-Werke,Nuernberg,Flossenburg (Ger.) 44-45	WITNESS	U.S.
SAINT-POL	121861		Ger.		Doctor,Civilian,C.C.Hinzert (Ger.)	TORTURE	BEL.
SAISSE, Heinrich	138748	M	Ger.		SS-Sgt.,Gestapo,Lyon (Fr.)	MURDER	FR.
SAJONIS, Isidorius	254247	M		19.10.23	Camp Harzungen,Nordhausen (Ger.)	MURDER	U.S.
SAKEL	260145	M	Ger.		Capt.,11 Pz.Div.,Massif du Vercors, Isere et Drome (Fr.) 20.7.-5.8.44	SUSPECT	FR.
SAKOURS (or ZAKOURS)	253336	M			Cpl.,C.C.Ellrich,Nordhausen (Ger.)	MURDER	U.S.
SALABAN	135308	M			SS-Uschfhr.,SS,C.C.Auschwitz-Birkenau (Pol.) 42	MURDER	U.S.
SALBEI	10338	M			Major,Stabschef d.Ordnungspolizei,Prague (Czech.) 39-44	TORTURE	CZECH.
SALBERG, Rudolf	139081	M	Ger.		Interpreter,Russian Labour Camp,C.C.Hof (Ger.)	TORTURE	U.S.
SALER	164738	M	Ger.		Adj.,Feldgendarmerie,Montigny en Vesoul (Fr.) 16.7.44	MURDER	FR.
SALETINGEN	167898	M	Ger.		Pvt.,9 Res.Gren.Rgt. 1 Coy,Magny d'Anigon (Fr.) 9.44	MURDER	FR.
SALETZKI	188354	M	Ger.		Member,SS,Schonefeld (Ger.) 44-45	TORTURE	POL.
SALEWSKI, Otto	301/39	M	Ger.		Uschfhr.,SS-Cpl.,C.C.Buchenwald (Ger.) 16.5.38-9.10.43	MURDER	BEL.
SALFELD, Otto	251282	M	Ger.		Cmdt., of Jewish Gratto,Civilian,Opatow (Pol.) 43	INTERR.	POL.
SALFEPT	256036	M	Ger.		SS-Mann,SS,Muhldorf	WITNESS	U.S.
SALGE, Fritz	251531	M	Ger.		Guard,C.C.Lahde-Weser (Ger.)	INTERR.	BEL.
SALIGAT	142224	M	Ger.		Lageraeltester,Waldlager V and VI,C.C.Muhldorf Ampfing (Ger.) 44-45	TORTURE	U.S.
SALIMAIER	256506	M		94	Rapportfhr.,SS	MURDER	U.S.
SALINGA, Gerhard	1474		Ger.		Army,H.Q. Coy,Engineer Bn.,Inf.Rgt.274,305 Div.,	MISC.CRIMES	U.K.
SALM, August	153236	M	Ger.		Cpl.,Army,1 Coy 1082 Sichr.Bn.	WITNESS	U.S.
SALMEN, Theodor	251255	M		4.1.06	Polizeimann,Polizei,Luxemburg (Lux.)	INTERR.	LUX.
SALMIN	124973				Wachtmeister,Gestapo,C.C.Bremen-Farge (Ger.) 6.43	MISC.CRIMES	U.K.
SALMON	141854	M	Ger.		Sgt.,Major,Army,Berlin (Ger.) 11.5.41	MISC.CRIMES	U.K.
SALOMON	261393	M	Ger.		C.C.Auschwitz (Pol.) 42-45	SUSPECT	POL.
SALOMON	302122	M	Ger.		Capt.,Member,of the Standgericht, 1 Bn.24 Rgt.of Fallschirmjg.Huebner, 7 Div.General Major Huebner,Roermond (Neth.) 12.44-1.45	MURDER	NETH.
SALOMON, Heinrich	181004	M	Ger.		(Ger.) 7.44	MURDER	U.S.
SALMUTH	776	M	Ger.		Lt.General,Stabschef v.General Bock,Army,nordl.Armeegruppe, 9.39	MURDER	POL.
SALPETER, Walter	258542	M	Ger.	83	Dr.,SS-Oberfhr.,SS,WVHA, (Ger.) 40-45	BRUTALITY	U.S.
SALSIGNER	301356	M	Ger.		N.C.O.,Allershausen nr.Freising Bav.(Ger.) 4.41	BRUTALITY	FR.
SALWEGNART, Wera	189190	F			Block-Warden,SS woman C.C.Uckermark (Ger.) 42-45	MURDER	FR.
SALZBRENNER, Alfred	253337	M			Rottfhr.,C.C.Harzungen,Nordhausen (Ger.)	MURDER	U.S.
SALZBURGER	187651	M	Ger.		Cpl.,Feldgendarmerie,Gourdriaan (Neth.) 22.5.44	MURDER	U.K.
SALZMANN, Friedrich	142247	M		84	Capt.,Gendarmerie,Schwiokerhausen, (Ger.) 9.44	MURDER	U.S.
SALZMANN, Oscar	142031	M	Ger.		N.C.O.,German Army,Medical Corps,Laterina Camp (It.) 6.44	MISC.CRIMES	U.K.
SAMBOR	261957	M	Ger.		Car-driver,SS,Belgrade,Valjevo (Yugo.) 15.8.42-10.9.44	SUSPECT	YUGO.
SAMEK	146715	M			SS-Hptschfhr.,SS,C.C.Flossenburg (Ger.)	TORTURE	U.S.
SAMEL	777	M			Lt.or Capt.,Gestapo,Waffen SS,Wolfenhoek (Neth.) 2.41	TORTURE	NETH.
SAMEL, D.	214029	M	Ger.	14	SS-Capt.,SD,Sipo,Hertogenbosch (Neth.) 44	TORTURE	U.S.
SAMLAND, Erich	193160	M	Ger.	10.5.04	Sgt.,Guard,Reichsjustizministerium Feldstraflager,Waffen SS,Finmark (Nor.) 9.3.45	MISC.CRIMES	NOR.
SAMLAND, Siegfried	256046	M	Ger.	07	SS-Oschfhr.,Town Hall of De Bilt,Utrecht (Neth.) 10.44	MURDER	NETH.
SAMMELDIENER, Michel	173287	M			Capo,C.C.Natzweiler (Fr.) 42-5.43	MURDER	U.K.
SAMMENTINGER	187787	M			C.C.Natzweiler (Fr.) 5.41	TORTURE	U.S.
SAMMER	129945	M			Dr., C.C. Mauthausen (Aust.) 41 - 45.	MURDER	U.S.
SAMMLER	302123	M	Ger.		Chauffeur,Sicherheitsdienst,Apeldoorn,Woeste Hoeve,Hoogsoeren,Lager "Mia",(Neth.) 10.-12.44, 7.4.45	MURDER	NETH.
SAMS	779	M	Ger.		Dr.,Perigueux (Fr.) 6.44	MURDER	FR.
SAMSOHN	305804	M	Ger.		Dr.,Capt.,Chief of Camp Hospital Oflag VI-C,Osnabrueck-Ewersheide (Ger.) 41-45	MURDER	YUGO.
SAMSON, Karl	253919	M			Member,Gestapo,G.F.P.,Lille (Fr.) 40-44	MISC.CRIMES	FR.
SAMUEL	780	M	Ger.		Official,medical officer,C.C.Oswiecim-Birkenau (Pol.) 39-45,40-43 Prof.,Dr.	MURDER	CZECH.,POL.,BEL.
SAN	261099	M	Ger.		Lt.Col.,Commander,Air Force,Garrison,Cerekvice near Vysoke Myto, (Czech.) 5.5.45	MURDER	CZECH.
SAND	17213	M	Ger.		Officer,Waffen SS,Chief Administration,C.C.Mauthausen (Aust.)	MISC.CRIMES	U.S.
SANDEL	300475	M	Ger.		Customs official,Urbes (Upper Rhine) (Fr.) 5.10.44	MURDER	FR.
SANDER	108927	M	Ger.	81	Major,Army,Puschkinsky Gory (Sov.Un.) 42 or 43	MURDER	U.S.
SANDER	133243	M			Usturmfhr.,Waffen SS 2 Pion.Ausbildungsbn.,Passau (Ger.) 4.45	MURDER	U.S.
SANDER	186227	M	Ger.		Guard,C.C.Sachsenhausen (Ger.)	TORTURE	FR.
SANDER	255688	M	Ger.	05	SS-Hptschfhr.,SS Bn.26006,Cornillon Confaux (Fr.) 23.8.43	INTERR.	FR.
SANDER	257246	M	Ger.		Generallt.,Div.Commander of Brugge,Beernem Flandre Occidentale (Bel.) 5.-6.9.44	INTERR.	BEL.
SANDER	301024	M	Ger.		Warden,Camp III,C.C.Oranienburg-Sachsenhausen (Ger.) 42-45	MURDER	FR.
SANDER	301280	M	Ger.		Crim.Oberasst.,Abt. IV A,SD,Bruessel (Bel.) 6.40-9.44	MURDER	BEL.
SANDER	301902	M	Ger.		Hptsturmfhr.,I b, 6 SS Div.Nord,20 Army, Finmark 10.11.44	MURDER	NOR.
SANDER, Emile	306651	M	Ger.		N.C.O.,Feldgendarmerie Chateaubriant (Loire-Inf.),St.Julien de Mouvantes,Soudan,Juigne les Moutiers,Les Teillais (Fr.) 21.7.44	MURDER	FR.
SANDER, Hermann	12496	M	Ger.		Pvt.,Army;110 Br 111.Pz.Gren.Rgt. 2 Coy,Albine (Fr.) 29.6.44	MURDER	FR.
SANDER, Knist	139715	M	Ger.		SS-Oschfhr.,Guard,Waffen SS,C.C.Nordhausen (Ger.) 5.4.45	MURDER	U.S.
SANDER, Rudolf	188182	M	Ger.	05	Leading Member,NSDAP,Praha (Czech.)	MISC.CRIMES	CZECH.
SANDER, Wilhelm	191258	M	Ger.		General,Governor,Civil-Servant,Poznan (Pol.)	PILLAGE	POL.
SANDERMANN	188777	M	Ger.		Agent,Railway,Le Bourget Triage (Fr.) 24.8.44	WITNESS	FR.
SANDERS	156929	M	Ger.		Lt.General,Div."Hermann Goering",Bellengreville (Fr.) 31.8.44	WITNESS	FR.
SANDERS	173549	M	Ger.		SS-Oschfhr.,SS,C.C.Dora (Ger.) 43-4.45	MURDER	FR.
SANDERS	301738	M	Ger.		Capt.,Command at the Camp 102,Aquila (It.) 8.12.43	MURDER	U.K.
SANDERS, Heinrich	253319	M	Ger.		Sgt.,10 Coy,377 Jg.Rgt.,Vinkt,Meigem (Bel.) 25.-31.5.40	MURDER	BEL.
SANDERS, Wilhelm	108928	M	Ger.		Guard,C.C.Boegermoor (Ger.)	TORTURE	U.S.
SANDIG	1745				Sturmbannfhr.,SS Pz.Div.Leibst."Adolf Hitler",Turin (It.) 9.43	MURDER	U.K.
SANDIG	31560	M	Ger.		Lt.,Army,Gren.Ers.Rgt.mot 209,Inf.Div.174,Warschau,Lemberg,Bilgoraj (Pol.) 44	MURDER	U.S.
SANDIC	124315	M			SS-Sturmbannfhr.,SS Army,1 SS Pz.Div.,2 SS Pz.Gren.Rgt.,Malmedy (Bel.) 17.12.44	MURDER	U.S.

SAN - SAU

NAME	C.R. FILE NUMBER	SEX	NATIO-NALITY	DATE OF BIRTH	RANK	OCCUPATION	UNIT	PLACE AND DATE OF CRIME	REASON WANTED	WANTED BY
SANDMANN, Bernhard (see SANDSTEDE, Gottfried)	214030									
SANDNER	253339	M				Pvt.,C.C.,Ellrich,Nordhausen (Ger.)			MURDER	U.S.
SANDNER, Johann	29723	M	Ger.			Landgerichtsrat,Justiz-Ministerium,Cheb (Czech.)			MURDER	CZECH.
SANDREUTER, Hans	143097	M	Ger.			Civilian,City Councillor,Fuerth (Ger.)			TORTURE	U.S.
SANDSTEDE,Gottfried(or SANDMANN, Bernhard)	214030	M	Ger.			Official,Gestapo,Buenos Aires (Argentine) 41			MISC.CRIMES	U.S.
SANDTNER, Rudolf	250469	M	Ger.	17.6.06		Civilian,Liberec (Czech.) 39-45			BRUTALITY	CZECH.
SANETZKI	252695	M			Oschfhr.,Leibstandarte Adolf Hitler,C.Q.M.S.,3.Coy.,Wormhoudt (Fr.,Bel.) 27.5.40				INTERR.	U.K.
SANFT	185330	M	Ger.	98	Lt.,Gendarmerie,Rawa near Tomaszow (Pol.) 7.-8.43				MURDER	POL.
SANGER, Heinrich	133250	M			Hptschfhr.,Waffen SS,C.C.,Flossenburg (Ger.)				TORTURE	U.S.
SANIZER	129944	M			Agent,Gestapo,Vienna (Aust.) 1.12.44				TORTURE	U.S.
SANN	181005	M			Lt.,Army,Annecy between Thonon (Fr.)				MURDER	FR.
SANNITZER (see STUNITZER)	131647									
SANONA (or ZANONA)	253338	M			Rottfhr.,C.C.,Harzungen,Nordhausen (Ger.)				MURDER	U.S.
SANTHOVEL, Ferdinand	164736	M	Ger.		Chief,Working Kdo. 767,Wolferlingen (Ger.) 43				TORTURE	FR.
SANT, Richard	188184	M	Ger.		Capt.,Army,Mayor,public official,Altiano (Grc.) 1.45				MURDER	GRC.
SANTLLBEN	257496	M			Factory worker,C.C.,Nordhausen (Ger.)				MURDER	U.S.
SANY, Josef	255223	M	Ger.	09	Employee,State service,Gestapo,Kolin (Czech.) 39-42				MURDER	CZECH.
SAPCR, Franz	187870	M		08	Miner,Adolf Mine,Merkstein (Ger.) 8.42-10.44				WITNESS	U.S.
SAFTER, Albert	189189	M			Customs officer,Zollgrenzschutz,near Plaine s-Mer (Fr.) 12.5.42				TORTURE	FR.
SAFFK, Wilhelm	184284	M			Mayor,public official,Vlotho,Herkmissen (Ger.)				MURDER	U.S.
SARCK	141996	M	Ger.	95	Civilian,Wiesbaden (Ger.) 42-45				MISC.CRIMES	POL.
SARCRANN	194405	M	Ger.		Blockleader,C.C.,Mauthausen (Aust.)				TORTURE	FR.
SARESER	152107	M	Ger.		Lt.,Air-force,Bousquet d'Orb (Fr.) 17.8.44				MURDER	FR.
SARETZLI, Elisabeth	306866	F	Ger.	22	Overseer,SS,C.C.,Auschwitz (Pol.) 40-45				MURDER	FR.
SARETZKI, Ewald	254039	M			Pvt.,C.C.,Ellrich,Nordhausen (Ger.)				MURDER	U.S.
SARHAN, Wenzl	258103	M	Ger.	26.12.13	Informer,Civilian,Gestapo,Nova Dubce (Czech.) 6.42				MURDER	CZECH.
SARHEK, Leo	167897	M	Ger.		Pvt.,9.Res.Gren.Rgt.,1.Ccy.,Magny d' Anigon (Fr.) 18.9.44				MURDER	FR.
SARTOW	156011	M	Ger.	10-11	Oschfhr.,SS,C.C.,Sachsenhausen,Oranienburg (Ger.) 43				TORTURE	U.K.
SASBACH (see SHOSBACH)	252670									
SASCHIN, Johann	193868	M	Ger.		Guard,4.SS Totenkopf-Sturmbann,C.C.,Dora-Mittelbau,Monowitz,Nordhausen (Pol.,Ger.) 43-45				INTERR.	U.S.
SASCS	253476	M	Ger.		Col.,President Torgau Mil.Court,Halle (Ger.) 4.2.44				INTERR.	FR.
SASINSKY	136193	M			Pvt.,SS,2.Pz.Div.,2.Coy.,2 AA A7,Albine (Fr.) 12.3.44				MURDER	FR.
SASMANNSHAUSEN, Wilhelm	121718	M	Ger.	6.7.97	Osturmfhr.,NSKK,Org.Todt,Staffel 71,La Fleche (Fr.) 28.6.44				MURDER	FR.
SASS, Arnold	194366	M	Ger.		Pvt.,2-188 Rgt.,Arb.Bn.,between Lekanger and Ervik (Nor.) 10.42				MURDER	NOR.
SASSE	189536	M	Ger.		Civilian,Lipperscheiderhelt,Flebour (Lux.)				MURDER	LUX.
SASSE, Heinrich	132737	M		06	Chief,Gestapo,Barcus (Fr.) 23.6.43				MURDER	FR.
SASSE, Walter	188374	M		01	Sgt.,Gendarmerie,Rawa near Tomaszow (Pol.) 7.-8.43				MURDER	POL.
SASSEN	253347	M	Ger.		Medicin Controleur,Camp Hinzert (Ger.)				INTERR.	POL.
SATLER	125530	M			SS,Ostheim (Ger.)				TORTURE	POL.
SATOW	156010	M	Ger.	10-15	SS guard,C.C.,Sachsenhausen,Oranienburg (Ger.)				TORTURE	U.K.
SATOW	167881	M	Ger.		Oschfhr.,SS,guard,C.C.,Oranienburg,Sacgsenhausen (Ger.) 39-45				MURDER	POL.
SATOW	253478	M			Coy cmdt.,3.Bn.,338.Div.Heeres Unteroffizier Schule,La Bresse (Fr.) 9.-11.44				MISC.CRIMES	FR.
SATR	133948	M	Ger.		Rottfhr.,SS,C.C.,Buchenwald (Ger.)				TORTURE	FR.
SATRAN, Franz	256037	M	Ger.		SS-Mann,Muhldorf (Ger.)				WITNESS	U.S.
SATTLER	190270	M	Ger.		Sturmbannfhr.,Gestapo,C.C.,Banjica,Beograd (Yugo.,Serb.) 41-44				MURDER	YUGO.
SATTLER	260848	M			Lt.,Elversberg (Ger.) 17.-19.7.44				MURDER	U.S.
SATTLER, Johann	174127	M			Guard,labor-camp,C.C.,Graylitz (Ger.)				TORTURE	U.S.
SATTMANN	253789	M	Ger.		Grave-digger,Ferlach (Aust.) 44-45				MURDER	YUGO.
SAUBER	300857	M			Pvt.,1.AufklAbt.,3.Coy.,2.Column,XV.Div.,Afrika Korps,Saint-Leger,(Arlon) 5.9.44				MISC.CRIMES	BEL.
SAUBER, Karl	261004	M			Member,SA,Frankenhofen (Ger.) 42-44				MISC.CRIMES	U.S.
SAUDISCH	190255	M			Usturmfhr.,SS "Prinz Eugen" Div.,Sinj Drasnice (Yugo.)5.11.43-17.4.44				MURDER	YUGO.
SAUER	781	M			Hptsturmfhr.,SS,C.C.,Treblinka B(Pol.) 42-43				MURDER	POL.
SAUER	31448	M			Sturmbannfhr.,SS,C.C.,Sachsenhausen (Ger.) 42				MURDER	U.S.
SAUER	62093	M	Ger.		Agent,Gestapo,3a41es (Fr.) 15.4.43				MURDER	FR.
SAUER	123968	M		10	Pvt.,515 Coy.,C.C.,Szerzewadna (Czech.) 31.3.45				MURDER	U.K.
SAUER	129943	M		90 or 95	Sturmbannfhr.,Waffen SS,C.C.,Mauthausen (Aust.) 39				MURDER	U.S.
SAUER	136598	M	Ger.		Lt.,SS,Kamp on the Rhine (Ger.)				MURDER	U.S.
SAUER	139083	M	Ger.		Sturmbannfhr.,SS Totenkopf,Riga,Auschwitz (Pol.)				MURDER	U.S.
SAUER	189188	M			Sturmbannfhr.,SS,C.C.,Ravensbrueck (Ger.) 42-45				MURDER	FR.
SAUER	191480	M			Hptsturmfhr.,SS,C.C.,Sachsenhausen,Oranienburg (Ger.) 39-4.45				MURDER	POL.
SAUER	192127	M			Sturmbannfhr.,SS,C.C.,Ravensbrueck (Ger.) 3.45				MURDER	U.K.
SADER	253790	M			Pvt.,3.Jaeger Bn.,738.Rgt.,Off Supetar (Yugo.) 10.3.44				MURDER	YUGO.
SAUER	254040	M			Flyer,C.C.,Ellrich,Nordhausen (Ger.)				MURDER	U.S.
SAUER, Albert	190256	M	Ger.		Major,Army,Kadinjaca (Yugo.) 29.11.41				MURDER	YUGO.
SAUER, Georg Paul	260525	M	Ger.	18.10.11	Oschfhr.,Waffen SS,guard Coy.,3.C.,Auschwitz (Pol.) 3.42-1.45				BRUTALITY	POL.
SAUER, Gertrud	171273	F	Ger.		SS,C.C.,Bergen-Belsen (Ger.)				MURDER	U.N.W.C.C.
SAUER, Hedwig	252691	F			SS Woman guard,C.C.,Geislingen (Ger.) 40-45				INTERR.	POL.
SAUER, Josef Karl	188335	M	Ger.	13	Lt.,Pi.Bn.98,or 898,Kamp St.Goar (Ger.) 29.12.44				MURDER	U.S.
SAUER, Karl	159115	M	Ger.	00-05	Pvt.,Army,3.Coy.,188.Kgf.Arb.Bn.,Fure (Nor.) 21.10.44				WITNESS	NOR.
SAUER, Otto	254041	M			Uschfhr.,C.C.,Harzungen,Nordhausen (Ger.)				MURDER	U.S.
SAUER, Willi	142223	M	Ger.	22	SS guard,C.C.,Mittergars,Muhldorf (Ger.) 44-45				TORTURE	U.S.
SAUERBIER, Joachim	259838	M	Ger.		Officer,Ger.submarine,Atlantic ocean on the route between Cardiff and New-York, 23,2.43				WITNESS	NETH.
SAUERBORN	256098	M	Ger.		Org.Todt,Muhldorf (Ger.)				WITNESS	U.S.
SAUERBRUCH, Ferdinand	79945	M			Geheimrat Professor,Surgeon,C.C.,Auschwitz (Pol.)				MURDER	DEN.
SAUERBRUCH, Peter	261109	M			Lt.Col.,Army				MURDER	U.S.
SAUERHOEFFR, Heinrich(or SAUERHOFFER)	255755	M	Ger.	01	Kreisleiter,NSDAP,Krs.Schlettstadt (Selestat) Muttersholtz(Fr.)21.7.44				MURDER	U.S.
SAUERITZ	253920	M	Ger.		Cpl.,Air-force,Entzheim (Fr.) 42-44				TORTURE	FR.
SAUERLAND	124387	M	Ger.		Lt.,Army,unknown A.A.A. Btty.,Neuss (Ger.) 24.12.44				MURDER	U.S.
SAUERMANN	39797	M	Ger.		SS-Mann,17.SS Pz.Gren.Div.,Segre-Renaze (Fr.)				MURDER	FR.

SAU - SCHA

NAME	C.R.FILE NUMBER	SEX	NATIO- NALITY	DATE OF BIRTH	RANK OCCUPATION UNIT PLACE AND DATE OF CRIME	REASON WANTED	WANTED BY
SAUERMANN	152120	M	Ger.		Guard,Arb.-Kdo.2021,Neuhof(Ger.)	MURDER	FR.
SAUERWALD, Klaus	255685	M			Flyer,C.C.Ellrich,Nordhausen(Ger.)	MURDER	U.S.
SAUGER, Josef	161656	M			Cpl.,C.C.Leipzig,Torgau(Ger.)	SUSPECT	U.S.
SAUHETTL	192648	M	Ger.		C.C.Falstad near Drontheim(Nor.) 9.-10.42	MURDER	NOR.
SAUL or SAWL	123967	M	Ger.		Sgt.,Army,5-635 Landesschuetzen-Bn.,Camp 35B,Stalag IXC, Erfurt(Ger.) 1.u.2.45	TORTURE	U.K.
SAULTER	906867	M			SS-Sturmfhr.,C.C.Auschwitz(Pol.) from 40	MURDER	FR.
SAUMANN, Willy	194406	M	Ger.	02	Agent,Gestapo,Savigny En Septaine(Fr.) 7.-8.44	MURDER	FR.
SAUPE, Fritz	190223	M	Ger.	00	Kriminal-Kommissar,Krim.-Pol.,Mlada-Boleslav(Czech.) 39-45	MURDER	CZECH.
SAUR, Adam	260685	M	Ger.		Pvt.,Guard-Chief Stalag 325,Stryj(Pol.) 7.,8.,9.42	MURDER	FR.
SAUR, Hans	179795	M	Ger.	17.2.22	SS-Uschfhr.,SS-Totenkopfverband,Kampfgruppe Oberdonau,C.C.Gusen (Aust.) 25.7.44	MURDER	U.S.
SAURER	180874	M	Ger.		Chief SS,C.C.Mauthausen(Aust.)	MURDER	FR.
SAURIG, Kurt	181006	M	Ger.	9.4.04	Cpl.,Prison,C.C.Vannes(Fr.) 42-44	TORTURE	FR.
SAUTER, Bernhard	121712	M	Ger.		Pvt.,Army,Greachmaout Pleubian(Fr.) 7.8.44	MURDER	FR.
SAUTTER	25464	M	Ger.		SS-Usturmfhr.,SS,C.C.Auschwitz-Birkenau(Pol.) 10.42	MURDER	YUGO.
SAUTTER, Karl	257498	M	Ger.	31.3.11	SS-Oschfhr.,SS-Gestapo,Mor.Ostrava(Czech.) 40-45	MISC.CRIMES	CZECH.
SAVATZKI	254046	M			Gestapo,Kragujevac(Yugo.)	MURDER	YUGO.
SAVELLI	190586	M			Lt.,Army,Ile Oleron(Fr.) 44-7.4.45	TORTURE	FR.
SAVER	139083	M	Ger.		Sturmbannfhr.,SS Totenkopf-Div.,C.C.Riga,C.C.Auschwitz(Latv.,Pol.)41-43	MURDER	U.S.
SAWADZKI	256491		Ger.		Employee,Mittelwerk Camp Nordhausen(Ger.)	MURDER	U.S.
SAWATZKI	133199	M			Doctor,C.C.Dora,Nordhausen(Ger.)	MURDER	U.S.
SAWATZKY or SANITSKI	179008				Cpl.,Kgf.Arb.Bn.184,3 Coy.,Kraakmoen(Nor.) 3.44	MURDER	NOR.
SAWBILL see SAYBILL	135557						
SANITSKI see SAWATZKY	179008						
SAWL see SAUL	123967						
SAX or SACHS, Johann	255684			21.12.19	Pvt.,C.C.Ellrich,Nordhausen(Ger.)	MURDER	U.S.
SAYBILL,Frederik or SAWBILL	135557	M	Ger.		Sgt.,Army,C.C.Alsleben(Ger.) 44	MISC.CRIMES	U.K.
SAYDEL, Arthur	167912	M	Ger.		Treuhaender Firma Asko Opus Prainia,Warsaw(Pol.) 9.39-12.44	PILLAGE	POL.
SAYLA	255690	M	Ger.		Chief of Camp,C.C.Mauthausen(Aust.) 2.41	BRUTALITY	FR.
SCALWIG, Max	256488	M	Ger.	23.10.14	Employee,C.C.Nordhausen(Ger.)	MURDER	U.S.
SCARFARGE see HEIDKAMP	29854						
SCARFE	193409	M	Ger.		Capt.,Army,C.C.Akervika(Nor.) 42	MURDER	NOR.
SCARLACH	256489	M	Ger.		Factory Worker,C.C.Dora,Nordhausen(Ger.)	MURDER	U.S.
SCAUMANN	251271	M			Physician,Camp Auschwitz(Pol.)	INTERR.	FR.
SCAVISCHKL	188581	M	Ger.		Major,Army,Public Official,Leivada Jerapetra.8.44	MURDER	GRC.
SCEER	261485	M			Sgt.,SS,C.C.at Rimini,P.O.W.Camp,Bologna(Ital.) 28.-29.6.44	MURDER	U.S.
SCEIFERT	261486	M	Ger.		Sgt.,SS,C.C.at Rimini,P.O.W.Camp,Bologna(Ital.) 28.-29.6.44	MURDER	U.S.
SCEINIS see SCHEINIS	253985						
SCGURDERBAYER, Robert	255999	M		18	Pvt.,C.C.Ellrich,Nordhausen(Ger.)	MURDER	U.S.
SCHAAF or SCHAAP	136374		Ger.		SS-Schfhr.,SS,C.C.Hinzert(Ger.) 41-43	TORTURE	U.S.
SCHAAF	190271	M	Ger.	16	SS-Usturmfhr.,SS,C.C.Belsen(Ger.) 40-44	MURDER	YUGO.
SCHAAF	255991	M			Pvt.,C.C.Dora,Nordhausen(Ger.)	MURDER	U.S.
SCHAAF, George	72053				SS-Oschfhr.,SS-Official,C.C.Hinzert(Ger.) 42-43	TORTURE	U.S.
SCHAAF, Walter	124856	M			Civ.-Schachtmeister,Deutsche Erdoel Aktienges.,C.C.Stalag IVG, Regis Breitigen(Ger.) 1.44-4.45	MISC.CRIMES	U.K.
SCHAAL	180875	M			SS-Uschfhr.,Employee,SD,Gestapo,Saarbruecken(Ger.)	PILLAGE	FR.
SCHAAL	188587	M			Col.,C.C.Kdo.Stalag IXO,Berga-Elster(Ger.) 2.or.9.45	MURDER	U.S.
SCHAAL, Ferdinand	62904	M	Ger.		Gen.d.Pz.Tr.,Cmdt.Wehrkr.Boehmen-Mashren.	TORTURE	UNWCC
SCHAAP see SCHAAF	136374						
SCHAASCHMIDT	255932	M			Pvt.,C.C.Ellrich,Nordhausen(Ger.)	MURDER	U.S.
SCHAAT	186225	M			Lt.,Army,Macon(Fr.) 40-45	WITNESS	FR.
SCHABATKA	254441	M			Police,Maribor(Yugo.) 44	MURDER	YUGO.
SCHABEL	257985	M			Cpl.,150 Pz.Bde.,Meuse Bridge-Antwerp. 12.44 (Bel.)	MISC.CRIMES	U.S.
SCHABLE	149863	M			Guard,SS,C.C.Gardelegen(Ger.) 4.-14.4.45	MURDER	U.S.
SCHABSCHNEIDER, Franz	255998				Flyer,C.C.Ellrich,Nordhausen(Ger.)	MURDER	U.S.
SCHAS	128777	M			Lt.,Lageroffizial,C.C.Dington-Bocholt(Ger.) 6.11.44	TORTURE	POL.
SCHACHMAERKL	255937	M			Pvt.,C.C.Dora,Nordhausen(Ger.)	MURDER	U.S.
SCHACHP see SHAP	152116						
SCHACHTSCHNEIDER	1746	M	Ger.		SS-Rottfhr.,Waffen-SS,Totenkopf Pz.Div.,Dunkirk(Fr.) 40	MURDER	U.K.
SCHACK	188776	M	Ger.		Guard,Auxerre(Fr.)	TORTURE	FR.
SCHACK, Friedrich August	192429	M	Ger.	82	Gen.,Army,Haute Savoie(Fr.) 43-44	MURDER	FR.,U.S.
SCHACK, Kurt	193161	M	Ger.	5.11.01	Sgt.-Guard,Reichsjustizminist.Feldstraflager,Waffen-SS,Finmark(Nor.) 1942-45	MISC.CRIMES	NOR.
SCHACKE	214091	M	Ger.	15	SS-Staff-Sgt.,SD,Kusel(Ger.)	TORTURE	U.S.
SCHACKTNER, M.	192789	M	Ger.		Schupo,Stalag C.C.Falstad(Nor.) 41-44	MURDER	NOR.
SCHAD see SHAD	152116						
SCHAD, L.	174848	M			Civilian,Wieseck(Ger.)	MURDER	U.S.
SCHADECKE, Karl	72052	M			SS-Uschfhr.,SS Div.Totenkopf	TORTURE	U.S.
SCHADE, Karl	167896	M	Ger.		Pvt.,9 Red.Gren.Regt.,1 Coy.,Magny d'Avignon(Fr.) 18.9.44	MURDER	FR.
SCHADL, Franz	12497	M	Ger.		Pvt.,Army,110 or 111 Pz.Gren.Regt.,2.Coy.,Albine(Fr.) 29.6.44	MURDER	FR.
SCHADOK	174765	M			Sgt.,P.W.-Working-Bn.209,Aspfjord(Nor.)	TORTURE	NOR.
SCHAUT	155950	M	Ger.		Sgt.,Gestapo,Morlaix(Fr.) 44	MURDER	FR.
SCHAECKE	188542	M	Ger.		Member Gestapo,Luxemburg(Lux.)	MISC.CRIMES	LUX.
SCHAEDLICH, Moritz	906172	M	Ger.		Member Volkssturm,Bochum Laer(Ger.) 24.9.45	MURDER	U.K.
SCHAEFER	785	M	Ger.		Gestapo,Katowice(Pol.) 39-43	MURDER	POL.
SCHAEFER	12498	M	Ger.		Sgt.,110 or 111 Panz.Gren.Regt.,2 Group,Gourdon(Fr.) 29.6.44	MURDER	FR.
SCHAEFER	21449	M	Ger.		Pvt.,Waffen-SS,Div.Goets von Berlichingen,98 Regt.H.Q., Montmartinen Craighes(Fr.) 17.6.44	MURDER	U.S.
SCHAEFER	123966				Sonderoffizier-Capt.,Stalag XVIII,C.C.Wolfsberg-Kaernten(Ger.) 42-43,45	MISC.CRIMES	U.K.
SCHAEFER	128917	M	Ger.	15	SS-Oschfhr.,SS,C.C.Buchenwald(Ger.)	TORTURE	U.S.
SCHAEFER	155952	M	Ger.	95	Bde.-Fhr.,Reg.-Rat,SS,C.C.Emsland,Oranienburg(Ger.) 33-45	MURDER	U.S.
SCHAEFER	155953		Ger.	05	Ogruppenfhr.,SS,Aschendorf-Moor(Ger.) 40-41	TORTURE	U.S.
SCHAEFER	162913	M	Ger.		Obermeister,Organ.Todt,Fm.Heinrich Butzer,Aspfjord(Nor.)	TORTURE	NOR.
SCHAEFER	188353	M	Ger.	20	Cpl.,Volks-Gren.Regt.109,Mons(Bel.)	MISC.CRIMES	U.S.

SCHA-SCHA

NAME	C.R.FILE NUMBER	SEX	NATIO-NALITY	DATE OF BIRTH	RANK OCCUPATION UNIT PLACE AND DATE OF CRIME	REASON WANTED	WANTED BY
SCHAEFER	189777	M			Dr.,Major,Medecisl Capt.Army,Ile D'Oleron(Fr.)44-17.1.45	MISC.CRIMES	FR.
SCHAEFER	189557	M	Ger.		SS Osturmbannfhr.Gestapo,CC Dachau(Ger.)40-45	MURDER	BEL.
SCHAEFER	190545	M			Korvetten-Kapitaen,Navy,Ile D'Oleron(Fr.)6.40	TORTURE	FR.
SCHAEFER	240116	M	Ger.		Osturmbannfhr.Police at officer's school,Mariaschen,Warschau(Pol.)4.45	MISC.CRIMES	UNWCC
SCHAEFER	253149	M	Ger.		Agent Gestapo,Limoges(Fr.)	INTERR.	FR.
SCHAEFER	253418	M	Ger.	01	Pvt.Army,Land.Schtz.Bn.632 or 625,Guard at Oflag IX A-H.(Ger.)24.8.42	INTERR.	U.K.
SCHAEFER	300858	M	Ger.		Pvt.1 Aufkl.Abt.3 Coy.2 Column,XV Div.of the Afrika Korps,Saint-Leger (Arlon)5.9.44	MISC.CRIMES	BEL.
SCHAEFER	301604	M	Ger.		SS Osturmbannfhr.Ehief of the Geheime Staatspolizei at Munich,CC Dachau(Ger.)40-45	MURDER	BEL.
SCHAEFER	301980	M	Ger.		Courts Martial-Councillor,Kriegsgericht,Utrecht(Neth.)7.7.44	BRUTALITY	NETH
SCHAEFER	305258	M	Ger.		Sgt.Signal Platoon,670 Art.Regt.Tripolis(Afrika)3.44	MISC.CRIMES	GRC.
SCHAEFER, Willy or SCHAEFFER or SCHEFFER or SHAEDER	306187	M	Ger.		Warder,CC Esterwegen,Papenburg(Ger.)7.7.43-15.5.44	MISC.CRIMES	BEL.
SCHAEFER	306197	M	Ger.		Lt.Army,Opladen(Ger.)15.-30.3.45	MURDER	CAN.
SCHAEFER, Alois	128916	M		10	Sgt.Field Police	MURDER	U.S.
SCHAEFER, Berthold	255951	M			Sgt.CC Buchenwald(Ger.)	MURDER	U.S.
SCHAEFER, Emanuel	62306	M	Ger.		SS Standartenfhr.High Police Official(Serb.)	INTERR.	UNWCC
SCHAEFER, Franz	253426	M	Ger.		Asst.Police,Neunkirchen(Ger.)1.8.44	WITNESS	U.S.
SCHAEFER, Gerd	12500	M	Ger.		Pvt.110 or 111 Pz.Gren.Regt.2 Coy.Albine(Fr.)29.6.44	MURDER	FR.
SCHAEFE, Helmut	143267	M	Ger.		SS Scharfhr.SS Totenkopfverband,CC Buchenwald(Ger.)	MURDER	U.S.
SCHAEFER, Johannes	143266	M	Ger.		SS Hptscharfhr.SS Totenkopfverband,Barrack Leader,CC Buchenwald(Ger.) 38-45	MURDER	U.S.
SCHAEFER, Josef	125268	M			Kgf.Arbeitskommando,CC Enkenbach(Ger.)12.43-3.45	TORTURE	U.S.
SCHAEFER, Josef	195162	M	Ger.	5.11.03	Sgt.Guard,Reichsminist.Feldstraflager,CC Finmark(Nor.)4.45	MISC.CRIMES	NOR.
SCHAEFER, Joseph see SCHEAFER	257294						
SCHAEFER, Karl	262208	M	Ger.		Uschafhr.Gestapo,Rennes(Fr.)43-44	MISC.CRIMES	FR.
SCHAEFER, Leopold	240117	M	Ger.	30.10.82	Ministerialdirector,Ministerialdirigent in the Reichsministerium,Berlin(Ger.)12.44	MISC.CRIMES	UNWCC
SCHAEFER, Ludwig	188545	M	Ger.	19.12.91	Master,Gendarmerie,Luxembourg(Lux.)	MURDER	LUX.
SCHAEFER, Oswald	255954	M	Ger.	14.6.08	Dr.,Lt.Col.SS.Gestapo,Muenchen(Ger.)	MURDER	U.K.
SCHAEFER, Paul	195163	M	Ger.		Major,Land.Schtz.Bn.809,CC Orsa(Nor.)45	TORTURE	NOR.
SCHAEFER, Peter or WERTH	306129	M	Ger.		SS Sturmfhr.served with R.S.D.Abt.VI-S,Copenhagen(Den.)1.44	PILLAGE	DEN.
SCHAEFER, Richard	164006	M	Ger.	4.00	Civilian,Government Building Counsellor,CC Wuerzburg(Ger.)1.45	MISC.CRIMES	U.S.
SCHAEFER, Walter	251594	M	Ger.		SS Oschafhr.CC Auschwitz,Birkenau(Pol.)12.42	MURDER	YUGO.
SCHAEFER, Wilhelm Johannes	128914	M			SS Scharfhr.CC Buchenwald(Ger.)	MURDER	U.S.
SCHAEFFER	39834	M	Ger.		SS 29 Div.Panz.,151 Bn.,Mogneville,Robert-Espagne,Beurey,Couvonges(Fr.) 28.9.44	MURDER	FR.
SCHAEFFER	121216	M	Ger.	06	Employee,Administration,Perigueux(Fr.)6.-8.44	MURDER	FR.
SCHAEFFER	128808	M	Ger.	92	Capt.Abwehr Branch,Wolsberg(Ger.)12.43-4.45	MISC.CRIMES	U.K.
SCHAEFFER	251516	M	Ger.		Agent Gestapo,SS Rottenfhr.,Troyes,Loellites(Fr.)43-44	MISC.CRIMES	FR.
SCHAEFFER	260680	M	Ger.		Lt.1 Coy,179 Res.Gren.Bn.,Massif du Vercors,Isere et Drome(Fr.) 20.7.-5.8.44	MISC.CRIMES	FR.
SCHAEFFER	306868	M	Ger.		SS Uschafhr.Charge of crematorium,CC Auschwitz(Pol.)40-45	MURDER	FR.
SCHAEFFER, A.	259242	M	Ger.		Stabsarzt,Hospital,Sorau near Frankfurt-Oder(Ger.)7.-8,9.40	BRUTALITY	FR.
SCHAEFFER, Emanuel	784	M	Ger.	20.4.00	Dr. SS Osturmbannfhr.Befehlshaber des S.D.Serbien,H.Q.of Hoeh.SS and Polizeifhr.,Beograd(Serb.)41-44	MURDER	YUGO.
SCHAEFFER, Ernst	259049	M	Ger.	30.9.05	Dr.,SS Osturmbannfhr.NSDAP, SS,20.4.44	INTERR.	U.S.
SCHAEFFER, Friedrich	302125	M	Ger.		Crim.secretary,Gestapo,Hradec-Kralove(Czech.)	TORTURE	CZECH.
SCHAEFFER, Reinhold	173069	M	Ger.		Chief.Fieldpolice,Auberive Flagey Chalency(Fr.)43-44	MURDER	FR.
SCHAEFFER, Wilhelm	258189	M	Ger.		Capt.Army 5 Schupo Regt.322 Btty.,Kragujevac,Orasac,Gruza(Yugo.)42-44	MURDER	YUGO.
SCHAEFFER, Willy see SCHAEFER	306187						
SCHAEFFERT	250485	M	Ger.		Director of Giessener Braunsteinwerk,Com.Leader,Kommando 1270 St.IX A. Gr.Linden(Ger.)12.44	MURDER	FR.
SCHAEFFLER	253355	M	Ger.		SS Oschafhr.CC Swientochlovice near Auschwitz(Pol.)43-44	TORTURE	U.K.
SCHAEFFLER, Ernst (Alfred)	253413	M			SS Mann,2 Pl.3 Pz.Pi.1 SS Pz.Regt.1 Panz.Div.Leibstandarte Adolf Hitler Ligneuville and Stoumont(Bel.)17.-19.12.44	MURDER	U.S.
SCHAEFFNER	12499	M	Ger.		Member Gestapo,Cahors(Fr.)29.6.44	MURDER	FR.
SCHAEFFNER, Ambros	189613	M	Ger.		SS Uschafhr.S.D.,Toulouse(Fr.)21.11.43	MURDER	FR.
SCHAEFRENRK	155954	M	Ger.		Dr.,Stabsarzt,Army,CC Stalag VIII B,Landsdorf(Ger.)44	PILLAGE	U.K.
SCHAEFLEIN	193855	M	Ger.		SS Uschafhr.4 SS Totenkopfsturmbann,CC Dora-Mittelbau,Nordhausen(Ger.) 43-45	INTERR.	U.S.
SCHAEKEL, Fritz	253419	M	Ger.		Guard,CC Lahde-Weser(Ger.)	INTERR.	BEL.
SCHAEPE, Wilhelm	173067	M	Ger.	1.4.10	SS Mann,CC Natzweiler,Struthof(Fr.)43-44	MURDER	FR.
SCHAEPER, Helmut	300114	M	Ger.	07	SS Hptsturmfhr.Sicherheitsdienst,Groningen,Drente(Neth.)43-45	MISC.CRIMES	NETH.
SCHAER, Josef	260369	M	Ger.		Oberwachtmeister,SS Penitentiary(North Nor.)6.42-45	MURDER	YUGO.
SCHAERMAIER	260860	M	Ger.		Mayor,Public Administration,Malchin(Ger.)44	MURDER	U.S.
SCHAERTEL, Johann	179990	M	Ger.		Policeman,Police,Langenzenn(Ger.)43-45	TORTURE	U.S.
SCHAFENS	253798	M	Ger.		Sgt.Unit 35350 B,St.Remy Aux Bois(Fr.)5.9.-7.9.44	MISC.CRIMES	FR.
SCHAFER	786	M			SS Bdefhr.9.39-1.42	MURDER	POL.
SCHAFER	121746	M	Ger.		SS Hptscharfhr.CC Buchenwald(Ger.)	TORTURE	FR.
SCHAFER	164719	M	Ger.		Dr.,Oberfhr.S.D.Belgrad(Yugo.)41-44	MURDER	U.S.
SCHAFER	186224	M	Ger.		Chief,SS CC 17,Emslandsmoor,Oranienburg(Ger.)	MURDER	FR.
SCHAFER	187792	M	Ger.		SS Oschafhr.CC Ravensbrusck,Oranienburg(Ger.)44-45	MURDER	U.S.
SCHAFER	194375	M	Ger.		Officer,Geheime Feldpolizei 648,Liege(Bel.)	TORTURE	BEL.
SCHAFER	194758	M	Ger.		SS Bdefhr.Litzmannstadt(Pol.)9.39-1.42	MURDER	BEL.
SCHAFER	251785	M	Ger.		SS Untersturmfhr.Sipo Brussel Abt.III(Bel.)40-44	INTERR.	BEL.
SCHAFER	255936	M			SS Mann,CC Mackenrode,Nordhausen(Ger.)	MURDER	U.S.
SCHAFER	258704	M		16	Sturmfhr.Waffen SS,150 Panz.Bde. Meuse-Bridge Antwerpen(Bel.)12.44	INTERR.	U.S.
SCHAFER	301025	M	Ger.		Head of 17 Camps,CC Oranienburg-Sachsenhausen(Ger.)42-45	MURDER	FR.
SCHAFER	301261	M	Ger.		SS Usturmfhr.Abt.III B,S.D.,Bruessels(Bel.)6.40-9.40	MURDER	BEL.
SCHAFER	306804	M	Ger.		N.C.O.Feldgendarmerie,Montigny Les Vesoul Hte Saone(Fr.)16.7.44	MURDER	FR.
SCHAFER, Adam	143265	M	Ger.		Civilian,Schwerta(Ger.)	MURDER	U.S.
SCHAFER, Alfred	255935	M		04	Flyer,CC Ellrich,Nordhausen(Ger.)	MURDER	U.S.

SCHA-SCHA

NAME	C.R.FILE NUMBER	SEX	NATIO-NALITY	DATE OF BIRTH	RANK, OCCUPATION, UNIT, PLACE AND DATE OF CRIME	REASON WANTED	WANTED BY
SCHAFER, Alois	193864	M	Ger.	25. 2.01	Uschfhr., 4.SS-Totenkopf-Stuba., C.C., Dora-Mittelbau, Nordhausen (Ger.)	MURDER	U.S.
SCHAFER, August	256277	M	Ger.	1. 3.03	Flyer, C.C.Ellrich, Nordhausen (Ger.)	MURDER	U.S.
SCHAFER, Fritz	256275	M	Ger.	28. 4.01	Rottfhr., C.C. Harzungen, Nordhausen (Ger.)	MURDER	U.S.
SCHAFER, Hans Joachim	186687	M	Ger.	22	Sturmmann, SS-Nachrichtenzug, Wormhoudt (Fr.) 5.40	MURDER	U.K.
SCHAFER, Haro	143264	M	Ger.		Rottfhr., 2.Pz.Gren.Rgt.,3.Bn.,12.Coy., Stavelot,Malmedy (Bel.) 12.44	MURDER	U.S.
SCHAFER, Heinrich	256276	M			Cpl., C.C.Ellrich, Nordhausen (Ger.)	MURDER	U.S.
SCHAFER, Johannes	256274	M			Pvt., C.C.Ellrich, Nordhausen (Ger.)	MURDER	U.S.
SCHAFER, Oscar	39832	M	Ger.		Pvt., C.C., Stalag 9 C, Pothen (Ger.) 43	MURDER	U.K.
SCHAFER, Wilhelm	253425	M	Ger.		Schfhr., SS, C.C., Buchenwald (Ger.) 42-45	MISC.CRIMES	U.S.
SCHAFER, Wilhelm	256262	M		15. 5.03	Flyer, C.C.Ellrich, Nordhausen (Ger.)	MURDER	U.S.
SCHAFERSKI	259110	M	Ger.	95	Chief of all "Kapo", C.C., Dachau (Ger.) 42-44	MISC.CRIMES	YUGO.
SCHAFF	147055	M	Ger.		Pvt., SS-Pz.Div."Das Reich", 1.Pz.Rgt.,2.Coy., Tulle (Fr.) 44	MURDER	FR.
SCHAFF	253797	M			Medicin-SS, Dietz-Lahn (Ger.)	INTERR.	FR.
SCHAFF (or SCHATT)	260146	M			Lt., Div.Oberland, Unit. Russ.,Ger., Massif du Vercors, Isere et Drome (Fr.) 7.44-8.44	SUSPECT	FR.
SCHAFF, Iwan	253512	M		95	W.O., Oschfhr., SS, C.C., Hinzert (Ger.)	MISC.CRIMES	FR.
SCHAFF, Wilhelm	143200	M			Dr., Prison-Doctor, Strafgefaengnis Freiendiez, Diez-Lahn (Ger.)43-45	TORTURE	U.S.
SCHAFFAUER, Theophil	253369	M		9. 5.94	2.Lds.Schtz.Ausb.Bn.5,Nr.4263, Wehr-Nr.94-30-6, Donau Eschingen Wervick (Bel.) 4.9.44	INTERR.	BEL.
SCHAFFELHOFER, Josef (see NO-VOTNY)	181288						
SCHAFFER	108960	M		01	Sgt., Stalag	MISC.CRIMES	U.S.
SCHAFFER	128809	M			Capt., Stalag XVIII A, Conc.Camp, Wolfsberg (Aust.) 12.43-5.45	MISC.CRIMES	U.K.
SCHAFFER	133307	M			Dr., Uschfhr., Waffen-SS, Conc.Camp, Flossenburg (Ger.)	TORTURE	U.S.
SCHAFFER	142300	M	Ger.	17	Cook, Conc.Camp, Lahde-Weser (Ger.)	TORTURE	BEL.
SCHAFFER	167361	M			Cpl., Feldgend., Montigny en Vesoul (Fr.) 16.7.44	MURDER	FR.
SCHAFFER	194275	M	Ger.	05	Staff-Sgt., SS, Conc.Camp, Flossenburg (Ger.)	TORTURE	U.K.
SCHAFFER	240118	M	Ger.	00	Uschfhr., SD, Metz (Fr.) 43.44.45	MISC.CRIMES	U.S.
SCHAFFER	251778	M	Ger.		Oberfhr., Bn.W.O., 4.Parachute-Rgt., Div."Herm.Goering", Helchteren (Bel.) 5.-11.9.44	MISC.CRIMES	BEL.
SCHAFFER	254020	M	Ger.		Col., 28.Pz.Gren.Rgt.3.Div., Robert Espagne (Fr.) 29.8.44	PILLAGE	FR.
SCHAFFER	257983	M			Lt., 150.Pz.Bde., Meuse-Bridge-Antwerp (Bel.) 12.44	MISC.CRIMES	U.S.
SCHAFFER	261179	M	Ger.		Pvt., 139.Arbeitsbereich Liane,5.Ln.Rgt.211,Alleur-Lez-Liege (Bel.)9.44	MURDER	BEL.
SCHAFFER	300427	M			Member, SD, Gestapo, Gers, Tarn, Toulouse, Haute-Garonne (Fr.) 42-8.44	MISC.CRIMES	FR.
SCHAFFER	301981	M			Lt., 3.Coy.,179.Gren.Bn.,157.Bay.Res.Div.,Massif du Vercors,Isere (Fr.) 20.7.-5.8.44	MURDER	FR.
SCHAFFER	305475	M			Pvt., 01512 K, Marine-Inf. partly composed of Waffen-SS, Trebeurden-Groas or Gollot, Ste.Anne-en-Tregastel (Fr.) 6.44-7.44	MISC.CRIMES	FR.
SCHAFFER	305476	M	Ger.	10	Secretary to the Chief indexer, Indre-et-Loire and Gironde (Fr.)40-45	MISC.CRIMES	FR.
SCHAFFER	306652	M	Ger.		N.C.O., (Feldgend.) Chateaubriant Cloire-Inf.),.St.Julien de Mouvantes, Soudan Juigne les Moutiers (Fr.) 21.7.44	MURDER	FR.
SCHAFFER, Hermann	256353	M		11.10.99	Cpl., C.C.Ellrich, Nordhausen (Ger.)	MURDER	U.S.
SCHAFFER, Josef	256273	M		14. 3.98	Cpl., C.C.Ellrich, Nordhausen (Ger.)	MURDER	U.S.
SCHAFFER, Martin (see WEISS)	261606						
SCHAFFER, Otto	194276	M	Ger.		Pvt., Airforce, Cambrai, (Fr.) 40-41	WITNESS	FR.
SCHAFFER, Reinhold	1085	M			Sgt.,(Senior W.O.) Feldgend., Langres-Auberive (Fr.)	MISC.CRIMES	FR.
SCHAFFER, Robert	254433	M	Ger.	28. 5.00	SA-Mann, Mostar (Yugo.) 44	MURDER	YUGO.
SCHAFFER, Wilhelm	787	M	Ger.		Hazebrouck (Fr.) 1.9.44	MURDER	FR.
SCHAFNAGEL (or SCHALFNAGEL)	173224	M	Ger.	15	Pvt., 4.Coy.,515.Lds.Schtz.Bn., Prague (Czech.) 3-45	MURDER	U.K.
SCHAFNER	12335	M			Lt., Army, 991.Gren.Rgt.,5.Coy. (Fr.) 28.5.44	MURDER	U.K.
SCHAFNER	143263	M			Capt., Stalag VIII A, Conc.Camp, Goerlitz (Ger.)	MURDER	U.S.
SCHAFNER	253510	M			Uschfhr., Conc.Camp, Hinzert (Ger.)	TORTURE	FR.
SCHAFFNER (or KESSNER)	223325	M		15	Lt., SD-Official, Bad Wildungen (Ger.) 45	MISC.CRIMES	U.S.
SCHAFFNER	253982	M	Ger.		Hptschfhr., SS, Buchenwald (Ger.) 42-45	MURDER	U.S.
SCHAFFNER, Ambroise	252738	M	Ger.		Oschfhr., SD, Toulouse (Fr.) 11.42-8.44	MISC.CRIMES	FR.
SCHAFFNER, Werner	256260	M			Pvt., C.C.Ellrich, Nordhausen (Ger.)	MURDER	U.S.
SCHAFRATH	261255	M	Ger.		Cpl., 2.Col.,3.Coy.,1.Aufkl.Abt.,XV.Div.,Africa-Corps, St.Leger Distr. Arlon (Bel.) 5.9.44	MISC.CRIMES	BEL.
SCHAFT	302126	M	Ger.		Medical-Officer, Prison, Dietz-Lahn (Ger.) 40-45	MURDER	BEL.
SCHAIPER, Alfred	189848	M	Ger.		SS-Mann, 1.Reconn.Bn., Renardmont Stavelot (Bel.) 19.12.44	MURDER	BEL.
SCHAIRER, Alfred	110069	M			N.C.O., Army, 18.12.44	MURDER	U.S.
SCHAIRER, Alfred	125267	M	Ger.	27	Pvt.,1.SS-Pz.Gr.Div., Engineer Platoon, H.Q.'s Coy., Rec.Bn., Renardmont, Stavelot (Bel.) 19.12.44	MURDER	U.S.
SCHAKERT	186822	M	Ger.		Lt., 950.Gren.Rgt., Departm.Charente et Vienne (Fr.) 8.44	TORTURE	FR.
SCHAKO, Karl	181192	M	Ger.		Infirmier, Conc.Camp, Mauthausen (Aust.)	MURDER	FR.
SCHALAMAYER (see SCHALLER-MEIER, Georg)	256375						
SCHALCK (see CHALQUE)	39634						
SCHALFNAGEL (see SCHAFNAGEL)	173224						
SCHALIES	256261	M		7. 6. ?	Flyer, C.C.Ellrich, Nordhausen (Ger.)	MURDER	U.S.
SCHAIX, Hans	72051	M			Oschfhr., SS-Totenkopf, H.Q.6.SS-Mtn.Div.	TORTURE	U.S.
SCHAIX (see CHAIQUE, Helmut)	191670						
SCHAIX, Richard	62307	M	Ger.		Deputy, Public-Official	MURDER	UNWCC
SCHAIKA	258604	M	Ger.		SS-Guard, Wachtmstr.,Waffen-SS,Slave Labour Camp, Beisfjord nr. Narvik (Nor.) 6.-11.42	BRUTALITY	YUGO.
SCHALL, August	184979	M	Ger.		Guard, SS, SD, Conc.Camp, Frankfurt-Main (Ger.)	TORTURE	U.S.
SCHALL, Martin	174578	M			Conc.Camp, Natzweiler-Struthof (Fr.)	MURDER	FR.
SCHALLEK (or CHALLEK)	186820	M			See.Lt., Airforce-Bn., Jaures, Saint Gery Noaillac (Fr.)	MURDER	FR.
SCHALLER, H.	251320	M			Agent, Gestapo, Uschfhr., SS, Troyes la Chaise (Fr.) 28.and 30.7.44	BRUTALITY	FR.
SCHALLER, Helmuth, Max	260917	M	Ger.		Rottfhr., SS-Guard, Conc.Camp, Auschwitz (Pol.) 44-45	BRUTALITY	POL.
SCHALLERMEIER (or SCHALAMAYER) Georg	256375	M	Ger.		Oschfhr., SS, Mueldorf (Ger.)	WITNESS	U.S.
SCHALLES	147356	M	Ger.		Pvt.,11.Panz.Div.,Kampfgeschw."Wilde" (Fr.) 44	MURDER	FR.
SCHALLING, Alfred	301441	M		6. 2.22	SS-Mann, C.C., Buchenwald (Ger.) 16.5.38-19.10.43	MURDER	BEL.

SCHA-SCHA

NAME	C.R.FILE NUMBER	SEX	NATIO-NALITY	DATE OF BIRTH	RANK OCCUPATION UNIT PLACE AND DATE OF CRIME	REASON WANTED	WANTED BY
SCHAMBERGER	196226	M	Ger.		Sgt.,Oberwachtmeister,Schupo-Stuetzpunkt,Westerbork (Neth.) 9.44	MURDER	NETH.
SCHAMBERGER,Franz	194404	M	Ger.	15. 7.13	Member,Gestapo,Klatovy (Czech.) 39-45	TORTURE	CZECH.
SCHAMBOEK	149864	M	Ger.	8. 1.95	Baker,Ortsgruppenleiter,NSDAP,Starnberg (Ger.)	MURDER	U.S.
SCHAMMERT,Heinz	147054	M	Ger.		Rottfhr.,SS,Pz.Div."Das Reich",13 Coy.,Moissac (Fr.) 44	MURDER	FR.
SCHAMPEL	186686	M	Ger.	21	SS-Mann,SS-Nachrichtenzug,Wormhoudt (Fr.) 5.40	MURDER	U.K.
SCHAMPER,Josef	305775	M	Ger.	19.11.96	Sturmschfhr,Krim.-Sekr.,Si.Polizei,Oslo (Nor.) 4.43-5.45	TORTURE	NOR.
SCHANDLER,Mathias	140811	M	Ger.		Farmer,Innkeeper,Civ.,Mittenwald (Ger.) 22.6.44	TORTURE	U.S.
SCHANFELDER	141898	M	Ger.		Pvt.,Stalag XX B,Guard,C.C.Willenberg (Ger.) 16.6.42	MURDER	U.K.
SCHANTZ,Albert (or SHANTZ)	108885	M	Ger.		Member,Civ.NSDAP,Gemmerich (Ger.)	TORTURE	U.S.
SCHAPER	10340	M	Ger.		Staatsanwalt,Ministry of Justice,Brno (Czech.) 40-42	MURDER	CZECH.
SCHAPER (or"CAPT. WILLIAMS")	62040	M	Ger.	01	Sgt.,Interpreter,Chief interrogation officer at Luckenwalde,interrog. Camp Attached to Stalag III A,Luckenwalde (Ger.) 9.43-1.44	TORTURE	U.S.,U.K.
SCHAPER	126514	M	Ger.		Capt.,SS-Pz.Div.Totenk.,2 Coy.,C.C.Hamburg,Neuengamme (Ger.)	MURDER	U.S.
SCHA(R)PER	140849	M	Ger.		Renegade,Sgt.,Army	WITNESS	U.K.
SCHAPER	253892	M	Ger.		Builder, Engineer,C.C.Neuengamme (Ger.) 44	MURDER	FR.
SCHAPER	261843	M	Ger.		Cpl.,Unit At.H.D.V.199-2235,N.D.F. No. of F.P.27046 C.Lorgies (Fr.) 3.9.44	MURDER	FR.
SCHAPER,Rudolf	305260	M	Ger.		Engineer,Foreman,Bahnabteilung,C.C.Neuengamme (Ger.)	MURDER	FR.
SCHAPERLE	169653	M		06	Abteilungsleiter,Member,N.S.D.A.P.,SS,Braunschweig (Ger.)	TORTURE	U.S.
SCHAR	181193	M	Ger.		Osturmfhr.,SS,Chief of Camp,Linz 3,C.C.Mauthausen (Aust.)	MURDER	FR.
SCHARDT,August	788	M			Uschfhr.,Waffen-SS,Scheveningen (Neth.) 40-41	MURDER	NETH.
SCHARE	253178	M		99	Lt.,377 Jaeg.Regt.,Vinkt and Meigen (Bel.) 25.-31.5.40.	MURDER	BEL.
SCHAREIKO,Willi	128913	M			Scharfhr.,SS,C.C.Buchenwald (Ger.)	TORTURE	U.S.
SCHAREIN,Friedrich	121754	M	Ger.		N.C.O.,Police,Navy, Migne (Fr.) 14. - 18.8.44	MURDER	FR.
SCHARENBERG,Wilhelm	146753	M			SS,C.C.Flossenburg (Ger.)	TORTURE	U.S.
SCHARF	251801	M	Ger.	14. 2.07	Employee,Gestapo,Litomerice (Czech.) 39-45	SUSPECT	CZECH.
SCHARF	152146	M	Ger.		Director,Schachtmeister,D.E.A.-Grube,C.C.Ingen (Ger.) 4.45	TORTURE	U.K.
SCHARF	155956	M			Constable of Buttelstadt,Civ.,Dassdorf,Guthmannshausen(Ger.) 8.44	MURDER	U.S.
SCHARF	162912	M	Ger.		Standartenfhr.,W-SS,Totenk.Standarte,C.C.Buchenwald (Ger.)	TORTURE	U.S.
SCHARF	253375	M	Ger.		Major,Waldraasch (Ger.) 1.7.44	MURDER	U.S.
SCHARF	253511	M	Ger.		Oberleutnant,Romainville (Fr.) 19.-20.8.44	INTERR.	FR.
SCHARF,Alfred	181924	M	Ger.	3. 3.09	Oschfhr.,SS,Gestapo,Crim.-employee,Prague (Czech.)	MURDER	CZECH.
SCHARF,Georg	258434	M			SS-Mann,Guard,SS,C.C.Ohrdruf (Ger.) 12.44-4.45	MURDER	U.S.
SCHARF,Heinrich	136567	M			Civilian,Beltershain (Ger.)	WITNESS	U.S.
SCHARFENSTEIN	193397	M	Ger.		Stabsarzt,Festungs-Bn.630,Drag Area (Nor.)	MURDER	NOR.
SCHARFNAGEL	152145	M	Ger.		Pvt.,Army,Lässchtz.-Bn.515 (Czech.) 24.2.45	MURDER	U.K.
SCHARIZER,Karl	11754	M	Ger.	30. 7.01	Bde.-Fuehrer,Gauleiter,Waffen-SS,NSDAP,Vienna (Aust.) 3.41	MISC.CRIMES	U.S.
SCHARLACH,Kurt	161287	M	Ger.	07	Lt.,Gestapo,Chalon s.Saone (Fr.) 43-44	MURDER	FR.
SCHARNHORST	152110	M	Ger.		Major,21 Pz.Div.Hqrs.,Sessenheim (Fr.) 1.45	MURDER	U.S.
SCHARP (see SCHRAPPEL)	143103						
SCHARPER	1475	M	Ger.		Usturmfhr.,SS,36 SS-Pz.Gren.Regt.,3 Coy.	MISC.CRIMES	U.K.
SCHARPF (see SCHRAPPEL)	143103						
SCHARPING,Walter	305562	M	Ger.		Sgt.,German medical corps, In Charge of the administration at the Hospital of Enghien,Bel. (the College of St.Augustins),Hospital, 10.40	MISC.CRIMES	U.K.
SCHARR (or SCHORR)	158593	M	Ger.	00	Pvt.,Army,Wolstein (Pol.) 11.6.41	MURDER	U.K.
SCHARRENBERG,Ewald	256259	M		29. 1.13	Sgt.,C.C.Ellrich,Nordhausen (Ger.)	MURDER	U.S.
SCHARSCHINGER,Ernst	254212	M		23. 3.15	Cpl.,C.C.Ellrich,Nordhausen (Ger.)	MURDER	U.S.
SCHARSCHMIDT	789	M	Ger.		Hptschfhr.,W-SS,C.C.Falstadt (Nor.) 43	TORTURE	NOR.
SCHARSCHMIDT	192849	M			Sturmbannfhr.,SS,C.C.Falstadt (Nor.) 42-3.43	MURDER	NOR.
SCHARTZ	123957	M	Ger.		Army,870 Coy.,Pottenbrunn (Aust.) 11.44	MISC.CRIMES	U.K.
SCHARTZE,Heinrich	259693	M	Ger.	10	Lt.,Guard,Camp of Candau des Angles,Avignon,Vaucluse(Fr.) 15.8.44	SUSPECT	FR.
SCHARTZMANN	261395	M	Ger.		Sekr.,Kreiskommandantur,Vire,Calvados (Fr.) 8.7.44	INTERR.	FR.
SCHARVOGEL	184286	M			Osturmfhr.,SS-Fuehrungs-Hauptamt,C.C.Dora,Nordhausen,Krakau,Plaszo (Ger.-Pol.) 43-45	WITNESS	U.S.
SCHARWACHTER	186819	M	Ger.		Capt.,950 Inf.Regt.,1'Bn.,Charente,Vienne (Fr.) 8.44	TORTURE	FR.
SCHARZ	167362	M			Pvt.,Head-Quarter,Crest (Fr.) 3.8.44	MURDER	FR.
SCHARZ	186157	M	Ger.		Sgt.,Army,C.C.Buchenwald,Compiegne (Ger.-Fr.)	MURDER	FR.
SCHARZ,Jacob	253888	M	Ger.	93	Ortsgruppenleiter,NSDAP,Florheim (Ger.) 12.9.44	MURDER	U.S.
SCHARZE	305737	M	Ger.		Member of Staff,SS,C.C.Auschwitz,Birkenau (Pol.) from 40	MURDER	FR.
SCHASKO,Karl	141372	M	Ger.		Sanitaeter,Civ.,C.C.Mauthausen (Aust.) 31.3.45	MURDER	FR.
SCHASTURM,Kurt	12501	M	Ger.		Pvt.,Army,110 or 111 Pz.Gren.Regt.,2 Coy.,Albine (Fr.) 29.6.44	MURDER	FR.
SCHAT	253891	M	Ger.		Lt.,Gend. of Macon,L'Ain (Fr.) 10.-21.7.44	INTERR.	FR.
SCHATIGER	139695	M	Ger.		Capt.,Stalag X E,C.C.Sandbostel (Ger.) 1.-5.45	TORTURE	U.S.
SCHATOW	155957	M	Ger.		Major,General,Commander of Occupation troops,Warsaw (Pol.) 7.44	MURDER	U.S.
SCHATT (see SCHAFF)	260146						
SCHATT,Karl	258399	M			Guard,SS,C.C.Ohrdruf (Ger.) 12.44-4.45	MURDER	U.S.
SCHATT,Oscar	189565	M	Ger.		Chief of C.C.Dachau (Ger.) 19.6.42-29.4.45	MURDER	BEL.
SCHATTAUER	39792	M	Ger.		Pvt.,17.SS-Pz.Gren.Div."Goetz v.Berlichingen",Sturmgesch.Abt.17 or Pz.Jg.Abt.17,Segre-Renaze (Fr.) 6.8.44430.7.44	MURDER	FR.
SCHATTLER,Hans	192850	M	Ger.		Schupo,C.C.Falstad,near Drontheim (Nor.) 10.42	MURDER	NOR.
SCHATTNER	21475	M	Ger.	01	Cpl.,C.C.Hinzert (Ger.)	TORTURE	U.S.
SCHATZ (or SCHULTZ-SCHULTE)	136214	M	Ger.		Capt.,Oflag VI A,Soest (Ger.)	MURDER	FR.
SCHATZ	257451	M	Ger.		Factory-worker,Nordhausen (Ger.)	MURDER	U.S.
SCHATZ	302127	M	Ger.	17 or 15	Lt.,Zugfhr.,Ordnungspol.,stationed at Hengelo,Overijssel Province (Neth.) 5.43	MURDER	NETH.
SCHATZ,Karl	261008	M			Leader of Sheepfold,Beberbeck district Hofgeismar (Ger.) 2.4.45	MISC.CRIMES	POL.
SCHATZHAUER,Andreas	301442	M	Ger.		Uschfhr.,SS,C.C.Buchenwald (Ger.) 16.5.38-9.10.43	MURDER	BEL.
SCHAU	142002	M	Ger.		Kreisleiter,NSDAP,Camp de Kahla,Rudolstadt (Ger.) 44-45	MISC.CRIMES	U.S.FR.
SCHAU	143262	M		18	Staff-Sgt.,1 Pz.Coy.,7 Pz.Rgpl. and Tng.Bn.,Freilassing (Ger.)	WITNESS	U.S.
SCHAUB	236539	F			Supervisor of Women,Muehldorf (Ger.)	MURDER	U.S.
SCHAUB,Christian	254211	M	Ger.	6. 5.00	SS-Mann,Camp Harzungen,Nordhausen (Ger.)	MISC.CRIMES	U.S.
SCHAUB,Hans	193165	M	Ger.	3. 8.02	Sgt.,Guard,W-SS,Reichsminist.Feldstraflager,C.C.Finmark (Nor.)42-45	MISC.CRIMES	NOR.YUGO.
SCHAUB,Heinrich	124388	M	Ger.	90	Major,Public official,Mayor of Oberdorfelden,Niederdorfelden(Ger)42-45	MURDER	U.S.
SCHAUB,Olga	184283	F	Ger.	11.13	Warsaw,Warszawa (Pol.) 40-42	PILLAGE	POL.
SCHAUB,Wilhelm	136381	M			Major,Civ.,Hanau (Ger.) 2.42-3.45	TORTURE	U.S.

SCHA-SCHE

NAME	C.R.FILE NUMBER	SEX	NATIO-NALITY	DATE OF BIRTH	RANK OCCUPATION UNIT PLACE AND DATE OF CRIME	REASON WANTED	WANTED BY
SCHAUBAUM	39831	M			Cpl., C.C. Rakau (Ger.) 43-45	TORTURE	U.K.
SCHAUBERL or SCHWEBEL	121768	M	Ger.		Cpl., Army, Semaphore de Creach Maout (Fr.) 5.8.44	MURDER	FR.
SCHAUER, Heinrich	254213	M		23.8.07	Pvt., C.C. Ellrich, Nordhausen (Ger.)	MURDER	U.S.
SCHAUF	251779	M	Ger.		Lt., Coy.Fuehrer, 4.Parachutist-Rgt., Div. "Hermann Goering", Helchteren (Bel.) 5.-11.9.44	MISC.CRIMES	BEL.
SCHAUFELER, Emile	191713	M	Ger.		Major, Inf.Bn. 77, Foret-Liege (Bel.) 6.9.44	MURDER	BEL.
SCHAUFF	218961	M	Ger.	08	Dr., Physician, SS, C.C. Drustte (Ger.)	MURDER	U.S.
SCHAUFLER, Franz	251802	M	Ger.	26.9.91	Gruppenfhr., SA, Member Freikorps, Cesky-Krumlov (Czech.) 42-44	SUSPECT	CZECH.
SCHAUENECHT	253417	M	Ger.		Cpl., St.Huibrechts, Lille (Bel.) 16.9.44	MISC.CRIMES	BEL.
SCHAULAND, Oscar	174776	M	Ger.	93	Sgt., Arbeitsbn. Kriegsgefang.Lager 3-188, Fjell (Nor.)	TORTURE	NOR.
SCHAUMBAUCK	142298	M	Ger.	00	Guide, Gestapo, C.C. Thalheim (Ger.) 45	MURDER	U.S.
SCHAUMBURG	194373	M	Ger.	97	Capt., Gendarmerie, St.Avold (Fr.) 9.8.45	MURDER	U.S.
SCHAUNBURG	166878	M	Ger.		General, Army, Div., Vuickt (Bel.)	TORTURE	BEL.
SCHAUP, Albrecht	125266	M		22	SS Panz.Replacement Training Rgt. Sennelager, Pol.,Sov.Un.,Grc.	MURDER	U.S.
SCHAESPIELER	188942	M			SS, Karlovy, Vary (Czech.) 1.4.45	MURDER	U.S.
SCHAUSS see LOCHANS	177534						
SCHAUSS	193396	M	Ger.		Stabsarzt, Airforce, Uthang, Orlandet (Nor.)	WITNESS	NOR.
SCHAUTIS	189111	M			Pvt., 5.Parachutist-Rgt., 4.Coy., St.Laurent de Cuves (Fr.) 3.7.44	MURDER	FR.
SCHAUTIS, Horst	167360	M	Ger.	11.7.25	Pvt., 5.Parachutist-Rgt., 4.Coy., St.Laurent de Cuves (Fr.) 3.7.44	INTERR.	FR.
SCHAUVE	136195	M	Ger.		Capt., Army, Unit 48081, St.Floret (Fr.) 30.6.44	RAPE	FR.
SCHAUVE	189110	M			Capt., Army, St.Floret (Fr.) 30.6.44	PILLAGE	FR.
SCHAUWACHER, Franz or SCHAUWACKER, SCHOWACKER	120620	M	Ger.		SS Cmdt., Gestapo, Camp Farge-Bremen (Ger.) 4.2.43-6.4.45	TORTURE	U.K.
SCHAWZE	121770	M			Capt., C.C. Marienburg Stalag XX B, (Pol.) 5.-12.43	TORTURE	U.K.
SCHEAFER, Joseph or SCHAEFER	257294	M			Landrat of Kreis Backnang, Gschwend (Ger.) betw. 1.-4.45	MURDER	U.S.
SCHECHT	155955	M			Interpreter, Clerk, Pvt., 877.Landesschutzen-Bn., C.C. Stalag 18 A Leisen (Aust.) 9.44-4.45	TORTURE	U.K.
SCHECKE or SCHINKEL	300581	M	Ger.		Lt., Army, 377. Inf.Rgt., Vinkt-Meigem (Bel.) 25.-31.5.40	MISC.CRIMES	BEL.
SCHEDER or SCHEVER	306268	M	Ger.	about 15	Member NSDAP, Gadebusch (Ger.) 10.9.44	MURDER	U.K.
SCHEEL	142297	M	Ger.		Crim.Assessor, Gestapo, SS, C.C. Lahde-Weser (Ger.)	MURDER	BEL.
SCHEEL, Gustav Adolph	62476	M	Ger.		Dr., Reichsstatthalter, Gauleiter NSDAP, Lt.Gen., SS, Salzburg (Aust.) 3-45	MISC.CRIMES	U.N.W.C.C.
SCHEELE, Heinrich	252716			21.11.94	SS Uscharfhr., 4.SS Totenkopf-Stuba,C.C.Dora-Mittelbau,Nordhausen (Ger.)	INTERR.	U.S.
SCHEER	301701	M	Ger.		SS-Mann, 4.SS Felders.Bn. 9-SS Hohenstaufen-Panz.Div., Neuville-les-Bois (Fr.) 11.8.44	MURDER	FR.
SCHEER, Paul	139233	M	Ger.	4.4.89	Gen.Lt., SIPO, Paris, Kiew (Fr.,Sov.Un.) 44, 1.42-2.43	MURDER	U.S.
SCHEER, Philipp	252718	M	Ger.	6.11.98	SS-Mann, Guard, 4.SS Camp Nordhausen (Ger.) 43-45	INTERR.	U.S.
SCHEER, Henning	165232	M	Ger.		Civ. Sales-Manager 39-45	MISC.CRIMES	U.S.
SCHEEREN, Walter	262209	M	Ger.	29.8.?	Scharfhr., Gestapo, Rennes (Fr.) 43-44	MISC.CRIMES	FR.
SCHEESCHMIDT, Arthur	174577	M	Ger.	15.8.97	Cpl., C.C.-prison- Vannes (Fr.) 42-44	TORTURE	FR.
SCHEEWE	254210	M			Sturmfhr., Camp Rottleberode, Nordhausen (Ger.)	MURDER	U.S.
SCHEF	39890	M	Ger.		Lt.Col., Army, Lillestrom (Nor.)	TORTURE	U.K.
SCHEFE	252748	M			SS Osturmbannfhr., state service, police and Waffen SS, Lods (Pol.) 39-40	MISC.CRIMES	POL.
SCHEFER, Karl	195499	M	Ger.		Lt., Verbindungsstab, Opladen (Ger.)	MURDER	CAN.
SCHEFERHOFF	187791	M		90	Capt., Cossacks-Bde., (Neth.) 12.3.45	MURDER	NETH.
SCHEFFE, Julius	254446	M		2.4.97	Cpl., Camp Ellrich, Nordhausen (Ger.)	MURDER	U.S.
SCHEFFE, Wilhelm	133905	M	Ger.	10	SS Osturmfhr., Waffen SS, Outercamp S III, Thueringen (Ger.) 45	TORTURE	U.S.
SCHEFFER	102785	M			Abwehr official, Nachr.Rgt. 506, Rome (It.)	MISC.CRIMES	U.S.
SCHEFFER	126928	M			SS Scharfhr., SS Panz.Div. "Das Reich", Valence d'Agen (Fr.) 44	MURDER	FR.
SCHEFFER	156912	M			Lagerfuehrer, Frauenland 4.45	MURDER	FR.
SCHEFFER	162911	M			SS Osturmfhr., Waffen SS Totenkopf-Standarte, C.C.Ohrdruf (Ger.)	TORTURE	U.S.
SCHEFFER	254026	M	Ger.	95	Overseer, C.C. Buchenwald (Ger.)	INTERR.	FR.
SCHEFFER	260054	M			Pvt., Slave labour camp, Botn, nr.Rognan (Nor.) 8.42-3.43, 4.44-5.45	BRUTALITY	YUGO.
SCHEFFER, Willy see SCHAEFER	306187						
SCHEFFEREGGER	188408	F			Dr.,Civ., Bolzano (It.) 19.3.45	MURDER	U.S.
SCHEFFERS	258143	M			SS Osturmfhr., Waffen SS C.C. Dachau (Ger.)	MURDER	BEL.
SCHEFFERS, Joseph	259608	M			Pvt., Flak, Haplincourt P.D.C. (Fr.) 10.6.44	BRUTALITY	FR.
SCHEFLE, Alfons	187347	M	Ger.		Sgt., Army, nrMittenwald (Ger.) 6.44	TORTURE	U.S.
SCHEFLER, Albert	129961	M	Ger.		Civ., Farmer, Meismesrode-Ostpr. (Ger.) 41	TORTURE	BEL.
SCHEFMANN	253370	M	Ger.		6.Ccy. 16.Huebner-Rgt., Kinrodi (Bel.) 9.44	INTERR.	BEL.
SCHEFTER	252708	M	Ger.		Senior W.O., Gend. Les Sables d'Olonne, Benet (Fr.) 25.8.44	INTERR.	FR.
SCHEGEL	256150	M			Capt., C.C. Harzungen, Nordhausen (Ger.)	MURDER	U.S.
SCHEGGER see SCHEPPER	189562						
SCHEHLING	132695	M	Ger.		Capt., Army, Gerardmer (Fr.) 9.-11.44	PILLAGE	FR.
SCHEID, Ernst	256377	M	Ger.		SS Mann, C.C. Muehldorf (Ger.)	WITNESS	U.S.
SCHEIBE	176010	F	Ger.		Leader NSDAP, Mueggelheim (Ger.) 3.45	TORTURE	U.S.
SCHEIBE	254438	M			Pvt., Camp Rottleberode, Nordhausen (Ger.)	MURDER	U.S.
SCHEIBE, Rudolf	260004	M	Ger.	17.10.99	Informer, Gestapo, SD, Strakonice-Bohemia (Czech.) 40-45	MURDER	CZECH.
SCHEIBEL, Jean	165230	M	Ger.	85	Civ., Factory-worker, Rothenbach-Pegnitz (Ger.)	TORTURE	U.S.
SCHEIBER	305261	M			Lt., Cmdt. of a Transportcol., Driebergen-Rijseuburg (Neth.) 5.45	PILLAGE	NETH.
SCHEIBLECKER, Helene nee ANDER	251794	F	Ger.	6.2.24	Hairdresser, Civ., Jihlava (Czech.) 42	MURDER	CZECH.
SCHEIBNER	259501	M			Cpl., Military, 9.SS Panz.Div. "Hohenstaufen", office staff, Beekbergen (Neth.) 10.or 11.9.44	WITNESS	NETH.
SCHEID	129941	M			SS Uscharfhr., Waffen SS C.C. Mauthausen (Aust.) 41-45	MURDER	U.S.
SCHEID	139229	M		15	Oscharfhr., SIPO, SD, Toulouse and other towns (Fr.) 6.-8.44	MURDER	U.S.
SCHEID	162919	M	Ger.		Cpl., Army, Guard at mine, C.C. Auschz (Fr.) 10.4.44	MURDER	FR.
SCHEIDEL	253499	M	Ger.		N.C.O., Grend.Troop 533, Annecy, Le Chablais (Fr.) 19.-21.5.44	INTERR.	FR.
SCHEIDER	31248	M	Ger.		Major, 11-6.SS Geb.Div. Nord, SS Geb.Jaeg.Rgt., 20.Army, Finmark (Nor.) 44	MURDER	NOR.
SCHEIDERICH, Josef	190248	M	Ger.		Gestapo, H.Q. Koeln (Ger.) 43-45	MURDER	U.K.
SCHEIDT	149866	M	Ger.		SS Rottfhr., C.C. Hirzenhain (Ger.) 25.-26.9.45	MURDER	U.S.
SCHEIDT, Hans Wilhelm	258202	M	Ger.		Amtsleiter, SA Oberfhr., Aussenpolit.Amt, R.S.H.A. Abt. IV b, Oslo (Nor.) 39-45	WITNESS	NOR.
SCHEIDT, Jacob	252737	M	Ger.		Sturmscharfhr., SD, Toulouse (Fr.) 11.42-8.44	MISC.CRIMES	FR.
SCHEIDTMANN	12340	M	Ger.		Pvt., Army, 110.or 111.Panz.Gren.Rgt. 2.Coy., Albine (Fr.) 29.6.44	MURDER	FR.

SCHE-SCHE

NAME	C.R.FILE NUMBER	SEX	NATIO-NALITY	DATE OF BIRTH	RANK OCCUPATION UNIT PLACE AND DATE OF CRIME	REASON WANTED	WANTED BY
SCHEIKLEPSKI	162616	M	Ger.		Hptsturmfhr., W-SS C.C. Voeght (Neth.)	MURDER	FR.
SCHEIFFERT	174576	M	Ger.		Lt., Army Verbindungsstab, Vallince (Fr.)	MISC.CRIMES	FR.
SCHEIGER	256384	M			Civ., Major, Frein Landstall (Anst.) 8.44	MURDER	U.S.
SCHEILEN, Wilhelm	162240	M	Ger.		Guard, Kriegsgef.Arbeits Kdo. Adolf Mine C.C. Merkstein (Ger.) 42-44	TORTURE	U.S.
SCHEIN (see SCHOEN, Hubert)	132140						
SCHEINERT	120553	M	Ger.		SS Hptstfhr., C.O. SS Div. Vet.Ers. Abt. 1.Coy.	TORTURE	U.S.
SCHEINERT	256378	M			Camp Leader, O.T. C.C. Muhldorf (Ger.)	WITNESS	U.S.
SCHEINIG	141400	M	Ger.		Lt., Pion.Coy. Marckolsheim (Fr.) 23.11.44	MURDER	FR.
SCHEINIG	186222	M	Ger.		Sgt., Army, Condom (Fr.) 5.44	MURDER	FR.
SCHEINIG	187039	M	Ger.		Lt., Heeres Opl. Schule der Pioniere Pont De Marc kolsheim (Fr.)23.11.44	MURDER	FR.
SCHEINIG	189156	M			Lt., Pioneer Sappers, Marckolsheim (Fr.) 23.11.44	MURDER	FR.
SCHEINIS (alias SCHINIS)	253385	M	Ger.		Uschfhr., SS C.C. Buchenwald (Ger.) 42-45	MISC.CRIMES	U.S.
SCHEINITZER	121840	M	Ger.		Volkssturm Cpt., Koenigstein Elbe (Ger.)	MURDER	U.S.
SCHEISSER	301654	M			Krim.Oberassistent, Strassburg (Fr.) 17.2.43	MURDER	CZECH.
SCHEITHAUER, Karl	262419	M	Ger.	6.12.03	Suspect is alleged to have committed a political murder of Walter Rosensweig, Skrbkovice-Kunova (Csech.) 26.11.35	SUSPECT	CZECH.
SCHEIVENZUBER	259243				Agent Gestapo of Poitiers antenne of Angoulême (Fr.)40-45	MISC.CRIMES	FR.
SCHELBRUNCKE	31427				Army 139-S Geb.Div. Jaeg.Rgt. Finnmark (Nor.) 44	MURDER	NOR.
SCHELENBURG (or SCHELLENBURG)	9612				SS Brigadefhr., SD R.S.H.A., Theresienstadt (Csech.) 40-45	TORTURE	BEL. NETH.
SCHELEPPI, Emil	162920	M	Ger.		Civilian, Altstadt Saarbruecken, (Ger.)	MURDER	FR.
SCHELL	138275	M	Ger.		SS Sgt., Chief d. Garage, Gestapo SS service automobile, Lyon (Fr.)	MURDER	FR.
SCHELL	162905	M	Ger.		Member, Gestapo, Dun Les Plages (Fr.) 26.-25.6.44	MURDER	FR.
SCHELL	181121	M	Ger.		SS-Osturmfhr., SS C.C. Dora Nordhausen (Ger.)	MURDER	BEL.
SCHELL, Gottlieb	254437	M			Pvt., Camp Ellrich Nordhausen (Ger.)	MURDER	U.S.
SCHELLE, Kurt	135332	M	Ger.		Sgt., Geheime Feldpolisei, Montigny en Gohelle (Fr.) 14.3.44	MURDER	FR.
SCHELLENBERG	188231	M	Ger.		Chief Reichssicherheitshauptamt C.C. Buchenwald (Ger.) 41-45	MURDER	BEL.
SCHELLENBERG	259424	M			Colonel, high official of R.S.H.A. Gestapo	MURDER	U.N.W.C.C.
SCHELLENBERG, Ewald	175672	M	Ger.		Sgt., Feldgendarmerie De Langes, Auberive, Flagey Coiffy Chalency (Fr.) 43-44	MURDER	FR.
SCHELLENBURG (see SCHELENBERG)	9612						
SCHELLER	128910	M	Ger.		General Major, Ps.Div. 11, Tiliktpno (Sov.Un.)20.12.41	MURDER	U.S.
SCHELLER (alias SCHELLERER)	136588	M		13	Sgt., Wehrmacht 27.Fuss.Rgt. 12.Volksgren.Div,3.Coy., Petite Langville (Bel.)10.1.45	MURDER	U.S.
SCHELLER	143261	M			SS Usturmfhr., 2. SS Pz.Div. Das Reich, Tulle (Fr.) 5.44	MURDER	U.S.
SCHELLER	168958	M			Leader, Abt. Forsten Amt des Gouverneurs Lublin (Pol.) 9.39-44	MISC.CRIMES	POL.
SCHELLER	252736	M			SD-Mann, Civ. Functionary GZA., SD, Toulouse (Fr.) 11.42-8.44	MISC.CRIMES	FR.
SCHELLER, Adolf	143260	M			SS, Hohnebostel (Ger.) 7.5.44	TORTURE	U.S.
SCHELLER, Eric	259241	M			SS-Pvt., SS Muhldorf area (Ger.)	MURDER	U.S.
SCHELLERER	72049	M	Ger.		Sgt., Army Petit Langville (Bel,)	MURDER	U.S.
SCHELLERER (see SCHELLER)	136588						
SCHELLHASS, Ludwig	253513	M	Ger.		W.O. SD. Dun Le Places (Fr.) 6.-8.6.44	MISC.CRIMES	FR.
SCHELLHORN, Frants	155959	M	Ger.		N.C.O., Heeres N.C.O. Schule der Pioniere Ordonance Marckolsheim (Fr.)44	WITNESS	FR.
SCHELLIN	111009	M			Verwaltungsassist., Wirtschafts and Verwaltungs-Hauptamt (Bel.)	MISC.CRIMES	U.S.
SCHELLIN, Alfred	124749	M	Ger.	10	SS Usturmfhr., Krim.Sekretaer, Wassenberg and Nilens, Brussels (Ger.Bel.)	MURDER	U.S. BEL
SCHELLING, Albert	253400	M	Ger.	8.12.06	Osturmfhr., SA, Luxemburg (Lux.) 40-45	INTERR.	LUX.
SCHELLMANN	258605	M			SS-Guard, SS slave labour camp, Beisfjord near Narvik (Nor.) 6.-11.42	BRUTALITY	YUGO.
SCHELSKE, Friedrich	125265	M			N.C.O. Guard, SS C.C. Helmbrecht Volary (Csech.)	TORTURE	U.S.
SCHEMBECK	306669	M			SS Opl., Chief Provisions C.C. Auschwitz (Pol.) 40	MURDER	FR.
SCHEMEL	306870	M			SS Lt., C.C. Auschwitz (Pol.) 40	MURDER	FR.
SCHEMENAU, Georg	155970	M			Baker, Civ., Untsmassfeld (ger.) 41-45	TORTURE	U.S.
SCHEMM, Hans	262135	M	Ger.	6.9.11	Driver, Unterfeldmeister,-Civ.occup. RAD. Muenchen (Ger.) 39-45 ZOINAOD	SUSPECT	U.S.
SCHEMMEL	250490	M			SS-Usturmfhr., SS C.C. Auschwitz Birkenau (Pol.) 9.42	MURDER	YUGO.
SCHENCK, Frans (or SCHENK)	795	M		17	Rottfhr., Stalag VIII B, Milovics (Pol.) 2.9.43	MURDER	U.K.
SCHENDORF	254428	M			Pvt., C.C. Dora Nordhausen (Ger.)		
SCHENEDER (see CHNADER)	134832						
SCHENEWA, Paul	302129	M	Ger.		SS Rottfhr., Dog-trainer, Slave Labour Camp Schandelah Labour (Brunswick) (Ger.) 1.5.44-30.4.45	MURDER	U.K.
SCHENIS	255946	M			Opl., C/C Buchenwald (Ger.)	MURDER	U.S.
SCHENK	21448	M	Ger.		Opl., Army W-SS	MISC.CRIMES	CAN.
SCHENK	125010	M	Ger.	15	Interpreter, Gestapo, Poitiers, Chateau De Porteau (Fr.) 23.-24.8.44	MURDER	FR.
SCHENK	129948	M			Pvt., Fallschirmjaeger Rgt. Quaregnon Jemappes Ghlin (Bel.) 2.-3.9.44	MURDER	BEL.
SCHENK	139750	M			Major, Director, W-SS SD, Dep'T III, Lemberg (Pol.) 42-44	MISC.CRIMES	U.S.
SCHENK	155971	M			Pvt., Machine Gunner Army Sturm-Bn. AOK. I 2.Platoon 1.Coy. Courcelles sur Nied (Fr.) 11.44	MURDER	U.S.
SCHENK	162904	M	Ger.	95	SS Hptsturmfhr., W-SS Totenkopf Standarte C.C. Buchenwald Weimar (Ger.)	TORTURE	U.S.
SCHENK	187201	M		24	SS-Usturmfhr., 12. SS Pans.Div.Hitler Jugend, naer.Caen (Fr.) 6.-7.44	MISC.CRIMES	CAN.
SCHENK	187869	M			SS Uschfhr., Guard, SS C.C. Ravensbrueck (Ger.) -44-45	MURDER	U.S.
SCHENK	189564	M			Member, Schupe, Stanislawon (Pol.) 8.41-10.42	MURDER	POL.
SCHENK	194528	M			Usturmfhr., Major 12. SS Ps. Div. H.J. Chateau Andrieu (Fr.) 8.6.44	MURDER	FR.
SCHENK	253506	M	Ger.		Sgt., Gend. Vendome (Fr.) 9.8.44	INTERR.	FR.
SCHENK	256535	M	Ger.		SS Medic Attendant Camp Ellrich Nordhausen (Ger.)	MURDER	U.S.
SCHENK	256536	M	Ger.		Oberfaehnrich, Aspirant, Fallschirmjaeger Coy. Lesidy St. Connan Xerien (Fr.) 44	MURDER	FR.
SCHENK (alias BOUCHER, Francois)	173546	M	Ger.		Uschfhr., SD, Poitiers (Fr.) 24.-25.8.44	MURDER	FR.
SCHENK, Franz (see SCHENCK)	795						
SCHENK, Frits	259244	M	Ger.		Uschfhr., Gestapo of Poitiers (Fr.) 40-45	MISC.CRIMES	FR.
SCHENK, Joseph	306500	M			Pvt., belonging to 8.Coy. Schlanders Police Rgt. Roncegno (It.) 3.45	MURDER	U.K.
SCHENK, Karl	255945	M			Opl., C.C. Buchenwald (Ger.)	MURDER	U.S.
SCHENK, Otto	306717	M			German Civilian, Bremen (Ger.) 24.2.45	BRUTALITY	U.S.
SCHENK, Waldemar	257550	M			SS Sgt., C.C. Ellrich Nordhausen (er.)	MURDER	U.S.
SCHENK, Wilhelm	141915	M			Matrosen Pvt., German Navy U 852 19.3.44	WITNESS	U.K.
SCHENKE, Werner	253177	M			Lt., 377. Jaeger Rgt., Vinkt (Bel.) 25.-31.5.40	MURDER	BEL.
SCHENKEL	257877	M			Lt., 150. Pz. Brigade, Meuse Bridge Antwerp (Bel.) 12.44	MISC.CRIMES	U.S.
SCHEPERS	168959	M	Ger.		Dr., Laeder, Oberregierungsrat Abt.fuer Raumordnung (Pol.) 9.39-44	MISC.CRIMES	POL.
SCHEPERS, Wilhelm	177160	M	Ger.	25	SS Sturmann, 12. SS Pz.Div. Hitler Jugend near Caen (Fr.) 6.6.-8.7.44	TORTURE	CAN.

SCHE-SCHI

NAME	C.R.FILE NUMBER	SEX	NATIONALITY	DATE OF BIRTH	RANK OCCUPATION UNIT PLACE AND DATE OF CRIME	REASON WANTED	WANTED BY
SCHEPMANN, Wilhem	62323	M	Ger.	17.6.94	SA-Obergruppenfhr.,Reichsleiter,Reg.-Praesident,Festigung Deutschen Volkstums,Dresden (Ger.) 43	MISC.CRIMES	U.S.,UNWCC
SCHEPP, Josef (or SCHOPS)	129940	M			C.C.Senior, Mauthausen (Aust.) 11.41-3.42	MURDER	U.S.
SCHEPPER (or SCHEGGER)	189562	M	Ger.		SS-Hptschfhr.,Gestapo,C.C.Westerbork (Ger.) 9.-12.44	MURDER	NETH.
SCHEPPER, Edwig	1530	M	Ger.	30.5.26	Pvt.,Gren.Bn.77,Hainant Quevaucamps (Bel.) 3.9.44	MURDER	BEL.
SCHERBAUM	167359	M	Ger.		Feldgendarm,Feldgendarmerie Luneville (Fr.) 1.8.44	MISC.CRIMES	FR.
SCHERDING	251780	M	Ger.		Sturmbannfhr.,SS,Sipo,Bruessel Abt.III (Bel.) 40	TORTURE	BEL.
SCHERER	192851	M	Ger.		Sgt.,Schupo,C.C.Falstad near Drontheim (Nor.) 41-45	MISC.CRIMES	NOR.
SCHERER	240121	M	Ger.		Oberreg.Rat,Abwehr,Nachr.Rgt.506,Berlin-Steglitz (Ger.)	MISC.CRIMES	UNWCC
SCHERER	257549	M	Ger.		Employee,Chief of Section Mittelwerk C.C.Nordhausen (Ger.)	MURDER	U.S.
SCHERER	305563	M		95	Foreman,Construction for Hoch and Tief Bohlers Factory,Marien-en-Martzoul (Aust.) 10.43-5.45	MISC.CRIMES	U.K.
SCHEFF	176011	M	Ger.		SS-Oschfhr.,SS Gestapo Jail,C.C.Saarbruecken (Ger.) 38-39	TORTURE	U.S.
SCHERF, Kurt	188547	M	Ger.		Leader, Book-keeper,NSDAP,Landsberg,Laufering (Ger.) 44-45	MURDER	CZECH.
SCHERFENBERG, Louis	142296	M	Ger.		SS-Schfhr.,Gestapo,SSofficer,Cannes (Fr.) 43	MURDER	FR.
SCHERFER, Wilhelm	139226	M	Ger.		Civilian,C.C.Plettenberg (Ger.)	TORTURE	U.S.
SCHERFF	257876	M			Capt.,150 Pz.Bde.,Meuse Bridge-Antwerp.(Bel.) 12.44	MISC.CRIMES	U.S.
SCHERG	143259	M			SS-Osturmfhr.,2 SS Pz.Div."Das Reich",Tulle (Fr.) 5.44	MURDER	U.S.
SCHERGER	188774	M	Ger.		SS-Schfhr.,SD,Lyon (Fr.)	PILLAGE	FR.
SCHERKES	178192	M			Inspector,Gestapo,Bordeaux (Fr.) 43	PILLAGE	FR.
SCHERNECK	252725	M	Ger.		SS-Hptschfhr.,SS,Abt.III A.Sipo,Bruessel (Bel.)	INTERR.	BEL.
SCHERNER	797	M	Ger.		SS-Oberfhr.,Polizeifhr.,SS,Police,Cracow (Pol.) 42	MURDER	POL.
SCHERNER	798	M	Ger.		Lt.Col.,Army,Dijon (Fr.) 7.44	MISC.CRIMES	FR.
SCHERNER, Julian	35531	M	Ger.	23.9.95	Hptsturmfhr.,Oberst,SS Junker Schule,Polizei,Rgt."Dirlewanger",Toelz,Prague,Cracow,Warschau (Ger.,Pol.) 44	MURDER	UNWCC
SCHERNER, Rosita Johanna	260931	F	Ger.	1.5.99	Wife of the SS and police leader,C.C.Krakau,Plaszow,Zakopane (Pol.) 41-44	MURDER	POL.
SCHERPER	306952	M	Ger.		Col.,Feldkdtr., Dijon (Fr.) 7.44	INCENDIARISM	FR.
SCHERRER, Jakob	253377	M		90	Civilian,Langenlonsheim (Ger.) 4.12.44	WITNESS	U.S.
SCHERRWITZ, Eric	194527	M	Ger.	12	Uschfhr.,SS,Paris (Fr.) 20.8.44	MURDER	FF.
SCHERSACH, Philip	190305	M	Ger.		Civilian,Bebra (Ger.)	WITNESS	U.S.
SCHERSKY, Alfred	187675	M	Ger.	92	SS-Oschfhr.,SS,Oranienburg,Sachsenhausen (Ger.)	MURDER	U.K.
SCHERZ, Karl	254429	M		8.8.05	Flyer,Camp Ellrich,Nordhausen (Ger.)	MURDER	U.S.
SCHERZLER	152109	M			Capt.,H.Q.21 Pz.Div.,Sessheim (Fr.) 1.45	MURDER	U.S.
SCHESCICH	301026	M	Ger.		On staff,Oranienburg,Sachsenhausen (Ger.) 42-45	MURDER	FR.
SCHETER	173505	M	Ger.		SS-Uschfhr.,WaffenSS,C.C.Oswiecim-Birkenau (Pol.) 39-45	MURDER	CZECH.
SCHETTEL	124625				Camp leader,SS,C.C.Auschwitz Manowice (Pol.) 1.44	MURDER	U.S.
SCHETTEL, Vinzenz	133194	M			SS-Osturmfhr.,Waffen SS,C.C.Mittelbau Dora,Nordhausen (Ger.)	SUSPECT	U.S.
SCHEUBEL	167313	M	Ger.		Kommissarischer Verwalter,Kommerzialbank,Krakau (Pol.) 9.39-12.44	PILLAGE	POL.
SCHEUER	12341	M	Ger.		Lt.,Army,3 Bn. 4 Coy Inf.,Macon (Fr.) 8.6.44	MURDER	FR.
SCHEUER	194266	M	Ger.		Lt.,Schwers Art.Abt. 3 Coy,Pont de Vaux (Fr.) 8.6.44	MURDER	FR.
SCHEUER	250489	M	Ger.		SA,Gadenbusch (Ger.)	MURDER	U.S.
SCHEUERMANN	141073	M	Ger.		SS-Sturmmann,C.C.Natzweiler (Fr.)	MURDER	U.K.
SCHEUERMANN	254206	M	Ger.		Architect,Civilian,Alzin (Fr.)	PILLAGE	FR.
SCHEUN	129968	M			Chief of Camp,Wittenburg near Potsdam (Ger.) 44	TORTURE	BEL.
SCHEUN	165701	M	Ger.		Guard,Abt.Kommando,C.C.Usine Kdo.703,Mariaweiler (Ger.)	TORTURE	FR.
SCHEUNBERG	253800	M	Ger.		W.O.,Unit Birkerdorff,F.P.18810,Saint Laurent (Fr.) 5.-6.8.44	TORTURE	FR.
SCHEUERT, Oskar	165553	M	Ger.		Sturmschfhr.,SS,C.C.Buchenwald (Ger.) 38-45	WITNESS	U.S.
SCHEUNERT, Oswald	301443	M	Ger.	12.5.78	Hptschfhr.,SS,Nr.287341,C.C.Buchenwald (Ger.) 16.5.38-9.10.43	MURDER	BEL.
SCHEUNCRABER	129939	M			SS-Usturmfhr., Waffen SS,C.C.Mauthausen (Aust.) 39	MURDER	U.S.
SCHEUFURENBRAND	256029	M	Ger.		Org.Todt,Muhldorf Area (Ger.)	WITNESS	U.S.
SCHEUFER, Wilhelm	142295	M		05	Civilian,C.C.Hadamar (Ger.) 6.44-3.45	WITNESS	U.S.
SCHEURINGER	193728	M	Ger.		Crim.Insp.,Gestapo,Brno (Czech.) 39-45	MURDER	CZECH.
SCHEURMANN	121217	M	Ger.		Dachfhr.,SS,C.C.Struthof,Natzweiler (Fr.) 42-44	MURDER	FR.
SCHEVER (see SCHEOFR)	306268						
SCHEWE	156893	M			Chief-cook,Waffen SS,C.C.Gardelegen (Ger.)	MURDER	U.S.
SCHEWE	166675	M	Ger.		Chief,Gestapo, (Pol.) 42	MURDER	U.S.
SCHEWFBFRGER,Ludwig	799	M	Ger.		Cpl.,Gestapo,Valenciennes-Onnaing (Fr.) 43, 1.9.44	MURDER	FR.
SCHEWEDE, Ernest	253494	M	Ger.		Inspector,Political Agent,Radio Unit L 47780,Letaillan-Medoc (Fr.)9.43	INTERR.	FR.
SCHFRATH	300859	M	Ger.		N.C.O.,1 Aufkl.Abt.3 Coy 2 Col.XV Div.of the Afrika Corps,Saint Leger Arlon (Bel.) 5.9.44	MISC.CRIMES	BEL.
SCHGAGULER, Florian	194380	M	Ger.	23	Pvt.,SS Unit Nr.15541 F.P.Nr.10443,Fouron St.Martin (Bel.) 5.-6.9.44	WITNESS	BEL.
SCHIBRTS (see STIVITZ)	132008						
SCHIBURG, Heinz	251337	M	Ger.		Osturmfhr.,Sainte Sanie Aube (Fr.) 25.8.44	INTERR.	FR.
SCHICHTHOLZ, Fritz	143257	M	Ger.		SS-Oschfhr.,SS Totenkopf Verband,C.C.Buchenwald (Ger.)	MURDER	U.S.
SCHICHTHOLZ (see SCHIEBTHOLZ)	128900						
SCHICK	188773	M	Ger.		Member,Feldgendarmerie,Bar le Duc (Fr.) 20.-23.8.44	MURDER	FR.
SCHICK	253503				Dr., in charge of Farms,Marienthal (Ger.) 5.42	BRUTALITY	FR.
SCHICK, Andreas	186624	M	Ger.	00	Army,Oberweier (Ger.) 29.7.44	TORTURE	CAN.
SCHICK, Wilhelm	186585	M	Ger.	20	Army,Oberweier (Ger.) 29.7.44	TORTURE	CAN.
SCHICKELBERGER,Karl Franz	197477	M		1.10.79	NSDAP,Amstetten (Aust.) 20.3.45	SUSPECT	U.S.
SCHICKERT,Ludwig	189547	M		02	Mayor,Ortsgruppenleiter,NSDAP,Bechtheim (Ger.) 27.12.44	TORTURE	U.S.
SCHICKHOFER, Rupert	254426	M		7.6.03	Rottfhr.,Camp Harzungen,Nordhausen (Ger.)	MURDER	U.S.
SCHICKMEIER	256030	M	Ger.		Baufhr.,Org.Todt,Muhldorf (Ger.)	WITNESS	U.S.
SCHIEBER	62324	M			Ministerial Director,Public official,	TORTURE	UNWCC
SCHIEBINGER	306871	M			Member, Roumanian Kommando,Gestapo,Vichy (Fr.) 10.43-9.44	MURDER	FR.
SCHIEBTHOLZ (or SCHICHTHOLZ)	128900	M			SS-Schfhr.,SS,C.C.Weimar, Buchenwald (Ger.)	TORTURE	U.S.
SCHIEBUR, Heinz	262197	M	Ger.	5.12.20	SS-Osturmfhr.,5 Coy 51 SS Armoured Bde.,Sainte Savine,Troyes (Fr.) 25.8.44	MISC.CRIMES	FR.
SCHIECKER, Otto	72047	M			SS-Uschfhr.,SS Div.Totenkopf Verband,Af.Ers.Rgt.,Bad Tennstedt (Ger.)	TORTURE	U.S.
SCHIED, Georg	176009	M	Ger.	07	SS-Uschfhr.,SS Totenkopf Verband,C.C.Sachsenhausen (Ger.) 43	MISC.CRIMES	U.S.
SCHIEDEL	254427	M			Pvt.,Camp Harzungen,Rottleberode,Nordhausen (Ger.)	MURDER	U.S.
SCHIEDERING, Josef	166681	M	Ger.	96	Civilian, (Ger.) 11.12.44	MURDER	U.S.
SCHIEDLAUSKI (see SCHIEDLAUSKY)	128901						

SCHI-SCHI

NAME	C.R.FILE NUMBER	SEX	NATIO-NALITY	DATE OF BIRTH	RANK OCCUPATION UNIT PLACE AND DATE OF CRIME	REASON WANTED	WANTED BY
SCHIEDLAUSKY(or SCHIEDLAUS-KI or SCHIEDLOWSKY)	128901	M			Schfhr.,SS,C.C.,doctor,Weimar,Buchenwald (Ger.)	TORTURE	U.S.
SCHIEDLAUSKY (or SCHLIDAUSKI)	261208	M	Ger.		Member,staff of C.C.,Ravensbrueck (Ger.)	SUSPECT	BEL.
SCHIEDLAUSKY,Guenther	167323	M	Ger.		Doctor,Einsatzstab Rosenberg,department Valuer (Fr.) 40-44	PILLAGE	FR.
SCHIEDLOWSKY(see SCHIEDLAUSKY)	128901						
SCHIEDT, Wilhelm	260678	M			Capt.,Army.	WITNESS	U.S.
SCHIEFER	193069	M			Col.,Kgf.Arb.Bn.203, C.C.,Lappstorvik (Nor.) 7.44-45	MURDER	NOR.
SCHIEFER	252726	M	Ger.		Crim.Asst.,Abt.IV A,SIPO,Bruessels (Bel.)	INTERR.	BEL.
SCHIEFNER	156920	M	Ger.		Chief,Gestapo,Cabrespuies (Fr.) 22.4.44	MURDER	FR.
SCHIEGEL	257699	M	Ger.		Hptsturmfhr.,SS,C.C.,Harzungen,Nordhausen (Ger.)	MURDER	U.S.
SCHIEHLS (or SCHIELS)	186218	M			Sgt.,19.police Rgt.,D'Aurillac (Fr.) 6.44	MURDER	FR.
SCHIEKE	167358	M	Ger.		Member,Feldgendarmerie,De Moulins,La Roche Millay (Fr.) 11.8.44	PILLAGE	FR.
SCHIEL	189155	M			Lt.General,C.O.,198 Inf.Div.,Gerardmer (Fr.) 9.-11.44	MISC.CRIMES	FR.
SCHIELKEN	165231	M	Ger.		Manager,civilian, 39-45	MISC.CRIMES	U.S.
SCHIELMANN	259550	M	Ger.		Doctor,Wolfsburg (Ger.) 29.6.44	WITNESS	U.S.
SCHIELS (see SCHIEHLS)	186218						
SCHIELZ, Friedrich	306437	M	Ger.		Member,police,Idesheim, on or about 17.8.44	MURDER	U.S.
SCHIEMANN	253391	M	Ger.		Employee,SIPO,Abt.3 B,Bruessels (Bel.) 40-45	INTERR.	BEL.
SCHIEPER, Richard	262195	M	Ger.	18. 3.14	Oscfhr.,SS,commander of the 1.platoon,51.SS Armoured Bde.,Breviandes,Bucheres,St.Savine,La Riviere de Corps,(Troyes) (Fr.) 22.-25.8.44	BRUTALITY	FR.
SCHIER	252735	M	Ger.		SS-Mann,SD,Toulouse (Fr.) 11.42-8.44	MISC.CRIMES	FR.
SCHIER, Herbert	256178	M	Ger.		Hptschfhr..C.C.,Muhldorf (Ger.)	WITNESS	U.S.
SCHIERL	256047	M	Ger.		Org.Todt,Muhldorf (Ger.)	WITNESS	U.S.
SCHIERLAU, August	149868	M			Pvt.,Army,Bokum (Ger.) 4.8.44	MURDER	U.S.
SCHIERS	194361	M			Commandant,Army,Baix (Fr.) 22.8.44	MURDER	FR.
SCHIESSER	165699	M	Ger.	10	Kriminaloberasst.,SIPO,Strasbourg (Fr.) 16.2.43	MURDER	FR.
SCHIESSL	256307	M	Ger.		Org.Todt,Muhldorf (Ger.)	WITNESS	U.S.
SCHIESSLE	126926	M	Ger.	05	Zugwachtmeister,Schupo,C.C.,Schirmeck (Fr.) 43-44	TORTURE	FR.
SCHIESSLE, Egon	253409	M		13. 4.99	C.C.,Schirmeck (Fr.) 40-49	INTERR.	FR.
SCHIESTEL	1322	M	Ger.		Lt.,Abwehr,Intelligence Corps	MURDER	U.K.
SCHIESTL	194293	M	Ger.		Lt.,Gestapo,Santa Dona (It.) 30.12.43	MURDER	U.K.
SCHIETRICH	125051	M	Ger.	90	Civilian,Saechsische Blechwarenfabrik,Radebeul,Dresden (Ger.)4.42-4.45	MISC.CRIMES	U.K.
SCHIETSCH, Rudolf	189154	M		18. 9.17	Sgt.,leichte Marine Art.Abt.681,Manebos en Lanester (Fr.) 9.8.44	MURDER	FR.
SCHIEVELBUSH	120621	M	Ger.		Civilian,C.C.,Himmelfahrt,Fundgrube,Frieberg (Ger.)10.43-10.44	MURDER	U.K.
SCHIEWANG (or SCHIMANG)	306873	M	Ger.	10	Meister,Gendarmerie,attached to Abt.IV,3a,Gestapo,Vichy (Fr.)10.43-9.44	MURDER	FR.
SCHIFFBAUER	162552	M	Ger.		Civilian,Hoffmungsthal (Ger.) 7.7.44	MURDER	U.S.
SCHIFFER	141332	M	Ger.		Sturmbannfhr.,SS	MURDER	U.K.
SCHIFFERER	800	M	Ger.		Major,Air-force,Parachute unit,Morvilliers (Fr.) 11.8.44	MURDER	FR.
SCHIFFL	300860	M	Ger.		Pvt.,1.Aufkl.Abt.,3.Coy.,2.Column,XV. Div.,Afrika Korps,Saint-Léger (Arlon) 5.9.44	MISC.CRIMES	BEL.
SCHIFFLER, Hans	262134	M	Ger.		Murder of an american airman,Muenchen-Priel (Ger.)L.O.D.N.A O.D.	SUSPECT	U.S.
SCHIFFMANN	258104	M	Ger.	05	Osturmfhr.,SS,state service,police official,Val.Mezirici (Czech.)44-45	MURDER	CZECH.
SCHIFFMANN, Hans	260997	M	Ger.		Lt.,SS,Castel Franco,Emilia (Modena) (It.) 14.-18.12.44	MURDER	U.S.
SCHIFFNER	128902	M	Ger.		Chief-doctor,Standort Res.Laz.,Wuerzburg (Ger.) 14.10.43	MURDER	U.S.
SCHIFFNER	167324	M	Ger.		Chief,SD,Carcassone,Belcaire,Camurac (Fr.) 30.11.43	MURDER	FR.
SCHIFFNER	186217	M	Ger.		Schfhr.,SS,chief,Gestapo,Carcasonne,Villebazy (Fr.) 1.7.44	PILLAGE	FR.
SCHIFFNER	191519	M	Ger.		Chief,SD,Aude (Fr.) 30.11.43	MURDER	FR.
SCHIGA(Alias:SZIGE)	168961	M	Ger.		Uschfhr.,SS,guard,C.C.,Sachsenhausen,Oranienburg (Ger.) 39-4.45	MURDER	FR.
SCHIGETI	260974	M	Ger.		SS-Mann,C.C.,Vaihingen a.d.Enz (Ger.) 13.8.44-7.4.45	MURDER	U.S.
SCHIGG, Franz	257026	M			Lt.,Army,Amer.Zone (Ger.)	TORTURE	U.S.
SCHIKARA	122924	M	Ger.		Crim.Employee,Gestapo,C.C.,Cuxhaven (Ger.) 29.-30.3.45	MURDER	U.S.
SCHIKER	252721	M	Ger.		Major,Kreiskommandant,Tournai (Bel.)	INTERR.	BEL.
SCHIDBACH, Hans	251795	M	Ger.		Cpl.,Mil.Army,Utrecht (Neth.) 9.41	INTERR.	NETH.
SCHILCHER	258602	M	Ger.		Guard,Waffen SS,slave labour camp,Beisfjord near Narvik (Nor.)6.-11.42	BRUTALITY	YUGO.
SCHILD, Helmut	251326	M	Ger.		Rottfhr.,SS,C.C.,Auschwitz,Birkenau (Pol.) 1.43	MURDER	YUGO.
SCHILD, Karl	143268	M	Ger.		Betriebsobmann,DAF,Traechtlingen (Ger.)	TORTURE	U.S.
SCHILDAIER	194520	M			Lt.,Army,Plancher Les Mines (Fr.) 9.10.44	WITNESS	FR.
SCHILF, Wilhelm	262912	M	Ger.		Harbor-employee,Veltenhof (Ger.) 5.8.45 I.O.D.N.A.O.D.	SUSPECT	U.S.
SCHILI, Josef (orSCHILY,SCHULEY SCHULY,SCHUELY)	149869	M	Ger.	01	Hpttruppfhr.,Org.Todt,Muhldorf,Ampfing (Ger.)	SUSPECT	U.S.
SCHILINGER	259246	M			Officer,SS,Auschwitz (Pol.)	TORTURE	FR.
SCHILL (or SCHILLE)	136196	M	Ger.		Lt.General,Inf.,Ville Le Marclet (Fr.) 27.8.44	MURDER	FR.
SCHILLF,	167325	M	Ger.		Prof.,Member,Admin.staff,Einsatzstab Rosenberg (Fr.) 40-44	PILLAGE	FR.
SCHILLENGER	147355	M	Ger.		Pvt.,11.Pz.Div.,Kampfgr."Wilde", (Fr.) 44	MURDER	FR.
SCHILLER	141613	M	Ger.		Kreisleiter,NSDAP,Oberlangstein-Rh. (Ger.)	TORTURE	FR.
SCHILLER	143256	M			SA,Muhlberg (Ger.) 3.42	MURDER	U.S.
SCHILLER	149870	M			Returns officer,C.C.,Mauthausen (Aust.) 41-45	MURDER	U.S.
SCHILLER	186685	M	Ger.		Hptsturmfhr.,SS Leibstandarte "Adolf Hitler",3.Coy.,Wormoudt (Fr.)5.40	MURDER	U.K.
SCHILLER	188807	M	Ger.		Uschfhr.,SS,C.C.,Flossenburg (Ger.)	TORTURE	FR.
SCHILLER, Friedrich-Karl	173509	M	Ger.		Official,Gestapo,Governor,Prison,Jasika near Krusejac (Yugo.) 7.43	MURDER	YUGO.
SCHILLER, Johann	124626	M	Ger.		Member,Gestapo,Giessen (Ger.) 26.-27.3.45	MURDER	U.S.
SCHILLER, Martin	133304	M	Ger.	27. 4.19	Uschfhr.,Waffen SS,C.C.,Flossenburg (Ger.)	TORTURE	U.S.
SCHILLGLEL	186215	M	Ger.		Col.,Army,St.Nazaire,Massif de Vercors (Fr.) 20.7.-5.8.44	MURDER	FR.
SCHILLHORN, Hans	260456	M	Ger.	20. 8.11	Guard instructor,Waffen SS,Stabsschfhr.,C.C.,Auschwitz (Pol.) 9.41-1.45	BRUTALITY	POL.
SCHILLIFER	257546	M		12	Engineer,chief,C.C.,Dora,Nordhausen (Ger.) 8.44	BRUTALITY	U.S.
SCHILLING	139697	M	Ger.		Sonderfhr.,Stalag X B,C.C.,Sandbostel (Ger.) 1.-5.45	TORTURE	U.S.
SCHILLING	162551	M	Ger.	07	Civilian,C.C.,Buchenwald (Ger.)	WITNESS	U.S.
SCHILLING	186216	M	Ger.		Professor of Medecin,C.C.,Dachau (Ger.)	MURDER	FR.
SCHILLING	189612	M	Ger.		SD,Area Lyonnaise (Fr.)	MISC.CRIMES	FR.
SCHILLING	194518	M	Ger.		Civilian,Lepanges (Fr.) 27.9.44	PILLAGE	FR.
SCHILLING	251332	M	Ger.		Cmdt.,Gend.,Aleksandrovac (Yugo.) 42	INTERR.	YUGO.

SCHI-SCHI

NAME	C.R.FILE NUMBER	SEX	NATIO-NALITY	DATE OF BIRTH	RANK OCCUPATION UNIT PLACE AND DATE OF CRIME	REASON WANTED	WANTED BY
SCHILLING	255944	M			Kapo, CC Buchenwald (Ger.)	MURDER	U.S.
SCHILLING	301357	M	Ger.		Member, SS, CC Mauthausen (Aust.) 11.42-5.45	MURDER	FR.
SCHILLING, Gica	142294	M	Ger. Rum.	7896	SS Rottfhr, medical, CC Ebensee (Aust.) 44-45	MURDER	U.S.
SCHILLING, Gisela	252749	F	Ger.		Nurse, Wolfsburg (Ger.) 29.6.44	WITNESS	U.S.
SCHILLING, Otto	252730	M	Ger.		Sturmschfhr, SD, Toulouse (Fr.) 11.42-8.44	MISC.CRIMES	FR.
SCHILLING, Otto Erik	306559	M	Ger.	9. 7.12	Lt., Sicherheitspolizei, SD, Mosjoen (Nor.) 11.43-4.45	MURDER	NOR.
SCHILLING, Victor Hugo	149871	M	Ger.	77	Civilian, CC Dachau (Ger.)	MISC.CRIMES	U.S.
SCHILLINGER	137629	M	Ger.	80	Dr., Prof., Civilian, CC Dachau (Ger.)	TORTURE	U.K.
SCHILLINGER	161290	M	Ger.		2 Cmdt., CC Varsovie (Pol.)	TORTURE	FR.
SCHILLINGER	306872	M	Ger.		Cmdt., CC Auschwitz-Birkenau (Pol.) 40-45	MURDER	FR.
SCHILLMAYER, Fritz	194519	M	Ger.		Chief, Mayor, public official, Stalag II-A, Kdo.475,2, CC Klader(Ger.) 43-44	MURDER	FR.
SCHILY, Jupp (see CHILLI)	251995						
SCHILOER	39794	M	Ger.		Pvt., 17 SS Pz.Gren.Div."Goetz v.Berlichingen", Sturmgeschuetz or Pz.Jg.Abt.17, Segre-Renaze (Fr.) 6.8.44-30.7.44	MURDER	FR.
SCHILS	174570	M	Ger.		Sgt., police 19.Rgt., 6 Coy,Region d'Aurillac (Fr.) 13.-15.6 .44	MURDER	FR.
SCHILTHUIZEN	302131	M	Ger.		Member SD, Almelo district (Neth.) 9.44-2.45	PILLAGE	NETH.
SCHILTZ	257868	M			Lt., 150 Pz.Bde., Meuse Bridge, Antwerpen (Bel.) 12.44	MISC.CRIMES	U.S.
SCHILTZ, Guillaume	177576	M	Ger.		Pvt., SS "Deutschland", 3 Rgt., Aiguillon (Fr.) 17.-22.6.44	MURDER	FR.
SCHILY, Josef (see SCHILI)	149869						
SCHIMA, Johann	252743	M	Ger.	24. 8.15	Employee, SD, Gestapo, Klatovy (Czech.) 39-45	MISC.CRIMES	CZECH.
SCHIMANG (see SCHIEWANG)	306873						
SCHIMANN	125621	M	Ger.		Medical Lt.Col., CC La Pallice (Fr.) 45	TORTURE	FR.
SCHIMANSKI, Josef	256248	M		13.12.08	Staff Sgt., CC Ellrich, Nordhausen (Ger.)	MURDER	U.S.
SCHIMANSKY, Wilhelm (or SCHIMANSKI)	162238	M	Ger.		Miner, Adolf mine, Labour Cmdo., Merkstein(Ger.) 42-44	SUSPECT	U.S.
SCHIMEK, Arthur	252723	M	Ger.		CC Ellrich (Ger.)	BRUTALITY	BEL.
SCHIMEL	131921	M			SS Oschfhr, SS Cmdt., Berger-Elster, CC near Werdau (Ger.) 3.-4.45	MURDER	U.S.
SCHIMEL (see SCHIMMEL)	142292						
SCHIMETSCHEK, Leo	251783	M	Ger.	27. 7.07	Employee, state service, labour office, M.-Ostrau(Czech.) 43-45	MURDER	CZECH.
SCHIMIDT	39829	M	Ger.		Pvt., CC Pothon (Fr.) 3.43	MURDER	U.K.
SCHIMIG, Inge	136968	F	Ger.		CC Helmbrechts (Ger.)	MURDER	U.S.
SCHIMINGER, Leopold	173284	M	Ger.	05	Sgt., 891 Lds.Schtz.Bn., 6 Coy, Marien en Marzoul near Wolfsberg(Aust.) 1., 4.45	TORTURE	U.K.
SCHIMION	135558	M			Sgt., Army, 21.1.-12.4.45	MURDER	U.K.
SCHIMKORT	306285	M	Ger.		Member,Gestapo,Nove Mesto nr.Vahom,CC Auschwitz-Birkenau(Pol.)39-45	MURDER	CZECH.
SCHIMM, Johann	194521	M	Ger.	24. 8.15	Member Gestapo, Klatovy (Czech.)	TORTURE	CZECH.
SCHIMMECK	253416	M	Ger.		Uschfhr, SS, CC Oranienburg (Ger.)	MISC.CRIMES	BEL.
SCHIMMECK, Arthur	187786	M	Ger.		Civilian, Camp Ellrich (Ger.)	MURDER	U.S.
SCHIMMEL (or SCHIMEL)	142292	M	Ger.		Oschfhr, SSTotenkopf Stuba., SS Cmdt.,Schwalbe V, Berga-Elster, Buchenwald (Ger.) 43-45	MURDER	U.S., U.K.
SCHIMMEL (or PINKARD)	155973	M		05	Capt., Marinecorps, CC Stettin (Ger.) 7.44	TORTURE	U.S.
SCHIMMEL	256278	M			Rottfhr, CC Mackenrode, Nordhausen (Ger.)	MURDER	U.S.
SCHIMMEL, George	139699	M	Ger.	05	Guard, W-SS, CC Berga (Ger.) 4.45	TORTURE	U.S.
SCHIMMEL, Johann	802	M	Ger.		Dr., Reg.-Praesident, public official, Bydgoszcz (Pol.) 9.39-42	MURDER	POL.
SCHIMMELPFENNIG	262288	M	Ger.		SS Standartenfhr, SD, various places in Slovenia(Yugo.) 41-45	MISC.CRIMES	YUGO.
SCHIMMER, Hans (see TSCHIMMER)	36628						
SCHIMMER, Martin	12344	M	Ger.		Pvt., Army, 110 or 111 Pz.Gren.Rgt., 2 Coy, Albine (Fr.) 29.6.44	MURDER	FR.
SCHIMMER, Paul	258068	M	Ger.		Oberwachtmstr, Gend., Benesov (Czech.)	WITNESS	CZECH.
SCHIMPF	143255	M	Ger.		Oberstabsrichter, Kriegsgericht, Ansbach (Ger.) 15.4.45	MURDER	U.S.
SCHIMPF	188583	M	Ger.		Civilian, Bush-Ahorn (Ger.) 17.8.43	TORTURE	U.S.
SCHIMPFOSEL	129938	M			Usturmfhr, W-SS, Totenkopf Sturmbann, CC Mauthausen (Aust.) 41-45	MURDER	U.S.
SCHIMPL, Karl	262196	M	Ger.	18.11.20	SS Uschfhr, detachment of Art., 51 SS Armoured-Bde., Breviandes, Bucheres, St.Savine, La Riviere de Corps, Troyes (Fr.) 22.-25.8.44	BRUTALITY	FR.
SCHINBORN	193410	M	Ger.		Sgt., 2 Coy, PoW Work Bn.206, Revanimis, Mesjoen, Kretnemes(Nor.)5.45	MURDER	NOR.
SCHINCKE, Fritz	132792	M	Ger.		Gend., Feld-Gend., Clairvaux (Fr.)	MURDER	FR.
SCHINDEL, Rudolf	147052	M	Ger.		Schfhr, SS Pz.Div. "Das Reich", Queylus (Fr.) 44	MURDER	FR.
SCHINDLER	137485	M			SS-Mann, CC Buchenwald (Ger.)	MURDER	U.S.
SCHINDLER	252729	M	Ger.		Agent, SD, Hte. Garonne (Fr.) 11.42-8.44	MISC.CRIMES	FR.
SCHINDLER	253182	M	Ger.		SS Uschfhr, W-SS, Security Section, Auschwitz (Pol.) 43-44	MURDER	U.K.
SCHINDLER, Adolf	305943	M	Ger.	17. 6.05	Pvt. Res., Velks, Heraltice (Czech.) 7.8.44	ILL-TREATMENT	CZECH.
SCHINDLER, Adolf	251330	M	Ger.		Uschfhr, SS, CC Auschwitz (Pol.) 1.43	MURDER	YUGO.
SCHINDLER, Albert	260679	M			Crimes against peace, war crimes and crimes against humanity	WITNESS	U.S.
SCHINDLER, Anton	251777	M	Ger.	8. 2.99	Employee, Gestapo, Bruenn (Czech.) 39-45	MURDER	CZECH.
SCHINDLER, Franz-	193727	M	Ger.	13. 9.06	Gestapo-employee, driver, SS Schfhr, Klatovy (Czech.) 39-45	TORTURE	CZECH.
SCHINDLER, Hans	131997	M		09	SS Osturmfhr, CC, Camp-S 111, Thueringen (Ger.) 45	TORTURE	U.S.
SCHINDLER, Hans	162550	M	Ger.	08	SS, CC Auschwitz, Ohrdruf (Pol.) Ger.) 12.44	TORTURE	U.S.
SCHINDLER, Hans	257548	M			SS Schfhr, CC Ellrich, B 12, Nordhausen (Ger.)	MURDER	U.S.
SCHINDLER, Hugo	260507	M	Ger.	27.10.97	Uschfhr, W-SS, Guard Coy, CC Eintrachtshuette, Auschwitz(Pol.)8.41-1.45	BRUTALITY	POL.
SCHINDLER, Richard	174569	M	Ger.	18. 9.99	Sgt., Army, Vannes (Fr.) 42-44	TORTURE	FR.
SCHINDLER, Rudolf	178759	M	Ger.	05	Pvt., 2 Lds.Schtz.Bn.559, St.Bolten (Czech.) 14.12.42	TORTURE	U.K.
SCHINDLER, Rudolf	39828	M			Stalag VIII B, 2 Bn, 559 Lds.Schtz., CC Lamsdorf (Ger.) 14.12.42	TORTURE	U.K.
SCHINDLER, Sebastian	12343	M	Ger.		Pvt., 110 or 111 Pz.Gren.Rgt., 2 Coy, Albine (Fr.) 29.6.44	MURDER	FR.
SCHINEG	256268	M			Oschfhr, CC Dora, Nordhausen (Ger.)	MURDER	U.S.
SCHINELLAR	181118	M	Ger.		Group-Leader, 1 Pz.Div."Adolf Hitler", W-SS, 2 Zug, 1 Ers.Bn., Parfondruy Stavelot (Bel.) 18.-22.12.44	MURDER	U.S.
SCHINEMEYER	143254	M			Policeman, Police, Springe (Ger.) 26.11.44	MURDER	U.S.
SCHINER	306874	M			SS Schfhr, workshop, CC Auschwitz (Pol.) from 40	MURDER	U.S.
SCHINKE	803	M			Lt., Guard, PoW-camp, CC Stalag VIII C, Kunau(Ger.) 9., 12.39	TORTURE	POL.
SCHINKE, Fritz	260975	M	Ger.	05	Secretary, Chief of the Abwehrdienst, Stalowa-Wola (Pol.) 44-45	MISC.CRIMES	POL.
SCHINKEL (see SCHECKE)	1069				Senior W.O., Feld-Gend., Bar sur Aube (Fr.)	MURDER	FR.
SCHINLAUER	300581						
SCHINOWSKI (or SCHINOWSKY)	129937	M			Uschfhr, W-SS, Div. Totenkopf, CC Mauthausen (Aust.) 41-45	MURDER	U.S.
	136197	M	Ger.		Sgt., 6 Div. Parachut., Feld-Gend., Domart-Ponthieu (Fr.)	MURDER	FR.

SCHI-SCHL

NAME	C.R.FILE NUMBER	SEX	NATIO-NALITY	DATE OF BIRTH	RANK OCCUPATION UNIT PLACE AND DATE OF CRIME	REASON WANTED	WANTED BY
SCHIPP, Anton	258603	M	Ger.		Member,Org.Todt,Schutzkdo.,slave labour camp,Erlandet,Deusand, Trola (Nor.) 6.42-45	MURDER	YUGO.
SCHIPPER	253371	M	Ger.		6 Coy, 16 Hubner Rgt.,Kinrodi (Bel.) 9.44	INTERR.	BEL.
SCHIPPMANN, Heinrich	152150	M	Ger.		Fuehrer, SA,Poppentin (Ger.) 7.-8.44	MURDER	U.S.
SCHIPTZ	167357	M	Ger.		Sgt.,Army, Formation de Train,Thiel sur Acolin (Fr.)15.-16.8.44	MURDER	FR.
SCHIRANSKI	126918	M			SS-medical, C.C. Buchenwald (Ger.)	TORTURE	FR.
SCHIRK	173545	M	Ger.		Pvt.,Army, Thiers (Fr.) 25.8.44	PILLAGE	FR.
SCHIRM, Lothar	257547	M			Pvt.,Navy,Finmark, northern Nor.(Nor.) 6.5.45	MURDER	NOR.
SCHIRMACHER	253507	M	Ger.		Lt.,3 Coy,Ost Bn 654, Dun les Places (Fr.) 26.,28.7.44	PILLAGE	FR.
SCHIRMACHER, Herbert or SCHIRRMACHER	193068	M	Ger.	02	Secretary, Reichsjustizministerium, Strafgefangenenlager, Finmark (Nor.) 42-45	MISC.CRIMES	NOR.
SCHIRMANN see SCHUHMANN	123952						
SCHIRMBACHER	193411	M	Ger.		Lt.,PW work Bn 206, Revanimie,Mosjoen,Kretnemes(Nor.) 44	MURDER	NOR.
SCHIRMBRANDT	254436	M	Ger.	96	Capt.,392 Inf.Blue Div.,Lika (Yugo.) 44-45	MISC.CRIMES	YUGO.
SCHIRMER	133303	M	Ger.		Usturmfhr.,Waffen-SS, C.C. Flossenburg (Ger.)	MURDER	U.S.
SCHIRMER	251775	M	Ger.		Lt.,Beernem (Bel.) 5.-6.9.44	MURDER	BEL.
SCHIRMER	301359	F	Ger.		Wardress, C.C. Flossenburg (Ger.) 42-45	MURDER	FR.
SCHIRMER, Adolphe	259245	M	Ger.		Uscharfhr., Gestapo, Area Poitiers (Fr.) 40-44	MISC.CRIMES	FR.
SCHIRMER, Alphonse	161289	M	Ger.		Cpl., 159 Inf.Div.,Cernay (Fr.) 1.-2.45	MURDER	FR.
SCHIRMER, Georg	260691	M	Ger.	90	Gen.,Army	WITNESS	U.S.
SCHIRMER, Rudolf Max	260487	M	Ger.	1.6.91	Scharfhr.,Waffen-SS, guard Coy, C.C. Bobrek and Monowitz (Auschwitz)(Pol.) 8.44-1.45	BRUTALITY	POL.
SCHIRNER	136366	M	Ger.		Forestmaster, Ruppertschutten (Ger.) 12.9.44	WITNESS	U.S.
SCHIRRMACHER, Herbert see SCHIRMACHER	193068						
SCHISLER	148422	M	Ger.		Lt.,15 Pz.Rgt.,11 Pz.Div. (Fr.) 44	MURDER	FR.
SCHISSEL, Josef	256249	M			Pvt.,C.C.Bismarckhuette(Pol.), Nordhausen (Ger.)	MURDER	U.S.
SCHISSELE	132542	M	Ger.		SS, Vaihingen (Ger.)	MURDER	FR.
SCHISSELE, Egon	252722	M	Ger.		Prison guard, Prison C.C. Schirmeck (Fr.)	MISC.CRIMES	FR.
SCHISSLER, Paul	256279	M		16.1.98	Pvt.,C.C. Harzungen-Nordhausen (Ger.)	MURDER	U.S.
SCHITLER or SCHITIER	140921				Civilian, Hosche (Ger.) 3.45	TORTURE	U.K.
SCHITLIE	301444	M	Ger.		SS-Staff-Sgt.,C.C. Nordhausen-Dora (Ger.) 40-45	MURDER	BEL.
SCHITTAUF	188565	M			Osturmfhr.,SS,C.C. (Ger.)	TORTURE	U.S.
SCHITTELM	155975	M	Ger.		N.C.O.,Army, Arbeitskdo.E 173,C.C. Setzdorf (Czech.) 7.41	TORTURE	U.K.
SCHITTENHELM	167337	M	Ger.		Capt.,Kaukasien Bn,Pont l'Abbe,Plobaznalec (Fr.)7.,4.8.44	MURDER	FR.
SCHITTENHELM	261923	M	Ger.		Standartenfhr., SD,Various places in Slovenia (Yugo.) 41-45	MISC.CRIMES	YUGO.
SCHITZICK, Herbert	46132	M	Ger.	25	Uscharfhr.,12 SS-Pz.Div. Hitlerjugend,nr.Caen (Fr.)6.6.-8.7.44	TORTURE	CAN.
SCHIWITZ, Claus	194267	M	Ger.		Sicherungs-Rgt.95,8 or 13 Coy,Pulle (Fr.) 7.6.44	MURDER	FR.
SCHLACHTER	10341	M	Ger.		Osturmfhr.,SS, C.C. Natzweiler (Fr.) 42	TORTURE	CZECH.
SCHLACHTER	256281	M			Hptsturmfhr.,SS, Camp Dora-Nordhausen (Ger.)	MURDER	U.S.
SCHLACHTER, August	173068	M	Ger.		Osturmfhr.,SS, C.C. Struthof (Fr.) 42-45	MURDER	FR.
SCHLAG	257698	M	Ger.		Chief of section Mittelwerk,C.C. Nordhausen (Ger.)	MURDER	U.S.
SCHLAG	258913	M	Ger.		Member, typist, Task force at custom house,Lourdes(Fr.) 1.-8.44	MURDER	FR.
SCHLAGEL	194529	M	Ger.		Major,7 group Art.,le Percy,Esparron (Fr.) 3.2.44	MURDER	FR.
SCHLAGER	253497	M	Ger.		W.O.,Airforce, 3 Coy Nr.26769, Pierre (Fr.) 7.,8.44	PILLAGE	FR.
SCHLAGER, Alois	188359	M	Ger.		Rottenfhr.,SS, SS-Div."Das Reich",2 Reconnaissance Bn,2 Coy, near St.Vith (Bel.) 12.44	MURDER	U.S.
SCHLAGER, Erhard	133238	M			Civilian, 20.2.45	WITNESS	U.S.
SCHLAGER, Markus	193166	M	Ger.	00	Capt.,Oberregierungsrat,Reichsjustizministerium,Feldstraflager, Waffen-SS,Finmark (Nor.) 6.42-45	TORTURE	YUGO., CZECH.,NOR.
SCHLAMADINGER, Johann	142270	M	Ger.	93	SS Oberwachtmstr., Police, C.C. Reichenau (Aust.) 42-43	TORTURE	U.S.
SCHLAMANN	193408	M	Ger.		Cpl.,1 Kgs.Arb.Bn 41, C.C. Kristiansund,Norlandsdal(Nor.) 41-45	TORTURE	NOR.
SCHLANDT, Leon	194385	M	Ger.		SS-Mann, C.C. Breendonck (Bel.) 41	MURDER	BEL.
SCHLANGE	156894	M			Oscharfhr.,Waffen-SS, C.C. Aschendorfer Moor (Ger.)	TORTURE	U.S.
SCHLANGENHAUF, Eugen	256280	M		8.1.05	Flyer, Camp Ellrich-Nordhausen (Ger.)	MURDER	U.S.
SCHLANK	148421	M	Ger.		Major, 11 Pz.Div. South West France 44	MURDER	FR.
SCHLANZ	128909		Ger.		Lt.,Gespenster Div.,11 Pz.Div. Mjassojadow (Sov.Un.)3.-4.42	MURDER	U.S.
SCHLAPKA	137486	M		05 - 08	Pvt.,Geh.Feldpol. Gruppe 713	MURDER	U.S.
SCHLARP, Joseph	146752	M			SS, C.C. Flossenburg (Ger.)	TORTURE	U.S.
SCHLATZER	171955	M	Ger.		Crim.employee, Gestapo, Fouligny (Fr.) 9.8.44	MURDER	U.S.
SCHLATZER, Hans	143253	M	Ger.	28.6.12	Rottenfhr.,SS, crim.asst., Gestapo, near St.Avold, 8.-12.44	MURDER	U.S.,FR.
SCHLAVIN, Paul	261919	M	Ger.	1.11.20	SS-Mann, member, SS and SD at the time of occupation of Slovakia, Bratislava (Czech.) 2.-3.45	MURDER	CZECH.
SCHLAWIN, Paul	250486	M	Ger.		SS-Mann, SS, C.C. Auschwitz-Birkenau (Pol.) 10.42	INTERR.	YUGO.
SCHLECHSE, Karl or SCHLECHTE	194268	M	Ger.		W.O.-chief, Sicherungs-Rgt.194,Prada-la-Javis(Fr.)30.7.44	MURDER	FR.
SCHLECHTA	305944	M	Ger.		Informant, Gestapo, Bohemia (Czech.) 39-45	INTERR.	CZECH.
SCHLECHTA, Jan	190236	M	Ger.	16.10.97	Agent, Gestapo, Rapsach (Czech.)	MURDER	CZECH.
SCHLECHTA, Hans	193766	M	Ger.		Employee, Gestapo, Brno (Czech.) 39-45	MURDER	CZECH.
SCHLECHTE, Karl see SCHLECHSE	194268						
SCHLECHTINGER	128908	M			Department head of Reich.werke Hermann Goering,Hellendorf (Ger.)	WITNESS	U.S.
SCHLEE	301858	M	Ger.		Col.,O.C.497 Inf.Rgt. Stars la Bruyere (Hainaut) 4.-5.9.44	MURDER	BEL.
SCHLEESE, Karl	182493	M	Ger.	07	Pvt.,Abwehr official Fak 206, Kuestrin (Ger.)	MURDER	U.S.
SCHLEGEL	182067	M	Ger.	05	Chief,Reg.Assessor, Gestapo, SS, Praha (Czech.) 39-43	PILLAGE	CZECH.
SCHLEGEL, Karl	193168	M	Ger.		Pvt., 7 Btty,Kuesten Art.Rgt.792 (Nor.) 7.4.45	MISC.CRIMES	NOR.
SCHLEGEL, Kurt	132143	M	Ger.		Civilian, Bad Durrenberg (Ger.) 29.5.44	TORTURE	U.S.
SCHLEGELMICH, Michel	121849	M	Ger.		Cpl., Interpreter of Cmdtr., Landrecies (Fr.) 8.1.44	MURDER	FR.
SCHLAGER	190272	M	Ger.		Civilian, Meckovac-Kragujevac (Yugo.)	MURDER	YUGO.
SCHLEGER, Franz	251793	M	Ger.	10.8.16	Member, Gestapo, Hradec, Kralove (Czech.) 39-45	MURDER	CZECH.
SCHLEICH, Eugen Karl	306653	M	Ger.		Lt., W.O., POW Camp (Fr.) Nr.135, Quimper,Finistere (Fr.) 26.2.41	MURDER	FR.
SCHLEIDER	300861	M	Ger.		N.C.O.,1 Aufkl.Abt.,3 Coy, 2 Col., XV Div. Afrika Korps St.Lager Distr.Arlon (Bel.) 5.9.44	MISC.CRIMES	BEL.
SCHLEIER	124312	M	Ger.		Ger.Foreign office, 41	INTERR.	U.S.
SCHLEIER	188806	M	Ger.		Sgt.,Airforce, Bedarrides (Fr. 15.6.44	MURDER	FR.
SCHLEIER	194370	M	Ger.		Sgt.,Army,189 Kgf.Arb.Bn, Bassis Tunnel (Nor.)	WITNESS	NOR.
SCHLEIER, I.K.	260234	M	Ger.		Commander,Foreign-office attache,Inf.Stelle XIV,Cult.Affairs Dept. (ant.Jewish activities abroad),Paris (Fr.)	MISC.CRIMES	U.S.
SCHLEIF	173261	M	Ger.	10	Pvt.,Lds.Schz.,Stalag XXIII A, C.C. Dietmannsdorf, 3.43-3.45	TORTURE	U.K.

SCHL-SCHL

NAME	C.R.FILE NUMBER	SEX	NATIO-NALITY	DATE OF BIRTH	RANK OCCUPATION UNIT PLACE AND DATE OF CRIME	REASON WANTED	WANTED BY
SCHLEIMER, Leopold	806	M	Ger.		SS, Fort-Musson (Fr.) 3.8.44	MURDER	FR.
SCHLEINING	126919	M	Ger.		Scharfhr., 2.SS-Panz.-Div. "Das Reich" 44	MURDER	FR.
SCHLEINING	147051	M	Ger.		Scharfhr., SS-Panz.Div. "Das Reich", Valence D'Agen(Fr.) 44	MURDER	FR.
SCHLEINING	186197	M	Ger.		Civilian, Vergt de Brion (Fr.) 5.44	MISC.CRIMES	FR.
SCHLEINING, Hans	191536	M	Ger.	19	Sgt., Waffen SS, Div. "Das Reich " 1.Coy.,Oradour-sur-Glane(Fr.)10.5.44	MURDER	FR.
SCHLEIPEN	121850	M	Ger.		Pvt., Army, FP.Nr. 56.067 D,Creach-Maouten-Plenbian (Fr.) 7.44	MURDER	FR.
SCHLELEIN, Johann	132009	M	Ger.	87	Capt., Army, Hammelburg (Ger.)	MURDER	U.S.
SCHLEM	1476	M			Opl., SD, Aussenkommando	MISC.CRIMES	U.K.
SCHLEMER	306321	M	Ger.		Employee of Saint-Germain des Fosses (Allier) Billy-Allier (Fr.)8.44	PILLAGE	FR.
SCHLEMM, Alfred	258940	M	Ger.	94	Lt.,General, wanted as Defendant,possibly witness,Crimes Against Peace W.A.R.,crimes and crimes Against Humanity	INTERR.	U.S.
SCHLEMMER	807	M	Ger.		Oberscharfhr.,SS, C.C. Dachau (Ger.) 40 - 43	MURDER	FR.
SCHLEMMER	67047	M	Ger.		Kanonier, SS-Div.,Chateau Gontier,St.Suhlice Montmousson (Fr.) 8.44	MURDER	FR.
SCHLEMMINGER,Gerhard	256250	M			Sgt., C.C., Nordhausen (Ger.)	MURDER	U.S.
SCHLENSTEDT, Otto	187789	M	Ger.		Civilian, Eiestedt (Ger.) 18.7.44	TORTURE	U.S.
SCHLERETH	136637	M			Capt., Army,Abwehr,Stalag III C, C.C., Altredwitz (Ger.) 9.44-2.45	TORTURE	U.S.
SCHLESIER, Anton	256298	M		16. 8.07	Cpl., C.C. Ellrich, Nordhausen (Ger.)	MURDER	U.S.
SCHLESIK, Toni	141333	M	Ger.		Guard, BAB 21,Stalag VIII B, Army, Blechammer (Ger.) 10.42	MURDER	U.K.
SCHLESINGER	167356	M			Chief, Gestapo, Enzfeld (Aust.)	MURDER	FR.
SCHLESINGER, Karl	143252	M	Ger.		Hauptscharfhr., SS-Leibstandarte "Adolf Hitler" Ers.Bn.,1,Rosbach(Ger.) 4.3.45	SUSPECT	U.S.
SCHLESINGER, Ludwig	126921	M	Ger.		Scharfhr., SS,C.C.,Schirmeck(Fr.) 43	PILLAGE	FR.
SCHLESINGER, Ludwig	178286	M	Ger.	24. 9.13	Civilian, 6.-9.44	WITNESS	U.K.
SCHLESSINGER	301027	M	Ger.		Scharfhr., C.C. Struthof-Natzweiler (Fr.) 42 - 44	MURDER	FR.
SCHLETT, Valentin	12345	M	Ger.		N.C.O, 111.or 110.Panz.-Gren.Rgt.,2.Coy. Albine (Fr.) 29.6.44	MURDER	FR.
SCHLETTWEIN	152135	M			Colonel, Gestapo, Bretagne (Fr.)	MURDER	FR.
SCHLEUGER	177573	M			Lt., Feldkommandantur, Porteau a Poitiers (Fr.) 28.8.44	MURDER	FR.
SCHLEUPNER, Martha	139700	F	Ger.		Woman-Guard,Arbeitslager 101 Polte Dept. C.C.,Magdeburg (Ger.)44-45	TORTURE	U.S.
SCHLEUSSNER	168962	M	Ger.		Dr., manager, Ostdeutsche Revisions Treuhandges. Krakow (Pol.)39-44	MISC.CRIMES	POL.
SCHLEY	152124	M	Ger.		Oberwachtmeister, Police-Gendarmerie, Herzfelde (Ger.) 3.45	MURDER	U.S.
SCHLEYER	259248	M	Ger.		Lt., Feldgendarmerie, St. Denis, Fort of St.Ains (Fr.) 15.8.44	MURDER	FR.
SCHLICH,Richard	256299	M			Pvt., C.C. Ellrich, Nordhausen (Ger.)	MURDER	U.S.
SCHLICHT	162916	M	Ger.	05	Obersturmfhr., Waffen SS, Totenkopf-Stuba.C.C. Czenstochow(Pol.)	TORTURE	U.S.
SCHLICHT	188585	M	Ger.		Oberscharfhr., Pysely (Czech.) 6.5.45	TORTURE	CZECH.
SCHLICHTE, Hermann	149876	M	Ger.		Police, Wiesbaden (Ger.) 2.2.45	MURDER	U.S.
SCHLICHTING	253392	M	Ger.		Employee, Sipo Abt. I R,Bruessel (Bel.) 40 - 45	INTERR.	BEL.
SCHLICHTLING	141941	M	Ger.		Pvt., Guard, Tschausch,III.Lager, Brux Area (Czech.) 5.8.44	MURDER	U.K.
SCHLICK, Franz	301445	M	Ger.	1. 1.13	Scharfhr., SS, C.C. Buchenwald (Ger.) 5.38 - 10.43	MURDER	BEL.
SCHICKER	253368	M	Ger.		Kreisleiter, Luxemburg (Lux.) 40 - 45	MISC.CRIMES	LUX.
SCHLIDAUSKI (see SCHIEDLAUSKI)	261208						
SCHLIEF	194369	M			Sonderfhr., Cpl., Army,184.KGF.Arb.Bn.,Bassis Tunnel,(Nor.)	MURDER	NOR.
SCHLIEF, Hans	258544	M		02	Obersturmbannfhr.,W.V.H.A. (Ger.) 40-45	BRUTALITY	U.S.
SCHLIEFAKE, Reinhold	166672	M	Ger.		Civilian, Weckersleben (Ger.) 7.44	MURDER	U.S.
SCHLIEMANN	300927	M	Ger.		Dr.,Chief of children Clinic in Velpke (Ger.) 5.44-12.44	MURDER	U.K.
SCHLIEPER	62325	M	Ger.		Lt.,General, Army-Mission in Slovakia (Czech.)	TORTURE	UNWCC.
SCHLIER, Heinz	174770	M	Ger.		Capt., Army, Kuesten-Rgt. 972,7.Btty., Lattervik (Nor.) 7.4.45	MURDER	UK. NOR.
SCHLIERBACH	305790	M	Ger.		Stubafhr., Vosges area (Fr.) 44	MURDER	U.K.
SCHLIERECKE, Hans	162549	M	Ger.	22	Rottenfhr., SS, C.C. Buchenwald (Ger.) 42 - 45	WITNESS	U.S.
SCHLIESMANN	167238	M			Pvt., Kommandantur, Crest-Drome (Fr.) 7.-8.44	MURDER	FR.
SCHLIESMANN	191252	M	Ger.		Cpl.,Kommandantur, Crest (Fr.) 7.-8.44	MURDER	FR.
SCHLIEWER	184973	M			Uscharfhr, 4.SS-Totenkopfsturmbann,Dora Nordhausen,Rosen,Oslau (Ger.) 43 - 45	WITNESS	U.S.
SCHLIMME	173507	M	Ger.		Capt., Cmdt., Gendarmerie, Vrnjacka Banja (Yugo.) 42 - 44	MURDER	YUGO.
SCHLIMMER	253887	M	Ger.		Officer, Stalag IV B, Muehlberg (Ger.) 1.45	MURDER	U.S.
SCHLINGBACH	301028	M	Ger.		Member of Staff,C.C., Struthof-Natzweiler (Fr.) 42-44	MURDER	FR.
SCHLINGHOFF, Willi	256300	M			Cpl., Camp Ellrich, Nordhausen(Ger.)	MURDER	U.S.
SCHLINGMANN, Gerhard	253412	M			Pvt., 2.Pl.3.Pz.-Pionier.1.Pz.-Div."Leibstandarte Adolf Hitler" Ligneuville (Bel.) 12.44	MURDER	U.S.
SCHLINKE	136636	M			Interpreter, Stalag III B, C.C. (Ger.) 44	MURDER	U.S.
SCHLINN	174581	M	Ger.		Sgt., Flak-Unit, Cherbourg (Fr.) 23.6.44	MURDER	FR.
SCHLINN, Alfred	194270	M	Ger.		Sgt., Flak, Anderville (Fr.) 24.6.44	MURDER	FR.
SCHLIPF	261381	M	Ger.		SS-Sgt.,ChiefPolice Dirlewanger Brigade,Sluck (Pol.) 40 - 44	MURDER	POL.
SCHLIPPE	251161	M	Ger.		Lt., Stalag Luft IV, Gross Tychow (Pol.) 21.6.44	WITNESS	POL.
SCHLISSER	396270	M	Ger.		Pvt., Army, Bernayen Champagne (Fr.) 3.9.44	WITNESS	FR.
SCHLIZID	251773	M	Ger.		Div."Hermann Goering" 4.Parachute Rgt.,1.Bn.,1.Coy.Helchteren, Hechtel (Bel.) 9.44	TORTURE	BEL.
SCHLOCHTER	300862	M	Ger.		Pvt.,1.Aufkl.Abt.,2.Column,3.Coy.XV.Div. of the Afrika Korps, Saint Leger Arlon (Bel.) 5.9.44	MISC.CRIMES	BEL.
SCHLODER, Ludwig	256165	M			flyer, C.C., Ellrich,Nordhausen (Ger.)	MURDER	U.S.
SCHLODFELDT	141916	M	Ger.		Lt., Army, Bois de Guron,Rom Deux Sevres (Fr.) 7.7.44	WITNESS	U.K.
SCHLOEFFEL	193169	M	Ger.		Sgt.,Member,Schupo,SD ,C.C., Falstad (Nor.) 41 - 45	MURDER	NOR.
SCHLOEGL	31428	M	Ger.		Colonel, 20.Army 111.-112.Geb.Div.Geb.Art.Rgt.,Finmark (Nor.) 44	MURDER	NOR.
SCHLOFFEN	256164	M			Cpl., C.C., Ellrich,Nordhausen (Ger.)	MURDER	U.S.
SCHLOR, Jacob	193767	M	Ger.		Employee, Driver, Gestapo, Brno (Czech.) 39 - 45	TORTURE	CZECH.
SCHLOSCHEK, Arden	302136	M	Ger.		Obersturmfhr., SS, Falstad Slave Labour Camp, (Nor.) 42 - 43	MURDER	YUGO.
SCHLOSEN	186214	M	Ger.		SD de St.Etienne, Tournon (Fr.) 6.7.44	MURDER	FR.
SCHLOSSER	186818	M			Lt., Pionier Bn., Gestapo, Tournon (Fr.) 42 - 43	MISC.CRIMES	FR.
SCHLOSER	302137	M			Director of the Passavant Works,Kommando 1784,Kettenbach bei Michelbach-Hut (Ger.) 14.10.44	MURDER	FR.
SCHLOSSER	136198	M	Ger.		Lt., 11.Panz.Div. "Du Fantomes" St.Quirin, (Fr.) 9.und 10.44	MURDER	FR.
SCHLOSSER	137487	M	Ger.		Member SS, C.C., Weimar-Buchenwald (Ger.)	CRUELTY	U.S.
SCHLOSSER	168963	M	Ger.		General-Director, Leader of Abt.Wirtschaft, Amt des Gouverneurs, Warzow (Pol.) 9.39 - 44	MISC.CRIMES	POL.
SCHLOSSER	173543	M	Ger.		Amt fuer Rassenpolitik-Sippenamt, Strassbourg (Fr.) 44	PILLAGE	FR.

SCHL-SCHM

NAME	C.R.FILE NUMBER	SEX	NATIO-NALITY	DATE OF BIRTH	RANK OCCUPATION UNIT PLACE AND DATE OF CRIME	REASON WANTED	WANTED BY
SCHLOSSER	253429	M	Ger.	85	Sgt., Commando 44 Stalag IV G, Mugeln (Ger.) 15.11.44	MURDER	U.S.
SCHLOSSER	300982	M	Ger.		Mdical Officer, C.C. Buchenwald (Ger.) 42-45	MURDER	FR.
SCHLOSSER	306654	M	Ger.		Pvt., Feldgend. Chateaubriant (Loire-Onf.) St. Julien de Monvantes Soudan Juigne Les Montiers (Fr.) 21.7.44	MURDER	FR.
SCHLOSSER, Adolphe	165698	M	Ger.	21. 5.96	Landroff (Fr.) 11.44	PILLAGE	FR.
SCHLOSSER, Hans	162548	M	Ger.	04	SS-Standartenfhr., SS, C.C. Weimar-Buchenwald (Ger.) 43	MURDER	U.S.
SCHLOSSER, Hans	188005	M	Ger.		Arbeits Kdo., Regensburg (Ger.) 41-45	TORTURE	U.S.
SCHLOSSER, Heinz	193170	M	Ger.		Polizei-Asst., Staatspolizei, Trandum (Nor.) 43	MURDER	NOR.
SCHLOSSER, Josef	306778	M	Ger.		Ger. Civilian, Miel (Ger.) 7.10.44	BRUTALITY	U.S.
SCHLOSSER, Karl	254444	M			Uschfhr., C.C. Harzungen, Nordhausen (Ger.)	MURDER	U.S.
SCHLOSSER, Rainer	258938	M	Ger.	89	Dr., Ministerialdirektor, Reichsministerium of Propaganda, Reichsdramaturg. Reichstheater-Kammer, H.J. Gebietsfhr.	INTERR.	U.S.
SCHLOSSIG	173145	M	Ger.		C.C. Schirmeck-Saales (Fr.) Herbst 44	TORTURE	U.K.
SCHLOSTER, Werner	301817	M	Ger.		SS-Mann, 1. SS-Pz.Div.Leibstandarte "Adolf Hitler", Stavelot Region of Stavelot (Bel.) 19-20.12.44	MURDER	BEL.
SCHLOTT	306805	M	Ger.		SS-Schfhr., Abt. IV Gestapo Vichy (Fr.) 10.43-9.44	MURDER	FR.
SCHLOTT, Jakob	254448	M			SS-Sturmann, C.C. Harzungen, Nordhausen (Ger.)	MURDER	U.S.
SCHLOTTE	155977	M	Ger.		Regierungsrat, Police, NSDAP, Jauer near Glogau (Ger.) 42-45	TORTURE	U.S.
SCHLOTTERER, Gustav	260871	M	Ger.	1. 3.04	Ministerialdirigent, Dr.,R.W.M.	MISC.CRIMES	U.S.
SCHLOTTLER	166670	M	Ger.		Dr., Civilian, Reichelsheim (Ger.) 18.3.45	MURDER	U.S.
SCHLUCKEBIER	124447	M	Ger.		Major, Paratrooper Regt. z.b.V., Ardennes (Fr.) 12.44	MISC.CRIMES	U.S.
SCHLUCKEBIER	142291	M	Ger.		Lt. Colonel, Tank-Corps, Gravenwoehr (Ger.) 2.11.-1.12.44	MISC.CRIMES	U.S.
SCHLUENTZEN or SCHLUENZEL,Heinrich	254435	M	Ger.	11	SS-Hauptsturmfhr., SD Police, Fiume (Yugo.) 44-45	TORTURE	YUGO.
SCHLUETER	254217	M		19.10.13	Cpl., C.C. Ellrich, Nordhausen (Ger.)	MURDER	U.S.
SCHLUETTER, Ernst Friedrich August	300928	M	Ger.	14. 7.94	Employee, railway, Bochum (Ger.) 24.3.45	MISC.CRIMES	U.K.
SCHLUFTER, August	143251	M	Ger.		Civilian Miner	TORTURE	U.S.
SCHLUMPRECHT	62326	M	Ger.		Dr., Reichs-Official, High Economic Official, (Bel.)	MISC.CRIMES	U.N.W.C.C.
SCHLUMS, Friedrich	180894	M			Hauptsturmfhr., SS Chief of Staff to Stropp,(Rhein Westmark Ger.) 43-45	TORTURE	U.S.
SCHLUNDERMANN	194226	M			Unterscharfhr., SS, C.C. Flossenburg (Ger.)	TORTURE	U.S.
SCHLUPER	301984	M	Ger.		Oscharfhr., SS,C.C. Auschwitz (Pol.) 44	BRUTALITY	POL.
SCHLUPPER	139225	M			Obersturmfhr., SS, Sicherheitskdo. C.C. Tiraspol, Thekina (Sov.Un., Rum.) 41	MURDER	U.S.
SCHLUSSER	253405	M	Ger.		Lt., Chateau de la Riviere Bourdet Quevillon (Fr.) 12.40-1.41	PILLAGE	FR.
SCHLUSSMACHER	189414	M			SS-Oberscharfhr., SS, C.C. Falstad (Nor.) 43	TORTURE	NOR.
SCHLUT see SCHLUTT, Hans	173528						
SCHLUTER or SCHULLER	174580	M	Ger.		Lt. 16. Inf. Div. Unit No. 230059 Maille St. Maure (Fr.) 25.8.44	MURDER	FR.
SCHLUTER, Georg	262931	M			7. Pz.Reconnaissance Co Sillersdorf (Ger.) L.o.D.N.A.o.D.16.4.45	WITNESS	U.S.
SCHLUTER, Willy or SCHULLER	155978	M	Ger.	07	Lt., SS, Chief of the Kreis-Kommandantur Gestapo, 16. Inf. Div. NSDAP, Maille (Fr.) 44	MURDER	FR.
SCHLUTER, Wilhelm	169047	M	Ger.	13. 6.18	Oschfhr., W.-SS, C.C. Natzweiler (Fr.) 42-44	MURDER	FR.
SCHLUTT, Hans or SCHLUT or SCHULTZ	173528	M	Ger.		SS-Osturmfhr., Gestapo, Jasjka (Yugo.) 7.43	MURDER	YUGO.
SCHLUTTER	173146	M	Ger.		C.C. Natzweiler (Fr.) Herbst 44	INTERR.	U.K.
SCHLUTTER, Hans	253802	M	Ger.		Pvt., C.C. Buchenwald (Ger.)	INTERR.	FR.
SCHLUTZEN	251781	M	Ger.		Lt., W.O., 4. Paratrooper Regt., Div. "Hermann Goering" Helchteren (Bel.) 5.and 11.9.45	TORTURE	BEL.
SCHLUZ-NOVER	126516	M			Orpo Feldgend. Vendome (Fr.) 10.8.44	MURDER	U.S.
SCHMACH	155979	M			SS-Sturmfhr., (Lt.) SA, C.C. Emsland (Ger.) 44	MURDER	U.S.
SCHMACKE	194258	M	Ger.		Capt., Sicherungs-Regt., 198, Echassieres (Fr.) 10.9.44	MURDER	FR.
SCHMAHL	254218	M			Pvt., C.C. Nordhausen Ellrich (Ger.)	MURDER	U.S.
SCHMALE, Heinz	137488	M	Ger.	22	SS-Rottenfhr., SS, C.C. Buchenwald (Ger.)	TORTURE	U.S.
SCHMALENBACH, Kurt	188468	M	Ger.		Dr., Civilian, GC. (Czech.) 40-45	MURDER	CZECH.
SCHMALZ	134904	M	Ger.	20	Cpl., W.-SS, St. With (Bel.) 1.45	MURDER	U.S.
SCHMALZ, Kurt	809	M			Stellv. Gauleiter Gau Wartheland Fhr. d. H.J., (Pol.) 9.39-1.42	MURDER	POL.
SCHMALZ, Otto	188507	M	Ger.		Member, Crim.Secretary, Gestapo, Luxembourg (Lux.)	MISC.CRIMES	LUX.
SCHMALZ, Wilhelm	253181	M	Ger.	01	Major-General-Commander,Air Force, "Hermann Goering" (It.)44	WITNESS	U.K.
SCHMANSER, Ernst see SCHMAUSER, Heinrich	173551						
SCHMATZ	133242	M			Oberscharfhr., C.C. Flossenburg (Ger.)	MURDER	U.S.
SCHMAUSER	136372	M	Ger.	92	SS-Obergruppenfhr., SS (Ger.) 1.45	TORTURE	U.S.
SCHMAUSER	254440	M	Ger.		Sgt., Kragujevac (Yugo.) 21.10.41	MURDER	YUGO.
SCHMAUSER,Ernest Heinrich or SCHMANSER	173551	M	Ger.		SS-Obergruppenfhr., Polizeifhr., SS, Polizei, Auschwitz,Breslau (Ger.,Pol.) 39-45	MURDER	U.K.,BEL.CZECH.
SCHMAUTZER	131713	M	Ger.		General, Senate President, Supreme Military Court, Berlin(Ger.)	MURDER	U.K.,FR.
SCHMEDE, Joseph	259169	M			Oscharfhr., Gestapo, Limoges (Fr.)	MISC.CRIMES	FR.
SCHMEER, Rudolf	62327	M	Ger.		SA Gruppenfhr., Ministerial Direktor, Reichswirtschaftsministerium	TORTURE	U.N.W.C.C.
SCHMEIDER	12458	M			Sgt., SS Div. "Der Fuehrer", Oradour (Fr.) 10.6.44	MURDER	FR.
SCHMEISSER, Karl	136577	M	Ger.	16	SS Junker, SSLeader-school for Economical administration Arolsen Berlin (Ger.) 41	MURDER	U.S.
SCHMEISSNER, Heinz	306568	M			Oberbaurat later Stadtrat, Nuernberg, Cracow (Pol.) 10.40	PILLAGE	POL.
SCHMELCHER, Willi	62328	M			SS-Brigadefhr., Lt.General, Chief of Technic. Police Emergency Corps	TORTURE	U.N.W.C.C.
SCHMELING	167354	M			Capt., Army, Ruines (Fr.) 10.6.44	MURDER	FR.
SCHMELING, Max	126505	M			SS-Untersturmfhr., SS, C.C. Weimar-Buchenwald (Ger.)	MURDER	U.S.
SCHMELL	193171	M	Ger.	05	Inspector, O.T. Kgf.Arb.Bn.186,Trondenes,Harsted (Nor.)	MISC.CRIMES	NOR.
SCHMELL, Philipp	142001	M	Ger.	20	SS-Rottenfhr., SS, M 1 Mettenheim, Ampfing Waldlager 5-6 (Ger.)44-45	MURDER	U.S.
SCHMELL, Wilhelm	21492	M	Ger.		Capt., Army medical Corps, Heppenheim (Ger.) 9.44-5.45	TORTURE	U.S.
SCHMELLER	253986	M	Ger.		SS, C.C. Ravensbruck (Ger.)	INTERR.	FR.
SCHMELLING	306655	M			Capt., Ruines (Cantal) 10.6.44	MURDER	FR.
SCHMELLUNG	152143	M			Sgt., Army, C.C. Blechhammer (Ger.)	MURDER	U.K.
SCHMELT	162796	M			Arbeitskdo. C.C. Parzymiechi (Pol.) 41-44	TORTURE	U.S.
SCHMELZ, Henrich	254219	M			Flyer, C.C. Nordhausen, Ellrich (Ger.)	MURDER	U.S.
SCHMELZER, Kurt	72003	M	Ger.		Cpl., 502 Army Flak Bde., Darmstadt (Ger.) 5..6.44	MURDER	U.S.

SCHM-SCHM

NAME	C.R.FILE NUMBER	SEX	NATIO-NALITY	DATE OF BIRTH	RANK OCCUPATION UNIT PLACE AND DATE OF CRIME	REASON WANTED	WANTED BY
SCHMELZER, Louis	260486	M	Ger.	23. 4.08	Rottfhr., Waffen-SS, Guard-Coy., C.C.Monowitz,Auschwitz (Pol.)44-1.45	BRUTALITY	POL.
SCHMELZER, Rudolf	72045	M			Oschfhr., SS-Div1Nord, San.Abt., C.C., Dachau, Danzig (Ger.)	TORTURE	U.S.
SCHMELZLE, Otto	149877	M	Ger.	85	Oschfhr., Waffen-SS, Schleissheim (Ger.) 6.-9.44	MURDER	U.S.
SCHMERBITZ	137489	M			Schfhr., SS, C.C. Buchenwald (Ger.)	TORTURE	U.S.
SCHMERK	194399	M	Ger.		Sgt., SS, C.C., Dachau (Ger.)	MISC.CRIMES	FR.
SCHMERZ, Otto	1211	M	Ger.		Supervisor, Public-Official, C.C., Alsdorf (Ger.)	WITNESS	U.S.
SCHMETZ	253387	M	Ger.		Capt., Airforce Toulouse, Villars (Fr.) 29.8.44	INTERR.	FR.
SCHMETZER	139694	M	Ger.		Lt.Col., Stalag XB, C.C., Sandbostel (Ger.) 1.-5.45	TORTURE	U.S.
SCHMEYER, Alfred	174288	M	Ger.		Pvt., Panz.Gren.Rgt.125,(Serbia-Yugo.) 9.-12.41	MURDER	YUGO.
SCHMICH, Hans (or SCHMICHE)	193172	M	Ger.	18. 2.02	Sgt.-Guard, Reichsjustiz-Ministerium,Feldstraflager,Finmark (Nor.) 45	MISC.CRIMES	NOR.
SCHMID (see SCHMITT)	138021						
SCHMID	138022	M		00	Lt., Army prison guard at Limburg Prison, Wurgess (Bel.) 44-45	MISC.CRIMES	U.S.
SCHMID (see SCHMIDT)	152148						
SCHMID	167327	M	Ger.		Rottfhr., SS attached to C.C., Struthof-Natzweiler (Fr.) 42-44	MURDER	FR.
SCHMID	188805	M			Oschfhr., SD, Lyon (Fr.) 40-45	MURDER	FR.
SCHMID	189151	M			Chief of Gen.Staff, Army Oberkmdo., Paris (Fr.) 41	MURDER	FR.
SCHMID	194403	M	Ger.		Kapo, C.C., Mauthausen (Aust.)	MURDER	FR.
SCHMID	252702	M		13	Lt., Army (concerned with Allied P.W.'s) (It.)	INTERR.	U.K.
SCHMID	252746	M			Employee, Sipo Abt. I R., Brussels (Bel.)	INTERR.	BEL.
SCHMID	253508	M			N.C.O., SS, C.C., Mauthausen (Aust.)	BRUTALITY	FR.
SCHMID	254014	M			Oschfhr., 84.Rgt. Landsturm, Rhenen (Neth.) 20.-30.3.45	INTERR.	NETH.
SCHMID	257418	M			SS-Guard, SS-Slave Labour Camp, Beisfjord nr.Narvik (Nor.) 6.-11.42	BRUTALITY	YUGO.
SCHMID (see SCHMIDT)	300907						
SCHMID	306806	M	Ger.		Member of St.Quentin Gestapo, Vraignes en Vermandois Somme (Fr.)29.8.44	MURDER	FR.
SCHMID	306924	M	Ger.		Gaupropagandaleiter, NSDAP, 44	BRUTALITY	FR.
SCHMID, A.	300863	M	Ger.		Pvt., 1.Aufkl.Abt.,3.Coy.,2.Column, XV.Div. of the Africa-Corps, Saint Leger (Arlon) (Bel.) 5.9.44	MISC.CRIMES	BEL.
SCHMID, Armand	12346	M	Ger.		Sgt., Waffen-SS, Armentieres (Fr.) 12.8.44	RAPE	FR.
SCHMID, Franz	21494	M		97	Pvt., 2.Btty. Mar.Flak-Abt.819, Walcheren (Neth.) 10.44	WITNESS	U.S.
SCHMID, Franz	193768	M	Ger.		Employee, Driver, Gestapo, Brno (Czech.) 39-45	TORTURE	CZECH.
SCHMID, Georg	259021	M		30. 4.94	Gaustellenleiter, Kreisobmann, DAF, Muehldorf Area (Ger.)	MURDER	U.S.
SCHMID, Johann	251776	M	Ger.		Camp-leader, C.C., Kumpfmuhl (Ger.)	TORTURE	FR.
SCHMID, Kaspar	254220	M			Pvt., C.C. Ellrich, Nordhausen (Ger.)	MURDER	U.S.
SCHMID, Martin	256258	M		1.11.04	Rottfhr., SS, C.C.Harzungen, Nordhausen (Ger.)	MURDER	U.S.
SCHMID, Otto	256257	M			Pvt., C.C. Ellrich, Nordhausen (Ger.)	MURDER	U.S.
SCHMID, Paul	138023	M			Chief,Werkschutz Plant, Police at Factory, Mannheim (Ger.) 45	MURDER	U.S.
SCHMIDBERGER	142056	M	Ger.	90	Sturmschfhr., SS, Waldlager V and VI, C.C.Muehldorf nr.Ampfing (Ger.) 44-45	TORTURE	U.S.
SCHMIDBERGER	149878	M	Ger.		Sturmfhr., SS, Poing (Ger.)	MURDER	U.S.
SCHMIDBORN, Theo	143246	M	Ger.		Civilian, C.C., Hannover (Stahlwerk) (Ger.) 42-45	MURDER	U.S.
SCHMIDEL, Fritz	188467	M			SS-Officer, C.C., Berlin (Ger.) 40-45	MURDER	CZECH.
SCHMIDGEN, Otto	134922	M	Ger.	95	Civilian, C.C.Hartheim (Aust.) 40-44	MURDER	U.S.
SCHMIDHAMMER, Josefa	305693	F	Ger.		Civilian, Amstetten, 20.3.45	TORTURE	U.S.
SCHMIDL, Ludwig	187777	M	Ger.		Employee, Arb.Kdo., C.C., Regensburg (Ger.) 41-45	TORTURE	U.S.
SCHMIDT	811	M	Ger.		W.O., Army, Porto Farina (It.) 12.42-4.43	MURDER	FR.
SCHMIDT	814	M	Ger.		Osturmbannfhr., Waffen-SS, Breendonck (Bel.) 40-41	MURDER	BEL.
SCHMIDT (see SCHMITT)	816						
SCHMIDT (or SCHMITT)	1212	M	Ger.		W.O., Army,	MISC.CRIMES	U.S.
SCHMIDT	9613	M	Ger.		Osturmbannfhr., SS, SS-Cmdt., C.C., Breendonck (Bel.) 40-44	TORTURE	BEL.
SCHMIDT	10343	M	Ger.		Uschfhr., SS, C.C., Buchenwald (Ger.) 40-45	TORTURE	POL.,CZECH.
SCHMIDT	12347	M	Ger.		Pvt., 110.or 111.Panz.Gren.Rgt., Gourdon (Fr.) 29.6.44	MURDER	FR.
SCHMIDT	12457	M	Ger.		Major, Schnelle Abt.608, Bussac, Charroux, Le Vigeant (Fr.) 8.5.44	MURDER	FR.
SCHMIDT	12460	M	Ger.		Oschfhr., SS, Employed Gestapo H.Q., Bergen (Nor.) 41	TORTURE	NOR.
SCHMIDT	21498	M		91	Major, Airforce, Fliegerhorst-Coy.Rheine, 44,45	MURDER	U.K.
SCHMIDT	26697	M	Ger.		Oschfhr., SS, C.C., Struthof (Fr.) 44	MISC.CRIMES	FR.
SCHMIDT	31445	M	Ger.		SD, Theresienstadt (Pol.)	MURDER	U.S.
SCHMIDT	31446	M	Ger.		Guard, SS (Gestapo), Koeln (Ger.) 1.45 and 2.45	MURDER	U.S.
SCHMIDT	31552	M	Ger.		Capt., Army, 89.Div.,1055.Rgt.	MISC.CRIMES	U.S.
SCHMIDT	31553	M	Ger.		Capt., Army, Works-Officer, Stalag-Luft 4, March from Gr.Tychols to Fallingbostel (Ger.) 2.45-3.45	TORTURE	U.K.
SCHMIDT	31554	M			Hptwachtmstr., Police, Tulle (Fr.) 9.6.44	MURDER	FR.
SCHMIDT	36694	M	Ger.		Sgt., Camp-Officer No.I, Army, Stalag 183, Saloniki (Gre.) 6.41-8.41	MURDER	U.K.
SCHMIDT	67033	M	Ger.		Sgt., C.C., Marburg, Heydekrug, Swinemuende (Ger.) 42-44	MURDER	U.K.
SCHMIDT	100432	M	Ger.		Capt., Camp 22 A. Lager work Kdo., Brux-Sudeten (Czech.)	MURDER	U.K.
SCHMIDT	119996	M	Ger.		Uschfhr., SS, C.C., Oswiecim (Pol.) 6.40-1.45	MURDER	POL.
SCHMIDT	121827	M	Ger.		SS-W.O., SS-Kmdo. CC-Kdo. Laura. nr. Sassfeld (Ger.)	MURDER	FR.
SCHMIDT	121829	M		05?	Hptschfhr., SS, C.C., Buchenwald (Ger.) 40-45	TORTURE	FR.
SCHMIDT	121830	M	Ger.		Capt., Army, C.C., Heydebreck (Ger.) 42	MURDER	U.K.
SCHMIDT	123956	M			Sgt., Army, C.C. 1.41	TORTURE	U.K.
SCHMIDT	124143	M		22	Officer, Stalag 4 A, C.C., Hainsburg (Ger.) 18.12.43	MURDER	U.K.
SCHMIDT	124446	M	Ger.		Lt.Col., Oflag IV C, Colditz (Ger.)	MISC.CRIMES	U.K.
SCHMIDT	124448	M			Pvt., 375.Bn. Rheinland, Groy-Zeidel (Ger.)	TORTURE	U.K.
SCHMIDT	124659	M	Ger.		Sgt., Guard, C.C., Nirwa, Regensburg (Pol.), (Ger.) 19.1.45-24.3.45	MURDER	U.K.
SCHMIDT	126278	M	Ger.		Col., C.C., Buch nr.Berlin (Ger.) 5.44	MURDER	U.S.
SCHMIDT	126280	M	Ger.	00 - 09	Osturmbannfhr., SS, C.C.Weimar, Buchenwald (Ger.)	MURDER	U.S.
SCHMIDT	126281	M	Ger.		Guard, Camp at St.Ludwigs Monasterx, Roermond (Neth.)	MURDER	U.S.
SCHMIDT	126722	M	Ger.		Schfhr., SS, Officer, SD Gestapo, Paris (Fr.) 12.40	TORTURE	FR.
SCHMIDT (or HAM HANDS)	129891	M	Ger.		Sgt., Airforce, Stalag Luft 4,Kiefheide (Ger.) 18.7.45	TORTURE	U.S.
SCHMIDT	130055	M	Ger.		N.C.O, Stalag XXI D, Posen (Pol.) 1.41	TORTURE	U.K.
SCHMIDT	131998	M		87	Capt., Army, C.C. Outer Camp, Thueringen (Ger.)	BRUTALITY	U.S.
SCHMIDT	132195	M	Ger.		Cpl., Army,18.Panz.Gren.Div.,293.Rgt.,13.Coy., Malmedy (Bel.) 5.44	MURDER	U.S.
SCHMIDT	132557	M	Ger.		Oberwachtmeister, Orpo, Hoym (Ger.) 8.4.45	MURDER	FR.
SCHMIDT	135559	M	Ger.		Capt., Stalag IX C, Mellingen (Ger.) 2.45-3.45	MISC.CRIMES	U.K.,U.S.
SCHMIDT, Captaine (see RETSCHKK)	136282						

SCHM-SCHM

NAME	C.R.FILE NUMBER	SEX	NATIO-NALITY	DATE OF BIRTH	RANK	OCCUPATION	UNIT	PLACE AND DATE OF CRIME	REASON WANTED	WANTED BY
SCHMIDT or SCHMITT	136379	M	Ger.			Gendarmerie chief, Koenigshofen (Ger.) 44			MURDER	U.S.
SCHMIDT	139751	M	Ger.			Guard, Waffen SS, C.C. Dora-Nordhausen (Ger.) 2.3.44			MURDER	U.S.
SCHMIDT	140912	M		05	Pvt., Army, C.C. Breendonck (Bel.)				TORTURE	BEL.
SCHMIDT	141381	M			SS Odofhr., C.C. Steyr (Aust.)				TORTURE	FR.
SCHMIDT	141612	M			Policeman, Fieldpolice, Military-police, Mayence Kastel (Ger.)				TORTURE	FR.
SCHMIDT	142289	M	Ger.		Kapo, C.C. Schandelah (Ger.) 44-45				TORTURE	BEL.
SCHMIDT	142290	M	Ger.		SA Otruppfhr., Viernheim (Ger.) 8.43				TORTURE	U.S.
SCHMIDT	143249	M			Wachtmeister, City official, Frankfurt-M. (Ger.) 43-44				TORTURE	U.S.
SCHMIDT	143250	M			SS Osturmfhr., SD Abschnitt Weimar, Muelhausen (Ger.) 2.45				WITNESS	U.S.
SCHMIDT	148420	M			Lt., 11.Panz.Div., South-west Fr. 44				MURDER	FR.
SCHMIDT	149852	M	Ger.	00	Osturmfhr., SA, Bodenteich (Ger.)				MURDER	U.N.W.C.C.
SCHMIDT	152148	M	Ger.		Cpl., Gestapo, Bretagne, Anjou, Poitou (Fr.)				MURDER	FR.
SCHMIDT	155980	M			Shoe store proprietor, Civ., C.C. Gardelegen (Ger.) 4.45				WITNESS	U.S.
SCHMIDT	155981	M	Ger.	95	Capt., Volkssturm, Camp B.A.B. 20, Heydebreck (Ger.) 8.42				MURDER	U.K.
SCHMIDT	155982	M			Pvt., 301.Gren.Rgt., Lichtfelde (Ger.) 8.42				TORTURE	U.K.
SCHMIDT	155983	M			Lt., Gestapo, Morlaix-Brest (Fr.) 44				MURDER	FR.
SCHMIDT	158592	M	Ger.	about 93	Capt., 379. Landesschuetzen-Bn., Brux (Czech.) 5.44-8.45				TORTURE	U.K.
SCHMIDT	158695	M		92	Major, Army, Dueren, North-west of Zuelich (Ger.) 8.44				TORTURE	U.K.
SCHMIDT	162577	M	Ger.		Cpl., Army, C.C. Stalag IX B Bad Orb (Ger.) 44				MURDER	U.S.
SCHMIDT	165233	M	Ger.		Gen. C.O. 2.Panz.Army, Sov.Un. 42				MURDER	U.S.
SCHMIDT	165697	M			Cmdt., Schnelle Abt. 608 of Poitiers, Charroux le Vigeant (Fr.) 8.44				MISC.CRIMES	FR.
SCHMIDT	167952	M	Ger.		Lt., 14.Rgt.Parachutist, SS Div."Adolf Hitler", Villey, St.Etienne (Fr.) 4.9.44				MURDER	FR.
SCHMIDT	173054	M		83	Major, 71.Pion.Bau-Bn., Chartres, Dueren, Obermaubach (Fr.,Ger.) 7.-11.44				TORTURE	U.K.
SCHMIDT	173213	M	Ger.	00	Sgt., 397.Landesschuetzen-Bn. C.C. Stalag XX B Marienburg (Ger.) 41				TORTURE	U.K.
SCHMIDT	173504	M			Dr., Major, C.C. Oswiecim-Birkenau (Pol.) 39-45				MURDER	CZECH.
SCHMIDT	173527	M	Ger.		Officer, occup. territories, Jasko (Yugo.) 7.43				MURDER	YUGO.
SCHMIDT	173544	M	Ger.		SS Scharfhr., Lagerfuehrer Waffen SS, C.C. Thekla (Ger.) 18.4.45				MURDER	FR.
SCHMIDT	174767	M			Pvt., Kfg.Arb.Bn. 209, C.C. Aspfjord (Nor.)				TORTURE	NOR.
SCHMIDT	176930	M			Capt., Bn.of Georgian, Brive la Gaillarde (Fr.)				MISC.CRIMES	FR.
SCHMIDT	179195	M		90	Lord-mayor, SS public official, Gotha (Ger.) 45				MISC.CRIMES	FR.
SCHMIDT	179799	M		16	Oscharfhr., SS Totenkopfverband C.C. Gusen (Aust.) 25.7.-8.44				MURDER	U.S.
SCHMIDT	181202	M	Ger.		Guard, C.C. Ravensbruck (Ger.)				TORTURE	FR.
SCHMIDT	181203	M	Ger.		SS Rottfhr., C.C. Mauthausen (Aust.)				TORTURE	FR.
SCHMIDT	186211	M	Ger.		Nurse, C.C. Dachau (Ger.)				MURDER	FR.
SCHMIDT	186213	M	Ger.		Lt., Army, Hennebont (Fr.) 6.8.44				PILLAGE	FR.
SCHMIDT	186709	M	Ger.	90	Col., Oflag IX A, Ger. 10.44				TORTURE	U.K.
SCHMIDT	187784	M	Ger.		Agent, Gestapo, C.C. Neckarelz (Ger.)				TORTURE	U.S.
SCHMIDT	188230	M	Ger.		Cmdt., Camp official, C.C. Krefeld (Ger.)				TORTURE	BEL.
SCHMIDT	188984	M		16	SS Scharfhr., C.C. Buchenwald (Ger.) 41-4.45				MURDER	U.S.BEL. CZECH.
SCHMIDT or KRUEGER	188999	M	Ger.		Major, Luftgau 3 Airforce, Berlin (Ger.) 8.44				MURDER	U.K.
SCHMIDT	189150	M			SS Scharfhr., C.C. Drancy (Fr.)				MURDER	FR.
SCHMIDT	189495	M	Ger.		SS Oscharfhr., C.C. Struthof-Natzweiler (Fr.) 42-44				MURDER	FR.
SCHMIDT	189626	M	Ger.	00	Dr., Gen.Major, Kriegslaz., Krankenabt. prison-hospital,Berlin-Buch (Ger.)				TORTURE	U.K.
SCHMIDT	189790	M	Ger.	20	Pvt., Guard, Landesschuetzen-Bn. 393 Dresden, C.C. Stalag IV A Hainsberg (Ger.) 18.12.43				TORTURE	U.K.
SCHMIDT or SCHMITT	190274	M	Ger.		Lt., Camp official, C.C. Banjica (Yugo.)				MURDER	YUGO.
SCHMIDT	193392	M	Ger.		Capt., 240.Kgf.Arb.Bn. C.C. Moersry (Nor.) 44				MURDER	NOR.
SCHMIDT	194064	M			Sgt., Btty.-Fuehrer, SS, Charbonnieres (Fr.) 8.8.44				WITNESS	FR.
SCHMIDT	194378	M	Ger.	01	Major, Geheime Feldpolizei, Brussels (Bel.)				TORTURE	BEL.
SCHMIDT	194398	M	Ger.		Pvt. Feldgendarmerie, Ploermel (Fr.) 18.6.44				TORTURE	FR.
SCHMIDT	194400	M	Ger.		Sgt., SS police, 19.Rgt. 2.Coy., Dovaine (Fr.) 19.7.44				MURDER	FR.
SCHMIDT	196083	M	Ger.		Member Gestapo, St. Vid				MURDER	YUGO.
SCHMIDT	206476	M	Ger.		Officer, Arbeitskdo. SA, Deputy mine manager NSDAP, Erica Grube nr.Dresden (Ger.) 41-45				TORTURE	U.K.
SCHMIDT	251991	M	Ger.		SS Uscharfhr., C.C. Auschwitz-Birkenau (Pol.) 43				MURDER	YUGO.
SCHMIDT	252709	M			Capt., Bn.1210 or 1294, Georgines, Boulazag (Fr.) 11.6.44				INTERR.	FR.
SCHMIDT	252710	M			N.C.O., Legion Turkestan, Carmaux (Fr.) 18.7.44				INTERR.	FR.
SCHMIDT	252792	M			Lt., F.P. 01140 C, Fontvieille (Fr.) 25.8.44				MISC.CRIMES	FR.
SCHMIDT	252742	M			SS Oscharfhr., SD, Toulouse (Fr.) 11.42				INTERR.	BEL.
SCHMIDT	252747	M			Employee SIPO Abt. IV E, Brussels (Bel.)				INTERR.	BEL.
SCHMIDT	253395	M	Ger.		Employee, SIPO Abt. III D, Brussels (Bel.) 40-44				INTERR.	BEL.
SCHMIDT	253408	M	Ger.	05	Pvt., 559.Inf.Bn., Karlstahl (Czech.) 11.41				TORTURE	U.K.
SCHMIDT	253803	M	Ger.	05	Lt., Army, Venelles (Fr.) 20.8.44				MURDER	FR.
SCHMIDT	253890	M	Ger.		Sonderfhr., Gestapo, Lille (Fr.) 40-44				INTERR.	FR.
SCHMIDT	254024	M	Ger.		Capt., Ortscmdt., Military, Bergen op.Zoom (Neth.) 25.10.44				INTERR.	NETH.
SCHMIDT	254027	M	Ger.		SS Uscharfhr., Gestapo, Paris (Fr.) 41-44				TORTURE	FR.
SCHMIDT see KOUPTIS	254835									
SCHMIDT	255933	M	Ger.		Major, Fieldpolice, Trupp Motor 687, Vienne (Fr.) 14.4.44 Neckargerach (Ger.)				TORTURE MURDER	FR. FR.
SCHMIDT	255934	M	Ger.	19. 3.04	Lt. C.C. Mauthausen (Aust.) 8.44				MURDER	U.S.
SCHMIDT	255940	M			Dr., SS Hptsturmfhr., C.C. Nordhausen (Ger.)				MURDER	U.S.
SCHMIDT	256253	M			Cpl., 2.Coy.,Sturm-Bn. I A.O.K., Courcelles sur Neid (Fr.) 15.11.44				MURDER	U.S.
SCHMIDT	256386	M	Ger.		SS Mann, C.C. Nordhausen (Ger.)				MURDER	U.S.
SCHMIDT	256847	M	Ger.							BEL.
SCHMIDT (Mrs.)	257243	F	Ger.	15	Typist, SD and SIPO at Antwerpen Abt. IV D I, SD and SIPO, Anvers (Bel.) 40-44				SUSPECT	BEL.
SCHMIDT	257670	M			Crim.Rat, Ingersheim (Fr.) 9.1.44				MISC.CRIMES	FR.
SCHMIDT or SCHMIDT-HUBER	257867	M			Lt. Panz.Bds.150, Meuse-Bridge Antwerp (Bel.) 12.44				MISC.CRIMES	U.S.

SCHM-SCHM

NAME	C.R.FILE NUMBER	SEX	NATIO-NALITY	DATE OF BIRTH	RANK · OCCUPATION UNIT PLACE AND DATE OF CRIME	REASON WANTED	WANTED BY
SCHMIDT	257889	M			Lt.,Pz.-Bde.,Meuse Bridge-Antwerp(Bel.) 12.44	MISC.CRIMES	U.S.
SCHMIDT	259020	M		06	SS-Scharfhr.,SS,Muhldorf Area(Ger.) 01 - 06	MURDER	U.S.
SCHMIDT	259736	M	Ger.		Lt.,Gend.of Compiegne,Crisolles-Oise(Fr.) 23.-24.6.44	MURDER	FR.
SCHMIDT	259831	M	Ger.		Capt.,Army,Orts-Cmdt.,Dinteloord-Noord Brabant(Neth.) 10.44	BRUTALITY	NETH.
SCHMIDT	261838	M	Ger.		Sgt.,Gend.,Romilly sur Seine(Fr.) 10.5.44	MISC.CRIMES	FR.
SCHMIDT	261895	M	Ger.		SS Pz.Gr.Mantau,Gembloux(Bel.) 4.9.44	MURDER	BEL.
SCHMIDT	300115	M	Ger.		Member of Kriminalpolizei,Kriminalpol.of Strasbourg, Ingersheim-Haut Rhin(Fr.) 9.1.44	TORTURE	FR.
SCHMIDT	300383	M	Ger.		SD-Mann,Gestapo in Toulouse, Hte-Garonne,Cers & Tarn,South-West France, especially Toulouse(Fr.) 11.42-19.8.44	MURDER	FR.
SCHMIDT see SCHMID	300907	M	Ger.				
SCHMIDT	300929	M	Ger.	05	Pvt.,Guard,559 Inf.Bn.,AK.E 122,Karlstahl(Czech.) 11.41	MISC.CRIMES	U.K.
SCHMIDT	300950	M	Ger.		Sgt.,"The Oak Leaf" Div.Susak,Lic,Delnice,Fuzine(Yugo.) 43 & 44	MURDER	YUGO.
SCHMIDT	301029	M	Ger.		Rottfhr.,C.C.Struthof-Natzweiler(Fr.) 42-44	MURDER	FR.
SCHMIDT	301282	M	Ger.		Employee,Registratur und Personalkartei I.R.,SD,Bruessel(Bel.)6.40-9.44	MURDER	BEL.
SCHMIDT	301283	M	Ger.		Geschz.Angestellter,Abt.IIIB,SD,Bruessel(Bel.) 6.40-9.44	MURDER	BEL.
SCHMIDT	301284	M	Ger.		Geschz.Angestellter,Abt.IVE,SD,Bruessel(Bel.).6.40-9.44	MURDER	BEL.
SCHMIDT	301446	M	Ger.		Hptscharfhr.,SS-Staff-Sgt.,SS,Standesamt(Registry Office Marriages), C.C.Dachau(Ger.) 43	MURDER	BEL.
SCHMIDT	301447	M			Rottfhr.,SS,Totenkopf-Stand."Oberbayern",C.C.Dachau(Ger.) 43	MURDER	BEL.
SCHMIDT	301448	M			SS,Dora-Nordhausen(Ger.) 40-45	MURDER	BEL.
SCHMIDT	301646	M			Hilfsverwalter,Erbach nr.Amberg(Ger.) -45	MURDER	CZECH.
SCHMIDT	302138	M			Major,Kalamai(Grc.) 2.44	MURDER	GRC.
SCHMIDT	305262	M			Member Stab,C.C.Neskarelz and Neckargerach(Ger.) 42-45	MURDER	FR.
SCHMIDT	305739	M			SS-Uschfhr.,Geheime Feldpolizei,Hotel Bratford,Paris,Member of Sonder-Kdo.IV-A-2,rue des Saussaies,Paris(Fr.) 41-44	TORTURE	FR.
SCHMIDT	305791	M			Hptscharfhr.,SS,Pers.W.O. to Cmdt.of Sec.Police(Bd.S.) Gestapo, Dr., Paris,Noailles-Oise(Fr.) 9.8.44	MURDER	U.K.
SCHMIDT	305871	M	Ger.		Hptsturmfhr.,Pz.-Gren.,Gembloux(Bel.) 4.9.44	MURDER	BEL.
SCHMIDT	306663	M	Ger.		SS-W.O.,SS-Gestapo Saarbruecken, Folking-Mosel(Ger.) 11.44	MURDER	FR.
SCHMIDT or SMID	306288	M			Member,Gestapo at Trencin,Oswiecim-Birkenau(Pol.) 39-45	MURDER	CZECH.
SCHMIDT	306875	M			Capt.,1 Coy. of 223 Inf.Regt.,Yves-Char.Inf(Fr.) 20.9.44	INCENDIARIEM	FR.
SCHMIE, Adolf	193173	M			Sgt.,Schupo,Member SD,Drontheim(Nor.) 41-45	MURDER	NOR.
SCHMID, Albert	148812	M		27	Civilian,Berg Oberbach(Ger.) 15.3.45	WITNESS	U.S.
SCHMID, Albert	253989	M			Foreman,C.C.Neuengamme,Wilhelmshaven(Ger.)	MURDER	FR.
SCHMID, Albert	253894	M	Ger.		Krim.-Kommissar,Gestapo,Luxemburg(Lux.)	INTERR.	LUX.
SCHMID, Alfred	142064	M	Ger.		Uschfhr.,Waffen-SS Totenkopf-Sturmbann,C.C.Buchenwald(Ger.)	TORTURE	U.S.
SCHMIDT, Alfred	158565	M			Volkssturm-Bn.,1 Coy.,Gardelegen(Ger.) 10.-14.4.45	MURDER	U.S.
SCHMIDT, Alphons or SCHMITT	174568	M	Ger.		Pvt.,Army,Mailley Le Camp(Fr.) 23.4.44	MURDER	U.S.
SCHMIDT, Arthur	188509	M		12. 4.15	Member Gestapo,Luxemburg(Lux.)	MISC.CRIMES	LUX.
SCHMIDT, Artur	255224	M			Oberwachtmeister,Schutzpolizei,Prag(Czech.) 41	MURDER	CZECH.
SCHMIDT, August	1229	M			C.C.Stassfurt(Ger.)	MURDER	U.S.
SCHMIDT, August	192852	M			Schupo,C.C.Falstad-Drontheim(Nor.) 6.8.42	MURDER	NOR.
SCHMIDT, August	194382	M			Chief of Org.Todt,Employee by Firm Otto Menzel,Bittburg, Alle-Sur-Semois(Bel.)	PILLAGE	BEL.
SCHMIDT, August see FORSTNER,A.	261970						
SCHMIDT, August	301219	M	Ger.		Member,Schoolmaster,NSDAP,evacuated Buchenfeld(Ger.) 17.3.45	MURDER	U.K.
SCHMIDT, Berthold	193771	M			Chief Prison Warden,Gestapo,Brno(Czech.) 39-45	MURDER	CZECH.
SCHMIDT, Bruno	255948	M			Crim.-Com.,Gestapo,Opava(Czech.) 39-45	MISC.CRIMES	CZECH.
SCHMIDT, Carl	302140	M			SS-Usturmfhr.,SD Dienststelle in the Villa"Windekin"76 Nieuwe Parklaan,The Hague(Neth.) 42-3.8.44	MURDER	FR.
SCHMIDT, Charles	194401	M	Ger.		Lt.,Interpreter,Gestapo de Parigueux,Chateau Leveque(Fr.) 20.6.34	MURDER	FR.
SCHMIDT, Ed.	167307	M			Lt.,Army,77 Bn.,4 Coy.,Foret(Bel.) 6.9.44	MURDER	BEL.
SCHMIDT, Edmond	152128	M		17	Lt.,2 Luftw.Regt.,Trondes,Bouca,Henil,La Tour(Fr.) 44	MURDER	FR.
SCHMIDT, Elisabeth nee SEFILDT	188506	F			Guard,C.C.Terezin(Czech.) 6.9.44	MURDER	CZECH.
SCHMIDT, Elmar	256254	M			Sgt., Camp Ellrich,Nordhausen(Ger.)	MURDER	U.S.
SCHMIDT, Emil	257934	M			Pvt.,150 Panz.Bde.,Meuse Bridge-Antwerp(Bel.) 12.44	MISC.CRIMES	U.S.
SCHMIDT, Erich	124858	M	Ger.		Guard,Landesschuetzen-Bn.398 Stalag IVF,Chemnitz(Ger.) 10.43-14.3.45	MURDER	U.K.
SCHMIDT, Erna	136971	F	Ger.		Civ.-Guard,C.C.Helmbrechts(Ger.)	WITNESS	U.S.
SCHMIDT, Ernst	301449	M			Scharfhr.,SS,C.C.Buchenwald(Ger.) 16.5.38-9.10.43	MURDER	BEL.
SCHMIDT, Ernst Adolf	251789	M	Ger.	99	Dr., State Service Ministry of Agriculture,Prag(Czech.) 6.42	MURDER	CZECH.
SCHMIDT, F.	167328	F			I Commissariat of Einsatzstab Rosenberg,Paris(Fr.) 40-44	PILLAGE	FR.
SCHMIDT, F.	300864	M			Pvt.,1 Aufkl.Abt.,3 Coy.,2 Column,XV Div.of the Africa Corps, Saint Leger(Arlon)(Bel.) 5.9.44	MISC.CRIMES	BEL.
SCHMIDT, Ferdinand	21493	M	Ger.		Civilian,Beltershain(Ger.) 1.12.44	MURDER	U.S.
SCHMIDT, Florian	162578	M		18	Oschfhr.,1 SS-Panz.Div.(LAH),Feldgend.-Coy.,Weissenbach(Aust.)12.4.45	MURDER	U.S.
SCHMIDT, Franz	188524	M	Ger.		Assessor,Richter,Occupied Territories Sondergericht Legal Off., Luxemburg(Lux.)	MURDER	LUX.
SCHMIDT, Frederick	62329	M	Ger.		Stabsleiter,Party Work Rosenberg	MISC.CRIMES	UNWCC.
SCHMIDT, Friedrich	256255	M		1. 4.03	Flyer,C.C.Ellrich,Nordhausen(Ger.)	MURDER	U.S.
SCHMIDT, Fritz	137490	M	Ger.	05	Inspektor,Geheime Feldpolizei Gruppe 713	MURDER	U.S.
SCHMIDT, Fritz	252719	M	Ger.		Ortsgruppenleiter NSDAP,concerned with civil labour,Loerrach(Ger.)	BRUTALITY	BEL.
SCHMIDT, Georg	129969	M			SS-Rottfhr.,Oberkapo,C.C.Mauthausen(Aust.) 41-45	MURDER	U.S.
SCHMIDT, Georg	188320	M	Ger.	17. 4.97	SA-Sturmfhr.,(Civ.dealer in pigs),Dachsbach(Ger.) 43-45	TORTURE	POL.
SCHMIDT, Georg	188505	M	Ger.		Civilian,Luxemburg(Lux.) 40-45	PILLAGE	LUX.
SCHMIDT, Georg	192524	M	Ger.	16. 7.03	Cpl.,Army,Schussbach(Ger.) 14.3.45	TORTURE	U.K.

NAME	C.R.FILE NUMBER	SEX	NATIO- NALITY	DATE OF BIRTH	RANK OCCUPATION UNIT PLACE AND DATE OF CRIME	REASON WANTED	WANTED BY
SCHMIDT, Georg	259896	M			Major, 2.Bn., 13.SS-Police-Rgt., Ferlach (Aust.) 44-45	MURDER	YUGO.
SCHMIDT, Georg	256251	M		1. 5.12	Sgt., Conc.Camp Ellrich, Nordhausen (Ger.)	MURDER	U.S.
SCHMIDT, Georg	301450	M	Ger.	11. 2.04	SS-Mann, C.C., Buchenwald (Ger.) 16.5.38-9.10.43	MURDER	BEL.
SCHMIDT, George	122923	M	Ger.		Civ., Teacher in village, Fuerth (Ger.)	MISC.CRIMES	U.S.
SCHMIDT, Gerhard	158597	M			Civilian, Wallrode (Ger.) 7.44	TORTURE	U.S.
SCHMIDT, Guenter	256742	M	Ger.		Osturmfhr., SS, Chief, Grenzkommissariate of SD,Foix (Fr.) 11.42-44	MURDER	FR.
SCHMIDT, Gustave	139220	M			Civilian, Aufhausen (Ger.) 7.7.44	WITNESS	U.S.
SCHMIDT, Hans	126279	M	Ger.		Officer, Gestapo, C.C. at Ludwig's Monastery, Roermond (Neth.)17.11.44	MURDER	U.S.
SCHMIDT, Hans	142054	M		10 - 20	Oschfhr., Waffen-SS Totenkopf-Stuba., C.C., Buchenwald (Ger.) 41-43	TORTURE	U.S.
SCHMIDT, Hans	165533	M		93	Hptschfhr., SS, C.C., Natzweiler (Fr.) 27.4.45	PILLAGE	BEL.
SCHMIDT, Hans	187350	M	Ger.		Manager, Civilian, Windischenbach (Ger.) 41	TORTURE	POL.
SCHMIDT, Hans	256256	M			SS-Mann, C.C. Ellrich, Nordhausen (Ger.)	MURDER	U.S.
SCHMIDT, Hans	259022	M			Schfhr., Organ.Todt, Muehldorf Area (Ger.)	MURDER	U.S.
SCHMIDT, Hartung	174284	M			Lt. Gen., Armeeoberkommando, Toulouse, Tarbes (Fr.)	MURDER	FR.
SCHMIDT, Heinrich	167314	M			Trustee, Cafe and Restaurant "Italia", Poznan (Pol.) 9.39-12.44	PILLAGE	POL.
SCHMIDT, Heinz	142053	M			Waffen-SS, Oschfhr., Totenkopfverband, C.C., Buchenwald (Ger.)	TORTURE	U.S.
SCHMIDT, Helmut	162580	M	Ger.	11	Oschfhr., SS, Section I, C.C., Buchenwald (Ger.) 44-45	WITNESS	U.S.
SCHMIDT, Helmut	167315	M	Ger.		Trustee, Civilian, Cafe "Metropol", Poznan (Pol.) 9.39-12.44	PILLAGE	POL.
SCHMIDT, Helmuth	261424	M	Ger.	15	Admin.Officer, Laterina (It.) 6.44	WITNESS	U.S.
SCHMIDT, Hermann	139698	M		98	SS-Mann, Waffen-SS, Prague (Czech.) 43	MURDER	U.S.
SCHMIDT, Hermann	252733	M	Ger.		Farmer, Kdo.662, Stalag IX C, Kulma ueber Schleiz (Ger.) 43	BRUTALITY	FR.
SCHMIDT, Hermann	256269	M			Rottfhr., SS, C.C.Dora, Nordhausen (Ger.)	MURDER	U.S.
SCHMIDT, Hugo	252699	M			Member, concerned with Civil Labour NSDAP, Loerrach (Ger.)	INTERR.	BEL.
SCHMIDT, Jakob	258404	M			Guard, SS, C.C., Ohrdruf (Ger.) 12.44-4.45	MURDER	U.S.
SCHMIDT, Johann	120571	M			Lagerfhr., C.C., Lsau (Ger.)	MURDER	U.S.
SCHMIDT, Johann	139702	M	Ger.	85	Schfhr., Waffen-SS, Waldlager V and VI, C.C., Muehldorf (Ger.) 44-45	TORTURE	U.S.
SCHMIDT, Johann	164718	M	Ger.	97	Housemaster in the Municipal Bldg., Civilian, Rothenbach a.d.Pegnitz (Ger.) 26.2.45	TORTURE	U.S.
SCHMIDT, Johann	167350	M	Ger.		Officer, 9.SS-Panz.Gren.Rgt.21, Senonches and La Saucelle (Fr.) 8.44	WITNESS	FR.
SCHMIDT, Johann	261154	M	Ger.	25. 1.13	Member, Stabsccy., SD, Brussels (Bel.) 43-44	SUSPECT	BEL.
SCHMIDT, Johanna	252705	F	Ger.		Secretary, Einsatz-Kmdo.z.b.V.6 Dr.Ernst, St.Die Saales (Fr.) 44	MURDER	U.K.
SCHMIDT, Johannes	126277	M	Ger.	16	Camp-Commander, SS, C.C., Dessau Bernburg (Ger.) 14.4.45	MURDER	U.S.
SCHMIDT, Johannes	162581	M	Ger.	4. 1.96	Oschfhr., SS-Totenkopf Command Staff, Buchenwald (Ger.) 40-45	TORTURE	U.S.
SCHMIDT, Johannes	187775	M	Ger.	11 - 14	Oschfhr., SS, Ulven nr.Bergen (Nor.) 7.43	MURDER	NOR.
SCHMIDT, Jonathan	62330	M	Ger.		Dr., Reichsofficial, Chief of Admin., Minister of Economics and the Interior at Wuerttemberg - France	TORTURE	UNWCC
SCHMIDT, Josef	135310	M			Volkssturm, C.C., Poelling (Ger.)	TORTURE	U.S.
SCHMIDT, Josef	162582	M	Ger.	00	Uschfhr., SS, Security-Guard, C.C., Buchenwald (Ger.) 41-42	WITNESS	U.S.
SCHMIDT, Josef	253388	M	Ger.	20	Pvt., Navy, Brest (Fr.) 7.44-8.44	MURDER	FR.
SCHMIDT, Josef	259425	M			Foreman, Organ.Todt, Muehldorf (Ger.)	MURDER	U.S.
SCHMIDT, Josef	301985	M	Ger.		Sturmfhr., SS, SD, Brest, Plougasnou, Finistere (Fr.) 4.5.u.8.7.44	MURDER	FR.
SCHMIDT, Joseph	129970	M			Camp "Elder", C.C., Mauthausen (Aust.) 41-45	MURDER	U.S.
SCHMIDT, Joseph	193312	M	Ger.	00	Camp-Guard, Pvt., Army, Stalag VIII B, Lamsdorf (Ger.) 16.8.42	MURDER	U.K.
SCHMIDT, Joseph	254021	M	Ger.	05	Pvt., K.A.A. 13.Abt. Werkstatt, Wemeldinge (Neth.) 20.9.44	MISC.CRIMES	NETH.
SCHMIDT, Jost or Konrad	137492	M		02	N.C.O., SS Gestapo, Lussault, Indre-et-Loire (Fr.) 4.8.44	MURDER	U.S.
SCHMIDT, Julius	301451	M	Ger.	14. 8.14	Schfhr., SS, C.C., Buchenwald (Ger.) 16.5.38-9.10.43	MURDER	BEL.
SCHMIDT, Karl	120574	M	Ger.		G.F.P.Kommissar, Geh.Feldpolizei, Toropez (Sov.Un.) 41	MURDER	U.S.
SCHMIDT, Karl	133239	M			Policeman, Civilian	TORTURE	U.S.
SCHMIDT, Karl	177575	M			C.C.Chief, C.C., Neuengamme (Ger.)	TORTURE	FR.
SCHMIDT, Karl	301452	M	Ger.	26.12.92	Uschfhr., SS, C.C., Buchenwald (Ger.) 16.5.38-5.10.43	MURDER	BEL.
SCHMIDT, Karl	301986	M	Ger.		Lt., Ersatz-Kmdo., Way-Wavre (Bel.) 6.8.44	MURDER	BEL.
SCHMIDT, Karl Wilhelm	21496	M			Volkssturm Bn.822, 2.Mobile, Herdorf (Ger.) 44-45	TORTURE	FR., SOV.UN.
SCHMIDT, Kurt	252724	M	Ger.	29. 8.05	Employee, Gestapo, Klatovy (Czech.) 39-45	MISC.CRIMES	CZECH.
SCHMIDT, Kurt (or BLAUEL, Adolf)	254013	M	Ger.	25.12.05 or 06	Osturmfhr., SD, Admin., Textile-Factory, Weert (Neth.) 11.41	TORTURE	NETH.
SCHMIDT, Kurt	256252	M			Flyer, C.C.Ellrich, Nordhausen (Ger.)	MURDER	U.S.
SCHMIDT (see ROELLER, Leo)	261490						
SCHMIDT, Lothar	10342	M	Ger.		Dr., Chief of Admin., SS, SD, Ministerium fuer Arbeit und Wirtschaft, Prague (Czech.) 42-44	MISC.CRIMES	CZECH.
SCHMIDT, Marie	193772	F	Ger.		Clerk, Gestapo, Brno (Czech.) 39-45	TORTURE	CZECH.
SCHMIDT, Martin	258395	M			Guard, SS, C.C., Ohrdruf (Ger.) 12.44-4.45	MURDER	U.S.
SCHMIDT, Max	256857	M	Ger.		Funk-Mt., Navy, Hopseidet in Finmark (Nor.) 6.5.45	MURDER	NOR.
SCHMIDT, Max	301987	M	Ger.		Oschfhr., SS, C.C., Auschwitz (Pol.) 41-45	MURDER	POL.
SCHMIDT, Michael	147050	M	Ger.		Oschfhr., SS-Pz.Div."Das Reich", 13.Ccy., Moissac (Fr.) 44	MURDER	FR.
SCHMIDT, Oskar	256390	M	Ger.	9. 1.87	Dr., Manager, Firma "Dynamit Nobel", Civ., Bratislava (Czech.) 40-45	MISC.CRIMES	CZECH.
SCHMIDT, Otto	31429	M			Col., 20.Army 36.Geb.Korps, Finmark (Nor.) 44	MURDER	NOR.
SCHMIDT, Otto	253898	M	Ger.		Oschfkr., Zugwachtmstr., Schutzpolizei, Thiel (Neth.) 3.-4.45	PILLAGE	NETH.
SCHMIDT, Otto	300116	M	Ger.	14	Lt., Green-Police, Groningen and Drente (Neth.) 43	MISC.CRIMES	NETH.
SCHMIDT, Paul	140853	M	Ger.	10	Standartenfhr., SS	WITNESS	U.K.
SCHMIDT, Paul	173216	M			Civilian, Vippack Edelhausen (Ger.) 3.45	MURDER	U.S.
SCHMIDT, Paul	174371	M		02	Pvt., Army, 188.Kgf.Arb.Bn.,3.Coy., Ramsoey (Nor.) 20.2.44	WITNESS	NOR.
SCHMIDT, Peter	177163	M	Ger.	25	SS-Mann, 26.SS-Panz.Gren.Rgt.,12.SS-Panz.Div."Hitler-Jugend", near Caen (Fr.) 6.6.-8.7.44	TORTURE	CAN.
SCHMIDT, Peter	188512	M	Ger.		Civilian, 5.-6.4.45	MURDER	U.S.
SCHMIDT, Philipp	140913	M		00	Sturmbannfhr., C.C., SS, Breendonck (Bel.) 40-44	TORTURE	BEL.
SCHMIDT, Richard	121828	M		07	Capt., SS, Gestapo, Challes les Eaux Arbin (Fr.)	MURDER	FR.
SCHMIDT, Richard	143248	M	Ger.	05 - 10	Dairy-Manager, Civilian, Poischendorf (Ger.) 29.5.44	TORTURE	U.S.
SCHMIDT, Richard	167353	M		10	Capt., SS, SD, Breslav, Chambery (Fr.)	MISC.CRIMES	FR.
SCHMIDT, Richard Johann George	137491				Oschfhr., SS, C.C., Buchenwald (Ger.)	TORTURE	U.S.
SCHMIDT, Robert	167351	M	Ger.	98	Cmdt. of C.C., Eichen in Westfalen (Ger.)	TORTURE	FR.
SCHMIDT, Rodolf	812	M			Senior W.O., Gestapo, Valenciennes Onnaing (Fr.) 1.9.44	MURDER	FR.
SCHMIDT, Rodolph	158692	M			Sgt., Feldgend., Maclay (Fr.) 7.44	PILLAGE	FR.
SCHMIDT, Rodolphe	141611	M	Ger.		Sgt., Feldgend., Baune (Fr.) 42-44	TORTURE	FR.

SCHM-SCHM

NAME	C.R. FILE NUMBER	SEX	NATIO-NALITY	DATE OF BIRTH	RANK OCCUPATION UNIT PLACE AND DATE OF CRIME	REASON WANTED	WANTED BY
SCHMIDT, Rolland (or SCHMITT "Willi")	138221	M			Member, Adjutant SS Gestapo, Lyon (Fr.) 7.-8.44	MURDER	FR.
SCHMIDT, Rose	136369	F	Ger.		Guard, C.C. Helmbrechts (Ger.) 7.44-13.4.45	MURDER	U.S.
SCHMIDT, Rudolf	42971	M	Ger.	23.2.07	Hptsturmfhr., Krim.Rat SS Civ. Gestapo Luxembourg (Lux.) 40-45	MURDER	LUX.
SCHMIDT, Rudolf	161644	M	Ger.	95	Major, Luftwaffe Luftgau C.O. Honefoss Egemoen (Nor.)	MURDER	NOR.
SCHMIDT, Rupput	189148	M		19.6.23	Opl., Army Kerviherne en Merlen Evez (Fr.) 28.4.45	MURDER	FR.
SCHMIDT, Sebastian	181116	M		00	Erbach, (Ger.) 19.9.44	TORTURE	U.S.
SCHMIDT, Victor	62331	M	Ger.		Head of Department of Agricuztur of Reicnsprotector, Bohe.Mor. (Czech.)	MISC. CRIMES	UNWCC. CZECH.
SCHMIDT, W.	300865	M			Pvt., 1.Aufkl.Abt. 3.Coy. 2.Column XV.Div. of the Afrika Korps Saint Leger Arlon (Bel.) 5.9.44	MISC. CRIMES	BEL.
SCHMIDT, Walter	813	M	Ger.		SS-Uschfhr., 2.SS Pz.Div. 3.SS Pz. Gren.Rgt. (Fr.)	MURDER	FR.
SCHMIDT, Walter	21497	M	Ger.	95-00	Kapo, Clausthal Zellerfeld Braunlage (Ger.) 6.4.45	MURDER	U.S.
SCHMIDT, Walter	124090	M			Time-Keeper and General Labour Chief Stalag VI Hauptbahnhof Chemnitz (Ger.) 6.2.45	MURDER	U.K.
SCHMIDT, Walter	167895	M	Ger.		Opl., section leader 9. Res.Gren. Rgt. 1.Coy. Magny D'Avignon (Fr.)44	MURDER	FR.
SCHMIDT, Walter	174567	M	Ger.		Hptschfhr., SS Tulle (Fr.) 9.6.44	WITNESS	FR.
SCHMIDT, Walter	251162	M	Ger.	16.8.12	SS Uschfhr., SS Jihla va Moravia (Czech.) 42 .	MURDER	CZECH.
SCHMIDT, Walter	253373	M	Ger.		Guard C.C. Lahde Weser (Ger.)	INTERR.	BEL.
SCHMIDT, Walter	258152	M	Ger.	14.8.15	Guard C.C. Belsen (Ger.)	TORTURE	BEL.
SCHMIDT, Walther	174045	M	Ger.	99	Civilian, Stalag IV F, C.C. Chemnitz (Ger.) 10.43-3.45	MURDER	U.K.
SCHMIDT, Werner	174565	M	Ger.	00	Hptsturmfhr., SS Oraylitz (Ger.) 42-45	TORTURE	U.S.
SCHMIDT, Wilhelm	167316	M	Ger.		Civ., Trustee Cafe Pangrat, Poznan (Pol.) 9.39-12.44	PILLAGE	POL.
SCHMIDT, Wilhelm	187351	M	Ger.		Head, Stalag XIII D, Police C.C. Woernitz Ansbach (Ger.)	TORTURE	BEL.
SCHMIDT, Wilhelm	256272	M			Oschfhr., C.C. Artern Nordhausen (Ger.)	MURDER	U.S.
SCHMIDT, Willem	143269	M			Civ., Medical Attendant Strafgefaengnis Freien-Dies Lahn (Ger.)43-45	TORTURE	U.S.
SCHMIDT, Willy	167349	M			Adjutant, Inf. Div. 186, Chatel Guyon (Fr.) 6.6.44	MISC. CRIMES	FR.
SCHMIDT, Willy	188528	M	Ger.		SS-Schfhr., C.C. Teresin (Czech.) 40-45	MURDER	CZECH.
SCHMIDT, Xaver	187348	M			Gendarmeriemeister, Gend. Bayreuth (Ger.) 44-45	TORTURE	POL.
SCHMIDT-HUBER (see SCHMIDT)	257867						
SCHMIDT-SCHNEIDER	253793	M	Ger.		Lt., Air Force 49-591 (Fr.)	INTERR.	FR.
SCHMIDT-SCHWARZENBURG	256388	M	Ger.	96	Surgeon Stalag XII A, Limburg (Ger.)	MURDER	U.S.
SCHMIDT-STAEHLER	167329	M	Ger.		Einsatsstab Rosenberg, Senior Administrative Official, Berlin (Ger.) 1940-44	PILLAGE	FR.
SCHMIDTBAUER (or SCHNITTBAUER)	143247	M			Opt., Army Stalag 13 B near Hammelburg (Ger.) 21.3.45	WITNESS	U.S.
SCHMIDTBAUER, Otto	142301	M			Civ., Engineer	MISC. CRIMES	U.S.
SCHMIDTHUBER, August	260656	M			Brigadier General Army	MISC. CRIMES	U.S.
SCHMIDTHUBERT, Arthur	173526	M	Ger.		SS-Standartenfhr., W-SS Div. Prinz Eugen 14. Standarte 41-44	MURDER	YUGO.
SCHMIDTKOWSKY	815	M	Ger.		SS-Oschfhr., C.C. Struthof (Fr.) 9.39-4.41	MURDER	POL.
SCHMIDTS	142288	M	Ger.		Lagerfhr., C.C. Halle (Ger.)	MISC. CRIMES	U.S.
SCHMIDTS (or TUMEN)	194063	F	Ger.		Female Overseer, C.C. Ravensbrueck (Ger.) 1.43	MURDER	FR.
SCHMIDTS	194402	M	Ger.		Opt., Prison Fresnes (Fr.) 13.-15.4.42	WITNESS	FR.
SCHMIDTS, Adam	136367	M	Ger.		Guard, C.C. Helmbrechts (Ger.) 7.44-13.4.45	WITNESS	U.S.
SCHMIDTS, Helmut	133196	M			C.C. Mittelbau Dora Nordhausen (Ger.)	MURDER	U.S.
SCHMIDT	128810	M	Ger.		Korv.Kapitaen, C.C. Marlag Milag Nord, Bremen (Ger.) 8.10.42-10.10.43	TORTURE	U.K.
SCHMIDTZ	173148	M	Ger.		Wachtmeister, C.C. Schirmeck Rotenfels Gaggenau (Fr.Ger.) 44	INTERR.	U.K.
SCHMIDTZ, Gerard	139230	M	Ger.		Civilian, Wankun (Ger.) 12.44-1.45	TORTURE	U.S.
SCHMIDTZ, Oscar	174271	M	Ger.		SS-Mann, SS C.C. Bergen Belsen (Ger.)	MURDER	UNWCC.
SCHMIECH, Karl	260435	M	Ger.		Oberwachtmeister SS Penitentiary Nord Norway, 6.42 5.5.45	MURDER	YUGO.
SCHMIED	147049	M	Ger.		SS-Oschfhr., SS Panz.Div. Das Reich, Moissac (Fr.) 44	MURDER	FR.
SCHMIED	256928	M			Employee, C.C. Nordhausen (Ger.)	MURDER	U.S.
SCHMIED, Franz	193770	M	Ger.		Employee, Brno., (Czech.) 39-45	MURDER	CZECH.
SCHMIED, Martin	251786	M	Ger.	04	Guard, SS Oberndorf, (Ger.)	TORTURE	FR.
SCHMIED, S.	1755	M			Camp Guard, C.C. Dachau (Ger.)	MISC. CRIMES	U.K.
SCHMIEDEBERG	39826	M	Ger.		SS-Sturmfhr., SS Div. Feldpost No. 48963 B, St. Suspice, Chateau Bontier, Fortmusson (Fr.) 6.8.44	MURDER	FR.
SCHMIEDEL, Fritz	306919	M	Ger.		Officer, SS Berlin (Ger.) 40-45	MURDER	CZECH.
SCHMIEDEN	162617	M	Ger.		Guard, W-SS, C.C. Neubrenn, (Ger.) 43-44	TORTURE	FR. U.S.
SCHMIEDEN	255941	M	Ger.		Uschfhr., SS, SD, Mauthausen (Austr.)	INTERR.	FR.
SCHMIEDER	132128	M		15	Pvt., W-SS, C.C. near Plattling (Ger.) 2.-5.45	MURDER	U.S.
SCHMIEDER	257888	M			Lt., Panz.Brig. 150 Meuse Bridge Antwerp (Bel.) 12.44	MISC. CRIMES	U.S.
SCHMIEDER, Otto	29684	M	Ger.		Dr., Oberlandesgerichtsrat, Public Official, Litomerice (Czech.) 40	MURDER	CZECH.
SCHMIEDLER	254209	M			Rottfhr., C.C. Dora-Wiede Nordhausen (Ger.)	MURDER	U.S.
SCHMIEDT, Joseph	142049	M	Ger.	95	Rapportfhr., Arbeitskdo. Waldlager V and VI, Muhldorf, near Ampfing (Ger.) 44-45	MURDER	U.S.
SCHMIEGEL, Franz	256303	M	Ger.		SS-Mann W-SS, Muhldorf (Ger.)	WITNESS	U.S.
SCHMIEDORFER, Karl	188511	M	Ger.		Civ. Servant, Civ.Administration (Locas)	MURDER	U.S.
SCHMIERER	256270	M		24.10.06	Sturmann, C.C. Harzungen Nordhausen (Ger.)	MURDER	U.S.
SCHMIETEL	253795	M	Ger.		Oschfhr., Gestapo, Limoges (Fr.)	INTERR.	FR.
SCHMIETEN	181201	M	Ger.		Uschfhr., SS Gestapo, Saarbruecken (Ger.)	PILLAGE	FR.
SCHMILLER	251787	M			Uschfhr., SD, Sonder u. Wirtschaftskomm. Beeck, Gorssel (Neth.) 9.44	WITNESS	NETH.
SCHMIT (or SCHMID)	138021	M	Ger.	94	Lt. Col., Reserve, Air corps medical hospital Rerik, Neubukow Rerik (Ger.) 16.-17.3.44	MURDER	U.S.
SCHMIT	191533	M	Ger.		Opt., Bn. Georgian, Perigneux (Fr.) 6.4.44	MISC. CRIMES	FR.
SCHMIT (or SCHMITT)	253420	M	Ger.		Detectiv, Devisen Schuetz Kommando, Amsterdam (Neth.) 12.42	MURDER	NETH.
SCHMIT, Karl	300931	M	Ger.		Member, SS of Staff C.C. Bergen Belsen (Ger.) 42-45	MURDER	U.K.
SCHMIT, Richard	257239	M	Ger.		Gestapo, Luxembourg, (Lux.) 40-45	BRUTALITY	LUX.
SCHMIT, Willy	301030	M	Ger.		Sgt., Unit Fp.No. 0414664, Chatel Guyon Puy de Dome (Fr.) 6.6.44	INTERR.	FR.
SCHMITH	255942	M	Ger.		Kapo, C.C. Mauthausen (Aust.)	MISC. CRIMES	FR.
SCHMITLE	301049	M			Kapo, SS C.C. Neuengamme (Ger.) 22.9.41	MURDER	BEL.
SCHMITT (or SCHMIDT)	816	M	Ger.		Sgt., Army C.C. Saarbruecken (Ger.)	TORTURE	FR.
SCHMITT	817	M	Ger.		Adjutant Army, Xinville (Fr.) 8.-9.44	MURDER	FR.
SCHMITT (see SCHMIDT)	1212						

NAME	C.R.FILE NUMBER	SEX	NATIO-NALITY	DATE OF BIRTH	RANK	OCCUPATION UNIT	PLACE AND DATE OF CRIME	REASON WANTED	WANTED BY
SCHMITT	126917	M	Ger.		Blockfuehrer, CC Dora, Nordhausen (Ger.)			TORTURE	FR.
SCHMITT	136203	M	Ger.		Capt., Org.Todt, Fraize (Fr.) 9.-11.44			MISC.CRIMES	FR.
SCHMITT (see SCHMIDT)	136379								
SCHMITT	137587	M	Ger.		Sgt., 9 Paratrooper Rgt.,			MURDER	U.K.
SCHMITT	138259	M	Ger.		Usturmfhr, 14 Coy, SS Formation Walker, Gambsheim(Fr.) 9.1.45			MURDER	FR.
SCHMITT	141920	M	Ger.		Dr., SS Sanit.Corps, CC Flossenburg (Ger.) 5.2.45			MURDER	U.K.
SCHMITT	146751	M			SS Hptschfhr, CC Flossenburg (Ger.)			TORTURE	U.S.
SCHMITT	147047	M			Oschfhr, SS Pz.Div."Das Reich", Montauban(Fr.) 44			MURDER	FR.
SCHMITT	152142	M		10	Usturmfhr, SS, Folking (Fr.) 11.44			MURDER	FR.
SCHMITT	156930	M			Capt., Terv.Navy Bordeaux, Ingrandes (Fr.) 24.8.44			MURDER	FR.
SCHMITT	162571	M		95	Capt., Army, Nordlager CC Buchenwald, Ohrdruf (Ger.) 45			TORTURE	U.S.
SCHMITT	162572	M		08	Major, Air Force, CC Ohrdruf (Ger.)			WITNESS	U.S.
SCHMITT	162573	M	Ger.		SS-Mann, 1 SS Pz.Div., II Zug, 3 Gruppe, Stavelot, Parfondruy (Bel., Ger.) 18.-22.12.44			MURDER	U.S.
SCHMITT	174574	M			Capt., air-raid precaution police, Koblenz (Ger.)			BRUTALITY	U.S.
SCHMITT	186212				Medicine, CC Sachsenhausen (Ger.)			MURDER	FR.
SCHMITT	186898	M			Guard, CC Command Kradiscko, Flossenburg (Ger.)			TORTURE	FR.
SCHMITT	188513	M			SS Uschfhr			MURDER	U.S.
SCHMITT	188526	M			Crim.Commissary, Gestapo, Luxemburg			MISC.CRIMES	LUX.
SCHMITT	189494	M	Ger.		Lt., member of Gestapo, CC Perigueux (Fr.) 6.-8.44			MURDER	FR.
SCHMITT (see SCHMIDT)	190274								
SCHMITT	194592	M	Ger.		Capt., Army, Belle Isle en Terre (Fr.)			MISC.CRIMES	FR.
SCHMITT	253359	M	Ger.		Hptsturmfhr, SS, CC Lublin (Pol.)			MISC.CRIMES	POL.
SCHMITT (see SCHMIT)	253420								
SCHMITT	256042	M	Ger.		Supervisor, CC Flossenburg (Ger.)			TORTURE	FR.
SCHMITT	256043	M	Ger.		SS-Mann, St.Marie les Mines (Fr.) 7.44			MURDER	FR.
SCHMITT	256823	M	Ger.		Oberbaurat, Volkswagenwerk, Doubs Sochaux(Fr.) 40-44			INTER.	FR.
SCHMITT	259247	M			Chief of camp-prison, CC Auschwitz-Birkenau(Pol.) 40			MURDER	FR.
SCHMITT	301146	M	Ger.		Lt., Feld-Gend.,St.Cloud,Rueil-Malmaison -Seine et Oise(Fr.)20.8.44			MURDER	FR.
SCHMITT	301960	M	Ger.		SS-Mann, CC Mauthausen (Aust.) 11.42-5.45			MURDER	FR.
SCHMITT, Alphons(see SCHMIDT)	174568								
SCHMITT, Bruno	256282	M		7.12.17	Cpl., CC Ellrich, Nordhausen (Ger.)			MURDER	U.S.
SCHMITT, Ferdinand	12348	M	Ger.	23. 3.02	Miscellaneous, Sarrabie (Fr.) 9.44			MURDER	FR.
SCHMITT, Fritz	188514	M		02	Member Gestapo, Luxemburg			MISC.CRIMES	LUX.
SCHMITT, Georg	173525	M	Ger.		Cmdt., Org.Todt, Zemun (Yugo.) 14.8.42-10.10.42			MURDER	YUGO.
SCHMITT, H.	137493	M	Ger.		Civ., teacher, school, Arnstein, Wuerzburg (Ger.) 14.10.43			TORTURE	U.S.
SCHMITT, Hans	256041	M	Ger.		Kapo, CC Flossenburg (Ger.)			BRUTALITY	FR.
SCHMITT, Hans Erich	67001	M			Hptschfhr, SS, CC Struthof (Fr.)			MISC.CRIMES	FR.
SCHMITT, Jean	259794	M			Oschfhr, Gestapo, Limoges (Fr.)			INTER.	FR.
SCHMITT, Johann	188508	M	Ger.		Member, Gestapo, Luxemburg			MISC.CRIMES	LUX.
SCHMITT, Josef	256271	M			Flyer, CC Ellrich, Nordhausen (Ger.)			MURDER	U.S.
SCHMITT, Karl	256987	M	Ger.		Civilian, mining- Assessor of Wieke, Krs.Celle,Liege(Bel.) 41-43			MURDER	BEL.
SCHMITT, Karl	306656	M	Ger.		SS Staff Sgt., CC Flossenburg (Ger.) 42-45			MURDER	FR.
SCHMITT, Karl Joseph	168964	M	Ger.		Oberregierungsrat, section-leader, General Government Poland (Forest Office), official, Radom (Pol.) 9.39-44			PILLAGE	POL., UNWCC.
SCHMITT, Kaspar	122544	M	Ger.		Civilian, owner of a drug-store, Muehlheim and Dietesheim(Ger)25.2.45			MURDER	U.S.
SCHMITT, Lorenz	142052	M		12	Oschfhr, W-SS Totenkopf Standarte, CC Flossenburg (Ger.) 42-45			TORTURE	U.S.
SCHMITT, Otto	261214	M	Ger.		Pvt., 199 Arbeitsbereich Liane 5,I Rgt.211, Alleur-lez-Liege (Bel.) 4.9.44			MURDER	BEL.
SCHMITT, Peter	196983	M		05	Lt., Army, Oberbettingen, Hillesheim(Ger.) 12.9.44 - 5.3.45			TORTURE	U.S.
SCHMITT, Rolland (see SCHMIDT,Rolland)	198221								
SCHMITT, Willy	301147	M	Ger.		N.C.O., chief of SD at Creil, Salency - Oise (Fr.) 23.6.44			PILLAGE	FR.
SCHMITT-SCHNEIDER	174573	M	Ger.		Lt., Air Force, Gironcourt sur Vraine Repel - Poussay (Fr.) 24.8., 31.8., 1.9.44			WITNESS	FR.
SCHMITTEN	262460	M	Ger.		Manager, civ.firm of Auto-Union, Stettin (Ger.) 44-45			MURDER	POL.
SCHMITTER	189611	M	Ger.		Pvt., Zentral Ersatzteillager 206, Paris (Fr.) 21.8.44			MURDER	FR.
SCHMITTKAMP	188804	M	Ger.		Cpl., Lds.Schtz.Bn.4, 4 Coy, Lyon (Fr.) 24.8.44			MURDER	FR.
SCHMITZ	1482	M		90	Pol.Capt, Schupo (Barracks of Hoechst), Ruesselheim(Ger.) 9.44			TORTURE	U.S.
SCHMITZ	1800	M			SS Oschfhr, CC Dachau (Ger.)			TORTURE	U.K.
SCHMITZ	31447	M	Ger.		SS Guard, Gestapo, CC Klingenputs (Ger.) 1. and 3.45			TORTURE	U.S.
SCHMITZ	67669	M	Ger.		SS-Mann, SS Div. F.P.48963 B, St.Sulpice, Chateau Gontier Fort Musson (Fr.) 6.8.44			MURDER	FR.
SCHMITZ	143245	M			Member of Gestapo, Leipzig and Celle (Ger.) 42-45			TORTURE	U.S.
SCHMITZ	156915	M	Ger.		Capt., 111 Kampfgeschwader 100, Villaudric (Fr.) 20.8.44			MURDER	FR.
SCHMITZ	156918	M	Ger.		Pvt., Gestapo, Brive (Fr.) 44			MURDER	FR.
SCHMITZ	162576	M		04	Uschfhr, SS, CC Buchenwald (Ger.) 44-45			TORTURE	U.S.
SCHMITZ	164720	M	Ger.		Capt., Police, NSDAP, Bruehl (Ger.) 17.1.45			TORTURE	U.S.
SCHMITZ	164799	M	Ger.		SS-Mann, 10 SS Pz.Div., 36 Rgt., Revin (Fr.) 12.-19.6.44			MURDER	FR.
SCHMITZ	165543	M	Ger.		Employee, custom, Hombourg (Bel.) 25.5.44			MURDER	BEL.
SCHMITZ	190275	M	Ger.		Cpl., 892 Gren.Rgt., 264 Div., Muc - Imotski district, Sucura (Island) of Hvar (Yugo.) 5.10.43			MURDER	YUGO.
SCHMITZ	301361	M	Ger.		Medical officer, Head, CC Flossenburg (Ger.)			MURDER	FR.
SCHMITZ	301453	M	Ger.		Rottfhr, SS, CC Buchenwald (Ger.) 16.5.38-9.10.43			MURDER	BEL.
SCHMITZ	305945	M	Ger.		Gauamtsleiter, Bodenteich Krs.Uelzen (Ger.) 3-4.45			MURDER	CZECH.
SCHMITZ	306229	M	Ger.		Osturmfhr, Feld-Gend. SS "Adolf Hitler" Div., Mean 4.9.44			TORTURE	BEL.
SCHMITZ, Clemens	156919	M	Ger.		Adjutant, interpreter, Gestapo, Brive (Fr.) 44			MURDER	FR.
SCHMITZ, Edmund	240123	M	Ger.	15	Oberfunkmeister, official, Nachr.Rgt.506, 6 Coy, Abwehr official, Koeln (Ger.)			MISC.CRIMES	U.S.
SCHMITZ, Ferdinand	124449	M		13	Sgt., Pz.Bde., 150 Paratrooper Rgt., Ardennes (Fr.) 12.44			MISC.CRIMES	U.S.
SCHMITZ, Ferdinand	251335	M	Ger.		Pvt., II Pz.Div., Unit 36-185, Lautree (Fr.) 5.8.44			MURDER	FR.
SCHMITZ, Franz Johann	261106	M	Ger.	8. 2.90	Capt., Police, Bruehl (Ger.) 17.1.45			SUSPECT	U.S.
SCHMITZ, Fritz	256169	M		16. 3.11	Pvt., CC Ellrich, Nordhausen (Ger.)			MURDER	U.S.
SCHMITZ, Guenther	256170	M			Flyer, CC Ellrich, Nordhausen (Ger.)			MURDER	U.S.

SCHM-SCHN

NAME	C.R.FILE NUMBER	SEX	NATIO-NALITY	DATE OF BIRTH	RANK	OCCUPATION	UNIT	PLACE AND DATE OF CRIME	REASON WANTED	WANTED BY
SCHMITZ, Heinrich	188525	M	Ger.		Krim.Komm.,Gestapo,Riga,Luxemburg,Lativa (Lux.)				MISC.CRIMES	LUX.
SCHMITZ, Heinz	133245	M	Ger.	3.7.96	Dr.,SS,C.C.Flossenburg (Ger.)				MURDER	U.S.
SCHMITZ, Herbert	1320	M	Ger.		Pvt.,903 Festungs-Ers.Bn.				MISC.CRIMES	U.S.
SCHMITZ, Jakob	135311	M	Ger.		Civilian, Efferen (Ger.) 2.10.44				WITNESS	U.S.
SCHMITZ, Jakob	193773	M	Ger.		Crim.Com.,Gestapo,Brno (Czech.) 39-45				MURDER	CZECH.
SCHMITZ, Johann	72002	M			Farmers-leader,Civ.				TORTURE	U.S.
SCMITZ, Johann	149879	M	Ger.		Chief,Police,Rheinbach (Ger.) 28.6.45				TORTURE	U.S.
SCHMITZ, Josef	126593	M		4.14	Lt.,9 Pz.Div.,102 Pz.Art.Regt.,Fuerth near Neukirchen(Ger.) 9.4.44				MURDER	U.S.
SCHMITZ, Josef	149880	M			Sgt.,Army,Borkum (Ger.) 4.8.44				MURDER	U.S.
SCHMITZ, Julius	133197	M			C.C.Mittelbau Dora,Nordhausen (Ger.)				MURDER	U.S.
SCHMITZ, Karl	190276	M	Ger.		Befehlshaber,S.D.,Sipo,Gorizie (Yugo.) 30.12.44				MURDER	YUGO.
SCHMITZ, Karl (SCHMITZ)	260013	M		06	Sturmbannfhr.,Chief,SS,Gestapo,Trencin,Slovakia (Czech.) 45				MURDER	CZECH.
SCHMITZ, P.	180907	M			Pvt.,3 Sicherungs-Regt.16 (Bel.) 44				MURDER	BEL.
SCHMITZ, Paul	253895	M		22	Pvt.,Army,Wisbuhr (Ger.) 15.11.44				MURDER	U.S.
SCHMITZ, Peter	256171	M		12.3.99	Pvt.,C.C.Ellrich,Nordhausen (Ger.)				MURDER	U.S.
SCHMITZ, Theodor	129918	M			Uschfhr.,W-SS,in Med.service at C.C.Mauthausen (Aust.) 41-45				MURDER	U.S.
SCHMITZ, Wilhelm	132196	M	Ger.		Pvt.(Mechanic.),German Navy U 852,South of Freetown,Atlantic,Ocean,44				WITNESS	U.K.
SCHMITZ, Wilhelm	256172	M			C.C.Ellrich,Nordhausen (Ger.)				MURDER	U.S.
SCHMITZ, Willi	92001	M	Ger.		Customs-secr.,customs-service,Hombourg (Bel.)				MURDER	U.S.
SCHMITZ, Willi	152140	M	Ger.		Hptschfhr.,SS,S.D.,Creil (Fr.) 42-43				TORTURE	FR.
SCHMITZ-VOIGT	62332	M			Standartenfhr.,Pol.-Oberst,SS,W.K.R.VII				TORTURE	UNWCC
SCHMOLA, Bruno	135312	M		00	Gestapo,C.C.Theresienstadt (Czech.)				TORTURE	U.S.
SCHMOLDT, Heinrich Ewald	166680	M	Ger.		Civilian,Ostbarthausen (Ger.) 25.11.44				TORTURE	U.S.
SCHMOLKE	141610	M	Ger.		Guard,Stalag Kdo.1195 au Stalag VII C,C.C.Meiningen (Ger.)				INCENDIARISM	FR.
SCHMOLL	181200	M	Ger.		Usturmfhr.,Pol.Insp.,SS,Gestapo,Searbruecken (Ger.)				PILLAGE	FR.
SCHMOLL	256824	M		14	Blockfhr.,Rottfhr.,C.C.Muhldorf (Ger.)				MURDER	U.S.
SCHMOLL, Philipp	142290	M		20	Rottfhr.,SS				MURDER	U.S.
SCHMOLLIK, Rudolf	301454	M	Ger.	1.5.20	SS-Mann,SS,C.C.Buchenwald (Ger.) 16.5.38-9.10.43				MURDER	BEL.
SCHMUCK	253505	M	Ger.		Capt.,Section for Information I C.Le Favuet (Fr.)				TORTURE	FR.
SCHMUCK	256304	M	Ger.		O.T.,Muhldorf (Ger.)				WITNESS	U.S.
SCHMUCKING	251323	M			Dr.,Hptschfhr.,SS,C.C.Dachau (Ger.) 42				BRUTALITY	BEL.
SCHMUHL (or SCHMULH)	141609	M	Ger.		Sen.W.O.,Feldgend.,Manlay,Besune (Fr.) 43-44				MISC.CRIMES	FR.
SCHMUNDT, Hubert (Herbert)	259585	M			Admiral				WITNESS	U.S.
SCHMUNDT, Rudolf	62333	M			Lt.General,Chief of Army pers.off.Chefadjutant d.Wehrmacht to Hitler				MISC.CRIMES	UNWCC
SCHMUSTER, Max	181199	M			Sgt.,Army,Semoussau (Fr.)				MURDER	FR.
SCHNABEL	36660	M			Usturmfhr.,SS,C.C.Stalag Luft III (Ger.)				WITNESS	U.K.
SCHNABEL	48748	M			Dr.,Sturmbannfhr.,Waffen-SS,C.C.Flossenburg (Ger.)				TORTURE	U.S.
SCHNABEL	136380	M	Ger.		Kreis-Chef,Gendarmerie,Bruckenau (Ger.) 44				MURDER	U.S.
SCHNABEL	253502	M	Ger.	10	Hptschfhr.,SS,C.C.Schomberg (Ger.) 44-45				MISC.CRIMES	FR.
SCHNABEL	305489	M			Cmdt.,SS,C.C.Schomberg (Ger.) 44-45				MURDER	FR.
SCHNABEL, August	173480	M			Camp official,Prison-Director,C.C.Oslo (Nor.) 11.41-9.43				TORTURE	NOR.
SCHNABEL, Helmut	301455	M	Ger.		Oschfhr.,SS,C.C.Buchenwald (Ger.) 16.5.38-9.10.43				MURDER	BEL.
SCHNABEL, Othmar	255943	M	Ger.		Oschfhr.,SS,C.C.Mauthausen (Aust.)				MURDER	FR.
SCHNABEL, Walter	188521	M	Ger.	13.3.10	Factory-manager,Civ.,Bruenn (Czech.) 39-45				PILLAGE	CZECH.
SCHNAEGELBERGER, Karl	259048	M	Ger.	23.9.93	Osturmbannfhr.,NSDAP,SS				INTERR.	U.S.
SCHNAK, Wilhelm	180904	M		92	Lt.,Pol.,Greuesmuehlen (Ger.) 6.44				MURDER	U.S.
SCHNAKE, Fritz	301456	M	Ger.		Scharfhr.,SS,C.C.Buchenwald (Ger.) 16.5.38-9.10.43				MURDER	BEL.
SCHNAKENBURGER, Heinrich	143210	M			Ortsgruppenleiter,NSDAP,Hingenheim (Ger.) 44				TORTURE	U.S.
SCHNALZE, Alfred	149891	M		12	Sturmmann,SS,C.C.Gross-Rosen (Aust.)				MURDER	U.S.
SCHNAPOF, Christian	188803	M	Ger.		Feldgendarm,Feldgendarmerie,Buire,Cite (Fr.) 2.11.43				MURDER	FR.
SCHNAPP, Hermann	256168	M		2.10.20	Cpl.,C.C.Ellrich,Nordhausen (Ger.)				MURDER	U.S.
SCHNATH	138342	M	Ger.		Prof.,High-School,Paris (Fr.) 44				PILLAGE	FR.
SCHNAUBER	186209	M	Ger.		Inspector (Officer SS),C.C.Sachsenhausen (Ger.)				MURDER	FR.
SCHNAUER	818	M			Hptsturmfhr.,Adjutant of Chief,S.D.,SS,Gestapo,Locmine (Fr.)7.-8.44				MURDER	FR.
SCHNAUER	300119	M			Scharfhr.,S.D.,Pontivy,Morbihan (Fr.) 4.-8.44				MISC.CRIMES	FR.
SCHNAUZ	122547				Lt.,Gren.Coy.,Army,Hanau-Main (Ger.) 7.1.45				MURDER	U.S.
SCHNEEBAUER	300866	M	Ger.		Pvt.,1 Aufkl.-Abt.,3 Coy.,2 Colum,XV Div. of the Afrika Korps, St.Leger (Arlon),(Bel.) 5.9.44				MISC.CRIMES	BEL.
SCHNEEBERGER (see HEUBERGER)	250244									
SCHNEEMANN	253384	M			Oberarzt,Air Force,Buchenwald (Ger.) 42-45				MISC.CRIMES	U.S.
SCHNEEMANN, Guenther	254228	M		07	Dr.,C.C.Ellrich,Nordhausen (Ger.)				MURDER	U.S.
SCHNEEWEISS	142051	M			Dr.,Civ.,C.C.Dachau (Ger.)				WITNESS	U.S.
SCHNEFFER, Adolf	252741	M	Ger.		Pvt.,Searchligat Coy.I le de Re,Ribedoux-Plage (Fr.) 29.11.42				MURDER	FR.
SCHNEIDEN	189000	M	Ger.	05	Cpl.,805 Landesschuetzen-Bn.,Stalag XIII C,Holzberghof near Bischofsheim (Fr.-Ger.)				TORTURE	U.K.
SCHNEIDER	819	M	Ger.		Mayor,Public official,Leszno (Pol.)				MURDER	POL.
SCHNEIDER	820	M	Ger.		Hptschfhr.,Zugwachtmeister,Gestapo,Trondheim (Nor.)				MISC.CRIMES	NOR.
SCHNEIDER	822	M	Ger.		Cpl.,Army,C.C.Caen (Fr.)				MURDER	FR.
SCHNEIDER	1534	M			Hptschfhr.,SS,C.C.Dachau (Ger.)				TORTURE	U.K.
SCHNEIDER	10344	M	Ger.		Hptsturmfhr.,SS,C.C.Oranienburg (Ger.) 39-44				TORTURE	CZECH.
SCHNEIDER	12458				Sgt.,SS-Pz.Div."Das Reich",N.C.O.,Regt."Der Fuehrer",Oradon (Fr.)6.44				MURDER	FR.
SCHNEIDER	28868	M	Ger.		Pvt.,Army,Mountain Unit,Allemond (Fr.) 15.8.44				TORTURE	FR.
SCHNEIDER	29633	M			Capt.,Feldgendarmerie,St.Die (Fr.) 11.44				MURDER	FR.
SCHNEIDER	31546	M		18	Kapo,Clausthal,Zellerfeld,Braunlage (Ger.) 6.4.45				MURDER	U.S.
SCHNEIDER	31551				Pol.-Direktor,Polizei,Altenbourg (Bel.)				MURDER	U.S.
SCHNEIDER	67032	M	Ger.		Capt.,Stalag VIII A,Stalag IX B,Goerlitz,Bad Orb (Ger.) 2.-4.45				MISC.CRIMES	U.K.
SCHNEIDER	67809	M	Ger.		Pvt.,398 Lssschtz.-Bn.,Coy."Zeitz",Stalag XII A - IV B, Arb.Kdo.123,Limburg,Muhlburg,Gleina (Ger.) 9.44-2.45				TORTURE	U.K.
SCHNEIDER	72513	M	Ger.		Official,Gestapo,Fresnes,Paris (Fr.) 4.-5.43				TORTURE	U.K.
SCHNEIDER	125073				Seaman,Navy,41				MURDER	U.K.
SCHNEIDER	126916		Ger.		Scharfhr.,SS,Pz.Div."Das Reich" (Fr.) 44				MURDER	FR.
SCHNEIDER	126942		Ger.		Osturmfhr.,SS,Pz.Div."Das Reich",Regt."Deutschland",Venerque(Fr.)44				MURDER	FR.
SCHNEIDER (see SCHNYDEN)	128812									
SCHNEIDER	133198	M			Rottfhr.,Waffen-SS,C.C.Mittelbau Dora,Nordhausen(Ger.)				MURDER	U.S.
SCHNEIDER	135560				Cpl.,Arbeits-Kdo.114,Etzdorf (Ger.)				TORTURE	U.K.

SCHN - SCHN

NAME	C.R.FILE NUMBER	SEX	NATIO-NALITY	DATE OF BIRTH	RANK OCCUPATION UNIT PLACE AND DATE OF CRIME	REASON WANTED	WANTED BY
SCHNEIDER	136201	M	Ger.		2.SS Panz.Div."Das Reich",F.P. No. 28688, Sud Quest (Fr.)	MURDER	FR.
SCHNEIDER	136975	M	Ger.		SS Oscharfhr., C.C. Hinzert (Ger.) 41-43	TORTURE	U.S.
SCHNEIDER	136982	M	Ger.		Aussendienst-Commissar, SS Gestapo, Koeln (Ger.)	MURDER	U.S. IT.
SCHNEIDER	142287	M	Ger.		Major, Oberkommando der Wehrmacht, PW affairs	WITNESS	U.S.
SCHNEIDER see SCHUSTER	143218						
SCHNEIDER	143244	M	Ger.		C.O., German Marine Corps, St.Marine (Fr.) 30.6.44	MURDER	U.S.
SCHNEIDER	147042	M	Ger.		SS Mann, SS Panz.Div."Das Reich", Tulle (Fr.) 44	MURDER	FR.
SCHNEIDER	152112	M	Ger.		Col., Army, Oflag 64 C.C. Altburgund (Ger.) 15.-26.5.44	TORTURE	U.S.
SCHNEIDER	152191	M			Adjutant, Gestapo, Chenebier, Etobon (Fr.) 27.9.44	MURDER	FR.
SCHNEIDER	155984	M			Uscharfhr., Guard, SS, 3.SS Bau-Bde., C.C.Wieda, Gardelegen (Ger.) 4.45	WITNESS	U.S.
SCHNEIDER	156991	M			Sgt., Feldgendarmerie, Quimperle (Fr.)	MURDER	FR.
SCHNEIDER	162584	M			Cpl., Army, C.C. Torgau (Ger.)	TORTURE	U.S.
SCHNEIDER	165696	M	Ger.		Oberwachtmeister, prison, Surrebruck (Ger.)	TORTURE	FR.
SCHNEIDER	167397	M	Ger.		SA, Wintzenheim (Fr.) 1.45	PILLAGE	FR.
SCHNEIDER	167989	M	Ger.		Cpl., Bn.of Georgian 1.Coy., Tulle (Fr.) 6.4.44	MISC.CRIMES	FR.
SCHNEIDER	169761	M	Ger.	00	Justizhauptwachtmeister NSDAP, C.C.	TORTURE	U.N.W.C.C.
SCHNEIDER	173151	M	Ger.		Lt., Stalag 6 A, C.C. Hemer (Ger.) 41-45	TORTURE	U.S.
SCHNEIDER	173255	M	Ger.	05	Interrogator, Gestapo, SS, SD, Noailles (Fr.) 9.8.44	MURDER	U.K.
SCHNEIDER	173883	M	Ger.		Major, Panz.Rgt. 15, Malley le Camp, (Fr.) 23.4.44	MURDER	U.S.
SCHNEIDER	173884	M	Ger.	01	Lt., Feldgendarmerie, Plouaret Lorge (Fr.) 6.8.44	MURDER	FR.
SCHNEIDER	186156	M	Ger.		Agent, Gestapo, Err (Fr.) 5.-9.43, 5.-9.44	PILLAGE	FR.
SCHNEIDER	186208	M	Ger.		Cpl., Army, C.C. Dachau (Ger.)	TORTURE	FR.
SCHNEIDER	186710	M	Ger.		Cpl., Army, Guard, Stalag IV B C.C. Muehlberg-Elbe (Ger.) 27.3.44	WITNESS	U.K.
SCHNEIDER	188007	M	Ger.	about 97	Cpl., Army, Guard Stalag XIII C Gallmuthausen (Ger.) 2.45	WITNESS	U.K.
SCHNEIDER	188800	M	Ger.		Cpl., Kriegslazarett, C.C. Dury Amiens (Fr.) 44	WITNESS	FR.
SCHNEIDER	191824	M	Ger.	17	Pvt., Art.Abt. 409.Bn., nr.Aalst (Neth.) 9.41	TORTURE	U.K.
SCHNEIDER	191826	M	Ger.	05	Pvt., Army, Arbeitskommando C.C. Karlstall (Czech.)	TORTURE	U.K.
SCHNEIDER	193090	M	Ger.		Oberbauleiter, Org. Todt, Tonmeness (Nor.)	TORTURE	NOR.
SCHNEIDER	194363	M	Ger.		Lt., Army, Barret s.Lioure (Fr.) 22.2.44	MURDER	FR.
SCHNEIDER	194422	M	Ger.		Cmdt., Lager Fliegerhorst Villaroche, Combs-la-Ville (Fr.) 21.8.44	MURDER	FR.
SCHNEIDER	194426	M	Ger.		Sgt., Feldgendarmerie, Ploermel (Fr.) 18.6.44	TORTURE	FR.
SCHNEIDER	194428	M	Ger.		Lt., Anti-terroriste detachment No. 26565 stat.aux Taillades (Vaucluse), Vercoiran (Fr.) 9.3.44	MURDER	FR.
SCHNEIDER	205321	M	Ger.	95	N.C.O., 805. Bn., Gamelshausen (Ger.) end 12.45	WITNESS	U.K.
SCHNEIDER	251333	M			Police official, Bonn (Ger.) 43-45	WITNESS	U.S.
SCHNEIDER	253170	M	Ger.	96	Major, Flak, 25.Div. 137.Flak-Rgt. 287.Group, Selvaggio,Giareno (It.) 20.5.44	MURDER	U.K.
SCHNEIDER	253180	M	Ger.	02	Pvt., 3.Coy., 714.Landesschuetzen-Bn., Wangerau (Ger.) 12.43-1.44	BRUTALITY	U.K.
SCHNEIDER	253509	M	Ger.		Capt., 99.Bn. Alpine-Rgt., Mont de Lans (Fr.) 13.8.44	INTERR.	FR.
SCHNEIDER	253792	M	Ger.		Capt., Army, Rosendaele (Fr.) 12.44-1.45	MISC.CRIMES	FR.
SCHNEIDER	253889	M	Ger.		Capt., 99.Bn. 157.Div. Inf.Rgt., L'Ain (Fr.) 10.-21.7.44	INTERR.	FR.
SCHNEIDER	254492	M	Ger.		Lt., 6.Coy. II.Bn. 893.Inf.Rgt. 264.Div., Primosten (Yugo.) 7.7.44	MISC.CRIMES	YUGO.
SCHNEIDER	256167	M			SS Uscharfhr., C.C. Mackenrode, Nordhausen (Ger.)	MURDER	U.S.
SCHNEIDER	256302	M			SS Rottfhr., C.C. Nordhausen (Ger.)	MURDER	U.S.
SCHNEIDER	256369	M	Ger.		Capt., 157.Div. 99.Bn., Allemont (Fr.) 44	MURDER	FR.
SCHNEIDER	259210	M	Ger.		Agent, Gestapo, Antenne of Rochelle, Poitiers Area (Fr.) 40-44	MISC.CRIMES	FR.
SCHNEIDER	259336	M			SS Mann, Todt.Org., Muehldorf Area (Ger.)	MURDER	U.S.
SCHNEIDER	259337	M			SS Mann, Muehldorf Area (Ger.)	MURDER	U.S.
SCHNEIDER	260655	M	Ger.		SS Uscharfhr., C.C. Buchenwald (Ger.) 40-44	BRUTALITY	FR.
SCHNEIDER	301369	M	Ger.		Font Romeu, Err-Pyrenees (Fr.) 5.-9.43	PILLAGE	FR.
SCHNEIDER	301903	M	Ger.		Dr.,Lt.Col.,Comd.Gren.Rgt.324,163.Inf.Div.20.Army,Finmark 10-11.44	MURDER	NOR.
SCHNEIDER	301904	M	Ger.		Hptsturmfhr., Comd.II SS Geb.Jaeg.Rgt. 11-6.SS Geb.Div.Nord 20.Army, Finmark, 10.-11.44	MURDER	NOR.
SCHNEIDER	305490	M	Ger.		SS Usturmfhr., Hinzert C.C. Treves, 42-45	MURDER	FR.
SCHNEIDER	301362	F	Ger.		Wardress, C.C. Flossenburg (Ger.) 42-45	MURDER	FR.
SCHNEIDER	305491	M	Ger.		Uscharfhr., Le Harcholet com.de Moussey (Fr.) about 10.44	MURDER	U.K.
SCHNEIDER	305946	M	Ger.		Dr., SS Sturmbannfhr., Regierungsrat, attached to Befehlshaber d. SD and SIPO in la leading capacity, C.C. Oswiecim-Birkenau (Pol.)39-45	MURDER	CZECH.
SCHNEIDER	306232	M	Ger.		Sgt., Staff, St.Julien du Verdon (Fr.) 11.6.44	MURDER	FR.
SCHNEIDER	306876	M	Ger.		Civ. Director, C.C.Auschwitz (Pol.) 40-45	MURDER	U.S.
SCHNEIDER	306878	M	Ger.		SS Mann, Bloc-leader, C.C. Auschwitz (Pol.) from 40	MURDER	U.S.
SCHNEIDER, Albert	260418	M		27.12.09	SS Osturmfhr., Major, Fire-Bde.	BRUTALITY	U.K.
SCHNEIDER, Aloys	188801	M	Ger.		Pvt., 9.Panz.Div.,Panz.Gren.Rgt. 11, Mayenne (Fr.)	WITNESS	FR.
SCHNEIDER, Alwin	256389	M	Ger.	12. 6.06	Flyer, C.C. Ellrich, Nordhausen (Ger.)	MURDER	U.S.
SCHNEIDER, Arno	253390		Ger.		Capt., Sicherheits-Rgt. 199,Fandreville, Liguères, St.Mards en Othe, Marcilly-le-Hayer (Fr.) 20.6.44, 18.8.44, 2.8.44	INTERR.	FR.
SCHNEIDER, Arthur	188522	M	Ger.		Lt., Army, Kalborn (Lux.) 22.9.44	MURDER	LUX.
SCHNEIDER, August	256155			13. 7.01	SS Rottfhr., C.C. Harzungen, Nordhausen (Ger.)	MURDER	U.S.
SCHNEIDER, Carl	190906	M			C.C. Dachau (Ger.)	MURDER	U.S.
SCHNEIDER, Conrad	253489		Ger.	30. 1.07	Factory-worker, Kaiserslautern (Ger.) 27.10.44	MURDER	FR.
SCHNEIDER, Emil	161297	M		6.10.04	Driver, Army, Res.Transp.Bn. 12, Altenkirchen (Ger.) 13.9.44	WITNESS	U.S.
SCHNEIDER, Ernst	124623	M			Member, Gestapo, Giessen (Ger.) 26.-27.3.45	MURDER	U.S.
SCHNEIDER, Erwin	147046	M			SS Rottfhr., SS Panz.Div."Das Reich", Moissac (Fr.) 44	MURDER	FR.
SCHNEIDER, Ewald	251768	M		8. 6.96	Gendarm, Gendarmerie, Poustevna (Czech.) 4.45	MURDER	CZECH.
SCHNEIDER, Fernand	194362	M			Chef des Paysans, Weissenhasse ueber Bebra (Ger.) 18.6.41	WITNESS	FR.
SCHNEIDER, Friedel see FURMANN	261492	F	Ger.	30. 9.11	SS Guard, SS Totenkopfverband, C.C.Auschwitz,Ravensbrueck (Pol.)42-44	BRUTALITY	POL.
SCHNEIDER, Fritz	143243				Lt.,29.Flak-Rgt., betw. Hausen and Ginnheim (Ger.) 9.44	WITNESS	U.S.
SCHNEIDER, Fritz	155985	M	Ger.		Col., Oflag 64, C.C. Schoubin (Pol.) 1.45-9.45	TORTURE	U.K.
SCHNEIDER, Fritz	177574	M	Ger.		Civ. Engineer, Paris (Fr.) 11.43-8.44	PILLAGE	FR.
SCHNEIDER, Gustav	262166	M	Ger.	12. 9. ?	Uscharfhr., Gestapo, Rennes (Fr.) 43-44	MISC.CRIMES	FR.
SCHNEIDER, Hans ?	192853	M	Ger.		Zugwachtmeister, Schupo, C.C. Falstad nr.Drontheim (Nor.) 41-44	TORTURE	NOR.
SCHNEIDER, Hans	253372	M	Ger.		SS Rottfhr.,1.Panz.Div. Leibstand."Adolf Hitler" 1.SS Panz.Rgt. 6.Coy., Malmedy (Bel.) 17.12.44	MISC.CRIMES	U.S.
SCHNEIDER, Hans	256383	M	Ger.	18	Sgt., 7.Parachute-Div., Alsace (Fr.)	MURDER	U.S.

SCHN-SCHN

-114-

NAME	C.R.FILE NUMBER	SEX	NATIO-NALITY	DATE OF BIRTH	RANK OCCUPATION UNIT PLACE AND DATE OF CRIME	REASON WANTED	WANTED BY
SCHNEIDER, Hans	301364	M	Ger.		Wachtmstr.,SD,Member,Gend.,Clermont ferrand,Aulnat,Puy de Dome 6.-7.44	MURDER	FR.
SCHNEIDER, Hans Paul	137496	M			Rottfhr.,SS,Weimar,Buchenwald (Ger.)	TORTURE	U.S.
SCHNEIDER, Heinz	133246	M			Oschfhr.,Waffen SS,Flossenburg (Ger.)	MURDER	U.S.,FR.
SCHNEIDER, Heinz or Anton	256154	M	Ger.	07?	Sgt.,Field-police,Kessel (Neth.) 7.11.44	MURDER	NETH.
SCHNEIDER, Hermann Konrad	143242	M	Ger.	23. 5.03	Sturmfhr.,SA,Rothenburg or Rothenberg (Ger.) 3.45	MURDER	U.S.
SCHNEIDER, Johann	256301	M		31. 7.09	Sturmmann,C.C.,Dora,Nordhausen (Ger.)	MURDER	U.S.
SCHNEIDER, Johann Karl	188523	M	Ger.	29. 7.96	Foerster,Civilian,Luxemburg (Lux.)	MURDER	LUX.
SCHNEIDER, Josef	193750	M	Ger.	95	Employee,Gestapo,Brno (Czech.) 39-45	TORTURE	CZECH.
SCHNEIDER, Karl	193749	M	Ger.		Employee,Gestapo,driver,Brno (Czech.) 39-45	MURDER	CZECH.
SCHNEIDER, Karl	194427	M	Ger.		Cpl.,Stalag 13 C,Bad Neustadt-Saale (Ger.) 2.8.44	TORTURE	FR.
SCHNEIDER, Max(see KATHREIN)	191782						
SCHNEIDER, Michael	256166	M			Pvt.,C.C.,Ellrich,Nordhausen (Ger.)	MURDER	U.S.
SCHNEIDER, Oger-Robert	253414	M	Ger.	98	Flyer,3.Coy.,2.Zug,15.Div.,Africa Corps,St.Leger (Bel.) 3.9.44	MISC.CRIMES	BEL.
SCHNEIDER, Otto	132141	M	Ger.		Landwacht,civilian,Ruhen (Ger.) spring 44	TORTURE	U.S.
SCHNEIDER, Otto	188232	M	Ger.		Pvt.,Heeres Kuesten Art.Abt.,Oostduinkerke (Bel.) 8.9.44	MURDER	BEL.
SCHNEIDER, Peter	251769	M	Ger.	22. 8.89	Lt.,police,Burbach (Ger.) 24.8.44	TORTURE	U.S.
SCHNEIDER, Robert	258999	M	Ger.	30. 6.11	Sturmbannfhr.,SS,NSDAP, 9.11.43	INTERR.	U.S.
SCHNEIDER, Rudi	256382	M	Ger.		Sgt.,Gendarmerie,Chauffeur,Kessel (Neth.) 7.11.44	MURDER	NETH.
SCHNEIDER, Rudolf	185557	M	Ger.	15.8.99	Regierungsrat,Gestapo,Sturmbannfhr.,SD,SS,Praha (Czech.) 39-45	PILLAGE	CZECH.
SCHNEIDER, Rudy	136986	M		07	Capt.,Feldgendarmerie,Brueggen (Ger.)	WITNESS	U.S.
SCHNEIDER, Sebastian	12349	M	Ger.		Pvt.,Army,110.or 111.Panz.Gren.Rgt.,2.Coy.,Albine (Fr.) 29.6.44	MURDER	FR.
SCHNEIDER, Theodor	193091	M		07	Pvt.,Kgf,Arb.Bn.186, (Nor.) 40-45	MISC.CRIMES	NOR.
SCHNEIDER, Walter	12351	M	Ger.		N.C.O.,Army,110.or 111.Panz.Gren.Rgt.,2.Coy.,Albine (Fr.) 29.6.44	MURDER	FR.
SCHNEIDER, Walter	142268	M	Ger.	93	Civilian,Schwickerhausen (Ger.) 9.44	MURDER	U.S.
SCHNEIDER, Walter	192056	M	Ger.		Cpl.,Eis.Art.Bn. 77,F.P.No. 22380,St.Andries,Varsenare,Les Bruges (Bel.) 4.9.44	MURDER	BEL.
SCHNEIDER, Walter	261797	M	Ger.		Pvt.,9.field Coy.,G.L.A.103,Elsenborn-Eifel,Nieppe (Fr.) 3.9.44	MURDER	FR.
SCHNEIDER, Wilhelm	302163	M	Ger.		Pvt.,Air-force,Coy.151,Isled' Espagnac,Mainzac,Charente (Fr.)25.7.44	MURDER	FR.
SCHNEIDER, Willi	138196	M		16	SS Pz.Ers.Rgt.,Capt.,Flavigny le Petit (Fr.)	MURDER	FR.
SCHNEIDER, Willi	173143	M			SD Kommando "Wenger",Gestapo,Baccarat,Etival (Fr.)	MURDER	U.K.
SCHNEIDER, Willy	123869	M			Uschfhr., Pz.Div."Goetz v.Berlichingen",near Montmartin en Craignes (Fr.) 17. 6.44	MURDER	U.S.
SCHNEIDER, Willy	251800	M	Ger.	25. 6.06	Employee,Gestapo,Krumlov (Czech.) 39-45	TORTURE	CZECH.
SCHNEIDER, Willy	301655	M	Ger.		Capt.,Cmdr.,SS,Unit Hirson,Neuve Maison (Fr.) 16.6.44	MURDER	CZECH.
SCHNEIDER, Wolfram	258998	M	Ger.	12.11.12	Sturmbannfhr.,SS,NSDAP, 21.6.44	INTERR.	U.S.
SCHNEIDEREIT, Otto	188491	M			Kapo,SS,C.C.,Mauthausen (Aust.)	MISC.CRIMES	U.S.
SCHNEIDERMEISTER	169527	M	Ger.		Member,SS,C.C.,Zamosc (Pol.) 43	MURDER	POL.
SCHNEIDERREIT, Arwed	193748	M	Ger.		Employee,Gestapo,Bruenn (Czech.) 39-45	MURDER	CZECH.
SCHNEIDMUELLER	251318	M	Ger.	11. 7.03	Osturmfhr.,SS,Kraftfahrdepot,Hlaska (Czech.) 8.5.45	TORTURE	CZECH.
SCHNEIDT	126506	M			Oschfhr.,SS,C.C.,Weimar,Buchenwald (Ger.) 39-41	TORTURE	U.S.
SCHNEIFER, Willy	167396	M	Ger.	16	Hptsturmfhr.,SS,Neuve Maison (Fr.) 16.7.44	MURDER	FR.
SCHNEITER	261798	M	Ger.		Cpl.,Fieldgend.,Romilly sur Seine (Fr.) 10.6.44	MISC.CRIMES	FR.
SCHNEITMANN	121839	M	Ger.		Oberinspector,Gestapo,Indicateur,Clermont, Ferrand (Fr.) 1.44	TORTURE	FR.
SCHNEIWALD	124313	M	Ger.		Guard,Waffen SS,C.C.,Vogelsang-Torgau (Ger.) 10.42	MURDER	POL.,U.S.
SCHNELL	1321	M			Asst.,Laval Supply,	MISC.CRIMES	U.K.
SCHNELI	168091	M	Ger.		Doctor,leader,Gen.Government,Abt.Forsten,Krakow (Pol.) 39-44	MISC.CRIMES	POL.
SCHNELLE, Hilda	252720	F			Civilian,Tiddische (Ger.) 30.5.44	WITNESS	U.S.
SCHNELLENBERG, Karl	262418	M	Ger.	10.12.98	Doctor,Director,Civ.of National Museum and Library,Warsaw (Pol.)40-44	PILLAGE	POL.
SCHNELLER, Gustav	10345	M	Ger.		Usturmfhr.,Waffen SS,Gestapo,Jihlava (Rum.) 39-44	TORTURE	CZECH.
SCHNELLHAMMER	12352	M			Pvt.,110.or 111.Panz.Gren.Rgt.,2.Coy.,Albine (Fr.) 29.6.44	MURDER	FR.
SCHNELLINGER, Fritz	184602	M	Ger.		Police official,Ass.Supervisor,C.C.,Blechhammer,Lendringen (Ger.) 45	MURDER	POL.
SCHNELLMANN	109565	M			Physician,Civ.Kiew Institute,C.C.,Kiew (Sov.Un.) 41-42	MURDER	U.S.
SCHNELSUSE	12353	M	Ger.		Lt.,Army,Unit 726,Wascomposed mostlyot Momjols,Blaye les Mines (Fr.) 15.7.44	MURDER	FR.
SCHNEPF, Franz Xaver	262133	M	Ger.	26. 3.00	Clerk,Civ.Occup.,Muenchen (Ger.) L.O.D.N.A.O.D.	SUSPECT	U.S.
SCHNER	125612	M	Ger.		Capt.,Gestapo,Baccarat (Fr.) 8.,9.10.44	MURDER	FR.
SCHNERBITZ	253983	M	Ger.		Schfhr.,SS,Buchenwald (Ger.) 42-45	MISC.CRIMES	U.S.
SCHNERER, Harry Wilhelm Heinz	262366	M	Ger.	28. 2.87	Lt.,NSKK,Staffel VII,Munich-Trudering (Ger.) 19.7.44	SUSPECT	U.S.
SCHNESTER	306877	M	Ger.		Doctor,SS,experiments,C.C.,Auschwitz (Pol.) 40-45	MURDER	FR.
SCHNETT(alias: SCHNETZE)	174287	M	Ger.		Lt.,10.I.D.,motorized Panz.Rgt.,1.Bn.,Chilleurs aux Bois (Fr.) 15.8.44	MURDER	U.K.
SCHNEU	167988	M	Ger.		Cpl.,Georgian Bn.,1.Coy.,Tulle (Fr.) 6.4.44	MISC.CRIMES	FR.
SCHNEVOIGT	165695	M	Ger.		Gestapo,Dijon Dun,les Places (Fr.) 26.,27.,28.6.44	MURDER	FR.
SCHNEYER	162565	M	Ger.	00	Osturmfhr.,SS,security guard,C.C.,Buchenwald (Ger.)	WITNESS	U.S.
SCHNICHELS, Heinz	190250	M	Ger.	20	Oschfhr.,SS,Gestapo,H.Q.,Koeln (Ger.) 43-45	MURDER	U.K.
SCHNICKE	306129	M	Ger.		Chief,police at the shell factory (Polte II) Arnstadt-Thuer.(Ger.)	MISC.CRIMES	FR.
SCHNIDERS	301988	M	Ger.		SS-Mann,C.C.,Auschwitz (Pol.) 41-45	MURDER	POL.
SCHNIEBERT	306880	M	Ger.		Ortskommandant,Montenois (Doubs) (Fr.) 10.44	SUSPECT	FR.
SCHNIEDER	161296	M	Ger.		SS,Hennebont (Fr.) 44	MURDER	FR.
SCHNIEZT	152100	M	Ger.		Member,SS,Koeln (Ger.) 10.44	MURDER	U.S.
SCHNILZ	181198	M	Ger.		Miscell.,Semoussac (Fr.) 29.9.44	MURDER	FR.
SCHNITTBAUER (see SCHMIDTBAUER)	143247						
SCHNITTKER	1279	M	Ger.	24	Usturmfhr.,9.SS Pz.Div."Hohenstaufen",19.Rgt.,10.Coy.,Bastogne (Bel.) 45	MISC.CRIMES	U.S.,U.K.
SCHNITTLER, Kurt Fritz	259506	M	Ger.	25.12.08	Sonderfhr.,Mil.U.Stelle L.Abt.,Wassenaer (Neth.) 42-43	PILLAGE	NETH.
SCHNITZ	305947	M	Ger.		Doctor,Osturmfhr.,C.C.,Oranienburg (Ger.) 11.39-45	MURDER	CZECH.
SCHNITZELBAUMER, Simon	148556	M	Ger.	07	Hptsturmfhr.,SS,Flak Rgt.Freimann,Muenchen (Ger.) 7.44	MURDER	U.S.
SCHNITZLER	177572	M	Ger.		SS,C.C.,Breslau,Striegau (Ger.)	TORTURE	FR.
SCHNITZLER	240123	M	Ger.	15	Oberfunkmstr.,Nachr.Rgt.506,Abwehr official,6.Coy.,Koeln (Ger.) 45	MISC.CRIMES	U.S.
SCHNITZLER	254231	M	Ger.		Uschfhr.,C.C.,Osterode,Nordhausen (Ger.)	MURDER	U.S.
SCHNOEDER	306779	M	Ger.		Sgt.,Stalag Luft IV,Grosstychow (Ger.) 15.7.-5.8.44	BRUTALITY	U.S.
SCHNOEK, Charles August	161295	M	Ger.	2. 3.03	Interpreter,Kreiskommandantur,Jalhay,Svrister,Verviers (Bel.) 22.-23.10.43	TORTURE	BEL.

SCHN-SCHO

NAME	C.R.FILE NUMBER	SEX	NATIO- NALITY	DATE OF BIRTH	RANK OCCUPATION UNIT PLACE AND DATE OF CRIME	REASON WANTED	WANTED BY
SCHNOELL	823	M	Ger.		SS Osturmfhr.,Dachau(Ger.)40	MURDER	FR.
SCHNOOR, Richard	301606	M	Ger.		Commanding the Feldgendarmerie,Stavelot(Bel.)2.-4.9.44	MURDER	BEL.
SCHNUCK	132734	M	Ger.		Contre-Maitre dans une Kalkwerke,Civilian,Nenntmansdorf(Ger.)2.43	TORTURE	FR.
SCHNULLE, Gustav	180888	M	Ger.		Civilian,Railroad Employee,Castrop Rauxel(Ger.)10.3.45	TORTURE	U.S.
SCHNUR	260845	M			Dr.,Address: 12.Cacilian-Strasse,Friedrichsthal,Elversberg(Ger.) 17.-19.7.44	WITNESS	U.S.
SCHNURR	253410	M	Ger.	15	Employee,Gestapo,Kolin(Czech.)39-45	INTERR.	CZECH.
SCHNYDEN or SCHNEIDER	128812			95	N.C.O.Stalag,KL Gallmuthausen(Ger.)2.45	TORTURE	U.K.
SCHNYDEN see SCHNEIDEN	189000						
SCHNYDER see SCHNEIDER	143211						
SCHOBER	121841	M	Ger.		SS Stubafhr.CC Buchenwald(Ger.)42-45	MURDER	FR.
SCHOBER	188985	M	Ger.		SS Oschafhr.Deputy Commander,CC Buchenwald Ger.)39-45	MURDER	BEL.CZECH.
SCHOBER, Ruppert	188543	M	Ger.		Member Gestapo,Luxembourg(Lux.)	MISC.CRIMES	LUX.
SCHOBERT	146750	M	Ger.		Major,SS,CC Flossenburg(Ger.)	TORTURE	U.S.
SCHOBERT	155987	M	Ger.		SS Stubafhr.KL Buchenwald(Ger.)9.44	MISC.CRIMES	U.K.U.S.
SCHOBERT	162799	M			Guard,SS Member,KL Parzymiecki(Pol.)41-44	TORTURE	U.S.
SCHOBERT	250473	M	Ger.		Hptsturmfhr.Botschafter,Cmdt.SS,Auschwitz-Birkenau(Pol.)11.42	INTERR.	YUGO.
SCHOBERT, Arno(Fritz Rudolf) or SCHUBERT	137497	M			SS Hptscharfhr.KL Weimar-Buchenwald(Ger.)	MURDER	U.S.
SCHOBERT, Max	301457	M	Ger.	25.12.04	SS Hptsturmfhr.CC Buchenwald(Ger.)16.5.38-9.10.43	MURDER	BEL.
SCHOBERTH, Georg	174219	M	Ger.		Policeman,Gestapo,CC Langenzenn(Ger.)43-45	TORTURE	U.S.
SCHOBERTZ	126287	M			Stubafhr.SS,CC Guard,Buchenwald(Ger.)	TORTURE	U.S.
SCHOCHKNECHT, M.	192855	M	Ger.		Schupo,CC Falstad near Drontheim(Nor.)10.42	TORTURE	NOR.
SCHODER	253796	M	Ger.		Member Gestapo,Lille(Fr.)40-44	MISC.CRIMES	FR.
SCHOEBELIN	260434	M	Ger.		Owachtmeister,SS Penitentiary Nord-Norway,6.42-5.5.45	MURDER	YUGO.
SCHOEBER	257768	M	Ger.		SS Mann,Transportation Sect.Nordhausen(Ger.)	MURDER	U.S.
SCHOEDDER, Stephan	41360	M			Major,Public Official,Kuerten(Ger.)	TORTURE	U.S.
SCHOEDE	251788	M	Ger.		Reichsbahn-Oberinspector,Railway of Ger.and Neth.Bilthoven(Neth.Ger.)	MISC.CRIMES	NETH.
SCHOEDEL, Leopold	254232	M			Cpl.CC Ellrich,Nordhausen(Ger.)	MURDER	U.S.
SCHOEDER see SCHRELER	190279						
SCHOEFER	34430	M	Ger.		Capt.Army,99/7 Geb.Div.Nachr.Abt.20 Army,Finmark(Nor.)44	MURDER	NOR.
SCHOEFFEL	194379	M	Ger.		Major,Army,9.44,Chaudfontaine(Bel.)	PILLAGE	BEL.
SCHOEFFEL, Wolfgang	256381	M	Ger.	13.10.01	Manager,Civilian,Pilsen(Czech.)42-45	PILLAGE	CZECH.
SCHOEFFER, Julius	142286	M	Ger.		Cpl.,Forester,Public Official,Forestry Office,Bande(Bel.)14.6.42	MURDER	BEL.
SCHOELE, Rudolf	261953	M	Ger.		SS Usturmfhr.Various places in Slovenia(Yugo.)41-45	MISC.CRIMES	YUGO.
SCHOELER	162586	M	Ger.	00	Capt.Army,CC Buchenwald(Ger.)	TORTURE	U.S.
SCHOEM	252740	M	Ger.		Cmdt.Air Unit #34505,Berre-L'Etang(Fr.)20.8.44	MURDER	FR.
SCHOEN	124323	M	Ger.	03	Lt.Stalag 3 B.Asst.Abwehr-Officer,CC Fuerstenberg(Oder)(Ger.)43-2.45	MURDER	U.S.
SCHOEN	138286	M	Ger.		Sgt.Heeres-Verwaltung,P.C.of Regt.in Keuthen(Ger.)Armainvillers(Fr.) 25.7.44	MURDER	FR.
SCHOEN	150588	M	Ger.		Adjudant,Feldkommandantur 515,Granville(Fr.)44	MURDER	FR.
SCHOEN	189133	M			Sgt.Heeresverwaltung,Dienststelle C 39999 L.P.G.A.,Gretz,Armainvillers (Fr.)25.7.44	MURDER	FR.
SCHOEN	253501	M	Ger.		N.C.O.Fieldpolice Troop 533,Le Chablais(Fr.)19.20.21.5.44	INTERR.	FR.
SCHOEN	261037	M			SS Uschafhr.CC Vaihingen a.d.Enz.,(Ger.)13.8.44-7.4.45	MURDER	U.S.
SCHOEN	300867	M	Ger.		Pvt.1 Aufkl.Abt.3 Coy.2 Column,XV Div.of the Africa Korps,Saint Leger (Arlon)5.9.44	MISC.CRIMES	BEL.
SCHOEN	305492	M	Ger.		Commandant,Airforce,Berre L'Etang,Bouches-du Rhone Fr.)28.8.44	MURDER	FR.
SCHOEN, Bernhard	193093	M		00	Owachtmeister,Sgt.Guard,Reichsjustizministerium,Feldstraflager,CC Finmark(Nor.)45	MISC.CRIMES	NOR.
SCHOEN, Dora	143239	F	Ger.		Guard,SS,CC Volary(Czech.)41-45	MURDER	U.S.
SCHOEN, Emil	259469	M			Major,residing at Vienna,Illesheim(Ger.)1.12.43	MURDER	U.S.
SCHOEN, Filip	305496	M			Member of the Werkschutz,Skoda Works,Dubnica nad Vakom(Slov.)44-45	MURDER	CZECH.
SCHOEN, Hubert or SCHEIN	132140	M			Civilian,Farmer,Oberforsbach(Ger.)8.41	TORTURE	U.S.
SCHOEN, Johann	254222	M			Pvt.CC Nordhausen(Ger.)	MURDER	U.S.
SCHOEN, Paul	254017	M		25.12.17	Flyer,CC Nordhausen(Ger.)	MURDER	U.S.
SCHOENAU	253428	M	Ger.		Lt.Fieldpost #L6572,Pepingen(Bel.)2.44-3.9.44	MISC.CRIMES	BEL.
SCHOENAUER	72027			00	SS Adolf Hitler Div.Feldgendarmerie,Odet(Bel.)4.9.44	MURDER	U.S.
SCHOENBACH	143238	M			Civilian,Headteacher,Gross-Schoenebeck(Ger.)38-40	WITNESS	U.S.
SCHOENBERG	173501	M	Ger.		Dr.,Regierungsrat,Occupied territories,Opava,Oswiecim,Birkenau(Czech. Pol.)39-45	MURDER	CZECH.
SCHOENBERGER	39628	M	Ger.		Army,Pvt.F.P.33632,Bernay en Champagne(Fr.)3.9.41	WITNESS	FR.
SCHOENBOHM, Alfred	260509	M	Ger.	4.3.09	SS Uschafhr.SS Guard,CC Auschwitz(Pol.)40-45	BRUTALITY	POL.
SCHOENBORN	260996	M	Ger.		Col.Streif Korps,Sued France,Vaucluse,Bouches du Rhône,Prov.Var-Gard- Basses-Alpes(Fr.)44	MISC.CRIMES	FR.
SCHOENBUSCH	167348	M	Ger.	10	Cpl.Inf.Regt.1210,159 Inf.Div..Cernay(Fr.)1.-2.45	MURDER	FR.
SCHOENE, Helmut	142210	M	Ger.		Agent,Police,44	TORTURE	FR.
SCHOENE, Helmuth	139221	M	Ger.	00	Osturmfhr.SS,KL Gross-Beeren(Ger.)42-43	MURDER	U.S.
SCHOENEBERG	180906	M	Ger.		Pvt.3 Sicherungs Regt.16,(Bel.)44	MURDER	BEL.
SCHOENECKER, Hans	143236	M	Ger.		Civilian,CC Cunnersdorf near Dresden(Ger.)24.3.45	WITNESS	U.S.
SCHOENER, Erwin	206132	M	Ger.		Gestapo,Vosges(Fr.)44	MURDER	U.K.
SCHOENER	251339	M	Ger.	85	Kriminalkommissar,SS Osturmfhr.Offenburg(Ger.)6.11.44	MURDER	FR.
SCHOENESEIFFEN	183244	M			Dr.,S.D.Rsha Amt IV-3-1-b(Gestapo)Mauthausen(Aust.)1.45	MURDER	NOR.
SCHOENFELD	31431	M	Ger.		Capt.Inf.Div.163,Ary Regt.234,Feld-Ers.-Bn.,Finmark(Nor.)44	MURDER	U.S.
SCHOENFELD, Adolf	254022	M	Ger.		Sgt.CC Ellrich,Nordhausen(Ger.)	MISC.CRIMES	U.S.
SCHOENFELD, Amalie born VOLKENING	253981	F	Ger.	6.12.19	Stellvertretende Kreisfrauenschaftsleiterin,N.S.F.,Daun Krs.Daun(Ger.) 25.12.44	MISC.CRIMES	U.S.
SCHOENFELD, Heinz	174226	M	Ger.	06	SS Oschafhr.CC Mauthausen(Aust.)1.-18.4.45	MURDER	U.S.
SCHOENFELD, Rudolf	193737	M	Ger.		SS Sturmmann,4 SS Totenkopf Stuba,CC Mittelbau,Dora,Nordhausen(Ger.)43	MURDER	U.S.
SCHOENFELDER	167987	F	Ger.		Member,Einsatzstab Rosenberg(Fr.)40-44	PILLAGE	FR.
SCHOENFELDER, Hildegard	253415	F	Ger.		Medicial-Chief,CC Oranienburg(Ger.)	MURDER	BEL.
SCHOENFELDT	255071	M			Flyer,CC Harzungen,Nordhausen(Ger.)	MURDER	U.S.
SCHOENHABER, Rudolf	193094	M	Ger.	25.10.08	Reichsjustizministerium,Feldstraflager,CC Finmark(Nor.)	WITNESS	NOR.
SCHOENING	192856	M	Ger.		SS Sgt.CC Falstadt near Drontheim(Nor.)10.41-5.42	MURDER	NOR.
SCHOENKOCH,Kurt	257767	M	Ger.	9.11.15	Guard,State Service,Gestapo,Brno(Czech.)40-42	MURDER	CZECH.
SCHOENKOPF, Lore (Leiu)	167986	F	Ger.		Member,Einsatzstab Rosenberg(Fr.)40-44	PILLAGE	FR.

SCHO-SCHO   -116-

NAME	C.R.FILE NUMBER	SEX	NATIONALITY	DATE OF BIRTH	RANK OCCUPATION UNIT PLACE AND DATE OF CRIME	REASON WANTED	WANTED BY
SCHOENMAKERS	300121	M	Ger.		SS-Uschfhr.,in command of a firing squad composed of Ukrainians belonging to a Pion.Detachment of the 84 Rgt."Landsturm Niederlande", Rhenen and Vreewijk (Neth.) 2.45	MURDER	NETH.
SCHOENMEYER	261254	M	Ger.		Sgt.,2 Col.,3 Coy,1 Aufkl.Abt.XV Div.Africa-Corps,St.Leger,Arlon (Bel.) 5.9.44	MISC.CRIMES	BEL.
SCHOENROCK	12354	M	Ger.		Pvt.,Army,110 or 111 Pz.Gren.Rgt.,Gourdon (Fr.) 29.6.44	MURDER	FR.
SCHOENUNG	255072	M			Uschfhr.,C.C.Ellrich,Nordhausen (Ger.)	MURDER	U.S.
SCHOENWALDER,Heinrich	162557	M	Ger.	00	SS-Oschfhr.,SS,C.C.Buchenwald (Ger.) 42-45	WITNESS	U.S.
SCHOEPEL,Karl	185872	M	Ger.	16.11.99	Lt.,SA,NSDAP,Chief of Police,Neumarkt,Freystadt (Ger.) 40-45	TORTURE	POL.
SCH)EPKE	253364	M	Ger.		SS-Oschfhr.,SS,C.C.Auschwitz (Pol.) 42-43	MURDER	U.K.
SCHOER	300868	M	Ger.		Pvt.,1 Aufkl.Abt.3 Coy 2 Col., XV Div.of the Afrika Corps,Saint Leger (Arlon) 5.9.44	MISC.CRIMES	BEL.
SCHOETT,Heinrich Georg	255225	M	Ger.	20. 3.03	Head of Labour Exchange,Kolin (Czech.) 39-45	MURDER	CZECH.
SCHOETTL,Otto	193738	M	Ger.	22. 2.14	Block-leader,NSDAP,Bohemia (Czech.)	MISC.CRIMES	CZECH.
SCHOFF,Fr.	72019	M			SS-Oschfhr.,SS,C.C.Struthof (Fr.)	MISC.CRIMES	FR.
SCHOGGL	300562	M			Oberfaehnrich,3 Jg.Bn.,738 Rgt.,on Board Sailing Ship MB 16 off Supetar (Yugo.) 10.3.44	MISC.CRIMES	YUGO.
SCHOHUSEN	126595	M			Cpl.,Flakalarmabt.503,10 Coy,Hilden (Ger.) 16.4.45	MURDER	U.S.
SCHOLDER	190277	M	Ger.		Kreiskommandant,Kreiskommandantur,Dr.,Krusevac (Yugo.) 4.-12.42	MURDER	YUGO.
SCHOLEMBURG	174572	M	Ger.		Lageraeltester Nr.1,C.C.Wansleben am See,Buchenwald (Ger.) 43-45	TORTURE	FR.
SCHOLER,Wilhelm	149886	M			Civilian,Dortmund (Ger.)	TORTURE	U.S.
SCHOLL	142284	M			Officer,Army,	WITNESS	U.S.
SCHOLL	253176	M	Ger.		Cpl.,Gendarmerie,Vendome (Fr.) 9.8.44	MURDER	FR.
SCHOLL	254227	M			Pvt.,C.C.Dora,Nordhausen (Ger.)	MURDER	U.S.
SCHOLL,Kurt	254216	M			Cpl.,C.C.Ellrich,Nordhausen (Ger.)	MURDER	U.S.
SCHOLL,Martin	192857	M	Ger.		Schupo,C.C.Falstad near Drontheim (Nor.) 6.-8.42	MURDER	NOR.
SCHOLLEN,Theo	825	M	Ger.		SS-Rottfhr.,C.C.Maidanek (Pol.) 4.40-44	MURDER	POL.,BEL.
SCHOLLMEYER	253490	M	Ger.		Sonderfhr.,Esquerdes (Fr.) 1.-2.42	PILLAGE	FR.
SCHOLLOWS	255953	M			Chief of culture,La Neuville-Boismont (Fr.) 21.8.44	INTERR.	FR.
SCHOLTEN,Peter	123868	M	Ger.	00	Cpl.,Ldsch.Bn. 6 Coy Stalag VI B or VI G (Ger.) 44-45	TORTURE	U.S.
SCHOLTZ	57748	M			Capt.,Army,Oflag IV B,Koenigstein (Ger.) 19.1.45	WITNESS	FR.
SCHOLTZ	133200	M			Usturmfhr.,Waffen SS,C.C.Dora Mittelbau,Nordhausen (Ger.)	MURDER	U.S.
SCHOLTZ	167347	M	Ger.		Adj.,Army,Rgt.Clodius,Saulieu (Fr.) 6.9.44	WITNESS	FR.
SCHOLTZ	187344	M	Ger.		Civilian,Montgauthier,Dinant (Bel.) 20.9.43	MURDER	BEL.
SCHOLTZ	189559	M	Ger.		Foreman,C.C.Dachau (Ger.) 40-45	TORTURE	BEL.
SCHOLTZ	301221	M	Ger.		Pvt.,Guard at Camp 13 Stalag XX A,Thorn (Pol.) 27.10.40	TORTURE	U.K.
SCHOLZ (see SCHULTZ,Paul)	126521						
SCHOLZ	142285	M			Capt.,Army,Halchter (Ger.)	MURDER	U.S.
SCHOLZ	156932	M	Ger.		Lt.,Securite militare,Tours (Fr.)	MURDER	FR.
SCHOLZ	167346	M	Ger.		Member,Feldgendarmerie,Larochemillay (Fr.)	PILLAGE	FR.
SCHOLZ	167990	M	Ger.		Prof.,Chief,Member,Einsatzstab Rosenberg,Photographie staff, (Fr.)	PILLAGE	FR.
SCHOLZ	168969	M	Ger.		Dr., Deputy leader, Ansiedlungsstab, Lodz (Pol.) 9-39-44	MISC.CRIMES	POL.
SCHOLZ	173524	M	Ger.		Col.,2 Bde. of Kuban Cossacks (Yugo.)	MURDER	YUGO.
SCHOLZ	186813	M	Ger.		Chief,Gendarmerie,Bayonne (Fr.)	MISC.CRIMES	FR.
SCHOLZ	193092	M	Ger.		Cpl.,Waffen SS,SD,C.C.Falstad (Nor.) 41-45	MURDER	NOR.
SCHOLZ	253175	M	Ger.		Sgt.,Gendarmerie,Vendome (Fr.) 9.8.44	MURDER	FR.
SCHOLZ	254224	M			Usturmfhr.,C.C.Ellrich,Nordhausen (Ger.)	MURDER	U.S.
SCHOLZ (or SCOLCE)	305810	M	Ger.		Col.,O.C.Tank Div."Lehr" from Berlin,Dresnice (Yugo.) 11.43	MURDER	YUGO.
SCHOLZ,Erich	826	M			Schfhr.,SS,Gestapo,Alesund (Nor.)	TORTURE	NOR.
SCHOLZ,Erich	137498	M		01-03	Inspector,Geh.Feldpolisei Gruppe 713	MURDER	U.S.
SCHOLZ,Ernst	306786	M	Ger.		Lt.,SS Recomn.Bn.SS,Renardsmont Stavelot, (Bel.) 19.12.44	MURDER	BEL.
SCHOLZ,Erwin Fritz	260485	M	Ger.	12. 8.25	SS-Pvt.,Waffen SS,Guard,C.C.Auschwitz (Pol.) 44-45	BRUTALITY	POL.
SCHOLZ,Fritz	126596	M	Ger.	95	Sturmbannfhr.,SS 2 Pz.Div."Das Reich" 2 Rgt.,Tours (Fr.)	MURDER	U.S.
SCHOLZ,Gotthold Hans	305776	M	Ger.	12. 1.15	Oschfhr.,Sachbearbeiter,Sipo Trondheim in charge of political prisoners Aalesund (Nor.) 4.44-10.44	TORTURE	NOR.
SCHOLZ,Hermann	149887	M			Guard,Stalag II B,Hammerstein (Ger.) 27.8.43	WITNESS	U.S.
SCHOLZ,Karl	254225	M			Pvt.,C.C.Ellrich,Nordhausen (Ger.)	MURDER	U.S.
SCHOLZ,Karl	261907	M	Ger.		Has Participated in the Arrest of 42 Hostages 35 of them Died Later on in Germany,Pessoux-Ciney (Bel.) 27.8.44	MURDER	BEL.
SCHOLZ,Paul	194359	M			Cpl.,Army,C.C.Poitiers (Fr.) 1.-6.44	MURDER	U.S.
SCHOLZ,Reinhold	193745	M	Ger.	7.11.01	SS-Cpl.,SS-Guard,4 SS Totenkopf Sturmbann,C.C.Mittelbau Dora,Nordhausen (Ger.)	MURDER	U.S.
SCHOLZ,Robert	143233	M	Ger.		Territorial leader,Rosenberg's staff west,Paris (Fr.,Bel.,Ger.)40-45	PILLAGE	U.S.,FR.
SCHOLZ,Roman	162556	M	Ger.	09	SS-Oschfhr.,SS,C.C.Buchenwald (Ger.) 42-45	WITNESS	U.S.
SCHOLZ,Siegfried	142266	M	Ger.	26.12.10	Capt.,Feldzeugkdo.7,Heeresmunitionsanstalt St.Georgen,Palling (Ger.) 22.9.44	MURDER	U.S.
SCHOLZ,Siegfried	262337	M			7 Pz.Recomn.Coy,wanted for the murder of an American flyer,Sillersdorf (Ger.) 16.4.45 L.O.D.N.A.O.D.	WITNESS	U.S.
SCHOLZ,Walter	143232	M			Cpl.,Waffen SS Totenkopf Standarte,C.C.Buchenwald (Ger.)	TORTURE	U.S.
SCHOLZ,Walter	194425	M	Ger.	11. 4.10	SS-Osturmfhr.,SS,SD,Kolin (Czech.) 39-45	MURDER	CZECH.
SCHOLZ,Werner	10347	M	Ger.		Staatsanwalt,German County Court,Brno (Czech.) 40	MURDER	CZECH.
SCHOLZ,Werner	162914	M	Ger.	23. 7.07	Usturmfhr.,Waffen SS,Totenkopf Standarte,C.C.Weimar-Buchenwald (Ger.)	TORTURE	U.S.
SCHOLZ,Wilhelm	162915	M	Ger.		Usturmfhr.,Waffen SS,Totenkopf Standarte,C.C.Weimar-Buchenwald (Ger.)	TORTURE	U.S.
SCHOLZE	254434	M	Ger.	96	Col.,Armoured Div."Lehr",Ogulin (Yugo.) 27.10.-11.43	INTERR.	YUGO.
SCHOLZE,Pene (or SCHULTZ or SCHULZ)	167992	M	Ger.	94	Sgt.,Prison Guard,St.Lo (Fr.) 6.-7.6.44	MURDER	FR.
SCHOLZE,Walter	253411	M			Pvt.,Pion.2 Pl.,3 Pz.Pi.,1 SS Pz.Div.Leibst."Adolf Hitler",Ligneuville Stoumont (Bel.) 17.-19.12.44	MURDER	U.S.
SCHOMWECH,Artur	256846	M	Ger.	29. 1.08	Employee,Factory worker,Nordhausen (Ger.)	MURDER	U.S.
SCHOMMERS,Hans	188544	M	Ger.	21. 8.03	SS-Zoellner,SS Custom,Luxembourg,Maulusmuehle (Lux.) 25.12.44	MURDER	LUX.
SCHOMMERSCHUK	255950	M			Cpl.,C.C.Buchenwald (Ger.)	MURDER	U.S.
SCHON	260033	M	Ger.		Gendarm,Div.Oberland Unit Russian-German,Massif du Vercors Isere et Drome (Fr.) 20.7.-5.8.44	SUSPECT	FR.
SCHON	256306	M	Ger.		SS-Mann,SS,Muehldorf (Ger.)	WITNESS	U.S.
SCHON,Adolf	147041	M	Ger.		Sturmann,SS Pz.Div."Das Reich" 13 Coy,Moissac (Fr.) 44	MURDER	FR.
SCHONAVER	162907	M	Ger.		SS Leibst."Adolf Hitler",Odet (Bel.) 4.9.44	MURDER	BEL.

SCHO-SCHR

NAME	C.R.FILE NUMBER	SEX	NATIO- NALITY	DATE OF BIRTH	RANK, OCCUPATION, UNIT, PLACE AND DATE OF CRIME	REASON WANTED	WANTED BY
SCHONDORFF, Adolf	191859	M	Ger.		Dr.,Member,Civ. Staff of Didier Werke,Belgrad (Yugo.)	MISC.CRIMES	YUGO.
SCHONE, Heinrich	62334	M	Ger.		Obergruppenfhr.,SA,commissioner of Wolhynia,chief of SA group "Tannenberg"	TORTURE	UNWCC.
SCHONECK, Frantz	194490	M	Ger.	09	Sgt.,guard-chief,Prison Rouen (Fr.) 41	TORTURE	FR.
SCHONEMANN	306286	M	Ger.		Member,Gestapo Nove Mesto n.Vahom,Oswiecim C.C. Birkenau(Pol.)39-45	MURDER	CZECH.
SCHONENSEIFEN	170389	M	Ger.	15	SS-official,C.C. Mauthausen (Aust.)	TORTURE	UNWCC.
SCHONER	305612	M	Ger.		Commissioner, Gestapo Offenburg Prison Baden (Ger.) 6.11.44	MURDER	FR.
SCHONFELDER	181117	M	Ger.		Pvt.,1 Pz.Div."Adolf Hitler",1 SS Ers.Bn,Parfondrig,Stavelot(Bel.) 18.-22.12.44	MURDER	U.S.
SCHONFELDER, Alfred	254447	M	Ger.	00	Lt.,Unit Russo-Ger.,La Ferte sur Aube (Fr.) 15.6.44	MURDER	FR.
SCHONGARTH	827	M	Ger.		Dr.,SS-Bde-Fuehrer (Pol.) 41	MURDER	U.S.
SCHONHALS	188798	M	Ger.		Major, Colonne In.950 R.I.H.,Charente et Vienne(Fr.) 8.44	TORTURE	FR.
SCHONHERR	192858	M	Ger.		Major, Schupo, C.C. Falstad near Drontheim (Nor.) 40-45	MISC.CRIMES	NOR.
SCHONING	828	M	Ger.		Lt.,Army, Comblanchien (Fr.) 21.-22.8.44	MURDER	FR.
SCHONSTEIN, Wilhelm	124383	M	Ger.		Lt.,Crim.Pol.,Camp Linfort (Ger.) 2.43-11.44	MURDER	U.S.
SCHONWALDER, Heinrich	301458	M	Ger.	28.4.98	Uscharfhr.,SS,(Nr.197311),C.C. Buchenwald (Ger.)16.5.38-9.10.43	MURDER	BEL.
SCHONWETTER	9615	M	Ger.		Major, Breendonck (Bel.) 43-44	TORTURE	BEL.
SCHOF	125052	M			Lt.,Camp Tarnstedt Bez.Bremen (Ger.) 9.5.42	MISC.CRIMES	U.K.
SCHOFF, Erich	142211	M			Oscharfhr.,SS, C.C.Lublin (Pol.) 42-45	MURDER	FR.
SCHOOK, Michael	149885	M			Civilian, Heiningen (Ger.) 28.9.44	MURDER	U.S.
SCHOON	136199	M			Pvt.,11 Pz.Div.,2 Coy AA A7, Albine (Fr.) 12.3.44	MURDER	FR.
SCHOON, Gerd	12355	M	Ger.		Pvt.,N.C.O.,111 Pz.Gren.Rgt.,2 Coy,Albine (Fr.) 29.6.44	MURDER	FR.
SCHOONMEYER	300869	M	Ger.		Sgt.,1 Aufkl.Abt.,3 Coy,2 Col.,XIV Div.Afrika Korps, St.Leger Distr.Arlon (Bel.) 5.9.44	MISC.CRIMES	BEL.
SCHOOP	191298	M	Ger.		Feldgendarm, Feldgendarmerie,Stenay Savannes (Fr.) 40-44	MURDER	FR.
SCHOOP, Harry	161292	M	Ger.		Chief, Gestapo, Nitra (Czech.) 44-45	TORTURE	CZECH.
SCHOPE	176007	M	Ger.		Civilian, Helmstedt (Ger.) 9.44	TORTURE	U.S.
SCHOPE nee WOLF	176008	F	Ger.		Civilian, Helmstedt (Ger.) 9.44	TORTURE	U.S.
SCHOPF, Michael	193736	M	Ger.	3.9.99	Pvt.,guard, 4 SS Totenkopf Stuba, C.C. Mittelbau Dora-Nordhausen (Ger.) 43-45	MURDER	U.S.
SCHOPF, Willi	188321	M	Ger.	04	Oscharfhr., Waffen-SS, Kamp Krs.St.Goar (Ger.) 29.12.44	MURDER	U.S.
SCHOPMEYER	1756	M	Ger.		Oscharfhr., SS, C.C. Dachau (Ger.)	TORTURE	U.K.
SCHOPOHL, August	193744	M	Ger.		Uscharfhr.,SS, 4 SS-Totenkopf-Stuba,Nordhausen,Auschwitz (Ger.,Pol.) 43-45	MURDER	U.S.
SCHOPP	126933	M	Ger.		Feldgendarmerie de Verdun, Bethincourt (Fr.) 21.7.44	MURDER	FR.
SCHOPP	167318	M	Ger.		Osturmfhr., Gestapo, SD, Oslo (Nor.) 4.40	TORTURE	NOR.
SCHOPP	174583	M	Ger.		Civilian,Stalag VI Ag.,C.C.Hamer (Ger.) 41-42	MISC.CRIMES	FR.
SCHOPP, Walter	138019	M			Civilian, Woltorf (Ger.) 8.44	MURDER	U.S.
SCHOPPA	254229	M			Pvt.,C.C.Dora-Nordhausen (Ger.)	MURDER	U.S.
SCHOPPE	829	M	Ger.		Oscharfhr.,SS,Oswiecim,Ratsko (Pol.) 6.40	MURDER	POL.,BEL.
SCHOPPE	143231	M	Ger.	15	Cpl.,SS Totenkopf Standarte,C.C.Buchenwald (Ger.)	TORTURE	U.S.
SCHOPPE	173503	M	Ger.		Uscharfhr.,Waffen-SS, C.C.Oswiecim-Birkenau (Pol.) 39-45	MURDER	CZECH.
SCHOPPE	250488	M	Ger.		Oscharfhr.,SS, C.C. Auschwitz-Birkenau (Pol.) 3.44	MURDER	YUGO.
SCHOPPERLE	129919	M			Kapo, C.C. Mauthausen (Aust.) 41-45	MURDER	U.S.
SCHOPPLEIN, Theo	125012	M		03	Major, Turceman Legion, Rimont (Fr.) 21.8.44	MURDER	FR.
SCHOPS, Josef see SCHEPP	129940						
SCHRAEDER	156921	M	Ger.		Capt.,H.U.V. Rgt."Lisieux",Cabrespuies (Fr.) 8.8.44	MURDER	FR.
SCHORN, Hildegard	253403	F	Ger.	05	Employee, Gestapo, Kolin (Czech.) 42-45	MISC.CRIMES	CZECH.
SCHORR	126597	M			Dr.,Civilian, C.C.Birkenau-Oswiecim (Pol.)	MURDER	U.S.
SCHORR see SCHARR	158593						
SCHOSCHIK	192859	M	Ger.		Osturmbannfhr., SS, Falstad near Drontheim (Nor.) 41-44	MURDER	NOR.
SCHOSSIG, Alfred	152114	M	Ger.	16.1.05	Oscharfhr., Gestapo, Region d'Angers (Fr.) 42-44	MURDER	FR.
SCHOSSIG, Alfred	193514	M	Ger.		Sturmscharfhr.,SD, Saales le Harcholet (Fr.) 44	MURDER	U.K.
SCHOSSMANN	192860	M	Ger.		SS, C.C. Falstad near Drontheim (Nor.) 9.42-2.44	WITNESS	NOR.
SCHOT, Katrina	149888	F	Ger.		Blockfuehrerin,Waffen-SS,C.C.Ravensbrueck(Ger.)	MISC.CRIMES	U.S.
SCHOTT	125053	M	Ger.		Oberstabsarzt, Dulag 183, Salonika (Grc.) 1.-8.41	MISC.CRIMES	U.K.
SCHOTT	189566	M	Ger.		Member, Gestapo, Stanislawow (Pol.) 8.41-10.42	MURDER	POL.
SCHOTT	253376	M	Ger.		Crim.asst., Gestapo, C.C. Buchenwald (Ger.) 38-39	TORTURE	U.S.
SCHOTT	261799	M	Ger.		Cpl.,Fieldgend.,Romilly sur Seine (Fr.) 10.6.44	MISC.CRIMES	FR.
SCHOTT, Albert	141606	M	Ger.	12.2.23	Chennebier,Etobon (Fr.) 27.9.44	MURDER	FR.
SCHOTT, Martin	301459	M	Ger.		Usturmfhr.,SS (Nr.340059), C.C.Buchenwald (Ger.) 16.5.38-9.10.43	MURDER	BEL.
SCHOTT, Wilhelm	194802	M	Ger.		Pvt.,Army, Semaphore de Beach Maout (Fr.) 5.8.44	MURDER	FR.
SCHOTKE, Robert	174841	M			Policeman, Police, Vienenburg (Ger.) 5.44-45	MURDER	U.S.
SCHOTTL	153272	M			Osturmfhr.,SS, C.C. Buna-Auschwitz (Pol.)	MURDER	U.S.
SCHOTTLER	166671	F	Ger.		Civilian, Reichelsheim (Ger.) 18.3.45	TORTURE	FR.
SCHOTTMUHLER	121845	M	Ger.		Officer, Gewerbepol.,Neurod-Busenbach (Ger.)	WITNESS	U.S.
SCHOTWOGMOWA	256034	F	Ger.		Nurse, Muehldorf (Ger.)	INTER.	FR.
SCHOTZ	253496	M	Ger.		N.C.O.,connection with executions,Fort de Seclin (Fr.)29.-30.8.44	MURDER	FR.
SCHOUANER	174566	M	Ger.		Army, Unit 56497 E,Plouigneau (Fr.) 9.8.44	MURDER	CZECH.
SCHOULA, Anna or SOULA	256853	F	Ger.	9.7.99	Civilian,Gestapo,C.C.Budejovice(Czech.) 9.9.44	INTER.	FR.
SCHOULTZ, Friedrich (SCHUTZ)	259899	M	Ger.		Lt.,Colonne Russo-Ger.,Turenne l'Ain (Fr.)	TORTURE	FR.
SCHOUMSCKITT	251774	M	Ger.	23	Overseer, SS, C.C. Ravensbrueck (Ger.)	MURDER	U.S.
SCHOVEN	152111	M	Ger.		Osturmfhr., SS, Rheinbach (Ger.) 1.45		
SCHOWACKER, Franz see SCHAUWACHER	120620						
SCHOWACKER, Frans	120634	M	Ger.		C.C. Bremen (Ger.) 4.2.43-6.4.45	MURDER	U.K.
SCHOWMAKER, A.	189560	M	Ger.		Bainfleur (Neth.) 7.7.44	WITNESS	U.S.
SCHPISS, Willy	174579	M	Ger.		Sgt.,Army,F.P.Nr.N.R.L. L.9591 L.P.,Repel-Gironcourt sur Vraine (Fr.) 2.8.44, 31.8.44, 1.9.44	WITNESS	FR.
SCHPORENBERG alias SPORENBERG	72043	M			Osturmfhr.,SS-Cmdt.Camp Wittlich,asst.commander Camp Wittlich, Hinsert (Ger.) 41-43	TORTURE	U.S.
SCHRADER	124974		Ger.	93	Lt.,SS, C.C. Bremen (Ger.) 6.43	MURDER	U.K.
SCHRADER	132369	M	Ger.		Miscellaneous	MURDER	U.S.
SCHRADER	143828	M	Ger.		Col.,C.C.Spangenberg (Ger.)	TORTURE	U.S.
SCHRADER	162555	M	Ger.	22	Uscharfhr.,SS,Command Staff, C.C. Buchenwald (Ger.)	TORTURE	U.S.
SCHRADER	190278	M	Ger.		Hptsturmfhr.,SS, C.C. Belsen (Ger.) 40-44	MURDER	YUGO.

SCHR - SCHR

NAME	C.R.FILE NUMBER	SEX	NATIO-NALITY	DATE OF BIRTH	RANK, OCCUPATION, UNIT, PLACE AND DATE OF CRIME	REASON WANTED	WANTED BY
SCHRADER	261491	M	Ger.		Capt., Air Force L.52.511, Pau, Soumonton, Narp, Lescar (Fr.) 6.-8.44	MURDER	FR.
SCHRADER	301365	M	Ger.		Prisoner, was at Camp Sick-Bay, Flossenburg (Ger.) 42-45	MURDER	FR.
SCHRADER, Bodo	146749	M			SS, C.C.Flossenburg (Ger.)	TORTURE	U.S.
SCHRADER, Hans	258102	M	Ger.	08	SS-Hptsturmfhr., State Service, Pol.Official, Val.Mezirici (Czech.) 44-45	MURDER	CZECH.
SCHRADER, Herman	125614	M	Ger.	03	Paymaster, Gestapo, Nord (Fr.)	MISC.CRIMES	FR.
SCHRADER, Wilhelm	132362	M	Ger.		Civilian, Farmer, Tiddische (Ger.) 5.44	MURDER	U.S.
SCHRAEDER, Rolf	256973	M	Ger.		Dr., Med.Officer, Regt. "Grossdeutschland", 4.Bn., Pancevo(Yugo.)4.41	WITNESS	YUGO.
SCHRAFFEN, Herman	128903	M			Guard, Kriegsgef.Arbeitskommando, Member of Nazi-Party (Ger.)	TORTURE	U.S.
SCHRAGIE	155988	M			N.C.O., Army, Stalag 344, C.C.Lamsdorf (Ger.) 10.44-11.44	MURDER	U.K.
SCHRAGNER	260014	M	Ger.		SS-Uschfhr., SS-guard at the transport of prisoners from Zitteu to Flossenburg, Plana near Marianske Lazne, Bohemia (Czech.) 15.4.45	MURDER	CZECH.
SCHRAIBA	830	M	Ger.		Pvt., Army, Brebieres (Fr.) 1.9.44	MURDER	FR.
SCHRAM	187342	M	Ger.		Rapportfhr., C.C. Buchenwald (Ger.)	MURDER	BEL.
SCHRAMEK	178959	M	Ger.		Capt., Kriegsgef.Arbeits-Klo. 190, Bbtn, Bassis Tunnel (Nor.) 43-45	MURDER	NOR.
SCHRAMEK, Karl	29685	M			Dr., Landgerichtsrat, Ministry of Justice, Litomerice (Czech.) 40	MURDER	CZECH.
SCHRAMETZ (or SCHRMETZ)	194271	M		90	Major, Air Force, Cambrai (Fr.) 40-41	PILLAGE	FR.
SCHRAML	39827	M	Ger.		Sturmfhr., SS Div, St.Sulpice, Fort Misson, Chateau Gontier (Fr.) 8.44	MURDER	FR.
SCHRAMM	6121	M	Ger.		Major, SS-Div. "Das Reich", Regt. "Der Fuehrer", Buzet s.Tara (Fr.) 7.7.44	MURDER	FR.
SCHRAMM	6156	M	Ger.		Army, Unter Massfeld (Ger.) 6.1.44	TORTURE	U.K.
SCHRAMM	124754				Capt., Schupo, Lodz (Pol.) 2. or 3.40	MURDER	U.S.
SCHRAMM	137499	M		11	SS-Uschfhr., C.C. Weimar-Buchenwald (Ger.)	TORTURE	U.S.
SCHRAMM	173540	M	Ger.		SS-Oschfhr., Waffen-SS, C.C. Buchenwald (Ger.) 42-45	MURDER	FR.
SCHRAMM	173886	M			Sgt., 469.Inf.Regt., 2.Bn., 198 Inf.Div., Letholy (Fr.) 13.11.44	INCENDIARISM	FR.
SCHRAMM	253360	M	Ger.		Usturmfhr., SS, Lublin (Pol.) 40-44	MISC.CRIMES	POL.
SCHRAMM	301072	M	Ger.		SS-Osturmfhr., SS, C.C.Hamburg-Neuengamme (Ger.) 45	MURDER	CZECH.
SCHRAMM, Gerda	162611	F	Ger.	21	Woman-Guard, Waffen-SS, C.C. Sasel (Ger.)	TORTURE	U.K.
SCHRAMM, Hans	143207	M	Ger.		Kreisbauernschaftsamtsleiter, NSDAP, Neustadt (Ger.) 40-45	MURDER	POL.
SCHRAMM, Johann	174840	M	Ger.		Civilian, West-Essen (Ger.) 1.45	MURDER	U.S.
SCHRAMM, Josef	142283	M	Ger.	22.1.03	Uschfhr., Waffen-SS "Totenkopf", C.C.Buchenwald-Weimar (Ger.)	TORTURE	U.S.
SCHRAMM (see SLAMM, Matheus)	137511						
SCHRAMM, Max	193691	M	Ger.	16.7.03	Oberwachtmeister, Ministry of Justice, Strafgefangenenlager Nord, C.C. Finmark (Nor.) 6.42-4.45	MISC.CRIMES	NOR.
SCHRAMM, Walther	193734	M	Ger.	3.2.04	Uschfhr., 4. SS-Totenkopf-Sturmbann, C.C. Nordhausen (Ger.) 43-45	MURDER	U.S.
SCHRAMMEL	258439	M	Ger.		SS-Uschfhr., Commander of the C.C.Waldenburg (Ger.) 45	MURDER	POL.
SCHRANDT, Elisabeth	300932	F	Ger.	14	Housewife, Walsum (Ger.) 1.8.44-31.10.44	MISC.CRIMES	U.K.
SCHRANFF	187778	M	Ger.		SS-Hptsturmfhr., Guard, C.C. Ravensbrueck (Ger.) 42-45	MURDER	U.S.
SCHRANKEL, Agnes	142282	F	Ger.	07	Nurse, Civ. KL. Hadamar (Ger.) 6.44-3.45	WITNESS	U.S.
SCHRANZ	187800	M	Ger.		SS-Hptscharfr., C.C. Ravensbrueck (Ger.) 42-45	MURDER	U.S.
SCHRAPPEL (or SCHARP or SCHARFF)	143103	M			Sgt., Army, P.W.-Guard, Stalag 4 D, Kiefheide (Ger.) 7.44	TORTURE	U.S.
SCHRATT, Anton	256380	M	Ger.	15.3.11	Member, Gestapo, Breclav (Czech.) 7.4.45	MURDER	CZECH.
SCHRATT, Hans	256044	M	Ger.		Kapo, C.C. Flossenburg (Ger.)	BRUTALITY	FR.
SCHRATZ	174282	M	Ger.		Feldgendarm, Feldgendarmerie, Cormainville (Fr.) 8.44	TORTURE	FR.
SCHRAUF	147345	M	Ger.		Pvt., 11.Panz.Div. Kampfgr. "Wilde" (Fr.) 44	MURDER	FR.
SCHRAWWEL	146748	M			Civilian, C.C. Flossenburg (Ger.)	WITNESS	U.S.
SCHRECK	141918	M	Ger.		SS-Mann, Bau-Inspektion Reich-Nord der Waffen-SS und Polizei, Sachsenhausen (Ger.)	WITNESS	U.K.
SCHRECK, Hugo	254007	M		25.5.05	Sturmmann, C.C. Harzungen, Nordhausen (Ger.)	MURDER	U.S.
SCHREDEL	254008	M			C.C. Rottleberode, Nordhausen (Ger.)	MURDER	U.S.
SCHREDER	188186	M			Dr., Kreisleiter, NSDAP (Lux.) 40-45	MURDER	LUX.
SCHREDER	252727	M	Ger.		Lt., F.P.No.38594, St.Martin (Fr.) 3.44	INTERR.	FR.
SCHREDER	300544	M	Ger.		SS-Hptsturmfhr., Cmdt., SS, C.C. Bergen-Belsen (Ger.) 42-45	MISC.CRIMES	YUGO.
SCHREDER (or SCHROEDER) Josef	254011	M			Pvt., C.C. Ellrich, Nordhausen (Ger.)	MURDER	U.S.
SCHREER	305811	M	Ger.		Capt., Camp Cmdt. Oflag VI-C, Osnabrueck-Eversheide (Ger.) 3.42-2.45	MURDER	YUGO.
SCHREIBER	891	M	Ger.		Sturmbannfhr., SS. (Fr.) 5.44	MURDER	FR.
SCHREIBER	39892	M	Ger.		SS-Osturmfhr., Crim.commissar, Kripo, Stalag III, C.C.Breslau (Ger.) 3.44	MURDER	U.S.
SCHREIBER	67668	M	Ger.		Sturmbannfhr., SS-Div. "Das Reich", Bagneres de Bigorre Trebonz, Pouzat (Fr.)	MURDER	FR.
SCHREIBER	67670	M	Ger.		Capt., Abwehr, Stalag VIII A, Goerlitz, Lindersack (Ger.)	MURDER	U.K.
SCHREIBER	120573	M	Ger.		Hptscharfhr., SS Totenkopf-Sturmbann, C.C. Theresienstadt (Czech.)	MURDER	U.S.
SCHREIBER	124750	M		10	Hptscharfhr., SS, C.C. Theresienstadt (Czech.)	MURDER	U.S.
SCHREIBER	147039	M	Ger.		Osturmfhr., SS-Panzer Div. "Das Reich", Regt. "Deutschland", 5.Bn., Vernerque Le Vernet (Fr.) 44	MURDER	FR.
SCHREIBER	167995	M	Ger.		Officer, Gestapo, Briey (Fr.) 28.8.44	TORTURE	FR.
SCHREIBER	173991	M	Ger.	00	Kreisleiter, NSDAP, Ermsleben (Ger.) 5.42	MURDER	POL.
SCHREIBER	188797	M	Ger.		SS-Hptscharfhr., C.C. Flossenburg (Ger.)	MURDER	FR.
SCHREIBER	194247	M	Ger.	27	Chief of Camp, C.C. Oamiers (Fr.) 41-44	TORTURE	FR.
SCHREIBER	194538	M	Ger.		Cpl., Feldgendarmerie, Ploermel (Fr.) 18.6.44	TORTURE	FR.
SCHREIBER	252739	M	Ger.		Sturmmann, S.D., Toulouse (Fr.) 11.42-8.44	MISC.CRIMES	FR.
SCHREIBER	253492	M	Ger.		Gendarm, Feldgendarmerie, Chaumont, Chateauvillain (Fr.) 24.8.44	MISC.CRIMES	FR.
SCHREIBER	300870	M	Ger.		Pvt., 1.Aufkl.Abt., 3.Coy, 2.Col., XV. Div. of the Afrika Korps, Saint Leger (Arlon) 5.9.44	MISC.CRIMES	BEL.
SCHREIBER	301905	M	Ger.		Oberfhr., Comd. SS Geb.Jaeger Regt.TP, 6.SS Geb.Div. Nord, 20.Army, Finmark (Nor.) 10.11.44	MURDER	NOR.
SCHREIBER	305625	M	Ger.		Member of S.D., Amsterdam (Neth.) 24.10.44	MURDER	NETH.
SCHREIBER, Ernst	255947	M	Ger.	5.3.06	Crim.secretary, Gestapo, Opava (Czech.) 39-45	MISC.CRIMES	CZECH.
SCHREIBER, Franz	188191	M	Ger.	97	Leader, NSDAP, Prag (Czech.)	MISC.CRIMES	CZECH.
SCHREIBER, Franz	257319	M	Ger.	26.9.13	Crim.asst., Gestapo, Prague (Czech.) 43-45	MISC.CRIMES	CZECH.
SCHREIBER, George	1076	M	Ger.		W.O., Army, Feldgendarmerie, Chaumont (Fr.)	MISC.CRIMES	FR.
SCHREIBER, Kurt	132197	M	Ger.	25	Lt., Air Force, Germsbach or Rastatt (Ger.) 1.45	WITNESS	U.K.
SCHREIBKE, Georg	259829	M	Ger.	28.3.23	SS-Mann, SS, I.Zug, II.Group, probably stationed at Bergeyk, North Brabant (Neth.) 11.9.44	MURDER	NETH.
SCHREIBJ	67031	M	Ger.		Camp-Capt., C.C. Linderbach-Gotha (Ger.)	MURDER	U.K.

NAME	C.R.FILE NUMBER	SEX	NATIO-NALITY	DATE OF BIRTH	RANK OCCUPATION UNIT PLACE AND DATE OF CRIME	REASON WANTED	WANTED BY
SCHREIDER	832	M	Ger.		Hauptsturmfhr., SS-Pz.Div. "Das Reich" Deutschl.Regt., Marsoulas and Mazeres (Fr.) 10.6.44	MURDER	FR.
SCHREIDER	186710	M	Ger.		Cpl.-Guard, Army Stalag IV-B, Muehlberg on Elbe (Ger.) 27.3.44	WITNESS	U.K.
SCHREIDER	188796	M	Ger.	02	Feldgendarm, Feldgendarmerie, Buire Cite (Fr.) 2.11.43	MURDER	FR.
SCHREIDER, Franz	253356	M	Ger.		Agent, Gestapo, Limoges (Fr.) 40-44	INTERR.	FR.
SCHREIEDER	165556	M	Ger.		Feldgendarm, Feldgendarmerie, Vielsam (Bel.)	PILLAGE	BEL.
SCHREIER	189441	M			Member, Sipo, Scheveningen (Neth.)	MURDER	NETH.
SCHREIER, Hans	253401	M			Pvt., 6.Coy.1.SS Pz.Regt. 1.SS Pz.Div. L.A.H., Engelsdorf (Bel.) 17.-19.12.44	MURDER	U.S.
SCHREIER, Johann	188190	M			Manager, Arbeitskdo., Passau (Ger.) 43-45	TORTURE	U.S.
SCHREIER, Otto	254009	M		7. 6.14	Sgt., C.C. Ellrich, Nordhausen (Ger.)	MURDER	U.S.
SCHREINER	12356	M	Ger.		Pvt., Army, 110. or 111. Pz.Gren.Regt.2.Coy. Albine (Fr.)29.6.44	MURDER	FR.
SCHREINER	67030	M	Ger.		Capt., Camp Army Stalag 8 A, on March to Goerlitz (Ger.) 1.44	TORTURE	U.K.
SCHREINER	193693	M		05	SS-Untersturmfhr., Ortskommandant, Lt., SS, Rjukan (Nor.)11.44	MURDER	U.K.
SCHREINER	256379	M			SS-Rottenfhr., SS Bn. 9 Nachsch. Abtlg.Dolem-Breux (Bel.) 7.9.44	PILLAGE	BEL.
SCHREINER, Karl	121852	M	Ger.		Pvt. Feldp.No. 48009 A, Gognies-Chaussee (Bel.) 3.9.44	MURDER	BEL.
SCHREINER, Leopold	39789	M	Ger.		Sous-Officer, SS-Div. Feldp.No. 43963 B, St.-Sulpice, Montmusson Chateau-Gontier (Fr.) 2.-6.8.44	MURDER	FR.
SCHREIRER, Heinrich	173555	M	Ger.		SS-Mann, W.-SS, C.C. Bergen-Belsen (Ger.) 1.10.39-30.4.45	MURDER	U.N.W.C.C.
SCHREITER, Anna	148010	F		08	Overseer, SS,	TORTURE	U.S.
SCHREITZ, Heinrich	251299	M	Ger.		Mason, Civ., Stod (Fr.) 44	INTERR.	FR.
SCHREK, Paul	253499	M	Ger.		Doyen, C.C. No. 3, Buchenwald (Ger.)	INTERR.	FR.
SCHRELER or SCHOEDER	190279	M	Ger.		Chief, Gestapo, C.C. Bankica (Yugo.) 40-44	MURDER	YUGO.
SCHREMER	253357	M			W.O., Unit of Aviatic C 26 769 3.Coy., Pierre (Fr.) 7.-8.44	PILLAGE	FR.
SCHRENCK	194061	F			Overseer, C.C. Ravensbrueck (Ger.)	TORTURE	FR.
SCHRENDER, Werner	188482	M	Ger.		Cpl., Army, Grete (Grc.) 3.44	MURDER	GRC.
SCHRENK	162613	M	Ger.	15	Pvt., Army Inf.Stal.XVIII, Radmer (Austr.)9.-10.41	MURDER	U.K.
SCHRENRS, Hubert	833	M			SS-Stabscharfhr., Fortmesson (Fr.) 3.8.44	MURDER	FR.
SCHREODER, Franz	167308	M	Ger.		Member, Feldgend. Vielsam (Bel.) 44	PILLAGE	BEL.
SCHREPPER	253424	M			SS-U-Scharfhr., C.C. Buchenwald (Ger.)42-45	MISC.CRIMES	U.S.
SCHREY, Heinrich	188188	M	Ger.	3. 8.06	Unterscharfhr., SS Gestapo, (Lux.)	MISC.CRIMES	LUX.
SCHREYER, Georg	62374	M	Ger.		SA-Gruppenfhr., Volhynia (Pol.)	TORTURE	U.N.W.C.C.
SCHRIBA	259144	M	Ger.		Capt., Ger. Army, Kistanje,Krnete, Bezbradice, Trazivuke (Yugo.) 11.43	MISC.CRIMES	YUGO.
SCHRIEBER	72255		Ger.		Sgt., Stalag-Luft 3, Kripo Breslau, Sagan (Ger.) 25.9.44	MURDER	U.K.
SCHRIEDMANN, Willy or KORFF	177571	M	Ger.		Agent, Gestapo Melun, Fontainebleau (Fr.) 3.8.44	TORTURE	FR.
SCHRIGUEL	255952	M	Ger.		W.O., Mauthausen (Aust.)	INTERR.	FR.
SCHRIMER	155990	M			Guard, SS, Poitier (Fr.) 3.44	TORTURE	U.S.
SCHRIMPF, Else	253999	F	Ger.		Gau-leader, Women's League, Luxembourg (Lux.) Grand Duchy 40-44	INTERR.	LUX.
SCHRINOL	261215	M	Ger.		SS-Standartenfhr., SS, Fieldpost No. 17221, Alleur-les-Liege (Bel.) 4.9.44	WITNESS	BEL.
SCHRITTER	256045	M	Ger.		SS-Mann, Neckargerach (Ger.)	TORTURE	FR.
SCHRMETZ see SCHRAMETZ	194271		Ger.				
SCHRODER	39787				SS-Schuetze, SS 17.Pz.Div."Goetz von Berlichingen" Sturm Geschuetz Abt. 17. or Pz. Jaeger Abt. 17, Segre-Renaze (Fr.) 6.8.44-30.7.44	MURDER	FR.
SCHRODER	142281	M		05	Lt., Police, Koeln (Ger.) 3.3.45	MURDER	U.S.
SCHRODER	155991	M			Platoon-Leader,Sgt., Army, Sturmbn. AOK-1, 2.Plat.4.Coy. Courcelles-Sur-Nied (Fr.) 11.44	MURDER	U.S.
SCHRODER	155992	M			Gendarme Boumath (Fr.)	MISC.CRIMES	FR.
SCHRODER	174541	M	Ger.		Sgt., Stalag Luft VI C.C. Heydekrug (Pol.)2.44	WITNESS	U.K.
SCHRODER	252713	M	Ger.		Gend.Gendarmerie, Brumath (Fr.) 4.5.41	PILLAGE	FR.
SCHRODER	253358	M	Ger.		Uscharfhr., Gestapo, Limoges (Fr.) 39-40	INTERR.	FR.
SCHRODER	253402	M			SS-Mann, 6.Coy.1.SS Pz.Regt., Stoumont (Bel.) 17.-19.12.44	MURDER	U.S.
SCHRODER, Gottfried	306657	M	Ger.		Guard, Ger.3.Coy. 334 Bn., Stalag III-A, Ebensdorf 2.9.44	MISC.CRIMES	FR.
SCHRODER, Helmut	126254	M		14	Camp, (Direktor bei der Eisenbahn) Achim b. Bremen (Ger.)	TORTURE	U.S.
SCHRODER, Hermann	72042	M	Ger.		Pvt., 204 Oberwinkle Labour Det.on 3.2.44	MISC.CRIMES	FR.
SCHRODER, Karl	6111	M			N.C.O. Army, Plombieres (Fr.) 18.7.44	MURDER	FR.
SCHRODER, Kurt	301760	M		7. 8.22	SS-Mann, SS, C.C. Buchenwald (Ger.) 16.5.38-9.10.43	MURDER	BEL.
SCHRODER, Ld.	146747	M			Obersturmfhr., SS, C.C. Flossenburg (Ger.)	TORTURE	U.S.
SCHRODER, Wilhelm	143230	M	Ger.		Oberlagerleiter, SS,C.C.	TORTURE	U.S.
SCHRODT, Friedrich	184285	M			SD C.C., Frankfurt (Ger.)	TORTURE	U.S.
SCHROECK, Xaver	254010	M		30. 6.05	Sturmmann, C.C. Ellrich, Nordhausen (Ger.)	MURDER	U.S.
SCHROEDER	29634		Ger.		Lt., Army Abwehr, Calais (Fr.) 4.9.44	MISC.CRIMES	FR.
SCHROEDER	121854	M	Ger.		Factory Official, Public Official, Deuts (Ger.)	TORTURE	FR.
SCHROEDER	121855	F	Ger.		Manager of the factory "West Waggon", Deutz nr.Koeln (Ger.)	TORTURE	FR.
SCHROEDER	126598			25. 7.05	Member, Sipo N.C.O., Oplanden (Ger.)	MISC.CRIMES	U.S.
SCHROEDER	162612	M	Ger.	14	Sgt., CC Stalag-Luft IV, Army, near Grosstychow (Ger.)44	WITNESS	U.S.
SCHROEDER	165555	M	Ger.		Sgt., Geheime Feldpolizei Bruessel (Bel.)	TORTURE	BEL.
SCHROEDER	167893	M	Ger.		Member, SD, St. Lo (Manche Fr.) 6.-7.6.44	MURDER	FR.
SCHROEDER	173502	M	Ger.		Chief, Gestapo, Staatspolizeileitstelle, C.C. Reichenberg, Oswiecim Birkenau (Czech. Pol.) 39-45	MURDER	CZECH.
SCHROEDER	180885	M	Ger.		Insp.General, for water and power, Aulnat (Fr.)	MISC.CRIMES	FR.
SCHROEDER	193301	M	Ger.	85	Prison-Guard, Justizvollzugsanstalten, C.C. Preungesheim, Frankfurt-Main (Ger.) 42-44	TORTURE	FR.,U.K.
SCHROEDER	194365	M	Ger.	10	Leader, O.T. Aasane (Nor.) 42-45	TORTURE	NOR.
SCHROEDER	253363	M			Major, O.C. Ger. Unit, Bolgana Area, Marke Graffa (It.) 25.9.44	INTERR.	U.K.
SCHROEDER	253378	M			Lt., Army, Daun (Ger.) 23.12.44	WITNESS	U.S.
SCHROEDER	256153	M			Manager, Civ. Utrecht (Neth.) 42	INTERR.	NETH.
SCHROEDER	256902	M	Ger.		Dr., Mil. Comdt. Military, Amsterdam (Neth.) 23.10.44	MURDER	NETH.
SCHROEDER	260849	M	Ger.		Obersturmbannfhr., Gestapo-Chief, Weimar (Ger.) 43-45	MURDER	U.S.
SCHROEDER	261922	M	Ger.		Guard, at Stalag VI I, Krefeld-Fichtenhain, Duesseldorf (Ger.)43-2.44	MURDER	YUGO.
SCHROEDER	300557	M	Ger.		Dr., Commissioner, Reichskommissar Amsterdam (Neth.) 24.10.44	MURDER	NETH.
SCHROEDER	300596	M	Ger.		Dr., Attached Ger. Red Cross, Heusden (Neth.) 5.11.44	MURDER	NETH.
SCHROEDER	305948	M	Ger.		Obersturmfhr., C.C. Oranienburg (Ger.) 11.39-45	MURDER	CZECH.
SCHROEDER	306718	M	Ger.		Cmdt., Obersturmbannfhr., SS, Merleburg, Nr. Altenburg (Ger.)30.8.44	MURDER	U.S.
SCHROEDER, Andreas	306130	M	Ger.		Pvt., Kennel Guard Royallieu Camp, Campiegne Camp de Royallieu Oise (Fr.) 41-44	MURDER	FR.

SCHR-SCHU

NAME	C.R.FILE NUMBER	SEX	NATIO-NALITY	DATE OF BIRTH	RANK OCCUPATION UNIT PLACE AND DATE OF CRIME	REASON WANTED	WANTED BY
SCHROEDER, August	251925	M	Ger.		Manager of War Factory.(Ger.) 45	INTERR.	CZECH.
SCHROEDER, August	253379	M	Ger.		Guard,C.C.Lahde-Weser(Ger.)	INTERR.	BEL.
SCHROEDER, Gottfried	167343	M	Ger.		3.Coy.,334 Bn.Landesschuetzen,Ebendorf(Ger.) 2.9.44	MURDER	FR.
SCHROEDER, Hugo	126273	M			Ausb.Off.Reichsbauernfuehrer(Kreisbauernfuehrer),Schackstad(Ger.)	TORTURE	U.S.
SCHROEDER see SCHRODER, Josef	254011						
SCHROEDER, Kurt	62092	M	Ger.		SS-Sturmbannfhr.,SS Camp-Cmdt.Neckargerach(Ger.) 44	MURDER	U.S.
SCHROEDER, Kurt	188187	M	Ger.	06	Usturmfhr.,5 Regt.SS Div.Totenk.Regt.,2 Bn.,8 Coy.,Plock(Pol.) 2.-9.41	MURDER	POL.
SCHROEDER, Margarete	253398	F	Ger.		Guard,C.C.Neunbremm(Ger.)	WITNESS	FR.
SCHROEDER, Oscar	191332	M	Ger.		Block-Aeltester,KL.Guard,C.C.Jakuschowitz-Auschwitz(Pol.) 43	MURDER	U.S.
SCHROEDER, Otto	185257	M	Ger.	6.1.02	SS-Osturmfhr.,Crim-Obersecretary,SD,Gestapo,Prague,Chrudim(Czech.)39-45	MURDER	CZECH.
SCHROEDER, Severin or SCHWERIN	190260	M	Ger.		Gen.,Flak-Art.	MURDER	YUGO.,U.S.
SCHROEDER, W.	12415	M	Ger.		SS-Sturmbannfhr.,Regierungsrat,Leiter der Org.-Abt.,Prag(Czech.) 39-45	TORTURE	CZECH.
SCHROEDER, Walter	894	M			Sgt.,Feldgend.,Henin-Lietard(Fr.) 11.-14.8.44	MURDER	FR.
SCHROEDER, Walter	194060	M	Ger.		Member Army,Semaphore de Beach Mscout(Fr.) 5.8.44	MURDER	FR.
SCHROEDER, Werner	196698	M			SS-Uscharfhr.,SS,Mbtz(Fr.) 10.44	MURDER	U.S.
SCHROEDER, Wilhelm	251797	M	Ger.		Stableiter,Ger.Evacuating Forces,Arnheim(Neth.) 1.-2.44	PILLAGE	NETH.
SCHROEDL, Klaus	12357	M	Ger.		Pvt.,Army,110 or 111 Pz.Gren.Regt.,Albine(Fr.) 29.6.44	MURDER	FR.
SCHROER	306696	M	Ger.		Pvt.,331 Pion.Bn.,331 Inf.Div.,Mijnheerenland(Neth.) 5.45	PILLAGE	NETH.
SCHROER, Guenther	254019	M		19.4.25	Pvt.,C.C.Ellrich,Nordhausen(Ger.)	MURDER	U.S.
SCHROEGLER see SHROEGLER	187774						
SCHROEGLER, Karl	188189	M			Blockaeltester,Waffen-SS,C.C.Mauthausen(Aust.)	TORTURE	U.S.
SCHROELER	124452		Ger.		Sgt.,C.C.staff,Sachsenhausen-Oranienburg(Ger.) 42	MURDER	U.K.
SCHROER	124310			18	Lt.,Army	MURDER	U.S.
SCHROER	167342	M	Ger.		W.O.,Air Force,Troissereux-Oise(Fr.) 15.,16.,18.8.44	MURDER	FR.
SCHROER	177570	M	Ger.		Lt.,Army,Longueil(Fr.) 24.6.44	MURDER	FR.
SCHROER, Peter	256875	M	Ger.	20.12.05	Employee,Factory Worker,C.C.Nordhausen(Ger.)	MURDER	U.S.
SCHROERS	253393	M			Employee,Abt. Sipo IIID,Bruessel(Bel.) 40-44	INTERR.	BEL.
SCHROENER	138229	M	Ger.		Sgt.,Army,Chartres,St.Martin De Nigelle(Fr.) 42	TORTURE	FR.
SCHROETER	256903	M			Pvt.,Krs.Art.Btty 717,St.Andre et Varsenare-Lez-Bruges(Bel.) 4.9.44	MURDER	BEL.
SCHROETER, Erwin	126388	M	Ger.		Dr.,Hptsturmfhr.or Sturmbannfhr.,SS,Psychiatric Research Institute, Muenchen(Ger.)	MURDER	U.S.
SCHROETER, Karl see SCHROETTER	252707						
SCHROETER, Karl Hans	199703	M	Ger.	99	Master-Policeman,Harthau(Ger.) 6.9.45	MURDER	U.K.,U.S.
SCHROETER, Wilhelm	173598	M			Kapo(Civ.:Ingenieur),C.C.Neckarelz(Ger.) 3.-8.44	TORTURE	FR.
SCHROETTER	162554	M	Ger.	85	Maj.-Gen.,Army O.-Edo.,C.C.Ohrdruf(Ger.)	TORTURE	U.S.
SCHROETTER, Karl or SCHROETER	252707	M	Ger.	01	Lt.,1 Coy.,92 Inf.Div.,192 Signal Unit,Farnese(Ital.) 6.6.44	INTERR.	U.K.
SCHROETINGER	254023	M			Flyer,C.C.Ellrich, Nordhausen(Ger.)	MURDER	U.S.
SCHROEUDER	260995	M	Ger.		Lt., Cmdt., Unit Art.Nr. 04528D,Noisy-Le-Grand(Fr.) 12.or.18.8.40	MURDER	FR.
SCHROLDER, Willy	260994	M			Pvt.,Unit Art.Nr.40539,Plounez(Fr.) 5.,6.8.44	TORTURE	FR.
SCHROLLER, Walter	259376	M	Ger.		Rottfhr.,Gestapo of Poitiers,Poitiers Area(Fr.) 40-45	MISC.CRIMES	FR.
SCHROMMEK	254201	M			Pvt.,C.C.Ellrich,Nordhausen(Ger.)	MURDER	U.S.
SCHROSENBERG, Charles	194257	M	Ger.		Chief des Douanes,Zollgreazschutz,Gedre(Fr.) 9.6.44	PILLAGE	FR.
SCHROTBERGER, Walther	141906	M	Ger.	90	Capt.,214 Div.Regt.355,12 M.G.Co.,Egersund(Nor.) 42-43	WITNESS	U.K.
SCHROTER	173539	M	Ger.		Kapo,C.C.Buchenwald(Ger.) 43-4.45	MURDER	FR.
SCHROTER	192057	M	Ger.		Ober-Cmdt.,Eis.Art.Btty.717,Feldp.Nr.22380,St.Andries,Varsenarde-Lez Bruges(Bel.) 4.9.44	MURDER	BEL.
SCHROTER	194537	M	Ger.		Cpl.,Feldgend.,Ploernel(Fr.) 18.6.44	TORTURE	FR.
SCHROTER	306872	M	Ger.		Capt.,2 Coy.,223 Inf.Regt.,Yves.Char.Inf.(Fr.) 20.9.44	INCENDIARISM	FR.
SCHROTH	171597	M			Sgt.,2 Div.paratrooper,2 Bn.,Plouzane(Fr.) 44	MURDER	FR.
SCHROTH, Franz	166679	M	Ger.	90	Member,Gestapo,SA,Rutingen(Ger.) 29.7.44	MURDER	U.S.
SCHROTH, Heinz Friedrich Hermann	301990	M	Ger.	22.11.10	Deserter from German Armed Forces,Rotterdam, Amsterdam(Neth.) 43	PILLAGE	NETH.
SCHROTT, Egbert	256264	M	Ger.	8.11.09	Confid.Agent,SD,Pilsen(Czech.) 39-45	TORTURE	CZECH.
SCHROTT, Gerhard	193733	M	Ger.		Chief,Crim-Assist.,Gestapo, Bruenn(Czech.) 39-45	MURDER	CZECH.
SCHROTTER	152115	M	Ger.		Senior-W.O.,Gestapo,Grenoble(Fr.) 43-44	TORTURE	FR.
SCHROTTER, Kurt	166678	M	Ger.		Civilian,Legal Official,Muenchen(Ger.) 43	MISC.CRIMES	U.S.
SCHRUFER	163654	M			Pvt.10 SS-Pz.Div.,36 Regt.,Revin(Fr.)	MURDER	FR.
SCHRUMER	194259	M			Lt.,Army Ober-Kdo.,La Rochette(Fr.) 3.8.44	MURDER	U.K.
SCHNURS, Harry	256152	M			SS-Mann,Heusden(Neth.) 11.44	PILLAGE	NETH.
SCHTALL	253237	M			Lt.,Cmdt.,1 Bn.Unteroffizierschule,338 Div., La Bresse(Fr.) 9.-11.44	MISC.CRIMES	FR.
SCHTALL	900983	M	Ger.		Gestapo Nancy,La Bresse-Vosges(Fr.) 9.-11.44	MURDER	FR.
SCHTANICKE	174766	M			Cpl.,Arb.Bn.203,Kgf.C.C.Aspfjord(Nor.)	TORTURE	NOR.
SCHU, Jakob	167935	M	Ger.		Civilian,C.C.Stalag XIID,Schleich(Ger.)	TORTURE	FR.
SCHUBERNEY	193201	M			Sturmmann,C.C.Niedersachsenwerfen,Nordhausen(Ger.)	MURDER	U.S.
SCHUBEN	191709	M	Ger.		Lt.,Inf.77 Bn.,4 Coy.,Liege(Bel.) 6.9.44	MURDER	BEL.
SCHUBER	250475	M		05	Political Chief,SS,Auschwitz-Birkenau(Pol.) 42-45	INTERR.	YUGO.
SCHUBERT	166674	M	Ger.		Policeman,Police (Ger.) 9.4.45	MURDER	FR.
SCHUBERT	167319	M	Ger.		Sturmschaffhr.,SS,Gestapo,Second in Command of Section 4 B(Nor.) 4.40	TORTURE	NOR.
SCHUBERT	167341	M	Ger.		Official,Cmdt.,C.C.Oberhau-Grunenthal(Ger.) 26.4.45	MURDER	FR.
SCHUBERT	173523	M	Ger.		Official,Usturmfhr., Agent,Gestapo-SS,Belgrad,Banjica(Yugo.) 17.8.41	MURDER	YUGO.
SCHUBERT	173882	M			Lt.,Art.Mountain 79 Kommandantur Albertville, Tours(Fr.) 8.,29.6.44	MURDER	FR.
SCHUBERT	186800	M			Chief,Member, Feldgendarmerie,NSDAP,St.Jean Le Luz(Fr.) 40-45	MISC.CRIMES	FR.
SCHUBERT	186802	M	Ger.		SS-Osturmfhr.,C.C.Flossenburg(Ger.)	MISC.CRIMES	FR.
SCHUBERT	190261	M	Ger.		Agent,Osturmfhr.,Gestapo,SS,C.C.Banjaci,Belgrad(Yugo.)	MURDER	YUGO.
SCHUBERT	191274	M	Ger.		Guard,Sgt.,O.C. 59-4.45	MURDER	U.K.,POL.,CZECH.
SCHUBERT	194535	M	Ger.	10	Osturmfhr.,Crim-Com.,Einsatz-Kdo.,Gestapo,Troppau,Lublin(Czech.,Pol.) 39-41	TORTURE	POL.
SCHUBERT	194596	M	Ger.		Cpl.,Feldgend.,Ploernel(Fr.) 18.6.44	TORTURE	FR.
SCHUBERT	253980	M	Ger.		Guard,C.C.Lahde-Weser (Ger.)	INTERR.	BEL.
SCHUBERT	254214	M			Uschfhr.,C.C.Sachsenhausen,Nordhausen(Ger.)	MURDER	U.S.
SCHUBERT	257802	M	Ger.		Lt.,RAD,Hautefort(Fr.) 1.4.44	MURDER	FR.
SCHUBERT	259333	M			Master,Org.Todt,Mühldorf Area(Ger.)	MURDER	U.S.
SCHUBERT	260298	M	Ger.		Sturmschfhr.,SS,Belgrade(Yugo.) 14.9.44	MISC.CRIMES	YUGO.
SCHUBERT	301607	M	Ger.		Warder-Kapo,barrack senior C.C.Gusen,Mauthausen(Aust.) 40-45	MURDER	BEL.

SCHU-SCHU

NAME	C.R.FILE NUMBER	SEX	NATIO-NALITY	DATE OF BIRTH	RANK OCCUPATION UNIT PLACE AND DATE OF CRIME	REASON WANTED	WANTED BY
SCHUBERT	301660	M	Ger.		Le Bourget,Triage,Gare (Fr.) 24.8.44	MURDER	FR.
SCHUBERT, Alois	305694	M	Ger.		Administr.,Head of the Messerschmidt Plant,C.C.Flossenburg, Hersbruck,Wolkenburg,Ganacker,Leitmeritz(Ger.-Czech.)1.1.42-8.5.45	MURDER	U.S.
SCHUBERT (see SCHOBERT), Arno Fritz-Rudolf	137497						
SCHUBERT, Franz	126599	M	Ger.	98 or 02	Chief,Police,Vienenburg (Ger.) 5.44	MURDER	U.S.
SCHUBERT, Frans	259819	M	Ger.		Chief-engineer,German sub-marine,Atlantic,Ocean: on the route between Cardiff and New York, 23.2.42	WITNESS	NETH.
SCHUBERT, Frid	188480	M	Ger.		N.C.O.,Army,Crete (Grc.) 5.42-12.43	MURDER	GRC.
SCHUBERT, Fritz	188591	M	Ger.		Cpl.,Chief infamousband of "Hunters",Army,Crete (Grc.)	MURDER	GRC.
SCHUBERT, Johann	250472	M	Ger.	26.10.16	Civ.,Driver,Andelska,Hora (Czech.) 4.45	MURDER	CZECH.
SCHUBERT, Paul	253396	M	Ger.	8. 9.02	Sgt.,Deputy-Cmdt.,Gestapo,z.b.V.Kommando 31,Valasske,Mezirici (Czech.) 14.2.-4.5.45	MISC.CRIMES	CZECH.
SCHUBERT, Rudolf	188517	M			Oldest man of block,SS,C.C.Mauthausen (Ger.)	MISC.CRIMES	U.S.
SCHUBLAT	194260	M	Ger.		Osturmfhr.,C.C.Flossenburg (Ger.)	MURDER	FR.
SCHUBRING	301285	M	Ger.		Krim.Sekr.,Abtl.IV D,S.D.,Bruessel (Bel.) 6.-9.40-44	MURDER	BEL.
SCHUBRINGS	187346	M	Ger.		Civilian,Montgauthier (Bel.) 20.9.43	MURDER	BEL.
SCHUCHARD, Willy	257801	M	Ger.		Maat,German Navy,Hopseidet (Nor.) 6.5.45	MURDER	NOR.
SCHUCHNIG (see SUSCHNIG)	39835						
SCHUCHZGART	259737	M	Ger.		Lt.,Unit:22,942 C stationed at Faymoreau,Vasles,La Chapelle, Montreuil,Deux Sevres,Vienne (Fr.) 25.-28.8.44	MURDER	FR.
SCHUCK	189145				Capt.,C.O.3 Coy.,95 Regt.,1 Sicherungs-Bn.,Mission Afrika, Chamalieres (Fr.) 23.8.44	MISC.CRIMES	FR.
SCHUCKART, Adolf	253397	M	Ger.	14. 8.94	Custom-house,officer,Luxemburg (Lux.) 40-44	INTERR.	LUX.
SCHUDBERG	165558	M	Ger.		Lt.,4 Coy.,Chars.Parach."Hermann Goering"-Dienststelle, Reboset Lil-Herstal (Ger.) 5.9.44	MURDER	BEL.
SCHUDOEK	187546	M	Ger.		Dr.,Physician (Oberarzt),12 SS-Pz.Div."Hitler Jugend", 12 Pz.Reg.Unit,Caen (Fr.) 6.6.-8.7.44	TORTURE	CAN.
SCHUEBELIN, Fritz	193694	M	Ger.	05	Oberwachtmeister,Reichsjustizminister,Strafgef.Lager Nord,Finmark (Nor.) 42-45	MISC.CRIMES	NOR.
SCHUEFFLER, Georg	12359	M	Ger.		Pvt.,Army,110 or 111 Pz.Gren.Regt.,2 Coy.,Albine (Fr.) 29.6.44	MURDER	FR.
SCHUELER, Kurt	193705	M	Ger.		Sekr.,Reichssicherheitshauptamt,Staatspolizei,Trandum,Berlin(Nor.Ger)	MURDER	NOR.
SCHUELLER	194533	M	Ger.		Lt.,Army,Lepanges (Fr.) 27.9.44	PILLAGE	FR.
SCHUELLER, Gerhard	254226	M		11.11.20	Pvt.,C.C.Ellrich,Nordhausen (Ger.)	MURDER	U.S.
SCHUELMANN, Paul,Friedrich	260469	M	Ger.	29. 6.99	Uschfhr.,SS,C.C. SS-Guard,Auschwitz (Pol.) 42-45	BRUTALITY	POL.
SCHUELTZE	252968	M	Ger.		Major,III Inf.Regt.,6 Army,Roolskamp (Bel.)	INTERR.	BEL.
SCHUELY, Josef (see SCHILI)	149869						
SCHUEMERS	149905	M	Ger.		Standartenfhr.,SS,Kazani (Grc.)	MURDER	U.S.
SCHUERMANN, Wilhelm Fritz	262365	M			Osturmfhr.,SS,150 Pz.Bde.,Meuse Bridge,Antwerp (Bel.) 12.44 L.O.D.N.A.O.D.	SUSPECT	U.S.
SCHUESSLER, Karl	262459	M	Ger.	27. 1.01	Employee,Daimler-Benz-Werke,Mannheim (Ger.) 44-45	BRUTALITY	POL.
SCHUETTER	256835	M	Ger.		Cpl.,Medical Attendent Klosterwerk,Nordhausen (Ger.)	MURDER	U.S.
SCHUETZ	307194	M	Ger.		Capt.,Slot Moermond,Renesse (Neth.) 10.12.44	MURDER	NETH.
SCHUETZE	129882	M	Ger.	20	Uschfhr.,W-SS,C.C.Buchenwald (Ger.)	TORTURE	U.S.
SCHUETZE, Helmut	852	M	Ger.	22.11.13	Oschfhr.,SS-Totenk.Stuba.,C.C.Maidanek,Buchenwald (Pol.Ger.) 40-44	SUSPECT	BEL.POL.U.S.
SCHUETZE, Lothar	254203	M		24. 6.11	Pvt.,C.C.Ellrich,Nordhausen (Ger.)	MURDER	U.S.
SCHUFFNER, Fritz	12360	M	Ger.		Pvt.,Army,110 or 111 Pz.Gren.Regt.,2 Coy.,Albine (Fr.) 29.6.44	MURDER	FR.
SCHUFFNER (see JAENISCH)	169755						
SCHUG, Franz	255470	M	Ger.	19. 4.01	Civilian,Gossengrun,Haberspirk (Czech.) 9.39	MURDER	CZECH.
SCHUH	62375	M	Ger.		Osturmfhr.,SS	MISC.CRIMES	UNWCC
SCHUH	147037	M	Ger.		Oschfhr.,SS,Pz.Div."Das Reich",Montauban (Fr.) 44	MURDER	FR.
SCHUH, Felix	250482	M	Ger.	10.12.97	Civilian,HR.Kralove (Czech.) 40-45	PILLAGE	CZECH.
SCHUH, Georg	261683	M	Ger.		Landrat,Civ.,Adr.,18 Immelmann-Str.,Karlsruhe,Colmar (Fr.) 40-45	MURDER	FR.
SCHUH, Jacob	260844	M	Ger.		Miner,Pvt.,Army,Elversberg (Ger.) 17.-19.7.44	WITNESS	U.S.
SCHUHBAUER, Franz	12361	M	Ger.		Pvt.,Army,110 or 111 Pz.Gren.Regt.,2 Coy.,Albine (Fr.) 29.6.44	MURDER	FR.
SCHUHLE	192861	M	Ger.		Schupo,C.C.Falstad near Drontheim (Nor.) 41-44	MURDER	NOR.
SCHUHLER, Madeleine	191527	F	Ger.		Civilian,Tulle (Fr.) 6.4.44	MISC.CRIMES	FR.
SCHUHMACHER	173500	M	Ger.		Uschfhr.,W-SS,C.C.Oswiecim,Birkenau (Pol.) 39-45	MURDER	CZECH.
SCHUHMACHER, Theo	188479	M	Ger.	00	Sturmschfhr.,S.D.,Vorden,Arnheim (Neth.) 2.10.44	MISC.CRIMES	U.K.
SCHUHMANN (or SCHIRMANN)	123952		Ger.		Capt.,Air Force(U.K.)	MURDER	U.K.
SCHUHMANN	149889	M			Asst.-Dr.,SS,C.C.Auschwitz (Pol.) 43-44	TORTURE	U.S.
SCHUHMANN	254004	M			Guard,SS,C.C.Rottleberode,Nordhausen (Ger.)	MURDER	U.S.
SCHUHMANN	305966	M	Ger.		N.C.O.,Head of SS Group,Oranienburg,Sachsenhausen (Ger.) 42-45	MURDER	FR.
SCHUHMANN, Otto	186206	M	Ger.		Uschfhr.,Guard,SS,C.C.Sachsenhausen (Ger.)	TORTURE	FR.
SCHUITZEN	260724	M	Ger.		Inspector,Field-Police,Auch-Fr.,Saint Jean Pontgo (Fr.) 3.5.44	MISC.CRIMES	FR.
SCHUITZLANN	254028	M	Ger.		Pvt.,Saechs.Gusstahlwerke,Freital (Ger.) 7.43	INTERR.	NETH.
SCHUKA, Walter	251338	M	Ger.		Customs,Zollverein,Essen,Katernberg (Ger.) 15.3.45	INTERR.	FR.
SCHUKERT	301717	M	Ger.		Member,S.D. or Gestapo,Oslo,Trandum near Oslo (Nor.) 19.1.43	MURDER	U.K.
SCHUKO	155994	M	Ger.		Pvt.,SS-Div."Adolf Hitler",Maastricht (Neth.)	RAPE	NETH.
SCHULD, Georg	254215	M		9.10.03	Rottfhr.,C.C.Harzungen,Nordhausen (Ger.)	MURDER	U.S.
SCHULDE, Ernst	126601	M			Civ.,Arbeitskommando,C.C.Hagen (Ger.) 40-45	TORTURE	U.S.
SCHULDT, Adolf	72041	M			Uschfhr.,SS-Mounta in Div."North"	MISC.CRIMES	FR.
SCHULENBERG	167997	M	Ger.		Lt.,1 Coy. of Georgian-Bn.,Tulle (Fr.) 6.4.44	MURDER	FR.
SCHULENBERG	167239	M	Ger.		Sgt.,General Staff,Kommandantur,Crest,Drome (Fr.) 7.-8.44	MURDER	FR.
SCHULENBURG	167339	M	Ger.		Cpl.,Etat Major de Crest,La Rochette (Fr.) 3.8.44	MURDER	FR.
SCHULER	31432	M	Ger.		Oberst,Gebirgsjaeger-Regt.218-7,Finmark (Nor.) 44	MURDER	NOR.
SCHULER	72026	M			Major,Police,district police-leader "Mark Brandenburg",Potsdam(Ger.)	MISC.CRIMES	U.S.
SCHULER	130069	M			Civ.,C.C.Schladming (Aust.) 7.44	TORTURE	U.K.
SCHULER	253147	M	Ger.		Dr.,C.C.Buchenwald (Ger.) 44	TORTURE	FR.
SCHULER	259331				Uschfhr.,SS,Mühldorf Area (Ger.)	MURDER	U.S.
SCHULER	301718	M	Ger.		Member,S.D. or Gestapo,Trandum near Oslo (Nor.) 19.1.43	MURDER	U.K.
SCHULER, Erwin	29819	M	Ger.	19. 9.12	Dr.,Oberstabsarzt,Sturmbannfhr.,SS,C.C.Buchenwald,Mauthausen, Gusen (Ger.-Aust.)	MURDER	FR.
					SS-Mann,SS,C.C.Buchenwald (Ger.) 16.5.38-9.10.43	MURDER	BEL.
SCHULER, Eugen	301461	M	Ger.	22.12.19	Verwalter,Member,NSDAP,Amsterdam (Neth.) 1.9.42-9.44	PILLAGE	NETH.
SCHULER, H.	300128	M	Ger.	27. 7.91	Pvt.,N.C.O.,110.Pz.Gren.Regt.,2 Coy.,Albine (Fr.) 29.6.44	MURDER	FR.
SCHULER, Wilhelm (or SCHULLER)	12362	M	Ger.				
SCHULEY, Josef (see SCHILI)	149869						

SCHU-SCHU

NAME	C.R.FILE NUMBER	SEX	NATIO-NALITY	DATE OF BIRTH	RANK OCCUPATION UNIT PLACE AND DATE OF CRIME	REASON WANTED	WANTED BY
SCHULLER	839	M	Ger.		Lt., Army 16. Div., St.Maure (Fr.) 8.44	MURDER	FR.
SCHULLER	126389	M	Ger.		Pvt., the SS-men guarding this camp were supplied by Buchenwald Magdeburg (Ger.) 44-45	MURDER	U.S.
SCHULLER	138290	M	Ger.		Sgt., C.C. Stalag XIII C, Bochum Werne (Ger.) 25.3.45	TORTURE	FR.
SCHULLER	146746	M			Civ., employed by the C.C. as Labor-Foremann, C.C. Flossenburg (Ger.)	TORTURE	U.S.
SCHULLER (see SCHLUTER, Willy)	155978						
SCHULLER (see SCHLUTER)	174580						
SCHULLER	182578	M	Ger.	15	Civ., Prison, Frankfurt M. (Ger.)	WITNESS	U.K.
SCHULLER	188794	M	Ger.		Sgt., Feldgendarmerie, Louhans , (Fr.) 16.10.43	TORTURE	FR.
SCHULLER, Adam	254221	M			SS-Mann Camp Bodungen, Nordhausen (Ger.)	MURDER	U.S.
SCHULLER, Karl	252728	M	Ger.	5	Aspirant, Gestapo, Meurthe and Moselle (Fr.) 40	TORTURE	FR.
SCHULLER, Wilhelm (see SCHULZE)	12362						
SCHULLING	129920	M			Pvt., W-SS C.C. Mauthausen (Aust.) 41-45	MURDER	U.S.
SCHULLTEIS, Christophe	263796	M			Agent Gestapo of Amiens, Gentelles (Fr.) 6.-8.44	MURDER	FR.
SCHULPELZKI	301608	M	Ger.		SS-Sturmbannfhr., stationed at C.C. Mauthausen (Aust.) 40-45	MURDER	BEL.
SCHULT	253174	M	Ger.		Opt., Truppendienststelle 1.39079, Ferrieres en Brie (Fr.) 24.8.44	MURDER	FR.
SCHULTE (see SCHATZ)	136214						
SCHULTE	174120	M	Ger.		Assistent to Major, Stalag 6 A, C.C. Hemer (Ger.) 41-45	TORTURE	U.S.
SCHULTE, Cornelius	149900	M	Ger.		Civilian, Oltmannsfehn, Stapelmoor (Ger.) 20.11.43	MURDER	U.S.
SCHULTE, Erich	133306	M	Ger.	19	Osturmfhr., W-SS Outercamp S III Thueringen (Ger.) 45	TORTURE	U.S.
SCHULTE, Ernest	262162	M	Ger.	9.12.12	SS Osturmfhr., 3.Coy. 51.SS Armoured Brigade, Bucheres, Breviandes Ste Savine, La Riviere de Corps (Troyes) (Fr.) 22.-25.8.44	BRUTALITY	FR.
SCHULTE, Ferdinand	253404	M	Ger.	1. 1.12	SS Oschfhr., Employee, SS Gestapo, Kolin (Czech.) 39-45	INTERR.	CZECH.
SCHULTE, Fritz	12363	M	Ger.		Pvt., 110. Pans.Gren.Rgt. N.C.O. Albine (Fr.) 29.6.44	MURDER	FR.
SCHULTE, Fritz	139227	M	Ger.		Employee, Civilian, Plettenberg (Ger.) 4.45	TORTURE	U.S.
SCHULTE, F.W.	301992	M	Ger.		Employee, Beauftragter fuer die Niederlande d. Reichsmin. fuer Bewaffn. und Munit. Richard Fieburg Laboratory of N.V. Brocapharm Meppel (Neth.) 9.44	PILLAGE	NETH.
SCHULZE, Heinrich	260052	M	Ger.		SS-Hptsturmfhr., Strafgefangenenlager Nord-Nordway 6.42-5.45	MISC.CRIMES	YUGO.
SCHULZE, Siebrand	174774	M	Ger.		Sgt., III. Kgf.Arb. Bn. 188 C.C. Fjell (Nor.) 42-45	TORTURE	NOR.
SCHULZE, Wilhelm	174842	M	Ger.		Civilian, Businessman, Lengerich (Ger.) 24.8.44	TORTURE	U.S.
SCHULZE, W.	250476	M	Ger.	10	SS-Usturmfhr., SS C.C. Auschwitz Birkenau (Pol.) 42-45	INTERR.	YUGO.
SCHULZE-MINBERG	260976	M	Ger.	95	S.A. Oberfhr., Chief of Abwehrdienst, Stalowa Wola (Pol.) 44-45	MURDER	POL.
SCHULZE-SCHUEPPING	31433	M	Ger.		Major, Gebirgs Div. Army, Gebirgs Art.Rgt. 124-8, Finmark (Nor.)44	MURDER	NOR.
SCHULTER (or SCHUTTER)	152127	M	Ger.		Opl., Army Prison, Graudena (Pol.)	TORTURE	U.K.
SCHULTHEISS, Friedrich	256385	M	Ger.		Opl., 3. Coy. Sturm Bn. 1, Courcelles (Fr.) 15.11.44	MURDER	U.S.
SCHULTHEISS, Georg	143226	M	Ger.	99	Sgt., Army, En Route Renda to Netra (Neth.) 29.9.44	MURDER	U.S.
SCHULTIESS	256265	M			Major, Aveyron, Herault, Gard Ardeche (Fr.) 8.44	MISC.CRIMES	FR.
SCHULTOKEN, R.	105979				Arbeitskommando	MURDER	U.S.
SCHULT, Hans	190282	M	Ger.		Kptsturmfhr., Gestapo, Krasevac, Kraljevo (Yugo.)	MURDER	YUGO.
SCHULTZ	840	M			SS-Standartenfhr.,	MURDER	POL.
SCHULTZ	841	M	Ger.		Oschfhr., SS Gestapo, Locmine (Fr.)	MURDER	FR.
SCHULTZ	1126	M	Ger.		Opt., Inf.Rgt. 497	MURDER	U.S.
SCHULTZ	1480	M		05	SS-Officer, Warder by C.C. Dzaldowa (Pol.)	MISC.CRIMES	POL.
SCHULTZ	67026	M	Ger.		Agent, Gestapo, Graudens, Thorn, Collar (Pol.Ger.) 44	TORTURE	U.K.
SCHULTZ	67671	M	Ger.		Pvt., Army C.C. Englesward (Ger.)	BRUTALITY	U.K.
SCHULTZ	67672	M	Ger.		Opl., Army C.C. Nordhausen (Ger.) 11.42	BRUTALITY	U.K.
SCHULTZ (see SCHUTZ)	67674						
SCHULTZ	105881				Sgt., Army	MURDER	U.K.
SCHULTZ (or SCHUTEZ)	122617	M			Gestapo C.C. Thorn (Pol.) 3.44	TORTURE	U.K.
SCHULTZ	123951				Dr., Commandeur, Arbeitskdo., C.C. Bleihammer (Ger.)	MURDER	U.K.
SCHULTZ	124451	M	Ger.		Stabsarzt, Stalag IV A, Koenigswartha Hospital (Ger.) 15.8.44-13.2.45	TORTURE	U.K.
SCHULTZ	126518	M	Ger.		Schfhr., SS Leibstandarte Adolf Hitler Rgt.1 Malmedy (Bel.) 17.12.44	MURDER	U.S.
SCHULTZ	128796	M	Ger.		Opl., Lamsdorf (Ger.) 18.7.43	TORTURE	U.K.
SCHULTZ	128815		Ger.		Arbeitskdo. 179, Opl.,	MURDER	U.K.
SCHULTZ (see SCHATZ)	136214						
SCHULTZ	137078	M	Ger.	03	Pvt., 610. Land.Schuetz.Bn. 4.Coy. between East Prussia and Brunswick (Ger.) 1.-3.45	TORTURE	U.K.
SCHULTZ	137079	M	Ger.		Sgt., 718. Land.Schuets. Halberstadt, Neugersleben (Ger.) 1.3.44	MURDER	U.K.
SCHULTZ	141919	M	Ger.	15	Art.Opt., C.C. Laterina (It.)	TORTURE	U.K.
SCHULTZ	142050	M	Ger.		Opl., C.C. Stalag 9 B Bad Orb (Ger.) 19.1.45	TORTURE	U.S.
SCHULTZ	142058	M	Ger.		Pvt. Guard, Army, C.C. Gneizendorf Stalag 17 B (Aust.) 1.-7.44	TORTURE	U.S.
SCHULTZ	149901	M			Sturmfhr., SS 4. Baubde. Div. Totenkopf, C.C. Ellrich Gardelegen (Ger.) 4.-14.4.45	MURDER	U.S.
SCHULTZ	152147	M	Ger.		Stabsa. Army, Stalag 9 D, C.C. Niesdorf (Ger.)	TORTURE	U.K. SOV.UN.
SCHULTZ	155996	M			Civ., Er. Gardelegen (Ger.) 4.45	MURDER	U.S.
SCHULTZ	155997	M	Ger.	05	Army 527. Land.Schuets.Bn. Stalag XX A, Nessau (Pol.) 44	TORTURE	U.K.
SCHULTZ	155998	M	Ger.	98	Dr., Civ., Stalag XX B Doctor from Christburg Budisch West-Russia (Ger.) 5.41 - 29.2.45	MURDER	U.K.
SCHULTZ	158580	M	Ger.		Opl., Land.Schuets.Bn. 610, Leslau (Pol.) 16.10.40	TORTURE	U.K.
SCHULTZ	158689	M	Ger.		Major, Army Pass. Div. Nachschub Training 52 3.Coy. Banneux (Bel.)9.44	MURDER	BEL.
SCHULTZ	161301	M	Ger.		Lt., 74. Motor Schuets. Rgt. 1. Bn. Clavieres (Fr.) 10.6.44	MURDER	FR.
SCHULTZ	167892	M	Ger.		Agent, Gestapo, Biache Saint Vasst (Fr.) 29.8.44	MURDER	FR.
SCHULTZ	168102	M	Ger.		Civilian, Friesack (Ger.) 22.6.44	MURDER	U.S.
SCHULTZ	173482	M	Ger.		Clerk, P.O.W. Camp Tripeli (Trip.) 20.6.41-10.8.41	TORTURE	U.K.
SCHULTZ	174546	M	Ger.	95	Civ., Manager of Benzia Factory Camp Bab 20, Heydebreck (Ger.) 40-45	TORTURE	FR.
SCHULTZ	186168	M			Guard, C.C. Dora Nordhausen (Ger.)	TORTURE	FR.
SCHULTZ	186205	M	Ger.		Opt., 19. SS Rgt. Pol. Valliery (Fr.) 9.6.44	MURDER	FR.
SCHULTZ	186803	M	Ger.		Opl., Feldgend. Truppe 626 Peronne Licourt (Fr.) 24.8.44	MURDER	FR.
SCHULTZ	186805	M	Ger.		Opt., Army Negeve (Fr.) 18.6.44	PILLAGE	FR.
SCHULTZ	187966	M	Ger.	09	Oschfhr., SD Geb.Div. Edelweiss, Trieste (It.) 10.44-1.45	TORTURE	U.K.
SCHULTZ	187992	M	Ger.	00	Lt., 4. Coy. 427. Land.Schuets.Bn. Stalag 344 Katschwits (Ger.) 27.3.45	MURDER	U.K.
SCHULTZ	188515	M	Ger.		Guard, SS Police Athens (Grc.) 44	PILLAGE	GRC.
SCHULTZ	188793	M	Ger.		Prison Instruction d'Avignon (Fr.) 40-44	TORTURE	FR.
SCHULTZ	189039	M	Ger.	01	Colonel, 1. paratroop Div. near Cassino (It.) 44	TORTURE	U.K.
SCHULTZ	189610	M	Ger.		Major, Central Ersatzteillager 206, Paris (Fr.) 21.8.44	MURDER	FR.

SCHU-SCHU

NAME	C.R.FILE NUMBER	SEX	NATIO- NALITY	DATE OF BIRTH	RANK OCCUPATION UNIT PLACE AND DATE OF CRIME	REASON WANTED	WANTED BY
SCHULTZ	189854	M	Ger.		Interpreter,Pvt.,Gestapo,527 Ldsch.Bn.,C.C.Graudenz (Pol.) 44	TORTURE	U.K.
SCHULTZ	189856	M	Ger.	05	Pvt.,Punishment Camp,C.C.Nessau near Thorn (Pol.) 4.-8.44	TORTURE	U.K.
SCHULTZ	190284	M	Ger.		Kreiskommandant,Kriegskommandantur Pozarevac (Serbia) 41-42	MURDER	YUGO.
SCHULTZ	190285	M	Ger.		Member,Gestapo,C.C.Belgrade,Banjica (Yugo.) 41	MURDER	YUGO.
SCHULTZ (or SCHULZ)	191273	M	Ger.		SS-Uschfhr.,C.C.Sachsenhausen,Oranienburg (Ger.) 39-4.45	MURDER	POL.
SCHULTZ	192058	M	Ger.		Pvt.,Eisenbahn Bn.717,F.P.Nr.22380,St.Andries Varsenare les Bruges (Bel.) 4.9.44	MURDER	BEL.
SCHULTZ	193311	M	Ger.	95	Cpl.,Army,Stalag VIII B,Lamsdorf (Ger.) 7.43	TORTURE	U.K.
SCHULTZ	193674	M	Ger.	16	Cpl.,Army,Oberkdo.324,218 Bn.Stalag 20 B,Filehne near Dtsch.Eylau (Ger.) 6.42	TORTURE	U.K.
SCHULTZ	194374	M			N.C.O.,Geh.Feldpolizei 112,Bruessels (Bel.)	TORTURE	BEL.
SCHULTZ	195498	M	Ger.		Lt.,SD,SS,Zdolbunow (Pol.) 7.8.41	MURDER	POL.
SCHULTZ	253495	M	Ger.		Capt.,Cmdt.,Villard de Lans (Fr.) 14.8.44	INTERR.	FR.
SCHULTZ	253901	M			Guard,C.C.Neuengamme (Ger.) 44	MURDER	FR.
SCHULTZ	257800	M			Lt.,Fest.Stamm Ers.Res.A.K.25,Pontivy (Fr.) 3.8.44	MURDER	U.S.
SCHULTZ	259317	M			Ortsgruppenleiter,Camp Thekla near Leipzig (Ger.) 18.4.45	MURDER	U.S.
SCHULTZ (or SCHULZ)	261269	M	Ger.		Marine-Lt.,Unit 21843,Le Touquet,Paris,Plage (Fr.) 43-44	PILLAGE	FR.
SCHULTZ	261493	M	Ger.		Sgt.,Air Force L 52511,Pau,Soumonton,Narp,Lescar (Fr.) 6.-8.44	MURDER	FR.
SCHULTZ	301740	M	Ger.	05	Cpl.,596 Ldsch.Bn.with Coy H.Q.,Sonderhausen,11.11.42	BRUTALITY	U.K.
SCHULTZ	302146	M			Lt.,Rotterdam (Neth.) 15.1.45	PILLAGE	NETH.
SCHULTZ	305268	M			Hptsturmfhr.,Commandant of Osturmfhr.Pahnke,stationed at Geldermalsen or Elstand Opijnen,Gameren,15.9.44	MURDER	NETH.
SCHULTZ	305497	M	Ger.		Naval Lt.,Le Touquet Paris Plage (Fr.) 43-44	PILLAGE	FR.
SCHULTZ	305498	M	Ger.		Staff Capt.,Villard de Lans,Cours Berriat Grenoble Isere (Fr.)14.8.44	INTERR.	FR.
SCHULTZ	306883	M	Ger.		Head,SS, of women's labour service at C.C.Auschwitz (Pol.) 40-45	MURDER	FR.
SCHULTZ,Alfred Jules (or SEH- MISCH)	307197	M	Ger.	14. 7.11	Interpreter of the Sicherheitsdienst Nice,Colmars Basses-Alpes (Fr.) 30.1.44	INTERR.	FR.
SCHULTZ,Arthur	259209	M	Ger.		Oschfhr.,Gestapo,Poitiers Area (Fr.) 40-44	MISC.CRIMES	FR.
SCHULTZ,Ecke	259600	M	Ger.	01	Uschfhr.,Gestapo,Area Angers Maine and Loire (Fr.) 42-44	MISC.CRIMES	FR.
SCHULTZ,Egon	251322	M	Ger.		C.O.,SS,Police,Ugine (Fr.)	MURDER	FR.
SCHULTZ,Erfriedel	142033	M	Ger.	00	Oberbereitschaftsleiter,NSDAP,St.Helier,Jersey Channel Isles,42-44	TORTURE	U.K.,SOV.UN.
SCHULTZ,Ernst	258557	M	Ger.		SS-Hptsturmfhr.,SS,W.V.H.A., (Ger.) 40-45	BRUTALITY	U.S.
SCHULTZ,Ernst (see SCHULZ)	259311						
SCHULTZ,Erwin	9616	M	Ger.		Bfefhr.,SD official of Reich Sicherheitshauptamt, (Bel.) 40-44	TORTURE	BEL.
SCHULTZ,Fr.	262457	M			Member,Chief,Gestapo,SS Ghetto and several factories,Warschau (Pol.) 42-43	MURDER	POL.
SCHULTZ,Friedrich Fritz	253238	M	Ger.	19	Lt.,Russ.-Ger.Columm,Chaumont,La Ferte sur Aube (Fr.) 15.6.44	MURDER	FR.
SCHULTZ,Guntram	257347	M	Ger.		Cpl.,Org.Todt,slave labour camps,Erlandet,Oeusand,Trola (Nor.)6.42-45	MURDER	YUGO.
SCHULTZ,Hans (see SCHLUTT)	173528						
SCHULTZ,Hans-Joachim	258951	M	Ger.		Vice-Admiral,Crimes against peace,crimes against humanity	WITNESS	U.S.
SCHULTZ,Karl	136215	M	Ger.	00	Sgt.,Army,C.C.Marseille (Fr.) 43	TORTURE	FR.
SCHULTZ,Otto	156000	M			Army,3 Coy Sturmbn.AOK 1,Sgt.,Courcelles sur Nied (Fr.)	MURDER	U.S.
SCHULTZ,Otto	158581	M			Volkssturm Bn.,Gardelegen (Ger.) 5.-15.4.45	MURDER	U.S.
SCHULTZ,Otto	300545	M		95	Company Commander,SS-Usturmfhr.,SS,C.C.Auschwitz-Birkenau (Pol.)42-45	MISC.CRIMES	YUGO.
SCHULTZ,Paul (or SCHOLZ)	126521				Sipo,Feldgendarmerie,Vendome (Fr.) 10.8.44	MURDER	U.S.
SCHULTZ,Paul	142032	M		11.12.95	Disziplinarstelle Org.Todt,St.Helier,Jersey Channel Isles,42-44	TORTURE	U.K.,SOV.UN.
SCHULTZ,Paul	142277	M		14	Cpl.,Ldsch.Bn.635, 6 Coy,Wulfingerode (Ger.) 7.44	MURDER	U.S.
SCHULTZ,Paul	305645	M		31. 5.10	Schfhr.,Crim.-Asst.,Sipo,Aussendienststelle Larvik,Notodden,Telemark, Lifjell (Nor.) 3.-9.11.44,19.-26.3.45 and 10.-14.10.44	TORTURE	NOR.
SCHULTZ,Rudi	253423	M	Ger.		SS-Schfhr.,SS,C.C.Buchenwald (Ger.) 42-45	TORTURE	U.S.
SCHULTZ,Ruth	125255	F			Woman-Guard,SS,Helmbrecht Volary (Czech.)	MURDER	U.S.
SCHULTZ,Walter	129974				Col.,C.C.Mauthausen (Aust.) 41-45	MURDER	U.S.
SCHULTZ,Walter	149902	M			Hptsturmfhr.,SS,Mauthausen (Aust.) 41-45	MURDER	U.S.
SCHULTZE (or SCHUTZE)	24829	M			Social Welfare Officer,I.G.Farbenwerke,Heidebreck (Ger.) 1.8.44	MURDER	U.K.
SCHULTZE	125728	M	Ger.		Sgt.,Flak Btty.,Stalag XX B,C.C.Rosenburg (Pol.) 1.43-2.44	MURDER	U.K.
SCHULTZE	142278		Ger.		Dr.,Col.,C.C.Schandelah-Braunschweig (Ger.) 44-45	TORTURE	BEL.
SCHULTZE	162231	M	Ger.	20	Uschfhr.,C.C.Ohrdruf-Buchenwald (Ger.) 45	TORTURE	U.S.
SCHULTZE	168101	M	Ger.		Major,SS Medecin,Chambon-Lignon (Fr.) 44	MURDER	FR.
SCHULTZE	305949				Crim.-Rat,Theresienstadt Prison,small Fortress,from Police,H.Q.,Prague Oswiecim-Birkenau (Czech.) 1.10.38-44,39-45	MURDER	CZECH.,POL.
SCHULTZE,Adolf	186549	M	Ger.		Pvt.,2 Coy K.G.F.Arbeits Bn.187,Potthus and Korgen (Nor.)	MURDER	NOR.
SCHULTZE,Alphonse	189624	M	Ger.		C.C.Dachau (Ger.) 3.45	MURDER	BEL.
SCHULTZE,Maxim	158582	M	Ger.		Civilian,Karthaus (Pol.) 44	WITNESS	U.K.
SCHULTZE,Wilhelm	188520	M	Ger.	18. 9.09	Hptsturmfhr.,Crim.-Rat,SD,Gestapo office,Prague (Czech.) 39-45	MURDER	CZECH.
SCHULY,Josef (see SCHILL)	149869						
SCHULZ	10348	M	Ger.	17	SS-Rottfhr.,SS,Natzweiler (Fr.) 42	TORTURE	CZECH.
SCHULZ	10349	M	Ger.		Sturmbannfhr.,SS,Olomouc (Czech.) 39-44	TORTURE	CZECH.
SCHULZ	12364	M	Ger.		Capt.,Army,Dienststelle F.P.Nr.57205 B,Ugine (Fr.) 5.6.44	MURDER	FR.
SCHULZ	21445	M			Soldier,Army,12 SS Pz.Div.,	WITNESS	CAN.
SCHULZ	21446	M		08	SA,SS,NSDAP, (Ger.)	MURDER	U.S.
SCHULZ	31434	M			Major,Army,307-163 Inf.Div., II Gren.Rgt.,Finmark (Nor.) 44	MURDER	NOR.
SCHULZ	31557	M			Civilian,Doctor u.District Attorney,C.C.Klingelpuetz (Ger.)	TORTURE	U.S.
SCHULZ	36342	M			SS-Rottfhr.,C.C.Natzweiler (Fr.)	TORTURE	CZECH.
SCHULZ	62139	M			Soldier,SS,12 SS Pz.Div.(Hitler Jugend)	WITNESS	BEL.
SCHULZ	122545				Capt.,Luft Festungsabt.,7,Neuhof (Bel.) 9.10.44	MURDER	U.S.
SCHULZ	129922	M			Lt.Col.,Waffen SS,C.C.Mauthausen (Aust.) 41-45	MURDER	U.S.
SCHULZ	129976	M	Ger.		5 Fallschirmjg.Rgt.Nachrichtensug,Quaregnon,Jemappes,Ghlin (Bel.) 2.-3.9.44	MURDER	BEL.
SCHULZ	131999	M		16	Oschfhr.,SS,C.C.Outercamp S III Thueringen (Ger.) 45	TORTURE	U.S.
SCHULZ	132007	M			Osturmfhr.,Gestapo,SD,Zamdsch (Pol.)	MURDER	U.S.
SCHULZ	136378	M			Civilian Detain,Zilly,15.12.44	WITNESS	U.S.
SCHULZ	139696	M	Ger.		Stabsintendant,Stalag X B,Sandbostel (Ger.) 1.-5.45	TORTURE	U.S.
SCHULZ	143220	M	Ger.		Lt.,SS,C.C.Buchenwald (Ger.)	MURDER	U.S.
SCHULZ	143221	M	Ger.		Civilian,Weinbohla (Ger.) 23.3.45	MURDER	U.S.

SCHU - SCHU

NAME	C.R.FILE NUMBER	SEX	NATIO-NALITY	DATE OF BIRTH	RANK OCCUPATION UNIT PLACE AND DATE OF CRIME	REASON WANTED	WANTED BY
SCHULZ	143222	M	Ger.	05	Cpl.,W-SS,Div."Leibstandarte Adolf Hitler",1 Ers.Bn.,Rosbach(Ger.)3.45	MURDER	U.S.
SCHULZ	152149	M	Ger.		Gestapo, Bretagne Anjou Puitov (Fr.)	MURDER	FR.
SCHULZ	156001	M			Officer , SS Anti Espionage Squad Prague (Czech.) 10.41 - 2.42	TORTURE	U.K.
SCHULZ	162614	M	Ger.		Hauptsturmfhr., SS-Totenkopf-Standarte,Mauthausen-Linz (Aust.)8.or 9.44	MURDER	U.S.
SCHULZ	165229	M	Ger.	89	Standortenfhr., SS, SD, Zwinkel (Pol. Sov.Un.) 41 - 42	MURDER	U.S.
SCHULZ	167998	M	Ger.		Branch Director, Einsatzstab Rosenberg,Angers (Fr.) 40 - 44	PILLAGE	FR.
SCHULZ	173293	M	Ger.		Uscharfhr.,SS, C.C.,Bunzlau near Breslau (Ger.) 1.45	MURDER	POL.
SCHULZ	173879	M	Ger.	85	Capt., Stalag XIII D.Kommando 1600, Nuernberg (Ger.)	MURDER	FR.
SCHULZ	173880	M	Ger.		Pvt., Parachute Rgt.,2.Bn.,Plouzane (Fr.) 44	MURDER	FR.
SCHULZ	173881	M			Cmdt., Gebirgsjaeger-Bn., Annecy (Fr.)	PILLAGE	FR.
SCHULZ	174274	M	Ger.		Capt., Inf.Rgt.497,Sars la Bruyere (Bel.) 9.44	MURDER	BEL.
SCHULZ	174858	M		05	Secretary-Uscharfhr., Gestapo, SS, Locmine (Fr.) 7.-8.44	TORTURE	FR.
SCHULZ	179498	M			Rottenfhr., SS, C.C., Oswiecim-Birkenau (Pol.)	MURDER	CZECH.
SCHULZ	188792	M			Sgt., Gestapo, SD, Merbihan (Fr.)	WITNESS	FR.
SCHULZ (see SCHULTZ)	191273						
SCHULZ	193406	M	Ger.		Pvt., Kriegsgefangenen Arb.Bn.41,Kristiansund-Nerlandsdal(Nor.)41-45	TORTURE	NOR.
SCHULZ	193698	M	Ger.		Cpl.,Kriegsgef.Arb.Bn., 190, Bergholnes Nordland (Nor.) 43 - 45	TORTURE	NOR.
SCHULZ	253173	M	Ger.		Cpl., Feldgendarmerie of Vendome (Fr.) 8.44	SUSPECT	FR.
SCHULZ	253394	M	Ger.		Employee, Arb.IV.D.Sipo, Bruessels (Bel.) 40 - 44	INTERR.	BEL.
SCHULZ	254431	M	Ger.		Cmdt., C.C., Nis (Yugo.) 4.43	PILLAGE	YUGO.
SCHULZ	256267	M	Ger.		Chief, Political Dept. Mauthausen (Ger.)	MURDER	FR.
SCHULZ	259830	M	Ger.		Chief-pay-master, Army, Commando "Raumbot", Breda Noord-Brabant(Neth.)	PILLAGE	NETH.
SCHULZ (see SCHULTZ)	261493						
SCHULZ	261794	M	Ger.		Cpl., Artillerie H.D.V. 199-2235 F.P. 27.046 C, Lorgies (Fr.) 3.9.44	MURDER	FR.
SCHULZ	300129	M	Ger.		Head of Political Section,C.C.Mauthausen (Aust.) 11.42 - 5.45	MURDER	FR.
SCHULZ	300563	M	Ger.		Cpl., Army,3.Jaeger Bn.,738.Rgt.,Sailing Chip MB 16,off Supetar (Yugo.) 10.3.44	MISC.CRIMES	YUGO.
SCHULZ	301183	M	Ger.		Capt., Cmdt."Heavy" 13.Coy.84 Landsturm Neth. SS,Bennekom,Ede (Neth.) 3.44 - 4.45	MURDER	NETH.
SCHULZ	301859	M	Ger.		Capt., Adjoint to Col. Schlee,479.Inf.Rgt.at Sars-la Bruyere(Chainaut) 9.44	MURDER	BEL.
SCHULZ	301993	M	Ger.		Rttfhr.,SS Staffel Sanitaeter, C.C., Auschwitz (Pol.) 42 - 45	MURDER	POL.
SCHULZ	305269	M	Ger.		Warder, C.C., Neuengamme (Ger.)	MURDER	FR.
SCHULZ	305499	M	Ger.		N.C.O., Vendome Loir et Cher (Fr.) 9.8.44	MURDER	FR.
SCHULZ, Adolf	254002	M		3. 7.97	Pvt., C.C., Artern-Harzungen-Nordhausen (Ger.)	MURDER	U.S.
SCHULZ, Arthur	302147	M	Ger.		Oberscharfhr., SS,Section IV of the Poitiers Gestapo, Poitiers, Chatellerault,Angouleme (Fr.)	MURDER	FR.
SCHULZ, Emil	255471	M			Crim.Assistent, Gestapo, Saarbruecken (Ger.)	INTERR.	U.K.
SCHULZ, Emil	141607	M			SS, Gestapo, Sturmschfhr., Agent. Felking (Fr.)	MURDER	FR.
SCHULZ, Erich	119395	M		06	Arbeitsdienstfhr.,C.C., Oswiecim(Pol.) 6.40 - 1.45	MURDER	POL.
SCHULZ, Erich	250483	M	Ger.		Pvt., SS, Auschwitz-Birkenau (Pol.) 12.42	INTERR.	YUGO.
SCHULZ, Erich, Hugo	300933	M	Ger.		Kommandofhr.,SS of Staff at C.C., Neugraben-Tiefstak (Ger.) 44 - 45	MURDER	CZECH. U.K.
SCHULZ, Erik	132364	M				MURDER	U.S.
SCHULZ, Ernst	187345	M	Ger.		Lt., Police Bn., Praha (Czech.) 5.42	MURDER	CZECH.
SCHULZ, Ernst	254003	M	Ger.	16. 3.08	Uscharfhr., C.C., Ellrich-Nordhausen (Ger.)	MURDER	U.S.
SCHULZ (or SCHULTZ,Ernst)	259311	M			Uscharfhr., SS, Organ.Todt, Muehldcf - Area (Ger.)	MURDER	U.S.
SCHULZ, Erwin	33692	M	Ger.	27.11.00	Gruppenfhr., SD, Sipo, Hamburg und Berlin (Ger.) 42	TORTURE	UNWCC
SCHULZ, Erwin	166673	M	Ger.		Brigadefhr.,General-Major,Cmdt.of Security Police and Security Service SS, (Ger.) 44 - 45	MISC.CRIMES	U.S.
SCHULZ, Friedrich	262163	M	Ger.		Uscharfhr., Gestapo, Rennes (Fr.) 43 - 44	MISC.CRIMES	FR.
SCHULZ, Fritz	300130	M			Chief of Labour Propaganda and Labour office, Warsaw (Pol.)40-45	INTERR.	POL.
SCHULZ, Gertrud	300934	F	Ger.		Aufseherin, SS of Staff at C.C. Neugraben-Tiefstak (Ger.) 44-45	MURDER	CZECH.U.K.
SCHULZ, Gustav	137500	M			Oberscharfhr.,SS, C.C., Weimar-Buchenwald (Ger.)	TORTURE	U.S.
SCHULZ, Herbert	254001	M			Pvt., C.C., Ellrich,Nordhausen (Ger.)	MURDER	U.S.
SCHULZ, Hugo	126285	M	Ger.	91	Uscharfhr., SS-Panz.Div.Totenkopf,	TORTURE	U.S.
SCHULZ, Karl	29727	M	Ger.		Dr., Oberlandesgerichtsrat,Public Official,Litomerice (Czech.)40	MURDER	CZECH.
SCHULZ, Karl	129975	M			Lt., Waffen SS, Police Official,C.C., Mauthausen (Aust.)41 - 45	MURDER	U.S.
SCHULZ, Karl	133202	M		15	Pvt., Air-Force,Luftnachr.Ausbaust,II,Funkstelle Heiketaler-Warte Zilly (Ger.) 15.9.44	MURDER	U.S.
SCHULZ, Karl	182571	M	Ger.	01	Obersturmfhr., SS,Police,C.C. Mauthausen (Aust.) 1.45	MURDER	U.S.
SCHULZ, Karl	250477	M	Ger.	15	Usturmfhr.,SS, C.C. Auschwitz-Birkenau (Pol.) 42 - 45	INTERR.	YUGO.
SCHULZ, Kurt	151932	M	Ger.		SA,Hauptsturmfhr., Gruppe Berlin-Brandenburg,Berlin (Ger.)	MURDER	U.S.
SCHULZ, Kurt	252711	M	Ger.		Farmer, KDO 287 Stalag IV G, Rehbach (Ger.) 11.40	MURDER	FR.
SCHULZ, Leo	193407	M	Ger.		Capt.,SS, Army Transport-Officer on SS Gotha,See-Transport(Nor.)4.-5.45	MURDER	NOR.
SCHULZ, Max	250986	M	Ger.		Pvt., SS, Auschwitz-Birkenau (Pol.) 10.42	MURDER	YUGO.
SCHULZ, Otto	190283	M	Ger.	77	Usturmfhr.,SS, C.C. Neuengamme (Ger.) 43	MURDER	YUGO.
SCHULZ, Otto	254016	M	Ger.	05	Uscharfhr., SS, Rathenow (Ger.)	TORTURE	NETH.
SCHULZ, Paul	126390	M	Ger.		Crim.-Assistent, Gestapo Amt (IV) (Pol.)	MISC.CRIMES	U.S.
SCHULZ, Reinhardt	141335	M			Civilian, Stein-Kaspendorf (Ger.) 8.4.41	TORTURE	U.K.
SCHULZ, Rene (see SCHOLZE)	167992						
SCHULZ, Roland	842	M			N.C.O., Gestapo,Feldgendarmerie,Chateau du Logron,Valencienes(Fr.)8.44	MURDER	FR.
SCHULZ, Rolf	306884	M	Ger.		Cmdt., Crematorium C.C., Auschwitz (Pol.) 40 - 45	MURDER	FR.
SCHULZ, Roman	133248	M	Ger.	09	Oberscharfhr., Waffen SS, Thueringen (Ger.)	TORTURE	U.S.
SCHULZ, Rudolf	301462	M	Ger.		Rottenfhr., SS, (No.198952) C.C., Buchenwald (Ger.) 38 - 10.43	MURDER	BEL.
SCHULZ, Waldemar	167891	M	Ger.		Pvt., 9.Rgt.Res.-Gren.,1.Coy. Magny d'Avignon (Fr.) 18.9.44	MURDER	FR.
SCHULZ, Walter	251790	M	Ger.	10. 6.19	Employee, SD, Prague (Czech.) 39 - 45	MURDER	CZECH.
SCHULZ, Wilhelm	305793	M	Ger.		Uscharfhr.,Rapportfhr.,C.C. Sachsenhausen(Ger,) 40 - 45	MURDER	U.K.
SCHULZ, Willi	260653	M	Ger.		Oberwachtmeister, SS, Prison Camp North Norway(Nor.) 6.42 - 5.45	MURDER	YUGO
SCHULZ - AYCKE	134712	M	Ger.		Head, SD, Sipo, Le Mans,Nantes-Tours (Fr.)	MISC.CRIMES	U.S.
SCHULZE	844	M			Uscharfhr., Gestapo, Locmine (Fr.) 7. - 8.44	MURDER	FR.
SCHULZE	1758	M			Oberscharfhr., SS, Dachau (Ger.)	TORTURE	U.K.
SCHULZE	68885	M	Ger.		Colonel, Mil.Verw. Abteilungschef Army	MISC.CRIMES	U.S.
SCHULZE	133203	M		05 - 10	Lt., German-Army, Bande (Bel.) 24.12.44	MURDER	U.S.
SCHULZE	147036	M	Ger.		Uscharfhr., SS-Panz.Div."Das Reich",La Croix-Falbarde (Fr.) 44	MURDER	FR.
SCHULZE	181197	M	Ger.		Sturmscharfhr.,SS, Secretary, Gestapo, Sarrebruck (Ger.)	SUSPECT	FR.

SCHU - SCHU

NAME	C.R.FILE NUMBER	SEX	NATIO-NALITY	DATE OF BIRTH	RANK OCCUPATION UNIT PLACE AND DATE OF CRIME	REASON WANTED	WANTED BY
SCHULZE	253148	M	Ger.		SS Osturmfhr., C.C. Buchenwald (Ger.) 42-45	MURDER	FR.
SCHULZE	300131	M	Ger.		Member, Ortsgruppenleiter NSDAP from Doetinchen, Vrasselt, Emmerich (Neth.) 10.44-3.45	MISC.CRIMES	NETH.
SCHULZE, Charles	194534	M	Ger.		Cpl., customs and excise, Veigy, Foncenex (Fr.) 6.10.43	TORTURE	FR.
SCHULZE, Friedrich	124311	M		12	Osturmfhr.,SS Div."Hitler-Jugend",12.SS Panz.Div. 25.SS Rgt., C.O. 2.Bn.,Krinkelt-Rocherath (Bel.) 17.12.44	MURDER	U.S.
SCHULZE, Heinrich	132142	M			Civ., Bad Duerrenberg (Ger.) 29.5.44	MURDER	U.S.
SCHULZE, Heinrich	177569	M	Ger.	09	Sgt., Fieldpolice, Esquetecques (Fr.) 31.10.43	MURDER	FR.
SCHULZE, Helmuth	187998	M		25	SS Mann, 12.Panz.Div."Hitler-Jugend", nr.Caen (Fr.) 6.6.-8.7.44	MURDER	CAN.
SCHULZE, Josef	128905	M			SS Usturmfhr., Crim.secretary, Gestapo, Hanau (Ger.) 3.45	MURDER	U.S.
SCHULZE, Julius	306438	M	Ger.		Crim.secretary, state police, Hanau (Ger.) 17.2.45	MURDER	U.S.
SCHULZE, Ruth	196970	F			Civ. Guard, C.C.Helmbrechts (Ger.)	MURDER	U.S.
SCHULZE, Wilhelm	142276	M			Civ. Teacher, Buchhorst (Ger.) 44	TORTURE	U.S.
SCHULZE, Willi	1324	M			Sgt., Army, 194. Gr. 1.Coy.	MISC.CRIMES	U.K.
SCHULZE-LANGEMANN	173522	M	Ger.		Kreiskommandant, Kreiskommandantur, Zajecar (Yugo.) 8.41-1.42	MURDER	YUGO.
SCHULZER	251796	M			Doctor, C.C.Gusen (Austr.)	BRUTALITY	BEL.
SCHUMACHER	9617	M			Pvt., Army, Breendonck (Bel.) 40-41	TORTURE	BEL.
SCHUMACHER	131714	M			Gen. or Col., judge of german supreme military tribunal, Berlin, Torgau (Ger.) 40-45	MURDER	FR.
SCHUMACHER	165537	M			Pvt., Guard, C.C. Breendonck (Bel.) 40-41	MISC.CRIMES	BEL.
SCHUMACHER	167240	M	Ger.		Cpl., Commandantur Gen.staff, Crest-Drome (Fr.) 7.-8.44	MURDER	FR.
SCHUMACHER	167940	M			Pvt., etat major de Crest, "La Rochette" (Fr.) 3.8.44	MURDER	FR.
SCHUMACHER	188296	M	Ger.		Chief, camp official, C.C. Dora II Duisburg (Ger.) 8.44	TORTURE	BEL.
SCHUMACHER	253367	M	Ger.		Landgerichtsrat, Luxemburg (Lux.) 40-44	MISC.CRIMES	LUX.
SCHUMACHER	253422	M			SS Sturmbannfhr., C.C. Buchenwald (Ger.) 42-45	BRUTALITY	U.S.
SCHUMACHER	254000	M			Flyer, C.C. Ellrich, Nordhausen (Ger.)	MURDER	U.S.
SCHUMACHER	260032	M			Overseer, C.C. Dachau (Ger.) 42-44	BRUTALITY	FR.
SCHUMACHER	306885	M	Ger.		Uscharfhr., SS, institute of hygiene, C.C. Auschwitz (Pol.) 40-45	MURDER	FR.
SCHUMACHER, Fritz Werner Christian	301994	M	Ger.	19.6.08	SS Oscharfhr., Crim.assist.,Rotterdam (Neth.) 3.44	MURDER	NETH.
SCHUMACHER, Georg	185876	M	Ger.	01	Pvt., Army, 3.Coy., Landesschuetzen-Bn.,Oberweier (Ger.) 29.7.44	MURDER	CAN.
SCHUMACHER, Gerhard	192101	M	Ger.		SS Uscharfhr., 2.SS Panz.Gren.Rgt. 11.Coy., Ardennes (Bel.) 17.12.44	MURDER	U.S.
SCHUMACHER, Johann	190286	M			Warder, C.C. Banjica (Yugo.) 41-45	MURDER	YUGO.
SCHUMACHER, Josef	193697	M	Ger.	05	Oberwachtmeister, Reichsjustizministerium,Strafg.Lager Nord, Finmark (Nor.) 11.44	MISC.CRIMES	NOR.
SCHUMACHER, Peter	258410	M			SS Guard, C.C. Ohrdruf (Ger.) 12.44-4.45	MURDER	U.S.
SCHUMACHER, W.	174119	M	Ger.		Cpl., C.C. Hemer Stalag 6 A 11.42-4.45	TORTURE	U.S.
SCHUMACHER, Wilfred	251163	M			Public official, state service, Kutno (Pol.) 39-45	MURDER	POL.
SCHUMACKER	121847	M			Lt., Schupo, Thionville (Fr.) 8.-9.44	MURDER	FR.
SCHUMAHER	256833	M			Capt., 6.Coy. 322.Bn. 5.Schupo-Rgt.,Ljubljana,Cetje,Kranj (Yugo.) 42-43	MISC.CRIMES	YUGO.
SCHUMANN	847	M	Ger.	01	Prof.med., Med.chief at Grosseneck and Hadamar, C.C.Auschwitz, Birkenau, Berlin (Pol. Ger.) 43-45	MURDER	YUGO. FR. BEL.
SCHUMANN	138018	M			Capt. Army, C.O. Oflag, C.C. Parchim - Airport Stalag 11 (Ger.)3.-4.45	INTERR.	U.S.
SCHUMANN	147035	M			SS Panz.Div."Das Reich", Deutschland-Rgt.,Venerque le Vernet (Fr.) 44	MURDER	FR.
SCHUMANN	149904	M	Ger.		Factory-foreman, Nuernberg (Ger.) 45	MISC.CRIMES	U.S.
SCHUMANN	167317	M			Civ., Treuhaender, firm "Majde i Ska", Warsaw (Pol.) 9.39-12.44	PILLAGE	POL.
SCHUMANN	168968	M			Leader,Abt.Landwirtschaft und Ernaehrung, Radom (Pol.) 9.39-end 44	MISC.CRIMES	POL.
SCHUMANN	173147	M	Ger.		SS Osturmfhr., SD, Gestapo, H.Q. Baccarat, Vosges Area (Fr.) autumn 44	INTERR.	U.K.
SCHUMANN	177568	M	Ger.		Prof., C.C. Ravensbrueck (Ger.)	MURDER	FR. BEL.
SCHUMANN	178284	M	Ger.	17	SS Osturmfhr., 12.SS Panz.Div. Hitler-Jugend, H.Q. 25.SS P.G.R. Abbaye, Ardennes (Fr.) 6.6.-2.7.44	TORTURE	CAN.
SCHUMANN	189550	M	Ger.		Crim.Rat, SS Hptsturmfhr., Gestapo, C.C. Dachau (Ger.) 40-45	MURDER	BEL.
SCHUMANN	251321	M			Master, Gendarmerie, Hasselfelde (Ger.)	MURDER	U.S.
SCHUMANN	257979	M			Cpl., 150.Panz-Bde., Meuse-Bridge Antwerp (Bel.) 12.44	MISC.CRIMES	U.S.
SCHUMANN	259377	M	Ger.		SS Uscharfhr., Gestapo, Antenne of Niort, Poitiers Area (Fr.) 40-45	MISC.CRIMES	FR.
SCHUMANN, Egon	252701	M	Ger.	95	Pvt., Guard, Nav. Art., C.C. Wilhelmshaven, Lueneburg (Ger.)7.-10.4.45	MURDER	U.K.
SCHUMANN, Franz	143219	M		8.12.94	Sgt., Landesschuetzen-Ers.Bn. 24, Augsburg (Ger.) 44-4.45	MURDER	U.S.
SCHUMANN, Georg	173190	M			Civ., Nuernberg (Ger.)	TORTURE	U.S.
SCHUMANN, Heinrich	253172	M	Ger.		Cpl., Feldgendarmerie of Vendome (Fr.) 9.8.44	SUSPECT	FR.
SCHUMANN, Joseph	126941	M			Lagerfuehrer, C.C. Erfurt, Hochheim-Gruenestahl (Ger.)	MURDER	FR.
SCHUMANN, Joseph	186209	M	Ger.		Guard, C.C. Dachau (Ger.)	MURDER	FR.
SCHUMANN, Karl	300935	M	Ger.		Member SS, staff at C.C. Sasel (Ger.) 10.44-4.45	TORTURE	U.K.
SCHUMANN, Kurt	135913	M			Civ., Ampfing (Ger.)	TORTURE	U.S.
SCHUMANN, Walter	162890	M			Pvt., Army, Inf.Bn.187,1.Coy. Gren., Fort Mahon (Fr.) 22.10.43	MURDER	FR.
SCHUMANSKY	258141	M			Guard, C.C. Esterwegen (Ger.) 44	INTERR.	BEL.
SCHUMERCHER	12965	M	Ger.		Pvt., Army, 110.or 111.Panz.Gren.Rgt. 2.Coy., Albine (Fr.) 29.6.44	MURDER	FR.
SCHUMITZ, Mathias	188293	M	Ger.		Stabswachtmeister, Heeres-Kuestenart. Abt. 1240 Btty.,Oostduinkerke (Bel.)	MURDER	BEL.
SCHUMMAN	121848	M	Ger.		Officer, Legion Spandinava, SS, Montferrier (Fr.) 8.7.44	PILLAGE	FR.
SCHUMMER, Horst	250471	M	Ger.		Civ., Landratsamt, Helmstedt (Ger.) 6. or 7.44	WITNESS	U.S.
SCHUNFS	261470	M	Ger.		SS-Hptscharfhr., Member, SD, Ax les Thermes (Fr.) 11.42 and 8.44	MURDER	FR.
SCHUNZLAR	9618	M			Lt., C.C.Breendonck (Bel.) 44	TORTURE	BEL.
SCHUON	31435	M	Ger.		Lt.,Col., Inf.Div. 169,staff, Finmark (Nor.) 44	MURDER	NOR.
SCHUPFER	174280	M			SS Rottfhr. Gestapo official, Le Mans (Fr.) 12.43-1.44	MURDER	FR.
SCHUPP	260031	M	Ger.		Gendarm, Div.Oberland,-Unit Russian German, Massif du Vercors, Isère et Drôme (Fr.) 20.7.-5.8.44	SUSPECT	FR.
SCHUPPE	194059	F	Ger.	06	Blockleiterin, C.C. Ravensbrueck (Ger.) 3.43-10.43	TORTURE	FR.
SCHUPPEL, Erwin	62378	M			Gauamtsleiter NSDAP, Strassburg (Fr.)	MURDER	U.N.W.C.C.
SCHUR, Jacob	190242	M			Gestapo H.Q., Koeln (Ger.) 43-45	MURDER	U.K.
SCHURMANN, Heinrich	139065	M	Ger.		Obertruppfhr., NSKK, SS, Traffic-police-Rgt., Riga (Latv.) 7.41	MURDER	U.S.
SCHURO	189139	F			Female warder, C.C. Ravensbrueck (Ger.) 42-45	MURDER	FR.
SCHURSBUCH, Hermann	260030	M	Ger.		Lt., Luneville, Meurthe and Moselle (Fr.) 40-45	PILLAGE	FR.
SCHURSE, Hans	147034	M	Ger.		SS Rottfhr., SS Panz.Div."Das Reich", Moissac (Fr.) 44	MURDER	FR.

NAME	C.R.FILE NUMBER	SEX	NATIO-NALITY	DATE OF BIRTH	RANK OCCUPATION UNIT PLACE AND DATE OF CRIME	REASON WANTED	WANTED BY
SCHURTZ	256896	M	Ger.		Lt., political Sec. Dora, SS, Nordhausen (Ger.)	MURDER	U.S.
SCHURTZ, Franz	152144	M	Ger.		Civilian, Aken (Ger.) 4.44	WITNESS	U.S.
SCHURZ, Fritz	21443	M	Ger.		Usturmfhr, SS, Gestapo, CC Auschwitz (Pol.)	MURDER	U.S.
SCHURZIG	259679	M	Ger.	93	Member, Gestapo, Area of Angers, Maine and Loire(Fr.) 42-44	MISC.CRIMES	FR.
SCHUSSER, Alexander	254006	M			Pvt., CC Ellrich, Nordhausen (Ger.)	MURDER	U.S.
SCHUSSLER	28845		Ger.		Major, Army, 20 Geb.Jg.Rgt.206,7, Finmark (Nor.) 44	MURDER	NOR.
SCHUSSLER	189558	M	Ger.		Employee, CC Dachau (Ger.) 40-45	MURDER	BEL.
SCHUSSMANN	189415	M	Ger.		Hptschfhr, SS, Gestapo, R.S.H.A., Trondheim (Nor.) 44	TORTURE	NOR.
SCHUSTER	125088	M			Sgt., Camp Bautzen (Ger.) 21.1.45-10.5.45	MISC.CRIMES	U.K.
SCHUSTER	130180	M			Lt., Air Force, Ground Staff 85,VII, San Pancrazzio (It.) 18.1.-2.4.43	TORTURE	U.K.
SCHUSTER (or SCHNEIDER)	143218	M			Oberkriegsverw.Rat, Kriegsgericht, Nantes (Fr.) 9.41	MISC.CRIMES	FR., U.S.
SCHUSTER	153256	M	Ger.	22	Usturmfhr, SS Div."Gross Deutschland", Fuehrer-Begleit-Bde., Daun (Ger.) 23.12.44	MURDER	U.S.
SCHUSTER	167332	M	Ger.		Sgt., Feld-Gend., Corcieux (Fr.) 9.-11.44	INCENDIARISM	FR.
SCHUSTER	173521	M	Ger.		Dr., Kreiskommandant, Kreiskommandantur, Kragujevac (Yugo.) 42-44	MURDER	YUGO.
SCHUSTER	178061	M	Ger.	05	Pvt., Army, Stalag VIII-B, Beuthen (Ger.) 41	TORTURE	U.K.
SCHUSTER	188341	M			SS CC Karlovy Vary (Czech.) 1.4.45	MURDER	U.S.
SCHUSTER	188516	M	Ger.		Rottfhr, SS, Mauthausen (Aust.)	TORTURE	U.S.
SCHUSTER	199696	M	Ger.	08	Sgt., Lds.Schtz.Zug 127,17, Lista (Nor.)	WITNESS	NOR.
SCHUSTER	194261	M	Ger.		Member SD, Chateau Gaillard, Saintes (Fr.) 17.8.44	MURDER	FR.
SCHUSTER	253171	M	Ger.		Lt., Technical Director, San Domnissi Airfield, S.Pancrazio(It.)7-43	INTERR.	U.K.
SCHUSTER	300871	M	Ger.		N.C.O.,1 Aufkl.Abt., 3 Coy, 2 Col., XV Div. of Africa Corps, Saint Léger Arlon 5.9.44	MISC.CRIMES	BEL.
SCHUSTER	301995	M	Ger.		Uschfhr, SS, CC Auschwitz (Pol.) 40-44	MURDER	POL.
SCHUSTER, Anna	124696	F	Ger.		Nurse, Rgf.Lazarett, Heppenheim (Ger.) 9.44-5.45	TORTURE	U.S.
SCHUSTER, Anton	240124	M	Ger.		SS Oschfhr., SD official, Sipo, Turin (It.) 45	TORTURE	U.S.
SCHUSTER, Emil	149906	M	Ger.		SS Totenkopf Sturmbann, CC Flossenburg (Ger.)	MISC.CRIMES	U.S.
SCHUSTER, Erich	167334	M	Ger.		Inspector, Custom, St.Nazaire (Fr.) 44	PILLAGE	FR.
SCHUSTER, Fritz	253514	M	Ger.		Civilian, Hoffnungstal, Rosrath (Ger.) 15.2.45	MURDER	FR.
SCHUSTER, Hans	1127	M		20	Sgt., Air Force 41 F 129, Gonderange (Lux.) 25.12.44	MURDER	U.S.
SCHUSTER, Hans	187880	M	Ger.		Employee, CC Regensburg (Ger.) 41-45	TORTURE	U.S.
SCHUSTER, Hans	254443	M	Ger.		Lt., Army, Dreznice near Usice (Yugo.) 18.8.41	MURDER	YUGO.
SCHUSTER, Heinrich J.	253897	M	Ger.		Physician, CC Dachau (Ger.)	WITNESS	POL.
SCHUSTER, Helmuth	142035	M	Ger.	01	SA Hptsturmfhr, Chief, Org.Todt, St.Helier,Channel Islands 8.42-4.44	TORTURE	U.K., SOV.UN.
SCHUSTER, Herbert	39786	M	Ger.	15	Sturmbannfhr, SS 17 Pz.Gren.Div."Goetz von Berlichingen", Sturmgeschuetz-Abt.17, F.P.Nr.97476, 30.7.44, 6.8.44	MURDER	FR.
SCHUSTER, Karl Georg	258962	M			Admiral	WITNESS	U.S.
SCHUSTER, Konrad	253366	M	Ger.	6. 9.95	Chief, Wirtschaftskammer, Luxemburg 40-44	MISC.CRIMES	LUX.
SCHUSTER, Kurt	257354	M			Sgt., Inf.Repl., Bn.29, I Platoon, 9 Coy, 129 Pz.Gren.Rgt., San Giovanni Paolo near Galazzo (It.) 13.10.43	MURDER	U.S.
SCHUSTER, Michael	254005	M			Pvt., CC Harzungen, Nordhausen (Ger.)	MURDER	U.S.
SCHUSTER, Michael	261494	M	Ger.	8.12.13	Schfhr., SS Art. 9 Bn., 12 Rgt., Tourouvre (Fr.) 13.8.44	MURDER	FR.
SCHUSTER, Robert	158691	M	Ger.	5.12.07	Rottfhr NSKK, Honfleur (Fr.) 27.4.43	WITNESS	FR.
SCHUSTER, Wilhelm	305500	M	Ger.		SS-Mann, Remalard Orne (Fr.) 26.6.44	RAPE	FR.
SCHUT	307193	M	Ger.		Member of SD Maastricht, Limburg (Neth.) 9.43-10.44	MURDER	NETH.
SCHUTE, Franz	191331	M			Kapo, CC Jawischowitz, Auschwitz (Pol.) 43-44	MURDER	U.S.
SCHUTZ (see SCHULTZ)	122617						
SCHUTH, Walter	29726	M	Ger.		Dr., Landgerichtsrat, Ministry of Justice, public official, Litomerice (Czech.) 40	MURDER	CZECH.
SCHUTLENBERG	252712	M	Ger.		Lt., Bn.1210 (or 1294), Georgians, Boulazac (Fr.) 11.6.44	INTERR.	FR.
SCHUTTE	39790				SS-Mann, 17 SS Pz.Gren.Div."Goetz von Berlichin gen", Sturmgeschuets Abt.17, Pz.Jg.Abt.17, Segre Renaze (Fr.)30.7.,6.8.44	MURDER	FR.
SCHUTTE	256032	M	Ger.		N.C.O., Mahldorf area (Ger.)	WITNESS	U.S.
SCHUTTE, Hermann	261792	M	Ger.		Driver, Gestapo d'Amiens, Gentelles (Fr.) 6.-8.44	MURDER	FR.
SCHUTTER	121851	M	Ger.		Schfhr. SS, Carcassone (Fr.)	MISC.CRIMES	FR.
SCHUTTER (see SCHULTER)	152127						
SCHUTTER, Jean	9619	M	Ger.		Electrician, Breendonck (Bel.) 40-44	TORTURE	BEL.
SCHUTTLER, Wilhelm	849	M	Ger.	11. 6.01	SS Sturmmann, Maidanek (Pol.) 40-4.44	MURDER	BEL., POL.
SCHUTTLI	158690	M		15	Camp leader, SS, CC Neuengamme, Hamburg (Ger.) 1942	MURDER	U.K.
SCHUTTLING	186202	M	Ger.		Camp leader, SS Chief, Oranienburg, Sachsenhausen (Ger.)	TORTURE	FR.
SCHUTZ	851	M	Ger.		N.C.O., Feld-Gend., Army, Abbeville (Northern France) 91.8.44	MURDER	FR.
SCHUTZ	67673	M	Ger.		Sgt., Lds.Schtz.Bn.622, 4 Coy, Bischofferode (Ger.) 9.-12.44	TORTURE	U.K.
SCHUTZ (or SCHULTZ)	67674	M	Ger.		Doctor, CC Riegersfeld (Ger.) 5.44-1.45	TORTURE	U.K.
SCHUTZ	136656	M			Civilian work supervisor, Eurach (Ger.) 5.44	MURDER	U.S.
SCHUTZ	138017	M	Ger.	20	Army, Alencon (Fr.) 8.7.44	TORTURE	U.S.
SCHUTZ	161375	M	Ger.		Rottfhr, SS Pz.Div."Das Reich", Fillaudrig	MURDER	FR.
SCHUTZ (alias KELLER,Georges)	189119	M			Lt., Army, St.Germain d'Esteuil Hameau de Liard (Fr.) 25.7.44	MURDER	FR.
SCHUTZ (see SCHOULTZ)	253899						
SCHUTZ, Arnold	850	M	Ger.		Pvt., Gestapo, Valenciennes (Northern France) 43-44	MURDER	FR.
SCHUTZ, Fritz	158586	M	Ger.	99	Sgt., 622 Lds.Schts.Bn., Bischofgrode (Ger.) 44	TORTURE	U.K.
SCHUTZ, Karl	256266	M			Polit.Dep., Mauthausen (Aust.)	INTERR.	FR.
SCHUTZE (see SCHULTZE)	24829						
SCHUTZE	156006	M			Pvt., Army, Sturmbn. A.O.K.I, 1 Coy, 2 Platoon, Courdelles sur Nied (Fr.) 15.11.44	MURDER	U.S.
SCHUTZE	162232	M	Ger.	12	Uschfhr, SS, CC Buchenwald (Ger.) 42-45	TORTURE	U.S.
SCHUTZE	167999	M	Ger.		Cpl., Georgian Bn., 1 Coy, Tulle (Fr.) 6.4.44	MISC.CRIMES	FR.
SCHUTZE, Carl	156007	M			Civilian, CC Untermassfeld (Ger.)	MURDER	U.S.
SCHUTZE, Helmut	852	M		22.11.19	SS Oschfhr, CC Maidanek (Pol.) 40 - 9.44	MURDER	BEL., POL.
SCHUTZE, Rudolf	135914	M	Ger.		Civilian, Ampfing (Ger.)	TORTURE	U.S.
SCHUTZEN	39791				SS-Mann, 17 SS Pz.Gren.Div."Goetz von Berlichingen", Sturmgeschuetz Abt.17, Pz.Jg.Abt.17, Segre -Renaze(Fr.)30.7.,6.8.44	MURDER	FR.
SCHWARZBERG	260059	M	Ger.		Sgt., Div.Oberland Russian-German; Massif of Vercors, Isere and Drôme (Fr.) 20.7.-5.8.44	SUSPECT	FR.

SCHU-SCHW

NAME	C.R.FILE NUMBER	SEX	NATIO-NALITY	DATE OF BIRTH	RANK OCCUPATION UNIT PLACE AND DATE OF CRIME	REASON WANTED	WANTED BY
SCHUWERAK, Anton	187877	M		08	Civilian,Miner Adof Mine,CC Merkstein(Ger.)8.42-10.44	WITNESS	U.S.
SCHWAAB, Hermann	129956	M	Ger.		Pvt.Army,F.P.N. L.49215N,Luftg.P.Paris,Quaregnon,Jemeppes,Ghlin(Bel.) 2.-3.9.44	MURDER	BEL.
SCHWAABE	1325	M	Ger.		Sgt.Army,114 Div.721 Jaeger Regt.	MISC.CRIMES	U.K.
SCHWAATL	253361	M	Ger.		SS Hptsturmfhr.CC Auschwitz(Pol.)42-44	MURDER	U.K.
SCHWAB	124975	M	Ger.		Wachtmeister,SS or Gestapo,CC Bremen-Farge(Ger.)6.43	MURDER	U.K.
SCHWAB see SCHWAP	161288						
SCHWAB, Franz	138016	M			Penzberg(Ger.)28-29.4.45	INTERR.	U.S.
SCHWAB, Otto	259001	M	Ger.	7. 9.89	Dr.,Bde.-General,Waffen-SS,NSDAP	INTERR.	U.S.
SCHWAB, Wilhelm	166677	M	Ger.	01	Member SA,Gestapo,Eutingen(Ger.)29.7.44	MURDER	U.S.
SCHWABACH	162233	M	Ger.	80	Engineer,Civilian,Sec.I,Utilities,KL Buchenwald(Ger.)43-45	TORTURE	U.S.
SCHWABE	136202	M	Ger.		Doctor and procurator,CC Hirschberg Silesia(Siedlung)(Ger.)44-45	TORTURE	FR.
SCHWABE, Karl	10350	M	Ger.		Dr.,Standartenfhr.SS Police,Polizei-President,Brno(Czech.)39-44	TORTURE	CZECH.
SCHWABE, Reinhold	253239	M	Ger.		Hpscharfhr.Gestapo,Limoges(Fr.)40-44	INTERR.	FR.
SCHWABEDISEN, H.	256874	M		16. 1.11	Civilian,Brno(Czech.)42-44	PILLAGE	CZECH.
SCHWABEN	108882	M		11	Sonder Bn.Capt.	MURDER	U.S.
SCHWAEGERL	256873	M			Kreisleiter NSDAP, Muhldorf(Ger.)	MURDER	U.S.
SCHWAEGLER, Eugen	854		Ger.	16. 3.09	SS Hptscharfhr.CC Maidanek(Pol.)40-4.44	MURDER	BEL.PCL.U.S.
SCHWAIKO	173537	M	Ger.		Guard,Waffen SS,Neckarelz(Ger.)	TORTURE	FR.
SCHWALEK, Erwin	254198	M			Pvt.CC Dora,Nordhausen(Ger.)	MURDER	U.S.
SCHWALLER, Karl	10351	M	Ger.		Dr.,Staatsanwalt,Public Official,Staatsanwaltschaft beim Landgericht Brno(Czech.)40-42	MURDER	CZECH.
SCHWALM, Eduard	254199	M		20. 5.98	Cpl.CC Harzungen,Nordhausen(Ger.)	MURDER	U.S.
SCHWAM	186804	M			SS Hptscharfhr.CC Flossenburg(Ger.)	MISC.CRIMES	FR.
SCHWAN	254439	M			Rottenfhr.CC Mackenrode,Nordhausen(Ger.)	MURDER	U.S.
SCHWANBECK, Paul	108857	M	Ger.	26.10.94	Civilian,Formerly Police Officer,Priest(Ger.)15.8.44	WITNESS	U.S.
SCHWANDER, Karl	300135	M			Slave Labour Camp at Osen-Norway,6.42-3.43	MURDER	YUGO.
SCHWANDER, Rudolf	257353	M			SS Osturmfhr.Slave Labour Camp, Osen(Nor.)6.42-3.43	MISC.CRIMES	YUGO.
SCHWANDNER	124319	M			N.C.O.1 SS Panzer Regt.1 SS Panzer Div.Malmedy(Bel.)17.12.44	MURDER	U.S.
SCHWANK	152101	M	Ger.		Employee,Engineer,Arbeitskdo.Firm Hochtief,NSDAP,Brux,Tschauch(Czech.) 2.6.44	TORTURE	U.K.
SCHWANKE	251772	M	Ger.		SS Osturmfhr.CC Neuengamme,Wilhelmshaven(Ger.)	MURDER	FR.
SCHWANFL	136204	M			Pvt.2 Coy.11 Panz.Div.Albine(Fr.)12.3.44	MURDER	FR.
SCHWANZ, Alfred	254200	M		28. 7.29	Pvt.CC Ellrich,Nordhausen(Ger.)	MURDER	U.S.
SCHWANZ, Karl	46178	M			Pvt.(Chauffeur)S.D.Gestapo HQ.Hertogenbosch,Neth.Tilburg(Neth.)9.7.44	MURDER	U.K.
SCHWAP or SCHWAB	161288	M		95	Major,Army,Esteil and St.Floret(Fr.)10.-11.7.44	MISC.CRIMES	FR.
SCHWAR	132005	M			Uscharfhr.SS,CC Flossenburg(Ger.)	MURDER	U.S.
SCHWARCK	253902	M	Ger.		Chief, Guard,Monsheim(Ger.)	MURDER	FR.
SCHWARM	253179	M	Ger.		W.O.Feldgendarmerie of Vesoul,Favernay(Fr.)9.8.44	INTERR.	FR.
SCHWAHMER or SWARMER	72015	M			Sgt.Army,CC Blechhammer(Ger.)23.8.42	TORTURE	U.K.
SCHWART	253903	M	Ger.		Chief,Kdo.of Lichtafeld,Neuengamme(Ger.)44-45	INTERR.	FR.
SCHWARTING	146714	M			Paymaster,Oflag XI A,Wlodzimierez(Russ.)	WITNESS	U.S.
SCHWARTS	252734	M	Ger.		Chief,Block 5,CC Mauthausen(Aust.)	MURDER	BEL.
SCHWARTZ or SCHWARZ	855	M	Ger.	14 or 18	SS Oschafr.Grini(Nor.)10.41	TORTURE	NOR.
SCHWARTZ	21442	M	Ger.	00	Dr.,CC Bohlen(Ger.)Arbeitserziehungslager "Alpenrosa",7.-11.44	MURDER	U.S.
SCHWARTZ	62092	M			Agent,Gestapo,Sasles(Fr.)43	MURDER	FR.
SCHWARTZ	72038	M		10	Officer,SS Commandant at CC Auschwitz(Pol.)6.-7.43	MURDER	U.S.
SCHWARTZ or SWARTZ	100431	M	Ger.		Sgt.Army,CC Pottenbrunn 872 Coy.St.Poelten(Aust.)3.44-5.45	TORTURE	U.K.
SCHWARTZ	124457	M	Ger.		Civilian,Director A.S.W.Espenhain,Leipzig(Ger.)3.45	MISC.CRIMES	U.K.
SCHWARTZ	125605	M			Officer,Bourg-Lastig(Fr.)7.44	MURDER	FR.
SCHWARTZ	129923	M		95	SS CC Mauthausen(Aust.)41-45	MURDER	U.S.
SCHWARTZ	133205	M			Sturmfhr.S.A.,CC Dora-Mittelbau,Nordhausen(Ger.)	MURDER	U.S.
SCHWARTZ	137501	M			SS Scharfhr.CC Weimar-Buchenwald(Ger.)	TORTURE	U.S.
SCHWARTZ	139224	M	Ger.		SS Osturmbannfhr.Leader Political,Guschurtz(Ger.)42	MURDER	U.S.
SCHWARTZ	140059	M	Ger.		N.C.O.7 Panzer Jaeger Ersatz Abt.14 Coy.Ecole en Bauges(Fr.)	MURDER	FR.
SCHWARTZ	141334	M	Ger.		Cpl.Army,Klosterwalde(Ger.)5.43	TORTURE	U.K.
SCHWARTZ	146713	M			SS Capt.CC Flossenburg(Ger.)	TORTURE	U.S.
SCHWARTZ	173496	M	Ger.		Hptsturmfhr.Waffen SS,CC Oswiecim-Birkenau(Pol.)39-45	MURDER	CZECH.
SCHWARTZ	174860	M			Driver,S.D.Beauvoir and Royans(Fr.)26.7.44	MURDER	FR.
SCHWARTZ	187785	M			SS Hptsturmfhr.CC Natzweiler(Fr.)	MURDER	U.S.
SCHWARTZ	188478	M	Ger.		Leader,Reichsschatzmeister,NSDAP(Ger.)40-45	MISC.CRIMES	CZECH.
SCHWARTZ	189140	M			Lt.Army,Craponne s-Arzon Chomelix(Fr.)20.7.44-8.8.44	MURDER	FR.
SCHWARTZ or SWARTZ	189556	M	Ger.		SS Sturmfhr.CC Dachau(Ger.)40-45	MURDER	BEL.
SCHWARTZ	191294	M			Officer,Army,Bourg Lastic(Fr.)9.-15.7.44	MURDER	FR.
SCHWARTZ	192862	M	Ger.		Sgt.SS CC Falstad and Drontheim(Nor.)40-45	MISC.CRIMES	NOR.
SCHWARTZ	253240	M			Guard of prison,Rouen(Fr.)43-44	TORTURE	FR.
SCHWARTZ	254442	M			Pvt.443 Regt.Belgrad(Yugo.)9.10.41-25.12.41	MURDER	YUGO.
SCHWARTZ	257943	M			Lt.Army,Bourseul(Fr.)	MURDER	FR.
SCHWARTZ	300134	M	Ger.		Lt.Unit of Russians and Germans at Bourseul and at Matignon(Cotes-du-Nord)(Fr.)31.10.-23.11.43	MURDER	FR.
SCHWARTZ	301050	M	Ger.		Head of Block V,Black Triangle,Common Law Prisoner,CC Mauthausen(Aust.) 11.42	MURDER	BEL.
SCHWARTZ	305273	M	Ger.		Lt.Tripolis,3.44	MURDER	GRC.
SCHWARTZ, Adolf	133204	M		08	CC Dora-Mittelbau,Nordhausen(Ger.)	MURDER	U.S.
SCHWARTZ, Charles	259031	M			A Dulag Luft Hospital,(Ger.)43-4.45	BRUTALITY	U.S.
SCHWARTZ, Georg	189857	M			Capt.CC Auschwitz(Pol.)9.-10.40	TORTURE	U.K.
SCHWARTZ, Georg	194058	M			Pvt.Kommandantur,Rochelongue near D'Agde(Fr.)18.3.43	WITNESS	FR.
SCHWARTZ, Heinz	149908	M			SS Osturmfhr.(Pol.)43-44	MURDER	U.S.
SCHWARTZ, Henri	152134	M			Lt.Legion Tartare,Craponne,Arzon(Fr.)19.8.44	MURDER	FR.
SCHWARTZ, Hubert	121757	M			Schutzhaftlagerfhr.CC Auschwitz(Pol.)CC Ravensbrueck(Ger.)	MURDER	FR.
SCHWARTZ, Lazar	193861	M			SS Sturmmann,Guard,4 SS Totenkopf Stuba,CC Mittelbau,Dora,Nordhausen (Ger.)43-45	INTERR.	U.S.
SCHWARTZ, Paul	72263	M	Ger.		Adjutant,Army,Pionier,Lons le Saunier(Fr.)25.8.44	MURDER	BEL.
SCHWARTZKOPF	856	M	Ger.		Dr.,SS Osturmfhr.SS Div.Das Reich,Buzet(Fr.)6.7.44-20.8.44	MURDER	FR.

SCHW-SCHW

NAME	C.R.FILE NUMBER	SEX	NATIONALITY	DATE OF BIRTH	RANK	OCCUPATION	UNIT	PLACE AND DATE OF CRIME	REASON WANTED	WANTED BY
SCHWARTZMANN	173479	M	Ger.			SS-Mann,guard,Waffen SS,C.C.,Oslo (Nor.) 11.41-9.43			TORTURE	NOR.
SCHWARZ(or SCHWARZHUBER)	853	M	Ger.	10		Usturmfhr.,SS,Cmdt.,director,C.C.,Birkenau,Oswiecim (Pol.) 43-44			MURDER	POL.,YUGO.,FR. U.S.
SCHWARZ (see SCHWARTZ)	855									
SCHWARZ	1326	M	Ger.			Col.,Army,Monte Rosa Div.,			MISC.CRIMES	U.K.
SCHWARZ	67810	M	Ger.			Sgt.,Army,3.Coy.,610.Bn.,C.C.,Elbing (Pol.) 43			WITNESS	U.K.
SCHWARZ	124635	M				Officer,C.C. III,Manowice,Oswiecim (Pol.) 1.44			MURDER	U.S.
SCHWARZ	126943	M				Usturmfhr.,SS Pz.Div."Das Reich",South-West (Fr.) 44			MURDER	FR.
SCHWARZ(orSCHWAZ)	131324	M				Hptsturmfhr.,SS,C.C.,Jawischowitz,Auschwitz (Pol.) 43-44			MURDER	U.S.
SCHWARZ	137502	M				Capt.,Army,Munich (Ger.) 3.45			TORTURE	U.S.
SCHWARZ	161534	M	Ger.			Oschfhr.,SS,			MURDER	U.K.
SCHWARZ	162234	M	Ger.	19		Rottfhr.,SS,Command-staffel,C.C.,Buchenwald (Ger.)			TORTURE	U.S.
SCHWARZ	162239	M	Ger.	10		Osturmfhr.,SS Wirtschaftsverwaltungs-Hauptamtgruppe,C.C., Ohrdruf,Buchenwald (Ger.)			TORTURE	U.S.
SCHWARZ	165971	M	Ger.			Usturmfhr.,SS Pz.Div."Das Reich",Valence D'Agen (Fr.) 44			MURDER	FR.
SCHWARZ	189858	M	Ger.			Sgt.,C.C.,Loos (Fr.) 9.40-3.41			TORTURE	U.K.
SCHWARZ	191531	M	Ger.			Usturmfhr.,SS Div."Das Reich" 1.Coy. of Pioneer,St.Sixte (Fr.)			MURDER	FR.
SCHWARZ	192863	M	Ger.			Schupo,C.C.,Falstad,Trondheim (Nor.) 12.43			MURDER	NOR.
SCHWARZ	251164	M	Ger.			Reichsschatzleiter,State-service,Berlin,Sieradz (Ger.,Pol.)			MISC.CRIMES	PCL.
SCHWARZ	251324	M	Ger.	08		Osturmfhr.,SS,Auschwitz (Pol.) 42-45			MURDER	YUGO.
SCHWARZ	252706	M	Ger.			Hptsturmfhr.,C.C.,Struthof,Natzweiler (Fr.) 40-44			BRUTALITY	FR.
SCHWARZ	253421	M	Ger.			Usturmfhr.,C.C.,Buchenwald (Ger.) 42-45			MISC.CRIMES	U.S.
SCHWARZ	254197	M				Oschfhr.,C.C.,Dora,Nordhausen (Ger.)			MURDER	U.S.
SCHWARZ	258197	M	Ger.			Major,German Army,Kragujevac,Orasag,Gruza (Yugo.) 42-44			INTERR.	YUGO.
SCHWARZ	260029	M	Ger.			Lt.,7.Res.Art.Rgt.,Massif du Vercors,Isere et Drome (Fr.)20.7.-5.8.44			SUSPECT	FR.
SCHWARZ	261448	M	Ger.			SS-Mann,C.C.,Buchenwald (Ger.) 42-45			SUSPECT	U.S.
SCHWARZ	261958	M	Ger.			Car driver,SS,Belgrade,Valjevo (Yugo.) 15.8.42-10.9.44			SUSPECT	YUGO.
SCHWARZ	305274	M	Ger.			Capt.,Ortscommandant,Bor,district of Zajecar (Serb.)11.41-12.42			MURDER	YUGO.
SCHWARZ	305501	M	Ger.			Administrator,Werkschutz,Skoda works at Dubnica nad Vahom, 44-45			MURDER	CZECH.
SCHWARZ	306887	M	Ger.			Member,Roumanian Kommando,Gestapo,Vichy (Fr.) 10.43-9.44			MURDER	FR.
SCHWARZ	306888	M	Ger.			Rottfhr.,builder,C.C.,Auschwitz (Pol.) 40			MURDER	U.S.
SCHWARZ, Adolf	254195	M				Hptsturmfhr.,Lager Cmdt.,C.C.,Auschwitz,Monow,Nordhausen (Ger.,Pol.)			MURDER	U.S.
SCHWARZ, Adolf Paul	254196	M		12.9.17		Pvt.,C.C.,Ellrich,Nordhausen (Ger.)			MURDER	U.S.
SCHWARZ, Anton	132125	M				Group-leader,NSDAP,employee post office,civilian			TORTURE	U.S.
SCHWARZ, Edmond	142062	M	Ger.	00		Foreman,Org.Todt,Muhldorf near Ampfing (Ger.) 44-45			TORTURE	U.S.
SCHWARZ, Hans	133206	M	Ger.			Dahlen (Ger.) 20.12.43			TORTURE	U.S.
SCHWARZ, Heinrich	139231	M	Ger.	03		Hptsturmfhr.,SS,Auschwitz (Pol.) 40-45			MURDER	U.S.
SCHWARZ, Hermann	138040	M		13.2.96		Civilian to be detained,in command of jail at Rottenberg, Regensburg (Ger.) 4.45			TORTURE	U.S.,FR.
SCHWARZ, Hubert	188358	M		17		Hptsturmfhr.,SS,Lagerfhr.,C.C.,Auschwitz (Pol.) 42-44			MURDER	POL.
SCHWARZ, Hubert	250487	M		02		Usturmfhr.,SS,C.C.,Auschwitz,Birkenau (Pol.) 42-45			MURDER	YUGO.
SCHWARZ, Kurt	257816	M		05		Capt.,German Army,Zajecar (Yugo.) 41-44			MURDER	YUGO.
SCHWARZ, Louis	259677	M		04		Uschfhr.,SS,Gestapo,Area of Angers,Maine,Loire (Fr.) 42-44			MISC.CRIMES	FR.
SCHWARZBACH	143217	M	Ger.			Uschfhr.,Waffen SS,Totenkopf Standarte,C.C.,Buchenwald (Ger.)			MURDER	U.S.
SCHWARZBERG	306889	M	Ger.			Adjutant,to Hoessler,C.C.,Auschwitz (Pol.) 40-45			MURDER	FR.
SCHWARZBRAUN, Johann	256035	M	Ger.			Muhldorf (Ger.)			WITNESS	U.S.
SCHWARZEL, Willi	150578	M	Ger.			11.Pz.Div.,Valence (Fr.) 44			MURDER	FR.
SCHWARZEN, Erich	168970	M	Ger.			Hptsturmfhr.,SS,member of camp guard,C.C.,Sachsenhausen,Oranienburg (Ger.) 39-45			MURDER	POL.
SCHWARZER, (the Duce)	255467	M	Ger.	03-05		Driver,Gestapo,Zlin			INTERR.	U.K.
SCHWARZHUBER (see SCHWARZ)	853									
SCHWARZHUBER	173495	M	Ger.			Osturmbannfhr.,Waffen SS,C.C.,Oswiecim,Birkenau (Pol.) 39-45			MURDER	CZEC.,YUGO.,BEL.,FR.,POL.
SCHWARZHUBER, Hans	149909	M	Ger.			Osturmfhr.,C.C.,Auschwitz-Birkenau (Pol.) 43-44			MURDER	U.S.,CZECH.
SCHWARZKOFF	72020	M	Ger.			Osturmfhr.,SS Rgt."Der Fuehrer",Div."Das Reich",Buzet (Fr.) 7.7.44			MURDER	FR.
SCHWARZKOPF,Andreas(or SCHWARZKOPP)	194057	M				Army,Semaphore de Creach Maout (Fr.) 5.8.44			MURDER	FR.
SCHWARZMEIER, Franz	262160	M	Ger.	13.1.?		Hptschfhr.,SS,Gestapo,Rennes (Fr.) 43-44			MISC.CRIMES	FR.
SCHWARZSCHULZ	168000	M	Ger.			Doctor,Professor,senior official,Einsatzstab Rosenberg,Berlin(Ger.) 40-44			PILLAGE	FR.
SCHWARZT, Hubert	142216	M	Ger.			Lagerfhr.,C.C.,Ravensbrueck (Ger.)			MURDER	FR.
SCHWAZ (see SCHWARZ)	131324									
SCHWEBE	173535	M	Ger.			Pvt.,Stalag IX,C.C.,Bad Sulza (Ger.) 44-45			MURDER	FR.
SCHWEBEL (see SCHAUBERL)	121768									
SCHWEBICH, Alexander	162241	M	Ger.	10		Civilian,Schierstein (Ger.) 43-45			TORTURE	POL.
SCHWECKE, Paul	253885	M	Ger.			Kapo,C.C.,Neuengamme (Ger.) 45			MURDER	FR.
SCHWEDE, Ernest	305502	M	Ger.			Inspector,political Kommissar,wireless,Taillan-Medoc			MURDER	FR.
SCHWEDER	143214	M	Ger.			Osturmfhr.,SA,Bad Oeynhausen (Ger.) 44-45			TORTURE	U.S.
SCHWEDERER, Marie	253241	F	Ger.			Agentin,Gestapo,Limoges (Fr.) 40-44			INTERR.	FR.
SCHWEDLER, Hans	857	M	Ger.			Oberfhr.,SS,Polizeifhr.,District Krakow (Pol.) 41			MURDER	POL.
SCHWEDLER, Helmut	301463	M	Ger.	11.4.15		Oschfhr.,SS No.288148,C.C.,Buchenwald (Ger.) 16.5.38-9.10.43			MURDER	BEL.
SCHWEHER	858	M	Ger.			Lt.,Army,98.Rgt.Geb.Jg.,Regione de la Maurienne (Fr.)22.-31.8.44			MURDER	FR.
SCHWEICH, Eugen	258850	M	Ger.	11.6.96		Custom officer,Luxembourg (Lux.) 40-45			MISC.CRIMES	LUX.
SCHWEICHEL	108856	M	Ger.			Osturmfhr.,Waffen SS,Lodz (Pol.)			MURDER	U.S.
SCHWEIDE	168001	M	Ger.			Professor,member,office for supervision of Literature,Ostgebiets-ministerium,Einsatzstab Rosenberg,Berlin(Ger.) 40-44			PILLAGE	FR.
SCHWEIDER, Fritz	305275	M	Ger.			Oschfhr.,SS,SD,Troyes and Region (Fr.) 3.10.43-22.8.44			MURDER	FR.
SCHWEIER, Friedrich Kaspar	305777	M		30.10.07		Staffelschfhr.,SIPO,Reg.Sekretaer,Oslo (Nor.) 44-45			MURDER	NOR.
SCHWEIGER	129924	M		00		Chief foreman,Waffen SS,Reithofer Br. of C.C.,Mauthausen (Aust.)41-45			MURDER	U.S.
SCHWEIGER	143213	M		20		Civilian,Foreman of Mine tunnels,Stalag 9 C,Berga (Ger.)2.-4.45			MURDER	U.S.
SCHWEIGER	173519	M	Ger.			Doctor,official,Gestapo,C.C.,Maribor (Yugo.) 4.41-44			MURDER	YUGO.
SCHWEIGER	259212	M	Ger.			Oberststurmbannfhr., German police,Zagreb (Yugo.) 9.9.43			MURDER	YUGO.
SCHWEIGER, Josef	251766	M	Ger.	12.5.99		Farmer,Occ.Civ.,Prague (Czech.) 39-45			SUSPECT	CZECH.
SCHWEIGER, Josef	257810	M		10		Sturmschfhr.,Gestapo,Chaumont (Fr.) 23.9.43			MISC.CRIMES	FR.

NAME	C.R.FILE NUMBER	SEX	NATIO-NALITY	DATE OF BIRTH	RANK	OCCUPATION UNIT PLACE AND DATE OF CRIME	REASON WANTED	WANTED BY
SCHWEIGER, Otto	251784	M	Ger.			Executioner, Civ., Praha, (Czech.) 43-45	MURDER	CZECH.
SCHWEIGHOFER	153372	M	Ger.			Cpl.,3 SS Bau-Bde,near Gardelegen (Ger.) 5.-14.4.45	MURDER	U.S.
SCHWEIKART, Erika Emma	251767	F	Ger.	5.9.07		Civilian, Burbach,Saarbruecken (Ger.) 24.8.44	INTERR.	U.S.
SCHWEIM, Albert	173292	M	Ger.			Hptsturmfhr.,Crim.Comm.SS, Gestapo, Hamburg (Ger.) 13.3.42	MURDER	POL.
SCHWEINEBACKE	191278	M	Ger.			Sgt.,SS, C.C.Sachsenhausen-Oranienburg (Ger.) 39-4.45	MURDER	POL.
SCHWEINGRUBER, Walter	132198	M	Ger.			Pvt.,SS,10 Pz.Div."Frundsberg",Dunkirk, Lisieux (Fr.) 40-15.1.44	WITNESS	U.K.
SCHWEINICKE	156008	M				Groupleader-Javenitzy,NSDAP,Civ., teacher,C.C.Gardelegen (Ger.) 4.45	MURDER	U.S.
SCHWEIR, Fritz	251771	M	Ger.			Oscharfhr.,SS, Gestapo (Fr.) 43-44	MISC.CRIMES	FR.
SCHWEIRTZ	21474	M			10	Capt.,Army,110 Inf.Div.,Rzhev (Sov.Un.) 6.42-1.43	MURDER	U.S.
SCHWEISER	156936	M	Ger.			Sgt.Army, Saxony (Ger.)	MURDER	U.K.
SCHWEISER	253886	M	Ger.			Capt.,4 Coy, 99 Bn, 157 Res.Inf.Div.,1'Ain (Fr.) 10.-21.7.44	INTERR.	FR.
SCHWEITZER	859	M	Ger.			Lt.,Army,Einville (Fr.) 8.-9.44	MURDER	FR.
SCHWEITZER	143212	M				Capt.,Army, 621 Inf.Rgt.,Stalag 9 B, bei Bad Orb (Ger.) 28.1.45	TORTURE	U.S.
SCHWEITZER	149910	M				Sturmbannfhr.,SS, Graz,Wanzelsdorf (Aust.) 2.45	MURDER	U.S.
SCHWEITZER	167981	M	Ger.			Member, Gestapo, Toulouse, (Fr.) 43	MURDER	FR.
SCHWEITZER	301111	M	Ger.			Crim.Rat,Osturmfhr.,chief of section R.S.D. Abt.IV-1-6, Chellhuset,Copenhagen (Den.) 2.9.44	TORTURE	DEN.
SCHWEITZER, Wilhelm	136385	M	Ger.	03		Civilian, Oberbettingen near Hillesheim (Ger.) 12.9.44-5.3.45	TORTURE	U.S.
SCHWEIZER	252744	M	Ger.			Crim.employee,SD, Toulouse (Fr.) 11.42-8.44	MISC.CRIMES	FR.
SCHWEJDA, Anton	260009	M	Ger.	31.12.03		Employee, Wachtmstr., Schupo,6 Coy,20 Bn,Praha,Kobylisy(Czech.)42	MURDER	CZECH.
SCHWELMER	141331	M	Ger.			Cpl.,Army,C.O.Kundorf, Posen (Pol.) 41	TORTURE	U.K.
SCHWELMER, Joseph	169470	M	Ger.	00		Sgt.,Policeman,Div. guard,B.A.B.21,Ger.Army,C.C.Posen,Blechhammer (Pol.,Ger.) 5.41-44	TORTURE	U.K.
SCHWENK, Erwin	260458	M	Ger.	16.6.17		Uscharfhr.,Waffen-SS,guard Coy, C.C.Auschwitz (Pol.) 10.40-8.41	BRUTALITY	POL.
SCHWENKE, Werner	180887	M	Ger.	00		Groupleader, NSDAP,Clothe (Ger.) 6.44	MURDER	U.S.
SCHWENKREIS, Josef	12366	M	Ger.			Pvt.,Army,110 or 111 Pz.Rgt.,Albine (Fr.) 29.6.44	MURDER	FR.
SCHWER	260182	M	Ger.			Col., 1 Res.Jg.Rgt.,Massif du Vercors (Isere and Drome-Fr.)20.7.-8.44	SUSPECT	FR.
SCHWERDT, Hans	4723	M	Ger.			Districtleader,NSDAP,Offenbach (Ger.)	TORTURE	UNWCC.
SCHWERGER	142000	M	Ger.	00		Hpttruppfhr.,O.T.Airplane factory construction,Ampfing-Mittenheim (Ger.) 44-45	TORTURE	U.S.
SCHWERIN, Severin see SCHROEDER, Severin	190280							
SCHWERING, Heinrich	199699	M	Ger.	05		Official secr.,Strafgef.Lager Reichsjustizminist.,Finmark (Nor.)42-45	MISC.CRIMES	NOR.,YUGO.
SCHWERMER	189609	M	Ger.			Pvt.,Army, Charente-Maritime (Fr.) 1.5.45	MURDER	FR.
SCHWERTEL, Albert	257317	M	Ger.	06		Crim.secr., Gestapo, Prague and Tabor (Bohemia-Czech.)17.3.39-45	MISC.CRIMES	CZECH.
SCHWERTFEGER	301464	M	Ger.			Oscharfhr.,SS chief of SS-guards,C.C. Neuengamme (Ger.) 40-45	MURDER	BEL.
SCHWERTFERGER	259378	M	Ger.			Hptsturmfhr.,SS, Lierentz (Haut-Rhin-Fr.) 16.2.44	BRUTALITY	FR.
SCHWETZ, Karl	250481	M	Ger.	19.8.00		Informer, Gestapo, Ivancice (Czech.) 40-45	MURDER	CZECH.
SCHWICHTENBERG	174575	M	Ger.			Pol.Lt.,chief, 19 Rgt., Aurillac (Fr.)	MURDER	FR.
SCHWIEBERG	28847	M	Ger.			Major,Army, Nachr.Abt.169, Inf.Div.,Finmark(Nor.) 10.-11.44	MURDER	NOR.
SCHWIEBUS	166363	M		00		Major, GP Sicherungsabschnitt IV,Campomelon (It.) 2.45	MURDER	U.S.
SCHWIEGER, Rudolf	185873	M	Ger.	1.5.13		Hptscharfhr.,SS, 19 Pol.Rgt,1 Bn, Bleiburg (Aust.) 14.10.44	MURDER	U.S.
SCHWIENTER, Martin	254202	M	Ger.			Pvt., Camp Ellrich-Nordhausen (Ger.)	MURDER	U.S.
SCHWIER, Aug. Ewald Werner	181294	M	Ger.	26.4.07		Camp-Fuehrer, C.C. "Erika", Ommen (Neth.) 40-44	TORTURE	NETH.
SCHWIGETENBERG	253893	M	Ger.			Lt.,6 Coy, 2 Bn, 95 Rgt., SS-Police,Stria (Yugo.) 42-44	MURDER	YUGO.
SCHWILZ, Friedrich	194393	M	Ger.	92		policeman Police, Idesheim (Ger.) 17.8.44	MURDER	U.S.
SCHWIN, Hans or Lulu or SWINN, SCHWINN, SCHWIND.	162902	M	Ger.	10		Lt.,SS Div.Brandenburg "Unit Speciale", 8 Coy, Gestapo, Izon,la Bruisse, Sederon, Mezel,la Manon (Fr.) 22.2.-10.6.-18.7.44	MURDER	FR.
SCHWIND see SCHWIN	162902							
SCHWINDEL	305503	M	Ger.			Capt.,the Azerbeidjan Bn attached to the Streuber column, Lavilledieu and St.Germain Ardeche (Fr.) 25.8.44	MURDER	FR.
SCHWINDT	306210	M	Ger.			Member, Deputy to Camp Cmdt, SS, C.C. Lodz (Pol.) 41-44	MURDER	CZECH.
SCHWINGE	194262	M	Ger.			Civilian, Saint Rambert (Fr.) 2.44	MISC.CRIMES	FR.
SCHWINKENDORF, Erich	252745	M	Ger.	18.11.12		Employee, Gestapo, Vsetin (Czech.) 39-45	MISC.CRIMES	CZECH.
SCHWINN see SCHWIN	162902							
SCHWINN, Peter	136984	M	Ger.			Osturmfhr.,Allg.SS, Gestapo, Bensheim (Ger.)	WITNESS	U.S.
SCHWINN, Wilhelm	250474	M	Ger.			Civ.,Districtleader NSDAP	MURDER	U.S.
SCHWINTE	253406	M	Ger.			C.C. Struthof-Natzweiler (Fr.) 40-44	INTERR.	FR.
SCHWITTER	143215	M	Ger.			Sgt., W-SS, Totenkopf Stand.,C.C. Buchenwald (Ger.)	MURDER	U.S.
SCHWITZER	252714	M	Ger.			SS-officer, C.C. Auschwitz (Pol.)	INTERR.	FR.
SCHWITZGABEL, Joseph	173065	M	Ger.	86		Uscharfhr.,SS, C.C. Struthof (Fr.)	MURDER	FR.
SCHWOCHOF	126393	M	Ger.	00		Crim secr., Sipo, Leitstelle Duesseldorf (Ger.)	MISC.CRIMES	U.S.
SCHWOEING, Bernhard	169775	M	Ger.			Guard, Waffen-SS, C.C. Heppen (Ger.) 45	WITNESS	U.S.
SCHWOEN	167338	M	Ger.			W.O., Feldgend., Montigny en Vesoul (Fr.) 16.7.44	MURDER	FR.
SCHWOEN	257808	M	Ger.			Lt.Col., Waffen-SS, C.C. Nordhausen (Ger.)	MURDER	U.S.
SCHWOHEN	257809	M				Lt.,Waffen-SS,C.C. Nordhausen (Ger.)	MURDER	U.S.
SCHWOHEN, Vincent	254207	M				Osturmfhr., Camp Dora-Ellrich-Nordhausen (Ger.)	MURDER	U.S.
SCHWORBASL	187354	M	Ger.			Sgt.,Army, Mittenwald (Ger.) 6.44	TORTURE	U.S.
SCHWORN	133207	M	Ger.			Osturmfhr., Waffen-SS,C.C.Dora-Mittelbau, Nordhausen(Ger.)	MURDER	U.S.
SCHWRICHT, Arno	188488	M	Ger.			Sgt.,Army, Feldgend., Kriz-Vrissi (Czech.) 44	MURDER	GRC.
SCHWUERZER, Joseph	11874	M	Ger.			Pvt.,Army,110 or 111 Pz.Gren.Rgt.,Albine(Fr.) 29.6.44	MURDER	FR.
SCHYMALIK, Czeslaw	254208	M				SS-Mann, Camp Monowitz, Nordhausen (Ger.)	MURDER	U.S.
SCHYMCZYCK	194360	M				Guard, Stalag,C.C. Poitiers (Fr.) 1.6.44	MURDER	U.S.
SCITZECK, Walter	261484	M	Ger.		10	Scharfhr.,SS, Gestapo, Mende (Lozere-Fr.) 43-44	SUSPECT	FR.
SCKDONIE	124860					Camp, 355 Comp, Eilenburg (Ger.) 12.43-6.6.44	MISC.CRIMES	U.K.
SCKEILLE, Kurt	126738					Sgt., Geh.Feldpol., Lille (Fr.)	TORTURE	FR.
SCMAUSER, Karl	88318				86	Brigadier Gen.,Reich Military-Court	MISC.CRIMES	U.S.
SCNAUR	188802	M	Ger.			Usturmfhr., SS, Morbihan (Fr.)	WITNESS	FR.
SCOBL	254048	M	Ger.			Major,Army, Shock-Bn,392 Inf."Blue Div.", Lika (Yugo.) 44-45	INTERR.	YUGO.
SCOLCE or SCHOLZ	305810	M	Ger.			Col.,O.C. Tank Div."Lehr" from Berlin, Dreznice (Yugo.) 11.43	MURDER	YUGO.

NAME	C.R.FILE NUMBER	SEX	NATIO-NALITY	DATE OF BIRTH	RANK OCCUPATION UNIT PLACE AND DATE OF CRIME	REASON WANTED	WANTED BY
SCRIBER	67004	M			Capt., 2.45	MURDER	U.K.
SCROEDER, Erich	254018	M			Pvt. C.C.Ellrich, Nordhausen (Ger.)	MURDER	U.S.
SCWAN	146716	M			Sgt., SS, Conc.Camp, Flossenburg (Ger.)	MURDER	U.S.
SCZIERA, Franz	124721	M			SS-Mann, Leibstand."Adolf Hitler", Renardmont Stavelot, 19.12.44	MURDER	U.S.
SCZMALA, Fritz	253921	M	Ger.		Cpl. for Kitchen, C.C., Neuengamme (Ger.) 44	TORTURE	FR.
SDOECK	252646	M			Oschfhr., Conc.Camp, Mittelbau, Nordhausen (Ger.)	MURDER	U.S.
SEAMAN	152151	M	Ger.		Sgt., Army, Stalag Luft III, Sagan (Ger.) 7.42	TORTURE	U.K.
SEBASTIAN	132806	M	Ger.		N.C.O., Ger.Commander of Crim.Prison, Isles-Aegina (Grc.) 5.6.43	MISC.CRIMES	U.K.
SEBEKOWSKY	173494	M	Ger.		Dr., Regierungspraesident, Occ.Terr., Karlovy-Vary,Oswiecim-Birkenau (Czech., Pol.) 39-45	MURDER	CZECH.
SEBEL, Gunther	251764	M	Ger.		Camp-"Elder", Conc.Camp, Schomberg (Ger.) 44-45	INTERR.	FR.
SEBELIN, August	256490	M		24. 7.91	Naval-Office, Navy, Harbour-Cmdt., Maloey (Nor.)	WITNESS	NOR.
SEBERA, Siegfried	124320	M			Rottfhr., 1.SS-Pz.Div.,2.Pz.Gr.Rgt.,12.Coy., Malmedy (Bel.) 17.12.44	MURDER	U.S.
SEBREICHT, Rudolf	186193	M			Civilian, Terrasson (Fr.) 15.-31.3.44	MURDER	FR.
SECKEL, Paul	168227	M	Ger.		Sgt., Feldgend., Auberive Flageu, Coiffey Chalengey (Fr.)	MURDER	FR.
SEDDON	124536	M			Capt., Camp, 44	MISC.CRIMES	U.K.
SEDENMAIER	260051	M	Ger.		Lt., 157.Bayr.Res.Div., Isere and Drome (Fr.) 7.44-8.44	SUSPECT	FR.
SEDERER	12367	M	Ger.		Pvt., Army, 110.or 111.Panz.Gren.Rgt.,2.Coy., Albine (Fr.) 29.6.44	MURDER	FR.
SEDLATSCHEK	255352	M			Watchman, Conc.Camp, Buchenwald (Ger.)	MURDER	U.S.
SEDLIGER, Rudi (see SEELIGER)	39629						
SEDOU	129925	M			Cpl., Waffen-SS, Conc.Camp, Mauthausen (Aust.) 41-45	MURDER	U.S.
SEEBACH	188185	M			Hptschfhr., SS-Guard, Conc.Camp (Ger.)	MURDER	U.S.
SEEBAUER, Fritz	135315	M	Ger.	25. 4.95	Oberfrontfhr., Organ.Todt, near Ampfing and Muehldorf (Ger.) 8.44-5.45	MURDER	U.S.
SEEBEN, Horst	133208	M	Ger.		Pvt., Army, Bande (Bel.) 24.12.44	MURDER	U.S.
SEEBERGER	253340	M			Police-Staff, Conc.Camp Ellrich, Nordhausen (Ger.)	MURDER	U.S.
SEEBRECHT	186226	M	Ger.		Lt., Army, Macon (Fr.) 40-45	WITNESS	FR.
SEECK	251274	M			Osturmfhr., SS, Brussels (Bel.)	MURDER	BEL.
SEEDORF	251275	M			Crim.Secretary, Sipo., Brussels (Bel.)	INTERR.	BEL.
SEEDORF, Karl	253918	M	Ger.		Pvt., 377.Jaeger-Rgt., F.P.No.34430, Vinkt, Meigem (Bel.) 25.-31.5.40	MURDER	BEL.
SEEFELD	159103	M	Ger.		Sgt., Gestapo, Lorient-Belle-Ile (Fr.) 44	MISC.CRIMES	FR.
SEEFERS, Erich	137876	M	Ger.		Ortsgr.Propagandaleiter, NSDAP, Wolfenbuettel (Ger.)	MURDER	FR.
SEEFRIED	253332	M			Rottfhr., Conc.Camp, Osterhagen, Nordhausen (Ger.)	MURDER	U.S.
SEEGER (see WEIMER)	999						
SEEGER	116281	M	Ger.		Lt.Col., Army, Cmdt. of Conc.Camp, Stalag 20 A, 40	TORTURE	U.K.
SEEGER	121222	M	Ger.		Lt., 7.Rgt.Res.Art., Paul sur Isere (Fr.) 6.44	MURDER	FR.
SEEGER	121862	M	Ger.		Lt.Col., SS-Kommandantur, Metz (Fr.) 44	MURDER	FR.
SEEGER	181007	M	Ger.		Col., Cmdt., 7.Art.Rgt.Res., Albertville Tours (Fr.) 8.6.and 23.6.44	MURDER	FR.
SEEGER	260181	M	Ger.		Col., 7.Res.Art.Rgt., Massif du Vercors, Isere and Drome (Fr.) 20.7.-5.8.44	SUSPECT	FR.
SEEGER	306234	M			Gen., Cmdr., 205.Div.Strassbourg (Ger.) Vogesen-Area (Fr.) 44	MURDER	U.K.
SEEGER, Erwin	192864	M			Schupo., Conc.Camp, Falstad, Drontheim (Nor.) 7.42	MURDER	NOR.
SEEGER, Gerhard	861	M			Stellvertr.Gauleiter fuer Danzig-Westpr., Public-Official, Danzig (Ger.) 9.39-42	MURDER	POL.
SEEGER, Gustav	188549	M		5. 4.02	Factory-Manager, Civilian, Bruenn (Czech.) 39-45	PILLAGE	CZECH.
SEEGER, Ludwig	301465	M	Ger.		SS-Mann (No.7092) C.C., Buchenwald (Ger.) 16.5.38-9.10.43	MURDER	BEL.
SEEGERS	251265	M			G.O.C., 405.Inf.Div., Prov.Vosges (Fr.) 44	INTERR.	U.K.
SEEHAUSEN, Kurt	161661	M	Ger.	14	Hptschfhr., SS, Conc.Camp, Buchenwald (Ger.) 42	SUSPECT	U.S.
SEEHAUSER, Hans	152130	M	Ger.		Employee, Arb.Kmdo.III, Firm: Hochtief, Bruex (Czech.) 2.6.44	TORTURE	U.K.
SEEHOLZER, Georg	306057	M	Ger.		Aubing (Ger.) 14.6.44	MISC.CRIMES	U.S.
SEEL	306107	M	Ger.		Osturmfhr., SS, C.C., Hamburg-Neuengamme (Ger.) 45	MURDER	CZECH.
SEEL, Willy	252674	M	Ger.		Coy.Commander, Dachau (Ger.) 42	MURDER	YUGO.
SEELENBINDER, N.	136635	M			Civilian, Holzminden (Ger.)	WITNESS	U.S.
SEELENMEIER	181008	M			Capt., Army, Stalag XI B, Conc.Camp, Fallenbach (Ger.)	MURDER	U.S.
SEELHOEFER, Johannes	253331	M		2. 2.01	Pvt., Conc.Camp Ellrich, Nordhausen (Ger.)	MURDER	U.S.
SEELIGER, Rudi (or SEDLIGER)	39629	M	Ger.		Sgt., Feldpost L 49458 Lg.Pa. operating at Carhaix (Fr.) 8.or 9.6.44	MURDER	FR.
SEELING, Kurt	194526	M	Ger.		Dr., General-Manager, Civ., Glass-Industry,Firm: "Deutsche Tafelglas A.G.", Prague (Czech.) 39	MURDER	CZECH.
SEEMAN	306189	M	Ger.		Osturmfhr., C.C., Kahla (Ger.) 40-45	MURDER	BEL.
SEEMANN	137503	M	Ger.		Major, 11.Pz.Div., Iljino (Sov.Un.) 2.42	MURDER	U.S.
SEEMANN	168971	M	Ger.		Kapo., Warder, C.C. Sachsenhausen, Oranienburg (Ger.) 39-4.45	MURDER	POL.
SEEMANN	251910	M		96	Pvt., Feldgend., Cotes Vieville Socs-Les (Fr.)	TORTURE	FR.
SEEMAYR, Josef	256354	M	Ger.	7. 7.05	Chief, Abt.I A Komm., Suedost-Heeresgruppe F (Yugo.) 41-45	INTERR.	YUGO.
SEENE, David	253345	M			SS-Mann, C.C. Bodungen, Nordhausen (Ger.)	MURDER	U.S.
SEER	129883	M			Civilian, C.C., Buchenwald (Ger.)	TORTURE	U.S.
SEER	259272	M			Uschfhr., SS, Muehldorf Area (Ger.)	MURDER	U.S.
SEERICH, Gertrude	190272	F	Ger.	22	Crim.Secretary, Gestapo, Mlada Boleslav (Czech.) 44-45	WITNESS	CZECH.
SEETZEN	173550	M	Ger.		Official, Sipo., SD, C.C., Oswiecim, Birkenau (Pol.) 39-45	MURDER	CZECH.
SEEWALD	130054	M	Ger.		Cpl., Stalag VI G, Berg Neustadt (Ger.) 17.-18.2.45	TORTURE	U.S., U.K.
SEEWALD, Otto	197826	M	Ger.	17	Sgt., Duisdorf (Ger.) 17.2.45	MISC.CRIMES	U.S.
SEFF	194525	M	Ger.		Agent, Gestapo, Bourges, Savigny en Septaine (Fr.) 7.44-8.44	MURDER	FR.
SEFFLAR	108853	M	Ger.		Cpl., SA, Stalag 8 C, 8 B, Sagan and March Sagan to Bad Orb (Ger.)2.45	TORTURE	U.K.
SEFFNER, Erich	139216	M	Ger.	14	Oschfhr., SS, Work-Detail-Leader, C.C., Lublin (Pol.) 42-43	MISC.CRIMES	U.S.
SEFFNER, Erich	301466	M	Ger.		Schfhr., SS, C.C., Buchenwald (Ger.) 16.5.38-9.10.43	MURDER	BEL.
SEFTSCHNIG	173518	M	Ger.		Dienststellenleiter, C.C., Maribor (Yugo.) 4.41-44	MURDER	YUGO.
SEGEDY	261035	M			SS-Mann, C.C. Vaihingen (Ger.) 19.8.44-7.4.45	MURDER	U.S.
SEGEL	159102	M	Ger.	00	Cpl., 398.Lds.Schtz.Bn., Klausberg (Ger.) 1.41-1.45	TORTURE	U.K.
SEGELBRECHT	1327	M	Ger.		Osturmfhr., SS, 1.Coy.,16.SS-Recce.Bn.	MISC.CRIMES	U.K.
SEGREDNITZ	150577	M	Ger.		Pvt., 11.Panz.Div., Kampfgruppe "Wilde" (Fr.) 44	MURDER	FR.
SEGRODNIK	253341	M			Pvt., C.C. Rottleberode, Nordhausen (Ger.)	MURDER	U.S.
SEHAN, Janina	143098	F			Civilian Doctor, Lauf (Ger.)	WITNESS	U.S.
SEHLBACH	188995	M	Ger.		Pvt., 16.Pz.Art.Rgt., Salerno (It.) 9.43	MISC.CRIMES	U.K.

NAME	C.R.FILE NUMBER	SEX	NATIO-NALITY	DATE OF BIRTH	RANK OCCUPATION UNIT PLACE AND DATE OF CRIME	REASON WANTED	WANTED BY
SEHLE, Joseph	169757	M	Ger.	04	SS-Uschfhr., C.C.Struthof-Natzweiler (Fr.)	MURDER	FR.
SEHMANS	862	M	Ger.		Capt., Perpignan (Fr.) 8.44	PILLAGE	FR.
SEHMISCH, Alfred Jules (see SCHULTZ)	307197						
SEHN	195314	M	Ger.	00	Osturmfhr., SS, S.D., Rowno, Luck (Pol.) 13.7.42, 7.-8.11.42	MURDER	POL.
SEHNER, Herbert	251756			05	Hptsturmfhr., Spangenberg, Woudrichem, 9.44	MURDER	NETH.
SEHRT, Johannes	124631	M		95	Civilian, Miscellaneous, Belersha (Ger.) 1.12.44	MURDER	U.S.
SEIB, Wilhelm	123863	M			Civilian-Ortsgruppenleiter, Beltershain and Geilshausen(Ger)3.-4.u.12.44	MURDER	U.S.
SEIBEL	194073	M	Ger.	12	Lt., Schnelle Abt.602, Chambord (Fr.) 21.-22.8.44	MURDER	FR.
SEIBEL, Friedrich	190239	M	Ger.	1. 7.11	Gestapo and Sipo, Koeln (Ger.) 43-45	MURDER	U.K.
SEIBEL, Fritz	180516	M	Ger.	92	SS-Sturmfhr., Crim.-Secretary, S.D., Gestapo, Bonn (Ger.)	TORTURE	U.S.
SEIBEL, Helmuth	253323	M			Pvt., C.C.Harzungen, Ellrich, Nordhausen (Ger.)	MURDER	U.S.
SEIBEL, Lothar (or HABERSTROH)	182066	M		12. 3.14	Member, Krim.-Oberassist., SS-Leibstand."Adolf Hitler", S.D., Gestapo, Praha (Czech.) 39-45	MURDER	CZECH.
SEIBERT	168972	M	Ger.		SS-Oschfhr., C.C.-Guard, Muhldorf Area (Ger.) 12.39-4.45	MURDER	U.S.POL.CZECH.
SEIBERT	306658	M	Ger.		Lt., Commanding 9 Coy., SS-Verfuegungstr. 52 R.S.T.SS-Regt. SS Deutschland Div."Das Reich", Miremont Hte.-Garonne, 2.6.44	MURDER	FR.
SEIBERT, Adam	136600	M		91	Ruesselsheim-Hess.Nassau (Ger.) 25.8.44	MURDER	U.S.
SEIBERT, Josef	253335	M			SS-Mann, C.C.Bodungen, Nordhausen (Ger.)	MURDER	U.S.
SEIBLER, Otto	253914	M	Ger.		Capt., G.F.P., Lille (Fr.) 40-44	MISC.CRIMES	FR.
SEIBOLD, Franz	174847	M	Ger.	25. 3.96	Priest, Civilian, C.C.Buchenwald, Seppenberg (Ger.) 7.4.-3.5.45	WITNESS	U.S.
SEIBOLT (see SEIFERT)	181196						
SEIBT, Otto	129927	M		05	Rottfhr., W-SS, C.C.Mauthausen (Aust.) 14.5.44-7.5.45	MURDER	U.S.
SEICHT	12368	M	Ger.		N.C.O., Army, 13 Coy. of 950 Indian reg., Ruffec (Fr.) 28.8.44	MURDER	FR.
SEIDEL (or SEIDL, ZEIDEL)	863	M	Ger.	90 or 99	SS-Usturmfhr., Grini (Nor.) 41-3.43	MISC.CRIMES	NOR.
SEIDEL	12459	M	Ger.		N.C.O., Army, 110 or 111 Pz.Gren.Regt., 2 Coy., Albine (Fr.) 29.6.44	MURDER	FR.
SEIDEL	152129	M	Ger.		Sgt., Gestapo, Trondes, Bocca, Menil, La Tour (Fr.) 15.-18.4.44	MURDER	FR.
SEIDEL (see SEIL)	161665						
SEIDEL	162896	M	Ger.		Pvt., 360 Pz.Regt., 10 SS-Pz.Div.Frundsberg, Revin (Fr.) 6.44	MURDER	FR.
SEIDEL	255955	M	Ger.		Paymaster, Army, Huybergen (Neth.) 4.9.44	PILLAGE	NETH.
SEIDEL	300136	M	Ger.		SS-Hptschfhr., Kriminalsekr., S.D. and Sicherh.Pol. Antwerp, Abt.IV, Antwerp and the Province of Antwerp (Bel.)6.40-9.44	MURDER	BEL.
SEIDEL	300872	M	Ger.		Pvt., 1 Aufkl.Abt., 3 Coy., 2 Column, XV Div. of the Africa Corps, St. Leger (Arlon), (Bel.) 5.9.44	MISC.CRIMES	BEL.
SEIDEL (or SEIDL)	306431	M	Ger.		Kreisleiter, Bohmte (Ger.) 28.2.45	MURDER	U.K.
SEIDEL, Albert	253334	M			Oschfhr., SS, C.C.Dora Nordhausen (Ger.)	MURDER	U.S.
SEIDEL, Eberhard	257264	M	Ger.		SS-Sturmscharfhr., Crim.-Secr., Abt.IV,Sipo and SD,Anvers(Bel.) 40-45	BRUTALITY	BEL.
SEIDEL, Ernst	253333	M			Cpl., C.C.Ellrich, Nordhausen (Ger.)	MURDER	U.S.
SEIDEL, Fritz	167890	M	Ger.		Pvt., 9 Res.Gren.Regt., 1 Coy., Magny d'Avignon (Fr.) 18.9.44	MURDER	FR.
SEIDEL, Hano (see VEIDENE, Hans)	141435						
SEIDEL, Hans	251304	M	Ger.		Oberst-Feldmeister, RAD, Gebirgs-Schuetzen (Aust.) 13.2.45	INTERR.	U.S.
SEIDEL, Herbert	137505	M		10	Sgt., Feldgend., Abt. 521	MURDER	U.S.
SEIDEL, Werner	167982	M	Ger.	14	Lt., 2 Schwadron, Schnelle Abt.602, Ferte St.Aubin (Fr.) 25.-26.8.44	MURDER	FR.
SEIDEMANN	158591	M	Ger.		Med.-Doctor, Civilian, Borsdorf (Ger.) 8.44	WITNESS	U.S.
SEIDENSTICKER (or SEIDENSTUCKER or SEIDENSTUECKER)	125534	M			Lt., Army, 1945	INTERR.	U.S.
SEIDENSTUCKER (or SEIDENSTUECKER or SEIDENSTUCKER)	133209	M	Ger.		Chief-Engineer, C.C.Mittelbau Dora, Nordhausen (Ger.)	MURDER	U.S.,FR.
SEIDFREI (or SEIDFRIED)	194072	M	Ger.		Pvt., Army, Semaphore de Creach Maout (Fr.) 5.8.44	MURDER	FR.
SEIDL (see SEIDEL)	863						
SEIDL	128779	M			Oberstfeldmeister, RAD, Schutzen (Aust.) 20.-25.3.45	MURDER	U.S.
SEIDL	135562	M	Ger.		Capt., Oflag VII B, KL.Eichstatt (Ger.) 28.2.-23.5.44	MISC.CRIMES	U.K.
SEIDL	141897	M	Ger.	10	Oberarzt, Lamsdorf (Ger.) 42-44	TORTURE	U.K.
SEIDL	192110	M	Ger.		SS-Hptsturmfhr., Dr., C.C.Teresin (Czech.) 41-43	MURDER	CZECH.
SEIDL	252688	M	Ger.		Cpl., Pioneer Unit 02010, La Bresse (Fr.) 9.-11.44	MISC.CRIMES	FR.
SEIDL (see SEIDEL)	306431						
SEIDL, Albert	253322	M			Osturmfhr., Chief of Sonderabt., C.C.Dora, Nordhausen (Ger.)	MURDER	U.S.
SEIDL, Franz	192865	M	Ger.		Schupo, C.C.Falstad near Drontheim (Nor.) 8.42	MURDER	NOR.
SEIDL, Gunther	305504	M	Ger.		Lageraeltester, C.C.Schomberg (Ger.) 44-45	WITNESS	U.S.
SEIDL, Hans	181002	M	Ger.	12	Oberfeldmeister, RAD, 6-352, Dutskirts of Schuetzen, (Aust.) 3.45	MURDER	FR.
SEIDL, Johann	12369	M	Ger.		Pvt., 110 or 111 Pz.Gren.Regt., N.C.O., Albine (Fr.) 29.6.44	TORTURE	CZECH.
SEIDL, Leo	251263	M		12	Employee, Gestapo, Kolin (Czech.) 39-45	MURDER	U.S.
SEIDL, Max	129926	M	Ger.		Hptschfhr., W-SS, C.C.Mauthausen (Aust.) 41-45	MISC.CRIMES	U.S.
SEIDL, Max	149911	M	Ger.		Kreisleiter, NSDAP, Waldmuenchen (Ger.)	MURDER	U.K.
SEIDL, Walter	130053	M	Ger.		Inf.-Regt.145	MURDER	BEL.POL.CZECH.
SEIDLER	864	M.	Ger.		SS-Osturmfhr., Guard, C.C.Oswiecim and Rajsko (Pol.) 6.40-12.43	MISC.CRIMES	NOR.
SEIDLER (or ZEIDLER)	865	M	Ger.	05 or 10	SS-Hptsturmfhr., Grini (Nor.) 6.42	MISC.CRIMES	U.K.
SEIDLER	128778				Cpl., Abwehr, Wolfsberg (Ger.) 12.43-4.45	MURDER	U.S.
SEIDLER	129932				Hptsturmfhr., W-SS, official at C.C.Mauthausen (Aust.) 1.45	MURDER	FR.
SEIDLER	136212	M	Ger.		Senior-W.O., 11 Pz.Div. Dite(Gespenst), St.Quirin (Fr.) 9.-10.44	MURDER	U.S.
SEIDLER	161284	M	Ger.		Sturmbannfhr., Waffen-SS, Linz (Aust.) 8. or 9.44	MURDER	BEL.U.S.
SEIDLER	179798	M	Ger.	05	Hptsturmfhr., C.O., SS-Totenkopf-Stuba., C.C.Gusen-Mauthausen (Aust.)	MURDER	

SEI - SEI

NAME	C.R.FILE NUMBER	SEX	NATIO-NALITY	DATE OF BIRTH	RANK	OCCUPATION UNIT PLACE AND DATE OF CRIME	REASON WANTED	WANTED BY
SEIDLER	257980	M				Lt.,150 Pz.Bde., Meuse-Bridge-Antwerp (Bel.) 12.44	MISC.CRIMES	U.S.
SEIDLER, Fritz	129930	M				SS,C.C.Mauthausen, Gusen (Aust.) 25.7.44	MURDER	U.S.
SEIDLER, Konrad	306287	M	Ger.			Member,Gestapo at Trencin,Oswiecim-Birkenau (Pol.) 39-45	MURDER	CZECH.
SEIDZ	67676	M	Ger.			Res.Lazarett,Obermasfeld (Ger.) 1.-5.45	TORTURE	U.K.
SEIDZ (or STITTS or STITTO)	173989	M	Ger.	03		Foreman,Arbeitslager Vacha (Ger.) 6.44	MURDER	U.K.
SEIDZT	189123	M				Guard,C.C.Ravensbrueck (Ger.)	MURDER	FR.
SEIF	12370	M				Pvt., Army,Gourdon (Fr.) 29.6.44	MURDER	FR.
SEIF, Hermann	261791	M	Ger.			Member, Gestapo,Caen Department Calvados (Fr.) 40-44	MURDER	FR.
SEIFAHRT	128776		Ger.			Lt.,C.C.761 Poethen (Pol.) 16.5.43	TORTURE	U.K.
SEIFER	159101	M	Ger.	00		Civilian,Stalag IV C, (Ger.) 10.41-3.42	INTERR.	U.K.
SEIFEP, Karl	257356	M	Ger.			Lagerfhr.,Coyfhr.,Org.Todt,Erlandet Oeusand Trola (Nor.) 6.42-45	MURDER	YUGO.
SEIFEE, Martin	259313	M				Sturmmann,SS,Muhldorf Area (Ger.)	MURDER	U.S.
SEIFERT	10352	M	Ger.			Oschfhr.,SS,Oranienburg (Ger.) 39-44	TORTURE	CZECH.
SEIFERT	119394	M	Ger.			Lt.,Waffen SS, Penal Detachment,C.C.Auschwits (Pol.) 6.40-1.45	MURDER	POL.
SEIFERT	124902	M	Ger.			Capt.,Major,Ldsch.,Stalag Luft III,Sagan (Ger.) 4.44	MURDER	U.S.
SEIFERT	129928					Doctor,Dentist,C.C.Mauthausen (Aust.) -41	MURDER	U.S.
SEIFERT	129929	M				Lt.,Waffen SS,C.C.Mauthausen (Aust.) 41-45	MURDER	U.S.
SEIFERT (see SEUFERS)	137509							
SEIFERT	141413	M	Ger.			Sgt.,Feldgendarmerie,Dreux (Fr.) 44	WITNESS	FR.
SEIFERT	143099	M				Fuerth (Ger.)	MURDER	U.S.
SEIFERT (or SEIBOLT)	181196	M				Kapo,Arbeitskdo.,C.C.Leonberg (Ger.)	MURDER	FR.
SEIFERT	186195	M	Ger.			SS-Osturmfhr.,SS,C.C.Sachsenhausen (Ger.)	MURDER	BEL.,FR.
SEIFERT	191424	M				SS-Oschfhr.,Guard,C.C., 39-45	MURDER	POL.,CZECH.
SEIFERT	194368	M	Ger.			Cpl.,184 Kgf.Arb.Bn., Bassis Tunnel (Nor.)	MURDER	NOR.
SEIFERT	251268	M	Ger.		11	Secret Field Police,Avezzano-Area (It.)	INTERR.	U.K.
SEIFERT	251757	M	Ger.			Doctor,Luxembourg (Lux.) 40-44	MISC.CRIMES	LUX.
SEIFERT	259312	M	Ger.			Master,Org.Todt, Muhldorf Area (Ger.)	MURDER	U.S.
SEIFERT	301467	M	Ger.			Oschfhr.,SS,Camp Guard,C.C.Oranienburg, Sachsenhausen (Ger.) 40-45	MURDER	BEL.
SEIFERT	306211		Ger.			SS,Lodz (Pol.) 41-44	MURDER	CZECH.
SEIFERT	307198	M	Ger.			Member of the SD,Almelo District (Neth.) 9.44-2.45	MURDER	NETH.
SEIFERT, Erhard	197798	M	Ger.			Crim.Asst.,Gestapo,Brno, (Czech.) 39-45	MURDER	CZECH.
SEIFERT, Franz	305505	M	Ger.			Chief,Werkschutz Police,Skoda Works,Dubnica nad Vahom (Slov.) 44-45	MURDER	CZECH.
SEIFERT, Karl	261042		Ger.			Camp and Coy-leader,Totenkopf Org.,Schutzkdo.,Erlandet,Oeusand,Trola (Nor.) 7.42-45	MURDER	YUGO.
SEIFERT, Kurth (see CEYFERT)	195323							
SEIFERT, Martin	185565	M	Ger.		02	SS-Hptsturmfhr.,Polizei-Oberinsp.,SD,Gestapo,Prag (Czech.)	MURDER	CZECH.
SEIFERT, Richard	306700	M	Ger.			Capt.,Gend.Darmstadt,Dromersheim (Ger.) 11.9.44	MURDER	U.S.
SEIFERT, Rudolf	12371		Ger.			Pvt.,Army,110 or 111 Pz.Gren.Rgt.,2 Coy,Albine (Fr.) 29.6.44	MURDER	FR.
SEIFERT, Walter	136211	M	Ger.			Cpl.,Army,Ville le Marclet (Fr.) 44	WITNESS	FR.
SEIFFER	149574	M	Ger.			Lt.,11 Pz.Div.Kampfgruppe Wilde,(South-West Fr.) 44	MURDER	FR.
SEIFFERT	158590	M			17	C.C.Caen (Fr.) 6.6.44	MURDER	FR.
SEIFFERT	181195	M				Miscell.6.-7.3.44,27.7. and 5.8.44	MURDER	FR.
SEIFFERT	184603	M	Ger.			Police official, Transport-leader,C.C.Blechhammer,Lendringen (Ger.) 45	MURDER	POL.
SEIFFERT	252687	M	Ger.		15	Leader,Statistik of Work,C.C.Buchenwald (Ger.)	INTERR.	FR.
SEIFFERT	301148	F	Ger.			Chief of womens,C.C.Floha,Flossenburg (Ger.) 42-45	MURDER	FR.
SEIFFERT, Erhard	149575	M	Ger.			11 Pz.Div. (Fr.) 44	MURDER	FR.
SEIFFERT, Hans Otto Erich	305778	M	Ger.	18.5.94		Osturmfhr.,Sipo Aussendierststelle Drammen (Nor.) 18.10.44-45	MURDER	NOR.
SEIFFERT, Wilhelm	123864	M	Ger.	12.5.98		Member,NSDAP,Chief of Camp Gluckaufsegen near Dortmund (Ger.)	TORTURE	U.S.
SEIGER (see SIEGERT)	67677							
SEIGERT	257621	M				Lageraeltester,C.C.Muehldorf,Dachau (Ger.)	MURDER	U.S.
SEIGMUND	187878	M	Ger.			SS-Usturmfhr.,Driver,Civilian,C.C.Ravensbrueck (Ger.) 41-45	MURDER	U.S.
SEIHANZ, Josef	167889	M	Ger.			Pvt.,9 Res.Gren.Rgt.,1 Coy,Magny d'Avignon (Fr.) 18.9.44	MURDER	FR.
SEIL (or SFIDED)	161665	M	Ger.		20	SS-Uschfhr.,C.C.Buchenwald (Ger.)	SUSPECT	U.S.
SEILER	149808	M	Ger.			Uschfhr.,SS 2 Pz.Gren.Rgt. 3 Bn.,12 Coy, 1 Div.,Stavelot,Malmedy (Bel.) 22-23.12.44	MURDER	U.S.
SEILER	179744	M	Ger.		98	Major, Div."Hermann Goering",Cavriglis (It.) 11.7.44	MURDER	U.K.
SEILER (see SAILER)	188332	M						
SEILER	193395	M	Ger.			Pvt.,2 Coy P.W.Work Bn.206,Rovanimie Kvesmenes Mosjoen (Nor.) 7.44-5.45	MURDER	NOR.
SEILER	253326	M				Oschfhr.,Nordhausen (Ger.)	MURDER	U.S.
SEILER, Anton	301087	M	Ger.			Pvt.,Vendeuvre Aube (Fr.) 29.and 30.8.44	PILLAGE	FR.
SEILER, Enrich	253325	M		9.5.97		Cpl.,C.C.Ellrich,Nordhausen (Ger.)	MURDER	U.S.
SEILES, Gerhard	253324	M				Pvt.,C.C.Ellrich,Nordhausen (Ger.)	MURDER	U.S.
SEIME	173534	M	Ger.			Kreisleiter,NSDAP,Heidelberg (Ger.) 44	TORTURE	FR.
SEIPTSCHE	159111	M	Ger.			Sgt.,C.C.Kitzingen Stalag XIII C,Camp-leader,Kitzingen (Ger.) 3.45	INTERR.	U.K.,U.S.
SEIP, Wilhelm	187994	M	Ger.			Mayor,Ortsgruppenleiter,Public-official,Beltershain (Ger.) 12.44	MURDER	U.S.
SEIPELT, Josef	29728	M	Ger.			Dr.,Landgerichtsrat,Public-official,Opava (Czech.) 40	MURDER	CZECH.
SEIPPEL	12372	M	Ger.			N.C.O.,Army,950 Indian Rgt.,13 Coy,Ruffec (Fr.) 18.8.44	MURDER	FR.
SEIS	1753	M				Hptschfhr.,C.C.Dachau (Ger.)	TORTURE	U.K.
SEISS	158589	M				Oschfhr.,SS,Dachau (Ger.)	TORTURE	U.S.
SEITENBRICHER	251356	M				Interpreter,Stalag Luft IV,Gross-Tychow (Ger.) 21.6.44	WITNESS	U.S.
SEITERLE	28849	M	Ger.			Capt.,Army,11 Gren.Rgt.324,Finmark (Nor.) 10.-11.44	MURDER	TUN.
SEITL, Franz	251301	M	Ger.	28.6.99		Employee,Gestapo,Vsetin (Czech.) 39-45	MURDER	CZECH.
SEITZ	132002	M				Osturmfhr.,SS,C.C.Flossenburg (Ger.)	TORTURE	U.S.
SEITZ	162664	M	Ger.			Civilian,Ansbach (Ger.) 4.45	MURDER	U.S.
SEITZ	251261	M	Ger.			Camp Employee,C.C.Struthof-Natzweiler (Fr.)	INTERR.	FR.
SEITZ	251272	M	Ger.			Workman,Sipo,Bruessels (Bel.)	INTERR.	BEL.

SEI - SEN

NAME	C.R.FILE NUMBER	SEX	NATIO-NALITY	DATE OF BIRTH	RANK	OCCUPATION UNIT PLACE AND DATE OF CRIME	REASON WANTED	WANTED BY
SEITZ	252673	M	Ger.			Sgt.2.Bn.738 Regt.118 Alpen Div.Jajce-Montenegro(Yugo.)42-5.6.43	MURDER	YUGO.
SEITZ	253327	M				Sturmscharfhr.CC Nixei,Nordhausen(Ger.)	MURDER	U.S.
SEITZ	257725	M	Ger.			SS Scharfhr.CC Nordhausen(Ger.)	MURDER	U.S.
SEITZ	259324	M				SS Pvt.CC Thekla near Leipzig(Ger.)18.4.45	MURDER	U.S.
SEITZ	301286	M	Ger.			Gesch.Angestellter,Abt.I.A1,M.D.Brussels(Bel.)6.40-9.44	MURDER	BEL.
SEITZ	305742	M	Ger.			SS Oschafhr.S.D.Oyonnax,Ain Attignat,Ain,Lyons and Surroundings(Fr.) 11.43-12.44	MURDER	FR.
SEITZ	305967	M	Ger.			Member of Staff,CC Struthof-Natzweiler(Fr.)42-44	MURDER	FR.
SEITZ, Ignatz	126502	M		26		Pvt.SS Totenkopf Stuba,Buchenwald,Leau	MURDER	U.S.
SEITZ, Jakob	12373	M	Ger.			Pvt.Army,110 or 111 Panz.Gren.Regt.2 Coy.Albine(Fr.)29.6.44	MURDER	FR.
SEITZ, Matthias	261437	M	Ger.			SS Rottenfhr.CC Auschwitz-Birkenau(Pol.)42-45	MURDER	YUGO.
SEITZ, Max	12374	M	Ger.			Pvt.110 or III.Panz.Gren.Regt.Albine(Fr.)29.6.44	MURDER	FR.
SEITZ, Oscar	259291	M	Ger.			Uschafhr.89 Regt.Landsturm,Tiel(Neth.)45	PILLAGE	NETH.
SEITZ, Robert	139217	M		14.1.11		Scharfhr.CC,Crematory,Lublin(Pol.)40-44	MURDER	POL.U.S.
SEIVER	10078	M		95 or 05		Cpl.Army,622.Coy.Nr.4 Land.Schtz.Bn.Ilmenau(Ger.)8-8.43	TORTURE	U.K.
SEIWERTH	259379	M	Ger.			Agent,Gestapo,Antenne of Angouleme,Area Poitiers(Fr.)40-45	MISC.CRIMES	FR.
SEJKA, Marta nee PETRNOUSCHEF	250456	F	Ger.	07		Confident,Civilian,Gestapo,Ceske Bude Jovice(Czech.)42 Civilian,Lauf(Ger.)	MISC.CRIMES	CZECH.
SEK, Kasimir	143100	M					WITNESS	U.S.
SELB, Heinrich	12375	M	Ger.			Pvt.Army,110 or 111 Panz.Gren.Regt.2 Coy.Albine(Fr.)29.6.44	MURDER	FR.
SELBACH	143101	M	Ger.	10		Pvt.Waffen SS,Leibstandarte Adolf Hitler,Ers.Bn.No.1,Rosbach(Ger.)4.3.45	MURDER	U.S.
SELBACH or ZELLBACH, Paul	260060	M	Ger.			Foreman of works,SS Penitentiary-Official Nord(Nor.)642-45	MURDER	YUGO.
SELBERT	194074	M				Lt.SS Div.Das Reich,SS Regt.Deutschland,Miremont(Fr.)2.6.44	MURDER	FR.
SELBRECHT, Rudolf (or SELBRICHT or ZICHMIL)	186196	M		91		Commandant,Feldgendarmerie,St.Nazaire en Vercors(Fr.)29.7.-5.8.44	MURDER	FR.
SELDINGER, Ludwig	262305	M				7 Pz.Reconnaissance-Coy,Lives at Perach Germany US-Zone,Sillersdorf (Ger.)16.4.45.L.O.D.N.4.O.D.	WITNESS	U.S.
SELDMEYER, Joseph	167900	M	Ger.	22		SS Rottenfhr.CC Natzweiler(Fr.)42-44	MURDER	FR.
SELGE, Franz	256941	M	Ger.	15		Zugswachtmeister,7.Coy.322 Bn.S.Schutz Regt.Cetje(Kranj,Ljubljana(Yugo.) 42-43	MISC.CRIMES	YUGO.
SELIGER, Fritz	250467	M	Ger.			Ligny en Bauris-Marne(Fr.)7.5.43	MISC.CRIMES	FR.
SELISKO, Otto	250457	M	Ger.	20.2.00		High School Teacher,Civilian,Melnik(Czech.)44	PILLAGE	CZECH.
SELKE or SELQUET	167333	M	Ger.			Pvt.Paratrooper Regt.Tourch(Fr.)44	MURDER	FR.
SELL	869	M	Ger.			SS Usturmfhr.Waffen SS,CC Birkenau,Ravensbruck,Oswiecim,Rajsko(Pol. Ger.)39-45	MURDER	BEL.POL.CZECH
SELL	193743	M	Ger.			SS Uschafhr.4 SS Totenkopf.Stuba,CC Mittelbau-Dora,Nordhausen(Ger.)43-45	MURDER	U.S.
SELL	253328	M				Osturmfhr.CC Dora,Nordhausen(Ger.)	MURDER	U.S.
SELL, Max	149913	M	Ger.			SS Osturmfhr.(Pol.)43-44	MISC.CRIMES	U.S.
SELLE	257932	M				Lt.150 Panzer Bde.Meusebridge,Antwerpen(Bel.)12.44	MISC.CRIMES	U.S.
SELLE, Herbert Ernst	260548	M	Ger.	12.12.17		SS Oschafhr.Waffen SS,Death Head,CC Auschwitz(Pol.)43-45	BRUTALITY	POL.
SELLENGIT nee TOPMAYER	260414	F	Ger.			Member,Gestapo,Pelhrimov(Czech.)39-45	SUSPECT	CZECH.
SELLER	152132	M	Ger.			Commissar,Gestapo,Folkling(Fr.)11.44	MURDER	FR.
SELLER	177567	M		95		Usturmfhr.Inspector,S.D.Gestapo,Sarrebruck(Ger.)	MURDER	FR.
SELLER	253349	M	Ger.			Capt.Cmdt.1 C.Bn.137 Regt.Fauske(Nor.)19.12.44	MURDER	FR.
SELLER, Friedrich	135316	M				CC Sgt.Untertuerkheim(Ger.)	TORTURE	U.S.
SELLER, Peter	152141	M	Ger.	95		Usturmfhr.SS Gestapo,Folkling (Fr.)11.44	MURDER	FR.
SELLENBERG	180902	M	Ger.			SS Gruppenfhr.1 SS Panz.Div.Leibstandarte Adolf Hitler,2 Group,2.Zug Porfondruy,Stavelot(Bel.)18.-22.12.44	MURDER	U.S.
SELLGE	300139	M	Ger.			Zugswachtmeister,322 Bn.(3.Bn.of the 5 Schutzpolizei Regt.)at Kraguje-vac.in district of Kragujevac,Serbia.42 in Slovenia,10.42-43	MURDER	YUGO.
SELLINGER	193860	M	Ger.			SS Uschafhr.4 SS Totenkopf Stuba,CC Mittelbau Dora,Nordhausen(Ger.) 43-45	INTERR.	U.S.
SELNER	186834	M	Ger.			Member,Police - Insp.NSDAP,Zollgrenzschutz,St.Jean de Luz(Fr.)40-45	TORTURE	FR.
SELQUET see SELKE	167333							
SELSKA	253484	M		06		Capt.272.Guard Coy.Gambin(Pol.)28.8.43	INTERR.	U.S.
SELT	306890	M	Ger.			Osturmfhr.Work Chief,CC Auschwitz(Pol.)40-45	MURDER	FR.
SELTE, Raimond	257355	M	Ger.			SS Usturmfhr.Slave Labour Camps,Beisfjord near Narvik(Nor.)6.-11.42	BRUTALITY	YUGO.
SELTSAM, Gabriel	260008	M	Ger.	11.2.20		Waffen SS,Gestapo,Kremnica-Slov.(Czech.)8.-11.44	SUSPECT	CZECH.
SELZER	156933	M	Ger.			Sgt.Gestapo de Nancy,Trondes,Boucq,Menil,la Tour(Fr.)	MURDER	FR.
SELZER	251765	M	Ger.			Dr.,Oberreichsbahnrat,connected with railway construction(Neth.)	INTERR.	NETH.
SELZER	254044	M				Pvt.CC Dora,Nordhausen(Ger.)	MURDER	U.S.
SELZMEYER, Wilhelm	870	M	Ger.			SS Hptscharfhr.Maidanek(Pol.)40-4.44	MURDER	BEL.
SEMAR, Ludwig	156031	M	Ger.			Procureur Tribunal Special,Strasbourg(Fr.)44	MURDER	FR.
SEMBRAL, Edward	137672	M	Ger.	05 - 10		Pvt.Army,398 Land.Schtz.Bn.Stalag VIII B.Troplowitz(Ger.)9.40	TORTURE	U.K.
SEMIGODOW	193742	M	Ger.			Guard,SS Scharfhr.4 SS Totenkopf Stuba CC Mittelbau.Dora,Nordhausen (Ger.)43-45	MURDER	U.S.
SEMKE see SIMKE	123949							
SEMLER, Leopold	253929	M		4.2.20		Cpl.CC Ellrich,Nordhausen(Ger.)	MURDER	U.S.
SEMMELMANN, Heinrich	301468	M	Ger.	12.1.00		SS Mann,CC Buchenwald(Ger.)16.5.38-9.10.43	TORTURE	BEL.
SEMMER	164007	M	Ger.	90		Col.Army(Serb.)44	MURDER	U.K.
SEMMER, Franz	173208	M	Ger.			CC Niederbuehl(Ger.)44	MISC.CRIMES	FR.
SEMMET, Karl	259380	M	Ger.			SS Scharfhr.Gestapo of Poitiers antenne of Rochelle,Area Poitiers (Fr.)40-44	INTERR.	BEL.
SEMMER	251276	M	Ger.			Employee,Sipo,Abt.IV B1,Brussels(Bel.)6.-9.40-44	INTERR.	BEL.
SEMSCH	253917	M	Ger.			Kapo,CC Neuengamme(Ger.)45	MURDER	FR.
SENDER	258909	M	Ger.			SS Rottenfhr.CC Auschwitz(Pol.)40-45	MISC.CRIMES	FR.
SENE	260041	M	Ger.			Capt.Unit 19548 A,Pluduno,Cotes du Nord(Fr.)3.8.44	MURDER	FR.
SENER, Adam or SZENER	261921	M	Ger.			Sgt.Police,Gospodjinci(Yugo.)1.42	TORTURE	YUGO.
SENFTLEBEN	257933	M				Lt.150 Panzer Bde.Meuse-Bridge-Antwerp.(Bel.)12.44	MISC.CRIMES	U.S.

SEN - SHA

NAME	C.R.FILE NUMBER	SEX	NATIO- NALITY	DATE OF BIRTH	RANK OCCUPATION UNIT : PLACE AND DATE OF CRIME	REASON WANTED	WANTED BY
SENFTLEBEN	305280	M	Ger.		Hptwachtmeister,Strafgefangenen-Lager Nord,Northern(Nor.)43-45	MISC.CRIMES	CZECH.
SENGER (see STENGER)	254873						
SENGER	301647	M	Ger.		Wirtschaftsverwalter,Ebrach near Amberg (Ger.) 45	MURDER	CZECH.
SENGEROB	12376	M	Ger.		Sgt.,Army,2 Regt.,F.N.P.L.62546 A,Locmine (Fr.) 12.7.-3.8.44	MURDER	FR.
SENOSIS	1752	M			Oschfhr.,SS,Dachau (Ger.)	TORTURE	U.K.
SENKIV,Anton	156649	M	Ger.		Prison guard,Civ.,Gestapo,City Prison,Wittelsbacher-Palais,C.C. Munich (Ger.)	TORTURE	U.S.
SENKLER,Rudolf	252679	M			Pvt.,C.C.Ellrich,Nordhausen (Ger.)	MURDER	U.S.
SENN	261483	M			Major,Bologna (Ital.) 28.-29.6.44	MURDER	U.S.
SENNEFELDER,Alfred	254045	M		20.9.07	Pvt.,C.C.Harzungen,Ellrich,Nordhausen (Ger.)	MURDER	U.S.
SENNEQUIE (see ZENCKE)	1048						
SENNLZ	181001	M	Ger.		2 Bn.,469 Inf.Regt.,198 Inf.Div.,Le Tholy (Fr.) 13.11.44	PILLAGE	FR.
SENTSCH	152108	M	Ger.		Staff-Sgt.,Gestapo,Trondes,Bouco,Menil La Tour (Fr.) 15.-18.9.44	MURDER	FR.
SEOLE	305743	M	Ger.		Member of Staff,SS,C.C.Auschwitz,Birkenau (Pol.) 40	MURDER	FR.
SEPKE	259800	M		17	Zugwachtmeister,Green-police,1 or 2 Freiw.Pol.-Bn.Niederlande, Zwolle,Overijssel (Neth.) 3.10.44	MURDER	NETH.
SEPP	300546	M	Ger.	95	Osturmfhr.,Coy.-Commander,SS,C.C.Auschwitz,Birkenau (Pol.) 42-45	MISC.CRIMES	YUGO.
SEPP (see PENEDER)	70978						
SEPT,Johann	188340	M	Ger.	31.8.85	Member,NSV,Cemetery caretaker,Lauf (Ger.) 11.4.45	MURDER	POL.
SERANOWITCH,Gerald	255353	M		15	W.O.,Gend.,34.Div. (Gen.List),Saorge (Fr.) 24.10.44	MURDER	FR.
SERBULOW	167983	F	Ger.		Civilian,servant,Member of Administrative Staff,Ostgebiets- Ministerium Rosenberg (Fr.) 40-44	PILLAGE	FR.
SERIEZ	255464	M	Ger.		Cmdt.,C.C.Mauthausen (Aust.)	INTERR.	FR.
SERMANN	188790	M		99	Lt.,Feldgendarmerie,Bar le Duc (Fr.) 20.-23.8.44	MURDER	FR.
SERNE (or SERNO)	108883	M			Standartenfhr.,SS,C.C.Weimar,Buchenwald (Ger.) 42-45	MURDER	U.S.
SERVAES	131712	M	Ger.		Procureur,Tribunal Militaire Supreme,Torgau (Ger.) 5.40-45	MURDER	FR.
SERVATIUS,Albert	126603	M	Ger.	01	Oberwachtmeister,Gend.,Civ.,Oberkail (Ger.) 15.8.44	MISC.CRIMES	U.S.
SERVATY,Karl	251747	M	Ger.	30.6.02	Farmer-woodworker,Civ.,Seinsfeld (Ger.) 15.8.44	MISC.CRIMES	U.S.
SERVEN,Helmut	306891	M			W.O. under orders of commandant of Ardennes,Revin (Ardennes) (Bel.) 13.-14.6.44	MURDER	FR.
SERVET	189608	M	Ger.		Feldgendarm,Feldgendarmerie,Vittel (Fr.) 17.8.44	TORTURE	FR.
SESSON,Heinrch	872	M	Ger.		Adjutant,Army,Feldgend.,Mussy sur Seine (Fr.) 2.-4.8.44	PILLAGE	FR.
SESTER,Robert	161737	M			Pvt.,Army,Landesschutzen-Bn.,5 Coy.,Stalag VI-B or VI G, C.C.Flamersheim (Ger.)	TORTURE	U.S.
SETTLER	301469	M	Ger.		Uschfhr.,Op13,SS,C.C.Buchenwald (Ger.) 16.5.38-9.10.43	MURDER	BEL.
SETZEPFUND	133211	M			Uschfhr.,W-SS,C.C.Dora Mittelbau,Nordhausen (Ger.)	MURDER	U.S.
SETZER	259678	M	Ger.		Gendarm,German Gendarmerie,Tham,Haut-Rhin (Fr.) 19.-29.10.44	BRUTALITY	FR.
SEUBERT	132003	M			Uschfhr.,SS,C.C.Flossenburg (Ger.)	TORTURE	U.S.
SEUBERT,Adolf	154588	M	Ger.	12	Wachtmeister,Army,2 Heeres-Kuesten-Artillerie-Regt.981,Island, Halsor,Vaagso,Island (Ger.) 6.-7.12.44	MURDER	NOR.
SEUBERT,Minna	161654	F	Ger.	15	Civilian,Sommerhausen (Ger.)	WITNESS	U.S.
SEUERIN	149913 A	M			Lt.,Luftwaffe,C.C.Gardelegen (Ger.)	MURDER	U.S.
SEUFERS,Mme Heinrich (or SEIFERT)	137509	M			Uschfhr.,SS,C.C.Weimar,Buchenwald (Ger.)	TORTURE	U.S.
SEUFERT,Josef	301384	M	Ger.		Krim.Sekr.,Oslo,surroundings (Nor.) 44	MURDER	NOR.
SEUME	199704	M	Ger.		Capt.,6 Geb.Div.,C.C.Koesmenes (Nor.) 45	MURDER	NOR.
SEVEN,Helmut	162649	M	Ger.		SS-Aspirant,86 Pz.Regt.,10 Div.,Revin (Fr.) 12.-13.6.44	MURDER	FR.
SEVERIN,Georg	300936	M	Ger.		Member of Staff of Baby Clinic,Wolfsburg,Ruehen	MURDER	U.K.
SEWALD	72024	M			Cpl.,Clerk to Commandant,P.W.Colleg Pt.,Army,Flamersheim, Euskirchen (Ger.) 15.-17.2.45	TORTURE	U.S.
SEWEINBERG	260047	M	Ger.		Gendarm,Div.Oberland,Russian,German,Massif of Vercors, Isère and Drôme (Fr.) 20.7.-5.8.44	SUSPECT	FR.
SEWERA,Arno	255757	M		20.4.94	Finance official,State service,Kyjov,Moravio (Czech.) 40-45	PILLAGE	CZECH.
SEWERA,Karoline (nee PRAGER)	255756	F	Ger.	9.1.00	Collaborator,Gestapo,Kyjov (Czech.) 43-45	PILLAGE	CZECH.
SEWERA-GROTE,Helene	255723	F	Ger.	9.9.21	Collaborator,Gestapo,Kyjov,Moravia (Czech.) 43-45	PILLAGE	CZECH.
SEYBOLD,Hans	254686	M	Ger.		13 SS-Pol.-Regt.,Ferlach (Aust.) 44-45	INTERR.	YUGO.
SEYCHAB	132138	M	Ger.		Oberstabsintendant,Oflag XIII B,Hammelburg (Ger.) 40-44	MURDER	FR.U.S.
SEYDEL,Arthur	260457	M	Ger.	24.11.86	Rottfhr.,Waffen-SS,Guard Coy.,C.C.Monowitz,Eintrachtshuette, Auschwitz (Pol.) 8.44-2.45	BRUTALITY	POL.
SEYDLITZ	208006				Osturmfhr.,SS,C.C.Auschwitz (Pol.) 40-41	MURDER	POL.
SEYFARTH,Paul	261790	M	Ger.	85	Lt.,Fieldgend.de Arras,Bourlon (Fr.) 11.6.44	WITNESS	FR.
SEYFARTH,Werner	167888	M	Ger.		Pvt.,9 Gren.Res.Regt.,1 Coy.,Magny D' Avignon (Fr.) 18.9.44	MURDER	FR.BEL.
SEYFERT	874	M	Ger.		Gruppenfhr.,Cmdt.,C.C.Mauthausen (Aust.) 42	MURDER	POL.
SEYFERT	260028	M	Ger.		Oschfhr.,SS,Belgrad (Yugo.) 1.-9.44	MURDER	YUGO.
SEYFRIED	252690	M	Ger.		Capt.,338 Div.,La Bresse (Fr.) 9.-11.44	MISC.CRIMES	FR.
SEYFRITZ	167241	M	Ger.		Lt.,950 Gren.Regt.,Indian-Inf.,Ruffec (Fr.)18.-21.8.44	TORTURE	FR.
SEYH,August	135317	M			SS,C.C.Ohrdruf (Ger.) 12.44-4.45	MURDER	U.S.
SEYRICH,Wolfgang	252676	M			Pvt.,C.C.Ellrich,Nordhausen (Ger.)	MURDER	U.S.
SEZNA,George	188548	M	Ger.		Capt.,Major,Army,Public official,Boukolia (Grc.) 2.44	MURDER	GRC.
SHAAL	173548	M	Ger.		Cmdt.,Stalag IX,Bad Salza (Ger.) 44-45	MURDER	FR.
SHACK,Hans	174854	M			Manager,Civ.,Moncel sur Seille near Nancy (Fr.) 40-44	TORTURE	FR.
SHAD (or SHAD or SCHACHT)	152116	M	Ger.	97	Capt.,Stalag III E,Kirchhain (Ger.)	MISC.CRIMES	U.K.
SHAEDER,Willy (see SCHAEFFER)	306187						
SHAEFFER	108969	M	Ger.		Leader and Mayor,NSDAP,Public official,Gemmerich (Ger.)	MURDER	U.S.
SHAERF	152122	M	Ger.		Civilian,Mons (Fr.) 7.44	MURDER	FR.
SHAFFER,Leo	174773	M	Ger.	15	Lt.,Orpo,Schutzpolizei-Coy.,Ulven near Bergen (Nor.) 42	MURDER	NOR.
SHAL,Alfred	181417	M			Sgt.,Army	PILLAGE	FR.
SHANTZ,Albert (see SCHANTZ)	108885						
SHAPOSHNIK	187970	M	Ger.	14	Sgt.,SS,Gestapo,Triest (Ital.) 10.44-1.45	TORTURE	U.K.
SHARFF,Hans	259070	M			Chief-Interrogator,A Dulag Luft Hospital (Ger.) 43-45	BRUTALITY	U.S.
SHARP (or SCHARFF or SCHRAPPEL)	143103	M	Ger.		Sgt.,Guard,Stalag Luft IV,C.C.Kiefheide (Ger.) 7.44	TORTURE	U.S.

SHA - SIE

NAME	C.R.FILE NUMBER	SEX	NATIO-NALITY	DATE OF BIRTH	RANK	OCCUPATION	UNIT	PLACE AND DATE OF CRIME	REASON WANTED	WANTED BY
SHARPER	257972	M				Language instr., 150.Panz.Bde., Meuse-Bridge Antwerp (Bel.) 12.44			MISC.CRIMES	U.S.
SHEARER	141902	M	Ger.	about 06	Sgt., hospital, Cosel (Ger.) about 43.				TORTURE	U.K.
SHELE, Hans	188486	M	Pol.		Officer, administration of occupied territories, Athens (Gre.)				MISC.CRIMES	GRC.
SHERA	178753	M	Ger.	.95	Construction foreman, Marien en Murtzal (Aust.) autumn 42				MURDER	U.K.
SHERRIFF R.S.M.	196648	M			Camp leader, Civ. Stalag 344 Gross-Stein-Silesia (Ger.) 24.8.42				MISC.CRIMES	U.S.
SHEURNIG	12977	M	Ger.		Lt., Army, 110.or 111.Panz.Gren.Rgt., Gourdon (Fr.) 29.6.44				MURDER	FR.
SHIFFER, Carl	120693	M	Ger.		C.C. Bremen (Ger.) 4.2.43-6.4.45				MURDER	U.K.
SHIFFER, Wilhelm or SHIPPER, Wilhelm	905567	M	Ger.		Cmdt., C.C. Bremen-Farge, following Walhorne, C.C.Bremen-Farge (Ger.) 1.43-4.45				MURDER	U.K.
SHIMANN	186806	M	Ger.		Col., Kriegslazarett, Chef-Arzt, La Rochelle (Fr.) 44-45				TORTURE	FR.
SHIPPEL see STRIPPEL	10360									
SHIPPEL	137510	M			Hptscharfhr., SS, C.C. Buchenwald (Ger.)				TORTURE	U.K.
SHIPPER, Wilhelm see SHIFFER, Wilhelm	905567									
SHOMBOECK	257699			01	Lagerfuehrer, C.C. Muehldorf (Ger.)				MURDER	U.S.
SHOOP	196200	M	Ger.		Feldgendarm, Feldgendarmerie, Stenay (Fr.) 5.8.44				MURDER	FR.
SHOSBACH, Adam or SASBACH or SOSBACH	252670	M	Ger.	about 11	Cpl. on anti-partisan duties in Mesola Prov.of Ferrara, Mesola (It.) 12.44				TORTURE	U.K.
SHROEGLR, Willie or SCHROEGLER	187774	M	Ger.		Civ. Executor, Camp official, Neckargerach-Neckarelz (Ger.) 44				MURDER	U.S.
SHUBERT	188789	M	Ger.		Agent, railway, Le Bourget Triage (Fr.) 24.8.44				WITNESS	FR.
SHUREN	132200	M	Ger.		C.C.Cmdt., C.C.Ravensbrueck (Ger.) 10.44				TORTURE	U.K.
SIBERT	57749	M	Ger.		Cmdt., Oflag Koenigstein (Ger.) 1.45				MURDER	FR.
SIBERT	901150	M	Ger.		Schupo, Hofgeismar-Kassel (Ger.) 5.4.45				MURDER	FR.
SIBERT, Adam	121864	M	Ger.	90	Assistant, Org. Todt, C.C. Wagbern (Ger.)				TORTURE	FR.
SIBLA, Franz	256370	M	Ger.		SS Sturmbannfhr., Muehldorf (Ger.)				WITNESS	U.S.
SIBLA, Georg	256969	M	Ger.		SS Mann, Muehldorf (Ger.)				WITNESS	U.S.
SIBLER	188788	M	Ger.		SS Rottfhr., Dury les Amiens (Fr.) 44				WITNESS	FR.
SICHEL	252665	M			Pvt., C.C. Ellrich, Nordhausen (Ger.)				MURDER	U.S.
SICHERT, Georg	252664	M		4.12.05	Flyer, C.C. Ellrich, Nordhausen (Ger.)				MURDER	U.S.
SICHINGER	306659	M	Ger.		Oberfeldmeister, RAD (state labour service) Div. K.6-271 F.P.No. L 12 442, Hte.Garonne, Toulouse, La Flambelle (Fr.) 19.8.44				MURDER	FR.
SICHEANN, Wilhelm	31548	M	Ger.	96	Member NSDAP, C.C.Westhausen (Ger.)				MURDER	U.S.
SICK	259982	M	Ger.		Uscharfhr., Gestapo of Poitiers, Area Poitiers (Fr.) 40-45				MISC.CRIMES	FR.
SICK, Heinrich	307200	M	Ger.		SS Uscharfhr., pers.assist.to Dr.Linn, Poitiers Gestapo, La Rochelle, Charente (Fr.)				MURDER	FR.
SICKERT, Walter	108929	M	Ger.		Civ., Aderstedt (Ger.) 11.-12.9.44				MURDER	U.S.
SIDLER, Francesco	259756	M		about 12	Oberarzt, Bondeno nr.Bologna (It.) 25.2.45				MURDER	U.S.
SIDOSKI	128795	M		10	Sgt., 559.Gren.Rgt. 4.Coy., C.C. Schischitz (Ger.) 23.3.44-19.3.45				TORTURE	U.K.
SIEBAIT see SIEBOLT	124385									
SIEBAR, Gertrude	133212	F		21	C.C. Dora-Mittelbau Nordhausen (Ger.)				MURDER	U.S.
SIEBAUER, Kurt	257991	M			Cpl., 150.Panz.Bde., Meuse-Bridge Antwerp (Bel.) 12.44				MISC.CRIMES	U.S.
SIEBAUER, Kurt A.	133213	M	Ger.	22.12.07	Pvt., Signal-Corps, Interpreter-school, Grafenwoehr (Ger.) 2.11.-12.44				WITNESS	U.S.
SIEBE	132686	M	Ger.		Capt., Kraftfahrzeuginstandsetzungs-Park 532, Epinal (Fr.) 16.9.44				PILLAGE	FR.
SIBBE, Heinrich	259541	M	Ger.		Officer, Police, Lengerich (Ger.) 8.44				WITNESS	U.S.
SIEBEN	149809	M	Ger.		Civ. Oflag XI A, C.C. Wlodzimieroz (Sov.Un.) 41				WITNESS	U.S.
SIEBEN, Karl or SIEPEN	124984	M	Ger.		Lt., Army, unknow AAA-Btty., 24.12.44				MURDER	U.S.
SIEBENBACH	161657	M	Ger.		Pvt., Landesschuetzen-Bn. 789, Sinzig (Ger.) 20.12.41				WITNESS	U.S.
SIEBER	253916	M	Ger.		Lt.,Gendarmerie, Macon, L'Ain (Fr.) 10.-21.7.44				MURDER	FR.
SIEBER	256968	M	Ger.		O.W., Muehldorf (Ger.)				WITNESS	U.S.
SIEBER	260185	M	Ger.	about 10-15	Lt., Div.Oberland, Unit Russian German, Massif du Vercors, Isère et Drôme (Fr.) 20.7.-5.8.44				SUSPECT	FR.
SIEBER, Friedrich	185566	M	Ger.	4. 5.00	SS Hptscharfhr., Criminalrat, SD, Kripo, Praha (Czech.) 40				MURDER	CZECH.
SIEBER, Karl	132144	M	Ger.	11.10.95	Col., Inf., Stalag 9 B Bad Orb (Ger.) 3.2.45				MURDER	U.S.,U.K. FR. SOV.UN.
SIEBER, Kurt	257642	M	Ger.		Col.Cmdt.of Oflag 65/Strassburg, Barkenbrueck (Ger.) 44-45				MISC.CRIMES	YUGO.
SIEBERT	108851	M	Ger.		Major, probably Luftwaffe, Dulag Luft, Klosterwald ? (Ger.)				TORTURE	U.K.
SIEBERT	161658	M	Ger.		Capt., C.C. Buchenwald (Ger.) 42-45				SUSPECT	U.S.
SIEBERT	162774	M			Cmdt., Lager Cmdt. in C.C.Koenigstein (Ger.) 1.45				MURDER	FR.
SIEBERT	166876	M			Dr., Head of Internat.administration - G.G. Poland				MURDER	U.N.W.C.C.
SIEBERT	177566	M	Ger.		Hptscharfhr., Gestapo, SD, Sarrebruck (Fr.)				PILLAGE	FR.
SIEBERT	188787	M	Ger.		Member, Feldgendarmerie, Bar le Duc (Fr.) 20.-23.8.44				MURDER	FR.
SIEBERT	259353	M	Ger.		Usturmfhr., 2.Coy., Recon.Bn., 1.SS Panz.Rgt. 1.SS Panz.Div. L.S.A.H., Malmedy (Bel.) 17.12.44				MURDER	U.S.
SIEBERT, Fritz	876	M	Ger.		Landgerichtsrat, Leiter der Abteilung im Amt des Generalgouvernements Pol. 1.39-8.40, 15.2.42				MURDER	POL.
SIEBERT, Hans	188554	M	Ger.	29.7.10	SS Hptscharfhr., Member SS Gestapo, Prag, Lidice (Czech.) 39-45				MURDER	CZECH.
SIEBERT, Karol	186607	M	Ger.		Sgt., Feldgendarmerie Trupp 626, Peronne, Licourt (Fr.) 24.8.44				MURDER	FR.
SIEBERT, Max	193732	M	Ger.		SS-Mann, 4.SS Totenkopf-Stuba., C.C.Nordhausen-Dora (Ger.) 43-45				MURDER	U.S.
SIEBERT, Marx	253948	M	Ger.		SS-Mann, C.C. Buchenwald (Ger.) 42-45				INTERR.	FR.
SIEBOLZ	124086	M			Sgt., Dulag Major?, Alland (Aust.) 25.3.45				TORTURE	U.K.
SIEBOIT or SIEBALT	124385	M			Cpl., Army, 12.SS Panz.Div. Hitler-Jugend, 25.SS Rgt. 6.Coy. 2.Bn., Krinkelt-Rocherath (Bel.) 17.12.44				MURDER	U.S.
SIEBRECHT, Richard	260959	M	Ger.		Leader, Landwache, police, Beberbeck, Distr.Hofgeismar (Ger.) 3.4.45				BRUTALITY	POL.
SIEBURG	901288	M	Ger.		Crim.secretary, Abt. IV B, SD, Brussels (Bel.) 6.49.40, 40-44				MURDER	BEL.
SIECHERT, Rudolf	167887	M	Ger.	97	Pvt., 1.Coy. 9.Res.Gren.Rgt., Magny d'Anigon (Fr.) 18.9.44				MURDER	FR.
SIECK	181115	M	Ger.		SS Osturmfhr., SS Leibstandarte "Adolf Hitler" 1.Div. 1.Coy., Malmedy (Bel.) 17.12.44				MURDER	U.S.
SIEDEL	149917	M			Guard, 4.SS Bau-Bde. Div.Totenkopf, C.C. Ellrich, Gardelegen (Ger.) 4.-14.4.45				MURDER	U.S.
SIEDEL, Herbert	148761	M			Sgt., Army, Bannalec (Fr.) 8.44				MURDER	FR.
SIEDEL, Max	259840	M	Ger.	18.9.21	SS Rottfhr., 1.Zug, 2.Gruppe, probably stat.at Bergeyk Prov.Noord Brabant (Neth.) 11.9.44				MURDER	NETH.
SIEDENBORG, Karl	188553	M	Ger.	7.6.81	SS-Usturmfhr., Member Gestapo, (Lux.)				MISC.CRIMES	LUX.
SIEDL	197823	M	Ger.		Clerk, C.C. Flossenburg (Ger.) 3.44-4.45				TORTURE	BEL.

SIE - SIL

NAME	C.R.FILE NUMBER	SEX	NATIO-NALITY	DATE OF BIRTH	RANK OCCUPATION UNIT PLACE AND DATE OF CRIME	REASON WANTED	WANTED BY
SIEFERT	72037	M	Ger.		Usturmfhr.,SS-Div. "Das Reich" Regiment "Der Fuehrer" 6.Coy.30.7.44	MURDER	U.S.
SIEFERT	306190	M	Ger.		Sturmbannfhr.,C.C., Kahla (Ger.) 40 - 45	MURDER	BEL.
SIEFKE	300873	M	Ger.		Pvt.,1.Aufkl.Abt.3.Coy.,2.Column,XV Div.of the Afrika-Korps, Saint Leger (Arlon) (Bel.) 5.9.44	MISC.CRIMES	BEL.
SIEGEL	143104	M			Cpl., Stalag 2.42	MURDER	U.S.
SIEGEL	133214	M			Engineer at Camp, C.C. Dora,Mittelbau,Nordhausen (Ger.)	MURDER	U.S.
SIEGEL, Conrad	194071	M	Ger.		Chief, Zollgrenzschutz,Post of Douane,Alos-Plateau de Larrech·(Fr.) 9.12.43	MURDER	FR.
SIEGEL, Ernst	257640	M	Ger.	29.10.03	Guard, SS, C.C., Oranienburg (Ger.) 40 - 45	MURDER	CZECH.
SIEGEL, Leo	139218	M	Ger.	10-	Hauptscharfhr., SS, Lublin (Pol.) 40 - 44	MURDER	U.S. POL.
SIEGEL, Phiel	192866	M	Ger.		Schupo, C.C., Falstad near Drontheim (Nor.) 6.-8.42	MURDER	NOR.
SIEGEL, Richard	149576	M	Ger.		Cpl., 11.Panz.-Div.,(South-West Fr.) 44	MURDER	FR.
SIEGEL, Wolfgang	252666	M			Cpl., C.C., Ellrich-Nordhausen (Ger.)	MURDER	U.S.
SIEGELKOW	258556	M			Hauptsturmfhr.,SS, W.V.H.A. (Ger.) 40 - 45	BRUTALITY	U.S.
SIEGEMANN, Wilhelm	877	M		18.8.98	Untersturmfnr., SS, Maidanek (Pol.) 40 - 4.44	MURDER	POL.
SIEGER (see ZEAGER)	124132						
SIEGER	173533	M	Ger.		Pvt., Stalag IX, C.C., Bad Sulza (Ger.) 44 - 45	MURDER	FR.
SIEGER	306697	M	Ger.		Pvt., 331.Pion.Bn.,331.Inf.Div.,Mijnheeren Land (Neth.) 5.45	PILLAGE	NETH.
SIEGERS	255686	M	Ger.		Civilian Chief of office Dept.Berliner Paketfahrt-Speditions-und Lagerhaus Akt.-Ges., Middelburg - Berlin (Neth.Ger.)10.43 - 6.44	INTERR.	NETH.
SIEGERT	878	M			Colonel, Army, Biserta (Tun.Fr.) 12.42 - 4.43	MURDER	FR.
SIEGERT,(or SEIGER or ZIEGERT or SPIEGET)	67677	M	Ger.		Sgt., Stalag IX A.,C.C., Breslau-Ziegenhain (Ger.) 3.45	TORTURE	U.K.
SIEGERT	194522	M	Ger.		Sgt., Army, Chennevieres sur Marne (Fr.) 40 - 44	PILLAGE	FR.
SIEGERT	194997	M	Ger.		Dr., Standartenfhr.,SS-Sicherungshauptamt 40 - 4.44	TORTURE	BEL.
SIEGFRIED	194524	M	Ger.		Kapo, KGF.Arb.Kdo.C.C.,Steip Mauthausen (Aust.)	TORTURE	FR.
SIEGFRIED	253351	M	Ger.		Civilian, C.C. Buchenwald (Ger.)	BRUTALITY	FR.
SIEGFRIED	255695	M	Ger.		Capt., 3.Panz.Gren.Rgt.2.Panz.-Div.,Middelburg, Alban (Neth.Fr.)15.8.44	SUSPECT	FR.
SIEGISMUND	260859	M	Ger.	09	Chief, Security-guard, Weimar (Ger.) 44 - 45	MURDER	U.S.
SIEGLER, Ernst (or ZIEGLER)	156033	M	Ger.	00 - 03	Obersturmfhr., SS, C.C., Sachsenhausen-Oranienburg (Ger.)	MURDER	U.K.
SIEGLER, Josef	188552	M	Ger.		Guard, Arbeitskommando, Frankfurt-Main (Ger.) 42	TORTURE	U.S.
SIEGMANN (or SIEMANN-ZIEMAN)	12378	M	Ger.		Capt., Luftw.190.Corps, Covillon (Fr.) 2.8.44	MURDER	FR.
SIEGMANN, Karl	156946	M	Ger.		Sturmbannfhr., C.C., SS, Auschwitz (Pol.) 44	TORTURE	POL. U.S.
SIEGMUND	67048	M	Ger.		Major, Army,Ortskommandant, Dax (Fr.) 18.6.44	MURDER	FR.
SIEGMUND, Karl	260416	M	Ger.		Member, Gestapo, Pelhrimov,Bohemia (Czech.) 39 - 45	MISC.CRIMES	CZECH.
SIEGMUND, Oswald (or SIGMUND)	107822	M	Ger.	21	Uscharfhr., 11.Coy.2.Panz.Gren.Rgt.,Leibstandarte SS "Adolf Hitler" Malmedy (Bel.) 23.12.44	MURDER	U.S.
SIEGROTH, Georg	31547	M	Ger.	95	Colonel, Army,110.Inf.Div.,225.Rgt., Rzhew (Russ.) 6.42 - 1.43	MURDER	U.S.
SIEHLER	252663	M		3.9.96	Pvt., C.C., Nordhausen (Ger.)	MURDER	U.S.
SIEKMEIER	251257	M	Ger.		Gauleiter, Luxemburg (Lux.)	INTERR.	LUX.
SIEMANN-ZIEMANN (see SIEGMANN)	12378						
SIEMENSMEYER	138318	M			Lt.,SS,Member Gestapo, Lyon (Fr.)	MURDER	FR.
SIEMSEN	1328	M	Ger.		Cpl., Army, 2.Pl.5.Sec.194 GR	PILLAGE	U.K.
SIEMSEN	250459	M	Ger.		Senior W.O. Gend.Trupp 925, Troyes,Aube (Fr.) 2.-6.44	TORTURE	FR.
SIENNIEKI, Sigismund	167886	M			Pvt., Res.9.Rgt.Gren.,1.Coy. Magny D'Anigón (Fr.) 18.9.44	MURDER	FR.
SIEPE	252662	M			Sturmscharfhr., Gestapo, Nordhausen(Ger.)	MURDER	U.S.
SIEPE	253475	M			Major, Medical-Officer, 13.SS-Polizei-Rgt. Ferlach(Aust.)44 - 45	MURDER	YUGO.
SIEPEN (see SIEBEN, Karl)	124384						
SIEPER	251755	M			Stabsarzt,(Major) C.O. or Germ.Troops,Nieuwvliet(Neth.) 43 - 44	INTERR.	NETH.
SIEREL	136205	M			Pvt., 11.Panz.-Div.,2.Coy.2.AA - A 7, Bergerac and Albine(Fr.)7.-8.44	MURDER	FR.
SIERVOGEL	141329	M	Ger.		Sonderfhr., Stalag IV C, Saalhaus (Ger.) 5.45	TORTURE	U.S.
SIETZMANN, Peter	139082	M	Ger.		Farmer, Civilian, Grossenschwand (Ger.) 25.4.45	TORTURE	U.S.
SIEVEKE, Karl	257935	M			Maat, Navy, 150.Pt.Brig.,Meuse-Bridge-Antwerpen (Bel.)12.44	MISC.CRIMES	U.S.
SIEVELING	67678	M	Ger.	93	Sgt., Army,Landesschuetzen 4.Coy.714.Bn.H.Q. at Bromberg, Falkenberg-Bromberg (Ger.Pol.) 2.-6.43	MURDER	U.K.
SIEVER	188551	M	Ger.		Cpl.,Army, Voutes(Grec.) 3.44	MURDER	GREC.
SIEVERS	181114	M	Ger.		Lt.,C.O., 3.SS-Pion.Coy.Leibstandarte "Adolf Hitler" Div.1 Malmedy (Bel.) 19.12.44	MURDER	U.S.
SIEVERS	252667	M			Uscharfhr., C.C., Ellrich-Nordhausen (Ger.)	MURDER	U.S.
SIEVERS	301818	M	Ger.		Obersturmbannfhr., SS Research Institute "Ahnenerbe" Dachau u.Auschwitz (Ger. u.Pol.) 3.42 - 2.43	TORTURE	BEL.
SIEVERT,Willy	301366	M	Ger.		Pvt., Service of Gast at Loguivy de la Mer Nr.Paim-Pol.(Cotes du Nord) (Fr.) 14.2.45	PILLAGE	FR.
SIEVIG	39833	M	Ger.		Officer, Army, Unit S.P.15201,Chenebier (Fr.) 27.9.44	MURDER	FR.
SIEWART	300986	M	Ger.		Cpl., Heeres-Uffz.-Schule, La Bresse,Vosges (Fr.) 9.-11.44	MURDER	FR.
SIEWERT	252689	M	Ger.		Sgt., 338 Div. La Bresse (Fr.) 9.-11.44	MISC.CRIMES	FR.
SIEWERT, Samuel	252660	M			Pvt., C.C., Ellrich-Nordhausen (Ger.)	MURDER	U.S.
SIFI	188485	M	Ger.		N.C.O., Army-Legion, Foye (Grec.) 8.44	MURDER	GRC.
SIGFRIED (or BAUMANN)	152106	M	Ger.		Lt., Army, Chenebier Etobon (Fr.) 27.9.44	MURDER	FR.
SIGHY	181282	M	Ger.		Cpl., Army, St.Barthelomy de Oun (Fr.) 7.44	MURDER	FR.
SIGL	301470	M	Ger.		Oscharfhr.,SS, (Nr.44 155) C.C. Buchenwald (Ger.) 5.38 - 10.43	MURDER	IZL.
SIGMOND	121414	M	Ger.		Oberkapo, C.C., Yaworzno(Selesie)(Czech.)	MURDER	FR.
SIGMUND	159110	M	Ger.	18.12.98	Army,Gestapo,Lt.,Member,Deauville (Fr.)	MURDER	FR.
SIGMUND (see SIEGMUND,Oswald)	197822						
SIGRIST, Charles	132733	M			Member, Gestapo, Colmar (Fr.)	MURDER	IRAQ
SIHWLTSE	188550	M	Ger.		Lt., Army,Territories Occupied,Reichs Official,Athen (Grc.)	TORTURE	GRC.
SIKINGEN	156917	M	Ger.		Oberfeldmeister, R.A.D., Villaudric (Fr.) 20.8.44	MURDER	FR.
SI KOFSKI	123950	M	Ger.		Lt., Gestapo, Salonica (Grec.) 10.44	MURDER	U.K.
SIKORA	300874	M	Ger.		Pvt., 1.Aufkl.Abt.3.Coy.2.Column, XV Div. of the Afrika-Korps Saint Leger (Arlon) (Bel.) 5.9.44	MISC.CRIMES	BEL.
SIKORSKI, Pawel	261480	M	Ger.		Civilian, Bromberg (Pol.) 39 - 45	MURDER	POL.
SILBERICH	188786	M			Lt., Army, Beaurepaire (Fr.) 5.8.44	MURDER	FR.
SILBERMANN	124616	M	Ger.		C.C., Hannover-Limmer (Ger.)	TORTURE	BEL.

SIL - SIP

NAME	C.R. FILE NUMBER	SEX	NATIO- NALITY	DATE OF BIRTH	RANK, OCCUPATION, UNIT, PLACE AND DATE OF CRIME	REASON WANTED	WANTED BY
SILBERMANN	156030	M			Volkssturm Member, C.C. Gardelegen, Vicinity of Kreis Gardelegen (Ger.)	MURDER	U.S.
SILBERNAGEL	167984	M	Ger.		Lt., Army F.P. No. 12329 0., Force en Charnie (Mayenne) (Fr.) 6.-7.8.44	MURDER	FR.
SILBERSDORF, Otto	226103	M	Ger.		Leader, DAF, Mains, (Ger.) 4.45	MISC.CRIMES	U.S.
SILINKA	121417	M	Ger.	19	Civ., Supervisor of Tailor-work shop C.C. Ravensbrueck (Ger.) 42-45	MURDER	FR. BEL.
SILOWSKY	121416	M	Ger.		Medicin SS C.C. Buchenwald (Ger.)	TORTURE	FR.
SILS, Frits	143105	M	Ger.		Lt., SS	MURDER	U.S.
SIMAS	256316	M			SS Mann Muhldorf (Ger.)	WITNESS	U.S.
SIMBERSKI	252661	M			Pvt., C.C. Nordhausen, Wolfleben (Ger.)	MURDER	U.S.
SIMHOF	173207	M	Ger.		Usturmfhr. SD, Vosges (Fr.)	INTERR.	U.K.
SIMKE (or SEMKE)	123949				Osturmfhr. SS Pz.Div. Das Reich SS Pans. Rgt. 2 Caylus (Fr.)	MURDER	FR. U.S.
SIMKUS	174564	M			Major, Lithuan.Army 13. Inf.Bn. Vilianpole (Lith.) 10.41	MURDER	U.S.
SIMM	130176	M			Opt., Stalag III A, Luckenwalde OFLAG 21 b Waldenhos (Ger.Pol.) 10.42-4.43	TORTURE	U.K.
SIMM, Paul, Max	138012	M	Ger.		Civilian, Ahlen (Ger.)	TORTURE	U.S.
SIMMER, Ernst	161659	M		05	Oschfhr., SS Buchenwald (Ger.) 39-45	SUSPECT	U.S.
SIMMES	300875	M			Pvt., 1.Aufkl.Abt. 3.Coy. 2.Column XV. Div. of the Afrika Korps Saint L'eger (Arlon) (Bel.) 5.9.44	MISC.CRIMES	BEL.
SIMOLEIT	139884	M			Major, Army Flak (Ger.)	MURDER	U.K.
SIMON (or SIMONS)	879	M			SS-Obergruppenfhr., SS Commandant of Rotterdam (Neth.) 42	MISC.CRIMES	NETH.
SIMON	31559	M			Lt.Col., Army Schleiden (Ger.) 6.9.44	WITNESS	U.S.
SIMON	121415	M	Ger.		Sgt., SS C.C. Buchenwald (Ger.)	TORTURE	FR.
SIMON	123868 A			85	SS Standartenfhr.	MURDER	U.S.
SIMON	126927	M		07	Usturmfhr., SS C.C. Mittelbau Dora Nordhausen (Ger.)	SUSPECT	U.S. FR.
SIMON	147029	M			Interpreter SS Pz.Div. Das Reich Queylus (Fr.) 44	MURDER	FR.
SIMON	159109	M			Col., Commander of Stalag 369 Kobiernyn (Pol.) 6.8.44	MURDER	FR.
SIMON	164735	M			W.O. 15.Div. Africa Corps, 33. Pionniers, Vaucourt et Xbuase (Fr.) 44	PILLAGE	FR.
SIMON	166619	M			Civilian Administrator of Luxembourg (Lux.) 40-45	TORTURE	U.S.
SIMON	169471	M			Cpl. Guard Army Stalag Luft III Sagan (Ger.) 7.42	TORTURE	U.K.
SIMON	189606	M			Lt., Army Ortafa (Fr.) 5.-7.44	MISC.CRIMES	FR.
SIMON	194070	W	Ger.		Lt., Airforce, L'isle sur la Sorgue (Fr.) 5.8.44	MURDER	FR.
SIMON	194376	M	Ger.		Commissar, Gestapo Arlon (Bel.)	TORTURE	BEL.
SIMON	194628	M	Ger.		SS Obergruppenfhr., Rotterdam (Neth.)	MISC.CRIMES	NETH.
SIMON	253913	M	Ger.		Org. Todt Rosny-Bois (Fr.) 20.8.44	WITNESS	FR.
SIMON	306660	M			Lt., G.A.F. Unit L 05062, Hameau des Cats Commune de l'isle de la Sorgue (Fr.) 5.8.44	MISC.CRIMES	FR.
SIMON, Alfred	62393	M	Ger.		Gauleiter NSDAP, Luxemburg	TORTURE	U.N.W.C.C.
SIMON, Alwin	194523	M	Ger.		Civilian Feldpost No. 53291 and 34234, Chateau de Badinghem (Fr.) 8.44	WITNESS	FR.
SIMON, Ernst	180788	M		15.10.99	Cpl., Prison C.C. Vannes (Fr.) 42-44	TORTURE	FR.
SIMON, Ernst	192916	M	Ger.	10	Cpt., III. Bn. 12. Police Rgt. Montorio san Michele (It.) 6.11.43	MURDER	U.K.
SIMON, Francois	258851	M	Ger.	25.8.11	Member, Gestapo Luxembourg 40-44	MISC.CRIMES	LUX.
SIMON, Friedrich	252680	M	Ger.		Civilian, Kragujevac (Yugo.)	MURDER	YUGO.
SIMON, Gerhard	124330	M	Ger.	10	SS Hptsturmfhr.	MURDER	U.S.
SIMON, Gerhard	208573	M	Ger.		Crim. Commissar Gestapo, Luxembourg (Lux.) 40-44	MISC.CRIMES	LUX.
SIMON, Gustav	880	M	Ger.	2.8.00	Gauleader, NSDAP, Gau Moselland Chief of Civil Administration (Public Officer) Luxembourg, Onulands and Coblens (Lux.Ger.) 40-44	MURDER	LUX.
SIMON, Hans	167885	M	Ger.		Pvt., 1.Coy. 9. Res. Gren.Rgt.Magny D'Avignon (Fr.) 15.9.44	MURDER	FR.
SIMON, Karl	168224	M	Ger.	4.11.06	SS Sturmann C.C. Struthof Natzweiler (Fr.) 42-44	MURDER	FR.
SIMON, Otto	192655	M	Ger.	97	Foreman, Civilian, Grossensnglis (Ger.) 40-45	SUSPECT	POL.
SIMON, Otto	252658	M		4.11.04	Rottenfhr., C.C. Ellrich Nordhausen (Ger.)	MURDER	U.S.
SIMON, Philipp	260473	M	Ger.	5.4.94	SS Uschfhr., SS Guard C.C. Auschwitz (Pol.) 41-42	BRUTALITY	POL.
SIMON, Simon	252659	M			Oschfhr., C.C. Dora Nordhausen (Ger.)	MURDER	U.S.
SIMON, Wilhelm	143106	M	Ger.	23.4.00	Sgt., W-SS Totenkopf Standarte C.C. Buchenwald (Ger.)	MURDER	U.S.
SIMOND	141404	M	Ger.		Cpl., 28. R.J. 116.Bn. 1.Coy. Sembrun Maubourguet (Fr.) 27.7.44	MURDER	FR.
SIMONEN	256664	M	Ger.	11	SS Oschfhr., C.C. Nordhausen (Ger.)	INTERR.	FR.
SIMONIS	174277	M	Ger.		SS Pvt. SS Gestapo Official Le Mans (Fr.) 12.43-1.44	MURDER	FR.
SIMONIS, Arnold	124393	M	Ger.	89	Civ., Butcher, Funderich (Ger.) 22.7.44	TORTURE	U.S.
SIMONS (see SIMON)	879						
SINAI, Louis	259467	M	Ger.		Gardener, Civ., Frankfurt M. (Ger.)	TORTURE	POL.
SINDELAR, Johann	251259	M	Ger.	07	Rptschfhr., Employee Gestapo SS, Kolin (Czech.)	TORTURE	CZECH.
SINDJELOV, Novak, Spavov	190287	M	Ger.		Agent Gestapo, Vladicin Han (Yugo.) 43-44	MURDER	YUGO.
SINDSISCH, Johann	108858	M			S.A. C.C. Wulfen (Ger.) 25.3.45	WITNESS	U.S.
SINGELDONK	305507	M	Ger.		Prison Warder, Prison at Utrecht (Neth.) 12.3.45	MISC.CRIMES	NETH.
SINGER	29635				Doctor, German Army Staff 2. Rgt. Locmine (Fr.) 44	MURDER	FR.
SINGER	193701	M	Ger.		Pvt., 3.Land.Schuetz.Bn. 809 C.C. Orsa (Swed.)	MURDER	NOR.
SINGER	250443	M	Ger.		Dr., C.C. Dachau (Ger.) 42	MURDER	BEL.
SINGER	252650	M			Uschfhr., SS C.C. Mittelbau Dora Nordhausen (Ger.)	MURDER	U.S.
SINGER	257352	M	Ger.		Guard, SS slave labour Camp, Beisfjord near Narvik (Nor.) 6.-11.42	BRUTALITY	YUGO.
SINGER, Eduard	188557	M	Ger.	13.9.98	Civilian, Cpt., Gendarmerie, Luxemburg (Lux.)	MURDER	LUX.
SINGER, Josef	125884	M			Dulag Sgt.	TORTURE	U.K.
SINGER, Karl	305968	M			Member Landwacht, (Edge of Achensee) Coffee Room of Gasthof Pfandler-Pertisan-Maurach (Aust.) 13.7.44	MURDER	FR.
SINGER, Maks	254047	M	Ger.		Sgt., Military Station Rukavac (Yugo.) 44-45	INTERR.	YUGO.
SINKPIEL, Jakob	126604	M	Ger.	05	Major, Schupo C.C. Saarbruecken (Ger.) 1.-2.45	MURDER	U.S.
SINN	252682	M			Cmdt., Kanton Standort, E'dtur. Mareilly le Hayer (Fr.) 8.-9.40	INTERR.	FR.
SINN, Otto	174547	M	Ger.	00	Cpl., 427.Land.Schuetz.Bn. 4.Coy. Bautzen (Ger.) 3.-45	MURDER	U.K.
SINNIG	881	M		00	Feldgend., Army Feldgendarmerie Locmine (Fr.) 7.-8.44	MURDER	FR.
SINOFZIK (or SINOVSKI)	192868	M			Schupo, C.C. Falstad, (Nor.) 11.42	MURDER	NOR.
SINSEMEISTER, August	251284	M		21	SS Rptschfhr., L.A.H. 12. Pz.Div. Hitler Jugend, Div. Panzer Spach Coy. "V" Coy. St. Sulpice (Fr.) 6.6.44	WITNESS	U.S.
SIOB	158585	M		05	Employee, C.C. Railway Bitterfeld 10.43-4.45	TORTURE	U.K.
SIR, Premysl	300971	M			Employee at the Junkers aircraft factory at Vysocany Prague (Czech.) 1.42-45	MURDER	CZECH.
SIPPACH	251752	M	Ger.		Uschfhr., SS C.C. Buchenwald (Ger.) 44-45	MISC.CRIMES	U.S.

-137-

SIR - SMI

NAME	C.R.FILE NUMBER	SEX	NATIO- NALITY	DATE OF BIRTH	RANK OCCUPATION UNIT PLACE AND DATE OF CRIME	REASON WANTED	WANTED BY
SIRAU	139709	M	Ger.		Capt., Stalag X-B, C.C. Sandbostel (Ger.) 1.-5.45	MURDER	U.S.
SISCHKE	253915	M	Ger.		Member, Gestapo, Lille (Fr.) 40-44	MISC.CRIMES	FR.
SISCHKE, Max Otto	251761	M	Ger.	22. 8.01	Sgt., Driver, Member, NSDAP, Secret Fieldpolice, Deventer, Zwolle (Neth.) 10.44-4.45	MURDER	NETH.
SISNIS, Karl	251267	M	Ger.		Gend.Gend. Romorantin No.577 F.P.22501, Orgay (Fr.) 8.8.44	MURDER	FR.
SISOWSKI, Sepp	121418	M	Ger.		Adjutant, Nice, (Fr.) 22.7.-7.8.44	MURDER	FR.
SISTERMANN, Richard	162908	M	Ger.		Agent, Arb.Kdo., C.C. Aachen (Ger.)	TORTURE	BEL.
SITERLING	259188	M	Ger.	25. 1.02	Cpl.-Chief, Technical Bn. 3. Coy., Saint-Macaire (Fr.) 24.8.44	MISC.CRIMES	FR.
SITTENBERGER	188784	M	Ger.		Capt., Army.Ruestung and Kriegsproduktion, Belfort (Fr.) 11.u.12.44	PILLAGE	FR.
SITTER	252675	M			C.C. Rottleberode, Nordhausen (Ger.)	MURDER	U.S.
SITTOF	253782	M	Ger.		Hptsturmfhr., Gestapo, Lille (Fr.) 40-44	MISC.CRIMES	FR.
SITZ	186165	M	Ger.		Chief, Gendarmerie, Rodemack (Fr.) 44	MURDER	FR.
SIX	255691	M	Ger.		C.O., SS Nachschub Bn., Dolem-Breux (Bel.) 5.u.7.9.44	MISC.CRIMES	BEL.
SIXENMEYER	1751	M			Sgt., Army-II. A.R. 959	MURDER	U.K.
SKATTLOSKI	251290	M	Ger.		Doctor, C.C. Ravensbrueck (Ger.)	TORTURE	FR.
SKALA, Wilhelm	174126	M			C.C. Schirmeck (Fr.) 44	TORTURE	U.K.
SKALAK, Jan	251286	M	Ger.	09	Member, Gestapo, Lidice (Czech.) 10.6.42	MURDER	CZECH.
SKANK, Josef	251313	M	Ger.	10. 1.09	Confident, Gestapo, Zlin (Czech.) 41-43	MURDER	CZECH.
SKAU	139764	M			SS-Mann, W-SS, C.C.	MURDER	U.S.
SKAZIDGORA	125074	M		05-10	Stalag VIII N.C.O., Milowicz (Ger.) 2.9.43	MURDER	U.K.
SKENEY	261155	M			Member Staff of C.C., Ravensbrueck (Ger.)	SUSPECT	BEL.
SKIBBE, Helmuth	252683	M	Ger.	06	Hptsturmfhr., Chief, Gestapo, Epinal, Abonsourt (Fr.)26.8.44	INTERR.	FR.
SKIBE	156028	M			Pvt., Guard in KL. Army, Zarnowitz (Pol.)	TORTURE	U.K.
SKIRDE, Max	188567	M	Ger.		Kapo, SS, C.C. Mauthausen (Ger.) 10.44	TORTURE	U.S.
SKIPKA	186808	M			Lt., Army, Flossenburg (Ger.)	MURDER	FR.
SKOBERLE	173516	M	Ger.		Governor, Prison C.C., Celje (Yugo.) 4.41-44	MURDER	YUGO.
SKOCHI, Paul	131309	M			Guard, C.C.	MURDER	U.S.
SKOERELS	253786	M	Ger.		Forman, Neuengamme (Ger.) 42-45	TORTURE	FR.
SKOPEK, Erich	252652	M			SS-Mann, C.C. Dora, Nordhausen (Ger.)	MURDER	U.S.
SKOPNIK, Hermann	158583	M			Hauptscharfhr., SS, Oranienburg (Ger.)	MURDER	U.S.
SKORGRONEK	36633	M			Public Official, Mayor Kaziniera (Pol.) Arbeit Kdo. E 713, Stalag-VIII B 1.44	TORTURE	U.K.
SKORZENY	251273	M	Ger.		SS Sturmbannfhr., SS, Prag (Czech.) 43-45	MURDER	CZECH.
SKOWRONSKI	126605	M	Ger.		Flakalarmabt. 503 2.Light Army A.A. Bde. 503, Hilden (Ger.) 16.4.45	MURDER	U.S.
SKRADE	261399	M	Ger.		Chief-paymaster, Unit L 52511, Pau, Soumoulen, Narp, Lescar (Fr.) 6. and 8.44	MURDER	FR.
SKREPTSCHUK-HEMMERLING, Stefan	256607			96	Lt., Einsatzstaffel, Slavonia (Yugo.) 41-44	MISC.CRIMES	YUGO.
SKROCKI, Paul	156027	M	Ger.		Lagerealtester, KL. Jawischowitz (Pol.)	MURDER	FR.
SKUBOVIUS	156909	M			Capt., Pz.Gren.Regt. 192-21.Pz.Div. Sessenheim (Fr.) 1.45	MURDER	U.S.
SKUPI	251751	M			Rottfhr., SS, C.C. Buchenwald (Ger.) 42-45	MISC.CRIMES	U.S.
SKURRAH	305508	F	Ger.		Head of the Vertrauungsbuero, Schomberg C.C. 44-45	MURDER	FR.
SKURT, Martin	252648	M			Pvt., C.C. Ellrich, Nordhausen (Ger.)	MURDER	U.S.
SLADON, Paul	250460	M	Ger.		SS Pvt., SS, C.C. Auschwitz-Birkenau (Ger.,Pol.) 9.44-	MURDER	YUGO.
SLADON, Paul	306892	M	Ger.		SS-Mann, Camp at Struthof nr.Natzweiler (Bas-Rhin) Struthof nr. Natzweiler (Fr.) from 40	MURDER	FR.
SLAKOVIC	256608	M		29.12.99	C.C. Nordhausen (Ger.)	MURDER	U.S.
SLAMM er SCHRAMM, Mathews	137511	M			Rottenfhr., SS, KL. Weimar-Buchenwald (Ger.)	TORTURE	U.S.
SLAVIK see STEUER, Maxmilian	262426						
SLAVING	188483	M			Pvt., Territories Occupied, Army, Salonika, Athens (Grc.)9.43	TORTURE	GRC.
SLAVITINSKY, Josef	29729	M			Dr., Landgerichtsrat, Public Official Brno (Czech.)40	MURDER	CZECH.
SLAWEK, Emil	305952	M	Ger.		Obersturmfhr., C.C. Oranienburg (Ger.) 11.39-45	MURDER	CZECH.
SLEVOOT see SLEVORT	189599						
SLEVORT er SLEVOOT	189599	M	Ger.		Capt. Art. Feldpost 40.539, Paimpol (Fr.)	WITNESS	FR.
SLEYER, George	259159	M	Ger.		SS-Rottenfhr., SS, C.C. Dachau (Ger.) 11.42-45	MISC.CRIMES	YUGO.
SLEYFER	301998	M	Ger.		Member, Sicherheitsdienst, Leeuwarden District (Neth.) 20.10.40 and 4.11.43	MURDER	NETH.
SLINAGEL	168226	M	Ger.		Cpl., Field-Police De Langes, Auberive, Flagey, Coiffy Chalensey (Fr.) 43-44	MURDER	FR.
SLINARSKY, Vincent	252655	M			Pvt., C.C. Ellrich, Nordhausen (Ger.)	MURDER	U.S.
SLIWINSKY, Stefan	143108	M			Civilian, Pattensen (Ger.) 12.3.45	WITNESS	U.S.
SLIZEK, Frans see STUERMER	251341						
SLOITER, Ernest	305295	M	Ger.		Lt., Reserve Navy Officier of the Naval Base Cerfu (Grc.)9.10.10.44	MURDER	GRC.
SLOMKA, Viktor	193741	M	Ger.	22. 3.01	Guard, Rottenfhr., 4.SS-Totenkopf Sturmbann, C.C. Nordhausen-Dora Mittelbau (Ger.) 43-45	MURDER	U.S.
SLOTANA, Fritz	198322	M			Adjutant, Gestapo Sect. IV, Lyon (Fr.) 20.-8.44	MURDER	FR.
SLOTNIKI	240094	M	Ger.	26	Official SS Crim.Asst. SS Obersturmfhr., Gestapo, Koblenz (Ger.)	MURDER	U.N.W.C.C.
SLOTTOWA	306661	M	Ger.		Section IV SD Lyons, surroundings (Fr.) 11.43-8.44	MURDER	FR.
SLOUKA, Alfred	162909	M	Ger.		W.O. 10.SS-Pz.Div. 36.Pz.Regt., Revin (Fr.)1.44	MURDER	FR.
SLOWIK, Joseph	167884	M	Ger.		Pvt., 9.Gren.Ers.Regt.1.Coy., Magny D'Andigon (Fr.) 18.9.44	MURDER	FR.
SLUPSKY	188579	M			SS-Sturmbannfhr., SS, C.C. Mauthausen (Aust.)	MURDER	U.S.
SLUPINSKY	255594	M			Lt., C.C. Mauthausen (Aust.)	MISC.CRIMES	FR.
SLUSZKER	882	M		90-95	Regional Officier, Public Official, Official of Baerem Expositur Amsterdam (Neth.)	MISC.CRIMES	NETH.
SLUSZKER-RAPPAPORT	883	M	Ger.	10-13	Public-Official, Official of Baeren Expositur, Amsterdam (Neth.)42		NETH.
SMEKAL, Emil	29682	M	Ger.		Landgerichtsdirektor, Public Official Opava (Czech.) 40	MURDER	CZECH.
SMELES, Max	259187	M	Ger.		Cpl.-Guard, C.C. Lamets (Fr.) 5.1.41	INTERR.	FR.
SMELKA	187790	M			Master Arbeitskdo.Firm of Heinrich Butzer, Aspfjord (Nor.)	TORTURE	NOR.
SMENT	124537	M			Oberarzt, Ex Police Surgeon in Hamburg	MISC.CRIMES	U.K.
SMETANA	10354	M	Ger.		Untersturmfhr., SS Gestapo, Morava-Ostrava (Czech.) 38-44	TORTURE	CZECH.
SMETANA, Alexander	250452	M	Ger.	8. 9.07	Dr., Civilian Chief, City Admin. Taber (Czech.) 1.43	MURDER	CZECH.
SMETS	251277	M			Interpreter, Sipo, Bruxxels (Bel.)	INTERR.	BEL.
SMETZEN	62394	M	Ger.		SS Lt., SS Police, Ukr. Kom.8	TORTURE	U.N.W.C.C.
SMID see SCHMIDT	306288						
SMILEVSKY	129917	M			Capt., W-SS, C.C. Mauthausen (Aust.) 41-45	MURDER	U.S.
SMIDEK, Friedericke	258101	F	Sex.	7. 9.13	Informer, Clerk, Gestapo, State Service Post Office, C.Budejovice (Czech.) 42	MURDER	CZECH.
SMIT, Hans	186497	M	Ger.	10	N.C.O., Army, Zutphen (Neth.) 2.10.44	TORTURE	NETH.

SMI-SOL

NAME	C.R.FILE NUMBER	SEX	NATIO-NALITY	DATE OF BIRTH	RANK OCCUPATION UNIT PLACE AND DATE OF CRIME	REASON WANTED	WANTED BY
SMITH	139216	M			Sturmbannfhr., W-SS, CC Dora, Mittelbau, Nordhausen (Ger.)	MURDER	U.S.
SMITH	156905	M	Ger.		Capt., Army, Cabrespines (Fr.) 22.4.45	MURDER	FR.
SMITH	255683	M	Ger.		Secretary of Cmdt., SS, Mauthausen (Aust.)	BRUTALITY	FR.
SMITH, Heinz (or HAMMETMER)	167985	M	Ger.		Pvt., Abw.Kdo.343, Landerneau (Fr.) 15.4.-29.8.44	MURDER	FR.
SMITHS-PORTEN (or POORTEN)	307202	M	Ger.		Lt., Ortskommandant at Zoelen (Neth.) 24.10.44	TORTURE	NETH.
SMITT	306912	M	Ger.		Guard, Fort 13 att. to Stalag XX-A, Thorn(Pol.) 12.1.42	BRUTALITY	U.K.
SMITTH	141436	M	Ger.		Uschfhr, SS, CC Gusen (Aust.)	TORTURE	FR.
SMITZ	251754	M	Ger.		Sgt., 6 Coy, Unit 10180, Evergem (Bel.) 7.9.44	INTER.	BEL.
SMITZ, Armand	306807	M	Ger.		Member St.Quentin Gestapo, Vraignes en Vermandois Somme (Fr.)29.8.44	MURDER	FR.
SMITZ, Fritz	306808	M	Ger.		Member St.Quentin Gestapo, Vraignes en Vermandois Somme (Fr.)29.8.44	MURDER	FR.
SMITZER	305759	M	Ger.		Prison guard, Chaidari CC (Athen) Greece, 10.43-10.44	MURDER	GRC.
SMOGER, Georges	160544	M	Ger.		Cpl., Customs frontier guard, La Plaine (Fr.) 12.5.42	TORTURE	FR.
SMOL, Albert	253317	M	Ger.	18	10 Coy, 377 Jg.Rgt., Vinkt Meigem (Bel.) 25.-31.5.40	MURDER	BEL.
SMOLA	1330				Major, Army	MURDER	U.K.
SMOLENSKY	306108	M	Ger.		Uschfhr, SS, CC Hamburg Neuengamme (Ger.) -45	MURDER	CZECH.
SMOLL	121422	M	Ger.		Director, CC Neu-Brann.(Ger.) 43-44	MISC.CRIMES	FR.
SMOLLNY	152133	M	Ger.		Dr., Kriegsgericht, 432 Div., Neisse (Ger.) 44	MISC.CRIMES	U.K.
SMOLNIK, Erich	260455	M		2.4.22	Uschfhr, W-SS, Guard-Coy, CC Monowitz-Auschwitz (Pol.)8.42-2.45	BRUTALITY	POL.
SMOLSKI, K.	252197	M			Capt., Brask (Ger.) 10.1.44 L.O.D.N.A.O.D.	WITNESS	U.S.
SMUTSCH	306447	M	Ger.		SS-Mann, SS, CC Oranienburg (Ger.) 11.39-45	MURDER	CZECH.
SMUTZ	124080	M			Agent, Gestapo, Brux (Czech.)	TORTURE	U.K.
SNADTNER, Eduard	255463	M		7.9.97	Civilian, Gossengrun, Haberspirk (Czech.) 9.39	MURDER	CZECH.
SNAIDER, Kurt	188492	M			SS Interrogator, 20 Department, Skaramanga Athens (Grc.)	MURDER	GRC.
SNELLER, Ferry	300142	M			Sgt., Feld-Gend., Alkmar Heer Hugowaard Wieringermeerdijk(Neth.) 9.-12.44	TORTURE	NETH.
SNELLING	36692	M	Ger.		Civilian, CO Kemberg, Stalag 4-D (Ger.)	TORTURE	U.K., SOV.UN.
SNIDER	124538	M			Capt., Stalag XX-B, Marienburg (Pol.)	RAPE	U.K.
SNIJDERS, Walter	306698	M	Ger.		331 Pion.Bn., 331 Inf.Div., Mijnheerenland(Neth.) 5.45	PILLAGE	NETH.
SNYDER	139215	M	Ger.		Guard at Ilag 7, Laufen (Ger.) 6.8.44	TORTURE	U.S.
SOBALA, Karl	192870	M	Ger.		Schupo, CC Falstad (Nor.) 11.42	MURDER	NOR.
SOBANIA	252651	M			Pvt., CC Rottleberode, Nordhausen (Ger.)	MURDER	U.S.
SOBANSKI, Hans	143109	M	Ger.		Member NSDAP, chief electrician, Weserhuette-factory, Bad Oeynhausen (Ger.) 44-45	TORTURE	U.S.
SOBECK	253481	M	Ger.		Rptschfhr, SS, Hospital, Laag-Soeren (Neth.) 5.9.44	BRUTALITY	NETH.
SOBINSKI	36603	M	Ger.	07	SS Sonderfhr, CC Stalag 3-B, Czenstochowa (Pol.) 12.41	MURDER	SOV.UN.
SOBOTKA, Leopold	251911	M		84	Civilian, Forester, Vihlava (Czech.) 39-45	INTER.	CZECH.
SOBOTTKA	192059	M	Ger.		Pvt., Eis.Art.Bn. 717, F.P.No.22380, St.Andries Varsenare, Lesbruges (Bel.) 4.9.44	MURDER	BEL.
SOBOTTKA	253482	M	Ger.		Sgt., Air Force, Ground service, Gitze Rijen Airfield, Ulvenhout, Nieuw-Ginneken (Neth.) 10.9.44	BRUTALITY	NETH.
SOCHMITZ (see SCHMITZ, Karl)	260013						
SOCHUREK, Karl	250458	M	Ger.	30.11.03	Schfhr, SS, Velke Svatonovice (Czech.) 42	TORTURE	CZECH.
SOCKEL, Fritz	129957	M	Ger.		Head, Camp Kahla (Ger.)	MURDER	BEL.
SODDEMANN	252653	M			CC Dora, Nordhausen (Ger.)	MURDER	U.S.
SODERMANN, Wilhelm	307205	M	Ger.		Railway official, Fernmeldemeisterei office at Amersfoort(Neth.) 4.10.44-5.45	PILLAGE	NETH.
SOECKEL, Johanna (see JOECKEL)	192669						
SOEDERMAN (see FISCHERMANN)	189431						
SOEHN, Paul	252654	M		25.12.17	Flyer, Air Force, Nordhausen (Ger.)	MURDER	U.S.
SOEHNEL, Kurt	250468	M	Ger.		Sturmfhr, SS, Pol.Res., Drakova (Czech.) 7.1.45	MURDER	CZECH.
SOERNGEN, Alfred	152126	M	Ger.		Doctor, Civilian, CC Tangerhuette, Goerlits (Ger.)	TORTURE	U.K.
SOEHRLEIN, Wolfgang Heinrich Poulus	301119	M	Ger.	25.9.19	Usturmfhr, SS, served with the SD Aarhus, Esbjerg and Odense, Fyn, Odense, Svendborg, (Den.) 4.1.44-45	MISC.CRIMES	DEN.
SOEHRING	259676	M	Ger.		Kriegsgerichtsrat, Air Force, Paris - Seine (Fr.) 24.6.42	INTER.	FR.
SOEKTING	260049	M	Ger.		Chief of guard, prison, Charleville, Ardennes (Fr.) 7.44	TORTURE	FR.
SOELCH, Georg	250470	M	Ger.	22.9.03	Civilian, confident, Gestapo, SD, Pilsen (Czech.) 43-45	MISC.CRIMES	CZECH.
SOELL	140926	M		00	Hptsturmfhr, SS, CC Ravensbrueck (Ger.)	TORTURE	U.K.
SOELL	156026	M			SS-Mann, W-SS, CC Magdeburg (Ger.) 10.44-4.45	TORTURE	U.S.
SOELLNER, Anton	189132	M			Schfhr, SS, CC Drancy (Fr.) 6.43	MURDER	FR.
SOELLNER, Michael (or SOLLNER)	180876	M	Ger.		Hptwachtmstr, administrator, guard at prison, Ebrach(Ger.) 39-45	SUSPECT	CZECH., FR.
SOELTER, Friedrich	301471	M	Ger.	1.6.94	Uschfhr SS, CC Buchenwald (Ger.) 16.5.38-9.10.43	MURDER	BEL.
SOELTER, Fritz	252656	M			Oschfhr, CC Mittelbau, Nordhausen (Ger.)	MURDER	U.S.
SOENK (or SUHN)	12379	M	Ger.		Lt., head of Feld-Gend., Lure (Fr.) 1.4.44	MURDER	FR.
SOERENS, Ernst	10355	M	Ger.		Sturmbannfhr, SA, commissary of Gestapo, Prague (Czech.) 38-44	TORTURE	CZECH.
SOERGONI	72014	M	Ger.		SS-Sturmmann, Struthof (Fr.)	TORTURE	FR.
SOETE, Willy	253390	M			Cpl., 10 Coy, 377 Jg.Rgt., Vinkt Meigem (Bel.) 25.-31.5.40	MURDER	BEL.
SOGL, Anton	188566	M	Ger.	17.2.92	Member NSDAP, Mikulow, Praha (Czech.) 4.45	MISC.CRIMES	CZECH.
SOHL, Fritz	123862	M		05	Guard, Kapo (long-term prisoner) Clausthal-Zellerfeld (Ger.)6.4.45	MURDER	U.S.
SOHMANN	189176	M		1895-00	Oberfhr. and commanding officer, SD, SS, for Rhine Westmark, Wiesbaden, Metz, Koblenz (Ger., Fr.) 44	MISC.CRIMES	U.S.
SOHN	252647	M			Oschfhr, CC Ellrich, Nordhausen (Ger.)	MURDER	U.S.
SOHRNY	139705	M	Ger.		Employee, main labour office (Pol.) 41-44	MISC.CRIMES	U.S.
SOIKO, Rudolf	252643	M			Flyer, Air Force, C.O, Ellrich, Nordhausen(Ger.)	MURDER	NOR.
SOKEL, Fritz	173477	M	Ger.		Chief, CC Ehlba (Ger.) 44-45	MURDER	BEL.
SOKELAND	194590	M			Cpl., driver, 12 Coy, Feldersatz Bn.114, II Pz.Div., Montesquieu de Lauragais (Fr.) 9.8.44	PILLAGE	FR.
SOKULOWSKI	199413	M			Pvt., 1 POW work Batl., CC Nerlandedal,Kristiansund (Nor.) 41-45	TORTURE	NOR.
SOLD, Heinz	99798	M			SS-Mann, Guard camp, Struthof (Fr.)	TORTURE	FR.
SOLDAN, Wilhelm	149110	M	Ger.		SA Sgt., Bochum (Ger.) 8.4.45	MURDER	U.S.
SOLDERS	256590	M			Hptsturmfhr, leader, CC Dora, Nordhausen (Ger.)	MURDER	U.S.
SOLICH, Franz	252657	M			Pvt., CC Ellrich, Nordhausen (Ger.)	MURDER	U.S.
SOLINSKI	156025	M	Ger.		Capt., CC Vitebsk (Sov.Un.) 43	MURDER	U.S.
SOLKEN	256317	M	Ger.		Oschfhr, SS, CC Muhldorf (Ger.)	WITNESS	U.S.

SOL - SOR

NAME	C.R.FILE NUMBER	SEX	NATIO- NALITY	DATE OF BIRTH	RANK OCCUPATION UNIT PLACE AND DATE OF CRIME	REASON WANTED	WANTED BY
SOLL, Walter	262159	M	Ger.	9.10.09	Uschfhr.,SS,51.SS Armoured Bde.,Bucheres,Breviandes,St.Savine La Riviere de Corps,Troyes (Fr.) 22.-25.8.44	BRUTALITY	FR.
SOLLANECK, Heinrich	193700	M	Ger.	1.11.94	Straflager,Reichsjustizministerium Finmark (Nor.)	WITNESS	NOR.
SOLLE, Karl	251521	M	Ger.		Sgt.,Stab Nachschubtruppe Feld Div.,Amsterdam (Neth.)	MURDER	NETH.
SOLLER, Georg	188322	M	Ger.		Director,Prison,Nuernberg (Ger.) 43-45	WITNESS	CZECH.
SOLLERMANN, Alfred	137512	M	Ger.	15	Pvt.,Geheime Feldpolizei,Gruppe 713	MURDER	U.S.
SOLLICH, Theophile	72010	M		28.12.07	Annonay (Fr.) 4.8.44	MURDER	FR.
SOLLIG, Martin	188783	M	Ger.		Oberstabsarzt,Kriegslazarett,Dury les Amiens (Fr.) 44	WITNESS	FR.
SOLLING	137518	M			Doctor,SS member (private),C.C. Buchenwald (Ger.)	MURDER	U.S.
SOLINER	126512	M	Ger.	15	Oschfhr.,SS,Buchenwald (Ger.) 39-41	TORTURE	U.S.
SOLINER, Michael (see SOELLNER)	180876						
SOLMES, Hienrich	139207	M	Ger.		Civilian,Plettenburg (Ger.)	TORTURE	U.S.
SOLOMON	188484	M	Ger.		Admin. of Territories occupied,Athens Peloponese (Grc.)	MURDER	GRC.
SOLOMONS	152113	M	Ger.		Major,Air force,Memel,Swinemuende (Lat.) 7.44	MISC.CRIMES	U.K.
SOLPER	164734	M	Ger.		W.O.,Army,Pont Labbe,Plobannalec (Fr.) 6.-8.44	MURDER	FR.
SOMANN, Otto	180895	M	Ger.		Oberfhr.,SS,Police,chief of security police,Wiesbaden,Rhein-Westmark (Ger.) 7.44	TORTURE	U.S.
SOMANN, Willy	39617	M	Ger.		Member,SD,Gestapo,Bourges (Fr.) 23.9.44	TORTURE	FR.
SOMERES	256048	M	Ger.		Hauptbauleiter,Org.Todt,Muhldorf (Ger.)	WITNESS	U.S.
SOMERS	108855	M	Ger.		Doctor,S-Arzt,C.C.,Stalag Luft 4,Gross-Tychow (Ger.) 44	TORTURE	U.K.
SOMMEL (or SOMMERS)	173258	M	Ger.		Lt.Col.,Army,Gestapo,Controlling Reichspost,Leipzig (Ger.)6.43-9.44	TORTURE	U.K.
SOMMER	884	M	Ger.		SD official,C.C.,Auschwitz,Birkenau (Pol.) 39-45	MURDER	CZECH.,FR.
SOMMER	12380	M	Ger.		Lt.,Marine Art.4.Bn.,Quiberan (Fr.) 7.-8.44	MURDER	FR.
SOMMER	12417	M	Ger.		Schfhr.,SS,C.C.,Buchenwald (Ger.) 38-44		FR.,U.S.,CZECH
SOMMER	149807	M	Ger.		Uschfhr.,SS 2.Panz.Gren.Rgt.,3.Bn.,12.Coy.,Stavelot,Malmedy (Bel.) 22.-23.12.44	MURDER	U.S.
SOMMER	156948	M			Member,SS,commd.,C.C.,Auschwitz (Pol.)	MURDER	U.S.
SOMMER	159106	M			Adjutant,74.Sicherungs Rgt.,1.Bn.,Clavieres (Fr.) 10.-11.6.44	MURDER	FR.
SOMMER	180787	M	Ger.		Pvt.,Stalag XIII D,Kommando 1600,C.C. Coy 1-624,Nuernberg (Ger.)	MURDER	FR.
SOMMER	188782	M			Lt.,74.Rgt.Sich.mot.,1.Bn.,SS Pz.Rgt.,Chaudes Aigues (Fr.) 20.6.44	MURDER	FR.
SOMMER	189567	M		97	Guard,Navy,C.C.,Luneburg (Ger.) 7.-10.4.45	MURDER	U.K.
SOMMER	252644	M			Oschfhr.,SS,Camp Ellrich,Nordhausen (Ger.)	MURDER	U.S.
SOMMER	253185	M	Ger.		Hptsturmfhr.,SS,Gestapo,Paris (Fr.) 41	PILLAGE	FR.
SOMMER	253483	M	Ger.		Sgt.,17.Rgt.,6.Div.Paratroopers,A.P.O.No. L 61021,Nienwaal (Neth.) 14.-15.1.45	WITNESS	NETH.
SOMMER	260048		Ger.		Gendarm,Div."Oberland",Russian-German,Massif of Vercors,Isere,Drome (Fr.) 20.7.-5.8.44	SUSPECT	FR.
SOMMER	300980	M	Ger.		Sgt.,17.Rgt.6.Div.,Paratroopers,F.P.No. L 61021,Nisuwaal Prov. of Gelderland (Neth.) 14.1.-15.1.45	MURDER	NETH.
SOMMER, Ernst	22047	M		18	Sgt.,Waffen SS,C.C.,Buchenwald (Ger.)	MURDER	U.S.
SOMMER, Josef	156938	M	Ger.		Sgt.,Landesschuetzen Bn.395,3.Coy.,Muehlberg (Ger.)	TORTURE	U.S.
SOMMER, Joseph	301472	M	Ger.	15.8.05	Rottfhr.,SS,C.C.,Buchenwald (Ger.) 16.5.38-9.10.43	MURDER	BEL.
SOMMER, Martin	143111	M	Ger.	8.2.15	Hptschfhr.,Waffen SS,Totenkopf Standarte,Barracks-leader,C.C. Buchenwald (Ger.) 8.2.45	TORTURE	U.S.
SOMMER, Meinhol	259667	M	Ger.		Guard,1.Coy.,624.Bn.,command of guard 2640,Stalag XIIID,Klein Seebach,Bayern,(Ger.) 18.8.44	MURDER	FR.
SOMMERFELD	253912	M			Oschfhr.,SS,Gestapo,Paris (Fr.) 41-43	MISC.CRIMES	FR.
SOMMERFELD, Helmuth	252645	M			Flyer,Camp Ellrich,Nordhausen (Ger.)	MURDER	U.S.
SOMMERFELD, Hermann	305697	M	Ger.		Member of C.C. Personnel,Flossenburg,Hersbruck,Wolkenburg,Genacker Leitmeritz (Ger.,Sov.Un.) 1.1.42-8.5.45	MURDER	U.S.
SOMMERFELD, Julius	254042	M	Ger.	02	Pvt.,Camp Ellrich,Nordhausen (Ger.)	MURDER	U.S.
SOMMERHAUSER	129959	M	Ger.		C.C.	MURDER	BEL.
SOMMERMANN, Max	262158	M	Ger.	30.6.?	Uschfhr.,SS,Gestapo,Rennes (Fr.) 43-44	MISC.CRIMES	FR.
SOMMERMEIER, Wilh.	256591	M	Ger.	22.4.81	Member,SS,Genthin (Ger.) 12.44	BRUTALITY	U.S.
SOMMERS	123948	M	Ger.	05	Civilian post official,Stalag IV G,Working camp 124,Oschatz (Ger.) 9.43-4.45	TORTURE	U.K.
SOMMERS (see SOMMEL)	173258						
SOMMERS, Ludwig	254049	M		20.8.02	Rottfhr.,SS,Camp Harzungeh,Nordhausen (Ger.)	MURDER	U.S.
SOMMERSCHUH	251744	M	Ger.		Schfhr.,SS,C.C.,Buchenwald (Ger.) 42-45	MURDER	U.S.
SOMMERSTHAL, Gustav	62175	M	Ger.		Nancy (Fr.) 19.8.44	MURDER	FR.
SOMOTZKY	133218	M			C.C.,Dora,Mittelbau,Nordhausen (Ger.)	MURDER	U.S.
SONETAG	179481	M	Ger.		Pvt.,20.Bau u.Arb.Bn.,3.Coy.,Reigersfeld (Pol.) spring 42	MURDER	U.K.
SONIA	260960	F	Ger.		Female-guard,C.C.,Hirtenberg (Ger.) 44-45	TORTURE	POL.
SONNECK	251753	M	Ger.		Werkmeister,Kalk und Zementwerke,Braunschweig (Ger.)	INTERR.	BEL.
SONNEFELD	161535	M	Ger.	95	Osturmfhr.,C.C.,Wuestegiersdorf	TORTURE	U.K.
SONNENLEITERN	187339	M	Ger.		Major,Army,Montgauthier (Bel.) 20.9.43	MURDER	BEL.
SONNENWEND, Frantisek	185259	M	Ger.	15.7.02	Leiter,Beauftragter fuer Ruestungs & Kriegsproduction,Duhnice-Vahom (Czech.) 41-45	MURDER	CZECH.
SONNEVELD	31540	M	Ger.		Supervisor,C.C.,Bohlen (Ger.) 7.44-11.44	MURDER	U.S.
SONNTAG	126612	M	Ger.		20.Bau u.Arb.Bn.,3.Coy.,Reigersfeld (Ger.) 4.42	SUSPECT	U.S.
SONNTAG	180877	M	Ger.		Chefarzt,Camp official,C.C.,Ravensbrueck (Ger.) 40	TORTURE	FR.,BEL.
SONNTAG	190220	M	Ger.		Crim.Secretary,Gestapo,SS,C.C.,Dachau (Ger.) 40-45	MURDER	BEL.
SONNTAG	251270	M	Ger.		Capt.,Commandant of Fontenay le Comte,Benet (Fr.) 25.8.44	INTERR.	FR.
SONTAG, Fritz	251258	M	Ger.		Kdo.Fhr.,Kdo.106 of Borna Stalag IV G,Leipzig (Ger.) 40-42	BRUTALITY	FR.
SONTGERATH, Willi	193669	M	Ger.	11.5.16	Reichsjustizministerium,Strafgefangenenlager,C.C.,Finmark (Nor.)	WITNESS	NOR.
SORENSEN	160545	M	Ger.		Capt.,Army,Lancieux (Fr.) 5.44	PILLAGE	FR.
SOREK, R.	147028	M	Ger.		SS,Pz.Div."Das Reich",Deutschland Rgt.,Venerque le Vernet (Fr.) 44	MURDER	FR.
SORG, Hugo	301222	M	Ger.		Leader,SA,Buchenfeld (Ger.) 17.3.45	MURDER	U.K.
SORGALLA, Fritz	260459	M	Ger.	18.5.99	Rottfhr.,Waffen SS,Blockfhr.,guard Coy.,C.C. Lublin,Kielce, Auschwitz (Pol.) 42-45	BRUTALITY	POL.
SORGATZ, Heinz	162906	M	Ger.		Rottfhr.,SS,La Calamine (Bel.) 6.9.44	MURDER	BEL.
SORGDIT, Gustav (see SORGE)	885						
SORGE	886	M	Ger.		Sturmbannfhr.,Charge of work details C.C.,Dachau,Sachsenhausen(Ger.)9.41	MURDER	FR.
SORGE	121421	M	Ger.	95	Major,C.C.,Heydebreck (Ger.) 5.42-1.44	MISC.CRIMES	U.K.
SORGE	124751	M			Hptschfhr.,SS,C.C.,Sachsenhausen (Ger.) 9.41	MURDER	U.S.

NAME	C.R.FILE NUMBER	SEX	NATIO-NALITY	DATE OF BIRTH	RANK OCCUPATION UNIT PLACE AND DATE OF CRIME	REASON WANTED	WANTED BY
SORGE	137514	M			Oschfhr., SS, C.C. Weimar-Buchenwald (Ger.)	TORTURE	U.S.
SORGE	139084	M	Ger.		Hptschfhr., SS Totenkopf, C.C., Riga Auschwitz (Latv., Pol.) 41-43	MURDER	U S.
SORGE	186811	M	Ger.		Conc.Camp, Flossenburg (Ger.)	MURDER	FR.
SORGE	191425	M	Ger.		Usturmfhr., SS, Conc.Camp, Oranienburg, Sachsenhausen (Ger.)	MURDER	POL.
SORGE	254241	M	Ger.		Hptsturmfhr., SS, Camp Dora, Nordhausen (Ger.)	MURDER	U S.
SORGE	301473	M	Ger.		Sturmbannfhr., SS-T.K.Stand."Oberbayern", C C , Dachau (Ger) 43	MURDER	BEL.
SORGE, Gustav (or poss.SORGDIT, Gustav)	885	M	Ger.	10	Hptschfhr., or Osturmfhr., SS-Totenkopfstandarte, Dachau, Sachsenhausen (Ger) 36-45	MURDER	POL.,U S, CZECH ,BEL , FR., U.K.
SORGE, Gustav	156898	M		13	Sgt., Waffen-SS, 12.Bau-Bde., Boppard (Ger) 1 -10.1.45	MURDER	U S.
SORGE, Walter	168973	M	Ger.		Usturmfhr., SS, C.C Sachsenhausen, Oranienburg (Ger.)	MURDER	POL.
SORGE, Walter	168974	M	Ger.		Warder or Kapo, SS, Conc.Camp, Sachsenhausen, Oranienburg (Ger.)39-4.45	MURDER	POL.
SORIN	64835	M	Ger		Camp-Cmdt., SS, Conc.Camp, Auschwitz (Pol.)	MURDER	DEN
SORKO, Rudolf (or SROKO)	138011	M			Kapo at Conc.Camp, Civilian, Hohenrheim (Ger) 2.45-3.45	MURDER	U.S.
SORMENLEITER	301474	M	Ger.		Major, Montgauthier-Dinant, 20.9.43	MURDER	BEL.
SOROWKA, Sepp	39800	M			Uschfhr., SS-Guard, C.C., Struthof (Fr.)	TORTURE	FR.
SOSBACH (see SHOSBACH)	252670						
SOSNOWSKI	124454	M	Ger.		Hptschfhr., SS, Conc.Camp Staff, Sachsenhausen, Oranienburg (Ger.) 42	MURDER	U.K.
SOSSNA	177564	M			Pvt., Army, Longueil (Fr.) 24. 6.44	MURDER	FR.
SOUESCHTECK, Anton	256592	M			Lt., Army, Lajecar (Yugo.) 41-44	MISC.CRIMES	YUGO.
SOUGER	162903	M	Ger.		Stabsschfhr., SS, 36.Pz.Rgt.,10.SS-Pz.Div., Revin (Fr.) 12.-13.6.44	MURDER	FR.
SOUKUP, Josef	180487	M			Gend. Feldgend., Crete (Grc.)	MURDER	GRC
SOULA, Anna (see SCHOULA)	256853						
SOUPAN-MEYER, Charles	164731	M			Interpreter, SS-Detachment, Busset (Fr.) 7.8.44	MURDER	FR.
SOWA, Friedrich	185258	M	Ger.	96	Standartenfhr., SA, Prague and Lidige (Czech.)	MURDER	CZECH.
SOWER, Franz	120637	M	Ger.		Conc.Camp, Bremen (Ger.) 2.43-4.45	BRUTALITY	U.K
SOYKE	194591	M	Ger.		SS-Div."Adolf Hitler" Inf., Rousseloy (Fr.)	MURDER	FR.
SPAN, Theo	133219	M	Ger.		Usturmfhr., Waffen-SS, Bande (Bel.) 24.12.44	MURDER	U.S.
SPAATZ (see PLAATZ)	196610						
SPAATZ, Franz	137515	M			Lagerfhr., Conc.Camp, Public-Official, near Friedrichsfeld (Ger.)	TORTURE	U S.
SPACEK-WIEDMANN, Eduard Josef Anton	255465	M	Ger.	5. 2.96	Informer, Gestapo, Tabor (Czech.) 43-45	MISC.CRIMES	CZECH
SPACHTHOLZ	253911	M	Ger.		Dr., Parachutist, 9.or 10.Div., Area d'Ussel (Fr.) 7.4.44	PILLAGE	FR.
SPACTHER (see SPAETHER)	255692						
SPAEHLER	147027	M	Ger.		SS-Mann, SS-Pz.Div."Das Reich", Tulle (Fr.) 44	MURDER	FR.
SPAEHT	159100	M	Ger.	98	Cpt., Lds.Schtz.Bn.439, 1.Coy., Detachment Bayreuth (Ger.) 11.4.45	BRUTALITY	U.K.
SPAET	252696	M	Ger.		Osturmfhr., SS-Commander, Leibstandarten-Coy., Wormboudt (Fr or Bel) 27.5.40	INTERR	U.K.
SPAETER, Georg	192098	M			Hptsturmfhr., 1.SS-Pz Rgt.,6.Coy., Ardennes (Bel.) 44	MURDER	U S
SPAETH	141999	M	Ger.	17	Schfhr. or Oschfhr., SS, M-1 Lager, C.C., Ampfing,Mueldorf.Mettenheim (Ger.) 44-45	MURDER	U.S.
SPAETH, Wilhelm	193057	M		31. 8.18	Reichsjustizministerium,Feldstraflager,Finmark (Nor.) 42-45	WITNESS	NOR.
SPAETHER (or SPACTHER)	255692	M	Ger.		Lt., 125.Aust.Gren.Bn., Hablainville (Fr.) 10.44	PILLAGE	FR.
SPAGENBERG, Richard	68903	M	Ger.		Stabswachtmstr., Signal-Sect.466.Inf., Doerigsen (Ger.)	MURDER	U.S.
SPAHL	300876	M	Ger.		N.C.O., 1.Aufkl.Abt ,3.Coy.,2.Column,XV.Div.of the Africa-Corps, Saint Leger (Arlon) 5.9.44	MISC.CRIMES	BEL.
SPAHL, Walter	188568	M	Ger.		Member, Gestapo, Luxembourg, Grand Duchy (Lux.)	MISC.CRIMES	LUX
SPAHN	141605	M	Ger.		Cpl., Chief, Feldgend., Beaune Manley (Fr.) 42-44	TORTURE	FR.
SPALLECK, Theo	257248	M	Ger.	08	Hptschfhr., SS, Crim.Secr., Abt.VI, Sipo and SD, Anvers (Bel.) 40-45	BRUTALITY	BEL.
SPAITMEIER, Franz	253994	M	Ger.	16	Sgt., SD, Milan (It.) 10.8.44	INTERR.	U.K.
SPAMER	252685	M	Ger.		Major, D.C.-works in San Pangrazio, San Donnissi (It.) 7.43	INTERR.	U.K.
SPAN-SPANN, Hermann	156937	K	Ger.		Capt., Gestapo, Region d'Angers (Fr.)	MURDER	FR.
SPANAGEL, Erich	262079	M	Ger.		N.C.O., Former SS, "Brandenburg-Div.", St.Truppert, 21.4.45	MURDER	FR.
SPANCK	195946	M	Ger.		General, Army, Plouvenez Medec (Fr.)	MISC.CRIMES	FR.
SPANG, Alois	254242	M			Pvt., Conc.Camp Ellrich, Nordhausen (Ger.)	MURDER	U.S.
SPANG, Heinrich	190068	M	Ger.		Pvt., 8.Flugsich.Coy.,Luftw.Rgt.35, Conc.Camp, Hamburg-Altona (Ger.)44	WITNESS	U.S.
SPANIOL	67679	M	Ger.	00	Pit-Manager, Civ., Hohenzollerngrube, C.C., Beuthen (Ger.) 9.40-1.45	TORTURE	U.K.
SPANIOL, Josef	190237	M	Ger.	18	Member, SS, SD, Kripo, Crim.Employee, Prague and Klatovy (Czech.)40-45	TORTURE	CZECH.
SPANJAR, Gerhard	305953	M	Ger.		Guard, C.C., Neugraben and Tiefstak (Ger.) 44-5.2.45	BRUTALITY	CZECH.
SPANN, Hermann	307206	M	Ger.		Hptsturmfhr., SS, Commissioner of Police Angers-Gestapo, Sarthe-et-Mayenne (Fr.) 42-3.8.44	MURDER	FR.
SPANNAUS, Wilhelm	133220	M			Secretary, Police	MURDER	U.S.
SPANNENBERG	1331	M	Ger.		Army, 903.Fortress-Bn.	MURDER	U.K.
SPANNER	194389	M	Ger.	00	Doctor, Anatomy-Institute Danzig (Ger.)	MISC.CRIMES	POL.
SPARBRODT	156899	M	Ger.	95	Capt., Army, Bruex (Czech.) 5.44-5.45	TORTURE	U.K.
SPARENBERG	31644	M			Groupleader, SS, C.C. Bukow-Warschau (Pol.) 43-44	MURDER	U.S.
SPARENBERG	240062	M	Ger.	90 - 00	Local-Group-Leader, NSDAP, Nottleben Gotha (Ger.) 4.45	TORTURE	U.S.
SPARER (see SPORER)	253350						
SPARING	143113	M	Ger.	10	Sgt., Waffen-SS, Totenkopf-Standarte, C.C., Buchenwald (Ger.)	TORTURE	U.S.
SPATE	67680	M	Ger.		Capt., C.C., Blechhammer (Ger.) 7.44-1.45	TORTURE	U.K.
SPATER, Georg	192098	M			Hptschfhr., 1.SS-Panz.Rgt., Ardennes (Bel.)	MURDER	U.S.
SPATH, Michael	258579	M	Ger.	5. 7.96	Sgt., Army, Murnau Oflag VII A (Ger.)	BRUTALITY	POL.
SPATHE	251278	M			Crim.Secretary, Sipo., Brussels (Bel.)	INTERR.	BEL.
SPATTER, Heinz	164728	M			Lt., 21.Pz.Div., Rehherry	MURDER	FR.
SPATZ (see PLATZ)	136206						
SPATZ	251415	M			Oschfhr., SS, Mauthausen (Aust.)	BRUTALITY	BEL.
SPATZ, Hans	125997	M	Ger.		Dr., Doctor.	MISC.CRIMES	U.S.
SPATZEK, Eduard Josef	256516	M	Ger.	5. 2.96	Factory-Manager, Civilian, Tabor (Czech.) 39-45	MURDER	CZECH.
SPATZENECKER	255693	M			SS-Cmdt., C.C., Mauthausen (Aust.)	MURDER	FR.
SPATZENEGG	141391	M	Ger.	98	Osturmfhr., SS-Chief, C.C., Mauthausen (Aust.)	TORTURE	FR.
SPATZENKOPF	142240	M			Hptschfhr., SS-Totenkopf, Dest (Ger.) 39	MURDER	U.S.
SPATZENEGGER	306853	M	Ger.		Cpl., SS, Camp-Guard at C.C., Mauthausen (Aust.) 40-44	MURDER	POL.
SPATZNAGER (see SPATZNEGGE)	180878						
SPATZNEGGE (or SPATZNAGER)	180878	M	Ger.	00	Oschfhr., SS, C.C., Mauthausen (Aust.)	MURDER	FR.
SPECHA, Kurt	254243	M		14. 8.07	Sgt., Camp Harzungen, Nordhausen (Ger.)	MURDER	U.S.
SPECHT	261061	M	Ger.		Hptsturmfhr., Gestapo, Strasbourg and Environs (Fr.) 43-1.44	MURDER	FR.

SPE-SPI

NAME	C.R.FILE NUMBER	SEX	NATIO-NALITY	DATE OF BIRTH	RANK	OCCUPATION	UNIT	PLACE AND DATE OF CRIME	REASON WANTED	WANTED BY
SPECHT, Henri	121426	M	Ger.		Sgt., Army, Clermont-Ferrand (Fr.) 13.-14.11.43				MURDER	FR.
SPECHTEINHAUSER	142063	M			Asst.Dr., Stalag XVI, Kaisersteinbruch (Aust.)				TORTURE	U.S.
SPECK	132469	M	Ger.	17	Uschfhr., SS, Camp Staff, C.C.Neuengamme near Hamburg (Ger.)				MURDER	U.K.
SPECK	132552	M	Ger.	10	Cpl., SS, Neuengamme (Ger.)				MURDER	YUGO.
SPECK	190288	M	Ger.		Official, Member of Staff, C.C.Neuengamme (Ger.) 43				MURDER	YUGO.
SPECK	256364	M	Ger.	15	Scharfhr., SS, C.C.Dora (Ger.)				INTERR.	FR.
SPECK	305298	M	Ger.		Scharfhr., SS, Serving in Dora Camp, 2 factory employing men from C.C.Buchenwald (Ger.) 43-4.45				MURDER	FR.
SPECK, Erich	198019	M	Ger.		Crim.Asst., Gestapo, Bruenn (Czech.) 39-45				MURDER	CZECH.
SPECKMANN, Gustav	143115	M	Ger.		Civ., C.C.Bielefeld (Ger.) 9.44				TORTURE	U.S.
SPECKMEIER, Werner	147026	M	Ger.		Osturmfhr., SS, Pz.Div."Das Reich", Tonneins (Fr.) 44				MURDER	FR.
SPECKSACK	131785	M	Ger.		Osturmfhr., SS, Saulgau (Ger.)				MURDER	U.S.
SPEER	136646	M	Ger.	18	Civ., Hospital orderly, C.C.Nuernberg (Ger.) 41-45				TORTURE	U.S.
SPEER	254244	M	Ger.		Pvt., C.C.Dora, Nordhausen (Ger.)				MURDER	U.S.
SPEER, Albert	130021	M		05	N.C.O., Feldgendarmerie, Arlon (Bel.) 25.8.44				MURDER	BEL.
SPEER, Max	259383	M			Scharfhr., Gestapo of Poitiers Area (Fr.) 40-45				MISC.CRIMES	FR.
SPEIDEL	888	M			Cmdt., Commander in Chief, Army (Grc.) 1.-4.44				MURDER	GRC.
SPEIGHT	189862	M	Ger.		Lt., official, C.C.Kanca (Grc.) 41				MURDER	U.K.
SPEISER (or SPEISSER)	889	M	Ger.		Capt., Army, F.P. No.12095 A, Bonneville (Fr.) 17.8.44				MURDER	FR.
SPEISER	262283	M	Ger.		Major, SS (Sturmbannfhr.), Unit: L 50656 A, Steene (Fr.) 5.-7.44				MISC.CRIMES	FR.
SPEISSER (see SPEISER)	889									
SPEISSER	156916	M	Ger.		8 Coy."Brandenburg", Pont St.Esprit (Fr.) 44				MURDER	FR.
SPEITZ, Hugo	198018	M	Ger.		Crim.-Employee, Gestapo, Bruenn(Czech.) 39-45				MURDER	CZECH.
SPEK	72036	M			Pol.Asst., NSDAP, Asst.Commander, Pol., Roermond (Neth.) 9.-11.44				MISC.CRIMES	NETH.,U.S.
SPEKTHOLZ	193071	M	Ger.		Sgt., 2 Leichte Flak-Abt.823, Malm (Nor.) 9.44				MURDER	NOR.
SPELGIER	193042	M	Ger.		Capt., Army, Leibnitz (Aust.) 14.11.44				TORTURE	U.K.
SPELTEAN	305510	M	Ger.		Interpreter, Vendome Loir et Cher (Fr.) 9.8.44				MURDER	FR.
SPELTERN	253184	M	Ger.		Sgt., Feldgendarmerie of Vendome (Fr.) 9.8.44				INTERR.	FR.
SPENGEL	180870	M	Ger.		Lt.Col., Feldkommanda..., Feldkommandantur de Tours, Maille (Fr.)25.8.44				MURDER	FR.
SPENGER	141604	M	Ger.		Police, Mayence, Kastel (Ger.)				TORTURE	FR.
SPENNMATH	121427	M	Ger.		Member, Gestapo, Vichy (Fr.)				TORTURE	FR.
SPENNRATH	10356	M	Ger.		Usturmfhr., SS, Gestapo, Prague (Czech.)				TORTURE	CZECH.
SPERK, Hans	251315	M	Ger.	6. 6.98	Wirtschaftsberater, Confidential, NSDAP, Gestapo, Holder of the "Blutorden", Pilsen (Czech.)				PILLAGE	CZECH.
SPERL	254246	M			Flyer, C.C.Ellrich, Nordhausen(Ger.)				MURDER	U.S.
SPERL	259775	M		88	Lt.Col., Army, Commander of Stalag IV B, Muhlberg (Ger.) 28.8.41				MURDER	U.K.
SPERLING	142263	M	Ger.		Haupttruppfhr., Org.Todt, C.C.Ampfing (Ger.)				MURDER	U.S.
SPERLING	300877	M	Ger.		Schirrmeister, 1 Aufkl.-Abt., 3 Coy., 2 Column, XV Div. of the Afrika Korps, St.Léger (Arlon) 5.9.44.				MISC.CRIMES	BEL.
SPERLING, Erich	188584	M	Ger.	14. 8.84	Member, Oberstaatsanwalt, NSDAP, Reichsjustiz-Ministerium, Prague (Czech.) 41-45				MURDER	CZECH.
SPERLING, Otto	140805	M	Ger.		Laborer, Civ., C.C.Muehldorf (Ger.) 44-45				TORTURE	U.S.
SPERRENDIANO	254245	M			Rottfhr., C.C.Osterhagen, Nordhausen (Ger.)				MURDER	U.S.
SPERZEL, Johann	143116	M	Ger.		Civ., near Ruppertshausen (Ger.) 12.9.44				WITNESS	U.S.
SPETH, Edwin	128797	M	Ger.		Civ., C.C.Stetten-Thuer.(Ger.) 8.42				MURDER	SOV.UN.
SPEYER	167229	F	Ger.		Civ., Einsatzstab "Rosenberg" (Fr.) 40-45				PILLAGE	FR.
SPEYER, Moritz	253343	M		6. 3.10	Pvt., C.C.Ellrich, Nordhausen (Ger.)				MURDER	U.S.
SPICKNIEPREUTHER, Karl	194050	M	Ger.		C.C., Weiden (Ger.) 43				TORTURE	POL.
SPIDZER	186200	M	Ger.		Sgt., Army, Honfleur (Fr.) 24.8.44				WITNESS	FR.
SPIEDEL	194254	M	Ger.		General, Army, Mil.Commander Greece, Averoff Prison, C.C.Athens (Grc.) 43-44				MISC.CRIMES	U.K.
SPIEGEL, Paul	192871	M	Ger.		Schupo, C.C.Falstad (Nor.) 10.42				MURDER	NOR.
SPIEGEL, Walter	253344	M		94	Sgt., S.C.C.Ellrich, Nordhausen (Ger.)				MURDER	U.S.
SPIEGELBERGER, Hans	162626	M	Ger.	03	Foreman, Fa.Behrens & Sohns, Engineering & Building, Bruex (Czech.)44-45				TORTURE	U.K.
SPIEGET (see SIEGERT)	67677									
SPIEGLER, Georg	193072	M	Ger.	07	Kriegsgef.Arb.Bn.186 (Nor.) 40-45				MISC.CRIMES	NOR.
SPIEKER	126606	M	Ger.	97	Lt.Col., Schupo, C.C.Saarbruecken (Ger.) 1.-2.45				TORTURE	U.S.
SPIEKER	156900	M			Sgt., W-SS, C.C.Gleiwitz (Ger.)				TORTURE	U.S.
SPIEL (or SPIELZ)	305970	M	Ger.		Member of the Sicherheitsdienst, Section 1 (Post and Archives Annecy), Annecy, Hte.Savoie (Fr.) 43-8.44				MURDER	FR.
SPIELBERG, Elmuth	305969	M	Ger.		Commanding Feld-Ersatz-Bn.1059, Esquiule, Basses,Pyrenees (Fr.)10.7.44				PILLAGE	FR.
SPIELHAGEN, Hans	251497	M	Ger.	22. 3.04	Manager, Civ., Cooperative, Mechrisch-Ostrau (Czech.) 39-45				MURDER	CZECH.
SPIELLMANN	136207	M			Ortsgruppenleiter, NSDAP, Oberseebach (Fr.) 7.44				MURDER	FR.
SPIELMANN	12381	M			Adjudant, SS, 2 Coy. of SS-Div."Der Fuehrer", Oradour (Fr.) 10.6.44				MURDER	FR.
SPIELVOGEL, Alois	301475	M	Ger.	27. 9.12	Oschfhr., SS, C.C.Buchenwald (Ger.) 16.5.38-9.10.43				MURDER	BEL.
SPIELZ (see SPIEL)	305970	M								
SPIER	258187		Ger.		Employee, Reichskommissariat "Den Haag", Amsterdam (Neth.) 7.2.45				SUSPECT	NETH.
SPIES	253479	M	Ger.	15	Oschfhr., SS, C.C.Buchenwald (Ger.)				INTERR.	FR.
SPIESS	39661	M	Ger.		Hschfhr., SS, Oberfw., C.C.Emden (Ger.) 45				MISC.CRIMES	YUGO.,U.S.
SPIESS (see WOLSTERMANN, Bernard)	150838									
SPIESS, Franz	252671	M		10. 7.99	Sgt., C.C.Ellrich, Nordhausen (Ger.)				MURDER	U.S.
SPIESS, Hans	193073	M	Ger.	13.12.03	Oberwachtmeister, Sgt., Reichsjustiz-Minist., W-SS, Feldstraflag., Finmark (Nor.) 42-45				MISC.CRIMES	NOR.,YUGO.
SPIESS, Hermann	164729	M	Ger.		Adjutant, 197 Inf.Div., Vercheny la Plaine (Fr.) 21.7.44				MURDER	FR.
SPIESS, Karl (or SPISS)	256521	M			Meister, O.T., C.C.Muehldorf (Ger.)				MURDER	U.S.
SPIESS, Walter	252672	M		25.12.20	Pvt., C.C.Ellrich, Nordhausen (Ger.)				MURDER	U.S.
SPIESSEL (see SPIESSL, Josef)	193074									
SPIESSL, Josef (or SPIESSEL)	193074	M	Ger.	04	Hauptwachtmeister, Sgt., Guard, Reichsjustiz-Ministerium, Feldstraf-Lager, W-SS, C.C.Finmark (Nor.) 42-45				MISC.CRIMES	NOR.,YUGO.
SPIESZ, Philipp	255351	M		2.11.97	Pvt., SS, Gren.Div.31, II Art.Regt., Nordhausen (Ger.)				MURDER	U.S.
SPIKER	250461	M			Cmdt., Unit: SS,12095 A, Wormhoudt (Fr.) 14.5.44				WITNESS	FR.
SPILLNER, Alfred	253346	M			Block-Chief, C.C.Buchenwald (Ger.) 42-45				MISC.CRIMES	U.S.
SPILLNER, Karl	301476	M	Ger.	3.11.90	Sturmschfhr., W.O., SS, C.C.Buchenwald (Ger.) 16.5.38-9.10.43				MURDER	BEL.
SPINDLER	138291	M	Ger.		Capt., Stalag XIII C, C.C.Bochum, Werne (Ger.) 25.3.45				TORTURE	FR.

SPI-STA

NAME	C.R.FILE NUMBER	SEX	NATIO-NALITY	DATE OF BIRTH	RANK OCCUPATION UNIT PLACE AND DATE OF CRIME	REASON WANTED	WANTED BY
SPINDLER	251291	M	Ger.	05	Lt., Navy, Brest (Fr.) 7.and 8.44	TORTURE	FR.
SPINDLER, Karl	252668	M			Pvt., C.C. Ellrich, Nordhausen (Ger.)	MURDER	U.S.
SPINGER	142269	M			SS Scharfhr. C.C.Weimar, Buchenwald (Ger.)	TORTURE	U.S.
SPINNRAD, Jean	152125	M	Ger.		Chief, C.C. Sandelack (Ger.)	MURDER	FR.
SPIRE	251292	M	Ger.		Chief of Atelier, Ravensbrueck (Ger.)	BRUTALITY	FR.
SPISS	141998	M	Ger.		O.T.Meister, airplant factory construction, C.C.Ampfing,Muehldorf, Mettenheim (Ger.) 44-45	TORTURE	U.S.
SPISS see SPIES	256521						
SPITT, Wilhelm	251294	M	Ger.	19.10.98	Civ. SS, NSDAP, Prag (Czech.)	INTERN.	CZECH.
SPITALER	257905	M			Cpl., Panzer-Bde., Meuse-Bridge Antwerp (Bel.) 12.44	MISC.CRIMES	U.S.
SPITTKA, Egon	891	M			Cpl., Airforce (Luftnachrichten), Poissons (Fr.) 17.8.44	TORTURE	FR.
SPITZ, Aleys	892	M	Ger.	6.12.11	SS Hptscharfhr., Maidanek (Pol.) 40-4.44	MURDER	POL.
SPITZBART, Gerd	139205	M			Civ., Stendal (Ger.) 35-45	TORTURE	U.S.
SPITZBAUER, Fritz	193707	M	Ger.		Pvt., 7.Heeres-Kuesten-A.t Rgt. 792, C.C.Lattervik (Nor.)	WITNESS	NOR.
SPITZER	300144	M	Ger.		Panz.Jaeger Abt.240, Chateau de Vallieres-Oise (Fr.) 10.40	PILLAGE	FR.
SPITZNAGEL	194377	M	Ger.	99	Officer, Geheime Feldpolizei, Brussels (Bel.)	MISC.CRIMES	BEL.
SPENGLER, Alfred	142226	M	Ger.	85	Hptsturmfhr., SS, C.C.Muehldorf, Ampfing (Ger.) 44-45	TORTURE	U.S.
SPLETSTOESSER, Willy	167310	M	Ger.		Sgt., Medical-corps, Bn.staff III, Inf.Rgt.517, Virolles les Chimay, Hainaut (Bel.) 6.40	PILLAGE	BEL.
SPLETZER, Georg	253791	M	Ger.		SS Oscharfhr., Radolfzell Distr.Konstanz (Ger.) 20.7.44	MURDER	U.S.
SPLITT	136369	M			Kreisstellenamtsleiter NSDAP, Karlsruhe (Ger.) 21.3.45	MURDER	U.S.
SPOERL	300878	M	Ger.		Pvt., 1.Aufkl.Abt. 3.Coy. 2.Col. XV.Div.Afrika-Corps, St.Leger (Arlon) 5.9.44	MISC.CRIMES	BEL.
SPOETH, Johann	252681	M		3. 3.03	Flyer, C.C. Ellrich, Nordhausen (Ger.)	MURDER	U.S.
SPOHL	189127	M			Pvt., SS Pol.Rgt. Todt 19, 4.Coy., Les Puisots (Fr.) 15.6.44	MURDER	FR.
SPONZEL	253354	M	Ger.	about 00	Kreisleiter, Kuchen (Ger.) 30.11.44	MURDER	U.S.
SPORENBERD	136358	M	Ger.		Sgt., SS, Wittlich, Hinzert (Ger.) 41-43	TORTURE	U.S.
SPORENBERG see SCHPORENBERG	72043						
SPORENBERG	136820	M	Ger.	about 97	SS Hptsturmfhr., SS, C.C. Sonderlager Hinzert (Ger.) 4.45	MURDER	U.S.
SPORENBERG	156019	M	Ger.		Chief of SS and police, SD, Hoeherer SS police-leader, Lublin (Pol.)44	MURDER	U.S.
SPORER	190218				Official, C.C. Dachau (Ger.) 40	MURDER	BEL.
SPORER alias SPARER	253950	M	Ger.		SS, C.C. Buchenwald (Ger.) 42-45	MURDER	U.S.
SPORER	301477	M	Ger.		Official, C.C. Dachau (Ger.) 43	MURDER	BEL.
SPORINBERG	253321	M	Ger.		SS Cmdt., C.C. Hinzert (Ger.) 42-45	MURDER	U.S.
SPORK	259691	M	Ger.		Capt., Guard, Camp of Candau des Angles, Avignon-Vaucluse (Fr.) 8.44	SUSPECT	FR.
SPORNBERGER	28851	M			Major, Army, Finmark (Nor.)	MURDER	NOR.
SPORRENBERG	251750	M	Ger.		SS Hptsturmfhr., C.C. Buchenwald (Ger.) 42-45	MISC.CRIMES	U.S.
SPORTK, Daedoa	143120	F	Ger.		Civ., Schapdetten (Ger.) 10.*11.44	TORTURE	U.S.
SPORTK, Josef	143121	M	Ger.		Civ., Schapdetten (Ger.) 10.-11.44	TORTURE	U.S.
SPRAABOOM, Simon	167290	M			Adjutant, Army, C.C. Tour la ville (Fr.) 2.44	TORTURE	FR.
SPRINGER, Friedrich Otto	251283	M	Ger.	27. 3.11	Chief assist., Gestapo, Crim.police, Sect.I, Tesin (Czech.) 42-45	MURDER	CZECH.
SPRAWE, Wilhelm	39973	M	Ger.		Cmdt., C.C. Eschweiler, Buchweiden (Ger.)	TORTURE	SOV.UN.
SPRECKENSEN	251266	M			SS Oscharfhr., SS, SD, Toulouse (Fr.) 11.42, 8.44	MURDER	FR.
SPREMBERG, Hans	253480	M	Ger.		SS Sgt., 4.Coy., SS-No. 089923, Urbes (Fr.) 4. and 5.10.44	MISC.CRIMES	FR.
SPRENGEL, Karl	180790	M	Ger.	10.12.97	Cpl., Prison C.C. Vannes (Fr.) 42-44	TORTURE	FR.
SPRENGER	139708	M			Capt., Kdo.Supervisor, Stalag II B, C.C. Hammerstein (Ger.) 8.43-2.45	TORTURE	U.S.
SPRENGER	188580	M			Chief of secret police at Meiros, Vasiliki (Grc.) 12.42	TORTURE	GRC.
SPRENGER, Jakob	62395	M			Gauleiter und Reichsstatthalter NSDAP Hessen-Nassau (Ger.)	MISC.CRIMES	U.N.W.C.C.
SPRENGER, Josef	260543	M	Ger.	1. 3.06	SS Rottfhr., Waffen SS, SS Guard, C.C. Auschwitz (Pol.) 44-45	BRUTALITY	POL.
SPRENGLER, Alfred	256510	M			Hpttruppfhr.	MURDER	U.S.
SPRENNUNGHAR	250462	M	Ger.		Capt., 4.Coy., 563.A.N.R., Boissaise la Bertrand (Fr.) 9.40	PILLAGE	FR.
SPREITER	190217	M	Ger.		Member Gestapo C.C. Dachau (Ger.) 40-45	MURDER	BEL.
SPRIECK	164005	M	Ger.		Civ. Manager, Hermann Goering works "Westmark", 39-45	WITNESS	U.S.
SPRINER	137516	M			Bloc-chief, C.C. Weimar, Buchenwald (Ger.)	MURDER	U.S.
SPRINGER	100383	M			Oberpraesident, C.C. Nassau (Ger.)	MURDER	U.S.
SPRINGER	137517	M			Scharfhr., SS, C.C. Buchenwald, Weimar (Ger.)	TORTURE	U.S.
SPRINGER, or SPRUGER	156018	M	Ger.		Capt., Army, C.C. Hammerstein (Ger.) 44-45	TORTURE	U.S.
SPRINGER	261069	M	Ger.		SS-Mann, 10.Panz.Gren.Rgt. Frundsberg, Boyelles (Fr.) 1.9.44	MURDER	FR.
SPRINGER	306289	M	Ger.		Member Gestapo at Trencin, C.C. Oswiecim, Birkenau (Pol.) 39-45	MURDER	CZECH.
SPRINGER, Adolf	250451	M	Ger.	27. 7.05	Civ., Lidice (Czech.) 6.42	MISC.CRIMES	CZECH.
SPRINGER, Alfred	301478	M	Ger.	24. 3.90	SS Oscharfhr., C.C. Buchenwald (Ger.) 16.5.38-9.10.43	MURDER	BEL.
SPRINGER, Erwin	142262	M	Ger.	10	SS Oscharfhr., Waffen SS Totenkopf-Standarte, C.C. Buchenwald, Weimar (Ger.)	BRUTALITY	U.S.
SPRINGER, Friedrich	253904	M			Flyer, C.C. Ellrich, Nordhausen (Ger.)	MURDER	U.S.
SPRINGER, Martin	161475	M	Ger.	90	Hptscharfhr., Waffen SS, C.C. Buchenwald (Ger.) 42-45	TORTURE	U.S.
SPRINGORIUM	893	M	Ger.		Regierungspraesident, public official,Oberschlesien (Pol.) 9.39-42	MURDER	POL.
SPRINTZ	143122	M	Ger.		Sturmbannfhr., SS, Gestapo, Oedenburg (Ger.)	MURDER	U.S.
SPRITZBACH	145832	M		95	Dr. SS Sturmbannfhr., C.C. Mauthausen (Aust.) 41-45	MURDER	U.S.
SPRONK, Johann	253905	M		27. 8.15	Cpl., C.C. Ellrich, Nordhausen (Ger.)	MURDER	U.S.
SPROTTER von KRAUTENSTEIN	190216	M	Ger.		Member, Gestapo C.C. Dachau (Ger.) 40-45	MURDER	BEL.
SPRUGER see SPRINGER	156018	M					
SPYRKA	261793	M	Ger.		Pvt., Ordonnanz at Major Stolz, Fontaine le Pin (Fr.) 12.7.44	MURDER	FR.
SQUEAKY	156017	M			Sgt., C.C. Hammerstein Stalag II B (Ger.) 44-45	TORTURE	U.S.
SRAESAKER	260050	M			Major, 157.Bayr.Res.Div., Massif du Vercors (Fr.) 7.44-8.44	SUSPECT	FR.
SRECHER	901999	F			Guard, SS, C.C. Auschwitz (Pol.) 42-45	BRUTALITY	POL.
SRELHOFER, Johann	256593	M			Scharfhr., SS, Camp Guard, C.C. Nordhausen (Ger.)	MURDER	U.S.
SRIMBERSKI	253906	M			Pvt., C.C. Ellrich, Nordhausen (Ger.)	MURDER	U.S.
SROKO see SORKO, Rudolf	198011						
SRUBA, Rudolf	259899	M	Ger.	6. 5.88	SS Rottfhr., 1.Zug, 2.Gruppe, prob. stat. at Bergeyk Prov.Noord Brabant (Neth.) 11.9.44	MURDER	NETH.
SRUETZ, Emil	62425	M		15.11.92	NSKK Gruppenfhr., Oberpraesident, Gauleiter of Mark Brandenburg (Ger.)	TORTURE	U.N.W.C.C.
STAAB, Andreas	254238	M	Ger.	19. 1.12	Pvt., C.C. Harzungen, Nordhausen (Ger.)	MURDER	U.S.
STAABEN, Wilhelm	192834	M	Ger.		Pvt.,7.Btty.Heer.-Kuest.-Art.Rgt.792, Lattervik (Nor.) 7.4.45	WITNESS	NOR.
STAAFER	194068	M	Ger.		Assistant, Customs and Excise, Veigy, Fonceney (Fr.) 6.10.43	TORTURE	FR.

STA - STA

NAME	C.R.FILE NUMBER	SEX	NATIO-NALITY	DATE OF BIRTH	RANK OCCUPATION UNIT PLACE AND DATE OF CRIME	REASON WANTED	WANTED BY
STABE (or STALE)	307207	M	Ger.		Superior officer,Mean (Bel.) 4.9.44	MISC.CRIMES	BEL.
STABE,B (see STRABE)	254233						
STABENON	254730	M	Ger.		Lt.Col.,Colonne Russia-Ger.,L'Ain (Fr.) 21.7.44	PILLAGE	FR.
STABER,Michal	252754	M	Ger.	95	Employee,Gestapo,Kolin (Czech.) 39-45	MISC.CRIMES	CZECH.
STABERNACH	132561	M	Ger.	97	Miscell.,Giessen,Burg-Gemuenden (Ger.)	MURDER	FR.
STABLE	130178	M			Pvt.,Army,Ldsch.Bn.559,2 Coy,Stalag 8 B Stalag 344,Lamsdorf,Mankendorf (Ger.) 11.11.43-18.11.43	TORTURE	U.K.
STABLE,Heinz	895	M	Ger.		SS-Rottfhr.,Waidanek (Pol.) 40-4.44	MURDER	BEL.,POL.
STABLER	147025	M	Ger.		Sturmbannfhr.,SS Pz.Div."Das Reich",Montauban (Fr.) 44	MURDER	FR.
STABREY	896	M	Ger.		Sgt.,Warder Army Prison Camp, Caen (Fr.) 44	MURDER	FR.
STACH,Karl	259473	M	Ger.		Wolfsburg (Ger.) 29.6.44	WITNESS	U.S.
STACHEL,Alfons	252755	M	Ger.	15	SS-Usturmfhr.,Employee,Gestapo,Kolin (Czech.) 39-45	MISC.CRIMES	CZECH.
STACHT (see STHACT)	260085						
STADEL,Karl	252766	M	Ger.	10	N.C.O.,Gestapo,Briey (Fr.)	TORTURE	FR.
STADL	29636	M	Ger.		Lt.,Army,Abwehr,St.Die (Fr.) 11.44	MURDER	FR.
STADLER	897		Ger.		SS-Standartenfhr.,SS Pz.Gren.Rgt.4,"Der Fuehrer",Div."Das Reich", Limoges (Fr.) 5.-6.44	MURDER	FR.
STADLER	100388	M			SS 9 Pz.Div.,C.C.Arnheim (Neth.)	MURDER	U.S.
STADLER	188781	M	Ger.		Sgt.,Adj.-chief,Feldgendarmerie,St.Sauveur (Fr.) 11.6.44	MURDER	FR.
STADLER	194251	M	Ger.		Guard,C.C.de juifs,Camiers (Fr.) 41-44	TORTURE	FR.
STADLER	301673	M	Ger.		Officer,Unit XI G.P.,SS "Der Fuehrer",3 Rgt.,Mesnil-St.-Blaise (Bel.) 5.-6.9.44	MURDER	BEL.
STADLER	305745	M	Ger.		Rottfhr.,C.C.Auschwitz-Birkenau (Pol.) 40	MURDER	FR.
STADLER	306448	M	Ger.		Foreman,Fa.Brandl,Eprach near Amberg (Ger.) 45	MURDER	CZECH.
STADLER,Ilse	190224	F	Ger.	21	Secr.,Gestapo,Mlada Boleslav (Czech.) 44-45	WITNESS	CZECH.
STADLER,Sylvester	67241	M	Ger.	30.12.10	Oberfhr.,Waffen SS,9 SS Pz.Div.Hohenstaufen,Arnheim (Neth.)	MURDER	U.S.
STADLINGER,Karl	12301	M	Ger.		Pvt.,110 or 111 Pz.Gren.Rgt.,2 Coy,N.C.O.,Albine (Fr.) 29.6.44	MURDER	FR.
STADTEGGER	192872	M	Ger.		Sgt.,SS,C.C.Falstad,Harstad (Nor.) 11.43	MURDER	NOR.
STADTHULLER	12302	M	Ger.		Pvt.,110 or 111 Pz.Gren.Rgt.,Albine (Fr.) 29.6.44	MURDER	FR.
STADTMULLER	192873	M	Ger.		Schupo,C.C.Falstad (Nor.) 9.-10.42	MURDER	NOR.
STAEBE,Willie	253486	M			Rottfhr.,1 Pion.Bn.,3 Pz.Pion.Rgt.,1 SS Pz.Div.Leibst.Adolf Hitler, Lineuville (Bel.) 17.-19.12.44	INTERR.	U.S.
STAEDKE,Helmut	260660	M		06	Bde.General,Army	WITNESS	U.S.
STAEFNER	12303	M	Ger.		N.C.O.,110 or 111 Pz.Gren.Rgt.,2 Coy,Albine (Fr.) 29.6.44	MURDER	FR.
STAEGLICH	143124	M	Ger.		C.O.,Schupo,C.C.Muehlheim-Ruhr (Ger.)	TORTURE	U.S.
STAEMPFEL	257712	M	Ger.		Paymaster,Army,Oflag 65,Strasburg,Barkenbruegge (Ger.) 44, 45	MISC.CRIMES	YUGO.
STAERFL,Franz	254735	M			Hptschfhr.,C.C.Bodungen,Nordhausen (Ger.)	MURDER	U.S.
STAFFA,Josef	194046	M	Ger.	23.11.96	Lt.,Police,Vhersky Brod (Czech.) 39-45	MURDER	CZECH.
STAFFELD	141376	M			Pvt.,Zollgrenzschutz,Paris (Fr.)	MISC.CRIMES	FR.
STAFFELDT	301481	M	Ger.	12.2.20	Uschfhr.,SS-Cpl.,SS,C.C.Buchenwald (Ger.) 16.5.38-9.10.43	MURDER	BEL.
STAFFELT	68911	M	Ger.		Major,Devisenschutzkdo.	MISC.CRIMES	U.S.
STAFNER,Johann	12304	M	Ger.		Pvt.,110 or 111 Pz.Gren.Rgt.N.C.O.,2 Coy,Albine (Fr.) 29.6.44	MURDER	FR.
STAH, (see STHAL,Henri, aliases Pudi)	138256						
STAHL	190289	M	Ger.		Officer,SD,Kraljevo (Yugo.) 43	MURDER	YUGO.
STAHL,Adolphe	67690	M			Adj.chief,Feldgendarmerie,Maubeuge (Fr.) 19.8.44	MURDER	FR.
STAHL,Hugo	72011	M	Ger.		SS-Uschfhr.,SS,Struthof (Fr.)	MISC.CRIMES	FR.
STAHL,Wilhelm	254718	M		27.2.13	Pvt.,C.C.Ellrich,Nordhausen (Ger.)	MURDER	U.S.
STAHLE (see STEELE)	254688						
STAHLAECKER	167320	M	Ger.		Dr.,Befehlshaber,SD, (Nor.) 4.40	TORTURE	NOR.
STAHLE	125608	M	Ger.	19	Lt.,Luftnachrichtenschule 4 Coy,Lyon (Fr.) 24.8.44	MURDER	FR.
STAHLE (see STIEHL)	143136						
STAHLECKER	173487	M	Ger.		Chief,SS-Osturmbannfhr.,Gestapo,Staatspolizeistelle,Brno,Oswiecim-Birkenau (Czech.,Pol.) 39-45	MURDER	CZECH.
STAHLENBERG	164733	M	Ger.		Lt.,Kreiskommandantur De Luneville,Vitrimont (Fr.)	PILLAGE	FR.
STAHLER,Alois	898	M	Ger.		Warder,SS Sturmbann,C.C.Oswiecim-Birkenau (Pol.) 39-45,40-44	MURDER	FR.,CZECH., BEL.
STAHLSCHMIED,Karl	139208	M	Ger.		Civilian,Plettenberg (Ger.) 6.44	TORTURE	U.S.
STAHN	158705	M	Ger.		Usturmfhr.,Gestapo,H.Q.,Berlin (Ger.) 39-45	MURDER	CZECH.
STAHNKE	193706	M	Ger.	05	Sgt.,Strafgef.Lager,Reichsjustizministerium,Finmark (Nor.)	MISC.CRIMES	NOR.
STAHR	301841	M			SD,Vichy (Fr.) 10.43-9.44	MURDER	FR.
STAIB	180879	M			Lt.,2 Jg.Bn.,7 Coy,Region Dela Maurienne (Fr.)	MURDER	FR.
STAINGRAND (or STEINGRAD)	254421	M	Ger.		W.O.,10 Coy,3 Bn.,SS Pol.Rgt.Todt,Mont Saxonnes (Fr.) 3.1.44	INTERR.	FR.
STAIR	899	M	Ger.		Lt.,Army,98 Sturmrgt.Pz.Dok.2 Coy (Fr.) 22.-31.8.44	MURDER	FR.
STALDIMEYER,Xavier	141330	M	Ger.	11	SS-Rottfhr.,SD,Sipo,SS,San Vittore-Milan (It.) 30.4.44-1.7.44	TORTURE	U.K.
STALE (see STABE)	307207						
STALING	256319	M	Ger.		Mayor,Pobing,Muhldorf (Ger.)	WITNESS	U.S.
STALL	156593	M			Sgt.,Waffen SS,Magdeburg (Ger.) 10.44-4.45	TORTURE	U.S.
STALLHEINRICH,Joseph	31642	M	Ger.		Work Overseer,Public-official,C.C.Westhausen (Ger.)	TORTURE	U.S.
STALLMANN,Johann	254719	M	Ger.	5.6.17	Pvt.,C.C.Ellrich,Nordhausen (Ger.)	MURDER	U.S.
STALTE	300879	M	Ger.		Pvt.,1 Aufkl.Abt.,3 Coy 2 Col.XV Div.of the Afrika Corps,Saint Léger (Arlon) 5.9.44	MISC.CRIMES	BEL.
STAWARA,Joseph	143125	M	Ger.		Civilian,Poischendorf (Ger.) 29.5.44	WITNESS	U.S.
STAWARIUS,Walter	173476	M			C.C.Halha (Ger.) 44-45	MURDER	BEL.
STAMM	1332	M	Ger.		Capt.,20 SS Police Rgt.,	MISC.CRIMES	U.S.
STAMM	1750	M	Ger.		Officer,326 Inf.Div.,752 Gren.Rgt.,6 Coy,Caumont (Fr.) 44	MURDER	U.K.
STAMM	143126	M			Major,SS and Gestapo,Oedenburg (Hung.) 10.-11.44	MURDER	U.S.
STAMM,Franz Gert	162917	M			SS-Pvt.,Unit 12611,La Calamine (Bel.) 6.9.44	MURDER	BEL.
STAMMATER (see STAMMEYER)	259386						
STAMMAH	259384	F	Ger.		Typist,Gestapo of Poitiers Area (Fr.) 40-44	SUSPECT	FR.
STAMMAN,Fritz	262191	M	Ger.	12.1.19	Lt.,51 SS Armoured Bde.,Bucheres,Breviandes,Le Stavine,Riviere de Corps,Troyes (Fr.) 22.-25.8.44	BRUTALITY	FR.
STAMMEL	153254	M	Ger.		Capt.,German Army,Oflag XIII B,Hammelburg, 44-45	MURDER	U.S.

NAME	C.R.FILE NUMBER	SEX	NATIO-NALITY	DATE OF BIRTH	RANK OCCUPATION UNIT PLACE AND DATE OF CRIME	REASON WANTED	WANTED BY
STAMMEYER, Gustave (or STAMMAIER)	259986	M	Ger.		Rottenfhr., Member of Gestapo, Poitiers Area (Fr.) 40-45	MISC.CRIMES	FR.
STAMMICH, Werner	259985	M	Ger.		Oschfhr., Gestapo of Poitiers, Area Poitiers (Fr.) 40-45	MISC.CRIMES	FR.
STAMMINGER	173155	M	Ger.		C.C. Natzweiler (Fr.) 9.44	INTERR.	U.K.
STAMMUNGER	12305	M	Ger.		Pvt., Army, Albine (Fr.)	MURDER	FR.
STAMPFER	28852	M	Ger.		Lt.Col., Army, Finmark (Nor.)	MURDER	NOR.
STAND, Hermann	194048	M			Cpl., SS 4.Totenkopf-Sturmbann. C.C.Dora, Nordhausen (Ger.) 43-45	INTERR.	U.S.
STANDIGER, Hans (see STAUDINGER)	136357						
STANEK, Jan Juray	300733	M	Ger.		Major in the Slovakian Army, Slovakia 44.	BRUTALITY	CZECH.
STANEK, Paul	190215	M	Ger.	07	Criminal-secretary, Gestapo, Tomazow Mazowiki (Pol.) 6.42	MURDER	U.K.
STANGE, Alfred	192833	M	Ger.	04	Sgt., Guard, Strafgefangenen-Lager, Ministry of Justice, C.C. Finmark (Nor.) 6.42-45	TORTURE	NOR., CZECH
STANGE, Hans	900	M	Ger.		Sgt., Army-Feldgendarmerie (Pol.) 39	MURDER	POL.
STANGE, Rudi	152105	M	Ger.		Pvt., Port Protection Commando, Salces (Fr.) 44	MURDER	FR.
STANGEL, Fritz	138924	M	Ger.		Sgt. SS-Gestapo, Lyon (Fr.) 6.8.44	MURDER	FR.
STANGELMAIER, Oscar	258100	M	Ger.	24. 2.07	Informer, Gestapo, Prague (Czech.) 43-45	MURDER	CZECH.
STANGER	39618	M	Ger.		Lt.Col., Army-Feldkommandantur, St.Avertin (Fr.) 22.8.44	MISC.CRIMES	FR.
STANGL, Heinz	252750	M	Ger.		Administrator, Jewish Business, Amsterdam (Neth.) 15.9.42	PILLAGE	NETH.
STANGL, Jiří	188504	M	Ger.	89	Member, NSDAP, Prague (Czech.)	MISC.CRIMES	CZECH.
STANGL, Johann	12306	M	Ger.		Pvt., Army, 110. or 111.Panz.Gren.Regt., Albine (Fr.) 29.6.44	MURDER	FR.
STANIEBERT	164724	M	Ger.		Officer, Ortskommandant, Montenois (Fr.) 10.44	MISC.CRIMES	FR.
STANNARIUS, Walter	129958	M	Ger.	05	Camp Kahla (Ger.)	TORTURE	BEL.
STANNEBEIN, Karl	301481	M	Ger.	12.10.86	Sturmscharfhr., SS-W.O., SS, C.C. Buchenwald (Ger.) 16.5.38-9.10.43	MURDER	BEL.
STANNEKER	173475	M	Ger.		Arbeitskommando, C.C. Braunschweig (Ger.) 44	TORTURE	BEL.
STANNUL	259692	M	Ger.	about 91	SS-Uschfhr., Gestapo, Area of Angers, Maine and Loire (Fr.) 42-44	MISC.CRIMES	FR.
STANZEL, Johann	194051	M	Ger.		Guard, SS-Mann, 4.SS Totenkopf-Sturmbann, C.C.Dora, Nordhausen (Ger.) 43-45	INTERR.	U.S.
STANZL	251878	M	Ger.		Member, Gestapo, S.D., Toulouse (Fr.) 11.42-8.44	MISC.CRIMES	FR.
STAPATELATUS	301482	M	Ger.		SS-Sturmmann, SS, C.C.Buchenwald (Ger.) 16.5.38-9.10.43	MURDER	BEL.
STAPEL, Helmut	149577	M			Cpl. 11. Panzer Div., South-West-France 44	MURDER	FR.
STAPELFELDT, Hertha	305698	F	Ger.		Civ. Housewife, Luebeck-Siems (Ger.) about 6.8.44	MURDER	U.S.
STAPLER, Erika (or STAPLES)	139706	F	Ger.		Supervisor, SS-Guard, Polte Munitions Factory, Magdeburg, Labour Camp 101, Buchenwald (Ger.) 44-45	SUSPECT	U.S.
STAPPER, Josef	26049	M	Ger.	26. 6.95	SS-Rottenfhr., Waffen-SS, Guard-Coy., C.C.Auschwitz (Pol.) 6.44-1.45	BRUTALITY	POL.
STAPS, Albert	257340	M	Ger.	20.12.02	Lt., Gendarmerie, Kr.Lotha (Czech.) 2.43	MURDER	CZECH.
STAR	133948	M			SS-Rottenfhr. and Blockfhr., C.C.Buchenwald (Ger.)	TORTURE	FR.
STARCK	254731	M	Ger.		Chief, Equipment, Monsheim (Ger.)	INTERR.	FR.
STARCK, Erhardt	301094	M	Ger.		Member, Kdo.z.b.V.6, stationed at St.Die (Fr.) 9.44	MURDER	U.K.
STARCK, Philip	180791	M	Ger.		Guard, Prison C.C. Vannes (Fr.) 44	MURDER	FR.
STARCKE	167243	M	Ger.		Officer, Indian Inf. 950.Regt., Ruffec (Fr.) 8.44	MURDER	FR.
STARFEL	36631	M	Ger.		Capt., Army, C.C.Belsen-Bodungen (Ger.) 6.4.45	MURDER	POL., FR.
STARK	137521	M	Ger.		Major, Mil. 2.Panz.Gren., 148.Landesschuetzen Bn., 5.Coy., Kl.Gnixendorf (Aust.) 4.10.41-4.42	MURDER	U.S.
STARK	194053	M	Ger.		Guard, 4.SS Totenkopf-Sturmbann, C.C.Dora, Nordhausen (Ger.)	MURDER	U.S.
STARK	261098	M	Ger.		Major, Cmdt., SS Garrison, Carekvice near Vysoke Myto (Czech.) 5.5.45	SUSPECT	CZECH.
STARK, August	91695	M			Stabsintendant, Army, Prison Camp Stalag 6, Muenster (Ger.)	MISC.CRIMES	U.S.
STARK, Emil Willy Walter	137520	M	Ger.	21. 9.10	Art.Bde. 503, Hilden (Ger.) 16.4.45	WITNESS	U.S.
STARK, Gerhard	259655	M	Ger.	about 13	SS-Scharfhr., Gestapo, Area Angers, Maine and Loire (Fr.) 42-44	MISC.CRIMES	FR.
STARK, Leonard	156595	M	Ger.	85	Sgt., SS, C.C. Sasel (Ger.)	MISC.CRIMES	U.K.
STARK, Rudolf	261270	M	Ger.	19. 7.12	Pvt., Camp Ellrich, Nordhausen (Ger.)	MURDER	U.S.
STARK, Willy	145524	M	Ger.	3. 2.11	SS,.C.C. Auschwitz (Pol.)	MISC.CRIMES	FR.
STARKAERT (see STARKER)	254727						
STARKE, Heinz	254877	M			Pvt., C.C.Ellrich, Harzungen, Nordhausen (Ger.)	MURDER	U.S.
STARKE, Hermann	120622	M	Ger.		Civ., C.C. Wittenberg (Ger.) 10.43-1.44	BRUTALITY	U.K.
STARKER (or STARKAERT)	254727	M	Ger.		Usturmfhr., Gestapo, SS, Paris (Fr.) 41-44	INTERR.	FR.
STARK-STINY, Anton	251353	M	Ger.	11. 6.11	Employee, Gestapo, Vestin (Czech.) 39-45	MURDER	CZECH.
STAROSTKA, Stanislawa	301483	F	Ger.		SS-Woman, Employee, SS, C.C.Bergen-Belsen (Ger.) 40-45	MURDER	BEL.
STARZONEK, Alfred Franz	260479	M	Ger.	5. 8.06	SS-Mann, Waffen-SS, Guard Coy., C.C.Auschwitz (Pol.) 9.44-1.45	BRUTALITY	POL.
STASCHEN	254875	M			Sgt., C.C. Ellrich, Nordhausen (Ger.)	MURDER	U.S.
STASSIK	162625	M	Ger.		Crim.asst., Gestapo, C.C. Schirmeck (Fr.) 6.44	MURDER	U.K.
STATTLER	902	M			N.C.O., Air Force, Rodez (Fr.) 8.44	MURDER	FR.
STATTMANN, Franz-Karl	188501	M	Ger.	17. 5.11	Member, Gestapo, Crim.asst., Luxembourg (Lux.)	MISC.CRIMES	LUX.
STAUBE	173514	M	Ger.		Major, Ortskommandantur, Valjevo (Yugo.) 8.41-1.42	MURDER	YUGO.
STAUDACKER, Karl	306662	M			Cpl., 21. En. Sicherheits-Regt. No.194, Prads et la Javie, Mezel (Basses-Alpes) 18.7.44 and 30.7.44	MURDER	FR.
STAUDE, Paul	254876	M			Pvt., C.C. Ellrich, Nordhausen (Ger.)	MURDER	U.S.
STAUDET	162791	M	Ger.		SS-Mann, 10.SS Div. Frundsberg,360.Panz.Regt., Revin (Fr.) 12.-13.6.44	MURDER	FR.
STAUDINGER, Anton	194052	M	Ger.		SS-Mann, Guard, 4.SS Totenkopf-Sturmbann, C.C. Nordhausen, Dora-Mittelbau, Monowitz (Ger., Czech.) 43-45	INTERR.	U.S.
STAUDINGER, Georg	142257	M	Ger.	12. 2.85	Schoolmaster, Civ., Seyboldsdorf and Vilsbiburg (Ger.) 28.4.45	WITNESS	U.S.
STAUDINGER, Hans (or STANDIGER)	136357	M		02	Kreisamtsleiter, NSDAP, Freising, Attenkirchen (Ger.) 13.6.44	MURDER	GRC.
STAUFER, Nikolas	188556	M			Member, SS, Asproryrges Eleusis (Grc.) 44	MURDER	U.S.
STAUPENDA	254682	M			Capt., C.C.Dora, Nordhausen (Ger.)	MISC.CRIMES	BEL.
STAUPENTHAL	31641	M			Capt., Waffen-SS, C.C.Weimar (Ger.)	WITNESS	U.K.
STAVINOCCA, Emil	141940	M			1252. Heereskuesten-Art.Abt. 2.Btty., Champs Rabats (Fr.) 7.44	MISC.CRIMES	U.S.
STAWITZKY	139704	M	Ger.		Capt., SS-Gestapo, (Pol.) 42-44	MURDER	U.S.
STEBER, Josef	254683	M			Pvt., C.C.Ellrich, Nordhausen (Ger.)	MURDER	CZECH.
STEBRICH, Berthold	190225	M	Ger.	15	Crim.asst., S.D., SS, Gestapo, Mlada, Boleslav, Kolin and Prag (Czech.) 40-45	MISC.CRIMES	BEL.
STECHER	300880	M	Ger.		Sgt., 1.Aufkl.Abt., 3.Coy., 2.Col., XX. Div. of the Afrika Korps, Saint-Leger (Arlon) 5.9.44	MURDER	NOR.
STECKAN	193412	M	Ger.		Capt., Army, C.C.Sunndal Sora (Nor.) 6.42	TORTURE	U.K.
STECKER, Hans	188006	M	Ger.	15 - 19	SS-Uschfhr., SS, C.C. Unterluess (Ger.)	MURDER	FR.
STECKITCH	39619	M			Feldgendarmerie de Laval (Fr.)		

STE-STE

NAME	C.R.FILE NUMBER	SEX	NATIO-NALITY	DATE OF BIRTH	RANK OCCUPATION UNIT	PLACE AND DATE OF CRIME	REASON WANTED	WANTED BY
STICKMANN	9621	M	Ger.		Lt., Breendonck (Bel.) 42-44		TORTURE	BEL.
STEDTLER, Fritz	255226	M	Ger.	03	Member, Firing Squad, Oberwachtmstr.,Schutzpol.,Prag-Kobylisy(Czech.)		MURDER	CZECH.
STEEGER	31640	M			SS-Capt.,Army, 12 SS Pz.Div. "Hitlerjugend"		MURDER	CAN.
STEEK	186192	M	Ger.		Officer, SS-guard, C.C. Sachsenhausen (Ger.)		TORTURE	FR.
STEELE see STIEHL	143136							
STEELE or STEHLE, STAHLE,STIDE	254688	M	Ger.	87	Lt.Col., Airforce, Nuernberg (Ger.) 20.1.45		MURDER	U.S.
STEEN, Hans	191391	M	Ger.		Sgt.,5 Coy,Bn Loewer, 3 Coy,Bn Helhmund,Kampfgr.Oberst Ulewis, St.Etienne de Montlug (Fr.) 8.44		MURDER	FR.
STEENCKE, Paul	259995	M			Pvt., Toulon (Fr.) 19.7.44		MURDER	FR.
STEFAN	24828	M			Lt.,Prison, SS Officer, Portland 13.3.41		MURDER	U.K.
STEFAN	188590	M		00	Capt., Police, Athen (Grc.) 44		MISC.CRIMES	GRC.
STEFAN, Erich	192835	M	Ger.	15.7.97	Feldstraflager Reichsjustizminin.,C.C. Finmark (Nor.)		WITNESS	NOR.
STEFAN, Josef	254708	M			Pvt., C.C. Ellrich-Nordhausen (Ger.)		MURDER	U.S.
STEFANI, Jonann	254671	M			Rottenfhr., C.C. Rossla, Bodungen, Nordhausen (Ger.)		MURDER	U.S.
STEFEL, Franc	256495	M	Ger.		Oscharfhr.,SS, 5 Coy, Klein Bodungen,C.C.Nordhausen (Ger.)		MURDER	U.S.
STEFELS, Albert	903	M			Pvt.,Army, Inf., Merville (Fr.) 9.6.44		MURDER	U.K.
STEFFA see STEFFEN	194272							
STEFFEN or STEFFA	194272	M	Ger.	10 or 14	W.O.,Feldgend, Unit 17491, Mimet (Fr.) 14.6.44		INCENDIARISM.	FR.
STEFFEN or STEPHEN	253456	M			Capt., Airforce Clothing Store, Enschede (Neth.) 42-45		INTERR.	NETH.
STEFFEN	260890	M			Flag-Cpl., SS, Eppstein-Taunus (Ger.) 19.10.44		MURDER	U.S.
STEFFENS	904	M			Pvt.,Army,O.C.3 Planton of 3 Coy,Sicherungs-Bn,Henbern 7.8.44		MURDER	U.K.
STEFFENS, Albert	124456	M			Pvt.,Sicherungs-Bn, 3 Zug, Merville-Henbern (Fr.)9.6.44-1.8.44		TORTURE	FR.
STEFFENS, Fritz	188325	M	Ger.	89 - 92	Sgt., Police, Aachen (Ger.) 9.8.44		TORTURE	U.S.
STEFFENS, Johanna	174114	F		05	Civilian, Lauenau (Ger.) 11.44		WITNESS	U.S.
STEFFENS, Leonhard	174214	M		08	Civilian, Lauenau (Ger.) 11.44		WITNESS	U.S.
STEFFENS, Walter	72012	M	Ger.		Scharfhr., SS, C.C. Struthof (Fr.)		TORTURE	FR.
STEFL	188498	M	Ger.		Member, NSDAP, Amtsgerichtsrat,Amtsgericht, Prag (Czech.) 40-44		MURDER	CZECH.
STEG, Johann	251342	M	Ger.	2.3.91	Schoolmaster, Civilian, Haj, Opava (Czech.) 5.45		INTERR.	CZECH.
STEGEMANN	251344	M			Hptscharfhr.,SS, chief, Abt.1 R., Sipo, Brussels (Bel.)		TORTURE	BEL.
STEGEMANN	307208	M			Hptscharfhr.,SS, C.C. Auschwitz (Pol.) 41-45		BRUTALITY	POL.
STEGEMANN, Heinrich Karl Gustav	254723	M	Ger.	29.3.11	Sgt., 4 Coy, Pol.-Waffen-Schule, Arnhem (Neth.) 3.45		INTERR.	NETH.
STEGENER, Karol	186801	M	Ger.		Sgt., Feldgend., Trupp 626, Peronne,Liquourt (Fr.) 24.8.44		MURDER	FR.
STEGER	253996	M			Uscharfhr.,3 Coy, 1 Bn "Das Reich",Oradour sur Glane (Fr.) 10.6.44		INTERR.	FR.
STEGER	257716	M			Lt.,Ger.Army, Orts-Cmdt.Donji Milanovac,Zajecar(Yugo.) 41-44		MURDER	YUGO.
STEGHERR, Peter	12307	M			Pvt.,Army, 110 or 111 Pz.Gren.Rgt.,2 Coy, Albine (Fr.) 29.6.44		MURDER	FR.
STEGMANN, Harry	174122	M			Civilian, Vippachedelhausen Distr.Weimar (Ger.) 3.45		MURDER	U.S
STEGMEIER, Franz	173142	M			Wachtmstr., C.C. Schirmeck,Rothenfels,Gaggenau (Fr.,Ger.)Autumn 44		INTERR.	U.K.
STEHL, Karl	158584	M			Scharfhr.,SS, Aschendorfer Moor (Ger.)		TORTURE	U.S.
STEHLE see STEELE	254688							
STEHR	189570	M	Ger.		Crim.secr. Gestapo Muenchen, C.C.Muenchen,Dachau (Ger.) 40-45		MURDER	BEL.
STEIB	129950	M	Ger.		C.C.Kaisheim (Ger.) 44-45		TORTURE	BEL.
STEIBETS see STIVITZ	132008							
STEIBITZ see STIWITZ	916							
STEIDL, Josef	192836	M	Ger.		Pvt.,Kgf.Bau-Arb.Bn 188, 2 Coy,Aasane (Nor.) 42-43		MISC.CRIMES	NOR.
STEIDL	186809	M			C.C. Flossenburg (Ger.)		MURDER	FR.
STEIDL, Vendelin	188206	M			Agent, SD (Security Service),Marianske,Lazne (Czech.) 39-45		MURDER	CZECH.
STEIG, Karl	166617	M	Ger.	16.4.04	Civilian, Farmer, Reiffenhausen (Ger.) 8.44		TORTURE	U.S.
STEIGELE	133221	M			Uscharfhr., Waffen-SS, C.C.Dora-Mittelbau, Nordhausen (Ger.)		MURDER	U.S.
STEIGEMANN or STEIMANN	194412	M	Ger.		Cpl.,Feldgendarmerie,Ploermel (Fr.) 18.6.44		TORTURE	FR.
STEIGER	133222	M			Osturmfhr.,SS,		MURDER	U.S.
STEIGER	256494	M			Lt.,SS,C.C.Ellrich-Nordhausen (Ger.)		MURDER	U.S.
STEIGER, Karl	143128	M	Ger.	08	Pvt.,SS-Leibstandarte "Adolf Hitler" Rgt., Feld Ers.Bn 1, Rosbach (Ger.) 4.3.45		MURDER	U.S.
STEIGERWALD	72033	M	Ger.		SS-Mann,SS-foreman,C.C.Wittlich (Ger.) 41-42		TORTURE	U.S.
STEIGERWALD, Michael	193770	M			SS-Pvt.,guard, 4 SS Totenkopf Stuba,C.C.Mittelbau-Dora, Osterode, Monowitz (Ger.,Czech.) 43-45		MURDER	U.S.
STEIGLER, Wend	192874	M	Ger.		Schupo, C.C.Falstad near Drontheim (Nor.) 9.-10.42		MURDER	NOR.
STEIGMANN	258912	M		90	Guard, Prison Preungesheim (Ger.) 42-44		BRUTALITY	FR.
STEILER, Josef	254734	M			Pvt., C.C.Ellrich-Nordhausen (Ger.)		MURDER	U.S.
STEIMAN	257510	M	Ger.		Osturmfhr.,SS, Plant manager, Ghetto Warsaw,Poniatowo,Treblinka (Pol.) 41-45		MURDER	POL.
STEIMANN see STEIGEMANN	194412							
STEIMEL, William	133223	M			Civilian in Camp		MURDER	U.S.
STEIMER	180491			00 - 05	Capt.,Army, Padulivo (It.) 10.-11.7.44		INTERR.	U.K.
STEIN	905	M	Ger.		Pvt.,Airforce,1 Coy Sch.Jaeg.Lftw.,Feld-Div.16 (Fr.)		MURDER	FR.
STEIN	906	M	Ger.		Brigadier-Gen., Pol.(SS),Danzig-Westpreussen (Pol.) 9.39-42		MURDER	POL.
STEIN	28867	M	Ger.		Capt.,Gestapo de Nancy, Badonvillier (Fr.) 11.9.44		MURDER	FR.
STEIN	39796	M			W.O.,2 Coy, Div.B,Noailles (Fr.) 3.4.44		MURDER	FR.
STEIN	68914	M			Cpl.,Army, C.C. Portland, 41		MURDER	U.K.
STEIN	121430	M		06	Lagerfuehrer,C.C.Buchenwald,Busenbach,Neurod(Ger.) 42-45		TORTURE	FR.
STEIN	121431	F	Ger.		Camp Cmdt's wife, Camp Civilian (Fr.)		TORTURE	FR.
STEIN	121432	M			Sgt.,C.C.Stalag XX B Marienburg (Pol.) 5.-12.43		TORTURE	U.K.
STEIN	122647	M		81	Major, Milit.Amt Abt.E, C.C.Stores Nischwitz (Ger.)1.45		MISC.CRIMES	U.S.
STEIN	124455	M			Cpl.,Airforce,Feld-Div.16,1 Co.(Fr.) 18.7.44		TORTURE	U.K.
STEIN	132793	M		20	Kapo, C.C. Mauthausen (Ger.)		MURDER	U.S.
STEIN	173531	M			Hauptgemeinschafts-Ltr.,Kreisltr.,NSDAP,Bruchsal(Ger.) 44		TORTURE	FR.
STEIN	254411	M			Lt.Col., Cmdt, Grenoble (Fr.) 14.8.44		INTERR.	FR.
STEIN	256366	M			Capt.,Gestapo,Nancy (Fr.) 9.9.44		MURDER	FR.
STEIN	257908	M			Usturmfhr.,SS,150 Pz.Bde, Meuse-Bridge Antwerp (Bel.) 12.44		INTERR.	U.S.
STEIN or STERN	260179	M	Ger.		Sgt.,Unit Russia-Ger.,Div.Oberland,Massif du Vercors. (Isère et Drôme-Fr.) 20.7.-5.8.44		SUSPECT	FR.
STEIN	300881	M	Ger.		Pvt.,6 Coy, 16 Hubner Rgt.,Kinrooi,Limburg(Bel.) 9.44		MURDER	BEL.

STE-STE

NAME	C.R.FILE NUMBER	SEX	NATIO- NALITY	DATE OF BIRTH	RANK OCCUPATION UNIT PLACE AND DATE OF CRIME	REASON WANTED	WANTED BY
STEIN, Ernest	186201	M	Ger.		Ortsgruppenleiter, N.S.D.A.P. Grostenquim Bertraing Hellimer (Fr.)44	LOOTING	FR.
STEIN, Ernst	142259	M	Ger.	19. 5.93	Hptsturmfhr., Gestapo, Amt Allg.SS, Bensheim (Ger.) 45	MURDER	U.S.
STEIN, Hans	139204	M	Ger.	1. 7.82	Osturmfhr., SA, Marburg (Ger.) 10.11.38	PILLAGE	U.S.
STEIN, Hans	168225	M	Ger.		Camp Official, C.C. Natzweiler Struthof (Fr.) 42-44	MURDER	FR.
STEIN, Heini	137522	M			Cpl., Army to Stalag III A C.C. Luckenwalde (Ger.) 13.2.45	TORTURE	U.S.
STEIN, Helmuth	181091	M		19. 8.91	Civilian, Factory Manager, Brno. (Czech.) 39-45	PILLAGE	CZECH.
STEIN, Hermann	173150	M	Ger.		Cpt., Gestapo, Vicinity of Pexonne (Fr.) 9.44-10.44	INTERR.	U.K.
STEIN, Hermann	186500	M		06	Sgt., Army, Kampen (Neth.) 2.10.44	TORTURE	NETH.
STEIN, Kurt	181111	M			Pvt., 669. Bn. 1.Coy. of Pos, Ferrieres, Burmontige, Villers Ste Gertrude Verbemont (Bel.) 9.44	MURDER	BEL.
STEIN, Max	168977	M			Warder or Kapo, C.C. Sachsenhausen Oranienburg (Ger.) 39-4.45	MURDER	POL.
STEIN, Robert	173532	M		17	Oberkapo, C.C. Neckarelz (Ger.)	TORTURE	FR.
STEIN, Willi	254869	M			Cpl., C.C. Ellrich Nordhausen, (Ger.)	MURDER	U.S.
STEINACHER	28746	M	Ger.		Major, Army, Finmark (Nor.) 11.44	MURDER	NOR.
STEINAU, Rudolf	254106	M			Cpl., C.C. Ellrich Nordhausen (Ger.)	MURDER	U.S.
STEINBACH	254728	M	Ger.		Lt., Cmdt., Artill. Bn. Tiel (Neth.) 45	PILLAGE	NETH.
STEINBACH	257247	F		10	Employee, Sipo and SD at Anvers Abt. IV DZ, Anvers (Bel.)	SUSPECT	BEL.
STEINBACH	257513	M			Chief of Sec. Mittelwerk C.C. Nordhausen (Ger.)	MURDER	U.S.
STEINBACH, Hans	259656	M			SS-Mann, Gestapo area Angers Maine and Loire (Fr.) 42-44	MISC.CRIMES	FR.
STEINBACH, Jean	256695	M			Kommdtr. De Viks, Beny Boccage (Fr.) 12.7.44	MURDER	FR.
STEINBACH, Walter	142061	M			Civilian, Prison Official, Waldheim (Ger.)	TORTURE	U.S.
STEINBAUER	149578	M			Sgt., 2. Panz. Div. Kampfgruppe Wilde, South West (Fr.) 44	MURDER	FR.
STEINBECHER	67681	M			Pvt., C.C. Swinemuende Marburg Heydekrug (Ger.) 42-44	MURDER	U.K.
STEINBECK, Georges	12308	M			N.C.O. Army 110. or.111. Panz.Gren.Rgt. 2. Coy. Albine (Fr.) 29.6.44	MURDER	FR.
STEINBEIN, Heinrich	256493	M			Uschfhr., SS Kitchen C.C. Dora Nordhausen, (Ger.)	MURDER	U.S.
STEINBERG	164742	M	Ger.		Lt., Artillerie Raville (Fr.) 16.8.44	TORTURE	FR.
STEINBERG	252768	M	Ger.		Oschfhr., C.C. Auschwitz Birkenau (Pol.)	INTERR.	FR.
STEINBERGER	124331	M			Pvt., Stalag	TORTURE	U.S.
STEINBOK	39784	M	Ger.		Adjutant, 2. Coy. Div. B, Noailles (Fr.) 3.4.44	MURDER	FR.
STEINBRECHER	161477	M		05	Lt., W-SS, C.C. Ohrdruf Buchenwald (Ger.)	WITNESS	U.S.
STEINBRINCK, Wilhelm	261345	M		26. 3.06	Chief, at Wharf, L'O.T. St. Aulin S-Mer (Fr.) 40-41	INCENDIARISM	FR.
STEINBRINK, Otto	60960	M		12	SS-Obergruppenfhr., SD, Duesseldorf (Ger.)	MISC.CRIMES	U.S.
STEINBUSCH, Georg	12309	M			Pvt., Army 110. or 111. Panz.Gren.Rgt. 2. Coy. Albins (Fr.) 29.6.44	MURDER	FR.
STEINCKE	180825	M			Pvt., Paratrooper Rgt. 2. Bn. Plonzane (Fr.) 44	MURDER	FR.
STEINCKE	192837	M			Hptsturmfhr., SD, C.O. Drontheim Vollan Falstadt (Nor.) 41-45	MURDER	NOR.
STEINDAMM, Najar	305954	M			Staatspolizei H.Q. Prague, Oswiecim Birkenau (Pol.) 39-45	MURDER	CZECH.
STEINDL	12310	M	Ger.		Pvt., Army 110.or 111. Panz.Gren.Rgt. 2.Coy. Albine (Fr.) 29.6.44	MURDER	FR.
STEINDL, Hermann	252753	M			Pvt., Fort De Vincennes (Fr.) 20.8.44	MISC.CRIMES	FR.
STEINED	306809	M			N.C.O. Feldgend. Vesoul, Montigny Les Vesoul Hte Saône (Fr.) 16.7.44	MURDER	FR.
STEINEL	124141	M	Ger.	95	Pvt., Land.Schuetz.Bn. 369 1 Coy. Labour Cdo. 39, Leipzig (Ger.)1.44-45	TORTURE	U.K.
STEINEL	161478	M	Ger.	21	Cpl., SS C.C. Buchenwald (Ger.)	TORTURE	U.S.
STEINEN, Heinrich	255293	M			Rottfhr., C.C. Harsungen Nordhausen (Ger.)	MURDER	U.S.
STEINER	67682	M			Cpt., C.C. Klausberg (Ger.) 41-45	MURDER	U.K.
STEINER	122618	M			Sgt., Army Stalag 18 A C.C. Lietzen (Aust.) 10.44	TORTURE	U.K.
STEINER	124066	M			Cpt., Stalag XVIII, Wolfsberg (Ger.) 42-43	TORTURE	U.K.
STEINER	137076	M	Ger.		Sgt., Airforce, San Pancratzia (It.) 13.4.43 - 6.43	MISC.CRIMES	U.K.
STEINER	139712	M		95	Gruppenfhr., Lt.General, W-SS Westland Lemberg Tarnopol (Pol.)	MURDER	U.S.
STEINER	141900	M		00	Cpt., Stalag VIII B,Gleiwitz (Ger.) 1.45	MURDER	U.K.
STEINER	156592	M			Sgt., 16. SS Inf.Div. Maille (Fr.) 25.8.44	MURDER	FR.
STEINER	158578	M			Cpt., Army 6. Coy. 398. Bn. Schlesien (Ger.) 21.1.45	TORTURE	U.K.
STEINER	255297	M			Flyer, C.C. Ellrich Nordhausen (Ger.)	MURDER	U.S.
STEINER	302000	M	Ger.		N.C.O. Member of the Geheime Feldpolice (taken from the 6. Parachuter Div.) Velp and Arnheim (Neth.) 1.45	BRUTALITY	NETH.
STEINER	306230	M	Ger.		Rottfhr., Feldgend. SS Div.Adolf Hitler Mean, 4.9.44	TORTURE	BEL.
STEINER, Erich	136640	M	Ger.		Civilian Germany	MISC.CRIMES	U.S.
STEINER, Franz	190352	M		90	Civilian, Stalag VII A, C.C. Muenchen (Ger.) 41-42	TORTURE	U.K.
STEINER, Friedrich	300731	M	Ger.		Hptsturmfhr., 13.SS Pol.Rgt. Commanding M T Coy. Ferlach (Aust.) 4.44-5.45	MURDER	YUGO.
STEINER, Johann	254860	M		22	Cpl., Anti-Partisan Duties, Mesola (It.) 12.44	MURDER	U.K.
STEINER, Karl	129987	M		02	SS-O.C. Mauthausen (Aust.) 41-45	MURDER	U.S.
STEINER, Karl	142261	M	Ger.	22. 2.18	Member, NSDAP, Brunswick (Ger.) 8.3.45	MURDER	U.S.
STEINER, Pavel	255630	M	Ger.	24. 2.03	Civ. Member, NSDAP, Bratis-Lava, (Czech.) 40-45	MISC.CRIMES	CZECH.
STEINERS, Hans	253430	M	Ger.	15.11.22	Pvt., Flak Ers.Abt. 6, St. Rijpen (Bel.) 3.9.44	MURDER	BEL.
STEINERT	193414	M	Ger.		Sgt., 1. Kgf. Arb. Bn. 41, Nerlandsdal Kristiansund (Nor.) 41-45	TORTURE	NOR.
STEINERT, Franz	251886	M	Ger.	25.12.15	Chief Assist. Gestapo, Tesin (Czech.) 42-45	SUSPECT	CZECH.
STEINERT, Joseph	137523	M			Uschfhr., SS C.C. Weimar Buchenwald (Ger.)	BRUTALITY	U.S.
STEINERTH	158579	M			Major, Kgf. Arf. Bn. 188 C.C. Bratthofmen, (Nor.) 44	MURDER	NOR.
STEINFALT	255296	M			Pvt., C.C. Ellrich Nordhausen (Ger.)	MURDER	U.S.
STEINFELER	162895	M	Ger.		SS-Lt., SS Lasalle (Fr.) 16.6.44	MURDER	FR.
STEINGRAD (see STEINGRAND)	254421						
STEINGROBE, Karl	194407	M	Ger.		Lt., Army F.P.No. 48987, Hucqueliers (Fr.) 44	TORTURE	FR.
STEINHARDT	136643	M			SS-Lt., SS Graz (Aust.) 45	MURDER	U.S. U.K.
STEINHAUS	908	M			Kreisleiter NSDAP, for Posnan (Pol.) 10.39-41	MISC.CRIMES	POL.
STEINHAUS	193775	M			SS-Pvt., 4.SS Totenkopf Sturmbann C.C. Mittelbau Gross Rosen C.C. Nordhausen (Ger.) 43-45	TORTURE	U.S.
STEINHAUSEL, Johann	260005	M	Ger.	27.10.05	Member, Gestapo of Kladno, Lidice Bohemia (Czech.) 10.6.42	MURDER	CZECH.
STEINHAUSER	162894	M	Ger.		Sgt., Army C.C. Markt Pongau, Stalag 18 C, (Ger.)	TORTURE	FR.
STEINHAUSER	164744	M	Ger.		Adjutant Chief, Feldgend., Laroche, Millay, (Fr.)	PILLAGE	FR.
STEINHILBER	261939	M	Ger.		Oschfhr., SS Belgrad and Valjewo (Yugo.) 15.8.42-10.9.44	SUSPECT	YUGO.
STEINHILER, Georg	156951	M	Ger.	1.11.01	Cpt., W-SS, Schleissheim (Ger.)	MURDER	U.S.
STEINHOFF	1333	M	Ger.		Assistent Naual Supply	TORTURE	U.K.
STEINHOFFEL, Otto	189569	M	Ger.	01	Civilian, C.C. Klettendorf (Ger.)	MURDER	POL.
STEINHUBER, Johann	252756	M	Ger.		Official, Gestapo, Brno. (Czech.) 39-45	MISC.CRIMES	CZECH.
STEINHUPEL, Ladislaus	193776	M	Ger.		Pvt., Guard, 4.SS Totenkopf Sturmbann C.C. Dora Mittelbau Nordhausen (Ger.) 43-45	MURDER	U.S.

STE - STE

NAME	C.R.FILE NUMBER	SEX	NATIO- NALITY	DATE OF BIRTH	RANK OCCUPATION UNIT	PLACE AND DATE OF CRIME	REASON WANTED	WANTED BY
STEINIGER	174216	M	Ger.		Dr.,Stalag 6A,C.C.Homer(Ger.) 41-45		TORTURE	U.S.
STEININGEN, Hans	126607	M			Lager 3 RD Coy.,2 Bn.Sauerland,CC.Hagen(Ger.) 11.40-2.45		MURDER	U.S.
STEININGER	240064	M	Ger.		Cpl.,Nachr.Regt.506-W-I,Abwehr Official,Zagreb(Yugo.) -44		MISC.CRIMES	U.S.
STEININGER	240065	M		93	Dr.,Agent,SD-Gestapo,Landwirtschaftsschule,Akum.		MISC.CRIMES	U.S.
STEININGER	255295	M			Rottfhr.,C.C.Mackenrode,Nordhausen(Ger.)		MURDER	U.S.
STEINKE	255294	M			Flyer,C.C.Ellrich,Nordhausen(Ger.)		MURDER	U.S.
STEINKE, Helmut K.	306561	M	Ger.	2.7.14	SS-W.O.,Kriminalangestellter,employed first in section IV, later IV N,Trondheim,Alesund(Nor.) 15.2.43		MURDER	NOR.
STEINKELLER, K.	192875	M	Ger.		Schupo,C.C.Falstad near Drontheim(Nor.) 6.-8.42		MURDER	NOR.
STEINKRAUS	190707	M			Pvt. Eisenb.Art. Btty.717,St.Andries,Varsenare Les Bruges(Bel.) 4.9.44		MURDER	BEL.
STEINKRAUTER	179233	M	Ger.	00	SS-Osturmfhr.,SS,Graudenz(Pol.) 44		TORTURE	U.K.
STEINLECHNER	305971	M	Ger.		Member of the Maurach Landwacht,Borders of Achensee,Pertisau-Maurach (Aust.) 13.7.44		MURDER	FR.
STEINMANN	129986				Sgt.,SS-Pz.Div.Totenkopf,C.C.Mauthausen(Aust.) 41-45		MURDER	U.S.
STEINMANN	240066	M	Ger.	15	SS-Sonderfuehrer-Capt.,SS,Kraftfahrpark,Bukow(Pol.)Warschau. 4.45		MURDER	U.S.
STEINMANN	258185	M	Ger.		Lt.,Feldgend.,Kragujevac(Yugo) 42-44		INTERR.	YUGO.
STEINMANN	260366	M	Ger.		Army-Employee,SS,PenitentaryNord-Norway(Nor.) 6.42-45		MURDER	YUGO.
STEINMANN, Helmuth	12311	M	Ger.		Pvt.,Army,110 or 111 Panz.Gren.Regt.,2 Coy.,Albine(Fr.) 29.6.44		MURDER	FR.
STEINMANN, Hermann	142244	M	Ger.	08	Truppfuehrer,Org.Todt,Ampfing-Mahldorf(Ger.)		MURDER	U.S.
STEINMANN, Karl	161480	M	Ger.	85	Mayor,Public Official,Sommerhausen(Ger.) 13.3.45		WITNESS	U.S.
STEINMETZ	184455	M			SS-Osturmbannfhr.,SSFuehrungshauptamt,C.C.Dora,Nordhausen(Ger.) 43-45		WITNESS	U.S.
STEINMETZ, Jakob	192898	M	Ger.	98	O.T.Truppfuehrer,Org.Todt,Abschnittsbauleitung,Harstad(Nor.) 42-43		MISC.CRIMES	NOR.
STEINMUELLER	72009	M			Hauptwachtmeister,Police,Tulle(Fr.) 9.6.44		MURDER	FR.
STEINMUELLER, Herbert	251346	M	Ger.	27	Foreman,RAD,Kreis Eisenstadt(Aust.) 13.2.45		MURDER	U.S.
STEINNEBECHER, Friedrich	306058	M	Ger.		Policeman,Aachen City Police,Aachen(Ger.) 9.8.44		MISC.CRIMES	U.S.
STEINO	164745	M	Ger.		Cpl.,Feldgend.Vesoul,Montigny en Vesoul(Fr.) 16.7.44		MURDER	FR.
STEINPECK, Emmi	194066	F	Ger.		C.C.Warder,C.C.Ravensbrueck(Ger.)		TORTURE	FR.
STEINRUECK	124752				Ascist.Camp-Cmdt.,SA Stand.Emsland,C.C.Neusustrum(Ger.)		MURDER	U.S.
STEINSICH	28747	M	Ger.		Major,Army,Finmark(Nor.) 11.44		MURDER	NOR.
STEINWARD, Adolf	185564	M	Ger.	23.7.05	Member-Kriminalsekretaer,SS,SD,Gestapo,Benesov,Jicin,Praha(Czech.) 39-45		MURDER	CZECH.
STEINWENDER, Herbert	304484			26.12.13	Oschfhr.,SS(Nr.139476),C.C.Buchenwald(Ger.) 16.5.38-9.10.43		MURDER	BEL.
STEINWENDTNER, Leopold	252757	M	Ger.	10	Employee,Gestapo,Kolin(Czech.) 42		MISC.CRIMES	CZECH.
STEIRNEIZ, Otto	136355	M	Ger.	10	Capt.,SS Totenkopf-Div.,3 Regt.,Poltawa(Sov.Un.) 2.-3.43		MURDER	J.S.
STEJSKAL	179815	M	Ger.	13	Usturmfhr.,12 SS Pz.Div.H.J.25,Abbaye-Ardenns,Caen(Fr.) 6.6.-2.7.44		TORTURE	CAN.
STEKES, Jacob	12312	M	Ger.		Cpl.,Army,110 or 111 Pz.Gren.Regt.,2 Coy.,Albine(Fr.) 29.6.44		MURDER	FR.
STELAU	142258	M		04	Lt.,Signal Corps,Gravenwoehr(Ger.) 2.11.-1.12.44		MISC.CRIMES	U.S.
STELLING, Karl	122908	M			Civilian in Camp		TORTURE	U.S.
STELLMACH, Viktor	240125	M	Ger.		Sgt.,Nachr.Regt.506,Abwehr Official,Belgrad(Yugo.) 11.43		MISC.CRIMES	U.S.
STELLMACHER	900882	M			Pvt.,1 Aufkl.Abt.,3 Coy,2 Column,XV Div. of the Africa Corps, Saint L'eger(Arlon) 5.9.44		MISC.CRIMES	BEL.
STELLO	136641	M			Lt.,SS,150 Pz.Bde.,Malmedy,Liege,Stavelot(Bel.) 12.44-1.45		MISC.CRIMES	U.S.
STELLRECHT, Helmut	259582	M	Ger.	21.12.98	Member SS and NSDAP, Asst. to Rosenberg, Flensburg (Ger.) 5.45		MISC.CRIMES	U.S.
STELLWAG, Theo	188499	M	Ger.	23.11.05	Factory Manager, Civ., Bruenn (Czech.) 39-45		PILLAGE	CZECH.
STELSTE	133225				SS-Cschfhr.		MURDER	U.S.
STELTER, Otto	260478	M	Ger.	14.6.93	SS-Rottenfhr., Waffen-SS, Guard-Coy., C.C.Auschwitz (Pol.) 6.44-5.45		BRUTALITY	POL.
STELTNER	31633	M			Lt., Army, Civ.occ.: Inspector of Berl.Kindl Brauerei, La Ferte, Mace (Fr.) 8.44		MISC.CRIMES	FR.
STELTNER, Karl	72005	M	Ger.	00	Lt., Ortskommandant, La Ferte Mace, Mayenne (Fr.) 6.44		MURDER	FR.
STELTNER, Karl	167232	M	Ger.	99	Lt., Ortskommandantur, Lignieres La Doucelle (Fr.) 6.44		MURDER	FR.
STELZ, Philip	124532	M	Ger.		Civilian, Stalag XIII C, Krum (Ger.) 10.41-2.43		MISC.CRIMES	U.K.
STELZIG	132694				Oberarzt, Stalag IV C, C.C.Wistriz (Czech.)		MURDER	FR.
STELZMANN, Rudie	253165	M			Block-Chief, Waffen-SS, C.C.Buchenwald (Ger.) 42-45		MURDER	U.S.
STELZNER	146717	M			Capt., SS, C.C. Flossenburg (Ger.)		TORTURE	U.S.
STELZNER	164721	M	Ger.		Lt., Kommandantur, Pont L'Abbe-Plobaznalec (Fr.) 6.-8.44		MURDER	FR.
STEMLER, Antonia	191996	F	Ger.	91	C.C. Ravensbrueck (Ger.) 2.45		TORTURE	FR.
STEMMER	254416	M	Ger.		Capt., Waffen-SS, Gouda-Utrecht (Neth.) 10.44		MURDER	NETH.
STEMMER (see STENNER)	256318							
STEMMLER, Wilhelm	253164	M		2.12.99	Standartenfhr., Waffen-SS, Neunkirchen (Ger.) 1.8.44		MURDER	U.S.
STEMPEL	189555	M			Crim.Commissar, SS Usturmfhr., Crim.Pol., Rechlin (Ger.) 21.6.44		MURDER	U.S.
STEMPNAKONSKI, Heinz	255629	M			Foreman, Army, Muenchen (Ger.) 10.4.45		MURDER	U.S.
STENCL, Leopold	164722	M	Ger.		Feldgendarm, Feldgendarmerie Luneville-Maize (Fr.) 16.-17.8.44		MURDER	FR.
STENDER, Adolf	132367	M	Ger.		Duesseldorf (Ger.)		MURDER	U.S.
STENG	166906			05 - 07	Lt., Geheime Feldpolizei, Recovro (It.) 1.45		INTERR.	U.S.
STENCKL	193393	M			Cpl., Kriegsgef.Arb.Bn.41, C.C.Nerlandsdal, Kristiansund (Nor.) 41-45		TORTURE	NOR.
STENCKL	261475	M	Ger.		SS-Sgt., Investigating-Magistrate, Warsaw-Sluck and other places (Pol.) 40-44		MURDER	POL.
STENGEL	301719	M			Member, S.D. or Gestapo, Oslo, Trandum near Oslo (Nor.) 19.1.43		MURDER	U.K.
STENCKEL, Hans	173530	M	Ger.		SS-Uschfhr., SS, C.C. Thekla (Ger.) 18.4.45		MURDER	FR.
STENGER	909	M			Lt.Col. C.O. 16. Inf.Div.Feldkdtr. 788 Tours, Maille (Fr.) 25.8.44		MURDER	FR.
STENGER	141896	M			Lt.Col., Army, Rom (It.) 7.7.44		WITNESS	U.K.
STENGER (or SENGER)	254873	M	Ger.		Col., Army, Nuernberg-Langwasser (Ger.) 41-45		MURDER	YUGO
STENGL, Adolphe	164743	M			Feldgendarm, Feldgendarmerie Luneville-Maize (Fr.) 16.-17.8.44		MURDER	FR.
STENGLE, Hans	192899	M			Usturmfhr., S.D. Administration, Trandum (Nor.) 1.43		MURDER	NOR.
STENGRITT	198347	M			Sgt., SS, Gestapo, Interpreter, Lyon (Fr.)		MURDER	FR.
STENK, Emil	260233	M	Ger.		Major, Member of Crim.Pol. in Berlin, Receare Terme (It.) 10.1.45		MURDER	U.S.
STENKE, Willi	255420	M	Ger.	24.11.11	Uschfhr., C.C.Harzungen, Nordhausen (Ger.)		MURDER	U.S.
STENKE	300883	M	Ger.		Pvt., 1 Aufkl.Abt. 3.Coy., 2.Col., XV. Div. of the Afrika Korps, Saint Leger (Arlon) 5.9.44		MISC.CRIMES	BEL.
STENKEL, Kristien	259184	M	Ger.		Member, SS, C.C. Dachau (Ger.)		MISC.CRIMES	YUGO.
STENLER, Antonia	180880	M	Ger.	91	Camp Official, C.C. Ravensbrueck (Ger.)		TORTURE	FR.
STENNER (or STEMMER)	256318	M	Ger.		Org.Todt, Mahldorf area (Ger.)		WITNESS	U.S.

NAME	C.R.FILE NUMBER	SEX	NATIO-NALITY	DATE OF BIRTH	RANK OCCUPATION UNIT PLACE AND DATE OF CRIME	REASON WANTED	WANTED BY
STENNER, Philipp	161106	M	Ger.	98	Sgt., Army, 102 or 107 Lds.Schtz.Bn., Hadamar (Ger.) 11.43	WITNESS	U.K.
STENZEL	164723	M			Officer, Kommandantur, Ammensee (Fr.)	WITNESS	FR.
STENZEL, Albert	158574	M			Oschfhr, SS, CC Gleiwitz (Ger.)	TORTURE	U.S.
STENZEL, Max	906705	M	Ger.		Deserter, Army, Leglantiers-Oise (Fr.) 13.7.44	RAPE	FR.
STENZEL, Paul Martin	143129	M	Ger.	17. 7.10	Pvt., Lds.Schtz.Ers.Bn., Augsburg (Ger.) 40-4.45	MURDER	U.S.
STENZELL	1749	M			Pvt., Army	MURDER	U.K.
STEPE (see STEPPE)	194408						
STEPELMANN	129978	M			Cmdt, SS, Gneisenau (Ger.) 40-45	MURDER	BEL.
STEPHAN	12913	M	Ger.		Lt., 950 Indian Rgt.,13 Coy,Ruffec (Fr.) 18.8.44	MURDER	FR.
STEPHAN	141327	M	Ger.		Sgt., Stalag 357, Coy Staff, CC Fallingbostel (Ger.) 1.-4.45	MISC.CRIMES	U.K.
STEPHAN, Karl	156590	M	Ger.	5.01	Chief, Feld-Gend., Hettange-Grande (Fr.) 7.9.44	MURDER	FR.
STEPHANIE, Hugo	156589	M			Civilian, Daasdorf and Guttmannshausen (Ger.) 7.-8.44	WITNESS	U.S.
STEPHEN	188779	M	Ger.		Officer, Gestapo, Sigee (Fr.) 7.44	TORTURE	FR.
STEPHEN (see STEFFEN)	253456						
STEPLER, Hans	910	M			Pvt., Gestapo, Onnainy, Valenciennes (Fr.) 43, 1.9.44	MURDER	FR.
STEPPE (or STEPE)	194408	M	Ger.		Lt., Army, St.Prest (Fr.) 12.6.44	WITNESS	FR.
STERH	189802	M			Political Dept. Kreiskommandantur, Krusevac (Yugo.) 4.12.42	MURDER	YUGO.
STERK	125245	M		1910- 15	Hptsturmfhr, SS Div."Gross-Deutschland", Daun (Ger.) 23.12.44	MURDER	U.S.
STERLING, Christian	224070	M			SS Oschfhr, Sipo and SD, Abt.III.Anvers (Bel.) 6.40-9.44	SUSPECT	BEL.
STERM	156922	M	Ger.		Capt., Army, Cabrespruies 22.4.45	MURDER	FR.
STERMAN, Josef	173513	M	Ger.		Guard, SS Pol.Rgt., CC Sajmiste-Zemun-Belgrad (Yugo.) 26.4.43	MURDER	YUGO.
STERMANN, Wilhelm	301967	M	Ger.		Sgt., service of la Gast at Loguivy de la Mer near Paim-Pol, Côtes du Nord (Fr.) 14.2.45	PILLAGE	FR.
STERN	189803	M	Ger.		Sgt., Feld-Kommandantur, CC Uglijarevo (Yugo.) 5.43	TORTURE	YUGO.
STERN (see STEIN)	260179						
STERNHUBER, Otto	257907	M			150 Pz.Bde., Meuse Bridge, Antwerpen (Bel.) 12.44	MISC.CRIMES	U.S.
STERNKOP	306212	M	Ger.		Member of staff, small fortress, CC Theresienstadt (Czech.)1.10.38-44	MURDER	CZECH.
STERNKOPF, Josef	251358	M	Ger.	20.10.01	Civilian-Guard, member of firing squad. CC Terezin(Czech.) 40-45	MURDER	CZECH.
STERZENBACH, Theo	111723	M	Ger.	12.12.06	Gestapo, Kripo, Luxembourg 40-45	MISC.CRIMES	LUX.
STESE, Johann	256179	M	Ger.		O.T., Muhldorf (Ger.)	WITNESS	U.S.
STESKA	186684	M		10	Uschfhr, SS Nachrichtenzug, Wormhouit (Fr.) 5.40	MURDER	U.K.
STESSEL	306894	M	Ger.		Male Nurse, in charge of Formol injections, CC Auschwitz(Pol.)40-45	MURDER	FR.
STESSEL, Henri Jean	174289	M			Capt., Army, Supreme Command, Namur (Fr.)	MURDER	FR.
STETNER, Bernhard	31699	M	Ger.	04	Uschfhr, W-SS, Pz.Abt.17, 1 Coy, St.Aubin du Perron (Fr.) 20.-21.6.44	MISC.CRIMES	U.S.
STETTELS	137508	M			Officer, Secret Field Police, Group 713	MURDER	U.S.
STETTENFELD, Conrad	250496	M			Wassertrudingen (Ger.) 1.3.45	MURDER	U.S.
STETTER, Fritz	257463	M	Ger.		SS Sgt., Camp Dora, Nordhausen (Ger.)	MURDER	U.S.
STETTIN	913	M			Gestapo, Rodez (Fr.) 8.44	MURDER	FR.
STETTNER	250497	M			Agent, Gestapo, Alencon (Fr.) 40-44	MURDER	FR.
STETZKOW, Anatol	255423	M		30. 1.07	CC Harzungen, Nordhausen (Ger.)	MURDER	U.S.
STEUBEN, Vincenz	192840	M	Ger.	00	Guard, Feldstraflager, CC Finmark (Nor.) 40-45	SUSPECT	NOR.
STEUBER	914	M	Ger.		Col., Army, Rodes (Fr.) 8.44	MURDER	FR.
STEUER	139212	M		15	Usturmfhr, SD, Sipo, Toulouse and other towns(Fr.) 6.-8.44	MURDER	U.S.
STEUR	149579	M	Ger.		Major, 11 Pz.Div., Nachr.Abt., South West France 44	MURDER	FR.
STEUER, Maximilian(or SLAVIK)	262426	M	Ger.	14.10.00	Chief secretary, criminal police, Olomouec(Czech.) 41-45	SUSPECT	CZECH.
STEVER, Ehrenreich	305794	M	Ger.		Kapitaen-Leutnant, Navy Submarine 1277(U), Atlantic near Portugal 2.6.45	INTERR.	U.K.
STEY	152139	M	Ger.		Adjutant, Army, Chenebier Etobon (Fr.) 27.9.44	MURDER	FR.
STEZKO, Isidore	187398	M	Ger.	15. 1.23	Guard, SS CC Buchenwald (Ger.)	TORTURE	BEL.
STEZL, Franz	142256	M		05	Pvt., Nachschub Bn. 612 K, supply Coy, Les Hogues Bure (Fr.) 25.8.44	WITNESS	U.S.
STHACT (or STACHT)	260085	M	Ger.		Gend., Russian German Div."Oberland", Massif du Vercors, Isere, Drome (Fr.) 20.7. - 5.8.44	SUSPECT	FR.
STHAL	261161	M	Ger.		Cpl., 139 Arbeitsbereich Liase, 5.I Rgt.211,Alleur-lez-Liège (Bel.) 4.9.44	MURDER	BEL.
STHAL (or STAHL, Henri alias Rudi)	138256	M			Interpreter, Gestapo, Section IV spionage, Lyon(Fr.)	MURDER	FR.
STHOK	254415	M	Ger.		Master of Police, military police, Arnheim,Oosterbeck(Neth.)	MURDER	NETH.
STIANSKY	124067	M	Ger.		Civ., Capt., mine, CC Brux (Ger.) 1.11.43	TORTURE	U.K.
STIBITZ (see STIWITZ)	916						
STIBITZ	250495	M			SS Medical Asst., Auschwitz-Birkenau Pol.) 42-45	MURDER	YUGO.
STIBITZ, Fritz	258911	M		14	Camp-chief, SS Commander, Ohrdruf (Ger.) 44-45	MURDER	FR.
STICH	162897	M	Ger.		Adjutant, Army, Ravin (Fr.) 13.-14.6.44	MURDER	FR.
STICHELBURMER	900589	M	Ger.		N.C.O., Army, 10 Coy, 377 Inf.Rgt.,Vinkt-Meigem(Bel.)25.-31.5.40	MISC.CRIMES	BEL.
STICHER	256694	M	Ger.		Crim.Asst., Oschfhr, Field Police, Foix (Fr.) 12.42-8.44	BRUTALITY	FR.
STICHER	901875	M	Ger.		Second Command of Gestapo at Foix, operating at Paivert(Aude)Fr.14.4.44	MURDER	FR.
STICHLER, Wilhelm	256699	M	Ger.		Oschfhr, SD, Foix (Fr.) 11.42-8.44	MURDER	FR.
STICHLING, Heinrich	31698	M			Mayor, civil administration (local) Gernsbach(Ger.)	WITNESS	U.S.
STICHFER	136959	M	Ger.		Civilian, Trier (Ger.) 42-44	TORTURE	U.S.
STICKLE	126504	M			Uschfhr, 1 SS Pz.Div."Adolf Hitler", 1 SS Pz.Rgt., 9 Coy, Malmedy (Bel.) 17.12.44	MURDER	U.S.
STICKLER, Johann	156744	M	Ger.		Pvt.,Army,299 Inf.Div.,Volks-Gren.Rgt.529,4 Coy,Muelheim,Dietesheim (Ger.) 25.2.45	WITNESS	U.S.
STIEB, Robert	143132	M	Ger.		Oberwachtmeister, CC Bielefeld (Ger.) 9.44	MURDER	U.S.
STIEBER, Theodor	174129	M	Ger.	20.12.78	Civilian, Saloon Keeper, Guttmanhausen (Ger.) 29.7.44	WITNESS	U.S.
STIEBERITZ	901485	M	Ger.		Sturmschfhr, SS, CC Buchenwald (Ger.) 16.5.38-9.10.43	MURDER	BEL.
STIEBERT	174788	M		00	Pvt., Army, Bronzolo (It.) 9.43	WITNESS	U.K.
STIEBITZ	125148	M			CC Auschwitz (Pol.)	MURDER	U.S.
STIEHLER	915	M	Ger.		Capt., Army, CC Loos (Fr.) 40-41	TORTURE	U.K.
STIERITZ	143134	M	Ger.		Oschfhr, W-SS, Totenkopfstandarte, CC Buchenwald (Ger.)	TORTURE	U.S.
STIEDING, Arao	125607	M	Ger.	21.10.02	Gend., Reitwiller (Fr.) 5.8.44	MURDER	FR.
STIEFEL	136642	M			Civilian, act. to be imprisoned	WITNESS	U.S.
STIEFL	143135	M	Ger.		Civilian, Frankenberg (Ger.) 20.9.45	TORTURE	U.S.
STIEFLING, Friedrich	174111	M	Ger.	14. 9.88	Capt., Police, Aken -Elbe (Ger.) 30.5.44	MURDER	U.S.
STIEFFLER	252763	M	Ger.	15	Pvt., Guard, Army, at camp 2780, Langwied(Ger.) 8.41,6.42	BRUTALITY	U.K.
STIEG, Karl	306439	M			Reiffenhausen 14.8.44	BRUTALITY	U.S.

STI - STO   -150-

NAME	C.R.FILE NUMBER	SEX	NATIO- NALITY	DATE OF BIRTH	RANK	OCCUPATION	UNIT	PLACE AND DATE OF CRIME	REASON WANTED	WANTED BY
STIEGELE	254715	M			Unterscharfhr., C.C. Nordhausen (Ger.)				MURDER	U.S.
STIEGER, Franz	305699	M	Ger.		Civilian, Amstetten (Aust.) 20.3.45				MISC.CRIMES	U.S.
STIEGER, Gustav	254716	M			Pvt. C.C. Ellrich, Nordhausen (Ger.)				MURDER	U.S.
STIEGLEK	250491	M	Ger.		Wassertrudingen (Ger.) 1.3.45				MURDER	U.S.
STIEGLER	174781	M	Ger.		Lt., Div. Brandenburg 16.Coy., Communanza (It.) 2.5.44				WITNESS	U.K.
STIEHL or STEELE or STAHLE	143136	M	Ger.		Major, Stalag C.C. Luft 4, Tichow-Fallingbostel, Kiefheide (Ger.)				MURDER	U.S.
STIEHL	254419	M			Pvt., Field-Police, Vendome (Fr.) 9.8.44				INTERR.	FR.
STIEHLE see STEELE	254688									
STIELAU	125244	M	Ger.		Oberleutnant, Army, Muskulus 1. Task Force C.C. Grafenwoehr (Ger.)				MISC.CRIMES	U.S.
STIELAU	257924	M			O-Lt., Pz.Bde.150, Meuse Bridge, Antwerp (Bel.) 12.44				MISC.CRIMES	U.S.
STIENENS	255628	M	Ger.		Pvt., Eyne (Bel.) 4.u.6.9.44				INTERR.	BEL.
STIENITZ see STIWITZ	916									
STIER	62396	M	Ger.		Dr., Sturmbannfhr., SS High Off. Of Commissariat for Ger. Racialism				MISC.CRIMES	U.N.W.C.C.
STIERTZ, Hermann	129960	M	Ger.		Chief, Zentrale der O.T. Firm Wiener & Trachter, Hemme (Ger.)43				TORTURE	BEL.
STIKLER	194414	M	Ger.		Foreman, Factory Wasag Reinsdorf near Wittenberg (Ger.) 29.1.44				MURDER	FR.
STIKLER or STILLER	261682	M	Ger.		Foreman, Factory, Wasag-Reinsdorf (Ger.) 29.1.44				MURDER	FR.
STILKENBOEHMER, Heinrich	253999	M	Ger.		Cpl., 377 Jaeg. Regt. 10. Coy., Vinkt (Bel.) 25.-31.5.40				MISC.CRIMES	BEL.
STILLE, Fritz	131328	M	Ger.		Unterscharfhr., Report-leader, SS, C.C. Arnstadt, Espenfeld (Ger.)				MURDER	U.S.
STILLER	36630	M	Ger.		Scharfhr., SS, C.C. Oxerhof near Deventer (Neth.) 5.-6.4.45				MURDER	NETH.
STILLER see STIKLER	261682									
STILLER, Paul	139214	M	Ger.		Member, SA				TORTURE	U.S.
STILLERICH	193306	M	Ger.		Guard, Justizvollzugsanstalten, C.C. Preungesheim,Frankfurt-Main (Ger.) 7.-10.44				TORTURE	U.K.
STILLGER, Hermann	124914	M	Ger.		Warden, Prison Justizvollzugsanstalt (Ger.) Diez-Lahn 43-20.3.45				TORTURE	U.S.
STILLNER	189554	M	Ger.		Civilian Trieben (Aust.) 5.5.45				MURDER	U.S.
STILP	12914	M	Ger.		Pvt., Army 110. or 111. Pz.Gren.Regt. 2. Coy., Albine (Fr.)29.6.44				MURDER	FR.
STILP, Max	194409	M	Ger.		Chief of block, C.C. Mauthausen (Austr.)				TORTURE	FR.
STIMPFLE	193305	M	Ger.	02	Pvt., Army, I-427 Landesschuetzen Bn., C.C. Stalag 344, Oppeln (Ger.) 1.-5.45				WITNESS	U.K.
STIMPL, Josef	166907	M			SS-Oberscharfhr., SS Hauptamt H.Q. C.C. Bolzano (It.)				MURDER	U.K.,U.S.,IT.
STINDT	301224		Ger.		Doctor, under Ob.Gruppenfhr., Oberg.Chief of Police and SS for France Vosges, Aera (Fr.) 44				MURDER	U.K.
STINGEL, Alfred	186828	M	Ger.		SS, Posing-Baviere (Ger.) 4.45				MISC CRIMES	FR.
STINGEL, Franz	192841	M	Ger.	08	Sgt., Reichsjustizministerium, Strafgefangenen-Lager Nord, C.C.-Finmark (Nor.) 42-45				MISC.CRIMES	NOR.
STINGEL, Karl	186829	M	Ger.	08	SS, Posing-Baviere (Ger.) 4.45				MISC.CRIMES	FR.
STINGHER, Hans	178289	M		90	Major, Stalag VIII C, Army, Sagan Bad Orb (Ger.) 2.u.3.45				MURDER	U.K.
STINGLAGWAGNER, Albert	251877	M	Ger.		Lt., 515 Inf.Regt. 1. Coy., Niellie (Fr.) 20.-21.10.44				PILLAGE	FR.
STINGLE, Alfred	146718	M			SS,C.C. Flossenburg (Ger.)				TORTURE	U.S.
STIRLICH	258891	M	Ger.		Guard, Prison of Preungesheim (Ger.) 42-44				BRUTALITY	FR.
STIRNWEISS, Christian	188331	M	Ger.		Civilian, Arb.Kdo. Dachsbach Kreis Neustadt (Ger.) 43-45				TORTURE	POL.
STIRTZ	257715	M	Ger		Cpl., Army, Blazevo (Yugo.) 3.u.4.12.42				MURDER	YUGO.
STIRZING	191390	M			Cmdt., Kommandantur, La Bourboule le mont D'ore (Fr.) 27.4.44				MURDER	FR.
STITTO see SEIDZ	173989									
STITTS	128794	M	Ger.		Civilian, Foreman, Stalag IX C, Exinberch, Vacha (Ger.) 1.,12.44-5.45				MURDER	U.K.
STITTS see SEIDZ	173989									
STIVA, Endrich	180903	M	Ger.		Miscell., Wittenberg (Ger.) 8.44				MURDER	U.S.
STIVITZ or SCHIBETS, STEIBETS	132008	M			Chief-Leader, SS, C.C. Ohrdruf (Ger.) 44-45				MURDER	U.S.
STIWETT see STIWITZ	916									
STIWETZ see STIWITZ	916									
STIWITZ or STIBITZ or STEIBITZ STIWETT,STIENITZ STIWETZ	916	M	Ger.	13	O-Scharfhr., SS Guard at C.C. Auschwitz-Birkenau (Pol.) 40-45				MURDER	U.S.,CZECH., U.K.FR.POL.BEL. YUGO.
STIWITZ	142260	M	Ger.		Unterscharfhr., SS, C.C., Pankofen near Plattling (Ger.) 22.4.45				MURDER	U.S.
STIX	162910	M	Ger.		Pvt., Army, Revin (Fr.) 13.-14.6.44				MURDER	FR.
STIX, Johann	254717	M			Pvt., C.C. Ellrich, Nordhausen (Ger.)				MURDER	U.S.
STJASSNER, Georg	142237	M		11	Public Official				TORTURE	U.S.
STNOWE	164725	M			Cpl., Etat-Mayor of Crest, La Rochelle (Fr.) 3.8.44				MURDER	FR.
STNOWE	167244	M	Ger.		Sgt., Kommandantur General Staff, Crest-Drome (Fr.) 7.-8.44				MURDER	FR.
STOBBE, Herbert	161481	M	Ger.		Unterscharfhr., W.-SS, C.C. Buchenwald (Ger.)				WITNESS	U.S.
STOBE	254871	M	Ger.		Major, District-Kommandant, Army at Valjevo (Yugo.) 6.-10.41				MURDER	YUGO.
STOBER, Julius	192842	M	Ger.	25.11.11	Exconvict, Reichsjustizministerium, Feldstraflager Nord, Finmark (Nor.) 42-45				WITNESS	NOR.
STOBZ	121433	M	Ger.		Pvt., Stalag 20 B, C.C. Marienburg (Pol.) 5.-12.43				TORTURE	U.K.
STOCHLIN, Rudolf or STOECKLIN	132685	M	Ger.		Sgt., Army, Miellin (Fr.) 17.,18.,19.9.44				RAPE	FR.
STOCK	167311	M	Ger.		W.O. Adjutant, 77.Inf.Bn. 4.Coy., Forest (Bel.) 6.9.44				MURDER	BEL.
STOCK	188778	M	Ger.		Lt., Army, La Rochelle (Fr.) 18.11.44				MURDER	FR.
STOCK, Werner	254869	M	Ger.	10. 1.24	Pvt., C.C. Ellrich, Nordhausen (Ger.)				MURDER	U.S.
STOCK	259807	M	Ger.	07-97	Meister der Schutzpolizei, Green-Police, I.or2. Coy. Freiwillige Pol.Btt. Zwolle, Overijssel (Neth.) 3.10.44				MURDER	NETH.
STOCKEL see STOECKL, Aloys	141997									
STOCKEL	194273	M	Ger.		Capt., Chasseurs Alpins 98, Cognin les Georges Malleval, Le Chablais (Fr.) 15.-16.12.43,29.1.44,10.-21.7.44				MISC.CRIMES	FR.
STOCKEL see STOCKL	256967									
STOCKEL, Alois	901720	M	Ger.		Fehrbauer, Civilian about 17.12.44				BRUTALITY	U.K.
STOCKEL, Emil	250492	M			SS-Hauptstfhr., SS, Auschwitz-Birkenau (Ger.) 42				MURDER	YUGO.
STOCKER, Emil	173484	M	Ger.		SS-Hauptsturmfhr., C.C. Oswiecim, Birkenau (Pol.) 39-45				MURDER	CZECH.
STOCKHAMMER, Georg	139206	M			Civilian, (Pol.) 39-40				MURDER	U.S.
STOCKHAUS, Heinrich Wilhelm	305779	M	Ger.	11. 6.06	Crim.-Secretary, Chief of Si.Polizei, Haugesund (Nor.)1.42-4.45				TORTURE	NOR.
STOCKHAUSEN	189804	M	Ger.		Bde.-General, Feldkommandantur C.C. Kadin Jaca (Yugo.)				MURDER	YUGO.
STOCKHOVER	162893	M	Ger.		Sgt., Army, Revin (Fr.) 13.-14.6.44				MURDER	FR.
STOCKING	256180	M			O.T. Muhldorf (Ger.)				WITNESS	U.S.
STOCKINGER, Franz	254865	M		19. 7.06	Flyer, C.C. Ellrich, Nordhausen (Ger.)				MURDER	U.S.
STOCKL or STOECKEL or STOCKEL	256967		Ger.		98 Bn. Alpine, Allevard- Massifdu Vercors (Fr.) 10.7.44,20.7.44-5.8.44				PILLAGE	FR.

NAME	C.R.FILE NUMBER	SEX	NATIO- NALITY	DATE OF BIRTH	RANK OCCUPATION UNIT PLACE AND DATE OF CRIME	REASON WANTED	WANTED BY
STOCKMAN	67683	M	Ger.		Major, Army,Krs.Zempleburg (Pol.) 9.-11.44	TORTURE	U.K.
STOCKMAN, Toni	301051	M	Ger.		Kapo, Klinkerwerk, C.C., Neuengamme (Ger.) 22.9.41	MURDER	BEL.
STOCKMANN	194415	M	Ger.		Pvt., Feldgendarmerie, Ploermel (Fr.) 18.6.44	TORTURE	FR.
STOCKMANN, Johnny	129949	M	Ger.		C.C., Neuengamme (Ger.)	TORTURE	BEL.
STOCKMEIER (or STOCKMIER)	142252	M		99	Oberscharfhr.,Foreman,SS,C.C. at Landshut,Loibersdorf(Ger.)2.5.45	WITNESS	U.S.
STODICK (or STODIECK)	257925	M			Lt., 150 Panz.-Brigade,Meuse-Bridge-Antwerpen (Bel.)12.44	MISC.CRIMES	U.S.
STOECK	254864	M			Sgt., C.C., Dora,Nordhausen (Ger.)	MURDER	U.S.
STOEBCKEL	917	M	Ger.		Capt.,98.Rgt. of mountain troops.1.Bn. 8.44	MURDER	FR.
STOECKEL	137518	M			Kapo, C.C., Buchenwald (Ger.)	TORTURE	U.S.
STOECKEL	180881	M			Capt., 1.Jaeger Bn., Region de la Maurienne (Fr.)	MURDER	FR.
STOECKEL (see STOCKL)	256367	M					
STOECKER	256692	M			Stellvertreter des Sonderbevollmaechtigten d.Ausw.Amtes f.d.Sued-Osten, Civilian German Foreign Office,Belgrad(Yugo.) 11.43-9.44	MISC.CRIMES	YUGO.
STOECKL	180785	M			Major, Jaeger -Bn.Btty.-Chef,Les Glieres (Fr.)	MURDER	FR.
STOECKL, Aloys (or STOCKEL)	141997	M		29. 6.98	Civilian, Fahrhauer, Kommert near Rhede (Ger.) 2.45	TORTURE	U.S.
STOECKLEIN, Hermann	254868	M			Pvt., C.C., Ellrich,Nordhausen (Ger.)	MURDER	U.S.
STOECKLIN,Rudolf (see STOCHLIN)	132685	M					
STOEGER, Hermann	254866	M		13. 1.07	Flyer, C.C., Ellrich,Nordhausen (Ger.)	MURDER	U.S.
STOEGNER	300884	M	Ger.		Pvt.,1.Aufkl.Abt.,3.Coy.,2.Column,XV.Div.of the Afrika Korps, Saint Léger (Arlon)(Bel.) 5.9.44	MISC.CRIMES	BEL.
STOEHEN, Wilhelm	260367	M	Ger.		Oberwachtmeister, SS,Penitentiary (Nor.) 6.42-45	MURDER	YUGO.
STOEHR, Heinrich	142060	M	Ger.		Civilian, C.C., Dachau (Ger.)	WITNESS	U.S.
STOEHR, Wilhelm	93802	M	Ger.	6.11.03	Gauleiter, NSDAP, Gau Westmark	TORTURE	UNWCC
STOELZ, Hans	254234	M	Ger.	19	Pvt., 400.Landsch.Bn., Eisleben (Ger.) 11.43	TORTURE	U.K.
STOEPMANN (Nicknamed "DE STEENPUIST"	252752	M	Ger.		Worked under Max Brand,SA, Eps and Vreden (Ger.) 10.44 - 2.45	INTERR.	NETH.
STOESSEL	156583	M	Ger.		Dr.,Oberstabsarzt,Hitler Jugend, C.C.,Hohenstein-Ernstthal (Ger.)	MURDER	FR.
STOESSEL	254418	M			Lt., Pionier Bn. 31 308 A, Le Touquet,Paris,Plage (Fr.) 43 - 44	PILLAGE	FR.
STOETLER	133226	M			Hauptsturmfhr., SS,	MURDER	U.S.
STOETZIER	122909	M	Ger.		Hauptsturmfhr., SS-Div.Totenkopf, C.C. Dora,Nordhausen, Auschwitz, Ellrich (Ger.Pol.) 10.44 - 2.45	MURDER	U.S.
STOETZLER	257460	M			Capt., SS, Camp-Leader and Asst.to Foerschner, Nordhausen (Ger.)	MURDER	U.S.
STOEVE	255076	M			Flyer, C.C., Ellrich,Nordhausen (Ger.)	MURDER	U.S.
STOEVER (or NELIS)	920	M			C.C., Leusderheide (Neth.) 42	MURDER	NETH.
STOEWE	300885	M			Pvt., 1.Aufkl.Abt., 3.Coy.,2.Column,XV.Div.of the Afrika Korps, Saint Léger (Arlon)(Bel.) 5.9.44	MISC.CRIMES	BEL.
STOEWER	254852	M			Lt., C.C., Dora,Nordhausen (Ger.)	MURDER	U.S.
STOEWSAND	300147	M	Ger.		Sicherheitsdienst man at Breda, Haaren,Utrecht (Neth.)10.42,31.5.43	INTERR.	NETH.
STOFFBERG, Paul	254235	M		10	Cpl., Army or Gestapo,Prison, Salonika (Grc.) 5.44 - 6.44	TORTURE	U.K.
STOFFEL	253997	M	Ger.		Capt., 3.Bn.Heer.Unt.-Offizierschule 338.Div.,La Bresse (Fr.)9.-11.44	MURDER	FR.
STOFFERMAIER, Willi	119390	M			Civilian, Settler, Olekszyn (Pol.) 12.39	INCENDIARISM	POL.
STOHF	33128	M			Kreisredner, NSDAP, Treutte (Aust.)	MURDER	FR.
STOHF, Fritz	188496	M	Ger.	7. 1.17	Crim.-Commissar, Gestapo, Luxemburg (Gra Duchy)(Lux.)	MISC.CRIMES	LUX.
STOHLBERG, Graf	173512	M			W.O., Cmdt., Cossack-Brigade (Yugo.) 11.43 - 8.44	MURDER	YUGO.
STOHR	1334	M	Ger.		Assistant, Naval Supply	MISC.CRIMES	U.K.
STOHR	12315	M	Ger.		Adjudant, SS-Div. "Der Fuehrer" 2.Coy. Oradour (Fr.) 10.6.44	MURDER	FR.
STOITSEF	305304	M	Ger.		Police Officer, Drama Area,(Grc.) 2.40 - 41	MURDER	GRC.
STOJAN, Rudolf	252762	M	Ger.		SS - Mann, Kolin (Czech.) 39 - 42	MISC.CRIMES	CZECH.
STOKITZT	67684	M			Sgt., Army, Argentan (Fr.) 7.44	MURDER	U.S.
STOLDT	158699	M	Ger.		Pvt.,Army Commando 602-1,Guard Coy.Neuwegersleben (Ger.) 1.3.44.	MURDER	FR.
STOLENBERG	194416	M			Pvt., Feldgendarmerie, Ploermel (Fr.) 18.6.44	TORTURE	FR.
STOLFA	143137	M			Pvt., Air-Force, C.C. Leipzig-Thekla (Ger.)	MURDER	U.S.
STOLL	33054	M	Ger.	20	Cpl., Waffen SS, C.C., Buchenwald (Ger.)	TORTURE	U.S.
STOLL	131327	M			Uscharfhr., SS, C.C., Arnstadt (Ger.)	MURDER	U.S.
STOLL (see STOLTON)	137526						
STOLL	140846	M			Pvt., 111. Bn., Parachute-Rgt., Calcar (Ger.) 15.5.45	MURDER	CAN.
STOLL, Friedrich	254867	M		29. 9.04	Flyer, C.C. Ellrich, Dora-Nordhausen (Ger.)	MURDER	U.S.
STOLL, Fritz (see STOLLBERG)	137519						
STOLL, Heinrich	142235	M	Ger.		Uscharfhr., Waffen SS, Totenkopf, C.C., Buchenwald (Ger.) 39 - 42	BRUTALITY	U.S.
STOLLBERG, Fritz (or STOLL)	137519	M	Ger.	19	Hauptscharfhr.,C.C.Totenkopf-Sturmbann, Weimar-Buchenwald (Ger.)	TORTURE	FR.
STOLLE	194418	M	Ger.	19	Cpl., Army, Rouen (Fr.) '41	MURDER	U.S.
STOLLE, Otto	142225	M		05	Sturmscharfhr. SS, Mittergarslager C.C., Muehldorf Area (Ger.)	MURDER	U.S.
STOLLER, Karl - Heinz	255074	M		9.11.21	Pvt., C.C., Ellrich,Nordhausen (Ger.)	MISC.CRIMES	FR.
STOLMANN	177563	M	Ger.		Capt., Prison, Montluc Lyon (Fr.)	MURDER	U.S.
STOLLMANN	194411	M	Ger.		Capt., Army, Rouen (Fr.) 43 - 44	TORTURE	U.S.
STOLOFF	31436	M			Kriegslazarett, Heppenheim (Ger.)	MURDER	U.S.
STOLTE	139711	M	Ger.		Obergruppenfhr., SS-Stalag X B, C.C. Sandbostel (Ger.) 1.-5.45	MURDER	U.S.
STOLTEN	120555	M	Ger.		Oberscharfhr., SS, Gleiwitz (Ger.)	MURDER	U.S.
STOLTEN	131126	M	Ger.		Oberscharfhr., Leader, SS, C.C., Arnstadt (Ger.) 3.4.45	MURDER	U.S.
STOLTEN	137525	M	Ger.		Oberscharfhr., SS-Totenkopfstandarte, C.C. Norowitz,Dora (Ger.)	MURDER	U.S.
STOLTEN	258475	M			Leader, Labour - Service, Ohrdruf (Ger.) 12.44 - 4.45	MURDER	FR.
STOLTEN	306895	M	Ger.		Hauptscharfhr., Labour-office, C.C., Auschwitz (Pol.) 40	MURDER	U.S.
STOLTEN, Richard	142253	M	Ger.	8. 3.10	Oberscharfhr., SS, C.C., Seyboldsdorf,Vilsbiburg (Ger.) 28.4.45	MURDER	U.S.
STOLTON (or STOLL)	137526	M			Scharfhr., SS, C.C., Weimar-Buchenwald	MURDER	U.S.
STOLTZ	261024	M			Rttfhr., SS, C.C., Vaihingeh (Ger.) 8.44 - 4.45	WITNESS	U.S.
STOLTZ, Harry	174124	M			Civilian, Near Graz (Aust.) 10.2.45	TORTURE	U.K.
STOLTZ, Heinz	67685	M	Ger.		Sgt., Army, Lillestrom (Nor.)	TORTURE	FR.
STOLTZE (or STOLZE)	194230	M	Ger.	95	Capt., SS, 12. SS-Panz.Div. "Hitler Jugend",26.Pz.-Gren.Rgt.14.Coy. Caen (Fr.) 6.-7.44	PILLAGE	FR.
STOLZ	164726	M	Ger.	18. 7.84	Ortsgruppenleiter, NSDAP, Moulins,Metz (Fr.)	MURDER	FR.
STOLZ	252760	M	Ger.		Pvt., 100.Rgt.,Alpins, Feissons sur Isere (Fr.) 5.8.42	MURDER	FR.
STOLZ	256050	M	Ger.		W.O.,Forthe Kriegs-Navy,Werkendam-Z-H (Neth.)	MURDER	NETH.
STOLZ	261845	M	Ger.		Major, Fontaine Le Pin, Manche (Fr.) 12.7.44	MURDER	FR.

STO - STR

NAME	C.R.FILE NUMBER	SEX	NATIO-NALITY	DATE OF BIRTH	RANK OCCUPATION UNIT PLACE AND DATE OF CRIME	REASON WANTED	WANTED BY
STOLZ, Hermann	254732	M		13 or 15	Kapo, C.C. Dora, Nordhausen (Ger.)	BRUTALITY	FR.
STOLZ, Otto	156907	M	Ger.	15	Civilian, Ruesselsheim (Ger.) 25.8.44	MURDER	U.S.
STOLZE (see STOLTZE)	194230						
STOLZE	254872	M	Ger.		Lt., Army, 443.Jaeger-Rgt., Serbia (Yugo.) 3.10.41-25.12.41	MURDER	YUGO.
STOMBER	139213	M			Civilian (Ger.)	TORTURE	U.S.
STOMMEL, Willy	194383	M	Ger.		Civilian, Servant, Organ.Todt, Firm: Otto Menzel of Bittburg, Alle sur Semois (Bel.) 5.-6.40	PILLAGE	BEL.
STONZE, Hans	260084	M	Ger.		Pvt., Navy, Sore - Landes - (Fr.) 23.-24.7.44	MISC.CRIMES	FR.
STOPFER, Hans	258892	M	Ger.		Member, Gestapo, Valenciennes (Fr.) 40-44	MURDER	FR.
STORATH, Heinrich	255073	M			Uschfhr., SS, C.C. Ellrich, Nordhausen (Ger.)	MURDER	U.S.
STORCH (see WILFRIED LA CIQOYNE)	1526						
STORCH	72031	M			SD, C.C. Theresienstadt (Czech.) 12.41	TORTURE	U.S.
STORCH	132807	M	Ger.	02	Capt., Stalag 317-XVIIIc- C.C., Markt-Pongau (Ger.) 6.44-3.45	MISC.CRIMES	U.K.
STORCH	162898	M			Agent, SD, Chappes (Fr.) 28.7.44	MURDER	FR.
STORCH	306213	M	Ger.		Uschfhr., Small Fortress, C.C., Theresienstadt (Czech.) 1.10.38-44	MURDER	CZECH.
STORCHMANN, Fritz	1335				Pvt., Army, 194.GR.	MURDER	U.K.
STORCK	251876				Agent, Gestapo, Paris (Fr.) 12.8.44	MURDER	FR.
STOREDIDANO, Walter	919	M	Ger.		N.C.O., Army, Hazebrouck (Fr.) 1.9.44	MURDER	FR.
STORK	173257	M	Ger.	95	Hptschfhr., SS, Member, Gestapo, Noailles (Fr.)	MURDER	U.K.
STORK	180492	M	Ger.	05	Sgt., Kraftfahr-Bn.611, Tpt.Bn.4.Coy., Partina (It.) 13.4.44	INTERR.	U.K.
STORM, Willi	255075	M			Pvt., C.C. Ellrich, Nordhausen (Ger.)	MURDER	U.S.
STORMANN	132691	M			Richter, Ger. War Court, Besancon (Fr.) 18.9.44	MURDER	FR.
STORMS	255420	M	Ger.		Lt., Garnisoncommand.at Wemeldinge (Neth.) 20.9.44	MISC.CRIMES	NETH.
STORSBERG	174218	M			Capt., Stalag VI A, C.C., Hemer (Ger.)	TORTURE	U.S.
STOSSARD (see STOSSIER)	137075						
STOSSEL	251881	M	Ger.		Crim.Secretary, 1.Abt.,IV.E, Sipo, Brussels (Bel.) 40-45	SUSPECT	BEL.
STOSSIER (or STOSSARD)	137075	M	Ger.	90	Lt.Col., Stalag IV B, Army, Cmdt., Muehlberg (Ger.) 1.1.44	MISC.CRIMES	U.K.
STOTACH	257464	M			SS-Sgt., C.C. Nordhausen (Ger.)	MURDER	U.S.
STOTZ	189175	M			Sturmschfhr., SS, Gestapo, Montauban, Commander, Montauban-Montech (Fr.) 26.7.44	MURDER	FR.
STOTZEL	174217	M	Ger.		Capt., Stalag VI A, C.C., Hemer (Ger.) 41-45	TORTURE	U.S.
STOTZEL, Richard	189605	M			Cmdt., Police-Gebiets-Kommandantur, Pozaverac - Serbia (Yugo.) 41-43	MURDER	YUGO.
STOTZEM	137081	M	Ger.		Pvt., SD, C.C., Wesselring (Ger.)	WITNESS	U.K.
STOTZER, Raimund	262222	M	Ger.	31.10.19	Usturmfhr., SS, 4.Coy.,1.Platoon, 51.Armoured Bde., Breviandes, Bucheres, Ste.Savine, La Riviere de Corps-Troyes (Fr.)22.-25.8.44	BRUTALITY	FR.
STOVER	31439	M			Lt., Waffen-SS, C.C. Amersfoort (Neth.) 42	WITNESS	U.S.
STOVES, Wilhelm	259542	M	Ger.		Rector, Lengerich (Ger.) 8.44	WITNESS	U.S.
STOVHASE, Karl	901486	M	Ger.		Rottfhr., SS, No. 7437 C.C., Buchenwald (Ger.) 16.5.38-9.10.45	MURDER	BEL.
STOW, Liselotte	194065	F	Ger.		Surveillante, C.C., Ravensbrueck (Ger.)	TORTURE	FR.
STOWASSER	132826	M	Ger.		Capt., Army, near Ostrowo (Pol.) 15.7.43	MISC.CRIMES	U.K.
STOXEN, Wilhelm	192846	M	Ger.	23.4.06	Police-Sgt., Reichsjustizministerium,Feldstraflager Nord, C.C., Finmark (Nor.) 4.45	MURDER	NOR.
STOYA (or STOYER)	180493	M	Ger.	06 or 10	Lt., 51.or 61.Flak-Bn., Montemignato (It.) 21.6.44	MURDER	U.K.
STRAATMAN, Franz Karl	122907	M	Ger.		Agent, Gestapo, Bensheim (Ger.) 2.45	MURDER	U.S.
STRABE (or STABE, B.)	254233	M	Ger.		Major, Field H.Q.1018, Orvieto (It.) 10.43	INTERR.	U.K.
STRABMANN, Theodor	254931	M		20.6.04	Pvt., C.C., Harzungen, Nordhausen (Ger.)	MURDER	U.S.
STRACH, Wilhelm	29730	M	Ger.		Dr., Landgerichtsrat, Public-Official, Prague (Czech.) 40	MISC.CRIMES	CZECH.
STRACHER	141326	M	Ger.		Cpl., Guard, Army, 48.Working-Bn., Kundorf, Posen (Pol.) 7.41	TORTURE	U.K.
STRACK	257711	M	Ger.		Gen.Major, Army, Cacak (Yugo.) 27.6.44	INTERR.	YUGO.
STRACK, Gerhard	255958	M	Ger.	06	Oschfhr., SS, Lodz (Pol.) 40	INTERR.	POL.
STRACKA, Josef	254969	M			Pvt., C.C. Dora, Nordhausen (Ger.)	MURDER	U.S.
STRACKE, Heinrich	254925	M		11.4.13	Flyer, C.C. Ellrich, Nordhausen (Ger.)	MURDER	U.S.
STRADE	161796	M	Ger.		Civilian, Farmer, Teplitz (Czech.)	WITNESS	U.S.
STRADNER, Karl	124534	M	Ger.		Policeman, Klagenfurt, Villach (Aust.) 10.-11.44	MURDER	U.S.
STRAEHELE, Karl	173149	M	Ger.		Pol.Leader, C.C., Schirmeck-Gaggenau (Fr., Ger.) 44	WITNESS	U.K.
STRAHAMMER	187545	M	Ger.	83 or 85	Cpl., 65.Inf.Div., O.C.Rgt.146, Cisapass (It.) 3.10.43	WITNESS	U.K.
STRAHBERGER, Karl	261120	M	Ger.	87	Crim.Inspector, Gestapo, Pilsen (Czech.) 39-40	MURDER	CZECH.
STRAHLBERG	901487	M	Ger.	29.10.77	Hptschfhr., SS-Staff-Sgt., C.C., Buchenwald (Ger.) 16.5.38-9.10.43	MURDER	BEL.
STRAHLEMDORF (or STRAHLENDORF)	147024	M	Ger.		Cpl., 11.Pz.Div., Kampfgruppe "Wilde", Rox (Fr.) 44	MURDER	FR.
STRAHLER	124535	M			Col., Army, Maehr.Trusbau (Czech.)	MURDER	U.K.
STRAHLER, Robert	251351	M	Ger.		Sgt., Parachute-Coy., Erauy (Fr.) 3.8.44	MURDER	FR.
STRAK, Stephan	260526	M	Ger.	14.7.22	Sturmmann, SS, Guard, Waffen-SS, C.C., Leitmeritz (Czech.) 9.44-5.45	TORTURE	CZECH.
STRAMMER	167883	M	Ger.		Lt., Army, 104.Gren.Rgt., La Rochette, Crest (Fr.) 7.-8.44	MURDER	FR.
STRANDERS, Vivian	140855	M	Ger.	8.4.08	SS-Major, SS-Public-Official	WITNESS	U.K.
STRANEL	180872	M	Ger.		Sgt., Feldgend., Locmine (Fr.) 7.-8.44	TORTURE	FR.
STRANGE, Rudi	189113	M			Sgt., Army, Hafenschutz-Coy.,Port Vendres nr.Salec (Fr.) 20.8.44	MURDER	FR.
STRANSKY, Max	10357	M			Dr., Staatsanwalt, Public-Official, Opava (Czech.) 40	MURDER	CZECH.
STRASDIN, Hans	124322	M			Pvt., Army, 1.SS-Pz.Div.,2.Coy.1.SS-Pz.Rgt.,Malmedy (Bel.) 17.12.44	MURDER	U.S.
STRASS, Max	254738	M		18.2.05	Rottfhr., C.C.Harzungen, Nordhausen (Ger.)	MURDER	U.S.
STRASSBERGER, F.	192876	M	Ger.		Schupo, C.C. Falstad nr. Drontheim (Nor.) 6.-8.42	MURDER	NOR.
STRASSBURGER	126399	M	Ger.		Gruppenfhr., SS, Gestapo, Head of Amt IV, Dr., (Pol.)	MISC.CRIMES	U.S.
STRASSE	307210	M	Ger.		Lt., Dienststelle F.P.No.58042 G, Zoelen (Neth.) 24.10.44	TORTURE	NETH.
STRASSENBERGER	192877	M	Ger.		Wachtmeister, Schupo, C.C. Falstad nr. Drontheim (Nor.) 41-44	WITNESS	NOR.
STRASSER	10958	M	Ger.		Oschfhr., SS. In charge of Mot.Pool, C.C.Natzweiler (Fr.) 42	TORTURE	U.K., CZECH.
STRASSER	31555	M	Ger.		Sgt., Waffen-SS, C.C. Struthof (Fr.)	MISC.CRIMES	FR.
STRASSER	164727	M			Lt., Army, Brionde (Fr.) 22.6.44	MURDER	FR.
STRASSER	180882	M			Member, SS, C.C., Mauthausen (Aust.)	MURDER	FR.
STRASSER	254859	M			Cpl., C.C. Ellrich, Nordhausen (Ger.)	MURDER	U.S.
STRASSGESCHWANDER	143138	M	Ger.		Cpl., 1.SS-Panz.Div."Adolf Hitler",2.Pz.Rgt.,3.Bn.12.Coy.,Stavelot Malmedy (Bel.) 22.-23.12.44	MURDER	U.S.
STRASSNER	149769	M			Cpl., C.C. Stavern (Nor.) 11.43	MURDER	NOR.
STRATENBURG	126609	M	Ger.		Civilian, C.C., Hagen (Ger.) 40-45	MURDER	U.S.
STRATMANN, Kurt	194384	M			SS-Pz.Rgt."Deutschland", Achens (Bel.) 7.9.44	MURDER	BEL.
STRATMANN (or STRATTMANN,Rud.)	257926	M			Pvt., 150.Panz.Bde., Meuse-Bridge-Antwerp (Bel.) 12.44	MISC.CRIMES	U.S.
STRAUB	6157	M			Pvt., Army, C.C., Thorn (Pol.)	MURDER	U.K.

NAME	C.R.FILE NUMBER	SEX	NATIO-NALITY	DATE OF BIRTH	RANK OCCUPATION UNIT PLACE AND DATE OF CRIME	REASON WANTED	WANTED BY
STRAUB, Franz	124748	M	Ger.	95	Sturmbannfhr., SS, Crim.Director, Gestapo, Brussels (Bel.) 40-44	MURDER	BEL.
STRAUB, Franz	250493	M	Ger.		SS-Mann, C.C., Auschwitz, Birkenau (Ger.) 12.42	MURDER	YUGO.
STRAUB, Genhilf	152138	M	Ger.	24.10.15	Chenebier, Etobon (Fr.) 27.9.44	MURDER	FR.
STRAUB, Marcus	254420	M	Ger.	12. 5.10	Sgt., 5.Techn.Bn., 3.Coy., Saint-Macaire (Fr.) 24.8.44	BRUTALITY	FR.
STRAUB, Peter	141074	M	Ger.		Hptschfhr., SS, Conc.Camp (Crematorium) Natzweiler (Fr.) 1.,2.9.44	MURDER	U.K.
STRAUBE	251880	M	Ger.		Cpl., F.P.Nr.23434 C, Balan (Fr.) 4.9.44	MURDER	FR.
STRAUCH (see STRAUSS)	1336						
STRAUCH (see HAUCH)	147323						
STRAUCH	156913	M	Ger.		Chief, Tribunal Military, Tours (Fr.) 43	MURDER	FR.
STRAUCH,	251357	M	Ger.		Dr., Sturmbannfhr., SS, Sipo and Waffen-SS, State Service, Baranowieze (Pol.) 43	INTERR.	POL.
STRAUCH	306290	M	Ger.		Member, Gestapo at Trencin, C.C., Oswiecim, Birkenau (Pol.) 39-45	MURDER	CZECH.
STRAUCH, Eduard	187337	M	Ger.		Obersturmbannfhr., SS, SD, Gestapo, Luettich (Bel.) 8.44	MURDER	BEL.
STRAUCH, Fritz	254742	M		25. 4.02	Sgt., C.C. Harzungen, Nordhausen (Ger.)	MURDER	U.S.
STRAUCH, Kurt	142246	M		10	Standartenfhr., SS, SD, Minsk (Sov.Un.)	MURDER	U.S.
STRAUCH, Peter	240067	M	Ger.	96	Head-Operator-Fuehrer of DASD, Abwehr-Nachr.Rgt.506,6.Coy., Bad Wildungen (Ger.) 3.45	MISC.CRIMES	U.S.
STRAUCK, Robert	254410	M	Ger.		Pvt., 5.Rgt. of Parachutistes, Savannes (Fr.) 31.8.44	MURDER	FR.
STRAUD (see STROUD)	72018						
STRAUHOFF	188495	M	Ger.		Member, Gestapo, Luxembourg (Grand Duchy) (Lux.)	MISC.CRIMES	LUX.
STRAUMEYER, Karl	194381	M	Ger.		Hptsturmfhr., SS-Div."Das Reich", Bra sur Lienne (Bel.)	MURDER	BEL.
STRAUS, Hartmond	124709	M	Ger.		Rottfhr., 1.SS-Aufkl.Bn.,Leibstandarte "Adolf Hitler", 1.Panz.Gren.Div., 1.Ers.Bn.Eng.Platoon, Renardmont Stavelot (Bel.) 19.12.44	MURDER	BEL.
STRAUS, Julius	181119	M	Ger.		Rottfhr., SS-Leibstandarte "Adolf Hitler.", Aufkl.Abt., Stavelot Renardmont (Bel.)	MURDER	BEL.
STRAUSBOURG	128793	M	Ger.		Feldw., Stalag VI J. W.O.D., Gerrisheim (Ger.) 5.44-1.45	TORTURE	U.K.
STRAUSS (or STRAUCH)	1336	M		15	Capt., Aufkl.Abt.26, 26.Panz.Div. (It.) 23.8.44	MISC.CRIMES	U.K.
STRAUSS	36629	M	Ger.		Guard, Army, 805.Bn.Coy., Stalag 13 C (Ger.) 5.1.45	TORTURE	U.K.
STRAUSS	124069	M	Ger.		N.C.O., 438.Lds.Schtz.Bn., C.C., Gursdorf (Ger.) 10.44-11.44	TORTURE	U.K.
STRAUSS	259160	M	Ger.		Oschfhr., SS-Div."Prinz Eugen", Niksic Distr.Montenegro (Yugo.)5.-6.43	MISC.CRIMES	YUGO.
STRAUSS, Adolf	12316	M	Ger.		N.C.O., 110.or 111.Pz.Gren.Rgt.,2.Coy., Albine (Fr.) 29.6.44	MURDER	FR.
STRAUSS, Fritz	126401	M	Ger.		Pvt., Sicherungs-Rgt.192, Mont Lucon (Fr.) 13.8.44 ?	MURDER	U.S.
STRAUSS, Gerhard	255422	M	Ger.		Flyer, C.C.Ellrich, Nordhausen (Ger.)	MURDER	U.S.
STRAUSS, Johann	169506	M	Ger.	17	Cpl., Lds.Schtz.Bn.438., 4.Coy., Gursdorf (Ger.) 10.44	TORTURE	U.K.
STRAUSS, Josef	135320	M			Civilian, Biertringen (Lux.) 7.44	WITNESS	U.S.
STRAUSS, Rudolf	254740	M			Pvt., C.C. Ellrich, Nordhausen (Ger.)	MURDER	U.S.
STRAUSS, Xaver	129993	M	Ger.		Hptsturmfhr.,.Waffen-SS, Conc.Camp. Mauthausen (Aust.) 41-45	MURDER	U.S.
STRAUT (see STROUD)	72018						
STRAYHER, Jacques	300389	M	Ger.		Officer-commanding, Ger.Detachment stationed at Bretignolles, Vendes, Bretignolles-sur-Mer Venedes (Fr.) 22.8.44	MURDER	FR.
STRAZER (see STRAZZER)	256181						
STRAZMANN, Curt	252751	M	Ger.		Pvt., Airforce, Soesterberg (Ger.)	PILLAGE	NETH.
STRAZZER (or STRAZER)	256181	M	Ger.		Organ.Todt, Muehldorf Area (Ger.)	WITNESS	U.S.
STREB	253998	M	Ger.	01 - 06	Sgt. - Major, Marine-Bord-Flak-Coy., Bogliaslo (It.) 12.12.44	MURDER	U.K.
STREBER	254874	M	Ger.		Capt., Army, Nuernberg-Langwasser (Ger.) 41-45	MURDER	YUGO.
STRECHER, Fritz	180784	M	Ger.		198.I.Div.469.I.R.,2.Bn., Le Tholy (Fr.) 19.11.44	MURDER	FR.
STRECKE	194420	M	Ger.		Sgt., Feldgend., Ploermel (Fr.) 18.6.44	TORTURE	FR.
STRECKE, Walter	254741	M			Rottfhr., C.C. Dora, Nordhausen (Ger.)	MURDER	U.S.
STRECKENBACH	921	M		03	Bde.Fhr., SS, SD, SS-Befehlshaber, C.C., Buchenwald,Crakow (Ger.,Pol.) 39-40, 40-45	MURDER	U.S., BEL. POL.
STRECKENBACH	166154	M	Ger.	95	Standartenfhr., SS, SD (Pol.) 39	MISC.CRIMES	U.S.
STRECKER, Bruno	259664	M		10. 5.05	Rottfhr., SS, Gestapo, Area of Angers, Maine and Loire (Fr.) 42-44	MISC.CRIMES	FR.
STRECKFUSS, Heinz	257981	M			Capt., 150.Pz.Bde., Meuse-Bridge-Antwerp (Bel.) 12.44	MISC.CRIMES	U.S.
STREESE	189800	M	Ger.	89	Usturmfhr., SS, C.C., Belsen (Ger.)	MURDER	YUGO.
STREGE	190214	M	Ger.		Head, Schupo., Stanislawow (Pol.) 8.41-10.42	MURDER	POL.
STREHE (see STREHLE)	922						
STREHLE	167233	F	Ger.		Member, Civ., Einsatz Rosenberg, Admin.Staff (Fr.) 40-44	PILLAGE	FR.
STREHLE (or STREHE)	922	M	Ger.	00	Osturmfhr., SS, SD, Sipo, Falstad, Aalesund (Nor.) 41-44	TORTURE	NOR., U.S.
STREHLE	156585	M	Ger.	90	Col., Oflag VIII F and later of Oflag C.C., Brunswick, Maehrisch-Trubau (Czech.)	MURDER	U.K.
STREHLKE	251945	M	Ger.		Capt., Bn.Fhr., Div.Herm.Goering,4.Rgt.Parachute, 1.Bn., Helchteren (Bel.) 5. and 11.9.44	PILLAGE	BEL.
STREHLOW	192879	M	Ger.		Col., Police-Rgt.27, C.C., Falstad, near Drontheim (Nor.) 41-44	MURDER	NOR.
STREIBECK	136208	M	Ger.		Lt., Airforce, 3.Rgt., Blenod Les Touls (Fr.) 7.44	MURDER	FR.
STREIBEL	306322	M	Ger.		Former Station Master or Employee at the station of Breslau, St.Germain des Fosses (Allier) Billy-(Allier) (Fr.) 8.44-28.8.44	PILLAGE	FR.
STREICH	1337	M	Ger.		Lt., Army, 9.P.Gr. 6.Coy.	MISC.CRIMES	U.K.
STREICHER	177605	M	Ger.	95	Army, Stalag XVIII, C.C., Markt Pongau (Ger.) 6.44	TORTURE	U.K.
STREICHER	188003	M	Ger.		Civilian, Mallinitz (Aust.) 8.41-4.43	TORTURE	U.K.
STREIN, Hermann	152137	M		4. 4.23	Chenebier Etobon (Fr.)	MURDER	FR.
STREISVISSER	141377	M			Chief, SS, Conc.Camp, Mauthausen (Aust.)	MURDER	FR.
STREIT	301236	M			Dr., Militaer-Verwaltungsoberrat, Abwehr-Beauftragter, Abwehr, Brussels (Bel.) 40-44	MURDER	BEL.
STREIT	306291	M	Ger.		Member, Gestapo at Trencin, C.C., Oswiecim, Birkenau (Pol.) 39-45	MURDER	CZECH.
STREIT, Emil	189553	M	Ger.	85 - 87	Civilian, Trieben (Aust.) 5.5.45	MURDER	U.S.
STREITWEISER	165972	M	Ger.		Hangman and Executioner, C.C., Sachsenhausen (Ger.)	MURDER	U.S.
STREITWIESSER, Toni	129992	M			Osturmfhr., SS, C.C., Mauthausen (Aust.) 41-45	MURDER	U.S.
STREJA	254743	M			Pvt., C.C., Mackenrode, Nordhausen (Ger.)	MURDER	U.S.
STREK	189781	M	Ger.		Major, Army, Feldzeug-Bn.18, Krasne White Ruthen (Sov.Un.) 19.3.43	MURDER	U.K.
STREKKER	159420	M			Engineer, Organ.Todt, Chief of Group Kirkenes (Nor.) 43-44	MURDER	NOR.
STRELLER	10359	M			Public Prosecutor, Ger.Country Court, Brno (Czech.) 40	MURDER	CZECH.
STRELOW	258155	M			1.SS-Rgt."Adolf Hitler" - Oschfhr. - 1.Coy., Wanne near Stavelot (Bel.) 19.-21.12.44	MURDER	BEL.
STREMME, Willy	121436	M	Ger.		Usturmfhr., SS-Pz.Div."Hitler-Jugend" F.P.Nr.58497, Hardencourt (Fr.) 4.44-5.44	MURDER	FR.

NAME	C.R.FILE NUMBER	SEX	NATIO-NALITY	DATE OF BIRTH	RANK OCCUPATION UNIT PLACE AND DATE OF CRIME	REASON WANTED	WANTED BY
STREMPEL, Herbert	31444	M			Lt.,Waffen SS, 2.Bn.Geb.A.R. "R.H."	MURDER	U.S.
STRENGER, Willi	262223	M	Ger.	30.7.?	Oscharfhr., Gestapo, Rennes (Fr.) 43-44	MISC.CRIMES	FR.
STRENZEL	260089	M	Ger.		Gendarm, Unit Russ.Ger. Div. "Oberland" Massif du Vercors, Isere and Drôme (Fr.) 20.7.-5.8.44	SUSPECT	FR.
STREU	156883	M	Ger.		Major, Panz.Gren.Rgt. 192, 21.Panz.Div., Sessenheim (Fr.) 1.45	MURDER	U.S.
STREUFERT	257982	M			Sgt., 150.Panz.Bde., Meuse-Bridge Antwerp (Bel.) 12.44	MISC.CRIMES	U.S.
STREZELENSKI	302002	M	Ger.		Pvt., Guard, Botn C.C. nr.Rognan (Nor.) 8.42-45	MURDER	YUGO.
STRICKER	124070	M			Capt., Stalag C.C. Markt Pongau (Aust.) 6.44-45	MISC.CRIMES	U.K.
STRIFGEL	129995	M			Sgt., Waffen SS,Panz.Div.Totenkopf C.C. Mauthausen (Aust.) 41-45	MURDER	U.S.
STRIEGEL	147023	M	Ger.		SS-Mann, SS Panz.Div."Das Reich", Tulle (Fr.) 44	MURDER	FR.
STRIGEL or STRLEGEL	261405	M	Ger.		Lt.,Gend.of Bethune, Hinges (Fr.) 12.8.44	TORTURE	FR.
STRIEPPEL	152123	M	Ger.	12	Osturmfhr., SS, C.C. Hamburg - Neuengamme (Ger.)	MURDER	U.K.
STRIEZEL	12317	M	Ger.		Lt., Army, 110.or 111.Panz.Gren.Rgt., Gourdon (Fr.) 29.6.44	MURDER	FR.
STRIGEL	180884	M	Ger.		SS Hptscharfhr., Comm.Melk C.C. Mauthausen (Aust.) 44	MURDER	FR.
STRIPPEL or SHIPPEL	10960	M			SS Rottfhr., C.C.Weimar, Buchenwald (Ger.) 38-44	TORTURE	U.S.
STRIPPEL	253485	M	Ger.		SS Osturmfhr., Lublin (Pol.) 40-44	MISC.CRIMES	POL.
STRIPPEL, A.	300688	M	Ger.		Uscharfhr., Bloc-leader, C.C. Neuengamme (Ger.) from 40	MISC.CRIMES	BEL.
STRIPPEL, Arnold	142233	M	Ger.	10	Usturmfhr., C.C. Buchenwald (Ger.) until 39	TORTURE	U.S.
STRISCH, Ferdinand	251883	M	Ger.	13.12.98	Forester, state service, Pilsen (Czech.) 39-45	TORTURE	CZECH.
STRIZ, Anton or VOJTA or JAS	258098	M	Ger.	6.11.15	Informer, Gestapo, Kyjov (Czech.) 39-45	MISC.CRIMES	CZECH.
STRLEGEL see STRIEGEL	261405						
STROBEL	1748	M	Ger.		SS Oscharfhr., C.C. Dachau (Ger.)	TORTURE	U.K.
STROBEL	254725	M	Ger.		Org. Todt, Rosny - Bois (Fr.) 20.8.44	MURDER	FR.
STROBEL, Ernst Friedr.	256540	M	Ger.	23.7.00	Factory worker, Nordhausen (Ger.)	MURDER	U.S.
STROBEL, Karl	259323	M			Oberfhr., SA, Camp Thekla nr.Leipzig (Ger.) 18.4.45	MURDER	U.S.
STROBEL, Valentin	31442	M	Ger.		Civ. Servant, post-office, Weissenbach (Ger.) 6.44	MURDER	U.S.
STROBER	126608	M	Ger.		Crim.secretary, SIPO, Aachen (Ger.) 9.8.44	MISC.CRIMES	U.S.
STROBI	190307	M			C.C. Dachau (Ger.)	MURDER	U.S.
STROBL	10361	M	Ger.		Obersturmbannfhr., SS, C.O., Garrison Benesov (Czech.) 38-45	TORTURE	CZECH.
STROBL	147022	M	Ger.		SS Mann, SS Panz.Div."Das Reich", Tulle (Fr.) 44	MURDER	FR.
STROBL	190351	M	Ger.		Employee, C.C. Muenchen Stalag VII A (Ger.) winter 41 - 42	TORTURE	U.K.
STROBL, Hans	252765	M	Ger.	12.7.08	SS Scharfhr., Crim.secretary, Crim.police Kolin (Czech.) 39-45	MISC.CRIMES	CZECH.
STROBL, Kurt	179168	M	Ger.	15	SS Hptsturmfhr., Capt., SS Ordnungspol. Kradschuetzen-Coy., Stavern (Nor.)	MURDER	NOR.
STROBLE	67687	M	Ger.		Col., POW Camp Oflag 79, C.C. Bary, Brunswick (It.,Ger.) 5.-9.44	MURDER	U.K.
STROEBEL	923	M	Ger.		Gestapo, Nazi prison official in Maastricht (Neth.) 1.-4.44	TORTURE	NETH.
STROEBEL	137528	M	Ger.		Hptscharfhr., SS, C.C. Buchenwald, Weimar (Ger.)	TORTURE	U.S.
STROEBEL	156582	M	Ger.	10	Capt.,commander of SD Maastricht, Helden (Neth.) 10.8.44	MURDER	NETH.
STROESSNREUTHER	28745	M	Ger.		Lt.Col., Army IV a 20.staff, Finmark (Nor.) 10.-11.44	MURDER	NOR.
STROFBECH, Gerd	256492	M			Oberbootsmaat, German Navy, Nor.	MURDER	NOR.
STROHFAHRT	125609	M			SS Rottfhr., SS Panz.Div."Hitler-Jugend",1.Pz.Aufkl.Abt.12, Ascq (Fr.) 1.4.44	MISC.CRIMES	FR.
STROHKIRCHEN, Werner	252764	M	Ger.	15	Pvt. Guard at C.C. Wilhelmshaven, Lueneburg (Ger.) 7.-10.4.45	MURDER	U.K.
STROHLER	301368	M	Ger.		SS Staff-Sgt., Kommandostab at Mauthausen CC. (Aust.) 11.42-5.45	MURDER	FR.
STROHMAIER, Richard	156914	M	Ger.		Employee, Gestapo, Goeppingen (Ger.)	MURDER	FR.
STROHMAYER, Josef	254870	M	Ger.		SS Hptsturmfhr., SS and Gestapo, Maribor (Yugo.) 44	MURDER	YUGO.
STRCHMEYER, Karl	188497	M	Ger.		Inspector, Gestapo, police, Luxembourg (Lux.)	MISC.CRIMES	LUX.
STROHMEYER, Karl	194381	M	Ger.		Hptscharfhr., SS-Div. "Das Reich", Bra sur Lienne (Bel.)	MURDER	BEL.
STROHNIG see STROENIG	253163						
STROENIG or STROHNIG	253163	M	Ger.		SS Scharfhr., C.C. Buchenwald (Ger.) 42-45	MURDER	U.S.
STROINK, Hermann	139219	M	Ger.	13	SS Hptscharfhr., work detail leader, C.C. Lublin (Pol.) 42-43	TORTURE	U.S.
STROK	254417	M	Ger.		Org. Todt, Rosny-Bois (Fr.) 20.8.44	INTERR.	FR.
STROLER, Karl	132369	M	Ger.	90	Capt., Army, Oflag XIII B, C.C. Hammelburg (Ger.) 44-45	MURDER	U.S.
STRONIK, Hermann	253487	M	Ger.		SS Hptscharfhr., Lublin (Pol.) 40-44	MISC.CRIMES	POL.
STROOP, Juergen	924	M	Ger.	26.9.95	SS Bde.Fhr., Major - General, Waffen SS, state service police, Gestapo, Wiesbaden, Koblenz, Metz, Warsaw (Ger. Pol.)	MISC.CRIMES	U.S. POL. GRC.
STROOP, Karl	62397	M	Ger.		Major - General, chief of SS and police, Baden (Ger. Grc.)	TORTURE	U.N.W.C.C.
STRORGH	162892	M	Ger.		Capt., Abwehr, C.C. Markt Pongau (Aust.)	TORTURE	FR.
STROTH, Albert	250356	M	Ger.		Help overseer, SS Penitentiary Nord-Nor. 6.42-45	MURDER	YUGO.
STROTHARM, Fritz	149131	M			Rottfhr., SS Panz.Div.Leibstandarte "Adolf Hitler" 2.Panz.Rgt. 3.Bn. 12.Coy., Stavelot, Malmedy (Bel.) 22.-23.12.44	MURDER	U.S.
STROUD or STRAUD or STRAUT	72018	M	Ger.	09	Pvt., Army 1-515.Coy. H.Q. Sosnowice, Grutewasser (Pol.) 19.2.45	MURDER	U.K.
STROWEL	138289	M	Ger.		Pvt., 7.Inf.Div., Garbeck (Ger.) 1.4.45	MURDER	FR.
STRUBE, Karl	254744	M			Pvt., C.C. Harzungen, Nordhausen (Ger.)	MURDER	U.S.
STRUCHWITZ see GRUSCHWITZ, Paul	252324						
STRUCK	191907	M	Ger.		Pvt., Eisenbahn-Art.Bn. 717, St.Andries, Varsenare, Les Bruegge (Bel.) 4.9.44	MURDER	BEL.
STRUCK	252758				Secretary of customs, Evian les Bains (Fr.) 16.1.44	INTERR.	FR.
STRUCK	305812	M	Ger.		N.C.O., Camp-cmdt., Oflag VI C, Disciplinary chief of Camp Orderlies, Osnabrueck-Ewersheide (Ger.) 41-45	MURDER	YUGO.
STRUCKHARDT	192880	M	Ger.		Schupo, C.C. Falstad nr.Drontheim (Nor.) 6.-8.42	MURDER	NOR.
STRUCKMANN	254745	M	Ger.		Pvt., C.C. Ellrich, Nordhausen (Ger.)	MURDER	U.S.
STRUCOVSKY, Josef	260710	M	Ger.	12.1.11	Member SA, SD, Praha (Czech.) 41	MISC.CRIMES	CZECH.
STRUEBLING, Hans	125243	M	Ger.		Uscharfhr., Gestapo, Berlin (Ger.)	TORTURE	U.S.
STRUEMF or STRUMF, Henry	67688	M	Ger.	00	610. Landesschuetzen-Bn. 2.Coy. Army, C.C. Losendori Stalag 20 B (Ger.) 2.4.42	TORTURE	U.K.
STRUING	121437	M	Ger.		SS Hptscharfhr.,C.C. Buchenwald (Ger.)	TORTURE	FR.
STRUK	251350	M	Ger.		Guard, Fort prison, Siegburg (Ger.) 41-45	MURDER	FR.
STRULLER, Karl	129990	M			Stabsscharfhr., SS Panz.Div.Totenkopf, C.C. Mauthausen (Aust.) 41-45	MURDER	U.S.
STRULLER, Otto	257923	M		6.11.12	Pvt., 150.Panz.Bde., Meuse-Bridge Antwerp (Bel.) 12.44	MISC.CRIMES	U.S.
STRUMBERGER, Josef	261404	M	Ger.		SS Mann, Guard, C.C. Auschwitz (Pol.) 43-44	BRUTALITY	POL.
STRUMF, Henry see STRUEMF	67688						
STRUNK	251348	M	Ger.		Overseer, Prison Siegburg (Ger.) 7.41-45	TORTURE	FR.
STRUNK, Paul	240068	M	Ger.	10	Pvt., Nachrichten-Rgt.506, SD official, Bad Wildungen (Ger.) 3.45	MISC.CRIMES	U.S.

NAME	C.R.FILE NUMBER	SEX	NATIO-NALITY	DATE OF BIRTH	RANK OCCUPATION UNIT PLACE AND DATE OF CRIME	REASON WANTED	WANTED BY
STRUNK, Richard	254687	M			98 Army, Gerardmer (Fr.) 29.5.44	WITNESS	U.S.
STRUPAT, Friedrich	254746	M			Pvt.,C.C.Ellrich,Nordhausen (Ger.)	MURDER	U.S.
STRUPP	254733	F	Ger.		Employee,Volkswagen-Factory,Fallersleben (Ger.)	WITNESS	U.S.
STRUSCHKA	181120	M	Ger.		SS-Mann,I.SS-Panz.Div."Adolf Hitler",1 Ers.-Bn.,2 Zug, Parfondry,Stavelot (Bel.) 18.-22.12.44	MURDER	U.S.
STRUSS, Xavier	253488	M	Ger.		Hptsturmfhr.,SS,C.C.Mauthausen (Ger.)	MURDER	U.S.
STRUUCK	194419	M	Ger.		Cpl.,Gestapo,Pornichet (Fr.)	MISC.CRIMES	FR.
STRUVE	156040	M	Ger.	00	Dir. of Labor office,Gen.Gouv.Polen,Gouvernement official(Pol.)43-44	MISC.CRIMES	U.S.
STRUVE, Gustav	258442	M	Ger.	7.7.99	Dr.,Chief,Cultur-Div. of the German Embassy,Warsaw (Pol.) 37-39	MISC.CRIMES	POL.
STRYJ, Konrad	260468	M		28.12.07	White Collar-worker,Rottfhr.,SS,Allg.SS,C.C.Auschwitz (Pol.) 42-45	BRUTALITY	POL.
STUBBE	186191	M			Chief,C.C.Sachsenhausen (Ger.)	TORTURE	FR.
STUBBS	192844	M	Ger.		Sturmschfhr.,SS,S.D.,C.C.Falsted,Drontheim (Nor.) 41-45	MURDER	NOR.
STUBBS, Werner	240069	M		12.1.18	Official,L.Abwehr-Amt,Abwehr-Nachr.Regt.506,Belzig (Ger.) 44	MISC.CRIMES	U.S.
STUBE, Erich	251879	M	Ger.		Osturmfhr.,SS,S.D.,Toulouse (Fr.) 11.42-8.44	PILLAGE	FR.
STUBEN	68917	M	Ger.		Sgt.,Army,85 Inf.Div.(Potsdam-Inf.Div.),2 Inf.-Regt.,1 Btty., 1 Coy.,Hasselfelde (Ger.) 18.4.45	MURDER	U.S.
STUBENRAUCH	926	M	Ger.		Sgt.,Army,738 Regt.,2 Bn.,Bosnia,Montenegro, 7.43	MURDER	YUGO.
STUBER, Heinrich	189116	M			Civilian,Toulon (Fr.) 25.8.44	MURDER	FR.
STUBINGER	192843	M	Ger.		Member,Army,Firing Sqad.(Nor.) 7.4.45	MISC.CRIMES	NOR.
STUBNER	167234	F	Ger.		Civ. Servant,Ostgebietsministerium,Einsatzstab Rosenberg (Fr.) 40-44	PILLAGE	FR.
STUBNER (see STUBZER)	256182						
STUBZER (or STUENER,H.W.)	256182	M	Ger.		Organisation Todt,Muhldorf Area (Ger.)	WITNESS	U.S.
STUCK	254413	M	Ger.		Sturmmann,S.D.,Toulouse (Fr.) 11.42-8.44	INTERR.	FR.
STUCKA (or STUKA)	126980	M			Zugwachtmeister,Camp Schirmeck (Ger.)	TORTURE	FR.
STUCKEL, Wilhelm	260082	M	Ger.		Uschfhr.,SS,Slave-labour-camp,Botn near Rognon (Nor.)8.42-5.45	BRUTALITY	YUGO.
STUCKLE	301369	M	Ger.		Pvt.,Region of Heimerdingen (Ger.) 3.4.45	MURDER	FR.U.
STUCKLER	300391	M	Ger.		Sturmbannfhr.,2 SS-Pz.Div.,H.Q.,La Roche,Wibrin, 10.-12.1.45	MURDER	BEL.
STUCKMANN, August	11872	M	Ger.		Oschfhr.,W-SS,Employed Gestapo H.Q.,Lillehammer (Nor.) 40	TORTURE	NOR.
STUD, Erich Albert	260659	M		89	Lt.General,Army	WITNESS	U.S.
STUDEMANN	254729	M	Ger.	15	Cmdt.,Paratrooper-Army,Tiel (Neth.) 3.-4.45	PILLAGE	NETH.
STUDENT	121434	M	Ger.		Oberwachtmeister,C.C.Bochum,Esterwegen (Ger.)	TORTURE	BEL.
STUDENT	189782	M	Ger.		Lt.Col.,7 Luftlande-Div.,Zeehaven,Rotterdam,Dortrecht s.Gravendeel (Neth.) 13.5.40,15.5.42-1.4.45	MISC.CRIMES	NETH.
STUDENT	254249	M	Ger.		Lt.,Feldbekleidungsamt der Luftwaffe I-XI,Enschede (Neth.) 42-45	INTERR.	NETH.
STUDHOFF	192050	M	Ger.	93	Dr.,Civ.,Lusohkau near Waldau (Pol.) 27.4.44	MURDER	U.K.
STUEBER, Josef	118097	M	Ger.		Major,Regierungsrat,Gestapo-Chef,SS,Stalag Luft III,Oppeln(Ger)4.43	MURDER	U.S.
STUECK	254748	M			Oschfhr.,C.C.Dora,Nordhausen (Ger.)	MURDER	U.S.
STUECKLE	152104	M	Ger.		Pvt.,Army,522 Wach-Bn.,5 Coy.,C.C.Heimerdingen (Ger.) 3.4.45	MURDER	UNWCC
STUECKLER	156039	M	Ger.	15	Lt.,German Air Force,Katsdorf (Aust.) 25.4.45	WITNESS	U.S.
STUEDE	300149	M	Ger.		Member,Green Police,Groningen,Drente (Neth.) 43-45	MURDER	NETH.
STUEDEMANN	254722	M	Ger.	15	Cmdt.,Parachustists,Tiel (Neth.) 3.-4.45	PILLAGE	NETH.
STUEMLER, Willy	12318	M	Ger.		Pvt.,Army,110 or 111 Pz.Gren.Regt,2 Coy.,Albine (Fr.) 29.6.44	MURDER	FR.
STUENDE	123945	M			Lt.,Stalag,Heeres-Kuesten-Art.,Lehr-Abtl.152,Champs Rabats (Fr.) 7.44	MURDER	U.K.
STUEPFERT, Heinz	254737	M			Pvt.,C.C.Ellrich,Nordhausen (Ger.)	MURDER	U.S.
STUERM	29638	M	Ger.		Feldgendarmerie 577,Pomorantin (Fr.) 17.8.44	MURDER	FR.
STUERMER (or SLIZEK,Franz)	251341	M		31.5.95	Employee,Gestapo,Vsetin (Czech.) 39-45	TORTURE	CZECH.
STUERTZ	189801	M	Ger.		Sgt.,Feldkommandantur,Ugljarevo (Yugo.) 5.43	TORTURE	YUGO.
STUERZENACKER, Erich	168976	M	Ger.		Dr.,Leader,office of Raumordnung,Lwow,Galizia (Pol.) 9.39-44	MISC.CRIMES	POL.
STUESSGEN	254736	M			Rottfhr.,C.C.Osterhagen,Nordhausen (Ger.)	MURDER	U.S.
STUETZLE, Anton	255627	M	Ger.	11.6.02	State official,Agriculturel Affairs,German (Government), Hredes,Kralove (Czech.) 42-45	PILLAGE	CZECH.
STUHL, Johann	254747	M			Pvt.,C.C.Herzungen,Nordhausen (Ger.)	MURDER	U.S.
STUHLKE, Adolf (of SUHLKE)	143148	M		89	Member,Farmer,NSDAP,Asst.Mayor,Lomitz (Ger.)	TORTURE	U.S.
STUHLMACHER, Gustav	254878	M			Flyer,C.C.Ellrich,Nordhausen (Ger.)	MURDER	U.S.
STUHLMULLER	158577	M			Oschfhr.,3 SS-Bau-Bde.,C.C.Wieda,Gardelegen (Ger.) 5.-14.4.45	MURDER	U.S.
STUHR	156038	M	Ger.		Oberwachtmeister,C.C.Emsland (Ger.) 44	WITNESS	NOR.
STUIBER, Heinrich	193343	M	Ger.		Inspector,230 Inf.Div.,Area Drag (Nor.)		
STUIBLE, Erich	259725	M			Country-commissary of Wissembourg (Bas-Rhin),Riedseltz,Bas-Rhin (Fr.) 3.41	INTERR.	FR.
STUKA (see STUCKA)	126980						
STUKART	194252	M	Ger.	19	Guard,Internment Camp,Condette-Camiers (Fr.) 41-44	TORTURE	FR.
STUMER	136365	F	Ger.		Guard,C.C.Helmbrechts (Ger.) 7.44-13.4.45	TORTURE	U.S.
STUMM, Curt Hugo	165710	M	Ger.	04	Police,Moy s.-Aisne (Fr.) 30.8. und 1.9.44	PILLAGE	FR.
STUMME	257514	M	Ger.		Chief of sub.sec.Mittelwerk,C.C.Nordhausen (Ger.)	MURDER	U.S.
STUMMEL	67689	M	Ger.		Pvt.,C.C.Marburg,Heydekrug,Swinemuende,Stalag XVIII D (Ger.)10.41-42-45	MURDER	U.K.
STUMMER, Josef	254861	M			Pvt.,C.C.Ellrich,Nordhausen (Ger.)	MURDER	U.S.
STUMP	173511	M	Ger.		Major,Cmdt.,Hilfspolizei,III Bn. (Yugo.) 42-44	MURDER	YUGO.
STUMPF	929	M	Ger.		Usturmfhr.,W-SS,C.C.Dachau (Ger.) 40-43	MURDER	FR.
STUMPF	156954	M			Rottfhr.,SS,Asst.to Camp Comdr. at Ilfeld,Gardelegen (Ger.)	MURDER	U.S.
STUMPF, Adolf	129989	M			Camp-Senior,Block 18,C.C.Mauthausen (Aust.) 11.41-3.42	MISC.CRIMES	CZECH.
STUMPF, Heinrich	257320	M	Ger.	circa 90	Crim.Secr.,Gestapo,Tabor,Bohemia (Czech.) 14.3.39-43	MURDER	U.K.
STUMPF, Heinz	300150	M	Ger.		Oberst-Feldmeister,2-370 Reichsarbeitsdienst,Flak-Btty. at Bemerode (Ger.) 9.4.45	MURDER	U.S.
STUMPF, Karl	174215	M	Ger.	4.2.00	Director,C.C.Kislau (Ger.) 41-45	MURDER	U.S.
STUMPF, Karl	31441	M	Ger.		Dr.,Kapo,Police,Clausthal-Zellerfeld to Braunlage (Ger.) 6.4.45	WITNESS	U.S.
STUMPF, Matthias	251885	M	Ger.		Sgt.,Straelen (Ger.) 11.44	WITNESS	U.S.
STUMPFEGGER	133241	M	Ger.	09	Obersturmbannfhr.,SS,(Ger.)		
STUN, Leopold	1747	M	Ger.	25	Oschfhr.,SS,Army,12 SS-Panzer-Div."Hitler Jugend",12 SS-Pz.Recce Unit,Ascq,Chateau Andrieu near Caen (Fr.) 6.6.-8.7.44	MURDER	CAN.FR.U.K.
STUNDE	1759	M			Lt.,Army,Aufkl.-Abt.1252,Comd.Lehrg.-Bn.H.K. (Fr.) 44	MURDER	U.K.
STUNGEN	156037	M	Ger.		Lt.,SS,Inf.Div.16,Maille (Fr.) 25.4.44	MURDER	FR.
STUNITZER (or SANNITZER)	131647	M			Dir.,Gestapo,Counsel for Crim.Affairs,Vienna (Aust.) 44	MISC.CRIMES	U.S.

STU-SUR

NAME	C.R.FILE NUMBER	SEX	NATIO-NALITY	DATE OF BIRTH	RANK OCCUPATION UNIT PLACE AND DATE OF CRIME	REASON WANTED	WANTED BY
STUNTZ	29637	M	Ger.		Lt.,Army,Art.Einheit,Kerbabu near Lanillis (Fr.) 6.-9.8.44	MURDER	FR.
STUPAREK, Alois	254862	M			Pvt.,C.C.,Ellrich,Harzungen,Nordhausen (Ger.)	MURDER	U.S.
STUPLER, Joachim(or STUPPLER)	125611	M	Ger.		Pvt.,Army,special section of Gendarmerie,Bourg-Lastic (Fr.)15.7.44	MURDER	FR.
STUPP	930	M	Ger.		Sgt.,Army,C.C.,Caen (Fr.) 6.44	MURDER	FR.
STUTTLER, Joachim(see STUFLER)	125611						
STURBECK, Otto	143145	M	Ger.	.13	Hptschfhr.,Waffen SS,Leibstandarte A.H.,Ers.Bn.1,Rosbach (Ger.)4.3.45	WITNESS	U.S.
STURCKLZ	162899	M	Ger.		Pvt.,Army,Heimerdingen (Ger.) 3.4.45	MURDER	FR.
STURM	254412	M	Ger.		Cpl.,Feldgend.577,Romorantin,Orcay (Fr.) 8.8.44	INTERR.	FR.
STURM, Anton	261956	M	Ger.		Interpreter,various places in Slovenia (Yugo.) 41-45	MISC.CRIMES	YUGO.
STURM, Franz	252761	M	Ger.	.08	Doctor,SS,C.C.,Dachau (Ger.) 39-45	INTERR.	CZECH.
STURM, Fritz	158697	M	Ger.	95	Capt.,Army,779.Landesschuetzen Bn.,3.Coy.,Altenkirchen (Ger.) 13.9.44	TORTURE	U.K.
STURM, Georg	194423	M	Ger.	1. 9.89	Member,NSDAP,locksmith,Darmstadt,Hessen (Ger.) 39-45	TORTURE	POL.
STURMEL (or STURMER)	165709	M			Member,Police,Montigny (Fr.) 28.9.44	MURDER	FR.
STURMFELS	124134	M	Ger.	10.	Sgt.,Commando 436,guard,Stalag IX C,C.C.,Weimar (Ger.) 9.40	MURDER	U.K.
STURR	136209	M	Ger.		Capt.,Feldgendarmerie,parachutist,Domarten,Ponthieu,Abbeville (Fr.) 31.8.44	MURDER	FR.
STURZENACKER, Erich	191535	M	Ger.		Doctor,occupied territories,Galizia Livow (Pol.) 9.39-44	PILLAGE	POL.
STURZKOPF	130177	M	Ger.		Major,Oflag 6 B,German Army,(Ger.) 10.41-10.42	TORTURE	U.K.
STUTA, Bruno (or STUTE)	156906	M	Ger.	98	Sgt.,Gestapo,Angers (Fr.) 21.7.44	MURDER	FR.
STUTOFF, Erich(or SUTHOFF)	46135	M	Ger.	25	SS-Mann,12.SS Pz.Div."Hitler-Jugend",near Caen (Fr.) 6.6.-8.7.44	TORTURE	CAN.
STUTZ, Georg	301515	M	Ger.		Quarry foreman,Vacha Krs.Eisenach (Ger.) 3.43-4.45	MURDER	U.K.
STUTZ, Oskar	29731	M	Ger.		Landgerichtsrat,public official,Cheb (Czech.) 40	MURDER	CZECH.
STUTZLE, Johannes	186717	M	Ger.		Gestapo,Vosges area Strassbourg (Fr.) 8.44	WITNESS	U.K.
STUVEN	251882	M	Ger.		Osturmfhr.,SD,Toulouse (Fr.) 44	PILLAGE	FR.
STUWER	156036	M			Farmer,civilian,Daasdorf,Outhmannhausen (Ger.) 7.-8.44	MURDER	U.S.
SUBKINO	152136	M	Ger.		Chief,Gestapo,Chenebier,Etobon (Fr.) 27.9.44	MURDER	FR.
SUBORG, Karl	250465	M			Civilian,St.Sauvier (Fr.) 7.6.44	MURDER	U.S.
SUCHANEK (see DJURIN)	305883						
SUCHARD	259164	M	Ger.		Osturmfhr.,German police for Croatia at Zagreb (Yugo.) 8.-9.9.43	MISC.CRIMES	YUGO.
SUCK	253907	M			Rottfhr.,C.C.,Osterhagen,Nordhausen (Ger.)	MURDER	U.S.
SUDDER, Karl (or SUDER)	72029	M	Ger.	4. 8.07	Crim.secretary,Gestapo,Luxembourg (Lux.)	MISC.CRIMES	U.S.
SUDE	253908	M			Uschfhr.,C.C.,Rottleberode,Nordhausen (Ger.)	MURDER	U.S.
SUDE, Karl	262224	M	Ger.	5.12.12	Oschfhr.,SS,commandant,3.Platoon,51.SS Armoured Bde.,Breviandes,Bucheres,St.Savine,La Riviere de Corps,(Troyes) (Fr.) 22.-25.8.44	BRUTALITY	FR.
SUDEKUM, Emil(see SAHL)	161655						
SUDER, Karl (see SUDDER)	72029						
SUDHOFF, Wilhelm	143146	M	Ger.		Civilian,Atten,Bochum (Ger.) 24.3.45	MURDER	U.S.
SUEHS, Josef	251299	M	Ger.	6. 2.94	Mason,civilian,Stod (Czech.) 44	MURDER	CZECH.
SUELDT, Walter	254240	M			Pvt.,Camp Ellrich,Nordhausen (Ger.)	MURDER	U.S.
SUELINER, Anton	251287	M	Ger.		Hauptwachtmeister,Lidice (Czech.) 10.6.42	MURDER	CZECH.
SUEPLITZ	1398	M	Ger.		N.C.O.,SD,Aussenkommando	MISC.CRIMES	U.K.
SUERTH, Hertha	300998	F	Ger.		Member,SS of staff at C.C.,Neugraben,Tiefstak (Ger.) 44-45	MURDER	U.K.,CZECH.
SUESS	10363	M			1.Staatsanwalt,publ.official,Litomerice (Czech.) 40	MURDER	CZECH.
SUESS, Ferdinand	262221	M	Ger.	22. 7. ?.	Oschfhr.,Gestapo,Rennes (Fr.) 43-44	MISC.CRIMES	FR.
SUESS, Wolfgang	190308	M			C.C.,Dachau (Ger.)	MURDER	U.S.
SUESSKOHL, Ludwich	259808	M	Ger.	23.12.14	Rottfhr.,SS,1.Zug,2.Group,probably stationed at Bergeyk,Noord-Brabant,(Neth.) 11.9.44	MURDER	NETH.
SUHLKE, Adolf(see STUHLKE)	143148						
SUHOLD (see SURCHOLD)	256594						
SUHR	139211	M		.15	Criminal rat,Sturmbannfhr.,SD,SIPC,Toulouse and other towns (Fr.),6.-8.44	MURDER	U.S.
SUHR	165712	M	Ger.		Lt.,Feldgendarmerie,Montignyen,Vescul (Fr.) 16.7.44	MURDER	FR.
SUHR	166905	M		14	Lt.,Adjutant to Major,Army,Sich.Abschnitt IV,Schwiebus,Compomelen.(It.) 2.45	MURDER	U.S.
SUHR	190213	M	Ger.		Lt.Col.,SS,police,Colmar (Fr.) 21.1.45	TORTURE	U.S.
SUHR	254239	M			Rottfhr.,Camp Rottleberode,Nordhausen (Ger.)	MURDER	U.S.
SUHR	301225	M	Ger.		Doctor,Obersturmbannfhr.,B.D.S. under Ogruppenfhr.,Oberg,chief of police,end SS for France,Vosges area (Fr.) 44	MURDER	U.K.
SUHREN	187782	M			Sturmbannfhr.,SS,Gestapo,Ravensbrueck,Mecklenburg (Ger.) 42-45	MURDER	U.S.
SUHRIG, Heinz	251909	M			Kapo,Wilhelmshaven (Ger.)	MURDER	FR.
SUHRVEN	141405	M			SS commandant,C.C.,Uckermarck (Ger.)	MURDER	FR.
SULBERG, Karl	129977	M	Ger.		Architect,civilian,Chemical works,Marguels (Ger.) 43-44	TORTURE	BEL.
SULKI	251760	M	Ger.		16.Hiebner Rgt.,6.Coy.,Kinrooi (Bel.) 9.44	MISC.CRIMES	BEL.
SULTZER	189799	M	Ger.		Member of staff,C.C.,Banjica (Yugo.)	MURDER	YUGO.
SULZBACH	161660	M	Ger.	00	Hptsturmfhr.,Waffen SS,guard,C.C.,Buchenwald (Ger.)	WITNESS	U.S.
SULZE	251280	M	Ger.		Sturmschfhr.,SD,Toulouse (Fr.)	MISC.CRIMES	FR.
SURCHOLD, Harry	251279	M	Ger.		Inspector,SD,Gestapo,Charleville,Etalle (Fr.) 6.7.44	MURDER	FR.
SUMISCH, Hermann	162900	M	Ger.	27. 9.21	Pvt.,1.Ost Bn.447,Freiwillige Div.,Plouvien (Fr.) 8.44	TORTURE	FR.
SUMMER, Gerhardt	132735	M	Ger.		Cpl.,Feldgend.Interpr.,Chartres (Fr.) 1.7.42	TORTURE	FR.
SUMMERLETT	251293	M	Ger.		W.O.,Stalag Luft III,Sagan (Ger.) 9.4.44	MURDER	U.S.
SUNDCHEN, Josef	132126	M	Ger.		Civilian,K.C.,Arb.Edo.,Eschweiler (Ger.) 9.42-11.44	MURDER	U.S.
SUNDERLAND, Heinrich	161474	M	Ger.	05	Civilian,C.C.,Buchenwald (Ger.)	TORTURE	U.S.
SUNDERMAJER, Walter	188205	M	Ger.	28. 6.00	Doctor,Landrat,territories occupied,Marianske Lazne (Czech.) 39-45	PILLAGE	CZECH.
SUNDERMANN	199710	M	Ger.		Lt.,Stalag X B,C.C.,Sandbostel (Ger.) 1.-5.45	MURDER	U.S.
SUNDERMANN	253352	M	Inter.		Guard,C.C.,Lahde-Weser (Ger.)	INTER.	BEL.
SUNDMAKER, Karl	306719	M	Ger.		German civilian,Bremen (Ger.) 24.2.45	BRUTALITY	U.S.
SUNKLER, Georg	260484	M	Ger.	17.10.07	Rottfhr.,Waffen SS,guard Coy.,C.C.,Auschwitz (Pol.) 2.42-1.45	BRUTALITY	POL.
SUNTAG	156035	M	Ger.		Pvt.,Army,guard,C.C.,Heydebreck (Ger.) 4.-8.42	MURDER	U.K.
SUPARITSCH, Hans	255227	M	Ger.	1. 5.05	Member,Gestapo,Zlin (Czech.) 40-45	MISC.CRIMES	CZECH.
SUPIA	251744	M	Ger.		Schfhr.,SS,C.C.,Buchenwald (Ger.) 42-45	MISC.CRIMES	U.S.
SUPPELL	251748	M	Ger.		Schfhr.,SS,C.C.,Buchenwald (Ger.) 42-45	MISC.CRIMES	U.S.
SUPPLIETH	256148	M	Ger.		Uschfhr.,SS,Muhldorf (Ger.)	BRUTALITY	U.S.
SURBERG, Karl	136960	M	Ger.		Pvt.,Army,709.Inf.Div.,Cherbourg (Fr.) 6.6.44	WITNESS	U.S.
SURBROCK	255722	M	Ger.		Innkeeper,Civilian,Frein Landstall (Aust.) 8.44	MURDER	U.S.

NAME	C.R.FILE NUMBER	SEX	NATIO- NALITY	DATE OF BIRTH	RANK OCCUPATION UNIT PLACE AND DATE OF CRIME	REASON WANTED	WANTED BY
SURCHOLD (or SUHOLD)	256594				Maschinenmeister, Org.Todt, C.C.Dachau, Muhldorf Area (Ger.)	MURDER	U.S.
SUREN	110364	M	Ger.	09	Lagerfhr., SS-Hptsturmfhr., C.C.Oranienburg, Ravensbrueck (Ger.) 39-44	MURDER	FR.,U.K., CZECH.,POL.
SURGAU	253784	M	Ger.		Cpl., Air Force, Entzheim (Fr.) 42-44	TORTURE	FR.
SUPH (see SOENK)	12379						
SUPIN	189316	M	Ger.		Attached, C.C.Ravensbrueck (Ger.) 42-45	MISC.CRIMES	FR.
SURING, Fans	305311	M	Ger.		Member, Wilhelmshavenkdo., C.C.Neuengamme, 42-45	MURDER	FR.
SUSCHNIG (or SCHUCHNIG)	39835	M	Ger.		Osturmfhr., 30 SS Div.Caucasien Bn., Tournon, St.Donat (Fr.) 15.6.-6.7.44	MURDER	FR.
SUSKO, Janina	143149	F			Civilian, Lauf (Ger.) 5.44	WITNESS	U.S.
SUSS	259665	M			Fieldpolice of Jonsac, Marignac, Charentes-Maritimes (Fr.) 21.8.44	TORTURE	FR.
SUSS, Franz	259276	M			Oschfhr., SS, Muhldorf Area (Ger.)	MURDER	U.S.
SUSS, Gerhard	126501	M	Ger.		SS-Sturmmann, 1 SS Pz.Div., 1 SS Pz.Rgt., 9 Coy, Malmedy (Bel.) 14.12.44	MURDER	U.S.
SUSS, Oscar,	250466	M	Ger.		Pvt., II Pz.Div.Unit 36-185, Lautrec (Fr.) 5.8.44	MURDER	FR.
SUSSER, Fichard	162901	M		15. 3.07	Pvt., 1-East Bn., 447 Freiwillig.Div., Plouvien (Fr.) 8.44	TORTURE	FR.
SUSSIEK, Paul	180890	M			Civilian, Berlin-Marienfelde (Ger.) 1.45 L.O.D.N.A.O.D.	WITNESS	U.S.
SUSSIEK, Walter	180889	M			Civilian, Berlin-Marienfelde (Ger.) 1.45 L.O.D.N.A.O.D.	WITNESS	U.S.
SUSTEP	180871	M			Lt., Army, Unit Nr.452806, Cervon (Fr.) 5.4.and 8.9.44	MURDER	FR.
SUTHOFF, Erich (see STUTOFF)	46135						
SUITER	194277		Ger.		Member, SD, Chateau Gaillard and Saintes (Fr.) 17.8.44	MURDER	FR.
SUTTOR	259267	M	Ger.		Schfhr., Gestapo of Poitiers, Antenne of Rochelle, Poitiers Area (Fr.) 40-44	MISC.CRIMES	FR.
SUUER, Fritz	261846	M	Ger.		Insp., Gestapo of Amiens, Gentelles (Fr.) 6.-8.44	MURDER	FR.
SUVER	251307	M	Ger.		Capt., Air Force, 77 Schwadron, Seguret and Vaison (Fr.) 10.6.44	MURDER	FR.
SUWELACK, Richard	305312	M	Ger.		Verwalter, Enschede (Neth.) 8.10.41-1.4.45	PILLAGE	NETH.
SVECKER	1760	M	Ger.		SS-Hptsturmfhr., SS, C.C.Prison S.Vittore Milan (It.)	TORTURE	U.K.
SVOBODA (or SWOBODA)	10365	M	Ger.		Dr., SS-Osturmfhr., Prague (Czech.)	MURDER	U.S.
SVOBODA (see PODE, Karl)	187658						
SVOBODA, Rupert	251312	M	Ger.	19. 9.99	Chief, Freikorps, Lednice (Czech.) 39	TORTURE	CZECH.
SWADE	12320	M	Ger.		Lt., Army, 110 or 111 Pz.Gren.Rgt., Gourdon (Fr.) 29.6.44	MURDER	FR.
SWADE	190704	M			Lt., 2 Coy, 11 Pz.Div., Bergerac and Albine (Fr.) 7.-8.44	MURDER	FR.
SWAELENS	251289	M	Ger.		Interpreter, Sipo, Brussels (Bel.)	INTERR.	BEL.
SWARMER (see SCHWARMER)	72015						
SWARTZ (see SCHWARTZ)	100431						
SWARTZ	141334	M	Ger.		Cpl., Army, C.C.Osterwälde (Ger.)	TORTURE	U.K.
SWAPIZ, Albert	301488	M	Ger.	11. 5.05	Osturmfhr., SS, C.C.Buchenwald (Ger.) 16.5.38-9.10.43	MURDER	BEL.
SWATERLING	173256	M	Ger.	02	Lt., 1-693 Ldsch.Bn., C.C.Brandenburg, Graudens (Ger., Pol.) 1.-3.45	TORTURE	U.K.
SWEN	72021			15	SS-Oschfhr., Berlin (Ger.) 5.43	MURDER	U.S.
SWEN (see MEPHISTO)	1533						
SWENGHAMMER	156903	M	Ger.	17	Hptsturmfhr., Waffen SS, Verona (It.) 3.-8.44	TORTURE	U.K.
SWENSSON	931	M	Ger.		SS-Usturmfhr., SD, Aalesund (Nor.) 42	TORTURE	NOR., U.K.
SWERDTMANN, Willy	194253	M	Ger.		Pvt., Arbeitskdo., C.C.Landerneau (Fr.)	TORTURE	FR.
SWERHOFF	256765	M			SS-Sgt., Nordhausen (Ger.)	MURDER	U.S.
SWIENTY, Willi	300152	M		9. 2.15	Capo, Peenemunde C.C.Common Law.prisoner, Peenemunde (Ger.) 6.43-3.45	MISC.CRIMES	POL.
SWIETEK, Johann	138010	M	Ger.		Gruppenfhr., SA, Erkenschwik-Bocholt (Ger.)	TORTURE	U.S.
SWIMMER (see ZWIMMER)	67675						
SWINGLER	174834	M	Ger.		Capt., Stalag XVIII A or XVIII C, C.C.Markt Pongau, Wolfsberg (Aust.) 4.45	TORTURE	U.K.
SWINN (see SCHWIN)	162902						
SWINQUIER	165557	M	Ger.		Lt., 4 Coy, Chars Parach. "Hermann Goering" Dienststelle L.X., Raboset-Lez-Herstal (Bel.) 5.9.44	MURDER	BEL.
SWOBOCA	187355	M	Ger.	98	Schfhr., Employee, SD, Gestapo, Brno (Czech.)	MURDER	CZECH.
SWOBODA (see SVOBODA)	10365						
SWOBODA	122911	M	Ger.		Col., Stalag XII A, C.C.Limburg (Ger.) 21.9.40 and 27.3.45	MURDER	U.S.
SWOBODA	132201	M			Pvt., Army, Gren.Rgt.731, 9 Coy, Touques, Trouville (Fr.) 4.44	WITNESS	U.K.
SWOBODA	173510	M	Ger.		Official, Gestapo, C.C.Maribor (Yugo.) 4.41-44	MURDER	YUGO.
SWOBODA, Fritz	258682	M		29. 3.22	SS-Oschfhr., Kennat (Ger.) 20.10.44	WITNESS	U.S.
SYLAGY	251759	M	Ger.		Member, SD, Meppel (Neth.) 18.12.44	MURDER	NETH.
SYMALIA, Josef	301489	M	Ger.	22. 7.91	Sturmscharfhr., SS W.OV., SS, C.C.Buchenwald (Ger.) 16.5.38-9.10.43	MURDER	BEL.
SYMANN, Otto	31637	M		95	Leader, NSDAP. (Ger.)	MISC.CRIMES	U.S.
SYORCH	71031	M			SD, C.C.Theresienstadt (Czech.)	TORTURE	U.S.
SYRING, Heinz	254237	M			Pvt., C.C.Ellrich, Nordhausen (Ger.)	MURDER	U.S.
SYRUP, Friedrich	932	M	Ger.		Dr., Staatssecr., Publfc-official, Reichsarbeitsministerium	INCENDIARISM	POL.,U.S.
SYSKA	259266	M	Ger.		Agent, Gestapo of Poitiers area (Fr.) 40-44	MISC.CRIMES	FR.
SYSKOWSKI, Wilhelm	193876	M	Ger.		SS-Rottfhr., Guard, 4 SS Totenkopf-Sturmbann, C.C.Mittelbau, Dora, Nordhausen (Ger.) 43-45	INTERR.	U.S.
SZARO, Stefan	193875	M	Ger.		Guard, 4 SS Totenkopf-Sturmbann, C.C.Dora, Mittelbau, Nordhausen (Ger.)	MURDER	U.S.
SZAKADICZ, Stefan	193874	M	Ger.		Guard, 4 SS.Totenkopf-Sturmbann, C.C.Dora, Mittelbau.Nordhausen, Monowits (Ger., Pol.) 43-45	INTERR.	U.S.
SZAMEITAT, Alfred (or SZEIMEI-TAZ, Willy)	164740	M			Senior W.O., Capt., Army, Pol.Rgt.19, St.Gingolph (Fr.) 22.7.44	MURDER	FR.
SZAMI	256149	M	Ger.		Org.Todt, Muhldorf (Ger.)	WITNESS	U.S.
SZAMY	193873	M			SS-Oschfhr., Oberwachtmeister, 4 SS Totenkopf-Sturmbann, SS Camp Fahrbereitschaft Plaszow, C.C.Dora, Mittelbau, Nordhausen (Pol., Ger.) 43-45		
SZAROLETTA, Maria	300939	F	Ger.		Member, SS or staff at C.C.Neugraben-Tiefstak (Ger.) 44-45	MURDER	U.K.
SZARUJEW	193872	M	Ger.		SS-Oschfhr., 4 SS Totenkopf-Sturmbann, C.C.Dora, Mittelbau, Nordhausen, Plaszow (Ger., Pol.) 43-45	TORTURE	U.S.
SZATZ	120623	M	Ger.		Lt., Army, Dingden (Ger.) 6.11.44	BRUTALITY	U.K.,POL.
SZECKA, Kraus	253783	M	Ger.		Member, Gestapo, Geh.Feldpolizei, Lille (Fr.) 40-44	MISC.CRIMES	FR.

SZE - TAU

NAME	C.R.FILE NUMBER	SEX	NATIO- NALITY	DATE OF BIRTH	RANK	OCCUPATION	UNIT	PLACE AND DATE OF CRIME	REASON WANTED	WANTED BY
SZEIMKITAZ, Willy (see SZAMKITAT, Alfred)	164740									
SZENER, Adam (see SENER)	261921									
SZIGE (see SCHIGA)	168961									
SZIHN	261252	M	Ger.		Pvt., 2. Obl. 3. Coy. 1. Aufklaer. Abt. XV. Div. Africa Corps, St. Lager, Distr. Arlon (Bel.) 5.9.44				MISC. CRIMES	BEL.
SZIMANSKI, Robert	188203	M	Ger.	31.7.08	Agent, SD, Security Service, Marimasko Lazne (Czech.) 39-45				MURDER	CZECH.
SZIMMITAT, Ewald	12321	M	Ger.		Lt., Feldgend. Truppe B 687 Moto., Charroux Le Vigeant, Lussac (Fr.) 3.-5.8.44				MURDER	FR.
SZMULEWICZ, Michael	257740	M		16.2.14	Employee, C.C. Nordhausen (Ger.)				MURDER	U.S.
SZPENDLER	257741	M			Oschfhr., C.C. Muhldorf Dachau (Ger.)				MURDER	U.S.
SZPET	257735	M			SS-Oschfhr., C.C. Dachau Muhldorf (Ger.)				MURDER	U.S.
SZUBERT, Jerzy	167662	M	Ger.		Pvt., 9. Res. Gren.Rgt. 1. Coy. Magny D'Anigon (Fr.) 18.9.44				MURDER	FR.
SZUKALA, Bernhard	143153	M			Civilian, Lauf (Ger.)				WITNESS	U.S.
SZUERIN	933	M	Germ		Lager Commander, C.C. Ravensbrueck (Ger.) 10.42				MURDER	POL.
SZWABE	119389	M	Ger.		Cpl., Army C.C. Auschwitz (Pol.) 6.40-1.45				MURDER	POL.
SZWARE, Helmut	156957	M			Leader, C.C. Mauthausen Gusen (Aust.)				MURDER	U.S.
SZYLI (or OZULI, Joseph)	256744	M			Oschfhr., C.C. Muhldorf Dachau (Ger.)				MURDER	U.S.
SZYMALIK, Czesla	193671	M	Ger.		Guard, Pvt., 4.SS Totenkopf sturmbann C.C. Dora Mittelbau Nordhausen (Ger.) 43-45				MURDER	U.S.
SZYMEK, Artur	256740	M		29.6.08	Employee, Camp Dora Block 109 Nordhausen (Ger.)				MURDER	U.S.
TAAG	193755	M	Ger.		SS-Rottfhr. 4. SS Totenkopf Sturmbann C.C. Mittelbau Dora Nordhausen (Ger.) 43-45				MURDER	U.S.
TAAKS (see TACKS)	186707									
TAAKS	187544	M		04	Doctor, 191.Arb.Kdo. Stalag IX C, C.C. Ochenberg Volkershausen (Ger.) 43-45				TORTURE	U.K.
TABOR	196242	M	Ger.		Lt., Dr., C.C. Dachau (Ger.)				TORTURE	BEL.
TABORY, Vinzenz	195711	M	Ger.		Driver, Gestapo, Brno., (Czech.) 39-45				TORTURE	CZECH.
TACHAKS (see TAKACS)	124133									
TACHAZI	29732	M	Ger.		Senatspraesident, Public Official, Litomarice (Czech.) 40				MURDER	CZECH.
TACHNER	124990	M	Ger.		Inspecteur des Customs (Fr.) 9.40-7.41				MURDER	FR.
TACK	902005	M	Ger.		Guard, SS C.C. Auschwitz (Pol.) 42-45				BRUTALITY	POL.
TACKS (or TAAKS)	186707	M	Ger.	95	Stabs-Arzt, Army C.C. Massbach near Vacha, (Ger.) 11.12.44				MURDER	U.K.
TADEUSZ, Demitrak	151023	M			Civ., Lauf, (Ger.)				WITNESS	U.S.
TAENDLER, Mathias	258580	M	Ger.		Pvt., Guard, Army Murnau Oflag VII A (Ger.) 18.7.41				MURDER	POL.
TAEUSNER, Wors	138261	M			SS-Rottfhr., Gestapo, Lyon (Fr.)				MURDER	FR.
TAGEDICK	261162	M	Ger.		Pvt. 139. Arbeitsbereich Lianes 5. Inf.Rgt. 211, Alleur Lez Liege (Bel.) 4.9.44				MURDER	BEL.
TAHLER	192219	M	Ger.		Sgt., Army staffs, La Rochette (Fr.) 3.8.44				INTERR.	FR.
TAIDEL	165973	M	Ger.		Civilian, Budesheim (Ger.) 6.44				TORTURE	U.S.
TAIG, Heinrich	192778	M	Ger.		Schupo, C.C. Falstad, (Nor.) 41-44				MURDER	NOR.
TAKACS, Eugen (or TACHAKS) Nickname: The big long Bastard	124133	M	Gen.		Sgt., Stalag XVII A, Arb.Kdo. Seyring near Vienna (Aust.) 21.12.44				MURDER	U.K.
TAMASCHKE	162849	M	Ger.		SS-Standartenfhr., SS Totenkopf Standarte Chief of the Camp Buchenwald (Ger.) 2.39				TORTURE	U.S.
TAMBOSI, Anton	179772	M	Ger.	97	Cpt., 611, Transport Begleit Bn. 4. Cby. Partimo (It.) 13.4.44				MURDER	U.K.
TAMCHIN	189762	M	Ger.		Zollinspector, Zollgrensschutz Suedost, Belgrade and Bela Crkva (Yugo.) 45				MURDER	YUGO.
TAMM	147021	M	Ger.		SS-Uschfhr., SS Panz.Div. Das Reich, Rgt. Deutschland, Venarque Le Vernet (Fr.) 44				MURDER	FR.
TAMM, Robert	307212	M	Ger.		SS Uschfhr., 2.Bn.Landsturm Niederlande, Apeldoorn near Bohnen Lager Wia. (Neth.) 10.12.44				MURDER	NETH.
TAMOS	62176	M	Ger.		Agent, Gestapo, Saales (Fr.) 15.4.43				MURDER	FR.
TANCKE	195413	M	Ger.		Grensschutz, Elfhijk (Neth.) 1.9.45				PILLAGE	NETH.
TANDLER	185494	M			SS-Oschfhr., Guard, C.C. SS (Ger.)				TORTURE	U.S.
TANERT, Heinz	39702	M	Ger.		Pvt., Army, Argentan, (Fr.) 6.44				MURDER	U.S.
TANG	124991	M	Ger.	15	Agent, Gestapo, Poitiers Chateau De Porteau (Fr.) 24.8.44				MURDER	FR.
TANGERMANN, Heinz	151021	M	Gen		Marinecorps, St. Marine (Vis) (Fr.) 30.6.44				MURDER	U.S.
TANGERMANN, Heinz	194292	M	Ger.	25.1.12	SS Lt., SD, Radwyn-Radom (Pol.) 43-44				TORTURE	POL.
TANK, Ernst	10025	M	Ger.		Public Prosecutor, Public Official, Cheb (Czech.)				MURDER	CZECH.
TANNEBAUM, Alfred	149581	M	Ger.		Cpl., 11. Panz.Div. South West (Fr.)				MURDER	FR.
TANNEBAUM, Josef	251369	M			Kapo, Army, Buchenwald (Ger.)				BRUTALITY	U.S.
TANNENBERG	251920	M			Pvt., C.C. Ellrich Nordhausen (Ger.)				MURDER	U.S.
TANNERT	174833	M			Cpt., Paratrooper Rgt. 2. Bn. 2.Div. Plouzanxe (Fr.) 44				MURDER	FR.
TANNHAUSEN, Mathias	260462	M	Ger.	21.9.87	SS Sgt., W-SS Guard Coy. C.C. Auschwitz (Pol.) 9.39-1.45				BRUTALITY	POL.
TANNKRIF	25277b	M	Ger.		Member, Gestapo Geh.Feld.Pol., Lille (Fr.) 40-44				MISC. CRIMES	FR.
TANZ, Harold	167742	M	Ger.		Pvt., 9. Res.Gren.Rgt. 1.Cby. Magny D'Anigon (Fr.) 18.9.44				MURDER	FR.
TANZA	259304	M			Uschfhr., SS Camp Thekle near Leipzig (Ger.) 18.4.45				MURDER	U.S.
TANZER, Josef	29733	M	Ger.		Dr., Landgerichtsrat, Public Official, Opava (Czech.) 40				MURDER	CZECH.
TANZER, Otto	190309	M	Ger.	8.9.96	SS-Member, SS Troppau (Czech.) 38-43				MURDER	CZECH.
TANZER, Walter	139236	M	Ger.		Official, discharge of Wehrmacht, Oberplan (Czech.) 29.4.45				MURDER	U.S.
TANZER, Walter	196241	M	Ger.	24.4.25	Pvt., Baker, German Army				INTERR.	FR.
TANZHAUS	72068	M			SS-Oschfhr., SS C.C. Lublin (Pol.) 43				TORTURE	U.S.
TANZMANN	139743	M	Ger.		Dr., Lt.Col. Chief Government Counsel W-SS General.Gov. Lemberg Roullons (Pol.Fr.) 42-44				MURDER	U.S., FR.
TANZMANN	261852	M	Ger.	circa 95	Ostunbannfhr., SD. of Montpellier, Clerval (Fr.) 28.8.44				MURDER	FR.
TANZMANN	306096	M	Ger.		Chief of Sicherheitsdienst of Montpellier succeeded Boemelberg at Vichy (Fr.) 10.43-9.44				MURDER	FR.
TAP, Hans	124617	M	Ger.		C.C. Elisabeth Stuerznal, (Ger.)				TORTURE	BEL.
TARACH, Karl	62280	M	Ger.	00	NSDAP, DAF, Augerburg (Ger.)				TORTURE	U.S.
TARNOFF	104843	M	Ger.		K.C.C. Gem Winiza (Sov.Un.) 41				MURDER	U.S.
TARZAN	185167	M	Ger.		Chief de bloc SS C.C. Sachsenhausen (Ger.)				TORTURE	FR.
TASCH, Jacob	130125	M		16	SS Sturmmann, SS C.C. Mauthausen (Aust.) 25.10.43				MURDER	U.S.
TATGE	306810	M	Ger.		Uschfhr., SD, Vichy, (Fr.) 10.43-9.44				MURDER	FR.
TAUBE	151019	M	Ger.		SS-Pvt., SS C.C.Volary, SS Guard Germ. Prison Camps (Czech.) 41-45				MURDER	U.S.
TAUBE, Adolf	62281	M			SS-Uschfhr., W-SS, C.C. Auschwitz (Pol.)				MURDER	U.K.
TAUBE, Heinrich	260464	M	Ger.	1.4.90	SS Pvt., W-SS Guard Coy. C.C. Blechhammer Auschwitz (Pol.) 7.44-4.45				BRUTALITY	POL.

TAU-TEL

NAME	C.R.FILE NUMBER	SEX	NATIO-NALITY	DATE OF BIRTH	RANK OCCUPATION UNIT PLACE AND DATE OF CRIME	REASON WANTED	WANTED BY
TAUBER	934	M	Ger.		SS Uscharfhr., Record clerk, C.C.Birkenau-Auschwitz (Pol.) 39-45	MURDER	U.S. POL. BEL. YUGO. CZECH.
TAUBER	130126	M			SS Rottfhr., C.C. Mauthausen (Aust.) 41-45	MURDER	U.S.
TAUBER	188351	M			SS Osturmfhr., formerly at disciplinary labor camp, Frankfurt-M.(Ger.)	MURDER	U.S.
TAUBER	300547	M	Ger.		SS Rapportfuehrer und Arbeitsdienstfuehrer, C.C.Auschwitz, Birkenau (Pol.) 42-43	MISC.CRIMES	YUGO.
TAUBER, Erhard	251919	M			SS Usturmfhr., C.C. Ellrich, Nordhausen (Ger.)	MURDER	U.S.
TAUBER, Karl Heinz	144975	M	Ger.		SS Hptsturmfhr., C.C. Auschwitz (Pol.) 43-44	TORTURE	U.S.
TAUBERICH	257854	M			O.C., Assault-gun unit, 2.K.F.G. Panz.Bde., Meuse-Bridge Antwerp (Bel.) 12.44	MISC.CRIMES	U.S.
TAUBERSHUFER see TAUBERTSHOFER	121292						
TAUBERT	192692	M	Ger.		SS Oscharfhr., C.C. Buchenwald (Ger.)	TORTURE	U.S.
TAUBERT	256580	M	Ger.		Usturmfhr., SS Pers.Sec.Mittelbau-Dora C.C. Nordhausen (Ger.)	MURDER	U.S.
TAUBERT, Alfred	185295	M	Ger.		N.C.O., Army, Myron Orovsidi (Grc.)43	MURDER	GRC
TAUBERT or TEUBERT, Max	250513	M	Ger.	about 98	Sgt., 8.Coy. 9.Bn. 192.Rgt., Cher-Allier-Loir (Fr.) 6.-8.44	PILLAGE	FR.
TAUBERTS, Alfred	185296	M	Ger.		Pvt., Army, Ancyea (Grc.) 8.44	MURDER	GRC.
TAUBERTSHOFER or TAUBERSHUFER or TAUFRATSCHOFER or TAUFRARSCHOFER or TEICHRATSHOFER	121292	M	Ger.	8. 9.90 or 94	Hptsturmfhr., C.C. Buchenwald (Ger.) 42-45	MISC.CRIMES	FR. U.S.
TAUBNER, Worz	300723	M	Ger.		Uscharfhr., Gestapo Sub-section IV F, Oyonnax, Ain, Lyon and surroundings. (Fr.) 11.43-8.44	MURDER	FR.
TAUCH, Michael	261347	M	Ger.		SS Guard, C.C. Auschwitz (Pol.) 42-44	BRUTALITY	POL.
TAUDT, Ewald	196376	M	Ger.	18. 5.09	Kriminalrat, Gestapo, Brno (Czech.) 39-45	SUSPECT	CZECH. U.K.
TAUER	192064	M	Ger.	00	Civ. Professor, anatomy institute, Danzig (Pol.)	TORTURE	POL.
TAUER, Hans	251962	M	Ger.	20.12.10	Employee, Gestapo, Vsetin (Czech.) 39-45	MURDER	CZECH.
TAUER, Georg I	192779	M	Ger.		Schupo, C.C. Falstad (Nor.) 41-44	MURDER	NOR.
TAUER, Georg II	192780	M	Ger.		Schupo, C.C. Falstad Stalag (Nor.) 41-44	MURDER	NOR.
TAUFFMANN, Fredy	256543	M			SA Gruppenfhr., Luftwaffe, SS, C.C.Dora Nordhausen (Ger.) 17.7.44	INTERR.	FR.
TAUFRARSCHOFER see TAUBERTSHOFER	121292						
TAUFRATSCHOFER see TAUBERTSHOFER	121292						
TAURER, Anton	188940	M			Landwacht, Ebenberg (Aust.) 16.11.44	MURDER	U.S.
TAUS	301491	M	Ger.		SS Oberfhr., C.C. Buchenwald (Ger.) 16.5.38-9.10.43	MURDER	BEL.
TAUSCH	11284	M	Ger.		Pvt., 110 or 111.Panz.Gren.Rgt. 3.Gruppe, Gourdon (Fr.) 29.6.44	MURDER	FR.
TAUSCH	188938	M			Member Gestapo, Stanislawow (Pol.)	MURDER	POL.
TAUSENDFREUND	262290	M	Ger.		SS Hptsturmfhr., Belgrad, Valjevo (Yugo.) 15.8.42-10.9.44	MISC.CRIMES	YUGO.
TAUSS, Christian	251918	M	Ger.		SS Mann, C.C. Bodungen, Nordhausen (Ger.)	MURDER	U.S.
TAUSS, David	251917	M			Pvt., C.C. Bodungen, Nordhausen (Ger.)	MURDER	U.S.
TAUTHE, Willi	251916	M			Pvt., C.C. Ellrich, Nordhausen (Ger.)	MURDER	U.S.
TAX, Johann	193498	M			SS Mann, 4.SS Totenkopf Stuba, C.C. Dora-Mittelbau Nordhausen (Ger.) 43-45	WITNESS	U.S.
TAZ	193499	M			Wachtmeister, 4.SS Totenkopf Stuba, C.C. Dora-Mittelbau Nordhausen (Ger.) 43-45	WITNESS	U.S.
TAZIA, Kaete	161279	F	Ger.	about 15	SS overseer, C.C. Sasel	MURDER	U.K.
TCHECHER	900724	M	Ger.		Oberinspector, C.C. Auschwitz, Birkenau (Pol.) from 40	MURDER	FR.
TCHEMERETZ, Michael	186104	M	Ger.	7.10.21	SS Guard, C.C. Buchenwald (Ger.)	TORTURE	BEL.
TCHERBINSKY	177561	M	Ger.		Chief, C.C. Neuengamme (Ger.)	MURDER	FR.
TEBBE	900887	M	Ger.		Pvt., 1.Aufkl.Abt. 3.Coy. 2.Col. XV.Div.Afrika-Corps, St.Léger (Arlon) 5.9.44	MISC.CRIMES	BEL.
TECHENTIN	151018	M			SS Rottfhr., 2.Panz.Gren.Rgt. 3.Bn., Staveldt-Malmedy (Bel.) 22.-23.12.44	MURDER	U.S.
TECHMEIER, Eberhard	240096	M	Ger.	13	Pvt., Nachrichten-Rgt. 506, 6.Coy., Bad Wildungen (Ger.) 45	MISC.CRIMES	U.N.W.C.C.
TECHMIER, H.	197529	M			Sgt., Stalag III A C.C. Luckenwalde (Ger.) 13.2.45	TORTURE	U.S.
TECLENZ, Ludwig	251915	M			Legionar, C.C. Harzungen, Nordhausen (Ger.)	MURDER	U.S.
TEEGEN see TEGEN, Hans	195932						
TEEWIS or TEWES	905919	M	Ger.		Sturmscharfhr., SD Utrecht (Neth.) 44	MURDER	NETH.
TEFFEL, Fritz	192166	M	Ger.		Obermaschinist, Org.Todt Firm Otto Menzel of Bittburg, Alle sur Semois (Bel.) 5.-6.40	PILLAGE	BEL.
TEFOEST	251912	M			Rottenfhr., C.C.Mackenrode, Nordhausen (Ger.)	MURDER	U.S.
TEGEN, Hans or TEEGEN	195932	M	Ger.		Usturmfhr., SD, Dienststelle Zwolle, Kampen (Neth.) 9.44-4.45	MURDER	NETH.
TEGETHOFF, Heinrich	251964	M	Ger.		SS Rottfhr., Clerk, Gestapo, Aube (Fr.) 43-44	INTERR.	FR.
TEHN, Edward	152950	M		20	Cpl., Army, 1.Plat. 4.Coy. Sturm-Bn. AOK 1, Gourcelles sur Nied (Fr.) 15.11.44	MURDER	U.S.
TEICHMAN	259264	M			Lt., F.P.No. 32 136 D., La Bassée-Nord (Fr.) 1.-3.9.44	MURDER	FR.
TEICHMANN	935	M	Ger.		Osturmfhr., Befehlshaber, SIPO SD (Serb.) 18.11.42	MURDER	YUGO.
TEICHMANN	196917	M			Pvt., 11.Panz.Div. 2.Coy. 2. AA-A7. Albine (Fr.) 12.8.44	MURDER	FR.
TEICHMANN	182108	M	Ger.	10	Obersturmbannfhr., SD, SS, Brussels (Bel.) 44	MURDER	BEL. U.S.
TEICHMANN, Karl	167741	M	Ger.		Pvt., Army, 1.Coy. 9.Res.Gren.Rgt., Magny d'Anigon (Fr.) 18.9.44	MURDER	FR.
TEICHMANN, Karl	190690	M			Pvt., 11.Panz.Div. 2 AAA 7, Bergeras, Albine (Fr.) 7.-8.44	MURDER	FR.
TEICHMUT, Albert see REICHMUT	261919						
TEICHRATSHOFER see TAUBERTSHOFER	121292						
TEIKE, Walter	262164	M	Ger.	6. 9. ?	Oscharfhr., Gestapo, Rennes (Fr.) 43-44	INTERR.	FR.
TEILEIS, Willi	256627	M	Ger.	21. 7.09	Employee, C.C. Nordhausen (Ger.)	MURDER	U.S.
TEISCHMANN	124458		Ger.		Col., Camp-Cmdt., Stalag VIII A Goerlitz (Ger.) 18.12.44-9.4.45	TORTURE	U.S.
TEISEN, Josef	162853	M	Ger.	about 19	Sgt., Kriegsgefang.Arb.Bn. 181, 3.Coy. C.C. Hsen (Ger.) 7.-25.12.44	MURDER	NOR.
TEITGE, Walter	151016	M	Ger.	20.10.92	Civ., Lockstedt (Ger.) 8.2.44	MURDER	U.S.
TEKEMAYER, Heinrich	256628	M	Ger.	19. 4.09	Employee, C.C. Nordhausen (Ger.)	MURDER	U.S.
TELLANTONYO, Martha	151017	F	Ger.		Chief-guard, asst.Camp-commander, SS, C.C. Volary (Czech.) 41-45	MURDER	U.S.
TELLER, Martin	193500	M			SS Mann, 4.SS Totenkopf Stuba, C.C.Nordhausen -Mittelbau-Dora (Ger.) 43-45	MURDER	U.S.
TELLMANN, Hans	192704	M	Ger.	2. 6.21	Reichsjustizministerium, Feldstraflager Nord, C.C.Finmark (Nor.)42-45	MISC.CRIMES	NOR.
TELSCH, Charles Joseph	255272	M			1.Coy. Six SS-Dep.Nachschub.Coy., Dolembreux (Bel.)	INTERR.	BEL.
TELSCHOVY	258149		Ger.		Prisoner, C.C. Natzweiler, Schoerzingen (Fr.)	SUSPECT	BEL.
TELSCHOW, Walter	251387	M	Ger.	about 08	Officer, Internment camp, Schoerzingen (Ger.)	BRUTALITY	FR.

NAME	C.R.FILE NUMBER	SEX	NATIO-NALITY	DATE OF BIRTH	RANK OCCUPATION UNIT PLACE AND DATE OF CRIME	REASON WANTED	WANTED BY
TELSCOW	251929	M			Uschfhr., SS, CC Nordhausen, Rottlsberode (Ger.)	MURDER	U.S.
TELTHOERSTER	146755	M	Ger.		Civilian, Oflag VI-A, Wlodizimiercz (Sov.Un.) 41	WITNESS	U.S.
TEMEL, Josef	901666	M	Ger.		House owner near Mostar 44	MURDER	YUGO.
TEMMLER, Helmuth	195412	M	Ger.		Army, Arnheim (Neth.) 1.-2.2.44	PILLAGE	NETH.
TEMNOFF	259179	M	Ger.		Hptsturmfhr, SS, CC Dachau (Ger.) 9.42-45	MISC.CRIMES	YUGO.
TEMPEL	153500	M		85	Sturmfhr, W-SS, Gardelegen (Ger.) 5.-14.4.45	MURDER	U.S.
TEMPEL, Willi	936	M	Ger.	1.11.08	Rottfhr, SS, CC Maidanek (Pol.) 40-4.44	TORTURE	BEL., POL.
TEMPLIN, Max	251911	M			Pvt., CC Ellrich, Nordhausen (Ger.)	MURDER	U.S.
TEN BRINK, Wilhelm	192691	M	Ger.		Rottfhr, SS Totenkopf-Verband, CC Buchenwald-Moringen(Ger.) 42-45	TORTURE	U.S.
TENDLER, Karl	196240	M	Ger.		Police secretary, Gestapo, Brno (Czech.) 39-44	MURDER	CZECH.
TENGELER, Christian	251910	M	Ger.		Flyer, CC Ellrich, Nordhausen (Ger.)	MURDER	U.S.
TENIZEL	937	M	Ge..		Lt., Army, 897 Rgt., 2 Bn., 3 Coy, Danilovgrad (Yugo.) 7.43	MURDER	YUGO.
TENK	194076	M	Ger.		Adjutant Chief, SS Div."Das Reich", Rgt."Deutschland", 9 Coy, Verfuegungstruppe, Miremont (Fr.) 2.6.44	MURDER	FR.
TENNER	300153	M	Ger.		Sgt. Major of Aegion district (Grc.) 42-43	MURDER	GRC.
TENNEYSEN	177562		Ger.		Secretary, police	MISC.CRIMES	U.N.W.C.C.
TENTLER, Heinrich	72067	M			Rottfhr, SS Mountain Totenkopf Div.,6 SS Pz.Jg.Abt.	TORTURE	U.S.
TENZAR	104944	M			SS Uschfhr., CC Thekla (Ger.)	MURDER	U.S.
TEPLI	251924	M			Stabsscharfhr, CC Rottleberode, Nordhausen (Ger.)	MURDER	U.S.
TEPS	189577	M	Ger.		Pvt., Army Unit 40599 (France)	PILLAGE	FR.
TERBECK, Karl	251923	M			Pvt., CC Ellrich, Nordhausen (Ger.)	MURDER	U.S.
TERBOVEN, Joseph. (see TERHOFEN)	166271						
TERBRAGH	252772	M	Ger.		O.T., Rosny - Bois (Fr.) 20.8.44	WITNESS	FR.
TERHOFEN (or TERBOVEN)	166271	M	Ger.	98	Ogruppenfhr SS, official, occupied territories, Strafgefangenenlager Northern Norway 40-45	TORTURE	U.S.
TRITSCHE (see ZIERNIECHE)	128892						
TERKER	251981	M	Ger.		3 Coy, Rgt.Ludendorf, Petie Synthe (Fr.)	INTERR.	FR.
TERLE	192690	M	Ger.		Uschfhr, SS, CC Buchenwald (Ger.) 43-45	TORTURE	U.S.
TERNES, Ferdinand	251922	M			Pvt., CC Ellrich, Nordhausen (Ger.)	MURDER	U.S.
TERPE	307215	M	Ger.		Guard, CC Auschwitz (Pol.) 9.44-1.45	BRUTALITY	POL.
TERRENES	306191	M	Ger.		Osturmfhr, CC Kahla (Ger.) 40-45	MURDER	BEL.
TERRNES	260958	M			Osturmfhr, SS, CC Vaihingen (Ger.) 13.8.44-7.4.45	MURDER	U.S.
TERVEEN, Claas	151015	M	Ger.		Group-leader NSDAP, Mayor, Kutno (Pol.)	TORTURE	U.S.
TERZENBACH, Walter	193501	M			Uschfhr, 4 SS Totenkopf Sturmbann, CC Dora, Mittelbau, Nordhausen (Ger.) 43-45	WITNESS	U.S.
TESARZ, Anton	196505	M	Ger.		Crim.Asst., Gestapo, Brno (Czech.) 39-45	MURDER	CZECH.
TESCH, Carl	104945	M	Ger.	98	Pvt., Sunder Command, CC Warstein-Suttrop (Ger.) 22.3.45	MURDER	U.S.
TESCH, Guenther	193759	M	Ger.	21.10.07	Dr., civilian, deputy chief of the "Lebenshorn",Lidice(Czech.)42-44	MISC.CRIMES	CZECH.
TESCH, Kurt	132521	M	Ger.	10	Schfhr, W-SS, Laubenheim (Ger.) 15.10.44	MURDER	U.S.
TESCHMANN	252771	M			Oberinsp., 13 SS Police Rgt., Ferlach (Aust.) 44-45	MURDER	YUGO.
TESCHNER	300796	M	Ger.		Pvt., 1 Aufkl.Abt., 3 Coy, 2 Col., XV Div. of Africa Corps, Saint Léger (Arlon) (Bel.) 5.9.44	MISC.CRIMES	BEL.
TESKE, Karl	192705	M	Ger.	12	Ministry of Justice, Feldstraflager Nord, CC Finmark(Nor.)42-45	MISC.CRIMES	NOR.
TESKE, Willy	168978	M	Ger.	23	Rottfhr, CC Natzweiler (Fr.)	MURDER	FR.
TESS, George	1340	M	Ger.		Pvt., 903 Festungs Bn.	MISC.CRIMES	U.K.
TETARD, Karl	189318	M	Ger.	6.2.24	SS-Mann, La Desmardiere, Les Bois (Fr.) 3.7.44	MISC.CRIMES	FR.
TETLOFF	251921	M			Flyer, CC Ellrich, Nordhausen (Ger.)	MURDER	U.S.
TETSCH	195931	M	Ger.		SS Sturmbannfhr., Pz.Rgt.2, Tulle (Fr.) 9.6.44	MURDER	FR.
TETZLAFF, Longin	151014	M			Cadet, Polish Army	WITNESS	U.S.
TETZNER	938	M	Ger.		Leiter der Devisenstelle, public official (Pol.) 39-6.40	PILLAGE	POL.
TEUBERT	190311	M			CC Dachau (Ger.), civ.occ.: physician, Dr.	MURDER	U.S.
TEUBERT, Max (see TAUBERT)	250513						
TEUBNER	174291		Ger.		Lt.Col., camp Cmdt., Oflag 55 V D, Aulendorf (Ger.) 8.42	MURDER	YUGO.
TEUCHERT	250517	M	Ger.		Dr., Capt., Bn.Kommandantur, premier Ortskommandant Ruisselede Vinkt Meigen (Bel.) 25.-31.12.40	MURDER	BEL.
TEUER	161268	M		21	Uschfhr, W-SS, CC Ohrdruf (Ger.) 9.4.45	TORTURE	U.S.
TEUERKORN (see TOJERKORN)	256208	M					
TEUFEL	196215	M	Ger.		Osturmfhr, SD, Kdo. z.b.V. 6, St.Die (Fr.) 44	MURDER	U.K.
TEUFEL	257705	M	Ger.		Gend., Feld-Gend.Trupp No.307, Pontivy(Fr.) 44	TORTURE	FR.
TEUFEL, Bernhard	260482	M	Ger.	15.12.12	Uschfhr, W-SS, Guard Coy, CC Auschwitz (Pol.) 7.44-1.45	BRUTALITY	POL.
TEUFEL, Willy	258058	M	Ger.		Capt. (Fr.)	MURDER	FR.
TEUFFEL	179479	M		03	Usturmfhr, W-SS, Gestapo, Le Mans (Fr.) 29.12.43-7.1.44	MURDER	FR.
TEUFFEL, Herbert	228240	M	Ger.	02	Crim.Asst, Gestapo,Gdynia (Pol.) 5.44	MURDER	U.S.
TEUNER, Franz	261097	M	Ger.	6.3.11	Chief of N.C.Y.O., General-secretary, SD, Curatory of Youth, Nazi Czech Youth Organisation, Prague (Czech.)41-45,civ.occ:physician	MISC.CRIMES	CZECH.
TEUSCH, Peter	130127	M	Ger.	25	Pvt., 3 Luftw.Jg.Rgt.35, Quaregnon, Jemappes, Ghlin (Bel.)2.-3.9.44	MURDER	BEL.
TEUTEBERG, Fritz	166262	M	Ger.		Group-leader NSDAP, Reiffenhausen (Bel.)	TORTURE	U.S.
TEUTEN, Jakob	255725	M			Kapo, CC Buchenwald (Ger.)	MURDER	U.S.
TEWES (see TEEWIS)	305319						
TEWES, Paul	141894	M	Ger.	10	Civilian, Essen (Ger.) 13.12.44	MURDER	U.K.
TEXT	260961	M			SS-Pvt., AA, CC Vaihingen (Ger.) 13.8.44-7.4.45	MURDER	U.S.
TEXTOR	138272	M	Ger.		Schfhr. SS, Gestapo, Lyon (Fr.)	MURDER	FR.
THAELER, Fritz	165536	M	Ger.	26	7 SS Pz.Div., Noorbeek (Neth.) 3.9.44	MURDER	BEL.
THAENN	192392	M	Ger.		Member NSDAP, CC Flossenburg (Ger.) 44-45	MURDER	U.S.
THAISS, Adolf	251927	M	Ger.	95	SS Guard, CC Oberndorf (Ger.)	TORTURE	FR.
THALENHORST, Walter	300154	M	Ger.		Foreman in Lohman Werke, Pabianice (Pol.), afterwards transferred to Herford-Sundern (Ger.) 6.40-8.44, -4.45	MISC.CRIMES	POL.
THALER	192629	M	Ger.		Dr.,Physician, Luftw.Sanit.Abt., CC Buchenwald (Ger.) 42-45	TORTURE	U.S.
THALER, Fritz	256515	M		1905 -10	Sturmfhr, W-SS, Automot.techn.training-school, Freia s.d.Muers(Aust.) 29.8.44		
THALHAMMER	251926	M	Ger.		Employee, 1 Abt.IV C Sipo, Brussels (Bel.)	MURDER	U.S.
THALHAUS	189321	M	Ger.		Wachtmstr, Art.Rgt.191, 91 Inf.Rgt., 3 Bn.,St.Maria du Mont,Fr.)5.6.44	INTERR.	BEL.
THALHOFER, Anton	257702	M	Ger.		Osturmfhr, SD, Stavanger, Kristiansund(Nor.) 41-44	MURDER	U.S.
THALLER	205069	M	Ger.		Dr., Civilian, St.Margarethen (Aust.) 5.44	WITNESS	NOR.
THALMANN, Helmut	142312	M	Ger.	19	Rptschfhr, W-SS Totenkopf Sturmbann, CC Buchenwald (Ger.) -43	MISC.CRIMES	U.K.
						MURDER	U.S.

THA-THI

NAME	C.R.FILE NUMBER	SEX	NATIO- NALITY	DATE OF BIRTH	RANK OCCUPATION UNIT PLACE AND DATE OF CRIME	REASON WANTED	WANTED BY
THALMEIER, Joseph	11285	M	Ger.		N.C.O., Panz.Gren.Regt. 110 or 111, 2.Coy., Albine (Fr.) 29.6.44	MURDER	FR.
THAMER	167092	M			Sgt., A.O.K., La Rochette (Fr.) 3.8.44	MURDER	FR.
THAMER	167745	M	Ger.		W.O., Kommandantur, Crest (Fr.) 7.8.44	MURDER	FR.
THAMM	300737	M	Ger.		Pvt., 1.Aufkl.Abt., 3.Coy., 2.Col., XV. Div. of the Afrika Korps, Saint Leger (Arlon) 5.9.44	MISC.CRIMES	BEL.
THAMM, Werner	258242	M	Ger.	24. 5.24	SS-Usturmfhr., SS-Div."Das Reich", Regt."Deutschland" (Fr.)	MURDER	FR.
THE, Werner	39701	M			SS-Usturmfhr., 2.SS Panz.Div."Das Reich" (1.Bn.), Trebons, Pouzat,Bagne- res, De Bigorre (Fr.) 11.6.44	MURDER	FR.
THEIHS, Wilhelm	136387	M	Ger.	06	Farmer, Civilian, Oberbettingen (Ger.) 12.9.44-5.3.45	TORTURE	U.S.
THEINER, Margarethe (nee JANDEK)	195710	F	Ger.		Clerk, Gestapo, Brno (Czech.) 39-45	TORTURE	CZECH.
THEIS, Heinrich	193758	M	Ger.	12. 6.92	Farmer, Civilian, Romersberg (Ger.)	TORTURE	POL.
THEISS	300599	M	Ger.		Pvt., Army, Landesschuetzen-Bn., Arbeitskommando Allendorf (Ger.) 3.43	MURDER	YUGO.
"THE JEW" Nickname (see LUETICH, Ernst)	72278						
THELEN, Christian	260483	M	Ger.	26. 3.93	SS-Sturmmann, Waffen-SS, Guard Coy., C.C.Auschwitz (Pol.) 6.44-1.45	BRUTALITY	POL.
THELL (see THIELE)	256630						
THELLIER	104947	M			Member, Wirtschaftl. and Devisen-Schutzkdo., Lille (Fr.)	WITNESS	U.S.
THEMEL, Richard	196184	M	Ger.		Employee-asst., Gestapo, Brno (Czech.) 39-44	MURDER	CZECH.
THEN, Albert Horst	153501	M	Ger.	27	Pvt., Army, Frankfurt a.Main (Ger.) 21.1.45	MURDER	U.S.
THEOBALD, Edmond	174835	M			Cpl., Dienststelle Giromcourt-Vraine, Repel Poussay (Fr.) 24.8.44-1.9.44	WITNESS	FR.
THEOBALD, Hermann	305972	M			Ortsgruppenleiter and Mayor, Hemina-Moselle (Fr.) 40-44	PILLAGE	FR.
THERBUEREN	104946	M			Civilian.	MISC.CRIMES	U.S.
THEUBERT	252781	M	Ger.		Dr., Gruppen-Sturmfhr., C.C.Dachau (Ger.) 11.42-45	MISC.CRIMES	YUGO.
THEUER	300738	M	Ger.		Pvt., 1.Aufkl.Abt., 3.Coy., 2.Col., XV. Div. of the Afrika Korps, Saint-Leger (Arlon) 5.9.44	MISC.CRIMES	BEL.
THEURING, Emile	162948	M	Ger.		Work Cdo., C.C. Halle (Ger.)	MURDER	BEL.
THEYER	258890	M	Ger.		SS-Hptscharfhr., SS, Ohrdruf (Ger.) 44-45	MURDER	FR.
THIALMANN	256629	M			Lt., Camp Dora, Nordhausen (Ger.)	MURDER	U.S.
THIBETS	306897	M	Ger.		Rottenfhr., SS, C.C.Auschwitz (Pol.) 40-45	MURDER	FR.
THIEBE	180035	M			N.C.O., Panz.Div.SS "Adolf Hitler", 1.Recon.Bn., Stavelot, Parfondruy (Bel.)	MURDER	U.S.
THIEDE	180034	M	Ger.	00 - 05	Capt., 205. Nachr.Regt., 12.Nachtjagd-Corps (Ger.) 5. or 6.44	TORTURE	U.S.
THIEDE, Karl	149152	M	Ger.		Member, Gestapo, Luxembourg (Lux.)	TORTURE	LUX.
THIEDE, Paul	196214	M	Ger.	12	4.Pol.Coy., Waffenschule III, Arnheim (Neth.) 43	MURDER	NETH.
THIEDECKE	251382	M	Ger.		SS-Hptsturmfhr., State Service R.S.H.A., Berlin (Ger.)	MURDER	POL.
THIEDEMANN, Kurt	149582	M	Ger.		11. Panz.Div., Valence (Fr.)	MURDER	FR.
THIEDEMANN, Willi	251909	M			Cpl., C.C. Ellrich, Nordhausen (Ger.)	MURDER	U.S.
THIEDT, Hans	939	M			Sgt., Army, Bizerta (Tun.) 12.42-4.43	MURDER	FR.
THIEKE, Harold	196229	M	Ger.	2. 1.23	Pvt., 3.Coy., Inf.Rspl.Bn.29, 1.Platoon, 129.Panz.Gren.Regt., San Giovanni, E.Paolo near Caia (It.) 13.10.43	MISC.CRIMES	U.S.
THIEL	173464	M	Ger.		Official, Kreiskommandantur F.369, Valjevo (Yugo.) 42-43	MURDER	YUGO.
THIEL	192706	M	Ger.	00	Hilfsaufseher, Ministry of Justice, Strafgefangenenlager Nord, C.C. Finmark (Nor.) 42-45	MISC.CRIMES	NOR.
THIEL	192707	M	Ger.	about 80	Camp Official, Strafgefangenlager Nord (Nor.)	MISC.CRIMES	NOR.
THIEL	259434	M	Ger.		SS-Oschfhr., Gestapo, Paris (Fr.) 41-44	TORTURE	FR.
THIEL	251366	M	Ger.		Kreisleiter, NSDAP, Prison of Camp Siegburg (Ger.) 41-45	MURDER	FR.
THIEL	260359	M	Ger.		Army-employee, SS-Penitentiary Nord-Norway (Nor.) 6.42-5.45	MURDER	YUGO.
THIEL	301906	M	Ger.		Capt., Cmd.Panz.Jaeger Abt.230, 169.Inf.Div., 20.Army, Finmark (Nor.) 10.11.44	MURDER	NOR.
THIEL, Gerhard	192781	M	Ger.		Oberwachtmeister, Schupo, Stalag, C.C.Falstad (Nor.) 41-44	MURDER	NOR.
THIEL, Gerhard	255789	M			Rottenfhr., C.C.Nordhausen (Ger.)	MURDER	U.S.
THIEL, Gerhart	72466	M			Kreisleiter, NSDAP, SS Landesschuetzen Regt.17	MURDER	U.S.
THIEL, Willi	251908	M			Pvt., C.C.Ellrich, Nordhausen (Ger.)	MURDER	U.S.
THIELE	11286	M	Ger.		Capt., Army, C.C. Valdahon (Fr.) 28.8.44	MURDER	FR.
THIELE	62427	M			Oberst d.Pol., SS,	MURDER	UNWCC
THIELE	100264	M		00	Lt., SS, Bremen (Ger.) 38	TORTURE	U.S.
THIELE	124325	M			SS-Hptscharfhr., 1.SS Panz.Div., 2.Panz.Gren.Regt., 12.Coy., Malmedy (Bel.) 17.12.44	MURDER	U.S.
THIELE	142315	M	Ger.	10	SS-Stabsscharfhr., SS, C.C. Neuengamme (Ger.)	BRUTALITY	U.S.
THIELE	191299	M	Ger.		Cpl., Eis.Art.Btty.717, Saint-Andre et Varsenare, Lez-Bruges (Bel.)9.44	MISC.CRIMES	BEL.
THIELE (or THELL)	256630	M			Sgt., SS-Judge, C.C.Ellrich, Nordhausen (Ger.)	MURDER	U.S.
THIELE, Gerhard	62283	M	Ger.		Kreisleiter, NSDAP, Lt.Col., SS, Gardelegen (Ger.) 13.4.45	MURDER	U.S.
THIELE, Hans (see VON THIELE, Hans Dr.)	112854						
THIELE, Hans	121233	M	Ger.	99	Arbeitsleiter, Org.Todt, Boulogne sur Mer (Fr.) 44	MURDER	FR.
THIELE, Joachim	151012	M	Ger.		Osturmfhr., 2.Panz.Gren.Regt., 3.Bn., Stavelot-Malmedy (Bel.) 22.12.44	MURDER	U.S.
THIELE, Julius	10026	M	Ger.		Staatsanwalt,Doctor,Public-Official,County Court,Litomerice (Czech.)	MURDER	CZECH.
THIELE, Wilhelm	135321	M	Ger.		Lagerfhr., Labour-Camp (Ger.)	TORTURE	U.S.
THIELE, Wilhelm	251394	M	Ger.	15.10.98	Pvt., z.b.V.Kommando 31, Valasske Mezirici (Czech.) 2.-5.45	TORTURE	CZECH.
THIELEBEIN	136389	M	Ger.	89	Col., Army (Ger.) 1.45	TORTURE	U.S.
THIELEMANN, R.	151011	M			Civilian?	WITNESS	U.S.
THIELEMANN	251907	M			Usturmfhr., C.C.Dora, Nordhausen (Ger.)	MURDER	U.S.
THIELER, Hans	124326				SS-Hptscharfhr., 1.SS Panz.Div., 2.Panz.Gren.Regt., C.O. 12.Coy., Malmedy (Bel.) 17.12.44	MURDER	U.S.
THIELKER (or THILKER)	195415	M	Ger.	00	SS-Rottenfhr., SS,S.D.Gestapo at Angers, St.Die and Saales (Fr.) 42-44	WITNESS	U.K.
THIELL (or THILL)	252774	M	Ger.		Capt., Enschede (Neth.) 9.-10.44	PILLAGE	NETH.
THIEM	189812	M	Ger.		Lt., Army, Kadinjaca (Yugo.) 29.11.41	MURDER	YUGO.
THIEM (or THIEME)	191195	M	Ger.		Sgt., SS-Guard, C.C.Oranienburg-Sachsenhausen (Ger.) 39-45	MURDER	POL.
THIEMAN, A.	62284	M	Ger.		Public Official, Aschersleben (Ger.) 6.4.45	TORTURE	U.S.
THIEMAN, Karl	251363	M	Ger.	22.10.94	Factory-Manager, Pers.Section, Pilsen (Czech.) 44	INTER.	CZECH.
THIEMANN	142026	M		09	Sturmmann, 12.Panz.Div."Hitler Jugend" and Feldgendarmerie, Abbaye near Caen (Fr.) 6.6.-2.7.44	TORTURE	FR.
THIEMANN	192218	M	Ger.		SS-Osturmfhr., 2.SS Panz.Div."Hohenstaufen", 4.Feld Ers.Bn., Neuville les Bois (Fr.) 11.8.44	MURDER	FR.

THI-THO

NAME	C.R.FILE NUMBER	SEX	NATIO-NALITY	DATE OF BIRTH	RANK	OCCUPATION	UNIT	PLACE AND DATE OF CRIME	REASON WANTED	WANTED BY
THIEMANN	259666	M	Ger.		Lt.(N.S.F.O.), 242 Inf.Div.,Ponteres (Var-Fr.) 27.7.44				MURDER	FR.
THIEMANN, Helmut	192627	M	Ger.		Dr., supervisor, Prisoner hospital,C.C.Buchenwald (Ger.) 42-45				MURDER	U.S.
THIEME	167739	M	Ger.		Dr., leader,occupied territores Gen.Governement Pol., Unterabt.Treuhandstelle,Lublin (Pol.) 9.39 to end of 44				PILLAGE	POL.,NOR.
THIEME see THIEM	191195									
THIEME, Herbert	168222	M	Ger.		Civilian, C.C.Struthof-Natzweiler (Fr.) 40-44				MURDER	FR.
THIEME, Herbert	301493	M	Ger.		SS-Staff-Sgt.,SS,C.C.Buchenwald (Ger.) 16.5.38-9.10.43				MURDER	BEL.
THIER	142314	M	Ger.	00	Chief, SS and Police, Cracow (Pol.) 39-44				MURDER	U.S.
THIERBACH, Herbert	192331	M	Ger.	11	Engineer,Army,Zinna,Torgau (Ger.) 2.-4.45				WITNESS	U.S.
THIERBACH, Martin	301494	M	Ger.	11.6.13	SS-Sgt. (Nr.287324)C.C.Buchenwald (Ger.) 16.5.38-9.10.43				MURDER	BEL.
THIERHOFF, Willi	72059	M	Ger.		Civ.,public official,Civ.internee,C.C.Sachsenhausen (Ger.) 41-43				MURDER	U.S.
THIERNAGEL	144971	M	Ger.		Osturmfhr.,SS, Muenchen (Ger.) 26.-29.7.44				MURDER	U.S.
THIERRY see EISCHINGER,Franz	250711									
THIES, Heinrich	250504	M	Ger.	99	Lt.,377 Jg.Rgt.,1 Inf.Bn., Vinkt (Bel.) 28.-31.5.40				INTERR.	BEL.
THIESS, Franz Hermann.	104949	M	Ger.		Capt.,Army, Stormtrooper,Rheydt (Moers section)(Ger.) 1.45				MISC.CRIMES	U.S.
THIESS, Sigmund	306898	M	Ger.		C.C. Struthof-Natzweiler (Fr.) 42-44				MURDER	FR.
THILE	29639	M	Ger.		Lt.,Army, Bannalec (Fr.) 4.-6.8.44				MURDER	U.S.
THILKEN see THIELKER	195415									
THILKER	307217	M	Ger.		Rottenfhr.,SS,Angers Gestapo,Departments-Sarthe et Mayenne (Fr.) 42-3.8.44				MURDER	FR.
THILL see TIEL	251712									
THILL see THIELL	252774									
THILLE	257474	M		10	Lt.,Ger.Army,Unit Nr.41039,Zajecar(Yugo.) 41-44				MURDER	YUGO.
THILO	126613	M	Ger.		Dr.,Osturmfhr.,SS, C.C.Birkenau,Auschwitz (Pol.) 43-44				MURDER	U.S.,FR.
THILO	251376	M	Ger.		Usturmfhr.,SS,C.C. Auschwitz-Birkenau (Ger.) 11.42				INTERR.	YUGO.
THIMM, Max	173472	M	Ger.		Kapo, C.C. Dora (Ger.) 43-4.45				MURDER	FR.
THIMM, Paul	138008	M	Ger.		Member, Civ. to be detained SA since 32,Erkenschwick(Ger.)				TORTURE	U.S.
THINIUS, Karl	151010	M	Ger.		Civilian,Rothenberg or Rothenburg (Ger.) 3.45				WITNESS	U.S.
THODE	162850	M	Ger.		Hptsturmfhr.,Waffen-SS, Totenkopf-Standarte,C.C.Buchenwald,Weimar (Ger.) 42-45				TORTURE	U.S.
THODE	196235	M	Ger.		Osturmfhr.,C.C.Neuengamme (Ger.)				TORTURE	BEL.
THOLE	941	M	Ger.		Sgt.,Feldgendarmerie,Army,Darracq (Fr.)				TORTURE	FR.
THOLE	39700	M	Ger.		Sgt.,Army,Dar (Fr.), 13.6.44				MURDER	FR.
THOELERT, Hugo	112888	M	Ger.		Gestapo,Quimper (Fr.)				TORTURE	FR.
THOENE, Hans	194291	M	Ger.	11	Lt.,SS,SD, Kolin (Czech.) 39-45				MURDER	CZECH.
THOERMANN, Heinrich	306811	M	Ger.		Cpl.,Kermassenet in Kervignac,Morbihan (Fr.) 20.8.44				MURDER	FR.
THOMA	94640	M	Ger.		Lt.Gen.,432 Div. Nachschub (Neisse (Ger.) 44				TORTURE	U.K.
THOMA see THOMAS, Max	139298									
THOMA	144979	M	Ger.		Lt.Col.,Army, Ludwigsburg (Ger.) 11.8.44				MISC.CRIMES	U.S.
THOMA	193502	M	Ger.		SS-Pvt.,4 SS Totenkopf-Stuba,C.C.Mittelbau-Dora,Nordhausen (Ger.) 43-45				MURDER	U.S.
THOMA	260027	M	Ger.		Sturmscharfhr.,SS,Belgrad (Yugo.) 1.-9.44				MURDER	YUGO.
THOMA, Hubert	135322	M	Ger.		Civilian, Neumarkt (Ger.)				TORTURE	U.S.
THOMA, Max	251906	M	Ger.		SS-Mann, C.C.Harzungen,Nordhausen (Ger.)				MURDER	U.S.
THOMA, Michael	257029	M	Ger.	06	Guard, Lds.Schz.Bn 827, 2 Coy, Grasseth (Ger.) 27.10.44				MURDER	U.S.
THOMAS	62629	M	Ger.		Gen.,head of Wehrwirtschaftsamt				TORTURE	UNWCC.
THOMAS	62430	M	Ger.		Dr.,SS-Gruppenfhr.,SS-Police with B.d.S. (Ukr.) 44				TORTURE	UNWCC.
THOMAS	104951	M	Ger.	00	Civilian,Luisenhoehe in Hullenberg (Ger.) 4.-5.8.44, 4.-5.12.44				MURDER	U.S.
THOMAS	132490	M		08	W.O.,Medical Corps,C.C.Stalag IV B,Muehlberg (Ger.)				TORTURE	U.K.
THOMAS	137530	M			Pvt.,Stalag XIII B,C.C.Weiden,Hau and Grasseth (Ger.,Czech.)9.44,4.45				MURDER	U.S.
THOMAS	138007	M			Lt.,Army,2 Coy, Festungs-Maschinen Bn, Mertert (Lux.) 6.1.45				MURDER	U.S.
THOMAS	139746	M			SS-Mann,Waffen-SS, C.C.Arbeits-Kdo.A-6 (Ger.)				TORTURE	U.S.
THOMAS	144970	M	Ger.		Usturmfhr.,Waffen-SS, Kazani (Grc.)				TORTURE	U.S.
THOMAS	161125	M	Ger.	98	Dr., Bde-Fhr., Police,SS,SD (Sov.Un.) 41-42				MURDER	U.S.
THOMAS	187676	M	Ger.	17	SS-Oberjunksr,C.C.Oranienburg,Sachsenhausen (Ger.)				MURDER	U.K.
THOMAS	251396				Member,SD,Meppel (Neth.) 18.12.44				TORTURE	NETH.
THOMAS, Albert	261612	M	Ger.	7.5.22	Brick-layer,domicile:Wendstrasse 44,Darmstadt,Tunnel Bruttig-Treis				BRUTALITY	FR.
THOMAS, Carolina	251395	F	Ger.		Head of female, C.C.Ravensbrueck (Ger.)				BRUTALITY	FR.
THOMAS, Ernest	124861	M	Ger.	10	Civilian in a Camp,Stalag IV D,Bitterfeld (Ger.) 11.44-4.45				MURDER	U.K.
THOMAS, Judith	104950	F	Ger.		Civilian,secr., C.C. Hadamar (Ger.) 6.44-3.45				WITNESS	U.S.
THOMAS, Karl	162110	M	Ger.		Cpl., 263 Inf.Div.,Finistere,Landernau(Fr.) 44				MURDER	FR.
THOMAS, Karl	168246	M	Ger.		Pvt.,Kdo 943,Landerneau (Fr.) 15.4.,m. 29.8.44				MURDER	FR.
THOMAS, Lydia	142311	F	Ger.		Civilian-nurse, C.C. Hadamar (Ger.) 6.44-3.45				WITNESS	U.S.
THOMAS, Max or THOMA	139298	M	Ger.	4.8.91	Dr.,Obergruppenfhr.,Sipo,SD,SS,RSHA Ukraine, Insbruck and other towns (Aust.) 4.44				MURDER	U.S.
THOMAS, Paul	124138	M	Ger.	05	Civilian,Dr.,C.C.Bitterfeld (Ger.) 6.44-4.45				TORTURE	U.K.
THOMASILIEWICZ, Marian	191197	M	Ger.		SS-Mann, SS, C.C.Sachsenhausen (Ger.) 39-45				MURDER	POL.
THOMER, Josef	193503	M	Ger.		SS-Mann,4 SS Totenkopf-Stuba,C.C.Dora-Mittelbau,Nordhausen(Ger.) 43-45				MURDER	U.S.
THOMEZ	191857	M	Ger.		Capt.,Pz.Truppen Tank,Malestrott (Fr.) 11.3.44				MURDER	FR.
THOMME	177560	F			SS-overseer, C.C. Neu Brenn (Ger.)				TORTURE	FR.
THOMMER	137645	M	Ger.		Hptsturmfhr., SS, C.C. Neuengamme (Ger.)				WITNESS	U.K.
THOMS	149583	M	Ger.	12	Capt.,11 Pz.Div.Nachrichten Abt. (South-West-Fr.) 44				MURDER	FR.
THOMS, Adolf	139749	M	Ger.		Civilian, Buchhorst (Ger.) 6.44				TORTURE	U.S.
THOMSEN	1276	M	Ger.	92	Civilian, Public official,Saules-Monclin (Fr.)				TORTURE	U.S.
THOMSEN	126403		Ger.	00.-08	Civilian,foreman of Chesnoy Farming Enterprise,Chesnoy-Boncourt (Bel.) 6.42-9.45				MURDER	U.S.
THOMSEN	137531	M	Ger.	09	Cpl.,Geh.Feldpol. Gruppe 713				MURDER	U.S.
THOMSEN	151026	M	Ger.	00	Stabsscharfhr.,SS,C.C. Neuengamme (Ger.)				MURDER	U.K.
THOMSEN, Artur	112917	M	Ger.	25.12.00	Hptsturmfhr.,SS,Sipo,Gestapo,RSHA,Reg.Rat,Graudenz(Pol.) Duesseldorf, Berlin (Ger.) 39-45, 11.44				MISC.CRIMES	UNWCC.,POL.
THOMSEN, Carl Albrecht	174782	M	Ger.	90	Capt.,Army,Inf., Bronzolo (It.) 9.43				WITNESS	U.K.
THOMSEN, Thomas	179807	M	Ger.	25.7.08	Usturmfhr.,SS, Crim.secr.,SD, Gestapo, Prague,Kladno,Lidice(Czech.) 39-45				MURDER	CZECH.

NAME	C.R.FILE NUMBER	SEX	NATIO- NALITY	DATE OF BIRTH	RANK OCCUPATION UNIT PLACE AND DATE OF CRIME	REASON WANTED	WANTED BY
THOMSON	300155	M	Ger.		Hauptsturmfhr., and Head of Sicherheitsdienst at Groningen Between Usquert and Warffun-Breede Parish of Baflo (Neth.) 1.4.45	MURDER	NETH.
THON, Willi	72064	M			Civilian, Public Official, Quirnbach, Helferskirchen (Ger.)16,.17.3.MURDER 45	MURDER	U.S.
THONON, Emil	307219	M	Ger.	6.12.96	Member, of the Sicherheitsdienst, Apeldoorn, Woeste Hoog-Soeren (Neth.) 10.,12.44-7.4.45	MURDER	NETH.
THORN	192390	M	Ger.		Commandant, Afrika Corps, Aubriguy Pas De Calais (Fr.) 12.-22.5.40	MURDER	BEL.,FR.
THORN	260726	M	Ger.	98	Major, Ordnungspolizei, Hague (Neth.) 8.41	PILLAGE	NETH.
THORN, Adolf	256514	M	Ger.		Stadtkommissar, Civilian, Altherik (Fr.) 40-44	BRUTALITY	FR.
THORNER	943	M	Ger.		Major, Army 118 Jaeger Div.,738.Regt., Brac (Yugo.)7.43-1.44	MURDER	YUGO.
THORWACHER, Kurt	301495	M	Ger.	17.5.12	Oscha, SS Sgt., SS (No.277546) C.C. Buchenwald (Ger.)16,5.38-9.10.43MURDFR	MURDER	PEL.
THORWEST	167093	M	Ger.		Lt., C.C., Sonnenberg near Kuestrin (Ger.)	TORTURE	FR.
THRON, Wilhelm	142313	M	Ger.	97	Rottenfhr., W.-SS, Totenkopf,C.C. Buchenwald (Ger.)	MISC.CRIMES	U.S.
THRONIER or TROMIER	191289	M	Ger.	96	Lt., Police, Negotin Zajecar (Yugo.) 41-43	TORTURE	YUGO.
THUDE, Gunther	301089	M	Ger.	27.10.20	Cpl., Vendeuvre, Aube (Fr.) 29.u.30.8.44	PILLAGE	FR.
THUKLAN, Rene	226315	M	Ger.	10-15	Agent, Abwehr Fst. 357, Ebersberg near St.Ingbert (Ger.) 11.44	PILLAGE	U.S.
THUEMEL, Paul or TUMMEL	306597	M	Ger.		Chief, SD, Meppel (Neth.) 12.44	TORTURE	NETH.
THUEMMLER, Hans	228097	M	Ger.	10	Major, Oberleiter, Gestapo SD Einsatz Kdo. 16, Chemnitz (Ger.)4.43	MISC.CRIMES	U.S.
THUERMANN, Walter see DURR- MANN	169464						
THUESING	185299	M	Ger.	05	Counceller of the Country Court, Occupied Territories of Bohemia Prague (Czesh.) 40-45	TORTURE	CZECH.
THULE, Kurt	11287	M	Ger.		Pvt., Army 110.or111. Pz.Gren.Regt. 2.Coy. Albine (Fr.)29.6.44	MURDER	FR.
THULKE	189351	M	Ger.		C.C. Dachau (Ger.)	MURDER	BEL.
THÜM	166270	M	Ger.		Sturmbannfhr., Reichsrichter, SS Ministry of Justice, Theresien- stadt (Czech.) 43	MISC.CRIMES	U.S.
THÜM	257959	M			Fin.Off., 150. Pz.Bde., Meuse-Bridge, Antwerp (Bel.) 12.44	MISC.CRIMES	U.S.
THUMA	142305	M	Ger.		Oberscharfhr., W.-SS Totenkopf Sturmbann C.C.Wernigerode (Ger.)	MISC.CRIMES	U.S.
THUMANN	121234	M	Ger.		SS-Sturmfhr., SS, C.C. Neuengamme Hamburg (Ger.)	WITNESS	BEL.
THUMANN	196232	M	Ger.		Untersturmfhr., Campleader, C.C. Gross-Rosen (Ger.) Until 43	TORTURE	BEL.
THUMM, Hans	251371	M	Ger.	28.10.94	Chief-Guard, Plant of Waldenmaier, Heidenheim (Ger.) 41-45	BRUTALITY	POL.
THUN	301721	M	Ger.		Member, SD or Gestapo, Oslo, Trandum nr. Oslo (Nor.) 19.1.43	MURDER	U.K.
THUN, Herbert	112954	M	Ger.		SS-Hauptscharfhr., SD, R.S.H.A. Berlin Amt VI, Trandum near Oslo Berlin (Ger.Nor.) 43	MURDER	NOR.
THUN, Walter	192097	M	Ger.		Civilian, Guard, Lidice (Czech.) 10.6.42	MURDER	CZECH.
THUNAMANN	132523	M	Ger.		SS Oberscharfhr. C.C. Nordhausen, Mittelbau-Dora (Ger.)	MURDER	U.S.
THUNECKE	162200	M	Ger.	20	SS-Untersturmfhr., C.C. Buchenwald (Ger.)	WITNESS	U.S.
THURANDT, Otto	300993	M	Ger.		SS-U-Scharfhr., S.D.-Section II Gestapo,Toulouse,Haute Garonne, (oers Sued West France,especially Toulouse and Tarm (Fr.) 42-44	MURDER	FR.
THURING	256218	M	Ger.		O.T. Muhldorf (Ger.)	WITNESS	U.S.
THURMANN	127101	M	Ger.		Oberwachtmeister, Schutzpolizei, C.C. Schirmeck (Fr.) 43-44	TORTURE	FR.
THURMANN	259146	M	Ger.		Company Commander, SS Hauptsturmfhr., SS Div."Prinz Eugen" Niksic District Montene-Gro (Yugo.) 5.-6.43	MISC.CRIMES	YUGO.
THURN, Karl	192708	M	Ger.	10	Dr., Member Chief Med.Off. Reichs-Justizmin.Medizinalrat, Straf- gefangenenlager Nord, Finmark (Nor.) 9.44	MISC.CRIMES	NOR.
THURNSTADTER, Johann	256217	M	Ger.		SS-Rottenfhr., SS, Muhldorf (Ger.)	WITNESS	U.S.
THURO, Peter	145758	M			C.C. SS, Flossenburg (Ger.)	TORTURE	U.S.
THURS, Max	193479	M	Ger.		Pvt., Army, Akervika (Nor.) 42	MURDER	NOR.
THURSTADT	192626	M	Ger.		SS, C.C. Buchenwald (Ger.) 42-45	MURDER	U.S.
THYLEN	153010	M	Ger.		Owner, of Brickworks, Holzheim (Ger.) 10.40	TORTURE	U.S.
THYROLF	192049	M			Major, Army, Bolzano Tyrol (It.) 19.3.45	MURDER	U.K.
THYROLF J.B.	173458	M	Ger.		Chief, Staatspolizeistelle C.C. Reichenberg,Oswiecim,Birkenau (Czech., Pol.) 39-45	MURDER	CZECH.
THYROLF, Rudolf	162851	M		28.7.06	SS-Sturmbannfhr., Regierungsrat, SS	SUSPECT	U.S.
THYSE	251905	M			Rettleberode, Nordhausen (Ger.)	MURDER	U.S.
THYSSEN	130128	M			SS-Rottenfhr., SS, Mauthausen (Aust.) 41-45	MURDER	U.S.
THYSSEN	301114	M	Ger.		Major, 2.in-commandant, Chief, in the Army, of the Standortskomman- dantur,40-42u.43, Aalborg (Den.) 23.8.43- Abt.1.10.43	MISC.CRIMES	DEN.
TIAKOV	195929	F	Ger.		Wardress, Factory-Scheuring, Krefeld (Ger.) 1.42-3.44	MISC.CRIMES	NETH.
TIATOR	945	M	Ger.		Capt., Feldkommandantur 755, Le Mans (Fr.)	PILLAGE	FR.
TICHATSCHEK, Franz	260427	M	Ger.	10	Member,Gestapo, Polhrimov (Bohemia Czech.) 39-45	MISC.CRIMES	CZECH.
TICHAVSKI, Josef W.	151009	M	Ger.		Civilian-Teacher, C.C. Volary (Czech.)	WITNESS	U.S.
TICHER	250510	M	Ger.		Unterscharfhr., C.C. Buchenwald (Ger.)	TORTURE	FR.
TICHLER, Erwin	252770	M	Ger.		Sgt., 13. Police Regt., Werlach (Aust.) 44-45	MURDER	YUGO.
TICKES or TIGGES	258183	M	Ger.		Uschfhr., 1.SS Pz.Regt."Adolf Hitler" 1.Coy., Wanne near Stavelot (Bel.) 19,21.12.44	MURDER	BEL.
TICKMANN	192217	M	Ger.		Ingenieur, Arbeits-Kdo. 2461, C.C. Stalag 7A, Muenchen (Ger.) 41-45	MURDER	FR.
TIE, Hans	194895	M	Ger.	15.9.02	Member, Oberzoll-Sekr., SD, Luxembourg (Lux.)	MURDER	LUX.
TIECHLER	194822	M	Ger.		Lt.Colonel, Army, C.C. Averoff, Athens-Averoff (Grc.)43-44	MISC.CRIMES	U.K.
TIEDCHEN	946	M	Ger.		Gestapo-Kommissar, C.C. Dachau (Ger.) 40-43	MISC.CRIMES	BEL.
TIEDEL	260080	M	Ger.		SS-Uschfhr., SS, Slave labour-camp, Botn near Rognan (Nor.)	BRUTALITY	YUGO.
TIEDEMANN	112970	M	Ger.		Oberwachtmeister, C.C. Ulven near Bergen (Nor.)	MURDER	NOR.
TIEDEMANN	300156	M	Ger.		Sgt.Member, Sonderkommando Dienststelle L 51685 V L.G.P.A. Amsterdam u.Bentheim Hermann Goering Div. of Admin.Staff,Noordwijk (Neth.) 27.and 28.9.44	TORTURE	NETH.
TIEDEMANN, Kurt	251914	M			Sgt., C.C. Ellrich, Nordhausen (Ger.)	MURDER	U.S.
TIEDLER	947	M	Ger.		Bde.Fuehrer, W.-SS, 9.39-1.42	MURDER	POL.
TIEDTKE, Paul	251988	M	Ger.		Capt. 134. Le.Flak Batt., Ciacomo (It.) 3.1.44	INTERR.	U.K.
TIEFENBACHER	180266	M	Ger.	90	Kreisleiter, NSDAP Arastätt, Oberweier (Ger.)29.7.44	MURDER	CAN.
TIEFENTHAL	124327	M			Capt., 1.SS Pz.Div. 2.Pz.Gr.Regt. G.D. 3.Bn., Malmedy (Bel.)17.12.44MURDER	MURDER	U.S.
TIEFER	167094	M			Cpl.Chief, Gebirgsjaeger Bn.100, Col Petit St. Bernard (Fr.)	MURDER	FR.
TIEFFENBACHER	174896	M	Ger.		Kreisleiter, NSDAP, Hagenau (Fr.)	MURDER	U.N.W.C.C.
TIEFT	164127	M			Capt., Stalag II B, Hammerstein (Ger.) 12.44	MURDER	U.S.
TIEL or THILL	251712	M	Ger.		Capt., L 55800, Army, Enschede (Neth.)	PILLAGE	NETH.
TIELE	192625	M	Ger.		SS-Capt., C.C. Buchenwald (Ger.) 42-45	TORTURE	U.S.
TIELEKEN	257958	M	Ger.		Lt. SA B, 150. Pz.Bde., Meuse-Bridge, Antwerp (Bel.) 12.44	MISC.CRIMES	U.S.
TIELECKE	948	M	Ger.		Cpl., Army, C.C. Caen (Fr.) 6.44	MURDER	FR.

NAME	C.R.FILE NUMBER	SEX	NATIO-NALITY	DATE OF BIRTH	RANK OCCUPATION UNIT PLACE AND DATE OF CRIME	REASON WANTED	WANTED BY
TIELKE	250511	M	Ger.		Chief of Atelier,Wismar(Ger.)42-43	TORTURE	FR.
TIELMAN	305807	M	Ger.		Major,Deputy Commandant at Oflag VI-C,Osnabrueck-Ewersheide(Ger.)42-45	MURDER	YUGO.
TIELS	305324	M	Ger.		Local Commandant Organisation Todt,Member NSDAP, Rhenen(Neth.) 17.11.44-17.4.45	PILLAGE	NETH.
TIEMAN	257457	M.	Ger.		Lt.Naval,Army Div.North Btty.A.A.Feldpost No.00232A,Texel(Neth.)2.2.45	MURDER	U.S.
TIEMANN	259623	M	Ger.		Oschafhr.Gestapo,Area Angers,Maine and Loire(Fr.)42-44	MISC.CRIMES	FR.
TIERBACH	192624	M	Ger.		SS Sgt.CC Buchenwald(Ger.)42-45	MURDER	U.S.
TIERGAERTNER	251913	M			Pvt.CC Ellrich,Nordhausen(Ger.)	MURDER	U.S.
TIERNEY, Jon or BASQUITO	39703	M			Singapore,Malaya(Jap.)	TORTURE	U.K.
TIESCH	135564	M	Ger.	10 or 15	Cpl.714 Land.Schtz.Bn.Stalag XX A,Zoppen(Pol.)12.3.44	MURDER	U.K.
TIESSLER, Stefan	251901	M			Pvt.CC Bodungen,Nordhausen(Ger.)	MURDER	U.S.
TIETENU	307220	M	Ger.		Member of Diez-Lahn Prison Staff(Ger.)40-45	MURDER	BEL.
TIETKA or TITKA	307221	M	Ger.		Cpl.Slot Moermond at Renesse,Zierikzee(Neth.)8.12.44-10.12.44	TORTURE	NETH.
TIETKE	136581	M			Member,Volkssturm,Lichtenberg(Ger.)	MURDER	U.S.
TIETKE, Friedrich	185702	M	Ger.	93	Hptsturmfhr.Polizeirat,S.D.Gestapo,Praha(Czech.)40-45	PILLAGE	CZECH.
TIETL, Willi see TITL	192698						
TIETSCHEN	196233	M			Lt.Police-Waffenschule,Arnheim(Neth.)3.45	MURDER	NETH.
TIETZ	28854	M			Col.20.Army,XVI¹¹ Geb.Corps,Finmark(Nor.)10.-11.44	MURDER	NOR.
TIETZ, Guenther	252484	M		24	Oschafhr.Jailor,State Service,SS,Prague(Czech.)42	TORTURE	CZECH.
TIETZ, Gunther	104952	M			SS Sgt.Totenkopf Div.Army,Bruggen(Ger.)12.44	WITNESS	U.S.
TIETZE'	949				SS Guard,CC Oswiecim,Rajsko,Birkenau(Pol.)6.40-43	MURDER	POL.BEL.
TIETZE	173457	M			Raportfhr.CC Oswiecim,Birkenau(Pol.)39-45	MURDER	BEL.POL.CZECH.
TIEVES, Fritz	251900	M			Sgt.CC Ellrich,Nordhausen(Ger.)	MURDER	U.S.
TIEZER	256219	M	Ger.		SS Mann,Muhldorf(Ger.)	WITNESS	U.S.
TIGER see VINTZER	189815						
TIGGES see TICKES	258183						
TIHANYI, Marina	176929	F			Civilian,between Sur and Aka-Gyor(Hung.)7.3.45	WITNESS	U.S.
TILO, Hans	251383	M	Ger.	12.2.06	SS Scharfhr.Sumperk(Czech.)31.3.45	MURDER	CZECH.
TILI	192697	M	Ger.		Sgt.Friegs-Gefangen.Arb.Bn.190,Bergholnes(Nor.)44-45	TORTURE	NOR.
TILF	151029	M	Ger.		Dr.,Ward,Civilian,P-W.ward Airforce Lazarett,Athen(Grc.)6.7.44	MURDER	U.K.
TILL, Fred	250501	M			Pvt.9 Panz.Pi.Coy.1 SS Panz.Regt.Malmedy(Bel.)17.12.44	MURDER	U.S.
TILLENBECK or TILLENBREK	195437	M	Ger.		Civilian,Schwelm(Ger.)21.3.45	WITNESS	U.S.
TILLER, Friedrich	261403	M	Ger.		Lt.Army,Inf.Regt.642,4 Coy.Aigne(Sarthe)(Fr.)3.8.44	MURDER	FR.
TILLH, Alfred	167025	M			Cpl.Army,Cheveuges(Fr.)6.42	WITNESS	FR.
TILLICH, Erich	305647	M		99	Hptscharfhr.Crim.secretary,Sicherheitspolizei,Aussendienststelle Lanwik Notodden,Telemark,Lifjell(Nor.)3-9.11.44,19.-26.3.45,10.-14.10.44	TORTURE	NOR.
TILLINGER, Franz	193204	M	Ger.		SS Pvt.4 SS Totenkopf Stuba,CC Nordhausen,Mittelbau-Dora(Ger.)43-45	MURDER	U.S.
TILLMANN	28756	M	Ger.		Lt.Waffen SS,CC Struthof(Fr.)44	MURDER	FR.
TILLMANN	124136	M	Ger.		Pvt.Army 4-559 L.8.3.45	MURDER	U.K.
TILLMANN	259724	M	Jer.		Lt.Collective-Coy.La Baffe,Vosges(Fr.)12.-16.-17.-18.9.44	MISC.CRIMES	FR.
TILLMANN, Fritz	256207	M			Baufhr.O.T.,Muhldorf(Ger.)	WITNESS	U.S.
TILLMANN, Joseph	124137	M	Ger.		Pvt.559 Inf.Div.4 Regt.Kornhaus(Czech.)3.45	MURDER	U.K.
TILMETZ	132524	M			Civilian,CC Mittelbau-Dora,Nordhausen(Ger.)	MURDER	U.S.
TILLO, O.	173456	M	Ger.		Dr.,SS Osturmbannfhr.Medical-Officer,Waffen SS,CC Oswiecim-Birkenau (Pol.)39-45	MURDER	CZECH.
TILMES, Marie	179923	F	Ger.	8.12.09	Kanzlie-Angestellte,Gestapo,Praha(Czech.)39-45	TORTURE	CZECH.
TILO	41695	M		13	Dr.,CC Asst.by Dr.Mengele,Possible in SS,Ravensbrueck,Auschwitz(Pol.)	MURDER	DEN.
TILOT	251384	M	Ger.		SS Medical,CC Auschwitz-Birkenau(Pol.)42-45	TORTURE	YUGO.
TILSNER	196291	M	Ger.		Capt.D.C.A.Germany,Beseea,Wiesbaden,Etampes(Fr.)18.8.44	MURDER	FR.
TIMM	62431	M			Gauleiter,Head of Sauckel's Central Depart	MISC.CRIMES	UNWCC
TIMM	251367	M	Ger.		Lt.Gend.Troup 925,Aube(Fr.)3.45	INTERR.	FR.
TIMME	261924	M	Ger.		SS Sturmscharfhr.Belgrad and Veljevo(Yugo.)15.8.42-10.9.44	SUSPECT	YUGO.
TIMMER II(Brother of the I)	28755	M	Ger.		SS Oschsfhr.CC Blockleiter,Chief of the Waescherei,Sachsenhausen(Ger.) 9.41-5.43	MURDER	U.S.
TIMMER, August	258689	M	Ger.		Gendarm,Former Gendarm Lelm(Ger.)Landrstamt Helmstedt(Ger.)6.or 7.44	MURDER	U.S.
TIMMERMAN, Karl	192247	M	Ger.		Civilian,Farmer	TORTURE	CAN.
TIMMERMANN	192782	M	Ger.		SS Lt.Schupo,CC Stalag,Felstad near Drontheim(Nor.)41-44	MURDER	NOR.
TIMMIJANN or TIMMIJMANN	253434	M	Ger.		Pvt.Parachute-Regt.St.Michielsgestel(Neth.)9.-10.44	INTERR.	NETH.
TIMMLER, Fritz	251899	M	Ger.		Pvt.CC Ellrich,Nordhausen(Ger.)	MURDER	U.S.
TIMMYMANN, Herbert	253435	M	Ger.		Pvt.St.Michielsgestel(Neth.)9.44	PILLAGE	NETH.
TIMPFLER	194839	M	Ger.		Pvt.Police 8 Coy.2 Bn.Regt.Schlanders,Roncegno(It.)2.45	MURDER	U.K.
TIPOLSMANN, Charles	251379	M	Ger.	14	Lt.Gend.Unit No.48563,Avignon(Fr.)20.8.44	MURDER	FR.
TIRAY	180008	M			SS Osturmbannfhr.12 SS Panz.Div. Hitler Jugend,25 SS Panz.Regt.near Caen(Fr.)6.6.-8.7.44	TORTURE	CAN.
TIRICH	251389	M	Ger.	00	Col.Army,Giacomo(It.)3.1.44	INTERR.	U.K.
TIRPITZ, Wilhelm	257295	M		13.10.91	Commander,Lt.Col.SS,Kassel(Ger.)1.4.45	MURDER	U.S.
TIRSCH	162852	M			Kriegsgefang.Arbeits Bn.184,4 Coy.Bassis Tunnel near Kobbelveid(Nor.) 4.44	MURDER	NOR.
TISCH	251391	M		06	Scharfhr.Gend.Borgo(It.)20.12.44	INTERR.	U.K.
TISCHBEIN	260683	M			Dr.	WITNESS	U.S.
TISCHBERICHT	124670	M	Ger.		Pvt.Guard,443 Land.Schtz.Bn.4 Coy.Arb.Kdo.780,Grosse Krosse-Widenau (Czech.)16.2.45	MURDER	U.K.
TISCHER	301907	M	Ger.		Capt.Comd.Bau Bn.405,6 Geb.Div.20 Army(Fin.)10.11.44	MURDER	NOR.
TISCHER, Bedrich	186106	M	Ger.	74	Leader,NSDAP,Praha(Czech.)	MISC.CRIMES	CZECH.
TISCHER, Max	262077	M	Ger.		Dr.,SS Sturmfhr.Chief,NSDAP,"Bodenamt",Prag(Czech.)40-44-	SUSPECT	CZECH.
TISCHER, Paul	144973	M			Civilian,Employee,CC Mauthausen(Aust.)11.44-5.45	TORTURE	U.S.
TISCHL	256212	M	Ger.		Employee,Crim.Commissar,SS Osturmfhr.Gestapo,Sumperk(Czech.)42-44	TORTURE	CZECH.
TISCHWITZ	151008	M			Major,3 Bn.15 Panz.Gren.Regt.between Capizzi and San Fratello(Sicily) 7.8.43	WITNESS	U.S.
TISLAU	251392	M	Ger.		SS Kommandofhr.CC Auschwitz(Pol.)	INTERR.	FR.
TISSER	251898	M			Cpl.CC Ellrich,Nordhausen(Ger.)	MURDER	U.S.
TITELUS see TITTLUS	62094						
TITELUS, Henri	306518	M	Ger.		Interpreter att.Feldgendarmerie Chateaubriant,Loire-Inferieure, St.Julien de Mouvantes(Fr.)21.7.44	MURDER	FR.
TITIMAN	162207	M	Ger.		Civilian,Punschau(Ger.)	WITNESS	U.S.
TITL, Willi or TIETL	192498	M	Ger.	circa 86	Prison-Doctor,Reichsjustizministerium,Strafgef.Lager Nord,Finmark(Nor.) 9.3.45	MURDER	NOR.

TIT-TOS

NAME	C.R.FILE NUMBER	SEX	NATIONALITY	DATE OF BIRTH	RANK OCCUPATION UNIT PLACE AND DATE OF CRIME	REASON WANTED	WANTED BY
TITKA (see TIETKA)	307221	M					
TITMANN, G.	191270	M	Ger.		Treuhaender,Fa.J.Diener Porcelana,Krakow (Pol.) 9.39-44	PILLAGE	POL.
TITO	950	M	Ger.	20	Sgt.,Waffen SS,C.C.,Deputy commander,Leusdenheide,Amersfoort (Neth.) 5.42-11.42	TORTURE	U.S.,NETH.
TITO, Karl	179810	M	Ger.		Usturmfhr.,SS,SD,RSHA,Bolzano (It.) 44-45	MURDER	U.S.
TITSE	141344	M	Ger.		Sgt.,Army,Gogolin (Ger.) 8.43	TORTURE	U.K.
TITSER	39704	M	Ger.		Pvt.,Army,Weismusser (Ger.) 12.43-2.45	TORTURE	U.K.
TITTEL	305326	M	Ger.		Doctor,Strafgefangenenlager Nord,Northern Norway (Nor.) 43-45	MISC.CRIMES	CZECH.
TITTEL, Josef	251368	M	Ger.		SS-Mann,Gestapo,La Chaise (Fr.) 28.-30.7.44	BRUTALITY	FR.
TITTEL, Oswald	161273	M	Ger.		SS Div.A.H.,Bois,Barsu,Hamlet,Odet (Bel.) 4.9.44	WITNESS	BEL.
TITTELBACH, Heinz	251897	M			Pvt.,C.C.,Ellrich,Nordhausen (Ger.)	MURDER	U.S.
TITTELBACH, Wilhelmine	255632	F		21. 2.96	Informer,Gestapo,Pilsen (Czech.) 42-45	MISC.CRIMES	CZECH.
TITTLUS, Henri (or TITELUS)	62094	M			Pvt.,Feldgendarmerie,Kripo 794,Ruffigne (Fr.) 6.7.44	MURDER	FR.
TITTMANN, G.	167733	M	Ger.		Treuhaender,civilian,firm J.Diener,Krakow (Pol.) 9.39-44	MISC.CRIMES	POL.
TITZE	951	M	Ger.		Col.,Army,118.Jaeger Div.,738.Rgt.,Montenegro (Yugo.) 7.43-1.44	MURDER	YUGO.
TITZE, Alois	260716	M		7. 6.05	Member,Werwolf,Krnov (Czech.) 4.45	MURDER	CZECH.
TKOTZ	251904	M			Pvt.,C.C.,Rottleberode,Nordhausen (Ger.)	MURDER	U.S.
TLHERS	188823				Major,C.C.,Souges (Fr.) 11.40-43	MURDER	FR.
TOBIAS, Hedwig	184501	F		5. 7.00	Privat seqretary,Gestapo,Praha (Czech.) 39-45	WITNESS	CZECH.
TOBIJ (or TOBOJ)	305986	M	Ger.		Capt.,commandant,of a block of Oflag X A,Sandbostel (Ger.) 40-41	MURDER	POL.
TOBLER, Helmut	129152	M			Capt.,Haupt-Ing.,civilian official,Dulag Luft,Frankfurt-Main, Oberursel (Ger.)	TORTURE	U.K.
TOBOJ (see TOBIJ)	305986						
TOBOLA	193505	M	Ger.		SS-Mann,4.SS Totenkopf Sturmbann,C.C.,Dora-Mittelbau,Nordhausen(Ger.) 43-45	MURDER	U.S.
TOBOLSKI	149584	M			Interpreter,11.Pz.Div.,South-West (Fr.) 44	MURDER	FR.
TOBROVSKY	186175	M	Ger.		Lt.,Navy,De Vaisseau,St.Andre,Le Caz (Fr.) 8.7.44	MURDER	FR.
TODA	256626	M			Employee,Camp,Nordhausen (Ger.)	MURDER	U.S.
TODHE (or TODKE)	184582	M	Ger.		Oschfhr.,SS,C.C.,Huggelheim,Sachsenhausen (Ger.)	TORTURE	FR.
TODT	952	M	Ger.		Intendant,Gestapo,Tunis (Tunisia)	INCENDIARISM	FR.
TODT	28855	M	Ger.		Lt.Col.,20.Army,36.Geh.Korps Staff,Finmark (Nor.) 10.-11.44	MURDER	NOR.
TOEKE	261844	M	Ger.		Cpl.,Unit Art.H.D.V. 199-2295,N.D.F.No. of F.P. 27046 C, Lorgies (Fr.) 3.9.44	MURDER	FR.
TOELLE	189040	M		10	Major,Army,Shio (It.) 1.45	WITNESS	U.K.
TOELLE, Hans	144978	M	Ger.		Civilian,Pfarrkirchen (Ger,)	MURDER	U.S.
TOENNIES, Ernst	250505	M,	Ger.	08	Hptscharfhr.,SS,Gestapo,Frankfurt-Main (Ger.) 10.6.44	BRUTALITY	U.S.
TOEPFER	250507	M	Ger.		Oschfhr.,3.Coy.,1.Bn.,"Das Reich",Oradour sur Glane (Fr.) 10.6.44	MURDER	FR.
TOEPFER, Emil	196230	M	Ger.	05	Lt.,Gend.,Cochem (Ger.) 6.1.45	MISC.CRIMES	U.S.
TOERNIG, Josef	185901	M	Ger.	7. 3.00	Oberstsatsanwalt,occupied territories of Bohemia,Prague (Czech.)40-45	TORTURE	CZECH.
TOERR	251928	M	Ger.		Major,SS,Standarte "Der Fuehrer",Lidice (Czech.) 10.6.42	MURDER	CZECH.
TOETER, Hans	195709	M	Ger.		Pvt.,1.SS Pz.Div.L.A.H.,3.Pi.Coy.,Pi.Bn.,Ligneuville (Bel.)17.-19.12.44	MURDER	U.S.
TOJERKORN (or TEUERKORN)	256208	M	Ger.		Baufhr.,Org.Todt,Muhldorf (Ger.)	WITNESS	U.S.
TOKARSKI	167096	M			Pvt.,Army staff,La Rochette (Fr.) 3.8.44	MURDER	FR.
TOLIUS, Albert	219354	M	Ger.	11	Sturmbannfhr.,Waffen SS,36.Standarte,Zoppot (Pol.) 45	TORTURE	U.S.
TOLL	62126	M	Ger.		Lt.,SS,12.SS Pz.Div."Hitler-Jugend".	WITNESS	U.S.,CAN.
TOLLE	192216	M			Troop-physician,9.SS Pz.Div."Hohenstaufen",4.Feld Ers.Bn.,Neuville les Bois (Fr.) 2.8.44	WITNESS	FR.
TOLLENAAR	252775	M	Ger.		SD-Mann,Terneuzen (Neth.)	PILLAGE	NETH.
TOLLGREVE, Hans	259265	M	Ger.		Rottfhr., active member of Poitiers Gestapo,Civ.Occ.Driver to Hamburg,district of Poitiers (Fr.) 40-45	MISC.CRIMES	FR.
TOLLKUEN	256942	M	Ger.		Sturmschfhr.,Gestapo,Saimiste C.C.,(Yugo.) 20.5.44	MURDER	YUGO.
TOLINER, Hansen	251903	M		18. 8.23	Flyer,C.C.,Ellrich,Nordhausen (Ger.)	MURDER	U.S.
TOLTZEN (see MOLTZEN)	163220						
TOMALA	251902	M			Pvt.,C.C.,Nordhausen (Ger.)	MURDER	U.S.
TOMALI	36699	M	Ger.		Sgt.,Army,515.L.S.Bn., 19.1.-20.3.45	TORTURE	U.K.
TOMALI (see TOMALLEY)	173276						
TOMALLA	193763	M	Ger.		SS-Mann,guard,4.Totenkopf Sturmbann,C.C.,Nordhausen,Dora-Mittelbau (Ger.) 43-45	MURDER	U.S.
TOMALLEY (or TOMALI)	173276	M	Ger.	05 - 10	Sgt.,1-115.Ld.Sch.Bn.Stalag VIII B,C.C. Sosnowitz (Pol.) 44-45	TORTURE	U.K.
TOMAN, Anton	152955	M	Ger.		Oberststurmfhr.,SS,C.C.,Gross-Rosen (Pol.)	MURDER	U.S.
TOMANEK, Rudi	196190	M			Guard or Kapo,C.C.,Gusen (Aust.)	TORTURE	BEL.
TOMARLE	123941	M	Ger.		Sgt.,515.Inf.Rgt.,1.Coy.,Regensburg (Ger.) 20.4.45	MURDER	U.K.
TOMASILIEWICZ, Marien	167738	M	Ger.		SS-Mann,C.C.,Oranienburg,Sachsenhausen (Ger.) 9.39-44	MURDER	POL.,NOR.
TOMASZEWSKI	193761	M	Ger.		Rottfhr.,4.SS Totenkopf Sturmbann,C.C.,Nordhausen,Mittelbau, Auschwitz (Ger.,Pol.) 43-45	MURDER	U.S.
TOMBERS, Lambert	193760	M	Ger.	14. 8.04	Cpl.,Army,electrician and farmer,Oberkail (Ger.) 15.8.44	TORTURE	U.S.
TOMBROWSKI	252780	M	Ger.		Cmdt.,C.C.,Dachau (Ger.) 42	MISC.CRIMES	YUGO.
TOMS	192215	M			Capt.,Army,formation O. 176 B,de Jonzac,Marignac (Fr.) 21.8.44	MURDER	FR.
TOMSC, Giuseppe	145098	M			Lt.,It.Army,Loski Potok (Yugo.) 42	PILLAGE	YUGO.
TONHAUSEROVA, Frony	306292				Member,Gestapo,Trencin,C.C.,Oswiecim,Birkenau (Pol.) 39-45	MURDER	CZECH.
TONI	259322	M			Pvt.,SS,Camp Thekla near Leipzig (Ger.) 18.4.45	MURDER	U.S.
TONN	252773	M			Doctor,Dental officer,Army,Ferlach (Aust.) 44-45	MURDER	YUGO.
TONNINGER, Peter	194950	M	Ger.	95	Member,Gestapo,Kolin (Czech.) 39-45	MURDER	CZECH.
TOCTOW	300739	M	Ger.		Sgt.,1.Aufkl.Abt.,3.Coy.,2.Column,XV. Div.,Afrika Korps,Saint Leger (Arlon) 5.9.44	MISC.CRIMES	BEL.
TOPERT	29734	M	Ger.		Doctor,Vizepresident,public official,Prague (Czech.) 40	MURDER	CZECH.
TOPP	125691	M	Ger.		Sonderfhr.,Feldkommandantur, (Fr.)	MISC.CRIMES	FR.
TOPPE, Alfred	260682	M	Ger.		General,Quartermaster,	WITNESS	U.S.
TOPRANOVSKY	301722	M	Ger.		Blockfhr.,C.C.,Wilhelmshaven (Ger.) 3.44	MURDER	U.K.
TORCK (or TUERCK)	259163	M	Ger.		Member,SS,C.C.,Dachau (Ger.) 12.42-45	MISC.CRIMES	YUGO.
TORKE (see SCHMIDTS)	194063						
TORKLER	194844	M	Ger.		Commissar,Geheime Feldpolizeigruppe,leader of G.F.P. group,C.C. Athens,Averoff prison,(Grc.) 43-44	MISC.CRIMES	U.K.
TORLE, Michael	161270	M	Ger.	19	Uschfhr.,Waffen SS,C.C.,Buchenwald (Ger.)	TORTURE	U.S.
TORMER, Paul	151004	M		1.12.12	Kapo,C.C.,Flossenburg (Ger.)	TORTURE	U.S.
TOROCK	121236	M			Chief,SD,Clermont-Ferrand (Fr.)	TORTURE	FR.
TOST	104953	M		95	Interpreter,Stalag Luft,C.C.,Sagan (Ger.) 25.3.44	MURDER	U.K.

TOT - TRE

NAME	C.R.FILE NUMBER	SEX	NATIO-NALITY	DATE OF BIRTH	RANK OCCUPATION UNIT PLACE AND DATE OF CRIME	REASON WANTED	WANTED BY
TOT	259109	M	Ger.		Coy.Commander, Sturmfhr., 2.Geb.Jaeger-Rgt., SS-Div."Prinz Eugen" Niksic distr.Montenegro (Yugo.) 5.6.43	MISC.CRIMES	YUGO.
TOTZAUER, Fritz	189813	M	Ger.	13	Usturmfhr., SS, C.C., Neuengamme (Ger.) 43	MURDER	YUGO.
TOUNAINT	144980	M	Ger.		Gen., Army, Plenipotentiary in Boehmen-Maehren, Lidice (Czech.)	MURDER	U.S.
TOUR	174548	M	Ger.	95	Capt., Camp BA,B 20, Heydebreck (Ger.) 40-42	TORTURE	U.K.
TOURY	194075	M	Ger.	00	Chief of Police, C.C., Ravensbrueck (Ger.)	TORTURE	FR.
TOWACHT (see KOWACHT)	173735						
TOYFL, Franz	255635	M	Ger.	14.10.98	Cmdt., Gestapo, Breclav (Czech.) 7.4.45	MISC.CRIMES	CZECH.
TOYKA	136584	M	Ger.	07	Dr., Counsellor, Ministry of finance, Posen (Pol.) 42	MISC.CRIMES	U.S., POL.
TRABANT	186683	M	Ger.		Sturmbannfhr., SS-Leibstandarte Adolf Hitler, Commander of III.Bn., Worm Houdt (Fr.) 5.40	MURDER	U.K.
TRABER	153011	M			Sgt., Army, Daasdorf (Ger.) 7.8.44	INTERR.	U.S.
TRACELER	141616	M			Sgt., Sarras and Andance (Fr.) 13.6.44	MURDER	FR.
TRAEFER	195928	M	Ger.		Capt., Waffen-SS-Chief, Izon la Bruisse Sederon (Fr.) 22.2.44	MISC.CRIMES	FR.
TRAEGER	252769	M	Ger.		Dr., Dental-Officer (P.W.'s.), Army, Ferlach (Aust.) 44-45	INTERR.	YUGO.
TRAEGER	300157	M	Ger.		Head of Block 15, 11.42 - 5.45	MURDER	FR.
TRAEGER, Francois	167099	M	Ger.		Driver, Army, Reichshoffen (Fr.) 45	WITNESS	FR.
TRAGENAPP	250516	M	Ger.		Capt., 2.Coy., 338.Div., La Bresse (Fr.) 9.44-11.44	MURDER	FR.
TRAGER	180033	M			Civilian, Palleben (Ger.) 10.44 or 11.44	WITNESS	U.S.
TRAGER, Franz	251377	M	Ger.		Police-Department, Ligny en Barrais (Fr.) 1.3.43	INTERR.	FR.
TRAGSCHUTZ	251896	M			Flyer, C.C.Ellrich, Nordhausen (Ger.)	MURDER	U.S.
TRAMNAU	305747	M	Ger.		Uschfhr., SS, Geh.Feldpol., Hotel Bratford, Paris, later 11,rue des Saussaies, Paris (Fr.) 41-44	TORTURE	FR.
TRAMP, Gerhard	130164	M		22	Pvt., Army, Eichstatt (Ger.) 25.2.44	MURDER	U.K.
TRAMPE	1341	M	Ger.		Lt., Army, 2.Pl.,194.Gr.	MISC.CRIMES	U.K.
TRAMPERT, Adam	187804	M	Ger.		Civilian, Wehrden-Saar (Ger.) 8.44	TORTURE	U.S.
TRAMPLER, Oskar	256213	M	Ger.	19.10.94	Lt., Police, Velke Mezirici (Czech.) 7.5.45	MURDER	CZECH.
TRAMPP	256139	M	Ger.		Hptschfhr., 3.Coy., 1.Bn., SS-Rgt."Das Reich", Oradour sur Glans (Fr.) 10.6.44	INTERR.	FR.
TRAN, Raqul	251393	M			Rottfhr., C.C., Auschwitz (Pol.)	BRUTALITY	FR.
TRANKEL	305572	M	Ger.		Lt., Muehlhausen and Frankfurt am Main (Ger.) 1.45-3.45	MURDER	U.K.
TRANKLE, Camill	192783	M	Ger.		Schupo., C.C., Stalag, Falstad nr.Drontheim (Nor.) 41-44	MURDER	NOR.
TRAPP, Johann	250502	M	Ger.	7.3.23	Pvt., 102.Flak-Abt.,95.K.A.B., Strijpen (Bel.) 3.9.44	MURDER	BEL.
TRAPP, Willi	165977	M	Ger.		Sgt., Army, Munition-Verwaltung, Cloyes (Fr.) 11.8.44	MURDER	FR.
TRASSER	179926	M	Ger.		SS-Mann, C.C., Ravensbrueck (Ger.)	MURDER	FR., BEL.
TRASSER	251895	M			Uschfhr., C.C., Woffleben, Nordhausen (Ger.)	MURDER	U.S.
TRASSL	953	M	Ger.		Commandant de Place, Army, SS-Div."Das Reich", Rgt."Der Fuehrer", Buzet (Fr.) 7.8.44	MURDER	FR.
TRATT, Karl	193764	M		03	Blockleiter,(NSDAP) (Czech.)	MISC.CRIMES	CZECH.
TRAUB	250514	M	Ger.		Unit: F.P.Nr.06459, Romilly (Fr.) 8.44	PILLAGE	FR.
TRAUB, Paul	252779	M	Ger.		Osturmbannfhr., SS, SD, Police, Fiume (Yugo.) 44-45	TORTURE	YUGO.
TRAUCH	152975	M	Ger.		Col., Feldkommandantur, Tours (Fr.) 42-43	MURDER	FR.
TRAUDE	152954	M	Ger.		SS, C.C., Auschwitz (Pol.)	MURDER	U.S.
TRAUER	162801	M	Ger.	11	SS-Officer, Trie le Chateau (Fr.) 14.8.44	MURDER	FR.
TRAUMNAU	253433	M	Ger.		Uschfhr., SS, Gestapo, Paris (Fr.) 41, 42, 43, 44	TORTURE	FR.
TRAUNER, Leopold	144974	M	Ger.	12.12.83	Civilian, Conc.Camp, Mauthausen (Aust.)	TORTURE	U.S.
TRAUT, Rudolf	192091	M	Ger.	2.7.02	Civilian, Guard, Lidice (Czech.)	MURDER	CZECH.
TRAUT	1761	M			8.Coy., 2.Bn., 148.I.R., Amiens (Fr.) 44	MURDER	U.K.
TRAUT	162111	M	Ger.	85	Sgt., 635.Lds.Schtz.Bn., Stalag IX e, 3.Coy., Romhild (Ger.) 41	TORTURE	U.K.
TRAUT, Hermann	148763	M	Ger.	16	Uschfhr., SS, Conc.Camp, Struthof (Fr.) 44	MURDER	FR.
TRAUTE	306900	M	Ger.		Hptschfhr., political-section, C.C., Auschwitz (Pol.) 40	MURDER	FR.
TRAUTMAN	153053	M	Ger.		Cpl., Army, Blechhammer (Ger.) 3.43	TORTURE	U.K.
TRAUTMAN, Max	179167	M	Ger.		Pol.Secr., Gestapo, Police, Conc.Camp, Niederbuehl-Gaggenau (Ger.) 44	MURDER	U.K.
TRAUTMANN, Otto	251894	M		19.10.05	Pvt., C.C. Ellrich, Nordhausen (Ger.)	MURDER	U.S.
TRAUTMANN, Werner (see THIELE VON, Hans)	112854						
TRAUTRAT, Fritz	262165	M	Ger.	11.6.13	Oschfhr., Coy.for Cars and Motorbicysles, 51.SS-Armoured-Bde., Breviandes,Bucheres, Ste.Savine,La Riviere de Corps (Troyes) (Fr.) 25.8.44	BRUTALITY	FR.
TRAUTWEIN, Emile	1089	M	Ger.		Sub.Officer, SD, Chalons (Fr.)	TORTURE	FR.
TRAXCELLER (or TRAXZELLER)	189283	M			Sgt.,9.Pz.Div.,20.Bn.,5.Coy., Andance (Fr.) 13.6.44	MURDER	FR.
TREATHER	258705	M	Ger.		Uschfhr., SS, 2.Bn., 38.SS-Rgt.,"G.v.B.-Div.", Kennat (Ger.) 20.10.44	WITNESS	U.S.
TREB	186773	M	Ger.		Osturmfhr., SS, C.C., Flossenburg (Ger.)	TORTURE	FR.
TRECHSEL	256138	M	Ger.		Guard, C.C., Flossenburg (Ger.)	TORTURE	FR.
TRECHSEL	305328	F	Ger.		Head Superintendent, C.C., Flossenburg (Ger.) 42-45	MURDER	FR.
TRECK (or TREK)	170544	M	Ger.		Dr., Capt., Army, Physician, Oflag 65,C.C.,Strasbourg Barkenbruegge,45	TORTURE	YUGO.
TREEN	124459	M	Ger.		N.C.O., Navy, Prison ship, Portland, 4.194?	MURDER	U.K.
TREFF	131143	B	Ger.		Pvt., 627.Wolga Tartares Legion	MURDER	BEL.
TREFZ	195343	M			Col., Commander of the Ger.P.W.Camp,Stalag 9 C,Bad Sulza (Ger.)44-45	MURDER	CZECH.
TREIBER	189041	M	Ger.	12	Lt., 1.Paratroop-Div., Intelligence-Officer, nr.Cassino (It.) 44	TORTURE	U.K.
TREICHEL, Ferdinand	261795	M	Ger.		Inspector, Gestapo of Amiens, Gentelles (Fr.) 6.-8.44	MURDER	FR.
TREICHTER	121237	M	Ger.		Doctor, Conc.Camp, Ravensbrueck (Ger.)	TORTURE	FR.
TREIMANN	177559	M			Conc.Camp, Neuengamme (Ger.)	TORTURE	FR.
TREIS	179738	M	Ger.	09	Sgt., 76.Panz.Armee-Korps, Cavriglia (It.) 11.7.44	MURDER	U.K.
TRETTER	188560	M	Ger.	10	SS-Physician, C.C., Ravensbrueck (Ger.)	TORTURE	U.K.
TREK (see TRECK)	170544						
TRENCKEL	180036	M	Ger.		SS-Mann,Leibstan."A.Hitler", Aufkl.Abt., Renardmont Stavelot (Bel.)12.44	MURDER	BEL.
TRENCZEK	188558	M	Ger.	13	Lt., 1047.Inf.Rgt., Marzana Canfanaro (It.) 3.45	MURDER	U.K.
TRENDELKAMP, Heinrich	169837	M	Ger.		Leader, NSDAP, Lengerich (Ger.) 24.8.44	TORTURE	U.S.
TRENGZEK	139066	M	Ger.		Ital.Army, Marzano Canfanco (It.)	MURDER	U.K.
TRENK, Heinrich	251891	M			Pvt., C.C. Nordhausen (Ger.)	MURDER	U.S.
TRENKEL	184583	M	Ger.		Officer, Gestapo, C.C., Dachau (Ger.)	MURDER	FR.
TRENKER, Hans	251890	M			Cpl., C.C. Woffleben, Nordhausen (Ger.)	MURDER	U.S.
TRENKLE	27412	M	Ger.	2.8.99	Hptschfhr., SS, C.C., Dachau, Neuengamme (Ger.) 43	MURDER	U.S.
TRENKLER	300740	M	Ger.		Pvt.,1.Aufkl.Abt.,3.Coy.,2.Col., XV.Div.Africa-Corps,St.Leger,Arlon,9.44	MISC.CRIMES	BEL.
TRENKLER, Hans	193851	M	Ger.	25.6.05	Uschfhr.,4.SS-Totenk.Stuba.,C.C.,Dora-Mittelbau,Nordhausen (Ger.)43-45	MURDER	U.S.

NAME	C.R.FILE NUMBER	SEX	NATIO-NALITY	DATE OF BIRTH	RANK OCCUPATION UNIT PLACE AND DATE OF CRIME	REASON WANTED	WANTED BY
TRENNHAUGER	255790	M	Ger.		Cpl., 2.Coy.Sturm Bn., AOK Lt.MG, Near Courcelles (Fr.) 15.11.44	MURDER	U.S.
TRENTMANN, Hermann	195927	M	Ger.		Pvt.,1.Inf.-Art.Div.,8.Bn.,Monterre Silly (Fr.) 25.6.40	MISC.CRIMES	FR.
TRENZ, Johann	191379	M	Ger.	1. 8.13	Civilian, Tephonist, Schwalbach (Ger.) 8.44	TORTURE	U.S.
TRECZYK, Jerzy (alias JUREK, George)	140816	M	Ger.		Lager-Officer,Blockleiter, C.C., Flossenburg (Ger.)	TORTURE	U.S.
TREPKAU	300741	M	Ger.		Pvt., 1.Aufkl.Abt.,3.Coy.,2.Column,XV.Div.of the Afrika Korps, Saint Leger (Arlon) (Bel.)5.9.44	MISC.CRIMES	BEL.
TREPKE	193480	M	Ger.		Lt., Army, Sunndalsora (Nor.) 42	MURDER	NOR.
TREPP, Grete	195708	F	Ger.		Employee, Gestapo, Bruenn (Czech.) 39 - 43	TORTURE	CZECH.
TRESCHLER	256346	M	Ger.		Cpl., 1.Coy. 1.SS-Panz.Div. Leibstandarte SS "Adolf Hitler" Malmedy (Bel.) 17.12.44	MISC.CRIMES	U.S.
TRESS, Albert	954	M			Pvt., Army, Baudrigues (Fr.)	MURDER	FR.
TRESS, Helmuth	194949	M	Ger.	13. 9.03	Member, Unterfhr. Gestapo, SS, Kolin (Czech.) 39 - 45	MURDER	CZECH.
TRESTER	39705	M			N.C.O.,Waffen SS, Div. Feldpost Nr. 48 763 B,St.Sulpice,Fortmusson, Chateau Gontier (Fr.) 8.44	MURDER	FR.
TRETTIN ,Karl	955	M	Ger.	21. 8.01	Pvt., Army, Feldgendarmerie de Cassel, Hazebrouck(Fr.) 8.-9.44	MURDER	FR.
TREU, Karl	196808	M	Ger.		Gestapo-Criminal-Employee, Border-Police, Brno (Czech.) 39 - 45	SUSPECT	CZECH.
TREUCH, Fritz	255791	M	Ger.		Feldgendarmerie, Annay s-Lens,Bully Grenay (Fr.) 8.44 - 9.44	WITNESS	FR.
TREUTZ, Arnold (or TROITSCH or TROITCH)	193650	M	Ger.		Uscharfhr., Aussendienststelle der Sipo und SD, Leeuwarden (Neth.) 9.44 - 4.45	MURDER	NETH.
TREYER, Joseph	72060	M	Ger.		Uscharfhr., Waffen SS, C.C. Struthof (Fr.)	MISC.CRIMES	FR.
TRIBE (see TRIEBE, Arno)	126406						
TRIBUS	179925	M	Ger.		Guard, C.C., Ravensbrueck (Ger.)	TORTURE	BEL.
TRIBUS, Joseph	306317	M	Ger.		Pvt., belonging to 8.Coy. Schlanders,Police Rgt.,Roncegno (It.)3.45	MURDER	U.K.
TRICKE	255724	M	Ger.		Hauptscharfhr., C.C., Buchenwald (Ger.)	MURDER	U.S.
TRIEB	257408	M	Ger.		Guard, Oberwachtmeister, SS, slave labour camp,Narvik (Nor.) 6.11.42	BRUTALITY	YUGO.
TRIEBE (or TRIBE, Arno)	126406	M	Ger.		Rottenfhr., SS-Guard, C.C., Buchenwald (Ger.) 44 - 45	TORTURE	U.S.
TRIEBEL	196221	M	Ger.		Gend.Master, Civilian, Poppenhausen (Ger.) 11.5.42	MURDER	POL.
TRIEBEL, Gustav	307222	M	Ger.		Reichsbahn official-employed, Fernmeldemeisterei office,Amersfoort (Neth.) 10.44 und 5.45	PILLAGE	NETH.
TRIEBENBERGER, Fritz	11288	M	Ger.		Pvt., Army, 110.or 111.Pz.Gren.Rgt.,2.Coy. Albins (Fr.) 29.6.44	MURDER	FR.
TRIEBLER, Wilhelm	251893	M			Sgt., C.C., Ellrich,Nordhausen (Ger.)	MURDER	U.S.
TRIEPINSKY	250506	M	Ger.		Obersturmfhr.,SS, C.C., Neuengarvme (Ger.)	INTERR.	BEL.
TRIER, Otto	251892	M			Rttfhr., C.C., Harzungen,Nordhausen (Ger.)	MURDER	U.S.
TRIERL, Willi	188715	M	Ger.		Inf.Bn., 18, Busset (Fr.) 7.8.44	MURDER	FR.
TRIES, Hans	72062	M	Ger.	13	Cpl., Army,10.Pz.Gr.Rgt.,1.Coy. Rochefort (Bel.) 29.12.44	MURDER	U.S.
TRIESCH, Adolf	141617	M	Ger.	28. 6.93	Capt., Gendarmerie, Bischwiller (Fr.) 1.12.44	MURDER	FR.
TRIESCHMANN	174026	M	Ger.		Capt., Stalag VI A, C.C., Hemer (Ger.) 41 - 45	TORTURE	U.S.
TRIESE, Hans	185303	M	Ger.		Dr.,Medizinalrat,Member, Reichsaerztekammer, Berga (Pol.)	MURDER	POL.
TRIETE	173277	M	Ger.	10	Chief-physician, C.C., Ravensbrueck (Ger.) 8.44	TOETURE	U.K.
TRIETZEL	126937	M	Ger.		11.Pz.Div.,2.Cie. Z.A.A. A.7, Albine (Fr.) 12.8.44	MURDER	FR.
TRIFTMANN, Ernst	258706	M	Ger.		Uscharfhr., SS, 2.Bn.,38.SS-Rgt."Goetz von Berlichingen" Div. Kennat (Ger.) 20.10.44	WITNESS	U.S.
TRILL, Victor	196219	M	Ger.		Kriminal-Clerk, Gestapo, Brno (Czech.) 39 - 43	MURDER	CZECH.
TRIMBUCH, Emil	251373	M	Ger.	30. 7.03	Employee, Gestapo, Litomerice (Czech.) 39 - 45	TORTURE	CZECH.
TRIMMEL	72056	M	Ger.	96	Lt., Verbindungsstab, Stalag 377, C.C., Gerolstein (Ger.) 12.44 - 2.45	TORTURE	U.S.
TRIMMEL	173463	M	Ger.		Ortsgruppenleiter, NSDAP, Golldorf (Yugo.) 4.41 - 44	MURDER	YUGO.
TRINKBERGER (or TRINKLBERGER)	256209	M	Ger.		O.T., Muehldorf (Ger.)	WITNESS	U.S.
TRINKEL, Michael	192329	M	Ger.		Member, Army, Prisonner, Zinna,Torgau (Ger.) 45	WITNESS	U.S.
TRINKELS	189322	M	Ger.		Hauptscharfhr., SS, C.C., Dachau (Ger.) 40 - 45	TORTURE	BEL.
TRINKHAUS	151002	M			Lt., 29.Panz.Gren.Div.,15.P.G.Rgt.,7.Coy.,Between Capizzi and San Fratello (Grc.) 1.8.43	WITNESS	U.S.
TRINKHAUSS (or TRINKHAUS)	12061	M		15	Rottenfhr., Kitchen-Chief, C.C.,Hinzert (Ger.) 43	MISC.CRIMES	U.S. FR.
TRINKLBERGER (see TRINKBERGER)	256209						
TRINKS	133996	M	Ger.	95. - 99	Lt., Army, Sicherungs Bn. 1082, Prum (Ger.) 22.12.44	MISC.CRIMES	U.S.
TRION, Horst	251386	M	Ger.		Sturmscharfhr., SS, SD, Toulouse (Fr.) 11.42 - 8.44	MISC.CRIMES	FR.
TRIPKE	168223	M	Ger.		Civilian, Leiter des Amtes f.Raumordnung, Lwow (Pol.) 9.39 - 44	MISC.CRIMES	POL. NOR.
TRIPKE, Rudolf	257410	M	Ger.		Rottenfhr., SS, slave Labour camp, Osen (Nor.) 6.42 - 3.43	MISC.CRIMES	YUGO.
TRIPPE	196218	M	Ger.	95	Cpl., Guard, KDO 7012.Dinkler, Attache "Pioneer" Hilversheim, Dinklar (Ger.) 11.44	TORTURE	U.K.
TRIPPE, Friedrich	141343	M	Ger.		Civilian, Gleiwitz (Ger.) 1.44	MURDER	U.K.
TRIPPEN, Maria	135323	F	Ger.		Efferen (Ger.) 2.10.44	WITNESS	U.S.
TRIPPLER, Otto	161278	M	Ger.		Civilian, Electrician at Adolf Mine,Merkstein (Ger.) 42 - 44	TORTURE	U.S.
TRISCHLER, Franz	252777	M	Ger.		Staffelhauptscharfhr., SS, Belgrade (Yugo.) 42 - 43	MISC.CRIMES	YUGO.
TRISHMANN	124139	M	Ger.		Major, Stalag 31 F,XVIII,C.C., Markt-Tongau (Aust.) 6.44 - 45	MISC.CRIMES	U.K.
TRISKA, Adolf	195707	M	Ger.		Attache, Locksmith, Gestapo, Civilian, Bruenn (Czech.) 39 - 45	TORTURE	CZECH.
TRITSCHLER, Eugen	302006	M	Ger.		Engineer,Ex-Director,techn.Director, Electrical Society,Zittau,Saxony Motorised Transport,Muelhausen,Haut-Rhin (Fr.) 1.1.44	PILLAGE	FR.
TRITTNER, Anna	195706	F	Ger.		Employee, Gestapo, Bruenn (Czech.) 39 - 45	TORTURE	CZECH.
TRKOVSKY, Josef	260426	M	Ger.		Civilian, Tabor (Czech.) 39 - 41	MISC.CRIMES	CZECH.
TROCKER (or TROCOURT or TROPCOURT or DROKUR)	177586	M	Ger.	80	Cmdt., Deputy, SS, C.C., Neu-Brenn(Ger.) 43 - 44	MISC.CRIMES	FR. U.K.
TROEGER,Fritz (alias Martin)	189677	M	Ger.		Abwehr, Vannes (Fr.)	MISC.CRIMES	FR.
TROEHLER	306925	M	Ger.		Amt fuer Rassenpolitik, Strassburg (Fr.) 44	BRUTALITY	FR.
TROELZ (or TROLZ)	253437	M	Ger.		Capt., Artillerie Div.Staff Hoek v.Holland,Heeres Kuesten Btty. Schouwen (Neth.) 5.11.43	MISC.CRIMES	NETH.
TROESCHEL, Otto	195926	M	Ger.		Sgt., Stalag VI.D. C.C., Dortmund (Ger.) 7.43	TORTURE	FR.
TROFFER, Karl	194289	M	Ger.		Pvt., Army, Unit 48 097, Vie la Gardiole (Fr.) 19.8.44	PILLAGE	FR.
TROGE, Richard	180259	M		98	Major, 1.Bn., 13.SS-Police Rgt., Bleiburg (Aust.) 14.10.44	MURDER	U.S.
TROHS, Rudolph	167827	M	Ger.		Pvt., 9.Res.Rgt.Gren. 1.Coy., Magny d'Anigon (Fr.) 18.9.44	MURDER	FR.
TROITER	251889	M			Flyer, C.C., Ellrich,Nordhausen (Ger.)	MURDER	U.S.
TROITSCH - TROITCCH, Arnold (see TREUTZ, Arnold)	193650						

TRO - TSC

NAME	C.R.FILE NUMBER	SEX	NATIO-NALITY	DATE OF BIRTH	RANK OCCUPATION UNIT PLACE AND DATE OF CRIME	REASON WANTED	WANTED BY
TROJAN	193481	M	Ger.		Pvt.,1Kgf.Arb.Bn.41,Neerlandsdel,Kristiansund (Nor.) 41-45	TORTURE	NOR.
TROLL	194843	M	Ger.		Oschfhr.,SS,C.C.Lublin (Pol.) 40-44	MURDER	POL.
TROLL	260984	M			Hptschfhr.,SS,C.C.Vaihingen (Ger.) 13.8.44-7.4.45	MURDER	U.S.
TROLSEN	147207	M	Ger.		Oschfhr.,SS,Cmdt.of C.C.Begunje (Yugo.) 43	MURDER	YUGO.
TROLZ (see TROELZ)	253437						
TROMA,Richard,Dr. (see TROMMER)	121239						
TROMER	256216	M	Ger.	29. 1.98	Capt.,Arvant,Bournoncle (Fr.) 13.8.44	MURDER	FR.
TROMER,August	147996	M		00	Dr.,W-SS,C.C.Ravensbrueck (Ger.)	MURDER	U.S.
TROMER,Otto	150587	M	Ger.	98	Capt.,Army,Arvant (Fr.) 44	MURDER	FR.
TROMIER	173462	M	Ger.		Chief-official,Gestapo,Negotin (Yugo.) 42-43	TORTURE	YUGO.
TROMMER	956	M	Ger.		Lt.,Army,Art.,OC,L 49300,L.G.P.A.Bruessel,Brabieres (Bel.)1.9.44	MURDER	FR.
TROMMER	186772	M.	Ger.		Lt.,C.C.Flossenburg (Ger.)	MURDER	FR.
TROMMER	189807	M	Ger.		Dr.,SS-Oberarzt,C.C.Ravensbrueck (Ger.)	TORTURE	BEL.
TROMMER,Fritz	192699	M	Ger.	circa 08	Reichsjustizminist.,Strafgef.Lager Nord,C.C.Finmark (Nor.)	MISC.CRIMES	NOR.
TROMMER,Richard (or TROMA)	121239	M	Ger.		Dr.,Hptsturmfhr.,Camp-Dr.,C.C.Ravensbrueck (Ger.) 42-45	MURDER	FR.U.K.
TROMMLER,Hans	258709	M			Dr.,Chief,Gestapo,Wiesbaden (Ger.)	INTERR.	U.S.
TROMPETER,Heinrich	251888	M			Pvt.,C.C.Harzungen,Nordhausen (Ger.)	MURDER	U.S.
TRONDLE	251385	M	Ger.		Uschfhr.,S.T.Mann,S.D.,Toulouse (Fr.) 11.42-8.44	MISC.CRIMES	FR.
TRONDLER,Wilhelm	152952		Ger.		Chief,Org.Todt,Ervik (Nor.) 42-43	TORTURE	NOR.
TRONE	194288	M	Ger.		Officer,Army,Cmdt. the place of Marck (Fr.),(P.d.C.) 9.44	MURDER	FR.
TRONER	152953	M	Ger.	20 or 25	SS-Mann,C.C.Reichenau (Aust.) 44	MURDER	U.S.
TRONER	186771	M	Ger.		Osturmbannfhr.,SS,C.C.Flossenburg (Ger.)	TORTURE	FR.
TRONIE	192623	M	Ger.		Cpl.,SS,C.C.Buchenwald (Ger.) 42-43	TORTURE	U.S.
TRONIER (see THRONIER,Georg)	191289	M					
TRONIER,Georg	306293	M	Ger.		Member,Gestapo,Nove Mesto n-Vahom,C.C.Oswiecim,Birkenau (Pol.) 39-45	MURDER	CZECH.
TRONNIER	192622	M	Ger.		Cpl.,SS,C.C.Buchenwald (Ger.) 42-45	TORTURE	U.S.
TROPCOURT (see TROCKER)	177586						
TROPITSCH,Rolf	251380	M	Ger.		Dr.,Dir.,Chemical Factory,Marktredwitz (Ger.) 40-45	BRUTALITY	POL.
TROPSCHUJ,Maximilian	255637	M	Ger.	5. 4.01	Forester,Member,Civ.,S.A.,Luzice (Czech.) 44	MURDER	CZECH.
TROSBACH	957	M	Ger.		Pvt.,Army,Koenigsberg (Ger.) 27.1.42	TORTURE	FR.
TROSCHKE	193765	M	Ger.	circa 11	Osturmfhr.,SS,Chief of Economic Section of C.C.Terezin (Czech.)39-45	TORTURE	CZECH.
TROSSEN	161269	M	Ger.		Pvt.,Ldsschtz.-Bn.789,Sinzig Krs.Ahrweiler, 20.12.44	TORTURE	U.S.
TROSSMANN,Ludwig	251887	M			Sturmmann,C.C.Ellrich,Nordhausen (Ger.)	MURDER	U.S.
TROSTER	174028	M	Ger.		Capt.,Stalag VI A,C.C.Hemer.(Ger.) 41-45	TORTURE	U.S.
TROTHE,Fritz	255640	M	Ger.	21.10.87	Ortskommandant,Sabac,Macva and Jarak (Yugo.) 41	MISC.CRIMES	YUGO.
TROTTER,Theo	29640	M	Ger.		Feldgendarm.,Abwehr,Feldgendarmerie,Pont Audemer (Fr.) 5.6.44	MURDER	FR.
TROUK,K.H.	136370				Minister of State in Bohemia and Moravia,Lidice (Czech.)	MURDER	U.S.
TROULE	161271	M	Ger.	85	Uschfhr.,Waffen-SS,Command Staff,C.C.Buchenwald (Ger.) 43-45	SUSPECT	U.S.
TROX,Fritz	139747		Ger.	03	Officer,Manager of A Plent,SA,Prag (Czech.)	TORTURE	U.S.
TRUCHEL	138333	M	Ger.		Uschfhr.,SS,Schendelah,Braunschweig (Ger.)	MURDER	FR.
TRUCKENBRODT	130131	M			Oschfhr.,SS,Pz.Div.Totenkopf,C.C.Mauthausen (AUST.) 41-45	MURDER	U.S.
TRUEBEL,Oskar	193852	M	Ger.		Pvt.,Guard,SS,4 SS-Totenk.-Sturmbann,C.C.Dora Mittelbau,Nordhausen (Ger.) 43-45	INTERR.	U.S.
TRUEBER (or TRUPER)	300158	M	Ger.		Major,officer-commanding,1 Bn.,16 Inf.Regt.,Crete (Grc.) 9.43	MISC.CRIMES	GRC.
TRUETTNER	259155	M	Ger.		Stabsscharfhr.,SS,Div."Prinz Eugen",Niksic district Montenegro(Yugo)43	MISC.CRIMES	YUGO.
TRUJAN,P.	195411	M	Ger.		Army,3 Coy.,II Bn.,Brandenburg-Regt.,Montelparo (Ital.)21.3.44	WITNESS	U.K.
TRULZSCH	256210	M	Ger.		Sgt.,Muhldorf Area (Ger.)	WITNESS	U.S.
TRUM,Andreas	130132	M			Oschfhr.,SS,C.C.Mauthausen (Aust.) 41-43	MURDER	U.S.
TRUMANN (see TUHMAN)	192554						
TRUMLER	165979	M	Ger.		Oberfuehrer,Gestapo of Saarbruecken,Folkling (Fr.) 11.44	MURDER	FR.
TRUMMEL	300742	M	Ger.		Oberfeldmeister,Reichsarbeitsdienst 174,Beauvechain (Bel.) 4.9.44	MISC.CRIMES	BEL.
TRUMMER	256211	M	Ger.		Sturmmann,SS,Muhldorf Area (Ger.)	WITNESS	U.S.
TRUMMER	256511	M			SA,Gratkorn (Aust.) 2.45	MURDER	U.S.
TRUMMER,Rupert	162802	M		14. 9.07	Freiw.I Ost-Bn.447,Plouvien (Fr.) 8.44	TORTURE	FR.
TRUMMLER,Hans (or TUMMLER)	179901	M		95	Oberfhr.,Chief,SS,Security-police,C.C.Drogen-Mecklenbg.,Rhein-Westmark (Ger.) 5.-6.44	TORTURE	U.S.
TRUMPF	141403	M			Chief,C.C.Mauthausen (Aust.)	MURDER	FR.
TRUNK	251361	M	Ger.		Lt.,Div."Herm.Goering",4 Regt.,Parachut-Regt.,Regt."Grassmel", Belchteren (Bel.) 5.-11.9.44	INTERR.	BEL.
TRUNKEL	184583	M	Ger.		Officer,Gestapo,C.C.Dachau (Ger.)	MURDER	FR.
TRUPER (see TRUEBER)	300158						
TRURANDT,Otto	251390	M	Ger.		Uschfhr.,SS,S.D.,Toulouse (Fr.) 11.42-8.44	MISC.CRIMES	FR.
TRUSCHEL	156825	M			Pvt.,Army,6 Para-Artl.Regt.,1 Btty.,Xanten (Ger.) 8.3.45	MURDER	CAN.
TRUTZ,Heinz	196216	M	Ger.		Krim.Clerk,Gestapo,Brno (Czech.) 39-44	MURDER	CZECH.
TRUXA	180037	M	Ger.		SS-Mann,Leibstand."Adolf Hitler",Aufkl.-Abt.,Renardmont,Stavelot(Bel.) 19.12.44	MURDER	BEL.
TRZEBINSKY,Alfred	189809	M	Ger.	04	Dr.,Hptsturmfhr.,SS,C.C.Neuengamme (Ger.) 43	MURDER	YUGO.BEL.
TSCHAIKE (or TSCHEIKE)	190702	M	Ger.		Uschfhr.,SS,Pz.Div."Das Reich",3 Coy.,1 Bn.,Oradour-Glane(Fr.)10.6.44	MURDER	FR.
TSCHAKEL	151013	M			Capt.,Medical office,15 Pz.Gren.Regt.,3 Bn.,Capizzi,San Fratello (Sicily) 7.8.43	WITNESS	U.S.
TSCHAKERT,Robert	186105	M	Ger.	82	Leader,NSDAP,Praha (Czech.)	MISC.CRIMES	CZECH.
TSCHAPKE	250508	M	Ger.		Civilian,Fort de Seclin,Nord (Fr.) 29.-30.8.44	WITNESS	FR.
TSCHARNKE,Walther	300159	M	Ger.	circa 05	Employed-first at Hamm,Westphalia,Kirchlengern Krs,Herford(Ger.)	TORTURE	NETH.
TSCHECE,Otto	1066	M	Ger.		Cpl.,Feldgendarmerie,Vitry le Francois (Fr.)	MISC.CRIMES	FR.
TSCHEKE (see TSCHAIKE)	190702						
TSCHEKE,Alfred	958	M	Ger.		Pvt.,Guard,Army,Ldsschtz.-Bn.749,4 Coy.,Stalag VIII B,C.C.Teschen (Czech.) 10.5.43	MURDER	U.K.
TSCHERMY	305516				Col.,Camp-Cmdt.,Stalag XI B,Fallingbostel (Ger.) 10.44-4.45	MISC.CRIMES	U.K.
TSCHERNKO,Franz	192700	M	Ger.	29.12.08	Reichsjustizminist.,Strafgef.Lager Nord,Finmark (Nor.)	MISC.CRIMES	NOR.
TSCHERSICH	257728	M			Employee,O.T.,C.C.Dachau,Muhldorf Area (Ger.)	MURDER	U.S.
TSCHERWENKA,Friedrich	255631	M	Ger.	16.10.02	Informer,Gestapo,Prag (Czech.) 44-45	MISC.CRIMES	CZECH.
TSCHETSCH,Otto	257465	M	Ger.	23. 3.01	Policeman,State service,C.Trebova (Czech.) 28.10.41	MURDER	CZECH.
TSCHICK	153012	M	Ger.	00	Pvt.,3-877 Ldsschtz.-Bn.,Liezen (Aust.) 10.44	TORTURE	U.K.

NAME	C.R.FILE NUMBER	SEX	NATIO-NALITY	DATE OF BIRTH	RANK	OCCUPATION	UNIT	PLACE AND DATE OF CRIME	REASON WANTED	WANTED BY
TSCHIMMER, Hans (or SCHIMMER)	36628	M	Ger.	10	Pvt., 559.Landesschuetzen-Bn. Arb.Kdo. E 497, Freiwaldau (Czech.) 43				TORTURE	U.K.
TSCHOL, Joh.	167743	M	Ger.		SS Regt. "Germania", Verfuegungs-Div., Nieppe (Fr.) 28.5.40				MURDER	U.K.
TSCHRESNER	252778	M	Ger.		Lt., 118.Coy. 1.Bn. Alpenjaeger Div. 738.Regt., Imotski (Yugo.) 7.43				MISC.CRIMES	YUGO.
TSHAGE	306812	M			Member of St.Quentin-Gestapo, Vraignes en Vermandois (Somme) (Fr.) 29.8.44				MURDER	FR.
TSHECHER	251397	M	Ger.		Oberinspektor, C.C. Auschwitz (Pol.)				INTERR.	FR.
TSORK	167100	M			Field-Police Moulins, Laroche-Millay (Fr.) 11.8.44				PILLAGE	FR.
TUBESTLOK	196522	M		04	Major.				MISC.CRIMES	U.S.
TUCEK	162202	M			Cpl., 263. D.I. Kommando de Landerneau, Finistere Landerneau (Fr.) 8.44				MURDER	FR.
TUCEK, Ladislav	251370	M		11. 8.04	Guard, N.S.F.K., Gestapo, Satalice (Czech.) 41				INTERR.	CZECH.
TUCHEL	139235	M	Ger.		Schutzoberwachtmeister, SS-Totenkopf Div.,Auschwitz,Riga (Pol.,Latv.)41-43				MURDER	
TUCHEL	194287	M	Ger.		Chief of Gestapo Melun (Fr.) 9.41-8.11.43				TORTURE	FR.
TUCHEL, Hans	261833	M	Ger.		Driver, Gestapo of Amiens, Gentelles (Fr.) 6.-8.44				MURDER	FR.
TUCHSCHERER	252785	M			Uschfhr., C.C. Rottleberode, Nordhausen (Ger.)				MURDER	U.S.
TUCK	151005	M			Capt., 15.Panz.Gren.Regt.,3.Bn., between Capizzi and San Tratella (Sicily)				WITNESS	U.S. 7.8.43
TUELLER	257469	M			Sonderfhr., Army, Zajecar (Yugo.) 41-44				MISC.CRIMES	YUGO.
TUEMMEL, Otto	300612	M	Ger.		Osturmfhr., SS-Aussenkommandos, C.C. Neuengamme (Ger.) 44-45				MURDER	U.K.
TUENGLER, Helmut	144976	M		7.11.15	Hptscharfhr., Waffen-SS, Schleissheim (Ger.) 6.-9.44				MURDER	U.S.
TUERCK (see TORCK)	259163									
TUERINGER, Karl	256204	M	Ger.		Foreman, Org.Todt, Mühldorf Area (Ger.)				WITNESS	U.S.
TUETEN, Jacob	192601	M	Ger.		Kapo, C.C. Buchenwald (Ger.) 42-45				TORTURE	U.S.
TUGEND	11289	M		.	Maat, Navy, Art. 4.Bn., Quiberon (Fr.) 44				MURDER	FR.
TUGGES	256205	M			SS-Uschfhr., SS, C.C.Mühldorf (Ger.)				WITNESS	U.S.
TUHMAN (or TRUMANN)	132554	M	Ger.	15	SS-Osturmfhr., C.C. Neuengamme (Ger.)				MURDER	FR.
TUIGI	959	M			Col., Waffen-SS, Toulon (Fr.) 10.-13.8.44				PILLAGE	FR.
TUKLL	137584	M	Ger.		Lt., Cmdt., Stalag XV B, C.C.Putlitz,Mecklenburg (Ger.) 24.4.45				WITNESS	U.K.
TULLA, Anton	128896	M		09	SS-Uschfhr., SS, Commando-Staff, C.C.Weimar-Buchenwald (Ger.)				TORTURE	U.S.
TUIZER, Otto	185304	M	Ger.	5. 3.95	Leiter Civ. Factory-Manager of Bohemia-Moravia, Brno (Czech.)				PILLAGE	CZECH.
TUMA, Otto	196809	M	Ger.		Employee, Asst., Gestapo-Section IV I a I, Brno (Czech.) 39-45				SUSPECT	CZECH.
TUMANN	132470	M	Ger.	13	Cmdt., SS-Camp Staff, C.C. Neuengamme (Ger.)				MURDER	U.K., YUGO.
TUMANN	257700	M	Ger.		SS-Lagerfhr., C.C.Dora, Nordhausen (Ger.) 7.4.44				MURDER	FR.
TUMAYER	137642	M	Ger.	10					TORTURE	U.K.
TUMFAHRT	251925	M			Sipo, Abt.V D, Brussels (Bel.) 40-45				INTERR.	BEL.
TUMMEL, Paul	189287	M			Secretary of Pol.-Lt., Gestapo, Douai (Fr.) 6.3.44				MURDER	FR.
TUMMEL, Paul (see THUEMEL)	306537									
TUMMLER (see TRUMMLER)	179301									
TUNAK, Erich	162803	M	Ger.		Lt., Gestapo, Chalons sur Saone (Fr.) 43-44				MURDER	FR.
TUNAKE	301428	M	Ger.		Member, Gestapo, operating at Chalons sur Saone, Dun-Les-Places (Fr.) 26.-28.6.44				MURDER	FR.
TUNGER	39698	M	Ger.		Cmdt., Army, Chenebier (Fr.) 27.9.44				MURDER	FR.
TUNGHANS, Willy	141404	M	Ger.		Lt., Feldgendarmerie, Dreux (Fr.) 44				TORTURE	FR.
TUNMIS, Alfons	139234	M	Ger.		S.A.-Oberstummann. (Czech.)				TORTURE	U.S.
TUNST	193778	M	Ger.		Member, Waffen-SS, C.C.Araiburg (Ger.)				MURDER	CZECH.
TUPPER	--	M	Ger.		Civ., Overseer in C.C. Svatoborice (Czech.)				MURDER	FR.
TURAN	960	M	Ger.		Lt., Army.					
TURBA, Alfred	135565	M	Ger.		Lt., Army, St.Brieuc (Fr.) 8.44				TORTURE	FR.
TURECK	256206	M	Ger.		Pvt., 320. Volks-Gren.Div. 22.9.44				WITNESS	U.K.
TURJERHUT (see FINGERHUX)	38955				SS-Mann, SS, Mühldorf (Ger.)				WITNESS	U.S.
TURK	144955	M	Ger.	10	Sgt., Sonder-Kommando C.C.Warstein, Arnsberg, Suttrop, Lippstadt (Ger.) 22.3.45				MURDER	U.S.
TURNER	258151	M	Ger.		SS-Uschfhr., C.C.Dachau (Ger.)				MISC.CRIMES	BEL.
TURNER, Harold	189806	M	Ger.		Dr., Befehlshaber, Mil.Verw., Ljubljana-Belgrad (Yugo.) 41-44				MURDER	YUGO.
TURNWALD, Johann	192328	M	Ger.	22. 4.04	S.A.-Obersturmmann. (Czech.)				MISC.CRIMES	CZECH.
TURNWALD, Karl	192327	M	Ger.	17. 1.14	Member, NSDAP, Civ.Tailor. (Czech.)				MISC.CRIMES	CZECH.
TURSZYK, Johann	195417	M			Pvt., 3.Coy., Brandenburg II.Bn., Montelparo (It.) 21.4.44				INTERR.	U.K.
TOSCHMANN	162204	M			Sgt., SS 10. Security Regt., Braine Le Comte (Bel.) 3.and 6.8.44				TORTURE	BEL.
TUST, Josef	260498	M		28. 6.06	SS-Rottenfhr., Waffen-SS, Guard Coy., C.C. Kobieszyn, Jawiszowice, Auschwitz (Pol.) 8.41-10.43				BRUTALITY	POL.
TUTTAS, Eduard	162205	M		98	Osturmfhr., Crim.Inspector, SS-Sipo, Stettin (Ger.)				MISC.CRIMES	BEL.
TUTTER, Werner	251378	M	Ger.		Kreispropagandaleiter, NSDAP, Bratislava (Czech.) 44				MISC.CRIMES	CZECH.
TUYMAYER	138301	M	Ger.		Master, Hallosches Salzbergwerk, Engesdorf (Ger.)				MURDER	FR.
TWOROWSKI, Franz	252783	M			Pvt., C.C.Ellrich, Nordhausen (Ger.)				MURDER	U.S.
TWORUSCHKA, Ignatz	141336	M			Civilian, Gleiwitz (Ger.) 1.44				MURDER	U.K.
TYBUREC, Franz	255693	M		08	Gestapo-Informer, Railway-Clerk, Prague (Czech.) 43				MURDER	CZECH.
TYBUSECK, Walter	151002	M		24	SS-Rottenfhr., SS-Leibstandarte "Adolf Hitler", Rosbach (Ger.) 4.3.45				MURDER	U.S.
TYCHMAYER, Hermann	1762	M		05	Pvt., Nachschub 475.Bn.5.Coy., St.Malo, Dieppe (Fr.) 19.8.42				MURDER	U.K., CAN.
TYCHSEN, Christian	195925	M		.	Osturmbannfhr., Panz.Regt.2 "Das Reich", Tulle (Fr.) 9.6.44				WITNESS	FR.
TYLE, Otto	300743	M			Officer or Sgt., 377. Inf.Regt.serving under Capt. Lohmann, Viakt-Meigen (Bel.) 25.5.40-31.5.40				MURDER	BEL.
TYLINSKI, Johann	252782	M		23. 1.04	Pvt., C.C.Ellrich, Nordhausen (Ger.)				MURDER	U.S.
TYPKY, Rudolf	138006	M			Member, NSDAP since 1930, Gagel (Ger.)				TORTURE	U.S.
TYROLD, George	139744	M	Ger.		Pers.Director, Volkswagen-Factory, Civ., Ruhen (Ger.) 44-45				MISC.CRIMES	U.S.
TZANNER	11290	M			Pvt., Army, 110. or 111.Panz.Gren.Regt., 2.Coy., Albine (Fr.) 29.6.44				MURDER	FR.
TZIGANE	306132	M			Foreman, at Zwil-Hall, C.C.Flossenburg (Ger.) 42-45				MURDER	FR.
TZULER	133252	M			SS-Official, Brunswick (Ger.) 40-42, 44-45				MURDER	U.S.
UAEGERLE	305957	M			Uschfhr., C.C.Oranienburg (Ger.) 11.39-45				MURDER	CZECH.
UBACH, Hubert	159047	M			Prison-Guard, C.C. Reinsbach (Ger.)3.40-3.45				WITNESS	U.S.
UBEBRUCK, Arthur	195924	M			Sgt., Jard sur Mer (Fr.) 21.1.44				WITNESS	FR.
UBEL	195421	M	Ger.		Org.Todt, Assen (Neth.) 12.44				MURDER	NETH.
UBELMANN, Johann	257322	M	Ger.	22. 6.14	Crim.Inspector, Gestapo, Pilsen, Klatovy, Tabor (Czech.) 40-45				MISC.CRIMES	CZECH.
UBER (see HEBER)	100521									
UBERLAKER, Joseph	186777	M	Ger.		Feldgendarm, Feldgendarmerie-Truppe 626, Peronne,Licourt (Fr.) 24.8.44				MURDER	FR.
UCKERT	257553	M			Hospital C.C.Dora, Nordhausen (Ger.)				MURDER	U.S.
UDE, Otto	250529	M		19.11.19	Pvt., C.C.Ellrich, Nordhausen (Ger.)				MURDER	U.S.
UDER	21323	M	Ger.		SS-Cmdt., C.C.Weimar (Ger.)				MISC.CRIMES	U.S.
UDER	128666	M	Ger.		Sgt., C.C. Herschbach near Selters (Ger.)				TORTURE	BEL.

UDE - ULL

- 170 -

NAME	C.R.FILE NUMBER	SEX	NATIO- NALITY	DATE OF BIRTH	RANK OCCUPATION UNIT PLACE AND DATE OF CRIME	REASON WANTED	WANTED BY
UDET see HEEBER	100521						
UEBELHACK, Friedrich	260658	M			Col., Army	WITNESS	U.S.
UEBELHOR or UEBELHOER	961	M	Ger.		Dr., Regierungspraesident, General-Government, Wartheland, Lodz (Pol.) 39-41	MURDER	POL.
UEBELMANN, Johann	250520	M	Ger.	22. 6.94	Employee, Gestapo, Prag (Czech.) 39-45	MURDER	CZECH.
UEHLENDAHL	195705	M	Ger.		Capt., SIPO, Member NSDAP, Kowno (Pol.) 42-43	MURDER	POL.
UEIX	138078	M		11	SS Usturmfhr., Budzyn, Kransnik (Pol.)	MURDER	
UELTZHOEFFER	139742	M			Sonderfhr., C.C. Sandbostel Stalag X B (Ger.) 1.5.45	MISC.CRIMES	U.S.
UELTZHOFFER	72079	M			SS Scharfhr., C.C.Struthof, Natzweiler (Fr.) 42-44	MISC.CRIMES	FR.
UERLIMGS	256221	M			SS Oscharfhr., Muehldorf (Ger.)	WITNESS	U.S.
UERSCHBAUMER	149586	M	Ger.		Pvt., 11.Panz.Div., South-west Fr., 44	MURDER	FR.
UFERKAMPF	307223	M	Ger.		Capt., Member of the Standgericht 1.Bn. 24.Rgt.Paratrooper Huebner 7.Div. Brigadier General Erdmann, Roermond-Kinroy, Maasbracht(Neth.) 44-45	MURDER	NETH.
UFFENKAMP, Werner	178064	M	Ger.	17	Guard, Arbeitslager Stalag XX B, Halberstadt (Ger.) 7.41	MURDER	U.K.
UHBIG	161282	M	Ger.		SS Hptsturmfhr., SS Totenkopf-Standarte Wien, Nonovitz via Gleiwitz to Dora (Ger.)	MURDER	U.S.
UHDE	188559	M		23	Pvt., 16.Panz.Aufkl.Abt., Bautzen (Ger.) 1.44	WITNESS	U.K.
UHE	257847	M			O.cand.,150.Panz.Bde., Meuse-Bridge Antwerp (Bel.) 12.44	MISC.CRIMES	U.S.
UHL	136659	M	Ger.		Capt., C.O. of Arbeitskdo. C.C. Stalag 3 B, Trattendorf bei Spremberg (Ger.) 7.-8.43	INTERR.	U.S.
UHL, Hans	146722	M			SS Leader, C.C.Flossenburg, Straubing (Ger.) 19.-20.4.45	MURDER	U.S.
UHL, Walter	161275	M	Ger.	18	Waffenwart, Ordnungspolizei, 1.Kradschuetz.Coy.,Stawern (Nor.) 11.43	MURDER	NOR.
UHLE	189329	M	Ger.		SS Oscharfhr., Leczyck (Pol.) 3.42	MURDER	POL.
UHLEMANN, Herbert or ULLMANN or ULEMAN	123174	M	Ger.	16	SS Hptscharfhr., C.C. Weimar, Buchenwald (Ger.) 39-45	TORTURE	CZECH.FR. BEL. U.S.
UHLENBROCK	254110	M	Ger.		Dr.,SS Hptsturmfhr., C.C.Auschwitz, Birkenau (Pol.) 9.42	MISC.CRIMES	YUGO.
UHLENDCRF	173470	M	Ger.		Sgt., Fallschirm-Pion-Ers.Bn.,Deloize (Fr.) 10.-11.7.44	MURDER	FR.
UHLENHAUT	259284	M			SS Hptsturmfhr., Camp Thekla nr.Leipzig (Ger.) 15.4.45	MURDER	U.S.
UHLICH	1943	M			Naval-inspector, Navy supply	MISC.CRIMES	U.K.
UHLIG	120556	M			SS Usturmfhr., Gleiwitz (Ger.)	MURDER	U.S.
UHLIG	126746	M			Officer Lagerfuehrer, Org. Todt, C.C. Camiers (Fr.) 43-44	PILLAGE	FR.
UHLIG	137568	M	Ger.		SS Usturmfhr., SS Totenkopf-Standarte C.C.Novowitz-Dora (Ger.)	MURDER	U.S.
UHLIG or ULICH	153041	M			Col.Com., 29.Panz.Gren.Div., 15.Panz.Gren.Rgt. nr. Capizzi (It.) 8.45	WITNESS	U.S.
UHLMANN	186682	M		23	SS Rottfhr., SS Nachrichtenzug, nr.Wormhoudt (Fr.) 5.40	MURDER	U.K.
UHLMANN	228002	M			Pvt., C.C. Neuengamme (Ger.) 42	MURDER	BEL.
UHLMANN	257554	M			F.P. No. 22 980, Eis.Art.Btty. 717, St.Andre (Bel.) 4.9.44	MURDER	BEL.
UHLMEIJER	254079	M			Lt., 10.Marine-Kraftfahrabt. 1.Coy., Soest (Neth.) 22.-25.10.44	PILLAGE	NETH.
UHLORN, Wilhelm	174067	M			Civ., Chief, Dept.resp,for building underground shelters at Junkers works, Halberstadt (Ger.) 2.-4.44	TORTURE	U.K.
UHLRICH, Heinrich	255784	M			SS Osturmfhr., Heusden (Neth.) 11.44	PILLAGE	NETH.
UHM see OHM	251207						
UHRIG, Friedrich	261346	M	Ger.		Dentist, SS Hptsturmfhr., Waffen SS, Gestapo, Strassburg (Fr.) 40-44	TORTURE	FR.
UHRIG, Friedrich	306269	M	Ger.	5. 3.12	Usturmfhr., SS, 8.E.G. teaching Btty., Langlinger (Fr.) 29.12.44	MURDER	U.K.
UIBERMACHER	250523	M	Ger.		SS Uscharfhr., C.C. Mauthausen (Aust.) 12.44	MURDER	U.S.
UIBERRETTER	166269	M	Ger.		Public official, chief, Civ. administration, Aust. 39-45	TORTURE	U.S.
UKELS	186775	M			SS Oscharfhr., Mont Morency (Fr.) 21.8.44	MURDER	FR.
UKENA, Hans	153050	M			Seaman, Navy, St.Marine (Fr.) 30.6.44	INTERR.	U.S.
UKRAINE, Joe	104956	M	Ger.		Civ., 43	TORTURE	U.K.
ULBICH see ULRICH Werner	128899						
ULBING, Richard	67712	M	Ger.	92	Dr., Hptsturmfhr.,SS Panz.Div."Das Reich", Gestapo of Limoges, St.Crepin de Richemont, Cantillac (Fr.) 26.-27.9.44	MURDER	FR.
ULBRECHT	124135	M	Ger.		Sgt., Inf.Coy L 983, Brotteswitz (Ger.) 12.11.43	MURDER	U.K.
ULBRICH	189810	M	Ger.		Lt., Army, Pozarevac (Yugo.) 41-43	MURDER	YUGO.
ULBRICH	255786	M			SS Osturmfhr., C.C. Buchenwald (Ger.)	MURDER	U.S.
ULBRICH	301397	M	Ger.		SS Leutnant, Employee, C.C. Buchenwald (Ger.) betw.16.5.38 and 9.10.43	MURDER	BEL.
ULBRICH, Karl	161283	M	Ger.	00	Hptsturmfhr., Waffen SS Wach-Bn. 1.Coy., C.C.Buchenwald (Ger.) till 43	TORTURE	U.S.
ULBRICH, Kurt	962	M	Ger.	16. 2.98	SS Osturmfhr., C.C.Maidanek (Pol.) 40-4.44	MURDER	POL. BEL.
ULBRICH, Otto	301398	M	Ger.		SS Uscharfhr. (No. 58377), C.C. Buchenwald (Ger.) 16.5.38-9.10.43	MURDER	BEL.
ULBRICHT, Hermann	254115	M	Ger.	5. 5.12	Employee, Gestapo, Litmerice (Czech.) 39-45	MISC.CRIMES	CZECH.
ULBRICHT, Kurt	193739	M	Ger.	26. 9.14	SS Hptscharfhr., C.C. Terezin (Czech.) 39-45	TORTURE	CZECH.
ULBRUEF, Otto	161281	M			Pvt., Gren.Ers.Bn. 440, Aulnois (Bel.) 3.9.44	WITNESS	BEL.
ULEMAN	10027	M			Uscharfhr., Waffen SS, C.C. Buchenwald (Ger.) 39-44	TORTURE	CZECH.
ULEMAN, Herbert see UHLEMANN	123174						
ULFFT see FAUREE	305107						
ULFORD, Baszyl	189575	M	Ger.		Pvt., Army, 11.Coy., Bauge (Fr.)	PILLAGE	FR.
ULHENDCRF	125684	M			Sgt., Paratrooper Abt. Pion.Ers.Bn. S.P. N 49 925 A, Montaron, Vandenesse (Fr.) 11.8.44	MURDER	FR.
ULICH see UHLIG	153041	M					
ULICH or ULRICH	306929	M	Ger.		Lt., Prov.of Macva and in Sabac Yugo., F.P. No. 22379 A, 41	MURDER	YUGO.
ULIK, Karl	167735	M	Ger.		Warder or Kapo, C.C.Sachsenhausen, Oranienburg (Ger.) 9.39-44	MURDER	POL. NOR.
ULITZKA, Max (?)	100041	M	Ger.		SS Oscharfhr., Gestapo, Kristiansand (Nor.) 41-44	MURDER	U.K.
ULKAN	195422	M	Ger.		SA - Politischer Einsatz, Eppe, Vreden (Ger.) 10.44-2.45	TORTURE	NETH.
ULLE, Arno	169310	M	Ger.		Baker, Civ. SA, Ulrichshalben (Ger.) 20.7.44	TORTURE	U.S.
ULLHERR, Thomas or ULLHERR	162807	M	Ger.	30. 8.98	Civ., Montigny en Metz (Fr.) 40-44	TORTURE	FR.
ULLMANN, Erich	184584	M			Pvt., 7.Gebirgs-Art. Ers.Rgt., 79.Detachm. Mountain-Artillery, Albertville (Fr.) 20.6.44	MURDER	FR.
ULLMANN, Herbert see UHLEMANN	123174						
ULLMANN, Walter	194948	M		15	Member, Scharfhr., Gestapo, SS, Kolin (Czech.) 39-45	MURDER	CZECH.
ULMER,Jean-Pierre (Joh.Peter)	256220	M			Foreman, C.C. Neckargerach, Neckarelz (Ger.) 42-45	INTERR.	FR.
ULRICH	153051	M		10	SS Osturmfhr., Guard, Waffen SS, C.C. Buchenwald (Ger.)	MURDER	U.S.
ULRICH	173165	M	Ger.		Wachtmeister, Staff at C.C. Schirmeck, Rotenfels, Gaggenau (Fr.,Ger.) 25.11.44	MURDER	U.K. U.S.
ULLRICH	195923	M	Ger.		Guard, C.C. Compiegne, Royallieu (Fr.) 41-44	MURDER	FR.
ULLRICH, Gustav	254116	M	Ger.	14.12.02	Employee, Gestapo, Bruenn (Czech.) 39-45	MISC.CRIMES	CZECH.
ULLRICH, Hans	142322	M	Ger.	08	Osturmfhr., Waffen SS Totenkopf, C.C. Buchenwald (Ger.)	BRUTALITY	U.S.

ULL-URB

NAME	C.R.FILE NUMBER	SEX	NATIO-NALITY	DATE OF BIRTH	RANK OCCUPATION UNIT PLACE AND DATE OF CRIME	REASON WANTED	WANTED BY
ULLRICH, Karl	195418	M	Ger.		SS-Osturmbannfhr., SS Totenkopf Div., Le Paradis (Fr.) 27.5.40	INTERR.	U.K.
ULM	963	M	Ger.		Lt., Army, SS Div. "Das Reich" Rgt. "Der Fuehrer", Buzet (Fr.) 7.-8.44	MURDER	FR.
ULM, Ernst	250524	M		29. 3.03	Pvt., C.C.Ellrich, Nordhausen (Ger.)	MURDER	U.S.
ULMANN	132529	M	Ger.		SS-Oschfhr., SS, C.C.Dora, Mittelbau, Nordhausen (Ger.)	MURDER	U.S.
ULMANN, Erich	192223	M	Ger.		Cpl., Army, Vineuil (Fr.) 17.8.44	WITNESS	FR.
ULMANN, Horst	192222	M	Ger.		Sgt., Army, Soissons (Fr.) 15.8.45	WITNESS	FR.
ULMANN, Rudolf	29641	M			Cpl., Gestapo, Josselin (Fr.) 44	MURDER	FR.
ULMANN, Rudolf	250525	M		13.11.12	Oschfhr., C.C.Dora, Nordhausen (Ger.)	MURDER	U.S.
ULMER, Friedrich	254114	M	Ger.	19. 5.22	Pvt., 4 Ldsch.Pi.Bn.515, Wervick (Bel.) 4.9.44	MISC.CRIMES	BEL.
ULRICH	126510	M	Ger.	10	Osturmfhr. or Oschfhr., SS, C.C.Buchenwald (Ger.) 42-45	SUSPECT	U.S.
ULRICH	196513	M			Lt., 5-3 Brandenburg Rgt.,	MISC.CRIMES	U.S.
ULRICH (see ULICH)	306929						
ULRICH, Adolf	192168	M	Ger.		Pvt., SS, F.P.Nr.11707 E, Veriee (Bel.) 7.9.44	MURDER	BEL.
ULRICH, Hermann	196224	M	Ger.	10	Sgt., Army, St.Marguerite des Loges (Fr.) 10.8.44	WITNESS	CAN.
ULRICH, Kurt	254178	M	Ger.		SS-Schfhr., SD, Toulouse (Fr.) 11.42-8.44	MISC.CRIMES	FR.
ULRICH, Otto	306901	M	Ger.		Ortsgruppenleiter, NSDAP, Peltre Moselle (Fr.) 40-44	INTERR.	FR.
ULRICH, Werner (or ULBICH)	128899	M			SS-Oschfhr., SS, C.C.Buchenwald (Ger.)	TORTURE	U.S.
ULPING	153052	M			Capt., Gestapo, Brive (Fr.) 44	MURDER	FR.
ULRISCHKA	250527	M			C.C.Ellrich, Nordhausen (Ger.)	MURDER	U.S.
ULTRA (or ULTZE)	250528	M			Cpl., C.C.Ellrich, Nordhausen (Ger.)	MURDER	U.S.
ULZHÖFER, Peter	153042	M	Ger.		Sgt., Chief, Waffen SS, NSDAP, Propaganda, Natzweiler (Fr.) 41-45	MURDER	U.S.
UMANN, Hugo	254084	M	Ger.	12.10.10	Employee, Gauleiter K.Behnlein, Liberec (Czech.) 40-45	MISC.CRIMES	CZECH.
UMAVAR	185305	M	Ger.		SS, Dep.for Communism Athen (Grc.)	TORTURE	GRC.
UMBACH	196243	M	Ger.		Policeman, Gestapo, Hofgeismar (Ger.) 5.4.45	TORTURE	FR.
UMBBE	28748	M	Ger.		Capt., 20 Army, 139-8 Geb.Jg.Rgt., Finmark (Nor.) 10.-11.44	MURDER	NUR.
UMHOLD	254080	M	Ger.		Major, 7 Res.Pion.Bn., Meylan (Fr.) 17.6.44	INTERR.	FR.
UMIERDJE	305958	M	Ger.		Osturmfhr., C.C.Oranienburg (Ger.) 11.39-45	MURDER	CZECH.
UMM, Karl	139239	M	Ger.		Employee, Civilian, Plettenberg (Ger.) 4.45	TORTURE	U.S.
UMSIATTER, Franz	305700	M	Ger.		Member, Army, nr. Russelsheim (Ger.) 26.8.44	MURDER	U.S.
UMUELLER	305959	M	Ger.		Uschfhr., C.C.Oranienburg (Ger.) 11.39-45	MURDER	CZECH.
UNAND	179902	M			Civilian, Berlin-Marienfelde (Ger.) 1.45	MURDER	U.S.
UNCK	180130	M	Ger.		Chief, C.C.Mauthausen (Aust.)	MURDER	FR.
UNDER, Emil	195922	M	Ger.		Custom-official, Zollgrenzschutz, Chaum (Fr.) 3.6.44	MURDER	FR.
UNTEFORST	179900	M	Ger.		Pvt., Army, Sich.Rgt.16 (Bel.)	MURDER	BEL.
UNEK, Franz	144967	M		01	Block-Elder, C.C.Mauthausen (Aust.) 41-45	MURDER	U.S.
UNFICHT, Otto	142321	M	Ger.	95	Civilian, Organ repairer, C.C.Loiberadorf (Ger.) 2.5.45	WITNESS	U.S.
UNGAR, Franz	257556	M	Ger.	16. 7.00	Civilian, SDP, NSDAP, SS, Prostejov (Czech.) 40	BRUTALITY	CZECH.
UNGER	138273	M	Ger.		SS-Sgt., Gestapo, Lyon (Fr.)	MURDER	FR.
UNGER	188716	M	Ger.		Member, Feldgendarmerie, Bar-le-Duc (Fr.) 8.44	MURDER	FR.
UNGER	189290	F	Ger.		Woman Supervisor, C.C.Ravensbrueck (Ger.)	TORTURE	BEL.
UNGER	192326	M	Ger.		Capo, C.C.Flossenburg (Ger.) 5.44-4.45	MURDER	BEL.
UNGER	255783	M	Ger.		Lt., 1 Coy Pion.Bn.46, Budinci-Croatia (Yugo.) 9.43	MISC.CRIMES	YUGO.
UNGER	301399	M	Ger.		Female-Warder, C.C.Ravensbrueck (Ger.) 40-45	MURDER	BEL.
UNGER, Adam	255787	M	Ger.	5.12.02	Civilian, Gossengrun, Habersbirk (Czech.) 9.39	MURDER	CZECH.
UNGER, Fritz	256679	M	Ger.		Oschfhr., SS, SD, Foix (Fr.) 11.42	MURDER	FR.
UNGER, Joseph	250526	M	Ger.		Member, Gestapo, Lille (Fr.) 40-44	MISC.CRIMES	FR.
UNGER, Ludwig	255788	M	Ger.	5. 5.10	Civilian, Gossengrun (Czech.) 9.39	MURDER	CZECH.
UNGER, Walter	153045	M	Ger.		Uschfhr., Waffen SS, Totenkopf-Sturmbann, C.C.Weimar, Buchenwald (Ger.) 11.39	MURDER	U.S.
UNGERECHTS	250532	M		26. 3.14	C.C.Ellrich, Nordhausen (Ger.)	TORTURE	U.K.
UNGERTHUM, Alfred	128789	M	Ger.	98	N.C.O., Yard-master, C.C.Stuetzengruen-Sa. (Ger.) 6.11.43	WITNESS	U.S.
UNGEWITTER	146757	M			Civilian, Frankfurt-Main (Ger.) 3.45	MURDER	U.S.
UNGLAUBE, Otto	250533	M		19. 9.25	Flyer, C.C.Ellrich, Nordhausen (Ger.)	MURDER	FR.
UNGLEHRT, Alois	11291	M			N.C.O., Pz.Gren.Rgt.110 or 111, 2 Coy, Albine (Fr.) 29.6.44	MURDER	U.S.
UNGNAD	153049	M	Ger.		Capt., POW Camp XI A, C.C.Altengrade (Ger.) 17.4.45	TORTURE	U.S.
UNITIS, Otto	166268	M			Bucha (Ger.) 7.7.44	MURDER	U.S.
UNRFLBACH, August	250530	M		26. 6.13	Sgt., C.C.Ellrich, Nordhausen (Ger.)	MURDER	FR.
UNLIG, Fenil	167731	M	Ger.		Pvt., 9 Res.Gren.Rgt., 1 Coy, Magny d'Anigon (Fr.) 18.9.44	MURDER	U.S.
UNPATH, Georg	193753	M	Ger.		Rottfhr., 4 SS Totenkopf-Sturmbann, C.C.Dora-Mittelbau, Nordhausen (Ger.) 43-45	MURDER	U.S.
UNPATH, Robert	162107	M	Ger.	14	Oschfhr., SS, C.C.Command staff, Buchenwald (Ger.)	TORTURE	U.S.
UNRAU, Horst (or ANRAU)	1342	M	Ger.		Lt., 12 Coy, 29 Gr., 3 Pz.Gr.Div., Communanza (It.) 2.5.44	MURDER	U.K.
UNRUH	254083	M	Ger.		SS-Rottfhr., Gestapo, SD, Troyes de L'Aube (Fr.) 3.10.43-22.8.44	MURDER	FR.
UNTERBERGER, Adolf	305973	M	Ger.		Member of the Landwacht of Maurach, Borders of Achensee, Coffee Room of Gasthof Pfandler, Pertisan-Maurach (Aust.) 13.7.44	MURDER	FR.
UNTERBOFRSCH, Hans	194960	M	Ger.	15	Member, Oschfhr., Gestapo, SS, Kolin (Czech.) 39-45	MURDER	CZECH.
UNTERICHT, Franz	179751	M	Ger.	21	Sgt., Army, Stia Garrison (It.) 18.4.44	MURDER	U.K.
UNTERFELZ, Valter Johann	307224	M	Ger.		Capt., Coyfhr., 517 Inf.Rgt.from 5.41-6.43 Croatia, Sabac and Macva (Serbia) 11.41	MURDER	YUGO.
UNTFECHT, Joseph	142003	M		12	Lager-Capo, German Prisoner in Waldlager V and VI, near Muehldorf (Ger.) 44-45	TORTURE	U.S.
UNTSCH, Wilhelm	257610	M		06	Cpl., SS, C.C.Muehldorf, Dachau (Ger.)	MURDER	U.S.
UNVERHAU	261800	M	Ger.		Cpl., Artillerie H.D.V.199-2235, H.D.F.Nr.de F.P.27046 C, Lorgies (Fr.) 3.9.44	MURDER	FR.
UNVERICHT, Berta	135325	F	Ger.		Civilian, Efferen (Ger.) 2.10.44	WITNESS	U.S.
URBAN	126967	M			SS-Usturmfhr., 2 SS Pz.Div. "Das Reich", Valence A'Agers (Fr.) 44	MURDER	FR.
URBAN	135958	M		05	Civilian	PILLAGE	U.S.
URBAN	188937	M	Ger.		Prison Guard, C.C.Kaisheim (Ger.) 39-45	TORTURE	CZECH.
URBAN	191467	M	Ger.		Usturmfhr., SS Div. "Das Reich", St.Sixte (Fr.) 44	MURDER	FR.
URBAN	259263	M	Ger.		Sturmschfhr., Gestapo, area Poitiers (Fr.) 40-45	MISC.CRIMES	FR.
URBAN, Antonin	250521	M	Ger.	01	Pvt., Ortsgruppenleiter, Informer, NSDAP, Gestapo, Ricancy, Uhrinekes (Czech.)	MISC.CRIMES	CZECH.
URBAN, Ernst	135326	M			Civilian, Miner, Arbeitskdo., Politish Leader if his District, C.C. (Ger.)	TORTURE	U.S.
URBAN, Gotthard	168243	M	Ger.	1. 3.05	Prof.Dr., Einsatzstab Rosenberg, Paris (Fr.) 40-44	PILLAGE	FR.
URBAN, Josef or Anton	254086	M	Ger.		Member, Gestapo-official, Prag (Czech.) 39-45	MISC.CRIMES	CZECH.
URBAN, Karlo	250534	M	Ger.		Lt., Gend., Kragujevac (Yugo.) 21.10.41	MURDER	YUGO.
URBAN, Rudolf	254081	M	Ger.	3. 2.10	Doctor, Civilian, Official of German Foreign Ministry, Prag (Czech.) 43	PILLAGE	CZECH.

URB - VAN

NAME	C.R.FILE NUMBER	SEX	NATIO-NALITY	DATE OF BIRTH	RANK OCCUPATION UNIT PLACE AND DATE OF CRIME	REASON WANTED	WANTED BY
URBANEK, Karl Martin	260513	M	Ger.	11.11.08	Guard, SS, CC Litomerice (Czech.) 9.44-4.45	MISC.CRIMES	CZECH.
URBANSKI, Kasimir	168247	M	Ger.		Pvt., 9 Res.Gren.Rgt., 1 Coy, M.G.Schtz.3, Magay d'Anigon(Fr.)18.9.44	MURDER	FR.
URBANTKE	189811	M	Ger.		Usturmfhr. SS, Ljubljana (Yugo.) 41-43	MURDER	YUGO.
URFAY	259610	M	Ger.		W.O., Unit F.N. 07382,Villequiers - Cher (Fr.) 7.40-6.41	INCENDIARISM	FR.
URFEHR	189330	M	Ger.		Uschfhr. SS, C.C.Dachau (Ger.)	MURDER	BEL.
URFELS	189328	M	Ger.		Member Gestapo, Uschfbr SS, Dachau (Ger.)	MURDER	BEL.
URLICHS	67704	M	Ger.		Army, F.P. 15201, Chenebier (Fr.) 27.9.44	MISC.CRIMES	LUX.
URMES, Albert	194894	M	Ger.		Leader, Propaganda, Luxembourg	TORTURE	U.K.
URSHMAN	128768	M	Ger.		Uschfhr, SS, Muenchen (Ger.) 12.44	MURDER	FR.
URTENOV	254082	M	Ger.		Sturmmann, Gestapo, S.D, Toulouse (Fr.) 11.42-8.44	MISC.CRIMES	FR.
USE	1344	M			Sgt.SS-Hitler-Jugend Div.,8 Coy, 11Bn.	MISC.CRIMES	U.K.
USMER (see USUER)	132827						
USNER	192620	M	Ger.		Uschfhr. SS, CC Buchenwald (Ger.) 42-45	TORTURE	U.S.
USUER (or USMER)	132827	M	Ger.	00	Stabs Schfhr. SS. Noailles (Fr.) 9.8.44	MURDER	U.K.
USUER	190005	M			Sgt., Guard, Paris (Fr.) 8.9.44	MURDER	U.K.
UTECH, Werner	195921	M	Ger.		Sgt., St.Anne-d'Auray, Bretagne (Fr.)	MURDER	FR.
UTECHT	138282	M	Ger.		SS Sgt., Gestapo, Lyon (Fr.)	MURDER	FR.
UTECHT, Hanna	256056	F	Ger.		O.T., Muhldorf (Ger.)	WITNESS	U.S.
UTERMARK, Siegfried	306721	M	Ger.		Oberarbeitsdienstfuehrer, R.A.D., Gross-Liedern (Ger.) 23.8.44	MURDER	U.S.
UTH (see ORTH)	72072						
UTKE, Hermann	250590	M		26. 2.95	Oschfhr, CC Harzungen, Nordhausen (Ger.)	MURDER	U.S.
UTPADEL, Gerhard	250522	M	Ger.	22. 7.11	Gestapo, Bradec Kralove (Czech.) 39-45	MURDER	CZECH.
UTZ	12447	M	Ger.		Army, Pz.Gren.Rgt., 110 or 111, 2 Coy, Albine (Fr.) 29.6.44	MURDER	FR.
UTZ	255785	M	Ger.		Oschfhr. SS, CC Buchenwald (Ger.)	MURDER	U.S.
UTZ	964	M			Sanitaetswachtmeister, Army, CC Falstad (Nor.) 42	TORTURE	NOR.
UTZ, Karl	192784	M	Ger.		Schupo, CC (Stalag)4 Falstad (Nor.) 41-44	MURDER	NOR.
UTZ, Willibald	260657	M	Ger.		Lt.General, Army	WITNESS	U.S.
UWER, Hans	256057	M	Ger.		Schfhr. SS, Muhldorf (Ger.)	WITNESS	U.S.
VAARST	307225	M	Ger.		Engineer Flyer belonging to Einheit F.P. L 55975, LGPA Unna-Westf., Laren (Neth.) 4.11.44-22.2.45	PILLAGE	NETH.
VABUSEG, Otto	250540	M		19.11.02	Pvt., CC Harzungen, Nordhausen (Ger.)	MURDER	U.S.
VACHMIN, Ernest	153026	M	Ger.	31. 8.07	Hptschfhr, Gestapo, Font-Romeu (Fr.) 1.-7.44	TORTURE	FR.
VACKNER, Aug. (or WAGNER)	181456	M	Ger.	09	Agent, Gestapo, Arles s-Tech (Fr.) 27.6.44	MURDER	FR.
VADEN, Herbert	254191	M	Ger.		Cmdt., 119 Art.Rgt., 11 Pz.Div., Confouleux (Fr.) 9.8.44	MURDER	FR.
VADJA	176931	M			SS-Mann, Sur - Akm (Hung.)	WITNESS	U.S.
VAGNER, Fritz	191894	M	Ger.		Major, public official, Weisenhassel (Ger.) 18.6.41	WITNESS	FR.
VAIDTINGER, Heinrich	146580	M			Commander, CC Eberstadt (Ger.) 43	TORTURE	POL.
VAINER	67724	M			Sgt., Luft IV, CC (Ger.)	TORTURE	U.K.
VAKERBARDT, V.	153022	M	Ger.		Major, Army, Siwerkaja (Russia) 42-44	MURDER	U.S.
VALDIGE, Herbert	165980	M	Ger.		Sgt., Army, 44	LOOTING	BEL.
VALDMULLER	147033	M	Ger.		Cmdt., SS Pz.Gren.Div."Hitler Jugend", Dinant-Namur (Bel.) 44	MURDER	BEL.
VALENTA, Karl	258110	M	Ger.	24. 8.84	Master of the rural police, commander of a rural police station, Stary Postrekov (Czech.) 9.8.44-45	MURDER	CZECH.
VALENTIN	192322	M			SS Sturmbannfhr, CC Flossenburg (Ger.) 44-45	SUSPECT	U.S.
VALENTIN (or NENOEIL)	162834	M	Ger.		Pvt., Lds.Schtz.Bn.740, 1 Coy, Kdo.102,3 Bodendorf (Ger.) 11.44	MURDER	FR.
VALENTIN, Erich	186103	M	Ger.		Sturmschfhr, SD, Montgauthier (Bel.) 20.9.43	MURDER	BEL.
VALENTIN, Max	251409	M			Cpl., CC Ellrich, Nordhausen (Ger.)	MURDER	U.S.
VALERIUS	124619		Ger.		Member Gestapo, CC Flussbach (Ger.)	MURDER	BEL.
VALERIUS, Theodore	258854	M	Ger.	30. 6.16	Member Gestapo, Luxembourg 40-45	MISC.CRIMES	LUX.
VALIS	306294	M	Ger.		Member Gestapo at Trencin, CC Auschwitz-Birkenau (Pol.) 39-45	MURDER	CZECH.
VALLAND	301985	M	Ger.		Oslo (Nor.) from 5.42	TORTURE	NOR.
VALLESCO, Victor	124128	M	Ger.	ca. 20	Pvt., Army, Inf. Lds.Schtz.427 Bn, 4 Coy, Katschwitz(Ger.)27.3.45	MURDER	U.K.
VALLET	254698	M	Ger.	15	Cmdt., SS, CC Ravensbrueck (Ger.)	TORTURE	FR.
VALMICHRAT	153024	M			Gestapo, Bretagne, Anjou, Poitou (Fr.)	MURDER	FR.
VALNUS, Hans	185308	M	Ger.		SS occupied territories, department of communism, Athen(Grc.)	MISC.CRIMES	GRC.
VALROTH	128787	M	Ger.		Civilian, worked in firm Himmelfahrt Funde Grube, CC Freiberg(Ger.) 11.44	TORTURE	U.K.
VAN BASZHOSEN, Hilde	193175	F		25	Asst., German Navy girl, Wilhelmshaven (Ger.) 15.10.44	WITNESS	CAN.
VAN BEBBER	257940	M			SAB 1,C 3,4 TRK Pz.Ede., Meuse Bridge,Antwerpen(Bel.) 12.44	MISC.CRIMES	U.S.
VAN BODMER	27760	M			Dr., CC Struthof-Natzweiler (Fr.) 40-44	MURDER	FR.
VAN BRIKENBEUL	192303	M	Ger.		Guard, CC Siegburg, Bautzen (Ger.) 1F-24.9.44	TORTURE	BEL.
VAN DE LOO (or VAN DER LOO, or VANDELOV)	132725	M	Ger.		Public prosecutor, military tribunal, Berlin and Torgau (Ger.)5.44-45	MURDER	FR.
VAN DEN BOSCH, Emiel	301936	M	Ger.	30. 3.15	Driver, SD, Apeldoorn district (Neth.) 9.44-4.45	MURDER	NETH.
VANDENER (see GESCHWANDTNEP)	147799						
VAN DEN HOEK	252185	M			Driver, CC Harzungen, Nordhausen (Ger.)	MURDER	U.S.
VAN DEN WIJNGAARD, Robert	305119	M			Member SD Groningen and Drente (Neth.) 43-45	MURDER	NETH.
VAN DER BERG	300018		Ger.		Member special command "Feldmeier", Groningen,Drente (Neth.) 43-45	MISC.CRIMES	NETH.
VANDEREYNDE, Efran	132525	M	Ger.		CC Mittelbau, Nordhausen (Ger.)	MURDER	U.S.
VAN DER HEYDTE	125737	M	Ger.		Lt.Col., Paratrooper Kampfgruppe v.d.Heydte, Normandy (Fr.)	WITNESS	U.S.
VAN DER LOO (see VAN DE LOO)	132725						
VAN DER MOSEL	625	M	Ger.		Lt., Feld-Gend.Trupp 5, Locmine (Fr.) 7.-8.44	MURDER	FR.
VAN DER SPEK	300987		Ger.		Member SS Sonder-Kdo."Feldmeier", Blaricum-Beemster (Neth.) 18.10.43-4.8.44		
VAN DETZEN	109	M			SS Oschfhr, CC Dachau (Ger.) 40	MURDER	NETH.
VAN DEURSEN, Petrus G.	306908	M	Ger.		Almelo (Neth.) 21.-24.3.45	MISC.CRIMES	FR., BEL.
VAN DE VIEN	305573	M	Ger.		Guard, SS or Gestapo at CC Bremen-Farge (Ger.) 1.43-4.45	MURDER	U.K.
VAN EHPEN	139151	M	Ger.		Hptsturmfhr, SS, leader of labour-camp, CC Treblinka (Pol.) 41-43	MURDER	U.K.
VAN GOGH, L.Th.	305409	M	Ger.	8.10.16	Member SS, Sonder-Kdo."Feldmeier", Blaricum, Beverwijk, Velsen, Westwoud, Berkhout, Purmerend, Beemster (Neth.)4.12.43-9.4.44-2.6.44	MURDER	U.S.
VAN HOBERG	179745	M	Ger.		Major, Army, Div."Hermann Goering", 11 Art.Rgt., Bucine (It.)9.7.44	MURDER	NETH.
VAN HOUTUM, Johann	254516	M	Ger.	4. 3.22	Lt., 83 Rgt., 1 Bn.Freiw.SS Gren.Landsturm (Neth.),Tiel(Neth.) 45	PILLAGE	NETH. U.K.

NAME	C.R.FILE NUMBER	SEX	NATIO-NALITY	DATE OF BIRTH	RANK OCCUPATION UNIT PLACE AND DATE OF CRIME	REASON WANTED	WANTED BY
VAN KILLINGER, Manfred	104237	M	Ger.	86	Member of people's court, German minister, Bucarest (Rum.)	MISC.CRIMES	U.N.W.C.C.
VAN KNAPFEN	24880	M			Sturmfhr.,SA,Gestapo,C.C.,Klingelpustz (Ger.)10.44-1.45	TORTURE	U.S.
VAN LENT, Franz	132187	M	Ger.		Pvt.,SS 12.Pz.Gren.Div.,1.Coy.,Pz.Abt.17,St.Aubin,Duperron (Fr.) 20.-21.6.44	WITNESS	U.S.
VANLOSCHEGG	173461	M	Ger.		Doctor,H.Q.,Graz (Aust.) 4.41-44	MURDER	YUGO.
VANLOSEN	306854	M			Warder,Kapo,Gusen,C.C.,(Aust.) spring 40-44	MURDER	POL.
VAN MEGEN	250374	M	Ger.		Uschfhr.,83.Rgt.Landsturm Neth.,Tiel (Neth.) spring 45	PILLAGE	NETH.
VAN OPPEL	675	M	Ger.		Major,Gestapo,Onnaing,Valenciennes (Fr.) 1.9.44-44	MURDER	FR.
VAN PEE	157984	M	Ger.		Feldgendarmerie D 966,Balcaire (Fr.) 29.11.43	TORTURE	FR.
VAN SAST	137583	M	Ger.		SD,SS,Gestapo,Hertogenbosch,Tilburg (Neth.) 9.7.44	MURDER	U.K.
VAN VECK, Franz	9674	M	Ger.		Driver,C.C.,Breendonck (Bel.) 40-2.3.44	TORTURE	BEL.
VAN WATTER	10966	M		5. 5.03	Oberlandrat,Justizabt.,Prague (Czech.) 39-45	MISC.CRIMES	CZECH.
VAN WERDEN	1345	M	Ger. 93 - 95		Major,99.Inf.Div.,Platoon commandant,Palazzo del Peron (It.) 23.6.44	MURDER	U.K.
VAN WINGERDEN	301293	M	Ger.		Hilfspolizeibeamter,interpreter,Abt.VD,SD,Brussels and other towns (Bel.) 6.40-9.44	MURDER	BEL.
VAN WULFFT (see FAUREE)	905107						
VANZO, Joseph	146737	M			SS,C.C.,Flosenburg (Ger.)	TORTURE	U.S.
VARGA nee SPACZEK, Wilma	192304	F	Ger.		Member,SD,leader,Gestapo,NSDAP,Novy,Neu Oderberg (Czech.)	MURDER	CZECH.
VARTNER	162491	M	Ger.		Sgt.,Army,Stalag Luft IV,Gross Tychow (Ger.) 44-45	TORTURE	U.S.
VARNAR (see FAHRNARD)	142527						
VARNE	141842	M	Ger.	90	Sgt.,Army,Stalag Air IV,C.C.,Kaifheide (Ger.) 7.44-2.45		U.K.
VARNER	72071	M	Ger.		Sgt.,Air-force,C.C.,Gross Tychow (Ger.) 19.7.44	TORTURE	U.K.
VASSUM	162847	M	Ger.		Lt.,Army,Rivin (Fr.) 13.-14.6.44	MURDER	FR.
VATER	67723	M	Ger.	00	Sgt.,C.C. XX A,Mielub,Bricsen (Ger.) 6.44	TORTURE	U.K.
VATER	139242	M			Kripo,Rupperts-Hutten (Ger.) 12.9.44	MURDER	U.S.
VATER	153021	M	Ger.		Camp commander,C.C.,Finkenheerd (Ger.) 42	MURDER	U.S.
VAUBEL (or FAUBEL or FAUBL)	187810	M	Ger.	15	Pvt.,Landesschuetzen Bn.827,2.Coy.,Falkenau (Czech.) 10.44	MURDER	U.S.
VAUCTERL, Vincent	192701	M	Ger.		Pvt.,Kgf.Arb.Bn.184,Engen-Nordland (Nor.) 6.-7.44	MURDER	NOR.
VAUTH (or FAUTH)	252980	M	Ger.		Guard,C.C.,Lahde-Weser (Ger.)	INTERR.	BEL.
VAVRA, Vaclav	260425	M	Ger. 11. 6.15		Member,Nazi Org.,Vlajka,Praha (Czech.) 40-45	MISC.CRIMES	CZECH.
VEES, Joseph	307226	M	Ger.		Interpreter,subsection,Gestapo,La Rochelle,Poitiers (Fr.)	MURDER	FR.
VEESE, Joachim	196369	M	Ger.		Osturmfhr.,SS,SD,Kdo.z.b.V., St.Die (Fr.) 8.44	MURDER	U.K.
VEESSEN, Heinz	179797	M	Ger. 98 - 00		Oschfhr.,SS Totenkopfverband,C.C.,Gusen (Aust.) 23.7.44	MURDER	U.S.
VEHLOW, Bernhardt	188718	M	Ger.		Pvt.,Army,Dury les Amiens (Fr.) 44	WITNESS	FR.
VEHSE	254192	M	Ger. 05 - 10		Osturmfhr.,Gestapo,Savannes (Fr.) 42-44	MURDER	FR.
VEHZE	905517	M			Osturmfhr.,SD,Angers,Tavannes,Meuse (Fr.) 31.8.44	MURDER	FR.
VEICHERT, Friede	153009	F	Ger.		Guard,Waffen SS,C.C.,Volary (Czech.) 41-45	MURDER	U.S.
VEID	141619	M			Abschnittsleiter,NSDAP,Bischwiller (Fr.) 1.12.44	MURDER	FR.
VEID (see FEIT)	191927	M	Ger.		Kreispropagandaleiter,NSDAP,Mofsheim (Fr.) 41	MISC.CRIMES	FR.
VEIDFNE, Hans (or SEIDEI)	141435	M	Ger.		Lt.,SS,Gestapo,Douai (Fr.) 8.44	TORTURE	FR.
VEIDT, (see FEIT)	142046						
VEIDTINGER, Heinz	125544	M			Civilian,Camp official,Eberstadt (Ger.) summer 43	TORTURE	FCL.,U.S.
VEIGEL	256231	M	Ger.		Chief Sgt. of the kitchen,C.C.,Mauthausen (Aust.) 11.42-5.45	MURDER	FR.
VLIHT, Karl	256058	M	Ger.		Abt.chief,C.C.,Flossenburg (Ger.)	TORTURE	FR.
VEISHAUPT	1766	M			Police-man,Geheime Fieldpolice	MURDER	U.K.
VEISS	141320	M	Ger.		Sturmbannfhr.,SS,C.C.,Dachau (Ger.) 4.43	TORTURE	U.K.
VEIT	124334	M	Ger.		Capt.,Army,6.Punishment Bn.,z.b.V.,Ostrov (Sov.Un.) 2.9.43	MURDER	U.S.
VEIT, Josef	254706	M	Ger. 10. 5.21		Cpl.,SS,Lidice (Czech.) 6.42	MURDER	CZECH.
VEITTES, Paul	260475	M	Ger. 7.12.03		Uschfhr.,Waffen SS,Guard Coy.,C.C.,Monowitz,Auschwitz (Pol.) 43-45	BRUTALITY	POL.
VELCHER	153007	M	Ger.		Lt.,Legion Azerbaidjan,La Parade (Fr.)	MURDER	FR.
VELTEN	139741	M			Betriebsobmann,DAF,Glanzstoffwerke Koeln (Ger.) 40	MURDER	U.S.
VELTEX	251407	M			Rottfhr.,C.C.,Dora,Osterhagen,Nordhausen (Ger.)	MURDER	U.S.
VENAUER	260079	M	Ger.		Sgt.,Russia-Germany, Div."Oberland",Massif du Vercors,Isere,Drome (Fr.) 20.7.-5.8.44	SUSPECT	FR.
VENCE	10079	M			Capt.,security officer,Stalag 21 D, Posen (Pol.) 44	MURDER	U.K.
VENDOR	174550	M	Ger.		Capt.,Landesschuetzen Bn.400,Stalag IV,C.C.,Eisleben (Ger.)19.6.44	WITNESS	U.K.
VENEDIGER	166267	M		07	Chief,Gestapo,Danzig (Pol.) 39-45	MURDER	U.S.
VENTEGERTS	1346	M	Ger.		Pvt.,Army,1.Pl.,3.Sec.149.G.R.	MISC.CRIMES	U.K.
VENTER, Karl	194841	M	Ger.		Kreisleiter,NSDAP,Luxembourg (Lux.)	MISC.CRIMES	LUX.
VETZKY, Heinz Borovin	966	M	Ger.		Officer,Army,Kavallerie Mot.,(Pol.) 1.9.-30.10.39	MURDER	POL.
VENZEL	195349	M	Ger.		Member,Gestapo,near Audun-Le-Tiche,Metz (Fr.) 20.8.44	MURDER	U.S.
VEPCH	251709	M	Ger.		Lt.,Mil.Dienststelle,Enschede (Neth.) 1.4.45	WITNESS	NETH.
VERDIER	120593	M		15	Abwehr,Agent,Brest (Fr.)		FR.
VERDURME	254694	M	Ger.		Hilfspolizeibeamter,Abt.V.D.,SIPO,Bruessel (Bel.) 40-45	INTERR.	BEL.
VEREZ, Robert	251711	M	Ger.		Sgt.,SD,Raon L'etape (Fr.) 4.9.44	MURDER	FR.
VERFZ, Robert	254763	M	Ger.	10	Group-commander,Kommando "Retzek",North Africa,Hamean,La Trouche (Fr.) 6.-9.10.44	MURDER	FR.
VERFUHRT, Johann	126410	M	Ger. 25.-3.94		Farmer,civilian,Moers (Ger.) 17.2.45	MISC.CRIMES	U.S.
VERFUHRT, Robert	126411	M	Ger. 7. 6.28		Civilian,Moers (Ger.) 17.2.45	MISC.CRIMES	U.S.
VERG'S	141365	M	Ger.		Capt.,Army,Inf.Rgt.869,348.Div.,7.Coy.,Pont a Marcq (Fr.) 3.9.44	MURDER	FR.
VERHULSDONCK, Theo	257241	M	Ger.		Hptschfhr.,SS,Crim.Secretery,Abt.IV,SIPO,SD,Anvers (Bel.)40-45	BRUTALITY	BEL.
VERMAGTEN, Josef(elias JUPP)	251399	M	Ger.		Kapo,Internment Camp,Neuengamme (Ger.) 44	TORTURE	FR.
VERMANN	188719	M	Ger.		Pvt.,Army,La Bourget,Triage (Fr.) 24.8.44	MURDER	FR.
VERNACH	184268	M	Ger.		Commandant,commandantur,Forges,Les Eaux (Fr.) 10.6.40	WITNESS	FR.
VERNEKOG	257853	M			Lt.,Pz.Bde.150,Meuse Bridge, Antwerp. (Bel.) 12.44	MISC.CRIMES	U.S.
VERNICKE, Albert	184267	M	Ger.		Agent,C.C.,Dachau (Ger.)	TORTURE	FR.
VERNIER	124140	M	Ger.		Capt.,Arbeitskdo.,C.C.,Hennesdorf O.-S.,(Ger.) 8.44	MURDER	U.K.
VIRSCHBAUMER	190699	M	Ger.		Pvt.,11.Pz.Div.,2.Coy.,2.A.A.A.7,near Bergerac and Albine (Fr.)7.-8.44	MURDER	FR.
VERSICK, Herbert	196016	M	Ger.		Rottfhr.,SS,1.Pl.3.Pz.Pi.,Ligneuville,Stoumont (Bel.)17.-19.12.44	MURDER	U.S.
VERTFURTH	967	M	Ger.		Lt.,Army,Feldschule Art.,Autun (Fr.) 7.44	PILLAGE	FR.
VERLOST	254695	M	Ger.		Interpreter,SIPO,Abt.IV A,Bruessel (Bel.) 40-45	INTERR.	BEL.

VER-VIN

NAME	C.R.FILE NUMBER	SEX	NATIO-NALITY	DATE OF BIRTH	RANK	OCCUPATION UNIT	PLACE AND DATE OF CRIME	REASON WANTED	WANTED BY
VERWEE	305344	M	Ger.			Member, SD at Heerenvoen, Luinjeberd (Neth.) 12.,13.4.45		MURDER	NETH.
VERWORST	259268	F	Ger.			Typist, Gestapo at Poitiers, Antenne of Angouleme,Poitiers (Fr.) 40-45		SUSPECT	FR.
VESCE	153003	M	Ger.			Chief, Gestapo, Angers (Fr.)		MURDER	FR.
VESEN, Heinz	306059	M	Ger.			SS-Mann, Gusen (Aust.) 25.7.44		MURDER	U.S.
VETSCHER, Olga	195704	F	Ger.			Employee, Gestapo, Brno (Czech.) 39-45		TORTURE	CZECH.
VETTER, Helmuth	67372	M		21. 3.10		Dr., Hptsturmfhr., SS, C.C., Mauthausen (Aust.)		MURDER	U.S.
VETTER	141620	M	Ger.			Cmdt., Bde.Gend., Bischwiller (Fr.) 44		MURDER	FR.
VETTER	146740	M				Civilian, Frankfurt-Main (Ger.)		MISC.CRIMES	U.S.
VETTER	153002	M	Ger.			Polizeipraesident, Police, Muelheim-Ruhr (Ger.) 12.43		MURDER	U.S.
VETTER	181524	M	Ger.			Medecin, C.C., Gusen I, Mauthausen (Aust.) 44		MURDER	FR.
VETTER	185312	M	Ger.			Landgerichterat, Country-Court, Occ.Territories,Prague,Brno (Czech.) 45		MURDER	CZECH.
VETTER	257615	M				Inspector, SD, Caen (Fr.) 42		INTERR.	FR.
VETTER	306521	M	Ger.			Kreisamtsleiter, Bischwiller Bas-Rhin (Fr.) 1.12.44		MURDER	FR.
VETTER, Gustav	254704	M		11		Dep.-Chief, Gestapo, Alencon (Fr.) 40-44		MURDER	FR.
VETTER, Josef	251410	M		14. 3.06		Pvt., C.C. Ellrich, Nordhausen (Ger.)		MURDER	U.S.
VETTER, Karl	153001	M				Sturmschfhr., Gestapo, SS		MURDER	U.S.
VETTER, Karl	251408	M				Pvt., C.C. Ellrich, Nordhausen (Ger.)		MURDER	U.S.
VETTER, Kurt	194054	M		28. 7.06		Sgt., SS, Crim.Secr., Gestapo, Landskron (Czech.) 38-45		MURDER	CZECH.
VETTER, Rudolf	250538	M		14. 9.24		Flyer, C.C. Ellrich, Nordhausen (Ger.)		MURDER	U.S.
VETZNER	11292	M	Ger.			Sgt., Feldgend., Chaumont (Fr.) 24.8.44		MURDER	FR.
VHIRTZ	167152	M				Cmdt., Army, Geb.Jg.Bn.,100.Alpin, Montgirod (Fr.) 8.44		MURDER	FR.
VICKART (I)	124480	M	Ger.			Hptschfhr., SS, C.C. Sachsenhausen (Ger.) 42		MURDER	U.K.
VICKART (II)	167736	M	Ger.			Hptschfhr., SS, C.C. Sachsenhausen, Oranienburg (Ger.) 42		MURDER	U.K.
VICKER, Franz	132526	M				Osturmfhr., SS, C.C. Dora-Mittelbau, Nordhausen (Ger.)		MURDER	U.S.
VICKERS	125238	M				Guard, C.C. Sachsenhausen (Ger.)		MURDER	U.S.
VICKUS, Franz	254194	M	Ger.			Pvt., F.P.Nr.11178, Romilly-Seine (Fr.) 8.44		PILLAGE	FR.
VICTOR, Kurt	162118	M				Pvt., Army, Wehrmachtgefaengnis, Leipzig, Torgau (Ger.)		TORTURE	U.S.
VIDEBACH, Hans	305518	M				Schfhr., Chauffeur, Gestapo Limoges, Hte.Vienne, Indre Loire Gironde (Fr.) 40-45		MURDER	FR.
VIDSKE	167151	M	Ger.			Senior W.O., Army, Pont L'Abbe, Ploubaznalec (Fr.) 6.44		MURDER	FR.
VIEBAHN	184585	M	Ger.			Lt., Sich.Rgt.192., Foret Deyaix (Fr.) 2.9.44		MURDER	FR.
VIEBIG	11545	M	Ger.			Head, Public-Official, Ruestungs-Inspektion, 44		INCENDIARISM	NETH.
VIEDLER (see FIEDLER)	245								
VIEDLER	246	F				Camp-Secretary to Cmdt., C.C., Grini (Nor.)		TORTURE	NOR.
VIEDNER	137674	M	Ger.			Sgt., Official,Arb.Kmdo.51, C.C. Klaussberg (Ger.) 22.1.45		MURDER	U.S.
VIEGER	146738	M				Oschfhr., SS, C.C. Flossenburg (Ger.)		MURDER	U.S., FR.
VIEHAGEN	138074	M	Ger.	09		Uschfhr., SS, Arb.Dienstfhr., RAD, Druette (Ger.)		MURDER	FR.
VIEHAGEN (see WIEHAGEN)	251723								
VIEHAGEN	301052	M	Ger.			Member, SS, C.C., Neuengamme (Ger.) 40		MURDER	BEL.
VIEHL, August	104961	M	Ger.	99		Civilian, Conc.Camp (Ger.)		MURDER	U.S.
VIEHWEGER	194284	M				Pvt., Feldgend., Ploermel (Fr.) 18.6.44		TORTURE	FR.
VIELHABER	174030	M				Capt., Stalag VII A, C.C. Hemer (Ger.) 41-45		TORTURE	U.S.
VIELHAUER	124129	M		94?		Cpl., Guard, Inf., 383.Coy., Arbeits-Kmdo.L.25, Lauchhammer (Ger.) 9.44-4.45		TORTURE	U.K.
VIENZIERL	256163	M	Ger.			SS, Mauthausen (Ger.)		MURDER	FR.
VIERBACH, Leo	254189	M		07		Pvt., Gestapo, Epinal (Fr.)		BRUTALITY	FR.
VIERBAUM	143321	M		00		Member, Organ.Todt, St.Helier, Jersey, 42-44		TORTURE	U.K.
VIEREGG	254406	M	Ger.	16		Lt., Army-Flak,197.Rgt.,25.Flak-Div., Selvaggio (It.) 20.5.44		INTERR.	U.K.
VIERHEILIG	250539	M				Pvt., C.C., Mackenrode, Nordhausen (Ger.)		MURDER	U.S.
VIERK, Karl	257242	M				Oschfhr., SS, Crim.Chief-Asst., Abt.I, Sipo and SD, Anvers (Bel.) 40-45		BRUTALITY	BEL.
VIERKANT	306449	M	Ger.			Sturmbannfhr., SS, C.C., Oranienburg (Ger.) 11.39-45		MURDER	CZECH.
VIERLING, August	159026	M				Guard, C.C., Untermassfeld (Ger.) 41-45		MURDER	U.S.
VIERLING, Emil	300941	M				SS-Anwaerter, Truck-driver, Struthof-Natzweiler (Fr.) 8.44		MURDER	U.K.
VIERLINGER, Albert	192703	M	Ger.	29. 9.06		Sgt., Guard, Reichsjustiz-Ministerium, Strafgef.Lager Nord, Finmark (Nor.)		MISC.CRIMES	NOR., YUGO.
VIERMETZ, Marie Inge nee LAUBMEISTER	193854	F	Ger.	7. 3.08		Employee, Territ.Occup., Lidice (Czech.) 42-44		MISC.CRIMES	CZECH.
VIERNOW	173460	M	Ger.			Lt.General, Feldkmdtr., Belgrad (Yugo.) 42-44		MURDER	YUGO.
VIEROW, Walter	188047	M	Ger.	1. 5.92		General, Cmdt., Army (Fr.) 41-44		MURDER	FR.
VIESE, Ludwig	251404	M				Pvt., C.C. Ellrich, Nordhausen (Ger.)		MURDER	U.S.
VIESELER, Hermann	130165	M		09 - 10		Sgt., 744.Inf.Rgt., 711.Inf.Div., Dives-sur-Mer (Fr.) 6.6.44		MURDER	U.K.
VIETH (or FIETH)	72069	M				Schfhr., SS, C.C. Hinzert (Ger.) 42		TORTURE	U.S.
VIETOR, Friedrich	140814	M	Ger.			Guard, Gestapo, Arbeitserziehungslager, C.C. Mainz (Ger.) 45		TORTURE	U.S.
VIETS, Helmuth	124744	M		12		Crim.Employee, Crim.Police, Abt.IV, Brussels (Bel.)		MURDER	U.S.
VIGOLZ, Anton	259496	M	Ger.			Custom-house-officer, Military, SD, Grouw (Neth.) 4.2.44		MURDER	NETH.
VIKLIP	305748	M				Uschfhr., SS, C.C., Auschwitz, Birkenau (Pol.) 40		MURDER	FR.
VIKTORIN, Edith nee JAECKEL	195703	F	Ger.			Employee, Gestapo, Brno (Czech.) 39-42		TORTURE	CZECH.
VILERI (or WILLERY)	185293	M	Ger.			N.C.O., 65.Inf.Rgt., Kerassow (Crete) (Grc.) 8.44		TORTURE	GRC.
VILL	254409	M	Ger.			Lt.-Chief, Section, 10.Coy., Pol.Rgt.Todt,3.Bn., Mont Saxonnex (Fr.) 3.1.44		INTERR.	FR.
VILL, Franziska	262333	F				Secretary to Dr.Falthauser, Kaufbeuren (Ger.) 29-45		SUSPECT	U.S.
VILLECHNER, Hans Robert	136572	M	Ger.	15		Kreisleiter, NSDAP, Attenkirchen, near Sillerthausen (Ger.) 13.6.44?		MURDER	U.S.
VILLECHNER, Margarete(see HUBER)	136393								
VILLEY (or VILLY)	162114	M	Ger.			W.O., Feldgend., Olixy (Fr.) 44		MURDER	FR.
VILLNOOK, Karl	254696	M	Ger.	5.11.08		Civilian, Prague (Czech.) 42		MURDER	CZECH.
VILLY (see VILLEY)	162114								
VILZENBERG, Friedrich	135327	M				Conc.Camp (Ger.)		TORTURE	U.S.
VINCE	67727	M				Capt., Stalag 21 D, Cmdt., Posen (Pol.) 6.44		MURDER	U.K.
VINDERHOETS	254705	M	Ger.			Hilfspolizei-Beamter, Sipo, Brussels (Bel.) 40-45		INTERR.	BEL.
VINKEMSTRADT	300585	M	Ger.			Lt., Army, 10.Coy.,377.Inf.Rgt., Vinkt-Meigem (Bel.) 25.-31.5.40		MISC.CRIMES	BEL.
VINKESTEIN	300584	M	Ger.			Army,9.,10.,11.or 12.Coy.Westende,192.Inf.Rgt., Vinkt-Meigem (Bel.)5.40		MISC.CRIMES	BEL.
VINSBERGER, Karl	262265	M	Ger.	29.10.19		Oschfhr., 51.SS-Armoured Bde.,7.Coy.,Chief of 4.Platoon, Breviandes, Bucheres, Ste.Savine, La Riviere de Corps (Troyes) (Fr.) 22.-25.8.44		BRUTALITY	FR.

NAME	C.R.FILE NUMBER	SEX	NATIO-NALITY	DATE OF BIRTH	RANK OCCUPATION UNIT PLACE AND DATE OF CRIME	REASON WANTED	WANTED BY
VINTSISELI	185526	M	Ger.		Pvt.Army,Oberkdo.Dep.Section for the persecutions of Jews,Athens Salonika(Athens)(Grc.)9.45	PILLAGE	GRC.
VINTZ	305347	M	Ger.		Agricultural Engineer at Strassburg,Neckarelz and Neckargerach CC(Ger.) 42-45	BRUTALITY	FR.
VINTZER or TIGER	189815	M	Ger.		Official,Gestapo,CC Banjica(Yugo.)	MURDER	YUGO.
VINZENS, Kurt	250535	M			Flyer,CC Ellrich,Nordhausen(Ger.)	MURDER	U.S.
VINZENZ	132527	M		07	Osturmfhr.CC Mittelbau,Dora-Nordhausen(Ger.)	MURDER	U.S.
VIRNICH	135566	M	Ger.		Pvt.Luftgau Kdo.XI.5.44	WITNESS	U.S.
VIRUS, Bruno	185700	M	Ger.	9.1.08	Sturmscharfhr.Crim.secretary,Gestapo,SS,Praha(Czech.)39-45	MURDER	CZECH.
VISKA	254700	M	Ger.		Army,Muehlberg(Ger.)1.45	MURDER	U.S.
VISSER, Alfons	100429	M	Ger.	00	Stabsfeldwebel,Feldgendarmerie,Lockeren(Bel.)	TORTURE	U.K.BEL.
VISSNER	136910	M	Ger.		Sgt.Army,St.Floret(Fr.)30.7.44	PILLAGE	FR.
VITCH	162115	M	Ger.	21	Lt.SS Panz.Gren.Regt.Condorcet(Fr.)19.3.44	MURDER	FR.
VITESSKA	162113	M	Ger.		SS Osturmfhr.SS,Gestapo,Bratislava(Czech.)	MURDER	CZECH.
VITISKA, Josef	194958	M	Ger.		Dr.SS Standartenfhr.Official,SS,S.D.Gestapo,Prag,Bratislava(Czech.)39-45	TORTURE	CZECH.
VITS, Helmut	162112	M	Ger.	12	Crim.Employee,SS,Sipo,Abt.IV-Ia,Brussels(Bel.)	MURDER	BEL.
VITT	124978	M			Member,Gestapo CC Bremen-Farge(Ger.)6.43	TORTURE	U.K.
VITTORF, Karl Heinz	254408	M	Ger.		10 Coy.377 I.R.,Vinkt,Meigem(Bel.)25.-31.5.40	INTERR.	BEL.
VITZTUM, Andreas	174031	M	Ger.	10	Foreman,Arb.Kdo.CC Feucht(Ger.)40-45	TORTURE	U.S.
VLADECK or WLADECK	301372	M	Ger.		SS Chef de Salle,Kdo.Wansleben am See nr.Buchenwald(Ger.)43-45	MURDER	FR.
VLEIGERS	9675	M	Ger.		Medical Service,CC Breendonck(Bel.)40	TORTURE	BEL.
VLIEGS alias FLIES	126465	M	Ger.		Hilfsgendarm,Civilian,Member of Landwacht,Dueren(Ger.)26.6.41	TORTURE	U.S.
VOBUSCH, Georges	121230	M	Ger.		Gestapo secteur postal 03063 CC 48252 D.Challes les Eaux et Arvin(Fr.)	MURDER	FR.
VOCF	142065	M	Ger.		Capt.German Army,Kaisersteinbruch(Aust.)5.43	TORTURE	U.S.
VOCKENRETH, Paul Konrad	260449	M	Ger.	9.10.91	SS Oschafhr.Waffen SS,Guard-Coy.CC Auschwitz(Pol.)6.44-1.45	BRUTALITY	POL.
VOCZ	250537	M			SS,CC Rottleberode,Nordhausen(Ger.)	MURDER	U.S.
VOECELE	153017	M	Ger.		Capt.Kommandantur at Millau,Rodezmillau(Fr.)6.8.44	MURDER	FR.
VOEGLER, Albert	254707	M		8.2.77	Gen.Director.Factory Vereinigte Stahlwerke,Duesseldorf(Ger.)	BRUTALITY	FR.
VOEGLER, Kurt	190252	M	Ger.	11	Crim.Asst.Gestapo,Dortmund(Ger.)	TORTURE	U.K.
VOELENER, Karl	256222	M			Osturmfhr.CC Buchenwald(Ger.)	MURDER	U.S.
VOELKEL	1754	M			Capt.Army,Canossa(It.)	TORTURE	U.K.
VOELKEL	254102	M	Ger.		Secretary,13 SS Police Regt.Ferlach(Aust.)44-45	MURDER	YUGO.
VOELKEL	260095	M	Ger.		Hptwachtmeister,SS Strafgefangenenlager Nord Norway,6.42-45	MURDER	YUGO.
VOELKER	970	M	Ger.		Gestapo,Lyon(Fr.)27.7.44	MURDER	FR.
VOELKER	104957	M	Ger.	95	Capt.Adjutant,Kraftfahrpark,Wuersburg(Ger.)8.44	WITNESS	U.S.
VOELKER see FOLKER	138222						
VOELKER, Leopold	113114	M	Ger.		Official,Gestapo,Interpreter in Abt.IV,S.D.Lyon(Fr.)44	MURDER	U.S.
VOELKNER, Karl	126461	M	Ger.		SS Osturmfhr.SS Div.Totenkopf Stuba 5,CC Buchenwald,Koeln-Deutz(Ger.) 5.or 6.44	MURDER	U.S.
VOEIPEL, Johannes	21494A	M	Ger.		Pvt.363 J.Div.Gren.Regt.959(Fr.)16.8.44	MURDER	U.K.
VOELZER, Herbert	307227	M	Ger.		Pvt.1 Bn.24 Rgt.of Fallschirmjaeger Huebner,7 Div.Gen.Major Erdmann Maasbracht Castle Hattem(Neth.)20.or 21.1.45	MURDER	NETH.
VOETZ or DOETZ	139820	M			Lt.Army,Salzburg,Leipzig(Ger.)4.45	MISC.CRIMES	U.S.
VOGNDES	971	M			Sgt.Airforce,Baudrigues(Fr.)19.8.44	MURDER	FR.
VOGEL	162116	M	Ger.	15	Usturmfhr.SS Standarte "Thueringen",Guard,Buchenwald(Ger.)	TORTURE	U.S.
VOGEL	162849	M	Ger.		Pvt.Army,Revin(Fr.)13.-14.6.44	MURDER	FR.
VOGEL	168241	M	Ger.		Pvt.Army,Courlandon(Fr.)20.8.44	MURDER	FR.
VOGEL	186102	M	Ger.		SS Oschafhr.CC Charels,Neckarelz(Ger.)	TORTURE	U.S.
VOGEL	192069	M	Ger.	10	Chief,Gestapo,Guard,CC Posen(Pol.)6.44	TORTURE	U.K.
VOGEL	195920	M	Ger.		Adjutant-Chief,Army,Lille(Fr.)28.4.44	MURDER	FR.
VOGEL	254193	M	Ger.		Sturmmann,CC Buchenwald(Ger.)	INTERR.	FR.
VOGEL	254710	M	Ger.		Capt.Army,Hengelo,Borne(Neth.)4.5.43	MURDER	NETH.
VOGEL	261148	M	Ger.		Member,Staff of CC Ravensbrueck(Ger.)	SUSPECT	BEL.
VOGEL	300744	M	Ger.		Pvt.1 Aufkl.Abt.3 Coy.2 Col.XV Div.Afrika Korps,Saint Leger(Arlon) 5.9.44	MISC.CRIMES	BEL.
VOGEL	301648	M	Ger.		Owachtmeister,Ebrach nr.Amberg(Ger.)45	MURDER	CZECH.
VOGEL	305112	M	Ger.	circa 05	Member,Feldgend.Ger.Political Serv.Alkmaar,Hugowaard,Wieringermeerdijk (Neth.)9.-12.44	TORTURE	NETH.
VOGEL	306912	M	Ger.		Capt.Bet.Hengelo end Borne(Neth.)4.5.43	MURDER	NETH.
VOGEL	306813	M	Ger.		Cpl.Chief Rutzko(Wege)Bn.of 896 R.I,Kermassenet in Kervignac Morbinan44	MURDER	FR.
VOGEL, Bonifacy	260450	M	Ger.	16.5.10	SS Rottenfhr.Waffen SS,Guard-Coy.CC Auschwitz,Charlottengrube(Pol.)40-45	BRUTALITY	POL.
VOGEL, Erich	192619	M	Ger.		CC Kapo,CC Buchenwald(Ger.)42-45	TORTURE	U.S.
VOGEL, Ewald Rudolf	195919	M	Ger.	21.5.99	Leader NSDAP,Verwelter,Textil Factory"Tweka"Geldrop(Neth.)	MURDER	NETH.
VOGEL, Fritz or VOGL or VOGT	259842	M	Ger.	10.4.09	SS Rottenfhr.Scharfschtz.SS,1 Zug.2 Group,Bergeyk(Neth.)11.9.44	MURDER	NETH.
VOGEL, Gunther	67589	M	Ger.		SS Sturmfhr.SS Div.Fp.48963 B.Chateau-Contier,Laval,St.Sulpice,Fort-Mousson(Fr.)6.8.44	MURDER	FR.
VOGEL, Hans	29845	M	Ger.		Sgt.Army,Kerlatz,La Roche,Maurice(Fr.)7.44	TORTURE	FR.
VOGEL born FEUSTL, Hedwig	194283	F	Ger.	13	Employee,S.D.Kolin(Czech.)39-45	MURDER	CZECH.
VOGEL, Heinrich	258545	M	Ger.	01	SS Osturmbannfhr.W.V.H.A.(Ger.)40-45	BRUTALITY	U.S.
VOGEL, Jrgna	195702	F	Ger.		Employee,Gestapo,Brno(Czech.)39-45	TORTURE	CZECH.
VOGEL, Johanne	137799	M			Civilian,Eberndorf(Aust.)	WITNESS	U.K.
VOGEL, K.	256228	M	Ger.		Manager of the Utrechtsche Machinale Stoellen Moebel-Fabrik,Utrecht (Neth.)44-45	PILLAGE	NETH.
VOGEL, Karl	193858	M	Ger.		Camp Guard(Capo)CC Gross Rosen(Ger.)1.-2.45	MURDER	YUGO.POL.
VOGEL, Kurt	192220	M	Ger.	29.9.13	Feldgendarme,Feldgendarmerie,Hazebrouck(Fr.)30.8.44	MURDER	FR.
VOGEL, Paul	192323	M	Ger.		CC Flossenburg(Ger.)44-45	MURDER	U.S.
VOGEL, Rudolf	194959	M	Ger.	14	Member Gestapo,SS Uschafhr.Kolin(Czech.)39-45	MURDER	CZECH.
VOGELBEIN	165551	M	Ger.		Guard,Damag Werke,Dessau(Ger.)10.44-3.45	TORTURE	BEL.

VOG-VOL

NAME	C.R.FILE NUMBER	SEX	NATIO-NALITY	DATE OF BIRTH	RANK	OCCUPATION	UNIT	PLACE AND DATE OF CRIME	REASON WANTED	WANTED BY
VOGELER, Friedrich	173474	M	Ger.		Dr., Praesidialchef-Reichsstatthalter, Gen.Gov.Pol., C.C.Oswiecim-Birkenau (Pol.) 39-45				MURDER TORTURE	CZECH. U.S.
VOGELSAND KUKELHEIN	139243	M	Ger.		Civilian, Plettenburg (Ger.)				MURDER	U.K.
VOGELSANG	10161	M			Civilian, Stalag IV, Arb.Kdo.M-73, Muehlbach(Ger.) 21.6.44				MURDER	FR.
VOGELSANG	254188	M	Ger.		Dir., Waggonfabrik, Wismar (Ger.) 11.42-9.43				WITNESS	U.S.
VOGELSANG, Gustav	259544	M	Ger.		Tailor, Lengerich (Ger.) 8.44				MURDER	U.K.
VOGELSBERG	153016	M		10	Hptscharfhr., Waffen-SS, C.C.Sachsenhausen (Ger.)				TORTURE	U.S.
VOGELSBERGER	153023	M			Oscharfhr., SS, Waffen-SS, C.C.Dachau (Ger.)				TORTURE	U.S.
VOGELSBERGER	192617	M	Ger.		Uscharfhr., SS, C.C.Buchenwald (Ger.) 42-45				MURDER	U.S.
VOGEZ	128889	M			Civilian in a camp official, C.C. Weimar, Buchenwald (Ger.)				MURDER	NETH.
VOGG	195948	M	Ger.		Sgt., Schupo-Revier, C.C.Westerberk (Neth.) 9.-12.44				MURDER	NOR.
VOGG, Leonhard	192785	M	Ger.		Member, Schupo, C.C.Falstad, Stalag (Nor.) 41-44					
VOGHT see VOGT	193646									
VOGL see VOGEL, Fritz	259842									
VOGL, Max	257614		Ger.	14.3.09	Oscharfhr., State Service, SA, Zamosc (Pol.) 40				MURDER	POL.
VOGL, Oskar	62433	M	Ger.		Gen., Army, Chairman of Armistic Commission Fr., Malans(Fr.) 41-42				MISC.CRIMES	FR.
VOGLER alias VOGLEN	199195	M	Ger.		Pvt., Army, C.C.Akervika (Nor.) 42				MURDER	NOR.
VOGLER	251406	M			Pvt., C.C. Ellrich-Nordhausen (Ger.)				MURDER	U.S.
VOGLER, Bill	259065	M			Dr., A Dulag Luft Hospital, A Dulag Luft (Ger.) 43-4.45				BRUTALITY	U.S.
VOGLER, Fritz	254187	M	Ger.		Lt., La Bresse (Fr.) 9.-11.44				MURDER	FR.
VOGLER, Hans	306820	M		2.9.09	Head of Ger.Police force at Nice (Fr.) 11.1.44				PILLAGE	FR.
VOGLEN, Robert	305960	M		28	Locksmith-apprentice, Velke Haraltice (Czech.) 7.8.44				BRUTALITY	CZECH.
VOGT	1765	M			Oscharfhr., SS, SS-Div.L.A.H., Turin (It.)				MURDER	U.K.
VOGT	68495	M	Ger.		Paratrooper-Rgt., 5 Nachrichtenzug, Quaregnon, Jemappes-Ghlin(Bel.)				MURDER	BEL.
VOGT	104959	M	Ger.		Civilian, C.C. Stiege (Ger.) 13.4.45				MURDER	U.S.
VOGT	152985	M	Ger.		Oscharfhr., SS, 1 SS Pz.Div., 2 Pz.Gren.Rgt., 3 Bn, 12 Coy, Stavelot Malmedy (Bel.) 22.-23.12.44				MURDER	U.S.
VOGT	189578	M	Ger.		Sgt., Feldgendarmerie, Vittel (Fr.) 17.8.44				TORTURE	FR.
VOGT	193857	M			SS-Rottenfhr., guard, 4 SS Totenk.Stuba, C.C.Dora-Mittelbau, Nordhausen (Ger.) 43-45				INTERR.	U.S.
VOGT	251398	M	Ger.		N.C.O., Airforce, Entzheim (Fr.) 42-44				TORTURE	FR.
VOGT	251403	M	Ger.		Osturmbannfhr., SS and Gestapo, Maribor (Yugo.) 44				MISC.CRIMES	YUGO.
VOGT	254761	M	Ger.		Former Major, Bagneres de Bigorre (Fr.)				MURDER	FR.
VOGT see VOGEL, Fritz	259842									
VOGT	305949	M	Ger.		Cpl., Airforce Aerodrome Entzheim, Bas-Rhin (Ger.) 42-44				MURDER	FR.
VOGT	306699	M	Ger.		Pvt., 331 Pion.Bn., 331 Inf.Div., Mijnheerenland (Neth.) 5.45				PILLAGE	NETH.
VOGT, August	167732	M	Ger.		Gruppenfhr., 9 Gren.Res.Rgt., 1 Coy, Magny d'Anigon (Fr.) 18.9.44				MURDER	FR.
VOGT, Ernest	173275	M	Ger.		Member, SS, Gestapo, SD, Noailles (Fr.) 9.8.44				MURDER	U.K.
VOGT, Friedrich	251405	M			Pvt., C.C.Ellrich-Nordhausen (Ger.)				MURDER	U.S.
VOGT, Heinz	104958	M			Civilian				WITNESS	U.S.
VOGT, Johann	174789	M	Ger.	9.3.91	Oscharfhr., Waffen-SS, C.C. Stutthof (Ger.) 11.41-1.45				MURDER	POL.,U.K.
VOGT, Joseph	258564	M	Ger.	83	Standartenfhr., SS, W.V.H.A., (Ger.) 40-45				BRUTALITY	U.S.
VOGT, Oskar see VOIGT, Oskar	256484									
VOGT, Thed or VOGHT	193646	M	Ger.		Usturmfhr., SD, Aussendienststelle der Sipo, Leeuwarden (Neth.) 13.9.44-14.4.45				MURDER	NETH.
VOGTLAENDER, Arno	126462	M	Ger.	04	Uscharfhr., SS-Totenkopf, C.C.Buchenwald, Weimar (Ger.)				MURDER	U.S.
VOHLAND, Josef	305520	M	Ger.		Member of the Werkschutz in Skoda works at Dubnica nad Vahom (Slovakia) 44-45				MURDER	CZECH.
VOHS	195347	M		94	Gestapo, Kassel, Hanau, Marburg, Hainmuehle-Niederdorfelden(Ger.) 42				MURDER	POL.
VOHSE, Herbert	187269	M	Ger.		Sturmscharfhr., SS, C.C. Kassel (Ger.)				MURDER	POL.
VOIGES, Fritz	152983	M			Civilian, Hohenbostel (Ger.) 7.5.44				TORTURE	U.S.
VOIGGT, Fritz	12091	M	Ger.		Pvt., C.C.				MISC.CRIMES	U.K.
VOIGHT, Willi	305701	M	Ger.		Civilian near Luebeck-Siems (Ger.) 6.8.44				MURDER	U.S.
VOIGT	195918	M	Ger.		Major, 669 Pion.Bn Mtz., Les Ponnes, Chirolet (Fr.) 25.6.44				MURDER	FR.
VOIGT	254186	M	Ger.		Major, Pleucadeuc and St.Marcel (Fr.) 18.-28.6.44				INTERR.	FR.
VOIGT	254709	M	Ger.		Referats-Leiter, State Service RSHA, Berlin (Ger.) 40-45				INTERR.	POL.
VOIGT	260662	M	Ger.		Aspirant, 5 Coy, 867 Batt. of DCA of Navy, Lanriec (Fr.) 24.8.44				MURDER	FR.
VOIGT	29844	M	Ger.		W.O., Ger.Gdo. Punish C.O. Haut Clos Troyes (Fr.) 12.43				MURDER	FR.
VOIGT, Ferdinand	136671	M	Ger.	05	Civilian, Lawyer (Ger.) 42				MISC.CRIMES	U.S.
VOIGT, Ferdinand	189250	M	Ger.		Lawyer, occupied territories, Poznan (Pol.) 39-44				PILLAGE	POL.
VOIGT, Frederic	136912	M	Ger.		Agent, Gestapo, St.Flour (Fr.) 14.6.44				MISC.CRIMES	FR.
VOIGT, Gustav	193859	M	Ger.		Guard-Pvt., 4 SS Totenk.Stuba, C.C.Dora-Mittelbau, Nordhausen(Ger.)43-45				INTERR.	U.S.
VOIGT or VOGT, Oskar	256484	M	Ger.		Mayor, State Service, Ottmannshausen (Ger.) 8.44				MURDER	U.S.
VOIGT, Richard	260499	M	Ger.	29.5.06	Rottenfhr., Waffen-SS, guard, C.C.Auschwitz (Pol.) 44-45				BRUTALITY	POL.
VOIGT, Rudolf	255781	M		18.4.02	Rottenfhr., C.C. Harzungen-Nordhausen (Ger.)				MURDER	U.S.
VOIGT, Wilhelm	11294	M	Ger.		Pvt., Army, 110 or 111 Pz.Gren.Rgt., 2 Coy, Albine (Fr.) 29.6.44				MURDER	FR.
VOIR RAFFIN see CHAFFIN	120028									
VOIT	251710	M	Ger.		Cpt., Parachutist, 6 Div. Paratroopers, 17 Rgt., Nieuwaal (Neth.) 14.-15.1.45				WITNESS	NETH.
VOIT, Georg	259002	M	Ger.	11.9.10	Usturmfhr.				INTERR.	U.S.
VOJTA, Anton see STRIZ	258098									
VOLANDER	167150	M	Ger.		Lt., Navy, Montamise (Fr.) 14.-17.8.45				MURDER	FR.
VOLCHIONDORF, Konsta	185268	M	Ger.		Cmdt., Ortskommandantur, Spilion (Gre.) 2.43				MURDER	GRC.
VOLCKHEIM	28857	M			Lt.Col., Army, 20 Army Staff, Finmark (Nor.) 10.,11.44				MURDER	UNWCC.
VOLDIGE, Herbert	121229	M	Ger.		Sgt., Dienststelle L 13359 F, Chièvres (Bel.) 2.9.44				MURDER	BEL.
VOLFINGER see WOELFINGER	1094									
VOLGKL	192615	M	Ger.		Usturmfhr., SS, C.C. Buchenwald (Ger.) 42-45				TORTURE	U.S.
VOLINER	256223	M			Uscharfhr., SS, C.C. Buchenwald (Ger.)				MURDER	U.S.
VOLK	10028	M	Ger.		Chief-Gestapo, C.C. Oranienburg (Ger.) 39-44				MURDER	CZECH.
VOLK	195346	M	Ger.		Crim.Comm., Gestapo, C.C. Sachsenhausen (Ger.)				MURDER	BEL.
VOLK	254711	M	Ger.		Cpl., Pepingen (Bel.) 2.44-3.9.44				WITNESS	BEL.
VOLK, Arno	255794	M		01	Rottenfhr., C.C. Harzungen-Nordhausen (Ger.)				MURDER	U.S.

NAME	C.R.FILE NUMBER	SEX	NATIO-NALITY	DATE OF BIRTH	RANK OCCUPATION UNIT	PLACE AND DATE OF CRIME	REASON WANTED	WANTED BY
VOLK, Jakob	301400	M	Ger.		SS-Cpl.Employee, C.C. Buchenwald (Ger.) Between 16.5.38-9.10.43		MURDER	BEL.
VOLK, Leo	261611	M	Ger.	10	Hsturmfhr.		MISC.CRIMES	U.S.
VOLKEL see VOLKER, Ernst	142318							
VOLKEL, Ernst	152979	M	Ger.		SS-Sturmmann, SS, C.C. Volary (Czech.) 44-45		MURDER	U.S.
VOLKENBOORN	147206	M			Chief, Bled (Yugo.) SS, Nachrichtendienst Regt., 43		MURDER	YUGO.,U.S.
VOLKENRADT	174838	M	Ger.		Unterscharfhr., SS, Osterode, Seesen (Ger.)6.4.45		MURDER	FR.
VOLKER	300395	M	Ger.		SD-Mann, Gestapo Toulouse, South-West France, especially, Toulouse Haute-Garonne, cersand Tarn (Fr.) 11.42-19.8.44		MURDER	FR.
VOLKER, Ernst or VOLKEL	142318	M		85	Police-Chief, Police, Watenbuttel (Ger.)7.-8.44		BRUTALITY	U.S.
VOLKER, Leopold	196089	M	Ger.		Interpreter, Gestapo SS, Lyon (Fr.)		MURDER	FR.
VOLKER, Otto	256232	M	Ger.		Pvt., C.C. Ellrich, Nordhausen (Ger.)		MURDER	U.S.
VOLKER, Richard	301401	M	Ger.		SS-Cpl.-Employee, C.C. Buchenwald (Ger.) Between 16.5.38-9.10.43		MURDER	BEL.
VOLKERT, Heinrich	139241	M	Ger.		Civilian, Ansbach (Ger.) 15.4.45		WITNESS	U.S.
VOLKHOFF	301152	M	Ger.		Staff at C.C. Struthof-Natzweiler (Fr.)42-44		MURDER	FR.
VOLKMANN	126464	M	Ger.		SS-Obersturmfhr., SS, C.C. Hauenstetten, Dachau (Ger.)3.7.-9.44		MURDER	U.S.
VOLKMANN	142004	M	Ger.		C.C. Kahla near Rudolstadt (Ger.) 44-45		MISC.CRIMES	U.S.
VOLKMANN	196100	M	Ger.		C.C. Guard, Adjutant, C.C. Royallieu (Fr.)41-44		INTERR.	FR.
VOLKMANN	301237	M	Ger.	10	SS-Hauptsturmfhr., Crim.Commissar, Leiter d. Abt. IV A Kommunismus u. Marxismus, Passfaelschungen, Feindpropaganda u. Belgische Polizei, Brussels (Bel.) 6.40-9.44		MURDER	BEL.
VOLKMANN, Kurt	973	M	Ger.	13.11.11	SS-Untersturmfhr., SS, C.C. Lublin, Maidanek (Pol.) 40-44		MURDER	POL.,U.K.
VOLKMANN, Willi	256233	M			Pvt., C.C. Ellrich, Nordhausen (Ger.)		MURDER	U.S.
VOLKMAR	192616	M			Staff-Sgt., SS, C.C. Buchenwald (Ger.) 42-45		MURDER	U.S.,FR.
VOLKMARR	29843	M			SS-Unterscharfhr., SS, C.C. Struthof (Fr.) 42-44		MURDER	FR.
VOLKMER	136911	M	Ger.		Interpreter, Army, St. Floret (Fr.)30.6.44		MISC.CRIMES	FR.
VOLKOFF	125616	M	Ger.		C.C. Natzweiler (Ger.)		MURDER	U.S.
VOLLAND, Georg	256234	M		04	Rottenfhr., C.C. Harzungen, Nordhausen (Ger.)		MURDER	U.S.
VOLLBACH	174837	M	Ger.		Pvt., 2.Bn.Paratroops-Regt., Plouzane (Fr.) 44		MURDER	FR.
VOLLBEHR, Friedrich	306780	M	Ger.		Iserbrook nr. Osdorf 20.6.44		BRUTALITY	U.S.
VOLLBRECHT, Richard	1347	M	Ger.		Pvt., Army, 194.Gr.		MISC.CRIMES	U.K.
VOLLERT, Ernst	254699	M	Ger.	25. 8.90	Ministry Official, State Service, Prague (Czech.) 39-45		MURDER	CZECH.
VOLLERTHUN, Lena	36602	F	Ger.		Civilian, Farm r. Klackendorf (Pol.)6.-11.41		MURDER	POL.
VOLLET	11295	M			Sgt., Army, 110 or 111. Pz.Gren.Regt.2.Coy., Albine (Fr.) 44		MURDER	FR.
VOLLMANN, Paul	259639	M	Ger.	95	SS-Hptschfhr., Gestapo, Area of Angers (Maine and Loire Fr.)42-44		MISC.CRIMES	FR.
VOLLMANN, Wilhelm	139244	M	Ger.		Employee, Civilian, Flettenberg (Ger.) 4.45		TORTURE	U.S.
VOLLMEN, Rudi	195419	M			SS-Pvt., SS, Arnheim (Neth.) 9.44-4.45		PILLAGE	NETH.
VOLLMER	166382	M			Lt., SS-Police-Regt., Record (It.) 1.45		MURDER	U.S.
VOLLMER, Anton	173203	M			C.C. Gaggenau, Rotenfels, Schirmeck (Fr.,Ger.) 44		INTERR.	U.K.
VOLLMER	255535	M	Ger.	10. 7.04	Military, Enschede and Haaksbergen (Neth.)10. or 11.44		INTERR.	NETH.
VOLLMER, Herbert	306930	M			SS-Sturmbannfhr., Cmdt. des I. Sturmbannes der 13 Stand.d. SS-Div. "Prinz Eugen" (F 364), 41-44		MURDER	YUGO.
VOLLMER, Hermann	161645	M		03	Sgt., Airforce, Luftgau C.C. Eggemoen,Honefoss (Nor.)		MURDER	NOR.
VOLLMER, Theo	300597	M	Ger.		Brother of Anton Vollmer, Painter, Enschede (Neth.) 9.or10.42		PILLAGE	NETH.
VOLLMERING, Kurt	140813	M	Ger.	08	Civilian, Dentist, Reichelsheim, Winter-Kasten (Ger.) 18.3.45		MURDER	U.S.
VOLLMERINGER see WOLLMERINGER	189764							
VOLLMERS, Jack	166265	M	Ger.	03	Geheime Fieldpolice, Recouro (It.) 1.45		INTERR.	U.S.
VOLLNER	128888	M			SS-Unterscharfhr., SS, C.C. Weimar, Buchenwald (Ger.)		TORTURE	U.S.
VOLLRATH	152981	M			Kreisleiter and Landrat, NSDAP, C.C. Muehlhausen (Fr.) 2.45		TORTURE	U.S.
VOLLSTEDT, Ernst	256224	M			Sturmfhr., SS, Opava (Czech.) 40-45		TORTURE	CZECH.
VOLLTEIN	188262	M		15	Major, 7. Para Div., Gristede (Ger.)		MURDER	CAN.
VOLLWEIDER or VOLLWEILER	256235	M			Rottenfhr., C.C. Nordhausen (Ger.)		MURDER	U.S.
VOLPERT	974	M	Ger.		General, Army, Valence (Fr.) 2.-7.44		MURDER	FR.
VOLRAP	256225	M	Ger.		Apotkecary, in a Hospital, Mauthausen (Aust.)		MURDER	FR.
VOLKMANN	186693	M	Ger.	10-15	Sturmfhr., SS, Lublin (Pol.) 40-44		TORTURE	U.K.
VOLSKY, Ernest	305350	M	Ger.		Capt., Turkestans Legion 1. Regt. of Volunteer turkestans, Albi, Tarn (Fr.) 19.8.44		MURDER	FR.
VOLTE	256236	M			Rottenfhr., C.C. Osterhagen, Nordhausen (Ger.)		MURDER	U.S.
VOLTER	146739	M			Dr., SS, C.C. Flossenburg (Ger.)		TORTURE	U.S.
VOLTZ	153014	M			Lt., Air Corps, Stettin (Ger.) 15.-18.7.44		TORTURE	U.S.
VOLTZ	161274	M	Ger.	95	Lt., Army, Stalag Luft IV, Grosstychow (Ger.) 44		TORTURE	U.S.
VOLTZ	191893	M		00	Major, Stalag Luft 6, Hagdeburg (Ger.) 27.4.44-27.5.44		MURDER	U.S.
VOLTZ, Arthur Karl	188613	M	Ger.		Miscellaneous		WITNESS	BEL.
VOLUCIDE	188722	M			Brigadier, Army, Le Bourget Triage (Fr.) 24.8.44		WITNESS	FR.
VOLZER, Ernest	306060	M	Ger.		Member, Kriminalpolizei Dessau, Bernburg (Ger.) 7.7.44		MURDER	U.S.
VON ALDRINGEN, Alfons Clary	254922	M	Ger.	12. 3.87	Civil, Teplice-Sanov (Czech.) 39-45		MISC.CRIMES	CZECH.
VON ALLWOEHREN (Baron)	250601	M	Ger.		SS-Sturmbannfhr., SS, Pysely (Czech.) 7.5.45		MURDER	CZECH.
VON ALLWORDEN, Reinhardt	149353	M			Stalag Kdo. 637 Stalag X, Badrachlersen (Ger.)		TORTURE	FR.
VON ALT	133978	M		95	Major, Cmdt., 1.Bn.Regt. de Securite No.1000, Grandeyrolles, Verrières (Fr.) 10.8.44		LOOTING	FR.
VON ALT	141498	M	Ger.		Cpl., Army, Chenebier-Etobon (Fr.) 27.9.44		MURDER	FR.
VON ALT	172895	M	Ger.		Major, 74 Sicherungs Regt. 1.Bat. C.Lavières (Fr.) 10.,11.6.44		MURDER	FR.
VON ALTEN	196165	M	Ger.		Major, of Gen. St. 62. Officier Luftflotte 4 (Hung.) Kisber (Hung.)		WITNESS	U.S.
VON ALVENSLEBEN	44625	M			Lt. Colonel, Army Ger. Military Command, H.Q., Schouwen-Duiveland (Neth.) 11.44		MURDER	NETH.
VON ALVENSLEBEN, Werner,Count	39	M			Police Commanding Officer Lublin (Pol.) 15.6.40		MURDER	POL.
VON AMMON, Wilhelm	261114	M	Ger.	3.03	Ministerial Councillor, Ministry of Justice,		SUSPECT	U.S.
VON ANNAMM	162083	M	Ger.		Major, Public Official, Augestowa (Pol.)		TORTURE	U.S.
VON APPEN	129245	M	Ger.		Oberlt., Nachrichten-Zug, Feldpost No. L. 49215 (N) L.P.A.Paris Hainaut (Bel.) 2.-3.9.44 (Geheim.Schrb.)		MURDER	BEL.
VON ARNIM, Juergen	259029	M	Ger.	89	Gen.Oberst		INTERR.	U.S.
VON AULOCK	259078	M	Ger.		Gen.		WITNESS	U.S.
VON BACH see VON BOCH	257182							
VON BAER	186467	M			Colonel, Army, Isere (Fr.)		PILLAGE	FR.

VON - VON

NAME	C.R.FILE NUMBER	SEX	NATIO-NALITY	DATE OF BIRTH	RANK OCCUPATION UNIT PLACE AND DATE OF CRIME	REASON WANTED	WANTED BY
VON BAHR	190024	M			Lt.,892 Gren.Regt.,264 Div.,Sucuraj-Croatia (Yugo.) 5.10.43	MURDER	YUGO.
VON BARBIER	189021	M	Ger.		Osturmbannfhr.,Chief,S.D.,Gestapo,Lyon (Fr.)	TORTURE	U.K.
VON BARGEN (see VON DETZEN)	167919						
VON BARGON	192074	M	Ger.	11	Oberpreparatur,Anatomy-Institute,Danzig (Pol.)	TORTURE	POL.
VON BARISANI	179789	M			Major,Army,St.Martin (Aust.)	INTERR.	U.S.
VON, BASSEWHITE, Graf	21408	M			Lons Le Saulnier (Fr.)	MURDER	FR.
VON BAUCH (see VON BUCH)	257182						
VON BAUMBACH	70	M	Ger.		Public official,Landrat Lezno (Pol.)9.-10.39	MURDER	POL.
VON BAUM-MUHLENBURY,Walter	250964	M		7. 2.13	Dr.,Pvt.,13 Coy.,558 Regt.,Rde.,Bruay en Artois (Fr.) 1.9.44	MURDER	FR.
VON BECHTOLSTEIN,Gustav,Frh. (gen.:MAUCHENHEIM)	260611	M			Major-General,Army	WITNESS	U.S.
VON BECKER	190027				Member of Staff,Banjica (Yugo.) 40-45	MURDER	YUGO.
VON BEGUSCH	126723	M			Dr.,Member,Gestapo,N.C.O.,Paris (Fr.) 42	TORTURE	FR.
VON BEHFER	146930	M			Adjutant du General Bader,Army,Savoie (Fr.)	TORTURE	FR.
VON BEHLER, Baron	78	M	Ger.		Officer,90 Motor-Inf.Div., 22.-31.8.44	MURDER	FR.
VON BEHR	123925	M	Ger.		General-Major,Army,Lebenhan (Ger.) 4.-5.42	MISC.CRIMES	U.K.
VON BEHR	135136	M	Ger.	97	Col.,C.C. (Ger.) 1.45	TORTURE	U.S.
VON BEHR	151708	M		87	Capt.,Nevy,Coy. Stielau Musculus Capt.,Gravenwoehr (Ger.) 11.-12.44	MISC.CRIMES	U.S.
VON BEHR (Baroness)	167640	F	Ger.		Civ.,Ostgebietsministerium Rosenberg,Reichs-official,Paris(Fr.)44	PILLAGE	FR.
VON BEHR	257941	M			Korv.-Kptn.,150 Pz.-Bde.,Meuse Bridge,Antwerp (Bel.) 12.44	MISC.CRIMES	U.S.
VON BEHR,Baron,Kurt	49098	M	Ger.	87	SS-Oberfhr.,and DRK-Feldfhr.,Einsatzstab "Rosenberg",Paris(Fr.Ger.)45	MISC.CRIMES	FR.U.S.BEL.
VON BENTIVEGNI,Franz	261729	M	Ger.		Oberst,Ministerialrat,Abwehr,Berlin (Ger.)	WITNESS	LUX.
VON BERG	146917	M			Gestapo,Salon (Fr.)	TORTURE	FR.
VON BERG,Kurt	260609	M			Major-General,Army	MISC.CRIMES	U.S.
VON BERLICHINGEN,Goetz	28735	M	Ger.		Major,Gebirgs-Armee-Korps 36 Staff I A,Finmark (Nor.) 11.44	MURDER	NOR.
VON BERLICHINGEN,Goetz	124510	M			Civilian	MURDER	U.S.
VON BERNUTH	21327	M	Ger.		Lt.Col.,Army,Cmdt.,Stalag II B,Hammerstein,Wiesenberg (Ger.) 9.-12.43	MURDER	U.S.
VON BERTHOLDI,Herbert	85	M			Inspector,S.D.,Caen (Fr.) 6.44	MURDER	FR.
VON BIRCHAAN	252447	M	Ger.		W.O.-Lt.,377 Jaeg.-Regt.,Vinkt,Meigem (Bel.) 25.-31.5.40	MISC.CRIMES	BEL.
VON BLANKENBURG	194732	M			Lt.,SS,Div."Das Reich",Regt."Gross Deutschland",Chasselay(Fr.)20.6.40	WITNESS	FR.
VON BLUCKER	196119	M		22	Lt.,Schnelle Abteilung,Div.602,Chambord (Fr.)	MURDER	FR.
VON BOCK (or BACH-BAUCH, Wilhelm)	257182	M	Ger.	98 or 96	Camp-Commander,Ziegenhain (Ger.) 29.3.44	MURDER	U.S.
VON BOCK,Wilhelm	148536	M		90	Capt.,Stalag IX A,Ziegenhain (Ger.) 3.45	MISC.CRIMES	U.S.
VON BODMANN	27765	M	Ger.		Osturmfhr.,SS,C.C.,Struthof,Natzweiler,Auschwitz,Birkenau (Fr.-Pol.) 39-45	MURDER	U.K.FR.CZECH.
VON und ZU BODMAN,Freiherr	159357	M	Ger.		Lt.Col.,Army,Nantes (Fr.) 9.41	INTERR.	U.S.
VON BOESCHTAL	120627	M	Ger.		Inspector,Army (Ger.) 8.44	TORTURE	U.K.CAN.
VON BOESTCHEL	190349	M	Ger.	10	Inspector,SS,Krazeen (Ger.) 8.44	TORTURE	CAN.
VON BOHAN (see BOHUN)	186704						
VON BOHEIM	167674	M	Ger.		Leader,Administration of Poland,Krakau (Pol.) 39-44	MISC.CRIMES	POL.
VON BOHUN (or BOHAN)	36663	M			Major,Army,C.C.Limburg,Aspach,Sagan (Ger.)	MURDER	U.K.
VON BOMBACH	159381	M	Ger.	05	Lt.Col.,Camp-Commander,Stalag Luft IV,Kiefheide (Ger.) 7.44-3.45	MURDER	U.S.
VON BONIN,Albert	159364	M	Ger.	93	Administrator,W-SS,C.C.Stutthof,Buchenwald (Ger.) 43	TORTURE	U.S.
VON BORGEN (or VON BORKE)	261387	M	Ger.	circa 85	Lt.Col.,Chief of Unit L 52511,Pau,Soumoulon,Narp,Lescar (Fr.)6.-8.44	MURDER	FR.
VON BORKE	166280	M	Ger.		Dr.,Occupied Territories (Latv.) 41-44	MISC.CRIMES	U.S.
VON BORRIES	173350	M	Ger.		Oberlandrat,Reichsprotector,Bohemia Moravia,Prague,Oswiecim,Birkenau (Czech.-Pol.)	MURDER	CZECH.
VON BORSTEL	251972	M	Ger.		Interpreter,Sipo,Bruessel (Bel.)	INTERR.	BEL.
VON BORSTEL,Heinrich	194112	M	Ger.		Kommandofhr.,C.C.Flossenburg (Ger.)	TORTURE	FR.
VON BOSSE	173339	M			Col.,Cossack-Bde.,Croatia (Yugo.) 11.43-8.44	MURDER	YUGO.
VON BOSSI,Anton,Graf	196271	M			Staff officer,Propaganda Hesselrings,HQ-Cmmd,South-West	MISC.CRIMES	U.S.
VON BRANDENBURG,Eric (see HOCKER,Harry)	11244						
VON BRAUCHITSCH,Walter	125	M	Ger.	81	Generaloberst,Army,German Army Poland,9.-10.39	MURDER	POL.
VON BRENTZ,Walter	253527	M			Lt.,Alencon (Fr.) 40-44	INTERR.	FR.
VON BULOW	132723	M	Ger.		Chief,Stalag II A,C.C.Neu-Brandenburg (Ger.)	MURDER	U.S.
VON BULOW	254276	M			Capt.,6 Coy.,377 Jaeg.-Regt.,Vinkt (Bel.)	INTERR.	BEL.
VON BURGSDORF	53155	M			Dr.,SA-Bde.-Fuehrer,official and SA,Prag (Czech.) 39-45	MURDER	CZECH.
VON BURSTINI	254275	M	Ger.		Capt.,4 Paratroop.-Regt."Grassmel",Div."Hermann Goering",Helchteren and Hechtel (Bel.) 5.-11.9.44	BRUTALITY	BEL.
VON BUSCH	254492	M			Oschfhr.,C.C.Mackenrode,Nordhausen (Ger.)	MURDER	U.S.
VON BUSSCHER,Hermann	139807 A	M	Ger.	10	Uschfhr.,SS	MURDER	U.S.
VON BUTLER	306116	M	Ger.		Col.,Standorts-Cmdt.,Army,Aalborg 1.12.42-44 (Den.) 23.8.43	MURDER	DEN.
VON BYDuROFSHAUSEN	189993	M			Capt.,Kreiskommandant,Kragujevac (Yugo.) 19.10.41	MURDER	YUGO.
VON CAPRI (or KAPRI)	173274	M	Ger.-Rum.		Member,Gestapo,Noailles (Fr.)	MURDER	U.K.
VON GARISMAR,Ernst Arnold Eugen Peter	252053	M		2. 2.01	Proxy Lippmann Rosental and Cie,Germ.R.A.D.,Amsterdam(Neth.)9.43	MISC.CRIMES	NETH.
VON CLAASS	190070	M	Ger.		Kommissar,Gestapo Gau Danzig,Kattowitz (Pol.) 39	MURDER	POL.
VON CLAASS	195734	M			Reg.-Praesident,Governor-General,Ziechenau (Pol.) 39-42	MURDER	POL.
VON CLASSEN	306949	M	Ger.		Pol.-Praesident at town Warschau,Warszawa (Pol.) 39	MURDER	POL.
VON CLEAR	185338	M			Bde.-General,Oberfeld-Kommdtr.,Liege (Bel.)	MISC.CRIMES	FR.
VON COSSEL	188934	M	Ger.		Major,Army,Remilly (Fr.) 8.43	TORTURE	FR.
VON DACHAU	166949	M			Lt.,15 Div.Afrika-Corps,33 Pion.,Vaucourt Xousse (Fr.) 9.-10.44	MISC.CRIMES	FR.
VON DAUBERSCHMIDT (RITTER)	251493	M	Ger.	25	Lt.Col.,Army,Karan (Yugo.)	INTERR.	YUGO.
VON DE TADEN	261344	M			Secr.,Kreiskommandantur,Vire (Fr.) 8.7.44	INTERR.	FR.
VON DEM BACH-ZELEIOSKI	142308	M	Ger.	95	Obergruppenfhr.,W-SS (Pol.)	INTERR.	U.S.
VON DEM KNESEBECK,DIETZ	254960	M	Ger.	13	Col.,Army,Gen.St.,65 Div.,Poivzano Magra (Ital.) 9.43	INTERR.	U.K.
VON DEM LARGE	151344	M			Capt.,Ldaschtz.-Bn.316,Friesack (Ger.) 22.6.44	MURDER	U.S.
VON DEN EICHEN,Werner	140873			05	Zahlmeister,21 Festungsnachrichtenstab,Elten (Ger.) 16.9.44	MURDER	CAN.U.K.
VON DEN HEYDEN,Karl	261496	M	Ger.		Supervisor,Post-office,W-SS,Gestapo,C.C.Auschwitz (Pol.) 41-45	MURDER	POL.
VON DER DECKER	258904	M	Ger.	23. 6.94	Capt.,Kdo.1784 of Stalag XII F,Kettenbach b.Michelbach-Hut(Ger)10.44	MURDER	FR.
VON DER EINDER	185678	M	Ger.		Pvt.,Heereskuesten-Art.(Grc.) 5.44	MURDER	GRC.

VON-VON

NAME	C.R.FILE NUMBER	SEX	NATIO- NALITY	DATE OF BIRTH	RANK, OCCUPATION, UNIT, PLACE AND DATE OF CRIME	REASON WANTED	WANTED BY
VON DER GOLTZ	185946	M	Ger.		Lt., Army, Charente et Vienne (Fr.) 17.-30.8.44	TORTURE	FR.
VON DER GROEBEN, Peter	260631	M			Bde.-General, Army.	WITNESS	U.S.
VON DER HAGEN	196627	M			Med. Kdo. 56 F, Essen-Katernberg (Ger.) 4.2.44	MURDER	FR.
VON DER LIPPE	252446	M	Ger.		Judge, SS, Duesseldorf (Ger.) 40-45	MISC.CRIMES	LUX.
VON DER MOSEL	625	M	Ger.		Lt., Army, Feldgendarmerie-Trupp 5, Locmine (Fr.)	MURDER	FR.
VON DER OSTEN	144489	M			Major, Army-Oberkommando.	WITNESS	U.S.
VON DER RECKE, Hilmar	122683	M	Ger.	91 - 96	Col., Army, C.C. Stammlager XII A, Limburg (Ger.)	MURDER	U.S.
VON DER ROPP	62212	M	Ger.		Head of the "E.R.R." Rosenberg-Looting offices.	PILLAGE	UNWCC
VON DER ROPP, Baron	138336	M	Ger.		Civilian (Fr.) 44	TORTURE	FR.
VON DER RUPP	167473	M	Ger.		Chief of Legal Section, Einsatzstab Rosenberg, Paris (Fr.) 40-44	PILLAGE	FR.
VON DER SCHULENBURG	898	M			General, Army-Camp. 42-44	WITNESS	U.K.
VONDETRODE	257616	F			Civilian, Genthin (Ger.) 12.44	MURDER	U.S.
VON DETZEN (or VON BARGEN)	167919	M	Ger.		Hptscharfhr., SS, C.C.Guard, C.C.Oranienburg (Ger.) 39-4.45	MURDER	POL.
VON DEVEN	256227	M			Pvt., C.C.Dora, Nordhausen (Ger.)	MURDER	U.S.
VON DEVILLE, Valere	196361	M			Chimay and St.Remy (Bel.) 22.4.44	MURDER	FR.
VON DIERINGSHOFEN	195812	M	Ger.		Dr., Oberstarzt, Prof.,Director, Med.Institute for the Air Force, Frankfurt-Main, Dachau, Neuengamme-Hamburg (Ger.) 42-43	MURDER	BEL.
VON DITFURTH	253618	M	Ger.		SS-Ustumfhr., 9.SS Panz.Gren."Das Reich" 20092, Mormont (Bel.)	MURDER	BEL.
VON DORNBERG	148931	M			SS-Gruppenfhr.,SS.	TORTURE	FR.
VON DORP	142012	M	Ger.		Obermaat, Navy, Fort Prins Hendrik near Ooltemsplaat (Neth.) 12.6.45	MURDER	NETH.
VON DULONG	62068	M			Lt., Army, Chateauneuf du Faou (Fr.)	MURDER	FR.
VON DULONG	155749	M			Capt., Parachute Units, Landebau (Fr.) 44	MURDER	FR.
VON EBELSTEIN, Friedrich Karl	301556	M	Ger.		Head of Police of the Wehrkreis, in which the Camp at Dachau was situated C.C.Dachau (Ger.) 40-45	MURDER	BEL.
VON EBERSTEIN, Frhr.Friedr.	187597	M	Ger.		General, Pol.leader, Waffen-SS-Pol., State Service, Munich (Ger.)	WITNESS	UNWCC, U.S.
VON EHRENREICH, Kurt Ludwig	210	M			Public Official, Gov. of Cracow (Pol.)	MURDER	POL.
VON EIBEN, Gerald	194092	M	Ger.	05	Pvt., Navy-Art. C.C.Guard, Wilhelmshaven (Ger.) 7.-10.4.44	MURDER	U.K.
VON EICKEN, Graf	21324	M	Ger.		Dr., Prof., Civ., C.C.Hohenlychen-Ravensbrueck (Ger.) 16.-18.5.44	TORTURE	FR.
VON EICKSTADT, Graf	257906	M	Ger.		Lt., Panzer Bde. 150, Meuse Bridge-Antwerp (Bel.) 12.44	MISC.CRIMES	U.S.
VON EISFELD	9652	M	Ger.		Sturmbannfhr., SS, C.C.Dachau (Ger.) 39	TORTURE	BEL., CZECH.
VON EKSTET, Alexander Graf Vitztum	250734	M	Ger.		Cmdt., Col., P.W.Camp Oflag V B, Biberach (Ger.) 41-45	TORTURE	YUGO.
VON ELTZ, Graf	173756	M	Ger.		Chief of Intelligence Service, Cossak Div. (Yugo.) 11.43-8.44	MURDER	YUGO.
VON EMMERICH, Nagy	147069	M	Ger.		Gen., Army-Oberkommando, Krasiska, Koruska (Yugo.) 43	MURDER	YUGO.
VON EMMERICK, Gustav	186431	M	Ger.	4. 5.90	S.A.-Sturmfhr., NSDAP, Bergwerksdirektor, Beauftragter fuer Eisenerz- Gewinnung u.-Verteilung, Luxembourg (Lux.)	MISC.CRIMES	LUX.
VON ENCKEVORT	173231	M	Ger.		Bde-General, Cmdt., Stalag III D, Rudow (Ger.) 11.41	TORTURE	U.K.
VON ENTZEN (or VON OERTZEN)	193882	M	Ger.	90	SS-Cmdt., Air Force, Dienststelle L 49, 193.Luftgaupostamt Pari., Seguret (Fr.) 10.6.44	MURDER	FR.
VON EPP	252077	M			Capt., SS, Popovice (Czech.)	MURDER	CZECH.
VON ERNEST (see EDWIN)	24780						
VONETZ, Heinrich	177557	M	Ger.	20	SS-Guard, SS, C.C.Neu-Benn (Ger.)	TORTURE	FR.
VON EVEN, Hans	171959	M	Ger.		Civilian, C.C. Osterhagen (Ger.)	TORTURE	U.S.
VON FABER DU FAUR, Moritz	195779	M	Ger.		Major-General, Chief of Administration Mil., Bordeaux (Fr.) 25.10.41	MURDER	FR., U.S.
VON FABRICE, Eberhard	258694	M	Ger.		Major-General, Replacement Div. No.172, Darmstadt (Ger.)	INTERR.	U.S.
VON FALKENHAUSEN,	141531	M	Ger.		Dr., Prof., Oberstarzt, Hohenlychen (Ger.) 16.-18.5.44	TORTURE	FR.
VON FALKENHEIM	72091	M	Ger.		Lt., 130.Panz.Lehr-Regt., H.Q.Coy.	MURDER	U.S.
VON FALKENSTEIN, Frhr. Sigismund	260875	M			Bde.-Gen., Army.	WITNESS	U.S.
VON FALKOWSKI, Leo	239	M	Ger.		SS Pol.Bde.Fhr., Pol.Praesident Danzig (Pol.) 9.39-42	MURDER	POL.
VON FALTHAMSER	133372A	M			Civilian.	MURDER	U.S.
VON FARSCH, Vincent	125449	M	Ger.		Pvt., Landesschuetzen Bn., 3.Coy., Hennersdorf-Sudetenland (Czech.) 17.10.44	MURDER	U.K.
VON FESSER, Wilhelm	148407	M	Ger.		Civilian, Eichstadt (Ger.)	TORTURE	U.S.
VON FEULBERS	161334	M	Ger.		Headquarter-Officer, Folkling (Moselle) (Fr.)	MURDER	FR.
VON FLOTOW	160185	M	Ger.		Col., Cmdt. Oflag VIII F, Maehrisch-Truebau (Czech.) 5.44	WITNESS	U.K.
VON FLOTOW, Hans	191862	M	Ger.		Dr.Civ.Geh.Oberreg;Vorsitzender des Aufsichtsrates of Didier-Werke A.G., Belgrad (Yugo.) 42-45	MISC.CRIMES	U.K.
VON FODOR, Luise (nee SLAMA)	188238	F	Ger.	27. 5.98	Chancery-employee, Member of Gestapo,S.D., Brno (Czech.) 39-45	MISC.CRIMES	CZECH.
VON FOELKERSAM, Adrian	257890	M			SS-Hptsturmfhr., 150.Panzer Bde., Meuse Bridge-Antwerp (Bel.) 12.44	MISC.CRIMES	U.S.
VON FRAUENBACHER	306075	M	Ger.		Former Director, International Agricultural Institute "Rom" (Pol.)45	PILLAGE	POL.
VON FRICKEN	133782	M	Ger.	05	Lt., Army, Kom.5, C.C.Fuerstenberg (Ger.) 8.44-1.45	MURDER	U.S.
VON FRICKENDORF	137016	M	Ger.		Major, Cmdt. of SS Troops, C.C. Stalag 10 B Sandbostel (Ger.) 4.45	MURDER	U.S.
VON FRICKING	253835	M			Lt., Stalag XX A, Marienburg (Ger.)	INTERR.	U.S.
VON FRIEZEN	121255	M	Ger.		Lt.Col., Army, Koenigstein-Elbe (Ger.)	WITNESS	FR.
VON FRINGANS	148265	M	Ger.		Arbeitskommando C.C.Dortmund (Ger.)	MISC.CRIMES	FR.
VON FRITZ	190604	M	Ger.		SS-Officer, SS Panz.Gren.Regt."Deutschland", La Parad (Fr.)	MURDER	FR.
VON FUCHS	161669	M	Ger.		Col., Oflag C.C.Fischbeck near Hamburg (Ger.) 10.5.41 and 5.42	TORTURE	UNWCC
VON FUECHTBAUER, Ritter, Heinrich	62341	M	Ger.		Lt.General, Army-Oberkommando (Fr.)		
VON FURSTENBERG, Elimar	147945	M	Ger.		Lt., Usturmfhr.,Waffen-SS,Besançon (Fr.)	MURDER	FR.
VON GALLE	256919	M		03	Major, Cmdt., Army, 125.Div., Ub (Yugo.) 6.1.42	INTERR.	YUGO.
VON GEISO (or VON PHELSO)	256920	M	Ger.		Kreiskommandant, Army, Uzice (Yugo.) 12.41	PILLAGE	YUGO.
VON GEITNER, Ritter	189978	M			Bde.-General, Army, Staff, District of Pozareval (Yugo.)	MURDER	YUGO.
VON GEYER	167617	M	Ger.		Lt.Gen., SS Panz.Troops West (Fr.) 1.44	MISC.CRIMES	U.S.
VON GEZANI, Leon	173435	M	Ger.		Official, Kulturbund, C.C. Maribor (Yugo.) 4.41-44	MURDER	YUGO.
VON GIANELLA, Gilbert	194970	M	Ger.		Lt., Army, St.Laurent des Eaux (Fr.) 18.-19.8.44	MURDER	FR.
VON GIENANTH, Kurt, Frhr.	253003	M	Ger.	6.12.76	Gen.of Cavalry, Mil.-Oberbefehlshaber, several towns of Poland 39-43	MISC.CRIMES	POL.
VON GLAISE-HORSTENAU,Edmund	62350	M	Ger.		Gen.Lt., Army, Croatia (Yugo.)	TORTURE	UNWCC
VON GLANDSTATTEN	199676	M	Ger.	circa05	SS-Hptsturmfhr., SS Pol.Coy., Poggio Mirteto (It.) 28.5.44	MURDER	U.K.
VON GLANSTATTEN	254509	M		96	SS-Hptsturmfhr., SS, Risti (Esth.)	MISC.CRIMES	U.S.
VON GLISZIZYNSKI	129635	M	Ger.		Lt., Ortskommandantur, Vlamertinge (Bel.) 1.-2.6.44	RAPE	BEL.
VON GOECKEL	126466	M			Major-Gen.Oflag, Cmd.Officer, Hammelburg (Ger.) 21.1.45	MURDER	U.S.
VON GOEDEL, Hans	67591	M	Ger.	90	General, Army, Cmdt.d.Verbindungsstabes (Valences), St.Donat (Fr.) 15.6.44	MURDER	FR.
VON GOLDACKER, Heinz or Heino	253014	M	Ger.	06	SS-Sturmbannfhr., SS-Regt. "Germany" 3.Bn., Alibunar (Yugo.)	MURDER	YUGO.

VON - VON

NAME	C.R.FILE NUMBER	SEX	NATIO-NALITY	DATE OF BIRTH	RANK OCCUPATION UNIT PLACE AND DATE OF CRIME	REASON WANTED	WANTED BY
VON GOLDBECK	251558	M	Ger.	01	Col.Town Commander of Milan (It.) 10.8.44	MURDER	U.K.
VON GONTHAL	252109	M	Ger.		Lt., Feldgendarmerie, Andel (Neth.) 4.-5.45	WITNESS	NETH.
VON GOSLAR, George	137020	M	Ger.		Major, 22.Pz.Rgt. 1.-2.Bn, Sessheim (Fr.) 1.45	MURDER	U.S.
VON GOTTBERG	125233	M	Ger.		Obergruppenfhr., Waffen-SS, Offizier, Minsk (Russ.) 43 - 44	MURDER	U.S.
VON GOTTBERG	147746	M	Ger.		Lt.General, Army, Sluzk (Pol.)	PILLAGE	FR.
VON GOTTBERG, Horst	106959	M			Capt., Sonder-Kommando,C.C.Langenbach,Hohenlichte,Suttrop (Ger.) 3.45	MURDER	U.S.
VON GOTZ VON SCHWANENWEISS	147753	M	Ger.		Capt., Panzer Div., Benewka (Latv.)	MURDER	FR.
VON GRAFENSTEIN	259054	M			General, crimes against peace, war crimes and crimes against humanity	WITNESS	U.S.
VON GRAVENSTEIN	250793	M	Ger.		General, Div.-Commander, Tiger-Inf.Div. 373	MISC.CRIMES	YUGO.
VON GRIMM	174972	M	Ger.		Lt., Army, Plouvigneau (Fr.)	MURDER	FR.
VON GRIENBERGER, Rupert	142029	M	Ger.		Regierungsbaurat, O.T., St. Helier,Chanel Jersey Isles (U.K.) 42 - 44	TORTURE	U.K. SOV.UN.
VON GROS	186007	M	Ger.		Capt., Army, La Roche-Posay (Fr.) 8.44	MURDER	FR.
VON GUILLEAUME	257489	M	Ger.		Direktor, Society Adler, Frankfurt-Main, Sochaux (Fr.) 40 - 44	INTERR.	FR.
VON HAEDING, Petrovic	259115	M	Ger.		Coy.-Cmdt.,Usturmfhr., SS, Div. "Prinz Eugen ",Miksic district, Montenegro (Yugo.) 6.-7.42	MISC.CRIMES	YUGO.
VON HAHNKE	300710	M	Ger.		Cadet, 3.Coy.Georgian Legion, Teillet, Tarn (Fr.) 21.6.44	MISC.CRIMES	FR.
VON HALVEN	149514	M	Ger.		SA, Kettenburg (Ger.)	TORTURE	FR.
VON HAMMERSTEIN, Eduord	337	M	Ger.	77	Lt.-General, Army,Brussels (Bel.) 43 - 44	MURDER	BEL.
VON HANSTEIN	190465	M	Ger.		Capt., NSDAP, C.C., Beelitz (Ger.) 40 - 45	MURDER	CZECH.
VON HAPPEN	174235	M	Ger.		Oberkriegsgerichtsrat,Justizministerium, Brive (Fr.) 44	MURDER	FR.
VON HARPEN, Ulrich	257954	M	Ger.		Sgt., 150.Pz.-Brig., Meuse-Bridge-Antwerpen (Bel.) 12.44	MISC.CRIMES	U.S.
VON HASSEL	254785	M	Ger.		Capt., 376.Jaeger Rgt., Vinkt (Belg.)	MISC.CRIMES	BEL.
VON HASSELBACH, Karl-Heinz	105924	M	Ger.	05	Oberfeldarzt, Panzer Army Corps "Gross Deutschland"	WITNESS	U.S.
VON HASSELT	351	M	Ger.		Kommissar Official, Zentralstelle juedische Auswanderung, Amsterdam (Neth.) 42	MISC.CRIMES	NETH.
VON HASSELT, H.	1348	M	Ger.		Pvt., Army, 194 Gr.,	MURDER	U.K.
VON HASSNER	255108	M	Ger.	circa 96	Col., SS, Born (Bel.) 12.1.45	MURDER	U.S.
VON HAUCK	173556	M	Ger.		Feldkommandant, Feldkommandantur, Poitiers (Fr.) 24.-25.8.44	MURDER	FR.
VON HAUSEN	142948	M			Group - Leader, NSDAP, Ginnheim (Ger.) 9.44	MURDER	U.S.
VON HAUSER (or HANSEK)	253850	M	Ger.		Pvt., 9.SS - Totenkopf-Stuba, Auschwitz-Birkenau (Pol.) 1.43	MURDER	YUGO.
VON HEGENER	188285	M	Ger.		Oberreichsleiter, Arbeitsgem.fuer erbbedingte Leiden, 40-45	MURDER	CZECH.
VON HEILDE	173570	M	Ger.		Chief, Sanitaets-Korps Dr., Croatia (Yugo.)	MURDER	YUGO.
VON HEINDL, Wolf	251051	M	Ger.		SS - Mann, Army,SS, Norgia (It.) 4.5.44	INTERR.	U.K.
VON HENNING	250249	M	Ger.	21	Gen.-Major, (Fr.) 10.-21.7.44	MISC.CRIMES	FR.
VON HIRSCHFELD	389	M	Ger.		Public official, Landrat, Inowroclaw (Pol.) 22.10.39	MURDER	POL.
VON HOERAUF, Franz	135186	M	Ger.	16.6.78	Brigadegeneral a.D., Cmdt., Lutz (Pol.) 43	MISC.CRIMES	U.S.
VON HOEREN, Wilhelm (Willi)	192141	M	Ger.	27.1.09	Hauptscharfhr., SS, Gestapo, Anvers (Bel.) 40 - 45	TORTURE	BEL.
VON HOFFMANN	189868	M	Ger.		Chief, Administration of Occ.Territories (It.)	SUSPECT	IT.
VON HOLLACK, Otto	34668	M	Ger.	83	Major, SS, SD, Sipo, C.C., Drontheim (Nor.) 2.43	MISC.CRIMES	U.S.
VON HOLSTEIN	255121	M	Ger.		General, Army, (Bel.)	MISC.CRIMES	BEL.
VON HORMANN, Hans	105955	M	Ger.	6.81	Colonel, Air-Force ,Stalag Luft VI, C.C. Heidekrug (Ger.) 3.44 - 5.44	MURDER	U.S.
VON HORN	167172	M	Ger.		Feldkommandant, Feldkommandantur,Montigny En Vesoul (Fr.)16.7.44	MURDER	FR.
VON HOUVALT	124338	M	Ger.	95	Oberstleutnant, Stalag, 3B, Asst.C.O.,Fuerstenberg (Ger.) 43 - 10.44	TORTURE	U.S.
VON HOUWALD, Karl, Friedrich	105956	M	Ger.	1.10.91	Colonel, Army, Stalag XIII, C.C., Ruppertsbusch-Wuerzburg (Ger.) 23.4.45	MURDER	SOV.UN.
VON HOVE, Albrecht	252880	M		18.4.13	Sgt., C.C., Ellrich, Nordhausen (Ger.)	MURDER	U.S.
VON HOVE (see HOVEN,Waldemar)	121047						
VON HUETZ	188265	M	Ger.		Major, 7.Para-Div., Cristede (Ger.) 29.4.45	MURDER	CAN.
VON HULST	119444	M	Ger.		Dr., 20.Army 378-169.Inf.Div., Gren.Rgt., Finmark (Nor.) 44	MURDER	NOR.
VON HUMBOLDT	137770	M			Capt.,15.Pz.Gren.Rgt.,29.Pz.Gren.-Div.,2.Bn.	WITNESS	U.S.
VON HUMMEL, Helmut,Herbert	258538	M	Ger.		Dr., Ministerialrat, Cracow (Pol.)	PILLAGE	POL.
VON IBACH (see IBACH,Friedrich)	135192						
VON INCHOF	251057	M	Ger.		Lt.-Col., Army, Nuernberg (Ger.) 41 - 45	INTERR.	YUGO.
VON IHRENBURGH, Prince	137602	M	Ger.		Welfare Officier,Arbeitskommando, Laim-Munich (Ger.)	TORTURE	U.K.
VON JENA	9694	M	Ger.		Obersturmbannfhr., SS, Oranienburg (Ger.) 39 - 44	MURDER	CZECH.
VON JENA	195318	M	Ger.		Cmdt., C.C., Sachsenhausen, (Ger.)	MURDER	BEL.
VON JESSER	195655	M	Ger.		Lt, General, 74.Sicherungs-Brigade, Clermont-Ferrand (Fr.) 11.7.44	MURDER	FR.
VON JOSEF, Baron	251634	M		15	Dr.,Capt.,Army, Zvizdar (Yugo.) 28.8.43	MURDER	YUGO.
VON JUTERZENKA, Erich	301500	M	Ger.	8.3.22	Uscharfhr., SS, C.C., Buchenwald (Ger.) 5.38 - 10.43	MURDER	BEL.
VON KAISERBERG	190212	M	Ger.		Cmdt., Feldkommandantur 599, Banjica District of Pozaverac (Serb.) 41	MURDER	YUGO.
VON KALMACH	440	M	Ger.		Stellvertretender Polizeipraesident, Police, Warszawa (Pol.)9.39-1.42	MURDER	UNWCC
VON KAMITZ	162561	M	Ger.		Capt., Army, C.C., Maehrisch-Trubau (Czech.) 5.44	WITNESS	U.K.
VON KAMP	254563	M			Lt., Stalag XX A, Marienburg (Ger.)	MURDER	U.S.
VON KAMPTZ	31902	M	Ger.		Generalmajor, SS, Police, (It.)	MURDER	U.K.
VON KAPRI,Alfred (see CAPRI)	173274						
VON KARGER, Walter	306988	M	Ger.	10.8.89	General-Managing-Director, Firm Lippmann Rosenthal, Amsterdam (Neth.) 8.41 - 5.43	PILLAGE	NETH.
VON KARMINSKY	442	M	Ger.		Colonel, Army, Feldkommandantur, Melun (Fr.) 42 - 44	MURDER	FR.
VON KEISENBERG	253859	M	Ger.		Major-Bn.-Leader,4.Rgt., Div."Hermann Goering",2.Bn., Parachute Rgt. Helchteren und Hechtel (Bel.) 9.44	MISC.CRIMES	BEL.
VON KELLERSPERG	29778	M	Ger.		Capt., Army, Geb.Jg.Rgt. 218, 7.Geb.Div., Finmark (Nor.) 11.44	MURDER	NOR.
VON KERL	167954	M			Member, Einsatzstab Rosenberg,Administrative Staff, (Fr.) 40 - 44	PILLAGE	FR.
VON KETTLER	139753	M	Ger.		Colonel, Cmdt. of Camp, Stalag II B, C.C., Hammerstein (Ger.) 8.43-2.45	TORTURE	U.S.
VON KIPPENAU (see KIPTENAU)	24911						
VON KLAPR, Baron	194712	M	Ger.		Colonel, Army, Bout Des Vergnes (Fr.) 7.-8.8.44	MURDER	FR.
VON KLATTE, Hermann (or KLATTE)	194581	M	Ger.		Hauptwachtmeister, Grenzschutz,Pol., Gallantsoog (Neth.) 9.41 - 3.42	TORTURE	U.K.
VON KLAUTCEK	157803	M	Ger.	90	Army, Military Head of Arbeitseinsatz, Brux (Czech.) 5.44 - 5.45	TORTURE	U.K.
VON KLEEMANN, Ritter	12224	M	Ger.		Landes-Forstmeister, Public Official, Saarbruecken, Saargemuend (Ger.)	MISC.CRIMES	U.K.

NAME	C.R.FILE NUMBER	SEX	NATIO-NALITY	DATE OF BIRTH	RANK OCCUPATION UNIT PLACE AND DATE OF CRIME	REASON WANTED	WANTED BY
VON KLEMM	305805	M	Ger.		Gen., O.C. of Prison Camp, Oflag VI-C, Osnabrueck-Ewers-Heide (Ger.)44	MURDER	YUGO.
VON KLEMM, Kuno	193352	M	Ger.	81	Brig.Gen., Kgf.Arb.Kdo., C.C. Oslo (Nor.) 10.44-5.45	TORTURE	U.K. U.S.
VON KLITZING	150591	M	Ger.		Major, Army, Courciual (Fr.) 40	MURDER	FR.
VON KLUGE, Gunther	474	M	Ger.		General, Armeegruppe 4 Befehlshaber, (Ger.) 9.-10.39	MURDER	POL.
VON KLUGE, Gunther	195732	M			SS Scharfhr., Waffen SS, C.C. Stutthof (Fr.) 39-41	MURDER	POL.
VON KNOHRR	256128	M	Ger.		Cmdt., C.C. Flossemburg (Ger.)	MURDER	
VON KOCHENHAUSIN	185856	M	Ger.		Major, Army, Chief of German Bn., Pyrgos (Grc.) 8.44	MURDER	FR.
VON KOCHENHAUSEN	257016	M	Ger.		Major, 22.Inf.Div., Strumica (Yugo.) 11.44	MURDER	GRC.
VON KONSBERGT	186744	M	Ger.		Capt., Army, Homblieres (Fr.) 1.8.40	PILLAGE	YUGO.
VON KONZMANN, Ritter	188814	M	Ger.		Major, Army, C.C. Souges (Fr.) 27.3.40-11.40	MISC.CRIMES	FR.
VON KCRAB	258082	M	Ger.		Cmdt., Prague (Czech.) 45	MURDER	FR.
VON KRALIK	12444	M	Ger.		Cmdt of place, Army, Pontivy (Fr.) 44	MURDER	CZECH.
VON KRAUS	300275	M	Ger.		Town-major of Thebes (Grc.) 3.7.44	MURDER	FR.
VON KREZMAR or VON KRETCHMAR	260672	M	Ger.		Lt., S.P. 08291, Neuville-en Ferrain (Fr.) 2.9.44	MISC.CRIMES	GRC.
VON KRISTEN	195064	M	Ger.		SS Usturmfhr., SS Div.Leibstand. "Adolf Hitler" 1.Bn., Wormhoudt (Fr.) 27.5.40-	SUSPECT	FR.
VON KRUDENER	261076	M	Ger.		C.C. Natzweiler (Fr.)	MURDER	U.K.
VON KUECHLER	189786	M	Ger.		Gen.d.Art., 18.Army Group, Oeffelt, Gennep (Neth.) 10.5.40	MURDER	FR.
VON KUNSBERGT	901425	M	Ger.		Capt., commanding Ortskommandantur, Homblieres-Aisne (Fr.) 1.8.40	MISC.CRIMES	NETH.
VON LAUCHET, Meinrad (Meinhard)	132959	M	Ger.	05	Brig.Gen., 2.Panz.Div., Bande (Bel.) 24.12.44	BRUTALITY	FR.
VON LAUSSMANN	122991	M	Ger.		Cmdo.Fhr., Waffen SS, C.C. Jaworzno	MURDER	U.S.
VON LEER	251696	M	Ger.		Officer, SS, C.C. Oswiecim, Auschwitz (Pol.) 42	MURDER	FR.
VON LE LEIRE	173686	M	Ger.		Brig.Gen., 117.Jaeger-Div., (Yugo.) 42-44	MURDER	POL.
VON LE SUIRE	305910	M	Ger.		Major Gen., General officer commanding, 117.Lt.Div., Tripolis (Afr.)44	MURDER	YUGO. U.S.
VON LETTOW	10304	M	Ger.		SA Sturmfhr., Kommissar der Gestapo, Brno (Czech.) 39-44	MISC.CRIMES	GRC.
VON LIEDERMANN	12579	M	Ger.		Lt., commanding detachm. Colonne Meyer of Africa-Corps, Sermaize les Bains (Fr.) 29.8.44	TORTURE	CZECH.
VON LILIENFELD	142573	M			Lt., Army Oberkommando (chief of PW affairs)	MURDER	FR.
VON LINDEINER	146447	M	Ger.	90	Col., Stalag Luft 3 Sagan (Ger.) 1.44	WITNESS	U.S.
VON LOSEN, Baron	581	M	Ger.		Land-owner, Drzeczkow (Pol.) 9.-10.39	TORTURE	U.K.
VON LOSEN see LOSEN	151940					MURDER	POL.
VON LOSEBERG, Bernard	260707	M			Gen., Army	MISC.CRIMES	U.S.
VON LUCK	152825	M	Ger.		Col., Army, 125.Panz.Gren.Coy. 2.Bn., Seesheim (Fr.) 1.45	MURDER	U.S.
VON LUCK	25555P	M	Ger.	10	Col., Hablainville (Fr.) 10.44	PILLAGE	FR.
VON LUEDINGHAUSEN (Baron)	255009	M	Ger.		Civ., Malomerice nr.Brno (Czech.) 39	PILLAGE	CZECH.
VON LUETTWITZ, Heinrich	254990	M	Ger.	96	Lt.Gen., Commander Tanks 26.Panz.Div., (It.) 44	BRUTALITY	U.K.
VON LUETTWITZ, Smilo see LEUETTWITZ	260654						
VON LUTGENDORFF	31614	M	Ger.		Major, Gebirgs-Div. 2, 20.Army, (Nor.) 10.-11.44	MURDER	NOR.
VON LUTZOW, Freiherr	150635	M	Ger.	95 - 97	Capt., SS Div. Leibstandarte Adolf Hitler, Rosbach (Ger.) 4.3.45	WITNESS	
VON MACK, Baron	251137	M	Ger.		Dr., F.P. No. L 06459, Romilly sur Seine (Fr.) 8.44	PILLAGE	FR.
VON MACK	252541	M	Ger.		Staff-Sgt., F.P. No. 96278 A (K), Vinkt, Meigem (Bel.) 25.-31.5.40	MISC.CRIMES	BEL.
VON MALOTTKI, Otto Rudolf	307146	M	Ger.		Crim.Polizist, Gestapo, Cracow (Pol.) 5.-12.42	MURDER	POL.
VON MALTZAHN, Hasso	306461	M	Ger.		SS Sgt., C.C. Buchenwald (Ger.) betw.16.5.38 and 9.10.43	MURDER	BEL.
VON MANNSTEIN	139686	M	Ger.		Osttruppen Fieldmarshall, Donez and Dnjepr (Sov.Un.)	MISC.CRIMES	U.S.
VON MANSTEIN, Fritz Erich	21394	M	Ger.	87 - 96	Generalfeldmeister, Commissioner of Kiew, NSDAP, betw.Donez and Dnjepr, (Sov.Un.) 42-43	MURDER	U.N.W.C.C.
VON MARCOVITZ, Ulrich	169494	M	Ger.		Pvt., Interpreter, Army, Waffen SS Div.Hohenstaufen, Arnheim, Zutfen (Neth.) 23.9.44	MURDER	U.K.
VON MARSO, Julius	255049	M	Ger.	16.5.08	Recruting officer, SS, NSDAP, Bratislava (Czech.) 40-44	BRUTALITY	CZECH.
VON MASSOW	146476	M	Ger.		Stalag Luft 3, Sagan, 3-44	WITNESS	U.K.
VON MASSOW	194398	M	Ger.	00	Capt., Schnelle. Abt.602, F.P. No. 27690 A, Chamborf (Fr.)21.-22.8.44	MURDER	FR.
VON MASSOW, Ruediger	196623	M	Ger.	circa 25	Lt., Army, 7.Panz.Recon.Replacem.and Training Bn., Berchtesgaden, LAUFEN (Ger.) 16.4.45	MURDER	U.S.
VON MEDEAZZA, Julius or MEDEAZZA	599	M	Ger.		Dr., Leader, Justiz-Abt. des General-Governments	MISC.CRIMES	POL.
VON MEERKATZ	156878	M	Ger.		Lt., Flak, Oursbekille (Fr.) 7.6.44	MISC.CRIMES	FR.
VON MELE	188382	M	Ger.		Chief, SD Einsatzgruppe, Nadrin (Bel.) 23.-25.12.44	MURDER	BEL.
VON MELLE see MELLE	257007						
VON MEYER	254258	M	Ger.		Lt.Col., Deputy to Brig.Gen. von Schramm, Head of the Feldkommändentur, L'Aube, Troyes Region (Fr.) 3.10.43-22.8.44	MURDER	FR.
VON MILLER see MILLER	252526						
VON MUELLER	104866	M	Ger.		Major, Army, Gestapo, O.C. Flushing Stalag Luft I (Neth.) 20.5.44	TORTURE	U.S.
VON MUELLER	136617	M	Ger.	00	Lt.Col., Army S-3 at Stalag Luft I C.C. Barth (Ger.) 20.11.44-13.5.45	MISC.CRIMES	U.S.
VON MUELLER	256723	M	Ger.		Major, German Army, Greifswald (Ger.) 10.-15.3.45	MURDER	U.S.
VON MULLER	251134	M	Ger.		Cmdt., Roche sur Yon, Boüin (Fr.) 5.44	INTERR.	FR.
VON MULLER, Hagen	167097	M	Ger.		Lt., Army, Sanatorium Kerpape (Fr.) 44	PILLAGE	FR.
VON NEUBRONN	151515	M	Ger.		Cmdt., 9.SS Panz.Div. Hohenstaufen, Nimes (Fr.)	MURDER	FR.
VON NEUMANN	194511	M	Ger.		Col., Stg. II A Neu-Brandenburg (Ger.) 5.-7.40	TORTURE	FR.
VON NEURAHT	261804	M	Ger.		Lt., St.Quentin (Fr.) 7.4.44	INTERR.	FR.
VON NOLCKEN	174490	M	Ger.		Col., Commander of Siberian Cossack Rgt., Croatia(Yugo.) 11.43-8.44	MURDER	YUGO.
VON OBERG	185943	M	Ger.		SS Oberstgruppenfhr., Gestapo, Paris (Fr.) 41-44	PILLAGE	FR.
VON OBERKAMPF, Ritter Carl Ferdinand Joseph	152340	M	Ger.	30.10.93	Bde.Fhr. and Brig.Gen., Waffen SS "Wiking" and "Prinz Eugen" Div., YUGO. 41-44	TORTURE	U.S.
VON OCHAFEN	174169	M	Ger.		Major Gen., Orpo O.C. Oswiecim, Birkenau (Pol.) 39-45	MURDER	CZECH.
VON OELHAFEN	139060	M	Ger.		Major, SD, SIPO, Ukraine (Sov.Un.) 7.-11.41	MURDER	U.S.
VON OELHAFEN	194515	M	Ger.		Col. Verbindungsstab de Foix, Chief Feldgendarmerie, Loubens (Fr.) 23.5.44	MURDER	FR.
VON OERTZEN see VON ENTZEN	193882						
VON OPPEL	167109	M	Ger.		Capt., Army, Athienville (Fr.) 5.9.44	TORTURE	FR.
VON OPPEL	250420	M	Ger.		Major, Cmdt. of Gorinchem (Neth.) 2.10.44	MURDER	NETH.
VON OPPELN	165703	M	Ger.	00	Lt.Gen., C.O. 35.Pz.Rgt.,(Sov.Un.) 42	MURDER	U.S.
VON ORERAY	196445	M	Ger.		Gen., Ht.Bugay, Valroney (Fr.) 2.44	MISC.CRIMES	FR.
VON PAAPE see PAAPE, Wilhelm	162687						
VON PAGAN	180490	M	Ger.	05 - 10	Lt., Jaeger-Div. 114.Lt.Div., (It.) 22.6.44	MURDER	U.K.

VON-VON

NAME	C.R.FILE NUMBER	SEX	NATIO-NALITY	DATE OF BIRTH	RANK OCCUPATION UNIT PLACE AND DATE OF CRIME	REASON WANTED	WANTED BY
VON PALEZIEUX, Ernst Wilhelm	149066	M	Ger.	02	Referent, General Gouvernement, Cracow (Pol.) 42-45	PILLAGE	U.S.
VON PANNWITZ, Helmut	174147	M	Ger.		Lt.General, 1 Cossack Div., district of Metlika (Yugo.) 43-44	MURDER	YUGO.
VON PAUMGARTEN	31411	M	Ger.		Lt.Col., Army, 7 Geb.Div.Staff, 20 Army, Finmark(Nor.) 44	MURDER	NOR.
VON PFAFFENROTH	164534	M	Ger.	00	Col. 15 Mountain Army Corps, Banja Luka (Yugo.) 1.-9.1.44	MURDER	U.S.
VON PHEISO (see VON GEISO)	256920						
VON PLANITZ, Edler Karl Ferd.	174080	M	Ger.		Reg.Praesident, public official, Opawa, Auschwitz-Birkenau (Czech., Pol.) 21.4.43	MURDER	CZECH.
VON POLC	259279	M	Ger.		Rittmeister, Capt., 1 Squ.Ukr.Cav., Loc.Maria en Candon (Fr.)10.8.44	INTERR.	FR.
VON POSCHINGER	140803	M			Major, 902 Pz.Gren.Rgt., Wardin (Bel.) 19.12.44	MURDER	U.S.
VON POSCHINGER	190092	M	Ger.		Lt.Col., Stalag VIII/B	MURDER	U.K.
VON POTT, Eugen	261925	M	Ger.	00	Major, Army, Cav., Zagreb (Yugo.) 41-42	SUSPECT	YUGO.
VON PRALIK	179866	M	Ger.		Officer, Kommandantur, Locmine (Fr.) 7.-8.44	MURDER	FR.
VON PRENKEN	153126	M	Ger.		Camp leader, Stalag 319., Cholm (Pol.) 1.43	MURDER	SOV.UN.
VON PRITZ	141593	M	Ger.		Cmdt., 3 SS Pz.Gren.Rgt."Deutschland", La Parade (Fr.) 12.7.44	MURDER	FR.
VON PRITZLEWITZ, Franz Alexander	122543	M	Ger.	05	Civilian, personnel-secretary, manager of a large munition-plant, CC Magdeburg (Ger.) 44-45	TORTURE	U.S.
VON PRONCK	712		Ger.		Police-Vice-President, Police Bydgoszcz (Pol.) 9.39-42	MURDER	POL.
VON PUTT	191744	M	Ger.		Usturmfhr, SS Pz.Div."Das Reich", Mongiscard.(Fr.) 43-44	MURDER	FR.
VON RADENITZ	142080	M	Ger.	95	Hptsturmfhr., SS, CC Dachau (Ger.) 40-45	MURDER	POL.
VON RAISON	167135	M	Ger.		Col., 15 Div.Africa Corps, Vaucourt Vousse(Fr.) 9.-10.44	MISC.CRIMES	FR.
VON RATH	900096	M	Ger.		SS, Adjutant-Lt., to Kreisleiter Pott and Korte at Hummelo and Keppel (Neth.) 1.1.45-31.5.45	PILLAGE	NETH.
VON RAVEN	174048	M	Ger.	1895-00	Civilian, pensioned Major, Gross Luchow near Pasewalk(Ger.) 9.45	MURDER	U.S.
VON RECKOW	725	M			Lt.Col., Stalag 18-A, CC Spittal (Aust.) 16.10.43	MURDER	U.K.
VON REIBNITZ	193021	M	Ger.		Maj.General, Commander, Army, PoW Labour Bn., Drag(Nor.) 44	MISC.CRIMES	NOR.
VON REICHENAU, Walter	732	M	Ger.		Col.General, Army, 10 Army group, Buggenum, Urmond Roosteren (Neth.)40	MURDER	NETH., POL.
VON REMLINGER (see VON RIMLEGER)	109624						
VON RENNENBERG	740	M	Ger.		Ritmeister, Feldkommandantur 755, Le Mans (Fr.) 40-44	PILLAGE	FR.
VON RENTELEN	152352	M	Ger.		Lt., Georgians Inf.Bn., Perigueux (Fr.) 44	MURDER	FR.
VON RENTELN, Theodor Adrian	62207	M	Ger.		Dr., regional official, public official, commissioner general of Lithuania	TORTURE	U.N.W.C.C.
VON RESECKE (or VON RIESSICKE)	193904	M	Ger.		Major, 157 Res.Div., Malleval Cognin Grenoble(Fr.) 2.2.43,29.1.44, 20.7.44, 5.9.44	MISC.CRIMES	FR.
VON RETTLEN	250434	M	Ger.		Col., 360.Gren.Rgt., Xylias (Fr.) 16.8.44	MURDER	FR.
VON RETTNER	186451	M	Ger.		Col., Army, Autun (Fr.) 8.9.44	MURDER	FR.
VON REDMOND	144488	M			Lt.Col., Army, Supreme Command	WITNESS	U.S.
VON RICHTER	259209	M	Ger.		Lt., Section AA 179, Landreville (Fr.) 40-41	PILLAGE	FR.
VON RICHTER, Willy	133293	M			Hptschfhr, W-SS, CC Flossenburg (Ger.)	TORTURE	U.S.
VON RIESSICKE (see VON RESECKE)	193904						
VON RIMLEGER (or VON REMLINGER)	109624	M	Ger.	87	Cmdt., Col., military prison, CC Torgau (Ger.) 40-42	TORTURE	U.K.
VON ROCKTESCHELL, Helmut	188080	M			Fregatten-Kapitaen, Navy	MURDER	U.K.
VON RODEN, Otto	252620	M	Ger.		Sgt., 377 Jg.Rgt., Vinkt (Bel.) 25.-31.5.40	MISC.CRIMES	BEL.
VON ROEDER	195309	M			Reichsprotektor, public official, Prague (Czech.) 39-45	MURDER	CZECH.
VON ROEM (see VON ROEHN,Hans)	128946						
VON ROEMER	755	M	Ger.		Col., CC Oflag 9.A.H., Spangenburg (Ger.) 9.-11.42	TORTURE	U.K.
VON ROEMER	124992	M	Ger.		Gestapo, Charlsville (Fr.) 43-44	MISC.CRIMES	FR.
VON ROEHN, Hans (or VON ROEM)	128946	M		10	Crim.Secretary, Gestapo, Lodz (Pol.) 40-42	MURDER	U.S.
VON ROHLEN	261487	M	Ger.		Lt.Col., PoW camp, Bologna (It.) 28.-29.6.44	MURDER	U.S.
VON ROPPER (or VON ROPPERT)	138335	M	Ger.		Civilian, Director, Immobilien, Paris (Fr.)	TORTURE	FR.
VON ROQUES, Franz	62211	M	Ger.		General of Infantry, Army group south	MURDER	U.N.W.C.C.
VON SALM (or VON SAM)	186188	M	Ger.		Col., Army, Terrasson (Fr.) 15.-31.9.44	MURDER	FR.
VON SALMUTH, Hans	62902	M	Ger.	88	Col.General, chief of staff to Gen.Bock (N.Army Group)	TORTURE	U.S.
VON SAM (see VON SALM)	186188						
VON SAMMER	778	M	Ger.		Gestapo-chief, Warschau (Pol.) 43	MURDER	POL.
VON SANDEN	251303	M	Ger.		KP-officer, Lt., Div.Goering, 4 Paratrooper Rgt., (Rgt. Grassmel), Grassmel, Helchteren (Bel.) 5.and 11.9.44	INTERR.	BEL.
VON SAST	137583	M	Ger.		Official, SD and Gestapo, Hertogenbosch,Tilburg(Neth.) 9.7.44	MURDER	U.K.
VON SAUCKEN, Dietrich	259008	M	Ger.	92	Lt.Gen.	WITNESS	U.S.
VON SCHEELE	132722	M	Ger.		General-President, court-martial, Torgau (Ger.) 5.40-45	MURDER	FR.
VON SCHER-TOSCH	156891	M			Lt.Col., Army, Gardelegen (Ger.) 10.-14.4.45	MURDER	U.S.
VON SCHILLING	36652	M			Cpl., camp Welfau,Stalag Luft III, CC Bonn (Ger.)	WITNESS	U.K.
VON SCHILZENDORF	259900	M	Ger.		Officer, Army, Fonda (It.) 9.43, 10.43	INTERR.	YUGO
VON SCHLICHT	173508	M	Ger.		Ober-Militaerverwaltungsrat, Verwaltungsgruppe Vrnjacka, Banja(Yugo.) 42-44	MURDER	YUGO.
VON SCHLICHTING	190279	M	Ger.		Oberkriegsverwaltungsrat,Feldkommandantur,Ljubljana(Yugo.)4.41-44	MURDER	YUGO.
VON SCHLIEB, RITTER	174364	M	Ger.	89	Lt.General, Air Force, Luftgau-Commander Norway (Nor.)	MURDER	NOR.
VON SCHMIELEWSKY	158596	M			Hptsturmfhr, SS, Hertogenbosch(Neth.)	TORTURE	U.S.
VON SCHNEBEN, Hans	158595	M	Ger.	18.5.93	Lt.Col., Ilag XIII,Army, Wulsburg (Ger.) 22.4.45	WITNESS	U.K.
VON SCHNEIDER	821	M	Ger.		SS, Luzoir (Fr.) 22.8.44	MISC.CRIMES	FR.
VON SCHOLZ, Fritz	259000	M	Ger.	9.12.96	SS-Oberfhr., SS-No.195698, NSDAP No.1304071, 1.10.41	INTERR.	U.S.
VON SCHOENENSEIFEN	161293	M	Ger.		Dr., Sturmbannfhr., SS,Gestapo, head office, Berlin (Ger.) 39-45	MURDER	CZECH.
VON SCHOTZ (or VON SHOTZ)	257971	M			Lt., 150 Pz.Bde., Meuse Bridge, Antwerpen (Bel.) 12.44	MISC.CRIMES	U.S.
VON SCHRAMM	305267	M	Ger.		Bde.General, head of the Feldkommandantur, Troyes region(Fr.) 3.10.43-22.8.44		
VON SCHRECK	186896	M	Ger.		Lt., Army, Hte.Savale. (Fr.)	MURDER	FR.
VON SCHROETTER (or VON SCJRPEDER,Ferdinand)	257992	M			Major, 150 Pz.Bde., Meuse Bridge, Antwerpen(Bel.) 12.44	MISC.CRIMES	FR.
						MISC.CRIMES	U.S.
VON SCHUBEN	167309	M	Ger.		Lt., 77 Bn.Inf., 4 Coy, Foret (Bel.) 6.9.44	MURDER	BEL.
VON SCHUMACHER	301182	M	Ger.		Dr., Dienstaufsicht, Oberstkrgs.Gerichtsrat,German Army.		
VON SCHULENBURG, Bodo Siegfried Ulrich	135561	M	Ger.		Court Martial, Utrecht (Neth.) 43-44	MURDER	NETH.
					Capt., G.A.F.	WITNESS	U.K.
VON SCHULTZ, Hans-Juergen	255956	M	Ger.	14	Usturmfhr, SS and Gestapo -44	TORTURE	POL.
VON SCHULZENDORF	1754	M			Major, Army, 3.Div. Pz.Rgt.29	MISC.CRIMES	U.K.

VON-VON

NAME	C.R.FILE NUMBER	SEX	NATIO-NALITY	DATE OF BIRTH	RANK OCCUPATION UNIT PLACE AND DATE OF CRIME	REASON WANTED	WANTED BY
VON SCHURA	190453	M	Ger.		Doctor,Assessor,C.C.,Beelitz,Vienna (Ger.,Aust.) 40-45	MURDER	CZECH.
VON SCHWARZENSTEIN, Berno	182890	M	Ger.		Doctor, Official, SD.,(Ger.)	MURDER	FR.
VON SCHWEINITZ	259824	M	Ger.		Col.,Recesre Terme.(It.) 10.1.45	INTERR.	U.S.
VON SCHWEPPENBURG, Eyck	164099	M	Ger.		General,Army-Russia	MURDER	U.S.
VON SCHWERLING, Graf	900952	M	Ger.		Lt.General,O.C. 116:Pz.Div.,GIons (Bel.) 7.9.44	MURDER	BEL.
VON SCHROEDER(seeSCHROETTER)	257992						
VON SENSBURG	251264		Ger.		Lt.Col.,Army,Leiter of Abt.,after Lt.Col.Tiechler,Athens (Gre.) 43-44	INTERR.	U.K.
VON SEYDLITZ, (nee DUDON)Maria	259381	F	Ger.		Police,SD of Digue,Colmar (Fr.) 30.1.44	INTERR.	FR.
VON SHOTZ (see VON SCHOTZ)	257971						
VON SOLLEN	305296	M	Ger.		Lt.,Col.,Wehrmachtskommandant at Tilburg and Middelburg,stationed at Culemborg (Neth.) 10.11.44	PILLAGE	NETH.
VON SOLMS, Graf	307204	M	Ger.		Lt.Col.,Ortskommandant,Dordrecht (Neth.) 1.45	PILLAGE	NETH.
VON SOMMERFELD	164741	M	Ger.	87	Col.,Abwehr,Belgrad (Yugo.) 44	MURDER	U.S.
VON SORWELL-OPITZ, Eduard	196442	M	Ger.		Col.,Mil.Records office,Prague (Czech.) 39-45	MISC.CRIMES	CZECH.
VON SPECK-STERNBERG,Spiegel	136356	M	Ger.		Consul General,public official,Marseille(Fr.) 43	WITNESS	U.S.
VON STECHOW, Hans	189991	M	Ger.	13	Polizei Praesident,Gestapo,Berlin (Ger.)	MURDER	U.S.
VON STECKE	167291	M	Ger.		Civilian,Einsatzstab Rosenberg,Paris (Fr.) 40-44	PILLAGE	FR.
VON STEIN,Ritter	300767	M	Ger.		Generalstaatsanwalt:Oberlandesgericht,Litomerice(Leitmeritz)(Czech.) 21.2.40	MURDER	CZECH.
VON STEIN, Fritz	173144	M	Ger.	88 - 90	Ortsgruppenleiter,NSDAP,Gross-Rohrheim (Ger.) 9.40-3.41	TORTURE	U.S.
VON STERNBERG,Freiherr Gerhard	251954	M	Ger.		Col.,Com. of the POW-Camp,Stalag XII D,Trier (Ger.)	BRUTALITY	YUGO.
VON STEUBEN, Kurt Liborius	143131	M	Ger.	86	Lt.Col.,Army.	MISC.CRIMES	U.S.
VON STOCKAUSEN	194410	M	Ger.		Col.,General,SS Div."Das Reich",SS Rgt."Grossdeutschland ,Chasselay (Fr.) 20.6.40	MURDER	FR.,YUGO.
VON STOCKHAUSEN	305302	M	Ger.		General,Rgt."Grossdeutschland",stationed at Pancevo and other places in that area (Yugo.) 4.41	MURDER	YUGO.
VON STREIT	156911	M	Ger.		Capt.,Panz.Gren.Rgt.192,21.Pz.Div.,supply troops,Sessenheim (Fr.)1.45	MURDER	U.S.
VON STROSER	261064	M	Ger.		Capt.,Patrol-corps,Sued-Frankreich (General Kriess) Vaucluse-Var-Bouche du Rhone (Fr.) 44	MISC.CRIMES	FR.
VON STUELPNAGEL, Otto	62424	M	Ger.		General,Mil.Gouverneur,Paris (Fr.) 9.-11.44	MURDER	FR.
VON STURDT	188279	M	Ger.		Sturmbannfhr.,SS,chief,SD,Einsatzgruppe L de La,SIPO,Nadrin (Bel.) 23.-25.12.44	MURDER	BEL.
VON SVOBODA, Robert	162659	M	Ger.	95	Lt.Col.,Air-force,46.Flak Rgt.,Dorsten (Ger.) 10.44	TORTURE	U.S.
VON TANN	147208	M	Ger.		Chief,Gestapo,Radouljica (Yugo.) 43	MURDER	YUGO.
VON TARBUCK	192096	M	Ger.	05	Lt.Col.,Gestapo,Prag (Czech.)	TORTURE	CZECH.
VON TEUSCH-BUTTLAR-BRANDENFELS, Freiherr	260629	M			Bde.General,Army	MISC.CRIMES	U.S.
VON THAL	189808	M			Interpreter,Admin.of occupied territories,Pozaverac (Yugo.) 41-43	MURDER	YUGO.
VON THIELE, Hans (alias: TRAUTMANN, Werner,THIELE, Hans Doctor)	112854	M	Ger.	4. 7.95	Lt.Col. or Col.,Abwehr,Funkleiter Uebersee I i,Engineer,Hamburg (Ger.) 5.44	MISC.CRIMES	U.S.
VON THOMAS	186774	M	Ger.		Oberstgruppenfhr.,SS,chief,General,SS,Gestapo,Paris,(Fr.)26.8.40-41	PILLAGE	FR.
VON TIEHLBERG(or VON TIEHBERG)	259823	M	Ger.		Major,Recesre Terme (It.) 10.1.45	INTERR.	U.S.
VON TIESCHOWITZ	138340	M	Ger.		Civilian,Paris (Fr.) 44	PILLAGE	FR.
VON TODDEN	195344	M	Ger.		Crim.secretary,Gestapo,C.C.,Sachsenhausen (Ger.)	MURDER	BEL.
VON TOUSSAINT, Rudolf	240033	M	Ger.	84 - 85	Col. or Capt.,Amt III c (V.O.) Berlin (Ger.) 1.42	MISC.CRIMES	U.N.W.C.C.
VON TREUENFELD	193989	M	Ger.	00 - 05	Bdefhr.,Waffen SS,Inf.Bds.1,Borissow (Sov.Un.) 8.-9.42	PILLAGE	U.S.
VON TREUENFELD, Karl	226544	M	Ger.	31. 3.85	Gruppenfhr.,Waffen SS,Div.Frundsberg,General,SIPO,SD,Kiew (Sov.Un.) 9.43	MURDER	U.S.
VON TROLL	189814	M	Ger.		Legationsrat,Legation,Lubljana (Yugo.) 4.41-5.43	MURDER	YUGO.
VON TROTT	306519	M	Ger.		Lt.,1.Bn.,P.G.,Poitiers,Depts. of Vienne,Charente (Fr.)17.-30.8.44	MURDER	U.S.
VON TSCHIRNHAUS	174029	M	Ger.		Staff officer,Stalag 6 A.C.C.,Hemer (Ger.) 41-45	TORTURE	U.S.
VON TURNHEIM	149585	M	Ger.		Lt.,11.Panz.Div.,South-West (Fr.) 44	MURDER	FR.
VON TZEBRIKOW, Georges	261075	M	Ger.	02	Interpreter,SD of Draguignan,Var (Fr.) 9.43-8.44	SUSPECT	FR.
VON ULM	152982	M			Col.,29.Panz.Gren.Div.,15.Pz.Gren.Rgt..	WITNESS	U.S.
VON VERE, Baron	965	M	Ger.		Commandant,C.C.,Oswiecim,Birkenau (Pol.) 40	MURDER	U.S.
VON VERSCHUER, Freiherr Otman	126412	M	Ger.		Doctor,member,NSDAP,(Kaiser-Wilhelm Institut Bln.-Dahlem) (Ger.)	MISC.CRIMES	NOR.
VON VIEBAHN, Gerhard	192702	M	Ger.	02	Lt.Col.,Kgf Art.Bn.186,Narvik (Nor.) 40	MISC.CRIMES	U.S.
VON VILMOWSKI	240080	M	Ger.	78	Beurat,public official,Deutsche Reichsbahn,Berlin,Nuernberg (Ger.)	MURDER	FR.
VON VITTERSBADEN	181523	M			90.Div.,1.Bau Pion.,Region of Maurienne (Fr.)	MURDER	FR.
VON VITTERSBAIEN	969	M			O.C.,Army,90.mot.Inf.Div.,1.Pion.Bn.,Savoie (Fr.)22.-31.8.44	MURDER	FR.
VON VOKOUR	306814	M	Ger.		Interpreter,SD,Vichy (Fr.) 10.43-9.44	TORTURE	U.K.
VON WACHTMEISTER, Freiherr	124064	M	Ger.		Col.?,Oflag X G,Luebeck (Ger.) 40-7.41	MURDER	FR.
VON WALLENBERG	250542	M	Ger.		Col.,chief,F.M. of Dijon,L'Ain (Fr.) 10.-21.7.44	MURDER	BEL.,U.S.
VON WALTHER, Erich	987	M	Ger.	03	Oberfeldkommandant,Army,Mons Namur (Bel.) 26.11.42	MURDER	FR.
VON WALTER, Georg (or WATHER)	262188	M	Ger.		Oschfhr.,SS,Gestapo,Rouen and district (Fr.) 40-44	MISC.CRIMES	BEL.
VON WANGENHEIM (Ritter)	252835	M	Ger.	85	Administrator,Gand (Bel.)		
VON WATHER (see VON WALTER)	262188						
VON WATTER	10366	M	Ger.		Doctor,Oberlandrat,public official,Prag (Czech.) 39-44	TORTURE	CZECH.
VON WEBSKY	165568	M	Ger.		Staff commander,Oberfeldkommandantur,Liege (Bel.)	MURDER	BEL.
VON WEDEL, Hasso	260627	M		88	General	WITNESS	U.S.
VON WEDELSTADT, Erich	62440	M	Ger.		Reichsprotector,public official,head of department of economics office Bohemia,Moravia (Czech.)	TORTURE	U.N.W.C.C.
VON WEGMANN, Klaus Dyka	149686	M	Ger.		Civilian,Borkum (Ger.) 4.8.44	MURDER	U.S.
VON WELICK, Baron	194850	M	Ger.		Capt.,Field Art.,Dussen (Neth.) 30.10.44	PILLAGE	NETH.
VON WELTZIEN	142720	M			Lt.Col.,OKW, 10.44	WITNESS	U.S.
VON WERNER, Max	257389	M	Ger.		Cpl.,Org.Todt,slave labour camps,Erlandet,Oeusand,Trola (Nor.) 6.42-45	MURDER	YUGO.
VON WESTERHAGEN	104973	M			Army,(Bel.) 20.12.44	MURDER	U.S.
VON WESTERHOLT, Graf	251742	M	Ger.		Sonderfhr.,7-3 Kommandantur,Le Touquet,Paris,Plage (Fr.) 43-44	PILLAGE	FR.
VON WICKEDE	300754	M	Ger.		Lt.,1.Aufkl.Abt.,3.Coy.,2.Column,XV.Div.,Afrika Korps,Saint Léger (Arlon) 5.9.44	MISC.CRIMES	BEL.

VON-WAC

NAME	C.R.FILE NUMBER	SEX	NATIO-NALITY	DATE OF BIRTH	RANK OCCUPATION UNIT PLACE AND DATE OF CRIME	REASON WANTED	WANTED BY
VON WIKTORIN ZU HAINBURG, Mauriz Alois	131600	M	Ger.	83	Lt.General, Oflag, Commanding 20.mot.Div., C.C., Hammelburg (Ger.) 25.7.44	MURDER	U.S., U.K.
VON WILGORSKI	260061	M	Ger.		Sohfhr., SS, Interpreter, Belgrad (Yugo.) 1.44-9.44	MISC.CRIMES	YUGO.
VON WILM	194086	M	Ger.		Lt., Flak-Rgt. Hermann Goering N.1, Coy.of D.C.A., La Bastide D'Armagnac (Fr.) 22.-25.2.43	PILLAGE	FR.
VON WILMOWSKY, Tilo	260401	M	Ger.	3.3.78	Dep.Ch.Ar.-Mem.Ar., Friedrich Krupp A.G. Reichs-Kredit-Ges.A.G., Essen, Berlin (Ger.)	MISC.CRIMES	U.S.
VON WINCKLER	194929	M	Ger.	90	Lt.Colonel, Feldkommandantur, Ornisto (It.) 10.43	MURDER	U.K.
VON WITTERSHEIM	1031	M	Ger.		Gen.Major, Panz.Div.1, Pz.Rgt.3, Basse Maurienne (Fr.) 22.-31.8.44	MURDER	FR.
VON WITTINGHOFF	1032	M	Ger.		Gen.Lt., Panz.Div.V.des XVI.Panz.Corps, Berlin.(Ger.) 9.39-10.39	MURDER	POL.
VON WITZLEBEN	1364	M	Ger.		Col., Army, 26.Div.,9.Pz.Gr.Rgt.	MISC.CRIMES	U.K.
VON WOLF, Baron	173846	M	Ger.		Lt.Col., Commander, Army, Kuban-Rgt. (Yugo., Croatia) 11.43-8.44	MURDER	YUGO.
VON WOLFF	166979	M	Ger.	10	Major, Army (Yugo.) 44.	TORTURE	
VON WOLMAR, Wolfgang Wolfram	196734	M	Ger.	9.6.16	Hptsturmfhr., Head of Press in Protectorate, Prague (Czech.) 39-45	MISC.CRIMES	CZECH.
VON ZEILBERG	187842	M	Ger.		Gen., 65.Inf.Div., Gisa Pass Senda (It.) 3.10.43	MURDER	U.K.
VON ZIELBERG	130167	M	Ger.		Gen., Inf.Div.65, Parma La Spezia (It.) 3.10.43	MURDER	U.K.
VON ZOLLIKOFFER	186786	M	Ger.		Civilian, Director of Factory Aivorex, Clichy.(Fr.) 40-44	MISC.CRIMES	FR.
VON ZOTTMANN, Ritter	138052	M	Ger.		Col. of Pol., Sipo and SD, Kiew (Sov.Un.) 15.2.43	MURDER	U.S.
VON ZYDOWITZ	28865	M	Ger.		Hptsturmfhr., 6.SS-Geb.Div.Nord, Finmark (Nor.) 10., 11.44	MURDER	NOR.
VORBACH, Walter	195350	M	Ger.	19.6.11	Member, SS, Moravske Budejovice (Czech.) 39-45	MISC.CRIMES	CZECH.
VORBERG	188377	M	Ger.		Oberreichsleiter, SS, Conc.Camp (Ger.) 40-45	MURDER	CZECH.
VORBUCH	167149	M			SD of Chambery (Fr.) St.Jean de Maurienne (Fr.)	MURDER	FR.
VORMANN	186552	M	Ger.	07	Pvt., 714.Lds.Schtz.Bn.,2.Coy., Zempelburg, Hildesheim (Ger.) 3.45	TORTURE	U.K.
VORMANN, Nikolaus	259581	M	Ger.	95	Gen.	WITNESS	U.S.
VORMBAUM	189478	M	Ger.		Sgt., Army, Busigny (Fr.) 23.8.44	MURDER	FR.
VORNLOCKER	301649	M	Ger.		Hilfsverwalter, Ebrach nr.Amberg (Ger.) 45	MURDER	CZECH.
VORNOF (see FAHRNARD)	142527						
VORRATH, Paul	193752	M	Ger.	1.6.01	Rottfhr., SS, 4.SS-Totenkopf-Stuba., C.C. Dora-Mittelbau, Nordhausen (Ger.) 43-45	TORTURE	U.S.
VORSTER, Gerhard	153031	M	Ger.		Capt., 21.Panz.Div. H.Q.'s, Sessenheim (Ger.) 1.45	MURDER	U.S.
VOSCH	153013	M	Ger.		Cpl., Army, Hospital, Muehlberg (Ger.) -5.44	MISC.CRIMES	U.K.
VOSNITZA	975	M	Ger.		Usturmfhr., SS, C.C., Oswiecim, Raisko, Birkenau (Pol.) 6.40-43	MURDER	POL., BEL.
VOSS	124620	M	Ger.		Conc.Camp, Hannover-Limmer (Ger.)	TORTURE	BEL.
VOSS	254762	M	Ger.	circa 15	SS-Navy-Police, C.C. Bremen-Farge (Ger.)	MISC.CRIMES	U.K.
VOSS, Alfons	255796	M	Ger.		Pvt., C.C.Ellrich, Nordhausen (Ger.)	MURDER	U.S.
VOSS, Bernhard	10029	M	Ger.		Standartenfhr., SS-Totenkopf-Standarte, Cmdt., Prague (Czech.) 38-44	MURDER	CZECH.
VOSS, Bernhard	254407	M	Ger.		Cpl., 377.Jaeger-Rgt., Vinkt (Bel.) 25.-31.5.40	INTERR.	BEL.
VOSS, Franz	37947	M	Ger.		Uschfhr., SS, Conc.Camp., Oxerhof near Deventer (Neth.) 5.,6.4.45	MURDER	U.K.
VOSS, Franz E.	976	M			Camp-Cmdt., Gruppenfhr., SS, C.C., Weimar-Buchenwald (Ger.) 9.39-44	MURDER	POL.,CZECH. U.S., FR.
VOSS, Hans	142316	M	Ger.		Uschfhr., SS, Conc.Camp, Neuengamme (Ger.)	BRUTALITY	U.K.
VOSS, Hermann	132528	M	Ger.		Civilian	PILLAGE	U.S.
VOSS, Joseph	161276	M	Ger.	95	Lt., Army, Pion.Ausb.Bn.71, 2.Coy., Chartres Ob.Maubach Dueren (Fr. Ger.) 7.44-11.44	TORTURE	U.K.
VOSS, Paul	255795	M		15.7.94	Pvt., C.C. Harzungen, Nordhausen. (Ger.)	MURDER	U.S.
VOSS, Peter	139245	M	Ger.	08	Oschfhr., SS, C.C., Auschwitz (Pol.) 40-45	MURDER	U.S.
VOSS, Richard	193740	M	Ger.		Crim.Commissar, Sipo, Dorgen (Ger.) 5.44 or 6.44	MURDER	U.S.
VOSSENACKER, Alfred	108859	M	Ger.	07	Pvt., Feldgend., Lockeren (Bel.)	TORTURE	U.K., BEL.
VOSTREL, Hans	194045	M	Ger.	10.8.04	Sgt., SS, Conc.Camp, Terezin (Czech.) 39-45	TORTURE	CZECH.
VOTH	137651	M	Ger.	05	Oschfhr., SS, Conc.Camp, Stutthof (Ger.)	TORTURE	U.K.
VOULLAIRE, Hans	255793	M		23.9.21	Sgt., C.C. Ellrich, Nordhausen	MURDER	U.S.
VOYRSCH, Udo	260424	M	Ger.	24.7.95	Obergruppenfhr., SS, Warsaw and other towns (Pol.) 39	MURDER	POL.
VRBA, Jan	254697	M		1.7.94	Agent, Gestapo, Jiloyice (Czech.) 42-45	MISC.CRIMES	CZECH.
VRIMMER	305615	M	Ger.		Lt., Unit: 19548 A - formation of Parachutist, Pluduno, Cotes-du-Nord (Fr.) 3.8.44	MURDER	FR.
VROBRICH	173465	M	Ger.		Pvt., Guard, Army, Briey (Fr.) 40-45	MURDER	FR.
VRUCK	258122	M	Ger.		Osturmbannfhr., Waffen-SS, C.C., Dachau (Ger.)	MISC.CRIMES	BEL.
VUKICH, Johann	254709	M	Ger.	95	Col., Army, Bjelovar Vrbica (Yugo.) 10.43-2.44	MURDER	YUGO.
VUSTER, Adolf	168244	M	Ger.		Civilian, Artistic adviser to Ger.Embassy, Paris (Fr.) 40-44	PILLAGE	FR.
WAASZ	191308	M	Ger.		Pvt., Eisenb.Art.Btty.717, St.Andries les Bruges (Bel.) 4.9.44	MURDER	BEL.
WABER, Bernhardt	189816	M	Ger.		Cmdr., Airforce, Bjelusa Visoki Sevcina (Yugo.) 9.43-12.43	WITNESS	YUGO., U.S.
WABERSICH	257849	M			SS-Lt., Panz.Bde., Meuse-Bridge-Antwerp (Bel.) 12.44	MISC.CRIMES	U.S.
WACBOLS	11296	M	Ger.		Sgt., 110.or 111.Pz.Gren.Rgt., 1.Gruppe, Gourdon (Fr.) 29.6.44	MURDER	FR.
WACHE	300396	M	Ger.		Osturmfhr., SS, H.Q., 2.SS-Panz.Div., La Roche and Wibrin (Bel.)12.1.45	MURDER	BEL.
WACHE	305114	M	Ger.		Formerly Cashier, Ger.shop in Leczno, Sroda (Pol.) 39-40	MISC.CRIMES	POL.
WACHENREDET (see WACKENRODER, Erich)	240087						
WACHHOLZ, Elfriede	252788	F	Ger.	08	Guard, C.C. Terezin (Czech.) 40-45	MISC.CRIMES	CZECH.
WACHHOLZ, Kurt	185577	M	Ger.	10.8.09	Osturmfhr., SS, SD, C.C., Chief-Guard, Terezin (Czech.) 39-45	MURDER	CZECH.
WACHIDON, Sumbil	193660	M	Ger.		Guard, 4.SS-Totenkopf-Stuba., C.C. Dora-Mittelbau, Nordhausen, Bismarckhuette, (Ger.) 43-45	WITNESS	U.S.
WACHMIN	196431	M	Ger.		Hptschfhr., SS, Gestapo, De Font-Romeu, Err (Fr.) 5.44-9.44	MISC.CRIMES	FR.
WACHSMOTH	62118	M	Ger.		SS-Col.	WITNESS	U.S.
WACHTEN, Peter	255840	M	Ger.		Pvt., C.C. Ellrich, Nordhausen (Ger.)	MURDER	U.S.
WACHTER	188770	M	Ger.		Member, Feldgend., Bar Le Duc (Fr.) 20.-23.8.44	MURDER	FR.
WACHTER, Engelm.	29687	M	Ger.		Dr., Vice-President, Public-Official, Litomerice (Czech.) 40	MISC.CRIMES	CZECH.
WACHTER, Stefan	193661	M	Ger.	20.7.99	Guard, 4.SS-Totenkopf-Stuba., C.C. Dora-Mittelbau, Nordhausen (Ger.) 43-45	WITNESS	U.S.
WACHTERL, Vinzenz (or WUCHTER)	193445	M	Ger.	10.1.00	Pvt., Kgf.Arb.Bn.184, Kalvik (Nor.) 6.44-7.44	MURDER	NOR.
WACHTERS, J.C.	189271	M	Ger.		Dr., Civilian, Bainflair (Neth.) 7.7.44	WITNESS	U.S.
WACHTIN-KREUTZ	156648	M	Ger.		Sgt., Army, Ville le Marclet (Fr.) 27.8.44	MURDER	FR.
WACHTLER, Fritz	62435	M	Ger.		Gauleiter, NSDAP, Head-Office for Teachers, Bayreuth (Ger.)	TORTURE	UNWCC
WACHTLER, Stefan	255839	M	Ger.	29.7.99	Pvt., C.C., Nordhausen (Ger.)	MURDER	U.S.
WACKE	258176	M	Ger.		Capt., Army, Kragujevac, Orasac, Gruza (Yugo.) 42-44	MURDER	YUGO.

WAC-WAG

NAME	C.R.FILE NUMBER	SEX	NATIO- NALITY	DATE OF BIRTH	RANK OCCUPATION UNIT PLACE AND DATE OF CRIME	REASON WANTED	WANTED BY
WACKERODER, Erich (or WACHEN-FELDT)	240087	M	Ger.		Ortsgruppenleiter,NSDAP,Scharnhorst-Celle (Ger.) 39	TORTURE	U.S.
WACKER	28858	M	Ger.		Major,20 Army,Comd.Nach.Coy 99-7 Geb.Div.,Finmark (Nor.) 10.-11.44	MURDER	NOR.
WACKER	195531	M	Ger.		Meister,Gendarmerie,Miaocz (Pol.) 14.10.42	MURDER	POL.
WACKER, Ernest	167852	M	Ger.		Cpl.,Feldgendarmerie,Coiffy,Langes,Chalencey,Auberive,Flagey (Fr.) 43-44	MURDER	FR.
WACKERZAPP	166986	M		15	SS-Hptschfhr.,15 Pz.Div.,Waffen SS Lettland 15,C.C.Dachau (Ger.) 42	MISC.CRIMES	U.S.
WACKNER, August	121669	M	Ger.		Official,Gestapo,Arles s-Tech (Fr.) 29.6.44	MURDER	FR.
WACKNER, August	131763	M	Ger.		Official,Zollgrenzschutzpolizei,Velmanya (Fr.) 1.8.44	MURDER	FR.
WADEBACH	139155	M			Commander,C.C.Siegburg (Ger.) 3.-9.42	MURDER	BEL.
WAECHNER	189817	M	Ger.		Driver,C.C.Banjica (Yugo.)	MURDER	YUGO.
WAECHTER	139733	M	Ger.		Dr.,G.Governor,Administration of Occ.Territ.Poland	MISC.CRIMES	U.S.
WAECHTER, Otto	15	M	Ger.		SS-Bde.General,SS,Krakau (Pol.)	MURDER	POL.
WAECHTLER, Fritz	259009	M	Ger.	91	SS-Obergruppenfhr.,SA-Fuehrer,Gauschulungsleiter,Member of Reichstag	INTERR.	U.S.
WAFKE, Richard	301115	M	Ger.		Crim.-Rat,Stabsscharfhr.,SS served with the R.S.D.Abt.IV-1-6,Shellhuset Copenhagen (Den.) 28.2.45	TORTURE	DEN.
WAELDE	142704	M			Col.,Air Force	MISC.CRIMES	U.S.
WAEM, Julius	168021	M	Ger.	28.3.15	Sicherheitspolizei,Marseilles (Fr.) 4.44	PILLAGE	FR.
WAENKE, Anton	185576	M	Ger.	22.5.11	Schfhr.,Crim.-Asst.,SD,Gestapo,Prague (Czech.) 41-45	MURDER	CZECH.
WAERTER	988	M	Ger.		SS-Uschfhr.,Guard,Waffen SS,C.C.Auschwitz-Birkenau,Baiskow (Pol.) 6.40-43	MURDER	NETH.,BEL., POL.
WAERTMANN, Harry	196435	M	Ger.		35 R.A.D.,Perigueaux,Tourtoirac (Fr.) 1.-2.4.44	MURDER	FR.
WAESCH, Alfred	136409	M	Ger.		Pvt.,709 Inf.Div.,Bakery Coy,Cherbourg (Fr.) 6.6.44	MURDER	U.S.
WAETZMANN, Walter	240034	M	Ger.	20	Pvt.,Abwehr Nachr.Rgt.506,6 Coy,Bad Wildungen (Ger.) 45	MISC.CRIMES	U.S.
WAFFEN	191309	M	Ger.		Sgt.,Eisenb.Art.Btty.717,F.P.Nr.22380,St.Andries les Bruges (Bel.) 4.9.44	MURDER	BEL.
WAFFNER, F.	158399	M			Army,F.P.Nr.32038 C,Plouvien (Fr.) 8.44	TORTURE	FR.
WAGEL	153317	M		05	Sgt.,Army,6-635 Ldsch.Bn.,C.C.Niederorschel (Ger.) 3.1.43	TORTURE	U.K.
WAGENER	191359	M	Ger.		Doctor,4 Air Force Div.,Pz.Jg.Coy,Lonsdal,Krokelva,Bjornelva (Nor.)	MURDER	NOR.
WAGENER, August K.	149679	M	Ger.	1.94	SS-Sturmschfhr.,SS,Gestapo,Kripo,NSDAP,Duesseldorf (Ger.)	WITNESS	U.S.
WAGENER, Ludwig (see WAGNER)	251443						
WAGENFUEHRER, Gerard	136395	M	Ger.	05	Feldgendarmerie,Bruggen (Ger.) 27.2.45	WITNESS	U.S.
WAGENFURT	196428	M	Ger.		Cmdt.,Etat Major,De Valence (Fr.) 40-44	WITNESS	FR.
WAGENHAUSER, Alfred	136660	M	Ger.		Farmer,Civilian (Ger.)	TORTURE	U.S.
WAGENPLAST	183933	M	Ger.		Member,SD,Gestapo,Plzen (Czech.) 39-45	MURDER	CZECH.
WAGERL, Jacob	21421	M	Ger.		Capt.,Army,2 Btty.Mar.Flak Abt.810,Walcheren (Neth.) 10.44	WITNESS	U.S.
WAGNER	978	M	Ger.		Lt.,Army,118 Jg.Div.,378 Rgt.,3 Btty., (Yugo.) 7.43-1.44	MURDER	YUGO.
WAGNER	979	M	Ger.		SS-Hptschfhr.,SS,C.C.Dachau (Ger.) 40-43	MURDER	FR.
WAGNER	980	M	Ger.		Capt.,Army,197 Sicherungsrgt.,Tours,Gare De Langeais (Fr.) 8.44	MURDER	FR.
WAGNER	981	M	Ger.		SS-Guard,C.C.Raisko,Oswiecime (Pol.) 40-43	MURDER	POL.,BEL.
WAGNER	1350	M	Ger.		Lt.,Army,1059 Gr.,3 Coy	MISC.CRIMES	U.K.
WAGNER	1351	M	Ger.		Capt.,Army,20 SS Police Rgt.,2 Coy	MISC.CRIMES	U.K.
WAGNER	29842	M	Ger.		Lt.,Army,Menton (Fr.) 9.44	MURDER	FR.
WAGNER	135568	M	Ger.		Sgt.,Army,Torgau (Ger.) 21.1.-1.11.42	TORTURE	U.K.
WAGNER	136267	M	Ger.		Pvt.,11 Pz.Div.,2 Coy AA-A 7,Albine (Fr.) 12.9.44	MURDER	FR.
WAGNER	136401	M	Ger.		Gendarmerie-Kreis-Chief,Gendarmerie-Police,Kitzingen (Ger.) 44	MURDER	U.S.
WAGNER	137532	M			Lt.,416 Volks-Gren.Div.	TORTURE	U.S.
WAGNER	141910	M	Ger.		Cpl.,Rgt.355,12 Coy,C.C.Sletteb (Nor.) 12.42	WITNESS	U.K.
WAGNER	142705	M			Commissar,Abwehr-Army,Geh.Feldpolizei,Gruppe 727,Idriza,Sebesch and Nowa-Fschew (Pol.) 43-44	MURDER	U.S.
WAGNER	149588	M	Ger.		Lt.,11 Pz.Div.Kampfgruppe Wilde, (Fr.) 44	MURDER	FR.
WAGNER	149680	M		12	SS-Lagerfhr.,C.C.Kaufbeuren (Ger.) 27.9.-27.11.44	MURDER	U.S.
WAGNER	150823	M			Osturmfhr.,III.SS-Pz.Gren.Rgt.4,Div."Das Reich",Tulle (Fr.) 5.44	MURDER	U.S.
WAGNER	150824	M	Ger.		Stalag Hauptmeister,C.C.Hammerstein,Stalag II B,Hammerstein (Ger.)	MURDER	U.S.
WAGNER	151459	M	Ger.		Lt.,19 SS Pol.Rgt."Todt" 4 Coy,Cran (Fr.) 15.6.44	MURDER	FR.
WAGNER	158400	M			Uschfhr.,SS 3 SS Baubde.,C.C.Wieda, Gardelegen (Ger.) 5.-14.4.45	MURDER	U.S.
WAGNER	158214	M	Ger.		Cpl.,Army,355 Rgt.,12 Coy,Egersund (Nor.) 42	MURDER	UNWCC
WAGNER	161691	M			Lt.,Army,C.C.Leipzig (Ger.)	SUSPECT	U.S.
WAGNER	162537	M	Ger.	06	Oberfeldrichter,Reich Military Court,Leipzig (Ger.) 10.44	MURDER	U.S.
WAGNER	164124	M	Ger.		Adj.,Army,Revin (Fr.) 13.-14.6.44	MURDER	FR.
WAGNER	166721	M	Ger.		Chief,Civil Administration,Alsace,40-45	TORTURE	U.S.
WAGNER	166916	M	Ger.		Lt.,15 Div.Afrika Corps,33 Pion.,Vancourt Xousse (Fr.) 9.and 10.44	MISC.CRIMES	FR.
WAGNER	173844	M	Ger.		Cpl.,C.C.Auschwitz-Birkenau (Pol.) 39-45	MURDER	CZECH.,BEL., POL.
WAGNER	173853	M	Ger.		Capt.,Kreiskommandantur,Kragujevac (Yugo.) 42-44	MURDER	YUGO.
WAGNER	173854	M	Ger.		Lt.Col.,Commander of Don Rgt., (Yugo.) 11.43-8.44	MURDER	YUGO.
WAGNER (see VACKNER)	181456						
WAGNER	189270	M	Ger.		Blockleiter,C.C.Dachau (Ger.) 40-45	MURDER	BEL.
WAGNER	189818	M	Ger.		Major,Commander,Army,Pozarevac (Yugo.) 41-43	MURDER	YUGO.
WAGNER	189819	M	Ger.		Kreiskommandant,Kreiskommandantur,Meskovac,Serbia (Yugo.) 19.10.41	MURDER	YUGO.
WAGNER	191373	M	Ger.	05	Major General,194 Div.,Fjell (Nor.)	TORTURE	BEL.
WAGNER	192131	M	Ger.		Police-chief,Police,Herstal-les-Liege (Bel.)	MISC.CRIMES	POL.
WAGNER	192228	M	Ger.	86	Civilian,Anatomy institute,Danzig (Pol.)	MURDER	FR.
WAGNER	192696	M	Ger.		C.C.Mauthausen (Aust.) 44	TORTURE	U.S.
WAGNER	192943	M	Ger.		SS-Oschfhr.,SS,C.C.Buchenwald (Ger.) 42-45	MURDER	U.S.
WAGNER	192945	M	Ger.		Hptsturmfhr.,SS-Doctor,SS,C.C.Buchenwald (Ger.) 42-45	PILLAGE	FR.
WAGNER	195893	M	Ger.		Custom-House-Officer,Customs-Frontier-Guard,Chaum (Fr.) 3.6.44	MURDER	NETH.
WAGNER	196960	M			Capt.,Cdt.of II Bn.,near Arnheim (Neth.) 3.45		

WAG - WAH

NAME	C.R.FILE NUMBER	SEX	NATIONALITY	DATE OF BIRTH	RANK, OCCUPATION, UNIT, PLACE AND DATE OF CRIME	REASON WANTED	WANTED BY
WAGNER	240035	M	Ger.	20	Cpl.,Abwehr, Rovereto (It.)	MISC.CRIMES	U.S.
WAGNER	250567	M	Ger.		Capt.,Gestapo, Lechelle (Fr.) 23.8.44	INTERR.	FR.
WAGNER	251422	M	Ger.		Lt.,F.P.16157,St.Nicolas,de Brem (Fr.) 28.8.44	MISC.CRIMES	FR.
WAGNER	251423	M	Ger.		Major-General, sector Cmit., la Bresse (Fr.) 9.-11.44	MISC.CRIMES	FR.
WAGNER	252818	M	Ger.	15	Sgt.,guard of Bridge River "de Noord" at H.T.Ambacht, Ridderkerk (Neth.) 5.5.45	MURDER	NETH.
WAGNER	253448	M	Ger.		Officer,14.885 RAD Labour Unit l'Etoile (Fr.) 43-44	PILLAGE	FR.
WAGNER	256294	M	Ger.		Lagerfhr.,Neckargerach (Ger.)	MURDER	FR.
WAGNER	256645	M	Ger.		Capt.,formation Bode, St.Pierre (Fr.) 19.6.-22.7.44	MISC.CRIMES	FR.
WAGNER	257529		Ger.		Employee, C.C.Nordhausen (Ger.)	MURDER	U.S.
WAGNER	257676	M	Ger.	12	Sgt.,guard Coy,Military Detention Prison,Fort Zinna,Torgau (Ger.) 11.41 and 11.42	BRUTALITY	U.K.
WAGNER	261832	M	Ger.		Capt.,Fronstalag 141,Vesoul (Fr.) 41-42	BRUTALITY	FR.
WAGNER	300745	M	Ger.		N.C.O.,1 Aufkl.Abt.,3 Coy,2 Col., XV Div.Afrika Korps, St.Leger Distr.Arlon(Bel.) 5.9.44	MISC.CRIMES	BEL.
WAGNER	301289	M	Ger.		Crim.secr.,Abt.V.D.,Sicherheitsdienst,Brussels and other towns (Bel.) 6.40-9.44	MURDER	BEL.
WAGNER	301847	M	Ger.		Major,commander of Ger.troops at Smederevska Palanka, District of Pozarevac (Serb.) 41, 42, 43	MURDER	YUGO.
WAGNER	301880	M	Ger.		Hptsturmfhr.,Gestapo (Nor.) 4.40	TORTURE	NOR.
WAGNER	301908	M	Ger.		Lt.Col. Ic 169 Inf.Div.Staff,20 Army,Finmark (Nor.) 10.11.44	MURDER	NOR.
WAGNER	302008	M	Ger.		Obermast,Navy,attached to the Army,Leeuwarden(Neth.)27.10.44	MURDER	NETH.
WAGNER	305355	M	Ger.		Member,C.C.Valley,Baden,Neckargerach,Neckarelz(Ger.) 42-45	MURDER	FR.
WAGNER	305523	M	Ger.		Capt.,Gestapo,Lechelle,Seine et Marne (Fr.)23.8.44	MURDER	FR.
WAGNER	306242	F	Ger.		Female Superintendant,C.C.Mauthausen (Aust.) 11.42-5.45	MURDER	FR.
WAGNER	306902	M	Ger.		Member,Gestapo Vichy (Fr.) 10.43-9.44	MURDER	FR.
WAGNER, Alfons	168239	M	Ger.		Dr., kommissarischer Verwalter "Hęta Pokoj" (Coalmine) Nowy Bytom (Pol.) 9.39-44	PILLAGE	POL.
WAGNER, Alfred	192007	M	Ger.		Major, Gestapo, C.C.Edelbach,Oflag XVII (Ger.),16.11.42	MURDER	FR.
WAGNER, Barbara	135328	F	Ger.		Civilian, Efferen (Ger.) 2.10.44	WITNESS	U.S.
WAGNER, Edmund	255852	M			Flyer, C.C.Ellrich-Nordhausen (Ger.)	MURDER	U.S.
WAGNER, Ernst	260535	M	Ger.	II. 9.25	Hptscharfhr.,Waffen-SS,guard Coy,C.C.Auschwitz (Pol.) 7.41-1.45	BRUTALITY	POL.
WAGNER, Franck	252815	M	Ger.		Gestapo, St.Die,Allermont (Fr.) 18.8.44	INTERR.	FR.
WAGNER, Franz	191960	M			C.C.Dachau (Ger.)	MURDER	U.S.
WAGNER, Freddy	195892	M	Ger.		Interpreter, Noailles (Fr.) 9.8.44	WITNESS	FR.
WAGNER, Fritz	191015	M			Oscharfhr.,SS, Totenkopf-Div., C.C.Mauthausen (Aust.) 41-45	MURDER	U.S.
WAGNER, Fritz	258565	M	Ger.		Capt.,SS,W.V.H.A. (Ger.) 40-45	BRUTALITY	U.S.
WAGNER, Fritz	306706	M	Ger.		Mayor of Weissenhassel Stalag IX A Kdo.805 (Ger.) 18.6.41	MURDER	FR.
WAGNER, Georg	193525	M	Ger.		Policeman, Police, Dillingen (Ger.) 40-45	TORTURE	POL.
WAGNER, Georg	196748	M	Ger.		Policeman, Police, Ahrweiler (Ger.) 5.-6.44	MISC.CRIMES	POL.
WAGNER, Hans	150822	M	Ger.	85 or '90	Cpl.,Army, C.C.Fuerstenburg,Buchenwald (Ger.) 2.45	MURDER	U.S.
WAGNER, Harald	168236	M	Ger.		Pvt.,9 Res.Gren.Rgt.,1 Coy,Magny d'Anigon (Fr.) 18.9.44	MURDER	FR.
WAGNER, Heinrich	167853	M	Ger.	13. 9.08	Rottenfhr.,SS, C.C.Struthof-Natzweiler (Fr.) 43-44	MURDER	FR.
WAGNER, Hermann	251436	M	Ger.	94	In charge Ration Store, Gamblin (Pol.) 28.8.43	WITNESS	U.S.
WAGNER, Ignaz	10030	M	Ger.		Dr.,Staatsanwalt, Public official, Brno (Czech.) 21.2.40	MURDER	CZECH.
WAGNER, Josef	16	M	Ger.		Praesident, Public official, Silesia (Pol.)	MURDER	POL.
WAGNER, Josef	31631	M	Ger.		Civilian, Nancy (Fr.) 19.8.44	MURDER	FR.
WAGNER, Josef	196730	M	Ger.		Leader of Prison warden, Gestapo, Brno (Czech.) 39-45	MURDER	CZECH.
WAGNER, Josef	307230	M	Ger.		Former Cpl.W-SS,Oberwachltr.,Werkschutz Deutsche Waffen u. Munitionsfabriken (DWM),Herstal-lez-Liège(Bel.)22.11.42-3.9.44	TORTURE	BEL.
WAGNER, Kanie	251716	M	Ger.		Probablement 377 Jg.Rgt.,Vinkt-Meigem (Bel.) 25.-31.5.40	PILLAGE	BEL.
WAGNER, Karl	12448	M	Ger.		Agent,Gestapo,Org.Todt,Hazebrouck (Fr.) 1.9.44	MURDER	FR.
WAGNER, Karl	250571	M	Ger.		Scharfhr., C.C.Buchenwald (Ger.)	BRUTALITY	FR.
WAGNER, Karl	259575	M	Ger.		Kapo, C.C.Dachau (Ger.) 44-45	MISC.CRIMES	YUGO.
WAGNER, Kurt	11297	M	Ger.		Pvt.,Army,110 or 111 Pz.Gren.Rgt.,2 Coy,Albine(Fr.) 44	MURDER	FR.
WAGNER, Kurt	252799	M	Ger.	3. 5.05	Civilian, Laborer, Saarbruecken (Ger.) 5.or 6.44	MURDER	U.S.
WAGNER, Ludwig	161697	M	Ger.	10	Uscharfhr.,SS, C.C.Buchenwald (Ger.)	WITNESS	U.S.
WAGNER, Ludwig	185913	M	Ger.	89	Leader, NSDAP,Praha (Czech.)	MISC.CRIMES	CZECH.
WAGNER, Ludwig or WAGENER	251443		Ger.		N.C.O.,Service-Luftwaffen, Listening and observation post, Liessel (Neth.) 8.9.44	MURDER	NETH.
WAGNER, Max	255318	M	Ger.	15	Employee, Gestapo, Breclav (Czech.) 7.4.45	MISC.CRIMES	CZECH.
WAGNER, Otto	24845	M	Ger.		Rottenfhr.,SS, C.C. Struthof (Fr.)	MISC.CRIMES	FR.
WAGNER, Paul	260661	M	Ger.	07.- 10	Sgt.,Gestapo of Epinal, Environ (Fr.) 40-44	MURDER	FR.
WAGNER, Richard	136272 A	M	Ger.		Cpl., Feldgendarmerie,Itenag (Fr.)	MURDER	FR.
WAGNER, Richard	240036	M	Ger.	(2.12.02	Dr.,Bde-Fhr.,SS,13 Freiw.Geb.Div.,SS-Hauptamt,Frankfurt, Crumstadt (Ger.) 45	MISC.CRIMES	U.S.
WAGNER, Richard	258889	M	Ger.		Capt., Heereswaffenamt, Paris (Fr.) 40-44	MISC.CRIMES	FR.
WAGNER, Robert	261086	M	Ger.		Mistreatment of french and allied PWS,Residence:Tauberbischofsheim near Darmstadt (Ger.)	BRUTALITY	FR.
WAGNER, Rudi	252794	M	Ger.		Osturmfhr.,SS, Command C.C. Auschwitz-Birkenau (Pol.) 42-45	MURDER	YUGO.
WAGNER, Rupert	131014	M	Ger.		Oscharfhr.,SS, Totenkopf Div.,C.C. Mauthausen (Aust.) 41-45	MURDER	U.S.
WAGNER, Stefan	193100	M	Ger.		Schupo, C.C.Falstad (Nor.) 41-44	MURDER	NOR.
WAGNER, Viktor	67728	M	Ger.		Guard-Rottenfhr.,SS,C.C.Struthof(Fr.)	MISC.CRIMES	FR.
WAGNER, Walter (Erich)	128939	M			Dr.,Uscharfhr.,SS, C.C.Weimar-Buchenwald(Ger.)	TORTURE	U.S.
WAGNER, Wilhelm	173878	M	Ger.		Feldgend.,Feldgendarmerie,Loomine (Fr.) 7.-8.44	MURDER	FR.
WAGNER, Willi	131013	M			Oscharfhr.,SS, C.C. Mauthausen (Aust.) until 39	MURDER	U.S.
WAGNER, Willi	142066	M			Hptscharfhr.,SS, C.C. Dachau (Ger.)	MURDER	U.S.
WAGNER, Willi	139247	M	Ger.		Driver,Kraftfahrpark Wuerzburg, Pechbrunn(Ger.) 15.4.45	WITNESS	U.S.
WAGNER-NARGANG	29686	M	Ger.		Dr.,Landgerichtsrat, Public official,Opava (Czech.) 40	MURDER	CZECH.
WAHL	21420	M			Hptsturmbannfhr.,SS "Goetz von Berlichingen"38, Montmartin en Craignes (Fr.) 17.6.44	MURDER	U.S.
WAHLEN, Josef see WALLEN	196736						
WAHLER	104968	M			Hptsturmfhr.,SS,C.C.Gerolstein, Dockweiler, SS as MP of Army (Ger.) 2.45	MURDER	U.S.

WAH-WAL

NAME	C.R.FILE NUMBER	SEX	NATIO- NALITY	DATE OF BIRTH	RANK, OCCUPATION, UNIT, PLACE AND DATE OF CRIME	REASON WANTED	WANTED BY
WAHLSTAB, Kurt	193125	M	Ger.		Lt., S.D., RSHA, Berlin (Ger.) 19.1.43	MURDER	NOR.
WAHOLZ	24851	M	Ger.		S.D., C.C.Theresienstadt (Pol.) 12.41	TORTURE	U.S.
WAHRENBURG, Heinrich	138350	M			Adjutant, SS, Gestapo, Lyon (Fr.)	MURDER	FR.
WAHRIG, Artur	131012	M		13.12.93	Sturmmann, SS, C.C. Mauthausen (Aust.) 14.5.44-7.5.45	MURDER	U.S.
WAHRMANN (see WOHRMANN)	1036						
WAILE	256343	M	Ger.		Obertruppfhr., Lagerfhr., O.T., Muehldorf (Ger.)	WITNESS	U.S.
WAIMANN, Horst	185575	M	Ger.	15.7.09	Oschfhr., Krim.Oberasst., S.D., Gestapo, Praha (Czech.) 39-43	MURDER	CZECH.
WAITZL	250553	M	Ger.		Sturmbannfhr., C.C.Dachau (Ger.) 42	MURDER	YUGO.
WAIZENEGGER, Erich	260874	M			Dr., Lt.Col., Army	WITNESS	U.S.
WAIZNER, Walter Leo	260536	M		29.9.99	Pvt., W-SS, Guard Coy., C.C.Monowitz, Rydultau, Auschwitz (Pol.) 7.44-1.45	BRUTALITY	POL.
WAKSENBERGER, Max	139248	M	Ger.		Obergruppenfhr., SA, Velden (Ger.)	TORTURE	U.S.
WALASHEK (or WALOCHEK)	158396	M		13	Pvt., 714 Lds.schtz.-Bn., Stalag XX A, 4 Coy., Falkenburg (Pol.) 2.43-8.43	TORTURE	U.K.
WALAT, Hans	21419	M		08	Member, SS, NSDAP (Ger.)	MISC.CRIMES	U.S.
WALBAUM	62437	M	Ger.		Dr., Leader, Head of Dept. of Health of Gen.Gouvernm.	MURDER	UNWCC
WALBAUM, Joseph	136272	M	Ger.		Cpl., Feldgendarmerie de Verdun, Steney (Fr.) 5.8.44	MURDER	FR.
WALBECK	252799	M	Ger.		Pvt., A.N.R.563, 4 Coy., Boissise La Bertrand (Fr.) 9.40	PILLAGE	FR.
WALBERT	173106	M			C.C.Natzweiler (Fr.) 44	WITNESS	U.K.
WALBERT, Erich	301402	M	Ger.		Sgt., Employed, SS, C.C. Buchenwald (Ger.) 16.5.38-9.10.43	MURDER	BEL.
WALBURG	138257	M			Capt., Gestapo, SS, Lyon (Fr.)	MURDER	FR.
WALBURG, Ernst	306403	M	Ger.		Secr., C.C.Dachau (Ger.) 43	MURDER	BEL.
WALCH, Hans	252829	M	Ger.	17	Hptsphfhr., SS, Graz (Aust.) 4.45	MURDER	U.K.
WALCH, Wilhelm	195891	M		14.12.08	Official, Krim.Kommissar, Gestapo, Pol., Brno (Czech.) 39-41	MURDER	CZECH.
WALCHER	261927	M	Ger.		Crim.Commissary, Gestapo, Various place at Slovenia (Yugo.) 41-45	MISC.CRIMES	YUGO.
WALCHER, Karl	261363	M			Guard, SS, C.C. Auschwitz (Pol.) 42-45	BRUTALITY	POL.
WALD	125617	M	Ger.		Wachtmeister, Gendarmerie, Koenigshofen (Ger.) 8.4.45	MURDER	U.S.
WALD	164123	M	Ger.	15	Capt., SS, Einsatzkdo 1, Lemberg, Kiev (Pol.-Sov.Un.) 41-42	MURDER	U.S.
WALD, Gustav	194872	M	Ger.	24.2.04	Amtsinspector, Occupied Territories, Luxembourg (Lux.)	MISC.CRIMES	LUX.
WALD, Konrad Ludwig	162619	M	Ger.	15.11.96	Oberwachtmeister, Member, Gestapo, S.D., Giessen (Ger.) 27.9.45	MURDER	U.S.
WALDE	252800	M	Ger.		Agent, Gestapo, SS, Offenburg (Ger.) 6.11.44	MURDER	FR.
WALDE, Hermann	190575	M			Member, Gestapo, S.D., Einsatzkommando Schoner, Belval (Fr.) 18.44	MURDER	U.K.
WALDE, Hermann (alias Wilhelm Helmut)	259744	M	Ger.	17.8.15	Crim.Asst., Gestapo, Strassburg, Bas-Rhin (Fr.) 8.12.43	MISC.CRIMES	FR.
WALDECK	256539	M	Ger.		Chief of sub.sect., C.C. Mittelwerk, Nordhausen (Ger.)	MURDER	U.S.
WALDECK, Hanns	194160	M	Ger.		Cpl., SS, C.C. Buchenwald (Ger.) 42-45	MISC.CRIMES	U.S.
WALDECK, Wilhelm	190409	M	Ger.		Civilian, Wiesbaden (Ger.) 43-45	WITNESS	U.S.
WALDEISS	191969	M	Ger.		Inspector, Zentral-Ersatzteillager 206, Paris (Fr.) 21.8.44	MURDER	FR.
WALDEN	149589	M	Ger.		Col., 11 Pz.Div., South-West (Fr.) 44	MURDER	FR.
WALDEN, Heinrich	188769	M	Ger.		Officer, Stalag VIII C, Kdo.1308, C.C. Rosenig (Ger.)	TORTURE	FR.
WALDENBERGER, Heinz	150818	M	Ger.		Uschfhr., 1 SS-Pz.Div., 2 Pz.Gren.Regt., Stavelot, Malmedy (Bel.) 12.44	MURDER	U.S.
WALDENMAIER, Erhard	253452	M	Ger.	07	Managing-Director of Plant, Heidenheim (Ger.) 41-45	BRUTALITY	POL.
WALDER, Hans (see WALDNER)	250564						
WALDHOEFER, L.	259841	M	Ger.		Uschfhr., SS, 1 Zug, 2 Gruppe, Probably stationed at Bergeyk, Bergeyk, Prov. Noord, Brabant (Neth.) 11.9.44	MURDER	NETH.
WALDHOFER	135329	M	Ger.		Policeman, Gend. at Ettlebruck, Bertrange (Lux.) 7.44	TORTURE	U.S.
WALDKIRCH	6113	M			Lt., Army, 14 Coy., Pz.Jg.-Ers.Bn.7, Ecoles en Bauge (Fr.)	MURDER	FR.
WALDMANN	194684	M	Ger.		Member of Personnel, C.C. Drancy (Fr.)	MURDER	FR.
WALDMANN	250541	M	Ger.		SS, Kaltenkirchen, Neuengamme (Ger.) 21.12.45	MURDER	FR.
WALDMANN, Robert	305356	M	Ger.		Member, Guard, SS, C.C. Neuengamme (Ger.)	MURDER	FR.
WALDMANN	251421	M	Ger.		Sgt., Interpreter, Pleucadeul, St Marcel (Fr.) 18.-28.6.44	MISC.CRIMES	FR.
WALDMUELLER, Hans	188239	M	Ger.	12 or 13	Sturmbannfhr., SS, 12 SS-Pz.Div., Hitler Jugend, 25 SS-Pz.Gren.Regt., Co. I Bn., near Caen (Fr.) 6.6.-8.7.?	WITNESS	CAN.
WALDNER	194682	M	Ger.	00	Usturmfhr., SS, S.D., Lukow, Hrubieszow, (Pol.) 40-43	SUSPECT	POL.
WALDNER	306295	M	Ger.		Member, Gestapo at Nove Mesto n. Vahom, Oswiecim, C.C. Birkenau (Pol.) 39-45	MURDER	CZECH.
WALDNER, Hans (or WALDER)	250564	M	Ger. Aust.	01	S.I.T.-Interpreter, N.C.O., on Anti-Partisan Duties at Masola, Ariano, Polesine (Ital.) 12.44	INTERR.	U.K.
WALDON	1352				Major, SS, 20 SS-Pol.Regt., 1 Bn.	MISC.CRIMES	U.K.
WALDORF	259654	M	Ger.		W.O., 242 Inf.Div., Pontevès, Var (Fr.) 27.7.44	MURDER	FR.
WALDSCHMIDT	122859	M	Ger.		Capt., Dulag Luft, C.C. Frankfurt-M. (Ger.)	TORTURE	U.K.
WALDSCHMIDT, Ernst	128802	M	Ger.	90	Major, Army, Oberursel, Frankfurt-M. (Ger.) 10.43	TORTURE	U.K.
WALDSCHMIDT, Pierre	151464	M	Ger.	05	Capt., Flyer-Regt.2, 2 Regt. de l'Air, Trondes, Bouxq, Henil, le Tour (Fr.) 15.-18.8.44	MURDER	FR.
WALDVOGEL, Walter	193124	M	Ger.		Sgt., Air Force, C.C. Lattervik (Nor.) 45	MISC.CRIMES	NOR.
WALECKI, Anton	151469	M	Ger.		SS-Guard, Stalag X B, C.C. Sandbostel (Ger.) 4.45	MURDER	U.S.
WALEN, Wilhelm	194863	M	Ger.		Crim.-Employee, Gestapo, Bruenn (Czech.)	TORTURE	CZECH.
WALENDA, Franz	197350	M	Ger.		Dr., Landgerichtsrat, Public official, Litomerice (Czech.) 40	MURDER	CZECH.
WALENSKI	193897	M			Custom-house-officer, Zollgrenzschutz, Creach Maout (Fr.)	MURDER	FR.
WALENTA	257695	M			Employee, C.C. Nordhausen (Ger.)	MURDER	U.S.
WALENTSCHKA, Rudolf	194163	M	Ger.	3.11.08	SS-applicant, C.C. Terezin (Czech.) 39-45	TORTURE	CZECH.
WALESZYNSKI, Stanislav	152738			09	Civ., political prisoner, C.C. Hannover, Gardelegen (Ger.) 5.-14.4.45	WITNESS	U.S.
WALETTSKO (see WALETZKO)	128936						
WALETZKO (or WALETTSKO), Albin	128936	M	Ger.	21.2.15	Uschfhr., Scharfhr., SS-Totenk. Sturmbann, C.C. Buchenwald, Weimar (Ger.)	TORTURE	U.S.
WALKOWIACK	252636	M	Ger.		N.C.O., Pepingen (Bel.) 25.2.44-9.9.44	WITNESS	BEL.
WALKOWIAK, Gerhard	196015	M	Ger.		Schuetze, 1 SS-Div., 2 Pl., 3 Pz.Pi., Ligneuville (Bel.) 17.-19.12.44	MURDER	U.S.
WALKOWITZ, Fritz	150816	M	Ger.	21.12.98	Sgt., Ldschtz.-Ers.Bn.24, 3 Coy., C.C. Augsburg (Ger.) 40-4.45	MURDER	U.S.
WALL, Johann	255848	M			Cpl., C.C. Ellrich, Nordhausen (Ger.)	TORTURE	U.S.
WALLACH, Alfred	136397	M	Ger.	08	Kapo, C.C. Flossenburg (Ger.) 3.-4.45	MURDER	U.S.
WALLASCH	255850	M			Pvt., C.C. Dora, Nordhausen (Ger.)	MISC.CRIMES	BEL.
WALLEK	196897	M	Ger.		Uschfhr., SS, C.C.-Guard, Gusen (Aust.)		

WAL-WAL

NAME	C.R.FILE NUMBER	SEX	NATIO-NALITY	DATE OF BIRTH	RANK	OCCUPATION	UNIT	PLACE AND DATE OF CRIME	REASON WANTED	WANTED BY
WALLEN, Josef (or WAHLEN)	196736	M	Ger.	10	Farmer Civilian, Member S.A., Hof near Frauenstein (Ger.) 41-45				MISC.CRIMES	POL.
WALLENDORFER	255851	M			C.C. Rottleberode, Nordhausen (Ger.)				MURDER	U.S.
WALLENHAUER, Georg	193659	M	Ger.		Guard, 4.SS Totenkopf-Sturmbann, C.C.Nordhausen-Dora, Auschwitz (Ger., Pol.) 43-45				WITNESS	U.S.
WALLER	173852	M	Ger.		Chief of German Pol. Amt III, Reichsfhr.d.SS. (Yugo.) 42-44				MURDER	YUGO.
WALLER	300746	M	Ger.		Pvt., 1.Aufkl.Abt., 3.Coy., 2.Col. XV. Div. of the Afrika Korps, Saint Leger (Arlon) 5.9.44				MISC.CRIMES	BEL.
WALLER, Friedrich	194875	M	Ger.	29.3.94	Cmdt., C.C.Dachau and Luxembourg (Lux., Ger.)				MURDER	LUX.
WALLER, Karl	256577	M	Ger.	06	Sgt., Pol., Praha-Kobylisy and Rakovnik (Czech.) 42				MURDER	CZECH.
WALLERACHER, Heinrich	177802	M	Ger.		SS-Rottenfhr., SS, C.C. Osterhofen-Darmstadt (Ger.)				MURDER	U.S.
WALLICH, Josef	255849	M			Pvt., C.C.Ellrich, Nordhausen (Ger.)				MURDER	U.S.
WALLING, August	261364	M	Ger.		SS-Hptscharfhr., Camp-Cmdt., C.C.Hessenthal (Ger.)				BRUTALITY	FR.
WALLINGER	255824	M			Pvt., C.C.Harzungen, Nordhausen (Ger.)				MURDER	U.S.
WALLIS, Karl	251719	M	Ger.		Sgt., Feldgendarmerie 577, Orsay (Fr.) 8.8.44				MURDER	FR.
WALLNER	151460	M			Pvt., Org.Todt, SS-Pol.Regt., Oran (Fr.) 15.6.44				MURDER	FR.
WALLNER	189398	M			SS-Mann, 19.SS Pol.Regt. (Todt), Hameau des Puisots (Fr.) 15.6.44				MURDER	FR.
WALLNER, Rudolf	192229	M	Ger.	18	Oberfaehnrich, 599.Flak Unit Feldpost Nr.52272, Schwalbach (Ger.) 8.44				TORTURE	U.S.
WALLNISCH, Erich	193522	M	Ger.		Pvt., Army, Leipzig (Ger.) 11.3.45				MURDER	U.S.
WALLOSCH	124401	M			Major, Schupo 1.Bn., 27.Pol.Regt.Schutzpol.Halle. Lodz (Pol.) 2. or 3.40				MURDER	U.S.
WALLOT	252837	M	Ger.		Lt., F.P.16572, Pepingen (Bel.) 2.44-3.9.44				PILLAGE	BEL.
WALLRAT	255917	M			Employee, Gestapo, Sart-Lez-Spa (Bel.) 3.6.42				MURDER	BEL.
WALLS, Karl	11298				Sgt., Feldgendarmerie 577, Romorantin (Fr.) 43-44				TORTURE	FR.
WALLS, Karl	251715	M	Ger.		Gen.-Cmdt., 21.Panzer Div., 7.Bn., Quevy Le Grand (Bel.) 3.9.44				INTERR.	BEL.
WALLUCH, Aleis (or WALLUSCH)	191470				Pvt., Arbeitskommando 343, Landernau (Fr.) 15.4.44-8.44				MURDER	FR.
WALLUS	196729	M	Ger.		Guard, C.C.Struthof-Natzweiler (Fr.) 40-44				TORTURE	FR.
WALLUSCH see WALLUCH, Aleis	305974	M	Ger.		Member of Staff, C.C.Struthof-Natzweiler (Fr.) 42-44				MURDER	FR.
WALLUSCH see WALLUCH, Aleis	191470									
WALLUSCH, Alexis	158450	M	Ger.		Cpl., 263.Inf.Div., Finistere (Fr.) 44				MURDER	FR.
WALMANN, Helmuth	250543	M	Ger.		SS-Officer, 2.SS Panz.Div., Das Reich, Montpezat du Quercy (Fr.) 2.5.44				MURDER	FR.
WALMICHRAT	259651	M	Ger.		Member, Gestapo, Area Angers (Maine and Loire) (Fr.) 42-44				MISC.CRIMES	FR.
WALOCHEK	67730	M	Ger.		Pvt., Army, C.C. Bromberg (Pol.) 2.43				MURDER	U.K.
WALOCHEK (see WALASHEK)	158396									
WALS	11299	M	Ger.		N.O., Feldgendarmerie, St.Germain en Laye (Fr.) 21.8.44				MURDER	FR.
WALSSHAM	983	M	Ger.		Capt., Army, Feldschule Art., Autun (Fr.) 7.44				MISC.CRIMES	FR.
WALTE	141423	M	Ger.		Cpl., Army, 28.Inf.Regt. 116.Bn., I.Coy., Maubourget (Fr.) 27.7.44				MURDER	FR.
WALTER	984	M	Ger.		Army, C.C. Caen (Fr.) 6.44				MURDER	FR.
WALTER	986	M	Ger.		Lt., Gestapo, Bizerte (Tun.) 12.42-4.43				MURDER	FR.
WALTER	31534	M			Interpreter, S.D., Vichy (Fr.)				MURDER	FR.
WALTER	126965	M		97	Kapo-Chief, C.C. Blechhammer (Ger.)				MURDER	FR.
WALTER	141950	M			Cpl., Gestapo of Belfort, Chenebier-Etobon (Fr.) 27.9.44				MURDER	FR.
WALTER	142708	M			Commissar, Kraftwagentransport-Regt., Cannes (Fr.)				PILLAGE	FR.
WALTER	147020	M	Ger.		Chief, Gestapo, Marquixanes (Fr.) 44				MURDER	FR.
WALTER	149590	M	Ger.		Lt., 11.Panz.Div., 15.Panz.Regt., South-West-France 44				MURDER	FR.
WALTER	151461	M	Ger.		Lt., Air Force, Bousquet d'Orb (Fr.) 17.8.44				MURDER	FR.
WALTER	151463	M	Ger.		Member, Gestapo, Angers (Fr.)				MURDER	FR.
WALTER	158413	M	Ger.		Pvt., Army, Vraignes en Vermandois (Fr.) 29.8.44				MURDER	FR.
WALTER	161696	M	Ger.	05	SS-Oschfhr., C.C. Buchenwald (Ger.) 42-45				WITNESS	U.S.
WALTER	162575	M	Ger.		Civilian, Schliersee (Ger.)				WITNESS	U.S.
WALTER	177798	M			Professional Criminal (wore SS uniforms) on the march between Flossenburg and Straubing (Ger.) 19.-20.4.45				MURDER	U.S., FR.
WALTER	182330	M	Ger.		Kapo, C.C.Leonberg-Stuttgart (Ger.)				MISC.CRIMES	FR.
WALTER	186860	M	Ger.		Guard, Kradischko C.C.Flossenburg (Ger.)				TORTURE	FR.
WALTER	188376	M	Ger.		Lt., (Ger.) 40-45				MURDER	CZECH.
WALTER	189042	M	Ger.	05	Col., Army, near Cassino (Italy) 44				WITNESS	U.K.
WALTER	189820	M	Ger.		SS-Usturmfhr., SS Administration, Geta, Kovno (Yugo.) 40-44				MURDER	YUGO.
WALTER	191958	M		10	Dr., SS Hptsturmfhr., C.C.Dachau (Ger.) 4.4.45				MURDER	U.S.
WALTER	192006	M			Major, Geb.Jaeger Regt.85, Lus la Croix Haute (Fr.) 10.7.44				MURDER	FR.
WALTER	192424	M	Ger.		W.O., Army, Chesnimieres (Fr.) 8.44				MURDER	FR.
WALTER	193657	M	Ger.		SS-Usturmfhr., SS, Lidice (Czech.) 10.6.42				MURDER	CZECH.
WALTER	194869	M	Ger.		SS-Usturmfhr., SS, C.C. Lublin (Pol.) 40-44				MURDER	POL.
WALTER	195565	M	Ger.		Osturmfhr., S.D. and Gestapo, Perpignan (Fr.)				MURDER	FR.
WALTER	195698	M	Ger.		Sgt., Waffen-SS, Zdolbunow (Pol.) 13.10.42				MURDER	POL.
WALTER	195890	M	Ger.		Guard, C.C. Royallieu (Fr.) 41-44				MURDER	FR.
WALTER	250544	M	Ger.		Cpl., Air Force (Fr.) 42-44				TORTURE	FR.
WALTER	50568	M	Ger.		Lt.Col., Army-Unit "Brandenburg", Kistianje (Yugo.) 44				MISC.CRIMES	YUGO.
WALTER	50569	M	Ger.		Interpreter, Gestapo, Saulscures (Fr.) 22.9.-2.10.44				PILLAGE	FR.
WALTER	52814	M	Ger.		S.D.-Mann, S.D.-Gestapo, Toulouse, Haute-Garonne (Fr.) 11.42-19.8.44				MURDER	FR.
WALTER	52825	M	Ger.		Gend., Feldgendarmerie, Romorantin Nr.577, F.P.No.22501, Orsay (Fr.) 8.8.44				MISC.CRIMES	FR.
WALTER	52831	M	Ger.		Cmdt., 9.Inf.Div. 85.Regt., Luz La Croix (Fr.) 10.7.44				MURDER	FR.
WALTER	53438	M	Ger.		Employee, Sipo IV E, Brussels (Bel.) 40-44				INTERR.	BEL.
WALTER	53460	M	Ger.		W.O. in charge Guard, Prison St.Quentin (Fr.)				INTERR.	FR.
WALTER	55823	M	Ger.		Cpl., SS Med.Asst., C.C.Dora, Nordhausen (Ger.)				MURDER	U.S.
WALTER	56344	M	Ger.		Hptscharfhr., SS, Muehldorf Area (Ger.)				WITNESS	U.S.
WALTER	57391	M	Ger.		Truppenfhr., Organisation Todt at the camps for forced labour in Norway Erlandet, Oeusand Trola (Nor.) 6.42-45				MURDER	YUGO.
WALTER	259261	M		17.2.01	Agent, Gestapo of Poitiers, Poitiers Area (Fr.) 40-45				MISC.CRIMES	FR.
WALTER	259262	M	Ger.		Kapo, C.C.Auschwitz (Pol.)				MURDER	FR.
WALTER	261036	M			SS-Oberamtmann, SS, C.C.Vaihingen a.d.Enz (Ger.) 13.8.44-7.4.45				MURDER	U.S.
WALTER	261071	M	Ger.		Capt., St.Gingolph (Fr.) 23.7.44				MURDER	FR.
WALTER	261365	M			Inspector, Air Force-Unit L.52511, Pau, Soumoulon, Narp, Lescar (Fr.) 6. and 8.44				MURDER	FR.

WAL - WAN

NAME	C.R.FILE NUMBER	SEX	NATIO-NALITY	DATE OF BIRTH	RANK OCCUPATION UNIT PLACE AND DATE OF CRIME	REASON WANTED	WANTED BY
WALTER	305357	M	Ger.		Major, German Forces, Dovraina, Hostia, Thisvy, Thebes (Grc.) 8.43	MURDER	GRC.
WALTER	306110	M	Ger.		SS-Oschfhr., SS C.C. Hamburg Neuengamme (Ger.) 45	MURDER	CZECH.
WALTER	306782	M	Ger.		Lt., Col., Einheit, Brandenburg, Kristanje (Yugo.) 44	TORTURE	YUGO.
WALTER	307232	M	Ger.		Member, C.C. Auschwitz Birkenau (Pol.) 40	MURDER	FR.
WALTER, Albert	168060	M	Ger.		Stellvertr.Leiter, Hauptabteilung Ernaehrung u.Landwirtschaft 9.39-44	PILLAGE	POL.NOR.
WALTER, Alfred	251411	M	Ger.		Schfhr., SS Div. Gestapo, La Bresse (Fr.) 9.-11.44	MURDER	FR.
WALTER, Alois	29649	M	Ger.		Oberlandgerichtsrat, Public Official, Litomerice (Czech.) 40	MURDER	CZECH.
WALTER, Anton	10031	M	Ger.		Dr., Staatsanwalt, Public Official, Litomerice (Czech.) 21.2.40	MURDER	CZECH.
WALTER, Anton	193123	M	Ger.	22.8.00	Sgt., Guard, Reichsjustizministerium, Feldstraflager W-SS Finmark (Nor.) 42-45	MISC.CRIMES	YUGO.NOR.
WALTER, Edgar	255822	M			Flyer, C.C. Ellrich Nordhausen (Ger.)	MURDER	U.S.
WALTER, Edmund	255821	M			Cpl., C.C. Ellrich Nordhausen (Ger.)	MURDER	U.S.
WALTER, Erich	255798	M		2.10.98	Cpl., C.C. Ellrich Nordhausen (Ger.)	MURDER	U.S.
WALTER, Ernst	11300	M	Ger.		Pvt., Pz.Gren.Rgt. 110 or 111, 2. Coy. Albine (Fr.) 29.8.44	MURDER	FR.
WALTER, Franz	260983	M	Ger.		Rapportfhr., C.C. Hirtenberg (Ger.) 44-45	MURDER	POL.
WALTER, Fritz	255800	M		12.5.21	Pvt., C.C. Harzungen Nordhausen (Ger.)	MURDER	U.S.
WALTER, Gottfried	131011	M			SS-Uschfhr., SS C.C. Mauthausen (Aust.) 41-45	MURDER	U.S.
WALTER, Guenther	255799	M	Ger.	21.1.24	Pvt., C.C. Ellrich Nordhausen (Ger.)	MURDER	U.S.
WALTER, Gustav	193122	M	Ger.	-00	Sgt., Guard, Reichsjustizministerium, Feldstraflager W-SS, Finmark (Nor.) 42-45	MISC.CRIMES	YUGO.NOR.
WALTER, Hans	136273	M	Ger.	13	Pvt., Stalag XII A. C.C. OF. French P.O.W. 1289 Coy. Stamfersbuch (Ger.)	MURDER	FR.
WALTER, Heinz	255801	M			Pvt., C.C. Harzungen Nordhausen (Ger.)	MURDER	U.S.
WALTER, Helmuth, Willi	253461	M	Ger.	13.12.13	Osturmfhr., or Schfhr., Gestapo, De Troyes Aube (Fr.) 8.44	MISC.CRIMES	FR.
WALTER, Nikolaus	260918	M	Ger.	20.4.15	Sturmmann, SS Guard C.C. Auschwitz (Pol.) 43-45	BRUTALITY	POL.
WALTER, Norbert	256975	M			Sgt., 2. Nachr. Coy. Holmes (Neth.) 8.5.45	INTERR.	NETH.
WALTER, Otto	175697	M	Ger.		SS-Mann, C.C. Bergen Belsen (Ger.) 1.10.39-30.4.45	MURDER	U.N.W.C.C.
WALTER, Otto	182339	M	Ger.		Civilian, Grosswange (Ger.) 9.44	WITNESS	U.S.
WALTER, Otto	256022	M			Bauleiter, O.T. Muehldorf (Ger.)	WITNESS	U.S.
WALTER, Otto	256416	M	Ger.	26.9.05	Probably, SS Major, SS C.C. Mauthausen (Aust.) 45	BRUTALITY	U.S.
WALTER, Peter	193524	M	Ger.		Officer, Airforce, Brusthem (Bel.) 11.7.44	MURDER	BEL.
WALTER, Philippe	177581	M	Ger.		Police, Porteau Poitiers (Fr.) 28.8.44	MURDER	FR.
WALTER, Raimund	255803	M		8.9.98	Cpl., C.C. Ellrich Nordhausen (Ger.)	MURDER	U.S.
WALTER, Rudolf (or WOLTER)	182326	M			Member of SD, Seyssinet (Fr.) 22.7.44	MURDER	FR.
WALTER, Rudolf	255828	M			Pvt., C.C. Harzungen, Nordhausen (Ger.)	MURDER	U.S.
WALTER, Willi	305356	M	Ger.		SS-Schfhr., Chauffeur, Member Sicherheitsdienst Troyes Rennes Gestapo Troyes and region (Fr.) 3.10.43-22.8.44	MURDER	FR.
WALTERS	36601	M	Ger.		Cpl., Guard Bn. L 565 Landesschutz. Bn. 565, C.C. Grulich (Czech.) 3-4.45	TORTURE	U.K.
WALTERS	131010	M			SS-Sturmbannfhr., SS C.C. Mauthausen (Aust.) 41-45	MURDER	U.S.
WALTERS	132698	M	Ger.		Camp Chief, C.C. Vaihingen (Ger.) 43-44	MURDER	FR.
WALTEUFFEL	261186	M	Ger.		Member, Staff of C.C. Ravensbrueck (Ger.)	SUSPECT	BEL.
WALTHER	1353	M	Ger.		Pvt., Army	MISC.CRIMES	U.K.
WALTHER	120605	M		05 or 08	Osturmfhr., 35. SD. Kommando, Rennes (Fr.)	INTERR.	FR.
WALTHER	124739	M	Ger.		Dr., Civilian C.C. Barka (Ger.)	MISC.CRIMES	U.S.
WALTHER	142709	M		85	Usturmfhr., W-SS, Lublin (Pol.) 42-44	MURDER	POL.
WALTHER, Erich	256855	M	Ger.	10	Lt., Comm. of z.b.V. Coy. at Bommersum, Gennar (Neth.) 3.40	INTERR.	NETH.
WALTHER	306723	M			Cpl., SS near Frickenhorst (Ger.) 11.44	BRUTALITY	U.S.
WALTHER, Gernard	138858	M			Lt., Col., Sipo. and SD, Kiev (Sov.Un.) 15.9.42	MURDER	U.S.
WALTHER, Karl - Heinz	257706	M		17.12.15	Lt., Stabsquartier d.Pz.Jg.Abt. 240, Chateau De Vallieres (Fr.) 10.40	PILLAGE	FR.
WALTHER, Norbert	140895	M	Ger.		Verbindungsabteilung 2. Coy. 331.Bn., Bolnes (Neth.) 8.5.45	MURDER	NETH.
WALTHER, Paul	138547	M			Dr., Civ., NSDAP, Lazart, Wiesloch (Ger.) 44	TORTURE	U.S.
WALTHER, Johann	255217	M	Ger.	14.10.09	Employee, Gestapo, State Service, Hradiste (Czech.) 39-45	MURDER	CZECH.
WALTZ	198500	M			Major, H.Q. Geheime Feldpolice, Vicenza (It.)	WITNESS	U.S.
WALZ	150819	M			Civilian, C.C. Schubin, Oflag 64 19.12.44	PILLAGE	U.S.
WALZ	255826	M			Pvt., C.C. Nottleberode, Nordhausen (Ger.)	MURDER	U.S.
WALZ	256359	M	Ger.		Sturmbannfhr., SS, Muehldorf area (Ger.)	WITNESS	U.S.
WALZBERGER, Leopold	196740	M	Ger.		Krim.Assistent, Gestapo, Brno. (Czech.) 39-43	MURDER	CZECH.
WALZEL, Adolf	193121	M	Ger.	15.12.93	Sgt., Guard, Reichsjustizministerium, Feldstraflager W-SS Finmark (Nor.) 42-45	MISC.CRIMES	YUGO. NOR.
WALZER	255825	M			Pvt., C.C. Mackenrode Nordhausen (Ger.)	MURDER	U.S.
WANDEL	151468	M	Ger.		Civilian, Neunkirchen (Ger.)	MURDER	U.S.
WANDEL	188768	M	Ger.		Feldgendarm, Feldgendarmerie, Bar Le Duc (Fr.) 20.-29.8.44	MURDER	FR.
WANDELT, Otto	255830	M		21.1.91	Pvt., C.C. Harzungen, Nordhausen (Ger.)	MURDER	U.S.
WANDER, Georg	305959	M	Ger.		Plapeville des Metz Moselle (Fr.) 41-43	PILLAGE	FR.
WANDERLEIGH	67731	M			C.C. Wortlah	TORTURE	U.K.
WANDERS, Wilhelm	135330	M	Ger.		Civ., Miner (Ger.)	TORTURE	U.S.
WANDKEN, Nicolas	29839	M	Ger.		Sgt., Chief Warder at Prison, C.C. Lafayette, Nantes (Fr.) 6.8.44	MURDER	FR.
WANDT, Rudolf	188729	M		00	Hptschfhr., C.C. Unterluess, (Ger.)	TORTURE	U.K.
WANDTZEN, August	29643	M			Feldgendarmerie 577, Brig. Romorantin (Fr.) 17.8.44	MURDER	FR.
WANEN, Karol	185899	M		17	N.C.O. Police 25. section, Department for Comm. Athens (Grc.)	MURDER	GRC.
WANGEMANN, Julius	135331	M	Ger.	93	Osturmfhr., Gestapo Allg.SS, Bensheim (Ger.) 9.-3.45	TORTURE	U.S.
WANIEK (or WANJEK)	193521	M	Ger.	11.10.97	SS-Mann, 4.SS Totenkopf Stuba. C.C. Mittelbau Dora Nordhausen (Ger.) 43-45	MURDER	U.S.
WANK	192423	M	Ger.		SS-Cpl., SS Pz.Div., Hohenstaufen, Neuville les Bois (Fr.) 11.8.44	MURDER	FR.
WANKDEN, Nicolas	189491	M			Cpl., Prison, Mantes (Fr.) 6.8.44	MURDER	FR.
WANKO, Ernst	188605	M	Ger.		Member, Employee, H.J. Gestapo SD SS, Brunn, Prag (Czech.) 39-45	MURDER	CZECH.
WANLOSEN	196910	M	Ger.		Guard or Kapo C.C. Gusen (Ger.)	MISC.CRIMES	BEL.
WANNAMACHER	177551	M	Ger.		Osturmfhr., SD, Gestapo, Saarbruecken (Ger.)	MISC.CRIMES	FR.
WANNEMACHER	126727	M		08	SS Osturmfhr., Gestapo, Lyon Plateau des Glieres, Paris (Fr.) 43	TORTURE	FR.

WAN-WAY

-190-

NAME	C R FILE NUMBER	SEX	NATIO-NALITY	DATE OF BIRTH	RANK OCCUPATION UNIT PLACE AND DATE OF CRIME	REASON WANTED	WANTED BY
WANNENACHER	189401	M	Ger.		SS-Osturmfhr., C.C.Drancy (Fr.)	MURDER	FR.
WANNENACHER, Rudolf	189257	M	Ger.		Obersturmfhr., Engineer,SA,Parschnitz (Czech.) 39-42	TORTURE	POL.
WANNENBACHER	121672	M	Ger		Agent,Gestapo, Gueret Aubusson (Fr.)	MURDER	FR.
WANNER, Josef	196898	M	Ger.		Crim.-Asst.,Gestapo, Brno (Czech.)	INTERR	CZECH.
WANNER, Josef	255832	M			Pvt.,C.C.Ellrich,Nordhausen (Ger.)	MURDER	U S
WANNING, Folzo	262189	M	Ger.	8. 5.15	SS-Hptschfhr.,51 SS Armoured Bde., Art Detachment,Breviardes,Bucheres, Ste Savine,La Riviere De Corps,Troyes (Fr) 22.-25 8 44	BRUTALITY	FR
WANSOHN, P	256173	M	Ger.		SS, Muhldorf (Ger.)	BRUTALITY	U S
WANSUNG	142006	M	Ger.		SS-Guard,C C.Muhldorf Area near Wittergars, (Ger.) 45	MURDER	U S
WANTON, Hans	256702	M		20	Sturmmann,C.C.Muehldorf (Ger.)	MURDER	U S
WAOELKI	151462	M	Ger.		Lt.,Army,Pioneer,Chenebier Etobon (Fr) 27 9.44	MURDER	FR
WAPPENHANS	185900	M	Ger	95	SS Bdefhr.,SD,official,Gestapo,Rowno (Pol.) 41-42	MURDER	U S
WAPPLER	196839	M	Ger		Hauptwachtmeister,8 Coy Schutzpolizei,near Arnheim (Neth) 3.45	INTERR	NETH
WARCZYN, Heinrich	193127	M	Ger.	05	Sgt.,Guard,Reichsjustizministerium,Feldstraflager,Finmark (Nor.) 1 45	MISC CRIMES	NOR
WAFENBERG	186174	M	Ger		Guard,C C.Rottenburg (Ger.)	TORTURE	FR
WARMBACH, Hans	149683	M	Ger	3 8.22	Pvt.,SS Totenkopf,C.C. Buchenwald (Ger.) 44-45	MURDER	U S
WARMBOLD, Erich	193520	M	Ger.		SS-Uschfhr.,4 SS Totenkopf-Sturmbann,C C Dora-Mittelbau,Nordhausen (Ger.) 43-45	MURDER	U S
WARMSTAEDT, Walter	128935	M	Ger.	.14	Hptschfhr.,SS,C.C.Buchenwald (Ger.)	WITNESS	U.S
WARMUND	255841	M			Pvt.,C.C.Osterhagen,Nordhausen (Ger.)	MURDER	U S
WARMUTH, Anna	151466	F	Ger.	09	Nurse,Civilian,near Ruppertshutten (Ger.) 12.9.44	WITNESS	U S
WARNECKE	193099	M	Ger.		Sgt.,Schupo,C.C.Falstad (Nor.) 41-44	MURDER	NOR
WARNECKE	257841	M	Ger	.16	SS-Uschfhr., Waffen SS,Rgt.37,Div. "Goetz v.Berlichingen", St.Eny (Fr) 3.7 44	MURDER	U S
WARNECKE, Friedrich	125619	M	Ger.	03	Civilian, Seesen (Ger.) 6.44	MURDER	U S
WARNECKE, Fritz	185901	M	Ger		Lt.,Gendarmerie, Seesen-Harz,Neuenkrug (Ger.) 44	MURDER	U K
WARNECKE, Wilhelm Dietrich	260532	M	Ger	19.12.90	Truppfhr.,Volkssturm,Hastedt (Ger.) 22.or23.4.45	MURDER	POL
WARNER	251412	M	Ger.		Interpreter,Rouen (Fr.) 43-44	MISC CRIMES	FR.
WARNFRT	195889	M	Ger.		Sgt.,Army,Selles s-Cher (Fr.) 31.8.44	WITNESS	FR.
WARNICKE	189437	M	Ger.		Capt.,Army,NSDAP,Zwolle (Neth) 9.44	MURDER	NETH
WARNKE	162536	M	Ger	05	SS-Oschfhr.,SS,Command staff,Section I,C.C.Buchenwald (Ger.) 39-44	TORTURE	U S
WARNKE, Ludwig	255833	M		22 10.18	Cpl.,C.C.Harzungen,Nordhausen (Ger.)	MURDER	U S
WARNKEN, Johann	255843	M			Flyer,C.C Ellrich Nordhausen (Ger.)	MURDER	U S
WARNSTAEDT (or WAUNSTEDT)	194119	M	Ger		SS-Oschfhr.,C.C.Buchenwald (Ger.) 42-45	MURDER	U S
WARNSTAEDT, Walter (or WARN-STEDT)	128935	M			SS-Hptschfhr.,SS Totenkopf-Sturmbann,C.C.Weimar,Buchenwald (Ger.)	TORTURE	U S
WARNSTEDT (See WARNSTAEDT, Walter)	128935						
WARNSTEDT	150826	M	Ger.		Col ,Air Force,Stalag 1 A,C C.Barth (Ger.) 17.or 18 2 45	MURDER	U S
WARNUNG, Raoul	138330	M	Ger		Policeman,Geh.Feldpolizei,Montigny-Gohelle (Fr.) 14.3 44	MURDER	FR
WAPSITZ	136402	M			Lt ,19 SS Police Rgt ,2 Bn.,5 Coy,C.C.Gaun,Tulle (Yugo.,Fr.)5.41-3 44 3.-10.44	MURDER	FR
WAPTEN	191326	M	Ger		N C.O., Eisenb.Art.Btty.717,F.P.Nr.22380,St Andries Varsenare les Bruges (Bel.) 4.9 44	MURDER	BEL
WAPTENBERG, Benita	253451	F	Ger.		Nurse,Wolfsburg (Ger.) 29 6.44	WITNESS	U S
WARTHER	142711	M	Ger.		Engineer,Civilian,Ingelheim (Ger.)	MURDER	FR
WARTIN	191325	M	Ger		N C.O., Eisenb.Art Btty.717,F.P.Nr.22380,St Andries Varsenare les Bruges (Bel.) 4.9 44	MURDER	BEL
WARTLIK, Erich	192442	M	Ger	20.11.98	Truppfhr., teacher,SA,Education,Bohemia (Czech)	SUSPECT	CZECH
WARTZ	11501	M	Ger.		Pvt.,Army,110 or 111 Pz Gren.Rgt., Albine (Fr.) 29.6.44	MURDER	FR
WARTZEL	192944	M	Ger		Capo,C.C.Buchenwald (Ger.) 42-45	TORTURE	U S
WARZEN, Erik	1527	M	Ger		Army,Kledia (Tun.) 13 4 43	MURDER	FR
WASCHKE	195999	M	Ger		Major,Gendarmerie,C.C.Westerbork (Ger) 9.-12 44	MURDER	NETH
WASCHUM	164121	M	Ger.	15	Pvt.,Asst.to Capt.Schmidt,SA,Army Straf.Col.,near Brux (Czech.) 44-45	BRUTALITY	U K
WASELER, Hermann	251418	M	Ger.	09	W O., Troop Train,Grangues (Fr.) 5 -6 6.44	MURDER	FR
WASENBERGER, Johann	195713	M	Ger.		Pvt.,1 SS Pz.Div.Leibst Adolf Hitler,3 Pion.Coy,Pion.Bn ,Ligneuville (Bel.) 17.-19.12.44	MURDER	U S
WASERMAN	137533	M	Ger.		Capt.,Gestapo,SS,Zakopane (Pol.) 3.-8.9 41	TORTURE	U S
WASIZTKY, Erich	131009	M	Ger		SS-Hptsturmfhr.,SS,Druggist at C C Mauthausen (Aust.) 41-43	MURDER	U.S
WASLER, Hermann	158415	M	Ger		Civilian,Buch (Ger., 4 44	MURDER	U S
WASSER	989	M	Ger.		Sgt ,Air Force, Baudrigues (Fr.) 19.8.44	MURDER	FR
WASSER	255820	M			Flyer,C C.Ellrich,Nordhausen (Ger.)	MURDER	U S
WASSER	300747	M	Ger		Pvt.,1 Aufkl Abt 3 Coy 2 Col.XV Div.of the Afrika Corps,Saint Leger (Arlon) 5 9 44	MISC CRIMES	BEL
WASSERMANN	193098	M	Ger		Sgt.,Schupo,C C Falstad (Nor) 41-44	TORTURE	NOR
WASSERMANN, Karl	11502	M	Ger.		Sgt.,Army,110 or 111 Pz Gren.Rgt., 2 Coy,Albine (Fr.) 29.6.44	MURDER	FR
WASSILAWSKI, Max	251459	M		11-16	Printer,Civilian,D.A.U.A.,Gerardmer (Fr.) 29.5 44	MURDER	U S
WASSILI	191968	M	Ger		Sgt.,Army,Orst Bn.Nr 59034,L'Epine Habet en Etables (Fr.)	MURDER	FR
WASSMANN, Ferdinand	262190	M	Ger.	12 10.13	SS-Hptschfhr.,Chief of Platoon 3, 51 SS Armoured Bde., 9 Coy Arti-Air Craft Group,Breviandes,Sucheres,Ste.Savine,La Riviere De Corps Troyes (Fr.) 22.-25.8.44	BRUTALITY	FR
WASZINIAK	192992	M	Ger		Capo,C C Buchenwald (Ger.) 42-45	TORTURE	U S
WATHER, Georg (see VON WALTER)	262188						
WATKE	62439	M	Ger.		Dr.,Head,Dept.of Science and Education of G.G	MISC CRIMES	UNWCC
WATMAN	188268				Member,Camp-official,C.C.Woippy (Fr)	MISC CRIMES	BEL ,FR
WATSACK	21432	M	Ger		Town Clerk,Civilian,Aschersleben (Ger) 4 45	TORTURE	U S
WATSON, Richard	129939	M	Ger		Coal Mine 17 km North Schornivitsch, 8.3.45	WITNESS	U.K.
WATZEL (see WENZEL)	191356						
WATZINGER	193097	M	Ger		C.C.Falstad (Nor.) 41-44	MURDER	NOR.
WATZLAVECK, Alfred	22841	M	Ger		Pvt.,P-714 Coy,C.C.Hildesheim (Ger.) 3.45	TORTURE	U K.
WAUBAN, Peter	193519	M	Ger.		SS-Schuetze,4 SS Totenkopf-Sturmbann,C.C Mittelbau-Dora,Nordhausen (Ger.) 43-45	MURDER	U S
WAUNSTEDT (see WARNSTEDT)	194119						
WAUTE, Michel	11504	M	Ger		Sgt.,Army,110 or 111 Pz Gren.Rgt., Gourdon (Fr.) 29 6 44	MURDER	FR
WAWRSZINOVSKI	194873	M	Ger.		Osturmfhr.,SD,SS, Averoff,Athens (Grc.) 43-44	MISC CRIMES	U.K
WAWPZYNIAK, Helmuth	168061	M	Ger.		Warder,Capo,C.C Sachsenhausen,Oranienburg (Ger.) 39-4 45	MURDER	POL
WAYAND, Emile	256295	M			Capo,C C.Neckargerach (Ger.) 44	BRUTALITY	FR
WAYRSCH	21434			05	SS-Obergruppenfhr.,Upper Silesia (Ger)	TORTURE	U S.

WAZ-WEB

NAME	C.R.FILE NUMBER	SEX	NATIO- NALITY	DATE OF BIRTH	RANK	OCCUPATION UNIT PLACE AND DATE OF CRIME	REASON WANTED	WANTED BY
WAZ, Ciniak	158995	M				Chief CC Warsaw (Pol.)	MURDER	U.S.
WAZEK	257944	M	Ger.	05	Lt. Adj., 922 Bn.,5 Schtz-Rgt.,Ljubljana, Cetje and Kranj(Yugo.) 42-43		MURDER	YUGO.
WDOWENKO, Iwan	255760	M		11. 27.19		CC Harzungen, Nordhausen (Ger.)	MURDER	U.S.
WEAVER, Erich	195947	M				SS-Mann,-1 SS Pz.Div., Stoumont (Bel.)	MURDER	U.S.
WEBEL	174793	M	Ger.	90	Staff-Sgt., Stalag 383, CC Hohenfels (Ger.) 42-45		TORTURE	U.K.
WEBEL, Gustav	21437	M	Ger.			Civilian, Beltersheim (Ger.) 1.12.44	MURDER	U.S.
WEBER	993	M	Ger.		Capt., Army, Neufchateau, Rollainville (Fr.) 9.9.44		MURDER	FR.
WEBER (alias BEHEING)	994	M	Ger.		Col., Army, CC Stalag IX-C (Ger.) 2.42		TORTURE	U.K.
WEBER	995	M	Ger.		Dr., member medical, CC Auschwitz (Pol.) 6.40-45		MURDER	BEL.,POL.
WEBER	11505	M	Ger.		Member, Gestapo, Cahors (Fr.) 29.6.44		MURDER	FR.
WEBER	21555	M	Ger.		Capt., Army, CC Bitterfeld (Ger.) 10.43		TORTURE	U.K.
WEBER	36611	M			Sgt., Army, Guard Bn. L 565, Grulich (Czech.) 3.-4.45		TORTURE	U.S.
WEBER	39658	M			Lt., Army, Borkum (Ger.)		MURDER	U.S.
WEBER	129937	M	Ger.		Sgt., Stalag 383, CC Hohenfels (Ger.) 42-45		MURDER	U.K.
WEBER	128934	M			Hptschfhr, SS, CC Weimar, Buchenwald (Ger.)		TORTURE	U.S.
WEBER	133910	M	Ger.		Doctor (Ger.)		WITNESS	U.S.
WEBER	199792	M	Ger.		Employee, main labour office (Pol.) 41-44		MISC.CRIMES	U.S.
WEBER	159467	M			Kreisleiter NSDAP, Ottmanedorf (Ger.)		MURDER	U.S.
WEBER	162792	M	Ger.	07	Hptsturmfhr, SS, CC Sasel (Ger.)		MURDER	U.K.
WEBER	166726	M	Ger.	93	Civ., formerly physician in prison, CC Rositten (Ger.) 42		WITNESS	U.S.
WEBER	166727	M		00	Hptsturmfhr, SS, 3 Coy, 5 SS Sign.and Depot Bn.,SS HQ,Vipitero(It.)		WITNESS	U.S.
WEBER	173843	M	Ger.		Dr.,medical officer, CC Auschwitz-Birkenau (Pol.) 39-45		MURDER	CZECH.,BEL.
WEBER	189821	M	Ger.		Cpl., 264 Inf.Div., 892 Gren.Rgt.,Sucaray,Mne(Yugo.) 5.10.-12.43		MURDER	YUGO.
WEBER	193096	M	Ger.		Oschfhr, SS, CC Falstad (Nor.) 41-44		MISC.CRIMES	NOR.
WEBER	196744	M	Ger.		Uschfhr, SS, office of local NSDAP, Barcelona (Spain)43-44		WITNESS	BEL.
WEBER	250566	M	Ger.	20	Capt., armoured Div., Tuk near Ogulin (Yugo.) 27.10.43-12.43		INTERR.	YUGO.
WEBER	251419	M	Ger.		Capt., Magnac-Laval-Hospital, Hte.Vienne (Fr.) 8.7.44		MISC.CRIMES	FR.
WEBER	251718	M	Ger.		6 Coy, 6 Huebner Rgt., Kinrooi (Bel.) 9.44		MURDER	BEL.
WEBER	253466	M	Ger.		Crim.Secretary, Sipo Abt.IV-E,Brussels (Bel.) 40-45		INTERR.	BEL.
WEBER (or WIEBER)	253466	M	Ger.		Agent, Gestapo, Offenburg (Ger.) 6.2.44		MURDER	FR.
WEBER	255222	M	Ger.		Oschfhr, SS, Gestapo, SD, Toulouse, Gers and Tarn (Fr.) 11.42-8.44		MURDER	FR.
WEBER	260096	M	Ger.		Lt., 157 Res.Div. Bavaria, Massif du Vercors, Isère and Drôme(Fr.) 20.7.44-5.8.44		SUSPECT	FR.
WEBER	261184	M	Ger.		Sgt., 199 Arbeitsbereich Liane, 5 In Rgt.211, Alleur-lez-Liege(Bel.) 4.9.44		MURDER	BEL.
WEBER	261401	M	Ger.		Oschfhr, SS, near Pfundres (It.) 13.6.44		MURDER	U.S.
WEBER	305962	M	Ger.		Member Sipo, The Hague, Scheveningen (Neth.) 12.1.44, 22.3.44		MURDER	NETH.
WEBER	305808	M	Ger.		Capt., Adj. of O.C. Tank Div."Lehr", Dresnice (Yugo.) 11.43		MURDER	YUGO.
WEBER	305975	M	Ger.		Wachtmeister, CC Struthof-Natzweiler (Fr.) 42-44		MURDER	FR.
WEBER, Adolf	120606	M		1905-08	Hptschfhr, SS, SD, 35 Kdo., Cirey (Fr.)		MURDER	FR.
WEBER, Alfred	165548	M	Ger.		Civ., foreman, Julius Koehler Werke, Limbach(Ger.) 43-45		TORTURE	BEL.
WEBER, Alois (or Friedrich)	260622	M		circa 98	Bde.General		WITNESS	U.S.
WEBER, Arno	990	M	Ger.	9. 1.97	Uschfhr, W-SS, CC Maidanek (Pol.) 40, 4.44		MURDER	U.S.,POL.,BEL.
WEBER, Arno	162529	M	Ger.	95	Hptschfhr, SS, Sec.II, administration,CC Buchenwald(Ger.)43		TORTURE	U.S.
WEBER, August	168234	M	Ger.		Sgt., 9 Res.Gren.Rgt., 1 Coy, Magny d'Avignon(Fr.) 18.9.44		MURDER	FR.
WEBER, Bruno	194690	M	Ger.	21. 5.15	Dr., Hptschfhr, SS, CC Auschwitz (Pol.) 43-45		SUSPECT	CZECH.
WEBER, Carl	185744	M	Ger.	22. 1.02	Factory-manager, Civilian, Brno (Czech.) 39-45		PILLAGE	CZECH.
WEBER, Christoph	255761	M			Sturmmann, CC Bodungen, Nordhausen (Ger.)		MURDER	U.S.
WEBER, Erich	196433	M	Ger.		Sturmfhr, SS, factory-manager, Pilsen (Czech.)		PILLAGE	CZECH.
WEBER, Erwin	185745	M	Ger.		Osturmfhr, chief, SS and Abwehr, Prague (Czech.) 39-45		MURDER	CZECH.
WEBER, Eugen	191852	M	Ger.		Pvt., Army, Mouleydier Pressigeac (Fr.)		MURDER	FR.
WEBER, Eugen	256575	M	Ger.		Kapo, CC Dora, Nordhausen (Ger.)		MURDER	FR.
WEBER, Franz	150809	M	Ger.		Wachtmeister, Schupo, Frankfurt (Ger.) 43-44		TORTURE	U.S.
WEBER, Franz	199448	M	Ger.		Pvt., Army, Akervika (Nor.) 42		WITNESS	NOR.
WEBER, Franz	196894	M	Ger.	31. 8.89	Member SA, Koeln (Ger.)		INTERR.	LUX.
WEBER, Fritz	185746	M	Ger.		Sturmbannfhr, SS		MURDER	LUX.
WEBER, Fritz or Franz	251724	M		circa 18	Uschfhr, Malmedy (Bel.) 17.12--		MURDER	U.S.
WEBER (or GUIGELE)	196909	M	Ger.		CC Schirmeck (Fr.) 40-44		MISC.CRIMES	FR.
WEBER, Gustav	196900	M	Ger.	16.10.08	Police-inspector, Gestapo, Brno (Czech.) 39-45		SUSPECT	CZECH.
WEBER, Hans	261072	M	Ger.	circa 00	Chief-guard, Arbois (Fr.) 30.10.42		MURDER	FR.
WEBER, Heinz	124335	M	Ger.	21	SS-Mann, Leibstandarte Adolf Hitler, near Bastogne (Fr.) 25.12.44		MURDER	U.S.
WEBER, Heinz	251720	M	Ger.		377 Jg.Rgt., Vinkt Meigen (Bel.) 25.-31.5.40		MURDER	BEL.
WEBER, Helmut	255763	M			Sturmmann, CC Bodungen, Nordhausen (Ger.)		MURDER	U.S.
WEBER, Helmut	257850	M			Lt., Pz.Bde., Meuse Bridges, Antwerpen (Bel.) 12.44		MISC.CRIMES	U.S.
WEBER, Herman	255762	M		2. 5.02	Pvt., CC Ellrich, Nordhausen (Ger.)		MURDER	U.S.
WEBER, Hermann	300400	M	Ger.		Kapo, CC Buchenwald (Ger.) 42-45		MURDER	FR.
WEBER, Johann	991	M	Ger.		Foreman, civ. asst. Annamine, Alsdorf (Ger.) 42-44		TORTURE	U.S.
WEBER, Johann	257321	M	Ger.	31. 1.04	Chief, crim.secretary, Gestapo, Havlickuv Brod (Czech.) 40-45		MISC.CRIMES	CZECH.
WEBER, Johann Georg	262250	M	Ger.		Uschfhr, 51 SS Armoured Bde., Bucheres, Breviandes, St.Savine, La Riviere De Corps, Troyes (Aube) (Fr.) 22.-23.8.44		BRUTALITY	FR.
WEBER, Josef	185747	M	Ger.	10	SS, Luxembourg		MURDER	LUX.
WEBER, Josef	189335	M	Ger.		Zoellner, SS, Maulusmuehle(Fr.) 25.12.44		MISC.CRIMES	LUX.
WEBER, Joseph	162709	M	Ger. or Aust.		Dr., Osturmfhr, SS, CC Melk (Ger.)		TORTURE	U.S.
WEBER, Karl	149685	M			Lt., Army, Borkum (Ger.) 4.8.44		MURDER	U.S.
WEBER, Karl (see CZERNICKI)	150962	M						
WEBER, Karl	256159	M	Ger.		Chief-secretary, CC Mauthausen (Aust.)		INTERR.	FR.
WEBER, Karl	259700	M	Ger.	circa 00	Hptschfhr, SS, Gestapo, area of Angers (Maine and Loire)Fr.42-44		MISC.CRIMES	FR.
WEBER, Ludwig	11506	M	Ger.		Pvt., Army, 110 or 111 Pz.Gren.Rgt., 2 Coy, Albine (Fr.) 29.6.44		MURDER	FR.
WEBER, Ludwig	190452	M			Capt., Stiftung CC Beelitz (Ger.) 40-45		MURDER	CZECH.
WEBER, Michel	167851	M	Ger.	18	SS-Mann, CC Struthof-Natzweiler (Fr.)		MURDER	FR.
WEBER, Oskar Felix (see WEIL, Otto)	189131							
WEBER, Rudolph	158419	M	Ger.		Cpl., 269 Inf.Div., Finistere (Fr.) 44		MURDER	FR.
WEBER, Walter	182940	M	Ger.		Civilian, Gernsbach, Weissenbach (Ger.) 9.8.44		MURDER	U.S.

WEB-WEH

NAME	C.R.FILE NUMBER	SEX	NATIO-NALITY	DATE OF BIRTH	RANK, OCCUPATION, UNIT, PLACE AND DATE OF CRIME	REASON WANTED	WANTED BY
WEBER, Wilhelm	135332	M	Ger.		Civ.,mine foreman,C.C.(Ger.)	TORTURE	U.S.
WEBER, William	150811	M	Ger.		Major,Airforce,C.C.Stalag Luft IV,Kiefheide(Ger.)2.-5.45	TORTURE	U.S
WEBER, Willy	305363	M	Ger.		Former member,Waffen-SS,C.C.Mauthausen(Aust.) between 43-45	MURDER	NETH.
WEBER, Wladislaus	258431	M			Guard,SS,C.C.Ohrdruf(Ger.) 12.44-4.45	MURDER	U.S.
WEBERSTADT	996	M	Ger.		Pol.leader,Police,Thorn (Pol.) 9.39-42	MURDER	POL.
WEBRENBACH, Heinz	255858	M	Ger.	01	Cpl.,C.C.Harsungen-Nordhausen (Ger.)	MURDER	U.S
WEBSCH or WOBER	67737	M	Ger.		Oscharfhr. SS Div.,F.P.48963 B,St.Sulpice-Montmusson. Chateau-Gontier(Fr.) 6.8.44	MURDER	FR.
WECHESSER, Jacob	166915	M		22	Cpl.,5 Coy,Alpine Jg.Bn,Bourg St.Maurice (Fr.) 22.7.45	MURDER	FR.
WECHLIN	146742	M			Hptscharfhr.,SS,C.C.Flossenburg(Ger.)	MURDER	U.S.
WECHLIN, Willy	167858	M	Ger.	30. 9.17	Hptscharfhr.,SS,C.C.Struthof-Natzweiler(Fr.)42-44	MURDER	FR.
WECHSELBERGER, Kurt	259833	M			Sgt.,Geb.Feldpol.,stationed Koningdlaan 74,Utrecht(Neth.)8.3.45	SUSPECT	NETH.
WECHSLER	194683	M	Ger.		Member,C.C.Drancy (Fr.) 43-44	MURDER	BEL.
WECHTER, Wilhelm	251717	M		22. 5.04	131-3 Bn Res.Flak Abt.144, Strijpen (Bel.) 3.9.44	MURDER	BEL.
WECKER	1354	M			Pvt.,Army, 903 fortress Bn	MISC.CRIMES	U.K.
WECKER	195998	M			SS-Propaganda-chief,C C.Arnstadt (Ger.)	MISC.CRIMES	FR.
WECKERLE	251429	M			Sgt.,Unit 17630, Mouchamps (Fr.) 6.8.44	INTERR.	FR.
WECKERLEIN, Karl	26108	M	Ger.	19.12.07	Chief Crim.secr. Nat. Ministry of Food(Normandie,Fr.,Ukr.,Sov.Un.) 41-42	MISC.CRIMES	U.S.
WECKERNAGEL	256527	M			Chief,section Mittelwerk-Nordhausen(Ger.)	MURDER	U.S.
WECKESSER, Rudolf	189905	M		07	Member,Police,Prague(Czech.) 7..8.42	MURDER	CZECH.
WECKMANN, Willi	168235	M	Ger.		Pvt.,9 Res.Gren.Rgt.,1 Coy, Magny d'Avignon (Fr.) 18.9.44	MURDER	FR.
WEDEMEYER	186173	M	Ger.		Sgt.,Agent,Army,SD,Lyon (Fr.) 40-44	MURDER	FR.
WEDEKIND, Heinrich	255859	M		18	Pvt.,C.C.Ellrich-Nordhausen(Ger.)	INTERR.	FR.
WEDEL	306404	M			SS-Lt.,C.C.Buchenwald (Ger.) 16.5.38-9.10.43	MURDER	BEL.
WEDEL, Josef	132700	M	Ger.		Sgt.guard,Stalag 141 Vescul (Fr.) 3.1.41	MURDER	FR.
WEDELEIN	126453	M			Oscharfhr.,I SS-Pz.Div.,I Pz.Rgt.,9 Coy(engineer)Malmedy(Bel.)17.12.44	MURDER	U.S.
WEDELEIT	126455	M			Oscharfhr.,I SS Pz.Div.,I Pz.Rgt. Penal Unit I Pl.9 Coy, Malmedy (Bel.) 17.12.44	MURDER	U.S.
WEDEL	301909	M			Sturmbannfhr.,IV=,6 SS Geb.Div.Nord,20 Army,Finmark(Nor.)10.11.44	MURDER	NOR.
WEDEMEYER, Richard Wilhelm	307297	M			Member,Self Defence Org.(Selbstschutz)Turon Distr.(Lulkow village) (Pol.) 39-42	BRUTALITY	POL.
WEDES, Otto	194087	M		97	Cpl.,Army,Costelsarrasin (Fr.) 16.8.44	MURDER	FR.
WEDIG	136274	M	Ger.		Feldgend.,Feldgendarmerie,Stenay-Verdun(Fr.) 40-44	MURDER	FR.
WEDOF	250560	M			Gen. in command Venice to Ancona,Mesola and Ariano Polesine (It.) 12.44	INTERR.	U.K.
WEDRAL, Ferdinand	256708	M			Ger.Army, Zajecar (Yugo.) 41-44	INTERR.	YUGO.
WEES, Joseph	259260	M			Interpreter, Gestapo Poitiers, Antenne of Rochelle (Fr.) 40-44	MISC.CRIMES	FR.
WEFING see WELFING	158410						
WEGE	306815	M	Ger.		Capt.,C O Rutsko Bn of 896 R.I.,Kermassenet in Kervignac Morbahan (Fr.) 20.8.44	MURDER	FR.
WEGELE	11508	M			Pvt.,110 or 111 Pz.Gren.Rgt.,2 Coy,Albine (Fr.) 29.6.44	MURDER	FR.
WEGELIN	251730	M			Major Cmdt.,376 Inf.Rgt.,Vinct-Moigen (Bel.) 25.-31.5.40	BRUTALITY	BEL.
WEGENER	997	M			Dr.,Osturmfhr.,SS, Waffen-SS, 9.39-1.42	MURDER	POL.,UNWCC.
WEGENER	138283				Cashier, Gestapo section III Police question judiciaire, Lyon (Fr.)	MURDER	FR.
WEGENER	149592	M	Ger.		Sgt.,11 Pz.Div.,Pz.Aufklaerungs-Abt.2(South-West-Fr.)44	MURDER	FR.
WEGENER	164131	M	Ger.		Capt.,Airforce,Nydelstedt Krs.Diepholz(Ger.) 7.4.15	MURDER	U.K.
WEGENER	191355	M	Ger.		Capt.,7 Pol.Rgt.,3 Pol.Bn,10 Coy,Junkerdal(Nor.) 10.44	TORTURE	NOR.
WEGENER	125997	M	Ger.		Capt.,C.C.Compiegne of Royallieu (Fr.) 41-44	MURDER	FR.
WEGENER, Guenther	255860	M			Pvt.,C.C.Ellrich-Nordhausen(Ger.)	MURDER	U.S.
WEGENER, Gustav	162528	M		99	Capo, C.C.Buchenwald (Ger.) 41-44	TORTURE	U.S.
WEGENER, Karl	196912	M		3. 5.99	Butler, Luxembourg (Lux.) 40-45	PILLAGE	LUX.
WEGENER, Theodor	126413	M		14. 6.07	Civilian, locate but do not detain,Moers(Ger.) 17.2.45	MISC.CRIMES	U.S.
WEGER, Adolph	150812	M		10	Chief,Gestapo,Hanau(Ger.)	MURDER	U.S.
WEGERICH	166914	M		95	Cpl., 2 Coy,Inf.Bn631,Oferode (Ger.) 31.5. or 1.4.45	MURDER	FR.
WEGERIS	252801	M			Uscharfhr.,SD,section IV,Gestapo Toulouse (Fr.) 11.42-8.44	MISC.CRIMES	FR.
WEGESCHNEIDER	251451	M			Sgt.,Fieldpol.,Vendome (Fr.) 9.8.44	MURDER	FR.
WEGMANN, Richard	306724	M			Ger.Civilian, near Elm (Ger.) 28.5.44	MURDER	U.S.
WEGNER	11559	M			Reg.Oberinsp.,Reichskommissariat for Evacuations,Finmark(Nor.)44	MISC.CRIMES	NOR.
WEGNER	192437	M			SS-Sgt.,C.C.Flossenburg (Ger.) 44-45	SUSPECT	U.S.
WEGNER	196958	M			Member,SD,Kdo."Wenger", Baccarat,Etival (Fr.) Autumn 44	WITNESS	U.K.
WEGNER	300748	M			Pvt.,1 Aufkl.Abt.,3 Coy, 2 Col., XV Div. Afrika Korps, St.Leger Distr.Arlon (Bel.) 5.9.44	MISC.CRIMES	BEL.
WEGNER, Artur	255861	M			Pvt.,C.C.Ellrich-Nordhausen (Ger.)	MURDER	U.S.
WEGNER, Friedrich	151448	M	Ger.		Civilian,Weiwiocki-Chelmo (Pol.) 10.39	MURDER	U.K
WEGNER, Gustav	300730	M			Sturmbannfhr., commandet, guard,SS Bn, Area of Sachsenhausen(Ger.) 1.40-4.45	MURDER	U.K.
WEGNER, Hermann	253439	M	Ger.	77	Civilian, Stalag II B Krs.Stolp (Ger.) 10.44	BRUTALITY	U.S.
WEGNER, Kuno Ernst Friedrich	260500	M	Ger.	5. 3.12	Rottenfhr.,Waffen-SS,guard-Coy,C.C.Anschwitz(Pol.) 9.41-9.44	BRUTALITY	POL.
WEGNER, Otto	139246	M	Ger.		Scharfhr.,SA (since 43) Lensing (Aust.)	TORTURE	U.S.
WEGSCHNEIDER, Josef	255862	M			Flyer, C.C.Ellrich-Nordhausen (Ger.)	MURDER	U.S.
WEH, Albert	998	M			Dr.,leader, Public official,Amt fuer Gesetzgebung-Gen.Gov. Warschau(Pol.) 9.39-43	MISC.CRIMES	POL.
WEHHOFER	256561	M			Major, Schutzpol.,Gradetin u.Nisch (Serb.) 7.43	MISC.CRIMES	YUGO.
WEHLE, Otto	11509	M			Pvt.,Army,110' or 111 Pz.Gren.Rgt.,2 Coy, Albine (Fr.) 29.6.44	MURDER	FR.
WEHLER, Hermann	139726	M	Ger.		Guard,Waffen-SS, C.C.	MURDER	U.S.
WEHMAYER	121685	M	Ger.	06	Officer, Gestapo Chambery, Challes les Eaux,Arbin (Fr.)	MURDER	FR.
WEHMAYER or WEHMEHLER	136275	M	Ger.	07	Oscharfhr.,SS,SD, Chambery (Fr.)	TORTURE	FR.
WEHMAYER, Horst	255768	M		1.10.25	Flyer, C.C.Ellrich-Nordhausen (Ger.)	MURDER	U.S.
WEHMELER see WEHMELER	136275						
WEHNELT, Richard	193126	M	Ger.	31..1.07	Sgt.,guard,Reichsjustizministerium Feldstraflg.,C.C.Finmark(Nor.) 42-45		
WEHNER	300558	M	Ger.		Member,Sachbearbeiter,SD, Sicherheitspol., Amsterdam(Neth.)24.3.44	MISC.CRIMES	NOR.,YUGO.
						MURDER	NETH.

WEH-WEI

NAME	C.R.FILE NUMBER	SEX	NATIO-NALITY	DATE OF BIRTH	RANK OCCUPATION UNIT PLACE AND DATE OF CRIME	REASON WANTED	WANTED BY
WEHNER	301876	M	Ger.		In charge of special operations Einsatzstab Rosenberg, Paris (Fr.) 40-44	PILLAGE	FR.
WEHNER	305961	M	Ger.		Osturmfhr., SS, Leading Official of Department of the SD, Leitabschnitt, Prague (Czech.) Oswiecim, C.C.Birkenau (Pol.) 39-45	MURDER	CZECH.
WEHNER, Ernst	11546	M	Ger.		Leader, Aussendienststst. d.Sipo, Alkmaar (Neth.) 44	MURDER	NETH.
WEHOVSKI, Alfred	253168	M	Ger.	25.5.82	Barrister,-Civilian, Bruenn (Czech.) 39-45	MISC.CRIMES	CZECH.
WEHRES, Robert	67733	M	Ger.	1.3.08 or 1.7.09	Officer, Army, Neuvic, Espinasse, St.Martin de Riberae (Fr.)	MURDER	FR.
WEHRES, Robert	194678	M	Ger.		Agent, Gestapo, Chateau Leveque (Fr.) 20.6.44	MURDER	FR.
WEHRLE	1357	M	Ger.		305.Div.,578.Gr.,5.Coy. 1 Cpl. -	MISC.CRIMES	U.K.
WEHRMANN	251727	M	Ger.		Lt., 1.Bn.Inf. 377.Jaeger-Rgt., Vinkt Meigem.(Bel.) 25.-31.5.40	MISC.CRIMES	BEL.
WEHRMANN	261185	M	Ger.		Member, Staff of C.C. Ravensbruck (Ger.)	SUSPECT	BEL.
WEHRMANN, T.	259845	M		3.9.04	Member, SD, SS, Leader, NSV, stationed at Hertogenbosch, Raamsdon Kveer Noord Brabant (Neth.) 9.44	PILLAGE	NETH.
WEHRMEISTER, Hans	251414	M	Ger.		Wachtmeister, Police-Bn.72, Rouen (Fr.) 6.40-7.40	MISC.CRIMES	FR.
WEHRMUTH	196841	M	Ger.		Zugwachtmstr., 8.Coy. Schupo, Arnheim (Neth.) 9.45	INTERR.	NETH.
WEHRSTEDT	251434	M	Ger.		N.CO., Fort de Seclin (Fr.) 29.-30.8.44	MURDER	FR.
WEIAND, Werner	181124	M	Ger.		SS-Mann, SS-Leibstandarte A.H., Aufkl.Abt., Renard - Mont Stavelot (Bel.) 19.12.44	MURDER	BEL.
WEIBEL	262157	M	Ger.		Schfhr., SS, Gestapo, Rouen (Fr.) 41-44	MURDER	FR.
WEIBEL, Oscar	11510	M	Ger.		Lt., SS-Div. Der Fuehrer, Oradour (Fr.) 29.6.44	MURDER	FR.
WEIBER	259232	M	Ger.		Kapo, Ger.Prisoner, Auschwitz (Pol.) 40	MURDER	FR.
WEIBGEN, Hans	10967	M	Ger.		Dr., Standartenfhr., Waffen-SS, Stand.108, Abwehr, Leader of the Werwolf-Organization, Prague (Czech.) 39-44	MURDER	U.S., CZECH.
WEIBRAUCH (or WEYRAUCH)	128933	M			Schfhr., SS, C.C. Weimar-Buchenwald (Ger.)	TORTURE	U.S.
WEICHBILLIG, Jacob	168024	M	Ger.		N.C.O., C.C. Mauthausen (Aust.) 4.44	TORTURE	FR.
WEICHELSDORFER, Karl	194162	M	Ger.		Major, Capt. SS, C.C. Admin., Buchenwald (Ger.) 42-45	TORTURE	U.S.
WEICHENBERGER, Theodor	259844	M	Ger.	30.7.07	SS, 1.Zug, 2.Gruppe, Probably stationed at Bergeyk Prov.Noord Brabant (Neth.) 11.9.44	MURDER	NETH.
WEICHFOLD	306664	M	Ger.		Bde.Chief, 05-243 Mongolian "Oberland" Unit, St.Nazaire en Royans (Fr.) 20.7.-5.8.44	MURDER	FR.
WEICHS	166720	M	Ger.	85	Feldmarschall, Army (Yugo.) 41-44	MURDER	U.S.
WEICHSEL	188259	M	Ger.		Army, Rundstedt-Offensive, Tavigny (Bel.) 12.-17.5.44	MISC.CRIMES	BEL.
WEICHSELDORFER, Karl	306405	M	Ger.		SS-Lt., C.C., Buchenwald (Ger.) 16.5.38-9.10.43	MURDER	BEL.
WEICK	305525	M	Ger.	13	Schfhr., Special in Jewish Affairs, attached to the Political Section at the Gestapo Limoges, Hte.-Vienne de Gironde (Fr.) 40-45	MURDER	FR.
WEICKE	302010	M	Ger.		Member, SD, Guard at the SD Camp Vught, Ravenstein (Neth.) 5.44-9.44	MURDER	NETH.
WEIDA, Max	192991	M	Ger.		Allgemeine SS Totenkopfverband, C.C. Buchenwald (Ger.) 42-45	TORTURE	U.S.
WEIDEMAN	1355	M			Pvt., Army, 9.P.G.R.	MISC.CRIMES	U.K.
WEIDEMANN, Johannes	240038	M	Ger.	15.8.87	Dr., Oberbuergermeister, Vice-President, NSDAP, Deutscher Parteitag, Halle, Leipzig, Muenchen, Berlin (Ger.) - 44	MISC.CRIMES	UNWCC
WEIDEMANN, Karl	162620	M	Ger.	12	Obersturmfhr., Waffen-SS, C.C. Sasel (Ger.)	MURDER	U.K.
WEIDEN (or MULLER, or WEIDEN-MULLER)	262156	M	Ger.		Sturmschfhr., SS, Gestapo, Rennes (Fr.) 43-44	MISC.CRIMES	FR.
WEIDENBACH	250555	M	Ger.		Osturmfhr., SD, Vaassen near Epe (Neth.) 3.5.43	MURDER	NETH.
WEIDENMULLER (see WEIDEN)	262156						
WEIDER, Ursule	306665	F	Ger.		05-243 Mongolian "Oberland" Unit, St. Nazaire en Royans (Fr.) 20.7.-5.8.44	MURDER	FR.
WEIDERBAIN	142712	M			Lt., Army, 2.Panz.Armee, Chanas (Fr.) 44	MURDER	FR.
WEIDERMANN	67735	M			Stabsarzt, Stalag XX A, Graudenz, Thorn (Pol.) 1.43-4.44	MURDER	U.K.
WEIDERMANN	173842	M	Ger.		Police-President, Police, C.C. Prague, Auschwitz-Birkenau (Czech.) (Pol.) 39-45	MURDER	CZECH.
WEIDICH (or WEIDIG)	149687	M			SS-Guard, C C, Ehrlich and Gärdelegen (Ger.) 4.-14.4.45	MURDER	U.S.
WEIDICH, Gustav	193528	M	Ger.	8.6.96	Uschfhr., SS, 4.SS-Totenkopf-Stuba., C.C. Dora-Mittelbau, Nordhausen (Ger.) 43-45	MURDER	U.S.
WEIDIG (see WEIDICH)	149687						
WEIDINGER	174491	M			Unterarzt, Stalag 383, C.C. Hohenfels (Ger.)	TORTURE	U.K.
WEIDINGER	195995	M	Ger.		Standartenfhr., SS-Div. Das Reich, SS-Rgt. Der Fuehrer, Tulle (Fr.) 9.6.44	MURDER	FR.
WEIDINGER, Richard	195003	M	Ger.	31.1.88	Guard, C.C. Vranovska Ves, Danzig (Czech., Ger.) 38-45	MISC.CRIMES	CZECH.
WEIDLER	300749	M			N.C.O., 1.Aufkl.Abt., 3.Coy, 2.Column, XV.Div. of the Africa-Corps, Saint Leger l-Arion (Bel.) 5.9.44	MISC.CRIMES	BEL.
WEIDLICH	162524	M	Ger.	95	Capt., Security-Guard, Army, C.C. Buchenwald (Ger.) 44	TORTURE	U.S.
WEIDLICH	173851	M	Ger.		Interpreter, Ortskommandantur, Cacak (Yugo.) 42-44	MURDER	YUGO.
WEIDLICH	191967	M	Ger.		Major, SD-Chief, Region Lyonnaise (Fr.) 40-45	MISC.CRIMES	FR.
WEIDLICH	193447	M	Ger.		Capt., Lds.Schtz.Ers.Bn.11 190.-190.P.W.Pion.Bn., 3210.Coy., O.C., Brønne Rognan (Nor.) 7.44	WITNESS	NOR.
WEIDLICH	194085	M	Ger.		Civilian, St.Rambert (Fr.) 27.44	MURDER	FR.
WEIDLICH, Otto	259847	M	Ger.	5.8.06	Rottfhr., SS, 2.Group, 1.Zug, Probably stationed at Bergeyk, Noord Brabant (Neth.) 11.9.44	MURDER	NETH.
WEIDLING	253459	M	Ger.		Lt., Fieldpolice, Romilly sur Seine Aube (Fr.) 10.6.44	MISC.CRIMES	FR.
WEIDLING	305366	M	Ger.		Lt., Head of Truppe 744 Feldgend., Romilly sur Seine, Troyes and Region (Fr.) 3.10.43-22.8.44	MURDER	FR.
WEIDMANN	162533	M	Ger.		Civilian (Ger.)	WITNESS	U.S.
WEIDMANN	162574	M	Ger.	00	Rottfhr., SS, Section F Personnel, C.C. Buchenwald (Ger.) 44-45	TORTURE	U.S.
WEIDMANN	301238	M	Ger.		Hptschfhr., SS, Crim.Secr., Leiter d.Abt.IV B.4, Judentum, SD Brussels (Bel.) 6.40-9.44	MURDER	BEL.
WEIDMANN, Artur	306296	M	Ger.		Member, Gestapo at Trencin, Oswiecim, C.C. Birkenau (Pol.) 39-45	MURDER	CZECH.
WEIDMANN, Fritz	196459	M	Ger.	16.6.03	Gend., Fieldpolice 625, Fresnes-au-Mont (Fr.) 22.8.44	MURDER	FR.
WEIDMANN, Hans	196434	M	Ger.	15	Lt., SS-Officer-School, Bresse, St.Maurice-Moselle (Fr.) 11.9.44	TORTURE	FR.
WEIDMANN, Ludwig	255764	M	Ger.	9.2.19	Cpl., C.C., Rottlsberode, Nordhausen (Ger.)	MURDER	U.S.
WEIDMANN, Otto	11512	M	Ger.		Pvt., Army, 110.or 111.Pz.Gren.Rgt., 2.Coy., Albine (Fr.)	MURDER	FR.

WEI-WEI

NAME	C.R.FILE NUMBER	SEX	NATIO-NALITY	DATE OF BIRTH	RANK OCCUPATION UNIT PLACE AND DATE OF CRIME	REASON WANTED	WANTED BY
WEIDMANN, Robert	11511	M	Ger.		Agent, Gestapo, Sizun (Fr.) 6.7.44	MURDER	FR.
WEIDNER	190400	M	Ger.		Employee, Crim.police, Wiesbaden (Ger.) 43-45	TORTURE	U.S.
WEIDNER	258994	M			Cpl., 2.Coy., 1559.Nachr.Abt. 559.Volksgren.Div., Fr. 10.44	MURDER	U.S.
WEIDT, Werner	255220	M	Ger.	05	C.O., Hafenueberwachungsstelle, Hoek van Holland, Wassenaar nr. the Hague (Neth.) 17.11.44	WITNESS	NETH.
WEIGAND	150803	M	Ger.		Sgt., 7.Panz.Rgt. Repl.Training Bn., Freilassing (Ger.) 16.4.45	WITNESS	U.S.
WEIGAND	191354	M	Ger.		Sonderfhr., Interpreter, 184.POW working Bn., Bassis Tunnel (Nor.)	WITNESS	NOR.
WEIGAND	195912	M	Ger.		Leader, Prof. of chemistry, Strassburg (Fr.)	MURDER	FR.
WEIGAND	900750	M	Ger.		Pvt.,1.Aufkl.Abt., 3.Coy., 2.Col. XV.Div.Africa-Corps, St. Leger (Arlon) 5.9.44	MISC.CRIMES	BEL.
WEIGAND, Konrad	906406	M	Ger.		SS Sgt., C.C. Buchenwald (Ger.) 16.5.38-9.10.43	MURDER	BEL.
WEIGAND, Ludwig	195994	M			Cpl., Barbezieux (Fr.)	MURDER	FR.
WEIGANT, Otto	150891	M	Ger.	00	Farmer, Member NSDAP, Klopenheim nr. Wiesbaden (Ger.) 43-45	TORTURE	POL.
WEIGEN, (S)	134716	M			SS Oberfhr., SS Sec.Police Wehrkreis XIII, Ger. 43-45	MISC.CRIMES	U.S.
WEIGEL	192990	M	Ger.		Sgt., SS, C.C. Buchenwald (Ger.) 42-45	MURDER	U.S.
WEIGEL	196743	M	Ger.		Sturmbannfhr., C.C. Neuengamme (Ger.)	TORTURE	BEL.
WEIGEL	258067	M	Ger.		Osturmbannfhr., Waffen SS, Benesov (Czech.) 7.5.45	MURDER	CZECH.
WEIGEL	900751	M	Ger.		Pvt.,1.Aufkl.Abt., 3.Coy., 2.Col. XV.Div. Africa-Corps, St.Leger (Arlon) 5.9.44	MISC.CRIMES	BEL.
WEIGEL, Gerhard	195378	M	Ger.		SS Sturmbannfhr., C.C. Sachsenhausen (Ger.)	MURDER	BEL. CZECH.
WEIGELT, Ernst	162594	M	Ger.	90	SS Sturmscharfhr., Weapons SS Sec.I, C.C. Buchenwald (Ger.) 42-45	SUSPECT	U.S.
WEIGELT, Heinz	255767	M		20.9.22	Cpl., C.C. Harzungen, Nordhausen (Ger.)	MURDER	U.S.
WEIGELT, Paul	195993	M	Ger.	96	Agent, SD, Maisons Laffitte, Seine et Oise (Fr.) 15.12.41-10.6.44	MURDER	FR.
WEIGELT, Willi	255766	M		19.1.26	Flyer, C.C. Ellrich, Nordhausen (Ger.)	MURDER	U.S.
WEIGERS	153466	M	Ger.		Sturmscharfhr., Waffen SS, Enschede (Neth.)	MURDER	U.K.
WEIGL, Martin	255765	M		2.11.00	Cpl., C.C. Ellrich, Nordhausen (Ger.)	MURDER	U.S.
WEIGLEIN	162530	M			Pvt., Army, Leipzig, Torgau (Ger.)	TORTURE	U.S.
WEIHAS	191008	M			SS Hptscharfhr., C.C. Mauthausen (Aust.) 41-45	TORTURE	U.S.
WEIHE	30359	M	Ger.	92	Sgt., Waffen SS Totenkopfverband, C.C. Flossenburg (Ger.) 44	MURDER	FR.
WEIHERS	21436	M	Ger.		Civ., Castrop-Rauxel (Ger.), 15.5.45	TORTURE	U.S.
WEIHOLD	258175	M	Ger.		Capt., Schupo, Village de Brzane (Yugo.) 7.-8.41	MURDER	YUGO.
WEIHRAUCH	195977	M	Ger.		Lt., Scharfschuetzen-Ausbildungs-Coy. 64 R, Mugron Lahosse (Fr.) 8.-12.7.44	MURDER	FR.
WEIHRAUCH, Heinrich	194879	M		25.7.11	SS Hptscharfhr., Gestapo, SS, Kolin (Czech.) 39-45	MURDER	CZECH.
WEIHRE, Richard	131007	M			Civ., C.C. Mauthausen (Aust.) 41-45	MURDER	U.S.
WEIHSELDORFER, Karl	162592	M	Ger.	10	SS Sturmbannfhr., C.C. Buchenwald (Ger.) 10.40	TORTURE	U.S.
WEIKEL	149593	M	Ger.		Major, 11.Panz.Div. 15.Panz.Rgt., South-west Fr., 44	MURDER	FR.
WEIKER, Karl	166913	M	Ger.		Sgt., Army, Rgt. 1210, 159. I.D., Cernay (Fr.) 45	MURDER	FR.
WEIKERT	191966	M			Adjutant, Army, Schuetzen-Bn. 981, 4.Coy., Welferding-Moselle (Fr.) 6.1.44	MURDER	FR.
WEIKIM	194158	M			Local group-leader NSDAP, Sandhofen (Ger.) 12.44	TORTURE	POL.
WEIL	146749	M			SS Scharfhr., C.C. Flossenburg (Ger.)	TORTURE	U.S.
WEIL	173850	M	Ger.		Rittmeister, Cosak-Div., Croatia (Yugo.) 11.43-8.44	MURDER	YUGO.
WEIL	256803	M	Ger.		German Military Government, Lask (Pol.) 41	MURDER	POL.
WEIL see WEILL	195996						
WEIL, Charlie see WEIL, Otto	189131						
WEIL, Hermann	256059	M			Kapo, C.C. Flossenburg (Ger.)	BRUTALITY	FR.
WEIL, Otto or WEIL, Charlie or WEBER, Oskar Felix	189131	M		31.9.11	Cpl., Abwehr official, Abwehrtrupp 363, Liege (Bel.) 45	TORTURE	U.S.
WEIL, Wilhelm	255673	M			Pvt., C.C. Ellrich, Nordhausen (Ger.)	MURDER	U.S.
WEILAND	181126	M	Ger.		SS Osturmfhr., SS Leibstandarte Adolf Hitler, 1.Panz.Gren.Div.9.Coy. Stavelot (Bel.) 19.-20.12.44	MURDER	BEL.
WEILAND	260097	M	Ger.		Lt. Cmdt., Detachment of Transmission, Massif of Vercors, Isere and Drome (Fr.) 20.7.-5.8.44	SUSPECT	FR.
WEILAND, Richard	905976	M	Ger.		Adjutant, Interpreter, Exquiule-Basses Pyrenees (Fr.) 10.7.44	PILLAGE	FR.
WEILANDS, Truda	158411	F	Ger.		Civ. Farmworker, Lichnau Konitz (Ger.) 10.6.44	INTERR.	U.K.
WEILBACH	146744	M			Kapo, Stone quarry, C.C. Flossenburg (Ger.) 5.44-4.45	TORTURE	BEL. U.S.
WEILER	6119	M			SS Hptsturmfhr., SS Div."Das Reich", Rgt."Der Fuehrer", Buzet (Fr.)7.44	MURDER	FR.
WEILER	192699	M	Ger.		Lagerfuehrer, C.C. Buchenwald (Ger.)	TORTURE	FR.
WEILER, Heinrich	905367	M	Ger.		Commando chief, Prison Monsheim nr. Rollwald (Fr.) 45	MISC.CRIMES	FR.
WEILER	166974	M			SS Osturmfhr., Teacher, Bruehl (Ger.) 17.1.45	TORTURE	U.N.W.C.C.
WEILER, Walter	199120	M		27.1.07	Ex convict, Reichsjustizministerium, Feldstraflager, C.C. Finmark (Nor.) 42-45	WITNESS	YUGO.NOR.
WEILERSHUS	159468	M	Ger.		Lt., Gestapo, Brive (Fr.) 44	MURDER	FR.
WEILHART, Ernst	11514	M	Ger.		Pvt., Army, 2.Coy. 110. or 111.Panz.Gren.Rgt., Albine (Fr.) 29.6.44	MURDER	FR.
WEILL or WEIL	195996	M	Ger.		Capt., Guingamp, Cotes du Nord (Fr.) 44	MURDER	FR.
WEILL, Hermann	162531	M		03	Oberfeldrichter, Reich, Military Comt., Leipzig (Ger.)	MURDER	U.S.
WEILER	250545	M	Ger.		Chief, Equipment, Monsheim (Ger.)	BRUTALITY	FR.
WEIMANN	153469	M			Member Gestapo, Rodez (Fr.) 8.8.44	MURDER	FR.
WEIMAR, Herbert	255669	M		20	Pvt., C.C. Harzungen, Nordhausen (Ger.)	MURDER	U.S.
WEIMBERGER	260968	M	Ger.		Owner, Civ. Coal firm, Nuernberg (Ger.)	BRUTALITY	POL.
WEIMER alias SKEGER	999				Lt.Col., Stalag 20 A, C.C. Thorn (Pol.) 7.40	MURDER	U.N.W.C.C. U.K.
WEIMER, Karl Ludwig	149688			00	SS Hptsturmfhr., Camp commander, C.C. Hirzenhain (Ger.) 25.-26.3.45	MURDER	U.S.
WEIN	190962	M	Ger.	43	Official, Gestapo, Bukovo (Yugo.) 43	MURDER	YUGO.
WEINART	195976	M	Ger.		Sgt., Parachute-Pion.Bn. 8, St.Amand Montrond (Fr.) 8.6.44	MURDER	FR.
WEINART	104970	M	Ger.		Capt., Airforce, Stalag Luft 4 Kiefheide C.C. (Ger.) 8.44-3.45	WITNESS	U.S.
WEINBERGER see WYNBERGER	124057						
WEINBERGER	186859	M	Ger.		SS Rapportfuehrer, C.C. Spephanskirchen bei Rosenheim (Ger.)	TORTURE	FR.
WEINBERGER, Josef	252804	M		23	Cpl., D.A.U.A 709.Inf.Rgt., St.Sauvier (Fr.) 7.6.44	MURDER	U.S.
WEINBERGER, Rudolf	255671	M			Pvt., C.C. Ellrich, Nordhausen (Ger.)	MURDER	U.S.
WEINBERGER, Willi	194688	M			Member Gestapo, Paris (Fr.) 9.6.44	TORTURE	FR.
WEINDISCH, Johann	252828	M	Ger.	05	Pvt., 3.Coy. 891.Landesschutzen-Bn., Retznei (Aust.) 5.2.42	INTERR.	U.K.
	193669			91	SS Uscharfhr., 4.SS Totenkopf-Stuba, C.C.Dora-Mittelbau Nordhausen, Auschwitz (Ger.,Pol.)	WITNESS	U.S.

NAME	C.R.FILE NUMBER	SEX	NATIO- NALITY	DATE OF BIRTH	RANK OCCUPATION UNIT PLACE AND DATE OF CRIME	REASON WANTED	WANTED BY
WEINECKE, Fritz	255670	M			Pvt., C.C. Harzungen, Nordhausen (Ger.)	MURDER	U.S.
WEINELT, Wilhelm	29650	M	Ger.		Landgerichtsrat, Ministry of Justiz, Prague (Czech.) 40	MURDER	CZECH.
WEINER	21435	M	Ger.		SS-Obersturmfhr., SS 12.SS Pz.Div.(H.J.)	MISC.CRIMES	CAN.
WEINER	301985	M	Ger.		SS-Hptsturmfhr., Oslo and surroundings (Nor.) 44	MURDER	NOR.
WEINER, Bonifacius	259158	M	Ger.		SS-Untersturmfhr., SS Dachau (Ger.) 10.42-45	MISC.CRIMES	YUGO.
WEINERT	46221	M	Ger.		Lt. Colonel, Army, Landsul (Fr.) 30.4.44	MURDER	FR.
WEINERT	128782	M	Ger.		Capt., Stalag Official Luft IV, Gross Tychow, Fallingbostel (Ger.) 6.2.45-1.4.45	MISC.CRIMES	U.K.
WEINERT	256565	M	Ger.		Lt. Col., Army, Braudrion and Landsul (Fr.) 30.4.44	MURDER	FR.
WEINERTH, Friedrich	196014	M	Ger.	15. 9.85	NSDAP, Amstetten (Aust.) 20.3.45	MISC.CRIMES	U.S.
WEINFURTNER, Wolfgang	137594	M	Ger.		Pvt., Army, Art. 999, 3de., Honsfeld (Bel.) 17.12.44	WITNESS	U.S.
WEINGAERTNER, Michael	153462	M	Ger.	30. 9.08	Oberscharfhr., W.-SS,.Totenkopf-Stuba, C.C. Auschwitz, Kreischenberg Buchenwald (Ger.Pol.),42	MURDER	U.S.
WEINGAERTNER	153458	M			Technical Sgt., W.-SS, Schlossberg (Ger.) 29.4.45	MURDER	U.S.
WEINGERTNER, Michel	136399	M			SS-Guard, CC Helmbrechts (Ger.) 7.44-19.4.45	MURDER	U.S.
WEINGRILL, Karl	255672	M		15. 1.15	Flyer, C.C. Ellrich, Nordhausen (Ger.)	MURDER	U.S.
WEINHUEBEL	305962	M			Obersturmfhr., C.C. Oranienburg (Ger.) 11.39-45	MURDER	CZECH.
WEINICH, Albert	255804	M			C.C. Buchenwald (Ger.)	BRUTALITY	U.S.
WEINKAM, Lise	187853	F	Ger.		Wes. Army, Bruchsal (Ger.) 2.-9.2.45	WITNESS	U.S.
WEINKOFF see GAUTHIER,Wolfram	257479						
WEINLEIN, Alfred	255665	M			Pvt., C.C. Harzungen, Nordhausen (Ger.)	MURDER	U.S.
WEINMAN, Erich	62442	M	Ger.		SS-Standartenfhr., SS Head of security-Police, (Czech.)	TORTURE	U.N.W.C.C.
WEINMANN	10968	M			Crim.Asst., Gestapo 2-B, Prague (Czech.) .39-44	TORTURE	CZECH.
WEINMANN	179841	M			Befehlshaber, Sipo, C.C. Auschwitz, Birkenau (Pol.) 39-45	MURDER	CZECH.
WEINMANN	187757	M			Dr., SS Standartenfhr., SS Wehrkreis Boehmen und Maehren (Czech.)	TORTURE	U.N.W.C.C.
WEINMANN, S.	189822	M			Dr., SS-Sturmbannfhr., SS, Ljubljana (Yugo.) 4.41-44	MURDER	YUGO.
WEINPRECHT	136405	M			Kreisleiter, NSDAP, Karlsruhe (Ger.) 3.3.45	MURDER	U.S.
WEINRAUCH	192989	M			Sgt., SS, C.C. Buchenwald (Ger.) 43-45	MURDER	U.S.
WEINRICH, Felix or Max	137535	M			SS-Sonderfhr., Member, SS, Gestapo, Lassault (Fr.) 4.8.44	MURDER	U.S.
WEINRICH, Hans	306192	M	Ger.		Hauptsturmfhr., C.C. Kahla (Ger.) 40-45	MURDER	BEL.
WEINRICH, Konrad	142714	M	Ger.		Tinsmith, Civilian, Badersleben (Ger.) 12.9.44	MURDER	IT.,U.S.
WEINTZEL	132590	M			Major, Chief of Service of Gestapo, Paris (Fr.)	MURDER	FR.
WEINZIERL	301609	M			C.C. Mauthausen (Aust.) 40-45	MURDER	BEL.
WEIR	167004	M			Techn.Sgt., Army, Berga-Elster, (Ger.) 2.45	MURDER	U.S.
WEIRANTER	28859	M	Ger.		Lt.Col. 20.Army, 137 Geb.Jaeg.Regt. 2. Geb.Div., Finmark (Nor.)11.44	MURDER	U.N.W.C.C.
WEIRE	192988	M	Ger.		Cpl. SS, Buchenwald (Ger.) 42-45	TORTURE	U.S.
WEIRENER	188767	M			Paris (Fr.) 19.8.44	MURDER	FR.
WEIRICH, Fritz	252648	M			Pvt., Unit 09899 A, Avelgem (Bel.) 6.9.44	WITNESS	BEL.
WEIRMSLER	153463	M			Sgt., Arbeitskdo. 101 E., Eisleben (Ger.) 8.44	TORTURE	U.K.
WEIS	196429	M			Pvt., I.Ps.Div. L.A.H.2.Pz.Gren.Regt.II. Coy., Malmedy (Bel.)17.12.44	MURDER	U.S.
WEIS	250554	M			Chief, Prison of Frankenthal, Neuengamme (Ger.) 44-45	BRUTALITY	FR.
WEIS	251428	M			Dr., Krefet-Factory, Gewelaberg (Ger.) 43	MURDER	FR.
WEIS, Andre	169772	M			Civilian, Directeur, Weiden (Ger.)	TORTURE	FR.
WEIS, Martin	139253	M	Ger.	02	Obersturmbannfhr., Lublin (Pol.) 42	MURDER	U.S.
WEIS, Martin Jakob	258881	M	Ger.	25. 1.87	Mayor, Luxembourg (Lux.)	SUSPECT	LUX.
WEISBACH	190008	M			Sgt., Prison C.C. Loos (Ger.) 23.9.40-8.3.41	MISC.CRIMES	U.K.
WEISBACH, Wilhelm	192226	M	Ger.	06	Cpl., Anatomy Institut, Danzig (Pol.)	TORTURE	POL.
WEISE	6123	M			SS-Doctor, SS Div."Das Reich" Regt. "Der Fuehrer", Buzet (Fr.)7.7.44	MURDER	FR.
WEISE	139731	M			Major, Ordnungs-Schutz-Polizei, Lemberg (Pol.) 40-44	MISC.CRIMES	U.S.
WEISE	175690	F	Ger.		Gauleiterin,B.D.M., Strasbourg (Fr.) 44	TORTURE	FR.
WEISE	300752	M	Ger.		Pvt., I.Aufkl.Abt. 3. Coy.2nd.Column XV Div.of the Afrika Korps Saint Leger (Arlon) (Bel.) 5.9.44	MISC.CRIMES	BEL.
WEISE	305749	M	Ger.		N.C.O., Caucasian Regt. of Volunteers, Fieldpost No.121700 Gambounee, Tarn (Fr.) 28.7.44	MURDER	FR.
WEISE, Adalbert	262266	M	Ger.		Dr., SS-Sturmbannfhr., Gestapo, Rennes (Fr.) 43-44	SUSPECT	FR.
WEISE, Erich	259283	M			Police Secretary, Police Camp, Thekla near Leipzig (Ger.) 18.4.45	MURDER	U.S.
WEISE, Kurt	255666	M		14. 1.07	Driver, C.C. Harzungen, Nordhausen (Ger.)	MURDER	U.S.
WEISE, Paul	185939	M	Ger.		Officer, Army, Geraards-Bergen (Bel.) 1.9.43	WITNESS	BEL.
WEISEL, Karl Heinz	260209	M	Ger.		Head of Dep. III. Of Ministry of Labor (Sauckel)	MISC.CRIMES	U.S.
WEISEMANN	197675	M	Ger.		Member, Engineer, NSDAP, Factory, 715.Arb.Kdo. Auschwitz (Pol.)2.44	TORTURE	U.K.
WEISENBORN	142716	M	Ger.		Hauptsturmfhr., Camp-Commander, W.-SS, Buchenwald (Ger.)	TORTURE	U.S.
WEISENBORN, Hans	195975	M			Sgt., Geheime Feld-Polizei, Zwolle (Neth.) 9.44	MURDER	NETH.
WEISENSEHL	193095	M			Schupo, C.C., Falstad (Nor.) 41-44	MURDER	NOR.
WEISER	306666	M			Adj., 05-243 Mongolian "Oberland" Unit, St.Nazaire en Royans (Fr.) 20.7.-5.8.44	MURDER	FR.
WEISER, Emma	185934	F	Ger.	97	Kreisabteilungsleiterin, NSV, NSDAP, Marianske, Lagne (Czech.)39-45	MISC.CRIMES	CZECH.
WEISER, Eric	261786	M	Ger.		Driver, Gestapo of Amiens, Gentelles (Fr.) 6.-8.44	MURDER	FR.
WEISERMANN see WEISSEMANN	186864						
WEISFLOCH, Hans	133309	M		07	Sturmscharfhr., W.-SS, RSHA, Lager, Langenzenn, Nuernberg (Ger.)43. 4.45	TORTURE	U.S.
WEISGERBER	149594	M			Cpl. II.Ps.Div. 2.Gruppe "Kampfgruppe Wilde", South-West France 44	MURDER	FR.
WEISHAUPT	123994	M		99	Sgt., Geheime Feld-Polizei, Lille (Fr.)	MURDER	U.K.
WEISKOEPPEL	175689	M			Ministry of Labour, Osnarbeitsamt, Strasbourg (Fr.) 44	TORTURE	FR.
WEISKOPF, Ernst	29651	M			Dr., Landgerichtsrat, Public Official, Opava (Czech.) 40	MURDER	CZECH.
WEISMANN, Harald	156731	M	Ger.		SS-Hauptsturmfhr., SS Gestapo, Kladno (Czech.) 27.9.41-9.7.42	MURDER	CZECH.
WEISMINGER, Georges	192439	M			Guard, C.C. Oberdingen (Ger.) 43-45	MURDER	BEL.
WEISMULLER, Paul	187456	M			SS Guard, SD, SS, Frankfurt (Ger.)	TORTURE	U.S.
WEISS	1002	M			SS Sturmbannfhr., C.C. Maidaneck (Pol.) 4.44	MURDER	POL.
WEISS	1009	M			Lt., Army, 738.Regt., 2.Battr.3. Coy.7.43	MURDER	YUGO.
WEISS	21438	M			Officer, Camp Official, Dachau Compiegne (Ger.,Fr.)	TORTURE	U.S.
WEISS	21439	M	Ger.		SS Hauptsturmm., C.C. Oranienburg (Ger.)	WITNESS	U.S.
WEISS	29641	M	Ger.		Adjutant, Army, Kerbabu near Lannilis (Fr.) 6.-9.8.44	MURDER	FR.
WEISS	29642	M	Ger.		Dr., Oberlandesgerichtsrat, Public Official, Prague (Czech.)40	MURDER	CZECH.
WEISS	120561	M	Ger.	00-05	Wachtmeister, Schutz-Polizei, Aken (Ger.) 7.44	MURDER	U.S.

NAME	C.R. FILE NUMBER	SEX	NATIO-NALITY	DATE OF BIRTH	RANK	OCCUPATION	UNIT	PLACE AND DATE OF CRIME	REASON WANTED	WANTED BY
WEISS	121673	M	Ger.		Sgt., Feldgendarmerie, Truppe 754, D'Appenay, St. Aubin, (Fr.) 16.6.44				PILLAGE	FR.
WEISS	131586	M	Ger.		Oschfhr., SS, C.C., Flossenburg (Ger.)				TORTURE	U.S.
WEISS	138276	M	Ger.		Sgt., SS, chief Gestapo, Lyon (Fr.)				MURDER	FR.
WEISS	141621	M	Ger.		Guard, Kommando 1066, CIC, Gross-Bodungen (Ger.)				MURDER	FR.
WEISS (alias: WISE)	142067	M	Ger.	10	Cpl., guard, Stalag IX B, Bad Orb (Ger.) 12.44-4.45				WITNESS	U.S.
WEISS	153460	M			Constable, police, Daasdorf, Guthmannshausen (Ger.) 7.-8.44				MURDER	U.S.
WEISS	153464	M	Ger.		Engineer, Arbeitskommando 121, Civilian, Gems (Aust.) 4.-10.44				TORTURE	U.K.
WEISS	158988	M	Ger.		Adjutant, Art. Einheit, Lannilis (Fr.) 6.8.44				MURDER	FR.
WEISS	166911	M	Ger.		Doctor, civilian, Gevelsberg				MURDER	FR.
WEISS	168233	M	Ger.		Adjutant, Kerbabu near Lannilis (Fr.) 6.-9 8.44				MURDER	FR.
WEISS	173840	M	Ger.		Commandant, C.C., Auschwitz, Birkenau (Pol.) 39-45				MURDER	CZECH.
WEISS	175702	M	Ger.		Pvt., Army, Thiers (Fr.) 25.8.44				PILLAGE	FR.
WEISS	177548	M	Ger.	10	Officer, Gestapo, C.C., Neubrenn (Ger.) 43				TORTURE	FR., U.K.
WEISS	177553	M			Employee, Gestapo, Saarbruecken (Ger.)				MURDER	U.N.W.C.C.
WEISS	177799	M	Ger.		Sgt., Army, Ebnet (Ger.) 3.45				MURDER	U.S.
WEISS	178763	M	Ger.	00	Sgt., 4. Coy. 1714 Landesschuetzen Bn., Gresse (Ger.) 20.3.45				MURDER	U.K.
WEISS	186869	M	Ger.		Sgt., 285 Inf. Bn., Lamor Plage (Fr.)				MURDER	FR.
WEISS	187477	M			Pvt., guard, 4. SS Totenkopfsturmbann, C.C., Dora, Nordhausen (Ger.) 43-45				TORTURE	U.S.
WEISS	191360	M	Ger.		Hptsturmfhr., Army, C.C., Ostrast (Nor.)				MURDER	NOR.
WEISS	192986	M	Ger.		SS, C.C., Buchenwald (Ger.) 42-45				TORTURE	U.S.
WEISS	196962	M	Ger.		Deputy Cmdt., C.C., Dachau (Ger.) 9.42				TORTURE	BEL.
WEISS	250551	M	Ger.		Sturmbannfhr., SS, C.C., Dachau (Ger.) 42				MURDER	YUGO.
WEISS	250562	M	Ger.	16	Capt., 14 police Res. Rgt., Tuk (Yugo.) 27.10.43				INTERR.	YUGO.
WEISS	251435	M			Capt., Unit 33748, Thonars (Fr.) 29.8.44				INTERR.	FR.
WEISS	253453	M			Engineer, plant of Waldenmaier, Heidenheim (Ger.) 41-45				BRUTALITY	POL.
WEISS	257409	M	Ger.		Foreman, Org. Todt, "Schutzkommando, slave labour camps, Erlandet, Oeusand, Frola (Nor.) 6.42-45				MURDER	YUGO.
WEISS	257851	M			Hptsturmfhr., Admin. off., 150. Pz. Bde., Meusebridge Antwerpen (Bel.) 12.44				MISC. CRIMES	U.S.
WEISS	258896	M	Ger.		Inspector, member, "Aktions Kommando", custom-house, Lourdes (Fr.) 1.-8.44				MURDER	FR.
WEISS	259018	M			Werkmeister, Daimler Benzwerke, Mannheim (Ger.) 9.44				MURDER	U.S.
WEISS	301116	M	Ger.		Lt. Col., commandant, Garrison, Odense (Den.) summer 43-8.43				MISC. CRIMES	DEN.
WEISS	305750	M	Ger.		Hptschfhr., SS, Broadcasting service, SD, Oyonnax-Ain Attinat, Ain, Lyons and surroundings, (Fr.) 11.43-8.44				MURDER	FR.
WEISS	306822	M	Ger.		SS-Mann, Blockfhr., C.C. Auschwitz (Pol.) from 40				MURDER	FR.
WEISS, Adolf	142718	M			Osturmfhr., Waffen SS, Camp commander, Waldlager 2, Muehldorfer Hart (Ger.)				MURDER	BEL.
WEISS, Adolph or Martin	139845	M	Ger.	-05	Sturmbannfhr., Waffen SS, C.C., Muhldorf (Ger.) 6.44-4.45				MURDER	U.S.
WEISS, Alexander	193668	M		23. 5.99	SS-Mann, guard, 4. SS Totenkopf Sturmbann, C.C., Dora, Nordhausen (Ger.) 43-45				WITNESS	U.S.
WEISS, Alois	255668	M			Flyer, C.C., Ellrich, Nordhausen (Ger.)				MURDER	U.S.
WEISS, Ernst	252819	M	Ger.		N.C.O., Army, Buister Heide (Neth.) 12.6.44				INTERR.	NETH.
WEISS, Franz	253296	M	Ger.	02	Sgt., Air-force, Nachschub Unit 12-VII, Ebnet (Ger.) 27.2.45				MURDER	U.S.
WEISS, Friedrich	305527	M			Kreiskommandant, Jagodina, village of Jasenova near Svilajnac (Serb.) 18.4.44				MURDER	YUGO.
WEISS, Fritz	153459	M			Sgt., Gendarmerie, Daasdorf, Guthenkopfshausen (Ger.) 7.-8.44				MURDER	U.S.
WEISS, Georg	193667	M	Ger.		SS-Mann, 4. SS Totenkopf Stubs., C.C., Dora, Nordhausen (Ger.) 43-45				WITNESS	U.S.
WEISS, Johann	259310	M			Sturmbannfhr., SS, Muhldorf area, (Ger.)				MURDER	U.S.
WEISS, Johann	259939	M	Ger.	17.10.91	Leader, NSDAP, leader of the FS-Freiwillige Schutzstaffel, German Nazi organization at Slovakia, SD, subject is believed to be at Weiden, Bayern, living at house of Baeumler, Bratislava (Czech.)				MURDER	CZECH.
WEISS, Johann Heinrich	149691	M	Ger.	10. 7.01	Capt., Sturmfhr., Army, SA, prison guard, Fresnes (Fr.) 40-45				MISC. CRIMES	U.S., FR.
WEISS, Josef	173290	M	Ger.	06	Crim. Asst., Gestapo, Hamburg-Poppenbuettel, (Ger.) 13.3.42				MURDER	POL.
WEISS, Karl	194692	M		29. 3.89	Hptsturmfhr., SS, head, SD, Gestapo, Jihlava (Czech.) 8.39-12.40				SUSPECT	CZECH.
WEISS, Karl	305752	M			Sgt., 3. Coy., 285 Bn., (Russian Cyclists) at Larmor plage, Morbihan (Fr.) 28.8.44				MURDER	FR.
WEISS, Kurt	251426	M	Ger.		Capt., Estivareilles (Fr.) 21.8.44				MISC. CRIMES	FR.
WEISS, Louis	151445	M			Member, Gestapo de Saarbruck, Folkling (Fr.) 11.44?				MURDER	FR.
WEISS, Martin	252840	M			Chief of SS, C.C., Neuengamme (Ger.)				MISC. CRIMES	BEL.
WEISS, Martin (or SCHAFFER)	261606	M	Ger.	circa 03	Hptschfhr., SS, Agent, Gestapo, Wilno (Pol.) 41-44				MURDER	POL.
WEISS, Michael	193666	M		5. 9.08	Guard, 4. SS Totenkopf Stuba., C.C., Mittelbau, Dora, Nordhausen (Ger.) 43-45				WITNESS	U.S.
WEISS, Otto	149692	M	Ger.		Farmer, civilian, (Ger.)				MURDER	U.S.
WEISS, Richard	168232	M	Ger.		Pvt., 9. Res. Gren. Rgt., 1. Coy., Magny D'Anigon (Fr.) 18.9.44				MURDER	FR.
WEISS, Rudolf	193119	M	Ger.	3. 1.03	Reichsjustizministerium, Feldstraflager Nord, C.C., Finmark (Nor.)				WITNESS	NOR.
WEISS, Stefen	306046	M	Ger.	31. 1.21	Pvt., Bochum (Ger.) 24.3.45				MURDER	U.K.
WEISS, Theodor	142149	M	Ger.		Cpl., Army, Kriegsgefangenenarbeits Bn. 188, Ramsoy-Nordland (Nor.) 10.-20.3.44				MURDER	U.K.
WEISSBACH, Henri	250557	M	Ger.		Gestapo, Lille (Fr.) 40-44				MURDER	FR.
WEISSBACHER	256177	M			Org. Todt, Muhldorf				BRUTALITY	U.S.
WEISSBAECKER	162525	M		10	Doctor, camp official, C.C., Buchenwald (Ger.)				WITNESS	U.S.
WEISSBAH, Hermann	194089	M	Ger.		Custom-house officier, Zollgrenzschutz, Semaphore, Deereaqh, Maout (Fr.) 5.8.44				MURDER	FR.
WEISSBORN	185101	M	Ger.		SS, C.C., Sachsenhausen, Oranienburg (Ger.)				TORTURE	FR.
WEISSEL	3767	M			Sturmbannfhr., SS, C.C., Dachau (Ger.)				TORTURE	U.K.
WEISSELT, Eugene Henri	198317	M	Ger.	14. 8.04	Sgt., SS, member, Gestapo, Lyon (Fr.)				MURDER	FR.
WEISSEMANN	186864	M	Ger.		Sgt., Navy Inf., Queten (Fr.)				WITNESS	FR.
WEISSENBACH, Karl	306221	M	Ger.		Rottfhr., NSDAP, Buchenfeld (Ger.) 17.3.45				MURDER	U.K.
WEISSENBERG	104971	M			General, Army, Wehrkreiskommando XIII, near Ochsenfurt (Ger.) 8.44				MURDER	U.K.
WEISSENBORN, Johann	189269	M		89	Pvt., Marine Art., C.C., Lueneburg, Wilhelmshaven (Ger.) 7.-10.4.45				MURDER	U.K.
WEISSENBORN, Willi	189405	M	Ger.	03	SS-Mann, Totenkopfverband, C.C., Flossenburg (Ger.) 44				MURDER	FR.
WEISSENFELD, Kurt	255667	M			Pvt., C.C., Ellrich, Nordhausen (Ger.)				MURDER	U.S.
WEISSHAAR, Baptist	180597	M	Ger.		Guard, C.C., Osterhagen (Ger.)				TORTURE	U.S.
WEISSHAUPT	13515	M	Ger.		Pvt., Army, 11. or 111. Pz. Gren. Rgt., 2. Coy., Albine (Fr.) 29.6.44				MURDER	FR.
WEISSHUHN, Karl	306725	M	Ger.		German civilian, Witscherzdorf (Ger.) 2.11.44				BRUTALITY	U.S.
WEISSKER	196665	M	Ger.		Reichstatthalter, Administrative Director, Govt. official to Gauleiter, (Ger.) 42				MISC. CRIMES	U.S.

WEI-WEN

NAME	C.R.FILE NUMBER	SEX	NATIO- NALITY	DATE OF BIRTH	RANK OCCUPATION UNIT PLACE AND DATE OF CRIME	REASON WANTED	WANTED BY
WEISSMAN	177603	M	Ger.	05	Pvt.,Army,Stalag VIII B,C.C.Lamsdorf (Ger.) 3.-4.43	TORTURE	U.K.
WEISSMAN	193041	M	Ger.		Pvt.,5 Coy.,891 Ldsschtz.-Bn.,Leitring (Aust.) 11.-29.5.43	MURDER	U.K.
WEISSMANN	137631	M		10	Capt.,Gestapo,Zakopane (Pol.) 12.42	TORTURE	U.K.
WEISSMANN	177603	M	Ger.	05	Pvt.,Army,Stalag VIII B,891 Ldsschtz.,5 Coy.,Lamsdorf (Ger.) 5.43	TORTURE	U.K.
WEISSMANN,Peter	193665	M	Ger.	24. 1.98	Schuetze,Guard,4 SS-Totenk.Stuba,C.C.Mittelbau Dora,Nordhausen, Wieda (Ger.) 43-45	WITNESS	U.S.
WEISSMANN,Robert	255322	M	Ger.		Sturmbannfhr.,SS,Gestapo,Brusx (Czech.)	MURDER	U.K.
WEISSMENTEL,Engelhart	168231	M	Ger.		Pvt.,9 Res.Gren.Regt.,1 Coy.,Magny B' Anigon (Fr.) 18.9.44	MURDER	FR.
WEISSNICHT	124063	M	Ger.		Capt.,Army,Dortmund (Ger.) 2.6.40	MISC.CRIMES	U.K.
WEISSPFENNING	136562	M			Capt.,Army	WITNESS	U.S.
WEISSWELLER,Herr.	188226	M	Ger.		Mayor,Public official,Weissensee (Ger.) 17.11.44	WITNESS	U.S.
WEISTERMANN,Wilhelm	300972	M	Ger.		Hptsturmfhr.,SS,official of S.D.,Leitabschnitt Prague, Oswiecim,Birkenau (Pol.) 39-45	MURDER	CZECH.
WEISZ	166912	M	Ger.		Cpl.,Feldgendarmerie,Montigny en Vezoul (Fr.) 16.7.44	MURDER	FR.
WEISZ,Gertrude	195701	F	Ger.		Employee,Gestapo,Bruenn (Czech.) 39-45	TORTURE	CZECH.
WEISZ,Willy	138001	M	Ger.		Arbeits-Inspector,Labor-Insp. for R.A.D. for Gau Westphalis, North (Ger.)	TORTURE	U.S.
WEIT	132702	M	Ger.		Capt.,Front Stalag 141,Vesoul (Fr.) 3.1.43	WITNESS	FR.
WEITEMEYER	21418	M			Major,Army,631 Ldsschtz.-Bn.,Stalag IX A,Ziegenhain (Ger.) 44-45	TORTURE	U.S.
WEITENDORF,Richard	255844	M		6. 8.00	Sgt.,C.C.Ellrich,Nordhausen (Ger.)	MURDER	U.S.
WEITER	300548	M	Ger.	circa 05	Kapo,C.C.Dachau (Ger.) 44-45	MISC.CRIMES	YUGO.
WEITER,Edmund	149693	M	Ger.		Osturmbannfhr.,SS,C.C.Dachau (Ger.) 43-45	TORTURE	U.S.
WEITER,Eduard	196742	M	Ger.		Lt.Col.,C.C.Dachau (Ger.)	TORTURE	BEL.
WEITH-GERBER	11516	M	Ger.		Cpl.,Army,110 or 111 Gren.Regt.,2 Gruppe,Gourdon (Fr.) 29.6.44	MURDER	FR.
WEITMANN	194852	M	Ger.		Cook,SS,Dussen (Neth.) 30.10.44	PILLAGE	NETH.
WEITSER,Fritz	252841	M	Ger.	1. 1.11	Pvt.,Leichte Flak-Abt.I,No.1215,Strijpen (Bel.) 3.9.44	BRUTALITY	BEL.
WEITZ	24849	M	Ger.		Sturmfhr.,Gestapo,C.C.Klingelputz (Ger.) 1.45	TORTURE	U.S.
WEITZ	253471	M	Ger.		Dr.,Dir.,Instit. for Air Force,Medicine Munich and Freising, C.C.Dachau (Ger.) 42	MURDER	BEL.
WEITZEL	259143	M		96	Sturmbannfhr.,SS,C.C.Dachau (Ger.) 44-45	MISC.CRIMES	YUGO.
WEITZIG	141078	M	Ger.		Oschfhr.,SS,C.C.Natzweiler (Fr.) 42-44	TORTURE	U.K.
WEIZEL	121674	M	Ger.	15	Scharfhr.,SS,C.C.Drancy (Fr.) 43-44	TORTURE	FR.
WEIZL	191954	M			C.C.Dachau (Ger.)	MURDER	U.S.
WEKER	175688	M	Ger.		Pvt.,Army,Briey (Fr.) 40-45	MURDER	FR.
WEKLIN	10369	M	Ger.		Hptschfhr.,SS,Command Steinbruch,C.C.Natzweiler (Ger.) 14.3.-4.8.42	TORTURE	CZECH.
WEKWERT	260637	M	Ger.		Lt.,157 Res.Div.Bavaroise,Massif du Vercors (Fr.) 20.7.-5.8.44	MISC.CRIMES	FR.
WELAUSCHUETZ	259932	M	Ger.		Uschfhr.,SS,Guard at the transport of prisoners from Zittau to Flossenburg,Plana near Matianske,Lazne,Bohemia (Czech.)15.4.45	MURDER	CZECH.
WELDHAGEN	147019	M	Ger.		Sturmbannfhr.,SS,Pz.Div."Das Reich",Queylus (Fr.) 20.4.-2.6.44	MURDER	FR.
WELFING (or WEFING)	158410	M	Ger.		Politischer Leiter,NSDAP,Dortmund,Asseln (Ger.) 25.3.45	MURDER	U.S.
WELKER,Wilhelm	194167	M	Ger.	26.11.90	Zellenleiter,SA,Sandhofen (Ger.) 12.44	TORTURE	POL.
WELKERLE	195974	M	Ger.		Cpl.,Director,Prison,C.C.Compiegne,Royallieu (Fr.) 41-44	MURDER	FR.
WELKERT,Otto	193118	M	Ger.	00	Inspector,Strafgef.-Lager Nord,Finmark (Nor.) 42-45	MISC.CRIMES	NOR.
WELLENDORFF,Herman	140897	M	Ger.		Verbindungs-Abtl.,331,2 Coy.,Bolnes,Ridderkerk (Neth.) 8.5.45	MURDER	NETH.
WELLER	142719	M	Ger.		Member,NSDAP,C.C.Plauen (Ger.)	TORTURE	FR.
WELLER	175677	M	Ger.		Officer,Stalag VI A,C.C.Hemer (Ger.) 41-45	TORTURE	U.S.
WELLER	255221	M	Ger.		Lt.,2 Coy.,658 Inf.Bn.,Sennecey Les Macon (Fr.) 20.7.44	MURDER	FR.
WELLER,Bedrich	185935	M	Ger.	80	Leading Member,NSDAP,Praha (Czech.)	MISC.CRIMES	CZECH.
WELLER,Georg	251427	M	Ger.		Pvt.,Unit 35250 B,St.Remy s.-Bois (Fr.) 5.-7.9.44	MISC.CRIMES	FR.
WELLER,Johann Georg	196906	M	Ger.	25.11.96	Painter,Guard at Welzheim (Ger.)	MISC.CRIMES	FR.
WELLES	258893	M	Ger.		Lt.,L.F.F.No.49060 E Lg.P.R.,Parcoul (Fr.) 21.8.44	INTERR.	FR.
WELLHAUSEN	255842	M			Pvt.,C.C.Dora,Nordhausen (Ger.)	MURDER	U.S.
WELLHOFER	1356	M			Inspector,Naval Supply	MISC.CRIMES	U.K.
WELLINITZ	138275	M	Ger.		Sgt.,Member,SS,Gestapo,Lyon (Fr.)	MURDER	FR.
WELLMANN	137536	M			Insp.,Chief of Gestapo,near Braunschweig,Hellendorf (Ger.)	MURDER	U.S.
WELLMANN	138000	M	Ger.		Guard in Mines,Erkenschwick (Ger.)	TORTURE	U.S.
WELLNER	136404	M	Ger.		Lt.,Air Force,Moosining,Erding, (Ger.) 20.7.44	MURDER	U.S.
WELLPOTT,Erich	191353	M	Ger.		Oberwachtmeister,3 Pol.Bn.,7 Pol.Regt.,10 Coy.,Junkerdal (Nor.)10.44	TORTURE	NOR.
WELMANN	252642	M	Ger.		Kapo,SS,C.C.Neuengamme (Ger.)	INTERR.	BEL.
WELNITZ	251420	M	Ger.		Lt.,Pion.-Bn., Formation 31308 A,Le Touquet (Fr.) 43-44	MISC.CRIMES	FR.
WELNITZKI,Paul	128932	M	Ger.		Uschfhr.,SS,C.C.Buchenwald,Weimar (Ger.)	TORTURE	U.S.
WELSCH	307240	M	Ger.		Lt.,F.P.No.06805,Ortskommandant at Renesse,Slot Moermond (Neth.) 10.12.44	MURDER	NETH.
WELSCH,Johann	142017	M	Ger.	12. 7.03	Gendarm,Gend.,Guenviller (Fr.) 8.44	MURDER	FR.
WELSCH,Karl	185936	M	Ger.		Chief,Stalag XIII D,bei Gunzenhausen,Meinheim (Ger.)	MURDER	BEL.
WELSCH,Peter	258894	M	Ger.	17. 3.05	Locksmith,Chief Hospital Birkenau (Pol.) 40-45	MURDER	FR.
WELSER	173877	M	Ger.		Sgt.,Army,Unit,Plouigneau (Fr.) 9.8.44	MURDER	FR.
WELSS,Rudolf	300943	M	Ger.		Member,SS,Staff at C.C.Sasel (Ger.) 10.44-4.45	TORTURE	U.K.
WELTER	77	M			Oschfhr.,Guard,SS,C.C.Dachau (Ger.)	TORTURE	U.K.
WELTI	305753	M	Ger.		Member of Gestapo,Gestapo at Lyons,(Fr.) 11.43-8.44	MURDER	FR.
WELTMANN	136403	M			Capt.,19 SS-Pol.Regt.,2 Bn.,8 Coy.,Vigaun,Tulle (Yugo.-Fr.)5.41-3.44	MURDER	U.S.
WELTZ (or WOLTZ)	256526	M	Ger.		Hptsturmfhr.,SS,C.C.,Nordhausen,Dora (Ger.)	MURDER	U.S.
WELTZ,A.G.	301820	M	Ger.		Dr.,Director,Institut for Luftfahrtmedizin,Muenchen,Freising, Dachau,Auschwitz (Ger.-Pol.) 3.42-26.2.43	TORTURE	BEL.
WELTZIN	150802	M			Lt.,Stalag XI A,C.C.Altengrabow (Ger.) 17.4.45	MURDER	U.S.
WELZ	255853	M			Capt.,C.C.Harzungen,Nordhausen (Ger.)	TORTURE	U.S.
WELZ,Gerhard	104972	M	Ger.	05	Asst.,Civ.,C.C.Magdeburg (Ger.) 44-45	MURDER	U.S.
WELZEL	255854	M			Oschfhr.,SS,C.C.Rossla,Nordhausen (Ger.)	MURDER	U.S.
WELZEL,Peter	188604	M	Ger.		Employee,Krim.Angestellter,Gestapo,S.D.,Brno (Czech.) 39-45	MURDER	CZECH.
WELZL,Gertrude	188603	F	Ger.		Kanzlei-Angestellte,Gestapo,Brno (Czech.) 39-45	WITNESS	CZECH.
WENC	67736	M	Ger.		Capt.,Stalag XXI D,Posen to Lamsdorf (Pol.) 8.44	TORTURE	U.K.
WENDEL	142721	M			Lagerfhr.,C.C.Kaisergarten,Solingen (Ger.) 44-45	TORTURE	BEL.
WENDEL	153456	M			Political-prisoner,C.C.Estedt (Ger.) 12.-14.4.45	WITNESS	U.S.
WENDEL	168025	M	Ger.		Interpreter,Gestapo of Foix,Puivert (Fr.) 14.4.44	MURDER	FR.

WEN-WER

NAME	C.R.FILE NUMBER	SEX	NATIO-NALITY	DATE OF BIRTH	RANK OCCUPATION UNIT PLACE AND DATE OF CRIME	REASON WANTED	WANTED BY
WENDEL, Oskar	256710	M	Ger.		Interpreter, SD, Foix (Fr.) 11.42	MURDER	FR.
WENDELIN	257390	M	Ger.		Sgt., guard, SS, Slave Labour Camp, Beisfjord near Narvik(Nor.)6.-11.42	BRUTALITY	YUGO.
WENDELROTH, Hans	193636	M	Ger.		Schupo, C.C., Falstad (Nor.) 41 - 44	MURDER	NOR.
WENDERING	24899	M			Lt.Col., Army, Stalag VI.G, Duisdorf (Ger.)	TORTURE	U.S.
WENDERS	132701	M	Ger.		Rittmeister, Stalag VI G, C.C. Buchenwald (Ger.) 15.9.44	MISC.CRIMES	FR.
WENDL	305369	M			Polizei-Oberleutnant, Town Mayor, Dienststelle Nr. 12085, Vrastamites near Livadia, Beotia (Grc.) 8.1.44	MURDER	GRC.
WENDLAND	251452	M	Ger.		Capt., C.C., Fonda (It.) 9.-10.43	INTERR.	YUGO.
WENDLER	257031	M	Ger.		Capt., Army, Belfort (Fr.) 7.44	MURDER	U.S.
WENDLER, Alfred	181125	M			Sgt., 3.Sich.Rgt. 16, (Bel.) 40 - 44	MURDER	BEL.
WENDLER, Ernst	252824	M	Ger.	6.4.05	Agent, Gestapo, Cheb (Czech.) 39 - 45	INTERR.	CZECH.
WENDLER, Richard	18	M	Ger.	22.1.98	Brigadefhr., Governor, Gen.Major, Police, Kielce,Cracow,Lublin (Pol.) 39 - 45	MURDER	UNWCC
WENDLER, Willy	182835	M	Ger.	30.5.08	Hauptsturmfhr., SS, C.C. Hardistro (Czech.) 42 - 45	MURDER	CZECH.
WENDLIK, Hubert	259930	M	Ger.	12.10.01	Leader, leading employee of Ceskomoravska Strojrrny in Prague, Praha-Vysocany (Czech.) 41 - 45	MURDER	CZECH.
WENDLIN, End	67753	M			Sgt., Guard, Waffen SS, C.C. Struthof (Fr.)	MURDER	FR.
WENDT	124204	M			Verwalter, Schupo, Prison Dreibergen, C.C., Buetzow	TORTURE	NOR.
WENDT (or WENZEL)	258895	M	Ger.		Custom-house-officer, Actions-Kommando Lourdes (Fr.) 1. - 8.44	MURDER	FR.
WENDT	301292	M			Crim. Secretary, Abteilung V D, Sicherheitsdienst, Bruessels and other towns(Bel.) 6.40 - 9.44	MURDER	BEL.
WENDT	305370	M	Ger.		Warder, C.C., Neuengamme (Ger.)	MURDER	FR.
WENDT, Franz	21422	M	Ger.		Civilian, near Aschersleben, (Ger.)	TORTURE	U.S.
WENDT, Hermann	250547	M	Ger.		Guard, C.C., Neuengamme (Ger.)	MURDER	FR.
WENERT	141944	M	Ger.		Dr., Civilian, Kripo, R.S.H.A, 5, Berlin, Vildage near Chance (Grc.) 7.41	MURDER	U.K.
WENEZIO	10370	M	Ger.		Sturmbannfhr., SS, Gestapo, Maehrich-Ostran-Moravia (Czech.)	TORTURE	CZECH.
WENGEFELD	193664	M	Ger.		Oberscharfhr., 4.SS-Totenkopf-Stuba, C.C. Mittelbau Dora, Nordhausen-Auschwitz (Ger, Pol.) 43 - 45	WITNESS	U.S.
WENGENROTH, Anna	192444	F	Ger.		Member, NSDAP, Salzburg (Aust.) 6.44	SUSPECT	U.S.
WENGER	125652	M			Capt., Gestapo, Pexonne, Baccarat (Fr.) 6.8.44	MURDER	FR.
WENGERN, Josef	11517	M	Ger.		Pvt., Pz.-Gren.Rgt. 110. or 111. 2.Coy. Albine (Fr.) 29.6.44	MURDER	FR.
WENGLORZ (see WENNGLORZ)	136666						
WENIG	1007	M			Lt., Army, Bizerta (Tun.) 12. 42 - 4.43	MURDER	FR.
WENIG	195380	M	Ger.		Guard, Pvt., German P.W. Camp, Stalag 9 C, Bad Sulza (Ger.) 45	MURDER	CZECH.
WENIG	196903	M	Ger.	13	Lt., 755.Rgt., 334 Inf.Div.	SUSPECT	U.S.
WENIG	251731	M	Ger.	86	General, Legion of Lombardia, Milan (It.) 10.8.44	WITNESS	U.K.
WENIGER	306823	M	Ger.		Auschwitz C.C., Auschwitz (Pol.) 40 - 45	MURDER	FR.
WENIGER, Alexander	258319	M	Ger.	9.5.06	Lt., II.Abt., SS Police Rgt. 13, Tury (Pol.) 43	BRUTALITY	POL.
WENIGER, Franz	149695	F	Ger.		Civilian, she is the wife of CR.Nr. 149696, Borkum (Ger.) 4.8.44	MURDER	U.S.
WENIGER, Franz	149696	M	Ger.		Civilian, Borkum (Ger.) 4.8.44	MURDER	U.S.
WENKE	255855	M	Ger.		Rttfhr., C.C. Wieda, Nordhausen (Ger.)	MURDER	U.S.
WENKEL, Martin	150830	M			Lt. Colonel, Gendarmerie, Berlin (Ger.) 38 - 40	WITNESS	U.S.
WENKEL, Walter	150829	M			Inspizient, O.K.W., Dep. Heeresmusik, Berlin (Ger.) 38 - 40	WITNESS	U.S.
WENKEL, Walter	162731	M	Ger.		Civilian, C.C., Emsland (Ger.) 9.44 - 45	MURDER	U.S.
WENNGLORZ (alias WENGLORZ)	136666	M			Major, Army, C.C., Offz.Stalag XVII B, Krems Gneixendorf (Aust.)10.43-4.44	MURDER	U.S.
WENTSINISEL	185907	M	Ger.	05	Capt., Police, Section of the Persecution of Jews,Salonika, Athens (Grc.) 43	MURDER	GRC.
WENTZ, Bernhard	1070	M	Ger.		Adjutant, Army, Feldgendarmerie, Bar-Aube (Fr.)	TORTURE	FR.
WENTZ, Werner	305371	M	Ger.		Sgt., Feldgendarmerie at Bar-suer-Aube, Troyes (Fr.) 10.43 - 8.44	MURDER	FR.
WENTZEK	262267	M	Ger.	22.9.?	Secretary, Gestapo, Rennes (Fr.) 43 - 44	SUSPECT	FR.
WENTZEL	166910	M	Ger.		Cmdt., C.C., Fallersleben (Ger.) 45	MURDER	FR.
WENTZEL	182307	M			Civilian, Falleben (Ger.) 10 or 11.44	WITNESS	U.S.
WENTZEL	301186	M	Ger.		Tiel, Gelderland, Utrecht (Neth.) 45	PILLAGE	NETH.
WENTZLAU, Karl	252802	M	Ger.		Scharfhr., SD, Toulouse (Fr.) 11.42 - 8.44	MISC.CRIMES	FR.
WENZ	147018	M			Pvt., SS-Pans.Div. " Das Reich", Tulle (Fr.) 44	MURDER	FR.
WENZ	192224	M	Ger.	05	Capt., Stalag XXI D, C.C., Posen (Pol.) 44	TORTURE	U.K.
WENZEL	121675	M	Ger.		Uscharfhr., SS, Aude (Fr.)	SUSPECT	FR.
WENZEL	142722	M		05	Sgt., Nachschub-Bn., 612 K, Supply-Coy., Les Hogues (Fr.) 25.8.44	WITNESS	U.S.
WENZEL	142723	M			Inspector, Army-Abwehr, Geh.Feldpolizei,Gruppe 727, Idriza-Sebesch, Nowo-Beschew (Sov.Un.) 43 - 44	MURDER	U.S.
WENZEL (or WATZEL)	191356	M	Ger.		Capt., 2.Coy., Kgf.Arb.Bn.202, Krckelva (Nor.)	WITNESS	NOR.
WENZEL	250548	M	Ger.		Cmdt., C.C., Neuengamme (Ger.) 44	MURDER	FR.
WENZEL	256753	M	Ger.		Hauptscharfhr., SD, Pontley (Fr.) 44	MURDER	FR.
WENZEL (see WENDT)	258895						
WENZEL	300564	M	Ger.		Pvt., 3.Jaeger Bn., 738.Rgt., Sailing Ship MB 16, Off Supetar (Yugo.) 10.3.44	MISC.CRIMES	YUGO.
WENZEL, Adolf	261108	M	Ger.		SS – Mann, SS, Penitentiary Nord Norway (Nor.) 6.42 - 5.45	MURDER	YUGO.
WENZEL, Barthelmus	305754	M	Ger.		Member of Sicherheitsdienst, Oyonnax, Ain, Attignat, Lyons and Surroundings (Fr.) 11.43 - 8.44	MURDER	FR.
WENZEL, Franz	188199	M	Ger.	17.12.08	Agent, SD, Marianske Lazne (Czech.) 39 - 45	MURDER	CZECH.
WENZEL, Hermann	253468	M	Ger.		Hauptscharfhr., Gestapo, Aube (Fr.) 10.44	MISC.CRIMES	FR.
WENZEL, Hermann (surnamed "Mexicano")	262268	M	Ger.	23.9.?	Dr., Hauptscharfhr., Gestapo, Rennes (Fr.) 43 - 44	MURDER	FR.
WENZEL, Karl	301429	M	Ger.		Uscharfhr., SS, Villebazy (Aude) (Fr.) 7.44	PILLAGE	FR.
WENZEL, Kurt, Friedrich, Franz	260461	M	Ger.	16.10.11	Oberscharfhr., Waffen SS, Guard Coy., C.C., Auschwitz (Pol.) 11.40-8.41	BRUTALITY	POL.
WENZEL, Werner	250550	M	Ger.		Sgt.-Major, 443.Jaeger Rgt., Belgrad (Yugo.) 10.41 - 12.41	MURDER	YUGO.
WENZELPINK	306135	M	Ger.		Scharfhr., SS, Zwickau Kommando, C.C., Flossenburg (Ger.) 42 - 45	MURDER	FR.
WERBELOW	1485	M	Ger.		Untersturmfhr., SS, 11.Coy.	MISC.CRIMES	U.S.
WERBER	256160	M	Ger.		Chief-Secretary, C.C., Mauthausen (Aust.)	INTERR.	FR.
WERBOCK	133186	M			Member SS, planing Staff, Waffen SS, C.C., Dora-Nordhausen(Ger.)	MURDER	U.S.
WERDIER	139738	M	Ger.		Sonderfhr., Stalag X B, C.C., Sandbostel (Ger.) 1. - 5.45	MISC.CRIMES	U.S.
WERECK	256534	M	Ger.		Sgt., C.C.Osterhagen, Nordhausen (Ger.)	MURDER	U.S.

NAME	C.R.FILE NUMBER	SEX	NATIO- NALITY	DATE OF BIRTH	RANK, OCCUPATION, UNIT, PLACE AND DATE OF CRIME	REASON WANTED	WANTED BY
WERFURT	260098	M	Ger.		Lt., Transport-Commando, Chissey en Morvan (Saone and Loire) (Fr.) 26.6.44	MURDER	FR.
WERK	194876	M	Ger.		Capt., Abwehr, Army, Averoff, Athens (Gre.) 43-44	MISC.CRIMES	U.K.
WERKMANN	165983	M	Ger.		Civilian, C.C. Charleroi (Bel.) 44	TORTURE	BEL.
WERKMEISTER (or WIRKMEISTER)	187636	M	Ger.		Staff physician, Stalag XXI A, Army med.Corps, Mischmiroff near Schieratz,(Pol.) 1.-3.42	MURDER	U.K.
WERKMEISTER, Carl	260477	M	Ger.	21.12.01	SS-Mann, Waffen-SS, Guard Coy., C.C.Auschwitz (Pol.) 1.44-45	BRUTALITY	POL.
WERLE see WOERLE, Otto	128924						
WERLE, Helmut	255857	M			Pvt., C.C.Harzungen, Nordhausen (Ger.)	MURDER	U.S.
WERLE, Otto	142724	M	Ger.		10 SS-Hptscharfhr., SS, C.C.Buchenwald (Ger.) 43-44	TORTURE	U.S.
WERLER	195973	M	Ger.		Meister, Gendarmerie, C.C. Westerbork (Neth.) 9.-12.44	MURDER	NETH.
WERMAQETEL, Joseph (Nickname: "Jupp")	305373	M	Ger.		Kapo - Political Internee, C.C. Neuengamme (Ger.)	TORTURE	FR.
WERMANN	251735	M			Capt., 29.Panz.Gren.Regt., 3.Panz.Gren.Div. Robert-Espagne, Hogneville, Convognes, Bevrey (Fr.) 29.8.44	MURDER	FR.
WERMANN, Margarete	194881	F	Ger.	03.	Member, Gestapo, Kolin (Czech.) 44-45	MURDER	CZECH.
WERNER	19	M	Ger.		Gauleiter, NSDAP, Oberschlesien (Pol.) 40	MURDER	POL.
WERNER	1010	M	Ger.		Lt.Col. or Lt., Sicherungsverbindungsstab, probably Gestapo, Ligueil, Vou, Betz Le Chateau (Fr.) 20.8.and 28.8.44	MURDER	FR.
WERNER	1233	M	Ger.	10	Stassfurt (Ger.)	TORTURE	U.S.
WERNER	1769	M	Ger.		Osturmfhr., O.C. Gren.Regt.25, 16.Coy., Roetz (Ger.) 10.6.44	MURDER	U.K.
WERNER	11518	M	Ger.		Lt.Col., Army, Essen (Ger.)	MURDER	FR.
WERNER	120592	M	Ger.		Kriminalrat, Officer, SS, S.D., C.C. Berlin (Ger.) 43-45	MISC.CRIMES	BEL., UNWCC
WERNER	131005	M			SS-Oschfhr., Kasernierte Polizei, C.C.Mauthausen (Aust.) 41-45	MURDER	U.S.
WERNER	131006	M			Criminal-secretary, O.R.P.O.	MURDER	U.S.
WERNER	136269	M	Ger.		Sgt., Inf.Regt. 15, 3.Coy., St.Avit-Parsac (Fr.) 8.6. and 8.7.44	TORTURE	FR.
WERNER	140845	M		22	Pvt., near Calcar (Ger.) 15.3.45	MURDER	CAN.
WERNER	141841	M			10 Commissar, Gestapo, Brunswick (Ger.) 8.42	MURDER	U.K.
WERNER	141846	M		22	Pvt., Paratrooper-Regt.16	WITNESS	U.K.
WERNER	142726	M			Oberstabsarzt, O.K.W. Subsection IV-P.W.Affairs.	WITNESS	U.S.
WERNER	146745				SS-Oschfhr., C.C. Flossenburg (Ger.)	TORTURE	U.S., FR.
WERNER	162526	M	Ger.	92	SS-Uschafhr., Waffen-SS, C.C.Buchenwald (Ger.)	TORTURE	U.S.
WERNER	166909	M			Sgt., Armee-Oberkommando, La Rochette (Fr.) 3.8.44	MURDER	FR.
WERNER	168036	M	Ger.		W.O., General-Staff, Kommandantur, Crest-Drome (Fr.) 7.-8.44	MURDER	FR.
WERNER	186857	M	Ger.		Lt.Col., Sicherungs-Bde., Ligueil (Fr.)	WITNESS	FR.
WERNER	189260	M	Ger.		Usturmfhr., SS, Leczyca (Pol.) 3,42	MURDER	POL.
WERNER	192134	M	Ger.		Secretary, Geheime Feldpol., Brussels (Bel.)	MISC.CRIMES	BEL.
WERNER	194165	M	Ger.		Cpl., 167.Feld Ers.Bn., Stavelot, La Gleize (Bel.)	WITNESS	U.S.
WERNER	194238	M	Ger.		12 SS Staff-Sgt., 12.SS Panz.Div. "Hitler Jugend", 26.SS Panz.Gren.Regt., 6.Coy., Caen (Fr.) 6.6.-8.7.44	TORTURE	CAN.
WERNER	196735	M	Ger.	05 - 10	Capt., Staff to SS, Verona (It.) 5.45	WITNESS	U.K.
WERNER	251433	M	Ger.		Lt., Naval Airforce, Ingrandes (Fr.) 24.8.44	MURDER	FR.
WERNER	251743	M	Ger.		Overseer, C.C. Buchenwald (Ger.)	INTERR.	FR.
WERNER	252893	M	Ger.		Sgt., 3.Coy., 15.Regt.Gren., Saint-Avit (Fr.) 9.6.44	INTERR.	FR.
WERNER	256709	M	Ger.	05	Employee, C.C.Dora, Nordhausen (Ger.)	BRUTALITY	FR.
WERNER	301430	M	Ger.		Lt., Head of Sector of Ia Cast Lezardieux, Loguivy de la Mer nr.Paim-Pol Cotes-du-Nord (Fr.) 14.2.45	BRUTALITY	FR.
WERNER	301431	M	Ger.		SS Sgt., C.C. Flossenburg (Ger.) 42-45	MURDER	FR.
WERNER	301674	M	Ger.		SS-Hptsturmfhr., Unit XI, 3.Regt.SS "Der Fuehrer", Mesnil-St.Blaise (Bel.) 5.-6.9.44	MURDER	BEL.
WERNER	301911	M	Ger.		Dr., Generalvet., G.O.C. Vet.Corps,20.Army, Finmark (Nor.) 10.11.44	MURDER	NOR.
WERNER	305118	M	Ger.		S.D. at Pontivy, District of Pontivy (Morbihan) (Fr.) 4.-8.44	MURDER	FR.
WERNER	305374	M	Ger.		Attached Dora Camp and Factory, employing men from C.C. Buchenwald (Ger.) 43-4.45	BRUTALITY	FR.
WERNER	306816	M	Ger.		Member, St.Quentin-Gestapo, Vraignes en Vermandois-Somme (Fr.) 29.8.44	MURDER	FR.
WERNER	306903	M	Ger.		Interpreter, Naves (Savoie) (Fr.) 10.6.44		FR.
WERNER, Anna	194433	F	Ger.		Member, Gestapo, Brno (Czech.) 39-45	WITNESS	CZECH.
WERNER, Anton-Martin	255218	M	Ger.	22.9.14	Electrician Civ., Gosselgrub, Eberspirk (Czech.) 9.39	MURDER	CZECH.
WERNER, Anton	262259	M		16.4.12	SS-Osturmfhr., 4.Coy., 51. armoured Bde., Breviandes, Bucheres, St.Savine, La Riviere de Corps, Troyes (Fr.) 22.-25.8.44	BRUTALITY	FR.
WERNER, Christian	177547	M	Ger.		Camp-Official, C.C. Neuengamme (Ger.)	TORTURE	FR.
WERNER, Franz	29653	M	Ger.		Dr., Oberlandgerichtsrat, Ministry of Justice, Litomerice (Czech.) 39-45	MURDER	CZECH.
WERNER, Friedrich	262967	M	Ger.	2.9.91	Lt.Col., Army and Gestapo, Chief of a Section of Gestapo, Prag (Czech.) 43-44	SUSPECT	CZECH.
WERNER, Fritz	173876	M	Ger.		Pvt., 15.Parachuts-Regt., 8.Coys., St. Lo (Fr.) 26.7.44	MURDER	U.S.
WERNER, Gustav	166376	M	Ger.	28.12.12	Sgt., Geheime Feldpol., Recoaro Valdagno (It.) 1.45	MURDER	U.S.
WERNER, Hans	301117	M	Ger.		Crim.secretary, Oschfhr., SS served with the R.S.D. Abt.IV-2a, Shellhuset, Copenhagen (Den.) 25.2.45	TORTURE	DEN.
WERNER, Heinrich	260055	M	Ger.		Chief, Railway-station Madeleine (North), Hallebecke (Bel.) 9.44	MURDER	FR.
WERNER, Hermann	259330	M			Rottenfhr., SS, Muehldorf Area (Ger.)	MURDER	U.S.
WERNER, Jacob	1008	M	Ger.		Sgt., Army, Candresse, Dax (Fr.) 11.6.44	INCENDIARISM	FR.
WERNER, Josef	193117	M	Ger.		Cpl., 7.Btty., Heeres-Kuesten Art.Regt.972, Lattervik (Nor.) 45	WITNESS	NOR.
WERNER, Karl	142727	M	Ger.	13.3.04	Member, Geheime Feldpol., S.D., Gestapo	WITNESS	U.S.
WERNER, Kurt	185937	M	Ger.		13 SS-Hptscharfhr., Guard, C.C. Sachsenhausen, Dachau (Ger.) 44	MURDER	POL.
WERNER, Kurt	195972	M	Ger.		Uschfhr., S.D., Maison Lafitte (Fr.) 15.12.41-10.8.44	MURDER	FR.
WERNER, Luise	162710	F	Ger.		24 SS-Overseer, SS, C.C. Sasel (Ger.)	MURDER	U.K.
WERNER, Max	194845	M	Ger.	17.12.07	Pvt., Army, W.B.K. Oo. Ausland oz Zuerich 110-1, Vlissingen (Neth.) 9.44	WITNESS	NETH.
WERNER, Peter	139153	M			Chief, Organisation Todt, Hnzgen (Ger.) 43	TORTURE	BEL.

WER-WET

NAME	C.R.FILE NUMBER	SEX	NATIO-NALITY	DATE OF BIRTH	RANK OCCUPATION UNIT PLACE AND DATE OF CRIME	REASON WANTED	WANTED BY
WERNER, William	132979	M	Ger.	7.11.99 or 21.4.92	Dr.,Wehrwirtschaftsfuehrer,Standartenfhr.,Legal official, NSKK, Reichs-Ministry for armament and warproduct, Berlin,Chemnitz (Ger.) 43	MISC.CRIMES	U.S.
WERNER-STEINER	121677	M	Ger.		Chief, Gestapo (Spionage),Challes-les Eaux (Fr.)	MURDER	FR.
WERNET	306667	M	Ger.		Interpreter, I.Bn. 74, R.S.M., Neuvaglise-Dept.Cantal (Fr.) 15.-29.6.44	MURDER	FR.
WERNETTE see BERNETTE	196270						
WERNICH, Wilhelm	187505	M			Guard,4.SS Totenkopf-Stuba, C.C.Dora - Nordhausen,Osterode (Ger.) 43-45	TORTURE	U.S.
WERNICKE	255896	M			C.C.Rottleberode, Nordhausen (Ger.)	MURDER	U.S.
WERNO, Peter	255856	M			Prt., C.C. Arteri, Nordhausen (Ger.)	MURDER	U.S.
WERTGEN, Wilhelm	252792	M	Ger.		SS Rottfhr., C.C.Auschwitz, Birkenau (Pol.) 11.42	MURDER	YUGO.
WERSBASCH, Henck or LE CANADIEN	138329	M	Ger.		Policeman, Geheime Feldpolizei, Montigny-en-Gohelle (Fr.) 14.9.44	MURDER	FR.
WERSCH	255895	M			Sgt., C.C. Osterhagen, Nordhausen (Ger.)	MURDER	U.S.
WERST	194121	M	Ger.		Sgt., SS, C.C. Buchenwald (Ger.) 42-45	TORTURE	U.S.
WERTEMANN	261326	M	Ger.		Senior W.O., Gendarmerie of Bethune, Hinges (Fr.) 12.8.44	TORTURE	FR.
WERTGANNER	131004	M			SS Hptscharfhr., Totenkopf SS Div., C.C. Mauthausen (Aust.) 41-45	MURDER	U.S.
WERTH, Henrick	258950	M	Ger.		Lt.Gen.	WITNESS	U.S.
WERTH see SCHAEFER, Peter	306129						
WERTHER	252846	M	Ger.		Admin.officer, Civ. Leather firm of Carl Loewe, Koeln, Brussels (Bel.) 3.9.44	INTERR.	BEL.
WERTHMANN	191324	M	Ger.		Pvt., Kis.Art.Bn.717, F.P. No. 22380, St.Andries, Varsenare, Lez Bruges (Bel.) 4.9.44	MURDER	BEL.
WERTHMANN, Eduard	151435	M	Ger.		Civ., Ruppertshuetten (Ger.) 12.9.44	MURDER	U.S.
WESE	306111	M			SS Uscharfhr. at Alderney C.C. (Channel Is) and Kortemark C.C. 42-45	MURDER	CZECH.
WESEMANN	1358	M			N.C.O., SD Aussenkdo.	MISC.CRIMES	U.K.
WESEMEIER	189823	M			Dr., German Legation of Zagreb, Ljubljana (Yugo.) 4.41-43	MURDER	YUGO.
WESER, Arno	62089	M	Ger.	00	Osturmfhr., SD Abt. IV Gestapo de Vichy, Bourboure, Vichy, Le Mont Dore (Fr.) 27.4.44	TORTURE	FR.
WESIERSKI	300753	M	Ger.		Pvt. 1.Aufkl.Abt. 3.Coy. 2.Col. XV.Div.Africa-Corps, St. Leger (Arlon) 5.9.44	MISC.CRIMES	BEL.
WESKAINY, Arnost	192249	M	Ger.		Member SS, Lidice (Czech.) 10.6.42	MURDER	CZECH.
WESKISCH	166908	M			Civ., Director, Trustees of work, Ger., Clermont-Ferrand (Fr.)	MISC.CRIMES	FR.
WESP, Michael	255216	M	Ger.	18.4.07	Civ., Gossengrun, Haberspirk (Czech.) 9.39	MURDER	CZECH.
WESPHALEN	256566	M			Lt., Formation Bode, St.Pierre d'Eyraud, Pressignac, Beaumont (Fr.) 19.6.-22.7.44	MISC.CRIMES	FR.
WESS	1011	M	Ger.		Member Gestapo, Lyon (Fr.) 27.7.44	MURDER	FR.
WESS	167855	M	Ger.		Cpl. chief, Fieldpolice, Auberive, Flagey, Coiffy, Chalencey (Fr.) 43-44	MURDER	FR.
WESS	257694	M	Ger.		Col., Army, Strassburg, Barkenbruegge (Ger.) 44-45	INTERR.	YUGO.
WESS (Rudolph)	306817	M	Ger.		SS Mann, SD Vichy (Fr.) 10.43-9.44	MURDER	FR.
WESSEING	188720	M	Ger.		Brig., Army, Letriage, Bourget (Fr.) 24.8.44	WITNESS	FR.
WESSEL	195938	M	Ger.	04	Osturmbannfhr., SS, C.C. Sachsenhausen, Oranienburg (Ger.)	MISC.CRIMES	U.K.
WESSEL	252843	M	Ger.	10	Hptsturmfhr., C.C. Oranienburg (Ger.)	INTERR.	BEL.
WESSEL, Karl	135333	M	Ger.		Baker, Labour camp, C.C. Gelsenkirchen (Ger.)	TORTURE	U.S.
WESSEL, Willi	257679	M	Ger.	21.5.99	Hptwachtmeister, police, Genthin (Ger.) 12.44	BRUTALITY	U.S.
WESSELAK, Johann	185998	M	Ger.		Employee, Gestapo C.C.Budejovice,(Czech.)	MURDER	CZECH.
WESELER, H.	306598	M	Ger.		Civ., Winterswisk (Neth.) 1.6.42	TORTURE	NETH.
WESSELY	185931	M	Ger.	07	Dr., SS Hptsturmfhr., C.C. Gross Rosen (Ger.)	TORTURE	U.K.
WESSELY	255837	M			Cpl., C.C. Rottleberode, Nordhausen (Ger.)	MURDER	U.S.
WESSHING, E.	133313 A	M			Hptscharfhr., SS	MURDER	U.S.
WESSIG, Max Wilhelm Franz	10679	M	Ger.	11.4.75	Geh.Regierungsrat, Chem.Industrie, Berlin (Ger.)	MISC.CRIMES	U.S.
WESSLEY, Georg	177801	M			Pvt., 190.Inf.Rgt., Winterspelt (Ger.) 20.12.44	MURDER	U.S.
WESSLING, Erwin	133911	M	Ger.		Civ. Lager Langenzenn, Nuernberg (Ger.) 43-4.45	TORTURE	U.S.
WESNER, Lorenz	11519	M			Pvt., Army, 110. or 111.Panz.Gren.Rgt. 2.Coy., Albine (Fr.) 29.6.44	MURDER	FR.
WESSOLEK, Gustav	257388	M			Cpl., Org.Todt, slave labour camp, Krlandet, Oeusand, Trola (Nor.) 6.42-45	MURDER	YUGO.
WESTCOTT	130064	M	Ger. Aust.		Civ. Engineer, Arb.Kdo, A 91 G.W., C.C. Judenburg (Aust.) 27.2.45-4.45	TORTURE	U.K.
WESTMAYER	196904	M			Capt.	SUSPECT	U.S.
WESTENDORFF	192132	M	Ger.		Member, Geheime Feldpolizei, Brussels (Bel.)	TORTURE	BEL.
WESTERBERGER, Johann	1012	M	Ger.		Hptscharfhr., Waffen SS, Oslo (Nor.) 41-44	TORTURE	NOR.
WESTEREIDE	153457	M	Ger.		Commander, Oflag XI Wladsimierec (Sov.Un.) 41	MURDER	U.S.
WESTERKAMPF	20	M	Ger.		Leader, Public official, Abt. Innere Verwaltung d.General-Gouvernem. 40-90.1.44	MURDER	POL.
WESTERLING	257962	M			Lt., 150.Pz.Bde., Meuse-Bridge Antwerp (Bel.) 12.44	MISC.CRIMES	U.S.
WESTERMAYER, Paul	258397	M	Ger.	96	Capt., Infantry, San Benedetto,Monte Buno (It.) 19.4.44	MURDER	U.S.
WESTERMEIER, Ludwig	185567	M	Ger.	30.3.15	SS Oscharfhr.,Crim.assist.,SD, Gestapo,Praha,Kolin (Czech.) 40-45	MURDER	CZECH.
WESTERMEYER	195916	M	Ger.		Owachtmeister,Schupo,C.C.Muehldorf,Westerbork (Neth.)	MURDER	NETH.
WESTERTEIGER	189268	M			Civ. Castrop (Ger.) 24.9.45	WITNESS	U.S.
WESTHOFF or WETZHOFF	125601				Civ.	MURDER	U.S.
WESTHOFF, Hans	142005	M	Ger.	93	Major Gen.,OKW Oflag XIII B, Hammelburg (Ger.) 11.44-45	MURDER	U.S.
WESTMAR, Engelbert	194880	M	Ger.	6.6.16	SS Scharfhr., Gestapo, Kolin (Czech.) 39-45	MURDER	CZECH.
WESTMEYER	186791	M	Ger.		Sgt., Army, Hemer (Ger.) 41-45	TORTURE	U.S.
WESTPFAHL	139734	M			Lt.Col., Stalag X B, Sandbostel (Ger.) 1.-5.45	TORTURE	U.S.
WESTPHAL	136271	M	Ger.	08	Sgt., Army, C.C. Dora - Nordhausen (Ger.)	MURDER	FR.
WESTPHAL	150804	M	Ger.		Civ., Budisheim (Ger.) 6.44	TORTURE	U.S.
WESTPHAL	193116	M		15	Oberbauleiter, Org.Todt, Narvik (Nor.) 42-43	MISC.CRIMES	NOR.
WESTPHAL	255858	M			Oscharfhr., C.C. Dora - Nordhausen (Ger.)	MURDER	U.S.
WESTPHAL	306407	M	Ger.		SS-Mann, C.C. Buchenwald (Ger.) 16.5.38-9.10.43	MURDER	BEL.
WESTPHALEN	185185	M	Ger.		Corvetten-Capt., Navy, Landhau1 (Fr.) 30.4.44	MURDER	FR.
WESTWEBER	306824	M	Ger.		SS Uscharfhr., Member of SS institute of hygiene,Auschwitz (Pol.)40-45	MURDER	FR.
WETZ, Fritz or Eris	191965	M	Ger.		SS Stabsscharfhr.,Adjutant,SS Div."Das Reich" F.P.No.29573. Flamarens (Fr.) 10.7.44	MURDER	FR.
WET-STEIN, Peter	258409	M			Guard, SS, C.C. Ohrdruf (Ger.) 12.44-4.45	MURDER	U.S.
WETTMANN	252609	M	Ger.		Rottfhr., SD, Toulouse (Fr.) 11.42-8.44	MISC.CRIMES	FR.
WETENGEL, Alfred	29654	M	Ger.		Dr.,Landgerichtsrat, public official, Cheb (Czech.) 40	MURDER	CZECH.

NAME	C.R.FILE NUMBER	SEX	NATIO-NALITY	DATE OF BIRTH	RANK OCCUPATION UNIT PLACE AND DATE OF CRIME	REASON WANTED	WANTED BY
WETTENGEL, Ottomar	188198	M	Ger.	16.11.12	Official, Gestapo, Marianske Lazne (Czech.) 39-45	TORTURE	CZECH.
WETTER	252817	M	Ger.		Dr., Usturmfhr., SS, C.C. Auschwitz-Birkenau(Pol.)42-45	INTERR.	YUGO.
WETTER, Josef	253457	M	Ger.		Dir.for Prison, Gestapo, Troyes(Fr.) 43-44	BRUTALITY	FR.
WETTERMANN	132703	F	Ger.		Overseer, C.C.Ravensbrueck(Ger.)	TORTURE	FR.
WETTSCHUREK	259609	M	Ger.		Lt.,Cdt.Place of Bethune,Noeux les Mines,Verquin-Drouvin-Houchain (Pas de Calais-Fr.) 31.8.40	INTERR.	FR.
WETZ	257852	M			Lt.,150 Pz.Bde, Meuse Bridge,Antwerp(Bel.)12.44	MISC.CRIMES	U.S.
WETZEL	186171	M	Ger.	00	Guard,C.C. Rottenburg (Ger.)	TORTURE	FR.
WETZEL	252807	M	Ger.		SS-Mann, Civil Admin., SD,Toulouse (Fr.) 11.42-8.44	MISC.CRIMES	FR.
WETZEL	306047	M	Ger.		Attached to Cdo.of Dr.Ernst,St.Die(Fr.) 9.44	MURDER	U.K.
WETZEL, Ewart	21423	M			Pvt.,Army,Pz.12 SS Pz.Div.(H.J.)	WITNESS	CAN.
WETZEL, Rudolf or WETZLER	255894	M			Cpl.,C.C.Bodungen-Nordhausen(Ger.)	MURDER	U.S.
WETZEL, Wilhelm	1013	M	Ger.	88	Gen.Army,L XVI Res.Corps,Clermont-Ferrand(Fr.) 8.3.44	MURDER	U.S.,FR.
WETZHOFF see WESTHOFF	125601						
WETZIMAYR	189422				Oscharfhr.,SS Pz.Div.H.J.,1.Coy,2 or 3 Coy,Asequ (Fr.) 1.4.44	MURDER	FR.
WETZKE	188766	M	Ger.		Lt.Col.,Army, Ruestung u.Kriegsproduktion,Belfort(Fr.)10.-11.44	PILLAGE	FR.
WETZL, Fritz	189824	M	Ger.	01	Hptsturmfhr.,SS, C.C. Neuengamme (Ger.) 43	MURDER	YUGO.
WETZLER see WETZEL, Rudolf	255894						
WETZLING, Wolfgang	104974	M		07	Osturmbannfhr.,sunder Kdo.,C.C. Stuttrop (Ger.)22.3.45	MURDER	U.S.
WEUSTENFELD	260078	M			Hptsturmfhr.,SS,Cmdt, slave labour camp, C.C.Botn near Rognan (Nor.) 8.42 - 1945	BRUTALITY	YUGO.
WEWEL, Heinrich or Friedrich	193115	M	Ger.	17. 5.05	Sgt.-guard,Reichsjustizmin.,Feldstraflg.,C.C.Finmark(Nor.) 45	MISC.CRIMES	NOR.,YUGO.
WEWINGER, Alois	173875	M	Ger.		Oberwachtmstr.,Police,Mailley le Camp (Fr.) 23.4.44	MURDER	U.S.
WEYDENHAMMER, Rudolph	151444	M			Stabsleiter, NSDAP,Gen.mgr.and Pres.of several industrial organisation (Aust.)	MURDER	U.S.
WEYER, Willi	162527	M	Ger.	05	Cpl.,Waffen-SS, command Staff,C.C.Buchenwald(Ger.) 42-45	TORTURE	U.S.
WEYLAND	261074	M	Ger.		Col.,Feld-Cmdt.,Field-Cmdtr.678,Lille, Environs(Fr.) 42-43	MURDER	FR.
WEYLAND, Robert	255323	M	Ger.		Sturmbannfhr.,SS, Gestapo, Liberec,Brnex (Czech.)	MURDER	U.K.
WEYMANN, Hans	10371	M	Ger.		Hptsturmfhr.,SS,C.C. Oranienburg (Ger.) 39-44	TORTURE	CZECH.
WEYMANN, Karl-Heinz	1086	M	Ger.		W.O.,chief,Army,Feldgend.,Langres,Coifey-le-Hault (Fr.) 43-44	TORTURE	FR.
WEYMERSCHAUS, Franz	251741	M	Ger.		Usturmfhr.,SS,Gestapo,Limoges(Fr.) 40-45	INTERR.	FR.
WEYRALKER	191844	M			Col., Army, La Rochelle (Fr.) 11.2.44	MURDER	FR.
WEYRAUCH see WEIBRAUCH	128933						
WEYRAUCH, Karl	142729	M	Ger.		Hptscharfhr.,Waffen-SS,Totenk.Stuba,C.C.Buchenwald(Ger.) 40-44	TORTURE	U.S.
WEYRAUTER	158387	M	Ger.		Col.,Army,Inf., la Rochelle (Fr.) 11.2.45	MURDER	FR.
WEYSKOOLT	307242	M	Ger.		Member of Staff, Diez-Lahn (Ger.) 40-45	MURDER	BEL.
WEZES, Fritz	307243	M	Ger.		Sgt.,Renesse,F.P.Nr.06085,Slot Moermond at Renesse (Neth.) 18.12.44	MURDER	NETH.
WEZNER	250563	M	Ger.		Cmdt.,Army,Merezosoe of Brac.Island(Czech.) 44	MISC.CRIMES	YUGO.
WHALL, Willi	24840	M		19	Scharfhr.(Coy-Fhr.)SS,Kriegsgef.Lg.20,C.C.Bremen (Ger.)	TORTURE	U.S.
WHIRTZ	191972	M			Capt.,Geb.Jg.Bn100, Montgirod(Fr.) 23.8.44	MURDER	FR.
WIARD, Albert	258849	M	Ger.	11. 5.08	Custom-officer,custom house office,Luxemburg 44	MISC.CRIMES	YUGO.
WIBENS	192443	M		05	Head,Major,SD,SS, Koblens,Rengsdorf(Ger.) 12.44	SUSPECT	U.S.
WIBMER, Martin	255677	M			Sturmmann, C.C. Harzungen (Ger.)	MURDER	U.S.
WIBORG	195913	M	Ger.		Agent,Secret,Waffen-SS,Ixon la Bruisse (Fr.) 22.2.44	MURDER	FR.
WICHER, Ernest	252806	M	Ger.		Uscharfr.,SD, Toulouse (Fr.)	MISC.CRIMES	FR.
WICHERT, Herbert	255845	M		27. 4.22	Pvt.,C.C.Ellrich-Nordhausen(Ger.)	MURDER	U.S.
WICHLER	147017	M	Ger.		Osturmfhr.,SS, Pz.Div."Das Reich", Moissac(Fr.) 44	MURDER	FR.
WICHMAN	251453	M	Ger.		Waffenmstr.,19 SS Pol.Rgt.,Ferlach (Aust.) 44-45	MURDER	YUGO.
WICHMAN, Erich or WICHMANN	251444	M	Ger.		Pvt.,Parachutist Unit St.Michielsgestel (Neth.) 9.-10.44	PILLAGE	NETH.
WICHMAN, Gerhard	179750	M	Ger.	29	Lt.,590 Pz.Jg.Abt.,Fucecchio Marshes (It.) 7.-8.44	MURDER	U.K.
WICHMANN	256061	M	Ger.		Capt.,Div.Inf."Treue und Ehre", Dampierre (Fr.) 41	PILLAGE	FR.
WICHMANN see WICHMAN, Erich	251444						
WICHMANN, Friedrich Wilhelm	21413	M	Ger.		Usturmfhr.,Army,Allg.SS	TORTURE	U.S.
WICHT	261787	M	Ger.		Interpreter, SD Besancon (Doubs),Rion (Fr.) 24.7.44	BRUTALITY	FR.
WICHT, Bernhard	158989	M			Civilian, Eisleben (Ger.) 41-45	TORTURE	U.S.
WICK	1360	M			Lt.Army	MISC.CRIMES	U.K.
WICK	124471	M			Officer-Stabsarzt, Dr.,Stalag III D Berlin(Ger.) 41-43	MURDER	U.K.
WICK	255846	M			Sgt.,C.C.Wolfsleben-Nordhausen(Ger.)	MURDER	U.S.
WICK, Stefan	131003	M			Uscharfr.,SS,C.C.Mauthausen (Ger.) 41-45	TORTURE	U.S.
WICK, Walter	162790	M	Ger.		Lt.,Army,Art.,F.P.Nr.21309 E,Monterre Silly(Fr.) 6.40	MURDER	FR.
WICKE	257229	M	Ger.		Capt.,Army,PW-camp deputy-Cmdt,Oflag XII A,Hadamar(Ger.)18.4.41	MURDER	POL.
WICKE, Rudolf	158439	M	Ger.		Sailor, Navy,Stellendam (Neth.)4.29-45	MURDER	NETH.
WICKENBERG	104975	M	Ger.	11	Lt.,Army,293 Rgt.,18 V.G.Div., Bleialf(Ger.) 44	WITNESS	U.S.
WICKERMANN	136276	M	Ger.		Capt.,Army,la Ferte sur Aube (Fr.) 15.4.44	MURDER	FR.
WICKERS	158440	M	Ger.		Capt.,Gestapo,Brive(Fr.) 44	MURDER	FR.
WICKERS	251740	M	Ger.		Usturmfhr.,Gestapo,Limoges(Fr.) 40-45	INTERR.	FR.
WICKERT	252813	M	Ger.		Worker, SD, Toulouse (Fr.) 11.42-8.44	MISC.CRIMES	FR.
WICKLEIN	255847	M			Pvt.,C.C.Mixel-Nordhausen(Ger.)	MURDER	U.S.
WICKMANN	167047	M	Ger.		Chief,Prison,Amenasse (Fr.) 25.and 27.4.44	MURDER	FR.
WICKNER see WIEGNER	305529						
WIDDISCH	166982	M	Ger.	00	Capt.,Army,2 Lds.Schz.Bn, Lager A 22 near Bruex (Ger.) 16.1.45	TORTURE	U.K.
WIDEMANN	173874	M	Ger.		Major,Georgian Inf.Bn,Locmine (Fr.) 7.-8.44	MURDER	FR.
WIDERROD, Wilhelm	150846	M	Ger.		Civilian, Hohnebostel (Ger.) 7.5.44	TORTURE	U.S.
WIDERA	195914	M	Ger.		Pvt.,Wach-Einheit, Royallieu (Fr.) 41-44	MURDER	FR.
WIDERMAIL	179733	M	Ger.	90	Col.,114 Jg.Div., Gubbie (It.) 22.6.44	MURDER	U.K.
WIDHALM, Michael	174366	M		25. 2.10	Statspol.Mstr.,Staatspol.,Reinitz-Gendarmerie, Weidmannsdorf-Klagenfurt(Aust.) 28.2.45	MURDER	U.K.
WIDHELM	306270	M	Ger.	25 - 05	Gend.master,Gendarmerie,Post at Viktring,Carinthia(Aust.) 2.45	MURDER	U.K.

WID - WIE

NAME	C.R.FILE NUMBER	SEX	NATIONALITY	DATE OF BIRTH	RANK OCCUPATION UNIT PLACE AND DATE OF CRIME	REASON WANTED	WANTED BY
WIDMANN	11520	M	Ger.		Pvt., Panz.Gren.Rgt. 110 or 111. 2. Coy., Albine (Fr.) 29.6.44	MURDER	FR.
WIEBE	142040	M	Ger.		Korvetten Kapitain, Navy O.C.U. 516. 28.9.42	MISC.CRIMES	U.K.
WIEBE, Antonius, Hendrijus	301095	M	Ger.	98	Detective, Police Nijmegen attached to the SD. Arnheim, Vorden (Neth.) 10.44	MURDER	U.K.
WIEBECK, Gerhard	192979	M	Ger.		Lt., SS C.C. Buchenwald (Ger.) 42-45	WITNESS	U.S.
WIEBECKE	194090	M	Ger.		Lt., Feldgendarmerie, Tourcoing (Fr.) 2.9.44	MURDER	FR.
WIEBENS, Wilhelm	170548	M	Ger.	06	SS Osturmbannfhr., SD, SS Rengsdorf Koblenz (Ger.) 23.12.44-14.2.45	MURDER	U.K. U.S.
WIEBENS, Wilhelm	194123	M	Ger.		Lt., SS C.C. Buchenwald (Ger.) 42-45	TORTURE	U.S.
WIEBER	137577	M	Ger.		SS-Officer, SS Leibst. Adolf Hitler C.C. Marienburg (Pol.) 14.8.40	MISC.CRIMES	U.S.
WIEBER (see WEBER)	253466						
WIEBER	305617	M	Ger.		Agent of the Gestapo, Offenburg Prison Baden, (Ger.) 6.11.44	MURDER	FR.
WIEBERNEIT, Kurt	251728	M	Ger.		Staff Sgt., 377. Jaeg.Rgt. Vinkt Heigem, (Bel.) 25.-31.5.40	MISC.CRIMES	BEL.
WIEBERSHEIM	166980	M	Ger.		General, Army 11. Panz.Div., (Sov.Un.) 43	PILLAGE	U.S.
WIEBOLD	261073	M	Ger.		Senior W.O. St. Gingolph (Fr.) 23.7.44	MURDER	FR.
WIEBUSCH, Fritz	194199	M	Ger.	10	Pvt., 2110 MKA 8. Zug Texel, Den Burg (Neth.) 4.45	WITNESS	NETH.
WIECH, Johann	128930	M			SS-Rottfhr., SS C.C. Weimar Buchenwald (Ger.)	TORTURE	U.S.
WIECHMANN, Wilhelm	307244	M	Ger.		Sgt., Quartiermacher, Rotterdam (Neth.) 15.1.45	PILLAGE	NETH.
WIECKBERG	1016	M	Ger.		Sturmbannfhr., W-SS, 9.39-1.42	MURDER	POL.
WIECKER (see W'EGNER)	305529						
WIECZOREK	255325	M		97	Crim.Rat. Gestapo, Pruex (Czech.)	MURDER	U.K.
WIECZOVEK, (or WITTASIK)	128929	M			Oschfhr., SS C.C. Weimar Buchenwald (Ger.)	TORTURE	U.S.
WIEDAUER, Anna	260715	F	Ger.-Aust.		C.C. Hallein.(Aust.)	MURDER	U.S.
WIEDE	256161	M			Furniture Factory, Utrecht, (Neth.) 44-45	PILLAGE	NETH.
WIEDEMANN	259746	M	Ger.		Gestapo, Dijon, (Fr.) 8.44	INTERR.	FR.
WIEDEMANN	252808	M	Ger.		Hptschfhr., SS SD, Toulouse (Fr.) 11.42-19.8.44	MISC.CRIMES	FR.
WIEDEMANN, Andreas	124829	M	Ger.		Cpt., Army Kriegsgefangenen Re.Laz, C.C. Heppenheim (Ger.) 9.44-5.45	TORTURE	U.S.
WIEDEMANN, Anton	1017	M	Ger.		Cpl., Army, Baudrigues (Fr.) 19.8.44	MURDER	FR.
WIEDEMANN, Xaver	260463	M	Ger.	21. 6.08	SS Rottfhr., W-SS Guard Coy. C.C. Auschwitz, (Pol.) 3.41-6.44	BRUTALITY	POL.
WIEDEN, Otto	123936	M	Ger.	06	Capo, Kalfaktor, C.C. Flossenburg (Ger.) 44-45	MURDER	U.S.
WIEDERMANN	1018	M	Ger.		Cpt., Army Kavallerie, Locmine (Fr.) 7.44	MURDER	FR.
WIEDERMERTH, Karl	196899	M	Ger.		Crim. Assist., Gestapo Section IV 1 b 2 a, Brno., (Czech.) 39-40	SUSPECT	CZECH.
WIEDMAN, Georg	110852	M	Ger.		Truppfhr., S.A.	TORTURE	U.S.
WIEDMANN	186865	M	Ger.		Frontfhr., Army, Bayonne (Fr.)	TORTURE	FR.
WIEDMANN	301156	M	Ger.		General at H.Q. of O.T. Organis. Eins.Gruppe West Cons la Granville MAM. (Fr.) 1.9.44	MISC.CRIMES	FR.
WIEDMANN, Ernst	255676	M		23. 8.04	Pvt., C.C. Harzungen Nordhausen (Ger.)	MURDER	U.S.
WIEDMANN, Hans	251425	M	Ger.		Lt.,338. Div. 3. Bn. School La Bresse (Fr.) 9.-11.44	MURDER	FR.
WIEDNER	1019	M	Ger.	01	Lt., Army 1. Bn. Montenegro (Yugo.) 7.43	MURDER	YUGO.
WIEDOM, Friedrich, Wilhelm	306787	M	Ger.		Stamm Coy.Gr.E.B.366 Bonn from 8.7.43 3.Res.Gren.366 Bn. Sars-la Bruyere Hainaut, (Bel.) 9.44	TORTURE	BEL.
WIEGAND	187455	M			SS-Usturmfhr., SS C.C. Nordhausen Auschwitz (Ger.Pol.) 43-45	TORTURE	U.S.
WIEGAND	192985	M	Ger.		Sgt., SS C.C. Buchenwald (Ger.) 42-45	TORTURE	U.S.
WIEGAND	305376	M	Ger.	07	SS Osturmfhr., Gestapo Sicherheitsdienst Troyes, Chauffour les Bailly (Fr.) 5.44	MURDER	FR.
WIEGAND, Clemens	136663	M	Ger.		Ortsgruppenleiter NSDAP, Civ., Teacher, Frankfurt M, Gimnheim (Ger.)11.44	MURDER	U.S.
WIEGAND, Konrad, (Ernst)	128928	M			SS Rottfhr., SS C.C. Weimar Buchenwald (Ger.)	TORTURE	U.S.
WIEGAND, Konrad	253469	M	Ger.		SS-Hptschfhr., C.C. Auschwitz Birkenau (Pol.) 11.42	MISC.CRIMES	YUGO.
WIEGAND, Ludwig	179734	M	Ger.	14	Major, 15. Pz.Gr.Rgt. 33. Bn. San Quistino (It.) 6.7.44	MURDER	U.K.
WIEGAND, Oskar	185909	M	Ger.	12. 5.07	Standortarzt SS and Pol. for the Grand Duchy, Luxembourg (Lux.)	MURDER	LUX.
WIEGARTNER, Johann	255807	M			Cpl., C.C. Ellrich Nordhausen (Ger.)	MURDER	U.S.
WIEGELE	250570	M	Ger.		Gestapo, Maribor, (Yugo.) 44	MURDER	YUGO.
WIEGLER, Richard	306408	M	Ger.		SS-Sgt., C.C. Buchenwald (Ger.) 16.5.38-9.10.43	MURDER	BEL.
WIEGMANN	195739	M	Ger.		SS-Uschfhr., W-SS C.C. Scheveningen (Neth.) 41-42	MURDER	NETH.
WIEGNER (or WIECKER or WICKNER)	305529	M			Pvt., 3. Rgt. 8. Coy. Guidel, Morbihan (Fr.) 10.44	MURDER	FR.
WIEHAGEN (or VIEHAGEN)	251723	M	Ger.		Uschfhr., SS, C.C. Neuengamme (Ger.)	INTERR.	BEL.
WIEHBERG, Joseph (or FIEBERG)	251430	M	Ger.		Sgt., 2. Inf.Coy. 658. Bn.Semnoccy Les Macon (Fr.) 20.7.44	MURDER	FR.
WIEHL, August	104961	M		99	Civilian, C.C.	MURDER	U.S.
WIELAND	104976	M			Civ., Presumable Civilian, Gernsbach (Ger.) 8.8.44	MURDER	U.S.
WIELAND (see WYLAND)	257455						
WIELAND, Kurt	194157	M	Ger.		Krim.Angestellter Gestapo, Prague (Czech.) 39-45	MURDER	CZECH.
WIELEN	31883	M			Lt., Col., Head of Kripo Leitstelle Breslau, Stalag Luft 3 Sagan (Ger.) 25.3.44	MURDER	U.K.
WIELER	11521	M			Lt., Pz.Gr.Rgt. 110 or 111 9. Coy., Gourden (Fr.) 29.6.44	MURDER	FR.
WIELING	142730	M			Oschfhr., W-SS C.C. Vught (Neth.) 43-44	TORTURE	BEL.
WIEMAN, Herbert (alias WYMAN, Karl)	179780	M			Krim.Kommissar, Gestapo Police Staag Markt Bongau Salzburg(Aust.) 10.44	MURDER	U.S.
WIEMANN, Konrad	255811	M		22.12.09	Sgt., C.C. Ellrich Nordhausen, (Ger.)	MURDER	U.S.
WIEMMER (see WIDMER)	139255						
WIEM	180640	M	Ger.		SS-Uschfhr., 1.SS Pz.Rgt. Leibstandarte Adolf Hitler 2. or 3. Platoon 6. Coy. Malmedy (Bel.) 17.12.44	MURDER	U.S.
WIEMANT	195915	M	Ger.	00	Cpt., Rgt. d'aviation No. 71 Fieldpost L 13883 Bressols et Montbeton (Fr.) 18.8.44	MURDER	FR.
WIEMANZ	21414	M	Ger.	19	Sgt. Schirrmeister 1.SS Panz.Div. 1.Pz. Rgt. Malmedy (Bel.) 17.12.44	MURDER	U.S.
WIENECKE	28751	M	Ger.		Cpt., 20. Army Comd. 1.Gren. Rgt. 510-163 Inf.Div. Finnmark (Nor.)10.44	MURDER	NOR.
WIENECKE	186486	M	Ger.	22 or 23	Usturmfhr., 12. SS Pz. Div.H.J. near Caen (Fr.) 4.6.-8.7.44	TORTURE	CAN.
WIENECKE	258073	M	Ger.	96	SS Osturmfhr., State Service Police Official, Val.Mezirici (Czech.) 44-45	MURDER	CZECH.
WIENECKE, Hans	259167	M	Ger.	4. 6.09	SS Hptschfhr. Gestapo Olomouc (Czech.) 39-42	MURDER	CZECH.
WIENECKE, Josef	185690	M	Ger.	8. 8.06	Official, 2. Staatsanwalt beim Sondergericht Luxembourg, Hamburg (Lux.) 40-9.44	MURDER	LUX.
WIENER, Eduard	196901	M	Ger.		Chief Prison Warden, Gestapo Section I S, Brno. (Czech.) 39-45	MISC.CRIMES	CZECH.
WIENERS, Konrad	21415	M	Ger.	6. 5.98	Assistant Chief and Guard, C.C. Alexander Work Witten (Ger.)	MISC.CRIMES	U.S.

NAME	C.R.FILE NUMBER	SEX	NATIO-NALITY	DATE OF BIRTH	RANK, OCCUPATION, UNIT, PLACE AND DATE OF CRIME	REASON WANTED	WANTED BY
WIENERT	126467	M	Ger.	03	Capt., Stalag Official, Stalag IV, C.C. Grosstychow (Ger.) 6.2.44-4.44	TORTURE	U.S.
WIENKE	193114	M	Ger.		Pvt., Kgf.Arb.Bn. 184, Kobbelvik (Nor.) 6.44	MURDER	NOR.
WIENKE, Walter	255810	M	Ger.		Flyer, C.C. Ellrich, Nordhausen (Ger.)	MURDER	U.S.
WIENZ	125076	M	Ger.		Capt., Staff of Stalag XXI D in 1942	TORTURE	U.K.
WIENZ, Peter	255809	M	Ger.	9. 9.11	Pvt., C.C. Ellrich, Nordhausen (Ger.)	MURDER	U.S.
WIEPKING, Jurgens	168063	M	Ger.		Prof., Reichskommissar, Fuer die Festigung des Deutschtums Berlin (Ger.) 9.39-end of 44	PILLAGE	POL.
WIER, Heinrich	193113	M	Ger.	00	Sgt.,Guard, Reichsjustizministerium, Strafgefangenenlager, Finmark (Nor.) -9.43	MISC.CRIMES	NOR.
WIERTNER	253445	M	Ger.		Employee, Abt. III C. Sipo, Bruessel (Bel.) 40-44	INTERR.	BEL.
WIERZ, Jan	306765	M	Ger.		Landholder, Ihlewerfehn, Friesland (Ger.) Summer 44	MURDER	YUGO.
WIESBADE	195992	M	Ger.		Chief of Kdo., Gestapo, Wurzach Schmieden near Stuttgart (Ger.) 3.4.44	MURDER	FR.
WIESE	253444	M	Ger.		Employee, Abt. IV Sipo, Bruessel (Bel.) 40-44	INTERR.	BEL.
WIESE, Friedrich	258939	M	Ger.	92	Lt.-Gen.	WITNESS	U.S.
WIESE, Gert	124795	M	Ger.	20	SS-Reichsfhr., Unterscharfhr., 16.Pz.Gn.Div. SS	MURDER	U.S.
WIESE, Walter	180634	M	Ger.		Member, Gestapo, Err (Fr.) 5.-9.43	PILLAGE	FR.
WIESEJAHN	253443	M	Ger.		Crim. Secretary, Abt. IV E. Sipo, Brusselsreter (Bel.) 40-44	INTERR.	BEL.
WIESEL	187482	M	Ger.		Unterscharfhr., Guard, SS Totenkopfsturmbann, Dora, Nordhausen (Ger.)43-45	WITNESS	U.S.
WIEGENBACH, Wilhelm	253440	M	Ger.		Ortsgruppenleiter, Civilian, Dudesheim (Ger.) 10.44	TORTURE	U.S.
WIESENBERG	16833	M	Ger.		Obersturmfhr., 12.Pz.Div. H.J. 25. Regt. SS-H.Q. 25 SS PGR, Abbaye Ardenne near Caen-Normandy (Fr.)6.-7.44	TORTURE	CAN.
WIESENPERG	251442	M	Ger.		Sgt., Gen.Trupp 593, Feldgend. Le Chablais (Fr.) 19.-21.5.44	MISC.CRIMES	FR.
WIESENBERGER	192438	M	Ger.		SS-Sgt., Flossenburg (Ger.) 44-45	SUSPECT	U.S.
WIESENFELD	151442	M	Ger.		SS-Untersturmfhr., Lt., SS and Army 150. Pz.Bde., Malmedy, Liege,Stavelot (Bel.) 12.,1.45	MISC.CRIMES	U.S.
WIESER	11522	M	Ger.		Cpl., Army 110. or 111. Pz. Gr. Regt. 2. Coy., Albine (Fr.) 29.6.44	MURDER	FR.
WIESER	173849	M	Ger.		Official Governor, Gestapo Official, Prison, Belgrad (Yugo.) 17.8.41	MURDER	YUGO.
WIESER	187481	M			Unterscharfhr., SS, Dora, Nordhausen (Ger.)43-45	MURDER	U.S.
WIESER, Johann	257387	M	Ger.		SS-Guard, Sgt., SS slave Labour Camp, Beisfjord near Narvik (Nor.)11.42	BRUTALITY	YUGO.
WIESINGER, Josef	260932	M	Ger.	27.10.05	SS-Uschfhr., Allg.-SS since 38, Army-SS since 41, C.C. Auschwitz (Pol.)41	MISC.CRIMES	POL.
WIESKORT, Paul	255816	M			Pvt., C.C. Harzungen, (Ger.)	MURDER	U.S.
WIESNER, Adolf	191953	M	Ger.	86	Official-Agent, Capt., Gestapo, SD Army, Pisek (Czech.)	MURDER	CZECH.
WIESNER, Max	255817	M		00	Cpl., C.C. Harzungen, Nordhausen (Ger.)	MURDER	U.S.
WIESMANN, Gudula Maria	166719	F	Ger.		Chief, Gestapo, Lezaky, Lidice (Czech.) 9.41-7.42	MURDER	CZECH.
WIESMANN, Harald	166717	M	Ger.	22. 4.09	Chief,SS-Hauptsturmfhr., Crim.Police and SS Chief of Gestapo Kladno Lidice, Lezaky, Kladno (Czech.) 9.41-7.42	MURDER	CZECH.
WIESMEIER	253464	M	Ger.		Chief-Postal, State Service, Leutershausen (Ger.) 43-45	BRUTALITY	POL.
WIESSINGER	147016	M	Ger.		SS-Rottenfhr., SS Pz.Div. "Das Reich" 1. Pz.Regt., Tulle (Fr.) 44	MURDER	FR.
WIESSMANN	158441	M	Ger.		Pvt., Luftnachrichten Coy. 21, Marseille (Fr.)18.8.44	MURDER	FR.
WIETEMAN	1022	M	Ger.		Capt., Army, 118. Jaeger Div. 7.43-1.44	MURDER	YUGO.
WIETER	1023	M	Ger.		Lt., Army 738. Regt., (Yugo.) 7.43	MURDER	YUGO.
WIETH	149595	M	Ger.		Pvt., 11. Pz. Div. 1. Group Kempfgr."Wilde", (South WestFr.) 44	MURDER	FR.
WIETING	306668	M	Ger.		05-243 Mongolian "Oberland" Unit, St.Nazaire En Royans (Fr.)20.7.-5.8.44	MURDER	FR.
WIEWIRENSKI, Waldemar	168230	M	Ger.		Pvt., 9. Res.Grenadier Regt. 1. Coy., Magny D' Avignon (Fr.) 18.9.44	MURDER	FR.
WIEZE	36626	M	Ger.		Sgt., Army, C.C., 714. Landessch.Bn., Stalag 20 A, Thorn (Pol.)18.3.45	MURDER	U.K.
WIGGER	261927	M	Ger.		Farmer, SS U.Sturmfhr., C.C. Hessenthal (Ger.)	BRUTALITY	FR.
WIGGER, August	253234	M	Ger.	5.11.96	Crim.Employee, Abt. IV O Sipo, Bruessels (Bel.)	INTERR.	BEL.
WIGGER, Hubert	258756	M	Ger.	02	Usturmfhr., Crim.Employee, R.S.H.A. Sipo, Anvers (Bel.)	TORTURE	BEL.
WIGGERS	139737	M	Ger.		Officer, Stalag X B, Sandbostel (Ger.) 5.45	MISC.CRIMES	FR.
WIJNBERGER, Hans	251438	M	Ger.		Pvt., Parachutist Unit, St. Michielsgedal (Neth.) 9.,10.44	INTERR.	NETH.
WIKLEIN	139154	M	Ger.		C.C. Kahla (Ger.)	TORTURE	BEL.
WIKORSKY	125650	M	Ger.		Cpl., Army, Bandekow 9.10.43	MURDER	FR.
WIKTORIN, Mauriz	194762	M	Ger.		Lt.-General, Pz.Gren.Div. 20. Motoriced Div., 27.5.40	MURDER	U.K.
WILBERT, Willic	195991	M	Ger.		Custom-house-Douanier at Cierp, Chaum (Fr.) 3.7.44	MURDER	FR.
WILBUR or WILBUER	162539	M	Ger.		SS-Unterscharfhr., Weapons SS, C.C., Command Staff, Buchenwald (Ger.)42-45	TORTURE	U.S.
WILCK	67741	M	Ger.		SS-Unterscharfhr., 17.Pz.Div."Goetz v. Berlichingen" Sturmgeschuetz Abt. 17 or Pz.Jaeger Abt. 17, Segre-Renaze (Fr.) 6.8.44-30.7.44	MURDER	FR.
WILCKE, Jochem	174221	M	Ger.	21. 3.25	Leader, H.J., Hessen (Ger.) 3.10.44	MURDER	U.S.
WILCZEK, Alois	255818	M	Ger.		Pvt., C.C. Ellrich, Nordhausen (Ger.)	MURDER	U.S.
WILD	185571	M	Ger.		Sgt., Prison, Guard, C.C. Ebrach (Ger.) 39-45	TORTURE	CZECH.
WILD	255806	M	Ger.		Pvt., C.C. Ellrich, Nordhausen (Ger.)	MURDER	U.S.
WILD	259202	M	Ger.		Untersturmfhr., SS Div. "Prinz Eugen ", Niraic (Yugo.) 5.-6.43	MISC.CRIMES	YUGO.
WILD, Eric	125651	M	Ger.		Adjutant, Gestapo, Baccarat (Fr.) 8.,9.,10.44	MURDER	FR.
WILD, Georges	250549	M	Ger.		Pvt., Instandsetzungszug 01, Toussus (Fr.) 2.8.44	MURDER	FR.
WILDBOUR see WILLBOUR	192983						
WILDBRAND	142731	M	Ger.		Member, Gestapo, Bielefeld (Ger.)	TORTURE	BEL.
WILDE	151441	M	Ger.		Untersturmfhr., Sipo-Section V, Paris (Fr.) 13.6.44	MURDER	FR.
WILDE	186866	M	Ger.		Lt.-Colonel, 2.Pz.Div. Kampfgruppe "Wilde", Tarn Dordogne (Fr.)	MURDER	FR.
WILDE, Erich	196896	M	Ger.		Sgt., SD Commander Wenger, Baccarat (Fr.)	MISC.CRIMES	U.K.
WILDE, Hans	262251	M	Ger.		SS-Rottenfhr., Gestapo, Rennes (Fr.) 43-44	MISC.CRIMES	FR.
WILDEN, Hans	21	M	Ger.		Leiter, Public Official, Leiter der Kirchenangelegenheiten Gen.Gov. 9.39-42	MURDER	POL.
WILDEN, Hendrick	131595	M	Ger.		Officer-Director, Labour, Civilian, Eschweiler (Ger.) 9.42-11.44	MURDER	U.S.
WILDENBLANCK	185187	M	Ger.		Capt., Feldgend., Macon (Fr.)	WITNESS	FR.
WILDENHAIN	191323	M	Ger.		N.C.O. Ers.Bn. 717, St.Andries, Varsenare Les Bruges (Bel.) 4.9.44	MURDER	BEL.
WILDERMANN, Heinrich	168229	M	Ger.		Pvt., 9. Reserve Gren.Regt. 1. Coy., Magny D' Avignon (Fr.) 18.9.44	MURDER	FR.
WILDERMUTH	1768	M	Ger.		Colonel, C.C. Dachau (Ger.)	MISC.CRIMES	U.S.
WILDET	195990	M	Ger.		Pvt., SS 12. Pz.Art. F.P.57 666 A, Tourouves (Fr.) 13.8.44	MURDER	FR.
WILDFANG, Jakob	193112	M	Ger.	12	Hauptfrontfhr., Org.Todt, Oberbauleitung, Narvik (Nor.) 42-43	MISC.CRIMES	NOR.
WILDFANG, Walter	252839	M	Ger.		Pvt., 2. Train 3. Coy.15.Div.Afrika Corps, St.L'eger (Bel.)3.,5.9.44	MISC.CRIMES	BEL.

NAME	C.R.FILE NUMBER	SEX	NATIO- NALITY	DATE OF BIRTH	RANK OCCUPATION UNIT PLACE AND DATE OF CRIME	REASON WANTED	WANTED BY
WILDFUHR	11560	M	Ger.		SS-Schfhr.,SS,Gestapo,Kristiansand (Nor.) 43	TORTURE	NOR.
WILDHAGE, Kurt	196425	M	Ger.	26. 4.05	Dr.,District-Capt.,Civilian,Mistek (Czech.) 39-45	MISC.CRIMES	CZECH.
WILDKRAUT	67816	M	Ger.		Civilian,Himmelfahrt,Funderube,Friedberg (Ger.) 26.10.43-17.4.45	MISC.CRIMES	U.K.
WILDMANN, Ernst	307246	M	Ger.		Reichsbahn-official employed,Fernmeldemeisteref office at Amersfoort (Neth.) 4.10.44 and 5.45	PILLAGE	NETH.
WILDRAUT (or WILROHYD)	180581	M		95	Arbeitskdo.,Stalag IV F,Freiburg (Ger.) 10.43-10.44	TORTURE	U.K.
WILDSCHUTZ	28860	M	Ger.		Major,20 Army staff,Finmark (Nor.) 10.-11.44	MURDER	UNWCC
WILEY	255819	M			C.C.Osterhagen (Ger.)	MURDER	U.S.
WILFERT, Joseph	125004	M	Ger.		Innkeeper,Civilian (Fr.) 40-44	PILLAGE	FR.
WILFERT, Josef	255219	M	Ger.	19. 3.22	Butcher,Civilian,Gossengrun Haberspirk (Czech.) 9.39	MURDER	CZECH.
WILFRUER, Frederik	179732	M	Ger.	10	Pvt.,Army,Stia Garrison (It.) 18.4.44	MURDER	U.K.
WILFING, Jakob	167046	M	Ger.	11	Camp official,C.C.Walchum (Ger.)	TORTURE	FR.
WILFLING	257399	M	Ger.		SS-Guard,Sgt.,SS slave labour camp,Beisfjord near Narvik (Nor.)6.-11.42	BRUTALITY	YUGO.
WILFRIED (alias:STORCH or LA CIGOYNE)	1526	M			Pvt.,Marignane (Fr.)	MURDER	FR.
WILHAUS	1025	M	Ger.		Commanding officer,C.C.Auschwitz-Birkenau,Lwow (Pol.) 43-45	MURDER	POL.,BEL.
WILHELM	255319	M	Ger.		Guard,Glaswerke Ruhr,Karnapp-Essen (Ger.) 44	TORTURE	BEL.
WILHELM	28863	M	Ger.		Major,20 Army Reported Comd.a Ldsch.Bn.,Finmark (Nor.) 10.-11.44	MURDER	NOR.
WILHELM	121682	M	Ger.		SS-Hptschfhr.,SS,C.C.Buchenwald (Ger.)	TORTURE	FR.
WILHELM	130183	M	Ger.		Pvt.,635 Ldsch.Bn.,5 Coy,Camp Commandantur Kdo.26,Erfurt (Ger.) 9.43	MISC.CRIMES	U.K.
WILHELM	136662	M	Ger.	09	SS-Uschfhr.,C.C.Flossenburg (Ger.) 42	TORTURE	U.S.
WILHELM	175685	M	Ger.		SS,C.C.Buchenwald (Ger.) 42-45	MURDER	FR.
WILHELM (see RUDI)	190363						
WILHELM	261325	M	Ger.		Cpl.,Bn.Spielberg,Rgt.2 z.b.V.,Colonel-Wolff,vinicity of Mauleon-Navarreux (Fr.) 6.-8.44	MURDER	FR.
WILHELM, Friedrich	240040	M	Ger.	22. 2.89	Vorstand,Public-official,Schuldenverwaltung,Konversions Kasse fuer Deutsche Auslandsschulden,Berlin (Ger.) 8.44	MISC.CRIMES	U.S.
WILHELM, Hans	31958	M	Ger.		Pvt.,Army,Gouesnou (Fr.)	WITNESS	FR.
WILHELM, Kurt	128805	M	Ger.		Officer,Arbeitskdo.,	TORTURE	U.K.
WILHELM, Ludwig	137537	M	Ger.		Truppfhr.,NSKK,NSV,DAF,Gross Gerau (Ger.) 29.8.44	MURDER	U.S.
WILHELM, Michael	259117	M	Ger.		SS-Usturmfhr.,Company-Commander, SS Div."Prinz Eugen",Niksic (Yugo.) 5.,6.43	MISC.CRIMES	YUGO.
WILHELM, Peter	194870	M	Ger.	8. 8.05	Amtsinspector,Occ.Territories,Luxembourg (Lux.)	MISC.CRIMES	LUX.
WILHELMI	125716	M	Ger.		SS-Uschfhr.,SS,C.C.Flossenburg (Ger.) 44-45	MURDER	FR.
WILHELMI	164118	M	Ger.	12	Organisationsleiter,NSDAP,Hunspach (Fr.) 26.11.44	MURDER	FR.
WILHELMS	142732	M	Ger.	95	Frauenkrietzen (Ger.) 5.43	BRUTALITY	FR.
WILHELMSNE, Helmut (see WALDE, Hermann)	259744						
WILHEM	300403	M	Ger.		Supervisor,Glaswerke Ruhr Works,Karnapp-Essen (Ger.) 7.44	MISC.CRIMES	BEL.
WILDMZIG	104977	M	Ger.		SS-Osturmfhr.,Gestapo,SS,Cuxhafen (Ger.) 3.45	MURDER	U.S.
WILDMZIG, Georg	195383	M	Ger.	30. 3.12	Crim.-Commissary,Osturmfhr.,Gestapo Kassel,SS,Niederdorfelden,Hanau,Hainmuehle near Marburg (Ger.) 42	MURDER	POL.
WILIN, Christel or Christian	1251	M	Ger.		Adj.to Camp Cmdt.,C.C.Beaupwy (Fr.) 21.4.44	MISC.CRIMES	FR.
WILKE	1362	M	Ger.		Major,SS 20 SS Police Rgt.,1 Bn.,	MISC.CRIMES	U.K.
WILKE	21416	M	Ger.	00	Obersecr.,Gestapo,C.C.Hinsert (Lux.)	TORTURE	U.S.
WILKE	142734	M			Major,Oberkdo.Army,Chief of PW Affairs	SUSPECT	U.S.
WILKE	150849	F			Civilian (Ger.) 38-40	WITNESS	U.S.
WILKE	168037	M	Ger.		Adj.,General staff Kommandantur,Crest (Fr.) 7.-8.44	MURDER	FR.
WILKE	192429	M	Ger.		Sgt.,Army,Oberkdo.,La Rochette (Fr.) 3.8.44	MURDER	FR.
WILKE	251454	M			Capt.,Air Force,Nacht-Dienststelle,Blaricum (Neth.) 9.44	PILLAGE	NETH.
WILKE	255815	M			Pvt.,C.C.Osterhagen-Nixei,Nordhausen (Ger.)	MURDER	U.S.
WILKE	252820	M	Ger.	15	Sgt.,Army Inf.Baustab stationed in Sept.44 at Roosendaal (Neth.)5.9.44	PILLAGE	NETH.
WILKE, Adolf	307247	M			Dr.,Head of the Town Hospital,Lueneburg (Ger.) 1.43-4.45	MURDER	YUGO.
WILKE, Arthur	142733	M		13	Hptsturmfhr.,SS and SD,Danzig (Ger.)	MURDER	U.S.
WILKE, Eva	137999	F	Ger.		Civilian	TORTURE	U.S.
WILKE, Gerd	150848	M			Dr.,Civilian (Ger.) 38-40	WITNESS	U.S.
WILKE, Heinrich	21416	M			Crim.-Obersecr.,Gestapo,Luxemburg (Lux.)	MURDER	LUX.
WILKE, Heinz	139725	M	Ger.	15	Civilian,Schutzpolizei at Polte Munitions Factory,Arbeitslager,Magdeburg (Ger.) 44-45	MURDER	U.S.
WILKELMANN	257680	M			SS,C.C.Muehldorf,Dachau (Ger.)	MURDER	U.S.
WILKEN	104978	M	Ger.		Crim.-Secr.,Gestapo,Cuxhaven (Ger.) 29.-30.3.45	MURDER	U.S.
WILKEN	306409	M	Ger.		SS-Cpl.,C.C.Buchenwald (Ger.) 16.5.38-9.10.43	MURDER	BEL.
WILKENING	194120	M	Ger.		SS-Schutze,SS,Stavelot (Bel.) 19.-20.12.44	MURDER	BEL.
WILKENS	1026	M	Ger.		Sonderfhr.,Army,Hauptverbindungstab 588,Clermont-Ferrand (Fr.) 1.2.44-15.7.44	MURDER	FR.
WILKENS, Erich	307248	M		1. 2.09	Pvt.,Guard,Arbeitskdo.121 at Luetzen (Ger.) 43-45	BRUTALITY	YUGO.
WILKIE	142735	M			Capt.,Inf.Rgt.46,Oflag 64 (Fr.) 6.-7.44	TORTURE	U.S.
WILKINS	139736	M	Ger.		Finance-Superintendent,Stalag X B,Sandbostel (Ger.) 1.-5.45	MISC.CRIMES	U.S.
WILL	188764	M	Ger.	95	Major,Stalag V A,C.C.Steinbrueck (Ger.) 22.7.44	MURDER	FR.
WILL	257691			86	SS-Schmetze,C.C.Muhldorf,Dachau (Ger.)	MURDER	U.S.
WILL, Michael	252790	M	Ger.		SS-Mann,C.C.Auschwitz-Birkenau (Pol.) 12.42	MURDER	YUGO.
WILLARD	195989	M	Ger.		Pvt.,O.C.Royallieu (Fr.) 41-44	MURDER	FR.
WILLBOUR (or WILDBOUR)	192983	M	Ger.		Cpl.,SS,C.C.Buchenwald (Ger.) 42-45	TORTURE	U.S.
WILLE, Wilhelm	22				Leader,Public-office,Abt.Justiz,Gen.Gouv.,39-43	MISC.CRIMES	POL.
WILLE, Wilhelm (see HEENE, Wilhelm)	142442						
WILLEHENS, Klaus	150797	M			Civilian,Pattensen (Ger.) 12.3.45	WITNESS	U.S.
WILLEK	261770	M	Ger.		Cpl.,Art.H.D.V.199-2235,N.D.F.Nr.S.P.27046 C,Lorgies (Fr.) 3.9.44	MURDER	FR.
WILLEK, Herbert	158442	M			Civilian,C.C.Wieda (Ger.) 5.-14.4.45	WITNESS	U.S.
WILLEM	251437	M			Administrator,C.C.Torgau (Ger.) 43-45	MURDER	U.S.
WILLEMS, Friedrich Wilhelm	158438	M	Ger.	20.11.14	Civilian,Nexine (Bel.) 6.9.44	MURDER	BEL.

NAME	C.R.FILE NUMBER	SEX	NATIO- NALITY	DATE OF BIRTH	RANK OCCUPATION UNIT PLACE AND DATE OF CRIME	REASON WANTED	WANTED BY
WILLEMS, Heinz	136407	M	Ger.	22	Cpl., Army, Erdorf (Ger.) 8.44	TORTURE	U.S.
WILLENBROCK	151478	M	Ger.	25.8.01	Uschfhr, SS, SD, Abt.IV, 3 a, Vichy (Fr.) 44	MURDER	FR.
WILLERY (see VILERI)	185299						
WILLEYE	252809	M	Ger.		Oschfhr, SS, SD, Toulouse (Fr.) 11.42-19.8.44	MISC.CRIMES	FR.
WILLI	191964	M	Ger.		Sgt., Army, Royan (Fr.) 11.44	PILLAGE	FR.
WILLI	300973	M	Ger.		Dr., CC Stettin-Poelitz, (Ger.) 44	MISC.CRIMES	CZECH.
WILLI, Alfons	255814	M		15.1.03	Rottfhr, CC Harzungen, Nordhausen (Ger.)	MURDER	U.S.
WILLIAMS (see SCHAPER)	62040						
WILLICH	62444	M	Ger.		Bie.leader, Maj.Gen. of police, inspector of security police and security service, Wehrkreis 20 Danzig, Thorn (Pol.) 41	MURDER	POL.
WILLICH, Helmut	187325	M	Ger.	2.5.95	Police.Maj.Gen., SD, W-SS, Sipo, Danzig 45	MISC.CRIMES	U.S.
WILLIE	158390	M	Ger.	10	Rottfhr, SS, CC Rawisk (Pol.) 42-43	TORTURE	U.K.
WILLIG	121686	M	Ger.		Customs-officer, frontier police, Creach Maout en Pleubian 5.8.-7.8.44	MURDER	FR.
WILLINGER, Josef	253166	M	Ger.	25.12.99	Dr., leading official,Reichsprotector in the Ministry of Education, Prag (Czech.) 40-45	MURDER	CZECH.
WILLIS	191963	M	Ger.		Col., Army, Rynst, Villamblard, Correges (Fr.)	MURDER	FR.
WILLKIE	124336	M			Obermeister, Guard, Stalag II A, Cordshagen near Neubrandenburg (Ger.) 2.-4.45	TORTURE	U.S.
WILLMANN	191322	M	Ger.		Pvt., Eis.Art.Btty 717, F.P. No.22980, St.Andries, Varsenare, Lez Bruges (Bel.) 4.9.44	MURDER	BEL.
WILLMANN, Heinz	191261	M	Ger.		Pvt., Gren.Ers.Rgt., Magny d'Anigon (Fr.) 18.9.44	MURDER	FR.
WILLMANN, Hermann	193663	M	Ger.		Guard, SS, CC Thekla (Ger.)	MURDER	POL.
WILLMES	126750	M			Lt., Africa Mission, 95 Sicherungs-Bn., Chamalieres (Fr.) 23.8.44	MURDER	FR.
WILLOWITZER, Franz	10372	M	Ger.		Dr., public prosecutor, P.O. county court, Litomerice(Czech.)21.2.40	MURDER	CZECH.
WILLY	1027	M			Gestapo, Perigueux (Fr.) 6.44	MURDER	FR.
WILLY	126964	M	Ger.		Capt., Sipo, Expo chief Block 7, CC Flossenburg, Gleiwitz(Ger.)	MURDER	FR.
WILLY	127080	M			Chief Block 108, CC Dora, Nordhausen (Ger.)	TORTURE	FR.
WILLY (see SCHMIDT, Rolland)	13822						
WILLY	141486	M	Ger.		Chief, SS, CC Mauthausen (Aust.)11.5.42-5.45	TORTURE	FR.
WILLY	151475	M	Ger.		Member Gestapo, Angers (Fr.)	MURDER	FR.
WILLY	185891	M	Ger.		N.C.O., Army, Cherehonosos-Creta- (Grc.)	MURDER	GRC.
WILLY	301610	M	Ger.		Customs official, employed in May 43 on the Franco-Belgian frontier, in particular at Vieux-Conde, Peruwelz(Hainaut) 29.5.43	MISC.CRIMES	BEL.
WILLY	906522	M	Ger.		Agent, IV Section Gestapo Angers, Flossenburg (Ger.) 42-45	MURDER	FR.
WILLZMANN	1026	M	Ger.		Hptsturmfhr, SS, Payzac (Fr.) 16.2.44	MURDER	FR.
WILMANN	104979	M	Ger.		SS-Mann, Guard, W-SS, CC, vicinity of Leipzig, Thekla (Ger.) 18.4.45	MURDER	U.S.
WILMOUTH, Mitty (or Metty)	306904	M	Ger.		Interpreter, Kommandantur, Abbeville-Somme (Fr.) 31.8.44	MURDER	FR.
WILNZIG	126966	M	Ger.		Usturmfhr, SS, Pz.Div."Das Reich", Valence d'Agen (Fr.) 23.6.44	MURDER	FR.
WILROYD (see WILDRAUT)	180581						
WILS	151474	M	Ger.	90	Bn.-leader, Army, Aixe la Chapelle (Ger.) 9.43	MURDER	FR.
WILSDORF	1963	M	Ger.		Pvt., Army, 903 fortress Bn.	MISC.CRIMES	U.K.
WILSDORF, Arthur	306410	M	Ger.		SS Sgt., CC Buchenwald (Ger.) 16.5.38-9.10.42	MURDER	BEL.
WILTSCHNIG (or WINSCHNIG)	192290						
WILTSCHKO, Johann	252789	M	Ger.		Zellenleiter, NSDAP Freikorps, Dolni (Czech.) 42	TORTURE	CZECH.
WILTZER, Frederic	185188	M	Ger.		Secretary, Navy, Moselle (Fr.) 44	PILLAGE	FR.
WILWERSIN	196727	M	Ger.		W.O., unit stationed at Wiesbaden, Etampes (Fr.) 17.-18.8.44	WITNESS	FR.
WILZ, Gerard	253232	M	Ger.		Pvt., Straslem (Ger.) 11.44	WITNESS	U.S.
WIMMER	21417	M			Pvt., Army, CC Jessen (Ger.) 17.8.44	MURDER	U.S.
WIMMER	67740	M	Ger.		Osturmfhr, 17.SS Pz.Gren.Div."Goetz von Berlichingen", Sturmgeschuets Abt.17, Pz.Jg.Abt.17, Segre-Renaze (Fr.) 6.8.44,30.7.44	MURDER	FR.
WIMMER	193111	M	Ger.		Lt.Col., KGF.Arb.Bn.189, Drag (Nor.) 44	MURDER	NOR.
WIMMER	258150	M	Ger.		Professor, CC Natzweiler (Fr.)	SUSPECT	BEL.
WIMMER, Charles (Karl)	195988	M	Ger.		Dr., Physician, SS medical officer to airforce, Asst. to Dr.August Hirt, Fort Ney Strassburg (Fr.) 40-44	MURDER	FR.
WIMMER, Josef	12449	M	Ger.		Pvt., Army, 110 or 111 Pz.Gren.Rgt., 2 Coy, Albine(Fr.) 29.6.44	MURDER	FR.
WIMMER, Josef	255813	M			Pvt., CC Ellrich, Nordhausen (Ger.)	MURDER	U.S.
WIMMER, Wastel or WIEMMER	139255	M	Ger.	00	Camp-leader, Hptsturmfhr, SS, CC Lublin (Pol.) 40-43	MURDER	U.S.;POL.
WIMMERS, Peter	187479	M			Guard, SS-Mann, 4 SS Totenkopf-Sturmbann, CC Monowitz,Nordhausen,Dora (Pol., Ger.) 43-45	TORTURE	U.S.
WIMPEL	193110	M	Ger.		Lt., 3 Coy, POW Work Bn.,184, CC Drag (Nor.) 11.-12.44	TORTURE	NOR.
WINCKELMANN, Hans	906826	M	Ger.		Pvt. operating near Gambsheim (Lower Rhine) Ger. 5.1.45	MURDER	FR.
WINCKLER	194088	M	Ger.		Agent, Gestapo, Lisle Perigueux (Fr.) 21.6.44	MURDER	FR.
WINCKLER	259640	M	Ger.		SS Scharfhr, chief of Kdo.272, Torgelow (Ger.) 43	BRUTALITY	FR.
WINCKLER, Jacob	251447	M	Ger.		SS Hptsturmfhr, CC Mauthausen (Aust.)	BRUTALITY	FR.
WINCKLER, Paul	149596	M	Ger.		Cpl., 11 Pz.Div., South West France 44	MURDER	FR.
WIND, Josef	251460	M	Ger.		13 SS Police Rgt., Ferlach (Aust.) 44-45	MURDER	YUGO.
WIND, Reinhard	256756	M	Ger.	1.1.11	Kapo, CC Nordhausen (Ger.)	MURDER	U.S.
WIND, Rolf	185892	M	Ger.	9.1.14	Clerk, CC Auschwitz (Pol.) 43-45	MURDER	U.S.
WINDAU	251736	M		26.7.99	Major, Urbes (Fr.) 24.9.44-5.10.44	TORTURE	FR.
WINDECK	192435	M	Ger.		Guard, CC Bautzen (Ger.) 18.-24.9.44	TORTURE	BEL.
WINDERLICH	257945	M	Ger.		Lt., Army, Valognes (Fr.) 6.6.44	MURDER	U.S.
WINDHOFEL	142737	M	Ger.	10	Usturmfhr, W-SS, CC Lublin (Pol.)	MURDER	POL.
WINDHORST, Karl	124736	M	Ger.	93	Crim.Secretary, Kripo, Brussels (Bel.)	TORTURE	BEL.
WINDIG	21411	M	Ger.	01	Uschfhr. W-SS, CC Hinzert (Ger.)	MURDER	U.S.
WINDMULLER	149699	M	Ger.		Lt., Air Force, CC Poing Muhldorf area (Ger.) 22.2.45	MURDER	U.S.
WINDOLF	24844	M	Ger.	12	Osturmbannfhr, SS, Tulle (Fr.) 9.6.44	MURDER	FR.
WINDOLPH	124062	M	Ger.		Inspector, Arbeits-Kdo., CC Leipzig (Ger.) 10.43-4.45	MISC.CRIMES	U.K.
WINDOLPH	186718	M	Ger.	88	Civilian, Stalag IV G, CC near Ammelshain (Ger.) 10.44-4.45	TORTURE	U.K.
WINDSTOSSER, Elisabeth (nee MITTER)	162724	F	Ger.	21.3.13	Civilian, Milk-Insp., Lampertsham (Ger.) 6.44	WITNESS	U.S.
WINEBERGER	151451	M	Ger.		Pvt. - Guard, Army, working command, Retanie(Aust.) 7.2.42	MURDER	U.K.
WINFURTHER, Anton	11525	M	Ger.		N.C.O., Pz.Gren.Rgt.110 or 111, 2 Coy, Albine (Fr.) 29.6.44	MURDER	FR.
WINGERT, Peter	255829	M	Ger.	4.12.16	Cpl., CC Ellrich, Nordhausen (Ger.)	MURDER	U.S.
WINGLER	166722	M	Ger.		Dr., regional official, civilian, Ministry of Justice, Muenchen(Ger.) 43	MISC.CRIMES	U.S.

NAME	C.R.FILE NUMBER	SEX	NATIO-NALITY	DATE OF BIRTH	RANK	OCCUPATION UNIT PLACE AND DATE OF CRIME	REASON WANTED	WANTED BY
WINGLER, Paul	192434	M	Ger.	81	Coaler-worker,Civ.,Limbach (Ger.) 44-45		MURDER	BEL.
WINGRUPPER	189261	F	Ger.		Member,Gestapo,C.C.Dachau (Ger.) 40-45		MURDER	BEL.
WINHAUZEN, Paul	149701	M			Capt.,SA,Work-Camp,Erfurt (Ger.)		MISC.CRIMES	U.S.
WINICKE	21412		Ger.		Usturmfhr.,SS,12 SS-Pz.Div."Hitler Jugend"		MISC.CRIMES	CAN.
WINIGER	191962	M	Ger.		Pol.-Chief,Zollgrenz-Pol.,Abondance (Fr.) 45		MURDER	FR.
WINIMOLLER	251431	M	Ger.		Col.,F.P.No.06459,Romilly (Fr.) 44		PILLAGE	FR.
WINIWARTER, Franz	125618	M	Ger.	1.6.87	Oberst,Stalag VII B,C.C.Memmingen (Ger.)		MISC.CRIMES	U.S.
WINKELMANN, Josef	256717	M		23	Pvt.,SS,C.C.Mühldorf,Dachau (Ger.)		MURDER	U.S.
WINKEL (see WINKLER)	192225	M						
WINKELHOFER, Heinrich	191950	M	Ger.	02	Osturmfhr.,Chief,Gestapo,S.D.,Klatovy (Czech.) 39-45		MURDER	CZECH.
WINKELMANN	121684	M			Lt.,Dr.,C.C.Ravensbrueck (Ger.)		MISC.CRIMES	BEL.
WINKELMANN	142007	M		20	SS,Waldlager V and VI,O.C.Ampfing (Ger.) 6.44-45		TORTURE	U.S.
WINKELMANN	147988	M		91	Dr.,Osturmfhr.,W-SS,C.C.Sachsenhausen,Oranienburg (Ger.)		TORTURE	U.K.
WINKELMANN	158391	M	Ger.		Chief,Gestapo,C.C.Stettin,Politz (Ger.)		MURDER	FR.
WINKELMANN	175695	M	Ger.		General-Lt.,Chief,SS,Hauptamt Orpo,C.C.Oswiecim,Birkenau (Pol.) 39-45		MURDER	CZECH.
WINKELMAYER	255674	M			Uschfhr.,C.C.Nordhausen (Ger.)		MURDER	U.S.
WINKELNKEMPER, Toni	240081	M	Ger.	18.10.05	Dr.jur.,Gauredner,official,Public official,Presse and Propaganda, Koeln-Lindenthal,(Ger.)		MISC.CRIMES	U.S.
WINKEN, Wilhelm	149702	M	Ger.		Farmer,Civ.,Oltmannsfehn,Stapelmoor (Ger.) 20.11.43		MURDER	U.S.
WINKER, Arno	256597	M	Ger.	23.8.06	Employee,C.C.Nordhausen (Ger.)		MURDER	U.S.
WINKHAUS, Hermann	240079	M	Ger.	97	Bergwerks-Dir.,Dr.Ing.,Public official,Warproduction,Duesseldorf (Ger.)		INTERR.	U.S.
WINKLER	1029	M			Bde.-Fuehrer,Pol.,Orpo,Befehlshaber SS, 42		MURDER	POL.
WINKLER	1087	M	Ger.		Capt.,Chief,Feldgendarmerie,Langres (Fr.)		TORTURE	FR.
WINKLER	124337	M	Ger.		Capt.,Abwehr Offizier,Stalag III B,C.C.Fuerstenberg-Oder(Ger.) 43-45		MISC.CRIMES	U.S.
WINKLER	127081	M	Ger.		Director,Civ.,C.C.Dora,Nordhausen (Ger.)		TORTURE	FR.
WINKLER (or WINCKLER)	130992	M	Ger.		Kapo,C.C.Mauthausen (Aust.) 41-45		SUSPECT	U.S.,FR.
WINKLER	136661	M	Ger.	80	Dr.,Mayor,Public official,Graudenz (Pol.) 42		MISC.CRIMES	U.S.,POL.
WINKLER	142738	M	Ger.		Civ.,C.C.Halle (Ger.)		TORTURE	U.S.
WINKLER	142739	M	Ger.	97	Stabsscharfhr.,W-SS,C.C.Lahde-Weser (Ger.) 43-45		MURDER	BEL.
WINKLER	167857	M			Opl.,Sturmmann,Lt.,Feldgendarm.,9 Inf.Div.,85 Regt.,SS,Auberive, Flagny,Coiffey,Chalencey (Fr.) 43-44		MURDER	FR.
WINKLER	191201	M	Ger.		Dr.,Mayor,Public official,Beauftragter f.d."Vierjahresplan" Kattowitz (Pol.) 39-44		PILLAGE	POL.
WINKLER	191971	M			Lt.,9 Inf.Div.,361 Regt.,Lus La Croix Haute (Fr.) 10.7.44		MURDER	FR.
WINKLER (or WINKEL)	192225	M	Ger.	97	Civ.,Arbeitskommando 959,Groditz (Ger.) 44-45		TORTURE	U.K.
WINKLER	195987	M	Ger.		Adjudant-Chief,2 Coy.,Feldausb.-Bn.189,116 Inf.Regt.,Clermont-Dessus,La Magistere (Lot et Garonne).(Fr.) 15.-17.8.44		MURDER	FR.
WINKLER	252810	M			SS-Mann,C.C.Sentry,Schurzingen (Ger.)		BRUTALITY	FR.
WINKLER	252822	M	Ger.		Capt.,leader,Arbeits-Kontrolldienst,Overijsel,Ommen(Neth.) 44		INTERR.	NETH.
WINKLER	256788		Ger.		Employee,C.C.Nordhausen (Ger.)		MURDER	U.S.
WINKLER, Alois	162540	M	Ger.	19	Rottfhr.,W-SS,1 Pz.Div."Lah",Feldgend.,Weissenbach (Aust.)12.4.45		MURDER	U.S.
WINKLER, Anton	255812	M		20.4.05	Pvt.,Rottfhr.,C.C.Harzungen,Nordhausen (Ger.)		MURDER	U.S.
WINKLER, Bruno	119387	M	Ger.		Settler,Olekszyn (Pol.) 12.39		INCENDIARISM	POL.
WINKLER, Edmund	301053	M	Ger.		Guard,Labour Camp,Lahde-Weser (Ger.) 43-45		MURDER	BEL.
WINKLER, "Fernandel"	250546	M			Blockfhr.,SS,C.C.Neuengamme (Ger.)		TORTURE	FR.
WINKLER, Franz	305379	M	Ger.		Civ.,Ebenberg,Krs.Spittal an der Drau,Carinthia Province (Aust.) 16.11.44		MURDER	U.S.
WINKLER, Gerhard	240078	M	Ger.	30.10.88	Bde.-Fuehr.,Pol.-Fuehr.,Befehlshaber,Hoehere SS,Polizei, Berlin,Krakau (Ger.Pol.) 42		MURDER	UNWCC
WINKLER, Heinz	259757	M	Ger.		Oberarzt,Sondeno near Bologna (Ital.) 25.2.45		WITNESS	U.S.
WINKLER, Herbert	187478	M			Guard,4 SS-Totenkopf-Sturmbann,C.C.Dora,Nordhausen,Auschwitz (Pol.Ger.)		TORTURE	U.S.
WINKLER, Jacob	305531	M	Ger.		Hptsturmfhr.,SS,Loibl-Pass Camp,Kdo.,Attached to Mauthausen C.C., (Ger.)43-45		MURDER	FR.
WINKLER, Karl	262252	M	Ger.	31.10.?	Uschfhr.,SS,Gestapo,Rennes (Fr.) 43-44		MISC.CRIMES	FR.
WINKLER, Klaus	173838	M	Ger.		Crim.Asst.,Stapo-Leitstelle,Dep.II B,C.C.Oswiecim,Birkenau, Prag (Pol.-Czech.) 35-45		MURDER	CZECH.
WINKLER, M.	136277				SS-Mann,SS-Pz.Div."Das Reich",Vernaque le Vernet (Fr.) 44		MURDER	FR.
WINKLER, Max	191358	M	Ger.	10	Pvt.,190 Kgf.-Bn.,2 Coy.,C.C.Russaones (Nor.) 11.44-5.45		MURDER	NOR.
WINKLER, Paul	104982	M	Ger.	99	Civ.,Mine Pol.-Insp.,C.C.Niedershausen,Sontra,Weissenhasel (Ger.) 12.44		MURDER	U.S.
WINKLER, Richard	260712	M		21.9.89	Employee-Manager,Reichsauftragsverwaltung,Savingsbank, Pilsen (Czech.) 2.45		PILLAGE	CZECH.
WINKLER, Rudolf	128927	M	Ger.	17.9.95	Oschfhr.,SS,W-SS,Totenkopf-Sturmbann,C.C.Buchenwald,Weimar (Ger.)		TORTURE	U.S.
WINKS, John	34628	M			Krim.Obersekr.,Pol.,Aachen (Ger.) 9.8.44		WITNESS	U.S.
WINNER, Rupert	11526	M	Ger.		Pvt.,Pz.Gren.Regt.,110 or 111, 2 Coy.,Albine (Fr.) 29.6.44		MURDER	FR.
WINNECKE	196745	M			Lt.Col.,Osturmbannfhr.,leader of Gestapo at Nis,Gardetin and Nis, Serbia (Yugo.) 4.43		MISC.CRIMES	YUGO.
WINNECKE, Friedrich	252811	M	Ger.		Hptfhr.,S.D.,Toulouse (Fr.) 11.42-19.8.44		MISC.CRIMES	FR.
WINNER, Olivier	151454	M	Ger.		Secr. de entreprise,civ.,Hagen (Ger.)		MISC.CRIMES	FR.
WINNEWASSER, Alfred	259235	M	Ger.		Oschfhr.,Gestapo of Poitiers antenne of Angouleme, (Einrichter in Heidelberg), Poitiers Area (Fr.) 40-45		MISC.CRIMES	FR.
WINNIGER	252823	M	Ger.		Lt., Army,Unit Brandenburg (Ital.)		INTERR.	U.K.
WINNINBERG, Willy	167042	M	Ger.		Pvt.,Air Force,Troissereux (Fr.) 15.-18.8.44		MURDER	FR.
WINSCHNIG (or WILTSCHNIG or WISCHNIG)	192230	M	Ger.		Sturmbannfhr.,SS,Volkssturm-Training-school,Villach,Wald an der Sava (Aust.-Yugo.) 22.11.44		MURDER	U.S.
WINTERHALTER, Emil	150837	M			Bauernfhr.,Public official,Schollach (Ger.)		MURDER	U.S.
WINTER	24856	M		00	Scharfhr.,SS,Asst.Camp-Commander at C.C.Wittlich, Trier (Ger.) 41-45		TORTURE	U.S.
WINTER	24857	M			Pvt.,Inf.,Oschatz (Ger.)		MURDER	U.K.
WINTER	67742	M	Ger.	11	Pvt.,Guard,Army,Stalag IV G,Leipzig (Ger.) 18.12.42		MURDER	U.K.
WINTER	100428	M			Cpl.,Army,872 Coy.,C.C.St.Poelten,Pottenbronn (Aust.) 3.44-5.45		TORTURE	U.K.
WINTER	124061	M	Ger.		Sgt.,4.Bn.,610 Inf.Regt.,Brambach,Bramburg (Ger.) 21.2.45		MISC.CRIMES	U.K.
WINTER	126400	M	Ger.		Oschfhr.,SS,C.C.Hinzert (Ger.) 41-43		TORTURE	U.S.

NAME	C.R FILE NUMBER	SEX	NATIO-NALITY	DATE OF BIRTH	RANK OCCUPATION UNIT PLACE AND DATE OF CRIME	REASON WANTED	WANTED BY
WINTER	142740	M			Oberwachtmeister, Police, Halchter (Ger.) 28.9.44	MURDER	U.S.
WINTER	150896	M			Sgt., Army, L Coy.,714. C C., Stargard, Neubrandenburg (Ger.) 1-3.45	TORTURE	U.S.
WINTER	186868	M	Ger		Pvt., Army, Beaumenil (Fr.)	PILLAGE	FR.
WINTER	186869	M	Ger.		Sgt., Feldgend., Trupp 626, Peronne Licourt (Fr.) 24.8.44	MURDER	FR
WINTER	189826	M	Ger.		Sgt, Feldgend., Bajnia Basta (Yugo) 7.43	RAPE	YUGO.
WINTER	192133	M	Ger.		Lt., Geh.Feldpolizei, Interpreter, Brussels (Bel.)	MISC.CRIMES	BEL.
WINTER	192428	M	Ger		Lt , Army, Bruay en Artois (Fr.) 24.8.44	MURDER	FR.
WINTER	256578	M	Ger.		Oschfhr., SS, Pers.Sec., Dora-Mittelbau, Nordhausen (Ger.)	MURDER	U.S.
WINTER	260059	M	Ger.		Sturmfhr., SS, Gestapo-Prison, Cmdt., Belgrad (Yugo.) 1.44-9.44	MISC.CRIMES	YUGO.
WINTER, August	257705	M	Ger	18.1.97	General, Asst.Chief of Staff, Supreme Command, Armed Forces, Brandenburg (Ger.)	WITNESS	U.S.
WINTER, Fritz	253441	M	Ger.		Civilian, Budesheim (Ger.) 10.44	WITNESS	U.S.
WINTER, Fritz	305381	M			SS-O'Sturmfhr.,Einsatzkdo.,S.D.,Sipo,Wierden,Zwolle (Neth.) 29.3.45, 31.3.45	MURDER	NETH.
WINTER, Gunther	151437	M	Ger.		Lt., 21.Panz.Div. H.Q.'s, Sessenheim (Fr.) 1.45	MURDER	U.S.
WINTER, Hans	151452	M	Ger.		Overseer, Ex-Cpl.invalided, D.E.A.Grube Regis-Breit, Ex-Army, Ingen nr.Altenburg (Ger.) 4.44-4.45	MISC.CRIMES	U K.
WINTER, Hans	158446	M	Ger.	00	Pvt., Stalag XX A, C.C., Nessau (Pol.) 44	TORTURE	U.K.
WINTER, Hans	306222	M	Ger.	15-17	N.C.O., Head of Detachment, B 2021 G.V. Kdo , Stalag XVII B, Pottenbrunn, St. Poelten (Aust.) 3.44-3.45	BRUTALITY	U.K.
WINTER, Heinz	307251	M			Asst., belonging to the operational Commando, attached to the Lourdes Custom-House, Htes.-Pyrenees (Fr.) 1.44-8.44	MURDER	FR.
WINTER, Jacob	163489	M			Civilian, C.C. Monsheim,Allier (Fr.) 44	MURDER	FR.
WINTER, Johann	11527	M	Ger.		Pvt., Army, 111.or 110.Panz.Gren.Rgt., Albine (Fr.) 29.6.44	MURDER	FR
WINTER, Josef	255675	M		18	Cpl., C.C.Ellrich, Nordhausen (Ger.)	MURDER	U.S.
WINTER, Josef	906297	M	Ger.		Member, Gestapo at Trencin, Oswiecim, C.C.Birkenau (Pol.) 39-45	MURDER	CZECH.
WINTER, Ladislaus	260527	M	Ger.	27.1.14	Rottfhr., SS, Waffen-SS, Guard-Coy., C.C Auschwitz (Pol) 41-43	BRUTALITY	POL.
WINTER, Ludwig	251737	M	Ger.		SS-Officer, C.C , Buchenwald (Ger.) 44-45	MISC.CRIMES	FR.
WINTER, Vinzenz	1030	M	Ger.		Worker, Civilian, Mine Conc.Camp, Alsdorf (Ger.) 42-44	TORTURE	FR.
WINTERBAUER	252812	M	Ger.	95	Uschfhr., SS, Schorzingen (Ger.)	MISC.CRIMES	FR.
WINTERBURG, Heinz	151453	M	Ger.		Sturmmann, SS, SS-Pz.Div."Das Reich", Standarte "Der Fuehrer", Flammenrens (Fr.) 44	MURDER	FR.
WINTERER, Anna	194159	F	Ger.	25.10.12	Waitress, Civilian, Amstetten (Aust.) 20.3.45	MISC.CRIMES	U.S.
WINTERHAGEN, Artur	255457	M	Ger.	25.4.01	Rottfhr., SS, C.C. Harzungen, Nordhausen (Ger.)	MURDER	U.S.
WINTERHALTER	136406	M		96	Policeman, Police, Karlsruhe (Ger) 31.3.45	WITNESS	U.S.
WINTERHALTER (Weber)	150842	M			Civilian, Schollach (Ger.)	MURDER	U.S.
WINTERHAUSER (or WINTHAUSER)	136410	F			Girl, SS, Conc.Camp, Erfurt (Ger.) 44	TORTURE	U.S.
WINTERLING, Max	194699	M	Ger.	10	Agent, Gestapostelle, Savigny en Septaine (Fr.) 7.44-8.44	MURDER	FR.
WINTERMANTEL, Fritz	240076	M	Ger.	26.4.82	Civ.Manager, Public-Official, Vorstand, Deutsche Bank, Betriebs-finanzierung, Berlin (Ger.)	MISC.CRIMES	U.S.
WINTERMAYER	174549	M	Ger.	96	Sgt., 515.Lds.Schtz.Bn.,2.Coy., Niwka nr.Bensburg (Pol.) 12.4.43	BRUTALITY	U.K.
WINTERMAYR, Karl	193109	M	Ger.	00	Sgt., Guard, Reichsjustiz-Ministerium, Feldstraflager,C.C., Finmark (Nor.) - 10.44	MISC.CRIMES	NOR.
WINTERS	124060	M	Ger.	89	Sgt., 714.Lds.Schtz.Bn.,1.Coy., Neubrandenburg-Gallin (Ger.) 3.45	BRUTALITY	U K
WINTERSHAGEN, Artur	256595	M	Ger.		Uschfhr., C.C. Dora, Nordhausen (Ger.)	MURDER	U S.
WINTERSTEIN	131606	M	Ger.	10	Osturmfhr., SS, Sicherheits-Kommando 11 b, Thekina (Rum.) Tiraspol (Sov.Un.) 41	MURDER	U S.
WINTERWATER, Franz	162538	M	Ger.	1.6.87	Camp-Official, Col., C.C., Stalag VII (Ger.) 6.44-10.44	MISC.CRIMES	U.S.
WINTGEN	252821	M	Ger.		Hptschfhr., SS, SD, Halfweg (Neth.) 11.44	PILLAGE	NETH.
WINTHAUSER (see WINTERHAUSER)	136410						
WINTHER, Gerta	28752	M	Ger.		Lt.Gen., Army, Comd.210.Geb.Div., 20.Army, Finmark (Nor.) 10.44-11.44	MURDER	NOR.
WINTJES	256501	M	Ger.		Military, Sipo, Amsterdam (Neth.) 23.10.44	MURDER	NETH.
WINTZE	194081	M	Ger.		Major, Army, Loire and Ampuis (Fr.) 28.,31.8 44	MURDER	FR.
WINTZER	251432	M	Ger.		Capt., Unit L 21228, Kormainville (Fr.) 17.8.44	TORTURE	FR.
WINZEN, Erich	253467	M			Pvt., Khledia, (Fr.) 13.-14.4.44	MURDER	FR.
WINZER, Bernhard	174224	M	Ger.	94	Head, Gestapo, Giessen (Ger.) 3.10.44	MURDER	U.S.
WINZHAUSEN, Paul	135335	M	Ger.		Hptsturmfhr., SS, C.C. near Erfurt (Ger.) 44	TORTURE	U.S.
WIPF, Eugene	251416	M	Ger.		Kapo, C.C , Hinzert (Ger.)	MISC.CRIMES	FR.
WIPPER, Ludwig	142068	M	Ger.		Dr.,O'Sturmbannfhr.,SS,Head Dental Surgeon at C.C. Dachau (Ger.)	TORTURE	U.S.
WIPPERMAN, Erich	104981	M	Ger.	18	Lt., 2.Army-Art.,503.Bde.,10.Btty , Hilden (Ger.) 16.4.45	MURDER	U.S.
WIPPERMANN	168072	M	Ger.		Lt., Feldgend., Feldkommandantur 595, Lebrell near Saumur (Fr)21.8.44	MURDER	FR.
WIPPLER, Gerharde (or FRANK)	253463	F	Ger.	17.3.24	Saleswoman, Civilian, K.Dvur (Czech.) 42	MURDER	CZECH.
WIRGES, August	189426	M			Member, Gestapo, Cannes, (Fr.) 44	PILLAGE	FR.
WIRENWEIN, Hedwig	194882	F	Ger.	22	Member, Gestapo, Kolin (Czech.) 39-45	MURDER	CZECH.
WIRINGER, Alphons	195986	M	Ger.		Chief, Kdo.711 St.VII., Moosburg (Ger.) 7.44-12.44	TORTURE	FR.
WIRISCH, Kuno	240075	M	Ger.		Dr., Hptsturmfhr., SS-Head of Legal Department Reichskommissariat fuer die Festigung Deutschen Volkstums (Section 2-C) Schweikelberg (Ger.) 3.44	MISC.CRIMES	U.S.
WIRKMEISTER	151449	M	Ger.		Dr., Stabsarzt, Army, Medical-Officer, Stalag XXI A, Schieratz (Pol.)42	MISC.CRIMES	U.K.
WIRKMEISTER (see WERKMEISTER)	187636						
WIRNITZER, Adolf	255324	M	Ger.	1.3.07	Civilian, Gossengrun-Haberspirk (Czech.) 9.39	MURDER	CZECH.
WIRSCHING, Wilhelm	161694	M	Ger.		Civilian, Steinbach (Ger.) 2.44	WITNESS	U.S.
WIRT (see WUERTH)	1043				Dr.		
WIRT (see WOITH)	185189						
WIRTH	12450	M	Ger.		Commissar, Geh.Feldpolizei, 737.Gruppe, Arras (Fr.) 44	TORTURE	FR.
WIRTH	168026	M	Ger.		Dr., Civilian, Einsatzstab Rosenberg (Fr.) 40-44	PILLAGE	FR.
WIRTH	196895	M	Ger.		Uschfhr., SS, C.C.-Guard, Gusen (Aust.)	MISC.CRIMES	BEL.
WIRTH	255456	M	Ger.		Sgt., C.C. Ellrich, Nordhausen (Ger.)	MURDER	U.S.
WIRTH	301370	M	Ger.		Capt., Police in-C.C. Lublin, Treblinka, Maidenak (Pol.)	MURDER	FR.
WIRTH	306523	M	Ger.		Capt., Commanding 5.Coy.,100.Bn.Geb.Jaeg.,Vilette - Savoie (Fr.)9.6.44	MURDER	FR.
WIRTH, Christian	134924	M	Ger.	85	Capt., Schupo, SS, C.C., Hartheim (Aust.) 40-44	MURDER	U.S.
WIRTH, Christian	188457	M	Ger.		Major, Army, C.C., (Ger.) 40-45	MURDER	CZECH.
WIRTH, Hans	11528	M	Ger.		Pvt., 110.or 111.Pz.Gren.Rgt.,2.Coy., Albine (Fr.) 29.6.44	MURDER	FR.
WIRTH, Hans	150601	M	Ger.		Cpl., 11.Pz.Div.(South West France) 44	MURDER	FR
WIRTHS	256596	M	Ger		Dr , Sturmbannfhr ,SS-Garrison Physician, C C Dora ,Nordhausen (Ger)	MURDER	U S.
WIRTHS, Erich	149703	M	Ger		Sturmbannfhr., SS, C C , Auschwitz (Pol.) 43-44	MURDER	U S

WIR - WIT

NAME	C.R.FILE NUMBER	SEX	NATIO-NALITY	DATE OF BIRTH	RANK OCCUPATION UNIT PLACE AND DATE OF CRIME	REASON WANTED	WANTED BY
WIRTMANN	260982	M	Ger.		Sturmmann, SS, C.C., Vaihingen, a.d.Enz (Ger.) 8.44 - 4.45	MURDER	U.S.
WIRTS	24848	M			Sgt., Army, 340.Inf.Div., 2.San.Coy.	TORTURE	U.S.
WIRTT	133188	M			Scharfhr., SS-Inf.Div. 340, C.C. Dora, Nordhausen (Ger.)	MURDER	U.S.
WIRTZ	104983	M	Ger.		Lt.Colonel, Waffen SS, C.C. Lublin Nordhausen (Ger.Pol.)	MURDER	U.S.
WIRTZ, Adolf	240072	M	Ger.	3. 3.72	Wehrwirtschaftsfhr., Member, NSDAP, Muehlheim-Ruhr (Ger.)	MISC.CRIMES	U S
WISCHER, Willi	255455	M		31. 3.05	Pvt., C.C., Harzungen, Nordhausen (Ger.)	MURDER	U S.
WISCHINSKY (or KISCHINSKY)	180641	M			Uscharfhr., SS-Div.Leibstandarte "Adolf Hitler", Stabscoy.,Aufklaerungs-stab, Renardmont Stavelot (Bel.) 19 12.44	MURDER	BEL.
WISCHNIG (see WINSCHNIG)	192230						
WISCOAT, Max	150810	M			Dr., Probably, Civilian Doctor	WITNESS	U.S.
WISE (see WEISS)	142067						
WISEE	29645	M	Ger.		Inspector, Police, Kerbabu, Lannilis (Fr.) 8.44	MURDER	FR.
WISLICENY, Dieter	253450	M	Ger.		Adviser on racial matters to the Slovakian Puppet Govt.,Bratislava (Czech.) 41 - 44	MURDER	CZECH
WISLING, Johann	142009	M	Ger.		Civilian, Farmer, Rehde near Bocholt (Ger.) 44	MURDER	YUGO.
WISNIEWSKI	193446	M	Ger.		Pvt., 1.Kriegsgef.Arb.Bn.41, C.C. Nerlandsdal, Kristiansund (Nor.) 41 - 45	TORTURE	NOR.
WISNIOWSKI	300755	M			Pvt., 1.Aufkl.Abt.3.Coy., 2.Column, XV Div.of the Afrika Korps, Saint Leger (Arlon) (Bel.) 5.9.44	MISC.CRIMES	BEL.
WISOCKI, Erich	192427	M	Ger.		Cpl., Army, C.C., Batterie Lux, near St. Nazaire (Fr.) 8.44	MURDER	FR.
WISSATA, Franz	255320	M	Ger.		Agent, Lt.Col., Gestapo, Pribram (Czech.) 39 - 45	MISC.CRIMES	CZECH.
WISSEL	251448	M	Ger.		Capt., Ortskommandantur, Savannes (Fr.) 31.8.44	MURDER	FR.
WISSEL, Bernhard	131607	M	Ger.	06	Pvt., 1.Wach-Coy., 77.Volksgren.Rgt , C.C. Stalag 28275, Euskirchen (Ger.) 3. -10.44	TORTURE	U S.
WISSEL, Theodor	255454	M			Cpl., C.C. Ellrich, Nordhausen (Ger.)	MURDER	U S.
WISSELMANN, Heinrich	260398	M	Ger.	14. 1.89	Gen.Dir., Preussische Bergwerks-und Huetten A.G., Berlin (Ger.)	MISC.CRIMES	U S.
WISSEMBOURG, Hermann	195985	M	Ger.	94	Oberscharfhr., SD, Maison-Lafitte (Fr.) 12.41 - 6.44	TORTURE	FR.
WISSICKEIT, Emil	1771	M		95	Miscellan Laeger	TORTURE	U.K. U.S.
WISSLER	138302	M	Ger.		Cpl., Army, Mannheim (Ger.)	MURDER	FR.
WISSMANN	193108	M	Ger.	00	Capt., Kgf.Arb.Bn., 186, Abwehr, Narvik (Nor.) 42	MISC.CRIMES	NOR.
WISSNER	175684	M			Kreisleiter, NSDAP, Tann (Ger.) 44	TORTURE	FR.
WITE, Willi	132697	M		12	Major, Standort Kommandantur, Gerardmer (Fr.) 9.-11.44	MISC.CRIMES	FR.
WITEK, Ignaz	257400	M	Ger.		Oberscharfhr., SS, slave labour camp, Osen (Nor.) 6.42 - 3.43	MISC CRIMES	YUGO
WITEKE, Heinz	158444	M			Pvt., Army, Borkum (Ger.) 4.8.44	MURDER	U S
WITERBING, Heinz	306669	M	Ger.		Cpl., Cie de Pontonniers SS " Das Reich" F.P.No. 29 573,Flamarens (Fr.) 7.44	MURDER	FR.
WITH	300371	M	Ger.		Senior Dr., Convalescent centre Font-Romeu, Saillagouse Pyr.Or.(Fr.) 7.6.43	PILLAGE	FR
WITISKA	139730	M	Ger.		Chief, Stapo-Gouvernment,Counsel Dept.C.C., Lemberg,Prag,Auschwitz, Birkenau (Pol. Czech.) 39 - 45	MURDER	U S CZECH
WITISKA, Josef	185568	M	Ger.	5. 7.94	Standartenfhr., Oberregierungsrat, SD, Gestapo,Prague, Lidice (Czech.) 42 - 45	MURDER	CZECH
WITKE, Richard	195699	M	Ger.	30. 8.06	Leader, NSDAP, Civilian, Valasske, Mezirici (Czech.) 39 - 45	MISC.CRIMES	CZECH
WITKOWSKI, Josef (Sepp)	195712	M	Ger.		Cpl., 1.SS-Panz.Div.Leibstandarte "Adolf Hitler" 3.Pl Coy., Ligneuville, (Bel.) 12.44	MURDER	U.S.
WITLAND, Wilhelm	255802	M	Ger.		Civilian, working in Dues clog factory, Wessum (Ger.) 7.44	INTERR	NETH
WITMANN	141431	M	Ger.	80	Sgt., Kommandantur, Bordeaux und Souges (Fr.)	MURDER	FR.
WITMANN, Franz	167850	M	Ger.		Sgt., Feld-Police, Auberive, Flagey, Coiffey, Chalancy (Fr.) 43 - 44	MURDER	FR.
WITSCHEL	300756	M	Ger		Pvt , 1.Aufkl.Abt.,3.Coy.,2.Column, XV.Div of the Afrika Korps, Saint Leder (Arlon) (Bel.) 5.9.44	MISC CRIMES	BEL
WITSCHER, Oscar	302014	M	Ger.	20. 4.82	Verwaltungs-Treuhaender und Stellvertreter,Firm Lippmann,Rosenthal & Co Amsterdam (Neth.) 7.43 - 9.44	PILLAGE	NETH.
WITT	180598	M	Ger.		SS - Mann, SS Div. Leibstandarte "Adolf Hitler", Aufklaerungsabt., Renardmont-Stavelot (Bel.) 12.44	MURDER	BEL
WITT (see WITTE)	256579						
WITT	302015	F	Ger.		Guard, SS, C.C., Auschwitz (Pol.) 40 - 44	MURDER	POL.
WITT, Fritz, Hermann	260442	M	Ger.		Uscharfhr., SS-Guard, C.C. Auschwitz (Pol.) 41 - 45	BRUTALITY	POL.
WITT, Hans	194698	M			Dr., C.C., Neuengamme (Ger.) 44	MURDER	FR.
WITT, Josef	255453	M			Pvt., C.C., Ellrich, Nordhausen (Ger.)	MURDER	U.S
WITT, Wilhelm	256240	M	Ger.	19. 1.98	Sturmscharfhr., SS, Opava (Czech.)	TORTURE	CZECH.
WITTAN	250558	M			Hauptwerkmeister, Feldbekleidungsamt d. Luftwaffe T-XI, Enschede (Neth.) 5 42 - 4 45	PILLAGE	NETH.
WITTASIK (see WIECZOVEK)	128929						
WITTATATT	167041	M	Ger.		Col., Army Leffinc-Krnrouke (Fr.) 44	MURDER	FR.
WITTE	104984	M			Lt.Col. Army, Volks Gren.Div.18, 293 Rgt , Bleialf (Ger.) 12.44	MURDER	U.S.
WITTE	174857	M	Ger.	01	Doctor, C C, Anrath (Ger.) 41 - 45	MURDER	FR.
WITTE	191970	M	Ger.		Chief, NSDAP, Volkssturm,C.C., Wattenstedt (Ger.) 45	MURDER	FR.
WITTE (or WITT)	256579	M			Colonel, Festungsstamm-Ers.Res.A.K.25, Pontivy (Fr.) 3.8.44	MURDER	FR.
WITTE, Erich	305780	M	Ger.	14. 1.11	Oberscharfhr., Si.Polizei, Aussendienststelle, Drammen (Nor.) 10.44-45	TORTURE	NOR.
WITTE, Otto	193107	M	Ger.	08	Ex Convict, Reichsjustizministerium, Feldstraflager C.C. Finmark (Nor.) 45	WITNESS	NOR.
WITTEBORG	258174	M			Cpl., 2.Signal Coy. Bolnes (Neth.) 8.5.45	INTERR.	NETH.
WITTEBORN	158393	M			Sgt., 379.Landesschuetzen Bn., Bruax (Czech.) 44 - 45	TORTURE	U.K.
WITTEK, Oskar	162729	M	Ger.	20	Sgt., Air-Force 1.Coy. C.C., Bau-Bn.133-3, Quistebo (Nor.)	MURDER	NOR.
WITTENHAGEN	256062	M	Ger.		Senior WO, dt.Abschnitt Stg.X B., Westerrecht (Ger.) 6.2.44	MURDER	FR.
WITTGRABE	175700	M			Rottenfhr.-Official, SS, Gestapo, Lemans (Fr.) 12.43 - 1.44	MURDER	FR.
WITTHAUS, Willy	251450	M	Ger.		Sturmscharfhr., Gestapo, Limoges (Fr.)	INTERR.	FR.
WITTICH, Karl	192440	M	Ger.		Guard, C.C., Flossenburg (Ger.) 44 - 45	SUSPECT	U.S.
WITTICH, Kurt	192431	M	Ger.	20. 5.07	SS - Pvt., 2.SS-Panz.Gren.Ausb.u.Ers.Bn. 4, Yves-Gomezee (Bel) 3.9.44	MURDER	BEL.
WITTIG	29840	M	Ger.		Major, Army, Vacqué (Fr.)	MURDER	FR
WITTIG	125715	M			SS - Mann, C.C. Flossenburg (Ger.) 29.3.45	MURDER	U.K.
WITTIG	173848	M	Ger.		Lt., Schupo 5.Pol.Rgt. III.Bn. 10 Coy. Todorovci-pistr.Leskovac (Yugo.) 16.7.43	MISC.CRIMES	YUGO
WITTIG	192441	M	Ger.		Guard, C.C., Flossenburg (Ger.) 44 -45	SUSPECT	U.S.

WIT-WOH

NAME	C.R.FILE NUMBER	SEX	NATIO-NALITY	DATE OF BIRTH	RANK OCCUPATION UNIT PLACE AND DATE OF CRIME	REASON WANTED	WANTED BY
WITTIG, Johann	257707	M	Ger.	3. 2.98	Civ. Miner, Most (Czech.) 44	MURDER	CZECH.
WITTIJK	142741	M	Ger.		Dr., Member Waffen SS, Professor University, C.C.Schandelah Braunschweig (Ger.) 44-45	MURDER	BEL.
WITTKE, Karl	260443	M	Ger.	20.10.95	SS Mann, Waffen SS, Guard-Coy. C.C. Charlottengrube Auschwitz (Pol.) 10.44-1.45	BRUTALITY	POL.
WITTKUHN, Ewald	193106	M	Ger.	27. 5.01	Sgt. Guard,Reichsjustizministerium, Feldstraflager, C.C.Finmark (Nor.) 9.3.45	MISC.CRIMES	NOR.
WITTMAACK, Jakob	149704	M			Obermaat, Navy, Borkum (Ger.) 4.8.44	MURDER	U.S.
WITTMAN	165565	M	Ger.		Lt., Army, Grand Menil (Bel.)	MURDER	BEL.
WITTMAN, Rudi	138245	M	Ger.		Uscharfhr., SS, sorting centre Levitan, Paris, St.Martin (Fr.) 7.44	TORTURE	FR.
WITTMANN	187652	M	Ger.	00	Col., Army, Stalag XXI A Nischmiroff (Pol.) 1.-3.42	TORTURE	U.K.
WITTMANN	194082	M	Ger.		Lt., Art.Ers.Rgt. 7, 79.D.A.M., Albertville (Fr.) 29.6.44	MURDER	FR.
WITTMANN	252795	M	Ger.		SS Mann, SD, Toulouse (Fr.) 11.42-8.44	MISC.CRIMES	FR.
WITTMANN	259236	M	Ger.		SS Oscharfhr., Gestapo, Poitiers Area (Fr.) 40-44	MISC.CRIMES	FR.
WITTMANN, Frantz	167861	M	Ger.		Chief cpl., Fieldpolice, Auberice, Flagey, Goiffey, Chalencey (Fr.)44	MURDER	FR.
WITTMANN, Hans	126471	M	Ger.	04 or 07	Pvt., Landesschuetzen-Bn. 814, C.C.Wolstein Warthegau (Pol.)	MURDER	U.S.
WITTMANN, Josef	150834	M	Ger.	10. 4.05	Civ. Supervisor, Schwartzenfeld (Ger.) 39-45	TORTURE	U.S.
WITTMANN, Rudi	138245	M	Ger.		Cpl., N.C.O. I-C of sorting centre Levitan,Magazin Levitan,St.Martin, Paris (Fr.) 7.44	TORTURE	FR.
WITTMANN, Rudolf	300974	M	Ger.		SS Usturmfhr., official of SD, Leitabschnitt Prague, C.C.Oswiecim, Birkenau (Pol.) 39-45	MURDER	CZECH.
WITTNER, Johann	186741	M	Ger.		Employee, Gestapo, Budejovice (Czech.) 39-45	MURDER	CZECH.
WITTOR	1033	M	Ger.		Cpl., SS Panz.Div."Das Reich", Rgt."Der Fuehrer", Buzet (Fr.) 7.7.44	MURDER	FR.
WITTREICH	173847	M	Ger.		Oberinspector, Reichsbahn, 4.41-5.43	PILLAGE	YUGO.
WITTRICH, Gertrude	195700	F	Ger.		Employee, Gestapo, Brno (Czech.) 39-45	TORTURE	CZECH.
WITTSCHNIG see WINSCHNIG	192290						
WITTSCHONNEK, Kurt	192436	M		26	SS Rottfhr., Rosbach (Ger.)	SUSPECT	U.S.
WITTVRE, Frank	139156	M	Ger.		Sgt., Guard, Army, C.C. Neuengamme (Ger.) 41-42	TORTURE	BEL.
WITUSCHER, Adam	253468	M	Ger.		SS Mann, C.C.Auschwitz, Birkenau (Pol.) 1.43	MISC.CRIMES	YUGO.
WITZ	150600	M	Ger.		Pvt., 11.Panz.Div., South-west Fr. 44	MURDER	FR.
WITZANY, Josef	142742	M		1. 9.01	Mayor, Civ., Oppolz (Czech.) 12.44	MURDER	U.S.
WITZEL, Hugo	11529	M	Ger.		Pvt., Panz.Gren.Rgt. 110.or 111., 2.Coy.,Albine (Fr.) 29.6.44	MURDER	FR.
WITZEL, Karl	255682	M	Ger.	6. 8.08	Pvt., C.C.Harzungen, Nordhausen (Ger.)	MURDER	U.S.
WITZELSBERGER, Karl	193105	M	Ger.		Pvt., Army, Nor. 4.45	MURDER	NOR.
WITZIG	10973	M		22. 5.11	SS Uscharfhr., Kdo.Steinbruch, C.C. Natzweiler (Fr.) 14.3.42-4.8.42	TORTURE	CZECH. FR. BEL.
WITZIG	194080	M	Ger.		Cmdt., Parachute-Pion.Bn. 8, St.Amand, Montrond, Izeure (Fr.) 10.6.44	MURDER	FR.
WITZINGER, Florian	177803	M			Civ., C.C. Inphl (Ger.)	WITNESS	U.S.
WITZKE, Heinz	149705	M			Pvt., Army, Mil.Guard,Borkum (Ger.) 4.8.44	MURDER	U.S.
WITZMANN	158445	M			Officer, Army, Sturm-Bn. AOK.1, 5 Coy.,Courcelles s.Nied (Fr.) 15.11.44	MURDER	U.S.
WITZMANN	300757	M	Ger.		Pvt.,1.Aufkl.Abt. 3.Coy. 2.Col. XV.Div. Africa-Corps, St.Leger (Arlon) 5.9.44	MISC.CRIMES	BEL.
WITZMANN, Adolf	161693	M	Ger.	94	Judge, P.O. Justizministerium, Leipzig (Ger.) 10.44	SUSPECT	U.S.
WLACH, Josef	161635	M	Ger.	08	SS Osturmfhr., C.C. Buchenwald (Ger.)	WITNESS	U.S.
WLADECK see VLADECK	301372						
WLASAK, Otto	188602	M	Ger.		Crim.secret. SS, SD, Gestapo, Brno (Czech.) 39-45	MURDER	CZECH.
WLASTOW, Jleuka	139252	M	Ger.		Civ., Plettenberg (Ger.) 6.44	TORTURE	U.S.
WLATHER, Filip or Philip	255827	M		16. 1.97	Cpl., C.C. Harzungen, Nordhausen (Ger.)	MURDER	U.S.
WLOKA, Franz	130996	M			SS Hptscharfhr., C.C. Mauthausen (Aust.) 41-45	MURDER	U.S.
WLOTAKA	130994	M			SS Uscharfhr., SS Panz.Div.Totenkopf, C.C. Mauthausen (Aust.) 41-45	MURDER	U.S.
WLOTZKA	130995	M			SS Uscharfhr., SS Panz.Div.Totenkopf, C.C. Mauthausen (Aust.) 41-45	MURDER	U.S.
WOCHNER	173100	M	Ger.	95	SS Oscharfhr., C.C. Gaggenau, Natzweiler (Ger.,Fr.) autumn 44	MURDER	U.K.
WODEMANN	162888	M			Member SD, Montlucon, Chappes (Fr.) 28.7.44	MURDER	FR.
WOEFL see WOELFL	158409						
WOEHLER, Otto	166981	M	Ger.	94	Gen., 8.Army, Sov.Un. 43	MISC.CRIMES	U.S.
WOELFEL, Karl	146762	M			SS Rottfhr., C.C.Flossenburg (Ger.)	MURDER	U.S.
WOELFINGER or VOLFINGER	1034	M			Col., Army, 717.Inf.Div. 749.Jaeg.Rgt., Grc. 12.43	MURDER	GRC.
WOELFL or WOEFL	158403	M			Pvt., Army, Sturmbn. AOK 1, Courcelles s.Nied (Fr.) 15.11.44	MURDER	U.S.
WOELFL	300975	M			SS Hptscharfhr., official of SD Leitabschnitt Prague, Oswiecim, Birkenau (Pol.) 39-45	MURDER	CZECH.
WOELFLINGSEDER, Franz	221961	M	Ger.		Wachtmeister, NSDAP, C.C. Papenburg (Ger.) 4.45	MURDER	U.S.
WOELKE	142747	M			Capt., O.K.W.	WITNESS	U.S.
WOELKER (Boby)	129007	M	Ger.		Interpreter, S.D., Lyon (Fr.) 40-44	MURDER	FR.
WOELKI	306905	M	Ger.		Lt., Pioneers, Etobon (Hte.Saone) Chenebier (Fr.) 27.9.44	--	FR.
WOELLER	173102	M	Ger.		C.C.Schirmeck, Rotenfels, Gaggenau (Fr.,Ger.) 44	INTER.	FR. U.K.
WOERBER, Georges	188763	M			Sgt., Adjutant, Dienststelle 14 653 E, Contes (Fr.)	MURDER	FR.
WOERLE or WORLE or WERLE,Otto	128924	M		10	SS Uscharfhr., Waffen SS, Totenkopf-Stuba, C.C. Buchenwald (Ger.)42-45	MURDER	U.S.
WOERLE, Eva	190419	F	Ger.		Civ., Innsbruck (Aust.) 25.12.44	WITNESS	U.S.
WOERLEIN or WORLEIN, WORRLEIN, WUERLEIN	240049	M	Ger.	08 or 09	Hptsturmfhr., SD, Zentralstelle fuer juedische Auswanderung, SIPO, Amsterdam (Neth.) 10.42	MISC.CRIMES	FR. U.S.
WOERNE, O	168297	M	Ger.		Treuhaender, Firm S.Menne, Krakau (Pol.) 9.39	PILLAGE	POL.
WOERNER	1095	M			Capt. Lt., Navy, Standort-Cmdt., Gray (Fr.) 28.7.44	PILLAGE	FR.
WOERRLE, Mathias	166987	M	Ger.		Member Civ., NSDAP, City official, Pensberg (Ger.)	TORTURE	U.S.
WOERSDORFER, Hermann	174856	M	Ger.		SS Mann, Fr.	MURDER	U.S.
WOEST	306073	M	Ger.		SS Hptsturmfhr., 12.SS Panz.Div. Hitler-Jugend, Panz.Jaeg.Abt., Waremme, 20.8.44	PILLAGE	BEL.
WOGE, Edo	135336	M				MISC.CRIMES	U.S.
WOGEL	191961	M	Ger.		Adjudant, Army, Chaumont en Vexin (Fr.) 12.8.44	WITNESS	FR.
WOHER see WEBSCH	67737						
WOHL	173103	M	Ger.		Gestapo Strassburg, Vosges Area (Fr.)	MURDER	U.K.
WOHLBRUCK, Lothar	6108	M	Ger.		Cpl., Army, Yseures s.Creuse (Fr.) 29.-30.8.44	WITNESS	FR.
WOHLE, Wilhelm	305121	M	Ger.		Administrator of Polish estates of Poland, Western parts of Pol.	MISC.CRIMES	POL.
WOHLENTIN	11590	M	Ger.		Sgt., Army, Hafenueberwachungsstelle, Calais (Fr.) 4.9.44	TORTURE	FR.
WOHLER, Marius see HANNOT	251046						
WOHLERS	151772	M			Official, Gestapo, Hamburg (Ger.) 38	MURDER	U.S.

WOH-WOL

NAME	C.R.FILE NUMBER	SEX	NATIONALITY	DATE OF BIRTH	RANK OCCUPATION UNIT PLACE AND DATE OF CRIME	REASON WANTED	WANTED BY
WOHLFAHRT, Alfred	138002	M	Ger.		Guard in Mines, Erkenschwick (Ger.)	TORTURE	U.S.
WOHLFAHRT, Georg	255681	M		15. 8.04	Pvt., C.C. Harzungen, Nordhausen (Ger.)	MURDER	U.S.
WOHLFAHRT, Jean (see WOLFART)	142745						
WOHLGEMUTH	194079	M	Ger.		Rottfhr., SS, 1.Panz.Aufkl.Abt.12, Ascq (Fr.) 1., 2.4.44	MURDER	FR.
WOHLLEBEN, Georg	182317	M	Ger.	30. 7.02	Toolmaker, Arbeits-Kmdo. Conc.Camp, Nuernberg (Ger.) 40-45	MISC.CRIMES	U.S.
WOHLMACHER, Ferdinand	167854	M	Ger.	-03	Uschfhr., SS, Natzweiler (Fr.) 43-44	MURDER	FR.
WOHLMUT, Josef	138003	M	Ger.		Civilian, Silbert in Mozart (Ger.) 15.3.45	MURDER	U S
WOHLRAB, Franz	136408	M	Ger.		Capt., Army, Ruppertsbuch (Ger.) 23.4.45	MURDER	U.S.
WOHLRABE	11531	M	Ger.		Capt., Army, Conc.Camp, Valdahon (Fr.) 28.8.44	MURDER	FR
WOHLRAP	186740	M			N.C.O., Army, Master, Firm of Heinrich Butzer, Aspfjord (Nor.)	TORTURE	NOR
WOHRMANN (or WAHRMANN)	1036	M			Lt.Col., Schupo, Posen (Pol.)	MURDER	POL.
WOHSMEYER, Heinrich	166977	M	Ger.	08	Chef du culture, Civilian, Donchery (Fr.) 19.8.44	MURDER	FR.
WOICZEK, Walter (see WOITSCHEIK)	104962						
WOIKE	1365				Pvt, Army, 2.Pl., 4.Sec., 194.Gr	MISC.CRIMES	U.K.
WOISCHKE	186711	M		99	Sgt., 4 Coy, 515.Lds.Schtz.Bn., Jedibab (Czech.) 2.45	MURDER	U.K.
WOITASCHEK	175683	M	Ger.		Pvt., Stammlager Conc.Camp, Bad Sulza (Ger)	MURDER	FR.
WOITH (or WIRT)	185189	M	Ger.		Capt., SD of Moutiers, St.Bernard Col du Petit (Fr)	MURDER	FR.
WOITMANN, Johann	188539	M	Ger.		Farmer, Civilian, Estrup (Ger) 26 2.45	PILLAGE	U.S
WOITSCHEIK, Walter (or WOICZEK)	104962	M	Ger.		SS-Guard, Sturmmann, SS Conc.Camp, Thekla,Vic.of Leipzig (Ger.) 18.4.45	MURDER	U.S., POL
WOJTECH, Karl	189232	M	Ger.		Dr , Landgerichtsrat, Occup.Territ., Opava (Czech.)	MISC.CRIMES	CZECH.
WOLANEK, Anton	188601	M	Ger		Aushilfsangestellter, Gestapo, SD, Brno (Czech.) 39-45	MURDER	CZECH.
WOLBERG	196497	M	Ger.		General. Verbindungsstab 990, Valence (Fr.) 40-45	MISC.CRIMES	FR.
WOLBRING, Julius	260725	M		86	Uschfhr.or Oschfhr., SS, C.C., Hallein (Aust.)	MURDER	U.S.
WOLD	146761	M			Uschfhr., SS, C.C., Flossenburg (Ger.)	MURDER	U.S.
WOLDA, Hans	259233	M	Ger.		Uschfhr., Gestapo of Poitiers Antenne d'Angouleme (Fr.)	MISC.CRIMES	FR.
WOLDEMAR	256238	M			Oschfhr., SS, C.C.,"Buchenwald (Ger.)	MURDER	U S
WOLDT	256598	M	Ger.		Chief of sub-sect., Mittelwerk C.C., Nordhausen (Ger.)	MURDER	U.S.
WOLF	1037	M	Ger.		Oberfhr., SA,"Director, Police, Wloclawek (Pol.) 9.39-1.42	MURDER	POL.
WOLF	1098	M	Ger.		Hptsturmfhr., SD de Rennes, Locmine (Fr.) 7.44-8.44	MURDER	FR.
WOLF	1367	M	Ger.		Uschfhr., SS, Inf.Gren.Pl..5.Squd.	MISC.CRIMES	U.K.
WOLF	28760	M			Secretary, Asst.to Political Section Chief, C.C. Auschwitz (Pol.)41-43	MURDER	U.S.
WOLF	67744	M	Ger.		Col.' or Lt., Army, Hemeyes (Fr.) 6.6.44	MURDER	U.S.
WOLF	67745	M	Ger. circa 95-00		Gen.Major, Cmdt.of Field-Commandantur 529,"Bordeaux"(Fr.) 25.10.41	MURDER	U.K., FR
WOLF	67746	M	Ger.		Stabsarzt, Hospital, Conc.Camp, Elbing (Ger.) 10.44	TORTURE	U.K.
WOLF	104963	M	Ger.		General der Flieger, Luftgau XI (Ger.)	MURDER	U.S., U K.
WOLF	104964	M			Capt., Lager B Stalag Luft-IV, C.C., Kiefheide (Ger) 8.44-3.45	WITNESS	U.S.
WOLF	124628	M		16	Uschfhr., SS, C.C., Birkenau (Pol.)	MURDER	U.S.
WOLF	126474	M			Sturmbannfhr., SS, Gestapo, C.C., Buchenwald-Weimar (Ger.)	TORTURE	U.S.
WOLF	133998	M			Usturmfhr., SS-Pion.Ausb.Bn.2, Passau (Ger.) 4.45	MURDER	U.S.
WOLF	139729	M		99	Cpl., Waffen-SS; Member, NSDAP, C C Arbeitskmdo A - 6	TORTURE	U.S.
WOLF	142743	M	Ger	91	Oschfhr., Waffen-SS, Conc.Camp, Buchenwald (Ger.)	TORTURE	U.S.
WOLF	150840	M			Sturmbannfhr.,"SS and SD, Pragues (Czech) 39-45	TORTURE	CZECH.
WOLF	161692	M	Ger.		Gestapo, Unterhaid (Ger.) 12.44	SUSPECT	U S
WOLF	162523	M	Ger.	08	Oschfhr., SS, C.C., Buchenwald (Ger)	WITNESS	U.S.
WOLF	167040	M			Pvt , Etat-Major, Army, Station Crest (Fr.) 3.8.44	MURDER	FR.
WOLF	168038	M			General Staff, Kommandantur, Cpl., Crest-Drome (Fr) 7.-8.44	MURDER	FR.
WOLF (or DIT "LA GIRAF")	174852	M	Ger		Cpl , Airforce, Member, SS, C., Wansleben (Ger.) 45	MURDER	FR.
WOLF	182090	M			Uschfhr , SS-Leibstandarte "Adolf Hitler", Staff-Coy., Aufkl.Abt., Renardmont Stavelot (Bel.) 19.12.44	MURDER	BEL.
WOLF	188761	M	Ger		Hptsturmfhr., Gestapo, Morbihan (Fr.)	WITNESS	FR.
WOLF	188762	M			Uschfhr., SS, C.C., Flossenburg (Ger.)	MURDER	FR.
WOLF	190460	M			Lt., Eis.Btty.717, Feldpost-Nr.22380, St.Andries, Varsenare, Les Bruges (Bel.) 4.9.44	MURDER	BEL.
WOLF	191357	M	Ger.		Major, Army, C.C. Gossen (Nor.) 42-45	MURDER	NOR.
WOLF	192426	M	Ger.		O.K.P.R., Etat-Major, Army, Oberkommando, La Rochette (Fr.) 3.8.44	MURDER	FR.
WOLF	250556	M	Ger.		Capt., Field-Police, Kragujevac (Yugo.) 21.10.41	MURDER	YUGO.
WOLF	251441	M	Ger.		Uschfhr., SS, Gestapo, Paris (Fr.) 41-44	TORTURE	FR.
WOLF	251739	M	Ger.		Uschfhr., SS, C.C., Buchenwald (Ger.)	BRUTALITY	FR.
WOLF	252797	M	Ger.		Member, SD, Interpreter, Toulouse (Fr.) 11.42-8.44	MISC.CRIMES	FR.
WOLF	255660	M			Pvt., Waffen-SS, C.C., Osterhagen, Nordhausen (Ger.)	MURDER	U S
WOLF	256237	M			Kapo, C.C., Buchenwald (Ger.)	MURDER	U.S.
WOLF	256646	M	Ger.		Employee, Factory-worker, Camp Nordhausen (Ger.)	MURDER	U.S
WOLF	258148	M	Ger.		Employee, C.C. Belsen (Ger.)	TORTURE	BEL.
WOLF	258897	M	Ger.		Inspector of Custom-House, Custom-Command.Action,Lourdes (Fr) 1.-8.44	MURDER	FR.
WOLF	259477	M			Capt., probably living at Velden, Fraenk.Schweis,Illesheim(Ger)1.12.43	MURDER	U S
WOLF (see WULF)	259601						
WOLF	260992	M	Ger.		Member, SS, Abwehrdienst, Stalowa Wola (Pol.) 44-45	MISC.CRIMES	POL.
WOLF	300406	M	Ger.		Schfhr., SS, SD section II, Toulouse,Gestapo, Gers and Tarn South-West-France especially Toulouse, Hte.-Garonne (Fr.) 11.42-19.8.44	MURDER	FR.
WOLF	301973	M	Ger.		Uschfhr., SS on Staff of Wkg.Kdo.,Wansleben am See nr Buchenwald (Ger.) 43-45	MURDER	FR.
WOLF	306112	M			SS-Mann, C.C., Alderney (Channel Is.) and Kortemark, 42-45	MURDER	CZECH.
WOLF	306136	M			Hptsturmfhr., SS, Unit 322, Ris-Orangis,Seine et Oise (Fr) 21.8.44	MURDER	FR.
WOLF	306827	M			Uschfhr., SS, Builder, C.C., Auschwitz (Pol.) 40	MURDER	FR.
WOLF, Adolf	29656	M			Dr., Landgerichtsrat, Public-Official, Cheb (Czech.)	MURDER	CZECH.
WOLF, Albert	166984	M		25. 9.09	Pvt., I.Ost-Ba.447, freiwillig, Plouvien (Fr.) 8.44	TORTURE	FR.
WOLF, Alfred	300758	M			Pvt., 1.Aufkl.Abt.,3.Coy.,2.Column, XV.Div. of the Africa-Corps, Saint Leger (Arlon) 5.9.44	MISC.CRIMES	BEL.
WOLF, Anton	162734	M			Foreman, Civ. C.C. "Adolf-Mine, Merkstein (Ger.) 42-45	TORTURE	U.S.
WOLF, Bruno	10374	M	Ger.		Staatsanwalt, Public-Official, Prague (Czech.) 21. 2.40	MURDER	CZECH.
WOLF, David	251458	M			Police-Officer, Geradmer (Fr.) 29.5.44	WITNESS	U.S.
WOLF, Dunnibier	179731	M	Ger.	10	Lt., 26.Panz.Div., 26.Recce., Fucecchio Marshes (It.) 23.8.44	MURDER	U.K.
WOLF, Franz	253447	M		21. 2.97	Policeman, State-Service, Breclav (Czech.) 24.1.45	INTERR.	CZECH.
WOLF, Franz	300759	M	Ger.		Pvt., 1.Aufkl.Abt.,3.Abt.,3.Coy., 2.Column, XV.Div. of the Africa-Corps, Saint Leger (Arlon) 5.9.44	MISC.CRIMES	BEL.

NAME	C.R.FILE NUMBER	SEX	NATIO- NALITY	DATE OF BIRTH	RANK	OCCUPATION UNIT PLACE AND DATE OF CRIME	REASON WANTED	WANTED BY
WOLF, Friedrich	175682	M	Ger.			Dr., public official, Amt fuer Volkstumsfragen,Strassburg(Fr.)44	TORTURE	FR.
WOLF, Fritz	189934	M				Uschfhr, 4 SS Totenkopf Sturmbann, CC Dora, Mittelbau,Nordhausen (Ger.) 43-45	WITNESS	U.S.
WOLF, Fritz	189269	M	Ger.			Deserter, Army, Colmar (Fr.) 21.4.45	WITNESS	U.S.
WOLF, Fritz	257963	M				Cpl., 150 Pz.Bde., Meuse Bridge, Antwerpen (Bel.) 12. 44	MISC.CRIMES	U.S.
WOLF, Gerhard	150599	M	Ger.			11 Pz.Div., South West France	MURDER	FR.
WOLF, Gerhardt	192439	M	Ger.		99	Uschfhr. SS, CC Flossenburg (Ger.) 44-45	MISC.CRIMES	U.S.
WOLF, Hans	257626	M	Ger.			Crim.Secretary, SD, Bodoe (Nor.) 41-49	WITNESS	NOR.
WOLF, Hans	259671	M	Ger.			Staff Sgt., Gend. of Morlaix, Plougasnou,Finistere (Fr.) 5.7.44	TORTURE	FR.
WOLF, Heinrich	900600	M	Ger.			Pvt., Army, Lds.Schtz.Bn., working command, Allendorf(Ger.) 14. or 16.9.43	MURDER	YUGO.
WOLF, Herman	306726	M				Civilian, near Wittmar (Ger.) 28.9.44	BRUTALITY	U.S.
WOLF, Hugo	151473	M	Ger.		07	Uschfhr, SS Pz.Div."Hitler Jugend",St.Sulpice sur Risle,Eure(Fr.)	MISC.CRIMES	CAN.
WOLF, Hugo	256242	M	Ger.			Sgt., III Pz.Gren.Rgt., II Pz.Div., Faycelles (Fr.) 24.7.44	INTERR.	FR.
WOLF, Johann	12451	M				Army, Pz.Gren.Rgt.110 or 111, 2 Coy, Albine (Fr.) 29.6.44	MURDER	FR.
WOLF, Johann	258396	M				Guard, SS, CC Ohrdruf (Ger.) 12.44-4.45	MURDER	U.S.
WOLF, Karl W.	259442	M	Ger.			Hanau (Ger.) 10.44	MISC.CRIMES	U.S.
WOLF, Kurt	136575	M	Ger.		00	Civilian, forester, CC Flossenburg (Ger.) 42	MISC.CRIMES	U.S.
WOLF, Kurt	300976	M	Ger.			Osturmfhr..SS., official of SD, Leitabschnitt Prague, CC Auschwitz-Birkenau (Pol.) 39-45	MURDER	CZECH.
WOLF, Martin	193104	M	Ger.			Pvt., 7 Btty, Heeres-Kuesten Art.Rgt.792, Lattervik(Nor.)-45	WITNESS	NOR.
WOLF, Max	260201	M	Ger.	25.9.88		MDR Daimler Benz Motoren-GmbH., Genshagen Krs.Teltow (Ger.)	MISC.CRIMES	U.S.
WOLF, Norbert	135337	M		29		Civilian, Bieringen (Lux.) 7.44	WITNESS	U.S.
WOLF, Otto (see WOLFF TAETS, Freiherr VON AMERONGEN)	240071							
WOLF, Otto	251417	M	Ger.			Cpl., Gend., Vendome (Fr.) 9.8.44	INTERR.	FR.
WOLF, Otto Wilhelm	258859	M	Ger.		95	Major-General	WITNESS	U.S.
WOLF, Paul	134714	M	Ger.			Interpreter, Sipo, Paris (Fr.) 42	TORTURE	FR.
WOLF, Paul	187270	M	Ger.	26.8.89		Guard, CC Rehmsdorf, Brieg (Ger.) 45	MURDER	CZECH.
WOLF, Richard	255921	M	Ger.	8.11.02		Hptschfhr, SS, Police, Mor.Ostrova and Zlin (Czech.) 39-45	INTERR.	CZECH.
WOLF, Rudolf	194694	M	Ger.			Cpl., Army, Chateau Regnault, Levreay (Fr.) 9.9.45	WITNESS	FR.
WOLF, Rudolf	262247	M	Ger.	26.7.--		Uschfhr, SS, Gestapo, Rennes (Fr.) 43-44	MISC.CRIMES	FR.
WOLF, Walter	142744	M	Ger.		15	Hptschfhr, W-SS, Agent, Gestapo, Kaplitz (Czech.) 9.12.44	MURDER	CZECH.
WOLF, Walter	150807	M	Ger.			Navy corps, St.Marine (Vic.) Fr.)	MURDER	U.S.
WOLF, Willi	193109	M	Ger.		08	Sgt.-Guard, Reichsjustiz-Feldstraflager,N-SS.,C.C.Finmark (Nor.) 45	MISC.CRIMES	NOR.
WOLFARD (or WOLFHARDT)	158404	M	Ger.		02	Pvt., 610 Lds.Schtz.Bn., Stalag 20-B, Rosemberg (Ger.) 24.11.42	TORTURE	U.K.,
WOLFAPT, Jean (or WOHLFAHRT)	142745	M			05	Member S.D., Cannes (Fr.) 43	MISC.CRIMES	FR.
WOLFE	103101	M	Ger.			Lt., field-police,.Prov.Vosges (Fr.)	MURDER	U.K.
WOLFE	104965	M	Ger.		05	Pvt., 565 Lds.Schtz.Bn., Stalag VIII-B, Arb.Kdo.E 241,Goldmoor(Ger.) 8.42-1.43	BRUTALITY	U.K.
WOLFE	125092	M	Ger.			Capt., L 375 Coy, CC Elbe (Ger.) 16.4.-5.45	MISC.CRIMES	U.K.
WOLFE	259470	M				Capt., Stalag Luft IV., Gr.Tychow (Pol.) 21.7.44	WITNESS	U.S.
WOLFEL, Bernhard	29657	M	Ger.			Dr., Oberlandesgerichtsrat, public official, Litomrices(Czech.)40	MURDER	CZECH.
WOLFER, Leo	126414	M				Doctor, Director, Civ., Mental-Hospitals "Salzburg" (Aust.)	MURDER	U.S.
WOLFERSDORF, Guenther	194876	M	Ger.	26.7.15		Sgt. SS, Gestapo, Kolin (Czech.) 39-45	MURDER	CZECH.
WOLFERT	301657	M	Ger.			Pvt., Stamm Coy, GR E.B., Aulndis(Bel.) 3.9.44	MURDER	BEL.
WOLFF	133189	M				Rottfhr, W-SS, CC Dora, Nordhausen (Ger.)	MURDER	U.S.
WOLFF	136398	M	Ger.		88	Lt.General, Army (Ger.)	TORTURE	U.S.
WOLFF	166985	M	Ger.			SS, CC Weimar, Referat IV- 1-c Ost, Weimar (Ger.) 45	MURDER	U.S.
WOLFF	187549	M	Ger.			Capt., 65 Inf.Div., Cisa Pass Senda (It.)	MURDER	U.K.
WOLFF	189293	M			99	Uschfhr. SS Totenkopfverband, CC Flossenburg (Ger.) 44	MURDER	FR.
WOLFF	194689	M				Sgt., Feld-Gend., Ploermel (Fr.) 18.6.44	TORTURE	FR.
WOLFF	219380	M	Ger.			Sturmbannfhr, 11 SS Mountain Inf.Rgt., 1 Coy, 44	MURDER	U.S.
WOLFF	228650	M	Ger.		07	Official, Oberregierungsrat, SS, Gestapo Amt IV.44	TORTURE	U.S.
WOLFF TAETS FREIHERR VON AMERONGEN (alias WOLF, Otto)	240071	M	Ger.	6.8.18		Agent, Lt.Res., Abwehr, of I H Kreis Organisation,Lissabon(Por.)10.42	MISC.CRIMES	U.S.
WOLFF	253472	M	Ger.			Feld-Gend., Marche (Bel.) 40-44	BRUTALITY	BEL.
WOLFF	253473	M	Ger.			SS Ogruppenfhr, CC Dachau (Ger.) 9.42	BRUTALITY	BEL.
WOLFF	261393	M	Ger.			Col., Rgt.z.b.V.(Col.Wolff), Environs,Mauleon-Navarreux(Fr.)7.-8.44	MURDER	FR.
WOLFF	261898	M	Ger. Or Rum.			SS-Mann, W-SS, Pijnacker near Delft (Neth.) 7.44	PILLAGE	NETH
WOLFF	301912		Ger.			Sturmbannfhr, Comd.I-SS Geb.Jg.Rgt.11, 6 SS Geb.Div.Nord, 20 Army, Finmark (Nor.) 10.-11.44	MURDER	NOR.
WOLFF	305122	M	Ger.	circa 00		SS-Mann, belonging to an SS unit in which he served as a Motor Mechanic, Pijnacker (Neth.) 4.9.44	PILLAGE	NETH.
WOLFF, Albert	240047	M	Ger.			Prof.Dr.ing., Wehrwirtschaftsfuehrer, SD official, Speer SS Berlin, Luebeck, Wesermuende (Ger.) 9.43	MISC.CRIMES	U.S.
WOLFF, Hugo	165535	M	Ger.	15		7 SS Pz.Div., Noorbeek (Neth.) 3.9.44	MURDER	BEL.
WOLFF, Otto	240046	M	Ger.	26.10.07		Dr.,SS Standartenfhr, Gauhauptstellenleiter, SS Stab Oberabschnitt Nordsee, Hamburg, Breslau (Ger.) 11.44	MISC.CRIMES	U.S.
WOLFF, Werner	253465	M	Ger.	21.7.11		Employee, Gestapo, Litomerice (Czech.) 39-45	MISC.CRIMES	CZECH.
WOLFF, Wilhelm	24859	M	Ger.			SS Oschfhr, CC Natzweiler, Struthof (Fr.) 42-44	MURDER	FR.
WOLFFE	6158	M				Lt., Army, CC Stalag XX-B, Marienburg (Ger.) 3.45	TORTURE	U.K.
WOLFHARDT, Friedrich	142746	M	Ger.	7.12.99		Member NSDAP, Linz (Aust.) 40-45	WITNESS	U.S.
WOLFGANG	306325	M	Ger.			Pvt., Mijnsheerenland, Oud-Beverland(Neth.) 4.-5.5.45	MURDER	NETH.
WOLFHARDT (see WOLFARD)	158404							
WOLFHART, Henri	135570	M	Ger.			Cpl., Arbeits-Kdo. 7006, Aisleben, Koenigshofen (Ger.)	TORTURE	U.K.
WOLFINEK	1039	M	Ger. or Aust.			Lt., Army, 118 Jg.Div. (Yugo.) 7.43-1.44	MURDER	YUGO.
WOLFRAM	301611	M	Ger.			CC Mauthausen (Aust.) 40-45	MURDER	BEL.
WOLFRAM, Alexander	260949	M	Ger. or Pol.	24.2.02		Police-Major, Inspector, Fire-Bde., Town-Mayor, German Police, present living at Heidenheim-Brens-Wuerttemberg. Warschau,Kattowitz (Pol.) 40-44	TORTURE	POL.
WOLFRAM, Josef	150808	M	Ger.			Civilian, in the vicinity of Bruch (Ger.) 4.45	MURDER	U.S.
WOLFRUM	185574	M	Ger.			Hptwachtmstr, Hursch (Ger.) 39-45	TORTURE	CZECH.
WOLFRUM, Gerhard	240045	M	Ger.			Pvt., Abwehr official, W-T operator and mechanic, Kreis-Organisation Speim, Trinidad 10.43	MISC.CRIMES	U.S.
WOLFS, Johannes	121685		Ger.			Pvt., Army, Crench-Macut en Pleubian (Fr.) 5.8.44 , 7.8.44	MURDER	FR.
WOLFRABE	301374	M	Ger.			SS-Schfhr., CC Mauthausen (Aust.) 11.42-5.45	MURDER	FR.

NAME	C.R.FILE NUMBER	SEX	NATIO-NALITY	DATE OF BIRTH	RANK	OCCUPATION	UNIT	PLACE AND DATE OF CRIME	REASON WANTED	WANTED BY
WOLHRAF	158405	M	Ger.		Cpl.,263 D.J.,Arbeitskommando 343,Landerneau,Finistere (Fr.)4.-8.44				MURDER	FR.
WOLKER,Willy	136394	M	Ger.	09	Lt.,Feldgendarmerie,Bruggen (Ger.) 27.2.45				WITNESS	U.S.
WOLL	175681	M	Ger.		Kreisleiter,NSDAP,Konstanz (Ger.) 44				TORTURE	FR.
WOLL,Albert	306061	M	Ger.		Civ.,Dudweiler (Ger.) 31.7.44				MISC.CRIMES	U.S.
WOLLEIX	150598	M	Ger.		Adjutant,11 Pz.Div.,South-West (Fr.) 44				MURDER	FR.
WOLLENBERG	306524	M	Ger.		Pvt.,Feldgendarmerie,Chateaubriant (Loire-Inf.),St.Julien de Mouvantes (Fr.) 21.7.44				MURDER	FR.
WOLLENWEBER	141371	M			Lt.,SS-Div."Der Fuehrer",Theil sur Vanne (Fr.) 44				WITNESS	FR.
WOLLER (see WULLER)	240131									
WOLLF	67743				Civ.,Mine-Manager,C.C.Heiligenrodn (Ger.)				TORTURE	U.K.
WOLLHEBER (or WOLLHUEBNER)	194691	M	Ger.		Interpreter,Feld-Ers.-Bn.114,2 Panz.-Div.,12 Coy.,Montesquieu de Lauragais (Fr.) 9.8.44				PILLAGE	FR.
WOLLMAN,Franz	142748	M			Arbeitskdo.,C.C.Jena (Ger.)				TORTURE	U.S.
WOLLMERINGER (or VOLLMERINGER)	189764	M	Ger.		Zollkommissar,Zollgrenzschutz Suedost,Bela-Crkva (Yugo.) 43				MURDER	YUGO.
WOLLSCHLAEGER	21329	M	Ger.		Oberjaeger,Army,Paratrooper,Roermond (Neth.) 11.44-1.45				TORTURE	U.S.
WOLLSTADT	11867	M	Ger.	19	N.C.O.,Marsch-Bn.418,3 Coy.,Gastungs (Fr.) 25.8.44				MURDER	FR.
WOLLUNG,Gerhard	147106	M	Ger.		Rottfhr.,SS,Pz.Div."Das Reich",13 Coy.,Moissac (Fr.) 44				MURDER	FR.
WOLMER	1040	M	Ger.		Chief of Police,Police,Sfax (Tun.) 1.-8.43				PILLAGE	FR.
WOLNY	253233	M	Ger.		Crim.Secr.,Abt.IV E,Sipo,Bruessel (Bel.) 40-45				INTERR.	BEL.
WOLPERS	257398	M	Ger.		Sgt.,Org.Todt,slave labour camps,Erlandet,Ousand,Trola(Nor.)1.42-45				MURDER	YUGO.
WOLSEGGER,Ferdinand	62445	M	Ger.		Ministerialrat,Dir. of the Govt. Chancellary Gen.Gouv.(Pol.)				TORTURE	UNWCC
WOLSTERMANN,Bernhard (or SPIESS)	150838	M	Ger.	10 or 15	Truppfhr.,SA-Bie.,Feldherrnhalle,Weilbach (Aust.) 15.4.45				MURDER	U.S.
WOLTE	182091	M	Ger.		Pvt.,3 Sicherungs-Regt.Z-6 (Bel.) 40-45				MURDER	BEL.
WOLTER	131002	M			Dr.,Osturmfhr.,Chief-Dr.,SS,C.C.Mauthausen (Aust.) 41-45				MURDER	U.S.
WOLTER (see WOLTHER)	137538									
WOLTER	185897	M	Ger.		N.C.O.,Army,65 Inf.Regt.,Kerrasson (Grc.)				TORTURE	GRC.
WOLTER	188772	M	Ger.		Capt.,Army,Saltris (Fr.) 24.8.44				MURDER	FR.
WOLTER,	189264	M	Ger.		Dr.,Hptsturmfhr.,SS,C.C.Dachau (Ger.)				TORTURE	BEL.
WOLTER	195983	M	Ger.		Lt.,Army,Barbezieux (Fr.) 27.-28.8.44				MURDER	FR.
WOLTER,Fritz Karl W.	260492	M	Ger.	13. 3.09	Hptsturmfhr.,Constution Engineer,SS,Guard Coy.,C.C.Auschwitz(Pol.) 10.40-1.45				BRUTALITY	POL.
WOLTER,Karl	255679	M		28. 7.03	Pvt.,C.C.Harzungen,Nordhausen (Ger.)				MURDER	U.S.
WOLTER,Rudolf (see WALTER)	182326									
WOLTERS	104966	M	Ger.		Member,Gestapo,near Westerode (Ger.) 7.7.44				WITNESS	U.S.
WOLTERS	139735	M	Ger.		Capt.,Adjutant,Stalag X B,C.C.Sandbostel (Ger.)1.-8.45				TORTURE	U.S.
WOLTERS	151470	M		97	Sgt.,Stabsfeldw.,Army,Paris (Fr.)				TORTURE	U.K.
WOLTERS	182092	M			O.T.Leiter,Sturmfhr.,C.C.Ellrigh,Nordhausen (Ger.)				TORTURE	BEL.
WOLTERS	195982	M	Ger.		Sgt.,Chief,Gestapo,SS,Grenoble et la Region (Fr.)				MURDER	FR.
WOLTERS	255678	M	Ger.		Sturmfhr.,C.C.Dora,Nordhausen (Ger.)				MURDER	U.S.
WOLTERS,Hans	39621	M	Ger.		Crim.Secr.,Gestapo,Strassburg|Shales,Schirmeck (Fr.) 9.-11.44				MURDER	FR.U.K.
WOLTERSDORF	168064	M	Ger.		Dr.,leader,Treuhandverwaltung fuer Privatgrundstueske,Lwow,Galizia (Pol.) 9.39-44				PILLAGE	POL.
WOLTERSDORG	62446	M	Ger.		Leader,Bureau of Estates Management in Dept.of Finance of Gen.Gouv. (Pol.)				MISC.CRIMES	UNWCC
WOLTHER (or WOLTER)	137538	M	Ger.	19	Uschfhr.19 SS-Pz.Div.Hohenstaufen,3 Bn.,Petite Leuglir(Bel.)10.1.45				MURDER	U.S.
WOLTZ (see WELTZ)	256526									
WOLZ	173855	M	Ger.		Official,Gauarbeitsamt,Strassburg (Fr.) 44				TORTURE	FR.
WOMBERG	138247	M	Ger.		Col.,Army,Paris (Fr.) 7.44				TORTURE	FR.UNWCC
WOMBERG	251733	M	Ger.		Major,Group of Railway,Station Amberieu,St.Denis en Bugsy(Fr)16.8.44				INTERR.	FR.
WONDERLICH	29852	M	Ger.		Kommissar Chief of Customs,St.Michel de Maurienne (Fr.) 9.3.44				MURDER	FR.
WONDERS,Hans	174853	M	Ger.		Lt.,Dienststelle,Repel,Poussay,Gironcourt (Fr.)24.8.-1.9.44				WITNESS	FR.
WONDRAK,Heinrich	252816	M	Ger.	30. 5.09	Chief,S.D.,State service,Liberec (Czech.) 39-45				MISC.CRIMES	CZECH.
WONDZIMSKI,Johannes	257530	M		8.10.96	Factory-worker,C.C.Nordhausen (Ger.)				MURDER	U.S.
WONEROW	150584	M	Ger.		Gestapo,C.C.Fredrikstad (Nor.) 44				TORTURE	NOR.
WONIAN,Willy H.	150839	M			Guard,Stalag work-Kdo.625,Stalag IX C,C.C.Berga (Ger.) 2.-4.45				MURDER	U.S.
WONS,Josef	196732	M	Ger.	23. 4.03	Wachtmeister,Reservist with Carinthian Provincial Police,Velden (Aust.) 20.-22.11.41				WITNESS	U.K.FR.
WONSCHUTZ	150597	M	Ger.		Pvt.,11 Pz.Div.Kampfgruppe "Wilde",South-West (Fr.) 44				MURDER	FR.
WOOL-SCHMIT	186872	M	Ger.		Officer,Commander,Air Force,2 F.B.K.,Evreux (Fr.) 40-41				PILLAGE	FR.
WOOLFE	123931	M	Ger.		General,Arbeits-Kdo.,C.C.Blechhammer (Ger.)				MURDER	U.K.
WORBACH	255461	M			Lt.,Usturmfhr.,C.C.Dora,Nordhausen (Ger.)				MURDER	U.S.
WOROUL,Emil	139728	M	Ger.		Civilian,C.C.Nordhausen (Ger.) 39-45				MISC.CRIMES	POL.
WORDELMANN	183937	M	Ger.	9. 3.94	Uschfhr.,4 SS-Sturmbann,C.C.Dora,Nordhausen (Ger.) 43-44				MURDER	U.S.
WORDENSTMANN,August	139251	M	Ger.		Commandant,C.C.Plettenberg (Ger.) 4.42-45				TORTURE	U.S.
WOREL,Lidja	188600	F	Ger.		Kanzleiangestellte,Gestapo,Brno (Czech.) 39-45				WITNESS	CZECH.
WORHOFF (or WOTOFF)	142749	M	Ger.	10	Osturmfhr.,W-SS,C.C.Lublin (Pol.) 42-45				MURDER	POL.
WORHOFF	194685	M	Ger.		Pvt.,Feldgendarmerie,Ploermel (Fr.) 18.6.44				TORTURE	FR.
WORLE,Otto-(see WOERLE)	128924									
WORLEIN (see WOERLEIN)	240049									
WORMA	168028	M			Revenue Officer,Ostgebiets-Minist.,Einsatzstab Rosenberg,Bayonne (Fr.) 40-44				PILLAGE	FR.
WORMBAUM	29642	M	Ger.		Stabsfeldw.,Army,Busigny (Fr.) 23.8.44				MURDER	FR.
WORMS	306670	M	Ger.		Bie.,05-243 Mongolian "Oberland" Unit,St.Nazaire en Royans(Fr)7.-8.44				MURDER	FR.
WORN,Philipp	139157	M	Ger.		Civilian,Frankfurt-Main (Ger.)				TORTURE	BEL.
WORNER,Valentin	255460	M		17.11.08	Pvt.,C.C.Harzungen,Nordhausen (Ger.)				MURDER	U.S.
WORNOW (see FAHRNARD)	142527									
WOROFSKY,J.	29658	M			Dr.,Landgerichtsrat,Ministry of Justice,Public official,Cheb (Czech)40				MURDER	CZECH.
WORRLEIN (see WOERLEIN)	240049									
WORSTER,Heinrich or Henri	1042	M	Ger.	27.11.09	Hptsturmfhr.,Chief of Administr.sect.,C.C.Maidanek,Dachau Lublin (Pol.-Ger.) 38-44				MURDER	FR.U.S. BEL.POL.
WORTHMANN	168240	M	Ger.		Krim.Asst.,Hptschfhr.,SS,Gestapo (Nor.) 4.40				TORTURE	NOR.UNWCC
WORTHMANN,Hans	193102	M	Ger.		Crim.Asst.,Kripo,RSHA,Tradum,Berlin (Nor.Ger.) 43				MURDER	NOR.
WORTMANN	137539	M			Hptsturmfhr.,Schutzstaffel,C.C.Hellendorf (Ger.)				MURDER	U.S.
WORTMANN	306731	M	Ger.		Member,S.D. or Gestapo,Oslo,Trandum near Oslo (Nor.) 19.1.43				MURDER	U.K.
WORUCH	166973	M	Ger.		Lt.,Army,Révin (Fr.)				MURDER	FR.

NAME	C.R.FILE NUMBER	SEX	NATIO-NALITY	DATE OF BIRTH	RANK OCCUPATION UNIT PLACE AND DATE OF CRIME	REASON WANTED	WANTED BY
WOSCHENEK	104967	M	Ger.	14. 1.92	Capt., Commander I.Bn., W.SS Sturm Bn. A.O.K. No.I, Courcelles sur Nied (Fr.) 15.11.44	WITNESS	U.S.
WOSHAU	195980	M	Ger.		Guard, Sgt., C.C. Royallieu (Fr.) 41-44	MURDER	FR.
WOSNICA	306828	M	Ger.		SS-Lt., Political Chief, C.C. Auschwitz (Pol.) from 40	MURDER	FR.
WOSNITZA, Johann	256357	M			Unterschfhr., Muhldorf (Ger.)	WITNESS	U.S.
WOSTAL	255459	M			Pvt., C.C. Dora, Nordhausen (Ger.)	MURDER	U.S.
WOSTE, Conrad	305123	M			Cmdt., Kommando-Westphalia, Mastholte (Ger.) 42-45	TORTURE	BEL.
WOSTECH, Karl	29655	M	Ger.		Dr., Landgerichtsrat, Public Official, Opava (Czech.)40	MURDER	CZECH.
WOSTENMEYER, Eugene	6104	M	Ger.		Army, Rennes (Fr.) 44	WITNESS	FR.
WOTNECKE see MOTNECKE	141584						
WOTOFF see WORHOFF	142749						
WOTREL, Otto	194679	M	Ger.		Employee, SD, Kolin (Czech.) 39-45	SUSPECT	CZECH.
WOUTERSE	307253	M	Ger.		Member of the Sicherheitsdienst, Almelo District (Neth.)9.44-2.45	MURDER	NETH.
WOZASEK, Walter	306818	M	Ger.		Sgt., D.C.A., Kermassenent in Kervignac,Morbihan (Fr.) 20.8.44	MURDER	FR.
WOZNICA	255458	M			Pol.Abt.Gestapo, C.C. Auschwitz, Nordhausen (Pol.,Ger.)	MURDER	U.S.
WOZNY, Wlodzimiers	158416	M		23	Civilian Political Prison, Osternhagen, Gardelegen (Ger.)5.-14.4.45	WITNESS	U.S.
WRBA, Johann	252786	M	Ger.	1. 7.94	Teacher, Civilian, Jilovice (Czech.) 39-45	MISC.CRIMES	CZECH.
WREDE, Anton	182321	M			SS-Sturmbannfhr., SS Adjutant to Trummler (Ger.) 44-45	MISC.CRIMES	U.S.
WRESTT	136278	M	Ger.		Cmdt., Army Unit No. 48081, St. Floret (Fr.) 30.6.44	MURDER	FR.
WRICKE, Kurt	256243	M	Ger.		Abt.Chief, C.C. Nord Mauthausen (Aust.)	INTERR.	FR.
WRIGHT, Edwin, Martens	262341	M			Medical Doctor, Wanted as a Witness to the shooting of an unarmed American Soldier, Appen (Ger.) 18.1.44 or 18.6.44 (L.o.D.N.A.o.D.)	WITNESS	U.S.
WRIMMER	260077	M	Ger.		Lt., Unit 19548 A, Pludono (Ger.) 3.8.44	MURDER	FR.
WROBEL, Gustav	302017	M	Ger.	20. 8.20	Lt., Army, 7. Parachute Div. H.Q., Gristede Abt.20.4.45	MURDER	U.K.
WROBEL, Ludwig	159293	M		15	Farmer, Political Prisoner from C.C. Wieda-Gardelegen (Ger.)5.-14.4.45	WITNESS	U.S.
WROBEL, Martin	260493	M	Ger.	21. 7.06	SS-Rottfhr., SS Guard-Coy. and supply service C.C. Auschwitz and Budy (Pol.) 3.41-1.45	BRUTALITY	POL.
WRONSKI	185192	M	Ger.		SS-Hauptscharfhr., SS Police, Org Todt 3.III Bn. 9. Coy., Bernex, Annemasse (Frankfurt, Ger.) 17.12.43 u.29.1.44	WITNESS	FR.
WROUCK	175699	M	Ger.		Fieldgend., Field-Police, Cormainville, Chateaudun, Logron (Fr.) 9.8.44-17.8.44	TORTURE	FR.
WUCHNER	189265	M	Ger.		Member, Hauptsturmfhr .. Gestapo, C.C. Dachau (Ger.) 40-45	MURDER	BEL.
WUCHTER see WACHTERL, Vinzenz	193445						
WUDKE	192981	M	Ger.		SS-Sgt., SS, C.C. Buchenwald-Allendorf (Ger.)	TORTURE	U.S.
WUENENBURG or WUENENBERG Alfred	62447	M		90	Police-Colonel, (General) SS Obergruppenfhr., Chief of order Police H.Q. in Berlin W.-SS, Berlin (Ger.) 43-45	MURDER	U.S.,UNWCC
WUENSCH, Robert	162624	M	Ger.		Untersturmfhr., W.-SS, Gaggenau (Ger.)25.11.44	MURDER	U.K.,U.S.
WUENSCHE	159294	M	Ger.		Capt., Landesschuetz.Bn. 398 2.Coy., East Sudetenland (Czech.)1.-3.45	TORTURE	U.K.
WUENSCHER, Hans	256239	M	Ger.		Factory Manager, Civilian (Ing.) Prag (Czech.) 39-45	MISC.CRIMES	CZECH.
WUERFLER	190451	M	Ger.		Dr., Generalarzt, Beelitz Stiftung C.C. (Ger.) 40-45	MURDER	CZECH.
WOERLEIN see WOERLEIN	240049						
WUERSTER, Eugen	189827	M	Ger.		Colonel, Army, Pozarevac (Serbia) 41-43	MURDER	YUGO.
WUERTH or WIRT	1043	M			Dr., Medical Group Employed in Experimental C.C. Oswiecim (Pol.)	MURDER	POL.,BEL.
WUERTHS, Eduard	250552	M	Ger.		Dr., SS-Obersturmfhr., C.C. Dachau (Ger.) 42	MURDER	YUGO.
WUESCHER or WUSSER	307254	M	Ger.		Lt. Head, Ordnungspol. of a unit stationed at Borne May 43 with H.Q. Hotel De Keizerskroom. Overijssel-Province (Neth.) 5.43	MURDER	NETH.
WUEST	259156	M	Ger.		SS-Obersturmbannfhr., SS, C.C. Dachau (Ger.) 9.42-45	MISC.CRIMES	YUGO.
WUETSCHER, Ludwig	123932	M	Ger.		SS-Obersturmbannfhr., SS, Mellrichstadt (Ger.) 21.9.44	TORTURE	U.K.
WUGGENICK, Richard	185741	M	Ger.		Kapo or Guard, SS, C.C. Gusen, Mauthausen (Aust.)	MURDER	U.S.,BEL.
WULF	252844	M			Cpl., Pepingen (Bel.) 2.44-3.9.44	WITNESS	BEL.
WULF	257964	M			Lt.Colonel, Jagdverb.150. Pz.Bde., Meuse Bridge, Antwerp (Bel.)12.44	MISC.CRIMES	U.S.
WULF or WOLF	259601	M	Ger.		Lt., Railway at Agen, Aude,Herault,Gard (Fr.) 8.44	MISC.CRIMES	FR.
WULF, Andreas	183936	M	Ger.	26. 9.12	SS-Haupttruppfhr., Org.Todt, (Pol.) 40-42	MISC.CRIMES	POL.
WULF, Hans	257677	M	Ger.		Capt., Army, Zajecar (Yugo.) 41-44	MURDER	YUGO.
WULF, Helmut	67748	M	Ger.		Miscellaneous.	TORTURE	U.K.
WULF, Petra	251714	F	Ger.	13	Overseer, C.C. Oranienburg (Ger.)	BRUTALITY	BEL.
WULFF	125223	M	Ger.		Lt.Colonel, Tank Corps Coy. of I.Assault Brig Co. Stielau-Musculus Gravenwoehr (Ger.) 2.11.-1.12.44	MISC.CRIMES	U.S.
WULFF, Heinrich	251734	M	Ger.		Leader, Gend. Erndtebrueck (Ger.) 15.3.45	MURDER	FR.
WULFF, Hermann	262216	M	Ger.	2. 2.15	SS-Usturmfhr., 7.Coy. 5.SS Amoured Bde., Bucheres, Breviandes, Ste Savine, La Riviere de Corps Troyes (Fr.) 22.-25.8.44	BRUTALITY	FR.
WULFFEN	195379	M	Ger.		SS-Lt., C.C. Sachsenhausen (Ger.)	MURDER	BEL.
WULFFT see FAUREE	305107						
WULFSTAFF see WULSTAFF	194686						
WULKAN	189267	M			Member, Gestapo, Stanislawow (Pol.) 8.41-1.10.42	WITNESS	POL.
WULLER or WOLLER	240131	M		10	SS-Stubannfhr., head of Abt.III/C, SD Leitabschn., Posen (Pol.)5.44	MURDER	U.S.
WULSTAFF or WULFSTAFF	194686	M			Member, C.C. Drancy Seine (Fr.) 43-44	MURDER	FR.
WUNDEL	194693	M	Ger.		Guard, Stalag 17 B, Marbach (Ger.) 17.12.43	PILLAGE	FR.
WUNDER, Johann	251721	M			Gend., Reichshoffen (Fr.) 16.2.45	MURDER	FR.
WUNDER, Johann	255462	M			Oberscharfhr., C.C. Harzungen, Nordhausen (Ger.)	MURDER	U.S.
WUNDERER	11592	M			Cpl., Army 110. or 111. Pz.Gren.Regt. 2. Coy., Albine (Fr.)29.6.44	MURDER	FR.
WUNDERLE, Franz	196430	M			Untersturmfhr., SS, Prag (Czech.) 39 - 45	MURDER	CZECH.
WUNDERLICH	141366	M	Ger.		Capt., 86% Gren.Regt. 348. 2. Bn. Pont a Marcq (Fr.) 3.9.44	MURDER	FR.
WUNDERLICH	192425	M		95	Officer, General Staff, Warsaw (Pol.) 39	SUSPECT	POL.
WUNDERLICH	251722	M			Civilian, Plainfaing (Fr.) 10.-11.44	PILLAGE	FR.
WUNDERLICH, Alfred	1772	M			Capt., Army, Comd.2.Bn. Gren.Regt. 869, Lille (Fr.) 44	MURDER	U.K.
WUNDERLICH, Otto	159292	M	Ger.		SA Hauptsturmfhr., C.C. Wulfen (Ger.)	MURDER	U.K.
WUNDERLISCHER	124460	M	Ger.		Volkssturm at Aseling (Aust.) 11.44	MURDER	U.S.
WUNGE	195979	M	Ger.		Member, Gestapo St. Etienne (Fr.)	MISC.CRIMES	FR.
WUNNENBERG see WUENENBURG,Alfred	62447						
WUNNENBERG, Ernst	162541	M	Ger.	3. 6.21	SS-Unterscharfhr., W.SS, 1. Pz.Div. L."A.H.", Weissenbach (Aust.) 12.4.45	MURDER	U.S.
WUNSCH	166903	M	Ger.		Camp-leader, C.C. Schirmeck (Fr.)	MURDER	FR.
WUNSCH	305755	M	Ger.		Oberscharfhr., C.C. Auschwitz-Birkenau (Pol.) from 40	MURDER	FR.
WUNSCHE, Erwin	255913	M		17. 9.05	Rottenfhr., C.C. Harzungen, Nordhausen (Ger.)	MURDER	U.S.

WUN-YUN

-214-

NAME	C.R.FILE NUMBER	SEX	NATIO- NALITY	DATE OF BIRTH	RANK OCCUPATION UNIT PLACE AND DATE OF CRIME	REASON WANTED	WANTED BY
WUNSCHMANN	193101	M	Ger.		Cpt., 3. Coy. Kgf. Arb.Bn. 204 C.C. Bassis Tunnel (Nor.) 44	MURDER	NOR.
WUPPERMANN	251729	M	Ger.	15	Lt., Vinkt, (Bel.) 25.-31.5.40	MURDER	BEL.
WURCH, Herman	159295	M	Ger.		Sailor, Navy, Stellemden on the Island of Goedereede (Neth.)29.4.45	MURDER	NETH.
WURGLER, Eduard, Oskar	167039	M	Ger.	6.4.02	Pvt., Rebaupaul, (Fr.) 9.9.44	MURDER	FR.
WURM	196733	M	Ger.		C.C. Struthof Matzweiler (Fr.) 40-44	TORTURE	FR.
WURMSER, Karl	253462	M	Ger.	11	Capo, C.C. Dora Nordhausen (Ger.)	TORTURE	FR.
WURST	173845	M	Ger.		Director, Bor Mines (Yugo.) 42	TORTURE	YUGO.
WURST, Joseph	305705	M	Ger.		Guard SS, C.C. Flossenburg, Hersbruck, Wolkenburg, Ganacker Leitmeritz (Ger. Czech.) 1.1.42-8.5.45	MURDER	U.S.
WURSTLIN, Emil	255914	M			Sgt., C.C. Ellrich Nordhausen (Ger.)	MURDER	U.S.
WURTH, Eugen	256063	M	Ger.		Kommandofhr., SS, Sainte Maire Aux Mines (Fr.) 7.44	MURDER	FR.
WURZ, E.	24847	M	Ger.		SS-Schfhr., SS C.C. Struthof Natzweiler (Fr.)	MISC.CRIMES	FR.
WURZ	305756	M			Hptsturmfhr., Senior medical officer of all the camps attached to C.C. Auschwitz Birkenau (Pol.) 40	MURDER	FR.
WURZEN, Otto	194166	M	Ger.	15	Civilian, Leipzig (Ger.) 11.3.45	MURDER	U.S.
WUSCHA	21433	M			SS-Uschfhr., C.C. Amersfoort (Neth.) 11.42	WITNESS	U.S.
WUSSER (see WUESCHER)	307254						
WUSSING	177543	M	Ger.		Cpl., Army St. Germain Les Corbeil (Fr.)	WITNESS	FR.
WUST, Josef	255316	M		13.5.04	Rottfhr., C.C. Harzungen Nordhausen (Ger.)	MURDER	U.S.
WUSTER	255315	M			Cpt., C.C. Dora Nordhausen (Ger.)	MURDER	U.S.
WUSTER, Adolf	191478	M	Ger.		Foreign Office, Paris (Fr.) 40-44	PILLAGE	FR.
WUSTHALZ	128804	M	Ger.		Pvt., Arbeitskommando Stalag V B, Allmendingen (Ger.) 6.3.44	MURDER	U.K.
WUSTRAU	300977	M	Ger.		SS-Oscnfhr., Official of SD. Leitabschnitt, Prague, Owiecim Birkenau (Pol.) 39-45	MURDER	CZECH.
WUTEL	142752	M		10	SS Oschfhr., W-SS C.C. Lublin (Pol.) 42-44	MURDER	POL.
WUTER	1368	M			Cpl., SD. Aussenkdo.	MISC.CRIMES	U.K.
WUTHENOW	193443	M			General Major, Army C.C. Oslo (Nor.) 10.43-6.44	TORTURE	U.K.
WUTNI, Henry	185742	M			SS-Interrogator,SS Department for Comm. 18. Section, Athens (Grc.)	TORTURE	GRC.
WUTSHKE	142753	M		95	Sturmschfhr., C.C. W-SS Lublin (Pol.) 42-44	MURDER	POL.
WUTTE	250561	M			Cpt., Army Lehr.Div.Mut. Ink near Ogulin (Yugo.) 27.10.43-11.43	INTERR.	YUGO.
WUTTIN	166983	M		00	Army, Sgt., Inf.Staff Stalag VIII B, Tarnowitz (Ger.) 12.43	TORTURE	U.K.
WUTTKE	162542	M		90	SS Hptschfhr., SS C.C. Buchenwald Tarnowitz (Ger.Pol.)	WITNESS	U.S.
WUTTKE	306526	M			Sgt., Interpreter, Chateaubriant (Loire Inf.), St. Julienne de Mouvantes (Fr.) 21.7.44	MURDER	FR.
WUTTKE, Willy	167038	M			Sgt., Abwehr Oflag XIII A, Nuernberg (Ger.) 13.7.41	TORTURE	FR.
WUTZ	166978	M		07	SS Hptsturmfhr., SS, SD, Kiew, Zwiakel, Lemberg (Ukr.Pol.) 41-42	MURDER	U.S.
WUTZEL, Wolfgang	67747	M			N.C.O. Pvt., SS 17.Grem.Div.II Goets von Berlichingen Sturm Gesch. Abt. 17, Segre Renaze (Fr.) 6.6.44-30.7.44	MURDER	U.K. FR.
WYBART	185743	M			Sgt., C.C. Mauthausen Gusen (Aust.)	TORTURE	U.S.
WYDLEDATZ, Emil	257528	M		18.7.09	Employee, C.C. Block 110 Dora Nordhausen (Ger.)	MURDER	U.S.
WYERSTRAUS, Christian	135533	M	Ger.		Civ., Efferen (Ger.) 2.10.44	BRUTALITY	U.S.
WYKLEFF	1044	M	Ger.		Schfhr., W-SS C.C. Auschwitz Birkenau (Pol.) 39-45	MURDER	BEL. YUGO.
WYLAND (or WIKLAND)	251455	M	Ger.		Feld.Gend. Borms (Neth.) 11.44	MURDER	NETH.
WYMAN, Karl (see WIEMAN, Herbert)	179780						
WYNBERGER or WEINBERGER	124057	M			Guard, C.C. Retzwey Leipnitz (Ge.) 10.1.42	MURDER	U.K.
WYS	192980	M			SS C.C. Buchenwald (Ger.) 42-45	TORTURE	U.S.
WYSOCKY	232354	M		05	SS Colonel SD, Essen (Ger.) 44	MURDER	U.S.
WYTSCHIGHLO, Anton	29659	M	Ger.		Landgerichtadir.Public Official, Litomerice (Czech.) 40	MURDER	CZECH.
XANEK	305987	M			Cpt. Adjutant of Camp X-A, Sandbostel (Ger.) 39-45	MURDER	POL.
YAAHILS	139463	M			N.C.O. 2.SS Panz.Div. Das Reich, Venerque le Vernet (Fr.)	MURDER	FR.
YAGER	161484	M			Lt., Police, Sebesch Tals. en Karisa (Latv.) 44-45	MURDER	U.S.
YAHNE	152056 A	M	Ger.		Cpl., Arbeits Kdo. Beuthen (Ger.) 12.42-1.43	TORTURE	U.K.
YAMAGATA, Tsuyuo	186915				Major General, Japanese Army 21 the Independent Mixed Brigade (New Guinea) 27.2.42-24.1.43	MURDER	AUSTL.
YANICK	196049	M	Ger.		Pvt., Airforce 8, 9, 10, Coy., Maizzag (Fr.) 25.7.44	MURDER	FR.
YANKE (see JANKE)	250850						
YANNIS (or Jaanis	305200	M	Ger.		Sgt., Geheime Staatspolizei Gruppe 510 Dienststelle No. K/661 Gestapo Livadia, Distromon Vrastamites (Grc.) 10.6.44-8.1.44	MISC.CRIMES	GRC.
YAROLIN	173825	M	Ger.		SS Mann, SS C.C. Dachau (Ger.) 3.5.41	TORTURE	FR.
YAROSTAWSKA, Lili	152057	F		23	(Pol.)	TORTURE	U.K.
YEALEGER	125056	M	Ger.		Officer, Stalag IX C, Merkers (Ger.)	MURDER	U.K.
YEDYSTINE, Katharina	162547	F	Ger.	24	Civilian, Ruedesheim (Ger.)	WITNESS	U.S.
YEKEL	141341	M			Cpt., Stalag IV C, Bruex (Czech.) 7.44-5.45	MISC.CRIMES	U.K.
YENTSCH	184576	M	Ger.		SS Oschfhr., SS C.C. Dachau (Ger.)	MURDER	FR.
YESKE, Hermann	193573	M		02	Agent, Gestapo, Savigny en Septaine, Bourges (Fr.) 7.44	MURDER	FR.
YEUNESS, Hermann	194572	M		00	Agent, Gestapo, Savigny en Septaine, Bourges (Fr.) 7.44	MURDER	FR.
YOACHMI	161486	M	Ger.		SS Div.Das Reich III P.G.R. Group Wilde Tulle Gamdom (Fr.) 6.44	TORTURE	FR.
YOCKL (see JOCKELOVI)	157497						
YOSTEN	172463	M	Ger.		SS-Osturmfhr., C.C. Auschwitz (Pol.) 42-45	MURDER	U.S.
YOUNG, Alfred	256018	M	Ger.		Customer, Custom House Campy Lamorans (Fr.) 22.7.41	INTERR.	FR.
YOUNG, Sid	257609				Civilian, Gratkorn (Aust.) 2.45	WITNESS	U.S.
YOUNGER (or JUNKER)	67754	M			Chefarzt, Stalag IX A, C.C. Kloster Haina (Ger.) 6.43	TORTURE	U.K.
YROVOI, Aleksej	156982				Civilian, Eischweiler and Bruchweiden (Ger.)	MISC.CRIMES	U.S.
YSEL	11533	M	Ger.		Member, Gestapo, Cahors (Fr.) 29.6.44	MURDER	FR.
YUNCK	166780	M	Ger.		General Army Cmdt. the places of St. Nazaire, La Roche S-Yom. (Fr.) 28.8.44	PILLAGE	FR.
YUNG	147105	M	Ger.		SS Panz. Div. Das Reich Rgt. Deutschland 3. Bn. Vener Que Le Vernet (Fr.) 44	MURDER	FR.
YUNG	184577	M	Ger.		Officer, Gestapo, C.C. Dachau (Ger.)	MURDER	FR.
YUNG	256019	M	Ger.		Senior N.C. Feldkommandantur Dax, (Fr.) 13.6.44	TORTURE	FR.
YUNG (see JUNG)	301418						

NAME	C.R.FILE NUMBER	SEX	NATIO-NALITY	DATE OF BIRTH	RANK OCCUPATION UNIT PLACE AND DATE OF CRIME	REASON WANTED	WANTED BY
YUNG, Ludwig	106907	M	Ger.		W.O.,15 Div. Africa Corps,33 pioniers,Vaucourt,Xousse(Fr.)9..10.44	MISC.CRIMES	FR.
YUNG, Norbert	161483	M	Ger.		Gestapo, Morlaix,St.Pol de Leon Brest (Fr.) 44	MURDER	FR.
YUNG, Rene	125681	M	Ger.		Policeman, Geh.Feldpol.,Lille,Montigny-en Gohelle(North-Fr.)14.3.44	MISC.CRIMES	FR.
YUSSEN, Paul	260086	M	Ger.		Paymaster,Dept.of Ger.Pay-office,Luneville(Meurt and Moselle-Fr.)40-44	PILLAGE	FR.
ZAADE	194342	M	Ger.		Civilian,St.Rambert (Fr.) 2.44	MISC.CRIMES	FR.
ZAAR	189828	M	Ger.	11	Usturmfhr.,SS,C.C.Neuengamme (Ger.) 43	MURDER	YUGO.
ZABASTA, Ferdinand	195197	M	Ger.	95	Member,employee,Gestapo,Kolin(Czech.) 39-45	MURDER	CZECH.
ZABCEK	168029	M	Ger.		Member-Staff,Ostgebietsministerium,Einsatzstab Rosenberg(Fr.)40-44	PILLAGE	FR.
ZABEL	11534	M	Ger.		Pvt.,Army,110 or 111 Pz.Gren.Rgt.,2 Coy,Albine(Fr.) 29.6.44	MURDER	FR.
ZABEL	156979	M			Cpl.,SS, 3 Baubde, C.C.Wieda and Gardelegen(Ger.)	MURDER	U.S.
ZABEL	305787	M	Ger.		Osturmfhr.,SS,town Major,Stab 1 Pz.Gren.Rgt.Nr.7 Lavadia, Kalamion Beotia (Gre.) 10.-12.6.44	MURDER	GRC.
ZABEL, Erich	138197	M	Ger.		SS,C.C.Neuengamme (Ger.)	MURDER	U.S.
ZABEL, Hermann	132961	M			Uscharfhr.,SS,C.C.Nordhausen,Mittelbau-Dora(Ger.)	MURDER	U.S.
ZABEL, Johannes	306829	M	Ger.		Uscharfhr.,SS-Institute of Hygiene,C.C.Auschwitz(Pol.) 40-45	MURDER	FR.
ZABEL, Wilhelm	256199	M		4. 2.07	Pvt.,C.C.Ellrich-Nordhausen(Ger.)	MURDER	U.S.
ZABEN, Subki	240044	M		08	Agent,Gestapo, Beirut(Syria) 41	MURDER	FR.
ZABOJNIK, Johann	306113	M	Ger.		Member of Staff C.C.Hamburg-Neuengamme (Ger.) up to 45	MURDER	CZECH.
ZABRANSKA, Hedwig	258074	F	Ger.	22. 8.06	Informer,clerk,Gestapo,C.C.Budejovice (Czech.) 42	MURDER	CZECH.
ZABWECKR or ZABWECKER	1046	M	Ger.		Capt.,SS,Tunis (Tunisia) 43	MURDER	FR.
ZACEK, Johann	194467	M	Ger.	2. 4.26	SS-Mann,SS (Bohemia-Czech.)	MISC.CRIMES	CZECH.
ZACEK, Josef	194466	M	Ger.	22. 1.22	Uscharfhr.,SS (Bohemia-Czech.)	MISC.CRIMES	CZECH.
ZACHARIAS	132962	M	Ger.		Lt.,Army,326 V.G.Div.,Eastern Front (Ger.,Sov.Un.)	MURDER	U.S.
ZACHARIDAS, Franz	256340	M			Cpl.,C.C.Ellrich-Nordhausen(Ger.)	MURDER	U.S.
ZACHER, Josef	152031	M			Foreman,Building Coy,Civilian	MURDER	U.S.
ZACHERT, Otto	256336	M			Pvt.,C.C.Ellrich-Nordhausen (Ger.)	MURDER	U.S.
ZACHMANN, Johann	251490	M	Ger.		Guard,SD,C.C.Lahde-Weser(Ger.)	INTERR.	BEL.
ZACHO, Minna	142306	F	Ger.		Civilian-nurse,C.C. Hadamar (Ger.) 6.44-3.45	WITNESS	U.S.
ZACHOW, Hans	186781	M	Ger.		Lt.,Pionier Nr.02502,Beaufai Par Aube (Fr.) 17.-21.8.44	PILLAGE	FR.
ZACK	257397	M	Ger.		SS-guard,Sgt.,slave labour camp,Beisfjord near Narvik(Nor.)6.-11.42	BRUTALITY	YUGO.
ZACKEL	250572	M			Sturmmann, 1 Coy,SS Pz.Rgt., Malmedy(Bel.) 17.12.44	MURDER	U.S.
ZADO	130046	M	Ger.		Civilian (farmer) Stalag XX B,Marienburg (Pol.),Summer 41	TORTURE	U.K.
ZAFELBERG	196026	M	Ger.		Sgt.,2 Coy,100 Bn de Chasseurs de Montagne,St.Germain de Joux (Fr.) 12.-18.7.44	MURDER	FR.
ZAGER, Hans Georg Willm	195649	M		27. 2.03	Lt.,Police,Offenbach (Ger.) 25.2.45	MURDER	U.S.
ZAGERMANN	251489	M	Ger.		Cpl. (Fr.) 29.-30.8.44	MISC.CRIMES	FR.
ZAH, Georg	11535	M	Ger.		Pvt.,Army,110 or 111 Pz.Gren.Rgt.,2 Coy,Albine(Fr.) 27.6.44	MURDER	FR.
ZAHATKA, Rudolf	251932	M	Ger.	29. 1.98	Agent, Gestapo, Prag (Czech.) 39-44	SUSPECT	CZECH.
ZAHL	128891	M			Dr.,Civilian,C.C.Weimar-Buchenwald (Ger.)	MURDER	U.S.
ZAHLI	192126	M	Ger.		Arbeitsfhr.,SS, C.C.Breendonck (Bel.) since 41	TORTURE	BEL.
ZAHMEL, Herbert	195097	M	Ger.		Uscharfhr.,SS,SD,Sonder-und Wirtschaftskdo,Beeck,Gorsselbeck(Neth.) 23.24.9.44	MURDER	NETH.
ZAHN	62170	M	Ger.		Agent,Gestapo,Seales(Fr.) 15.4.43	WITNESS	FR.
ZAHN or ZIEL	136254	M	Ger.		2 SS Pz.Div."Das Reich" Rgt."Deutschland",3 Bn,F.P.Nr.28688, Verneque,le Vernet (Fr.) 44	MISC.CRIMES	FR.
ZAHN	196027	M	Ger.		Feldgend.,Feldgendarmerie,Morlaix Plougasnou (Fr.) 5.7.44	MURDER	FR.
ZAHN	306732	M	Ger.		Policeman,Jugesheim near Frankfurt a.M.(Ger.) 6.1.45	BRUTALITY	U.K.
ZAHN, Heinz	262219	M	Ger.	3. 5.20	Uscharfhr.,SS, 3 Coy, 3 Platoon,51 Armoured Bde.,Breviandes,Buchares, St.Savine,la Riviere de Corps (Troyes) (Fr.)	BRUTALITY	FR.
ZAHN, Konrad	133384	M			Sturmfhr.,Waffen-SS	WITNESS	SOV.UN.
ZAHNEN, Mathias	194194	M	Ger.	11. 8.98	Sgt.,Pionier 23,Oberkail Bitburg (Ger.) 15.8.44	MURDER	U.S.
ZAHNLEITNER	11536	M	Ger.		Pvt.,Army,110 or 111 Pz.Gren.Rgt.,2 Coy,Albine(Fr.) 29.6.44	MURDER	FR.
ZAHNWEH, Xaver	195648	M	Ger.	81	Farmer, Civilian, Motzing (Ger.) 4.41	MURDER	POL.
ZAHRER, Hans	250587	M	Ger.		Lt.Col.,Gestapo,La Bresse (Fr.) 9.-11.44	MURDER	FR.
ZAISER, Eduard	140817	M	Ger.		Civilian, Railroad worker,Miesbach (Ger.)	TORTURE	U.S.
ZAJUCEK	256183	M			Oscharfhr.,C.C. Buchenwald (Ger.)	MURDER	U.S.
ZAJZEK, Alois	161947	M	Ger.	12	Oscharfhr.,SS,command Staff,C.C.Buchenwald (Ger.)	WITNESS	U.S.
ZAKEL, Hans	161946	M	Ger.	02	Standartenfhr.,SS,Medical-Detachment,C.C.Buchenwald(Ger.) 37-39	MURDER	U.S.
ZAKOURS see SAKOURS	253336						
ZAKOWSKI	140882	M		80 - 85	Sgt.,208 Fliegerhorst,Hobsten(Ger.) 15.3.45	MURDER	CAN.
ZALEL	306411	M			Capt.,SS,C.C. Buchenwald (Ger.) 16.5.38-9.10.42	MURDER	BEL.
ZALEWSKI	132809	M	Ger.		Capt.,Abwehr Stalag Luft VI Heydekrug (Ger.) 44	MISC.CRIMES	U.K.
ZALL or ZILL, Wilm	191388	M			C.C.Dachau (Ger.)	SUSPECT	U.S.
ZAILMANN	104986	M	Ger.		Major, Stalag Luft 4,C.C.Kiefheide (Ger.) 8.44-3.45	MURDER	U.S.
ZALTO, Josef	192250	M	Ger.	1.11.06	Oscharfhr., SA (Bohemia-Czech.)	MISC.CRIMES	CZECH.
ZALYRINGER	259707	M	Ger.	10 - 14	Uscharfhr.,SS, Gestapo, Area of Angers (Maine and Loire-Fr.)42-44	TORTURE	FR.
ZAMBREGL	156978	M			Pvt.,SS, C.C.Aschendorfer Moor (Ger.)	MURDER	U.S.
ZAMECNIK, Jan	251993	M	Ger.	2. 7.95	Civilian,Roznow,Ceske Budejovice (Czech.) 39-45	SUSPECT	CZECH.
ZAMERT	1214	M	Ger.		Pvt.,406 Inf.Div.,1075 Sec.Bn,Sellerich (Ger.) 4.1.45	MURDER	U.S.
ZAMYSLICKY	256347	M	Ger.		Oscharfhr.,SS, C.C. Muhldorf (Ger.)	WITNESS	U.S.
ZANDER	250581	M	Ger.		Cpl.,Gend.Trupp 533,Le Chablais (Fr.) 19.-21.5.44	MISC.CRIMES	FR.
ZANDER, Fu.	162546	M			Crim.secr.,Fieldpol.-commissar,Gestapo,Fieldpolice, C.C.Theresienstadt (Czech.)	TORTURE	U.S.
ZANDER, Gunther	191399	M			SS-Pvt.,1 SS Pz.Rgt. L.A.H.,Lignseuville,Stoumont (Fr.)17.-19.12.44	WITNESS	U.S.
ZANDER, Henri	29851	M	Ger.		Capt.,Army,189 Res.Div.,38 Jg.Bn on foot,Castelnav-Magnec, Beaupuy (Fr.)21.4.-21.6.44	TORTURE	FR.
ZANDER, Hermann	179890	M		10	SS-Sturmfhr.,Crim.secr.,SD Gestapo,Praha (Czech.) 39-45	MURDER	CZECH.
ZANDONAI, Johanna	900902	F	Ger.		Servant, Gasthof Pfendler,Pertisau-Maurach (Aust.,Tyrol)13.7.44	MURDER	FR.
ZANDT, Ernst	257488	M	Ger.		Member,NSDAP, DAF, Lorrach (Ger.)	TORTURE	BEL.
ZANDT, Johann	256337	M		6. 9.23	Pvt.,C.C.Harsungen-Nordhausen (Ger.)	MURDER	U.S.
ZANDY	257454	M	Ger.		Lt.,Ger.Army Unit 43088, Zajecar (Yugo.) 41-44	MURDER	YUGO.
ZANGEN, Wilhelm	62448	M	Ger.	30. 9.91	Leader,Reichsgruppe Industrie,Chairman Mannesmann-Roehrenwerke, Deutsche Bank,Duesseldorf-Berlin (Ger.)	MISC.CRIMES	UNWCC.,U.S.

ZAN-ZEI

NAME	C.R.FILE NUMBER	SEX	NATIO- NALITY	DATE OF BIRTH	RANK OCCUPATION UNIT PLACE AND DATE OF CRIME	REASON WANTED	WANTED BY
ZANGL	250591	M	Ger.		Gestapo, Maribor (Yugo.) 44	MURDER	YUGO.
ZANK, Arthur	194571	M	Ger.		Asst., Custom-House, Veigy Foncenex (Fr.) 6.10.43	TORTURE	FR.
ZANONA (see SANONA)	253338						
ZANT	122082	M	Ger.		Pvt., Army, Creach Maout (Fr.)	MURDER	FR.
ZAP	194146	M	Ger.		Camp Guard, C.C. Kaisheim (Ger.) 40-45	MURDER	CZECH.
ZAPF, Michael	256338	M			Rottfhr., C.C. Artern, Nordhausen (Ger.)	MURDER	U.S.
ZAPFL, Siegfried	261332	M	Ger.		N.C.O., SS, near Pfundres (It.) 13.6.44	MURDER	U.S.
ZAPKA	160948	M			Pvt., Guard, 3 SS Baubde., C.C. Wieda and Gardelegen (Ger.) 5.-14.4.45	MURDER	U.S.
ZAPPAR	147103	M	Ger.		Rottfhr., SS Pz. Div. "Das Reich", Villaudric (Fr.) 44	MURDER	FR.
ZAPFNFL, Marie	188144	F	Ger.		Member, Gestapo, Brno (Czech.) 39-45	WITNESS	CZECH.
ZAPPE	189829	M			SS-Sturmfhr., SS, Gestapo, Posarevac (Serb.) 41-43	MURDER	YUGO.
ZAPPI, Adolf	260470	M	Ger.	20.8.11	SS-Rottfhr., Waffen SS Guard Coy, Supply Service, Auschwitz (Pol.) 5.42-1.45	BRUTALITY	POL.
ZAPUDCK, Albert	168008	M	Ger.		Pvt., Army, 9 Res. Gren. Rgt., 1 Coy, Magny d'Anigon (Fr.) 18.9.44	MURDER	FR.
ZAPINGER	152033	M		17	Gestapo, Bretagne Anjou Poitou (Fr.)	MURDER	FR.
ZAPSKE, Karl	168065	M	Ger.		Cpl., Fieldpolice of Langes, Auberivg Flagey Coiffy Chalorcey (Fr.) 43-44	MURDER	FR.
ZARUBA, Hans	147102	M	Ger.		Dr., Lt., 5 Tank Div., Longwy-Haut (Fr.) 44	PILLAGE	FR.
ZARZUNOS	257493	M			Factory Worker, Camp Dora, Nordhausen (Ger.)	MURDER	U.S.
ZARZUPTI, Vanda	205534	F	Ger.	26	Gestapo Limoges, Hte-Vienne of Gironde, 40-44	MURDER	FR.
ZASSIEK (see ZASSIEF)	67721						
ZASSIEF, F. (or ZASSIEK)	67721	M	Ger.		SS-Pvt., SS Div.F.P.48963 B, St. Sulpice Fortousson Chateau-Gontier, Laval (Fr.) 2.-6.8.44	MURDER	FR., UNWCC
ZASTROW, Fritz	251484	M	Ger.	18	Lt., 165 Gend., 65 Div., Ponzano-Magra (It.) 21.9.43	INTERR.	U.K.
ZATI (see ZATTI)	144988						
ZATTI (or ZATI)	144988	M			Lt. General, Lombardia Div., Fuzane (Yugo.) 43	MURDER	UNWCC, YUGO.
ZAUER	194348	M	Ger.		SS-Capt., SS Commandant, C.C. Ravensbruck (Ger.)	MURDER	FR.
ZAUNER	257396	M	Ger.		SS-Guard, Sgt., SS slave labour camp, Beisfjord near Narvik (Nor.) 6.-11.42	BRUTALITY	YUGO.
ZAUNER	305386	M	Ger.		Lt., Voutes Cretes (Grc.) 12.8.44	MISC.CRIMES	GRC.
ZAUNER, Kaethi	136576	F	Ger.		Civilian, near Freilassing-Obb., (Ger.)	MURDER	U.S.
ZAVAFI, Victor	250575	M			Policeman, C.C. Buchenwald (Ger.)	TORTURE	FR.
ZAVAR	300768	M	Ger.		Judge, Landesgericht Prague (Czech.) 21.2.40	MURDER	CZECH.
ZAVAPSKI (see ZAVATZKY)	132657						
ZAVATSKY (or ZAVAPSKI)	132657	M	Ger.		SS-Mann, C.C. Woippy (Fr.) 44	MISC.CRIMES	BEL., FR.
ZAVATSKI	173826	M			SS-Sturmbannfhr., SS Director of factory employing men for C.C. Buchenwald, C.C. Dora (Ger.) 43-4.45	MURDER	FR.
ZAPADZINSKI, Otto	251464	M	Ger.	16.7.08	Gestapo, Moravska-Ostrava (Czech.) 42-45	MISC.CRIMES	CZECH.
ZAWAP	186385			05	Landgerichtsrat, County Court, Prague (Czech.) 39-44	MURDER	CZECH.
ZAWODNIK, Anton	188145	M	Ger.	27.2.99	Member, Clerk, SD, Gestapo, SS, Brno (Czech.) 39-45	MURDER	CZECH.
ZAYC, Karl	300978	M	Ger.		SS-Hotschfhr., official of SD Leitabschnitt, Prague (Czech.), Auschwitz-Birkenau (Pol.) 39-45	MURDER	CZECH.
ZAZENBACH	251483	M	Ger.		Chief, NSDAP, NSV, Lorrach (Ger.)	BRUTALITY	BEL.
ZCFALER	161487	M	Ger.		Sgt., Army, Morlaix, St. Pol de Leon (Fr.) 44	MURDER	FR.
ZCHMIELEVSKY, Karl	129723	M		circa 05	SS-Uschfr., SS, C.C. Mauthausen (Aust.) 41-45	MURDER	U.S.
ZCZIERA, Franz	190462	M	Ger.		SS-Mann, 1 SS Recconnaissance Bn., SS Ausb. and Ers. Abt., Renardmont Stavelot (Bel.) 19.12.44	MURDER	BEL.
ZDROJEWSKI, Edmund	260514	M	Ger.	29.8.15	SS-Sgt., State Service, Waffen SS 15 Coy 1 Bn. C.C. Krakow, Plaszow (Pol.) 43-44	MURDER	POL.
ZEAGER (or STEGER)	124132	M	Ger.		Cpl., Inf.5-388, Hindenberg-Els. (Ger.) 17.12.41	MURDER	U.K.
ZEBPECK	165566	M	Ger.		Commandant, Fieldpolice, Tournai (Bel.) 28.5.44	TORTURE	BEL.
ZEBROWSKI	29646	M			Lt., Army, Locmine (Fr.)	MURDER	FR.
ZECFK, Rudolf	29661	M	Ger.		Oberlandesgerichtsrat, Dr., Public-official, Prague (Czech.) 40	MURDER	CZECH.
ZECH	24	M			SS-Gruppenfhr., Befehlshaber d. SS and Police, Cracow (Pol.) 39-9.40	MURDER	POL.
ZECH	256339	M			Uschfhr., C.C. Nixei, Nordhausen (Ger.)	MURDER	U.S.
ZECH, Emil	260471	M	Ger.	30.11.90	SS-Rottfhr., Waffen SS, Guard Coy, C.C. Auschwitz (Pol.) 9.44-12.44	BRUTALITY	POL.
ZECHA, Alice	194570	F	Ger.	22	Employee, SD, Kolin (Czech.) 39-45	MURDER	CZECH.
ZECHE	300760	M	Ger.		N.C.O., 1 Aufkl. Abt. 3 Coy 2 Col. XV Div. of the Afrika Corps, Saint Leger (Arlon) 5.9.44	MISC.CRIMES	BEL.
ZECHMANN, Otto	11537	M	Ger.		Pvt., Army, 2 Coy, 110 or 111 Pz.Gren.Rgt., Albine (Fr.) 29.6.44	MURDER	FR.
ZECHNER	129722	M			SS-Sturmbannfhr., SS, C.C. Personnel Mauthausen (Aust.) 41-45	MURDER	U.S.
ZECHNER, Hermann	29660	M	Ger.		Dr., Amtsgerichtsrat, Ministry of Justice, Prague (Czech.) 40	MURDER	CZECH.
ZECINER, Karl	138005	M			Liezen (Aust.)	WITNESS	U.S.
ZETNIK, Karl	188146	M	Ger.	4.1.09	Oberwachtmeister, SD, Gestapo, Brno (Czech.) 39-45	MURDER	CZECH.
ZEEP	191952	M	Ger.		Chief, C.C. Dachau (Ger.) 19.6.42-29.4.45	MURDER	BEL.
ZEFFIS	172466	M			SS-Osturmbannfhr., C.C. Mauthausen (Aust.)	MURDER	U.S.
ZEGLER	192386	M	Ger.		Major, 9 SS Pz. Div. "Hohenstaufen", Neuville les Bois (Fr.)	WITNESS	FR.
ZEH, Friedrich	193133	M	Ger.	00	Sgt., Kgf.Bau-Arb.Bn.186, (Nor.) 40-45	MISC.CRIMES	NOR.
ZEHAK	257394	M	Ger.		Director, Engineer, Org.Todt., slave labour camp, Osen (Nor.) 6.42-3.43	MISC.CRIMES	YUGO.
ZEHENTMEIER, Hans	188147	M	Ger.	28.4.09	Member, Gestapo, SD, Brno (Czech.) 39-45	MURDER	CZECH.
ZEHFUSS, Johannes	306728	M	Ger.		German Civilian, nr. Dromersheim, 28.9.44	BRUTALITY	U.S.
ZEHNER	173834	M			Investigating officer, Gestapo, Jasika Krusevac (Yugo.) 7.43	MURDER	YUGO.
ZEHNER, Herbert	259794	M	Ger.	circa 20	Sgt., 2 Coy, 331 Ger.Pion.Bn., Woudrichem (Neth.) 5.5.45	SUSPECT	NETH.
ZEHNER, Willy	186782	M		97	Adj., Feldgendarmerie, Meroy le Bas (Fr.) 27.8.44	PILLAGE	FR.
ZEIBIG, Albin	124130				Civilian, Proprietor, Stalag 4 G, Weisses Ross, C.C. Stalag 4 G, Ammelshain Grimma-Sa. (Ger.) 44	MISC.CRIMES	U.K.
ZEICHENKOV, Ivan	258006	M			Farmer, Civilian, Reichertsdorf (Ger.) 8. or 9.44	WITNESS	U.S.
ZEICHNER	160939	M	Ger.		Member, Waffen SS, Totenkopf-Sturmbann, Weimar, Buchenwald (Ger.)	MURDER	U.S.
ZEIDEL (see SFIDEL)	863						
ZEIDELBERGER	260362	M	Ger.		Oberwachtmeister, SS Penitentiary Nord-Norway (Nor.) 6.42-45	MURDER	YUGO.
ZEIDLER (see SFIDLER)	865						
ZEIDLER	104938	M	Ger.		School-teacher, Civilian, Mansfeld (Ger.)	TORTURE	U.S.
ZEIDLER	191951	M			SS-Pvt., SS, C.C. Mauthausen (Aust.) 25.7.44	MURDER	U.S.
ZEIDLER, Helmut	152035	M	Ger.		Zeugmeister, RAD, (H.551) F.P.Nr.12442, Purpan (Fr.) 44	WITNESS	FR.
ZEIDLER, Josef	194465	M	Ger.	1.10.22	SS-Rottfhr., SS, Bohemia (Czech.)	MISC.CRIMES	CZECH.
ZEIDNER, Feketchami	138357	M			General, SS 25 Hungadi Div., Ulvider (Hung.)	MURDER	U.S.
ZEIGE, Frederick	144986	M			SS-Mann, SS Trooper, Bad Kozen (Ger.) 11.45	MURDER	U.S.

ZEI-ZER

NAME	C.R.FILE NUMBER	SEX	NATIO-NALITY	DATE OF BIRTH	RANK OCCUPATION UNIT PLACE AND DATE OF CRIME	REASON WANTED	WANTED BY
ZEIGER	67749	M	Ger.		Sgt.,Inf.,6 Coy.	TORTURE	U.K.
ZEIGER, Heinrich	193207	M	Ger.		Guard,Schupo,C.C.Falstad,Trondheim(Nor.) 41-44	MURDER	NOR.
ZEIGERT, Joseph	142008	M	Ger.	00	Camp Elder,SS,C.C.Waldlager V and VI,Mühldorf Area,nr.Ampfing (Ger.) 44-45	TORTURE	U.S.
ZEIGLER, Carl	67752	M	Ger.		Steiger,C.C.Arb.-Kdo.7009 (Ger.) 3.45	TORTURE	U.K.
ZEIKGEBER	11598	M	Ger.		Pvt.,Army,1 Gruppe,110 or 111 Pz.Gren.Regt.,Gourdon(Fr.) 29.6.44	MURDER	FR.
ZEILER	256348	M	Ger.		SS-Uschfhr.,C.C.Mühldorf(Ger.)	WITNESS	U.S.
ZEINE	173266	M	Ger.	89	Sgt.,Army,Putlitz(Ger.) 24.4.45	WITNESS	U.K.
ZEINECKER, Eduard	194145	M	Ger.	24.7.08	SS-Scharfhr.,Oberwachtmeister,SS,Police,C.C.Terezin(Czech.) 44-45	TORTURE	CZECH.
ZEININGER	257395	M	Ger.		SS-Guard,Sgt.,SS slave labour camp,Beisfjord near Narvik(Nor.)6.-11.42	BRUTALITY	YUGO.
ZEIPP	28864	M	Ger.		Hptsturmfhr.,Army 111,6 SS Geb./Div.Nord Staff,Finmark(Nor.) 10.-11.44	MURDER	NOR.
ZEISLHER	152036	M			Lt., Armenian Legion, Cap de nae(Fr.) 23.6.44	MURDER	FR.
ZEISS	1047	M	Ger.		SS-Hptschfhr.,C.C.Dachau(Ger.) 40-43	MURDER	FR.
ZEISS see ZEUSS	29850						
ZEISS	39622	M	Ger.		Pvt.,Army, 3 Coy.,179 Bn.,Gilly s-Isere(Fr.) 14.8.44	MURDER	FR.
ZEISS	168030	M	Ger.		Member,Administrature-staff,Einsatzstab Rosenberg (Fr.) 40-44 (Dr.)	PILLAGE	UNWCC.,FR.
ZEISS, Emil	260069	M	Ger.		Cmdt.,Dept.of German Pay-office,Luneville(Fr.) 40-45	PILLAGE	FR.
ZEIST	122079	M	Ger.		Hptsturmfhr.,SS,C.C.Ravensbrueck(Ger.)	TORTURE	FR.
ZEIST	189298	M			Guard,C.C.Ravensbrueck(Ger.) 42-45	TORTURE	FR.
ZEISZNITZ	192125	M	Ger.		SS-Osturmfhr.,SS Div."Müller" F.P.Nr.10443,Fouron St.Martin(Bel.) 5.-6.9.44	PILLAGE	BEL.
ZEITKE	126472		Ger.		Sgt.,Military Prison Tegel, C.C.Tegel near Berlin(Ger.) 11.43-5.44	TORTURE	U.S.
ZEITLER	1969	M	Ger.		Pvt.,Army,5 Coy.,578 Gren.Regt.,305 Div.	MISC.CRIMES	U.K.
ZEITLER	195352	M	Ger.		SS-Cmdt.,C.C.Mauthausen(Aust.) 43-6.44	MURDER	BEL.,FR.
ZEITLER	305124	M	Ger.		Head of Prison 11.42-5.45	MISC.CRIMES	FR.
ZEITLER, Fritz or OLIVERO or OLIVIERO	166381	M	Ger.	14.7.12	Lt.,Interpreter,Gren.Regt.1047,Police H.Q.,Recoare(Ital.) 1.45	MURDER	U.S.
ZEITSCHKE, Franz	29662	M	Ger.		Dr.,Landgerichtsrat,Ministry of Justice,Litemerice(Czech.) 40	MURDER	CZECH.
ZEITTER	256249	M	Ger.		SS-Mann,C.C.Mühldorf (Ger.)	WITNESS	U.S.
ZEITZ	123622	M	Ger.		Official,SD,Wien(Aust.)	MISC.CRIMES	U.S.
ZEITZ	128277	M	Ger.		SS-Mann,Gestapo,Lyon(Fr.)	MURDER	FR.
ZEITZ	306527	M	Ger.		Pvt.,Feldgend.Chateaubriant(Loire-Inf.),St.Julien de Mouvantes(Fr.) 21.7.44	MURDER	FR.
ZEITZ, H.	255607	M			Sgt.,C.C.Nordhausen(Ger.)	MURDER	U.S.
ZEITZLER, Kurt	62449	M	Ger.		Major,Chief of Staff	TORTURE	UNWCC.,FR.
ZEIZER	25073	M	Ger.		Cpl.,157 Res.Div.,98 Bn., Mountain Troops,Mens(Fr.) 3.7.44	PILLAGE	FR.
ZEKLER	194211	M	Ger.		SS C.C.Buchenwald(Ger.) 42-45	MURDER	U.S.
ZELDER, Thomas	255610	M		14.12.07	Pvt.,C.C.Harzungen, Nordhausen(Ger.)	MURDER	U.S.
ZELENTKOV, Nicholas	305989	M	Ger.		Sgt.,Gend.,Sidirocastron(Grc.) 41	MURDER	GRC.
ZELINKA, Theresia	188148	F	Ger.		Women-Guard,Gestapo Women Prison,Brno(Czech.) 39-45	WITNESS	CZECH.
ZELL	257475	M	Ger.		SS-Arbeitsdienstfhr.,C.C.Auschwitz-Birkenau(Pol.) 42-45	MURDER	YUGO.
ZELLBACH see SEIBACH, Paul	26060						
ZELLENKOWITSCH, Georg	195199	M	Ger.	20	Member,Employee,Gestapo,Kolin(Czech.) 39-45	MURDER	CZECH.
ZELLENKOWITSCH, Michal	195198	M	Ger.	95	Member,Employee,Gestapo,Kolin(Czech.) 39-45	MURDER	CZECH.
ZELLER	192541	M	Ger.	95	Vaihingen(Ger.) 43-44	MISC.CRIMES	FR.
ZELLER	152098	M	Ger.	00	Police,C.C.Klopenheim near Wiesbaden(Ger.) 40-45	TORTURE	POL.
ZELLER	261939	M	Ger.		Pvt.,Unit Air Force L.52511,Pau,Soumouton,Narp,Lescar(Fr.) 6.-8.44	MURDER	FR.
ZELLER, Anton	255609	M		28.2.08	Rottfhr.,C.C.Dora,Nordhausen(Ger.)	MURDER	U.S.
ZELLER, Charles	166905	M	Ger.		Chief,Gend.,Ottmarsheim(Fr.) 31.10.44	MURDER	FR.
ZELLER, Friedrich	257994	M	Ger.		Crim.-Assist.,Abt.IVC Sipo,Bruxelles(Bel.)	INTER.	BEL.
ZELLER, Wolf-Dieter	259848	M	Ger.	10.5.21	SS-Rottfhr.,SS 2 Group,I Zug,Wurfbahm,Probably stationed at Bergey X, Bergeyk-Noord Brabant(Neth.) 11.9.44	MURDER	NETH.
ZELLHOFER see BOLLHOFER	1280						
ZELLMAN, Bernhard	192400	M	Ger.		Agent,Gestapo,Bad Hersburg(Ger.) 7.7.44	MURDER	U.S.
ZELLMANN	255608	M			Rottfhr.,C.C.Dora,Nordhausen(Ger.)	MURDER	U.S.
ZELLMEIER	11599	M			Cpl.,2 Coy.,110 or 111 Panz.Gren.Regt.,Albine(Fr.) 29.6.44	MURDER	FR.
ZELLNER	259329	M			Rottfhr.,SS,Mühldorf Area(Ger.)	MURDER	U.S.
ZELLNER	305988	M	Ger.		Sgt.,attached to Capt.Rademacher(Abwehroffiser)Oflag VI-B, Doessel nr.Warburg(Ger.) 39-45	MURDER	POL.
ZELLSMANN	196029		Ger.		Aspirant,SS,12 Art.Regt.,Tourouvres(Fr.) 13.8.44	MURDER	FR.
ZEMEK	300761	M	Ger.		Cpl.,1 Aufkl.Abt.,3 Coy.,2 Col.,IV Div.of the Africa Corps, Saint L'eger(Arlon) 5.9.44	MISC.CRIMES	BEL.
ZEMER	256350	M	Ger.		O.T.Mühldorf(Ger.)	WITNESS	U.S.
ZEMKE	261764	M	Ger.		Member,Assist. Gestapo of Amiens,Gentelles(Fr.)6.-8.44	MURDER	FR.
ZEMKE, Kurt	306412	M	Ger.	25.9.14	SS-Cpl.,C.C.Buchenwald(Ger.) 16.5.38-9.10.43	MURDER	BEL.
ZEMKIE	128825	M			Col.,Camp-Cmdt. Stalag Luft I,C.C.Barth(Ger.) 3.45	MURDER	U.K.
ZEMS	31959	M	Ger.		Sgt.,Army,F.P.Nr.50750,Hannalec(Fr.) 4.-6.8.44	MURDER	FR.
ZEMSCH, Alfred	129264	M	Ger.		Pvt.,Luftgaupostamt Paris,F.P.Nr.L 49215 N,Quaregnon,Jemappes,Ghlin (Bel.) 2.-3.9.44	MURDER	BEL.
ZENCKE or ZENKE or SENNEQUIE	1048	M	Ger.		Osturmfhr.,Waffen-SS,F.P.Nr.50604B,Eguill(Fr.)23.4.44	MURDER	FR.
ZENKER	194198	M	Ger.		Sgt.,SS,C.C.Buchenwald(Ger.) 42-45	MURDER	U.S.
ZENKER, Rudolf	257485	M	Ger.		Guard,Pvt.,K.D.O. D 3 Stg.IV F,Hartannsdorf(Ger.) 41-45	TORTURE	FR.
ZENNER	104987	M	Ger.		Pvt.,Army,1082 Sich.-Bn.,Sellerich(Ger.) 4.1.45	WITNESS	U.S.
ZENNER, Josef	194464	M	Ger.		SS-Sturmmann,Guard,4 SS Totenkopf Sturmbann,C.C.Nordhausen-Dora-Mittelbau, Nordhausen(Ger.) 43-45	MURDER	U.S.
ZENNHOF	196030		Ger.		Pvt.,C.C.Compiegné(Fr.) 41-44	TORTURE	FR.
ZENS, Fritz	135938	M	Ger.	90	Civilian,Brertring(Lux.) 7.44	WITNESS	U.S.
ZENS, Margarethe	135939	F	Ger.		Civilian,Brertring(Lux.) 7.44	MISC.CRIMES	FR.
ZEPEIK	196031	M	Ger.		SS-Sgt.,SS Regt.Art.,F.P.Nr.57666A,Tourouvres(Fr.) 13.8.44	MURDER	U.S.
ZEPP	192069				SS-Rottfhr.;	MURDER	U.K.
ZEPP	199679	M	Ger.		Capt.,Army,Sulmona(Ital.) 30.9.43	MURDER	U.S.
ZEPP, Paul	21430	M	Ger.	95	SS,C.C.Dachau(Ger.)	MURDER	FR.
ZEPUSCH, Franz	168009	M	Ger.		Pvt.,Army,9 Res.Gren.Regt.,1 Coy.,MG-Schuetze 2,Magny d'Anigon(Fr.) 18.9.44	MURDER	FR.
ZERAVIK, Alois	257930	M	Ger.	5.5.00	Employee,SD Bratislava(Czech.) 39-45	SUSPECT	CZECH.
ZERBIAN	256357	M	Ger.		SS-Mann,C.C.Mühldorf(Ger.)	WITNESS	U.S.

ZER-ZIE

NAME	C.R.FILE NUMBER	SEX	NATIO-NALITY	DATE OF BIRTH	RANK OCCUPATION UNIT PLACE AND DATE OF CRIME	REASON WANTED	WANTED BY
ZEREMBA	144982	M	Ger.		Capo C.C., Mauthausen (Aust.) 41 - 45	MURDER	U.S.
ZERESS	251471	M	Ger.		Lt., Miribel (Fr.) 10.8.44	INTERR.	FR.
ZERM, Anni	251476	F	Ger.		SS - Helper, C.C., Geisenheim (Ger.) 12.44 - 4.45	TORTURE	POL.
ZERMAHR, Leo	162947	M	Ger.		Inspector, Labour-Kdo., C.C., Aachen (Ger.)	TORTURE	BEL.
ZERNIKOW	256529	M	Ger.		Military, Sipo, Amsterdam (Neth.) 23.10.44	SUSPECT	NETH.
ZERNO	122078	M	Ger.		Hauptscharfhr., SS, C.C., Buchenwald (Ger.)	TORTURE	FR.
ZERVES	305536	M	Ger.		Uscharfhr., Etival Moussey (Fr.) 10.44	MURDER	U.K.
ZERWECK, Hans	152039	M	Ger.		Personalamtsleiter, NSDAP, Sinzenich (Ger.) 40 - 45	TORTURE	U.S.
ZERWES	306830	M	Ger.		Member of Rounanian Kommando, Gestapo, Vichy (Fr.) 10.43 - 9.44	MURDER	FR.
ZETSER (see KRULL)	194003						
ZETTEL, Franz	261340	M	Ger.		Senior W.O., Gend. of Bethune, Hinges (Fr.) 12.8.44	TORTURE	FR.
ZETTELMEYER, Josef	231275	M	Ger.		Uscharfhr., Crim.-Secretary, SS, Gestapo, Bingen (Ger.) 44	MURDER	CZECH.
ZETTL, Karl	29663	M	Ger.		Dr., Landgerichtsrat, Public-Official, Cheb (Czech.) 40	MURDER	CZECH.
ZETZSCHE	168034	M	Ger.		Dr., Leiter Hauptabteilung Wirtschaft, Amt des Generalgouverneur (Pol.) 9.39 - 44	PILLAGE	POL.
ZETZSCHE	191321	M	Ger.		Pvt., Eis.Art.Bn.717, Feldpost Nr. 22380, St.Andries, Varsenare, Bruegge (Bel.) 4.9.44	MURDER	BEL.
ZEUNER, Anton	256500	M	Ger.		Uscharfhr., SS, Desinfection Camp Dora, Nordhausen (Ger.)	MURDER	U.S.
ZEUS	258147	M	Ger.		Cmdt., C.C., Belsen (Ger.)	MURDER	BEL.
ZEUSEN	251491	M	Ger.		Capo, C.C., SS, Neuengamme (Ger.)	MURDER	BEL.
ZEUSS (or ZEISS)	29850	M	Ger.		Sturmfhr., SA, C.C. Struthof (Fr.) 42 - 44	MURDER	FR.
ZEUSS	141363	M	Ger.		SS, C.C. Natzweiler (Fr.) 43 - 44	MURDER	U.K.
ZEUSS, Joseph	72271	M			Lt., Waffen SS, C.C. , Struthof (Fr.)	MISC.CRIMES	FR.
ZEUSS, Wolfgang	72270	M	Ger.		Hauptsturmfhr., Waffen SS, C.C., Struthof (Fr.)	MISC.CRIMES	FR.
ZEUSS, Wolfgang	251474	M	Ger.		Hautscharfhr., Inspecteur, C.C., Schortingen (Ger.)	INTERR.	FR.
ZEYER	301869	M	Ger.		Senior W.O., Ge nd.Thionville (Fr.) 8. - 9.44	MURDER	FR.
ZEYNEK, Wolfgang	10377	M	Ger.		Dr., Public Prosecutor, Prague (Czech.) 21.2.40	MURDER	CZECH.
ZHEMALITE	161949	M	Ger.		Major, Army, C.C., Stalag Luft III, near Sagan (Ger.) 42 - 43	TORTURE	U.S.
ZIBIEL, Edmund	261825	M	Ger.		Gend., Fieldgen.Lens, Bouvigny Boyeffls (Fr.) 9.8.44	MURDER	FR.
ZIBIEL, Helmut	256185	M	Ger.		N.C.O., Gend. Anny s.-Bois (Fr.)	WITNESS	FR.
ZIBUS	306298	M	Ger.		Member, Gestapo at Trencin, C.C., Oswiecim,Birkenau)Pol.) 39-45	MURDER	CZECH.
ZICCAVO, Ferrucio	262424	M	It.		General of Div. 1.Army, Udine and Gorizia (It.) 42	MURDER	YUGO.
ZICH, Joseph	301821	M	Ger.		SS - Mann, 1.Panz.Div. SS-Leibstandarte "Adolf Hitler", Region of Stavelot (Bel.) 12.44	MURDER	BEL.
ŽICHMIL (see SELBRECHT, Rudolf)	186196						
ZICK	152040	M			Pvt., Stalag II B, C.C. Guard, Hammerstein (Ger.)	MURDER	U.S.
ZIDECK	129721	M			Uscharfhr., SS, Skull and Crossbone Organisation,C.C.,Mauthausen(Aust.) 41 - 45	MURDER	U.S.
ZIEBERT, Willy	256672	M	Ger.		Military, Nuland (Neth.) 9.-10.44	SUSPECT	NETH.
ZIEBLER	180040	M	Ger.		Obersturmfhr., SS, C.C. Gusen-Mauthausen (Aust.) 7.44	MURDER	FR.
ZIEBRICH, Rudolf	196032	M	Ger.		Major, Feldgendarmerie, Voreppe (Fr.) 7.-8.44	MURDER	FR.
ZIEDEK, Georges	306528	M	Ger.		Pvt., Feldgendarmerie, Chateaubriant (Loire-Inf.), St.Julien de Mouventes (Fr.) 21.7.44	MURDER	FR.
ZIEDEL	160947	M			Member, Volkssturm, Gardelegen (Ger.) 4.45	WITNESS	U.S.
ZIEDEL, Albert	256670	M	Ger.		Sgt.,Register's Office, C.C. Dora Nordhausen (Ger.)	MURDER	U.S.
ZIEDRICH	25	M	Ger.		Police Praesident, Warschau (Pol.) 9.39 - 1.42	MURDER	POL.
ZIEFGLER, Karl	259328	M			Shaft-master, O.T., Miehldorf Area (Ger.)	MURDER	U.S.
ZIEGEL	162945	M	Ger.		Capt., Army, C.C. Markt Pongau (Ger.)	TORTURE	FR.
ZIEGEL	196033	M	Ger.		Lt., Fliegerrgt.71, Dienststelle Feldpost-Nr.13 883,Bressols,Mont Beton (Fr.) 18.8.44	INTERR.	FR.
ZIEGEL, Simeon	168031	M	Ger.		Treuhaender, General Governor of Poland,Poznan (Pol.) 9.39-44	PILLAGE	POL.
ZIEGELBERGER	28837	M	Ger.		Cpl., Army, Belonging to Air Unit, Feldpost Nr. 49060 B, Perigueux(Fr.)	MURDER	FR.
ZIEGENHERN	300762	M	Ger.		N.C.O., 1.Aufkl.Abt.,3.Coy.,2.Column, XV.Div. of the Afrika Korps, Saint Leger (Arlon) (Bel.) 5.9.44	MISC.CRIMES	BEL.
ZIEGENHIRT	192397	M	Ger.		Lt., Zentral-Ersatzteillager 206, Paris (Fr.) 21.8.44	MURDER	FR.
ZIEGERT (see SIEGERT)	67677						
ZIEGERT, Richard	262218	M	Ger.	28.12.19	Oberscharfhr., 8.Coy.,51.SS Armoured Brigade, Chief of Group of officers of Lance Grenaders ,Bucheres,Breviandes,Ste.Savine,La Riviere de Corps (Troyes) (Fr.) 8.44	BRUTALITY	FR.
ZIEGEUMEYER	196034	M	Ger.	04	Sgt., Sicherungs-Rgt. 618, St.Marcel (Fr.) 13.9.44	WITNESS	FR.
ZIEGLER	152041	M	Ger.		Lt., Army, Feldpost Nr. 13883, Monbeton (Fr.) 24.8.44	MURDER	FR.
ZIEGLER	184579	M	Ger.		Colonel, Army, Feldpost Nr. 48180, Bavent (Fr.) 2.4.44	WITNESS	FR.
ZIEGLER	186784	M	Ger.		Feldgendarm, Feldgendarmerie, St. Lambert (Fr.) 16.7.44	MISC.CRIMES	FR.
ZIEGLER	194453	M	Ger.		Lt., Army, Molde (Nor.) 11.42	WITNESS	NOR.
ZIEGLER	256671	M	Ger.		Sgt., C.C. Osterhagen, Nordhausen (Ger.)	MURDER	U.S.
ZIEGLER	261899	M	Ger.		Building-leader-engineer, Civilian, Hamm and Kirchlengern(Ger.)40 - 45	BRUTALITY	NETH.
ZIEGLER, Ambrosius	256187	M			Cpl., C.C., Ellrich, Nordhausen (Ger.)	MURDER	U.S.
ZIEGLER, Arno	256191	M			Pvt., C.C. Osterhagen-Nixei,Nordhausen(Ger;)	MURDER	U.S.
ZIEGLER, Ernst (see SIEGLER)	156033						
ZIEGLER, Georg	256193	M			C.C. Ellrich, Nordhausen (Ger.)	MURDER	U.S.
ZIEGLER, Hans	254820	M	Ger.	16. 2.89	Chief, Gestapo, State Service, Zlin (Czech.) 39 - 45	MURDER	CZECH.
ZIEGLER, Heinz	192088	M	Ger.	00	Capt., Gestapo, Danzig (Pol.)	TORTURE	POL.
ZIEGLER, Heinz	256192	M	Ger.	1. 3.23	Flyer, C.C. Harzungen, Nordhausen (Ger.)	MURDER	U.S.
ZIEGLER, Karl	178280	M	Ger.	97	Under Foreman, Stalag XI B. C.C. Ohlendorf (Ger.)	TORTURE	U.K.
ZIEGLER, Max	262217	M	Ger.		Interpreter, Rttfhr., SS, Gestapo, Rennes (Fr.) 43 - 44	MISC.CRIMES	FR.
ZIEGLER, Victor	305706	M	Ger.		Civilian, Amstetten (Aust.) 20.3.45	MISC.CRIMES	U.S.
ZIEHAUS, Fritz	251472	M		04	Chief, Gestapo, Alencon (Fr.) 40 - 44	MISC.CRIMES	FR.
ZIEHE	183846	M			Oberscharfhr., 4.SS-Totenkopf-Sturmbann, C.C., Dora Mittelbau, Nordhausen, Rosen Aslau (Ger.) 43 - 45	WITNESS	U.S.
ZIEHEISEN	132964	M			Uscharfhr., SS, C.C. Dora-Nordhausen (Ger.)	MURDER	U.S.
ZIEHL	72273	M	Ger.	04	Oberscharfhr., C.C. Hinzert (Ger.) 41 - 43	MISC.CRIMES	U.S.
ZIEHREIS	261341	M	Ger.		Standartenfhr., Commanding Officer C.C., Mauthausen, Bologna(It.) 28.-29.6.44	MURDER	U.S. POL. CZECH.
ZIEL (see ZAHN)	136254						
ZIEL	142069	M	Ger.	05	Hauptsturmfhr., C.C., Dachau (Ger.) 40 - 45	TORTURE	POL.
ZIEL	147104	M	Ger.		SS Panz.-Div. "Das Reich", Deutschland Rgt.,Verneraue le Vernet(Fr.)	MURDER	FR.

- 219 -

ZIE-ZIM

NAME	C.R.FILE NUMBER	SEX	NATIO- NALITY	DATE OF BIRTH	RANK OCCUPATION UNIT PLACE AND DATE OF CRIME	REASON WANTED	WANTED BY
ZIEL	259214	M	Ger.		SS Sturmbannfhr., Dachau (Ger.) 11.42-43	MURDER	YUGO.
ZIEL, Emil	119921	M	Ger.	95	Civ. Foreman, Schellerbau, Hildesheim (Ger.)	TORTURE	U.S.
ZIELER	184152	M	Ger.		SS Mann, 4.SS Totenkopf-Stuba, C.C. Dora - Nordhausen (Ger.) 43-45	WITNESS	U.S.
ZIELFELD	188149	M	Ger.		Crim.Commissar, Member SD, Gestapo, Brno (Czech.) 99-40	MURDER	CZECH.
ZIELINSKI	128806	M	Ger.		Pvt., 4-383.Coy. Stalag IV D Annaburg (Ger.) 11.44-4.45	TORTURE	U.K.
ZIELKE, Hans	192350	M	Ger.	3. 7.26	Flyer, Airforce, F.P. No. 63 194 B, Vineuil (Fr.) 17.8.44	WITNESS	FR.
ZIELKE, Paul	132041	M	Ger.	10	SS Mann, Tuchold (Pol.) 39-44	MURDER	POL.
ZIEMANN, Hans	255612	M	Ger.	8. 1.94	Civ., Estate-manager, Roudnice (Czech.) 4.45	PILLAGE	CZECH.
ZIEMANN, Inge	250584	F	Ger.	19	Employee, Gestapo, Mail office, Limoges (Fr.)	MISC.CRIMES	FR.
ZIEMEKA	194197	M	Ger.		SS Uscharfhr., C.C. Buchenwald (Ger.) 42-45	TORTURE	U.S.
ZIEMER	144981	M	Ger.		SS Rottfhr., Muenchen (Ger.) 29.7.44	MURDER	U.S.
ZIEMER, Fritz	141624	M	Ger.		Paris (Fr.) 42-45	INCENDIARISM	FR.
ZIEMESEN	173833	M	Ger.		SS Hptsturmfhr., Chief of camp administration, C.C. Auschwitz, Birkenau (Pol.) 99-45	MURDER	CZECH.
ZIEMSHEN	300763	M	Ger.		N.C.O.,1.Aufkl.Abt. 3.Coy. 2.Col. XV. Div.Africa-Corps, St.Leger (Arlon) 5.9.44	MISC.CRIMES	BEL.
ZIEMSSEN	251467	M	Ger.		SS Hptsturmfhr., C.C. Auschwitz, Birkenau (Pol.) 5.42	MISC.CRIMES	YUGO.
ZIEMSSEN, Dietrich	161945	M	Ger.	11	SS Osturmbannfhr., Waffen SS, 1.SS Panz.Div. (L.A.H.) Feldgend.Coy., Weissenbach (Aust.) 4.45	MURDER	U.S.
ZIEMPEK, Herbert	195165	M	Ger.	24	Member SS	WITNESS	U.S.
ZIENERT	34291	M	Ger.	12	Kreisleiter NSDAP, Ingolstadt (Ger.) 10.9.44	MURDER	U.S.
ZIER	179824	M	Ger.		Counsellor, Kommandantur, Perpignan, Velmanya (Fr.)	MURDER	FR.
ZIER, Alfred	168010	M	Ger.		Pvt., Army, 9.Res.Gren.Rgt. 1.Coy. M.G.Schuetze 2, Magny d'Anigon (Fr.) 18.9.44	MURDER	FR.
ZIERBEL	1486	M	Ger.		SS Osturmfhr., 12.Coy.	MISC.CRIMES	U.S.
ZIREIS	1049	M		09	SS Osturmbannfhr., C.C. Mauthausen (Aust.) 9.39-1.42	MURDER	POL. U.S.
ZIEREIS, Franz	189130	M	Ger.		SS Standartenfhr., C.C. Mauthausen (Aust.)	MURDER	CZECH.
ZIEREIS, Franz	256184	M	Ger.		SS Hptsturmfhr., C.C. Buchenwald (Ger.)	MURDER	U.S.
ZIERELSEN, Otto	184151	M	Ger.	26. 9.02	SS Uscharfhr., 9.SS Totenkopf-Stuba, C.C. Dora - Nordhausen, Auschwitz (Ger.,Pol.) 43-45	WITNESS	U.S.
ZIERGER	189890	M	Ger.		Army German Punitive Expedition, Meckovac nr.Kragujevac (Serb.)10.41	MURDER	YUGO.
ZIERL	301161	M	Ger.		Staff at Struthof-Natzweiler C.C. (Fr.) 42-44	MURDER	FR.
ZIERNICHE or TERITSCHE	128892	M			Arbeitsdienstfhr., C.C. Buchenwald (Ger.)	TORTURE	U.S.
ZIESE	133900	M	Ger.	05	Crim.secretary, Gestapo, Ahlen (Ger.)	MURDER	U.S.
ZIESOWITZ	122081	M	Ger.		Lt., Btty.Fhr., SS-Div. "Adolf Hitler", Coulonges (Fr.) 25.6.44	MURDER	U.K. FR.
ZIESSING, Willi	250590	M			German Army, Gerardmer (Fr.) 29.5.44	INTER.	U.S.
ZIEZELLER	198280	M	Ger.		SS Usturmfhr., SS Gericht Gestapo, Lyon (Fr.)	MURDER	FR.
ZIEZENITZ, Karl	250583	M	Ger.		Lt. 2.Coy. Lance grenades Div. Hitler-Jugend, Hellenvilliers (Fr.) 9.7.44	TORTURE	FR.
ZIEZER	260068	M	Ger.		Lt., Bn. II-98, I.Gebirgsjaeger-Res.Rgt., Massif of Vercors, Isere and Drome (Fr.) 20.7.-5.8.44	SUSPECT	FR.
ZIGA, Alfred	256190	M		11. 1.14	Pvt., C.C. Ellrich, Nordhausen (Ger.)	MURDER	U.S.
ZIGLER	131617	M			Sgt., Airforce, C.C. Gardelegen, Osterhagen (Ger.)	MURDER	U.S.
ZIGLOWSKI	21429	F	Ger.		Civ., Faulen, Rosenberg (Ger.) 40-45	MISC.CRIMES	U.K.
ZIGLREIN, Otto	31225	M	Ger.		Feldgendarmerie, Pont Audemer (Fr.) 5.-6.6.44	MURDER	FR.
ZILL, Egon	10378	M	Ger.	30. 5.01	SS Sturmbannfhr., Camp-Cmdt., C.C. Natzweiler, Flossenburg (Fr.,Ger.) 42-45	MURDER	CZECH. FR. BEL. U.S.
ZILL, Johann	192525	M	Ger.	25. 6.21	Sgt., Army, Schussbach (Ger.) 14.3.45	TORTURE	U.K.
ZILL see ZALL, Willi	191388						
ZILLE	1050	M	Ger.		SS Hptsturmfhr., Waffen SS, C.C. Dachau (Ger.) 40-43	MURDER	FR.
ZILLE, Gerhard	190366	M	Ger.	17	SS Osturmfhr., Gestapo, Negotin, Zajekar (Yugo.) 41-43	TORTURE	YUGO.
ZILLING, Hans	301650	M	Ger.		Pvt., Ebrach nr.Amberg (Ger.) up to 45	MURDER	CZECH.
ZILLIS, Martin	306413	M	Ger.	7. 8.13	SS Sgt., C.C. Buchenwald (Ger.) 16.5.98-9.10.43	MURDER	BEL.
ZILLMER	160949	M			Lt.Col., Airforce, Vic.of Distr.Gardelegen (Ger.) 10.-14.4.45	MURDER	U.S.
ZILS	161944	M	Ger.		Pvt., Inf. Landesschuetzen-Bn. 789, Sinzig Distr.Ahrweiler.(Ger.)12.41	TORTURE	U.S.
ZIMA	188760	M	Ger.		Feldgendarm, Feldgendarmerie, Bar le Duc (Fr.) 20.-23.8.44	MURDER	FR.
ZIMELITE	139724	M			Major, C.C. Sagan Stalag Luft III (Ger.) 27.1.45	BRUTALITY	U.S.
ZIMMELIN	262334	M			Capt., Army, Wulfingerode (Ger.) 7.44 L.o.D.N.A.o.D.	SUSPECT	U.S.
ZIMMERER see ZIMMERER	250577						
ZIMMER	1051	M	Ger.		Capt., Army, Garnison commander, Rollainville (Fr.) 9.9.44	MURDER	FR.
ZIMMER	1052	F	Ger.		Oberin, C.C. Ravensbrueck (Ger.) 42	MURDER	POL.
ZIMMER	1053		Ger.		Warder, C.C. Oswiecim, Birkenau, Raiska (Pol.) 40-42	MURDER	FR.POL. YUGO.
ZIMMER	147101	M	Ger.		SS Oscharfhr., St.Germain (Fr.)	MURDER	FR.
ZIMMER	194761	M	Ger.		CC.officer, C.C. Ravensbrueck (Ger.)	MURDER	POL.
ZIMMER	258204	M	Ger.		District leader, Agriculture, Radzymin (Pol.) 39-45	MISC.CRIMES	POL.
ZIMMER, Hans	900899	M	Ger.		Sentinel, SS Adolf Hitler, Leignon - Dinant (Bel.) 6.9.44	MURDER	BEL.
ZIMMER, Jakob	194196	M	Ger.	90	Hauptwachtmeister, Gendarmerie, Dudweiler (Ger.)	MISC.CRIMES	U.S.
ZIMMER, Joseph	12452	M	Ger.		Cpl., Army, F.P. No. L 45438 Breslau, Mas de Breteuil (Fr.) 25.8.44	MURDER	FR.
ZIMMERER	133902	M	Ger.	04	Uscharfhr., Waffen SS, C.C. Hohenrheim nr.Plattling (Ger.)	MURDER	U.S.
ZIMMERER, Gerhard or ZIMMER	250577	M	Ger.	11	Scharfhr., Gestapo, Limoges (Fr.) 40-44	MISC.CRIMES	FR.
ZIMMERMAN	72720			08	SA Standartenfhr., Kreisleiter, SA, Grenzpolizei, Roermond (Neth.) 24.9.44-27.10.44	TORTURE	U.S.
ZIMMERMAN	128807	M	Ger.		Sgt., C.C. Trondhjem (Nor.) 7.40	MISC.CRIMES	U.K.
ZIMMERMAN	129716	M	Ger.		Blockfuehrer, C.C. Neuengamme (Ger.)	TORTURE	BEL.
ZIMMERMAN	199129	M	Ger.	04	Pvt., 4.Coy. Kgf.Bau-Arb.Bn. 188 C.C. Fjell (Nor.)	MURDER	NOR.
ZIMMERMANN	1054	M	Ger.		Police, SIPO, St.Quentin (Fr.) 4.43	MURDER	FR.
ZIMMERMANN	1773	M	Ger.		SS Hptscharfhr., C.C. Sachsenhausen (Ger.)	MISC.CRIMES	U.K.
ZIMMERMANN	6102	M	Ger.		Sgt., Army, Yzeures s.Creuse (Fr.)	WITNESS	FR.
ZIMMERMANN	12982	M	Ger.		Cpl., C.C. Breendonok (Bel.) 40-42	MISC.CRIMES	BEL.
ZIMMERMANN	21428	M	Ger.		Sgt., Army, Arbeitskommando, Jessen (Ger.) 17.8.44	MURDER	U.S.
ZIMMERMANN	29848	M	Ger.		Schupo, Stalag 6 A Ko.555, 28.2.42	MURDER	FR.
ZIMMERMANN	36625	M	Ger.	15	C.C. Belsen, Klein Bedungen, Osterode (Ger.) 6.4.45	MURDER	FR. POL.
ZIMMERMANN	72719	M	Ger.		Guard Pvt., Army, 2.Coy. 714.Bn., Stalag XX A Watsum(Ger.) 45	TORTURE	U.K.
ZIMMERMANN	122080	M	Ger.		Adjudant, Army, Feldgendarmerie Trupp 986, St.Illide (Fr.) 15.3.44	PILLAGE	FR.
ZIMMERMANN	124469	M	Ger.		SS Scharfhr., Guard C.C. Sachsenhausen, Oranienburg (Ger.) end 39-4.45	MURDER	POL. U.K.
ZIMMERMANN	124862	M	Ger.	95	Capt., NSDAP, Camp Security Officer, Oflag 64 Schubin (Pol.) 19.12.44	TORTURE	U.S.

ZIM-ZIM

NAME	C.R.FILE NUMBER	SEX	NATIO-NALITY	DATE OF BIRTH	RANK OCCUPATION UNIT PLACE AND DATE OF CRIME	REASON WANTED	WANTED BY
ZIMMERMANN	136668	M	Ger.		Pvt.,Inf.Kampfgruppe "Sachs",1 Coy. "Schwaben-Bn.",Billingsbach (Ger.) 17.4.45	WITNESS	U.S.
ZIMMERMANN	142141	M	Ger.		Agent,Gestapo	MISC.CRIMES	FR.
ZIMMERMANN	146727	M			Uschfhr.,SS,C.C.Flossenburg (Ger.)	TORTURE	FR.U.S.
ZIMMERMANN	152042	M	Ger.		Capt.,Abwehr,Stalag XXI A,Schieratz (Pol.) 23.1.-12.3.42	MISC.CRIMES	U.K.
ZIMMERMANN	152043	M	Ger.		Interpreter,Feldgendarmerie 958,Sisteron (Fr.) 6.6.44	MURDER	FR.
ZIMMERMANN	152044	M	Ger.		Oberfhr.,Gestapo,Folkling (Fr.) 11.44	MURDER	FR.
ZIMMERMANN	152045	M	Ger.		Rottfhr.,SS,C.C.Hamburg (Ger.)	MURDER	U.K.
ZIMMERMANN	160946	M	Ger.		Employee,tomb stone maker,prison,Civ.,Dettenhausen (Ger.) 42-45	TORTURE	U.S.
ZIMMERMANN (see FASSBINDER)	176707						
ZIMMERMANN,De.	177523	M		00	Doctor,Oberfhr.,SS,Gestapo,SD.,Saarbruecken (Ger.)	MURDER	FR.
ZIMMERMANN	180039	M	Ger.		Oberwachtmeister,Gendarmerie,Them,Haut-Rhin (Fr.) 42-24.2.43	TORTURE	FR.
ZIMMERMANN	191398	M			Capt.,Krgsgef.Arbeits-Bn.202,Abwehr,Krokelva,Bjornelva,Lousdal(Nor.)	WITNESS	NOR.
ZIMMERMANN	192349	M	Ger.		Osturmfhr.,SS,Div."Das Reich",Regt."Der Fuehrer",1 Bn.,Frayssinet Le Gelat (Fr.) 21.5.44	MURDER	FR.
ZIMMERMANN	192367	M	Ger.		Lt.,Army,Feldpost 41518 D,Pyrenes Orientale (Fr.) 7.-8.44	PILLAGE	FR
ZIMMERMANN	194347	M	Ger.		Major,Commandant de la Place de Rochelongus (Fr.) 18.4.43	WITNESS	FR.
ZIMMERMANN	194539	M	Ger.		Capt.,SS,Dussen (Neth.) 30.10.44	PILLAGE	NETH.
ZIMMERMANN	194568	M	Ger.		Sgt.,Feldgendarmerie,Ploermel (Fr.) 18.6.44	TORTURE	FR.
ZIMMERMANN	250592	M	Ger.		Civilian,Dachau (Ger.)	MURDER	YUGO.
ZIMMERMANN	251473	M	Ger.		Lt.,Unit Art.-Stuetzpunkt 266,Jere-Btty.,Feldpost No.56524, Thermes (Fr.) 3.8.44	MISC.CRIMES	FR.
ZIMMERMANN	259426	M			Uschfhr.,SS,Muhldorf Area (Ger.)	MURDER	U.S.
ZIMMERMANN	259689	M	Ger.		Gendarm,Gendarmerie,Them,Haut-Rhin (Fr.) 19.-29.10.44	BRUTALITY	FR.
ZIMMERMANN	261874	M	Ger.		Hptwachtmeister,Prison,Jauer near Glogau (Ger.) 42-45	SUSPECT	U.S.
ZIMMERMANN	301612	M	Ger.	6. 4.20	Pvt.,SS,official in Amt I or II of W.V.H.A.,Zentrale Bauinspektion, C.C.Mauthausen,Gusen (Aust.) 40-45	MURDER	BEL.POL.
ZIMMERMANN	301913	M	Ger.		Osturmfhr.,Cmdt.,SS-Aufkl.-Abtl.,6 SS-Geb.-Div."Nord",20 Army. Finmark (Nor.) 10.-11.44	MURDER	NOR.
ZIMMERMANN	305391	M	Ger.		Hptwachtmeister,Strafgefangenen-Lager "Nord",Northern (Nor.), Administr. official,Northern (Nor.) 43-45	MISC.CRIMES	CZECH.
ZIMMERMANN	305977	M	Ger.		Sturmschfhr.,C.C.Struthof,Natzweiler (Fr.) 42-44	MURDER	FR.
ZIMMERMANN	306540	M	Ger.		Lt.,391 Pion.-Bn.,331 Inf.Div.,Zuid-Holland (Neth.) 4.-5.5.45	MURDER	NETH.
ZIMMERMANN,Anton	262215	M	Ger.	9. 3. ?	Uschfhr.,Gestapo,Rennes (Fr.) 43-44	MISC.CRIMES	FR.
ZIMMERMANN,Arnold	129715	M	Ger.	17	C.C.Kahla (Ger.)	TORTURE	U.S.
ZIMMERMANN,Arthur	259003	M	Ger.	31. 3.83	Sturmbannfhr.,Standartenfhr.,SS	INTERR.	U.S.
ZIMMERMAN(N),Bruno	251486	M	Ger.		TelephoneFitter,Civ.,Zwolle (Ger.)	PILLAGE	NETH.
ZIMMERMANN,Fritz	162946	M	Ger.	23. 8.03	Pvt.,Army,Devin (Fr.) 13.-14.6.44	MURDER	FR.
ZIMMERMANN,Georg	62450	M	Ger.		General-Lt.,Army,Plenipotentiary (Ital.)	TORTURE	UNWCC
ZIMMERMANN,Georg	142304	M	Ger.	90	Agent,Gestapo,Remscheid (Ger.)	WITNESS	U.S.
ZIMMERMANN,Gerhard Anton	251463	M	Ger.		Scharfhr.,Gestapo,Troyes,Aube (Fr.) 8.44	MISC.CRIMES	FR.
ZIMMERMANN,Guenther or Otto	193130	M	Ger.	04	Sgt.,Guard,W-SS,Reichsjustizministerium,Feldstraflager, Finmark (Nor.) 12.44	MISC.CRIMES	YUGO.NOR.
ZIMMERMAN,Hans	57711	M	Ger.		SS,Gestapo,Mielec (Pol.) 42-44	MURDER	POL.
ZIMMERMANN,Hans	192368	M	Ger.		Sgt.,Feldgendarmerie,Mauriac (Fr.) 23.5.45	MISC.CRIMES	FR.
ZIMMERMANN,Hans	240041	M	Ger.	96	Osturmfhr.,S.D.official,Wehrwirtschaftsstelle VI,Bad Wildungen (Ger.) 45	MISC.CRIMES	U.S.
ZIMMERMANN,Heinrich	260709	M	Ger.		Farmer,Civ.,Farm,Stapelburg (Ger.) 16.8.45	WITNESS	U.S.
ZIMMERMANN,Heinrich	262214	M	Ger.		Crim.Secr.,Gestapo,Neustedt (Ger.) 1.41	MURDER	FR.
ZIMMERMANN,Herbert (or ZOELLNER)	125218	M	Ger.	05 or 10	Osturmfhr.,Reg.-Rat,SS,Gestapo,Bialystok,Koenigsberg (Ger.-Pol.)42-45	MURDER	U.S.
ZIMMERMANN,Hugo	257393	M	Ger.		Osturmfhr.,SS,slave labour camp,Osen(Nor.) 6.42-3.43	MISC.CRIMES	YUGO.
ZIMMERMANN,Jakob	125217	M	Ger.	98	Mayor,Public official,Efferen (Ger.) 2.10.44	MISC.CRIMES	U.S.
ZIMMERMANN,Joseph	190696	M	Ger.		Interpreter,Feldgendarmerie,Sisteron (Fr.) 6.6.44	MURDER	FR.
ZIMMERMANN,Karl	132656	M	Ger.		Sturmscharfhr.,Commandant du camp,SS,C.C.Vaihingen (Ger.) 3.45	MURDER	FR.
ZIMMERMANN,Karl	176623	M	Ger.		Scharfhr.,SS,C.C.Gaggenau (Ger.) 25.11.44	SUSPECT	U.S.
ZIMMERMANN,Karl	250578	M	Ger.	06	Lt.,784 Bn.,autonome Turkestans,Clairac (Fr.) 14.-21.8.44	MISC.CRIMES	FR.
ZIMMERMANN,Karl	256198	M			Pvt.,C.C.Rottleberode,Nordhausen (Ger.)	MURDER	U.S.
ZIMMERMANN,Karl Friedrich	259934	M	Ger.	21. 7.92	Lt.Col.,Regular officer,Military,WMA Dirschau,P.O.W. Camp, Bologna (Ital.) 28.-29.6.44	INTERR.	U.S.
ZIMMERMANN,Katharina	250574	F	Ger.	81	Civilian,Langenlosch (Ger.)	WITNESS	U.S.
ZIMMERMANN,Kurt	306243	M	Ger.		Lt.,Commanding P.O.W.-Coy.,12 Coy.,Feld-Ers.-Bn.114,11 Pz.Div.01-857, Montesquieu du Lauragais (Fr.) 9.8.44	PILLAGE	FR.
ZIMMERMANN,Marie	169964	F	Ger.		Civ.,Gotha (Ger.) 4.45	MURDER	U.S.
ZIMMERMANN,Max	62412	M	Ger.	95	Cpl.,Guard,W-SS,C.C.Hinzert (Ger.)	MURDER	U.S.
ZIMMERMANN,Max	169963	M	Ger.		Volkssturmfhr.,Volkssturm "Werwolf",Gotha (Ger.) 4.45	MURDER	U.S.
ZIMMERMANN,Max	240042	M	Ger.	1. 1.89	Crim.Secr.,SS-Fuehrer,Gestapo,Radom (Pol.) 11.43	MISC.CRIMES	U.S.
ZIMMERMANN,Max	251480	M	Ger.		Pvt.,C.C.Auschwitz (Pol.)	MURDER	FR.
ZIMMERMANN,Otto or Guenther	193130	M	Ger.	04	Sgt.,Guard,W-SS,Justiz-Minist.,Feldstraflag.,Finmark (Nor.) 12.44	MISC.CRIMES	NOR.YUGO.
ZIMMERMANN,Richard	1801	M	Ger.		Pvt.,Army	TORTURE	FR.
ZIMMERMANN,Rudolf	256673	M	Ger.	1. 2.97	Miner,Civ.,Most (Czech.) 44	MURDER	CZECH.
ZIMMERMANN,Werner	21427	M	Ger.		Gastrop-Rauxel (Ger.)	WITNESS	U.S.
ZIMMERMANN,Wilhelm	135340	M			Lt.,SA,Stadtinsp. u. Sturmabtlg.-Fuehrer	TORTURE	U.S.
ZIMMERMANN,Wilhelm	180041	M			Civ.,Polleben (Ger.) 10. or 11.44	MURDER	U.S.
ZIMMERMANN,Wilhelm	188150	M		10	Crim.Asst.,S.D.,Gestapo,Brno (Czech.) 39-45	MURDER	CZECH.
ZIMMERMANN,Willy	251487	M	Ger.	23	Uschfhr.,SS,Stationed,Graz (Aust.) 4.45	WITNESS	U.K.
ZIMMERMANN-FLEISCHHACKER	240043	M	Ger.		Cpl.,Abwehr official,Nachr.-Regt.506,Zagreb (Yugo.) 44	MISC.CRIMES	U.S.
ZIMMERMANS	258145	M	Ger.		Employee,C.C.Esterwegen (Ger.) 40	MISC.CRIMES	BEL.
ZIMMERN,Joseph	1055	M	Ger.		Cpl.,Army,Valenciennes (Fr.) 25.8.44	MURDER	FR.
ZIMMERS	258131	M	Ger.	circa 00	Guard,C.C.Esterwegen (Ger.) 40	MISC.CRIMES	BEL.
ZIMMES	162228	M	Ger.		Coal-miner,Civ.,Abwehr Grube Mine,C.C.Klausberg0/S,(Ger.) 3.9.44	TORTURE	U.K.
ZIMNIAK	168032	M	Ger.		Sturmbannfhr.,SS,Commissioner for the Liquidation of the Property of Semi Military Association,Rybnik (Pol.) 9.39-44	PILLAGE	POL.
ZIMPEL,Karl Wilhelm	306198	M	Ger.		Major,Army,Hagen (Ger.) 3.4.45	MURDER	CAN.

ZIM-ZOL

NAME	C.R.FILE NUMBER	SEX	NATIO-NALITY	DATE OF BIRTH	RANK OCCUPATION UNIT PLACE AND DATE OF CRIME	REASON WANTED	WANTED BY
ZIMPRICH, Marie	191922	F	Ger.	5.11.22	Employee, Gestapo, Brno (Czech.) 39-45	WITNESS	CZECH.
ZINDERHOFF	123928	M	Ger.		Capt., Inf..398.Bn., Silexa (Ger.) 45	TORTURE	U.K.
ZINECKER	306214	M	Ger.		Member of Staff, Small Fortress, C.C., Theresienstadt (Czech.)10.38-44	MURDER	CZECH.
ZING, Hans	125689	M	Ger.		W.O., Gestapo, Onnaing (Fr.) 1.9.44	MURDER	FR.
ZINGLI, Alfred	72274	M	Ger.		Pvt., Army, Lds.Schtz.Bn.H., 6.Coy., Coeln-Ehrenfeld (Ger.) 11.44	WITNESS	U.S.
ZINGRAF	257744	M	Ger.		Lt., Pol.Waffen-Schule III, Arnheim (Neth.) 3.45	MURDER	NETH.
ZINK (or ZINNEKE, ZINNERER)	128893	M			Uschfhr., SS, C.C. Weimar-Buchenwald (Ger.)	TORTURE	U.S.
ZINKER	125706	M	Ger.	13	Cpl., Stalag XVIII, C.C., Wolfsberg (Aust.)	TORTURE	U.K.
ZINKL	188759	M	Ger.		9.Panz.Div. Panz.Gren.Rgt.14 (Fr.)	WITNESS	FR.
ZINN, Artur	251477	M	Ger.		C.C. Auschwitz-Birkenau (Pol.) 1.43	MURDER	YUGO.
ZINN, Bruno	152047	M	Ger.	15. 1.21	Uschfhr., SS, Totenkopf-Stuba., Waffen-SS, C.C., Buchenwald (Ger.)	TORTURE	U.S.
ZINNEKE (see ZINK)	128893						
ZINNECKE	161943	M	Ger.	08	Uschfhr., SS, Section I, Conc.Camp, Buchenwald (Ger.) 4.45	WITNESS	U.S.
ZINNECKER	300979	M	Ger.		Oschfhr., SS, Official of SD, Leitabschnitt, Prague, Oswiecim-Birkenau (Pol.) 39-45	MURDER	CZECH.
ZINNECKER, Wilhelm	256189	M	Ger.	2.12.07	Flyer, C.C. Ellrich, Nordhausen (Ger.)	MURDER	U.S.
ZINNER	306819	M	Ger.		Member, St.Quentin Gestapo, Vraignes en Vermandois-Somme (Fr.)29.8.44	MURDER	FR.
ZINNERER (see ZINK)	128893						
ZINSER	126473	M			N.C.O., Civilian, State Policeman, C.O.Gend.at Ettelbrueck, Birtringen-Muehle (Lux.) 7.44	TORTURE	U.S.
ZINSER, Karl	251931	M	Ger.		Crim.Asst., Abt.IV.C, Sipo, Brussels (Bel.)	INTERR.	BEL.
ZINSS	256020	M	Ger.		Organ.Todt, Muehldorf (Ger.)	WITNESS	U.S.
ZINT, Hans	1056	M	Ger.		W.O., Gestapo, Valenciennes (Fr.) 43-44	MURDER	FR.
ZINZELMAYER, Georg	184150	M		1. 4.98	Uschfhr., SS, 4.Totenkopf-Stuba., C.C. Dora, Nordhausen, Auschwitz (Ger., Pol.) 43-45	WITNESS	U.S.
ZINZIG, Alfred	162222	M			Army, 6.Coy.Lds.Schtz.Bn., Stalag VI G, VI B, Bonn (Ger.) 44-45	TORTURE	U.S.
ZIOBRO, Honorata	152048	F ?			Sturmfhr., NSDAP, NSKK, Lauf (Ger.)	WITNESS	U.S.
ZIOLA, Ewald	301822	M	Ger.		SS-Mann, 1.Panz.Div., SS-Leibstandarte "Adolf Hitler", Region of Stavelot (Bel.) 19.,20.12.44	MURDER	BEL.
ZIPFEL	1057	M	Ger.		Uschfhr., Waffen-SS, Fontvielle (Fr.) 14.9.43	MURDER	FR.
ZIPFEL, Fritz	152050	M	Ger.		Uschfhr., SS, Tarascon (Fr.) 14.9.43	MURDER	FR.
ZIPPEL	192335	M	Ger.		Usturmfhr., SS, Conc.Camp, Flossenburg (Ger.) 44-45	MURDER	U.S.
ZIPPEL	256674	M	Ger.		SS-Sgt., Guard, Camp Ellrich B B IV, Nordhausen (Ger.)	MURDER	U.S.
ZIPPELIUS, Fritz	173828	M	Ger.		D.LT. Regierungs-Praesident, Official, District-President Bohemia-Moravia, Oswiecim, Opava, Troppau (Pol., Czech.) 39-43	MURDER	CZECH.
ZIPPERT, Willy	152051	M	Ger.	20.12.04	Member, Gestapo, SS-Totenkopf, Krakau, Warschau, Sokal, Tarnopol (Pol., Sov.Un.) 34-45	TORTURE	U.S.
ZIRKE, Erich	256197	M		16.10.04	Pvt., C.C. Harzungen, Nordhausen (Ger.)	MURDER	U.S.
ZIRNGIBL	129714	M	Ger.		Hptschfhr., SS-Panz.Div. Totenkopf, Conc.Camp,Mauthausen (Aust.)41-45	MURDER	U.S.
ZISCHKA, Josef	256196	M			Pvt., C.C. Ellrich, Nordhausen (Ger.)	MURDER	U.S.
ZISLER	307260	M	Ger.		Dr., Regierungsrat, Chairman of the Commission for Recr. of Forced Labour for Germany, Zagreb (Yugo.) 6.41	BRUTALITY	YUGO.
ZISTERER, Willi	184149	M			Rottfhr., SS, 4.SS-Totenkopf-Stuba., C.C. Dora-Mittelbau, Nordhausen Osterode (Ger.) 43-45	WITNESS	U.S.
ZITA, Anton	122084	M	Ger.	13	Oschfhr., SS, C.C., Drancy (Fr.) 43-44	TORTURE	FR.
ZITOWSKI, Alois	259931	M	Ger.		Crim.Secretary, Gestapo, Leskovec (Moravia, Czech.) 2.4.45	MURDER	CZECH.
ZITTERBART, Gerhardt	11540	M	Ger.		Pvt., Army, 110.or 111.Pz.Gren.Rgt.,2.Coy., Albine (Fr.) 29.6.44	MURDER	FR.
ZITTLAU	306529	M	Ger.		Sgt., Interpreter, Feldgend. Chateaubriant (Loire-Inf.) St.Julien de Mouvantes (Fr.) 21.7.44	MURDER	FR.
ZITZELSBERGER	256021	M	Ger.		Asst., Police, O.T.Police, Muehldorf (Ger.)	WITNESS	U.S.
ZITZKE, Ursula	152052	F			SS-Overseer, Work-Camp 101, C.C., Magdeburg, Buchenwald (Ger.) 44-45	TORTURE	U.S.
ZITZMANN, Michael	187802	M		21.11.92	Leader, Volkssturm, Innkeeper and miller, Civilian, Dechsbach, nr. Neustadt (Ger.) 43-45	TORTURE	POL.
ZIX, Otto	196035	M	Ger.		Uschfhr., SD, Maisons-Lafitte (Fr.) (Seine and Oise) 15.12 41-0.6.44	MISC.CRIMES	FR.
ZIZZER	174828	M			Lt., Army, Mens (Fr.)	MURDER	FR.
ZLOUNDER	186383	M			Lt., Army, Voutes (Grc.) 3.44	MURDER	GRC.
ZMARSLY, Wincent	256195	M			Pvt., C.C.Ellrich, Nordhausen (Ger.)	MURDER	U.S.
ZOBEK, Franz	192334	M			Kapo, Conc.Camp, Flossenburg (Ger.) 44-45	MURDER	U.S.
ZOBLEIN	260125	M	Ger.	circa 85	Capt., Engergy Reference Rouen, Cantellen (Fr.) 9.-11.7.44	INCENDIARISM	FR.
ZOCTHE	300764	M			Pvt., 6.Coy., 16.Hubner-Rgt., Kinrooi-Limourg (Bel.) 9.44	MURDER	BEL.
ZOEHRL, Karl	255616	M	Ger.	1. 5.04	Civilian, Gossengruen-Haberspirk (Czech.) 9.39	MURDER	CZECH.
ZOELCH	179823	M			Lt., Army, Blaye (Fr.) 15.6.44	TORTURE	FR.
ZOELLER, Hermann Mano	255615	M	Ger.	31. 7.06	Engineer, Civilian, Manager of the firm Ringhafer-Taha,Roudnice n-L. (Czech.) 40-44	INTERR.	CZECH.
ZOELLNER (see ZIMMERMANN, Herbert)	125218						
ZOELLNER, Ewald	142307	M	Ger.		Schfhr., Waffen-SS Totenkopf, Conc.Camp, Buchenwald (Ger.)	TORTURE	U.S.
ZOEPFEL, Richard	194463	M	Ger.		Guard, Civilian, Lidice (Czech.) 10.6.42	MURDER	CZECH.
ZOERNACK	156981	M	Ger.	00	Leiter, DAF, Restaurant-keeper, Civilian, Poznan (Pol.) 9.39-12.44	MISC.CRIMES	POL.
ZOERNER, Ernst	134207	M	Ger.	91	Governor, Public-Official in the District, Lublin (Pol.) 40	TORTURE	U.S.
ZOETHE	251492	M			6.Coy., 16.Hubner-Rgt., Kinrooi (Bel.) 9.44	MISC.CRIMES	BEL.
ZOETSKE	1370	M			Major, SS-Pz.Div., Police 4	MISC.CRIMES	U.K.
ZOGALLA	256194	M			Oschfhr., SS, C.C., Nordhausen (Ger.)	MURDER	U.S.
ZOHLER	142020	M	Ger.		Sgt., Army, Koenigshofen (Ger.)	TORTURE	U.K.
ZOLBRAT-KOLLIBAY (or KILIBAY)	39625	M	Ger.		Counsellor, Pbl.Official, Customs, Ville La Grand (Fr.) 2.44-7.44	MURDER	FR.
ZOLDERN	261193	M			Lt., Unit 37214 b, Maldegem (Bel.) 4.9.44	SUSPECT	BEL.
ZOLLER	34580	M			Capt., Waffen-SS,Conc.Camp, Mauthausen (Aust.) 41-45	MURDER	U.S.
ZOLLER, Hans	259238	M			Sgt., NSDAP, Dortmund (Ger.) 3.45	MURDER	FR.
ZOLLER, Johann	11541	M			Pvt., Army, 110.or 111.Pz.Gren.Rgt.,2.Coy., Albine (Fr.) 29.6.44	MURDER	FR.
ZOLLERMAN	161950	M		90	Major, Airforce, Stalag Luft, Stalag 357, Hannover (Ger.) 2.-4.45	TORTURE	U.S.
ZOLLHOFER (or ZELLHOFER)	1280	M			Lt.Col., 9.SS-Div."Hohenstaufen",19.Pz.Gren.Rgt.	TORTURE	U.S.
ZOLLICOFFER, H.	123927	M			N.C.O., Inf.Rgt.301, Znin (Pol.) 8.40	MISC.CRIMES	U.K.
ZOLLIG	31224	M	Ger.		Lt., Army, Art.Unit Fp.Nr.44818 E, Kerbabu nr.Lannilis (Fr.) 8.44	MURDER	FR.

ZOL-ZYN

NAME	C.R.FILE NUMBER	SEX	NATIONALITY	DATE OF BIRTH	RANK OCCUPATION UNIT PLACE AND DATE OF CRIME	REASON WANTED	WANTED BY
ZOLLNER	256203	M			SS-Rottfhr.,C.C.Dora,Nordhausen (Ger.)	MURDER	U.S.
ZOLLNER, Anton	122083	M	Ger.	15	SS-Schfhr.,SS,C.C.Drancy (Fr.) 43-44	TORTURE	FR.
ZOLLNER, August	306068	M	Ger.		Usturmfhr.,Chief,Gestapo,Prison Dubrovnik and surroundings (Yugo.) 44	MURDER	YUGO.
ZOLTY	306832	M	Ger.		Barrackduties-selection,C.C.Auschwitz (Pol.) 40-45	MURDER	FR.
ZOMER	195351	M	Ger.		Capt.,Stalag Luft IV,C.C.Grosstychow (Ger.)	TORTURE	U.S.
ZOPES, Peter	256202	M		14. 7.22	Pvt.,C.C.Ellrich,Nordhausen (Ger.)	MURDER	U.S.
ZOPP	184580	M	Ger.		Chief of Block,C.C.Dachau (Ger.) 5.1.45	MURDER	FR.
ZORBACH	301073	M	Ger.		SS-Uschfhr.,Personal Secretary to SS-Osturmfhr."Moritz" Luetkemeier at C.C.Hamburg-Neuengamme (Ger.) 45	MURDER	CZECH.
ZOPEN, Heinz	193206	M	Ger.		Schupo,C.C.Falstad,Trondheim (Nor.) 41-44	MURDER	NOR.
ZORCATT, Hugo	194452	M	Ger.		Sgt.,Arb.Bn.180,1 Coy,Strinda (Nor.) 4.4.45	WITNESS	NOR.
ZORGIEBEL	205393	M	Ger.		Member,Prison staff Monsheim nr.Rollwald (Fr.) 44 and 45	MISC.CRIMES	FR.
ZORGIEBEL	250596	M	Ger.		Guard,C.C.Monsheim (Ger.)	BRUTALITY	FR.
ZORN	256619				Col.,Doubs (Fr.) 9.-11.44	PILLAGE	FR.
ZORN	258203	M	Ger.		Capt.,17 SS Div.,37 Rgt.,Merzig (Ger.)	MURDER	U.S.
ZORN, Julius	169966	M	Ger.	03	Army,Butingen (Ger.) 29.7.44	TORTURE	U.S.
ZORNEF	34560	M			Dr.,Lublin (Pol.)	MURDER	POL.
ZSCHALER, Albert	262220	M	Ger.		Sgt.,Manager,"Soldatenheim" of Morlaix,St.Pol de Leon (Fr.) 26.and 27. 6.44, 5.-8.44	MURDER	FR.
ZSCHERNITZ, Otto	152053	M	Ger.		Sturmfhr.,SA, (Ger.)	TORTURE	U.S.
ZSCHICHNER	196036	M	Ger.		Oberwachtmeister,Schupo,Stuetzpunkt Groningen,C.C.Westerbork (Neth.) 9.44	MURDER	NETH.
ZSCHIMER, Erhart	256620	M		26. 5.10	Employee,Factory Worker,Camp Nordhausen (Ger.)	MURDER	U.S.
ZSCHUNKE	22836	M	Ger.		Capt.,Army,Locmine (Fr.)	MURDER	FR.
ZUBER	305964	M	Ger.		SS-Hptsturmfhr.,Leading official of Department of Sicherheitsdienst Leitabschnitt Prague,Oswiecim-Birkenau (Pol.) 39-45	MURDER	CZECH.
ZUBEF, Johann	29664	M	Ger.		Dr.,Landgerichtsrat,Public-official,Cheb (Czech.) 40	MURDER	CZECH.
ZUBER, Josef	193128	M	Ger.		Pvt.,Kriegsgef.Arb.Bau Bn.190,Sundbi (Nor.) 28.4.45	MURDER	NOR.
ZUCKAU	125704	M	Ger.		Forester,Civilian,Stalag XX B,Kdo.365,C.C.Rosenberg (Pol.) 1.43-2.44	MISC.CRIMES	U.K.
ZUCKER, Erwin	250595	M	Ger.		Capo,C.C.Neuengamme (Ger.) 44	MURDER	FR.
ZUCKER, Karl	255613	M	Ger.	19. 9.92	Regierungsrat,District head,Kladno (Czech.) 42-45	MISC.CRIMES	CZECH.
ZUCKER, Marie	255614	F	Ger.	11. 1.03	Civilian,Kladno (Czech.) 42-45	MISC.CRIMES	CZECH.
ZUCKPIEGEL	187435	M	Ger.		Member,SD,Gestapo,SS,NSDAP,Pilsen (Czech.) 39-45	MURDER	CZECH.
ZUELICHS	132655	M	Ger.		Cpl.,Police,Stalag II A,C.C.Neubrandenburg (Ger.)	MURDER	FR.
ZUFLE	301162	M	Ger.		Guard at Kdo.2786,Stalag VII A,Landshut-Bayern (Ger.) 6.3.43	MURDER	FR.
ZUG	191512	M	Ger.		SS-Sturmschfhr.,SS,Gestapo, (Nor.) 4.45	TORTURE	NOR.
ZU GUTTENBERG, Freiherr Karl Theodor	132820	M	Ger.	22	Lt.,4 Q 711 Inf.Div.,Wissant Bay. 1.2.44	WITNESS	U.K.
ZULL, Johann	11542	M	Ger.		Pvt.,Army,110 or 111 Pz.Gren.Rgt.,2 Coy,Albine (Fr.) 29.6.44	MURDER	FR.
ZULZFACHER, Karl	144983	M			Block-leader,C.C.Mauthausen (Aust.) 41-45, 12.44	MURDER	U.S.
ZUM BROCK	72272	M	Ger.		SS-Rottfhr.,C.C.Struthof-Natzweiler (Fr.) 42-44	MURDER	FR.
ZUNDEL	194346	M	Ger.		Adj.,Chief,SS Div."Das Reich" Rgt."Deutschland",Miremont (Fr.) 2.6.44	MURDER	FR.
ZUNDEP, Emil	11543	M	Ger.		Pvt.,Army,110 or 111 Pz.Gren.Rgt.,2 Coy,Albine (Fr.) 29.6.44	MURDER	FR.
ZUNKER, Emil	160970	M	Ger.		Sgt.,Army,Stalag XX A,Strassburg (Fr.) 11.40	TORTURE	U.K.
ZUNKEWSKI, Alfons	168011	M	Ger.		Army, 9 Gren.Rgt.Res.,1 Coy,M.G.Schuetse 5,Magny d'Avignon(Fr.) 18.9.44	MURDER	FR.
ZUNNDORF (or ZUNNDORFF)	1371	M	Ger.	17-18	Lt.,Platzkommandant, II-1003,Palazzo-Bd-Per,near Arnezzo (It.) 23.6.44 24.6.45	MURDER	U.K.,IT.
ZUNTER, Arnold	11544	M	Ger.		Hptsturmfhr.,Waffen SS,Div."Der Fuehrer" 2 Coy,Oradour (Fr.) 10.6.44	MURDER	FR.
ZUPFEIDE	141625	M	Ger.		Adj.-chief,Feldgendarmerie,Beaune (Fr.) 42-44	MURDER	FR.
ZURSEE, Johann Hans	188758	M	Ger.		Capt.,Army,Village de Grandes Acheres (Fr.) 25.1.45	MURDER	FR.
ZU STOLBERG, Fuerst Wolf Heinrich	132277	M	Ger.		Obersturmfhr.,SA,Leiter d.Forst Abt.Sachsen-Anhalt	TORTURE	U.S.
ZUTTER	129765	M			Hptsturmfhr.,Adj.,Waffen SS,C.C.Mauthausen (Aust.) 41-45	MURDER	U.S.
ZWAHLEN	300765	M			N.C.O.,1 Aufkl.Abt.3 Coy,2 Col.XV Div.of the Afrika Corps,Saint Leger (Arlon) 5.9.44	MISC.CRIMES	BEL.
ZWECK	257392	M	Ger.		SS-Guard,Sgt.,SS slave labour camp,Beisfjord near Narvik (Nor.) 6.-11.42	BRUTALITY	YUGO.
ZWEIN, Adolf (see MALKOVSKY)	305965						
ZWEINIGER	6107	M	Ger.		Schirrmeister,Army,Div."Freies Indien",Yseuves s-Creuse (Fr.) 29.-30. 8.44	MURDER	FR.
ZWEIPFENNIG	152054	M	Ger.		Lt.,Army,Feldgendarmerie,Dreux (Fr.) 42-43	MURDER	FR.
ZWPISTER, Wilby	189630	M			11 SS Pz.Gren.Ausb.Training Bn.,Graz (Aust.) 3.45	MURDER	U.K.
ZWFRENZ, Josef	194462	M	Ger.	13. 7.94	Local Group Leader,NSDAP,NSV,Sorghof (Czech.) 38-45	MISC.CRIMES	CZECH.
ZWERGER	256201	M			Cpl.,C.C.Dora,Nordhausen (Ger.)	MURDER	U.S.
ZWERGER, Joseph	168066	M	Ger.	11	SS-Rottfhr.,C.C.Natzweiler,Struthof (Fr.) 43-44	MURDER	FR.
ZWESPER, Johann	256200	M			Pvt.,C.C.Ellrich,Nordhausen (Ger.)	MURDER	U.S.
ZWICK, Paul	259239	M			Uschfhr.,Gestapo of Poitiers Area (Fr.) 40-44	MISC.CRIMES	FR.
ZWJCKEL, Johann	184148	M		10. 5.99	SS-Mann,Schuetse,4 SS Totenkopf-Sturmbann,C.C.Dora-Mittelbau,Nordhausen (Ger.) 43-45	WITNESS	U.S.
ZWICKEPT	138199	M	Ger.		Faisait partie,C.C.Woippy (Fr.) 44	TORTURE	FR.
ZWIEG, Erich	195164	M	Ger.		Feldgendarm,Feldgendarmerie,F.P.Nr.43800,Tourcoing (Fr.) 2.9.44	MURDER	FR.
ZWIMMER (see SWIMMER)	67675						
ZWIN	129724	M	Ger.		Arbeitskdo.,Buessing-Nag.-Werke,Braunschweig (Ger.) 44	TORTURE	BEL.
ZWINER	256188	M	Ger.	15	Lt.,Army,Heusden (Ger.)	PILLAGE	NETH.
ZWINER, Willy	172462	M	Ger.		Civilian,C.C.Dora,Nordhausen (Ger.)	MURDER	U.S.
ZWINGER, Matthias	140718	M	Ger.	23	SS-Usturmfhr.,SS Junkerschule Toelz,5 Lehrgang,Toelz (Ger.)	MURDER	NOR.
ZWIRNER	250588	M	Ger.		Dr.,Army,13 SS Police Rgt.,Ferlach (Aust.) 44-45	INTERR.	YUGO.
ZWIRNER, Hans	258996	M	Ger.	22. 2.06	SS-Osturmbannfhr.,SS, 20.4.44	INTERR.	U.S.
ZYGULA, Wladislaw	152055	M		19.11.93	Capt.,Interpreter,Ldsch.Ers.Bn.24,1 Coy,Augsburg (Ger.) 45	MURDER	U.S.
ZYLL	192399	M	Ger.		Leader,C.C.Dachau (Ger.) 39-41	MURDER	U.S.
ZYMFLKA	193205	M	Ger.		Schupo,C.C.Falstad,Trondheim (Nor.) 41-44	MURDER	NOR.
ZYNGLER, Hgt.	256621	M			Chief of section Mittelwerke,Camp Nordhausen (Ger.)	MURDER	U.S.

SPECIAL SECTION (Giving Particulars of Crime in lieu
of Rank & Occupation etc.)

1.   This List contains the names of persons of Germans or Unknown Nationality wanted in connection with War Crimes regarding whom very little is known as to their Ranks and Occupations. It is therefore considered that if these names were listed under the usual headings there would be insufficient information to lead to the identification and apprehension of the Wanted Persons.

2.   The column of the List which normally includes details of Rank and Occupation has therefore been changed for this purpose to " ALL AVAILABLE INFORMATION AS TO THE RANK, OCCUPATION (CIVIL, PARTY OR MILITARY). PARTICULARS OF CRIME AND PHYSICAL DESCRIPTION - (IF KNOWN)" and the column includes every available scrap of information concerning the Wanted Person and the circumstances of the Crime. It is hoped that thereby this List may provide Screening Authorities with more useful information.

MAN-OBE
-224-

NAME	C.R.FILE NUMBER	SEX	NATIO-NALITY	DATE OF BIRTH	ALL AVAILABLE INFORMATION AS TO THE RANK, OCCUPATIONS (CIVIL, PARTY OR MILITARY), PARTICULARS OF CRIME AND PHYSICAL DESCRIPTION - IF KNOWN.	WANTED BY
MANN	259391	M			Murder. Very brutal and blood-thirsty. Responsible for the death of several prisoners at Auschwitz (Pol.) Source of information: Bacherach, 22 rue de Fbg. Montmartre (Paris).	FR.
MAREK	259549	M	Ger.		Lt. of City-Police (at Wolfsburg). Witness. The murder of an American airman believed to be Sidney L.Newson, Wolfsburg(Ger.)	U.S.
MARIENFELD, Gerhard	258400	M	Ger.		Capt., Army, Perpetrator in the alleged murder of seven unknown unarmed American PW's at Hemmevez (Fr.)	U.S.
MARZ	259041	M			Murder and atrocities at Muhldorf Area.	U.S.
MATTKE	255480	M	Ger.		Suspect. Subject took part in murder of 61 czechs from Velke Mezirici (Czech.) on 7 May 45.	CZECH.
MATZLOFF (or MATZLUFF)	259492	M	Ger.		No personal data available spelling may be wrong and incorrect. Believed to have been a member of the SS, E.D.S. or Gestapo at Strasbourg. Complicity as the leader in the murder of an unidentified U.S. aviator during the night of 14-15 August 44 at Wolfisheim.	U.S.
MATZLUFF (see MATZLOFF)	259492					
MAYER	259763	M	Ger.		Suspect. Commander-in-chief of occupying forces at Annecy. Suspected to be connected with the shooting of 3 people at Eloise on 11 June 44 and the shooting of 4 people at Eloise on 14 June 44.	FR.
MAYER, Stefan	259089	M			SS Murder and atrocities at Muhldorf Area.	U.S.
MEHDEN, Karl	261157	M	Ger.		Murder. Execution of 20 hostages at Gosselies, on August 24, 44.	BEL.
MELBOECK, Hermann	260713	M	Ger.	01 or 06	Witness. Wanted for the murder of 5 American flyers at near Kaplice (Czech.) on 9 Dec.44. Hair: dark brown.	U.S.
MELIUS, Georg	259321	M			Suspect lives at Bechtheim (Ger.). Wanted for participation in the murder of an American airman and the believed murder of three other airmen. Area of Bechtheim (Ger.) betw. Sept. and Dec. 44/	U.S.
MERKEL, Johann	259138	M			Murder and atrocities at Muhldorf Area.	U.S.
MERKLE, Franz	258590	M	Ger.	01	Wanted for participation in the murder of three American airmen at Bernbach (Ger.) on August 9, 44.	U.S.
MERSEBURGER, Artur	257976	M			Suspect. Wanted for participation in the alleged beating of 4 unknown American airmen on or about 12 Sept. 44 at Hornhausen (Ger.), Russian Zone. Suspect was residing at Hornhausen on 17 May 45, believed to be still residing there.	U.S.
MERTE, Gustav	259340	M	Ger.		Opl..Wanted for participation in the murder of an unknown American airman in the vicinity at Martin Camp (Fr.) 43.	U.S.
METZDORF	257005	M	Ger.		Mil. 2. Nachr.Coy. Interr., Bolnes	NETH.
MEYER, Otto	254265	M			Wanted as a witness to the shooting of American airman at Tiddische (Ger.) on or about 30 May 44.	U.S.
MITSCHE	254675	M	Ger.		Wanted as a witness to the murder of three men in civilian clothes, believed to be political prisoners in Hasselfeld (Ger.) (GSGS 4346 Sheet M-52, Coordinates D-15) Russian Zone on or about the end of March or beginning of April 45. Witness is the wife of Mitsche, FNU, Ger. Landsjaeger-Stiege, Germany.	U.S.
MLYNARCZYK, Julius	258020	M			Brutality. Inflicted very harsh treatment on prisoners under his command.	FR.
MOLLER	259140	M			O.T. Murder and atrocities at Muhldorf Area.	U.S.
MONGEL, Georg	261088	M	Ger.		Brutality. Mistreatment of French Slave Labourers in Sossenheim (Ger.) from 43 to 45.	FR.
MUEHRER, Heinz	261158	M	Ger.		Murder. Execution of 20 hostages at Gosselies, on August 24, 44.	BEL.
MUELLER	259765	M	Ger.		Wanted as witness to the murder of Messrs.Courville, Massin and Vauche, committed at Balan on Sept. 4. 44, by Capt. Straube.	FR.
MUELLER, Wilhelm	261167	M	Ger.		Murder. Execution of 20 hostages at Gosselies, on August 24, 44.	BEL.
MUGGE, Robert	250391	M	Ger.		Wanted as a witness to the murder of Sgt.George.R. Michael, then an unarmed, surrendered prisoner of war, at Holzhausen-Ortsteil Tosbusch (Ger.) (GSGS 4346, Sheet L 53, Coord. W71) in the British Zone on or about 30 Sept. 44. Residing at Waldenhausen (Ger.) (GSGS 4346, Sheet 150, Coord.N 22.)	U.S.
MULLER	258685	M	Ger.	99	Lt. Brutality, Darmstadt on July 4, 44.	U.S.
MULLER	258697	M	Ger.		Lt.Col. Wanted for interrogation concerning order allegedly given the troops of said 3 Regt., to commit civilians to violence on captured allied airmen, Darmstadt (Ger.) on May or June 44.	U.S.
MULLER	258777	M	Ger.	99	Lt. Suspect believed to live in Mannheim. Wanted for participation in giving the orders to kill enemy airmen without warning in the Darmstadt area, also not protecting the airmen from the civilians.	U.S.
MULLER	259765					
MULLER, Kurt	259037	M	Ger.		O.T. Murder at Muhldorf area.	U.S.
NEUBRICH	256876	M	Ger.		Wanted for participation in the alleged burying alive of two American airmen at Oberndorf, Pfalz (Western Ger.) (GSGS 4346, Sheet K 50, Coord.M 02) French Zone. Supposedly living at Cologne-Beierfeld (Ger.). (The only Beierfeld, Ger. to be found in the Gazetteer is GSGS 4346, Sheet N 51, Coord. K 53, Russian Zone.)	U.S.
NICHSNER, Jakob	258035	M	Ger.		Wanted reports issued on the basis of possible perpetrator or witness for the development of Muhldorf area Case No. 000-50-136.	U.S.
NIEDERMEIER, August	258034	M	Ger.		Wanted reports issued on the basis of possible perpetrator or witness for the development of Muhldorf area Case No. 000-50-136.	U.S.
NIGGETIEDT	259572	F	Ger.		Wanted as a witness to the beating of ten (10) American airmen sometime at Lengerich (Ger.) on Aug. 44.	U.S.
NOBIS, Karl	251204	M		17.10.20	Civilian. Wanted as a witness to the shooting of an American airman near Laufen, on Feb. 22, 44.	U.S.
NOGLI, Gerhart	258033	M	Ger.		Wanted reports issued on the basis of possible perpetrator or witness for the development of Muhldorf area Case No. 000-50-136.	U.S.
NORDHOFF	257000	M	Ger.		Suspected of the shooting down of 5 Dutchmen.	NETH.
NOWAK, Ludwig	255475	M	Ger.	20. 8.97	As informer of Gestapo at Pelhrimov (Czech.), he is responsible for imprisonment, torture and death of Czechs.	CZECH.
NUESSEL	261945	M	Ger.		Suspect. Participated in crimes committed by Seidel or perpetrated them personally.	YUGO.
NUSSBAUM, George	257301	M		26	Wanted as a perpetrator in the murder by shooting of two surrendered unarmed PW's near Blechhammer near Pullenried (Ger.) on April 22, 45.	U.S.
OBERHAUS	196315	M	Ger.		Dr. - Doctor at Ravensbrueck Camp. Co-responsible for tortures and massacres of Belgian prisoners.	BEL.

NAME	C.R. FILE NUMBER	SEX	NATIO-NALITY	DATE OF BIRTH	ALL AVAILABLE INFORMATION AS TO THE RANK, OCCUPATIONS (CIVIL, PARTY OR MILITARY), PARTICULARS OF CRIME AND PHYSICAL DESCRIPTION - IF KNOWN.	WANTED BY
OCHSENMEYER or OSCHMEYER	251213	M	Ger.		Member of the Feldgendarmerie. He is wanted as a Suspect.	BEL.
OEHLERKING, Wilhelm	258220	M			Wanted for participation in the alleged beating of an unknown American flyer believed to be Krebs (FNU), after he had parachuted to earth in the vicinity of Abbensen (Ger.), (GSGS 4346, sheet 153, coord. X 62) British Zone on or about 8 April 1944. Suspect lives at Abbensen.	U.S.
OEHMIG, Walter	261169	M	Ger.		Execution of twenty hostages at Gosselies, on August 24, 1944	BEL.
OELTERMANN, Friedrich, Karl ("Fritz")	250419	M	Ger.	08	Oeltermann was in charge of a camp for foreign forced workers at Klein Scharrel near Oldenburg in 1942, where apart from numerous cases of ill-treatment and beatings, three Russians died. The blame for above deaths must rest on Oeltermann.	SOV.UN.
OMMERBORN, Hans	261131	M	Ger.		Execution of twenty hostages at Gosselies, on August 24, 1944	BEL.
OSCHMEYER see OCHSENMEYER	251213					
PACKHAUSER, Wilhelm	258030	M	Ger.		Wanted reports issued on the basis of possible perpetrator or witness for the development of Muehldorf area case No.000-50-136.	U.S.
PAETZ	259295	M			O.T., murder and atrocities at Muehldorf area	U.S.
PAPLEO	196417	M	Ger.		Wanted for alleged atrocities committed at Struthof C.C. at Natzweiler on May 1944, employee at C.C. Struthof-Natzweiler	FR.
PEER	196406	M			Wanted for alleged atrocities committed at Struthof C.C. at Natzweiler, Employee at C.C. Struthof-Natzweiler, 40-44	FR.
PEST	259475	M		07	Subject lives at Trier (Ger.), wanted as a perpetrator to the alleged murder of four American PW's at Issel (Ger.) 15.1.45	U.S.
PETERS	259338	M	Ger.		Capt., wanted as a witness to the murder of an unknown American Airman in the vicinity at Martin-Camp (Fr.)	U.S.
PETRENKO, Michael	259471	M			Witness lives at Mainz-Kastel (Ger.) (DP-Camp), wanted as a witness to the murder of an American Airman by beating after he was wounded at Burg (Ger.) 2.45	U.S.
PFEFFERL, Gottard	259016	M		16	Dark brown hair, brown eyes, complexion pale, built stocky and fleshy, scar one inch long on upper left arm. Wanted for participation in the beating and murder of French, Czech, Russian, Polish, Yugoslavian, Italian and German nationals. Wolfe (Ger.), between Febr.44 and April 45	U.S.
PFIEGER, Georg	258052	M	Ger.		Wanted reports issued on the basis of possible perpetrator or witness for the development of Muehldorf area case No.000-50-136.	U.S.
PFUHER	259670	M	Ger.		Subject authorized looting of Mr. Ziffermann's apartment at Paris, 1943	FR.
PIUM	259766	M	Ger.		Administrative officer at Chalon-sur-Saone in 1941. Guilty of arresting jews, then pillaging and confiscation of their property.	FR.
POTEMPA, Homar	258031	M	Ger.		Wanted reports issued on the basis of possible perpetrator or witness for the development of Muehldorf area case No.000-50-136.	U.S.
QUINTEN, Jacob	250431	M	Ger.		Previous camp leader of C.C. of Neuenbrem. Mistreatment and killing of many French nationals. Confined: POW hospital center No.4, Postleitzahl 14, Frankensaal Block III-I B1 No.67 Bad Margentheim	FR.
RASP, Siegfried	258984	M	Ger.	98	Lt.Gen., wanted as defendant, possibly witness. Crimes against Peace, War Crimes and Crimes against Humanity.	U.S.
REGER	259302	M			Uscharfhr., murder and atrocities at Muehldorf area	U.S.
REIDE, Arthur	257472	M			Wanted for the alleged beating to death of an American Airman, who had landed safely at Teplice-Sanov (Czech.) (GSGS 4346, N 51 F 34) on or about 23 July 1944. Last reported living in Saxony (GSGS 4346, N 51 F 05) or at Neu-Wernsdorf No.1, Saxony, (Ger.), Russian Zone	U.S.
REINDL, Johann	258039	M	Ger.		Wanted reports issued on the basis of possible perpetrator or witness for the development of Muehldorf area case No.000-50-136.	U.S.
RETTER, Franz	258038	M	Ger.		Wanted reports issued on the basis of possible perpetrator or witness for the development of Muehldorf area case No.000-50-136.	U.S.
REUSS	259211	M			Wanted for participation in the murder of fifteen American soldiers and many other Allied personnel. Also for mistreatment of American and Allied Prisoners of War at Fort Zinna, Torgau-Elbe (Ger.) (GSGS series 4346, sheet N-52, coord. E-64), Russian Zone. Improper administration of military justice by German Military Courts in many cases of Allied Prisoners of War at Fort Zinna, Torgau-Elbe (Ger.) from 1943 to April 1945. To be confined in IC 29, Dachau (Ger.) after being apprehended. Last reported in Wuerzburg (Ger.) (GSGS 4346 L 50, N-59) U.S.Zone	U.S.
REUTHER, Fritz	259903	M			O.T., murder and atrocities at Muehldorf area	U.S.
RHEIN or VON RHEIN	261160	M	Ger.		Execution of twenty hostages at Gosselies, on August 24, 1944	BEL.
RICHARZ	259292				O.T., murder and atrocities at Muehldorf area	U.S.
RIEDEL	256696	M	Ger.		Chief of defence at the Peugeot-Works at Sochaux. Was responsible for arrests, deportations and pillages.	FR.
RIEDL, Artur	252586	M	Ger.	1. 5.95	Wanted for alleged murder of an American Airman. Suspect is alleged to have beaten to death an unidentified American Airman, member of the crew of an American bomber, that was downed after an air attack on the plant Hydrierwerke in Most (Czech.) on July 23, 1944. Suspect is believed to be living either at Neu-Wernsdorf No.1, Saxony, or at Bienenmuehle No.10 Postplatz, Saxony	CZECH.
RIENZ	258884	M	Ger.		Officer, wanted as a witness. To be responsible for the slaughter of five Frenchmen, at Taisnieres s. Hon (Nord)	FR.
ROGGE	258684	M			SS-Pvt., about the middle of Jan. 1945 at Staines near Lenden (Ger.). Also believed to have killed twenty-three other Americans.	U.S.
ROHN, Hanns	259042	M		10	Murder and atrocities at Muehldorf area	U.S.
ROHRBACHER	257192	M	Ger.		SS, murder and atrocities at C.C. Nordhausen, (witness)	U.S.
RUDERT, Helmuth	252602	M	Ger.		On September 3, 1944 German soldiers driving through Strijpen in four military cars, threw hand-bombs and fired at a group of Belgian civilians without any reason. Four persons were killed and one wounded. The identity of the authors of the crime has not been established, but a short time later, German cars were attacked and the soldiers wounded and captured. Rudert is one of the soldiers, suspected of participation in the crime. Residence: Eschenlach, Vogtland (Ger.)	BEL.
RUDOLPH	259767	M	Ger.		Could give information about the shooting of five F.F.I.-prisoners, committed at Varaignes, on July 24, 1944	FR.
RUPP, Rene	258017	M	Ger.		Could give informations on the destruction of the installations of the weaving factory in Longpre-les-Amiens on September 1943, and to identify the officers responsible for the crime.	FR.
RUTKOWSKI	259279	F			Murder and atrocities at Muehldorf area	U.S.

RUX - SEM

NAME	C.R.FILE NUMBER	SEX	NATIO-NALITY	DATE OF BIRTH	ALL AVAILABLE INFORMATION AS TO THE RANK, OCCUPATIONS (CIVIL, PARTY OR MILITARY), PARTICULARS OF CRIME AND PHYSICAL DESCRIPTION - IF KNOWN.	WANTED BY
RUX, Ernst	260861	M		6.10.05	Wanted as a witness to the murder of two unknown American airmen at CC Buchenwald in April 45. Witness believed to be friendly. Resides at 45 Ackerstrasse, Brunswick, British Zone.	U.S.
SACHS, Ursula	259334	F			Wanted as a witness to the alleged murder of 2 or 3 American airmen in the vicinity of Mansfeld (Ger.) on March 15, 44. Witness lives in Grossorner (Ger.)	U.S.
SANER, Wilhelm	259281	M	Ger.		Rottenfhr., murder and atrocities at Mühldorf area	U.S.
SATTLER, Karl	250455	M	Ger.		Lootings in France during occupation. Present location: Obertrotzingen, Kreis Heidenheim (Wuerttemberg)	FR.
SCHACHTNER, Max	258060	M	Ger.		Wanted report issued on basis of possible perpetrator or witness for the development of Mühldorf area case No.000-50-136.	U.S.
SCHAFFER, Willy (Nickname CHARLOT)	253362	M	Ger.		Wanted for brutality of prisoners, CC Papenburg. Moustache a la Charlot.	BEL.
SCHAFFNER, Philipp	260348	M	Ger.	18. 3.99	Subject is responsible for mass-murder of Polish nationals committed at the plant of Wilhelm Fischer in Poland. Subject is presently living at Moerfelden.	POL.
SCHANK, Theodor	258059	M	Ger.		Wanted report issued on basis of possible perpetrator or witness for the development of Mühldorf area case No.000-50-136	U.S.
SCHARTEL, Ludwig	250484	M	Ger.	24. 1.00	Wanted for alleged torture and deportation of civilians, Hagondange 40-44	FR.
SCHEFFER	259768	M	Ger.		Was present when Mr.Mailloux was murdered on 15th of August 1944 at "Les Allends" (Deux-Sevres) N.C.O.-Unit 03420	FR.
SCHERBAUM	259240	M			O.T., murder and atrocities at Mühldorf area	U.S.
SCHERER, Karl Heinz	262143	M	Ger.		Wanted for murder - Exact place and date unknown.	U.S.
SCHINKE	259255	M			Capt., wanted for participation in the shooting of four American airmen after they were forced to dig their own graves, at near Schweidnitz(Ger.) 3-45	U.S.
SCHLEISSL, Josef	251770	M	Ger.	29. 1.26	Subject is responsible for shooting of 11 Slovak nationals at Cepcin and Turosko, Slovakia on 30 November 1944.	CZECH.
SCHLEMER, Hans (alias SCHLEMMER)	259769	M	Ger.		Should disclose the identity of the German officer, nick-named "The Lieutnant with green eyes", responsible for numerous crimes, committed in Haute-Savoie from 27.1.44 to 1.9.44	FR.
SCHLEMMER, Hans (see SCHLEMER)	259769					
SCHLESINGER, Ludwig	259770	M	Ger.	14. 9.13	Murder and torture against civilians, Urbes (Haut-Rhin) 24.9.44, 4.and 5.10.44	FR.
SCHMALACKER, Oskar	251792	M	Ger.	98	Former Guard, PW-Camp Oberndorf, illtreatment of French PWs. Residence: Stuttgart-Obertuerkheim (Ger.)	FR.
SCHMIDT-AUF-DER-GUENNE	259573	M	Ger.		Dr., Wanted as a witness to the beating of ten (10) American airmen sometime at Lengerich (Ger.), August 44	U.S.
SCHMIDT, Theodor	258114	M	Ger.		Wanted as witness to the murder of two American airmen in the vicinity of Erkrath (Ger.), British Zone, 4.11.44. Resides at No.3 Gartenstrasse, Mettmann (Ger.)	U.S.
SCHMIDTKONZ, Michael	256743	M	Ger.		Wanted as a witness to the alleged murder of an U.S. parachutist in the spring of 1944 in the vicinity of Ramersdorf, Germany, U.S.Zone (GSGS 4346, sheet M-49, Coord Y-85). Present whereabouts unknown.	U.S.
SCHMIEDEL, Walter	251798	M	Ger.	3. 5.80	Is guilty of the defalcation and fraud of a sum to the amount of fl.3000 for the benefit of the Germans. Address: Boulevard Heuvelink 39, Arnheim (Neth.)	NETH.
SCHMITT, Otto	251799	M	Ger.		Member of NSDAP since 1927. - Mistreatment of a French PW in his shop 27 Siemensstrasse, Nuernberg (Ger.) in 1942-1943. Residence: Huettenbach 45 near Markt Schmaittach (Ger.)	FR.
SCHMITT, Reinhard	251317	M	Ger.	27. 1.11	Wanted for murder, torture and atrocities committed at Camp Dachau. Information is that Schmitt is at present in custody at Bamberg County Jail (Coordinates M 50,024, G.S.G.S. 4346 Germany, 1:250.000) or was in custody at Bamberg as of 1 May 1946. Also wanted in other cases.	U.S.
SCHNEIDER, Othon	258852		Ger.	20. 7.15	Wanted as a war criminal. Denunciations of Luxembourg subjects, Grand Duchy Luxembourg during German occupation.	LUX.
SCHNELL, Simon	259332	M			Murder and atrocities at Mühldorf area	U.S.
SCHNOCH	259482	M			SD, wanted for participation in the alleged murder of four American PWs at Issel (Ger.) 15.1.1945	U.S.
SCHOFBOCK, Heinrich	258040	M	Ger.		Wanted report issued on basis of possible perpetrator or witness for the development of Mühldorf area case No. 000-50-136.	U.S.
SCHROFT, Hermann	258026	M	Ger.		Wanted report issued on basis of possible perpetrator or witness for the development of Mühldorf area case No. 000-50-136.	U.S.
SCHUBERT, Karl	250478	M	Ger.	6. 1.95	Subject is wanted as war criminal responsible for persecuting and murdering of Poles in Poland as well as in Germany. Subject was recently detained at P.W.E. 22 Regensburg.	POL.
SCHUCKERT, Wilhelmine	259540	F	Ger.		Wanted as a witness to the beating of ten (10) American airmen sometime in August 1944 at Lengerich (Ger.).	U.S.
SCHUMMER, Heinrich Jacob	256834	M	Ger.		Wanted for participation in the alleged beating and mistreatment of an unidentified U.S. airman, who had safely parachuted to earth, in the vicinity of Saarbruecken (Ger. - French Zone) - (G.S.G.S. 4346, sheet K-50, Coord.Q-47) in July or August 1944.	U.S.
SCHWALM, Helmuth	259274	M			Murder and atrocities at Mühldorf area.	U.S.
SCHWARTS	259843	M	Ger.	about 1926	Ill-treatment and deportation to Germany of Dutch nationals. Black hair, looks like a Chinese type and a sadist.	NETH.
SCHWARTS	260016	M	Ger. (or Russ.)		Military (corpulent, broad), ill-treatment, deportation of Dutchmen to Germany. Mongolian appearance.	NETH.
SCHWEIGER	259273	M			O.T., murder and atrocities at Mühldorf area.	U.S.
SCHWING	259771	M	Ger.		Capt., participated in the execution of 6 Frenchmen detained in the Citadel of Calais on 4.9.44. According to a witness this officer was a PW in British hands in the U.K. 19.4.46.	FR.
SEDLMEIER, Anselm	258061	M	Ger.		Wanted report issued on basis of possible perpetrator or witness for the development of Mühldorf area case No. 000-50-136.	U.S.
SIEGLER	259799	M	Ger.	about 40 years	Hptsturmfhr., Neck scars; suspected of murder on 6.10.44	NETH.
SEEKAMP, Albert	258690	M	Ger.		Wanted as a witness to the murder of an unknown American airman believed to be Sgt. Leon Synfelt at or near Bad Salzdet-Fuerth, British Zone on Nov.4.44	U.S.
SELLNER, Franz	261159	M	Ger.		Execution of 20 hostages at Gosselies, on August 24, 1944.	BEL.
SEMP	259476	M			Lt.Col., Illesheim, 1.Dec.43, wanted because of murder, probably living at Velden, Fraenkische Schweiz	

NAME	C.R.FILE NUMBER	SEX	NATIO-NALITY	DATE OF BIRTH	ALL AVAILABLE INFORMATION AS TO THE RANK, OCCUPATION (CIVIL, PARTY OR MILITARY), PARTICULARS OF CRIME AND PHYSICAL DESCRIPTION - IF KNOWN.	WANTED BY
SETTELS, Anne (nee SCHON)	258853	F	Ger.	11. 7.15	Civilian. Denunciation of Luxembourg subjects. (Lux.) 40-45	LUX.
SHATLE	250454	M	Ger.		Wanted as a witness to the murder of T-Sgt. Aubrey E. Teague, A.S.N. 1813989 at Stalag Luft IV, Gross-Tychow, in what is now Poland (GSGS Series 4346, Sheet O-54, Coordinates M-62).	U.S.
SIEGL	259772	M	Ger.		Witness. Could give particulars of the persons responsible for burning the farm of Bec-Thomas, at La-Saussaye (Eure) on August 11, 44.	FR.
SILAFF, Arthur	261156	M	Ger.		Murder. Execution of 20 hostages at Gosselies, on August 24, 44.	BEL.
SIMON, Nikolaus	251256	M	Ger.		Wanted as a war criminal. Denounced a good many Luxembourg citizens who were sent to C.C. and deported.	LUX.
SINGER, Andreas	259275	M			Murder and atrocities at Mühldorf area.	U.S.
SLABINAK, Friedrich (see KAMMLER)	260717					
SLIZEK (see STUERMER,Franz)	251341					
SLOTTA, Georges	258910	M	Ger.		Unit L 10.107. Wanted as a witness. Should give particulars of officers or non-commissioned officers responsible for the murder of Fatrez, Georges and for looting civilians' houses on August 25, 44 at La Croix,St.Quen (Oise)(Fr.)	FR.
SMRZ, Wilhelm	198017	M	Ger.		Member of the Gestapo. In Brno he used very cruel methods of interrogation. Suspect is alleged to have caused the death of several Czechoslovak political prisoners. Smrz was transferred to Russia.	CZECH.
SOMMER, Irene	259574	F	Ger.		Wanted as a witness to the beating of ten American airmen sometime at Lengerich (Ger.) on August 44.	U.S.
SOMMER, Josef	259773	M	Ger.		Lt. He participated in the execution of 6 Frenchmen detained in the citadel on Sept. 4, 44. According to a witness this officer was a POW in British hands in the U.K. 19.4.46. Witness.	FR.
SONNTAG, Emil	250453	M	Ger.		Wanted as a witness to the beating to death of three crew members of a B 17 which crashed at Polleben (Ger.) (GSGS Series 4346, Sheet M 52 - D 63) Russian Zone. Home address: Sylitz (Ger.)	U.S.
SOPELSA, Ernst	258027	M	Ger.		Wanted report issued on basis of possible perpetrator or witness for the development of Mühldorf area Case No. 000-50-136.	U.S.
SPATH, Herbert	258028	M	Ger.		Wanted report issued on basis of possible perpetrator or witness for the development of Mühldorf area Case No. 000-50-136.	U.S.
STADTMULLER, Hans	256039	M	Ger.		Wanted report issued on basis of possible perpetrator or witness for the development of Mühldorf area Case No. 000-50-136.	U.S.
STAHLSCHMIDT	251343	M	Ger.		Policeman. Official and interpreter at Abteilung III R (Geschaeftsstelle Sipo, Brussels). Suspect.	BEL.
STALLER, Michael	258037	M	Ger.		Wanted report issued on basis of possible perpetrator or witness for the development of Mühldorf area Case No. 000-50-136.	U.S.
STAUDAHER, Edo	259182	M	Ger.	02	Clerk. The accused denounced a Yugoslav citizen, one Alfred Mojzes, a Jew, to the Gestapo at Varazdin (Yugo.).	YUGO.
STAUDAHER, Marija	259183	F	Ger.	80	Civ.: Housewife. The accused denounced her son-in-law, Jew, to the Gestapo at Varazdin (Yugo.) Suspect.	YUGO.
STEGERER, Albert	256062	M	Ger.		Interrogation. Accomplice of Rug, Paul, in commanding various war crimes.	FR.
STEIN	260892				Wanted for participation in the murder of an American airman. Lt. James E.Dale was shot with a shotgun before he even reached the ground at Landsberg (Ger.) U.S.Zone on the 11 July 44.	U.S.
STEIN, Karl	260825	M			Wanted for participation in the murder of an American airman. Lt. James E.Dale was shot in the air by a shotgun before he even reached the ground. On or about 11 July 44 in the vicinity at Landsberg (Ger.) U.S.Zone.	U.S.
STELLJES, Dietrich	250500	M	Ger.		Subject is accused of mistreatment, beating and murdering of Polish inmates of the C.C. Geisenheim. Subjects present address is unknown.	POL.
STIER	258683	M			SS-Lt. Wanted for participation in the murder of an American soldier after he had struck him with a rifle but, on or about January 45, at Staines near Lenden (Ger.). Also believed to have killed twenty three other Americans.	U.S.
STOL	259494	M			Wanted for the beating to death of an American airman at Burg (Ger.) on Febr.45	U.S.
STORCK, Edgar	253431	M	Ger.		Director for Adlerwerke at Hannover. Took part in brutalities against Belgian prisoners. Denounced workers to the Gestapo.	BEL.
STRAKA, Engelbert (aliases: BURGHARD, Karl)	251349	M	Ger.	9. 9.21	Member of SS. Subject murdered a Czech peasant in the forest of Vlastejov near Susice (Czech.) on May 17, 45. Suspect.	CZECH.
STRUCKER	258184	M	Ger.		Major, at Varazdin (Yugo.). Interrogation.	YUGO.
STUERMER, Franz (aliases: SLIZEK)	251341	M	Ger.	31. 5.95	Member of Gestapo at Vsetin (Czech.), he is responsible for imprisonment torture and death of Czechs. Suspect.	CZECH.
SUDENT (Nickname: "Le Chinois")	251555	M			Employee. Wanted for alleged brutality of belgian and French prisoners of war.	BEL.
SURIG, Hans	251308	M	Ger.		Wanted for brutality towards deported foreign workers.	FR.
SUTSCH	258053	M	Ger.		Wanted report issued on basis of possible perpetrator or witness for the development of Mühldorf area Case No. 000-50-136.	U.S.
TARRACH, Franz	258045	M	Ger.		Wanted report issued on the basis of possible perpetrator or witness for the development of Mühldorf area Case No. 000-50-136.	U.S.
TEPKE, Hugo	256892	M			Suspect. Wanted for participation in the alleged beating of 4 unknown American airmen on or about 12 Sept.44 at Hornhausen (Ger.) Russian Zone. Residence: Hornhausen (Ger.); present whereabouts unknown.	U.S.
TEUFEL, Willy	258058	M	Ger.		Capt. Murder, pillaging and arson in the village of La Tranche on the 6. and 9. of October, 44.	FR.
THOMA, Jean Pierre	258855	M	Ger.	23. 5.14	Denunciations of Luxembourg subjects (Lux.) 40-45.	LUX.
THURMANN, Kurt	196234	M	Ger.		Wanted for alleged atrocities committed at Shirmeck C.C.	FR.
TICKES (or TIGGES)	258183	M	Ger.		SS-Unterscharfhr. 1.SS Panzer Regt. "Adolf Hitler", 1.Coy. Wanted for participation in the murder of two Belgian civilians. During the Rundstaedt offensive at Wanne near Stavelot (Bel.). 19-21. Dec.44.	BEL.
TIENECKEN	259543	F	Ger.		Wanted as a witness to the beating of ten American airmen sometime in Aug.44 at Lengerich (Ger.)	U.S.

NAME	C.R. FILE NUMBER	SEX	NATIO- NALITY	DATE OF BIRTH	ALL AVAILABLE INFORMATION AS TO THE RANK, OCCUPATIONS (CIVIL, PARTY OR MILITARY), PARTICULARS OF CRIME AND PHYSICAL DESCRIPTION - IF KNOWN.	WANTED BY
TIGGES see TICKES	258183					
TILL, Peter	255634	M	Ger.		Farmer, above accused flogged, starved and humiliated POW's on his farm at Dittlingen, Kreis Saarburg, Bezirk Trier (Ger.)	YUGO.
TRIES	251360	M			Dr., coroner. Suspect believed to have signed false death certificate on a murdered American Airman at Kelkheim (Ger.) on October 19, 1944. Signed that death was caused by fall from plane when caused by shooting. Formerly the coroner of Kelkheim (Ger.) (GSGS Series 4346, Sheet L 51, Coord. M-17). Exact address and description unknown. Attitude unknown.	U.S.
TRINKLEIN, August	196185	M	Ger.		Wanted for the hanging of an Allied national in some woods near Fischbach (Ger.) (GSGS Series 4346, Sheet M 50, Coord. T 59, American Zone). Date of crime unknown. Home address: 12 Wilhelm Marx-Str., Nuernberg (Ger.) (GSGS Series 4346, Sheet M-50, Coord. O-40, American Zone) Germany I-250-000. Suspect has not been apprehended and is believed to be living at the address.	U.S.
UNRECHT, Joseph	259052	M	Ger.	12	Sexual pervert, gold filed teeth, arms and hands tattooed, erect posture, round face, thick upper lip, fat neck, loud voice, small stocky body. Murder and atrocities and brutality at Muehldorf area.	U.S.
VATHER	259495	M	Ger.		Military, murder, shooting down of a Dutchman, 4.2.44	NETH.
VEIL	258042	M	Ger.		Wanted reports issued on basis of possible perpetrator or witness for the development of Muehldorf area case No.000-50-136.	U.S.
VETTER, Franz	258066	M	Ger.		On Sept.3, 1944, at about 12.15 p.m., two German officers driving in a motor-car along the road Renaix-Kwaremont (Prov. East Flanders) fired at a group of men and killed a Belgian civilian, Mr. Richard Van den Abeele of Kwaremont. These Germans belonged to the same unit as Vetter. The latter had been ordered by them to blow up flying bombs deposited in the garden of Behaegel mansion at Bueren. Soon afterwards Vetter was taken prisoner in this place. He should be able to give useful information about the identity of the two German officers, authors of the above-detailed-crime. He is wanted as a witness. (Perhaps a suspect.) Residence: Berlin-Oberschoeneweide, Wattstr.22.	BEL.
VIERKOETTER, Henriette	196367	F	Ger.		Wanted as a War Criminal, Looting of Luxembourg properties.	LUX.
VOEKL, Hans	258043	M	Ger.		Wanted as a witness to the alleged murder of an unknown wounded American POW. by Schneider, Hans, on or about Febr. 1945 in the vicinity of Alsace (Fr.). Last known to have been in custody at 2228 PW-camp, Overitsche (GSGS 4042, Sheet 2 A, Coord. V-02) Netherlands.	U.S.
VOGEL, Michael	258041	M	Ger.		Wanted reports issued on basis of possible perpetrator or witness for the develop-ment of Muehldorf area case No.000-50-136.	U.S.
VON RHEIN see RHEIN	261160					
WAGNER	259277				O.T., murder and atrocities at Muehldorf area	U.S.
WALTER, Friederich	252826	M		97	Beating of unknown Canadian pilot at Eschwege (Ger.).	CAN.
WANNER, Heinrich	257627	M	Ger.	22.2.25	Wanted for participation in the alleged mistreatment of an American Airman Annallo (?) George, near Viernheim (GSGS 4346, Sheet L-50, Coord. M-60), U.S. Zone on 5 Sept. 1944. Victim was Annallo, George, rank and serial number unknown. Born in New York.	U.S.
WEBER	259437	M			Former town-official at Grossorner (Ger.). Wanted as a witness to the alleged murder of two or three American Airmen. Area of Mansfield (Ger.), 15.3.44	U.S.
WECKERLE, Josef	258048	M	Ger.		Wanted reports issued on basis of possible perpetrator or witness for the development of Muehldorf area case No.000-50-136.	U.S.
WEDERMANN	258036	M	Ger.		Wanted reports issued on basis of possible perpetrator or witness for the development of Muehldorf area case No.000-50-136.	U.S.
WEILAND, Franz	257300	M	Ger.	89	Wanted for participation in the murder of three American Airmen at Bernbach (Ger.) 9.8.44	U.S.
WEINBRACHT, Max	258046	M	Ger.		Wanted reports issued on basis of possible perpetrator or witness for the development of Muehldorf area case No.000-50-136.	U.S.
WEINERT, Friedrich	251726	M	Ger.		Wanted for murder of Belgian civilian prisoners at Lahde-Weser.	BEL.
WEISS	256711	M	Ger.		Member of the German Commission responsible for pillaging the Peugeot-Works in Sochaux from Sept. to Nov. 1944	FR.
WEISS, Hermann	259305	M			Murder and atrocities at Muehldorf area	U.S.
WELLER	259254				Wanted for the shooting of an American Airman at near Buendheim (Ger.)	U.S.
WENCK, Walter	258959	M	Ger.	00	Lt.Gen., crimes against Peace, crimes against Humanity.	U.S.
WENDT, Walter	259282	M			Wanted for participation in the murder of Allied nationals by shooting at camp Thekla (Area of Leipzig), 18.4.45	U.S.
WERBANATZ, Franz	258049	M	Ger.		Wanted reports issued on basis of possible perpetrator or witness for the development of Muehldorf area case No.000-50-136.	U.S.
WERDATH, Johann	258050	M	Ger.		Wanted reports issued on basis of possible perpetrator or witness for the development of Muehldorf area case No.000-50-136.	U.S.
WERIKA	258051	M	Ger.		Wanted reports issued on basis of possible perpetrator or witness for the development of Muehldorf area case No.000-50-136.	U.S.
WERNER	259253	M			Sgt., wanted for participation. The murder of four American Airmen, after they were forced to dig their own graves near Schweidnitz, 3.45	U.S.
WERNER	259790	M	Ger.		N.C.O., could possibly give information on the murder of Mr. Metreau, murdered on 29.1.44 at St.Pierre de Palais (Charente Maritime).	FR.
WERNER, Josef	259454	M	Ger.		Wanted as a witness to the murder of an American flyer at Amerod, on or about October 1944. Address: Merkelsdorf 209, Kreis Braunau, Sudetenland, (Czech.)	U.S.
WERRING, Joseph	258024	M	Ger.		Could give informations on the destruction of the installations of the weaving factory in Longpre Les Amiens in September 1943, and to identify the officers, responsible for the crime.	FR.
WESTMEIER, Jakob	259325	M			Murder and atrocities at Muehldorf Area	U.S.
WETTER	252791	M	Ger.		SS-Osturmfhr., about ten thousand Yugoslavian citizens of both sexes were tortured and killed at the Auschwitz-Birkenau SS C.C. Only one hundred Yugoslav citizens survived the regime of torture, starvation, murder and killings.	YUGO.
WIELANDER, Ludwig	258054	M	Ger.		Wanted reports issued on basis of possible perpetrator or witness for the development of Muehldorf area case No.000-50-136.	U.S.
WIEBER, Julius	253230	M	Ger.		Lootings in Metz (Fr.) during German occupation. Residence: Neckarelz near Heidelberg (Ger.)	FR.
WILDSCHITZ, Ignatz	258055	M	Ger.		Wanted reports issued on basis of possible perpetrator or witness for the development of Muehldorf area case No.000-50-136.	U.S.
WILLKOMMER, Ludwig	258056	M	Ger.		Wanted reports issued on basis of possible perpetrator or witness for the development of Muehldorf area case No.000-50-136.	U.S.

WIL-ZIV

NAME	C.R.FILE NUMBER	SEX	NATIO-NALITY	DATE OF BIRTH	ALL AVAILABLE INFORMATION AS TO THE RANK, OCCUPATIONS (CIVIL, PARTY OR MILITARY), PARTICULARS OF CRIME AND PHYSICAL DISCRIPTION - IF KNOWN.	WANTED BY
WILLY	259234	M			Kapo, Bigamist (?) - replaced "Peter". Equally savage. Beat deportees to death, Auschwitz (Pol.). Murder.	FR.
WINKLER, Karl	258956	M	Ger.		Manager of the Party Chancellory. Wanted for trial under Control Law No.10. Int-arr.	U.S.
WOERSDOERFER	257678	M	Ger.		Wanted for participation in the alleged murder of an American airman, Lt.Jack Rives, O-832696, of the 507th fighter squadron on 20 March 1945 near Helferskirchen, Germany. Victim was captured by the local Gestapo and two Gestapo agents who took him to a nearby wood that same day and murdered him. Suspect is possibly in custody at Billy Mitchell Field, Milwaukee, Wisconsin.	U.S.
WOHLER (see HANMOT)	259792					
WOHLER, Fritz	261188	M	Ger.		Execution of 20 hostages at Gosselies, on August 24, 1944.	BEL.
WOLF, Gottfried	259421	M			Murder and atrocities at Muhldorf Area.	U.S.
WOLF, Guenther	257194	M	Ger.		Guard, wanted as a perpetrator in the alleged murder of seven unarmed American PWs in the vicinity of Hemevez (Fr.) 6.6.44. Suspect.	U.S.
WOLF, Gustav	257197	M	Ger.		Wanted as a perpetrator in the alleged murder of seven unarmed American PWs at Hemevez, France. 6.6.44. Suspect.	U.S.
WOLF, Hans	257196	M	Ger.		Wanted as a perpetrator in the alleged murder of seven unarmed American PWs at Hemevez, France. 6.6.44. War Criminal.	U.S.
WOLF, Siegfried	257195	M			Wanted as a perpetrator in the alleged murder of seven unarmed American PWs at Hemevez, France. 6.6.44. War Criminal.	U.S.
WOLFRAMY, Johann	258057	M	Ger.		Wanted report issued on basis of possible perpetrator or witness for the development of Muhldorf Area case No. 000-50-136. Suspect.	U.S.
ZAGRANICZNY, Nikolaj	259497	M			Wanted as a witness to the murder of an American airman by beating at Burg (Ger.) 2.45.	U.S.
ZAPLETAL, Franzl	250585	M			Wanted as a witness to the murder of an American airman, Dean N.Post jr., O-807603, at Gerardmer, France (GSGS 4346, sheet K-49, coordinates V-34) on 29 May 1944. Address: Semperstrasse, Vienna (GSGS 4346, sheet O-49, coordinates X-49.)	U.S.
ZAVADINSKI, Otto	256528	M	Ger.	16. 7.08	Wanted for the alleged beating and torturing of prisoners and is responsible for several murders at Frydet (Czech.).	U.S.
ZEISE, Gustav	259259	M	Ger.		Wanted for murder of an American aviator at Friesack (Ger.). 26.6.44	U.S.
ZENTER (or ZENNER)	259327	M			O.T., murder and atrocities at Muhldorf Area.	U.S.
ZENNER (see ZEMMER)	259327					
ZIEBERT, Willi	258021	M	Ger.		Could give information about the plundering committed by Jurgens and Optier, of the office and house of Hubert Nederveen at Nuland, in September and October 1944. Home address: Duesseldorf-Gerresheim, Hegenerstrasse 47. Interr.	NETH.
ZIEGLER	250594	M	Ger.		Took part in the massacre of 7.000 people at Kragujevac (Serbia) on the 21 October 1941. On duty at the Gestapo in October 1941 at Kragujevac.	YUGO.
ZIMMER	259287	M			O.T., murder and atrocities at Muhldorf Area.	U.S.
ZIMMERMANN, Otto	259489	M	Ger.	28.10.86	Merchant, looting of Luxembourg property during German occupation.	LUX.
ZIVNUSTKA, Ernst	251478	M	Ger.	23. 5.96	As member of SD at Hr.Kralove and Major of Horice and Modrany, Czech., he is responsible for imprisonment, torture and death of many Czechs. He is living someplace at Passau, U.S.Zone of Germany.	CZECH.

APPENDIX - 'A'

Number of Germans Wanted in Part I of List, VOL.-A-L.		19,557
Number of Germans Wanted in Part I.of List, VOL.-M-Z.		16,198
TOTAL NUMBER OF PERSONS WANTED IN CONSOLIDATED WANTED LIST (PART I - GERMANS).		35,755 *

NUMBER WANTED BY NATIONS.	VOL. A-L	VOL. M-Z	Total
AUSTRALIA	1	1	2
ARGENTINE	-	1	1
BELGIUM	1,499	1,227	2,726
BULGARIA	1	-	1
CZECHOSLOVAKIA	1,259	1,147	2,406
CANADA	72	77	149
DENMARK	20	17	37
FRANCE	6,362	4,749	11,111
GREAT BRITAIN (U.K.)	1,679	1,504	3,183
GREECE	85	94	179
HOLLAND (NETH.)	542	360	902
HUNGARY	7	4	11
IRAN	1	-	1
IRAQUE	-	1	1
ITALY	7	4	11
LUXEMBOURG	106	88	194
NORWAY	617	536	1,153
POLAND	747	635	1,382
SOVIET UNION (RUSSIA)	24	23	47
U.S.A.	6,121	5,317	11,438
YUGOSLAVIA	634	630	1,264
U.N.W.C.C.	204	151	355
TOTAL NUMBER OF NAMES LISTED AS WANTED BY ABOVE COUNTRIES			36,544 *

* **NOTE.** The disparity between Number of Germans Wanted and Total Sought by Individual Countries, is due to the fact that 726 persons are sought by two or more countries.

APPENDIX - 'B'

PERSONS INCLUDED IN CONSOLIDATED WANTED LIST AND EITHER NOW DETAINED OR NO LONGER WANTED

I. Consolidated Wanted List, Vol. A-L.

NAME	C.R.FILE NUMBER	PAGE	IF NO LONGER WANTED	WHERE DETAINED	DETAINED BY
BAAR, Hans	187454	9	Yes	-	-
BAIER, Otto	260466	11	Yes	-	-
BECKER, Fritz M.K.	190491	20	Yes	-	-
BEISSWENGER, Walter	144568	22	-	P.W.E.27 Zimming	U.S.
BELZ, Helmut	172907	23	Yes	-	-
BERTRAM, Georg	258967	27	-	C.I.C.Munster Lager	U.K.
BIERSACK, Martin	139115	29	Yes	-	-
BIRLI	173982	30	Yes	-	-
BOERNER	173319	36	-	P.W.E.29 Dachau	U.S.
BOHN, Richard	152493	37	Yes	-	-
BORCH see BORSCH, Johann	174849	39	-	P.W.E.29 Dachau	U.S.
BORSCH (BOSCH,BORCH),Johann	174849	40	-	P.W.E.29 Dachau	U.S.
BOSCH see BORSCH, Johann	174849	40	-	P.W.E.29 Dachau	U.S.
BRACK, Victor or JENNERWEIN	134913	41	-	6 C.I.C.Moosburg transferred to Nuernberg	U.S.
BRACK, Viktor	188277	41	-	6 C.I.E.Moosburg transferred to Nuernberg	U.S.
BRAUN, Wilhelm	187525	44	Yes	-	-
BUTTINGER, Josef	173973	56	Yes	-	-
DANNHAUSER, Johann	186735	63	Yes	-	-
DAR Victor Heinr. see EBELING, Karl	142336	64	Yes	-	-
DEPPE, Wilhelm	151179	67	-	5 C.I.C.Natternberg	U.K.
DERN	189640	67	-	75 C.I.E.Kornwestheim	U.S.
DING	72345	71	Yes (now dead)	-	-
DING	253610	71	Yes (now dead)	-	-
DITTMAYER, Julius	252057	71	Yes	-	-
DREIWURST, Josef	187298	76	Yes	-	-
DVORAK, Alfred	251327	79	Yes	-	-
EBELING, Karl or EBERLEIN, EBERLING, Dar Victor Heinrich	142336	79	Yes	-	-
EBERLEIN see EBELING, Karl	142336	80	Yes	-	-
EBERLING see EBELING, Karl	142336	80	Yes	-	-
EBERLING, Otto	162827	80	Yes	-	-
EICHLINGER, Thomas	262335	83	Yes	-	-
EISENHOEFER	147179	84	Yes (sentenced to death by hanging)	-	-
EISENHOFER	142146	84	Yes (sentenced to death by hanging)	-	-
ENGELHARDT, Otto	134839	86	Yes	-	-
EXNER, Theodore	193224	90	-	78 C.I.E.Zuffenhausen	U.S.
FASSBINDER or ZIMMERMANN	176707	92	Yes	-	-
FAUDE	193484	92	-	8356 Lab.Serv.Coy.APO 228	-
FOERSTE, Erich	259073	102	Yes	-	-
FOTTER, Karl aliases VOTTER	261911	102	Yes	-	-
FRITZ, Phillip	133362	110	Yes	-	-
FUCHS	279	111	-	P.W.E.27 Zimming transferred to 10 P.W.E.Heilbronn	U.S.
FUCHS, Dr.	62340	111	-	P.W.E.27 Zimming transferred to 10 P.W.E.Heilbronn	U.S.
FUCHS	139813	111	Yes	-	-
FUCHS, Dr.	222568	111	-	P.W.E.27 Zimming transferred to 10 P.W.E.Heilbronn	U.S.
GEISSER	192925	118	-	9 C.I.E.Hammelburg	U.S.
GLANDSTATTER	195128	123	Yes	-	-
GRESSE, Rudolf	188255	131	Yes	-	-
GRONAU	193490	133	-	7036 Lab.Serv.Coy.(130)APO 168	U.S.
GROSS, Josef	67599	134	Yes	-	-
HEINZ, Dr.	154962	157	Yes	-	-
HEROLD, Walter	306391	163	-	5 C.I.C.Natternberg	U.K.
HERZOG, Kate	194775	165	Yes	-	-
HESS, Fritz	24965	165	Yes	-	-
IMMING, Valentin	142085	185	Yes	-	-
ISKRA, Mathews	145357	185	Yes	-	-
JAKOB	194767	187	Yes	-	-
JENNERWEIN see BRACK, Victor	134913	190	-	6 C.I.E.Moosburg transferred to Nuernberg	U.S.
JOSTEN	192660	192	-	P.W.E.29 Dachau	U.S.
JOSTEN	173564	192	-	P.W.E.29 Dachau	U.S.
KITTEL, Gerhard	150670	209	Yes	-	-
KORN	232455	225	-	Groningen State Jail Nord Singel Prison	NETH.
KRAUSKOPF, Edmond	143174	230	-	5 C.I.C.Natternberg	U.K.
LANGE	185132	246	Yes	-	-

APPENDIX - 'B'

PERSONS INCLUDED IN CONSOLIDATED WANTED LIST AND EITHER-NOW DETAINED OR NO LONGER WANTED.

I. Consolidated Wanted List, Vol. M-Z.

NAME	C.R.FILE NUMBER	PAGE	IF NO LONGER WANTED	WHERE DETAINED	DETAINED BY
MARTENS, Fritz	196019	6	-	Prison The Hague	NETH.
MASHOFF, Karl	156858	7	Yes	-	-
MATHES see MATTHES, Max	170071	7	-	P.W.E.29 Dachau	U.S.
MATTHES or MATHES, Max	170071	8	-	P.W.E.29 Dachau	U.S.
MERKER, Peter	141979	15	-	78 C.I.E.Zuffenhausen	U.S.
MEYER, Hans	174702	18	Yes	-	-
MIKA, Emanuel	253883	19	Yes	-	-
MOENNICH, Willy	196499	22	Yes	-	-
MUELLER	10312	25	Yes (now dead)	-	-
MUELLER	132254	25	Yes (now dead)	-	-
MULLER-BRAND, Hermann	163222	28	Yes	-	-
NIEDNER	104887	39	Yes	-	-
NIEZOLDI	39592	40	-	P.W.E.29 Dachau	U.S.
PANNWITZ, Walther	149068	49	Yes	-	-
PELLENGAHR	190042	51	Yes	-	-
PETRI	153175	54	-	Held at Nuernberg	U.S.
PRONATH, George	192506	64	-	78 C.I.E.Zuffenhausen	U.S.
PULFER, Martin	262132	65	Yes	-	-
RADLOFF, Heinrich	190324	67	-	P.W.E.29 Dachau	U.S.
RECH, Richard	152333	70	Yes	-	-
REINKENSMEIER, Friedrich	152092	73	Yes	-	-
REUTTER, Dr.	10928	76	Yes	-	-
RIKO	158233	78	-	4 C.I.E.Recklinghausen	U.K.
RINGEISEN, Edmund	259814	80	-	72 C.I.E.Ludwigsburg	U.S.
ROGALA, Helmut	156051	83	Yes	-	-
SCHAUB, Heinrich	124388	97	Yes	-	-
SCHAUP, Albrecht	125266	98	Yes	-	-
SCHAMBOEK	149864	97	Yes	-	-
SCHAUSS	193396	98	Yes	-	-
SCHINDLER, Hugo	260507	102	-	78 C.I.E.Zuffenhausen	U.S.
SCHLEGEL, Kurt	132143	103	-	P.W.E.29 Dachau	U.S.
SCHLUNDERMANN	194226	105	-		
SCHMIDT, Karl	133239	109	Yes	-	-
SCHMIDT, Marie	193772	109	Yes	-	-
SCHMITZ, Franz Johann	261106	111	Yes	-	-
SCHOLZ	251791	116	Yes	-	-
SCHRIMPF, Else	253399	110	Yes	-	-
SCHULTHEISS, Georg	143226	122	Yes	-	-
SCHWENN, Friedrich Karl	198013	120	Yes	-	-
SCHWENDT, Hans	4723	129	Yes	-	-
SEITZ, Robert	139217	133	Yes	-	-
SIEBER, Karl	132144	135	Yes	-	-
SPEIDEL	888	142	Yes	-	-
STEIN, Ernst	142259	147	Yes	-	-
STROBL, Hans	252765	154	Yes	-	-
SUDHOFF, Wilhelm	143146	156	Yes	-	-
VON GLANDSTATTEN	193676	179	Yes	-	-
VON GLANSTATTEN	254509	179	Yes	-	-
WEBER, Dr.	173843	191	Yes	-	-
WEBER, Johanna	149684	191	-	P.W.E.29 Dachau	U.S.
WECHLIN, Willy	167858	192	Yes	-	-
WIEGAND	1020- 206647	202	-	2 C.I.C.Sandbostel	U.K.
WIENERS, Konrad	21415	202	Yes	-	-
WIGAND, Arpad	206647	203	-	2 C.I.C.Sandbostel	U.K.
WINKHAUS, Hermann	240079	206	-	5 C.I.C.Natternberg	U.K.
WITTMANN, Peter	137998	209	Yes	-	-
WOLF, Johann	258396	211	Yes	-	-
WOROFSKY, J. Dr.	29658	212	Yes	-	-
ZELLNER	305988	217	-	4 C.I.C.Recklinghausen	U.K.
ZIMMERMANN see FASSBINDER	176707	220	Yes	-	-
ZWIRNER, Hans	258996	222	Yes	-	-

THE CENTRAL REGISTRY OF WAR CRIMINALS AND SECURITY SUSPECTS

CONSOLIDATED WANTED LIST – PART 2

NON – GERMANS ONLY

NOTE: ALL PREVIOUS CROWCASS WANTED LISTS SHOULD BE DESTROYED

CROWCASS
ALLIED CONTROL AUTHORITY
APO 742,
U.S. ARMY

TELEPHONE: BERLIN (TEMPELHOF) 5336, 5775
TELEPRINTER: BERLIN / STATION DHBP.

MARCH 1947

INDEX.

	PAGE.
FRONTISPIECE	(i)
CONCERNING THE UNITED NATIONS WAR CRIMES COMMISSION.	(ii)
PERSONS LISTED ALPHABETICALLY ACCORDING TO SURNAMES.	1
PERSONS LISTED ALPHABETICALLY ACCORDING TO NATIONALITY.	41
Albania	41
Arabia	41
Argentine	41
Austria	41
Belgium	46
Bulgaria	47
Czechoslovakia	52
Denmark	52
France	52
Hungary	53
Italy	56
Luxembourg	74
Netherlands	75
Norway	75
Poland	75
Rumania	77
Russia	78
Spain	79
Stateless	79
Switzerland	79
Turkey	79
Yugoslavia	79
APPENDIX - 'A': PERSONS ESPECIALLY LISTED UNDER DIFFERENT HEADINGS	81
APPENDIX - 'B': UNKNOWNS (GERMANS AND NON-GERMANS) CATEGORISED ACCORDING TO RANK OR STATUS	89
APPENDIX - 'C': TABLE SHOWING TOTAL NUMBER OF PERSONS IN CONSOLIDATED WANTED LIST PART II (NON-GERMANS) AS WANTED BY EACH OF THE ALLIED NATIONS	129

ABBREVIATIONS OF COUNTRIES.

UNITED STATES OF AMERICA	U.S.	GREECE	GRC.
GREAT BRITAIN (UNITED KINGDOM)	U.K.	ITALY	IT.
		FINLAND	FIN.
FRANCE	FR.	HUNGARY	HUNG.
SOVIET UNION (RUSSIA)	SOV.UN.	AUSTRIA	AUST.
BELGIUM	BEL.	CANADA	CAN.
HOLLAND (NETHERLANDS)	NETH.	AUSTRALIA	AUSTL.
POLAND	POL.	NEW ZEALAND	N.Z.
DENMARK	DEN.	SOUTH AFRICA	S.A.
NORWAY	NOR.	UKRAINE	UKR.
CZECHOSLOVAKIA	CZECH.	SLOVENIA	SLOV.
LUXEMBOURG	LUX.	ROUMANIA	RUM.
YUGOSLAVIA	YUGO.	LATVIA	LATV.
GERMANY	GER.		

GENERAL ABBREVIATIONS.

ARMY RANKS.		ARMY FORMATIONS.		GENERAL TERMS.	
PRIVATE	PVT.	SECTION	SEC.	MILITARY	MIL.
CORPORAL	CPL.	COMPANY	COY.	DIRECTOR	DIR.
SERGEANT	SGT.	BATAILLON	BN.	COMMANDANT	CMDT.
NON COMMISSIONED OFFICER	NCO	REGIMENT	REGT.	OFFICER COMMANDING	O.C.
WARRANT OFFICER	W.O.			GENDARME	GEND.
OFFICER CANDIDATE	O/CAND.			CONCENTRATION CAMP	C.C.
LIEUTENANT	LT.			ASSISTANT	ASST.
CAPTAIN	CAPT.			SABOTAGE UNIT	SAB.
COLONEL	COL.				
GENERAL	GEN.				

SPECIAL ABBREVIATION.

L.O.N.A.O.D.   Locate only - do not arrest or detain.

NOTE. German Party Ranks are too numerous to list and any abbreviations used in this Publication should be easily recognisable.

CONSOLIDATED WANTED LIST (PART II - NON-GERMANS)

IT IS IMPORTANT THAT YOU READ THIS.

1. This List is the second Part of the Consolidation of the names of all persons in CROWCASS Records who are wanted in connection with War Crimes and includes all Wanted Reports received up to 31 Jan.1947 plus a few additional names not published in previous lists.

2. This list contains the names of all persons stated to be of nationality other than German who according to the information passed to CROWCASS are still wanted by the Allied Nations in connection with War Crimes. Persons of German nationality have been published in Part I.

3. This list also includes the names of all persons of nationality other than German who have been listed in the United Nations War Crimes Commission Lists Nos. 1 - 50 who, so far as CROWCASS is aware, are still wanted in connection with war crimes perpetrated against the nationals of any other of the United Nations.

4. It is considered probable that some of the persons listed have been detained, some tried, some sentenced and others may be no longer wanted. If this is so, CROWCASS has not been informed and the various Allied Authorities who can supply such information are requested to do so immediatley in orde. that CROWCASS Records may be adjusted. It is also possible that some Wanted Reports went astray during the move of CROWCASS from Paris to Berlin and the names are therefore not included in this list. If such is the case new Wanted Reports should be submitted immediately and the names will be published in a supplementary List.

5. Names of persons known to be detained, and where the Wanting Authority has been informed accordingly, are not included in this list.

6. It is hoped that by now all authorities receiving a copy of this List will also have received and read the pamphlet entitled "What is CROWCASS?" in order that a better understanding may be reached concerning the functions of this organisation and the service given to and required from all using agencies.

7. All recipients of this List are reminded of the following requirements as previously set out in the frontispieces of CROWCASS Wanted Lists:

    (I) If any person listed should be located and detained the CROWCASS Detention Report (to be invariably submitted in respect of all Detainees) should be completed showing Reason for Arrest as "CROWCASS Consolidated Wanted List (Part II) CR.NO. ..." or "Possibly CROWCASS Consolidated Wanted List (Part II) CR.NO. ...". If a Wanted Person is located only and not detained as full a description as possible of the person located should be set out in letter form and forwarded to CROWCASS including the reason for non-detention.

    (II) In the event of CROWCASS thus receiving information of a match or possible match between a Wanted Person and a Detained or located Person the wanting nation is immediately informed, even although the Detainee may be held in the custody of that nation. In some cases where the person's name has not been listed by the UNWCC and where extradition is applied for considerable delay may be unavoidable. (See page (II)). If and when the extradition of a CROWCASS Wanted Personality has taken place CROWCASS should be informed immediately.

    (III) If a Detaining Authority receives instructions to Release or Transfer any Detainee who is possibly or definitely a CROWCASS Wanted Personality a check should first be made with that Authority's War Crimes Group HQ. and a copy of the communication endorsed to CROWCASS.

    (IV) The information given in this list about each person is all that is contained on the Wanted Reports filed with CROWCASS. The descriptions given are not summaries.

8. It is particulary requested that the War Crimes HQ's of all the Allied Nations endeavour to make special arrangements to have this List distributed to all Detaining Authorities, Prisoner of War Information Bureaus (or the equivalent) and all other HQ.'s or Formations which may be able to assist in locating the persons listed.

9. No doubt the Inter-Allied National policy as regards the probable duration of the Investigation of War Crimes will depend to quite a considerable extent upon the number of Alleged War Criminals "still at large" in the sense of not being in the custody of the nation who wants them. To help to reduce this period of duration and the enormous expenditure and man power involved all Allied Nations are again requested to exploit every means within their power to reduce this List as quickly as possible.

10. At Appendix 'A' will be found the names of persons, especially listed under different headings owing to a lack of detailed information suitable for listing under the normal headings.

11. At Appendix 'B' will be found a list of all persons of unknown name whatever their nationality.

12. At Appendix 'C' will be found a table showing the total number of persons included in this list who are wanted by each of the Allied Nations.

13. CROWCASS has a teleprinter station in its office. It is "Station DHEP - Berlin". Using agencies are requested to make use of it as it greatly speeds up replies to requests for information.

14. CROWCASS holds large stocks of Blank Wanted and Detention Reports and they can be had on application by TPM, Signal or letter.

15. Whilst every effort has been made to eliminate error from this List there may still be left a few discrepancies which although unavoidable are regretted.

(ii)

CONCERNING THE UNITED NATIONS WAR CRIMES COMMISSION.

The following is quoted from Section X of Information Paper No. 1 issued by the Reference Division of the United Nations Information Organisation, London:

INTER-ALLIED DECLARATION OF DECEMBER 17, 1942

On December 17, 1942, a Declaration was made simultaneously in London, Moscow, and Washington in connection with reports that the German authorities were engaged in exterminating the Jewish people in Europe. In this Declaration, the Governments of Belgium, Czechoslovakia, Greece, Luxembourg, the Netherlands, Norway, Poland, the United States of America, the United Kingdom, the Soviet Union and Yugoslavia and the French National Committee reaffirmed their solemn resolution that those responsible should not escape retribution and their intention to press on with the necessary practical measures to that end.

There was some delay in setting up the United Nations War Crimes Commission, but it was eventually brought into being by a meeting of Government representatives at the British Foreign Office on October 20, 1943.

COMPOSITION OF THE COMMISSION

The Commission consists of seventeen members: the representatives of the Governments of Australia, Belgium, Canada, China, Czechoslovakia, Denmark, France, Greece, India, Luxembourg, the Netherlands, New Zealand, Norway, Poland, the United Kingdom, the United States of America and Yugoslavia. The representatives are all distinguished lawyers or diplomats.

If a representative is unable to act, or for some other special reason, he may be replaced.

The Commission may hear experts.

The first Chairman was the United Kingdom representative, Sir Cecil Hurst, Vice-President of the Permanent Court of International Justice, formerly legal Adviser to the Foreign Office. After his resignation on account of illhealth, he was replaced by the Right Hon. Lord Wright, Lord of Appeal in Ordinary, who represents Australia on the Commission. Lord Wright has been Chairman since January 31, 1945.

TERMS OF REFERENCE OF THE COMMISSION

The Commission has limited functions. It is primarily a fact-finding body, though it has also advisory functions.

Its terms of reference were defined in the Lord Chancellor's statement of October 7, 1942. Its purpose, he said is to investigate war crimes committed against nationals of the United Nations, recording the testimony available, and to report from time to time to the Governments of those nations cases in which such crimes appear to have been committed, naming and identifying wherever possible the persons responsible.

After its creation, it was entrusted with advisory functions, namely to make recommendations to the Governments on the methods to be adopted to ensure the surrender or capture of the persons wanted for trial as war criminals and on the tribunals by which they should be tried.

HOW THE COMMISSION OPERATES

The United Nations War Crimes Commission prepares lists of war criminals on the basis of evidence submitted by National War Crimes Offices which have been set up to detect, investigate and record evidence of war crimes committed against the citizens or subjects of their own countries.

The lists are furnished to the apprehending authorities - at present the military authorities - in order that the persons accused of crimes against people or property may be sent back to the country against which they have offended. This was the procedure contemplated in the Moscow Declaration on Atrocities by President Roosevelt, Mr. Winston Churchill and Marshal Stalin which was issued on November 1, 1943 and by the Foreign Secretaries of their three countries, who had been attending the Moscow Conference of October 16 to 30.

After referring to the atrocities, massacres and mass executions which were being perpetrated by the Hitlerite forces, the Declaration said:

"The United Kingdom, the United States and the Soviet Union ....

"... speaking in the interests of the thirty-two United Nations ... solemnly declare and give full warning of their declaration as follows: At the time of the granting of any armistice to any Government which may be set up in Germany, those German officers and men and members of the Nazi Party who have been responsible for or who have taken a consenting part in the above atrocities, massacres and executions will be sent back to the countries in which their abominable deeds were done in order that they many be judged and punished according to the laws of these liberated countries and of the Free Governments which will be erected therein. Lists will be compiled in all possible detail from all these countries ..."

Offences against members of the Allied armed forces will be dealt with summarily by military courts, in accordance with international custom.

The following is a Statement issued by UNWCC especially for incorporation in this Consolidated Wanted List:

"All Allied Authorities concerned are reminded that in order to secure extradition they should submit to the United Nations "War Crimes Commission in London dossiers with charges concerning the offences committed by persons wanted. The United "Nations War Crimes Commission in accordance with its terms of reference decides whether there appears to be either prima "facie evidence sufficient to justify the handing over for trial of individuals accused of War Crimes or else sufficent "ground to consider the wanted persons as suspects or material witnesses"

ALPHABETICAL SECTION
(See NATIONALITY SECTION for the same names listed in order of nationality.)

ABE-ARR

NAME	C.R.FILE NUMBER	SEX	NATIO-NALITY	DATE OF BIRTH	RANK OCCUPATION UNIT PLACE AND DATE OF CRIME	REASON WANTED	WANTED BY
ABEL, Wolfgang	142405	M	Aust.		Oschfhr., Gestapo, SS	TORTURE	U.S.
ABELSON	147085	M	Nor.		Guard, Boten Camp, Rohnan (Nor.) 43	MURDER	YUGO.
ABLEIDINGERF, Friedrich	132816	M	Aust.		Feldgendarm., Feldgendarmerie Trupp 648, Conde (Fr.)	WITNESS	U.K.,U.S.
ABRAMCZYK, Isidor	140340	M	Pol.	15	Chief, C.C.Auschwitz (Pol.)	TORTURE	FR.
ABRAMOWITCH, Gesel	259405	M	Pol.	05	Leader, SS, Block 7, Auschwitz (Pol.)	SUSPECT	FR.
ACQUA, Fredda	190871	M	Ital.		Crim.-Commissar., Italian Police, Susak Podhum (Yugo.) 41-4.43	MURDER	YUGO.
ADAMCZICK, Janek	140354	M	Pol.	15	Blockleiter, Buchenwald (Ger.)	MURDER	FR.
ADAMER	196267	M	Aust.		Capt., Camp Laterina (Ger.)	WITNESS	U.S.
ADAMI-ROSSI, E.	129135	M	Ital.		General-Lt., Armee Corps 2142, Sulmona (It.) 26.12.41	MISC.CRIMES	U.K.
ADAMO, Fernando	190872	M	Ital.		Member, Blackshirt Unit, Vodice, Sibenik (Yugo.) 2.4.43	MURDER	YUGO.
ADDARI, Ranieri	250029	M	Ital.		Vice-Brigadier, Dazlina, Dubrava (Yugo.) 24.7.42	MURDER	YUGO.
ADDESST, Giovanni	250010	M	Ital.		Political Secretary, C.C.Fonda (Yugo.) 9.-10.43	INTERR.	YUGO.
ADERMOUSSIAK, Karl	174914	M	Aust.		Guard, SS, C.C.Schoerzingen (Ger.)	MISC.CRIMES	FR.
ADOTTO, Duchetti	190873	M	Ital.		Major, Italian Army, Biograd-on-Sea (Yugo.) 12.4.43	MURDER	YUGO.
AFRI, Bruno	250025	M	Ital.		Commissar, Prov.Vodice (Yugo.) 42-43	MURDER	YUGO.
AGAZZI, Giovanni	250022	M	Ital.		Capellano militare, Army, 10 Flottielia-Mass, Conegliano (Slov.) 21.12.44 - 3.1.45	INTERR.	YUGO.
AGOSTINO	36677	M	Ital.		Tenente Colonello, Army, Castel San Pietro, Bologna (It.)	MISC.CRIMES	U.K.
AIGNER, Toni	132545	M	Aust.	20	Uschfhr., SS, Hallein (Aust.)	MURDER	YUGO.
ALACEVIC, Josip	190874	M	Ital.		Secretary, Fascio Italian SS, Sibenik (Yugo.) 41-43	MURDER	YUGO.
ALBERTAZZI, Augusto	146105	M	Ital.		Capt., Italian Army, Cetigne (Yugo.) 43	MURDER	YUGO.
ALDO	152498	M	Ital.		Lt., Italian Army, 313. Inf.Regt., C.C.Larissa (Grc.) 8.43	TORTURE	U.K.
ALDO, Cicero	152497	M	Ital.	17	Cpl., Italian Army, Guard, Thebes (Grc.) 8.42	TORTURE	U.K.
ALESSANDRI, Guiseppe	250607	M	Ital.		Ital.Air Force, Av.A.Mot.119, Sosici (Yugo.) 12.7.43	MISC.CRIMES	YUGO.
ALESSANDRO	189917	M	Ital.		Lt., Italian Army, Bizerte (Tunisia)	MURDER	FR.
ALEXIUS, Adolf	152490	M	Rum.	17	Uschfhr., SS staff, Buchenwald (Ger.) 1.11.44	WITNESS	U.S.
ALFAREZ	193910A	M	Ital.		Sgt.,Chief, Jg.-Bn., Fontaine-Par-Grenoble (Fr.)	TORTURE	FR.
ALIENZO, Luiggi	257458	M	Ital.		Brigadier, Carabinieri Regt., Pisnottoli (Fr.) 9.5.43	MURDER	FR.
ALLERT	196457	M	Aust.		W.O., Gestapo, Valence (Fr.) 40-44	INTERR.	FR.
ALLEVI, Vittorio	146098	M	Ital.		Dr., Major, Army, Mil.Hospital, Treviglio (It.) 42-43	TORTURE	U.K.
ALLMANN, Stefan	258415	M	Hung.	25.8.95	Waffen-SS, C.C.Ohrdruf (Ger.) 12.44-4.45	MURDER	U.S.
ALONGI, Francesco	125709	M	Ital.		Dr., Camp of civilian, Camp Commandant, Corropoli (It.) 42	TORTURE	FR.
ALROLDI, Alberto	250021	M	Ital.		Capt., Italian Army, Susak (Yugo.) 41-43	MISC.CRIMES	YUGO.
ALVISI, Alessandro	307336	M	Ital.		Consul, Judge of special Tribunal for defence of State Rom (It.) 4.41-9.43	MURDER	YUGO.
ALZETTA	146104	M	Ital.		Lt., Italian Army, "Lombardia" Div., Slovenia,Croatia (Yugo.) 43	MURDER	YUGO.
AMADASI	190876	M	Ital.		Commissar,Capo, Sibenik (Yugo.) 43	MURDER	YUGO.
AMATO, Attilio	195528	M	Ital.		General, Italian Army, Div."Messina", Korcula (Yugo.) 15.1.43	MURDER	YUGO.
AMBROSIO, Nittorio	146102	M	Ital.		General, Army, Fusina (Yugo.) 42	MURDER	YUGO.
AMBROSIO, N.	146103	M	Ital.		Col., Italian Army, Groinicko Polje (Yugo.) 43	MURDER	YUGO.
AMEDEO, Constantino	190877	M	Ital.		Major, Italian Army, Commander of Carabinieri, Sibenik (Yugo.) 41-43	MURDER	YUGO.
AMEDORO, Francesco	190878	M	Ital.		Marshall, Italian Army, 15.Regt., Cabar (Yugo.) 7. and 8.42	MURDER	YUGO.
ANARELLI	146101	M	Ital.		Commissar, Police, Dalmatia (Yugo.) 43	MURDER	YUGO.
ANCONA, Francesco	302155	M	Ital.		Capt., Carabinieri, stationed at Ploce near Metkovic, 42-43	TORTURE	YUGO.
ANDING, Alwin	259806	M	Aust.	8.10.14	Sgt., Staff-pioneer Bn.331, Raid (Neth.) 4.5.45	BRUTALITY	NETH.
ANDRESCH	185969	M	Rum.		SS-Sturmmann, C.C. Neu Brem near Saarbruecken (Ger.)	TORTURE	FR.
ANDRITSCHEK, Adam	134719	M	Hung.	18.9.98	Pvt.,Guard, SS, 3.SS Gren.Div., 2.Art. Regt., Dora-Nordhausen (Ger.) 43-45	MURDER	U.S.
ANEV	190715	M	Bulg.		Lt., Army Bulgarian, 7.Cavalry Squadron (Yugo.) 42-43	MURDER	YUGO.
ANGELLINI	146100	M	Ital.		Col., Army, 1.Regt. (Yugo.) 43	MURDER	YUGO.
ANGOLZI, Salvatore	190880	M	Ital.		Carabiniere, Italian Army, Sibenik,Vodice (Yugo.) 41-43	MURDER	YUGO.
ANGONA, Francesco	190879	M	Ital.		Capt., Italian Army, C.C.Ploce (Yugo.) 42-43	MURDER	YUGO.
ANKER, Daniel or Samuel	118706	M	Pol.	02	C.C.Buchenwald (Ger.)	MISC.CRIMES	FR.
ANNUSKY	157155	M	Russ.		Sgt., Army, Morlaix (Fr.) 44	MURDER	FR.
ANTANAS	190716	M	Bulg.		Pvt., Bulgarian Army, 27.Div., Blaca (Yugo.)	MURDER	YUGO.
ANTIMANTO, Vittorio	300006	M	Ital.		Lt. of Res., 7.Inf.Regt., "Cuneo" Div., Serifos, 11.41-9.43	MISC.CRIMES	GRC.
ANTONIOLLI, Alvaris	256979	M	Ital.		Cpl.,Fascist Republican Army, Tagl.VIII Alp.Regt., Dorenberg (Yugo.) 43-4.45	INTERR.	YUGO.
ANTONOF, Lazaros	300164	M	Bulg.		Member of the Drama Secret Police, Drama Area (Grc.) 28.9.-20.10.41	MURDER	GRC.
ANUSCHEWSKI, Stanislas	258903	M	Pol.		Feldgendarm., Feldgendarmerie, Valenciennes (Fr.) 40-44	MURDER	FR.
APATINI-FERNBACH, Peter	189956	M	Hung.		Governor, Government, Novi Sad (Yugo.)	MURDER	YUGO.
APOSTOLOV, Aleksander	190717	M	Bulg.		Lt.Col.,Commander, Frontier Detachment, Bulgarian Army, Poljanice, Kriva, Reca, Vladicinti (Yugo.) 2.43	MURDER	YUGO.
APRICHKINE	189121	M	Russ.		Camp-Guard, C.C.Dachau (Ger.)	MURDER	BEL.
ARALDI, Alberto	190881	M	Ital.		Vice-Brigadier, Italian Army, Sibenik, Vadenise (Yugo.) 41-43	MURDER	YUGO.
ARCHER, Umberto	162747	M	Ital.		Capitane, Italian Army, Administration Officer at C.C.Benevento (It.) 42	TORTURE	U.K.
ARESTA (see TISANI)	194290						
ARMANDO, Enrico	190882	M	Ital.		Lt.-General, Italian Army, Corps D'Armata, Sibenik (Yugo.) 43	MURDER	YUGO.
ARMELLINI, Q.	195529	M	Ital.		General, Italian Army, Brundno Fromnid Bukovica (Yugo.) 6.-7.42	MURDER	YUGO.
ARNAUDOV, Anastas Mihajlov	190718	M	Bulg.		Sgt., Bulgarian Army, 27.Inf.Div., Prokoplje (Yugo.) 43-44	MURDER	YUGO.
ARNOLD	23923	M	Czech.		Sgt., Waffen-SS, Lyon, Annecy, St.Gervais (Fr.)	PILLAGE	FR.

ART-BAU

NAME	C.R.FILE NUMBER	SEX	NATIO-NALITY	DATE OF BIRTH	RANK OCCUPATION UNIT PLACE AND DATE OF CRIME	REASON WANTED	WANTED BY
ARTMANN	186571	M	Aust.		Capt., Army, Athen (Grc.)	TORTURE	GRC.
ARTS, Suze	148428	F	Dut.		Guard, SS, C.C. Vught (Neth.)	MURDER	BEL.
ASANGER, Peter	156726	M	Aust.		NSDAP-Ortsgruppen-Propagandaleiter	MURDER	U.S.
ASCARI	250009	M	Ital.		Sgt.,Carabinieri, Split (Yugo.) 14.-16.4.42	BRUTALITY	YUGO.
ASCOLI, Arturie	72181	M	Ital.		Marseille (Fr.)	PILLAGE	FR.
ATANOSOV	190719	M	Bulg.		Lt., Bulg.Army, Art. Unit 5765 (Yugo.) 42-43	MURDER	YUGO.
ATHANASOV, Athanas	300167	M	Bulg.		Lawyer, Sidicrocastron (Grc.) 15.10.41	TORTURE	GRC.
ATZINGER	136319	M	Aust.	16	Interpreter, public official, prison Marseille (Fr.) 43-44	WITNESS	FR.
AUMAYR, Rupert	148751	M	Aust.	11	SS-Usturmfhr., C.C. Mauthausen (Aust.)	TORTURE	U.S.
AUSTONI	251946	M	Ital.		Dr., physician, Civilian, Split (Yugo.) 17.4.42	INTERR.	YUGO.
AVELKA	148240	M	Aust.		Scharfhr., SS, Nancy (Fr.) 43	TORTURE	FR.
AVRAMOV, Boris	190720	M	Bulg.		Mayor, municipality of Jelasnica, Surdulica (Yugo.) 22.3.42	MURDER	YUGO.
BACH, Franz	135120	M	Aust.	03	Cpl.,19 SS-Police-Rgt., Oberkrain (Yugo.), Toulouse, Compiegne, Tulle (Fr.) 5.41-3.44, 9-10.44	WITNESS	U.S.
BACHUTOW	261367	M	Russ.		Capt., Inf. 11.424 A, Rieux (Fr.) 2.9.44	MURDER	FR.
BADINI, Andrea	255507	M	Ital.		Major, 291 Inf.Rgt.,Zara-Div.,Kistanje (Yugo.) 42	BRUTALITY	YUGO.
BADIRIAN, Jakob	185401	M	Armenian		Interpreter in the occupied territory, Saloniki (Grc.)	MISC.CRIMES	GRC.
BAIG, Johann	185285	M	Hung.	12.2.98	SS-Mann, guard, 31 SS-Gren-Div., Art.Rgt., C.C. Dora-Nordhausen (Ger.) 43-45	WITNESS	U.S.
BAITCHEFF	300171	M	Bulg.		Lt., police, Sidicrocastron (Grc.) 5.43	MURDER	GRC.
BAJC, Andor	307267	M	Hung.	circa 00	Major, chief of counter-espionage, Backa and Baranja 41-44	MURDER	YUGO.
BAJKUSEV	189973	M	Alb.		Agent, police, Pirot (Yugo.)	TORTURE	YUGO.
BALABANOV	190721	M	Bulg.		Lt., Bulg.Army (Yugo.) 43-44	MURDER	YUGO.
BALAS	189955	M	Hung.		Agent, police (Hung.)	MURDER	YUGO.
BALBIS, Marco	190889	M	Ital.		Commander, Cpl.,Italian Army, Sibenik (Yugo.) 43	MURDER	YUGO.
BALDESCHI	162319	M	Ital.		Tenente, Italian Army, Art., Padula (It.) 42	TORTURE	U.K.
BALDI, Remido	250065	M	Ital.		Vice Brig. Etat Major, Carabinieri-Div., Santo Pietro di Tenda (It.) 19.-31.8.43	TORTURE	FR.
BALDUCCI	192075	M	Ital.		Lt., Fascist Army, Cupramontana (It.) 20.5.44	MURDER	U.K.
BALE, Leopold	72656	M	Aust.		Interpreter Adjutant, Army, St.Laurent du Manoir (Fr.) 13.-19.8.44	MURDER	FR.
BALKANSKI, Konstantin	190722	M	Bulg.		Chief of police, Agent, Police, Vladicin (Yugo.) 43-44	MURDER	YUGO.
BAMBERGER see BREMBERGER	162328						
BANCALARI	149624	M	Ital.		Army, 23 Rgt. "Fant Coma", "Isonzo" Div., Cernomelj(Yugo.) 43	MURDER	YUGO.
BANCALARI, Andreas	190884	M	Ital.		Bde-General, Ital.Army, XI Bn Carabinieri,Cetinje,Orna (Yugo.) 41-43	MURDER	YUGO.
BANDI, Sagi	261926	M	Hung.		See Consolidated List Part II - Appendix "A"		
BANKOV, Djordje	190723	M	Bulg.		Mayor, Veliko Bobince (Yugo.) 8.43	TORTURE	YUGO.
BAR, Willy	259406	M	Aust.		SS-Sturmscharfhr., Gestapo, area Poitiers (Fr.) 40-45	MISC.CRIMES	FR.
BARASI	189910	M	Ital.		Col., Italian Army	PILLAGE	FR.
BARBA	190885	M	Ital.		Capt., Italian Army, VI Rgt. of "Aosta Cavalry", Prapatnice Prgomet, Trogir-Dalmatia (Yugo.) 43	MURDER	YUGO.
BARBA	250049	M	Ital.		Major, Sassari Div., Kistanje (Yugo.) 6.41	PILLAGE	YUGO.
BARBALIA, Pietro	190886	M	Ital.		Lt.,Italian Army, Gracac (Yugo.) 41-43	MURDER	YUGO.
BARBERA, Gaspero	149623	M	Ital.		General, Army, Prefekt of Province Zara (Yugo.) 43	MURDER	YUGO.
BARBERO, Pietro	250048	M	Ital.		Col.,XVIII Corpodi Armata Sassari Div.,Biograd, Betina, Vodice (Yugo.) 42	MURDER	YUGO.
BARBIERI, Mario	300661	M	Ital.		Agent, prison of Krk (Yugo.) 41-43	TORTURE	YUGO.
BARCIA, Mario see BARELLI	169500						
BARDELLI, Renaldo	149621	M	Ital.		Lt., commander of garrison, Army, Gren.Rgt.,Losk, Potok (Yugo.) 43	MURDER	YUGO.
BARDINI, Karel	256983	M	Ital.		Sgt., Italian Army, Plave Anhovo (Yugo.) 13.-23.2.45	INTERR.	YUGO.
BARDOSSY	189954	M	Hung.		Prime Minister, public official (Hung.)	MURDER	YUGO.
BARDOVAGNI, Guido Ubaldo	250045	M	Ital.		Major, Italian Army, Ljubljana (Yugo.) 41-43	MISC.CRIMES	YUGO.
BARELA, Mario see BARELLI	169500						
BARELLI, Mario or BARELA or BARCIA	169500	M	Ital.		Lt.Col., Army, Chisti (It.) 7.42-9.43	TORTURE	U.K.
BARSA	144619	M	Czech.		C.C. Buchenwald (Ger.) 44	MISC.CRIMES	FR.
BARTELME	176558	M	Aust.		Oscharfhr., SS, Div.Totenkopf, C.C. Landweier (Ger.)	BRUTALITY	FR.
BARTHA	189953	M	Hung.		Minister of Defence, public official (Hung.)	MURDER	YUGO.
BARTOLINI, Alphonco	300168	M	Ital.		Lt.,Italian Army, Kymi Evea 3.42	MURDER	GRC.
BARTOLUCCI, Athos	190888	M	Ital.		Dr.,secretary, Governor General Secretario Federale,Sibenik (Yugo.) 41-11.42	MURDER	YUGO.
BASCIONI, Gino	149607	M	Ital.		Member Fasciste Italian, Belmonts (It.)	MURDER	U.K.
BASOLCHI	259134	M	Ital.		Maggiore, Commandant, Venezia-Div., Bn Bijelo Polja (Montenegro) 41-43	MISC.CRIMES	YUGO.
BASSANOW, Michel	261350	M	Russ.		Pvt., Unit 11424 A Inf., Rieux (Fr.) 2.9.44	MURDER	FR.
BASSI, E.	250634	M	Ital.		President, military court, Susak (Yugo.) 41-43	MISC.CRIMES	YUGO.
BASTIANINI, Giuseppe	149620	M	Ital.		Dr., Governor, public official, Sibenik (Yugo.) 8.41-7.42	MURDER	YUGO.
BATIK, Willi	192686	M	Aust.		Hptscharfhr., SS, SD, Wien (Aust.)	MURDER	NOR.
BATOLA, Carlo	190889	M	Ital.		Agent, Ital. Press Official of Cattaro (Yugo.) 41-43	MURDER	YUGO.
BATTISTI, Frederico	256995	M	Ital.		Cpl., Italian Army, Plave Anhovo (Yugo.) 13.,23.2.45	INTERR.	YUGO.
BATZIAVANOV, Theodoros	300338	M	Bulg.		Governor of the Bulg.Prefecture in Drama Area (Grc.)28.9.-20.10.41	MURDER	GRC.
BAUER	187527	M	Aust.	05	Agent, Abwehr, Lisbon (Port.)	MISC.CRIMES	U.S.
BAUER	189952	M	Hung.		Agent, police, Novi-Sad (Yugo.)	MURDER	YUGO.
BAUER, Johann	185280	M	Hung.	3.3.98	SS-Mann, 3 SS Gren.Art., C.C. Nordhausen (Ger.)	WITNESS	U.S.
BAUER, Josef	193971	M	Aust.		Truppfhr., SA, Hallein (Aust.) 43-45	TORTURE	CZECH.
BAUHOFER, Otto	170553	M	Aust.	12	Osturmfhr., SS, SD, Strassenhaus (Ger.)	MURDER	U.K.

BAU - BIA

NAME	C.R.FILE NUMBER	SEX	NATIO-NALITY	DATE OF BIRTH	RANK OCCUPATION UNIT PLACE AND DATE OF CRIME	REASON WANTED	WANTED BY
BAUMANN, Albert	195878	M	Inx.		Agent, SD, Maisons-Laffette (Fr.) 15.12.41-10.6.44	MISC.CRIMES	FR.
BAUMHOFER, Otto	192286	M	Aust.	09	Osturmfhr., SS, Rangsdorf (Ger.) 12.44	MURDER	U.S.
BAYOR, Vitez Ferenc	189951	M	Hung.		Gen., Army, Novi-Sad (Yugo.)	MURDER	YUGO.
BAZZOCCHI, Carlo	190890	M	Ital.		Commissar Governor General Italy, Podgorica, Trebrljevo, Sirogosto, Kolasin, Majkovac (Yugo.) 11.41	MURDER	YUGO.
BECHMANN, Willy	196126	M	Dut.		D.C.F., SD Kdo.z.b.V. 7 "Pullmer" BDS-France, Cirey (Fr.) 9.44	TORTURE	U.K.
BECKER	176565	M	Pol.		SS-Mann, C.C. Krispl (Aust.) 44	TORTURE	FR.
BECOCCI, N.	149619	M	Ital.		Officer, Army, Grobnicko Polje (Yugo.) 43	MURDER	YUGO.
BEGUCCI	190891	M	Ital.		Gen. Italian Army, Island of Brac (Yugo.) 6.8.43	MURDER	YUGO.
BEIGLBOECK	258567	M	Aust.		Dr. med., Stabsarzt, Army, Dachau (Ger.) 40-45	BRUTALITY	U.S.
BEKIAROF, Josef	300172	M	Bulg.		Lt.Col., Cmdt., 57 Bulgarian Army, Head of the Bulgarian Army and Armed Civil Servants, Drama Area (Grc.) 28.9.-20.10.41	MURDER	GRC.
BEKA	255568	M	Rum.		SD, Mauthausen (Aust.)	BRUTALITY	FR.
BELE	190892	M	Ital.		Agent, Italian Press Official of Cattaro, Kotor (Yugo.) 41-43	MURDER	YUGO.
BELEV, Aleksander	302150	M	Bulg.		Dr., Commissioner for Jewish Affairs, Sofia (Bulg.) 41-12.3.43	MISC.CRIMES	YUGO.
BELIANOF, Sevas	300173	M	Bulg.		Policeman, Bulgarian Police, Drama Area (Grc.) 28.9.-20.10.41	MURDER	GRC.
BELIONI, Luigi	190893	M	Ital.		Blackshirt, Italian SS, 215 Bn.Nizza, Sezane (Yugo.) 2.9.42	MURDER	YUGO.
BELLINI, Giovanni	300616	M	Ital.	12	Lt., Cmdt., Mayor and Secretary, Cmdt. of the Guardia Nazionale Republicana and of the Black Bde.at Mesola, Fascist Republican Party, Mesola, Ferrara, Adria, Rovigo (It.) 12.44	MURDER	U.K.
BELLINI, Luigi	307272	M	Ital.		Member of the Italian Fascist Black Bde., near Caselle Pressana Prov. Verona (It.) 6.1.45	MURDER	U.K.
BELIOMO, N.	193598	M	Ital.		Lt.Gen., Italian Army, Bari (It.) 11.41	MURDER	U.K.
BELLOSI, Luigi	191143	M	Ital.		Judge, Italian Special Court, Sibenik (Yugo.) 41-43	MURDER	YUGO.
BELOZZI	189909	M	Ital.		Major, Italian Army, Montenegro (Yugo.)	MURDER	FR.
BELTRAME, Giulio	252394	M	Ital.		Capt., Italian Army, Ljubljana (Yugo.) 41-43	MISC.CRIMES	YUGO.
BELTRAME, Livio	252925	M	Ital.		Lt., Ufficiale Osservator, Ital.Airman 113 Squadriglia O.A. Sosici (Yugo.) 12.7.43	INTERR.	YUGO.
BENDER, Friedrich	134750	M	Hung.	7.11.99	Pvt., Camp-Guard, SS, 31 Gren.Regt., 2 Artl.Regt., Nordhausen (Ger.) 43-45	WITNESS	U.S.
BENDER, Peter	134760	M	Hung.	16.10.99	Pvt., 4 SS Totenkopfsturmbann, Camp Dora Mittelbau Nordhausen (Ger.) 43-45	WITNESS	U.S.
BENECASA	162485	M	Ital.	98	Capt., Army Ital., C.C. Padula (It.) 7.42	TORTURE	U.K.
BENELI or BENELLI	300174	M	Ital.		Lt.Col., "Pinerolo"-Div., C.C. Larissa and Area. 41-43	MURDER	GRC.
BENINCASA, Antonio	196931	M	Ital.		Col., Military Tribunal, Ljubljana (Yugo.) 41-43	INTERR.	YUGO.
BENKO	261943	M	Hung.		Lt., 38 Regt.from Budapest, near the village of Belje (Yugo.) 18.4.41	MURDER	YUGO.
BENKO, Georg	162484	M	Aust.	15	Civilian, Arlon (Fr.) 3.9.44	MURDER	BEL.
BENSCH (Nickname JEEP)	191895	M	Czech.	05	Sgt., 5 Coy., 559 Landesschuetzen-Bn., C.C. (Czech., Ger.) 3.45	TORTURE	U.K.
BENTIVOGLIO, N.	252924	M	Ital.		Sgt.Maj., Pilot, Ital.Air Force, Visnja (Yugo.) 17.3.43	INTERR.	YUGO.
BENVENUTI, Leone	255506	M	Ital.		Lt. of the customs guard, Kistanje (Yugo.) 41	INTERR.	YUGO.
BERANI	149618	M	Ital.		Lt., Army "Lombarda"-Div., 79 Regt., 3 Bn., (Yugo.) 43	MURDER	YUGO.
BERARDI, Manlio	149617	M	Ital.		Lt.Col., Isonzo-Div., 24 Inf.Regt. "Como", (Yugo.) 43	MURDER	YUGO.
BERARDI, Paolo	149616	M	Ital.		Gen., Cmdt., Sassari-Div., (Yugo.) 43	MURDER	YUGO.
BEREOZ	189950	M	Hung.		Lt., Army Hungarian, Stari Becej (Yugo.)	MURDER	YUGO.
BERG	82	M	Aust. or Ger.		Lager Official, C.C. Lauderheide (Neth.) 5.42	TORTURE	NETH.
BERGER	158957	M	Aust.	95	Civilian, C.C. Khulengraben (Aust.) 12.43	TORTURE	U.K.
BERGER	173153	M	Fr.		Chief, Milice, C.C. Saales-Vosges (Fr.) 9.44	INTERR.	U.K.
BERGER, Josef	193459	M	Aust.	04	Pvt., 4-188 Kriegsgef.Arb.Kdo., C.C. Fjell (Nor.) 5.44	TORTURE	U.S.
BERGMEISTER, Otto	162486	M	Aust.	95	Capt., 2 Heer.Kuestenartl.Regt.981, Halsor, Vaagso (Nor.-Island) 6.-7.12.44	MURDER	NOR.
BERGONZI, A.	262425	M	Ital.		Corps-Gen., Cmdt., Ital.Army, Udine and Gorisia (It.) 42	MURDER	YUGO.
BERNACCHI	190894	M	Ital.		Carabinieri, Ital.Army, C.C. Montalbano (It.) 41-43	MISC.CRIMES	YUGO.
BERTELLI	190895	M	Ital.		Col., Ital.Army, Budva (Yugo.) 17.7.41	MURDER	YUGO.
BERTI, Giuseppe	300617	M	Ital.	15	Lt., Unit of the Italian Republican Army stationed at Rocca San Stefano, Prov.of Roma (It.) 14.5.44	MURDER	U.K.
BERTICO	149615	M	Ital.		Carabinieri, Army, Isle of Ebroula (Yugo.) 43	MURDER	YUGO.
BERTIZOLO	158350	M	Ital.		Civilian, Solagne (It.) 4.11.44	MURDER	U.K.
BERTONI	173242	M	Ital.		Col., Ital.Army, C.C. Caserta (It.) 9.42	MURDER	U.K.
BERTORELIX	190896	M	Ital.		Maj.Col., Ital.Army, Crna Gora (Yugo.) 41	MURDER	YUGO.
BERTOSI, Umberto	252299	M	Ital.		Cmdt., 10 Flottiglia Mas., St.Peter (Czech.) 16. Jand 24.1.45	MISC.CRIMES	YUGO.
BERZ, Artur	131164	M	Arg.		SA-Mann	TORTURE	BEL.
BESTA, Fabio	149613	M	Ital.		Col., Army, Lombardia-Div., 73 Inf.Regt., (Yugo.) 43	MURDER	YUGO.
BETTONI	172910	M	Ital.	07	Interpreter, Army, C.C. Tahuna (Africa) 2.42	MISC.CRIMES	U.K.
BEVELTSOF, Christos	300178	M	Bulg.		Officer, Bulgarian Army of Drama during 1941, Drama Area (Grc.) 28.9-20.10.41	MURDER	GRC.
BIANCHERI, Giovanni	256984	M	Ital.		Secretary of Town-Administration, Kastav (Yugo.) 41-43	SUSPECT	YUGO.
BIANCHI	300179	M	Ital.		Cpl., Medical Orderly, Inf.at Averof Prison, Athens (Grc.) 41-43	MURDER	GRC.
BIANCHI, Angel Antonio	259600	M	Ital.		Cmdt., Squadra d'Azione del Partito Fascista Republicano, Fonda-Littoria (It.) 9. - 10.43	TORTURE	YUGO.
BIANCHI, Arturo	259275	M	Ital.	05	See Consolidated List Part II Appendix "A"	PILLAGE	YUGO.
BIANCHI, Giovanni	149612	M	Ital.		Carabinieri, Ital.Army (Dalmatia-Yugo.) 7.42-8.43	MURDER	YUGO.
BIANCHI, Guido	149611	M	Ital.		Capt., Army, Kriegsgericht, Cettige (Yugo.) 43	MURDER	YUGO.
BIANCO, Ferruccio	300669	M	Ital.		Col., President of War Military Tribunal, Second Army Sezione di Sebenico, Sibenik-Dalmatia (Yugo.) 41-43	MISC.CRIMES	YUGO.

BIA-BOY

NAME	C.R.FILE NUMBER	SEX	NATIO-NALITY	DATE OF BIRTH	RANK OCCUPATION UNIT PLACE AND DATE OF CRIME	REASON WANTED	WANTED BY
BIAVATI, Guiseppe	256985	M	Ital.		See Consulidated List Part II Appendix "A"		
BIDJURI	29828	M	Russ.		Pvt.,Legion Georgian Castres,Castres (Fr.) 6.44	TORTURE	FR.
BIEBERHOFER, Theodor	192297	M	Aust.		Civilian, Salzburg (Aust.) 6.44	WITNESS	U.S.
BIGLINO, Eraldo	252862	M	Ital.	26.12.02	Milic. 2 Coy.,60.Bn.black shirt,Grosicchia (It.)13.7.43	PILLAGE	FR.
BIGLIO, Felice	307261	M	Ital.		Seniore,commandante,117 Bn.Mouronog 98 Fascist Legion attached to "Isonzo Div." 42-43	MURDER	YUGO.
BILAKOWA, Martha	167645	F	Hung.		Guard, Jail, St.Lo (Fr.) 7.6.44	MURDER	FR.
BINDER, Heinrich	240134	M	Aust.	28.11.96	Polizeirat, office of the Pol.President, Vienna (Aust.) 9.43	TORTURE	U.S.
BINDOLO	144942	M	Ital.		Carabinieri, Army (Yugo.) 43	MURDER	YUGO.
BINGEVSKI, Bosco	190724	M	Bulg.		Agent, Police, Vladidin Han. (Yugo.)	MURDER	YUGO.
BINNA	190897	M	Ital.		Dr.,prefetto,administration of occupied territories, Sibenik (Yugo.) 41-43	MURDER	YUGO.
BISANTI, J.	144941	M	Ital.		Major, Military Station, St.Anton (Yugo.) 42	MISC.CRIMES	YUGO.
BIRBAN, Wladimir	187977	M	Pol.	18.9.18	Civilian, Bruchsal (Ger.) 2.-3.2.45	WITNESS	U.K.
BISENNIUS, Leo (alias DUBOIS, Jean)	125151	M	Lux.		SD, La Bourboule, Leincot Dore (Fr.) 27.4.44	MURDER	FR.
BITFLINGMEYR, Jakob	185270	M	Hung.	95	SS-Mann, 3 SS Gren.Div.,C.C. Nordhausen-Dora,Dachau (Ger.)43-45	WITNESS	U.S.
BIZARRI, Vicenzo	259099	M	Ital.		Capt.,It.Army 56 Rgt."Marche" Div.,Stolac (Yugo.) 4.41-9.42	MURDER	YUGO.
BJORDJE	190725	M	Bulg.		Cpl.,Bulgarian Army, Inf.Rgt. Leskovac (Yugo.) 42-43	MURDER	YUGO.
BLAHA	258125	M	Aust.		Employee, C.C. Dachau (Ger.) 45	MURDER	BEL.
BLOSKEVITCH, Sabina	306906	F	Pol.	25	POW,employed as a servant by Mr.Lehrbass,Farm Gut Freydeck (Ger.) 2.7.45	MURDER	U.K.
BOBBER	132475	M	Yugo.		Col., Zagreb (Yugo.) 7.-8.5.45	MURDER	U.K.
BOBIN, Sigmund	193591	M	Pol.		Guard, C.C. Flossenburg (Ger.)	TORTURE	BEL.
BOCCA	190899	M	Ital.		Col., It.Army 82.Bn.Div. "Ferrara", Sarnik (Montenegro-Yugo.) 43	MURDER	YUGO.
BOCQUET	159370	M	Bel.		Militia, Folkling (Fr.) 11.44	MURDER	FR.
BODO	193595	M	Ital.		Col.Chief It.Army Police, Nice (Fr.) 43	TORTURE	FR.
BOETTI, Pier, Antonio	307285	M	Ital.		Centurione, judge, Military Court 2.Army section of Ljubljana (Yugo.) 41-43	MURDER	YUGO.
BOGDANOV	190727	M	Bulg.		Lt.Gen.Cmdr.of 7 Inf.Div. "Rila" Bulg.Army (Yugo.) 7.42-3.43	MURDER	YUGO.
BOGDANOV, Asen	190726	M	Bulg.		District Chief of Police, Skoplje (Yugo.) 43	MISC.CRIMES	YUGO.
BOJADZIJEV	190728	M	Bulg.		Lt., 7 Cavalry Squadron Bulg.Army Veliki Plana (Yugo.) 42-43	MURDER	YUGO.
BOLJOTINAC, Bajasit, Isa	189975	M	Alb.		Major, Albanian Army Kosuobes Mitrowica (Yugo.)	MURDER	YUGO.
BOLL	140394	M	Bel.	00	Agent, Gestapo, Bruxelles (Bel.) 15.6.43	MURDER	FR.
BOLLO	190900	M	Ital.		Capt., It.Army, Kistanje, Rogomaice (Yugo.) 42	MURDER	YUGO.
BOLO	190901	M	Ital.		Col., It.Army Makarska Ploca, Bari (Yugo.) 22.12.42	PILLAGE	YUGO.
BOLOGNE, Vittorio	144940	M	Ital.		Capt., 24.Inf.Rgt."Como", "Isonzo" Div.(Yugo.) 43	MURDER	YUGO.
BOLTAKJIS, Viktors	257788	M	Latv.		See Consulidated List Part II Appendix "A"		
BOLDUEV, Zarco	190729	M	Bulg.		Agent, Police Predejan, Repiste Distr.of Vladidin H_n (Yugo.) 22.2.43-23.3.43	MURDER	YUGO.
BONATTI, Bruno	259178	M	Ital.	15	Tenente, W.O. of Batt.Cmdr.Andrijevica (Yugo.) 41-43	MISC.CRIMES	YUGO.
BOMAYUTO, Felice	300187	F	Ital.		Marecniallo with Carabinieri Reali at Corfu (Political Department)1044	TORTURE	GRC.
BONES, Kathi	187978	F	Aust.		Civilian, St. Lorenzen (Aust.) 2.4.44	WITNESS	U.S.
BONGIOVANNI, Guiseppe	190902	M	Ital.		Col., It.Army 1.Bn.83 Rgt. Div. "Venetia" Podgorica (Montenegro-Yugo.) 9.-11.42, 8.43	MURDER	YUGO.
BONIFACI	259125	M	Ital.		Camp leader, head of internment camp Pistici (It.) 41-43	BRUTALITY	YUGO.
BONITO-OLIVA, Achille	163285	M	Ital.		Col., It.Army Inf.C.C. Capua (It.) 27.1.43	TORTURE	U.K.
BONOMO, Giovanni	149630	M	Ital.		Tenente Medico, Army 24. Inf.Rgt. "Como", "Isonzo" Div. (Yugo.) 43	MURDER	YUGO.
BONONI, Felice	252011	F	Ital.		Judge, investigator Civilian Splitt (Yugo.) 17.4.42	MURDER	YUGO.
BONPACE or BONNAPACE, Renzo	193939	M	Ital.	09	Capt., Chass.Alp.chief S.R.It.Div. "Pusteria" Fontaine Par Grenoble (Fr.) 3.3.43	MISC.CRIMES	FR.
BOPPE-BIANCO	194111	M	Ital.		Civilian chief,physician Prison Military Cuneo (It.) 9.-10.44	TORTURE	FR.
BORDON, Luigi	300618	M	Ital.		Milite Black Bde, Mesola Ferrara Adria Rovigo (It.) 12.44	MURDER	U.K.
BORELLI, Vincenzo	190903	M	Ital.	11.5.11	Carabiniere, It.Army Sibenik Lezovak (Yugo.) 41-43	MURDER	YUGO.
BORGHESE, Prince Valerio	252014	M	Ital.		Cmdt., Army X Flottiglia MAS, Comagliano (It.) 12.43-4.45	MISC.CRIMES	YUGO.
BORRINI, Carlo	300619	M	Ital.		Vice Brigadier, order of public security, Mesola, Ferrara, Adria, Rovigo, (It.) 12.44	MURDER	U.K.
BORRUZO, Pietro	190904	M	Ital.		Major, It.Army, 3.Btty. 151 Rgt. Fanteria "Sassari" Div., Fara Slovenia (Yugo.) summer 41	MURDER	YUGO.
BORSI, Sebastiano	259133	M	Ital.		Vice Brigadiere of C.C. R.R., IV It.Partisan Bde,Bera-Podjorica, Berane (Montenegro-Yugo.) 41-43	MISC.CRIMES	YUGO.
BOSDARI, Avv. Francesco Saverio	255510	M	Ital.		Capt., member, Tribunal, Kotor (Yugo.) 41-43	INTERR.	YUGO.
BOSSANT, Gustav	27708	M	Bel.		Agent, Gestapo, Bruges (Bel.)	MURDER	FR.
BOTA	256986	M	Ital.	10	Cmdt., Albania Fascist Milita, Nikiforovo,Mavrove-Leunovo (Yugo.)9.43	PILLAGE	YUGO.
BOTCHER (see BOTKER)	174763						
BOTH, Philipp	193532	M	Hung.	27.5.96	SS-Mann, SS Totenk.Stuba,C.C.Mittelbau-Dora-Nordhausen (Ger.) 43-45	MURDER	U.S.
BOTSVAROF,Pervan (or PETSVAROF)	305224	M	Bulg.		Major,Engineer,Ferdinand-Bulgaria,Drama Area (Grc.) 28.9.-20.10.41	MURDER	GRC.
BOTTIGLIANI (or MONTIGLIANI)	300190	M	Ital.		Capt.,or Lt., "Forli" Div. C.C. Larisa, 41-43	MURDER	GRC.
BOTKER (BOTCHER)	174763	M	Pol.		Interpreter, Kriegsgefangenen Arb.Bn. 185, Aspfjord (Nor.)	TORTURE	NOR.
BOTSEV, Bonef (or VOTSEF)	305351	M	Bulg.		Capt.,engineer Corps, (Transport) Sidirocastron (Grc.) 41	MURDER	GRC.
BOUQUET, Carlos	193564	M	Bel.	13	SS-Mann, SD, Sipo, Leeuwarden (Neth.) 13.9.44-14.4.45	MURDER	NETH.
BOUTOURIAN	185421	M	Ital.		Civil.serv.Territ. Occupied Athen (Grc.) 9.43	MURDER	GRC.
BOUXIL, Alexandre	159385	M	Ital.		Pvt., Army stationed at Moncontour, Monteise (Fr.) 1.8.44	PILLAGE	FR.
BOYDES, Axel	176144	M	Dan.		Member, Gestapo	MURDER	FR.
BOYLAN, Angelef	305002	M	Bulg.		Lt., Cmdr.of a Coy. Psychico, Serres, 43-44	MURDER	GRC.

BOZ-CAM

NAME	C.R. FILE NUMBER	SEX	NATIONALITY	DATE OF BIRTH	RANK OCCUPATION UNIT PLACE AND DATE OF CRIME	REASON WANTED	WANTED BY
BOZILOV	190730	M	Bulg.		Lt., Commander of police unit attached to 27 Inf.Div., Prokuplje (Yugo.) 43-44	MURDER	YUGO.
BOZZI	300620	M	Ital.		Capt., Campo 52, Chiavari (It.) 12.41-10.42	TORTURE	U.K.
BRAGGA	150583	M	Csech.		SD official, Marseille (Fr.)	MISC. CRIMES	FR.
BRANCATI, Corrado	190905	M	Ital.		SS Oberstgruppenfhr., Fascist, Miliz, Sibenik (Yugo.) 41-43	MURDER	YUGO.
BRAND, Stephan	195667	M	Ukr.	7.11.27	SS-Mann, Waffen SS, Pecany (Czech.) 1.2.45	MURDER	CZECH.
BRANDL, Franz	140764	M	Aust.		NCO, member SA, Hallein (Aust.) 38-45	MISC. CRIMES	U.S.
BRANDL, Fritz	257187	M	Aust.		Sturmbannfhr., Waffen SS, 1 Bn., 3 Coy, Rgt."Der Fuehrer", Fort de Nieppe (Fr.) 5.40	SUSPECT	U.K.
BRANDT, Josef	185368	M	Hung.	96	Pvt., SS Totenkopf Stuba, CC Dachau, Dora-Nordhausen (Ger.)	WITNESS	U.S.
BRANDT, Leonie	149718	F	Dut.		CC Ravensbrueck (Ger.) 8.43-11.44	TORTURE	FR.
BRANDSTAETTER, Anton	159810	M	Aust.-Ger.	10.1.01	SS Mann, SS Totenkopf, Dest (Ger.) 39	WITNESS	U.S.
BRAUN, Martin	174227	M	Rum.	21.8.12	SSGuard, between Wien and Mauthausen (Aust.) 1.-18.4.43	WITNESS	U.S.
BRAUN, Michael	260934	M	Hung.	4.11.22	SS-Mann, SS Guard, CC Auschwitz (Pol.) 42-44	BRUTALITY	POL.
BRAUNER, Karl	258381	M	Aust.	05	Civ., Employee of Sauerwerke, Vienna (Aust.) autumn 44, spring 45	MURDER	U.S.
BRAUNITZER, Joseph	135220	M	Hung.	19	Hungarian army, Belsen (Hung.) 15.4.45	MURDER	U.K.
BRAVO	194706	M	Span.		Guard, CC Mauthausen (Aust.)	TORTURE	FR.
BREDAROS	253823	M	Ital.	4.4.27	Agent, SD Toulouse (Fr.) 11.42-8.44	MISC. CRIMES	FR.
BREDOUL	187648	M	Dut.		Pvt., Army, Goudrian (Neth.) 22.5.44	MURDER	U.K.
BREIER, Alois	253809	M	Aust.		Pvt., Guard, Camp 139-L, Middle Steyrmark (Aust.) 41	INTERR.	U.K.
BREITFUSS, Matthias	159843	M	Aust.	1.10.99	Civ., NSDAP, Maishofen (Aust.) 2.44	TORTURE	U.S.
BREMBERGER or BAMBERGER	162328	M	Csech.	circa95	Pvt., 3 Coy, Lds.Schtz.Bn.877, CC Liexen (Aust.) 44-45	TORTURE	U.K.
BREZZI	190906	M	Ital.		Maggiore, Ital.Army, Vosnic (Yugo.) 7.41	PILLAGE	YUGO.
BRION, Marcel	196108	M	Bel.		SD, Prison, CC Heerenveen Crackstate (Neth.) 15.4.45	MURDER	NETH.
BRUCCIAMONTE	193547	M	Ital.		Brig., Ital.Army, Carabinieri, Petrovac (Yugo.) 8.41	MURDER	YUGO.
BRUCKNER, Leopold or Josef	190355	M	Aust.	06	Detachment leader, 3 Coy, 891 or 391 Lds.Schtz.Bn., Stalag XVIII A Wolfsberg-Marburg (Ger.) 2.-3.44	MISC. CRIMES	U.K.
BRUGGLER, Joseph	196109	M	Aust.		Leader NSDAP, CC Krispl (Aust.)	TORTURE	NETH.
BRUNO	149629	M	Ital.		Carabiniere, Army, Isle of Korkula (Yugo.) 43	MURDER	YUGO.
BRUNNER	148497	M	Aust.	15	SS Hptsturmfhr., Drancy (Fr.) 43-44	TORTURE	FR.
BRUNNER	148516	M	Aust.-Ger.		SS Hptsturmfhr., SD, CC Drancy (Fr.) 44	TORTURE	FR.
BRUNNER, Hans	187980	M	Aust.		Civ., Sankt Lorenzen (Aust.) 2.4.44	WITNESS	U.S.
BRUNO, Camillo	190907	M	Ital.		Deputy Prefect, Zara Province, Sibenik (Yugo.) 6.42-9.42	MURDER	YUGO.
BUCARI, Giorgio	259106	M	Ital.		Lt., Ital.Army, 56 Rgt. "Marche"-Div., Stolac (Yugo.) 4.41-9.42	MURDER	YUGO.
BUCCERINI	149628	M	Ital.		Col., Army, Kriegsgericht, Cettigne (Yugo.) 43	MURDER	YUGO.
BUCCILLI, Renato	254485	M	Ital.		Major, Ital.Army, Tribunal, Ljubljana (Yugo.) 41-43	INTERR.	YUGO.
BUCHER	194787	M	Aust.	95	Lagerfuehrer, 107 Grenzwacht, CC Wetzeldorf (Aust.) 2.45	TORTURE	U.K.
BUEHLER	147956	M	Aust.		Sgt., Waffen SS, Nancy (Fr.) 43	TORTURE	FR.
BUGATTI	254287	M	Csech.		SS, CC Auschwitz (Pol.)	BRUTALITY	FR.
BUIOLI	149627	M	Ital.		Carabiniere, Army Fasciste, Isle of Korcula (Yugo.) 43	MURDER	YUGO.
BULIONI, Italo	259132	M	Ital.		Major, Venezia Div., 1 Bn., 84 Rgt., Andrijevica-Montenegro (Yugo.) 8.41-9.42	MISC. CRIMES	YUGO.
BULLO, Atillio	259194	M	Ital.		Lt., Ital.Army, "Marche"-Div., 56 Rgt., Stolac (Yugo.) 4.41-9.42	MURDER	YUGO.
BUNGARA, Guiseppe	190908	M	Ital.		Capt., Ital. Army, officer of carabinieri, Sibenik (Yugo.) 41-43	MURDER	YUGO.
BUORO, Antoine	185647	M	Ital.		Pvt., Member, Ital.Army, Gestapo, Dordogne (Fr.)	MISC. CRIMES	FR.
BURASSO	254285	M	Ital.		Photographer, Air Force, Ital., Slovenia (Yugo.) 8.-9.42	INTERR.	YUGO.
BURGER, Konrad	255085	M	Hung.	14.7.99	SS Mann, Waffen SS, Nordhausen (Ger.)	MURDER	U.S.
BURGERMEISTER, Stefan	185230	M	Hung.	95	SS Mann, 31 SS Inf.Rgt., CC Nordhausen (Ger.) 43-45	WITNESS	U.S.
BURGIO, Francesco	149626	M	Ital.		Commander, Army, 98 Fascist Legion, "Isonzo"-Div., Trebnje (Yugo.) 43	MURDER	YUGO.
BURK, Frans	149750	M	Yugo.	5.12.21	19 SS Polizei Rgt., 2 Bn.	MISC. CRIMES	FR.
BUSSIERI, Antonio	259167	M	Ital.		Head of Banda Volontaria Anticommunista, Biovixcino, Selo, Kistanje, Ivosevci (Yugo.) 5.-6.42	SUSPECT	YUGO.
BUTTI, Giuseppe	149625	M	Ital.		Cmdt., Army, Carabinieri Reali, Dalmatia (Yugo.) 43	MURDER	YUGO.
BUZDUGAN, Gheorghe	307334	M	Rum.		Sgt. Major, Timisul de Jos near Brasov (Rum.) 4.-5.44	BRUTALITY	U.K.
CAGNE	192238	M	Ital.		Lt., Ital.Army, 10 Bn. Chasseurs alpins, Hauteville, Gondon (Fr.) 8.43	PILLAGE	FR.
CAINE, Cesarino	256990	M	Ital		Pvt., Ital.Army, Execution Squad, Plave (Yugo.) 13.2.45-23.2.45	INTERR.	YUGO.
CAIVTER	301552	M	Rum.-Hung.		SS Overseer at Breendonck CC, 44	MURDER	BEL.
CAKABOV, Peter	190731	M	Bulg.		Deputy Director, District Police, Vranje, Vladicin Han (Yugo.) 43-44	MURDER	YUGO.
CALANCHI, Umberto	137618	M	Ital.		Capt., Ital.Army, CC San Guiseppe-Sicily (It.) 12.42-1.43	MISC. CRIMES	U.K.
CALCATERRA V.E.	106973	M	Ital.		Col., Cmdt., Camp 57, Udine (It.) 20.5.43, 9.43, 45	MURDER	U.K.
CALCETERA	125362	M	Ital.		Camp Col., CC Bindasi (It.) 42-43	TORTURE	U.K.
CALDONE, Firrao N.	178326	M	Ital.	95	Major Gen., Army, Athens (Grc.) autumn 41, autumn 42	TORTURE	U.K.
CALETTI, Nello	190927	M	Ital.		Pvt., Ital.Army, Brigadiere Carabinieri, Susak (Yugo.) 41-42, 4.43	MURDER	YUGO.
CALLIGARIS, Mario	252002	M	Ital.		Observer, Ital.Airforce, Gruppe 240, 43.Sturm Bn. 98, Polica, Podpesek, Metnaj, Babna (Yugo.) 8.-9.42	INTERR.	YUGO.
CALZA, Carlo	145741	M	Ital.		Lt., 24 Inf.Rgt. "Como" II Bn. "Isonzo"-Div. (Yugo.) 43	MURDER	YUGO.
CAMBA, Charlie	252045	M	Fr.		F.C.F., SD Kdo. "Wenger", Baccarat Etival (Fr.)	MURDER	U.K.
CAMBIBASIO, Angelo	185907	M	Ital.	10.-15	Fascist, Trescore (It.) 4.1.45	MURDER	U.S.
CAMELLI, Guido	190909	M	Ital.		Secretary, Fascio at Blato of Korcula Island (Yugo.), first half of 43	MURDER	YUGO.
CAMILLO	169474	M	Ital.		Dr., Capt., Ital.Army, CC Capua (It.) 4.41-6.43	TORTURE	U.K.
CAMMER	137617	M	Alb.	13 - 15	Civ., Tirana (Alb.) 8.1.44	MISC. CRIMES	U.K.
CAMOUSSO, Cesare	300203	M	Ital.		Maresciallo, Chief of the Carabinieri Reali, of CC warders, Averof Prison, Athens (Grc.) 41-43	MURDER	GRC.
CAMPASSI	256991 A	M	Ital.		Pvt., Ital.Army, Plave Anhovo (Yugo.) 13.-23.2.45	INTERR.	YUGO.
CAMPELLI, Enrico	120005	M	Ital.	2.1.05	Supervisor, Prison, San Remo (It.) 16.7.43-3.44	TORTURE	YUGO. FR.

CAN-CHA

NAME	C.R.FILE NUMBER	SEX	NATIO-NALITY	DATE OF BIRTH	RANK OCCUPATION UNIT PLACE AND DATE OF CRIME	REASON WANTED	WANTED BY
CANADA, Calcedonis	190910	M	Ital.		Lt.Col., Commandor, Ital.-Army, XI Bn. of Carabinieri, Cetinje Orna Gora (Yugo.) 41.42.43	MURDER	YUGO.
CANATA	300368	M	Ital.		Lt.,26 Bn. Royal Carabinieri, Casta Hamlet Corsica(Fr.)19.-31.8.43	TORTURE	FR.
CANATA, G.	145740	M	Ital.		Lt.Col.,3 Btty. Metlika, Cernomelj (Yugo.) 43	MURDER	YUGO.
CANCEV, Georgie	190756	M	Bulg.		Lt., Bulg.-Army,27 Inf.Div.,67 Regt., Blaca Serbia (Yugo.) 43-44	MURDER	YUGO.
CANDIDA, Renato	190911	M	Ital.		Kapo, Ital.-Army del Posto de Carabinieri, Kotor (Yugo.) 41-43	MURDER	YUGO.
CANEV, Jlija	190732	M	Bulg.		Chief of Police, Bulg.-Army, 27 Inf.Div. (Yugo.) 43-44	MURDER	YUGO.
CANINO, Ignacio	190912	M	Ital.		O.C., Ital.-Army,259 Regt. of Murge-Div., Trebine Boski, Jubine(Yugo)43	MURDER	YUGO.
CANIONI	251987	M	Ital.		Cmdt.,Lt.Col.,60 Bn."Black Chemises", Croicchia (Fr.) 13.7.43	PILLAGE	FR.
CANKOV, Hristo	190733	M	Bulg.		Mayor, occupied territories, Ciradesnica, Pirot (Yugo.) 42-43	MISC.CRIMES	YUGO.
CANTARELLA, Roberto	250088	M	Ital.		Lt., Cmdt., La Temenza di Zaravecchia (Yugo.) 43	INTERR.	YUGO.
CANTATORE, Vittorio	145739	M	Ital.		Lt., Carabinieri Reali, XIV Bn., Cernomelj (Yugo.) 42	MURDER	YUGO.
CAPELINI (see Toneti)	191130						
CAPIGATI, Guiseppe	259105	M	Ital.		Lt.Col., Ital.-Army,56 Regt. "Marche"-Div., Stolag (Yugo.),4.41-9.42	MURDER	YUGO.
CAPITANO, Gino	190913	M	Ital.		Major, Ital.-Army,55 Regt. "Marche"-Div., Trebine (Yugo.)20.4.41-8.9.43	MURDER	YUGO.
CAPO, Luigi	193891	M	Ital.		Leader,Ital.Red Cross,C.C.Cuneo (It.) 9.43	MURDER	FR.
CAPOBIANCO, Donato	162752	M	Ital.		Lt.Col., Ital.-Inf.,O.C.Fermo (It.) 43	TORTURE	U.K.
CAPOGROSSO (or CAVAGNIN)	145738	M	Ital.		Major, Army, Dalmatia (Yugo.) 43	PILLAGE	YUGO.
CAPORALI, Dante	252040	M	Ital.		Lt.Col., Cmdt., Chiesanuova (It.) 42-43	INTERR.	YUGO.
CAPPELLI	193892	M	Ital.		General,Military Court, Breil s-Roya (Fr.) 9.43	MURDER	FR.
CAPRIOLO, Georgio	190914	M	Ital.		Adjutant,Div. "Messina" aide de Camp Bfrane (Yugo.) 7.-9.41	MURDER	YUGO.
CAPURSO	163282	M	Ital.	circa 95	Col., Ital.-Army,O.C.Macerata (It.) 6.-9.43	MISC.CRIMES	U.K.
CAPUTI, Pietro	250086	M	Ital.		See Part II Appendix A		
CARATINI, Amlete	162751	M	Ital.		Col., Cmdt. of PG 87,Ital.-Cav.,O.C.Benevento (It.) 7.-11.42	TORTURE	U.K.
CARBONARI	145736	M	Ital.		Carabiniere, Army, Isle of Koroula (Yugo.) 43	MURDER	YUGO.
CARBONI	145735	M	Ital.		Carabiniere, Army, Isle of Koroula (Yugo.) 43	MURDER	YUGO.
CARELLI, Guiseppe	190915	M	Ital.		Major, Ital.-Army,53 Regt. "Marche"-Div., Trebinje (Yugo.)4.41-9.43	MURDER	YUGO.
CARETTO, Anunzio	190916	M	Ital.		Col., Ital.-Army, Bersaglieri, Trogir (Yugo.) 5.41	TORTURE	YUGO.
CARIGNANI, Ferdinando	250085	M	Ital.		Lt.Col., Ital.-Army, Ljubljana (Yugo.) 41-43	MISC.CRIMES	YUGO.
CARINCIA	259124	M	Ital.		Member, staff of internment camp, Jstonic-Marina, Pistici, Fabriano(It.) 41-43	BRUTALITY	YUGO.
CARLETTO, Achili	300664	M	Ital.		Agent, Prison at Krk, (It.) 41-43	TORTURE	YUGO.
CARLI	250935	M	Ital.		Agent, Police, Split (Yugo.)	TORTURE	YUGO.
CARLI, Giovanni	145734	M	Ital.		Lt.Col., "Isonzo"-Div., Novo Mesto (Yugo.) 43	MURDER	YUGO.
CARLUCCI	152020	M	Ital.		Lt., Ital.-Army,58 R.A., Frejus (Fr.) 7.1.43	PILLAGE	FR.
CARLUCCI	192078	M	Ital.		Capt., Fascist Military, Sap Vicino near Cerretto d' Esi (It.)	MURDER	U.K.
CARONE	190918	M	Ital.		Agent, Press and Propaganda Italian, Kotor (Yugo.) 41	MURDER	YUGO.
CAROSSI	256992	M	Ital.		Vice-Ble., Ital.-Army, Plave Anhovo (Yugo.) 13.-23.2.45	INTERR.	YUGO.
CAROZZI	300204	M	Ital.	97	Capt., Interpreter, Campo PG-57, Gruppignano and Udine (It.)10.42-10.43	MISC.CRIMES	U.K.
CARR, William	155764	M	Dan.		Consul-General, Civ., Wilhelmshaven (Ger.)	MURDER	U.K.
CARRETTO	300678	M	Ital.		Capt., Medical-officer,40 Bn., Italian Republican Guard, Stationed at San Michele (It.) 6.11.43	MURDER	U.K.
CARRUSO, Pietro	190919	M	Ital.		Cpl. of Ital."Extraor Dinary Court", Sibenik (Yugo.) 41-43	MURDER	YUGO.
CASABUONI, Conrado	191144	M	Ital.		Judge, Ital.Special Court, Sibenik (Yugo.) 41-43	MURDER	YUGO.
CASAGRANDE	256994	M	Ital.		Pvt., Ital.-Army, Plave, Anhovo (Yugo.)13.-23.2.45	INTERR.	YUGO.
CASANEGRO	191163	M	Ital.		Official, Engineer, operating in Yugo. (Yugo.) 42	TORTURE	YUGO.
CASCI, Giovanni	190920	M	Ital.		Pvt., Ital.-Army, Sibenik (Yugo.) 41-43	MURDER	YUGO.
CASELLI	190921	M	Ital.		Pvt., Ital.-Army,O.C.Montalbano (Yugo.) 41-43	MISC.CRIMES	YUGO.
CASSETTO, Pietro	145729	M	Ital.		Major,24 Inf.Regt."Como", "Isonzo"-Div. (Yugo.) 43	MURDER	YUGO.
CASSU, Giovanni	145727	M	Ital.		Carabiniere, Carabinieri-Station, Sibenik (Yugo.) 42	MURDER	YUGO.
CASULLO, Filipo di Guissepe	137615	M	Ital.		Pvt., Guard, Ital.-Army,O.C., Bari (It.) 16.7.42	MURDER	U.K.
CASTAGLIONI, Massimo	191145	M	Ital.		General-Consul, Vice-Chairman of Italian "Special Court" in Sibenik (Yugo.) 41-43	MURDER	YUGO.
CASTAGNOLI, Bruno	145728	M	Ital.		Lt., Army, Novo Mesto (Yugo.) 42	MURDER	YUGO.
CASTELLANI, Leopoldo	195625	M	Ital.		Bde.-Gen.,Military, 41-43	MURDER	YUGO.
CASTELLI-TADDEI, Mario	173273	M	Ital.		Col., Ital.-Army,O.C.Chiavari (It.)	TORTURE	U.K.
CASTIGLINI, Alfredo	251482	M	Ital.		Lt., Ital.Air Force,113 Squadriglia,63 Gruppe,21 Stormo,Village Hrastov-Dol and Trnovica (Yugo.) 31.7.43	INTERR.	YUGO.
CATALDI, Giovanni Battista	189904	M	Ital.		Capt., Ital.-Army, Montenegro (Yugo.)	MURDER	YUGO.
CATARY, Vitez	189949	M	Hung.		Lt., Hungary-Army, Senta (Yugo.)	MURDER	YUGO.
CATTANI, Anna Maria (Nick-name: "Donna Paola")	300621	F	Ital.	circa 15	Nurse, Mesola, Ferrara, Adria, Rovigo (It.) 12.44	MURDER	U.K.
CAVAGNIN (see CAPOGROSSO)	145738						
CAVALERRI, Giorgio	259123	M	Ital.		Lt., Ital.-Army,56 Regt. "Marche"-Div., Stolag (Yugo.) 4.41-9.42	MURDER	YUGO.
CAVANO	300205	M	Ital.		Capt., "Forli"-Div.,O.C.Larissa, 41-43	MURDER	GRC.
CAVAZZONI	190923	M	Ital.		Member,Fascist.Military,Sibenik (Yugo.) 41-43	MURDER	YUGO.
CAVENDA	148914	M	Pol.	95	Guard,C.C.Morderney (Ger.)	TORTURE	FR.
CAWTER	192320	M	Rum.		Guard,O.C.Breendonck (Bel.) 4.-5.44	MURDER	BEL.
CECCHINI, Attilio	258165	M	Ital.		Sgt., Tagliamento VIII Alp.-Regt.,2 Bn., Fasc.-Republ.-Army, Dorenberg (Yugo.) 12.43-4.45	INTERR.	YUGO.
CECCIONI,	190924	M	Ital.		Dr., Commissar, Ital.-Army, Fraschette O.C. for div. at Alatri(It.)41-43	MURDER	YUGO.
CECCONI	141463	M	Ital.		Lt., Ital.-Army, Petreto, Bicchisane, Corse (Fr.)	MURDER	FR.
CELLINI, Candido	193548	M	Ital.		Sgt., Ital.-Army, Carabinieri, Banovina, Zevska (Yugo.) 41	MURDER	YUGO.
CENEV, N.	190734	M	Bulg.		Director, Police, Babusnica, Pirot district (Yugo.) 41-44	MURDER	YUGO.
CENKOV, Mirko	190735	M	Bulg.		Deputy, Director of district Police, Vranje, Vladicin, Han(Yugo.) 43-44	MURDER	YUGO.
CENOV, Ivan	190736	M	Bulg.		Chief of Police, Vladicin, Han (Yugo.) 43-44	MURDER	YUGO.
CENTONZE, Francesko	190925	M	Ital.		Dr., Fascist-Party, Army, Sibenik (Yugo.) 41-43	MURDER	YUGO.
CERETANI	189902	M	Ital.		Major, Venezia-Army, Montenegro (Yugo.)	PILLAGE	YUGO.
CERKEZOV	190737	M	Bulg.		Lt., Bulg.-Army,1 Coy.,122 Bn., Litni Potek (Yugo.) 43-44	MURDER	YUGO.
CERUTTI, Guido	145722	M	Ital.		Brigadier, Ink.-Div., Novo Mesto (Yugo.) 42	MURDER	YUGO.
CERVANTES (alias:FERNANDES)	167915	M	Span.		S.D., St.Lo (Fr.) 6.-7.6.44	MURDER	FR.
CESI, Antonio	189901	M	Ital.		Capt., Ital.-Army, Montenegro (Yugo.)	MURDER	YUGO.
CESNOVAR, Joseph	120031	M	Yugo.		Bethune (Fr.)	MURDER	FR.
CHAKANOF, Kusek	186676	M	Russ.		Lt., Army, Russ., Plozevet (Fr.)	MURDER	FR.

CHA-CON

NAME	C.R.FILE NUMBER	SEX	NATIO-NALITY	DATE OF BIRTH	RANK OCCUPATION UNIT PLACE AND DATE OF CRIME	REASON WANTED	WANTED BY
CHAPINSKY	194322	M	Pol.		Camp-doctor, C.C., Mauthausen (Aust.) 44	MURDER	FR.
CHELOTTI, Carlo	307273	M	Ital.		Lt.,Off.in charge of Detachm.,C.PG-106 Vercelli West of Milan(It.)42	MURDER	U.K.
CHERMIZA see ZCHEMITZA	196028						
CHIARPAGRINI	252000	M	Ital.		Capt.,1 Coy.,59 Rgt.,Santo-Pietro-Di-Tenda (Fr.) 19.8.-31.8.44	TORTURE	FR.
CHIBIDZIURA	149182	M	Aust.		Civilian, Graz (Aust.)	MURDER	FR.
CHIDOROW, Kurban	120049	M	Russ.	14	Pvt.,Turcoman Legion,C.C., Poornet (Sov.Un.)	MURDER	FR.
CHIMIELEVSKY	250966	M	Ital.		Fiscist "Federale",Split (Yugo.) 6.1.41	TORTURE	YUGO.
CHINICI, Dominico	189900	M	Ital.		General, Italian Army, Montenegro (Yugo.)	MURDER	YUGO.
CHIODI	145718	M	Ital.		Lt., Army, (Yugo.) 42	MURDER	YUGO.
CHITTER, Lydia	149183	F	Lux.		Conc.Camp,Ravensbrueck (Ger.)	MISC.CRIMES	FR.
CHMIMIELEVSKI, Alfred	252003	M	Ital.		Merchant,Civilian, Split (Yugo.)	PILLAGE	YUGO.
CHOROCHI, Siegmund	251989	M	Pol.		Guard, C.C., Auschwitz (Pol.)	TORTURE	FR.
CHOURA	149184	M	Russ.		Conc.Camp,Ravensbrueck (Ger.)	TORTURE	FR.
CHRISTEF, Christos	300206	M	Bulg.		Lt.Col.,Head,Military Command,Drama,Head of Section of the Bulgarian Army and Armed Civil Servants,Drama (Grc.) 28.9.-20.10.41	MURDER	GRC.
CHRISTEF, Kyrillos	300207	M	Bulg.		Sgt.-Major,Bulgarian Army,Drama Area (Grc.) 28.9.-20.10.41	MURDER	GRC.
CHRISTIANINI, Nello	300211	M	Ital.		Black Bde.,Frasinelle,Rovigo (It.) 2.8.44	MISC.CRIMES	U.K.
CHROMIK	193893	M	Pol.		Civilian,St.Rambert (Fr.)	MURDER	FR.
CIACCIO, Luigi	190926	M	Ital.		Col.,Italian Army,Lustica-Dalm,Djurasevic (Yugo.) 9.9.43	MURDER	YUGO.
CIAMPAULO, Rolando	259104	M	Ital.		Lt.,Italian Army,56 Rgt., "Marche"-Div.,Stolac (Yugo.) 4.41-9.42	MURDER	YUGO.
CIANCABILLA	189899	M	Ital.		Col.,Italian Army,Ljubljana (Yugo.)	TORTURE	YUGO.
CIANCOLLINI, Piero	190927	M	Ital.		Commissar,Italian Municipal-Admin., Sibenik (Yugo.) 41-43	MURDER	YUGO.
CIANI, Fernando	250087	M	Ital.		See Consolidated List Part II Appendix A		
CIBROV, Boris	190738	M	Bulg.		Agent,Police,Predejan,Vladicin Han (Yugo.) 22.2.43-23.4.43	MURDER	YUGO.
CIGALA, Fulgosi Alfonso	190929	M	Ital.		Lt.Gen., Italian Army,Sibenik (Yugo.) 41-43	MURDER	YUGO.
CIHANEK, Ferdinand	258090	M	Ger.	3. 5.20	Agent,Gestapo,Olomouc (Czech.)	MISC.CRIMES	CZECH.
CILOTTI,S.	163283	M	Ital.		Col.,Italian Army,Conc.Camp,Macerate (It.) 28.2.43	MURDER	U.K.
CIMINO, Giovanni	254930	M	Ital.		Capt., Judge,Italian Special Tribunal,Zadar,Sibenik,Kotor (Yugo.) 41-43	INTERR.	YUGO.
CIOLEK	250664	M	Pol.		Civilian,Chatou (Fr.) 27.8.44	WITNESS	FR.
CIONE, Vincenso	173272	M	Ital.		Col.,Italian Army,Conc.Camp 63,Aversa (It.) 42-3.43	TORTURE	U.K.
CIPOLETTI, Nicolo	190930	M	Ital.	circa 06	Kapo,Italian Army,Conc.Camp,Tribune (Yugo.) 42	MURDER	YUGO.
CIPRIANI	190932	M	Ital.		Cpl.,Italian Army,Div."Ferrera",Kepno-Polje (Yugo.) 6.43	MURDER	YUGO.
CIPRIANI, Nanni	190931	M	Ital.		Col.,Italian Army,O.C.of Bn."Bolzano", "Pusteria"-Div.,Cetinji-Savrik Podgorica (Yugo.) 11.41	MURDER	YUGO.
CIRILO, Antonio	145712	M	Ital.		Lt.,Doctor,"Isonzo" Div.,24 Inf.Rgt."Como" (Yugo.) 43	MURDER	YUGO.
CIRILO, Antonio	190933	M	Ital.		Lt.Col., Italian Army,51 Rgt. of "Murge" Div.,Trebinje (Yugo.) 42-43	MURDER	YUGO.
CIROTTI, Mario	190934	M	Ital.		Lt.Gen.,Italian Army,"Alpi Grae"-Div.,Savnik Montenegro (Yugo.) 5.42-9.42	TORTURE	YUGO.
CISOTTI, Carlo	307286	M	Ital.		General-Consul,Judge,Special Tribunal for defense of State Rom (It.) 4.41-9.43	MURDER	YUGO.
CISSEL, Josef	158	M	Russ.		N.C.O.,Camp Stalag VIII B, 8.42	MISC.CRIMES	U.K.
CITERNI, Teodorico	178323	M	Ital.		Col.,Italian Army,Conc.Camp PG-82,Loterina (It.) 8.42-9.43	TORTURE	U.K.
CITTATI, Gaetano	307287	M	Ital.		Capt., Judge,Military Court 2 Army-Section di Lubiana,Ljubljana (Yugo.) 41-43	MURDER	YUGO.
CIUPPA, Francois	185333	M	Pol.	26	Agent,SS,Gestapo,Rattingen (Ger.)	MISC.CRIMES	FR.
CLASEN	137616	M	Dan.		Pvt.,Conc.Camp	TORTURE	U.K.
CLERICI, N.	145704	M	Ital.		Prefect of Pola,Trieste Pola (It.) 43	MURDER	YUGO.
COBELLI, Giovanni	300623	M	Ital.		Pvt.,40 Bn.Italian Republican Guard,Stationed at San-Michele (It.) 43	MURDER	U.K.
COCCIA, Angelo	193549	M	Ital.		Col.,Garrison Commander,Italian Army,Nikaic (Yugo.) 11.11.41	MURDER	YUGO.
COCCMARELLA, Vicenzo	145703	M	Ital.		Col.,24 Inf.Rgt."Como", "Isonzo"-Div., Novo Mesto, 43	MURDER	YUGO.
CODA, N.	252001	M	Ital.		Lt.,Observer,Italian-Airforce,43 Sturm-Bn.98,Gruppe 240,Metnaj Babna,Polica,Podpesek (Yugo.) 8.42 and 9.42	MISC.CRIMES	YUGO.
COIAZZI, Emilio	307288	M	Ital.		Doctor,Lt.Col.,Judge,Military Court,Susak (Yugo.) 41-43	MURDER	YUGO.
COIALILLO, Gaetano	190935	M	Ital.		N.C.O.,Italian-Army,Novo Mesto Metleka (Yugo.) 42	MURDER	YUGO.
COLINO, Quiseppe	250967	M	Ital.		Agent,Police,Split (Yugo.) 2.42	MURDER	YUGO.
COLIZZA, Ugo	307289	M	Ital.		General-Consul,Judge,Special Tribunal for defense of State Rom (It.) 4.41-9.43	MURDER	YUGO.
COLLEONI, Antonio	162753	M	Ital.		Major,Italian Inf.Major,Cmdt.of PG-41,C.C.,Montalbo (It.)12.41-5.43	TORTURE	U.K.
COLNAGHI, Ettore	300209	M	Ger. Ital.		Lt.,Quartermaster, PG-57 Camp,Gruppignano and Udine (It.) 10.42-43	MISC.CRIMES	U.K.
COLO, Luigi	307274	M	Ital.		Italian Fascist,Campo Longo Padus (It.) 5.11.44	MURDER	U.K.
COLOMBO	193890	M	Ital.		Chief,Guard,Prison,Conc.Camp,Cuneo (It.) 9.43	TORTURE	FR.
COLOMBO, Tenente	193289	M	Ital.	10	Official,Arbeits-Kommando,64 Camp Bergamo Gardone V.T.Brescia (It.) 8.43	TORTURE	U.K.
COLOTTO, Emilio	190936	M	Ital.		Member,Italian Army,Metlika (Yugo.) 1.2.42	MURDER	YUGO.
COMELLA, E.	307290	M	Ital.		Capt., Judge,Correspondent Military Court,Susak (Yugo.) 41-43	MURDER	YUGO.
CONCEV, N.	190761	M	Bulg.		Asst.of Police-Director,Police, Pirot (Yugo.) 41-45	MURDER	YUGO.
CONCINA, Giovanni	190937	M	Ital.		Official,Italian Army,"Black shirts",Susak,Podheim (Yugo.) 41,42,43	MURDER	YUGO.
CONCINA, Roberto	190938	M	Ital.		Capt.,Italian Army,XXII Bn.Zadar,Zara,Veliki (Yugo.) 28.7.42	MURDER	YUGO.
CONCINI, Ause	145697	M	Ital.		Capt.,Army,Zadar (Yugo.) 43	MURDER	YUGO.
CONEV (or KONEV)	189970	M	Bulg.		Agent,Police,Pirot (Yugo.)	MISC.CRIMES	YUGO.
CONEV, Gono	190740	M	Bulg.		Cmdt.,Bulgarian Army,25 Inf.Rgt.,2 Bn., Mbdra Stena (Yugo.) 41-43	MURDER	YUGO.
CONRAD, Klaus	147761	M	Aust.		Dr., SS,SD,Oberarzt,Marburg (Ger.)	MURDER	FR.
CONSINI, Alberto or CONSOLMI, Alberto	305008	M	Ital.		Lt.Col., Italian Gend.,Vonitza and Xyromeri-district,10.-15.11.42,4.43	MISC.CRIMES	GRC.

CON - DEC

NAME	C.R.FILE NUMBER	SEX	NATIO-NALITY	DATE OF BIRTH	RANK OCCUPATION UNIT PLACE AND DATE OF CRIME	REASON WANTED	WANTED BY
CONSTANTINI,Constantino	145695	M	Ital.		Doctor,Tenente medico,25 Inf.Regt.,"Como","Isonzo" Div.Cernomelj (Yugo.) 43	MURDER	YUGO.
CONTI (see CORTI)	178324						
CONTI,Alfredo	190939	M	Ital.		Civ.,commissioner,political department,Questura-Naples(Ital.) 28.9.43	MURDER	YUGO.
CONTICELLI,Giuseppe	195626	M	Ital.		Official,Mil.,Rom (It.) 41-43	TORTURE	YUGO.
COOLEN,Willy	39580	M	Lux.	05	SD,Gestapo,Chateau,Gontier (Fr.) 4.-5.8.44	MURDER	FR.
COPIL (or KOPIL)	189794	M	Rum.		Sgt.,Major,Rum.Army,Timisul de Jos (Rum.) 4.-8.44	TORTURE	U.K.
COPIL	189870	M	Rum.		Major,Rum.Army,Brasov (Rum.)	MISC.CRIMES	U.K.
COPPA	189898	M	Ital.		Medical officer,Ital.Army,Ponza (It.)	TORTURE	YUGO.
COPPI (or GOPP)	145694	M	Ital.		Carabiniere,Army,Dalmatia (Yugo.) 43	MURDER	YUGO.
COPPOLA	132482	M	Ital.		Col.,Ital.Army,commandant of camp 65,Gravina (It.) 43	TORTURE	U.K.
CORDOPATRI,Antonio	190940	M	Ital.		Lt.,Ital.Army,Carabiniere XXII Bn.,Veliki (Yugo.) 28.7.42	MURDER	YUGO.
CORNACCHIA,Giuseppe	300624	M	Ital.		Paratrooper,Coricone,Comune,Amandola (It.) 2.5.44	MURDER	U.K.
CORONATI,Emilio(or COVINATI)	145690	M	Ital.		Genral,Inf.Div.,"Isonzo" part of XI Corpo d'Armata,Novo Mesto(Yugo)42	MURDER	YUGO.
CORRIAS,Ugo	190941	M	Ital.		Carabiniere,Ital.Army,Sobenik (Yugo.) 41-43	MURDER	YUGO.
CORSI,Candino	190942	M	Ital.		Commander,C.C.,Montalbano (It.) 41-43	TORTURE	YUGO.
CORTE,Giovanni	250680	M	Ital.		Lt.Genral,Commander,Army,Trieste (It.) 42	MISC.CRIMES	YUGO.
CORTI (or CONTI) Guido	178324	M	Ital.	85	Commandant,Major,Army,C.C. Aver of prison,Athens (Grc.) 42	WITNESS	U.K.
COSCI,Furio	300210	M	Ital.		Black-Bis.,Frasinelle,Rovigo,Province (It.) on or about 2.8.44	MISC.CRIMES	U.K.
COSMIN,Pietro	188537	M	Ital.	15.10.03	Mayor,Police public,Prefect Praesident,Fascist Federation,Member Grezzana-Verona (It.) 12.11.43	MURDER	U.K.
COSSU,Garino	190943	M	Ital.		Carabiniere,Ital.Army,Sibenik (Yugo.) 41-43	MURDER	YUGO.
COTZI,Vittorio	178322	M	Ital.	95	Governor,civilian,C.C.,Bari (It.) 1.-2.43	TORTURE	U.K.
COVINATI,Emilio (see CORONATI)	145690						
CRISTICIANI,David	259174	M	Ital.	18	Tenente,deputy Carabinieri,commander,Venezia Div.,Berane,Montenegro (Yugo.) 41-43	MISC.CRIMES	YUGO.
CRISTINI,Giuseppe	169475	M	Ital.		Capt.,Ital.Army,medical officer at Camp 82,Caterina(It.) 8.42-9.43	TORTURE	U.K.
CROCE,Mario (see GROCE)	169487						
CROFOLLO (Alias:OROFOLO)	193539	M	Ital.		Col.,C.C.,POW Camp 75,Cmdt.,Bari (It.)	MURDER	U.K.
CUIULI	190944	M	Ital.		Col.,C.C.,Italian RAB Island, (Yugo.) 4.41-8.43	TORTURE	YUGO.
CVETAN	190741	M	Bulg.		Pvt.,Bulg.Army,H.Q. of Frontier guard,Sinjac-Pirot (Yugo.) 20.2.44	MURDER	YUGO.
DAGLI,Alberi Delio	259100	M	Ital.		Lt.,Ital.Army,56 Regt.,"Marche" Div.,Stolac (Yugo.) 4.41-9.42	MURDER	YUGO.
DAKOV,Marinov (or DAKO)	190742	M	Bulg.		Capt.,Bulg.Army,52 Inf.Regt.,Vranje (Yugo.) 5.43	TORTURE	YUGO.
D'ALESSANDRO,Italo	307337	M	Ital.		General Consul,special Tribunal for de fense of State,Rom (It.) 4.41-9.43	MURDER	YUGO.
DALESSIO	300212	M	Ital.		Capt. or Lt.,"Forli" Div.,C.C.,Larissa, 41-43	MURDER	GRC.
DALLA-FRIA,Agostino	307275	M	Ital.		Italian Fascist,Camp Longo Padua (It.) on or about 5.11.44	MURDER	U.K.
DALLOLIO	155751	M	Ital.		Ital.Army,commander,Bassano (It.) 11.44	MURDER	U.K.
DALMAZZO,Renzo	190945	M	Ital.		General,Ital.Army,VI Corps D'Armata,Solin,Dalmatia (Yugo.) 24.1.42	MURDER	YUGO.
D'ALOISI,Ruggero	190875	M	Ital.		Member,Ital.Army,Sibenik (Yugo.) 41-43	MURDER	YUGO.
D'AMBROSIO,G.	193537	M	Ital.	30.3.88	Medical officer,Ital.Army,Coserta hospital,(It.)	MURDER	U.K.
DAMIANI DE VERGADA,Pietro	259168	M	Ital.	13	Commandant,291 Regt.Zara Div.,Kistanje,Piramatovci,Banja (Yugo.) 17.8.42, 3.43, 22.4.43	MISC.CRIMES	YUGO.
DAMICO	300213	M	Ital.		Officer,Art.Ital.Army,Naxos (Grc.) 41-43	MISC.CRIMES	GRC.
D'AMICO,Angelo Beppino	153868	M	Ital.	20.3.21	457 Unit,Ital.Army,ospidale da Lampo (Tunisia)	TORTURE	FR.
D'AMIGO,Angelo	189916	M	Ital.		Civ.,Bizerte (Tunisia)	MURDER	FR.
DAMISCH,Eduard	255090	M	Pol.		See Consolidated List Part II, Appendix "A"		
DAMM,Piet	140413	M	Dut.		Chief,Gestapo,Bruxelles (Bel.)	MURDER	FR.
DANDONGEN,Pieter	170712	M	Dut.	02	Agent,Gestapo,Schiebroek (Neth.)	MISC.CRIMES	UNWCC
DANIEF,Christos	300215	M	Bulg.		Member of the Secret police,Drama area (Grc.) 28.9.-20.10.41	MURDER	GRC.
DANIEF,Stefanos	300214	M	Bulg.		Employee,Railway from Tsirpan,Drama area(Bulg.,Grc.)28.9.-20.10.41	MURDER	GRC.
DANIEL,Jacob	182733	M	Hung.-Ger.	2.3.99	Pvt.,31 Waffen-Gren.Div.,2 Art.Regt.,C.C.Nordhausen-Dora (Ger.) 43-45	WITNESS	U.S.
D'ANTILIO (see D'AUTILIO), Salvatore	146099						
DARNEN	141502	M	Aust.		Political leader,NSDAP,Vienna (Aust.)	MISC.CRIMES	FR.
DASKALOV,Assen Anguelof	300217	M	Bulg.		Bulg.Sgt.,Serres, 10.41	MURDER	GRC.
DASKALOV,Nikola	190743	M	Bulg.		Sgt.,Bulg.Army,Mcma-Lovgrad (Bulg.) 2.44	TORTURE	YUGO.
DATSEF,Alexandros	300218	M	Bulg.		Lt.,Bulg.Army,Drama area (Grc.) 28.9.-20.10.41	MURDER	GRC.
D'AUTILIO,Salvatore (or D'ANTILIO)	146099	M	Ital.		Carabiniere,Army,Carabinieri station "Sebenico Sued",Sibenik (Yugo.) 12.4.42	MURDER	YUGO.
DAVANA,António	305012	M	Ital.		Lt.,Crete (Grc.) 42-43	MISC.CRIMES	GRC.
DAVELA,Giuseppe	190946	M	Ital.		Officer,Ital.Army,Div."Ferrara",Rastok,Montenegro (Yugo.) 3.42	MURDER	YUGO.
DAVID,Eduard	132173	M	Pol.-Ger.		Opl.,SS-Pz.Div."Hohenstaufen",(Fr.) 7.-8.44	WITNESS	U.K.
DAVIKOFF,Stephen	305013	M	Bulg.		Official,Achladikis,Kavalla area, 6.43	MISC.CRIMES	GRC.
DEAK,Ladislaus	189946	M	Hung.		Col.,Hung.Army	MURDER	YUGO.
DEAK,Leo	189945	M	Hung.		Civil,Governor Off.,Backa,Sombor (Yugo.)	MURDER	YUGO.
DEANA	252938	M	Ital.		Lt.,59 Regt., black shirts,1 Coy.,St.Pietro (It.) 19.-31.8.43	MISC.CRIMES	FR.
DE BAZI,George	300220	M	Ital.		Lt.Col.,officer commanding,Carabinieri Reali in Corfu 10.41-9.43	MISC.CRIMES	GRC.
DE BLASIO	190898	M	Ital.		Doctor,Lt.General,Ital.Army,Promina,Bruvno (Yugo.) 24.7.42	MURDER	YUGO.
DE BONDT,Joris	193563	M	Bel.	11.3.21	SS-Mann,SD,Sipo,Leeuwarden (Neth.) 13.9.44-10.4.45	MISC.CRIMES	NETH.
DECEV (see DECKO)	190744						
DE CICCO,Michele	307276	M	Ital.		Pvt.,guard,Camp 66,at or nr. Capua (It.) 27.1.43	BRUTALITY	U.K.
DECKER,Jos.	141515	M	Lux.	15	Member,NSDAP, 44	MISC.CRIMES	FR.

DEC - DIE

NAME	C.R.FILE NUMBER	SEX	NATIONALITY	DATE OF BIRTH	RANK OCCUPATION UNIT PLACE AND DATE OF CRIME	REASON WANTED	WANTED BY
DECKER, Peter	185597	M	Lux.		Chief, Arbeitslager Block 2, C.C.Leonberg nr.Stuttgart (Ger.)	MURDER	FR.
DECKER, Pierre	184270	M	Lux.		Chief, C.C. Dachau (Ger.)	TORTURE	FR.
DECKO or DECEV, Ivanow	190744	M	Bulg.		Lt. Army, Gujilane (Serb.Yugo.) 1.-2.43	MURDER	YUGO.
DECUYPER	145549	M	Bel.		Civilian, 41	MISC.CRIMES	FR.
DEFRAY	72448	M	Bel.		Agent, Gestapo, Roosebeke (Bel.)	MISC.CRIMES	FR.
DE FRETELLE	72449	M	Bel.		Indicateur, Gestapo, Cahors-Gramat (Fr.)	MISC.CRIMES	FR.
DECK or TINTIN	141518	M	Pol.		Agent, Milice and Gestapo, Autun-Munster (Fr. Ger.)	MURDER	FR.
DE GENDT, Emil	193629	M	Bel.	21. 8.07	SS Mann, S.D.Gent, Aussendienststelle der Sipo, Leeuwarden (Neth.) 13.4.44-14.4.45	MURDER	NETH.
DE GUIDA	190981	M	Ital.		Col.,Ital.Army,51.Rgt.of "Marche" Div.,Trebinje (Yugo.) 42-43	MURDER	YUGO.
DE HEYN	194279	M	Bel.	20	SS Mann, S.D.Heerenveen (Neth.) 2.1.-15.4.45	MURDER	NETH.
DELATTI	178920	M	Ital.		Capt.,Army, Italian Medical Corps, CC PG-53,Mascerata (It.) 1.-2.43	TORTURE	U.K.
DELREKE, Gaston	193568	M	Bel.	25. 2.13	SS Mann, Aussendienststelle Sipo and S.D.,Assen (Neth.) 13.9.44-14.4.45	TORTURE	NETH.
DELCEV, Nedeljko	190745	M	Bulg.		Commandant, Int.Camp Plovdiv (Bulg.)	TORTURE	YUGO.
DELETZ	155753	M	Aust.		Butcher, Civilian, Spittal (Aust.) 6.44	MISC.CRIMES	U.S.
DEL GIUDICE	300613	M	Ital.		Col., Major-General, Commd.of the Pinerolo Div. Town Major of Kastoria, Officer commanding Occupation Army, Kastoria,Nestorion, Argos,Crestikon (Grc.) 42-43	MURDER	GRC.
DELICH, Ugo	259131	M	Ital.		see Consolidated List Part II Appendix "A"		
DE LITALA, Giuseppe	307291	M	Ital.		Police officer, Spalato (Split) C.C.Lipari (It.) 41-43	BRUTALITY	YUGO.
DELLA, Mano Francesco	300221	M	Ital.		Brig.Carabinieri of Vrhnika nr.Ljubljana (Yugo.) 41 and 42	MISC.CRIMES	YUGO.
DELLE-VENERI, Edouardo	162340	M	Ital.		Capt. Army (Italian) Medical Corps, Benevento (It.) 7.-11.42	MISC.CRIMES	U.K.
DELMANTO, Osvaldo	150895	M	Ital.		Sottotenente, Italian Army Isonzo Div. (Yugo.) 42-43	MURDER	YUGO.
DELMOND	192079	M	Fr.	05	Civilian, Professor, Anatomy Institute Danzig	MURDER	POL.
DELOGU, Giovanni	190947	M	Ital.		Carabinieri, Italian Army, Sibenik (Yugo.) 41-43	MURDER	YUGO.
DEL OLMO	150904	M	Span.	00	Sous Chef de Banague, C.C.Hinzert (Ger.) 43	TORTURE	FR.
DE LORENZIO or DE LORENZIS	261331	M	Ital.		General, Pietralba (Fr.) 10.9.43	BRUTALITY	FR.
DE LUCA	900665	M	Ital.		Major, Judge, Military Tribunal of war of second Army, Sezione di Sebenico, Sibenik (Yugo.) 41-43	TORTURE	U.K.
DE LUCA, Mario	253775	M	Ital.		Carabinieri, Brigade, Police, Split (Yugo.) 26.6.43	TORTURE	YUGO.
DELUSSI	142036	M	Ital.	12	Lt. Col., Italian Army, 313.Inf.Rgt., Larissa (Grc.) 10.42-8.43	TORTURE	U.K.
DEMARCHI, Frederico	150894	M	Ital.		Lt., Italian Army, Carabiniere Bde. Lt., Isle of Vis (Yugo.) 7.3.43	MURDER	YUGO.
DE MARCO	191002	M	Ital.		Dr., Lt.,Italian Prison C.C. Cetinje and Crna Gora (Yugo.) 41-43	MURDER	YUGO.
DE MARTINO, G.	145474	M	Ital.		Lt. Col. (Yugo.) 42	PILLAGE	YUGO.
DEMETRIEF, Jovtzief	300222	M	Bulg.		Lt.,Bulgarian Army, Xylagani-Rodope 9.4.44	MURDER	GRC.
DENEDV, Kira	190746	M	Bulg.		Deputy Major, Jovac, Vladicen Han.(Yugo.) 43-44	MURDER	YUGO.
DENNER, Karl	187220	M	Stateless	20	Rottenfhr., S.D., Vorden (Neth.) 2.10.44	MURDER	U.K.
DENTCHEF, Alexis	300223	M	Bulg.		Bulg.Major, Commanding Officer of the Gendarmerie, Serres (Fr.) 44	MURDER	GRC.
DE PAOLI, Giovanni or DE PAOLO, Giambat-Tista	191053	M	Ital.		Gen.Major, Commander of Carabinieri, Sibenik (Yugo.) 41-43	MURDER	YUGO.
DE PUNEK, Conte	255027	M	Aust.		Guard, Gestapo, Limoges (Fr.) 40-45	INTERR.	FR.
DE REYK see DE RIJCK	194106						
DE RIJCK, Adolf or DE RIJK or REYK	194106	M	Bel.		Cpl. S.D., Steenwijk, Heerenveen (Neth.) 12.1.45-15.4.45	MURDER	NETH.
DERING	145563	M	Pol.		SS Doctor, C.C. Birkenau (Pol.) 42-43	TORTURE	FR.
DE ROY	145565	M	Dut.		Guard, C.C. Hersbruck (Ger.)	MISC.CRIMES	FR.
D'ERRICO, Francisco	150889	M	Ital.		Centurione, Isonzo Army, 98.Fasc.Legion, Rakovnik (Yugo.) 43	MURDER	YUGO.
DESPREE, Georges	145569	M	Bel.		SS, C.C. Camp de Siegmar-Schonau (Ger.) 7.44	MISC.CRIMES	FR.
DESSANTIS, Domenico	190948	M	Ital.		C.C. Director, C.C. Fraschette for Civilians at Alatri (It.) 41-43	TORTURE	YUGO.
DESSY, Carlo	252857	M	Ital.		Tenente Colonello,Observer, Italian Airforce, 43 Storm, B.T.98 Gruppe 240, Metnaj, Babna, Polica, Podpesek (Yugo.) 8.-9.42	INTERR.	YUGO.
DE TANDT, Edmond Helmut or Helmont	132724	M	Bel.		Agent, Gestapo, Douai (Fr.) 6.3.44	MURDER	FR.
DE TURRIS	191134	M	Ital.		Col., Italian Army, Garrison Commander at Omis, Gata near Omis (Yugo.) 8.42	MURDER	YUGO.
DEVA or DEVE	189974	M	Alb.		Civilian	MURDER	YUGO.
DEVECASI, Edalo	126894	M	Ital.		Civilian, 9.43-2.44	MISC.CRIMES	U.K.
DE VECCHI, Pietro	191159	M	Ital.		Major, Judge of Italian Special Court, Sibenik (Yugo.) 41-43	MURDER	YUGO.
DE VECCHIS, Ennio	191160	M	Ital.		Legal Official, Judge of Italian Special Court, Sibenik (Yugo.) 41-43	MURDER	YUGO.
DE VESOVI, A.	900969	M	Ital.		Capt, Army from Zadar, Kistanje, Northern Dalmatia (Yugo.) 9.42	MURDER	YUGO.
DE VITO, Giovanni	305111	M	Ital.		Guard at P.O.W. working commando near Brindisi Airfield (It.) 8.43	MURDER	U.K.
DE WACHTER	194848	M	Bel.		Guard, SS Mann, S.D., Heerenveen, Meppel (Neth.) 2.1.45-15.4.45	MURDER	NETH.
DE WERD, Jules	145575	M	Bel.		Civilian, 44	MISC.CRIMES	FR.
D'HOLLANDER, Alfons	194126	M	Bel.	7. 9.14	Pvt. Aussendienststelle der Sipo and S.D.,Leeuwarden (Neth.) 13.9.44-14.4.45	MURDER	NETH.
DIANA, Evelino	258164	M	Ital.		Alpino, Fasc.Rep.Army,Tagliamento VIII Alp.Rgt. 2.Bn. Dorenberg (Yugo.) end of 43 to 4.45	INTERR.	YUGO.
DICHAVITZ, Fabian	154448	M	Aust.		Cpl. Wehr Arb.Kdo.22, Resident Vienna, Stalag XVIII A, Leoben (Aust.)	TORTURE	U.K.
DICKENS, Josephine see DICKENS	150897						
DICKENS, Josephine or DICKEN	150897	F	Dut.	22	Kapo, Guard, Hermann Goering Werk, C.C. Wattenstedt, Braunschweig (Ger.) 8.44 and 4.45	TORTURE	FR.
DIEHL, Kristian see DIEL	182763						
DIEL, Kristian or DIEHL	182763	M	Hung.	24. 9.99	Pvt. 4.SS Totenkopf-Sturmbann, C.C. Dora Mittelbau Nordhausen (Ger.) 43-44	WITNESS	U.S.
DIETICH see DIETRICH	157084						

DIE-DUS

NAME	C.R.FILE NUMBER	SEX	NATIO-NALITY	DATE OF BIRTH	RANK	OCCUPATION	UNIT	PLACE AND DATE OF CRIME	REASON WANTED	WANTED BY
DIETRICH or DIETRIK or DIETICH	137084	M	Pol.		Arb.Kdo.E 715,Stalag VIII-B,Auschwitz (Pol.) 2.44				MURDER	U.K.
DIFALCO	300227	M	Ital.		Lt.,Carabinieri Reali,Xironomi,Thebes (Grc.) 22.6.42				MURDER	GRC.
DIFRANCESCO,Antonio	150893	M	Ital.		Brig.,Ital.Army,Carabinieri,Isle of Koscula (Yugo.) 43				MURDER	YUGO.
DI IONNO,Antonio	194309	M	Ital.	23.5.20	Pvt.,Ital.Army,Camp Calabre,Toulon (Fr.) 16.7.44				MURDER	FR.
DI MARCO	300625	M	Ital.		Carabieniere,Territorial Legion of the Royal Carabinieri of Ancona, Station of Comunanza,Ascoli,Picena (It.) 25.12.43				MURDER	U.K.
DI MARTINI	300626	M	Ital.		Carabiniere,Camp 52,Chiavari (It.) 12.41-10.42				TORTURE	U.K.
DIMATTEO,Francesco	300228	M	Ital.		Pvt.,Collaborated with the secret fieldpolice,Vrastamites near Livadia,Beotia (Grc.) 8.1.44				MURDER	GRC.
DIMITROF	300229	M	Bulg.		Major in the Bulg.Police-Force,Drama area (Grc.) 28.9.-20.10.41				MURDER	GRC.
DIMITROV,Kristiv Kresimir	190747	M	Bulg.		Cpl.,Bulg.Army,Garrison Distr.of Vranje,Vlase (Yugo.) 7.44				MURDER	YUGO.
DIMITROV,Milko Stanojev	190748	M	Bulg.		Official,Police,Vladicin,Han (Yugo.) 43-44				MURDER	YUGO.
DIMOF	300230	M	Bulg.		Member of the Secret Police,Drama area (Grc.) 28.9.-20.10.41				MURDER	GRC.
DI NEGRO	145637	M	Ital.		Col.,1 Gren.Rgt., (Yugo.) 42				MURDER	YUGO.
DINO-CASTELLI,Taddei	300627	M	Ital.		Cmdt.,Camp 52,Chiavari (It.) 12.44				TORTURE	U.K.
DI PAOLI	188956	M	Ital.		Lt.,Ital.Army,Grenoble (Fr.)				TORTURE	FR.
DISCHEKOV	166955	M	Russ.		Inf.Div.,Unit 23209,Plozevst (Fr.) 4.8.44				MURDER	FR.
DJORDJEN	191180	M	Bulg.		Official,Police at Vladicin,Han (Yugo.) 43-44				MURDER	YUGO.
DJOREV,Vlajko or ILIJEV	190749	M	Bulg.		Official,Police,Stublo,Vladicin,Han (Yugo.) 41-44				MURDER	YUGO.
DJUMURDJIJEV,Georgijev Dimitrije	190750	M	Bulg.		Secretary,Occupied Territories,Pirot (Yugo.) 41-43				TORTURE	YUGO.
DODA,Argeo	190949	M	Ital.		Member,Ital.Army,IV Legion,Confinaria C.C.NN. "Monte Nevoso" Metlika (Yugo.) 42				MURDER	YUGO.
DOEHRING	258901	M	Pol.		Doctor,Block 10,Auschwitz (Pol.) 40-45				MURDER	FR.
DOIMI,Elena	150892	F	Ital.		Tescher,P.O.Education,Vis (Yugo.) 9.3.43				TORTURE	YUGO.
DOITSINOV,Stoyan Myref	300234	M	Bulg.		Prefect,Skopoi,Lefkon near Serres (Grc.) 41-42				MURDER	GRC.
DOLADA	148944	M	Pol.		Director,C.C.Sontra (Ger.)				TORTURE	FR.
DOLD,Paul	148941	M	Yugo.	15	Member,SS-Totenkopf-Div.,Natzweiler (Fr.) 7.43-4.44				MURDER	FR.
DOMBROWSKI,Kurt	155754	M	Pol.		Merchant,Civ.,Elbing (Pol.) 42				TORTURE	U.K.
DOMENICI	256988	M	Ital.		Cpl.,Ital.Army,Plave (Yugo.) 13.-23.2.45				INTERR.	YUGO.
DOMENICO,Giusto	150891	M	Ital.		Carabiniere,Ital.Army,Babno Polje near Prezid (Yugo.) 2.-25.7.42				TORTURE	YUGO.
DOMO,Otto	189944	M	Hung		Lt.,Hung.Army				MURDER	YUGO.
DONATI,Domenico	190950	M	Ital.		Governor,Prison Poggio Reale,Naples (It.) 28.9.43				MURDER	YUGO.
DONHOFFER	169456	M	Aust.	05	Pvt.,Army,Stalag XVIII-A,Premstatten (Aust.) 2.44				MURDER	U.K.
DONIMIRSKI	194312	M	Pol.		Kapo,SS,C.C.Mauthausen (Aust.) 3.44-5.45				MURDER	FR.
DONNABELLA	252474	M	Ital.		Agent,Police,Split (Yugo.) 30.4.43				TORTURE	YUGO.
DONNAMURA	307292	M	Ital.		N.C.O.,Member,Carabinieri,Trieste (It.) 12.41				MURDER	YUGO.
"DONNA PAOLA" (nick-name) see GATTANI,Anna Maria	300621									
D'ORAZIO,Rafaele	188959	M	Ital.		Capt.,Ital.Army,Grenoble (Fr.)				PILLAGE	FR.
DORLANO	252064	M	Ital.		Capt.,Ital.Army,Village of Tribanj (Yugo.) 7.-8.41				BRUTALITY	YUGO.
D'ORO	150890	M	Ital.		Capt.,Ital.Army,Div.Lombardia,Fuzine (Yugo.) 42				MURDER	YUGO.
DORSTLER	62022	M	Ger.or Aust.		Lt.,Airforce, (tunnel du coudray Dise) Andeville, Boncourt Noeilles (Fr.)				MURDER	FR.
DOTA,Pasquale	169476	M	Ital.		Capt.,Ital.Army,Capua (It.) 4.41-6.43				TORTURE	U.K.
DOUBROVSKY,Irene	147974	F	Russ.	15	Civ.,Grueneberg (Ger.) 44				MISC.CRIMES	FR.
DOULA	147975	M	Czech.	10	Kapo,Ersbrueck (Ger.)				MURDER	FR.
DRAGANOV	190751	M	Bulg.		Lt.,Bulg.Army,7 Cavalry Squadron (Yugo.) 42-43				MURDER	YUGO.
DRAGIG,Hinke	192939	M	Aust.		Lt.Col.,Yugo.Airforce,C.C.Flossenburg (Ger.) 44-45				WITNESS	U.S.
DRAGUITS,Raiko	300237	M	Bulg.		Bulg.Soldier,Xylagani-Rodopi (Grc.) 9.4.44				MURDER	GRC.
DRANKEF	300238	M	Bulg.		Major,Head,Bulg.Army,Section of the Bulg.Army and of Armed Civil Servants,Drama area (Grc.) 28.8.-20.10.41				MURDER	GRC.
DRAS	137614	M	Dan.		Wachtmeister,Stafgefaengnis,C.C.Hamburg (Ger.)				TORTURE	U.K.
DRASCOVIC	194957	M	Hung.		Lt.,Airforce,Kormend (Hung.) 8.44				MISC.CRIMES	U.K.
DRASER,Andreas	147977	M	Rum.	12	Unterscharfhr.,Waffen SS,C.C.Auschwitz (Pol.)				MURDER	FR.
DRASKOWITCH or MATHIAS	62030	M	Hung.or Yugo.	07	Member,Gestapo,Chalons sur Marne (Fr.)				TORTURE	FR.
DRENT,Marinus	162861	M	Dut.		Sturmmann,SS, Asche (Bel.)				MURDER	BEL.
DRUZEIC-KOSIC,Vicko	259169	M	Ital.		Member,Ital.Fascist,Mil.,Split (Yugo.) 4.41, 7.42, 8.42				SUSPECT	YUGO.
DUBOIS	161702	F	Bel.	03	Gestapo,Koeln (Ger.) 44				MURDER	FR.
DUCHETTI,Adotto	190873	M	Ital.		Major,Ital.Army,Biograd Namorn (Yugo.) 12.4.43				MURDER	YUGO.
DURANTI,Azelio	254937	M	Ital.		Judge,Member,Tribunal,Kotor (Yugo.) 41-43				INTERR.	YUGO.
DURANTI,Vincenzo	254936	M	Ital.		Member,Seniore,Tribunal,M.V.S.N.,Kotor (Yugo.) 41-43				INTERR.	YUGO.
DURELLO,Natale	173271	M	Ital.	10	Ital.Army,Campolongo,Venice (It.) 2.-5.11.44				MURDER	U.K.
DUSKOV,Peter	190752	M	Bulg.		Head,Police,Vladicin,Han (Yugo.) 43-44				MURDER	YUGO.
DUSTI,Benito	189897	M	Ital.		Carabiniere,Ital.Army,Vela Luka (Yugo.)				MURDER	YUGO.

DUV-FAR

NAME	C.R.FILE NUMBER	SEX	NATIO-NALITY	DATE OF BIRTH	RANK OCCUPATION UNIT PLACE AND DATE OF CRIME	REASON WANTED	WANTED BY
DUVAL, Ludo	149361	M	Bel.	12	Civilian	MISC.CRIMES	FR.
EBERLE, Hans	24769	M	Aust.	09	S.R.A., Dijon (Fr.)	MURDER	FR.
EBNER	155741	M	Aust.	00	Police Obermeister, Gusen (Aust.)	MURDER	FR.
EBNER, Franz	151221	M	Aust.		N.S.D.A.P., (Pol.) 39-40	MURDER	U.S.
EBSER, Joseph	185504	M	Aust.		Civ., St. Martin (Aust.) 16.11.44	PILLAGE	U.S.
ECHMETIKOV, George	300240	M	Bulg.		Gendarme, Gendarmerie Sidirodastron (Grc.) 5.41	PILLAGE	GRC.
EDELMANN, Ferdinand	193788	M	Aust.	13. 3.87	Civilian, Merchant, Amstetten (Aust.) 20.3.45	TORTURE	U.S.
EDINI	250998	M	Ital.		Gestapo, Limoges (Fr.) 40-45	MURDER	FR.
EGERTS, Franz	182778	M	Hung. Ger.	31. 5.97	SS-Mann, 4 SS Totenkopfsturmbann C.C. Dora Mittelbau Nordhausen (Ger.) 43-45	WITNESS	U.S.
EGNER, Johann	182780	M	Hung. Ger.	7. 8.95	SS-Mann, 4 SS Totenkopfsturmbahn C.C. Dora Mittelbau Nordhausen (Ger.) 43-45	WITNESS	U.S.
EGNER, Peter	182736	M	Hung. Ger.	20.12.95	SS-Mann, SS 31 Waffen Gren.Div., 2 Art.Rgt. C.C. Nordhausen, Dora (Ger.)	WITNESS	U.S.
EIBISBERGER, Alois	115674	M	Aust.		Criminal Secretary, Kripo, Linz Donau (Aust.) 43	MURDER	U.K.
EIGRUBER, August	135159	M	Aust.	07	Gauleiter (Gruppenfuehrer) N.S.D.A.P. Arlt, Aussee (Aust.) 4.45	MISC.CRIMES	U.S.
EINFALD	187034	M	Aust.	17 or 18	Pvt., 3-188 P.O.W. working Bn., Bratholmen, Hordeland (Nor.) 5.43	MURDER	NOR.
EISENMANN, Rudolf	260928	M	Yugo.		SS-St. Mann, SS Guard, C.C. Auschwitz (Pol.) 42-45	BRUTALITY	POL.
ELDICO	145368	F	Hung.		Nurse, Budapest (Hung.) 9.44	MISC.CRIMES	U.S.
ELIAS	149202	F	Pol.	95	Interpreter, Factory, Berlin (Ger.)	MISC.CRIMES	FR.
ELMI, Antonio	190951	M	Ital.		Pvt., Ital.Army, Isle of Viz (Yugo.) 9.9.43	TORTURE	YUGO.
EMATHINGER, Emma	147174	F	Aust.		Frauenschaftsleiterin, Civ., NSF., Wife of Major	TORTURE	U.S.
EMMA	251522	F	Hung.		Nurse, C.C. Auschwitz (Pol.)	INTERR.	FR.
EMOEDY, Philipp	183112	M	Hung.	29.12.94	SS-Mann, 31 SS Gren.Div., C.C. Dora Nordhausen, Dachau (Ger.) 43-45	MURDER	U.S.
EMSBERGER, Georg	183113	M	Hung.	10. 4.98	SS-Mann, 4 SS Totenkopf-Sturmbann, C.C. Dora Nordhausen, Dachau (Ger.) 43-45	MURDER	U.S.
ENEV	189969	M	Hung. Bulg.		Agent, Police, Pirot (Yugo.)	MISC.CRIMES	YUGO.
ENGELBERT, Max	167130	M	Yugo.		Pvt., Army, Etreux (Fr.) 2.9.44	WITNESS	FR.
ENGLAENDER, Josef	260926	M	Yugo.	17. 3.19	Sturmmann, SS Guard, C.C. Auschwitz (Pol.) 42-45	BRUTALITY	POL.
ENGLANDER, Joseph	183903	M	Hung. Ger.	21. 2.95	SS-Mann, 4 SS T.Stuba, C.C. Mittelbau Nordhausen Dora, Dachau (Ger.) 43-45	WITNESS	U.S.
ENGL-PUTZEDER, Erwin	154338	M	Aust.		Kameradschaftsfhr., H.J.	TORTURE	U.S.
ENTICO, Papa	194240	M	Ital.		Colonel, Ital.Army Cmdt. POW. Camp No. 70, Ferme Ancona (It.) 12.42-1.43	TORTURE	U.K.
ENZO, Giovanni	252960	M	Ital.	18	Brigadier, Customs Police, Kistanje (Yugo.) 25.5.42	MURDER	YUGO.
ESPINOSA	300245	M	Ital.	25	Lt., Interpreter, POW., Camp 75, Member of the Fascist Militie and Intelligence, Bari (It.) 22.1.43	MISC.CRIMES	U.K.
ESPOSITO, Giovanni	190952	M	Ital.		General, Italian Army Div. "Pusteria", Montenegro Savnik (Yugo.) 41	MURDER	YUGO.
ESSO	189943	M	Hung.		Major, Colonel, Hungarian Army, public official	MURDER	YUGO.
ETLINGER (or HAAKNEUS)	233	M	Aust.-Ger.	05	Hptsturmfhr., Cmdt. C.C. Mauthausen, Vught (Aust., Neth.) 40-43	MURDER	NETH. BEL.
ETTL, Fritz	188288	M	Aust.		Civilian, St.Lorenzen (Aust.) 2.4.44	WITNESS	U.S.
EUSTAT, Nicholas	300247	M	Bulg.		Head of the Sidirocastion District, Sidirocastron (Grc.) 41	BRUTALITY	GRC.
EVROP	190753	M	Bulg.		Sgt., Bulgarian Army, Distr. of Pirot, Sinjac, Village (Yugo.) 20.2.44	MURDER	YUGO.
EXPOSITO, Pepino	251513	M	Ital.		Carabiniere, Unit of Carabiners, San Gavinodi Di Carbini (It.) 43	INTERR.	FR.
FABBRI	148318	M	Ital.		General, Staff of 2 Army, (Yugo.) 43	MURDER	YUGO.
FABERIES, Ottorino	300628	M	Ital.		Sgt., Black Bde. Villamovo Marchesana on detachment at Ariano, Mesola Ferrara, Adria, Rovigo (It.) 12.44	MURDER	U.K.
FABIANI	256932	M	Ital.	10 or 15	Lt., Valle (Gace) Garrison Cmdt., Krmed (Yugo.) 25.8.43-11.43	INTERR.	YUGO.
FABRI, Augusto	148317	M	Ital.		Lt., Carabiniere Reali, Crnomelj (Yugo.) 42	MURDER	YUGO.
FACCIN	148316	M	Ital.		Col.Commander, Army "Lombardia Div." Inf.Rgt. 73, 41-43	MURDER	YUGO.
FADDA, Gioachimo	148315	M	Ital.		Maresciallo, Army "Sebenico Sued" Carabinieri station, Sibenik (Yugo.) 1942	MURDER	YUGO.
FAGGIANI, Rino	307277	M	Ital.		Member, Ital.Fasc.Black Bde., Nr. Caselle Pressana, Prov. Verona (It.) 6.1.45	MURDER	U.K.
FAHRNGRUBER	155409	M	Aust.	15	Cpt., Army Panz.Jaeg.Ersatz Abt. 10, 2 Coy., Metting (Ger.) 28.12.44	TORTURE	U.S.
FAINI, Virgilio	307278	M	Ital.		Member, Italian Fascist Federation, Grezzana, Verona PG-73, Capri (It.) 8.43	MURDER	U.K.
FAIS, Giovanni	190953	M	Ital.		Marshal, Italian Army, Sibenik (Yugo.) 41-43	MURDER	YUGO.
FAJECKA	259351	M	Rum.		Lt., General of the Camp Auschwitz (Pol.)	SUSPECT	FR.
FALAVOLTI	141406	M	Ital.		Lt., Carabinieri, Sfax (Tunisia)	WITNESS	FR.
FALCOMARE, Marcello	259193	M	Ital.		Lt., Italian Army "Marche" Div. 56 A Rgt., Stolac (Yugo.) 41-9.42	MURDER	YUGO.
FALETTI	251541	M	Ital.		N.C.O. Carabinier, Unit Tenenza Sebenico, Sibenik (Yugo.)	BRUTALITY	YUGO.
FALTISCHEA, Ludwig	141596	M	Hung.	10. 9.18	Agent, SD, Headaye, (Fr.)	WITNESS	FR.
FANTACCI, Clemente	300629	M	Ital.		Member of the Italian Army, Campo PG-53, Macerata, Sfor Zancosta (It.) 28.2.43	MURDER	U.K.
FANFOGNA - GARAGNIN, Nino	190954	M	Ital.		Civilian, Commissar, Trogir, Kasteli (Yugo.) 41-43	TORTURE	YUGO.
FANTINI, Ferdinando	148314	M	Ital.		Officer, Army, (Yugo.) 43	MURDER	YUGO.
FANTOLI	148313	M	Ital.		Fascist Commissioner (Yugo.) 43	MURDER	YUGO.
FANTUSSATTI, Giovanni (or Giuseppe)	190955	M	Ital.		Director, C.C. Fraschetti Alatri (It.) 41-43	TORTURE	YUGO.
FAPRINI, Enrico	187766	M	Ital.		Pvt., Fascist, near Trescore (It.)	MURDER	U.S.
FARACHO	135215	M	Hung.		Lt., Police Hungary, Sopron (Hung.) 3.45	MURDER	U.S.
FARESSIN, Emilio	259192	M	Ital.		Lt., Italian Army "Marche" Div. 56 Rgt., Stolac (Yugo.) 4.41-9.42	MURDER	YUGO.
FARINA, Guido	148312	M	Ital.		Col., Army Inf.Rgt. 23 "Como", "Isonzo" Div., Crnomelj (Yugo.) 43	MURDER	YUGO.
FARNETI, Carlo	188573	M	Ital.		Cpt., Italian Army, PG 35, Padula (It.) Summer 43	MISC.CRIMES	U.K.
FARNIK, Alois	141312	M	Pol.		Civilian (Aust.)	WITNESS	U.K.

FAU-FRA

NAME	C.R.FILE NUMBER	SEX	NATIO-NALITY	DATE OF BIRTH	RANK OCCUPATION UNIT PLACE AND DATE OF CRIME	REASON WANTED	WANTED BY
FAUST, Walter	162018	M	Pol.		Truppfhr., Org.Todt, Le Rove (Fr.) 20.8.44	MURDER	FR.
FEAUX, Henriette	141546	F	Bel.	10	C.C. Sommerfeld (Ger.) 44	MISC.CRIMES	FR.
FEICHT, Armand	144721	M	Swiss.	2.12.11	Interpreter, Gestapo, Charleville (Fr.)	MISC.CRIMES	FR.
FEKETISCH, Johann or PEKETISCH	144719	M	Yugo.	12	Sturmann, SS-Div. Totenkopf C.C. Natzweiler (Fr.) 13.7.43-22.4.44	MURDER	FR.
FEKTOR, Franz or Frank	187420	M	Hung.	16.7.95	SS-Mann, Guard, 4. SS Totenk.Sturm, C.C. Dachau, Dora, Nordhausen (Ger.)	MURDER	U.S.
FELICE, Mario	190956	M	Ital.		Civilian, Commander, of Railway Militia, Nova Mesto Metlika (Yugo.) 42	MURDER	YUGO.
FELICIANI	253634	M	Ital.		Commander, Cdiecima Flottiglia Mass, Fulmine (Slovenia.) 2.1.45	MISC.CRIMES	YUGO.
FELLER	144753	F	Pol.	09	Civilian, Paris (Fr.) 3.43	MISC.CRIMES	FR.
FELLER, Philipp	187421	M	Hung.		SS-Mann, Guard, 4. SS Totenk. Sturm C.C. Dachau, Nordhausen, Dora (Ger.)	TORTURE	U.S.
FELLINGER, Franz	171674	M	Yugo.	22.5.09	SS-Rttfhr., C.C. Natzweiler (Fr.) 42-44	MURDER	FR.
FELZIOVANI, Franz	121244	M	Hung.	22	Agent, Gestapo of Chambery, Challes les Eaux et Arbin (Fr.)	MURDER	FR.
FERRARI, Attilio	169479	M	Ital.		Dr., Capt., Ital.Army, Laterina (It.) 8.42-9.43	TORTURE	U.K.
FERENCZY	135216	M	Hung.		Lt.Col. Police,Ministry of Interior, Councillor, Budapest (Hung.)45	MISC.CRIMES	U.S.
FERIZIANE	192067	M	Ital.	00	Landrat, Prefect of Macerata (It.) 2.-5.44	MURDER	U.K.
FERLAN, Antonio	255134	M	Ital.		Pvt., Army, Radunic (Yugo.) 43	PILLAGE	YUGO.
FERNANDEL	166975	M	Bel.		SS Rottenfhr., C.C. Wattensted (Ger.)	MURDER	FR.
FERNANDES see CERVANTES	167915						
FERRARESE	188891	M	Ital.		Indicator, Gestapo, Commupay (Fr.) 9.6.44	MURDER	FR.
FERRARI	258154	M	Ital.		Pvt., Ital.Army, Execution Squad, Plave Anhovo (Yugo.) 13.2.45-23.2.45	INTERR.	YUGO.
FERRARI, Arturo	148311	M	Ital.		Lt., Army "Isonzo" Div., 24. Inf.Regt. "Como", (Yugo.) 43	MURDER	YUGO.
FERRARI, Giovanni	163284	M	Ital.		Capt., Ital.Army, Inf. C.C. Capri (It.) 27.1.43-1.45	TORTURE	U.K.
FERRATA	190957	M	Ital.		Dr., Commissar, C.C. Fraschetti Alatri (It.) 41-43	TORTURE	YUGO.
FERRERO, Alberto	253957	M	Ital.		Lt. Gen.,Cmdt., XXIII Army-Corps, Julian March (It.) 42	INTERR.	YUGO.
FERRETI, Dante	190958	M	Ital.		Member, Ital.Army,Fascist Militia, Schenilz (Yugo.) 41-43	MURDER	YUGO.
FERRONI	148310	M	Ital.		Col.Commander, Army 74 Inf. Regt., "Lombardia"-Div., (Yugo.) 43	MURDER	YUGO.
FERULLO	141864	M	Ital.		Lt., Staleg Beng Hazi (Africa) 42	MISC.CRIMES	U.K.
FERVANTI	173254	M	Ital.		Lt. Colonel, Army, Capri (It.) 6.-7.43	TORTURE	U.K.
FESTI, Antonio	300249	M	Ital.		Major Commanding a Bn. "Blackshirts","Pinerolo" Div., Elassona Area, Domenika, Livadia 1.10.42-16.2.43	MURDER	GRC.
FEUCHT	253640	M	Aust.		Cpl., Chief of Kdo. H.V.X., Blumau-Austrich (Aust.)	INTERR.	FR.
FEULA, Antonio	300250	M	Ital.		Member of the Ital.Police, Xironomi Thebes 22.6.42	MURDER	GRC.
FIENGA, Giovanni	148309	M	Ital.		Capt., Bicovo (Yugo.) 42	TORTURE	YUGO.
FILIPOV	190754	M	Bulg.		Lt., Bulg. Army, Pistr. of Zupa Stupenj, Gornji (Yugo.)2.-6.8.43	TORTURE	YUGO.
FILIPPOF, Kirof Christof	300252	M	Bulg.		Bulg.-Officer, of the Kavalla Security, Kavalla 9.41-9.43	MISC.CRIMES	GRC.
FILOFF	148395	M	Bulg.		Civilian, C.C. Mauthausen (Aust.) 41-45	MURDER	U.S.
FINAGUERRA	192073	M	Ital.	05	Lt., Fascist Milice, Braccano (It.) 24.3.44	MURDER	U.K.
FINK	161748	M	Russ.		Lt.Army, Morlaix St. Pol De Leon (Fr.) 44	MURDER	FR.
FIOCHI	193550	M	Ital.		Capt., Ital.Mountain Unit, Petrovac, Banovina, Zevska (Yugo.)8.41	MURDER	YUGO.
FIORDIPONTE	148308	M	Ital.		Col. Fascist Legion 137, (Yugo.) 43	MURDER	YUGO.
FIORENZA, Giuseppe	307293	M	Ital.		Major, Judge, Correspondent of Military Tribunal, Susak (Yugo.)41-43	MURDER	YUGO.
FIREIK	142673	M	Pol.		Agent, Gestapo, Roswik (Nor.) 4.44	MISC.CRIMES	FR.
FISCHERLEN	143407	M	Aust.	10	Falkenhain (Ger.) 44	TORTURE	FR.
FISCHETTI, Ettore	190959	M	Ital.		Lt., Ital.Army 56. Inf.Regt. 1.Bn. I A Coy. Div.Marche, Mostar (Yugo.) 42	PILLAGE	YUGO.
FISTER, Hans	142487	M	Aust.	25	Sturmann, W.-SS 1.SS Div. Leibstandarte "Adolf Hitler" Rosbach (Ger.) 4.3.45	WITNESS	U.S.
FLAVONI, Giulio	255135	M	Ital.		Major, Army, Zara-Div., 291. Regt., Kistanje (Yugo.) 42	BRUTALITY	YUGO.
FLECK, Ludwig	144739	M	Pol.		Doctor, Civilian and Former P.W. at Buchenwald C.C. (Ger.) 44-45	TORTURE	FR.
FLORENTINI	148307	M	Ital.		Major, "Lombardia"-Div. 73.Regt., 3. Bn., (Yugo.)	MURDER	YUGO.
FLOUE or FLUHE	258140	M	Lux.		Employee, C.C. Natzweiler (Fr.)	MURDER	BEL.
FLUCHER	171666	M	Aust.	02 or 05	Capt., 2.-189 Kgf.Arb.Bn., Fjell (Nor.) 5.44	MURDER	NOR.
FLUHE see FLOUE	258140						
FOGGLEIN, Andreas	255588	M	Hung.	9.7.03	SS, Civ. Farmer, Nordhausen (Ger.)	MURDER	U.S.
FOGGIA, G.	254153	M	Ital.		Pilot, Ital. Army, Airforce, 69.Group 21.Sturm, Baronje Selo (Yugo.) INTERR. 26.6.43	INTERR.	YUGO.
FOLDESI	189941	M	Hung.		Agent, Hung.Police, Novi Sad (Yugo.)	MURDER	YUGO.
FOPIANO, Mario	190960	M	Ital.		Major, Ital.Army Bn.of "Venezia" Div., Kolasin and Area (Yugo.)8.43	MURDER	YUGO.
FORESIO	190961	M	Ital.		Commandant, Ital.Army, Div. Bergamo, Sibenik (Yugo.) 9.6.43	MURDER	YUGO.
FORGIONNE, Rosario	194979	M	Ital.	28.10.13	Pvt., Army, Toulon (Fr.) 6.7.44	MURDER	FR.
FORNACIARI, Raul	190962	M	Ital.		Capt., Ital.Army, St.Marten Podstrava (Yugo.)Middle of 8.42	MURDER	YUGO.
FORNARA, N.	252095	M	Ital.		Pilot, Ital.Airforce 43. Sturm Bn. 98 Group 240. Squadriglia Bn Metnaj, Babna Polica Podpesek (Yugo.) 8.-9.42	MISC.CRIMES	YUGO.
FORTUNATO, L.	307294	M	Ital.		Major, Judge, Military Tribunale, Susak (Yugo.) 41-43	MURDER	YUGO.
FOSCO, Gianni	258157	M	Ital.		Civ.Commiss. Admin. District of Kastav (Yugo.) 41-43	MURDER	YUGO.
FRACASSI	148306	M	Ital.		Lt.Col.137.Fascist Legion Deputy Commander (Yugo.) 43	MURDER	YUGO.
FRACASSO, Arsenio	148905	M	Ital.		"Isonzo" Div., 24. Inf.Regt. "Como" (Yugo.) 43	MURDER	YUGO.
FRANC	254145	M	Ital.		Civilian, School-Official, Split (Yugo.) 15.5.42	TORTURE	YUGO.
FRANCESCHETTI	189896	M	Ital.		Commissar, Ital.-Public-official, Spalato (It.)	MURDER	YUGO.
FRANCESCHINI	300631	M	Ital.		Lt., 40. Bn. Italian Republican Guard stationed at San-Michele (It.) 11.43	MURDER	U.K.
FRANCESCHINI, Mario	190963	M	Ital.		General, Ital.Army " Div. Ferrara" Savnik (Montenegro Yugo.)5.-6.42	MURDER	YUGO.
FRANCESCO, Turco	148319	M	Ital.		Cmdt., Col., Army, C.C. 62 Bergamo (It.) 42	TORTURE	U.K.
FRANCESCONI Umberto	255141	M	Ital.		Col. Judge, Zadar Sibenik Split, Kotor (Yugo.) 41-43	INTERR.	YUGO.
FRANCESQUI, Sancho	254123	M	Ital.		Agent, Member, Gestapo SD of Toulouse (Hte.-Garonne Fr.)11.42-8.44	MISC.CRIMES	FR.
FRANCIOSINI, Mario	191146	M	Ital.		Judge, Italian Special Court, Sibenik (Yugo.) 41-43	MURDER	YUGO.
FRANCK, Robert	193628	M	Bel.	1.9.11	Member, Sipo, Leeuwarden (Neth.) 13.9.44-14.4.45	MURDER	NETH.
FRANCONI, E.	300632	M	Ital.		Marshal, 40.Bn. Italian Republican Guard, stationed at San-Michele (It.) 6.11.43	MURDER	U.K.

FRA - GAT

NAME	C.R.FILE NUMBER	SEX	NATIO-NALITY	DATE OF BIRTH	RANK, OCCUPATION, UNIT, PLACE AND DATE OF CRIME	REASON WANTED	WANTED BY
FRANGIPANE, Francesco	190964	M	Ital.		Lt., Italian Army, Sibenik (Yugo.) 41-43	MURDER	YUGO.
FRANGIPANE, Francesco	251536	M	Ital.		Dr., Civilian, Lt.,Cmdt., Della Teneza Vodice (It.) 41-43	MURDER	YUGO.
FRANGIPANE, Michele	190965	M	Ital.		Lt.,Cmdt., of a Unit at Sibenik (Yugo.) 41-43	MURDER	YUGO.
FRANK	254155	M	Czech.		C.C. Buchenwald (Ger.)	INTERR.	FR.
FRANZ	72084	M	Aust.		Scharfhr., SS, C.C.Lublin (Pol.)	TORTURE	U.S.
FRANZINI	300633	M	Ital.		Capt., 30 Bn. Italian Republican Guard, San Michele (It.) 6.11.43	MURDER	U.K.
FRAUENHOFER, Josef	142518	M	Rum.		Army, C.C. Oberplan (Czech.) 29.4.45	MURDER	U.S.
FREISLER	155402	M	Czech.		Army, Landesschuetzen Bn 391, 3 Coy, (Pol.) 2.2.45	MURDER	U.K.
FREISLER	193309	M	Czech.	20	Pvt., guard, 3.-997 Landesschnetzen Bn, Graudenz (Pol.) 45	MURDER	U.K.
FREISSESS, Ludwig	148922	M	Croat.	21.10.13	Chief-guard, Civilian, Friedrichshafen (Ger.) 44-45	TORTURE	FR.
FREIWALD, Franz	155408	M	Stateless	10	Gypsy, Civilian Farmer, Pol. Prisoner. C.C. Ilfeld near Gardelegen (Ger.) 12.-14.4.45	MURDER	U.S.
FREUND, Philipp	187363	M	Hung.	10.12.94	Pvt., 4 SS-Totenkopf-Stuba, C.C. Dora-Nordhausen,Dachau (Ger.) 43-45	MURDER	U.S.
FREY, Fritz	185125	M	Aust.		Chief du Block, SS, C.C. Sachsenhausen (Ger.)	PILLAGE	FR.
FRICH (see FRISCH, Frantz)	186842						
FRICH, Franz Francois (see FRISCHOU)	167116						
FRIEDL, Joseph	148193	M	Aust.		Chief, C.C.Hartenberg, Nieder-Donau (Aust.)	TORTURE	FR.
FRIEDMANN	148199	M	Pol.		Eldest of Block 27, C.C.Auschwitz-Birkenau (Pol.) 40		
FRIESSNEGG, Bruno	162029	M	Aust.	21	Zugwachtmeister, Ordnungs-Police, Krad-Schuetzen-Coy, Stavern (Nor.)43	MURDER	NOR.
FRISCH, Frantz (or FRICH)	186842	M	Lux.		(Fr.)	WITNESS	FR.
FRISCHKNECHT	148267	M	Swiss.		Agent, SS, (Fin.)	TORTURE	FR.
FRISCHOU (or FRICH, Franz Francois)	167116	M	Lux.		Interpreter, Civilian, Saone, Loire (Fr.) 40-44	WITNESS	FR.
FRITSCH	147777	M	Aust.		SS-Mann, Waffen-SS, Panz.Div."Das Reich", Tonneins (Fr.) 44	MURDER	FR.
FRITZ (or FRIZZI)	256101	M	Aust.		Senior of the Block 15, C.C. Mauthausen (Aust.)	INTERR.	FR.
FRITZ	259429	M	Aust.		Kapo, C.C. Auschwitz (Pol.)	MURDER	FR.
FRIZARI, Nito	189895	M	Ital.		Capt., Italian Army, Montenegro (Yugo.)	MURDER	YUGO.
FRIZZI (see FRITZ)	256101						
FROSINI, Remo	254168	M	Ital.		Carabinieri, Royany Carabiniera, 2 Coy, 29 Bn, Calacuccia(Fr.) 5.43	INTERR.	FR.
FUCHS, Max	133914	M	Aust.	92	Capt., Ger. Army, Oflag XIII B, Hammelburg (Ger.) 44-45	MURDER	U.S.
FURIA, Fernando	189894	M	Ital.		Dr., Carabinieri, Capt., Italian Army, Ljubljana (Yugo.)	MURDER	YUGO.
FURLOTTI, Nicola	307279	M	Ital.		Member, Italian Fascist, Federation, Grezzana Verona (It.) 12.11.43	MURDER	U.K.
GABEL, Jacob	182997	M	Hung.	1.7.99	SS-Mann, Guard, 31 SS-Gren.Div., Waffen-SS, C.C.Dora-Nordhausen, Dachau (Ger.) 43-45	WITNESS	U.S.
GABEL, Leonhard	183128	M	Hung.-Ger.	31.1.95	SS-Mann, 4 SS-Totenkopf-Stuba, C.C. Dora-Nordhausen, Mittelbau, Dachau (Ger.) 43-45	WITNESS	U.S.
GABUTI, Aldo	190966	M	Ital.		Colonel, Italian Army, 93 Rgt.,Fanteria, Dalmatia,(Yugo.) 42	MURDER	YUGO.
GAETANI, Giuseppe	147287	M	Ital.		Lt., Italian Army, (Yugo.) 43	MURDER	YUGO.
GALANTIA, Charlico	185947	M	Russ.		Lt., Army, 4 Coy, Unit 20988, Mont-Martin-Mer (Fr.) 8.6.44	MURDER	FR.
GALDIERI	161201	M	Ital.	15	Lt., Army, Padua (It.) 8.43	TORTURE	U.K.
GALEF, Anguelos	350137	M	Bulg.		Major, Commanding officer, 42 Rgt.,Mikri, Deria, Thrace (Grc.) 41	MURDER	GRC.
GALEV	190755	M	Bulg.		Pvt., Bulgarian Army, (Yugo.) 42-43	MURDER	YUGO.
GAILHOFER, Raimund	251572	M	Aust.	92	Sgt.,SD, worked at Goes at the Ortskom.Wemelding (Z-B) (Neth.) 9.44	INTERR.	NETH.
GAILI, Giuseppe	147286	M	Ital.		Sottotenente, 29 Rgt."Como" Ital.Army, "Isonzo" Div., 1 Bn, Cernomelj (Yugo.) 43	MURDER	YUGO.
GAILINI, Giuseppe	147285	M	Ital.		Major, Italian Army, 73 Inf.Rgt."Lombardia" Div. (Yugo.) 43	MURDER	YUGO.
GALLO, Annibale	147284	M	Ital.		Col., Italian Army, XI Corps (Yugo.) 41	MURDER	YUGO.
GALLO, Rufino	147283	M	Ital.		Sottotenente, 24 Inf.Rgt.,It.Army, "Como" "Isonzo" Div.,(Yugo.) 43	MURDER	YUGO.
GALLUS, Sandor	137611	M	Hung.	10	Lt., Cmdt.,Govern.Archologist, Budapest Museum, C.C.Leled (Hung.) 44	TORTURE	U.K.
GALTERIO, Enrico	189893	M	Ital.		Lt., Italian Army, Montenegro (Yugo.)	MURDER	YUGO.
GALVAGNI, Mario	190967	M	Ital.		Cmdt.,Italian Army, Unit of Carabiniere, Sibenik (Yugo.) 41-43	MURDER	YUGO.
GAMBERINI	307295	M	Ital.		Gendarm, Tenenza di Curzola, Island of Curzola (Yugo.) 5.12.42	MURDER	YUGO.
GANCAROLLI, Antonio	190968	M	Ital.		Brigadier, Italian Army, Carabinieri, Kotor (Yugo.) 41-43	MURDER	YUGO.
GANDINI, Tomaseo	190969	M	Ital.		Lt. Col., Italian Army, XI Bn, Carabinieri, Cetinje Drna Gora (Yugo.) 41-43	MURDER	YUGO.
GANGEMI, Giovanni	307296	M	Ital.		General-Consul, Judge, Spécial Tribunal for defense of State Rom, Rom (It.) 4.41-9.43	MURDER	YUGO.
GANGER, Johann	161199	M	Aust.	95	Obersteiger, Arb.Kdo.951, Civilian, C.C. Kogl,Eisenertz (Aust.) 2.42-4.43	TORTURE	U.K.
GARCIA	257562	M	Spain.		Chief of bloc, C.C. Dora-Nordhausen (Ger.) 2.44	BRUTALITY	FR.
GARDINI, J.	147282	M	Ital.		Major, Italian Army, Velika Lusca (Yugo.) 42	PILLAGE	FR.
GARFENSTEIN, Josee	149355	M	Pol.	23	Civilian, 43-45	MISC.CRIMES	FR.
GARGIULO (see SCHMIDT, Ema)	191100						
GARGIULO, Enzo	190970	M	Ital.		Lt., Italian Army, I Bn, 56 Rgt., Mostar (Yugo.) 7.42	PILLAGE	YUGO.
GARIBALDI	161309	M	Ital.		Lt., Italian Army, Padula (It.) 42	TORTURE	U.K.
GARLICH	29878	M	Pol.		Major, Publ. official (Pol.)	MURDER	U.K.
GAROFOLO (see GAROLFO)	147281						
GAROLFO (or GAROFOLO)	147281	M	Ital.		Lt., Italian Army, "Lombardia" Div.,73 Rgt.,1 Bn, (Yugo.) 43	MURDER	YUGO.
GASS, Mathias	183118	M	Hung.-Ger.	2.10.99	SS-Mann, SS-Totenkopf-Stuba, C.C. Dora-Mittelbau, Nordhausen and Dachau (Ger.) 43-45	WITNESS	U.S.
GASTNER	186561	M	Aust.	85	Lt., Arb.Kdo 107, Stalag 18 A, C.C. Wolfsberg (Aust.)	TORTURE	U.K.
GATTELANO	189903	M	Ital.		Capt., Italian Army, Raumikal (Yugo.)	MURDER	YUGO.
GATTERNIGG, Erich	53453	M	Aust.-Ger.	20.7.07	Sturmbannfhr., SS, 12 SS-Pz.Div. "Hitler Jugend", 25 Rgt., Normandy, Abbaye, Ardenne near Caen (Fr.)	Torture	FR.

GAT-GOL

NAME	C.R.FILE NUMBER	SEX	NATIO-NALITY	DATE OF BIRTH	RANK OCCUPATION UNIT PLACE AND DATE OF CRIME	REASON WANTED	WANTED BY
GATTI	161231	M	Ital.	00	Capt., Ital.Army, on staff of camp 35 and at P.O.W. camp Bergoma between Padula and Bologna (It.) 13.8.43	TORTURE	U.K.
GATTI	1693	M	Ital.		Capt., Venice (It.)	TORTURE	U.K.
GATTNING	129793	M	Aust.		Commander, Lt., Stalag 18 A, C.C. Spittal (Aust.) 16.10.43	MURDER	U.S.
GAUTTIERI, Filippo	195622	M	Ital.		Official, Justizministerium, Rom. (It.) 41-43	TORTURE	YUGO.
GAVINO see MORO GARINO	145470						
GAZZINI or GAZZINO	190971	M	Ital.		Col., Ital.Army Rgt.of Sassari Div. (F 559), Udbing Gracac (Yugo.) 1.-2.43	MURDER	YUGO.
GEBURA	255988	M	Pol.		Hairdresser, C.C. Block 16, Mauthausen (Aust.)	MURDER	FR.
GEHMES	161525	M	Hung.		Interpreter, Gestapo, Bretagne, Anjou, Poitou (Fr.)	MURDER	FR.
GEISENDORFER, Annie	147823	F	Czech.	05	Woman-guard, C.C. Ravensbrueck (Ger.)	TORTURE	FR.
GELOZA, Luigi	190972	M	Ital.		Marschall, Ital.Army, Berane, Montenegro (Yugo.) 3.42	TORTURE	YUGO.
GELTSCH, Edward Georg	145387	M	Bulg.	27.7.08	Businessman, civilian	MISC.CRIMES	U.S.
GEMELLI	189892	M	Ital.		Major, Ital.Army, Brodarevo (Yugo.)	MURDER	YUGO.
GENOVESI	190973	M	Ital.		Chief, Ital.Police, Prem (Yugo.) 42	TORTURE	YUGO.
GENTILE, Pasquale	190974	M	Ital.		Tenente, Ital.Army, Officer commanding port at Omia, Jesenica, 8.42	INCENDIARISM	YUGO.
GEORGI	190757	M	Bulg.		Pvt., Bulg.Army, H.Q. of frontier guard, village of Sinjac, Pirot (Yugo.) 20.2.44	MURDER	YUGO.
GEORGIEF, Georgios	305143	M	Bulg.		Prefect, Bulg. Prefectuer in Drama (Grc.) 28.9.-20.10.41	MURDER	GRC.
GEORGIEV, Marin Vasilow	190758	M	Bulg.		Agent, Police. Prekodolac, Vladicin Han (Yugo.) 43-44	MURDER	YUGO.
GERACI, Guiseppe	190975	M	Ital.		Camp-leader, C.C. Lipari (It.) 41-43	TORTURE	YUGO.
GERLITZER	133346	M	Aust.	10	Rottenfhr., Waffen-SS, C.C. Hohenrheim near Plattling (Ger.) 2.-5.1945	MURDER	U.S.
GERMANO, Francesco	190976	M	Ital.		Col., Ital.Army, Unit "Ferrara" Div., Montenegro (Yugo.) 5.43	MURDER	YUGO.
GERMANO, T.	147280	M	Ital.		Capt., Army, Cetijne (Yugo.) 43	MURDER	YUGO.
GERMI	147289	M	Ital.		Sottotenente, Ital.Army Bersaglieri, C.C. Treviglio (It.) 42-43	TORTURE	U.K.
GERRITSEN, Gerrit	231273	M	Neth.	23	Agent, Gestapo, SD.	MISC.CRIMES	CZECH.
GESNOWACK, Joseph	189597	M	Yugo.		Feldgendarm, Feldgendarmerie, Bethune (Fr.) 25.8.44	MURDER	FR.
GETTZI	169483	M	Ital.		Adjutant, Ital.Army, C.C. Capua (It.) 4.41-6.43	TORTURE	U.K.
GEYER, Friedrich	183108	M	Hung.	95	Pvt., 4. SS-Totenkopf-Sturmbann, C.C. Nordhausen, Dachau (Ger.)	MURDER	U.S.
GEYRHOFER, Rudolf	252306	M	Aust.	7.2.85	Member, NSDAP, Amstetten (Aust.) 20.3.45	MISC.CRIMES	U.S.
GEZA, Bondi	161214	M	Hung.	07	Civilian, Political prisoner, C.C. Dora-Nordhausen, from Dora to Gardelegen (Ger.) 5.-14.4.45	WITNESS	U.S.
GHELLERO, Giovanni	300634	M	Ital.		Kapo, Gr.Black Bde., Conche di Codevigo, Piove di Sacco, Province of Padua (It.) 20.2.45	MURDER	U.K.
GHELLERO, Renato	300635	M	Ital.		Member of Black Bde., Conche di Codevigo, Piove di Sacco, Province of Padua (It.) 20.2.45	MURDER	U.K.
GHI, Giovanni	147279	M	Ital.		Capt., Ital.Army, Cetijne (Yugo.) 43	MURDER	YUGO.
GHIRARDELLI, Edwards	1694	M	Ital.		Venice (It.)	TORTURE	U.K.
GHIY, Giovanni	189891	M	Ital.		Major, Ital.Army, Montenegro (Yugo.)	MURDER	YUGO.
GIACOBELLI, Ettore	261237	M	Ital.		Col., Army, Military Tribunal, Lubljana (Yugo.) 41-43	MURDER	YUGO.
GIANGRECO, Francesco	147278	M	Ital.		General, Ital.Army, "Sassari" Div., (Yugo.) 43	MURDER	YUGO.
GIANNEY, Petko Ch.	305144	M	Bulg.		Member, secret police of Drama (Grc.) 28.9.-20.10.41	MURDER	GRC.
GIANNERINI, Giuseppe	169484	M	Ital.		Capt., Ital.Army, Inf., C.C. Laterina (It.) 8.42-9.43	TORTURE	U.K.
GIANNERINI, Velio	178063	M	Ital.		Capt., Ital.Army, P.O.82, C.C. Caterina (It.) 8.42-9.43	TORTURE	U.K.
GIERAGGI, Vitto	190977	M	Ital.		Finance-officer, Ital. Finanze Ministry official, Sibenik (Yugo.)43	MURDER	YUGO.
GIGANTE, Antonio	253006	M	Ital.		Pvt., Ital.Army, (Yugo.) 6.43	BRUTALITY	YUGO.
GIGANTE, Mario	259130	M	Ital.		Capt., Garrison Commandant, Biovicino Selo, Kistanje, Ivosevei (Yugo.) 5.-6.42	MISC.CRIMES	YUGO.
GIGLIOLI	189045	M	Ital.		Lt., General, Ital.Army, Benghazi (Africa) 42	TORTURE	U.K.
GILLICH, Kasper	183109	M	Hung.	6.5.95	Pvt., 31 SS-Gren.Div., C.C. Dora-Nordhausen, Dachau (Ger.)	MURDER	U.S.
GIMELLI, Fernando	259129	M	Ital.		Maggiore, Commandant, II Bn., 84 Rgt., Venezia Div., Berane, Montenegro (Yugo.) 41-43	MISC.CRIMES	YUGO.
GIORDANO, Guiseppe	258162	M	Ital.		Carabiniere, Ital.Army, Cerknica (Yugo.) 2.11.41	TORTURE	YUGO.
GIORRI, Antonio	190978	M	Ital.		Commander, Ital.Army, Sibenik (Yugo.) 41-43	MURDER	YUGO.
GIOVANETTI, Dante	147277	M	Ital.		Sgt., Ital.Army, 14 Inf. Batt. (Yugo.) 42	MURDER	YUGO.
GIOVANNI, J.	147276	M	Ital.		Capt., Ital.Army, Lubljana (Yugo.) 43	TORTURE	YUGO.
GIOVARELLI, Fernando.	147275	M	Ital.		Sottotenente, Ital.Army, 23 Inf.Rgt. "Como", "Isonzo"-Div., Cernomeli (Yugo.) 43	MURDER	YUGO.
GIUFFRIDA, Giuseppe	169486	M	Ital.		Doctor, Capt., Ital.Army, C.C. Laterina (It.) 8.42-9.43	TORTURE	U.K.
GIULIANI	178762	M	Ital.	17	Cpl., Army, P.G.35, Padula (It.) 8.43	TORTURE	U.K.
GIULIANI, Guiseppe	147274	M	Ital.		Capt., Ital.Army, Army Dalmatia (Yugo.) 43	MURDER	YUGO.
GIULIETTI or GUILETTI, Giulio	300637	M	Ital.		Marescialo, 40 Bn. of the Ital. Republican guard stationed at San Michele. (It.) 6.11.43	MURDER	U.K.
GIURA, Luigi	147273	M	Ital.		Centurione, Ital.Army, "Isonzo"-Div., 98 Fasc.Leg., 3 Coy., Trebnie (Yugo.) 43	MURDER	YUGO.
GIUSEPPE	254098	M	Ital.		Agent, C.C. Corropola (It.) 41	TORTURE	YUGO.
GIUSEPPE, Paolo	189890	M	Ital.		Lt., Col., Ital.Army, Montenegro (Yugo.)	MURDER	YUGO.
GIUSFREDI, Gino	191147	M	Ital.		Legal official, Doctor, Ing., Vice-chairman of Ital. "Special" court in Sibenik (Yugo.) 41-43	MURDER	YUGO.
GLENSKI, Bogdan	147814	M	Pol.	19	Kapo, C.C. Laura (Ger.) 44	TORTURE	FR.
GLIGORCA, N.	190759	M	Bulg.		Policeman, Police, Surdulica (Yugo.) 2.8.42	MURDER	YUGO.
GLIGOROV, Stojan	190760	M	Bulg.		Sgt., Police, Vladicin Han (Yugo.) 43-44	MURDER	YUGO.
GLINZ, Anton	129662	M	Aust.	09	Civilian, Alt Aussee (Aust.) 4.45	INCENDIARISM	U.S.
GLOCK, Jacob	183294	M	Hung.	27.11.99	SS-Schuetze, 4 SS-Totenkopf-Sturmbann, C.C. Dora-Nordhausen, Dachau (Ger.)	WITNESS	U.S.
GLOGOWSKI, Jacob Jack	251554	M	Pol.	16.9.09	Police, (Bel.)	INTERR.	BEL.
GLORIA	147272	M	Ital.		General, Ital.Army, "Lombardia"-Rgt., "Sassari"-Div. (Yugo.) 43	MURDER	YUGO.
GNOSKA, Franz	147719	M	Czech.		Agent, Gestapo, (Ger.)	MISC.CRIMES	FR.
GOBATZ, Henri	39642	M	Bel.		Sgt., Feldgendarmerie de Laval (Fr.) 31.7.44	MURDER	FR.
GOBBO	147271	M	Ital.		Doctor, Tenente Medico, It.Army 23 Inf.Rgt. "Como", "Isonzo" Div. Cernomeli (Yugo.) 43	MURDER	YUGO.
GOEHMES	259612	M	Hung.	circa 10	Member, Gestapo, Area Angers (Fr.) 42-44	MISC.CRIMES	FR.
GOERTZ, Franz-Michael	252307	M	Aust.	26.12.15	NSDAP, S.A., Amstetten (Aust.) 20.3.45	MISC.CRIMES	U.S.
GOLBERG	147787	M	Rum.	00	C.C. Blechmar (Ger.)	TORTURE	FR.

GOL - GYA

NAME	C.R.FILE NUMBER	SEX	NATIO-NALITY	DATE OF BIRTH	RANK OCCUPATION UNIT. PLACE AND DATE OF CRIME	REASON WANTED	WANTED BY
GOLDENBERG, Simon	162708	M	Aust.	20. 9.10	Chief, Gestapo, Montelimar (Fr.)	MISC.CRIMES	FR.
GOMEZ	185129	M	Spain		Nurse, C.C., Bad Gandersheim (Ger.)	MURDER	FR.
GONEV, Anastas	190762	M	Bulg.		Civil servant, occup. territ., Jelasnica, Surdulica district (Yugo.) 21.10.43	MURDER	YUGO.
GONZALES or GONZALO	143270	M	Spain	23	Stalag 2-B, Camp Hammerstein (Ger.)	MISC.CRIMES	FR.
GOPP see COPPI	145694						
GORCILOV, Aleksander	190763	M	Bulg.		High official, commander of Lowna Druzina (Yugo.) 43-44	MURDER	YUGO.
GORFEL	255990	M	Aust.		Uscharfhr., SS, state service, Poznan (Pol.) 7.-8.7.42	WITNESS	POL.
GORI, Giuseppe	190979	M	Ital.		Commander, Ital. Army, Carabinieri-station, Sibenik (Yugo.)	MURDER	YUGO.
GORI, Mario	173250	M	Ital.		Col., Ital. Army, C.C. Padula (It.)	TORTURE	U.K.
GORKI	163311	M	Ital.	90	Tenente Colonnello, Padula (It.) 42-43	TORTURE	U.K.
GORONDY-NOVAK, Elemer	307268	M	Hung.	circa 95	Vice-Fieldmarshal Commander, 3 Army Group, Backa (Yugo.) 1941	MURDER	YUGO.
GOSTOURKOF, Demetrios	305147	M	Bulg.		Bulg. Commanding Officer, Serres Security, Serres (Grc.) 9.41-8.42	MURDER	GRC.
GOTTARDI	307280	M	Ital.		Member Italian Fascist Fed. Verona, Grezzana (It.) 12.11.43	MURDER	U.K.
GOTTSCHALL, Michel	162044	M	Rum.	21. 6.16	Member, SS-Totenkopf, Mauthausen (Aust.) 8.43-5.45	TORTURE	U.S.
GOTWITZ, Henny	193915	F	Dut.	23	Blockleiterin, C.C. Ravensbrueck (Ger.)	TORTURE	FR.
GOUP or JOUP	174973	M	Pol.		Camp-eldest, C.C. Wansleben am See (Ger.) 43-45	TORTURE	FR.
GRABSKA	193916	F	Pol.		Medecin, C.C. Ravensbrueck (Ger.)	TORTURE	FR.
GRAF	190764	M	Bulg.		Pvt., Agent, special police from Sofia, 27 Inf. Div. at Prokuplje (Yugo.) 43-44	MURDER	YUGO.
GRAIA	148141		Pol.		Doctor, C.C. Auschwitz (Pol.) 42-44	TORTURE	FR.
GRANDI, Antonio	251022	M	Ital.		Brig., mixed detachment of Carabinieri, P.M.64, Pianottoli (Fr.) 9.5.43	MURDER	FR.
GRASEGGER, Vinzenz see VINZENZ	188291						
GRASSI, Giovanni	250783	M	Ital.		Major, Carabinieri, Vodice (Yugo.) 1.2.43	MURDER	YUGO.
GRASY, Matias	149321	M	Hung.	19	Sturmmann, SS, SD, Hendaye (Fr.)	PILLAGE	FR.
GRAUS, Marianna	192177	F	Aust.		Civilian, Salzburg (Aust.) 6.44	WITNESS	U.S.
GRAZHOFER	53542	M	Aust.	02	Dr., SS-Osturmbannfhr., Graz (Aust.)	TORTURE	NETH.
GRAZIANI, Fernando	189889	M	Ital.		Col., Ital. Army, 83 Inf.Div., Montenegro (Yugo.)	MURDER	YUGO.
GRECO	169485	M	Ital.		Interpreter, Army, C.C. Tarhuna, Transit Camp, Libya, North Africa. 10.42	TORTURE	U.K.
GRIEB, Tommaso	300666	M	Ital.		Capt., Judge, Special Correspondent of Military Tribunal of War of Second Army, Sezione di Sebenico, Dalmatia (Yugo.) 43-43	TORTURE	U.K.
GRIFFINI, Mario	307338	M	Ital.		General Consul, Court President of special tribunal for defence of State Rom (It.) 4.41-9.43	MURDER	YUGO.
GRIFOS, Antonelo	305151	M	Ital.		Sgt., Ital. Carabinieri in Larissa, Aya, Thessaly, village of Yarakari (Grc.) 12.9.42, 5.1.43, 7.1.43, 12.1.43, 3.5.43	MURDER	GRC.
GRIGNOLO	147269	M	Ital.		Col., chief of staff, Ital. Army, Susak (Yugo.) 1941	MURDER	YUGO.
GRILIO, Giovanni	253009	M	Ital.		Brig., customs police, Kistanje (Yugo.) 5.42	MURDER	YUGO.
GRIMALDI	132532	M	Ital.		Lt.Col., Army	MISC.CRIMES	FR.
GRIMALDI, Paolo	190980	M	Ital.		Lt.General, Ital. Army, Div. Berjamo, Sibenik (Yugo.) 41-43	MURDER	YUGO.
GRINBERG, Zigi	157560	M	Rum.		C.C. Auschwitz (Pol.) 7.42-10.43	MURDER	FR.
GRISL, Alois Josef	145403	M	Aust.	1. 5.12	Medical Councillor, civilian, physician, Molln (Aust.) 26.7.44	MISC.CRIMES	U.S.
GROCE, Mario or CROCE	169487	M	Ital.		Capt., Ital. Army, Chieti (It.) 7.42-9.43	TORTURE	U.K.
GROH, Michael	260940	M	Yugo.	15. 3.08	Pvt., SS-Guard, C.C. Auschwitz (Pol.) 43-45	BRUTALITY	POL.
GROS, Joseph	171676	M	Aust.	21	SS-Sturmmann, C.C. Natzweiler (Fr.)	MURDER	FR.
GROSSI, Arnaldo	307297	M	Ital.		Capt., judge, military tribunal for 2nd army, section of Lubiana (Yugo.) 41-43	MURDER	YUGO.
GROUGEROF, Matsef	305157	M	Bulg.		Secret Agent, Bulg. Security of Drama-area (Grc.) 28.9.-20.10.41	MURDER	GRC.
GSNADI, Navay Irme	189948	M	Hung.		Dr., Lt., Hung. Army, Art., Novi-Sad (Yugo.)	TORTURE	YUGO.
GUALTIERI, Enrico	173248	M	Ital.		Capt., Adjutant, Inf., C.C. Udine (It.) 20.5-8.7.43	MURDER	U.K.
GUAZZINI, Francesco	254100	M	Ital.		Capt., Ital. Airforce, 240 Squadriglia Bn., 43 Stormo Bn., 98 Gr., Metnaj, Babna (Yugo.) 8.-9.42	INTERR.	YUGO.
GUAZZO, Angelo	147267	M	Ital.		Col., Ital. Army, 6 Artl.Regt., "Isonzo"-Div., Novo Mesto (Yugo.) 1943	MURDER	YUGO.
GUBSCHOKDV or KUSCHOKDV	39645	M	Russ.		Pvt., Feldpost Nr.23209, Pauldreuzic (Fr.) 4.8.44	MURDER	FR.
GUDWEIN, Peter	183310	M	Hung.	23.12.94	SS-Mann, 4 SS-Totenkopf-Sturmbann, C.C. Dora, Mittelbau, Nordhausen, Dachau (Ger.) 43-45	WITNESS	U.S.
GUELLI, N.	147266	M	Ital.		Capo del Inspettorato Generale, Ital. Army, Cavalry, Trieste (It.) 1943	MURDER	YUGO.
GUENOW, Iwan	305160	M	Bulg.		Leader, Merchant at Comitadji, secret police at Drama (Grc.) 28.9.-20.10.41	MURDER	GRC.
GUERRINI, Remo	147265	M	Ital.		Centurione, Ital. Army, "Isonzo"-Div., 98 Fascist Legion, Velaloka (Yugo.) 1943	MURDER	YUGO.
GUGLIAIMINO, Antonio	259103	M	Ital.		Lt., Ital. Army, 56 Regt., Maroñe-Div., Stolac (Yugo.) 4.41-9.42	MURDER	YUGO.
GUGLIOTTI	302151	M	Ital.		Lt., 8 Coy., 2 Bn., 83 Regt., "Venezia"-Div., Montenegro (Yugo.) 9.-11.41, 8.43	MURDER	YUGO.
GUGOV, Velicko	190765	M	Bulg.		Mayor, occupied territories, Gnjilan district of Pirot (Yugo.) 41-43	TORTURE	YUGO.
GUIDO	189888	M	Ital.		Carabinieri, Ital. Army, Vela Luka (Yugo.)	MURDER	YUGO.
GUIDO, Francesco	190982	M	Ital.		Sgt., Ital. Army, Div. "Ferrara", Kapino, Polje, Montenegro (Yugo.) 6.43	MURDER	YUGO.
GUILIETTI see GIULIETTI	300637						
GUNDE	189998	M	Hung.		Col., Hung. Army, Backa (Yugo.)	MURDER	YUGO.
GURILEA, Ioan	307335	M	Rum.		Sub-Lt., Brasov 4.-5.44, Timisulde, Jos near Brasov (Rum.) 22.8.44	BRUTALITY	U.K.
GUSCHOROW	188834	M	Russ.		Army Unit 23.209, Pouldreuzig (Fr.) 4.8.44	MURDER	FR.
GUTIERREZ, A.	147264	M	Ital.		Ital. Army, "Isonzo"-Div., 23 Regt., "Como", Cernomeli (Yugo.) 1943	MURDER	YUGO.
GUTONIOLI	254099	M	Ital.		Capt., Observer, Ital. Air-Force, Vismja (Slovenia, Yugo.) 17.3-43	INTERR.	YUGO.
GYARIG	161244	M	Hung.		Sgt., police, Myling (Hung.) 1.11.44	TORTURE	U.S.
GYARMATY, Gabor	259918	M	Hung.	15. 1.12	Member Nyclas Party, high ranking civilian official, district Kosice, Tahanovce, Slovakia (Czech.) 1.45	MURDER	CZECH.

HAA - HOL

NAME	C.R.FILE NUMBER	SEX	NATIO- NALITY	DATE OF BIRTH	RANK OCCUPATION UNIT PLACE AND DATE OF CRIME	REASON WANTED	WANTED BY
HAAGEN, Gustav	144493	M	Aust.	24. 3.04	Standartenfhr., NSKK	TORTURE	FR.
HAAKNEUS see ETLINGER	239						
HAAS, Peter	186601	M	Hung.	7. 8.98	SS-Mann, Guard, 4.SS Totenkopf-Stuba, C.C.Nordhausen (Ger.) 43-45	WITNESS	U.S.
HAEERL	151653	M	Aust.		Sgt., Army, C.C. Graudens (Pol.) 1.45	TORTURE	U.K.
HABSBURG, Archduke Albrecht	261952	M	Hung.		Col., 98.Regt. from Budapest, nr. Belje (Yugo.) 18.4.41	MURDER	YUGO.
HADABRA, Josef	253698	M	Aust.		Lt., Sicherheits-Regt. 199, Troyes, Marcilly, Fandreville (Fr.) 44	MISC.CRIMES	FR.
HADJIJSKI	190766	M	Bulg.		Lt.Col., Bulg.Army, Cdr. of Garrison, Surdulica Velasrica (Yugo.) 21.10.43	MURDER	YUGO.
HADZI-ILIJEV, Boja	189967	M	Bulg.		Lt., Army Reserve, Goro, Selo, Trateno (Yugo.)	MURDER	YUGO.
HAGEMANN	259827	M	Ital.		Sonderfhr., Recoare Terme (It.) 10.1.45	INTERR.	U.S.
HAGER, Johann	145928	M	Aust.	27. 4.01	Groupleader NSDAP, Civ., MolIn (Aust.) 26.7.44	MURDER	U.S.
HAIDER, Karl	188157	M	Aust.		Civ., Sankt Lorenzen (Aust.) 2.4.44	TORTURE	U.S.
HAJEK	177346	M	Aust.		Sgt., Army, 999.Inf.Div.	MURDER	SOV.UN.
HAJNAL, Vitez	189937	M	Hung.		Officer, Hung.Army, Senta (Yugo.)	MURDER	YUGO.
HAIASCHA	185110	M	Czech.		Civ., SS, C.C.Dachau (Ger.)	MURDER	FR.
HALINKA	259228	M	Aust.		SS Uscharfhr., Gestapo, Area Poitiers (Fr.) 40-44	MISC.CRIMES	FR.
HALITAROF, Groum	305163	M	Bulg.		Municipal Servant, Drama Area (Gre.) 28.9.-20.10.41	MURDER	GRC.
HAMATMA, Jakob	186608	M	Hung.	99	SS-Mann, 4.SS Totenkopf-Stuba, C.C. Nordhausen (Ger.)	WITNESS	U.S.
HAMICH	167193	M	Aust.		Sgt., Feldgendarmerie, Briey (Fr.) 28.8.44	TORTURE	FR.
HAMM, John	253046	M	Nor.		Guard, Quisling Norwegian Bn. "Norway", Boten-Rognan (Nor.) 42	MURDER	NOR.
HAMMER, Mariechen	257798	F	Aust.		Hausfrau, Gratkorn (Aust.) 2.45	WITNESS	U.S.
HANDZIEV	190767	M	Bulg.		Col., Bulg.Army, Deputy Cdr. of 7.Inf.Div. of "Rila", Seskovac (Yugo.) 42-43	MURDER	YUGO.
HANNAK, Wendel	186615	M	Hung.	19. 3.98	SS-Mann, Guard, 4.SS Totenkopf-Stuba, C.C. Nordhausen (Ger.) 43-45	WITNESS	U.S.
HANOT	194282	M	Bel.		SS Sgt., SD, Transport-Commander, Heerenveen (Neth.) 13.4.45	MURDER	NETH.
HANOT, Leon	188651	M	Bel.		Agent, Gestapo, Douai (Fr.) 6.9.44	MURDER	FR.
HANSEN, Hans Peter	341	M	Dan.		Guard, Boten C.C. (Nor.)	MURDER	NOR.
HARALAMPIEV, Ilatan	190768	M	Bulg.		Custom officer, Custom and Excise Police, Vladicin han District (Yugo.) 43-44	MURDER	YUGO.
HARASIMOWICZ	255584	M	Ukr.		Pol.Cmdt. of Ukrain.Police under the Ger.,Wilchowic,Delatya,Nadworna (Pol.) 41-42	MURDER	POL.
HARKAI, Jozsef	307269	M	Hung.	circa 00	Lt.Col., Cmdt. Gendarmerie, 5-1 Investigating Section Gendarmerie, Backa and Baranja during the Hung.occupation (Yugo.) 41-44	MURDER	YUGO.
HARKER	195214	M	Aust.	00	Capt., Arbeitskdo., 6.Coy. Land.Schuetz.Bn. 891, St.Marein Murstal (Aust.)	TORTURE	U.K.
HARRASSER	169523	M	Aust.		Dr., Aerstekammer	MISC.CRIMES	U.S.
HARRESER	251621	M	Aust. or Ger.	circa 11	Pvt., Fieldpolice-troop 532, Nave (It.) 1.8.44	INTERR.	U.K.
HASENFLUCHT	187639	M	Dut.		Pvt., Army, Goudriaan (Neth.) 22.5.44	MURDER	U.K.
HAUNOLD, Carl	196662	M	Aust.	05	Lt., Military Security Police, F.P.No.02039, Turin (It.) 9.12.43	WITNESS	U.K.
HAUSSER, Adam	186623	M	Hung. or Ger.	5. 9.98	SS-Mann, Guard, 4.SS Totenkopf-Stuba, C.C.Nordhausen (Ger.) 43-45	WITNESS	U.S.
HAYNDEL	173587	M	Aust.		SS-Oscharfhr., Waffen-SS, C.C.Theresienstadt (Czech.) 44-45	TORTURE	NETH.
HEGEL	305058	M	Russ. or Ger.		SS Rottenfhr., 84.Landst. Niederlande-Regt., Rhenen, Vreewijk (Neth.) 2.45	MURDER	NETH.
HEGYI	189936	M	Hung.		Agent, Hungarian Police, Novi-Sad (Yugo.)	MURDER	YUGO.
HEIDFOGEL, Anton or HIDEFOGEL	161174	M	Aust.	95	Cpl., Army Arbeitskdo. 951, Kogl, Eisenerz (Aust.) 2.42-4.43	TORTURE	U.K.
HEININGER	254944	M	Aust.	16	Cpl., SD, Gestapo, Milan (It.) 10.8.44	INTERR.	U.K.
HEINS, Jakob	187015	M	Hung. or Ger.	98	SS-Mann, Guard, 31.SS Gren.Div., 2.Art.Regt., C.C.Nordhausen (Ger.) 43-45	WITNESS	U.S.
HELMREICH, Otto	193208	M	Aust.	08	Farmer, Pvt., 4-188.Kgf.Arb.Bn., Fjell (Nor.) 5.44	MURDER	NOR.
HENKEL, Andreas	185974	M	Hung.	24. 8.97	SS-Mann, Guard, C.C. Dora-Nordhausen, Dachau (Ger.) 43-45	WITNESS	U.S.
HENSEL	197609	M	Dan.		Wachtmeister, Justisvollzugsanstalten, C.C. Hamburg (Ger.) 12.42	TORTURE	U.K.
HERNANDEZ	254547	M	Span.	00	Sonderkommandofhr., Gestapo Angers, Savannes (Fr.) 31.8.44	MISC.CRIMES	FR.
HERTZ	197727	M	Rum.		SS Guard, C.C. Buchenwald, Flossenburg (Ger.)	MURDER	U.S.
HESS, Lukas	187097	M	Hung.	26. 9.95	SS-Mann, Guard, 4.SS Totenkopf-Stuba, C.C.Dora-Nordhausen (Ger.) 43-45	TORTURE	U.S.
HEYERMANN	194280	M	Bel.	20	SS-Mann, Warder, SD, SS, Heerenveen (Neth.) 15.4.45	MURDER	NETH.
HIDEFOGEL, Anton see HEIDFOGEL	161174						
HIMMLER, Karl	154573	M	Aust.	05 - 10	Scharfhr., SS, C.C. Reichenau nr. Innsbruck (Aust.) 44-45	TORTURE	U.S.
HINTERSEER, Heinz	179794	M	Aust.		Civ., Lofer (Aust.)	WITNESS	U.S.
HODJEK	192135	M	Czech.	15	Member, Geheime Feldpolizei, Brussels (Bel.)	TORTURE	BEL.
HODVINA	261928	M	Hung.		Solicitor, nr.Belje (Yugo.) 4.41	MURDER	YUGO.
HOEDL, Franz	134916	M	Aust.	07	Civ., C.C. Hartheim (Aust.) 40-44	MURDER	U.S.
HOELZEL	174772	M	Aust.	05	Capt., Police-Coy., Ordnungspolizei, Ulven nr.Bergen (Nor.) 42	MURDER	NOR.
HOFER, Josef or HOFFO	192469	M	Aust.	02	Groupleader NSDAP, Weilbach (Aust.) 14.4.45	MURDER	U.S.
HOFER, Josef	188162	M	Aust.		Civ., Sankt Lorenzen (Aust.) 2.4.44	TORTURE	U.S.
HOFFMANN, Ernst	255589	M	Lux.		C.C. Neckargerach (Ger.)	BRUTALITY	FR.
HOFFMANN, Georg	192769	M	Hung.	21.11.98	SS-Mann, 4.SS Totenkopf-Stuba, C.C. Nordhausen-Dora, Dachau (Ger.) 43-45	WITNESS	U.S.
HOFFMANN, Philipp	192768	M	Hung.	13. 2.97	Guard, SS-Mann, 4.SS Totenkopf-Stuba, C.C.Dora-Mittelbau-Nordhausen, Dachau (Ger.) 43-45	WITNESS	U.S.
HOFFO, see HOFER, Josef	192469						
HOFMANN, Bruno	194848	M	Aust.	22.11.09	Hauptbauleiter, Org.Todt, Volkssturm-Bn. in Ampfing, Muehldorf, Mittergras (Ger.) 6.44-5.45	MURDER	U.S.
HOLBACK see KOLBACK	259729						

HOL-JAN

NAME	C.R.FILE NUMBER	SEX	NATIO- NALITY	DATE OF BIRTH	RANK OCCUPATION UNIT PLACE AND DATE OF CRIME	REASON WANTED	WANTED BY
HOLENIA	168855	M	Aust.		Major, Pz.Pion.Bn., Godinne (Bel.)	MURDER	BEL.
HOLLBACHER, Maria	194301	F	Aust.		C.C. Krispl (Aust.)	WITNESS	NETH.
HOLLIN, Josef	166614	M	Aust.	28.12.97	Civ., Oberndorf (Aust.) 22.11.44	WITNESS	U.S.
HOMER	256862	M	Bel.		Head, C.C. Dora - Nordhausen (Ger.)	MISC.CRIMES	FR.
HOPALONG, Cassidy see MERCH	192915						
HOPPY see MERCH	192915						
HORNETZKI	177595	M	Czech.	12	C.C. Neu Brenn nr. Saarbrucken (Ger.)	TORTURE	FR.
HORVATH	195207	M	Hung.		Col., Army, Kormend (Hung.) 8.44	WITNESS	U.K.
HORWATH, Kazmel	189935	M	Hung.		Mayor (Deputy), Dr., Hung. official, Novi-Sad (Yugo.)	MURDER	YUGO.
HRYNA	134882	M	Aust.	85	Dr., Major, Army, Advisor to chief of security police for Hung. Sopron (Hung.) 3.45	MURDER	U.S.
HRISTOV, Slavov Dono	190769	M	Bulg.		Pvt., Bulg.Army, Frontier Coy., Repiste, Predejan (Yugo.) 22.2.43-23.3.43	MURDER	YUGO.
HUBER, Anton	166612	M	Aust.	12. 8.87	Civ., Oberndorf Kr. Salzburg (Aust.) 22.11.44	WITNESS	U.S.
HUBERT	194300	M	Bel.	15	Rottenfhr., Driver, SD., Heerenveen (Neth.) 15.4.45	TORTURE	NETH.
HUBERT, Joseph	194565	M	Rum.		Cpl., Army, St.Laurent du Manoir (Fr.) 13., 19.8.44	MURDER	FR.
HUGO see JURY	132026						
HUNZINGER, Georg	192680	M	Hung.	96	Pvt.,Guard,31.SS Waffen-Gren.Div.,CC.Dora-Nordhausen,Dachau(Ger.)43-45	MISC.CRIMES	U.S.
HUSS, Gregor	132533	M	Aust.or Ger.		Gestapo de St.Quentin, Chauny (Fr.)	MISC.CRIMES	FR.
IANUZZI	300638	M	Ital.		Lt.,Commander, Black Bde., Codigoro, Adria, Mesola, Ferrara, Rovigo (It.) 12.42	MISC.CRIMES	U.K.
ILEV, Cvetay Ivanov	190770	M	Bulg.		Deputy Mayor, Occupied Territories, Stublo, Vladicin, Han (Yugo.) 43-44	MURDER	YUGO.
ILIEF, Ilias	305194	M	Bulg.		Secret Agent, Bulg.Security, Drama area (Grc.) 28.9.-20.10.41	MURDER	GRC.
ILIJA	190771	M	Bulg.		Pvt., Bulg. Army, H.Q. of Frontier Guard, Sinjac Pirot (Yugo.) 20.2.44	MURDER	YUGO.
ILIJEV see DJOREV	190749	M					
ILIJEVSKI, Krsta Vasov	190772	M	Bulg.		Official, Police at Stublo, Vladicin, Han (Yugo.) 43-44	MURDER	YUGO.
IMPELLIZZERI	67705	M	Ital.		Col., Enfidaville (Tunisia) 42-43	TORTURE	FR.
IMREI	186910	M	Hung.		Unterwachtmeister, 13.SS Pol.Rgt., Bleiburg (Aust.) 14.10.44	MISC.CRIMES	U.S.
INA	301754	F	Pol.		SS-Polish-Woman, Staff of C.C. Auschwitz (Pol.) 40-45	MURDER	FR.
INCHIOSTRI, Ruggero	190983	M	Ital.		Member,Fascio, Sibenik (Yugo.) 41-43	MURDER	YUGO.
INFANTE, Adolfo	305195	M	Ital.		Lt., General, Commander, "Pinerolo" Div., Almiros, Thessaly (Grc.) 15.8.-18.8.43	MISC.CRIMES	GRC
INGEGNI, Pasquale	259121	M	Ital.		Lt., Ital. Army, 56.Rgt., "Marche" Div., Stolac (Yugo.) 4.41-9.42	MURDER	YUGO.
INGLESE	191148	M	Ital.		Col., Chief Prosecutor, Zadar (Yugo.) 41-43	MURDER	YUGO.
INTRECCIALAGLI, Antonio	300679	M	Ital.		Chaplain, 63.Tagliamento Bn., Varallo, Province of Vercelli (It.) 15.4.44	MURDER	U.K.
ISASCA	191164	M	Ital.		Lt. General, Ital. Army, Podgorica (It.) 4.42	MURDER	U.K.
ISASCA, Carlo	190984	M	Ital.		Lt. General, Ital. Army, Div."Venezia", Andrijevica (Montenegro-Yugo.) 5.43-7.43	MURDER	YUGO.
ISMAILOV, Saban	190773	M	Bulg.		Pvt., Bulg.Army, 52.Inf.Rgt., Vranje, Jelasnica, Surdulica (Serbia-Yugo.) 22.3.43	MURDER	YUGO.
IVAN, Hristo see IVANOV	190774						
IVANOF, Ivan	305197	M	Bulg.		Member, Bulg. Security, Drama area (Grc.) 28.9.-20.10.41	MISC.CRIMES	GRC.
IVANOFF	261468	M	Russ.		Major, Inf. II 4.24.A.,Rieux (Fr.) 2.9.44	MURDER	FR.
IVANOV, Hristo or IVAN	190774	M	Bulg.		Lt., Bulg.Army, 6-2 Frontier Sector at Vitnia, Gnjilane (Yugo.) 1.-2.43	MURDER	YUGO.
IVANOV, Vasil Anastasov	190775	M	Bulg.		Lt., 52.Inf.Rgt. at Frontier garrison, Vlase, Distr. of Vrenji (Yugo.) 7.44	MURDER	YUGO.
IVKOVITSCH, Josef	183912	M	Hung.	18. 8.99	SS Mann, 31.SS Gren.-Div., C.C. Dora, Dachau (Ger.)	MURDER	U.S.
IWANOWA	250259	M	Russ.		Pol.prisoner, C.C. Ravensbrueck (Ger.)	INTERR.	FR.
JAHNSRUD, Otto	416	M	Nor.		Camp Guard, C.C. Beten (Nor.) 3.42-43	MURDER	YUGO.
JAKAB, Lajos Ludovit	261975	M	Hung.	2. 8.11	Member, Nyilas-Party, Kosice (Czech.) 1.45	MURDER	CZECH.
JAKOB	258926	M	Aust.		Interpreter, Aktions Kdo. of Custom-house, Lourdes (Fr.) 1.-8.44	MURDER	FR.
JAKOB, Michels	255529	M	Hung.	14.11.98	SS Mann, C.C. Nordhausen (Ger.)	MURDER	U.S.
JAMADJIJEV	190776	M	Bulg.		N.C.O., Bulg.Army, 27. Inf.Div., Prokuplje (Serbia-Yugo.) 43-44	MURDER	YUGO.
JANCE, Josef or JANZ	183452	M	Hung.-Ger.	4. 7.95	SS Mann, 4.SS Totenkopf-Stuba, C.C. Dora-Mittelbau Nordhausen, Dachau (Ger.) 43-45	WITNESS	U.S.
JANKOV, Jordan Pop	190777	M	Bulg.		Mayor, Cmdt., Bulg.Army, Frontier Sector, "Zegra", Gnjilane (Serbia-Yugo.) 1.-2.43	MURDER	YUGO.
JANKOVITCH	257571	M	Aust.		Engineer, Montage VII, Camp Dora - Nordhausen (Ger.) 23.3.44-2.4.45	INTERR.	FR.
JANTSCH	188011	M	Czech.	98	Cpl., 396. Landesschtz.Bn., Stalag IV-A, 5.Coy., near Dresden (Ger.) 3.45	WITNESS	CAN.
JANZ, Josef see JANCE	183452						

JAR - KIM

NAME	C.R.FILE NUMBER	SEX	NATIO-NALITY	DATE OF BIRTH	RANK OCCUPATION UNIT PLACE AND DATE OF CRIME	REASON WANTED	WANTED BY
JARSKO	251063	M	Aust.	11 or 16	RSM,SD,Gestapo,Milan (It.) 10.8.44	INTERR.	U.K.
JASMAKOV,Stanimir	190778	M	Bulg.		Lt.,Bulg.Army,Commandant of Frontier Guard,Sector of Pirot (Yugo.,Serb.) 20.2.44	MURDER	YUGO.
JAWORSKI,Wlodzimierz	189071	M	Ukr.		Member,Gestapo,Stanislawow (Pol.) 8.41-10.42	MURDER	POL.
JELENSKI,Kolev Konstantin	190779	M	Bulg.		Lt.,Bulg.Army,52 Regt. Vranje,Jelasnica sur Dulica (Yugo.) 22.3.43	MURDER	YUGO.
JOERSTL	132030	M	Aust.	18	SS,C.C.Hohenrheim,Plattling (Ger.) 2.-5.45	MURDER	U.S.
JOHANSEN,Tideman	429	M.	Nor.		Lager-Guard,C.C.Boten (Nor.) 3.42-43	MURDER	YUGO.
JOHN	141877	M	Ital.		Sgt.,Major,Camp staff,Tobruk (Africa) 7.42	TORTURE	U.K.
JOHNSRUD,Otto	250862	M	Nor.		Guard,Quisling Norwegian Bn."Norway",Boten-Rognan (Nor.)	MURDER	YUGO.
JONKE,Elise	165914	F	Aust.	3. 4.10	Civilian,Oberndorf (Aust.) 22.11.44	MURDER	U.S.
JORDAN	190780	M	Bulg.		Pvt.,Guard,Bulg.Army,H.Q. of Frontier Guard at Pirot Sinjac,Distr. of Pirot (Yugo.) 20.2.44	MURDER	YUGO.
JOSEF	301759	M	Rum.		Kapo,C.C.Auschwitz (Pol.) 40-45	MURDER	FR.
JOUP (see GOUP)	174973						
JUND,Charles Auguste	196344	M	Fr.	22. 2.22	Uscha,Gestapo,Strassburg (Fr.) 44	MURDER	U.K.
JUNG,Philipp	183506	M	Hung.	7.11.97	Pvt.,4 SS-Totenkopfsturmbann SS Camp Guard,Dora, Nordhausen, Dachau (Ger.) 43-45	WITNESS	U.S.
JUNGWIRTH	146758		Aust.		Civilian,Lietzen (Aust.)	WITNESS	U.S.
JURASZIK,Josef	165915	M	Hung.	15. 3.13	SS-Unterscharfhr.,SS "Kampfgruppe Ney",sur and Aka (Hung.) 7.3.45	MURDER	U.S.
JURY (or HUGO)	132026	M	Aust.	95	Gauleiter,NSDAP,Budapest (Hung.) 44	MISC.CRIMES	U.S.
KAEFSGAARD,Niels	137605	M	Dan.		Wachtmeister,Justizvollzugsanstalten KL.Hamburg (Ger.) 12.42	MURDER	U.K.
KAGEK	174666	M	Pol.	21	Lager Schutz C.C.Wansleben am See (Ger.) 43-45	BRUTALITY	FR.
KAISER,Cornelius (or KAYSER)	170552	M	Lux.-Ger.	03	SS-Unterscharfhr.,SS,SD,H.Q.,Strassenhaus near Rengsdorf (Ger.) 23.12.44-14.2.45	WITNESS	U.K.
KALLAY,Niklos	307270	M	Hung.		Minister,Hung. Prime,Backa,Baranja,Medjumurje,Prekomurje (Yugo.) 9.3.42-19.3.44	MURDER	YUGO.
KALTSEISS,Josef (and Sepp)	29808	M	Pol.	10	SS-Uscharfhr.,SD and Crim.Asst.,Clermont-Ferrand (Fr.) 11.43, 3.44, 9.44, 11.45	MURDER	FR.
KALUTZAN	151329	M	Pol.		Sgt.,Discipline at Stalag 4 A,C.C.Hohnstein (Ger.)	MISC.CRIMES	U.K.
KAMBOURIS see KAVALDJIEF	300029						
KANEV,Kanca	190781	M	Bulg.		Lt.,Bulg.Army,Commander of Unit in 27.Inf.Div.Prokuplje (Yugo.)43-44	MURDER	YUGO.
KANTOR,Janos	189934	M	Hung.		Dr.,Member,Hung.Police,Novi Sad (Yugo.)	MURDER	YUGO.
KAPRI (see VON CAPRI)	173274						
KAROKISA,Konstantin	186757	M	Russ.	17. 2.20	Cpl.,Army Unit 20988, 4 Coy.,Montmartin s-Mer. (Fr.) 8.6.44	MURDER	FR.
KARIUS,Adam (or KARJUS)	183582	M	Hung.-Ger.	5. 4.96	SS-Mann,4 SS-Sturmbann,C.C.Nordhausen,Dora,Mittelbau (Ger.) 43-45	WITNESS	U.S.
KARLIX,Emmanuel	186756	M	Czech.		Oberkapo,C.C.Stephanskirchen near Rosenheim (Ger.)	TORTURE	FR.
KARNER,born EHNER,Stefanie (see KORNER)	194007						
KAROLIJEV	190782	M	Bulg.		Lt.Col.,Bulg.Army,Commander of 52 Inf.-Regt. at Vranje Vlase, Jelasnica, sur Dulica (Yugo.) 22.3.43	MURDER	YUGO.
KASOBOWSKI,John	162563	M	Pol.		Civilian,Dairy worker,Montan nr. Graudenz (Pol.) 3.43	MISC.CRIMES	U.K.
KASUM-CHAN-VELI	187334	M	Turk.	15. 7.04	Civilian,Marianske Lazne (Czech.) 39-45	MISC.CRIMES	CZECH.
KASZ,Josef Daniel	167228	M	Hung.	18	SS-Oberscharfhr.,Hung.Kampfgruppe "Ney",Sur-Aka Gyor (Hung.) 3.45	MURDER	U.S.
KATJA	150678	F	Dut.	27	Oberaufseherin,SS,C.C.Vught (Neth.) 43-44	MURDER	BEL.
KATSCHEFSKY	167089	M	Pol.		Rehaupaul (Fr.) 9.9.44	MURDER	FR.
KAUNS	137606	M	Dan.		Wachtmeister,Justizvollzugsanstalten,KL.Hamburg (Ger.) 12.42	TORTURE	U.K.
KAVALEK,Joseph	257517	M	Czech.		Guard,C.C.Dora,Nordhausen (Ger.)	MURDER	FR.
KAVALDJIEF,Demetrios (or KAMBOURIS)	300039	M	Bulg.		Member of the Bulg.Ochrana Security Service,Kavalla, 43-44	TORTURE	GRC.
KAYSER,Cornelius (see KAISER)	170552						
KAZAKOF,Christos	300261		Bulg.		Command. of the Bulg.Security in Drama - Area, 28.9.-20.10.41	MURDER	GRC.
KEJZ	257292	M	Aust.	circa 26	SS-Mann,Aid Stat.Regt.37, SS-Div."Goetz von Berlichingen",W-SS near St. Eny (Fr.) 3.7.44	WITNESS	U.S.
KEREMITSKI,Cena Petrov	190783	M	Bulg.		Police-man,Police at Babusnica and Surronding Villages (Yugo.) 44	MURDER	YUGO.
KERN,Christian	186122	M	Hung.	17. 2.98	Pvt.,31 SS Gren.Div,2 Art.Regt.,C.C.Dora,Nordhausen, Dachau (Ger.)	WITNESS	U.S.
KERN,Joachim	161259	M	Aust.	28.10.95	Civilian,Meishofen (Aust.) 25.2.44	WITNESS	U.S.
KERN,Peter	186121	M	Hung.	23.11.95	Pvt.,31 SS Gren.Div.,C.C.Dora,Nordhausen,Dachau (Ger.) 43-45	WITNESS	U.S.
KERZENBERGER,Konrad	137789	M	Aust.	8. 2.98	Truppfhr.,SA,Liezen (Aust.) 43	MURDER	U.S.
KEYL,Joseph	193652	M	Bel.	2.11.08	SS-Rottfhr.,SD Gent,Aussend.,der Sipo,Leeuwarden (Neth.) 19.9.44 14.4.45	MURDER	NETH.
KHAN	188754	M	Hung.		Colonne Indoue,950,Charente Et Vienne (Fr.) 25.8.44	TORTURE	FR.
KIENAST,Helmuth	260618	M	Aust.	10 or 14	SS-Sgt.,Member of NSDAP,Promoted to Gestapo Lt., Environs de St. Flour (Fr.) 14.6.44	MURDER	FR.
KIESIEL,Josef	187172	M	Pol.-Ger.	95	Cpl.,565 L.Sch.Bn.,C.C.Stalag 8 B,Lamsdorf (Ger.) 42-44	TORTURE	U.K.
KILBACHER,Peter	194098	M	Aust.		Forman,.C.C.Krispl (Aust.)	Torture	NETH.
KIMOURJIEF,Jordan	300263		Bulg.		Guard,Police, Rural at Makri-Evros, 7.45	TORTURE	GRC.

NAME	C.R.FILE NUMBER	SEX	NATIO-NALITY	DATE OF BIRTH	RANK	OCCUPATION UNIT	PLACE AND DATE OF CRIME	REASON WANTED	WANTED BY
KIPFER, Franz	187986	M	Czech.	05	Pvt., Army 561.Land.Schuetz.Bn., Bauerwitz (Ger.) 12.11.41			MURDER	U.K.
KIRALY, Franz	259566	M	Hung.		SS-Mann, C.C. Buchenwald (Ger.) 40-43			MURDER	BEL.
KIRCHEIM	137603	M	Russ.		German Army, Holds Ironcross 2. Class, Belgrade (Yugo.) 4.44			MISC.CRIMES	U.K.
KISELICKI, Kiril	190784	M	Bulg.		Col.,Bulg.Army, Chief of staff of 27.Inf.Div.(Yugo.) (Serb.) 43-44			MURDER	YUGO.
KJOSTEBEKOV, P.	191022	M	Bulg.		Director, State Security of Sofia, Pirot (Yugo.) 4.42			MISC.CRIMES	YUGO.
KLEESZ, Karl	186291	M	Hung.	25.4.97	SS-Mann, 4.SS Totenkopf Sturmbann, C.C. Dora Nordhausen (Ger.) 43-45			WITNESS	U.S.
KLEIN, Nikolaus	186278	M	Hung.-Ger.	24.10.95	SS-Mann, 4.SS Totenkopf Sturmbann, C.C. Nordhausen,Dora,Dachau (Ger.)			TORTURE	U.S.
KLEIN, Stephan	250937	M	Hung.		Doctor, C.C. Buchenwald (Ger.)			INTERR.	FR.
KLEINE	186762	M	Czech.		Kapo, C.C. Stephanskirchen near Rosenheim (Ger.)			TORTURE	FR.
KLEPP, Jacob	186274	M	Hung.	14.8.99	SS-Mann, Guard, 31 SS Gren.Div.,2.Art.Rgt. C.C. Dora,Nordhausen, Dachau (Ger.) 43-45			WITNESS	U.S.
KLETSOCK	150673	M	Rum.-Ger.		Guard, SD, C.C. Lahde Weser (Ger.)			TORTURE	BEL.
KLIM, Alois	185689	M	Aust.		Interrogator official, SS interrogation center, department for communism Byron, Kalithea, Athens (Grc.)			MURDER	GRC.
KLJUNAK, Emelija	190986	F	Ital.		Civilian, Daughter of Commissario Del Fascio (Jakov Kljunak) Blato (Yugo.) 41-43			MURDER	YUGO.
KLJUNAK, Jakov	190985	M	Ital.		Commissario, Ital.Party Fascio, Island of Korcula, Blato, Veli, Luki (Yugo.) 41-43			MURDER	YUGO.
KLUTE	102948	M	Ital.		Major, Oflag C.C. Graudenz (Pol.) 7.44			MURDER	U.K.
KNEIP	185860	M	Rum.		Rottfhr., SS, C.C. Mauthausen (Aust.)			TORTURE	U.S.
KNOLL, Karl	253725	M	Aust.		Major, Air-Force, Enns. (Ger.): 27.2.45			WITNESS	U.S.
KNY	192372	M	Czech.		Pvt., Army Unit 26033, Soissons (Fr.) 15.8.44			WITNESS	FR.
KOCEV	190785	M	Bulg.		High police official, Village of Zavidinac, Pirot (Yugo.) 41-43			MURDER	YUGO.
KOCZAK, Franz	145188	M	Aust.		Oschfhr., SS Leibstandarte "Adolf Hitler", Rosbach (Ger.) 4.5.45			MURDER	U.S.
KOEBERL, Erwin	137794	M	Aust.		Schfhr., SA, Bad Aussee (Aust.)			TORTURE	U.S.
KOGON, Eugen	161516	M	Aust.	02	Civilian, C.C. Buchenwald (Ger.)			TORTURE	U.S.
KOHLER, Adam	187185	M	Hung.	19.9.96	SS-Mann, SS Totenkopf Sturmbann C.C. Nordhausen,Dora,Dachau (Ger.) 43-45			TORTURE	U.S.
KOHLBES, Florian	185844	M	Hung.	7.7.96	SS-Mann,C.C.,Guard,Dachau,Nordhausen,Dora,(Ger.) 43-45			WITNESS	U.S.
KOHOUTEK, Wenzel	165247	M	Aust.	88	Standartenfhr., SS, SD, Sipo, Belgrad (Yugo.) 44			MURDER	U.S.
KOKAIL	152506	M	Aust.		Col, Stalag XX A, C.C. Thorn (Pol.) 26.7.44			MURDER	U.S.
KOLB	88819	M	Aust.		Sturmbannfhr., SS C.C. Sachsenhausen (Ger.)			MURDER	FR.
KOLBACK (or HOLBACK)	259729	M	Lux.		Interpreter,Unit F.P. VL 05811,St.Pierre de Semilly,Manche (Fr.) 9.42			WITNESS	FR.
KOLTAI	189933	M	Hung.		Doctor, Asst. Hung.Police, Novi Sad (Yugo.)			MURDER	YUGO.
KOMMATNY	255543	M	Russ.		See Consolidated List Part II Appendix "A"				
KONEV (see CONEV)	189970								
KONIG, Oskar	145179	M	Rum.	00	Civilian, C.C. Buchenwald (Ger.)			TORTURE	U.S.
KONSTANTINOV	189966	M	Bulg.		Major, Bulg.Army, Public official, Pirot (Yugo.)			MISC.CRIMES	YUGO.
KONYOKY, Josef	189932	M	Hung.-Ger.		Counsellor, Hung.Police, Novi Sad (Yugo.)			MURDER	YUGO.
KOPECKY, Jan	255160	M	Pol.	29.7.23	See Consolidated List Part II Appendix "A"				
KOPIL (see COPIL)	189794								
KOPJAN, Imrich	253751	M	Hung.	4.11.06	Civilian, Komarno (Czech.) 44			MURDER	CZECH.
KOPROWIAK, Michel	256130	M	Pol.		Guard, C.C. Flossenburg (Ger.)			MURDER	FR.
KORB	259761	M	Aust.		See Consolidated List Part II Appendix "A"				
KOREIL, Rupert	185843	M	Hung.	13.5.97	Pvt.,31 SS Gren.Div.2 Art.Rgt.,Guard, C.C.Dachau,Nordhausen,Dora,(Ger.)			TORTURE	U.S.
KOREIL, Robert or Rupert	185816	M	Hung.-Ger.		SS-Mann,4.SS Totenk.Stuba.,C.C.Mittelbau Dora,Nordhausen (Ger.)43-45			WITNESS	U.S.
KORNER(nee ERNER) (or KARNER)	194007	F	Aust.	14	Civilian, Saleswoman, Amstetten (Aust.) 20.9.45			TORTURE	U.S.
KURNER, Stefanie)									
KOSMANOF, Lasaros	300271	M	Bulg.		Member, of the secret police, Drama area (Yugo.) 26.9.-20.10.41			MURDER	GRC.
KOSSIAR	132486	M	Aust.-Ger.		Doctor, Civilian, Kindberg, (Aust.) 10.43-4.44			MISC.CRIMES	U.K.
KOSTOV, Ilija (see KRESTEV)	190786	M	Bulg.		Commander, Bulg.Army, Unit, 27. Inf.Div., Prokuplje (Yugo.) 43-44			MURDER	YUGO.
KOSTOV, Ilija (see KRESTEV)	190788								
KOTZEV, Slesco Kosta	300272		Bulg.		Lt., Commanding officer of the Garrison of Scutari Serres, 9.43-44			MURDER	GRC.
KOTZIK	178309	M	Pol.		SS-Mann,12.SS Pz.Div.,25.Pz.Gren.Rgt.,15.Coy, Abbaye-Ardenne (Fr.) 6.6.-2.7.44			TORTURE	CAN.
KOURTOF	300273	M	Bulg.		Lt., Bulg. serving in Mikri, Daria, Thrace, 5.42-9.43			MISC.CRIMES	GRC.
KOUTCHEFF	167070	M	Russ.-Ger.		Medicin, Army, Blobasmalec Pont L'Abbe (Fr.) 6.-8.44			WITNESS	FR.
KOWATZ	905758	M	Hung.		Pvt.,prison guard, C.C. Chaidari (Athens) (Grc.) 10.43-10.44			MURDER	GRC.
KOZAROV, Hristo	190787	M	Bulg.		General Major, Bulg.Army, commander of 27.Inf.Div.Prokuplje(Yugo.)43-44			MURDER	YUGO.
KRACHER, Max	179790	M	Aust.		Civilian, St.Martin. (Aust.) 16.11.44			PILLAGE	U.S.
KRACHLER	164135	M	Aust.	09	Cpl.,3-188 ArbBn. Brattholmen. (Nor.) 5.45			MURDER	NOR.
KRACIUM, Karl	132043	M	Rum.		Wachtmeister,Civilian, last known home address: Lebenstedt, Reppenerschestr.2			TORTURE	U.S.
KRACIUM, Stephan	132061	M	Rum.		Wachtmeister,police, Camp Hallendorf, home address: Lebenstedt, Reppenerschestr.2			TORTURE	U.S.
KRAFT	192455	M	Rum.-Hung.		Guard, C.C. Breendonck (Bel.) 4.-5.44			TORTURE	BEL.
KRAFT, Bruno	164049	M	Czech.		Uschfhr., SS, Brussels (Bel.)			MURDER	BEL.
KRAIGER	165250	M	Aust.	95	Capt., Abwehr, Belgrade (Yugo.) 44			MURDER	U.S.

KRA - LAN   -20-

NAME	C.R.FILE NUMBER	SEX	NATIO-NALITY	DATE OF BIRTH	RANK	OCCUPATION UNIT PLACE AND DATE OF CRIME	REASON WANTED	WANTED BY
KRAUSE	302073	M	Pol.			Doctor, Head of Block 7, C.C.Birkenau (Pol.) 40-45	MURDER	FR.
KRAUSS, Joseph or Jupp	251666	M	Pol.			Kapo, C.C.Buchenwald (Ger.) 43-44	TORTURE	FR.
KRAVAJK	255549	M	Pol.			Gendarm, Fieldpolice, Annay sur Bois (Fr.) 2.7.44-21.8.44	INTERR.	FR.
KREGERSMAN	261916		Bel.			See Consolidated List Part II - Appendix "A"		
KREIL, Franz	143176	M	Aust.			Civilian, Locomotive Fireman	MURDER	U.S.
KREMER, Anton	167964	M	Yugo.	31.8.08		Schuetze, SS, C.C.Natzweiler (Fr.) 42-44	MURDER	FR.
KRESTEV, Ilija or KOSTOV	190788	M	Bulg.			Head, Police, Vitina Gnjilane (Yugo.) 1.-2.43	MURDER	YUGO.
KREUTZER, Georg	260935	M	Yugo.	28.11.09		SS-Sturmmann, SS-Juard, Farmer, Civilian, Auschwitz (Pol.) 42-45	BRUTALITY	POL.
KREUZER, Franz	137795	M	Aust.			Country Pol.Man, Zellenleiter, Army, NSV, DAF, Altmuenster (Aust.) 6.44	MURDER	U.S.
KRIEG, Anton	185845	M	Hung.	20.1.96		Guard, 31 SS Gren., 2 Art., Dora-Nordhausen, Dachau (Ger.) 43-45	WITNESS	U.S.
KRIEGER, Daniel	187152	M	Ger.-Hung.	6.7.95		SS-Pvt., Guard, 4 SS Totenkopf-Sturmbann, C.C.Dora-Nordhausen (Ger.)	TORTURE	U.S.
KRIVAN, Sepp Joseph	257503	M	Aust.	96		Sgt., North Btty., AA, Texel (Neth.) 3.2.45	MURDER	U.S.
KROLL	125065	M	Pol.			Capt., Kgf.Arb.Kdo., C.C.Sosnowitz (Pol.) 43	TORTURE	U.K.
KROLL, Christian	178757	M	Bess.			Farmer, Civilian, Fedelhausen (Pol.) 20.2.44	MURDER	U.K.
KRONHOLZ, Robert	251679	M	Aust.			Secret Agent, Gestapo, Belgrad (Yugo.) 4.41-10.44	INTERR.	YUGO.
KROPIVEEC	192450	M	Rum.-Hung.			Guard, C.C.Breendonck (Bel.) 4.-5.44	MURDER	BEL.
KRUEGER, Heinz	256912	M	Aust.-Ger.			Zugwachtmeister, 7 Coy.322 Bn., 5 Schtz.Rgt., Ljubljana, Cotje und Kranj (Yugo.) 42-43	MISC.CRIMES	YUGO.
KRUG, Maria	188294	F	Aust.			Civilian, Sant Lorenzen (Aust.) 2.4.44	WITNESS	U.S.
KRUPKA, Oskar Wilhelm	189447	M	Czech.			Civilian, Eindhoven (Neth.)	MISC.CRIMES	NETH.
KRUPKA, Rudolf	189446	M	Czech.	11.8.04		Civilian, Eindhoven (Neth.)	MISC.CRIMES	NETH.
KUDLER, Karl	145169	M	Aust.	11		SS-Uschfhr., Waffen SS, Leibst."Adolf Hitler", Rosbach (Ger.) 4.3.45	MURDER	U.S.
KUENZEL, Karl	174104	M	Aust.	05		Usturmfhr., Allg.SS, Gestapo, Member Camp Commander of work reformatory C.C.Vienna, Mauthausen (Aust.) 1.-18.4.45	MURDER	U.S.
KUIPERS, Lammert	150681	M	Dut.-Ger.			C.C.Vugt (Neth.) 43-44	MURDER	BEL.
KULA	261043	M	Czech.			Sgt., Unit.of.Art.Nr.40539, Plounez (Fr.) 5.-6.8.44	TORTURE	FR.
KULA, Georg	186107	M	Hung.	96		SS-Mann, Guard, C.C.Dora-Nordhausen, Dachau (Ger.) 43-45	WITNESS	U.S.
KULUFAKAS, Kosta	141929	M	Ital.			Interpreter, C.C.Larissa (Grc.) 7.-10.42	MISC.CRIMES	U.K.
KUN	189931	M	Hung.			Lt.Col., Hungarian Gestapo, Novi Sad (Yugo.)	MURDER	YUGO.
KUNICK (or KUNIK) Maria	143184	F	Aust.			Female Member, Guard, Waffen.SS, C.C.Sensing (Ger.) 1.45	MISC.CRIMES	U.S.
KURCHBAUM, A.	132487	M	Aust.-Ger.			Guesthousekeeper, Civilian, Wagendorf near Liebnitz (Aust.) 25.2.44	TORTURE	U.S.
KURNER (nee EBNER, Stefanie) (see KORNER)	194007							
KUSCH-CHAKANOV	167049	M	Russ.			Lt., Army, Inf.Unit Nr.23209, Plozevet (Fr.) 4.8.44	MURDER	FR.
KUSCHOKOW (see GUBSCHOKOV)	39645							
KUTSCH, Georg	186111	M	Hung.	93		SS-Mann, Guard, 4 SS Totenkopf-Sturmbann, C.C.Mittelbau-Nordhausen, Dora, Dachau (Ger.) 43-45	INTERR.	U.S.
KUTSCHERA	145167	M	Aust.			SS-Bdefhr., White Russia, Pol. 40	MISC.CRIMES	U.S.
KWANIEWSKI, Marian	192333	M	Pol.			Member, SS, C.C.Flossenburg (Ger.)	MISC.CRIMES	FR.
KWARDA, Karl	145296	M	Aust.			Lagerfuehrer, Civilian, (Aust.)	TORTURE	U.S.
KYROF	300286	M	Bulg.			Lt., Bulgarian served in the Polygyro Area, Taxiarchis Polygyros 7.-8.44	MURDER	GRC.
LABONIA, Enrico	190987	M	Ital.			Major, Italian Stalag, C.C.Gravina (It.) 29.9.43	MURDER	YUGO.
LACCIE (see LEACCIE)	132186							
LAFARINA	190988	M	Ital.			Commissar, Police, Susak, Podlum (Yugo.) 41-4.43	MURDER	YUGO.
LAHNER, Franz	192742	M	Aust.	circa 05		Sgt., Guard, Feldstraflager Nord, Reichsjustizministerium, C.C.Finmark (Nor.)	MISC.CRIMES	NOR.
LALOEV, Stephan	190789	M	Bulg.			Bulgarian Army, 27 Inf.Div., Prokuplje (Yugo.) 43 and 44	MURDER	YUGO.
LA MARCA, Giacomo	307298	M	Ital.			Capt., Judge, Military Tribunal for 2 Army Section of Ljubljana (Yugo.) 41-43	MURDER	YUGO.
LANARI, Pietro	307299	M	Ital.			Prosecutor, Military, Judge, Correspondent of Special Tribunal for defence of State Rom (It.) 4.41-9.43	MURDER	YUGO.
LANCESCO	257644	M	Ital.			Major, Italian Army, PW Camp 115, Marisciano (It.) 3.43-9.43	BRUTALITY	U.K.
LANDINI, Luciano	145143	M	Ital.			Capt., Army, Giudiredel Tribunale militare di Guerra, Dettigne (Yugo.) 43	MURDER	YUGO.
LANG, Rupert	72318	M	Aust.			Pvt., Army, 377 Dulag, Guard, Coy.Dulag 377 (Ger.) 1.45	TORTURE	U.S.
LANGER, Fritz	259935	M	Aust.	13.1.04		Crim.-officer, NSDAP, Crim.-Police, Wien, Home Adress: Wien XXI, Angererstr.3 Austria, Castel del Rio (It.)	MURDER	U.S.
LANTIERI	145429	M	Ital.			Col., Army, "Re" Div., Art.Rgt., Slovenia, Croatia (Yugo.) 43	MURDER	YUGO.

NAME	C.R.FILE NUMBER	SEX	NATIO-NALITY	DATE OF BIRTH	RANK OCCUPATION UNIT PLACE AND DATE OF CRIME	REASON WANTED	WANTED BY
LAPO, Adam	187062	M	Hung.-Ger.	3.12.95 or 9.12.95	SS Mann, Guard, 9.SS Gren.Div.,C.C. Nordhausen-Dora (Ger.) 43-45	TORTURE	U.S.
LARISO, Giuseppe	259191	M	Ital.		Lt.,Ital.Army "Marche" Div.56.Rgt.,Stolac (Yugo.) 4.41-9.42	MURDER	YUGO.
LARSEN, Flemig	162072	M	Dan.	15	Oberscharfhr., Waffen SS,"Wiking"-Div.,Arnheim (Neth.) 24.9.44	MURDER	U.K.
LARSSON	250917	M	Nor.		Guard at Boten-Rognan, Nor.Bn.Norway Quisling (Nor.) 42	INTERR.	YUGO.
LA SPADA, Michelangelo	146308	M	Ital.		Lt., Ital.Army,"Isonzo"Div. 23.Inf.Rgt.,Cernomels (Yugo.) 43	MURDER	YUGO.
LA SPINA	300652	M	Ital.	21	Member Black-Bde.,Mesola Ferrara Adria Rovigo, 12.44	MURDER	U.K.
LASTRETIO	259101	M	Ital.		Capt. Carabinieri, Mostar (Yugo.) 12.7.42	INTERR.	YUGO.
LASZLO, Marton	172076	M	Hung.		SS Guard, C.C. Auschwitz, Buchenwald (Pol. Ger.) 4.45	MURDER	U.S.
LATANZIA	173235	M	Ital.		Lt.Col., Oflag, C.C. Bari, (It.)	TORTURE	U.K.
LATANZIA	193540	M	Ital.		Italian Army, C.C. Ancone (It.) 12.42-1.43	TORTURE	U.K.
LATARNIK, Alois	162870	M	Pol.	7. 6.04	Sturmfhr., S.A., Louperhouse (Fr.) 1.11.44	MURDER	FR.
LATTANCIO see LATTAUGIO	67570						
LATTARULA, Leonardo	151345	M	Ital.		Sgt. Major, Italian Army, C.C. Tradate-Varese (It.)	TORTURE	U.K.
L'ATTAUGIO or LATTANCIO	67570	M	Ital.		Col.,Oflag 79, Brunswick (Ger.) 5.-9.44	MURDER	U.K.
LATTE	253126	M	Aust.	04	Major, Airforce, 734.Flak Btty., Ciacomo (It.) 3.1.44	INTERR.	U.K.
LAUBAISE, Leonie	252381	F	Bel.		BCF,BDS France SD-Kdo.z.b.V. 7 "Pullmer", Cirey (Fr.) 44	WITNESS	U.K.
LAUWAERT, Florimond	193656	M	Bel.	11. 4.86	SS Mann, SIPO, SD. Gent, Leeuwarden (Neth.) 13.4.44-14.4.45	MURDER	NETH.
LEACCIE or LEZZIE or LACCIE	132186	M	Ital.	90	Sgt. Major, Italian Army, Trigtarhuna (North Africa) 7.42	TORTURE	U.K.
LEBEDOV, Ivan	190790	M	Bulg.		Civilian, Tax Collector, Belisevo Vladicin Han (Yugo.) 43-44	MURDER	YUGO.
LECHNER	192740	M	Aust.	00	Sgt., Reichs-Justizministerium,Feldstraflager, C.C. Finmark (Nor.) 6.42-45	MISC.CRIMES	NOR.
LEDRAPPIER, Jean	195056	M	Fr.		SD. Einsatz Kdo.(FPN 03069 C), Wenger, Pexonne (Fr.) autumn 44	MURDER	U.K.
LEFTHEROF see MALINOF	300310						
LEHNARD	254988	M	Aust.	circa 00	Col.Cmdt.,P.G.77, Spoletto (It.) 13.11.43	INTERR.	U.K.
LEHRER, Franz	178756	M	Aust.	05	Pvt., Landesschtz.Bn. 373, 1.Coy., Leonhard (Aust.) 2.44	MISC.CRIMES	U.K.
LEINWEBER, Reno	259171	M	Ital.	circa 10	Commander, 291.Rgt.,Zara Div. Kistanje, Piramatovci, Banja (Yugo.) 17.8.42, 9.43, 22.4.43	MISC.CRIMES	YUGO.
LEIPOLD, Georg	187046	M	Hung.-Ger.	3. 9.95	SS Mann, Guard, 4.SS Totenkopf Sturmbann, C.C. Mittelbau Dora-Nordhausen (Ger.) 43-45	MURDER	U.S.
LEITNER, Fritz	188298	M	Aust.		Civilian, Sant Lorenzen (Aust.) 2.4.44	WITNESS	U.S.
LE METRE, Gaetano	195624	M	Ital.		Official, Justizministerium, Rom (It.) 41-43	TORTURE	YUGO.
LENTI, Nicholas	300295	M	Ital.		Major and Governor, Inf.7 Italian Rgt. - "Cuneo"Div. Military of Naxos, during the Italian Occ., Island of Naxos, 41-43	MISC.CRIMES	GRC.
LEONARDI	190989	M	Ital.		Col.,Italian Army, O.C.Rgt. Sassari-Div. (F.561),Udbina Gracac (Yugo.) 1. and 2.43	MURDER	YUGO.
LEONARDI	251122	M	Ital.		Col. C.O. of Rgt. "Sassari", Fara-Slovenia	MURDER	YUGO.
LEONARDI, Nicola	307300	M	Ital.		Consul Judge of Special Tribunal for defense of State Rom (It.) 4.41-9.43	MURDER	YUGO.
LEOPARDI, Alberto	190990	M	Ital.		Cdt., Italian Army, 151.Rgt.Fanteria "Sassari" Div., Fara (Yugo.)	PILLAGE	YUGO.
LEOPOARDI, Sergio	145428	M	Ital.		Brigadiere of Customs Guard, Commander of Customs Guard at Kuzalj in District of Banja Luka on Border Croatia, Slovenia (Yugo.) 41-15.8.42	PILLAGE	YUGO.
LEPROWSKI	253767	M	Russ.		Interpreter, Gestapo, Paris (Fr.) 41-44	TORTURE	FR.
LETTIERI, Roberto	300667	M	Ital.		Major, Judge, Military Tribunal of war of Army, Sezione di Sebenico, Sibenik, Dalmatia (Yugo.) 41-43	TORTURE	U.K.
LEUTENS, Joseph	67575	M	Bel.	28	Member, Organisation Todt, Boulogne-sur-Mer (Fr.) 44	MURDER	FR.
LEVI, Lorenzo	187972	M	Ital.	95	Col.,Army, C.C. Tahuna (North Africa) 7.-11.42	TORTURE	U.K.
LEVY, Elie	162708	M	Aust.	20. 9.10	Chief, Gestapo, Montelimar (Fr.)	MISC.CRIMES	FR.
LEX, Alfred (Fred)	257189	M	Aust.		Hauptsturmfhr., Waffen SS, 3.Coy. 1.Bn. Rgt."Der Fuehrer", Foret de Nieppe (Fr.) 5.40	SUSPECT	U.K.
LEZZIE see LEACCIE	132186						
LICEV	190791	M	Bulg.		Capt.,Bulgarian Army, Commander of 1.Coy. 122.Bn.,Zitni Potok (Yugo.) 43-44	MURDER	YUGO.
LICHKA, Georges or LISCHKA	48446	M	Pol.		Pvt., Army, Tulle (Fr.) 4.6.44	MURDER	FR.
LIDO	254142	M	Ital.		Agent, C.C. Corropola (It.) 41	TORTURE	YUGO.
LIETO, Achille	253774	M	Ital.		Brigadiere, Police, Public Security, Split (Yugo.) 26.6.43	BRUTALITY	YUGO.
LIGAS	190991	M	Ital.		Major, Italian Army, XXII Bn. Isle of Is Veliki (Yugo.) 28.7.42	MURDER	YUGO.
LILLA, Wilhelm	134801	M	Aust.	03	Sgt., 19.SS Police Rgt.,Vigaun, Toulouse, Campiegne, Agen Tulle (Yugo. Fr.) 5.41-10.44	Torture	U.S.
LINDENBERGER, Gustav	190653	M	Aust.		Farmer, Ortsbauernfuehrer, Public official, SS, C.C.	MURDER	U.S.
LINDZE, Benedikt	156097	M	Ger.-Aust.		Civilian, C.C. Klagenfurt (Aust.) 23.11.43	TORTURE	U.K.
LINEMANN, Fritz	188292	M	Czech.		Lt. Army, Athens (Grc.)	TORTURE	GRC.
LIPARI, Ignazio	145427	M	Ital.		Lt. Medico, "Isonzo"-Div. 23.Inf.Rgt. Como, Cernomelj (Yugo.) 43	MURDER	YUGO.
LIPINSKI	253132	M	Pol.		Lt., Gendarmerie, Valence (Fr.)	INTERR.	FR.
LIPPI	261323	M	Ital.		Cmdt. 88.Bn, Black shirt, Pietralba (Fr.) 10.9.43	BRUTALITY	FR.
LISCHKA, Georges see LICHKA	48446						
LJUPCV	190792	M	Bulg.		Capt., Bulgarian Army, Zupa (Yugo.) 2.-6.8.43	TORTURE	YUGO.
LOCCI, Nicodemo	190992	M	Ital.		Member of Fascist Directorat in Sibenik (Yugo.) 41-43	MURDER	YUGO.
LODI, Georgio	145426	M	Ital.		Lt.-Col., "Isonzo"-Div. 23.Inf.Rgt. "Como" (Yugo.) 43	MURDER	YUGO.
LOERINCZ, Albert	261897	M	Hung.	19	Member, Nyilas Party, Kosice (Czech.) 1.45	MURDER	CZECH.
LOGAGLIO	189914	M	Ital.		Bizerta (Tunisia)	MURDER	FR.
LOIALI, Adalberto	255288	M	Ital.		Judge, Ital.Special Trib., Zadar, Sibenik,Split,Kotor (Yugo.) 41-43	INTERR.	YUGO.
LOLLA	190993	M	Ital.		Capt., Ital.Army, 11.Bn. Carabinieri, Cetinje, Crna.Gora (Yugo.) 41-43	MURDER	YUGO.
LOMONACH, Guido	145425	M	Ital.		Headmaster, Primary School, Isle of Vis (Yugo.) 43	TORTURE	YUGO.
LOPEZ	194647	M	Span.		Kapo, C.C. Mauthausen (Aust.) 44-45	MISC.CRIMES	FR.
LOTHALER, Hans	134918	M	Aust.		SA Member, Civilian, Reichspost of Linz, C.C.Hartheim (Ger.) 40-44	MURDER	U.S.

LOT-MAR

NAME	C.R.FILE NUMBER	SEX	NATIO-NALITY	DATE OF BIRTH	RANK OCCUPATION UNIT PLACE AND DATE OF CRIME	REASON WANTED	WANTED BY
LOTTI, Pietro	255287	M	Ital.		Civilian, Questore of Cattaro, Kotor (Yugo.) 41-43	MISC.CRIMES	YUGO.
LOTURGO	259125	M	Ital.		Questore di Messina, C.C.Lipari (It.) 42	BRUTALITY	YUGO.
LOUVIER, Rene	253128	M	Fr.		FGF, SD, Kom'Do "Wenger", Bds.Baccarat,Etival (Fr.) 44	MURDER	U.K.
LO VULLO, Luigi	145429	M	Ital.		Major, "Isonzo" Div., 24.Inf.Regt. "Como" (Yugo.)	MURDER	YUGO.
LOUVIER, Eduardo	145424	M	Ital.		Capt., "Isonzo" Div., 98.Fascist Legion, Trebnje (Yugo.) 43	MURDER	YUGO.
LUBINI, Alfredo	145422	M	Ital.		Port customs official, Dalmatio (Yugo.) 43	MURDER	YUGO.
LUCCHETTI, Augusto	251190	M	Ital.		Col.,292.Regt. Fanteria, Cmdr.,Brima near Sibenik (Yugo.) 9.12.42	PILLAGE	YUGO.
LUCCHETTI, Nilo	189046	M	Ital.	20	Civilian, Black shirt, near Magliano (It.) 10.10.43	TORTURE	U.K.
LUCI	145432	M	Ital.		Col.,chief of Intelligence II.Army, Susak (Yugo.) 41	MURDER	YUGO.
LUCIANO	259190	M	Ital.		Lt., It.Army, "Marche" Div.,56.Regt., Stolac (Yugo.) 4.41-9.43	MURDER	YUGO.
LUCINI, Bruno	145421	M	Ital.		Col., Army, chief of staff, XI.Army Corps, Ljubljana (Yugo.) 41	MURDER	YUGO.
LUCKANZ, Johann	134809	M	Aust.	22 - 24	Pvt., Air Force, Ahrweiler (Ger.) 26.12.44	WITNESS	UNWCC.
LUNDAL, Randulf	257399	M	Nor.		Pvt., SS, slave labour camp, Korgen (Nor.) 6.42-43	MURDER	YUGO.
LUPARELLI, Enzo	259189	M	Ital.		Lt., It.Army, "Marche" Div., 56.Regt., Stolac (Yugo.) 4.41-9.42	MURDER	YUGO.
LUPI, Giuseppe	300699	M	Ital.		Cpl., Italian Fascist, Pogio Mirteto (It.) 28.5.44	MURDER	U.K.
LURUDAC, Palmiro	145420	M	Ital.		Capt., Cmdr.25 Sector Copertura Timavo, St.Peter nr.Krasu (Yugo.) 42	TORTURE	YUGO.
LUSANO, Alexandro	190994	M	Ital.		Lt.Gen., It.Army, 55.Regt., "Marche" Div., Trebinje (Yugo.) 41-43	MURDER	YUGO.
LUWITZKI, Kasimir	199149	M	Rum.		Pvt., SS Totenkopf-Verband, C.C.Buchenwald, Flossenburg, Oranienburg (Ger.) 42-45	TORTURE	U.S.
LUZENTE	145419	M	Ital.		Major, Lombardia Div.,73.Regt., I.Bn., Slovenia-Croatia(Yugo.) 43	MURDER	YUGO.
LWJTROFF	252452	M	Russ. or Ger.		Lt., 190. Legion Armenienne, Chanac (Fr.) 16.8.44	PILLAGE	FR.
MACARIO, Alessandro	189886	M	Ital.		Gen., Italian Army, Ljubljana (Yugo.)	MISC.CRIMES	YUGO.
MACCHI, Antonio	145480	M	Ital.		Capt., 24.Inf.Regt."Como", III.Bn., "Isonzo" Div.(Yugo.)43	MURDER	YUGO.
MACHATSCHEK, Josef	190584	M	Czech.		Sgt.,SD,Einsatz-Kdo. z.b.V.6, La Grande Fosse (Fr.) 15.10.44	MURDER	U.K.
MACHIELSE, Anton	141398	M	Dut.	26.5.13	Fireman, C.C.Mauthausen (Aust.)	TORTURE	FR.
MACIEJEWSKI, Jan	167032	M	Pol.		Pvt., Army, Equerdreville (Fr.)	WITNESS	FR.
MACIS	190995	M	Ital.		Lt.Col., It.Army,Tribunale Militare, Ljubljana (Yugo.) 42-43. Dr.	MURDER	YUGO.
MADERAZZI	145481	M	Ital.		Brigadiere, Dalmatia (Yugo.) 43	TORTURE	YUGO.
MADILE	145482	M	Ital.		Sgt.,Cerknica (Yugo.) 43	TORTURE	YUGO.
MADVARSKI	190793	M	Bulg.		Lt., Bulg.Army, 7.Cavalry Squadron (Yugo.-Serb.) 42-43	MURDER	YUGO.
MADOGLIO, Luigi	145483	M	Ital.		Marschall, It.Carabinieri, Cmdt.of prison, Ljubljana (Yugo.) 43	TORTURE	YUGO.
MAENE, Albert	194446	M	Bel.	17.12.21	SS-Mann, Foreign Post of Sipo and SD, Leeuwarden-Gent (Neth.) 13.9.44-14.4.45	MURDER	NETH.
MAGALDI, Cherardo	190996	M	Ital.		Cmdt., Chairman of the It.Extra Ordinary Court, Sibenik (Yugo.) 41-43	MURDER	YUGO.
MAGG, Manfredone	100509	M	Ital.		Cpl., owner of a milan amusement park, C.C.San Vittore (It.)	TORTURE	U.K.
MAGGIORA VERGANE NOBILE, Ernesto	191149	M	Ital.		Legal official, Chairman of It."Special Court" in Sibenik (Yugo.) 41-43	MURDER	YUGO.
MAGIELANSKI, Stepan	900907	M	Bulg.		Chief of Security in Drama-Area (Grc.) 28.9.-20.10.41	MURDER	GRC.
MAGNARINI, Mevio	307301	M	Ital.		Capt.,Judge, Sibenik section, Military Tribunal section of Ljubljana (Yugo.) 41-43	MURDER	YUGO.
MAINERI	193553	M	Ital.		Lt.Gen., It.Army, Cmdt. of 29 "Ferrara" Div.,Niksic (Yugo.)	MURDER	YUGO.
MAIZONI	190997	M	Ital.		Member, C.C. Carropoli (It.) 43	TORTURE	YUGO.
MAJER, Gusband	261978	M	Pol.		Former Haeftlingsfunktionaer in C.C.Vaihingen (Ger.)	MURDER	FR.
MAJJIGRI, Vittorio	178904	M	Ital.		Medico Lt., It.Army, Treviglio (It.) 42-43	TORTURE	U.K.
MAJOR, Vites	307271	M	Hung.		Gen.Cmdt., Hung.light motorised Bde., Novi Sad and other towns of Northern (Yugo.) 4.41	MURDER	YUGO.
MAKEDONAKI, Sotirios	900909	M	Bulg.		Member, Secret Police, Sidirokastron (Grc.) 5.43	MURDER	GRC.
MALENTACCI	190998	M	Ital.		Cmdt., Prisons It.Army. Marescialli XI. Bn., C.C.Cetinje, Crnogona (Yugo.) 41-43	MURDER	YUGO.
MALEVANY	255048	M	Ukr.		Confidential Agent, Gestapo, Pribram (Czech.) 39-45	MISC.CRIMES	CZECH.
MALEWICZ, Henri	29765	M	Pol.	08 or 09	Army, Inf.Regt., Waziers (Fr.) 1.11.41	MURDER	FR.
MALINOF, Stoyan or LEFTHEROF	900910	M	Bulg.		Servant, Municipal of Drama-Area (Grc.) 28.9.-20.10.41	MURDER	GRC.
MALISCHECK	124818	M	Aust.	86	Col., Army (Ger.)	TORTURE	U.S.
MALORCHI, Ernesto	307302	M	Ital.		Capt. of Grenadiers, C.C.Molat (Yugo.) 42-43	MURDER	YUGO.
MALTESE, Giuseppe	307303	M	Ital.		Lt.Col., Judge, Military Tribunal, Susak (Yugo.) 41-43	MURDER	YUGO.
MANASIJEV, Cira	190794	M	Bulg.		Official in occupied administration of Krusevac (Yugo.) 42	TORTURE	YUGO.
MANCA, Francesco	305099	M	Ital.		Pvt., Italian, Basis Abis, POW-Camp Sardinia. 10.4.43	MURDER	U.K.
MANCHA	145484	M	Ital.		Major, Garrison Cmdt., Low (Yugo.) 42	MURDER	YUGO.
MANCINELLI, Ivo	900668	M	Ital.		Major, Judge, Military Tribunal of war Army, Sesione di Sebenico, Sibenik, Dalmatia (Yugo.) 41-43	TORTURE	U.K.
MANDEL	190999	M	Ital.		Major, head of medical section attached to Governor at Cetinja Crna Gora (Yugo.) 41-43	MURDER	YUGO.
MANEV	190796	M	Bulg.		Dr., Head, Crim.Police, Skoplje, Gnjilane (Yugo.) 1.-2.43	MURDER	YUGO.
MANEV	190797	M	Bulg.		Lt., Bulg.Army, 27.Div. at Blaca (Yugo.) 15.-30.6.44	MURDER	YUGO.
MANEV, Alexander	190795	M	Bulg.		Col., Bulg.Army, Cdo. of Garrison at Prokuplje (Yugo.) 42-43	MURDER	YUGO.
MANFRE, Luigi	900312	M	Ital.		Lt., Carabinieri Reali, Davlia (Grc.) 5.5.43	MURDER	GRC.
MANIANELLI, Angelo	191000	M	Ital.		Vice Brigadiere, Station at Maled sta, Sibenik (Yugo.) 41-43	MURDER	YUGO.
MANOUTZIEF, Dimos	900913	M	Bulg.		Employee, Railway from Bulg., Drama-Area (Grc.) 28.9.-20.10.41	MURDER	GRC.
MANZANI	300641	M	Ital.		Carabinieri, Camp 52, Chiavari (It.) 12.41-10.42	BRUTALITY	U.K.
MARANGIO, Ezio	191001	M	Ital.		Capt., Police, XXII.Bn., Veliki (Yugo.) 28.7.42, Dr.	MURDER	YUGO.
MARASCO, M.	307304	M	Ital.		Major, Judge, correspondent of Military Tribunal, Susak (Yugo.) 41-43	MURDER	YUGO.
MARAZZA, A.	145471	M	Ital.		Maggiore Aitante, "Isonzo", Div.29.Inf.Regt. "Como", Cernomelj (Yugo.) MURDER 43		YUGO.
MARCHETTI, Vincenzo	145472	M	Ital.		Lt., "Isonzo" Div., 24.Inf.Regt. "Como" (Yugo.) 43	MURDER	YUGO.

MAR-MCZ

NAME	C.R.FILE NUMBER	SEX	NATIO-NALITY	DATE OF BIRTH	RANK OCCUPATION UNIT PLACE AND DATE OF CRIME	REASON WANTED	WANTED BY
MARENGONI	261376	M	Ital.		Capt.,88 Bn.of black-shirt,Pietralba (Fr.) 10.9.43	BRUTALITY	FR.
MARI	178303	M	Ital.		Lt.,Ital.Army,C.C.Macerata (It.) 43	TORTURE	U.K.
MARIACHER,Hans	138044	M	Aust.	2. 9.98	Scharfhr.,SS,Innsbruck (Aust.) 40-45	MISC.CRIMES	U.S.
MARIANELLO	307281	M	Ital.		Guard,Carabinieri,Camp 57,Udine Gruppigano (It.) 20.5.43	MURDER	U.K.
MARIANNE	194610	M	Pol.		Kapo,C.C.Mauthausen (Aust.)	TORTURE	FR.
MARIANNE	257521	M	Pol.		Kapo,C.C.Dora,Nordhausen (Ger.)	BRUTALITY	FR.
MARIANZUCK	192266	M	Rum.or Hung.		Guard,C.C.Breendonck (Bel.) 4.-5.44	MURDER	BEL.
MARICKA	253805	F	Pol.		Woman-Guard,C.C.Auschwitz (Pol.)	MISC.CRIMES	FR.
MARIN	253548	M	Ital.		Commissary,Zlarin (Yugo.) 25.6.42	INTERR.	YUGO.
MARINELLI	253547	M	Ital.		Official,Ital.-Police,Split (Yugo.) 17.4.42	MURDER	YUGO.
MARINI,Mario	191003	M	Ital.		Ital.-Army,XI Bn.,Police,Cetinje,Crna Gora (Yugo.) 41-43	MURDER	YUGO.
MARINO,Umberto	191004	M	Ital.		Comdt.,Ital.Army,II Bn.,8 Coy.,Div."Venezia",Trebzljevo-Kolasin (Yugo.) 41	MURDER	YUGO.
MARINOF,Ivan	305461	M	Bulg.		Lt.General,Commanding officer,15 Bulgarian-Div.in Monastir,Western Macedonia (Grc.) 43-44	MURDER	GRC.
MARINOF,Marinos	300915	M	Bulg.		Policeman,Bulgarian in Drama Area (Grc.) 28.9.-20.10.41	MURDER	GRC.
MARINOF,Pelko	300316	M	Bulg.		Lt.,Bulg.in charge of security at Pravala,Serres Area (Grc.) 41-42	MURDER	GRC.
MARINOV	190798	M	Bulg.		Lt.,Bulg.Army,27 Div.,Blace (Yugo.) 15.-30.6.44	MURDER	YUGO.
MARINOV	190799	M	Bulg.		Agent,Police,Vladicin Han (Yugo.) 43-44	MURDER	YUGO.
MARINOV,Nina Pelov	190800	M	Bulg.		State Forester,Belisevo,district of Vladicin Han (Yugo.) 43-44	MURDER	YUGO.
MARIOTTI,Giorgio	257003	M	Ital.		Pvt.,Army,Plave Anhovo (Yugo.) 23.2.45	INTERR.	YUGO.
MARIOTTI,Pasquale	251157	M	Ital.		Carabinier,2 Coy.,29 Carabin.-Bn.,Calacuccia (Fr.) 30.5.43	BRUTALITY	FR.
MARISCHA	194341	F	Pol.		Camp-Aufseherin,C.C.Ravensbrueck (Ger.)	TORTURE	FR.
MARKOV	190802	M	Bulg.		Head,Pol.at Kacanick,Gnjilane (Yugo.) 1.-2.43	MURDER	YUGO.
MARKOV,Dimitrije	190801	M	Bulg.		Head,Bulg.Police,Pirot (Yugo.) 43-44	MURDER	YUGO.
MAROSI,Koloman	260000	M	Hung.	3. 4.10	Leader,Civ.,Hung.Nylas-party organization,Guta district Komarno-Slov. (Czech.) 19.2.45	MURDER	CZECH.
MAROTTA,Antonio	145473	M	Ital.		General,Ital.Military Tribunal,Cetinje (Yugo.) 43	MURDER	YUGO.
MARRANZUCK	301581	M	Rum.or Hung.		Overseer,SS,C.C.Breendonck (Bel.) 44	MURDER	BEL.
MARSILI,Dino	300642	M	Ital.		Sgt.,Black-Bde.,Villanova Marchesana on detachment at Ariano,Mesola, Ferrara Adria Rovigo (It.) 12.44	MISC.CRIMES	U.K.
MARSILI,Giorgio	300643	M	Ital.		Member,Black-Bde.,Villanova Marchesana on detachment at Ariano,Mesola Ferrara Adria Rovigo (It.) 12.44	MISC.CRIMES	U.K.
MARTAETSCHLAEGER	167001	M	Aust.		Dr.,Civ.,(Fr.-Czech.-Aust.-Neth.) 38-45	MISC.CRIMES	U.S.
MARTELOTTA	191005	M	Ital.		Capt.,Ital.-Army,Orebic (Yugo.) 8.42	MURDER	YUGO.
MARTETSCHLAEGER	39848	M	Aust.		Civ.,F.P.Nr.40566 B, Conlie (Fr.) 7.8.44	MURDER	FR.
MARTIN,Fredrich	157016	M	Rum.	11. 7.13	Civ.Linz (Aust.) 42-45	TORTURE	U.S.
MARTINELLI	188179	M	Ital.	03	Member,NSDAP,Ital.,Grezzana (It.)	MURDER	U.K.
MARTINELLI	259088	M	Ital.		Member of Staff,Internment camp at Jstonio-Marina (It.) 41-43	BRUTALITY	YUGO.
MARTINETTO,Fanny	254776	F	Ital.	9. 8.16	Agent,Orra S.D.,Toulouse (Fr.) 12.42-8.44	MISC.CRIMES	FR.
MARTINETTO,Guiseppe	254775	M	Ital.	21.11.19	Agent,S.D.,14 Ovra,Toulouse (Fr.) 11.42-8.44	MISC.CRIMES	FR.
MARTORELLI	178301	M	Ital.		General,Kriegsgericht,Army,Athens (Grc.) 42	MISC.CRIMES	U.K.
MARUSIC (see MARUSSICH)	191008						
MARUSSICH (or MARUSIC)	191008	M	Ital.		Agent,Capt.,Pol.-Ital.,Div."Messina",C.C.Montenegro,Fraschette,Alatri (Yugo.-It.) 41-42	MURDER	YUGO.
MARZUCCHI,Mario	300644	M	Ital.		Maresciallo,Black-Bde.,Villanova Marchesana on detachment at Ariano Mesola Ferrara Adria Rovigo (It.) 12.44	MISC.CRIMES	U.K.
MASAN,Franco	300317	M	Ital.	circa 20	Guardia,Frontiera,Mavrovo,Lennovo,Nikiforovoni,Tetovo, 9.43	INTERR.	YUGO.
MASCHERONI	194339	M	Ital.	16	Capt.,Ital.Alpen-Jaeg.,Div."Fusteria",Fontaine (Fr.) 9.3.43	TORTURE	FR.
MASLAROF	300318	M	Bulg.		Chief of the 2 Bulg.-Police sector in Drama Area, 28.9.-20.10.41	MURDER	GRC.
MASSI,Giuseppe	130184	M	Ital.		Lt.Col.,Ital.Army,C.C. PG-21,Chieti (It.) 1.43	MISC.CRIMES	U.K.
MASSIMO,Tosti	185213	M	Ital.		Capt.,Carabinieri,Army,St.Gervais Chambéry (Fr.) 8.43	TORTURE	FR.
MASTROIANI,Ottavio	191150	M	Ital.		Col.,Italian special court,State Prosecutor,Sibenik, (Yugo.) 41-43	MURDER	YUGO.
MATAREZE,Rosario	191006	M	Ital.		Head,Prison Guards,C.C.Naples,Poggio Reale (It.) 28.9.43	MURDER	YUGO.
MATHIAS (see DRASKOWITCH)	62030						
MATIESCU	189795	M	Rum.		Major,Roumanian-Army,Brasov,Timisul de Jos (Rum.) 4.-8.44	MISC.CRIMES	U.K.
MATTEI	191007	M	Ital.		Agent,della Iquadra Politica,Split (Yugo.) 2.-3.43	TORTURE	YUGO.
MATTHIAS,Hubert	157012	M	Rum.or Ger.	21	Rottfhr.,Leibstandarte "Adolf Hitler",Probably,1 SS-Div., Field-Ers. Bn.1,Rabach (Ger.) 4.3.45	MURDER	U.S.
MATZINI (see MAZZINI)	173267						
MAURY,Carmen	194337	F	Swiss.	16	Capo,C.C.Ravensbrueck (Ger.)	MURDER	FR.
MAX	255889	M	Pol.		Chief,Block II,C.C.Mauthausen (Aust.)	INTERR.	FR.
MAXIMOF	300321	M	Bulg.		Member of the Drama Secret-Police,Drama Area (Grc.) 28.9.-20.10.41	MURDER	GRC.
MAYER	104878	M	Aust.	circa 10	Pvt.,Army,2 Coy.,337 Ldsch.-Bn.,C.C.Stalag VI 6, Holotious (Czech.) 2.45	BRUTALITY	U.S.
MAYER	259937	M	Aust.	10	Doctor,C.C.Auschwitz (Ger.)	INTERR.	FR.
MAYER (see MEYER)	259764						
MAZZA	305465	M	Ital.		Gendarm,Mixed Detachment of Royal Gendarmerie (It.),PM 64,Pianottoli, Corsica, 9.5.43	MURDER	FR.
MAZZA,Antonio	300669	M	Ital.		Ital.-Soldier,Kastel Kambelovas Garrison,Split and neighbouring towns (Yugo.) 42	MURDER	U.K.
MAZZANTINI	261374	M	Ital.		Capt.,88 Bn. of black-shirt,Pietralba (Fr.) 10.9.43	BRUTALITY	FR.
MAZZINI (or MATZINI,Pietro)	173267	M	Ital.	circa 90	Civ.,Political office,Piazenza (It.) 1.44	TORTURE	U.K.
MAZZOLINI,Idelma	259461	M	Ital.		Agent,Teacher,S.D.Longwy,Herserange (Fr.)	MISC.CRIMES	FR.
MCZK	196024	M	Pol.		Pvt.,12 SS Pz.Art.Rgt.,Tourouvres (Fr.) 13.8.44	MURDER	FR.

MED-MON

NAME	C.R.FILE NUMBER	SEX	NATIO-NALITY	DATE OF BIRTH	RANK OCCUPATION UNIT PLACE AND DATE OF CRIME	REASON WANTED	WANTED BY
MEDICI, Carmine	191010	M	Ital.		Director, C.C. Corrpoli, Bagna, Ripoli (It.) 41-43	TORTURE	YUGO.
MELCA, Pietro	188178	M	Ital.	14	Member NSDAP, Grezzana (It.) 12.11.43	MURDER	U.K.
MELE	109523	M	Ital.		Guard, C.C. S.Vittore Prison, Milano (It.)	TORTURE	U.K.
MELINI	191011	M	Ital.		Major, Ital.Army,Div. "Taro",Gradjame,Radomir,Montenegro (Yugo.) 5.42	PILLAGE	YUGO.
MELIS	145475	M	Ital.		Lt., "Lombardia"-Div., 23 Rgt., 3 Bn. (Yugo.) 43	MURDER	YUGO.
MELOCHI, Ernesto	145476	M	Ital.		Capt., (Dalmatia-Yugo.) 43	MURDER	YUGO.
MENAIDO, Luigi	191012	M	Ital.		Pvt., Ital.Army, Carabinieri Bde., Susak,Podhum, (Yugo.) 41-43	MURDER	YUGO.
MENICHELLI, Amorino	307306	M	Ital.		Major,Judge,Correspondent of Military Tribunal, Susak (Yugo.) 41-43	MURDER	YUGO.
MENTASTI, Luigi	191013	M	Ital.		Gen., Ital.Army XIV Corps D'Armata, Berane (Yugo.) 4.43	MISC.CRIMES	YUGO.
MENUCCI, Enzo	305306	M	Ital.		Major, Judge, Military Tribunal, 2 Army Section of Lubiana (Yugo.)41-43	MURDER	YUGO.
MERANGHINI, Umberto	254888	M	Ital.		Lt.-Gen., Member of Tribunale,Zadar,Split,Kotor 41-43	INTERR.	YUGO.
MERCH or HOPALONG, Cassidy or Hoppy	192915	M	Yugo.	85	Cmdtr., Capt., Yugo.Army, Sikloss (Hung.) 43	TORTURE	U.K.
MERCURIO, Renato	251154	M	Ital.		Lt., 4 Coy., 29 Bn.Carabinieri, Sartene-Corso (Fr.) 2.-5.43	TORTURE	FR.
MERLINI, Aurelio	257006	M	Ital.		Alpine Troop, Tagliamento VIII Alp.Rgt., 2 Bn., Fasc.Republ.Army Dorenberg (Yugo.) 43-4.45	MISC.CRIMES	YUGO.
MEROLA, Luigi	145463	M	Ital.		Capt., Carabinieri Reali, Novo Mesto (Yugo.) 42	MURDER	YUGO.
MESSANA, Ettore	191024	M	Ital.		Civilian, Ljubljana (Yugo.) 40-44	MURDER	YUGO.
MESSINA	145461	M	Ital.		Lt.-Gen., Italian Army, C.C. Treviglio (It.) 42-43	TORTURE	U.K.
METELSKY	142564	M	Rum.	13	SD-Guard, C.C. Lahde-Weser (Ger.) 43-45	TORTURE	BEL.
MEYER or MAYER	38867	M	Aust.		Schfhr., SS, C.C. Lublin (Pol.) 43	TORTURE	U.S.
MEYER or MAYER	259764	M	Aust.		See Consolidated List Part II Appendix "A"		
MEYERSHUBER	120529	M	Aust.		Police-Chief, C.C. Auschwitz (Pol.)	MISC.CRIMES	FR.
MEYERSHUBER	191208	M	Aust.		Lt.,Police C.C. Hartheim (Ger.) 43-45	MURDER	BEL.
MEZZANA, Cesare	191025	M	Ital.		Cmdt., Ital.Army,IV Legion Monte Nevoso,Novo Mesto-Metlika (Yugo.)42	MURDER	YUGO.
MEZZI, Adraste	145464	M	Ital.		Lt.-Col., "Isonzo"-Div., 24 Inf.Rgt. "Como" (Yugo.) 43	MURDER	YUGO.
MICAN, Francesco	196512	M	Ital.		See Consolidated List Part II Appendix "A"		
MICHALKE, Franz	166274	M	Aust.		SS-Fuehrer, (Fr.,Neth.,Aust.,Czech.) 38-45	WITNESS	U.S.
MICHELI, Mario	191151	M	Ital.		Capt., Cmdt., of Stari Trg and Village of Dane (Yugo.) 3.43	MURDER	YUGO.
MICHELS, Jacob	183678	M	Hung.-Ger.	14.11.98	SS-Mann, 91 SS Gren.Inf.Div., 2 Art.Rgt., C.C. Dachau,Nordhausen - Dora (Ger.) 43-45	TORTURE	U.S.
MICHERZINSKI, Michel	192353	M	Pol.	20	Kapo, C.C. Flossenburg (Ger.)	MURDER	FR.
MIETKA	121179	M	Pol.	20	Kapo, Yaworzno-Silesia (Ger.)	TORTURE	FR.
MIGNANI	262431	M	Ital.	05	Major, Fascist Militia at Pola, Bokardica (Yugo.) 8.-9.1.44	MURDER	YUGO.
MIHAILOF, Mihos	300329	M	Bulg.		Col., Governor of the Bulgarian Inf.Military,Drama Area, 28.9.-20.10.41	MURDER	GRC.
MIHALOVICS	189930	M	Hung.		Dr., Counsellor, Hungarian Police, Novi-Sad (Yugo.)	MURDER	YUGO.
MIHOV, Stejan	190803	M	Bulg.		Inspector, Occ.Territories Service of Confiscation of Food Stuffs, Gnjilane, (Yugo.) 1.-2.43	MURDER	YUGO.
MILAN, Carlo	145465	M	Ital.		Capt., Army, Dalmatia (Yugo.) 43	MISC.CRIMES	YUGO.
MILANOV, Kiril Ivanov	190804	M	Bulg.		Civil, Servant, Occ. Territories, Tax-Collector,Kalane,Pirot (Yugo.)43	MURDER	YUGO.
MILANOVITSCH, Adam	173897	M	Rum.-Ger.	22	Uschfhr., SS, between Wien and Mauthausen (Aust.) 1.-4.45	MURDER	U.S.
MILAZZI, Paola	191026	F	Ital.		Manageress, C.C. Pollenza (Yugo.) 43	TORTURE	YUGO.
MILAZZO, Gioacchino	307339	M	Ital.		Prof., Dr. Prosecuter,Judge,Special-Tribunal for de Fense of State, Rom (It.) 4.41-9.43	MURDER	YUGO.
MINAFRA, Vincenzo	254771	M	Ital.		Capt., Army Gravina (It.) 42-43	BRUTALITY	U.K.
MINEV, Anastas (see NOJEV)	190812						
MINGONI, Mario	307307	M	Ital.		Consul, Judge of Special Tribunal for Defense of State Rom (It.) 4.41-9.43	MURDER	YUGO.
MINTSEV, Jvan (see PENTSEF)	300332						
MINUTELLI, Fabio	145466	M	Ital.		Capt., Dalmatia (Yugo.) 43	MURDER	YUGO.
MIRABELLA, Bartolomea	145467	M	Ital.		Lt.-Col. (Yugo.)41	MURDER	YUGO.
MIRAGO, Leonida	191027	F	Ital.		Agent, Italian Police, C.C. Corropoli (It.) 43	TORTURE	YUGO.
MIRANDA	255885	M	Spain		Hairdresser, Block 19, C.C. Mauthausen (Aust.)	INTERR.	FR.
MIRCEV, Archimede	190805	M	Bulg.		Deputy-Chief, Police of Kacanik Gnjilane (Yugo.) 1.-2.43	MURDER	YUGO.
MISCHI, Archimede	191028	M	Ital.		Lt.,Gen., Ital.Army, Cmdt. of Carabinieri and Milizia Confin., Fiume (It.) 41-43	MURDER	YUGO.
MISKA, Rudolf	196064	M	Lux.		Agent, SD, Maisons-Lafette (Fr.)	TORTURE	FR.
MITKOF	300333	M	Bulg.		Secret-Agent, Bulgarian Security, Drama Area, 28.9.-20.10.41	MURDER	GRC.
MITOV, Boris	190806	M	Bulg.		Customs-Officer, Zollgrenzschutz, Osmakovo (Yugo.) 43-44	MURDER	YUGO.
MIZI, Aurelio	191029	M	Ital.		Doctor, C.C. Fraschette Alatri (It.) 41-43	TORTURE	YUGO.
MOCCIA, Alfonso	145468	M	Ital.		Major, "Isonzo" Div.98 Fascist Legion 117 Bn. 1943	MURDER	YUGO.
MOLARO, Cesare	257004	M	Ital.		Sgt., Tagliamento VIII Alp.Rgt. Fasc.Republ.Army, Dorenberg (Yugo.) 12.43-4.45	INTERR.	YUGO.
MOLDINGER	156861	M	Aust.		Major, Civilian, Krispl (Aust.) 44	MISC.CRIMES	NETH.
MOLINARI	174694	M	Ital.	10	Capt., Geb.Jaeg.Bn.2, Annecy (Fr.)	MURDER	FR.
MOLNAR, Pal	156999	M	Hung.	22	Lt.Army, C.C. Belsen (Ger.)	MURDER	U.K.
MOLOTOW (see REGULSKI)	177578						
MONDIAN	300335	M	Ital.		Capt., C.C. Larissa, 41-43	MURDER	GRC.
MONFORTINI	300336	M	Ital.		Maresciallo Carabinieri Reali, Thebes. 14.8.43	MURDER	GRC.
MONICA, Vittorio	191030	M	Ital.		Dr., Commissioner, Ital.Public Security (Sipo),Sibenik (Yugo.) 41-43	MURDER	YUGO.
MONTALTO, Rino	191031	M	Ital.		Capt., of Carabinieri, Ital.Army, 55 Rgt. "Marche" Div. Trebinje (Yugo.) 20.4.41-9.43	MURDER	YUGO.
MONTANELLE	162074	M	Ital.		Major, Ital.Army, Camp 4, Montalbo (It.) 12.41-3.43	TORTURE	U.K.
MONTAROTTI	191037	M	Ital.		Capt. 2 Ital.Army, Chief of operational Office, Susak (Yugo.) 41-43	MURDER	YUGO.
MONTARULI, Sabino	145469	M	Ital.		Capt., Guidice del Tribunale Militare di Guerra, Cettigne (Yugo.) 43	MURDER	YUGO.

NAME	C.R.FILE NUMBER	SEX	NATIO- NALITY	DATE OF BIRTH	RANK OCCUPATION UNIT PLACE AND DATE OF CRIME	REASON WANTED	WANTED BY
MONTEDORO, Renato	254889	M	Ital.		Capt., Judge, Tribunal Spec., Dalmatia, Split (Yugo.) 41-43	INTERR.	YUGO.
MONTEMURRO	169492	M	Ital.		Capt., Italian-Army, C.C., Juane-Ben-Adem, (North-Africa) 5.42-1.43	TORTURE	U.K.
MONTESSI, Enzo	259122	M	Ital.		Lt., Italian-Army, 56.Rgt., "Marche"-Div., Stolac (Yugo.) 4.41-9.42	MURDER	YUGO.
MONTIGLIANI (see BOTIGLIANI)	300190						
MONTUORI, Guiseppe	191032	M	Ital.		Member, Fascio Directory, Sibenik (Yugo.) 41-43	MURDER	YUGO.
MONTUORO, Vittorio	191033	M	Ital.		Col., Italian-Army, Commander of Carabinieri, Centinje Crno Gora (Yugo.) 41-43	MURDER	YUGO.
MORATTI, Stephan	130857	M	Aust.or Ital.	05	SS-Mann, Interpreter at the Gestapo SD, Bonnert Arlon (Bel.) 1.9.44	MURDER	BEL.
MORELLI, Giuseppe	253546	M	Ital.		Chief-Police of Political Department, Italian-Police, Split (Yugo.) 17.4.42	MURDER	YUGO.
MORGLIA, Piero	191034	M	Ital.		Secretary, Prefect of Zara, Sibenik (Yugo.) 41-43	MURDER	YUGO.
MORI, Mario	191035	M	Ital.		General, Commander of Presidio at Podgorica (Yugo.) 4.42	MURDER	YUGO.
MORO, Carino or Gavino	145470	M	Ital.		Carabiniere, "Sebenica Sud" Carabinieri Station, Sibenik (Yugo.) 42	MURDER	YUGO.
MORONI, Giovan Battista	185922	M	Ital.		Fascist, near Trescore (It.) 4.1.45	MURDER	U.S.
MORRA, Eugenio	191036	m	Ital.		Col., Chief of military government Italian-Army at Zara, Zadar Dalmatia (Yugo.) 41-43	MURDER	YUGO.
MORTAROTTI	196515	M	Ital.		Capt., Ital. 2.Army, Susak (Yugo.) 41-43	MISC.CRIMES	YUGO.
MORTICELLI	193541	M	Ital.		Capt., Italian-Army, Conc.Camp-57, Gruppignamo (It.) 12.41	MURDER	U.K.
MOSCA	191152	M	Ital.		Maresciallo Guardia Financia, Lopud, Miset (Yugo.) 42	TORTURE	YUGO.
MOSCATELLI, Guiseppe	133443	M	Ital.		Col. of "Carabinieri", Camp-Cmdt., Conc.Camp, Gavi (It.) 5.42-9.43	MISC.CRIMES	U.K.
MOUNTROF, Stetko	300337	M	Bulg.		Member of the Drama Secret Police, Drama Area (Yugo.) 41	MURDER	GRC.
MOULAPTCHIEV, Demetrios	305077	M	Bulg.		Bulgarian Gend. from Philippopolis-Bulgaria, Old Kavalla (Grc.) 7.6.44	MURDER	GRC.
MOUTZVANOF, Tontor	300338	M	Bulg.		Governor, Bulgarian Prefecture in Drama, Drama Area (Yugo.) 28.9.-20.10.41	MURDER	GRC.
MUEHLBACH	138268	M	Aust.		Sgt., Gestapo SS, Chief of Office of Courrier, Lyon (Fr.)	MURDER	FR.
MUEHLMANN, Kajetah (Kai)	154823	M	Aust.	90	State-Secretary (honarytitle) Director for Confiscations of art and cultural Treasures (Pol.) 39-44	PILLAGE	U.S.
MUELLER	156990	M	Aust.	95	877.Lds.Schtz.Bn. 3.Coy. - Prvt - Conc.Camp, Liexen (Aust.)	TORTURE	U.K.
MUELLER, David	183687	M	Hung.	98	SS-Mann, SS-Camp-Guard, 31.SS-Gren.Inf.Div., C.C., Nordhausen, Dora, Dachau (Ger.)	TORTURE	U.S.
MUELLER, Willy	257345	M	Nor.		SS-Guard, Uschfhr., Slave Labour Camp, Korgen (Nor.) 6.42-43	MURDER	YUGO.
MULLER	194544	M	Rum.	05 - 15	SS-Mann, Guard, SD, Heerenween (Neth.) 15.4.45	MURDER	NETH.
MULLER, Michel	188964	M	Lux.		Chief of Culture, Civilian, Raucourt (Fr.) 41	PILLAGE	FR.
MURGANTI	189884	M	Ital.		Carabinieri, Italian-Army, Vela-Lucca (Yugo.)	MISC.CRIMES	YUGO.
MURIGI, Natale	145597	M	Ital.		Carabinieri, Italian-Army, Isle of Corcula (Yugo.) 43	MURDER	YUGO.
MUSCATELLI, Pietro	145596	M	Ital.		Carabinieri, Italian-Army, Babno Polja near Prezad (Yugo.) 42	TORTURE	YUGO.
MUSEMECI, Antonio	307308	M	Ital.		Major, Judge, Military Tribunal for 2.Army Section of Ljubljana (Yugo.) 41-43	MURDER	YUGO.
MUSSI, Bruno	259188	M	Ital.		Lt., Italian-Army, "Marche"-Div. 56.Rgt., Stolac (Yugo.) 4.41-9.42	MURDER	YUGO.
MUSTAFO	188963	M	Russ.		Sgt., Army, Penhors en Pouldreuzig (Fr.)	TORTURE	FR.
MUTTERER, Renatus	230268	M	Fr.		SS-Cpl., SD, Moussey (Fr.) 44	MURDER	U.K.
MYNHA, Fritz	174829	M	Aust.	17	Hpttruppfhr., RAD 6-352, Schuetzen (Aust.) 3.45	WITNESS	U.S.
MYREV, Nicolov Demetrius	300346	M	Bulg.		Prefect of Serres during 1944, North Souli and Ag.Pnevma, 10.3.44	MURDER	GRC.
NACCI, Gaetano	170922	M	Ital.	18.10.09	Supervisor, Prison,-Conc.Camp, San Romeo (It.) 16.7.43-3.44	TORTURE	FR., YUGO.
NADI (see NAGI, Miklos)	189929						
NAGERL, Jacob	62406	M	Aust.	95	Prt., Army, Btty.Nord-M.Fla.Abt.810 (Neth.)	WITNESS	U.S.
NAGI, Miklos (or NADI)	189929	M	Hung.		Mayor, Public-Service, Novi-Sad (Yugo.)	MURDER	YUGO.
NAMNCI	191038	M	Ital.		Agent, Questura of Cattaro, Kotor (It.) 41-43	MURDER	YUGO.
NANI, Repato	191039	M	Ital.		Col., Owner of a Coffee-House, Commander of Carabinieri, Kistanje Split (Yugo.) 41-42	MURDER	YUGO., U.K.
NANTA	191040	M	Ital.		Commissary, Chief of Italian Civil Admin., Cabar (Yugo.) 41-43	MURDER	YUGO.
NAPOLITANO, Vincenzo	191153	M	Ital.		Judge, Italian Special Court, Sibenik (Yugo.) 41-43	MISC.CRIMES	YUGO.
NATCHERSKIN, Leonil	196436	M	Mong.		Formation stat.Macon, St.Laurent (Fr.) 31.5.44	INTERR.	FR.
NATIVI, Sergio	300347	M	Ital.		Lt. and Director of the Aver of Prison, Athen (Grc.) 41-43	MURDER	GRC.
NAUDOR, Pal	138207	M	Hung.		Dr., Chief, Police, Kolozsvar (Hung.) 44	MISC.CRIMES	FR.
NEDELIKOV	190813	M	Bulg.		Capt., Bulgar.Army "Lovna Druzina" (Yugo.) - Serbia) 40-44	MURDER	YUGO.
NEDWED	163114	M	Aust.	07	Chief, Gestapo, Innsbruck (Aust.), Ger.) 43-45	MURDER	U.S.
NEEDLE, Expert	129045	M	Aust.	15	SS-Osturmfhr., C.C., Mauthausen (Aust.)	MURDER	U.S.
NEGRI, Jasques	151519	M	Fr.		Conc.Camp, Civilian, Schrobeshausen (Ger.) 44-45	WITNESS	UNWCC
NEGRO	194513	M	Span.		Member, Police, C.C., Mauthausen (Aust.) 44-45	TORTURE	FR.
NEIDER, Peter	183280	M	Hung.-Ger.		SS-Mann, 31.SS-Gren.Div.2.Art.Rgt., Conc.Camp, Dachau, Dora, Nordhausen (Ger.) 43-45	WITNESS	U.S.
NEMET, Laszlo	189928	M	Hung.		Agent, Hung.Police, Novi-Sad (Yugo.)	MURDER	YUGO.
NENOF, Neiko	300349	M	Bulg.		Major (Bulg.) of Xylagani Rodopi, 9.4.44	MURDER	GRC.
NEROU	139870	M	Fr.	22	Gestapo, Vichy (Fr.) 5.44	TORTURE	U.K.
NESSER, Max	12569	M	Swiss.		Interpreter, Gestapo, Veldalon C.C. (Fr.) 28.8.44	MURDER	FR.
NEVITZANOV, Demetrios	305206	M	Bulg.		Lt.Col., Gend. (Bulg.), Serres (Grc.) 5.41-8.41	PILLAGE	GRC.
NEZVAL, Josef	261979	M	Hung.	14. 5.02	Member, Nyilas-Party, Kosice (Czech.) 1.45	MURDER	CZECH.
NICITA	252562	M	Ital.	90	Col., Carabinieri-Cmdt., P.G.107, Porpetto (It.) 5.43	BRUTALITY	U.K.
NICOLAIEFF, Alex (see NICOLAYE)	250401						
NICOLAYE (or NICOLAIEFF, Alex)	250401	M	Russ.or Ger.		Capt., Colonne Russo-Allemande, Chaumont, Caserne Fuch, L'Ain (Fr.) 10.-21.7.44	MISC.CRIMES	FR.
NICOLETTI	169496	M	Ital.		Col., Ital.Army, Capua (It.) 4.41-6.43	TORTURE	U.K.
NICOLETTI, Tulio	191041	M	Ital.		Dr., Civilian, Sibenik (Yugo.) 41-43	MURDER	YUGO.
NICOSTA, Salvatore	191154	M	Ital.		Major, Inf.Div. "Messina", Procuratore del Imperatore, Cetinge (Yugo.) 1941	MURDER	YUGO.
NIEDAN, Friedrich	193282	M	Hung.	28. 6.97	SS-Mann, Guard, 4.SS-Totenkopf-Sturmbann, C.C., Nordhausen, Dora-Mittelbau, Dachau (Ger.) 43-45	MURDER	U.S.

NIE - PAL

NAME	C.R.FILE NUMBER	SEX	NATIO- NALITY	DATE OF BIRTH	RANK OCCUPATION UNIT PLACE AND DATE OF CRIME	REASON WANTED	WANTED BY
NIEDAN, Philipp	183278	M	Hung.	8.7.94	SS Mann, 31.SS Gren.Div., C.C. Dora Nordhausen, Dachau (Ger.)	WITNESS	U.S.
NIEDERWANGER, Karl	166630	M	Aust.	31.10.18	Civ., Innsbruck (Aust.) 20.4.45	TORTURE	U.S.
NIKIFOROV	190807	M	Bulg.		Lt., Bulg. Army, 7.Cavalry-Squadron (Yugo.) 42-43	MURDER	YUGO.
NIKOLOV	190808	M	Bulg.		Major-Gen., Commander of 1.Bulg.Corps (Yugo.) 42-43	MURDER	YUGO.
NIKOLOV, Georgi	190809	M	Bulg.		Lt., Bulg.Army, 7.Cavalry Squadron (Yugo.) 42-43	MURDER	YUGO.
NIKOLOV, Nikola-Krstev	190810	M	Bulg.		Secret Agent, Teacher, Bulg.Gestapo, Vladicin Han (Yugo.) 43-44	MURDER	YUGO.
NIKOLOV, Zodor	190811	M	Bulg.		Customs officer, Zollgrenzschutz-Polizei, Osmakovo (Yugo.) 43-44	MURDER	YUGO.
NOHEL, Vinzenz	134919	M	Aust.	00	Civ., C.C. Hartheim (Aust.) 40-44	MURDER	U.S.
NOTEV or MINEV, Anastas	190812	M	Bulg.		Lt., Bulg.Army, Mijajlovac (Yugo.) 15.12.42	MURDER	YUGO.
NOLDE, Rudy	192549	M	Rum.		SS Rgt. 56993, Braine le Comte,(Bel.) 18.2.44	MURDER	BEL.
NOLFOI, Giovanni	255698	M	Ital.		Brig.of Finance Guard, Customs, Radunic nr.Kistanje (Yugo.) 17.3.42	INTERR.	YUGO.
NOLLI, Stefano	259120	M	Ital.		Lt., Ital.Army, 56.Rgt., "Marche"-Div., Stolac (Yugo.) 4.41-9.42	MURDER	YUGO.
NONNI, Carlo	145636	M	Ital.		Dr. Lt., "Isonzo"-Div. 24.Inf.Rgt. "Como" (Yugo.)	MURDER	YUGO.
NOVACO, Carlo	191042	M	Ital.		Agent, Questura of Cattaro, Kotor (Yugo.) 41-43	MURDER	YUGO.
NOWAK, Conrad (Gerad)	136288	M	Dut.	23	SS Usturmfhr., Gueret (Fr.)	MURDER	FR.
NOVAK, Jean	177531	M	Pol.	18	Camp official, C.C. Neubrenn (Ger.)	TORTURE	FR.
NOVAKOVICS, Bela	189927	M	Hung.		General, Hung.Army, Backa Novi-Sad (Yugo.)	MURDER	YUGO.
OBERREITER, Josef	155503	M	Aust.	3.2.93	Carpenter, Civ., Katzdorf (Aust.) 4.45	MURDER	U.S.
OBERZAUCHNER, Anton	251217	M	Aust.	04 or 05	Ortsgruppenleiter, Bruggen-Greifenberg, Ebenberg,Kaernten (Aust.) 16.11.44	MURDER	U.S.
OBLA, Vincenzo	256972	M	Ital.		Sgt., Ital. Army, Plave, Anhovo (Yugo.) 13.-23.2.45	INTERR.	YUGO.
OGIONE, Giovanni	191043	M	Ital.		Major, Ital.Army, Commander of Btty."Busano", Podgorica,Berane, Cetinje,Savnik (Yugo.) 7.-11.41	MURDER	YUGO.
OGRIS	155499	M	Aust.	00	SS Chief, Gusen (Aust.) 44-45	TORTURE	FR.
OGRISSEC	191044	M	Ital.		Capt., Ital.Army, Div. "Messina", Montenegro (Yugo.) 13.7.41-spring 42	MURDER	YUGO.
OLAH, Elemer	189926	M	Hung.		Dr., Counsellor, Hung.Police, Novi-Sad (Yugo.)	MURDER	YUGO.
OLASZY, Alexander	144394	M	Hung.	02	Lt.Gen., Hung.Army (Hung.)	MURDER	U.S.
OLDANI, Guilo	137599	M	Ital.	95	Col., POW Camp, C.C. San Guiselle (It.) 12.42- 1.43	TORTURE	U.K.
OLERT	179861	M	Aust.		Adjutant, Gestapo SD, Valence (Fr.)	TORTURE	FR.
OLIVIERI, Edmondo	191155	M	Ital.		Legal official, Primo (I) Seniore Judge of Italian "Special Court", Sibenik (Yugo.) 41-43	MURDER	YUGO.
OLIVIERI, Francesco	162078	M	Ital.		Lt., Ital.Army, Inf., C.C. Montalbo (It.) 42	TORTURE	U.K.
OMELANOVIC-PAVLENKO, Nikolaj	251205	M	Ukr.	22	SS Unterstumfhr., Mnichovice (Czech.) 45	MURDER	CZECH.
ONELIO, Manone	256971	M	Ital.		Vice-Brig., Carabiniere, Kastav (Yugo.) 4.43	MURDER	YUGO.
OPDEBECK, Marcel or OPDEBEEK	193565	M	Bel.	15.8.12	Cpl., SD, SIFO, Leeuwarden (Neth.)	MURDER	NETH.
OPRIKOV, Petko	190814	M	Bulg.		Deputy Chief, Bulg.Police, Vladicin Han (Yugo.) 43-44	MURDER	YUGO.
ORASI, U.	307309	M	Ital.		Capt., Judge, Military Tribunale, Susak (Yugo.) 41-43	MURDER	YUGO.
ORAZI, Vizio	191045	M	Ital.		Official, Prefect of Province of Zara-Sibenik (Yugo.) 41-43	MURDER	YUGO.
ORFATTI, Emilio	250416	M	Ital.		Maresciallo pilot, Airforce, 21. Storm Camp, Avazione, Hrastov, Dol, Trnovica (Yugo.) 31.7.43	MISC.CRIMES	YUGO.
ORIDLI, Antonio	148665	M	Ital.		Capt., "Isonzo"-Div. 98.Fascist Legion, 1.Coy., Rakovnik (Yugo.) 43	MURDER	YUGO.
ORIFICI, Domenico	148666	M	Ital.		Col., "Isonzo"-Div., 24.Inf.Rgt. "Como" (Yugo.) 43	MURDER	YUGO.
ORIOLI, E.	191046	M	Ital.		Major, Ital.Army, Deputy Chief of Staff "Taro"-Div.,Crna Gora (Yugo.) 41	MURDER	YUGO.
ORLANDO, Luigi see ROLANDO	132194						
ORLANDO, Taddeo (Tadeo)	148664	M	Ital.		Gen., "Granattieri di Sardegna" Div. XI.Army Corps (Yugo.) 43	MURDER	YUGO.
ORLICH, Gualtiero	191047	M	Ital.		Dr., Member Squadrist, Ital.Party, Sibenik (Yugo.) 41-43	MURDER	YUGO.
OROFOLO see CROFOLLO	193539						
OROSZ	189925	M	Hung.		Dr., Counsellor, Hung.Army, Police, Novi-Sad (Yugo.)	MURDER	YUGO.
OROTALO	193542	M	Ital.		Col., Commander of POW Camp 75 Bari (It.)	MURDER	U.K.
ORSICK	144392	M	Hung.		Hung.Pilot, Budapest (Hung.) 18.9.44	TORTURE	U.S.
ORSINI	155500	M	Ital.	15	Cpl., Inf.Rgt. 319, C.C. Larissa (Grc.) 10.42-6.43	TORTURE	U.K.
ORSONI, Jose	148669	M	Ital.		Lt. (Med.) "Isonzo"-Div., 23.Inf.Rgt. "Como", Cernomelj (Yugo.) 43	MURDER	YUGO.
ORTNER, Lorenz	142105	M	Aust.		Lagerfuehrer, C.C. Voecklabruck-Traunkirchen (Aust.)	TORTURE	U.S.
OSMANN, Franz	193390	M	Hung.	30.8.98	SS Mann, 4.SS Totenkopf-Stuba, C.C. Nordhausen Dora-Mittelbau (Ger.) 43-45	MURDER	U.S.
OSMIANI	307311	M	Ital.		N.C.O. Member, Gendarmerie of Ovra Trieste, 12.41	MURDER	YUGO.
OSTER, Michael	193329	M	Hung.	4.7.99	SS Mann, 4.SS Totenkopf-Stuba, O.C.Nordhausen Dora-Mittelbau (Ger.) 43-45	MURDER	U.S.
OSTI, Giovanni	196924	M	Ital.		Col.Pres., Military Tribunal, 41-43	MISC.CRIMES	YUGO.
OSWALD, Anton	193599	M	Hung.		Guard, C.C. Flossenburg (Ger.) 2.-3.45	WITNESS	BEL.
OSWALD, Joseph	167759	M	Hung.	8.12.09	SS Mann, C.C. Natzweiler (Fr.) 43-44	MURDER	FR.
OTTAWA, Rudolph	174453	M	Czech.		Interpreter under orders of Kowacht, 4.40	PILLAGE	FR.
OTTENHEIMER, Kaspar	193327	M	Hung.	4.4.99	Guard, 4.SS Totenkopf Stuba, C.C. Nordhausen Dora-Mittelbau (Ger.)43-45	MURDER	U.S.
OTTONE, Giorgio	307312	M	Ital.		Major Judge, Military Tribunal, 2.Army, Sect.of Lubiana (Yugo.) 41-43	MURDER	YUGO.
PACE, Pasquale	307313	M	Ital.		Major Judge, Military Tribunal, Susak (Yugo.) 41-43	MURDER	YUGO.
PACIFICI, Riccardo	191048	M	Ital.		Lt., Ital.Army, Commander of Carabinieri, Sibenik (Yugo.) 41-43	MURDER	YUGO.
PACIFICO, Luigi	178295	M	Ital.		Lt., Army, Arb.Kommando, Sesto SanGiovanni (Ital.) spring 43	TORTURE	U.K.
PACSIUS	192494	M	Rum.-Hung.		Guard, C.C. Breendonck (Bel.) 4.-5.44	MISC.CRIMES	BEL.
PALA, Misie	191049	M	Ital.		Sgt.,Ital.Army, Deputy Commander of Carabinieri Unit Vodice-Sibenik (Yugo.) 41-43	MURDER	YUGO.
PALAMARA, Giovanni	307314	M	Ital.		Doct.Capt. Judge, Military Tribunal, Susak (Yugo.) 41-43	MURDER	YUGO.
PALEREO	141894	M	Ital.		Capt., C.C. Benghazi (North Afr.) 11.42	MISC.CRIMES	U.K.
PALERMO	191050	M	Ital.		Capt. of Carabinieri, Ital.Army, Div. "Re" Otocac (Yugo.) 41-43	MURDER	YUGO.
PALERMO	302153	M	Ital.		Capt., Cmdt. Benghazi POW Camp (North Afr.) 6.42-9.42	MURDER	U.K.
PALLOTTA, E.	129147	M	Ital.		Col., Army, Sulmona (It.) 26.12.41	MISC.CRIMES	U.K.
PALMA, Giuseppe	149015	M	Ital.		Lt.Col., Army, Military Court, Cettigne-Montenegro (Yugo.)	MURDER	YUGO.

PAL-PER

NAME	C.R.FILE NUMBER	SEX	NATIO-NALITY	DATE OF BIRTH	RANK, OCCUPATION, UNIT, PLACE AND DATE OF CRIME	REASON WANTED	WANTED BY
PALMENTOLA, Aldo	307315	M	Ital.		General-Consul, Judge of special Tribunal for defense of State Rom (It.) 4.41-9.43	MURDER	YUGO.
PALMERI, Gaetano	307316	M	Ital.		General-Consul, Judge of special Tribunal for defense of State Rom (It.) 4.41-9.43	MURDER	YUGO.
PALOMBA, Ignatio	305213	M	Ital.		Capt., Director, Ital. Section, Averof prison, Athens (Grc.) 41-43	MURDER	GRC.
PALPINELLI	149073	M	Ital.		Lt., Ital.Army, "Lombardia"-Div., 73 Rgt., 3 Bn., Slov. Croat.(Yugo.)	MURDER	YUGO.
PANAJOTOV, Rusan	190815	M	Bulg.		Member, mounted police, Pirot (Yugo.) 7.43	TORTURE	YUGO.
PANARA, Francesco	300671	M	Ital.		Capt., Judge, Military Tribunal of War,Army,Sezione di Sebenico Sibenik, Dalmatia (Yugo.) 41-43	TORTURE	U.K.
PANARELLI, Francesco	149074	M	Ital.		Lt., Ital. Army, "Ferrara"-Div., Carabinierie, Montenegro (Yugo.)	MURDER	YUGO.
PANATELLO, Francesco	191051	M	Ital.		Official, Ital.Army, Div.6 "Alpi Grac", Montenegro (Yugo.) 42	TORTURE	YUGO.
PANCONI, Giovanni	256970	M	Ital.		Capt., Fascist Militia, Kastav (Yugo.) 41-43	MURDER	YUGO.
PANDOLERI	193543	M	Ital.		Capt., P.O.W. Camp, 7 O, Ferno Ancona (Ital.) 12.42-1.43	TORTURE	U.K.
PANDOZZI, Aldo	253272	M	Ital.		Cmdt., Nat.Sicilian Volum Teers, Fonda (It.) 9.-10.43	INTERR.	YUGO.
PANEV (see PANOV)	190819	M					
PANEV, Andonov	190816	M	Bulg.		Policeman, Vladicin Han, (Yugo.) 42-44	MURDER	YUGO.
PANEV, Milan, Nikolov	190817	M	Bulg.		Mayor, Paklestice, Velika-Lika, Pirot (Yugo.) 41-43	TORTURE	YUD
PANEV, Peter	189963	M	Bulg.		Col., Bulg. Army, Kriva Reka (Yugo.)	MURDER	YUGO.
PANEV, Vasil	190818	M	Bulg.		Dep. Mayor, Municipality of Jelasnica,Surdulica (Yugo) 22.3.43	MURDER	YUGO.
PANICUCCI, Gina	189883	M	Ital.		Capt., Ital. Army, Montenegro (Yugo.)	MISC.CRIMES	YUGO.
PANOV, T.H. or T.N. (or PANEV)	190819	M	Bulg.		Chief of security, Gestapo, Skolplje (Yugo.) 43-44	MURDER	YUGO.
PANNUTI, Vicenzo	255425	M	Ital.		Judge, Member, Ital. special Tribunal, Zadar, Sibenik, Kotor,Split (Yugo.) 41-43	INTERR.	YUGO.
PANSINI	149075	M	Ital.		Col., Ital. Army, 15 Inf.Rgt., Cabar (Yugo.)	MURDER	YUGO.
PANSOLA	149076	M	Ital.		Col., C.C.Zlarin (Yugo.)	TORTURE	YUGO.
PANTSEF	305215	M	Bulg.		Lt., Bulg. Army, Xylagani-Rodopi (Grc.) 9.4.44	MURDER	GRC.
PANZERGRUBER	258134	M	Yugo.		Prisoner Yugoslave,asst. of Doctor, C.C.Dachau (Ger.)	MURDER	BEL.
PANZIERI	155528	M	Ital.		Gestapo, Bassano (It.) 11.44	MURDER	U.K.
PAOLINI, Enrico	251224	M	Ital.		Carabinier, 147 Section carabiniers, Sartens (Fr.) 2.-5.43	MISC.CRIMES	FR.
PAPAEVANGELOF, George,Popof	305097	M	Bulg.		Tax collector, Bulg. government, Kavalla (Grc.) 8.42	PILLAGE	GRC.
PAPANTONIO, Guiseppe	188865	M	Ital.	10	Guard., Ital. Army Camp 49, Rimini (It.) 5.43	MURDER	U.K.
PAPINCAK, Eugen	261896	M	Hung.	9. 9.03	Member, Nyilas Party, Kosice (Czech.) 1.45	MURDER	CZECH.
PARACUOLLO, Salvatore	300646	M	Ital.		Vice-Brigadiere of the carabinieri, near Bracigliano, Volturare, Prov. Salerno (It.) 2.44	MISC.CRIMES	U.K.
PARDO	300672	M	Ital.		Active Fascist, Island of Vis (Yugo.) 41-43	MURDER	U.K.
PARINI	191056	M	Ital.		Officer, Lt., C.C.Montalbano (It.) 41-43	TORTURE	YUGO.
PARKDJIJEV, Kristo	189972	M	Bulg.		Local Commissar, Jewish Affairs, Pirot (Yugo.)	MISC.CRIMES	YUGO.
PAROUBEK, Hans	153190	M	Aust.	25. 2.13	Civilian, Linz (Aust.) 42-45	WITNESS	U.S.
PASQUALE, Guiseppe	253276	M	Ital.		Chief, 21 Bn., Sardinia Gren.Div. Executive Section, Ljubljana (Yugo.)	MISC.CRIMES	YUGO.
PASQUALI, Rocco	307317	M	Ital.	circa 05	Cpl., Gen. Molat, C.C.Molat (Meleda) 42-43	MURDER	YUGO.
PASQUALINO	191054	M	Ital.		Agent, Police, Fraschette, Alatri (It.) 41-43	TORTURE	YUGO.
PASQUALUCCI, Renato	307318	M	Ital.		General-Consul, Judge, of special Tribunal for defense of State Rom (It.) 4.41-9.43	MURDER	YUGO.
PASSARELLO, Cosimo	193554	M	Ital.		Sgt., Carabinieri, Budva, Rijeka, Crnojevika (Yugo.) 9.41	MURDER	YUGO.
PAST, Johann	155533	M	Aust.	0. 3.85	Jail warden, civilian, Garsten (Aust.) 4.43-5.45	TORTURE	U.S.
PASTOREK	156834	M	Aust.	04	Rottenfhr., Feldgendarmerie, 12 SS-Pz.-Div., "H.-J.", D'Abbaye (Fr.) 6.6.-2.7.44	WITNESS	CAN.
PATTRACHINI, Vittorio	254150	M	Ital.		Formerly member of black Bde.,Ariano Polesine (It.) 12.44	INTERR.	U.K.
PATYRINIERI, Nunzio	162077	M	Ital.		Capt., Ital. Army,Fermo (It.) 41-43	TORTURE	U.K.
PAULOVICH	191055	M	Ital.		District commissioner, Sibenik (Yugo.) 41-43	MURDER	YUGO.
PAUNOV, Georgi	190820	M	Bulg.		Head, District police at Vranje, Vladicin Han, (Yugo.) 43-44	MURDER	YUGO.
PAVANINI	300647	M	Ital.		Member, Black Bde., Mesola, Ferrara, Adria Rovigo (It.) 12.44	MISC.CRIMES	U.K.
PAVISSICH	191057	M	Ital.		Capt., Ital. Army, Div. "Messino", Montenegro (Yugo.) 13.7.41-42	MURDER	YUGO.
PAVLOF, Georgios	305218	M	Bulg.		Member, security Drama (Grc.) 28.9.-20.10.41	MURDER	GRC.
PAWELL (Query as to spelling)	132803	M	Czech.		Cmdt.,Artl.-officer, C.C. II D,Stargard (Ger.) 20.1.45	TORTURE	U.K.
PECIS, A.	191058	M	Ital.		Lt. Col., Ital. Army, Solin, Dalmatia (Yugo.) 24.1.42-21.2.42	MURDER	YUGO.
PECKMANN, Hans	193594	M	Aust.		Sgt., 2 SS-Pz.Gren.Ausb. & Ers. Abt., 12, Berneau,(Bel.) 5.9.44	MURDER	BEL.
PEDINI, Pio	169290	M	Ital.		Lt. Col., Administ.officer, Camp P.G. 82, Laterina,(It.) 8.42-9.43	TORTURE	U.K.
PEDRAZOLI	149077	M	Ital.		General, Ital. Army, Tarro Div., Montenegro (Yugo.)	MURDER	YUGO.
PEDROTTI, Aldo	256969	M	Ital.		Capt., Commandant, 4 Coy., Milizacoost, Plave Anhovo (Yugo.) 13.-23.2.45	INTERR.	YUGO.
PEITSEF, Dimitrios	305219	M	Bulg.		Major, Police, Drama (Grc.) 28.9.-20.10.41	MURDER	GRC.
PEKETISCH (see FEKETISCH)	144719	M					
PELAZZI, Antonio	149078	M	Ital.		Col., Ital. Army, "Isonzo"-Div, Trebaje (Yugo.)	MURDER	YUGO., UNWCC.
PELEGRINO, Allessandro	259187	M	Ital.		Lt., Ital. Army, "Marche"-Div., 56 Div.,Stolac (Yugo.) 4.41-9.42	MURDER	YUGO.
PELEGRINO (or PELLEGRIMOS)N.	191059	M	Ital.		Commissary, Sipo, Ljubljana (Yugo.)	MURDER	YUGO.
PELIGRA (see PELLIGRA)	148979						
PELIKAN	120564	M	Aust.		Doctor, Sturmfhr., N.S.K.K., Semi-Military, Odessa (Sov.Un.)41-42	MURDER	U.S.
PELIZZARI, Giovanni	193287	M	Ital.		Guard, C.C. 6, Verchili (It.) 43	MURDER	U.K.
PELLEGRIMOS, N. (see PELEGRINO)	191059						
PELLIGRA (alias:PELIGRA)	148979	M	Ital.		General, "Re" Div., Gornji-Kotar, Kotar-Caberin (Yugo.) 43	MURDER	YUGO.
PENEF, Panayotis	305101	M	Bulg.		Policeman, Kavalla, 19.11.43	TORTURE	GRC.
PENSENTHEIMER (see PESENTHEIMER)	686						
PENTSEF, Ivan (or MINTSEF)	300332	M	Bulg.		Guard, Bulg. Rural police, Hydromili-Kavalla, 1942	PILLAGE	GRC.
PEPPI	259170	M	Ital.		Agent, later Director, It. Questura, Split, prison, Parma (It.) Split (Yugo.) 1.42	SUSPECT	YUGO.
PERDON, Louis	196700	M	Fr.	10. 2.09	F.C.F., SD., Kommando "Wenger", Etival (Fr.) 44	WITNESS	U.K.

PER-PIT

NAME	C.R.FILE NUMBER	SEX	NATIO-NALITY	DATE OF BIRTH	RANK OCCUPATION UNIT PLACE AND DATE OF CRIME	REASON WANTED	WANTED BY
PERILLO, Emilio	307319	M	Ital.		Consul,Judge,Special Tribunal for defence of State Rom(Ital.) 4.41-9.43	MURDER	YUGO.
PERIN, Italo	305220	M	Ital.		Black Bde.,Frasinelle,Rovigo Prov.(Ital.) 2.9.44	MISC.CRIMES	U.K.
PERMA, U.	191010	M	Ital.		Cmdt.,Ital.Army,2 "Granatlieri" di Sardigne,Blocice(Yugo.) 25.-28.6.42	PILLAGE	YUGO.
PERODI, Gino	169505	M	Ital.		Capt.,Ital.Army,Laterina(Ital.) 8.42-9.43	TORTURE	U.K.
PERONCINI, Giovanni Battista	300673	M	Ital.		Lt.-Col.,President and Judge of Military Tribunal,Sibenik-Dalmatia (Yugo.) 41-43	TORTURE	U.K.
PERONI	141939	M	Ital.	05	Major,Army,Public Prosecutor to the Procuratore Generale,Athen(Grc.)42	MISC.CRIMES	U.K.
PERSTERER, Alois	185025	M	Aust.	29.9.09	Osturmbannfhr.,SS,Caucasus(Russ.) 42	MURDER	U.S.
PESCARA see TISANI	194290						
PESODA see TISANI	194290						
PESENTHEIMER or PENSENTHEIMER	686	M	Aust.or Ger.		Oschfhr.,SS,Gestapo,Loomine(Fr.) 7.-8.44	MURDER	FR.
PESKENS, Marcel	193567	M	Bel.		Cpl.,SD,Sipo,Leeuwarden(Neth.) 13.9.44-14.4.45	MURDER	NETH.
PETAKI, Jeno	199924	M	Hung.		Lt.,Hungarian Army,Novi Sad(Yugo.)	TORTURE	YUGO.
PETER, Aladar	166624	M	Hung.	02	Hptsturmfhr.,SS,Hungarian SS,SS Kampfgruppe"Ney", between Sur and Aka (Hung.) 7.5.45	MURDER	U.S.
PETERBAUER see WIESER	179781						
PETERKA, Rudolph	186770	M	Czech.		Kapo,Camp Stephanskirchen near Rosenheim(Ger.)	TORTURE	FR.
PETKOF, Peter	305221	M	Bulg.		Secret Agent,Security,Drama Area(Grc.) 28.9.-20.10.41	MURDER	GRC.
PETKOV, Angel	190821	M	Bulg.		Sgt.,Bulg.Army,Pirot(Yugo.) 11.5.44	MURDER	YUGO.
PETKOV, G.	189962	M	Bulg.		Chief,Bulg.Police,Pirot(Yugo.) 4.42	TORTURE	YUGO.
PETKOV, Peter	305222	M	Bulg.		Servant,Civilian,Sidirocastron(Macedonia) 5.41	PILLAGE	GRC.
PETKOV, Tryfon	305223	M	Bulg.		Officer,Police,Chryssopolis-Kavalla(Grc.) 4.43	MURDER	GRC.
PETRAELLO, Svanco-Cucoz	254089	M	Ital.		Fascist Militioner,Split(Yugo.) 1.41-5.42	TORTURE	YUGO.
PETRAGNANI	189090	M	Ital.		Col.,Cmdt.of P.G.53,Macerata(Ital.) 9.-9.43	TORTURE	U.K.
PETRECK	155991	M	Russ.		Block-Leader,C.C.Mauthausen(Aust.) 11.5.42-10.5.45	MURDER	BEL.
PETRELLI, Mazzarero	132191	M	Ital.	10	River Manocchia(Ital.) 25.11.43	MURDER	U.K.
PETRICIONI, Domenico	191061	M	Ital.		Camp-Cmdt.,Women's C.C.,Pallenza-Macerata(Ital.) 43	TORTURE	YUGO.
PETRINA, Karl	155519	M	Aust.	99	Block-Elder, C.C.Ebensee(Aust.)	MURDER	U.S.
PETRINI, Dante	191062	M	Ital.		Carabinieri,Ital.Army,Sibenik and District Vodice(Yugo.) 41-43	MURDER	YUGO.
PETROF, Elie	205104	M	Bulg.		Sgt.,Serving at Ehinos,Xanthi during 1942,Melivia(Grc.) 9.42	PILLAGE	GRC.
PETROSSI, Verdi	149083	M	Ital.		Civilian Municipal Commissioner (Yugo.) 43	MURDER	YUGO.
PETROV	190824	M	Bulg.		Major, Bulgarian Army,Intelligence Officer of 27 Inf.Div.,Prokuplje (Yugo.) 43-44	MURDER	YUGO.
PETROV, Andreja	190822	M	Bulg.		Sgt.,Bulgarian Army,Gnjilane(Yugo.) 1.-2.43	MURDER	YUGO.
PETROV, Hristo	191141	M	Bulg.		County Director,Sofia's Police Directorate,Pirot(Yugo.) 4.42	MISC.CRIMES	YUGO.
PETROV, J.Simeun	190823	M	Bulg.		Forester,Village of Krupac near Nis,Pirot(Yugo.) 43	TORTURE	YUGO.
PETROV, Nikolaj	190825	M	Bulg.		Capt.,Bulgarian Army,Cmdt.of 6 Machine-Gun Coy.,117 Inf.Div. (Yugo.) 42-44	MURDER	YUGO.
PETRUNOV, Ivan	190826	M	Bulg.		Forester, Pirot(Yugo.) 41-43	MURDER	YUGO.
PETRUNOV, Nenko	190827	M	Bulg.		Inspector,Polizei, Vrenje,Vladicin-Han(Yugo.) 43-44	MURDER	YUGO.
PETSCHNER, Josef	193264	M	Hung.	6.3.99	Guard,SS-Mann,4 SS Totenkopf-Stuba,C.C.Dora,Nordhausen,Dachau(Ger.) 43-45	MURDER	U.S.
PETSVAROF see BOTSVAROF	305224						
PETZ, Maria	188243	F	Aust.		Civilian,Saint Lorenzen(Aust.) 2.4.44	WITNESS	U.S.
PEZZANO	191063	M	Ital.		Col.,Cmdt.of 2 Gruppe "Alpini del Valle",Ital.Army, Povisa,Stubica. Kuuk,Medjedja,Praprat(Yugo.) 9.41	MISC.CRIMES	YUGO.
PFAFF, Jakob	193266	M	Hung.	28.7.99	Guard, SS-Mann, 4 SS-Totenkopf-Stuba, Nordhausen(Ger.) 43-45	MURDER	U.S.
PFEIFFER	156831	M	Pol.	16	Uschfhr.,SS,Feldgend.,12 SS Pz.Div."Hitler-Jugend", Abbaye Ardenne near Caen-Normandy(Fr.) 6.6.-2.7.44	TORTURE	CAN.
PFENNIG	173184	M	Fr.		Interpreter,Gestapo,Vosges Area (Fr.)	TORTURE	U.K.
PFESTERER	155696	M	Aust.	98	Kdo.-Fhr.,Cmdt.Landesschuetzen Bn.3-788,C.C.Kuhlengraben(Aust.) 43	MURDER	U.K.
PHILLIS	254911	F	Dut.		Overseer,C.C.Ravensbrueck(Ger.)	INTERR.	FR.
PIACENTI, Nicolo	149084	M	Ital.		Maresciallo del Carabinieri,Ital.Army,Vis(Yugo.) 43	MURDER	YUGO.,UNWCC.
PIAMONTE	305225	M	Ital.		Carabinieri,Vrhnika,Ljubljana(Yugo.) 41 and 42	PILLAGE	YUGO.
PIAZZA, Vito	166625	M	Ital.	18	Agent,SD,Campomelon(Ital.)	WITNESS	U.S.
PIZZONI	149085	M	Ital.		Lt.-Gen.,Ital.Army "Bergamo"-Div.,Bickovo(Yugo.) 42	TORTURE	YUGO.
PICCAJA, Valerian	261980	M	Russ.	5.6.92	Member Gestapo Kutajs,Bratislava,Banska,Bystrica,Trencin(Czech.)	MURDER	CZECH.
PICCININI	191064	M	Ital.		Carabinieri,C.C.Pallenza(Ital.) 41-43	TORTURE	YUGO.
PICCINI, Sergio	253183	M	Ital.		Sgt.,Pilot,Air Force,21 Stormo,63 Group,Sosici(Yugo.)	INTERR.	YUGO.
PICOLOGIO, Vani	189881	M	Ital.		Lt.,Italian Army,Montenegro(Yugo.)	MISC.CRIMES	YUGO.
PIEER	146143	M	Aust.		Capt.,C.C.Stalag Luft III (Ger.)	WITNESS	U.K.
PIERRO-PARINI	305226	M	Ital.		Political Governor of the Jonia Islands,Corfu(Corsica) 1.6.41-11.9.43	PILLAGE	GRC.
PIGNATELLI, Antonio	191065	M	Ital.		Col.,Ital.Army,55 Regt."Marche" Div.,Trehinje(Yugo.) 41-43	MURDER	YUGO.
PILLER, Josef	260480	M	Yugo.	5.8.09	SS-Mann,Waffen-SS,C.C.Auschwitz(Pol.) 44-45	BRUTALITY	POL.
PILLERI	191066	M	Ital.		Member of Ovra(Ital.Secret Police) Chief of Police,Susak-Podhum(Yugo.)	MURDER	YUGO.
PILOT, Pietrot	39669	M	Ital.	29.6.24	Opl.,Unit 15201,Chenebier(Fr.) 27.9.44	MURDER	FR.
PILOTTI, Ugo	191156	M	Ital.		Capt.,Deputy State Prosecutor, Extraordinary Military Tribunal, Sibenik(Yugo.) from 41	MURDER	YUGO.
PINELLI, Corrado	149086	M	Ital.		Capt.,Isonzo-Div.,23 Regt.Fant"Como",Ital.Army,Cernomelj(Yugo.)	MURDER	YUGO.
PINI	121271	M	Ital.		Lt. de Vaisseau,Ital.Navy Cmdt.,d'Asmara. 10.7.40	MURDER	FR.
PINI	258201	M	Ital.		Lt.,Ital.Army,Plave Anhovo(Yugo.) 13.,23.2.45	INTERR.	YUGO.
PIOTT, Florian	260488	M	Yugo.	2.4.09	Pvt.,Waffen-SS,Guard,Totenkopf-Stuba,C.C.Auschwitz(Pol.) 43-45	BRUTALITY	POL.
PIROZZI, Vito	191067	M	Ital.		C.C.-Director,C.C.Ariano-Irpino(Ital.) 41-43	TORTURE	YUGO.
PISKIOROF	305227	M	Bulg.		Major,Bulgarian,Xylagani-Rodopi(Grc.) 9.4.44	MURDER	GRC.
PISTOGLIESI	259108	M	Ital.		Carabinieri,Venezia Div.,Berane(Yugo.) 8.41-9.43	MISC.CRIMES	YUGO.
PITARRELO, Romoaldo	259186	M	Ital.		Lt.,Ital.Army,"Marche" Div.,56 Regt.,Stolac(Yugo.) 4.41-9.42	MURDER	YUGO.
PITAU	149087	M	Ital.		Lt.-Gen.,Ital.Army "Lombardia"-Div. (Yugo.) 43	MURDER	YUGO.
PITHURNIJ, Eugen	195560	M	Ukr.	31.7.20	Rottfhr.,Waffen-SS,Pecany(Czech.) 1.2.45	MURDER	CZECH.

PIV-RAD

NAME	C.R.FILE NUMBER	SEX	NATIO-NALITY	DATE OF BIRTH	RANK OCCUPATION UNIT PLACE AND DATE OF CRIME	REASON WANTED	WANTED BY
PIVANO	191068	M	Ital.		General, Ital.Army, Commander of "Cacciatori del Alpi", Kubide-Niksic (Yugo.) 10.8.41	TORTURE	YUGO.
PIVIDORI, Eligio	191069	M	Ital.		Member, Fascist Militia, Sibenik (Yugo.) 41-43	MURDER	YUGO.
PIVIDORI, N.	253278	M	Ital.		Observer, It.Air Force 21, Stormo-69, Group-41, Squadriglia O.A., Baronje Selo (Yugo.) 28.6.43	INTERR.	YUGO.
PIZZI, Enrico	191070	M	Ital.		Col., Ital.Army, Commander of Rgt. "Alpini del Valle",Podgorica Berane Cetinje Savnik (Yugo.) 7.-11.41	MURDER	YUGO.
PIZZI, Guiseppe	189880	M	Ital.		Major, Ital.Army, Brodarevo (Yugo.)	MISC.CRIMES	YUGO.
PIZZILIO, Giovanni	191071	M	Ital.		Lt., Judge at Military Tribunal of War, Cetinje (Yugo.) 7.41- 9.43	MURDER	YUGO.
PIZZILLO, Carlo	196695	M	Ital.		Col., Military Tribunal, Sibenik (Yugo.) 41-43	MISC.CRIMES	YUGO.
PLANGER, Josef	164136	M	Aust.	03	Cpl., 3-188 POW Working Bn.,Brathalmen (Nor.) 5.40	MURDER	NOR.
PLASCHKA	36696	M	Pol.or Ger.		Pvt., Army, Lds.Schtz.Bn.875, 2.Coy. (Pol.) 17.2.45	MURDER	U.K.
PLATTNER, Franz	192603	M	Aust.	1897-98	Cpl., Kgf.Arb.Bn.II-188 C.C. Fjell (Hordaland, Nor.) 42-43	TORTURE	NOR.
PLAZZA	142126	M	Czech.	10	Osturmfhr., SS, C.C. Dora - Nordhausen (Ger.) 9.43	MURDER	FR.
PLIEM, Bernhard	144402	M	Aust.		Clerk, NSV-Office, Hallein (Aust.) 45	MISC.CRIMES	U.S.
PLOS	258200	M	Ital.		Pvt., Ital.Army, Plave-Anhovo (Yugo.) 12. and 23.2.45	INTERR.	YUGO.
POBORNIKOV, Fordor	190928	M	Bulg.		Lt., Bulg.Army, Gnjilane (Yugo.) 1.-2.43	MURDER	YUGO.
PODNIK	139868	M	Aust.	10	Dr., surgeon, Flugplatz-Kdo. A 3-XI, Romoe (Den.)	MURDER	U.K.
POLANSKI	130331	M	Aust.	21	SS Osturmfhr., 12.SS Pz.Div., 26.Rgt., 13.Coy.,Caen (Fr.) 6.44	TORTURE	CAN.
POLANYI, Josef	161638	M	Aust.	04	Cpl., Army, 2.Coy., 188 POW Working Bn., Furt (Nor.)	TORTURE	NOR.
POLVERINI, Alessandre	162623	M	Ital.		Capt., Ital. Army, Fermo (It.) 41-43	MISC.CRIMES	U.K.
POMPERL	137590	M	Aust.		Col., Stalag XVII-A, C.C. Dollersheim (Aust.) 7.6.44	TORTURE	U.K.
POMPERL	178764	M	Aust.		Col., Oflag IV C, 8.44	TORTURE	U.K.
POMPILI, Torello	307320	M	Ital.		Consul, Judge of special Tribunal for Defence of State Rom (It.) 4.41-9.43	MURDER	YUGO.
PONSINI, I.	190052	M	Ital.		Col., Ital.Army, Commander of 15 Inf.Rgt., Cabar - Slovenia (Yugo.) 7.-8.42	MURDER	YUGO.
POPOF, Ivan	305230	M	Bulg.		Cpl., 1 police sector of Drama (Grc.) 28.9.-20.10.41	MURDER	GRC.
POPOF, Joseph	305231	M	Bulg.		Deputy Major, Inspector, Jewish Community, Kavalla (Grc.) 42-43	MISC.CRIMES	GRC.
POPOF, Traiko	305232	M	Bulg.		Secret Agent, Security in Drama area (Grc.) 28.9.-20.10.41	MURDER	GRC.
POPOV	190831	M	Bulg.		Lt.,Bulg.Army, 25.Inf.Rgt., 3.Coy., 2.Bn. Modra Stena, district of Pirot (Yugo.) 41-43	MURDER	YUGO.
POPOV, Georgi, Lazarov	190829	M	Bulg.		Deputy Mayor, Prekodolac, Zitoradje, Poloma, Vladicin Han (Yugo.) 43-44	MURDER	YUGO.
POPOV, Ivan	190830	M	Bulg.		Col., Bulg.Army, Commander of a Div. at Vranje, Jelasnica-Vlase (Yugo.) 21.10.43	MURDER	YUGO.
PORMA, Joseph	257664	M	Czech.		Police, Block 107, C.C. Dora Nordhausen (Ger.)	MURDER	FR.
POSCHKE, Max Ferdinand	240015	M	Aust.	75	Wehrwirtschaftsfuehrer, NSDAP, Stuttgart (Ger.)	MISC.CRIMES	U.S.
POSERT, Eduard	255868	M	Pol.		Guard, Neckargerach (Ger.)	TORTURE	FR.
POSI, Camillo	251243	M	Ital.		Capt., Carabinieri, Srima near Sibenik (Yugo.)	INTERR.	YUGO.
POTOSKIE, Johnie	178291	M	Ital.	10	Cpl., Ital. Army, C.C. Gravina, Camp 65 (It.) 6.42	MURDER	U.K.
POUEL, Otto	191854	M	Aust.		Civilian, Secretary, Change (Fr.)	WITNESS	FR.
POURRAIN, Guy	185553	M	Fr.	11.9.24	Member NSKK, Geeraardsbergen (Bel.) 5.9.43	MURDER	BEL.
POZZUOLI, Angelo	149088	M	Ital.		Lt., Ital. Army "Isonzo", 24.Inf.Rgt. "Como" (Yugo.)	MURDER	YUGO. UNWCC.
PRECIOSO	259119	M	Ital.		Head of internment camp at Istonic-Marina (It.) 41-43	BRUTALITY	YUGO.
PRENNER, Anton	253280	M	Aust.	9.2.02	Employee, Gestapo, Vsetin (Czech.) 39-45	MISC.CRIMES	CZECH.
PRESTI, Giovanni	307321	M	Ital.		Prosecutor (Military), special Tribunal for defence of State Rom (It.) 4.41-9.43	MURDER	YUGO.
PROCOPIEF, Valento	305235	M	Bulg.		Member of Bulg. Security at Kavalla (Grc.) 12.42	PILLAGE	GRC.
PROPERZI, Claudio	191072	M	Ital.		Ital Army, Podhum near Susak (Yugo.) 41-43	MURDER	YUGO.
PROSTREDNIK, Josef	173865	M	Aust.	21.3.09	Oberstfeldmeister, RAD 6-352 Unit, Schuetzen am Gebirge (Aust.) 3.45	WITNESS	U.S.
PULTAR, Anna	189443	F	Czech.	11.11.11	Civilian, Eindhoven (Neth.)	MISC.CRIMES	NETH.
PUSCH, Friedrich	194118	M	Aust.		Osturmbannfhr., SS, 2.Pion.Ausb.Bn., Passau (Ger.) 4.45	MURDER	U.S.
QUACARI, Guiseppe	259107	M	Ital.		see Consolidated List Part II - Appendix "A"		
QUARANTOTTO, Paolo	191079	M	Ital.		Secretary, Zadar, Sibenik (Yugo.) 41-43	MURDER	YUGO.
QUATTRINI, Arturo	300416	M	Ital.	circa 00	Sgt., Fascist Republican Guard, Andorno Micco (Vercelli Prov.) (It.) 24.4.44	MURDER	U.K.
RABAGLIOLI	191074	M	Ital.		Vice-Cmdt.,Ital.Army, Posto du Carabinieri at Krtoli (Yugo.) 9-43	MURDER	YUGO.
RACEV, Raco	189958	M	Bulg.		Cmdt., police, Pirot (Yugo.)	TORTURE	YUGO.
RACS	189923	M	Hung.		Dr., Counsellor, Hung. Police, Novi-Sad (Yugo.)	MURDER	YUGO.
RADET, Jean	195191	M	Fr.	02	Member SD, Einsatz-Kdo. Wenger (F.P.No.03069 C), Baccarat Etival (Fr.) 44	WITNESS	U.K.
RADINI-TEDESCHI, Francesco	191157	M	Ital.		Legal-Official, Judge of Ital."Special Court", Sibenik (Yugo.) 41-43	MURDER	YUGO.
RADL, Karl	259289	M	Aust.	12.11.11	Major, 150.Pz.Bde., Meuse Bridge, Antwerp (Bel.) 12.44	SUSPECT	U.S.
RADOMIRSKI, Botja	190832	M	Bulg.		Lt., Bulg.Army, 52.Inf.Rgt., Frontier Garrison at Vlase, District of Veranje Vlase (Yugo.) 7.44	MURDER	YUGO.
RADOMIRSKI, Georgije	190833	M	Bulg.		Deputy Mayor, occupied territories, village of Vojnegovac, District of Pirot (Yugo.) 6.44	TORTURE	YUGO.
RADOVANI, Plinio	255037	M	Ital.		Secretary, leader, Fascio, Biovicino, Selo, Kistanje, Ivosevei (Yugo.) 6.42	MURDER	YUGO.

RAF - ROC

NAME	C.R. FILE NUMBER	SEX	NATIONALITY	DATE OF BIRTH	RANK OCCUPATION UNIT PLACE AND DATE OF CRIME	REASON WANTED	WANTED BY
RAFFELLI, Giuseppe	169498	M	Ital.		Ital.Army, Camp of Prison.of War, Suani-Ben-Adem (Africa) 5.42-1.43	TORTURE	U.K.
RAGOZZI, Guido	191075	M	Ital.		Lt.Col., Ital.Army, Cmdt.of Bn.of the Div. "Messine", Prov.Montenegro (Yugo.) 31.7.41-3.9.42	MURDER	YUGO.
RAHM	173938	M	Aust.		Osturmfhr., SS, 44-45	TORTURE	NETH.
RAMEZANI	300649	M	Ital.		Carabinieri, Camp 52, Chisvari (It.) 12.41-10.42	MISC.CRIMES	U.K.
RAMPONI, Mario	191076	M	Ital.		Major, Cmdt.of Bn.G.A.F., Vice-Commissary at Susak, Susak and Podhum (Yugo.) 41-4.43	MURDER	YUGO.
RAPUSNIK	144969	M	Rum.	05	Guard, SD, C.C.Lahde-Weser (Ger.) 43-45	TORTURE	BEL
RASO see ROSSO, Luigi	191087						
RAUCH, Josef	196003	M	Aust.	1. 8.97	Hptsturmfhr., SS, SD, Arnheim (Neth.) 3.45	MURDER	NETH.
RAUER, Karl	261239	M	Aust.	7. 8.13	Maj., Cmdt.of Air Field, Hopsten (Ger.) 25.3.45	MURDER	U.S.
RAUSCHER	253194	M	Aust.		Oscharfhr., 3 Coy., 1 Bn., Regt."Der Fuehrer", Div."Das Reich", Oradour (Fr.) 10.6.44	INTERR.	FR.
RAUTER, Darius	121404	M	Ital.		17 Pz.Gren.Div., G.V.B.Sturmgeschuetz Abt.17, Segre Renale (Fr.) 30.7.44	MURDER	FR.
RAVENI	148643	M	Ital.		Col.,Army, "Lombardie"-Div., 57 Artl.Regt., (Yugo.)	MURDER	YUGO.
RAVERA, Joseph	121406	M	Ital.		17 SS-Pz.Gren.Div.G.V.B.Sturmgeschuetz Abt.17, Segre Renale (Fr.) 30.7.44	MURDER	FR.
RAVILL	300099	M	Russ.		Lt., Unit of Russ. and Ger. stationed at Bourseul and Matignon, Cotes-du-Nord, Bourseul (Fr.) 31.10. and 23.11.43	MISC.CRIMES	FR.
RAZZINI	253309	M	Ital.		Lt.,Chars Legers, 21 Bn., Aiti (Fr.) 10.6.-11.7.43	MISC.CRIMES	FR.
RE, Giuseppe	300650	M	Ital.		Sentry, at Camp PG-70, Fermo (It.) 4.1.43	TORTURE	U.K.
REA, Gianfranco	258196	M	Ital.		Capt., Fascist Republ.Army Tagliamento VIII Alp.Regt., 2 Bn., Dorenberg (Yugo.) 12.43-4.45	INTERR.	YUGO.
RECHENPRATER	156049	M	Aust.	00	Foreman (SS-Civil), Factory Georgen-Muehle, Gusen II-Oberdonau (Aust.) 44-45	TORTURE	FR.
REGULSKI al.MOLOTOW, Edouard Charles	177578	M	Pol.	22. 8.11	C.C.Newbrenn nr. Saarbruecken (Ger.)	MURDER	FR.
REICH, Oscar	121389	M	Aust.	22	Civilian (Fr.) 43-44	MISC.CRIMES	FR.
REICHERT, Hans	162708	M	Aust.	20. 9.10	Chief, Gestapo, Montelimar (Fr.)	MISC.CRIMES	FR.
REICHLEITNER, Franz	134920	M	Aust.	05	Schupo-Capt., SS Member, C.C.Harthein (Aust.) 40-44	MURDER	U.S.
REICHMANN, Hans	193022	M	Aust.	1. 5.03	Sgt., Guard, Werkfuehrer, Reichsjustizministerium, Strafgefangenenlager W-SS, C.C.Finmark (Nor.) 8.44	MISC.CRIMES	YUGO., NOR.
REINER, Karl	193901	M	Aust.		Pvt., SS Publ.Official, Maire Weigesdorf (Aust.) 25.9.43	MURDER	FR.
REINISCH, Pierre	252640	M	Aust.		Uscharfhr., Gestapo, Limoges (Fr.)	MISC.CRIMES	FR.
REISER see RIESER	136633						
REISINGER, Josef	173927	M	Aust.	25	Vormann, RAD 6-352, Area Schuetzen (Aust.) 3.45	MURDER	U.S.
REITTMANN, Anton	193434	M	Hung.	11.12.98	Pvt., 4 SS-Totenkopf sturmbann, C.C.Dora-Mittelbau, Nordhausen, Dachau (Ger.) 43-45	MURDER	U.S.
REK, Ander	189922	M	Hung.		Civil-Governor, Hungarian Public Official, Subotica (Yugo.)	MURDER	YUGO.
RELEV, Alexander	189971	M	Bulg.		Dr., Commission for Jewish Affairs, Sofia (Bulg.)	MISC.CRIMES	YUGO.
RENATH, Hans	193028	M	Aust.	12	Sgt.-Guard, Justizministerium Feldstraflager, C.C.Finmark (Nor.) 8.44	MISC.CRIMES	NOR.
RENHART	255774	M	Hung.		Kapo, Neckargerach (Ger.)	INTERR.	FR.
RENTZ, Johann	260524	M	Rum.	31. 5.08	SS-Mann, Waffen-SS, Guard-Coy., C.C.Lublin, Auschwitz (Pol.) 7.43-1.45	BRUTALITY	POL.
RENZO, Edwardo	148642	M	Ital.		Capt., Army "Isonzo"-Div., 24 Inf.Regt. "Como", (Yugo.) 43	MURDER	YUGO.
RETCHEAL, Henry	193320	M	Aust.	05	Dr., Interpreter, Gesundheitsamt, Vienna (Aust.) 5. or 8.44	MURDER	U.S.
REUL, Karl	139069	M	Aust.		Foreman, C.C.Krispl (Aust.)	TORTURE	NETH.
REWAY, Julius	260012	M	Hung.	26. 7.99	Civilian, Founder of the Terrorist Organisation SIC in Ruthenia, Suspect is believed to be living in Frankfurt-Main, Ushorod, Mukacevo-Ruthenia (Czech.) 39-44	MISC.CRIMES	CZECH.
RICCI	253292	M	Ital.		Lt., 1 Coy., 59 Regt.of Black Shirts, St.Pietro (Fr.) 31.8.43	MISC.CRIMES	FR.
RICCI, Settino	300420	M	Ital.	96	Sgt.-Major, Fascist Republican Guard, Andorno Micca (Vercelli Prov.) (It.) 24.4.44	MURDER	U.K.
RICCIO, Gennaro	306340	M	Ital.		Consul, Judge of Special Tribunal for Defense of State, Rom (It.) 4.41-9.43	MURDER	YUGO.
RICCIOTTI	191077	M	Ital.		Lt., Ital.Army, C.C.R.R., Isle of Veliki (Yugo.) 28.7.42	MURDER	YUGO.
RICHTER, Herman	148550	M	Aust.	13. 8.15	Osturmfhr., SS, C.C.Mauthausen (Aust.), 41-45	MURDER	U.S.
RICHTER, Wilhelm	186723	M	Aust.	04 - 09	Rottenfhr., Chief, Allg.SS, Gestapo, Sturm I, Steyr (Aust.) 45	MURDER	FR.
RICUCCI, Dario	253295	M	Ital.		Lt., Observer, Ital.Air Force, 21 Stormo, 63 Gr.41A, Baronje (Yugo.) 26.6.43	INTERR.	YUGO.
RIEDEL, Josef	186702	M	Pol.	85	Foreman, Civ.Saw mills, Beuthen (Ger.)	MURDER	U.K.
RIEGLER, Josef	180727	M	Hung.		Unterwachtmeister, 13 SS Police Regt., 1 Bn., Bleiburg (Aust.) 14.10.44	WITNESS	U.S.
RIESER or REISER	136633	M	Aust.		Capt., Unit Garding P.W.at Stalag XVIIB, Krems-Gneisendorf (Aust.) 10.43-4.45	MURDER	U.S.
RIESS, Johannes	161636	M	Aust.	06	Pvt., Army, 3 Coy., 188 Kgf.Arb.Bn., Herdla (Nor.)	MURDER	NOR.
RIESS, Leonhart	260537	M	Rum.	11.12.20	SS-Mann, Waffen-SS, Guard-Coy., C.C.Auschwitz (Pol.) 8.43-1.45	BRUTALITY	POL.
RILL, Samuel	192568	M	Rum.		Pvt., Army, Chatou (Fr.) 25.8.44	WITNESS	FR.
RINGELS, Paul	252594	M	Hung.	7.12.08	Farmer, Army, Buchenwald (Ger.)	MISC.CRIMES	U.S.
RISTERUCCI	173930	M	Ital.	00	Cmdt., Police, Pontoharra (Fr.)	MURDER	UNWCC.
RITZAL, Heinrich	148548	M	Aust.	20. 9.04	SS-Sgt., SS-Totenkopf-Stand., C.C.Mauthausen (Aust.) 41-45	TORTURE	U.S.
RIZOV, Cyril	305247	M	Bulg.		Lt.Col., District Porria-Serres (Gre.) 10.41	MURDER	GRC.
RIZZATO, Francesco	300674	M	Ital.		Cpl., 130 Regt., Stanza Zopovica, Split and neighbouring towns, 42	MURDER	U.K.
RIZZI see RIZZO, Luigi	191078						
RIZZO, Luigi or RIZZI	191078	M	Ital.		Director, Prison Poggio Reale, Naples (It.) 28.9.43	MURDER	YUGO.
ROATTA	307322	M	Ital.		N.C.O., Gend., C.C. Molat, 42-43	MURDER	YUGO.
ROBICKA, Jovan	261929	M	Hung.		Near the village of Belje (Yugo.) 18.4.41	MURDER	YUGO.
ROCCAFORTE, Filadelfo	191079	M	Ital.		Capt., Ital.Army, 6 Artl.Regt."Isonzo"-Div., Cmdt., Straza (Yugo.) 43	MURDER	YUGO.
ROCCHETTI, Nello	300421	M	Ital.	26	Pvt., Fascist Republ.Guard, Andorno Micca (It.) 24.4.44	MURDER	U.K.
ROCCHI, Armando	148641	M	Ital.		Col., Dalmatia (Yugo.) 43	MURDER	YUGO.
ROCCO, G.	148640	M	Ital.		Capt. (Dr.) "Isonzo"-Div., 23 Regt."Como", Cornomelj (Yugo.) 43	MURDER	YUGO.

ROC-SAM

NAME	C.R.FILE NUMBER	SEX	NATIO- NALITY	DATE OF BIRTH	RANK OCCUPATION UNIT PLACE AND DATE OF CRIME	REASON WANTED	WANTED BY
ROCHBERG, Jean	162708	M	Aust.	20. 9.10	Chief, Gestapo, Montelimar (Fr.)	MISC.CRIMES	FR.
ROCI, Viciano	191080	M	Ital.		Lt., Army Italian, 259.Regt., "Murge"-Div. at Trebinje, Ljubine (Yugo.) 42 - 43	MURDER	YUGO.
ROGL, Emerich	139076	M	Aust.	30. 4.09	Staffelfhr., NSKK, DAF, Steyr (Aust.) 40 - 45	TORTURE	U.S.
ROHNER, Babtiste	188812	M	Swiss.		Civilian, Vitry (Fr.) 24. 8.44	PILLAGE	FR.
ROIA, Roberto	255036	M	Ital.		Judge, Member of the Tribunal, Split (Yugo.) 41 - 43	INTERR.	YUGO.
ROLANDO (or ROWLANDO or ORLANDO, L.)	132194	M	Ital.	about 95	Capt., Ital.Army, Tahuna (N.-Africa) 9.42	TORTURE	U.K.
ROMANELLI, Giovanni	148646	M	Ital.		Fascist Italian Army, Grottazzolina (It.)	MURDER	U.K.
ROMANELLI, Giovanni	173244	M	Ital.		Civilian, Fermo (It.)	MURDER	U.K.
ROMANO	192573	M	Ital.		Cmdt., Ital.Army, 10.Gebirgs-Jaeger-Bn., Haute Ville, Gondon (Fr.) 8.43	PILLAGE	FR.
ROMEO, Caesare	132824	M	Ital.	93	Mareschiallo di Carabiniere, Athen (Grc.) 11.41 - 5.42	TORTURE	U.K.
ROMEO, Pietro	148638	M	Ital.		Colonel, Dalmatia (Yugo.) 43	TORTURE	YUGO.
ROMETSCH	260437	M	Yugo.	29. 8.12	SS-Uschfhr., Waffen-SS, Guard-Coy., C.C., Auschwitz (Pol.) 11.42 - 12.44	BRUTALITY	POL.
RONCAGLIA, Ercole	191081	M	Ital.		Lt. General, XIV.Corps D'Armata, Commander, Montenegro (Yugo.) 5.43 - 9.43	MURDER	YUGO.
RONCO	193544	M	Ital.		Lt., P.O.W.Camp No.70, Gruppignano (It.) 12.41	MURDER	U.K.
RONCORONI, Alfredo	148637	M	Ital.		Capt., Carabiniere, Dolmatia Isle of Korcyla (Yugo.) 43	MURDER	YUGO.
RONNER, Robert	191082	M	Ital.		N.C.O., Ital.Army, Carabiniere, Peninsula of Peljesce and Orebic (Yugo.) 42 - 43	MURDER	YUGO.
ROOCKE	173245	M	Ital.		Lt., Ital.Army, C.C., Camp 63, Aversa (It.) 42 - 43	TORTURE	U.K.
ROSA, Giuseppe	305251	M	Ital.		Police-Officer, Livadia, Davlia (Grc.) 5. 5.43	MURDER	GRC.
ROSADI, Gino	191083	M	Ital.		Lt., Ital.Army, Commander of a Unit at Sibenik and District (Yugo.) 41 - 43	MURDER	YUGO.
ROSANO, Raffaello	148636	M	Ital.		Capt., "Isonzo"-Div.98, Fascist-Legion, 43	MURDER	YUGO.
ROSATI, Filippo	191084	M	Ital.		Capt., Ital.Army, Sibenik (Yugo.) 41 - 43	MURDER	YUGO.
ROSA-ULIANA, Riccardo	307323	M	Ital.		Consul-Judge, of Speciale Tribunal for defence of State, Rom (It.) 4. 41 - 9. 43	MURDER	YUGO.
ROSCIOLI, Guiseppe	191085	M	Ital.		Colonel, Ital.Army, 47.Regt. Dolla Div."Ferrara", Savnik (Yugo.) (Montenegro) 43	MURDER	YUGO.
ROSENBERGER, Colestin	173932	M	Aust.	10	Hpttruppfhr., RAD-Arbeitsgau, Schutzen (Aust.) 3.45	MURDER	U.S.
ROSETI	191086	M	Ital.		Lt., Ital.Army, "Murge"-Div., 51.Regt., Trebinje (Yugo.) 42 - 43	MURDER	YUGO.
ROSI, Guiseppe	129150	M	Ital.		Pvt., Guard, C.C., Sulmona (It.) 26.12.41	MURDER	U.K.
ROSSAMANDO	189044	M	Ital.	95	Colonel, Ital.Art., Benghazi (Africa) Summer 42	TORTURE	U.K.
ROSSI	156053	M	Ital.	19	Cpl., 313.Inf.Regt., C.C., Larissa (Grc.) 10.42 - 6.43	TORTURE	U.K.
ROSSI, Romolo	307283	M	Ital.		Member, Ital.Fascist Federation at Verona, Grezzana (It.) 12.11.43	MURDER	U.K.
ROSSI, Umberto	307324	M	Ital.		General, Consul-Judge of Special Tribunal for defence of State, Rom (It.) 4. 41 - 9. 43	MURDER	YUGO.
ROSSINI	152350	M	Ital.		Sgt., Ital.Army, 313.Inf.Regt., Larissa (Grc.) 8. 42	TORTURE	U.K.
ROSSO, Luigi (or RASO)	191087	M	Ital.		Civilian, Provost Marshal, Fraschette Alatri (Yugo.) 41 - 43	TORTURE	YUGO.
ROTH, Ludwig	193530	M	Hung.	8.10.95	SS-Schuetze, 4.SS-Totenkopf-Sturmbann, C.C. Nordhausen, Mittelbau Dora (Ger.) 43 - 45	MURDER	U.S.
ROTH, Nikolaus	184127	M	Hung.	97	SS-Sturmmann, 31.SS-Inf.Div., C.C.Dora, Nordhausen (Ger.)	MURDER	U.S.
ROUNTZOFF, George	305254	M	Bulg.		Gendarme, Sidirocastron (Macedonia) 5. 41	PILLAGE	GRC.
ROVER, Giuseppe	193555	M	Ital.		Ital.Army, Carabiniere, Budva (Yugo.) 6. - 8.41	MURDER	YUGO.
ROVERO	189912	M	Ital.		Prison Doctor, C.C., San Remo (It.)	TORTURE	FR.
ROWLANDO, Luigi (see ROLANDO)	132194						
ROZHON, Rudolf	193011	M	Aust.	14.12.97	Reichsjustiz-Ministerium, C.C., Finmark (Nor.) 5. 45	WITNESS	NOR.
RUDOLF, Franz-Siegesmund	138042	M	Aust.	25. 2.92	Bde.General, Oberkommando d.Army, Foreign-Div. Germ. and Occupied Countries, 39 - 45	TORTURE	U.S.
RUGGERI	191088	M	Ital.		Sgt., Ital.Army, IX.Btty., Sibenik (Yugo.) 41 - 43	MURDER	YUGO.
RUGGERO, Vittorio	148635	M	Ital.		General, "Cacciatori delle Alpi"-Division, Ljubljana (Yugo.) 43	MURDER	YUGO.
RUGGI	253516	M	Ital.		Officer, Security Police, Sibenik (Yugo.) 12.41	BRUTALITY	YUGO.
RUGGIERO	191089	M	Ital.		Commissary, Public-Safety, Metlika-Slovenia (Yugo.) 42	MURDER	YUGO.
RUJU, Francesco	191090	M	Ital.		Tenente, Ital.Army, Commander of Tenenza of Vodice Sibenik a District (Yugo.) 41 - 43	MURDER	YUGO.
RUMPE, Josef	253248	M	Yugo.		SS-Mann, C.C. Cmdo. Klosterwerk, Buchenwald (Ger.)	INTERR.	FR.
RUNG	253249	M	Yugo.		SS-Mann, Cmdo. Klosterwerk, C.C., Buchenwald (Ger.)	INTERR.	FR.
RUSEV	190834	M	Bulg.		Lt., Bulg.Army, 7. Cavalry-Squadron (Yugo.) 42 - 43	MURDER	YUGO.
RUSSA, Salvatore	137588	M	Ital.		Pvt., Army, Gruppigniano (It.) 5. 43	MURDER	U.K.
RYBATSELMT, Warilli	12493	M	Russ.	21	Miscell., 23. 7.44	RAPE	FR.
SABA, Michele	258190	M	Ital.		Lt., Army, Plave Anhovo (Yugo.) 23. 2.45	INTERR.	YUGO.
SABATINI, Ciaccomi	173260	M	Ital.		Lt.Colonel (Med.) Ital.Army, Treviglio (It.)	MURDER	U.K.
SABATINI, Giaccomo	146171	M	Ital.		Col., Army, Mil.Hosp. for Tuberculosis, Treviglio (It.) 42 - 43	TORTURE	U.K.
SADULA (or SABDULA)	261394	M	Russ.		Lt.Commander, Garrison of Caucasian soldiers, Ronces near Valle in the community of Arta (Udine It.) 4. 4.45	WITNESS	NETH.
SACCESE, Luigi	169501	M	Ital.		Capt., Ital.Army, Capua (It.) 4. 41 - 6. 43	TORTURE	U.K.
SAGNOTTI, Augusto	259128	M	Ital.		Capt., Carabiniere Commandant, Berane (Montenegro Yugo.) 8. 41 - 7. 42	MISC.CRIMES	YUGO.
SALAMONE, Angelo	307325	M	Ital.		Court-President of Military Tribunal 2.Army, Section oi Lubiana (Yugo.) 41 - 43	MURDER	YUGO.
SALATEO, Max	191091	M	Ital.		Agent, Ital.Party, (Squadra politica) Split (Yugo.) 2. - 3.43	TORTURE	YUGO.
SALATIELLO, Luigi	256352	M	Ital.		Cmdt., Carabiniere Reali, Benkovac (Yugo.) 6. - 10.42	MISC.CRIMES	YUGO.
SALICCIA, Giovanni	129151	M	Ital.		Guard, Carabiniere, C.C., Sulmona (It.) 26.12.41	MURDER	U.K.
SALTINGER, Max	139080	M	Aust.		Untermeister, Spinnerei Richdorf (Aust.) 22. 2.44	MURDER	U.S.
SALVATELLI	146321	M	Ital.		Brigadier, Army Ital., Vela Luka (Yugo.)	MURDER	YUGO.
SALVATORE, Russo	146320	M	Ital.		Guard, Ital.Army, Isle de Korcula (Yugo.) 43	MURDER	YUGO.
SAMOLJ	261944	M	Hung.		Lt., 38.Regt., from Budapest, near the Village of Belje (Yugo.) 18. 4.41	MURDER	YUGO.

SAN - SCHU

NAME	C.R. FILE NUMBER	SEX	NATIO-NALITY	DATE OF BIRTH	RANK OCCUPATION UNIT PLACE AND DATE OF CRIME	REASON WANTED	WANTED BY
SANDLES	193869	M	Hung.	24. 9.08	Guard,SS-Mann,4 SS-Totk.-Stuba.,C.C.Dora Mittelbau,Nordhausen(Ger.)43-45	MURDER	U.S.
SANDLES, Philipp	184369	M	Hung.	18. 2.99	SS-Mann,31 SS-Gren.Div.,2 Artl.Regt.,C.C.Dora,Nordhausen,Dachau (Ger.)	WITNESS	U.S.
SANTAMARIA, Giovanni	191092	M	Ital.		Doctor,Director, C.C.Corrpoli (It.) 41-43	TORTURE	YUGO.
SANTARO, Pasquale	173262	M	Ital.		Col., Ital.Army, C.C. Padulla (It.)	TORTURE	U.K.
SANTINI, Umberto	191158	M	Ital.		Dr., Legal-official,Primo (I) Senior Judge of Ital."Special Court", Sibenik (Yugo.) 41-43	MURDER	YUGO.
SANTIS de Vincenzo, Eugenio	191165	M	Ital.		Commander,III Btty.,14 Artl.Regt."Ferraro"-Div.,Savnik, Montenegro (Yugo.) 5.-6.43	MURDER	U.K.
SANTOJEMA	191093	M	Ital.		Capt.,Head of police at Cetinje,XI Bn.,Carabiniere,Cetinje,Crna, Gora (Yugo.) 41-43	MURDER	YUGO.
SAPANO	253788	M	Ital.		Teacher,Civ.,Ital.-School,Split (Yugo.) 9.5.43	TORTURE	YUGO.
SAPUNDZIEV	190835	M	Bulg.		Col.,Bulg.Army,Commander of 17 Inf.Div.,Prokuplje (Yugo.) 42-43	MURDER	YUGO.
SARLENO	194286	M	Ital.		Major,Ital.-Police,Nice (Fr.) 1.-6.43	TORTURE	FR.
SAUER	174559	M	Pol.	10	Prt.,Ldsschtz.-Bn.515, Stalag 344, C.C.nr. Prague (Czech.) 3.45	MURDER	U.K.
SAURO	146318	M	Ital.		Capt.,Ital.Army,Marine,Biekovo (Yugo.) 42	MURDER	YUGO.
SAVALLI, Joseph	189911	M	Ital.		Civilian, Bizerte (Tun.)	MURDER	FR.
SAVARINO, F.	191094	M	Ital.		Major,Commander II Bn.32, Inf.Regt. "Como", Isonzo-Div.,District of Cernomelj (Yugo.) 11.8.42	MURDER	YUGO.
SAVIOLA, Giorgie or Giorgio	191095	M	Ital.		Lt.Col.,Ital.Army, 51 Rgt. of "Murge"-Div.,Trebuije Area,(Yugo.) 42-43	MURDER	YUGO.
SAVO, Diovanni	253474	M	Itsl.		Vice-Federale, Split (Yugo.) 8.41	INTERR.	YUGO.
SAVOV	190836	M	Bulg.		Capt.,Bulg.Army,Commander of Artl.at Prokuplje (Yugo.) 43-44	MURDER	YUGO.
SAWATSKI, Josef	187218	M	Hung.	10.10.17	Uschfhr.,SS,S.B.,C.C.Metz,Wouppy (Fr.) 6.-7.44	MISC.CRIMES	CAN.
SCALAMOGNA, Francesco	191096	M	Ital.		Director,Civ.,C.C.Lipari (It.) 41-43	TORTURE	YUGO.
SCALCHI, Giovanni	261032	M	Ital.		Col.Army, 107 Squadristi Legion, Bezbradica (Yugo.) 30.5.42	MURDER	YUGO.
SCALCHI, Jvan	191097	M	Ital.		Consul,Head of Political Investigation office,U.S.S,Zade, Sibenik (Yugo.) 41-43	MURDER	YUGO.
SCALPA, Guiseppe	189879	M	Ital.		Capt.,Ital.Army, Montenegro (Yugo.)	MISC.CRIMES	YUGO.
SCALZO, Michele	146317	M	Ital.		Major,Mil.Tribunal,Cettigne (Yugo.) 43	MURDER	YUGO.
SCARANO	307326	M	Ital.		Marshall,Member,Gendarmerie,OVRA,Trieste (It.) 12.41	MURDER	YUGO.
SCARANO, Alfredo	162067	M	Ital.		Capt.,Ital.Army,C.C.Fermo (It.) 11.41-43	MISC.CRIMES	U.K.
SCARPA, Guiseppe	191098	M	Ital.		Capt.,Judge of Military Tribunal of Cetinje (Yugo.) 7.41-9.43	MURDER	YUGO.
SCARPA	191099	M	Ital.		Agent,Questura of Cattaro,Kotor (Yugo.) 41-43	MURDER	YUGO.
SCARPERIA, G.	146316	M	Ital.		Lt.Col.,Ital.Army,"Isonzo"-Div.,23 Rgt.,Cernomels (Yugo.) 43	MURDER	YUGO.
SCASELATI, Franco	189878	M	Ital.		Prefect,Ital.Public official,Kotor (Yugo.)	MISC.CRIMES	YUGO.
SCHADE, Johann	193867	M	Hung.	9. 1.98	Guard,SS-Mann,4 SS-Totk.-Stuba,C.C.Dora Mittelbau,Nordhausen, Dachau (Ger.) 43-45	TORTURE	U.S.
SCHADT, Jakob	155951	M	Hung.	18. 7.91	Guard,W-SS,C.C.Mauthausen (Aust.) 10.44- 5.45	TORTURE	U.S.
SCHAFFER, Johann	253374	M	Pol.		See Consolidated List-Part II Appendix "A"		
SCHALIER, Hans	149875	M	Aust.		Kreisamtsleiter,NSDAP,Hallein (Aust.),45	MISC.CRIMES	U.S.
SCHARF, Karl (I)	184282	M	Hung.	30. 6.98	SS-Mann,31 SS-Gren.Div.,2 Artl.Rgt.,C;C.Dora,Nordhausen,Dachau (Ger.) 45	MURDER	U.S.
SCHARF, Karl (II)	184481	M	Hung.	11.10.97	SS-Mann,31 SS-Gren.Div.2 Artl.Regt.,C.C.Dora,Nordhausen,Dachau(Ger.)43-45	WITNESS	U.S.
SCHARINGER, Arthur	250480	M	State-less	16. 8.01	Member,Civ. Bratislava (Czech.) 42-45	MURDER	CZECH.
SCHEER, Ludwig	184982	M	Hung.-Ger.	6.10.99	SS-Mann,Guard,31 SS-Gren.-Div.,2 Art.Regt.1 C.C.Dora,Nordhausen (Ger.) 45	WITNESS	U.S.
SCHEKEMOV	39626	M	Russ.		Lt.,Army,Pouldreuzig (Fr.) 3.8.44	MURDER	FR.
SCHEPPESCH	186220	M	Hung.		SS,C.C.Dachau (Ger.)	MISC.CRIMES	FR.
SCHILLING	181194	M	Rum.	05	Nurse,C.C.Ebensee,Mauthausen (Aust.) 4 4	MURDER	FR.
SCHILLING, Gica	142294	M	Rum.-Ger.	06	Rottfhr.,SS-Medical, C.C.Ebensee (Aust.) 44-45	MURDER	U.S.
SCHILLING, Karl	255758	M	Hung.	95	Prt.,Guard, 2 Artl.Rgt.,SS-Gren.-Div. 31, Nordhausen (Ger.)	MURDER	U.S.
SCHLEBES, Erich	142057	M	Rum.		Uschfhr., SS-Totk.,Camp-Guard,C.C.Ebensee,Mauthausen (Aust.)	TORTURE	U.S.
SCHLEINING, Hans	167326	M	Aust.	18	Sgt.,SS-Div."Das Reich", 1.Coy., 1.Bn.,Oradour sur Glane (Fr.) 10.6.44	MURDER	FR.
SCHLIMER	62106	M	Rum.	10	Sturmmann,S.D.Vichy (Fr.) 8.44	MURDER	U.S.
SCHLOSSER, Franz	156896	M	Aust.		Cpl.,2 Coy., 188 POW Work-Bn., Ervik (Nor.) 42-43	MURDER	NOR.
SCHMIDT, Ema (or GARGIULO)	191100	F	Ital.		Wife,Civ.,Sub.Lt.,Gargiulo,Mortar (Yugo.) 7.42	PILLAGE	YUGO.
SCHMIDT, Friedrich	184980	M	Hung.	19. 6.97	SS-Mann, 4 SS-Totk.Stuba., C.C.Dora,Nordhausen (Ger.) 43-45	WITNESS	U.S.
SCHMIDT, Gustav	166676	M	Hung.		Lt.,27 SS-Div. Langemark,between Sur and Aka (Hung.) 7.3.45	MURDER	U.S.
SCHMIDT, Wilhelm	184981	M	Hung.	2.10.97	Prt.,SS-guard, 31 SS-Gren.Div.,2 Artl.Rgt.,C.C.Dora,Nordhausen (Ger.) 43-45	WITNESS	U.S.
SCHNEIDER (or SNEIDER)	301605	M	Rum.-Hung.		Overseer,SS,C.C.Breendonck (Bel.) 44-45	MURDER	BEL.
SCHNEIDER, Dominique	173066	M	Yugo.	5. 4.10	Sturmmann,SS, C.C.Natzweiler (Fr.) 42-44	MURDER	FR.
SCHOECKEL	306188	M	Aust.	97	Uschfhr.,aide de camp to Cmdt., C.C.Kahla (Ger.) 40-45	MURDER	BEL.
SCHORG, Karl	193690	M	Aust.	97	O'Wachtmeister,Reichsjustizministerium,Strafgefangenenlager Nord, C.C.Finmark (Nor.) 8.45	MISC.CRIMES	NOR.
SCHRITTWEISER	257199	M	Aust.		N.C.O., W-SS, Regt., "Der Fuehrer", 1.Bn.,3 Coy., Nieppe (Fr.) 5.40	SUSPECT	U.K.
SCHRUNER, Ludwig	193678	M	Aust.		Cpl.,Army,Stalag XVIII, A, C.C.Kaiserburg,Lesben (Aust.) 10.43	TORTURE	U.K.
SCHUCKERT, Anton	193695	M	Aust.		Hptschfhr., S.D.Security service, Wien,Trandum (Aust. Nor.)	MURDER	NOR.
SCHULEIN	837	M	Ger.-Aust.		Oberfaehnrich,Army, 118 Jg.Div. 738 Regt., Kalinwich,Montenegro (Yugo.) 8.43	MURDER	YUGO.
SCHULZE	845	M	Ger.-Aust.		Lt.,Army,38 Regt.-Jaeg.,1 Bn., 1 Coy., Montenegro (Yugo.) 7.43	MURDER	YUGO.
SCHURA	132730	M	Russ.		Surveillante, C.C.Ravensbrueck (Ger.)	TORTURE	FR.

SCHU - SLA

NAME	C.R.FILE NUMBER	SEX	NATIO-NALITY	DATE OF BIRTH	RANK	OCCUPATION UNIT PLACE AND DATE OF CRIME	REASON WANTED	WANTED BY
SCHUTZ, Martin	157015	M	Aust.	02	Pvt.,Ldsch.Bn 3-788, 3 Coy, C.C.khulengraben (Aust.)		MURDER	U.K.
SCHWABE	129921	M	Hung.		Guard, Waffen-SS, C.C.Mauthausen (Aust.) 41-45		MURDER	U.S.
SCHWAMBERGER, Josef	256872	M	Aust.		Uscharfhr.,Ghetto and Comp.Lab.Camp,SS,Przemysl,Rozwadow (Pol.)42-43		MURDER	POL.
SCHWARNER	161285	M	Czech.	00	Sgt.,Bau Bn 21,48, Blechhammer (Ger.) 12.12.44		MURDER	U.K.
SCHWARTS	260016	M	Russ.-Ger.		See Consolidated List Part II Appendix "A"			
SCHWARZENBERG	143216	M	Aust.		Kriegsgerichtsrat, Kriegsgericht, Nantes (Fr.) 9.41		WITNESS	U.S.
SCHWEMMER, Wilhelm	860	M	Pol.-Ger.		Wachtmstr., Sgt., Police, Prison Camp official,Oswiecim (Pol.) 40		MURDER	FR.
SCIPIONE	146915	M	Ital.		General, Italian Army, Deputy Commander (Yugo.) 43		MURDER	YUGO.
SCLOBLACK (see SCOBLIN)	252684							
SCOBLIN (or SCOBLACK)	252684	M	Ital.		Capt.,It. Troops stationed at Collonges, Archampa (Fr.) 11.6.43		INTERR.	FR.
SCOLARI	256974	M	Ital.		Pvt.,Italian Army, Plave Anhovo (Yugo.) 13.-23.2.45		INTERR.	YUGO.
SCOMBOLI, Hector	305277	M	Ital.		Sgt., Carabinieri Reali, Corfu (Corsica) 9.43		TORTURE	GRC.
SCONOCHI, Paulo	259127	M	Ital.	11	Capt.,Commandant,Carabinieri,Venezia Div., Berane (Yugo.) 8.42-9.43		MISC.CRIMES	YUGO.
SCROBOGNA, Giovanni	146314	M	Ital.		Italian Army, 98 Fascist Legion, Trebnje (Yugo.) 43		MURDER	YUGO.
SCUTELI	189877	M	Ital.		Carabinieri, Italian Army, Vela Luka (It.)		MISC.CRIMES	YUGO.
SECCHI	258191	M	Ital.		Pvt., Italian Army, Plave-Anhovo (Yugo.) 13.-23.2.45		INTERR.	YUGO.
SEDIVY, Pal.	261951	M	Hung.	31. I.12	Member, Nyilas Party, Kosice (Czech.) 1.45		MURDER	CZECH.
SEIFE, Matis	148007	M	Rum.	20	Posten, SS, C.C. Wattenstedt (Ger.)		TORTURE	U.S.
SEMERTZIEV	305279	M	Bulg.		Lt., Sidirocastron (Macedonia) 5.41		PILLAGE	GRC.
SEMKO	190837	M	Bulg.		Sgt., Bulgarian Army, Village of Sinjac, Pirot (Yugo.) 20.2.44		MURDER	YUGO.
SENATORE, Aldo	191101	M	Ital.		Major, Italian Army,Commander of Inf.Div."Zara",Sibenik(Yugo.)41-43		MURDER	YUGO.
SENEIDER, Kurt	121860	M	Aust.		Member, Gestapo, Clermont Ferrand (Fr.)		MURDER	FR.
SEPPILLI, Ilicio	146313	M	Ital.		Major, Italian Army, Mil.Tribunal, Cettigne (Yugo.) 43		MURDER	YUGO.
SERACCHIOLI, Luigi	307327	M	Ital.		Lt.,Col.,President,Judge,Mil.Tribunal for 2 Army section of Lubiana (Yugo.) 41-43		MURDER	YUGO.
SERAFINI (see SERAFINO)	162069							
SERAFINO, Guido (or SERAFINI)	162069	M	Ital.		Capt.,Italian Army, Camp 87, Benevento (It.) 7.-11.42		TORTURE	U.K.
SERAFOV, Penco	190838	M	Bulg.		Lt.,Col., Inf.Div.,Cmdr. of Art.Unit Nr.5765 of 1779 Serbia (Yugo.) 42-43		MURDER	YUGO.
SERAPIGLIA, Antonio	191102	M	Ital.		Fascist, C.C.N.N.134 Bn "Larino",Czaljon,Kupa,Novo Mesto(Yugo.) 43		PILLAGE	YUGO.
SERRENTINO, Pietro	259098	M	Ital.		Lt.,Italian Army,56 Rgt.,"Marche"Div.,Stolac (Yugo.) 4.41-9.42		MURDER	YUGO.
SERRENTINO, Vincenco	191103	M	Ital.		Judge, Ital.Extra Ordinary Court, Sibenik (Yugo.) 41-43		MURDER	YUGO.
SERVIDORI	258188	M	Ital.	00	Secretary, Fascist Party at Rijeka, Kastav (Yugo.) 41-43		INTERR.	YUGO.
SESTIILI, Gualterio	191104	M	Ital.		Lt.Col., C.O.Carabinieri, Sibenik (Yugo.) 42-43		MURDER	YUGO.
SEVAROF, Petros	305281	M	Bulg.		Financial-Inspe., Drama Area (Grc.) 28.9.-20.10.41		MURDER	GRC.
SFERCO, Massimiliano	253787	M	Ital.		Agent, Police, Split (Yugo.) 42-43		TORTURE	YUGO.
SIDDI, R.	146312	M	Ital.		General-Major, Italian Army, Praesident of Mil.Tribunal, Cettigne (Yugo.) 43		MURDER	YUGO.
SIDOSKI	120638	M	Yugo.		Guard, Army, C.C. Schishchitz (Pol.)		BRUTALITY	U.K.
SIEGEL, Herbert	139086	M	Aust.		Osturmfhr., Waffen-SS, Floc (Pol.) 8.42		MURDER	U.S.
SIFFREDI, G.	191108	M	Ital.		Col.,Commando Sector of Castelmoro,Bakovci,Zelenika,Presjeka, Lastovo (Yugo.) 41		MURDER	YUGO.
SIGMUND	192867	M	Aust.		Lt., Schupo, C.C. Falstad (Nor.) 4.43		MURDER	NOR.
SIHLER, Georg	184599	M	Hung.	96	Guard, Pvt., 4 SS-Totenkopf-Sturmbann, C.C.Dora-Mittelbau, Nordhausen, Dachau (Ger.) 43-45		INTERR.	U.S.
SILESAROV, Venca	190839	M	Bulg.		Agent, Bulgarian Army, Bulgarian Police,27 Inf.Div., (Yugo.) 43-44		MURDER	YUGO.
SIMEONOFF	305282	M	Bulg.		Major, Sidirocastron (Macedonia) 41		MURDER	GRC.
SIMON, Johann	260916	M	Yugo.	26.12.08	Farmer, Pvt., SS-guard, C.C. Auschwitz (Pol.) 43-45		BRUTALITY	POL.
SIMONEILI	191109	M	Ital.		Civilian, Commissary in municipality of Preko,Island Dugi Otok (Yugo.) 42-43		MURDER	YUGO.
SIMONETO, Guglielmo	300675	M	Ital.		Italian Soldier, Kastel-Kambelovac Garrison, Split and neighbouring towns (Yugo.) 42		MURDER	U.K.
SINGER	9620	M	Aust.		Doctor, employed as male nurse at C.C. Breendonck(Bel.) 40-44		TORTURE	BEL.
SINOKAPOVITS, Joannis	305283	M	Bulg.		Member, Secret Police of Drama Area (Grc.) 28.9.-20.10.41		MURDER	GRC.
SIOB	72016	M	Pol.		Civilian, employee, Camp Bitterfeld (Ger.) 10.43-4.45		TORTURE	U.K.
SIPOS, Tibor	135218	M	Hung.		Hungarian Army, Belsen (Ger.) 15. 4.45		MURDER	U.K.
SIPSEN, Tihomir	305284	M	Bulg.		Deputy-in-commandant, Security, Drama (Grc.) 28.9.-20.10.41		MURDER	GRC.
SIRACUSA, Vincenzo	191105	M	Ital.		Capt.,XI Bn, Carabinieri, Chief of Police, Cetinje Crna Gura (Yugo.) 41-43		MURDER	YUGO.
SIRAKOV	305285	M	Bulg.		General, Bulgarian Army, Commanding officer of the "Drama" Div., Drama Area (Grc.) 28.9.-20.10.41		MURDER	GRC.
SIRRES, Marcel	187340	M	Lux.		Interpreter, Civilian, Montgauthier, Dinant (Bel.) 20.9.43		MURDER	BEL.
SISKOV, St.	191142	M	Bulg.		Director, Gestapo, Sofia Pirot (Yugo.)		MISC.CRIMES	YUGO.
SIUBA, Enzo	191107	M	Ital.		Dr., Civilian, Head of Agents of prefecture, Kotor (It.) 41-43		MURDER	YUGO.
SIZEMBEYEF	125732	M	Russ.	21	II,9 R. 959, Caen (Fr.) 16.8.44		MURDER	U.K.
SKATINI	177604	M	Ital.		Official General, SD, Army, Athens (Grc.) 41-43		TORTURE	U.K.
SKETINI, Vicenzo	305291	M	Ital.		Colonel, Bn C, Carabinieri Reali, Davlia (Grc.) 5.5.43		MURDER	GRC.
SKOPP	186198	M	Pol.		Civilian, Bruay en Artois (Fr.) 1.-2.9.44		WITNESS	FR.
SKOWRONEK	188001	M	Pol.	circa 95	Mayor, Leader, SA, Nience nr.Sosnowitz, Kazimierz (Pol.) 12.42-6.44		TORTURE	U.K.
SLATANOF, Vangel	305293	M	Bulg.		Officer, Abdira Garnison Xanti 3 Bn,58 Bulgarian Rgt., Abdira, Canti (Grc.) 44		MURDER	GRC.
SLAVOV	190841	M	Bulg.		Capt., Bulgarian Army,5 Bulg.Cavalry Rgt.,Strelce (Yugo.) 4.43		RAPE	YUGO.
SLAVQV (or SLAVTSO)	305294	M	Bulg.		Officer, Security at Serres (Grc.) 41-44		MURDER	GRC.
SLAVOV, Slave	190842	M	Bulg.		Agent, Bulgarian Police, Predejan District of Vladicin-Han, (Yugo.) 22.2.43-23.4.43		MURDER	YUGO.
SLAVTSO (see SLAVOV)	305294							

SLA-STE

NAME	C.R.FILE NUMBER	SEX	NATIONALITY	DATE OF BIRTH	RANK OCCUPATION UNIT PLACE AND DATE OF CRIME	REASON WANTED	WANTED BY
SLAWING, Alfred	188481	M	Aust.	11	Lt., Occupied Territories, Army, Athen (Grc.) 43	MURDER	GRC.
SMALDINI, Vincenzo	191110	M	Ital.		Vice Brigadier, Cmdr. of Carabinieri at Mandolini, Sibenik(Yugo.)41-42	MURDER	YUGO.
SMARAGLIA	253785	M	Ital.		Lt., I.O.V.R.A., Commissaire, Aitti (Fr.) 10.6.-11.7.43	TORTURE	FR.
SMERDEL	253477	M	Croat.		SS, C.C. Buchenwald (Ger.)	BRUTALITY	FR.
SMOLEN, Hans	261400	M	Yugo.		SS-guard, SS-Totenkopf, C.C. Auschwitz (Pol.) 42-44	BRUTALITY	POL.
SMOLIK	6127	M	Pol.		SS-Div. "Das Reich", Buzet-Tann, Haute Garonne (Fr.) 6.-7.44	MURDER	FR.
SNAIDER, Karol	188493	M	Aust.		SS-Interregater, 13 Department, Byron, Stagalea, Athen (Grc.)	MURDER	GRC.
SNEIDER (see SCHNEIDER)	301605						
SOFIA, Mario	146311	M	Ital.		Lt., Ital. Army, "Isonzo" Div. 24 Inf. Regt., 1 Bn. (Yugo.) 45	MURDER	YUGO.
SOKOLOV	305509	M	Russ.		Capt., 634 Inf. Regt. (Sov.Un.), Belz, Morbihan	INTERR.	FR.
SOLDANO, Vincenzo	191111	M	Ital.		Major, 259 Regt., "Murge" Div. Trebrinse, Iboski, Sume, Lubine, Ljubomir (Yugo.) 42-43	MURDER	YUGO.
SOLDINI, Marinello	137585	M	Ital.	10	Carabinieri, Gruppigriamo (It.) 5.43	MURDER	U.K.
SOLEF, Gregory	300143	M	Bulg.		Lt., Bulg. Serving in Provata, Serres (Grc.)	MURDER	GRC.
SOMAUILLE, Angelo	146310	M	Ital.		Col., Ital. Army, Gracao (Yugo.)	MURDER	YUGO.
SOMMER	140809	M	Rum.		Sturmmann, SS, Frankfurt-Main. (Ger.) 25.3.45	MURDER	U.S.
SOMMER	194250	M	Aust.		Civilian, C.C. Change d' Auvour (Fr.)	WITNESS	FR.
SORA, Josef	142250	M	Aust.	16. 3.10	Dr., Air Force Staff, C.C. Ebensee (Aust.) 44-45	WITNESS	U.S.
SORCETTI, Corrado	300651	M	Ital.	23. 8.27	Ger. colaborator, Goriconi Comune Amandola (It.) 2.5.44	MURDER	U.K.
SORDI	178288	M	Ital.	95	Col., Ital. Army, Athen (Grc.) autumn 41 - autumn 42	TORTURE	U.K.
SORDI, Giuseppe	146309	M	Ital.		Lt.Col., Ital. Army, 24 Inf. Regt., III Bn. (Yugo.) 43	MURDER	YUGO.
SORDI, T.	189876	M	Ital.		Col., Ital. Army, Ljubljana (Yugo.)	MISC.CRIMES	YUGO.
SORENTINI	259172	M	Ital.		Member of Staff, internment camp at fabriano (It.) 41-43	BRUTALITY	YUGO.
SOTIROF, Georgios	305297	M	Bulg.		Major, Bulg. Army, Drama-Area (Grc.) 28.9.-20.10.41	MURDER	GRC.
SPAGNA	191112	M	Ital.		Capt., 56 Inf. Regt., 1 Bn., 1 Coy., Div. "Marche", Mostar (Yugo.) 7.42	PILLAGE	YUGO.
SPAGNOLO	156022	M	Ital.		Ital.Army, Fascist Commissionier, Bassano (It.) 4.11.44	MURDER	U.K.
SPALATINI (see SPOLETI)	191117						
SPAMPINETTI, Giovanni	191113	M	Ital.		Civilian, C.C. Fraschette, Alatri (It.) 41-43	TORTURE	YUGO.
SPASOV, Panta	190844	M	Bulg.		Deputy-chief, Police, Vladicin-Han (Yugo.) 43-44	MURDER	YUGO.
SPECCHIALE, Francesco	191114	M	Ital.		Brigadiere, Ital. Army, Togir, Dalmatia, Prapatnice, Prgomet (Yugo.) spring 43	MURDER	YUGO.
SPEISS, Philip	194047	M	Hung.	2.11.97	Guard, Pvt., SS 4 Totenk. Stuba, C.C. Mittelbau-Dora, Nordhausen, Dachau (Ger.) 43-45	INTERR.	U.S.
SPERANDIO, Rinaldo	146307	M	Ital.		Cpl., Ital. Army, "Isonzo" Div., 98 Legion, 3 Coy., 117 Bn., 43	MURDER	YUGO.
SFIGO, Umberto	189875	M	Ital.		Gen., Ital. Army, Dalmatia (Yugo.)	MISC.CRIMES	YUGO.
SPINELLI	191116	M	Ital.		Col., Cmdr. of Art. at Delnice, Gorski, Kotar, Vrata, Croatia (Yugo.) 25.8.43	INCENDIARISM.	YUGO.
SPINELLI, Filippo	191115	M	Ital.		Civilian, Censor, C.C. Casoli (It.) 42-43	PILLAGE	YUGO.
SPIOTTA, Vito	137077	M	Ital.		Ingegnere, Silvio Parodi Black-Bde. of Chiaveri(C.O.)Carasco(It)10.44	MURDER	U.K.
SPITALERI	193556	M	Ital.		Major, Ital. Army, Div. "Tarro", Budve, Banoviane, Zevska (Yugo.) 41	MURDER	YUGO.
SPOERRY, Anne Marie	194069	F	Swiss.		C.C. Ravensbrueck (Ger.)	TORTURE	FR.
SPOGNIOLI	141899	M	Ital.		Dr., Capt. Stalag, C.C. Benghazi (Africa) 42	MISC.CRIMES	U.K.
SPOLERO, Olinto	258186	M	Ital.		Maresciallo, Fasc. Republ.-Army, Tagliamento, VIII Alp. Regt., 2 Bn. Dorenberg and neighbouring villages (Yugo.)	INTERR.	YUGO.
SPOLETI (or SPALATINI)	191117	M	Ital.		Lt., 51 Regt. Div. "Murge", Iboski, Lubine, Sume (Yugo.) 42-43	MURDER	YUGO.
SPOR	146306	M	Ital.		Interpreter, Ital. Army, Trieste (It.) 43	TORTURE	YUGO.
STAHLE	130178	M	Pol.		Guard, 559 Lds.Sch.Bn., 2 Coy., C.C. Lamsdorf (Ger.) 11.-18.11.43	TORTURE	U.K.
STALTERI, G.	191118	M	Ital.		Mayor, Mayors-office of Cattaro, Kotor (Yugo.) 43	TORTURE	YUGO.
STAMENOV	190845	M	Bulg.		Lt., Deputy-chief, Bulg. Army, Police official, Pirot (Yugo.) 43-44	MURDER	YUGO.
STAMOV, Nikifor Petrov	190846	M	Bulg.		Policeman, Bulg.Pol., Vladicin Han (Yugo.) 43-44	MURDER	YUGO.
STANGOFF, Nickolas (or TSANGOFF)	305332	M	Bulg.		Pol.Capt., Sidirocastron-Macedonia (Grc.) 41	MURDER	GRC.
STANIMIROV, Zodor	190847	M	Bulg.		Capt., Bulg. Army, Cmdr. of 7 Caval.Squadron, Velika Plana (Yugo.) 42-43	MURDER	YUGO.
STANKOV	190848	M	Bulg.		Lt., Bulg.Army (Yugo.) 42-43	MURDER	YUGO.
STAREK, Rudolf	166303	M	Aust.	3. 7.24	Civilian, formerly NavymObenrndorf Krs. Salzburg (Aust.) 22.11.44	WITNESS	U.S.
STASSI, Geremio	191119	M	Ital.		Ital. Army, Carabinieri, Sibenik and District (Yugo.) 41-43	MURDER	YUGO.
STATHIEF, Stathis	305299	M	Bulg.		Member, Drama Secret Police during 41, Drama-Area(Grc.) 28.9.-20.10.41	MURDER	GRC.
STEFAN, Josef	250494	M	Hung.	6.10.24	Civilian, Komarno (Czech.) 44	MURDER	CZECH.
STEFAN, Martin	250499	M	Hung.	24. 1.22	Civilian, Komarno (Czech.) 44	MURDER	CZECH.
STEFAN, Zoltan	250498	M	Hung.	5. 6.23	Civilian, Komarno (Czech.) 44	MURDER	CZECH.
STEFANO	146305	M	Ital.		Lt., Ital. Army, 23 Inf. Regt. "Como" (Yugo.) 43	MURDER	YUGO.
STEIGER, Mathias	158573	M	Hung.	20	SS-Sturmmann, SS-Totenk. Stuba, C.C. Buchenwald, Pawiak(Ger.-Pol.)42-43	TORTURE	U.K.
STEIN	158572	M	Hung.	25	SS-Mann, SS, C.C. Reichenau (Aust.) 44	MURDER	U.S.
STEINBERGER	252692	M	Aust.	00	Cpl., Police, 532 Gend.Trupp, Nave (It.) 1.8.44	INTERR.	U.K.
STEINER	128799	M	Aust.		Capt., Stalag XVIII A, Wolfsberg (Aust.) 6.1-3.45	TORTURE	U.K.
STEINER	158461	M	Aust.	95	Sgt., Army, 877 Lds.Schz.Bn., 3 Coy., Liezen (Aust.) 44-45	TORTURE	U.K.
STEINHAUSEN (see STENHAUSEN)	180826						
STEINHAUSER, J.	116811	M	Aust.		Civ., Inkeeper, Arb.-Kdo., St.Margarethen (Aust.) 1.-11.5.44	TORTURE	U.K.
STELLAS, Panayotis	305300	M	Ital.		Interpreter, leader, Gazale-Regt., stationed at Carpenissi in the Lamia Area (Grc.) 10.42-4.43	MISC.CRIMES	GRC.
STENHAUSEN (or STEINHAUSEN)	180826	M	Czech.		Chief-paymaster of Commandantur, 7 Regt.Art. d. Res., Tours and Albertville (Fr.) 8.-23.6.44	MURDER	FR.
STENIA	305600	F	Pol.		Woman-Lageraelteste, C.C. Belsen (Ger.) 40	MISC.CRIMES	BEL.
STEPANIAK, Ivan (Josef)	260540	M	Russ.	13. 3.12	Civilian, Merchant, Rzeszow (Pol.) 41	MISC.CRIMES	POL.

STE-TAL

NAME	C.R.FILE NUMBER	SEX	NATIONALITY	DATE OF BIRTH	RANK OCCUPATION UNIT PLACE AND DATE OF CRIME	REASON WANTED	WANTED BY
STERN, Samuel	306893	M	Rum.		Male nuse, C.C.Auschwitz Block 28 (Pol.) 40-45	MURDER	FR.
STIFT, Erich	188002	M	Aust.	09 - 10	SS-Obersturmbannfhr., 25 SS-Pz.Gren.Regt., 12 SS-Pz.Div.(Hitl.Jugend) nr. Caen (Fr.) 6.6.-8.7.44	TORTURE	CAN.
STIGLER, Josep	261930	M	Hung.		Mayor of Beli Manastir, nr.Village of Belje (Yugo.) 4.41	MURDER	YUGO.
STILOV, Hrito L.	190849	M	Bulg.		Head, Police of Skoplje Distr,Vladicin Han (Yugo.) 43-44	MURDER	YUGO.
STIPLIEF, Demetrios	305301	M	Bulg.		Mayor of Kavalla (Bulg.) 9.42	MURDER	GRC.
STOCKER, Alois	188407	M	Aust.		Civ., St. Lorenzen (Aust.) 2.4.44	WITNESS	U.S.
STOCKER, Karl	188406	M	Aust.		Civ., St. Lorenzen (Aust.) 2.4.44	WITNESS	U.S.
STOFFNER, Paul	140808	M	Hung.		SS-Mann, Waffen-SS Totenkopf-Verband, C.C.Zipf (Aust.) 43-45	MISC.CRIMES	U.S.
STOICKOV, Sergije	190850	M	Bulg.		Mayor, occupied Territories, Osmakovo (Yugo.) 42-43	MURDER	YUGO.
STOJANOV, Aleksander	190851	M	Bulg.		Lt., Bulg.Army, Vladicin Han (Yugo.) 22.2.43-23.9.43	MURDER	YUGO.
STOJANOV, Vasil	190852	M	Bulg.		Agent, Police, Vladicin Han (Yugo.) 43-44	MURDER	YUGO.
STOLP	300676	M	Ital.		Agent,Prison of Krk (Yugo.) 41-43	TORTURE	U.K.
STOMKA, Hubert	252759	M	Pol.	2. 2.12	Warder, C.C.Auschwitz (Aust.)	MISC.CRIMES	FR.
STORICH	191120	M	Ital.		Dr.,Civ.Commissioner, Head of Municipality, Sibenik (Yugo.) 41	MURDER	YUGO.
STORZER, Josef	260474	M	Czech.	7. 2.12	SS-Mann, Waffen-SS,Guard-Coy.,C.C.Golleschau,Auschwitz (Pol.) 43-45	BRUTALITY	POL.
STOUYANOF, Georgief Atanas	305305	M	Bulg.		Policeman,Bulgarian,Xylagani-Rodopi, 9.4.44	MURDER	GRC.
STOUYANOF, Yankof Atanas	305306	M	Bulg.		Policeman,Bulgarian,Xylagani-Rodopi, 9.4.44	MURDER	GRC.
STRACCA	307328	M	Ital.		Deputy to Governor of Dalmatia,Zara (Yugo.) 2.42	Interr.	Yugo.
STRACHER	141326	M	Czech.	05	Cpl.,Kgf.Arb.Bn.,48 Working-Bn., C.C.Posen (Pol.) 7.41	TORTURE	U.K.
STRAHLNOF	305307	M	Bulg.		Capt., Bulg.Army, Drama Area (Grc.) 28.9.-20.10.41	MURDER	GRC.
STRAMMER	260188	M	Czech.		Lt.,19 Gren.Regt., Massif du Vercors, Isere et Drôme (Fr.)20.7.-5.8.44	SUSPECT	FR.
STRANSKI, Nikola	190853	M	Bulg.		Commander, Bulg.Army, 2 Coy.,50 Regt. (Yugo.) 43-44	MURDER	YUGO.
STRIEF, Anton	132465	M	Aust.	02	Innkeeper and Farmer,Civ.,Weilbach (Aust.) 15.4.45	MURDER	U.S.
STROPPOLATINI	162068	M	Ital.		Lt.,Ital.Army,C.C.Benevento (It.) 7.11.42	MISC.CRIMES	U.K.
STRUNG, Stefan	193877	M	Hung.	19. 8.99	Guard,4 SS-Totenkopf-Stuba,C.C.Dachau, Dora-Mittelbau, Nordhausen (Ger.)	INTERR.	U.S.
STUCKLIK	158698	M	Czech.		Interpreter,Gestapo, Saone and Loire (Fr.) 43-44	MURDER	FR.
STUMPILICH, Jakob	259439	M	Rum.		Farmer,Joiner,SS-Mann,Waffen-SS Totenkopf-Bn., C.C.Buchenwald (Ger.)	MISC.CRIMES	U.S.
STUNSKI	252767	M	Aust.		Judge,Military Court,Finistere (Fr.)	INTERR.	FR.
SUCAROTY (or SWCAROTY)	142238	M	Hung.		Capt.,Hung.Army,Budapest (Hung.) 9.44	MURDER	U.S.
SULAS, Giovanni	146303	M	Ital.		Policeman,Ital.Army, Korenja (Yugo.) 43	MURDER	YUGO.
SULIKA	255721	M	Ukr.		Agent,Gestapo,Pribram (Czech.) 39-45	MISC.CRIMES	CZECH.
SUPPIEJ, Giorgio	307341	M	Ital.		General-Consul,President,Judge of Special Tribunal for defence of state, Rom (It.) 4.41-9.43	MURDER	YUGO.
SURCI, Tancredi	255957	M	Ital.		Judge,Lt.Col., Military Courts,Split,Zadar, Kotor (Yugo.) 41-43	INTERR.	YUGO.
SVERKO, Aleksander	191121	M	Ital.		Interpreter,Ital.occ.terr."Squadra Politica",Split(Yugo)2.-9.43	TORTURE	YUGO.
SWCAROTY (see SUCAROTY)	142238						
SWIDA	186189	M	Pol.		Guard, C.C.Dachau (Ger.)	TORTURE	FR.
SYKA, Willibald	251260	M	Ger.-Aust.	00	Capt., Cuneo (It.) 12.12.43	INTERR.	U.K.
SYLVESTRI	305313	M	Ital.		Capt.,C.C.Larissa (Grc.) 41-43	MURDER	GRC.
SYMANSKI	167245	M	Pol.		Interpreter,Schnelle Abt. 602, Forte St. Aubin (Fr.)	MURDER	FR.
SZAPU, Matej	250463	M	Hung.	19. 2.05	Civ.,Member,"Nyilasparty" Hung.SS,firing squad in Komarno (Czech.)44	MURDER	CZECH.
SZEIDL, Johann	251749	M	Hung.		Guard,SS-Mann, C.C.Buchenwald (Ger.) 42-45	BRUTALITY	U.S.
SZENTGYOGYI	149775	M	Hung.		General,Sombor (Yugo.) 41	MURDER	YUGO.
SZIKORA, Caspar	175934	M	Hung.		SS-Guard,C.C.Buchenwald,Auschwitz (Ger.-Pol.) 4.45	MURDER	U.S.
SZILAGYI	185874	M	Hung.		SS-Uscharfhr., SS 13 Police-Regt.,1 Bn.,Bleiburg (Aust.) 14.10.44	MURDER	U.S.
SZOBEL, Aurel	158696	M	Hung.	19	Civ., Political,Prisoner, C.C.Illfeld-Gardelegen (Ger.) 5.-14.4.45	WITNESS	U.S.
SZOMBACHELJI, Ferrai (or SZOMBATHELJI)	136571	M	Hung.		Lt.Gen.,Chief of staff,Hung.Army, 41-44	MISC.CRIMES	U.S.
SZOMMER, Carlo	307329	M	Ital.		Director of C.C.Molat (Meleda) 42-43	MURDER	YUGO.
SZYDLOWSKI	140915	M	Pol.		Doctor,SS, C.C.Ravensbrueck,Auschwitz (Ger.-Pol.)	TORTURE	U.K.
TABANELLI	191122	M	Ital.		Fascist,Officer of C.C. N.N. at "Ferrara"-Div.,Kapino, Polje, Nikso-Montenegro (Yugo.) end of 6.43	MURDER	YUGO.
TACCHINI, Pietro	191123	M	Ital.		Officer,Commander of Military Naval Sector,Sibenik (Yugo.) 41-43	MURDER	YUGO.
TADDEO, Sergio	191124	M	Ital.		Lt.,55 Regt. "Marche"-Div.,Trebinje (Yugo.) 20.4.41, 8.9.43	MURDER	YUGO.
TAGLIAMOTTI	300677	M	Ital.		Superintendent,Store House at the C.C. at Ponza,Island of Ponza (It.) 42-43	TORTURE	U.K.
TAGLIO, Pietro	259465	M	Ital.		Lt.,Ital.Army, "Marche"-Div.,56 Regt, Stolac (Yugo.) 4.41-9.42	MURDER	YUGO.
TAMIANTI	121231	M	Ital.		Capt.,Army,30 Div.,1 Coy.,Tobruk (North Afr.) 10.7.42	MURDER	U.K.
TARINI, Carlo	191125	M	Ital.		Commander, Carabinieri at Sibenik a.District (Yugo.) 41-43	MURDER	YUGO.
TASKOV, Petar Joucev	190854	M	Bulg.		Agent,Police Bulgarian, Vladicin Han (Yugo.) 43-44	MURDER	YUGO.
TAUSCH, Felix	259468	M	Aust.	10.11.95	Dr.,Director,Plant Radom and Krakau (Pol.) 39-42	INTERR.	POL.
TAUSS, Gottfried	193756	M	Hung.	17. 5.96	Guard,SS-Mann,4 SS-Totenkopf-Stuba, C.C.Mittelbau Dora,Nordhausen, Dachau (Ger.) 43-45	MURDER	U.S.

TCH - TYT

NAME	C.R.FILE NUMBER	SEX	NATIO-NALITY	DATE OF BIRTH	RANK OCCUPATION UNIT PLACE AND DATE OF CRIME	REASON WANTED	WANTED BY
TCHEKOV, Stavros	305316	M	Bulg.		Employee, Sofia Propaganda office in charge of Bulg. Propaganda in district of Odessa, Florina, Kosani, Macedonia (Bulg.) 41-44	MISC.CRIMES	GRC.
TEICHMANN, Ernst	134717	M	Aust.	27.11.05	Doctor, Kriminalrat, Kripo (Ger.) 43-45	WITNESS	U.S.
TEOFEF, Stergios	305318	M	Bulg.		Security service, Chryssopolis (Grc.) 17.4.43	MURDER	GRC.
TERRANOVA, Ignazio	191126	M	Ital.		Ital.Army, Carabiniere, Lt., Sibenik (Yugo.) 41-43	MURDER	YUGO.
TERZI, Flamminio	191127	M	Ital.		Lt. Col., Commandant of 114.Bn.,Mitraglieri,Djurasevic, Lustica, Dalmatia (Yugo.) 9.9.43	MURDER	YUGO.
TESTA, Massimo	145097	M	Ital.		Capt.,Ital.Army, 24.Inf.Rgt. "Como" (Yugo.) 43	MURDER	YUGO.
THALKMANN, Yvan	165975	M	Russ.	3.7.20	Chenebier-Etobon (Fr.) 27.9.44	MURDER	FR.
THALER, Herbert	133251	M	Aust.	10	Doctor, Airforce, Outercamp S-III, Thueringen (Ger.)	TORTURE	U.S.
THEODOROFF	305320	M	Bulg.		Agriculturist, Sidirocastron E. Macedonia (Grc.) 41	MURDER	GRC.
THEODOSIOS, Gerassimos	305321	M	Bulg.		Served in the Polygyros town, Taciarchis (Grc.) 7. and 8.44	MURDER	GRC.
TIEFENTHALER, Friedrich	189906	M	Hung.	98	Guard, SS, C.C. Nordhausen - Dora, Dachau (Ger.)	MURDER	U.S.
TINTIN see DEGE	141518						
TINTZEN, Peter	305325	M	Bulg.		Cpl., Gendarmerie, Village of Orphanos, Kavalla (Grc.) 41-44	MURDER	GRC.
TISANI or PESCARA or ARESTA or PESCADA	194290	M	Ital.		Capt., Carabinieri, Ovra (Police Politique Italienne) Nice (Fr.) 1.-6.43 or 44	TORTURE	FR.
TOBOLEZYK	136318	M	Russ.		Guard, C.C. La Ciotat (Fr.)	MURDER	FR.
TODOROV, Nikola	190855	M	Bulg.		Lt., Bulg. Army, 7.Kav.Schwadron (Yugo.) 42-43	MURDER	YUGO.
TOMASELLI	191128	M	Ital.		Doctor, head, police, Susak (Yugo.) 4. and 6.43	MURDER	YUGO.
TOMASO, David	191129	M	Ital.		Capt., Fascist Militia, Benkovac (Yugo.) 7.42 and 1.43	MURDER	YUGO.
TOMASSO	307330	M	Ital.		Gend., on service at Molat (Meleda) C.C. Camp Molat, 42-43	MURDER	YUGO.
TOMED, Imrich Imre	261967	M	Hung.	24.1.09	Member, Nyilas party, Kosice (Czech.) 1.45	MURDER	CZECH.
TOMOV, Ljuben	190856	M	Bulg.		Agent, Bulg.Police, Vladicin Han (Yugo.) 43-44	MURDER	YUGO.
TONETI or CAPELINI	191130	M	Ital.		Capt., Ital.Army, 51.Rgt. "Murge" Div., Trebinje area, Villages of Iboski, Ljubins, Sume, Ljubomir (Yugo.) 42-43	MURDER	YUGO.
TONILIO	152949	M	Ital.		Civilian, Bassano (It.) 4.11.44	MURDER	U.K.
TONTOROF, Simeon	305927	M	Bulg.		Secret Agent, secret police of Drama area (Grc.) 28.9.-20.10.41	MURDER	GRC.
TORIELIE, Emilio	191131	M	Ital.		Camp-doctor, C.C. Fraschette-Alatri (It.) 41-43	TORTURE	YUGO.
TORMENE, Alessandro	307284	M	Ital.		Member, Italian Fascist Federation at Verona, Grezzana (It.) 12.11.43	MURDER	U.K.
TOROCK	167098	M	Aust.		Chief, SS, Clermont Ferrand (Fr.) 22.-29.11.44	MURDER	FR.
TORRACA, Rocco	196238	M	Ital.		Col.,Mil.Courts, Ljubljana (Yugo.) 41-43	MISC.CRIMES	YUGO.
TORREGROSSA, Pasquale	300653	M	Ital.		Lt.Col., Commander of the 110.Legion of the Natinal Republican guard and officer in charge Mil.H.Q. Ascoli Piceno (It.) 2.44	MURDER	U.K.
TORSIELLA, Mario	191132	M	Ital.		Major, Ital. Army, chief of staff of Garrison at Niksic (Yugo.) 27.6.42	MURDER	YUGO.
TOSARELLI, Mario or TOSCARELLI	258182	M	Ital.		Capt., Fasc.Mil., Bn.,Squadristi Emiliano, District of Kastav (Yugo.) 41-43	MURDER	YUGO.
TOSCANO, Gaetano	145095	M	Ital.		Col., Ital. Army, Gottigne-Montenegro (Yugo.) 43	MURDER	YUGO.
TOSCARELLI see TOSARELLI)	258182						
TOSEV, Fodor	190857	M	Bulg.		Police-man, Jelaslica sur Dulica (Yugo.) 22.3.43	MURDER	YUGO.
TOSKANINO, Antonio	189874	M	Ital.		Col.,Ital.Army, Montenegro (Yugo.)	MISC.CRIMES	YUGO.
TOSONI, Lixvio	162079	M	Ital.		Lt., Ital.Army, Inf. Fermo (It.) 11.41-8.43	TORTURE	U.K.
TOSTI, Massimo	194078	M	Ital.		Capt., Ital. Army, Carabiniere, Chambery (Fr.) 8.43	TORTURE	FR.
TOTANI, Olvio	259492	M	Ital.		Pvt., 2.Coy.,29. Bn. Royank, Calac-Uccia (Fr.) 30.5.43	MISC.CRIMES	FR.
TOTEV, Georgi Ganoer	190858	M	Bulg.		N.C.O.,Bulg.Army, 27.Inf.Div. (Yugo.) 43-44	MURDER	YUGO.
TOTOMANOV	190859	M	Bulg.		Lt., Bulg. Army, Dirot (Yugo.) 43-44	MURDER	YUGO.
TRAGEISER, Michael	260448	M	Yugo.	14.3.09	SS Mann, Waffen SS, C.C. Auschwitz (Pol.) 11.43-5.45	BRUTALITY	POL.
TRENTI	250448	M	Ital.		Cpl., 29.Bn. Carabiniere, Sartene (Fr.) 2.-5.43	TORTURE	FR.
TRINGALI-CASANUAVA, Antonio	195627	M	Ital.		Official, Justizministerium, Rom (It.) 41-43	TORTURE	YUGO.
TRUPIANI, Francesco	191133	M	Ital.		Civilian, Civil Commissary at Berane, Cetinje, Savnik, Pidgerica (Yugo.) 7.-11.41	MURDER	YUGO.
TRUBSCHNICK	138346	M	Aust.		Adjutant, SS, Gestapo, Lyon-Rhone (Fr.)	MURDER	FR.
TSAKIROF, Baikosta	305329	M	Bulg.		Secret Agent, Bulg.security, Drama area (Grc.) 28.9.-20.10.41	MURDER	GRC.
TSAKIROF, Constantinos	305330	M	Bulg.		Market inspector, Drama area (Grc.) 28.9.-20.10.41	MURDER	GRC.
TSAKLAROV, Stephen	305331	M	Bulg.		Mayor, Orphanos near Kavalla (Grc.) 41.-44	MURDER	GRC.
TSANGOFF, Nicholas see STANCOFF	305332						
TSEKOF, Licupen	305333	M	Bulg.		Member, Drama, secret police during 41, Drama area (Grc.) 28.9.-20.10.41	MURDER	GRC.
TSERNOSEMSKI, Boris	305334	M	Bulg.		President, Community of Sidirohorion, Kavalla (Grc.) 42	MURDER	GRC.
TUCCI, Carlo	193558	M	Ital.		Lt.General, G.O.C.,"Messina" Div.,Montenegro (Yugo.) 7.41	MURDER	YUGO.
TUFFANELLI-DISAVINA, Arturo	257466	M	Ital.	12.1.99	Squad.,Capt.,Fascist Republican Militia, Fiume (Yugb.) 2.4.45	MURDER	YUGO.
TULIO, Gino	258181	M	Ital.		Sgt.,Fasc.Republican Army, Tagliamento VIII Alpine Rgt., 2.Bn., Dorenberg, Villages (Yugo.) 43-4.45	INTERR.	YUGO.
TUMA	191329	M	Aust.	95	Guard.,Kriegsgefangenen-Arb.Bn.220, 1.Coy.,Bjornelva (Nor.)	MURDER	NOR.
TURCHET	258180	M	Ital.	circa 15	Sgt.,Major, Ital.Army,Lupoglava-Istria (Yugo.) 43-44	INTERR.	YUGO.
TURCHI, Ottorino	193536	M	Ital.	3.28	Cpl., chief, Ital.Army,7.Coy.,3.Bn.,Cais, Frejus (Fr.) 8.43	MURDER	FR.
TURCO, Francesco	141845	M	Ital.		Col.,Camp commandant PG 62, Bergamo (It.) 7.43	MURDER	U.K.
TURESIN	104910	M	Bel.	00	Lt.Col.,SD official, Abwehr, Bad Ems (Ger.)	MURDER	UNWCC
TYTECA, Maurice	195416	M	Bel.	15.8.93	Agent, SD, Loehne (Ger.) 9.44	MURDER	NRTH.

TZE-VER

NAME	C.R.FILE NUMBER	SEX	NATIO-NALITY	DATE OF BIRTH	RANK OCCUPATION UNIT PLACE AND DATE OF CRIME	REASON WANTED	WANTED BY
TZEFSKY	183890	M	Czech.		Occupied territories official, Athens (Grc.)	MURDER	GRC.
TZETZEF, Petrof	305335	M	Bulg.		Pvt., Bulgarian, Xylagani-Rodopi (Grc.) 9.4.44	MURDER	GRC.
TZUPANI, Stephane	305336	M	Ital.		Capt., C.C. Larissa (Grc.) 41-43	MURDER	GRC.
UGOLINI	169473	M	Ital.		Capt., Italian Army, C.C. Laterina (It.)	TORTURE	U.K.
UGOLINI	305337	M	Ital.		Lt., Cmdt. della Lavanderia at Vrhnika, nr.Ljubljana, Slovenia (Yugo.) 41-42	MISC.CRIMES	YUGO.
UGOLINI, Renato	305996	M	Ital.		Cmdt., 42.Regt. "Forli" Div., Davlia (Grc.) 5.5.43	MURDER	GRC.
UHRING, Robert	100028	M	Fr.		Kriminalrat, Sturmbannfhr., Kripo, Amt VI, Strassburg (Fr.) 8.-11.44	MURDER	U.F.SZ.
UNGHERETTI	191135	M	Ital.		Cav. Higher official, Fasust Police, Split-Dalmatia (Yugo.) 41-43	TORTURE	YUGO.
UTASI	195420	M	Aust.		Col., Army, Kormend (Hung.) 8.44	WITNESS	U.K.
VACARO, Carmello	148383	M	Ital.		Carabiniere, Italian Army, Isle of Korenla (Yugo.) 43	MURDER	YUGO.
VACCA	191136	M	Ital.		Lt., Italian Army, Carabinieri, Kistanje (Yugo.) 42	MURDER	YUGO.
VACCARI, Umberto	195628	M	Ital.		Lt., General, Military, 41-43	MURDER	YUGO.
VACHINI, Carlo	259126	M	Ital.	15	see Consolidated List Part II - Appendix 'A'		
VAKOSKY (or VAKOVSKI)	167153	M	Pol.		Chief, SS, Omenau, Limburg (Ger.)	TORTURE	FR.
VALDINANS	121268	M	Swiss		Agent, Gestapo, Banvillars (Fr.) 10.10.44	MURDER	FR.
VALENTE	194286	M	Ital.		Major, Italian Police, Nice (Fr.) 1.-6.43	TORTURE	FR.
VALENTE, Nicola	300655	M	Ital.		Capporale Maggiore in Command of Platoon Public Security, Adria Mesola, Ferrara, Adria, Rovigo (It.) 19.44	MURDER	U.K.
VALENTINI	251712 A	M	Ital.		Capt., 2.Coy., 96.Bn., 59.Regt., Santo Pietro (Fr.) 1°.-31.8.43	TORTURE	FR.
VALI, Antonio	305340	M	Ital.		Major,Commanding Officer, 120.Bn. of Blackshirts quartered at Elassona Pinerolo Div., Elassona Area (Grc.) 42-43	MISC.CRIMES	GRC.
VALLISTER, Josef	134923	M	Aust.	11	Civilian, C.C.Hartheim (Ger.) 40-44	MURDER	U.S.
VALPREDO, Giuseppe	258170	M	Ital.		Soldier, Carabiniere, District of Kastav (Yugo.) 41-43	INTERR	YUGO.
VAN DEN DORPE, Alfred	229076	M	Bel.	20. 9.19	SS-Mann, SD, Sipo, Assen (Neth.) 13.9.44-14.4.45	MURDER	NETH.
VAN DER WAL, Ebeltje nee DE VRIES	306915	F	Dut.	20. 9.91	Almelo (Neth.) 44-45	MURDER	U.K.
VAN DER WAL, Grietja A.	306014	F	Dut.		Almelo (Neth.) 44-45	MURDER	U.K.
VAN HOUTTE, Bobby	196419	M	Fr.		Pvt., SD, Kdo. Wenger, Baccarat, Etival (Fr.) 44	MURDER	U.K.
VAN HOVE, Karl Emil	140034	M	Bel.	18	N.C.O., Volunteer in German Army, Cleder (Fr.) 8.8.44	MURDER	FR.
VANINI, Guiseppe	148384	M	Ital.		Maresciallo, Italian Army, Carabiniere, Isle of Forcula (Yugo.) 43	MURDER	YUGO.
VAN KOL	194101	M	Bel.		Sturmmann, SD, Heerenveen, Crakstats Prison (Neth.) till 15.4.45	MURDER	NETH.
VAN LAERE, Firmin Gustaaf	193655	M	Bel.	15. 3.23	SS-Mann, Aussendienststelle der Sipo, SD., Gent, Leeuwarden (Neth.) 13.9.44-14.4.45	MURDER	NETH.
VAN MARCKE	141076	M	Bel.		Civilian, C.C.Natzweiler (Fr.)	MURDER	U.K.
VAN MEERSCHAUT	194543	M	Bel.	25	SS-Mann, Driver, SD., Heerenveen (Neth.) 15.4.45	TORTURE	NETH.
VAN MOL	194542	M	Bel.		Rottfhr., SD., Heerenveen (Neth.) 2.1.45-15.4.45	MURDER	NETH.
VANNI	251713	M	Ital.		Lt., 2.Coy., 96.Bn., 59.Regt., Santo Pietro Ci-Tenda (Fr.) 19.-31.8.43	PILLAGE	FR.
VAN WEINSBERG (H)EN, Walter or WIJNSBERGHEN	302011	M	Bel.	25 or 23	SS-Mann, Guard, Einsatzkommando of the Sipo, Steenwijk (Neth.) 1.10.44	MURDER	NETH.
VARESTE, Robert	196374	M	Fr.		Pvt., SD, Kdo. Retzek, Pexonne (Fr.) 44	MURDER	U.K.
VARIO, Antonio	194285	M	Ital.	21	Pvt., Italian Army, Toulon (Fr.) 16.7.44	MURDER	FR.
VARKOLY, Denes, Bela Daniel	260006	M	Hung.	30. 3.11	Chief, Political Department, Kosice (Czech.) 5.1.45-17.1.45	MURDER	CZECH.
VASAROV (or VAZAROV)	189957	M	Bulg.		Agent, Police, Pirot (Yugo.)	MISC.CRIMES	YUGO.
VASILJEV, Angel	190861	M	Bulg.		Pvt., Bulgarian Army, 27.Inf.Div., Prokuplje (Yugo.) 43-44	MURDER	YUGO.
VASILJEV, Zlate Simeonov	190862	M	Bulg.		Pvt., Bulgarian Army, 27.Inf.Div. (Yugo.) 43-44	MURDER	YUGO.
VASSALLO, Silverio	189873	M	Ital.		Director, Ital.Public Official, Split (Yugo.) 41-43	MISC.CRIMES	YUGO.
VASSEUR, Jacques	196370	M	Fr.		F.C.F. SD, Kdo.z.b.V., St.Die Saales (Fr.) 44	MURDER	U.K.
VASSILIEF, Grecef Christof	305342	M	Bulg.		Major, Stavroupolis, Xanthi (Grc.) 44	INTERR.	GRC.
VASTLE	184266	M	Aust.		Chief, C.C.Dachau (Ger.)	MURDER	FR.
VECCHIARELLI	148385	M	Ital.		General, Army Korps Italian, Fuzine (Yugo.) 43	MURDER	YUGO.
VEDANI, Mario	307931	M	Ital.		General Consul, Judge of Special Tribunal for defence of State Rom (It.) 4.41-9.43	MURDER	YUGO.
VELDHUIS, Jan Hendrick	306913	M	Dut.		Prison Warder, Almelo (Neth.) 21.-24.3.45	MURDER	U.K.
VELKOV, Kiril Marinov	190863	M	Bulg.		Agent, Bulgarian Police, Vladicin Han (Yugo.) 43-44	MURDER	YUGO.
VELKOV, Ljubomir	190864	M	Bulg.		Civilian, Pirot (Yugo.) 4.42	MISC.CRIMES	YUGO.
VENCHI, Mario	305343	M	Ital.		Major, Commanding Officer, Carabinieri in Corfu (Grc.) 41	MISC.CRIMES	GRC.
VENEZANDI, Luigi	259118	M	Ital.		Col., Carabiniere, IX.Bn., Split (Yugo.) 41-43	MISC.CRIMES	YUGO.
VENIERI, Aldo	300614	M	Ital.		Col., Commanding officer of the Italian Occupation Army at Kastoria, Nestorion, Argos, Orestikon (Grc.) 42-43	MURDER	GRC.
VENTI, Carlo	257617	M	Ital.		Lt., Italian Army, P.W.Camp 115, Marisciano (It.) 3.-9.43	BRUTALITY	U.K.
VENTORINI	300657	M	Ital.		Capt., 69. Tagliamento Bn., Prov. Varallo Vercelli (It.) 15.4.44	MURDER	U.K.
VENTORUZZO	258178	M	Ital.		Vice Brig. Army, Plave Anhovo (Yugo.) 2.45	INTERR.	YUGO.
VENTURELLA	141844	M	Ital.		Lt., Medical Staff, Benghazi (Africa) 42	MISC.CRIMES	U.K.
VERBESSELT, Julius	199647	M	Bel.		SS-Mann, SD., Aussendienststelle der Sipo,. Leeuwarden (Neth.) 13.9.44-14.4.45	MURDER	NETH.
VERCELLINO, Mario	153004	M	Ital.		General, IV.Italian Army, Nive, Antibes, Cannes, Grasse (Fr.) 43	MISC.CRIMES	FR.
VERDECCHIA, Olindo	148382	M	Ital.		Fasciste, Fermo (It.) 3.5.44	MURDER	U.K.
VERDI, Hugo	191137	M	Ital.		Col., Italian Army, 51.Regt. of "Murge" Div., Sibenik (Yugo.) 41-43	MURDER	YUGO.

VER - WAL

NAME	C.R.FILE NUMBER	SEX	NATIO- NALITY	DATE OF BIRTH	RANK OCCUPATION UNIT PLACE AND DATE OF CRIME	REASON WANTED	WANTED BY
VERES, Vitez Lajos	189921	M	Hung.		General, Hung.Army, Novi Sad (Yugo.)	MURDER	YUGO.
VERGNA	148386	M	Ital.		Lt., Italian Army, Babno Polje (Yugo.) 42	TORTURE	YUGO.
VERNONI, Luigi	256145	M	Ital.		Judge, Member of the Tribunal, Kotor (Yugo.) 41-43	INTERR.	YUGO.
VERRARI	148387	M	Ital.		Tenente, Italian Army, Cerknica (Yugo.) 43	TORTURE	YUGO.
VERWEE	194122	M	Bel.		Rottfhr., SD, Heerenveen Steenwijk (Neth.) -15.4.45	MURDER	NETH.
VESCOVI	255769	M	Ital.		Capt., Army, Kistanje-Dalmatia (Yugo.) 9.42	MURDER	YUGO.
VESELOVSKY	255797	M	Ukr.		Agent, Gestapo, Pribram (Czech.) 39-45	MISC.CRIMES	CZECH.
VIALE, Carlo	191198	M	Ital.		General, Ital.Army, Com.of "Zara"-Div., Sibenik (Yugo.) 41-43	MURDER	YUGO.
VIARENGO, Giorgio	258177	M	Ital.		Major, Italian Army, Garrison Commander, Tetowo, Marovo, Leunovo, Nikiforovo (Yugo.) 9.43	PILLAGE	YUGO.
VICENTINI, Olivio	305346	M	Ital.		Sgt., Carabinieri Reali Security Department, Corfu (Grc.) 9.43	MISC.CRIMES	GRC.
VICTOR	254714	M	Pol.		Kapo, Conc.Camp, Auschwitz (Pol.)	TORTURE	FR.
VIDEBACH, Hans	254190	M	Arab.		Schfhr., Gestapo, Limoges (Fr.) 40-45	INTERR.	FR.
VIDOVICH	191139	M	Ital.		Capt., Intelligence Dept. for Vodice Sector, Vodice (Yugo.) 41	MURDER	YUGO.
VIERLINGER, Albrecht	192703	M	Aust.	29. 9.06	Sgt., Reichsjustiz-Ministerium, Feldstraflager "Nord", Finmark (Nor.) 6.42 - 45	MISC.CRIMES	NOR., YUGO.
VIGAN, Johann	152995	M	Aust.	19	Kapo, Conc.Camp. Flossenburg (Ger.)	TORTURE	U.S.
VIGNERI, Achille	191161	M	Ital.		Col., Judge of Italian "Special Court", Sibenik (Yugo.) 41-43	MURDER	YUGO.
VILIAGNO, Antonio	152999	M	Ital.		Lt., Italian Army, Tradate, Varese (It.)	TORTURE	U.K.
VILIERO	148388	M	Ital.		Lt.Col., Chief. Staff, "Lombardia"-Div. (Yugo.) 43	MURDER	YUGO.
VILLACI, Edoardo	256144	M	Ital.		Member of the Tribunal, Kotor (Yugo.) 41-43	INTERR.	YUGO.
VILLASANTA, Carlo	191140	M	Ital.		Chief-Secretary, Government of Dalmatia, Zadar, Dalmatia (Yugo.) 41-43	MURDER	YUGO.
VILLELIA, G.	191017	M	Ital.		Cmdt., Italian Army, 169.Bn. C.C.N.N., Gruda (Yugo.)	MURDER	YUGO.
VINCENZO	189872	M	Ital.		Dr., Commisser, Ital.Public-Official, Spalato (It.)	MISC.CRIMES	YUGO.
VINZENZ (or GRASEGGER, Vinzens)	188291	M	Aust.		Civilian, Sankt-Lorenzen (Aust.) 2.4.44	WITNESS	U.S.
VIOLA	254713	F	Hung.		Guard, C.C. Auschwitz (Pol.)	TORTURE	FR.
VIRGHILIO	191018	M	Ital.		Sgt., Italian Army, Cetinae, Crnagora (Yugo.) 41-43	MURDER	YUGO.
VISCARDI, Giuseppe	191014	M	Ital.		Vice-Brigadiere, Italian Army, Sibenik (Yugo.) 41-43	MURDER	YUGO.
VISCUSI, Paolo	251401	M	Ital.		Italian Airforce A.V.A.A.rma 119 A, Sosici (Yugo.) 12.7.43	INTERR.	YUGO.
VITALE, Arturo	191015	M	Ital.		Lt., Cmdt., Italian Army, Solin (Yugo.) 24.1.42	MURDER	YUGO.
VITTORELLI	159018	M	Ital.		Civilian, Bassano (It.) 4.11.44	MURDER	U.K.
VLACHOV, George	305348	M	Bulg.		Officer, Military Police of Drama, Emmanuel Papa nr.Serres (Grc.) 11.41	MURDER	GRC.
VLADEK	174839	M	Pol.	2?	Arbeits-Kndo., Wansleben am See (Ger.) 43-45	MURDER	FR.
VODENICAROV, Panca	190865	M	Bulg.		Major, Admin.of Occupied Territories, Vladicinhan (Yugo.) 43-44	MURDER	YUGO.
VOGG, Hugo	257198	M	Aust.		Hptschfhr., Waffen-SS, 1.Bn., 3.Coy., Regt. "Der Fuehrer", Foret de Nieppe (Fr.) 5.40	SUSPECT	U.K.
VOJTOVICH, Richard	254760	M	Hung.	12. 1.80 or 19.10.14	Hungarian-SS, Komarno (Czech.) 44	MURDER	CZECH.
VOJTOVICHOVA-BOROS, Romalia	258299	F	Hung.		Civilian, Hungarian-SS, Komarno (Czech.) 44	MURDER	CZECH.
VOLLMANN, Alois	152978	M	Aust.	97 - 98	Sgt., Army, Kriegsgef.Bezirks-Kommandentur, Verst.Kgf.Arb.Bn.188, II.Coy., Aasane Hjortland-Bergen (Nor.) 42-43	MURDER	NOR.
VOLPI, Adomo	148389	M	Ital.		Capt., Italian Army, Znostrog (Yugo.) 43	TORTURE	YUGO.
VOLTURNO, Patrizie	191016	M	Ital.		Italian Army, Conc.Camp Fraschette Alatri (It.) 41-45	TORTURE	YUGO.
VON BATIZFALVY, Fernau	128010	M	Hung.		Head, Police-Officer, Koeroesmezde (Hung.) 41	MURDER	POL.
VON CAPRI (or KAPRI)	173274	M	Rum. or Ger.	20	Member, Gestapo, Noailles (Fr.) 9.8.44	MURDER	U.K.
VON GILBERT, Gianella	191874	M	Aust.		Lt., Army, St.Hilaire, St.Mesmin (Fr.) 19.-25.8.44	MURDER	FR.
VON KRAUSS	252097	M	Rum.		Pvt., SS, C.C. Buchenwald (Ger.)	INTERR.	FR.
VON ROSLBERG	67016	M	Czech.		Osturmfhr., SS, 17.Pz.Gren.Div."Goetz von Berlichingen", Sturm- Gesch.Abt.17, Segre-Renaze (Fr.) 30.7.44-6.8.44	MURDER	FR.
VON SCHOLZ, Harald	196194	M	Aust.	23	Osturmfhr., SS, Gueret (Fr.)	MURDER	FR.
VON TENIISAKOF, Boris	305317	M	Bulg.		Security-Officer, Bulgarian-Serres (Grc.) 4.41-9.41	INTERR.	GRC.
VORMITTAG, Paul	159092	M	Rum.	10	Rottfhr., Waffen-SS, Leibstandarte "Adolf Hitler", 1.SS-Div.Field-Res. Bn.1, Rosbach (Ger.) 4.3.45	WITNESS	U.S.
VOTHEY, Vonef (see BOTHEY)	305351						
VOULTSIEF	305952	M	Bulg.		Member, Secret Police in Drama 1941, Drama Area (Grc.) 28.9.-20.10.41	MURDER	GRC.
VRBANOV, Nikola	190868	M	Bulg.		Chief, Police, Vladisin Han (Yugo.) 43-44	MURDER	YUGO.
VUKOVARY	189920	M	Hung.		Dr., Civilian-Servant, Occ.Territories, Zabailj (Yugo.)	MURDER	YUGO.
WACHLEWSKI	252892	M	Pol.		Physician, C.C. Auschwitz (Pol.)	BRUTALITY	FR.
WACHSMANN, Ernst	261888	M	Hung.	21.10.13	Member, SD, Prague (Czech.) 4.43-45	SUSPECT	CZECH.
WAECHTER	188269	M	Aust.	95	Lt., 7. Pars-Div., H.Q., Gristede (Ger.)	WITNESS	CAN.
WAGNER, Alfred	136268	M	Aust.		Gestapo-Chief, Oflag XVII A, C.C. Edelbach (Aust.)	MURDER	FR.
WAGNER, Joseph	251424	M	Hung.		Gestapo, Limoges (Fr.) 40-45	BRUTALITY	FR.
WALCHER, Ferdinand	179782	M	Aust.		Civilian, Ramsau (Aust.)	MURDER	U.S.
WALDNER (or WALDER)	250564	M	Aust. or Ger.	01	N.C.O., Interpreter, Anti-Partisan Duties, Mesda and Ariano Polesine (It.) 12.44	INTERR.	U.K.
WALDNER, Mathias	150617	M	Aust.		Civ.Admin., Labour-Camp, C.C. Krispl (Aust.) 44	TORTURE	U.S.
WALKNER, Rupert	194849	M	Aust.		Civilian, C.C. Krispl (Aust.)	WITNESS	NETH.

NAME	C.R.FILE NUMBER	SEX	NATIO-NALITY	DATE OF BIRTH	RANK OCCUPATION UNIT PLACE AND DATE OF CRIME	REASON WANTED	WANTED BY
WALLER, Ludwig	193523	M	Hung.	29. 1.98	Schuetze, 4 SS-Totenkopf-Stuba, C.C.Dora Mittelbau, Nordhausen (Ger.) 43-45	MURDER	U.S.
WALLNER, Matthias	152739	M	Aust.	22. 2.86	Civilian, R.R.worker, Railroad, Maishofen (Aust.) 25.2.44	WITNESS	U.S.
WALTER	150820	M	Hung.		Guard, SS-Mann, C.C.Valory (Czech.) 41-45	MURDER	U.S.
WALZER	192430	M	Rum. or Hung.		Guard, C.C.Breendonck (Bel.) 4.-5.44	TORTURE	BEL.
WARTHA, Georg	240037	M	Aust.	12. 7.07	Sturmscharfhr., Antipartisan office, SD, Turin (It.) 45	TORTURE	U.S.
WASICKI	194695	M	Aust.		SS-Hauptsturmfhr., C.C.Mauthausen (Aust.)	MURDER	FR.
WATTELSKI	300398	M	Pol.		Wachtmeister, Arbeits-Erziehungs-Lager, Lahde near Hannover (Ger.) 11.2.-24.3.45	MISC.CRIMES	NETH.
WATZLAWEK, Franz	135569	M	Pol.		Miner, Civilian labour, C.C.Jaqorzna (Pol.) 25.2.43	MURDER	U.K.
WAUTERS, Marcel	193518	M	Bel.		SS-Mann, SD, Sipo, Leeuwarden (Neth.) 13.9.44-14.4.45	MURDER	NETH.
WEBER, Heinrich	193527	M	Hung.	17. 2.97	SS-Schuetze, 4 SS-Totenkopf-Stuba, C.C.Dora Mittelbau, Nordhausen (Ger.) 43-45	MURDER	U.S.
WEBER, Johann	193526	M	Hung.	21. 2.95	SS-Schuetze, 4 SS-Totenkopf-Stuba, C.C.Dora Mittelbau, Nordhausen (Ger.) 43-45	MURDER	U.S.
WEBER, Joseph	162709	M	Aust. or Ger.		Obersturmfhr., SS, C.C.Melk (Ger.)	TORTURE	U.S.
WEBER, Joseph	260440	M	Rum.	20.11.06	SS-Pvt., SS-guard, C.C.Auschwitz (Pol.) 44-45	BRUTALITY	POL.
WEGER	192422	M	Aust.		Lt., Wach-Coy., Cheminieres (Fr.) 8.44	MURDER	FR.
WEILBACHER, Johann	179792	M	Aust.		Civilian, Lofer (Aust.)	WITNESS	U.S.
WEICHAND, Mathias	252787	M	Hung.		SS-Sturmmann, C.C.Buchenwald (Ger.)	MISC.CRIMES	U.S.
WEIERMANN, Karl	252627	M	Aust.	00	Pvt., 5 Coy., Lds.Sch. Tanzelsdorf (Aust.) 7.3.42	INTERR.	U.K.
WEIMANN	146741	M	Aust.		Pol.Inspector, Police, Grafendorf (Aust.) 3.45	TORTURE	U.S.
WEIMANN, Anton	260491	M	Yugo.	28.10.09	SS-Pvt., Waffen-SS, guard-Coy., C.C.Auschwitz (Pol.) 43-1.45	BRUTALITY	POL.
WEITENTHALER, Johann	139249	M	Aust.		Revier-Inspector, Member, Gendarmerie, NSDAP, Mitterndorf (Aust.)	TORTURE	U.S.
WENZEL, Erich	260476	M	Czech.	3. 6.28	SS-Pvt., Waffen-SS, guard-Coy., C.C.Auschwitz (Pol.) 3.43-8.44	BRUTALITY	POL.
WENZL, Friedrich	153455	M	Aust.	29.12.11	Sgt., Waffen-SS, Totenkopf-Stand., C.C.Mauthausen (Aust.) 9.44-5.45	MURDER	U.S.
WERTH, Daniel	187504	M	Hung.	4. 9.96	SS-Mann, 4 SS-Totenkopf-Stuba, C.C.Dora Mittelbau, Nordhausen (Ger.) 43-45	TORTURE	U.S.
WESTCOTT	130064	M	Aust. or Ger.		Civilian, Enginner, C.C.Arb.Kdo. A 91 G.W., Judenburg (Aust.) 2.45-1.4.45	TORTURE	U.K.
WEU	194083	M	Czech.		Civilian, St.Rambert (Fr.)	MURDER	FR.
WIEDAUER, Anna	260715	F	Aust. or Ger.		C.C.Hallein (Aust.)	MURDER	U.S.
WIENERZ, Jean	256162	M	Aust.		Imprison of the Bloc 10, C.C.Mauthausen (Aust.)	INTERR.	FR.
WIESER, Hedwig	187855	F	Aust.		Civilian, St.Lorenzen (Aust.) 2.4.44	WITNESS	U.S.
WIESER, Heinrich (or PETERBAUER)	179781	M	Aust.		Ramsau (Aust.)	MURDER	U.S.
WIESINGER, Josef	260932	M	Aust. or Ger.	27.10.05	SS-Unterscharfhr., Allg.SS, Waffen-SS, C.C.Auschwitz (Pol.) 41	MISC.CRIMES	POL.
WIJNBERGEN	194847	M	Bel.	25	SS-Mann, SD, Heerenveen (Neth.)	MURDER	NETH.
WIJNSBERGHEN (see WEINSBERGHEN, VAN)	302011	M					
WILLE, Joseph	260445	M	Rum.	9. 2.02	SS-Sturmmann, Waffen-SS, guard-Coy., C.C.Monowitz, Jarwischowitz, Auschwitz (Pol.) 8.43-1.45	BRUTALITY	POL.
WILLY	180582	M	Pol.		Kapo, C.C.Dachau, Bad Gandersheim (Ger.) 42-4.45	MURDER	FR.
WILLY	194084	M	Pol.		Blockmann, C.C.Flossenburg (Ger.)	MURDER	FR.
WILMET, Jose	193517	F	Bel.		Guard, SD, Leeuwarden (Neth.) 13.9.44-14.4.45	MURDER	NETH.
WIMMER, Johann	179793	M	Aust.		Civilian, gravedigger at St.Martin near Lofer (Aust.)	WITNESS	U.S.
WOLLMANN, Fritz	192227	M	Aust.	06	Doctor, Civ., Doctor Gynacologist, Anatomy Inst., Danzig (Pol.)	MISC.CRIMES	POL.
WLADEK	251738	M	Pol.	25	Leader, C.C.Buchenwald (Ger.)	BRUTALITY	FR.
WODAL, Gustav	158406	M	Aust.	98	Cpl., Kriegsgefangenen Bezirks-Kdo., 2 Coy., Assans (Nor.) 42-43	MURDER	NOR.
WOLF, Georg	260444	M	Yugo.	16.10.14	SS-Guard, Waffen-SS, Guard-Coy., C.C.Auschwitz (Pol.) 10.42-1.45	BRUTALITY	POL.
WOLF, Hugo	151473	M	Aust.	07	SS-Unterscharfhr., 12 SS-Pz.Div. "Hitler Jugend", St. Sulpice sur Risle, Eure (Fr.) 10.6.44	MURDER	U.S.
WOLFF	194846	M	Bel.		SS-Mann, Motor Cycle Driver, SD, Heerenveen(Neth.) 2.1.45-15.4.45	TORTURE	NETH.
WOLFF	261898	M	Rum. or Ger.	circa 00	SS-Mann, Waffen-SS, Pijnacker near Delft (Neth.) 7.44	PILLAGE	NETH.
WOLFF, Johann	186739	M	Rum.	03	Guard, Waffen-SS, labour camp, Arb.Kdo., Innsbruck(Aust.) 44-5.45	TORTURE	U.S.
WOLFINEK	1039	M	Aust.		Lt., Army, 118 Jg.Regt., (Yugo.) 7.43-1.44	MURDER	YUGO.
WONSCHINA	195981	M	Russ.	24	Agent, guard, SD, prisoner, Maisano, Lafitte(Fr.) 15.12.41-10.6.44	TORTURE	FR.
WOOS, Stephan	194687	M	Pol.	17	Guard, C.C.Mauthausen (Aust.) 3.-5.44	MURDER	FR.
WORM, Franz	158407	M	Aust.		Cpl., 2-186 Kriegsgefangenen Arb.Bn., Ervik (Nor.) 42-43	MURDER	NOR.
WULKENSTEIN	137576	M	Dän.		Wachtmeister, C.C.Hamburg (Ger.) 12.42	TORTURE	U.K.
WURGLER, Eduard Oskar	167039	M	Swiss.or Ger.	6. 4.02	Rshaupaul (Fr.) 9.9.44	MURDER	FR.
WUTTKE, Willibald	190573	M	Fr.	12	Unterscharfhr., SD, Einsatz-Kdo. 6, La Grande (Fr.) 15.10.44	MURDER	U.K.

YAB - ZWI

NAME	C.R.FILE NUMBER	SEX	NATIO-NALITY	DATE OF BIRTH	RANK OCCUPATION UNIT PLACE AND DATE OF CRIME	REASON WANTED	WANTED BY
YABLONSKY	261765	M	Czech.		Senior W.O., 3.Coy., 393.Bn. Stalag XVII A Cmdo. 1004 G.W. Pitten (Aust.) 2. 5.43	MURDER	FR.
YUSYSTA, Selina	188177	F	Pol.		Civilian, Fedelhausen (Pol.) 20. 2.44	WITNESS	U.K.
ZAENNGUT (or ZEHNGUT)	259237	M	Czech.		Camp-Master, C.C. Auschwitz (Pol.) 40	MURDER	FR.
ZAHAROF, Grigorios	305388	M	Bulg.		Municipal Servant, Drama Nevrokopio, Bulgaria, Drama Area (Grc.) 28. 9. - 20.10.41	MISC.CRIMES	GRC.
ZAMBONI, Giorgio	300658	M	Ital.		Capt., Guardia Nazionale Republicana of the 2.Coy., Order of Public Security Adria, Mesola, Ferrara Rovigo (It.) 12.44	MURDER	U.K.
ZANATTA, Riccardo	191019	M	Ital.		Agent, Security Public, Metlika (Yugo.) 42	MURDER	YUGO.
ZANINI	250586	M	Ital.		Chief Ex.Off., 21.Bn. Saroinia Gren.Div.,Ljubljana (Yugo.) 42	TORTURE	YUGO.
ZANKOVITCH	257455	M	Aust.		Engineer, C.C. Dora, Nordhausen (Ger.)	BRUTALITY	FR.
ZANNI, Enzo	144989	M	Ital.		Lt.,Italian Army "Isonzo"-Div.24, Inf.Rgt."Coma" (Yugo.) 43	MURDER	YUGO.
ZANONI	142021	M	Ital.	08	Lt.,83.Fascist Militia,stationed at Garribaldi Barracks, Piacenza (It.) 11.43 - 1. 44	TORTURE	U.K.
ZANOTTI	191020	M	Ital.		Col., Italian Army, O.C.Rgt. Sassari Div.F 562, Udbina, Gracac (Yugo.) 2., 3.43	MURDER	YUGO.
ZANZI, Giovanni	191162	M	Ital.		Col., Deputy State Prosecutor of Italian Special Court, Sibenik (Yugo.) 41 - 43	MURDER	YUGO.
ZAPPI, Adolf	260470	M	Rum., Ger.	20. 8.11	SS-Rottfhr., Waffen-SS, Guard-Coy., Supply-Service, C.C.Auschwitz (Pol.) 5. 42 - 1. 45	BRUTALITY	POL.
ZARONE, Gerardo	307332	M	Ital.		Capt., Judge, Mil.Tribunal for 2.Army, Section of Lubiana (Yugo.) 41 - 43	MURDER	YUGO.
ZARTL, Ernst	194540	M	Aust.		Official Stabsarzt, Police, C.C.Altenrode, Tilburg (Ger., Neth.) 13. 4.44 - 25. 5.44	TORTURE	NETH.
ZARUTI, Wandax	250580	M	Pol.		Gestapo, Limoges (Fr.)	MISC.CRIMES	FR.
ZATI (see ZATTI)	144988						
ZATTI (alias ZATI)	144988	M	Ital.		Lt.General, Italian Army, Lombardier-Div., Fuzine (Yugo.) 43	MURDER	YUGO.
ZAUER	250593	M	Aust.	13	Capt., Army, 14.Pol.Rgt., Iuk (Czech.) 27.10.43	INTERR.	YUGO.
ZAVATARI, Filippo	300659	M	Ital.		Lt., Camp 52, Chiavari (It.) 12.41 - 10.42	BRUTALITY	U.K.
ZAVATSKY	132657	M	Hung.		SS-Mann, C.C. Woippy - Moselle - (Fr.) 44	TORTURE	FR., BEL.
ZCHEMITZA (alias CHERMIZA)	196028	M	Russ.		Paris (Fr.)	TORTURE	FR.
ZEHNGUT (see ZAENNGUT)	259237						
ZEITELSBERGER	193132	M	Aust.	10	Sgt., Guard, Reichsjustiz-Ministerium, Feldstraflager, Finmark (Nor.) 43	MURDER	NOR.
ZEKOV	190866	M	Bulg.		Major, Sebane (Yugo.) 42 - 43	MURDER	YUGO.
ZELENGOROV	190867	M	Bulg.		Chief, Bulgarian Gestapo, Vladecin Han (Yugo.) 43 - 44	MURDER	YUGO.
ZELESKOV, Alexander	190868	M	Bulg.		Lt., Bulgarian Army, 25.Inf.Rgt., Pirot (Yugo.) 6. 44	MURDER	YUGO.
ZENKTELLER	258919	M	Pol.		Doctor, Hospital, Birkenau (Pol.) 40 - 45	MISC.CRIMES	FR.
ZENTA, Massimiliano	191021	M	Ital.		Dr., Member, Fascist Militia, Sibenik (Yugo.) 41 - 43	MURDER	YUGO.
ZERBINO, Paolo	189871	M	Ital.		Prefect, Italian Public Official, Spalato (It.)	MISC.CRIMES	YUGO.
ZEUTLER	306831	M	Pol.		Dr., C.C. Auschwitz (Pol.) 40 - 45	MURDER	FR.
ZIMMERMANN, Joseph	132538	M	Ital.		Feldgend., Sisteron (Fr.) 6. 6.44	MURDER	FR.
ZIMPROCH, Josef	260923	M	Yugo.	20. 3.13	SS-Sturmmann, Pvt. SS-Guard, C.C. Auschwitz (Pol.) 42.- 43	BRUTALITY	POL.
ZINCTLER	251481	M	Pol.		Chief Doctor, C.C. Auschwitz (Pol.)	MURDER	FR.
ZINGALEZ	194323	M	Ital.		General, Italian Army, Cuneo (It.) 43	MISC.CRIMES	FR.
ZINKOVSKI, Sergej Alexe Jevitsch	195647	M	Russ.		Agent, Gestapo, Sezimovo-Usti (Czech.)	PILLAGE	CZECH.
ZIPF, Josef	152049	M	Hung.		Pvt., SS-Guard, C.C. Volary (Czech.)	MURDER	U.S.
ZLATAROV, Kosta	190869	M	Bulg.		Officer, Bulgarian Army, Prokuplje (Yugo.) 43 - 44	MURDER	YUGO.
ZOBOLI, Remo	250589	M	Ital.		Capt., 113a Squadriglia Lia, 63.Gruppe, 21.Stormo, C.C. Avazione di Ljublaja Hrastov Dol, Trnovica (Yugo.) 31. 7.43	INTERR.	YUGO.
ZOELDI, Marton	124563	M	Hung.		Hptsturmfhr., SS, 26.Hun.Div., Ujvidek (Hung.) 45	MURDER	U.S.
ZOLDI, Martin	189919	M	Hung.		Capt., Gend., Backa (Yugo.)	MURDER	YUGO.
ZOLLA-CANNONERO, Pietro	307333	M	Ital.		Capt., Judge, Mil.Tribunal for 2.Army, Section of Lubiana (Yugo.) 41 -43	MURDER	YUGO.
ZOMBORI, Gyula	189918	M	Hung.		Commandant, Hungarian Police, Novi Sad (Yugo.)	MURDER	YUGO.
ZONI, Francesco	144987	M	Ital.		Officer, Italian Army, Ferrara Div., Montenegro (Yugo.) 43	MURDER	YUGO.
ZSIROSS, Hadaprod Jstran	195096	M	Hung.		Interpreter, C.C. Leled (Hung.) 11.44	TORTURE	U.K.
ZUCCARI	300660	M	Ital.		Col., Commander of the 63.Tagliamento-Btty., Varollo Prov.Vercelli (It.) 15. 4.44	MURDER	U.K.
ZUCKAU	125704	M	Pol., Ger.		Forester, Civilian, Stalag XX B, Cmdo.365, C.C. Rosenberg (Pol.) 1. 43 - 2. 44	MISC.CRIMES	U.K.
ZULIANNI, Emilio	256976	M	Ital.		Col., Army Fasc.Republ., Comm. of Tagliamento 8, Alpine-Rgt., Dorenberg and neighbouring villages (Yugo.) 11.43 - 4. 45	INTERR.	YUGO.
ZWICK, Michael	251468	M	Rum.		Cpl., Waffen-SS, SS Death's Head-Bn., Buchenwald (Ger.)	BRUTALITY	U.S.

NATIONALITY SECTION
(See ALPHABETICAL SECTION for the same names listed in alphabetical order.)

ALBANIA - ARABIA - ARGENTINE - AUSTRIA

NAME	C.R.FILE NUMBER	SEX	DATE OF BIRTH	RANK	OCCUPATION	UNIT	PLACE AND DATE OF CRIME	REASON WANTED	WANTED BY
					ALBANIA.				
BAJKUSEV	189973	M		Agent, Police, Pirot (Yugo.)				TORTURE	YUGO.
BOLJOTINAC, Bajsait Isa	189975	M		Maj., Albanian Army, Kosouba-Mitrovica (Yugo.)				MURDER	YUGO.
CAMMER	137617	M	13 - 15	Civilian, Tirana (Alb.) 8.1.44				MISC.CRIMES	U.K.
DEVA or DEVE	189974	M		Civilian				MURDER	YUGO.
DEVE see DEVA	189974								
					ARABIA.				
VIDEBACH, Hans	254190	M		Scharfhr., Gestapo, Limoges (Fr.) 40-45				INTERR.	FR.
					ARGENTINE.				
BERZ, Artur	131164	M		S.A.-Mann				TORTURE	BEL.
					AUSTRIA.				
ABEL, Wolfgang	142403	M		Oscharfhr., SS, Gestapo				TORTURE	U.S.
ABLEIDINGERF, Friedrich	132816	M		Feldgendarm., Feldgendarmerie, Trupp 648, Conde (Fr.)				WITNESS	U.K., U.S.
ADAMER	196267	M		Capt., Camp Laterina (Ger.)				WITNESS	U.S.
ADERMOUSSIAK, Karl	174914	M		Guard, SS, C.C. Schoerzingen (Ger.)				MISC.CRIMES	FR.
AIGNER, Toni	132545	M	20	Uscharfhr., SS, C.C. Hallein (Ger.)				MURDER	FR.
ALLERT	196457	M		W.O., Gestapo, Valence (Fr.) 40-45				INTERR.	FR.
ANDING, Alwin	259806	M	8.10.14	Sgt., staff-pioneer-Bn.331, blacksmith, civilian, Zuid (Neth.) 5.45				BRUTALITY	NETH.
ARTMANN	186571	M		Capt., Army, Athen (Grc.)				TORTURE	GRC.
ASANGER, Peter	156726	M		Ortsgruppen-Propagandaleiter, N.S.D.A.P.				MURDER	U.S.
ATZINGER	136919	M	16	Interpreter, public official, prison, Marseille (Fr.) 43-44				WITNESS	FR.
AUMAYR, Rupert	148751	M		Usturmscharfhr., SS, C.C. Mauthausen (Aust.)				TORTURE	U.S.
AVELKA	148240	M		Scharfhr., SS, Nancy (Fr.) 1943				TORTURE	FR.
BACH, Franz	135120	M	03	Cpl., 19 SS-Police-Regt., Oberkrain, Toulouse, Compiegne, Tulle (Yugo., FR.) 5.41-9.44. 3.-10.44				WITNESS	U.S.
BALL, Leopold	72656	M		Interpreter, Adjutant, Army, St. Laurent du Manoir (Fr.) 8.44				MURDER	FR.
BAR, Willy	259406	M		Sturmscharfhr., SS, Gestapo, area Poitiers (Fr.) 40-45				MISC.CRIMES	FR.
BARTELME	176558	M		Oscharfhr., SS-Div.Totenkopf, C.C. Landweier (Ger.)				BRUTALITY	FR.
BATIK, Willi	192686	M		Hptscharfhr., SD, Wien (Aust.)				MURDER	NOR.
BAUER	187527	M	05	Agent, Abwehr, Lisbon (Port.)				MISC.CRIMES	U.S.
BAUER, Josef	193971	M		Truppfhr., S.A., Hallein (Aust.) 43-45				TORTURE	CZECH.
BAUHOFER, Otto	170553	M	12	Osturmfhr., SS, SD, Strassenhaus (Ger.)				MURDER	U.K.
BAUMHOFER, Otto	192286	M	09	Osturmfhr., SS, Rengsdorf (Ger.) 12.44				MURDER	U.S.
BEIGIBOECK	258567	M		Surgeon, Dr.med., Army, Dachau (Ger.) 40-45				BRUTALITY	U.S.
BENKO, Georg	162484	M	15	Civilian, Arlon (Fr.) 3.9.44				MURDER	BEL.
BERG	82	M		Austrian or German, camp official, C.C. Leusderheide (Neth.) 5.42				TORTURE	NETH.
BERGER	158957	M	95	Civilian, C.C. Khulengraben (Aust.) 1943				TORTURE	U.K.
BERGER, Josef	193459	M	04	Pvt., 4-188 Kriegsgef.Arb.Bn., C.C. Fjell (Nor.) 5.44				TORTURE	U.S.
BERGMEISTER, Otto	162486	M	95	Capt., 2 Heer.Kuesten-Artl.Regt.981, Halsor Vaagso Island (Nor.) 6.-7.12.44				MURDER	NOR.
BIEBERHOFER, Theodor	192297	M		Civilian, Salzburg (Aust.) 6.44				WITNESS	U.S.
BINDER, Heinrich	240134	M	28.11.96	Polizeirat in the office of the Police President, Vienna (Aust.) 9-43				TORTURE	U.S.
BLAHA	258125	M		Employee, C.C. Dachau (Ger.) 1945				MURDER	BEL.
BONES, Kathi	187978	F		Civilian, St. Lorenzen (Aust.) 2.4.44				WITNESS	U.S.
BRANDL, Franz	140764	M		N.C.O., member, S.A., Hallein (Aust.) 38-45				MISC.CRIMES	U.S.
BRANDL, Fritz	257187	M		Sturmbannfhr., Waffen-SS, 1 Bn., 3 Coy., Regt. "Der Fuehrer", Fort de Nieppe (Fr.) 5.40				SUSPECT	U.K.
BRANDTSTAETTER, Anton or BRANDSTAETTER	159810	M	10. 1.01	SS-Mann, SS-Totenkopf, Dest (Ger.) 1939 Austrian or German				WITNESS	U.S.
BRAUNER, Karl	258981	M	05	Employee of Sauerwerke, civilian, Vienna (Aust.) fall 1944, spring 1945				MURDER	U.S.
BREIER, Alois	253809	M		Pvt., guard, camp 139-L, Middle-Steyrmark (Aust.) 1941				INTERR.	U.K.
BREITFUSS, Matthias	159843	M	1.10.99	Civilian, N.S.D.A.P., Maishofen (Aust.) 2.44				TORTURE	U.S.
BRUCKNER, Leopold or Josef	190355	M		Detachment-leader, 3 Coy., 891 or 391 Landesschuetzen-Bn. Stalag XVIII A. Wolfsberg-Marburg (Ger.) 2.-3.44				MISC.CRIMES	U.K.
BRUGGLER, Joseph	196109	M		Leader, N.S.D.A.P., C.C. Krispl (Aust.)				TORTURE	NETH.
BRUNNER	148497	M	15	Hptsturmfhr., SS, Drancy (Fr.) 43-44				TORTURE	FR.
BRUNNER	148516	M		Austrian or German, SS-Hptsturmfhr., SD, C.C. Drancy (Fr.) 1944				TORTURE	FR.
BRUNNER, Hans	187980	M		Civilian, St. Lorenzen (Aust.) 2.4.44				WITNESS	U.S.
BUCHER	194787	M	95	Lagerfhr., 107 Grenz-Wacht., C.C. Stalag XVIII A, Wetzeldorf (Aust.) 2.45				TORTURE	U.K.
BUEHLER	147956	M		Oscharfhr., Waffen-SS, Nancy (Fr.) 1943				TORTURE	FR.
CHIBIDZIURA	149182	M		Civilian, Graz (Aust.)				MURDER	FR.
CONRAD, Klaus	147761	M		Dr., Oberarzt, SS, SD, Marburg (Ger.)				MURDER	FR.
DARNEN	141502	M		Political leader, N.S.D.A.P., Vienna (Aust.)				MISC.CRIMES	FR.
DELETZ	155753	M		Butcher, civilian, Spittal (Aust.) 6.44				MISC.CRIMES	U.S.
DICHAVITZ, Fabian	154448	M		Cpl., Wehr-Arb.Kdo.22, Stalag XVIII A, Resident Vienna, Leoben (Aust.)				TORTURE	U.K.
DONHOFFER	169456	M	05	Pvt., Army, Stalag XVIII A, Premstatten (Aust.) 2.44				MURDER	U.K.
DORSTLER	62022	M		Austrian or German, Lt., Airforce, (Tunnel du coudray Oise), Andeville, Boncourt, Moailles (Fr.)				MURDER	FR.

AUSTRIA

AUSTRIA. (Cont.)

NAME	C.R. FILE NUMBER	SEX	DATE OF BIRTH	RANK, OCCUPATION, UNIT, PLACE AND DATE OF CRIME	REASON WANTED	WANTED BY
DRAGIC, Hinko	192939	M		Lt.Col., Yugosl. Airforce, C.C. Flossenbürg (Ger.) 44-45	WITNESS	U.S.
EBERLE, Hans	24763	M	09	S.R.A., Dijon (Fr.)	MURDER	FR.
EBNER	155741	M	00	Obermeister, Police, Gusen (Aust.)	MURDER	FR.
EBNER, Franz	151221	M		N.S.D.A.P., (Pol.) 39-40	MURDER	U.S.
EBSER, Joseph	185504	M		Civilian, St. Martin (Aust.) 16.11.44	PILLAGE	U.S.
EDELMANN, Ferdinand	193788	M	13. 3.87	Merchant, civilian, Amstetten (Aust.) 20.3.45	TORTURE	U.S.
EIBISBERGER, Alois	115674	M		Crim. secretary, Kripo, Linz-Donau (Aust.) 1943	MURDER	U.K.
EIGRUBER, August	135159	M	07	Gauleiter (Gruppenfhr.), N.S.D.A.P., Alt Aussee (Aust.) 4.45	MISC.CRIMES	U.S.
EINFALD	187034	M	17 - 18	Pvt., 3-188 POW-working-Bn., Bratholmen Hordaland (Nor.) 5.43	MURDER	NOR.
EMATHINGER, Emma	147174	F		Frauenschaftsleiterin, N.S.F., civilian, wife of mayor	TORTURE	U.S.
ENGLFUTZEDER, Erwin	154338	M		Kameradschaftsfhr., Hitler-Jugend	TORTURE	U.S.
ETLINGER or HAAKNEUS	233	M	05	Austrian or German, Hptsturmfhr., commandant, C.C. Mauthausen, Vught (Aust., Neth.) 40-45	MURDER	NETH. BEL.
ETTL, Fritz	188288	M		Civilian, St. Lorenzen (Aust.) 2.4.44	WITNESS	U.S.
FAHRNGRUBER	155409	M	15	Capt., Army, 2 Coy., Pz.Jaeger-Ers.Abt.10, Metting (Ger.) 28.12.44	TORTURE	U.S.
FEUCHT	253640	M		Cpl., chief of Kdo.H.V.X., Blumau-Austrich (Aust.)	INTERR.	FR.
FISCHERLEN	143407	M	10	C.C. Falkenhain (Ger.) 1944	TORTURE	FR.
FISTER, Hans	142487	M	25	Sturmmann, Waffen-SS, I SS-Div. Leibstandarte "Adolf Hitler", Rosbach (Ger.) 4.3.45	WITNESS	U.S.
FLUCHER	171666	M	02 - 05	Capt., 2-189 Kgf.Arb.Bn., Fjell (Nor.) 5.44	MURDER	NOR.
FRANZ	72084	M		SS-Scharfhr., C.C. Lublin (Pol.)	TORTURE	U.S.
FREY, Fritz	185125	M		Chief of Block, SS, C.C. Sachsenhausen (Ger.)	PILLAGE	FR.
FRIEDL, Joseph	148193	M		Chief, C.C. Hirtenberg-Niederdonau (Aust.)	TORTURE	FR.
FRIESSNEGG, Bruno	162029	M	21	Zugwachtmeister, Ordnungspolizei, Kradschuetzen-Coy., Stavern (Nor.) 1943	MURDER	NOR.
FRITSCH	147777	M		SS-Mann, Waffen-SS, Pz.Div. "Das Reich", Tonneins (Fr.) 1944	MURDER	FR.
FRITZ	259429	M		Kapo, C.C. Auschwitz (Pol.)	MURDER	FR.
FRITZ aliases FRIZZ	256101	M		Senior of the block 15, C.C. Mauthausen (Aust.)	INTERR.	FR.
FUCHS, Max	133314	M	92	Capt., German Army, Oflag XIII B, Hammelburg (Ger.) 44-45	MURDER	U.S.
GALIHOFER, Raimund	251572	M	92	Sgt., SD, worked at Goes at the Ortskmdtr., Wemeldinge (Z-B) (Neth.) 20.9.44	INTERR.	NETH.
GANGER, Johan	161199	M	95	Obersteiger, Arb.Kdo.951, civilian, C.C. Kogl. Eisenertz (Aust.) 2.-4.42	TORTURE	U.K.
GASTNER	186561	M	85	Lt., Arb.Kdo.107, Stalag XVIII A, Wolfsberg (Aust.)	TORTURE	U.K.
GATTERNIGG, Erich	53453	M	20. 7.07	Austrian or German, SS-Sturmbannfhr., 12 SS-Pz/Div. "Hitler-Jugend", Dr., 25 Regt., Abbaye, Ardenne near Caen, Normandy (Fr.)	TORTURE	CAN.
GATTNING	129793	M		Lt., commander, Stalag XVIII A, C.C. Spittal (Aust.) 16.10.43	MURDER	U.S.
GERLITZER	133346	M	10	Rottenfhr., Waffen-SS, C.C. Hohenrheim near Plattling (Ger.) 2.-5.45	MURDER	U.S.
GEYRHOFER, Rudolf	252306	M	7. 2.85	Member, N.S.D.A.P., Amstetten (Aust.) 20.3.45	MISC.CRIMES	U.S.
GLINZ, Anton	129662	M	09	Civilian, Alt Aussee (Aust.) 4.45	INCENDIARISM	U.S.
GOETZ, Franz-Michael	252307	M	26.12.15	N.S.D.A.P., S.A., Amstetten (Aust.) 20.3.45	MISC.CRIMES	U.S.
GOLDENBERG, Simon	162708	M	29. 9.10	Chief, Gestapo, Montelimar (Fr.)	MISC.CRIMES	FR.
GORFEL	255990	M		Uscharfhr., SS, state service, Poznan (Pol.) 7.-8.7.42	WITNESS	POL.
GRAUS, Marianna	192177	F		Civilian, Salzburg (Aust.) 6.44	WITNESS	U.S.
GRAZHOFER	53542	M	02	SS-Osturmbannfhr., Graz (Aust.), Dr.	TORTURE	NETH.
GRISL, Alois, Josef	145403	M	1. 5.12	Medizinalrat, physician, civilian, Molln (Aust.) 26.7.44	MISC.CRIMES	U.S.
GROS, Joseph	171676	M	21	SS-Sturmmann, SS, C.C. Natzweiler (Fr.)	MURDER	FR.
HAAGEN, Gustav	144493	M	24. 3.04	Standartenfhr., N.S.K.K.	TORTURE	FR.
HAAKNEUS see ETLINGER	233					
HABERL	151653	M		Sgt., Army, C.C. Graudenz (Pol.) 1.45	TORTURE	U.K.
HADABRA, Josef	253698	M		Lt., Sicherheits-Regt.199, Troyes, Marcilly, Fandreville (Fr.) 1944	MISC.CRIMES	FR.
HAGER, Johann	145328	M	27. 4.01	Ortsgruppenleiter, N.S.D.A.P., civilian, Molln (Aust.) 26.7.44	MURDER	U.S.
HAIDER, Karl	188157	M		Civilian, St. Lorenzen (Aust.) 2.4.44	TORTURE	U.S.
HAJEK	177346	M		Sgt., Army, 999 Inf.Div.	MURDER	SOV.UN.
HALINKA	259228	M		Uscharfhr., SS, Gestapo of Poitiers (Fr.) 40-45	MISC.CRIMES	FR.
HAMICH	167193	M		Sgt., Feldgendarmerie, Briey (Fr.) 28.8.44	TORTURE	FR.
HAMMER, Mariechen	257798	F		House-wife, Gratkorn (Aust.) 2.45	WITNESS	U.S.
HARKER	195214	M	00	Capt., Arbeitskdo., 6 Coy., Landesschuetzen-Bn.891, St. Marein Murztal (Aust.)	TORTURE	U.K.
HARRASSER	169523	M		Doctor, Aerztekammer	MISC.CRIMES	U.S.
HARRESER	251621	M	11	Austrian or German, pvt., Feldgendarmerie, Trupp 532, Nave (It.) 1.8.44	INTERR.	U.K.
HAUNOLD, Carl	196662	M	05	Austrian or German, Lt., Military, Security Police, Feldpostnr. 02099, Departm. Turin (It.) 9.12.43	WITNESS	U.K.
HAYNDEL	173587	M		SS-Oscharfhr., Waffen-SS, C.C. Theresienstadt (Czech.) 44-45	TORTURE	NETH.
HEIDFOGEL, Anton or HIDEFOGEL	161174	M	95	Cpl., Army, Arbeitskdo.951, Kogl Eisenertz (Aust.) 2.42-4.43	TORTURE	U.K.
HEININGER	254944	M	16	Cpl., SD, Gestapo, Milan (It.) 10.8.44	INTERR.	U.K.
HELMREICH, Otto	193208	M	08	Pvt., 4-188 Kgf.Arb.Bn., farmer, Fjell (Nor.) 5.44	MURDER	NOR.
HIDEFOGEL, Anton see HEIDFOGEL	161174					
HIMMLER, Karl	154373	M	05 - 10	Scharfhr., SS, C.C. Reichenau near Innsbruck (Aust.) 44-45	TORTURE	U.S.
HINTERSEER, Heinz	179794	M		Civilian, Lofer (Aust.)	WITNESS	U.S.
HOEDL, Franz	134916	M	07	Civilian, C.C. Hartheim (Aust.) 40-44	MURDER	U.S.
HOFER, Josef	188162	M		Civilian, St. Lorenzen (Aust.) 2.4.44	TORTURE	U.S.
HOFER, Josef (HOFFO)	132463	M	02	Ortsgruppenleiter, N.S.D.A.P., Weilbach (Aust.) 14.4.45	MURDER	U.S.
HOFMANN, Bruno	134848	M	22.11.09	Hauptbauleiter, O.T., Volkssturm-Bn. in Ampfing, Miehldorf Mittergras (Ger.) 6.44-5.45	MURDER	U.S.
HOLENIA	168855	M		Maj., Pz.Pion.Bn., Godinne (Bel.)	MURDER	BEL.
HOLLBACHER, Maria	194301	F		C.C. Krispl (Aust.)	WITNESS	NETH.
HOLLIN, Josef	166614	M	28.12.97	Civilian, Oberndorf (Aust.) 22.11.44	WITNESS	U.S.
HOELZEL	174772	M	05	Capt., Police-Coy., Ordnungspolizei, Ulven near Bergen (Nor.) 1942	MURDER	NOR.
HORYNA	134882	M	85	Maj., Army, advisor to chief of Security Police for Hungary, Dr., Sopron (Hung.) 3.45	MURDER	U.S.
HUBER, Anton	166612	M	12. 8.87	Civilian, Oberndorf, Kreis Salzburg (Aust.) 22.11.44	WITNESS	U.S.
HUSS, Gregor	132533	M		Austrian or German, Gestapo of St. Quentin, Chauny (Fr.)	MISC.CRIMES	FR.

AUSTRIA

AUSTRIA. (Cont.)

NAME	C.R.FILE NUMBER	SEX	DATE OF BIRTH	RANK	OCCUPATION UNIT PLACE AND DATE OF CRIME	REASON WANTED	WANTED BY
JAKOB	258926	M			Interpreter, Aktions-Kdo. of custom-house, Lourdes (Fr.) 1.-8.44	MURDER	FR.
JANKOVITCH	257571	M			Engineer, Montage VII, Camp Dora, Nordhausen (Ger.) 3.44-4.45	INTERR.	FR.
JARSKO	251063	M	11 - 16		RSM, SD, Gestapo, Milan (It.) 10.8.44	INTERR.	U.S.
JOESTL	132090	M	18		SS, C.C. Hohenrheim, Plattling (Ger.) 2.-5.45	MURDER	U.S.
JONKE, Elise	165914	F	3. 4.10		Civilian, Oberndorf (Aust.) 22.11.44	MURDER	U.S.
JUNGWIRTH	146758	M			Civilian, Lietzen (Aust.)	WITNESS	U.S.
JURY, Hugo	132026	M	95		Gauleiter, Dr., N.S.D.A.P., Budapest (Hung.) 1944	MISC.CRIMES	U.S.
KARNER, Stefanie nee EBNER see KORNER	194007						
KEJZ	257292	M	26		SS-Sturmmann, Aid station, Regt.37, SS-Div. "Goetz von Berlichingen" Waffen-SS, near St. Eny (Fr.) 9.7.44	WITNESS	U.S.
KERN, Joachim	161259	M	28.10.95		Civilian, Maishofen (Aust.) 25.2.44	WITNESS	U.S.
KERZENBERGER, Konrad	137789	M	8. 2.98		Truppfhr., S.A., Liezen (Aust.) 1943	MURDER	U.S.
KIENAST, Helmuth	260618	M	10 - 14		SS-Sgt., member of N.S.D.A.P., promoted to Gestapo-Lt., vicinity of St. Flour (Fr.) 14.6.44	MURDER	FR.
KILBACHER, Peter	194098	M			Foreman, C.C. Krispl (Aust.)	TORTURE	NETH.
KLIM, Alois	185689	M			Interrogator official, SS Interrogation Center, department for communism, Byron, Kalithea, Athens (Grc.)	MURDER	GRC.
KNOLL, Karl	253725	M	90 - 00		Maj., Airforce, Ebnet (Ger.) 27.2.45	WITNESS	U.S.
KOCZAK, Franz	145188	M	15		Oscharfhr., SS-Leibstandarte "Adolf Hitler", Rosbach (Ger.) 4.3.45	MURDER	U.S.
KOEBERL, Erwin	137794	M			S.A.-Scharfhr., Bad Aussee (Aust.)	TORTURE	U.S.
KOGON, Eugen	161516	M	02		Civilian, C.C. Buchenwald (Ger.)	TORTURE	U.S.
KOHOUTEK, Wenzel	165247	M	88		Standartenfhr., SS, SD, Sipo, Belgrad (Yugo.) 1944	MURDER	U.S.
KOKAIL	152506	M			Col., Stalag XX A, C.C. Thorn (Pol.) 26.7.44	MURDER	U.S.
KOIB	88819	M			SS-Sturmbannfhr., C.C. Sachsenhausen (Ger.)	MURDER	FR.
KOPS	259761	M			See Consolidated List Part II - Appendix "A"		
KORNER, Stefanie nee EBNER or KARNER or KURNER	194007	F	14		Saleswoman, civilian, Amstetten (Aust.) 20.9.45	TORTURE	U.S.
KOSSIAR	132486	M			Austrian or German, doctor, civilian, Kindberg (Aust.) 10.43-4.44	MISC.CRIMES	U.K.
KRACHER, Max	179790	M			Civilian, St. Martin (Aust.) 16.11.44	PILLAGE	U.S.
KRACHIER	164135	M	09		Cpl., 3-188 Arb.Bn., Brattholmen (Nor.) 5.45	MURDER	NOR.
KRAIGER	165250	M	95		Capt., Abwehr, Belgrad (Yugo.) 1944	MURDER	U.S.
KREIL, Franz	143176	M			Civilian, Locomotive fireman	MURDER	U.S.
KREUZER, Franz	137795	M			Country policeman, Army, Zellenleiter, N.S.V., D.A.F., Altmuenster (Aust.) 6.44	MURDER	U.S.
KRIWAN, Sepp (Joseph)	257503	M	96		Sgt., North-Btty.AA, Texel (Neth.) 3.2.45	MURDER	U.S.
KRONHOLZ, Robert	251679	M			Secret Agent, Gestapo, Belgrad (Yugo.) 4.41-10.44	INTERR.	YUGO.
KRUEGER, Heinz	256912	M			Austrian or German, Zugwachtmeister, 7 Coy., 322 Bn., 5 Schutz-Regt., Ljubljana, Cetje and Kranj (Yugo.) 42-43	MISC.CRIMES	YUGO.
KRUG, Maris	188294	F			Civilian, St. Lorenzen (Aust.) 2.4.44	WITNESS	U.S.
KUDLER, Karl	145169	M	11.		Uscharfhr., Waffen-SS, Leibstandarte "Adolf Hitler", Rosbach (Ger.) 4.3.45	MURDER	U.S.
KUENZEL, Karl	174104	M	05		Usturmfhr., Allg.SS, Gestapo, member camp commander of work reformatory (Vienna 23), C.C. between Vienna and Mauthausen (Aust.) 1.-18.4.45	MURDER	U.S.
KUNICK, Maria or KUNIK	143184	F			Female member and guard of Waffen-SS, C.C. Sensing (Ger.) since 1.45	MISC.CRIMES	U.S.
KURCHBAUM, A.	132487	M			Austrian or German, civilian, guesthousekeeper, Wagendorf near Liebnitz (Aust.) 25.2.44	TORTURE	U.S.
KURNER, Stefanie nee EBNER see KORNER	194007						
KUTSCHERG	145167	M			SS-Brigadefhr., (White Russia, Pol.) 1940	MISC.CRIMES	U.S.
KWARDA, Karl	145296	M			Lagerfhr., civilian, (Aust.)	TORTURE	U.S.
LAHNER, Franz	192742	M	05		Sgt., guard, Feldstraflager Nord, Reichsjustizministerium, C.C. Finmark (Nor.)	MISC.CRIMES	NOR.
LANG, Rupert	72318	M			Pvt., Army, 377 Dulag, guard-Coy., (Ger.) 1.45	TORTURE	U.S.
LANGER, Fritz	259935	M	13. 1.04		Crim.officer, Crim.Police Wien, N.S.D.A.P., home address: Wien XXI, Angererstr.3 (Aust.), Castel del Rio (It.)	MURDER	U.S.
LATTE	253126	M	04		Major, Airforce, 734 Flak-Btty., Ciacomo (It.) 3.1.44	INTERR.	U.K.
LECHNER	192740	M	00		Sgt., Feldstraflager Nord, Reichsjustizministerium, C.C. Finmark (Nor.) 6.42-45	MISC.CRIMES	NOR.
LEHNARD	254388	M	00		Col., cmdt., P.G.77, Spoletto (It.) 13.11.43	INTERR.	U.K.
LEHNER, Franz	178756	M	05		Pvt., 1 Coy., Landesschuetzen-Bn.373, Leonhard (Aust.) 2.44	MISC.CRIMES	U.K.
LEITNER, Fritz	188298	M			Civilian, St. Lorenzen (Aust.) 2.4.44	WITNESS	U.S.
LEUBE, Hans	259481	M			Dr., see Consolidated List Part II - Appendix "A"		
LEVY, Elie	162708	M	20. 9.10		Chief, Gestapo, Montelimar (Fr.)	MISC.CRIMES	FR.
LEX, Alfred (Fred)	257189	M			Hptsturmfhr., Waffen-SS, 3 Coy., 1 Bn., Regt."Der Fuehrer", Foret de Nieppe (Fr.) 5.40	SUSPECT	U.K.
LILIA, Wilhelm	134801	M	03		Sgt., 19 SS-Police-Regt., Vigaun, Toulouse, Campiegne, Agen, Tulle (Yugo., Fr.) 5.41-3.44 and 3.-10.44	TORTURE	U.S.
LINDENBERGER, Gustav	150653	M			Farmer, Ortsbauernfhr., public official, SS, C.C.	MURDER	U.S.
LINDZE, Benedikt	156097	M			Austrian or German, civilian, C.C. Klagenfurt (Aust.) 23.11.43	TORTURE	N.L.
LOTHALER, Hans	134918	M	00		Member, S.A., civilian, Reichspost of Linz, C.C. Hartheim (Ger.) 40-44	MURDER	U.S.
LUCKANZ, Johann	134809	M	22 - 24		Pvt., Airforce, Ahrweiler (Ger.) 26.12.44	WITNESS	UNWCC.
MALISCHECK	124818	M	86		Col., Army, (Ger.)	TORTURE	U.S.
MARIACHER, Hans	138044	M	2. 9.98		Scharfhr., SS, Innsbruck (Aust.) 40-45	MISC.CRIMES	U.S.
MARTAETSCHLAEGER	167001	M			Civilian, Dr., (Fr.,Czech.,Aust.,Neth.) 38-45	MISC.CRIMES	U.S.
MARTETSCHLAGER	39848	M			Civilian, Feldpostnr.40566 B, Conlie (Fr.) 7.8.44	MURDER	FR.
MAYER	104878	M	10		Pvt., Army, 2 Coy., 337 Landesschuetzen-Bn., C.C., Stalag VI G, Holotous (Czech.) 2.45	BRUTALITY	U.S.
MAYER	253937	M	10		Doctor, C.C. Auschwitz (Pol.)	INTERR.	FR.
MAYER see MEYER	259764						
MEYER	38867	M			Scharfhr., SS, C.C. Lublin (Pol.) 1943	TORTURE	U.S.
MEYER or MAYER	259764	M			See Consolidated List Part II - Appendix "A"		

AUSTRIA

AUSTRIA. (Cont.)

NAME	C.R.FILE NUMBER	SEX	DATE OF BIRTH	RANK, OCCUPATION, UNIT, PLACE AND DATE OF CRIME	REASON WANTED	WANTED BY
MEYERSHUBER	120529	M		Police-chief, C.C. Auschwitz (Pol.)	MISC.CRIMES	FR.
MEYERSHUBER	191208	M		Lt., Police, C.C. Hartheim (Ger.) 43-45	MURDER	BEL.
MICHALKE, Franz	166274	M		SS-Fuehrer, SS, (Fr.,Neth.,Aust.,Czech.) 38-45	WITNESS	U.S.
MOLDINGER	156861	M		Mayor, civilian, Krispl (Aust.) 1944	MISC.CRIMES	U.S.,NETH.
MORATTI, Stephan	130857	M	05	SS-Mann, interpreter at the Gestapo, SD, Bonnert Arlon (Bel.) 1.9.44	MURDER	BEL.
MUEHLBACH	198268	M		Sgt., SS, Gestapo, chief of office of courrier, Lyon (Fr.)	MURDER	FR.
MUEHLMANN, Kajetah (Kai)	154823	M	90	Staatssekretaer (honorary title), Director for confiscations of art and Cultural Treasures, (Pol.) 39-44	PILLAGE	U.S.
MUELLER	156990	M	95	Pvt., 3 Coy., 877 Landesschuetzen-Bn., C.C. Liexen (Aust.)	TORTURE	U.K.
MYNHA, Fritz	174829	M	17	Hpttruppfhr., R.A.D. 6-352, Schuetzen (Aust.) 3.45	WITNESS	U.S.
NAGERL, Jacob	62406	M	95	Pvt., Army, Btty.Nord, M.Flak-Abt.810, (Neth.)	WITNESS	U.S.
NEDWED	163114	M	07	Chief, Gestapo, Innsbruck, Kassel (Aust., Ger.) 43-45	MURDER	U.S.
NEEDLE	129045	M	15	Expert, SS-Osturmfhr., C.C. Mauthausen (Aust.)	MURDER	U.S.
NIEDERWANGER, Karl	166630	M	31.10.18	Civilian, Innsbruck (Aust.) 20.4.45	TORTURE	U.S.
NOHEL, Vinzenz	134919	M	00	Civilian, C.C. Hartheim (Aust.) 40-44	MURDER	U.S.
OBERREITER, Josef	155503	M	3. 2.93	Carpenter, civilian, Katzdorf (Aust.) 4.45	MURDER	U.S.
OBERZAUCHNER, Anton	251217	M	04 or 05	Ortsgruppenleiter, Bruggen-Greifenberg, Ebenberg-Kaernten (Aust.) 16.11.44	MURDER	U.S.
OGRIS	155499	M	00	SS-Chief, SS, Gusen (Aust.) 44-45	TORTURE	FR.
OLERT	173861	M		Adjutant, Gestapo, SD, Valence (Fr.)	TORTURE	FR.
ORTNER, Lorenz	142105	M		Lagerfhr., C.C. Voecklabruck-Traunkirchen (Aust.)	TORTURE	U.S.
PAROUBEK, Hans	153190	M	25. 2.13	Civilian, Linz (Aust.) 42-45	WITNESS	U.S.
PAST, Johann	155533	M	10. 3.85	Jail-warder, civilian, Carsten (Aust.) 4.34-5.45	TORTURE	U.S.
PASTOREK	156834	M	04	Rottenfhr., Feldgendarmerie, 12 SS-Pz.Div. "Hitler-Jugend", The Abbaye (Fr.) 6.6.-2.7.44	WITNESS	CAN.
PECKMANN, Hans	193594	M		Austrian or German, Oscharfhr., SS, 2 SS-Pz.Gren.Ausb.u.Ers.Bn.12, Berneau (Bel.) 5.9.44	MURDER	BEL.
PELIKAN	120564	M		Sturmfhr., N.S.K.K., Dr., Semi-Military, Odessa (Sov.Un.) 41-42	MURDER	U.S.
PENSENTHEIMER see PESENTHEIMER	686			Austrian or German		
PERSTERER, Alois	185025	M	29. 9.09	Obersturmbannfhr., SS, Caucasus (Sov.Un.) 1942	MURDER	U.S.
PESENTHEIMER or PENSENTHEIMER	686	M		Austrian or German, SS-Oscharfhr., Gestapo, Locmine (Fr.) 7.-8.44	MURDER	FR.
PETERBAUER see WIESER	179781					
PETRINA, Karl	155519	M	99	Camp-blockelder, C.C. Ebensee (Aust.)	MURDER	U.S.
PETZ, Maria	188243	F		Civilian, St. Lorenzen (Aust.) 2.4.44	WITNESS	U.S.
PFESTERER	155696	M	98	Kdo.-Fhr., omdt., Landesschuetzen-Bn.3-788, C.C. Kuhlengraben (Aust.) 1943	MURDER	U.K.
PIEBER	146143	M		Capt., Stalag Luft III, C.C., (Ger.)	WITNESS	U.K.
PLANGER, Josef	164136	M	03	Cpl., 3-188 POW-working-Bn., Brathalmen (Nor.) 5.43	MURDER	NOR.
PLATTNER, Franz	192603	M	97 or 98	Cpl., Kgf.Arb.Bn.II-188, C.C. Fjell (Nor.) 42-43	TORTURE	NOR.
PLIEM, Bernhard	144402	M		Clerk, N.S.V.-office, Hallein (Aust.) 1945	MISC.CRIMES	U.S.
PODNIK	139868	M	10	Surgeon, Dr., Flugplatz-Kdo.A 9-XI, Rome (Den.) 4.43	MURDER	U.K.
POLANYI, Josef	161698	M	04	Cpl., Army, 2 Coy., 188 Kgf.Arb.Bn., Furt (Nor.)	TORTURE	NOR.
POLANSKI	130931	M	21	SS-Osturmfhr., 12 SS-Pz.Div., 26 Regt., 13 Coy., Caen (Fr.) 6.44	TORTURE	CAN.
POMPERL	137590	M		Col., Stalag XVII A, C.C. Dollersheim (Aust.) 7.6.44	TORTURE	U.K.
POMPERL	178764	M		Col., Oflag IV C, 8.44	TORTURE	U.K.
POSCHKE, Max.Ferdinand	240015	M	75	Wehrwirtschaftsfhr., N.S.D.A.P., Stuttgart (Ger.)	MISC.CRIMES	U.S.
PAUKL, Otto	191854	M		Secretary, civilian, Change (Fr.)	WITNESS	FR.
PRENNER, Anton	253280	M	9. 2.02	Employee, Gestapo, Vsetin (Czech.) 39-45	MISC.CRIMES	CZECH.
PROSTREDNIK, Josef	173865	M	21. 3.09	Oberstfeldmeister, R.A.D. 6-352 unit, Schuetzen am Gebirge (Aust.) 3.45	WITNESS	U.S.
PUNKE, Conte de	255027	M		Guard, Gestapo, Limoges (Fr.) 40-45	INTERR.	FR.
PUSCH, Friedrich	194118	M		Lt.Col., Osturmfhr., SS, 2 Pion.Ausb.Bn., Passau (Ger.) 4.45	MURDER	U.S.
RADL, Karl	259289	M	12.11.11	Maj., 150 Pz.Bde., Meuse-Bridge, Antwerp (Bel.) 12.44	SUSPECT	U.S.
RAEM	173938	M		Osturmfhr., SS, 44-45	TORTURE	NETH.
RAUCH, Josef	196003	M	1. 8.97	SS-Hptsturmfhr., Sicherheitspolizei, Arnheim (Neth.) 3.45	MURDER	NETH.
RAUER, Karl	261239	M	7. 8.13	Maj., omdt., of Airfield, Hopsten (Ger.) 25.3.45	MURDER	U.S.
RAUSCHER	253194	M		Oscharfhr., 3 Coy., 1 Bn., Regt. "Der Fuehrer", Div. "Das Reich", Oradour (Fr.) 10.6.44	INTERR.	FR.
RECHENFRATER	156049	M	00	Foreman (SS-civil), factory Georgen-Miehle, Gusen II (Aust.) 44-45	TORTURE	FR.
REICH, Oscar	121389	M	22	Civilian, (Fr.) 43-44	MISC.CRIMES	FR.
REICHERT, Hans	162708	M	20. 9.10	Chief, Gestapo, Montelimar (Fr.)	MISC.CRIMES	FR.
REICHLEITNER, Franz	134920	M	05	Schupo-Capt., SS-member, C.C. Hartheim (Aust.) 40-44	MURDER	U.S.
REICHMANN, Hans	193022	M	1. 5.03	Sgt., guard, Werkfuehrer, Waffen-SS, Strafgefangenenlager, Reichsjustizministerium, C.C. Finmark (Nor.) 8.45	MISC.CRIMES	YUGO.,NOR.
REINER, Karl	193901	M		Pvt., SS, public official, Maire Weigesdorf (Aust.) 25.9.43	MURDER	U.S.
REINISCH, Pierre	252640	M		Uscharfhr., Gestapo, Limoges (Fr.)	MISC.CRIMES	FR.
REISER see RIESER	136633					
REISINGER, Josef	173927	M	25	Vormann, R.A.D. 6-352, Area Schuetzen (Aust.) 3.45	MURDER	U.S.
RENATH, Hans	193028	M	12	Sgt., guard, Feldstraflager, Justizministerium, C.C. Finmark (Nor.) 8.44	MISC.CRIMES	NOR.
RETCHKAL, Henry	193320	M	05	Interpreter, Dr., Gesundheitsamt, Vienna (Aust.) May or August 1944	MURDER	U.S.
REUL, Karl	139069	M		Foreman, C.C. Krispl (Aust.)	TORTURE	NETH.
RICHTER, Herman	148550	M	13. 8.15	SS-Osturmfhr., C.C. Mauthausen (Aust.) 41-45	MURDER	U.S.
RICHTER, Wilhelm	186723	M	04 - 09	Rottenfhr., Allg.SS, chief, Gestapo, Sturm I, Steyr (Aust.) 1945	MURDER	FR.
RIESER or REISER	136633	M		Capt., Unit guarding PW at Stalag XVII B, Krems-Gneisendorf (Aust.) 10.43-4.45	MURDER	U.S.
RIES, Johannes	161636	M	06	Pvt., Army, 3 Coy., 188 Kgf.Arb.Bn., Herdla (Nor.)	MURDER	NOR.
RITZAL, Heinrich	148554	M	20. 9.04	SS-Sgt., SS-Totenkopf-Standarte, C.C. Mauthausen (Aust.) 41-45	TORTURE	U.S.
ROCHBERG, Jean	162708	M	20. 9.10	Chief, Gestapo, Montelimar (Fr.)	MISC.CRIMES	FR.
ROGL, Emerich	139076	M	30. 4.09	Staffelfhr., N.S.K.K., D.A.F., Steyr (Aust.) 40-45	TORTURE	U.S.
ROSENBERGER, Colestin	179932	M	10	Hpttruppfhr., R.A.D.-Arbeitsgau XXXV, Schuetzen (Aust.) 3.45	MURDER	U.S.
ROZHON, Rudolf	193011	M	14.12.97	Reichsjustizministerium, C.C. Finmark (Nor.) 5.45	WITNESS	NOR.
RUDOLF, Franz-Siegesmund	138042	M	25. 2.92	Brig.Gen., O.K.W., foreign-Div., (Ger. occupied countries) 39-45	TORTURE	U.S.
SAITINGER, Max	139080	M		Untermeister, spinning-mill, Richdorf (Aust.) 22.2.44	MURDER	U.S.

AUSTRIA

NAME	C.R. FILE NUMBER	SEX	DATE OF BIRTH	RANK OCCUPATION UNIT PLACE AND DATE OF CRIME	REASON WANTED	WANTED BY
				AUSTRIA. (Cont.)		
SCHALDER, Hans	149875	M		Kreisamtsleiter, N.S.D.A.P., Hallein (Aust.) 1945	MISC.CRIMES	U.S.
SCHLEINING, Hans	167326	M	18	Sgt., 1 Coy., 1 Bn., SS-Div. "Das Reich", Oradour sur Glane (Fr.) 10.6.44	MURDER	FR.
SCHLOSSER, Franz	156896	M		Cpl., 2 Coy., 188 POW-work-Bn., Ervik (Nor.) 42-43	MURDER	NOR.
SCHOECKEL	306188	M	95	Uscharfhr., aide-de-camp to cmdt., C.C. Kahla (Ger.) 40-45	MURDER	BEL.
SCHORG, Karl	193690	M	97	Oberwachtmeister, Reichsjustizministerium, Strafgefangenenlager Nord, C.C. Finmark (Nor.) 8.45	MISC.CRIMES	NOR.
SCHRITTWEISER	257199	M		N.C.O., Waffen-SS, Regt. "Der Fuehrer", 1 Bn., 3 Coy., Nieppe (Fr.) 5.40	SUSPECT	U.K.
SCHRUNER, Ludvic	193678	M		Cpl., Army, Stalag 18 A, C.C. Kaiserburg Lesben (Aust.) 10.43	TORTURE	U.K.
SCHUCKERT, Anton	193695	M		Hptscharfhr., SD. (Security Service), Wien, Trandum (Aust., Nor.)	MURDER	NOR.
SCHULEIN	837	M		Austrian or German, Oberfaehnrich, Army, 738 Regt., 118 Jaeger-Div. Kalinwich Montenegro (Yugo.) 7.43	MURDER	YUGO.
SCHULZE	845	M		Austrian or German, Lt., Army, 1 Coy., 1 Bn., 138 Jaeger-Regt., Montenegro (Yugo.) 7.43	MURDER	YUGO.
SCHUTZ, Martin	157015	M	02	Pvt., 3 Coy., Landesschuetzen-Bn.768, C.C. Khulengraben (Aust.)	MURDER	U.K.
SCHWAMBERGER, Josef	256872	M		Uscharfhr., ghetto and comp. lab. camp, Przemysl and Rozwadow (Pol.) 42-43	MURDER	POL.
SCHWARZENBERG	143216	M		Kriegsgerichtsrat, Kriegsgericht, Nantes (Fr.) 9.41	WITNESS	U.S.
SENEIDER, Kurt	121860	M		Member, Gestapo, Clermont Ferrand (Fr.)	MURDER	FR.
SIEGEL, Herbert	139086	M		Osturmfhr., Waffen-SS, Ploc (Pol.) 8.42	MURDER	U.S.
SIGMUND	192867	M		Lt., Schupo, C.C. Falstad (Nor.) 4.43	MURDER	NOR.
SINGER	9620	M		Doctor, employed as male nurse at C.C., Breendonck (Bel.) 40-44	TORTURE	BEL.
SLAWING, Alfred	188481	M	11	Lt., Army, occupied territories, Athens (Grc.) 1943	MURDER	GRC.
SNAIDER, Karol	188493	M		SS-Interrogator, 13 Department, Byron Stagelon Athens (Grc.)	MURDER	GRC.
SOMMER	194250	M		Civilian, C.C. Change d'Auvours (Fr.) 1944	WITNESS	FR.
SORA, Josef	142250	M	16. 3.10	Doctor, Airforce, staff, C.C. Ebensee (Aust.) 44-45	WITNESS	U.S.
STAREK, Rudolf	166303	M	3. 7.24	Civilian, formerly Navy, Oberndorf, Kreis Salzburg (Aust.) 22.11.44	WITNESS	U.S.
STEINBERGER	252692	M	00	Cpl., Police, 532 Gend. Trupp, Nave (It.) 1.8.44	INTERR.	U.K.
STEINER	158461	M	95	Sgt., Army, 877 Landesschuetzen-Bn., 3 Coy., Liexen (Aust.) 44-45	TORTURE	U.K.
STEINER	128799	M		Capt., Stalag XVIII A, Wolfsberg (Aust.) 6.41-3.45	TORTURE	U.K.
STEINHAUSER, J.	116811	M		Innkeeper, civilian, Arbeitskdo., St. Margarethen (Aust.) 1.-11.5.44	TORTURE	U.K.
STIFT, Erich	188002	M	09 - 10	SS-Osturmbannfhr., 25 SS-Pz.Gren.Regt., 12 SS-Pz.Div. "Hitler-Jugend", near Caen (Fr.) 6.6.-8.7.44	TORTURE	CAN.
STOCKER, Alois	188407	M		Civilian, St. Lorenzen (Aust.) 2.4.44	WITNESS	U.S.
STOCKER, Karl	188406	M		Civilian, St. Lorenzen (Aust.)	WITNESS	U.S.
STRIEF, Anton	132465	M	02	Innkeeper and farmer, civilian, Weilbach (Aust.) 15.4.45	MURDER	U.S.
STUNSKI	252767	M		Judge, Military Court, Finistere (Fr.)	INTERR.	FR.
SYKA, Willibald	251260	M	00	Austrian or German, Capt., Cuneo (It.) 12.12.43	INTERR.	U.K.
TAUSCH, Felix	259468	M	10.11.95	Director, plant, Dr., Radom and Krakau (Pol.) 39-42	INTERR.	POL.
TEICHMANN, Ernst	134717	M	27.11.05	Crim.investigation officer, Dr., Kripo, (Ger.) 43-45	WITNESS	U.S.
THALER, Herbert	133251	M	10	Dr., Airforce, Outercamp S-III, Thuringia (Ger.)	TORTURE	U.S.
TOROCK	167098	M		SS-Chief, SS, Clermont Ferrand (Fr.) 22. and 29.11.44	MURDER	FR.
THUTSCHNICK	138946	M		SS-Adjutant, SS, Gestapo, Lyon (Rhone) (Fr.)	MURDER	FR.
TUMA	191329	M	95	Capt., Kgf.Arb.Bn.202, 1 Coy., Bjornelva (Nor.)	MURDER	NOR.
VALLISTER, Josef	134923	M	11	Civilian, C.C. Hartheim (Ger.) 40-44	MURDER	U.S.
VASTLE	184266	M		Chief, C.C. Dachau (Ger.)	MURDER	FR.
VIERLINGER, Albrecht	192703	M	29. 9.06	Sgt., Reichsjustizministerium, Feldstraflager Nord, Finmark.(Nor.) 6.42-45	MISC.CRIMES	NOR., YUGO.
VIGAN, Johann	152995	M	13	Kapo, C.C. Flossenburg (Ger.)	TORTURE	U.S.
VINZENZ (or GRASEGGER, Vinzenz)	188291	M		Civilian, St. Lorenzen (Aust.) 2.4.44	WITNESS	U.S.
VOGG, Hugo	257198	M		Hptscharfhr., Waffen-SS, 3 Coy., 1 Bn., Regt. "Der Fuehrer", Foret de Nieppe (Fr.) 5.40	SUSPECT	U.K.
VOLLMANN, Alois	152978	M	97 or 98	Sgt., Army, Kriegsgef.Bezirkskmdtr., Verst.Kgf.Arb.Bn.188, II Coy., Aasane Hjortland-Bergen (Nor.) 42-43	MURDER	NOR.
VON GILBERT, Gianella	191874	M		Lt., Army, St. Hilaire, St. Mosmin (Fr.) 19.-25.8.44	MURDER	FR.
VON SCHOLZ, Harald	136194	M	23	Usturmfhr., SS, Gueret (Fr.)	MURDER	FR.
WAECHTNER	188263	M	95	Lt., 7 para-Div., H.Q., Gristede (Ger.)	WITNESS	CAN.
WAGNER, Alfred	136268	M		Chief, Gestapo, Oflag XVII A, C.C. Edelbach (Aust.)	MURDER	FR.
WALCHER, Ferdinand	179782	M		Civilian, Ramsau (Aust.)	MURDER	U.S.
WALDNER, Hans or WALDER	250564	M	01	Austrian or German, N.C.O., interpreter, Anti-Partisan Duties, Masola and Ariano Polesine (It.) 12.44	INTERR.	U.K.
WALGNER, Mathias	150817	M		Civilian administrator, labour-camp, C.C. Krispl (Aust.) 1944	TORTURE	U.S.
WAIKNER, Rupert	194849	M		Civilian, C.C. Krispl (Aust.)	WITNESS	NETH.
WALLNER, Matthias	152739	M	22. 2.86	Civilian, railroad worker, Maishofen (Aust.) 25.2.44	WITNESS	U.S.
WARTHA, Georg	240037	M	12. 7.07	SD-Sturmscharfhr., Antipartisan office, SD, Turin (It.) 1945	TORTURE	U.S.
WASICKI	194695	M		SS-Hptsturmfhr., C.C. Mauthausen (Aust.)	MURDER	FR.
WEBER, Joseph	162709	M		Austrian or German, Osturmfhr., SS, C.C. Melk (Ger.)	TORTURE	U.S.
WEGER	192422	M		Lt., Guard-Coy., Cheminieres (Fr.) 8.44	MURDER	FR.
WEIBBACHER, Johann	179792	M		Civilian, Lofer (Aust.)	WITNESS	U.S.
WEIKMANN, Karl	252827	M	00	Pvt., 5 Coy., 891 Landesschuetzen-Bn., Tanzelsdorf (Aust.) 7.3.42	INTERR.	U.K.
WEIMANN	146741	M		Police-inspector, Police, Grafendorf (Aust.) 3.45	TORTURE	U.S.
WETTENTHALER, Johann	139249	M		Revierinspektor, Gendarmerie, member, N.S.D.A.P., Mitterndorf (Aust.)	TORTURE	U.S.
WENZL, Friedrich	153455	M	29.12.11	Sgt., Waffen-SS, Totenkopf-Standarte, C.C. Mauthausen (Aust.) 9.44-5.45	MURDER	U.S.
WESTCOTT	130064	M		Austrian or German, engineer, civilian, Arb.Kdo.A 91 G.W., C.C. Judenburg (Aust.) 27.2.-1.4.45	TORTURE	U.K.
WIEDAUER, Anna	260715	F		Austrian or German, C.C. Hallein (Aust.)	MURDER	U.S.
WIENER, Jean	256162	M		Imprisoner of the bloc 10, C.C. Mauthausen (Aust.)	INTERR.	FR.
WIESER, Hedwig	187855	F		Civilian, St. Lorenzen (Aust.) 2.4.44	WITNESS	U.S.
WIESER, Heinrich or PETERBAUER	179781	M		Ramsau (Aust.)	MURDER	U.S.
WIESINGER, Josef	260932	M	27.10.05	Austrian or German, SS-Uscharfhr., Allg. SS, Waffen-SS, C.C. Auschwitz (Pol.) 1941	MISC.CRIMES	POL.
WIMMER, Johann	179793	M		Gravedigger, civilian, St. Martin near Lofer (Aust.)	WITNESS	U.S.
WODAL, Gustav	158406	M	98	Cpl., 2 Coy., Kriegsgefangenen-Bezirks-Kmdtr., Aasane (Nor.) 42-43	MURDER	NOR.

AUSTRIA - BELGIUM

NAME	C.R.FILE NUMBER	SEX	DATE OF BIRTH	RANK	OCCUPATION UNIT PLACE AND DATE OF CRIME	REASON WANTED	WANTED BY

AUSTRIA. (Cont.)

NAME	C.R.FILE NUMBER	SEX	DATE OF BIRTH	OCCUPATION / UNIT / PLACE AND DATE OF CRIME	REASON WANTED	WANTED BY
WOLF, Hugo	151473	M	07	SS-Uschfhr., 12.SS-Pz.Div."Hitler-Jugend", St.Sulpice sur Risle, Eure (Fr.) 10.6.44	MURDER	U.S.
WOLFINEK	1039	M		Austrian or German, Lt., Army, 118.Jg.Div.(Yugo.) 7.43-1.44	MURDER	YUGO.
WOLLMANN, Fritz	192227	M	06	Dr., Civilian, Gynaecologist, Anatomy Inst., Danzig (Pol.)	MISC.CRIMES	POL.
WORM, Franz	158407	M		Cpl., 2-188 Kgf.Arb.Bn., Ervik (Nor.) 42-43	MURDER	NOR.
ZANKOVITCH	257455	M		Engineer, C.C.Dora, Nordhausen (Ger.)	BRUTALITY	FR.
ZARTL, Ernst	194540	M		Official, Police, surgeon, C.C.Altenrode, Tilburg (Ger.,Neth.) 13.4.44, 25.5.44	TORTURE	NETH.
ZAUER	250593	M	13	Capt., Army, 14.Pol.Rgt., Tuk (Czech.) 27.10.43	INTERR.	YUGO.
ZEITELSBERGER	193132	M	10	Sgt., Guard, Reichsjustizministerium, Feldstraflager, C.C.Finmark (Nor.) 43	MURDER	NOR.

BELGIUM.

NAME	C.R.FILE NUMBER	SEX	DATE OF BIRTH	OCCUPATION / UNIT / PLACE AND DATE OF CRIME	REASON WANTED	WANTED BY
BOCQUET	159970	M		Militia, Folkling (Fr.) 11.44	MURDER	FR.
BOLL	140394	M	00	Agent, Gestapo, Bruxelles (Bel.) 15.6.43	MURDER	FR.
BOSSANT, Gustav	27708	M		Agent, Gestapo, Bruges (Bel.)	MURDER	FR.
BOUQUET, Carlos	193564	M	13	SS-Mann, SD, Sipo, Leeuwarden (Neth.) 13.9.44-14.4.45	MURDER	NETH.
BRION, Marcel	196108	M		SD, Prison, C.C.Heerenveen Crackstate (Neth.) 15.4.45	MURDER	NETH.
DE BONDT, Joris	193563	M	11.3.21	SS-Mann, SD, Sipo, Leeuwarden (Neth.) 13.9.44-10.4.45	MISC.CRIMES	NETH.
DECUYPER	145549	M		Civilian, 1941	MISC.CRIMES	FR.
DETANDT, Edmond Helmut or Helmont	132724	M		Agent, Gestapo, Douai (Fr.) 6.3.44	MURDER	FR.
DEFRAY	72448	M		Agent, Gestapo, Roosebeke (Bel.)	MISC.CRIMES	FR.
DEFRETELLE	72449	M		Indicateur, Gestapo, Cahors-Gramat (Fr.)	MISC.CRIMES	FR.
DE GENDT, Emil	193629	M	21.8.07	SS-Mann, SD, Gent Aussendienststelle der Sipo, Leeuwarden (Neth.) 13.9.44-14.4.45	MURDER	NETH.
DE HEYN	194279	M	-20	SS-Mann, SS, SD, Heerenveen (Neth.) 2.1. - 15.4.45	MURDER	NETH.
D'HOLLANDER, Alfons	194126	M	7.9.14	Pvt., Assendienststelle der Sipo and SD, Leeuwarden (Neth.) 13.9.44-14.4.45	MURDER	NETH.
DELBEKE, Gaston	193568	M	25.2.13	SS-Mann, Aussendienststelle der Sipo and SD, Assen (Neth.) 13.9.44-14.4.45	TORTURE	NETH.
DE REYK (see DE RIJCK)	194106					
DE RIJCK, Adolf (or DE REYK or DE RIJK)	194106	M		Cpl., SD, Steenwijk, Heerenveen (Neth.) 12.1.45-15.4.45	MURDER	NETH.
DE RIJK (see DE RIJCK)	194106					
DESPREZ, Georges	145569	M		SS, C.C.Siegmar-Schonau (Ger.) 7.44	MISC.CRIMES	FR.
DE WACHTER	194848	M		SS-Mann, Guard, SD, Heerenveen, Meppel (Neth.) 2.1.45-15.4.45	MURDER	NETH.
DE WERD, Jules	145575	M		Civilian, 1944	MISC.CRIMES	FR.
DUBOIS	161702	F	03	Gestapo, Koeln (Ger.) 1944	MURDER	FR.
DUVAL, Ludo	149961	M	12	Civilian	MISC.CRIMES	FR.
FEAUX, Henriette	141546	F	10	C.C.Sommerfeld (Ger.) 1944	MISC.CRIMES	FR.
FERNANDEL	166975	M		SS-Rottfhr., C.C.Wattensted (Ger.)	MURDER	FR.
FRANCK, Robert	193628	M	1.9.11	Member, Sipo, Leeuwarden (Neth.) 13.9.44-14.4.45	MURDER	NETH.
GOBATZ, Henri	39642	M		Sgt., Feldgend., Laval (Fr.) 31.7.44	MURDER	FR.
HANOT	194282	M		SS-Sgt., SD, transport-commander, Heerenveen (Neth.) 13.4.45	MURDER	NETH.
HANOT, Leon	188651	M		Agent, Gestapo, Douai (Fr.) 6.3.44	MURDER	FR.
HELMONT (see DETANDT)	132724					
HEYERMANN	194280	M	20	SS-Mann, Warder, SS, SD, Heerenveen (Neth.) 15.4.45	MURDER	NETH.
HOMER	256862	M		Head, Camp Dora, Nordhausen (Ger.)	MISC.CRIMES	FR.
HUBERT	194300	M	15	Rottfhr., driver, SD, Heerenveen (Neth.) 15.4.45	TORTURE	NETH.
KEYL, Joseph	193652	M	2.11.08	SS-Rottfhr., SD Gent, Aussenstelle der Sipo, Leeuwarden (Neth.) 13.9.44-14.4.45	MURDER	NETH.
KREGERSMAN	261916			See Consolidated List Part II - Appendix 'A'		
LAUBAISE, Leonie	252381	F		BdF, BDS France, SD-Kmdo.z.b.V. 7 "Pullmer", Cirey (Fr.) 44	WITNESS	U.K.
LAUWAERT, Florimond	193656	M	11.4.86	SS-Mann, foreign post of Sipo and SD, Gent, Leeuwarden (Neth.) 13.9.44-14.4.45	MURDER	NETH.
LEUTENS, Joseph	67575	M	28	Member, Organ.Todt, Boulogne sur Mer (Fr.) 1944	MURDER	FR.
MAENE, Albert	194446	M	17.12.21	SS-Mann, foreign post of Sipo and SD, Leeuwarden (Neth.) 13.9.44-14.4.45	MURDER	NETH.
OPDEBECK, Marcel (or OPDEBEECK)	193565	M	15.8.12	Cpl., SD, Sipo, Leeuwarden (Neth.)	MURDER	NETH.
OPDEBEECK, Marcel (see OPDEBECK)	193565					
PESKENS, Marcel	193567	M	19.1.21	Cpl., SD, Sipo, Leeuwarden (Neth.) 13.9.44-14.4.45	MURDER	NETH.

BELGIUM - BULGARIA

NAME	C.R.FILE NUMBER	SEX	DATE OF BIRTH	RANK	OCCUPATION UNIT PLACE AND DATE OF CRIME	REASON WANTED	WANTED BY
					BELGIUM. (Cont.)		
TURKSIN	104910	M	00		Lt.Col., SD Official, Abwehr, Bad Ems (Ger.)	MURDER	UNWCC
TYTECA, Maurice	195416	M	15. 8.93		Agent, SD, Loehne (Ger.) 9.44	MURDER	NETH.
VAN DEN DORPE, Alfred	223076	M	20. 9.19		SS-Mann, SD, Sipo, Assen (Neth.) 13.9.44-14.4.45	MURDER	NETH.
VAN HOVE, Karl Emil	140034	M	18		N.C.O., volunteer in German Army, Cleder (Fr.) 8.8.44	MURDER	FR.
VAN KOL	194101	M			Sturmmann, SD, Heerenveen, Crakstate Prison (Neth.) till 15.4.45	MURDER	NETH.
VAN LAERE, Firmin Gustaaf	193655	M	15. 3.23		SS-Mann, Aussendienststelle der Sipo und SD, Gent, Leeuwarden (Neth.) 13.9.44-14.4.45	MURDER	NETH.
VAN MARCKE	141076	M			Civilian, C.C. Natzweiler (Fr.)	MURDER	U.K.
VAN MEERSCHAUT	194543	M	25		SS-Mann, driver, SD, Heerenveen (Neth.) 15.4.45	TORTURE	NETH.
VAN MOL	194542	M			Rottfhr., SD, Heerenveen (Neth.) 2.1.-15.4.45	MURDER	NETH.
VAN WEINSBERG(H)EN, Walter (or WIJNSBERGHEN)	302011	M	23 - 25		SS-Mann, Guard, Einsatzkmdo.d. Sicherheitspolizei, Steenwijk (Neth.) 1.10.44	MURDER	NETH.
VERBESSELT, Julius	193647	M			SS-Mann, SD, Aussendienststelle der Sipo, Leeuwarden (Neth.) 13.9.44-14.4.45	MURDER	NETH.
VERWEE	194122	M			Rottfhr., SD, Heerenveen, Steenwijk (Neth.) till 15.4.45	MURDER	NETH.
WALTERS, Marcel	193518	M			SS-Mann, SD and Sipo, Leeuwarden (Neth.) 13.9.44-14.4.45	MURDER	NETH.
WIJNBERGEN	194847	M	25		SS-Mann, SD, Heerenveen (Neth.)	MURDER	NETH.
WIJNSBERGHEN (see WEINSBERG(H)EN VAN, Walter)	302011						
WILMET, Jose	193517	F			Guard, SD, Leeuwarden (Neth.) 13.9.44-14.4.45	MURDER	NETH.
WOLFF	194846	M			SS-Mann, SD, motorcycle-driver, Heerenveen (Neth.) 2.1. - 15.4.45	TORTURE	NETH.
					BULGARIA.		
ANEV	190715	M			Lt., Army Bulgarian, 7.Cavalry Squadron, (Yugo.) 42-43	MURDER	YUGO.
ANTANAS	190716	M			Pvt., Army Bulgarian, 27.Div., Blaca (Yugo.)	MURDER	YUGO.
ANTONOF, Lazaros	300164	M			Member of the Drama Secret Police, Drama Area (Grc.) 28. 9. - 20.10.41	MURDER	GRC.
APOSTOLOV, Aleksander	190717	M			Lt.Col., Commander, Frontier Detachment, Bulgarian Army Poljanico, Kriva, Reca, Vladicinttan (Yugo.) 2. 43	MURDER	YUGO.
ARNAUDOV, Anastas Mihajlov	190718	M			Sgt., Bulgarian Army, 27.Inf.Div., Prokoplje (Yugo.) 43 - 44	MURDER	YUGO.
ATANASOV	190719	M			Lt., Bulgarian Army, Artl.Unit No.5765, (Yugo.) 42 - 43	MURDER	YUGO.
ATHANASOV, Athanas	300167	M			Lawyer, Sidicrocastron, 15.10.41	BRUTALITY	GRC.
AVRAMOV, Boris	190720	M			Mayor, municipality of Jelasnica, Surdulica (Yugo.) 22. 3.43	MURDER	YUGO.
BAITCHEFF	300171	M			Lt., Police, Sidicrocastron, 5.43	MURDER	GRC.
BALABANOV	190721	M			Lt., Bulgarian Army, (Yugo.) 43 - 44	MURDER	YUGO.
BALKANSKI, Konstantin	190722	M			Chief of Police-Agents, Police, Vladicin (Yugo.) 43 - 44	MURDER	YUGO.
BANKOV, Djordje	190723	M			Mayor, Veliko Bobince (Yugo.) 8.43	TORTURE	YUGO.
BATZIAVANOV, Theodoros	300338	M			Governor of the Bulgarian Prefecture in Drama Area 28.9. - 20.10.41	MURDER	GRC.
BEKIAROF, Josef	300172	M			Lt.Col., Commander, 57.Bulgarian Army, head of the Bulgarian Army and Armed Civil Servants, Drama Area (Grc.) 28.9. - 20.10.41	MURDER	GRC.
BELEV, Aleksander	302150	M			Commissioner for Jewish Affairs at Sofia (Bulg.) 41 - 12.3.43	MISC.CRIMES	YUGO.
BELIANOF, Sevas	300173	M			Policeman, Bulgarian Police, Drama Area (Grc.) 28.9. - 20.10.41	MURDER	GRC.
BEVELTSOF, Christos	300178	M			Officer, Bulgarian Army of Drama Area (Grc.) 28.9. - 20.10.41	MURDER	GRC.
BINGEVSKI, Bonce	190724	M			Agent, Police, Vladicin Han (Yugo.)	MURDER	YUGO.
BJORDJE	190725	M			Cpl., Bulgarian Army, Inf.Rgt., Leskovac (Yugo.) 42 -43	MURDER	YUGO.
BOGDANOV	190727	M			Lt.Gen., Bulgarian Army, Commander of 7.Inf.Div. of "Rila" (Yugo.) 7.42 - 3.43	MURDER	YUGO.
BOGDANOV, Asen	190726	M			District-Chief of Police, Bulgarian Police, Skoplje (Yugo.) 1943	MISC.CRIMES	YUGO.
BOJADZIJEV	190728	M			Lt., Bulgarian Army, 7.Cavalry Squadron, Veliki Plana (Yugo.) 42 - 43	MURDER	YUGO.
BOLUCEV, Zarco	190729	M			Agent, Police, Repiste and Predejan, District of Vladicin Han (Yugo.) 22.2. - 23.3.43	MURDER	YUGO.
BOTSEV, Bonef	305351	M			Capt., engineering, corps transport, Sidirocastron (Grc.) 1941	MURDER	GRC.
BOTSVAROF, Pervan (or PETSVAROF)	305224	M			Major, Engineer, Ferdinand-Bulgaria, Drama Area (Grc.) 28. 9. - 20.10.41	MURDER	GRC.
BOYIAN, Angelef	305002	M			Lt., Commander of a Coy. at Psychico Serres, 43 - 44	MURDER	GRC.
BOZILOV	190730	M			Lt., Commander of Police Unit attached to 27.Inf.Div., Prokuplje (Yugo.) 43 - 44	MURDER	YUGO.
CAKAROV, Peter	190731	M			Deputy-Director, District-Police, Vranje, Vladicin Han (Yugo.) 43 - 44	MURDER	YUGO.
CANCEV, Georgie	190756	M			Lt., Bulgarian Army, 27.Inf.Div., 67.Rgt., Blaca Serbia (Yugo.) 43 - 44	MURDER	YUGO.

BULGARIA

NAME	C.R.FILE NUMBER	SEX	DATE OF BIRTH	RANK	OCCUPATION	UNIT	PLACE AND DATE OF CRIME	REASON WANTED	WANTED BY
							BULGARIA. (Cont.)		
CANEV, Ilija	190732	M					Chief of Police, Bulgarian Army, 27 Inf.Div., (Yugo.) 43-44	MURDER	YUGO.
CANKOV, Hristo	190733	M					Mayor, occupied territories, Ciradesnica, Pirot (Yugo.) 42-43	MISC.CRIMES	YUGO.
CENEV, N.	190734	M					Director, Police, Babusnica, Pirot district (Yugo.) 41-44	MURDER	YUGO.
CENKOV, Mirko	190735	M					Deputy director of district Police, Vranje, Vladicin Han (Yugo.) 43-44	MURDER	YUGO.
CENOV, Ivan	190736	M					Chief of Police, Vladicin Han (Yugo.) 43-44	MURDER	YUGO.
CERKEZOV	190737	M					Lt., Bulgarian Army, 1 Coy., 122 Bn., Litni Potok (Yugo.) 43-44	MURDER	YUGO.
CHRISTEF, Christos	300206	M					Lt.Col., head, Military Command. Drama, head of section of the Bulgarian Army and Armed Civil Servants, Drama (Grc.) 28.9.-20.10.41	MURDER	GRC.
CHRISTEF, Kyrillos	300207	M					Sgt.-Maj., Bulgarian Army, Drama Area (Grc.) 28.9.-20.10.41	MURDER	GRC.
CIBROV, Boris	190738	M					Agent, Police Predejan, Vladicin Han (Yugo.) 22.2.43-23.4.43	MURDER	YUGO.
CONCEV, N.	190761	M					Asst. of Police director, Police, Pirot (Yugo.) 42-44	MURDER	YUGO.
CONEV or KONEV	189970	M					Agent, Police, Pirot (Yugo.)	MISC.CRIMES	YUGO.
CONEV, Cono	190740	M					Cmdt., Bulgarian Army, 25 Inf.Regt., 2 Bn., Modra Stena (Yugo.) 41-43	MURDER	YUGO.
CVETAN	190741	M					Pvt., Bulgarian Army, H.Q. of Frontier Guard, Sinjac-Pirot (Yugo.) 20.2.44	MURDER	YUGO.
DAKO see DAKOV	190742								
DAKOV, Marinov or DAKO	190742	M					Capt., Bulgarian Army, 52 Inf.Regt., Vranje (Yugo.) 5.43	TORTURE	YUGO.
DANIEF, Christos	300215	M					Member of the Secret Police, Drama Area (Grc.) 28.9.-20.10.41	MURDER	GRC.
DANIEF, Stefanos	300214	M					Employee, railway from Tsirpan (Bul.), Drama Area (Grc.) 28.9.-20.10.41	MURDER	GRC.
DASKALOV, Assen, Anquelof	300217	M					Bulgarian Sgt., serving in Serres, 10.41	MURDER	GRC.
DASKALOV, Nikola	190743	M					Sgt., Bulgarian Army, Momci-Lovgrad (Bul.) 2.44	TORTURE	YUGO.
DATSEF, Alexandros	300218	M					Lt., Bulgarian Army, Drama Area (Grc.) 28.9.-20.10.41	MURDER	GRC.
DAVIKOFF, Stephen	305013	M					Official, Achladikis-Kavalla district. 6.43	MISC.CRIMES	GRC.
DECEV see DECKO	190744								
DECKO, Ivanow or DECEV	190744	M					Lt., Army, Gujilane Serb. (Yugo.) 1.-2.43	MURDER	YUGO.
DELCEV, Nedeljko	190745	M					Cmdt., Int.Camp Plovdiv (Bul.)	TORTURE	YUGO.
DEMETRIEF, Jovtzief	300222	M					Lt., Bulgarian Army, Xylagani-Rodopi, 9.4.44	MURDER	GRC.
DENKOV, Kira	190746	M					Deputy Mayor, Jovac, Vladicin Han (Yugo.) 43-44	MURDER	YUGO.
DENTCHEF, Alexis	300223	M					Bulgarian Major, commanding officer of the Gendarmerie at Serres, 1944	MURDER	GRC.
DIMITROF	300229	M					Major in the Bulgarian Police Force, Drama Area (Grc.) 28.9.-10.41	MURDER	GRC.
DIMITROV, Kristiv, Kresimir	190747	M					Cpl., Bulgarian Army, garrison of Vlase, village in district of Vranje (Yugo.) 7.44	MURDER	YUGO.
DIMITROV, Milko, Stanojev	190748	M					Official, Police, Vladicin Han, (Yugo.) 43-44	MURDER	YUGO.
DIMOF	300230	M					Member of the Secret Police, Drama Area (Grc.) 28.9.-20.10.41	MURDER	GRC.
DJORDJEN (First name)	191180	M					Official, Police at Vladicin Han (Yugo.) 43-44	MURDER	YUGO.
DJOREV, Vlajko or Ilijev	190749	M					Official, Police Stublo, Vladicin Han (Yugo.) 41-44	MURDER	YUGO.
DJUMURDJIJEV, Georgijev, Dimitrije	190750	M					Secretary, occupied territories, Pirot (Yugo.) 41-43	TORTURE	YUGO.
DOITSINOV, Stoyan, Myref	300234	M					Prefect at Serres, Skopoi and Lefkon near Serres, 41-42	MURDER	GRC.
DRAGANOV	190751	M					Lt., Bulgarian Army, 7 Cavalry Squadron, (Yugo.) 42-43	MURDER	YUGO.
DRAGUITS, Raiko	300237	M					Bulgarian soldier, Xylagani-Rodopi, 9.4.44	MURDER	GRC.
DRANKEF	300238	M					Major, Bulgarian Army, head of the section of the Bulgarian Army and of Armed Civil Servants, Drama Area (Grc.):28.8.-20.10.41	MURDER	GRC.
DUSKOV, Peter	190752	M					Head, Police, Vladicin Han (Yugo.) 43-44	MURDER	YUGO.
ECHMETIKOV, George	300240	M					Gendarm, Gendarmerie, Sidiroccastron, 5.41	PILLAGE	GRC.
EUSTAT, Nicholas	300247	M					Head of the Sidiroccastron district, 1941	BRUTALITY	GRC.
EVROP	190753	M					Sgt., Bulgarian Army, district of Pirot, village Sinjac (Yugo.) 20.2.44	MURDER	YUGO.
FILIPOV	190754	M					Lt., Bulgarian Army, Gornji, Stupanj, district of Zupa (Yugo.) 2.-6.8.43	TORTURE	YUGO.
FILIPPOF, Kirof, Christof	300252	M					Bulgarian officer of the Kavalla Security, Kavalla, 9.41-9.43	MISC.CRIMES	GRC.
FIOFF	148395	M					Civilian, C.C. Mauthausen (Aust.) 41-45	MURDER	U.S.
GAIEF, Anguelos	350137	M					Bulgarian Major, commanding officer of the 42 Regt., Mikri Deria, Thrace (Grc.) 1941	MURDER	GRC.
GAIEV	190755	M					Pvt., Bulgarian Army, (Yugo.) 42-43	MURDER	YUGO.
GEITSCH, Edward, Georg	145387	M	27.7.08				Businessman, civilian	MISC.CRIMES	U.S.
GEORGI	190757	M					Pvt., Bulgarian Army, H.Q. of Frontier Guard, village of Sinjac, Pirot (Yugo.) 20.2.44	MURDER	YUGO.
GEORGIEF, Georgios	305143	M					Prefect, Bulgarian Prefecture in Drama (Grc.) 28.9.-20.10.41	MURDER	GRC.
GEORGIEV, Marin, Vasilov	190758	M					Agent, Police Prekodolac, Vladicin Han (Yugo.) 43-44	MURDER	YUGO.
GIANNEF, Petko, Ch.	305144	M					Member, Secret Police, Drama Area (Grc.) 28.9.-20.10.41	MURDER	GRC.
GLIGORCA, N.	190759	M					Policeman, Police, Surdulica (Yugo.) 2.8.42	MURDER	YUGO.
GLIGOROV, Stojan	190760	M					Sgt., Police, Vladicin Han (Yugo.) 43-44	MURDER	YUGO.
GONEV, Anastas	190762	M					Civil Servant, occupied territories, Jelasnica, Surdulica district, (Yugo.) 21.10.43	MURDER	YUGO.
GORCILOV, Aleksandar	190763	M					High official, commander of Lowna Druzina (Yugo.) 43-44	MURDER	YUGO.
GOSTOURKOF, Demetrios	305147	M					Bulgarian commanding officer, Serres Security, Serres (Grc.) 9.41-8.42	MURDER	GRC.
GRAF	190764	M					Pvt., Agent, Special Police from Sofia, 27 Inf.Div. at Prokuplje, Prokuplje (Yugo.) 43-44	MURDER	YUGO.
GROUGEROF, Matsef	305157	M					Member, Secret Agent, Bulgarian Security of Drama (Grc.) 28.9.-20.10.41	MURDER	GRC.
GUENOW, Iwan	305160	M					Member, leader, Secret Police, merchant at Comitadji, Drama (Grc.) 28.9.-20.10.41	MURDER	GRC.
GUGOV, Velicko	190765	M					Mayor, occupied territories, Gnjilan, district of Pirot (Yugo.) 41-43	TORTURE	YUGO.
HADJIJSKI	190766	M					Lt.Col., Bulgarian Army, cmdr. of garrison of Surdulica Felasrica (Yugo.) 21.10.43	MURDER	YUGO.
HADZI-JLIJEV, Boja	189967	M					Lt., Army-Reserve, Goro, Selo, Trsteno (Yugo.)	MURDER	YUGO.
HALITAROF, Groum	305163	M					Municipal servant of Drama (Grc.) 28.9.-20.10.41	MURDER	GRC.
HANDZIEV	190767	M					Col., Bulgarian Army, deputy commander of 7 Inf.Div. of "Rila", Seskovac (Yugo.) 42-43	MURDER	YUGO.

BULGARIA

NAME	C.R.FILE NUMBER	SEX	DATE OF BIRTH	RANK OCCUPATION UNIT PLACE AND DATE OF CRIME	REASON WANTED	WANTED BY
				BULGARIA. (Cont.)		
HARALAMPIEV, Ilatan	190768	M		Customs officer, Zollgrenzschutzpolizei, Vladicin Han district (Yugo.) 43-44	MURDER	YUGO.
HRISTOV, Slavov, Dono	190769	M		Pvt., Bulgarian Army, stationed at Predejan, Frontier-Coy., Repiste and Predejan (Yugo.) 22.2.43-23.3.43	MURDER	YUGO.
ILEV, Cvetay, Ivanov	190770	M		Deputy Mayor, occupied territories, Stublo, Vladicin Han (Yugo.) 43-44	MURDER	YUGO.
ILIEF, Ilias	305194	M		Secret Agent, Bulgarian Security, Drama Area (Grc.) 28.9.-20.10.41	MURDER	GRC.
ILIJA	190771	M		Pvt., Bulgarian Army, H.Q. of Frontier Guard, Sinjac Pirot (Yugo.) 20.2.44	MURDER	YUGO.
ILIJEV see DJOREV	190749					
ILIJEVSKI, Krsta, Vasov	190772	M		Official, Police at Stublo, Vladicin Han (Yugo.) 43-44	MURDER	YUGO.
ISMAILOV, Saban	190773	M		Pvt., Bulgarian Army, 52 Inf.Regt., Vranje, Jelasnica, Surdulica Serb. (Yugo.) 22.3.43	MURDER	YUGO.
IVAN, Hristo see IVANOV	190774					
IVANOF, Ivan	305197	M		Member, Bulgaria Security, Drama Area (Grc.) 28.9.-20.10.41	MISC.CRIMES	GRC.
IVANOV, Hristo or IVAN	190774	M		Lt., Bulgarian Army, 6-2 Frontier Sector at Vitnia, Gnjilane (Yugo.) 1.-2.43	MURDER	YUGO.
IVANOV, Vasil, Anastasov	190775	M		Lt., 52 Inf.Regt. at frontier garrison, Vlase, district of Vrenje (Yugo.) 7.44	MURDER	YUGO.
JAMADJIJEV	190776	M		N.C.O., Bulgarian Army, 27 Inf.Div., Prokuplje (Yugo.) 43-44	MURDER	YUGO.
JANKOV, Jordan, Pop	190777	M		Major, Bulgarian Army, cmdt. Frontier Sector "Zegra", Gnjilane Serb. (Yugo.) 1.-2.43	MURDER	YUGO.
JASMAKOV, Stanimir	190778	M		Lt., Bulgarian Army, cmdt. of Frontier Guard, Sector of Pirot, Pirot Serb. (Yugo.) 20.2.44	MURDER	YUGO.
JELENSKI, Kolev, Konstantin	190779	M		Lt., Bulgarian Army, 52 Regt., Vranje, Jelasnica, Surdulica (Yugo.) 22.3.43	MURDER	YUGO.
JORDAN	190780	M		Pvt., guard, Bulgarian Army, H.Q. of Frontier Guard at Pirot, Sinjac, district of Pirot (Yugo.) 20.2.44	MURDER	YUGO.
KANEV, Kanca	190781	M		Lt., Bulgarian Army, commander of Unit in 27 Inf.Div., Prokuplje (Yugo.) 43-44	MURDER	YUGO.
KAROLIJEV	190782	M		Lt.Col., Bulgarian Army, commander of 52 Inf.Regt. at Vranje, Vlase, Jelasnica, Surdulica (Yugo.) 22.3.43	MURDER	YUGO.
KAVAIDJIEF, Demetrios or Kambouris	300039	M		Member of the Bulgarian Ochrana Security Service, Kavalla, 43-44	TORTURE	GRC.
KAZAKOF, Christos	300261	M		Second in command of the Bulgarian Security in Drama (Grc.) 28.9-20.10.41	MURDER	GRC.
KEREMITSKI, Cena, Petrov	190783	M		Policeman, Police at Babusnica and surronding villages (Yugo.) 41-44	MURDER	YUGO.
KIMOURJIEF, Jordan	300263	M		Guard, Rural Police at Makri-Evros, 7.45	TORTURE	GRC.
KISELICKI, Kiril	190784	M		Col., Bulgarian Army, chief of staff of 27 Inf.Div., Serb. (Yugo.)	MURDER	YUGO.
KJOSTEBEKOV, P.	191022	M		Director, State Security of Sofia, Pirot (Yugo.) 4.42	MISC.CRIMES	YUGO.
KOCEV	190785	M		High Police official, Police, village of Zavidince, Pirot (Yugo.) 41-43	TORTURE	YUGO.
KONEV see CONEV	189970					
KONSTANTINOV	189966	M		Major, Bulgarian Army, public official, Pirot (Yugo.)	MISC.CRIMES	YUGO.
KOSMANOF, Lazaros	300271	M		Member of the Secret Police, Drama Area (Grc.) 28.9.-20.10.41	MURDER	GRC.
KOSTOV	190786	M		Commander, Bulgarian Army, Unit of 27 Inf.Div., Prokuplje (Yugo.) 43-44	MURDER	YUGO.
KOSTOV, Ilija see KRESTEV	190788					
KOTSEV, Slesco, Kosla	300272	M		Lt., commanding officer of the garrison of Soutari Serres, 9.43-44	MURDER	GRC.
KOURTOF	300273	M		Lt., Bulgarian serving in Mikri, Deria, Thrace, 5.42-9.43	MISC.CRIMES	GRC.
KOZAROV, Hristo	190787	M		Gen.Maj., Bulgarian Army, commander of 27 Inf.Div., Prokuplje (Yugo.) 43-44	MURDER	YUGO.
KRESTEV, Ilija or KOSTOV	190788	M		Head, Police, Vitina, Gnjilane (Yugo.) 1.-2.43	MURDER	YUGO.
KYROF	300286	M		Lt., Bulgarian served in the Polygyro Area, Taxiarchis-Polygyros 7.-8.44	MURDER	GRC.
LALCEV, Stephan	190789	M		Bulgarian Army, 27 Inf.Div., Prokuplje (Yugo.) 1943 and 1944	MURDER	YUGO.
LEBEDOV, Ivan	190790	M		Tax collector, civilian, Belisevo, Vlodicin Han (Yugo.) 43-44	MURDER	YUGO.
LEFTHEROF see MALINOF	300310					
LICEV	190791	M		Capt., Bulgarian Army, commander of 1 Coy., 122 Bn., Zitni Potok (Yugo.) 43-44	MURDER	YUGO.
LJUBOV	190792	M		Capt., Bulgarian Army, Zupa (Yugo.) 2.-6.8.43	TORTURE	YUGO.
MADJARSKI	190793	M		Lt., Bulgarian Army, 7 Cavalry Squadron, Serb. (Yugo.) 42-43	MURDER	YUGO.
MAGIELANSKI, Stepan	300307	M		Chief of the Security, Drama Area (Grc.) 28.9.-20.10.41	MURDER	GRC.
MAKEDONAKI, Sotirios	300309	M		Member of the Secret Police, Sidirokastron, 5-43	MURDER	GRC.
MALINOF, Sloyan or LEFTHEROF	300310	M		Servant, municipal of Drama (Grc.) 28.9.-20.10.41	MURDER	GRC.
MANASIJEV, Cira	190794	M		Official, Occupat. administration of Krusevac (Yugo.) 1942	TORTURE	YUGO.
MANEV	190796	M		Head, Crim. Police, Skoplje, Gnjilane (Yugo.) 1.-2.43	MURDER	YUGO.
MANEV	190797	M		Lt., Bulgarian Army, 27 Div. at Blaca (Yugo.) 15.-30.6.44	MURDER	YUGO.
MANEV, Alexander	190795	M		Col., Bulgarian Army, Kdo. of garrison at Prokuplje (Yugo.) 42-43	MURDER	YUGO.
MANOUTZIEF, Dimos	300313	M		Employee, railway from Bulgaria, Drama Area (Grc.) 28.9.-20.10.41	MURDER	GRC.
MARINOF, Ivan	305461	M		Lt.Gen., commanding officer, 15 Bulgarian Div. in Monastir, Western, Macedonia (Grc.) 43-44	MURDER	GRC.
MARINOF, Marinos	300315	M		Policeman, Bulgarian in Drama, Drama Area (Grc.) 28.9.-20.10.41	MURDER	GRC.
MARINOF, Petko	300316	M		Lt., Bulgarian in charge of Security at Pravala, Serres Area, 41-42	MURDER	GRC.
MARINOV	190798	M		Lt., Bulgarian Army, 27 Div. at Blaca (Yugo.) 15.-30.6.44	MURDER	YUGO.
MARINOV	190799	M		Agent, Police, Vladicin Han (Yugo.) 43-44	MURDER	YUGO.
MARINOV, Nina, Pelov	190800	M		State Forester, Belisevo, district of Vladicin Han (Yugo.) 43-44	MURDER	YUGO.
MARKOV	190802	M		Head, Police at Kacanick, Gnjilane (Yugo.) 1.-2.43	MURDER	YUGO.
MARKOV, Dimitrije	190801	M		Head, Bulgarian Police, Pirot (Yugo.) 43-44	MURDER	YUGO.
MASIAROF	300318	M		Chief of the second Bulgarian Police sector in Drama (Grc.) 28.9.-20.10.41	MURDER	GRC.
MAXIMOF	300321	M		Member of the Drama Secret Police, Drama Area (Grc.) 28.9.-20.10.41	MURDER	GRC.
MIHAILOF, Mihos	300329	M		Col., Governor of the Bulgarian Infantry, Military of Drama, Drama Area (Grc.) 28.9.-20.10.41	MURDER	GRC.

BULGARIA

BULGARIA. (Cont.)

NAME	C.R.FILE NUMBER	SEX	DATE OF BIRTH	RANK OCCUPATION UNIT PLACE AND DATE OF CRIME	REASON WANTED	WANTED BY
MIHOV, Stojan	190803	M		Inspector, Service of confiscation of food stuffs, occupied territories, Gnjilane (Yugo.) 1.-2.43	MURDER	YUGO.
MILANOV, Kiril, Ivanov	190804	M		Civil servant, tax collector, occupied territories, Kalane, Pirot (Yugo.) 1943	MURDER	YUGO.
MINEV, Anastas see NOJEV	190812					
MINTSEF, Ivan see PENTSEF	300332					
MIRCEV	190805	M		Deputy chief, Police of Kacanik, Gnjilane (Yugo.) 1.-2.43	MURDER	YUGO.
MITKOF	300333	M		Secret Agent of the Bulgarian Security in Drama (Grc.) 28.9.-20.10.41	MURDER	GRC.
MITOV, Boris	190806	M		Customs officer, Zollgrenzschutz, Osmakovo (Yugo.) 43-44	MURDER	YUGO.
MOUNTHOF, Sfetko	300337	M		Member of the Drama Secret Police, Drama Area (Grc.) 28.9.-20.10.41	MURDER	GRC.
MOUTAPICHIEV, Demetrios	305077	M		Bulgarian Gendarm from Philippopolis (Bul.), Old Kavalla (Grc.) 7.6.44	MURDER	GRC.
MOUTZVANOF, Tontor	300338	M		Governor of the Bulgarian prefecture in Drama (Grc.) 28.9.-20.10.41	MURDER	GRC.
MYREV, Nicolov, Demetrius	300346	M		Prefect of Serres, North Souli and Ag. Pnevma, 10.3.44	MURDER	GRC.
NEDELJKOV	190813	M		Capt., Bulgarian Army, Lovna Pruzina Serb. (Yugo.) 43-44	MURDER	YUGO.
NENOF, Neiko	300349	M		Major (Bulgarian), Xylagani Rodopi, 9.4.44	MURDER	GRC.
NEVITZANOV, Demetrios	305206	M		Lt.Col., Gendarmerie (Bulgarian), Serres (Grc.) 5.-8.41	PILLAGE	GRC.
NIKIFOROV	190807	M		Lt., Bulgarian Army, 7 Cavalry Squadron, (Yugo.) 42-43	MURDER	YUGO.
NIKOLOV	190808	M		Gen.Lt., commander of 1 Bulgarian corps, (Yugo.) 42-43	MURDER	YUGO.
NIKOLOV, Georgi	190809	M		Lt., Bulgarian Army, 7 Cavalry Squadron, (Yugo.) 42-43	MURDER	YUGO.
NIKOLOV, Nikola-Krstev	190810	M		Secret Agent, Bulgarian Gestapo, teacher, Vladicin Han (Yugo.) 43-44	MURDER	YUGO.
NIKOLOV, Zodor	190811	M		Customs officer, Zollgrenzschutzpolizei, Osmakovo (Yugo.) 43-44	MURDER	YUGO.
NOJEV, Anastas or MINEV	190812	M		Lt., Bulgarian Army, Mijajlovac (Yugo.) 15.12.42	MURDER	YUGO.
OPRIKOV, Petko	190814	M		Deputy chief, Bulgarian Police, Vladicin Han (Yugo.) 43-44	MURDER	YUGO.
PANEV see PANOV	190819					
PANAJOTOV, Risan	190815	M		Member, Mounted Police, Pirot (Yugo.) 7.43	TORTURE	YUGO.
PANEV, Andonov	190816	M		Policeman, Vladicin Han (Yugo.) 42-44	MURDER	YUGO.
PANEV, Milan, Nikolov	190817	M		Mayor, Paklestice, Velika-Luka, Pirot (Yugo.) between 1941 and 1943	TORTURE	YUGO.
PANEV, Peter	189969	M		Col., Bulgarian Army, Kriva Reka (Yugo.)	MURDER	YUGO.
PANEV, Vasil	190818	M		Deputy Mayor, municipality of Jelasnica, Surdulica (Yugo.) 22.3.43	MURDER	YUGO.
PANOV or PANEV,T.H. or T.N.	190819	M		Chief of Security, Gestapo, Skolplje (Yugo.) 43-44	MURDER	YUGO.
PANTSEF	305215	M		Lt., Bulgarian Army, Xylagani-Rodopi (Grc.) 9.4.44	MURDER	GRC.
PAPAEVANGELOF, George, Popof	305097	M		Tax collector, Bulgarian Government, Kavalla (Grc.) 8.42	PILLAGE	GRC.
PARKDJIJEV, Kristo	189972	M		Local Commissioner, Jewish Affairs, Pirot (Yugo.)	MISC.CRIMES	YUGO.
PAUNOV, Georgi	190820	M		Head, District Police at Vranje, Vladicin Han (Yugo.) 43-44	MURDER	YUGO.
PAVLOF, Georgios	305218	M		Member, Security, Drama Area (Grc.) 28.9.-20.10.41	MURDER	GRC.
PEITSEF, Dimitrios	305219	M		Major, Police, Drama Area (Grc.) 28.9.-20.10.41	MURDER	GRC.
PENEF, Panayotis	305101	M		Policeman, Bulgarian, Kavalla, 19.11.43	TORTURE	GRC.
PENTSEF, Ivan or MINTSEF	300332	M		Guard, Bulgarian Rural Police, Hydromili-Kavalla, 1942	PILLAGE	GRC.
PETKOF, Peter	305221	M		Secret Agent, Security, Drama Area (Grc.) 28.9.-20.10.41	MURDER	GRC.
PETKOV	189962	M		Chief, Police, Pirot (Yugo.)	TORTURE	YUGO.
PETKOV, Angel	190821	M		Sgt., Bulgarian Army, Pirot (Yugo.) 11.5.41	MURDER	YUGO.
PETKOV, G.	191023	M		Director, Bulgarian Police, Pirot (Yugo.) 4.42	MISC.CRIMES	YUGO.
PETKOV, Peter	305222	M		Servant, civilian, Sidirocastron Macedonia, 5.41	PILLAGE	GRC.
PETKOV, Tryfon	305223	M		Officer, Police of Chryssopolis-Kavalla (Grc.) 4.43	MURDER	GRC.
PETROF, Elie	305104	M		Sgt., serving at Eninos, Melivia-Xanthi, 9.42	PILLAGE	GRC.
PETROV	190824	M		Major, Bulgarian Army, Intelligence officer of 27 Inf.Div., Prokuplje (Yugo.) 43-44	MURDER	YUGO.
PETROV, Andreja	190822	M		Sgt., Bulgarian Army, Gnjilane (Yugo.) 1.-2.43	MURDER	YUGO.
PETROV, Hristo	191141	M		County director, Sofia's Police Directorate, Pirot (Yugo.) 4.42	MISC.CRIMES	YUGO.
PETROV, I.Simeun	190823	M		Forester, village of Krupac near Nis, Pirot (Yugo.) 1943	TORTURE	YUGO.
PETROV, Nikolaj	190825	M		Capt., Bulgarian Army, commander of 6 Machine-Gun-Coy.,117 Inf.Div., (Yugo.) 42-44	MURDER	YUGO.
PETRUNOV, Ivan	190826	M		Forester, Pirot (Yugo.) 41-43	MURDER	YUGO.
PETRUNOV, Nenko	190827	M		Inspector, Police, Vranje, Vladicin Han (Yugo.) 43-44	MURDER	YUGO.
PETSVAROF see BOTSVAROF	305224					
PISKIOROF	305227	M		Major, Bulgarian, Xylagani-Rodopi (Grc.) 9.4.44	MURDER	GRC.
POBORNIKOV, Fordor	190828	M		Lt., Bulgarian Army, Gnjilane (Yugo.) 1.-2.43	MURDER	YUGO.
POPOF, Ivan	305230	M		Opl. 1 Police Sector of Drama (Grc.) 28.9.-20.10.41	MURDER	GRC.
POPOF, Joseph	305231	M		Deputy Major, inspector, Jewish community of Kavalla (Grc.) 42-43	MISC.CRIMES	GRC.
POPOF, Traiko	305232	M		Secret Agent, Security, Drama Area (Grc.) 28.9.-20.10.41	MURDER	GRC.
POPOV	190831	M		Lt., Bulgarian Army, 25 Inf.Regt., 3.Coy., 2 Bn., Modra Stena, district of Pirot (Yugo.) 41-43	MURDER	YUGO.
POPOV, Georgi, Lazarov	190829	M		Deputy Mayor, Prekodolac, Zitoradje, Poloma, Vladicin Han (Yugo.) 43-44	MURDER	YUGO.
POPOV, Ivan	190830	M		Col., Bulgarian Army, commander of a Div. at Vranje, Jelasnica, Vlase (Yugo.) 21.10.43	MURDER	YUGO.
PROCOPIEF, Valento	305235	M		Member, Bulgarian Security at Kavalla (Grc.) 12.42	PILLAGE	GRC.
RACEV, Raco	189958	M		Cmdt., Police, Pirot (Yugo.)	TORTURE	YUGO.
RADOMIRSKI, Botja	190832	M		Lt., Bulgarian Army, 52 Inf.Regt., frontier garrison at Vlase, district of Veranje, 7.44	MURDER	YUGO.
RADOMIRSKI, Georgije	190833	M		Deputy Mayor, occupied territories, village of Vojnegovac, district of Pirot (Yugo.) 6.44	TORTURE	YUGO.
RELEV, Alexander	189971	M		Dr., Commission for Jewish Affairs, Sofia (Bul.)	MISC.CRIMES	YUGO.
RIZOV, Cyril	305247	M		Lt.Col., district Porria-Serres (Grc.) 10.41	MURDER	GRC.
ROUNTZOFF, George	305254	M		Gendarm, Sidirocastron Macedonia, 5.41	PILLAGE	GRC.
RUSEV	190834	M		Lt., Bulgarian Army, 7 Cavalry Squadron, (Yugo.) 42-43	MURDER	YUGO.
SAPUNDZIEV	190835	M		Col., Bulgarian Army, commander of 17 Inf.Div., Prokuplje (Yugo.) 42-43	MURDER	YUGO.
SAVOV	190836	M		Capt., Bulgarian Army, commander of Artillery at Prokuplje (Yugo.) 43-44	MURDER	YUGO.
SEMERTZIEV	305279	M		Lt., Sidirocastron Macedonia, 5.41	PILLAGE	GRC.
SEMO	190837	M		Sgt., Bulgarian Army, village of Sinjac, Pirot (Yugo.) 20.9.44	MURDER	YUGO.
SERAFOV, Penco	190838	M		Lt.Col., Inf.Div., commander of Artillery, Unit No.5765 of 1779, Serb. (Yugo.) 42-43	MURDER	YUGO.

BULGARIA

NAME	C.R.FILE NUMBER	SEX	DATE OF BIRTH	RANK	OCCUPATION	UNIT	PLACE AND DATE OF CRIME	REASON WANTED	WANTED BY

BULGARIA. (Cont.)

NAME	C.R.FILE NUMBER	SEX	PARTICULARS	REASON WANTED	WANTED BY
SEVAROF, Petros	305281	M	Financial inspector, Drama Area (Grc.) 28.9.-20.10.41	MURDER	GRC.
SILESAROV, Venca	190839	M	Agent, Bulgarian Army, Bulgarian Police, 27 Inf.Div., (Yugo.) 43-44	MURDER	YUGO.
SIMEONOFF	305282	M	Major, Sidirocastron Macedonia, 1941	MURDER	GRC.
SINOKAPOVITS, Joannis	305283	M	Member, Secret Police, Drama Area (Grc.) 28.9.-20.10.41	MURDER	GRC.
SIPSEV, Tihomir	305284	M	Deputy-in-commandant, Security at Drama (Grc.) 28.9.-20.10.41	MURDER	GRC.
SIRAKOV	305285	M	General, Bulgarian Army, commanding officer of the "Drama"-Div., Drama Area (Grc.) 28.9.-20.10.41	MURDER	GRC.
SISKOV, St.	191142	M	Director, Gestapo (Bulgarian), Sofia, Pirot (Bul., Yugo.)	MISC.CRIMES	YUGO.
SLATANOF, Vangel	305293	M	Lt.Col., officer, Abdira-Garnison Xanthi 3 Bn., 58 Bulgarian Regt., Abdira, Xanthi (Grc.) 1944	MURDER	GRC.
SLAVOV	190841	M	Capt., Bulgarian Army, 5 Bul. Cavalry Regt., Strelce (Yugo.) 4.43	RAPE	YUGO.
SLAVOV or SLAVTSO	305294	M	Officer, Security at Serres (Grc.) 41-44	MURDER	GRC.
SLAVOV, Slave	190842	M	Agent, Bulgarian Police, Predejan, district of Vladicin Han (Yugo.) 22.2.-23.4.43	MURDER	YUGO.
SLAVOV, Vasil	190843	M	Agent, Bulgarian Army, staff, 27 Inf.Div., Prokuplje (Yugo.) 43-44	MURDER	YUGO.
SLAVTSO see SLAVOV	305294				
SOLEF, Gregory	300143	M	Lt., Bulgarian, serving in Provata (Serres) (Grc.) 1941	MURDER	GRC.
SOTIROF, Georgios	305297	M	Major, Bulgarian Army, Drama Area (Grc.) 28.9.-20.10.41	MURDER	GRC.
SPASOV, Panta	190844	M	Deputy chief, Police, Vladicin Han (Yugo.) 43-44	MURDER	YUGO.
STAMENOV	190845	M	Deputy chief, Police official, Lt., Bulgarian Army, Pirot (Yugo.) 43-44	MURDER	YUGO.
STAMOV, Nikifor, Petrov	190846	M	Policeman, Bulgarian Police, Vladicin Han (Yugo.) 43-44	MURDER	YUGO.
STANGOFF, Nicholas or TSANGOFF	305332	M	Capt., Police, Sidirocastron Macedonia (Grc.) 1941	MURDER	GRC.
STANIMIROV, Zodor	190847	M	Capt., Bulgarian Army, commander of 7 Cavalry Squadron, Velika Plana (Yugo.) 42-43	MURDER	YUGO.
STANKOV	190848	M	Lt., Bulgarian Army, (Yugo.) 42-43	MURDER	YUGO.
STATHIEF, Stathis	305299	M	Member of the Drama Secret Police, Drama Area (Grc.) 28.9.-20.10.41	MURDER	GRC.
STILOV, Hrito, L	190849	M	Head of Police of Skoplje, district of Vladicin Han (Yugo.) 43-44	MURDER	YUGO.
STIPLIEF, Demetrios	305301	M	Mayor of Kavalla (Bul.) 9.42	MURDER	GRC.
STOIGKOV, Sergije	190850	M	Mayor, occupied territories, Osmakovo (Yugo.) 42-43	MURDER	YUGO.
STOJANOV, Aleksander	190851	M	Lt., Bulgarian Army, Vladicin Han (Yugo.) 22.2.43-23.3.43	MURDER	YUGO.
STOJANOV, Vasil	190852	M	Agent, Police, Vladicin Han (Yugo.) 43-44	MURDER	YUGO.
STOUYANOF, Georgief, Atanas	305305	M	Policeman, Bulgarian, Xylagani-Rodopi, 9.4.44	MURDER	GRC.
STOUYANOF, Yankof, Atanas	305306	M	Policeman, Bulgarian, Xylagani-Rodopi, 9.4.44	MURDER	GRC.
STRAHLINOF	305307	M	Capt., Bulgarian Army, Drama Area (Grc.) 28.9.-20.10.41	MURDER	GRC.
STRANSKI, Nikola	190853	M	Commander, Bulgarian Army, 2 Coy., 50 Regt., (Yugo.) 43-44	MURDER	YUGO.
TASKOV, Petar, Joucev	190854	M	Agent, Bulgarian Police, Vladicin Han (Yugo.) 43-44	MURDER	YUGO.
TCHEKOV, Stavros	305316	M	Employee, Sofia Propaganda Office in charge of Bulgarian Propaganda in district of Edessa-Florina-Kozani Macedonia (Bul.) 41-44	MISC.CRIMES	GRC.
TENTEF, Stargios	305318	M	Security Service, Chryssopolis-Kavalla (Grc.) 17.4.43	MURDER	GRC.
THEODOROFF	305320	M	Agriculturist, Sidirocastron E. Macedonia (Grc.) 1941	MURDER	GRC.
THEODOSIOS, Gerassimos	305321	M	Served in the town Polygyros, Taciarchis (Grc.) 7. and 8.44	MURDER	GRC.
TINTZEN, Peter	305325	M	Cpl., Gendarmerie, village of Orphanos Kavalla (Grc.) 41-44	MURDER	GRC.
TODOROV, Nikola	190855	M	Lt., Bulgarian Army, 7 Cavalry Squadron, Serb. (Yugo.) 42-43	MURDER	YUGO.
TOMOV, Ljuben	190856	M	Agent, Bulgarian Police, Vladicin Han (Yugo.) 43-44	MURDER	YUGO.
TONTOROF, Simeon	305327	M	Secret Agent, Secret Police at Drama (Grc.) 28.9.-20.10.41	MURDER	GRC.
TOSEV, Fodor	190857	M	Policeman, Police, Jelaslica Sur Dulica (Yugo.) 22.3.43	MURDER	YUGO.
TOTEV, Georgi, Cancer	190858	M	N.C.O., Bulgarian Army, 27 Inf.Div., Serb. (Yugo.) 43-44	MURDER	YUGO.
TOTOMANOV	190859	M	Lt., Bulgarian Army, Pirot (Yugo.) 43-44	MURDER	YUGO.
TSAKIROF, Baikosta	305329	M	Secret Agent, Bulgarian Security, Drama Area (Grc.) 28.9.-20.10.41	MURDER	GRC.
TSAKIROF, Constantinos	305330	M	Market inspector, Drama Area (Grc.) 28.9.-20.10.41	MURDER	GRC.
TSAKLAROV, Stephen	305331	M	Mayor, village of Orphanos near Kavalla (Grc.) 41-44	MURDER	GRC.
TSANGOFF, Nicholas see STANGOFF	305332				
TSENEF, Licoupen	305333	M	Member, Secret Police, Drama Area (Grc.) 28.9.-20.10.41	MURDER	GRC.
TSERNOSEMSKI, Boris	305334	M	President, Community of Sidirohorion Kavalla (Grc.) 1942	MURDER	GRC.
TZETZEF, Petrof	305335	M	Pvt., Bulgarian, Xylagani-Rodopi (Grc.) 9.4.44	MURDER	GRC.
VASAROV or VAZAROV	189957	M	Agent, Police, Pirot (Yugo.)	MISC.CRIMES	YUGO.
VASILJEV, Angel	190861	M	Pvt., Bulgarian Army, 27 Inf.Div., Prokuplje (Yugo.) 43-44	MURDER	YUGO.
VASILJEV, Zlate, Simeonov	190862	M	Pvt., Bulgarian Army, 27 Inf.Div., Prokuplje (Yugo.) 43-44	MURDER	YUGO.
VASSILIEF, Grecef, Christhof	305342	M	Major, Stavroupolis Xanthi (Grc.) 1944	INTERR.	GRC.
VAZAROV see VASAROV	189957				
VELKOV, Kiril, Marinov	190863	M	Agent, Bulgarian Police, Vladicin Han (Yugo.) 43-44	MURDER	YUGO.
VELKOV, Ljubomir	190864	M	Civilian, Pirot (Yugo.) 4.42	MISC.CRIMES	YUGO.
VLACHDV, George	305348	M	Officer, Military Police of Drama, Emmanuel Papa near Serres (Grc.) 11.41	MURDER	GRC.
WODENICAROV, Pansa	190865	M	Major, admin. of occupied territories, Vladicin Han (Yugo.) 43-44	MURDER	YUGO.
VON TENITSAROF, Boris	305317	M	Security officer, Bulgarian, Serres (Grc.) 4.-9.41	INTERR.	GRC.
VOTSEV, Vonef	305351	M	Capt., engineering corps (transport), Sidirocastron (Grc.) 1941	MURDER	GRC.
VOULTSIEF	305352	M	Member, Secret Police, Drama Area (Grc.) 28.9.-20.10.41	MURDER	GRC.
VRBANOV, Nikola	190860	M	Chief, Police, Vladicin Han (Yugo.) 43-44	MURDER	YUGO.
ZAHAROF, Grigorios	305388	M	Municipal servant, Nevrokopio (Bul.), Drama Area (Grc.) 28.9.-20.10.41	MISC.CRIMES	GRC.
ZEKOV	190866	M	Major, Sebane (Yugo.) 42-43	MURDER	YUGO.
ZELENGOROV	190867	M	Chief, Bulgarian Gestapo, Vladicin Han (Yugo.) 43-44	MURDER	YUGO.
ZELESKOV, Alexander	190868	M	Lt., Bulgarian Army, 25 Inf.Regt., Pirot (Yugo.) 6.44	MURDER	YUGO.
ZLATAROV, Kosta	190869	M	Officer, Bulgarian Army, Prokuplje (Yugo.) 43-44	MURDER	YUGO.

CZECHOSLOVAKIA - DENMARK - FRANCE   -52-

NAME	C.R.FILE NUMBER	SEX	DATE OF BIRTH	RANK OCCUPATION UNIT PLACE AND DATE OF CRIME	REASON WANTED	WANTED BY
				CZECHOSLOVAKIA.		
ARNOLD	23923	M		Sgt., Waffen-SS, Lyon, Annecy, St.Gervais (Fr.)	PILLAGE	FR.
BARSA	144619	M		C.C.Buchenwald (Ger.) 44	MISC.CRIMES	FR.
BENSCH (Nick-Name: JEEP)	191835	M	05	Sgt., 5.Coy., 559.Ld.Sch.-Bn., C.C.Czech. Frontier Area and Upper Silesia, 9.45	TORTURE	U.K.
BRAGGA	150583	M		SD.-Official, Marseille (Fr.)	MISC.CRIMES	FR.
BREMBERGER (or BAMBERGER)	162328	M	circa 95	Pvt., 3.Coy., Ld.Sch.-Bn. 877, C.C.Liexen (Aust.) 44-45	TORTURE	U.K.
BUGATTI	254287	M		SS, C.C. Auschwitz (Pol.)	BRUTALITY	FR.
DOULA	147975	M	10	Kapo, Ersbrueck (Ger.)	MURDER	FR.
FRANK	254155	M		C.C. Buchenwald (Ger.)	INTERR.	FR.
FREISLER	155402	M		Pvt., Army, 3.Coy., Ld.Sch.-Bn. 301 (Pol.) 2.45	MURDER	U.K.
FREISLER	193909	M	20	Pvt. Guard, 3-997, Ld.Sch.-Bn., Graudenz (Pol.) 45	MURDER	U.K.
GEISENDORFER, Annie	147823	F	05	Woman-Guard, Waffen-SS, C.C. Ravensbrueck (Ger.)	TORTURE	FR.
GNOSKA, Franz	147719	M		Agent, Gestapo (Ger.)	MISC.CRIMES	FR.
HALASCHA	185110	M		Civilian, SS, C.C.Dachau (Ger.)	MURDER	FR.
HODJEK	192135	M	15	Member, Geh.Feldpolizei, Brussels (Bel.)	TORTURE	BEL.
HORNETZKI	177595	M	12	C.C.Neu Brenn near Saarbruecken (Ger.)	TORTURE	FR.
JANTSCH	188011	M	98	Cpl., 5.Coy., 396.Ld.Sch.-Bn., Stalag IV A, near Dresden (Ger.) 45	WITNESS	CAN.
KARLIK, Emmanuel	186756	M		Oberkapo, C.C. Stephanskirchen near Rosenheim (Ger.)	TORTURE	FR.
KAVALEK, Joseph	257517	M		Guard, C.C.Dora-Nordhausen (Ger.)	MURDER	FR.
KIPFER, Franz	187986	M	05	Pvt., Army, 561.Ld.Sch.-Bn., Bauerwitz (Ger.) 12.11.41	MURDER	U.K.
KLEINE	186762	M		Kapo, C.C.Stephanskirchen near Rosenheim (Ger.)	TORTURE	FR.
KNY	192372	M		Pvt., Army, Unit 26033, Soissons (Fr.) 15.8.44	WITNESS	FR.
KRAFT, Bruno	164049	M	15	Uscharfhr., SS, Brussels (Bel.)	MURDER	BEL.
KRUPKA, Oskar Wilhelm	189447	M		Civilian, Eindhoven (Neth.)	MISC.CRIMES	NETH.
KRUPKA, Rudolf	189446	M	11. 8.04	Civilian, Eindhoven (Neth.)	MISC.CRIMES	NETH.
KULA	261043	M		Sgt., Unit of Artl. No. 40539, Plounez (Fr.) 5.-6.8.44	TORTURE	FR.
LINEMANN, Fritz	186292	M		Lt., Army, Athens (Gre.)	TORTURE	GRC.
MACHATSCHEK, Josef	190584	M		Sgt., SD., Einsatzkdo. z.b.V. 6, La Grande Fosse (Fr.) 15.10.44	MURDER	U.K.
OTTAWA, Rudolph	174153	M		Interpreter, under orders of Kowacht, 4.40	PILLAGE	FR.
PAWELL (Query as to spelling)	132803	M		Cmdt., Artl.officer, C.C. II D, Stargard (Ger.) 21.1.45	TORTURE	U.K.
PETERKA, Rudolph	186770	M		Kapo, Camp Stephanskirchen nar Rosenheim (Ger.)	TORTURE	FR.
PIAZZA	142126	M	10	SS-Osturmfhr., SS, C.C.Dora-Nordhausen (Ger.) 9.43	MURDER	FR.
PORMA, Joseph	257664	M		Police, Block 107, C.C. Dora (Ger.)	MURDER	FR.
PULTAR, Anna	189443	F	11.11.11	Civilian, Eindhoven (Neth.)	MISC.CRIMES	NETH.
SCHWARNER	161285	M	00	Sgt., Bau-Bn., 21.48, C.C.Blechhammer (Ger.) 12.42-44	MURDER	U.K.
STEINHAUSEN (or STEINHAUSEN)	180826	M		Chief-paymaster of Cmdtr., 7.Regt. Art.d.Res., Tours and Albertville (Fr.) 8.-23.6.44	MURDER	FR.
STORZER, Josef	260474	M	7. 2.12	SS-Mann, Waffen-SS, Guard Coy., C.C. Gollaschau, Auschwitz (Pol.) 43-45	BRUTALITY	POL.
STRACHER	141326	M	05	Cpl., Kgf.Arb.Bn., 48 Working Bn., Posen (Pol.) 7.41	TORTURE	U.K.
STRAMMER	260188	M		Lt., 19.Gren.Regt., Massif du Vercors Isere et Drome (Fr.) 20.7.-5.8.44	SUSPECT	FR.
STUCKLIK	158698	M		Interpreter, Gestapo, Saone and Loire (Fr.) 43-44	MURDER	FR.
TZEFSKY	183380	M		Official, occupied territories, Athens (Gre.)	MURDER	GRC.
VON ROSIBERG	67016	M		Osturmfhr., SS, 17.Pz.Gren.Div."Goetz von Berlichingen", Sturmgeschuetz-Abt.17, Segre-Renaza (Fr.) 30.7.-6.8.44	MURDER	FR.
WENZEL, Erich	260476	M	3. 6.28	SS-Mann, Waffen-SS, Guard-Coy., C.C.Auschwitz (Pol.) 9.43-8.44	BRUTALITY	POL.
WEU	194083	M		Civilian, St.Rambert (Fr.)	MURDER	FR.
YABLONSKY	261765	M		Senior W.O., 3.Coy., 399.Bn., Stalag XVII A, Cdo.1004 G.W., Pitten (Aust.) 2.5.43	MURDER	FR.
ZAENNGUT or ZEHNGUT	259237	M		Camp-master, C.C.Auschwitz (Pol.) 40	MURDER	FR.
				DENMARK.		
BOVING, Axel	176144	M		Member, Gestapo	MURDER	FR.
CARR, William	155764	M		Consul-General, Civilian, Wilhelmshaven (Ger.)	MURDER	U.K.
CLASEN	137616	M		Pvt., Camp	TORTURE	U.K.
DRAS	137614	M		Wachtmeister, Staatsgefaengnis, C.C.Hamburg (Ger.)	TORTURE	U.K.
HANSEN, Hans Peter	341	M		Guard, C.C.Boten (Nor.)	MURDER	YUGO.
HENSEL	137609	M		Wachtmeister, Justizvollzugsanstalten, C.C.Hamburg (Ger.) 12.42	TORTURE	U.K.
KAERSGAARD, Niels	137605	M		Wachtmeister, Justizvollzugsanstalten, C.C.Hamburg (Ger.) 12.42	MURDER	U.K.
KAUNS	137606	M		Wachtmeister, Justizvollzugsanstalten, C.C.Hamburg (Ger.) 12.42	TORTURE	U.K.
LARSEN, Flemig	162072	M	15	Oschfhr., Waffen-SS, "Wiking"-Div., Arnheim (Neth.) 24.9.44	MURDER	U.K.
WULKENSTEIN	137576	M		Wachtmeister, C.C.Hamburg (Ger.) 12.42	TORTURE	U.K.
				FRANCE.		
BERGER	173153	M		Chief, Milice, C.C.Saales Vosges (Fr.) autumn 44	INTERR.	U.K.
CAMBA, Charlie	252045	M		F.C.F., SD, Kdo. "Wenger", Baccarat Etival (Fr.)	MURDER	U.K.
DELMOND	192079	M	05	Professor, civilian, Anatomy Institute, Danzig	MURDER	POL.
JUND, Charles Auguste	196344	M	22. 2.22	Uschfhr., Gestapo, Strassburg (Fr.) 44	MURDER	U.K.
LEIRAPPIER, Jean	195056	M		SD-Einsatz-Kdo., Feldpostnr.03069 C, Wenger, Pexonne (Fr.) autumn 44	MURDER	U.K.
LOUVIER, Rene	253128	M		F.C.F., SD-Kdo. "Wenger", B.D.S., Baccarat, Etival (Fr.) 44	MURDER	U.K.
MUTTERER, Renatus	290268	M		SS Uschfhr., SD, Moussey (Fr.) 44	MURDER	U.K.
NEGRI, Jacques	151519	M		Civilian, C.C. Schrobeshausen (Ger.) 44-45	WITNESS	UNWCC.
NEROU	139870	M		Gestapo, Vichy (Fr.) 5.44	TORTURE	U.K.
PERDON, Louis	196700	M	10. 2.09	F.C.F., SD-Kdo. "Wenger", Etival (Fr.) 44	WITNESS	U.K.
PFENNIG	173184	M		Interpreter, Gestapo, Vosges area (Fr.)	TORTURE	U.K.
POURRAIN, Guy	185553	M	11. 9.24	Member NSKK, Geeraardsbergen (Bel.) 5.9.43	MURDER	BEL.
RADET, Jean	195191	M	02	Member, SD, Einsatz-Kdo. "Wenger", Feldpostnr. 03069 C, Baccarat, Etival (Fr.) autumn 44	WITNESS	U.K.
UHRING, Robert	100028	M		Crim.investigation officer, Sturmbannfhr., Kripo, Amt VI, Strassburg (Fr.) 8.11.44	MURDER	U.K.
VAN HOUTTE, Bobby	196419	M		Pvt., SD, Kdo. "Wenger", Baccarat, Etival (Fr.) autumn 44	MURDER	U.K.
VARESTE, Robert	196374	M		Pvt., SD, Kdo. "Ratzek", Pexonne (Fr.) autumn 44	MURDER	U.K.
VASSEUR, Jacques	196370	M		F.C.F., SD, Kdo. z.b.V., St.Die and Saales (Fr.) autumn 44	MURDER	U.K.
WUTTKE, Willibald	190573	M	12	Uschfhr., SD, Einsatz-Kdo. 6, La Grande Fosse (Fr.) 15.10.44	MURDER	U.K.

HUNGARY

HUNGARY.

NAME	C.R. FILE NUMBER	SEX	DATE OF BIRTH	RANK, OCCUPATION, UNIT, PLACE AND DATE OF CRIME	REASON WANTED	WANTED BY
ALLMANN, Stefan	258415	M	25. 8.95	Waffen-SS, C.C. Ohrdruf (Ger.) 12.44-4.45	MURDER	U.S.
ANDRYTSCHEK, Adam	134719	M	18. 9.98	Pvt., guard, SS, 31 SS-Gren.Div., 2 Artl. Regt., Camp Dora, Nordhausen (Ger.) 43-45	MURDER	U.S.
APATINI-FERNBACH, Peter	189956	M		Governor, Government, Novi Sad (Yugo.)	MURDER	YUGO.
BAIG, Johann	185285	M	12. 2.98	SS-Schuetze, guard, 31 SS-Gren.Div., Artl. Regt., Camp Dora, Nordhausen (Ger.) 43-45	WITNESS	U.S.
BAJC, Andor	307267	M	00	Major, chief of Counter-Espionage, Backa and Baranja (Yugo.) 41-44	MURDER	YUGO.
BALAS	189955	M		Agent, Police, (Hung.)	MURDER	YUGO.
BANDI, Sagi	261926	M		See Consolidated List Part II - Appendix "A"		
BARDOSSY	189954	M		Prime minister, public official, (Hung.)	MURDER	YUGO.
BARTHA	189953	M		Minister of defence, public official, (Hung.)	MURDER	YUGO.
BAUER	189952	M		Agent, Police, Novi Sad (Yugo.)	MURDER	YUGO.
BAUER, Johann	185280	M	3. 3.98	SS-Schuetze, 3 SS-Gren.Art., C.C. Nordhausen (Ger.)	WITNESS	U.S.
BAYOR, Vitez, Ferencz	189951	M		General, Army, Novi Sad (Yugo.)	MURDER	YUGO.
BENDER, Friedrich	134750	M	7.11.99	Pvt., guard, SS, 31 Gren.Regt., 2 Artl.Regt., Nordhausen (Ger.) 43-45	WITNESS	U.S.
BENDER, Peter	134760	M	16.10.99	Pvt., 4 SS-Totenkopfsturmbann, Camp Dora-Mittelbau, Nordhausen (Ger.) 43-45	WITNESS	U.S.
BENKO	261943	M		Lt., 98 Regt. from Budapest, near the village of Belje (Yugo.) 18.4.41	MURDER	YUGO.
BERECZ	189950	M		Lt., Hung. Army, Stari, Becej (Yugo.)	MURDER	YUGO.
BILAKOWA, Martha	167645	F		Guard, Jail, St. Lo (Fr.) 7.6.44	MURDER	FR.
BITTLINGMEYR, Jakob	185270	M	95	SS-Mann, 3 SS-Gren.Div., C.C. Dora, Nordhausen, Dachau (Ger.) 43-45	WITNESS	U.S.
BOTH, Philipp	193532	M	27. 5.96	SS-Mann, SS-Totenkopfsturmbann, C.C. Dora-Mittelbau, Nordhausen (Ger.) 43-45	MURDER	U.S.
BRANDT, Josef	185368	M	96	Pvt., SS-Totenkopfsturmbann, C.C. Dachau, Dora, Nordhausen (Ger.)	WITNESS	U.S.
BRAUN, Michael	260934	M	4.11.22	SS-Mann, guard, C.C., Auschwitz (Pol,) 42-44	BRUTALITY	POL.
BRAUNITZER, Joseph	135220	M	19	Hung. Army, Belsen (Hung.) 15.4.45	MURDER	U.K.
BURGER, Konrad	255085	M	14. 7.99	Schuetze, Waffen-SS, Nordhausen (Ger.)	MURDER	U.S.
BURGERMEISTER, Stefan	185290	M	95	SS-Mann, 31 SS-Inf.Regt., C.C. Nordhausen (Ger.) 43-45	WITNESS	U.S.
CAIVTER	301552	M		Hung. or Rum., SS-overseer, C.C. Breendonck (Bel.) from 1944 onwards	MURDER	BEL.
CATAHY, Vitez	189949	M		Lt., Hung. Army, Senta (Yugo.)	MURDER	YUGO.
DANIEL, Jacob	182733	M	2. 3.99	Pvt., 31 Waffen-Gren.Div., 2 Artl.Regt., C.C. Dora, Nordhausen (Ger.) 43-45	WITNESS	U.S.
DEAK, Ladislaus	189946	M		Col., Hung. Army	MURDER	YUGO.
DEAK, Leo	189945	M		Civil Governor Off., Backa, Sombor (Yugo.)	MURDER	YUGO.
DIEHL, Kristian see DIEL						
DIEL, Kristian or DIEHL	182763	M	24. 9.99	Hung. or Ger., Pvt., 4 SS-Totenkopfsturmbann, C.C. Dora-Mittelbau, Nordhausen (Ger.) 43-44	WITNESS	U.S.
DOMO, Otto	189944	M		Lt., Hung. Army	MURDER	YUGO.
DRASCOVIC	194957	M		Lt., Airforce, Kormend (Hung.) 8.44	MISC.CRIMES	U.K.
DRASKOWITCH or MATHIAS	62030	M	07	Hung. or Yugo., Member, Gestapo, Chalons sur Marne (Fr.)	TORTURE	FR.
ECKERTS, Franz	182778	M	31. 5.97	Hung. or Ger., SS-Mann, 4 SS-Totenkopfsturmbann, C.C. Dora-Mittelbau, Nordhausen (Ger.) 43-45	WITNESS	U.S.
EGNER, Johann	182780	M	7. 8.95	Hung. or Ger., SS-Mann, 4 SS-Totenkopfsturmbann, C.C. Dora-Mittelbau, Nordhausen (Ger.) 43-45	WITNESS	U.S.
EGNER, Peter	182736	M	20.12.95	Hung. or Ger., SS-Mann, SS, 31 Waffen-Gren.Div., 2 Artl.Regt., C.C. Dora, Nordhausen (Ger.)	WITNESS	U.S.
ELDIGO	145368	F		Nurse, civilian, Budapest (Hung.) 9.44	MISC.CRIMES	U.S.
EMMA	251522	F		Nurse, C.C. Auschwitz (Pol.)	INTERR.	FR.
EMOEDY, Philipp	189112	M	23.12.94	SS-Schuetze, 31 SS-Gren.Div., C.C. Dora, Nordhausen, Dachau (Ger.) 43-45	MURDER	U.S.
EMSBERGER, Georg	189113	M	10. 4.98	SS-Schuetze, 4 SS-Totenkopfsturmbann, C.C. Dora, Nordhausen, Dachau (Ger.) 43-45	MURDER	U.S.
ENEV	189969	M		Hung. or Bulg., Agent, Police, Pirot (Yugo.)	MISC.CRIMES	YUGO.
ENGLANDER, Joseph	183903	M	21. 2.95	Hung. or Ger., SS-Mann, 4 SS-Totenkopfsturmbann, C.C. Dora-Mittelbau, Nordhausen, Dachau (Ger.) 43-45	WITNESS	U.S.
ESSO	189943	M		Major, Col., Hung. Army, public official	MURDER	YUGO.
FAITISCHKA, Ludwig	141596	M	10. 9.18	Agent, SD, Hendaye (Fr.)	WITNESS	FR.
FARACHO	135215	M		Lt., Hung. Police, Sopron (Hung.) 3.45	MURDER	U.S.
FEKTOR, Franz or Frank	187420	M	16. 7.95	SS-Mann, guard, 4 SS-Totenkopfsturmbann, C.C. Dora, Nordhausen, Dachau (Ger.)	MURDER	U.S.
FELLER, Philipp	187421	M		SS-Mann, guard, 4 SS-Totenkopfsturmbann, C.C. Dora, Nordhausen, Dachau (Ger.)	TORTURE	U.S.
FELZIOVANI, Franz	121241	M	22	Agent, Gestapo of Chambery, Challes les Eaux et Arbin (Fr.)	MURDER	FR.
FERENCZI	135216	M		Lt. Col., Police, Counciller, Ministry of Interior, Budapest (Hung.) 1945	MISC.CRIMES	U.S.
FOGELEIN, Andreas	255588	M	9. 7.03	SS-Mann, SS, farmer, civilian, Nordhausen (Ger.)	MURDER	U.S.
FOLDESI	189941	M		Agent, Hung. Police, Novi Sad (Yugo.)	MURDER	YUGO.
FREUND, Philipp	187363	M	10.12.94	Pvt., 4 SS-Totenkopfsturmbann, C.C. Dora, Nordhausen, Dachau (Ger.) 43-45	MURDER	U.S.
GABEL, Jakob	182997	M	1. 7.99	SS-Mann, guard, Waffen-SS, 31 SS-Gren.Div., C.C. Dora, Nordhausen, Dachau (Ger.) 43-45	WITNESS	U.S.
GABEL, Leonhard	183128	M	31. 1.95	SS-Mann, 4 SS-Totenkopfsturmbann, C.C. Dora-Mittelbau, Nordhausen, Dachau (Ger.) 41-45	WITNESS	U.S.
GALIUS, Sandor	137611	M	10	Lt., cmdt., C.C., Govern. Archeologist, Budapest Museum, Leled (Hung.) 12.44	TORTURE	U.K.
GASS, Mathias	183118	M	2.10.99	SS-Mann, 4 SS-Totenkopfsturmbann, C.C. Dora-Mittelbau, Nordhausen, Dachau (Ger.) 43-45	WITNESS	U.S.
GERMES	161525	M		Interpreter, Gestapo, Bretagne, Anjou, Poitou (Fr.)	MURDER	FR.

HUNGARY

HUNGARY. (Cont.)

NAME	C.R.FILE NUMBER	SEX	DATE OF BIRTH	RANK, OCCUPATION, UNIT, PLACE AND DATE OF CRIME	REASON WANTED	WANTED BY
GEYER, Friedrich	183108	M	95	Pvt., 4 SS-Totenkopfsturmbann, C.C. Dora, Nordhausen, Dachau (Ger.)	MURDER	U.S.
GEZA, Bondi	161214	M	07	Civilian, political prisoner, C.C. Dora, Nordhausen, from Dora to Gardelegen (Ger.) 5.-14.4.45	WITNESS	U.S.
GILLICH, Kasper	183109	M	6. 5.95	Pvt., 31 SS-Gren.Div., C.C. Dora, Nordhausen, Dachau (Ger.)	MURDER	U.S.
GLOCK, Jacob	183294	M	27.11.99	SS-Schuetze, 4 SS-Totenkopfsturmbann, C.C. Dora, Nordhausen, Dachau (Ger.)	WITNESS	U.S.
GOEHMES	259612	M	about 10	Member, Gestapo, Area Angers Maine and Loire (Fr.) 1942,1944	MISC.CRIMES	FR.
GORONDY-NOVAK, Elemer	307268	M	about 95	Vice-Fieldmarshal, commander, 3 Army Grp., Backa (Yugo.) 1941	MURDER	YUGO.
GRASY, Matias	149321	M	19	Sturmmann, SD and SS, Hendaye (Fr.)	PILLAGE	FR.
GSNADI, Navay, Irme	189948	M		Dr., Lt., Hung. Army, Artl., Novi Sad (Yugo.)	TORTURE	YUGO.
GUDWEIN, Peter	183310	M	23.12.94	Pvt., 4 SS-Totenkopfsturmbann, C.C. Dora-Mittelbau, Nordhausen, Dachau (Ger.) 43-45	WITNESS	U.S.
GUNDE	189938	M		Col., Hung. Army, Backa (Yugo.)	MURDER	YUGO.
GYARIC	161244	M		Sgt., Police, Myling (Hung.) 1.11.44	TORTURE	U.S.
GYARMATY, Gabor	259918	M	15. 1.12	Member, Nyilas Party, high ranking civilian official, district Kosice, Tahanovce Slovakia (Czech.) 1.45	MURDER	CZECH.
HAAS, Peter	166601	M	7. 8.98	Pvt., 4 SS-Totenkopfsturmbann, Camp-guard, Nordhausen (Ger.) 43-45	WITNESS	U.S.
HABSBURG, Archducke, Albrecht	261952	M		Col., 38 Regt. from Budapest, near the village of Belje (Yugo.) 18.4.41	MURDER	YUGO.
HAJNAL, Vitez	189937	M		Officer, Hung. Army, Senta (Yugo.)	MURDER	YUGO.
HAMATMA, Jakob	186608	M	99	Pvt., 4 SS-Totenkopfsturmbann, C.C. Nordhausen (Ger.)	WITNESS	U.S.
HANNAK, Wendel	186615	M	13. 3.98	Pvt., 4 SS-Totenkopfsturmbann, Camp-guard, Nordhausen (Ger.) 43-45	WITNESS	U.S.
HARKAI, Jozsef	307269	M	about 00	Lt.Col., cmdt., Gendarmerie, 5-I Investigating Section, Backa and Baranja (Yugo.) from 1941-1944	MURDER	YUGO.
HAUSSER, Adam	186623	M	5. 9.98	Pvt., 4 SS-Totenkopfsturmbann, Camp-guard, Nordhausen (Ger.) 43-45	WITNESS	U.S.
HEGYI	189936	M		Agent, Hung. Police, Novi Sad (Yugo.)	MURDER	YUGO.
HEINS, Jakob	187015	M	98	SS-Mann, guard, 31 SS-Gren.Div., 2 Artl.Regt., C.C. Nordhausen (Ger.) 43-45	WITNESS	U.S.
HENKEL, Andreas	185974	M	24. 8.97	SS-Mann, guard, C.C. Dora, Nordhausen, Dachau (Ger.) 43-45	WITNESS	U.S.
HESS, Lukas	187097	M	26. 9.95	SS-Mann, guard, 4 SS-Totenkopfsturmbann, C.C. Dora, Nordhausen (Ger.) 43-45	TORTURE	U.S.
HODJINA	261928	M		Solicitor, near the village of Belje (Yugo.) 4.41	MURDER	YUGO.
HOFFMANN, Georg	192769	M	21.11.98	SS-Schuetze, 4 SS-Totenkopfsturmbann, C.C. Dora, Nordhausen, Dachau (Ger.) 43-45	WITNESS	U.S.
HOFFMANN, Philipp	192768	M	13. 2.97	SS-Mann, guard, 4 SS-Totenkopfsturmbann, C.C. Dora-Mittelbau, Nordhausen, Dachau (Ger.) 43-45	WITNESS	U.S.
HORVATH, Kazmel	195207	M		Col., Army, Kormend (Hung.) 8.44	WITNESS	U.K.
HORWATH, Kazmel	189935	M		Dr., Mayor (Deputy), Hung. official, Novi Sad (Yugo.)	MURDER	YUGO.
HUNZINGER, Georg	192680	M	96	Pvt., guard, 31 SS-Waffen-Gren.Div., C.C. Dora, Nordhausen, Dachau (Ger.) 43-45	MISC.CRIMES	U.S.
IMREI	186310	M		SS-Unterwachtmeister, 13 SS-Police-Regt., Bleiburg (Aust.) 14.10.44	MISC.CRIMES	U.S.
IVKOVITSCH, Josef	183312	M	18. 8.99	SS-Mann, 31 SS-Gren.Div., C.C. Dora, Dachau (Ger.)	MURDER	U.S.
JAKAB, Lajos, Ludovit	261975	M	2. 8.11	Member, Nyilas Party, Kosice (Czech.) 1.45	MURDER	CZECH.
JAKOB, Michels	255529	M	14.11.98	SS-Mann, SS, C.C. Nordhausen (Ger.)	MURDER	U.S.
JANCZ, Josef or JANZ	183452	M	4. 7.95	SS-Mann, 4 SS-Totenkopfsturmbann, C.C. Dora-Mittelbau, Nordhausen, Dachau (Ger.) 43-45	WITNESS	U.S.
JANZ, Josef see JANCZ	183452					
JUNG, Philipp	183506	M	7.11.97	Pvt., 4 SS-Totenkopfsturmbann, SS-Camp-guard, C.C. Dora, Nordhausen Dachau (Ger.) 43-45	WITNESS	U.S.
JURASZIK, Josef	165915	M	15. 3.13	SS-Uscharfhr., SS, Kampfgruppe "Ney", Sur and Aka (Hung.) 7.3.45	MURDER	U.S.
KALLAY, Miklos	307270	M		Minister, Hung.Prime, Backa, Baranja, Medjumurje, Prekomurje (Yugo.) 9.3.42-19.3.44	MURDER	YUGO.
KANTOR, Janos	189994	M		Dr., member, Hung. Police, Novi Sad (Yugo.)	MURDER	YUGO.
KARIUS, Adam or KARJUS	183582	M	5. 4.96	SS-Mann, 4 SS-Totenkopfsturmbann, C.C. Dora-Mittelbau, Nordhausen (Ger.) 43-45	WITNESS	U.S.
KARJUS, Adam see KARIUS	183582					
KASZ, Josef, Daniel	167228	M	18	SS-Oscharfhr., Hung. SS-Kampfgruppe "Ney", Sur and Aka near Gyor (Hung.) 7.3.45	MURDER	U.S.
KERN, Christian	186122	M	17. 2.98	Pvt., 31 SS-Gren.Div., 2 Artl.Regt., C.C. Dora, Nordhausen, Dachau (Ger.)	WITNESS	U.S.
KERN, Peter	186121	M	23.11.95	Pvt., 31 SS-Gren.Div., C.C. Dora, Nordhausen, Dachau (Ger.) 43-45	WITNESS	U.S.
KHAN	188754	M		"Colonne Indoue 950", Charente et Vienne (Fr.) 25.8.44	TORTURE	FR.
KIRALY, Franz	259566	M		SS-Mann, C.C. Buchenwald (Ger.) 40-43	MURDER	BEL.
KLEESZ, Karl	186231	M	25. 4.97	SS-Mann, 4 SS-Totenkopfsturmbann, C.C. Dora, Nordhausen (Ger.) 43-45	WITNESS	U.S.
KLEIN, Nikolaus	186278	M	24.10.95	SS-Mann, 4 SS-Totenkopfsturmbann, C.C. Dora, Nordhausen, Dachau (Ger.)	TORTURE	U.S.
KLEIN, Stephan	250337	M		Doctor, C.C. Buchenwald (Ger.)	INTER.	FR.
KLEPP, Jacob	186274	M	14. 8.99	SS-Schuetze, guard, 31 SS-Gren.Div., 2 Artl.Regt., C.C. Dora, Nordhausen, Dachau (Ger.) 43-45	WITNESS	U.S.
KOHLER, Adam	187185	M	13. 9.96	SS-Mann, SS-Totenkopfsturmbann, C.C. Dora, Nordhausen, Dachau (Ger.) 43-45	TORTURE	U.S.
KOHLHEB, Florian	185844	M	7. 7.96	SS-Mann, guard, SS, C.C. Dora, Nordhausen, Dachau (Ger.) 43-45	WITNESS	U.S.
KOLTAI	189933	M		Dr., asst., Hung. Police, Novi Sad (Yugo.)	MURDER	YUGO.
KONYOKY, Josef	189932	M		Dr., Counsellor, Hung. Police, Novi Sad (Yugo.)	MURDER	YUGO.
KOPJAK, Imrich	253751	M	4.11.06	Civilian, Komarno (Czech.) 1944	MURDER	CZECH.
KOREIL, Rupert	185843	M	13. 5.97	Pvt., 31 SS-Gren.Div., 2 Artl.Regt., guard at C.C. Dachau, Dora, Nordhausen (Ger.)	TORTURE	U.S.
KORELL, Robert or Rupert	185816	M		Hung. or Ger., SS-Mann, 4 SS-Totenkopfsturmbann, C.C. Dora-Mittelbau, Nordhausen (Ger.) 43-45	WITNESS	U.S.
KOWATZ	305758	M		Pvt., prison guard, C.C. Chaidari (Athens) (Grc.) 10.43-10.44	MURDER	GRC.
KRAFT	192455	M		Hung. or Rum., Guard, C.C. Breendonck (Bel.) 4.5.44	TORTURE	BEL.
KRIEG, Anton	185845	M	20. 1.96	Guard, 31 SS-Gren.Div., 2 Artl.Regt., C.C. Dora, Nordhausen, Dachau (Ger.) 43-45	WITNESS	U.S.
KRIEGER, Daniel	187152	M	6. 7.95	SS-Mann, guard, 4 SS-Totenkopfsturmbann, C.C. Dora, Nordhausen (Ger.)	TORTURE	U.S.

HUNGARY

HUNGARY. (Cont.)

NAME	C.R.FILE NUMBER	SEX	DATE OF BIRTH	RANK OCCUPATION UNIT PLACE AND DATE OF CRIME	REASON WANTED	WANTED BY
KROPIVSEC	192450	M		Hung. or Rum., Guard, C.C. Breendonck (Bel.) 4.5.44	MURDER	BEL.
KUIA, Georg	186107	M	96	SS-Mann, guard, C.C. Dora, Nordhausen, Dachau (Ger.) 43-45	WITNESS	U.S.
KUN	189931	M		Lt.Col., Hung. Gestapo, Novi Sad (Yugo.)	MURDER	YUGO.
KUTSCH, Georg	186111	M	93	SS-Mann, guard, 4 SS-Totenkopfsturmbann, C.C. Dora-Mittelbau, Nordhausen, Dachau (Ger.) 43-45	INTERR.	U.S.
LAPO, Adam	187062	M	3.12.or 9.12.95	SS-Mann, guard, 3 SS-Gren.Div., C.C. Dora, Nordhausen (Ger.) 43-45	TORTURE	U.S.
LASZLO, Marton	172076	M		SS-Guard, C.C. Auschwitz (Pol.), C.C. Buchenwald (Ger.) 4.45	MURDER	U.S.
LEIPOLD, Georg	187046	M	3. 9.95	SS-Mann, guard, 4 SS-Totenkopfsturmbann, C.C. Dora-Mittelbau, Nordhausen (Ger.) 43-45	MURDER	U.S.
LOERINCZ, Albert	261897	M	19	Member, Nyilas Party, Kosice (Czech.) 1.45	MURDER	CZECH.
MAJOR, Vitez	307271	M		General commander, Hung. light motorised Bde., Novi Sad and other towns of Northern Yugo., 4.41	MURDER	YUGO.
MARIANZUCK	192266	M		Hung. or Rum., Guard, C.C. Breendonck (Bel.) 4.-5.44	MURDER	BEL.
MAROSI, Koloman	260000	M	3. 4.10	Civilian, leader, Hung. Nyilas Party, organization of Guta, district Komarno Slovakia (Czech.) 19.2.45	MURDER	CZECH.
MATHIAS see DRASKOWITCH	62030					
MICHELS, Jacob	183678	M	14.11.98	SS-Schuetze, 31 SS-Gren.Inf.Div., 2 Artl.Regt., C.C. Dora, Nordhausen, Dachau (Ger.) 43-45	TORTURE	U.S.
MIHAIOVICS	189930	M		Dr., Counsellor, Hung. Police, Novi Sad (Yugo.)	MURDER	YUGO.
MOLNAR, Pal	156999	M	22	Lt., Army, C.C. Belsen (Ger.)	MURDER	U.K.
MUELLER, David	183687	M	98	SS-Schuetze, SS Camp-guard, 31 SS-Gren.Inf.Div., C.C. Dora, Nordhausen, Dachau (Ger.)	TORTURE	U.S.
NADI see NAGI, Miklos	189929					
NAGI, Miklos or NADI	189929	M		Mayor, Public Service, Novi Sad (Yugo.)	MURDER	YUGO.
NAUDOR, Pal	138207	M		Dr., Chief, Police, Kolozsayar (Hung.) 1944	MISC.CRIMES	FR.
NEIDER, Peter	183280	M	3. 9.98	SS-Schuetze, 31 SS-Gren.Div., 2 Artl.Regt., C.C. Dora, Nordhausen, Dachau (Ger.) 43-45	WITNESS	U.S.
NEMET, Laszlo	189928	M		Agent, Hung. Police, Novi Sad (Yugo.)	MURDER	YUGO.
NEZVAL, Josef	261979	M	14. 5.02	Member, Nyilas Party, Kosice (Czech.) 1.45	MURDER	CZECH.
NIEDAN, Friedrich	193282	M	28. 6.97	SS-Mann, guard, 4 SS-Totenkopfsturmbann, C.C. Dora-Mittelbau, Nordhausen (Ger.) 43-45	MURDER	U.S.
NIEDAN, Philipp	183278	M	97	SS-Schuetze, 31 SS-Gren.Div., C.C. Dora, Nordhausen, Dachau (Ger.)	WITNESS	U.S.
NOVAKOVICS, Bela	189927	M		General, Hung. Army, Backa, Novi Sad (Yugo.)	MURDER	YUGO.
OLAH, Elemer	189926	M		Dr., Counsellor, Hung. Police, Novi Sad (Yugo.)	MURDER	YUGO.
OLASZY, Alexander	144394	M	02	Lt.Gen., Hung. Army, (Hung.)	MURDER	U.S.
OROSZ	189925	M		Dr., Counsellor, Hung. Army, Police, Novi Sad (Yugo.)	MURDER	YUGO.
ORSICK	144392	M		Hung. Pilot, Budapest (Hung.) 18.9.44	TORTURE	U.S.
OSMANN, Franz	193330	M	30. 8.98	Pvt., 4 SS-Totenkopfsturmbann, C.C. Dora-Mittelbau, Nordhausen (Ger.) 43-45	MURDER	U.S.
OSTER, Michael	193329	M	4. 7.99	SS-Mann, 4 SS-Totenkopfsturmbann, C.C. Dora-Mittelbau, Nordhausen (Ger.) 43-45	MURDER	U.S.
OSWAID, Anton	193599	M		Guard, C.C. Flossenburg (Ger.) 2.-3.45	WITNESS	BEL.
OSWAID, Joseph	167759	M	8.12.09	SS-Mann, SS, C.C. Natzweiler (Fr.) 43-44	MURDER	FR.
OTTENHEIMER, Kaspar	193327	M	4. 4.99	Guard, 4 SS-Totenkopfsturmbann, C.C. Dora-Mittelbau, Nordhausen (Ger.) 43-45	MURDER	U.S.
PACSIUS	192494	M		Hung. or Rum., Guard, C.C. Breendonck (Bel.) 4.5.44	MISC.CRIMES	BEL.
PAPINCAK, Eugen	261896	M	9. 9.03	Member, Nyilas Party, Kosice (Czech.) 1.45	MURDER	CZECH.
PETAKI, Jeno	189924	M		Lt., Hung. Army, Novi Sad (Yugo.)	TORTURE	YUGO.
PETER, Aladar	166624	M	02	SS-Hptsturmfhr., Hung. SS, SS-Kampfgruppe "Ney" between Sur and Aka (Hung.) 7.3.45	MURDER	U.S.
PETSCHMER, Josef	193264	M	6. 3.99	SS-Mann, guard, 4 SS-Totenkopfsturmbann, C.C. Dora-Mittelbau, Nordhausen, Dachau (Ger.) 43-45	MURDER	U.S.
PFAFF, Jakob	193266	M	28. 7.99	SS-Mann, guard, 4 SS-Totenkopf-Sturmbann, C.C. Dora-Mittelbau, Nordhausen, Dachau (Ger.) 43-45	MURDER	U.S.
RACS	189923	M		Dr., Counsellor, Hung. Police, Novi Sad (Yugo.)	MURDER	YUGO.
REITMANN, Anton	193434	M	11.12.98	Pvt., 4 SS-Totenkopfsturmbann, C.C. Dora-Mittelbau, Nordhausen, Dachau (Ger.) 43-45	MURDER	U.S.
REK, Ander	189922	M		Civil Governor, Hung. Public official, Subotica (Yugo.)	MURDER	YUGO.
RENHART	255774	M		Kapo, Neckargerach (Ger.)	INTERR.	FR.
REWAY, Julius	260012	M	26. 7.99	Civilian, teacher, Founder of the terrorist organization SIC in Ruthenia. Suspect is believed to be living in Frankfurt-Main, Uzhorod, Mukacevo, Ruthenia (Czech.) 39-44	MISC.CRIMES	CZECH.
RIEGLER, Josef	180727	M		Unterwachtmeister, 13 SS-Police-Regt., 1 Bn., Bleiburg (Aust.) 14.10.44	WITNESS	U.S.
RINGELS, Paul	252594	M	7.12.08	Farmer, Army, Buchenwald (Ger.)	MISC.CRIMES	U.S.
ROBICKA, Jovan	261929	M		Near the village of Belje (Yugo.) 18.4.41	MURDER	YUGO.
ROTH, Ludwig	193530	M	8.10.95	SS-Schuetze, 4 SS-Totenkopfsturmbann, C.C. Dora-Mittelbau, Nordhausen (Ger.) 43-45	MURDER	U.S.
ROTH, Nikolaus	184127	M	97	SS-Sturmann, 31 SS-Inf.Div., C.C. Dora, Nordhausen (Ger.)	MURDER	U.S.
SANDLJ	261944	M		Lt., 38 Regt. from Budapest, near the village of Belje (Yugo.) 18.4.41	MURDER	YUGO.
SANDLES, Heinrich	193869	M	24. 9.08	SS-Mann, guard, 4 SS-Totenkopfsturmbann, C.C. Dora-Mittelbau, Nordhausen (Ger.) 43-45	MURDER	U.S.
SANDLES, Philipp	184369	M	18. 2.99	SS-Schuetze, 31 SS-Gren.Div., 2 Artl.Regt., C.C. Dora, Nordhausen, Dachau (Ger.)	WITNESS	U.S.
SAWATSKI, Josef	187218	M	10.10.17	SS-Uscharfhr., SD, C.C. Metz-Woippy (Fr.) 6.-7.44	MISC.CRIMES	CAN.
SCHADE, Johann	193867	M	9. 1.98	SS-Mann, guard, 4 SS-Totenkopfsturmbann, C.C. Dora-Mittelbau, Nordhausen, Dachau (Ger.) 43-45	TORTURE	U.S.
SCHADT, Jakob	155951	M	18. 7.91	Guard, Waffen-SS, C.C. Mauthausen (Aust.) 10.44-5.45	TORTURE	U.S.
SCHARF, Karl (I)	184282	M	30. 6.98	SS-Schuetze, 31 SS-Gren.Div., 2 Artl.Regt., C.C. Dora, Nordhausen, Dachau (Ger.) 43-45	WITNESS	U.S.
SCHARF, Karl (II)	184281	M	11.10.97	SS-Schuetze, 31 SS-Gren.Div., 2 Artl.Regt., C.C. Dora, Nordhausen, Dachau (Ger.) 43-45	WITNESS	U.S.
SCHEER, Ludwig	184982	M	6.10.99	SS-Schuetze, 31 SS-Gren.Div., 2 Artl.Regt., Guard, C.C. Dora, Nordhausen (Ger.) 43-45	WITNESS	U.S.

HUNGARY - ITALY (Acq - Ado)

NAME	C.R. FILE NUMBER	SEX	DATE OF BIRTH	RANK OCCUPATION UNIT PLACE AND DATE OF CRIME	REASON WANTED	WANTED BY
				HUNGARY. (Cont.)		
SCHEPPESCH	186220	M		SS, C.C. Dachau (Ger.)	MISC.CRIMES	FR.
SCHILLING, Karl	255758	M	95	Pvt., guard, 2 Artl.Regt., SS-Gren.Div.31, Nordhausen (Ger.)	MURDER	U.S.
SCHMIDT, Friedrich	184980	M	19. 6.97	SS-Mann, 4 SS-Totenkopfsturmbann, C.C. Dora, Nordhausen (Ger.) 43-45	WITNESS	U.S.
SCHMIDT, Gustav	166676	M	14	Lt., 27 SS-Div. "Langemark", between Sur and Aka (Hung.) 7.3.45	MURDER	U.S.
SCHMIDT, Wilhelm	184981	M	2.10.97	Pvt., guard, 31 SS-Gren.Div., 2 Artl.Regt., C.C. Dora, Nordhausen (Ger.) 43-45	WITNESS	U.S.
SCHNEIDER or SNEIDER	301605			Hung. or Rum., SS-Overseer, C.C. Breendonck (Bel.) from 1944 onw.	MURDER	BEL.
SCHWABE	129921	M		Guard, Waffen-SS, C.C. Mauthausen (Aust.) 41-45	MURDER	U.S.
SEDIVY, Pal	261951	M	31. 1.12	Member, Nyilas Party, Kosice (Czech.) 1.45	MURDER	CZECH.
SIHLER, Georg	184599	M	96	Pvt., guard, 4 SS-Totenkopfsturmbann, C.C. Dora-Mittelbau, Nordhausen, Dachau (Ger.) 43-45	INTERR.	U.S.
SIPOS, Tibor	135218	M		Hung. Army, Belsen (Hung.) 15.4.45	MURDER	U.K.
SNEIDER see SCHNEIDER	301605					
SPEISS, Philip	194047	M	2.11.97	Pvt., guard, 4 SS-Totenkopfsturmbann, C.C. Dora-Mittelbau, Nordhausen, Dachau (Ger.) 43-45	INTERR.	U.S.
STEFAN, Jozef	250494	M	6.10.24	Civilian, Komarno (Czech.) 1944	MURDER	CZECH.
STEFAN, Martin	250499	M	24. 1.22	Civilian, Komarno (Czech.) 1944	MURDER	CZECH.
STEFAN, Zoltan	250498	M	5. 6.23	Civilian, Komarno (Czech.) 1944	MURDER	CZECH.
STEIGER, Mathias	158573	M	20	Sturmmann, SS-Totenkopfsturmbann, C.C. Buchenwald, Pawiak near Warsaw (Ger., Pol.) 42-43	TORTURE	U.K.
STEIN	158572	M	25	SS-Mann, SS, C.C. Reichenau (Aust.) 1944	MURDER	U.S.
STIGLER, Josep	261930	M		Mayor of Beli Manastir near the village of Belje (Yugo.) 4.41	MURDER	YUGO.
STOFFNER, Paul	140808	M		SS-Mann, Waffen-SS, Totenkopf-Verband, C.C. Zipf (Aust.) 43-45	MISC.CRIMES	U.S.
STRUNG, Stefan	193877	M	19. 8.99	Guard, 4 SS-Totenkopfsturmbann, C.C. Dora-Mittelbau, Nordhausen, Dachau (Ger.)	INTERR.	U.S.
SUCAROTY or SWCAROTY	142238	M		Capt., Hung. Army, Budapest (Hung.) 9.44	MURDER	U.S.
SZAPU, Matej	250463	M	19. 2.05	Civilian, member, Nyilas-Party, Hung. SS, firing squad in Komarno (Czech.) 1944	MURDER	CZECH.
SZEIDL, Johann	251749	M		Pvt., guard, SS, C.C. Buchenwald (Ger.) 42-45	BRUTALITY	U.S.
SZENTGYOCYI	149775	M		General, Sombor (Yugo.) 1941	MURDER	YUGO.
SZIKORA, Caspar	175934	M		SS-Guard, C.C. Buchenwald, Auschwitz (Ger., Pol.) 4.45	MURDER	U.S.
SZILAGYI	185874	M		SS-Uscharfhr., SS, 13 Police-Regt., 1 Bn., Bleiburg (Aust.) 14.10.44	MURDER	U.S.
SZOBEL, Aurel	158696	M	19	Civilian, Political Prisoner, C.C. Illfeld-Gardelegen (Ger.) 5.-14.4.45	WITNESS	U.S.
SZOMBACHELJI, Ferrai or SZOMBATHELJI	136571	M		Lt.Gen., Hung. Army, chief of staff, 41-44	MISC.CRIMES	U.S.
SZOMBATHELJI, Ferrai see SZOMBACHELJI	136571					
TAUSS, Gottfried	193756	M	17. 5.96	SS-Mann, guard, 4 SS-Totenkopfsturmbann, C.C. Dora-Mittelbau, Nordhausen, Dachau (Ger.) 43-45	MURDER	U.S.
TIEFENTHALER, Friedrich	183906	M	98	SS-Guard, SS, C.C. Dora, Nordhausen, Dachau (Ger.)	MURDER	U.S.
TOMEO, Imrich, Imre	261967	M	24. 1.09	Member, Nyilas Party, Civilian, locksmith, Kosice (Czech.) 1.45	MURDER	CZECH.
UTASI	195420	M		Col., Army, Kormend (Hung.) 8.44	WITNESS	U.K.
VARKOLY, Denes, Bela, Daniel	260006	M	30. 3.11	Chief, political department, Kosice (Czech.) 5.1.-17.1.45	MURDER	CZECH.
VERES, Vitez, Lajos	189921	M		General, Hung. Army, Novi Sad (Yugo.)	MURDER	YUGO.
VIOLA	254713	F		Guard, C.C. Auschwitz (Pol.)	TORTURE	FR.
VOJTOVICH, Richard	254760	M	12. 1.80 or 19.10.14	Hung. SS, Komarno, (Czech.) 1944	MURDER	CZECH.
VOJTOVICHOVA-BOROS, Rozalia	258299	F		Civilian, Hung. SS, Komarno (Czech.) 1944	MURDER	CZECH.
VON BATIZFALVY, Fernau	128010			Head, Police officer, Koeroesmezde (Hung.) 1941	MURDER	POL.
VUKOVARY	189920	M		Civil.Serv., Dr., occupied territories, Zabalj (Yugo.)	MURDER	YUGO.
WACHSMANN, Ernst	261888	M	21.10.13	Member, SD, Civilian, clerk, Prag (Czech.) 4.43-45	SUSPECT	CZECH.
WAGNER, Joseph	251424	M		Gestapo, Limoges (Fr.) 40-45	BRUTALITY	FR.
WALLER, Ludwig	193523	M	29. 1.98	SS-Schuetze, 4 SS-Totenkopfsturmbann, C.C. Dora-Mittelbau, Nordhausen, (Ger.) 43-45	MURDER	U.S.
WALTER	150820	M		SS-Mann, guard, SS, C.C. Valory (Czech.) 41-45	MURDER	U.S.
WAIZER	192430	M		Hung. or Rum., Guard, C.C. Breendonck (Bel.) 4.5.44	TORTURE	BEL.
WEBER, Heinrich	193527	M	17. 2.97	SS-Schuetze, 4 SS-Totenkopfsturmbann, C.C. Dora-Mittelbau, Nordhausen (Ger.) 43-45	MURDER	U.S.
WEBER, Johann	193526	M	21. 2.95	SS-Schuetze, 4 SS-Totenkopfsturmbann, C.C. Dora-Mittelbau, Nordhausen (Ger.) 43-45	MURDER	U.S.
WEICHAND, Mathias	252787	M		SS-Sturmmann, C.C. Buchenwald (Ger.)	MISC.CRIMES	U.S.
WERTH, Daniel	187504	M	4. 9.96	SS-Mann, 4 SS-Totenkopfsturmbann, C.C. Dora, Nordhausen, Dachau (Ger.) 43-45	TORTURE	U.S.
ZAVATSKY	132657	M		SS-Mann, C.C. Woippy (Moselle) (Fr.) 1944	TORTURE	FR., BEL.
ZIPF, Josef	152019	M		Pvt., SS-Guard, C.C. Volary (Czech.)	MURDER	U.S.
ZOELDI, Marton	124563	M		Hptsturmfhr., SS, 26 Hung. Div., Ujvidek (Hung.) 1945	MURDER	U.S.
ZOLDI, Martin	189919	M		Capt., Gendarmerie, Backa (Yugo.)	MURDER	YUGO.
ZOMBORI, Gyula	189918	M		Cmdt., Hung. Police, Novi Sad (Yugo.)	MURDER	YUGO.
ZSIROSS, Hadaprod, Istran	195096	M		Interpreter, C.C. Leled (Hung.) 11.44	TORTURE	U.K.
				ITALY.		
ACQUA, Fredda	190871	M		Crim.Comm., Italian Police, Susak Podhum (Yugo.) 41-4.43	MURDER	YUGO.
ADAMI-ROSSI, E.	129135	M		Maj.Gen., Armee-Corps 2142, Sulmona (It.) 26.12.41	MISC.CRIMES	U.K.
ADAMO, Fernando	190872	M		Member, Black shirt Unit, Vodice, Sibenik (Yugo.) 2.4.43	MURDER	YUGO.
ADDARI, Ranieri	250029	M		Vice-Brig., Dazlina, Dubrava (Yugo.) 24.7.42	MURDER	YUGO.
ADDESST, Giovanni	250010	M		Political secretary, C.C. Fonda (Yugo.) 9.,10.43	INTERR.	YUGO.
ADOTTO, Duchetti	190873	M		Major, Italian Army, Biegrad-On-Sea (Yugo.) 12.4.43	MURDER	YUGO.

ITALY (Afr-Bel)

NAME	C.R.FILE NUMBER	SEX	DATE OF BIRTH	RANK	OCCUPATION	UNIT	PLACE AND DATE OF CRIME	REASON WANTED	WANTED BY

ITALY. (Cont.)

NAME	C.R.FILE NUMBER	SEX	DATE OF BIRTH	RANK, OCCUPATION, UNIT, PLACE AND DATE OF CRIME	REASON WANTED	WANTED BY
AFRI, Bruno	250025	M		Commissar, Provinz Vodice (Yugo.) 42-43	MURDER	YUGO.
AGAZZI, Giovanni	250022	M		Capellano militare, Army, 10 Flottielia-Mass, Conegliano (Slov.) 21.12.44-3.1.45	INTERR.	YUGO.
AGOSTINO	36677	M		Tenente colonnello, Army, Castel San Pietro, Bologna (It.)	MISC.CRIMES	U.K.
ALACEVIC, Josip	190874	M		Secretary, Fascio Italian SS, Sibenik (Yugo.) 41,42,43	MURDER	YUGO.
ALBERTAZZI, Augusto	146105	M		Capt., Italian Army, Cettigne (Yugo.) 1943	MURDER	YUGO.
ALDO	152498	M.		Lt., Italian Army, 313 Inf.Regt., C.C. Larissa (Grc.) 8.42	TORTURE	U.F.
ALDO, Cicero	152497	M	17	Cpl., Italian Army, Guard, Thebes (Grc.) 8.42	TORTURE	U.K.
ALESSANDRI, Guiseppe	250607	M		Italian Airforce, Av.A.Mot.113, Sosici (Yugo.) 12.7.43	MISC.CRIMES	YUGO.
ALESSANDRO	189917	M		Lt., Italian Army, Bizerte (Tunisia)	MURDER	FR.
ALFAREZ	193910A	M		Sgt.-Chief, Jaeger-Regt., Fontaine-Par-Grenoble (Fr.)	TORTURE	FR.
ALIENZO, Luiggi	257458	M		Brig., Carabinieri-Regt., Pianottoli (Fr.) 9.5.43	MURDER	FR.
ALLEVI, Vittorio	146098	M		Dr., Major, Army, Mil. Hospital, Treviglio (It.) 42-43	TORTURE	U.K.
ALONGI, Francesco, Dott.	125703	M		Camp-Cmdt., Camp of civilian, Corropoli (It.) 1942	TORTURE	FR.
ALFOLDI, Alberto	250021	M		Capt. Italian Army, Susak (Yugo.) 41-43	MISC.CRIMES	YUGO.
ALVISI, Alessandro	307336.			Consul, Judge of Special Tribunal for defense of State, Rom (It.) 4.41-9.43	MURDER	YUGO.
ALZETTA	146104	M		Lt., Italian Army, "Lombardia-Div.", Slovenia Croatia (Yugo.) 1943	MURDER	YUGO.
AMADASI	190876	M		Commissar, Kapo, Sibenik (Yugo.) 41-43	MURDER	YUGO.
AMATO, Attilio	195528	M		General, Italian Army, Div."Messina", Korcula (Yugo.) 15.1.43	MURDER	YUGO.
AMBROSIO, Nittorio	146102	M		General, Army, Fuzine (Yugo.) 1942	MURDER	YUGO.
AMBRCSIO, N.	146103	M		Col., Italian Army, Grcinicko Polje (Yugo.) 1943	MURDER	YUGO.
AMEDEO, Constantino	190877	M		Major, Italian Army, Commander of Carabinieri, Sibenik (Yugo.) 41-43	MURDER	YUGO.
AMEDORO, Francesco	190878	M		Marschall, Italian Army, 15 Regt., Cabar (Yugo.) 7. and 8.42	MURDER	YUGO.
ANARELLI	146101	M		Commissar, Police, Dalmatia (Yugo.) 1943	MURDER	YUGO.
ANCONA, Francesco	302155	M		Capt., Carabinieri, Ploce near Metkovic, 42-43	TORTURE	YUGO.
ANGELLINI	146100	M		Col., Army, 1 Regt., (Yugo.) 1943	MURDER	YUGO.
ANGOIZI, Salvatore	190880	M		Carabinieri, Italian Army, Sibenik, Vodice (Yugo.) 41-43	MURDER	YUGO.
ANCONA, Francesco	190879	M		Capt., Italian Army, C.C. Ploce (Yugo.) 42-43	MURDER	YUGO.
ANTIMANTO, Vittorio	300006	M		Lt.of Res., 7 Inf.Regt., "Cuneo"-Div., Serifos, 11.41-9.43	MISC.CRIMES	GRC.
ANTONIOLLI, Alvaris	256979	M		Cpl., Fascist Republ. Army, Tagl. VIII, Alp.Regt., Dorenberg (Yugo.) 43-4.45	INTERR.	YUGO.
ARALDI, Alberto	190881	M		Vice-Brig., Italian Army, Sibenik, Vadenice (Yugo.) 41-43	MURDER	YUGO.
ARCHER, Umberto	162747	M		Capitano, Italian Army, Administration officer at C.C. Benevento (It.) summer 1942	TORTURE	U.K.
ARESTA see TISANI	194290					
ARMANDO, Enrico	190882	M		Lt.Gen., Italian Army, Corps D'Armata, Sibenik (Yugo.) 1943	MURDER	YUGO.
ARMELLINI, Q.	195529	M		General, Italian Army, Brundno-Promnij Bukovica (Yugo.) 6.-7.42	MURDER	YUGO.
ASCARI	250009	M		Mareschiallo (Sgt.), Carabinieri, Split (Yugo.) 14.-16.4.42	BRUTALITY	YUGO.
ASCOLI, Arturie	72181	M		Marseille (Fr.)	PILLAGE	FR.
AUSTONI	251946	M		Dr., physician, civilian, Split (Yugo.) 17.4.42	INTERR.	YUGO.
BADINI, Andrea	255507	M		Major, 291 Inf.Regt., Zara-Div., Kistanje (Yugo.) 1942	BRUTALITY	YUGO.
BALBIS, Marco	190883	M		Commander, Cpl., Italian Army, Sibenik (Yugo.) 1943	MURDER	YUGO.
BALDESCHI	162319	M		Tenente, Italian Army, Artl., Padula (It.) 1942	TORTURE	U.K.
BALDI, Remido	250065	M		Vice-Brig., Etat Major, Carabinieri-Div., Santo-Pietro-di Tenda (It.) 19.-31.8.43	TORTURE	FR.
BALDUCCI	192075	M		Lt., Fascist Army, Cupramontana (It.) 20.5.44	MURDER	U.K.
BANCAIARI	149624	M.		Army, 23 Regt. "Fant Coma", "Isonzo"-Div., Cernomelj (Yugo.) 1943	MURDER	YUGO.
BANCAIARI, Andreas	190884	M		Brig.Gen., Italian Army, XI Bn., Carabinieri, Cetinje, Orna (Yugo.) 41,42,43	MURDER	YUGO.
BARASI	189910	M		Col., Italian Army	PILLAGE	FR.
BARBA	190885	M		Capt., Italian Army, VI Regt. of "Aosta Cavalry", Prapatnise, Prgomat Trogir-Dalmatia (Yugo.) spring of 1943	MURDER	YUGO.
BARBA	250049	M		Major, Sassari-Div., Kistanje (Yugo.) 6.41	PILLAGE	YUGO.
BARBALIA, Pietro	190886	M		Lt., Italian Army, Gracac (Yugo.) 41-43	MURDER	YUGO.
BARBERA, Gaspero	149623	M		General, Army, Prefekt of Province, Zara (Yugo.) 1943	MURDER	YUGO.
BARBERO, Pietro	250048	M		Col., XVIII Corpodi Armata Sassari Div., Biograd, Betina, Vodice (Yugo.) 1942	MURDER	YUGO.
BARBIERI, Mario	300661	M		Agent, Prison of Krk (It.) 41-43	TORTURE	YUGO.
BARCIA, Mario see BARELLI	169500					
BARDELLI, Renaldo	149621	M		Lt., commander of garrison, Army, Gren.Regt., Losk, Potok (Yugo.) 1943	MURDER	YUGO.
BARDINI, Karel	256983	M		Sgt., Italian Army, Plave Anhovo (Yugo.) 13.-23.2.45	INTERR.	YUGO.
BARDOVAGNI, Guido, Ubaldo	250045	M		Major, Italian Army, Ljubljana (Yugo.) 41-43	MISC.CRIMES	YUGO.
BARELA, Mario see BARELLI	169500					
BARELLI, Mario or BARELA or BARCIA	169500	M		Lt.Col., Army, Chieti (It.) 7.42-9.43	TORTURE	U.F.
BARTOLINI, Alphonso	300168	M		Lt. Italian Army, Kymi, Evea, 3.42	MURDER	GRC.
BARTOLUCCI, Athos	190888	M		Dr., secretary, Governor General Secretario Federale, Sibenik (Yugo.) 41-11.42	MURDER	YUGO.
BASCIONI, Gino	149607	M		Member, Fascists Italian, Belmonte (It.)	MURDER	U.K.
BASOLCHI	259134	M		Maggiore, cmdt., Venezia-Div., Bn. Bijelo Polje, Montenegro, 41-43	MISC.CRIMES	YUGO.
BASSI, E.	250634	M		President, Military Court, Susak (Yugo.) 41-43	MISC.CRIMES	YUGO.
BASTIANINI, Giuseppe	149620	M		Dr., Governor, Public official, Sibenik (Yugo.) 8.41-7.42	MURDER	YUGO.
BATOIA, Carlo	190889	M		Agent, Italian Press. official of Cattaro (Kotor) (Yugo.) 41-43	MURDER	YUGO.
BATTISTI, Frederico	256995	M		Cpl., Italian Army, Plave Anhovo Venezia (Yugo.) 13.,23.2.45	INTERR.	YUGO.
BAZZOCCHI, Carlo	190890	M		Commissar, Governor General Italy, Podgorica, Trebrljevo, Sirogosto, Kolasin, Majkovac, Montenegro (Yugo.) 11.41	MURDER	YUGO.
BECOCI, N.	149619	M		Officer, Army, Grobnicko Polje (Yugo.) 1943	MURDER	YUGO.
BECUCCI	190891	M		General, Italian Army, Island of Brac (Yugo.) 6.8.43	MURDER	YUGO.
BEIE	190892	M		Agent, Italian Press. official of Cattaro, Kotor (Yugo.) 41-43	MURDER	YUGO.
BELICNI, Luigi	190893	M		Blackshirt, Italian SS, 215 Bn. Nizza, Sezane (Yugo.) 2.9.42	MURDER	YUGO.
BELLINI, Giovanni	300616	M	12	Lt., commander, Mayor and Secretary, commander of the Guardia Nazionale Republicana and of the Black Brigade at Mesola. Fascist Republican Party, Mesola, Ferrara, Adria, Rovigo (It.) 12.44	MURDER	U.K.

ITALY (Bel- Bot)

ITALY. (Cont.)

NAME	C.R.FILE NUMBER	SEX	DATE OF BIRTH	RANK OCCUPATION UNIT PLACE AND DATE OF CRIME	REASON WANTED	WANTED BY
BELLINI, Luigi	307272	M		Member of the Italian Fascist Black Bde., near Caselle Pressana Prov. Verona (It.) 6.1.45	MURDER	U.K.
BELIOMO, N.	193538	M		Lt.Gen., Italian Army, Bari (It.) 11.41	MURDER	U.K.
BELLOSI, Luigi	191143	M		Judge, Italian Special Court in Sibenik (Yugo.) 41-43	MURDER	YUGO.
BELOZZI	189909	M		Major, Italian Army, Montenegro (Yugo.)	MURDER	FR.
BELTRAME, Giulio	252394	M		Capt., Italian Army, Ljubljana (Yugo.) 41-43	MISC.CRIMES	YUGO.
BELTRAME, Livio	252925	M		Lt., Ufficiale Osservatore, Ital. Airman 113, Squadriglia O.A., Sosici (Yugo.) 12.7.43	INTERR.	YUGO.
BENECASA	162485	M	.98	Capt., Italian Army, C.C. Padula (It.) summer 1942	TORTURE	U.K.
BENELI or BENELLI	300174	M		Lt.Col., C.O., "Pinerolo"-Div., C.C. Larissa Andares, 41-43	MURDER	GRC.
BENELLI see BENELI	300174					
BENINCASA, Antonio	196139	M		Col., Military Tribunal, Ljubljana (Yugo.) 41-43	INTERR.	YUGO.
BENTIVOGLIO, N.	252924	M		Sgt.Maj., Pilot, Italian Airforce, Vianja)Slov.) 17.3.43	INTERR.	YUGO.
BENVENUTI, Leone	255508	M		Lt., of the customs guard, Fistanje (Yugo.) 1941	INTERR.	YUGO.
BERANI	149618	M		Lt., Army, "Lombardia"-Div., 73 Regt., 3 Bn., (Yugo.) 1943	MURDER	YUGO.
BERARDI, Manlio	149617	M		Lt.Col., Isonzo-Div., 24 Inf.Regt. "Como", (Yugo.) 1943	MURDER	YUGO.
BERARDI, Pholo	149616	M		General, commander, Sassari-Div., (Yugo.) 1943	MURDER	YUGO.
BERGONZI, A.	262425	M		Corps-General, commander, Italian Army, Udine and Gorizia (It.) 1942	MURDER	YUGO.
BERNACCHI	190894	M		Carabinieri, Italian Army, C.C. Montalbano (It.) 41-43	MISC.CRIMES	YUGO.
BERTELLI	190895	M		Col., Italian Army, Budva (Yugo.) 17.7.41	MURDER	YUGO.
BERTI, Giuseppe	300617	M	circa 15	Lt., Unit of the Italian Republican Army, Rocca San Stefano Prov. Roma (It.) 14.5.44	MURDER	U.K.
BERTIOTO	149615	M		Carabiniere, Army, Isle of Korcula (Yugo.) 1943	MURDER	YUGO.
BERTIZOLO	158350	M		Civilian, Solagne (It.) 4.11.44	MURDER	U.K.
BERTONI	173242	M		Col., Italian Army, C.C. Caserta (It.) 9.42	MURDER	U.K.
BERTORELLE	190896	M		Major, Col., Italian Army, Crna Gora (Yugo.) 1941	MURDER	YUGO.
BERTOSI, Umberto	252263	M		Cmdt., 10 Flottiglia Mas., St. Peter (Slov.) 16. and 24.1.45	MISC.CRIMES	YUGO.
BESTA, Fabio	149613	M		Col., Army, Lombardia-Div., 73 Inf.Regt., (Yugo.) 1943	MURDER	YUGO.
BETTONI	172910	M		Interpreter, Army, C.C. Tahuna (Africa) 2.42	MISC.CRIMES	U.K.
BIANCHIERI, Giovanni	256984	M		Secretary of town, administration, Kastav (Yugo.) 41-43	SUSPECT	YUGO.
BIANCHI	300179	M		Cpl., Medical Orderly, Inf. at Averof Prison, Athens (Grc.) 7.41-4.42	MURDER	GRC.
BIANCHI, Angel, Antonio	253600	M		Cmdt., Squadra d'Azione del Partito Fascista Republicano, Fonda (Littoria) (It.) 9.,10.43	TORTURE	YUGO.
BIANCHI, Arturo	259175	M	05	See Consolidated List Part II - Appendix "A"		
BIANCHI, Giovanni	149612	M		Carabiniere, Italian Army, Dalmatia (Yugo.) 7.42-8.43	PILLAGE	YUGO.
BIANCHI, Guido	149611	M		Capt., Army, Kriegsgericht, Cettigne (Yugo.) 1943	MURDER	YUGO.
BIANCO, Ferruccio	300663	M		Col., President of War Military Tribunal, Second Army, Sezione di Sebenico, Sibenik Dalmatia (Yugo.) 41-43	MISC.CRIMES	YUGO.
BIAVATI, Guiseppe	256985	M		See Consolidated List Part II - Appendix "A"		
BIGLINO, Eraldo	252862	M	26.12.02	Milicien, 2 Coy., 60 Bn., black shirt, Grocicchia (It.) 13.7.43	PILLAGE	FR.
BIGLIO, Felice	307261	M		Seniore, cmdt., 117 Bn. at Mouronog, 98 Fascist Legion attached to "Isonzo"-Div., 42-43	MURDER	YUGO.
BINDOLO	144942	M		Carabiniere, Army, (Yugo.) 1943	MURDER	YUGO.
BINNA	190897	M		Dr., prefetto, Administration of Occupied Territories, Sibenik (Yugo.) 41-43	MURDER	YUGO.
BISANTI, J.	144941	M		Major, Military Station, St. Anton (Yugo.) 1942	MISC.CRIMES	YUGO.
BIZARRI, Vicenzo	259099	M		Capt., Italian Army, 56 Regt., "Marche"-Div., Stolac (Yugo.) 4.41-9.42	MURDER	YUGO.
BOCCA	190899	M		Col., Italian Army, 82 Bn., Div. "Ferrara", Sarnik Montenegro (Yugo.) 5.,6.43	MURDER	YUGO.
BODO	193535	M		Col., chief, Italian Army, Police, Nice (Fr.) 1943	TORTURE	FR.
BOETTI, Pier Antonio	307285	M		Centurione, Judge, Military Court, 2 Army, section of Ljubljana (Yugo.) 41-43	MURDER	YUGO.
BOLLO	190900	M		Capt., Italian Army, Kistanje Rogoznica (Yugo.) 1942	MURDER	YUGO.
BOLO	190901	M		Col., Italian Army, Makarska Ploce Bari (Yugo.) 22.12.42	PILLAGE	YUGO.
BOLOGNE, Vittorio	144940	M		Capt., 24 Inf.Regt. "Como", "Isonzo"-Div., (Yugo.) 1943	MURDER	YUGO.
BONATTI, Bruno	259178	M	15	Tenente, Adjutant of Btty.-Commander, Andrijevica (Yugo.) 41-43	MISC.CRIMES	YUGO.
BONAYUTO, Felice	300187	M		Maresciallo with Carabinieri Reali at Corfu (Political Department) Corfu, 10.44	TORTURE	GRC.
BONGIOVANNI, Guiseppe	190902	M		Col., Italian Army, 1 Bn., 83 Regt., Div. "Venetia", Podgorica Montenegro (Yugo.) 9.,10.,11.41, 8.43	MURDER	YUGO.
BONIFACI	259125	M		Camp leader, Head of internment camp, Pistici (It.) 41,42,43	BRUTALITY	YUGO.
BONITO-OLIVA, Achille	163285	M		Col., Italian Army, Inf., C.C. Capua (It.) 27.1.43	TORTURE	U.K.
BONNAPACE (or BONPACE), Renzo	193939A	M		Cpt., Alp.Chasseurs, Fusterier, Chief S.R. Grenoble, Fontaine 3.3.43	MISC.CRIMES	FR.
BONOMO, Giovanni	149630	M		Tenente Medico, Army, 24 Inf.Regt. "Como", "Isonzo"-Div., (Yugo.) 1943	MURDER	YUGO.
BONONI, Felice	252011	M		Judge, Investigator, civilian, Split (Yugo.) 17.4.42	MURDER	YUGO.
BOPPE-BIANCO	194411	M		Civilian, chief, physician, Prison Military, Cuneo (It.) 9.,10.44	TORTURE	FR.
BORELLI, Vincenzo	190903	M	11.5.11	Carabiniere, Italian Army, Sibenik Lezovak (Yugo.) 41-43	MURDER	YUGO.
BORDON, Luigi	300618	M		Milite, Black Bde., Mesola, Ferrara, Adria, Rovigo (It.) 12.44	MURDER	U.K.
BORGHESE, Prince Valerio	252014	M		Cmdt., Army X, Flottiglia Mas., Conegliano (It.) 12.43-4.45	MISC.CRIMES	YUGO.
BORRINI, Carlo	300619	M		Vice-Brig., Order of Public Security, Mesola, Ferrara, Adria, Rovigo (It.) 12.44	MURDER	U.K.
BORRUZO, Pietro	190904	M		Major, Italian Army, 3 Btty., 151 Regt. Fanteria, "Sassari"-Div., Fara Slovenia (Yugo.) summer 1941	MURDER	YUGO.
BORSI, Sebastiano	259133	M		Vice-Brig. of C.C. R.R., IV It. Partisan Bde., Beri-Podjorica, Berane Montenegro (Yugo.) 41-43	MISC.CRIMES	YUGO.
BOSDARI, Avv., Francesco, Saverio	255510	M		Capt., member of the Tribunal, Kotor (Yugo.) 41-43	INTERR.	YUGO.
BOTA	256986	M	10	Cmdt., Albania Fascist Milita, Nikiforoun, Mavrove-Leunovo (Yugo.) 9.43	PILLAGE	YUGO.
BOTIGLIANI or MONTIGLIANI	300190	M		Capt. or Lt., "Forli"-Div., C.C. Larissa, 41-43	MURDER	GRC.

ITALY (Bou-Car)

ITALY. (Cont.)

NAME	C.R.FILE NUMBER	SEX	DATE OF BIRTH	RANK	OCCUPATION UNIT PLACE AND DATE OF CRIME	REASON WANTED	WANTED BY
BOUTOURIAN	185421	M			Civil. Serv., Occupied Territories, Athen (Grc.) 9.43	MURDER	GRC.
BOUZIL,Alexandre	159385	M			Pvt., Army, stationed at Moncontour (Fr.), Monteize (Fr.) 1.8.44	PILLAGE	FR.
BOZZI	300620	M			Capt., Campo 52, Chiavari (It.) 12.41-10.42	TORTURE	U.F.
BRANCATI,Corrado	190905	M			SS-Oberstgruppenfhr., General, Fascist-Miliz, Sibenik (Yugo.) 41-43	MURDER	YUGO.
BREDAROS	253823	M			Agent, SD, Toulouse (Fr.) 11.42-8.44	MISC.CRIMES	FR.
BREZZI	190906	M			Maggiore, Italian Army, Vosnic (Yugo.) 7.41	PILLAGE	YUGO.
BRUCCIAMONTE	193547	M			Brig., Italian Army, Carabinieri, Petrovac (Yugo.) 8.41	MURDER	YUGO.
BRUNEC	149629	M			Carabiniere, Army, Isle of Korcula (Yugo.) 1943	MURDER	YUGO.
BRUNO,Camillo	190907	M			Deputy Prefect, Zara Province, Sibenik (Yugo.) 6.42-9.42	MURDER	YUGO.
BUCARI,Giorgio	259106	M			Lt., Italian Army, 56 Regt., "Marche"-Div., Stolag (Yugo.) 4.41-9.42	MURDER	YUGO.
BUCCERINI	149628	M			Col., Army, Kriegsgericht, Cettigne (Yugo.) 1943	MURDER	YUGO.
BUCCILLI,Renato	254485	M			Major, Italian Army, Tribunal, Ljubljana (Yugo.) 41-43	INTERR.	YUGO.
BUIOLI	149627	M			Carabiniere, Army-Fasciste, Isle of Korcula (Yugo.) 1943	MURDER	YUGO.
BULIONI,Italo	259132	M			Major, Venezia-Div., 1 Bn., 84 Regt., Andrijevica Montenegro (Yugo.) 8.41-9.42	MISC.CRIMES	YUGO.
BULLO,Atillio	259194	M			Lt., Italian Army, "Marche"-Div., 56 Regt., Stolac (Yugo.) 4.41-9.42	MURDER	YUGO.
BUNGARO,Guiseppe	190908	M			Capt., Italian Army, officer of Carabinieri, Sibenik (Yugo.) 41,42,43	MURDER	YUGO.
BUORO,Antoine	185647	M			Pvt., member, Italian Army, Gestapo, Dordogne (Fr.)	MISC.CRIMES	FR.
BURASSO	254285	M			Photographer, Italian Airforce, Slovenia (Yugo.) 8.-9.42	INTERR.	YUGO.
BURGIO,Francesco	149626	M			Commander, Army, 98 Fascist Legion, "Isonzo"-Div., Trebnje (Yugo.) 1943	MURDER	YUGO.
BUSSIERI,Antonio	259167	M			Head of Banda Volontaria Anticommunista, Biovixcino, Selo, Kistanje, Ivosevci (Yugo.) 5.-6.42	SUSPECT	YUGO.
BUTTI,Giuseppe	149626	M			Cmdt., Army, Carabinieri Reale, Dalmatia (Yugo.) 1943	MURDER	YUGO.
CAGNE	192238	M			Lt., Italian Army, 10 Bn., Chasseurs Alpins, Hauteville Gondon (Fr.) 8.43	PILLAGE	FR.
CAIER,Cesarino	256990	M			Pvt., Italian Army, Execution Squad, Plave (Yugo.) 13.2.-23.2.45	INTERR.	YUGO.
CAIANCHI,Umberto	137618	M			Capt., Italian Army, San Guiseppe, Sicily (It.) 12.42-1.43	MISC.CRIMES	U.K.
CALCATERRA,V.E.	106973	M			Col., cmdt., Camp 57, Udine (It.) 20.5.43, 9.43, 1945	MURDER	U.F.
CALCETERA	125362	M			Col., C.C. Bindau (It.) 42-43	TORTURE	U.K.
CALDONE,Firrao,N.	178326	M		95	Maj.Gen., Army, Athens (Grc.) autumn 1941, autumn 1942	TORTURE	U.K.
CALETTI,Nello	190917	M			Pvt., Italian Army, Brigadiere Carabinieri, Susak (Yugo.) 41-42, 4.43	MURDER	YUGO.
CALLIGARIS,Mario	252002	M			Observer, Italian Airforce, Gruppe 240, 43 Sturm-Bn.98, Polica, Podpesek, Metnaj, Babna (Yugo.) 8.-9.42	INTERR.	YUGO.
CALZA,Carlo	145741	M			Lt., 24 Inf.Regt. "Como", II Bn., "Isonzo"-Div., (Yugo.) 1943	MURDER	YUGO.
CAMBIRASIO,Angelo	185977	M	10 - 15		Fascist, Trescore (It.) 4.1.45	MURDER	U.S.
CAMELLI,Guido	190909	M			Secretary, Fascio at Blato of Korcula Island (Yugo.) during first half of 1943	MURDER	YUGO.
CAMILLO	169474	M			Dr., Capt., Italian Army, Capua (It.) 4.41-6.43	TORTURE	U.K.
CAMOUSSO,Cesare	300203	M			Maresciallo, chief of the Carabinieri Reali, of C.C. Warders, Averof Prison, Athens (Grc.) 41-43	MURDER	GRC.
CAMPASSI	256991A	M			Pvt., Italian Army, Plave Anhovo (Yugo.) 13.-23.2.45	INTERR.	YUGO.
CAMPELLI,Enrico	120005	M	2.1.05		Supervisor, Prison, San Remo (It.) 16.7.43-3.44	TORTURE	YUGO.,FR.
CANADA,Calcedonis	190910	M			Lt.Col., commander, Italian Army, XI Bn. of Carabinieri, Cetinje, Crna Gora (Yugo.) 41,42,43	MURDER	YUGO.
CANATA	300368	M			Lt., 26 Bn. Royal Carabinieri, Casta Hamlet Corsica (Fr.) 19.-31.8.43	TORTURE	FR.
CANATA,G.	145740	M			Lt.Col., 3 Btty. Metlika, Cernomelj (Yugo.) 1943	MURDER	YUGO.
CANDIDA,Renato	190911	M			Kapo, Italian Army, del Posto de Carabinieri, Kotor (Yugo.) 41-43	MURDER	YUGO.
CANINO,Ignacio	190912	M			O.C., Italian Army, 259 Regt. of Murge-Div., Trebine Boski Jubine (Yugo.) 42-43	MURDER	YUGO.
CANIONI	251987	M			Cmdt., Lt.Col., 60 Bn. "Black Chemises", Croicchia (Fr.) 13.7.43	PILLAGE	FR.
CANTARELLA,Roberto	250088	M			Lt., cmdt., La Tenenza di Zaravecchia (Yugo.) 1943	INTERR.	YUGO.
CANTATORE,Vittorio	145739	M			Lt., Carabinieri Reali, XIV Bn., Cernomelj (Yugo.) 1942	MURDER	YUGO.
CAPELINI see TONETI	191130	M					
CAPIGATI,Guiseppe	259105	M			Lt.Col., Italian Army, 56 Regt., "Marche"-Div., Stolag (Yugo.) 4.41-9.42	MURDER	YUGO.
CAPITANO,Gino	190913	M			Major, Italian Army, 55 Regt. "Marche"-Div., Trebine, 20.4.41-8.9.43	MURDER	YUGO.
CAPO,Luigi	193891	M			Leader, Italian Red Cross, C.C. Cuneo (It.) 9.43	MURDER	FR.
CAPOBIANCO,Donato	162752	M			Lt.Col., Italian Inf., C.C. Fermo (It.) 11.41-43	TORTURE	U.K.
CAPOGROSSO or CAVAGNIN	145738	M			Major, Army, Dalmatia (Yugo.) 1943	PILLAGE	YUGO.
CAPORALI,Dante	252040	M			Lt.Col., cmdt., Chiessanuova (It.) 42-43	INTERR.	YUGO.
CAPPELLI	193892	M			General, Military Court, Breil s-Rova (Fr.) 9.43	PILLAGE	FR.
CAPRIOLO,Georgio	190914	M			Adjutant, Div. "Messina", aide de camp, Bfrane (Yugo.) 7.-9.41	MURDER	YUGO.
CAPURSO	163282	M	circa 95		Col., Italian Army, C.C. Macereta (It.) 6.-9.43	MISC.CRIMES	U.K.
CAPUTI,Pietro	250086	M			See Consolidated List Part II - Appendix "A"		
CARATINI,Amlete	162751	M			Col., cmdt. of PG 87, Italian Cav., C.C. Benevento (It.) 7.11.42	TORTURE	U.K.
CARBONARI	145736	M			Carabiniere, Army, Isle of Korcula (Yugo.) 1943	MURDER	YUGO.
CARBONI	145735	M			Carabiniere, Army, Isle of Korcula (Yugo.) 1943	MURDER	YUGO.
CARELLI,Guiseppe	190915	M			Major, Italian Army, 53 Regt., "Marche"-Div., Trebinje (Yugo.) 20.4.41-8.9.43	MURDER	YUGO.
CARETTO,Anunzio	190916	M			Col., Italian Army, Bersaglieri, Trogir (Yugo.) 5.41	TORTURE	YUGO.
CARIGNANI,Ferdinando	250085	M			Lt.Col., Italian Army, Ljubljana (Yugo.) 41-43	MISC.CRIMES	YUGO.
CARINCIA	259124	M			Member, Staff of internment camp at Istonio-Marina, Pistici, Fabriano (It.) 41-43	BRUTALITY	YUGO.
CARLETTO,Achili	300664	M			Agent, Prison at Krk (It.) 41-43	TORTURE	YUGO.
CARLI	250935	M			Agent, Police, Split (Yugo.)	TORTURE	YUGO.
CARLI,Giovanni	145734	M			Lt.Col., "Isonzo"-Div., Novo Mesto (Yugo.) 1943	MURDER	YUGO.

ITALY (Car-Coc)

ITALY. (Cont.)

NAME	C.R. FILE NUMBER	SEX	DATE OF BIRTH	RANK OCCUPATION UNIT PLACE AND DATE OF CRIME	REASON WANTED	WANTED BY
CARLUCCI	152020	M		Lt., Italian Army, 58 R.A., Frejus (Fr.) 7.1.43	PILLAGE	FR.
CARLUCCI	192078	M		Capt., Fascist Military, San Vicino near Cerretto d'Esi (It.) 20.2.44	MURDER	U.K.
CARONE	190918	M		Agent, Press and Propaganda Italian, Kotor (Yugo.) 1941	MURDER	YUGO.
CAROSSI	256992	M		Vice-Brig., Italian Army, Plave Anhovo (Yugo.) 13.-23.2.45	INTERR.	YUGO.
CAROZZI, Enrico	300204	M	97	Capt., interpreter, Campo PG-57, Gruppignano and Udine (It.) between 10.42. and 10.43	MISC.CRIMES	U.K.
CARRETTO	300678	M		Capt., Medical officer, 40 Bn., Italian Republican Guard, stationed at San-Michele (It.) 6.11.43	MURDER	U.K.
CARUSO, Pietro	190919	M		Judge, Cpl., of Italian Extraordinary Court, Sibenik (Yugo.) 41.42.43	MURDER	YUGO.
CASABUONI, Conrado	191144	M		Judge, Italian Special Court, Sibenik (Yugo.) 41-43	MURDER	YUGO.
CASAGRANDE	256994	M		Pvt., Italian Army, Plave Anhovo (Yugo.) 13.2.45-23.2.45	INTERR.	YUGO.
CASANEGRO	191163	M		Official, engineer, operating in Yugo., 1942	TORTURE	U.K.
CASCI, Giovanni	190920	M		Pvt., Italian Army, Sibenik (Yugo.) 41-43	MURDER	YUGO.
CASELLI	190921	M		Pvt., Italian Army, C.C. Montalbano (Yugo.) 41-43	MISC.CRIMES	YUGO.
CASCETTO, Pietro	145729	M		Major, 24 Inf.Regt. "Como", "Iconzo"-Div., (Yugo.) 1943	MURDER	YUGO.
CASSU, Giovanni	145727	M		Carabiniere, Carabinieri Station, Sibenik (Yugo.) 1942	MURDER	YUGO.
CASULIO, Filipodi, Guiseppe	137615	M		Pvt., guard, Italian Army, C.C. Bari (It.) 16.7.42	MURDER	U.K.
CASTAGLIONI, Massimo	191145	M		General-Consul, Vice-Chairman of Italian "Special Court" in Sibenik (Yugo.) 41-43	MURDER	YUGO.
CASTAGNOLI, Bruno	145728	M		Lt., Army, Novo Mesto (Yugo.) 1942	MURDER	YUGO.
CASTELLANI, Leopoldo	195625	M		Brig.Gen., Military, 41-43	MURDER	YUGO.
CASTELLI-TADDEI, Dino	173273	M		Col., Italian Army, C.C. Chiavari (It.)	TORTURE	U.F.
CASTIGLINI, Alfredo	251482	M		Lt., Italian Airforce, 113 Squadriglia, 63 Gruppe, 21 Stormo, Village Hrastov-Dol and Trnovica (Yugo.) 31.7.43	INTERR.	YUGO.
CATALDI, Giovanni, Battista	189904	M		Capt., Italian Army, Montenegro (Yugo.)	MURDER	YUGO.
CATTANI, Anna, Maria Nick-Name "Donna Paola"	300621	F	circa 15	Nurse, Mesola, Ferrara, Adria, Rovigo (It.) 12.44	MURDER	U.K.
CAVAGNIN see CAPOGROSSO	145738					
CAVALERRI, Giorgio	259123	M		Lt., Italian Army, 56 Regt., "Marche"-Div., Stolag (Yugo.) 4.41-9.42	MURDER	YUGO.
CAVAI'O	300205	M		Capt., "Forli"-Div., C.C. Larissa, 41-43	MURDER	GRC.
CAVAZZONI	190923	M		Member, Fascist Military, Sibenik (Yugo.) 41-43	MURDER	YUGO.
CECCHINI, Attilio	258165	M		Sgt., Tagliamento VIII Alp.Regt., 2 Bn., Fasc.Republ.Army, Dorenberg (Yugo.) 12.43-4.45	INTERR.	YUGO.
CECCIONI	190924	M		Dr., Commissar, Italian Army, Fraschette C.C. for civilians at Alatri, Fraschette, Alatri (It.) 41-43	MURDER	YUGO.
CECCONI	141463	M		Lt., Italian Army, Petreto, Bicchisano, Corse (Fr.)	MURDER	FR.
CELLINI, Candido	193548	M		Sgt., Italian Army, Carabinieri, Banovina-Zevaka (Yugo.) 1941	MURDER	YUGO.
CEMONZE, Francesko	190925	M		Dr., Fascist-Party, Army, Sibenik (Yugo.) 41-43	MURDER	YUGO.
CERETANI	189902	M		Major, Venezia-Army, Montenegro (Yugo.)	PILLAGE	YUGO.
CERUTTI, Guido	145722	M		Brig., Divisional Infantry, Novo Mesto (Yugo.) 1942	MURDER	YUGO.
CESI, Antonio	189901	M		Capt., Italian Army, Montenegro (Yugo.)	MURDER	YUGO.
CHELOTTI, Carlo	307273	M		Lt., officer in charge of Detachment, Campo PG-106, Vercelli West of Milan (It.) 6. or 7.42	MURDER	U.K.
CHIARPAGRINI	252000	M		Capt., 1 Coy., 59 Regt., Santo-Pietro-di-Tenda (Fr.) 19.-31.8.44	TORTURE	FR.
CHINICI, Dominico	189900	M		General, Italian Army, Montenegro (Yugo.)	MURDER	YUGO.
CHIODI	145718	M		Lt., Army, (Yugo.) 1942	MURDER	YUGO.
CHIMIELEVSKY	250966	M		Fascist "Federale", Split (Yugo.) 6.1.41	TORTURE	YUGO.
CHMIMIELEVSKI, Alfred	252003	M		Merchant, civilian, Split (Yugo.)	PILLAGE	YUGO.
CHRISTIANINI, Nello	300211	M		Black Bde., Frasinelle, Rovigo, (It.) on or about 2.8.44	MISC.CRIMES	U.K.
CHRISTINI, Guiseppe	169475	M		Dr., Lt., Italian Army, Laterina (It.) 8.42-9.43	TORTURE	U.K.
CIACCIO, Luigi	190926	M		Col., Italian Army, Lustica-Dalmatia, Djurasevic (Yugo.) 9.9.43	MURDER	YUGO.
CIAMPAULO, Rolando	259104	M		Lt., Italian Army, 56 Regt., "Marche"-Div., Stolac (Yugo.) 4.41-9.42	MURDER	YUGO.
CIANCABILLA	189899	M		Col., Italian Army, Ljubljana (Yugo.)	TORTURE	YUGO.
CIANCOLLINI, Piero	190927	M		Commissar, Italian Municipal Administration, Sibenik (Yugo.) 41-43	MURDER	YUGO.
CIANI, Fernando	250087	M		See Consolidated List Part II - Appendix "A"		
CIGALA, Fulgosi, Alfonso	190929	M		Lt.Gen., Italian Army, Sibenik (Yugo.) 41-43	MURDER	YUGO.
CILOTTI, S.	163283	M		Col., Italian Army, C.C. Macerate (It.) 28.2.43	MURDER	U.K.
CIMIMO, Giovanni	254930	M		Capt., Judge, Italian Special Tribunal, Zadar, Sibenik, Kotor (Yugo.) 41-43	INTERR.	YUGO.
CIONE, Vincenzo	173272	M		Col., Italian Army, Camp 63, Aversa (It.) 42. 3.43	TORTURE	U.K.
CIPOLETTI, Nicolo	190930	M	circa 06	Kapo, Italian Camp, C.C. Tribune (Yugo.) 1942	MURDER	YUGO.
CIPRIANI	190932	M		Cpl., Italian Army, Div. "Ferrara", Kapino-Polje (Yugo.) 6.43	MURDER	YUGO.
CIPRIANI, Nanni	190931	M		Col., Italian Army, O.C. of Bn. "Bolzano", "Pusteria"-Div., 11.41 Cetinji-Savrick, Podgorica' (Yugo.) 7.,11.41	MURDER	YUGO.
CIRILO, Antonio	145712	M		Lt., Doctor, "Isonzo"-Div., 24 Inf.Regt. "Como", (Yugo.) 1943	MURDER	YUGO.
CIRILO, Antonio	190933	M		Lt.Col., Italian Army, 51 Regt. of "Murge"-Div., Trebinje (Yugo.) 42-43	MURDER	YUGO.
CIROTTI, Mario	190934	M		Lt.Gen., Italian Army, "Alpi Grae"-Div., Savnik Montenegro (Yugo.) 5.,6.,9.42	TORTURE	YUGO.
CISOTTI, Carlo	307286	M		General-Consul, Judge of Special Tribunals for defence of State, Rom (It.) 4.41-9.43	MURDER	YUGO.
CITERNI, Teodorico	178323	M		Col., Italian Army, C.C. PG-82, Loterina (It.) 8.42-9.43	TORTURE	U.K.
CITTATI, Gaetano	307287	M		Capt., Judge, Military Court, Second Army section di Lubiana, Ljubljana (Yugo.) 41-43	MURDER	YUGO.
CLERICI, N.	145704	M		Prefect of Pola, Trieste Pola (It.) 1943	MURDER	YUGO.
COBELLI, Giovanni	300623	M		Pvt., 40 Bn. Italian Republican Guard, stationed at San-Michele (It.) 6.11.43	MURDER	U.K.
COCCIA, Angelo	193549	M		Col., Garrison Commander, Italian Army, Niksic (Yugo.) 11.11.41	MURDER	YUGO.
COCCMARELLA, Vicenzo	145703	M		Col., 24 Inf.Regt. "Como", "Isonzo"-Div., Novo Mesto (Yugo.) 1943	MURDER	YUGO.

ITALY (Cod-Del)

NAME	C.R.FILE NUMBER	SEX	DATE OF BIRTH	RANK	OCCUPATION	UNIT	PLACE AND DATE OF CRIME	REASON WANTED	WANTED BY

ITALY. (Cont.)

NAME	C.R.FILE NUMBER	SEX	DATE OF BIRTH	OCCUPATION, UNIT, PLACE AND DATE OF CRIME	REASON WANTED	WANTED BY
CODA, N.	252001	M		Lt., observer, Italian Airforce, 43 Sturm-Bn.98, Gruppe 240, Metnaj, Babna, Polica, Podpesek (Yugo.) 8. and 9.42	MISC.CRIMES	YUGO.
COIAZZI, Emilio	307288	M		Doctor, Lt.Col., Judge, Military Court, Susak (Yugo.) 41-43	MURDER	YUGO.
COIALILIO, Gaetano	190935	M		N.C.O., Italian Army, Novo Mesto, Metleka (Yugo.) 1942	MURDER	YUGO.
COLINO, Giuseppe	250967	M		Agent, Police, Split (Yugo.) 2.42	MURDER	YUGO.
COLIZZA, Ugo	307289	M		General-Consul, Judge of Special Tribunal for defense of state. Rom (It.) 4.41-9.43	MURDER	YUGO.
COLLEONI, Antonio	162753	M		Major, Italian Inf., Cmdt. of PG-41, C.C. Montalbo (It.) 12.41-5.43	TORTURE	U.K.
COLNACHI, Ettore	300209	M		Lt., Quartermaster, PG-57 Camp, Gruppignano and Udine (It.) 10.42-10.43	MISC.CRIMES	U.K.
COLO, Luigi	307274	M		Italian Fascist, Camp Longo Padua (It.) on or about 5.11.44	MURDER	U.K.
COLOMBO	193890	M		Chief, guard, Prison, C.C. Cuneo (It.) 9.43	TORTURE	FR.
COLOMBO, Tenente	199289	M	10	Official, Arbeits-Kdo., 64 Camp Bergamo, Gardone V.T.Brescia (It.) 8.43	TORTURE	U.K.
COLOTTO, Emilio	190936	M		Member, Italian Army, Metlika (Yugo.) 1.2.42	MURDER	YUGO.
COMELIA, E.	307290	M		Capt., Correspendent, Military Court, Susak (Yugo.) 1943	MURDER	YUGO.
CONCINA, Giovanni	190937	M		Official, Italian Army, "Black shirts", Susak, Podheim (Yugo.) 41-42, until 1943	MURDER	YUGO.
CONCINA, Roberto	190938	M		Capt., Italian Army, XXII Bn. Zadar, Zara, Veliki (Yugo.) 28.7.42	MURDER	YUGO.
CONCINI, Ante	145697	M		Capt., Army, Zadar (Yugo.) 1943	MURDER	YUGO.
CONSINI, Alberto	305008	M		Lt.Col., Italian Gendarmerie, Vonitza, Xyromer district, 10.-15.11.42, 11.4.43	MISC.CRIMES	GRC.
CONSCIMI, Alberto	305008	M		Lt.Col., Italian Gendarmerie, Vonitza, Xyromer district, 10.-15.11.42, 11.4.43	MISC.CRIMES	GRC.
CONSTANTINI, Constantino	145695	M		Dr., Tenente medico, 25 Inf.Regt. "Como", "Isonzo"-Div., Cernomelj (Yugo.) 1943	MURDER	YUGO.
CONTI see CORTI	178324					
CONTI, Alfredo	190939	M		Civilian, Commissioner, Political Department of Questura-Naples (It.) 28.9.43	MURDER	YUGO.
CONTICELLI, Giuseppe	195626	M		Official, Military, Rom (It.) 41-43	TORTURE	YUGO.
COPPA	189898	M		Medical officer, Italian Army, Ponza (It.)	TORTURE	YUGO.
COPFI or GOPP	145694	M		Carabiniere, Army, Dalmatia (Yugo.) 1943	MURDER	YUGO.
COPPOLA	132482	M		Col., Italian Army, Cmdt. of Camp 65, Gravina (It.) 1943	TORTURE	U.K.
CORDOPATRI, Antonio	190940	M		Lt., Italian Army, Carabinieri XXII Bn., Veliki (Yugo.) 28.7.42	MURDER	YUGO.
CORNACCHIA, Giuseppe	300624	M		Paratrooper, Corioeni, Comune, Amandola (It.) 2.5.44	MURDER	U.K.
CORONATI, Emilio or COVINATI	145690	M		General, Inf.Div. "Isonzo"-part of XI Corpo d'Armata, Novo Mesto (Yugo.) 1942	MURDER	YUGO.
CORRIAS, Ugo	190941	M		Carabiniero, Italian Army, Sobenik (Yugo.) 41-43	MURDER	YUGO.
CORSI, Candino	190942	M		Commander, C.C. Italian, Montalbano Sicily (It.) 41-43	TORTURE	YUGO.
CORTE, Giovanni	250680	M		Lt.Gen. Cmdt., Army, Trieste (It.) 1942	MISC.CRIMES	YUGO.
CORTI, Guido or CONTI	178324	M		Cmdt., Major, Army, Aver of Prison, Athens (Grc.) 1942	WITNESS	U.Y.
COSCI, Furio	300210	M		Black Bde., Frasinelle, Rovigo Province (It.) on or about 2.8.44	MISC.CRIMES	U.K.
COSMIN, Pietro	188597	M	15.10.03	Mayor, Prefect Praesident, Police Public, Member, Fascist Federation, Grezzana-Verona (It.) 12.11.43	MURDER	U.K.
COSSU, Carino	190943	M		Carabiniero, Italian Army, Sibenik (Yugo.) 41-43	MURDER	YUGO.
COTZI, Vittorio	178322	M	95	Civilian, Governor, C.C. Bari (It.) 1.-2.43	TORTURE	U.K.
COVINATI, Emilio see CORONATI	145690					
CRISTICIANI, David	259174	M	18	Tenente, deputy Carabinieri Commander, Venezia-Div., Berane Montenegro (Yugo.) 41-43	MISC.CRIMES	YUGO.
CRISTINI, Guiseppe	169475	M		Capt., Italian Army, Medical officer at Camp 82, Laterina (It.) 8.42-9.43	TORTURE	U.K.
CROCE, Mario see GROCE	169487					
CROFOLIO aliases OROFOLO	193539	M		Col., C.C. Italian, P.O.W. Camp Nr. 75, Cmdt., Bari (It.)	MURDER	U.K.
CUIULI	190944	M		Col., C.C. Italian, Rab-Island (Yugo.) 4.41-9.43	TORTURE	YUGO.
DAGLI, Alberi, Delio	259100	M		Lt., Italian Army, 56 Regt., "Marche"-Div., Stolac (Yugo.) 4.41-9.42	MURDER	YUGO.
D'ALESSANDRO, Italo	307337	M		General-Consul, Special Tribunal for defense of State, Rom (It.) 4.41-9.43	MURDER	YUGO.
DALESSIO	300212	M		Capt., or Lt., "Forli"-Div., C.C. Larissa, 41-43	MURDER	GRC.
DALLA-PRIA, Agostino	307275	M		Italian Fascist, Camp Longo Padua (It.) on or about 5.11.44	MURDER	U.K.
DALIOLIO	155751	M		Commander, Italian Army, Bassano (It.) 11.44	MURDER	U.K.
DAIMAZZO, Renzo	190945	M		General, Italian Army, VI Corps d'Armata, Solin Dalmatia (Yugo.) 24.1.42	MURDER	YUGO.
D'ALOISI, Ruggero	190875	M		Member, Italian Army, Sibenik (Yugo.) 41,42,43	MURDER	YUGO.
D'AMBROSIO, G.	193537	M	30. 3.88	Medical officer, Italian Army, Coserta Hospital (It.)	MURDER	U.K.
DAMIANI DE VERGADA, Pietro	259168	M	circa 13	Cmdt., 291 Regt. of the Zara-Div., Kistanje, Piramatovci, Banja (Yugo.) 17.8.42, 3.43, 22.4.43	MISC.CRIMES	YUGO.
DAMICO	300213	M		Officer, Artl., Italian Army, Naxos, 41-43	MISC.CRIMES	GRC.
D'AMICO, Angelo, Beppino	153868	M	20. 3.21	Italian Army, 457 Unit, Ospidale da Lampo (Tunisia)	TORTURE	FR.
D'AMICO, Angelo	189916	M		Civilian, Bizerte (Tunisia)	MURDER	FR.
D'ANTILIO see D'AUTILIO, Salvatore	146099					
D'AUTILIO, Salvatore or D'ANTILIO	146099	M		Carabiniere, Army, Carabinieri Station "Sebenico Sud", Sibenik (Yugo.) 12.4.42	MURDER	YUGO.
DAVANA, Antonio	305012	M		Lt., Crete (Grc.) 42-43	MISC.CRIMES	GRC.
DAVELA, Giuseppe	190946	M		Officer, Italian Army, Div. "Ferrara", Rastok Montenegro (Yugo.) 3.42	MURDER	YUGO.
DEANA	252998	M		Lt., 59 Regt. "Black shirts", 1 Coy., St. Pietro (It.) 19.-31.8.43	MISC.CRIMES	FR.
DE BAZI, George	300220	M		Lt.Col., Officer Commanding, the Carabinieri Reali in Corfu (Korsika) 10.41-9.43	MISC.CRIMES	GRC.
DE BLASIO	190898	M		Dr., Lt.Gen., Italian Army, Promina Bruvno (Yugo.) 24.7.42	MURDER	YUGO.
DE CICCO, Michele	307276	M		Prt., guard, Camp 66, Ator near Capua (It.) 27.1.43	BRUTALITY	U.K.
DE GUIDA	190961	M		Col., Italian Army, 51 Regt. of "Marche"-Div., Trebinje (Yugo.) 42-43	MURDER	YUGO.
DELATTI	178320	M		Capt., Army, Italian Medical Corps, C.C. PG-53 Macerata (It.) 1.-2.43	TORTURE	U.K.

ITALY (Del-Fag)

NAME	C.R.FILE NUMBER	SEX	DATE OF BIRTH	RANK, OCCUPATION, UNIT, PLACE AND DATE OF CRIME	REASON WANTED	WANTED BY
				ITALY. (Cont.)		
DEL GIUDICE	300613	M		Col., Maj.-Gen., Commander of the Pinerolo Div., Town-Mayor of Kastoria, Officer Commanding Occupation Army, Kastoria, Nestorion, Argos, Orestikon (Grc.) 42-43	MURDER	GRC.
DELICH, Ugo	259131	M		See Consolidated List Part II - Appendix "A"		
DE LITALA, Giuseppe	307291	M		Police Officer, Spalato (Split), C.C. Lipari (It.) 41-43	BRUTALITY	YUGO.
DELLA, Mano, Francesco	300221	M		Brig., Carabinieri of Vrhnika near Ljubljana (Yugo.) 41 and 42	MISC.CRIMES	YUGO.
DELLE-VENERI, Edoardo	162340	M		Capt., Italian Army, Medical Corps, Benevento (It.) 7.-11.42	MISC.CRIMES	U.F.
DEIMANTO, Osvaldo	150895	M		Sottotenente, Italian Army, "Isonzo"-Div., (Yugo.) 42-43	MURDER	YUGO.
DEIOGU, Giovanni	190947	M		Carabinieri, Italian Army, Sibenik (Yugo.) 41-43	MURDER	YUGO.
DE LORENZIO or DE LORENZIS	261331	M		General, Pietralba (Fr.) 10.9.43	BRUTALITY	FR.
DE LORENZIS see DE LORENZIO.	261331					
DE LUCA	300665	M		Major, Judge, Military Tribunal of War of Second Army, Sezione di Sebenico, Sibenik (Yugo.) 41-43	TORTURE	U.K.
DE LUCA, Mario	253775	M		Carabinieri, Bde. Police, Split (Yugo.) 26.6.43	TORTURE	YUGO.
DELUSKI	142036	M	12	Lt.Col., Italian Army, 313 Inf. Regt., Larissa (Grc.) 10.42-8.43	TORTURE	U.K.
DEMARCHI, Federico	150894	M		Lt., Italian Army, Carabiniere Bde., Isle of Vis (Yugo.) 7.3.43	MURDER	YUGO.
DE MARCO	191002	M		Dr., Lt., Italian Prison, C.C. Cetinje and Crna Gora (Yugo.) 41-43	MURDER	YUGO.
DE PAOLI, Giovanni or DE PAOLO, Giambattista	191059	M		Brig.Gen., Commander of Carabinieri, Sibenik (Yugo.) 41-43	MURDER	YUGO.
DE PAOLO, Giambattista see DE PAOLI, Giovanni	191059					
D'ERRICO, Francesco	150889	M		Centurione, "Isonzo"-Army, 98 Fasc. Legion, Rakovnik (Yugo.) 1943	MURDER	YUGO.
DESSANTIS, Domenico	190948	M		C.C. Director, C.C. Fraschette for civilians at Alatri, Fraschette, Alatri (It.) 41-43	TORTURE	YUGO.
DESSY, Carlo	252857	M		Tenente Colonello, Observer, Italian Airforce, 43 Stormo, Bn. 98, Gruppe 240, Metnaj, Babna, Polica, Podpesek (Yugo.) 8.-9.42	INTERR.	YUGO.
DE TURRIS	191134	M		Col., Italian Army, Garrison Commander of Omis, Gata near Omis (Yugo.) 8.42	MURDER	YUGO.
DEVECASI, Edalo	126894	M		Civilian, (It.) 9.43-2.44	MISC.CRIMES	U.K.
DE VECCHI, Pietro	191159	M		Major, Judge of Italian Special Court, Sibenik (Yugo.) 41-43	MURDER	YUGO.
DE VECCHIS, Ennio	191160	M		Legal Official, Judge of Italian Special Court, Sibenik (Yugo.) 41-43	MURDER	YUGO.
DE VESOVI, A.	300369	M		Capt., Army from Zadar, Kistanje, Northern Dalmatia (Yugo.) 9.42	MURDER	YUGO.
DE VITO, Giovanni	305111	M		Guard at P.O.W. Working Cdo. near Brindisi Airfield, at or near Brindisi (It.) 8.43	MURDER	U.F.
DIANA, Evelino	258164	M		Alpino, Fasc. Rep. Army, Tagliamento VIII Alp. Regt., 2 Bn., Dorenberg (Yugo.) End of 1943 to April 1945	INTERR.	YUGO.
DIFALCO	300227	M		Lt., Carabinieri Reali, Xironomi, Thebes, 22.6.42	MURDER	GRC.
DIFRANCESCO, Antonio	150893	M		Brig., Italian Army, Carabinieri, Isle of Kosoula (Yugo.) 1943	MURDER	YUGO.
DI IONNE, Antonio	194309	M	23. 5.20	Pvt., Italian Army, Camp Calabre, Toulon (Fr.) 16.7.44	MURDER	FR.
DI MARCO	300625	M		Carabiniere, Territorial Legion of the Royal Carabinieri of Ancona, Station of Cominanza, Ascoli, Picena (It.) 25.12.43	MURDER	U.K.
DI MARTINI	300626	M		Carabiniere, Campo 52, Chiavari (It.) 12.41-10.42	TORTURE	U.K.
DIMATTEO, Francesco	300228	M		Pvt., Collaborated with the Geheime Feldpolizei, Vrastamites near Livadia, Beotia. 8.1.44	MURDER	GRC.
DI NEGRO	145637	M		Col., Army, 1 Gren.Regt., (Yugo.) 1942	MURDER	YUGO.
DINO-CASTELLI, Taddei	300607	M		Cmdt., Campo 52, Chiavari (It.) 12.44	TORTURE	U.K.
DI PAOLI	188956	M		Lt., Italian Army, Grenoble (Fr.)	TORTURE	FR.
DODA, Argeo	190949	M		Member, Italian Army, IV Legion, Confinaria, C.C. N.N. "Monte Nevoso", Metlika (Yugo.) 1942	MURDER	YUGO.
DOIMI, Elena	150892	F		Teacher, P.O. Education, Vis (Yugo.) 9.3.43	TORTURE	YUGO.
DOMENICI	256988	M		Cpl., Italian Army, Plave (Yugo.) 13.-23.2.45	INTERR.	YUGO.
DOMENICO, Giusto	150891	M		Carabiniere, Italian Army, Babno Polje near Prezid (Yugo.) 2.7.-25.7.42	TORTURE	YUGO.
DONATI, Domenico	190950	M		Governor, Prison Poggio Reale, Naples (It.) 28.9.43	MURDER	YUGO.
DONNA BELIA	252474	M		Agent, Police, Split (Yugo.) 30.4.43	TORTURE	YUGO.
DONNAMURA	307292	M		N.C.O., member, Carabinieri, Trieste (It.) 12.41	MURDER	YUGO.
D'ORAZIO, Rafaele	188959	M		Capt., Italian Army, Grenoble (Fr.)	PILLAGE	FR.
DORIANO	252064	M		Capt., Italian Army, Village of Tribanj (Yugo.) 7.-8.41	BRUTALITY	YUGO.
D'ORO	150890	M		Capt., Italian Army, Div. Lombardia, Fuzine (Yugo.) 1942	MURDER	YUGO.
DOTA, Pasquale	169476	M		Capt., Italian Army, Capua (It.) 4.41-6.43	TORTURE	U.K.
DRUZEIC-EDSIC, Vicko	259169	M		Member, Ital. Fasc. Mil., Split (Yugo.) 4.41, 7.42, 8.42	SUSPECT	YUGO.
DUCHETTI, Adotto	190879	M		Major, Italian Army, Biograd Namorbr (Yugo.) 12.4.43	MURDER	YUGO.
DURANTI, Aselio	254937	M		Judge, member, Tribunal, Kotor (Yugo.) 41-43	INTERR.	YUGO.
DURANTI, Vincenzo	254936	M		Member, Seniors, Tribunal, M.V.S.N., Kotor (Yugo.) 41-43	INTERR.	YUGO.
DURELIO, Natale	173271	M	10	Italian Army, Campolongo, Venice (It.) 2.-5.11.44	MURDER	U.K.
DUSTI, Benito	189897	M		Carabiniere, Italian Army, Vela Luka (Yugo.)	MURDER	YUGO.
EDINI, Mme.	250998	M		Gestapo, Limoges (Fr.) 40-45	MURDER	FR.
ELMI, Antonio	190951	M		Pvt., Italian Army, Isle of Viz (Yugo.) 9.3.43	TORTURE	YUGO.
ENTICO, Papa	194240	M		Col., Italian Army, Cmdt. P.O.W. Camp Nr. 70, Ferno Ancona (It.) 12.42-1.43	TORTURE	U.K.
ENZO, Giovanni	252960	M	18	Brig., Customs-Police, Kistanje (Yugo.) 25.5.42	MURDER	YUGO.
ESPINOSA	300245	M	circa 20	Lt., interpreter, P.O.W. Camp 75, Member of the Fascist Militia and Intelligence, Bari (It.) 22.1.43	MISC.CRIMES	U.K.
ESPOSITO, Giovanni	190952	M		General, Italian Army, Div. "Pusteria", Montenegro, Savnik (Yugo.) 1941	MURDER	YUGO.
EXPOSITO, Pepino	251513	M		Carabiniere, Unit of Carabiniers, San Gavinodi di Carbini (It.) 43	INTERR.	FR.
FABBRI	148318	M		General, Staff-Off. Second Army, (Yugo.) 1943	MURDER	YUGO.
FABERIES, Ottorino	300628	M		Sgt., Black Bde., Villanova Marchesana on detachment at Ariano, Mesola, Ferrara, Adria, Rovigo (It.) 12.44	MURDER	U.K.
FABIANI	256992	M	10 - 15	Lt., Valle (Gale), Garrison Cmdt., Armed, 25.8.-11.43	INTERR.	YUGO.
FABRI, Augusto	148917	M		Lt., Carabiniere Reali, Crnomelj (Yugo.) 1942	MURDER	YUGO.
FACCIN	148916	M		Col., Commander, Army, Inf.Regt.73, "Lombardia"-Div., 41-43	MURDER	YUGO.
FADDA, Giacchimo	148915	M		Maresciallo, Army, "Sebenico Sued", Carabinieri Station, Sibenik (Yugo.) 1942	MURDER	YUGO.
FAGGIANI, Rino	307277	M		Member of the Italian Fascist Black Bde., near Caselle, Pressana Prov. Verona (It.) 6.1.45	MURDER	U.K.

ITALY (Fai-Gal)

NAME	C.R.FILE NUMBER	SEX	DATE OF BIRTH	RANK OCCUPATION UNIT PLACE AND DATE OF CRIME	REASON WANTED	WANTED BY
				ITALY. (Cont.)		
FAINI, Virgilio	307278	M		Member of the Italian Fascist Federation at Verona, Grezzana PG-73 Capri (It.) 6.-8.43	MURDER	U.K.
FAIS, Giovanni	190953	M		Marshal, Italian Army, Sibenik (Yugo.) 41-43	MURDER	YUGO.
FALAVOLTI	141406	M		Lt., Carabinieri, Sfax (Tunisie)	WITNESS	FR.
FALCOMARE, Marcello	259193	M		Lt., Italian Army, "Marche" Div.,56 Rgt., Stolac (Yugo.) 41-9.42	MURDER	YUGO.
FALETTI	251541	M		N.C.O., Carabinier, Unit Tenenza Sebenico, Sibenik (Yugo.)	BRUTALITY	YUGO.
FANFOGNA-GARAGNIN, Nino	190954	M		Civilian, Commissar, Trogir, Kastelli (Yugo.) 41-43	TORTURE	YUGO.
FANTACCI, Clemente	300629	M		Member of the Italian Army, Campo PG-53, Macerata, Sforza Costa (It.) 28.2.43	MURDER	U.K.
FANTINI, Ferdinando	148314	M		Officer, Army, (Yugo.) 43	MURDER	YUGO.
FANTOLI	148313	M		Fascist Commissioner, Army (Yugo.) 43	MURDER	YUGO.
FANTUSSATTI, Giovanni or Giuseppe	190955	M		Director, C.C.Fraschetti, Alatri (It.) 41-43	TORTURE	YUGO.
FAPRINI, Enrico	187766	M		Pvt., Fascist, near Trescore (It.)	MURDER	U.S.
FARESSIN, Emilio	259192	M		Lt., Italian Army, "Marche" Div.,56 Rgt., Stolac (Yugo.) 4.41-9.42	MURDER	YUGO.
FARINA, Guido	148312	M		Col., Army, Inf.Rgt.23,"Como", "Isonzo" Div.,Cernomelj (Yugo.) 43	MURDER	YUGO.
FARNETI, Carlo	188573	M		Capt., Italian Army, PG 35, Padula (It.) 43	MISC.CRIMES	U.K.
FELICE, Mario	190956	M		Civilian of Railway, Commander, Militia, Nova Mesto, Metlika (Yugo.)42	MURDER	YUGO.
FELICIANI	253634	M		Commander, Cdiecima Flottiglia Mass, Fulmine (Slov.) 2.1.45	MISC.CRIMES	YUGO.
FERIZIANE	192067	M		Landrat, Prefect of Macerata (It.) 2.-5.44	MURDER	U.K.
FERLAN, Antonio	255134	M		Pvt., Army, Radunic (Yugo.) 43	PILLAGE	YUGO.
FERRARESE	188831	M		Indicator, Gestapo, Communay (Fr.) 9.6.44	MURDER	FR.
FERRADI	258154	M		Pvt., Italian Army, Execution Squad, Plave Anhovo (Yugo.) 13.2.45-23.2.45	INTERR.	YUGO.
FERRARI, Arturo	148311	M		Lt., Army, "Isonzo" Div.,24 Inf.Rgt."Como" (Yugo.) 43	MURDER	YUGO.
FERRARI, Attilio	169479	M		Dr., Capt., Italian Army, Laterina (It.) 8.42-9.43	TORTURE	U.K.
FERRARI, Giovanni	163284	M		Capt., Italian Army, Inf., C.C.Capri (It.) 27.1.43-1.45	TORTURE	U.K.
FERRATA	190957	M		Dr., Commissar, C.C.Fraschetti Alatri (It.) 41-43	TORTURE	YUGO.
FERRERO, Alberto	253957	M		Lt.General, Cmdt., XXIII Army Corps, Julian March (It.) 42	INTERR.	YUGO.
FERRETI, Dante	190958	M		Member, Italian Army, Fascist Militia, Schenils (Yugo.) 41-43	MURDER	YUGO.
FERRONI	148310	M		Col.Commander, Army, 74 Inf.Rgt., "Lombardia" Div. (Yugo.) 43	MURDER	YUGO.
FERULLO	141864	M		Lt., Stalag, Beng Hazi (Africa) 42	MISC.CRIMES	U.K.
FFFVANTI	173254	M		Lt.Col., Army, Capri (It.) 6.-7.43	TORTURE	U.K.
FESTI, Antonio	300249	M		Major, Commanding a Bn., "Blackshirts", "Pinerolo" Div., Elassona Area, Domenika, Livadia, 1.10.42-16.2.43	MURDER	GRC.
FEULA, Antonio	300250	M		Member of the Italian Police, Xironomi, Thebes, 22.6.42	MURDER	GRC.
FIENGA, Giovanni	148309	M		Capt., Bicovo (Yugo.) 42	TORTURE	YUGO.
FINAGUERRA	192073	M		Lt., Fascist Milice, Braccano (It.) 24.3.44	MURDER	U.K.
FINCHI	193550	M		Capt., Ital.Mountain Unit, Petrovac, Banovina, Zevska (Yugo.) 8.41	MURDER	YUGO.
FIORDIPONTE	148308	M		Col.,137 Fascist Legion (Yugo.) 43	MURDER	YUGO.
FIORENZA, Giuseppe	307293	M		Major, Judge, Corespendent of Military Tribunal, Susak (Yugo.)41-43	MURDER	YUGO.
FISCHETTI, Ettore	190959	M		Lt., Italian Army,56 Inf.Rgt.,1 Bn., I A Coy,Div.Marche, Mostar (Yugo.) 42	PILLAGE	YUGO.
FLAVONI, Giulio	255135	M		Major, Army, Zara Div.,291 Rgt., Kistanje (Yugo.) 42	BRUTALITY	YUGO.
FLORENTINI	148307	M		Major, "Lombardia" Div.,73 Rgt.,3 Bn., (Yugo.)	MURDER	YUGO.
FOGGIA, G.	254153	M		Pilot, Italian Air Force,63 Group,21 Sturm, Baronje Selo (Yugo.) 26.6.43	INTERR.	YUGO.
FOPIANO, Mario	190960	M		Major, Italian Army, Bn. of "Venezia", Div., Kolasin and Area (Yugo.) 8.43	MURDER	YUGO.
FOPESIO	190961	M		Commandant, Italian Army, Div.Bergamo, Sibenik (Yugo.) 9.6.43	MURDER	YUGO.
FORGIONNE, Rosario	194979	M	28.10.13	Pvt., Army, Toulon (Fr.) 6.7.44	MURDER	FR.
FORNACHAPI, Raul	190962	M		Capt., Italian Army, St.Marten, Podstrava (Yugo.) 8.42	MURDER	YUGO.
FORNARA, N.	252095	M		Pilot, Italian Air Force,43 Sturm B.T.,98 Group,240 Squadriglia B.T. Vetnaj Babna Polica Podpesek (Yugo.) 8.9.42	MISC.CRIMES	YUGO.
FORTUNATO, L.	307294	M		Major, Judge, Military Tribunale, Susak (Yugo.) 41-43	MURDER	YUGO.
FOSCO, Gianni	258157	M		Civil Commiss., Admin., District of Kastav (Yugo.) 41-43	MURDER	YUGO.
FRACASSI	148306	M		Lt.Col.,137 Fascist Legion, Deputy Commander (Yugo.) 43	MURDER	YUGO.
FRACASSO, Arsenio	148305	M		Dr., "Isonzo" Div.,24 Inf.Rgt."Como" (Yugo.) 43	MURDER	YUGO.
FRANC	254145	M		Civilian, School-Official, Split (Yugo.) 15.5.42	TORTURE	YUGO.
FRANCESCPETTI	189896	M		Commissar, Italian Public-official, Spalato (It.)	MURDER	YUGO.
FRANCESCHINI	300631	M		Lt.,40 Bn., Italian Republican Guard, stationed at San-Michele (It.) 6.11.43	MURDER	U.K.
FRANCESCHINI, Mario	190963	M		General, Italian Army, Div.Ferrara, Savnik Montenegro (Yugo.) 5.-6.42	MURDER	YUGO.
FRANCESCO, Turco	148319	M		Cmdt., Col., Army, C.C.62, Bergamo (It.) 42	TORTURE	U.K.
FRANCESCONI, Umberto	255141	M		Col., Judge, 7adar, Sibenik, Split, Kotor (Yugo.) 41-43	INTERR.	YUGO.
FRANCESQUI, Sancho	254338	M		Agent, Member, Gestapo, SD of Toulouse, Hte.-Garonne (Fr.) 11.42-8.44	MISC.CRIMES	FR.
FRANCIOSINI, Mario	191146	M		Judge, Italian Special Court, Sibenik (Yugo.) 41-43	MURDER	YUGO.
FRANCONI, B.	300632	M		Marshal,40 Bn., Italian Republican Guard, stationed at San-Michele (It.) 6.11.43	MURDER	U.K.
FRANGIPANE, Francesco	190964	M		Lt., Italian Army, Sibenik (Yugo.) 41-43	MURDER	YUGO.
FRANGIPANE, Francesco	251536	M		Dr., Lt., Commandante Delle Teneza Vodice, 41-43	MURDER	YUGO.
FRANGIPANE, Michele	190965	M		Lt., Cmdt., Commander of a Unit at Sibenik (Yugo.) 41-43	MURDER	YUGO.
FRANZINI	300633	M		Capt.,40 Bn., Italian Republican Guard, stationed at San-Michele (It.) 6.11.43	MURDER	U.K.
FRIZARI, Nito	189895	M		Capt., Italian Army, Montenegro (Yugo.)	MURDER	YUGO.
FROSINI, Remo	254168	M		Carabiniere, Royaux Carabiniers, 2 Coy, 29 Bn., Calacuccia (Fr.) 30.5.43	INTERR.	FR.
FUPIA, Fernando	189894	M		Dr., Carabinieri Capt., Italian Army, Ljubljana (Yugo.)	MURDER	YUGO.
FURLOTTI, Nicola	307279	M		Member, Italian Fascist Federation at Verona, Grezzana (It.) 12.11.43	MURDER	U.K.
GABUTI, Aldo	190966	M		Col., Italian Army,93 Rgt.Fanteria, Dalmatia (Yugo.) 42	MURDER	YUGO.
GAETANI, Giuseppe	147287	M		Lt., Italian Army (Yugo.) 43	TORTURE	U.K.
GALDTEPI	161201	M		Lt., Italian Army, Padua (It.) 8.43	MURDER	YUGO.
GALLI, Giuseppe	147286	M		Sottotenente,23 Rgt. "Como", Italian Army, "Isonzo" Div.,1 Bn., Cernomelj (Yugo.) 43	MURDER	YUGO.
GALLINI	147285	M		Major, Italian Army,73 Inf.Rgt. "Lombardia" Div.,(Yugo.) 43	MURDER	YUGO.

ITALY (Gal-Gra)

NAME	C.R.FILE NUMBER	SEX	DATE OF BIRTH	RANK OCCUPATION UNIT PLACE AND DATE OF CRIME	REASON WANTED	WANTED BY
				ITALY. (Cont.)		
GALLO, Annibale	147284	M		Col., Italian Army, XI Corps (Yugo.) 41	MURDER	YUGO.
GALL, Rufino	147283	M		Sottotenente, 24 Inf.Rgt., Italian Army, "Como", "Isonzo" Div., (Yugo.) 43	MURDER	YUGO.
GALTERIO, Enrico	189893	M		Lt., Italian Army, Montenegro (Yugo.)	MURDER	YUGO.
GALVAGNI, Mario	190967	M		Commander, Italian Army, Unit of Carabiniere, Sibenik (Yugo.) 41-43	MURDER	YUGO.
GAMBETINI	307295	M		Gendarm, Tenenza di Cursola, Island of Cursola, 5.12.42	MURDER	YUGO.
GANCAROLLI, Antonio	190968	M		Brigadier, Italian Army, Carabinieri, Kotor (Yugo.) 41-43	MURDER	YUGO.
GANDINI, J.	147282	M		Major, Italian Army, Velika Lusca (Yugo.) 42	PILLAGE	YUGO.
GANDINI, Tomaseo	190969	M		Lt.Col., Italian Army, XI Bn.of Carabinieri, Cetinje Orna Gora (Yugo.) 41-43	MURDER	YUGO.
GANGEMI, Giovanni	307296	M		General-Consul, Judge of Special Tribunal for defense of State Rom (It.) 4.41-9.43	MURDER	YUGO.
GAROIULO, Enzo	190970	M		Lt., Sottotenente, Italian Army,1 Bn.,56 Rgt., Mostar (Yugo.) 7.42	PILLAGE	YUGO.
GAROIULO (see SCHMIDT, Ema)	191100					
GARIBALDI	161309	M		Lt., Italian Army, Padula (It.) 42	TORTURE	U.K.
GAROFOLO (see GAROFOLO)	147281					
GAROLFO (or GAROFOLO)	147281	M		Lt., Italian Army, "Lombardia" Div.,73 Rgt.,1 Bn., (Yugo.) 43	MURDER	YUGO.
GATTELANO	189903	M		Capt., Italian Army, Raunikal (Yugo.)	MURDER	YUGO.
GATTI	1693	M		Capt., Venice (It.)	TORTURE	U.K.
GATTI	161231	M		Capt., Italian Army, on staff of camp 35 and at POW camp Bergoma, Padula and Bologna (It.) 13.8.43	TORTURE	U.K.
GAUTTIERI, Filippo	195622	M		Official, Justizministerium, Rom (It.) 41-43	TORTURE	YUGO.
GAVINO (see MORO GARINO)	145470					
GAZZINI (or GAZZINO)	190971	M		Col., Italian Army, Rgt.of Sassari Div.(F 559), Udbina Gracac (Yugo.) 1. and 2.43	MURDER	YUGO.
GELOZA, Luigi	190972	M		Marshal, Italian Army, Berane Montenegro (Yugo.) 3.42	TORTURE	YUGO.
GEMELLI	189892	M		Major, Italian Army, Brodarevo (Yugo.)	MURDER	YUGO.
GENOVESI	190973	M		Chief, Italian Police, Prem (Yugo.) 42	TORTURE	YUGO.
GENTILE, Pasquale	190974	M		Tenente, Italian Army, Officer commanding port at Omis, Jesenica (Yugo.) 8.42	INCENDIARISM	YUGO.
GEPACI, Giuseppe	190975	M		Camp-leader, C.C.Lipari (It.) 41-43	TORTURE	YUGO.
GERMANO, Francesco	190976	M		Col., Italian Army, Unit Ferrara Div., Montenegro (Yugo.) 5.43	MURDER	YUGO.
GERMANO, T.	147280	M		Capt., Italian Army, Cetijne (Yugo.) 43	MURDER	YUGO.
GERVI	147289	M		Sottotenente, Italian Army, Bersaglieri, C.C.Treviglio (It.) 42-43	TORTURE	U.K.
GETTI	169483	M		Adj., Italian Army, Capua (It.) 4.41-6.43	TORTURE	U.K.
GHELLERO, Giovanni	300634	M		Capo, Gruppo of Black Bde., Conche di Codevigo, Piove di Sacco, Province of Padua (It.) 20.2.45	MURDER	U.K.
GHELLERO, Renato	300635	M		Member of Black Bde., Conche di Codevigo, Piove di Sacco, Province of Padua (It.) 20.2.45	MURDER	U.K.
GHI, Giovanni	147279	M		Capt., Italian Army, Cetijne (Yugo.) 43	MURDER	YUGO.
GHIRARDELLI, Edwards	1694	M		Venice (It.)	TORTURE	U.K.
GHIY, Giovanni	189891	M		Major, Italian Army, Montenegro (Yugo.)	MURDER	YUGO.
GIACOBELLI, Ettore	261237	M		Col., Army, Military Tribunal, Ljubljana (Yugo.) 41-43	MURDER	YUGO.
GIANCPECO, Francesco	147278	M		General, Italian Army "Sassari" Div., (Yugo.) 43	MURDER	YUGO.
GIANNEFINI, Giuseppe	169484	M		Capt., Italian Army, Inf., Laterina (It.) 8.42-9.43	TORTURE	U.K.
GIANNEFINI, Velio	178063	M		Capt., Italian Army, C.C. P.G.82, Caterina (It.) 8.42-9.43	TORTURE	U.K.
GIERAGCI, Vitto	190977	M		Finance officer, Italian Finance Ministry official, Sebenik (Yugo.) 41-43	MURDER	YUGO.
GIGANTE, Antonio	253006	M		Pvt., Army (Yugo.) 6.43	BRUTALITY	YUGO.
GIGANTE, Mario	259130	M		Capt., Garrison Commandant, Biovicino Selo, Area Kistanje, Ivosevci (Yugo.) 5., 6.42	MISC.CRIMES	YUGO.
GICLIDLI	189045	M		Lt.General, Italian Army, Benghazi (North-Africa) 42	TORTURE	U.K.
GINELLI, Fernando	259129	M		Maggiore, Commandant, II Bn.,84 Rgt., Venezia Div., Berane Montenegro 41-43	MISC.CRIMES	YUGO.
GIORDANO, Giuseppe	258162	M		Carabiniere, Italian Army, Cerknica (Yugo.) 2.11.41	TORTURE	YUGO.
GIPPI, Antonio	190978	M		Commander, Italian Army, Sibenik (Yugo.) 41-43	MURDER	YUGO.
GIOVANETTI, Dante	147277	M		Sgt., Italian Army,14 Inf.Bn. (Yugo.) 42	MURDER	YUGO.
GIOVANNI, J.	147276	M		Capt., Italian Army, Ljubljana (Yugo.) 43	TORTURE	YUGO.
GIOVARELLI, Fernando	147275	M		Sottotenente, Italian Army,23 Inf.Rgt. "Como", "Isonzo" Div., Cernomeli (Yugo.) 43	MURDER	YUGO.
GIUFFRIDA, Giuseppe	169486	M		Dr.,Capt., Italian Army, Laterina (It.) 8.42-9.43	TORTURE	U.K.
GIULIANI	178762	M	17	Cpl., Army P.G.35, Padula (It.) 8.43	TORTURE	U.K.
GIULIANI, Giuseppe	147274	M		Capt., Italian Army, Dalmatia (Yugo.) 43	MURDER	YUGO.
GIULIETTI, Giulio (or GUILLETTI)	300637	M		Maresciallo, 40 Bn. of the Italian Republican Guard, stationed at San-Michele (It.) 6.11.43	MURDER	U.K.
GIUPA, Luigi	147273	M		Centurione, Italian Army, "Isonzo" Div.,98 Fasc.Leg.,3 Coy, Trebnie (Yugo.) 43	MURDER	YUGO.
GIUSEPPE	254098	M		Agent, C.C.Corropola (It.) 41	TORTURE	YUGO.
GIUSEPPE, Paolo	189890	M		Lt.Col., Italian Army, Montenegro (Yugo.)	MURDER	YUGO.
GIUSFREDI, Gino	191147	M		Legal Official, Dr.Ing., Vice-Chairman of Italian "Special" Court in Sibenik (Yugo.) 41-43	MURDER	YUGO.
GLORIA	147272	M		General, Italian Army, "Lombardia" Rgt., "Sassari" Div., (Yugo.) 43	MURDER	YUGO.
GOBBO	147271	M		Dr., Tenente Medico, Italian Army,23 Inf.Rgt. "Como", "Isonzo" Div., Cernomeli (Yugo.) 43	MURDER	YUGO.
GOPP (see COPPI)	145694					
GORI, Giuseppe	190979	M		Commander, Italian Army, Carabinieri-Station, Sibenik (Yugo.)	MURDER	YUGO.
GORI, Mario	173250	M		Col., Italian Army, C.C.Padula (It.)	TORTURE	U.K.
GORKI	161311	M	90	Tenente Colonnello, Padula (It.) 42-43	TORTURE	U.K.
GOTTARDI	307280	M		Member, Italian Fascist Fed.Verona, Grezzana (It.) 12.11.43	MURDER	U.K.
GRANDI, Antonio	251022	M		Brigadier, Mixed Detachment of Carabinieri P.M.64, Pianottoli (Fr.) 9.5.43	MURDER	FR.
GRASSI, Giovanni	250783	M		Major, Carabinieri, Vodice (Yugo.) 1.2.43	MURDER	YUGO.
GRAZIANI, Fernando	189889	M		Col., Italian Army,83 Inf.Div., Montenegro (Yugo.)	MURDER	YUGO.

ITALY (Gre-Leo)

ITALY. (Cont.)

NAME	C.R. FILE NUMBER	SEX	DATE OF BIRTH	RANK, OCCUPATION, UNIT, PLACE AND DATE OF CRIME	REASON WANTED	WANTED BY
GRECO	169485	M		Interpreter, Army, Transit Camp, Tarhuna Libya (North Africa) 10.42	TORTURE	U.K.
GRIEB, Tommaso	300666	M		Capt., Judge, Special Correspondent of Military Tribunal of War of second Army, Sezione di Sebenico, Sibenik, Dalmatia (Yugo.) from 1941 till 1943	TORTURE	U.F.
GRIFFINI, Mario	307338	M		General-Consul, Court President of Special Tribunal for defense of State, Rom (It.) 4.41-9.43	MURDER	YUGO.
GRIFOS, Antonelo	305151	M		Sgt., Italian Carabinieri in Larissa, Ava, Thessaly, village of Warakari-Aya (Grc.) 12.9.42, 5.1.43, 7.1.43, 12.1.43, 3.5.43	MURDER	GRC.
GRIGNCIO	147269	M		Col., Chief of Staff, Italian second Army, Susak (Yugo.) 1941	MURDER	YUGO.
GRILIO, Giovanni	253009	M		Brig., Customs Police, Kistanje (Yugo.) 25.5.42	MURDER	YUGO.
GRIMALDI	132532	M		Lt.Col., Army	MISC.CRIMES	FR.
GRIMALDI, Paolo	190980	M		Lt.Gen., Italian Army, Div. Bergamo, Sibenik (Yugo.) 41-43	MURDER	YUGO.
GROCE, Mario or CROCE	169487	M		Capt., Italian Army, Chisti (It.) 7.42-9.43	TORTURE	U.F.
GROSSI, Arnaldo	307297	M		Capt., Judge, Military Tribunal for second Army, section of Lubiana (Yugo.) 41-43	MURDER	
GUALTIERI, Enrico	173248	M		Capt., Inf. Adjutant, C.C. Udine (It.) 20.5.-8.7.43	MURDER	U.K.
GUAZZINI, Francesco	254100	M		Capt., Italian Airforce, 240 Squadriglia Bn., 43 Stormo-Bn., 98 Gruppe, Metnaj, Babna (Yugo.) 8.-9.42	INTERR.	YUGO.
GUAZZO, Angelo	147267	M		Col., Italian Army, 6 Artl.Regt., "Isonzo"-Div., Novo Mesto (Yugo.) 1943	MURDER	YUGO.
GUELLI, N.	147266	M		Capo del Inspettorato Generale, Italian Army-Cavallery, Trieste (It.) 1943	MURDER	YUGO.
GUERRINI, Remo	147265	M		Centurione, Italian Army, "Isonzo"-Div., 98 Fascist Legion, Velaloka (Yugo.) 1943	MURDER	YUGO.
GUGLIALMINO, Antonio	259103	M		Lt., Italian Army, 56 Regt., "Marche"-Div., Stolac (Yugo.) 4.41-9.42	MURDER	YUGO.
GUGLIOTTI	302151	M		Lt., 8 Coy., 2 Bn., 83 Regt., "Venezia"-Div., Montenegro (Yugo.) 9.-11.41, 8.43	MURDER	YUGO.
GUIDO	189888	M		Carabinieri, Italian Army, Vela Luka (Yugo.)	MURDER	YUGO.
GUIDO, Francesco	190982	M		Sgt., Italian Army, Div. "Ferrara", Kapino Polje Montenegro (Yugo.) 6.43	MURDER	YUGO.
GUILIETTI see GIULIETTI	300637					
GUTIERREZ, A.	147264	M		Italian Army, "Isonzo"-Div., 23 Regt. "Como", Cernomeli (Yugo.) 43	MURDER	YUGO.
GUTCNIOLI	254099	M		Capt., Observer, Italian Airforce, Visnja (Slovenia) 17.9.43	INTERR.	YUGO.
HAGEMANN	259827	M		Sonderfhr., Recoare Terme (It.) 10.1.45	INTERR.	U.S.
IANUZZI	300638	M		Lt., Commander, Black Bde., Codigoro, Adria, Mesola, Ferrara, Rovigo (It.) 12.42	MISC.CRIMES	U.K.
IMPELLIZZERI	67705	M		Col., Enfidaville (Tunisia) 42-43	TORTURE	FR.
INCHIOSTRI, Ruggero	190983	M		Member of Fascio in Sibenik (Yugo.) 41-43	MURDER	YUGO.
INFANTE, Adolfo	305195	M		Lt.Gen., Commander, "Pinerolo"-Div., Almiros, Thessaly (Grc.) 15.8.-18.8.43	MISC.CRIMES	GRC.
INGEGNI, Pasquale	259121	M		Lt., Italian Army, 56 Regt., "Marche"-Div., Stolac (Yugo.) 4.41-9.42	MURDER	YUGO.
INGLESE	191148	M		Col., Chief Prosecutor in Zadar (Yugo.) 41-43	MURDER	YUGO.
INTRECCIALAGLI, Antonio	300679	M		Chaplain, 63 Tagliamento Bn., Varallo, Province of Vercelli (It.) 15.4.44	MURDER	U.K.
ISASCA	191164	M		Lt.Gen., Italian Army, Podgorica (It.) 4.42	MURDER	U.K.
ISASCA, Carlo	190984	M		Lt.Gen., Italian Army, Andrijevica Montenegro (Yugo.) 5.-7.43	MURDER	YUGO.
JOHN	141877	M		Sgt.-Major, Camp Staff, Tobruk (Africa) 7.42	TORTURE	U.K.
KLJUNAK, Emalija	190986	F		Civilian, Daughter of Commissario del Fascio (Jakov Kljunak), Veli luki, Island of Korcula, Blato (Yugo.) 41-43	MURDER	YUGO.
KLJUNAK, Jakov	190985	M		Commissario, Ital. Party Fascio, Veli luki, Island of Korcula, Blato (Yugo.) 41-43	MURDER	YUGO.
KLUTE	102948	M		Major, Oflag, C.C. Graudenz (Pol.) 7.44	MURDER	U.K.
KULUFAKAS, Kosta	141929	M		Interpreter, C.C. Larissa (Grc.) 7.-10.42	MISC.CRIMES	U.K.
LABONIA, Enrico	190987	M		Major, Italian Stalag, C.C. Gravina (It.) 29.9.43	MURDER	YUGO.
LACCIE see LEACCIE	132186					
LAFARINA	190988	M		Commissar, Police, Susak (Yugo.) 41-4.43	MURDER	YUGO.
LA MARCA, Giacomo	307298	M		Capt., Judge, Military Tribunal for second Army, section of Lubiana (Yugo.) 41-43	MURDER	YUGO.
LANARI, Pietro	307299	M		Prosecutor, (Military) Judge, Correspondent of Special Tribunal for defense of State, Rom (It.) 4.41-9.43	MURDER	YUGO.
LANCESCO	257644	M		Major, Italian Army, P.W. Camp 115, Marisciano (It.) 3.-9.43	BRUTALITY	U.K.
LANDINI, Luciano	145430	M		Capt., Army Ciudjre del Tribunale militare di Guerra, Dettigne (Yugo.) 1943	MURDER	YUGO.
LANTIERI	145429	M		Col., Army, "Re"-Div., Artl.Regt., Slovenia, Croatia (Yugo.) 1943	MURDER	YUGO.
LARISO, Giuseppe	259191	M		Lt., Italian Army, "Marche"-Div., 56 Regt., Stolac (Yugo.) 4.41-9.42	MURDER	YUGO.
LA SPADA, Michelangelo	146908	M		Lt., Italian Army, "Isonzo"-Div., 23 Inf.Regt., Cernomels (Yugo.) 1943	MURDER	YUGO.
(LA) SPINA	300652	M	21	Member, Black Bde., Mesola, Ferrara, Adria, Rovigo, 12.44	MURDER	U.K.
LASTRETIO	259101	M		Capt., Carabinieri, Mostar (Yugo.) 12.7.42	INTERR.	YUGO.
LATANZIA	173235	M		Lt.Col., Oflag, C.C. Bari (It.)	TORTURE	U.K.
LATANZIA	193540	M		Italian Army, C.C. Ancone (It.) 12.42-1.43	TORTURE	U.F.
LATTANCIO see LATTAUGIO	67570					
LATTARULA, Leonardo	151345	M		Sgt.-Major, Italian Army, C.C. Tradate-Varese (It.)	TORTURE	U.K.
L'ATTAUGIO or LATTANCIO	67570	M		Col., Oflag 79, Brunswick (Ger.) 5.-9.44	MURDER	U.K.
LEACCIE or LEZZIE or LACCIE	132186	M	90	Sgt.-Major, Italian Army, Trigtarhuna (North Africa) 7.42	TORTURE	U.K.
LEINWEBER, Reno	259171	M	circa 10	Commander, 291 Regt., Zara-Div., Kistanje, Piramatovci, Banja (Yugo.) 17.8.42, 3.43, 22.4.43	MISC.CRIMES	YUGO.
LE METRE, Gaetano	195624	M		Official, Justizminhisterium, Rom (It.) 41-43	TORTURE	YUGO.
LENTI, Nicholas	300295	M		Major and Governor, Inf., 7 Italian Regt. "Cuneo" Div. Military of Naxos during the Italian Occ., Island of Naxos, 41-43	MISC.CRIMES	GRC.
LEONARDI	190989	M		Col., Italian Army, O.C.Regt., Sassari-Div. (F.561), Udbina Gracac (Yugo.) 1. and 2.43	MURDER	YUGO.

ITALY (Leo-Mar)

ITALY (Cont.)

NAME	C.R.FILE NUMBER	SEX	DATE OF BIRTH	RANK, OCCUPATION, UNIT, PLACE AND DATE OF CRIME	REASON WANTED	WANTED BY
LEONARDI	251122	M		Col., C.O. of Rgt. "Sassari", Fara-Slovenia (Slov.)	MURDER	YUGO.
LEONARDI, Nicola	307300	M		Consul, Judge of Special Tribunal for defense of State Rom (It.) 4.41-9.43	MURDER	YUGO.
LEOPARDI, Alberto	190990	M		Commandant, Italian Army, 151 Rgt. Fanteria "Sassari" Div., Fara (Yugo.)	PILLAGE	YUGO.
LEOPOARDI, Sergio	145428	M		Brigadiere of Customs Guard, Commander of Customs Guard at Kuzalj in District of Banjaluka, on Border Croatia, Slovenia (Yugo.) 41-42		YUGO.
LETIFFI, Roberto	300667	M		Major, Judge, Military Tribunal of War of Army, Sezione di Sebenico, Sibenik, Dalmatia (Yugo.) 41-43	TORTURE	U.K.
LEVI, Lorenzo	187972	M		Col., Army, C.C. Tahuna (North Africa) 7.-11.42	TORTURE	U.K.
LEZZIE (see LEACCIE)	132186					
LIDO	254142	M		Agent, C.C. Corropola (It.) 41	TORTURE	YUGO.
LIETO, Achille	253774	M		Brigadiere, Police, Public Security, Split (Yugo.) 26.6.43	BRUTALITY	YUGO.
LIGAS	190991	M		Major, Italian Army, XXII Bn., Isle of Is Veliki (Yugo.) 28.7.42	MURDER	YUGO.
LIPARI, Ignazio	145427	M		Lt., medico, "Isonzo" Div., 23 Inf.Rgt. "Como", Gernomelj (Yugo.) 43	MURDER	YUGO.
LIPPI	261323	M		Cmdt., 88 Bn., "Blackshirt", Pietralba (Fr.) 10.9.43	BRUTALITY	FR.
LOCCI, Nicodemo	190992	M		Member of Fascist Directorate in Sibenik (Yugo.) 41-43	MURDER	YUGO.
LODI, Georgio	145426	M		Lt.Col., "Isonzo" Div., 23 Inf.Rgt. "Como" (Yugo.) 43	MURDER	YUGO.
LOGAGLIO	189914	M		Biserte (Tunisia)	MURDER	FR.
LOIALI, Adalberto	255288	M		Judge, Italian Special Tribunal, Zadar, Sibenik, Split, Kotor (Yugo.) 41-43	INTERR.	YUGO.
LOLLA	190993	M		Capt., Italian Army, 11 Bn. Carabinieri, Cetinje, Crna, Gora (Yugo.) 41-43	MURDER	YUGO.
LOMONACH, Guido	145425	M		Headmaster, Primary School, Isle of Vis., (Yugo.) 43	TORTURE	YUGO.
LOTTI, Pietro	255287	M		Civilian, Questore of Cattaro, Kotor (Yugo.) 41-43	MISC.CRIMES	YUGO.
LOTURGO	253125	M		Questore di Messina, C.C. Lipari (It.) 42	BRUTALITY	YUGO.
LOUFIER, Eduardo	145424	M		Capt., "Isonzo" Div., 98 Fascist Legion, Trebnje (Yugo.) 43	MURDER	YUGO.
LO VULLO, Luigi	145423	M		Major, "Isonzo" Div., 24 Inf.Rgt. "Como" (Yugo.)	MURDER	YUGO.
LUBINI, Alfredo	145422	M		Port Customs Official, Dalmatio (Yugo.) 43	MURDER	YUGO.
LUCCHETTI, Augusto	251130	M		Col., 292 Rgt. Fanteria, Commander, Srima near Sibenik (Yugo.) 9.12.42	PILLAGE	YUGO.
LUCHETTI, Nilo	189046	M		Civilian, Blackshirt, near Magliano (It.) 10.12.43	TORTURE	U.K.
LUCI	145432	M		Col., Chief of Intelligence II Army, Susak (Yugo.) 41	MURDER	YUGO.
LUCIANO	259190	M		Lt., Italian Army, "Marche" Div., 56 Rgt., Stolac (Yugo.) 4.41-9.42	MURDER	YUGO.
LUCINI, Bruno	145421	M		Col., Army, Chief of Staff, YI Army Corps, Ljubljana (Yugo.) 41	MURDER	YUGO.
LUPARELLI, Enzo	259189	M		Lt., Italian Army, "Marche" Div., 56 Rgt., Stolac (Yugo.) 4.41-9.42	MURDER	YUGO.
LUPI, Giuseppe	300639	M		Cpl., Italian Fascist, Pogio Mirteto (It.) 28.5.44	MURDER	U.K.
LUPUDAC, Palmiro	145420	M		Capt., Commander of 25 Sector Copertura Timavo, St. Petar near Krasu (Yugo.) 42	TORTURE	YUGO.
LUSANO, Alexandro	190994	M		Lt.General, Italian Army, 55 Rgt. "Marche" Div., Trebinje (Yugo.) 41-43	MURDER	YUGO.
LUZENTE	145419	M		Major, "Lombardia" Div., 73 Rgt., 1 Bn., Slovenia Croatia (Yugo.) 43	MURDER	YUGO.
MACARIO, Alessandro	189886	M		General, Italian Army, Ljubljana (Yugo.)	MISC.CRIMES	YUGO.
MACCHI, Antonie	145480	M		Capt., 24 Inf.Rgt. "Como", III Bn. "Isonzo" Div., (Yugo.) 43	MURDER	YUGO.
MACIS	190995	M		Dr., Lt.Col., Italian Army, Tribunale Militare, Ljubljana (Yugo.) 41-43	MURDER	YUGO.
MADERAZZI	145481	M		Brigadiere, Dalmatia (Yugo.) 43	TORTURE	YUGO.
MADILE	145482	M		Sgt., Cerknica (Yugo.) 43	TORTURE	YUGO.
MAFOGLIO, Luigi	145483	M		Marshal, Italian Carabinieri, Commander of Prison Ljubljana (Yugo.) 43	TORTURE	YUGO.
MAGALDI, Cherardo	190996	M		Commandant, Chairman of the Ital. Extraordinary Coury, Sibenik (Yugo.) 41-43	MURDER	YUGO.
MAGG, Manfredone	100509	M		Cpl., owner of a Milan Amusement Park, C.C. San Vittore (It.)	TORTURE	U.K.
MAGGIORA, Vergane Nobile Ernesto	191149	M		Legal Official, Chairman of Ital. "Special Court", Sibenik (Yugo.) 41-43	MURDER	YUGO.
MAGNARINI, Vavio	307301	M		Capt., Judge of Sibenik Section, Military Tribunal Section of Ljubljana (Yugo.) 41-43	MURDER	YUGO.
MAINERI	193553	M		Lt.General, Italian Army, Commander of 23 "Ferrara" Div., Niksic (Yugo.)	MURDER	YUGO.
MAIZONI	190997	M		Member, C.C. Carropoli (It.) 43	TORTURE	YUGO.
MAJJIDRI, Vittorio	178304	M		Medico Lt., Italian Army, Treviglio (It.) 42-43	TORTURE	U.K.
MALENTACCI	190998	M		Commandant, Prisons Italian Army, Maresciallo XI Bn., C.C. Cetinje Ornogona (Yugo.) 41-43	MURDER	YUGO.
MALORCHI, Ernesto	307302	M		Capt. of Grenadiera, Molat C.C. Molat (Meleda) 42-43	MURDER	YUGO.
MALTESE, Giusenpe	307303	M		Lt.Col., Judge, Military Tribunal, Susak (Yugo.) 41-43	MURDER	YUGO.
MANCA, Francesco	305039	M		Pvt., Italian, Bacu Abis POW Camp Sardinia, 10.4.43	MURDER	U.K.
MANCHA	145484	M		Major, Garrison Commander, Loz (Yugo.)	MURDER	YUGO.
MANCINELLI, Ivo	300668	M		Major, Judge, Military Tribunal of War Army, Sezione di Sebenico, Sibenik, Dalmatia (Yugo.) 41-43	TORTURE	U.K.
MANDEL	190999	M		Major, Head of medical Section attached to Governor at Cetinje, Dr., Crna Gora (Yugo.) 41-43	MURDER	YUGO.
MANFRE, Luigi	300312	M		Lt. of the Carabinieri Reali, Davlia, 5.5.43	MURDER	GRC.
MANGANELLI, Angelo	191000	M		Vice Brigadiere at Station at Malacista, Sibenik (Yugo.) 41-43	MURDER	YUGO.
MANZANI	300641	M		Carabiniere, Camp 52 Chiavari (It.) 12.41-10.42	TORTURE	U.K.
MAPANGIO, Frio	191001	M		Dr., Capt., Police, XXII Bn., Veliki (Yugo.) 28.7.42	MURDER	YUGO.
MARASCO, M.	307304	M		Major, Judge, Corespendent of Military Tribunal, Susak (Yugo.) 41-43	MURDER	YUGO.
MAPAZZA, A.	145471	M		Maggiore Aitante, "Isonzo" Div., 23 Inf.Rgt. "Como", Gernomelj (Yugo.) 43	MURDER	YUGO.
MARCHETTI, Vincenzo	145472	M		Lt., "Isonzo" Div., 24 Inf.Rgt. "Como" (Yugo.) 43	MURDER	YUGO.
MAPENGONI	261376	M		Capt., 88 Bn. of black-shirt, Pietralba (Fr.) 10.9.43	BRUTALITY	FR.
MARI	178303	M		Tenento, Lt., Italian Army, C.C. Macerata (It.) 43	TORTURE	U.K.
MARIANELLO	307281	M		Guard, Carabinieri, Camp 57 Undine Gruppignano (It.) 20.5.43	MURDER	U.K.
MARIN	253548	M		Commissary, Zlarin (Yugo.) 25.6.42	INTERR.	YUGO.
MARINELLI	253547	M		Official, Italian Police, Split (Yugo.) 17.4.42	MURDER	YUGO.
MARINI, Mario	191003	M		Italian Army, XI Bn., Police, Cetinje, Crna Gora (Yugo.) 41-43	MURDER	YUGO.
MARINO, Umberto	191004	M		Commandant, Italian Army, II Bn., 8 Coy, Div. "Venezia", Trebaljevo-Kolasin (Yugo.) 41	MURDER	YUGO.
MARIOTTI, Giorgio	257003	M		Pvt., Army, Plave Anhovo (Yugo.) 23.2.46	INTERR.	YUGO.
MARIOTTI, Pasquale	251157	M		Carabinier, 2 Coy, 29 Carabinieri Bn., Calacuccia (Fr.) 30.5.43	BRUTALITY	FR.
MAROTTA, Antonio	145473	M		General, Italian Military Tribunal, Cettigne (Yugo.) 43	MURDER	YUGO.
MARSILI, Dino	300642	M		Sgt., Black Bde., Villanova Marchesana, on detachment at Ariano, Mesola, Ferrara, Adria Rovigo (It.) 12.44	MISC.CRIMES	U.K.
MARSILI, Giorgio	300643	M		Member, Black Bde., Villanova Marchesana or detachment at Ariano, Mesola Ferrara Adria Rovigo (It.) 12.44	MISC.CRIMES	U.K.
MARTELOTTA	191005	M		Capt., Italian Army, Orebic (Yugo.) 42	MURDER	YUGO.
MARTINELLI	188179	M	03	Member, NSDAP Italian, Crezzana (It.)	MURDER	U.K.

ITALY (Mar-Mon)

ITALY. (Cont.)

NAME	C.R.FILE NUMBER	SEX	DATE OF BIRTH	RANK, OCCUPATION, UNIT, PLACE AND DATE OF CRIME	REASON WANTED	WANTED BY
MARTINELLI	259088	M		Member of Staff, Int.Camp at Istonic-Marina (It.) 41-43	BRUTALITY	YUGO.
MARTINETTO, Fanny	254776	F	9. 8.16	Agent, Ovra S.D., Toulouse (Fr.) 11.42-8.44	MISC. CRIMES	FR.
MARTINETTO, Guiseppe	254775	M	21.11.19	Agent, S.D. 14 Ovra, Toulouse (Fr.) 11.42-8.44	MISC. CRIMES	FR.
MARTINO, G.	145474	M		Lt.Col., (Yugo.) 1942	PILLAGE	YUGO.
MARTORELLI	178901	M		General, Army, Kriegsgericht, Athens (Grc.) summer 1942	MISC. CRIMES	U.F.
MARUSIC see MARUSSICH	191008					
MARUSSICH or MARUSIC	191008	M		Agent, Capt., Pol.-Ital., C.C.,Div. "Messina", Montenegro, Fraschette, Alatri (Yugo., It.) 41-42	MURDER	YUGO.
MARZUCCHI, Mario	300644	M		Maresciallo, Black Bde., Villanova Marchesana on detachment at Ariano, Mesola, Ferrara, Adria, Rovigo (It.) 12.44	MISC. CRIMES	U.K.
MASAN, Franco	300917	M	20	Guardia. Frontiera. Mavrovo, Leunovo, Nikiforovo near Tetovo, 9.43	INTERR.	YUGO.
MASCHERONI	194339	M	16	Capt., Ital. Alpen-Jaeger, Div. "Pusteria", Fontaine (Fr.) 3.3.43	TORTURE	FR.
MASSI, Giuseppe	130184	M		Lt.Col., Ital. Army, C.C. PG 21, Chisti (It.) 1.43	MISC. CRIMES	U.K.
MASSIMO, Tosti	185213	M		Capt., Carabinieri, Army, St. Gervais Chambery (Fr.) 8.43	TORTURE	FR.
MASTROIANI, Ottavio	191150	M		Col., Italian Special Court, State Prosecutor, Sibenik (Yugo.) 41-43	MURDER	YUGO.
MATAREZE, Rosario	191006	M		Head, Prison-guards, C.C. Naples, Poggio Reale (It.) 28.9.43	MURDER	YUGO.
MATTEI	191007	M		Agent, della Squadra Politica, Split (Yugo.) 2.-9.43	TORTURE	YUGO.
MATZINI see MAZZINI	173267					
MAZZA	305465	M		Gendarm, Mixed Detachment of Royal Gendarmerie (Italian) FM 64, Pianottoli, Corsica, 9.5.43	MURDER	FR.
MAZZA, Antonio	300669	M		Italian soldier, Kastel Kambelovac Garrison, Split and neighbouring towns (Yugo.) 1942	MURDER	U.K.
MAZZANTINI	261374	M		Capt., 88 Bn. of black-shirt, Pietralba (Fr.) 10.9.43	BRUTALITY	FR.
MAZZINI or MATZINI, Pietro	173267	M	circa 90	Civilian, Political Office, Piazenza (It.) 1.44	TORTURE	U.F.
MAZZOLINI, Idelma	259601	M		Agent, S.D., Longwy-Herserange (Fr.)	MISC. CRIMES	FR.
MEDICI, Carmine	191010	M		Director, C.C. Corrpoli, Bagna, Ripoli (It.) 41-43	TORTURE	YUGO.
MEICA, Pietro	188278	M	14	Member, N.S.D.A.P., Grezzana (It.) 12.11.43	MURDER	U.K.
MELE	109523	M		Guard, C.C. S. Vittore Prison, Milan (It.)	TORTURE	U.F.
MELINI	191011	M		Major, Ital. Army, Div. "Taro", Gradjame, Radomir, Montenegro (Yugo.) 5.42	PILLAGE	YUGO.
MELIS	145475	M		Lt., "Lombardia"-Div., 23 Regt., 3 Bn., Slovenia, Croasia (Yugo.) 1943	MURDER	YUGO.
MELOCHI, Ernesto	145476	M		Capt., Dalmatia (Yugo.) 1943	MURDER	YUGO.
MENAIDO, Luigi	191012	M		Pvt., Ital. Army, Carabinieri Bde., Susak, Podhum (Yugo.) 41-43	MURDER	YUGO.
MENICHELLI, Amorino	307305	M		Major, Judge, Correspondent of Military Tribunal, Susak (Yugo.) 41-43	MURDER	YUGO.
MENTASTI, Luigi	191013	M		General, Ital. Army, XIV Corps D'Armata, Berane (Yugo.) 4.43	MISC. CRIMES	YUGO.
MENUCCI, Enzo	307306	M		Major, Judge, Military Tribunal, second Army, Section of Lubiana (Yugo.) 41-43	MURDER	YUGO.
MERANGHINI, Umberto	254888	M		Gen.Lt., Member of Tribunale, Zadar, Split and Kotor (Yugo.) 41-43	INTERR.	YUGO.
MERCURIO, Renato	251154	M		Lt., 4 Coy., 29 Bn. Carabinieri, Sartene - Corse (Fr.) 2. and 5.43	TORTURE	FR.
MERLINI, Arcilio	257006	M		Alpine Troop, Tagliamento VIII Alp. Regt., 2 Bn., Fasc.Republ. Army, Dorenberg (Yugo.) 43-4.45	MISC. CRIMES	YUGO.
MEROLA, Luigi	145463	M		Capt., Carabinieri Reali, Novo Mesto (Yugo.) 1942	MURDER	YUGO.
MESSANA, Ettore	191024	M		Civilian, Ljubljana (Yugo.) 40-41	MURDER	YUGO.
MESSINA	145461	M		Lt.General, Ital. Army, C.C. Treviglio (It.) 42-43	TORTURE	U.K.
MEZZANA, Cesare	191025	M		Commander, It.Army, IV Legion, Monte Nevoso, Novo Mesto, Metlika, Slovenia (Yugo.) 1942	MURDER	YUGO.
MEZZI, Agraste	145464	M		Lt.Col., "Isonzo"-Div., 24 Inf.Regt. "Como", (Yugo.) 1943	MURDER	YUGO.
MICAN, Francesco	196512	M		See Consolidated list Part II - Appendix "A"		
MICHELI, Mario	191151	M		Capt., Commander of Stari Trg and village of Dane (Yugo.) 3.43	MURDER	YUGO.
MIGNANI	262431	M	circa 05	Major, Fascist Militia Atpola, Bokardica (Yugo.) 8.-9.1.44	MURDER	YUGO.
MIIAN, Carlo	145465	M		Capt., Army, Dalmatia (Yugo.) 1943	MISC. CRIMES	YUGO.
MIIAZZI, Paola	191026	F		Manageress, C.C. Pollenza (It.) 1945	TORTURE	YUGO.
MILAZZO, Gioacchino	307339	M		Proff. Doct. Prosecutor, Judge, Special Tribunal for defence of State, Rom (It.) 4.41-9.43	MURDER	YUGO.
MINAFRA, Vincenzo	254771	M		Capt., Army, Gravina (It.) 42-43	BRUTALITY	U.K.
MINGONI, Mario	307307	M		Consul, Judge of Special Tribunal for defence of State, Rom (It.) 4.41-9.43	MURDER	YUGO.
MINUTELLI, Fabio	145466	M		Capt., Dalmatia (Yugo.) 1943	MURDER	YUGO.
MIRABELLA, Bartolomea	145467	M		Lt.Col., (Yugo.) 1941	MURDER	YUGO.
MIRACO, Leonida	191027	F		Agent, Ital. Police, C.C. Corropoli (It.) 1943	TORTURE	YUGO.
MISCHI, Archimede	191028	M		Lt. Gen., Ital. Army, Commander of Carabinieri and Milizia Confinaria, Fiume (It.) 41-43	MURDER	YUGO.
MIZI, Aurelio	191029	M		Dr., C.C. Fraschette, Alatri (It.) 41-43	TORTURE	YUGO.
MOCCIA, Alfonso	145468	M		Major, "Isonzo"-Div., 98.Fascist Legion, 117 Bn., 1943	MURDER	YUGO.
MOLARO, Cesare	257004	M		Sgt., Tagliamento VIII Alp.Regt., Fascist Republ. Army, Dorenberg (Yugo.) End of 1943 to April 1945	INTERR.	YUGO.
MOLINARI	174694	M		Capt., Gebirgsjaeger-Bn.2, Annecy (Fr.)	MURDER	FR.
MONDIANI	300335	M		Capt., C.C. Larissa, 41-43	MURDER	GRC.
MONFORTINI	300336	M		Maresciallo, Carabinieri Reali, Thebes, 14.8.43	MURDER	GRC.
MONICA, Vittorio	191030	M		Dr., Commissioner, Ital. Public Security (Sipo), Sibenik (Yugo.) 41-43	MURDER	YUGO.
MONTALTO, Rino	191031	M		Capt. of Carabiniere, Ital. Army, 55 Regt., "Marche"-Div., Trebinje (Yugo.) 20.4.41-8.9.43	MURDER	YUGO.
MONTANELLI	162074	M		Major, Ital. Army, Camp 41, Montalbo (It.) 12.41-3.43	TORTURE	U.K.
MONTAROTTI	191037	M		Capt., Second Ital. Army, Chief of operational Office, Susak (Yugo.) 41-43	MURDER	YUGO.
MONTARULI, Sabino	145469	M		Capt., Guidice del Tribunale Militare di Guerra, Cettigne (Yugo.) 43	MURDER	YUGO.
MONTEDORO, Renato	254889	M		Capt., Judge, Tribunal Spec., Dalmatia, Split (Yugo.) 41-43	INTERR.	YUGO.

ITALY (Mon-Pal)

ITALY. (Cont.)

NAME	C.R.FILE NUMBER	SEX	DATE OF BIRTH	RANK OCCUPATION UNIT PLACE AND DATE OF CRIME	REASON WANTED	WANTED BY
MONTEMURRO	169492	M		Capt., Ital. Army, C.C. Juane-Ben-Adem, Suani-Ben-Adem (North-Africa) 5.42-1.43	TORTURE	U.K.
MONTESSI, Enzo	259122	M		Lt., Ital. Army, 56 Regt., "Marche"-Div., Stolac (Yugo.) 4.41-9.42	MURDER	YUGO.
MONTIGLIANI see BOTIGLIANI	300190					
MONTUORI, Giuseppe	191032	M		Member, Fascio Directory, Sibenik (Yugo.) 41-43	MURDER	YUGO.
MONTUORO, Vittorio	191033	M		Col., Ital. Army, Commander of Carabinieri, Centinje Crno Gora (Yugo.) 41-43	MURDER	YUGO.
MORELLI, Giuseppe	253546	M		Chief-Police of Political Department, Italian Police, Split (Yugo.) 17.4.42	MURDER	YUGO.
MORGLIA, Piero	191034	M		Secretary, Prefect of Zara, Sibenik (Yugo.) 41-43	MURDER	YUGO.
MORI, Mario	191035	M		General, Commander of Presidio at Podgorica (Yugo.) 4.42	MURDER	YUGO.
MORO, Garino (or Gavino)	145470	M		Carabiniere, "Sebenico Sud", Carabinieri Station, Sibenik (Yugo.) 1942	MURDER	YUGO.
MORONI, Giovan, Battista	185922	M		Fascist, near Trescore (It.) 4.1.45	MURDER	U.S.
MORRA, Eugenio	191036	M		Col., Chief of Military Government at Zara, Ital. Army, Zadar Dalmatia (Yugo.) 41-43	MURDER	YUGO.
MORTAROTTI	196515	M		Capt., Ital. second Army, Susak (Yugo.) 41-43	MISC.CRIMES	YUGO.
MORTICELLI	193541	M		Capt., Ital. Army, C.C. 57, Gruppignamo (It.) 12.41 and after	MURDER	U.K.
MOSCA	191152	M		Maresciallo Guardia Financia, Iopud, Miset (Yugo.) 1942	TORTURE	YUGO.
MOSCATELLI, Giuseppe	133443	M		Col. of Carabinieri, Camp-Cmdt., C.C. Gavi (It.) 5.42-9.43	MISC.CRIMES	U.K.
MURGANTI	189884	M		Carabinieri, Ital. Army, Vela-Lucca (Yugo.)	MISC.CRIMES	YUGO.
MURIGI, Natale	145597	M		Carabiniere, Ital. Army, Isle of Corcula (Yugo.) 1943	MURDER	YUGO.
MUSCATELLI, Pietro	145596	M		Carabiniere, Ital. Army, Babno Polje near Prezad (Yugo.) 1942	TORTURE	YUGO.
MUSEMECI, Antonio	307308	M		Major, Judge, Military Tribunal for second Army, Section of Lubiana, Ljubljana (Yugo.) 41-43	MURDER	YUGO.
MUSSI, Bruno	259188	M		Lt., Ital. Army, "Marche"-Div., 56 Regt., Stolac (Yugo.) 4.41-9.42	MURDER	YUGO.
NACCI, Gaetano	170922	M	18.10.09	Supervisor, Prison, C.C. San Romeo (It.) 16.7.43-3.44	TORTURE	FR., YUGO.
NAMUCI	191098	M		Agent, Questura of Cattaro (Kotor), Kotor (It.) 41-43	MURDER	YUGO.
NANI, Repato	191039	M		Col., Commander of Carabinieri, Kistanje, Split (Yugo.) 41-42	MURDER	YUGO.
NANI, Renato	300670	M		Owner of a Coffee-House, Split (Yugo.?) 8.41	TORTURE	U.K.
NANTA	191040	M		Commissary, Chief of Italian Civil Administration, Cabar (Yugo.) 41-42	MURDER	YUGO.
NAPOLITANO, Vincenzo	191153	M		Judge, Italian "Special Court", Sibenik (Yugo.) 41-43	MISC.CRIMES	YUGO.
NATIVI, Sergio	300347	M		Lt., Director of the Aver of Prison, Athens (Grc.) 41-43	MURDER	GRC.
NICITA	252562	M	90.	Col., Carabinieri-Cmdt., PG 107, Porpetto (It.) 5.43	BRUTALITY	U.K.
NICOLETTI	169496	M		Col., Ital. Army, Capua (It.) 4.41-6.43	TORTURE	U.K.
NICOLETTI, Tulio	191041	M		Dr., Civilian, Sibenik (Yugo.) 41-43	MURDER	YUGO.
NICOSIA, Salvatore	191154	M		Major, Inf.Div. "Messina", Procuratore del Imperatore, Cetinge (Yugo.) 1941	MURDER	YUGO.
NOIFOI, Giovanni	255698	M		Brig. of Finance Guard, Customs, Radunic near Kistanje (Yugo.) 17.3.42	INTERR.	YUGO.
NOLLI, Stefano	259120	M		Lt., Ital. Army, 56 Regt., "Marche"-Div., Stolac (Yugo.) 4.41-9.42	MURDER	YUGO.
NONNI, Carlo	145636	M		Lt., Doctor, "Isonzo"-Div., 24 Inf.Regt., "Como", (Yugo.)	MURDER	YUGO.
NOVACO, Carlo	191042	M		Agent, Questura of Cattaro (Kotor), Kotor (Yugo.) 41-43	MURDER	YUGO.
OBLA, Vincenzo	256972	M		Sgt., Ital. Army, Plave Anhovo (Yugo.) 13.-29.2.45	INTERR.	YUGO.
OGIONE, Giovanni	191043	M		Major, Ital. Army, Commander of Btty. "Basano", Podgorica Berane Cetinje Savnik (Yugo.) 7.-11.41	MURDER	YUGO.
OGRISSEO	191044	M		Capt., Ital. Army, Div. "Messina", Montenegro (Yugo.) 13.7.41, spring 1942	MURDER	YUGO.
OLDANI, Guilo	137593	M		Col., P.O.W. Camp, C.C. San Guiselle (It.) 12.42-1.43	TORTURE	U.K.
OLIVIERI, Edmondo	191155	M		Legal official, Primo (I) Seniore-Judge of Italian "Special Court", Sibenik (Yugo.) 41-43	MURDER	YUGO.
OLIVIERI, Francesco	162078	M		Lt., Ital. Army, Inf., Montalbo (It.) 1942	TORTURE	U.K.
OLVIERI, Edmondo	302157	M		Primo (I), Seniore, Judge of Ital. "Special Court" in Sibenik (Yugo.) 41-43	MURDER	YUGO.
ONELIC, Manone	256971	M		Vice-Brig., Carabiniere, Kastav (Yugo.) 4.43	MURDER	YUGO.
ORASI, U.	307309	M		Capt., Judge, Military Tribunale, Susak (Yugo.) 41-43	MURDER	YUGO.
ORAZI, Vizio	191045	M		Official, Prefect of Province of Zara, Sibenik (Yugo.) 41-43	MURDER	YUGO.
ORFATTI, Emilio	250416	M		Maresciallo pilot, Airforce, 21 Storm Camp, Avazione, Hrastov, Dol Trnovica (Yugo.) 31.7.43	MISC.CRIMES	YUGO.
ORIDLI, Antonio	148665	M		Capt., "Isonzo"-Div., 98 Fascist Legion, 1 Coy., Rakovnik (Yugo.) 1943	MURDER	YUGO.
ORIFICI, Domenico	148666	M		Col., "Isonzo"-Div., 24 Inf.Regt. "Como", (Yugo.) 1943	MURDER	YUGO.
ORIOLI, E.	191046	M		Major, Ital. Army, Deputy Chief of Staff "Taro"-Div., Crna Core (Yugo.) 1941	MURDER	YUGO.
ORLANDO, Luigi see ROLANDO	132194					
ORLANDO, Taddeo (Tadeo)	148664			General, "Granattieri di Sardegna" Div., XI Army-Corps, (Yugo.) 43	MURDER	YUGO.
ORLICH, Gualtiero	191047	M		Dr., Member, Squadrist, Ital. Army, Sibenik (Yugo.) 41-43	MURDER	YUGO.
OROFOLO see CROFOLLO	193539					
OROTALO	193542	M		Col., Commander of P.O.W. Camp 75, Bari (It.)	MURDER	U.Y.
ORSINI	155500	M	15	Cpl., Inf.Regt.313, C.C. Larissa (Grc.) 10.42-6.43	TORTURE	U.K.
ORSONI, Jose	148663	M		Lt. (Med.), "Isonzo"-Div., 23 Inf. Regt. "Como", Cernomelj (Yugo.) 1943	MURDER	YUGO.
OSMANI	307311			N.C.O., Member, Gendarmerie, of OVRA, Trieste, 12.41	MURDER	YUGO.
OSTI, Giovanni	196324	M		Col.Pres., Military Tribunal, 41-43	MISC.CRIMES	YUGO.
OTTONE, Giorgio	307312	M		Major, Judge, Military Tribunal, second Army, Section of Lubiana (Yugo.) 41-43	MURDER	YUGO.
PACE, Pasquale	307313	M		Major, Judge, Military Tribunal, Susak (Yugo.) 41-43	MURDER	YUGO.
PACIFICI, Riccardo	191048	M		Lt., Ital. Army, Commander of Carabinieri, Sibenik (Yugo.) 41-43	MURDER	YUGO.
PACIFICO, Luigi	178295	M		Lt., Army, Arb.Kdo., Sesto San Giovanni (It.) spring 1943	TORTURE	U.K.
PALA, Efisin	191049	M		Sgt., Ital. Army, Deputy Commander of Carabinieri Unit, Vodice, Sibenik (Yugo.) 41-43	MURDER	YUGO.
PALAMARA, Giovanni	307314	M		Doctor, Capt., Judge, Military Tribunal, Susak (Yugo.) 41-43	MURDER	YUGO.
PALEREO	148894	M		Capt., C.C. Benghazi (North-Africa) 11.42	MISC.CRIMES	U.K.
PALERMO	191050	M		Capt. of Carabinieri, Ital. Army, Div. "Re", Otocac (Yugo.) 41-43	MURDER	YUGO.
PALERMO	302153	M		Capt., Cmdt., Benghazi, P.O.W. Camp, Benghazi (North-Africa) 1942	MURDER	U.K.

ITALY (Pal-Pie)

NAME	C.R.FILE NUMBER	SEX	DATE OF BIRTH	RANK, OCCUPATION, UNIT, PLACE AND DATE OF CRIME	REASON WANTED	WANTED BY

ITALY. (Cont.)

NAME	C.R.FILE NUMBER	SEX	DATE OF BIRTH	Particulars	REASON WANTED	WANTED BY
PALLOTTA, F.	129147	M		Col., Army, Sulmona (It.) 26.12.41	MISC.CRIMES	U.K.
PALMA, Giuseppe	149015	M		Lt.Col., Army, Military Court, Cettigne, Montenegro (Yugo.)	MURDER	YUGO.
PALMENTOLA, Aldo	307315	M		General Consul Judge of Special Tribunal for de-fense of State Rom (It.) 4.41-9.43	MURDER	YUGO.
PALMERI, Gaetano	307316	M		General Consul Judge, Special Tribunal for defense of State Rom (It.) 4.41-9.43	MURDER	YUGO.
PALOMBA, Ignatio	305213	M		Capt., Dir., Italian Section, Averof Prison Athens (Grc.) 41-43	MURDER	GRC.
PALPINELLI	149073	M		Lt., Italian Army, Lombardia Div., 73 Rgt., 3 Bn., Slovenia Croatia (Yugo.)	MURDER	YUGO.
PANAPA, Francesco	300671	M		Capt., Judge, Military Tribunal of War Army, Sezione di Sebenico, Sibenik, Dalmatia (Yugo.) 41-43	TORTURE	U.K.
PANARELLI, Francesco	149074	M		Lt., Italian Army "Ferrara" Div., Carabinieri, Montenegro (Yugo.)	MURDER	YUGO.
PANAIELLO, Francesco	191051	M		Official, Italian Army, Div.6 "Alpi Grae", Montenegro (Yugo.) 42	TORTURE	YUGO.
PANCONI, Giovanni	256970	M		Capt., Fascist Militia, Kastav (Yugo.) 41-43	MURDER	YUGO.
PANDOLERI	193543	M		Capt., POW Camp 70, Fermo-Ancona (It.) 12.42-1.43	TORTURE	U.K.
PANDOZZI, Aldo	253272	M		Cmdt., Nat. Sicilian Voluntaeers, Fonda (It.) 9.-10.43	INTERR.	YUGO.
PANICUCCI, Gina	189883	M		Capt., Italian Army, Montenegro (Yugo.)	MISC.CRIMES	YUGO.
PANNUTI, Vicenlo	255425	M		Judge, Member, Italian Special Tribunal, Zadar, Sibenik, Kotor, Split (Yugo.) 41-43	INTERR.	YUGO.
PANSINI	149075	M		Col., Italian Army, 15 Inf.Rgt., Cabar (Yugo.)	MURDER	YUGO.
PANSOLA	149076	M		Col., C.C. Zlarin (Yugo.)	TORTURE	YUGO.
PANZIERI	155528	M		Gestapo, Bassano (It.) 11.44	MURDER	U.K.
PAOLINI, Enrico	251224	M		Carabinier, 147 Section Carabiniers, Sartene (Fr.) 2.-5.43	MISC.CRIMES	FR.
PAPANTONIO, Guiseppe	188465	M		Guard, Italian Army, Camp 49 Rimini (It.) 5.43	MURDER	U.K.
PAPACUOLLO, Salvatore	300646	M		Vice Brigadiere of the Carabinieri, nr. Bracigliano, Volturare Prov. Salerno (It.) 2.44	MISC.CRIMES	U.K.
PARIO	300672	M		Activ Fascist, Island of Vis. (Yugo.) 41-43	MURDER	U.K.
PAPINI	191056	M		Officer, Lt., C.C. Montalbano (It.) 41-43	TORTURE	YUGO.
PASQUALE, Guiseppe	253276	M		Chief, 21 Bn. Sardinia Gren. Div. Executive Section, Ljubljana (Yugo.) 42	MISC.CRIMES	YUGO.
PASQUALI, Focco	307317	M	05	Cpl., Gend. Molat, C.C. Molat (Meleda) 42-43	MURDER	YUGO.
PASQUALINO	191054	M		Agent, Police, Fraschetta Alatri (It.)	TORTURE	YUGO.
PASQUALUCCI, Renato	307318	M		General Consul, Judge of Special Tribunal for defense of State Rom (It.) 4.41-9.43	MURDER	YUGO.
PASSARELLO, Cosimo	193554	M		Sgt., Carabinieri, Budva Pijeka, Crnojevika (Yugo.) 9.41	MURDER	YUGO.
PATTRACHINI, Vittorio	254150	M		Formerly Member of Black Bde., Ariano Polesine (It.) 12.44	INTERR.	U.K.
PATYPINIERI, Nunzio	162077	M		Capt., Italian Army, Fermo (It.) 41-43	TORTURE	U.K.
PAULOVICH	191055	M		District Commissioner, Sibenik (Yugo.) 41-43	MURDER	YUGO.
PAVANINI	300647	M		Member, Black Bde., Mesola Ferrara Adria Rovigo (It.) 12.44	MISC.CRIMES	U.K.
PAVISSICH	191057	M		Capt., Italian Army, Div. "Messino", Montenegro (Yugo.) 13.7.41-42	MURDER	YUGO.
PECIS, A.	191058	M		Lt.Col., Italian Army, Solin, Dalmatia (Yugo.) 24.1.42-21.2.42	MURDER	YUGO.
PEDINI, Pio	169290	M		Lt.Col., Administ.Officer Camp P.G.82, Laterina (It.) 8.42-9.43	TORTURE	U.K.
PEDRAZOLI	149077	M		General, Italian Army, Tarro-Div., Montenegro (Yugo.)	MURDER	YUGO.
PEDROTTI, Aldo	256969	M		Capt., Commandant, IV Coy, Milizao Cost, Plave Anhovo (Yugo.) 13.-23.2.45	INTERR.	YUGO.
PELAZZI, Antonio	149078	M		Col., Italian Army, "Isonzo" Div., Trebnje (Yugo.)	MURDER	YUGO., UNWCC
PELEGRINO (or PELLEGRIMOS) N.	191059	M		Commissary, Sipo, Ljubljana (Yugo.) 41-43	MURDER	YUGO.
PELEGRINO, Alessandro	259187	M		Lt., Italian Army, "Marche" Div. 56 Div., Stolac (Yugo.) 4.41-9.42	MURDER	YUGO.
PELIGRA (see PELLIGRA)	148979	M				
PELIZZARI, Giovanni	193287	M		Guard, C.C.6, Verchili (It.) 43	MURDER	U.K.
PELLEGRIMOS, N. (see PELEGRINO)	191059					
PELLIGRA (alias: PELIGRA)	148979	M		General, "Re." Div., Gornji-Kozar, Kotar-Caber (Yugo.) 43	MURDER	YUGO.
PEPPI	259170			Agent later Director, Italian Questura, Prison Parma, It., Split (Yugo.) 1.42	SUSPECT	YUGO.
PEPILLO, Emilio	307319	M		Consul, Judge, Special Tribunal for defense of State Rom (It.) 4.41-9.43	MURDER	YUGO.
PERIN, Italo	305220	M		Black Bde., Frasinelle, Rovigo Prov. (It.) 2.8.44	MISC.CRIMES	U.K.
PERMA, U.	191060	M		Commander, Italian Army, 2 "Granattieri" di Sordigne, Blocice Slovenia (Yugo.) 25.-28.6.42	PILLAGE	YUGO.
PERODI, Gino	169505	M		Capt., Italian Army, Laterina (It.) 8.42-9.43	TORTURE	U.K.
PERONCINI, Giovanni Battista	300673	M		Lt., Col., President and Judge of Military Tribunal of War Army Sezione di Sebenico, Sibenik Dalmatia (Yugo.) 41-43	TORTURE	U.K.
PERONI	141939	M		Major, Army, Public Prosecution to the Procuratore Generale, Athens (Grc.) 5.42	MISC.CRIMES	U.K.
PESCARA (see TISANI)	194290					
PESCDA (see TISANI)	194290					
PETRAELLO, Svanco-Cucos	254089	M		Fascists, Fascist Militioner, Split (Yugo.) 1.41-5.42	TORTURE	YUGO.
PETRAGNANI	189030	M		Col., Commander of P.G.53, Macerata (It.) 3.-9.43	TORTURE	U.K.
PETRELLI, Nazzarero	132191	M	10	River Manocchia (It.) 25.11.43	MURDER	U.K.
PETRICIONI, Domenico	191061	M		Camp Commander, Women's C.C. Pallenze Macerata (It.) 43	TORTURE	YUGO.
PETRINI, Dante	191062	M		Carabiniere, Italian Army, Sibenik and District Vodice (Yugo.) 41-43	MURDER	YUGO.
PETROSSI, Verdi	149083	M		Civilian, Municipal Commissioner (Yugo.) 43	MURDER	YUGO.
PEZZANO	191063	M		Col., Commander of 2 Gruppo Alpini del Valte, Italian Army, Povisa, Stubica Funk Hedjedja Praprat (Yugo.) 9.41	MISC.CRIMES	YUGO.
PIACENTI, Nicolo	149084	M		Maresciallo dei Carabinieri, Carabinieri Station, Italian Army, Vis (Yugo.) 43	MURDER	YUGO., UNWCC
PIAMONTE	305225	M		Carabiniere, Vrhnika, Ljubljana, Slovenia (Yugo.) 41 and 42	PILLAGE	YUGO.
PIAZZA, Vito	166625	M	18	Agent, SD, Campomelem (It.)	WITNESS	U.S.
PIAZZONI	149085	M		Lt.General, Italian Army, "Bergamo" Div., Bickovo (Yugo.) 42	TORTURE	YUGO.
PICCINI, Sergio	253183	M		Sgt., Pilot, Air Force, 21 Stormo, 63 Groupe, 113 Squadriglia O.A., Sosici (Yugo.)	INTERR.	YUGO.
PICCININI	191064	M		Carabiniere, C.G. Pallenza (It.) 41-43	TORTURE	YUGO.
PICOLOGIO, Vani	189881	M		Lt., Italian Army, Montenegro (Yugo.)	MISC.CRIMES	YUGO.
PIERRO-PAPINI	305226	M		Political Governor of the Jonia Islands, Corfu (Corsica) 1.6.41-11.9.43	PILLAGE	GRC.

ITALY (Pig - Rom)

NAME	C.R.FILE NUMBER	SEX	DATE OF BIRTH	RANK	OCCUPATION UNIT PLACE AND DATE OF CRIME	REASON WANTED	WANTED BY
					ITALY. (Cont.)		
PIGNATELLI,Antonio	191065	M			Col., Ital. Army, 55 Regt., "Marche"-Div., Trehinje (Yugo.) 20.4.41-8.9.43	MURDER	YUGO.
PILLERI	191066	M			Member of Ovra (Ital. Secret Police), Chief of Police at Susak, Podhum (Yugo.) 41-43	MURDER	YUGO.
PILOT,Pietrot	39669	M	29.6.24		Cpl., Unit 15201, Chenebier (Fr.) 27.9.44	MURDER	FR.
PILOTTI,Ugo	191156	M			Capt., Deputy State Prosecutor, Extraordinary Military Tribunal, Sibenik (Yugo.) from 1941	MURDER	YUGO.
PINELLI,Corrado	149086	M			Capt., "Isonzo"-Div., 23 Regt. Fant. "Como", Ital. Army, Cerhomelj (Yugo.)	MURDER	YUGO.
PINI	121271	M			Lt. de Vaisseau, Ital. Navy, Commander, D'Asmara, 10.7.40	MURDER	FR.
PINI	258201	M			Lt., Ital. Army, Plave Anhovo (Yugo.) 23.2.45	INTERR.	YUGO.
PIROZZI,Vito	191067	M			C.C.-Director, C.C. Ariano-Irpino (It.) 41-43	TORTURE	YUGO.
PISTOCLIESI	259108	M			Carabiniere, Venezia-Div., Berane Montenegro (Yugo.) 8.41-9.43	MISC.CRIMES	YUGO.
PITARRELO,Romoaldo	259186	M			Lt., Ital. Army, "Marche"-Div., 56 Regt., Stolac (Yugo.) 4.41-9.42	MURDER	YUGO.
PITAU	149087	M			Lt.General, Ital. Army, "Lombardia"-Div., (Yugo.) 1943	MURDER	YUGO.
PIVANO	191068	M			General, Ital. Army, Commander of "Cacciatori del Alpi", Nubide Niksic (Yugo.) 10.8.41	TORTURE	YUGO.
PIVIDORI,Eligio	191069	M			Member, Fascist Militia, Sibenik (Yugo.) 41-43	MURDER	YUGO.
PIVIDORI,N.	253278	M			Observer, Ital. Airforce 21, Stormo-63, Group-41a, Squadriglia O.A., Baranje Selo (Yugo.) 28.6.43	INTERR.	YUGO.
PIZZI,Enrico	191070	M			Col., Ital. Army, Commander of Regt. "Alpini del Valle", Podgorica, Berane, Cetinje, Savnik (Yugo.) 7.-11.41	MURDER	YUGO.
PIZZI,Guiseppe	189880	M			Major, Ital. Army, Brodarevo (Yugo.)	MISC.CRIMES	YUGO.
PIZZILIO,Giovanni	191071	M			Lt., Judge at Military Tribunal of War, Cetinje (Yugo.) 7.41-9.43	MURDER	YUGO.
PIZZILIO,Carlo	196695	M			Col., Military Tribunal, Sibenik (Yugo.) 41-43	MISC.CRIMES	YUGO.
PLOS	258200	M			Pvt., Ital. Army, Plave Anhovo (Yugo.) 12. and 23.2.45	INTERR.	YUGO.
POLVERINI,Alessandre	162623	M			Capt., Ital. Army, Fermo (It.) 41-43	MISC.CRIMES	U.K.
POMPILI,Torello	307320	M			Consul, Judge of Special Tribunal for defense of State, Rom (It.) 4.41-9.43	MURDER	YUGO.
PONSINI,I.	190052	M			Col., Ital. Army, Commander of 15 Inf.Regt., Gabar (Slovenia) (Yugo.) 7.-8.42	MURDER	YUGO.
POSI,Camillo	251243	M			Capt., Carabinieri, Srima near Sibenik (Yugo.)	INTERR.	YUGO.
POTOSKIE,Johnie	178291	M			Cpl., Ital. Army, C.C. Gravina (It.) 6.42	MURDER	U.K.
POZZUOLI,Angelo	149088	M			Lt., Ital. Army, "Isonzo"-Div., 24 Inf.Regt. "Como", (Yugo.)	MURDER	YUGO.,UNWCC.
PRECIOSO	259119	M			Head of internment camp at Istonia-Marina (It.) 41-43	BRUTALITY	YUGO.
PRESTI,Giovanni	307321	M			Prosecutor (Military), Special Tribunal for defense of State, Rom (It.) 4.41-9.43	MURDER	YUGO.
PROPERZI,Claudio	191072	M			Lt., Ital. Army, Podhum near Susak (Yugo.) 41-4.43	MURDER	YUGO.
QUACARI,Guiseppe	259107	M			See Consolidated List Part II - Appendix "A".		
QUARANTOTTO,Paolo	191073	M			Secretary, Zadar, Sibenik (Yugo.) 41-43	MURDER	YUGO.
QUATTRINI,Arturo	300416	M	00		Sgt., Fascist Republican Guard, Andorno Micco (Vercelli Prov.) (It.) 24.4.44	MURDER	U.F.
RABAGLIOLI	191074	M			Vice-Cmdt., Ital. Army, Posto du Carabinieri at Krtoli (Yugo.) 9.43	MURDER	YUGO.
RADINI-TEDESCHI,Francesco	191157	M			Legal official, Judge of Ital. "Special Court", Sibenik (Yugo.) 41-43	MURDER	YUGO.
RADOVANI,Plinio	255037	M			Secretary, leader, Fascio, Biovicino Selo Kistanje Ivosevei, 6.42	MURDER	YUGO.
RAFFELLI,Giuseppe	169498	M			Ital. Army, P.O.W.Camp, Suani-Ben-Adem (North-Africa) 5.42-1.43	TORTURE	U.F.
RAGOZZI,Guido	191075	M			Lt.Col., Ital. Army, Commander of Bn. of the Div. "Messina", Prov. Montenegro (Yugo.) 31.7.41-spring 1942	MURDER	YUGO.
RAMEZANI	300649	M			Carabiniere, Camp 52, Chiavari (It.) 12.41-10.42	MISC.CRIMES	U.K.
RAMPONI,Mario	191076	M			Major, Ital. Army, Commander of Bn. G.A.F., Vice-Commissary at Susak, Podhum (Yugo.) 41-4.43	MURDER	YUGO.
RASO see ROSSO,Luigi	191087						
RAUTER,Darius	121404	M			17 SS-Pz.Gren.Div., G.V.B.Sturmgeschuetz Abt.17, Segre-Renale (Fr.) 30.7.44	MURDER	FR.
RAVENI	148643	M			Col., Army, "Lombardia"-Div., 57 Artl.Regt., Slovenia, Croatia (Yugo.)	MURDER	YUGO.
RAVERA,Joseph	121406	M			17 SS-Pz.Gren.Div., G.V.B.Sturmgeschuetz Abt.17, Segre-Renale (Fr.) 30.7.44	MURDER	FR.
RAZZINI	253309	M			Lt., Chars Legers, 21 Bn., Aiti (Fr.) 10.6.-11.7.43	MISC.CRIMES	FR.
RE,Giuseppe	300650	M			Sentry at Camp PG-70, Fermo (It.) 4.1.43	TORTURE	U.K.
REA,Gianfranco	258196	M			Capt., Fasc.Republ.Army,Tagliamento VIII Alp.Regt., 2 Bn., Dorenberg (Yugo.) End of 1943 to April 1945	INTERR.	YUGO.
RENZO,Edwardo	148642	M			Capt., Army, "Isonzo"-Div., 24 Inf.Regt. "Como", (Yugo.) 1943	MURDER	YUGO.
RICCI	253292	M			Lt., 1 Coy, 59 Regt. of Black Shirts, St. Pietro (Fr.) 31.8.43	MISC.CRIMES	FR.
RICCI,Settino	300420	M	96		Sgt.-Major, Fascist Republ. Guard, Andorno,Micca (Vercelli Prov.) (It.) 24.4.44	MURDER	U.K.
RICCIO,Gennaro	306349	M			Consul, Judge of Special Tribunal for defense of State, Rom (It.) 4.41-9.43	MURDER	YUGO.
RICCIOTTI	191077	M			Lt., Ital. Army, C.C.R.R., Isle of Veliki (Yugo.) 28.7.42	MURDER	YUGO.
RICUCCI,Dario	253295	M			Lt., observer, Ital. Airforce, 21 Stormo, 63 Gr.41 A, Baronje (Yugo.) 26.6.43	INTERR.	YUGO.
RISTERUCCI	173930	M			Cmdt., Police, Pontocharra (Fr.)	MURDER	UNWCC.
RIZZATO,Francesco	300674	M			Cpl.,130 Regt.di Stanza Zrnovica,Split and neighbouring towns, 42	MURDER	U.F.
RIZZI see RIZZO,Luigi	191078						
RIZZO,Luigi or RIZZI	191078	M			Director, Prison, Poggio Reale, Naples (It.) 28.9.43	MURDER	YUGO.
ROATTA	307322	M			N.C.O.,Gendarmerie,C.C. Molat, 42-43	MURDER	YUGO.
ROCCAFORTE,Filadelfo	191079	M			Capt.,It.Army,6 Art.Regt.,"Isonzo"-Div.,Commander,Straza (Yugo.)43	MURDER	YUGO.
ROCCHETTI,Nello	300421	M	26		Pvt., Fascist Republ. Guard,Andorno Micca (It.) 24.4.44	MURDER	U.K.
ROCCHI,Armando	148641	M			Col., Dalmatia (Yugo.) 1943	MURDER	YUGO.
ROCCO,G.	148640	M			Dr., Capt., "Isonzo"-Div., 23 Regt. "Como", Cornomelj (Yugo.) 1943	MURDER	YUGO.
ROCI,Viciano	191080	M			Lt.,It.Army,259 Regt.,"Murge"-Div.,Trebinje, Ljubine (Yugo.) 42-43	MURDER	YUGO.
ROIA,Roberto	255036	M			Judge, Member of the Tribunal, Split (Yugo.) 41-43	INTERR.	YUGO.
ROLANDO or ROWLANDO or ORLANDO, L.	132194	M	circa 95		Capt., Ital. Army, Tahuna (North-Africa) 9.42	TORTURE	U.K.
ROMANELLI,Giovanni	148646	M			Marschall, Fascist Ital. Army, Grottazzolina (It.)	MURDER	U.K.
ROMANELLI,Giovanni	173244	M			Civilian, Fermo (It.)	MURDER	U.K.

ITALY (Rom-Sco)

NAME	C.R.FILE NUMBER	SEX	DATE OF BIRTH	RANK OCCUPATION UNIT PLACE AND DATE OF CRIME	REASON WANTED	WANTED BY
				ITALY. (Cont.)		
ROMANO	192575	M		Commandant,Italian Army,10 Geb.Jg.Div.,Heuteville Gondon (Fr.) 8.43	PILLAGE	FR.
ROMEO,Caesaro	132824	M		Mareschiallo di Carabinieri,Athen (Grc.) 11.41-5.42	TORTURE	U.S.
ROMEO,Pietro	148698	M		Col.,Dalmatia (Yugo.) 43	TORTURE	YUGO.
RONCAGLIA,Ercole	191081	M		Lt.General,XIV Corps D'Armata,Commander,Montenegro (Yugo.)5.-9.43	MURDER	YUGO.
RONCO	193544	M		Lt.,POW Camp 70,Gruppignano, (It.) 12.41	MURDER	U.K.
RONCORINI,Alfredo	148697	M		Capt.,Carabinieri,Dalmatia,Isle of Korcula (Yugo.) 43	MURDER	YUGO.
RONNER,Robert	191082	M		N.C.O.,Italian Army,Carabiniere,Peninsula of Peljesca and Orebic (Yugo.) 42-43	MURDER	YUGO.
ROOCKE	173245	M		Lt.,Italian Army,C.C.Aversa Camp 63 (It.) 42-43	TORTURE	U.K.
ROSA,Giuseppe	305251	M		Police Officer,Livadia,Davlia (Grc.) 5.5.43	MURDER	GRC.
ROSADI,Rino	191083	M		Lt.,Italian Army,Commander of a Unit at Sibenik and District (Yugo.) 41-43	MURDER	YUGO.
ROSANO,Raffaello	148636	M		Capt.,"Isonzo" Div.,98 Fascist Legion, 43	MURDER	YUGO.
ROSATI,Filippo	191084	M		Capt.,Italian Army,Sibenik (Yugo.) 41-43	MURDER	YUGO.
ROSA-ULIANA,Riccardo	307323	M		Consul-Judge of Speciale Tribunal for defense of State Rom (It.) 4.41-9.43	MURDER	YUGO.
ROSCIOLI,Guiseppe	191085	M		Col.,Italian Army,47 Rgt.Doila Div."Ferrara",Savnik,Montenegro (Yugo.) 43	MURDER	YUGO.
ROSETI	191086	M		Lt.,Italian Army,"Murge" Div.,51 Rgt.,Trebinje (Yugo.) 42-43	MURDER	YUGO.
ROSI,Guiseppe	129150	M		Pvt.,Guard,C.C.Sulmona (It.) 4.41-6.43	MURDER	U.K.
ROSSAMANDO	189044	M		Col.,Italian Artillery,Benghazi (Africa) 42	TORTURE	U.K.
ROSSI	156053	M		Cpl.,313 Inf.Rgt.,C.C.Larissa (Grc.) 4.41-6.43	TORTURE	U.K.
ROSSI,Romolo	307289	M		Member,Italian Fascist Federation at Verona,Grezzana (It.)12.11.43	MURDER	U.K.
ROSSI,Umberto	307324	M		General-Consul,Judge of Special Tribunal for defense of State Rom (It.) 4.41-9.43.	MURDER	YUGO.
ROSSINI	152350	M		Sgt.,Italian Army,313 Inf.Rgt.,Larissa (Grc.) 8.42	TORTURE	U.K.
ROSSO,Luigi (or RASO)	191087	M		Civilian,Provost Marshal at Fraschette Alatri (Yugo.) 41-43	TORTURE	YUGO.
ROVER,Giuseppe	193555	M		Carabiniere,Italian Army,Budva (Yugo.) 6.-8.41	MURDER	YUGO.
ROVERO	189912	M		Prison Doctor,C.C.San Remo (It.)	TORTURE	FR.
ROWLANDO,Luigi (see ROLANDO)	132194					
RUGGERI	191088	M		Sgt.,Italian Army,1 Btty.,Sibenik (Yugo.) 41-43	MURDER	YUGO.
RUGGERO,Vittorio	148635	M		General,"Cacciatori delle Alpi" Div.,Ljubljana (Yugo.) 43	MURDER	YUGO.
RUGGI	253516	M		Officer,Security Police,Sibenik (Yugo.) 12.8.41	BRUTALITY	YUGO.
RUGGIERO	191089	M		Commissary,Public Safety,Metlika Slovenia (Yugo.) 42	MURDER	YUGO.
RUJU,Francesco	191090	M		Tenente,Italian Army,Commander of Tenenza of Vodice,Sibenik and District (Yugo.) 41-43	MURDER	YUGO.
RUSSA,Salvatore	137588	M		Pvt.,Army,Gruppigniamo (It.) 5.43	MURDER	U.K.
SABA,Michele	258190	M		Lt.,Army,Plave Anhovo (Yugo.) 23.2.45	INTERR.	YUGO.
SABATINI,Ciaccomi	173260	M		Lt.Col.,med.,Italian Army,Treviglio (It.)	MURDER	U.K.
SABATINI,Giacomo	146171	M		Col.,Army,Mil.Hosp.for Tuberculosis,Treviglio (It.) 42-43	TORTURE	U.K.
SAGGESE,Luigi	169501	M		Capt.,Italian Army,Capua (It.) 4.41-6.43	TORTURE	U.K.
SAGNOTTI,Augusto	259128	M		Capt.,Carabinieri Commandant,Berane Montenegro (Yugo.) 8.41-7.42	MISC.CRIMES	YUGO.
SALAMONE,Angelo	307325	M		Court-Président,Military Tribunal 2 Army Section of Ljubljana (Yugo.) 41-43	MURDER	YUGO.
SALATEO,Max	191091	M		Agent,Italian Party Squadra politica,Split (Yugo.) 2.-3.43	TORTURE	YUGO.
SALATIELLO,Luigi	256352	M		Cmdt.,Carabinieri Reali,Benkovac (Yugo.) 6.-10.42	MISC.CRIMES	YUGO.
SALICCIA,Giovanni	129151	M		Guard,Carabiniere,C.C.Sulmona (It.) 26.12.41	MURDER	U.K.
SALVATELLI	146321	M		Brigadier,Italian Army,Vele Luka (Yugo.)	MURDER	YUGO.
SALVATORE,Russo	146320	M		Guard,Italian Army,Isle de Korcula (Yugo.) 43	MURDER	YUGO.
SANTAMARIA,Giovanni	191092	M		Doctor,Director,C.C.Corrpoli (It.) 41-43	TORTURE	YUGO.
SANTARO,Pasquale	173262	M		Col.,Italian Army,C.C.Padulla (It.)	TORTURE	U.K.
SANTINI,Umberto	191158	M		Dr.,Legal Official,Primo (I) Senior Judge of Italian"Special Court" Sibenik (Yugo.) 41-43	MURDER	YUGO.
SANTIS DE VINCENZO,Eugenio	191165	M		Commander,III Btty.14 Artillery Rgt.,"Ferrara" Div.,Savnik Montenegro (Yugo.) 5.-6.43	MURDER	U.K.
SANTOJEMA	191093	M		Capt.,Head of Police at Cetinje,XI Bn.Carabiniere,Cetinje Crna Gora (Yugo.) 41-43	MURDER	YUGO.
SAPANO	253788	M		Teacher,Civilian,Italian School,Split (Yugo.) 9.5.43	TORTURE	YUGO.
SARLENO	194286	M		Major,Italian Police,Nice (Fr.) 1.-6.43	TORTURE	FR.
SAURO	146918	M		Capt.,Italian Marine,Bickovo (Yugo.) 42	MURDER	YUGO.
SAVALLI,Joseph	189911	M		Civilian,Bizerte (Tunisia)	MURDER	FR.
SAVARINO,F.	191094	M		Major,Commander II Bn.23 Inf.Rgt."Como","Isonzo" Div.,District of Cernomelj (Yugo.) 11.8.42	MURDER	YUGO.
SAVIOLA,Giorgie or Giorgio	191095	M		Lt.Col.,Italian Army,51 Rgt.of "Murge" Prison,Trebuije Area (Yugo.) 42-43	MURDER	YUGO.
SAVO,Diovanni	259474	M		Vice-Federale,Split (Yugo.) 8.41	INTERR.	YUGO.
SCALAMOGNA,Francesco	191096	M		Civilian,Director of C.C.Lipari (It.) 41-43	TORTURE	YUGO.
SCALCHI,Giovanni	261032	M		Col.,Army,107 Squadristi Legion,Bezbradica (Yugo.) 30.5.42	MURDER	YUGO.
SCALCHI,Ivan	191097	M		Consul,Head of Political Inrestigation Office U.S.S.,Zede,Sibenik (Yugo.) 41-43	MURDER	YUGO.
SCALPA,Guiseppe	189879	M		Capt.,Italian Army,Montenegro (Yugo.)	MISC.CRIMES	YUGO.
SCALZO,Michele	146317	M		Major,Mil.Tribunal,Cettigne (Yugo.) 43	MURDER	YUGO.
SCARANO	307326	M		Marshal,Member,Gendarmerie,OVRA,Trieste,12.41	MURDER	YUGO.
SCARANO,Alfredo	162067	M		Capt.,Italian Army,Fermo (It.) 11.41-43	MISC.CRIMES	U.K.
SCARPA	191099	M		Agent,Questura of Cattaro,Kotor (Yugo.) 41-43	MURDER	YUGO.
SCARPA,Guiseppe	191098	M		Capt.,Judge of Military Tribunal of Cetinje (Yugo.) 7.41-9.43	MURDER	YUGO.
SCARPERIA,G.	146316	M		Lt.Col.,Italian Army,"Isonzo" Div.,23 Rgt.,Cernomels (Yugo.) 43	MURDER	YUGO.
SCASELATI,Franco	189878	M		Prefect,Italian Public Official,Kotor (Yugo.)	MISC.CRIMES	YUGO.
SCHMIDT,Emm or Carguila	191100	F		Civilian,Wife of Sub.Lt.Garguilo,Mostar (Yugo.) 7.42	PILLAGE	YUGO.
SCIPIONE	146315	M		General,Italian Army,Deputy Commander (Yugo.) 43	MURDER	YUGO.
SCLOBLACK (see SCOBLIN)	252684					
SCOBLIN (or SCLOBLACK)	252684	M		Capt.,It.Troops stationed at Collonges,Archamps (Fr.) 11.6.43	INTERR.	FR.
SCOLARI	256974	M		Pvt.,Italian Army,Plave Anhovo (Yugo.) 13.-23.2.45	INTERR.	YUGO.

ITALY (Sco - Szo)

ITALY. (Cont.)

NAME	C.R. FILE NUMBER	SEX	DATE OF BIRTH	RANK, OCCUPATION, UNIT, PLACE AND DATE OF CRIME	REASON WANTED	WANTED BY
SCOMBOLI, Hector	305277	M		Sgt., Carabinieri Reali, Corfu (Grc. from the beginning of Occ. to Sept. 1943	TORTURE	GRC.
SCONOCHI, Paulo	259127	M	circa 11	Capt., Cmdt., Carabinieri, Venezia-Div., Berane (Yugo.) 8.42-9.43	MISC.CRIMES	YUGO.
SCROBOGNA, Giovanni	146314	M		Ital. Army, 98 Fascist Legion, Trebnje (Yugo.) 1943	MURDER	YUGO.
SCUTELI	189877	M		Carabiniere, Ital. Army, Vela luka (It.)	MISC.CRIMES	YUGO.
SECCHI	258191	M		Pvt., Ital. Army, Plave Anhovo (Yugo.) 13. and 23.2.45	INTERR.	YUGO.
SENATORE, Aldo	191101	M		Major, Ital. Army, Commander of Inf. Div. "Zara", Sibenik (Yugo.) 41-43	MURDER	YUGO.
SEPPILLI, Ilicio	146313	M		Major, Ital. Army, Military Tribunal, Cettigne (Yugo.) 1943	MURDER	YUGO.
SERACCHICLI, Luigi	307327	M		Lt.Col., President, Judge of Military Tribunal for second Army, Section of Lubiana (Yugo.) 41-43	MURDER	YUGO.
SERAFINI see SERAFINO	162069					
SERAFINO, Guido or SERAFINI	152069	M		Capt., Ital. Army, Camp 87, Benevento (It.) 7.-11.42	TORTURE	U.K.
SERAFIGLIA, Antonio	191102	M		Fascist, C.C. N.N. 134, Bn. "Larino", Czaljon Kupa and Novo Mesto (Yugo.) 1943	PILLAGE	YUGO.
SERENTINO, Pietro	259098	M		Lt., Ital. Army, 56 Regt., "Marche"-Div., Stplac (Yugo.) 4.41-9.42	MURDER	YUGO.
SERRETINO, Vincenzo	191103	M		Judge, Ital. Extraordinary Court, Sibenik (Yugo.) 41-43	MURDER	YUGO.
SERVIDORI	258188	M	circa 00	Secretary, Fascist Party at Rijeka, Kastav (Yugo.) 41-43	INTERR.	YUGO.
SESTIILI, Gualterio	191104	M		Lt.Col., C.O. Carabinieri, Sibenik (Yugo.) 41-43	MURDER	YUGO.
SFERCO, Massimiliano	253787	M		Agent, Police, Split (Yugo.) 42-43	TORTURE	YUGO.
SIDDI, R.	146312	M		Generalmajor, Ital. Army, President of Military Tribunal, Cettigne (Yugo.) 1943	MURDER	YUGO.
SIFFREDI, C.	191108	M		Col., Commando Sector of Castelnovo, Bakovci, Zelenika, Presjeka, Lastovo (Yugo.) 1941	MURDER	YUGO.
SIMONELLI	191109	M		Civilian, Commissary in municipality of Preko, Island Dugi Otok (Yugo.) 42-43	MURDER	YUGO.
SIMONETO, Giglielmo	300675	M		Ital. soldier, Kastel-Kambelovac Garrison, Split and neighbouring towns (Yugo.) 1942	MURDER	U.K.
SIRACUSA, Vincenzo	191105	M		Capt., XI Bn. Carabinieri, Chief of Police, Cetinje-Crna Gura (Yugo.) 41-43	MURDER	YUGO.
SIUBA, Enzo	191107	M		Dr., Civilian, Head of Agents of Prefecture, Cattaro, Kotor (It.) 41-43	MURDER	YUGO.
SKATINI	177604	M		Official General, S.D., Army, Athens (Grc.) 41-42	TORTURE	U.K.
SKETINI, Vicenzo	305291	M		Officer, Bn. C, Carabinieri Reali, Davlia (Grc.) 5.5.43	MURDER	GRC.
SMALDINI, Vincenzo	191110	M		Vice-Brig., Commander of Carabinieri at Mandolini, Sibenik (Yugo.) 41-43	MURDER	YUGO.
SCARAGLIA	259785	M		Lt., I.O.V.R.A., Commissaire, Aitti (Fr.) 10.6-11.7.43	TORTURE	FR.
SOFIA, Mario	146311	M		Lt., Ital. Army, "Isonzo"-Div., 24 Inf.Regt., 1 Bn., (Yugo.) 1945	MURDER	YUGO.
SOLDANO, Vincenzo	191111	M		Major, 259 Regt., "Murge"-Div., Trebrinje Iboski Sume Ljubine Ljubomir (Yugo.) 42-43	MURDER	YUGO.
SOLDINI, Marinello	137585	M		Carabinieri, Gruppigriamo (It.) 5.43	MURDER	U.K.
SCMAUILIE, Angelo	146310	M		Ital. Army, Col., Gracac (Yugo.)	MURDER	YUGO.
SCROETTI, Corrado	300651	M	23.8.27	German Collaborator, Coriconi Comine Amandola (It.) 2.5.44	MURDER	U.K.
SORDI	178288	M		Col., Ital. Army, Athens (Grc.) autumn 1941 till autumn 1942	TORTURE	U.K.
SORDI, Giuseppe	146909	M		Lt.Col., Ital. Army, 21 Inf.Regt., III Bn., (Yugo.) 1943	MURDER	YUGO.
SORDI, T.	189876	M		Col., Ital. Army, Ljubljana (Yugo.)	MISC.CRIMES	YUGO.
SORENTINI	259172	M		Member of Staff, Int. Camp at Fabriano (It.) 41-43	BRUTALITY	YUGO.
SPAGNA	191112	M		Capt., 56 Inf.Regt., 1 Bn., 1 Coy., Div. "Marche", Mostar (Yugo.) 7.42	PILLAGE	YUGO.
SPAGNOLO	156022	M		Ital. Army, Fascist Commissionier, Bassano (It.) 4.11.44	MURDER	U.K.
SPAIATINI see SPOLETI	191117					
STAMPINETTI, Giovanni	191113	M		Civilian, Accountant at C.C. Fraschette, Alatri (It.) 41-43	TORTURE	YUGO.
SPECCHIALE, Francesco	191114	M		Brig., Ital. Army, Togir Dalmatia Trapatnice Prgomet (Yugo.) spring 1943	MURDER	YUGO.
SPERANDIO, Rinaldo	146307	M		Cpl., Ital. Army, "Isonzo"-Div., 98 Legion, 3 Coy., 117 Bn., 1943	MURDER	YUGO.
SFIGO, Umberto	189875	M		General, Ital. Army, Dalmatia (Yugo.)	MISC.CRIMES	YUGO.
SPINELLI	191116	M		Col., Commander of Artl. at Delnice Gorski Kotar, Vrata-Croatia (Yugo.) 25.8.43	INCENDIARISM	YUGO.
SPINELLI, Filippo	191115	M		Civilian, Censor, C.C. Casoli (It.) 42-43	PILLAGE	YUGO.
SPIOTTA, Vito	137077	M		Ingegnere, Silvio Parodi Black Bde.at Chiaveri (C.C.), Carasco (It.) 10.44	MURDER	U.K.
SPITALERI	193556	M		Major, Ital. Army, "Tarro"-Div., Budva, Banovina, Zevska (Yugo.) 41	MURDER	YUGO.
SPOTNICLI	141899	M		Dr., Capt., Stalag, Benghazi (Africa) 1942	MISC.CRIMES	U.K.
SPOLERO, Clinto	258186	M		Maresciallo, Essc.Republ.Army, Tagliamento VIII Alp.Regt., 2 Bn., Dorenberg and neighbouring villages (Yugo.)	INTERR.	YUGO.
SPOLETI or SPAIATINI	191117			Lt., 51 Regt. of "Murge"-Div., Iboski, Ljubine, Sume (Yugo.) 42-43	MURDER	YUGO.
SPOP	146305	M		Interpreter, Ital. Army, Trieste (It.) 1943	TORTURE	YUGO.
STALTERI, C.	191118	M		Mayor, Mayor's office of Cattaro, Kotor (Yugo.) 41-43	TORTURE	YUGO.
STASSI, Geremio	191119	M		Ital. Army, Carabinieri, Sibenik and district (Yugo.) 41-43	MURDER	YUGO.
STEFANO	146305	M		Lt., Ital. Army, 23 Inf.Regt. "Como", (Yugo.) 1943	MURDER	YUGO.
STELLAS, Panayotis	305300	M		Interpreter, leader to the Cazele Reg., stationed at Carp-nissi in the Lamia area, Carpenissi and district Lamia (Grc.) 10.42-4.43	MISC.CRIMES	GRC.
STOLP	300676	M		Agent, Prison of Krk (Yugo.) 41-43	TORTURE	U.K.
STORICH	191120	M		Dr., Civil Commissioner, Head of Municipality of Sibenik (Yugo.)41	MURDER	YUGO.
STRACCA	307328	M		Deputy to Governor of Dalmatia, Zara (Yugo.) 2.42	INTERR.	YUGO.
STROFFOLATINI	162068	M		Lt., Ital. Army, Benevento (It.) 7.-11.42	MISC.CRIMES	U.K.
SULAS, Giovanni	146303	M		Policeman, Ital. Army, Korenja (Yugo.) 1943	MURDER	YUGO.
SUPPIEJ, Giorgio	307341	M		General-Consul, President, Judge of Special Tribunal for defense of State. Rom (It.) 4.41-9.43	MURDER	YUGO.
SURCI, Tancredi	255957	M		Judge, Lt.Col., Military Courts, Split, Zadar, Kotor (Yugo.) 41-43	INTERR.	YUGO.
SVERKO, Aleksander	191121	M		Interpreter, Ital. Occupied Territories, "Squadra Politica" Split (Yugo.) 2. and 3.43	TORTURE	YUGO.
SYLVESTRI	305313	M		Capt., C.C. Larissa (Grc.) 41-43	MURDER	GRC.
SZOMMER, Carlo	307329	M		Director of C.C. Molat (Meleda), 42-43	MURDER	YUGO.

ITALY (Tab-Ver)

ITALY. (Cont.)

NAME	C.R.FILE NUMBER	SEX	DATE OF BIRTH	RANK, OCCUPATION, UNIT, PLACE AND DATE OF CRIME	REASON WANTED	WANTED BY
TABANELLI	191122	M		Fascist,Officer of C.C.,N.N.at "Ferrara" Div.,Kapino Polje Nikso,Montenegro (Yugo.) 6.43	MURDER	YUGO.
TACCHINI,Pietro	191123	M		Officer,Commander of Military Naval Sector,Sibenik (Yugo.) 41-43	MURDER	YUGO.
TADDEO,Sergio	191124	M		Lt.,55 Rgt.,"Marche" Div.,Trebinje (Yugo.) 20.4.41-8.9.43	MURDER	YUGO.
TAGLIAMOTTI	300677	M		Superintendant,Store House at the C.C.at Ponza,Island of Ponza (It.) 42-43	TORTURE	U.K.
TAJLIO,Pietro	259185	M		Lt.,Italian Army,"Marche" Div.,56 Rgt.,Stolac (Yugo.) 4.41-9.42	MURDER	YUGO.
TAMIANTI	121291	M		Capt.,Army,30 Div.,1 Coy.,Tobruk (North Africa) 10.7.42	MURDER	U.K.
TARINI,Carlo	191125	M		Commander,Carabinieri at Sibenik and District (Yugo.) 41-43	MURDER	YUGO.
TERRANOVA,Ignazio	191126	M		Lt.,Italian Army,Carabinieri,Sibenik (Yugo.) 41-43	MURDER	YUGO.
TERZI,Flamminio	191127	M		Lt.Col.,Commandante of 114 Bn.,Mitraglieri,Djurasevic,Lustica Dalmatia (Yugo.) 9.9.43	MURDER	YUGO.
TESTA,Massimo	145097	M		Capt.,Italian Army,24 Inf.Rgt."Como" (Yugo.) 43	MURDER	YUGO.
TISANI (or PESCARA or ARESTA or PESCADA)	194290	M		Capt.,Carabinieri Ovra,Police Politique Italienne,Nice (Fr.) 1.-6.43 and 44	TORTURE	FR.
TOMASELLI	191128	M		Dr.,Head,Police of Susak (Yugo.) 4. and 6.43	MURDER	YUGO.
TOMASO,David	191129	M		Capt.,Fascist Militia,Benkovac (Yugo.) 7.42 and 1.43	MURDER	YUGO.
TOMASSO	307330	M		Gend.on service at Molat Meleda C.C.,42-43	MURDER	YUGO.
TONETI (or CAPELINI)	191130	M		Capt.,Italian Army,51 Rgt. of "Murge" Div.,Trebinje Area,Villages of Iboski,Ljubine,Sume,Ljubomir (Yugo.) 42-43	MURDER	YUGO.
TONILIO	152949	M		Civilian,Bassano (It.) 4.11.44	MURDER	U.K.
TORDELLE,Emilio	191131	M		Camp Doctor,C.C.Fraschette Alatri (It.) 41-43	TORTURE	YUGO.
TORMENE,Alessandro	307284	M		Member,Italian Fascist Federation at Verona,Grezzana (It.)12.11.43	MURDER	U.K.
TORRACA,Rocco	196238	M		Col.,Military Courts,Ljubljane (Yugo.) 41-43	MISC.CRIMES	YUGO.
TORREJROSSA,Pasquale	300653	M		Lt.Col.,Commander of the 110 Legion of the National Republican Guard and Officer charge Militia H.Q.,Ascoli Piceno (It.) 2.44	MURDER	U.K.
TORSIELLO,Mario	191132	M		Major,Italian Army,Chief of staff of Garrison at Niksic (Yugo.) 27.6.42	MURDER	YUGO.
TOSARELLI,Mario (or TOSCARELLI)	258182	M		Capt.,Fascist Militia,Bn.Squadristi Emiliano,District of Kastav (Yugo.) 41-43	MURDER	YUGO.
TOSCANO,Gaetano	145095	M		Col.,Italian Army,Gottigne-Montenegro (Yugo.) 43	MURDER	YUGO.
TOSCARELLI (see TOSARELLI)	258182					
TOSKANINO,Antonio	189874	M		Col.,Italian Army,Montenegro (Yugo.)	MISC.CRIMES	YUGO.
TOSONI,Luvio	162079	M		Lt.,Italian Army,Inf.,Fermo (It.) 11.41-8.43	TORTURE	U.K.
TOSTI,Massimo	194078	M		Capt.,Italian Army,Carabinieri,Chambery (Fr.) 8.43	TORTURE	FR.
TOTANI,Olivio	253432	M		Pvt.,2 Coy,29 Bn.Royank,Calac-Uccia (Fr.) 30.5.43	MISC.CRIMES	FR.
TRENTI	250448	M		Cpl.,29 Bn.Carabinier,Sartene (Fr.) 2.-5.43	TORTURE	FR.
TRINGALI-CASANUOVA,Antonio	195627	M		Official,Justizministerium,Rom (It.) 41-43	TORTURE	YUGO.
TRUPIANI,Francesco	191133	M		Civilian,Civil Commissary at Berane,Cetinje,Savnik,Pidgerica (Yugo.) 7.-11.41	MURDER	YUGO.
TUCCI,Carlo	193558	M		Lt.General,G.O.C."Messina" Div.,Montenegro (Yugo.) 7.41	MURDER	YUGO.
TUFFANELLI DI SAVINA,Arturo	257466	M	12. 1.99	Squad.,Capt.,Fascist Republican Militia,Fiume (Yugo.) 2.4.45	MURDER	YUGO.
TULIO,Gino	258181	M		Sgt.,Fascist Republican Army,Tagliamento VIII Alpine Rgt.,2 Bn.,Dorenberg and Villages (Yugo.) 43-4.45	INTERR.	YUGO.
TURCHET	258180		circa 15	Sgt.,Major,Italian Army,Lupoglava Istria (Yugo.) 43-44	INTERR.	YUGO.
TURCHI,Ottorino	193536	M	3.28	Cpl.-chief,Italian Army,7 Coy 3 Bn.,Cais,Frejus (Fr.) 8.43	MURDER	FR.
TURCO,Francesco	141846	M		Col.,Camp Commandant PG 62,Bergamo (It.) 7.43	MURDER	U.K.
TZUPANI,Stefane	305396	M		Capt.,C.C.Larissa (Grc.) 41-43	MURDER	GRC.
UGOLINI	169473	M		Capt.,Italian Army,C.C.Isterina (It.)	TORTURE	U.K.
UGOLINI	305397	M		Lt.Commander,della Lavanderia at Vrhnika nr.Ljubljana Slovenia (Yugo.) 41-42	MISC.CRIMES	YUGO.
UGOLINI,Renato	305396	M		Commandant,42 Rgt."Forli",Div.,Davlia (Grc.) 5.5.43	MURDER	GRC.
UNGHERETTI	191125	M		Cav.Higher Official,Fascist Police,Split Dalmatia (Yugo.) 41-43	TORTURE	YUGO.
VACARO,Carmello	148383	M		Carabiniere,Italian Army,Isle of Korenla (Yugo.) 43	MURDER	YUGO.
VACCA	191136	M		Lt.,Italian Army,Carabinieri,Kistanje (Yugo.) 42	MURDER	YUGO.
VACCARI,Umberto	195628	M		Lt.General,Military,41-43	MURDER	YUGO.
VACHINI,Carlo	259126	M	15	see Part.II appendix A		
VALENTE	194286	M		Major,Italian Police,Nice (Fr.) 1.-6.43	TORTURE	FR.
VALENTE,Nicola	300655	M		Capporale Maggiore in Command of platoon,Public Security,Adria,Mesola Ferrara,Rovigo (It.) 12.44	MURDER	U.K.
VALENTINI	251712A	M		Capt.,2 Coy,96 Bn.,59 Rgt.,Santo Pietro (Fr.) 19.-31.8.43	TORTURE	FR.
VALI,Antonio	305340	M		Major,Commanding Officer,120 Bn.of Blackshirts quartered at Elassona Pinerolo Div.,Elassona Area (Grc.) 42-43	MISC.CRIMES	GRC.
VALPREDO,Giuseppe	258179	M		Soldier,Carabiniere,District of Kastav (Yugo.) 41-43	INTERR.	YUGO.
VANINI,Guiseppe	148384	M		Maresciallo,Italian Army,Carabiniere,Isle of Korcula (Yugo.) 43	MURDER	YUGO.
VANNI	251713	M		Lt.,2 Coy,96 Bn.,59 Rgt.,Santo Pietro,Oi-Tenda (Fr.)19.-31.8.43	PILLAGE	FR.
VARIO,Antonio	194285	M	21	Pvt.,Italian Army,Toulon (Fr.) 16.7.44	MURDER	FR.
VASSALLO,Silverio	189873	M		Director,Italian Public Official,Ponza (It.)	MISC.CRIMES	YUGO.
VECCHIARELLI	148385	M		General,Army Corps Italian,Fuzine (Yugo.) 42	MURDER	YUGO.
VEDANI,Mario	307391	M		General Consul,Judge,Special Tribunal for defense of State Rom (It.) 4.41-9.43	MURDER	YUGO.
VENCHI,Mario	305343	M		Major Commanding Officer,Carabienieri in Corfu (Grc.) 41	MISC.CRIMES	GRC.
VENEZANDI,Luigi	259118	M		Col.,Carabiniere IX Bn.,Split (Yugo.) 41-43	MISC.CRIMES	YUGO.
VENIERI,Alto	300614	M		Col.,Commanding Officer of the Italian Occupation Army at Kastoria Nestorion Argos Orestikon (Grc.) 42-43	MURDER	GRC.
VENTI,Carlo	257617	M		Lt.,Italian Army,PW Camp 115,Marisciano (It.) 3.-9.43	BRUTALITY	U.K.
VENTORINI	300657	M		Capt.,63 Tagliamento Bn.,Varallo Prov.Vercelli (It.) 15.4.44	MURDER	U.K.
VENTORUZZO	258178	M		Vice Brigadier,Army,Plave Anhovo (Yugo.) 13.,23.2.45	INTERR.	YUGO.
VENTURELLA	141844	M		Lt.,Medical Staff,Benghazi (Africa) 42	MISC.CRIMES	U.K.
VERCELLINO,Mario	153004	M		General,IV Italian Army,Nice,Antibes,Cannes,Grasse (Fr.) 5.-7.43	MISC.CRIMES	FR.
VERDECCHIA,Olindo	148382	M		Fasciste,Fermo (It.) 3.5.44	MURDER	U.K.
VERDI,Hugo	191137	M		Col.,Italian Army,51 Rgt.of "Murge" Div.,Sibenik (Yugo.) 41-43	MURDER	YUGO.
VERGNA	148386	M		Lt.,Italian Army,Babno Polje (Yugo.) 42	TORTURE	YUGO.
VERNONI,Luigi	256145	M		Judge,Member of the Tribunal,Kotor (Yugo.) 41-43	INTERR.	YUGO.

ITALY(VER-ZUL) - LUXEMBOURG

NAME	C.R.FILE NUMBER	SEX	DATE OF BIRTH	RANK OCCUPATION UNIT PLACE AND DATE OF CRIME	REASON WANTED	WANTED BY
				ITALY. (Cont.)		
VERRARI	148987	M		Tenente, Ital.Army, Cerknica (Yugo.) 1943	TORTURE	YUGO.
VESCOVI	255769	M		Capt., Army, Kistanje Dalmatia (Yugo.) 9.42	MURDER	YUGO.
VIALE, Carlo	191138	M		General, Ital.Army, Com. of "Zara"-Div., Sibenik (Yugo.) 41-43	MURDER	YUGO.
VIARENGO, Giorgio	258177	M		Major, Ital.Army, Garrison Commander Tetowo, Marovo, Leunovo, Nikiforovo (Yugo.) 9.43	PILLAGE	YUGO.
VICETINI, Olivio	305346	M		Sgt., Carabinieri Reali Security Department, Corfu (Grc.) 9.43	MISC.CRIMES	GRC.
VIDOVICH	191139	M		Capt., Intelligence Dept. for Vodice Sector, Vodice (Yugo.) 1941	MURDER	YUGO.
VIGNERI, Achille	191161	M		Col., Judge of Ital. "Special Court", Sibenik (Yugo.) 41-43	MURDER	YUGO.
VILLAGNO, Antonio	152999	M		Lt., Ital.Army, Tradate, Varese (It.)	TORTURE	U.K.
VILIERO	148988	M		Chief, Lt.Col., Staff, "Lombardia"-Div., (Yugo.) 1943	MURDER	YUGO.
VILLACI, Edoarde	256144	M		Member of the Tribunal, Kotor (Yugo.) 41-43	INTERR.	YUGO.
VILLASANIA, Carlo	191140	M		Chief-secretary, Government of Dalmatia, Zadar, Dalmatia (Yugo.) 41-43	MURDER	YUGO.
VILLELLA, G.	191017	M		Cmdt., Ital.Army, 163 Bn. C.C. N.N., Gruda (Yugo.)	MURDER	YUGO.
VINCENZO	189872	M		Dr., Commissar, Ital. Public Official, Spalato (It.)	MISC.CRIMES	YUGO.
VIRGHILIO	191018	M		Sgt., Ital. Army, Cetinje, Crnagora (Yugo.) 41-43	MURDER	YUGO.
VISCARDI, Giuseppe	191014	M		Vice-Brig., Ital.Army, Sibenik (Yugo.) 41-43	MURDER	YUGO.
VISCUSI, Paolo	251401	M		Ital.Airforce, AV.A.Arma 113 A, Sosici (Yugo.) 12.7.43	INTERR.	YUGO.
VITALE, Arturo	191015	M		Lt., Cmdt., Ital.Army, Solin (Yugo.) 24.1.42	MURDER	YUGO.
VITTORELLI	153018	M		Civilian, Bassano (It.) 4.11.44	MURDER	U.K.
VOLPI, Ademo	148989	M		Capt., Ital.Army, Zaostrog (Yugo.) 1943	TORTURE	YUGO.
VOLTURNO, Patrizio	191016	M		Ital.Army, C.C. Fraschette Alatri (It.) 41-45	TORTURE	YUGO.
ZAMBONI, Giorgio	300658	M		Capt., Guardia Nazionale Republicana of the 2 Coy., order of Public Security, Adria, Mesola, Ferrara, Rovigo (It.) 12.44	MURDER	U.K.
ZANATTA, Riggardo	191019	M		Agent, Security Public, Metlika (Yugo.) 1942	MURDER	YUGO.
ZANINI	250586	M		Chief, Ex-Off., 21 Bn., Sardinia Gren.Div., Ljubljana (Yugo.) 1942	TORTURE	YUGO.
ZANNI, Enzo	144989	M		Lt., Ital.Army, "Isonzo"-Div., 24 Inf.Regt. "Como", (Yugo.) 1943	MURDER	YUGO.
ZANONI	142021	M	08	Lt., 83 Fascist Militia, stationed at Garribaldi Barracks, Piacenza (It.) 11.43-1.44	TORTURE	U.K.
ZANOTTI	191020	M		Col., Ital.Army, O.C.Regt., Sassari-Div., F.562, Udbina, Gracac (Yugo.) 2. and 3.43	MURDER	YUGO.
ZANZI, Giovanni	191162	M		Col., Deputy Prosecutor of Ital. "Special Court", Sibenik (Yugo.) 41-43	MURDER	YUGO.
ZARONE, Gerardo	307332	M		Capt., Judge, Military Tribunal for second Army, Section of Lubiana (Yugo.) 41-43	MURDER	YUGO.
ZAVATARI, Filippo	300659	M		Lt., Camp 52, Chiavari (It.) 12.41-10.42	TORTURE	U.K.
ZATI see ZATTI	144988					
ZATTI aliases ZATI	144988	M		Lt.General, Ital.Army, "Lombardia"-Div., Fuzine (Yugo.) 1943	MURDER	YUGO.
ZENTA, Massimiliano	191021	M		Dr., Member, Fascist Militia, Sibenik (Yugo.) 41-43	MURDER	YUGO.
ZERBINO, Paolo	189871	M		Prefect, Ital.Public Official, Spalato (It.)	MISC.CRIMES	YUGO.
ZIMMERMANN, Joseph	132538	M		Feldgendarmerie, Sisteron (Fr.) 6.6.44	MURDER	FR.
ZINGALEZ	194323	M		General, Ital.Army, Cuneo (It.) 1943	MISC.CRIMES	FR.
ZOBOLI, Remo	250589	M		Capt., 113 a Squadriglia, 63 Gruppe, 21 Stormo, C.C.Avazione di Ljublaja, Hrastov Dol, Trnovica (Yugo.) 31.7.43	INTERR.	YUGO.
ZOLLA-CANNONERO, Pietro	307333	M		Capt., Judge, Military Tribunal for second Army, Section of Lubiana (Yugo.) 41-43	MURDER	YUGO.
ZONI, Francesco	144987	M		Officer, Ital.Army, "Ferrara"-Div., Montenegro (Yugo.) 1943	MURDER	YUGO.
ZUCCARI	300660	M		Col., Commander of 63 Tagliamento Btty., Varollo Prov.Vercelli (It.) 15.4.44	MURDER	U.K.
ZULIANNI, Emilio	256976	M		Col., Army, Fasc.Republ., Comm. of Tagliamento 8 Alp.Regt., Dorenberg and neighbouring villages (Yugo.) 11.43-4.45	INTERR.	YUGO.
				LUXEMBOURG.		
BAUMANN, Albert	195878	M		Agent, S.D., Maisons-Laffette (Fr.) 15.12.41, 10.6.44	MISC.CRIMES	FR.
BISENNIUS, Leo aliases DUBOIS, Jean	125151	M		Member, S.D., La Bourboule, Lamont Dore (Fr.) 27.4.44	MURDER	FR.
CHITTER, Lydia	149183	F		C.C. Ravensbrueck (Ger.)	MISC.CRIMES	FR.
COOLING, Willy	39580	M	05	S.D., Gestapo, Chateau-Gontier (Fr.) 4.-5.8.44	MURDER	FR.
DECKER, Jos.	141515	M	15	Member, N.S.D.A.P., 1944	MISC.CRIMES	FR.
DECKER, Peter	185597	M		Chief, Arbeitslager, Block 2, C.C. Leonberg near Stuttgart (Ger.)	MURDER	FR.
DECKER, Pierre	184270	M		Chief, C.C. Dachau (Ger.)	TORTURE	FR.
DUBOIS, Jean see BISENNIUS, Leo	125151					
FIQUE or FIUHE	258140	M		Employee, C.C. Natzweiler (Fr.)	MURDER	BEL
FRICH, Franz Francois see FRISCHOU	167116					
FRICH see FRISCH, Frantz	186842					
FRISCH, Frantz or Erich	186842	M		(Fr.)	WITNESS	FR.
FRISCHOU or FRICH, Franz Francois	167116	M		Interpreter, Civilian, Saone and Loire (Fr.) 40-44	WITNESS	FR.
HOFFMANN, Ernst	255583	M		C.C. Neckargerach (Ger.)	BRUTALITY	FR.
HOLBACK see KOLBACK	259729					
KAISER or KAYSER, Cornelius	170552	M	03	Lux. or Ger., SS-Uscharfhr., SS, S.D., H.Q., Strassenhaus near Rengsdorf (Ger.) 23.12.44-14.2.45	WITNESS	U.K.
KOLBACK or HOLBACK	259729			Interpreter, Unit F.P.VI 05811, St.Pierre de Semilly Manche (Fr.) 9.42	WITNESS	FR.
MISKA, Rudolf	196064	M		Agent, S.D., Maisons-Laffette (Fr.)	TORTURE	FR.
MULLER, Michel	188964	M		Chief du culture, Civilian, Raucourt (Fr.) 1941	PILLAGE	FR.
SIFFRES, Marcel	187340	M		Interpreter, Civilian, Montgauthier, Dinant (Bel.) 20.9.43	MURDER	BEL

NETHERLANDS - NORWAY - POLAND

NAME	C.R.FILE NUMBER	SEX	DATE OF BIRTH	RANK	OCCUPATION UNIT PLACE AND DATE OF CRIME	REASON WANTED	WANTED BY

NETHERLANDS.

NAME	C.R.FILE NUMBER	SEX	DATE OF BIRTH	OCCUPATION, UNIT, PLACE AND DATE OF CRIME	REASON WANTED	WANTED BY
ARTS, Suze	148428	F		Guard, SS, C.C., Vught (Neth.)	MURDER	BEL.
BECHMANN, Willy	196126	M		Sd-Kdo.z.b.V. 7 "Pullmer", BDS-France, Cirey (Fr.) autumn 1944	TORTURE	U.K.
BRANDT, Leonie	149718	F		C.C., Ravensbrueck (Ger.) 8.43-11.44	TORTURE	FR.
BREDOUL	187648	M		Pvt., Army, Goudrian (Neth.) 22.5.44	MURDER	U.K.
DAMM, Piet	140413	M		Chief, Gestapo, Bruxelles (Bel.)	MURDER	FR.
DANDONGEN, Pietet	170712	M	02	Agent, Gestapo, Schiebrock (Neth.)	MISC.CRIMES	UNWCC.
DEROY	145565	M		Guard, C.C. Hersbruck (Ger.)	MISC.CRIMES	FR.
DICKEN, Josephine see DICKENS	150897					
DICKENS, Josephine or DICKEN	150897	F	22	Kapo, Guard, Hermann Goering-Werk, C.C. Wattenstedt and Braunschweig (Ger.) 8.44 and 4.45	TORTURE	FR.
DRENT, Marinus	162861	M		SS-Sturmmann, Asche (Bel.)	MURDER	BEL.
GERRITSEN, Gerrit	231273		23	Agent, Gestapo, SD	MISC.CRIMES	CZECH.
GOTWITZ, Henny	193915	F	23	C.C.-Blockleiterin, C.C. Ravensbrueck (Ger.)	TORTURE	FR.
HASENFLUCHT	187639	M		Pvt., Army, Goudrian (Neth.) 22.5.44	MURDER	U.K.
KATJA	150678	F		Oberaufseherin, SS, C.C., Vught (Neth.) 43-44	MURDER	BEL.
KUIPERS, Lammert	150681	M		Dutch or Ger., C.C., Vught (Neth.) 43-44	MURDER	BEL.
MACHIELSE, Anton	141398	M	26.5.13	Fireman, C.C. Mauthausen (Aust.)	TORTURE	FR.
NOWAK, Conrad (Gerad)	196288	M	. 23	SS-Usturmfhr., SS, Gueret (Fr.)	MURDER	FR.
PHYLLIS	254911	F		Overseer, Camp Ravensbrueck (Ger.)	INTERR.	FR.
VAN DER WAL, Ebeltje nee DE VRIES	306915	F	20.9.91	Almelo (Neth.) 44-45	MURDER	U.K.
VAN DER WAL, Grietje A.	306914	F		Almelo (Neth.) 44-45	MURDER	U.K.
VELDHUIS, Jan Hendrick	306913	M		Prison-warder at Almelo (Neth.) 21. and 24.3.45	MURDER	U.K.

NORWAY.

NAME	C.R.FILE NUMBER	SEX	DATE OF BIRTH	OCCUPATION, UNIT, PLACE AND DATE OF CRIME	REASON WANTED	WANTED BY
ABELSON	147085	M		Guard, Boten Camp, Rohnan (Nor.) 1943	MURDER	YUGO.
HAMM, John	253046	M		Guard, Quisling Norwegian Bn. "Norway", Boten-Rognan (Nor.) 1942	MURDER	YUGO.
JAHNSRUD, Otto or JOHNSRUD	416	M		Guard, Camp Boten (Nor.) 3.42-43	MURDER	YUGO.
JOHANSEN, Tideman	429	M		Camp-Guard, C.C. Boten (Nor.) 3.42-43	MURDER	YUGO.
JOHNSRUD, Otto see JAHNSRUD	416					
LARSSON	250917	M		Guard at Boten-Rognan, Nor. Bn. "Norway", Quisling, (Nor.) 1942	INTERR.	YUGO.
LUNDAL, Randulf	257339	M		SS-Mann, SS, Slave Labour Camp, Korgen (Nor.) 6.42-43	MURDER	YUGO.
MUELLER, Willy	257345	M		SS-Guard, Uscharfhr., Slave Labour Camp, Korgen (Nor.) 6.42-43	MURDER	YUGO.

POLAND.

NAME	C.R.FILE NUMBER	SEX	DATE OF BIRTH	OCCUPATION, UNIT, PLACE AND DATE OF CRIME	REASON WANTED	WANTED BY
ABRAMCZYK, Isidor	140340	M	15	Chief, C.C. Auschwitz (Pol.)	TORTURE	FR.
ABRAMOWITCH, Gesel	259405	M	05	Leader, SS, Block 7, Auschwitz (Pol.)	SUSPECT	FR.
ADAMCZICK, Janek	140354	M	15	Blockleiter, C.C. Buchenwald (Ger.)	MURDER	FR.
ANKER, Daniel or Samuel	118706	M	02	C.C. Buchenwald (Ger.)	MISC.CRIMES	FR.
ANUSCHEWSKI, Stanislas	258903	M		Feldgendarm, Feldgendarmerie, Valenciennes (Fr.) 40-44	MURDER	FR.
BECKER	176565	M		SS-Mann, C.C. Krispl (Aust.) 1944	TORTURE	FR.
BIRBAN, Wladimir	187977	M	18.9.18	Civilian, Bruchsal (Ger.) 2.-3.2.45	WITNESS	U.K.
BIOSKEVITCH, Sabina	306906	F	25	Prisoner of War, employed as a servant by Mr. Lehrbass, Farm Gut Fraydeck (Ger.) 2.7.45	MURDER	U.K.
BOBIN, Sigmond	193591	M		Guard, C.C. Flossenburg (Ger.)	TORTURE	BEL.
BOTKER (BOTCHER)	174763	M		Interpreter, Kriegsgefangenen Arbeits-Bn.185, Aspfjord (Nor.)	TORTURE	NOR.
CAVENDA	148914	M	95	Guard, C.C. Norderney (Ger.)	TORTURE	FR.
CHAPINSKY	194322	M		Camp-Doctor, C.C. Mauthausen (Aust.) 1944	MURDER	FR.
CHOROCHJ, Siegmund	251989	M		Guard, C.C. Auschwitz (Pol.)	TORTURE	FR.
CHROMIK	193893	M		Civilian, St. Rambert (Fr.)	MURDER	FR.
CIOLEK	250664	M		Civilian, Chatou (Fr.) 27.8.44	WITNESS	FR.
CIUPPA, Francois	185333	M	26	Agent, SS, Gestapo, Rattingen (Ger.)	MISC.CRIMES	FR.
DANISCH, Eduard	255090	M		See Consolidated List Part II - Appendix "A"		
DAVID, Eduard	132173	M		Pol. or Ger., Cpl., SS-Pz.Div. "Hohenstaufen", Normandie (Fr.) 7.-8.44	WITNESS	U.K.
DEGE or "TINTIN"	141518	M		Agent, Milice and Gestapo, Autun, Muenster (Fr., Ger.)	MURDER	FR.
DERING	145563	M		SS-Doctor, C.C. Birkenau (Ger.) 42-43	TORTURE	FR.
DIETICH see DIETRICH	137084					
DIETRICH or DIETRIK or DIETICH	137084	M		Arbeitskdo.E 715, Stalag VIII B, Auschwitz (Pol.) 2.44	MURDER	U.K.
DIETRIK see DIETRICH	137084					
DOEHRING	258901	M		Doctor, Block 10, Auschwitz (Pol.) 40-45	MURDER	FR.
DOLADA	148944	M		Director, C.C. Sontra (Ger.)	TORTURE	FR.
DOMBROWSKI, Kurt	155754	M		Merchant, Civilian, Elbing (Pol.) 1942	TORTURE	U.K.
DONIMIRSKI	194312	M		Kapo, SS, C.C. Mauthausen (Aust.) 3.44-5.45	MURDER	FR.
ELIAS	149202	F	95	Interpreter, Factory, Berlin (Ger.)	MISC.CRIMES	FR.
FARNIK, Alois	141312	M		Civilian, (Aust.)	WITNESS	U.K.
FAUST, Walter	162018	M		Truppfhr., Organisation Todt, Le Rove (Fr.) 20.8.44	MURDER	FR.
FELLER	144753	F	09	Civilian, Paris (Fr.) 3.43	MISC.CRIMES	FR.
FIREIK	142673	M		Agent, Gestapo, Rosvik (Nor.) 4.44	MISC.CRIMES	FR.
FLECK, Ludwig	144739	M		Doctor, Civilian, PW. at C.C. Buchenwald (Ger.) 44-45	TORTURE	FR.
FRIEDMANN	148199	M		Eldest of Block 27, C.C. Auschwitz-Birkenau (Pol.) from 1940	MURDER	FR.
GARFERSTEIN, Josee	149355	F	23	Civilian, 43-45	MISC.CRIMES	FR.

POLAND

POLAND. (Cont.)

NAME	C.R.FILE NUMBER	SEX	DATE OF BIRTH	RANK OCCUPATION UNIT PLACE AND DATE OF CRIME	REASON WANTED	WANTED BY
GARLICH	29878	M		Mayor,Public Official. (Pol.)	MURDER	U.K.
GEBURA	255988	M		Hairdresser,C.C.,Block 15,Mauthausen (Aust.)	MURDER	FR.
GLENSKI,Bogdan	147814	M	29	Kapo,C.C. Laura (Ger.) 1944	TORTURE	FR.
GIOGOWSKI,Jacob Jack Jacques	251554	M	26. 9.09	Police, (Bel.)	INTERR.	BEL.
GOUP or JOUP	174973	M		Camp eldest,Civilian,Wansleben am See (Ger.) 43-45	TORTURE	FR.
GRABSKA	193916	F		Medicin,C.C.Ravensbrueck (Ger.)	TORTURE	FR.
GRAJA	148141	M		Doctor,C.C.Auschwitz (Pol.) 42-44	TORTURE	FR.
HORN,Hans	167187	M	3.10.13	Pol. or Ger.,trustees,Civilian,Firm "Jutrzenko",Krakow (Pol.) 9.39-44	PILLAGE	UNWCC.
INA	301754	F		SS-Police-Woman,Staff of Auschwitz,C.C.Auschwitz (Pol.) 40-45	MURDER	FR.
JOUP see GOUP	174973					
KACEK	174666	M	21	Lagerschutz,C.C.Wansleben am See (Ger.) 43-45	BRUTALITY	FR.
KAITSEISS,Josef or Sepp	29808	M	10	SS-Oscharfhr.,S.D. and Kriminalasst.,Clermont-Ferrand (Fr.) 11.43,3.44,9.44,11.45	MURDER	FR.
KAIUTZAN	151929	M		Sgt.,Stalag 4a,C.C.Hohnstein (Ger.)	MISC.CRIMES	U.K.
KASOBOWSKI,John	162563	M		Dairy worker,Civilian,Montan near Graudenz (Pol.) 3.43	MISC.CRIMES	U.K.
KATSCHEFSKY	167089	M		Rehaupaul (Fr.) 9.9.44	MURDER	FR.
KISIEL,Josef	187172	M	95	Pol. or Ger.,Cpl.,565 Landesschuetzen-Bn.,C.C.,Stalag VIII B, Lamsdorf (Ger.) 42-44	TORTURE	U.K.
KOPECKY,Jan	255160	M	23. 7.23	See Consolidated List Part II - Appendix "A"		
KOPROWIAK,Michel	256130	M		Guard,C.C.Flossenburg (Ger.)	MURDER	FR.
KOTZIK	178309	M		Pvt.,12 SS-Pz.Div.,25 SS-Pz.Gren.Regt.,15 Coy.,Abbaye-Ardenne (Fr.) 6.6.-2.7.44	TORTURE	CAN.
KRAUSE	302073	M		Dr.,Head of Block 7,C.C. Birkenau (Pol.) 40-45	MURDER	FR.
KRAUSS,Joseph or Jupp	251666	M		Kapo,C.C.Buchenwald (Ger.) 43-44	TORTURE	FR.
KRAVAJK	255549	M		Gendarm,Fieldpolice,Annay s-Bois (Fr.) 21.7.44-21.8.44	INTERR.	FR.
KROLL	125065	M	90	Capt.,Kriegsgefangenen-Arbeitskdo.,C.C.Sosnowitz (Pol.) summer 1943	TORTURE	U.K.
KWANIEWSKI,Marian	192333	M		Member,SS,C.C.Flossenburg (Ger.)	MISC.CRIMES	FR.
LATARNIK,Alois	162870	M	7. 6.04	SA-Sturmfhr.,Loupershouse (Fr.) 1.11.44	MURDER	FR.
LICHKA or LISCHKA,Georges	48446	M		Pvt.,Army,Tulle (Fr.) 4.6.44	MURDER	FR.
LIPINSKI	253132	M		Lt.,Gendarmerie,Valence (Fr.)	INTERR.	FR.
LISCHKA see LICHKA,Georges	48446					
MACIEJEWSKI,Jan	167032	M		Pvt.,Army,Equeurdreville (Fr.)	WITNESS	FR.
MAJER,Gusband	261378	M		Functionary among prisoners,Vaihingen (Ger.)	MURDER	FR.
MALEWICZ,Henri	29765	M	08 or 09	Army,Inf.Regt.,Waziers (Fr.) 1.11.41	MURDER	FR.
MARIANNE	194610	M		Kapo,C.C.Mauthausen (Aust.)	TORTURE	FR.
MARIANNE	257521	M		Kapo,C.C.Dora-Nordhausen (Ger.)	BRUTALITY	FR.
MARICKA	253805	F		Woman-guard,C.C.Auschwitz (Aust.)	MISC.CRIMES	FR.
MARISCHA	194341	F		Overseer,C.C.Ravensbruck (Pol.)	TORTURE	FR.
MAX	255889	M		Chief, Block II,C.C.Mauthausen (Aust.)	INTERR.	FR.
MCZK	196024	M		Pvt.,12 SS-Pz.Artl.Regt.,Tourouvres (Fr.) 13.8.44	MURDER	FR.
MICHERZINSKI,Michel	192353	M	20	Kapo,C.C.Flossenburg (Ger.)	MURDER	FR.
MIETKA	121179	M	20	Kapo,Yaworzno Silesia (Ger.)	TORTURE	FR.
MOLOTOW see REGULSKI	177578					
MOROZ,Kazimierz see MORAG	145978	*				
NOVAK,Jean	177531	M		Camp official,C.C.Neu-Brenn (Ger.)	TORTURE	FR.
PFEIFFER	156831	M	16	SS-Uscharfhr.,Feldgendarmerie,12 SS-Pz.Div."Hitler-Jugend", Abbaye Ardenne near Caen Normandie (Fr.) 6.6.-2.7.44	TORTURE	CAN.
PLASCHKA	36696	M		Pol. or Ger.,Pvt.,Army,Landesschuetzen-Bn.875,2 Coy., (Pol.) 17.2.45	MURDER	U.K.
POSERT,Eduard	255868			Guard,Neckargerach (Ger.)	TORTURE	FR.
REGULSKI,Edouard Charles aliases MOLOTOW	177578	M	22. 8.11	C.C.Neubrenn near Saarbruecken (Ger.)	MURDER	FR.
RIEDEL,Josef	186702	M	85	Foreman,Civilian,Saw-mills,Beuthen (Ger.)	MURDER	U.K.
SAUER	174559	M	10	Pvt.,Landesschuetzen-Bn.515,Stalag 344,C.C. near Prague (Czech.) 9-45	MURDER	U.K.
SCHAFFER,Johann	253374	M		See Consolidated List Part II - Appendix "A"		
SCHWEMMER,Wilhelm	860	M		Pol. or Ger.,Wachtmstr.d.Polizei,Prison Camp Official,Oswiecim (Pol.) 1940	MURDER	FR.
SIOB	72016	M		Civilian,employee,camp Bitterfeld (Ger.) 10.43-4.45	TORTURE	U.K.
SEOPP	186198	M		Civilian,Bruay en Artois (Fr.) 1. and 2.9.44	WITNESS	FR.
SKOWRONEK	188001	M	circa 95	Mayor,leader,SA,Nience near Sosnowitz,Kazimierz (Pol.) 12.42-6.44	TORTURE	U.K.
SMOLIK	6127	M		SS-Div."Das Reich",Buzet-Tarn,Haute Garonne (Fr.) 6.-7.44	MURDER	FR.
STABIE	130178	M		Guard,559 Landesschuetzen-Bn.,2 Coy.,C.C.Lamsdorf (Ger.) 11.11.43-18.11.43	TORTURE	U.K.
STENIA	305600	F		Woman,Camp eldest,C.C.Belsen (Ger.) from 1940	MISC.CRIMES	BEL.
STOMKA,Hubert	252759	M	2. 2.12	Warder,C.C.Auschwitz (Pol.)	MISC.CRIMES	FR.
SWIDA	186189	M		C.C.-guard,C.C.Dachau (Ger.)	TORTURE	FR.

POLAND - RUMANIA

NAME	C.R. FILE NUMBER	SEX	DATE OF BIRTH	RANK	OCCUPATION UNIT PLACE AND DATE OF CRIME	REASON WANTED	WANTED BY

POLAND. (Cont.)

NAME	C.R. FILE NUMBER	SEX	DATE OF BIRTH	OCCUPATION UNIT PLACE AND DATE OF CRIME	REASON WANTED	WANTED BY
SYMANSKI	167245	M		Interpreter, Schnelle Abtlg. 602, Ferte St. Aubin (Fr.)	MURDER	FR.
SZYDLOWSKI	140915	M		SS-Doctor, C.C. Ravensbrueck, Auschwitz (Ger., Pol.)	TORTURE	U.K.
"TINTIN" see DEGE	141518					
VAKOSKY or VAKOVSKI	167153	M		Chief, SS, Omenau, Limburg (Ger.)	TORTURE	FR.
VAKOVSKI see VAKOSKY	167153					
VICTOR	254714	M		Kapo, C.C. Auschwitz (Pol.)	TORTURE	FR.
VLADEK	174899	M	21	Arbeitskdo., Wansleben am See (Ger.) 43-45	MURDER	FR.
WACHILEWSKI	252832	M		Physician, C.C. Auschwitz (Pol.)	BRUTALITY	FR.
WATTELSKI	300398	M		Wachtmeister, Arbeitserziehungslager, Lahde near Hannover (Ger.) 11.2.-24.3.45	MISC.CRIMES	NETH.
WATZLAWEK, Franz	135569	M		Miner, Civilian, Labour C.C. Jaworzna (Pol.) 25.2.43	MURDER	U.K.
WILLY	180582	M		Kapo, C.C. Bad Gandersheim, Dachau (Ger.) 42-4.45	MURDER	FR.
WILLY	194084	M		Blockmann, C.C. Flossenburg (Ger.)	MURDER	FR.
WLADEK, Stephane	251738	M	25	Leader, C.C. Buchenwald (Ger.)	BRUTALITY	FR.
WOOS, Stephane	194687	M	17	Guard, C.C. Mauthausen (Aust.) 3.-5.44	MURDER	FR.
YUSYSTA, Selina	188177	F		Civilian, Fedelhausen (Pol.) 20.2.44	WITNESS	U.K.
ZARUTI, Wandax	250580	M		Gestapo, Limoges (Fr.)	MISC.CRIMES	FR.
ZENKTELIER	258919	M		Doctor, Hospital Birkenau (Pol.) 40-45	MISC.CRIMES	FR.
ZEUITELER	306891	M		Dr., C.C. Auschwitz (Pol.) 40-45	MURDER	FR.
ZINCTLER	251487	M		Chief-Doctor, C.C. Auschwitz (Pol.)	MURDER	FR.
ZUCKAU	125704	M		Pol. or Ger., Forester, Civilian, Stalag XX B, Kdo. 365, C.C. Rosenberg (Pol.) 1.43-2.44	MISC.CRIMES	U.K.

RUMANIA.

NAME	C.R. FILE NUMBER	SEX	DATE OF BIRTH	OCCUPATION UNIT PLACE AND DATE OF CRIME	REASON WANTED	WANTED BY
ALEXIUS, Adolf	152499	M	17	Uscharfhr., SS, Staff, C.C. Buchenwald (Ger.) 1.11.44	WITNESS	U.S.
ANDRESCH	185996	M		SS-Sturmmann, C.C. Neubrenn near Saarbruecken (Ger.)	TORTURE	FR.
BEKKA	255568	M		S.D., Mauthausen (Aust.)	BRUTALITY	FR.
BRAUN, Martin	174227	M	21. 8.12	SS-Guard, SS, between Wien and Mauthausen (Aust.) 1.-18.4.43	WITNESS	U.S.
BUZDUGAN, Gheorghe	307334	M		Sgt.-Major, Timisul de Jos near Brasov (Rum.) 4.-5.44	BRUTALITY	U.K.
CAIVTER	301552	M		Rum. or Hung., SS-overseer, C.C. Breendonck (Bel.) from 1944	MURDER	BEL.
CAWTER	192320	M		Camp Guard, C.C. Breendonck (Bel.) 4.-5.44	MURDER	BEL.
COPIL	189870	M		Major, Rum. Army, Brasov (Rum.)	MISC.CRIMES	U.K.
COPIL or KOPIL	189794	M		Sgt.-Major, Rum. Army, Timisul de Jos (Rum.) 4.-8.44	TORTURE	U.K.
DRASER, Andreas	147977	M	12	Uscharfhr., Waffen-SS, Auschwitz (Pol.)	MURDER	FR.
FAJECKA	259351	M		Lt.Gen. of the Camp, C.C. Auschwitz (Pol.)	SUSPECT	FR.
FRAUENHOFFER, Josef	142518	M		Army, C.C. near Oberplan (Czech.) 29.4.45	MURDER	U.S.
GOLBERG	147787	M	00	C.C. Blachmar (Ger.)	TORTURE	FR.
GOTTSCHALL, Michel	162044	M	21. 6.16	Member, SS-Totenkopf, Mauthausen (Aust.) 8.43-5.45	TORTURE	U.S.
GRINBERG, Zigi	157560	M		C.C. Auschwitz (Pol.) 7.42-10.43	MURDER	FR.
GURILEA	307335	M		Lt., Timisul de Jos near Brasov (Rum.) 4.-5.44, 22.8.44	BRUTALITY	U.K.
HERTZ	197727	M		SS-Guard, C.C. Buchenwald, Flossenburg (Ger.)	MURDER	U.S.
HUBERT, Joseph	194565	M		Cpl., Army, St. Laurent, Du Manoir (Fr.) 13. and 19.8.44	MURDER	FR.
JOSEF	301759	M		Kapo, C.C. Auschwitz (Pol.) 40-45	MURDER	FR.
KAPRI see VON CAPRI	173274					
KLETSOCK	150673	M		Rum. or Ger., Guard, S.D., C.C. Lahde-Weser (Ger.)	TORTURE	BEL.
KNEIP	185860	M		Rottenfhr., SS, C.C. Mauthausen (Aust.)	TORTURE	U.S.
KONIG, Oskar	145179	M	00	Civilian, C.C. Buchenwald (Ger.)	TORTURE	U.S.
KOPIL see COPIL	189794					
KRACIUM, Karl	132043	M		Civilian, Wachtmeister, last known home-address: Lebenstredt, Reppenerschestr. 2	TORTURE	U.S.
KRACIUM, Stephen	132061	M		Wachtmeister, Police, Camp Hallendorf, home-address: Lebenstredt, Reppenerschestr. 2	TORTURE	U.S.
KRAFT	192455	M		Guard, C.C. Breendonck (Bel.) 4.-5.44	TORTURE	BEL.
KROPIVSEC	192450	M		Rum. or Hung., Guard, C.C. Breendonck (Bel.) 4.-5.44	MURDER	BEL.
LUWITZKI, Kasimir	193149	M		Rottenfhr., SS-Totenkopfverb., C.C. Buchenwald, Flossenburg, Oranienburg (Ger.) 42-45	TORTURE	U.S.
MARIANZUCK or MARRANZUCK	192266	M		Rum. of Hung., Guard, C.C. Breendonck (Bel.) 4.-5.44	MURDER	BEL.
MARRANZUCK see MARIANZUCK	192266					
MARTIN, Fredrich	157016	M	11. 7.13	Civilian, Linz (Aust.) 42-45	TORTURE	U.S.

RUMANIA - RUSSIA

NAME	C.R.FILE NUMBER	SEX	DATE OF BIRTH	RANK OCCUPATION UNIT PLACE AND DATE OF CRIME	REASON WANTED	WANTED BY
				RUMANIA. (Cont.)		
MATIESCU	189795	M		Major,Rum.Army,Timisul de Jos,Brasov (Rum.) 4.-8.44	MISC.CRIMES	U.K.
MATTHIAS,Hubert	157012	M	21	Rum.or Ger.,Rottfhr.,Leibstandarte "Adolf Hitler",probably I SS-Div.,Field-Ers.Bn.I,Rosbach (Ger.) 4.3.45	MURDER	U.S.
METELSKY	142564	M	13	S.D.-Guard,C.C.Lahde-Weser (Ger.) 43-45	TORTURE	BEL.
MILANOVITSCH,Adam	173897	M	22	Rum.or Ger.,Uscharfhr.,SS,between Wien and Mauthausen (Aust.) 1.-4.45	MURDER	U.S.
MULLER	194544	M	circa 10	Guard,SS-Mann,S.D.,Heerenween (Neth.) 15.4.45	MURDER	NETH.
NOLDE,Rudy	192549	M		SS-Rgt.,56393,Brainele Comte (Bel.) 18.2.44	MURDER	BEL.
PACSIUS	192494	M		Rum.or Hung.,Guard,C.C.Breendonck (Bel.) 4.-5.44	MISC.CRIMES	BEL.
RAPUSNIK	144369	M	05	Guard,S.D.,C.C.Lahde Weser (Ger.) 43-45	TORTURE	BEL.
RENTZ,Johann	260524	M	31. 5.08	SS-Mann,Waffen SS,Juard-Coy.,C.C.Lublin,Auschwitz (Pol.)7.43-1.45	BRUTALITY	POL.
RIESS,Leonhart	260537	M	11.12.20	SS-Mann,Waffen SS,Guard-Coy.,C.C.Auschwitz (Pol.) 8.43-1.45	BRUTALITY	POL.
RILL,Samuel	192568	M		Pvt.,Army,Chatou (Fr.) 25.8.44	WITNESS	FR.
SCHILLING	181194	M	05	Nurse,C.C.Ebensee,Mauthausen (Aust.) 44	MURDER	FR.
SCHILLING,Gica	142294	M	06	Rum.or Ger.,SS-Rottfhr.,SS-Medical,C.C.Ebensee (Aust.) 44-45	MURDER	U.S.
SCHLEBES,Erich	142057	M		SS-Uschfhr.,SS-Totenkopf,Camp-Guard,C.C.Ebensee,Mauthausen (Aust.)	TORTURE	U.S.
SCHLIMMER	62106	M	10	Sturmmann,S.D.,Vichy (Fr.) 8.44	MURDER	U.S.
SCHNEIDER or SNEIDER	301605	M		Rum.or Hung.,SS-overseer,C.C.Breendonck (Bel.) from 44	MURDER	BEL.
SEIFE,Matis	148007	M	20	Warder,SS,C.C.Wattenstedt (Ger.)	TORTURE	U.S.
SNEIDER see SCHNEIDER	301605					
SOMMER	140809	M		Sturmmann,SS,Frankfurt-Main (Ger.) 25.3.45	MURDER	U.S.
STERN,Samuel	306893	M		Male nurse,Block 28,C.C.Auschwitz (Pol.) 40-45	MURDER	FR.
STUMPILICH,Jakob	259439	M		SS-Mann,Waffen SS,SS-Totenkopf-Bn.,Buchenwald (Ger.)	MISC.CRIMES	U.S.
VON CAPRI or KAPRI	173274	M	20	Rum.or Ger.,Member,Gestapo,Noailles (Fr.) 9.8.44	MURDER	U.K.
VON KRAUSS	252097	M		SS-Mann,SS,C.C.Buchenwald (Ger.)	INTERR.	U.S.
VORMITTAG,Paul	153032	M	10	Rottfhr.,Waffen SS,Leibstandarte "Adolf Hitler",1 SS-Div.Feld-Ers. Bn.I,Rosbach (Ger.) 4.3.45	WITNESS	U.S.
WALZER	192430	M		Rum.or Hung.Guard,C.C.Breendonck (Bel.) 4.-5.44	TORTURE	BEL.
WEBER,Josef	260440	M	20.11.06	SS-Mann,SS-Guard,C.C.Auschwitz (Pol.) 44-45	BRUTALITY	POL.
WILLE,Joseph	260445	M	9. 2.02	SS-Sturmmann,Waffen SS,Guard-Coy.,C.C.Monowitz,Jarwischowitz, Auschwitz (Pol.) 8.43-1.45	BRUTALITY	POL.
WOLFF	261898	M	circa 00	Rum.or Ger.,SS-Mann,Waffen SS,Pijnacker near Belft (Neth.) 7.44	PILLAGE	NETH.
WOLFF,Johann	186739	M	03	Guard,Waffen SS,Labor Camp,Arb.Kdo.,Innsbruck (Aust.) 2.44-5.45	TORTURE	U.S.
ZAPPI,Adolf	260470	M	20. 8.11	SS-Rottfhr.,Waffen SS,Guard-Coy.,Supply Service,C.C.Auschwitz (Pol.) 5.42-1.45	BRUTALITY	POL.
ZWICK,Michael	251468	M		Uschfhr.,Waffen SS,SS-Totenkopf-Bn.,Buchenwald (Ger.)	BRUTALITY	U.S.
				RUSSIA.		
ANNUSKY	157155	M		Sgt.,Army,Morlaix (Fr.) 44	MURDER	FR.
APRICHKINE	189121	M		Camp Guard,C.C.Dachau (Ger.)	MURDER	BEL.
BACHUTOW	261367	M		Capt.,Inf.II.4.24 A,Rieux (Fr.) 2.9.44	MURDER	FR.
BAIDRIAN,Jakob	185401	M		Interpreter in the Occupied Territories,Saloniki (Grc.)	MISC.CRIMES	GRC.
BASSANOW,Michel	261350	M		Pvt.,Inf.11 424 A,Rieux (Fr.) 2.9.44	MURDER	FR.
BIDJURI	29828	M		Pvt.,Legion Georgian,Caetres (Fr.) 6.44	TORTURE	FR.
BRAND,Stephan	195667	M	7.11.27	SS-Mann,Waffen SS,Pecany (Czech.) 1.2.45	MURDER	CZECH.
CHAKANOF,Kusek	186676	M		Lt.,Russ.Army,Plozevet (Fr.)	MURDER	FR.
CHIDOROW,Kurban	120049	M	14	Pvt.,Turcoman Legion,C.C.Poornet (Sov.Un.)	MURDER	FR.
CHOURA	149184	M		C.C.Ravensbruck (Ger.)	TORTURE	FR.
CISSEL,Josef	158	M		N.C.O.,Camp,Stalag VIII B, 8.42	MISC.CRIMES	U.K.
DISCHEKOV	166955	M		Inf.Div.,Unit 23209,Plozevet (Fr.) 4.8.44	MURDER	FR.
DOUBROVSKY,Irene	147974	F	15	Civilian,Grueneberg (Ger.) 44	MISC.CRIMES	FR.
FINK	161748	M		Lt.,Army,Morlaix,St.Pol de Leon (Fr.) 44	MURDER	FR.
GALANTIA,Charlico	185947	M		Lt.,Army,4 Coy.,Unit 20988,Montmartin s-Mer (Fr.) 8.6.44	MURDER	FR.
GUBSCHOKOV or KUSCHOKOV	39645	M		Pvt.,Feldpost Nr.23209,Pouldreuzic (Fr.) 4.8.44	MURDER	FR.
GUSCHOKOW	188834	M		Army,Unit 23209,Pouldreuzic (Fr.) 4.8.44	MURDER	FR.
HARASIMOW..	255584	M		Police-Cmdt.,of Ukr.Police under the German,Wilchowic,Delatyn, Nadworna (Pol.) 41-42	MURDER	POL.
HEGEL	305058	M		Russ.or Ger.,SS-Rottfhr.,84 Landst.Niederlande-Rgt.,Rhenen Vreewijk (Neth.) 2.45	MURDER	NETH.
IVANOFF	261468	M		Major,Unit of Inf.II 4.24 A, Rieux (Fr.) 2.9.44	MURDER	FR.
IWANOWA	250259	M		Pol.Prisoner,C.C.Ravensbruck (Ger.)	INTERR.	FR.
JAWORSKI,Wlodzimierz	189071	M		Member,Gestapo,Stanislawow (Pol.) 8.41-1.10.42	MURDER	POL.
KARCKISA,Konstantin	186757	M	17. 2.20	Cpl.,Army,Unit 20988, 4 Coy.,Montmartin s-Mer (Fr.) 8.6.44	MURDER	FR.
KIRCHEIM	137603	M		Iron-Cross-Holder,Second Class,Ger.Army,Belgrade (Yugo.) 4.44	MISC.CRIMES	U.K.
KOMNATNY	255543	M		See Consolidated List Part II - Appendix "A"		
KOUTSCHEFF	167070	M		Russ.or Ger.,Medicin,Army,Blobaznalec Pont L'Abbe (Fr.) 6.-8.44	WITNESS	FR.
KROLL,Christian	178757	M		Farmer,Civilian,Fedelhausen (Pol.) 20.2.44	MURDER	U.K.
KUSCH-CHAKANOV	167049	M		Lt.,Army,Inf.Unit 23209,Plozevet (Fr.) 4.8.44	MURDER	FR.
KUSCHOKOV see GUBSCHOKOV	39645					
LEPKOWSKI,Wladimir,Leonid see GAJEWSKY	187111					
LEPROWSKI	253767	M		Interpreter,Gestapo,Paris (Fr.) 41-44	TORTURE	FR.
LNJYROFF	252452	M		Russ.or Ger.,Lt.,190 Legion Armenienne,Chanac (Fr.) 16.8.44	PILLAGE	FR.
MALEVANY	255048	M		Confidential Agent,Gestapo,Pribram (Czech.) 39-45	MISC.CRIMES	CZECH.
MUSTAFO	188963	M		Sgt.,Army,Penhors en Pouldreuzic (Fr.)	TORTURE	FR.
NATCHERSKIN,Leonil	196436	M		Formation Stat.Macon,St.Laurent (Fr.) 31.5.44	INTERR.	FR.
NICOLAIEFF,Alex see NICOLAYE	250401					
NICOLAYE or NICOLAIEFF,Alex	250401	M		Russ.or Ger.,Capt.,Colonne Russo-Allemande,Chaumont Caserne Fuch L'Ain (Fr.) 10.-21.7.44	MISC.CRIMES	FR.
OMELANOVIC-PAVLENKO,Nikolaj	251205	M	22	SS-Usturmfhr.,SS,Maichovice (Czech.) 45	MURDER	CZECH.
PETRECK	195391	M		Blockleader,C.C.Mauthausen (Aust.) 11.5.42-10.5.45	MURDER	BEL.
PICCHAJA,Valerian	261980	M	5. 6.92	Member,Gestapo,Bratislava,Banska,Trencin (Czech.) 40-45	MURDER	CZECH.
PITHURNIJ,Eugen	195560	M	31. 7.20	SS-Rottfhr.,Waffen SS,Pecany (Czech.) 1.2.45	MURDER	CZECH.
RAVILL	300059	M		Lt.,Unit of Russians and Germans,stationed at Bourseul and at Matignon,Cotes-du-Nord,Bourseul (Fr.) 31.10. and 23.11.43	MISC.CRIMES	FR.
RYBATSELMT,Warilli	12493	M	21	23.7.44	RAPE	FR.
SADUIA or SABDULA	261394	M		Lt.,Commander,garrison of Caucasian soldiers,Ronces near Valle in the Community of Arta,Udine (It.) 4.4.45	WITNESS	NETH.

RUSSIA - SPAIN - SWITZERLAND - STATELESS - TURKEY - YUGOSLAVIA

NAME	C.R.FILE NUMBER	SEX	DATE OF BIRTH	RANK	OCCUPATION	UNIT	PLACE AND DATE OF CRIME	REASON WANTED	WANTED BY
					RUSSIA. (Cont.)				
SCHEKELOV	39626	M		Lt.,Army,Pouldreuzic (Fr.) 3.8.44				MURDER	FR.
SCHURA	132730	M		Surveillante,C.C.Ravensbrueck (Ger.)				TORTURE	FR.
SCHARTS	260016	M		Russ.or Ger.,See Consolidated List Part II - Appendix "A"					
SIKE,BEYEF	125732	M	21	II G.R.4959, Caen (Fr.) about 16.8.44				MURDER	U.K.
SOKOLOV	305509	M		Capt.,634 Inf.Rgt., (Russ.), Belz Morothan				INTERR.	FR.
STEPANIAK,Ivan (Josef)	260540	M	13. 3.12	Civilian,Rzeszow (Pol.) 41				MISC.CRIMES	POL.
SULIKA	255721	M		Agent,Gestapo,Pribram (Czech.) 39-45				MISC.CRIMES	CZECH.
THALEMANN,Yvan	165975	M	3. 7.20	Chenebier-Etobon (Fr.) 27.9.44				MURDER	FR.
TOBOLEZYK	136318	M		Guard,C.C.La Ciotat (Fr.)				MURDER	FR.
VDALOW,Ivan	254702	M		See Consolidated List Part II - Appendix "A"					
VESELOVSKY	255797	M		Agent,Gestapo,Pribram (Czech.) 39-45				MISC.CRIMES	CZECH.
WONSCHINA	195681	M	24	Agent,Guard,S.D., Prison,Maisons Lafitte (Fr.) 15.12.41-10.6.44				TORTURE	FR.
ZCHLMITZA alias CHERMIZA	196028	M		Paris (Fr.)				TORTURE	FR.
ZINKOVSKI,Sergej Alexejewitsch	195647	M		Agent,Gestapo,Sezimovo-Usti (Czech.)				PILLAGE	CZECH.
					SPAIN.				
BRAVO	194706	M		Guard,C.C.Mauthausen (Aust.)				TORTURE	FR.
CERUANTES alias FERNANDEZ	167915	M		S.D., St.Lo (Fr.) 6.-7.6.44				MURDER	FR.
DEL OLMO	150904	M	00	Chief of a camp,C.C.Hinzert (Ger.) 43				TORTURE	FR.
FERNANDEZ see CERUANTES	167915								
GARCIA	257562	M		Chief of Block,C.C.Dora,Nordhausen (Ger.) 2.44				BRUTALITY	FR.
GOMEZ	185129	M		Informer,C.C.Bad Gandersheim (Ger.)				MURDER	FR.
GONZALES or GONZALO	143270	M	23	Stalag 2 B,Camp Hammerstein (Ger.)				MISC.CRIMES	FR.
GONZALO see GONZALES	143270								
HERNANDEZ	254547	M	00	Sonderkdo.-Fuehrer,Gestapo,Angers,Savannes (Fr.) 31.8.44				MISC.CRIMES	FR.
LOPEZ	194647	M		Capo,C.C.Mauthausen (Aust.) 44-45				MISC.CRIMES	FR.
MIRANDA	255885	M		Hairdresser,Block 13,C.C.Mauthausen (Aust.)				INTERR.	FR.
NEGRO	194513	M		Member,Police,C.C.Mauthausen (Aust.) 44-45				TORTURE	FR.
					SWITZERLAND.				
FEICHT,Armand	144721	M	2.12.11	Interpreter,Gestapo,Charleville (Fr.)				MISC.CRIMES	FR.
FRISCHKNECHT	148267	M		SS-Agent (Fin.)				TORTURE	FR.
MAURY,Carmen	154337	F	16	Capo,C.C.Ravens brueck (Ger.)				MURDER	FR.
NESSER,Max	12569	M		Interpreter,Gestapo,C.C.Valdalon (Fr.) 28.8.44				MURDER	FR.
ROHNER,Baptiste	188812	M		Civilian,Vitry (Fr.) 24.8.44				PILLAGE	FR.
SPOERRY,Anne Marie	194065	F		C.C.Ravensbrueck (Ger.)				TORTURE	FR.
VALDINANZ	121268	M		Agent,Gestapo,Banvillars (Fr.) 10.10.44				MURDER	FR.
WURJLER,Eduard Oskar	167039	M	6. 4.02	Swiss or Ger.,Rehaupaul (Fr.) 9.9.44				MURDER	FR.
					STATELESS.				
DENNER,Karl	187220	M	20	Rottfhr.,S.D.,Vorden (Neth.) 2.10.44				MURDER	U.K.
FREIWALD,Franz	155408	M	10	Farmer,Civilian, Pol.Prisoner,C.C.Ilfeld near Gardelegen (Ger.)4.45				MURDER	U.S.
SCHARINJER,Arthur	250480	M	16. 8.01	Civilian,Member,Gestapo,Bratislava (Czech.)				MURDER	CZECH.
					TURKEY.				
KASUM-CHAN-VELI	187334	M	15. 7.04	Civilian,Marianske Lazne (Czech.) 39-45				MISC.CRIMES	CZECH.
					YUGOSLAVIA.				
BOBEER	132475	M		Col.,Zagreb (Yugo.) 7.-8.5.45				MURDER	U.K.
BURK,Franz	149750	M	5.12.21	19 SS Polizei-Rgt.,2 Bn.				MISC.CRIMES	FR.
CESNOVAR,Joseph	120031	M		Bethune (Fr.)				MURDER	FR.
DOLD,Paul	148941	M	15	Member,SS-Totenkopf-Div.,Natzweiler (Fr.) 7.43-4.44				MURDER	FR.
EIGENMANN,Rudolf	260928	M	6. 1.13	SS-Sturmmann,SS-Guard,C.C.Auschwitz (Pol.) 42-45				BRUTALITY	POL.
ENGELBERT,Max	167130	M		Pvt.,Army,Etreux (Fr.) 2.9.44				WITNESS	FR.
ENGLAENDER,Josef	260926	M	17. 3.19	SS-Sturmmann,SS-Guard,C.C.Auschwitz (Pol.) 42-45				BRUTALITY	POL.
FEKETISCH,Johann or PEKETISCH	144719	M	12	Sturmmann,SS-Totenkopf-Div.,C.C.Natzweiler (Fr.) 13.7.43-22.4.44				MURDER	FR.
FELLINJER,Franz	171674	M	22. 5.09	SS-Rottfhr.,C.C.Natzweiler (Fr.) 42-44				MURDER	FR.
FREISSESS,Ludwig	148922	M	21.10.13	Chief-Guard,Civilian,Friedrichshafen (Ger.) 44-45				TORTURE	FR.
GESNOWACK,Joseph	189597	M		Feldgendarm,Feldgendarmerie,Bethune (Fr.) 25.8.44				MURDER	FR.
GROH,Michael	260940	M	15. 3.08	SS-Mann,SS-Guard,C.C.Auschwitz (Pol.) 43-45				BRUTALITY	POL.
*HOPALONG,Cassidy see MERCH	192915								
HOPPY see MERCH	192915								
KREMER,Anton	167964	M	31. 8.08	Schuetze,SS,C.C.Natzweiler (Fr.) 42-44				MURDER	FR.
KREUTZER,Georg	260935	M	28.11.09	SS-Sturmmann,SS-Guard,Auschwitz (Pol.) 42-45				BRUTALITY	POL.
MERCH or HOPALONJ,Cassidy or HOPPY	192915	M	85	Cmdt.,Capt.,Yugo.Army,Sikloss (Hung.) 43				TORTURE	U.K.
PANZERGRUBER	258134	M		Prisoner,Asst.of Doctor,C.C.Dachau (Ger.)				MURDER	BEL.
PEKETISCH see FEKETISCH	144719								
PILLER,Josef	260480	M	5. 8.09	SS-Mann,Waffen SS,C.C.Auschwitz (Pol.) 44-45				BRUTALITY	POL.
PIOTT,Florian	260488	M	2. 4.09	SS-Mann,Waffen SS,Guard,Totenkopf Sturmbann,C.C.Auschwitz (Pol.) 43-45				BRUTALITY	POL.
ROMETSCH,Adam	260437	M	29. 8.12	SS-Uschfhr.,Waffen SS,Guard-Coy.,C.C.Auschwitz (Pol.)11.42-12.44				BRUTALITY	POL.
RUMPF,Josef	253248	M		SS-Mann,C.C.Kdo.Klosterwerk,Buchenwald (Ger.)				INTERR.	FR.
RUNG	253249	M		SS-Mann,C.C.Kdo.Klosterwerk,Buchenwald (Ger.)				INTERR.	FR.
SCHNEIDER,Dominique	173066	M	5. 4.10	SS-Sturmmann,C.C.Natzweiler (Fr.) 42-44				MURDER	FR.
SIDOSKI	120638	M		Guard,Army,C.C.Schischchitz (Pol.)				BRUTALITY	U.K.
SIMON,Johann	260916	M	26.12.08	SS-Mann,Guard,SS,C.C.Auschwitz (Pol.) 43-45				BRUTALITY	POL.
SMERDEL	253477			SS,C.C.Buchenwald (Ger.)					FR.
SMOLEN,Hans	261400	M		SS-Guard,SS-Totenkopf,C.C.Auschwitz (Pol.) 42-44				BRUTALITY	POL.
TRAGEISER,Michael	260448	M	14. 3.09	SS-Sturmmann,Waffen SS,C.C.Auschwitz (Pol.) 11.43-5.45				BRUTALITY	POL.
WEIMANN,Anton	260491	M	28.10.09	SS-Mann,Waffen SS,Guard-Coy.,C.C.Auschwitz (Pol.) 5.43-1.45				BRUTALITY	POL.
WOLF,Georg	260444	M	16.10.14	SS-Guard,Waffen SS,C.C.Auschwitz (Pol.) 10.42-1.45				BRUTALITY	POL.
ZIMPROCH,Josef	260923	M	20. 3.13	SS-Sturmmann,SS-Guard,C.C.Auschwitz (Pol.) 42-43				BRUTALITY	POL.

NAME	C.R. FILE NUMBER	SEX	NATIO- NALITY	DATE OF BIRTH	ALL AVAILABLE INFORMATION AS TO THE RANK, OCCUPATION (CIVIL, PARTY OR MILITARY), PARTICULARS OF CRIME AND PHYSICAL DESCRIPTION - IF KNOWN.	WANTED BY
BANDI, Sagi	261926	M	Hung.		Is responsible for the shooting of six peaceful Serbian citizens on April 18, 1941.	YUGO.
BIANCHI, Arturo	259175	M	Ital.	05	Maresciallodei CC.RR. The above accused was guilty of the massacre, torture, starvation and deportation of the civilian population at Berane, Andrijevica and Bijelo Polje. Further accused of pillaging, burning of houses and other buildings, destruction of property deliberate bombardment of undefended places. 8.41-9.43.	YUGO.
BIAVATI, Guiseppe	256985	M	Ital.		The accused participated in the arrest, deportation and murder of the people in the district of Kastav.	YUGO.
CAPUTI, Pietro	250086	M	Ital.		Judge at a special court for defence of the State. Murder and massacre; systematic terrorism. (Misc.Crimes)	YUGO.
CIANI, Ferdinando	250087	M	Ital.		General-Counsel at a special court for defence of State Rom. Murder and massacres, systematic terrorism. (Misc.Crimes)	YUGO.
DANISCH, Eduard	255090	M	Pol.		Suspected of plundering and blowing up houses in Heusden. Nov.44. (Pillage)	NETH.
DELICH, Ugo	259131	M	Ital.		Commissaria Prefetizio. As local head of one the Italian Occupying Authorities in Municipality at Kistanje the above accused initiated ordered and/or took part in a series of crimes against the Yugoslav.population. Kistanje, Biovicino Selo, Ivosevcl.	YUGO.
GRASEGGER, Vinzenz (see VINZENZ)	188291					
KOMNATNY	255543	M	Russ.		Wanted for alleged mistreatment,torture and deportation of prisoners, subject was a confidential agent of Gestapo in Pribram,Czech. and in this capacity is alleged to be responsible for the above mentioned crimes and even the death of many Czech. political prisoners. His mail is addressed to Luise Sechmann, Munich,Aeussere Prinz- regentenstrasse 9-11, so that it is probably that he is living at the address too.	CZECH.
KOPECKY, Jan	255160	M	Pol.	23. 7.23	Subject was arrested at Nyrested Czech. as a war criminal. While being escorted he succeeded in escape. He is believed to live with Babatta Wening at Roth, nr. Nuernberg (Ger.).	CZECH.
KOPS	259761	M	Aust.		On the 3rd and 4th of April 1944, at Treignac and Lonzac, ordered the shooting of 5 persons.	FR.
KREGERSMAN	261916		Bel.		Suspected of pillage of leather at factory in Waalwijk between companion of Walter Hohn and Denneborg.	NETH.
LEUBE, Hans	259481	M	Aust.		Doctor, Major, wanted for participation in the alleged murder of three American airmen at Illesheim, 1 Dec.1943.	U.S.
MAYER (see MEYER)	259764					
MEYER (or MAYER)	259764	M	Aust.		May give informations on the shooting of 5 F.F.I. prisoners on July 24, 1944., at Varaignes. Sgt. Airforce stationed at Rochefort nr. Angouleme,Varaignes, July 24, 1944.	FR.
MICAN, Francesco	196512	M	Ital.		Francesco Mican participated in the systematic terrorism of the slav inhabitants of Istria, especially at the time of the German operations there, and participated in murders, pillage and torture.	YUGO.
QUACARI,Guiseppe	259107	M	Ital.		N.C.O., Conduty with Frederico Cerestani, chief of Int. (The above accused was guilty of the massacre, torture, starvation and deportation of the civilian population. Berane and Rijevica and Bijelo Polje. Further accused of pillaging, burning of houses and other buildings, destruction of property, deliberate bombardment of undefended places.	YUGO.
SCHAFFER, Johann	253374	M	Pol.		Wanted for the illtreatment of prisoners and slaughter of Belgian civilians in Concentration Camp Ladhe-Weser.	BEL.
SCHWARTS	260016	M	Russ. or Ger.		Military (Corpulent broad). Illtreatment, deportations of Dutchman to Germany. Mongolian-appearance.	NETH.
TOSARELLI (TOSCARELLI)	258182	M	Ital.		Capt., Bataglione Squadristri Emiliano, Fascist Militia, Croatia. Above accused was responsible for Fascists and Carabinieri at 5 T. Mate arresting, deporting and murdering people in the district of Kastav.	YUGO.
VACHINI, Carlo	259126	M	Ital.	15	Tenente, C.C.R.R., Andrijevica, Montenegro. 8.41-8.42	YUGO.
VINZENZ (or GRASEGGER, Vinzenz)	188291	M	Aust.		Civilian, wanted as a witness to the alleged mistreatment and robbing of American airmen at St.Lorenzen.	U.S.

APPENDIX - 'A'.

SPECIAL SECTION - GIVING PARTICULARS OF CRIME IN LIEU OF RANK & OCCUPATION ETC.

1. This List contains the names of persons of NON-GERMAN Nationality wanted in connection with War Crimes regarding whom very little is known as to their Ranks and Occupations. It is therefore considered that if these names were listed under the usual headings there would be insufficient information to lead to the identification and apprehension of the Wanted Persons.

2. The column of the List which normally includes details of Rank and Occupation has therefore been changed for this purpose to "ALL AVAILABLE INFORMATION AS TO THE RANK, OCCUPATIONS (CIVIL. PARTY OR MILITARY), PARTICULARS OF CRIME AND PHYSICAL DESCRIPTION - IF KNOWN" and the column includes every available scrap of information concerning the Wanted Person and the circumstances of the Crime. It is hoped that thereby this List may provide Screening Authorities with more useful information.

---

1. ARMY RANKS (Officers) - Major and above.

C.R.FILE NO.	NATIO-NALITY	RANK OR STATUS	UNIT OR OCCUPATION	PLACE AND DATE OF CRIME	PARTICULARS OF CRIME OR REASON FOR WHICH WANTED FOLLOWED BY PHYSICAL DESCRIPTION IF KNOWN	WANTED BY
FR/1/1	Ger.	General	15 Tank Div. F.P.No. 29200	Rahon (M-ET-M) (8.9.44)	Pillage.	FR.
FR/1/2	Ger.	Colonel	748 Gren.Regt. operating in Alsace	Elsenhein, Orbey, Faing (11. and 12.44)	Pillage.	FR.
FR/1/3	Ger.	Lt.Col.	O.C. D'Einville-Bau area Hails from Cologne. Formerly O.C. Cassino citadel, then living in Pope's villa of Castelgondolfo.	(8.-9.44)	Murder. 1.75 m or more in height, fair, rather young, medium build.	FR.
UK/1/4	It.	Colonel, Cmdt.	P.O.W. Camp No. 70 P.M. 3300	Fermo Ancona (It.) (30.12.42, 1.1.43)	Brutality. Believed to be Enrico Papa.	U.K.
UK/1/5	Ger.-Aust.	Chief-surgeon	On medical staff of P.O.W. Camp, hospital XVIII A	Graz, Austria (1.2.44)	Ill-treatment.	U.K.
UK/1/6	Ger.	Major	Dr. in the prison "Wehrmachts Untersuchungsgefaengnis"	Berlin, Germany (8.43)	Ill-treatment. Aged about 65, height about 5'6", slight but corpulent build, hair white and thin. Wore spectacles. Face very wrinkled and clean shaved. Features aquiline.	U.K.

2. ARMY RANKS (Officers) - Captain and below.

C.R.FILE NO.	NATIO-NALITY	RANK OR STATUS	UNIT OR OCCUPATION	PLACE AND DATE OF CRIME	PARTICULARS OF CRIME OR REASON FOR WHICH WANTED FOLLOWED BY PHYSICAL DESCRIPTION IF KNOWN	WANTED BY
BEL/2/7	Ger.	Lt.	377 Jaeger-Regt. (Civil occupation: Teacher at Cologne Athenaeum)	Vinkt, Meigem and vicinity (East Flanders) Belgium (25.-31.5.40)	Pillage and Incendiarism. Terrorised the population.	BEL.
FR/2/8	Ger.	Capt.	O.C. 5 Coy., 522 Guard-Bn.	Near Heimerdingen, Germany (3.4.45)	Interrogation.	FR.
FR/2/9	Ger.	Capt.	O.C. 293 Inf.Coy., prison	Dillingen, Germany	Brutality.	FR.
FR/2/10	Ger.	Lt.,Oberarzt	Stalag VI F	Bocholt, Germany (16.5.41)	Brutality.	FR.
FR/2/11	Ger.	Lt.	2 Coy., 12 Working-Bn. Stalag XII D	Hamm, Germany (3.43)	Brutality.	FR.
FR/2/12	Ger.	Capt., Cmdt.	3 Coy., 586 Bn.,Stalag VIII C	Sagan, vicinity of Hamburg, Germany (2.45)	Torture.	FR.
FR/2/13	Ger.	Capt., Cmdt.	Stalag VIII C	Sagan, vicinity of Hamburg, Germany (2.45)	Torture.	FR.
FR/2/14	Ger.	Capt., Cmdt.	Camps for prisoners	Perigueux, (6.44)	Murder and other crimes.	FR.
NETH/2/15	Ger.	Lt.	Feldgendarmerie, O.C. the section of Feldgendarmerie to which the other accused belonged.	Heel, Kessel and Venlo, Prov. Limburg, (11.44)	Murder. Aged about 40.	NETH.
NETH/2/16	Ger.	Lt.	2 or 3 Btty., Artl. Abt. (Motor) 444 or 485, O.C. V-2 Weapon	Wassenaar (Duindigt) near the Hague, Netherlands (17.11.44)	Murder. 30-35 years of age.	NETH.
UK/2/17	Ital.	Lt.	Camp-Cmdt.	Derna, North Africa (1.7.42)	Brutality.	U.K.
UK/2/18	Ital.	Capt.	Camp-Cmdt., O.C.	Larissa, Greece (7.-10.42)	Looting. Aged about 45, weight: thin, height about 5'10".	U.K.
UK/2/19	Ital.	Capt.	Camp-Cmdt., O.C.	Larissa, Greece (10.42 onwards)	Miscellaneous crimes. Dark brown hair, dark complexion, additional characteristics: Young, short, dark and slim.	U.K.
UK/2/20	Ital.	Capt., Cmdt.	Prison	Averof, Athens, Greece (up to 1942)	Murder.	U.K.
UK/2/21	Ger.	Surgeon	Stalag XX A	Oberwalden near Konitz, Germany (12.3.44)	Ill-treatment of P.O.W.	U.K.
UK/2/22	Ger.	Lt.	Army	Oels near Breslau, Germany (12.43)	Ill-treatment. Aged about 40. Slim build and clean shaven. Close cropped fair hair, blue eyes, fair complexion. Weight: 11 stone, height: 5'9"	U.K.
UK/2/23	Ger.	Capt.	Query Alp.Regt., Query 5 Mountain-Div.	Sarsina and Martino, Italy, (28.9.44)	Murder. Aged about 37, height: 5'7", brown hair, glasses eyes, fresh complexion, scars, gold filled teeth.	U.K.
US/2/24	Ger.	Capt.	Stalag XII A	Limburg, Germany (1945)	Murder and ill-treatment of American and Allied P.O.W.'s. Weight 200 lbs, height 6'.	U.S.
US/2/25	Ger.	Capt.	Army, PW Camp	Flamersheim, Germany (21.3.45)	Miscellaneous crimes. Date of birth: 1895; height 5'11".	U.S.
US/2/26		Lt.	Army, Adjutant of Cheressy Caserne (A German Army barrack)	Konstanz, Germany (29.7.-3.8.44)	Murder. Date of birth: 1906-1909, weight: 65-68 K, height: 1.75 m. Thin face, dark blond hair. Appeared knockkneed, slim figure, and talks with a Wuerttemberger dialect.	U.S.
US/2/27		Capt.	Controlling officer. Stalag 357 (Civil occupation: Newspaper man)	Thorn, Poland (26.7.44)	Murder. Wanted for killing an American PW after an unsuccessful escape attempt.	U.S.

3. ARMY RANKS - All other ranks.

C.R.FILE NO.	NATIONALITY	RANK OR STATUS	UNIT OR OCCUPATION	PLACE AND DATE OF CRIME	PARTICULARS OF CRIME OR REASON FOR WHICH WANTED FOLLOWED BY PHYSICAL DESCRIPTION IF KNOWN	WANTED BY
BEL/3/28	Ger.	Batman	to Lt. Wuppermann	Vinkt-Meigem, Belgium (25.-31.5.40)	Murder.	BEL.
BEL/3/29	Ger.	Batman	to Capt. Lange, 1 Coy.B, 377 Inf. Regt.	Vinkt-Meigem, Belgium	Murder. Came from neighbourhood of Bremen, Germany. Christian Name: Kurt.	BEL.
FR/3/30	Ger.	Sgt.	1 Coy.B, 377 Jaeger-Regt.	Vinkt-Meigem and vicinity, Belgium (25.-31.5.40)	Murder, pillage, incendiarism. He was called "Spiess"	FR.,BEL.
FR/3/31	Ger.	N.C.O.	2 Pz.Div. called: Div.Des Fantômes	St. Quirin, (End of Sept. or beg. of Oct. 44)	Murder of Cecile Mathis; after a car accident. First Name: Helmut.	FR.
FR/3/32	Ger.	Cpl., sentinel	1 Coy., 632 Bn., I-G.Kdo. 805, St.IX A Kdo. 805	Weissenhassel	Murder.	FR.
FR/3/33	Ger.	Sgt., control officer	Kdo. 6-012	Siedenburg, Hannover, Germany (4.42)	Murder.	FR.
FR/3/34	Ger.	Sgt.		Flossenburg, Germany (42-45)	Murder.	FR.
FR/3/35	Ger.	Pvt., guard	Piennes mine	Bassin de Briey (M.ET.-M.) (40-44)	Murder.	FR.
FR/3/36	Ger.	Lt.	Feldgendarmerie	Longwy, (8.-9.42)	Torture.	FR.
FR/3/37	Ger.	Adjutant-chief	2 Pz.Div. called: Div.Des Fantômes	St. Quirin, France (End of Sept. or beg. of Oct. 44)	Witness. First Name: Werner.	FR.
FR/3/38	Ger.	N.C.O., chief-guard	1. Coy., 740 Landesschuetzen-Bn.	Haldensleben, Germany (11.44)	Ordered the murder of two French PW's of Fdo. 102-3. He lives at Homberg and his wife may be living in Bodendorf with wife of an ex-quarry foreman named Peters. Known as "BOBON".	FR.
UK/3/39	Ger.	Pvt.	in charge of, or a unit of those in charge of, Kdo. 29 from Stalag XX B	(3.2.42)	Murder.	U.K.
UK/3/40	Ger.	Pvt., Hundfuehrer	Stalag XVII B	Neupolla, Austria (about 18.4.45)	Brutality. About 5'6", average build, about 48 years old, fair hair, defect in one eye (possible left) or glass eye.	U.K.
UK/3/41	Ger.	Pvt.	Stalag XXI D	(15.7.43)	Murder.	U.K.
UK/3/42	Ger.-Aust.	Coy.Sgt.-Maj.	(Query) Alp.Regt., (Query) 5 Mountain-Div.	Sarsina and Martino, Italy (28.9.44)	Murder. The wanted German Feldwebel is alleged to have told the inhabitants that these were reprisals for the wounding by Italian Partisans of two soldiers of a German patrol which had visited Sarsina on the previous day (Sept. 27th). Date of birth: 1918, height: 5'8". First Name: Franz.	U.K.
UK/3/43	Ger.	Pvt.	Landesschuetzen-Bn.209 Coy. with H.Q., Arbeits-Kdo. 614	Pankendorf near Marienwerder, Germany (11.9.44)	Murder. First Name: Walter, Date of birth: about 1910, weight between 9-10 stone, height: 5'10". He was clean shaven, had deep set eyes and a thin pointed nose. He was round shouldered. He had been wounded in his left arm and could not hold his rifle properly.	U.K.
UK/3/44	Ger.	Cpl.	German Guard on Working Party, Army, Stalag VIII B	C.C. Auschwitz, Poland (6.3.44)	Murder.	U.K.
UK/3/45		Camp-cmdt., Cpl.	Arb.Kdo.R 104	Reichenberg, Czechoslovakia (12.41-8.42)	Miscellaneous crimes.	U.K.
UK/3/46	Ger.	Cpl.	Camp	C.C. Stalag IX C, C.C. Stalag Luft 3 (1942)	Murder or manslaughter of a prisoner of war; ill-treatment of prisoners of war.	U.K.
UK/3/47	Ger.	Pvt.	Detachment leader Joannitergut, Seubersdorff (Marienwerder)	C.C. Stalag XX B (3.2.43)	Murder of a prisoner of war.	U.K.
UK/3/48	Ger.	Sgt., Cmdt.	Army, 355 Coy., Camp B.E.2	Bitterfeld, Germany (10.43-1.44)	Wanted for ill-treatment of British Prisoners of War. Date of birth: 1885, weight: 12 stone, height: 5'8", grey hair, almost bald, blue eyes, complexion sallow. Long Service man with smart military carriage. Deep snarling voice.	U.K.
UK/3/49	Ger.	Cpl., guard	Army, Stalag IV B	Muehlberg-Elbe, Germany (27.3.44)	Murder. Date of birth: about 1905, weight: 11 stone, height: 5'7". The accused had a glide in one of his eyes and that eye was either blind or artificial. He had a rough skin.	U.K.
UK/3/50	Ger.	Pvt.	Army, 379 Landesschuetzen-Bn.	Bruex, Czechoslovakia (44-45)	Assault with intent to do grievous bodily harm on prisoners of war. Date of birth: 1895, weight: 10 stone, height: 5'6", turning grey hair, glasses eyes, pale complexion, moustache, medium build - full faced.	U.K.
UK/3/51	Ger.	Pvt.	Army, Stalag XVIII A	Wolfsberg, Austria (16.7.43)	Wanted for participation in the shooting of Pte. E.W. Dillon, A.I.F. on 16th July 1943. Date of birth: 1915, weight: 150 lbs, height: 5'10", dark brown hair, dark complexion.	U.K.
UK/3/52	Ger.	Sgt.	Army, Stalag XVIII A	Wolfsberg, Austria (16.7.43)	Wanted for the shooting of Pte. E.W. Dillon, A.I.F. Date of birth: 1900, weight: 130 lbs, height: 5'6". Turning grey hair, grey eyes, fresh complexion, bow bandy legs, corpulent build.	U.K.
UK/3/53	Ger.	Pvt., guard	Volksturm Unit at Goerlitz	Linderback (Stalag VIII A), Germany (4.3.45)	Murder. Date of birth: about 1890, height: 5'5". He has one eye only, corpulent build.	U.K.
UK/3/54	Ger.	Pvt.	in charge of Camp Prison Art 1.Regt.	Stalag IV B, (31.12.43 and 1.1.44)	Ill-treatment. Date of birth: about 1895, weight: about 13 stone, height: 5'5", grey hair, fresh complexion, moustache, corpulent build. His hair was close cropped as also his moustache which was squarish. He had very broad and powerful shoulders was thick set and getting a bit portly. He wore a last war Iron Cross and other last war medal ribbons and on one of them were small metal cross swords.	U.K.

APPENDIX - 'B'.

PERSONS OF UNKNOWN NAME - ALL NATIONALITIES.

After due consideration as to how best to list these persons in order to give the greatest possible convenience to all authorities referring to this List it has been decided to divide them into twelve groups.

The order of the groups is as follows:-

	Page.
1. ARMY RANKS (Officers) - Major and above	89
2. ARMY RANKS (Officers) - Captain and below	89
3. ARMY RANKS - All other ranks	90
4. ARMY - MISCELLANEOUS (Ranks not known)	93
5. WAFFEN S.S. and FIELD POLICE REGTS.	101
6. AIR FORCE - All Ranks	103
7. NAVY - All Ranks	104
8. NAZI PARTY MEMBERS - NSDAP etc.	105
9. NAZI PARTY MEMBERS - State Service, Gestapo, S.D. and Police	106
10. CIVILIANS - Occupation Known	121
11. CIVILIANS - Occupation Not Known	121
12. ALL CONCENTRATION CAMP PERSONNEL - Irrespective of Rank or Status	122

3. ARMY RANKS - All other ranks. (cont.)

C.R. FILE NO.	NATIONALITY	RANK OR STATUS	UNIT OR OCCUPATION	PLACE AND DATE OF CRIME	PARTICULARS OF CRIME OR REASON FOR WHICH WANTED FOLLOWED BY PHYSICAL DESCRIPTION IF KNOWN	WANTED BY
UK/3/55	Ger.	Pvt.	718 Landesschuetzen-Div. Arbeits-Kdo. 340, Stalag XI A	Gross Schierstedt near Aschersleben, Germany (12.44 to 4.45)	This man was responsible for an assault on Pvt. Mills (The Buffs). Date of birth: about 1905, weight: 11 stone, height: 5'10.5", dark brown hair, sallow complexion. Two very large protruding teeth in his upper jaw; spoke with a lisp; married.	U.K.
UK/3/56	Ger.	Regular soldier, Sgt.	Army, 814 Landesschuetzen-Div.	near Leipzig, Germany (2.45)	This man was responsible for giving orders to guards to fire upon POW from Stalag VIII C on the march from Sagan to Bad Orb in February 1945. This order was given when the column was in the Leipzig area. As a result, one POW was shot in the hip and severely wounded. Date of birth: about 1900, weight: 15 stone, height: 6'4", brown hair, turning grey, fair complexion.	U.K.
UK/3/57	Ger.	Pvt.	Army, 1-714 Bn., Landesschuetzen-Regt.	Hannover, Germany (6.4.45)	The accused was a guard on the march of POW from Stalag XX A into Germany; the column was commanded by Capt. Mackensen. The guard fired on several POW, because they tried to get some potatoes from a clamp situated in a field. Date of birth: about 1919, weight: 11 stone, height: 5'10", fair hair, blue eyes, fresh complexion.	U.K.
UK/3/58	Ger.	Pvt., guard	German Army, (Stalag XX A) Camp 142	Zeksin, Kreis Konitz, East Prussia (10.41)	First guard on duty after arrival of PW's. Alleged to have murdered L-Bdr. Ladler (wore thick rimmed glasses). Is engaged to a girl in village of Zeksin, East Prussia.	U.K.
UK/3/59	Ger.	Sgt.	Army, 635 Coy.	Milhausen Salt Mine, Germany (about 16.4.43)	Belabouring Pvt. James Murray (4 Camerons) with rifle butt. About 47 years old. Bald except for some dark hair graying on the sides of the head. Outstanding feature - piggy eyes always screwed up. Height about 5'11", weight about 13 stone.	U.K.
UK/3/60	Ger.	Pvt.	Army	Klausberg, Germany (1.41 to 1.45)	Wanted for generally ill-treating prisoners of war and in particular for bayonetting in the hand a British corporal in November 1944. Date of birth: 1908, weight: 10 st. 6lbs., height: 5'8", fair hair, blue eyes, squint in left eye, ruddy complexion, left limp leg. A very high pitched voice and speaks with an Upper Silesia accent.	U.K.
UK/3/61		Pvt.	379 Landesschuetzen-Bn. Posterns No. 384 D.	Brüx, Czechoslovakia (2.45)	Brutality. Height: 5'10", lean face, prominent cheek bones, swaggering walk throwing feet well forward, dark complexion, right finger (No.1) missing.	U.K.
UK/3/62	Ger.	Sgt.	Army, Inf.	Palatinate Erbach Krs. Konig Germany (21.-22.11.44)	Wanted in connection with the murder of two captured British Airmen. Date of birth: about 1920, weight: about 80 kg, height: 1.80 m, dark blond hair, tall and fat, full face, clean shaven; tanned complexion. Holder of the Iron Cross first and second Class and another medal.	U.K.
UK/3/63	Ger.	Cpl.	Kdo. Fuehrer of Camp 739	Sondershausen, Germany (13.8.41)	Bayonetted and wounded PW for talking on route. Date of birth: middleaged, height: 5'9", brown hair, blue eyes.	U.K.
UK/3/64	Ger.	Pvt.	Army, 1-714 Landesschuetzen-Bn.	Retzow, Germany (18.2.45)	Murder. Date of birth: about 1911, weight: 13 stone, height: 5'9", dark brown hair, blind in one eye, sallow complexion. Clean shaven, with sharp features but a heavy brow and eyebrows. Wore a medal which he had won in this war. His voice was deep when shouting and he wore a large ring on one of the fingers of his right hand.	U.K.
UK/3/65	Ger.	Sgt., Cmdt.		Branhau or Brandau or Braunau, Germany (4.40)	Brutality to POW. Date of birth: 1902-1905, height: 5'10", turning grey hair.	U.K.
UK/3/66	Ger.	Pvt.	Army, Landesschuetzen-Bn. Guard at Arb.Kdo. 176	Kolano, Poland (25.12.41)	The wounding by shooting of 4444811 C.Q.M.S. Patrick Gallogly D.L.I. and 7344239 Pvt. James Buchanan Richardson. Date of birth: about 1917, height: 5'10", black hair. The accused was of slim build. He was a keen boxer and claimed to be and had the reputation of being a very fine shot. He was very proud of his athletic ability and wore a National Socialist sports badge.	U.K.
UK/3/67	Ger.	Pvt.	Army, Landesschuetzen-Bn. Guard at Arb.Kdo. 176	Kolano, Poland (25.12.41)	The wounding by shooting of 4444811 C.Q.M.S. Patrick Gallogly D.L.I. and 7344239 Pvt. James Buchanan Richardson at Arb.Kdo. 175. Date of birth: about 1895 height: 5'11", grey moustache walrus type. The accused was broad and well built. He had very bad feet. It is thought he was a local man and lived at Karthaus.	U.K.
UK/3/68	Ger.	Pvt., guard	Straflager E 718 administered by Stalag VIII B	Gurschdorf near Freiwaldau, Czechoslovakia (about 6.43)	Brutality. Name believed to be Kessel. Nicknamed "Black Mamba" and "Schweinlander" on account of guttural voice and residence in the Rhineland. Age about 40, height: 5'10". Very dark hair, very dark complexion, dark brown eyes, flat nose, firm, straight mouth, short, bull neck, heavy build, about 13 or 14 stone, gnarled, stumpy fingers. Walked with a strut. Believed to have come from Landes Schutz 325.	U.K.

3. ARMY RANKS - All other ranks. (Cont.)

C.R.FILE NO.	NATIO-NALITY	RANK OR STATUS	UNIT OR OCCUPATION	PLACE AND DATE OF CRIME	PARTICULARS OF CRIME OR REASON FOR WHICH WANTED FOLLOWED BY PHYSICAL DESCRIPTION IF KNOWN	WANTED BY
UK/3/77	Ger.	Pvt., guard		Cosel, Stalag VIII B, Lamsdorf and known as "Pioneer Park", (6.40-1.41)	Brutality. Nickname "Cherry nose". About 5'4" in height and very slightly built; aged about 48-50, hair thin on stop, had been fair but was almost grey, complexion fresh, round face, red cheeks, grey eyes; came from Upper Silesia.	U.K.
UK/3/78	Ger.-Pol.	Pvt.	565 Landesschuetzen-Coy., probably Ex-SS	Silesia, Sudetenland (1.-3.45)	Appalling conditions on the march from Upper Silesia to West Sudetenland. Nickname "Scar face". Scars across jawbone.	U.K.
UK/3/79	Ger.	Pvt.	Arb.Kdo. B 51 Civ.occ.: ship steward	Klausberg, Germany (3.41)	Wanted for assault. Nickname "South American Joe". Height: 5'7", black hair, brown eyes, dark complexion, scars on right cheek. Spoke English with a strong American accent.	U.K.
UK/3/80	Ger.	Cpl., guard		Cosel, Stalag VIII B, Lamsdorf and known as "Pioneer Park", (6.40-1.41)	Brutality. Nickname "The ghoul". About 5'4" in height and of medium build, fair hair, aged about 45 sallow complexion, small grey eyes, face very ugly and repulsive. High cheekbones giving eyes; the appearance of receding into head, hollow cheeks, no teeth, skin of face was wrinkled and deeply pockmarked and that on his fore head seemed very taut; lived in Breslau.	U.K.
UK/3/81	Ger.	Cpl.	4 Coy., 559 Landesschuetzen-Bn.	Schishchitz near Welwern, Bohemia (13.3.45)	Wanted for brutal treatment of PW's on route from Upper Silesia to Central Germany. Age about 30. Nickname "The Jeep", weight: 13-14 stone, height: 6'1", fair hair, blue eyes. Has broad sloping shoulders, upright carriage and rather ungainly. Has soft speech and noticeable scar on the right side of the neck and throat. Believed to come from Aachen. Is believed to have been captured by the Americans in Bavaria about the end of April 1945.	U.K.
UK/3/82	Ger.	Pvt.	891 Landesschuetzen-Bn. Guard at Camp 132 G.W. attached to Stalag 18 D	Retznei, Austria (5.2.42)	Murder and custody. Known as "Weinberger Willi" this being the name of the Arbeitskdo. at which he had previously been a guard. About 37-38 years. 5'8"-10" in height, weight: 13 stone; stout round face, fresh complexion, fair hair, blue eyes.	U.K.
US/3/83		Pvt., guard	Stalag VII A	Mooseburg, Germany (3.45)	Wanted for alleged shooting of an American PW. Date of birth: 1903, weight: 150 lbs, height: 5'5". Suspect wore artillery markings on his uniform.	U.S.
US/3/84	Ger.	Cpl.	Army, medical orderly PW Camp	Flamersheim, Germany (21.3.45)	Suspect. Date of birth: 1900, height: 5'1".	U.S.
US/3/85		Sgt.	Army, Stalag 3-A	C.C. Buchenwald, Germany (1.-2.45)	Wanted for striking, without provocation, one Charles Di Christy, American prisoner of war, in the face, using his hands and a sharp stick, injuring the prisoner of war's face. Suspect had accused Di Christy of tearing up floor to make a fire. Date of birth: 1905-1907, weight: 180 lbs., turning grey hair, fairly tall. Middle-aged. Greyish at temples.	U.S.
US/3/86	Ger.	Sgt.	1 Coy., Gr. 921, Army	near Marigny, France (28.7.44)	Wanted in connection with murder of an American PW. Presence of American PW became embarrassing when German Unit was forced to retreat. American PW was then shot by unknown German Sergeant.	U.S.
US/3/87	Ger.	Sgt.	Army, in charge of Kdo., attached to Stalag IV A	Zittau, Germany (2.45)	Pvt. Orval Steffensen and three other American pw's died at the Kdo. for which this suspect was directly responsible, due to inadequate feeding and lack of proper medical attention. The deaths occurred in the month of February 1945. This suspect lived in a little town in the vicinity of the Kdo. and had been in the German Army in the last war. Height: 6', very heavy set.	U.S.
US/3/88	Ger.	Sgt.	Stalag XII A	Limburg, Germany	Wanted for participation in the murder and ill-treatment of American and Allied prisoners of war. Weight: 130 lbs., height: 5'4", small build, well marked scar running from ear to lower part of chin on left side of face about ¼" wide and looked as though it had been burned.	U.S.
US/3/89	Aust.	Sgt.	Army, Commander of Kdo. 416-0	Juterborg, Germany (15.2.-10.3.45)	Wanted for the alleged mistreatment and improper medical care and harsh disciplinary punishments at a German PW Camp. Date of birth: about 1911, weight: 180 lbs., height: 5'9", dark complexion, moustache, bow-legged.	U.S.

4. ARMY - MISCELLANEOUS (Rank not known).

C.R.FILE NO.	NATIO-NALITY	RANK OR STATUS	UNIT OR OCCUPATION	PLACE AND DATE OF CRIME	PARTICULARS OF CRIME OR REASON FOR WHICH WANTED FOLLOWED BY PHYSICAL DESCRIPTION IF KNOWN	WANTED BY
BEL/4/90	Ger.	Ordnance	Regt.B. - 377.Jaeger Regt.	Vinkt, Meigem and vicinity, Prov.Flandre Orientale, Belgium (25.-30.5.40)	First name Kurth. Batman of Capt. Lange. Alleged to have participated in the murder of more than 200 persons under the most atrocious circumstances at Vinkt, Meigem and vicinity (East Flanders) between May 25 and 31, 1940. Terrorised population, pillage, incendiarism. Place of birth: Bremen.	BEL.
BEL/4/91	Ger.	Oberfeldkommandant		Liege, Belgium (7.44).	Murder. (Probably VON CLAER)	BEL.
BEL/4/92	Ger.	Officers and men	Army: 192. Inf.Regt.	Vinkt-Meigem, Belgium (25.-31.5.40)	Murder.	BEL.
BEL/4/93	Ger.	O.C.	Artillery-Regt.	Louvain (16.5.40)	Incendiarism. Bombarding the University Library of Louvain from Kessel-Loo.	BEL.
BEL/4/94	Ger.	probably Lt.Gen. Sander,	General of Division in command of German Forces	Bruges, Belgium (4.- 8.9.44)	Murder.	BEL.
BEL/4/95	Ger.	Man	of 7.Coy. Inf.Regt.385; then Inf.Ers.Bn.385; then Nachschub Coy.(Besp.) 229, after 10.12.43 Nachschub Coy. 275.	Sars-La-Bruyere, Hainaut, Belgium (3.-4.9.44)	Brutality.	BEL.
BEL/4/96	Ger.		Afrika Korps. XV. Div. I.Aufkl., 3.Coy., 2.Col.	Saint-Leger, Prov.Luxemburg, Belgium (5.9.44)	On 5.9.44, about 100 Germans belonging to his unit put fire to 114 houses, massacred 3 inhabitants, pillaged and terrorized systematically the population.	BEL.
BEL/4/97	Ger.	Mil.Personnel	17. Inf.Regt.	Binderveld (Limbourg) (12.-13.5.40)	Mil.personnel of the German Red Cross pillaged the castle at Binderveld.	BEL.
BEL/4/98	Ger.	Officers, N.C.O.s and Men	192. Jaeger-Regt.	Vinkt, Meigem (East Flanders) and vicinity (25.-31.5.40)	Murder of more than 200 persons under atrocious conditions.	BEL.
BEL/4/99	Ger.	Officers and Men	4.Coy., 77. Inf.Bn.	Chaudfontaine and Troox (Prov.Liege) (6.9.44)	Brutality towards and murder of disarmed PWs and members of Red Cross. Unnecessary pillage and incendiarism.	BEL.
BEL/4/100	Ger.		Stabs-Coy.-Wolga-Tataren, Bn. 627	Quaregnon-Jemappes-Ghlin, Prov.Hainaut, Belgium (2.-9.9.44)	One member of Waffen-SS killed with his m.g. 6 civilians. Other German soldiers set fire to a mansion, and murdered 4 persons (2 of whom were priests) in another mansion. On next day, 3.9., members of Luftwaffe-Units perpetrated following crimes: 22 civilians were savagely murdered. Some time later joined by members of the Kriegsmarine-Unit, stationed in the locality 14 civilians were murdered. Proceeding towards Ghlin, they killed 10 other civilians. Military papers found on the spot included "Abmeldebuch des Nachrichtenzuges Fallschirm Jaeger Regt.5", a parcel with unopened letters addressed to Feldpostnr. L 49.215 N, Luftgaupostamt Paris, a parachute cask with the name of Schenk, several military books belonging to Luftwaffe Jaeger Regt./35 and to Stabs-Coy. Wolga/Tataren, Bn. 627.	BEL.
CZECH/4/101	Ger.	Chief officer	Schiess-Schule in Zella-Mehlis	C.C. Oswiecim-Birkenau, Poland (39-45)	Murder and massacres, systematic terrorism.	CZECH.
CZECH/4/102	Ger.	Chief officer	Nachrichten Ausb.Abt. Funkschule auf Schloss Gruenberg	Berlin, Germany. C.C.Oswiecim-Birkenau, Poland (39-45)	Murder and massacres, systematic terrorism.	CZECH.
FR/4/103	Ger.	Feldgendarm		Abbeville (Somme) (31.8.44)	Murder. First name "Alfred".	FR.
FR/4/104	Ger.	Feldgendarm		Abbeville (Somme) (31.8.44)	Murder. First name "Hans".	FR.
FR/4/105	Ger.	Feldgendarm		Abbeville (Somme) (31.8.44)	Murder. First name "Jupp".	FR.
FR/4/106	Ger.	W.O.		La Saucelle (Eure et Loire) (3.8.44)	Rape. First name "Robert".	FR.
FR/4/107	Ger.	O.C.		Maurienne (Savoy) (8.9.44)	Murder. O.C. troops operating at Maurienne (Savoy) Aiguebelle, Argentine and St.Michel de Maurienne possibly Bader, General commanding 90. Mot. Inf.Div.	FR.
FR/4/108	Ger.	O.C.	7.Coy., 745.Gren.Regt.	Don-Annoeuillin (Nord). (3.9.44)	Murder.	FR.
FR/4/109	Ger.	O.C.		Near Castres (12.5.44)	Murder. O.C. a unit of troops operating near Castres.	FR.
FR/4/110	Ger.	Officers, N.C.O.s and Men	of Unit F.P.No.48949 (about 100 Men)	Dolus Le Sec. Manthelan, Loches (Indre-et-Loire) (20. and 22.8.44)	Murder.	FR.
FR/4/111	Ger.	Officers, N.C.O.s and Men	of Sicherungsverbindungsstab	Ligueil and Betz Le Chateau (20. and 28.8.44)	Murder.	FR.
FR/4/112	Ger.	O.C.troops		Nice	Murder.	FR.
FR/4/113	Ger.	O.C.	Unit of Chasseurs Feldpost No.22.942 A	Vasles (Deux-Sevres) and La Tricherie (Vienne) (25. and 27.8.44)	Murder.	FR.
FR/4/114	Ger.	Cmdt.	P.O.W.-Camp at Hammerstein	Hammerstein, Germany (41-42)	Brutality.	FR.
FR/4/115	Ger.	Feldkommandant		Dijon (end of July, 44)	Misc.Crimes.	FR.

4. ARMY - MISCELLANEOUS (Rank not known). (Cont.)

C.R.FILE NO.	NATIO-NALITY	RANK OR STATUS	UNIT OR OCCUPATION	PLACE AND DATE OF CRIME	PARTICULARS OF CRIME OR REASON FOR WHICH WANTED FOLLOWED BY PHYSICAL DESCRIPTION IF KNOWN	WANTED BY
FR/4/116	Ger.	Cmdt.	P.O.W. Camp	Bad Orb, Germany (27.8.42)	Murder.	FR.
FR/4/117	Ger.	Gen., Commander	of 150 Div.	Vercors area, (7.-8.44)	Murder.	FR.
FR/4/118	Ger.	O.C. troops		Vercors, La Chapelle, St. Martin, Vassieux, Mure, La Bruitiere (Grotta), Presles, Labalme, Charasson, (7.-8.44)	Murder.	FR.
FR/4/119	Ger.	O.C. occupation troops		Saumur, (8.44)	Murder.	FR.
FR/4/120	Ger.	Chief	Feldgendarmerie	Clermont, (3.-4.44)	Murder.	FR.
FR/4/121	Ger.	O.C. occupation troops		Jura, (8.-17.3.44)	Murder.	FR.
FR/4/122	Ger.	O.C. troops		L'Isère, (17. and 18.6.44)	Murder.	FR.
FR/4/123	Ger.	O.C. occupation troops		Haute Saône, (27.7.44)	Murder.	FR.
FR/4/124	Ger.	O.C. troops		Clermont-Ferrand district (13.7.44)	Murder.	FR.
FR/4/125	Ger.	Commander	of troops	L'Ardeche, St. Feray, Touland, (8.-9.3.44) Sanilhac, (16.4.44)	Murder.	FR.
FR/4/126	Ger.	Chief	Kdo. 3452	Lustringen, vicinity of Osnabrueck, Germany	Torture.	FR.
FR/4/127	Ger.	Chief	Kdo. 6083 of Stalag X C	Rekum near Wildeshausen, Germany (17.8.44)	Shot at W.P. Eustace from near distance and wounded him severely.	FR.
FR/4/128		Men	of detachment No. 79, 7 Artl. Regt. (Reserve)	St. Paul sur Isere (Savoy) (14.6.44)	Murder, torture of civilians, and other crimes.	FR.
FR/4/129		All officers	Unit 15958 B	Montham near Dolhain, Belgium (11.9.44)	Murder and other crimes.	FR.
FR/4/130	Ger.	Cmdt.	3 Coy., Gren.Res.Bn.373, 221 Regt. of Gren.Res.	Le Liege, Orbigny, Nouans, France (1944)	Murder and other crimes.	FR.
FR/4/131	Ger.	Officers, Cpl.'s and men of troop	Unit F.P.No. 33632	Bernay En Champagne, France (3.9.41)	Miscellaneous crimes.	FR.
FR/4/132	Ger.	Officers	Army	Flexecourt, Ville-le-Marclet France (8.44)	Witnesses.	FR.
FR/4/133	Ger.	Coy.-leader	2 Coy., Div. B	Noailles, France (3.4.44)	Murder.	FR.
FR/4/134	Ger.	Officers, Cpl.'s and men of troop	Unit F.P.No. 28309	Lignieres La Doucelle, France (13.-14.6.44)	Miscellaneous crimes.	FR.
FR/4/135	Ger.	Cmdt.	of a fortress	Jauer, Germany	Murder.	FR.
FR/4/136		Cmdt.	2 Pz.Gren.Regt., 2 Pz.Div.	Landelles and Coupigny (Calvados) (6.43-17.8.44)	Murder.	FR.
FR/4/137			Feldgendarmerie 577 of Romorantin (Loir et Cher), attached to Feldgendarmerie of Blois		Murder.	FR.
FR/4/138			Detachment of Feldgendarmerie of Fontainebleau, subordinates to Korp (Gestapo of Melun)	(24.7.44)	Murder and other crimes.	FR.
FR/4/139	Ger.	Sentry	3 Coy., 439 Bn. Landschutz	Dittersbach, Czech. (2.45)	Murder of PW GOGA of Kdo. F.259, Stalag 344.	FR.
FR/4/140	Ger.	Chief sentry	Kdo. 453, Stalag X B	Westerrech, Germany (6.2.44)	Murder of PW SUCHET.	FR.
FR/4/141	Ger.	W.O.	1 Coy., 585 Landschutz Bn.	Tunzenhausen (district Weimar), Germany (1945)	Murder of two prisoners.	FR.
FR/4/142	Ger.	Capt.	O.C., 3 Coy., 439 Landschutz Bn.	Dittersbach, Czech. (2.45)	Responsible for the murder of PW GOGA, Jules of Kdo. F.259, Stalag 344.	FR.
FR/4/143	Ger.	Capt.	O.C., 3 Coy., 586 Inf.Bn.	Spremberg, Sagan, Bad Sulza, Germany (1.45)	Murder and ill-treatment of PW's in an evacuation column. Date of birth: 1905-1910, height: 1,75 m, fair hair.	FR.
FR/4/144	Ger.	Capt.	O.C., 5 Coy., 586 Inf.Bn.	Spremberg, Bad Sulza, Germany (1.45)	Murder and ill-treatment of PW's in an evacuation column. Date of birth: about 1895, height: 1,70 m, brown hair, glasses eyes.	FR.
FR/4/145	Ger.	Commander	of occupation troops, Army	Prov. Loir et Cher, France (1944)	Torture of civilians.	FR.
FR/4/146	Ger.	Commander	of occupation troops, Army	Doubs - Prov., France (1944)	Murder and other crimes.	FR.
FR/4/147	Ger.	Cmdt.	Stalag 325	Stryj, (20.9.42)	In that Camp, situated 60 kms from Hungarian frontier, discipline was extremely harsh. Many prisoners escaped to Hungary. Escapes were followed by shooting of other prisoners. That was the case on: Sept.20,1942, when War Prisoner LEMERLE and VIZIER were shot by the Chief Guard in a wood where they were working.	FR.
FR/4/148		All members of	Bn. AZERBAIDJAN	St. Donat, France (15.6.44)	Miscellaneous crimes.	FR.
FR/4/149			See Consolidated Wanted List Part I (Germans) BECKER, Emil Page 266-271		Suspect. Nickname: "Grand Mimile".	FR.
NETH/4/150	Ger.	O.C.	777 Landesschuetzen-Bn.	near Langsur, Germany (1944)	Ill-treatment of, and employment on unauthorised work of, POW's.	NETH.
NETH/4/151	Ger.	Cmdt.		Camp Beisfjord, Norway (1942)	Ill-treatment and murder of, and unauthorised employment of, POW's (Hague Regulations 1907, Geneva Convention 1929).	NETH.

4. ARMY - MISCELLANEOUS (Rank not known). (Cont.)

C.R.FILE NO.	NATIO-NALITY	RANK OR STATUS	UNIT OR OCCUPATION	PLACE AND DATE OF CRIME	PARTICULARS OF CRIME OR REASON FOR WHICH WANTED FOLLOWED BY PHYSICAL DESCRIPTION IF KNOWN	WANTED BY
NETH/4/152	Ger.	O.C.	Army	Camp Boten, Norway (1943)	Ill-treatment and murder of, and unauthorised employment of, POW's (Hague Regulations 1907, Geneva Convention 1929).	NETH.
NETH/4/153	Ger.	O.C.	Army, 1 Coy., E-Bn., 125 Pz.Regt.	(1944)	Incitement to murder.	NETH.
NOR/4/154	Ger.	Cmdt.		Camp Boten, Norway (from March 1943 onwards)	Murder, terrorism, ill-treatment of POW.	NOR.
POL/4/155	Ger.	Cmdt.	Polish Bn. 309 Coy.	Village of Okolniki, Poland (7.41).	Murder.	POL.
POL/4/156	Ger.	Commander	42 Inf.Div.	(1.9.-30.10.39)	Murder.	POL.
POL/4/157	Ger.	Commander	41 Inf.Div.	(1.9.-30.10.39)	Murder.	POL.
POL/4/158	Ger.	Commander	Landwehr der 8. Armee	(1.9.-30.10.39)	Murder.	POL.
POL/4/159	Ger.	Officer, Cmdt.	Fort VII at fortress of	Poznan, (39-42)	Murder.	POL.
POL/4/160	Ger.	Cmdt., Officer	Fort VII at fortress of	Poznan, (39-42)	Murder, execution of persons without trial and other crimes.	POL.
POL/4/161	Ger.	Cmdt.		Puszczykowo transit camp, Poland (39-40)	Murder, execution of persons without trial and other crimes.	POL.
POL/4/162	Ger.	Cmdt.		Obra transit camp, Poland (39-40)	Murder, execution of persons without trial and other crimes.	POL.
POL/4/163	Ger.	Cmdt.		Lublin transit camp, Poland (39-40)	Murder, execution of persons without trial.	POL.
POL/4/164	Ger.	Cmdt.		Lad transit camp, Poland (39-40)	Murder, execution of persons without trial.	POL.
POL/4/165	Ger.	Cmdt.		Konstantynow-Lodzki transit camp, Poland (39-40)	Murder, execution of persons without trial.	POL.
POL/4/166	Ger.	Cmdt.		Kazimierz Biskupi transit camp, Poland (39-42)	Murder, execution of persons without trial and other crimes.	POL.
POL/4/167	Ger.	Cmdt.		Goruszki transit camp, Poland (39-40)	Murder, execution of persons without trial and other crimes.	POL.
POL/4/168	Ger.	Cmdt.		Gorna Grupa transit camp, Poland (39-40)	Murder, execution of persons without trial and other crimes.	POL.
POL/4/169	Ger.	Cmdt.		Chludowo transit camp, Poland (39-40)	Murder, execution of persons without trial and other crimes.	POL.
POL/4/170	Ger.	Cmdt.		Bruczkow transit camp, Poland (39-40)	Murder, execution of persons without trial and other crimes.	POL.
POL/4/171	Ger.	Cmdt.		Bielsk PW-camp, Poland (10.10.39)	Murder of POW.	POL.
POL/4/172	Ger.	Cmdt.		Kunau Stalag VIII C, Germany (9.-12.39)	Torture of POW.	POL.
POL/4/173	Ger.	Cmdt.		Norderney Island PW-camp (Stalag VIII C), Germany (4.-5.42)	Murder and torture of POW.	POL.
POL/4/174	Ger.	Commander	Army, 183 Landwehr der 8 Armee	(1939)	Mass murder, torture, wanton destruction of property and other crimes.	POL.
POL/4/175	Ger.	Commander	Army, 41 Inf.Div.	Poland (1939)	Mass murder, torture, wanton destruction of property and other crimes.	POL.
POL/4/176	Ger.	Commander	42 Inf.Div.	Poland (1.9.-30.10.39)	Mass murder, torture, wanton destruction of property and other crimes.	POL.
UK/4/177	Ital.	Cmdt.	POW-Camp	Tobruk (29.6.42)	Murder.	U.K.
UK/4/178	Ital.	Cmdt.	POW-Camp	Tripoli (13.11.42)	Murder.	U.K.
UK/4/179	Ger.	German officer	in charge of prison at	Fresnes (10.5.-9.6.44)	Brutality.	U.K.
UK/4/180	Ger.	Ger. transportation officer	i-C of train, which left Apeldorn on or about 26.9.44 and arrived at Fallingbostel, Germany on or about 28.9.44.	(26.-28.9.44)	Brutality.	U.K.
UK/4/181	Ger.	Officer	i-C of dispatch by train of 600 British wounded POW's from Apeldoorn, Netherlands to Fallingbostel, Germany.		Brutality.	U.K.
UK/4/182	Ger.	Officer	i-C German troops at	Base, Tripoli (6.41-1.42)	Brutality.	U.K.
UK/4/183	Ger.	Q-M or other officers	i-C unloading military stores	Tripoli (6.41-1.42).	Brutality.	U.K.
UK/4/184	Ger.	O.C.	the Banska, Bystrica prison.	Kremnicka, Czechoslovakia (20.11.44)	Murder.	U.K.
UK/4/185	Ital.	Officer	concerned with embarkation of prisoners of war on SS "Scillin" or "Scillon".	(13.11.42)	Murder. Name of officer could be obtained from the cmdt., POW-Camp Tripoli, or from Capt. Parigi, or from Capt. Ugo Siviero, C.C.Naval Forces, Tripoli, or from Lt.Comm. Pietro Corrao, second in command.	U.K.
UK/4/186	Ger.	Guard, probably N.C.O.	on duty as patrol leader at	Stalag VIII B	Murder.	U.K.
UK/4/187	Ital.	Cmdt.	POW-Camp	Derna (about early 4.41)	Brutality.	U.K.
UK/4/188	Ital.	Officer	commanding troops at or near	Bomba (Libya) (23.-24.6.42)	Brutality.	U.K.
UK/4/189	Ger.	Cmdt.	POW-Camp	Kalamata, Greece (5.41)	Murder.	U.K.
UK/4/190	Ger.	Sgt., Camp-Cmdt.		Bitterfeld, Germany (1.-4.45)	Brutality.	U.K.
UK/4/191	Ital.	Officer	in command of sentries or guards in charge of POW's in train travelling from Chieti to Fonatenellato small railway station near Rimini	(1.5.43)	Murder.	U.K.

4. ARMY - MISCELLANEOUS (Rank not known). (Cont.)

C.R.FILE NO.	NATIO-NALITY	RANK OR STATUS	UNIT OR OCCUPATION	PLACE AND DATE OF CRIME	PARTICULARS OF CRIME OR REASON FOR WHICH WANTED FOLLOWED BY PHYSICAL DESCRIPTION IF KNOWN	WANTED BY
UK/4/192	Ital.	Officer	in charge of POW employed in building aerodrome at Camp 85	Tuturano, Italy (3.43)	Brutality.	U.K.
UK/4/193	Ital.	Second-in-command or adjutant	Camp 85	Tuturano, Italy (3.43)	Brutality.	U.K.
UK/4/194	Ital.	Cmdt.	Camp 85	Tuturano, Italy (prior to 3.43)	Brutality.	U.K.
UK/4/195	Ital.	Adjutant or second in-command	Camp 62, Bergamo, to which working camp of Falcke's factory, Sesto, San Giovanni was attached.	Sesto, San Giovanni (probably during 2. and 3.43)	Brutality.	U.K.
UK/4/196	Ital.	Officer	in command at Garibaldi barracks	Piacenza Bettola (12.43 and 1.44)	Miscellaneous crimes.	U.K.
UK/4/197	Ital.	Capt.	Inf., in charge of transfer of two British officers from POW-Camp at Alghero, Sardinia, to naval barracks at La Maddalena, North of Sardinia. Formerly schoolmaster on Island of La Maddalena	(8.43)	Brutality.	U.K.
UK/4/198	Ital.	Officer	in charge of guard, Camp P.G. 53	Macerata, Sforza Costa (28.2.43)	Murder.	U.K.
UK/4/199	Ital.	Adjutant or second in-command	Camp P.G. 53	Macerata, Sforza Costa (8.42-9.43)	Murder.	U.K.
UK/4/200	Ital.	Second-in-command	Camp 65	Gravina	Brutality.	U.K.
UK/4/201	Ital.	Second-in-command	Camp 63	Aversa (up to 3.43)	Brutality.	U.K.
UK/4/202	Ital.	Adjutant or second in-command	POW-Camp (No. P.G. 62)	Bergamo (1942 onwards)	Brutality.	U.K.
UK/4/203	Ger.	German sentry		Oflag 79, Germany (31.8.44)	Murder.	U.K.
UK/4/204	Ger.	Officer	in command of district of	Norcia, Italy (4.5.44)	Murder.	U.K.
UK/4/205	Ger.	Officer	in command of district "Quercette"	between Tor Lupara and Monte Gentile (27.-28.10.42)	Murder.	U.K.
UK/4/206	Ger.	Commander	of Bn., 20 Mot.Div.	(on or about 27.5.40)	Murder.	U.K.
UK/4/207	Ger.	Sentry		Oflag VII C-H	Murder.	U.K.
UK/4/208	Ger.	Adjutant or second in-command	at material times Camp P.G. 82	Laterina, Italy (between March and June 1944)	Murder.	U.K.
UK/4/209	Ger.	Cmdt.	Camp P.G. 82	Laterina, Italy (between March and June 1944)	Murder.	U.K.
UK/4/210	Ital.	Cmdt.	of Trigtarhuna transit camp	Tripoli (7.-8.42)	Brutality. Fair, clean shaven, age about 30-35. Spoke fluent English. Said he had been educated at Oxford. Wore civilian clothes, although not a civilian.	U.K.
UK/4/211	Ger.	Medical officer	at Waldheim prison on or about 7 February 1945	(between 14 March 1944 and February 1945)	Murder.	U.K.
UK/4/212	Ger.	Cmdt.	of Waldheim prison on or about 7 February 1945	(between 14 March 1944 and February 1945)	Murder.	U.K.
UK/4/213	Ger.	O.C.	district including Muelheim Germany	at or near Efringen, Germany (42-43)	Murder.	U.K.
UK/4/214	Ger.	Cmdt.	Camp 73	Carpi (from 9.9.43 onwards)	Murder.	U.K.
UK/4/215	Ger.	German officer	in command of district South of Cerignola	five miles South of Cerignola near Sulmona, Italy	Murder.	U.K.
UK/4/216	Ger.	Oberbefehlshaber	der Armee	Channel Islands (30.4.-20.7.1943)	Suspect.	U.K.
UK/4/217	Ger.	Camp-Cmdt.	Stalag III E	(9.9.41)	Brutality. Age about 48, height about 6'1", weight about 13 stone, fairish complexion, broad shoulders and well built, married. Possibly his son sent to Russian front in winter of 1941.	U.K.
UK/4/218	Ger.	Guard	belonging to construction and labour Bn. 21, defence area VIII	Blechhammer (20.10.42)	Murder.	U.K.
UK/4/219	Ger.		in charge of a working party from Stalag XX B	(23.5.42)	Murder.	U.K.
UK/4/220	Ger.	Chief	der Abteilung Organisation des Kriegsgefangenenwesens (PW-Welfare)	Fresnes, Paris, Chartres, Chalons sur Marne, France, C.C. Buchenwald, Germany (6.-9.44)	Ill-treatment of POW and other crimes. Responsible for railway journey of POW from Fresnes, Paris to C.C. Buchenwald.	U.K.
UK/4/221	Ital.	General commander	Italian Forces in Athens and prisons in Greece	Isle of Aegina, Greece (5.6.43)	Miscellaneous crimes.	U.K.
UK/4/222	Ital.	Cmdt.	Italian garrison	Bardia, North Africa (20.-22.10.42)	Brutality. Shackling and withholding of food and water.	U.K.
UK/4/223		Cmdt.		Stalag 315 Epinal, France (1944)	Murder of POW.	U.K.
UK/4/224	Ger.	Cmdt.	Army, Wehrkreis VIII	Germany (3.-5.44)	Mass murder.	U.K.
UK/4/225	Ger.	Doctor	Wehrmachtuntersuchungsgefaengnis	Berlin, Germany (4.43-5.44)	Ill-treatment of POW.	U.K.
UK/4/226	Ital.	Adjutant or second in-command	Camp P.G. 57	Udine, Gruppignano, Italy (20.5.43 and 8.7.43)	Murder of POW.	U.K.
UK/4/227	Ger.	Adjutant or second in-command	POW-Camp	Bari, Italy (about 17.7.42)	Murder and other crimes.	U.K.
UK/4/228		Adjutant or second in-command	POW-Camp P.G. 106	Vercelli, West of Milan, Italy (6. or 7.43)	Murder and other crimes.	U.K.

4. ARMY - MISCELLANEOUS (Rank not known). (Cont.)

C.R.FILE NO.	NATIO-NALITY	RANK OR STATUS	UNIT OR OCCUPATION	PLACE AND DATE OF CRIME	PARTICULARS OF CRIME OR REASON FOR WHICH WANTED FOLLOWED BY PHYSICAL DESCRIPTION IF KNOWN	WANTED BY
UK/4/229		Cmdt.	POW-Camp P.G. 106	Vercelli near Milan, Italy (6. or 7.43)	Murder and other crimes.	U.K.
UK/4/230	Ger.	Medical officer	POW-Camp P.G. 62	Bergamo, Italy (1942 onw.)	Ill-treatment of wounded POW.	U.K.
UK/4/231	Ger.	N.C.O., guard	on duty under patrol from Command of working Kdo.119 supplied from Stalag XXI A	Stalag VIII B (5.44)	Murder.	U.K.
UK/4/232	Ger.	Guard, acting as Camp leader		at or near Lichnau, Czechoslovakia (10.6.44)	Murder.	U.K.
UK/4/233	Ger.	Guard	Arb.Kdo.E.192, possibly 685 Landschutz-Bn., Army	Oels near Breslau, Germany (12.43)	Ill-treatment. Date of birth: about 1902, weight: 10 stone, height: 5'5", dark brown hair, sallow complexion. Accused was clean shaven and married.	U.K.
UK/4/234	Ger.		Army, Coy. L.439, Stalag 344	Heydebreck (Upper Silesia), Nuernberg, Germany (end Feb. to early March 1945)	Wanted for being concerned in beating British PW. with rifle butts. Nicknamed "Aachen" - town where he lived.	U.K.
UK/4/235	Ger.	Cmdt., probably Capt.		Stalag VIII B (10.5.43)	Murder or manslaughter or complicity in murder or manslaughter of a prisoner of war.	U.K.
UK/4/236	Ger.	German officer	in charge of prison	Angers, France (22.4.44 to 10.5.44)	Ill-treatment of POW.	U.K.
UK/4/237	Ger.	Doctor	of Army, Strafvollzug, Untersuchungsgefaengnis	Berlin, Lehrter Str. 3, Germany (4.43-5.44)	Ill-treatment of POW.	U.K.
UK/4/238	Ger.	O.C.	of prison, known as Wehrmachtuntersuchungsgefaengnis	Berlin, Germany (14.4.43-25.5.44)	Ill-treatment of POW.	U.K.
UK/4/239	Ger.	Officer or officers	Command Wehrmachtuntersuchungsgefaengnis, Strafvollzug	Berlin, Germany (4.43 onw.)	Ill-treatment of POW.	U.K.
UK/4/240	Ger.	Cmdt.	prison	Fresnes, France (6.5.-9.6.44)	Ill-treatment of POW.	U.K.
UK/4/241	Ger.	Cmdt.	prison	Frankfurt, Germany (3.6.44)	Ill-treatment of POW.	U.K.
UK/4/242	Ger.	O.C.	prison camp (Dulag 132)	Laterina, Italy (6.44)	Murder.	U.K.
UK/4/243	Ger.	Officer (Actg. Cmdt.)	P.W.Camp	Kanea, Greece (summer 1941)	Ill-treatment of prisoners of war. (Geneva Convent. 1929, Art. 2).	U.K.
UK/4/244	Ger.	Cmdt.	P.W.Camp	Salonika, Greece (6.41)	Ill-treatment of prisoners of war. (Geneva Convention 1929, Art. 2).	U.K.
UK/4/245	Ger.	Cmdt.	P.W.Camp	Corinth, Greece (1941)	Ill-treatment of prisoners of war. (Geneva Convent. 1929, Art. 2). Illegal employment of prisoners of war (Art. 31).	U.K.
UK/4/246	Ger.	O.C.	1 Coy., E-Bn., 125 Pz.Regt.	(6.44)	Issued orders to his Company to shoot Allied soldiers taken prisoner.	U.K.
UK/4/247	Ger.	Area Cmdt.	Army	Chartres, Paris, Chalons sur Marne, France (21.-30.6.44)	Ill-treatment of POW and other crimes.	U.K.
UK/4/248	Ger.	Cmdt.	prison	Tours, France (16.2.-22.4.44)	Ill-treatment of prisoners of war.	U.K.
UK/4/249	Ger.	O.C.	military prison	Torgau-Elbe, Germany (March 1944 onwards)	Ill-treatment of prisoners of war.	U.K.
UK/4/250	Ger.	Cmdt.	prison	Wiesbaden, Germany (9.6.-8.7.44)	Ill-treatment of POW.	U.K.
UK/4/251	Ger.	O.C.	military prison hospital	Berlin-Buch, Germany (period after March 1944)	Ill-treatment of POW.	U.K.
UK/4/252		Cmdt.	POW-Camp	Maribor and Wolsberg, Austria (7.41-8.43)	Murder and other crimes.	U.K.
UK/4/253	Ger.	Senior medical officer		Tobruk, Africa (from 21.6.42)	Ill-treatment of wounded POW.	U.K.
UK/4/254	Ger.	Officers	in charge of ammunition and store dumps at Cyrenaica camp	Fatma, Africa (6.41-1.42)	Ill-treatment of POW.	U.K.
UK/4/255	Ger.	Senior officer in charge		Tripoli, North Africa (41-42)	Ill-treatment of prisoners of war; employment of prisoners of war on unauthorised works.	U.K.
UK/4/256	Ger.	Area Cmdt.		Lille, France (40-41)	Ill-treatment of prisoners of war.	U.K.
UK/4/257	Ger.	O.C.	276 V.G.Div.	Western Front (7.44)	Directions to give no quarter.	U.K.
UK/4/258	Ger.		Charge of unit of those in charge of Kdo. 259	Stalag XX B (12.1.42)	Murder of a prisoner of war.	U.K.
UK/4/259	Ger.		Charge of unit of those in charge working party 357	Stalag XX B (16.6.42)	Murder of a prisoner of war.	U.K.
UK/4/260	Ger.		Charge of unit of those in charge of Kdo. Neudorf 229	Stalag XXIII (16. and 17. August 1942)	Threatening to shoot a prisoner of war; murder of a prisoner of war.	U.K.
UK/4/261	Ger.	Cmdt.		Stalag IV D (1941)	Complicity in murder of prisoners of war.	U.K.
UK/4/262	Ger.	Cmdt.		C.C. 13 A Nuremberg, Germany	Ill-treatment of prisoners of war.	U.K.
UK/4/263	Ger.	Kommandofuehrer	Army	Quarterberg, Germany (10.41)	Wanted for ill-treatment of prisoners of war - in particular assaulting Pvt. Josier of the Australian Imperial Forces at Stalag IV C and stationed at Quarterberg, Tetschen. Date of birth: 1910, weight: 12 stone, height: 5'10", black hair, brown eyes, dark complexion, hooked nose. Has a soldier-like bearing and is of good physique.	U.K.
UK/4/264	Ger.	Coy.-leader	adl. labour company from	Stalag XX B (26.4.41)	Murder of a prisoner of war; wounding of two prisoners of war.	U.K.
UK/4/265	Ger.	Officer	in charge of transport arrangements	Apeldoorn, Netherlands (26.,28.9.44)	Ill-treatment of wounded POW.	U.K.
UK/4/266	Ger.	Senior medical officer		Apeldoorn, Netherlands (26.,28.9.44)	Ill-treatment of wounded POW.	U.K.
UK/4/267	Ger.	Officer	in charge of prison camp	Graudenz, Poland (1.-4.43)	Slaughter and other crimes.	U.K.
UK/4/268	Ger.	Medical officer	at prison camp	Graudenz, Poland (1.-4.43)	Mass slaughter and other crimes.	U.K.

4. ARMY - MISCELLANEOUS (Rank not known). (Cont.)

C.R.FILE NO.	NATIONALITY	RANK OR STATUS	UNIT OR OCCUPATION	PLACE AND DATE OF CRIME	PARTICULARS OF CRIME OR REASON FOR WHICH WANTED FOLLOWED BY PHYSICAL DESCRIPTION IF KNOWN	WANTED BY
UK/4/269	Ital. or Ger.	Camp-Cmdt.	Camp 78	Sulmona, Italy (15.5.42-24.9.43)	Lack of food and fuel causing illness among POW.	U.K.
UK/4/270	Ger.	R.S.M.	Alp./-Regt.,5 Mountain Div. Inf.	Sarsina and Martino, Italy (28.9.44)	At SARSINA (Italy) and MARTINO - map ref. 108-F12-1:100,000, on 28 September 1944, sixteen Italian civilians were killed; five in the town itself between 0630 hours and 0730 hours; ten at MARTINO about one mile from SARSINO in the direction of SOREANO on the main S.Piero to SOREANO road (route 71), and one of the way to MARTINO. Shortly afterwards the town of SARSINO was set on fire. The wanted German Feldwebel is alleged to have told the inhabitants that these were reprisals for the wounding by Italian Partisans of two soldiers of a German patrol which had visited SARSINA on the previous day (September 27th). The victims were apparently selected at random. The accused is believed to have belonged to an Alpine Unit and was dressed in normal grey-green uniform with white lapels and a white metal Edelweiss badge worn on a Bustina a Visiera cap, and wore Alpine boots. It is suggested that if an Alpine Unit can be identified which operated in the area SARSINA - MARTINO - CA'DI NARDO, MONTE PIETRE on the 27th and 28th September 1944, the tracing of the accused might be facilitated. The accused is alleged personally to have supervised the killings. Date of birth: about 1895, height: 5'7", grey hair, brown eyes, fresh complexion, moustache.	U.K.
UK/4/271	Ger.	Commander	20 Pz.Div.	(27.5.40)	Mass murder.	U.K.
UK/4/272	Ger.	Chief	POW-Welfare	(1944)	Ill-treatment of POW.	U.K.
UK/4/273		Cmdt.	Mulberg,PW-Camp	Jacobstal (Zaiton) (12.43)	For failing to obey order to salute German under officers 1,000 prisoners of war sent to Ex-Jewish Concentration Camp for six weeks. Height: 5'8", false teeth, very thin, frail looking.	U.K.
UK/4/274		Cmdt.	Stalag 6 A	Dortmund, Germany (11.10.44)	Alleged to have been responsible for the beating and murder (by shooting) of a RAF Warrant Officer as a reprisal for the RAF bombing of Dortmund. Height: 5'8", grey moustache, medium build, high cheek bones.	U.K.
UK/4/275	Ger.	Camp-Cmdt.	Stalag XII A	Limburg, Germany (9.9.-10.10.44)	No arrangements for treatment of sick office PW's; no medical treatment given over night to wounded officer.	U.K.
UK/4/276	Ger.	Cmdt.	Prison	Paviak, Poland (42-43)	Ill-treatment of a prisoner of war.	U.K.
UK/4/277	Ital.	Cmdt.	Military prison	Patras, Greece (6.9.43)	Insufficient food, bad sanitary conditions, no medical attention and appalling treatment.	U.K.
UK/4/278	Ger.	Cmdt.	Prison	Angers, France (22.4.-10.5.44)	Ill-treatment of POW.	U.K.
UK/4/279	Ger.		Army, 379 Landschutz-Bn.	Obergeorgenthal, Czechoslovakia (20.7.44)	Wanted for the murder of Pte. I. Francis 2/5 Essex Regt. at Lager 22A attached to Stalag IV C. Date of birth: 1915, weight: 11 stone, height: 5'7", fair hair, blue eyes, ruddy complexion. His left eye was nearly obliterated as a result of a war wound, so that only the blue corner of the pupil showed. He had a face like a pig with a turned up nose like a snout.	U.K.
UK/4/280	Ger.	Guard	Stalag VIII-B, known as "Pioneer Park"	Cosel, Stalag VIII B, Lamsdorf, Germany, (6.40-1.41)	Brutality. Nicknamed "Black Bomber". Height 6' and of medium build, aged about 37, hair black and slightly wavy, brown eyes, whites of eyes also brownish colour; had a chocolate-coloured face and his hands were of the same colour and heavily covered with hair; broad snub nose, good white teeth and thick lips; gave the impression of having negroid blood in his veins; morose expression; was a Bavarian.	U.K.
UK/4/281	Yugo.	Guard		Schishchitz near Welwern, Poland (13.3.45)	Together with Feldwebel,two Unteroffiziere and three guards, severely beat with rifle butts sticks and fists five POW's on their recapture after escaping from a column of POW's. The wanted man was known by the nickname of "Tito". Very thick set, fat face. Very short sighted, blue eyes, fair hair, height: 5'5", ruddy complexion. Believed to be captured by Americans in Bavaria, April 1945.	U.K.
UNWCC/4/282	Ger.	Place-Commander		Rieti (9.4.44)	Suspected of the commission of a war crime in that he published a notice containing threats of action contrary to the laws and customs of war which was probably taken.	U.N.W.C.C.
US/4/283	Ger.	C.O.	Army, Stalag II B	Fallenbach, Germany	Wanted for alleged starvation of American PW's. PW's were not given sufficient food. Four starved to death.	U.S.
US/4/284	Ger.	Second-in-command	Stalag IX B	Bad Orb, Germany (12.44-4.45)	Wanted for mistreatment of American PW's. Made some of them stand in the snow for three hours.	U.S.

-93-

4. ARMY - MISCELLANEOUS (Rank not known). (Cont.)

C.R.FILE NO.	NATIO-NALITY	RANK OR STATUS	UNIT OR OCCUPATION	PLACE AND DATE OF CRIME	PARTICULARS OF CRIME OR REASON FOR WHICH WANTED FOLLOWED BY PHYSICAL DESCRIPTION IF KNOWN	WANTED BY
US/4/285		Ordinary guard	Army	Stalag II B, Hammerstein, Germany, Kdo. 1534, Gambin, Germany (8.43)	Wanted for alleged murder of two American PW's at Kdo. 1534, Gambin, Germany, which was under Stalag II B, Hammerstein, Germany. Two American PW's were apprehended after trying to escape and were shot. Bodies were left in latrine for three days. Suspect was one of the guards who did the shooting. Information obtained from statements of American PW's who were in the Stalag where incident occurred. Height: 5'7", slender build, badly scarred.	U.S.
US/4/286	Ger.	Officer	in charge of the convoy	En route from Normandy to Oflag 64, Altburgund, Germany (6.-7.44)	Wanted for the alleged mistreatment of American PW's.	U.S.
US/4/287		Guard	on the convoy	En route from Normandy to Oflag 64, Alburgund, Germany (6-.7.44)	Wanted for the alleged mistreatment of American PW's. Weight: 130.lbs, height: 5'8½", dark brown hair, tall slim build, dark complexion.	U.S.
US/4/288		All officers and men	Army, 1 Bn., 190 Volksgren.Regt., 62 Volksgren. Div.	Habscheid, Germany (19. or 20.12.44)	Capt. Kulger (also known as Kugler) CO 1st Bn., 190 Volksg.Regt., 62 Volksg.Div. at the village of Habscheid ordered the shooting of 40 American PW's who had been captured at this village. Shooting occurred on 19 or 20 Dec. 1944. Members of this organization should be questioned as to this offense.	U.S.
US/4/289		All officers and men	Transient Camp, Remount School, Gardelegen	En route to and at or near Gardelegen, Germany (10.-14.4.45)	Wanted for participation in the murder, torture and abuse of hundreds of political prisoners while en route to and at or in the vicinity of Gardelegen, Germany. Because of rapid advance of American troops, political prisoners from numerous concentration camps in Germany were evacuated to the vicinity of Kreis Gardelegen. En route many were starved, beaten and shot. Of those who arrived at the Isenshnibbe Barn, near Gardelegen, 1016 were killed by burning and shooting on 13.-14. April 1945.	U.S.
US/4/290		Guard, camp leader	Army	Stalag II B, Hammerstein, Germany, Kdo. 1534, Gambin, Germany (8.43)	Wanted for alleged murder of two American PW's at Kdo. 1534, Gambin, Germany which was under Stalag II B, Hammerstein, Germany. Two American PW's were apprehended after trying to escape and were shot. Bodies were then left in latrine for three days. Suspect was one of the guards who did the shooting. Information obtained from statements of American PW's who were in the Stalag where incident occurred. Weight: 180. lbs., height: 6 ft., dark complexion. Husky man.	U.S.
US/4/291		All members	of the Landesschuetzen-Bn. 739	Fallingbostel, Germany (1.-4.45)	PW's were given insufficient food at Stalag XI B, Fallingbostel, Germany, resulting in death by starvation of four American PW's, including Pfc. Titzloff. Landesschuetzen-Bn.739 was stationed in Fallingbostel and probably provided guards for Stalag XI B. It's members should be able to identify the CO of the Stalag and others responsible.	U.S.
US/4/292		All members	of the Landesschuetzen-Bn. 1012	Fallenbach, Germany (1.2.-16.4.45)	Wanted in connection with alleged starvation of American PW's. Two companies of subject unit. guarded Stalag (356) XI B, where crime was committed.	U.S.
US/4/293	Ger.	All officers	in command of or attached to Stalag II B	(11.44-2.45)	Wanted for alleged participation in killing of American PW's on march from Stolp to Swinemuende in Feb. 1945.	U.S.
US/4/294		All officers and men	of the 17 Landesschuetzen-Regt.	En route to and at or near Gardelegen, Germany (5.-14.5.45)	Wanted for participation in the murder, torture and abuse of hundreds of political prisoners while en route to and at or in the vicinity of Gardelegen, Germany. Because of rapid advance of American troops, political prisoners from numerous concentration camps in Germany were evacuated to the vicinity of Kreis Gardelegen. En route many were starved, beaten and shot. Of those who arrived at the Isenschnibbe Barn, near Gardelegen, 1016 were killed by burning and shooting on 13.-14. April 1945.	U.S.
US/4/295		All members	of the 470 Landesschuetzen-Bn.	Thorn, Poland (26.7.44)	An unknown German Capt. shot and killed an American PW, S/Sgt. Thomas Stephens at Camp No. 357 of Stalag XX A, Thorn, Poland. Landesschuetzen-Bn. 470 was stationed in Thorn, and probably provided guards for the PW-Camp. The members of the Bn. may therefore, be able to identify the Capt. and any others responsible.	U.S.
US/4/296		All members	of the 714 Landesschuetzen-Bn.	Thorn, Poland (26.7.44)	An unknown German Capt. shot and killed an American PW, S/Sgt. Thomas Stephens at Camp No. 357 of Stalag XX A, Thorn, Poland. Landesschuetzen-Bn. 714 was stationed in Thorn, and probably provided guards for the PW-Camp. The members of the Bn. may therefore, be able to identify the Capt. and any others responsible.	U.S.
US/4/297		All members	of the 368 Landesschuetzen-Bn.	Thorn, Poland (26.7.44)	An unknown German Capt. shot and killed an American PW, S/Sgt. Thomas Stephens at Camp No. 357 of Stalag XX A, Thorn, Poland. Landesschuetzen-Bn. 368 was stationed in Thorn, and probably provided guards for the PW-Camp. The members of the Bn. may therefore, be able to identify the Capt. and any others responsible.	U.S.

4. ARMY - MISCELLANEOUS (Rank not known). (Cont.)

C.R.FILE NO.	NATIO-NALITY	RANK OR STATUS	UNIT OR OCCUPATION	PLACE AND DATE OF CRIME	PARTICULARS OF CRIME OR REASON FOR WHICH WANTED FOLLOWED BY PHYSICAL DESCRIPTION IF KNOWN	WANTED BY
US/4/298		All members	of the 397 Landesschuetzen-Bn.	Thorn, Poland (26.7.44)	An unknown German Capt. shot and killed an American PW, S/Sgt. Thomas Stephens at Camp No. 357 of Stalag XX A, Thorn, Poland. Landesschuetzen-Bn. 397 was stationed in Thorn, and probably provided guards for the PW-Camp. The members of the Bn. may therefore, be able to identify the Capt. and any others responsible.	U.S.
US/4/299		All members	of the Landesschuetzen-Bn. 259	Thorn, Poland (26.7.44)	An unknown German Capt. shot and killed an American PW, S/Sgt. Thomas Stephens at Camp No. 357 of Stalag XX A, Thorn, Poland. Landesschuetzen-Bn. 259 was stationed in Thorn, and probably provided guards for the PW-Camp. The members of the Bn. may therefore, be able to identify the Capt. and any others responsible.	U.S.
US/4/300		All members	of the Wach-Bn. 561	Thorn, Poland (26.7.44)	An unknown German Capt. shot and killed an American PW, S/Sgt. Thomas Stephens at Camp No. 357 of Stalag XX A, Thorn, Poland. All these Units were stationed in Thorn, and probably provided guards for the PW-Camp. The members of the Bn. may therefore, be able to identify the Capt. and any others responsible.	U.S.
US/4/301	Ger.	All members	of the 7 Coy., 1200 Regt 286 Div.	Anzegem, Belgium (6.9.44)	Wanted for allegedly shooting American Airmen found in civilian clothes without trial.	U.S.
US/4/302		All members	of the Battle Group Diemer 3 companies of 130 each Vonalt	Reidwihr Forest, France (25.1.45)	The B.G. Diemer was at the tip of the Reidwihr Forest, The witness Pvt. Amos B.Feete, 20920539, of Co.A, 15th Infantry, 3rd Inf.Div., saw members of this battle group shoot four unknown American soldiers of the 15th Infantry while said soldiers were lying dead on the ground. Witness also heard a wounded American soldier call for water, and saw a German soldier advance towards him and fire several shots; the call was heard no more. Four American soldiers were taken prisoners, guarded by two or three Germans. They were marched into the woods; a machine gun was fired; yells and screams were heard.	U.S.
US/4/303		Platoon leader		Emsland, Germany (1944)	Wanted for participating in the alleged mistreatment and killing of Allied Nationals. He has beaten to death the 59 years old French citizen Romaise Renard, who was sick and asked to go to the medics. Nicknamed "Blonde Inge".	U.S.
YUGO/4/304	Ger.	Cmdt.	German Unit F.P.Nr.01072 A	Geugelia, Yugoslavia (1944)	Pillage.	YUGO.
YUGO/4/305	Ital.	O.C.	Bn. "Latisone"	Montenegro, Cetinje, Savnik, Podgorica, Berane (7.-11.41)	Murder.	YUGO.
YUGO/4/306	Ital.	O.C.	Bn. "Tagliamento"	Montenegro, Cetinje, Savnik, Podgorica, Berane (7.-11.41)	Murder.	YUGO.
YUGO/4/307	Bulg.	Commander	Bulgarian Div.	Krusevac, Serbia (6.42-43)	Murder.	YUGO.
YUGO/4/308	Ger.	Standortkommandant	at Petrovac	District of Pozarevac, Serbia (1941,1942,1943)	Murder.	YUGO.
YUGO/4/309	Ger.	German garrison commander		Naples (9.43)	Murder.	YUGO.
YUGO/4/310	Ital.	O.C.	48 Regimento D'Infanteria "Ferrara"-Div.	Montenegro (5.43)	Murder.	YUGO.
YUGO/4/311	Ger.	O.C.	777 Landesschuetzen-Bn.	near Langsur, Germany (22.9.-14.10.44)	Brutality.	YUGO.
YUGO/4/312	Ger.	Officer, O.C.		Boten Camp, Norway (from 1943 onwards)	Murder.	YUGO.
YUGO/4/313	Ger.	C.C.	118 German Div. carrying out "cleaning-up"	(27.3.44 and later)	Murder.	YUGO.
YUGO/4/314	Ger.	Officer, Kreis-Kmdt.		District Zajecar (8.41-1.42)	Murder.	YUGO.
YUGO/4/315	Ger.	C.C.	118 Jaeger-Div.	(27.3.44)	Murder and other crimes.	YUGO.

5. Waffen SS and FIELD POLICE REGTS.

C.R.FILE NO.	NATIO-NALITY	RANK OR STATUS	UNIT OR OCCUPATION	PLACE AND DATE OF CRIME	PARTICULARS OF CRIME OR REASON FOR WHICH WANTED FOLLOWED BY PHYSICAL DESCRIPTION IF KNOWN	WANTED BY
BEL/5/316	Ger.	O.C.	Waffen SS,F.P.Nr.58116	Anderlues (1.9.44)	Murder.	BEL.
BEL/5/317	Ger.		Identy disc with inscription:2 Pz.Jg.E.Abt.4688, Waffen SS	Sars-La-Bruyere, Hainaut, Belgium (3.-4.9.44)	Brutality.	BEL.
BEL/5/318	Ger.		3 Coy.,33 Pz.Gren.Rgt., Div."SS Hitlerjugend	Godinne,Riviere,Bouillon, Warnant,Belgium (4.-5.9.44)	Pillage.	BEL.
BEL/5/319	Ger.	Oschfhr.,	SS Pz.Div."Das Reich"	Gerard-Wez, Belgium (9.9.44)	Murder.	BEL.
BEL/5/320			7 A E R, 482 SS T.V. 3 Pz. "Das Reich"	Quenast, Belgium (4.9.44)	Murder.	BEL.
CZECH/5/321	Ger.	Chief	Sanitaetswesen der Waffen SS	Germany, C.C.outside Germany (40-45)	Murder.	CZECH.
CZECH/5/322	Ger.	SS-Member	6 SS Totenkopf-Standarte	Terezin (1.10.38-44)	Murder.	CZECH.
CZECH/5/323	Ger.	Reichsarzt	SS	Germany, C.C.outside Germany (40-44)	Misc.Crimes.	CZECH.
CZECH/5/324	Ger.	Chief	Sanitaetswesen der Waffen SS	Germany, C.C.outside Germany (40-44)	Murder.	CZECH.
FR/5/325	Ger.	N.C.O.	Coy. SS Div."Das Reich" F.P.Nr.24607,comes from Berlin	St.Lys (12.6.44)	Murder.	FR.
FR/5/326	Ger.	Officer,N.C.O.	1 and 3 Coy.,SS Pz.Gren. Rgt.4 "Der Fuehrer", Div."Das Reich"	Oradour-sur-Glane (10.6.44) Figeac (12.5.44),Cahors, Montauban,Noailles(15.5.44)	Murder.	FR.
FR/5/327	Ger.	Commandant	3 Coy.,SS Pz.Gren.Rgt.4 "Der Fuehrer",Div. "Das Reich"	Oradour-sur-Glane (10.6.44) Figeac (12.5.44),Cahors, Montauban,Noailles(15.5.44)	Murder.	FR.
FR/5/328	Ger.	O.C.	151 Bn.of 29 SS Pz.Div.		Murder.	FR.
FR/5/329	Ger.	Commandant	1 Coy.,SS Pz.Gren.Rgt.4 "Der Fuehrer",Div. "Das Reich"	Oradour-sur-Glane (10.6.44) Figeac (12.5.44),Cahors, Montauban,Noailles(15.5.44)	Murder.	FR.
FR/5/330	Ger.	Commander	SS Rgt."Adolf Hitler"	Aussonne (1.5.44)	Murder.	FR.
FR/5/331	Ger.	Commander	SS,Units operating in	Correze (2.4.44)	Murder.	FR.
FR/5/332	Ger.	Commandant	SS,troops operating in	Montauban area (6.5.44)	Pillage.	FR.
FR/5/333	Ger.	Commander,SS-Obersturmbannfhr.	SS,	Lyons District (12.43)	Torture. Dr.Werner Knab.	FR.
FR/5/334	Ger.	SS-personnel	Institute of Anatomy	Strasbourg and Fort Ney at Robertsau (40-44)	Murder.	FR.
FR/5/335	Ger.	O.C.	SS Rgt."Germania",operating on or about in Foret de Nieppe Sector	Foret de Nieppe Sector (28.5.40)	Murder.	FR.
FR/5/336	Ger.	O.C.	Units of the "Hohenstaufen" Waffen SS Div.stationed at Nimes and operating in the Le Gard area	Nimes,Le Gard area (2.-4.44)	Murder.	FR.
FR/5/337	Ger.	Patrol of about 15 men	6 Coy.,A.u.E.Bn.1,Bde.51, Waffen SS from Depot at Berlin-Lichterfelde, operating at	Fontvannes (Aube) (25.8.44)	Murder.	FR.
FR/5/338	Ger.		1 Bn.,SS Div."Das Reich", operating at	Trebons,Pouzac and Bagneres de Bigorre (Hautes-Pyrenees) (11.6.44)	Murder.	FR.
FR/5/339		Commandant	6 Coy.,A.u.E.Bn.1,Bde.51, Waffen SS	Fontvannes (Aube) (25.8.44)	Murder and other crimes.	FR.
FR/5/340	Ger.	Lt.	SS Tannenberg 5 and 6 Btty.	Champ le Duc (France) (5.9.44)	Looting.	FR.
FR/5/341	Ger.	Officers	SS,F.P.Nr.44181 A	Secondigny, France (25.5.44)	Suspect.	FR.
FR/5/342	Ger.	Obergruppenfhr.,	SS	Longwy Haut, France (44)	Murder and other crimes.	FR.
UK/5/343	Ger.	Commander	SS Verfuegungs Div.	Forest of Nieppe (28.5.40)	Murder.	U.K.
UK/5/344	Ger.	Chief,Prison-officer	SS	Portland (2.-3.41)	Murder.	U.K.
UK/5/345	Ger.	Officer	in command of SS	Portland (2.-3.41)	Murder.	U.K.
UK/5/346	Ger.	Osturmfhr.	Waffen SS,12 SS Pz.Div. Hitler Jugend,26 SS Pz. Gren.Rgt.,probably 3 Bn. F.P.Nr.L 56804	Les Fains,Calvados, France (12.-15.6.44)	Murder.Hair going from temples,black hair.Brown eyes. Oval face.Height:1,76	U.K.
UK/5/347	Ger.	SS-Mann or Junior N.C.O.	Waffen SS,12 SS Pz.Div. Hitler Jugend,26 SS Pz. Gren.Rgt.,probably 3 Bn. F.P.Nr.L 56804	Les Fains,Calvados, France (12.6.44)	Murder.Date of birth:1925-26.Height:1,65,fair auburn hair,brown eyes.Complexion:freckles.Slim figure. Slouching carriage,straight nose,pendant ear-lobes.	U.K.
UK/5/348	Ger.-Pol.	SS-Schuetze	SS Totenkopf Detachment	Karthaus,Poland (beginning of May 44)	Witness.Bushy eyebrowns,good teeth.Height:approx 5'8". Born and lives in Karthaus 25 kms West of Danzig.	U.K.
UK/5/349	Ger.	SS-Mann or Junior N.C.O.	Waffen SS,9 SS Pz.Div.	Near Arnhem,Netherland (23.9.44)	Murder.Medium build;clean shaven;pointed chin;rather jewish appearance.Date of birth:1925-27.Height:5'7". Black hair,light blue eyes.Complexion,fair fresh.	
UK/5/350	Ger.	Commander	Bn.SS,Verfuegungs Div., Rgt."Der Fuehrer"	Nieppe, France (40)	Murder.	U.K.
US/5/351		Assistant Doctor	SS	Schwarzenfeld,Germany (16.-25.4.45)	Murder.Date of birth:1923-1922.Weight:70-75 kilo, height:1,75,dark brown hair.Complexion fair.Non-military posture,clean shaven.	U.S.
US/5/352	Ger.	Commander,high SS rank	SS	Near Malmedy,France (6.44)	Murder.He was strongly built.Had a dark red scar on left side of face,running from temple to chin.Height: 1,80,dark hair.	U.S.

5. Waffen SS and FIELD POLICE REGTS. (Cont.)

C.R.FILE NO.	NATIO-NALITY	RANK OR STATUS	UNIT OR OCCUPATION	PLACE AND DATE OF CRIME	PARTICULARS OF CRIME OR REASON FOR WHICH WANTED FOLLOWED BY PHYSICAL DESCRIPTION IF KNOWN	WANTED BY
US/5/353		Osturmfhr.	SS	Damme, Germany (2.11.44)	Suspect. Date of birth: about 1922-23, weight: 165-170 height: 6'1", light brown hair, ruddy complexion, regular featured with stron white teeth; spoke English fluently	U.S.
US/5/354		Osturmfhr.	SS	Damme, Germany (2.11.44)	Suspect. Date of birth: about 1919, weight: 160-165, height: 5'11", dark hair, scar about 1/2 in. long running from the bottom of his cheek bone toward the bottom of his right ear.	U.S.
US/5/355		Sturmbannfhr.	SS	Damme, Germany (2.11.44)	Suspect. Date of birth: about 1906, weight: 210 lbs, height: 6'2", black hair, ruddy complexion, straight black hair combed straight back; heavy beard.	U.S.
US/5/356		Sturmbannfhr. or Osturmbannfhr.	SS	Damme, Germany (2.11.44)	Suspect. Date of birth: about 1901-1906, weight 190 lbs height 5'6", dark brown hair, thick neck; hair combed straight back with rather high line; pudgh countenance round nose and heavy jowls; wore pince-nez attached to a black string when reading.	U.S.
US/5/357		S/Sgt., Oschfhr.	Interrogation Center	Nuernberg, Germany (about 17.4.1945)	Torture. Subject admitted having lived in Chicago, USA, raised two (2) children there and wife was from Nebraska. Red hair, complexion moustache, height, medium	U.S.
US/5/358	Ger.	All members	Waffen SS, probably 1 SS Div. Leibstandarte Adolf Hitler Field Ers.Bn.1	Rosbach, Siegkreis, Germany (4.3.45)	Wanted as a witness in connection with murder of an American aviator who had been taken prisoner.	U.S.
US/5/359	Ger.	Oschfhr.	SS, 2 training Coy., Reserve & Training Bn.11	Wezelsdorf, Austria (3.45)	Murder. Date of birth: approx 1920, weight 85-90 k, height 1.85.	U.S.
US/5/360	Ger.	Osturmbannfhr.	SS, Reserve & Training Bn.11	Wezelsdorf, Austria (3.45)	Murder. Date of birth: approx 1911, weight 55 k, height 1.60.	U.S.
US/5/361		Osturmbannfhr.	SS	Near Polangen, Lithuania (6.44)	Murder.	U.S.
US/5/362		Uschfhr.	SS, 1 Coy. SS Vet.Ers.Abt.	Radom, Poland	Murder, (slaughter).	U.S.
YUGO/5/363	Ger.	O.C.	172 SS Div., stationed at	Donji Lapac croatian province of Lika, Districts of Obrovac, Korenica	Murder.	YUGO.
YUGO/5/364	Ger.	SS-Officer, Commandant		Beisfjord Camp, Norway (6.-11.42)	Murder.	YUGO.

6. AIR FORCE - All Ranks.

C.R.FILE NO.	NATIO-NALITY	RANK OR STATUS	UNIT OR OCCUPATION	PLACE AND DATE OF CRIME	PARTICULARS OF CRIME OR REASON FOR WHICH WANTED FOLLOWED BY PHYSICAL DESCRIPTION IF KNOWN	WANTED BY
Bel/6/365	Ger.	Commandant	Dienststelle F.P.No.L.13353 LGPA. Brussels	Bauffe (2.9.44)	Misc. Crimes	Bel.
Bel/6/366	Ger.		I Air Force Jaeger Regt. 35	Quaregnon/Jemappes-Ghlin (Bel.) 2.-3.9.44	Murder	Bel.
Bel/6/367	Ger.		Paratrooper Rgt. 5. Nachrichtenzug	Quaregnon/Jemappes/Ghlin (Bel.) 2.-3.9.44	Murder	Bel.
Fr/6/368	Ger.	Head/Pay-Master	German Air-Force Dienststelle, L 50-370 A. LGPA. Paris	Royge'val, Carentan, 12.6.44	Murder	Fr.
Fr/6/369	Ger.	Pvt.	4 Coy. Luftnachrichtenschule	Lyon (Fr.) 2 4.8.44	Murder	Fr.
Fr/6/370	Ger.	Commander	4 Coy. Luftnachrichtenschule	Lyon (Fr.) 24.8.44	Murder	Fr.
Fr/6/371	Ger.	O.C.	Luftnachrichten Rgt. 302	Poissons, Haute Marne (Fr.) 17.8.44	Miscellaneous Crimes	Fr.
Fr/6/372	Ger.	Head-Pay-Master	Army, Dienststelle L 50-370 A.	Roygeval-Carentan (Fr.) 44	Murder	Fr.
Fr/6/373		Officers, N.C.O's and men	Unit No. L 52750 H LGPA	Paris Lannedern (Fr.) 28.7.44	Looting and other crimes.	Fr.
Fr/6/374		Officers, N.C.O's and men	Air Unit F.P.No. 42432 LGPA. Paris	(Fr.) 9.8.44	Murder	Fr.
Fr/6/375		Officer	Air Unit L 49060 B F.P.No. 12826 and Stab 730	Perigueux (Fr.) 21.8.44	Murder	Fr.
Fr/6/376		Officers, N.C.O's and men	Unit No. L 52750 A LGPA. Paris	Paris Lannedern (Finistere) 28.7.44	Looting and other crimes	Fr.
Fr/6/377		Officers, N.C.O's and men	Unit L 52176 and L 54570	Kerlaz and La Roche Maurice (Finistere) 7.44	Murder and other crimes.	Fr.
Fr/6/378		Commandant	F.P.No. L 52750 A LGPA. Paris	Lannedern (Finistere)	Looting and other crimes.	UNWCC., Fr.
Fr/6/379	Ger.	Officers, N.C.O's and men	of the Troop of parachutist Unit F.P.No. L 31.184	Plouzane (Fr.) 24.-27.8.44	Murder and other crimes.	Fr.
Fr/6/380	Ger.	Officers, N.C.O's and men	of the Troop of parachutist Unit F.P.No. L 39714 D	Plouzane (Fr.) 24.-27.8.44	Murder and other crimes.	Fr.
Fr/6/381	Ger.	Officers, N.C.O's and men	of the Troop, of Unit F.P.No. L 49452 LGPA. Paris	Carhaix (Fr.) 8.-9.6.44	Murder and other crimes.	Fr.
UK/6/382	Ger.			Stalag IV	Ill-treatment of P.O.W., responsible for Transport of P.O.W. to Gross-Tychow (Ger.) from Kriefheide station.	U.K.
UK/6/383	Ger.	Lt., Provost Marshal	Air-Force, Interrogation Centre Oberursel	Frankfurt a.M. (Ger.) 16.-30.9.43	Third degree methods of interrogation at Gestapo Political prisoners Detention prison.	U.K.
UK/6/384	Ger.	Cpt.	In charge of Klesheim Air-Camp	Illesheim (Ger.) 14.-18.3.45	He has a badly burned face and wears dark glasses.	U.K.
UK/6/385	Ger.	Commander	Flak "Verfuegungs Reserve" Air Gau 3, Berlin-Mariendorf	Berlin (Ger.) 8.44	Gave orders to his Unit to fire on descending parachutists during air attack on Berlin.	U.K.
US/6/386		Lt.Col.	Air-Force	Budapest (Hung.) 5.5.44	Wanted for participation in the alleged murder of 2 American navigators and one Negro pilot at a Federal Penitentiary in Budapest.	U.S.
US/6/387	Ger.	Lt.	German A.A.Unit	Dorstem 20 miles north of Essen, 15.10.44	Wanted for participation in the alleged beating of Allied airman. Major Cheney, A.C. was badly beaten by officer and men at a A.A.Hdq. building in Dorsten. Suspect had Africa corps Band on cuff of left sleeve, also been wounded in Africa. Date of birth: 15-17. Weight: 190-200 lbs. Height: 6' 1".	U.S.
US/6/388		Col., Cmdt.	Flak school Rerik	Neubukow and Rerik (Ger.) 16.-17.3.44	Wanted for questioning in connection with the murder of 6 US AAF personnel. Witness was commandant of Flak-school at Rerik. Witness should be able to give full name of Dr.Schmid, commandant of Air-Corps hospital at Rerik, the Major in charge of PW's at Rerik, the District-leader of Bad Doberan. Date of birth: 95, Weight: 180 lbs, Height: 180 cm. Hair: dark brown-turning grey. Complexion: dark.	U.S.
US/6/389	Ger.	Capt., Cmdt.	Aigen, Air-Field	Steiermark (Aust.) 2.45	Refused medical attention to four captured U.S.-airman. Appalling treatment for 12 days.	U.S.
US/6/390		All officers and men	Probably Air-Force Ground Crews-Airfield	Gardelegen (Ger.) 10.-14.4.45	Wanted for participation in the murder, torture and abuse of hundreds of political prisoners while en route to and at in the vicinity of Gardelegen. En route many were starved, beaten and shot. Of those who arrived at the Isenschnibbe Barn, near Gardelegen, 1016 were killed by burning and shooting.	U.S.
US/6/391		All officers and men	Provisional Paratroop-Rgt. "Von Einem"	Vicinity of Krs.Gardelegen (Ger.) 10.-14.4.45	Wanted for participation in the murder, torture and abuse of hundreds of political prisoners while en route to and at or in the vicinity of Gardelegen. En route many were starved, beaten and shot. Of those who arrived at the Isenschnibbe Barn, near Gardelegen, 1016 were killed by burning and shooting.	U.S.
US/6/392	Ger.	Pvt., guard	Air-Force, Stalag Luft 4	Kiefheide (Gross Tuchow) (Ger.) 21.6.44	Murder - Wanted for murder of T/Sgt. Aubrey J. Teague, 18213989. Date of birth: about 05, Weight: 150 lbs, Height: 5' 7". Hair: turning grey. Complexion: fair. Medium build, wears dark, hornrimmed glasses with thick lens. Hitler-type, black moustache.	U.S.

6. AIR FORCE - All Ranks. (Cont.)

C.R.FILE NO.	NATIO- NALITY	RANK OR STATUS	UNIT OR OCCUPATION	PLACE AND DATE OF CRIME	PARTICULARS OF CRIME OR REASON FOR WHICH WANTED FOLLOWED BY PHYSICAL DESCRIPTION IF KNOWN	WANTED BY
US/6/393	Ger.	Pvt., guard	Dulag Luft	Frankfurt-Main (Ger.) 21.8.43	Wanted for the alleged shooting (not seriously) of an unknown American. Weight: 185 lbs. Height: 5' 6". Stocky build, wears tortoise shell glasses.	U.S.
US/6/394		Guard	Air-Force, Stalag Luft 3 (South Camp)	Sagan (Ger.) 9. or 10.44	Wanted for participation in alleged murder of American PW, S/Sgt."Ward". Suspect, a guard at camp, shot American PW. during an air alarm. The guard was on the outside of the compound fence and rested his rifle on the fence. Victim was standing in the kitchen doorway, a distance of approximately 150 yards away. Date of birth: about 15. Weight: 170 lbs. Height: 5' 8".	U.S.
US/6/395	Ger.	Major	German A.A.Unit	Dorsten, 20 miles north of Essen (Ger.) 15.10.44	Wanted for participation in the alleged beating of Allied airman. Major Cheney, A.C. was badly beaten by officer and men. Date of birth: 95-00. Weight: 160 lbs. Height: 5'8" Hair: black- turning grey. Eyes: blue. Complexion: ruddy; long pointed nose and a nasal voice.	U.S.

7. NAVY - All Ranks.

C.R.FILE NO.	NATIO- NALITY	RANK OR STATUS	UNIT OR OCCUPATION	PLACE AND DATE OF CRIME	PARTICULARS OF CRIME OR REASON FOR WHICH WANTED FOLLOWED BY PHYSICAL DESCRIPTION IF KNOWN	WANTED BY
CAN./7/396	Ger.	Obermaat	Navy A.A.	Wilhelmshaven (Ger.) 15.10.44	Wanted as a witness to the shooting of J-37830 F/O/ R A Roman, Royal Canadian Air-Force, near Wilhelmshaven. - Witnesses to Crime: 1. Ulferts, Hero, Wilhelmshaven,Edsardstr. 28 2. Bornert, Paul, Wilhelmshaven,Leuchtturmstr.11 3. Saueressig, Willi, Wilhelmshaven, Leuchturmstr.3 4. Jung, Wolfgang, Wilhelmshaven, Leuchturmstr.15. 5. Koch, Dora, Alt Voslapp - Ger. First name: Kurt. Weight: 150 lbs. Height: 170 cm. Hair: fair.	CAN.
FR/7/397	Ger.		2 Coy, 5 Rgt., Navy Art.	Lassicourt, Precy St. Martin (Aube) (Fr.) 27.8.44	Murder	FR.
UK/7/398	Ger.	Prison officer Thought to be U-Boot Cmdr.	Ger. Navy, Ger.ship "Orion"	At sea 26.11.40 onwards.	Illtreatment of British men and women, causing some deaths.	U.K.
UK/7/399	Ger.	Chief Navigation officer	Ger. Navy, S.S. "Rio Grande"	At sea 11.,12.40	Height: 5' 9". Complexion: sandy. Slight build. Appalling conditions and lack of food on Prison ship S.S. "Rio Grande"	U.K.

8. NAZI PARTY MEMBERS - NSDAP etc.

C.R.FILE NO.	NATIO-NALITY	RANK OR STATUS	UNIT OR OCCUPATION	PLACE AND DATE OF CRIME	PARTICULARS OF CRIME OR REASON FOR WHICH WANTED FOLLOWED BY PHYSICAL DESCRIPTION IF KNOWN	WANTED BY
UK/8/400		Leader	N.S.D.A.P.	Fermo, Italy (3.5.44)	Murder and other crimes.	U.K.
UK/8/401	Ger.	Ortsgruppenleiter		Frankfurt-Main Ginnheim, Germany, (12.44 or 1.45)	Murder.	U.K.
UK/8/402	Ger.	Ortsgruppenleiter		Sachsenburg, Germany, (3.45)	Murder.	U.K.
US/8/403		Ortsgruppenleiter	N.S.D.A.P.	Waldrach, Germany (9.44)	Murder.	U.S.
US/8/404		Ortsgruppenleiter	N.S.D.A.P.	Laubenheim, Germany (2.45)	Murder.	U.S.
US/8/405	Ger.	Ortsgruppenleiter, Civilian	N.S.D.A.P.	Geilhausen, Germany Beltershain, Germany (Early 45)	Murder.	U.S.
US/8/406	Ger.	Ortsgruppenleiter	Civilian	Ottmannhausen, Germany (2.-3.45)	Murder.	U.S.
US/8/407				St. Andreasberg, Harz, Germany, (3.3.45)	Murder. Aged about 45. Very thick, Horn rimmed, medium build, natural mean look, straight hair, deep lines from mouth to nose.	U.S.
US/8/408		Brigadefhr.	S.A.	Polangen, Lithuania (6.44)	Murder.	U.S.

9. NAZI PARTY MEMBERS - State Service, Gestapo, SD and Police.

C.R.FILE NO.	NATIO-NALITY	RANK OR STATUS	UNIT OR OCCUPATION	PLACE AND DATE OF CRIME	PARTICULARS OF CRIME OR REASON FOR WHICH WANTED FOLLOWED BY PHYSICAL DESCRIPTION IF KNOWN	WANTED BY
BEL/9/409	Ger.	Director	Prison	Siegburg, Germany	Illtreatment of Prisoners.	BEL.
BEL/9/410	Ger.	Director	Prison	Wolfenbuettel, Germany (44-45)	Torture.	BEL.
BEL/9/411	Ger.	Chief	Gestapo	Malmedy, Belgium (6.40-3.43)	Miscellaneous crimes.	BEL.
BEL/9/412	Ger.	Lt.	Geheime Feldpolizei	Brussels, Belgium (28.2.41-1.10.41)	Torture.	BEL.
BEL/9/413	Ger.	Governor	Prison	Ebrach, Bavaria (8.44-1.45)	Brutality.	BEL.
CAN/9/414		Chief	Gestapo	Paris, France (13.7.43)	Torture.	CAN.
CZECH/9/415	Ger.	7 Members	Gestapo, Con.Camp.	Oswiecim-Birkenau, Poland Nove Mesto-Vahom, Czechoslovakia, (39-45)	Murder.	CZECH.
CZECH/9/416	Ger.	18 Members	Gestapo, Con.Camp.	Oswiecim-Birkenau, Poland Trencin, Czechoslovakia (39-45)	Murder.	CZECH.
CZECH/9/417	Ger.	SS-Sgt., Member	Gestapo, Con.Camp.	Oswiecim-Birkenau, Poland Trencin, Czechoslovakia (39-45)	Murder.	CZECH.
CZECH/9/418	Ger.	All officials	Aussenstellen of the Staatspolizeistellen and Staatspolizeileitstellen, Con.Camp Oswiecim-Birkenau	Cesky, Krumlov, Kaplice, Ceske, Budejovice and Trebon, Czechoslovakia	Murder.	CZECH.
CZECH/9/419	Ger.	All officials	Aussenstellen of the Staatspolizeistellen and Staatspolizeileitstellen, Con.Camp, Ceske, Domazlice, Klatovy, Susice and Prachatice.	Con.Camp Oswiecim-Birkenau, Poland (39-45)	Murder.	CZECH.
CZECH/9/420	Ger.	All Regierungspraesidenten	Aussig	Con.Camp Oswiecim-Birkenau, Poland.(39-45)	Murder.	CZECH.
CZECH/9/421	Ger.	Chief	Sicherheitsdienst	Karlsbad, Karlovy Vary, Germany, Con.Camp Oswiecim-Birkenau, Poland (39-45)	Murder.	CZECH.
CZECH/9/422	Ger.	Staff	Of the Inspector of the Sicherheitspolice and the Sicherheitsdienst.	Reichsgau Sudetenland. Con.Camp Oswiecim-Birkenau, Poland (39-45)	Murder.	CZECH.
CZECH/9/423	Ger.	Staff	Of the Befehlshaber of the Sicherheitspolice in the Protectorate of Bohemia and Moravia.	Con.Camp Oswiecim-Birkenau, Poland (39-45)	Murder.	CZECH.
CZECH/9/424	Ger.	All Befehlshaber	Sicherheitspolizei in the Protectorate of Bohemia and Moravia.	Con.Camp Oswiecim-Birkenau, Poland (39-45)	Murder.	CZECH.
CZECH/9/425	Ger.	All officials, Kripo	Kriminalleitstellen and Kriminalpolizeistellen Sudetenland, Czechoslovakia, Poland	Con.Camp Oswiecim-Birkenau, Poland (39-45)	Murder. Massacres, systematic terrorism.	CZECH.
CZECH/9/426	Ger.	All officials, Kripo	Of other Kriminalpolizeileitstellen. Bohemia and Moravia, Czechoslovakia, Poland.	Con.Camp Oswiecim-Birkenau, Poland (39-45)	Murder. Massacres, systematic terrorism.	CZECH.

9. NAZI PARTY MEMBERS - State Service, Gestapo, SD and Police. (cont.)

C.R.FILE NO.	NATIO-NALITY	RANK OR STATUS	UNIT OR OCCUPATION	PLACE AND DATE OF CRIME	PARTICULARS OF CRIME OR REASON FOR WHICH WANTED FOLLOWED BY PHYSICAL DESCRIPTION IF KNOWN	WANTED BY
CZECH/9/427	Ger.	Head, civilian	Sportschule	Pretzsch, Czechoslovakia, Poland, Con.Camp Oswiecim-Birkenau, Poland (39-45)	Murder. Massacres, systematic terrorism.	CZECH.
CZECH/9/428	Ger.	All chiefs	Polizeipraesidien, Polizeidirektionen, Polizeiaemter.	Czechoslovakia, Poland, Hlucin Frystat, Cesky, Tesin, Con.Camp Oswiecim-Birkenau, Poland (39-45)	Murder. Massacres, systematic terrorism.	CZECH.
CZECH/9/429	Ger.	Regierungspraesidenten and their Deputies.	Public officials.	Hlucin, Frystat, Cesky, Tesin, Czechoslovakia, Poland, Con.Camp Oswiecim-Birkenau Poland (39-45)	Murder. Massacres, systematic terrorism.	CZECH.
CZECH/9/430	Ger.	All Oberlandraete, and Inspectors of the Reichsprotectors and their Deputies.		Con.Camp Oswiecim-Birkenau Poland (39-45)	Murder. Massacres, systematic terrorism.	CZECH.
CZECH/9/431	Ger.	All Regierungspraesidenten.	Karlouy, Vary.	Karlouy, Vary, Czechoslovakia Con.Camp Oswiecim-Birkenau Poland (39-45)	Murder. Massacres, systematic terrorism.	CZECH.
CZECH/9/432	Ger.	Regierungs-Vice-Praesidenten.		Karlouy, Vary, Czechoslovakia Con.Camp Oswiecim-Birkenau Poland (39-45)	Murder. Massacres, systematic terrorism.	CZECH.
CZECH/9/433	Ger.	Regierungspraesidenten.		Troppau, Czechoslovakia, Con.Camp Oswiecim-Birkenau Poland (39-45)	Murder. Massacres, systematic terrorism.	CZECH.
CZECH/9/434	Ger.	Deputies of the Regierungspraesidenten.		Troppau, Czechoslovakia, Con.Camp Oswiecim-Birkenau Poland (39-45)	Murder. Massacres, systematic terrorism.	CZECH.
CZECH/9/435	Ger.	Deputies of Reichsstatthalter.		Sudetenland, Czechoslovakia Con.Camp Oswiecim-Birkenau Poland (39-45)	Murder. Massacres, systematic terrorism.	CZECH.
CZECH/9/436	Ger.	Deputies of Regierungspraesidenten.		Aussig, Czechoslovakia Con.Camp Oswiecim-Birkenau Poland (39-45)	Murder. Massacres, systematic terrorism.	CZECH.
CZECH/9/437	Ger.	All officials	Of the Kriminalabt. of Staatliche Polizeiverwaltungen.	Bohemia and Moravia, Czechoslovakia, Con.Camp Oswiecim-Birkenau, Poland (39-45)	Murder. Massacres, systematic terrorism.	CZECH.
CZECH/9/438	Ger.	Staff	Of the Inspector of the Sicherheitspolizei and the Sicherheitsdienst.	Sudetenland, Czechoslovakia Con.Camp Oswiecim-Birkenau Poland (39-45)	Murder. Massacres, systematic terrorism.	CZECH.
CZECH/9/439	Ger.	All officials	Sicherheitsdienst Abschnitt	Karlouy Vary, Czechoslovakia Con.Camp Oswiecim-Birkenau Poland (39-45)	Murder. Massacres, systematic terrorism.	CZECH.
CZECH/9/440	Ger.	All officials	Sicherheitsdienst Leitabschnitt.	Liberec, Czechoslovakia Con.Camp Oswiecim-Birkenau Poland (39-45)	Murder. Massacres, systematic terrorism.	CZECH.
CZECH/9/441	Ger.		Sicherheitsdienst Abschnitt	Troppau, Czechoslovakia Con.Camp Oswiecim-Birkenau Poland (39-45)	Murder. Massacres, systematic terrorism.	CZECH.
CZECH/9/442	Ger.	All officials	Staatspolizeileitstellen	Liberec, Czechoslovakia Con.Camp Oswiecim-Birkenau Poland (39-45)	Murder. Massacres, systematic terrorism.	CZECH.
CZECH/9/443	Ger.	All officials	Of the Aussenstellen of the Staatspolizeileitstellen.	Liberec, Czechoslovakia Con.Camp Oswiecim-Birkenau Poland (39-45)	Murder. Massacres, systematic terrorism.	CZECH.
CZECH/9/444	Ger.	All officials	Staatspolizeistelle	Karlouy, Vary, Czechoslovakia Con.Camp Oswiecim-Birkenau Poland (39-45)	Murder. Massacres, systematic terrorism.	CZECH.
CZECH/9/445	Ger.	All officials	Of the Aussenstellen of the Staatspolizeileitstellen.	Karlouy, Vary, Czechoslovakia Con.Camp Oswiecim-Birkenau Poland (39-45)	Murder. Massacres, systematic terrorism.	CZECH.
CZECH/9/446	Ger.	All officials	Staatspolizeistelle.	Troppau, Czechoslovakia Con.Camp Oswiecim-Birkenau Poland (39-45)	Murder. Massacres, systematic terrorism.	CZECH.
CZECH/9/447	Ger.	All administrative officials	Of the Aussenstellen of the Staatspolizeistellen	Troppau, Czechoslovakia Con.Camp Oswiecim-Birkenau Poland (39-45)	Murder. Massacres, systematic terrorism.	CZECH.
CZECH/9/448	Ger.	All officials	Kriminalpolizeistellen	Liberes, Czechoslovakia Con.Camp Oswiecim-Birkenau Poland (39-45)	Murder. Massacres, systematic terrorism.	CZECH.
CZECH/9/449	Ger.	All officials	Kriminalpolizeistellen	Karlouy, Vary, Czechoslovakia Con.Camp Oswiecim-Birkenau Poland (39-45)	Murder. Massacres, systematic terrorism.	CZECH.
CZECH/9/450	Ger.	All officials	Kriminalpolizeistellen	Troppau, Czechoslovakia Con.Camp Oswiecim-Birkenau Poland (39-45)	Murder. Massacres, systematic terrorism.	CZECH.
CZECH/9/451	Ger.	All officials	Of the Kriminalabteilungen of the Staatlichen Polizeiverwaltungen.	Sudetenland, Czechoslovakia Con.Camp Oswiecim-Birkenau Poland (39-45)	Murder. Massacres, systematic terrorism.	CZECH.

9. NAZI PARTY MEMBERS - State Service, Gestapo, SD and Police.

C.R.FILE NO.	NATIO-NALITY	RANK OR STATUS	UNIT OR OCCUPATION	PLACE AND DATE OF CRIME	PARTICULARS OF CRIME OR REASON FOR WHICH WANTED FOLLOWED BY PHYSICAL DESCRIPTION IF KNOWN.	WANTED BY
CZECH/9/452	Ger.	Chief	Sicherheitsdienstabschnitt	Karlouy, Vary, Czechoslovakia Con.Camp Oswiecim-Birkenau, Poland (39-45)	Murder. Massacres, systematic terrorism.	CZECH.
CZECH/9/453	Ger.	All Praesidenten and their Deputies.	Police	Bruex, Czechoslovakas Con.Camp Oswiecim-Birkenau, Poland (39-45)	Murder. Massacres, systematic terrorism.	CZECH.
CZECH/9/454	Ger.	All Gestapo-officials	Staatspolizeileitstellen Staatspolizeistellen	Cesky Krumlov, Kaplice, Ceske Budejovice, Trebon, Czechoslovakia, Con.Camp Oswiecim-Birkenau, Poland (39-45)	Murder. Massacres, systematic terrorism.	CZECH.
CZECH/9/455	Ger.	All Befehlshaber	Ordnungspolizei	Bohemia-Moravia, Czechoslovakia, Con.Camp Oswiecim-Birkenau, Poland (39-45)	Murder. Massacres, systematic terrorism.	CZECH.
CZECH/9/456	Ger.	All Gestapo-officials	Aussenstellen of Staatspolizeileitstellen and Staatspolizeistellen.	Domazlice, Klatouy, Susice, Prachatice, Czechoslovakia Con.Camp Oswiecim-Birkenau, Poland (39-45)	Murder. Massacres, systematic terrorism.	CZECH.
CZECH/9/457	Ger.	All Gestapo-officials	Staatspolizeileitstellen and Staatspolizeistellen	Domazlice, Klatouy, Susice, Prachatice, Czechoslovakia Con.Camp Oswiecim-Birkenau, Poland (39-45)	Murder. Massacres, systematic terrorism.	CZECH.
CZECH/9/458	Ger.	All Gestapo-officials	Staatspolizeileitstelle	Prague, Czechoslovakia Con.Camp Oswiecim-Birkenau, Poland (39-45)	Murder. Massacres, systematic terrorism.	CZECH.
CZECH/9/459	Ger.	All Gestapo-officials	Staatspolizeileitstellen and Staatspolizeistellen	Hlucin, Frystat, Cesky Tesin, Czechoslovakia, Con.Camp Oswiecim-Birkenau, Poland (39-45)	Murder. Massacres, systematic terrorism.	CZECH.
CZECH/9/460	Ger.	All Chiefs	Polizeidirektionen, Polizeiaemter, Polizeipraesidien	Znojmo, Mikulou, Jindruchuv, Hradec, Dacice, Mor.Budejovice, Moravsky, Krumlov, Hustopec, Bratislava, Czechoslovakia, Con.Camp Oswiecim-Birkenau, Poland (39-45)	Murder. Massacres, systematic terrorism.	CZECH.
CZECH/9/461	Ger.	All Chief and Deputies	Verwaltungspolizei, Polizeipraesidien, Polizeidirektionen, Polizeiaemter	Domazlice, Klatouy, Susice, Prachatice, Czechoslovakia, Con.Camp Oswiecim-Birkenau, Poland (39-45)	Murder. Massacres, systematic terrorism.	CZECH.
CZECH/9/462	Ger.	All Chiefs	Polizeipraesidien, Polizeidirektionen, Polizeiaemter, Verwaltungspolizei	Cesky Krumlov, Kaplice, Ceske Budejovice, Trebon, Czechoslovakia, Con.Camp Oswiecim-Birkenau, Poland (39-45)	Murder. Massacres, systematic terrorism.	CZECH.
CZECH/9/463	Ger.	All Chiefs and their Deputies	Polizeipraesidien, Polizeidirektionen, Polizeiaemter	Bohemia and Moravia, Czechoslovakia, Con.Camp Oswiecim-Birkenau, Poland (39-45)	Murder. Massacres, systematic terrorism.	CZECH.
CZECH/9/464	Ger.	All Chiefs and their Deputies	Polizeipraesidien, Polizeidirektionen, Polizeiaemter	Sudetenland, Czechoslovakia, Con.Camp Oswiecim-Birkenau, Poland (39-45)	Murder. Massacres, systematic terrorism.	CZECH.
CZECH/9/465	Ger.	All Kripo officials	Kriminalpolizeileitstellen, Kriminalpolizeistellen	Domazlice, Klatouy, Susice, Prachatice, Czechoslovakia Con.Camp Oswiecim-Birkenau, Poland (39-45)	Murder. Massacres, systematic terrorism.	CZECH.
CZECH/9/466	Ger.	All Kripo officials	Kriminalpolizeileitstellen, Kriminalpolizeistellen	Cesky Krumlov, Kaplice, Ceske Budejovice, Trebon, Czechoslovakia, Con.Camp Oswiecim-Birkenau, Poland (39-45)	Murder. Massacres, systematic terrorism.	CZECH.
CZECH/9/467	Ger.	All Kripo officials	Kriminalpolizeileitstellen, Kriminalpolizeistellen	Znojmo, Mikulov, Jindrichuv, Hrades, Dacice, Mor.Budejovice, Moravsky, Krumlov, Hustopec, Bratislava, Czechoslovakia, Con.Camp Oswiecim-Birkenau, Poland (39-45)	Murder. Massacres, systematic terrorism.	CZECH.
CZECH/9/468	Ger.	All Kripo officials	Kriminalpolizeileitstellen, Kriminalpolizeistellen	Hlucin, Frystat, Cesky Tesin, Czechoslovakia, Con.Camp Oswiecim-Birkenau, Poland (39-45)	Murder. Massacres, systematic terrorism.	CZECH.
CZECH/9/469	Ger.	All Chiefs	Kriminalpolizeistellen Kriminalpolizeileitstellen	Bohemia and Moravia, Czechoslovakia, Con.Camp Oswiecim-Birkenau, Poland (39-45)	Murder. Massacres, systematic terrorism.	CZECH.
CZECH/9/470	Ger.	All Gestapo-officials	Kriminalabteilungen	Cesky Krumlov, Kaplice, Ceske Budejovice, Trebon, Czechoslovakia, Con.Camp Oswiecim-Birkenau, Poland (39-45)	Murder. Massacres, systematic terrorism.	CZECH.

9. NAZI PARTY MEMBERS - State Service, Gestapo, SD and Police. (cont.)

C.R.FILE NO.	NATIO-NALITY	RANK OR STATUS	UNIT OR OCCUPATION	PLACE AND DATE OF CRIME	PARTICULARS OF CRIME OR REASON FOR WHICH WANTED FOLLOWED BY PHYSICAL DESCRIPTION IF KNOWN.	WANTED BY
CZECH/9/471	Ger.	All Inspectors	Sicherheitspolizei and Sicherheitsdienst	Sudetenland, Czechoslovakia Con.Camp Oswiecim-Birkenau, Poland (39-45)	Murder. Massacres, systematic terrorism.	CZECH.
CZECH/9/472	Ger.	Chief	Sicherheitsdienstabschnitt	Troppau, Czechoslovakia Con.Camp Oswiecim-Birkenau, Poland (39-45)	Murder. Massacres, systematic terrorism.	CZECH.
CZECH/9/473	Ger.	All Inspectors	Ordnungspolizei	Sudetenland, Czechoslovakia Con.Camp Oswiecim-Birkenau, Poland (39-45)	Murder. Massacres, systematic terrorism.	CZECH.
CZECH/9/474	Ger.	Head	Of school of the Sicherheitspolizei und des Sicherheitsdienstes.	Prague, Czechoslovakia Con.Camp Oswiecim-Birkenau, Poland (39-45)	Murder. Massacres, systematic terrorism.	CZECH.
CZECH/9/475	Ger.	Head	Of Sicherheitsdienst-school	Bernau, Czechoslovakia Con.Camp Oswiecim-Birkenau, Poland (39-45)	Murder. Massacres, systematic terrorism.	CZECH.
CZECH/9/476	Ger.	All Stapo officials	Staatspolizeileitstellen, Staatspolizeistellen	Znojmo, Mikulov, Jindrichuv, Hrade, Dacice, Moravsky, Krumlov, Hustopec, Bratislava, Czechoslovakia, Con.Camp Oswiecim-Birkenau, Poland (39-45)	Murder. Massacres, systematic terrorism.	CZECH.
CZECH/9/477	Ger.	Staff	Of the Befehlshaber of the Sicherheitspolizei	Bohemia and Moravia, Czechoslovakia Con.Camp Oswiecim-Birkenau, Poland (39-45)	Murder. Massacres, systematic terrorism.	CZECH.
CZECH/9/478	Ger.	All Befehlshaber	Sicherheitspolizei	Bohemia and Moravia, Czechoslovakia, Con.Camp Oswiecim-Birkenau, Poland (39-45)	Murder. Massacres, systematic terrorism.	CZECH.
CZECH/9/479	Ger.	All Gestapo-officials	Aussenstellen of Staatspolizeileitstellen and Polizeistellen	Hlucin, Frystat, Cesky Tesin, Czechoslovakia, Con.Camp Oswiecim-Birkenau, Poland (39-45)	Murder. Massacres, systematic terrorism.	CZECH.
CZECH/9/480	Ger.	All Gestapo-officials	Aussenstellen of the Staatspolizeileitstellen, Staatspolizeistellen	Znojmo, Mikulov, Jindrichuv, Hradec, Hustopec, Bratislava, Dacice, Mor, Budejovice, Moravsky, Krumlov, Czechoslovakia, Con.Camp Oswiecim-Birkenau, Poland (39-45)	Murder. Massacres, systematic terrorism.	CZECH.
CZECH/9/481	Ger.	All Gestapo-officials	Aussenstellen of the Staatspolizeileitstellen, Staatspolizeistellen	Cesky Krumlov, Kaplice, Ceske Budejovice, Trebon, Czechoslovakia, Con.Camp Oswiecim-Birkenau, Poland (39-45)	Murder. Massacres, systematic terrorism.	CZECH.
CZECH/9/482	Ger.	All officials	Kriminalabteilung of the Polizeidirektion	Moravska, Ostrava, Czechoslovakia, Con.Camp Oswiecim-Birkenau, Poland (39-45)	Murder. Massacres, systematic terrorism.	CZECH.
CZECH/9/483	Ger.	All officials	Kriminalabteilung of the Polizeidirektion	Olomduc, Czechoslovakia, Con.Camp Oswiecim-Birkenau, Poland (39-45)	Murder. Massacres, systematic terrorism.	CZECH.
CZECH/9/484	Ger.	All officials	Kriminalabteilung	Aussig, Czechoslovakia Con.Camp Oswiecim-Birkenau, Poland (39-45)	Murder. Massacres, systematic terrorism.	CZECH.
CZECH/9/485	Ger.	All officials	Kriminalabteilung	Bruex, Czechoslovakia, Con.Camp Oswiecim-Birkenau, Poland (39-45)	Murder. Massacres, systematic terrorism.	CZECH.
CZECH/9/486	Ger.	All officials	Kriminalabteilung of the Polizeidirektion	Plzen, Czechoslovakia, Con.Camp Oswiecim-Birkenau, Poland (39-45)	Murder. Massacres, systematic terrorism.	CZECH.
CZECH/9/487	Ger.	Chief	Sicherheitsdienstleit-abschnitt	Prague, Czechoslovakia, Con.Camp Oswiecim-Birkenau, Poland (39-45)	Murder. Massacres, systematic terrorism.	CZECH.
CZECH/9/488	Ger.	All Kripo officials	Kriminalpolizeileitstelle	Prague, Czechoslovakia, Con.Camp Oswiecim-Birkenau, Poland (39-45)	Murder. Massacres, systematic terrorism.	CZECH.
CZECH/9/489	Ger.	All officials	Aussenstellen of the Staatspolizeileit-stellen	Prague, Czechoslovakia, Con.Camp Oswiecim-Birkenau, Poland (39-45)	Murder. Massacres, systematic terrorism.	CZECH.
CZECH/9/490	Ger.	All Gestapo officials	Staatspolizeileitstelle	Brno, Czechoslovakia, Con.Camp Oswiecim-Birkenau, Poland (39-45)	Murder. Massacres, systematic terrorism.	CZECH.
CZECH/9/491	Ger.	All officials	Kriminalabteilung of the Polizeidirektion	Brno, Czechoslovakia, Con.Camp Oswiecim-Birkenau, Poland (39-45)	Murder. Massacres, systematic terrorism.	CZECH.

9. NAZI PARTY MEMBERS - State Service, Gestapo, SD and Police, (cont.)

C.R.FILE NO.	NATIO-NALITY	RANK OR STATUS	UNIT OR OCCUPATION	PLACE AND DATE OF CRIME	PARTICULARS OF CRIME OR REASON FOR WHICH WANTED FOLLOWED BY PHYSICAL DESCRIPTION IF KNOWN	WANTED BY
CZECH/9/492	Ger.	All Stapo officials	Aussenstellen of the Staatspolizeistelle, Staatspolizei-leitstelle	Brno, Czechoslovakia, Con.Camp Oswiecim-Birkenau, Poland (39-45)	Murder. Massacres, systematic terrorism.	CZECH.
CZECH/9/493	Ger.	All Inspectors	Ordnungs polizei	Reichsgau Oberdonau, Austria, Con.Camp Oswiecim-Birkenau, Poland (39-45)	Murder. Massacres, systematic terrorism.	CZECH.
CZECH/9/494	Ger.	All Inspectors	Ordnungspolizei	Reichsgau Niederdonau, Austria, Con.Camp Oswiecim-Birkenau, Poland (39-45)	Murder. Massacres, systematic terrorism.	CZECH.
CZECH/9/495	Ger.	All hoeheren SS- und Polizeifhr.		XVII, Vienna, Austria, Con.Camp Oswiecim-Birkenau, Poland (39-45)	Murder. Massacres, systematic terrorism.	CZECH.
CZECH/9/496	Ger.	Staff, Sipo officials	Of the Inspectors of the Sicherheitspolizei, Sicherheitsdienst	XVII, Vienna, Austria, Con.Camp Oswiecim-Birkenau, Poland (39-45)	Murder. Massacres, systematic terrorism.	CZECH.
CZECH/9/497	Ger.	Inspectors	Sicherheitspolizei, Sicherheitsdienst	XVII, Vienna, Austria, Con.Camp Oswiecim-Birkenau, Poland (39-45)	Murder. Massacres, systematic terrorism.	CZECH.
CZECH/9/498	Ger.	All hoeheren SS- und Polizeifhr.		XVII, Salzburg, Austria, Con.Camp Oswiecim-Birkenau, Poland (39-45)	Murder. Massacres, systematic terrorism.	CZECH.
CZECH/9/499	Ger.	Inspectors	Sicherheitspolizei, Sicherheitsdienst	Reichsgau Oberdonau, Austria, Con.Camp Oswiecim-Birkenau, Poland (39-45)	Murder. Massacres, systematic terrorism.	CZECH.
CZECH/9/500	Ger.	Staff, Sipo official	Of the Inspectors of the Sicherheitspolizei, Sicherheitsdienst	Reichsgau Oberdonau, Austria, Con.Camp Oswiecim-Birkenau, Poland (39-45)	Murder. Massacres, systematic terrorism.	CZECH.
CZECH/9/501	Ger.	All Reichsstatthalter and their Deputies	Public officials	Reichsgau Oberdonau, Austria, Con.Camp Oswiecim-Birkenau, Poland (39-45)	Murder. Massacres, systematic terrorism.	CZECH.
CZECH/9/502	Ger.	All Reichsstatthalter and their Deputies	Public officials	Reichsgau Niederdonau, Austria, Con.Camp Oswiecim-Birkenau, Poland (39-45)	Murder. Massacres, systematic terrorism.	CZECH.
CZECH/9/503	Ger.	General-Inspectors	Schutzpolizei of the Reich. Reichsministerium des Inneren	Con.Camp Oswiecim-Birkenau, Poland (39-45)	Murder. Massacres, systematic terrorism.	CZECH.
CZECH/9/504	Ger.	Inspectors	Public-official, Ministry of Interior, Weltanschauliche Erziehung, Reichsministerium des Inneren.	Con.Camp Oswiecim-Birkenau, Poland (39-45)	Murder. Massacres, systemaito terrorism.	CZECH.
CZECH/9/505	Ger.	General-Inspectors	Gendarmerie, Schutzpolizei d. Gemeinden, Reichsministerium des Inneren.	Con.Camp Oswiecim-Birkenau, Poland (39-45)	Murder. Massacres, systematic terrorism.	CZECH.
CZECH/9/506	Ger.	General-Inspectors	Polizeischulen, Reichsministerium des Inneren	Con.Camp Oswiecim-Birkenau, Poland (39-45)	Murder. Massacres, systematic terrorism.	CZECH.
CZECH/9/507	Ger.	General-Inspectors	Feuerschutzpolizei, Reichsministerium des Inneren	Con.Camp Oswiecim-Birkenau, Poland (39-45)	Murder. Massacres, systematic terrorism.	CZECH.
CZECH/9/508	Ger.	All chiefs / All chiefs and officials	of the SS-Wirtschafts- and Verwaltungshauptamt of the Amtsgruppe D	Con.Camp Oswiecim-Birkenau, Poland (39-45)	Murder. Massacres, systematic terrorism.	CZECH.
CZECH/9/509	Ger.	Oberpraesidenten and their Deputies	Public-official, Occupied Territories Poland	Oberschlesien Con.Camp Oswiecim-Birkenau, Poland (39-45)	Murder. Massacres, systematic terrorism.	CZECH.
CZECH/9/510	Ger.	Chief, Hauptmann	Hauptamt Ordnungspolizei in the Reichsministerium des Inneren.	Con.Camp Oswiecim-Birkenau, Poland (39-45)	Murder. Massacres, systematic terrorism.	CZECH.
CZECH/9/511	Ger.	All Inspectors	Sicherheitsdienst, Sicherheitspolizei	Oberschlesien Con.Camp Oswiecim-Birkenau, Poland (39-45)	Murder. Massacres, systematic terrorism.	CZECH.
CZECH/9/512	Ger.	All hoeheren SS-Polizeifhr.	Wehrkreis Bohemia and Moravia.	Con.Camp Oswiecim-Birkenau, Poland (39-45)	Murder. Massacres, systematic terrorism.	CZECH.
CZECH/9/513	Ger.	Head	Sicherheitspolizei-schule	Con.Camp Oswiecim-Birkenau, Poland (39-45)	Murder. Massacres, systematic terrorism.	CZECH.
CZECH/9/514	Ger.	All Inspectors	Ordnungspolizei	Oberschlesien, Con.Camp Oswiecim-Birkenau, Poland (39-45)	Murder. Massacres, systematic terrorism.	CZECH.
CZECH/9/515	Ger.	All Deputies of Reichsstatthalter	Public-officials	Land Bayern, Con.Camp Oswiecim-Birkenau, Poland (39-45)	Murder. Massacres, systematic terrorism.	CZECH.
CZECH/9/516	Ger.	All Inspectors	Ordnungspolizei	Land Bayern, Con.Camp Oswiecim-Birkenau, Poland (39-45)	Murder. Massacres, systematic terrorism.	CZECH.
CZECH/9/517	Ger.	Staff	Of the Polizeiinspectors Sicherheitspolizei, Sicherheitsdienst	Oberschlesien, Con.Camp Oswiecim-Birkenau, Poland (39-45)	Murder. Massacres, systematic terrorism.	CZECH.
CZECH/9/518	Ger.	All officials	Reichssicherheitshauptamt	Con.Camp Oswiecim-Birkenau, Poland (39-45)	Murder. Massacres, systematic terrorism.	CZECH.
CZECH/9/518	Ger.	All officials	Reichssicherheitshauptamt	Con.Camp Oswiecim-Birkenau, Poland (39-45)	Murder. Massacres, systematic terrorism.	CZECH.

9. NAZI PARTY MEMBERS - State Service, Gestapo, SD and Police. (Cont.)

M.R.FILE NO.	NATIO-NALITY	RANK OR STATUS	UNIT OR OCCUPATION	PLACE AND DATE OF CRIME	PARTICULARS OF CRIME OR REASON FOR WHICH WANTED FOLLOWED BY PHYSICAL DESCRIPTION IF KNOWN	WANTED BY
CZECH/9/519	Ger.	Chief	Sicherheitspolizei, Sicherheitsdienst, Reichsfhr.-SS	Con.Camp Oswiecim-Birkenau, Poland (39-45)	Murder. Massacres, systematic terrorism.	CZECH.
CZECH/9/520	Ger.	Unterstaatssekretaer, Successor to Dr. von Borgsdorf	Public-official, Occupied Territories Poland	Con.Camp Oswiecim-Birkenau, Poland (39-45)	Murder. Massacres, systematic terrorism.	CZECH.
CZECH/9/521	Ger.	Head of Fuehrerschule	Sicherheitspolizei, Sicherheitsdienst	Berlin-Charlottenburg, Germany, Con.Camp Oswiecim-Birkenau, Poland (39-45)	Murder. Massacres, systematic terrorism.	CZECH.
CZECH/9/522	Ger.	All hoeheren SS- and Polizeifhr.		Nuernberg, Germany, Con.Camp Oswiecim-Birkenau, Poland (39-45)	Murder. Massacres, systematic terrorism.	CZECH.
CZECH/9/523	Ger.	All Regierungspraesidenten and their Deputies.	Public-officials	Domazlice, Klatouy, Susice, Prachatice, Czechoslovakia, Con.Camp Oswiecim-Birkenau, Poland (39-45)	Murder. Massacres, systematic terrorism.	CZECH.
CZECH/9/524	Ger.	All Regierungspraesidenten and their Deputies.	Public-officials, Occupied Territories Poland	Znojmo, Mikulov, Jindrichuv, Hradec, Dacicie, Mor, Budejovice, Moravsky, Krumlov, Hustopec, Bratislava, Czechoslovakia, Con.Camp Oswiecim-Birkenau, Poland (39-45)	Murder. Massacres, systematic terrorism.	CZECH.
CZECH/9/525	Ger.	All Regierungspraesidenten		Aussig, Czechoslovakia, Con.Camp Oswiecim-Birkenau, Poland (39-45)	Murder. Massacres, systematic terrorism.	CZECH.
CZECH/9/526	Ger.	All officials	Sicherheitsdienst Leitschnitt, Sicherheitsdienst Abschnitt	Cesky Krumlov, Kaplice, Ceske Budejovice, Czechoslovakia, Con.Camp Oswiecim-Birkenau, Poland (39-45)	Murder. Massacres, systematic terrorism.	CZECH.
CZECH/9/527	Ger.	All officials	Sicherheitsdienst Leitabschnitt, Sicherheitsdienst Abschnitt	Bohemia and Moravia, Czechoslovakia, Con.Camp Oswiecim-Birkenau, Poland (39-45)	Murder. Massacres, systematic terrorism.	CZECH.
CZECH/9/528	Ger.	All officials	Sicherheitsdienst Leitabsch.	Prague, Czechoslovakia, Con.Camp Oswiecim-Birkenau, Poland (39-45)	Murder. Massacres, systematic terrorism.	CZECH.
CZECH/9/529	Ger.	All officials	Sicherheitsdienst Leitabschnitt, Sicherheitsdienst Abschnitt	Domazlice, Klatouy, Susice, Prachatice, Czechoslovakia, Con.Camp Oswiecim-Birkenau, Poland (39-45)	Murder. Massacres, systematic terrorism.	CZECH.
CZECH/9/530	Ger.	All Chiefs	Sicherheitsdienst Leitabschnitt, Sicherheitsdienst Abschnitt	Znojmo, Mikulov, Jindrichuv, Hradec, Dacice, Mor, Budejovice, Moravsky, Krumlov, Hustopec, Bratislava, Czechoslovakia, Con.Camp Oswiecim-Birkenau, Poland (39-45)	Murder. Massacres, systematic terrorism.	CZECH.
CZECH/9/531	Ger.	All officials	Sicherheitsdienst Leitabschnitt, Sicherheitsdienst Abschnitt	Znojmo, Mikulov, Jindrichuv, Hradec, Dacice, Mor, Budejovice, Moravsky, Krumlov, Hustopec, Bratislava, Czechoslovakia, Con.Camp Oswiecim-Birkenau, Poland (39-45)	Murder. Massacres, systematic terrorism.	CZECH.
CZECH/9/532	Ger.	All officials	Sicherheitsdienst Leitabschnitt, Sicherheitsdienst Abschnitt	Hlucin, Frystat, Cesky Tesin, Czechoslovakia, Con.Camp Oswiecim-Birkenau, Poland (39-45)	Murder. Massacres, systematic terrorism.	CZECH.
CZECH/9/533	Ger.	All Chiefs	Sicherheitsdienst Leitabschnitt, Sicherheitsdienst Abschnitt	Cesky Krumlov, Kaplice, Ceske Budejovice, Czechoslovakia, Con.Camp Oswiecim-Birkenau, Poland (39-45)	Murder. Massacres, systematic terrorism.	CZECH.
CZECH/9/534	Ger.	All Chiefs	Sicherheitsdienst Leitabschnitt, Sicherheitsdienst Abschnitt	Hlucin, Frystat, Cesky Tesin, Czechoslovakia, Con.Camp Oswiecim-Birkenau, Poland (39-45)	Murder. Massacres, systematic terrorism.	CZECH.
CZECH/9/535	Ger.	All Chiefs	Sicherheitsdienst Leitabschnitt, Sicherheitsdienst Abschnitt	Domazlice, Klatouy, Prachatice Czechoslovakia, Con.Camp Oswiecim-Birkenau, Poland (39-45)	Murder. Massacres, systematic terrorism.	CZECH.
CZECH/9/536	Ger.	All officials	Kriminalabteilungen of the Staatlichen Polizeiverwaltungen	Hlucin, Frystat, Cesky Tesin, Czechoslovakia, Con.Camp Oswiecim-Birkenau, Poland (39-45)	Murder. Massacres, systematic terrorism.	CZECH.
CZECH/9/537	Ger.	All officials	Kriminalabteilungen of the Staatlichen Polizeiverwaltungen	Domazlice, Klatouy, Susice, Prachatice, Czechoslovakia, Con.Camp Oswiecim-Birkenau, Poland (39-45)	Murder. Massacres, systematic terrorism.	CZECH.

9. NAZI PARTY MEMBERS - State Service, Gestapo, SD and Police. (Cont.)

C.R.FILE NO.	NATIO-NALITY	RANK OR STATUS	UNIT OR OCCUPATION	PLACE AND DATE OF CRIME	PARTICULARS OF CRIME OR REASON FOR WHICH WANTED FOLLOWED BY PHYSICAL DESCRIPTION IF KNOWN	WANTED BY
CZECH/9/538	Ger.	All Gestapo officials	Kriminalabteilungen of the Staatlichen Polizeiverwaltungen	Znojmo, Mikulov, Jindrichuv, Hradec, Dacice, Mor. Budejovice, Moravsky, Krumlov, Hustopec, Bratislava, Czechoslovakia, Con.Camp Oswiecim-Birkenau, Poland (39-45)	Murder. Massacres, systematic terrorism.	CZECH.
CZECH/9/539	Ger.	All Polizeidirektoren and their Deputies	Police	Karlovy Vary, Czechoslovakia, Con.Camp Oswiecim-Birkenau, Poland (39-45)	Murder. Massacres, systematic terrorism.	CZECH.
CZECH/9/540	Ger.	All Polizeidirektoren and their Deputies	Police	Troppau, Czechoslovakia, Con.Camp Oswiecim-Birkenau, Poland (39-45)	Murder. Massacres, systematic terrorism.	CZECH.
CZECH/9/541	Ger.	All Polizeipraesidenten and their Deputies	Police	Brno, Czechoslovakia, Con.Camp Oswiecim-Birkenau, Poland (39-45)	Murder. Massacres, systematic terrorism.	CZECH.
CZECH/9/542	Ger.	All Polizeipraesidenten and their Deputies	Police	Aussig, Czechoslovakia, Con.Camp Oswiecim-Birkenau, Poland (39-45)	Murder. Massacres, systematic terrorism.	CZECH.
CZECH/9/543	Ger.	All Polizeipraesidenten and their Deputies	Police	Liberec, Czechoslovakia, Con.Camp Oswiecim-Birkenau, Poland (39-45)	Murder. Massacres, systematic terrorism.	CZECH.
CZECH/9/544	Ger.	All Polizeipraesidenten and their Deputies	Police	Moravska, Ostrava, Czechoslovakia, Con.Camp Oswiecim-Birkenau, Poland (39-45)	Murder. Massacres, systematic terrorism.	CZECH.
CZECH/9/545	Ger.	All Polizeipraesidenten and their Deputies	Police	Olomouc, Czechoslovakia, Con.Camp Oswiecim-Birkenau, Poland (39-45)	Murder. Massacres, systematic terrorism.	CZECH.
CZECH/9/546	Ger.	All Polizeipraesidenten and their Deputies	Police	Zlzen, Czechoslovakia, Con.Camp Oswiecim-Birkenau, Poland (39-45)	Murder. Massacres, systematic terrorism.	CZECH.
CZECH/9/547	Ger.	All Polizeipraesidenten and their Deputies	Police	Prague, Czechoslovakia, Con.Camp Oswiecim-Birkenau, Poland (39-45)	Murder. Massacres, systematic terrorism.	CZECH.
CZECH/9/548	Ger.	Chief	Sicherheitsdienst Leitabschnitte	Liberec, Czechoslovakia, Con.Camp Oswiecim-Birkenau, Poland (39-45)	Murder. Massacres, systematic terrorism.	CZECH.
FR/9/549	Ger.	Capt.	Gestapo	Perigueux, Auriac-de-Perigord France (30-3-44)	Murder. Unknown, first name "Hans" comes from Innsbruck Austria.	FR.
FR/9/550	Ger.	Sturmbannfhr. spec. Agent of Straub, Head	Gestapo	Breendonck, Brussels, Belgium (1944)	Murder. Home is in Antwerp. Born 1903, height 1.72m, fat round figure, bent slightly forward full oval face, brown hair, dark eyes, speaks French, Flemish, and German with a Flemish accent. Said to have gone to Germany after liberation.	FR.
FR/9/551	Ger.	German Director.	Women's prison	La Petite Roquette, France (1943)	Torture.	FR.
FR/9/552	Ger.	Chief	Gestapo	Lyons, France, (1.43, 1.44, 4. and 8.44)	Murder.	FR.
FR/9/553	Ger.	Chief	German Police	Haute, Savoie, France, (1.44 3. and 4.44)	Pillage.	FR.
FR/9/554	Ger.	Chief	Gestapo	Grenoble District, France (11.12.1942)	Murder.	FR.
FR/9/555	Ger.	Chief	Gestapo	Con.Camp Neubrenn, Saar, Germany, (1943-1944)	Miscellaneous crimes.	FR.
FR/9/556	Ger.	Chief	Gestapo	Eure-et-Loir, France (12.43-3.44)	Murder.	FR.
FR/9/557	Ger.	Chief	Of German Security Police	Clermont-Ferrand, France (24.2.1944)	Murder.	FR.
FR/9/558	Ger.	Chief	Gestapo	Clermont-Ferrand, France (11.43, 2.3.4. and 7.1944)	Murder.	FR.
FR/9/559	Ger.	Member	Of executive personnel, Gestapo	St.Martin de Nigelle, Chartres, France, (8. and 14.12.1943)	Murder.	FR.
FR/9/560	Ger.	Members	Of Gestapo	Poitiers, France (12.6.44)	Murder.	FR.
FR/9/561	Ger.	Commandant	Gestapo	Maisons Lafitte, France (7.-8.1943)	Torture.	FR.
FR/9/562	Ger.	Chief	Gestapo	Luebeck, Germany (between 20.4.44 and 1.5.44)	Murder.	FR.
FR/9/563	Ger.	Kreisleiter		Loerrach, Germany (1944)	Brutality.	FR.
FR/9/564	Ger.	Kreisleiter		Lahr, Germany (1944)	Brutality.	FR.
FR/9/565	Ger.	Kreisleiter		Kehl, Germany (1944)	Brutality.	FR.
FR/9/566	Ger.	Kreisleiter		Heidelberg, Germany (1944)	Brutality.	FR.
FR/9/567	Ger.	Kreisleiter		Donaueschingen, Germany (1944)	Brutality.	FR.
FR/9/568	Ger.	Kreisleiter		Muehlheim, Germany (1944)	Brutality.	FR.

9. NAZI PARTY MEMBERS - State Service, Gestapo, SD and Police. (Cont.)

C.R.FILE NO.	NATIO-NALITY	RANK OR STATUS	UNIT OR OCCUPATION	PLACE AND DATE OF CRIME	PARTICULARS OF CRIME OR REASON FOR WHICH WANTED FOLLOWED BY PHYSICAL DESCRIPTION IF KNOWN	WANTED BY
FR/9/568	Ger.	Kreisleiter		Muehlheim, Germany (1944)	Brutality.	FR.
FR/9/569	Ger.	Kreisleiter		Zabern, Germany (1944)	Brutality.	FR.
FR/9/570	Ger.	Kreisleiter		Strassburg, Germany (1944)	Brutality.	FR.
FR/9/571	Ger.	Kreisleiter		Kolmar, Germany (1944)	Brutality.	FR.
FR/9/572	Ger.	Kreisleiter		Stockach, Germany (1944)	Brutality.	FR.
FR/9/573	Ger.	Kreisleiter		Sinsheim, Germany (1944)	Brutality.	FR.
FR/9/574	Ger.	Kreisleiter		Saeckingen, Germany (1944)	Brutality.	FR.
FR/9/575	Ger.	Kreisleiter		Rastatt, Germany (1944)	Brutality.	FR.
FR/9/576	Ger.	Kreisleiter		Buchen, Germany (1944)	Brutality.	FR.
FR/9/577	Ger.	Governor	Sedan Prison	(8.-10.40, 3.-4.41)	Murder.	FR.
FR/9/578	Ger.	Customs-Officer		Le Cap Ferret, France (8.1944)	Murder.	FR.
FR/9/579	Ger.	Chief	Gestapo	Vesoul, France (27.7.44)	Murder.	FR.
FR/9/780	Ger.	Military Governor and Chief	Gestapo	Strassbourg, France (7.43)	Murder.	FR.
FR/9/581	Ger.	Chief	Gestapo	St. Etienne, France, (12.43, 2.44)	Murder.	FR.
FR/9/582	Ger.	Chief	Gestapo	Lyon, France (7.-8.44)	Murder.	FR.
FR/9/583	Ger.	SS and SD-leader	SS and SD	Lublin, Poland (40-44)	Murder. May be Globotschnik	FR.
FR/9/584	Ger.	Chief	Gestapo	Chambery, France (1.-6.5.1944)	Torture.	FR.
FR/9/585	Ger.	Chief	Gestapo	Tours, France (3.-4.8.44)	Murder.	FR.
FR/9/586	Ger.	Chief	Gestapo	Savoy, France (8.-9.1944)	Murder.	FR.
FR/9/587	Ger.	Chief	Gestapo	Nice, France (7.7.44)	Murder. Probably Keil	FR.
FR/9/588	Ger.	Chief	SD	Lyon, France (8.1944)	Murder.	FR.
FR/9/589	Ger.	Chief	Gestapo	Rennes, France (7. and 8.44)	Murder.	FR.
FR/9/590	Ger.	Chief	Gestapo	Caen, France (6.6.44)	Murder.	FR.
FR/9/591	Ger.	Chief	Gestapo	Ain, France (16.6.44)	Murder.	FR.
FR/9/592	Ger.	Warder	Prison	Wolfach, Black forest, Germany	Constant illtreatment of prisoners and letting them starve to death. First name Otto.	FR.
FR/9/593	Ger.	Member	Gestapo	Toulouse, France, South-west France, (11.42-8.44)	Murder. Torture, deportation, lootings, destructions of civilian property, detention of civilians under inhuman conditions. First name Volker.	FR.
FR/9/594	Ger.	SS-trooper, staunch nazi.	Gestapo, N.S.D.A.P.	Grenoble, France (43-44)	Mass murder and other crimes. Alias; Jose Born 1915 height 1.70m	FR.
FR/9/595		Member	Gestapo	Limoges, France (4.1944)	Murder.	FR.
FR/9/596	Ger.	Officers, N.C.O.'s. Agents.	Gestapo Angers	St.Sulpice, Fortmusson Chateau Gontier, France (31.7.-6.8.1944)	Torture. Complicity in arresting, torturing and savagely, executing eleven French civilians.	FR.
FR/9/597	Ger.	Policeman		Grossen-Linden, Hessen-Nassau Germany (12.44)	Murder of P.O.W., Monsenergue of Kdo. 1270 of Stalag 9 A.	FR.
FR/9/598	Ger.	Policeman	Gestapo Tiefenau	Tiefenau, Germany (20-3 45)	Murder of P.O.W., Courtesaire of Stalag 4 A. Born circa 1905. Height 1.68m	FR.
FR/9/599		Subordinates	Feldgendarmerie and Gestapo of Melun.	Fontainebleau, Melun, France (24.7.44)	Murder and other crimes.	FR.
FR/9/600	Ger.	Commandant	Prison	Diez-Lahn, Germany (17.3.45)	Responsible for the death of P.O.W. Thuau, Jean Georges Marie, through starvation and illtreatment	FR.
NOR/9/601	Ger.	Gebietskommissar	Arbeitslager Finmark	Narvik, Norway (1944)	Systematic terrorism and other crimes.	NOR.
NOR/9/602	Ger.	Gebietskommissar	Arbeitslager Finmark	Narvik, Norway (10.-11.44)	Systematic terrorism and other crimes.	NOR.
NOR/9/603	Ger.	Doctor	Wuehlbuettel prison	Hamburg, Germany	Murder of Norwegians and Danes.	NOR.

9. NAZI PARTY MEMBERS - State Service, Gestapo, SD and Police. (Cont.)

C.R.FILE NO.	NATIO-NALITY	RANK OR STATUS	UNIT OR OCCUPATION	PLACE AND DATE OF CRIME	PARTICULARS OF CRIME OR REASON FOR WHICH WANTED FOLLOWED BY PHYSICAL DESCRIPTION IF KNOWN	WANTED BY
POL/9/604	Ger.	Chiefs	Police, Gestapo and SS	Obrzycko (1939-1942)	Murder.	POL.
POL/9/605	Ger.	Chiefs	Police, Gestapo and SS	Gostyn (1939-1942)	Murder.	POL.
POL/9/606	Ger.	Head	Ger. Civ. Administration	District of Tuchel (21.and 22.10.1939)	Murder.	POL.
POL/9/607	Ger.	Leader der	Abt. Forsten, Amt des Reichsstatthalters	Jau Wartheland (9.1939-44)	Pillage.	POL.
POL/9/608	Ger.	Leader der	Abt. Forsten, Amt des Reichsstatthalters	Gau Danzig, Westpreussen (9.1939-to the end of 1944)	Pillage.	POL.
POL/9/609	Ger.	Chief	Police, Gestapo and SS	Barcin, Poland (39-42)	Deportation of civilians; execution of persons without trial.	POL.
POL/9/610	Ger.	Chief	Police, Gestapo and SS	Bogomin (1939-1942)	Deportation of civilians illtreatment and torture of internees torture of internees causing death violation of art.46 Hague convention (1907)	POL.
POL/9/611	Ger.	Chief	Gestapo	Borek, Poland (1939-1942)	Deportation of civilian; execution of persons without trial.	POL.
POL/9/612	Ger.	Leader	Treuhandstelle	Lodz, Poland (9.1939-to the end of 1944)	Confiscation of property.	POL.
POL/9/613	Ger.	Reichsofficial	Sondertreuhaender	Danzig (9.1939-to the end of 1944)	Confiscation of property.	POL.
POL/9/614	Ger.	Reichsofficial	Sondertreuhaender	Gau Oberschlesien (9.1939-to the end of 1944)	Confiscation of property.	POL.
POL/9/615	Ger.		Gauleiter, Reichsstatthalter	Prov. Ostpreussen (9.1939-1942)	Murder, torture and other crimes.	POL.
POL/9/616	Ger.	Chief	Police, Gestapo and SS	Zyglin (1939-1942)	Deportation of civilians illtreatment and torture of internees torture of internees causing death violation of art.46 of Hague convention.	POL.
POL/9/617	Ger.	Chief	Gestapo	Chorzew, Poland (1939-1942)	Deportation of civilians; illtreatment and torture of internees causing death, violation of art.46 of Hague convention (1907)	POL.
POL/9/618	Ger.	Chief	Police, Gestapo and SS	Gdynia (Gotenhafen), Poland (1939-1942)	Deportation of civilians; illtreatment and torture of internees causing death, violation of art.46 of Hague convention (1907).	POL.
POL/9/619	Ger.	Chief	Gestapo, SS	Gdansk (Danzig), Poland (1939-1942)	Deportation of civilians, illtreatment and torture of internees, torture of internees causing death, violation of art.46 of Hague convention (1907).	POL.
POL/9/620	Ger.	Chief	Police	Gdansk, Poland (1939-1942)	Deportation of civilians, illtreatment and torture of internees causing death, violation of art.46 Hague convention (1907).	POL.
POL/9/621	Ger.	Chief	Police, Gestapo and SS	Fordon (1939-1942)	Deportation of civilians, illtreatment and torture of internees, torture of internees causing death, violation of art.46 Hague convention (1907).	POL.
POL/9/622	Ger.	Chief	Police, Gestapo and SS	Dziedzice (1939-1942)	Deportation of civilians, illtreatment and torture of internees, torture of internees causing death, violation of art.46 of Hague convention (1907).	POL.
POL/9/623	Ger.	Chief	Police, Gestapo and SS	Drelow, Poland (1939-1942)	Deportation of civilians, illtreatment and torture of internees.	POL.
POL/9/624	Ger.	Chief	Police, Gestapo and SS	Czechowice (1939-1942)	Deportation of civilians, illtreatment and torture of internees causing death, violation of art.46 of Hague convention (1907).	POL.
POL/9/625	Ger.	Chief	Police, Gestapo and SS	Czarnkow (1939-1942)	Deportation of civilians, execution of persons without trial.	POL.
POL/9/626	Ger.	Chief	Police, Gestapo and SS	Cieszyn (1939-1942)	Deportation of civilians, illtreatment and torture of internees, torture of internees causing death, violation of art.46 of Hague convention (1907).	POL.
POL/9/627	Ger.	Chief	Police, Gestapo and SS	Ciechanow (1939-1942)	Deportation of civilians, illtreatment of internees and torture, torture of internees causing death, violation of art.46.	POL.
POL/9/628	Ger.	Chief	Gestapo, SS	Choszcz, Poland (1939-1942)	Deportation of civilians, execution of persons, without trial.	POL.
POL/9/629	Ger.	Chief	Police, Gestapo and SS	Chełtowice (1939-1942)	Deportation of civilians, illtreatment and torture of internees, torture of internees causing death, violation of art.46 of Hague convention.	POL.
POL/9/630	Ger.	Chief	Police, Gestapo and SS	Gniezno (1939-1942)	Deportation of civilians, execution of persons, without trial.	POL.
POL/9/631	Ger.	Chief	Police, Gestapo and SS	Gora Kalwaria, Warsaw district (1939-1942)	Deportation of civilians, illtreatment and torture of internees, torture of internees causing death, violation of art.46 of Hague convention (1907).	POL.
POL/9/632	Ger.	Chief	Police, Gestapo and SS	Dziecmorowice (1939-1942)	Deportation of civilians, illtreatment and torture of internees, torture of internees causing death, violation of art.46 of Hague convention.	POL.
POL/9/633	Ger.	Chief	Police, Gestapo and SS	Gora Kalwaria, Poland (1939-1942)	Deportation of civilians, illtreatment and torture of internees.	POL.
POL/9/634	Ger.	Chief	Police, Gestapo and SS	Gorna-Grupa, Poland (1939-1942)	Deportation of civilians, illtreatment and torture of internees causing death, violation of art.46 of Hague convention (1907).	POL.
POL/9/635	Ger.	Chief	Police, Gestapo and SS	Goscieszyn, Poland (1939-1942)	Deportation of civilians, execution of persons without trial.	POL.
POL/9/636	Ger.	Chief	Police, Gestapo and SS	Gostyn, Poland (1939-1942)	Deportation of civilians, execution of persons without trial.	POL.
POL/9/637	Ger.	Chief	Police, Gestapo and SS	Kicin (1939-1942)	Deportation of civilians, execution of persons without trial.	POL.
POL/9/638	Ger.	Chief	Police, Gestapo and SS	Kepno, Poland (1939-1942)	Deportation of civilians, execution of persons without trial.	POL.

9. NAZI PARTY MEMBERS - State Service, Gestapo, SD and Police. (Cont.)

C.R.FILE NO.	NATIO-NALITY	RANK OR STATUS	UNIT OR OCCUPATION	PLACE AND DATE OF CRIME	PARTICULARS OF CRIME OR REASON FOR WHICH WANTED FOLLOWED BY PHYSICAL DESCRIPTION IF KNOWN	WANTED BY
POL/9/639	Ger.	Chief	Police, Gestapo and SS	Katowice (1939-1942)	Deportation of civilians, illtreatment and torture of internees causing death, violation of art.46 of Hague convention.	POL.
POL/9/640	Ger.	Chief	Police, Gestapo and SS	Ledziny (1939-1942)	Deportation of civilians, Illtreatment and torture of internees, torture of internees causing death, violation of art.46 of Hague convention (1907).	POL.
POL/9/641	Ger.	Chief	Police, Gestapo and SS	Lechlin (1939-1942)	Deportation of civilians, execution of persons without trial.	POL.
POL/9/642	Ger.	Chief	Police, Gestapo and SS	Lazizka (1939-1942)	Deportation of civilians, illtreatment and torture of internees, torture of internees causing death, violation of art.46 of Hague convention (1907)	POL.
POL/9/643	Ger.	Chief	Police, Gestapo and SS	Laki (1939-1942)	Deportation of civilians, illtreatment and torture of internees, torture of internees causing death, violation of art.46 of Hague convention (1907).	POL.
POL/9/644	Ger.	Chief	Police, Gestapo and SS	Krzyzowniki, Poland (1939-1942)	Deportation of civilian, execution of persons without trial.	POL.
POL/9/645	Ger.	Chief	Police, Gestapo and SS	Kreznica (1939-1942)	Deportation of civilians, illtreatment and torture of internees.	POL.
POL/9/646	Ger.	Chief	Police, Gestapo and SS	Kossakow, Poland (1939-1942)	Deportation of civilians, illtreatment and torture of internees causing death, violation of art.46 of Hague convention (1907).	POL.
POL/9/647	Ger.	Chief	Police, Gestapo and SS	Koscian, Poland (1939-1942)	Deportation of civilians, execution of persons without trial.	POL.
POL/9/648	Ger.	Chief	Police, Gestapo and SS	Koziglowi (1939-1942)	Deportation of civilians, illtreatment and torture of internees.	POL.
POL/9/649	Ger.	Chief	Police, Gestapo and SS	Kossarow (1939-1942)	Deportation of civilians, illtreatment and torture of internees, torture of internees causing death, violation of art.46 of Hague convention (1907).	POL.
POL/9/650	Ger.	Chief	Police, Gestapo and SS	Konczyce Wielkie (1939-1942)	Deportation of civilians, illtreatment and torture of internees, torture of internees causing death, violation of art.46 of Hague convention (1907).	POL.
POL/9/651	Ger.	Chief	Police, Gestapo and SS	Konarzewo (1939-1942)	Deportation of civilian, execution of persons without trial.	POL.
POL/9/652	Ger.	Chief	Police, Gestapo and SS	Komorowka, Podlaska (1939-1942)	Deportation of civilians, illtreatment and torture of internees.	POL.
POL/9/653	Ger.	Chief	Police, Gestapo and SS	Mszczonow, Poland (1939-1942)	Deportation of civilians, illtreatment and torture of internees.	POL.
POL/9/654	Ger.	Chief	Police, Gestapo and SS	Mlawa (1939-1942)	Deportation of civilians, illtreatment of internees, torture of internees causing death, violation of art. 46 of Hague convention (1907).	POL.
POL/9/655	Ger.	Chief	Police, Gestapo and SS	Markowice (1939-1942)	Deportation of civilians, execution of persons without trial.	POL.
POL/9/656	Ger.	Chief	Police, Gestapo and SS	Lubliniec (1939-1942)	Deportation of civilians, illtreatment and torture of internees, torture of internees causing death, violation of art.46 of Hague convention (1907).	POL.
POL/9/657	Ger.	Chief	Police, Gestapo and SS	Lopienno, Poland (1939-1942)	Deportation of civilians, execution of persons without trial.	POL.
POL/9/658	Ger.	Chief	Police, Gestapo and SS	Leszna Goerna (1939-1942)	Deportation of civilians, illtreatment and torture of internees, torture of internees causing death, violation of art.46 of Hague convention (1907).	POL.
POL/9/659	Ger.	Chief	Police, Gestapo and SS	Lenice, Poland (1939-1942)	Deportation of civilians, execution of persons without trial.	POL.
POL/9/660	Ger.	Official, Gauleiter and Reichsstatthalter	Deutscher Gemeindetag, NSDAP	Baden, Germany (1941-1942)	Murder. Adress: Karlsruhe, Erbprinzenstr.15.	POL.
POL/9/661	Ger.	Chief	Police, Gestapo and SS	Karwina (1939-1942)	Deportation of civilians, illtreatment and torture of internees, torture of internees causing death, violation of art.46 of Hague convention (1907).	POL.
POL/9/662	Ger.	Chief	Police, Gestapo and SS	Kamienica-Polska, Poland (1939-1942)	Deportation of civilians, illtreatment and torture of internees.	POL.
POL/9/663	Ger.	Chief	Police, Gestapo and SS	Kalisz, Poland (1939-1942)	Deportation of civilians, execution of persons without trial.	POL.
POL/9/664	Ger.	Chief	Police, Gestapo and SS	Janowiec (1939-1942)	Deportation of civilians, execution of persons without trial.	POL.
POL/9/665	Ger.	Chief	Police, Gestapo and SS	Jaktorowo (1939-1942)	Deportation of civilians, execution of persons without trial.	POL.
POL/9/666	Ger.	Chief	Police, Gestapo and SS	Jablonkow (1939-1942)	Deportation of civilians, illtreatment and torture of internees, torture of internees causing death, violation of art.46 of Hague convention (1907).	POL.
POL/9/667	Ger.	Chief	Police, Gestapo and SS	Istebna (1939-1942)	Deportation of civilians, illtreatment and torture of internees, torture of internees causing death, violation.	POL.
POL/9/668	Ger.	Chief	Police, Gestapo and SS	Inowroclaw (1939-1942)	Deportation of civilians, execution of persons without trial.	POL.
POL/9/669	Ger.	Chief	Police, Gestapo and SS	Gromadno (1939-1942)	Deportation of civilians, execution of persons without trial.	POL.
POL/9/670	Ger.	Chief	Police, Gestapo and SS	Grodzisk, Poland (1939-1942)	Deportation of civilians, execution of persons without trial.	POL.
POL/9/671	Ger.	Kreisleiter	NSDAP	Wloclawek, Poland (10.1939-1941)	Deportation of civilians.	POL.
POL/9/672	Ger.	Chief	Police, Gestapo and SS	Torun, Poland (1939-1942)	Deportation of civilians, illtreatment and torture of internees causing death, violation of art.46 of Hague convention (1907).	POL.

9. NAZI PARTY MEMBERS - State Service, Gestapo, SD and Police. (cont.)

C.R.FILE NO.	NATIO-NALITY	RANK OR STATUS	UNIT OR OCCUPATION	PLACE AND DATE OF CRIME	PARTICULARS OF CRIME OR REASON FOR WHICH WANTED FOLLOWED BY PHYSICAL DESCRIPTION IF KNOWN	WANTED BY
POL/9/673	Ger.	Chief	Police, Gestapo and SS	Tarnowskie Gory (1939-1942)	Deportation of civilians, illtreatment and torture of internees, torture of internees causing death, violation of art.46 of Hague convention (1907).	POL.
POL/9/674	Ger.	Chief	Police, Gestapo and SS	Tarnow (1939-1942)	Deportation of civilians, illtreatment and torture of internees.	POL.
POL/9/675	Ger.	Chief	Police, Gestapo and SS	Tarnobrzeg (1939-1942)	Deportation of, civilians, illtreatment and torture of internees.	POL.
POL/9/676	Ger.	Chief	Police, Gestapo and SS	Skomielna (1939-1942)	Deportation of civilians, illtreatment of internees.	POL.
POL/9/677	Ger.	Chief	Police, Gestapo and SS	Skarzysko-Kamienna (1939-1942)	Deportation of civilians, illtreatment of internees.	POL.
POL/9/678	Ger.	Chief	Gestapo and SS	Siewierz-Konopiska, Poland (1939-1942)	Deportation of civilians, illtreatment and torture of internees.	POL.
POL/9/679	Ger.	Chief	Police, Gestapo and SS	Sierakowice, Poland (1939-1942)	Deportation of civilians, illtreatment and torture of internees causing death, violation of art.46 of Hague convention (1907).	POL.
POL/9/680	Ger.	Chief	Police, Gestapo and SS	Siemianowice (1939-1942)	Deportation of civilians, illtreatment of internees and torture, torture of internees causing death, violation of art.46 of Hague convention (1907).	POL.
POL/9/681	Ger.	Chief	Police, Gestapo and SS	Siedlce (1939-1942)	Deportation of civilians, illtreatment of internees and torture.	POL.
POL/9/682	Ger.	Chief	Police, Gestapo and SS	Rzeszow (1939-1942)	Deportation of civilians, illtreatment of internees.	POL.
POL/9/683	Ger.	Chief	Police, Gestapo and SS	Rzadkin, Poland (1939-1942)	Deportation of civilians, execution of persons without trial.	POL.
POL/9/684	Ger.	Chief	Police, Gestapo and SS	Rudne (1939-1942)	Deportation of civilians, illtreatment and torture of internees, torture of internees causing death, violation of art.46 of Hague convention (1907).	POL.
POL/9/685	Ger.	Chief	Police, Gestapo and SS	Roznowo, Poland (1939-1942)	Deportation of civilians, execution of persons without trial.	POL.
POL/9/686	Ger.	Chief	Police, Gestapo and SS	Rawicz, Poland (1939-1942)	Deportation of civilians, execution of persons without trial.	POL.
POL/9/687	Ger.	Chief	Police	Rzadkin (1939,1940)	Deportation of civilians, execution of persons without trial.	POL.
POL/9/688	Ger.	Chief	Police, Gestapo and SS	Przemysl (1939-1942)	Deportation of civilians, illtreatment and torture of internees.	POL.
POL/9/689	Ger.	Chief	Police, Gestapo and SS	Przasnysz (1939-1942)	Deportation of civilians, illtreatment and torture of internees, torture of internees causing death, violation of art.46 of Hague convention (1907).	POL.
POL/9/690	Ger.	Chief	Police, Gestapo and SS	Podzamcee, Poland (1939-1942)	Deportation of civilians, execution of persons without trial.	POL.
POL/9/691	Ger.	Chief	Police, Gestapo and SS	Pniewy, Poland (1939-1942)	Deportation of civilians, execution of persons without trial.	POL.
POL/9/692	Ger.	Chief	Police, Gestapo and SS	Plonkowo (1939-1942)	Deportation of civilians, execution of persons without trial.	POL.
POL/9/693	Ger.	Chief	Police, Gestapo and SS	Plock (Schroetterburg) (1939-1942)	Deportation of civilians, illtreatment and torture of internees, torture of internees causing death, violation of art.46 Hague convention (1907).	POL.
POL/9/694	Ger.	Chief	Police, Gestapo and SS	Plaski (1939-1942)	Deportation of civilians, execution of persons without trial.	POL.
POL/9/695	Ger.	Chief	Police, Gestapo and SS	Piotrkow Kujawski (1939-1942)	Deportation of civilians, execution of persons without trial.	POL.
POL/9/696	Ger.	Chief	Police, Gestapo and SS	Piotrowice (1939-1942)	Deportation of civilians, illtreatment and torture of internees, torture of internees causing death, violation of art.46 of Hague convention (1907).	POL.
POL/9/697	Ger.	Chief	Police, Gestapo and SS	Pieniazkowo, Poland (1939-1942)	Deportation of civilians, illtreatment and torture of internees causing death, violation of art.46 of Hague convention (1907).	POL.
POL/9/698	Ger.	Chief	Police, Gestapo and SS	Piekary (1939-1942)	Deportation of civilians, illtreatment and torture of internees, torture of internees causing death, violation of art.44 of Hague convention (1907).	POL.
POL/9/699	Ger.	Chief	Police, Gestapo and SS	Pelplin, Poland (1939-1942)	Deportation of civilians, illtreatment and torture of internees causing death, violation of art.46 of Hague convention (1907).	POL.
POL/9/700	Ger.	Chief	Police, Gestapo and SS	Pawlowice (1939-1942)	Deportation of civilians, illtreatment of internees and torture, torture of internees causing death, violation of art.46 of Hague convention (1907).	POL.
POL/9/701	Ger.	Member, Chief	SS; political Dept.	Oswiecim (6.1940-end 1943)	Murder, torture and other crimes.	POL.
POL/9/702	Ger.	Chief	Police, Gestapo and	Okrzeja (1939-1942)	Deportation of civilians, illtreatment and torture of internees.	POL.
POL/9/703	Ger.	Chief	Police, Gestapo and SS	Obrzycko (1939-1942)	Deportation of civilians, execution of persons without trial.	POL.
POL/9/704	Ger.	Chief	Police, Gestapo and SS	Nowe Miastro Lubawskie, Poland (1939-1942)	Deportation of civilians, illtreatment and torture of internees causing death, violation of art.46 of Hague convention (1907).	POL.
POL/9/705	Ger.	Chief	Police, Gestapo and SS	Noskow (1939-1942)	Deportation of civilians, execution of persons without trial.	POL.
POL/9/706	Ger.	Chief	Police, Gestapo and SS	Naklo, Poland (1939-1942)	Deportation of civilians, illtreatment and torture of internees causing death, violation of art.46 of Hague convention (1907).	POL.
POL/9/707	Ger.	Chief	Gestapo	Szubin, Poland (1939-1942)	Deportation of civilians, execution of persons without trial.	POL.
POL/9/708	Ger.	Chief	Gestapo	Szczepanowo, Poland (1939-1942)	Deportation of civilians, execution of persons without trial.	POL.

9. NAZI PARTY MEMBERS - State Service, Gestapo, SD and Police. (Cont.)

C.R.FILE NO.	NATIO-NALITY	RANK OR STATUS	UNIT OR OCCUPATION	PLACE AND DATE OF CRIME	PARTICULARS OF CRIME OR REASON FOR WHICH WANTED FOLLOWED BY PHYSICAL DESCRIPTION IF KNOWN	WANTED BY
POL/9/709	Ger.	Chief	Police, Gestapo and SS	Swietochlowice (1939-1942)	Deportation of civilians, illtreatment and torture of internees, torture internees causing death, violation of art.46 of Hague convention (1907).	POL.
POL/9/710	Ger.	Chief	Police, Gestapo and SS	Swiety Krzyz (1939-1942)	Deportation of civilians, illtreatment and torture of internees.	POL.
POL/9/711	Ger.	Chief	Police, Gestapo and SS	Sroda (1939-1942)	Deportation of civilians, execution of persons without trial.	POL.
POL/9/712	Ger.	Chief	Police, Gestapo and SS	Srem (1939-1942)	Deportation of civilians, execution of persons without trial.	POL.
POL/9/713	Ger.	Chief	Police, Gestapo and SS	Srebrniki, Poland (1939-1942)	Deportation of civilians, illtreatment and torture of internees causing death, violation of art.46 of Hague convention (1907).	POL.
POL/9/714	Ger.	Chief	Police, Gestapo and SS	Sliwice, Poland (1939-1942)	Deportation of civilians, illtreatment and torture of internees causing death, violation of art.46 of Hague convention (1907).	POL.
POL/9/715	Ger.	Chief	Police, Gestapo and SS	Slaboszewo, Poland (1939-1942)	Deportation of civilians, execution of persons without trial.	POL.
POL/9/716	Ger.	Leader	Treuhandstelle fuer Bezirk	Bialystok (9.1939-to the end of 1944)	Confiscation of property.	POL.
POL/9/717	Ger.	Leader	Abt. Forste, Amt des Reichsstatthalters	Gau Oberschlesien, Poland (9.1939-to the end of 1944)	Confiscation of property.	POL.
POL/9/718	Ger.	Reich-official, Governor General	Sonderbevollmaechtigte fuer die Erdoelwirtschaft, Amt des Generalgouverneurs	(9.1939-to the end of 1944)	Confiscation of property.	POL.
POL/9/719	Ger.	Leader	Abt. Ernaehrung und Landwirtschaft, Amt des Gouverneurs fuer District Lublin	Lublin (9.1939-to the end of 1944)	Confiscation of property.	POL.
POL/9/720	Ger.	Leader	Abt. Ernaehrung und Landwirtschaft, Amt des Reichsstatthalters	Gau Danzig (9.1939-to the end of 1944)	Confiscation of property.	POL.
POL/9/721	Ger.	Leader	Abt. Wirtschaft, Amt des Reichsstatthalters	Wartheland (9.1939-to the end of 1944)	Confiscation of property.	POL.
POL/9/722	Ger.	Leader	Abt. Wirtschaft, Amt des Reichsstatthalters, Wirtschaftsministerium	Oberschlesien, Germany (9.1939-to the end of 1944)	Confiscation of property.	POL.
POL/9/723	Ger.	Leader	Abt. Ernaehrung und Landwirtschaft, Amt des Reichsstatthalters	Oberschlesien (9.1939-to the end of 1944)	Confiscation of property.	POL.
POL/9/724	Ger.	Reich-official, Generalverwalter	Oeffentliche Bewirtschaftung Land-und Forstwirtschaftlicher Betriebe und Grundstuecke in den eingegliederten Ostgebieten	Poland (9.1939-to the end of 1944)	Confiscation of property.	POL.
POL/9/725	Ger.	Leader	Treuhandstelle fuer Staatliches Vermoegen im General Gouvernement Polen, Amt des Generalgouverneurs	Poland (9.1939-to the end of 1944)	Confiscation of property.	POL.
POL/9/726	Ger.	Leader	Treuhandaussenstelle	Ciechanow, Poland (9.1939-to the end of 1944)	Confiscation of property.	POL.
POL/9/727	Ger.	Chief	Police, Gestapo and SS	Zamosc (1939-1942)	Deportation of civilians, illtreatment and torture of internees.	POL.
POL/9/728	Ger.	Chief	Police, Gestapo and SS	Znin (1939-1942)	Deportation of civilians, execution of persons without trial.	POL.
POL/9/729	Ger.	Chief	Police, Gestapo and SS	Zbaszyn (1939-1942)	Deportation of civilians, execution of persons without trial.	POL.
POL/9/730	Ger.	Chief	Police, Gestapo and SS	Wrzesnia, Poland (1939-1942)	Deportation of civilians, execution of persons without trial.	POL.
POL/9/731	Ger.	Chief	Police, Gestapo and SS	Wozniki (1939-1942)	Deportation of civilians, illtreatment and torture of internees, torture of internees causing death, violation of art.46 of Hague convention (1907).	POL.
POL/9/732	Ger.	Chief	Gestapo und SS	Wola Sulowska, Poland (1939-1942)	Deportation of civilians, illtreatment and torture of internees.	POL.
POL/9/733	Ger.	Chief	Police, Gestapo and SS	Wiele (1939-1942)	Deportation of civilians, illtreatment of internees, torture of internees causing death, violation of art.46 Hague convention (1907).	POL.
POL/9/734	Ger.	Chief	Police, Gestapo and SS	Turek (1939-1942)	Deportation of civilians, execution of persons without trial.	POL.
POL/9/735	Ger.	Governor, Head	German civil administration district	Tichola, Poland (10.1939)	Murder, illegal employment.	POL.
POL/9/736	Ger.	Chief	Police, Gestapo and SS	Trzyniec (1939-1942)	Deportation of civilians, illtreatment and torture of internees, torture of internees causing death, violation of art.46 of Hague convention.	POL.
POL/9/737	Ger.	Leader	Treuhandstelle, territories occupied	Gdynia, Poland (9.1939-to the end of 1944)	Confiscation of property.	POL.
POL/9/738	Ger.	Leader	Treuhandstelle, occupied territory	Katowice, Poland (9.1939-to the end of 1944)	Confiscation of property.	POL.
POL/9/739	Ger.	Chief	Police, Gestapo and SS	Choron, Poland (1939-1942)	Deportation of civilians, illtreatment and torture of internees.	POL.
POL/9/740	Ger.	Chief	Gestapo and SS	Chometowo, Poland (1939-1942)	Deportation of civilians, execution of persons without trial.	POL.
POL/9/741	Ger.	Chief	Police, Gestapo and SS	Chobzow (1939-1942)	Deportation of civilians, illtreatment and torture of internees, torture of internees causing death, violation of art.46 of Hague convention (1907).	POL.

9. NAZI PARTY MEMBERS - State Service, Gestapo, SD and Police. (Cont.)

C.R.FILE NO.	NATIO-NALITY	RANK OR STATUS	UNIT OR OCCUPATION	PLACE AND DATE OF CRIME	PARTICULARS OF CRIME OR REASON FOR WHICH WANTED FOLLOWED BY PHYSICAL DESCRIPTION IF KNOWN	WANTED BY
POL/9/742	Ger.	Chief	Police, Gestapo and SS	Chelmno, Poland (1939-1942)	Deportation of civilians, illtreatment and torture of internees, torture of internees causing death, violation of art.46 of Hague convention (1907).	POL.
POL/9/743	Ger.	Chief	Police, Gestapo and SS	Chelm Lubelski, Poland (1939-1942)	Deportation of civilians, illtreatment and torture of internees.	POL.
POL/9/744	Ger.	Chief	SS	Bydgoszcz, Poland. (1939-1942)	Deportation of civilians, execution of persons without trial.	POL.
POL/9/745	Ger.	Chief	Police, Gestapo and SS	Bukowiec, Poland (1939-1942)	Deportation of civilians, execution of persons without trial.	POL.
POL/9/746	Ger.	Chief	Police, Gestapo and SS	Adamow, Poland (1939-1942)	Deportation of civilians, illtreatment and torture of internees.	POL.
POL/9/747	Ger.		Beauftragte fuer den Vierjahresplan bei der Haupttreuhandstelle Ost (HTO)	Berlin, Germany (9.1939-to the end of 1944)	Confiscation of property.	POL.
UK/9/748	Ger.	Mayor		of Steudnitz (1.-3.45) on a forced march from St.344 Lamsdorf to Goerlitz and from thence to Mellingen, Ziegenhain Muehlhausen and Frankfurt am Main, Germany	MURDER.	U.K.
UK/9/749	Ger.	Officer Commanding	Gestapo	in the Banska, Bystrica District, Czech. (20.11.44), Kremnika, Czech.	Murder.	U.K.
UK/9/750	Ger.	Governor	Prison	at Hirschberg, Silesia (between 25.3.44 and 8.5.44)	Murder.	U.K.
UK/9/751	Ger.	Official	SS commanding	Gestapo, H.Q. at Modlin. W. Poland (19.-22.1.44)	About 3'8.5'10" tall. Weight about 12 st.6. Dark hair, fresh complexion, round fat face, clean-shaven, straight nose, dark brown eyes, full lips, one top right tooth either gold or gold filled. Wore four gold signet rings on left hand. Speaks with Hamburg accent and has deep voice. Brutality.	U.K.
UK/9/752	Ger.	Governor	of Paviak Prison,	Poland (10.42-2.43)	Brutality.	U.K.
UK/9/753	Ger.	Policeman	a forest	Ostheim, Nordheim, Stettin, Ger. (7.44-8.42)	5'10" tall. Weight 11 st., dark complexion, born 1905 near Duesseldorf. Shot a British PW between Nordheim and Ostheim, than district, Thuringia, with a Ger.Civilian, shot two Russian PW's in a forest near the village at Stettin.	U.K., SOV.UN.
UK/9/754		Members	1010 Sicherheitsdienst-Regiment	Chilleurs-Aux-Bois, France (15.8.44)	On 3 July 1944, thirty-one members of this 1 SAS Rgt. were taken prisoner, removed to Poitiers, for interrogation, and thence to an isolated area in a forest near Rom, where they were executed by members of the Staff of the Poitiers Gestapo.	U.K.
UK/9/755	Ger.	Kreisleiter	NSDAP	of Muelheim (Baden) Germany (11.44)	Took custody of two R.A.F Lancaster pilots, shot down after attack on Standamm of Kembs/Alsace. When Luftwaffe guards arived to take these men to Oberursel, they were informed at the Kreisleiter's H.Q. that they had been "liquidated".	U.K.
UK/9/756	Ger.	Commandant	of Civilian Gestapo Prison	Belgrade (Yugo.) (8.42)	Ill-treatment of P.o.W. Torture.	U.K.
UK/9/757	Ger.	Commandant	of main Gestapo Prison	Belgrade, Yugo., (8.,7.42)	Ill-treatment of P.o.W. Torture.	U.K.
UK/9/758	Ger.	Commandant	of Civilian Gestapo Prison	Belgrade, Yugo., (1942)	Ill-treatment of P.o.W. Torture.	U.K.
UK/9/759	Ger.	Commandant (Major)	of main Gestapo Prison	Belgrade, Yugo., (1942)	Ill-treatment of P.o.W.	U.K.
UK/9/760	Ger.	N.C.O. Commanding guard	at main Gestapo Prison	Belgrade, Yugo., (1942)	Ill-treatment of P.o.W.	U.K.
UK/9/761	Hung.	Head warder	State Prison	Budapest (Hung.) (12.7.44-2.8.44)	About 1895. Dark brown thinning hair, Hitler moustache, thick red neck Brutality, lack of food, exercise, and ill-treatment during interrogation. State Prison, Budapest.	U.K.
UK/9/762	Hung.	Chief	Police	Zombor, Hung. (5.7.44)	Born about 1895, over 6 ft. Height, fair complexion Additional particulars, Burly, Prominent jew. Chaining and appalling brutality by officials at Zombor, in order to extract information.	U.K.
UK/9/763	Ger.	Burgomaster	Civilian	Leipzig, Germany (4.12.43-8.1.44)	Reprisals taken against PWs for RAF raid on Leipzig. Appalling conditions at Arb.Kmdo.39, attached Stalag IV c, Leipzig.	U.K.
UK/9/764	Ger.	Burgomaster	Civilian	Chemnitz, (Germany) (10.10.44-10.4.45)	Ordered PW's to work long terms on very little food. Arb.Kmdo.c 98. Firm: Mibag Ltd., Chemnitz.	U.K.
UK/9/765	Ger.	Commandant	of civil Gestapo	Frankfurt am Main, Germany (1943-1944)	Ill-treatment of Prisoners of War. Torture.	U.K.
UK/9/766	Ger.	Burgomaster	Civilian	Ludersberg, just south of River Elbe, North Germany, on the march from Fallingbostel to Lauenberg	Refused to help sick PW's who had dropped out of the column-heading for Lauenberg (Elbe).	U.K.
UK/9/767	Ger.	Burgomaster	Civilian	Sarendorf, Germany, (17.4.45)	Unjustified violence, beatings etc. Sarendorf, Germany.	U.K.
UK/9/768	Ger.	Regular policeman	Civilian	employed in Halles Prison, Germany, (25.7.44)	Halles, Germany, Prison, Struck English woman and illtreated an English PW. Accused is described as a big strong man.	U.K.

9. NAZI PARTY MEMBERS - State Service, Gestapo, SD and Police. (Cont.)

C.R.FILE NO.	NATIO-NALITY	RANK OR STATUS	UNIT OR OCCUPATION	PLACE AND DATE OF CRIME	PARTICULARS OF CRIME OR REASON FOR WHICH WANTED FOLLOWED BY PHYSICAL DESCRIPTION IF KNOWN	WANTED BY
UK/9/769	Ger.	Sgt.	Police	Ostheim vor der Rhoen, Germany, (8.1944)	Murder of two British PW's after their attempted escape. Ostheim von der Rhoen.	U.K.
UK/9/770	Ger.	Governor	of a Prison (Stated Gestapo Prison)	Goerlitz, Germany, (3.44-5.44)	Murder.	U.K.,FR.BEL.
UK/9/771		Governor	Prison	Hirschberg-Silesia, Germany, (between 25.3.44 and 8.5.44)	Murder.	U.K.
UK/9/772		Commandant	Gestapo H.Q.	Modlin W.Poland, (19.,22.1.44)	About 12 st.6, 5'10" tall, dark-brown Eyes, round fat face, straight nose, full lips, clean shaven, wore four gold signet rings on left hand, speak with Hamburg accent and has deepvoice. Born on 1907. Miscellaneous.	U.K.
UK/9/773	Pol.	Head Warder	Kattowitz Prison, Civilian	Kattowitz, Poland, (5.43-9.43)	Born between 1890 and 1895, 13 st.Weight, 5'6" - 5'7" Height, Light-brown hair. This man was Polish born and was employed at Kattowitz prison prior to 1939. He is thought to have handed over the prison to the Germans and entered their service. He was married and lived in a house behind the prison. He was responsible for assaulting and beating Sapper Arthur Walker, R.E. who was detained at the prison from May to September 1943.	U.K.
UK/9/774		Staff	of the Poitiers Gestapo	Poitiers, France Rom, Italy, (3.7.44)	Execution of thirty-one members of the 1.SAS Rgt.	U.K.
UK/9/775		Member	SD	Brussels, Belgium (5.44-9.44)	Height: 190 cms, hair: white, eyes: sometimes glasses, build: thin. A member of the SD in Brussels in 1944. Has an oval face and clean shaven. Speaks fluent Flemish, Dutch, Spanish and English. He is wanted for the ill-treatment of British officers in Brussels from May to September 1944 in PW's.	U.K.
UK/9/776	Ger.	Head	of Gestapo	at Rheims, France (9.1944)	Torture and 3rd degree methods at Gestapo H.Q. Rheims, September 1944 in order to extract information from a Canadian airman.	U.K.
UK/9/777	Ger.	Gestapo Agent	the only one in Beauvais Prison	Beauvais, France (27.10.1944)	Born: 1885-1895, hair: white. Beating with fists, rubber truncheon, kicking, to obtain information from P.W. in Beauvais prison.	U.K.
UK/9/778	Fr.	Gestapo Agent	Gestapo H.Q.	Avenue Foch, Paris, France, (4.43-6.43)	Born: 1917, about 5'7", hair: dark brown thick. The above man has a welleducated Parisian accent, and very French movements. He is of medium build, has a good-shaped head, good teeth and very beautiful eyes and eyelashes. He was always well dressed. Wanted for burning Eusigh Odette SANSOM, F.A.N.Y. in order to extract information from her.	U.K.
UK/9/779	Ger.	Interrogator	Geh.Feldpolizei	Rue des Saussaies, Paris, Seine, France (7. 9.1942)	Gestapo H.Q., Avenue Foch, April or June '43.Murder. Born: between 1910 and 1915, about 5'10". Slightly pointed chin, wavy hair well back from the forehead, always wore civilian clothes and spoke perfect French. Left British prisoner with a guard to be beaten up after interrogation. Torture.	U.K.
UK/9/780	Ger.	Governor	of Prison	Hirschberg-Silesia, Germany, (25.3.44-8.5.44)	Murder.	U.K.
US/9/781		Civilian-Guard		at Wiesbaden, Germany, (28.3.44-19.5.44)	Weight: 190 Lbs., Height: 5'10", characteristics: Heavy set. Veteran of first World War. Wanted for the beating of two American Officers at the Wiesbaden City Jail, Wiesbaden, Germany, U.S.Zone Suspect was guard at Wiesbaden Jail from 28 March 1944 to 19 May 1944. Miscellaneous.	U.S.
US/9/782	Ger.	Commissar	Gestapo	at Schwerin, Germany, (16.-17.3.44) Neubukow, Rerik, Mecklenburg	Weight: 170 Lbs., height: 175 cm, born: 1910, hair: partly bald, characteristics: slightly humped back, double chin, broad, slightly-hooked nose, small, hairy hands, short fingers. Wanted for questioning in connection with the murder of six US AAF personnel, on or about 17 or 16 March 1944 at or near Neubukow, Province Mecklenburg, Germany. Suspect was member of SS, who attempted to have records of death falsified. Suspect able to identify and name Gauleiter of Mecklenburg (W/R); District Leader of BAD DOBERAN (W/R).	U.S.
US/9/783		Member	SD	Radom, Poland, (1943)	Murder, Slaughter.	U.S.
US/9/784		Policeman	Civilian, Police, Military Government	Munstedt, Germany, (3.or 4.45)	Born: 1895-1900, 5'6", characteristics: Heavy build. Wanted for the alleged murder of two American flyers at Munstedt, Germany, BritishZone about a mile out of town. Suspect was a policeman for Military Government at the end of April 45. Suspect resides at Munstedt, Germany. Two American airmen parachuted from a plane and were beaten as they were marched through Munstedt, they were shot about a mile out of town.	U.S.

9. NAZI PARTY MEMBERS - State Service, Gestapo, SD and Police. (Cont.)

C.R.FILE NO.	NATIO-NALITY	RANK OR STATUS	UNIT OR OCCUPATION	PLACE AND DATE OF CRIME	PARTICULARS OF CRIME OR REASON FOR WHICH WANTED FOLLOWED BY PHYSICAL DESCRIPTION IF KNOWN	WANTED BY
US/9/785		Burgomaster	Civilian	Frohnhausen, Germany, (23.3.45)	On 23 March 1945 an American airman, believed to be Russel D. WADE, was killed when his parachute failed to open or shot and beaten to death upon landing in the vicinity of Frohnhausen, Germany. The Burgomaster of Frohnhausen states that the airman's parachute failed to open and that WADE died as a result of the fall. The witness wanted was the Burgomaster of Frohnhausen on or about the 23rd Mar.45.	U.S.
US/9/786	Ger.	Chief of Police, Officer	German Gestapo	Minden, Germany, (6.8.44)	Lt. W.A. Langenfeld, 469 Group, A.F. was severely beaten by a German Gestapo officer at Minden, Germany, on 6 August 1944. Lt. Langenfeld thought, German Officer was Chief of Police of Minden.	U.S.
US/9/787		Policeman	Civilian	the only one in Kirch-Muelzow, Poischendorf, Province Mecklenburg, Germany, (29.5.44)	Born: 1900, weight: 95 Kilos, height: 1,70 m, hair: black, eyes: blue. On 29 May 44 the crew of an American bomber, which bellied in near Poischendorf in Mecklenburg Province, were beaten and killed. The crew, guarded by an obergefreiter, Prussing, were being beaten by civilians when this police officer, the only one in Kirch-Muelzow, joined the civilians in stealing the money and property of the beaten crewmen. The French witness left the scene without observing the further conduct of the policeman. The crew were all later killed and buried possibly in the cemetery at Kirch-Muelzow.	U.S.
US/9/788		Mayor	Civilian	Oschatz-Saxony, Germany, (17.3.45)	Wanted for beating and possible killing of captured American aviators at Oschatz, Germany, on 17 March 1945. Subject, the burgomaster of the above town, led a mob in beating the above victims severely, and is alleged to have shot and killed one of them whose parachute had been caught in the telephone wires after bailing out of his plane.	U.S.
US/9/789	Ger.	District-leader	Civilian	Bad Doberan, near Nebukow, Germany, (17.3.44)	Wanted for the murder of 6 American fliers near Nebukow, Germany, 12 March 1944. A U.S. Air Crew of 7 men, captured in district of Bad Doberan, Germany, was handed over to suspect on orders of Gauleiter of Mecklenburg. Six were found dead near Nebukow the next day.	U.S.
US/9/790		Ex-Bauernfuehrer	Civilian	Lashorst, Krs.Lübbeck, Germany (3.1945)	Wanted for the mistreatment of two wounded and burned American pilots after they had descended to the ground by parachute. Witnesses: Jean Du Bourg - ex French P.o.W., now at Ste.Andre du Bois, par Ste.Macaire, Gironde.	U.S.
US/9/791		Mayor	Civilian	Friebus, Germany, (March)	Wanted for mistreating Allied prisoners of war. Subject, the burgomaster of Friebus, Germany, failed to furnish shelter to Allied prisoners of war when same passed his town on a march from Sagan to Spremberg, at a time when the temperature was below zero.	U.S.
US/9/792		Czech Police Chief		Marava-Ostrava, Czech. (29.8.44)	Born: between 1890 and 1900, height: 5'8", characteristics: Fairly fat man. Wanted in connection with the beating and exhibition to the public of S/Sgt.William G Hagat and other unnamed American PW's at Morava-Ostrava, Czechoslovakia, (GSGS A50/059), on or about 29 August, 44. Suspect that is wanted is Czech Police Chief on about 29 Aug.44.	U.S.
US/9/793		Captain	Gestapo	Marava-Ostrava, Czech., (29.8.44)	Born: 1895 - 1900. Characteristics: Slight build. Suspect is wanted for the beating and mistreatment of S/Sgt. William G. Hayett, ASN 16 006113, and another un-named airman at Marava-Ostrava, Czechoslovakia, on or about 29 August 1944. S/Sgt. Hayett and another soldier were taken to Marava-Ostrava, after being captured and turned over to the Captain of Gestapo and the local head of the Czech police, at the police station. (W/R issued 25 June 1945). They were driven in a truck through the streets and displayed to the public and were subject to severe beatings by various un-named civilians and soldiers. They were returned to the police station where the un-named airman was severely beaten by the Gestapo Captain and the Czech policeman. Sgt.Hayett was also beaten by another un-named German civilian. Torture.	U.S.

9. NAZI PARTY MEMBERS - State Service, Gestapo, SD and Police. (Cont.)

C.R.FILE NO.	NATIO-NALITY	RANK OR STATUS	UNIT OR OCCUPATION	PLACE AND DATE OF CRIME	PARTICULARS OF CRIME OR REASON FOR WHICH WANTED FOLLOWED BY PHYSICAL DESCRIPTION IF KNOWN	WANTED BY
US/9/794	Ger.	Burgomaster		Neubukow and Rerik, Mecklenburg, Germany, (16.-17.3.44)	Born: 1900, weight: 150 lbs, height: 5'10", hair: straight waved, eyes: blue, reading glasses, characteristics: Tall and straight. Wanted for questioning in connection with the murder of six (6) US AAF personnel on or about 16 or 17 March 44 at or near Neubukow, Prov. Mecklenburg, Germany. Witness should be able to identify and give full names of the following witness: Commandant of Flak School, Rerik (W/R); Commandant of Air Corps Hospital, Rerik (W/R); Major in charge of PW camp for transient PW's. at Rerik (W/R). District Leader of Bad Doberan (W/R); and SS men who participated in murder.	U.S.
US/9/795	Ger.	Burgomaster	Civilian, Publ.offic.	Hoffnungstahl, Germany, (7.7.44)	Wanted for alleged murder of American pilot at Hoffnungstahl, Germany, on 7 July 1944. Suspect is alleged to have been present at the brutal beating of American pilot who parachuted down in vicinity of Hoffnungstahl, Germany, along with other civilians and 10 members of Leibstandarte Adolf Hitler. Address: Hoffnungsthal, Germany. Murder.	U.S.
US/9/796		Burgomaster	Civilian	Strassgange, near Graz, Austria, (12.3.1945)	Wanted for alleged murder of 7 American airmen forced down near Graz, Austria in March 1945.	U.S.
US/9/797	Hung.	Mayor	Civilian	of City of Sarosg, Hungary, (2.7.44)	Lt. Vittorio O. Russo was severely beaten by Hungarian troopers at Sarosg, Hungary, (90, K - S.W. of Budapest). The civilian Mayor of Sarosg on July 2, 1944 received a snapshot of the victim and the two perpetrators at about that same date. The Mayor took no part in war crime but should be able to identify perpetrators. Sworn statement of Lt Vittorio O. Russo, 2nd Lt.AC. Witness.	U.S.
US/9/798	Ger.	Kreisleiter	NSDAP	of Eschborn, Bad Soden, Germany, (1.or 2.45)	Involved in shooting of an American Airman shot down between Steinbach and Weisskirchen and interned at Bad Soden, Jan.or Febr.1945.	U.S.
US/9/799	Ger.	Kreisleiter	NSDAP, Civilian	of Giessen, Beltershain, Germany, (early 1945)	"Tried" 4 American airmen at Beltershain and condemned them to death. The airmen were shot 500-800 meters from Beltershain and buried in the Northern third of the forest, approx. location G 8626 (GSGS 4346, Germany 1:250000, Frankfurt am Main, Final Edition, Army/Air, Sheet L-51).	U.S.
US/9/800		Bauernfuehrer	Probably a civilian	A Suburb on the west of Graz, Strassgang, Austria, (10. 2.1945)	Wanted for allegedly killing 3 American airmen at or near Graz, Austria, 10 February 1945. The shooting may have occurred in or near Puntigam or Strassgang, suburbs of Graz. Suspect probably resides at Strassgang, Austria (near Graz).	U.S.
US/9/801	Ger.	Hptsturmfhr., Chief Hoehere SS and Pol.Fuehrer	SD, of Stab der SS and Polizei Fuehrung	Villach, Austria Laipach, (1.12.44-1.45)	Height: 170 cm. characteristics: Blood type tattooed under left arm. Wanted for the alleged murder of 4 American flyers in the vicinity of Villach (GSGS 4346, 1:250,000, K51, F53) in the French Zone. Between 1 Dec.1944 and Jan. 1945 certain SS men and one SD man were responsible for the execution of many American Airmen. Suspect close personal friend and believed hiding out with HARMS (W/R) at Muhlstadt.	U.S.
YUGO/9/802	Bulg.	Police-Official	Police	at Vladicin Han, District of Vladicin Han, (1943-1944)	MURDER. Christian name: "Djordjen".	YUGO.

10. CIVILIANS (Occupation known.)

C.R.FILE NO.	NATIO-NALITY	RANK OR STATUS	UNIT OR OCCUPATION	PLACE AND DATE OF CRIME	PARTICULARS OF CRIME OR REASON FOR WHICH WANTED FOLLOWED BY PHYSICAL DESCRIPTION IF KNOWN.	WANTED BY
BEL./10/803	Ger.	Interpreter	Prison	Goerlitz, Ger.,25.3.44 and later.	Murder and other crimes.Speaks English with strong American accent.	BEL.,FR.,U.K.
FR./10/804	Ger.	Interpreter	to Capt.Pielmann,who comd. detachment,Feldpost No. 28637A.	St.Hilaire de' Court(Cher.), France,31.8.44	Should be questioned about Murders etc.	FR.
FR./10/805	Ger.	Gamekeeper	to the countess von Finken-stein at Schoenberg.Lived at Sommerau.	On the road from Schoenberg to Eylau Rosenberg,East Prussia.17.3.44	Murder of P.O.W.LECOQ.About 65 years of age; white hair;height 1,70	FR.
FR./10/806	Ger.		Personnel pay office of Artificial Silk Works "Clanzstoff"	Elsterberg,Sax.12.44	Pillage.	FR.
FR./10/808	Ger.	Staff	Firm of "HAAG"	Barbarsonstrasse,Kaiserlautern	Surrendered number of Polish Jews to Gestapo,who subsequently hung them.Among persons of responsibility in firm LESSING, SPIEGEL, WEBER.	FR.
FR./10/809	Ger.	Members	Todt Organisation	Cherbourg, 1943	Responsible for the working camp at Ile a Aurigny accused of torture,systematics terrorism and pillage.	FR.
FR./10/810	Ger.	Chief	Fire Service Delmer-Bentz factory	Wuertemberg Unterturkeis, 1943	Ill-treatment of P.O.Ws.	FR.
U.K./10/811	Ger.	Overseer	Domestic Administration	Stalag IX C, 2.42	Brutality	U.K.
U.K./10/812	Ger.or Pol.	Local Doctor	Stalag	Ratibor Harmer,Poland, 10.1943	Torture.Passed P/W fit for work when he had acute mastoiditis.About 14 stone.Height 5'8".	U.K.
U.K./10/814	Ital.	Mother Superior	P.O.W.T.B.Hospital	Treviglio,Italy,42-43	Pillage.Food and clothing stolen from P.O.Ws.and given to civilian patients.	U.K.
U.K./10/815	Ger.	Doctor	Arb.Kdo.E 173	Setzdorf, 1943	Ill-treatment.Death of P.O.W.Through lack of medical treatments.Old man, going bald,pock-marked, pearshaped head,thin legs.	U.K.
U.K./10/816	Ger.	Works manager	Graf Rennard Colliery. Poland	Sosnovitz,Poland,6.1.44-19.1.45	Cruelty;Compulsorily detaining prisoners and Poles in coal strips containing a high percentage of gas.	U.K.
U.K./10/817	Ger.	Lagerleiter	Reichsbahnlager,main station	Halle-Saale	General ill-treatment of Polish workers in the Lager forced polish woman to work the morning following the birth of her child.	U.K.
U.K./10/818	Ger.	Schoolmaster		Sachsenburg,Germany, 3.45	Ill-treatment of allied airmen.	U.K.
U.S./10/819		Physician		Waldrach,Ruwer,Germany	Could give information about the NSDAP Ortsgruppen-leiter accused of maltreatment and murder of American pilot.9.44.He lives in the only wooden house,situated in the outskirts of the village from Trier.	U.S.
U.S./10/820	Ger.	Local schoolteacher		Neu Wuhmsdorf,Germany,20.6.44	Together with one Ernst Bors or Bors Ernst,responsible for killing parachuted American aviator.	U.S.
U.S./10/821		Farmhand	Civilian Guard	Poischendorf,Mecklenburg, Germany,29.5.44	Witness.He probably knows who killed the crew of an American bomber after it had crash landed, and also their place of burial.One eye red and blind; height 1,65;weight 85-87 kg	U.S.
U.S./10/822		Barrelmaker		Munstedt,Germany,March or April 45	Wanted for the alleged murder of two American flyers. weight 1,70; height 5'9";born 1900;husky build.	U.S.
U.S./10/823		Engineers.	Company of Hoch Tief Essen	Menden,Auerland,Germany,1944	Wanted,without exception, for alleged mistreating and killing of Allied Nationals.Especially cruel to French,Belgian,Dutch and Russian P.O.Ws.Three or four of them died daily.	U.S.
U.S./10/824		Head foreman or Yard Superintendant	Kosterman Coalyard	Munich,Germany, 6.44	Participation in the beating to death American Capt. who had parachuted to the ground.Extremely fat.red fleshy face;height 5'9".Hitler type moustache,reads and speaks English.	U.S.
U.S./10/825		Chemist		Frohnleiten a.d.Muhr,Austria	Refused an injection to an injured American flyer so that he died.	U.S.
U.S./10/826		Farmer		Gadebusch,Germany,Between 19 and 21 Sep 1943	Wanted for participation in the alleged murder of two American fliers.To be confined in PWE 29	U.S.
YUGO./10/827		Daughter-in-law	of Benz,Heinrich	Summer 1944,village of Ihlower-fehn,Aurich(Friesland)	Murder	YUGO.

11. CIVILIANS (Occupation not known.)

C.R.FILE NO.	NATIO-NALITY	RANK OR STATUS	UNIT OR OCCUPATION	PLACE AND DATE OF CRIME	PARTICULARS OF CRIME OR REASON FOR WHICH WANTED	WANTED BY
BEL./11/828	Ger.				Nickname "Le Chinois".See Consolidated Wanted List Part I(Germans) SUDENT Page 224-229 Brutality	BEL.
U.S./11/829				Rockau,Germany,25.2.44	Wanted for letting an American airman bleed to death from a cuts in his leg. Murder	U.S.
U.S./11/830	Ger.	Local official		Basement of a large building, like a courthouse,in small town 6 kilometers NW of Cologne.	Wanted for participation in beating of three Allied airmen.Date of birth 1915.Powerfully built. Height 6'0" Torture	U.S.

12. ALL CONCENTRATION CAMP PERSONNEL-Irrespective of Rank or Status.

C.R.FILE NO.	NATIO-NALITY	RANK OR STATUS	UNIT&OR OCCUPATION	PLACE AND DATE OF CRIME	PARTICULARS OF CRIME OR REASON FOR WHICH WANTED FOLLOWED BY PHYSICAL DESCRIPTION IF KNOWN	WANTED BY
BEL/12/831	Ger.	Criminal	in charge of executions	Boelke-Kaserne, Nordhausen-Dora, Germany, (1940-45)	32 years old, blond, red nose, 6 ft. tall Murder. First name: "Franz"	BEL.
BEL/12/832	Ger.		in charge of execution at Boelke-Kaserne	C.C. Nordhausen-Dora, Germany (1940-45)	Murder. First name: "Hans"	BEL.
BEL/12/833	Ger.	Chief Capo		Camp Schandelah-Braunschweig, Germany, (1944-45)	Ill-treatment of prisoners. First name: "Hans"	BEL.
BEL/12/834	Ger.	Commandant	SA	C.C. Rheinbach, Germany, (betw. Sept. and end 41)	Murder and other crimes. Fair hair, height 1,80 First name: "Heinz".	BEL.
BEL/12/835	Ger.	Common law prisoner foreman	in command of a section of the Brick works, Auscharte 3	C.C. Neuengamme, Germany, (from 22.9.41)	Murder, 30-35 years old, height about 1,65 very stout dark hair, healther complexion reddish face. First name: "Joup."	BEL.
BEL/12/836	Ger.	Kapo		C.C. Dachau, Germany, (7.1.43)	Participated in tortures and brutalities Nick-name "Ludwig".	BEL.
BEL/12/837	Ger.	Guard		C.C. Mauthausen (Aust.) (since 1943)	Ill-treatment of civil internees. Stole a precious diamond from a prisoner. Nick-name "Paul". 40-45 years old.	BEL.
BEL/12/838	Pol.	Lageraelteste		C.C. Bergen-Belsen, Germany	Participation in tortures and brutalities Nick-name "Stenia"	BEL.
BEL/12-839	Ger.	Guards		C.C. Neuengamme, Germany,	Inhuman treatment of Belgian civilians, many of whom died as a consequence of innumerable acts of ferocity.	BEL.
BEL/12/840	Ger.	Political commissary		C.C. Neuengamme, Germany,	Murders and brutalities (author or co-operator)	BEL.
BEL/12/841	Ger.	Camp doctor	Gievenbeck camp	C.C. Muenster, Germany (27.3.45)	Ill-treatment of civilians	BEL.
BEL/12/842	Ger.	Chiefs	of disinfection house	C.C. Bergen-Belsen, Germany	Ill-treatment on Belgian prisoners	BEL.
BEL/12/843	Ger.	Chief	of kitchens 1 and 2	C.C. Bergen-Belsen, Germany	Participation in ill-treatment inflicted on Belgian prisoners.	BEL.
BEL/12/844	Ger.	Commandant	Erla camp	C.C. Chemnitz, Germany (1943)	Ill-treatment of civilians	BEL.
BEL/12/845		Blockaelteste	block 15	C.C. Dachau, Germany (since 7.1.43)	Tortures and brutalities.	BEL.
BEL/12/846	Ger.	Chief	of room 27/4, said disciplineroom	C.C. Dachau, Germany (2.-5.45)	Tortures and brutalities	BEL.
BEL/12/847		Kapo	block 27	C.C. Dachau, Germany (since 7.1.43)	Participation in tortures and brutalities.	BEL.
BEL/12/848		Kapo	block 20	C.C. Dachau, Germany (since 7.1.43)	Participation in tortures and brutalities.	BEL.
BEL/12/849	Ger.	Guard		C.C. Dachau, Germany	Ill-treatment and massacre of Belgian prisoners	BEL.
BEL/12/850	Ger.	Blockaeltester	Block 30	C.C. Dachau, Germany (since 7.1.43)	Author or co-operator of murder, tortures and brutalities.	BEL.
BEL/12/851		Blockaeltester	block 21	C.C. Dachau, Germany	Ill-treatments. Responsible for the death of numerous prisoners.	BEL.
BEL/12/852		Chief	of room 4 of block 20	C.C. Dachau, Germany (since 7.1.43)	Participation in tortures and brutalities.	BEL.
BEL/12/853	Ger.	Commandant	Camp Dora II	C.C. Duisburg, Germany, (8.44)	Ill-treatment of a Belgian prisoner, living at Hamborn	BEL.
BEL/12/854		Commandant		C.C. Esterwegen, Germany (since 24.5.43)	Responsible for slaughter and ill-treatment of Belgian prisoners.	BEL.
BEL/12/855	Ger.	Chief	of the "Autopark" block	C.C. Flossenburg, Germany	Accused of atrocities and murders	BEL.
BEL/12/856	Ger.	Chief	of block 18	C.C. Flossenburg, Germany	Accused of brutal treatment of prisoners	BEL.
BEL/12/857	Ger.	Asst. to Blockaeltester	block 18	C.C. Flossenburg, Germany	Accused of brutal treatment of prisoners	BEL.
BEL/12/858	Ger.	Lageraeltester		C.C. Flossenburg, Germany	Accused of atrocities and slaughter	BEL.
BEL/12/859	Ger.	Kapo	of the "Barackenbau"	C.C. Flossenburg, Germany	Blows, wounds and serious brutalities inflicted on prisoners.	BEL.
BEL/12/860		Blockaeltester	of block 9	C.C. Gross-Rosen, Germany	Murders, tortures and brutalities (author or part author)	BEL.
BEL/12/861	Ger.	Kommandofhr.	of the sporting-place	C.C. Mauthausen, Austria (8.7.42-8.11.42)	Ill-treatment of civil prisoners, with serious or fatal consequences for the victims.	BEL.
BEL/12/862	Ger.	Arbeitsdienstfhr.		C.C. Mauthausen, Austria	Accused of atrocities and murders,	BEL.
BEL/12/863	Ger.	Blockaeltester	of block 15	C.C. Mauthausen, Austria	Participated in tortures and violences. 35 years old	BEL.
BEL/12/864	Ger.	Blockaeltester	of block 16	C.C. Mauthausen, Austria (since 1942)	Participated especially in the murder of the Belgian police-inspector Bouddet de Bressoux. Participated, too, in serious violences against Mr. Bonnameau, from Liege.	BEL.
BEL/12/865	Ger.	Blockaeltester	of block 19	C.C. Mauthausen, Austria (since 1942)	Participated especially in the murder of the Belgian police-inspector BOUDET de BRESSOUX. Participated, too, in serious violences against Mr. BONRAMEAU, Joseph, from LIEGE.	BEL.
BEL/12/866	Ger.	Blockaeltester	of Block 31	C.C. Gusen-Mauthausen, Austria (since 1943)	Participation in murders and brutalities.	BEL.
BEL/12/867	Ger.	Kapos	of block 15	C.C. Mauthausen, Austria	Participated in tortures and violences.	BEL.
BEL/12/868	Ger.	Kitchen-personnel		Ebrach,	Co-responsibility for ill conditions in the penitentiary and sufferings inflicted on the prisoners.	BEL.
BEL/12/869	Ger.	Director		Penitentiary Ebrach	Responsible for ill conditions in the penitentiary and sufferings inflicted on the prisoners.	BEL.
BEL/12/870	Ger.	Chief of guards		Penitentiary Ebrach	Shares responsibility for ill conditions in the penitentiary and sufferings inflicted on the prisoners.	BEL.
BEL/12/871	Ger.	Nursing personnel		Penitentiary Ebrach	Nursing personnel at Ebrachs penitentiary (the Czech detained among them excepted) shares responsibility for ill conditions in that prison and sufferings inflicted on the prisoners.	BEL.

12. ALL CONCENTRATION CAMP PERSONNEL - Irrespective of Rank or Status (cont.)

C.R.FILE NO.	NATIO-NALITY	RANK OR STATUS	UNIT OR OCCUPATION	PLACE AND DATE OF CRIME	PARTICULARS OF CRIME OR REASON FOR WHICH WANTED FOLLOWED BY PHYSICAL DESCRIPTION IF KNOWN	WANTED BY
BEL/12/872	Ger.	Guard of camp		Woippy, Dept.Moselle, France (44)	Internment of civilians under inhuman conditions.	BEL., FR.
BEL/12/873	Ger.	SS-Guards	Staff of "Woippy-camp"	Camp de Woippy, Dept.Moselle, France (44)	Systematic terrorism against prisoners at Woippy Camp. (Many Belgians were among them.) Internment of civilians under inhuman conditions. Brutalities.	BEL.
BEL/12/874		SS-Guards	employed "Woippy-camp"	Woippy, Dept.Moselle, France (44)	Internment of civilians under inhuman conditions.	BEL., FR.
BEL/12/875	Ger.	Camp-Guard	SS	C.C. Oswiecim, Rajsko, Poland (43 to May 44)	Torture of civilians and other crimes.	BEL., POL.
BEL/12/876	Ger.	Chief	SS	C.C. Oswiecim, Rajsko, Poland (40-43)	Murder, torture, and other crimes.	BEL., POL.
BEL/12/877	Ger.	Cmdt. of camp		C.C.Rheydt, Germany (45)	Torture of civilians.	BEL., FR.
BEL/12/878	Ger.	Chief and factory employing men	Block 132	Camp Dora, C.C.Buchenwald, Nordhausen (40-45)	Murder.	BEL., FR.
BEL/12/879			At charge of kitchens 1 and 2	C.C. Belsen (40)	Murder.	BEL.
BEL/12/880	Ger.	Head	of Praesifix Camp	C.C. Dachau (43-45)	Murder.	BEL.
BEL/12/881	Ger.	Baraekaeltester No.22		C.C.Flossenburg (since 13.9.45)	Murder.	BEL.
BEL/12/882	Ger.	Blockfuehrer 21		C.C.Flossenburg (2.-9.45)	Murder.	BEL.
BEL/12/883	Ger.	Chief	of Block 8	C.C.Flossenburg (12.44-45)	Torture.	BEL.
BEL/12/884	Ger.	Kapo	of Block 5 1/e B Wing	C.C.Flossenburg (2.-3.45)	Murder. Age about 35.	BEL.
BEL/12/885	Ger.	Usturmfhr.		C.C. Buchenwald (41)	Brutality.	BEL.
BEL/12/886	Ger.	Cmdt.		C.C. Niederooden (6.-10.44)	Brutality.	BEL.
BEL/12/887	Ger.	Rapportfhr.		Floridsdorf and Moedling, Schwechat C.C. (since 44)	Murder.	BEL.
BEL/12/888	Ger.	SS-Lt., Cmdt.		Schwechat, Floridsdorf and C.C.Moedling (since 44)	Murder.	BEL.
BEL/12/889	Ger.	Blockfuehrer 23		C.C.Flossenburg (20.1.45-1.3.45)	Murder.	BEL.
BEL/12/890	Ger.	Blockfuehrer 9		C.C.Flossenburg (20.1.45-10.3.45)	Murder.	BEL.
BEL/12/891	Ger.	Blockfuehrer 21		C.C.Flossenburg (20.1.45-10.3.45)	Murder.	BEL.
BEL/12/892	Ger.	Kommandofuehrer	of the quarry	C.C. Mauthausen, Austria (18.4.43-28.4.45)	Murder.	BEL.
BEL/12/893	Ger.	Room-warder	of room 4, Block 17	C.C.Dachau, Germany (19.6.42-29.4.45)	Torture.	BEL.
BEL/12/894	Ger.	Room-warder	of room 9, Block 28	C.C.Dachau, Germany (19.6.42-29.4.45)	Torture.	BEL.
BEL/12/895	Ger.	Blockaeltester	of Block 20	Camp Neuengamme, Germany	Tortures and violences at Neuengamme (author or co-operator). Nicknamed: The "one-eyed".	BEL.
BEL/12/896		Member of Staff		Camp Woippy, Dept.Moselle, France (44)	Internment of civilians under inhuman conditions. Nicknamed "the fighter"	BEL.
BEL/12/897	Ger.			C.C.Papenburg.	Misc.crimes. Nickname: "Charlot"	BEL.
BEL/12/898	Ger.	N.C.O. and factory employing men	Camp Dora	C.C.Nordhausen and Buchenwald, Germany (40-45)	Murder. (Known as "Gueule en biais")	BEL., FR.
BEL/12/899	Ger.	Uscharfhr.		C.C.Dachau, Germany (40-45)	Murder. (Nicknamed: "Noir")	BEL.
BEL/12/900	Ger.	Lageraeltester		C.C.Flossenburg, Germany (12.44)	Murder.	BEL., FR.
BEL/12/901	Ger.	Blockaeltester	of Block 4	C.C.Neuengamme, Germany	Tortures and violences at Neuengamme (author or co-operator) (Nicknamed: "Le tatoué")	BEL.
BEL/12/902		Member of Staff	at Woippy Camp	Woippy, Dept. Moselle, France (45)	Internment of civilians, under inhuman conditions.	BEL.
CZECH/12/903	Ger.	Chief Medical Off.	of the Stammanstalt	Hadamar-Lahn, Germany	Murder, massacres and other crimes.	CZECH.
CZECH/12/904	Ger.	Head and Chief Med.Off.	of the Reichsarbeits-gemeinschaft	Germany	Murder, massacres and other crimes.	CZECH.
CZECH/12/905	Ger.	Chief Med.	Mental Home	Pirna-Elbe, Germany (40-45)	Murder, massacres and other crimes.	CZECH.
CZECH/12/906	Ger.	Senior wardress		C.C.Oswiecim-Birkenau, Poland (39-45)	Murder and massacres. Systematic terrorism. Formerly attached to C.C.Ravensbrueck	CZECH.
CZECH/12/907	Ger.	Members	of Totenkopf-Standarte, 6. SS	Terezin. (Czech.) (1.10.38-44)	Torture and ill-treatment causing death and other crimes.	CZECH.
CZECH/12/908	Ger.	SS-Hptscharfhr.		C.C.Dachau, Sachsenhausen, Germany.	Murder. Born 1910. Nickname "Eiserner Gustav"	BEL., CZECH., FR., POL., U.K., U.S.
FR/12/909	Ger.			Ravensbrueck, Germany.	Brutalities. 25 or 26 years. Height 1'78", fair compl.	FR.
FR/12/910				Camp de Minden, Germany.	Brutalities. 60 years. Height 1'65. Hair brown. (Aliases: French or Süram, Georges) Nose crooked	
FR/12/911	Ger.			Camp de Flossenburg, Germany	Had been a prisoner of the French in 1914-1918 and hated them. He used to beat the prisoners. "I" Gustav or Harry".	FR.
FR/12/912	Ger.	Kapo	Atelier N. 2	Camp Flossenburg, Germany, Kdo. of Floha. (15.4.45)	Murder.	FR.
FR/12/913	Ger.	Chief	Revier 4	Camp Neuengamme, Germany.	Torture. First name: Hans.	FR.
FR/12/914	Ger.	Kapo		Stephanskirchen, Krs. Rosenheim.	Brutality. First name: Hans Rudolph.	FR.

12. ALL CONCENTRATION CAMP PERSONNEL-Irrespective of Rank or Status. (Cont.)

C.R.FILE NO.	NATIO-NALITY	RANK OR STATUS	UNIT OR OCCUPATION	PLACE AND DATE OF CRIME	PARTICULARS OF CRIME OR REASON FOR WHICH WANTED FOLLOWED BY PHYSICAL DESCRIPTION IF KNOWN	WANTED BY
FR/12/915	Pol.		Overseer of prisoners	C.C.Neu-Brenn near Saarbruck,Germany	Participated in murders,tortures,ill-treatments of prisoners.	FR.
FR/12/916	Ger.	SS Rottenfhr.		C.C.Buchenwald,Germany	Torture	FR.
FR/12/917	Ger.	Foreman	Civilian	C.C.Sachsenhausen,Germany (42-45)	Brutality First name: Max.	FR.
FR/12/918	Ger.	Kapo,head	of block 31	C.C.Buchenwald,Germany(42-45)	Murder	FR.
FR/12/919	Ger.	Kapo	of block 7,Common law prisoner	C.C.Flossenburg,Bavaria,Germany, (42-45)	Murder First name: "Willy"	FR.
FR/12/920	Ger.	Commandant		C.C.Langenfeld,Germany	During the evacuation of camp Langenfeld,on 20.4.45 the sick of the hospital were fettered to their beds, then burnt.	FR.
FR/12/921	Ger.	Commandant		C.C.Klein Glattebach near Vaihingen,Germany	Responsible for all kinds of tortures towards the detained, whose physical misery was frightful. Out of 9000 detained who had passed through,3 quarters died.	FR.
FR/12/922	Ger.	Commandant		C.C.Hedderheim,Germany	Ill-treatment towards political deportees.	FR.
FR/12/923	Ger.	Commandant	Camp 21	C.C.Wattenscheid,Germany	Responsible for the murder of the French forced labourers;Bellier Marcel(13.July 44) and Bourjon Jacques (towards end of July 45) at Braunschweig mun.factory.	FR.
FR/12/924	Ger.	Zivilmeister (Edo.)		C.C.Sachsenhausen,Oranienburg Germany (42-45)	Lived in a village near camp,spoke Polish, escaped with the SS,murder	FR.
FR/12/925	Ger.	Deputy chief	of block 38	C.C.Oranienburg,Sachsenhausen Germany, (42-45)	Murder	FR.
FR/12/926	Ger.	Head	of block 38	C.C.Oranienburg,Sachsenhausen Germany (42-45)	Murder	FR.
FR/12/927	Ger.	Deputy-chief	of block 37	C.C.Oranienburg,Sachsenhausen Germany (42-45)	Murder	FR.
FR/12/928	Ger.	Head,German Detainee	of block 37	C.C.Oranienburg,Sachsenhausen Germany	Murder	FR.
FR/12/929	Ger.	Commandant	of Jawarzno Camp	(8.-9.43)	Murder	FR.
FR/12/930	Ger.	Commandant		C.C.Birkenau,Germany (7.43)	Murder	FR.
FR/12/931	Ger.	Commandant		C.C.Dachau,Germany(since 1940)	Murder	FR.
FR/12/932	Ger.	Commandant		of Tourlaville Penal camp (2.1944)	Torture	FR.
FR/12/933	Ger.	Oberkapo	at station	C.C.Auschwitz,Poland,(40-45)	Murder	FR.
FR/12/934	Ger.	Female warder		C.C.Uckermark,Germany(42-45)	Murder	FR.
FR/12/935	Ger.	Rapportfhr. X		C.C.Dachau,Germany	Brutality	FR.
FR/12/936	Ger.	Head	of block 7	C.C.Flossenburg,Germany, (42-45)	Murder	FR.
FR/12/937	Pol.	Employee	SS,internee	C.C.Neubrenn,Saar,Germany (43-44)	Misc.Crimes	FR.
FR/12/938	Ger.	Chief	of Gestapo	Munich,C.C.Dachau,Germany (from 1940)	Murder	FR.
FR/12/939	Ger.			C.C.Neuengamme,Germany,(2.40-4.45)	Murder	FR.
FR/12/940	Ger.	Head,German common law detainee	of block 2,at the camp hospital	C.C.Mauthausen,Austria,(11.42-till Liberation 5.45)	Murder	FR.
FR/12/941	Ger.	Head	of block 5	C.C.Mauthausen,Austria,(11.42 till 5.45)	Murder	FR.
FR/12/942	Ger.	Lageraeltester	Block 5	C.C.Mauthausen,Austria(11.42 till Liberation 5.45)	Murder	FR.
FR/12/943	Ger.	Oberkapo	No.50124 at Keller Bau, Kommando Steyr,	C.C.Mauthausen,Austria,(11.42 till Liberation 5.45)	Murder	FR.
FR/12/944	Ger.	Guard	at the home court mine	Bassin de Briey(M-ET-M)(40-44)	Murder	FR.
FR/12/945	Ger.	SS N.C.O.	worked in"mirador" No.2 of the camp	C.C.Dachau,Germany		FR.
FR/12/946	Ger.	Blockmann	of block 16	C.C.Flossenburg,Bavaria,Germany (1942-45)	Murder,Nicknamed:"Der grosse Fritz".Of gipsy origin	FR.
FR/12/947	Ger.	Political internee head	of block 4	C.C.Flossenburg,Bavaria, Germany, (1942-45)	Murder, Nicknamed:"l'etrangleur"	FR.
FR/12/948	Ger.	Camp leader	Loibl-Pass camp,Kdo. at	C.C.Mauthausen,Austria,(43-45)	Murder, Nicknamed:"Manciel"	FR.
FR/12/949	Ger.	Head	of block,South camp,Loibl-Pass camp,Kdo. at	C.C.Mauthausen,Austria,(43-45)	Murder,Nicknamed:"The Tattooed"	FR.
FR/12/950	Ger.	Commander	of the camp at Loibl-Pass		Called a Russian a bad worker.This Russian was then killed by an SS soldier.Without any reason he used to beat the prisoners with an iron rod,daily. About 44 years old. Alias:"Manceil".	FR.
FR/12/951	Ger.	Chief	of block at south camp.		In order to enforce work on the prisoners, he constantly beat them with a bull's pizzle. (Witness Capitole Pierre)	FR.
NETH/12/952	Ger.	Usturmfhr.head	of camp,Arbeitserziehungslager	Lahde near Hannover,Germany (11.2.45-24.3.45)	Had a stiff or wooden leg,Murder	NETH.
NETH/12/953	Ger.	Wachtmeister	Arbeitserziehungslager	Lahde near Hannover,Germany	Heavy build,Nicknamed:"The horse",Murder	NETH.
NETH/12/954	Ger.	Revierhauptwachtmeister	of the Green Police,Arbeitserziehungslager	Lahde near Hannover,Germany (11.2.45-24.3.45)	Nicknamed:"Tempo",Murder	NETH.
NOR/12/955		Doctor	SS Dreibergen prison	C.C.Buetzow,Mecklenburg, Germany	Responsible for a number of deaths of political prisoners.(Norwegians and Danes) He was a beast	NOR.
NOR/12/956		Head doctor	SS Hospital	Buetzow,Mecklenburg,Germany	Responsible for a number of deaths of political prisoners.(Norwegians and Danes)	NOR.

12. ALL CONCENTRATION CAMP PERSONNEL-Irrespective of Rank or Status. (Cont.)

C.R.FILE NO.	NATIO-NALITY	RANK OR STATUS	UNIT OR OCCUPATION	PLACE AND DATE OF CRIME	PARTICULARS OF CRIME OR REASON FOR WHICH WANTED FOLLOWED BY PHYSICAL DESCRIPTION IF KNOWN	WANTED BY
POL/12/957	Ger.	Commander	Lager	C.C.Sobibor for Jews, Poland (42 - 43)	Murder and other crimes.	POL.
POL/12/958	Ger.	Commandant		C.C.for Jews,Kosow,Podlaski Poland (42 - 43)	Murder and other crimes.	POL.
POL/12/959	Ger.	Commandant,Officer		C.C.for Jews,Maidanek near Lublin,Poland (42 - 43)	Murder and other crimes.	POL.
POL/12/960	Ger.	Commander		C.C.for Jews,Chelmo (Kulmhof) Poland (42 - 43)	Massmurder and other crimes.	POL.
POL/12/961		Blockfhr.		C.C.Auschwitz,Poland (41)	Inhuman treatment of Prisoners. Stoned to death a Polish priest.	POL.
POL/12/962	Ger.	Commander	Lager	C.C.Ravensbrueck,Germany (3.42)	Murder,Torture,ill-treatment of internees.	POL.
POL/12/963	Ger.	Commander	Lager	C.C.Opava,(Troppau),Czech. (39-42)	Massmurder.	POL.
POL/12/964	Ger.	Sturmbannfhr.	SS,in command of a detachment of the Landesschutz	Warsaw,Poland (39)	Massmurder,torture.	POL.
UK/12/965	Ger.	SS-Guard	Transit camp	C.C.Romainville, (8.44)	Wanted for ill-treatment of internees at Romainville camp, further particulars, well built, hard looking. About 1918 born.	UK.
UK/12/966	Ger.	Commandant,head Official	German SS, SD	C.C.Theresienstadt,Czech. (3.3.-4.4.45)	Illegal internment and ill-treatment of POW's.	UK.
UK/12/967	Ger.	Doctor	Prison	C.C.Cottbus,Germany, (14.3.44 and 2.45)	Murder.	UK.
UK/12/968	Ger.	Commandant or successor	Prison	C.C.Cottbus,Germany, (14.3.44 and 2.45)	Murder.	U.K.
UK/12/969	Ger.	Oschfhr.,	SS, in charge of	C.C.Torgau,Germany, (8.44)	Wanted for the ill-treatment of internees. Further particulars,square face,wore uniform of SS. About 1905 born.	U.K.
UK/12/970		Chief,commandant	of Camp	C.C.Auschwitz,Poland (9.or 10.44)	Ill-treatment of POW's.	U.K.
UK/12/971	Ger.	Nurse	at the hospital	C.C.Ravensbrueck,Germany (about 8.44)	Wanted for the ill-treatment of internees. Further particulars,spoke a little French. About 1885 born.	U.K.
UK/12/972	Yugo.	Officer		C.C.Jasenovac,Yugo. (25.4.45)	Wore epaulettes with 3 stars on each.Slight build, very soldierly bearing.Speaks fluent French. Suspected accused:Ill-treatment of POW's during interrogation at Jasenovac 24.4.45,while en route to No.1 POW Camp Zagreb,Yugo.About 1913 born.	U.K.
UK/12/973	Ger.	Wardress		C.C.Cottbus,Germany (14.3.44 and 2.45)	Brutality,Nicknamed: "The Cockatoo",but was generally called."La Gestapo".	U.K.
US/12/974		Officers and men	SS, 17.Landes-schuetzen-Rgt.	C.C.Gardelegen,Germany (13.4.45)	Regiment reffered to is claimed have participated in the massacre of 1100 Jews and Allied prisoners of war at Gardelegen.Murder.	U.S.
US/12/975		Officers and men	4.SS Bau-Bde. (Formerly SS-Div.Totenkopf)	en route to and at or near C.C.Gardelegen,Germany (5.-14.4.45)	Murder.Wanted for participation in the murder, torture and abuse of hundreds of political prisoners while en route to and at or in the vicinity of Gardelegen.Because of rapid advance of American troops, political prisoners from numerous concentration camps in Germany were evacuated to the vicinity of Kreis Gardelegen. En route many were starved,beaten and shot. Of those who arrived at the Isenschnibbe Barn, near Gardelegen,1016 were killed by burning and shooting on 13-14 April 1945.	U.S.
US/12/976		Officers and men	3.SS-Bau-Bde.(Formerly SS-Div.Totenkopf)	en route to and at or near C.C.Gardelegen,Germany, (5.-14.4.45)	Murder.Wanted for participation in the murder, torture and abuse of hundreds of political prisoners while en route to and at or in the vicinity of Gardelegen.Because of rapid advance of American troops,political prisoners from numerous concentration camps in Germany were evacuated to the vicinity of Kreis Gardelegen.En route many were starved,beaten and shot. Of those who arrived at the Isenschnibbe Barn,near Gardelegen,1016 were killed by burning and shooting on 13- 14. April 1945.	U.S.
US/12/978	Ger.	Camp-Policeman		C.C.St.Ludwig's-Monastery, Netherland, (17.11.44)	Murder.Wanted as the perpetrator of an alleged war crime in which seven (7) female Russian forced laborers were physically abused and finally shot and killed. Hans was a policeman at a camp at St.Ludwig's-Monastery located approximately 15 kilometers southeast of Roermond,Netherlands, on 17 November 1944, the date of the alleged war crime. At the camp, Hans was known as Policeman Hans, his surname has not been ascertained.	U.S.

-120-

12. ALL CONCENTRATION CAMP PERSONNEL - Irrespective of Rank or Status. (Cont.)

C.R.FILE NO.	NATIO-NALITY	RANK OR STATUS	UNIT OR OCCUPATION	PLACE AND DATE OF CRIME	PARTICULARS OF CRIME OR REASON FOR WHICH WANTED FOLLOWED BY PHYSICAL DESCRIPTION IF KNOWN	WANTED BY
US/12/979	Ger.	SS-Uschfhr.		C.C.Pankofen,Bavaria, Germany,(22.4.45)	Murder.Wanted in connection with the murder by shooting of nine (9) Allied nationals concentration camp prisoners,enroute from Buchenwald to another concentration camp,at Pankofen,near Plattling, Germany,on 22 April 1945.Subject was one of the guards on the train.Subject is alleged to have taken fifty (50) seriously injured prisoners from Freising to Munich,by truck on 28 April 1945.	U.S.
US/12/980	Serb.	SS-Sturmmann		C.C.Saal on the Danube,Kelheim,Germany,(1.12.44-22.4.45)	Wanted for murders, brutal beatings,starvation and cruel and inhumane treatment of political prisoners, Allied nationals,at the concentration camp at Saal on the Danube,Germany,between 1.12.44 and 22.4.45. Subject was a guard at above camp.Participated in the shooting and beating of prisoners.Surname of Perpetrator unknown.Born:1924.	U.S.
US/12/981	Ukr.	Policeman,Guard	Police Department Nuernberg,Gestapo,Nuernberg	C.C.Langenzenn,Bavaria, Germany,(1943-1945)	Wanted for beatings and other mistreatment of foreign workers at the concentration camp.Suspect was employed by the Gestapo in Nuernberg.First name: Nicolei.	U.S.
US/12/982	Ger.	Policeman		C.C.Ludwig's Monastery, Netherlands,(17.11.44)	Wanted as the perpetrator of an alleged war crime in which seven (7) female Russian forced laborers were physically abused and finally shot and killed. First name: Otto.	U.S.
US/12/983	Ger.	Kapo		Kamp Kreis St.Goar,Germany, (29.12.44)	Wanted for murder of 3 unknown United States airmen at Kamp (K50/WL 9280).Suspect known as "Kappo" was probably a professional criminal in charge of the prisoners. He acted as cook in the prison train. He was known in Kamp as being a rascal,brutal and arrogant. Place of his home,and other personal data, are unknown.First name: Otto.About 1917 born; High forehead,blond Eyebrows,long pointed nose, pointed chin,oval face,tall,strong,broad body,blue eyes,brutal,arrogant,appearance.	U.S.
US/12/984		Kapo		C.C.Flossenburg,Germany, (1944-1945)	Murder.Wanted for the participation in the killings brutal punishment and mistreatment of PW's at C.C. Suspect was Kapo of the potato peelers.First name: Paul.	U.S.
US/12/985		Commandant		C.C.Amersfoort,Netherlands, (6.1944)	Torture.Wanted for participating in the alleged mistreatment of Allied nationals.Between 8 June and 22 June 1944 prisoners were made to march from morning until evening while guards beat them with wooden clubs. The camp commander had a vicious dog which he often set upon the prisoners.	U.S.
US/12/986		Commandant		C.C.Vucht,Netherlands, (6.1944)	Wanted for participating in the alleged murder of Bommel, the son of the Mayor of either Tilburg or Breda.Bommel's execution was at the orders of the camp commandant.	U.S.
US/12/987		SS-Rottfhr., Guard		C.C.Saal on the Danube, Kelheim,Germany, (1.12.44-22.4.45)	Wanted for murders,brutal beatings,starvation, cremation and cruel inhumane treatment of political prisoners,Allied nationals,at the concentration camp. Small build. Height: 1,65. Blue eyes. Fair hair.	U.S.
US/12/988		Uschfhr., SS-Guard		C.C.Saal on the Danube, Kelheim,Germany, (1.12.44-22.4.45)	Wanted for murders,brutal beatings,starvations, cremation and cruel inhumane treatment of political prisoners,Allied nationals,at the concentration camp. Turning grey hair,blue eyes,height: 1,82,Bavarian Dialect.	U.S.
US/12/989	Aust.	Guard		Saal on the Danube,C.C., Kelheim,Germany, (1.12.44-22.4.45)	Wanted for murders,brutal beatings,starvations cremation and cruel inhumane treatment of political prisoners,Allied nationals,at the concentration camp.Weight:85 kilo,height:1,76,blue eyes, brown hair,thin face,talked out of side of mouth.	U.S.
US/12/990		Uschfhr., SS		C.C.Saal on the Danube, Kelheim,Germany, (1.12.44-22.4.45)	Wanted for murders,brutal beatings,starvations, cremation and cruel inhumane treatment of political prisoners,Allied nationals,at the concentration camp.Height:1,75,turning grey hair,brown eyes, false teeth.	U.S.
US/12/991		SS-Guard		Schwarzenfeld,Germany, (16.-25.4.45)	Wanted for murder by shooting,cruel and inhumane treatment and starvation of Allied civil nationals while on a transport of prisoners stopped in Schwarzenfeld.Responsible for shooting sick and starved prisoners and those who were wounded from an air attack.Weight:70 kilo,height:1,65,black hair,brown eyes,dark complexion,nonchalant posture, clean shaven,upper jaw, only one tooth. Born: 1910 - 1895.	U.S.
US/12/992		SS-Guard		Schwarzenfeld,Germany, (16.-25.4.45)	Wanted for murder by shooting,cruel and inhumane treatment and starvation of Allied civil nationals while on a transport of prisoners stopped.Responsible for shooting sick and starved prisoners and those who were wounded from an air attack.Weight: 60 kilo,height:1,70,dark complexion,non-military posture,clean shaven. Born: 1895 - 1905.	U.S.

12. ALL CONCENTRATION CAMP PERSONNEL-Irrespective of Rank or Status. (Cont.)

C.R.FILE NO.	NATIO-NALITY	RANK OR STATUS	UNIT OR OCCUPATION	PLACE AND DATE OF CRIME	PARTICULARS OF CRIME OR REASON FOR WHICH WANTED FOLLOWED BY PHYSICAL DESCRIPTION IF KNOWN	WANTED BY
US/12/993		Oberscharfhr.,SS Transport leader		Schwarzenfeld,Germany, (16.-25.4.45)	Wanted for the murder by shooting,cruel and inhumane treatment and starvation of Allied civil nationals while on a transport of prisoners stopped.Responsible for the many deaths that incurred while the train was halted,by the shooting and starvation of prisoners.Born 1905-1910.Weight 70-75 kilo,height 1,75,turning grey hair,fair hair,dark complexion,clean shaven, military posture.	U.S.
US/12/994		SS Oberscharfhr., train commander		Schwarzenfeld,Germany, (16.-25.4.45)	Wanted for the murder by shooting,cruel and inhumane treatment and starvation of Allied civil nationals while on a transport of prisoners stopped.Responsible for the many deaths that incurred while the train was halted,by the shooting of sick and starved prisoners.Born about 1910. Weight 80 kilo,height 1,84,black hair,dark complexion,smooth shaven,strong military posture.	U.S.
US/12/995		Scharfhr.,SS, guard.		Schwarzenfeld,Germany, (16.-25.4.45)	Wanted for the murder,by shooting,cruel and inhumane treatment and starvation of Allied civil natinals while on a transport of prisoners stopped.Responsible for shooting sick and starved prisoners and those who were wounded from an air attack.Born about 1905-1910.Weight 70 kilo, height 1,75,clean shaven,military posture, Prussian accent.	U.S.
US/12/996	Ger.	Chief nurse		Hadmar,Germany,C.C.	height 6 feet,	U.S.
US/12/997	Ger.	Head keeper		Hadmar,Germany,C.C.		U.S.
US/12/998	Ger.	Doctor		C.C.Hadmar,Germany	born 1875	U.S.
US/12/999	Ger.	Lagerkapo	Arbeitskommando	C.C.Jawiszoice,Auschwitz, Poland, (43-44)	Born 1915,Slim,medium height,very brutal,wore a green triangle.Suspect was one of those in charge of Jawiszoice C.C.,which was a subsidiary of Oswiecim.Work at this camp was mainly in coal mines. Every four to six weeks and select 100 or more of the sickest prisoners to be gassed at Birkehau. In November 1943,300 men were so selected, and in December 1943,400 more.About the middle of January 1945,the entire camp was evacuated in one column of 1500 men.They were taken first to Leslau where they arrived in two or three days and then by rail to Buchenwald where they arrived two days later. Nick-name: Karol.	U.S.
US/12/1000		Lageraeltester	Arbeitskommando	C.C.Jawiszoice,Auschwitz, Poland,(43-44)	Suspect was one of those in charge of Jawiszoice C.C.U.S. which was a subsidiary of Oswiecim. Every four to six weeks and select 100 or more of the sickest prisoners to be gassed at Birkenau. In November 1943,300 men were so selected, and in December 1943,400 more.About the middle of January 1945,the entire camp was evacuated in one column of 1500 men.They were taken first to Leslau where they arrived in two or three days and by rail to Buchenwald where they arrived two days later.Nick-name: "Paul".	
US/12/1001	Ital.	Agent		C.C.Corropola (1941)	Torture of civilians,Christian name:Giuseppe)	YUGO.
YUGO/12/1001	Ital.	Agent		C.C.Corropola (1941)	Murder	YUGO.
YUGO/12/1002	Ger.	Chemist		C.C.Dachau,Germany(during 1942)C.C.board Oranienburg Germany,(during 1945)		
YUGO/12/1003	Ital.	Commandant		C.C.Gonars, (1942-43)	Sanitaty Major Bettini Might supply name.Murder	YUGO.
YUGO/12/1004	Ital.	Commandant		C.C.Monigo province Treviso (1942-43)	Murder.	YUGO.
YUGO/12/1005	Ital.	Commandant		C.C.Rab (Yugo.) (1942-43)	Murder.	YUGO.
YUGO/12/1006	Ital.	Commandant		C.C.Renicci, (1942-43)	Murder.	YUGO.
YUGO/12/1007	Ital.	Commandant		C.C. Chiesa Nuova,Province Padova,(1942-43)	Murder.	YUGO.
YUGO/12/1008	Ital.	Commandant		C.C.Fraschette-Alatri,Province Frosinone,(1942-43)	Murder.	YUGO.
YUGO/12/1009	Ger.	Commandant		C.C.Capljina Yugo.,Cara (9.1.44)	Torture of civilians,Internment of civilians under inhuman conditions,illegal arrest and sending to C.C.	YUGO.

APPENDIX - 'C'

TOTAL NUMBER OF PERSONS, OF KNOWN NAME AND OF NON-GERMAN NATIONALITY, WHO ARE INCLUDED IN PART II.OF THE CONSOLIDATED WANTED LIST, AND WANTED BY AN ALLIED NATION OTHER THAN THEIR OWN :-   2,425*

TABLE SHOWING THE NUMBERS OF SUCH PERSONS WANTED BY THE ALLIED NATIONS.

WANTED BY	TOTAL
BELGIUM	48
CANADA	9
CZECHOSLOVAKIA	33
FRANCE	382
GREECE	159
NORWAY	28
NETHERLANDS	57
POLAND	31
UNITED KINGDOM (Great Britain)	365
SOVIET UNION (Russia)	1
U.S.A.	302
YUGOSLAVIA	1012
U.N.W.C.C.	9

TOTAL OF NUMBERS REGISTERED AS WANTED BY THE ABOVE NATIONS   2,436

* NOTE: THE DISCREPANCY IN THE TWO TOTALS IS DUE TO THE FACT THAT 11 PERSONS ARE SOUGHT BY MORE THAN ONE COUNTRY.

THE CENTRAL REGISTRY OF WAR CRIMINALS AND SECURITY SUSPECTS

SUPPLEMENTARY WANTED LIST Nº 2

PART 1 GERMANS

PART 2 NON GERMANS

NOTE: THIS IS THE SECOND SUPPLEMENT TO THE CONSOLIDATED WANTED LIST DATED MARCH 47

CROWCASS
ALLIED CONTROL AUTHORITY
APO 742
U.S. ARMY

TELEPHONES:	DIRECTOR	BERLIN 45246	
	INFORMATION	BERLIN 45246	
	BRITISH WAR CRIMES LIAISON	BERLIN 44616	
	FRENCH WAR CRIMES LIAISON	BERLIN 45249	SEPTEMBER 1947

TELEPRINTER: BERLIN / STATION DHBP

INDEX.

	Page.
FRONTISPIECE	(i)
CONCERNING THE UNITED NATIONS WAR CRIMES COMMISSION.	(ii)
PART I (GERMANS)	
NAMES LISTED UNDER NORMAL HEADINGS	1
NAMES LISTED UNDER SPECIAL HEADINGS	75
PART II (NON GERMANS)	81

ABBREVIATIONS OF COUNTRIES.

UNITED STATES OF AMERICA	U.S.	GREECE	GRC.
GREAT BRITAIN (UNITED KINGDOM)	U.K.	ITALY	IT.
		FINLAND	FIN.
FRANCE	FR.	HUNGARY	HUNG.
SOVIET UNION (RUSSIA)	SOV.UN.	AUSTRIA	AUST.
BELGIUM	BEL.	CANADA	CAN.
HOLLAND (NETHERLANDS)	NETH.	AUSTRALIA	AUSTL.
POLAND	POL.	NEW ZEALAND	N.Z.
DENMARK	DEN.	SOUTH AFRICA	S.A.
NORWAY	NOR.	UKRAINE	UKR.
CZECHOSLOVAKIA	CZECH.	SLOVENIA	SLOV.
LUXEMBOURG	LUX.	RUMANIA	RUM.
YUGOSLAVIA	YUGO.	LATVIA	LATV.
	GERMANY	GER.	

GENERAL ABBREVIATIONS.

ARMY RANKS.		ARMY FORMATIONS.		GENERAL TERMS.	
PRIVATE	PVT.	SECTION	SEC.	MILITARY	MIL.
CORPORAL	CPL.	COMPANY	COY.	DIRECTOR	DIR.
SERGEANT	SGT.	BATTALION	BN.	COMMANDANT	CMDT.
NON COMMISSIONED OFFICER	NCO.	REGIMENT	REGT.	OFFICER COMMANDING	O.C.
WARRANT OFFICER				GENDARME	GEND.
OFFICER CANDIDATE	O/CAND.			CONCENTRATION CAMP	C.C.
LIEUTENANT	LT.			ASSISTANT	ASST.
CAPTAIN	CAPT.			SABOTAGE	SAB.
COLONEL	COL.				
GENERAL	GEN.				

NOTE. German Party Ranks are too numerous to list and any abbreviations used in this Publication should be easily recognisable.

SUPPLEMENTARY WANTED LIST NO. 2

1. This List is the second Supplement to the Consolidated Wanted List dated March 1947. The first Supplement was published in June 1947.

2. It was hoped that this List would include "Amendments" to the Consolidated Wanted List and Supplement No. 1 but as the inclusion of "Amendments" (amounting to many thousands) would cause considerable delay in the publication of this List it has been decided to omit them.

3. As mentioned in the frontispieces of former Wanted Lists information that the subjects of Wanted Reports have been detained in custody, are no longer wanted or have been otherwise disposed of can only be processed, recorded and published by CROWCASS if the responsible authorities invariably pass such information to this office. It therefore follows that any discrepancies of this nature discovered by using agencies should be notified immediately, whereupon the necessary adjustment will be made.

4. All recipients of this List are reminded of the following requirements as previously set out in the frontispieces of CROWCASS Wanted Lists:

   (I) If any person listed should be located and detained the CROWCASS Detention Report (to be invariably submitted in respect of all Detainees) should be completed showing Reason for Arrest as "Supplementary Wanted List No.2 CR.NO. ....." or "Possibly Supplementary Wanted List No.2 CR.NO. .....". If a Wanted Person is located only and not detained as full a description as possible of the person should be set out in letter form and forwarded to CROWCASS including the reason for non-detention.

   (II) In the event of CROWCASS thus receiving information of a match or possible match between a Wanted Person and a Detained or located Person the wanting nation is informed immediately, even although the Detainee may be held in the custody of that nation. In some cases where the person's name has not been listed by the UNWCC and where extradition is applied for considerable delay may be unavoidable. (See page (II)). If and when the extradition of a CROWCASS Wanted Personality has taken place CROWCASS should be informed immediately.

   (III) If a Detaining Authority receives instructions to Release or Transfer any Detainee who is possibly or definitaly a CROWCASS Wanted Personality a check should first be made with that Authority's War Crimes Group H.Q. and a copy of the communication endorsed to CROWCASS.

5. CROWCASS has a teleprinter station in its office. It is "Station DHBP - Berlin". Using agencies are requested to make use of it as it greatly speeds up replies to requests for information.

6. CROWCASS holds large stocks of Blank Wanted and Detention Reports and they can be had on application by TPM, Signal or letter.

CONCERNING THE UNITED NATIONS WAR CRIMES COMMISSION.

The following is quoted from Section X of Information Paper No. 1 issued by the Reference Division of the United Nations Information Organisation, London:

INTER-ALLIED DECLARATION OF DECEMBER 17, 1942

On December 17, 1942, a Declaration was made simultaneously in London, Moscow, and Washington in connection with reports that the German authorities were engaged in exterminating the Jewish people in Europe. In this Declaration, the Governments of Belgium, Czechoslovakia, Greece, Luxembourg, the Netherlands, Norway, Poland, the United States of America, the United Kingdom, the Soviet Union and Yugoslavia and the French National Committee reaffirmed their solemn resolution that those responsible should not escape retribution and their intention to press on with the necessary practical measures to that end.

There was some delay in setting up the United Nations War Crimes Commission, but it was eventually brought into being by a meeting of Government representatives at the British Foreign Office on October 20, 1943.

COMPOSITION OF THE COMMISSION

The Commission consists of seventeen members: the representatives of the Governments of Australia, Belgium, Canada, China, Czechoslovakia, Denmark, France, Greece, India, Luxembourg, the Netherlands, New Zealand, Norway, Poland, the United Kingdom, the United States of America and Yugoslavia. The representatives are all distinguished lawyers or diplomats.

If a representative is unable to act, or for some other special reason, he may be replaced.

The Commission may hear experts.

The first Chairman was the United Kingdom representative, Sir Cecil Hurst, Vice-President of the Permanent Court of International Justice, formerly legal Adviser to the Foreign Office. After his resignation on account of illhealth, he was replaced by the Right Hon. Lord Wright, Lord of Appeal in Ordinary, who represents Australia on the Commission. Lord Wright has been Chairman since January 31, 1945.

TERMS OF REFERENCE OF THE COMMISSION

The Commission has limited functions. It is primarily a fact-finding body, though it has also advisory functions.

Its terms of reference were defined in the Lord Chancellor's statement of October 7, 1942. Its purpose, he said is to investigate war crimes committed against nationals of the United Nations, recording the testimony available, and to report from time to time to the Governments of those nations cases in which such crimes appear to have been committed, naming and identifying wherever possible the persons responsible.

After its creation, it was entrusted with advisory functions, namely to make recommendations to the Governments on the methods to be adopted to ensure the surrender or capture of the persons wanted for trial as war criminals and on the tribunals by which they should be tried.

HOW THE COMMISSION OPERATES

The United Nations War Crimes Commission prepares lists of war criminals on the basis of evidence submitted by National War Crimes Offices which have been set up to detect, investigate and record evidence of war crimes committed against the citizens or subjects of their own countries.

The lists are furnished to the apprehending authorities - at present the military authorities - in order that the persons accused of crimes against people or property may be sent back to the country against which they have offended. This was the procedure contemplated in the Moscow Declaration on Atrocities by President Roosevelt, Mr. Winston Churchill and Marshal Stalin which was issued on November 1, 1943 and by the Foreign Secretaries of their three countries, who had been attending the Moscow Conference of October 16 to 30.

After referring to the atrocities, massacres and mass executions which were being perpetrated by the Hitlerite forces, the Declaration said:

"The United Kingdom, the United States and the Soviet Union ....

" .... speaking in the interests of the thirty-two United Nations ... solemnly declare and give full warning of their declaration as follows: At the time of the granting of any armistice to any Government which may be set up in Germany, those German officers and men and members of the Nazi Party who have been responsible for or who have taken a consenting part in the above atrocities, massacres and executions will be sent back to the countries in which their abominable deeds were done in order that they many be judged and punished according to the laws of these liberated countries and of the Free Governments which will be erected therein. Lists will be compiled in all possible detail from all these countries ... "

Offences against members of the Allied armed forces will be dealt with summarily by military courts, in accordance with international custom.

The following Statement was issued by UNWCC especially for incorporation in the Consolidated Wanted List:

"All Allied Authorities concerned are reminded that in order to secure extradition they should submit to the United Nations
"War Crimes Commission in London dossiers with charges concerning the offences committed by persons wanted. The United
"Nations War Crimes Commission in accordance with its terms of reference decides whether there appears to be either prima
"facie evidence sufficient to justify the handing over for trial of individuals accused of War Crimes or else sufficient
"ground to consider the wanted persons as suspects or material witnesses"

PART I
(GERMANS ONLY)

ABE - AVR

NAME	C.R. FILE NUMBER	SEX	DATE OF BIRTH	RANK OCCUPATION UNIT PLACE AND DATE OF CRIME	UNWCC LIST/ SERIAL NO.	REASON WANTED	WANTED BY
ABERMASS	266024	M		Major., Feldkmdtr., Brest (Fr.) 8.9.44	-	MURDER	FR.
ABUDA, Erich	265925	M		SS-Mann, SS, Zylka, Tomaszow, Lubelski (Pol.) 4.10.42	-	MURDER	POL.
ACHELIUS, Erwin	308704	M		Member, "Selbstschutz" and SS, Pomorze (Pol.) 39-40	60/2	MISC.CRIMES	POL.
ACKERMANN, Alwin	265898	M		Butcher, Civilian, Halle-Saale (Ger.) 41-44	-	BRUTALITY	POL.
ACKERMANN, Emil	266500	M	circa 08	N.C.O., Feldgendarmerie d'Avallon, Yonne (Fr.) 44	-	MISC.CRIMES	FR.
ACKMANN, Bernhard	304090	M	17.12.03	Wachtmeister, Police, Lohne (Ger.) 3.4.45	58/3	BRUTALITY	POL.
ADAM, Adolf	303492	M	31.10.15	SS-Rottenfhr., C.C., Majdanek (Pol.) 40-44	57/3	BRUTALITY	POL.
ADAM, Gustav	302874	M		N.C.O., Gestapo staff, Kattowitz (Pol.) 39-42	56/2	BRUTALITY	POL.
ADAM, Karl	303493	M	10. 1.91	Guard, C.C., Majdanek (Pol.) 40-42	57/4	MURDER	POL.
ADAM, Karl	266348	M	20. 8.95	Chief, Culture, living at: Essen-Katenberg, Bruchweiherstr.246, Ardennen (Fr.) 41-44	-	MISC.CRIMES	FR.
ADLER, Josef	304091	M	28. 8.90	SS-Uscharfhr., member, SD, Hautes Alpes (Fr.) 43-44	58/4	MURDER	FR.
ADNER (see VON GREUZ)	144541						
ADRIAAN, A.	304495	M		Member of customs, Frontier-Defence, Zwartsluis (Neth.) 8.10.44	59/1	MURDER	NETH.
AHLBORN	266499	M		Major, Kampfgruppe Oberst Hartung, Mamey, Martincourt (Fr.) 1.-9.44		MURDER	FR.
AHLERT	266719	M		Feldpolizeikommissar, G.F.P., Gand and vicinity (Bel.) 40-45	-	TORTURE	BEL.
AIGNER, Johann	304496	M		Member, Gestapo, Krakau (Pol.) 11.39-2.45	59/2	BRUTALITY	POL.
AITEN	266498	M		Customs secr., Custom house, Foncine le Haut Castelblanc (Fr.) 30.8.44	-	INCENDIARISM	FR.
ALBER, Gotthold	304497	M		Member, Gestapo, Krakau (Pol.) 11.39-2.45	59/3	MURDER	POL.
ALBERT, Carl	267027	M		Employee, Metallwaren-Fabrik, Wuppertal-Barmen, Paris (Fr.) 12.-19.8.44	-	PILLAGE	FR.
ALBERT, Georg	302875	M		Crim.secretary, Gestapo staff, Kattowitz (Pol.) 39-42	56/3	BRUTALITY	POL.
ALBERTI	266349	M		Chief-Cpl., Africa-Corps, Regt. Ruxleben, 6 Coy., 1 Section, Hte.Marne-Aube (Fr.) 25.-31.8.44	-	MURDER	FR.
ALBRECHT	266347	M		Sturmscharfhr., Gestapo of Baccarat, Kdo. Toufel, Neufmaisons, Pexonne, Viombois (Fr.) 9.44	-	MURDER	FR.
ALBRECHT, Otto	304092	M		Eppstein-Taunus (Ger.) 44	58/8	BRUTALITY	U.S.
ALEDBERG	267337	M		Oscharfhr., Gestapo, Marseille and vicinity (Fr.) 44	-	MURDER	FR.
ALLKAMPFER, Wilhelm	304498	M		Member, Gestapo, Krakau (Pol.) 11.39-2.45	59/4	BRUTALITY	POL.
ALT, Adam	303494	M	23.12.07	SS-Mann, C.C., Majdanek (Pol.) 40-44	57/6	BRUTALITY	POL.
ALTEM	267026	M		Uscharfhr., SS-Police, 10 Coy., 3 Bn., 19 Regt., Brives, Limoges and vicinity (Fr.) 7.44	-	MURDER	FR.
ALTHAUS, Helmuth	266798	M		Agent, Gestapo, Rouen and region (Fr.) 40-44	-	MURDER	FR.
ALTHOF	266799	M		Officer, Waffen-SS, Div."Adolf Hitler", Saint Germain Langet (Fr.) 5.7.44	-	MURDER	FR.
ALTMANN	304093	M		Schutzpolizeimeister, Schutzpolizei, Piotrkow-Trybunalski (Pol.) 44	58/9	MURDER	POL.
AMBERG	266026	M		Major, Feldkmdtr., Brest (Fr.) 8.9.44	-	MURDER	FR.
AMBROSIUS, Georg	302877	M		Pvt., Group 530 of Geh. Feldpolizei, Bruessel (Bel.) 40-44	56/8	MURDER	BEL.
AMDERKA, Kurt	266350	M		N.C.O., SS-Div. "Das Reich", 2 Art1.Btty., 1 Section, Selles-sur-Cher (Fr.) 14.-15.8.44	-	MURDER	FR.
AMLER, Josef	265387	M	12. 8.07	Executive of an optical factory "Optikotechna", Prerov (Czech.) 5.45	-	MURDER	CZECH.
AMM, Ernst	304499	M		Member, Gestapo, Krakau (Pol.) 11.39-2.45	59-5	BRUTALITY	POL.
ANDERMANN, Heinrich	302878	M		Sgt., Group 530 of Geh. Feldpolizei, Bruessel (Bel.) 40-44	56/10	MURDER	BEL.
ANDRASCHEK	302879	M		Feldpolizei-Sekretaer, Group 530 of Geh. Feldpolizei, Bruessel (Bel.) 40-44	56/11	MURDER	BEL.
ANDRASUK	304500	M		Member, Gestapo, Krakau (Pol.) 11.39-2.45	59/6	MURDER	POL.
ANGERER, Karl	265332	M	circa 07	Chief, Gendarmerie Station, Pisece (Yugo.) 11.7.43	-	MURDER	YUGO.
ANGESTELFER, Jessnil	266351	M	18. 4.05	Agent, SS-Uscharfhr., SD of Marseille, Beaurecueil (Fr.) 4.44	-	PILLAGE	FR.
ANHAMMER, Hans	308706	M	10	Sgt., Gendarmerie, St.Barbara v Halozah (Slov.) 43-45	60/4	MURDER	YUGO.
ANKELM, Adolf	266352	M		Feldgendarm, Feldgendarmerie, Valenciennes (Fr.) 40-44	-	MURDER	FR.
ANSBERG (see HAMSBERG,Franz)	308851						
ANTHOR	304094	M		SS-Scharfhr., charge of stables, Jerozolimska-Krakau (Pol.) 43	58/12	MURDER	POL.
ANTKOFIAK	304095	M		Member, Schutzgruppen at "Laura-Mine", Eigelshoven (Neth.) 44	58/13	MISC.CRIMES	NETH.
ANTLINGER,Helmut-Anton	267440	M		Engineer, Messerschmitt-Plant, C.C., Leonberg (Ger.) 44-45	-	BRUTALITY	FR.
APEL	306114	M		Crim.Asst., Sicherheitspolizei, Kopenhagen (Den.) autumn 43	31/59	INTERR.	DEN.
APP, Hans	305096	M		Member of Gestapo, hangman or asst., Lublin (Pol.) 43	58/14	MURDER	POL.
APPEL, Georg	267262	M		Sturmmann, G.F.P., Gestapo, Paris, Marseille (Fr.) 4.3.43	-	MURDER	FR.
APPELBAUM	308707	M		Policeman, Lendringsen, Distr. Iserlohn (Ger.) 39-45	60/5	MISC.CRIMES	POL.
APPELHANS, Alex	303495	M	21.12.22	SS-Mann, C.C., Majdanek (Pol.) 40-44	57/10	BRUTALITY	POL.
APPOLD	304501	M		Cpl., Secr.Field-Police, Luettich (Bel.) 40-41	59/7	MURDER	BEL.
ARENC	308708	M		Member, Military Police, Czorkow near Lodz (Pol.) 39-42	60/6	MURDER	POL.
ARENDT, Joachim	266316	M		Lt., Stabs-Coy., 115 Gren.Regt., Hte.Marne-Aube (Fr.)25.-31.8.44	-	MURDER	FR.
ARLT, Fritz Dr.	264661	M	12. 4.12	See names listed under "special Headings"			
ARNDT	266315	M	circa 11	N.C.O.,1 Sect.,1 Coy., Afrika-Corps, Regt.Ruxleben, Hte.Marne-Aube (Fr.) 25.-31.8.44	-	MURDER	FR.
ARNDT, Theo	304097	M		Cpl.,Nachtjagd-Group 4, vicinity of Charleroi (Bel.) 44	58/15	MURDER	BEL.
ARNOLD	266025	M		Major, Feldkmdtr., belonged to Africa-Corps, Brest (Fr.) 8.9.44	-	MURDER	FR.
ARNOLD, Paul	304502	M		Cpl., Secr.Field-Police, Luettich (Bel.) 40-41	59/8	MURDER	BEL.
ARNS, Hubert	43	M		Mine-worker, Civilian, C.C., Alsdorf (Ger.) 42-44	-	BRUTALITY	FR.
ARTKER, Arthur	266581	M		Pvt., Feldgendarmerie 658, Paray le Monial and vicinity (Fr.)43-44	-	SUSPECT	FR.
ARTMANN (see CONRAD)	266269						
ASSMANN	266992	M		Sgt.-Major, Feldgendarmerie, Sisteron (Fr.) 44	-	MISC.CRIMES	FR.
ATZBERGER, Hans	265362	M	circa 10	Cpl., Ger. Army, Strzisce (Yugo.) 22.2.45	-	MURDER	YUGO.
AUER, Otto	23906	M	circa 05	Interpreter, Cpl., Feldgendarmerie, La Ferte sur Aube (Fr.) 44	42/16	TORTURE	FR.
AUERHANN (see GUCKENHANN, Ernst)	265713						
AUFMUTH, Jakob	303496	M	2. 2.08	SS-Mann, C.C., Majdanek (Pol.) 40-44	57/14	BRUTALITY	POL.
AUGUSTIN	266580	M	circa 20	Hptsturmfhr., SS-Unit "Sarnow", Braquis (Fr.) 30.8.44	-	MURDER	FR.
AUGUSTIN, Walter	304503	M		Member, Gestapo, Krakau (Pol.) 11.39-2.45	59/9	MURDER	POL.
AUTEM, Wilhelm	302881	M		Pvt., Group 530 of Geh.Feldpolizei, Bruessel (Bel.) 40-44	56/15	MURDER	BEL.
AVISIUS, Franz	304504	M		Member, Secr.Field-Police, Luettich (Bel.) 40-41	59/10	MURDER	BEL.
AVRIL	303497	M		Member, Gestapo, Warschau (Pol.) 10.39-1.45	57/16	MURDER	POL.

BAA - BAU

NAME	C.R.FILE NUMBER	SEX	DATE OF BIRTH	RANK OCCUPATION UNIT PLACE AND DATE OF CRIME	UNWCC LIST/ SERIAL NO.	REASON WANTED	WANTED BY
BAARS	266371	M		Cpl.,Africa-Corps Regt.Ruxleben,6 Coy.,1 Sect., Hte.Marne-Aube (Fr.) 25.-31.8.44		MURDER	FR.
BAAS	308712	M		Oschfhr. and Crim.Asst,SS,Radom (Pol.) 1.40-1.45	60/10	TORTURE	POL.
BAASCH, Hans	304505	M		Inspector of Customs,Zwartsluis (Neth.) 8.10.44	59/11	MURDER	NETH.
BAATZ, Louis	264662	M	15. 8.10	See names listed under special headings			
BABBEL, Nicolas	304506	M		Secretary,Secr.Field-Police,Luettich (Bel.) 40-41	59/12	MURDER	BEL.
BACH, Hans	302882	M	circa 10	SS-Uschfhr.,SD,Avignon (Fr.) 42-44	56/16	MURDER	FR.
BACHER, Konstantin	265363	M		Chief,Gendarmerie,Medvode (Yugo.) 21.10.43	-	MISC.CRIMES	YUGO.
BACHLET, Adam	303498	M	20. 6.08	SS-Mann,C.C.,Majdanek (Pol.) 40-44	57/18	BRUTALITY	POL.
BACHINGER, Johann	267136	M	17.10.06	Chief and SS-Mann,Gestapo and SS,In the village of Radovljica (Yugo.) 42-44	-	MURDER	YUGO.
BACHMANN	308713	M		SS-Sturmschfhr.and Crim.Secretary,Radom (Pol.) 1.40-1.45	60/11	BRUTALITY	POL.
BACHMANN, Vilhelm	304507	M		Member,Gestapo,Krakau (Pol.) 11.39-2.45	59/13	MURDER	POL.
BACHNER, Wilhelm	302883	M		Hpt.Kriminalsekretaer,Gestapo-Staff,Kattowitz (Pol.) 39-42	56/17	BRUTALITY	POL.
BACKER	303499	M		Member,Gestapo,Warschau (Pol.) 10.39-1.45	57/19	MURDER	POL.
BACKER, Leopold	304508	M		Member,Gestapo,Krakau (Pol.) 11.39-2.45	59/14	TORTURE	POL.
BACKER, Oskar	304509	M		Member,Gestapo,Krakau (Pol.) 11.39-2.45	59/15	MURDER	POL.
BACKES	302884	M		Sgt.,Mot.Inf.Bn.z.b.V.commanded by Cpt.Fleck,South-Limburg (Neth.) 10.5.40	56/18	SUSPECT	NETH.
BACKHAUSEN, Christa	72685	F		Employee,Gestapo,Carcassonne (Fr.)	-	SUSPECT	FR.
BACKOFEN	266579	M		Lt.,Chief,Feldgendarmerie of Angouleme,Chasseneuil and environs (Fr.) 43-44	56/19	MURDER	FR.
BADKE, Emanuel	303500	M	29. 2.12	SS-Mann,C.C.,Majdanek (Pol.) 40-44	57/20	BRUTALITY	POL.
BADLSTSHOFER, Alois	303501	M	8. 2.11	SS-Guard,C.C.,Auschwitz (Pol.) 40-45	57/21	BRUTALITY	POL.
BADTKE	267573	M		Lt.,Unit-No.34828,Renesse (Neth.) 10.12.44	-	SUSPECT	NETH.
BAECKER	308714	M		SS-Hptschfhr.,Crim.Secr.,Radom (Pol.) 1.40-1.45	60/12	TORTURE	POL.
BAER	308715	M		SS-Usturmfhr.,Secr.of Crim.,Radom (Pol.) 1.40-1.45	60/13	TORTURE	POL.
BAGANZ, Friedrich	308716	M	17. 3.02	Crim.Secr.,Gestapo,Bruessel (Bel.) 43	60/14	MISC.CRIMES	BEL.
BAHR	304510	M		Secretary,Secr.Field-Police,Luettich (Bel.) 40-41	59/16	MURDER	BEL.
BAIER, Walter	265307	M		See names listed under "Special Headings"			
BAIKOW	308717	M		Secretary,Fieldpolice,Antwerpen,Bruessel (Bel.) 40-44	60/15	MURDER	BEL.
BAJOR, Basilius	304511	M		Member,Gestapo,Krakau (Pol.) 11.39-2.45	59/16	BRUTALITY	POL.
BALDAUF	267499	M		Capt.,Feldgendarmerie,Besancon and region (Fr.) 44	-	MURDER	FR.
BALHORN	308718	M		SS-Sturmschfhr.and Crim.Secr.,Radom (Pol.) 1.40-1.45	60/16	TORTURE	POL.
BALKENKOL	266369	M		Osturmfhr.,SS-Div."Das Reich",2 Btty.,Art. 1 Sect., Selles-sur-Cher (Fr.) 14.-15.8.44	-	MURDER	FR.
BALLAS, Walter	265312	M	18.11.87	Official,Friedrich Krupp A.G.,Essen (Ger.)	-	MISC.CRIMES	U.S.
BALLHAUSE	308719	M		SS-Oschfhr.and Crim.Asst.,Radom (Pol.) 1.40-1.45	60/17	TORTURE	POL.
BALSA	267263	M		Sgt.,Airforce,91 Regt.,Chantraine (Fr.) 20.-22.8.44	-	MURDER	FR.
BALTRUSCH, Dr.	267004	M		Major (Commander of a/n Regt.) Pion.Bn.Unit 01696, Zwammerdam (Neth.) 21.11.42	-	WITNESS	NETH.
BALZER	304099	M		SS-Usturmfhr.,Member,SD,Sipo,Krakau (Pol.) 41-43	58/24	MISC.CRIMES	POL.
BALZER, Anna	267264	F	circa 23	Secretary,Gestapo,Bordeaux and vicinity (Fr.) 42-8.44	-	MURDER	FR.
BAMBERGER (or BREMBERGER)	125101	M	95	Pvt.,Army,3 Coy.,877 Landesschuetzen-Bn.,C.C.,Schladming, Leizen (Aust.) 44-45	16/858	TORTURE	U.K.
BANASCHAK	303502	M		Member,Gestapo,Warschau (Pol.) 10.39-1.45	57/24	MURDER	POL.
BANDEL, Martin	303503	M	17.10.99	SS-Mann,C.C.,Majdanek (Pol.) 40-44	57/25	BRUTALITY	POL.
BANGARTNER	304100	M		Adjutant,Feldgendarmerie,Arlon and surroundings (Bel.) 44	58/25	MURDER	BEL.
BANKIEL, Johann	302887	M		Crim.Official,Gestapo-Staff,Kattowitz (Pol.) 39-42	56/24	BRUTALITY	POL.
BANNERT	267265	M		350 Hindou-Regt.,Departm.Indre (Fr.) 8.44	-	MURDER	FR.
BANNERT, Alphonse	266827	M		Cpl.,Army,Groslezac,Carsac,Peyrillac,Calviac,Carlux (Fr.) 8.6.44	-	MISC.CRIMES	FR.
BANNES, Joachim	265299	M	circa 00	Sonderfhr.,Regt."Brandenburg" (It.)	-	SUSPECT	U.K.
BANNING	267266	M		Agent,Gestapo,Marseille and vicinity (Fr.)	-	MURDER	FR.
BANTSCHUK, Mieczyslaw	303504	M	23. 2.07	Kapo,C.C.,Hessenthal, 10.39-1.45	57/26	MURDER	POL.
BAR	302888	M		Member,Feldgendarmerie,Region of Cholet (Fr.) 7.and 8.8.44	56/25	MURDER	FR.
BARLIAN, Josef	303505	M	10. 4.10	SS-Mann,C.C.,Majdanek (Pol.) 40-44	57/27	BRUTALITY	POL.
BARNEFSKI	304101	M		Member,Schutzgruppen at "Laura-mine",Eigelshoven (Neth.) 44	58/26	PILLAGE	NETH.
BARNAR, Adalbert	266370	M	circa 02	Driver,gunsmith,Uschfhr.,Gestapo,Nantes and region (Fr.) 43-44	-	MURDER	FR.
BARON, Heinrich	302889	M		Crim.Secretary,Gestapo-Staff,Kattowitz (Pol.) 39-42	56/26	BRUTALITY	POL.
BARON, Paul	304512	M		Member,Gestapo,Krakau (Pol.) 11.39-2.45	59/18	PILLAGE	POL.
BARTCH, Oswald	267062	M		N.C.O.,19 SS-Pol.Regt.,3 Bn.,10 Coy., Limoges,Brive and environ (Fr.) 7.44	-	MURDER	FR.
BARTH, Friedrich	266001	M	21. 3.11	N.C.O.,Clerk,Stab.Artl.Regt.704,Feldgend.,Kreiskommandantur 595 (hospitalized 3.6.42 War-Hospital I/612 Nantes) Seine (Fr.)	-	SUSPECT	FR.
BARTH, Josef	303506	M	9. 3.09	SS-Mann,C.C.,Majdanek (Pol.) 40-44	57/29	BRUTALITY	POL.
BARTHELMOS	61	M		Officer,Gestapo,Lyon (Fr.) 27.7.44	-	MURDER	FR.
BARTON	303507	M		Member,Gestapo,Warschau (Pol.) 10.39-1.45	57/30	MURDER	POL.
BARTZ	304102	M		Lt.,Chief-Inspector,Airforce,Town-council,Sosnowiec (Pol.)	58/29	MURDER	POL.
BARYLKO, Zbigniew	304513	M		Member,Gestapo,Krakau (Pol.) 11.39-2.45	59/19	INTERR.	POL.
BARZION, Morris	303508	M	17. 7.19	Baracks-Attendant,C.C.,Auschwitz (Pol.) 40-45	57/31	MURDER	POL.
BASCHLEBEN, Hermann	185161	M	2.11.98	Sgt., Schfhr.or Oschfhr.,Employee,Gestapo,Civil Police Service, BDS IV, SD, Gruppe Geh.Feldpolizei 550,Paris,Vichy (Fr.) 11.42	-	SUSPECT	FR.
BASELE	304103	M		SS-Hptsturmfhr.,Member,Civil Admin.,Sosnowiec (Pol.) 43	58/30	MURDER	POL.
BASSLER	303509	M		Member,Gestapo,Warschau (Pol.) 10.39-1.45	57/33	MURDER	POL.
BASSLER, Robert	304514	M		Member,Gestapo,Krakau (Pol.) 11.39-2.45	59/20	RAPE	POL.
BASZMANN, Josef	303510	M	18. 3.10	SS-Mann,C.C.,Majdanek (Pol.) 40-44	57/34	MURDER	POL.
BATHEN, Hans	308727	M		Guard,Prison,Hagen (Ger.) 42-45	60/20	MISC.CRIMES	BEL.
BATMANN	267267	M		Feldgendarm,Feldgendarmerie,Hondschoote (Fr.) 41-45	-	MISC.CRIMES	FR.
BATZINGER	266800	M		Capt.,Airforce,Unit L 49193 L.G.P.A.,Camaret sur Aigues (Fr.) 44	-	MISC.CRIMES	FR.
BAUCH	303511	M	circa 95	Collaborator and Member,Gestapo,SS Dirlewanger-Bde.,Warschau (Pol.) 40-44	57/35	MURDER	POL.
BAUCH, Paul	302890	M		Crim.Secretary,Gestapo-Staff,Kattowitz (Pol.) 39-42	56/29	BRUTALITY	POL.
BAUER	21387	M		Member,SD,Pau (Fr.)	-	SUSPECT	FR.
BAUER	266826	M		Inspector,Staff-Coy.,3 J.G.Udet,Sours (Fr.) 7.,8.44	-	PILLAGE	FR.

BAU - BEI

NAME	C.R.FILE NUMBER	SEX	DATE OF BIRTH	RANK OCCUPATION UNIT PLACE AND DATE OF CRIME	UNWCC LIST/ SERIAL NO.	REASON WANTED	WANTED BY
BAUER,	266933	M		Feldgendarme, Feldgendarmerie, Sisteron (Fr.) 44	-	MISC.CRIMES	FR.
BAUER,	267268	M		Hptschfhr., Gestapo, Bordeaux and vicinity (Fr.) 42-8.44	-	MURDER	FR.
BAUER,	308721	M		Interpreter, Radom (Pol.) 1.40-1.45	60/21	MURDER	POL.
BAUER, Alfons	302891	M		Schfhr., Gestapo, Lodz (Pol.) 39-44	56/31	MURDER	POL.
BAUER, Franz	266768	M	91	Member, Gestapo, Telhrimov (Czech.) 39-45	-	MISC.CRIMES	CZECH.
BAUER, Franz	265981	M		Chief-Sgt., SD. Bayonne and vicinity (Fr.) 40-44	-	MURDER	FR.
BAUER, Gottfried	267115	M	09	Hptwachtmeister, Gendarmerie, St. Jurij on the river Scavnica (Yugo.) 7.42-5.45	-	MURDER	YUGO.
BAUER, Josef	303512	M	25. 1.21	SS-Mann, C.C. Majdanek (Pol.) 40-44	57/38	BRUTALITY	POL.
BAUER, Ludwig	267063	M	circa 00	Capt., Chief, Dienststellenleiter, Gestapo. Blois, Maves and vicinity (Fr.) 43-44	-	MURDER	FR.
BAUER, Pierre	304104	M		Electrician, SS, St.Anne D'Auray Morbihan (Fr.) 44	58/35	MURDER	FR.
BAUERLE	266376	M	circa 07	Chief, Schfhr., Gestapo Section IV, Angers and vicinity (Fr.)	-	MURDER	FR.
BAUM, Georg, Adalbert	304105	M		Member, NSDAP., Eppstein, Taunus (Ger.) 44	58/36	BRUTALITY	U.S.
BAUMANN	303513	M		Member, Gestapo, Warschau (Pol.) 10.39-1.45	57/41	MURDER	POL.
BAUMANN, Dr.	304215	M		Presumably "Stadtkrankenhaus" Kassel (Ger.) 16.1.44	59/23	MURDER	NETH.
BAUMANN	308722	M		SS-Usturmfhr., and Crim.Secretary, Radom (Pol.) 1.40-1.45	60/22	BRUTALITY	POL.
BAUMANN, Bernhard	308723	M		Secretary, Fieldpolice, Antwerpen, Bruessel (Bel.) 40-44	60/23	MURDER	BEL.
BAUMANN, Erich	72726	M		Sturmfhr., SS, C.C. Struthof-Natzweiler (Fr.) 44	10/72	MURDER	FR.
BAUMEISTER	144700	M		Capt., Member, SRA. Nizza (Fr.)	-	SUSPECT	FR.
BAUMGAERTNER, Karl	304106	M		Gendarmeriemeister, Gendarmerie, near Bauerbach (Ger.)21.7.44	58/37	BRUTALITY	U.S.
BAUMGARDT, Reinhold	303514	M	25. 7.06	Guard, C.C. Majdanek (Pol.) 40-42	57/43	MURDER	POL.
BAUMGART, Willi	308724	M		Civilian, vicinity of Halle (Ger.) 44	60/24	BRUTALITY	U.S.
BAUMGARTNER	303515	M		Member, Gestapo, Warschau (Pol.) 10.39-1.45	57/44	MURDER	POL.
BAUMGARTNER, Heinrich	266374	M	circa 00	Sgt., Feldgendarmerie, La Motte St Jean-Paray Le Monial (Fr.) 43-44	-	MISC.CRIMES	FR.
BAUSBACH, Ferdinand	267445	M	18.11.84	See names listed under "Special Headings"			
BAYER, Alfred (or BUJER, Alfred)	304516	M		Member, Gestapo, Krakau (Pol.) 11.39-2.45	59/24	BRUTALITY	POL.
BAYERLEIN	304107	M		Usturmfhr., Head, SD. Sipo., Miechow and sub-district (Pol.)-43	58/40	MURDER	POL.
BAYRHOFFER, Walter	265607	M	1. 2.90	Deutsche Industrie Bank A.R.	-	MISC.CRIMES	U.S.
BECHER, Oskar	304108	M		Osturmfhr., Head, Jewish Dept.of SD. and Sipo. at Krakau Bochnia (Pol.) 42	58/41	MURDER	POL.
BECK	302993	M		Cpl.,Univ.Professor, Feldgendarmerie at Angoulême at Muenchen Chasseneuil-Charente (Fr.) 43-22.3.44	56/34	MURDER	FR.
BECK	302895	M		Interpreter, Quimperle district Finistère (Fr.) 44	56/35	MURDER	FR.
BECK	304109	M		Wachtmeister, Gendarmerie, Bochnia (Pol.) 40-43	58/42	MURDER	POL.
BECK	185822	M	circa 12	Ordensjunker (Reichs-official) Deputy Gebietskommissar in charge of the Distr.General-Gouvernor-Waffen-SS,Rowno (Pol.)	-	MURDER	POL.
BECK, Erich, Max	267003	M	22.12.10	Kapo, C.C. Vught (Neth.) 40-45	-	BRUTALITY	NETH.
BECK, Martin	266815	M	23. 9.09	Revier-Ob.Wachtmeister, C.C. Schirmeck (Fr.) -5.45	-	MURDER	FR.
BECK, Paul (or BOCK)	266830	M		Sgt., Stabs Coy. 3 J.G. Udett, Sours (Fr.) 7.44-8.44	-	PILLAGE	FR.
BECKER	266578	M		W.O., Feldgendarmerie, Grattery-les-Vesoul (Fr.) 16.7.44	-	MURDER	FR.
BECKER	266721	M		SS-Mann, C.C. Grossenlendorf, Dinstadt near Buchenwald (Ger.)45	-	WITNESS	BEL.
BECKER	267572	M		Capt., Unit No. 40706, Renesse (Neth.) 10.12.44	-	SUSPECT	NETH.
BECKER	303516	M		Member, Gestapo, Warschau (Pol.) 10.39-1.45	57/47	MISC.CRIMES	POL.
BECKER	304110	M		SS-Oschfhr., Member, SD, Sipo. at Sanok, Ustrzyki Dl.Lutowska (Pol.) 42-13.1.43	58/43	MURDER	POL.
BECKER	304111	M		Member, Group 648, G.F.P., Boulevard Piercot Liege (Bel.)40-44	58/44	TORTURE	BEL.
BECKER	308728	M		SS-Usturmfhr., and Crim.Secr., Radom (Pol.) 1.40-1.45	60/28	RAPE	POL.
BECKER	267064	M	circa 00	High ranking officer, Paratrooper 5 Rgt., Carhaix (Fr.)10.6.44	-	SUSPECT	FR.
BECKER, Alfred	303529	M		Camp Commander, C.C. Auschwitz (Pol.) 40-45	57/49	MURDER	POL.
BECKER, Bruno, Dr.	167677	M		Leader, Economy-Gouvernor of Wirtschaft, Lublin (Pol.) 39-44	10/487	MISC.CRIMES	POL.
BECKER, Friedrich	303517	M	2. 11.09	SS-Mann, C.C. Majdanek (Pol.) 40-44	57/51	BRUTALITY	POL.
BECKER, Georg	183056	M		Army, P.O.W. now in Camp No. 218, C.C. Offoy (Fr.) 9.44	6/416	MURDER	FR.
BECKER, Gustave	266790	M	26. 4.68	Civilian, Brieulles a/Meuse (Fr.) 40-43	-	MISC.CRIMES	FR.
BECKER, Hermann	308729	M	19.12.98	Member, "Schutzgruppen", Brunssum (Neth.) 9.44	60/29	PILLAGE	NETH.
BECKER, Joachim	304289	M		SS-Usturmfhr.,Member,Krim.Polizei, Sosnowiec (Pol.) 40-42	58/46	MURDER	POL.
BECKER, Karl	268718	M		Cpl., G.F.P. Gand and vicinity, (Bel.) 40-45	-	TORTURE	BEL.
BECKER, Kurt, Adolf	302894	M		SS-Usturmfhr., Gestapo Staff, Katowice (Pol.) 39-42	56/39	BRUTALITY	POL.
BECKER, Mathias	303518	M	5. 3.13	SS-Mann, C.C. Majdanek (Pol.) 40-44	57/54	BRUTALITY	POL.
BECKER, Michael	265237	M	99	Osturmfhr., SA.-FW.Cage, Luensbach (Ger.) 10.44	-	MURDER	FR.
BECKER, Richard	266373	M		Prt., Afrika-Corps, Aube-Hte-Marne (Fr.) 25.-31.8.44	-	MURDER	FR.
BECKHAUZEN	302896	M		Member, Feldgendarmerie or Army, Breda (Neth.) 43-44	-	MURDER	NETH.
BECKLER	266813	M		Interpreter, SD, Brive, Correze (Fr.) 44	-	SUSPECT	FR.
BECKMANN	303519	M		Member, Gestapo, Warschau (Pol.) 10.39-1.45	57/56	MISC.CRIMES	POL.
BECKMANN, Heinrich	302897	M	5. 5.09	Guard, Kdo. 950, Rinteln (Ger.) 44-45	56/41	BRUTALITY	FR.
BEDLEWSKI	308731	M		Secretary, Field-Police, Antwerpen, Bruessel (Bel.)40-44	60/31	MURDER	BEL.
BEECK, Claus, Friedrich	302898	M		Ortsbauernfuehrer, Dakendorf, (Ger.) 6.42	56/43	BRUTALITY	POL.
BEGELE	266814	M		Oschfhr., Div. "Das Reich", Dordogne,Correze,Creuse, Hte Vienne (Fr.) 5.6.44	-	SUSPECT	FR.
BEHN	302899	M		Staff-Sgt., Feldgendarmerie at Angoulême, Chasseneuil (Charente), (Fr.) 43-22.3.44	56/44	BRUTALITY	FR.
BEHNKE, Hermann	303520	M	5. 1.08	SS-Guard, C.C. Majdanek (Pol.) 40-44	57/60	BRUTALITY	POL.
BEHRENDS	266985	M		Professor, Wehrgeologenstab, Paris (Fr.) 12.-13.2.43	-	PILLAGE	FR.
BEHRLING, Karl	303521	M	14. 4.23	SS-Usturmfhr., C.C. Auschwitz (Pol.) 40-45	57/65	BRUTALITY	POL.
BEIERKE, Alfred	303522	M	26.12.02	SS-Mann, C.C. Majdanek (Pol.) 40-44	57/66	MURDER	POL.
BEIERLEIN	144678	M		Hptschfhr., SS, C.C. Struthof (Fr.)	-	SUSPECT	FR.
BEIGER, Mieczislaus	304517	M		Member, Gestapo, Krakau (Pol.) 11.39-2.45	59/29	MURDER	POL.
BEILICH	265330	M		Commander, Police, Sorge Settendorf, near Greis (Ger.) 44	-	BRUTALITY	POL.
BEIN, Andreas, Karl	308732	M	23. 1.04	Crim.Secr., RSD. at the Gestapo,Esjerg (Den.) 12.43-4.45	60/32	TORTURE	DEN.
BEINING, Hubert	267142	M		Oschfhr., Gestapo, Auto-service, Marseille and vicinity (Fr.)	-	MURDER	FR.
BEITLICH	144567	M		Member, Gestapo, Einsatzkommandantur, Vichy (Fr.)	-	SUSPECT	FR.

BEI - BIC

NAME	C.R.FILE NUMBER	SEX	DATE OF BIRTH	RANK OCCUPATION UNIT PLACE AND DATE OF CRIME	UNWCC LIST/ SERIAL NO.	REASON WANTED	WANTED BY
BEITSCH, Ernst	304291	M		Member, deputy to mayor, Gestapo, Bydgoszcz (Pol.,Ger.) 39-45	58/49	MURDER	POL.
BELLINGHAUS	265224	M	circa 12	Capt.,Div. Hermann Goering, Partins,Moscaid (It.) 4.44	-	SUSPECT	U.K.
BELLOK, Georg	304518	M		Member, Gestapo, Krakau (Pol.) 11.39-2.45	59/30	MURDER	POL.
BELLSCHUSS, Paul	302901	M		Kriminalsekretaer, Gestapo Staff, Kattowitz (Pol.) 39-42	56/46	BRUTALITY	POL.
BELTZ	144564	M	99	Chief, Radio-Service, Dijon (Fr.)	-	SUSPECT	FR.
BENACK, Felix	266002	M		Hptscharfhr., S.D., Chalons sur Marne (Fr.) 43-44	-	MISC.CRIMES	FR.
BENDER, Fritz	266792	M	circa 15	see names listed under special headings			
BENDINGER, Alvin	304519	M		Member, Gestapo, Krakau (Pol.) 11.39-2.45	59/31	MURDER	POL.
BENDIX, Friedrich	267571	M		Lagerfuehrer, Org.Todt, Wageningen (Neth.) 3.45	-	PILLAGE	NETH.
BENDLER	302902	M		N.C.O., Sipo and S.D. Kommando, Rouen (Fr.) 42-44	56/47	MURDER	FR.
BENEFIS	308733	M		Member, Military Police, Czorkow nr.Lodz.(Pol.) 39-42	60/33	MURDER	POL.
BENESCH, Karl	302904	M	24. 1.98	Cpl.,Lagerfuehrer,Landesschuetzen-Bn.2-877 at Kaiser-Steinbruch Arbeitskommando, Veitsch-Styria (Aust.) 9.or 10.42	56/48A	BRUTALITY	U.K.
BENKO, Michael	303523	M	19. 3.24	SS-Mann, C.C. Majdanek (Pol.) 40-44	57/69	PILLAGE	POL.
BENKOWITZ	303524	M		Member, Gestapo, Warschau (Pol.) 10.39-1.45	57/70	MISC.CRIMES	POL.
BENNECKE, Bruno	266732	M	13	Substitute for commandant of penal labour camp, Krakau (Pol.) 42	-	MURDER	POL.
BENNEWITZ	266969	M	circa 95	Staff-Sgt., Feldgendarmerie, Maslives,Coulanges and Blois (Fr.) 1.39-8.44	-	MURDER	FR.
BENNEWITZ, Rudolf	304521	M		Member, Gestapo, Krakau (Pol.) 11.39-2.45	59/33	RAPE	POL.
BENTHACK, Otto Adolf	304521	M	26. 3.05	Customs-Commissioner, Head of Frontier-Defence-Unit,Zwartsluis (Neth.) 8.10.44	59/34	MURDER	NETH.
BERANG	266003	M	10	Cpl., Army, Biscarosse (Fr.) 13.8.44	-	MISC.CRIMES	FR.
BERENSZ	267269	M	circa 12	Sgt., Feldgendarmerie, Avallon (Fr.) 44	-	MISC.CRIMES	FR.
BERESNIEWICZ	303525	M		Member, Gestapo, Warschau (Pol.) 10.39-1.45	57/71	MISC.CRIMES	POL.
BERG	267182	M		Lt., 257.Art.Regt.,Arnaucourt (Fr.) 9.9.44	-	MURDER	FR.
BERG	304293	M		Lt.,Orts-Cmdt., Jagodina-Serbia (Yugo.) 5.9.41	58/57	BRUTALITY	YUGO.
BERGEMANN	303526	M		Member, Gestapo, Warschau (Pol.) 10.39-1.45	57/72	MISC.CRIMES	POL.
BERGER	308734	M		Cpl., Geh.Feldpolizei, Antwerpen,Bruessel (Bel.) 40-44	60/36	MURDER	BEL.
BERGER	308735	M		Commissioner, Field-Police, Antwerpen, Bruessel (Bel.) 40-44	60/37	MURDER	BEL.
BERGER	308736	F		Head of the Graphic sub-dept.of the Berlin "Stabshauptamt des Reichskommissars fuer die Festigung des Deutschtums in Berlin" (Yugo.) 41-45	60/38	MISC.CRIMES	YUGO.
BERGER, Arno	267270	M	7. 7.10	Cpl., 487.Inf.Regt.,Stab II, Oignies and Courrieres (Fr.) 28.5.40	-	SUSPECT	FR.
BERGER, Ernst	308737	M		Oscharfhr., SS, Gross-Rosen (Ger.) 43-45	60/39	MURDER	POL.
BERGER, Fabian	303527	M	1. 4.11	SS-Mann, C.C. Majdanek (Pol.) 40-44	57/73	BRUTALITY	POL.
BERGER, Franz	264563	M	16. 1.10	See names listed under "Special Headings"			
BERGER, Fritz	267035	M	circa 15	Capt., Unit Z.E.L. 206, No. 47.471, Paris (Fr.) 21.8.44	-	MURDER	FR.
BERGER, Gottlob	67156	M		General (SS-Ogruppenfhr.) Special Kdo."Dirlewanger", Punitive-Bn.,Warschau,Sluck,Lublin (Pol.) 40-1.45	-	MISC.CRIMES	POL., CZECH.
BERGER, Joseph	267183	M	22. 5.17	Oscharfhr.,Zentralersatzteillager 206, SS (6.43),Buchenwald (Ger.) 41-42	-	MURDER	FR.
BERGER, Paul	304523	M		Member, Gestapo, Krakau (Pol.) 11.39-2.45	59/36	RAPE	POL.
BERGER, Tony (see RACH,Max)	267071						
BERGES	265445	M		Major,Chief physician, Hospital, St.Anne d'Auray (Fr.) 5.8.44	-	MURDER	FR.
BERGES, Friedrich	266004	M	02	SS-Usturmfhr., S.D.,Section IV of Marseille, Bouches du Rhone (Fr.) 43-44	-	SUSPECT	FR.
BERGMANN	267122	M		Lt., Army, 893.Gren.Regt., Sinj (Yugo.) 8.9.43-10.44	-	MURDER	YUGO.
BERGMANN, Kurt	308739	M		Usturmfhr., SS, the Departm.of the Dordogne (Fr.) 10.43-19.8.44	60/41	MURDER	FR.
BERHOLD, Helmut	304524	M		Member, Gestapo, Krakau (Pol.) 11.39-2.45	59/37	TORTURE	POL.
BERKA	304295	M		Head of Labour Office, Bochnia (Pol.) 40-42	58/61	MURDER	POL.
BERLIN	267036	M		Capt.,350.Hindou-Regt., Lureuil, Linge,St.Michel-en-Brenne,Vendoeuvres,St.Maur,Imbrault,Ardentes and Neuilly-les-Blois (Fr.) End of 8.44	-	MURDER	FR.
BERLIN, Hugo	308740	M	2. 5.10	Member,"Schutzgruppen",Brunssum (Neth.) 9.44	60/42	PILLAGE	NETH.
BERNAUER, Max	302905	M		Sgt., Mixed German and Polish Unit, Luijkageltel (Neth.) 8.9.44	56/52	MURDER	NETH.
BERNHARDT, Charles	267500	M		Lt., Feldgendarmerie,Besancon and region (Fr.) 44	-	MURDER	FR.
BERNSCHER, Dr.	267301	M		Interpreter, Gestapo, Bordeaux and vicinity (Fr.) 42-8.44	-	MURDER	FR.
BERNSHAUSEN	266358	M		Capt., 3.Coy.,44.Section D.C.A., Vern s/Seiche (Fr.) 14.7.44	-	MURDER	FR.
BERRING	267037	M		Capt.,Airforce, Unit No. L 26769, Saint-Piat (Fr.) 6.40	-	PILLAGE	FR.
BERSTEIN	302906	M		Osturmfhr., Gestapo Lodz (Pol.) 39-44	56/53	PILLAGE	POL.
BERTEL, Michael	303528	M	23. 6.09	SS-Mann, C.C. Majdanek (Pol.) 40-44	57/77	BRUTALITY	POL.
BERTMAN	303530	M		Member, Gestapo, Warschau (Pol.) 10.39-1.45	57/78	MISC.CRIMES	POL.
BERTRAM, Friedrich Wilhelm Julius Otto	304296	M	29. 8.12	Member, S.D., Abt.II, Sauward, Zeist, Oldenzaal, The Haag (Neth.) 44-45	58/62 59/38	PILLAGE	NETH.
BERTRAM, Fritz	308741	M		Betriebsobmann, DAF, Lendringsen, Distr.of Iserlohn (Ger.) 39-45	60/43	BRUTALITY	POL.
BESCH	302907	M		Lt., Commanding the Feldgendarmerie at Granville-Manche, La Rochelle-Manche (Fr.) 29.7.44	56/54	MURDER	FR.
BESSE	308742	M		Capt., presumably Member of the V-weapon-troops, Wassenar (Neth.) 11.44	60/44	PILLAGE	NETH.
BEST, Walter	265468	M	circa 13	W.O., S.D.,Bayonne and vicinity (Fr.) 40-44	-	MURDER	FR.
BETJER	304297	M		Hptscharfhr., SS-Wach-Bn.3, Amersfoort (Neth.) 2.5.43	58/64	MURDER	NETH.
BETSCHER, Hans	304298	M		Oberfhr., Polizeifhr., SS, Radom and Distr.Woladow (Pol.) 41-43	58/65	MURDER	POL.
BETTICH, Georg (or BETTIGE)	266733	M		Member, Gestapo, Tomaszow Mazowiecki (Pol.) 39-45	-	MURDER	POL.
BETTIGE (see BETTICH, Georg)	266733						
BETTIN, Wilhelm	303531	M	23. 1.07	SS-Guard, C.C. Majdanek (Pol.) 40-44	57/80	BRUTALITY	POL.
BETZ, Erich	265675	M		Pvt., Army, Vatan (Fr.) 10.8.44	-	MURDER	FR.
BEUGEMANN	302908	M		Member Group 530 of Geh.Feldpolizei, Bruessel (Bel.) 40-44	56/56	MURDER	BEL.
BEUTHNER, Paul	304525	M		Member, Gestapo, Krakau (Pol.) 11.39-2.45	59/39	PILLAGE	POL.
BEVERNIK, Hermann	304526	M		Secretary, Secr.Field-Police, Luettich (Bel.) 40-41	59/40	MURDER	BEL.
BEYERN	266970	M		Feldgendarm, Feldgendarmerie, Sisteron (Fr.) 44	-	MISC.CRIMES	FR.
BIANSKI	304299	M		Member, S.D., Sneek (Neth.) 12.44, 13.4.45	58/70	MURDER	NETH.
BIRAU, Gustav	304300	M		Police-Master, Schutzpolizei, Weselburen Village	58/71	MURDER	POL.
BICHISKY	266005	M		Member, Feldgendarmerie, Cholet (Fr.) 7.and 8.8.44	-	MURDER	FR.

BIC - BOD

NAME	C.R.FILE NUMBER	SEX	DATE OF BIRTH	RANK	OCCUPATION UNIT PLACE AND DATE OF CRIME	UNWCC LIST/ SERIAL NO.	REASON WANTED	WANTED BY
BICHNISKY	302909	M			Member, Feldgendarmerie, Gholst (Fr.) 7.-8.8.44	56/57	MURDER	FR.
BICKELHAUPT, Leo	265673	M			Member, SD, Chalons sur Marne (Fr.) 43-44	-	MISC.CRIMES	FR.
BICKLER	267501	M			Member, Gestapo, Limoges and vicinity (Fr.) 44	-	SUSPECT	FR.
BIEDELBACH, Hans (or BIEDELMANN)	267502	M			Member, Gestapo, Limoges and vicinity (Fr.) 44	-	SUSPECT	FR.
BIEDELMANN (see BIEDELBACH, Hans)	267502							
BIEDENKAPP	303532	M			Member, Gestapo, Warschau (Pol.) 10.39- 1.45	57/81	MISC.CRIMES	POL.
BIEDER, Fritz	304527	M			Member, Gestapo, Krakau (Pol.) 11.39	59/41	PILLAGE	POL.
BIEGEL	304301	M			Sturmbannfhr., SS, Jerozolimska forced labour camp, Jerozolimska camp, Krakau (Pol.) 42-43	58/73	MURDER	POL.
BIEGLER, Carl	308743	M			SS-Usturmfhr. served in Bunce's section, Slagelse and Kopenhagen (Den.) 12. 2.45 and 3. 1.45	60/46	MURDER	DEN.
BIELAR	266728	M			Rapportfhr., C.C., Barth nr.Ravensbrueck (Ger.) 42-45	-	MURDER	POL.
BIERMEYER	304302	M			Regt."Deutschland," Div."Das Reich", Achene, 7.9.44	58/74	MURDER	BEL.
BIGLIER	266007	M	circa 07		Lt., Jagd-Kdo. of Grasse (Alpes Maritimes) Chaudon-Norante (Fr.) 5.7.44	-	MURDER	FR.
BIHLO	303533	M			Member, Gestapo, Warschau (Pol.) 10.39- 1.45	57/82	MISC.CRIMES	POL.
BILGERI, Georg, Dr.	264562	M	13. 2.98		See names listed under "Special Headings"			
BILHARTZ (see BILHARZ)	159404							
BILHARZ (or BILHARTZ)	159404	M	circa 05		Agent, Oscharfhr., SS, SD, Gestapo, Nice, Cannes (Fr.) 44	-	SUSPECT	FR.
BILHSE (see BOHSE)	267186							
BILLER	266791	M			Lt., Div. Bode, Bergerac, St.Pierre d'Eyraud, Beaumont (Fr.) 19.6.-22.7.44	-	MISC.CRIMES	FR.
BILOVITZKI, Otto	265338	M	9. 9.99		Manager, Secret Agent of the steel-works, of Gestapo, Ravne (Yugo.) 41-45	-	MISC.CRIMES	YUGO.
BINDER	308745	M			SS-Sturmscharfhr. and Crim.Secr., Radom (Pol.) 1.40-1.45	60/49	PILLAGE	POL.
BINDER, Stefan	303534	M	24.11.08		SS-Mann, C.C., Majdanek (Pol.) 40-44	57/84	BRUTALITY	POL.
BIRCKHOLZ, Ilse	302911	F			Wife of Sturmbannfhr. Schmitt, Commandant C.C. Breendonck Prov. Antwerpen (Bel.) 40-44	56/59	MURDER	BEL.
BIRKHOELZER, Johannes Hermann Echard	308746	M	11		Member, "Schutzgruppen", Brunssum (Neth.) 9.44	60/50	PILLAGE	NETH.
BIRKHOLZ (I)	303535	M			Member, Gestapo, Warschau (Pol.) 10.39- 1.45	57/86	BRUTALITY	POL.
BIRKHOLZ (II)	303536	M			Member, Gestapo, Warschau (Pol.) 10.39- 1.45	57/87	BRUTALITY	POL.
BIRKMAN (see BRENSKMAN)	263313							
BIRKNER	303537	M			Member, Gestapo, Warschau (Pol.) 10.39- 1.45	57/88	BRUTALITY	POL.
BIRKWOLF, Karl	266015	M			Capt., Customs official, Custom House, Montceau les Mines Saint Vallier (Fr.) 44	-	MURDER	FR.
BISCHOFF	265674	M			Oscharfhr., SD, Chalons Sur Marne (Fr.) 43-44	-	MISC.CRIMES	FR.
BISCHOFF, Peter	267184	M			Rottenfuehrer, Gestapo, Marseille and vicinity (Fr.)	-	MURDER	FR.
BISCHOFF, Walter	266948	M	22. 7.03		Member, Inf.Ers.Bn.600-Lissa-3.Inf.Ers.Bn.30, Geh.Feldpolizei	-	SUSPECT	FR.
BITNER (or BITTNER or BITTman or WALTER)	266840	M			Lt. Commanding a group of anti-aircraft, Francheville, Prairay (Fr.) 4.7.44	-	MISC.CRIMES	FR.
BITTER, Hermann	265470	M	24.12.20		SS-Sturmfhr. Adjutant, Instruction course of N.C.O.'s, Veron-Etigny (Fr.) 17.-19.8.44	-	MURDER	FR.
BITTMAN (see BITNER)	266840							
BITTNER (see BITNER)	266840							
BLAESCHKE	265477	M			Uscharfhr., Waffen-SS, 3.Coy.1.Bn.Regt. "Der Fuehrer" Div. "Das Reich", Qradour-S.Glane (Fr.) 10.6.44	-	MURDER	FR.
BLANKE, Reinhold	302912	M			Kriminal-Asst., Gestapo Staff, Kattowitz (Pol.) 39-42	56/60	BRUTALITY	POL.
BLASZEZYK, Franz	266012	M	11. 2.11		Pvt.,2.Coy.,Res.M.G,Bn.14, Divion (Fr.) 9.4.44	-	MURDER	FR.
BLATTNER	302913	M			Cpl., Group 530 Geh.Feldpolizei, Bruessel (Bel.) 40-44	56/62	MURDER	BEL.
BLAUFUSZ	303538	M			Oscharfhr., SS, C.C., Majdanek (Pol.) 40-44	57/94	BRUTALITY	POL.
BLEICH	265339	M			Gendarm, Gendarmerie, Medvode (Yugo.) 3.3.42	-	MISC.CRIMES	YUGO.
BLESSMANN, Hugo	302914	M			Clerk, Criminal Police, Brühl (Ger.) 1.45	56/63	BRUTALITY	U.S.
BLHUM (see BLUHM)	253591							
BLICK	267134	M			Lt.Col., Army,893.Gren.Regt., Sinj (Yugo.)8.9.43-10.44	-	MURDER	YUGO.
BLIDA	304305	M			Wachtmeister, member, Schutzpolizei, Krakau (Pol.) 39-43	58/81	MURDER	POL.
BLIM	304306	M			Sturmbannfhr., deputy of SS and Polizeifhr., SS, Radom and district (Pol.) 41-43	58/82	MURDER	POL.
BLOCHER, Willi (see BLOCKER, Willi)	304528							
BLOCK	303539	M	15. 7.96		Oscharfhr., SS, C.C., Majdanek (Pol.) 40-42	57/97	BRUTALITY	POL.
BLOCK, Josef	303540	M	23. 7.91		Uscharfhr., SS, C.C., Majdanek (Pol.) 40-42	57/98	BRUTALITY	POL.
BLOCKER, Willi (or BLOCHER, Willi)	304528	M			Member, Gestapo, Krakau (Pol.) 11.39- 2.45	59/43	BRUTALITY	POL.
BLOCKERS	302915	M			Member, Group 530 of Geh.Feldpolizei, Bruessel (Bel.) 40-44	56/64	MURDER	BEL.
BLOECHL, Walter	308748	M	21. 9.00		Member, SD, Hlohovec (Czech.) 44	60/54	INTERR.	CZECH.
BLOECKER, Johann	302916	M			Sgt., Group 530 of Geh.Feldpolizei, Bruessel (Bel.) 40-44	56/65	MURDER	BEL.
BLOM	303541	M			Member, Gestapo, Warschau (Pol.) 39-45	57/99	BRUTALITY	POL.
BLOSCHE	303542	M			Member, Gestapo, Warschau (Pol.) 39-45	57/100	BRUTALITY	POL.
BLUHM (or BLHUM)	253591	M	02		Agent, Officer, Gestapo, Sipo and SD, Limoges (Fr.)2.43-8.44	41/30	SUSPECT	FR.
BLUM	308749	M			Officer, Customs, Larmor (Fr.) 5.6. and 7.8.44	60/55	MURDER	FR.
BLUMHAGEN	304307	M			Civilian, nr. Muenchen (Ger.) 9.4.45	58/83	MURDER	U.S.
BOCH (or BOSCH)	266356	M			Engineer, Chief inspector, Railway, (Ger.)	-	BRUTALITY	FR.
BOCHMANN, Ilse	304308	F			Operating theatre sister, "Ost"Hospital, Luebeck (Ger.) 43-45	58/84	BRUTALITY	POL.
BOCK	111018	M			Member, SD Montlucon, Chappes (Fr.) 28.7.44	-	MURDER	FR.
BOCK	303543	M			Member, Gestapo, Warschau (Pol.) 10.39- 1.45	57/101	BRUTALITY	POL.
BOCK (see BECK, Paul)	266830							
BOCK, Willy (or CARL)	265685	M	circa 98		Hptscharfhr., SD, Gestapo of Mans, Sarthe and Mayenne (Fr.)42-44	-	SUSPECT	FR.
BOCKMANN, Gunther	267298	M	circa 10		Usturmfhr., Chief, Gestapo, Abt.VI, Bordeaux and vicinity (Fr.) 42- 8.44	-	MURDER	FR.
BOCKWOLDT	304309	M			Pvt., Geh.Feldpolizei, Bruessel (Bel.) 40-44	58/85	MURDER	BEL.
BODEMANN (see BOLLMANN)	266727							
BODMANN, Helmut	267300	M			SS-Guard, SS, Struthof-Natzweiler (Fr.) 40-44	-	MURDER	FR.

BOD - BOU

NAME	C.R.FILE NUMBER	SEX	DATE OF BIRTH	RANK OCCUPATION UNIT PLACE AND DATE OF CRIME	UNWCC LIST/ SERIAL NO.	REASON WANTED	WANTED BY
BODNARCZUK, Wilhelm	304529	M		Member, Gestapo, Cracow (Pol.) 11.39-2.45	59/44	BRUTALITY	POL.
BODZUM, Peter	265309	M	95	See names listed under "special headings"			
BOECK (see SOECK)	309094						
BOEHLECKE, Paul	304530	M		Member, Secr.Field-Police, Luettich (Bel.) 40-41	59/46	MURDER	BEL.
BOERM	308750	M		Capt.,Cmdt.of the V-weapontroops "Marlot", Wassenaar (Neth.) 11.44	60/58	PILLAGE	NETH.
BOEHM (or BOHM), Otto or Alex	304310	M	circa 00	Lt.or Capt.,Cmdt.,Fort Hatry, Belfort (Fr.) 44	58/87	MURDER	FR.
BOEHMFELD, Werner	124704	M	8.1.24	Schuetze, SS-Panz.Gren.A.u.E.12.Bn.,7.Stamm-Coy. or 1.SS-A.u.E.Panz.Gren.Bn.12, Anhee, Yvoir-Meuse (Bel.) 4.9.44	13/8	MURDER	BEL.
BOELER	266359	M		Agent, Gestapo, Nantes and region (Fr.) 43-44	-	MURDER	FR.
BOES, Hermann	265812	M	19.9.03	Lt., Police, Ostheim (Fr.) 40-44	-	MISC.CRIMES	FR.
BOGLER, Max	266540	M		Guard, Asst.chief, works, C.C. Buchloe-Landsberg	-	SUSPECT	FR.
BOGUSCH (I)	304311	M		Wachtmstr., Member, German Gendarmerie, Wieliczka (Pol.) 25.8.42	58/89	MURDER	POL.
BOGUSCH (II)	304312	M		Wachtmstr., Member, German Gendarmerie, Bochnia (Pol.) 43	58/90	MURDER	POL.
BOHIKEN, Reinhold	302917	M		Cpl., Group 530 Geh.Feldpolizei, Bruessel (Bel.) 40-44	56/70	MURDER	BEL.
BOHLARS	304531	M		Member, Secr.Field-Police, Luettich (Bel.) 40-41	59/47	MURDER	BEL.
BOHM	266934	M		Chief-Cpl., Flakmst 30/XII, Carcassonne (Fr.) 19.8.44	-	MURDER	FR.
BOHM	303544	M		Member, Gestapo, Warschau (Pol.) 39-45	57/105	MISC.CRIMES	POL.
BOHM, Karl	304532	M		Member, Gestapo, Krakau (Pol.) 11.39-2.45	59/48	MURDER	POL.
BOHM (see BOEHM), Otto or Alex	304310						
BOHM, Willi	304533	M		Member, Gestapo, Krakau (Pol.) 11.39-2.45	59/49	MURDER	POL.
BOHME,	266821	M		Pvt., Section I a. Feldkommandantur 641 of Blois, Seillac (Fr.) 22.6.44	-	MISC.CRIMES	FR.
BOHME, Hans Joachim	126901	M		Regierungsrat, SS-Stubafhr., Head, Gestapo, Tilsit (Ger.)	9	SUSPECT	UNWCC
BOHMER	303545	M		Member, Gestapo, Warschau (Pol.) 39-45	57/106	MISC.CRIMES	POL.
BOHMER, Siegfried	302918	M		Kriminalbeamter, Staff Gestapo, Kattowitz (Pol.) 39-42	56/72	BRUTALITY	POL.
BOHN	266541	M		Lt., Unit No. 59 182, Buzancais (Fr.) 8.0.44	-	MISC.CRIMES	FR.
BOHNE, Erich	302919	M		Feldpolizeiinspektor, Group 530 Geh.Feldpolizei, Bruessel (Bel.) 40-44	56/73	MURDER	BEL.
BOHNE, Wilhelm	302920	M		Cpl., Group 530 Geh.Feldpolizei, Bruessel (Bel.) 40-44	56/74	MURDER	BEL.
BOHNE, Willi	304534	M		Member, Gestapo, Krakau (Pol.) 11.39-2.45	59/50	BRUTALITY	POL.
BOHNERT, Alois	304535	M		Member, Gestapo, Krakau (Pol.) 11.39-2.45	59/51	MURDER	POL.
BOHNING, Hans	304536	M		Member, Gestapo, Krakau (Pol.) 11.39-2.45	59/52	TORTURE	POL.
BOHSE (or BIHSE)	267186	M		Capt., Navy, Le Trait (Fr.) 40-44	-	BRUTALITY	FR.
BORSE	301076	M		Kriminalrat, Leader, R.S.D., Odense (Den.)	31/140	TORTURE	DEN.
BOLDT	302921	M		Capt., Police Officer, Police in the Province of North Neth. Alkmaar (Neth.) 11.10.44	56/75	MURDER	NETH.
BOLK, called "Carl" Willy	304314	M	circa 98	SS-Hscharfhr., Inspector, Gestapo at Mans, Kriminal Polizei Departm.of Sarthe and Mayenne (Fr.) 8.42-8.44	58/92	MURDER	FR.
BOLLENSDORF,	303546	M		Member, Gestapo, Warschau (Pol.) 39-45	57/110	BRUTALITY	POL.
BOLLING, Emil	302922	M		Sgt., Feldgendarmerie at Angouleme, Chasseneuil (Charente) (Fr.) 43-44 (22.3.44)	56/76	MURDER	FR.
BOLLINGER	303547	M		Member, Gestapo, Warschau (Pol.) 39-45	57/111	BRUTALITY	POL.
BOLLMANN (or BODMANN)	266727	M		Hauptsturmfhr., Crim.secretary, chief, Sonderkommando Kulmhof (Pol.) 41-45	-	MURDER	POL.
BOLLREIT, Franz	197717	M	13	Agent, Gestapo at Calais and Amiens, Laglantiers (Fr.) 13.7.1944	A 28/42	RAPE	FR.
BOLNEY	308752	M		SS-Sturmscharfhr., Crim.secretary, Radom (Pol.) 1.40-1.45	60/62	BRUTALITY	POL.
BOLG, Otto	31596	M	15.9.01	Professor, Institute for Anatomie, Strassburg (Fr.) 44	30/147	MURDER	FR.
BONGARDS	266880	M		Sgt., Stabs-Coy., 3.J.G.Udet, Soeurs (Fr.) 7.-8.44	-	PILLAGE	FR.
BONGERS	304315	M		Member, SD Aussenstelle Maastricht, Limburg and Friesland (Neth.) 44-45	58/94	MURDER	NETH.
BONKOWSKI	308757	M		Hairdresser, Sipo, Radom (Pol.) 1.40-1.45	60/67	PILLAGE	POL.
BOSCH	195897	M	26.6.07	Officer, Unit No. 14653 D., Guillaumes (Fr.) 23.7.44	28/43	MURDER	FR.
BONTE	266879	M	8.12.96	Capt., Chief, Feldkommandantur 641 of Blois, Section I, Police affairs, Lavardin and Vendome (Fr.) 9.-10.8.44	-	MURDER	FR.
BOOTMANN, Hans (see BOTHMANN)	265329						
BORCHARDT, Siegfried	304537	M		Member, Gestapo, Krakau (Pol.) 11.39-2.45	59/53	BRUTALITY	POL.
BORGER, Wilhelm	304538	M		Member, Gestapo, Krakau (Pol.) 11.39-2.45	59/54	BRUTALITY	POL.
BORGMANN, Heinrich	304539	M		Member, Gestapo, Krakau (Pol.) 11.39-2.45	59/55	BRUTALITY	POL.
BORIS	267187	M		Oberscharfhr., Gestapo of Baccarat, Pexonne (Fr.) 27.8.44	-	MISC.CRIMES	FR.
BORK	159984	F	15	C.Z.A., Typist, Gestapo, SD, area Vichy (Fr.) 44	16/23	SUSPECT	FR.
BORKERT	259161	M		Rottenfhr., SS, C.C.Dachau (Ger.) 42	40/383	MISC.CRIMES	YUGO.
BORM, Paul	308758	M	8.2.05	Member, Gendarmerie, Holzheim 42-45	60/69	MURDER	POL.
BORMANN, Heinrich Arthur Walter	176405	M	29.9.93	SS-Scharfhr., staff of C.C. Auschwitz (Pol.) 40-45	16/231	MURDER	FR.
BORN, Johannes	304540	M		Member, Gestapo, Krakau (Pol.) 11.39-2.45	59/56	TORTURE	POL.
BORNEFELD, Wilhelm	265359	M		Chief, Lt.Col., Recruiting Commission I German Army Kranj (Yugo.) 42-44	-	MISC.CRIMES	YUGO.
BORNHOLT, Johann	304541	M		Member, Gestapo, Krakau (Pol.) 11.39-2.45	59/58	MURDER	POL.
BOSCH (see BOCH)	266956						
BOSCHECK	302923	M		Member, Group 530 of Geh.Feldpolizei, Bruessel (Bel.) 40-44	56/81	MURDER	BEL.
BOSSE, Paul Dr.	266565	M		See names listed under "Special Headings"			
BOTHMANN, Hans Johann (or BOOTMANN)	265329	M		Sturmbannfhr., Leader, Sonderkommando SS, Extermination camp Chelm (Pol.) 41-42	-	MURDER	POL.
BOTTCHER, Herbert	304543	M		Member, Gestapo, Krakau (Pol.) 11.39-2.45	59/61	BRUTALITY	POL.
BOUCH (or BUCH)	146513	M		Adjutant, Interpreter, Kommandantur, Dax (Landes) (Fr.) 13.6.44	13/4	MURDER	FR.
BOUILLON, Maurice (see ROTTLOF, Herbert or Ludwig)	304387						
BOUKMAKOWSKY (or BUKMAKOSKY or BUCHMAKOSKY)	265212	M	circa 09	Capt.or Major, Army, 10.leichte Inf.Regt., 114 Lt.Inf.Div. Gubbia (It.) 22.6.44	-	SUSPECT	U.K.
BOULARD (see BULHARD), Harris	266014						
BOULLION	302924	M		Agent, Gestapo, Kempen (Ger.) 25.10.41	56/83	MURDER	POL.

BRA - BRO

NAME	C.R.FILE NUMBER	SEX	DATE OF BIRTH	RANK OCCUPATION UNIT PLACE AND DATE OF CRIME	UNWCC LIST/ SERIAL NO.	REASON WANTED	WANTED BY
BRACHOC, Herbert	266542	M	circa 14	Pvt., Pioneer Unit, Saint Die (Fr.) 11.44	-	MURDER	FR.
BRACKSIEK	266607	M		Chief accountant, Ueberwachungsstelle, Organisation of the Black Market in France (Fr.) 42-44	-	PILLAGE	FR.
BRADER	267299	M		Member, Gestapo, Bordeaux and vicinity (Fr.) 42-8.44	-	MURDER	FR.
BRAEKOW, Ernst	148460	M		Head, Press and Propaganda Department in the Reich Propaganda Office	9/-	MISC.CRIMES	UNWCC
BRAEMER, Walter	62214	M		Lt.Gen., Army, Kav., Ostland	7	MISC.CRIMES	UNWCC
BRAUENING, Edmund	159807	M		SS-Hptscharfhr., Waffen SS, Totenkopf-Stuba., C.C.Buchenwald-Weimar (Ger.) 39, 42-45	25/63	MISC.CRIMES	BEL.
BRAHMANN	266657	M		Farmer, Civilian, Gueblange les Dieuze, (Fr.) 41-44	-	PILLAGE	FR.
BRAMEN	256426	M		SS-Uscharfr., C.C.Neuengamme (Ger.)	31/11	MURDER	BEL.
BRAND, Otto	266898	M		Cpl., Feldgendarmerie 624, Avallon, Yonne, (Fr.) 44	-	MISC.CRIMES	FR.
BRANDECKER	265331	M		Capt., Ger.Army, Nachr.Coy., District of Slovenjgradec (Yugo.) 8.-11.44	-	MISC.CRIMES	YUGO.
BRANDEL	266357	M		Mechanician at the Station of Buchloe-Landsberg (Ger.)	-	BRUTALITY	FR.
BRANDES	29836	M		Paymaster, Army, Evry (Fr.) 44	8/72	MISC.CRIMES	FR.
BRANDSTAETTER	308759	M		Secretary, Fieldpolice, Antwerpen and Bruessel (Bel.) 40-44	60/74	MURDER	BEL.
BRANDT	302925	M		N.C.O., Sipo and SD-Kdo.Rouen, Avranches Branch, Cherburg and Dep.La Manche (Fr.) 42-44	56/86	MURDER	FR.
BRANDT, Fritz	304544	M		Member, Gestapo, Krakau (Pol.) about 11.39-about 2.45	59/62	MURDER	POL.
BRANDT, Heinrich	264561	M	3. 5.01	See names listed under "Special Headings"	-		U.S.
BRANDTNER, Franz	265352	M	28. 9.06	SS-Mann, Crim.Secr., Sipo, SD, (Gestapo), Carinthi and Carniola (Yugo.) 7.42-5.45	-	MURDER	YUGO.
BRASS, Theodor	302926	M		Scharfhr., Kempen (Ger.) 25.10.41	56/87	MURDER	POL.
BRAUER, Fritz	304545	M		Member, Gestapo, Krakau (Pol.) about 11.39-about 2.45	59/63	PILLAGE	POL.
BRAUER, Walter	304546	M		Member, Gestapo, Krakau (Pol.) about 11.39-about 2.45	59/64	RAPE	POL.
BRAUER, Willi	304547	M		Member, Gestapo, Krakau (Pol.) about 11.39-about 2.45	59/65	PILLAGE	POL.
BRAULICH, Maurycy	266729	M	22. 9.92	Worker, "Solway" factory, Krakau (Pol.)	-	MISC.CRIMES	POL.
BRAUN	36660	M		Sgt., Army, 1010 mot.Regt., 2 Bn., 8 Coy., Lorient Orlenais(Fr.) 13.-15.8.44	13/791	MURDER	U.K.
BRAUN	266264	M		Cpl., Africa-Corps, Regt.Ruxleben, 6 Coy., 1 Sect., Hte.Marne-Aube (Fr.) 25.-31.8.44	-	MURDER	FR.
BRAUN	306414	M		SS-Mann, C.C.Oranienburg (Ger.) 39-45	25/750	MURDER	CZECH.
BRAUN, Joseph	132601	M	17	SS-Scharfhr., Waffen SS, SD, Vichy (Fr.)	16/233	SUSPECT	FR.
BRAUN, Otto	266931	M	circa 90	Sgt., Feldgendarmerie, Masleves, Coulanges, Blois (Fr.) 7.44, 10.8.44	-	MURDER	FR.
BRAUN, Willy	265296	M		Pvt. (It.)	-	SUSPECT	U.K.
BRAUNE, Rudolf Dr.	304114	M		Dr., Head, Treuhandstelle Ostoberschlesien, Bendzin (Pol.) 40-43	58/104	MURDER	POL.
BRAUNISCH, Georg	303548	M	25. 5.93	Guard, C.C. Majdanek (Pol.) 40-42	57/124	BRUTALITY	POL.
BRAUWEILER, Otto	304548	M		Member, Gestapo, Krakau (Pol.) about 11.39-about 2.45	59/66	MURDER	POL.
BREGER	303549	M		Member, Gestapo, Warschau (Pol.) 39-45	57/125	BRUTALITY	POL.
BREHMER, Georg	302927	M		Crim.Secr., Gestapo Staff, Kattowitz (Pol.) 39-42	56/90	BRUTALITY	POL.
BREINL, Franz Dr.	31985	M		District-court-counsellor, Public official, Litomerice (Czech.) 40	8/10	MURDER	CZECH.
BREITAULT (Colonel) (see FORN, Reinhold)	267148						
BREITER	266558	M		SS-Usturmfhr., Manager, Purchase office Textiles, Organisation of the Black Market (Fr.) 42-44	-	MISC.CRIMES	FR.
BREITHAUPT, Walter	308761	M	2. 2.08	Techn.Secr., Gestapo Headquarters Saarbruecken at various places in Germany and German occupied territory 25.3.44,13.4.44	60/79	MURDER	U.K.
BREMBERGER (see BAMBERGER)	125101						
BREMER	304549	F		Member, SD Section II, Oldenzaal, Sauwerd, Den Haag (Neth.) 45	59/67	PILLAGE	NETH.
BRENDEL, Wilhelm	208296	M	9. 8.06	Crim.Secr., Sturmscharfhr., Sipo, BDS Einsatzkdo.III-2, Mulhouse, Strassburg (Fr.) 16.2.43, 45	25/109	MURDER	FR.
BRENDLER	304115	M		SS-Oscharfhr., Head, Economic Dept.of SD and Sipo, Sanok (Pol.) 42	58/105	MISC.CRIMES	POL.
BRENNECKE	267188	M		Capt., Gestapo, Marseille and environ (Fr.)	-	MURDER	FR.
BRENNER	28737	M		Gruppenfhr., Comd. 6 SS Geb.Div.Nord, 20 Army, Finmark (Nor.) 11.44	8/230	MURDER	NOR.
BRENSCHEIDT, Hugo	308762	M		Member, 1 Coy., 1,2 or Schwaben Bn., nr.Billingsbach (Ger.) 17.4.45	60/80	MURDER	U.S.
BRENSFMAN (or BIRFMAN)	263913	M		See names listed under "Special Headings"			FR.
BRESFOW, Wilhelm Friedrich	303550	M	15. 5.10	Kapo, C.C.Auschwitz (Pol.) 40-45	57/129	BRUTALITY	POL.
BRETAG, Wilhelm	301679	M		Lt., Feldgendarmerie at Digne, Mezel, Pradsetla, Javie (Basses-Alpes) (Fr.) 18.7.44, 30.7.44	27/30	MURDER	FR.
BRETZ, Laure	267302	F		Secr., Interpreter, Gestapo, Bordeaux and vicinity (Fr.) 42-8.44	-	MURDER	FR.
BREUCHE, Paul	302928	M		Crim.Secr., Gestapo Staff, Kattowitz (Pol.) 39-42	56/93	BRUTALITY	POL.
BRIESEMEISTER	308763	M		SS-Hptscharfhr., probably an official, Radom (Pol.) 1.40-1.45	60/82	BRUTALITY	POL.
BRIESMEISTER, Paul	304550	M		Member, Gestapo, Kraukau (Pol.) 11.39-2.45	59/68	MURDER	POL.
BRITY	304116	M		Hauptwachtmeister, Gendarmerie, Bochnia (Pol.) 40-43	58/107	MURDER	POL.
BRINKMANN	266265	M	circa 00	Hptsturmfhr., Court of Justice, Dijon (Fr.) 1, u.3.44	-	MURDER	FR.
BRIX, Erhard	304551	M		Member, Gestapo, Krakau (Pol.) 11.39-2.45	59/69	MURDER	POL.
BROCHNIK (see PROCHNIK, Robert)	304342						
BROCK	146664	M		Cmdt. of Fort at Havre, Montvilliers (Fr.) 2.9.44	13/5	WITNESS	FR.
BROCK	303551	M		Member, Gestapo, Warschau (Pol.) 39-45	57/131	BRUTALITY	POL.
BROCK, Egbert	304552	M		Member, Gestapo, Krakau (Pol.) 11.39-2.45	59/70	MURDER	POL.
BROCKAUS	144669	M		Sgt., Gestapo, S R A, Bordeaux (Fr.)	-	SUSPECT	FR.
BROCKE	144670	M		Osturmfhr., SS Dienststelle No.34356 A, SS Div. "Das Reich" and SS Div. "Goetz von Berlichingen", Mirebeau.	-	SUSPECT	FR.
BROCKHAUS	266013	M		Interpreter, Cmdt., for Maneken, of Fireman at Brest (Fr.) 8.-9.44	-	MURDER	FR.
BROCKHOFF	144672	M		Commandant, Section Ic espionnage security 6-XII, Civ. doctor official of coal-mines, Salon (Fr.)	-	SUSPECT	FR.

BRO - BUK

NAME	C.R.FILE NUMBER	SEX	DATE OF BIRTH	RANK OCCUPATION UNIT PLACE AND DATE OF CRIME	UNWCC LIST/ SERIAL NO.	REASON WANTED	WANTED BY
BRODA, Emil	304117	M		Head, Price Control Office, Sosnowiec (Pol.) 40-42	58/108	MISC.CRIMES	POL.
BRODAR, Aribert, Dr.	265361	M		Wine-Merchant, Civ., Ormoz (Yugo.) summer 41	-	MISC.CRIMES	YUGO.
BRODMANN, Werner	304553	M		Member, Gestapo, Krakau (Pol.) 11.39-2.45	59/71	MURDER	POL.
BRODMEIER, Walter	302929	M		Sgt., Group 530 Geh.Feldpolizei, H.Q. Bruessel (Bel.) 40-44	56/94	MISC.CRIMES	BEL.
BRODOWSKI, Karl	302930	M		Staff-Sgt., Feldgendarmerie at Angouleme, Chasseneuil (Fr.) 43, 22.3.44	56/95	MURDER	FR.
BRODT, Friedrich	303552	M	4. 4.10	SS-Mann, C.C. Majdanek (Pol.) 40-44	57/132	BRUTALITY	POL.
BROKER	304118	M		N.C.O., Group 648 of the G.F.P., H.Q.Boulevard Piercot Liege (Bel.) 40-44	58/110	TORTURE	BEL.
BROKUF, Erhardt	124706	M	17.11.25	SS-Mann, SS-Pz.Gren.Ers.u.Ausb.Bn.12, 7.or 1.Coy., Anhee, Yvoir-Meuse (Bel.) 4.9.44	13/13	MURDER	BEL.
BRONEL	266935	M		Feldgendarm, Feldgendarmerie, Sisteron (Fr.) 44	-	MISC.CRIMES	FR.
BROSCH	267303	M	circa 14	Cpl., Army, Motoris.m.1000, Fournels (Fr.) 22.6.44	-	MURDER	FR.
BROSE	162093	M		Hptstubefhr., Pz.Div. "Das Reich", 1.Pz.Regt.,2.Coy., Tulle (Fr.) 44	11/43	MURDER	FR.
BROSOF	195727	M		Pvt., Pz.Div. SS "Das Reich", 2.Coy., F.P.No.27310 B, Tulle (Fr.) beginning 44	11/44	MURDER	FR.
BROTMAN, Alfons	265321	M	18. 2.16	Chief of Kripo, Tomaszow,Mazowiecki (Pol.) 39-45	-	MURDER	POL.
BROTZIG	302931	M		Lt.,Head of Quarters, Departm.Basses-Pyrenees (Fr.) 8.6.-8.44	56/98	MURDER	FR.
BROUCH	266996	M		Feldgendarm, Feldgendarmerie, Sisteron (Fr.) 44	-	MISC.CRIMES	FR.
BRUCHHAUSSER, Alois	198076	M		Works-Director, Member NSDAP, Busenbach, Neurod (Ger.) 43-45	16/239	BRUTALITY	FR.
BRUCK, Leopold	308764	M	23. 3.05	Gestapoman, Sipo and SD Aussenstelle, Jesenice-Slovenia 41-45	60/85	MURDER	YUGO.
BRUCKLER	267189	M		Hptscharfhr., Gestapo, Marseille and vicinity (Fr.)	-	MURDER	FR.
BRUCKLER (Nickname "Boxer")	146496	M	circa 05	Agent, SS-Hptscharfhr., SD, Nice (Fr.) 43-44	-	MURDER	FR.
BRUCKMANN, Dr.	265471	M		Interpreter, 18.446 R, Customes F.P.N.,Barcelonnette (Fr.) 6.44	-	MISC.CRIMES	FR.
BRUCKNER	147014	M		Pvt., Pz.Div. "Das Reich", 2.Coy. F.P.No.27310 B, Tulle (Fr.) 44	11/46	MURDER	FR.
BRUCKNER	304120	M		Major, Commander, Fort Macon, Saint Laurent-les Macons-Ain (Fr.) 13.-14.8.44	58/113	MURDER	FR.
BRUECKNER, Wilhelm	148462	M		Adjutant to the Fuehrer, Army	9	MISC.CRIMES	UNWCC
BRUHBASSE (see BRUHWASSER)	267038						
BRUHL, Hans	308521	M		Capt., Gestapo of Perigueux,Auriac-de-Perigord (Fr.) 30.3.44	10/410	MURDER	FR.
BRUHN, Fritz	304554	M		Member, Gestapo, Krakau (Pol.) 11.39-2.45	59/74	PILLAGE	POL.
BRUEN, Hans	11655	M		Oberdienstleiter, Head Political Training Dept.Reichsleitung (Party Directorate)	9/23	MISC.CRIMES	UNWCC
BRUHWASSER (or BRUHBASSE)	267038	M		19.SS-Pol.Regt., 3.Bn.,11.Coy.,Limoges,Brive and vicinity (Fr.) 9.7.-25.7.44	-	MURDER	FR.
BRUMMERLOCH, Helmut	304555	M		Member, Gestapo, Krakau (Pol.) 11.39-2.45	59/75	MURDER	POL.
BRUN	266937	M		Feldgendarm, Feldgendarmerie, Sisteron (Fr.) 44	-	MISC.CRIMES	FR.
BRUNDT	267297	M		SS-Guard, Struthof-Natzweiler (Fr.) 40-44	-	MURDER	FR.
BRUNKEN, Heinz	302932	M		Kriminalsekretaer, Gestapo Staff, Kattowitz (Pol.) 39-42	56/101	BRUTALITY	POL.
BRUNNER	125029	M		Member, Gestapo, Sipo, SD-Einsatz Kdo., Chalons s. Marne (Fr.)43-44	-	MISC.CRIMES	FR.
BRUNNER	266831	M		SS-Hptsturmfhr., SD, Nice (Fr.) 44	-	SUSPECT	FR.
BRUNNER, Friedrich	304556	M		Member, Gestapo, Krakau (Pol.) 11.39-2.45	59/76	PILLAGE	POL.
BRUNNLER, Paul	304557	M		Member, Gestapo, Krakau (Pol.) 11.39-2.45	59/77	BRUTALITY	POL.
BRUNS	267518	M		Capt.,Commandant,Wach-Coy.,Oflag X B,Stalag X C,Nienburg-Weser (Ger.) 7.43-11.44	-	MURDER	FR.
BRUNSTEIN	302933	M		Uscharfhr., Gestapo, Lodz,(Pol.) 39-44	56/104	BRUTALITY	POL.
BRUNSTEIN, Hans	302934	M		SS-Scharfhr., Gestapo Staff, Kattowitz (Pol.) 39-42	56/105	MURDER	POL.
BRUNTSCH, Herbert	302935	M		Kriminalsekretaer, Gestapo Staff, Kattowitz (Pol.) 39-42	56/106	Interr.	POL.
BRUSCH, Johann	304558	M		Member, Gestapo, Krakau (Pol.) 11.39-2.45	59/78	BRUTALITY	POL.
BRUTTEL, Emil	146343	M		Oscharfhr., C.C. Struthof-Natzweiler (Fr.) 40-44	38/371	MURDER	FR.,U.K.
BRYKTZINSKI	303553	M		Member, Gestapo, Warschau (Pol.) 39-45	57/138	BRUTALITY	POL.
BTIUK	303554	M	1. 2.23	SS-Mann, C.C. Majdanek (Pol.) 40-44	57/139	BRUTALITY	POL.
BUBELEBER	308765	M		Guard, Wolfenbuettel Prison (Ger.) betw. 42-45	60/86	TORTURE	BEL.
BUCARD, Max (see BURGARD)	41005						
BUCH (see BOUCH)	146513						
BUCH, Herbert Hans	308766	M	29.11.11	Crim.secret.(Crim.commissioner?) Dept.IV 2a Shell house,Copenhagen and other towns (Den.) 1.8.44-4.5.45	60/87	MURDER	DEN.
BUCHELT, Willy	195824	M		Sgt., NUTZ KO (Wege) Batt. of the 896.R.I., Kermassenet in Kervignac (Fr.) 20.8.44	16/241	MURDER	FR.
BUCHHOLD, Gerhard	304559	M		Member, Gestapo, Krakau (Pol.) 11.39-2.45	59/79	BRUTALITY	POL.
BUCHHOLZ	303555	M		Member, Gestapo, Warschau (Pol.) 39-45	57/140	BRUTALITY	POL.
BUCHHOLZ, Else	304560	F		Member, Gestapo, Krakau (Pol.) 11.39-2.45	59/80	BRUTALITY	POL.
BUCHINGER, Karl	308768	M		Insp., Fieldpolice, Antwerpen, Bruessel (Bel.) 40-44	60/89	MURDER	BEL.
BUCHMAIER	304121	M		Oscharfhr., SS, Radom (Pol.) 40-43	58/118	MURDER	POL.
BUCHMAROSA (see BOUKMAKOWSKY)	265212						
BUCHNER, Franz	60060	M		Deputy Gauleiter, NSDAP, Muenchen (Ger.)	9/24	MISC.CRIMES	UNWCC
BUCHWALD	266832	M		Lt., SD of Rennes, Cirey s.Vezouse (Fr.) 9.-11.44	-	MURDER	FR.
BUCK, Niklaus	266266	M	21. 8.05	Custom-secretary, Customs-service, Liebenswiller (Fr.) 29.3.42	-	MURDER	FR.
BUCKER	266522	M		See Names listed under "Special Headings"			
BUCKER, Johann	308767	M		Civ., Verne Distr.Buren 12.44	60/91	BRUTALITY	POL.
BUDE	303556	M		Member, Gestapo, Warschau (Pol.) 39-45	57/144	MURDER	POL.
BUDDENBERG	267190	M		Cpl., Unit-No. 05.744/A, Marines (Fr.) 16.8.44	-	INTERR.	FR.
BUETTNER	195005	M		Pvt., Army, Airforce Unit L 20968, Flakmant 30/XII Flakmunition Abgabestelle, Chateau de Baudrigues nr.Carrassone (Fr.) 19.8.44	3/49	MURDER	FR.
BUENTING, Dietrich	302937	M		Feldpolizeisekretaer, Group 530 of Geh.Feldpolizei, Bruessel (Bel.) 40-44	56/108	MURDER	BEL.
BUHL	304561	M		Secretary, Secr.Field-Police, Luettich (Bel.) 40-41	59/81	MURDER	BEL.
BUHL (or PUHL), Anna	131840	F		Civ., Bad Duerrenberg (Ger.) 29.5.44	16/971	TORTURE	U.S.
BUJER, Alfred (see BAYER, Alfred)	304516						
BUKLADA, Stanislaw	266730	M	24. 2.01	Worker, Electric railway, Krakau (Pol.) 39-45	-	MISC.CRIMES	POL.
BUKMAKOSKY (see BOUKMAKOWSKY)	265212						

BUL - CRO

NAME	C.R.FILE NUMBER	SEX	DATE OF BIRTH	RANK OCCUPATION UNIT PLACE AND DATE OF CRIME	UNWCC LIST/ SERIAL NO.	REASON WANTED	WANTED BY
BULHARD, Harris (or BOULARD)	266014	M	circa 90	Oschfhr., SD, Chalons sur Marne (Fr.) 43-44	-	MISC.CRIMES	FR.
BULLOW, Helmut	304562	M		Member, Gestapo, Krakau, (Pol.) 11.39-2.45	59/82	MURDER	POL.
BUM	265308	M		See names listed under "Special Headings"			
BUNK, Bruno	303557	M	17. 8.07	SS-Mann, C.C. Majdanek, (Pol.) 40-44	57/147	PILLAGE	POL.
BURANER	31373	M		Cpt., Army Comd.Pi.Bn.82-2, Gebirgs Div. 20 Army Finnmark (Nor.) 10.-11.44	8/234	MURDER	NOR.
BURCKHAUSEN	304122	M		Uschfhr., Member, SS-Gestapo, Sosnowiec, Bendzin (Pol.)41-43	58/122	MURDER	POL.
BURGARD, Max (or BUCARD)	41005	M	circa 90	Hptschfhr., SD, Chalons sur Marne (Fr.) 43-44	-	MISC.CRIMES	FR.
BURGER	147012	M		Waffen-SS, Pz.Div."Das Reich", Deutschland Rgt. 3 Bn. Venerque le Vernet (Fr.) 44	11/49	MURDER	FR.
BURGER	308769	M		Schfhr., Radom (Pol.) 1.40-1.45	60/94	MURDER	POL.
BURGER, Heinrich	267437	M		Foreman, Eckart Werke Plant, Velden near Hersbruck (Ger.)42-45	-	BRUTALITY	FR.
BURGIN, Hermann	304563	M		Member, Gestapo, Krakau (Pol.) 11.39-2.45	59/84	MURDER	POL.
BURKHARDT, Arthur	267446	M	10. 3.05	See names listed under "Special Headings"			
BURNIGER	266833	M	circa 92	Lt., Chief, of water communication and Forester,Licheres (Fr.)	-	MURDER	FR.
BURS	308770	M		Civilian, Verne district Buren (Ger.) 12.44	60/95	TORTURE	POL.
BURY, Eduard	266128	M	17. 8.95	Member, German Police, Civilian, Merchant,Mysowice (Pol.)40-45	-	MISC.CRIMES	POL.
BUSCH, Alfred	265608	M	3.12.93	See names listed under "Special Headings"			
BUSCH, Erna	304564	F		Member, Gestapo, Krakau (Pol.) 11.39- 2.45	59/85	PILLAGE	POL.
BUSCHKA, Max	304593	M		Member, Gestapo, Krakau (Pol.) 11.39- 2.45	59/86	PILLAGE	POL.
BUSS	303558	M		Member, Gestapo, Warschau (Pol.) 39-45	57/149	BRUTALITY	POL.
BUSSE	266267	M		Manager, Buying Service, (Fr.) 42-44	-	PILLAGE	FR.
BUSSERT	308771	M		Pvt., GFP., Antwerpen and Bruessel (Bel.) 40-44	60/96	MURDER	BEL.
BUTNER, Ernst (called "Storkneck")	267482	M		Member, Gestapo, Luchon and vicinity (Fr.) 1.43-7.44	-	MURDER	FR.
BUTTERLING,	304123	M		Sgt., Feldgendarmerie, Arlon and vicinity (Bel.) 8.44- 9.44	58/124	MURDER	BEL.
BUTTNER	131735	M		N.C.O. 2 SS Pz.Div. "Das Reich" F.P.No. 20727, La Croix-Falgarde (Hte-Garonne), (Fr.) 44	11/51	MURDER	FR.
BUTTNER	266523	M		Obermeister, Unit 2 L-38440, Lesquin (Fr.) 1.9.44	-	INCENDIARISM	FR.
BUTTOLD, Anne-Marie	308772	F		Camp-Leader, Women's dept. of the "Strafdienstpflichtlager" Sterntal near Ptui (Slov.) 1.45-4.45	60/97	BRUTALITY	YUGO.
BUTZ, Eduard	304592	M		Member, Gestapo, Krakau (Pol.) 11.39- 2.45	59/87	BRUTALITY	POL.
BUTZ, Victor	304591	M		Member, Gestapo, Krakau (Pol.) 11.39- 2.45	59/88	BRUTALITY	POL.
CALOW, Helmut	267099	M	circa 00	Member, Gestapo, Blois and Mavès (Fr.) 43-44	-	MURDER	FR.
CARGELL, N.	304124	M		Engineer and Manager, Vereinigte Jutespinnerei und Weberei A.G. Hamburg (Ger.) 40-45	58/124 A	BRUTALITY	POL.
CARL (see BOCK, Willy)	265685						
CARSTENS	266268	M		Chief-Cpl., Africa Corps, Rgt. "Ruxleben" 6 Coy. 1 Sect. Hte.Marne-Aube (Fr.) 25.-31.8.44	-	MURDER	FR.
CHAPLAIN	267525	M		Sgt.Major, 350 Hindou-Rgt., Departm.Indre (Fr.) 8.44	-	MURDER	FR.
CHARLAU, Lorens-Hans	267040	M		Agent, Gestapo, Arras (Fr.) 8.41	-	MURDER	FR.
CHICKINGER (or FICKINGER)	157406	M		Inspector, Gestapo, St.Quentin (Fr.) 40-44	16/50	MURDER	FR.
CHIELEWICZ	303559	M		Member, Gestapo, Warschau (Pol.) 39-45	-	BRUTALITY	POL.
CHIEMANN, Waldemar	304590	M		Member, Gestapo, Krakau (Pol.) 11.39-2.45	59/89	PILLAGE	POL.
CHIERTZ, Walter	304589	M		Member, Gestapo, Krakau, (Pol.) 11.39-2.45	59/90	PILLAGE	POL.
CHRISTENEJM	125025	M		Interpreter, Feldkommandantur, Poitiers,Chateau de Porteau (Fr.) 24.-25.8.44	13/7	MURDER	FR.
CHRISTENSEN, Herbert	304051	M	4.10.20	SS-Mann, C.C. Majdanek, (Pol.) 40-44	57/160	BRUTALITY	POL.
CHRISTIANSEN, Christian	304127	M		Former Mayor of Achtrup (Ger.) 6.5.45	58/129	MURDER	POL.
CHRISTOFERSON	308779	M		SS-Usturmfhr., and Crim.Secr., Radom (Pol.) 1.40-1.45	60/106	MURDER	POL.
CHROSTEK, Herbert	304588	M		Member, Gestapo, Krakau (Pol.) 11.39-2.45	59/92	MURDER	POL.
CHUJAR, Albert (see HUJER)	265750						
CHULEIN	267204	M		Sgt., 350 Rgt. "Hindou", l'Indre (Fr.) 8.44.	-	MURDER	FR.
CHURENAU (or CHURNAU)	167007	M		Cpl., Sgt., Etat Major,General staff Kommandantur Crest, La Rochette (Fr.) 7. and 8.44	10/4	MURDER	FR.
CHURNAU (see CHURENAU)	167007						
CHWALLEK, Gerhard	302998	M		Krim.Beamter, Gestapo Staff, Katowitz (Pol.) 39-42	56/112	INTERR.	POL.
CIELECKI, Alois	268834	M		Cpl., Unit No. 25061, St.Martin de Fressengeas (Fr.) 29.4.44	-	MURDER	FR.
CLAPEK, Karel	302939	M		Cpl. of a Mixed German and Polish Unit,Luijksgestel (Neth.) 8.9.44	56/113	MURDER	NETH.
CLAUZEN, Willy	302940	M		Presumably Member, 331 Inf.Div., Oud-Beijerland (Neth.) 17.10.44	56/116	PILLAGE	NETH.
CLAUSE	267577	M		Customhouse Secretary, Custom-house,Renesse and Zierikzee (Neth.) 12.10.44	-	BRUTALITY	NETH.
CLAUSEN, Honriks	304587	M		Member, Gestapo, Krakau (Pol.) 11.39-2.45	59/93	PILLAGE	POL.
CLAUSEN, Theodor	302941	M		Cpl., Group 530 Geh.Feld.Polizei, Bruessel (Bel.) 40-44	56/117	MURDER	BEL.
CLAUSS	303560	M		Member, Gestapo, Warschau (Pol.) 39-45	57/166	BRUTALITY	POL.
COGONI	308780	M		Lt., Carabinieri, Petreto-Biccisano and at Ajaccio, Corsica (Fr.) 43	60/107	MURDER	FR.
COHNEN, Willy	308781	M		Member, Gendarmerie, Holzheim (Ger.) 42-45	60/108	MURDER	POL.
COLLER, Siegfried, (or KELLER)	265216	M	18	Sgt., stationed at Goriano Valli (It.) 10.1.44	-	SUSPECT	U.K.
CONRAD (or ARTMANN)	266269	M	circa 10	See names listed under "Special Headings"			
CONRAD	266524	M	circa 10	Pvt., Kdo. coming from Rennes or d'Angers,Saint Die (Fr.)11.44	-	MURDER	FR.
CONRAD	304129	M		Member, SD, Dingjum Friesland (Neth.) 8.3.45	58/132	MURDER	NETH.
CORGNEL, Barker	147010	M		SS-Mann, Pz.Div. "Das Reich", K.13 Coy., Moissac (Fr.) 44	11/54	MURDER	FR.
CORS	154342	M		N.C.O., Pz.Jaeg.Ers.Bn.7, 14 Coy. Unit No. 15181 Ecole en Bauges (Fr.) 1.5. and 6.7.44	11/55	MURDER	FR.
COULD	267524	M		Member, Gestapo,Angers,Tours and vicinity (Fr.) 43	-	MURDER	FR.
COUSIN, Josef	303561	M	2.12.01	SS-Mann, C.C. Majdanek (Pol.) 40-44	57/167	BRUTALITY	POL.
COUTURIER	126982	M	00	Oberwachtmeister, Schupo.,C.C.Schirmeck (Fr.) 43-44	30/158	MURDER	FR.
CRAMER	266266	M		Inspector, Stabs Coy. 3 J.G. Udett, Sours (Fr.) 7.44-8.44	-	PILLAGE	FR.
CRAMER, Hans	308782	M		Member, Terrorgroup "Peter",Fredericia (Den.) 3.45	60/109	MURDER	DEN.
CREMER, Aleska	304565	M		Member, Gestapo, Krakau (Pol.) 11.39-2.45	59/95	PILLAGE	POL.
CROO	304131	M		Cpt., possibly of the Feldgendarmerie or the Pion.Abt. stationed at Fort Hoek van Netherlands Unit 45696 Honsersdijk near Naaldwijk (Neth.) 28.4.45	58/136	MURDER	NETH.

CUR - DEN

NAME	C.R.FILE NUMBER	SEX	DATE OF BIRTH	RANK	OCCUPATION	UNIT	PLACE AND DATE OF CRIME	UNWCC LIST/ SERIAL NO.	REASON WANTED	WANTED BY
CURBITZ	267483	M		Sgt., 350.Regt."Hindou",Department l'Indre (Fr.) 8.44				-	MURDER	FR.
CUSCH	266270	M		Cpl.,Africa-Corps,Regt.Ruxleben,6.Coy.1.Sect.,Hte.Marne - Aube (Fr.) 25.-31.8.44				-	MURDER	FR.
CVETNIK	304566	M		Gendarm,Gendarmerie,Selce,Skofja Loka (Slov.) end of 43				59/96	MURDER	YUGO.
CYROCKI	303562	M		Member, Gestapo, Warschau (Pol.) 39-45				57/169	BRUTALITY	POL.
CZAJA, Horst	304567	M		Member, Gestapo, Krakau (Pol.) Nov.39- 2.45				59/97	PILLAGE	POL.
CZECH, Hermann	266129	M	27.10.92	Camp senior, C.C., Goerlitz (Ger.) 44-45				-	MURDER	POL.
CZERNIN, Felix	265609	M		See names listed under "Special Headings"						
CZERWONY, Erwin	304568	M		Member, Gestapo, Krakau (Pol.) 11.39- 2.45				59/98	MURDER	POL.
CZOGALA	304082	M		Member, Gestapo, Warschau (Pol.) 39-45				57/170	BRUTALITY	POL.
CZORNY	303563	M		Member, Gestapo, Warschau (Pol.) 39-45				57/171	BRUTALITY	POL.
CZYCHOLT	308784	M		Official, Prison, Hagen (Ger.) between 42 and 45				60/111	TORTURE	BEL.
DAHL, Paul	308785	M	28. 2.86	Worksmanager, Member, NSDAP, Heerenberg (Neth.) 41-45				60/112	INTERR.	NETH.
DAHLHEIMER, Karl	302942	M		Polizei-Inspektor, Gestapo Staff, Kattowitz (Pol.) 39-42				56/120	INTERR.	POL.
DAHLMANN, Edmund	304132	M		Polizeimann, Polizei, Distr.Gleidorf (Ger.) 42-44				58/137	BRUTALITY	POL.
DAHNKE, Gustav	302943	M		Pvt.,Group 530 Geh.Feldpolizei,Bruessel (Bel.) 40-44				56/121	MURDER	BEL.
DAJNOWSKI, Jan	304133	M		Agent, Gestapo, Wilno (Pol.) 12.39				58/138	INTERR.	POL.
DALKE, Julius	303564	M	22. 1.16	SS-Mann,Blockfhr.,C.C., Majdanek (Pol.) 40-44				57/173	BRUTALITY	POL.
DALLENBERG, Fred	304134	M		Zugfhr., member, Schutzpolizei, Sosnowiec, Bendzin, Szrodula(Pol.)43				58/139	MURDER	POL.
DALSKI, Jeski	304135	M		Osturmfhr.,SS, Kielce (Pol.) 43				58/140	MURDER	POL.
DAMITZ	303565	M		Member, Gestapo, Warschau (Pol.) 39-45				57/174	MURDER	POL.
DAMM	304136	M		Lt. serving in Arta-Epiros and Western Thessalia area (Grc.) 10.43				58/141	MURDER	GRC.
DAMM, Ferdinand	308786	M		Betriebsobmann,Lendringsen distr.Iserlohn (Ger.) 39-45				60/114	BRUTALITY	POL.
DAMMANN	190676	M		Pvt.,Eis.Art.Btty.717 at Chateau de Peres Blancs,F.P.No.22380, St.Andries,Varsenare,le Bruges (Bel.) 4.9.44				14/8	MURDER	BEL.
DAMMER, Viktor	302944	M		Member, Gestapo, Namestovo-Slovakia (Czech.) 44 and 45				56/122	MISC.CRIMES	CZECH.
DAMMERS, Johann Josef	304137	M	9. 8.03	Head overseer,member, Julia state coal mine at Eigelshoven, Ger.Schutzgruppen, Eigelshoven (Neth.) 8.9.-13.9.44				58/142	MISC.CRIMES	NETH.
DAMS	304138	M		Member, Group 648 of the G.F.P.,HQ of G.F.P.Boulevard,Piercot, Liege (Bel.) between 40-44				58/143	TORTURE	BEL.
DANEKER, Jakob	303566	M	11.12.19	SS-Mann, C.C.,Majdanek (Pol.) 40-44				57/176	TORTURE	POL.
DANIELS, Johann	124729	M	1. 9.24	SS-Mann,SS Pz.Gren.A.u.E.Bn.12,7.Stamm-Coy. or 1.Coy., Anhee and Yvoir-Meuse (Bel.) 4.9.44				13/16	MURDER	BEL.
DANILLER, Anton	304139	M		Member, official, NSDAP, Firm Kirchhoff, Sanok (Pol.)41-42				58/144	MURDER	POL.
DANITZ, Walter	124730	M	14. 1.24	SS-Mann,SS Pz.Gren.A.u.E.Bn.12,7.Stamm Coy. or 1.Coy., Anhee and Yvoir-Meuse (Bel.) 4.9.44				13/17	MURDER	BEL.
DANNEGER (or DANZIGER), Joh.	174180	M	17. 8.05	Councellor of the County Court,Special Court,Prag (Czech.)40-45				38/64	MURDER	CZECH.
DANZIGER (see DANNEGER,Joh.)	174180									
DARKOW, Ewald	304569	M		Member, Gestapo, Krakau (Pol.) 11.39- 2.45				59/99	MURDER	POL.
DARNBERG	131737	M		N.C.O. or Cpl.,SS,2.SS Pz.Div."Das Reich" K-2,16.Coy. F.P.No.20727,La-Groix-Falgarde (Fr.) 44				11/56	MURDER	FR.
DASCH, Dr.	266731	M		Col.,Vetenary, Police Forces,Krakau,Brzuchowice (Pol.)39-45				60/115	PILLAGE	POL.
DATZ	131718	M		Secret Service (Customs Dept.)Perpignan,Vetmanya (Fr.)1.8.44				13/374	MURDER	FR.
DAUER	266521	M		Lt.,29.Regt.Panzergrenadiere, Mamey et Martincourt (Fr.)2.9.44				-	MURDER	FR.
DAVID, Ernst	303567	M	27. 6.99	SS-Mann,C.C.,Majdanek (Pol.) 40-44				57/180	MURDER	POL.
DE BOTH	304542	M		Driver,Security Police,Vollehove and Steenwijk (Neth.) 12.44- 4.45				59/60	PILLAGE	NETH.
DEBROSKY	266555	M		Sgt.,722.Inf.Regt.Guard detachment of Verdun prison, Verdun (Fr.) 29.6.44				-	SUSPECT	FR.
DEBUAN (see DEBUNAN)	266276									
DEBUNAN (or DEBUAN)	266276	M	circa 15	Lt.,Unit 15.483 B, Alleray (Fr.) 44				-	PILLAGE	FR.
DEBUS (see DEBUSE, Adolphe)	64847									
DEBUSE, Adolphe (or DEBUS)	64847	M	8.10.05	Interpreter, SD, Gestapo,Basses Pyrenees,Toulouse, Pau and vicinity (Fr.) 1.43-7.44				-	MURDER	FR.
DECKER	308788	M		SS-Sturmscharfhr. and First Secr.,Criminality,Radom (Pol.)1.40-1.45				60/116	TORTURE	POL.
DE CORTE, Josef	303568	M	24. 2.25	SS-Mann, Guard, C.C., Majdanek (Pol.) 40-42				57/182	BRUTALITY	POL.
DEDERDING	304140	M		Cpl., Geh.Feldpolizei, Bruessel (Bel.) 40-44				58/145	MURDER	BEL.
DEGENER, Richard	304141	M		Foreman, Herring packing factory,Cuxhaven (Ger.) 40-45				58/146	MISC.CRIMES	POL.
DEGENHARD	304570	M		Cpl.,Tank-soldier,Camp-leader, of the Italian P.W.'s employed in the firm "Henschel and Sohn" factory,Kassel (Ger.) 16.1.44				59/100	MURDER	NETH.
DEGENHART	304142	M		SS-Sturmbannfhr., member,SD and Sipo,Czestochowa and elsewhere in Radom district (Pol.) 40-45				58/147	MURDER	POL.
DEGENKOLBE, Georg	302945	M		Hptkriminal-Asst., Gestapo Staff,Kattowitz (Pol.) 39-42				56/126	PILLAGE	POL.
DEGUER	1254	M		Member, W.O., Army,SD,Unit 15483 A,Casteljaloux, La Rochelle, Gaujac,Beaupuy (Fr.) 43-44				-	MURDER	FR.
DEHNKE	303569	M		Member, Gestapo, Warschau (Pol.) 39-45				57/183	MURDER	POL.
DEIHER	157390	M		Member, Gestapo, St. Quentin (Fr.) 44				16/54	MURDER	FR.
DEICHEN, Hans	267231	M		Oscharfhr., Gestapo, Marseille and vicinity (Fr.)				-	MURDER	FR.
DEINASS, Martin	302946	M		Cpl., Group 530 Geh.Feldpolizei,Bruessel (Bel.) 40-44				56/127	MURDER	BEL.
DEKHEN	267229	M		See names listed under "Special Headings"						
DELANG	177	M		Kreisleiter, NSDAP, Ostrow (Pol.) 39-41				1/252	MISC.CRIMES	POL.
DELIOS (or DELIUS),Rudolph	266777	M		Chief of culture,Jonval-Ard. (Fr.) 41-44				-	BRUTALITY	FR.
DELIUS (see DELIOS,Rudolph)	266777									
DELMOTTE, Dr.	198079	M		SS-Osturmfhr.,C.C.Section Sterilisation,Auschwitz (Pol.)				16/258	MISC.CRIMES	POL.,FR.
DEMMERT, Willi	304144	M		Kapo,Labour Camps,Husum,Ladelund,Meppen,Dalum (Ger.)40-45				58/150	MURDER	POL.
DEMPWOLFF	308789	M		Cpl.,Member of the Feldgendarmerie at Utrecht (Neth.), Lage Vuursche (Neth.) 29.12.44				60/118	MISC.CRIMES	NETH.
DEMUTH	302947	M		Present in the Office at the C.H.F.Mueller "Roentgen" Factory, Hamburg (Ger.) 43-44				56/130	MURDER	NETH.
DENGLER	145580	M		SS-Uscharfhr., C.C., Auschwitz (Pol.)				16/260	MURDER	POL.,FR.
DENK, Pavel, Dr.	304145	M	20. 7.06	Chief, State Security Police, Bratislava (Czech.) 41-45				58/151	MURDER	CZECH.
DENKMANN, Artur	308790	M	31. 7.04	Driver, Gestapo HQ at Kiel (Ger.) at various places in Germany and Ger.occupied territory between 25.3.44 and 13.4.44				60/119	MURDER	U.K.
DENNAERT	198197	M		SD, Arnhem, Deventer (Neth.) 17.4.44				30/346	MURDER	NETH.

DEN - DOM

NAME	C.R.FILE NUMBER	SEX	DATE OF BIRTH	RANK OCCUPATION UNIT PLACE AND DATE OF CRIME	UNWCC LIST/ SERIAL NO.	REASON WANTED	WANTED BY
DENNER (or RENNER)	267232	M		See names listed under "Special Headings"			
DENTRICH (see DIETRICH, Kurt)	266845						
DENZEL I	303570	M		Member, Gestapo, Varrchau (Pol.) 39-45	57/185	MURDER	POL.
DENZEL II	303571	M		Member, Gestapo, Warschau (Pol.) 39-45	57/186	MURDER	POL.
DENZEL, Albert	302948	M		Cpl., Group 530 Geh.Feldpolizei, Bruessel (Bel.) 40-44	56/132	MURDER	BEL.
DERKSEN, Fritz	304571	M		Farmer at Steinberg, Kleve-District (Ger.) 39-45	59/101	MISC.CRIMES	POL.
DETER, Egon Dr.	302949	M	11. 5.09	I.O. with the 80 Corps, Poitiers (Fr.) 7.44	56/135	MURDER	U.K.
DETHLEFS, Charles	267511	M	07 - 10	SS-Uschfhr., Chief, Gestapo, Luchon and vicinity (Fr.) 1.43-7.44	-	MURDER	FR.
DEUKER, Johann	304146	M		Guard, Prison, Aachen (Ger.) 43-44	58/153	TORTURE	BEL.
DEUSSEN, August	264559	M	24.10.84	See names listed under "Special Headings"			
DEUTRICH (see DIETRICH, Kurt)	266845						
DEUTSCHMANN, Josef	267137	M	9. 2.95	Agent, Gestapo, St.Vid near Ljubljana (Yugo.) 43-45	-	MURDER	YUGO.
DEVEIKAS, Bronius	303572	M		Osturmfhr., C.C., Majdanek (Pol.) 39-42	57/190	BRUTALITY	POL.
DHEN	197470	M		Lt., Unit: 38349, Moliets (Fr.) 22.8.44	32/191	INCENDIARISM	FR.
DIBOLSMANN	72384	M		Chief, Feldgendarmerie, Avignon (Fr.) 40-44	25/853	BRUTALITY	FR.
DICHTEL, Erich	304594	M	20. 4.11	Member of Gestapo, SS-Oschfhr., Chief of the "Aussenstelle der Sipo and SD", Kranj (Slov.) 42-44	59/102	MURDER	YUGO.
DICKE, Hans	304147	M		SS-Hptschfhr., Member, Jewish Department of the Gestapo at Kattowitz, Bendzin, Sosnowiec and district (Pol.) 40-43	58/154	MURDER	POL.
DICKERHOFF, Dr. (or DYCKERHOFF, DYCKENHOF)	196048	M		Physician, Faculty, C.C., Strassburg, Auschwitz (Fr.,Pol.) 40-45	30/159 16/ 26	MURDER	POL., BEL. FR.
DICKESCHEID, Heinrich	264558	M	14.11.97	See names listed under "Special Headings"			
DICKMANN, Dr.	131695	M		Doctor, Airforce, C.C., Vaihingen (Ger.) 13.8.44-7.4.45	25/854	MURDER	FR.
DIDDEN(S), Fokke	304595	M		Customs-official, Frontier-defence, Zwartsluis (Neth.) 8.10.44	59/103	MURDER	NETH.
DIDRICH, Fritz	198199	M	circa 00	Head, C.C., Block 21, Flossenburg (Ger.) 42-45	30/ 44 31/197	MURDER	FR.,BEL.
DIEDERICH, Paul	159994	M	06	Director of Purchas, Member, Department in Busenbach Factory, NSDAP, C.C., Busenbach or Neurod (Ger.)	16/264	MURDER	FR.
DIEHM	303573	M		Member, Gestapo, Varschau (Pol.) 39-45	57/195	MURDER	POL.
DIEKMANN, Karl	304148	M	23. 8.78	Cmdt., Labour-Camp attached to Braunschweigische Blechwarenfabrik, Braunschweig (Ger.) 41-44	58/157	BRUTALITY	POL.
DIENEMANN	266525	M		Pvt., Gebirgsjaeger Unit: 64 874, 202 Bn., Vosges (Fr.) 11.44	-	MURDER	FR.
DIERDORF, Albert	303574	M	19.10.96	SS-Uschfhr., C.C., Majdanek (Pol.) 40-42	57/196	BRUTALITY	POL.
DIERG (or DIEZ)	141467	M		Sonderfhr., Feldgendarmerie, Montbelliard (Fr.) 10.u.19.8.44	13/381	MURDER	FR.
DIERMANN, Anton	44073	M		SS BF. Generalmajor der Polizei, SS, Successor to Winkelmann in the Kommandoamt in Hauptamt Ordnungspolizei, Reichsministerium des Inneren, C.C., Auschwitz-Birkenau (Pol.) 39-45	13/ 45	MURDER	CZECH.
DIETEL	304149	M		Member, Schutzgruppen at the "Laura-Mine", Eigelshoven (Neth.) 8.-13.9.44	58/159	PILLAGE	NETH.
DIETRICH	308791	M		SS-Sturmfhr. and Secretary of Admin., Radom (Pol.) 1.40-1.45	60/122	BRUTALITY	POL.
DIETRICH, Karl	302951	M		Kriminalkommissar, Gestapo-Staff, Kattowitz (Pol.) 39-42	56/138	PILLAGE	POL.
DIETRICH, Kurt (or DENTRICH or DEUTRICH)	266845	M	26. 4.25	Usturmfhr., Chief, Gestapo, Abwehr-Ers.Coy., Inf.Ers.Bn.600 Lissa Front-Aufkl.Nachschub-Dienststelle Ost, Paris (Fr.)	-	SUSPECT	FR.
DIETRICH, Otto	304596	M		Member, Gestapo, Krakau (Pol.) 11.39-2.45	59/104	MURDER	POL.
DIETRICH, Paul	266734	M	17. 2.88	Manager, Power station, Krakau (Pol.) 41-45	-	MISC.CRIMES	POL.
DIETZ, Rudolf	188	M		Pvt., Airforce, Unit: L 20368, Flakmant 30-XII, Flakmunitions-Abgabestelle, Chateau de Baudrigues (Fr.) 19.8.44	3/ 64	MURDER	FR.
DIEZ (see DIERG)	141467						
DILLE	266608	M		SS-Mann, SS, Unit:20188, Longwy (Fr.) 1.9.44	-	MURDER	FR.
DILLENBURGER	302952	M		Hptschfhr., Mielec (Pol.) 41-44	56/139	MURDER	POL.
DILLSCHNEIDER, Josef	304150	M	circa 10	Kapo, Hangman, Crematorium, C.C., Vught (Neth.) 40-44	58/160	MURDER	NETH.
DINANI	265467	M		SS-Uschfhr., 3 Coy.,1 Bn., Regt."Der Fuehrer", Div."Das Reich", Oradour s.Glane (Fr.) 10.6.44	-	MURDER	FR.
DINGEMANN	150902	M		SS-Rottfhr., C.C., Auschwitz (Pol.)	16/265	MURDER	POL.,FR.
DINGER	197469	M		V.O., 157 Div.Gebirgsjaeger (Reserve) Plateau des Glieres (Fr.) 22.3.44-5.4.44	38/265	PILLAGE	FR.
DIPALLA, Paul	265300	M		Pvt., Regt."Brandenburg" (It.)	-	SUSPECT	U.K.
DIRKS	266649	M	circa 00	Sgt., Feldgendarmerie d'Avallon, Yonne (Fr.) 44	-	MISC.CRIMES	FR.
DIRKSEN	197468	M		Pvt., Sentinel at Oflag X B, Nienburg-Weser (Ger.) 10.6.42	32/192	MURDER	FR.
DIRKSWETSCHKY	302953	M		Cpl., Gruppe 530 Geh.Feldpolizei, Bruessel (Bel.) 40-44	56/141	MURDER	BEL.
DISKAR, Hans	266760	M		Sturmbannfhr., Gestapo, Luebeck (Ger.) 44	-	MURDER	POL.
DITR (or LORENZ or LORENZ, Dieter)	147959	M		SS, Giesburg (Ger.)	-	SUSPECT	FR.
DITTMANN	308792	M		Commissioner, Fieldpolice, Antwerpen and Bruessel (Bel.) 40-44	60/127	MURDER	BEL.
DITTMANN, Heinrich	162297	M		Civilian, near Valsum (Ger.) 9.44	-	TORTURE	U.K.
DITTMANN, Hermann	308695	M		Civilian, Valsum (Ger.) 1.8.-31.10.44	32/432	BRUTALITY	U.K.
DITTMANN, Wilhelm	302955	M		Crim.Secretary, Gestapo-Staff, Kattowitz (Pol.) 39-42	56/143	INTERR.	POL.
DITTMAR, Georg	266761	M	1. 8.04	Chief, Cleaning Institution, Krakau (Pol.) 39-45	-	MISC.CRIMES	POL.
DIX, Georg	304598	M		Cpl., Secr.Field-Police, Luettich (Bel.) 40-41	59/107	MURDER	BEL.
DJURAN, Luppo	302956	M		Pvt., Group 530 Geh.Feldpolizei, Bruessel (Bel.) 40-44	56/144	MURDER	BEL.
DOBNER, Otto	187304	M		Propagandaleiter, NSDAP, Civ.waiter, Tri Sekery (Czech.) 39-45	-	SUSPECT	CZECH.
DOEHLER	304572	M		Sgt., Blechhammer, Wilkce, Strzelce, Slask (Pol.) 1.45-2.45	59/109	MURDER	POL.
DOEK, Paul	304573	M		Member, Gestapo, Krakau (Pol.) 11.39-2.45	59/110	MURDER	POL.
DOER	62001	M		Agent, Gestapo, Saales (Bas-Rhin) (Fr.) 15.4.43	10/ 10	MURDER	FR.
DOERING, Walter (or DORING)	9648	M		SS-Schfhr., Waffen-SS, C.C., Buchenwald (Ger.) 39-44	6/215 8/8 25/101	MURDER	CZECH., BEL.
DOERR	266225	M		Sgt., Army, 3 Coy., 441 Sect.B.C.A., Vern s.Seiche (Fr.) 14.7.44	-	MURDER	FR.
DOESCHER	266226	M	08	Chief, Osturmfhr., Gestapo, Nantes and region (Fr.) 43	-	MURDER	FR.
DOETSCH	267510	M		Uschfhr., Gestapo, St.Etienne and vicinity (Fr.) 43-44	-	MISC.CRIMES	FR.
DOHLEN, Leonard	303575	M	29. 4.00	SS-Mann, C.C., Majdanek (Pol.)	57/203	BRUTALITY	POL.
DOLF	266955	M		Sgt., Feldgendarmerie, Sisteron (Fr.) 44	-	MISC.CRIMES	FR.
DOLGER, Liselotte	304574	F		Member, Gestapo, Krakau (Pol.) 11.39-2.45	59/111	MURDER	POL.
DOLLE	308794	M		SS-Sturmfhr. and Crim.Secr., Radom (Pol.) 1.40-1.45	60/129	MURDER	POL.
DOMANSKI, Max	304575	M		Member, Gestapo, Krakau (Pol.) 11.39-2.45	59/112	MURDER	POL.
DOMECLE	303576	M		Member, Gestapo, Varschau (Pol.) 39-45	57/205	MURDER	POL.
DOMROSE	303577	M		Member, Gestapo, Varschau (Pol.) 39-45	57/207	MURDER	POL.

DON - EDL

NAME	C.R.FILE NUMBER	SEX	DATE OF BIRTH	RANK OCCUPATION UNIT PLACE AND DATE OF CRIME	UNWCC LIST/ SERIAL NO.	REASON WANTED	WANTED BY
DONNENBURG, Alfred	304152	M	15	Medical officer,Lt.,Airforce:attached to Raveredo Airforce command, Polcenigo, Udine (It.) 4.2.45	58/165	MURDER	FR.
DONOTHEK, Wilhelm	302957	M		Kriminalbeamter, Employee, Staff of Gestapo, Kattowitz (Pol.) 39-42	56/145	PILLAGE	POL.
DOOSE (or DOSE), August	305588	M		Sailor, Luebeck-Siems.(Ger.) 6.8.44	-	MURDER	U.S.
DOPPKE	304576	M		Oschafhr., Member of the secr.service and secr.police Ustrijkidl, Lutowiska, Sanok (Pol.) 42-43	59/113	MURDER	POL.
DORING	266227	M	05 - 10	Lt., Army, Vence (Fr.) 23. 8.44	-	MURDER	FR.
DORING, Walter (see DOERING)	9648						
DORNBACH	147009	M		SS-Mann, Waffen-SS, Panzer-Div."Das Reich", 2.Coy., F.P.No. 27.910 B, Tulle (Fr.)	11/58	MURDER	FR.
DORNIEDEN, Wilhelm	267034	M	circa 00	Member, Gestapo of Blois, in charge of Gen.Pol., Maves (Fr.) 43-44	-	MURDER	FR.
DOSE (see DOOSE), August	305588						
DOSE, Hans	304159	M	circa 95	SS-Usturmfhr., Krim.Sekretaer, Member, Einsatzkdo.of the Sipo Katerveer, Zwolle (Neth.) 10.4.45	58/167	MURDER	NETH.
DOSER, Georg	147008	M		Sturmmann, Waffen-SS, Pz.Div."Das Reich", K 13 Coy., F.P.No. 03669, Moissac (Fr.)	11/59	MURDER	FR.
DOSTAL	267503	M		W.O., Feldgendarmerie, Besancon and region (Fr.) 44	-	MURDER	FR.
DOSTER, H.	201	M		Col.(Flyer), Airforce, L 92688, L.G.P.A. O.C. Punitive expedition Paris, Andeville (Fr.) 27. 8.44	3/72	MURDER	FR.
DRABEICH, Hans	267230	M		Sgt., Army, Waffenwerkstatt 812, Chateaumeillant (Fr.) 27.6.44	-	MURDER	FR.
DRAEGER	267560	M		Present, C.H.F. Mueller Roentgenfactory, Hamburg Ger. 43-44	56/148	MURDER	NETH.
DRAEGER, Karl	302959	M		Leitender Feldpolizeidirektor, Westen (Bel.) 41-42	56/149	MURDER	BEL.
DRAHEIM,	304577	M		Member, Gestapo, Krakau (Pol.) 11.39-2.45	59/114	MURDER	POL.
DRAHT,	303578	M		Member, Gestapo, Warschau (Pol.) 39-45	57/212	MURDER	POL.
DRASE, Heinrich	301826	M		Civilian, Labour camp, Lahde-Weser (Ger.) 43-45	16/4	MURDER	BEL.
DRAXAL, Karel	304578	M	23. 6.97	Local Groupleader, Agent, NSDAP, Gestapo, Valasske, Mezirici (Czech.) 41	59/115	INTERR.	CZECH.
DRECHOLER	198081	M		Torturer, C.C. Auschwitz (Pol.) 40-45	16/273	MURDER	FR.
DREIER, Hans	302960	M		Kriminalkommissar, Gestapo Staff, Kattowitz (Pol.) 39-42	56/150	PILLAGE	POL.
DREISE, Willi	304579	M		Member, Gestapo, Krakau (Pol.) 11.39-2.45	59/116	BRUTALITY	POL.
DREISING, Kurt	304580	M		Member, Gestapo, Krakau (Pol.) 11.39-2.45	59/117	MURDER	POL.
DRESCH, Christian	198203	M		Chief, Block 16, C.C. Flossenburg (Ger.) 42-45	31/200	MURDER	FR.
DRESSLER,	308879	M		Pvt., Guards unit forming part of the crew of the V-weapon based at Hook van Holland, Wassenaar (Neth.) 11.44	60/131	PILLAGE	NETH.
DRESSLER, Josef Frantisek	197471	M	20. 2.99	Col., Gendarmerie, Bratislava (Czech.) 39-45	28/723	MISC.CRIMES	CZECH.
DRESSLER, Karl	157382	M	10. 8.13	Member, SS, Civ. Merchant later Tax-inspector, Gotha C.C. Moringen, Hinzert, Dachau (Ger.)	-	SUSPECT	FR.
DRESSLER, Karl	302961	M		Hptschfhr., SS, near Quirnbach (Ger.) 20. 3.45	56/151	MURDER	U.S.
DREWITZ,	267504	M		Member, Gestapo, Limoges and vicinity (Fr.) 44	-	SUSPECT	FR.
DREYER, Hans Dr.	304154	M		SS-Hschfhr., Head, Jewish Department of the Gestapo, Kattowitz (Pol.) 40-43	58/170	MURDER	POL.
DRIEHAUG, Georg	185369	M		Member, SS, Civ. had a linen drapery-shop, C.C. Osnabrueck (Ger.)	-	SUSPECT	FR.
DROSDZ, Konrad	302962	M		Employee, Factory, Mielec (Pol.) 41-44	56/152	MURDER	POL.
DROWS,	303579	M		Member, Gestapo, Warschau (Pol.) 39-45	57/215	MURDER	POL.
DROZD	198082	M		SS-Unterscharfhr., C.C. Auschwitz (Pol.)	16/275	MURDER	POL.,FR.
DRUM,	185606	M		Oscharfhr., Kommandostab, Mauthausen (Aust.) 42-45	25/860	MURDER	FR.
DUERR, August	308881	M	23. 3.90	Commissary, confiscated private, Governm.forests, Pohorje (Slov.) (Yugo.) 41-45	60/133	MISC.CRIMES	YUGO.
DUFEK, Alfred	304155	M	28.12.99	Rangiermeister, Railway at Hamburg, Pruszec 1.9.39	58/171	INTERR.	POL.
DULLBERG, Fritz	308882	M		Campleader, Lendringsen, distr.of Iserlohn (Ger.) 39-45	60/134	BRUTALITY	POL.
DUMKE, Wilhelm	266130	M		Member, SS-Staff, C.C. Giebow near Halle (Ger.) 42	-	MURDER	POL.
DUMONT,	308883	M		Member, Selbstschutz, Grudziadz (Pol.) 39	60/135	MURDER	POL.
DUNGER,	266842	M	circa 00	Lt., Chief of Gend., Feldgend., Troyes, St.Maurice-les-Riches-hommes (Fr.) 3.44	-	MURDER	FR.
DUNSCHER	266228	M		Unit:12988 A Colonne de Marche "Gen Fessart" Lamotte-Beuvron (Fr.) 23.,24.8.44	-	WITNESS	FR.
DUPS, Jakob	303580	M		SS-Mann, C.C. Majdanek (Pol.) 40-44	57/221	BRUTALITY	POL.
DURSTAMITZ, Engelhardt	124732	M	7. 2.25	SS-Mann, SS Pz.Gren.A.u.E.Bn.12,7.Stamm-Coy.or 1.Coy., Anhee Yvoir/Meuse (Bel.) 4.9.44	13/18	MURDER	BEL.
DWORSKI, Jakob	147006	M		SS-Mann, SS-Pz.Div."Das Reich", 13.Coy., Moissac (Fr.) 44	11/61	MURDER	FR.
DYCKENHOF (see DICKERHOFF)	196048						
DYCKERHOFF (see DICKERHOFF)	196048						
DZIOMBEK, Roman	302964	M		Uschfhr., SS, Gestapo Staff, Kattowitz (Pol.) 39-42	56/156	BRUTALITY	POL.
DZUBA, Adalbert	304581	M		Scharfhr., SS Secr.Police-school, Rabka (Pol.) 40-42	59/118	BRUTALITY	POL.
EBERECHT, Wilhelm	304156	M	2. 7.91	Ortsgr.Leiter, Fhr., Amtsleiter, NSDAP, SA, Rychtal 40-45	58/173	MISC.CRIMES	POL.
EBELING, Albert	157363	M	05	SS-Sturmschfhr., Pol.Secret., Abt.II B 2,SD, Bruessel (Bel.) 6.40	28/43	MURDER	BEL.
EBERLE,	24761	M		Uscharfhr., SS, C.C.Struthof-Natzweiler (Fr.) 40-44	32/196	MURDER	FR.
EBERLE	266246	M		Guard, Camp Buchloe	-	BRUTALITY	FR.
EBERLE, Hans	302965	M		Kriminalsekret., Gestapo Staff, Kattowitz (Pol.) 39-42	56/157	INTERR.	POL.
EBERLEIN,	308884	M		SS-Sturmscharfhr., Crim.Ob.Secret., Radom (Pol.) 1.40-1.45	60/136	TORTURE	POL.
EBERS	263319	M		Schfhr., SS, 1.Bn., Regt."Der Fuehrer", Div."Das Reich", Lacapelle Biron, Vergt de Biron, Devillac, St.Pierre de Clairac Monbalen Lot et Garonne (Fr.) 5.-7.44	54/96	BRUTALITY	FR.
EBERT	303581	M		Member, Gestapo, Warschau (Pol.) 39-45	57/225	MURDER	POL.
EBNER	266961	M		Chief Sgt.-Major, Feldgendarmerie, Sisteron (Fr.) 44	-	MISC.CRIMES	FR.
ECCARIUS	198264	M		Osturmfhr., C.C. Neuengamme (Ger.)	16/27	MURDER	BEL.
ECKARD	23996	M		Member, Gestapo, SD, Sipo, Einsatzkdo., Chalons s.Marne (Fr.)	-	SUSPECT	FR.
ECKARD	265700	M		Member, SD, Chalons s.Marne (Fr.) 43-44	-	MISC.CRIMES	FR.
ECKARD	266650	M		Sgt., Feldgend., Chassenseuil, Angoulome, Fr. 40-44	-	MURDER	FR.
ECKE	23997	M		Oscharfhr., C.C.Vaihingen (Ger.) 13.8.44-7.4.45	25/865	MURDER	FR.
ECKERT, Wilhelm	304582	M		Member, Gestapo, Krakau (Pol.) 11.39-2.45	59/119	BRUTALITY	POL.
ECKHARDT, Wilhelm	304583	M		Member, Gestapo, Krakau (Pol.) 11.39-2.45	59/120	MURDER	POL.
EDEL, Hans	304584	M		Member, Gestapo, Krakau (Pol.) 11.39-2.45	59/121	BRUTALITY	POL.
EDER, Gottfried	267088	M	circa 05	Sgt., Army, Belfort (Fr.) 41-42	-	PILLAGE	FR.
EDLINGER, Karl	304585	M		Member, Gestapo, Krakau (Pol.) 11.39-2.45	59/122	BRUTALITY	POL.

EDM - ENG

NAME	C.R.FILE NUMBER	SEX	DATE OF BIRTH	RANK OCCUPATION UNIT PLACE AND DATE OF CRIME	UNWCC LIST/ SERIAL NO.	REASON WANTED	WANTED BY
EDMEYER (or EPMAYER, called: HUMPBACK)	266604	M		Chief of works, C.C., Buchloe-Landsberg (Ger.)	-	BRUTALITY	FR.
EGEL	198217	M		Pvt., Army, Landesschuetzen-Bn.515, Lisany or Lisnay (Czech.) 2. or 3.45	38/363	MURDER	CZECH.
EGENHOFER, Hans	304586	M		Member, Gestapo, Krakau (Pol.) 11.39-2.45	59/123	RAPE	POL.
EGGER	308885	M		Instructor and employee, G.F.P., Antwerpen,Bruessel (Bel.)40-44	60/138	MURDER	BEL.
EGGER, Fritz	308886	M		Member, Gestapo, Leipzig, Mannheim, Berlin (Ger.) 11.41-4.43	60/139	MISC.CRIMES	CHINA
EGGERT, Ernst	302966	M	4.11.91	Head of Kdo.277 at Stalag X C, Anstedt (Ger.) 20.3.45	56/161	MURDER	FR.
EGGI, Ludwig	303583	M	11. 4.08	SS-Mann, C.C., Majdanek (Pol.) 40-44	57/228	BRUTALITY	POL.
EHLERS	157367	M	05	SS-Osturmbannfhr., Chief, C.C., Sipo, SD, C.C.Breendonck, Bruessel (Bel.) 44	27/36 28/11	MURDER	BEL.
EHLERT, Harta or Hertha	173776	F		SS-Woman, C.C., Plaszow, Auschwitz, Bergen-Belsen (Pol.,Ger.) 39-45	-	MURDER	UNWCC,POL.
EHNERT	303584	M		Member, Gestapo, Warschau (Pol.) 39-45	57/229	MURDER	POL.
EHRENTRAUT, Gustav	304599	M		Member, Gestapo, Krakau (Pol.) 11.39-2.45	59/124	RAPE	POL.
EHRLICH, Rudolf	302967	M		SS-Oscharfhr., SD at Rodez, Departm.of Aveyron (Fr.) 43-8.44	56/164	MURDER	FR.
EIBEL	198268	M		Member of Staff, C.C., Struthof-Natzweiler (Fr.) 42-45	32/197	MURDER	FR.
EIBENSTEINER, Anton	302968	M		Sgt., Group 530 of Geh. Feldpolizei, Bruessel (Bel.) 41-44	56/165	TORTURE	BEL.
EICHENAUER, Konrad Dr.	264557	M	13. 7.90	See names listed under "Special Headings"			
EICHENLAUB, Alfred	267226	M		Matrose, Navy, Senon (Fr.) 9.44	-	MURDER	FR.
EICHHORN, Franz	303585	M	12.12.12	SS-Mann, C.C., Majdanek (Pol.) 40-44	57/232	BRUTALITY	POL.
EICHMANN, Adolf	62241	M	19. 3.00	SS-Osturmbannfhr., Chief of the Sonderkdo., (Ger.,Hung.,Den.) 43-44	28/26 25/870	MURDER	CZECH.,FF
EICHMANN, Eduard or Edward	124727	M	29. 1.24	SS-Mann, 1 Coy., SS-Pz.Gren.Ausb.u.Ers.Bn.12,Anhee,Yvoir-Meuse (Bel.) 4.9.44	13/21	MURDER	BEL.
EICHSTAEDT, Friedrich	302969	M		Cpl., Group 530 of Geh. Feldpolizei, Bruessel (Bel.) 40-44	56/167	MURDER	BEL.
EIKER	266954	M		Feldgendarm, Feldgendarmerie, Sisteron (Fr.) 44	-	MISC.CRIMES	FR.
EIKHOLN, Dr.	147002	M		Cambery (Fr.) 44	11/68	MURDER	FR.
EIKLAGGERT	266659	M		SS-Feldpost-Nr.20188, Longwy (Fr.) 1.9.44	-	MURDER	FR.
EILEMANN, Hermann	266844	M		Lt., Feldgendarmerie of Saint Germain en Laye, Poissy (Fr.) 21.8.44	-	MURDER	FR.
EILENFUSS	304157	M		Inspector, Town Administration, Sosnowiec (Pol.) 39-43	58/176	MISC.CRIMES	POL.
EILERS	266571	M	circa 90-95	Lt.-Col.,Unit of "Craftuurffe"(?), stationed August 1944 at Beaume, Grosbois and Sechin (Fr.) 26.-28.8.44	-	MURDER	FR.
EILLERS, Hanna	304600	F		Member, Gestapo, Krakau (Pol.) 11.39-2.45	59/126	MURDER	POL.
EILLERS, Wilhelm	304601	M		Member, Gestapo, Krakau (Pol.) 11.39-2.45	59/127	MURDER	POL.
EINBERGER	267421	M		Sgt.,242 Inf.Div., Ampus (Fr.) 7.44	-	MURDER	FR.
EINENKEL	304158	M		Hptscharfhr.,SS-Wach-Bn.3, Amersfoort (Neth.) 2.5.43	58/177	MURDER	NETH.
EISFELDER	303586	M		Member, Gestapo, Warschau (Pol.) 39-45	57/236	MURDER	POL.
EITTER	266843	M		SS-Hptscharfhr., SD, Nice (Fr.) 44	-	SUSPECT	FR.
EKERLE	24809	M		Sub-Lt.,Commander, SD, Brive, Correze, Bourges (Fr.) 44	-	SUSPECT	FR.
EIBIN	304651	M		Kriminalrat, Head of the Criminal Police, Sosnowiec (Pol.)42-43	59/128	MISC.CRIMES	POL.
ELFERS, Georg	302970	M		Member, Group 530 of Geh. Feldpolizei, Bruessel (Bel.) 40-44	56/170	MURDER	BEL.
ELFRICH (see ELRICH)	266822						
ELGER, Hans	302971	M		Hptkriminalsekretaer, Gestapo, staff, Kattowitz (Pol.) 39-42	56/171	INTERR.	POL.
ELLENBERGER	266823	M	circa 91	Lt.,SD of Rennes, Cirey s. Vezouse (Fr.) 9.-11.44	-	MURDER	FR.
ELLERS, Josef	308887	M		SS-Policeman, Ploeger-Coy.,Carsten-Bn., Keppeln (Ger.) 18.9.44	60/142	MURDER	U.S.
ELLWANGER, Thomas	303587	M	3. 3.17	SS-Uscharfhr., Blockfhr., C.C., Majdanek (Pol.) 40-44	57/237A	BRUTALITY	POL.
EIPERT	301079	M		Krim.Rat, SS-Osturmfhr., Leader of the R.S.D., Abt.IV-3-a, Shellhuset, Kopenhagen (Den.) 27.2.45	31/146	TORTURE	DEN.
ELRICH (or ELFRICH)	266822	M		Cpl., Airforce, Eguilles (Fr.) 19.8.44	-	MURDER	FR.
ELSHOLZ	304159	M		Dep.Head, Sachbearbeiter, SD Aussenstelle at Maastricht, Limburg and Friesland (Neth.) 44-45	58/178	MURDER	NETH.
ELSNER	303588	M		Member, Gestapo, Warschau (Pol.) 39-45	57/238	MURDER	POL.
ELSTER, Rudolf	157365	M		Crim.employee, SD, Abt. IV A, Bruessel (Bel.) 40-44	28/45	MURDER	BEL.
ELTER, Karl	267228	M	31. 5.92	Uscharfhr., Ban-St.-Martin (Fr.) 41	-	PILLAGE	FR.
EMDE	266243	M		Capt., Feldgend. de Besancon, Le Vernois nr. Marchaux (Fr.) 21.7.44	-	MURDER	FR.
EMERIC	266244	M		Chief, Stationmaster, Labour-Camp, Buchloe (Ger.)	-	MISC.CRIMES	FR.
EMIACH	131658	M		Cpl. at Mines Bassin of Briey, Meurthet, Moselle (Fr.) 40-45	13/391	TORTURE	FR.
ENDERES (see ENDERS)	131657						
ENDERLEIN	303589	M		Member, Gestapo, Warschau (Pol.) 39-45	57/239	MURDER	POL.
ENDERS (or ENDERES)	131657	M		Cpl. at St. Pierremont Mines, at the Bassin of Briey, Meurthet, Moselle (Fr.) 40-45	13/393	TORTURE	FR.
ENDERS, Johann	303590	M	31. 1.04	SS-Mann, C.C., Auschwitz (Pol.) 40-45	57/240	MURDER	POL.
ENDRICH	223	M		Wachtmeister, C.C., Grini (Nor.) 9.41	3/498	TORTURE	NOR.
ENGEL	116600	M		Crim.secretary, SD, Abt. IV E, Bruessel (Bel.) 6.40-9.44	28/45	MURDER	BEL.
ENGEL	154333	M		SS, C.C., Auschwitz (Pol.) 6.40-1.45	8/209	MURDER	POL.
ENGEL	198211	M		Pvt., Royallieu camp, Compiegne (Fr.) 41-44	31/82	MURDER	FR.
ENGEL, Alex	267227	M		Agent, Gestapo, Marseille and vicinity (Fr.)	-	MURDER	FR.
ENGEL, Emil	157364	M	98	SS-Sturmscharfhr., Crim.secretary, Gestapo Aachen, Sipo, Abt. IV-3, Kdo.16 z.b.V., Bruessel (Bel.)	-	SUSPECT	BEL.
ENGELBRECHT	149480	M	97	SS-Sturmbannfhr., Crim.Director, Gestapo, Strassburg, Stuttgart (Fr., Ger.) 5.11.44	38/364	SUSPECT	FR.
ENGELBRECHT	198225	M		Capt., 19 SS-Police-Regt., Payzac (Dordogne) (Fr.) 16.2.44	38/129	MISC.CRIMES	FR.
ENGELBRECHT	303591	M		Member, Gestapo, Warschau (Pol.) 39-45	57/241	MURDER	POL.
ENGELHARDT	147001	M		Member, Waffen-SS, 3 Bn., Regt."Deutschland", Pz.Div. "Das Reich", Venerque Le Vernet (Fr.) 44	11/69	MURDER	FR.
ENGELHARDT	154339	M		SS-Oscharfhr. as repres. of Rapportfhr., C.C., Auschwitz (Pol.) 6.40-1.45	8/210	MURDER	POL.
ENGELHARDT	154340	M		Major (probably i/c supply), 20 Army, XVIII Geb.Corps Staff, Finmark (Nor.) 10.-11.44	8/250	MURDER	NOR.
ENGELHARDT, Karl	162865	M		Member, Feldgendarmerie, Vielsalm (Bel.) 40-44	10/9	PILLAGE	BEL.
ENGELS	9653	M		Oscharfhr., Camp Sgt.-Major, C.C., Natzweiler (Fr.) 42	6/220	TORTURE	CZECH.
ENGELS	308888	M		Guard at Wolfenbuettel Prison and attached commandos, Wolfenbuettel (Ger.) 42-45	60/144	MISC.CRIMES	BEL.

ENG - FEC

-14-

NAME	C.R.FILE NUMBER	SEX	DATE OF BIRTH	RANK OCCUPATION UNIT PLACE AND DATE OF CRIME	UNWCC LIST/ SERIAL NO.	REASON WANTED	WANTED BY
ENGERER	266245	M		See names listed under "Special Headings"			FR.
ENGERLMANN, Hans	304602	M		Member, Gestapo, Krakau (Pol.) 11.39-2.45	59/129	MURDER	POL.
ENGFER, Ewald	198085	M		SS-Mann,C.C.,8 SS Stuba.,Auschwitz (Pol.)	6/288 40/399	MURDER	POL.,FR. YUGO.
ENGLER-FUESSLIN, Fritz	124188	M	15.9.91	Standartenfhr., Reichsredner, Landesbauernfhr., SS, Race and Settlement office (RSHA), NSDAP, Laufen, Strassburg, (Ger.,FR.) 44	13/394	MURDER	FR.
ENGLERT	304169	M		Member, Gestapo at Chaions sur Marne, Dept. of Marne (Fr.) 43-44	58/180	MURDER	FR.
ENKERLE	198228	M		Lt.,2-111 Panzer, Brive (Fr.) 20.6.44	32/67	PILLAGE	FR.
ENNSBERGER	147000	M		Hptsturmfhr.,SS,Pz.Div."Das Reich" (Fr.) 44	11/70	MURDER	FR.
ENTZIAN, Joachim Dr.	265610	M	9.7.91	See names listed under "Special Headings"			U.S.
ENZELBERGER	304170			Gestapo, Bayonne and vicinity (Fr.) 44-45	58/181	MURDER	FR.
EPMAYER (see EDMEYER called; Humpback)	266604						
ERBE	266660	M		SS-Mann,SS Feldpost No.20188, Longwy (Fr.) 1.9.44	-	MURDER	FR.
ERBERL, Edmund	304603	M		Member, Gestapo, Krakau (Pol.) 11.39-2.45	59/130	BRUTALITY	POL.
ERBT	266953	M		Feldgendarm, Feldgendarmerie, Sisteron (Fr.) 44		MISC.CRIMES	FR.
ERDLINGER	266570	M		Lt.,112 R.I.,7 Coy., Custines (Fr.) 19.9.44	-	MURDER	FR.
ERDMANN	198257	M		SS-Rottfhr.,C.C.Neuengamme (Ger.) 40-44	16/30	MURDER	BEL.
EREN, Willi	302972	M		Oscharfhr., Gestapo, Lodz (Pol.) 39-44	56/177	BRUTALITY	POL.
ERFURT	267491	M		Sgt., Airforce, 91 Regt., Chantraine (Fr.) 22.9.44		MURDER	FR.
ERGH (see ERGK)	146999						
ERGK (or ERGH)	146999	M		SS-Sturmmann,SS Panz.Div."Das Reich", Feldpost No.48933, Villaudrix (Fr.) 44	11/71	MURDER	FR.
ERKERT	198270	M		Pvt., Paratroops, Feldpost No.L 60191, Babylonienbroek, Genderen, Woudrichen (Neth.) 4.-5.45	30/6	MURDER	NETH.
ERKINGER, Georg	124728	M	22.7.23	SS-Mann,SS Pz.Gren.A.u.E.Bn.12,7 or 1 Coy., Anhee, Yvoir-Meuse (Bel.) 4.9.44	13/23	MURDER	BEL.
ERKURT, Eva	304604	F		Member, Gestapo, Krakau (Pol.) 11.39-2.45	59/131	MURDER	POL.
ERLER	303592	M		Member, Gestapo, Warschau (Pol.) 39-45	57/243	MURDER	POL.
ERNST	198213	M	14	Counsellor, Feldkommandantur 529, Bordeaux (Fr.) 25.10.41	30/13	MURDER	FR.
ERNST, Hans-Dietrich	116735	M	3.11.08	SS-Osturmbannfhr., Kommandeur, Oberreg.Rat, Co. of Sipo Com.,Gestapo, Marseille, De Angers, Vosges, Paris (Fr.) 6.-9.44	31/203 27/777	MURDER	U.K.,FR., U.S.
ERTEL, Paul Walter	308890	M		Member, Gestapo, nr.Altwied b.Schwerte (Ger.) 1.or 2.45	60/147	MURDER	U.S.
ERTL, Otto	263491	M		See names listed under "Special Headings"			CZECH.
ERTNER	303593	M		Member, Gestapo, Warschau (Pol.) 39-45	57/244	MURDER	POL.
ESCHENBURG, Walter	304605	M		Member, Gestapo, Krakau (Pol.) 11.39-2.45	59/132	PILLAGE	POL.
ESCHERICH	144470	M		Cmdt.,II Pz.Div., Colombier-Fontaine, Montbellard (Fr.) 19.9.44	40/122	MURDER	FR.
ESCHRICH, Walter	304606	M		Member, Gestapo, Krakau (Pol.) 11.39-2.45	59/133	PILLAGE	POL.
ESSER	308891	M		Commissary, Fieldpolice, Antwerpen, Bruessel (Bel.) 40-44	60/149	MURDER	BEL.
ESSIG	308892	M		SS-Hptscharfhr.,Crim.Comm., Radom (Pol.) 1.40-1.45	60/150	BRUTALITY	POL.
ETTEL, Hans	167926	M		Pvt., Army, Res.Gren.Regt.,1 Coy., Magny d'Anigon (Fr.) 8.-9.44	10/36	MURDER	FR.
ETTWIEG, Johann	304607	M		Farmer at Kirsel, Kleve district (Ger.) 39-45	59/134	MISC.CRIMES	POL.
EUBE (or EULZ)	304608	M		Commissioner, Fieldpolice, Luettich (Bel.) 40-41	59/135	MURDER	BEL.
EUCHLER, Fritz	303594	M	22.3.94	SS-Mann,C.C.Majdanek (Pol.) 40-44	57/246	MURDER	POL.
EULZ (see EUBE)	304608						
EVERS, Heinz	304609	M		Member, Gestapo, Krakau (Pol.) 11.39-2.45	59/136	PILLAGE	POL.
EWALDS	198210	M		Senior Cpl.,SS-Uscharfhr., Camp Royallieu (Fr.) 41-44	31/83	MURDER	FR.
EXEL	267484	M		Sgt., Feldgendarmerie, Besancon and vicinity (Fr.) 44		MURDER	FR.
EXLER	31390	M		Capt.,20 Army Geb.Pion.Bn.99,7 Geb.Div., Finmark (Nor.) 10.-11.44	8/253	MURDER	NOR.
EXNER, Gustav Dr.	264556	M	9.10.08	See names listed under "Special Headings"			
EXNER, Rudolf	304610	M		Member, Gestapo, Krakau (Pol.) 11.39-2.45	59/137	PILLAGE	POL.
FABER	267481	M		Member, Gestapo, Luchon and vicinity (Fr.) 1.43-7.44	-	MURDER	FR.
FABRY	198163	M		SS-Hptsturmfhr., Waffen SS,SS Unit S.P.No.3664,La Capelle, St.Sulpice (Fr.) 25.8.44	32/200	MURDER	FR.
FADIKOW	198098	M		Uscharfhr., employed on painting, Auschwitz (Pol.) 40	16/292	MURDER	FR.
FAEHNDRICH, Ernst Dr.	264565	M	17.1.08	See names listed under "Special Headings"			
FAHL	146998	M		Obergruppenfhr.,SS Pz.Div."Das Reich" (Fr.) 44	11/72	MURDER	FR.
FAHNENSCHREIDER, Paul (or FAHNENSCHREIBER)	10009	M		Major, Ortskommandant, Ortskommandantur at Veliko Gradiste, Malce-Recica (Czech.) 7.43-2.44	14/630	MURDER	YUGO.
FAHNER	303595	M		Member, Gestapo, Warschau (Pol.) 39-45	57/248	MURDER	POL.
FAJFER	308893	M	21	Wachtmeister, Member, Gendarmerie, Jagikdo., Zancut (Pol.) 39-44	60/151	MURDER	POL.
FAJGS (or FEIGS) Hermann or Artur	308894	M		Commander at C.C. of the Sonderdienst, Janow Lubelski (Pol.) 40-43	60/152	MURDER	POL.
FALCENHAUER, Josef	304611	M		Member, Gestapo, Krakau (Pol.) 11.39-2.45	59/138	BRUTALITY	POL.
FALK, Artur	308895	M	circa 99	Mayor, Wieckowy, district of Koscierzyna (Pol.) 39-42	60/153	BRUTALITY	POL.
FALK, Wilhelm	308896	M	23.12.98	Cpl., Schutzgruppen Brunssum,Neth., (Neth.) 9.44	60/154	PILLAGE	NETH.
FALYE	308897	M		SS-Osturmfhr., Member, terror group "Peter", 31.1.44	60/155	MURDER	DEN.
FALKENBERG, Erwin Gustav	308898	M	22.11.08	Member, Ortsbauernfhr.,SS, manager of the estate at Debicz, District of Szoda (Pol.) 40-43	60/156	MURDER	POL.
FALKENBERG, Hans	308899	M	circa 02	Deputy Commander, German Police, Dzialdow (Pol.) 39-45	60/157	MURDER	POL.
FALKNER, Henryk	308900	M	8.7.07	Commander, Police, Zerkow (Pol.) 39-44	60/158	BRUTALITY	POL.
FARBER	302973	M		Sgt., Feldgendarmerie at Angouleme, Chasseneuil (Charente) (Fr.) 43-22.3.44	56/180	MURDER	FR.
FARBER, August	302974	M		Crim.Secr., Gestapo Staff, Kattowitz (Pol.) 39-42	56/181	INTERR.	POL.
FARBER, Erich	266242	M	circa 10	Lt.,86 Army Corps, Feldgend.Trupp 486, Candresse (Fr.) 11.6.44	-	PILLAGE	FR.
FARBER, Erna	304612	F		Member, Gestapo, Krakau (Pol.) 11.39-2.45	59/139	MURDER	POL.
FAST, Johannes	308795	M	15.9.98	Sturmbannfhr., Head,SS Labour office, Mogilin (Pol.) 39-44	60/160	INTERR.	POL.
FAUPEL	302975	M		Member, Group 530 Geh.Feldpolizei, Bruessel (Bel.) 40-44	56/183	MURDER	BEL.
FAUTE	304613	M		Watchman, Blechhammer, Wilkie, Strzelce, Slask (Pol.) 1.,2.45	59/140	MURDER	POL.
FAYKUS	205357			Crim.Employee, Dept.II G.Staatspolizeileitstelle Prag,C.C. Auschwitz-Birkenau (Pol.) 39-45	13/115	MURDER	CZECH.
FECHLER	304614	M		Storekeeper, Field-clothing-depot of the Airforce, Zawiercie (Pol.) 8.43	59/141	MURDER	POL.
FECHLING	302976	M		Oscharfhr., Gestapo Lodz (Pol.) 39-44	56/185	PILLAGE	POL.
FECHNER, Oskar	304615	M		Member, Gestapo, Krakau (Pol.) 11.39-2.45	59/141	MURDER	POL.

FEC - FIN

NAME	C.R.FILE NUMBER	SEX	DATE OF BIRTH	RANK OCCUPATION UNIT PLACE AND DATE OF CRIME	UNWCC LIST/ SERIAL NO.	REASON WANTED	WANTED BY
FECHTNER	304616	M		SS-Schfhr., (In charge of Jewish Labourers employed at Gas-works), Radom (Pol.) 40-43	59/143	BRUTALITY	POL.
FEDERLE	308796	M		Pvt., Geh.Feld.Polizei, Antwerpen and Bruessel (Bel.)40-44	60/161	MURDER	BEL.
FEHENIG	266884	M		Faehnrich, Div. "B", Dordogne,Correze,Hte.Vienne (Fr.)	-	SUSPECT	FR.
FEHLING	266545	M		Chief-Sgt., Div."B", 10 Btty. 4 Sect., Dordogne, Correze Hte.Vienne (Fr.) 6.44	-	SUSPECT	FR.
FEHLING, Hermann	72125	M		Agent, SD.section C.E. Lyons and vicinity (Fr.) 43-44	27/42	MURDER	FR.
FEIGS (see FAJGS, Hermann or Artur)	308894						
FEIL, Adolf	304617	M		Member, Gestapo, Krakau, (Pol.) 11.39-2.45	59/144	MURDER	POL.
FEINDT	302977	M		Pvt., Group 530 Geh.Feldpol., Bruessel (Bel.) 40-44	56/186	MURDER	BEL.
FELDER (see FELDES)	266546						
FELDES (or FELDER)	266546	M	circa 00	Sgt., Army, Coming from Rennes and d'Angers, Saint Die (Fr.)44	-	MURDER	FR.
FELDHOFF	308697	M		Cpt., Postal Section 20-768, Naives for Bar, Meuse (Fr.)29.8.44	27/304	MURDER	FR.
FELDMANN, Heinrich	308797	M	circa 12	Manager, Member, NSDAP., group of estates near Dzialyn (Pol.) 39-44	60/162	MISC.CRIMES	POL.
FELDMEIER, Franz	267233	M		Rottfhr., Gestapo, Marseille and vicinity, (Fr.)	-	MURDER	FR.
FELENS	304618	M		Hptsturmfhr., Deputy of SS-Polizei-Fuehrer at Krakau District (Pol.) 40-42	59/145	INTERR.	POL.
FELGNER, Paul	131904	M		Civilian, Bad Durrenburg (Ger.) 29.5.44	16/984	TORTURE	U.S.
FELL, Johann	267138	M		Hptwachtmeister, Gendarmerie, in the villages of Smartno ob Dreti,Smartno ob Paki,Velog and Bocna and Gornji Grad (Yugo.) 10.10.44-12.12.44	-	MURDER	YUGO.
FELLER	304619	M		Lt.Col.,Commander,Airforce,8 Gruppe Feldbekleidungsamt Zawiercie (Pol.) 43	59/146	MURDER	POL.
FELLMANN	266519	M		Pvt., Army, Saint Die (Fr.) 11.44	-	MURDER	FR.
FELLNER	265469	M		Capt., 99 Alpen Jaeg.Bn. 157 Jaeg.Div., Le Monetier les Bains (Fr.) 11.12.44	-	MURDER	FR.
FELSE, Fritz	198099	M		SS-Rottfhr., C.C. Auschwitz (Pol.)	16/296	BRUTALITY	POL., FR.
FELSEGGER	10010	M		Attached to Medical Corps C.C. Breendonck (Bel.) 40-44	5/29	MISC.CRIMES	BEL.
FELSKE	303596	M		Member, Gestapo, Warsaw, (Pol.) 39-45	57/252	MURDER	POL.
FELSKE, Erich	303799	M	19. 6.09	Member, political Leader, SS and Selbstschutz, NSDAP. Lopatki (Pol.) 39-43	60/163	MURDER	POL.
FINENIG	308799	M		Cadet, Bremer Div., Departm. of the Dordogne,Correze and Hte.Vienne (Fr.)26.3.44-20.4.44	60/164	MURDER	FR.
FEST	308800	M		Secretary of Fieldpolice, Antwerpen and Bruessel (Bel.)40-44	60/165	MURDER	BEL.
FETSCH, Ernst	38937	M		SS-Sturmbannfhr., 2 SS Pz.Div. "Das Reich" 1 Pz.Rgt. Montpezat (Fr.) 5.44	11/75 43/72	MURDER	FR.
FETTE, Walter	267420	M	19. 8.97	Capt., 8 Coy. 487 Inf.Rgt.,Oignies and Courrieres (Fr.)28.5.40	-	MURDER	FR.
FETTERMANN	304620	M		SS-Officer, Town Commander, SS, Bochnia (Pol.) 39-10.41	59/147	PILLAGE	POL.
FEUCHT	304621	M		Sturmfhr., H.Q. of SD. and Sipo.,Radom and district (Pol.)-43	59/148	MURDER	POL.
FEURING	266241	M	14	Cpl., Feldgend.658,Paray le Monial and vicinity (Fr.) 43-44	-	MISC.CRIMES	FR.
FEYERABEND	305848	M		SS-Uschfhr., C.C. Neuengamme (Ger.) 40	28/49	MURDER	BEL.
FIBIOR	303597	M		Uschfhr., Member, SS, Gluck (Pol.) 40-44	57/254	MURDER	POL.
FICKEN	302978	M		Cpl., Group 530 Geh.Feld Polizei,Bruessel (Bel.) 40-44	56/188	MURDER	BEL.
FICKER, Gerhard	308801	M	11. 9.94	Lt.Commander, Town-Police, Szamotuly (Pol.) 39-44	60/168	BRUTALITY	POL.
FICKERT, Fritz	12380	M		SS-Oschfhr., Blockfhr.,C.C.Sachsenhausen (Ger.) 40-45	38/365 25/133 6/222	MURDER	U.K.,BEL. CZECH.
FICKINGER (see CHICKINGER)	157406						
FIDLER, Erwin	308802	M	23. 7.97	Member, Mayor, SS, NSDAP., village of Ostrowiec, district of Konin (Pol.) 39-44	60/168	MURDER	POL.
FIEBES	304173	M		Member, Schutzgruppen at the "Laura Mine", Eigelshoven (Neth.) 8.-13.9.44	58/191	PILLAGE	NETH.
FIEBIG	304174	M		SS-Hptschfhr., Member of SD.Aussenstelle Maastricht. Culture and Press department. Resistance Organizations, Limburg and Friesland (Neth.) 44-45	58/192	MURDER	NETH.
FIEDLER	168953	M		Leader d.Grundstueckges., Gdynia (Pol.) 39-44	10/497	PILLAGE	POL.
FIEDLER	302979	M		W.O., Feldgend., district of Dinan C'Otes du Nord (Fr.) 8.44-11.44	56/189	MURDER	FR.
FIEDLER, Walter	304622	M		Member, Gestapo, Krakau (Pol.) 11.39-2.45	59/149	MURDER	POL.
FIEDRICH (see HIDRICH)	266606						
FIEGE	197796	M		Cpl., Camp Royallieu (Fr.) 41-44	31/86	MURDER	FR.
FIEREK, Jakob	304623	M		Member, Gestapo, Krakau (Pol.) 11.39-2.45	59/150	MURDER	POL.
FIETSCH, Reinhold	267248	M		Sturmschfhr., Gestapo, Marseille and vicinity (Fr.)	-	MURDER	FR.
FILCEK, Klemens	308803	M	23.11.97	Recruiting Agent, German Labour Office, Miedzyrzecz - Podlaski (Pol.) 39-44	60/169	MURDER	POL.
FILIETZ, Karl	308698	M		SS-Hptsturmfhr., Member, of SD. Kdo. operating at Apeldoorn (Neth.) 2.10.44	31/371	MURDER	U.K.
FILIPOWICZ, Florian	308804	M	circa 25	Foreman, Div. Monowice (so called "Buna") C.C. Auschwitz (Pol.) 39-44	60/170	TORTURE	POL.
FILIPS (or FILIIPS)	38949	M		Agent, Gestapo (Einsatzkdo.), Paris, Vichy (Fr.)	-	SUSPECT	FR.
FILIPS	198100	M		Member of Roumanian Kdo., Gestapo, Vichy (Fr.) 43-44	16/298	MURDER	FR.
FILLA, Werner	302980	M		Hptkrim.Assistant, Gestapo Chief, Kattowitz (Pol.) 39-42	56/191	INTERR.	POL.
FILLIPS (see FILIPS)	38949						
FINDEISEN, Marianne	304624	F		Member, Gestapo, Krakau (Pol.) 11.39-2.45	59/151	MURDER	POL.
FINDER, N.	308805	M	circa 18	Hptwachtmstr., Gendarmerie, Brzesk (Pol.) 43-44	60/171	MURDER	POL.
FINDL, Georg	267247	M	15	Uschfhr., Gestapo, Marseille and vicinity (Fr.)	-	MURDER	FR.
FINGER	171692	M		Police-Master, Police and SD., C.C. Metz and Mauthausen (Fr., Aust.) 4.44	19/131	MURDER	FR.
FINK, Wilhelm	303598	M	6. 6.08	SS-Mann, C.C. Majdanek (Pol.) 40-44	57/258	BRUTALITY	POL.
FINK, Wilhelm	303599	M	11. 9.08	SS-Mann, C.C. Majdanek (Pol.) 40-44	57/259	BRUTALITY	POL.
FINNER, Hans	308806	M	3. 5.93	Member, Police constable, SS Police, Ostrzeszow (Pol.) 39-44	60/172	MISC.CRIMES	POL.

FIN - FOR

NAME	C.R.FILE NUMBER	SEX	DATE OF BIRTH	RANK OCCUPATION UNIT PLACE AND DATE OF CRIME	UNWCC LIST/ SERIAL NO.	REASON WANTED	WANTED BY
FINNHER, Georg	267246	M		Member, Gestapo, Marseille and vicinity (Fr.)	-	MURDER	FR.
FISCHER, Dr.	72700	M		Chief, Gestapo, C.C., Strasbourg, Ballersdorf-Struthof (Fr.)	6/905	MURDER	FR.
FISCHER	131662	M		Sgt., Guard at Trieux and Trucquenieux, Bassin de Briey (Fr.) 40-45	13/398	MURDER	FR.
FISCHER	131912	M		SS-Oscharfhr., C.C. Sub-chief of quarry Kdo., Flossenburg (Ger.) 42-45	25/879	MURDER	FR.
FISCHER	197790	M		Cmdt., C.C. Ravensbrueck (Ger.) 40-45	25/138	MURDER	BEL.
FISCHER	197792	M		Staff-Sgt., 157.Gebirgs-Jaeg.Div., Plateau des Glieres (Fr.) 22.3. and 5.4.44	38/272	PILLAGE	FR.
FISCHER	197794	M	circa 94	Officer-Medical, Camp Gleiwitz (Ger.) 22.1.45	30/175	MURDER	FR.
FISCHER	254503	F		Woman-Police, Abt. Ia , SD, Brussels (Bel.) 41-45	28/53	INTERR.	BEL.
FISCHER	265575	M	17?	Osturmfhr., 16.SS-Pz.Div., Massa Carrara (It.) 8.44	-	MURDER	U.K.
FISCHER	265638	M	14. 8.21?	Customs official, F.P. No. 57 727 B, Larmor-Pleubian (Fr.) 5.,6.,7.8.44	-	MURDER	FR.
FISCHER	266240	M		Pvt., Africa-Corps, Regt. Ruxleben, 1.Sect.,6.Coy., Hte.Marne-Aube (Fr.) 25.-31.8.44	-	MURDER	FR.
FISCHER	266885	M	circa 03	Capt.,Feldgendarm.of Chaussin (Jura), Le Cheminot (Fr.) 10.4.44	-	MURDER	FR.
FISCHER	267001	M		Feldwebel, Navy, Calais (Fr.) 4.9.44	-	MURDER	FR.
FISCHER, Dr.	267124	M		Member, Camp-admin.,Camp-hospital at Stalag III A, Stalag III A 4.41	-	MURDER	YUGO.
FISCHER	267245	M		Agent, Gestapo, Marseille and vicinity (Fr.)	-	MURDER	FR.
FISCHER (see Sternfeld, Hans)	267361						
FISCHER	267422	M		Osturmfhr., Gestapo, Bordeaux and vicinity (Fr.) 42-8.44	-	MURDER	FR.
FISCHER	304625	M		Usturmfhr., C.C.(in charge of the training of SS-Men) Auschwitz (Pol.) 42-43	59/152	MURDER	POL.
FISCHER, Ernst	303600	M	16. 5.10	SS-Mann, C.C. Majdanek (Pol.) 40-44	57/261	BRUTALITY	POL.
FISCHER, Georg Franz	302982	M		Kommissar, Group 530, Geh.Feldpolizei,Bruessel (Bel.) 40-44	56/194	MURDER	BEL.
FISCHER, Heinrich	302983	M		Cpl., Geh.Feldpolizei (Bel.) 40-44	56/195	MURDER	BEL.
FISCHER, Hermann	308807	M		Member SS, SA, Mayor of the town of Slupcy (Pol.) 39-45	60/174	MISC.CRIMES	POL.
FISCHER, Johann	303602	M	7. 5.10	SS-Mann, C.C. Majdanek (Pol.) 40-44	57/263	BRUTALITY	POL.
FISCHER, Johann S.	265618	M		See names listed under "Special Headings"			
FISCHER, Josef	303602	M	23. 8.14	SS-Mann, C.C. Majdanek (Pol.) 40-44	57/264	BRUTALITY	POL.
FISCHER, Karl	267099	M	22. 9.05	Hptscharfhr., SS, Gestapo Paris BDS or KDS II C2, Paris (Fr.)44	-	SUSPECT	FR.
FISCHER, Otto	185123	M		Chief, Block 23 C.C. Dachau (Ger.)	25/882	TORTURE	FR.
FISCHER, Otto	303107	M		Hptscharfhr., SS, Kempen (Ger.) 25.10.41	56/196	MURDER	POL.
FISCHER, Walther	308808	M		Head-cook, Haaren Camp probably ditto at Hooge Boekel nr.Enschede (Neth.) 43-44	60/175	PILLAGE	NETH.
FISHMAYER (see FISHMEYER, Otto)	138258						
FISHMEYER, Otto (or FISHMAYER)	138258	M		SS-Scharfhr., Gestapo, Sub section IV f, Lyon (Fr.) 43-44	38/273	MURDER	FR.
FISTER, Weiter Albert	308809	M	7. 4.97	Head, Crim.Police Dept.at the Landratur, Wejherowo (Pol.) 39-45	60/176	BRUTALITY	POL.
FITTERER	57337	M		Oberbereichsleiter, Kreisleiter NSDAP, Mosbach (Ger.) 44	13/402	BRUTALITY	FR.
FITZ, Hans	303108	M		SS-Scharfhr., Gestapo Chief, Kattowitz (Pol.) 39-42	56/199	BRUTALITY	POL.
FITZKE, Arthur	308810	M	11. 4.17	Member, SS, Gestapo, Miloslaw Distr.of Wrzesnia (Pol.) 39-44	60/177	MURDER	POL.
FITZKE, Willi	308811	M	30.10.08	Member, SS, Miloslaw Distr.of Wrzesnia (Pol.) 40-45	60/178	MURDER	POL.
FLACH, Amelie	304626	F		Member, Gestapo, Krakau (Pol.) 11.39-2.45	59/154	MURDER	POL.
FLACHE (see FLASCHE)	303109						
FLAD	308812	M		SS-Usturmfhr., Secretary of Crim.,Radom (Pol.) 1.40-1.45	60/180	MURDER	POL.
FLASCHE (or FLACHE)	303109	M		Command of a unit of SS, Pantin Station - Seine (Fr.) 22.8.44	56/200	MURDER	FR.
FLASCHE, Franz	303603	M	14. 3.00	SS-Rottfhr., C.C. Majdanek (Pol.) 10.39- 1.45	57/266	MURDER	POL.
FLECK	303110	M		Capt., Comm.the motor.Inf.Bn. z.b.V. at Wahn nr.Koeln, Linnich nr.Aachen, Hillenberg on the German-Dutch frontier, South Limburg (Neth.) 10.5.40	56/201	MISC.CRIMES	NETH.
FLECKENSTEIN	267419	M	9. 4.03	Gendarmeriemeister, Feldgend., Thann (Fr.) 19.-22.10.44, 29.10.44	-	BRUTALITY	FR.
FLECKNER, Hans	254143	M		Ostubafhr., 13.SS Polizei-Regt., Ferlach (Aust.) 44-45	38/404	MURDER	YUGO.
FLEI	304627	M		Member, German railway Police (Bahnschutzpolizei), Sanok (Pol.) 40-42	59/155	MURDER	POL.
FLEISCHER, Georg	303604	M	15. 3.14	SS-Mann, C.C. Majdanek (Pol.) 40-44	57/268	BRUTALITY	POL.
FLEISCHMANN	197784	M		SS-Mann, Professor of physics, Fakulty of Medicine University, Strassbourg (Fr.) 40-44	30/176	MURDER	FR.
FLEISCHMANN, Alfred	267112	M		Verwaltungsrat, Energieversorgung Suedsteiermark A.G.,Trbovlje (Yugo.) 41-45	-	PILLAGE	YUGO.
FLEKATSCH	303605	M	30. 8.20	Member, Gestapo, C.C. Majdanek (Pol.) 40-44	57/269	BRUTALITY	POL.
FLEMING, Herbert	304628	M		Member, Gestapo, Krakow (Pol.) 11.39-2.45	59/156	MURDER	POL.
FLETZ	267092	M	circa 10	Lt. or Sgt., Feldgendarmerie,Clumanc and Tartonne (Fr.) 2.,3.2.44	-	MISC.CRIMES	FR.
FLINKERT, Hans	197535	M	5. 2.11	Pvt., Aube (Fr.) 20.-30.8.44	31/88	PILLAGE	FR.
FLOSSLER, Anton	304629	M		Member, Gestapo, Krakau (Pol.) 11.39- 2.45	59/157	BRUTALITY	POL.
FLOTER	303111	M		Employee, Gestapo, Lodz,(Pol.) 39-44	56/202	PILLAGE	POL.
FLUCH, Ulrich	267125	M	23. 6.07	Gendarmeriepostenfhr., Gend.,St.Marjeta on the river Pesnica (Yugo.) 7.44-2.45	-	MISC.CRIMES	YUGO.
FLUCHER, Joseph	198101	M		SS-Uscharfhr., C.C. Auschwitz (Pol.)	16/305 40/405	MURDER	POL.,FR. YUGO.
FLUGGE	266882	M		Osturmfhr., 4.SS-Unit, Feld-Ers.Bn.10 "Frundsberg" Unit No. 57.815 A, Oulins (Fr.)	-	INCENDIARISM	FR.
FOBACH	191659	M		Pvt., Guard, Piennes Mines, Bassin de Briey (Fr.) 40-45	13/406	MURDER	FR.
FOERSTER	303606	M		Member, Gestapo, Warschau (Pol.) 10.39- 1.45	57/270	BRUTALITY	POL.
FOERSTER, Wilhelm	303112	M		Sgt., Geh.Feldpolizei (Bel.) 40-44	56/203	MURDER	BEL.
FOFFMAN, Walter	303113	M		Chief secretary, Gestapo, Lodz (Pol.) 39-44	56/204	PILLAGE	POL.
FOJELIN	266883	M		Agent, Scharfhr., SD, SS, Nice (Fr.) 44	-	SUSPECT	FR.
FOLKMANN	303623	M		Member, Gestapo, Warschau (Pol.) 10.39-1.45	57/271	BRUTALITY	POL.
FOLTE	304630	M		Osturmfhr., Member, Gestapo, Oppeln (Ger.) 40-43	59/158	INTERR.	POL.
FORDON	267130	M		Lt., Army, 264.Div. 893.Gren.Regt. 3.Bn., Sinj (Yugo.) 8.9.43-1044	-	MURDER	YUGO.
FORESTER, Viktor	304691	M	22.10.11	Inspector, Gestapo, Krakau (Pol.) 11.39-2.45	59/159	MURDER	POL.
FORLER	197914	M		Member of staff, C.C. Struthof-Natzweiler (Fr.) 40-44	32/202	BRUTALITY	FR.

NAME	C.R.FILE NUMBER	SEX	DATE OF BIRTH	RANK	OCCUPATION	UNIT	PLACE AND DATE OF CRIME	UNWCC LIST/ SERIAL NO.	REASON WANTED	WANTED BY
FORSCHLER	198065	M			Sgt.,Waffen-SS,Izon la Bruisse-Sederon (Fr.)22.2.44			30/14	MISC.CRIMES	FR.
FORSTER	142688	M			Member, Gestapo, Cahors (Lot.) (Fr.) 29.6.44			6/483	MURDER	FR.
FORTZWANGLER	197538	M			Stabsarzt at Royallieu-Camp,Compiegne (Fr.) 41-44			31/208	MURDER	FR.
FRAAS	303607	M			Member, Gestapo, Warschau (Pol.) 10.39- 1.45			57/273	BRUTALITY	POL.
FRANC	251540	M			Capt.,Army,was with K.L.M.Dutch Air-Force before the war,Huybergen (Neth.) 4.9.44			40/89	MISC.CRIMES	NETH.
FRANCK	304632	M			Member,Secr.Field-Police,HQ.,G.F.P.,Luettich (Bel.)40-41			59/160	MURDER	BEL.
FRANCK (or FRANK),Arthur	267090	M			Osturmfhr., Civil Police Service Gruppe Geh.Feldpolizei 734 Gestapo,H.SS Pf.Transport Officer,Paris (Fr.) 11.42			-	SUSPECT	FR.
FRANCK, Pawel	308815	M	02		N.C.O.,Gendarmerie, Bochnia (Pol.) 41-45			60/184	MURDER	POL.
FRANK	197938	M			N.C.O., Oflag X B, Nienburg-Weser (Ger.) 6.10.42			32/203	MURDER	FR.
FRANK	265990	M			Member, Feldgendarmerie, Cholet (Fr.) 7.-8.8.44			-	MURDER	FR.
FRANK (see FRANCK,Arthur)	267090									
FRANK	303114	M			Member,Feldgend.,Region of Cholet (Fr.) 7.and 8.8.44			56/206	MURDER	FR.
FRANK	303608	M			Member, Gestapo, Warschau (Pol.) 10.39- 1.45			57/274	MURDER	POL.
FRANK	304175	M			SS-Usturmfhr.,SD attached to Kasse, Payofficer of BDS, Zeist,Oldenzaal,The Hague (Neth.) 44-45			58/195	PILLAGE	NETH.
FRANK, Josef	308816	M			Rottfhr.,7.Coy.1.Regt.SS-Div.Adolf Hitler,Tilly la Campagne (Fr.) 1.8.44			60/185	MURDER	U.K.
FRANK, Rudolf	266518	M	circa 00		Sgt.,Feldkommandantur,Saint Die (Fr.) 11.44			-	MURDER	FR.
FRANKE	265650	M			Capt.Cdt.1.Fallschirm-Pi.Abt.2.F.J.Div.,Brest (Fr.)8.9.44			-	MURDER	FR.
FRANKE, Horst	267418	M	7. 6.07		Lt.,487.Inf.Regt., Oignies and Courrieres (Fr.)28.5.40			-	MURDER	FR.
FRANKEINSTEIN (or HAUTHIER)	197939	M			Lt.,Gestapo at Avignon,Vercoiran,Drome (Fr.)			30/177	MURDER	FR.
FRANKEL	266917	M			Lt.,Brevands (Fr.) 8.6.44			-	WITNESS	FR.
FRANKEWITZ, Johannes	267244	M	05		Scharfhr., Gestapo,Marseille and vicinity (Fr.)			-	MURDER	FR.
FRANKOWITSCH	267207	M			Sturmmann,Gestapo,Marseille and vicinity (Fr.)			-	MURDER	FR.
FRANTZ	198102	M			Kapo,C.C.,Auschwitz (Pol.)			16/308	MURDER	POL.,FR.
FRANZ	39691	M			SS-Mann,SS-Kanonier,SS Div.F.P.No.48963 B,St.Sulpice, Chateau Gonthier (Fr.) 8.44			11/38	MURDER	FR.
FRANZ	143466	M			Agent,Gestapo at Cahors (Lot.)(Fr.) 29.6.44			6/484	MURDER	FR.
FRANZ	171698	M			Head, Gestapo, Orleans (Fr.)10.6.44			10/138	MURDER	FR.
FRANZ, Heinrich	300591	M			Driver,SS-Oscharfhr.,SD,Amsterdam (Neth.)24.3.44			40/126	MURDER	NETH.
FRANZEN, Jack	308817	M	circa 04		Member,NSDAP and Gendarmerie,Muszyn (Pol.) 39-44			60/186	MURDER	POL.
FRARI, Albert	131660	M			Cpl.-chief,Mines of St.Pierremont,Bassin of Briey (Fr.)40-45			13/409	TORTURE	FR.
FRAUENFELD,Alfred Eduard	62297	M			Formerly Gauleiter,Commissioner-Gen.for Crimes,Chief of Propaganda-Office,Wie n (Aust.)			-	MURDER	UNWCC
FRAUZEL	161193	M			Member of St.Quentin Gestapo,St.Quentin (Fr.) 44			16/60	MURDER	FR.
FREDERICH	304176	M			Feldwebel,Feldgend., Arlon and surroundings (Bel.)8.and 9.44			58/196	MURDER	BEL.
FREDOW, Fritz	267528	M			Gestapo,Limoges and vicinity (Fr.) 44			-	SUSPECT	FR.
FREDSICK (or FREDZICK)	173364	M			SS-Rottfhr.Block Senior, C.C.,Auschwitz (Pol.)			16/309	MURDER	POL.,FR.
FREDZICK (see FREDSICK)	173364									
FREI, Heinrich	308818	M	8. 2.20		Official,German Labour Office,Gostyn (Pol.) 40-43			60/187	BRUTALITY	POL.
FREIMANN, Friedrich	308819	M	14. 6.08		Ortsgr.Ltr., Mayor,NSDAP,Puck and Piasecznica (Pol.)39-44			60/188	MURDER	POL.
FREIMEIER, Jakob	303609	M	23.11.09		Guard,C.C.,Majdanek (Pol.) 40-42			57/278	BRUTALITY	POL.
FREISEN	308700	M			Farmer at Stein Kaspendorf -Deutsch-Eylau Krs.Rosenberg (Ger.) 8.4.41			27/42	BRUTALITY	U.K.
FREISINGER, I.	267117	M	circa 00		Gendarmeriepostenfhr.,Gendarmerie,Velenje (Yugo.) 43-44			-	MISC.CRIMES	YUGO.
FREISINGER, Sebastian	303610	M	15. 3.21		SS-Mann, C.C., Majdanek (Pol.) 40-44			57/279	MURDER	POL.
FRENKEL, Gustav	308820	M			Bailiff, Tuczno nr.Torun (Pol.) 39-45			60/189	INTERR.	POL.
FRENTZEL, Georg	304634	M			Member,Gestapo,Krakau (Pol.) 11.39- 2.45			59/162	BRUTALITY	POL.
FRENZEL	267409	M			350 Regt."Hindou", Department l'Indre (Fr.) 8.44			-	MURDER	FR.
FRESSMANN, Martin	198103	M			SS-Scharfhr.,SS,C.C., Auschwitz (Pol.)			16/310 40/406	MURDER	POL.,FR. YUGO.
FRESSMULLER	126795	M			Oscharfhr.,(Cpl.Chief),Gestapo and SD,Member des Formations Allemandes (Sipo-Einsatz-Kdo.),Chalons Sur Marne (Fr.)43-44			-	MISC.CRIMES	FR.
FREUND, Paul	173408	M	4. 8.25		SS-Uscharfhr.,SS,C.C.,Sachsenhausen,Calais, Arras (Ger.,Fr.)			32/205	TORTURE	FR.
FREUNDLICH, Paul	267308	M	15. 5.19		Sgt.,E.M.II,Inf.Regt.487,Oignies and Courrieres (Fr.)28.5.40			-	SUSPECT	FR.
FREY	197944	M			Officer,Organisation Todt,Bussang (Fr.)6.-9.40,10.44			32/206	PILLAGE	FR.
FREY, Fritz	304178	M			Head, German Labour Office,Sanok (Pol.)39-42			58/199	MURDER	POL.
FREY, Fritz	185125	M			Chief of block,C.C.,Sachsenhausen (Ger.)			32/207	PILLAGE	FR.
FREY, Richard	267307	M			Feldgendarm,Feldgend.,Le Mesnil-Thomas (Fr.)24.7.44			-	MURDER	FR.
FREYMEIER (see KREYMEIER)	267098									
FREYTAG, Johann	304179	M			SS-Hptscharfhr.,Member of Gestapo,Kattowitz and Distr.(Pol.)41-43			58/200	MISC.CRIMES	POL.
FREYTAG, Karl	303116	M			Krim.Secr.,Gestapo-Staff,Kattowity (Pol.) 39-42			56/211	PILLAGE	POL.
FRIB	186841	M			SS-Hptscharfhr.,SS Admin. of C.C.,Flossenburg (Ger.)			25/889	MURDER	FR.
FRICK, Helmuth	308821	M	4.11.07		Member,SA,NSKK and of the courtmartial,Szubin (Pol.)39-40			60/190	MURDER	POL.
FRICK, Wilhelm Reinhard	304635	M	22. 3.03		Mayor,Krs.Amtsltr.NSDAP,Kom.Polit.Zawiercie (Pol.)39-45			59/163	MISC.CRIMES	POL.
FRICKE	146995	M			SS-Mann,SS Pz.Div."Das Reich",Tulle (Fr.) 44			11/77	MURDER	FR.
FRIECK, Rudolf	308822	M	25. 9.98		Official,Labour Office,Ostrow Wlkp (Pol.) 39-45			60/191	MISC.CRIMES	POL.
FRIEDEL	265991	M			Hptscharfhr.,Div."Das Reich",Region of Rouen (Fr.)44			-	MURDER	FR.
FRIEDEL, Fritz Gustav	308823	M			SS Krim.Inspektor,Sipo,SD,Bialystok (Pol.) 42-44			16/192	MURDER	POL.
FRIEDEL, Paul Gerhard	266916	M	21. 4.09		See names listed under "Special Headings"					
FRIEDLEIN	308825	M			Instructor,employee,G.F.P.,Antwerpen and Bruessel (Bel.)40-44			60/194	MURDER	BEL.
FRIEDLT, Lydia	308699	F			Interpreter,Feldgendarmerie,Sens,Champigny s.Marne (Fr.)9.4.44			16/32	INTERR.	FR.
FRIEDRICH	266164	M			Cpl.,Afrika Corps,Regt.Ruxleben 6.Coy.,1.Sect., Hte Marne-Aube (Fr.) 25.-31.8.44			-	MURDER	FR.
FRIEDRICH	266165	M	circa 22		Usturmfhr.,Gestapo,Nantes and region (Fr.)43-44			-	MURDER	FR.
FRIEDRICH, Eduard	304636	M			Member, Gestapo, Krakau (Pol.) 11.39- 2.45			59/164	BRUTALITY	POL.
FRIEDRICH, Herbert	264607	M			See names listed under "Special Headings"					
FRIEDRICH, Otto	308826	M	19. 4.09		Oscharfhr.member,stellv.Commander,Gestapo,Gorlice (Pol.)40-43			60/195	MURDER	POL.
FRIES	197837	M			SS-Oscharfhr.member of Staff,C.C.,Struthof-Natzweiler(Fr.)40-44			32/208	MURDER	FR.
FRIESKE	303611	M			Member,Gestapo,Warschau (Pol.)10.39- 1.45			57/286	BRUTALITY	POL.
FRINDT, Max	306260	M			Meister,Gendarmerie,Bressanone (It.)			28/198	MURDER	U.K.
FRINKS	266160	M	circa 10		Oscharfhr.,Chief of drivers,Gestapo,Nantes and region (Fr.)43-44			-	MURDER	FR.
FRISCH	303612	M			Member,Gestapo,Warschau (Pol.) 10.39- 1.45			57/287	BRUTALITY	POL.

FRI - GAR

NAME	C.R.FILE NUMBER	SEX	DATE OF BIRTH	RANK OCCUPATION UNIT PLACE AND DATE OF CRIME	UNWCC LIST/ SERIAL NO.	REASON WANTED	WANTED BY
FRISCH, Josef	304637	M		Member, Gestapo, Krakau (Pol.) 11.39-2.45	59/166	BRUTALITY	POL.
FRISCHER, Robert	304638	M		Rottfhr., SS, Member, SD and Sipo, Krakau (Pol.) 42-43	59/167	MURDER	POL.
FRISKE, Julius	303613	M	18. 8.09	SS-Rottfhr., C.C. Majdanek (Pol.) 40-44	57/288	MURDER	POL.
FRITSCHE, Dr.	197839	M		Baurat, Cmdt., Field-build office the Airforce at Lille, Roubaix (Fr.) 11.41-7.42	32/210	PILLAGE	FR.
FRITSCHE, Franz	303614	M	24.10.96	SS-Rottfhr., C.C. Majdanek (Pol.) 40-44	57/289	MURDER	POL.
FRITZ	303117	M		Feldpolizei-Sekretaer, Group 530, Geh.Feldpolizei, Bruessel (Bel.) 40-44	-	MURDER	BEL.
FRITZ, Karl	266915	M	20. 9.05	Usturmfhr., Civil Police Service, Gruppe Geheime Polizei 603, Gestapo, Paris (Fr.) 11.42	-	SUSPECT	FR.
FRITZ, Kurt	308827	M	8. 9.13	Member, SS and Gendarmerie, Naklo (Pol.) 39	60/196	MURDER	POL.
FRITZER, Charlotte	304639	F		Member, Gestapo, Krakau (Pol.) 11.39-2.45	59/168	BRUTALITY	POL.
FROBOESE, Erich	31512	M	6. 4. °	Hptschfhr., Gestapo, Chief, Adjutant, SD, Section III, Rennes (Fr.) 43-44	8/173 52/164	MISC.CRIMES	FR.
FROCHBERG, Paul	308828	M	19. 8.85	Member, Commissioner, SS and NSDAP, Ostrowiec (Pol.) 40-44	60/197	MISC.CRIMES	POL.
FRODL, Ernst	304208	M		Cpl., Nachtjagd-Gr.No.4, vicinity of Charleroi (Bel.) 2.44	58/203	MURDER	BEL.
FROEHLICH, Hans Dr.	265693	M	8. 9.09	Kreisleiter, NSDAP, Stribro (Czech.) 40	-	MISC.CRIMES	CZECH.
FROH	303615	M	24. 4.21	SS-Mann, C.C. Majdanek (Pol.) 40-44	57/291	BRUTALITY	POL.
FROHBERG, Heinz	198025	M		Agent, SD, Maisons-Laffitte (Fr.) 15.12.41-10.6.45	30/178	MISC.CRIMES	FR.
FROHLICH, Michael	303616	M	23. 7.11	SS-Mann, C.C. Majdanek (Pol.) 40-44	57/292	BRUTALITY	POL.
FROLICH, Willi	304640	M		Member, Gestapo, Krakau (Pol.) 11.39-2.45	59/169	BRUTALITY	POL.
FROMHAGE	266508	M	circa 12	Lt., 15 Pz.Div., Semur (Fr.) 25.8.44	-	MURDER	FR.
FROMMER	304180	M		SS-Rottfhr., Member of Jewish Depart.of SD and Sipo, Krakau, Bochnia (Pol.) 42-43	58/204	MURDER	POL.
FRONTZEK, Wilhelm	304641	M		Member, Gestapo, Krakau (Pol.) 11.39-2.45	59/170	BRUTALITY	POL.
FROSCH	303118	M		W.O., Feldgend., Dinan, Cotes-Du-Nord (Fr.) 8.44 and 11.44	56/214	MURDER	FR.
FROSLER, Gerd	267206	M	15 or 17	Oschfhr., Gestapo, Marseille and vicinity (Fr.)	-	MURDER	FR.
FROTSCH	142494	M		SS-Uschfhr., C.C., Buchenwald (Ger.) 38-43	25/155	MURDER	BEL.
FRUCHTENICHT, Otto	304642	M		Member, Gestapo, Krakau (Pol.) 11.39-2.45	59/171	BRUTALITY	POL.
FUCHS	148026	M	98	SS-Hptsturmfhr., Cmdt., Camp Royallieu (Fr.) 41-44	30/179 31/210	MURDER	FR.
FUCHS	198027	M	14	SS-Sturmbannfhr., Adjutant, Camp-Commander Biebow, Radom, Lodz (Pol.) 42	-	MURDER	POL., CZECH.
FUCHS	265226	M		Sgt., Police, Albenga (It.) 44-45	-	MURDER	U.K.
FUCHS	304643	M		Oberwachtmstr., Commander, Crim.Police, Zawiercie (Pol.) 40-43	59/172	MURDER	POL.
FUCHS	304644	M		Capt., Commander, Schupo, Zawiercie (Pol.) 42-43	59/174	MURDER	POL.
FUCHS, Johann	304645	M		Member, Gestapo, Krakau (Pol.) 11.39-2.45	59/175	BRUTALITY	POL.
FUESSEL (see FUESSEZ)	265992						
FUESSSZ (or FUESSEL)	265992	M		Member, Feldgendarmerie, Cholet (Fr.) 7.,8.8.44	56/216	MURDER	FR.
FUGGER	198104	M		SS-Uschfhr., Guard, C.C., Member of SS-Institute of Hygiene, Auschwitz (Pol.) 40-45	16/319	MURDER	FR., POL.
FUHR, Hans	304646	M		Member, Gestapo, Krakau (Pol.) 11.39-2.45	59/176	BRUTALITY	POL.
FUHRMANN, Ilse	304647	F		Member, Gestapo, Krakau (Pol.) 11.39-2.45	59/177	MURDER	POL.
FULLRIEDE	198088	M		Lt.Col., Army, Airforce, Hermann Goering-Troops, Putten, Hardewijk (Neth.) 10.44	30/355	MURDER	NETH.
FUNCK	265472	M		SS-Sturmschfhr., SD, Chalons-sur-Marne (Fr.) 43-44	-	MISC.CRIMES	FR.
FUNDHELLER, Ernst	304648	M		Member, Gestapo, Krakau (Pol.) 11.39-2.45	59/178	MURDER	POL.
FUR	265686	M		Driver, SD, SS-Mann, Gestapo of Mans (Sarthe) Sarthe and Mayenne (Fr.) 42-44	-	SUSPECT	FR.
FURST, Peter	304649	M		Member, Gestapo, Krakau (Pol.) 11.39-2.45	59/179	MURDER	POL.
FURTINGER, Aurel	156655	M	25. 9.23	SS-Mann, Waffen-SS, Pz.Gren.A.u.E. 12 Bn.,7 Stamm-Coy. (or 1 SS-Pz.Gren.A.u.E.) Anhee, Yvoir-Meuse (Bel.) 4.9.44	13/27	MURDER	BEL.
FUSCHER	303120	M		Guard, C.C., Wolfenbuettel (Braunschweig) (Ger.) 44-45	56/220	TORTURE	FR.
FUSEL	303617	M		Member, Gestapo, Warschau (Pol.) 10.39-1.45	57/295	BRUTALITY	POL.
GAA, Gerhard	304652	M		Member, Gestapo, Krakau (Pol.) 11.39-2.45	59/181	BRUTALITY	POL.
GABERLE, Alois	140481	M		SS-Usturmfhr., Hospital, C.C., Oranienburg, Sachsenhausen (Ger.) 42-45	32/217	MURDER	FR.
GABLER	267345	M		Cpl., Waffenwerkstatt 812, Charteaumeillant (Fr.) 27.6.44	-	MURDER	FR.
GABO, Stefan	303121	M		Staff of C.C., Breendonck, Prov.Antwerpen (Bel.) 40-44	56/221	MURDER	BEL.
GACH	31953	M		Sgt., Feldgendarmerie 577, Bde. de Remorantin, 43-44	8/156	MURDER	FR.
GADE, Gustav	303122	M		Kriminalsekretaer, Gestapo-Staff, Kattowitz (Pol.) 39-42	56/223	INTERR.	POL.
GAEDT, Wilhelm	303123	M		Member, Group 530 Geh.Feldpolizei, Bruessel (Bel.) 40-44	56/224	MURDER	BEL.
GAHER, Willi	303618	M	27. 7.03	SS-Mann, C.C. Majdanek (Pol.) 40-44	57/297	BRUTALITY	POL.
GAHN	266968	M		Feldgendarm, Feldgendarmerie, Sisteron (Fr.) 44	-	MISC.CRIMES	FR.
GAIER, Hans	265239	M		Kapo, C.C., Sachsenhausen (Ger.)	-	BRUTALITY	FR.
GAJEWSKI	266507	M		Capt., Commander of sector Bergues (Fr.) 16.9.44	-	MURDER	FR.
GALITZ	267529	M		Sgt., Feldgendarmerie, Besancon and vicinity (Fr.) 44	-	MURDER	FR.
GALL	100605	M		Crim.Asst. in Dept.II B Staatspolizeistelle Prague, Auschwitz-Birkenau (Pol.) 39-45	-	MURDER	CZECH.
GALLASINSKI	304183	M		Member, Schutzgruppen at the Laura-mine, Eigelshoven (Neth.) 8.-13.9.44	58/209	PILLAGE	NETH.
GALLBACH	303125	M		Feldpolizeisekretaer, Group 530 Geh.Feldpolizei, Bruessel (Bel.) 40-44	56/226	MURDER	BEL.
GALLINGER	23831	M	circa 05	Hptsturmfhr., SD and Army, Vichy (Fr.) 8.44	-	MURDER	FR.
GALLISH	161200	F		Member, Gestapo St.Quentin, Vraignes en Vermandois-Somme (Fr.) 29.8.44	-	MURDER	FR.
GAM	265334	M		Major, Army, Sumetljica near Nova Gradiska (Yugo.) 28.7.43	-	INTERR.	YUGO.
GANDT	198105	M		Kapo, C.C., Auschwitz (Pol.)	16/323	MURDER	POL., FR.
GANSAR	266987	M		Chief-Cpl., Flakmast 30-XII, Baudrigues near Carcassonne (Fr.) 19.8.44	-	MURDER	FR.
GANSMANNS (see MANNS, Hans)	266222						
GANZ, Andreas	266940	M	7. 4.05	Uschfhr., Gestapo, Geh.Feldpolizei 733, Paris (Fr.) 7.41-44	-	SUSPECT	FR.
GAPPMAYER	267116	M		Gendarm, Gendarmerie, Sencur near Kranj (Yugo.) 8.3.-5.5.42	-	MURDER	YUGO.
GARAND	303619	M		Member, Gestapo, Warschau (Pol.) 39-45	57/300	BRUTALITY	POL.
GARBLER, Julius	304653	M		Member, Gestapo, Krakau (Pol.) 11.39-2.45	59/182	BRUTALITY	POL.

GAR - GIE

NAME	C.R.FILE NUMBER	SEX	DATE OF BIRTH	RANK OCCUPATION UNIT PLACE AND DATE OF CRIME	UNWCC LIST/ SERIAL NO.	REASON WANTED	WANTED BY
GAREIS, Georg	304185	M		Lt.,Commanding Officer of F.P.No.56 391, Argos (Grc.)9.44	58/212	BRUTALITY	GRC.
GAREISS, Rudolphe	267091	M		Capt.,19.Pol.SS-Regt.,3.Bn.,10.Coy.,Limoges,Brives (Fr.)44	-	MURDER	FR.
GARGAM	266161	M		Member,SS,Longeville,Villedieu (Fr.) 15.8.44	-	MURDER	FR.
GARSCHEM	266194	M		Sgt.,Feldgendarmerie,Valenciennes (Fr.) 40-44	-	MURDER	FR.
GARTNER, Paul	266162	M		Capt.,Albert (Fr.) 23.7.44	-	MURDER	FR.
GARTSKE, Herbert	267254	M	05 - 07	Chief Sgt.-Major,2.Paratrooper-Div.,Brest (Fr.) 7.-8.44	-	MURDER	FR.
GARUS, Peter	304654	M		Member,Gestapo,Krakau (Pol.) 11.39- 2.45	59/183	BRUTALITY	POL.
GASCHLER, Arthur	266735	M	12.11.00	Political controller,NSDAP,Fittings Works,Lagieniki (Pol.)39-44	-	BRUTALITY	POL.
GASTINGER	266986	M		Chief Sgt.-Major,Feldgendarmerie,Sisteron (Fr.) 44	-	MISC.CRIMES	FR.
GAUBATZ, Paul	185145	M		Chief,Block C.C. Oranienburg,Sachsenhausen (Ger.) 42-45	32/219	MURDER	FR.
GAUMANN, Johann	303129	M		Kriminalbeamter,Gestapo Staff,Kattowitz (Pol.) 39-42	56/230	BRUTALITY	POL.
GAUWEILER, Willy	198106	M		SS-Mann, C.C. Auschwitz (Pol.)	16/326 40/409	MURDER	POL. FR.
GAWELEK, Franz	303131	M		Kriminalbeamter,Staff of Gestapo,Kattowitz (Pol.) 39-42	56/232	BRUTALITY	POL.
GAWENDA, Fritz	304655	M		Osturmfhr.,Head,Gestapo,Sosnowiec-Bendzin (Pol.) 42	59/184	INTERR.	POL.
GAWLIK, Franz	303132	M		Kriminalsekretaer,Gestapo Staff,Kattowitz (Pol.) 39-42	56/233	INTERR.	POL.
GEBAUER	303133	M		Cpl.,Group 530 Geh.Feldpolizei,Bruessel (Bel.) 40-44	56/234	MURDER	BEL.
GEBAUER (I)	308829	F		Crim.Employee,Radom (Pol.) 1.40-1.45	60/201	MURDER	POL.
GEBAUER (II)	308830	M		Interpreter,Radom (Pol.) 1.40-1.45	60/202	MURDER	POL.
GEBAUER, Willi	308831	M		Member,Selbstschutz,Grudziadz (Pol.) 39	60/203	MURDER	POL.
GEBEL, Frantz	266517	M		Sgt.,G.F.P.,Arras (Fr.) 8.41	-	MURDER	FR.
GEBHART, Paul	267344	M		Hauptscharfhr.,Gestapo,Marseille and environ (Fr.)	-	MURDER	FR.
GEBRAERT	304186	M		Cpl.,Member,Group 648 of the GFP,Liege (Bel.) Betw.40 and 44	58/214	TORTURE	BEL.
GEERAERT (or GERARD or GERHARD)	266715	M		Director,Admin.service of highways,Mont s.Marchienne nr.Charleroi (Bel.) 9.4.41	-	WITNESS	BEL.
GEGKE	265453	M		W.O.,Sainte-Anne-D'Auray (Fr.) 5.8.44	-	MURDER	FR.
GEHL, Friedrich	266131	M		See names listed under "Special Headings"			
GEHRING	267343	M		Major,Feldkommandantur d'Epinal,Grandrupt-les-Nains & Hennezel (Fr.) 7.9.44	-	MURDER	FR.
GEHRMANN	265666	M		Sgt.,558 Regt.der Infanterie, 13.Coy.,Bruay en Artois (Fr.)9.44	-	SUSPECT	FR.
GEIDEL	308832	M		SS-Sturmscharfhr., Secretary of Administration,Radom (Pol.) 1.40- 1.45	60/205	PILLAGE	POL.
GEIKO	267493	M		Commanding Officer,Airforce,91.Regt.,Chantraine (Fr.)20.u.22.8.44	-	MURDER	FR.
GEILEN, Magda	196104	F		Member,Gestapo,St.Quentin,Vraignes en Vermandois (Somme) (Fr.) 29.8.44	-	MURDER	FR.
GEIPEL	303620	M		Member,Gestapo,Warschau (Pol.) 39-45	57/308	BRUTALITY	POL.
GEISLER (II)	303622	M		Member,Gestapo,Warschau (Pol.) 10.39-1.45	57/310	BRUTALITY	POL.
GEISSLER (I)	303621	M		Member,Gestapo,Warschau (Pol.) 10.39-1.45	57/309	BRUTALITY	POL.
GEISSLER, Karl	267342	M		Agent,Gestapo,Marseille and environ (Fr.)	-	MURDER	FR.
GELEHRT, Julius	304187	M		Supervisor,Polish workers,Schonau nr.Bergedorf (Ger.) 3.45	58/219	MURDER	POL.
GELMONT	265993	M		Lt.,5.Coy.,200.Mot.Gren.Regt.,90.Pz.Gren.Div.,La Condamine Chatelard (Fr.) 27.,28.,29.8.44	-	INCENDIARISM	FR.
GEMS, Erich	267338	M		Oscharfhr.,SD d'Epinal,Grandrupt-les-Bains and Hennezel (Fr.)9.44	-	MURDER	FR.
GENDZMAJER, Zenon	304656	M		Member,Gestapo,Krakau (Pol.) 11.39-2.45	59/185	PILLAGE	POL.
GENEK	303134	M		SS-Scharfhr.,Gestapo,Lodz (Pol.) 39-44	56/237	MURDER	POL.
GENG	304188	M		Member,Schutzgr.,Laura Mine,Eigelshoven (Neth.) 8.-13.9.44	58/222	PILLAGE	NETH.
GENL	267126	M		Capt.,Army,37.Regt.,118.Alpenjager Div.,Village of Borovec (Yugo.) 19.u. 21. 3.44	-	INCENDIARISM	YUGO.
GENSEL, Hermann (or GENZEL, Erik or GUNSLER, Hermann)	23833	M	28. 4.04	Oschfhr.,Civ.Police Service Gruppe Geh.Polizei 733,Gestapo KDS IV E 4, Paris (Fr.) 43-44	-	SUSPECT	FR.
GENZEL, Erik (see GENSEL, Hermann)	23833						
GEORG	304189	M		Driver,Town-Major,Piraeus (Grc.) 6.41	58/223	PILLAGE	GRC.
GERARD (see GEERAERT)	266715						
GERBER	265994	M		Engineer, Kodak factories Commission Koch,Bordes,Scues (Fr.)43	-	PILLAGE	FR.
GERCKE	303624	M		Member,Gestapo,Warschau (Pol.) 39-45	57/312	BRUTALITY	POL.
GERDUNG, Gustav	304190	M		Politischer Leiter,Rude,Distr.of Chelm (Pol.) 39	58/226	BRUTALITY	POL.
GERECKE, Albert	303135	M		Kriminalbeamter,Staff of Gestapo,Kattowitz (Pol.) 39-42	56/239	INTERR.	POL.
GERERHLEIN	304191	M		Cpl.,Nachtjagd Group No.4,Vicinity of Charleroi (Bel.) 2.44	58/227	MURDER	BEL.
GERHARD (see GEERAERT)	266715						
GERHARD	304657	M		SS-Gruppfhr.,Steenwijkerwold nr.Steenwijk (Kallenkote) (Neth.) 2.10.44-13.10.44	59/186	MURDER	NETH.
GERHARDT	131720	M		SS-Mann,SS, Velmenya (Fr.) 1.8.44	13/415	MURDER	FR.
GERHARDT	303136	M		Lt.,Feldgendarmerie, Reg.of Cholet (Fr.) 7.u.8.8.44	56/240	MURDER	FR.
GERHER (see GERNER)	263321			See names listed under "Special Headings"			
GERICKE	266516	M		W.O.,1.Coy.,6.Paratrooper-Div.,Panz.Jaeger,Chateau de Miannay (Fr.) 43-44	-	PILLAGE	
GERKE	303625	M		Member,Gestapo,Warschau (Pol.) 39-45	57/313	BRUTALITY	POL.
GERLACH, Otto	304658	M		Member,Gestapo,Krakau (Pol.) 11.39- 2.45	59/187	PILLAGE	POL.
GERNER (or GERHER)	263321	M		See names listed under "Special Headings"	-	MURDER	FR.
GERSTENMEYER, Rudolf	267341	M		Unterschfhr.,Interpreter,Gestapo,Marseille and environ (Fr.)	-	MURDER	FR.
GERSTL, Karl	303165	M		Hptkriminal-Asst.,Gestapo Staff,Kattowitz (Pol.) 39-42	56/243	MURDER	POL.
GERSTNER	265657	M		Major,Commandant 1 Fallschirmpionierabteilung 2 F.J.Div. Brest (Fr.) 8.-9.44	-	MURDER	FR.
GESTER, Eduard	303166	M		Cpl.,Group 530 Geh.Feldpolizei,Bruessel (Bel.) 40-44	56/244	MURDER	BEL.
GIEBEL, Wilhelm	308833	M		Pvt.,G.F.P.,Antwerpen,Bruessel (Bel.) 40-45	60/207	MURDER	BEL.
GIESE	266132	M		Member,SS-Staff,C.C. Giebow nr.Halle (Ger.) 42	-	MURDER	POL.
GIESE (see GUISE)	267519						
GIESE, Erich	303690	M	27.11.09	SS-Sturmann,C.C. Majdanek (Pol.) 40-44	57/317	PILLAGE	POL.
GIESS (or GIESSE)	265995	M	circa 95	Interpreter,German customs official,Custom house,Montceau le Mines,Saint Vallier (Fr.) 42-44	-	MURDER	FR.
GIESS, Robert Dr.	132299	M	02	SS-Standartenfhr.,SA,SD,Chief of the SD,State Service,Chief of the Ministeramt,Prag, Berlin (Czech.;Ger.) 39-45	-	MISC.CRIMES	CZECH.
GIESSE (see GIESS)	265995						

GIE - GOS

NAME	C.R.FILE NUMBER	SEX	DATE OF BIRTH	RANK OCCUPATION UNIT PLACE AND DATE OF CRIME	UNWCC LIST/ SERIAL NO.	REASON WANTED	WANTED BY
GIESSLER, Peter	304659	M		Member, Gestapo, Krakau (Pol.) 11.39-2.45	59/188	PILLAGE	POL.
GILBERG	144272	M	circa 04	SS-Rottenfhr.,SS, member, Gestapo, Abt.I, Vichy (Fr.) 44	16/63	MURDER	FR.
GILCH, Johann	304193	M		SS-Oscharfhr., Volkssturm, Mayor, near Mühldorf (Ger.) 15.4.45	58/234	BRUTALITY	U.S.
GILKEV, Martin	267255	M		Oscharfhr., Gestapo, Bordeaux and vicinity (Fr.) 42-8.44	-	MURDER	FR.
GINAL, Josef	303626	M	1.8.24	SS-Mann, C.C., Majdanek (Pol.) 40-44	57/320	BRUTALITY	POL.
GINDEL	110793	M	.98	SS-Sturmbannfhr.,Polizeirat,Chief, Gestapo, Abt.I, Bruessel and other towns (Bel.) 6.44-9.44	28/67	MURDER	BEL.
GLANER, Heinrich	304194	M		Cpl., 4 Coy., Pion.Bn.538, Otwock (Pol.) 39-45	58/236	MURDER	POL.
GIAS, Else	304660	F		Member, Gestapo, Krakau (Pol.) 11.39-2.45	59/189	MURDER	POL.
GLASER	304661	M		Oberwachtmeister, Schupo, Jerozolimska Camp, Krakau (Pol.) 43	59/190	MURDER	POL.
GLASS	266163	M		Pvt., 1 Sect., 6 Coy., Regt. Ruxleben, Afrika Corps, Hte. Marne-Aube (Fr.) 25.-31.8.44	-	MURDER	FR.
GLEICH, Dr.	304195	M		Solicitor, Civilian, Kommissar of F.P., Group 648, Liege (Bel.) 40-44	58/238	TORTURE	BEL.
GLIENKE	308835	M		SS-Hptsturmfhr., Kriminalrat, Radom (Pol.) 1.40-1.45	60/209	MURDER	POL.
GLIENKE, Friedrich	304662	M		Member, Gestapo, Krakau (Pol.) 11.39-2.45	59/191	BRUTALITY	POL.
GLIETSCH, Willi	303169	M		Kriminalbeamter, Gestapo staff, Kattowitz (Pol.) 39-42	56/250	PILLAGE	POL.
GLIETZ	29877	M	circa 10	Lt., Army, 4 Coy., Landesschuetzen-Bn.714, Stalag XX A, Camin, Hannover, Hildesheim (Ger.) 3.-4.45	27/794	BRUTALITY	U.K.
GLINDERMANN, Wilhelm	308836	M		Civilian, vicinity of Walle (Ger.) 44	60/210	BRUTALITY	U.S.
GLINZER, Josef	262512	M	94	See names listed under "Special Headings"			
GLOBISCH, Alois	304669	M		Member, Gestapo, Krakau (Pol.) 11.39-2.45	59/192	MURDER	POL.
GLOCKNER	303627	M		Member, Gestapo, Warschau (Pol.) 39-45	57/326	BRUTALITY	POL.
GLOCKNER, Lorenz	144281	M	31.5.02	Wm.d.Schutzpolizei d.R.,2 SS-Pol.Regt.19		SUSPECT	FR.
GLOECKNER	186413	M		SS-Hptsturmfhr., Gestapo, Offensive Rundstedt, Commander of Sec.Pol.z.b.V.Vianden, Luxemburg (Lux.) 12.44-1.45	16/774	MURDER	LUX.
GLOOS, Kurt	266378	M	circa 18	Lt., 1 Section, 6 Coy., Regt. Ruxleben, Africa Corps, Bar s-Seine, Mesnil St.Pere (Fr.) 25.-31.8.44	-	MURDER	FR.
GLOWIK, Heinz	265985	M	circa 12	SS-Mann, SS, Lapugnoy (Fr.) 31.5.40	-	MISC.CRIMES	FR.
GNADT, Paul	304664	M		Member, Gestapo, Krakau (Pol.) 11.39-2.45	59/193	MURDER	POL.
GOBBEL, Mathias	303628	M	10.10.08	SS-Mann, C.C., Majdanek (Pol.) 40-44	57/329	MURDER	POL.
GOBBEL, Michael	303629	M	30.7.10	SS-Mann, C.C., Majdanek (Pol.) 40-44	57/330	BRUTALITY	POL.
GODDECKE	267340	M		Oscharfhr., Gestapo, Marseille and vicinity (Fr.)	-	MURDER	FR.
GODE	144602	M		Chief, German Police, Briancon (Fr.)	-	SUSPECT	FR.
GODECKE	266377	M		Manager, Purchase Office, Black Market, (Fr.) 42-44	-	PILLAGE	FR.
GODENSCHWEGER, Olga	304665	F		Member, Gestapo, Krakau (Pol.) 11.39-2.45	59/194	MURDER	POL.
GODIREC (or GOUIDEC)	144598	M	23	Member, SD (formation "Perrot"), Rennes (Fr.)	-	SUSPECT	FR.
GOEBBEL	267339	M		Lt., Sqadron Udet, Air Force, L 34756, Senon (Fr.) 28.8.44	-	MURDER	FR.
GOEBBEL	304666	M		Wachtmeister, Gendarmerie, Bochnia (Pol.) 43	59/195	MURDER	POL.
GOEBBEL, Charles	265454	M		Appraiser, Customs Field Police, F.P.Nr.18446 R, Barcelonnette (Fr.) 6.44	-	MISC.CRIMES	FR.
GOEBBELE	144603	M		Member, Gestapo, Chambery (Fr.)	-	SUSPECT	FR.
GOEBEL (or GOEBBELS or WIRTH)	144600	M		Major-C.O., SD, Gestapo, Group 737, Arras and region (Fr.) 41-44	-	MURDER	FR.
GOEBEL, Paul	304196	M		Member, SS, near Salzburg (Aust.), 10. or 11.44	58/239	MURDER	U.S.
GOEBBELS (see GOEBEL)	144600						
GOECHEL (or GOECKEL)	266379	M		Sgt., Army, Heeresabnahmestelle, Besancon (Fr.) 8.44	-	PILLAGE	FR.
GOECKEL (see GOECHEL)	266379						
GOECKEL, Manfred	265295	M		Pvt., Regt. "Brandenburg", (It.)	-	SUSPECT	U.K.
GOEGTS, Henri	144597	M		Lt., Gestapo, Valenciennes (Fr.)	-	SUSPECT	FR.
GOEMANN, Reinhard	304667	M		Member, Secr.Field Police, (Bel.) 40-41	59/196	MURDER	BEL.
GOERING	265229	M		Lt., "Hermann Goering"-Div., Partina, Moscaio (It.) 4.44	-	SUSPECT	U.K.
GOETSCH, Werner	304668	M		SS-Hptsturmfhr., SS, SD, Stechovice near Prag (Czech.)	59/197	MURDER	CZECH.
GOETTING, Wilhelm	303170	M		Feldgendarmerie, Dinan, Cotes-du-Nord (Fr.) 8. and 11.44	56/254	MURDER	FR.
GOETZ, Hans	144593	M	99	Lt., Gestapo, Valenciennes (Fr.) 12.42	-	SUSPECT	FR.
GOETZ, Karl	264524	M	11.3.03	See names listed under "Special Headings"			
GOETZIOF, Helmut	267129	M		Lt., Army, 893 Regt., Sinj (Yugo.) 8.9.43-10.44	-	MURDER	YUGO.
GOGL	186009	M		SS-Oscharfhr., Kdo.-Stab at C.C. Mauthausen (Aust.) 11.42-5.45	25/903	MURDER	FR.
GOGOL, Heinrich	129358	M		Agent, Gestapo at Paris, Fontenay-Rohan and Mauze (Fr.) 3.6.43, 44	30/183	PILLAGE	FR.
GOHL, Albert	303631	M	7.4.04	SS-Mann, C.C., Majdanek (Pol.) 40-44	57/334	BRUTALITY	POL.
GOHLBERG	308837	M		Cpl., Antwerpen and Bruessel (Bel.) 40-44	60/212	MURDER	BEL.
GOHNWETS	198108	M		SS-Mann, C.C., Auschwitz (Pol.)	16/335	MURDER	POL.,FR.
GOLAK	304669	M		SS-Mann, SS, Camp near Lublin (Pol.) 43	59/198	MURDER	POL.
GOLDAMMER, Edmund	304670	M		Member, Gestapo, Krakau (Pol.) 11.39-2.45	59/199	BRUTALITY	POL.
GOLDBERG, Franz	125030	M	29.9.19	Cpl., Gestapo, Montbeliard (Doubs), Vandoncourt (Fr.) 10. and 19.8.44	13/422	MURDER	FR.
GOLDITZ, Ella	304671	F		Member, Gestapo, Krakau (Pol.) 11.39-2.45	59/200	MURDER	POL.
GOLL, Anton	303632	M	7.8.19	SS-Mann, C.C., Majdanek (Pol.) 40-44	57/337	BRUTALITY	POL.
GOLIAN	144570	M		Feldgendarm, Feldgendarmerie, Brive (Fr.)	-	SUSPECT	FR.
GOLIMANN, Paul	267118	M	12.1.94	Gendarmeriepostenfuehrer, Gendarmerie, Slov.Konjice (Yugo.)41-44	-	MISC.CRIMES	YUGO.
GOLINER, Erich	304672	M		Member, Gestapo, Krakau (Pol.) 11.39-2.45	59/201	BRUTALITY	POL.
GOLONKA, Josef	304673	M		Member, Gestapo, Krakau (Pol.) 11.39-2.45	59/202	MURDER	POL.
GONTCHAROFF	266302	M		Interpreter of Schellhorn, Agent, Gestapo, Nantes and region (Fr.) 43-44	-	MURDER	FR.
GONTOW	266303	M		Pvt., 1 Section, 6 Coy., Regt. Ruxleben, Africa-Corps, Hte. Marne-Aube (Fr.) 25.-31.8.44	-	MURDER	FR.
GOOS, Berend	148179	M		Chief, SA, Cacassonne (Fr.)	-	MISC.CRIMES	FR.
GORBACH	148875	M		SS-Usturmfhr., Waffen-SS, Pz.Div."Das Reich", (Fr.) 44	11/89	MURDER	FR.
GOREING, Friedrich	266850	M	17.1.11	Agent, SD, Nice (Fr.) 44	-	SUSPECT	FR.
GORJES	266971	M		Feldgendarm, Feldgendarmerie, Sisteron (Fr.) 44	-	MISC.CRIMES	FR.
GORLL, Fritz	303171	M		Crim.secretary, Gestapo-Staff, Kattowitz (Pol.) 39-42	56/255	MURDER	POL.
GORTZ	198109	F	circa 17	C.C., Auschwitz (Pol.)	16/336	MISC.CRIMES	POL.,FR.
GORZAWSKI, Josef	303172	M		Technical asst., Gestapo-Staff, Kattowitz (Pol.) 39-42	56/256	PILLAGE	POL.
GORZITZE, Guenther	304198	M		Pvt., Flak-Abt.4-815, Texel (Neth.) 10.4.45	58/242	MURDER	NETH.
GOSS	127084	M		Pvt. (Brigadier) of Customs at Delle-Belfort (Fr.) 23.4.42, 25.1.43, 22.7.44	13/424	MURDER	FR.
GOSTIK (see KOSTIK)	265876						

GOT - GRO

NAME	C.R.FILE NUMBER	SEX	DATE OF BIRTH	RANK OCCUPATION UNIT PLACE AND DATE OF CRIME	UNWCC LIST/ SERIAL NO.	REASON WANTED	WANTED BY
GOTMANN, Eugen	267346	M		Rottfhr., Gestapo, Marseille and vicinity (Fr.)	-	MURDER	FR.
GOTTMANN, Albin	156654	M	28.4.24	SS-Mann, Waffen SS, Pz.Gren.A.u.E., 12 Bn., 7 Stamm Coy. or 1 SS Pz.Gren.A.u.E., 12 Bn., Anhee-Yuoir-Meuse (Bel.) 4.9.44	13/29	MURDER	BEL.
GOTTSCHALK, Karl	266736	M		Stabsscharfhr., Crim.Secr., Gestapo, Luebeck (Ger.) 44	-	MURDER	POL.
GOTTSMANN, Herbert	304574	M		Member, Gestapo, Krakau (Pol.) 11.39-2.45	59/203	MURDER	POL.
GOTZ, Dr.	267294	M	18.8.07	Usturmfhr., BDS IV 2/3, Interpreter (Funkspiele), Paris (Fr.) 42-44	-	SUSPECT	FR.
GOTZ, Xaver	304199	M		Civilian, Gernsbach u.Oberstrot, nr.Weisenbach (Ger.) 9.8.44	58/244	MURDER	U.S.
GOUBERT GANDY, Hans	266897	M	circa 15	Pvt., Unit 12061-3, Hautmont (Fr.) 24.6.44	-	MISC.CRIMES	FR.
GOUIDEC (see GODIREC)	144598						
GRABE, Hans	266304	M	circa 05	Oscharfhr., Gestapo, Nantes and region, (Fr.) 43-44	-	MURDER	FR.
GRABOWSKI, Willi	303174	M		Kriminalbeamter, Gestapo, Kattowitz (Pol.) 39-42	56/260	INTERR.	POL.
GRACZYK	303633	M		Member, Gestapo, Warschau (Pol.) 39-45	57/342	BRUTALITY	POL.
GRADNIG	266305	M		Oscharfhr., SS-Div."Das Reich", 2 Art.Btty., 1 Section, Selles sur Cher (Fr.) 14.-15.8.44	-	MURDER	FR.
GRADZ, Karl Dr.	304675	M		Member, Gestapo, Krakau (Pol.) 11.39-2.45	59/204	BRUTALITY	POL.
GRAEF, Heinrich	303634	M	4.8.11	SS-Mann, C.C.Majdanek (Pol.) 40-44	57/343	MURDER	POL.
GRAEMER (see GRAMER)	95056						
GRAETER, Ludwig	148165	M	08	Employee, Gestapo, Strassburg (Fr.)	-	SUSPECT	FR.
GRAEWE	266250	M		German chief manager, Sendoux factories, Le Cateau (Fr.) 1.9.44	-	INCENDIARISM	FR.
GRAF	131719	M		Lt., Interpreter, Operating at Velmanya (Pyr.) (Fr.) 1.8.44	13/425	MURDER	FR.
GRAF	265785	M		C.C., Lublin-Majdanek (Pol.)	-	MISC.CRIMES	POL.
GRAF	303635	M		Member, Gestapo, Warschau (Pol.) 39-45	57/344	BRUTALITY	POL.
GRAF, Anny	266247	F	9.4.20	Meteorological asst., Meteorological Observatory, Le Bourget (Fr.)	-	SUSPECT	FR.
GRAF, Helmut	304676	M		Member, Gestapo, Krakau (Pol.) 11.39-2.45	59/205	MURDER	POL.
GRAF, Hermann	265783	M	15.3.20	Unterwachtmeister, C.C., Chelmno (Pol.) 42-44	-	MURDER	POL.
GRAFF	266972	M		Sgt., Gestapo, SD, Besancon, Numerous Towns in Doubs and Haute Saone Department (Fr.) 43-44	-	MISC.CRIMES	FR.
GRAFF (or GREEF)	304201	M		Member, G.F.P., Bruessel (Bel.) 40-44	58/247	MURDER	BEL.
GRAFF (or KRAFFT)	304202	M		Lt.Commander, Jagd-Kdo. at Grasse (Alpes-Maritimes), Chacedon-Norante (B.Alpes) (Fr.) 5.7.44	58/248	MURDER	FR.
GRAHN, Friedel	267386		05	Sgt., Waffenwerkstatt 812, Chateaumeillant (Fr.) 27.6.44	-	MURDER	FR.
GRAMER (or GRAEMER)	95056	M	10 or 13	Medical officer, Capt., Erica Grube Coal Mine, Army, Hoyerswerda nr.Dresden (Ger.) 3.41-4.45	31/377	TORTURE	U.K.
GRASSHOFF, Paul	267387	M	86	Manager, Agricultural Servies of Epinal, Belmont-sur-Vair (Fr.) 13.-14.5.45	-	MISC.CRIMES	FR.
GRASSL	265455	M		SS-Guard, C.C.Struthof-Natzweiler (Fr.) 15.7.43	-	MURDER	FR.
GRASSNER, Gunther	303176	M		Feldpolizeikommissar, Group 530, Geh.Feldpolizei, Bruessel (Bel.) 40-44	56/262	MURDER	BEL.
GRATZ, Peter	303636	M	9.4.08	SS-Mann, C.C.Majdanek (Pol.) 40-44	57/351	BRUTALITY	POL.
GRAUBERGER, Johann	303637	M	11.6.00	SS-Mann, C.C.Majdanek (Pol.) 40-44	57/353	BRUTALITY	POL.
GRAUL	265817	M		SS-Osturmfhr., Member, Sipo, Tarnow (Pol.) 43	-	MURDER	POL.
GRAUL, Hans Dr.	265784	M	4.7.09	Employee, Institut f.deutsche Ostarbeit, Krakau (Pol.)	-	PILLAGE	POL.
GRAUPNER	304677	M		Hauptwachtmeister, Schutzpolizei, Sosnowiec-Bendzin (Pol.) 42-43	59/206	MURDER	POL.
GREATSCHUTZ (or GREITSCHUTZ)	265816	M		SS-Oscharfhr., Extermination Camp, Sobibor (Pol.) 42-43	-	MURDER	POL.
GREEF (see GRAFF)	304201						
GREESE, Karl	304678	M		Member, Gestapo, Krakau (Pol.) 11.39-2.45	59/207	MURDER	POL.
GREGER, Gerhard	265815	M	10	Inspector, Post office, Lublin (Pol.)	-	BRUTALITY	POL.
GREISHEIMER (or GRIESHEIMER)	266836	M	circa 00	Member, Feldgendarmerie 624 of Avallon (Yonne), Avallon region (Fr.) 44	-	MISC.CRIMES	FR.
GREISNER	265763	M		Member, of Staff, C.C.Dachau (Ger.)	-	MURDER	POL.
GREITSCHUTZ (see GREATSCHUTZ)	265816						
GREMER	265813	M		Employee, Ministry of Propaganda and education (Pol.)	-	PILLAGE	POL.
GRESIALZ	127088	M		Osturmfhr., SS, 2 SS Pz.Div."Das Reich", F.P.No.27310, 28454, 29883, 28900, Caussade (Fr.) 44	11/92	MURDER	FR.
GRESSER, Adolph	267490			Chief Sgt.Major, Airforce, 71 Inf.Regt., Dept.Aude & Herault (Fr.) 5.-8.44	-	MISC.CRIMES	FR.
GRETA	198111	M		SS-Staff, C.C. Auschwitz (Pol.) 40-45	16/341	MURDER	POL., FR.
GRETT, Erwin	265762	M	2.1.05	Member, NSDAP, SS (Pol.)	-	MISC.CRIMES	POL.
GREUZER	144540	M		Feldgendarm, Feldgendarmerie, Brive (Fr.)	-	SUSPECT	FR.
GRIEBEL, Wilhelm Peter	267561	M	29.4.97	Working inspector, Manager, state-coal-mine "Maurits", Gelsen, Limburg (Neth.) 9.44	58/251	MISC.CRIMES	NETH.
GRIEGER	266249	M		Pvt., Africa-Corps, Regt.Ruxleben, 6 Coy., 1 Section, Hte.Marne Aube (Fr.) 25.-31.8.44	-	MURDER	FR.
GRIESCHKE	303638	M		Member, Gestapo, Warschau (Pol.) 39-45	57/357	BRUTALITY	POL.
GRIESE	144538	M		Colonel, SD, 17 Pol.Regt., Marseille (Fr.) 4.43	-	SUSPECT	FR.
GRIESHEIMER (see GREISHEIMER)	266836						
GRILLER	267489	M		Sgt., Feldgendarmerie, Besancon and vicinity (Fr.) 44	-	MURDER	FR.
GRIMM	265761	M		Representative, SS-Oscharfhr., Camp Commandant, C.C.Plaszow (Pol.)	-	MURDER	POL.
GRIMM	144532	M		Hauptmann der Gendarmerie, Police, Kommandantur Muelhausen (Fr.)	-	SUSPECT	FR.
GRIMM	144533	M		Agent, Gestapo, Rennes (Fr.)	-	SUSPECT	FR.
GRIMM	144534	M		Member, SD, Troyes (Fr.) 5.44	-	SUSPECT	FR.
GRIMM	144535	M		SS-Gruppenfhr.und General der Polizei	-	SUSPECT	FR.
GRIMM (I)	303639	M		Member, Gestapo, Warschau (Pol.) 39-45	57/359	BRUTALITY	POL.
GRIMM (II)	303640	M		Member, Gestapo, Warschau (Pol.) 39-45	57/360	BRUTALITY	POL.
GRIMM	308840	M		Sonderfhr., G.F.P., Antwerpen and Bruessel (Bel.) 40-44	60/218	MURDER	BEL.
GRIMM, Lorenz	303641	M	26.8.19	Member, Gestapo, Warschau (Pol.) 40-44	57/361	BRUTALITY	POL.
GRIMMINGER	266248	M		Commander, Regt.Stuttgart, Pz.Regt.of Unit 61629, Mont s-Meurthe (Fr.) 30.8.44, 18.-19.9.44	-	PILLAGE	FR.
GRIPPENKARB	304205	M		Policeman at Jewer nr.Wilhelmshaven (Ger.) 44	58/253	MURDER	POL.
GRIST, Friedel	144526			Member, Gestapo, L.61181 LGPA Paris, Josselin (Fr.)	-	SUSPECT	FR.
GROB, Rudolf	127089	M		Usturmfhr., SS, 2 SS Pz.Div."Das Reich", F.P.No.59544, 06660, 00560, Caussade (Fr.) 44	11/94	MURDER	FR.
GROBEL	303642	M		Member, Gestapo, Warschau (Pol.) 39-45	57/364	BRUTALITY	BEL.
GROBER, Otto	127956	M		Sturmscharfhr.and Crim.Secr., Kripo, Gestapo, SD, Abt.IV C, Duesseldorf, Bruessel and other towns (Ger., Bel.) 3.44	28/69	MURDER	BEL.

GRO - GSCH

NAME	C.R.FILE NUMBER	SEX	DATE OF BIRTH	RANK	OCCUPATION	UNIT	PLACE AND DATE OF CRIME	UNWCC LIST/ SERIAL NO.	REASON WANTED	WANTED BY
GROEBER	304679	M			Wachtmeister, Gend., Wieliczka (Pol.) 40-42			59/208	MURDER	POL.
GROEBIN	304680	M			Hptschfhr., SS and Polizeifuehrer, Radom (Pol.) 42-43			59/209	MURDER	POL.
GROENITZ, Minna	303179	F			Nursery Institution, Lefitz, 6.44-11.44			56/265	MURDER	POL.
GROES (see GROSS)	265760									
GROHE	303178	M			Sgt., Feldgend.Angoulême, Chasseneuil Charente (Fr.) 43-44			56/264	MURDER	FR.
GROHS	266366	M			Prt., Africa Cop. Rgt. Ruxleben, 6 Coy. 1 Section Hte.Marne-Aube (Fr.) 25.-31.8.44			-	MURDER	FR.
GROM, Alfred	144521	M	24. 7.00		Member, Abwehr AST			-	SUSPECT	FR.
GROM, Hans	144520	M			Agent,SD. Section IV Aon IV E, Annecy (Fr.)			-	SUSPECT	FR.
GROMALA	304681	M			Wachtmeister, Wieliczka (Pol.) 39-42			59/210	MURDER	POL.
GROND, Erich	267388	M			Oschfhr., Gestapo, Marseille and vicinity (Fr.)			-	MURDER	FR.
GROSBOS	267492	M			Member, Gestapo, Luchon and vicinity (Fr.) 1.43-1.44			-	MURDER	FR.
GROSCHECK	303180	M			Feldpolizei Kommissar, Group 530 Geh.Feldpol. Bruessel (Bel.) 40-44			56/267	MURDER	BEL.
GROSE	146871	M			SS-Mann, SS Pz.Div."Das Reich" 2 Coy., Tulle (Fr.) 44			11/96	MURDER	FR.
GROSS	129623	M			SS-Oschfhr., C.C. Gusen, Mauthausen (Aust.) 41-45			-	MURDER	POL., BEL
GROSS	131738	M			SS-Osturmfhr., 2 SS Pz.Div. "Das Reich" Unit No. 28688 Venerque le Vernet (Fr.) 44			11/97	MURDER	FR.
GROSS	138260	M			SS-Oschfhr., Gestapo, Sub Section IV F, Lyon (Fr.) 43-44			38/282	MURDER	FR.
GROSS (or GROES)	265760	M	95		Driver, Post-Office, Chelm (Pol.) 42-44			-	MISC.CRIMES	POL.
GROSS	301259	M			Krim.Assistant, SD. Abt.IV A, Bruessel (Bel.) 40-44			28/70	MURDER	BEL.
GROSS, Gustav	265759	M			SS-Sturmmann, C.C. Plaszow, (Pol.)			-	TORTURE	POL.
GROSS, Hans	144514	M	12. 5.07		2 SS Pol.Rgt. 19, Civilian Shoemaker			-	SUSPECT	FR.
GROSS, Johann	308841	M			Oschfhr., Krim.Assistant, Gestapo, near Altwied (Ger.) 1.45			60/219	MURDER	U.S.
GROSS, Walter	266506	M			Sgt., Feldgend. 658, Paray le Monial and vicinity (Fr.) 43-44			-	SUSPECT	FR.
GROSS, Wilhelm	303643	M	28. 5.22		SS-Mann, C.C. Majdanek (Pol.) 40-44			57/369	MURDER	POL.
GROSSE, Karl, Otto	304206	M	16. 1.96		Pol.Leiter, Dienstgruppenleiter NSDAP, Gruppenfhr.-SA. Oberfhr., Kommandant of Schutzgruppen, Eigelshoven (Neth.)9.44			58/255	PILLAGE	NETH.
GROSSELHAUSEN	267256	M			Feldgendarm, Feldgend. Coy., Villers s.Coudon (Fr.) 8.44			-	MURDER	FR.
GROSSER	144511	M			Officer, SD.Section IV, Marseille (Fr.) 7.43			-	SUSPECT	FR.
GROSSER, Wilhelm or Albert, or Williams (called: Double zero)	267390	M	05		Hptschfhr., Gestapo, Marseille and vicinity (Fr.)			-	MURDER	FR.
GROSSKOPF (see GRUSSKOPF)	147288									
GROSSLER, Dr.	267389	M			Agent, Gestapo, Marseille and vicinity, (Fr.)			-	MURDER	FR.
GROSSMAN	303181	M			SS-Schfhr., Gestapo Lodz (Pol.) 39-44			56/270	MISC.CRIMES	POL.
GROSSMANN	265748	M			SS-Schfhr., Chief, Gestapo Section IV-4, Wielun, Lodz (Pol.)45			-	MISC.CRIMES	POL.
GROSSMANN	304682	M			Member, Attached to "Sonderbeauftragter fuer Fremdvoelkischen Arbeitseinsatz Ost", Sosnowiece (Pol.) 40-43			59/211	INTERR.	POL.
GROSSMANN, Artur	303182	M			Agent, Gestapo, Selbstschutz, Thorn (Pol.) 39			56/271	MURDER	POL.
GROSSMANN, Paul	303183	M			Kriminalbeamter, Gestapo Staff, Katowice (Pol.) 39-42			56/272	INTERR.	POL.
GROSSWANDT, Hans	192108	M	10.12.08		Member, Employee, Gestapo at Jicin (Czech.) 43-44			32/16	TORTURE	CZECH.
GROT, Paul	265746	M			SS-Uschfhr., Extermination Camp Sobior (Pol.) 42-43			-	MURDER	POL.
GROTH, Wilhelm	303184	M			Cpl., Group 530 Geh.Feldpol.H.Q.G.F.P. Bruessel (Bel.) 41-44			56/273	MISC.CRIMES	BEL.
GROTHE, Hermann	265747	M			Guard, Prison administration Krakow (Montelupich) (Pol.) 42			-	MURDER	POL.
GROTHESLUESCHEN	305856	M			Sgt., Army 377 Jaeger Rgt. 1 Coy. Rgt.B served under Capt. Lohmann, Vinkt, Meigem and vicinity (Flandern) (Bel.) 31.5.40			38/59	MURDER	BEL.
GRUBE, Max	304683	M	circa 98		Oschfhr., Secr.Field Pol.Sipo., Zwolle (Neth.) 10.4.45			59/212	MURDER	NETH.
GRUBER, Fr.	144509	M	95		Agent, SRA. Bruessel (Bel.)			-	SUSPECT	FR.
GRUBER	144510	M			Chief, Gestapo, Fontainebleau (Fr.)			-	SUSPECT	FR.
GRUBER	265779	M			Member, SS Staff C.C. Majdanek Lublin (Pol.)			-	MURDER	POL.
GRUBER, Annelise	304684	F			Member, Gestapo, Krakau (Pol.) 11.39-2.45			59/213	MURDER	POL.
GRUBER, Simon	304685	M			Member, Gestapo, Krakau (Pol.) 11.39-2.45			59/214	MURDER	POL.
GRUBER, Stefan	304686	M			Member, Gestapo, Krakau (Pol.) 11.39-2.45			59/215	BRUTALITY	POL.
GRUBERET	266505	M			Major, 9 SS Pz.Div. "Hohenstaufen", Unit No. 23474 Nimes (Fr.) 2.3.44			-	MURDER	FR.
GRUCA, Marian	304687	M			Member, Gestapo, Krakau (Pol.) 11.39-2.45			59/216	BRUTALITY	POL.
GRUCHOTT, Franz	303185	M			Kriminalbeamter, Gestapo Staff, Kattowitz (Pol.) 39-42			56/275	MURDER	POL.
GRUDNO	303644	M			Member, Gestapo, Warschau (Pol.) 39-45			57/373	BRUTALITY	POL.
GRUEHN	144508	M	10		expert radio, SRA. Bruessel (Bel.)			-	SUSPECT	FR.
GRUEMMER	265778	M			SS-Oschfhr., Staff C.C. Sobibor (Pol.) 42-43			-	MURDER	POL.
GRUEN	265777	M			Finance-Inspector, Finance-office, Chelm (Pol.) 40			-	MISC.CRIMES	POL.
GRUEN	304688	M			SS-Mann, Jerozolimska Camp, Krakau (Pol.) 43			59/217	MURDER	POL.
GRUENER, Aleksander	266737	M	20. 3.02		Section-Chief, of the Power Station, Krakau (Pol.) 41-45			-	MISC.CRIMES	POL.
GRUMBERG (see GRUNBERG)	266367									
GRUN	265552	M			Major, Army, Civitella (It.) 7.44			-	MURDER	U.K.
GRUNBERG (or GRUMBERG)	266367				Unit L 61629, L.G.P.A. Frankfurt Main, Benamenil (Fr.) 31.8.44			-	PILLAGE	FR.
GRUNBERG, Max	303186	M			Sgt., Group 530 Geh.Feldpol., Bruessel (Bel.) 40-44			56/276	MURDER	BEL.
GRUNEAU, Wilhelm	144507	M			Officer, Gestapo, Nizza (Fr.)			-	SUSPECT	FR.
GRUNER	303645	M			Member, Gestapo, Warschau (Pol.) 39-45			57/375	BRUTALITY	POL.
GRUNERT	267512	M			Member, Gestapo, Limoges and vicinity (Fr.) 44			-	SUSPECT	FR.
GRUNET	267513	M			Member, Gestapo, Limoges and vicinity (Fr.) 44			-	SUSPECT	FR.
GRUNEWALD, Martin	144506	M			Agent, Gestapo, Clermont Fd. (Fr.)			-	SUSPECT	FR.
GRUNINGER, Hans	144505	M			Aspirant, SD, Montbeliard (Fr.)			-	SUSPECT	FR.
GRUNN	144504	M	10		Inspecteur radio, SRA., Paris (Fr.)			-	SUSPECT	FR.
GRUSSKOPF (or GROSSKOPF)	147288	M			SS-Sturmbannfhr., Head, Commander of Sec.Police for General-Government, Gestapo, Graz (Aust.) 40			1/290 9	MURDER	POL.
GRUTTNER	144502	M			Hptschfhr., SD Lyon (Fr.)			-	SUSPECT	FR.
GRUTZNER, Johann	304689	M			Member, Gestapo, Krakau (Pol.) 11.39-2.45			59/218	BRUTALITY	POL.
GRYNCZEL, Alexander	265691	M			Officers mess-servant, Warschau (Pol.)			-	MISC.CRIMES	POL.
GRZYMEK, Joseph	304690	M			SS-Hptschfhr., Commander, Forced Labour Camp, Jaktorow-Trzebinia Camp (Pol.) 41-43			59/220	MURDER	POL.
GSCHAIDER, Franz	267391	M			Agent, Gestapo, Marseille and vicinity (Fr.)			-	MURDER	FR.

NAME	C.R.FILE NUMBER	SEX	DATE OF BIRTH	RANK OCCUPATION UNIT PLACE AND DATE OF CRIME	UNWCC LIST/ SERIAL NO.	REASON WANTED	WANTED BY
GUCKENHANN, Ernst (or AUERHANN)	265713	M		Room-senior, political-prisoner, C.C., Oranienburg (Ger.)	-	MURDER	POL.
GUDAT	303646	M		Member, Gestapo, Warschau (Pol.) 39-45	57/376	BRUTALITY	POL.
GUDERIAN	308843	M		Krim.Angestellter, Interpreter(?), Radom (Pol.)1.40-1.45	60/222	MURDER	POL.
GUENTHER, Hans	137227	M	22. 8.10	SS-Sturmbannfhr., Waffen-SS,16.SS Panz.Gren.Div. Reichsfuehrer SS (Den.and Czech.)6.42-44	-	MURDER	FR.
GUENTHER, Paul	266133	M		Member, Gendarmerie, Rytel, Distr. Chojnice (Pol.)40-45	-	MURDER	POL.
GUGGENBERGER	308844	M		SS-Oscharfhr., Krim.Angestellter, Radom (Pol.)1.40-1.45	60/224	BRUTALITY	POL.
GUIBER	308845	M		Customs officer, Larmor, Creach-Maout (Fr.)5.-7.8.44	60/225	MURDER	FR.
GUISE (or GIESE)	267519	M	circa 92	Capt., Kommandantur at La Machine, La Machine (Fr.)11.44	-	BRUTALITY	FR.
GUKDEN	267067	M		Agent, Gestapo, Arras (Fr.) 8.41	-	MURDER	FR.
GULKE	265736	M		Kapo, C.C., Lublin-Majdanek (Pol.)	-	MURDER	POL.
GULZENT	267257	M		Lt.,2.Paratrooper-Div.stat.at Plomodiern,Unit No. 41 846, L.G.P.A., Brest and vicinity (Fr.) 7.-8.44	-	MURDER	FR.
GUNDERMANN	308846	M		SS-Sturmscharfhr., Interpreter(?), Radom (Pol.)1.40-1.45	60/226	MURDER	POL.
GUNDLACH, Heinz	162597	M	circa 98	F.Lt.(Hptsturmfhr.), Feldgendarmerie, Enghein Les Beins(Fr.)	25/917	MURDER	FR.
GUNKLER (or KUNKLER)	265734	F	05	SS-Aufseherin, C.C., Ravensbrueck (Ger.) 43-45	-	TORTURE	POL.
GUNSLER, Hermann (see GENSEL, Hermann)	23833						
GUNST	303647	M		Member,SS Dirlewanger Bde., Warschau, Lublin (Pol.) 40-44	57/379	MURDER	POL.
GUNTER	303187	M		On the staff of C.C.Breendonck Prov.Antwerpen (Bel.) 40-44	56/280	MURDER	BEL.
GUNTERG	267258	M		Sgt.,350.Hindou-Regt., Dpt.Indre (France) 8.44	-	MURDER	FR.
GUNTHER, Henri	266835	M		Faehnrich, Division "B", Dordogne, Correze, Hte.Vienne (Fr.)	-	SUSPECT	FR.
GUNTZLER, Herbert	265986	M	circa 07	Hptsturmfhr., SD, Chalons sur Marne (Fr.) 44	-	MISC.CRIMES	FR.
GUNZSCHEL, Walter	303188	M		Hpt.Kriminalsekretaer, Gestapo Staff, Kattowitz (Pol.)39-42	56/281	PILLAGE	POL.
GURKE, Oskar (or OGOREK)	266134	M		See names listed under "Special Headings"			
GURMANN, Max Stefan	303648	M	24.12.03	Guard, C.C., Auschwitz (Pol.) 40-45	57/381	BRUTALITY	POL.
GUSSMER	265987	M		Capt.,2.Paratrooper-Div., Brest (Fr.) 8.9.44	-	MURDER	FR.
GUT	303189	M		Lt., Feldgendarmerie, Dinan, Cotes-Du-Nord (Fr.)11.43-8.44	56/282	MURDER	FR.
GUTGLEISCH	267259	M		Member, Schutzpolizei, Elamont (Fr.) 9.44	-	MURDER	FR.
GUTLEBEN, Paul	267392	M		Sturmscharfhr., Gestapo, Marseille and vicinity (Fr.)	-	MURDER	FR.
GUTZ (see SUTZ)	267169						
GUZIAK, Zygmunt	303649	M		Medical Asst.,C.C. Dachau (Ger.)39-45	57/383	MURDER	POL.
HAAGEN	265731	M		Economical leader,SS-Uscharfhr., Extermination Camp, Treblinka (Pol.) 42-43	-	TORTURE	POL.
HAAGEN, Fritz	265735	M	10.12.08	Oberwachtmeister, Extermination Camp, Chelmo (Pol.) 41-45	-	MURDER	POL.
HAAK, Karl	304691	M		Member, Zollgrenzschutz, Zwartsluis (Neth.) 8.10.44	59/222	MURDER	NETH.
HAAS, Franz	303650	M	5. 4.12	SS-Mann, C.C., Majdanek (Pol.) 40-44	57/385	BRUTALITY	POL.
HAASE	303651	M		Member, Gestapo, Warschau (Pol.) 39-45	57/387	BRUTALITY	POL.
HAASE	308847	M		SS-Usturmfhr., Kriminaloberseksretaer, Radom (Pol.) 1.40-1.45	60/229	PILLAGE	POL.
HAASE, Willy	265814	M		SS-Sturmbannfhr.,C.C.,Krakau,Plaszow,Szebno (Pol.)	-	MURDER	POL.
HAAUGER	131666	M		N.C.O., Guard, Joeuf Mine, Bassin de Briey (Fr.) 40-45	13/443	TORTURE	FR.
HACKBARDT	265687	M		Commissar, Tarnow (Pol.) 43-44	-	MURDER	POL.
HACKE, Herbert	303190	M		Feldpolizeisekretaer, Group 530 G.F.P., Bruessel (Bel.) 40-44	56/288	MURDER	BEL.
HACKENBERG, Karl	267393	M		Scharfhr., Gestapo, Marseille and vicinity (Fr.)	-	MURDER	FR.
HACKENJOS, Adolf	303652	M	6. 2.10	Guard, C.C., Auschwitz (Pol.) 40-45	57/391	BRUTALITY	POL.
HAEGKEL, Ulrich	266504	M	6.10.05	Paymaster and dep.leader, Slaughter Unit No.151, Tuffe (Fr.) 8.8.44	-	MURDER	FR.
HAECKS	162409	M		Pvt., Standort Wach-Coy., La Rochelle (Fr.) 11.2.44	14/208	MURDER	FR.
HAENEL	303191	M		Sgt., Group 530 Geh.Feldpolizei, Bruessel (Bel.) 40-44	56/289	MURDER	BEL.
HAENSCH (see HEINSCH)	266868						
HAERIG, Theodor	308848	M		Secretary of Fieldpolice, Antwerpen and Bruessel (Bel.)40-44	60/232	MURDER	BEL.
HAFFLNER	266965	M	circa 15	Cpl., Feldgendarmerie, Masleves, Coulanges, Blois (Fr.)1.39/8.44	-	MURDER	FR.
HAFFMANN, Alexander Willi	265897	M	26. 2.84	Transportbeauftragter, Gov.d.District,civ.occ.:Engineer, Krakau (Pol.) 44-45	-	MISC.CRIMES	POL.
HAFFNER	303192	M	circa 00	Commandant, Basses-Pyrenees (Fr.)8.6.-8.44	56/290	MURDER	FR.
HAGE, Franz	162449	M		Member, Gestapo, St. Quentin (Fr.) 44	16/66	SUSPECT	FR.
HAGEMANN, Ernst	308850	M		Tradesman, Wolfenbuettel (Ger.) 42-45	60/234	MISC.CRIMES	BEL.
HAGEN, Dr.	196630	M		SS-Mann, Medical officer, Director, Institute of Hygiene, Strassburg (Fr.)	30/192 30/193	MURDER	FR.
HAGENMEISTER, Richard	265698	M		C.C., Auschwitz (Pol.)	-	MURDER	POL.
HAGENON, Ludwig	267394	M		Oscharfhr., Gestapo, Marseille and vicinity (Fr.)	-	MURDER	FR.
HAGER	72568	M		Hptwachtmstr., Gendarmerie Abt.IV 3a, Gestapo, Vichy (Fr.)	16/67	MURDER	FR.
HAGER, Willmar, Dr.	304692	M	14.12.03	Judge,appointed to investigate crimes committed against the German Reich, Plzen (Czech.) 40-42	59/223	BRUTALITY	CZECH.
HAHMANN	265699	M		Chief,SS-Hptsturmfhr., Gestapo, Commandantur IV, Nowy, Sacz, Krakau (Pol.) 40-44	-	MURDER	POL.
HAHN	266502	M		Major, Unit No.L 38-440, Air-Force, Lesquin (Fr.) 1.9.44	-	INCENDIARISM	FR.
HAHN, Franz Gunter, Dr.	304693	M		Member, Gestapo, Krakau (Pol.) 11.39- 2.45	59/224	MURDER	POL.
HAHNE	303193	M		General in command of Pau fortifications, Dep.Basses-Pyrenees, (Fr.) 8.6.- 8.44	56/291	MURDER	FR.
HAIDER, Simon	265692	M	16.12.04	Meister, Schupo, Chelmno (Pol.)	-	MISC.CRIMES	POL.
HAIM, Fritz (see HAUM)	266380						
HAINZ, Karl	198113	M		SS-Oscharfhr., C.C., Auschwitz, Birkenau (Pol.) 40-1.43	16/350 40/421	MURDER	POL.,FR. YUGO.
HAINZL, Leo	185530	M		Member, Gestapo, Ceske Budejovice (Czech.)	31/109 32/17	MURDER	CZECH.
HAETZLER, Maurus	304207	M		Ortsgr.Ltr., Hilpertsau, Weisenbach, Gernsbach, Oberstrot(Ger.)8.44	58/264	MURDER	U.S.
HALAT	303653	M		Member, Gestapo, Warschau (Pol.) 39-45	57/394A	BRUTALITY	POL.
HALLA	72547	M		Member, Oscharfhr., Gestapo Abt.VI, SS, Vichy (Fr.) 44	16/68	SUSPECT	FR.
HALLEN	185111	M		Member of Staff, C.C., Sachsenhausen-Oranienburg (Ger.)	32/229	SUSPECT	FR.
HALLENBERGER, Friedrich	264669	M	7. 6.11	See names listed under "Special Headings"			
HALLER	119427	M		Major,II b,XIX Geb.Korps Staff,20.Army, Finmark (Nor.)	8/276	MURDER	NOR.
HALLWACHS, Heinz, Dr.	265640	M		Col., veterinary surgeon, St. Just (Fr.) 12.5.42	-	PILLAGE	FR.
HALTER, Werner	266503	M	circa 13	Stabsfeldwebel,SS unknw.(wore air-force uniform)Collaborateur of S-Lt. Robert, Camp de Jhil (Fr.) 5.-9.44	-	BRUTALITY	FR.

HAM - HAU

NAME	C.R.FILE NUMBER	SEX	DATE OF BIRTH	RANK OCCUPATION UNIT PLACE AND DATE OF CRIME	UNWCC LIST/ SERIAL NO.	REASON WANTED	WANTED BY
HAMACHER, Dr.	265822	M		Leiter, Unterabt.Treuhandwesen, Lublin (Pol.)	-	PILLAGE	POL.
HAMAKEL	266964	M		Lt., Unit No. 36753 A,Cassenauil,Fougeres,St.Livrade, Cazeneuve (Fr.) 28.8.44	-	PILLAGE	FR.
HAMANN	265811	M	05	SS-Hptsturmfhr., Chief, Gestapo, Nowy Sacz (Pol.) 40-43	-	MURDER	POL.
HAMANN, Alfred	304694	M		Feldpolizeikommissar, Secr.Field-Police, H.Q.Boulevard Piercot or the Avenue Rogier Luettich (Bel.) 40-41	59/226	MURDER	BEL.
HAMANN, Eberhard	265809	M		Collaborator, Gestapo, Bydgoszcz (Pol.) 39-45	-	MISC.CRIMES	POL.
HAMED	267065	M		Capt., Unit No. L 26769 Airforce, Saint Piat (Fr.) 6.40	-	PILLAGE	FR.
HAMEL, Hermann	150308	M	21	Member, Gestapo, Hamburg (Ger.) 43-44	-	SUSPECT	FR.
HAMER	265639	M		Major, 7.Regt.Paratrooper, Cdt. I Bon, Brest (Fr.) 8.4.44	-	MURDER	FR.
HAMERLE, Heinrich	304695	M		Member, Gestapo, Krakau (Pol.) 11.39-2.45	59/227	BRUTALITY	POL.
HAMBERLI	303654	M		Member, Gestapo, Warschau (Pol.) 39-45	57/397	BRUTALITY	POL.
HAMMEL	267066	M		Capt., 350.Regt. Hindou, Lureuil,Linge,St.Michel,Brenne,Vendoeuvres,St.Maur,Ambrault,Ardentes,Neuilly les Blois (Fr.)8.44	-	MURDER	FR.
HAMMER, Joseph	265810	M		Member, Gestapo, Kazimierz Dolny (Pol.)	-	MURDER	POL.
HAMMER, Max	264664	M	27. 1.03	See names listed under "Special Headings"			
HAMMER, Schmith	266566	M		Usturmfhr., SS-School at Guebwiller, Lordon (Fr.) 6.9.44	-	MURDER	FR.
HAMMLER, Heinrich	304696	M		Pvt.,Member,Secr.Field-Police, H.Q.Boulevard Piercot or the avenue Rogier, Luettich (Bel.) 40-41	59/228	MURDER	BEL.
HAMSBERG, Franz (or ANSBERG)	308851	M	10. 6.04	Gestapo at Perigueux, Dept.de la Dordogne (Fr.) 9.43-8.44	60/235	MURDER	FR.
HAMUNTE	304697	M		Member, Secr.Field-Police, H.Q.Boulevard Piercot or the avenue Rogier, Luettich (Bel.) 40-41	59/229	MURDER	BEL.
HANAKE, Kurt	266609	M		Lt.,6.Paratrooper-Div., Pz.Jaeg. 1.Coy.,Chateau de Miannay (Fr.) 43-44	-	WITNESS	FR.
HANDT, Werner	303196	M		Kriminalbeamter, Gestapo, Kattowitz (Pol.) 39-42	56/298	INTERR.	POL.
HANENSTERN, Ernst	265786	M		Member, Gestapo, Biala Podlaska (Pol.)	-	MISC.CRIMES	POL.
HANKO	265823	M		Member, Gestapo, Lublin (Pol.)	-	BRUTALITY	POL.
HANNEMANN, Hermann	304209	M		Member of terror.Unit of militaer.Railway-Police,Pruszec (Pol.) 1.9.39	58/267	INTERR.	POL.
HANNIG, Gerhard	304725	M		Member, Gestapo, Krakau (Pol.) 11.39-2.45	59/258	BRUTALITY	POL.
HANNIG, Rudolf	304699	M		Member, Gestapo, Krakau (Pol.) 11.39-2.45	59/231	BRUTALITY	POL.
HANS	266509	M		Sgt., 29.Regt.Pz.Grenadiere,Mamey, Martincourt (Fr.) 1.-2.9.44	-	MURDER	FR.
HANS, Bruno	266914	M		Capt., Army, Ferrieres d'Aunis (Fr.) 19.9.44	-	MURDER	FR.
HANS, Ferdinand	266848	M		Lt., Div."B", Dordogne,Correze, Haute Vienne (Fr.)	-	SUSPECT	FR.
HANSEL	266610	M	circa 00	Member, Feldgendarmerie of Avallon-Yonne (Fr.) 44	-	MISC.CRIMES	FR.
HANSEL	303655	M		Member, Gestapo, Warschau (Pol.) 39-45	57/398	BRUTALITY	POL.
HANSEN, Josef	304700	M		Member, Gestapo, Krakau (Pol.) 11.39-2.45	59/232	MURDER	POL.
HANSFELD	304210	M		Member of Group 648 of the G.F.P., Boulevard Piercot, Liege (Bel.) betw. 40-44	58/268	TORTURE	BEL.
HANSLIK, Michael	303197	M		Hpt.Kriminalsekretaer, Gestapo, Kattowitz (Pol.) 39-42	56/299	INTERR.	POL.
HANSMANN, Ilse	304701	F		Member, Gestapo, Krakau (Pol.) 11.39-2.45	59/233	MURDER	POL.
HANTKE	265732	M		SS-Oscharfhr., Schupo, C.C. Budzyn,Krasnik (Pol.) 42-44	-	MURDER	POL.
HAOUSMIN	267520	M		Lt., Customs-House, Luchon and vicinity (Fr.) 1.43-7.44	-	MURDER	FR.
HAPP, Paul	266738	M	19.11.09	Inspector, Railway, Ostrowo (Pol.) 41-45	-	BRUTALITY	POL.
HAPPACH	266963	M		Inspector, Unit No. 32087, Saint Denis de Moronval (Fr.)15.8.44	-	INCENDIARISM	FR.
HARAUT	266847	M		Pvt., Div. "B", Dordogne, Correze, Haute Vienne (Fr.)	-	SUSPECT	FR.
HARBLISTA	266360	M		Chief Cpl., Army, Calais (Fr.) 4.9.44	-	WITNESS	FR.
HARBRECHT, Anna	304702	F	18.10.05	Probably attached to firm Henschel & Sohn, Factory, Kassel (Ger.) 16.1.44	59/234	MURDER	NETH.
HARDERS, Johann	303199	M		Member, Group 530 of Geh.Feldpolizei, Brussels (Bel.) 40-44	56/301	MURDER	BEL.
HARDONK	304211	M		Member of SD, Enschede (Neth.) 31.3.45	58/270	MURDER	NETH.
HARDT, Hermann	265795	M	26. 6.12	Member, Staff Extermination Camp,Chelmno (Pol.) 41-44	-	MURDER	POL.
HARDTDEGEN, Georg	304703	M		Vorarbeiter, Member (Blockhelfer),Werkzeugschmiede in the firm Henschel & Sohn, Factory, Kassel; DAF, NSV, Kassel (Ger.) 16.1.44	59/235	MURDER	NETH.
HARENDA	303656	M		Member, Gestapo, Warschau (Pol.) 39-45	57/402	BRUTALITY	POL.
HARMANSA	304704	M		Member, Gestapo, Krakau (Pol.) 11.39-2.45	59/236	BRUTALITY	POL.
HARMS	308852	M		Hptamtsleiter,SS-Stubafhr., Radom (Pol.) 1.40-1.45	60/238	RAPE	POL.
HARMS, Ewald	304212	M		Foreman at factory making torpedo parts,Blumenthal (Ger.)40-45	58/271	BRUTALITY	POL.
HARN, Franz Gunther	304705	M		Member, Gestapo, Krakau (Pol.) 11.39-2.45	59/237	BRUTALITY	POL.
HARRER, Hans	265772	M	circa 05	Oscharfhr., SD, Chalons s.Marne (Fr.) 43-44	-	MISC.CRIMES	FR.
HARSTENS	266567	M		Pvt., 59.Regt.Pz.Gren. Mamey and Martincourt (Fr.) 1.and 2.9.44	-	MURDER	FR.
HART, Otto	262593	M		See names listed under "Special Headings"			
HARTEL	265797	M		Official, Gestapo (Section IV 2-Sabotage), Lodz (Pol.) 41-44	-	MISC.CRIMES	POL.
HARTEMANN	267068	M		Capt.? Gestapo, Arras (Fr.) 8.41	-	MURDER	FR.
HARTER, August	304707	M		Member, Gestapo, Krakau (Pol.) 11.39-2.45	59/239	BRUTALITY	POL.
HARTER, Erich	265798	M	23. 6.20	Member, Staff Extermination-Camp, Chelmno (Pol.) 41-44	-	MURDER	POL.
HARTL, Bernhard	167833	M		Oberassistant, Reichsbahn or Reichsbank, Bertrix (Bel.) 4.3.44	-	MURDER	BEL.
HARTMANN	265676	M		Chief Cpl., Army, Montcontour (Fr.) 5.8.44	-	MISC.CRIMES	FR.
HARTMANN	267395	M		Sgt., Gestapo of Baccarat, Pexonne (Fr.) 27.8.44	-	MISC.CRIMES	FR.
HARTMANN	308853	M		Instructor and employee, G.F.P.,Antwerpen,Brussel (Bel.)40-44	60/241	MURDER	BEL.
HARTMANN, Friedrich	308854	M		Civ., nr.Michelfeld (Ger.) on or ab.25.4.44	60/242	MURDER	U.S.
HARTMANN, Kurt	304708	M		Member, Gestapo, Krakau (Pol.) 11.39-2.45	59/240	BRUTALITY	POL.
HARTMANN, Theobald	303657	M	23.12.22	Rottfhr., C.C.Majdanek (Pol.) 40-44	57/407	BRUTALITY	POL.
HARTUNG, Ernst	304709	M		Member, Gestapo, Krakau (Pol.) 11.39-2.45	59/241	BRUTALITY	POL.
HARTZLER, Klaus(or KARTZLER)	265997	M		Member, SD, Chalons s.Marne (Fr.) 43-44	-	MISC.CRIMES	FR.
HARY	265796	M		Prisoner and Block-senior, C.C. Sachsenhausen (Ger.)	-	BRUTALITY	POL.
HARZER	265219	M	21	Lt., Army, 26.Pz.Div., Foccechio Marshes (It.) 7.44	-	WITNESS	U.K.
HASENFUS, Hans	266568	M		Pvt., 29.Regt.Pz.Gren., Mamey and Martincourt (Fr.) 1.and 2.9.44	-	MURDER	FR.
HASENOHRL, Andreas	303658	M	7. 5.12	Guard, C.C. Auschwitz (Pol.) 40-45	57/408	BRUTALITY	POL.
HASSELBRUNG, Hans (or HASSENRING)	267553	M		Chief Sgt.Major, Feldgendarmerie, Besancon and vicinity (Fr.)44	-	MURDER	FR.
HASSENRING (see HASSELBRUNG, Hans)	267553						
HAUBL, Wilhelm	304710	M		Member, Gestapo, Krakau (Pol.) 11.39-2.45	59/242	BRUTALITY	POL.

HAU - HEI

NAME	C.R.FILE NUMBER	SEX	DATE OF BIRTH	RANK OCCUPATION UNIT PLACE AND DATE OF CRIME	UNWCC LIST/ SERIAL NO.	REASON WANTED	WANTED BY
RAUCIG, Erich	266789	M		Lt.,Commander,Feldgend.,St.Germain-en-Laye (S.O.) (Fr.) 3.7.42	-	MISC.CRIMES	FR.
HAUER	304711	M		Wachmann,Member,Sipo,Einsatzkdo.,Steenwijk,Steenwijkerwold (Kallenkote) (Neth.) 2.10.44-13.10.44.	59/243	MURDER	NETH.
HAUG, Josef	304712	M		Member,Gestapo,Krakau (Pol.) 11.39- 2.45	59/244	BRUTALITY	POL.
HAUGWITZ, Emil	309659	M	15. 9.00	SS-Mann, C.C. Majdanek (Pol.) 40-44	57/409	BRUTALITY	POL.
HAUK, Albert	266773	M	17. 1.95	SS-Usturmfhr.,Guard, SD, Nimes (Fr.) 44	-	MISC.CRIMES	FR.
HAUKE	265818	M		Member,Gendarmerie,Pulawy (Pol.) 43	-	MURDER	POL.
HAUM (or HAIM), Fritz	266980	M		See names listed under "Special Headings"			
HAUPELE	265819	M		Informer,Confidential Agent,SS,C.C.Dachau (Ger.)	-	MISC.CRIMES	POL.
HAUPTMANN, Norbert	267552	M		Gestapo,Limoges and vicinity (Fr.) 44	-	SUSPECT	FR.
HAURER	267260	M		Lt.,Army,Vienville (Fr.) 8.11.44	-	MISC.CRIMES	FR.
HAUSCH, Werner	304713	M		Member,Gestapo, Krakau (Pol.) 11.39- 2.45	59/245	BRUTALITY	POL.
HAUSER, Josef	309660	M	2.12.04	SS-Hauptsturmfhr.,C.C.Auschwitz (Pol.) 40-45	57/411	MURDER	POL.
HAUSLER, Alfred	303201	M		Kriminalsekretaer,Gestapo,Kattowitz (Pol.) 39-42	56/308	PILLAGE	POL.
HAUSMANN,	266762	M		Sturmbannfhr.,Kommandeur,SS Research office,Brzuchowice (Pol.)	-	PILLAGE	POL.
HAUSSCHILD, Waldemar	265781	M	21	Member,Gestapo,Bydgoszcz (Pol.) 39-40	-	MURDER	POL.
HAUSSER, Wilhelm	304714	M		Member,Gestapo,Krakau (Pol.) 11.39-2.45	59/246	BRUTALITY	POL.
HAUTHIER (see FRANKEINSTEIN)	197939						
HAVELOCK	265782	F		SS-overseer,C.C. Lublin-Majdanek (Pol.)	-	MURDER	POL.
HAWELKA, Leopold	303202	M		Kriminalsekretaer,Gestapo,Kattowitz (Pol.) 39-42	56/309	BRUTALITY	POL.
HAWRANKEN, Huart	303203	M		Cpl.,Geh.Feldpolizei (Bel.) 40-44	56/310	MURDER	BEL.
HAY	308855	M		SS-Stschfhr.,Secretary of Administration, Radom (Pol.) 1.40-1.45	60/245	BRUTALITY	POL.
HAYER (see HEYER), Karl	308868						
HAZELMANN	304214	M		Member,Group 648 of G.F.P., Boulevard Piercot,Liege (Bel.)40-44	58/279	TORTURE	BEL.
HEBECKER, Fritz	303204	M		Hpt.Polizeisekretaer,Gestapo,Kattowitz (Pol.) 39-42	56/311	PILLAGE	POL.
HEBELSPEIT	161965	M		Oschfhr., I-C. of prison trains (Fr.)	S 27/60	MISC.CRIMES	FR.
HEBERKORN, Erich	304715	M		Member,Gestapo,Krakau (Pol.) 11.39- 2.45	59/247	BRUTALITY	POL.
HECHT	266966	M		Hptsturmfhr., 18. SS Pz.Gren.Div."Horst Wessel" Oradour sur Glane (Fr.) 10. 6.44	-	MURDER	FR.
HECHT	308856	M		Instructor and employee, G.F.P., Antwerpen,Bruessel (Bel.)40-44	60/246	MURDER	BEL.
HECHT, Hans	308857	M		Oschfhr.,Gestapo, Korsr (Den.) 1.-2.45	60/247	TORTURE	DEN.
HECK	266251	M		Col.,Army,15.Regt. D.C.A.,Vern s.Seiche (Fr.) 14.7.44	-	MURDER	FR.
HECKEL	267551	M		Sturmbannfhr.,Gestapo,St.Etienne and vicinity (Fr.) 43-44	-	MISC.CRIMES	FR.
HECKEL, Fritz	267102	M		Interpreter,SD,Vicinity of Moulins departm.,Nevers (Fr.) 43-44	-	MISC.CRIMES	FR.
HECKMEIER	304716	M		Guard,Blechhammer,Wielkie,Strzelce,Slask (Pol.) 1.-2.45	59/248	MURDER	POL.
HEEP, Heinrich	304215	M	circa 15	Pvt.,Pi.Abt.I A-PI.,field-post-No.45696 Fort Hock Van Holland Houseleradijk nr.Naaldwijk (Neth.) 28. 4.45	58/282	MURDER	NETH.
HEES, Hermann (or HESS)	142439	M		Bezirksoberwachtmstr.,Gend.,Thionville (Fr.) 5.9.44	13/446	MURDER	FR.
HEETDERKS, Bernhard	304216	M		Obermaat,Probably member of Flak Abt.4-815,Texel (Neth.)10.4.45	58/283	MURDER	NETH.
HEFEKE, Horst	267400	M		Capt.,5.Regt., "Kouban" 2.Bn.,Dun les Places (Fr.) 26.-27.6.44	-	MURDER	FR.
HEFFELE, Alois	265743	M	95	Chief,SS-Usturmfhr.,Hauskdo., Extermination Camp Chelmno (Pol.) 41-44	-	MURDER	POL.
HEFFLE	265744	M		SS-Sturmbannfhr.,Gestapo,Lublin (Pol.)	-	TORTURE	POL.
HEFFNER	265590	M		Staatsanwalt,Civilian,Kattowitz,C.C.Blechhammer (Pol.) 45	-	MURDER	POL.
HEFTER, Otto Dr.	142467	M		Director,President,Schandelah Kalk-und Zementwerke,Institute for "Petrol-Bore-Attempts",Braunschweig (Ger.)	16/48	SUSPECT	BEL.
HEGEMANN, Franz-Josef	301732	M		Sipo,Almelo (Neth.) 15.2.-1.4.45	16/874	MURDER	U.K.
HEGENBART	303205	M		Pvt.,Feldgend.,Angouleme,Chasseneuil,Charents (Fr.) 43-44	56/312	MURDER	FR.
HEGENWALD, Eric	266534	M		Treasurer,Army,hospital,Lons-le-Saunier, La Charme (Fr.) 11.8.44	-	MISC.CRIMES	FR.
HEIDENBERG, Joseph	267401	M		Osturmfhr.,Gestapo,Bordeaux and vicinity (Fr.) 42-8.44	-	MURDER	FR.
HEIDER	303206	M		Polizeimstr.,Member,Sonderkdo.,Kulmhof (Pol.) 41-45	56/313	MURDER	POL.
HEIDER, Otto	264663	M	26. 5.96	See names listed under "Special Headings"			
HEIDORN, Wilhelm Friedrich	256443	M		Inspector,Gestapo,Langenhagen,Hannover (Ger.)	27/667	MISC.CRIMES	NETH.
HEIDRICH, Stanislaus	304717	M		Member,Gestapo,Krakau (Pol.) 11.39- 2.45	59/249	BRUTALITY	POL.
HEIDTMANN, Georg Klaus	305895	M		Guard,C.C.Neugraben,Tiefstak	32/52 32/452	BRUTALITY	CZECH. U.K.
HEIDUK	308858	M		SS-Hschfhr.,Krim.Ob.Asst.,Radom (Pol.) 1.40- 1.45	60/250	BRUTALITY	POL.
HEIL	11	M		Interpreter,Kommandantur,Finnmark	3/127	MURDER	FR.
HEILBRUNNER, Johann	265745	M	13.11.19	Policeman,C.C. Chelmno (Pol.)	-	TORTURE	POL.
HEILMANN	119434	M		Lt.Col.,Comd.Art.Regt.234-163,Inf.Div.,20.Army,Finmark (Nor.) 44	8/283	MURDER	NOR.
HEILMANN	131722	M		Customs-officer,Velmenya (Fr.) 1.8.44	13/447	MURDER	FR.
HEIM, Herbert	266605	M	circa 00	Chief Sgt.-Major,Feldgend.,Avallon,Yonne (Fr.) 44	-	MISC.CRIMES	FR.
HEIMSCH	308860	M		Gestapo at Perigueux,Dept. de la Dodogne (Fr.) 9.43- 8.44	60/252	MURDER	FR.
HEIN, Ewald	303661	M	1. 5.07	SS-Sturmmann,C.C. Majdanek (Pol.) 40-44	57/417	MURDER	POL.
HEINE	303662	M		Member,Gestapo,Warschau (Pol.) 39-45	57/418	BRUTALITY	POL.
HEINE	266772	M	circa 14	SS-Hptsturmfhr.,Chief of Montrignard Station,Feverolles (Fr.) 12.-13. 8.1944	-	MURDER	FR.
HEINE (or HEINTZ), Louise	267083	F	circa 15	Typist,Gestapo,Blois,Laves (Fr.) 43-44	-	MURDER	FR.
HEINECKE, Alfred	304718	M		Member,Gestapo,Krakau (Pol.) 11.39-2.45	59/249 a	BRUTALITY	POL.
HEINEMANN	304719	M		Member,Gestapo,Krakau (Pol.) 11.39-2.45	59/250	MURDER	POL.
HEINEMANN, Paul	267084	M	circa 00	Chief Sgt.-Major,Taratrooper 8.Regt., Carhaix (Fr.) 10.6.44	-	SUSPECT	FR.
HEINEN	265824	M		SS-Mann,Extermination Camp, Jenow (Pol.)	-	MURDER	POL.,U.K.
HEINRICH	265988	M		Interpreter-Sgt.,Army,Unit.No.15.483 B and E,La Reole (Fr.) 5.44	-	WITNESS	FR.
HEINRICH	265677	M	07	SS-Mann, SD,Gestapo,Mans (Sarthe),Mayenne (Fr.) 42-44	-	SUSPECT	FR.
HEINRICH, Joseph	265787	M		Member,Staff at extermination camp Chelmno,Fabianice (Pol.)41-44	-	MURDER	POL.
HEINRICHSBAUER, August	265636	M	15. 6.90	See names listed under "Special Headings"			
HEINRITZ	303663	M		Member,Gestapo,Warschau (Pol.) 39-45	57/420	BRUTALITY	POL.
HEINS	138294	M		Member,NSDAP,POW Working Commando 715 F at mine "Elisabethglueck", Dorchholz (Ger.)	-	TORTURE	FR.
HEINSCH (or HAENSCH)	266868	M		Member,Sipo, SD, Perigueux Gestapo,Dordogne (Fr.) 43-44	-	SUSPECT	FR.
HEINTZ (see HEINE), Louise	267083						
HEINTZ-HEINSON (see KARLENS, Henri)	267029						
HEINZ	304217	M		Lt.,Army or Schutztruppen,Geleen (L.)(Neth.) 9.44	58/286	MISC.CRIMES	NETH.

HEI - HES

NAME	C.R.FILE NUMBER	SEX	DATE OF BIRTH	RANK OCCUPATION UNIT PLACE AND DATE OF CRIME	UNWCC LIST/ SERIAL NO.	REASON WANTED	WANTED BY
HEINZ, Ferdinand	265456	M		Guard, Camp, Montvilliers (Fr.) 27.7.44	-	MURDER	FR.
HINZE, Dr.	265230	M		Former-Chief, SD, Prison, Caen (Fr.) 6.6.44	-	MURDER	FR.
HEINZE, Friedrich	304720	M		Member, Gestapo, Krakau (Pol.) 11.39-2.45	59/252	BRUTALITY	POL.
HEIS	303664	M		Member, Gestapo, Warschau (Pol.) 39-45	57/423	BRUTALITY	POL.
HEISER, Johann	303665	M	10.11.09	SS-Mann, C.C., Majdanek (Pol.) 40-44	57/426	MURDER	POL.
HEITZIG, Franz	304218	M		Estate-administrator, Civilian, Dreckburg (Pol.) 40-45	-	BRUTALITY	POL.
HELBERT	265788	M		SS-Uschfhr., functionary, Gestapo, Lodz (Pol.) 39-45	-	MISC.CRIMES	POL.
HELBIG	267554	M		Chief Sergeant Major, Feldgendarmerie, Besancon and vicinity (Fr.) 44	-	MURDER	FR.
HELBING, Helmuth	265789	M	95	Vice-director, Post-office-direction, Lublin (Pol.)	-	BRUTALITY	POL.
HALD	303666	M		Member, Gestapo, Warschau (Pol.) 39-45	57/429	BRUTALITY	POL.
HELL	266973	M		Chief-Cpl., Gendarmerie, Sisteron (Fr.) 44	-	MISC.CRIMES	FR.
HELL, Josef	303667	M	29. 3.12	SS-Mann, C.C., Majdanek (Pol.) 40-44	57/430	MURDER	POL.
HELLBERG, Hans	304219	M		Commander, block in Labour-Camp in "Hochbrucke" barracks, Lubeka, 44-45	58/289	BRUTALITY	POL.
HELLBRANDT	267530	M		Chief Sergeant Major, Feldgendarmerie, Besancon and vicinity (Fr.) 44	-	MURDER	FR.
HELLER	265790	M		Doctor, C.C., Auschwitz (Pol.)	-	MURDER	POL.
HELLER	303668	M		Member, Gestapo, Warschau (Pol.) 39-45	57/431	BRUTALITY	POL.
HELLWIG, Gunter	304721	M		Member, Gestapo, Krakau (Pol.) 11.39-2.45	59/254	BRUTALITY	POL.
HELLWIG, Heinz	304220	M		SS-Mann, Waffen-SS, 12 Aufklaer.Abt., 12 Pz.Div. "Hitler-Jugend", Ascq.Nord, 1.-2.4.44	58/291	MURDER	FR.
HELM, Leon	263132	M		See names listed under "Special Headings"			
HELMER	308861	M		Cpl., G.F.P., Antwerpen and Bruessel (Bel.) 40-44	60/253	MURDER	BEL.
HELMARCEN, Erwin Dr.	265566	M		Camp-Physician, Hptsturmfhr., SS, Auschwitz (Pol.) 43-45	-	MURDER	POL.
HELMERLIN, Heinrich	267531	M	circa 18	Cpl., 78 Gren.Regt.,26 Inf.Div., Wolkovisk (Sov.Un.)	-	MURDER	FR.
HELMERLING, Helena	304722	F	29. 7.19	Member, Gestapo, Krakau (Pol.) 11.39-2.45	59/255	MURDER	POL.
HELMERLING, Wilhelm Dr.	304723	M	12.11.14	Member, Gestapo, Krakau (Pol.) 11.39-2.45	59/256	MURDER	POL.
HEMPEN, Georg	266021	M		Hptschfhr., Gestapo, Metz,Fort de Queuleu (Fr.) 40-45	-	MURDER	FR.
HEMSING	304724	M		Member, Gestapo, Krakau (Pol.) 11.39-2.45	59/257	MURDER	POL.
HENCKEL VON DONNERSMARK, Graf	263325	M		See names listed under "Special Headings"			
HENDRICKS	308863	M		Sgt.-Major, prisoners camp, Missburg, 40-44	60/256	MURDER	BEL.
HENDSCHEL	265701	M		Member, Gestapo, Krasnik (Pol.)	-	MURDER	POL.
HENESBERGER, Leopold	303669	M	6. 9.11	SS-Rottfhr., C.C., Majdanek (Pol.) 40-44	57/433	BRUTALITY	POL.
HENK, Wilhelm	304221	M		Member of Flak-Abt.4-815, Miner,Civ., Texel (Neth.) 10.4.45	58/293	MURDER	NETH.
HENKEL	267368	M		Agent, Gestapo, Marseille and environ (Fr.)	-	MURDER	FR.
HENKEL	303670	M		Member, Gestapo, Warschau (Pol.) 39-45	57/434	BRUTALITY	POL.
HENNE	267532	M		Lt., Feldgendarmerie,Besancon and vicinity (Fr.) 44	-	MURDER	FR.
HENNES, Franz Josef	304222	M	23.11.94	Mine-overseer,Member, "Julia" State coal-mine,Schutzgruppen, Eigelshoven (Neth.) 8.-13.9.44	58/295	MISC.CRIMES	NETH.
HENNIG, Paul	304726	M		Member, Gestapo, Krakau (Pol.) 11.39-2.45	59/259	MURDER	POL.
HENNING, Georg	308864	M		Member, Selbstschutz, Manager, Factory "Fiebrandt", Bydgoszcz (Pol.) 39-44	60/258	INTERR.	POL.
HENSCHE, Otto	303671	M	16. 8.04	SS-Mann, C.C., Majdanek (Pol.) 40-44	57/435	BRUTALITY	POL.
HENSEL, Helmut	304727	M		Member, Gestapo, Krakau (Pol.) 11.39-2.45	59/260	MURDER	POL.
HENSEL, Karl	303672	M	6. 3.97	SS-Guard, C.C., Neudorf, Gusen (Pol.) 39-45	57/437	BRUTALITY	POL.
HENSSLING, Joachim	267369	M		Interpreter, Gestapo, Marseille and environ (Fr.)	-	MURDER	FR.
HERBERS	266962	M		Sgt., Feldgendarmerie, Sisteron (Fr.) 44	-	MISC.CRIMES	FR.
HERBERT	265741	M		Pvt., Lds.Schtz.Bn.71, 4 Coy., Gubin (Pol.)	-	MURDER	POL.
HERBERT, Karl	265774	M		SS-Oschfhr., C.C., Sachsenhausen-Oranienburg (Ger.)	-	MURDER	POL.
HERBST, Willi	265742	M		Chief, Gestapo, Sturmbannfhr., SS, Jaslo,Krosno (Pol.) 41-44	-	TORTURE	POL.
HERLF	265644	M	14. 8.21	Customs-Official, Feldpost-No.57 727 B, Larmor-Pleubian (Fr.) 5.,6.,7.8.44	-	MURDER	FR.
HERFURTH, Friedrich Karl	264670	M	30. 4.01	See names listed under "Special Headings"			
HERGERT	304223	M		Capt., Airforce, commanding Nachtjagd-Gr.No.4, Vicinity of Charleroi (Bel.) 2.44	58/298	MURDER	BEL.
HERING, Erich	266252	M		Cpl., H.V.Stelle Laon 609,meeting place Soissons,Admin.Coy. Laon 609 S.P. 26300 N, Soissons (Fr.) 28.8.44	-	INCENDIARISM	FR.
HERMANN	265645	M		Member, SD, Chalons sur Marne (Fr.) 43-44	-	MISC.CRIMES	FR.
HERMANN	265678	M		SS-Uschfhr., Agent, SD, Carcassonne (Aude) (Fr.) 43-44	-	SUSPECT	FR.
HERMANN	265799	M		Apothecary, C.C., Auschwitz (Pol.)	-	MURDER	POL.
HERMANN	266903	M		Major, Airforce,Unit L 49193 L.G.P.A., Camaret sur Aigues (Fr.) 44	-	MISC.CRIMES	FR.
HERMANN	267402	M		Feldgendarm, Feldgendarmerie, Villers s.Coudun (Fr.) 8.44	-	MURDER	FR.
HERMANN, Karl	266904	M		N.C.O., Army, Groslezac, Carsac, Peyrillac, Calviac, Carlux (Fr.) 8.6.44	-	MISC.CRIMES	FR.
HERMANN, Stefan	303673	M	26. 4.14	SS-Mann, C.C., Majdanek (Pol.) 40-44	57/443	BRUTALITY	POL.
HERMANN, Waltor	264671	M	29. 5.95	See names listed under "Special Headings"			
HERMANNS, Barbara	304728	F		Member, Gestapo, Krakau (Pol.) 11.39-2.45	59/262	MURDER	POL.
HERMER, Josef	303674	M	31.10.96	SS-Mann, C.C., Majdanek (Pol.) 40-44	57/445	BRUTALITY	POL.
HEROLD	267533	M		Sgt.Major,Feldgendarmerie,Besancon and Vicinity (Fr.) 44	-	MURDER	FR.
HERRMANN	265364	M		Crim.Secretary, Gestapo, Konin (Pol.) 39	-	MURDER	POL.
HERSTISE	266782	M		Member, Div."B", Dordogne-Correza-Hte.Vienne (Fr.)	-	SUSPECT	FR.
HERTEL, Hermann	267261	M	circa 17	Hptschfhr., Gestapo, Bordeaux and environ (Fr.) 42-8.44	-	MURDER	FR.
HERTNER	303211	M		Gardener at the C.H.F.Mueller "Roentgen" Factory, Member, NSDAP, Hamburg (Ger.) 43-44	56/323	MURDER	NETH.
HERWIG	304224	M		Member,Schutzgruppen at the "Laura-mine",Eigelshoven (Neth.) 8.-13.9.44	58/302	PILLAGE	NETH.
HESACK	308865	M		Pvt., G.F.P., Antwerpen, Bruessel (Bel.) 40-44	60/262	MURDER	BEL.
HESCHL, Dr.	265802	M	13	SS-Usturmfhr., C.C., Auschwitz (Pol.)	-	MURDER	POL.
HESS (see HEES, Hermann)	142439						
HESS	266783	M		Lt.,Agricultural-Service,Licheres (Fr.) 6.,7.44	-	MURDER	FR.
HESS, Adam	265800	M	05	Official,Kreishauptmann,Office food supply,Biala Podlaska (Pol.)	-	MISC.CRIMES	POL.
HESSE, Alfred	303212	M		Crim.Secretary, Gestapo, Kattowitz (Pol.) 39-42	56/324	BRUTALITY	POL.
HESSE, Franz-Paul	267403	M	circa 15	Member, Gestapo, Bordeaux and environ (Fr.) 42-8.44	-	MURDER	FR.
HESSEL	265801	M		Prisoner, Block-senior, C.C., Lublin-Majdanek (Pol.)	-	TORTURE	POL.

HET - HOF

NAME	C.R. FILE NUMBER	SEX	DATE OF BIRTH	RANK OCCUPATION UNIT PLACE AND DATE OF CRIME	UNWCC LIST/ SERIAL NO.	REASON WANTED	WANTED BY
HETSCH, Ernst	267534	M	circa 00	Member, Gestapo, Luchon and vicinity (Fr.) 1.43, 7.44	-	MURDER	FR.
HEUBERGER, Willy	267478	M	circa 17	Sgt., interpreter, Feldgendarmerie, Besancon and vicinity (Fr.).44	-	MURDER	FR.
HEUCKENKAMP, Rudolf Dr.	264668	M	16.11.00	See names listed under "Special Headings"			
HEUER	308866	M		Sgt., G.F.P., Antwerpen and Bruessel (Bel.) 40-44	60/264	MURDER	BEL.
HEUER, Hermann	267555	M	10. 4.10	SS-Scharfhr., Gestapo KDS IV, Paris (Fr.) 41-44	-	SUSPECT	FR.
HEUN, Wilhelm	304225	M	18. 7.04	Foreman, Hermann Goering-works, Hannover (Ger.) 40-45	58/304	BRUTALITY	POL.
HEUSER, Gerard	265984	M		Chief, Customs post, Saint Vallier (Fr.) 42-44	-	MURDER	FR.
HEUSER, Herbert	308867	M		Sgt., G.F.P., Antwerpen and Bruessel (Bel.) 40-44	60/265	MURDER	BEL.
HEUSS, Otto	267370	M	5.11.04	Usturmfhr., Gestapo, Marseille and vicinity (Fr.)	-	MURDER	FR.
HEYDERHOFF	267085	M		Agent, Gestapo, Arras (Fr.) 8.41	-	MURDER	FR.
HEYER	303243	M		Agent, Gestapo, member, "Selbstschutz", Torun (Pol.) 9.39	56/327	MURDER	POL.
HEYER, Friedrich	303244	M		Cpl., Group 530, Geh.Feldpolizei, Bruessel (Bel.)	56/328	MURDER	BEL.
HEYER, Karl (or HAYER)	308868	M		Betriebsobmann, Lendringsen, Distr.Iserlohn (Ger.) 39-45	60/266	BRUTALITY	POL.
HIDRICH (or FIEDRICH)	266606	M		Major, Pz.Gren.Regt.29, Mamey, Martincourt (Fr.) 1., 2.9.44	-	MURDER	FR.
HIEBL, Theresia Dr.	304226	F		Hospital for women, Ost-Hospital, Luebeck (Ger.) 43-45	58/305	BRUTALITY	POL.
HIEDREIDER	265764	M		SS-Uscharfhr., SS-Guard, C.C., Treblinka (Pol.)	-	MURDER	POL.
HIEGMANN	304227	M		Cpl., Air Force, Nachtjagd-Group 4, vicinity of Charleroi (Bel.) 2.44	58/306	MURDER	BEL.
HIERSCHE	303675	M		Member, Gestapo, Warschau (Pol.) 39-45	57/453	BRUTALITY	POL.
HILDEBRANDT	267357	M		Member, Gestapo, Marseille (Fr.)	-	MURDER	FR.
HILDEBRANT, Gisela	265739	F		Member, Institute for the Work in the East, Krakau (Pol.)	-	MISC.CRIMES	POL.
HILDEBRAND, Erwin	304729	M		Member, Gestapo, Krakau (Pol.) 11.39-2.45	59/263	BRUTALITY	POL.
HILGERS	308869	M		Possibly member of Schutzgruppen, Civilian, working in the fitters' work-shop at the "Hendrik" state mine, Brunssum (Neth.) 9.44	60/267	PILLAGE	NETH.
HILLER	303676	M		Member, Gestapo, Warschau (Pol.) 39-45	57/454	BRUTALITY	POL.
HILLER, Joseph	265740	M		Member, Gestapo, Kazimierz Dolny (Pol.) 42	-	MURDER	POL.
HILLIAT	303245	M		Cpl., Dep. of Basses-Pyrenees (Fr.) 8.6. and 8.44	56/330	MURDER	FR.
HILSCHAR, Rudolf	265769	M		Wachtmeister, Gendarmerie, Rynek Tarnogrod (Pol.) 2.11.42	-	MURDER	POL.
HILSENBEZ	265768	M		Kapo, C.C., Dachau (Ger.)	-	MURDER	POL.
HIMMEL, Richard	308870	M		Cpl., member of guard unit forming part of the crew of the V.-weapon based at Hook van Holland, Wassenaar (Neth.) 11.44	60/268	PILLAGE	NETH.
HIMPEL, Rudolf	303246	M		Crim.secretary, Gestapo, Kattowitz (Pol.) 39-42	56/331	INTERR.	POL.
HINGST, Heinrich	303247	M		Pvt., Group 530, Geh.Feldpolizei, Bruessel (Bel.) 40-44	56/332	MURDER	BEL.
HINKE	267477	M		Sgt.-Major, 350 Regt. Hindu, Department Indre (Fr.) 8.44	-	MURDER	FR.
HINRICHSEN, Heinrich	303248	M		Member, Group 530, Geh.Feldpolizei, Bruessel (Bel.) 40-44	56/333	MURDER	BEL.
HINTERNEDER, Eduard	304730	M		Member, Gestapo, Krakau (Pol.) 11.39-2.45	59/264	BRUTALITY	POL.
HINZ	303249	M		Hptscharfhr., Gestapo, Lodz (Pol.) 39-44	56/334	MURDER	POL.
HINZEN, Heinz	254535	M		See names listed under "Special Headings"			
HIOTZOT (see JANTZO)	267406						
HIPP	154372			Block-senior, C.C. Dachau (Ger.)	-	MURDER	POL.
HIRSCH	266598	M		W.O., Feldgendarmerie, Nimes (Fr.) 2.3.44	-	MURDER	FR.
HIRSCH, Robert	303250	M		Crim.asst., Gestapo, Kattowitz (Pol.) 39-42	56/335	PILLAGE	POL.
HIRSEKORN	303677	M		Member, Gestapo, Warschau (Pol.) 39-45	57/456	BRUTALITY	POL.
HIRT, Dr.	114849	M		SS-Hptsturmfhr., Physician, Professor of University SS, Auschwitz, Strassburg (Pol., Fr.) 45	-	MURDER	POL.
HIRT	303678	M		Member, Gestapo, Warschau (Pol.) 39-45	57/457	BRUTALITY	POL.
HITTNER	265765	M		SS-Hptscharfhr., SS, Extermination Camp, Sobibor (Pol.)	-	MURDER	POL.
HIOZHOMMER	267087	M		Farmer, Civilian, Unterferrieden (Ger.) 12.12.44	-	BRUTALITY	FR.
HOBEK	265767	M	19	SS-Scharfhr., official, SS, Gestapo, Section "Sabotage of work", Lodz (Pol.)	-	BRUTALITY	POL.
HOBEK, Max	265766	M	circa 19	SS-Scharfhr., official, interpreter, Gestapo, working for Neiller and Mueller (Gestapo), Lodz (Pol.)	-	MURDER	POL.
HOBER, Adolf	267317	M		Uscharfhr., Gestapo, Marseille and vicinity (Fr.)	-	MURDER	FR.
HOCHBERGER, Richard	265946	M		Engineer, Commission Koch, Bordes, Soues (Fr.) 1.-3.43	-	PILLAGE	FR.
HOCHGRAEBE, Hans-Joachim (or SCHMITT)	303253	M		Feldpolizeidirektor, Feldpolizei-Direktion, (Bel., Fr.) 40-44	56/340	MURDER	BEL.
HOCHSTRAISSER, Charles	266781	M		Interpreter, SD, Pau (Fr.) 12.42-8.44	-	MISC.CRIMES	FR.
HOEBEL, Dr.	265757	M		Physician, Concentration and Extermination Camp, Auschwitz (Pol.)	-	MURDER	POL.
HOECH, Wilhelm	265758	M	circa 90	Post-inspector, Civilian, Lublin (Pol.)	-	MURDER	POL.
HOEDLE	265756	M		SS-Osturmfhr., SS-Gestapo, Rowno (Pol.)	-	TORTURE	POL.
HOEFFLE	265792	M		Functionary, Gestapo, Warschau (Pol.) 40-45	-	MURDER	POL.
HOEFNER	309165	M		Manufacturer, Jicin (Czech.) 43	28/29	INTERR.	CZECH.
HOEHE, Karl Albert	267133	M		Major, Army, 3 Bn., 893 Gren.Regt., 264 Div., Sinj (Yugo.) 8.9.43-10.44	-	MURDER	YUGO.
HOEHN, Leon	309001	M		Kreutzwald (Moselle) (Fr.) 7.5.44	28/74	MURDER	FR.
HOELLER	304230	M		Member, Schutzgruppen at "Laura-Mine",Eigelshoven (Neth.)13.9.44	58/315	PILLAGE	NETH.
HOELLING, Alfred	265633	M	6.11.88	See names listed under "Special Headings"		PILLAGE	FR.
HOELZER, Prof.	191603	M		Member,Office for the supervision of literature,Einsatzstab Rosenberg, Berlin (Ger.) 40-44	10/192		
HOEPNER	265794	M		Leader,Abt.Wirtschaft im Gen.Government, (Pol.)	-	BRUTALITY	POL.
HOERA	304744	M		Usturmfhr., SD,Abt. II, Oldenzaal,Sauwerd,Den Haag (Neth.) 45	59/281	PILLAGE	NETH.
HOERINGER, Josef	263010	M	16. 6.06	See names listed under "Special Headings"			
HOESCH, Dr.	196553	M		SS-Mann, Institute of Anatomy, Strassburg (Fr.) 40-44	30/201	MURDER	FR.
HOETTOPEIS	266908	M		See names listed under "Special Headings"			
HOFER	267408	M	circa 95	Officer, 2 Paratrooper-Div., Brest and vicinity (Fr.) 7. and 8.44	-	MURDER	FR.
HOFER	303679	M		Member, Gestapo, Warschau (Pol.) 39-45	57/461	MURDER	POL.
HOFFEN, Alberts	266253	M		See names listed under "Special Headings"			
HOFFER	265791	M	17	SS-Scharfhr.,official,Chief political office,C.C.Auschwitz (Pol.) 42-45	-	MURDER	POL.
HOFFMAN, Gerhard	265773	M	10	Member, Gestapo, Radzyn (Pol.)	-	MISC.CRIMES	POL.
HOFFMANN	185117	M		SS-Mann, Kapo, C.C., Dachau (Ger.)	25/945	MURDER	FR.
HOFFMANN	265793	M		SS-Scharfhr., Functionary, C.C., Political Office, Auschwitz, Birkenau (Pol.) 41-45	-	MURDER	POL.
HOFFMANN	265820	M		Member, Gestapo, Turek (Pol.) 42	-	MURDER	POL.
HOFFMANN	265821	M		SS-Oscharfhr., guard, prison, Lublin (Pol.) 40-44	-	BRUTALITY	POL.

HOF - HOR

NAME	C.R.FILE NUMBER	SEX	DATE OF BIRTH	RANK OCCUPATION UNIT PLACE AND DATE OF CRIME	UNWCC LIST/ SERIAL NO.	REASON WANTED	WANTED BY
HOFFMANN (I)	303680	M		Member, Gestapo, Warschau (Pol.) 39-45	57/463	BRUTALITY	POL.
HOFFMANN (II)	303681	M		Member, Gestapo, Warschau (Pol.) 39-45	57/464	BRUTALITY	POL.
HOFFMANN (III)	303682	M		Member, Gestapo, Warschau (Pol.) 39-45	57/465	BRUTALITY	POL.
HOFFMANN	304731	M		Field-Pol.Secretary, Secr.Field Police, H.Q., Boulevard, Piercotor or the Avenue Rogier,Luettich (Bel.) 40-41	59/267	MURDER	BEL.
HOFFMANN	308872	M		Guard, Wolfenbuettel prison (Ger.) 42-45	60/273	MISC.CRIMES	BEL.
HOFFMANN, Artur, Heinrich	306587	M		Mayor, Jugesheim near Frankfurt (Ger.)	27/803	BRUTALITY	U.K.
HOFFMANN, Emile	265409	M	8. 4.07	Cpl., Coy. of Auxiliary Inf., Bernay (Sarthe) (Fr.) 3.9.41	-	MURDER	FR.
HOFFMANN, Ernst	162426	M	98	SS-Hptschfhr., Krim.Kommissar, Hoehere SS and Bde.Fuehrer Sipo.Abt. V B, Duesseldorf, Bruessel (Ger.Bel.) 40	28/90	MURDER	BEL.
HOFFMANN, Frantz	267442	M	circa 05	Hptsturmfhr., Chief, C.C. Neckarelz Wuerttemberg (Ger.) 44-45	-	MURDER	FR.
HOFFMANN, Franz	265776	M		SS-Usturmfhr., C.C. Dachau (Ger.)	-	MURDER	POL.
HOFFMANN, Herbert	267141	M		Uschfhr., Gestapo, Beziers (Fr.) 43-44	-	SUSPECT	FR.
HOFFMANN, Jacob	303683	M	2. 3.12	SS-Rottfhr., C.C. Majdanek (Pol.) 39-45	57/469	BRUTALITY	POL.
HOFFMANN, Joseph	266599	M	11. 9.92	Commander, Caen Prison, Alencon and region (Fr.) 6.44	-	MURDER	FR.
HOFFMANN, Karl	303254	M		Senior Adjutant, Mle. No. 874851, Chaute-Aulin (Finistere) (Fr.) 20.5.44	56/345	MISC.CRIMES	FR.
HOFFMANN, Karl, Heinz, Dr.jur.	301098	M		SS-Sturmbannfhr., Chief, Ob.Reg.Rat, SS of R.S.D. section Abt. IV (Den.) 44-45	31/153	MURDER	DEN.
HOFFMANN, Walter	265317	M	07	SS-Usturmfhr., C.C. Auschwitz (Pol.) 40-44	-	MISC.CRIMES	POL.
HOFFMANN, Walter	265775	M	00	SS-Mann, Member, Gestapo, Section IV, Lodz (Pol.)	-	MISC.CRIMES	POL.
HOFFMANN, Walter	308874	M		Secretary of Fieldpolice, Antwerpen,Bruessel (Bel.) 40-44	60/275	MURDER	BEL.
HOFFMEYER, Horst	264636	M	29. 5.03	See names listed under "Special Headings"			
HOFFNER	267086	M		Agent, Gestapo, Arras (Fr.) 8.41	-	MURDER	FR.
HOFLING, Fridrich	266543	M		See names listed under "Special Headings"			
HOFMAN	265710	M		SS-Hptsturmfhr., Gestapo-president, Gestapo Sondergericht Lublin (Pol.)	-	MURDER	POL.
HOFMANN	265948	M		Capt., Bordes, Soues (Fr.) 1.-3.43	-	PILLAGE	FR.
HOFMANN	303684	M		Member, Gestapo, Warschau (Pol.) 39-45	57/470	MURDER	POL.
HOFMANN, Georg	304732	M		Member, Gestapo, Krakau (Pol.) 11.39-2.45	59/268	MURDER	POL.
HOFMANN, Heinrich	304733	M		Member, Gestapo, Krakau (Pol.) 11.39-2.45	59/269	MURDER	POL.
HOFMANN, Karl	309164	M	8. 6.97	Police official, Sturmschfhr., Sipo. formerly at Sipo. and SD. Post, Terneuzen, Schoondijke (Neth.) 40-44	40/93	PILLAGE	NETH.
HOFMAYER, Walter	267139	M		Lt., Army, 893 Rgt. 3 Bn., Sinj (Yugo.) 8.9.43-10.44	-	MURDER	YUGO.
HOFMEISTER, Walther	162417	M	98	SS-Hptsturmf., Pol.Oberinspector, Leader, Sipo. Abt.I Administration, Bruessel, Koblenz (Bel.Ger.) 40-44	28/93	MURDER	BEL.
HOFT	303685	M	2. 7.09	SS-Sturmann, C.C. Majdanek (Pol.) 40-44	57/471	BRUTALITY	POL.
HOHMA, Erich	266544	M		Schfhr., SE School at Guebwiller, Lordon (Fr.) 6.9.44	-	MURDER	FR.
HOHMANN	303686	M		Member, Gestapo, Warschau (Pol.) 39-45	57/472	BRUTALITY	POL.
HOHMANN, Max	304734	M	circa 00	Oschfhr., G.F.P. attached to the Sipo., C.C. Zwolle (Neth.)	59/270	MURDER	NETH.
HOHN	162416	M		"Member", Gestapo, St.Quentin, Vraignesen Vermandois (Fr.)44	16/41	MURDER	FR.
HOHN, Franz	303687	M	20. 7.20	SS-Mann, C.C. Majdanek (Pol.) 40-44	57/473	MURDER	POL.
HOHN, Kurt	265705	M	15	Member, Gestapo, Lublin (Pol.)	-	MURDER	POL.
HOHNSTEIN, Richard	304736	M		Member, Gestapo, Krakau (Pol.) 11.39-2.45	59/272	MURDER	POL.
HOLDOWSKI, Stefan	303688	M	1. 1.24	SS-Guard, C.C. Buchenwald, Flossenburg (Ger.) 39-45	57/475	MURDER	POL.
HOLL, Kurt	303256	M		Adjutant, Bergues Nord, (Fr.) 16.9.44	56/347	MURDER	FR.
HOLLAND, Helmut	304737	M	14. 6.98	Chief Prosecutor, in Piotrkow (Pol.) 41-45	59/273	MURDER	POL.
HOLLBACH	265947	M		Member, Feldgend., Cholet (Fr.) 7. and 8.8.44	56/348	MURDER	FR.
HOLLER	265945	M		Oschfhr., SD., Chalons sur Marne (Fr.) 43-44	-	MISC.CRIMES	FR.
HOLLER	304829	M		Capt., Army, 118 Div., Gythion area (Pelepon.) Tripoli, Corinth (Grc.) 43-44	58/313	MURDER	GRC.
HOLLER	308875	M		SS-Oschfhr., Krim.Employee, Driver, Radom (Pol.) 1.40-1.45	60/277	PILLAGE	POL.
HOLLMANN	303689	M		Member, Gestapo, Warschau (Pol.) 39-45	57/477	MURDER	POL.
HOLM, Otto	264446	M	20. 5.99	Schfhr., Civilian Police Service, Group Geh.Feldpolizei Gestapo Paris KDS.IV (Fr.) 20.11.42-44	-	SUSPECT	FR.
HOLM, Otto	303258	M		Cpl., Group 530 Geh.Feldpol., Bruessel (Bel.) 40-44	56/349	MURDER	BEL.
HOLMOM, Geza	303690	M	17.12.20	SS-Mann, C.C. Majdanek (Pol.) 40-44	57/478	BRUTALITY	POL.
HOLST, Hans	303259	M		Sgt., Group 530 Geh.Feldpol., H.Q.G.F.P., Bruessel (Bel.)41-44	56/350	MISC.CRIMES	BEL.
HOLTMANN, Josef	304738	M		Member, Gestapo, Krakau (Pol.) 11.39-2.45	59/274	MURDER	POL.
HOLTZ	266364	M	circa 09	Lt., Unit stationed at camp of Varennes, Ligny Le Chatel (Yonne) (Fr.) 2.8.44	-	MURDER	FR.
HOLZ	267318	M	circa 08	Agent, Gestapo, Marseille and vicinity (Fr.)	-	MURDER	FR.
HOLZBERGER, Rudolf	304739	M		Member, Gestapo, Krakau (Pol.) 11.39-2.45	59/276	MURDER	POL.
HOLZE, Fritz	304740	M		Member, Gestapo, Krakau (Pol.) 11.39-2.45	59/277	RAPE	POL.
HOLZER, Adolf, Ludwig	301203	M		Member, NSDAP. at Huchenfeld,Dillweissenstein (Ger.) 17.-18.3.45	-	MURDER	U.K.
HOLZHAUSEN, Wilhelm	308876	M		SS-Officer, SS near Muenstadt (Ger.) 24.8.44	60/280	MURDER	U.S.
HOLZHOJMER	265707	M		Instructor, Wasser Wirtschafts Camp for Jews,Siedliszcze (Pol.)	-	MURDER	POL.
HOLZLER, Ludig	304741	M		Member, Gestapo, Krakau (Pol.) 11.39-2.45	59/278	RAPE	POL.
HOLZMANN	266365	M		Lt., Anti-Aircraft, Unit L 51151 or L 51157, at moment of Crime Quarteted at Muedes and Nouan sur Loire (Fr.) 18.9.44	-	MISC.CRIMES	FR.
HOMBRECHER, Fritz	265944	M		SS-Rottfhr., SD. Charleville Ardennes (Fr.) 45	56/352	MURDER	FR.
HOMMEL, Willy	266583	M		Pvt., SS 2 Pz.Jg.Ausb.u.Ers.Abt.No.1 "Rastenburg" East - Prussia, Omey (Fr.) 28.8.44	-	MURDER	FR.
HOMOLA, Josef	303261	M		Pol.Secretary, Gestapo, Kattowitz (Pol.) 39-42	56/353	INTERR.	POL.
HONIKE, Fritz	303262	M		Sgt., Feldgend. at Angouleme, Chasseneuil (Charente) (Fr.) 43-22.3.44	56/354	MURDER	FR.
HOPFNER, Anton	265706	M		SS-Schfhr., Krakau (Pol.)	-	MISC.CRIMES	POL.
HOPP	265714	M		Cmdt., Frontier-guard, Turek (Pol.)	-	MURDER	POL.
HOPPACH, Konrad	304742	M		Member, Gestapo, Krakau (Pol.) 11.39-2.45	59/279	RAPE	POL.
HOPPE, Fritz	303263	M		Krim.Sekr., Gestapo, Kattowitz (Pol.) 39-42	56/355	INTERR.	POL.
HOPPE, Paul	304743	M		Member, Gestapo, Krakau (Pol.) 11.39-2.45	59/280	RAPE	POL.
HORACH	266582	M		W.O., 9 SS Pz.Div. "Hohenstaufen" Unit No. 23474, Nimes (Fr.) 2.3.44	-	MURDER	FR.
HORETZKI, Johann	267475	M	circa 15	Cpl., Feldgend., Besancon and vicinity (Fr.) 44	-	MURDER	FR.
HORING	303691	M		Member, Gestapo, Warschau (Pol.) 39-45	57/479	BRUTALITY	POL.
HORING	304745	M		Member, Gestapo, Krakau (Pol.) 11.39-2.45	59/282	MURDER	POL.

HOR - ILC

NAME	C.R.FILE NUMBER	SEX	DATE OF BIRTH	RANK OCCUPATION UNIT PLACE AND DATE OF CRIME	UNWCC LIST/ SERIAL NO.	REASON WANTED	WANTED BY
HORLICH	267404	M		Lt., Army, St.Pierre de Varangeville (Fr.) 17.11.40	-	MURDER	FR.
HORMANN (I)	303692	M		Member, Gestapo, Warschau (Pol.) 39-45	57/480	BRUTALITY	POL.
HORMANN (II)	303693	M		Member, Gestapo, Warschau (Pol.) 39-45	57/481	BRUTALITY	POL.
HORN, Max, Dr.	265625	M		See names listed under "Special Headings"			
HORN, Otto	265715	M		Uscharfhr.,SS-staff Extermination-Camp, Treblinka (Pol.) 42-43	-	MURDER	POL.
HORNIG	303694	M		Member, Gestapo, Warschau (Pol.) 39-45	57/482	MURDER	POL.
HOSCHEK	303264	M		Member, Group 530 Geh.Feldpolizei,Bruessel (Bel.) 40-44	56/357	MURDER	BEL.
HOSER, Marianne	304746	F		Member, Gestapo, Krakau (Pol.) 11.39-2.45	59/283	MURDER	POL.
HOSSER, Paul	303265	M		Cpl., Group 530 Geh.Feldpolizei,Bruessel (Bel.) 40-44	56/359	MURDER	BEL.
HOTZER	304231	M		Lt. serving in Arta-Epiros and Western Thessalia area (Grc.) 10.43	58/318	MURDER	GRC.
HOUBEN	304232	M		Member,Feldgendarmerie at Fort Hoek Van Holland, Einheit IA. AK.30, Honselersdijk nr.Naaldwijk (Neth.) 28.4.45	58/319	MURDER	NETH.
HOUCHELAG	267405	M		Sgt.-Major, Feldgendarmerie of Compiegne, Villers s.Coudun (Fr.) 8.44	-	MURDER	FR.
HOVEN	265943	M		Capt., 2.F.J.Div.,Brest (Fr.) 8.9.44	-	MURDER	FR.
HOYER	309695	M		Member, Gestapo, Warschau (Pol.) 39-45	57/485	MURDER	POL.
HRUBE, Karol	266758	M	8.12.96	Commissary, owner of the factory "Pischinger", Krakau (Pol.) 39-45	-	MURDER	POL.
HUBER	266600	M		Lt., Art.Regt.?, Hesmond (Fr.) 4.9.44	-	MURDER	FR.
HUBER	266930	M		Chief Cpl., Flakmast 30-XII, Carcassonne (Fr.) 19.8.44	-	MURDER	FR.
HUBER	267465	M		Staff-Sgt.,Feldgend.,Besancon and vicinity (Fr.) 44	-	MURDER	FR.
HUBER	304233	M		Sgt., Feldgendarmerie Naaldwijk,Honsersdijk nr.Naaldwijk (Neth.) 28.4.45, 12.4-5.45	58/320	MURDER	NETH.
HUBER, Alfred	264638	M	18. 1.22	See names listed unter "Special Headings"			
HUBER, Hans	304747	M		Member, Gestapo, Krakau (Pol.) 11.39-2.45	59/284	MURDER	POL.
HUBERT (or HUEBER) called: The Chinese	266601	M		Guard (Works foreman), C.C. Buchloe (Ger.)	-	MISC.CRIMES	FR.
HUBERT, Josef	265335	M		Cmdt.,Gendarmerie, Praprotno nr.Skofja Loka (Yugo.) 1.43-5.45	-	MISC.CRIMES	YUGO.
HUBERT, Willi	304748	M		SS-Oscharfhr., Driver, Sich.Pol.Kolomea, to Leideritz, Commander of SD and Sipo, Zablotow,Kossow,Szeparowce,Kolomea (Pol.) 41-42	59/285	MURDER	POL.
HUBIG, Hermann	304749	M		Member, Gestapo, Krakau (Pol.) 11.39-2.45	59/286	BRUTALITY	POL.
HUBL, Kurt	304750	M		Member, Gestapo, Krakau (Pol.) 11.39-2.45	59/287	MURDER	POL.
HUBNER	303766	M		Scharfhr., Gestapo Lodz (Pol.) 39-44	56/361	BRUTALITY	POL.
HUBNER	308877	M		Feldpolizeikommissar, Antwerpen, Bruessel (Bel.) 40-44	60/282	MURDER	BEL.
HUBNER, Erich	121046	M	23. 1.23	Army, Sars-La-Bruyere Hainaut (Bel.) 44	16/9	WITNESS	BEL.
HUBNER, Otto	265403	M		Capt., Gestapo, SD, Bayonne and vicinity (Fr.) 40-44	-	MURDER	FR.
HUDEL-KOCH, Augustin	161631	M		SS-Uscharfhr.,No.Char.174/95 Bn.,Leibstandarte SS "Adolf Hitler", Bierwart (Bel.) 44	16/58	PILLAGE	BEL.
HUEBER (see HUBERT) called: The Chinese	266601						
HUEBLER	265755	M		SS-Scharfhr.,Guard, Staff C.C.,Extermination-Camp, Sobibor (Pol.) 42-43	-	MURDER	POL.
HUEBNER	265753	M		SS-Scharfhr.,Interpreter,Official, 4.Gestapo section,Lodz (Pol.)	-	MISC.CRIMES	POL.
HUEBNER, Werner	265960	M	5. 3.23	Oscharfhr., SS (327-1947), Horsens-Juetland (Den.) 13.1.45	-	MURDER	DEN.
HUEGE, Friedhelm	304752	M		Member, Gestapo, Krakau (Pol.) 11.39-2.45	59/289	MURDER	POL.
HUFFSCHMIDT, Hans	197111	M		N.C.O., Kdo.1502 Stalag XII B, Bubingen (Ger.) 28.4.41	30/206	MURDER	FR.
HUFING, Gustav	265752	M		Guard, Extermination-Camp, Chelmno (Pol.) 41-43	-	MURDER	POL.
HUG	303267	M		Cpl.,Group 530 Geh.Feldpolizei,Bruessel (Bel.) 40-44	56/362	MURDER	BEL.
HUGLER	266361	M		Pvt., Caen (Fr.) 6.44	-	MURDER	FR.
HUGU	265751	M		Member, Gestapo, Kazimierz Dolny (Pol.) 42	-	MURDER	POL.
HUGUELHE, Georges	197141	M		Pvt., 2.Coy. Feld-Ausb.Bn.189, F.P.No. 22732 D, Clermont-Dessus (Fr.) 17.8.44.	28/79	MURDER	FR.
HUITZ	179594	M		Member, Gestapo, St.Quentin (Fr.) 44	16/80	MURDER	FR.
HUJER, Albert (or ChUJAR)	267650	M		SS-Hptscharfhr., C.C. Plaszow (Pol.) 43	-	MURDER	POL.
HULLER	266906	M	22	Ordonnance Officer, Div. "Bode", Dordogne (Fr.) 19.6.,22.7.44	-	SUSPECT	FR.
HUMM	185959	M		Head Kdo.of C.C. Flossenburg - Hersbruck (Ger.) 42-45	25/953	MURDER	FR.
HUMMEL, Adam	306250	M		Pvt., Boedo (Nor.) 7.5.45	28/177	MURDER	NOR.
HUMMEL, Dr.	265749	M		Personal-Secretary, Reichsleiter Bormann, Krakau (Pol.)	-	MISC.CRIMES	POL.
HUMMITZSCH, Heinz	179478	M	08	SS-Stubafhr., Head SD, Abt.III Sipo, Bruessel (Bel.) 40-44	28/15	MURDER	BEL.
HUNDERTPFENNIG	266929	M		Hptscharfhr., 18.SS-Pz.Gren.Div."Horst Wessel", Oradour s.Glane (Fr.) 10.6.44	-	MURDER	FR.
HUNDT	303697	M		Member, Gestapo, Warschau (Pol.) 39-45	57/490	MURDER	POL.
HUNERFELD	266362	M	circa 00	Sgt.Major, Interpreter, Feldgendarmerie 662 at Beaune, Manlay (Fr.) 29.-31.7.44	-	MISC.CRIMES	FR.
HUNKO, Wasyl	304753	M		Member, Gestapo, Krakau (Pol.) 11.39-2.45	59/291	MURDER	POL.
HUNNICKE, Diderich	304754	M		Member, Geh.Feldpolizei, H.Q. Boulevard Piercot or the Avenue Rogier, Luettich (Bel.) 40-41	59/292	MURDER	BEL.
HUNSCHE, I.A.	303268	M		Polizeiassessor, Kempen (Ger.) 25.10.41	56/364	MURDER	POL.
HUNSER	197657	M	05	Feldgend., Feldgendarmerie, Reims (Fr.) 21.12.43	31/236	MURDER	FR.
HUNTELMAYER, Georg	267319	M		Agent, Gestapo, Marseille and vicinity (Fr.)	-	MURDER	FRA
HURBANN, Fritz	197143	M		Adjutant, Parachute-pioneer-Bn., F.P. No. L 50633 B,Airforce. St. Amand-Montrond (Fr.) 8.6.44	31/237	MURDER	FR.
HUT, N.	266759	M		Sgt., Mannschafts-Stammlager III A, Luckenwalde (Ger.) 39-45	-	TORTURE	POL.
HUTTEMAN, Peter	265949	M	circa 05	Hptscharfhr., SD, Chalons s.Marne (Fr.) 43-44	-	MISC.CRIMES	FR.
HUTTICH, Paul	266363	M	00	Sgt., Feldgendarmerie, St.Michel (Fr.) 3.3.44	-	MISC.CRIMES	FR.
HUTTIG, Helmut	309166	M		SS-Uscharfhr., (No.127673), C.C. Buchenwald (Ger.)betw.5.38-10.43	25/250	MURDER	BEL.
HYNCK	197145	M		Cpl.-Chief, SS-Uscharfhr., Camp Royallieu (Fr.) 41-44	31/99	MURDER	FR.
IBES (see ITES)	304237						
IBNER	265708	M		Member, Gestapo, Lublin, Hrubieszow (Pol.) 42-44	-	MURDER	POL.
IBORG (I)	265803	M		SS-Oscharfhr., Gestapo, Lodz (Pol.) 39-44	56/365	BRUTALITY	POL.
IBORG (II)	265804	M		SS-Scharfhr., Gestapo, Lodz (Pol.) 39-44	56/366	BRUTALITY	POL.
ICKS, Werner	308969	M		Lt., Feldgendarmerie, Tournai-Ville Pommeroeul (Bel.) 9.44	60/285	MURDER	BEL.
IFFLANDER, Klara	304755	F		Member, Gestapo, Krakau (Pol.) 11.39-2.45	59/294	MURDER	POL.
IHNE, Otto	304235	M		Cpl., Airforce, Nachtjagd-Group No.4, Vicinity of Charleroi (Bel.) 2.44	58/328	MURDER	BEL.
ILCHMANN	265402	M		SS-Mann, Regt. "Der Fuehrer", Div. "Das Reich", Oradour s.Glane (Fr.) 10.6.44	-	MURDER	FR.

ILK - JOH

NAME	C.R.FILE NUMBER	SEX	DATE OF BIRTH	RANK OCCUPATION UNIT PLACE AND DATE OF CRIME	UNWCC LIST/ SERIAL NO.	REASON WANTED	WANTED BY
ILKIW	265733	M		Member, Gestapo, Tarnow (Pol.) 40-45	-	BRUTALITY	POL.
ILLMER	308970	M		Ostuumbannfhr., Oberregierungsrat, Radom (Pol.)1.40-1.44	60/287	MURDER	POL.
IMERT	265998	M		Cápt., Feldkommandantur, Brest (Fr.) 8.9.44	-	MURDER	FR.
IMLER calles:THE SPITZ	266584	M	circa 10	Sgt., Unit SS No.A 75.794, Langoiran (Fr.) 10.4.40	-	MURDER	FR.
INFLIND	265729	M		SS-Mann, Chief, Factory of ammunition, Skarzysk (Pol.)	-	MURDER	POL.
IRIG	267132	M		Major, Bn.Commander, SS "Prinz Eugen" Div., Sinj (Yugo.) 8.9.43-10.44	-	MURDER	YUGO.
IRRMANN, Fritz	265730	M		Commandant, SS-Stabsscharfhr., Extermination camp, Belzec (Pol.) 42-44	-	MISC.CRIMES	POL.
IRZIG, Franz	264441	M	13. 3.01	Uscharfhr., Gestapo Paris KDS IV-2, Paris (Fr.) 44	-	SUSPECT	FR.
ISHORST, Horst	304236	M		Lt., Air-Force, Nachtjagd-Group No.4, vicinity of Charleroi (Bel.) 2.44	58/329	MURDER	BEL.
ITES (or IBES), Heiko	304237	M	circa 04	Lt., MA Btty-Fhr.in Flak-Abt.4-815, Texel (Neth.) 10.4.45	58/330	MURDER	NETH.
ITNER, Paul	265718	M		Guard, C.C., Chelmno (Pol.)	-	MISC.CRIMES	POL.
IWAN	265716	M		Kapo, C.C., Plaszow (Pol.)	-	MURDER	POL.
JABLOWSKI	266907	M		Uscharfhr., Waffen-SS, SS Div. "Das Reich", Dordogne, Correze, Creuse, Hte.Vienne (Fr.)5.-6.44	-	SUSPECT	FR.
JACKEL, Georg	266958	M	21. 2.03	Uscharfhr., Gestapo KDS IV A2, Paris (Fr.) 43-44	-	SUSPECT	FR.
JACOB	266299	M		Pvt., Africa-Corps,6.Coy., 1.Section, Hte.Marne-Aube (Fr.) 25.-31.8.44	-	MURDER	FR.
JACOBI, Helene	267464	F		Gestapo, Limoges and vicinity (Fr.) 44	-	SUSPECT	FR.
JACOBS, Walter	308973	M	3. 3.13	Krim.Asst., Gestapo H4 Kiel, various places in Germany and German occupied territory (Ger.) 25.3.and 13.4.44	60/291	MURDER	U.K.
JAECK	308974	M		SS-Sturmscharfhr., secretary of Administration, Radom (Pol.) 1.40- 1.45	60/292	BRUTALITY	POL.
JAECKEL, Gerhard	265320	M		Lt., Schutzpolizei, 32.Pol.Regt., Lublin (Pol.) 43	-	MURDER	POL.
JAEGER, Kurt	308975	M		Civilian, vicinity of Walle (Ger.) 44	60/294	BRUTALITY	U.S.
JAEGER, Wilhelm	266440	M		Mayor, Wiltz (Grand-Duchy-Lux.) 40-45	-	MISC.CRIMES	LUX.
JAENCHEN	303330	M		Sonderfhr., Group 530 of Geh.Feldpolizei, Bruessel (Bel.)40-44	56/368	MURDER	BEL.
JAGERHORST (or JAGERHOST)	267028	M		Lt., 19.SS-Pol.Regt., 3.Bn.10.Coy., Limoges, Brive and vicinity (Fr.) 7.44	-	MURDER	FR.
JAGERHOST (see JAGERHORST)	267028						
JAGIELSKI, Bruno	265719	M		SS, Szubin (Pol.) 39	-	MURDER	POL.
JAHN	265978	M		Engineer, Commission Koch, Bordes, Soues (Fr.) 1.-3.43	-	PILLAGE	FR.
JAHRKE	265722	M		Commandant, Lt., Police, (Schupoabt.), Warschau (Pol.) 39-42	-	MURDER	POL.
JAKOB, Hans	265723	M		Member, staff at extermination camp, Chelmno (Pol.) 41-44	-	MURDER	POL.
JAKOBY	266928	M	circa 10	Cpl., Feldgendarmerie of Blois, Masleves, Coulanges, Blois (Fr.) 7.44 and 10.8.44	-	MURDER	FR.
JAKOPASCHKE	303698	M		Member, Gestapo, Warschau (Pol.) 39-45	57/497	MURDER	POL.
JAKUBOWSKI, Felix	265724	M	20.11.11	Owachtmstr., guard, Extermination camp, Chelmno (Pol.) 41-44	-	BRUTALITY	POL.
JAMISCHEN, Rudolf	266804	M	31. 3.98	Sgt., Detachment which was stationed, Nuits sur Armancon (Yonne), Planay (Fr.) 6.9.44	-	MISC.CRIMES	FR.
JANES, Karl	265408	M	00	W.O., SD, Bayonne and vicinity (Fr.) 40-41	-	MURDER	FR.
JANKE	303331	M		SS-Uscharfhr., Factory, Mielec (Pol.) 41-44	56/371	MURDER	POL.
JANKE	303699	M		Member, Gestapo, Warschau (Pol.) 39-45	57/501	MURDER	POL.
JANKE, Erwin	265727	M		Member, Lt., Command Oflag, Army, Luckenwalde (Ger.) 45	-	MURDER	POL.
JANSEN	266298	M		N.C.O., Africa-Corps, Regt. Ruxleben, 6. Coy., 1. Section, Hte. Marne-Aube (Fr.) 25.-31.8.44	-	MURDER	FR.
JANSSEN	308976	M		SS-Guard, (attached to the hospital), Wolfenbuettel prison (Ger.) 42-45	60/296	MISC.CRIMES	BEL.
JANSSEN, Hans	303332	M		Pvt., Feldgendarmerie Angouleme, Chasseneuil (Fr.) 43-22.3.44	56/372	MURDER	FR.
JANSSEN, Johann	306162	M	3. 2.27	SS-Mann, Sicherheitsdienst, Apeldoorn-distr. (Neth.)44-45	45/245 31/391	MURDER	U.K., NETH.
JANTZO (or HIOTZOT)	267406	M		Chief of culture, Civilian, Avioth (Fr.) 15.8.44	-	MISC.CRIMES	FR.
JANULEWITSCH	267407	M		SS-Guard, C.C., Struthof-Natzweiler (Fr.) 40-45	-	MURDER	FR.
JANZ, Hans-Ulrich	265720	M	14. 9.04	SS-Rottfhr., Member, SS-Heimwehr, Vehiclegroup 8, NSDAP (from 1944), Gdansk, Inowroclaw (Pol.) 22.10.39	-	MURDER	POL.
JAQUES	265721	M		Kapo, C.C., Auschwitz (Pol.)	-	MURDER	POL.
JAROSCH	267119	M		Cpl., Chief, Gestapo, Sinj (Yugo.) 8.9.43-10.44	-	MURDER	YUGO.
JASCHKE, Alfred	303333	M		Gestapo, Siewers' Interpreter, Lodz (Pol.) 39-44	56/373	MURDER	POL.
JASCHKOWSKE, Ewald	303700	M	21. 4.13	SS-Sturmmann, C.C., Majdanek (1cl.) 40-44	57/507	BRUTALITY	POL.
JASCHKUS, Jonas	303701	M		SS-Uscharfhr., C.C., Majdanek (1cl.) 40-42	57/508	BRUTALITY	POL.
JEANSEN, Fernand	266297	M		Architect, Organisation Todt, Mesnois (Fr.) 2.6.44	-	MURDER	FR.
JECK, Eduard	304757	M		Member, Gestapo, Krakau (Pol.) 11.39- 2.45	59/296	MURDER	POL.
JEHL, Marcel	267347	M		Interpreter, Gestapo, Marseille and vicinity (Fr.)	-	MURDER	FR.
JENDE	266771	M		SS-Usturmfhr., Commandant, Group SS L 50539 Paris, Savigny sur Orge (Fr.) 19.8.44	-	MURDER	FR.
JENDREYCZAK, Wladimir	303702	M	7.12.94	SS-Guard, C.C., Majdanek (Pol.) 40-44	57/511	BRUTALITY	POL.
JENKE, Erich	303335	M		Kriminal-Asst., Gestapo, Kattowitz (Pol.) 39-42	56/375	MURDER	POL.
JENNERWEIN	267033	M		Capt., 350.Hindou-Regt., Lureuil, Linge, St.Michel-en-Brenne, Vendoeuvres, St. Maur, Ambrault, Ardentes, Neuilly-les-Blois(Fr.)8.44	-	MURDER	FR.
JENTSCH, Heinrich	308978	M		Feldpolizeikommissar, Antwerpen and Bruessel (Bel.) 40-44	60/298	MURDER	BEL.
JEPSEN	303703	M		Member, Gestapo, Warschau (Pol.) 39-45	57/512	MURDER	POL.
JESS, Paul	304784	M		Member, Gestapo, Krakau (Pol.) 11.39- 2.42	59/298	MURDER	POL.
JESSA	308980	M		SS-Sturmscharfhr., Krim.Angestellter, Radom (Pol.)1.40-1.45	60/300	TORTURE	POL.
JESSEN, Fritz	308981	M		Uscharfhr., Kopenhagen (Den.) 7.5.-19.12.44	60/301	MURDER	DEN.
JETTER	308982	M		SS-Oscharfhr., Krim.Asst., Radom (Pol.) 1.40-1.45	60/302	BRUTALITY	POL.
JIRSA, August	265694	M	88	Manager, Fisher's Trade Union, Lublin (Pol.)	-	MISC.CRIMES	POL.
JOB	265695	M		Room senior, Block No.45 C.C., Sachsenhausen (Ger.)	-	MISC.CRIMES	POL.
JOB	266563	M		Capt., 1.Coy., 6.Div.Paratrooper, Pz.-Jaeg., Chateau de Miannay (Fr.) 43-44	-	MISC.CRIMES	FR.
JOCHN	265696	M		Wachtmeister, Gendarmerie, Brzesko (Pol.)	-	BRUTALITY	POL.
JOHANNSEN, Heinrich	304238	M	17. 1.98	Farmer, Civilian, 42	-	BRUTALITY	POL.
JOHN, Aleksander	303337	M		Kriminaldirektor, Gestapo, Kattowitz (Pol.) 39-42	56/377	INTERR.	POL.
JOHN, Hans	303338	M		SS-Osturmfhr., Gestapo, Kattowitz (Pol.) 39-42	56/378	PILLAGE	POL.

JOH - KAP

NAME	C.R.FILE NUMBER	SEX	DATE OF BIRTH	RANK OCCUPATION UNIT PLACE AND DATE OF CRIME	UNWCC LIST/ SERIAL NO.	REASON WANTED	WANTED BY
JOHN, Robert	265697	M		Wachmann, Gendarmerie, Szczurowa, Brzesko (Pol.)	-	BRUTALITY	POL.
JOHNSDORF, Willy	304239	M	circa 03	Railway-employee, Guard duty of the Hilledijk, Parallelweg, Rotterdam (Neth.) 27.4.45	58/337	MURDER	NETH.
JOKISCH, Gustaw	265703	M		District head of farmers, Civilian, Biala Podlaska (Pol.)	-	MISC.CRIMES	POL.
JOOS	303704	M		Member, Gestapo, Warschau (Pol.) 39-45	57/515	MURDER	POL.
JOPKE	303705	M		Member, Gestapo, Warschau (Pol.) 39-45	57/515 A	MURDER	POL.
JOPPICH, Ergard	267279	M		Oscharfhr., Gestapo, Bordeaux and vicinity (Fr.) 42-8.44	-	MURDER	FR.
JORDAN	308984	M		Cpl., G.F.P., Antwerpen and Bruessel (Bel.) 40-44	60/304	MURDER	BEL.
JORDAN, Anton	265704	M	07	Official, member, County office, Gendarmerie, Lublin (Pol.) 43-44	-	MURDER	POL.
JORDENS, Hans	303339	M		Polizeisekretaer, Gestapo, Kattowitz (Pol.) 39-42	56/379	PILLAGE	POL.
JOSTEIN	265702	M		Member, Staff, C.C. Auschwitz (Pol.)	-	MURDER	POL.
JOTHANN	265738	M		SS-Osturmbannfhr., C.C. Oswiesim, Brzezinka (Pol.)	-	MURDER	POL.
JUDES, Kurtz	267278	M	13 or 15	Commander, Chief Sgt.Major, Prisoner Camp, Army, Lampaul-Guillimiau, Brest and vicinity (Fr.) 7.-8.44	-	MURDER	FR.
JUERGENS, Ludwig	265728	M	30. 7.80	Employee, Institute for German work in the East, Krakau (Pol.)	-	MISC.CRIMES	POL.
JUNG, Friedrich	303706	M	1. 9.08	SS-Mann, C.C. Majdanek (Pol.) 40-44	57/518	BRUTALITY	POL.
JUNG, Heinrich	267355	M		Lt., Gestapo, Pexonne (Fr.) 27.8.44	-	MISC.CRIMES	FR.
JUNG, Ludwig	265737	M	28. 2.20	Member, Wachtmeister, Schupo, C.C. Chelmno (Pol.) 41-44	-	MURDER	POL.
JUNG, Walter	304240	M		SS-Rottfhr., 12 Aufkl.Abt., 12 SS Pz.Div. "Hitler Jugend", Ascq Nord (Fr.) 1.-2.4.44	58/339	MURDER	FR.
JUNGE, Artur	303707	M	22. 2.01	SS-Rottfhr., C.C. Majdanek (Pol.) 40-44	57/519	MURDER	POL.
JUNGE, Max	303341	M		Pvt., Group 530, Geh.Feldpolizei, Bruessel (Bel.) 40-44	56/381	MURDER	BEL.
JUNGE, Wilhelm	265709	M		SS-Hptsturmfhr., Secretary, Gestapo, Lodz (Pol.)	-	MISC.CRIMES	POL.
JUNGINGER, Hans	304241	M		Ortsgruppenleiter in the area of Gernsbach, Weisenbach, Oberstrot, Hilpertsau (Ger.) 9.8.44	58/340	MURDER	U.S.
JUPKE, Erwin	265711	M		Lt., Sonderfhr., Army, POW Camp Stalag III A, Luckenwalde (Ger.) 43-45	-	BRUTALITY	POL.
JUNTZINGER, Frantz	267032	M		Member, Gestapo of Charleville, Revin (Fr.) 14.-15.6.44	-	MURDER	FR.
JURASTIF	308985	M		Pvt., member of guard unit forming part of the crew of the V-weapon based at Hook van Holland, Wassenaar (Neth.) 11.44	60/305	PILLAGE	NETH.
JURGENSEN	267277	M		Member, Gestapo, Bordeaux and vicinity (Fr.) 42-8.44	-	MURDER	FR.
JURGENSEN	303708	M		Member, Gestapo, Warschau (Pol.) 39-45	57/520	MURDER	POL.
JURGES, Gerda	304786	F		Member, Gestapo, Krakau (Pol.) 11.39-2.45	59/301	MURDER	POL.
JURIEFF, Johann	304787	M		Member, Gestapo, Krakau (Pol.) 11.39-2.45	59/302	MURDER	POL.
JURSCHEIT	308986	M		Feldpolizeikommissar, G.F.P., Antwerpen and Bruessel (Bel.) 40-44	60/306	MURDER	BEL.
JUTTNER	304242	M		Member, Gestapo at Chalons-sur-Marne, Dept.Marne (Fr.) 43-44	58/341	MURDER	FR.
KACZYSKA, Stanislaw	303709	M	23. 5.13	Kapo, C.C. Belsen (Ger.) 39-45	57/522	MURDER	POL.
KADDATZ, Otto	303710	M	25. 1.04	SS-Mann, C.C. Majdanek (Pol.) 40-44	57/523	BRUTALITY	POL.
KAEHLER	265977	M		Fregattenkapitaen, Commander of Seaport Brest (Fr.) 8.9.44	-	MURDER	FR.
KAEHLER, Hans	308987	M		Crim.Asst.Anwaerter, Gestapo HQ Kiel, Germany and German occupied territory 25.3.-15.4.44	60/308	MURDER	U.K.
KAESTNER	303961	M		Doctor, Firm of Deschimag Seebeck, Wesermuende Camp (Ger.) 44-45	56/385	BRUTALITY	FR.
KAH, Dr.	303711	M		Dr., Member, Gestapo, Warschau (Pol.) 39-45	57/524	MURDER	POL.
KAHLER, Karl, Heinz	304788	M		Member, 3 Coy.of Paratroops stat.at Relecq Kerhuon, Finistere (Fr.) 25.7. and 27.8.44	59/304	MISC.CRIMES	FR.
KAHNERT (or KANNER)	303962	M		Feldgendarme, Unit 740, Feldgendarmerie Jonzac, Marignac, Charente Maritime (Fr.) 21.8.44	56/386	MURDER	FR.
KAINER, Joseph	265899	M		Oberwachmann, Extermination Camp, Sobibor (Pol.) 42-43	-	MURDER	POL.
KAINRADL, Anton	303712	M	13. 1.09	SS-Uscharfhr., C.C. Majdanek (Pol.) 40-44	57/525	MURDER	POL.
KAISER	1705	M	12	SS-Hptsturmfhr., 12 Pz.Div. "Hitler Jugend", Caen (Fr.) 6.-7.44	-	MURDER	CAN.,U.K.
KAISER	265900	M		SS-Hptsturmfhr., Chief, Construction Branch, Lwow (Pol.)	-	MURDER	POL.
KAISER	266547	M		W.O.Sgt.Major, Feldgendarmerie 658, Paray le Monial and vicinity (Fr.) 44	-	SUSPECT	FR.
KAISER	266805	M	circa 00	Miller, Civilian, Gispersleben (Ger.) 14.4.41	-	MURDER	FR.
KAISER	267276	M		Hptscharfhr., Gestapo, Bordeaux and vicinity (Fr.) 42-8.44	-	MURDER	FR.
KAISER	267463	M		Member, Gestapo, Luchon and vicinity (Fr.) 1.43-7.44	-	MURDER	FR.
KAISER	303713	M		Member, Gestapo, Warschau (Pol.) 39-45	57/526	MURDER	POL.
KAISER, Walter	304789	M		Member, Gestapo, Krakau (Pol.) 11.39-2.45	59/305	BRUTALITY	POL.
KAJSER, Alex	265857	M	22	Interpreter, Chief, Extermination Camp, Sobibor (Pol.) 42-43	-	BRUTALITY	POL.
KALF	308988	M		Cpl., G.F.P., Antwerpen and Bruessel (Bel.) 40-44	60/311	MURDER	BEL.
KALKHOFEN, Fritz	264637	M	11.1.04	See names listed under "Special Headings"	-		
KALLENBORN	304790	M		Field-Pol.-Commiss., Secr.Field Police, Boulevard, Piercot or the Avenue Rogier, Luettich (Bel.) 40-41	59/306	MURDER	BEL.
KALLMEIER, Fritz	304791	M		Member, Gestapo, Krakau (Pol.) 11.39-2.45	59/307	BRUTALITY	POL.
KALMS, Arthur	303363	M		Kriminalbeamter, Gestapo, Kattowitz (Pol.) 39-42	56/388	BRUTALITY	POL.
KALON, Ruth	304792	F		Member, Gestapo, Krakau (Pol.) 11.39-2.45	59/308	BRUTALITY	POL.
KALTENBRAUNER, Anton	303364	M		Kriminalbeamter, Gestapo, Kattowitz (Pol.) 39-42	56/390	PILLAGE	POL.
KAMM (see KAMN)	266207						
KAMM, Peter	265858	M		SS-Rottfhr., C.C. Lublin-Majdanek (Pol.)	-	MURDER	POL.
KAMM, Rudolf	265877	M		SS-Uscharfhr., Extermination Camp, Sobibor (Pol.) 42-43	-	MURDER	POL.
KAMMANN (see KARMANT, Otto)	267275						
KAMPF	267354	M		Agent, Gestapo, Marseille (Fr.)	-	MURDER	FR.
KAMPLAIR (or KAMPLER) Friedrich	265646	M		Hptscharfhr., SD, Chalons sur Marne (Fr.) 43-44	-	MISC.CRIMES	FR.
KAMPLER, Friedrich (see KAMPLAIR)	265646						
KANDIAN	265574	M	17	SS-Hptsturmfhr., 16 SS Pz.Div., Massa Carrara (It.) 8.44	-	MURDER	U.K.
KANDZIA, Josef	304793	M		Member, Gestapo, Krakau (Pol.) 11.39-2.45	59/309	BRUTALITY	POL.
KANNENGIESSER, Rudolf	266999	M	11. 4.03	SS-Uscharfhr., Gestapo KDS IV E 3, Paris (Fr.) 43-44	-	SUSPECT	FR.
KANNER (see KAHNERT)	303362						
KAOFFER (or KLEFFER)	265404			Town-Major, Place at "Lecreusot", Larmagne, St.Pierre De Varenne (Fr.) 28.6.44	-	MURDER	FR.
KAPLAN	266300	M		Pvt., Africa-Corps, Regt.Ruxleben, 6 Coy., 1 Section, Hte.Marne Aube (Fr.) 25.-31.8.44	-	MURDER	FR.
KAPPENBERG, Gottfried	303365	M		SS-Scharfhr., Gestapo, Kattowitz (Pol.) 39-42	56/394	MURDER	POL.

KAP - KIP

NAME	C.R.FILE NUMBER	SEX	DATE OF BIRTH	RANK OCCUPATION UNIT PLACE AND DATE OF CRIME	UNWCC LIST/ SERIAL NO.	REASON WANTED	WANTED BY
KAPFES, Karl	303714	M	2. 4.14	SS-Mann,C.C.Majdanek (Pol.) 40-44	57/532	BRUTALITY	POL.
KAPUSCIK	308989	M		Interpreter ?, Radom (Pol.) 1.40- 1.45	60/312	MURDER	POL.
KAREL, Augustin	267140	M		Councillor,coal-mining establishment civ.,Trbovlje (Yugo.)41-45	-	MURDER	YUGO.
KARLENS, Henri (or HEINTZ-HEINSON)	267029	M	circa 07	Abteilungsleiter,Interpreter,Gestapo of Blois,Maves and vicinity (Fr.) 43-44		MURDER	FR.
KARMANN (or KAMMANN),Otto	267275	M		Capt.,Baker-Coy.,19.,unit-no.08 598,Chailles (Fr.) 6.-8.40	-	PILLAGE	FR.
KARSTEN	267274	M		Hptscharfhr.,Gestapo,Bordeaux and vicinity (Fr.) 42-8.44	-	MURDER	FR.
KARSTEN	303366	M		Lt.,Feldgend.,Angouleme,Chasseneuil (Fr.) 43-44 (22. 3.44)	56/398	MURDER	FR.
KARTEK, Maria	267467	F		Gestapo,Limoges and vicinity (Fr.) 44	-	SUSPECT	FR.
KARTH, Erwin	265232	M		Pvt.,26.Panzer-Div., Furbechio Marshes (It.) 7.44		WITNESS	U.K.
KARTH, Willi	304161	M		Member,Hilfspolizei at Janowiec,Znin distr. (Pol.) 39-44	58/350	MURDER	POL.
KARTZLER (see HARTZLER, Klaus)	265997						
KARWEGER, Ernst	265406	M		3.Coy.,1.Bn.,SS-Regt."Der Fuehrer",Div."Das Reich",Cradour s. Glane (Fr.) 10. 6.44	60/313	MURDER	FR.
KASANOW, Kasyk	304794	M		Member,Gestapo,Krakau (Pol.) 11.39-2.45	59/310	BRUTALITY	POL.
KASER, Willy	267030	M		Lt.,350.Hindou-Regt.,Lureuil,Linge,St.Michelen Brenne,Vendoeuvres St.Maur,Ambrault,Ardentes,Neuillay-les-Blois (Fr.) 8.44		MURDER	FR.
KASPRUSCH, Edmund	303715	M	27.10.07	Camp-Commander,C.C. Majdanek (Pol.) 40-42	57/535	MURDER	POL.
KASTLE, Wilhelm	266548	M		Commissary,Custom house,Foncine le Haut,Castelblanc (Fr.)30.8.44	-	INCENDIARISM	FR.
KASZUB, Emil	265924	M		Member,Guard,Sgt.,C.C. Auschwitz (Pol.)		BRUTALITY	POL.
KAUFMANN (I)	303716	M		Member,Gestapo,Warschau (Pol.) 39-45	57/537	BRUTALITY	POL.
KAUFMANN (II)	303717	M		Member,Gestapo,Warschau (Pol.) 39-45	57/598	BRUTALITY	POL.
KAUFMANN, Johann	304795	M		Member,Gestapo,Krakau (Pol.) 11.39- 2.45	59/311	BRUTALITY	POL.
KAUL, Willi	267031	M	9. 2.09	Hptscharfhr.,Gestapo B S IV, Paris (Fr.) 44	-	SUSPECT	FR.
KAULA, Johann	303354	M		Kriminalbeamter,Gestapo,Kattowitz (Pol.) 39-42	56/401	INTERR.	POL.
KAULFUSS	265920	M		SS-Uscharfhr., Penal camp, Janow (Pol.)		BRUTALITY	POL.
KAUSCH, Otto	303355	M		Secretary,Group 530,Geh.Feldpolizei,Bruessel (Bel.) 40-44	56/402	MURDER	BEL.
KAUTTER	265919	M		Chief,SS-Hptsturmfhr.,Gestapo office IV 1,Lodz (Pol.)	-	BRUTALITY	POL.
KAUTZ, Erich	303356	M		Kriminalsekretaer,Gestapo,Kattowitz (Pol.) 39-42	56/404	INTERR.	POL.
KAWIAK, Jan	266757	M	13.12.03	Manager,Electric Railway,Krakau (Pol.) 39	-	MISC.CRIMES	POL.
KEIL, Gustave	266549	M		Pvt.,Feldgend.,658.,Paray le Moniel and environ (Fr.) 43-44	58/354	SUSPECT	FR.
KEIMER, Claire	267468	F	circa 21	Secretary,Gestapo,Bordeaux (Fr.) 43-44	-	MISC.CRIMES	FR.
KEISER, Joseph	265921	M	99	Director,Trade Chamber,Lublin (Pol.)		BRUTALITY	POL.
KELBERT	265923	M		SS-Uscharfhr.,Interpreter,Gestapo,Lodz (Pol.) 39-45	56/406	MISC.CRIMES	POL.
KELER, Richard	265922	M		Wachtmeister,Gendarmerie,Dabrowa (Pol.) 43	-	MURDER	POL.
KELLER	265965	M		SS-Sturmfhr.,Police-Bn.,Balish (Pol.) 39-40	-	MURDER	POL.
KELLER	267075	M		Capt.,350.Regt.Hindou,Lureuil,Liece,St.Michel-en Brenne Vendoeuvres,St.Maur,Ambrault ?,Ardentes,Neuillay-les-Blois (Fr.) 8.44	-	MURDER	FR.
KELLER, Arno	264410	M	29. 4.10	SS-Schfhr.,Gestapo Paris BDS IV,Paris (Fr.) 44	-	SUSPECT	FR.
KELLER, Fillip	265896	M	29.12.97	Secretary,Amtskommissar,Office, (Pol.)	-	MISC.CRIMES	POL.
KELLER, Siegfried (see COLLER)	265216						
KELM	303719	M		Member,Gestapo,Warschau (Pol.) 39-45	57/545	BRUTALITY	POL.
KELNER, Paperl	267076	M		Agent,Gestapo,Arras (Fr.) 8.41	-	MURDER	FR.
KEMNITZ,	265680	M		Capt.,2.Paratrooper-Div.,Cdt.Paratrooper-Abt.,Brest (Fr.)8.9.44	-	MURDER	FR.
KEMPF, Wilhelm	303720	M	22. 3.09	SS-Rottenfhr.,C.C.Dora Nordhausen (Ger.) 39-45	57/546	BRUTALITY	POL.
KENDEL, Josef	303721	M	7. 8.20	SS-Mann,C.C. Majdanek (Pol.) 40-44	57/547	BRUTALITY	POL.
KERGER	267559	M		Twentsche Bank,Wageningen (Neth.) 3.45	-	PILLAGE	NETH.
KERLING, Hans	264564	M	5. 2.04	See names listed under "Special Headings"			
KERNER	265892	M		Member,Gendarmerie,Krasnik (Pol.)	-	MURDER	POL.
KERN	265893	M		Kapo and Guard,C.C. Gusen (Aust.)	-	MURDER	POL.
KERN, Fritz	304164	M		SS-Osturmfhr.,Rollkommando, Weisenbach,Gernsbach,Oberstrot (Ger.) 9.8.44	58/355	MURDER	U.S.
KERNER,	148791	M		Chief,Hauptsturmfhr.,SD, polit.section,Gestapo,Krakau (Pol.)	-	MURDER	POL.,U.K.
KERSCHIEPER, Berndt	308901	M		Sgt.-M.,G.F.P.,Antwerpen,Bruessel (Bel.) 40-44	60/317	MURDER	BEL.
KERSTEN	265641	M	circa 07	Major,244.Inf.Div., transferred 932.R-I,3.Bn.,Le Castellet (Fr.) 6.-8.44	-	MURDER	FR.
KERTING	265894	M		Chief,Post-office,Zamosc (Pol.)	-	BRUTALITY	POL.
KESSELKAMPF (see SESSELKAMPF, Bernard)	267459						
KESSLER	267273	M		Ruestungskdo.of Nancy,Blamont (Fr.) 9.44	-	MURDER	FR.
KETHER	265895	M		Standartenfhr.,Chief,SS and Police,Gen.Gov.,(Pol.)	-	MURDER	POL.
KETTLER	266301	M		Cpl.,Army,95.Security Regt.,Le Bugue,Journiac,Saint-Leon-sur-Vezere (Fr.) 6.44	-	MURDER	FR.
KEUSEN, Hellmuth	264616	M	11. 9.09	See names listed under "Special Headings"			
KHUN	197676	M	circa 05	Chief Artificer,Usturmfhr.,Flakmat 30-XII SS-officers school at Bresse, Baudrigues nr.Carcassonne,St.Maurice s.Moselle (Fr.) 19. 8.44-16.9.44	32/253	MURDER	FR.
KICKBUSCH	266938	M		Agent,Gestapo,Rouen and region (Fr.) 40-44	-	MURDER	FR.
KIEFER	267070	M	circa 00	Lt.,3.Coy.,Bn.199 at Creusot,Marmagne (Fr.) 28. 6.44	-	MURDER	FR.
KIEFFER (see KAOFFER)	265404						
KIEL (or KILL, Wilhelm also Willy)	185088	M	26. 1.06	Sturmschfhr.,Gestapo Paris BDS IV,SD,Paris,Vichy (Fr.) 44	-	SUSPECT	FR.
KIELEMANN	265934	M		SS-Mann,Chief, C.C. Skarzysko (Pol.) 44	-	BRUTALITY	POL.
KIELLEWSKI, Johann	267155	M		Uscharfhr.,Cook,Gestapo,Marseille and environ (Fr.)	-	MURDER	FR.
KIEPERT, Rudolf	264628	M		See names listed under "Special Headings"			
KIERSCHKE, T. Wally	303723	F	1. 8.10	Kapo, C.C. Auschwitz (Pol.) 40-45	57/550	BRUTALITY	POL.
KIES, Willy	304797	M		Member,Gestapo,Krakau (Pol.) 11.39- 2.45	59/314	BRUTALITY	POL.
KIKMANN	265902	M		Member,Gestapo,Krasnik (Pol.) 42-44	-	MURDER	POL.
KILL (see KIEL,Wilhelm also Willy)	185088						
KILSAR, Jean	266217	M		Gend.,Feldgend.,Valenciennes (Fr.) 40-44	-	MURDER	FR.
KINTZLER	303724	M		Member,Gestapo,Warschau (Pol.) 39-45	57/552	BRUTALITY	POL.
KIPP, Friedrich	308903	M	6. 7.95	Member,Landwacht,Borgel 1945	60/319	MURDER	POL.

NAME	C.R.FILE NUMBER	SEX	DATE OF BIRTH	RANK	OCCUPATION	UNIT	PLACE AND DATE OF CRIME	UNWCC LIST/ SERIAL NO.	REASON WANTED	WANTED BY
KIRCHBAUM (see KRICHBAUM)	303398									
KIRCHHAMMER, Willy-Eugen	267441	M			Employee, Messerschmitt Plant, C.C., Leonberg (Ger.) 44-45			-	MISC.CRIMES	FR.
KIRCHNER	265904	M	03	Capt., Army (Pol.) 39-40				-	MURDER	POL.
KIRCHNER, Hans	265935	M		SS-Oschfhr., C.C., Auschwitz (Pol.)				-	MURDER	POL.
KIRCHOF, Heinz Dr.	304166	M		Professor of "Ost"-Hospital, Luebeck (Ger.) 43-45				58/358	BRUTALITY	POL.
KIRCHSTEIN, Uhland	265911	M		SS-Usturmfhr., Gen.Secretary, Gestapo, Lodz,Kutno (Pol.) 40-45				56/415	MISC.CRIMES	POL.
KIRMACH, Julius	265405	M		Pvt., Army, Penhoet (Fr.) 8.1.43				-	MURDER	FR.
KIRMSE, Kurt	264408	M	28.11.08	Uschfhr., Member, Gestapo BDS IV E, Paris (Fr.) 44				-	SUSPECT	FR.
KIRSCHNER	265914	M	12	SS-Osturmfhr., Commandant, Sick Bay, C.C., Lublin,Majdanek, Auschwitz (Pol.) 41-45				-	MURDER	POL.
KIRSCHNER	265915	M		Kapo, C.C., Dachau (Ger.)				-	TORTURE	POL.
KIRSCHNER, Willi	266216	M		Cpl., H.V.Stelle Laon 609, Collecting Center Soissons,Admin.-Coy., Laon 609 S.P. 26 300 N, Soissons (Fr.) 28.8.44				-	MISC.CRIMES	FR.
KISCH	303725	M		Member, Gestapo, Warschau (Pol.) 39-45				57/557	BRUTALITY	POL.
KISCH	304168	M		SS-Sturmschfhr., Verwaltungsfhr., BDS, Uelzen, Zeist, Oldenzaal, The Hague (Neth.) 44-45				58/360	PILLAGE	NETH.
KISSEL, Franz	265913	M		SS-Hptschfhr., Gestapo, Lodz (Pol.)				56/416	MISC.CRIMES	POL.
KISSKALT, Wilhelm	265624	M	21. 8.73	See names listed under "Special Headings"						
KITZING, Arthur	265916	M		SS-Mann, C.C., Auschwitz (Pol.)				-	MURDER	POL.
KLAAS	308904	M		Owner, Firm of Klaas, Prison at Hagen (Ger.) 42-45				60/322	TORTURE	BEL.
KLAD	265912	M		Member of staff, Extermination camp, Sobibor (Pol.) 42-43				-	MURDER	POL.
KLAS	266905	M		Agent, Gestapo, Rouen and region (Fr.) 40-44				-	MURDER	FR.
KLATT	303726	M		Member, Gestapo, Warschau (Pol.) 39-45				57/561	BRUTALITY	POL.
KLAUSS, Wilhelm	304246	M	14. 2.02	SS-Schfhr., Mans Gestapo, Department of Sarthe and Mayenne (Fr.) 8.42-8.44				58/362	MURDER	FR.
KLAUSTERMEYER	303727	M		Member, Gestapo, Warschau (Pol.) 39-45				57/563	BRUTALITY	POL.
KLEEBERG	308905	M		Obannfhr., Reichsjugendfuehrung, Assessor, Volksgerichtshof, Saarbruecken (Ger.) 43				60/323	MURDER	FR.
KLEEMANN	303728	M		Member, Gestapo, Warschau (Pol.) 39-45				57/566	BRUTALITY	POL.
KLEIN	265866	M		Guard, Member, Prison, Tomaszow Mazowiecki (Pol.) 43-44				-	MURDER	POL.
KLEIN	266209	M		Agent, Gestapo, Nantes and region (Fr.) 43-44				-	MURDER	FR.
KLEIN	304247	M		Pvt., Member of Group 648 of the Geheime Feldpolizei, Boulevard Pierrot, Liege (Bel.) 40-44				58/364	TORTURE	BEL.
KLEIN, Armand	304798	M		Member, Secr.Field-Police, Boulevard Pierrot or the Avenue Rogier, Luettich (Bel.) 40-41				59/315	MURDER	BEL.
KLEIN, Karol	303368	M		Crim.Official, Gestapo, Kattowitz (Pol.) 39-42				56/420	PILLAGE	POL.
KLEIN, Paul	267078	M		Navy, 2 Coy., 3 Regt., Queven (Fr.) 18.8.44				-	MURDER	FR.
KLEIN, Willy	266215	M		Interpreter, SD Beauvais, Monceaux (Fr.) 8.8.44				-	MURDER	FR.
KLEINAUER, Hermann	266214	M	circa 05	Oschfhr., Gestapo, Nantes and region (Fr.) 43-44				-	MURDER	FR.
KLEINER	303729	M		Member, Gestapo, Warschau (Pol.) 39-45				57/570	BRUTALITY	POL.
KLEINERT	308906	M		Member of German Military-Police, Czorkow nr. Lodz (Pol.) 39-42				60/325	MURDER	POL.
KLEINKEIN, Heinrich	304799	M		Member, Gestapo, Krakau (Pol.) 11.39-2.45				59/316	BRUTALITY	POL.
KLEIS, Johann Albert	267097	M	10. 4.04	Member, Gestapo, Paris (Fr.)				-	SUSPECT	FR.
KLEIST	303730	M		Member, Gestapo, Warschau (Pol.) 39-45				57/573	BRUTALITY	POL.
KLEMENS, Gustav	264629	M		See names listed under"special headings"						
KLEMMER, Heinz	265553	M		Pvt., Polizei-Regt., San Pancrazio,Civitella,Cornia (It.) 7.44				-	MURDER	U.K.
KLEMM	265867	M		SS-Uschfhr., Gestapo, Lodz (Pol.) 39-45				56/423	BRUTALITY	POL.
KLEMMER, Werner	304800	M		Member, Gestapo, Krakau (Pol.) 11.39-2.45				59/317	BRUTALITY	POL.
KLENK	265940	M		Fw. or Hptschfhr., Ital.Freiw.Police-Regt.,2 Bn.,3 Coy., stationed at Ponte di Piave near Treviso (It.) 2.45				-	SUSPECT	U.K.
KLEYBOLT, Christof	266213	M	4. 7.00	Secretary, Police Resident, Metz (Fr.) 40-43				-	PILLAGE	FR.
KLEYER, Johann	304801	M		Member, Gestapo, Krakau (Pol.) 11.39-2.45				59/313	RAPE	POL.
KLEYN	267007	M		Lt., Pion.Bn. Unit No. 01696, Zwammerdam.(Neth.) 21.11.42				-	WITNESS	NETH.
KLICH, Hans	304802	M		Guard, Blechhammer, Wielkie, Strzelce, Slask (Pol.) 1.-2.45				59/319	MURDER	POL.
KLIEBER, Franz	304803	M		Member, Gestapo, Krakau (Pol.) 11.39-2.45				59/320	BRUTALITY	POL.
KLIEVA	308907	M		Member, Selbstschutz, Grudziadz (Pol.) 39				60/326	MURDER	POL.
KLIMCZOK, Erich	304804	M		Member, Gestapo, Krakau (Pol.) 11.39-2.45				59/321	BRUTALITY	POL.
KLIMSA, Alfred	188301	M	2. 3.03	Confidential-Agent, SD (Security Service) Marianske Lazne (Czech.) 39-45				-	MISC.CRIMES	CZECH.
KLINCKMANN	303731	M		Member, Gestapo, Warschau (Pol.) 39-45				57/574	BRUTALITY	POL.
KLINGER	265927	M		SS-Oschfhr., Crim.Police, Debica (Pol.) 42-44				-	BRUTALITY	POL.
KLINGER, Frantz	267469	M	circa 10	Chief of Culture, St.Fergeux (Fr.) 40-44				-	BRUTALITY	FR.
KLINKERT, Hugo	266212	M		See names listed under "Special Headings"						
KLIPP	139879	M	05 - 07	Usturmfhr.,Allg.SS,Lagerfuehrer Arb.Kdo.,C.C.,Blechhammer (Ger.)				-	SUSPECT	U.K.
KLIPPEL	267272	M		Uschfhr., Gestapo, Bordeaux and vicinity (Fr.) 42-8.44				-	MURDER	FR.
KLOCK	268806	M		Capt., Airforce,Unit:L 49193 L.G.P.A., Camaret sur Aigues (Fr.) 1.-6.44						
KLOODT, Friedrich	304248	M		Farmer, Luderhausen (Ger.) 42				58/367	BRUTALITY	POL.
KLOSE, Julius	264617	M	3. 1.93	See names listed under "Special Headings"						
KLOSTER-MEYER	266550	M		Capt.,9 SS-Pz.Div."Hohenstaufen" Unit No.23 474,Nimes (Fr.)2.3.44				-	MURDER	FR.
KLOSTERMEYER	265926	M		Guard, Ghetto, Warschau (Pol.) 43				-	MURDER	POL.
KLOUZAL, Erwin	266756	M		Member, Gestapo, Director,Electr.Railway,Krakau (Pol.) 39				-	MISC.CRIMES	POL.
KLUGE	303732	M		Member, Gestapo, Warschau (Pol.) 39-45				57/579	BRUTALITY	POL.
KLUNDER, Heinrich	303771	M		Member,Group 530 Geh.Feldpolizei,Bruessel (Bel.) 40-44				56/426	MURDER	BEL.
KLUTH, Eleonore	265642	F	circa 17	Employee, SD Du Mans, Sarthe, Mayenne (Fr.) 42-44				-	SUSPECT	FR.
KNAPCZYNSKI, Oskar (or KNAPPE, Oskar)	304249	M	8. 5.98	Member,SA, Supervisor,Ghetto, Strykow (Pol.) 40-43				58/369	MURDER	POL.
KNAPPE, Oskar (see KNAPCZYNSKI, Oskar)	304249									
KNAUER	266211	M	circa 90	Capt.,Russian Unit stationed at Morez,Le Vernois,nr.Marchaux (Fr.) 21.7.44				-	MURDER	FR.
KNAUF	308908	M		SS-Osturmfhr., Kriminal-Kommissar, Radom (Pol.) 40-45				60/329	PILLAGE	POL.
KNIECINSKI, Roman	304805	M		Member, Gestapo, Krakau (Pol.) 11.39-2.45				59/323	RAPE	POL.

KNI - KOL

NAME	C.R.FILE NUMBER	SEX	DATE OF BIRTH	RANK OCCUPATION UNIT PLACE AND DATE OF CRIME	UNWCC LIST/ SERIAL NO.	REASON WANTED	WANTED BY
KNICKELHEIN	267470	M		Sgt., Airforce, 91 Rgt., Chantraine (Fr.) 20.-22.9.44	-	MURDER	FR.
KNIESEL	303733	M		SS-Mann, C.C. Majdanek (Pol.) 40-44	57/582	BRUTALITY	POL.
KNIGGE	308910	M		SS-Usturmfhr. and Krim.Obersekretaer, Radom (Pol.) 40-45	60/331	MURDER	POL.
KNIPPEL (or KNUPPEL)	303374	M		Lt., Dept. of Basses Pyrenees (Fr.) 8.6.44-8.44	56/428	MURDER	FR.
KNIPSEL, Marian	304806	M		Member, Gestapo, Krakau (Pol.) 11.39-2.45	59/324	RAPE	POL.
KNITLER	265970	M		SS-Oschfhr., Chief of Camp "Dora", Sachsenhausen-Oranienburg (Ger.)	-	MURDER	POL.
KNITTEL	300537	M		Member, SS-Uschfhr., SS staff C.C. Auschwitz (Pol.)	-	MURDER	POL.
KNIZKI	265864	M		Member, Gestapo-Ghetto administration Lublin (Pol.) 42	-	MISC.CRIMES	POL.
KNOER, Georges	266210	M	circa 06	Sgt., 1212.Rgt., 2 Bn., Lomont (Fr.) 9.44	-	MURDER	FR.
KNOERZER, Friedrich	303373	M		Sgt., Group 530 Geh.Feldpol., Bruessel (Bel.) 40-44	56/431	MURDER	BEL.
KNOGL, Georg	266049	M	27	Oberkapo, C.C. Porta	-	MURDER	FR.
KNOLL	303731	M		Member, Gestapo, Warschau (Pol.) 39-45	57/586	BRUTALITY	POL.
KNOLL, Christian	265917	M		Kapo, C.C. Dachau (Ger.)	-	MURDER	POL.
KNOLL, Georg	265918	M		Kapo, C.C. Dachau (Ger.)	-	MURDER	POL.
KNOLI, Katarzyna (Kathe)	132670	F		Blockleader, C.C. Ravensbrueck (Ger.)	-	BRUTALITY	POL.
KNOLL, Leonhard	265971	M	circa 05	Driver, Post-office, Lublin (Pol.)	-	BRUTALITY	POL.
KNOP, Joachim	266281	M	9. 2.05	Chief, Culture, Marby (Fr.) 41-44	-	MISC.CRIMES	FR.
KNOPF, Otto	267439	M		Kapo, C.C. Leonberg (Ger.) 44-45	-	BRUTALITY	FR.
KNOPHIUS, Kathe	304807	F		Member, Gestapo, Krakau (Pol.) 11.39-2.45	59/325	MURDER	POL.
KNORR	267271	M		Capt., 350 Hindou Rgt., Departm. Indre (Fr.) 8.44	-	MURDER	FR.
KNOTH, Erich	304808	M		Member, Gestapo, Krakau (Pol.) 11.39-2.45	59/326	MURDER	POL.
KNOTHE	128991			SS-Usturmfhr., Secret. and official, SS Gestapo Section 4-2, Lodz (Pol.)	-	MISC.CRIMES	POL.
KNUPPEL (see KNIPPEL)	303374						
KOBOLD, Hermann	267312	M		SS-Guard, SS, C.C. Struthof-Natzweiler (Fr.) 40-44	-	MURDER	FR.
KOBLITZ	265869	M		Chief, "Ostinstitut", Krakau (Pol.) -44	-	MISC.CRIMES	POL.
KOBLITZ	304250	M		Member of the Schutzgruppen Eigelshoven (Neth.) 8.9.-13.9.44	58/371	PILLAGE	NETH.
KOCH	265556	M		Lt., Gendarmerie-chief, Debica (Pol.) 39-44	-	MURDER	POL.
KOCH	265979	M		Usturmfhr., Div. "Das Reich", Region de Rouen (Fr.) 8.44	-	TORTURE	FR.
KOCH	266279	M		Chief-Cpl., Africa-Corps, Rgt.Ruxleben 1 Sect. 6 Coy. Hte.Marne Aube (Fr.) 25.-31.8.44	-	MURDER	FR.
KOCH	267152	M		Lt., Squadron "Udet" L. 34756, Senon (Fr.) 28.8.44	-	MURDER	FR.
KOCH	304251	M		Feldwebel, Feldgend., Arlon and vicinity (Bel.) 25.8.44-3.9.44	58/372	MURDER	BEL.
KOCH	304252	M		Head Superintendent at the "Maurits" state coal-mine, Geleen (L) (Neth.) 9.44	58/373	MISC.CRIMES	NETH.
KOCH	304253	M		Stabs-Engineer with the Airforce H.Q., Bordes (Basses-Pyrenees) Soues (Hautes - Pyrenees) (Fr.) 43	-	PILLAGE	FR.
KOCH	308911	M		SS-Mann, Waffen-SS, Radom (Pol.) 40-45	60/333	MURDER	POL.
KOCH, Alfred	265968	M		See names listed under "Special Headings"			
KOCH, Fritz	266280	M		Cpl., Feldgend., St.Michel (Fr.) 3.3.44	-	MISC.CRIMES	FR.
KOCH, Karl, Otto	490	M	2. 8.97	SS-Standartenfhr., Camp Commandant C.C. Sachsenhausen, Buchenwald (Ger.) 40-45	1/337 6/280 8/32 13/503 25/306	MURDER	CZECH. BEL. POL. FR.
KOCH, Oskar	303376	M		Krim.Kommissar, Gestapo, Kattowitz (Pol.) 39-42	56/436	BRUTALITY	POL.
KOCH, Wilhelm	304810	M		Member, Gestapo, Krakau (Pol.) 11.39-2.45	59/328	MURDER	POL.
KOCHEL, Lorenz	265931	M		Wachtmeister, Gendarmerie, Debno, Brzesko (Pol.) 40-44	-	MISC.CRIMES	POL.
KOCUR (see KOTZUR)	265885						
KOEBE, Gerhard	304811	M		Member, Gestapo, Krakau (Pol.) 11.39-2.45	59/329	MURDER	POL.
KOEBERLE, Heinrich or Herne	266551	M	circa 05	Sgt., Army, came from Lyon, Saint Die (Fr.) 11.44	-	MURDER	FR.
KOEHLER, Richard	265928	M		SS-Uschfhr., Gestapo, Zamosc (Pol.) 40-44	-	BRUTALITY	POL.
KOELER, Friedrich	265886	M	23. 2.98	Inspector, Agricultural Comites of District, Raszkow (Pol.)-44	-	BRUTALITY	POL.
KOELLER, Hans	303377	M		Sgt., Group 530 Geh.Feldpol., Bruessel (Bel.) 40-44	56/438	MURDER	BEL.
KOELLNER, Josef	266717	M		Kdo.Fuehrer, Strafgefangenenlager Harsewinkel (Ger.) 43-45	-	SUSPECT	BEL.
KOENES, Willem	303914	M	11. 8.92	Member of Schutzgruppen, Brunssum (Neth.) 44	60/338	PILLAGE	NETH.
KOENIG, Berta	265953	F	circa 12	Official, Post, Lublin (Pol.)	-	BRUTALITY	POL.
KOENIG, Franz	308912	M		SS-Schfhr., Waffen-SS, Radom (Pol.) 40-45	60/335	TORTURE	POL.
KOENIG, Fritz	266881	M		Hptsturmfhr., Chief, SS Depot of German Railway-workers Limoges, Haute-Vienne (Fr.)	-	MURDER	FR.
KOENIG, Sepp	265854	M		SS-Oschfhr., SS Gestapo, Krakau (Pol.)	-	BRUTALITY	POL.
KOENTZ	267315	M		Lt., Unit No. 15483 B.&C., La Reole (Fr.) 7.-9.6.44	-	MISC.CRIMES	FR.
KOEPPEN, Paul	265326	M	14. 3.97	Chief, Gendarmerie, Raszkow (Pol.) 40	-	MISC.CRIMES	POL.
KOERBERLICH, Dr.	304820	M		Doctor, Firm Henschel & Sohn, factory, Kassel (Ger.) 16.1.44	59/338	MURDER	NETH.
KOERTEL, Heinr., August	304925	M	15. 1.90	Foreman, Member, Firm Henschel & Sohn, factory, DAF. Kassel (Ger.) 16.1.44	59/343	MURDER	NETH.
KOGARDT (see VON KOGARD)	165246						
KOGLIN	303735	M		Member, Gestapo, Warschau (Pol.) 10.39-1.45	57/592	BRUTALITY	POL.
KOHL	266957	M		Chief-Cpl., Flakmast 30-XII, Carcassonne (Fr.) 19.8.44	-	MURDER	FR.
KOHLASS, Oswald	303380	M		Krim.Assistent, Gestapo, Kattowitz (Pol.) 39-42	56/442	PILLAGE	POL.
KOHLENBUSCH	267154	M	90	Sub-manager, Agricultural Service, Vittel, Belmont s.Vair (Fr.) 13.-14.5.45	-	MISC.CRIMES	FR.
KOHLER, Franz	303381	M		SS-Rottfhr., Gestapo Lodz (Pol.) 39-44	56/443	PILLAGE	POL.
KOHLER, Helmuth	308913	M	21. 3.18	Denouncer, Gestapo, Prag (Czech.) 40	60/337	INTERR.	CZECH.
KOHLSDORF	303738	M		Member, Gestapo, Warschau (Pol.) 10.39-1.45	57/596	BRUTALITY	POL.
KOHRER	265390	M		Chief, SD, Bayonne and vicinity (Fr.) 40-44	-	MURDER	FR.
KOKOTHAKI, Rakan	267439	M		Commercial Director, Messerschmitt Plant, C.C.Leonberg (Ger.)	-	BRUTALITY	FR.
KOLARO (or KOICNKO)	265929	M		SS-Mann, C.C. Janow (Pol.) 42	-	MURDER	POL.
KOLB	265965	M		SS-Usturmfhr., Gestapo, Zamosc, Bilgoraj (Pol.) 39-44	-	MURDER	POL.
KOLBE	303739	M		Member, Gestapo, Warschau (Pol.) 10.39-1.45	57/597	MURDER	POL.
KOLBE, Ernst	303382	M		Cpl., Group 530 Geh.Feldpol., Bruessel (Bel.) 40-44	56/444	MURDER	BEL.
KOLBE, Waldemar	303383	M		Sonderfhr., Group 530 Geh.Feldpol., Bruessel (Bel.) 40-44	56/445	MURDER	BEL.

KOL - KRA

NAME	C.R.FILE NUMBER	SEX	DATE OF BIRTH	RANK OCCUPATION UNIT PLACE AND DATE OF CRIME	UNWCC LIST/ SERIAL NO.	REASON WANTED	WANTED BY
KOLBERG	267314	M	circa 13	Officer, Commander, Cayeux-sur-Mer (Fr.) 40-44	-	MISC.CRIMES	FR.
KOLBERG, Hans	303534	M		Kriminalsekretaer, Gestapo, Kattowitz (Pol.) 39-42	56/446	MURDER	POL.
KOLBIASZ, Roman	304812	M		Member, Gestapo, Krakau (Pol.) 11.39- 2.45	59/330	MURDER	POL.
KOLBL, Karl	265980	M		W.O., Feldgendarmerie, Region of Quimperle (Fr.) 44	-	MURDER	FR.
KOLL, Wilhelm	303385	M		Pvt., Group 530 Geh.Feldpolizei, Bruessel (Bel.) 40-44	56/447	MURDER	BEL.
KOLLE, Hans	303386	M		Member, Group 530 Geh.Feldpolizei, Bruessel (Bel.) 40-44	56/448	MURDER	BEL.
KOLLER	265827	M		SS-Uscharfhr., C.C., Auschwitz (Pol.)		MURDER	POL.
KOLLIGS, Karl	266946	M	22. 1.99	Sgt., Unit L 01032 Frontleitstelle,Le Bourget (Fr.)	-	SUSPECT	FR.
KOLMEDER	265828	M		Gendarm, Gendarmerie, Zamosz (Pol.) 17.2.44		MURDER	POL.
KOLMEL	265829	M		Kapo, C.C., Dachau (Ger.)		BRUTALITY	POL.
KOLONKO (see KOLANKO)	265929						
KOLREP, Horst	266283	M	09	Capt., 487.Inf.Regt.,Oignies and Courrieres (Fr.) 28.5.40	-	MURDER	FR.
KOLSKI, Berek	303740	M		On Staff C.C., Auschwitz (Pol.) 40-45	57/600	BRUTALITY	POL.
KOMACHAN (or KOMACHN)	265849	M		Wachtmeister, Gendarmerie, Brzesko,Debno (Pol.) 39-44	-	MISC.CRIMES	POL.
KOMACHN (see KOMACHAN)	265849						
KOMAREK	303741	M		Member, Gestapo, Warschau (Pol.) 39-45	57/601	MURDER	POL.
KOMPE, Paul (or KUMPEL)	265981	M	18.10.05	Chief,SS-Usturmfhr.,Sub-section 3 of section IV SD, Marseille,Bouches du Rhone (Fr.) 42-44	-	SUSPECT	FR.
KONDRITZ, Wilhelm	265851	M		SS-Oscharfhr., SS Gestapo (Section 4-1), Lodz (Pol.)	56/450	MISC.CRIMES	POL.
KONIER	267471	M		Gestapo, Limoges and vicinity (Fr.) 44	-	SUSPECT	FR.
KONIETSCHNY	265852	M		SS-Uscharfhr.,SS, C.C., Lublin-Majdanek (Pol.)		BRUTALITY	POL.
KONIG	303742	M		Member, Gestapo, Warschau (Pol.) 39-45	57/602	BRUTALITY	POL.
KONIG, Gustav	303388	M		Kriminalkommissar, Gestapo, Kattowitz (Pol.) 39-42	56/451	BRUTALITY	POL.
KONIG, Josef	304813	M		Member, Gestapo, Krakau (Pol.) 11.39- 2.45	59/331	MURDER	POL.
KONIG, Willy	267096	M		Agent, Gestapo, Arras (Fr.) 8.41	-	MURDER	FR.
KONINGER I	303743	M		Member, Gestapo, Warschau (Pol.) 39-45	57/603	BRUTALITY	POL.
KONINGER II	303744	M		Member, Gestapo, Warschau (Pol.) 39-45	57/604	BRUTALITY	POL.
KONNECKE, Willy	304814	M		Member, Gestapo, Krakau (Pol.(11.39- 2.45	59/332	BRUTALITY	POL.
KONOPINSKI, Tadeusz Jozef	308915	M	3. 7.08	Employee of Labour-Office, Czestochowa (Pol.) 41-45	60/340	MISC.CRIMES	POL.
KONRAD, Bruno	304815	M		Member, Gestapo, Krakau (Pol.) 11.39- 2.45	59/333	TORTURE	POL.
KOOLNNITZER, Siegfried	304816	M		Member, Gestapo, Krakau (Pol.) 11.39- 2.45	59/334	MURDER	POL.
KOOP, Friedrich	304255	M		Farmer, Duwensee Krs. Lauenburg (Ger.) 42	58/381	BRUTALITY	POL.
KOOP, Heinrich	303389	M		Policeman, Dakendorf, 6.42	56/452	MURDER	POL.
KOPKA, Max	267582	M		Cpl., G.F.P. Groups 3, 738, 739, Charleroi,Mons,Namur, Tournai,Ath (Bel.) 40-45	-	BRUTALITY	BEL.
KOPP	303745	M		Member, Gestapo, Warschau (Pol.) 39-45	57/606	MURDER	POL.
KOPPEK, Christian	304817	M		Member, Gestapo, Krakau (Pol.) 11.39- 2.45	59/335	TORTURE	POL.
KOPPING, Friedrich	304818	M		Member, Gestapo, Krakau (Pol.) 11.39- 2.45	59/336	TORTURE	POL.
KOPPISCH, Hans	304819	M		Member, Gestapo, Krakau (Pol.) 11.39- 2.45	59/337	TORTURE	POL.
KOPSEL, Erwin	303390	M		Kriminalsekretaer, Gestapo,Kattowitz (Pol.) 39-42	56/454	INTERR.	POL.
KORCZ	265830	M		Merchant, Owner of shop, Legjonow (Pol.)		MISC.CRIMES	POL.
KORDYS, Franz	304821	M		Member, Gestapo, Krakau (Pol.) 11.39- 2.45	59/339	TORTURE	POL.
KORING, Gerhard	304822	M		Member, Gestapo, Krakau (Pol.) 11.39- 2.45	59/340	TORTURE	POL.
KORK	304257	M		Wachtmeister at Gettorf,Distr.Eckernfoerde,Osdorf (Ger.)45	58/385	BRUTALITY	POL.
KORMANN, Albin	303746	M		SS-Mann, C.C.Majdanek (Pol.) 40-44	57/607	BRUTALITY	POL.
KORN,Reinhold (or BREITAULT,Colonel)	267148	M	circa 13	Oscharfhr., Gestapo, Marseille and vicinity (Fr.)	-	MURDER	FR.
KORNER, Rudolf	304823	M		Member, Gestapo, Krakau (Pol.) 11.39- 2.45	59/341	TORTURE	POL.
KORNFEIL	303747	M		Member, Gestapo, Warschau (Pol.) 39-45	57/608	MURDER	POL.
KORNRUMPF, Willy	304824	M		Member, Gestapo, Krakau (Pol.) 11.39- 2.45	59/342	TORTURE	POL.
KORREMANS	304258	M		N.C.O.,member of Group 648 of the Geheime Feldpolizei, Liege,Boulevard,Piercot (Bel.) 40-44	58/386	BRUTALITY	BEL.
KORTH	266514	M		Chief Cpl., Unit No. 24.884, Mezieres en Brenne (Fr.) 8.44	-	PILLAGE	FR.
KORUNF	265831	M		Official, Gestapo, Debica (Pol.)		BRUTALITY	POL.
KOSMALA	303748	M		Member, Gestapo, Warschau (Pol.) 39-45	57/609	MURDER	POL.
KOSSMANN, Hugo	265875	M	circa 03	Penal Inspector, Post Office, Lublin (Pol.)	-	MISC.CRIMES	POL.
KOSSNER, Anton	303391	M		Kriminalsekretaer, Gestapo, Kattowitz (Pol.) 39-42	56/456	INTERR.	POL.
KOSTEK (see KOSTIK)	265876						
KOSTIK (or GOSTIK or KOSTEK)	265876	M		Block-senior, C.C., Auschwitz (Pol.)		BRUTALITY	POL.
KOSTREWA	304259	M		Member of Schutzgruppen at the "Laura-mine", Eigelshoven (Neth.) 9.44	58/387	PILLAGE	NETH.
KOTALLA, Wilhelm	303392	M		Office employee, Gestapo, Kattowitz (Pol.) 39-42	56/457	PILLAGE	POL.
KOTTKE, Ernst	267153	M		Hptscharfhr., Gestapo, Marseille and vicinity (Fr.)	-	MURDER	FR.
KOTZUR (or KOCUR)	265885	M	05	SS-Oscharfhr.,Arbeitsdienstfhr.,C.C.,Gusen (Aust.)	-	MURDER	POL.
KOUSTOS	267095	M		SD, Nievres department and vicinity of Moulins (Fr.) 43-44	-	MISC.CRIMES	FR.
KOWALIK, Maria	304826	F		Member, Gestapo, Krakau (Pol.) 11.39- 2.45	59/344	MURDER	POL.
KOWALSKI, Wladislaus	304827	M		Member, Gestapo, Krakau (Pol.) 11.39- 2.45	59/345	MURDER	POL.
KOWOLLIK, August	304261	M	circa 08	Verwalter, "Julia" state coal mine,Eigelshoven (Neth.)9.44	58/390	MISC.CRIMES	NETH.
KOZA, Erika	304828	F		Member, Gestapo, Krakau (Pol.) 11.39- 2.45	59/346	MURDER	POL.
KRAATZ	303749	M		Member, Gestapo, Warschau (Pol.) 39-45	57/611	MURDER	POL.
KRACHT	303750	M		Member, Gestapo, Warschau (Pol.) 39-45	57/612	BRUTALITY	POL.
KRAETZ	308916	M		SS-Hptscharfhr.and Verw.inspector, Radom (Pol.) 40-45	60/341	PILLAGE	POL.
KRAFFT (see GRAFF)	304202						
KRAFT	267313	M	circa 95	Sturmmann, Gestapo, Bordeaux and vicinity (Fr.) 42-8.44	-	MURDER	FR.
KRAFT I	303751	M		Member, Gestapo, Warschau (Pol.) 39-45	57/613	BRUTALITY	POL.
KRAFT II	303752	M		Member, Gestapo, Warschau (Pol.) 39-45	57/614	BRUTALITY	POL.
KRAHE, Heinrich	303395	M		Kriminalbeamter, Gestapo, Kattowitz (Pol.) 39-42	56/462	INTERR.	POL.
KRAHN	265982	M		Member, Feldgendarmerie, Reg.of Cholet (Fr.)7.and 8.8.44	56/463	MURDER	FR.
KRAJEWSKI, Bernhard	308917	M		Betriebs-Obmann,Lendringen Distr.of Iserlohn (Pol.)39-45	60/342	BRUTALITY	POL.
KRAMER	266510	M		W.O.Sgt.-Major,9.SS Pz.Div."Hohenstaufen", Unit No.23.474 Nimes (Fr.) 2.3.44	-	MURDER	FR.
KRAMER	303753	M		SS-Hptscharfhr., C.C., Majdanek (Pol.) 40-44	57/615	MURDER	POL.
KRAMER (or KROMBER)	304262	M		SS-Scharfhr.,with the Gestapo at Chalons-sur-Marne, Department of Marne (Fr.) 43-44	58/391	MURDER	FR.

KRA - KRU

NAME	C.R.FILE NUMBER	SEX	DATE OF BIRTH	RANK OCCUPATION UNIT PLACE AND DATE OF CRIME	UNWCC LIST/ SERIAL NO.	REASON WANTED	WANTED BY
KRAML, Johann	303754	M	17. 3.06	SS-Mann, C.C., Majdanek (Pol.) 40-44	57/618	BRUTALITY	POL.
KRAMMER	267466	M		Lt., Feldgend.Kdo., Bonrencontre (Fr.) 6.9.44	-	MURDER	FR.
KRANKENREWIER	303755	M		Member, Gestapo, Warschau (Pol.) 39-45	57/619	BRUTALITY	POL.
KRANSCHER, Bernard	267472	M	23. 9.06	Werkschutzleiter, Werkschutz, Factory (Hermann Goering-Werke), Moyeuvre Grande (Fr.) 40-45	-	BRUTALITY	FR.
KRANTZ	266278	M		Interpreter, Gestapo, Nantes and region (Fr.) 43-44	-	MURDER	FR.
KRATCCHWIL, Karl	304829	M		Member, Gestapo, Krakau (Pol.) 11.39-2.45	59/347	BRUTALITY	POL.
KRATTEIT (or KRETTEIT)	308918	M		Feldpolizei-Insp., G.F.P., Antwerpen, Bruessel (Bel.) 40-44	60/344	MURDER	BEL.
KRATZ, Ferdinand	267156	M		Sgt.-Major, Coy. of Navy General Staff of C.D.T. of Marseille port postal sector 40930, Marseille (Fr.) 9.43	-	PILLAGE	FR.
KRAUDELT	308919	M		SS-Sturmscharfhr., Crim.secretary, Radom (Pol.) 40-45	60/345	PILLAGE	POL.
KRAUS, Gaston	266533	M		Pvt., SD Lyon, retreated to the Vosges, Saint Die (Fr.) 11.44	-	MURDER	FR.
KRAUS, Johannes	304830	M		Member, Gestapo, Krakau (Pol.) 11.39-2.45	59/348	BRUTALITY	POL.
KRAUS, Wilhelm	304263	M		Regt."Deutschland", Div."Das Reich", Aachen (Ger.) 9.44	58/392	MURDER	BEL.
KRAUSE	267094	M	circa 05	Capt., Carmes at Prepignan (East Pyrenees) (Fr.) 9.8.44	-	MISC.CRIMES	FR.
KRAUSE	267310	M		Cpl., Unit No. 15483 B and S, La Reole (Fr.) 7.-9.6.44	-	MISC.CRIMES	FR.
KRAUSS, Eleonore	266956	F		Member, Gestapo, Paris (Fr.)	-	MURDER	FR.
KRAUSS, Horst	265557	M	2. 1.26	Pvt., Army, Ers.u.Ausb.Regt.GG, Civitella area (It.) 7.44	-	MURDER	U.K.
KRAUSS, Johann	303756	M	20. 6.13	SS-Mann, C.C., Majdanek (Pol.) 40-44	57/622	BRUTALITY	POL.
KRAUT, Erwin Dr.	265382	M	30. 1.08	Chief, Civ.Service, District Office, Prerov (Czech.) 5.45	-	MURDER	CZECH.
KRAUT, Ludwig	304831	M		Member, Gestapo, Krakau (Pol.) 11.39-2.45	59/349	BRUTALITY	POL.
KRAUTINGER, Franz	304832	M		Member, Gestapo, Krakau (Pol.) 11.39-2.45	59/350	BRUTALITY	POL.
KRAUZE, Heinrich	304833	M		Member, Gestapo, Krakau (Pol.) 11.39-2.45	59/351	BRUTALITY	POL.
KRAUZE, Willy	304834	M		Member, Gestapo, Krakau (Pol.) 11.39-2.45	59/352	BRUTALITY	POL.
KRAUZER, Dr.	301779	M		Sturmbannfhr., C.C., Auschwitz (Pol.) 40	-	MURDER	POL.
KRAZER, Hans	266277	M		Lt., 3 Ostreiter-Bn., Augea (Fr.) 28.6.44	-	MURDER	FR.
KREBS, Hella	267309	F	23	Secretary, Gestapo, Bordeaux and vicinity (Fr.) 42-8.44	-	MURDER	FR.
KREIL	304265	M		Member, Gestapo, Chalons-sur-Marne (Fr.) 43-44	58/395	MURDER	FR.
KREIS	304862	M		Field-Pol.-Director, Secr.Field-Police,HQ., Boulevard Piercot or the Avenue Rogier, Luettich (Bel.) 40-41	59/353	MURDER	BEL.
KREISEL	303757	M		Member, Gestapo, Warschau (Pol.) 39-45	57/625	BRUTALITY	POL.
KREISSIG, Edmund	304863	M		Member, Gestapo, Krakau (Pol.) 11.39-2.45	59/354	MURDER	POL.
KREKELER, Robert	266984	M	30. 6.00	SS-Uscharfhr., Gestapo, BDS W I-a-Ib, Paris (Fr.)	-	SUSPECT	FR.
KREMER	308920	M		Major of Army Commandantur at Utrecht, Lage Vuursche (Neth.) 43	60/346	MISC.CRIMES	NETH.
KRENZ	266877	M		Sturmbannfhr., Commander, SS, Artl.Regt., Div."Das Reich", Tulle (Fr.) 44	-	MURDER	FR.
KRESSLER	303397	M		Sgt., Group 530 Geh.Feldpolizei, Bruessel (Bel.) 40-44	56/469	MURDER	BEL.
KRESSNER	303758	M		Member, Gestapo, Warschau (Pol.) 39-45	57/627	BRUTALITY	POL.
KRETSCHMANN, Reimund	304864	M		Member, Gestapo, Krakau (Pol.) 11.39-2.45	59/355	RAPE	POL.
KRETSCHMAR, Herbert	304865	M		Member, Gestapo, Krakau (Pol.) 11.39-2.45	59/356	MURDER	POL.
KRETSCHMAR, Willy	266238	M		Hptscharfhr., Gestapo, Metz, Fort de Queuleu (Fr.) 40-45	-	MURDER	FR.
KRETSCHMER, Gerda	304866	F		Member, Gestapo, Krakau (Pol.) 11.39-2.45	59/357	MURDER	POL.
KRETTEIT (see KRATTEIT)	308918						
KREUZER, Willy	267127	M		Lt., Army, Sinj (Yugo.) 8.9.43-10.44	-	MURDER	YUGO.
KREUZMAIER	267316	M		Hptscharfhr., Gestapo, Bordeaux and vicinity (Fr.) 42-8.44	-	MURDER	FR.
KREYMEIER (or FREYMEIER)	267098	M		3 Coy., Bn."Tirplitz", La Tremblade (Fr.) 9.44	-	MURDER	FR.
KRICH, Michael	303759	M	14. 8.17	SS-Mann, C.C., Majdanek (Pol.) 40-44	57/630	MURDER	POL.
KRICHBAUM (or KIRCHBAUM or KRIEGBAUM)	303398	M		Oberfeldpolizeichef, Army and Air Force, (Bel.) 40-44	56/470	MURDER	BEL.
KRIEGBAUM (see KRICHBAUM)	303398						
KRIER, Anton	303760	M	3. 7.09	SS-Mann, C.C., Majdanek (Pol.) 40-44	57/631	MURDER	POL.
KRIES, Eberhardt	308921	M		Ortsgruppenleiter and Commander, NSDAP, Selbstschutz, Kolonia, Ostrowite, Pomorze (Pol.) 39-45	60/347	MISC.CRIMES	POL.
KRISCHKE	304867	M		Member, Gestapo, Krakau (Pol.) 11.39-2.45	59/358	MURDER	POL.
KRISCHOK, Albert	304868	M		Member, Gestapo, Krakau (Pol.) 11.39-2.45	59/359	MURDER	POL.
KRIZONS, Helmut	303412	M		Crim.asst., Gestapo, Kattowitz (Pol.) 39-42	56/471	PILLAGE	POL.
KROGLER, Helmut	304869	M		Member, Gestapo, Krakau (Pol.) 11.39-2.45	59/360	PILLAGE	POL.
KROMAYER	303761	M		Member, Gestapo, Warschau (Pol.) 39-45	57/634	BRUTALITY	POL.
KROMBER (see KRAMER)	304262						
KROMER	303762			Member, Gestapo, Warschau (Pol.) 39-45	57/635	BRUTALITY	POL.
KRONAU, Bruno	303413			Kriminalbeamter, Gestapo, Kattowitz (Pol.) 39-42	56/473	INTERR.	POL.
KRONEN	304266	M		Cmdt. of the Schutzgruppen at the "Julia" state coal mine, Eigelshoven (Neth.) 9.44	58/396	MISC.CRIMES	NETH.
KRONERT, Erich	303414			Crim.asst., Gestapo, Kattowitz (Pol.) 39-42	56/474	INTERR.	POL.
KROPPE	304870			Member, Secr.Field-Police,HQ., Boulevard Piercot or the Avenue Rogier, Luettich (Bel.) 40-41	59/362	MURDER	BEL.
KROPPELOWSKI	303415			Member, Group 530 Geh.Feldpolizei, Bruessel (Bel.) 40-44	56/475	MURDER	BEL.
KROUTZRADT, Willy	266532	M		N.C.O., belonged at time of facts to formation, stationed at Panzer-School of Versailles (Fr.) 28.9.40	-	MURDER	FR.
KRUEGER, Heinrich, Wilhelm	514	M		SS-Obergruppenfhr., O.C. for District Krakau, Gestapo, Krakau (Pol.) 39-43	-	MURDER	UNWCC, NOR.,POL.
KRUG	266876	M		Unit of cosaks, stationed at Chatillon s.Seine, Essarois (Fr.), 11.6.44	-	MURDER	FR.
KRUGER	303416			Lt., 784 Turkestan Bn., Clairac, Marmande, La Reole (Fr.) 12.-21.8.44	56/476	MURDER	FR.
KRUGER, Ewald	303763	M	2. 2.17	Guard, C.C., Majdanek (Pol.) 40-42	57/638	BRUTALITY	POL.
KRUK, Reinhold	303417	M		Kriminalbeamter, Gestapo, Kattowitz (Pol.) 39-42	56/477	BRUTALITY	POL.
KRUMBECK	267311	M	circa 15	Uscharfhr., Gestapo, Bordeaux and vicinity (Fr.) 42-8.44	-	MURDER	FR.
KRUMBHOLZ	266235	M		N.C.O., 1 Sect., 6 Coy., Regt. Ruxleben, Africa-Corps, Hte.Marne-Aube (Fr.) 25.-31.8.44	-	MURDER	FR.
KRUMM	308923	M		SS-Sturmscharfhr., Krim.Obersekretaer, Radom (Pol.) 40-45	60/349	PILLAGE	POL.
KRUMMER, Edmund	308924	M		Civilian, Verne, distr.of Buren, 44	60/350	BRUTALITY	POL.
KRUPKA, Edmund	303418	M		Employee, Gestapo, Kattowitz (Pol.) 39-42	56/478	PILLAGE	POL.
KRUSE, Zanter	303419	M		Crim.secretary, Gestapo, Kempen, 25.10.41	56/479	MURDER	POL.
KRUX (or KRUZE)	266234	M		Paymaster, H.V.Stelle Laon 609, Collecting Center Soissons, Administration-Coy.Laon 609 S.P.26033 N, Soissons (Fr.) 28.8.44	-	MISC.CRIMES	FR.
KRUZE (see KRUX)	266234						

KRZ-LAN

NAME	C.R.FILE NUMBER	SEX	DATE OF BIRTH	RANK OCCUPATION UNIT PLACE AND DATE OF CRIME	UNWCC LIST/ SERIAL No.	REASON WANTED	WANTED BY
KRZYSANOWSKI, Karl	304872	M		Member, Gestapo, Krakau (Pol.) 11.39-2.45	59/365	PILLAGE	POL.
KRYSCHANIWSKY, Andreas	304871	M		Member, Gestapo, Krakau (Pol.) 11.39-2.45	59/364	PILLAGE	POL.
KUBACH, Adolf	266531	M		Occupying farmer, Civilian, Gueblange les Dieuze (Fr.) 41-44	-	PILLAGE	FR.
KUBE	308925	M		SS-Sturmscharfhr.and Crim.Secr. at Radom (Pol.) 40-45	60/351	TORTURE	POL.
KUBELKE, Heinz	264630	M		See names listed under "Special Headings"			U.S.
KUBIAK, Erich	304873	M		Member, Gestapo, Frakau (Pol.) 11.39-2.45	59/366	BRUTALITY	POL.
KUBITZ, Hans-Jochen	264631	M	6. 9.10	See names listed under "Special Headings"			U.S.
KUBITZA, Karl	303764	M	21. 3.99	SS-Mann, C.C.Majdanek (Pol.) 40-44	57/640	BRUTALITY	POL.
KUCZEVITSCH, Zarko	303765	M	14. 4.08	Camp Doctor, C.C.Majdanek (Pol.) 40-42	57/641	BRUTALITY	POL.
KUDLICH, Werner Dr.	265593	M		Director of Museum, Civilian, Krakau (Pol.) 40	-	PILLAGE	POL.
KUEHN I	308926	M		Interpreter at Radom (Pol.) 40-45	60/352	PILLAGE	POL.
KUEHN II	308927	M		Interpreter at Radom (Pol.) 40-45	60/352 A	PILLAGE	POL.
KUEHNE, Martin	265223	M		Major, Commander, 1 Bn., 2 Para.Regt., Refredi, Castello nr. Florence (It.) 5.8.44	-	SUSPECT	U.K.
KUEHNEL, Rudolf	264667	M	8. 2.06	See names listed under "Special Headings"			U.S.
KUGLER	265679	M	14. 8.21	Cpl., Unit No.57727, Lamor Pleubian (Fr.) 5.-7.8.44	-	MURDER	FR.
KUHL	267288	M		Guard, SS, Struthof-Natzweiler, (Fr.) 41-45	-	MURDER	FR.
KUHN	266239	M		See names listed under "Special Headings"			FR.
KUHN, Aleksander	304874	M		Member, Gestapo, Krakau (Pol.) 11.39-2.45	59/367	PILLAGE	POL.
KUHN, Arthur	265391	M		Capt., Customs Field Police, F.P.No.18446 R, Barcelonnette (Fr.) 6.44	-	MISC.CRIMES	FR.
KUHNE, Karl	303420	M		Office employee, Gestapo, Kattowitz (Pol.) 39-42	56/480	PILLAGE	POL.
KUHRING, Walter	304875	M		Member, Gestapo, Krakau (Pol.) 11.39-2.45	59/368	PILLAGE	POL.
KUJAT	308928	M		Krim.Angestellter and Interpreter, Radom (Pol.) 40-45	60/356	MURDER	POL.
KULEMANN, Alfred Dr.	264666	M	5. 9.97	See names listed under "Special Headings"			U.S.
KULL, Walter	304876	M		Member, Gestapo, Krakau (Pol.) 11.39-2.45	59/369	PILLAGE	POL.
KULMANN	266875	M		Cpl., Div.Brenner, Correze (Fr.) 3.4.44	-	MISC.CRIMES	FR.
KUMPEL, Paul (see KOMPE)	265981						
KUMPF	308929	M		Sgt., G.F.P., Antwerpen, Bruessel (Bel.) 40-44	60/358	MURDER	BEL.
KUN, Hans	267099	M	circa 03	Member, Gestapo of Blois (in charge of Gen.Pol.), Blois and Maves (Fr.) 43-44	-	MURDER	FR.
KUNA, Albert	267473	M	21.10.04	Scharfhr., Gestapo, St.Etienne & vicinity (Fr.) 43-44	-	MISC.CRIMES	FR.
KUNDE, Friedrich	264404	M	12. 5.01	Oscharfhr., Gestapo Paris RDS IV, Paris (Fr.) 44	-	SUSPECT	FR.
KUNESCH, Rudolf	267289	M		Usturmfhr., Chief, Gestapo, Section IV E, Bordeaux and vicinity (Fr.) 42-8.44	-	MURDER	FR.
KUNKLER (see GUNKLER)	265734						
KUNTZ	266586	M		W.O., Feldgendarmerie 658, Paray le Monial and vicinity (Fr.) 44	-	SUSPECT	FR.
KUNTZE, Wolfgang (or KUNZE)	308930	M		Sgt., G.F.P., Antwerpen, Bruessel (Bel.) 40-44	60/359	MURDER	BEL.
KUNZE (see KUNTZE, Wolfgang)	308930						
KUPPERSCHMIDT, Maria	304877	F		Member, Gestapo, Krakau (Pol.) 11.39-2.45	59/371	MURDER	POL.
KURH, Joseph	267290	M	circa 15	2 Paratrooper-Div., Brest and vicinity (Fr.) 7.-8.44	-	MURDER	FR.
KURT	267100	M		N.C.O.,19 SS Pol.Regt.,3 Bn.,11 Coy. Limoges, Brive and vicinity, (Fr.) 7.44	-	MURDER	FR.
KURT, Johann	266530	M	circa 20	Sgt., Kdo.coming from Lyon, Saint Die (Fr.) 11.44	-	MURDER	FR.
KURTEN	267431	M		C.C.Leonberg (Ger.) 44-45	-	MISC.CRIMES	FR.
KURTEN, Mathias	303422	M		Sgt., Geh.Feldpolizei Belgium (Bel.) 40-44	56/484	MURDER	BEL.
KURTH, Hans Josef (or TREY)	267149	M		Agent, Gestapo, Marseille and vicinity (Fr.)	-	MURDER	FR.
KURZ	267101	M		Lt., 148 Art.Regt., 1 Btty., Chalautre la Petite (Fr.) 27.8.44	-	MURDER	FR.
KURZE, Kurt	303766	M	27. 4.04	SS-Mann, C.C.Majdanek (Pol.) 40-44	57/649	BRUTALITY	POL.
KURZERA	304268	M		Member of the Schutzgruppen at the "Laura-mine", Eigelshoven (Neth.) 9.44	58/406	PILLAGE	NETH.
KURZYCA	308931	M		SS-Mann, Interpreter, Radom (Pol.) 40-45	60/360	MURDER	POL.
KUSCH	303423	M		Secr., Group 530 Geh.Feldpolizei, Bruessel (Bel.) 40-44	56/485	MURDER	BEL.
KUSS, Franz	308932	M		Watchmen, Blechhammer, Wielkie, Strzelce, Slask (Pol.) 45	60/361	MURDER	POL.
KUSTCHER, Fritz	266878	M		See names listed under "Special Headings"			FR.
KUTOWSKI, Theodor	304878	M		Member, Gestapo, Krakau (Pol.) 11.39-2.45	59/372	MURDER	POL.
KUTZ	266983	M		Sgt.Major, Feldgendarmerie, Sisteron (Fr.) 44	-	MISC.CRIMES	FR.
KUTZMANN	266513	M		W.O.,9 SS Pz.Div."Hohenstaufen",F.P.No.29474, Nimes (Fr.) 2.3.44	-	MURDER	FR.
KYLLMANN, Hans	264659	M		See names listed under "Special Headings"			U.S.
KYNAST	303424	M		Secr., Group 530 Geh.Feldpolizei, Bruessel (Bel.) 40-44	56/486	MURDER	BEL.
LAAF, Heinrich	304879	M		Member, Gestapo, Krakau (Pol.) 11.39-2.45	59/373	MURDER	POL.
LACHMANN, August	303425	M		Crim.Secr., Gestapo, Kattowitz (Pol.) 3.9.44	56/487	MURDER	POL.
LACHMANN, Walter	303426	M		Driver,623 Nachschub Bn., Petit-Enghien (Bel.) 3.9.44	56/488	MURDER	BEL.
LADDIG	266887	M		Lt., Air-Corps Coy.stationed at Ecot, Mathay-Ecot (Fr.) 9.44	-	MURDER	FR.
LADWIG, Bruno	304880	M		Member, Gestapo, Krakau (Pol.) 11.39-2.45	59/374	MURDER	POL.
LAGELBAUER, Bruno	304881	M		Member, Gestapo, Krakau (Pol.) 11.39-2.45	59/375	MURDER	POL.
LAHRFELD, M.	304269	M		Member, Schutzgruppen at the "Laura-mine", Eigelshoven (Neth.) 8.-13.9.44	58/408	PILLAGE	NETH.
LAHRFELD, O.	304270	M		Member, Schutzgruppen at the "Laura-mine", Eigelshoven (Neth.) 9.44	58/409	PILLAGE	NETH.
LAMBERT, Oskar	304882	M		Guard, Farmer, Strafgefangenenlager, Civilian, Harsewinckel, (Ger.) 44 and 45	59/376	TORTURE	BEL.
LAMBOY, Ludwig	304883	M		Member, Gestapo, Krakau (Pol.) 11.39-2.45	59/377	MURDER	POL.
LAND	308933	M		Member of German Military Police, Czorkow nr.Lodz (Pol.) 39-42	60/363	MURDER	POL.
LANDA, Franciszek (see TABAS, Antoni)	304006						
LANDWEHLE	265681	M		Osturmfhr., Member, SD, Chalons s.Marne (Fr.) 43	-	MISC.CRIMES	FR.
LANDWEHRLEN, Albert	304884	M		Field-Pol.-Director, Gestapo, HQ, Boulevard Piercot or the Avenue Rogier, Luettich (Bel.) 40-41	59/378	MURDER	BEL.
LANE, Helmut	303427	M		SS-Hptsturmfhr., Deputy to Tesmar Gestapo, Lodz (Pol.) 39-44	56/491	BRUTALITY	POL.
LANG, Friedrich	303767	M	21.11.08	SS-Mann, C.C.Majdanek (Pol.) 40-44	57/655	BRUTALITY	POL.
LANG, Ludwig	303428	M		Employee at a factory, Mielec (Pol.) 41-44	56/492	MURDER	POL.
LANG, Willi or Max	266232	M		Interpreter, Unit 12988 A, Lamotte-Beuvron (Fr.) 23.,24.8.44	-	WITNESS	FR.
LANG, Willy	304271	M		Farmer at or near Kemel (Ger.) 10.2.45	58/411	MURDER	U.S.
LANGANGE	266888	M		Oscharfhr., SS,10 Btty.,4 Section, Tulle (Fr.) 6.44	-	MURDER	FR.
LANGE	266231	M	circa 06	Sgt.-Major, Unit stationed at Camp Varennes, Ligny le Chatel (Fr.) 2.8.44	-	MURDER	FR.

LAN - LES

NAME	C.R.FILE NUMBER	SEX	DATE OF BIRTH	RANK OCCUPATION UNIT PLACE AND DATE OF CRIME	UNWCC LIST/ SERIAL NO.	REASON WANTED	WANTED BY
LANGE (I)	303768	M		Member, Gestapo, Warschau (Pol.) 39-45	57/657	BRUTALITY	POL.
LANGE (II)	303769	M		Member, Gestapo, Warschau (Pol.) 39-45	57/658	BRUTALITY	POL.
LANGELOH, Ernst	303429	M		Sgt., Group 530 Geh.Feldpolizei, Brussel (Bel.) 40-44	56/493	MURDER	BEL.
LANGEN, Alois	304885	M		Member, Gestapo, Krakau (Pol.) 11.39-2.45	59/379	MISC.CRIMES	POL.
LANGEN, Paul	266939	M	8.10.10	See names listed under "Special Headings"			
LANGER	303770	M		Member, Gestapo, Warschau (Pol.) 39-45	57/659	BRUTALITY	POL.
LANGER, Franz	266747	M	15. 7.96	Foreman, Electric Railway, Krakau (Pol.) 39		MISC.CRIMES	POL.
LANGFELD, Walter	304886	M		Member, Gestapo, Krakau (Pol.) 11.39-2.45	59/380	MURDER	POL.
LANHOLZ	303771	M		Member, Gestapo, Warschau (Pol.) 39-45	57/660	BRUTALITY	POL.
LANZ, Max	303430	M		Kriminalsekretaer, Gestapo, Kattowitz (Pol.) 39-42	56/496	PILLAGE	POL.
LANZER	265682	M		Lt., 558.Gren.Regt., 13.Coy., Bruay en Artois (Fr.) 1.9.44	-	SUSPECT	FR.
LAPRELL	303431	M		Member of Mot.Inf.Bn."z.b.V.", commanded by Capt.Fleck, School-master, German Franciscan Monastery at Sittard, German School at Heerlen (Neth.), Head of the German School in Utrecht, South Limburg (Neth.) 10.5.40	56/497	MISC.CRIMES	NETH
LARCHE, Erich	264621	M	19. 2.04	See names listed under "Special Headings"			
LASAI, Alfons	303432	M		Deputy Polizei-Kommissar, Gestapo Staff, Kattowitz (Pol.) 39-42	56/498	BRUTALITY	POL.
LASAI, Karls	303433	M		Kriminalbeamter, Gestapo, Kattowitz (Pol.) 39-42	56/499	BRUTALITY	POL.
LASKE	265667	M		Officer, Unit No. 23.176 ??, Mortemer (Fr.) 22.8.44	-	SUSPECT	FR.
LASNORJ	267474	M		Gestapo, Limoges and vicinity, (Fr.) 44	-	SUSPECT	FR.
LASSON, Peter	304887	M		Member, Gestapo, Krakau (Pol.) 11.39-2.45	59/381	MURDER	POL.
LAUBE, Klaus	265938	M	circa 02	Fw.or Hptscharfhr., Ital.Freiw.Police Regt.,2.Bn.,3.Coy.,stat. at Ponte di Piave nr.Treviso (It.) 2.45	-	SUSPECT	U.K.
LAUBENBERGER	267291	M		Usturmfhr., Gestapo, Bordeaux and vicinity (Fr.) 42-8.44	-	MURDER	FR.
LAUCHER	266974	M		Sgt., Feldgendarmerie, Sisteron (Fr.) 44	-	MISC.CRIMES	FR.
LAUDENBACH, Thomas	303772	M	4. 3.13	SS-Mann, C.C. Majdanek (Pol.) 40-44	57/663	BRUTALITY	POL.
LAUFENBERG	304272	M		Guard, Aachen (Ger.) 43-44	58/415	TORTURE	BEL.
LAUFF, Artur	303773	M	16. 8.94	SS-Uscharfhr., C.C. Majdanek (Pol.) 40-42	57/664	BRUTALITY	POL.
LAUKAN, Paul	265832	M		Obermeister, Stuetzpunkt, Szczurow (Pol.)		BRUTALITY	POL.
LAUNERT, Gottfried	303774	M	24. 8.98	SS-Mann, C.C. Majdanek (Pol.) 40-44	57/665	BRUTALITY	POL.
LAUPELT, Hermann	304273	M		Driver, to Dr. Leijer, Enschede (Neth.) 31.3.45	58/416	MURDER	NETH.
LAURUSCHKUS	266230	M		Lt.Col., Unit 12.988 A, Lamotte-Beuvron (Fr.) 23.,24.8.44	-	WITNESS	FR.
LAURENZEN	265833	F		SS-Guard, C.C. Ravensbrueck (Ger.)	-	MURDER	POL.
LEBECK	266889	M		Capt., Unit No.19.616 a,quartered at Nogent-le-Roi (Fr.) 7.7.40	-	SUSPECT	FR.
LECHNER	265340	M		Major, Army, 1218.Bn. 139.Regt. 188.Alpenjaeger-Div.,Skrapnje, Zvonici (Yugo.) 4.44	-	MURDER	YUGO.
LECHNER	303776	M		Member, Gestapo, Warschau (Pol.) 39-45	57/667	MURDER	POL.
LECKA, Wallerian	303434	M		Staff of C.C. Breendonck (Bel.) 40-44	56/503	MURDER	BEL.
LEDOCHOWSKI	266229	M		Cpl., Army, Calais (Fr.) 4.9.44	-	WITNESS	FR.
LEFFLER	265873	M		SS-Uscharfhr., C.C., Treblinka (Pol.)	-	BRUTALITY	POL.
LEFLER	265872	M		Member, Army, Wlodawa (Pol.) 41-44	-	MURDER	POL.
LEHMANN	265837	F		Wardress, C.C. Ravensbrueck (Ger.)	-	MURDER	POL.
LEHMANN	265838	M		SS-Usturmfhr., Gestapo, Rowne (Pol.) 41-44	-	BRUTALITY	POL.
LEHMANN	266529	M		Sgt., G.F.P., Arras (Fr.) 8.41	-	MURDER	FR.
LEHMANN	308935	M		Cpl., G.F.P., Antwerpen,Bruessel (Bel.) 40-44	60/366	MURDER	BEL.
LEHMANN, Hugo	308936	M		Kapo, Preusak-Kdo. Camp Missburg, 44-45	60/367	MURDER	BEL.
LEHMANN, Max (I)	304894	M		Member, Gestapo, Krakau (Pol.) 11.39-2.45	59/382	MURDER	POL.
LEHMANN, Max (II)	304888	M		Member, Gestapo, Krakau (Pol.) 11.39-2.45	59/383	MURDER	POL.
LEHMANN, Richard	303777	M	15. 3.92	SS-Mann, C.C. Majdanek (Pol.) 40-44	57/671	BRUTALITY	POL.
LEIBHERZ, Adam	303778	M	23. 9.09	Evacuation officer, C.C. Majdanek (Pol.) 40-42	57/672	BRUTALITY	POL.
LEIDERITZ, Heinrich	304889	M		SS-Osturmfhr., Head, SD and Sipo, Kolomea and Sub-district (Pol.) 9.41-42	59/384	MURDER	POL.
LEIDERITZ, Peter	304890	M		Member, Gestapo, Krakau (Pol.) 11.39-2.45	59/385	MURDER	POL.
LEIK	267292	F		Secretary, Gestapo, Bordeaux and vicinity (Fr.) 42-8.44	-	MURDER	FR.
LEIMANN, Max	265874	M		Member, Gestapo, Kazimierz Dolny (Pol.)	-	MURDER	POL.
LEINERLEPP	266890	M		Sgt.Major, Div. "Das Reich", Dordogne,Correze,Creuse,Hte.Vienne (Fr.) 5.-6.44	-	SUSPECT	FR.
LEINWEBER, Otto	304891	M		Member, Gestapo, Krakau (Pol.) 11.39-2.45	59/386	MURDER	POL.
LEIPOLD, Josef	265835	M		SS-Usturmfhr., Gestapo, Wieliczka, Plaszow (Pol.)	-	MURDER	POL.
LEISERING, Gertrud	304893	F		Member, Gestapo, Krakau (Pol.) 11.39-2.45	59/388	MURDER	POL.
LEISERING, Herbert	304895	M		Member, Gestapo, Krakau (Pol.) 11.39-2.45	59/389	MURDER	POL.
LEISS, Richard	304896	M		Member, Gestapo, Krakau (Pol.) 11.39-2.45	59/390	MURDER	POL.
LEISTERT	308938	M		Hptwachtmeister of Sipo,stat.at:"Marlot" flats building nr. Wassenaar Oct.44 but about the end of that month transf.to Hoock van Holland, Wassenaar (Neth.) 44	60/369	MURDER	NETH.
LEITER	267151	M		Lt.,Carpentras (Fr.) 7.44	-	INCENDIARISM	FR.
LEITUNG	304275	M		Cpl., G.F.P. Group 648, Liege (Bel.) 40-44	58/419	TORTURE	BEL.
LEIWAND	265836	M		SS-Uscharfhr., Extermination-Camp, Sobibor (Pol.) 42-43	-	MURDER	POL.
LEMASKI	303779	M		Member, Gestapo, Warschau (Pol.) 39-45	57/674	MURDER	POL.
LEMBACH, Fritz	265834	M		Member, Gestapo, Kazimierz Dolny (Pol.)	-	MURDER	POL.
LEMERTZ	265908	M		Member of staff, C.C. Dachau (Ger.)	-	MURDER	POL.
LEMPKE, Dr.	267562	M		Medical officer, Renesse and Zierikzee (Neth.) 10.12.44	-	BRUTALITY	NETH.
LEMPKE	303435	M		Sgt.,Group 530 Geh.Feldpolizei, H.Q. Bruessel (Bel.) 40-44	56/506	MISC.CRIMES	BEL.
LENGENFELDER, Engerbert	304897	M		Member, Gestapo, Krakau (Pol.) 11.39-2.45	59/391	MURDER	POL.
LENKE	266018	M		Member, Feldgendarmerie, Region of Cholet (Fr.) 7.and 8.8.44	56/507	MURDER	FR.
LENKOWSKI, Karl	267527	M		Gestapo, Limoges and vicinity (Fr.) 44	-	SUSPECT	FR.
LENNER, Franz	264620	M	27. 8.03	See names listed under "Special Headings"			
LENTSCH	266856	M		Staff-Sgt., Stabs-Coy. 3.J.G.Udet, Sours (Fr.) 7.-8.44	-	PILLAGE	FR.
LENZ	265328	M		Wachtmeister, Gendarmerie,Extermination Camp, Chelm (Pol.) 41-42	-	MURDER	POL.
LENZ	266763	M		Master police, Sonderkommando, Schupo, Gestapo, Kulmhof (Pol.) 41-45	-	MURDER	POL.
LENZ	267293	M		Lt.,Airforce, 91.Regt.,Chantraine (Fr.) 20.-22.9.44	-	MURDER	FR.
LENZNER, Herbert	304898	M		Member, Gestapo, Krakau (Pol.) 11.39-2.45	59/392	BRUTALITY	POL.
LEO, Rolf	304899	M		Member, Gestapo, Krakau (Pol.) 11.39-2.45	59/393	BRUTALITY	POL.
LESCH	308939	M		SS-Usturmfhr. and Krim.Sekretaer, Radom (Pol.) 40-45	60/371	MURDER	POL.
LESCH, Karl	304900	M		Member, Gestapo, Krakau (Pol.) 11.39-2.45	59/394	BRUTALITY	POL.

LES - LOE

NAME	C.R.FILE NUMBER	SEX	DATE OF BIRTH	RANK OCCUPATION UNIT PLACE AND DATE OF CRIME	UNWCC LIST/ SERIAL NO.	REASON WANTED	WANTED BY
LESCH, Max	304901	M		Member,Gestapo,Krakau (Pol.) 11.39- 2.45	59/395	BRUTALITY	POL.
LESCHEK, Rudolf	304903	M		Member,Gestapo,Krakau (Pol.) 11.39- 2.45	59/397	BRUTALITY	POL.
LESCHIK, Theophil	304902	M		Member,Gestapo,Krakau (Pol.) 11.39- 2.45	59/396	BRUTALITY	POL.
LESKEN	266224	M	circa 00	Guard,Interpreter,C.C.,Wattenstedt (Neuengamme) (Ger.)	-	MISC.CRIMES	FR.
LESSING	303780	M		Member,Gestapo,Warschau, (Pol.) 39-45	57/677	MURDER	POL.
LETTENMEYER, Georg	267235	M	00	Hptscharfhr.,Gestapo,Marseille and vicinity (Fr.)	-	MURDER	FR.
LETZGUS (or LETZKUS, Oskar)	266857	M	29. 3.98	Major,Airforce,Unit No.26769 and No.L.44766 (Luftgau-Post-amt Paris),Faverolles (Fr.) 12.-13.8.44	-	MURDER	FR.
LETZKUS (see LETZGUS,Oskar)	266857						
LEUCHTENBERGER	265983	M		Hptscharfhr.,Gestapo de Pau,Basses-Pyrenees (Fr.)	-	MURDER	FR.
LEUK	266858	M		Faehnrich,Div."B",Dordogne-Correze,Haute-Vienne (Fr.)	-	SUSPECT	FR.
LEUFEN (or LOIPEN), Karl	267103	M	circa 08	Driver,Gestapo,Blois and Maves (Fr.) 43-44	-	MURDER	FR.
LEUTTSCHAR	265220	M	95	Capt.,San Giacomo (It.) 3.1.44	-	SUSPECT	U.K.
LEVI, Franz	304276	M		Kapo,Labor Camps of Husum,Ladelund,Meppen,Dalum (Ger.) 40-45	58/421	MURDER	POL.
LEVEN, Heinrich	304904	M		Member,Gestapo,Krakau (Pol.) 11.39- 2.45	59/398	MURDER	POL.
LEWIN	265909	M	95	Member,Secretary,NSDAP,County Council, Lublin (Pol.) 40-44	-	MISC.CRIMES	POL.
LEY, Friedrich	304905	M		Member,Gestapo,Krakau (Pol.) 11.39- 2.45	59/399	MURDER	POL.
LEYDA	265968	M		Capt.,Feldkommandantur, Brest (Fr.) 8.9.44	-	MURDER	FR.
LEZOK, Leonhard	304906	M		Member,Gestapo,Krakau (Pol.) 11.39- 2.45	59/400	MURDER	POL.
LIDEKA, Fritz	304907	M		Member,Gestapo,Krakau (Pol.) 11.39- 2.45	59/401	MISC.CRIMES	POL.
LIEBELER	267104	M		Lt.,350.Regt."Hindou",Lureuil,Linge,St.Michel,Brenne,Vendoeuvres St.Maur,Ambrault,Ardentes,Neuilly les Blois (Fr.) 8.44	-	MURDER	FR.
LIEBER	265907			Cmdt.,C.C. Auschwitz (Pol.)	-	MURDER	POL.
LIEBHART, Wilhelm	265305	M		Sgt.,"Brandenburg" Regt., (It.)	-	SUSPECT	U.K.
LIEBIER, Willy	267224	M	circa 16	Sgt.,Waffenwerkstatt 812,Chatesumeillent (Fr.) 27. 6.44	-	MURDER	FR.
LIEBING, Herta	304908	F		Member,Gestapo,Krakau (Pol.) 11.39- 2.45	59/402	MURDER	POL.
LIEBL, Hermann	264622	M	30. 3.12	See names listed under "Special Headings"			
LIEDFE	303781	M		Member,Gestapo,Warschau (Pol.) 39-45	57/679	INTERR.	POL.
LIEDL, Sebastian	303782	M	9. 1.00	SS-Mann,C.C. Majdanek (Pol.) 40-44	57/680	BRUTALITY	POL.
LIEDTKE, Reinold	265905	M	05	Member,Security Unit,Chelmno (Pol.)	-	BRUTALITY	POL.
LIEDHAUS	303305	M		Supervisor or Gang Leader,C.H.F.Mueller "Roentgen" factory Hamburg (Ger.) 43-44	56/512	MURDER	NETH.
LIETKE	265906	M		Wachtmeister,Gendarmerie,Wlodawa (Pol.) 41-44	-	MURDER	POL.
LIGUDA, Johann	304909	M		Member,Gestapo,Krakau (Pol.) 11.39- 2.45	59/403	MURDER	POL.
LINCK, Richard	266585	M		Sgt.,Feldgend.658,Paray le Monial and environ (Fr.) 43-44	-	SUSPECT	FR
LINDEKE	265910	M		SS-Uscherfhr.,C.C. Treblinka (Pol.)	-	BRUTALITY	POL.
LINDER	265840	M		Hptwachtmeister,Gend.,Szczurowa (Pol.) 40-44	-	BRUTALITY	POL.
LINDER	304278	M		Member,G.F.P.Group 648,Liege (Bel.) 40-44	58/424	TORTURE	BEL.
LINDER, Richard	267243	M		Matrose,Navy,Senon (Fr.) 9.44	-	MURDER	FR.
LINDERT, Josef	304910	M		Member,Gestapo,Krakau (Pol.) 11.39- 2.45	59/404	BRUTALITY	POL.
LINDER	266989	M		Lt.,Flakmast 30-XII,Baudrigues nr.Carcassonne (Fr.) 19.8.44	-	MURDER	FR.
LINDNER	303783	M		Member,Gestapo,Warschau (Pol.) 39-45	57/682	INTERR.	POL.
LINENSCHLOSS, Otto	265839	M		Manager,Great estate,Serebryszcze-Community Kszywiczki (Pol.)	-	MURDER	POL.
LINGEN	304279	M		Member,Schutzgruppen at the "Laura-mine",Eigelshoven (Neth.) 8.-13.9.44	58/425	PILLAGE	NETH.
LINGNER, Friedrich	303784	M	19. 3.21	SS-Mann,C.C. Majdanek (Pol.) 40-44	57/684	MURDER	POL.
LINHARDT, Julius	264618	M	4. 3.05	See names listed under "Special Headings"			
LINHART, Walter	265984	M	22. 3.03	Leading official,Distr.office of Prerov (Czech.) 5.45	-	MURDER	CZECH.
LINTMANN	266909	M		Pvt.,Div."B",Haute-Vienne,Dordogne,Correze (Fr.)	-	SUSPECT	FR.
LINKENBACH	303306	M		N.C.O.,Feldgend.,Angouleme,Chassenueil,Charente (Fr.) 43- 3.44	56/514	MURDER	FR.
LINKER, Ludwig	267397	M		Lt., Baker-Coy.19, Unit No. 08598,Chailles, (Fr.) 6.7.and 8.40	-	PILLAGE	FR.
LINNER, Julian	265847	M		Gestapo,Rudki nr. Krzywiczki (Pol.) 4. 7.40	-	MURDER	POL.
LINNER, Julius	265846	M		Member,Gestapo,Chelm (Pol.) 4. 7.40	-	MURDER	POL.
LIPERT, Josef	303307	M		Crim.secretary,Gestapo at Kattowitz (Pol.) 39-42	56/515	BRUTALITY	POL.
LIPINSKI	265841	M		Member,Gend.,Warszawa (Pol.) 44	-	MURDER	POL.
LIPINSKI	265848	M		Camp senior, C.C. Lublin-Majdanek (Pol.)	-	BRUTALITY	POL.
LIPKE, Otto	265845	M		SS-Oscharfhr.,Gestapo,Lodz (Pol.) 39-44	56/516	BRUTALITY	POL.
LIPPART (see LIPPERT)	265915						
LIPPERT (or LIPPART)	265319	M	circa 11	SS-Mann, C.C. Auschwitz (Pol.) 40-44	-	MISC.CRIMES	POL.
LISCHKA, Georg	304911	M		Member,Gestapo,Krakau (Pol.) 11.39- 2.45	59/405	MISC.CRIMES	POL.
LISENKO, Nikolai	303785	M		Oberwaerter, C.C. Wattenstadt (Ger.) 39-45	57/686	BRUTALITY	POL.
LISKE, Dr.	265825	M		Finance Office, Zamosc (Pol.) 41-42	-	BRUTALITY	POL.
LISKE	265863	M		SS-Sturmbannfhr.,Represent of chief,Gestapo,Lublin (Pol.)	-	MURDER	POL.
LISKE, Ernst	267238	M	08	Lt.,1.Coy.of high-way police,Ban-St.Martin (Fr.) 41	-	PILLAGE	FR.
LISSNER, Josef	304912	M		Member,Gestapo,Krakau (Pol.) 11.39- 2.45	59/406	BRUTALITY	POL.
LITKE	304280	M		Capt.,Town-major, German Army of Piraeus (Gre.) 6.41	58/429	PILLAGE	GRC.
LITNU, Walter	267105	M		SS-Div."Das Reich",Unit No. 37746,South West France 1944	-	MURDER	FR.
LOBA, Ernst	264619	M	12.11.89	See names listed under "Special Headings"			
LOEBERLEIN, Alfred	265304	M		Sgt.,"Brandenburg" Regt.,(It.)	-	SUSPECT	U.K.
LOBIG	303786	M		Member,Gestapo,Warschau (Pol.) 39-45	57/687	INTERR.	POL.
LOBNER, Georg	303787	M	15.10.25	SS-Mann,C.C. Majdanek (Pol.) 40-44	57/688	BRUTALITY	POL.
LOC	265844	M		Official,Gestapo,Czostkow-Tluste (Pol.)	-	MISC.CRIMES	POL.
LOCH, Martin	303788	M	8. 11.21	SS-Mann, C.C. Majdanek (Pol.) 40-44	57/689	BRUTALITY	POL.
LOCHNER, Johann-Hans	264430	M	13. 7.01	Uscharfhr.,Civ.Pol.Service,Gruppe Geh.Feldpolizei,550, Gestapo Paris BDS IV E,Paris (Fr.) 20.11.42- 44	-	SUSPECT	FR.
LOCKERT, Heinrich	303309	M		Kriminalsekretaer,Gestapo,Kattowitz (Pol.) 39-42	56/517	BRUTALITY	POL.
LOEFING	266988	M		Usturmfhr.,Gestapo,Alencon and region (Fr.) 40-44	-	MURDER	FR.
LOEDEL	265843	M		Uscharfhr.,SS,C.C. Mauthausen-Gusen (Aust.)	-	MURDER	POL.
LOEFFEL, Ernst	265862	M	circa 01	Director,"Liegenschaften", Zalesie n.Biala Podlaska (Pol.)	-	BRUTALITY	POL.
LOEFFEL, Eva	265861	F	23	Daughter of Loeffel,Ernst,Dir.of "Liegenschaften" Zalesie nr.Podlaska (Pol.)	-	BRUTALITY	POL.
LOESCH	265969	M		See names listed under "Special Headings"			
LOESCHAK, Friedrich	303311	M		Pol.Wachtmeister,Member of Sonderkdo.,Kulmhof (Pol.) 41-45	56/519	MURDER	POL.
LOESER, Ewald Oskar Ludwig	265315	M	11. 4.88	Official,Friedrich Krupp A.G., Essen (Ger.)	-	MISC.CRIMES	U.S.

LOE - MAC

NAME	C.R.FILE NUMBER	SEX	DATE OF BIRTH	RANK OCCUPATION UNIT PLACE AND DATE OF CRIME	UNWCC LIST/ SERIAL NO.	REASON WANTED	WANTED BY
LOEWI	265859	M		SS-Usturmfhr., Guard, SS, C.C. Auschwitz (Pol.)	-	MURDER	POL.
LOFSBERG	303310	M		Member, Feldgend. or Army, Breda (Neth.) 43-44	56/518	MURDER	NETH.
LOHMANN	304281	M		Cpl., G.F.P. Bruessel (Bel.) 40-44	58/431	MURDER	BEL.
LOHR, Alfons	303312	M		Krim.Sekretaer, Gestapo at Kattowitz (Pol.) 39-42	56/521	BRUTALITY	POL.
LOHR, Ferdinand	264429	M	26.10.03	Hptsturmfhr., Civil.Police Service, Gruppe Geh.Feldpol., 633 Orleans Gestapo Paris BDS IV E, (Fr.) 20.11.42-44	-	SUSPECT	FR.
LOMP, Paul, Georg	304284	M		Uschfhr., Schutzgruppen State coal mine "Julia" Eigelshoven (Neth.) 8.-13.9.44	58/434	PILLAGE	NETH.
LONGRET	266910	M		Capt., Commandant, Standort Kmdtr., La Celle Saint Cloud (Fr.)	-	MISC.CRIMES	FR.
LOPFER	308941	M		Director, Prison, at Wolfenbuettel (Ger.) 40-45	60/379	TORTURE	BEL.
LOPPEN (see LEUPEN, Karl)	267103						
LOPSCH, N.	265360	M		Hptwachtmeister, Gendarmerie, Brzesko (Pol.)	-	BRUTALITY	POL.
LORENSCHAD, Christoph	304913	M		Member, Gestapo, Krakau (Pol.) 11.39-2.45	59/407	BRUTALITY	POL.
LORENTZ	266220	M		N.C.O., SS Div. "Das Reich", 2 Art.Btty. 1 Sect. Selles sur Cher (Fr.) 14.-15.8.44	-	MURDER	FR.
LORENZ (see DITR)	147959						
LORENZ	267505	M		Member, Gestapo, Limoges and vicinity (Fr.) 44	-	SUSPECT	FR.
LORENZ	303789	M		Member of Guard, Warschau (Pol.) 39-45	57/692	INTERR.	POL.
LORENZ, Dieter (see DITR)	147959						
LORENZ, Fritz	304914	M		Member, Gestapo, Krakau (Pol.) 11.39-2.45	59/408	BRUTALITY	POL.
LORENZ, Hermann	265882	M	circa 97	Post-official, Zamosc (Pol.)	-	BRUTALITY	POL.
LORENZ, Josef	264665	M	29.11.01	See names listed under "Special Headings"			
LORENZ, Wilhelm	265882	M	circa 83	Secretary, SS Gestapo, Lodz (Pol.) 39-44	56/522	MISC.CRIMES	POL.
LORENZE, Alfred	303314	M		SS-Schfhr., Gestapo, Lodz (Pol.) 39-44	56/522 A	PILLAGE	POL.
LORENZEN,	303315	M		Sonderfhr., Group 530 of GFP, Bruessel (Bel.) 40-44	56/523	MURDER	BEL.
LORENZEN, Fritz	304915	M		Member, Gestapo, Krakau (Pol.) 11.39-2.45	59/409	BRUTALITY	POL.
LORENZO, Alfred	265890	M		SS-Uschfhr., Official, SS Gestapo,Sect.4-1 Right-wing Parties (Lodz), (Pol.)	-	BRUTALITY	POL.
LORKE	267398	M		Interpreter, Gestapo, Bordeaux and vicinity (Fr.) 42-8.44	-	MURDER	FR.
LOS	267399	M		Interpreter, Gestapo, Bordeaux and vicinity (Fr.) 42-8.44	-	MURDER	FR.
LOSCHNIGG, Karl	266896	M		Member, Sipo. SD. Perigueux Gestapo, Dordogne (Fr.) 43-44	-	SUSPECT	FR.
LOSSACK, Helmut	304916	M		Member, Gestapo, Krakau (Pol.) 11.39-2.45	59/410	BRUTALITY	POL.
LOTH	308942	M		Instructor and Employee of GFP, Antwerpen, Bruessel (Bel.)	60/382	MURDER	BEL.
LOTHOLZ	303790	M		Member, Gestapo, Warschau (Pol.) 39-45	57/694	BRUTALITY	POL.
LOYSCHER, Alfons	265837	M	12.9.03	SS-Officer, C.C. Radogoszcz near Chelmno (Pol.)	-	MURDER	POL.
LUCK, Heinrich	303791	M	12.11.04	SS-Sturmmann, C.C. Majdanek (Pol.) 40-44	57/697	MURDER	POL.
LUDWICK, Medoc	266221	M	00	Capt., Unit stationed at Camp Varennes, Ligny-le-Chatel (Yonne), (Fr.) 2.8.44	-	MURDER	FR.
LUDWIG	267120	M		General SS "Prinz Eugen" Div., Dinj (Yugo.) 8.9.43- 10.44	-	MURDER	YUGO.
LUDWIG	303792	M		SS-Uschfhr., C.C. Majdanek (Pol.) 40-44	57/698	BRUTALITY	POL.
LUDWIG, Emil	265881	M		SS-Oschfhr., Extermination Camp Sobibor (Pol.) 42-43	-	MURDER	POL.
LUDWIG, Emil (or LUDWIK)	265891	M		SS-Oschfhr., SS C.C. Cmdt. of Gaschambers, Treblinka (Pol.)	-	MURDER	POL.
LUDWIG, Franz	266648	M		Pvt., Army, Dieppe (Fr.) 3.44	-	MURDER	FR.
LUDWIG, Helene	304917	F		Member, Gestapo, Krakau (Pol.) 11.39-2.45	59/411	MURDER	POL.
LUDWIG, Karl	265879	M	95	Propietor, Censor, "Deutsche Buecherei", Lublin (Pol.)	-	MISC.CRIMES	POL.
LUDWIG, Willy	304918	M		Member, Gestapo, Krakau (Pol.) 11.39-2.45	59/412	BRUTALITY	POL.
LUDWIK (see LUDWIG, Emil)	265891						
LUDWISCHKOSKI	267218	M		Leiter, Schupo., Gestapo, Bordeaux and vicinity (Fr.)42-8.44	-	MURDER	FR.
LUEBUSCH, Eduard	265880	M		SS-Mann, C.C.Auschwitz (Pol.)	-	MURDER	POL.
LUEFTERING, Johann, Wilhelm	304235	M		Pol.Leiter, at Helenenhoehe near Haltern District Recklinghausen (Ger.) 20.10.44	58/435	MURDER	U.K.
LUETHJE, Wilhelm	308943	M		Gendarmerie official, of Gend., near Cramme (Ger.) 44	60/383	MURDER	U.S.
LUGMAYR	303317	M		Gendarm, Feldgend., at Angouleme, Chasseneuil (Fr.)43-3.44	56/526	MURDER	FR.
LUIG, Wilhelm, Dr.	264613	M	30.9.00	See names listed under "Special Headings"			
LUJYROFF	266897	M	circa 15	Lt., Unit No. 47523 Armenian Unit stationed at Mende, Chanac (Fr.) 15.-16.8.44	-	MURDER	FR.
LUKAS	265889	M		SS-Osturmfhr., Gestapo, Luck (Pol.)	-	MISC.CRIMES	POL.
LUKAS	267416	M		SS-Guard, C.C. Struthof-Natzweiler (Fr.) 40-45	-	MURDER	FR.
LUKASCHWSKI	303793	M		Member, Gestapo, Warschau (Pol.) 39-45	57/700	BRUTALITY	POL.
LUMAN (or LUMANN)	266898	M	circa 10	SS-Mann, SD. Chatelleraut and vicinity (Fr.) 8.42-8.44	-	SUSPECT	FR.
LUMANN (see LUMAN)	266898						
LUTCKE, Albert	265970	M		Feldgend., Interpreter, Feldgend., Tredrez (Fr.) 9.1.44	-	MURDER	FR.
LUTER	265930	M		Wachtmeister, Gendarmerie, Wlodawa (Pol.)	-	MURDER	POL.
LUTGEN, Willy	267237	M	07	Hptschfhr., Gestapo, Marseille and vicinity (Fr.)	-	MURDER	FR.
LUTZ, Jacob	304919	M		Member, Gestapo, Krakau (Pol.) 11.39-2.45	59/413	MURDER	POL.
LUTZELBERGER, Rudolf	304920	M		Member, Gestapo, Krakau (Pol.) 11.39-2.45	59/414	MISC.CRIMES	POL.
LUTZOK	303794	M		Member, Gestapo, Warschau (Pol.) 39-45	57/702	BRUTALITY	POL.
LUX, Gustav	304286	M	31.10.19	Interpreter, Member, Gestapo, (Slov.) 44	58/437	MURDER	CZECH.
LYR	304921	M		Member, Secr.Field Pol., H.Q. Boulevard Piercot or the Avenue Rogier, Luettich (Bel.) 40-41	59/415	MURDER	BEL.
MAACK	308944	M		Feldpol.Kommissar, Antwerpen and Bruessel (Bel.) 40-44	60/384	MURDER	BEL.
MAAS, Erich	303319	M		Krim.Sekretaer, Gestapo at Kattowitz (Pol.) 39-42	56/531	PILLAGE	POL.
MAASEN	266352	M	17.8.89	Capt., Sect. I a,Feld-Kmdtr.641, Blois,Seillac (Fr.) 22.6.44	-	MISC.CRIMES	FR.
MACHDALS	266895	M		Lt., Infantry Unit. Neigne and Chauvigny (Fr.)14.-26.8.45	-	MURDER	FR.
MACHER	308945	M		SS-Usturmfhr. and Krim.Kommissar, at Radom (Pol.) 40-44	60/385	RAPE	POL.
MACHETEK, Sepp	304923	M		Member, Gestapo, Krakau (Pol.) 11.39-2.45	59/416	MISC.CRIMES	POL.
MACHNIK, Josef	304923	M		Member, Gestapo, Krakau (Pol.) 11.39-2.45	59/417	MISC.CRIMES	POL.
MACHNIK, Wilhelm	266093	M	10	Agent, Gestapo, Manager of the Coal Firm Lagenhausen,Lublin (Pol.)	-	MURDER	POL.
MACHNOWSKI, Heinrich	304924	M		Member, Gestapo, Krakau (Pol.) 11.39-2.45	59/418	MISC.CRIMES	POL.
MACHTZ	265392	M		Col., Legion Georgienne, Aveyron (Fr.) 18.6.44	-	MISC.CRIMES	FR.
MACHULE, Walter, Dr.	267306	M	circa 97	Sturmbannfhr., Chief, Gestapo, Bordeaux and vicinity (Fr.)-8.44	-	MURDER	FR.
MACK, Hans	304925	M		Member, Gestapo, Krakau (Pol.) 11.39-2.45	59/419	MISC.CRIMES	POL.
MACK, Karl	308992	M		Civilian, near Michelfeld (Ger.) 25.4.44	60/388	MURDER	U.S.
MACKEL, Walter	304926	M		Member, Gestapo, Krakau (Pol.)11.39-2.45	59/420	MISC.CRIMES	POL.
MACKENSEN	267044	M		See names listed under "Special Headings"			

MAC - MAT

NAME	C.R.FILE NUMBER	SEX	DATE OF BIRTH	RANK	OCCUPATION UNIT PLACE AND DATE OF CRIME	UNWCC LIST/ SERIAL NO.	REASON WANTED	WANTED BY
MACKUE, Franz	304287	M			Informer, Gestapo, Jaromer, Bohemia (Czech.) 42-45	58/438	INTERR.	CZECH.
MADEJA	303795	M			Member, Gestapo, Warschau (Pol.) 39-45	57/704	BRUTALITY	POL.
MADER, Franz	304927	M			Member, Gestapo, Krakau (Pol.) 11.39-2.45	59/421	MISC.CRIMES	POL.
MADERHOLZ, Friedrich	266092	M			Member of staff, Extermination Camp, Chelmno (Pol.) 41-43	-	MURDER	POL.
MADERUK, Iwan	304928	M			Member, Gestapo, Krakau (Pol.) 11.39-2.45	59/422	MISC.CRIMES	POL.
MAESER, Paul (or MESER)	266223	M			Sgt., Feldgendarmerie, Bucey-les-Gy (Fr.) 28.7.44	-	MURDER	FR.
MAGNER, Paul	303796	M	16. 6.87		SS-Rottfhr., C.C.Majdanek (Pol.) 40-44	57/705	MURDER	POL.
MAHLE, August	267506	M			Cpl., Feldgendarmerie, Besancon and region (Fr.) 44	-	MURDER	FR.
MAHNE, Georges	267414	M	circa 15		Oscharfhr., Gestapo, Bordeaux and vicinity (Fr.) 42-8.44	-	MURDER	FR.
MAIBAUER	308994	M			SS-Hptscharfhr., Crim.Oberasst., SS, Radom (Pol.) 1.40-1.45	60/390	TORTURE	POL.
MAIER	267521	M			Col., 71 Inf.Regt., Airforce, Aude and Herault Dept. (Fr.) 5.-8.44	-	MISC.CRIMES	FR.
MAIER, Albert	265578	M			Finance Director, Fa.Roechling (Fr.) -45	-	MISC.CRIMES	FR.
MAIER, Samuel	303797	M	4.10.08		SS-Mann, C.C.Majdanek (Pol.) 40-44	57/706	BRUTALITY	POL.
MAIER-KAIBITSCH, Alois	264611	M	20. 5.91		See names listed under "Special Headings"			
MAIER, Joseph (or MEIER)	265370	M	10. 1.98		Interpreter, Kommandantur, Delle (Fr.) 27.1.41	-	TORTURE	FR.
MAINZINGER, Ferdinand	266051				Major, Army, Camp Bitche (Fr.)	-	MURDER	FR.
MAJER	266091	M			Interpreter, Gestapo, Lodz (Pol.) 39-44	56/534	MISC.CRIMES	POL.
MAJOWSKI, Elise	304990	F			Member, Gestapo, Krakau (Pol.) 11.39-2.45	59/424	MURDER	POL.
MALCHER, Leonhard	304931	M			Member, Gestapo, Krakau (Pol.) 11.39-2.45	59/425	PILLAGE	POL.
MALCZYNSKI, Johann	303321	M			Employee at a factory in Mielec (Pol.) 41-44	56/535	MURDER	POL.
MALI, Wilhelm	304932	M			Member, Gestapo, Krakau (Pol.) 11.39-2.45	59/426	PILLAGE	POL.
MALIK	266106	M			SS-Uscharfhr., Penal Camp, Gundelsdorf (Ger.) 44	-	BRUTALITY	POL.
MALOUCK	266853	M			Lt., Unit No.19616 A, quartered at Nogent-le-Roi (Fr.) 7.7.40	-	SUSPECT	FR.
MALYNOWICZ, Theodor	304933	M			Member, Gestapo, Krakau (Pol.) 11.39-2.45	59/427	PILLAGE	POL.
MALZER	265971	M			Sgt.Major, Senior W.O., Feldgendarmerie, Quimperle (Fr.) 44	-	MURDER	FR.
MALZMUELLER, Teo	303322	M			Police-Wachtmeister, Member of Kulmhof Sonderkdo., Kulmhof (Pol.) 41-45	56/536	MURDER	POL.
MAMSCH	266869	M			Agent, Gestapo, Rouen and region (Fr.) 40-44	-	MURDER	FR.
MANEKEN	265972	M			Capt., Cmdt., Fire-Bde.at Metz, Brest (Fr.) 8.9.44	-	MURDER	FR.
MANG, Julius	303798	M	7.12.05		SS-Guard, C.C.Majdanek (Pol.) 40-44	57/709	BRUTALITY	POL.
MANKE	266105	M			Lt., Schutzpolizei, Lublin (Pol.)	-	MURDER	POL.
MANKOSUHUI	266854	M			Pvt., Div."Das Reich", Dordogne, Creuse, Hte.Vienne, Correze (Fr.) 5.,6.44	-	SUSPECT	FR.
MANN	304288	M			Cpl., Nachtjagd Group No.4, vicinity of Charleroi (Bel.) 2.44	58/441	MURDER	BEL.
MANN, Georg	303323	M			N.C.O., Group 530 Geh.Feldpolizei, Bruessel (Bel.) 40-44	56/537	MURDER	BEL.
MANNHEIM	267578	M			See names listed under "Special Headings"			
MANNICH, Walter	304934	M			Member, Gestapo, Krakau (Pol.) 11.39-2.45	59/428	PILLAGE	POL.
MANNS, Hans (or GANSMANNS)	266222	M			Sgt., Airforce, Unit L 49761, Nancy (Fr.) 40-45	-	SUSPECT	FR.
MANULIAK, Johann	304935	M			Member, Gestapo, Krakau (Pol.) 11.39-2.45	59/429	PILLAGE	POL.
MANZKE	267296	M			Capt., 71 Airforce Regt., La Tour-sur-Orb (Fr.) 17.8.44	-	MURDER	FR.
MARCEL (or MARCELL)	267523	M	circa 16		Lt., Army, Montmarin (Fr.) 1.9.44	-	MURDER	FR.
MARCELL (see MARCEL)	267523							
MAREK, Gustav	308995	M	14. 8.08		Usturmfhr., Chief of Gestapo, Gniezno (Pol.) 39-45	60/392	MURDER	POL.
MARFIEWICZ, Jan	266749	M	22.12.89		Labourer, Power Station, Krakau (Pol.) 39-1.43	-	MURDER	POL.
MARGART	304936	M			Field-Police-Director, Secr.Field-Police, HQ, Boulevard Piercot or the Avenue Rogiere, Luettich (Bel.) 40-41	59/430	MURDER	BEL.
MARIO	304316	M			Carabiniere, attached to 1 Bde., Levie, Corsica (Fr.) 6.43	58/443	BRUTALITY	FR.
MARDHL, Walter	303324	M			Hpt.-Crim.Asst., Gestapo, Kattowitz (Pol.) 39-42	56/539	BRUTALITY	POL.
MARSCHALL, Teo	266135	M			Member, Gendarmerie, Zambrow (Pol.) 42-44	-	MURDER	POL.
MARSCHANT, Hans	304937	M			Member, Gestapo, Krakau (Pol.) 11.39-2.45	59/431	PILLAGE	POL.
MARSCHNER, Dr.	267415	M	circa 10		Gestapo, Bordeaux and vicinity (Fr.) 42-8.44	-	MURDER	FR.
MARTEN, Wilhelm	266108	M	16. 4.07		Gendarm, Gendarmerie, Raszkow (Pol.)	-	MURDER	POL.
MARTENS, Max	303325	M			N.C.O., Group 530, Geh.Feldpolizei, Bruessel (Bel.) 40-44	56/540	MURDER	BEL.
MARTENS, Wilhelm	304317	M			Farmer, Heidenau (Ger.) 40-43	58/444	BRUTALITY	POL.
MARTHA	266855	M			SS-Nurse, SS Camp Ravensbrueck (Ger.) 43-45	-	MISC.CRIMES	FR.
MARTIN	197490	M			Member, SS-Scharfhr., SS staff, central recovery, C.C.Mauthausen, Gusen (Aust.)	-	MURDER	POL., BEL.
MARTIN (see RUMER, Ernst)	267193							
MARTIN, Friedrich	304938	M			Member, Gestapo, Krakau (Pol.) 11.39-2.45	59/432	PILLAGE	POL.
MARTIN, Johann	304939	M			Member, Gestapo, Krakau (Pol.) 11.39-2.45	59/433	PILLAGE	POL.
MARTINCEK, Anton	308998	M	13. 6.08		Liaison Officer, between the Hlinka Guard and the Gestapo, Trencin (Czech.) 41-45	60/397	MURDER	CZECH.
MARTINEC, Wladimir	304940	M			Member, Gestapo, Krakau (Pol.) 11.39-2.45	59/434	PILLAGE	POL.
MARTINS, F.H.F.	308999	M	4. 9.01		Member, Schutzgruppen Brunssum (Neth.) 9.44	60/398	PILLAGE	NETH.
MARTINSON	303327	M			SS-Scharfhr., Guard in Oldenburg Goal, Oldenburg (Ger.) 43-45	56/542	MURDER	POL.
MARTSCHKE, Gerhart	267220	M			Osturmfhr., Gestapo, Marseille and vicinity (Fr.)	-	MURDER	FR.
MARWEDE	303455	M			Major, Cologne "Abwehrstelle", situated in a house in the Bel- forstrasse, Koeln, Sued Limburg (Neth.) 10.5.40	56/543	MISC.CRIMES	NETH.
MARWEDE	303799	M			Member, Gestapo, Warschau (Pol.) 39-45	57/716	MURDER	POL.
MARX, Hans	266891	M			Sgt., Interpreter, Kommandantur, Campagne les Hesdins (Fr.) 10.12.43	-	MISC.CRIMES	FR.
MARZ (or MAX)	267221	M			Usturmfhr., Gestapo, Marseille and vicinity (Fr.)	-	MURDER	FR.
MARZELANIK, Johann	303456	M			Kriminalbeamter, Gestapo, Kattowitz (Pol.) 39-42	56/545	PILLAGE	POL.
MARZUK, Pierre	309000	M			Member, Gestapo, Perigueux (Fr.) 9.43-8.44	60/399	MURDER	FR.
MASCHNER, Viktor	266099	M			Chief, Sonderdienst, Camp "Dylle" (Pol.) 21.11.42	-	MURDER	POL.
MAST	304318	M			Lt., Member, Feldgendarmerie, F.P.No.45696, Fort Hoek van Holland, Naaldwijk, Honselrsdijk (Neth.) 28.4.45	58/446	MURDER	NETH.
MATERNA	266100				Member, Sonderdienst, Szczurowa (Pol.)	-	MURDER	POL.
MATHAEUS	266101	M			Physician, Extermination Camp, Chelmno, Radogoszcza (Pol.)	-	BRUTALITY	POL.
MATHAEUS (see MATHEUS, Walter)	266102							
MATHAUS	267522				Lt., 71 Inf.Regt., Airforce, Aude and Herault Dept. (Fr.) 5.-8.44	-	MISC.CRIMES	FR.
MATHEJ, Eduard	304941	M			Member, Gestapo, Krakau (Pol.) 11.39-2.45	59/436	PILLAGE	POL.
MATHES	309002	M			Cpl., Secret Field-Police, Antwerpen, Brussel (Bel.) 40-44	60/401	MURDER	BEL.
MATHEUS, Walter (or MATHAEUS)	266102	M			SS-Sturmscharfhr., Chief, Gestapo, of a Unit to fight adherents of the Polish Underground, Jaslo, Krosno (Pol.) 40-44	-	MURDER	POL.
MATHEUS, Walter	304942	M			Member, Gestapo, Krakau (Pol.) 11.39-2.45	59/437	BRUTALITY	POL.

MAT - MEL

NAME	C.R.FILE NUMBER	SEX	DATE OF BIRTH	RANK OCCUPATION UNIT PLACE AND DATE OF CRIME	UNWCC LIST/ SERIAL NO.	REASON WANTED	WANTED BY
MATHIAS	266103	M		SS-Scharfhr., Extermination Camp, Treblinka (Pol.) 42-43	-	MURDER	POL.
MATHIES, Wilhelm	266104	M		Deputy to Lane, Gestapo, Lodz (Pol.) 39-44	56/547	BRUTALITY	POL.
MATHIEU, Peter	267197	M		Member, Gestapo, Bordeaux vicinity (Fr.) 42-8.44	-	MURDER	FR.
MATL, Leopold	304943	M		Member, Gestapo, Krakau (Pol.) 11.39- 2.45	59/438	BRUTALITY	POL.
MATSCHEL, August	304944	M		Member, Gestapo, Krakau (Pol.) 11.39- 2.45	59/439	BRUTALITY	POL.
MATTAUSCH	303800	M		Member, Gestapo, Warschau (Pol.) 39-45	57/721	BRUTALITY	POL.
MATTES, Paul	304945	M		Member, Gestapo, Krakau (Pol.) 11.39- 2.45	59/440	BRUTALITY	POL.
MATTHES, Wilfrid	265569	M		Pvt., Army, Civitella area (It.) 7.44	-	MURDER	U.K.
MATTIS, Fritz	304946	M		Member, Gestapo, Krakau (Pol.) 11.39- 2.45	59/441	MURDER	POL.
MATUCH (see MATUCHA)	197491						
MATUCHA (or MATUCH)	197491	M		Guard or Kapo, C.C., Gusen (Aust.)	-	MURDER	POL., BEL.
MATYSIAK	266751	M		Cpl., Mannschafts-Stammlager III A, Luckenwalde (Ger.) 39-45	-	MISC. CRIMES	POL.
MATZ	303801	M		Member, Gestapo, Warschau (Pol.) 39-45	57/725	MURDER	POL.
MATZKE	266512	M		Chief manager of purchase service Organisation of the Black Market (Fr.) 42-44	-	PILLAGE	FR.
MAU, Gustav	265318	M		Employee, Railway, Danzig-Prauss (Pol.) 39	-	MISC. CRIMES	POL.
MAUER	309003	M		Krim.Angest.and Interpreter?, Radom (Pol.) 1.40-1.45	60/403	MURDER	POL.
MAUER, Willi	304947	M		Member, Gestapo, Krakau (Pol.) 11.39- 2.45	59/442	BRUTALITY	POL.
MAUKEL	266602	M		Pvt., Feldgendarmerie 658, Paray le Monial, vicinity(Fr.)43-44	-	SUSPECT	FR.
MAUMANN, Karl (or NEUMANN)	266096	M		Chief manager, "Economy and supply", Warschau (Pol.)	-	PILLAGE	POL.
MAURER	266097	M		Member, guard, Extermination camp, Sobibor (Pol.) 42-43	-	MURDER	POL.
MAUTHE, Erich	304948	M		Member, Gestapo, Krakau (Pol.) 11.39- 2.45	59/443	BRUTALITY	POL.
MAUZ, Herrold	265974	M	circa 05	Hptscharfhr., Belfort (Fr.) 8.9.44	-	MURDER	FR.
MAX (see MARZ)	267221						
MAYER (see MEYER)	266893						
MAYER	266990	M	circa 10	Cpl., Feldgendarmerie, Masleves, Coulanges and Blois (Fr.) 7.44 and 10.8.44	-	MURDER	FR.
MAYER	266991	M		SS-Oscharfhr.,18.SS Panz.Gren.Div. "Horst Wessel", Oradour sur Glane (Fr.) 10.6.44	-	MURDER	FR.
MAYER	267417	M		Sgt., 350 Regt. "Hindou", Department l'Indre (Fr.) Aug.44	-	MURDER	FR.
MAYER, Alois	304949	M		Member, Gestapo, Krakau (Pol.) 11.39- 2.45	59/444	BRUTALITY	POL.
MAYER, Eddi	303459	M		Hptscharfhr., Gestapo, Lodz (Pol.) 39-44	56/550	BRUTALITY	POL.
MAYER, Herich	267045	M		Uscharfhr., Member, Gestapo of Beziers, Herault (Fr.)43-44	-	SUSPECT	FR.
MAYER, Johann	304319	M		Keyenberg District Erkelenz (Ger.) 40-45	58/451	BRUTALITY	POL.
MAYER, Kurt, Dr.	264612	M	27. 6.03	See names listed under "Special Headings"			
MAYER, Lutschi	266750	M		Commandant, C.C., Neuengamme (Ger.) 43-44	-	MURDER	POL.
MAYER, Otto	265231	M	02?	Sgt., Army, Verona (It.) 5.44	-	SUSPECT	U.K.
MAYER, Wilhelm	266950	M	4.11.05	Member, Civil Police Service Group Geheime Feldpolizei 733, Buchenwald (Ger.) 11.42	-	SUSPECT	FR.
MAYET	266992	M		Sgt-Major, Feldgendarmerie, Sisteron (Fr.) 44	-	MISC. CRIMES	FR.
MAZIS, Willy	304950	M		Member, Gestapo, Krakau (Pol.) 11.39- 2.45	59/445	BRUTALITY	POL.
MAZON, Zygmunt	303802	M		Different C.C.'s (Pol.and Ger.) 39-45	57/732	MURDER	POL.
MAZURKIEWICZ, Bruno	266095	M		Member, SS-Scharfhr., Gestapo, Krakau (Pol.) 41-45	-	MISC. CRIMES	POL.
MEANZARLAN, Johann	266094	M		Kapo, informer, SS-Staff, C.C., Duchau (Ger.)	-	BRUTALITY	POL.
MEBERSCHAR, Arthur	266444	M	7. 5.09	Pvt., Luftgaukdo.VI,Raeumungsstab z.b.V. Kdo. Arnhem, Arnhem (Neth.) 1.-2.44	-	PILLAGE	NETH.
MECKLEMBERG	267074	M		Member, Div. "Das Reich", South West France (Fr.) 44	-	MURDER	FR.
MECKLENBURG	266894	M		Oscharfhr., Div. "Das Reich", Dordogne, Correze, Creuse, Hte.Vienne (Fr.) 5.-6.44	-	SUSPECT	FR.
MEHL, Otto	267507	M	18. 3.97	Oscharfhr.,Gruppe Geheime Feldpolizei 649,Paris (Fr.)20.11.42	-	BRUTALITY	FR.
MEHLER	265668	M		Major, Cmdt.,2.F.J.Div.-Fallschirm-Nachr.Abt., Brest (Fr.) 8.9.44	-	MURDER	FR.
MEHIKOPF	304320	M		Member,Schutzgruppen at the "Laura Mine", Eigelshoven (Neth.) 8.-13.9.44	58/456	PILLAGE	NETH.
MEHRING, Anton Otto	266110	M	25 3.20	Member, Staff, Extermination Camp, Chelmno (Pol.)	-	MURDER	POL.
MEIDINGER, Willy	267508	M	circa 10	Cpl., Pioneer school at cosne, Cosne-St.Pere (Fr.)6.7.44	-	MISC. CRIMES	FR.
MEIER, Emil (or MICHEL,Dr.)	265975	M	9. 1.14	Member, SD, Chalons-sur-Marne (Fr.) 43-44	-	MISC. CRIMES	FR.
MEIER, Gerhard	304321	M	24.12.17	Farmer, Zweidorf, Braunschweig (Ger.) 42-43	58/458	BRUTALITY	POL.
MEIER, Gustav Alfred	265976	M	95	Asst.,SS-Sturmbannfhr., Commander of Sipo and SD, Marseille, Bouches du Rhone (Fr.) 44	-	SUSPECT	FR.
MEIER (see MAIER, Joseph)	265370						
MEIER, Kurt	303460	M		Police-Wachtmeister, member, Sonderkommando, Kulmhof (Pol.)41-45	56/552	MURDER	POL.
MEIJER, Dr.	304322	M		Solicitor, Korvetten-Capt., Head of Office at Wilhelmshaven, Sonderkdo.Neth.Sect.of Abwehrstelle, Wilhelmshaven, Enschede (Neth.) 31.3.45	58/459	MURDER	NETH.
MEIJER, Hermann Bernhard	309006	M	19. 5.98	Stuetzpunktltr.,member,worksmanager,NSDAP, Ingenieurausschuss, N.V."Probat" Factory,'s-Heerenberg (Neth.) 41-45	60/407	INTERR.	NETH.
MEIJER ZUR KNOLLE	267576	M		Adjutant, Major Hornn, Renesse (Neth.) 10.12.44	-	MURDER	NETH.
MEINBERG, Otto	304324	M	23. 6.80	Supervisor of 50 villages, Distr.of Chelm (Pol.) 39	58/461	MURDER	POL.
MEINEL, Otto	266947	M	7.11.02	Uscharfhr., Civil Police Service Gruppe Geheime Feldpolizei 649 Paris BDS-IV-Ia-Ib, Paris (Fr.) 11.42	-	SUSPECT	FR.
MEINERS (or MINNERS), Heinz Werner	267052	M	3. 4.24	Oscharfhr.,SS,Gestapo, BDS IV 2-3, Paris (Fr.)	-	SUSPECT	FR.
MEINHARDT, Dr.	309005	M		Gau-Hauptstellenltr.,NSDAP Arnhem,'s-Heerenberg (Neth.)41-45	60/406	INTERR.	NETH.
MEISMER	267051	M		Lt.Col.,Anti-terrorist-Coy.unit No.26.565 STEIF-Corps, Robion (Fr.) 44	-	MURDER	FR.
MEISNER, Wilhelm	303461	M		SS-Oscharfhr., Gestapo, Lodz (Pol.) 39-44	56/553	MURDER	POL.
MEISSNER, Franz	304325	M	4.11.04	SS-Unterfhr., Ger.Schutzgruppen "Julia" state coalmine, Eigelshoven (Neth.) 8.9.-13.9.44	58/462	MISC. CRIMES	NETH.
MEISSNER, Willy Friedrich	267050	M	31. 8.01	Member, Gestapo, Paris (Fr.)	-	SUSPECT	FR.
MEISTER, Hermann	303463	M		Kriminalasst.,Gestapo, Kattowitz (Pol.) 39-42	56/555	BRUTALITY	POL.
MEISTER, Marta	303462	F		Gestapo agent, member of "Selbstschutz", Torun (Pol.) 9.39	-	MURDER	POL.
MEISTER, Richard	303464	M		Gestapo agent, member, "Selbstschutz", Torun (Pol.) 9.39	56/556	MURDER	POL.
MEIWALD	304951	M		Field-Pol.secretary, Secr.Field-Police,H.., Boulevard Piercot or the Avenue Rogier, Luettich (Bel.) 40-41	59/447	MURDER	BEL.
MELCHER, Emil	304952	M		Member, Gestapo, Krakau (Pol.) 11.39- 2.45	59/448	BRUTALITY	POL.

NAME	C.R.FILE NUMBER	SEX	DATE OF BIRTH	RANK	OCCUPATION UNIT PLACE AND DATE OF CRIME	UNWCC LIST/ SERIAL NO.	REASON WANTED	WANTED BY
MELCHIOR, Karl	265504	M			Uscharfhr., C.C. Lwow and Plaszow (Pol.) 42-43	-	MURDER	POL.
MELNICK, Zenobius	304953	M			Member, Gestapo, Krakau (Pol.) 11.39- 2.45	59/450	BRUTALITY	POL.
MELSER, Fritz	251834	M	18		SS-Oscharfhr., SD. and Gestapo, Sipo, Limoges (Fr.) 40-45	-	SUSPECT	FR.
MELZER	303803	M			Member, Gestapo, Warschau (Pol.) 39-45	57/736	MURDER	POL.
MEMPEL, Gerhard, Dr.	266112	M			Member, German Office for Agricultural Search, Krakau (Pol.) 1.45	-	PILLAGE	POL.
MENCKE	303465	M			Was in North-Netherlands, neighbourhood of Alkmaar (Neth.) 8.44, 11.10.44	56/557	MURDER	NETH.
MENDE	266111	M			Officer, SS-Usturmfhr., Sipo, Warschau (Pol.) 40-44	-	MISC.CRIMES	POL.
MENEMANN	304954	M			Guard, C.C. Mesum, Emsdetten Distr.Steinfurt (Ger.) 31.8.42, 42-19.10.44	-	MURDER	POL.
MENN, Hermann	303804	M	10. 6.01		SS-Guard, C.C.Majdanek (Pol.) 40-44	57/739	BRUTALITY	POL.
MENZ	303805	M			Member, Gestapo, Warschau (Pol.) 39-45	57/740	BRUTALITY	POL.
MENZEL	304955	M			Secretary, Secr.Field-Police,H.Q.Boulevard,Piercot or the Avenue Rogier, Luettich (Bel.) 40-41	59/452	MURDER	BEL.
MERKEL	303806	M			Member, Gestapo, Warschau (Pol.) 39-45	57/742	BRUTALITY	POL.
MERKENDORFER, Wilhelm	303807	M	2. 4.00		Guard, C.C. Majdanek (Pol.) 40-42	57/743	BRUTALITYT	POL.
MERKL, Josef	303808	M	13. 9.08		SS-Mann, C.C. Majdanek (Pol.) 40-44	57/744	BRUTALITY	POL.
MERKLE, Hans, Dr.	304326	M			SS-Sturmfhr., nr.Wiesenbach,Gernsbach and Oberstrot (Ger.), on or about 9.8.44	58/464	MURDER	U.S.
MERSMANN, Irmgard	304956	F			Member, Gestapo, Krakau (Pol.) 11.39-2.45	59/454	MURDER	POL.
MERTEN	303809	M			Member, Gestapo, Warschau (Pol.) 39-45	57/746	BRUTALITY	POL.
MERTENS	266321	M			SS-Oscharfhr., repres. Principal of Prison, Lwow (Pol.)	-	MURDER	POL.
MERTENS, Josef	304957	M			Member, Gestapo, Krakau (Pol.) 11.39-2.45	59/455	MURDER	POL.
MERTZ	265233	M	95		Bezirks-Gefaengnis No. 2, Karlsruhe (Ger.) 11.44	-	BRUTALITY	FR.
MESCHE, Heinz	303466	M			Kriminalsekretaer, Gestapo, Kattowitz (Pol.) 39-42	56/558	BRUTALITY	POL.
MESER (see MAESER, Paul)	266223							
MESSEL	266920	M			Gendarm, Gendarmerie, Wlodawa (Pol.)	-	MURDER	POL.
MESSINGSCHLAGER, Hans	266322	M			Member of staff, C.C. Chelmno (Pol.)	-	BRUTALITY	POL.
MESSIRICH	304327	M			Member, Schutzgruppen "Laura-Mine", Eigelshoven (Neth.)8.-13.9.44	58/466	PILLAGE	NETH.
METZELTHIN, Ernst	304958	M			Member, Gestapo, Krakau (Pol.) 11.39-2.45	59/456	MURDER	POL.
METZEN, Peter	267222	M			Uscharfhr., Gestapo, Marseille and vicinity (Fr.)	-	MURDER	FR.
METZGER, Heinrich	303810	M	15. 5.12		SS-Mann, C.C. Majdanek (Pol.) 40-44	57/747	BRUTALITY	POL.
METZGER, Josef	303811	M	6. 3.10		SS-Mann, C.C. Majdanek (Pol.) 40-44	57/748	PILLAGE	POL.
METZNER, Albert	304959	M			Member, Gestapo, Krakau (Pol.) 11.39-2.45	59/457	MURDER	POL.
METZNER, Erwin	264610	M	17. 7.90		See names listed unter "Special Headings"			
MEUER, Josef	266323	M	circa 85		Director, Chamber for Handicraft and Artisan, Lublin (Pol.)	-	MISC.CRIMES	POL.
MEUER, Philip	266324	M	circa 80		Official, Referent, Gestapo, Workshop-Section, Lublin (Pol.)	-	BRUTALITY	POL.
MEURER, Johann (Hans)	304328	M	18. 6.99		Overseer, Mine-Insp.,"Julia" State coal mine, Member,German Schutzgruppen, Eigelshoven (Neth.) 8.-13.9.44	58/467	PILLAGE	NETH.
MEYER	266765	M			Lt.Col., I c of AOK 15, Wissant Bay (Fr.) 2.-9.44	-	SUSPECT	U.K.
MEYER (or MAYER)	266893	M			Lt., Airforce, Eguilles (Fr.) 19.8.44	-	MURDER	FR.
MEYER	267305	M	circa 12		Uscharfhr., Gestapo, Bordeaux and vicinity (Fr.) 42- 8.44	-	MURDER	FR.
MEYER (I)	303812	M			Member, Gestapo, Warschau (Pol.) 39-45	57/749	BRUTALITY	POL.
MEYER (II)	303813	M			Member, Gestapo, Warschau (Pol.) 39-45	57/750	TORTURE	POL.
MEYER (III)	303814	M			Member, Gestapo, Warschau (Pol.) 39-45	57/751	TORTURE	POL.
MEYER, Dr.	309007	M			SS-Doctor, Haaren-Camp and Hooge Boekel (Neth.) 43-44	60/408	PILLAGE	NETH.
MEYER, Gustav	267223	M			Hptsturmfhr., Chief, Gestapo, Section II, Marseille and vicinity (Fr.)	-	MURDER	FR.
MEYER, Heinz	266892	M			Agent, Gestapo, Rouen and vicinity (Fr.) 40-44	-	MURDER	FR.
MEYER, Helmuth, Dr.	267565	M	96		Capt.Lt., Leader of "Abwehrstelle Wilhelmshaven" "Dienststelle Hengelo", Hengelo (Neth.) 31.3.45	-	SUSPECT	NETH.
MEYER, Karl	264609	M	7. 7.09		See names listed under "Special Headings"			
MEYER, Kurt	266271	M	circa 10		Rottfhr., Agent, Gestapo, Nantes and region (Fr.) 43-44	-	MURDER	FR.
MEYER, Rosa	266319	F			Official, Post, Lublin (Pol.)	-	BRUTALITY	POL.
MEYER, Wilhelm	304960	M			Member, Gestapo, Krakau (Pol.) 11.39-2.45	59/458	MURDER	POL.
MEYERBERGER	266272	M	circa 98		Capt., 1212.Inf.Regt., 2.Bn., Lomont (Fr.) 9.-11.44	-	MURDER	FR.
MICEL	266174	M	circa 10		Chief, Public Safety, Chelmno (Pol.)	-	BRUTALITY	POL.
MICHAEL	267413	M	circa 15		2.Paratrooper-Div.,Commanding the II.Coy. Unit No.54566 L.G.P.A. Brest and vicinity (Fr.) 7.-8.44	-	MURDER	FR.
MICHAEL	309008	M			SS-Hptsturmfhr. and Kriminalrat, SS, Radom (Pol.) 1.40-1.45	60/409	RAPE	POL.
MICHAEL, Eduard	304961	M			Member, Gestapo, Krakau (Pol.) 11.39-2.45	59/459	BRUTALITY	POL.
MICHAEL, Max	198118	M	circa 05		Hptsturmfhr., Chief, Gestapo, Abt. 1, Vichy, Marseille and vicinity (Fr.) 43-44	16/521	MURDER	FR.
MICHALLA, Gerhard	303467	M			Sekretaer, Group 530 of the Secr.Field-Police,Bruessel (Bel.) 40-44	56/563	MURDER	BEL.
MICHALSEN (see MICHELSEN)	266171							
MICHALSKI	266172	M			Osturmfhr., Commissar, Chief, SS, Gestapo, Section 4 "Sabotage of Work", Lodz, (Pol.) 39-44	56/564	MISC.CRIMES	POL.
MICHALSKI, Georg	263119	M			See names listed unter "Special Headings"			
MICHALSKI, Paul	303469	M			Police-Wachtmeister, Member Sonderkommando, Kulmhof (Pol.)41-45	56/565	MURDER	POL.
MICHEELS, Walter	304329	M	20.12.02		Member, former Police-Officer, SD and Gestapo, SD Aussenstelle Maastricht, "Staatspolizei"Department, Limburg and Friesland (Neth.) 44-45	58/468	MURDER	NETH.
MICHEL, Dr. (see MEIER)	265975							
MICHEL, Hermann	266173	M			Osturmfhr., SS, C.C. Sobibor (Pol.)	-	MURDER	POL.
MICHEL, Nicolas	266979	M			Chief of culture, Pure (Fr.) 40-44	-	BRUTALITY	FR.
MICHELBACH, Laurens	265369	M			Agent, SS-Uscharfhr.,Gap Gestapo, SD of Gap, Hautes-Alpes (Fr.) 10.43-9.44	-	SUSPECT	FR.
MICHELL	303470	M			Sonderfhr.,Group 530 Secr.Field-Police,Bruessel (Bel.) 40-44	56/566	MURDER	BEL.
MICHELSEN (or MICHALSEN)	266171	M			Member, SS, Gestapo, Warschau (Pol.)	-	MURDER	POL.
MIELKE	303815	M			Member, Gestapo, Warschau (Pol.) 39-45	57/756	TORTURE	POL.
MIESCH	266273	M			Cpl., 95.Sich.Regt. 4.Coy.,2.Sect.,2.Group, Journiac, Le Bugue,St.Leon s.Vezere (Fr.) 6.44	-	MURDER	FR.
MIETE, Franz	266170	M			Chief-Guard, Hospital in Extermination Camp, Treblinka (Pol.)	-	TORTURE	POL.
MIETZEL	266867	M			Capt., Stabs-Coy. 9.G.J. Udet, Sours (Fr.) 7.and 8.44	-	PILLAGE	FR.
MIKA	197380	M			Commandant, Major, 3.Regt. Turkestan 3.Coy. St.Laurent,Marsonnas (Fr.) 31.5.44-10.6.44	-	SUSPECT	FR.
MIKER	266175	M			Pvt., Army, Brzesko (Pol.)	-	BRUTALITY	POL.
MIKIETA, Adolf	304961	M			Member, Gestapo, Krakau (Pol.) 11.39-2.45	59/461	BRUTALITY	POL.
MIKLAS	266176	M			Member of staff, C.C. Auschwitz,Brzezinka (Pol.)	-	MISC.CRIMES	POL.
MIKOWSKI, Lucjan	309009	M			Member, Gestapo, Radom (Pol.) 1.40-1.45	60/410	MURDER	POL.

MIL - MUE

NAME	C.R.FILE NUMBER	SEX	DATE OF BIRTH	RANK	OCCUPATION	UNIT	PLACE AND DATE OF CRIME	UNWCC LIST/ SERIAL NO.	REASON WANTED	WANTED BY
MILBRADT, Arnold	304963	M			Member,Gestapo,Krakau (Pol.) 11.39- 2.45			59/462	MURDER	POL.
MILOH, E.	266119	M			Official,Member,Reichsluftfahrtministerium,Staff,C.C. Auschwitz (Pol.)			-	MURDER	POL.
MILEK, Joseph	266755	M	15. 2.91		Conductor of the Electric Railway, Krakau (Pol.) 39-?			-	MISC.CRIMES	POL.
MILKO	266118	F			Kapo,C.C. Lublin-Majdanek (Pol.)			-	MISC.CRIMES	POL.
MILLA, Franz	303816	M			SS-Guard,C.C. Auschwitz (Pol.) 40-45			57/758	BRUTALITY	POL.
MILLER	266117	M			Member,Staff,C.C. Lublin-Majdanek (Pol.)			-	MURDER	POL.
MINCHOW, Wilhelm	266116	M			Gendarmeriemeister,Gendarmerie,Dabrowa (Pol.)			-	MURDER	POL.
MINKWIS	266115	M			Official,Gestapo,Warszawe (Pol.)			-	MISC.CRIMES	POL.
MINNERS (see MEINERS, Heinz Werner)	267052									
MIRBACH	303817	M			Member,Gestapo,Warschau (Pol.) 39-45			57/759	TORTURE	POL.
MIRCKA, William	266274	M			Lt.,Unit 12.988 A,Lamotte-Beuvron (Fr.)			-	MURDER	FR.
LIROZ	266113	M			SS-Feldfhr.,Extermination Camp,C.C. Lublin-Majdanek (Pol.)			-	MISC.CRIMES	POL.
MISCA, Roudy	266556	M			SD,Rennes,retreated to Meurthe and Moselle,Pettonville (Fr.) 6.10.44			-	MISC.CRIMES	FR.
MISCHKE	303818	M			Member,Gestapo,Warschau (Pol.) 39-45			57/760	TORTURE	POL.
MISKA	266000	M			Capt.,2.Paratrooper-Div.,Brest (Fr.) 8.9.44			-	MURDER	FR.
MISNER, Wilhelm	266114	M			Oscharfhr., official,SS,Gestapo,Lodz (Pol.)			-	MURDER	POL.
MITAS	266120	M			Room-senior, Stuba,C.C,Penal section Block No.1,Auschwitz (Pol.)			-	TORTURE	POL.
MITTENGGER	267049	M			Div."Das Reich",South-west France 1944			-	MURDER	FR.
MITTERECKEN, Otto	267225	M			Matrose,Navy,Senon (Fr.) 9.44			-	MURDER	FR.
MITTMANN, Erich	304965	M			Member,Gestapo,Krakau (Pol.) 11.39- 2.45			59/464	BRUTALITY	POL.
MOBIUS	266978	M	circa 15		Staff-Sgt.,Feldgend.,Masleves,Coulanges,Elois (Fr.) 7.44-8.44			-	MURDER	FR.
MOCZ, Julius	304966	M			Member,Gestapo,Krakau (Pol.) 11.39- 2.45			59/465	BRUTALITY	POL.
MODELHAMMER, Alois	267249	M			Scherfhr.,Gestapo,Marseille and vicinity (Fr.)			-	MURDER	FR.
MOEBIS	266084	M			Driver,SS-Rottenfhr.,Extermination Camp,Treblinka (Pol.)42-43			-	BRUTALITY	POL.
MOECK	303819	M			Member,Gestapo,Warschau (Pol.) 39-45			57/763	TORTURE	POL.
MOELLER	265999	M			Lt.Col.,266.Inf.Div.,Brest (Fr.) 8.9.44			-	MURDER	FR.
MOELLER, Karl	304332	M			Cpl.,Gestapo,Bruessel (Bel.) 40-44			58/473	MURDER	BEL.
MOELLER, Lorenz	303471	M			Sgt.,Group 530 of the Geh.Feldpol.,Bruessel (Bel.) 40-44			56/567	MURDER	BEL.
MOENNICH, Bruno	266141	M			Member,SS-Scherfhr.,Gestapo,Krakau (Pol.)			-	MISC.CRIMES	POL.
MOERING, Paul	304337	M	circa 22		Uscharfhr.,Waffen-SS,Guard-Bn.3,Amersfoort (Neth.) 2.5.43			58/478	MURDER	NETH.
MOERS	266993	M	circa 05		Cpl.,Feldgend.,Masleves,Coulanges and Elois (Fr.) 7.44-10.8.44			-	MURDER	FR.
MOGDANS	309010	M			Interpreter ?,Radom (Pol.) 1.40- 1.45			60/813	MURDER	POL.
MOHAUPT	266275	M			Member,Gestapo,Nantes and region (Fr.) 43-44			-	MURDER	FR.
MOHR, Dr.	304333	M			Probably Head,EDS "Auffangleger",Uelzen,Zeist,Oldenzaal,Den Haag (Neth.) 44 - 45			58/474	PILLAGE	NETH.
MOHR, Hans Dr.	304334	M			Sgt.,Geh.Feldpolizei,Bruessel (Bel.) 40-44			58/475	MURDER	BEL.
MOKRYS, Dominik	303472	M			Kriminalbeamter,Gestapo,Kattowitz (Pol.) 39-42			56/569	BRUTALITY	POL.
MOKUET	266082	M			Wachtmeister,Gendarmerie,Debno,Brzezko (Pol.)			-	BRUTALITY	POL.
MOLAN, Fritz	304758	M			Member,Gestapo,Krakau (Pol.) 11.39- 2.45			59/466	BRUTALITY	POL.
MOLKE, Henri	267250	M			Sgt.,Army,Marseille and vicinity (Fr.) 43-44			-	MISC.CRIMES	FR.
MOLLENHAUER, Rudolf	304335	M			Owner,Herring Packing Factory,Cuxhaven (Ger.) 40-45			58/476	BRUTALITY	POL.
MOLLER	267251	M			Hptscharfhr.,Gestapo,Pezonne (Fr.) 27.8.44			-	MISC.CRIMES	FR.
MOLLER, Frantz	266569	M			Director of a purchase,office at Paris Organisation of the Black Market, France 1942-44			-	PILLAGE	FR.
MOLLERT	267252	M			Hptsturmfhr.,Gestapo,Marseille and vicinity (Fr.) 44			-	MURDER	FR.
MOLT, Peter Eugen	309011	M	circa 23		Lt.,Army,in charge of troops doing guard duty in connection with a V-base at Hoek van Holland,Wassenaar (Neth.) 11.44			60/415	MURDER	NETH.
MOLTER, Philippe	267509	M			Scharfhr.,Gestapo,St.Etienne and vicinity (Fr.) 43-44			-	MISC.CRIMES	FR.
MOLMSET	304759	M			Commissioner,Secr.Field-Police,Boulevard,Pierqot or the Avenue Rogier,Luettich (Bel.) 40-41			59/467	MURDER	BEL.
MONTEL, Gerhard Dr.	266083	M			Geolog and official,"Reichsamt fuer Bodenforschung" Krakau (Pol.) 1.45			-	PILLAGE	POL.
MONTSCHER, Franz	304336	M			Civilian,near Muenchen (Ger.) 4.45			58/477	MURDER	U.S.
MOCR	266140	M			Member,Schutzpolizei, C.C. Budzyn (Pol.)			-	MISC.CRIMES	POL.
MORAWIAK, Leon	304760	M			Member,Gestapo,Krakau (Pol.) 11.39- 2.45			59/468	BRUTALITY	POL.
MORGEL	265996	M			Major,Commanding of the 2.Bn.,200.Mot.Gren.Regt.,La Condamine Chatelard,Basses-Alpes (Fr.) 25.-29.8.44			56/572	MISC.CRIMES	FR.
MORGNER, Alfred	303474	M			Sgt.(Stabsfeldwebel),Feldgendarmerie,Angouleme,Chasseneuil,Charente (Fr.) 43 and 2.9.44			-	MURDER	FR.
MORITZ, Joseph	64	M	14. 6.06		Hptsturmfhr.,Gestapo Paris BDS IV B, Paris (Fr.) 42-44			-	SUSPECT	FR.
MORLOCK,	309012	M			Oscharfhr.,Krim.Asst.,Radom (Pol.) 1.40- 1.45			60/416	RAPE	POL.
MOSEL, Hans	303820	M	5.11.96		Camp-guard,C.C. Lustbokel 1999-45			57/774	BRUTALITY	POL.
MOSER, Enrich	266866	M	10		Driver,SD,Chatellerault and vicinity (Fr.) 8.42-8.44			-	SUSPECT	FR.
MOSER, Karl	266139	M	circa 09		Official,Police,Home-add....,Halle, Slomniki (Pol.)			-	MURDER	POL.
MOSLER, Hans	266090	M			Hptscharfhr.,SS-Uni ?ww (Pol.) 4.-43			-	MURDER	POL.
MOSMULLER	266865	M			Pvt.,Div."Das Reich",Dordogne,Correze,Creuse, Hte Vienne (Fr.)5.44			-	SUSPECT	FR.
MOTEL	267412	M			Lt.,350.Regt."Hindou",Department l'Indre (Fr.) 8.44			-	MURDER	FR.
MOUKA	303475	M			Sgt.,Department of Basses-Pyrenees (Fr.) 8.6.-8.44			56/574	MURDER	FR.
MOURMANN	267253	M			Oscharfhr.,Gestapo,Marseille and vicinity (Fr.)			-	MURDER	FR.
MROZEK, Franz	266138	M			Chief,Gestapo,Home-address:Silesia,Lodz (Pol.)			-	MISC.CRIMES	POL.
MUCHA, Gerhard	303477	M			Kriminalbeamter,Employee,Gestapo,Kattowitz (Pol.) 39-42			56/576	PILLAGE	POL.
MUDLE	266511	M			Asst.Chief,C.C. Buchloe (Fr.)			-	BRUTALITY	FR.
MUDRICH	31401	M			Capt.,comd.II-Gren.Regt.910-163.Inf.Div.20 Army,Finmark (Nor.)11.1944			-	MURDER	NOR.
MUEHLAUSLER, Hans	266941	M	18. 9.11		Uschfhr.,Released from Army 20.11.42,Civ.Police service, Gruppe Geh.Feldpolizei 734,Gestapo,Paris (Fr.) 11.42			-	SUSPECT	FR.
MUEHLBERGER, Erhard	266748	M	26. 7.06		Director,Power station,Krakau (Pol.) 41-45			-	MURDER	POL.
MUEHLE, Max Reinhold Rudolf	265901	M			Manager,factory "Pelze Syn","Hasag" "Granat",Ozestochowa,Kielce (Pol.) 41-45			-	MISC.CRIMES	POL.
MUEHLHAUSEN	266186	M			Member,Hilfspolizei,Inowroclaw (Pol.)			-	MISC.CRIMES	POL.
MUELHAUPT	303478	M			Pvt.,Group No.530,Geh.Feldpolizei,Bruessel (Bel.) 40-44			56/577	MURDER	BEL.

MUE - MUS

NAME	C.R.FILE NUMBER	SEX	DATE OF BIRTH	RANK OCCUPATION UNIT PLACE AND DATE OF CRIME	UNWCC LIST/ SERIAL NO.	REASON WANTED	WANTED BY
MUELLER	266089	M		Member SS Staff, C.C.,Giebow near Halle (Ger.) 42	-	MURDER	POL.
MUELLER	266121	M		SS-Oscharfhr., C.C. Lublin,Majdanek (Pol.) 40-43	-	MISC.CRIMES	POL.
MUELLER	266122	M		SS-Oscharfhr.,Extermination Camp, Treblinka (Pol.) 42-43	-	MURDER	POL.
MUELLER	266123	M		Commissar, Chief, SS-Osturmfhr., Section "Jews and Religion and intercourse of Poles with Germans",Gestapo, Lodz (Pol.) 40-44	-	MURDER	POL.
MUELLER	266126	M		Member, Gestapo, Wlodawa (Pol.) 41-43	-	MURDER	POL.
MUELLER	266127	M		SS-Mann, SS-Unit, Lwow (Pol.)	-	MURDER	POL.
MUELLER	303484	M		Employée,Sicherheitspolizei and SD, Kempen (Ger.) 25.10.41	56/585	MURDER	POL.
MUELLER	303821	M		Foreman, Warschau (Pol.) 40-44	57/778	MISC.CRIMES	POL.
MUELLER	304340	M		Inspector,Customs officer, Glanerbrug (Neth.) 24.10.44	58/484	MURDER	NETH.
MUELLER	309013	M		SS-Sturmscharfhr.,Crim.-Secretary, Radom (Pol.) 1.40-1.45	60/418	TORTURE	POL.
MUELLER, Eberhard	266184	M	98	Director, District Post Office,Lublin,Piaski (Pol.)	-	MURDER	POL.
MUELLER, Erich	303479	M		Cpl.,Group 530 of the Geh.Feldpolizei,Bruessel (Bel.) 40-44	56/508	MURDER	BEL.
MUELLER, Ernst	264608	M	17. 9.	See names listed under "Special Headings"			
MUELLER, Georg	266183	M	06	Secretary,SS-Hptscharfhr.,Gestapo, Lodz (Pol.)		MISC.CRIMES	POL.
MUELLER, Johann	304763	M		Watchman , Blechhammer, Wielkie, Strzelce, Slask (Ger.,Pol.) 1.-2.45	59/472	MURDER	POL.
MUELLER, Karl	266125	M		SS-Tscharfhr.,Extermination Camp, Sobibor (Pol.) 42-43	-	MURDER	POL.
MUELLER, Karl	267234	M	30. 6.01	Member,Gestapo, Paris (Fr.)	-	SUSPECT	FR.
MUELLER, Karl	304338	M		Incommand of a Hitler Youth Group,Blechhammer (Ger.) 22.4.45	58/479	MURDER	U.S.
MUELLER, N.	266740	M		Commandant of penal labour camp, building service "Liban Quarry", Krakau (Pol.) 42	-	TORTURE	POL.
MUELLER, Paul	303480	M		Member,Group 530 Geheime Feldpolizei, Bruessel (Bel.) 40-44	56/579	MURDER	BEL.
MUELLER, Reichard	303481	M		Feldpolizeisekretaer,Group 530 Geh.Feldpolizei,Bruessel(Bel.)40-44	56/580	MURDER	BEL.
MUELLER, Wilhelm	266124	M		Gardener, Botanic Garden, Krakau (Pol.)	-	MISC.CRIMES	POL.
MUELLERS, Heinz	266716	M		Pvt., Army, Mont sur Marchienne near Charleroi (Bel.) 9.4.41	-	WITNESS	BEL.
MUELNICHEL, Rudolf	266150	M	20.11.10	Member, Staff, Extermination Camp, Chelmno (Pol.) 41-44	-	MURDER	POL.
MUEUCH, Hans	198120	M		Officer,Member,SS-Usturmfhr.,SS-Staff,Hygienic Institute, C.C.Auschwitz (Pol.) 40-45	-	MURDER	POL. FR.
MUHLHEISEN	265388	M	10	W.O.,SD,Gestapo, Bayonne and Environs (Fr.) 40-44	-	MURDER	FR.
MUJAR	266185	M		SS-Oscharfhr., Extermination Camp, Plaszow (Pol.)	-	MURDER	POL.
MULLER	265367	M	15	W.O. SD,Gestapo, Bayonne and Environs (Fr.) 40-44	-	MURDER	FR.
MULLER	265368	M		Interpreter-Secretary, SD, Bayonne and Environs (Fr.) 40-44	-	MURDER	FR.
MULLER	266577	M		Col., 9 SS-Pz.Div."Hohenstaufen"Unit No.29474,Nimes (Fr.) 2.3.44	-	MURDER	FR.
MULLER	265637	M		N.C.O.,Ruestungskommando Montbeliard or Belfort, Sochaux,Valentigney,Arbouans (Fr.) 41-45	-	PILLAGE	FR.
MULLER	265951	M		Member,Feldgendarmerie,Cholet (Fr.) 7.-8.8.44	-	MURDER	FR.
MULLER	266326	M	ca. 10	Cpl.,Africa-Corps,Regt.Ruxleben,6 Coy.,1 Section, Hte.Marne-Aube (Fr.) 25.-31.8.44	-	MURDER	FR.
MULLER	266327	M		N.C.O. Africa-Corps, Regt. Ruxleben, 6 Coy.,1 Section, Hte.Marne-Aube (Fr.) 25.-31.8.44		MURDER	FR.
MULLER	267201	M	ca. 05	Hptscharfhr., Gestapo, Bordeaux and vicinity (Fr.) 42-8.44	-	MURDER	FR.
MULLER	267287	M		Chief, Gestapo, Section V,Marseille and vicinity (Fr.)	-	MURDER	FR.
MULLER	303482	M		SS-Osturmfhr., Gestapo at Lodz, Lodz (Pol.) 39-44	56/581	MURDER	POL.
MULLER	303483	M		Member,Feldgendarmerie, Region of Cholet (Fr.) 7.-8.8.44	56/584	MURDER	FR.
MULLER (I)	303822	M		Member, Gestapo, Warschau (Pol.) 39-45	57/785	TORTURE	POL.
MULLER (II)	303823	M		Member, Gestapo, Warschau (Pol.) 39-45	57/786	TORTURE	POL.
MULLER (III)	303824	M		Member, Gestapo, Warschau (Pol.) 39-45	57/787	TORTURE	POL.
MULLER	304339	M		SS-Stubafhr., W-SS commander of the Unit F.P.No.10443, Fouron St.Martin Liege (Bel.) 5.-6.9.44	58/481	INCENDIARISM	BEL.
MULLER	304769	M		Commander,Punitive Camp, Krakau (Pol.) 11.39-2.45	59/479	BRUTALITY	POL.
MULLER II	309014	M		Guard,Prison and Attached Kommandos, Wolfenbuettel (Ger.) 42 - 45	60/421	TORTURE	BEL.
MULLER, Albert	304765	M		Member, Gestapo , Krakau (Pol.) 11.39-2.45	59/474	BRUTALITY	POL.
MULLER, Alois	304766	M		Member, Gestapo, Krakau (Pol.) 11.39-2.45	59/475	BRUTALITY	POL.
MULLER, Arthur	267241	M	05	Hptscharfhr., Chief, Gestapo of the blackmarket section, Marseille and vicinity (Fr.)	-	MURDER	FR.
MULLER, Eduard	304767	M		Member, Gestapo, Krakau (Pol.) 11.39-2.45	59/476	BRUTALITY	POL.
MULLER, Edward	304341	M		Capo, C.C.Szandelech near Braunschweig,C.C.Weblin(Ger.) 44-45	58/485	MURDER	POL.
MULLER, Erich	303485	M		Hpt.-Crim.-Secretary,Gestapo staff, Kattowitz(Pol.) 39-42	56/586	PILLAGE	POL.
MULLER, Ernst	266325	M		Sgt.Major, Army, Longeville (Fr.) 15.8.44	-	MURDER	FR.
MULLER, Georg	303487	M		SS-Hptscharfhr., Gestapo, Lodz (Pol.) 39-44	56/588	MURDER	POL.
MULLER, Georg Herbert Willi	303825	M	3. 6.03	SS-Uscharfhr., C.C.Plaszow (Pol.) 39-45	57/789	BRUTALITY	POL.
MULLER, Johann	303826	M	2. 3.08	SS-Mann, C.C.Majdanek (Pol.) 40-44	57/790	BRUTALITY	POL.
MULLER, Josef	303489	M		Crim.-Secretary, Gestapo, Kattowitz (Pol.) 39-42	56/590	BRUTALITY	POL.
MULLER, Kurt	304768	M		Member, Gestapo, Krakau (Pol.) 11.39-2.45	59/477	MURDER	POL.
MULLER, Olga	304770	F		Member, Gestapo, Krakau (Pol.) 11.39-2.45	59/480	MURDER	POL.
MULLER, Otto	266864	M	10 or.15	Osturmfhr., SD de Lyon,Kom. retreated to the Vosges, Saint-Pierremont (Fr.) 14.9.44	-	MISC.CRIMES	FR.
MULLER, Walter	267242	M		Sturmscharfhr.,Gestapo, Marseille and vicinity (Fr.)	-	MURDER	FR.
MULLER, Walter	303490	M		Sgt.,Group 530 Geheime Feldpolizei, Bruessel (Bel.) 40-44	56/592	TORTURE	BEL.
MULLER, Wilhelm	267286	M		Usturmfhr., Gestapo, Marseille and environ (Fr.)	-	MURDER	FR.
MULLER, Wilhelm	303491	M	ca. 05	SS-Usturmfhr., head of Sicherheitsdienst at Avignon, Department of Vaucluse (Fr.) 12.42-8.44	56/593	MURDER	FR.
MUNINER	266902	M		SS-Mann, Waffen-SS,SS Div."Das Reich", Dordogne, Correze Creuse, Hte Vienne (Fr.) 5.-6.44	-	SUSPECT	FR.
MUNDT, Heinrich	264623	M	19. 3.00	See names listed under "Special Headings"			
MUNK	303828	M		Member, Gestapo, Warschau (Pol.) 39-45	57/795	TORTURE	POL.
MUNKWITZ	303829	M		Member, Gestapo, Warschau (Pol.) 39-45	57/796	TORTURE	POL.
MUNSTER	303399	M		Sgt.,Feldgendarmerie at Angouleme, Chasseneuil, Charente (Fr.) 43-44, 22.3.44	56/594	MURDER	FR.
MUNSTER, Ernst	304771	M		Member, Gestapo, Krakau (Pol.) 11.39-2.45	59/482	MURDER	POL.
MUNZER	303400	M		Member, Geh.Feldpol. Group 530, Bruessel (Bel.) 40-44	56/595	MURDER	BEL.
MUNZERT	303401	M		Cpl.,Feldgend.Angouleme,Chasseneuil,Charente(Fr.)43-44,22.3.44	56/596	MURDER	FR.
MUSALL, Kurt	304772	M		Member, Gestapo, Krakau (Pol.),11.39-2.45	59/482	MURDER	POL.

MUS - NIC

NAME	C.R.FILE NUMBER	SEX	DATE OF BIRTH	RANK OCCUPATION UNIT PLACE AND DATE OF CRIME	UNWCC LIST/ SERIAL NO.	REASON WANTED	WANTED BY
MUSCHALIK, Karl Heinz	303402	M		Krim.Beamter, Staff of Gestapo, Kattowitz (Pol.) 39-42	56/597	BRUTALITY	POL
MUTH, Johann	266152	M	88	Member, NSDAP, SS-Unit, Director, Chamber of Industry and Commerce, Lublin, Belrzec (Pol.) 40-44	-	MURDER	POL
MUTTERSBACH	266149	M		Member, Gendarmerie, Wachtmeister, Sicherheitsdienst, Krasnik (Pol.) 42-44	-	MURDER	POL
MUTZE, Heinz	304773	M		Member, Gestapo, Krakau (Pol.) 11.39-2.45	59/483	MURDER	POL
MYLAND	198122	F		Wardress, C.C., Auschwitz (Pol.) 40-45	-	MURDER	POL,FR.
MYSZ	266136	F		SS-Woman, C.C., Auschwitz, Brzezinka (Pol.)	-	BRUTALITY	POL
NAEGLER	309017	M		Member, Selbstschutz, Grudziadz (Pol.) 39	60/425	MURDER	POL
NANS (see NANZ, Rudolph)	266918						
NANZ, Rudolph (or NANS)	266918	M	1.12.03	Capo, Civil Police Service, Geheime Feldpolizei, Gruppe 734, C.C., Stephanskirchen (Ger.) 11.42	-	SUSPECT	FR.
NAPORRA	303830	M		Member, Gestapo, Warschau (Pol.) 39-45	57/800	TORTURE	POL
NARKWSKA, Walentyna	303403			Blockleiter, C.C., Ravensbruck (Ger.) 42-43	56/598	MURDER	POL
NASSAU	267048	M		Sgt.-Major, 19 SS-Pol.Regt.,3 Bn.,10 Coy., Limoges, Brive and vicinity (Fr.) 7.44	-	MURDER	FR.
NATSCHKE	309018	M		SS-Sturmscharfhr., Crim.secretary, SS, Radom (Pol.) 1.40-1.45	60/427	BRUTALITY	POL
NAUKEL	304342	M		Feldgendarm, Paray-Le-Manial and surroundings, Saone-et-Loire, (Fr.) 42-44	58/486	MURDER	FR.
NAUMANN, A.	304343	M		Air Force, Flak-Abt.4-815, Texel (Neth.) 10.4.45	58/487	MURDER	NETH.
NAUMANN, Heinrich	303404	M		Gefreiter, Geh. Feldpolizei, Group 530, Bruessel (Bel.) 40-44	56/600	MURDER	BEL
NAWIN	303831	M		Member, Gestapo, Warschau (Pol.) 39-45	57/801	TORTURE	POL
NEBEL	267536	M		Member, Gestapo, Limoges and vicinity (Fr.) 44	-	SUSPECT	FR.
NEDOBA, Dr. (or NIEDAUER), Ludvik	304344	M	16.8.02	Gestapo and SD, Zilina (Slov.) 41-45	58/488	MURDER	CZECH.
NEHLIS, Dr. Prof.	309020	M		SS-Sturmbannfhr., SS, member, Sipo, Lage Vuursche (Neth.) 29.12.43	60/432	MISC.CRIMES	NETH.
NEHLITZ	303832	M		Member, Gestapo, Warschau (Pol.) 39-45	57/802	TORTURE	POL
NEIDEK, Samuel	266154	M		Official, interpreter, SS-Rottenfhr., Gestapo, Lodz (Pol.)39-45	56/601	MISC.CRIMES	POL
NEILER, Alfred	266153	M	11	SS-Officer, SS-Usturmfhr., Gestapo, Lodz (Pol.) 41-45	56/602	MISC.CRIMES	POL
NEINZLING, Karl	304774	M		Member, Gestapo, Krakau (Pol.) 11.39-2.45	59/485	BRUTALITY	POL
NEITL, Hans	304345	M		Member, Gestapo, Chalons sur Marne (Fr.) 43-44	58/490	MURDER	FR.
NEKOLA	304775	M		Member, Gestapo, Krakau (Pol.) 11.39-2.45	59/486	MURDER	POL
NELIES	266996	M		Sgt.-Major, Feldgendarmerie, Sisteron (Fr.) 44	-	MISC.CRIMES	FR.
NEMETH, Josef	303833	M	3.3.21	SS-Mann, C.C., Majdanek (Pol.) 40-44	57/803	BRUTALITY	POL
NEMTZ	303834	M		Member, Gestapo, Warschau (Pol.) 39-45	57/804	TORTURE	POL
NESS, Paul	304346	M		SS-Hptscharfhr., Gestapo, Hendaye, Basses-Pyrenees (Fr.) 43-44	58/491	MURDER	FR.
NESS, Willy	266148	M		Kapo, C.C., Dachau (Ger.)	-	MISC.CRIMES	POL
NETCHER	267537	M		Interpreter, Grenzpolizeipost, Luchon and vicinity (Fr.)1.43-1.44	-	MURDER	FR.
NETH, Johann	302873	M		On Staff, C.C., Auschwitz (Pol.) 40-45	-	MURDER	POL
NETZEL, Ernest	266147	M		Extermination Camp, Chelmno (Pol.) 42-43	-	MISC.CRIMES	POL
NEUBACHER	650	M		General, Army, Patras, Calavryta, Mega Spileon, Aghia, Lavra, Skspasto, Clitoria (Grc.) 12.43	-	MURDER	U.S.,GRC.
NEUBAUER	309021	M		Member, Waffen-SS, Radom (Pol.) 1.40-1.45	60/434	MURDER	POL
NEUBAUER, Hans	304776	M		Member, Gestapo, Krakau (Pol.) 11.39-2.45	59/487	BRUTALITY	POL
NEUBAUER, Jan	265310	M	15.1.02	Member, SD, Tabor (Czech.) 42	-	MISC.CRIMES	CZECH.
NEUBAUER, Otto	266146	M		Officer, SS-Osturmfhr., Staff, Penal Camp, Kaiserhafen (Ger.) 41-44	-	MURDER	POL
NEUBERG, Franz	304777	M		Member, Gestapo, Krakau (Pol.) 11.39-2.45	59/488	BRUTALITY	POL
NEUBERT	309022	M		Cpl., Secr.Field-Police, Antwerpen, Bruessel (Bel.) 40-44	60/435	MURDER	BEL
NEUDEK, Franz	304778	M		Member, Gestapo, Krakau (Pol.) 11.39-2.45	59/489	BRUTALITY	POL
NEUGEBAUER	266929	M		Agent, Gestapo, Nantes and region (Fr.) 43-44	-	MURDER	FR.
NEUGEBAUER, Erich	303407	M		Crim.secretary, Staff of Gestapo, Kattowitz (Pol.) 39-42	56/603	INTERR.	POL
NEUGEBAUER, Valentin	266145	M	96	Official, Interpreter, Gestapo, Lodz (Pol.) 42-45	-	MISC.CRIMES	POL
NEUHAUS, Rudolf	303409	M		Cpl., Geh. Feldpolizei, Group 530, Bruessel (Bel.) 40-44	56/605	MURDER	BEL
NEUHOFF	265652	M		Lt., 558 Regt. der Infanterie, 13 Coy., Bruay en Artois (Fr.) 9.44	-	SUSPECT	FR.
NEUMAN (see NEUMANN)	266166						
NEUMANN	266143	M		Interpreter, Gestapo, Radzyn (Pol.)	-	MISC.CRIMES	POL
NEUMANN	266166	M	09	SS-Hptsturmfhr., Chief, SS, Gestapo, Section 4-1A, Lodz (Pol.)	-	MISC.CRIMES	POL
NEUMANN (I)	303895	M		Member, Gestapo, Warschau (Pol.) 39-45	57/809	TORTURE	POL
NEUMANN (II)	303896	M		Member, Gestapo, Warschau (Pol.) 39-45	57/810	MISC.CRIMES	POL
NEUMANN	309023	M		Cpl., Secr. Field-Police, Antwerpen, Bruessel (Bel.) 40-44	60/436	MURDER	BEL
NEUMANN	309024	M		SS-Uscharfhr., Crim.secretary, SS, Radom (Pol.) 1.40-1.45	60/437	BRUTALITY	POL
NEUMANN, Alfons	303897	M	11.8.24	SS-Mann, C.C., Majdanek (Pol.) 40-44	57/811	BRUTALITY	POL
NEUMANN, Anton	266142	M		Official, SS-Oscharfhr., Gestapo, SS, Krakau (Pol.) 41-44	-	MURDER	POL
NEUMANN (see MAUMANN, Karl)	266096						
NEUMANN, Karl	303411	M		Hpt.Krim.Sekr., Gestapo, Kattowitz (Pol.) 39-42	56/607	PILLAGE	POL
NEUMANN, Karl	303898	M	11.10.07	SS-Mann, C.C., Majdanek (Pol.) 40-44	57/814	BRUTALITY	POL
NEUMANN, Karl	304779	M		Member, Gestapo, Krakau (Pol.) 11.39-2.45	59/492	BRUTALITY	POL
NEUMANN, Kurt	304780	M		Member, Gestapo, Krakau (Pol.) 11.39-2.45	59/493	BRUTALITY	POL
NEUMANN, Rudolf	304781	M		Pvt., Secr. Field-Police, (Bel.) 40-41	59/494	MURDER	BEL
NEUMANN, Walter	266144	M		Member, SS-Unit, Szubin (Pol.) 9.-12.39	-	MURDER	POL
NEUMANN, Walter	304782	M		Secretary, Customs Official, Zwartsluis (Neth.) 8.10.44	59/495	MURDER	NETH.
NEUMAYER, Otto	304347	M		SS-Osturmfhr., Punitive Camp, Kaiserhaven (Ger.) 41-44	58/494	MURDER	POL
NEUSCHEL	266167	M		SS-Usturmfhr., SS, Chief, Workshop at C.C., Plaszow (Pol.)	-	MISC.CRIMES	POL
NEUTZE, Wilhelm	309025	M		Policeman, Police, near Mienstedt (Ger.) 24.8.44	60/438	MURDER	U.S.
NEUWERTH, Werner	302984	M		Member, Geh. Feldpolizei, Group 530, Bruessel (Bel.) 40-44	56/608	MURDER	BEL
NEUWIRT, Heinz	267575	M	11.3.12 or 13.3.12	Political Leader, Wageningen (Neth.) 3.45	-	PILLAGE	NETH.
NICKEL	265389	M		Pvt., 3 Coy., 1 Bn., Regt."Der Fuehrer", Div."Das Reich", Oradour s.Glane (Fr.) 10.6.44	-	MURDER	FR.
NICKEL	266741	M		Pvt., Army, prisoners of war camp - staff, Luckenwalde (Ger.) 39-45	-	TORTURE	POL
NICKEL	302985	M		Feldwebel, Feldgendarmerie at Angouleme, Chasseneuil, Charente (Fr.) 43-45, 22.3.44	56/609	MURDER	FR.

NIC - OPI

NAME	C.R.FILE NUMBER	SEX	DATE OF BIRTH	RANK OCCUPATION UNIT PLACE AND DATE OF CRIME	UNWCC LIST/ SERIAL NO.	REASON WANTED	WANTED BY
NICKIEL	302986	M		SS-Schfhr., Gestapo, Lodz (Pol.) 39-44	56/610	BRUTALITY	POL.
NICOLAUS	303839	M		Member, Gestapo, Warschau (Pol.) 39-45	57/815	MISC.CRIMES	POL.
NICOLOSI	266899	M		SS-Mann, Waffen-SS, Div."Das Reich", Dordogne, Correze, Creuse, Hte.Vienne (Fr.) 5.-6.44	-	SUSPECT	FR.
NIEDAUER, Dr. (see NEDOBA, Ludvik, Dr.)	304344						
NIEDERMEIER I	266169	M		Blockfhr., C.C., Dachau (Ger.)	-	MISC.CRIMES	POL.
NIEDERMEIER II	266195	M		Chief, SS-Oschfhr., Crematory, C.C., Dachau (Ger.)	-	MURDER	POL.
NIEDERMEIR (or WINDERNIAIL)	265211	M	circa 92	Lt., 114 Inf.Div., Gubbio (It.) 22.6.44	-	SUSPECT	U.K.
NIEDING, Kurt, Dr.	304783	M		Member, Gestapo, Krakau (Pol.) 11.39-2.45	59/496	MURDER	POL.
NIEDZIELA, Heinrich	304835	M		Member, Gestapo, Krakau (Pol.) 11.39-2.45	59/497	BRUTALITY	POL.
NIEHAUS, Hans	267123	M		Lt., Army, 893 Gren.Regt.,3 Bn., Sinj (Yugo.) 8.9.43-10.44	-	MURDER	YUGO.
NIEMANN, Friedrich	304836	M		Member, Gestapo, Krakau (Pol.) 11.39-2.45	59/498	BRUTALITY	POL.
NIEMANN, Jonny	266168	M		SS-Usturmfhr., Member, C.C., Sobibor (Pol.)	-	MURDER	POL.
NIEMEYER, Hermann	304837	M		Member, Gestapo, Krakau (Pol.) 11.39-2.45	59/499	BRUTALITY	POL.
NIETSCH, Georg	303840	M	16. 3.14	SS-Mann, C.C., Majdanek (Pol.) 40-44	57/819	BRUTALITY	POL.
NIGSCH	266997	M		Chief-Cpl., Flakmast 30-XII, Baudrigues nr.Carassonne (Fr.) 19.8.44	-	MURDER	FR.
NILCKE	266994	M		Usturmfhr., 18 SS-Pz.Gren.Div."Horst Wessel", Oradour sur Glane (Fr.) 10.6.44	-	MURDER	FR.
NINEMANN	302988	M		Secretary, Geh.Feldpol, Group 530, Bruessel (Bel.) 40-44	56/612	MURDER	BEL.
NISCHKE	266151	M		Lt., Official, Gestapo, Wlodawa (Pol.)	-	MURDER	POL.
NISCHKE, Richard	266193	M		Official, Gestapo, SS, Kazimierz Dolny (Pol.)	-	MURDER	POL.
NISCHT, Anton	303841	M	3. 6.11	SS-Mann, C.C., Majdanek (Pol.) 40-44	57/820	PILLAGE	POL.
NOACK, Fritz	304838	M		Member, Gestapo, Krakau (Pol.) 11.39-2.45	59/500	INTERR.	POL.
NOBEL, Herbert	304839	M		Member, Gestapo, Krakau (Pol.) 11.39-2.45	59/501	INTERR.	POL.
NOCZYNSKI	266192	M		Pvt., 1 Coy., Bau-Bn., Wawrze (Pol.) 27.12.39	-	MURDER	POL.
NOHLEN	265651	M		Cpl., 558 Regt. de Grenadiers, 13 Coy., Bruay en Artois (Fr.) 1.9.44	-	SUSPECT	FR.
NOLLE	265954	M	circa 05	Cmdt.,SS-Sturmbannfhr., Sicherheitspolizei SD of Marseille, Bouches du Rhone (Fr.) 7.-8.44	-	SUSPECT	FR.
NOLTE, Karl	304840	M		Member, Gestapo, Krakau (Pol.) 11.39-2.45	59/502	INTERR.	POL.
NONNEMACHER, Dr.	266191	M		Official, Institut fuer Deutsche Ostarbeit, Krakau (Pol.)	-	PILLAGE	POL.
NORDECK	303842	M		Member, Gestapo, Warschau (Pol.) 39-45	57/823	MISC.CRIMES	POL.
NOTZKE	309027	M		Oschfhr. and Crim.Asst., SS, Radom (Pol.) 1.40-1.45	60/444	BRUTALITY	POL.
NOVAK, Wladislaw	267538	M		Interpreter, Gestapo, St.Etienne and vicinity (Fr.) 43-44	-	MISC.CRIMES	FR.
NOWACK	303843	M		Member, Gestapo, Warschau (Pol.) 39-45	57/824	MISC.CRIMES	POL.
NOWAK	266187	M		Member, Gestapo, Tarnow (Pol.) 40-45	-	MISC.CRIMES	POL.
NOWAK	304842	M		Member, Gestapo, Krakau (Pol.) 11.39-2.45	59/504	MURDER	POL.
NOWAK, Berthold	303000	M		Kriminalbeamter, Staff of Gestapo, Kattowitz (Pol.) 39-42	56/617	INTERR.	POL.
NOWAK, Franz	266190	M		Member, Gestapo, Usturmfhr., SS, Krakau (Pol.)	-	MURDER	POL.
NOWAK, Hans	304843	M		Member, Gestapo, Krakau (Pol.) 11.39-2.45	59/505	INTERR.	POL.
NOWAK, Karl	302989	M		Crim.Secretary, Staff of Gestapo, Kattowitz (Pol.) 39-42	56/618	INTERR.	POL.
NOWAK, Kurt	266188	M		Uschfhr., SS, C.C., Sobibor (Pol.)	-	MURDER	POL.
NOWAK, Willi	266189	M	circa 00	Chief, Post-Office, Radom (Pol.)	-	MISC.CRIMES	POL.
NOWOTNY, Isle	304844	M		Member, Gestapo, Krakau (Pol.) 11.39-2.45	59/506	MURDER	POL.
NUMSEN, Hermann	304351	M		Farmer, Westerhausen nr.Heide-Holstein (Ger.) 45	58/499	MURDER	POL.
NURENBERG, August	304845	M		Member, Gestapo, Krakau (Pol.) 11.39-2.45	59/507	MURDER	POL.
NUSPERLING	303844	M		Member, Gestapo, Warschau (Pol.) 39-45	57/825	MISC.CRIMES	POL.
NUSSBAUM, Johann	304352	M		Member, Hitler-Youth-Group, Blechhammer nr.Pullenried (Ger.) 22.4.45	58/500	MURDER	U.S.
OBERENDER, Johann	302990	M	04	Gendarmerie-Meister, Gestapo, Kattowitz (Pol.) 39-42	56/618 A	MURDER	POL.
OBERLENT	266177	M		Wachtmeister, Gendarmerie, Debno, Brzesko (Pol.) 41-45	-	MISC.CRIMES	POL.
OBSCHITSCH (see OPSIC)	303848						
OCHMANN, Hildegard	304846	F		Member, Gestapo, Krakau (Pol.) 11.39-2.45	59/508	MURDER	POL.
OCKVENT	266900	M		Sturmbannfhr., SS, St.Jean du Corail (Fr.) 31.7.44	-	MURDER	FR.
OCZKO (see WILLY)	266709						
OEFFNER	266178	M		SS-Hptschfhr., C.C., Dachau (Ger.)	-	MURDER	POL.
OEHME	267213	M		Sturmbannfhr., Gestapo, Bordeaux and vicinity (Fr.) 42-8.44	-	MURDER	FR.
OERTWIG	303845	M		Member, Gestapo, Warschau (Pol.) 39-45	57/826	MISC.CRIMES	POL.
OESTER	266182	M		Member, Gestapo, Debica (Pol.) 40-44	-	MURDER	POL.
OETTING	266901	M	15.12.93	Lt.Col., Feldkommandantur 641, Blois, Seillac, Lavardin and Vendome (Fr.) 22.6.44-9.,10.9.44	-	MURDER	FR.
OGINSKI, Theodor	304847	M		Sgt., Secr.Field-Police, H.Q.G.F.P. Boulevard Piercot or the Avenue Rogier, Luettich (Bel.) 40-41	59/509	MURDER	BEL.
OGOREK (see GURKE, Oskar)	266134						
OHEIM, Reinhold	304848	M		Member, Selbstschutz and Gestapo, Bialachow (Grudziadz Dist.) (Pol.) 39-43	59/510	MURDER	POL.
OHL	266537	M		Chief of Purchase office, textiles, leathers Organization of the Black Market (Fr.) 42-44	-	MISC.CRIMES	FR.
OHLE, Hugo	264633	M	8. 3.91	See names listed under "Special Headings"	-	SUSPECT	U.K.
OHM, Hans	265215	M	23	Sonderfhr.(Interpreter) 33 Sign.Bn.,15 Pz.Gren.Div., San Giustino (It.) 6.7.44	-	SUSPECT	U.K.
OKON, Alexander	304849	M		Member, Gestapo, Krakau (Pol.) 11.39-2.45	59/511	MURDER	POL.
OLBERT	303846	M		SS-Uschfhr., C.C., Majdanek (Pol.) 40-44	57/830	MURDER	POL.
OLBRICH, Kurt	303847	M		SS-Uschfhr., C.C., Majdanek (Pol.) 40-44	57/831	BRUTALITY	POL.
OLDELAND, Magdalena	266179	F	11	Secretary, Chamber of Trade, Lublin (Pol.)	-	MISC.CRIMES	POL.
OLFF, Wilhelm	267240	M		Interpreter, Gestapo, Marseille and vicinity (Fr.)	-	MURDER	FR.
OLGEBRAND (or OLGEBRANDT)	266180	M		Member, Gestapo, Krakau (Pol.) 39-45	-	MURDER	POL.
OLGEBRANDT (see OLGEBRAND)	266180						
OLSEYER	266576	M		SD Rennes, retreated to: Meurthe and Moselle, Pettonville (Fr.) 6.10.44	-	MISC.CRIMES	FR.
OLSZEWSKI	266181	M		Member, SS-unit, Lublin (Pol.) 42-43	-	MURDER	POL.
OPITZ	304850	M		Pvt., Guard over Ital.PW's working in the "Firm Henschel & Sohn" Factory, Kassel (Ger.) 16.1.44	59/512	MURDER	NETH.

OPI - PET

NAME	C.R.FILE NUMBER	SEX	DATE OF BIRTH	RANK	OCCUPATION UNIT PLACE AND DATE OF CRIME	UNWCC LIST/ SERIAL NO.	REASON WANTED	WANTED BY
OPITZ, Martin	266156	M			SS-Oscharfhr., Gestapo, Krakau (Pol.) 40-45	-	MISC.CRIMES	POL.
OPPERMANN	266157	M			Member, SS-Oscharfhr., Gestapo, Ghetto, Tarnow (Pol.) 42-43	-	MURDER	POL.
OPPERMANN, Karl	304851	M			Member, Gestapo, Krakau (Pol.) 11.39-2.45	59/513	TORTURE	POL.
OPSIC (or OBSCHITSCH)	303848	M	22. 2.12		SS-Mann, C.C., Majdanek (Pol.) 40-45	57/832	MURDER	POL.
ORF	303849	M			Member, Gestapo, Warschau (Pol.) 39-45	57/833	MISC.CRIMES	POL.
ORLAND	266158	M			Oberkapo, C.C., Janow (Pol.)	-	MURDER	POL.
ORTEKO	266911	M			Major, Air Force, Eguilles (Bouches du Rhone) (Fr.) 19.8.44	-	MURDER	FR.
ORTLIEB, Johann	303850	M	22. 5.08		SS-Mann, C.C., Majdanek (Pol.) 40-44	57/834	MURDER	POL.
OSBORN	266155	M			Member, Gestapo, Wlodawa (Pol.) 41-43	-	MURDER	POL
OSIANDER, Friedrich, Wilhelm	264615	M	14. 9.03		See names listed under "Special Headings"			
OSSENBERG	266328	M			Agent, Gestapo, Nantes and region (Fr.) 43-44	-	MURDER	FR.
OSSOWICZ, Albin	304852	M			Member, Gestapo, Krakau (Pol.) 11.39-2.45	59/514	TORTURE	POL.
OSTER, Ignatz	303851	M	11. 6.08		SS-Mann, C.C., Majdanek (Pol.) 40-44	57/835	BRUTALITY	POL
OSTER, Philipp	304853	M			Member, Gestapo, Krakau (Pol.) 11.39-2.45	59/515	TORTURE	POL.
OSTERMEIER, Josef	302992	M			Pol.Wachtmeister, Pol.-Sonderkdo., Kulmhof (Pol.) 41-45	56/621	MURDER	POL.
OSTERWALD	266239	M			Member, Gestapo, Tarnow (Pol.) 41-44	-	MURDER	POL.
OSTHEIMER, Eduard	304854	M			Sgt., Secr. Field-Police, HQ., G.F.P., Boulevard Piercot or the Avenue Rogier, Luettich (Bel.) 40-41	59/516	MURDER	BEL
OSTKOP	266445	M			Member, SD, Almelo District (Neth.) 9.44-2.45	-	MURDER	NETH.
OTT, Josef	303852	M	4. 8.08		SS-Mann, C.C., Majdanek (Pol.) 40-44	57/841	BRUTALITY	POL.
OTTENHEIM, Hugo	266995	M	05		Oscharfhr., SS, SD, Sipo, Limoges (Fr.)	-	SUSPECT	FR.
OTTO	302993	M			Cpl., Kdo.440, Stalag IV-C, Neu-Wistritz (Ger.) 30.6.43	56/623	MURDER	FR.
OTTO	303853	M			Member, Gestapo, Warschau (Pol.) 39-45	57/842	MISC.CRIMES	POL.
OTYLLA (see WOLLHAUS)	266622							
OUCHY	251211	F			Wardress, C.C., Auschwitz (Pol.)	-	MURDER	POL.,FR.
OVERBECK, August	265623	M			See names listed under "Special Headings"			
OVERMANN	266980	M			Sgt., Flakmast.30-XII, Baudrigues near Carcassonne (Fr.) 19.8.44	-	MURDER	FR.
PAATZ, Paul	304855	M			Member, Gestapo, Krakau (Pol.) 11.39-2.45	59/517	PILLAGE	POL.
PACIEN, Alfred	304856	M			Member, Gestapo, Krakau (Pol.) 11.39-2.45	59/518	TORTURE	POL.
PACKEBUSCH	309029	M			Osturmfhr., SS, Grudziadz (Pol.) 39	60/450	MURDER	POL.
PACKERNIETH (or PATCHNECK or PATCHNEK)	37972	M	15		Sgt., Army, Staff of working party at Groppenstein of Wolfsberg prison camp, Groppenstein (Aust.) 42	-	BRUTALITY	U.F.
PADBERG, Ernst	302994	M			Crim.asst., Staff of Gestapo, Kattowitz (Pol.) 39-42	56/626	BRUTALITY	POL
PADBERG, Ernst	304857	M			Member, Gestapo, Krakau (Pol.) 11.39-2.45	59/519	TORTURE	POL
PAGEL	303854	M			Member, Gestapo, Warschau (Pol.) 39-45	57/844	BRUTALITY	POL
PAHL, Jonny	304354	M			First inspector, Railway at Emden, Pruszce (Pol.) 1.9.39	58/508	INTERR.	POL
PAHLKE	267539	M			Stabsfuehrer, Col., Div.Seiz, Nolay (Fr.) 3.9.44	-	MURDER	FR.
PALM	267540	M			Chief-Cpl., 71 Inf.Regt., Air Force Lisieux, 5 Coy., 2 Bn., Ldschtz.Regt., Aude and Herault (Fr.) 5.44-8.44	-	MISC.CRIMES	FR.
PANDUR, Stefan	302995	M			Member, Staff of C.C., Breendonck (Bel.) 40-44	56/629	MURDER	BEL
PANEWICZ, Genowefa	303855	F	21. 6.21		Kapo, C.C. Ravensbrueck (Ger.) 39-45	57/848	MURDER	POL.
PANKE	267541	M			Member, Gestapo, Limoges and vicinity (Fr.) 44	-	SUSPECT	FR.
PANSE, Friedrich	302996	M			Feldwebel, Geheime Feldpolizei, Group 530, Bruessel (Bel.) 40-44	56/630	MURDER	BEL
PANSNER, Otto	304355	M			Guard, Prison, Arlon and surroundings (Bel.) 24.-25.8.44, 1.-3.9.44	58/509	MURDER	BEL
PAPE, Josef	267239	M			Pvt., Army, Waffenwerkstatt 812, Chateaumeillant (Fr.) 27.6.44	-	MURDER	FR.
PARCHER, Karl, Franz, Friedrich	303856	M	6. 8.21		SS-Oscharfhr., C.C., Auschwitz (Pol.) 40-45	57/852	BRUTALITY	POL.
PASELOK, Walter	302997	M			Member, Geheime Feldpolizei, Group 530, Bruessel (Bel.) 40-44	56/632	MURDER	BEL
PASING, Heinrich	309091	M	13		Member, Schutzgruppen, Brunssum (Neth.) 9.44	60/452	PILLAGE	NETH.
PASTOR, Franz	303857	M	7.11.19		SS-Sturmmann, C.C., Majdanek (Pol.) 40-44	57/853	BRUTALITY	POL
PATCHNECK (see PACKERNIETH)	37972							
PATCHNEK (see PACKERNIETH)	37972							
PATRY	267542	M			Member, Gestapo, Limoges and vicinity (Fr.) 44	-	SUSPECT	FR.
PATZ, Eberhardt	267164	M			Matrose, Navy, Senon (Fr.) 9.44	-	MURDER	FR.
PAUER, Frans (or VAUER)	267574	M			Capt., Unit No. 6805, Renesse (Neth.) 10.12.44	-	MURDER	NETH.
PAUL	267535	M			Member, Gestapo, Limoges and vicinity (Fr.) 44	-	SUSPECT	FR.
PAUL, Wilhelm	266284	M	11. 6.05		See names listed under "Special Headings"			
PAUST	267550	M			Sgt., 350 Regt. "Hindou", Department L'Indre (Fr.) 8.44	-	MURDER	FR.
PAUZER, Hermann	304858	M			Member, Gestapo, Krakau (Pol.) 11.39-2.45	59/522	PILLAGE	POL.
PAWLIK	303858	M			Member, Gestapo, Warschau (Pol.) 39-45	57/858	BRUTALITY	POL.
PAWLOWSKI	303859	M			Member, Gestapo, Warschau (Pol.) 39-45	57/859	BRUTALITY	POL.
PECKHAUS	309092	M			Sgt., Secret Field Police, Antwerpen, Bruessel (Bel.) 40-44	60/454	MURDER	BEL
PECKMANN	266975	M			Osturmfhr., 18 SS-Pz. Gren.Div."Horst Wessel", Oradour sur Glane (Fr.) 10.6.44	-	MURDER	FR.
PEDERZANI, Alois	302999	M			Oberfeldwebel, Geheime Feldpolizei, Group 530, HQ., Bruessel (Bel.) 40-44	56/635	MISC.CRIMES	BEL
PEILER	303860	M			Member, Gestapo, Warschau (Pol.) 39-45	57/860	BRUTALITY	POL.
PELKER	309033	M			Member, Military Police, Czorkow near Lodz (Pol.) 39-42	60/455	MURDER	POL.
PENDEROK, Hermann	303001	M			Kriminalbeamter, Staff of Gestapo, Kattowitz (Pol.) 39-42	56/636	BRUTALITY	POL.
PENTEN, Jakob	303861	M	13.11.02		Kapo, C.C. Auschwitz (Pol.) 40-45	57/862	BRUTALITY	POL.
PERIBACH	303862	M			Member, Gestapo, Warschau (Pol.) 39-45	57/863	BRUTALITY	POL.
PERTHEN, Karl	264614	M	8.12.11		See names listed under "Special Headings"			
PERTL, Johann	265351	M	circa 10		Oberwachtmeister, Gendarmerie, Litija (Yugo.) 44-45	-	MURDER	YUGO.
PERTSCHI, Johann	303863	M	29. 3.25		SS-Mann, C.C., Majdanek (Pol.) 40-44	57/864	BRUTALITY	POL.
PERZANOWSKI	303864	M			Member, Gestapo, Warschau (Pol.) 39-45	57/865	BRUTALITY	POL.
PESCHT	266661	M			Chief, Purchase service - machines and tools, Organisation of the Black Market in France, (Fr.) 42-44	-	MISC.CRIMES	FR.
PETER	303865	M			Member, Gestapo, Warschau (Pol.) 39-45	57/866	BRUTALITY	POL.
PETER, Otto, Georg	266945	M	26. 4.92		See names listed under "Special Headings"			
PETERS	266285	M			Cpl., 1 Section, 6 Coy., Regt. Ruxleben, Africa-Corps, Hte.Marne-Aube (Fr.) 25.-31.8.44	-	MURDER	FR.
PETERS	304859	M			Secretary, Secr.Field Police, HQ., Boulevard Piercot or the Avenue Rogier, Luettich (Bel.) 40-41	59/523	MURDER	BEL
PETERS, A.	303003	M			SS-Scharfhr., Gestapo, Lodz (Pol.) 39-45	56/698	MURDER	POL.

NAME	C.R.FILE NUMBER	SEX	DATE OF BIRTH	RANK OCCUPATION UNIT PLACE AND DATE OF CRIME	UNWCC LIST/ SERIAL NO.	REASON WANTED	WANTED BY
PETERS, Josef	265227	M	26. 4.05	Lt.,Adjutant, Heavy Flak Abt. 575, from Flak Rgt. 137 Seluaggio-Giaveno (It.) 20.5.44	-	SUSPECT	U.K.
PETERS, L.	303002	M		SS-Hptschfhr., Gestapo, Lodz (Pol.) 39-44	56/639	MURDER	POL.
PETERSEN	303866	M		Member, Gestapo, Warschau (Pol.) 39-45	57/868	BRUTALITY	POL.
PETEPSKOWSKI, Fritz	303004	M		Krim.Sekretaer, Staff of Gestapo, Kattowitz (Pol.) 39-42	56/641	PILLAGE	POL.
PETERSON, Benno, Paul, Kurt	304356	M	18. 8.04	SA-Leader, SA, Kempno (Pol.) 40-1.45	58/514	BRUTALITY	POL.
PETRAS, Eidukas	303867	M		SS-Mann, C.C. Majdanek (Pol.) 40-42	57/870	BRUTALITY	POL.
PETRACCH, Robert	265688	M	6. 6.95	Chief, City Administration, Plzen (Czech.) 44-45	-	MISC.CRIMES	CZECH.
PETRI	266286	M		Sgt., Army, 3 Coy. 441 Sect. D.C.A., Vern s-Seiche (Fr.)14.7.44	-	MURDER	FR.
PETRI, Hans	303005	M		Krim.Beamter, Staff of Gestapo, Kattowitz (Pol.) 39-42	56/642	INTERR.	POL.
PETRIK, Heinrich	304360	M		Member, Gestapo, Krakau (Pol.) 11.39-2.45	59/524	TORTURE	POL.
PETZNICK	303868	M		Member, Gestapo, Warschau (Pol.) 39-45	57/871	BRUTALITY	POL.
PFAHL, Alfred	266287	M	14. 4.01	Lt., Div.Brehmer Sich.Rgt.1, commanded 2 Armoured Sect., Dordogne,Correze and Hte.Vienne (Fr.) 3.-4.44	-	MURDER	FR.
PFAHLS, Augen	190606	M		Pvt., II Panz.Div. 2 AA-A 7, 2 Coy., near Bergerac and Albine (Fr.) 7.-8.44	-	MURDER	FR.
PFALZER	304357	M		Cpl., Nachtjagd Group No.4, vicinity of Charleroi (Bel.) 2.44	58/515	MURDER	BEL.
PFEFFER	304861	M		Secretary, Secr.Field Pol., H.Q. GFP. Boulevard Piercot or the Avenue Rogier, Luettich (Bel.) 40-41	59/525	MURDER	BEL.
PFEIFER	265663	M		Sgt., 244 Inf.Div., Le Castellet (Fr.) 17.6.44	-	MURDER	FR.
PFEIFFER	265663	M		Lt.Col., 157 Alpen Div., Barcelonette (Fr.) 11.-16.6.44	-	MISC.CRIMES	FR.
PFEIFFER	266913	M	circa 00	Sgt.-Major, SD. Rennes, Cirey s-Vezouse (Fr.) 9.-11.44	-	MURDER	FR.
PFEIFFER, Hermann	265235	M		Lt., Inf.Rgt. 157, Vercors (Fr.) 40-45	-	MURDER	FR.
PFEIFFER, Paul	309034	M		Chief, Dept. Rheinisch-Westfaelische Kalkwerke,Lendringsen by Iserlohn (Ger.) 39-45	60/458	BRUTALITY	POL.
PFITZNER	309035	M		SS-Sturmschfhr. and Krim.Sekretaer, SS,Radom (Pol.)1.40-1.45	60/460	PILLAGE	POL.
PFITZNER, Gerhard	303006	M		Krim.Assistent, Staff of Gestapo, Kattowitz (Pol.) 39-42	56/643	INTERR.	POL.
PFLAUM, Filip	303969	M	20. 6.12	SS-Mann, C.C. Majdanek (Pol.) 40-45	57/876	BRUTALITY	POL.
PFLAUM, Paul	303870	M	2. 4.03	SS-Uschfhr., Guard, C.C. Majdanek (Pol.) 40-44	57/877	BRUTALITY	POL.
PHILIPP	303871	M		Member, Gestapo, Warschau (Pol.) 39-45	57/878	BRUTALITY	POL.
PICHA	265395	M		Uschfhr., Waffen-SS, 3 Coy. 1 Bn. Rgt. "Der Fuehrer" Div. "Das Reich", Oradour s-Glane (Fr.) 10.6.44	-	MURDER	FR.
PICHTER	21486	M		Militaerverwaltungsoberrat (Ger.) 44	-	WITNESS	BEL.
PICK	303007	M		Adjutant, Feldgend., Cholet (Fr.) 7.-8.8.44	56/644	MURDER	FR.
PICKERT, Franz	267046	M		Agent, Gestapo, Arras (Fr.) 8.41	-	MURDER	FR.
PIEKARSKI, Kurt	303872	M	circa 19	Camp Administrator, C.C. Wattenstaedt (Ger.) 39-45	57/880	MURDER	POL.
PIEL, Joachim	266288	M		Pvt., SS Div. "Das Reich", 2 Btty. Art.1 Sect., Selles-sur-Cher (Fr.) 14.-15.8.44	-	MURDER	FR.
PIELLA, Rosa	303008	F		Krimin.Official, Staff of Gestapo, Kattowitz (Pol.) 39-42	56/645	INTERR.	POL.
PIES	265396	M		Capt. or Commandant, Unit F.K. 2-455 or Unit "Dollenger" I 33, Cormainville (Fr.) 17.8.44	-	MURDER	FR.
PIETCHOTKA, Ulrich	304358	M		Lt., Army, 932 Inf.Rgt.,Pennes-Mirabeau (Fr.) 19.8.44	58/518	MURDER	FR.
PIETRUS	266289	M		N.C.O., Africa Corps Rgt. "Ruxleben", 6 Coy. 1 Sect. Hte.Marne-Aube (Fr.) 25.-31.8.44	-	MURDER	FR.
PIETZONKA, Erich	267212	M	4.10.06	Osturmfhr., former chief,Commander, of Quarter General, 2 Div.Paratrooper Unit 52326, Brest and vicinity (Fr.)7.-8.44	-	MURDER	FR.
PILAREK, Anzelm	303873	M	12. 6.03	Kapo, C.C. Auschwitz (Pol.) 40-45	57/882	MURDER	POL.
PILM	303009	M		Stabsfeldwebel,Feldgend. at Angouleme, Chasseneuil, Charente (Fr.) 43-45	56/647	MURDER	FR.
PINEL	267162	M	circa 15	Kapo, C.C. Melk (Ger.)	-	BRUTALITY	FR.
PINKAS, Franz	304967	M		Member, Gestapo, Krakau (Pol.) 11.39-2.45	59/526	MURDER	POL.
PINIOW	303874	M		Member, Gestapo, Warschau (Pol.) 39-45	57/884	BRUTALITY	POL.
PIPPER	266611	M		Lt., Department of Basses Pyrenees (Fr.) 6.-8.44	-	MURDER	FR.
PITSCH, Auguste	304968	F		Member, Gestapo, Krakau (Pol.) 11.39-2.45	59/527	MURDER	POL.
PITTER	303010	M		Lt., Department of Basses-Pyrenees (Fr.) 8.44	56/648	MURDER	FR.
PLATE	265327	M		Pol.Hptwacht.mstr., Extermination Camp Chelm (Pol.) 41-42	-	MURDER	POL.
PLANA	303875	M		Member, Gestapo, Warschau (Pol.) 39-45	57/887	BRUTALITY	POL.
PLATZ	266742	M		Member, SS-Usturmfhr., Gestapo,Sonderkdo.,Kulmhof (Pol.)41-45	-	MURDER	POL.
PLATE	266976	M		Korvettenkapitaen,Navy, Calais (Fr.) 4.9.44	-	MURDER	FR.
PLELI, Andreas	303876	M	29. 9.09	SS-Sturmmann, C.C. Majdanek (Pol.) 40-45	57/888	BRUTALITY	POL.
PLISCHKA	267211	M		Usturmfhr., Gestapo Border security and secret passages Bordeaux and vicinity (Fr.) 42-8.44	-	MURDER	FR.
PLIZBOUCH	267210	M		N.C. Feldgend. Coy., Villers S-Condon.(Fr.) 8.44	-	MURDER	U.K.
POERER, Ignatz	265294	M		Pvt., "Brandenburg" Rgt. (It.)	-	SUSPECT	U.K.
PLOETZ, Peter	266977	M	circa 00	Chief-Sgt.Major, Feldgend., Sisteron (Fr.) 44	-	MISC.CRIMES	FR.
PLON	304360	M		Farmer at Oadorf (Ger.) 45	-	BRUTALITY	POL.
POBIESKA, Roman	266912	M		Chief of Culture, Neuville les Bois (Fr.) 41-44	-	MISC.CRIMES	FR.
POBURSKI, Fritz	309037	M		Blockaeltester, C.C. Stutthof (Pol.) 42-44	60/464	MURDER	POL.
POCHERT, Gustav	304969	M		Member, Gestapo, Krakau (Pol.) 11.39-2.45	59/528	MURDER	POL.
POILECH	303877	M		Member, Gestapo, Warschau (Pol.) 39-45	57/889	BRUTALITY	POL.
POEPPELMANN, Bernard	266291	M		Manufacturer, Director, of Society (For the tanners) Paris (Fr.) 42-44	-	PILLAGE	FR.
POETERS	265222	M	circa 12	Lt., Div. "Hermann Goering", Partina Moscaio (It.) 4.44	-	SUSPECT	U.K.
POHL, Walter	266788	M		Chief of culture, Alland'huy (Fr.) 41-44	-	MISC.CRIMES	FR.
POLACZEK, Hortensia	303012	F		Office-Employee, Staff of Gestapo, Kattowitz (Pol.) 39-42	56/651	PILLAGE	POL.
POLH	266951	M		Sgt., Sisteron (Fr.) 44	-	MISC.CRIMES	FR.
POLLAK, Imrich, Emerich	265689	M	20. 6.97	Dance-teacher, Civilian, Krupina (Czech.) 42-44	-	MISC.CRIMES	CZECH.
POLTE, Ernst	304970	M		Member, Secr.Field Police, H.Q. GFP. Boulevard Piercot or the Avenue Rogier, Luettich (Bel.) 40-41	59/529	MURDER	BEL.
POLTEN, Josef	303013	M		Krim.Sekretaer, Staff of Gestapo, Kattowitz (Pol.) 39-42	56/652	INTERR.	POL.
POMMER, Hermann	303014	M		Hpt.Pol.Insp., Staff of Gestapo, Kattowitz (Pol.) 39-42	56/653	BRUTALITY	POL.
POMMERENKE	303015	M		Agent and Member, Gestapo "Selbstschutz", Torun (Pol.) 9.39	56/654	MURDER	POL.
POMORIA, Wilhelm	303016	M		Krim.Insp., Staff of Gestapo, Kattowitz(Pol.) 39-42	-	BRUTALITY	POL.

POO - RAM

NAME	C.R.FILE NUMBER	SEX	DATE OF BIRTH	RANK OCCUPATION UNIT PLACE AND DATE OF CRIME	UNWCC LIST/ SERIAL NO.	REASON WANTED	WANTED BY
POOTZ (or POUTZ)	266292	M		Sgt.Major,W.O.,Unit stationed at Camp Varennes,Ligny le Chatel (Fr.) 2.8.44	-	MURDER	FR.
POPP,Ernst	304971	M		Member,Gestapo,Krakau (Pol.) 11.39-2.45	59/530	MURDER	POL.
PORR,Albert	303878	M	14.10.21	SS-Mann,C.C.Majdanek (Pol.) 40-44	57/891	BRUTALITY	POL.
PORSEN	265643	M		Cpl.,Army,Royallieu (Fr.) 43-44	-	MURDER	FR.
POSNANSKI	36605	M	circa 95	Sgt.,610 Ldsch.Bn.,Halle,Willenburg to Fahrbinde (Ger.) 45	14/555	TORTURE	U.K.,U.S.
POSSELT,Walter Emile	266612	M	11. 9.89	Agent,SD at German Embassy (Fr.) 41-45	-	MISC.CRIMES	FR.
POST,Johannes	309038	M	11.11.08	Crim.Comm.,Gestapo HQ Kiel,various places in Germany and German occupied territory, 25.3.44-13.4.44	60/466	MURDER	U.K.
POTEMPA,Thomas	303879	M	20.12.04	SS-Guard,C.C.Majdanek (Pol.) 40-44	57/892	PILLAGE	POL.
POTING,August	266952	M	10	SS-Uscharfhr.,Member,SD,Sipo,Limoges (Fr.)	-	SUSPECT	FR.
POTRATZ	303880	M		Member,Gestapo,Warschau (Pol.) 39-45	57/893	BRUTALITY	POL.
POUTZ (see POOTZ)	266292						
PRAUSE,Gerhard	267151	M		Usturmfhr.,Gestapo,Marseille and vicinity (Fr.)	-	MURDER	FR.
PRAXMARER,Ivo	303107	M		Crim.Secr.,Staff of Gestapo,Kattowitz (Pol.) 30-42	56/655 A	INTERR.	POL.
PRECHTER,Georg	38842	M		Uscharfhr.,SS,C.C.Struthof (Fr.) 42-44	10/289	MURDER	FR.,UNWCC
PREISS,Otto	309039	M	21. 7.06	Crim.Secr.,Gestapo,HQ Karlsruhe,various places in Germany and German occupied territory, 25.3.44-13.4.44	60/467	MURDER	U.K.
PREUSS,Hugo	266949	M	29. 8.02	Chief Commissary,Gestapo Saarbruecken,Civil Police Service,Maison-Laffitte (Fr.)	-	SUSPECT	FR.
PREUSSNER	309040	M		Assessor to court for trial of French civilians,Saarbruecken (Ger.) 10.and 11.44	60/468	MURDER	FR.
PREYSS, Dr.	137302	M	02	Major-Stabsarzt,German Army Medical Service,German MO I/C Lazaretts,C.C.Cosel (Ger.) 43-45	-	TORTURE	U.K.
PRIESNER,Franz	304972	M		Member,Gestapo,Krakau (Pol.) 11.39-2.45	59/531	PILLAGE	POL.
PRIESS	266290	M		Member,SS,Kdo.Gestapo of Lyon,withdrawn Kdo.Nagler,Gerardmer and region (Fr.) 9.-10.44	-	MURDER	FR.
PRIMFE,Herbert	303018	M		Pol.Secr.,Staff of Gestapo,Kattowitz (Pol.) 39-42	56/657	PILLAGE	POL.
PRINZ,Johann	303019	M		Crim.Secr.,Staff of Gestapo,Kattowitz (Pol.) 39-42	56/658	BRUTALITY	POL.
PROBOSZCZ,Erwin	304973	M		Member,Gestapo,Krakau (Pol.) 11.39-2.45	59/532	PILLAGE	POL.
PROCHNIK,Robert (or BROCHNIK)	304362	M	15	On the staff of C.C.Theresienstadt confident of the SS (Czech.) 42-44	58/527	MURDER	CZECH.
PROIDL,Johann	267160	M		Sturmscharfhr.,Gestapo,Marseille and vicinity (Fr.)	-	MURDER	FR.
PROTZ	309041	M		SS-Hptscharfhr.and Fernschreiber,Radom (Pol.) 1.40-1.45	60/470	MURDER	POL.
PROTZBER,Franz	304974	M		Member,Gestapo,Krakau (Pol.) 11.39-2.45	59/533	PILLAGE	POL.
PRUCHNIEWSKI,Franz	304975	M		Member,Gestapo,Krakau (Pol.) 11.39-2.45	59/534	PILLAGE	POL.
PRUMMER	309042	M		SS-Usturmfhr.and Crim.Comm.,Radom (Pol.) 1.40-1.45	60/471	PILLAGE	POL.
PRUZA,Otto	304976	M		Member,Customs Official,Zwartaluis (Neth.) 8.10.44	59/535	MURDER	NETH.
PRYMELSKI,Jan	304364	M		Foreman at textile factory "Wilhelm Schlochauer",Hamburg (Ger.) 40-45	58/529	BRUTALITY	POL.
PRZYBILLA,Herbert	303020	M		Crim.Beamter,Staff of Gestapo,Kattowitz (Pol.) 39-42	56/659	BRUTALITY	POL.
PUCKNATH	309043	M		SS-Hptscharfhr.,Inspector of Administration,Radom (Pol.) 1.40-1.45	60/472	MURDER	POL.
PUDER,Arthur	265953	M		Senior W.O.,Unit L 50262,Rauzan (Fr.) 10.8.44	-	SUSPECT	FR.
PUFF,Richard	303022	M		Crim.Secr.,Staff of Gestapo,Kattowitz (Pol.) 39-42	56/661	MURDER	POL.
PUFKE,Walter	304977	M		Member,Gestapo,Krakau (Pol.) 11.39-2.45	59/536	PILLAGE	POL.
PUHL (see BUHL,Anna)	131840						
PUHL,Emil	265631	M	28. 8.89	See names listed under "Special Headings"			U.S.
PUHLMANN,Wilhelm	303023	M		SS-Sturmbannfhr.,Staff of Gestapo,Kattowitz (Pol.) 39-42	56/662	MURDER	POL.
PULS, Willi Walter Dr.	264655	M	9. 1.08	See names listed under "Special Headings"			U.S.
PULTAR	257047	M		General,Airforce,Belfort (Fr.) 43-44	-	PILLAGE	FR.
PURPER,Albert	265348	M	11.11.07	SS-Uscharfhr.,Cpl.,Befehlshaber der deutschen Sich.Pol.and SD Abt.IV 2 a (Case No.348/1947),Kopenhagen (Den.) 24.2.45	-	MURDER	DEN.
PUSACK,Erich	303881	M	11. 8.04	SS-Mann,C.C.Majdanek (Pol.) 40-44	57/895	BRUTALITY	POL.
PUZIK,Waldemar	303024	M		Pol.Secr.,Staff of Gestapo,Kattowitz (Pol.) 39-42	56/663	BRUTALITY	POL.
QUENOL	267543	M		Sgt.,350 Regt.Hindou,Dept.Indre (Fr.) 8.44	-	MURDER	FR.
QUINTUS,Peter	303882	M	18. 4.15	SS-Mann,C.C.Majdanek (Pol.) 40-44	57/898	BRUTALITY	POL.
QWEITSCH	303883	M		Member,Gestapo,Warschau (Pol.) 39-45	57/899	BRUTALITY	POL.
RAABE,Rudolf	304978	M		Member,Gestapo,Krakau (Pol.) 11.39-2.45	59/537	RAPE	POL.
RAACH (see RACH,Max)	257071						
RAASCHE,Gustav	303884	M	5. 7.20	SS-Mann,C.C.Majdanek (Pol.) 40-44	57/900	BRUTALITY	POL.
RABBE	265397	M		Lt.,Unit 41573 A,Valras (Fr.) 2.3.44	-	MISC.CRIMES	FR.
RACH,Max (or RAACH or BERGER,Tony)	267071	M	circa 05	Asst.Chief,Gestapo,Blois and region (Fr.) -12.43	-	MURDER	FR.
RADEMACHER,Alfred	304979	M		Member,Gestapo,Krakau (Pol.) 11.39-2.45	59/538	RAPE	POL.
RADEMACHER,Gustave	265684	M		Pvt.,Army,Vatan (Fr.) 10.8.44	-	MURDER	FR.
RADERSCHEIT	266787	M		Lt.,Feldkommandantur of Besancon,stationed at St.Laurent,Saint Pierre la Grande Riviere (Fr.) 3.7.44	-	MURDER	FR.
RADICKE	167489	M		SS-Oscharfhr.,Camp Guard,C.C.Sachsenhausen Oranienburg (Ger.) 39-4.45	-	MURDER	POL.
RADIKER,Wilhelm	304980	M		Member,Gestapo,Krakau (Pol.) 11.39-2.45	59/539	RAPE	POL.
RADKE,Kurt	304981	M		Member,Gestapo,Krakau (Pol.) 11.39-2.45	59/540	RAPE	POL.
RAENNER	265217	M	circa 92	Capt.,Commandant of SS Police Unit at Rocca Di Mezza,Goriano Valli (It.) 10.1.44-3.44	-	SUSPECT	U.K.
RAGALLER,Ernst	264657	M	10. 6.95	See names listed under "Special Headings"			U.S.
RAHN	266206	M		Counsillor,Embassy,Paris (Fr.) 41-44	-	MISC.CRIMES	FR.
RAHN (see RANN)	266207						
RAHSBACH,Thea	304983	F		Member,Gestapo,Krakau (Pol.) 11.39-2.45	59/542	MURDER	POL.
RAIMANN (or SCHIRMJAGER)	304366	M		SS-Oscharfhr.,Gestapo and possibly SD at Enschede,Glauerburg (Neth.) 24.10.44	58/532	MURDER	NETH.
RAIZNER,Paul	304984	M		Member,Gestapo,Krakau (Pol.) 11.39-2.45	59/543	MURDER	POL.
RAMACH,Bronislaus	304985	M		Member,Gestapo,Krakau (Pol.) 11.39-2.45	59/544	MURDER	POL.
RAMKE	267073	M		Agent,Gestapo,Arras (Fr.) 8.41	-	MURDER	FR.
RAMM	309045	M		SS-Oscharfhr.,Crim.Employee,Radom (Pol.) 1.40-1.45	60/477	PILLAGE	POL.
RAMS (or RAMSCH)	304367	M	circa 95	Major,Head of the Airforce Command Raveredo,Polcenigo,Udine (It.) 4.2.45	58/533	MURDER	FR.
RAMSCH (see RAMS)	304367						

NAME	C.R.FILE NUMBER	SEX	DATE OF BIRTH	RANK – OCCUPATION – UNIT – PLACE AND DATE OF CRIME	UNWCC LIST/ SERIAL NO.	REASON WANTED	WANTED BY
RAMZOCH	265326	M		SS-Oberfhr., Extermination Camp, Chelm (Pol.) 41-42	-	MURDER	POL.
RANN (or RAHN or KAMM)	266207	M	circa 10	Scharfhr., SD, Dijon (Fr.) 17.,18.8.44	-	MURDER	FR.
RANZ, Erwin	303025	M		Krim.Sekr., Staff of Gestapo, Kattowitz (Pol.) 39-42	56/666	BRUTALITY	POL.
RAPP	303026	M		Agent, Gestapo, Lot-et-Garonne, Gironde, Landes (Fr.) 3.-21.7.44	56/667	MURDER	FR.
RAPP	303885	M		Member, Gestapo, Warschau (Pol.) 39-45	57/905	PILLAGE	POL.
RASCHWITZ, Wilhelm	304986	M		Member, Gestapo, Krakau (Pol.) 11.39- 2.45	59/545	MURDER	POL.
RATHER	266613	M		Hauptscharfhr., SD of Rennes, retreated to Meurthe and Moselle, Pettonville (Fr.) 6.10.44	-	MISC.CRIMES	FR.
RATHMANN, Heinrich	303027	M		SS-Oscharfhr., Guard, Oldenburg Gaol, Oldenburg (Ger.) 4.40-44	56/668	MURDER	POL.
RATHS	303886	M		Member, Gestapo, Warschau (Pol.) 39-45	57/907	PILLAGE	POL.
RATKE, Paul	303887	M	27. 4.07	SS-Mann, C.C. Majdanek (Pol.) 40-44	57/908	MURDER	POL.
RATZ, Kurt	303028	M		Feldwebel, Geheime Feldpolizei, Belgium 1940-44	56/669	MURDER	BEL.
RATZKE, Julius	304370	M		Ortsgruppenleiter, area of Gernsbach, Wiesenbach, Obertsrot and Hilpertsau (Ger.) 9.8.44	58/536	MURDER	U.S.
RAU, Fritz	265214	M		Sgt., Army, 33.Sign.Bn., 15.Pz.Gren.Div., San Giustino (It.)6.7.44	-	SUSPECT	U.K.
RAU, Fritz	304987	M		Member, Gestapo, Krakau (Pol.) 11.39- 2.45	59/546	BRUTALITY	POL.
RAUBER	304371	M		Lt., German Army, Member of the staff of the Town-major of the Piraeus (Grc.) 6.41	58/537	PILLAGE	GRC.
RAUCH	265952	M		Major-General, Commander of 342 Div., Brest (Fr.) 8.9.44	-	MURDER	FR.
RAUCHEGGER, Johann	309046	M	19. 6.01	Member, Schutzgruppen, Brunssum (Neth.) 9.44	60/478	PILLAGE	NETH.
RAUDZUS, Friedrich	303029	M		Wachtmeister, Pol.-Sonderkdo., Kulmhof (Pol.) 41-45	56/670	MURDER	POL.
RAUSCH	265671	M	14. 8.21	Unit No. 57727 B, Larmor-Pleubian, (Fr.) 5.-7.8.44	-	MURDER	FR.
REBITZ	302030	M		Stabsfeldwebel, Geh.Feldpol., Group 530, Bruessel (Bel.) 40-44	56/673	MURDER	BEL.
RECCERT	304373	M		Works engineer, Maurits State coal mine, Geleen (L) (Neth.) 9.44	58/539	MISC.CRIMES	NETH.
RECHER	266785	M		Pvt., Div."B", Dordogne, Correze, Haute-Vienne (Fr.)	-	SUSPECT	FR.
RECKBERGER	266743	M		SS-Usturmfhr., C.C.command, Barth nr.Ravensbrueck (Ger.) 42-45	-	MURDER	POL.
RECKLAU	266614	M	circa 08	Staff-Sgt., Collaborator of Lt.Robert, SS unknown (had the uniform of aviators) Camp of Jhil (Fr.) 5.-9.44	-	BRUTALITY	FR.
REEDING	267205	M		Member, Gestapo, Bordeaux and vicinity (Fr.) 42-8.44	-	MURDER	FR.
REGNER	266784	M		Member, SD, Pau (Fr.) 12.42- 8.44	-	MISC.CRIMES	FR.
REH, Joseph	267544	M		Member, Gestapo, Limoges and vicinity (Fr.) 44	-	SUSPECT	FR.
REHM (see RHEM)	267060						
REICHARDT, Rudolf	304988	M		Member, Gestapo, Krakau (Pol.) 11.39- 2.45	59/547	BRUTALITY	POL.
REICHARDT, Willi	266203	M	circa 03	Agent, Rottfhr., Gestapo, Nantes and region (Fr.) 43-44	-	MURDER	FR.
REICHEL, Otto	304989	M		Member, Gestapo, Krakau (Pol.) 11.39- 2.45	59/548	BRUTALITY	POL.
REICHERT	309047	M		SS-Osturmfhr., Krim.Kommissar, Radom (Pol.) 1.40- 1.45	60/485	MURDER	POL.
REICHERT, Albert	304374	M		Capo, Labour Camps, Husum, Ladelund, Meppen, Dalum (Ger.) 40-45	58/542	MURDER	POL.
REICHMANN, Willy	304087	M	9. 7.00	Guard, C.C. Auschwitz (Pol.) 40-45	57/912	BRUTALITY	POL.
REIDSCHELL	266204	M		See names listed under "Special Headings"			
REIF, Leo	304378	M		Civilian, nr.Weisenbach, Gernsbach, Oberstrot (Ger.) 8.44	58/544	MURDER	U.S.
REIFF	266587	M	31. 5.03	Chief Cpl., Customs official at Mouthe, Foncine-le-Haut-Castelblanc (Jura) (Fr.) 30. 8.44	-	INCENDIARISM	FR.
REIGER, Michel	266205	M		Rottfhr., SS-Div."Das Reich", Art.Regt.,4.Sect.,10.Btty., Ferme de la Viesse, Buzet sur Tarn (Fr.) 7.7.44	-	MURDER	FR.
REIHE	303888	M	28.12.10	SS-Mann, C.C. Majdanek (Pol.) 40-44	57/913	BRUTALITY	POL.
REIMANN	303889	M		Member, Gestapo, Warschau (Pol.) 39-45	57/914	PILLAGE	POL.
REIMER, Wilhelm	265770	M		Pvt., Army, Vatan (Fr.) 10. 8.44	-	MURDER	FR.
REIN, Peter	303890	M	10. 6.14	SS-Mann, C.C. Majdanek (Pol.) 40-44	57/915	BRUTALITY	POL.
REINECKE	266588	M		W.O.,9.SS Pz.Div."Hohenstaufen", Unit No. 29.474, Nimes (Fr.) 2.3.44	-	MURDER	FR.
REINECKE, Heinrich	303893	M	18.11.04	Camp Guard, Arbeits-Kdo., Kohlenfeld 1939-45	57/920	BRUTALITY	POL.
REINECKER, Heinz	267204	M	circa 18	Cpl., Feldgend., d'Avallon (Fr.) 44	-	MISC.CRIMES	FR.
REINHARDT, Fritz	264660	M		See names listed under "Special Headings"			
REINHE	265592			Standartenfhr., (leader of the SS Einsatz) SS, Rowiez (Pol.)39-40	-	MISC.CRIMES	POL.
REINHOLD	302031	M		Cmdt., 1.Coy., 623.Nachschub-Bn., Petit Enghien (Bel.) 3.9.44	56/679	MURDER	BEL.
REINHOLD	303891	M		Member, Gestapo, Warschau (Pol.) 39-45	57/916	PILLAGE	POL.
REINICKE	266859	M		See names listed under "Special Headings"			
REINKE, Helmut	264654	M	23. 3.97	See names listed under "Special Headings"			
REINSCHARDT, Walter	304990	M		Member, Gestapo, Krakau (Pol.) 11.39- 2.45	59/549	BRUTALITY	POL.
REINZBURG, Mueller	21489	M		Lt.Col., Waffen-SS, 12.SS Pz.Div."Hitler Jugend",	-	WITNESS	CAN.
REISCH	303892	M		Member, Gestapo, Warschau (Pol.) 39-45	57/917	PILLAGE	POL.
REISCH, Ursula	304991	F		Member, Gestapo, Krakau (Pol.) 11.39- 2.45	59/550	MURDER	POL.
REISNER, Carl Friedrich	309048	M	25.12.13	Krim.Asst., Aarhus (Den.) 11.44- 45	60/488	MURDER	DEN.
REISMULLER,	252641	M	14	SS-Oschfhr., Gestapo, SD, Sipo, Limoges (Fr.) 40-45	41/374	SUSPECT	FR.
REISNER, Karl	304992	M		Member, Gestapo, Krakau (Pol.) 11.39- 2.45	59/551	BRUTALITY	POL.
REISS, Margarete	304380	F	11.10.00	Interpreter, Gap SD, Briancon detachment, Hautes-Alpes Department of Hautes-Alpes (Fr.) 9.43- 8.44	58/546	MURDER	FR.
REISSNER, Sepp	303032	M		Wachtmeister, Pol.Sonder-Kdo., Kulmhof (Pol.) 41-45	56/681	MURDER	POL.
REITH, Hans	304993	M		Member, Gestapo, Krakau (Pol.) 11.39- 2.45	59/552	MURDER	POL.
REITHOFER,	304381	M		Member of the Schutzgruppen at the "Laura-mine" State coal mine, Eigelshoven (Neth.) 9.44	58/547	PILLAGE	NETH.
REITMEIER,	309049	M		SS-Osturmfhr., Krim.Rat, Radom (Pol.) 1.40- 1.45	60/489	PILLAGE	POL.
REMBRARD	267545	M		Sgt.Major, 350.Regt."Hindou", Departm.Indre (Fr.) 8.44	-	MURDER	FR.
REMESIK, Vojtech	303093	M	28. 8.07	Founder of the Hlinka Guard Organisation in Uava during the Slovakian uprising in 1944 (Czech.)	56/682	MURDER	CZECH.
REMMERS, Hans Hermann	264653	M	13. 7.06	See names listed under "Special Headings"			
RENNER (see DENNER)	267292						
RENNER, Karl	303034	M		Office Asst., Staff of Gestapo, Kattowitz (Pol.) 39-42	56/684	PILLAGE	POL.
RENTSCH, Walter	267564	M	16. 8.10	Pvt., Abt.I Mess (Kriegskarten u.Vermessungsamt), Utrecht (Neth.) 41- 45	-	SUSPECT	NETH.
RENZ, Emil	302267	M	28. 2.11	Allg.SS, C.C., Escaped from 6 C.I.C.Neuengamme on 7.12.46 Auschwitz (Pol.) 40-45	51/261	TORTURE	POL.
RENZ, Otto	304994	M		Member, Gestapo, Krakau (Pol.) 11.39- 2.45	59/553	MURDER	POL.
RENZEL	303894	M		Member, Gestapo, Warschau (Pol.) 39-45	57/924	PILLAGE	POL.
RESCHKE	303895	M		Member, Gestapo, Warschau (Pol.) 39-45	57/925	PILLAGE	POL.

RET - ROL

NAME	C.R.FILE NUMBER	SEX	DATE OF BIRTH	RANK OCCUPATION UNIT PLACE AND DATE OF CRIME	UNWCC LIST/ SERIAL NO.	REASON WANTED	WANTED BY
RETTER, Fritz	303035	M		Sgt.,Feldgendarmerie at Angouleme,Chasseneuil,Charente (Fr.) 43-44	56/686	MURDER	FR.
RETTIGER	309050	M		SS-Osturmfhr. and Krim.Inspektor, Radom (Pol.) 1.40- 1.45	60/490	RAPE	POL.
RETZ, Fritz or Otto	267072	M	circa 07	Asst.Chief, Gestapo,Bois,Maves and vicinity (Fr.) 1.44	-	MURDER	FR.
RETZECK	304995	M		Commissioner, Secr.Field-Police,HQ.G.F.P,Boulevard Piercot, or the Avenue Rogier,Luettich (Bel.) 40-41	59/554	MURDER	BEL.
REUEN, Friedrich	304996	M		Sgt., Secr.Field-Police,HQ.G.F.P.Boulevard Piercot or the Avenue Rogier,Luettich (Bel.) 40-41	59/555	MURDER	BEL.
REUTER	303896	M		Member, Gestapo, Warschau (Pol.) 39-45	57/927	PILLAGE	POL.
RHEM (or REHM)	267060	M		Lt., Unit composed of Hindou soldiers,stationed at Jussey, Betaucourt (Fr.) 10.9.44	-	MURDER	FR.
RICHARD	265771	M	circa 05	Uscharfhr., SD Mans, Sarthe, Mayenne (Fr.) 42-44	-	SUSPECT	FR.
RICHTER	265726	M		Feldgendarm, Capt.,Feldkommandant of Pleurtuit,Ille and Vilaine (Fr.) 9.8.44	-	INCENDIARISM	FR.
RICHTER	267202	M		Sgt.,Air-Force, 91.Regt.,Chantraine (Fr.) 20.or 22.9.44	-	MURDER	FR.
RICHTER	303897	M		Member, Gestapo, Warschau (Pol.) 39-45	57/929	PILLAGE	POL.
RICHTER, Herbert	267147	M	circa 19	Rottfhr., Gestapo, Marseille and vicinity (Fr.)	-	MURDER	FR.
RICHTER, Rudolf	265297	M		Member, Regt."Brandenburg" (It.)	-	SUSPECT	U.K.
RICHTER, Rudolf	267061	M	27. 7.00	Member,Oscharfhr.,Gestapo, KDS IV, Paris (Fr.) 43	-	SUSPECT	FR.
RICKOFF, Helmuth	309051	M	circa 05	Krim.Sekr., Odense (Dan.) 10.43- 1.45	60/491	TORTURE	DEN.
RIDDER	309053	M		Inspector,"Hendrik"state mine Brunssum from Jan.44 and also at other mines,Brunssum (Neth.) 9.44	60/493	PILLAGE	NETH.
RIEBLINGER, Anton	303036	M		Pol.Wachtmeister,Pol.Sonderkommando,Kulmhof (Pol.)41-45	56/690	MURDER	POL.
RIECK, Friedrich, Dr.	161885	M		SS-Osturmfhr., Sipo and SD,official, Kassel (Ger.) 44	-	SUSPECT	FR.
RIECKEN, Gustav	304375	M		Farmer and innkeeper, Luderhausen (Ger.) 42	58/550	BRUTALITY	POL.
RIEDBERG, Erich	267159	M		Oscharfhr., Gestapo, Marseille and vicinity (Fr.)	-	MURDER	FR.
RIEDIGER, Guenter	264658	M	1.10.09	See names listed under "Special Headings"			
RIEELS	266237	M		Pvt., Unit: 01235 A., Hte.Marne-Aube (Fr.) 25.-31.8.44	-	MURDER	FR.
RIEGER	267198	M		Scharfhr., Gestapo, Bordeaux,vicinity (Fr.) 42-8.44	-	MURDER	FR.
RIEGER, Heinrich	309054	M		Feldpolizeisekretaer., Antwerpen and Bruessel (Bel.) 40-44	60/494	MURDER	BEL.
RIEKEN, Ricke	267517	M	28. 1.97	SS-Oscharfhr., Gestapo KDS V, Paris (Fr.) 43-44	-	SUSPECT	FR.
RIEMSER, Ludwig Georg	304376	M	14. 5.01	General manager of the Continental Trust, Krakau and Lwow (Pol.) 39-45	58/552	MURDER	POL.
RIETHMULLER, Hans	266314	M	circa 02	Rottfhr., Gestapo, Nantes and region.(Fr.) 43-44	-	MURDER	FR.
RIETZ	303898	M		Member, Gestapo, Warschau (Pol.) 39-45	57/934	INTERR.	POL.
RIETZINGER, Georg	303899	M	15. 1.92	Guard, C.C., Auschwitz (Pol.) 40-45	57/935	BRUTALITY	POL.
RIEWALD, Bodo	304997	M		Member, Gestapo, Krakau (Pol.) 11.39- 2.45	59/557	MURDER	POL.
RIFFERT	265398	M		Officer, Interpreter, Repression unit:Edelweiss, Barcelonnette (Fr.) 6.44	-	MISC.CRIMES	FR.
RIKOWSKI, Karl	304998	M		Member, Gestapo, Krakau (Pol.) 11.39- 2.45	59/558	MURDER	POL.
RINGWALD, Otto	266574	M	circa 97	Customs official at Mouthe, Custom house, Foncine le Haut, Castelblanc (Fr.) 30.8.44	-	INCENDIARISM	FR.
RINKELGAY	267546	M		Sgt.-Major, 350 Regt."Hindou",Department l'Indre (Fr.)8.44	-	MURDER	FR.
RINN, Hans	265634	M	4. 3.99	See names listed under "Special Headings"			
RINNE, Hans, Dr.	304377	M		Hospital Superintendent at Bad Segeberg, attached to the "Ost"-Hospital, Luebeck (Ger.) 43-45	58/555	BRUTALITY	POL.
RINTROP	267547	M		Lt., 350 Regt."Hindou",Department l'Indre (Fr.) 8.44	-	MURDER	FR.
RIPPER, Willi	304382	M		Foreman at Herring packing factory, Cuxhaven (Ger.) 40-45	58/556	MISC.CRIMES	POL.
RIPPERT	267158	M		Member, Gestapo, Marseille and vicinity (Fr.)	-	MURDER	FR.
RISTER	267285	M		350.Regt."Hindou", Department l'Indre (Fr.) 8.44	-	MURDER	FR.
RITTENHOFER, Johann	304999	M		Member, Gestapo, Krakau (Pol.) 11.39- 2.45	59/560	MURDER	POL.
RITTER, Karl	265303	M		Pvt., Regt."Brandenburg" (It.)	-	SUSPECT	U.K.
ROBERT	266654	M		Cpl.Chief, Camp de Jhil (Fr.) 5.-9.44	-	BRUTALITY	FR.
ROBRADE	308549	M		Commissioner, Secr.Field-Police,HQ.G.F.P. Boulevard Piercot or the Avenue Rogier,Luettich (Bel.)	59/561	MURDER	BEL.
ROCHR, Eugen	303038	M		SS-Uscharfhr., Gestapo, Lodz (Pol.) 39-44	56/697	PILLAGE	POL.
RODER	303900	M		Member, Gestapo, Warschau (Pol.) 39-45	57/936	INTERR.	POL.
RODOLPH	266615	M		N.C.O., chemist, Division "B",Dordogne,Correze,Hte.Vienne(Fr.)	-	SUSPECT	FR.
RODREGO	267563	M		Stabsleiter, Org.Todt,Wageningen (Neth.) 3.45	-	PILLAGE	NETH.
ROEDER, Georges	302506	M		Dienststellenleiter, SD Brest, Pettonville (Fr.) 6.10.44	-	PILLAGE	FR.
ROEHRICH, Dr.	264639	M	12.10.07	See names listed under "Special Headings"			
ROEHRS, Heinrich	303039	M		Feldwebel, Geh.Feldpolizei Group 530,Bruessel (Bel.)40-44	56/699	MURDER	BEL.
ROEREN, Josef	309058	M		Policeman, Salzkotten 1.12.44	60/500	MISC.CRIMES	POL.
ROESSLER	309059	M		Oscharfhr., Krim.Oberasst.,Radom (Pol.) 1.40- 1.45	60/501	PILLAGE	POL.
ROETTGER, Karl	309065	M		Uscharfhr., SS-Pz.Gren.Div.9 Hohenstaufen,Evelette(Bel.)7.9.44	60/509	MURDER	BEL.
ROEVER, Ernst	303040	M	16.11.83	Farmer at Klostergut, Northeim (Ger.) 40-44	56/700	BRUTALITY	POL.
ROEVER nee STEITMANN, Margot	303041	F		Wife of Ernst Roever,farmer at Klostergut,Northeim(Ger.)40-44	56/701	BRUTALITY	POL.
ROGGE	304384	M		Lt.,M.A. in charge of Flak-Abt.4-815,Texel (Neth.)4.45	58/558	MURDER	NETH.
ROHDE, Gustav	308524	M		Member, Gestapo, Krakau (Pol.) 11.39- 2.45	59/563	BRUTALITY	POL.
ROHDI (see ROHDR)	265210						
ROHDL (see ROHDR)	265210						
ROHDR (or ROHDI or ROHDL or ROLEDR)	265210	M	circa 03	Oberstabsvet.and Coy.-Chief, O.C. at Fara in Sabina (It.)12.43	-	SUSPECT	U.K.
ROHLING, Gustav	309060	M	4. 7.91	Cpl., Schutzgruppen, Brunssum (Neth.) 9.44	60/502	PILLAGE	NETH.
ROHLOFS, Albert	267157	M		Oscharfhr., Gestapo, Marseille and vicinity (Fr.)	-	MURDER	FR.
ROHR	303042	M		Lt.Adjutant,331.Inf.Div.Adj.to Gen.Diesel or Diestel,Ortskdt.of Oud-Beijerland (Neth.) 17.10.44	56/702	MISC.CRIMES	NETH.
ROHRBACHER, Oswald	308525	M		Member, Gestapo, Krakau (Pol.) 11.39- 2.45	59/564	BRUTALITY	POL.
ROHRMANN, Willi	309061	M	26. 6.02	Estate manager, SS member, SS, Uetze district 39-44	60/503	BRUTALITY	POL.
ROHRSDORFER, Andreas	303901	M	3. 9.21	SS-Mann, C.C. Majdanek (Pol.) 40-44	57/939	MURDER	POL.
ROHWER, Karl Heinz	308526	M		Member, Gestapo, Krakau (Pol.) 11.39- 2.45	59/565	BRUTALITY	POL.
ROIF	266981	M		Feldgendarm, Feldgendarmerie, Sisteron (Fr.) 44	-	MISC.CRIMES	FR.
ROJECK, Hans	266313	M		Sgt., Heeresabnahmestelle, Doubs,Besancon (Fr.) 8.44	-	PILLAGE	FR.
ROLEDR (see ROHDR)	265210						
ROLLAND, Fritz	266198	M		Interpreter,12.SS-Panz.Div."Hitler-Jugend",Chateauneuf-en-Thymerais (Fr.) 24.7.44	-	TORTURE	FR.

ROM-SAN

NAME	C.R.FILE NUMBER	SEX	DATE OF BIRTH	RANK	OCCUPATION	UNIT	PLACE AND DATE OF CRIME	UNWCC LIST/ SERIAL NO.	REASON WANTED	WANTED BY
ROMBACH, Erich	303043	M			Pol.Wachtmeister,Sonderkdo.at Kulmhof (Pol.) 41-45			56/703	MURDER	POL.
ROMER (see RUMER, Ernst)	267193									
ROMMEL, Anna	308527	F			Member, Gestapo, Krakau (Pol.) 11.39-2.45			59/566	BRUTALITY	POL.
ROOS	309062	M			Instructor and Employee, G.F.P., Antwerpen,Bruessel (Bel.)40-44			60/504	MURDER	BEL.
ROSA, Adolf	267444	M	15.10.93		See names listed unter "Special Headings"					
ROSCHLAU, Alfred	265399	M		Lt., Btty. Hamburg, Sainte Anne d'Auray (Fr.) 5.8.44				-	MURDER	FR.
ROSE	266575	M		Cpl., Feldgendarmerie, Chasseneuil, Angouleme and vicinity (Fr.) 43-44				-	MURDER	FR.
ROSEGGER, Otmar	303902	M	13.7.22		SS-Mann, C.C. Majdanek (Pol.) 40-44			57/944	TORTURE	POL.
ROSENBERG, Chaskiel	304385	M			Member of the Ordnungsdienst in the distr.of Nowy Sacz (Pol.) 40-45			58/561	MISC.CRIMES	POL.
ROSENTHAL (or ROZANSKI)	303903	M			Arbeitsdienstfhr., C.C. Auschwitz (Pol.) 40-45			57/946	MURDER	POL.
ROSNE	267548	M		Sgt., 350.Regt. "Hindou", Department l'Indre (Fr.) end of 8.44				-	MURDER	FR.
ROSS	304386	M			Beauftragter, prob.Head of "Ernaehrung und Landwirtschaft at Franeker, Leeuwarden,Dongjum,Friesland (Neth.) 3.45			58/562	MURDER	NETH.
ROSSMAN, Georg	308528	M			Hilfsaufseher at Blechhammer,Wielkie,Strzelce,Slask (Ger.,Pol.) 1.-2.45			59/567	MURDER	POL.
ROSTALSKI, Paul	303044	M			Lagerfhr.,Betriebsobmann, DAF, Plange (Ger.) 39-45			56/707	MISC.CRIMES	POL.
ROTBAUER, Karl	267146	M	circa 09	Rottenfhr., Gestapo, Marseille and vicinity (Fr.)				-	MURDER	FR.
ROTH	267194	M		Sgt., Waffenwerkstatt 812, Chateaumeillant (Fr.) 27.6.44				-	MURDER	FR.
ROTH, Albert	303045	M			Interpreter, SD Clermont-Ferrand,Chaux,Belfort,Planchez les Mines,Hte.Savoie (Fr.) 21.9.44			56/708	MURDER	FR.
ROTH, Erwin	309064	M			Member, Selbstschutz, Grudziadz (Pol.) 39			60/507	MURDER	POL.
ROTHER	303904	M			Member, Gestapo, Warschau (Pol.) 39-45			57/952	INTERR.	POL.
ROTTINGER, Michael	303905	M	30.8.08		SS-Mann, C.C. Majdanek (Pol.) 40-44			57/953	PILLAGE	POL.
ROTTLOF, Herbert or Ludwig (or BOUILLON, Maurice)	304387	M			SS-Hptscharfhr., Interpreter, Gestapo at Chalons s.Marne, Departm.of Marne (Fr.) 43-44			58/563	MURDER	FR.
ROUDY	267549	M		Sgt., 350.Regt. Hindou, Departm.l'Indre (Fr.) end of 8.44				-	MURDER	FR.
ROZANSKI (see ROSENTHAL)	303903									
ROZZCZKA, Karl	303046	M			Kriminalsekretaer, Staff of Gestapo, Kattowitz (Pol.) 39-42			56/709	BRUTALITY	POL.
RUCHE	266812	M		Pvt., Div. "B", Dordogne,Correze,Haute Vienne (Fr.)				-	SUSPECT	FR.
RUDA, Herbert	267581	M			Cpl., G.F.P., Groups 3, 738 and 739,Charleroi,Mons,Namur,Tournai,Ath (Bel.) 40-45			-	BRUTALITY	BEL.
RUDAITIS, Domas	303906	M			SS-Mann, C.C. Majdanek (Pol.) 40-42			57/955	BRUTALITY	POL.
RUDLER, Kurt	266196	M			Cpl., Panz.Div.Abt.115/15, 1.Coy. Blenod les Toul-Allain (Fr.) 1.9.44			-	MISC.CRIMES	FR.
RUDOLPH	303907	M			Member, Gestapo, Warschau (Pol.) 39-45			57/956	INTERR.	POL.
RUEDEBUSCH, Hermann	266052	M			See names listed unter "Special Headings"					
RUEGER, Otto	309066	M			Amtswalter, German Labour Front, nr.Bremen (Ger.) ab.28.5.44			60/511	BRUTALITY	U.S.
RUFF, Dr.	251866	M			Physician, C.C. Auschwitz (Pol.)			-	TORTURE	POL.
RUGER	266197	M		Sgt., Feldgend.662 at Beaune, Manley (Fr.) 29.,31.7.44				-	MISC.CRIMES	FR.
RUGER	304388	M			Capt.,Assist.Town-Major, German Army, Piraeus (Grc.) 6.41			58/565	PILLAGE	GRC.
RUHM, Walther	304389	M			Member, SD Aussenstelle Maastricht.Had the supervision of the industrial concerns, Limburg, Friesland (Neth.) 44-45			58/566	MURDER	NETH.
RUHR	265665	M			Member, SD, Chalons s.Marne (Fr.) 43-44			-	MISC.CRIMES	FR.
RUMELIN	303048	M			Lt.,Departm.of Basses-Pyrenees (Fr.) 8.6.-end of 8.44			56/712	MURDER	FR.
RUMER, Ernst (or ROMER or MARTIN)	267193	M	11		Scharfhr., Gestapo, Marseille and vicinity (Fr.)			-	MURDER	FR.
RUMMLER, Walter	303049	M			Chief, Police, Kampen (Ger.) 25.10.41			56/713	MURDER	POL.
RUNAU, Gustav	304390	M	2.11.98		Fahrdienstleiter at Hamburg, Pruszez (Pol.) 9.39			58/568	INTERR.	POL.
RUNDEL	309068	M			Instructor and Employee, G.F.P., Antwerpen,Bruessel (Bel.)40-44			60/514	MURDER	BEL.
RUNGE, Friedrich	264640	M	30.7.07		See names listed under "Special Headings"					
RUNGEL	266828	M		Pvt., Div. "B", Dordogne, Correze,Haute-Vienne (Fr.)				-	SUSPECT	FR.
RUPKEN	267284	M			Rottfhr., Gestapo, Bordeaux and vicinity (Fr.) 42-8.44			-	MURDER	FR.
RUPP	267283	F	circa 23		Secretary, Gestapo, Bordeaux and vicinity (Fr.) 42-8.44			-	MURDER	FR.
RUPP, Pierre or Peter	267192	M			Agent, Gestapo, Avignon (Fr.) 43-44			-	MURDER	FR.
RUPPS	266982	M			Feldgendarm, Feldgendarmerie, Sisteron (Fr.) 44			-	MISC.CRIMES	FR.
RUSCH	303908	M			Member, Gestapo, Warschau (Pol.) 39-45			57/963	INTERR.	POL.
RUSTIGE, Heinrich	303909	M	2.4.95		Camp-Guard, C.C. Lustbokel,39-45			57/965	MURDER	POL.
RUTCHEN	303050	M			Owner of a Garage at Breda (Neth.) 43-44			56/716	MURDER	NETH.
RUTGERS	309069	M			Civ.,Firm at Hagen, Haaren and Hooge Boekel (Neth.)			60/517	PILLAGE	NETH.
RUTZ, Walter	303910	M	16.2.14		SS-Rottfhr., C.C. Majdanek (Pol.) 40-44			57/967	MURDER	POL.
RUWOLT, Hermann	303051	M			Adjutant, Feldgendarmerie, Distr.of Dinan,Cotes-du-Nord (Fr.) 8. and 11.44			56/717	MURDER	FR.
RYBINSKI	303911	M			Member, Gestapo, Warschau (Pol.) 39-45			57/969	INTERR.	POL.
RYKALA, Franz	308530	M			Member, Gestapo, Krakau (Pol.) 11.39-2.45			59/570	BRUTALITY	POL.
SAAM	266199	M			Cpl., Africa-Corps,Rgt.Ruxleben,6.Coy.,1.Sect.,Hte.Marne-Aube (Fr.) 25.-31.8.44			-	MURDER	FR.
SABINSKI	309070	M			SS-Hptscharfhr., Administration, Radom (Pol.) 40-45			60/518	PILLAGE	POL.
SACEK	265967	M			Capt., Feldkommandantur, Brest (Fr.) 8.9.44			-	MURDER	FR.
SACHER, Gerhard	308531	M			Member, Gestapo, Krakau (Pol.) 11.39-2.45			59/571	BRUTALITY	POL.
SACK, Gerhard	264641	M	2.3.09		See names listed under "Special Headings"					
SADLER	267191	M			Officer, Org.Todt, Marseille (Fr.) 9.43			-	PILLAGE	FR.
SAEGER	267566	M			Lt., Unit No. 34828, Renesse (Neth.) 10.12.44			-	MURDER	NETH.
SALAW (or SALLAW)	309071	M			Feldpolizei-Kommissar, Antwerpen,Bruessel (Bel.) 40-44			60/519	MURDER	BEL.
SALECK	309072	M			SS-Oscharfhr. and driver, Radom (Pol.) 40-45			60/520	BRUTALITY	POL.
SALLAW (see SALAW)	309071									
SALZER, Franz	308532	M			Member, Gestapo, Krakau (Pol.) 11.39-2.45			59/572	BRUTALITY	POL.
SALZMANN	267282	M			See names listed under "Special Headings"					
SAMMELDIENER, Michel (or SAMMELDINGER,) (or SAMMENTINGER)	173287	M			Guard, SS Kapo of C.C. Natzweiler-Struthof (Fr.) 42-43			30/271	MURDER	FR.,U.K.
SAMMELDINGER, Michel (see SAMMELDIENER)	173287									
SAMMENTINGER, Michel (see SAMMELDIENER)	173287									
SANDER	267281	M			Osturmfhr., Gestapo, Bordeaux and vicinity (Fr.) 42-8.44			-	MURDER	FR.

SAN - SCHE

NAME	C.R.FILE NUMBER	SEX	DATE OF BIRTH	RANK OCCUPATION UNIT PLACE AND DATE OF CRIME	UNWCC LIST/ SERIAL NO.	REASON WANTED	WANTED BY
SANDER, Ernst	308533	M		Member, Gestapo, Krakau (Pol.) 11.39-2.45	59/573	BRUTALITY	POL.
SANDER, Willy	309073	M		Sgt.,Member,technicial troops forming part of the V.-weapon based at Hook van Holland,Wassenaar(Neth.)11.44	60/521	MURDER	NETH.
SANDLER	267042	M	ca. 00	Lt.,8 Paratrooper Regt.,Carhaix(Fr.) 10.6.44	-	SUSPECT	FR.
SANDROCK, Otto	267580	M		Cpl., G.F.P.Groups 3, 738 and 739, Charleroi, Mons, Namur, Tournai, Ath (Bel.) 40-44	-	BRUTALITY	BEL.
SAPOTOTZKY	303912	M		Member, Gestapo, Warschau (Pol.) 39-45	57/971	INTER.	POL.
SATURNUS, Erhard	308534	M		Member, Gestapo, Krakau (Pol.) 11.39-2.45	59/574	PILLAGE	POL.
SAUER	266662	M		Farmer, Civ., Moselle,Gueblange les Dieuze (Fr.) 41-44	--	PILLAGE	FR.
SAUER, Karl	303052	M		Cpl.,Feldgendarmerie Bruessel (Bel.) 40-44	56/721	MURDER	BEL.
SAUERBREY, Walter	308535	M		Member, Gestapo, Krakau (Pol.) 11.39-2.45	59/575	PILLAGE	POL.
SAUR, Otto	265573	M	22	Oscharfhr., 16 SS Pz.Div. Massa Carrara (It.) 8.44	-	MURDER	U.K.
SAVATSKY, Gustav	267196	M	05	Usturmfhr., Gestapo, Marseille and environ (Fr.)	-	MURDER	FR.
SAWCZYN, Anton	308536	M	30. 5.23	Member(SS-Guard),SS,Gestapo, Krakau (Pol.) 11.39-2.45	59/576	MURDER	POL.
SCHAAR (or SCHORR)	782	M		Cpl., Guard, POW Camp Stalag XXI (Ger.) 11.6.41	-	MURDER	U.K.
SCHABER	266829	M		Agent, Gestapo, Rouen and region (Fr.) 40-44	-	MURDER	FR.
SCHACK	267195	M		Chief of agricultural exploitation, Moncel sur Seille (Fr.) 5.43-8.44	-	MISC.CRIMES	FR.
SCHAD	265485	M		Kapo, C.C. Dachau (Ger.)	-	TORTURE	POL.
SCHADER, Erwin	265486	M		Official and Interpreter, Gestapo Sect.IV, Lodz (Pol.)	-	MISC.CRIMES	POL.
SCHAEFER (see SCHAEPER)	266825						
SCHAEFER	309074	M		Guard, Prison Wolfenbuettel (Ger.) 40-45	60/524	MISC.CRIMES	BEL.
SCHAEFER, Paul	304392	M	ca. 21	SS-Oscharfhr., SS-Wach-Bn.3, Amersfoort(Neth.) 4.-5.43	58/571	MURDER	NETH.
SCHAEFFER	265521	M		Principal, SS-Uscharfhr., Crematorium, C.C.Auschwitz(Pol.)	-	MURDER	POL.
SCHAEFFER, Walter	265487	M		SS-Oscharfhr.,Member of SS Staff, C.C.Auschwitz(Pol.)	-	MURDER	POL.
SCHAFER	267485	M		Member, Gestapo, Limoges and Vicinity(Fr.) 44	-	SUSPECT	FR.
SCHAFER	303053	M		Soldier, Kommando Sipo and SD at Rouen, Cherbourg and department of La Manche (Fr.) 42-44	56/724	MURDER	FR.
SCHAFER, Erich	308537	M		Member, Gestapo, Krakau (Pol.) 11.39-2.45	59/577	PILLAGE	POL.
SCHAFFRANIETZ, Egon	304393	M		Personalamtsltr.,Ortsgruppenltr.,NSDAP, Nowy-Bytom(Pol.)39-45	58/572	MURDER	POL.
SCHAFFSTEIN, Karl Friedrich	303054	M		Cpl., Geheime Feldpolizei Group 530, Bruessel (Bel.) 40-44	-	MURDER	BEL.
SCHAFNER, Hans	265525	M	23. 4.20	See names listed under "Special Headings"			
SCHAGULER, Florian	304394	M	3. 5.23	SS-Mann,Unit F.P.No.10443,Fouron St.Martin Liege(Bel.)9.44	58/574	INCENDIARISM	BEL.
SCHALKE, Johann (or SZALKE)	265524	M		SS-Scharfhr., Gestapo, Krakau (Pol.)	-	MISC.CRIMES	POL.
SCHALLMEYER, Luitpold	264642	M		See names listed under "Special Headings"			
SCHALLER, Herman	308538	M		Revier-Capt., Schupo, Krakau and Przemysl (Pol.) 43-45	59/578	MURDER	POL.
SCHALLUNG, Franz	265523	M	17. 9.10	O-Wachtmstr., C.C. Chelmno (Pol.)	-	MISC.CRIMES	POL.
SCHAMER (or SCHARMER)Wilhelm	267043	M	ca. 00	Driver, Gestapo, Blois & Mayes(Fr.) 43-44	-	MURDER	FR.
SCHANER	309075	M		Member, SS-Mann, Waffen-SS, Radom (Pol) 1.40-1.45	60/525	MURDER	POL.
SCHANNATH, Heinz	265386	M	3. 3.91	Local Officer, SS-Stubafhr. in Race and Settlement Problems in the Elbe District,SS, Dresden (Ger.)	-	MISC.CRIMES	U.S.
SCHAPENACY, Walter	267486	M		Sgt.Hospital Orderly Unit No.22256 LGPA,Paris, Auneau (Fr.) 14.5.43	-	MISC.CRIMES	FR.
SCHAPER, Hermann Gustav	304395	M		engineer,manager,Factory making torpedo parts, Plumenthal (Ger.) 40-45	58/575	MURDER	POL.
SCHARF, Paul	309076	M		Pvt., G.F.P. Antwerpen, Bruessel (Bel.) 40-44	60/526	MURDER	BEL.
SCHARMANN, Willy	265522	M		Official, SS-Rttscharfhr., Gestapo, Lodz (Pol.)	-	MURDER	POL.
SCHARMER (see SCHAMER)Wilhelm	267043						
SCHARPER (or SCHAEFER)	266825	M		Lt.,Unit stationed at Ecot (Doubs) Mathay-Ecot (Fr.) 9.44	-	MURDER	FR.
SCHARPWINKEL, Wilhelm Dr.	102742	M		Stubafhr.,O-Regierungsrat,Chief,Gestapo at Breslau, various places in Ger. 25.3.44-13.4.44	60/527	MURDER	U.K.
SCHARTZ	266811	M		Cpl., Div."B", Dordogne,Correze,Haute-Vienne (Fr.)	-	SUSPECT	FR.
SCHARZ (or SCHWARZ)	304396	M		Feldpolizei-Kommissar,Capt.,Member, Group 648 of G.F.P., Boulevard Piercot,Liege (Bel.) 40-44	58/576	TORTURE	BEL.
SCHATNER, Hermann	265526	M	2. 9.20	See names listed under "Special Headings"			
SCHATTI	308539	M		Wachtmstr., Member, Crim.-Pol.,Zawiercie (Pol.) 40-43	59/579	MURDER	POL.
SCHATZ	309913	M		Member, Gestapo, Warschau (Pol.) 39-45	57/974	RAPE	POL.
SCHAUB	265567	M		See names listed under "Special Headings"			
SCHAUBERGER, Simon	303914	M	27. 6.76	SS-Mann, C.C. Majdanek (Pol.) 40-44	57/975	BRUTALITY	POL.
SCHAUER	309915	M		Member, Gestapo, Warschau (Pol.) 39-45	57/976	RAPE	POL.
SCHAUH, Adolf	265488	M		Member, Gestapo, Kazimierz Dolny (Pol.)	-	MURDER	POL.
SCHAUMANN, Dr.	265489	M		Member of staff, C.C. Auschwitz (Pol.)	-	MURDER	POL.
SCHEEDE	303916	M		Member, Gestapo, Warschau (Pol.) 39-45	57/977	RAPE	POL.
SCHEEMANN, Alfred	308540	M		Member, Gestapo, Krakau (Pol.) 11.39-2.45	59/580	PILLAGE	POL.
SCHEERER	303917	M		Member, Gestapo, Warschau (Pol.) 39-45	57/978	RAPE	POL.
SCHEFEL, Hugo	265481	M		Member, Gestapo, Chelm (Pol.)	-	MURDER	POL.
SCHEFER	265482	M		Member, Gestapo, Borek, Chelm (Pol.)	-	MURDER	POL.
SCHEFFCZYK, Heinrich	303056	M		Employee, staff of Gestapo, Kattowitz (Pol.) 39-42	56/731	BRUTALITY	POL.
SCHEFFEL, Rudolf	266819	M	22.11.91	Physician, Unit-No.01047 Stab Pi.Bn.162,Soure(Fr.) 7.-8.44	-	PILLAGE	FR.
SCHEFFLER	303918	M		Member, Gestapo, Warschau (Pol.) 39-45	57/979	RAPE	POL.
SCHEIDT	265483	M		SS-Usturmfhr., Cmdt.,C.C.Plaszow,Szczebno (Pol.)	-	MURDER	POL.
SCHEINER	266200	M		Pvt.,Issy-les-Moulineaux (Fr.) 21.8.44	-	MURDER	FR.
SCHEINER, Karl	265234	M		Lt.,Inf.Regt.157, Vercors (Fr.) 40-45	-	MURDER	FR.
SCHEINERT	265484	M		SS-Oscharfhr., Sturmfhr., Gestapo,Sect.IV,Lodz,Kutno(Pol.)42-44	-	BRUTALITY	POL.
SCHEPEL	308541	M		Usturmfhr., Member,SD and Sipo, Radom (Pol.) 41-43	59/581	MURDER	POL.
SCHEI, Otto	266653	M		Sgt., Army Kdo.coming from Lyon (?), Saint Die (Fr.) 11.44	-	MURDER	FR.
SCHELLE, Walter	308542	M		Member, Gestapo, Krakau (Pol.) 11.39-2.45	59/582	BRUTALITY	POL.
SCHELLHORN, Kurt	266201	M	05	Oscharfhr., Gestapo, Nantes and region (Fr.) 43-44	-	MURDER	FR.
SCHELLING, Hans	265520	M	05	Official, Section "Supply", Lublin (Pol.)	-	MISC.CRIMES	POL.
SCHEMERINK	304399	M		Policeman, Jewer near Wilhelmshaven (Ger.) 44	-	MURDER	POL.
SCHENK, Ludwig	308543	M		Member, Gestapo, Krakau (Pol.) 11.39-2.45	59/583	BRUTALITY	POL.
SCHENKEL, Max	265478	M	8. 9.97	SS-Officer,C.C.Torun,Oranienburg (Pol.,Ger.)39-45	-	MURDER	POL.
SCLENKEMAYER	186221	M		Agent, Gestapo, Agen (Fr.) 41-45	-	SUSPECT	FR.

SCHE - SCHM

NAME	C.R.FILE NUMBER	SEX	DATE OF BIRTH	RANK OCCUPATION UNIT PLACE AND DATE OF CRIME	UNWCC LIST/ SERIAL NO.	REASON WANTED	WANTED BY
SCHERBEL, Dr.	303919	M		Member, Gestapo, Warschau (Pol.) 39-45	57/980	RAPE	POL.
SCHERINGER	308544	M		Usturmfhr., Head, of the SD. and Sipo. SS, at Sanok and Sub-District (Pol.) 41-43	59/584	MURDER	POL.
SCHERLACK	265479	M		SA-Osturmfhr., Camp Janow (Pol.)	-	MURDER	POL.
SCHERPE, Herbert	265480	M		Sanitary Assistant, SS Uschfhr., C.C. Auschwitz (Pol.)	-	MURDER	POL.
SCHERRER,	266202	M	circa 00	Lt., Feldgend., Manlay (Fr.) 29.-31.7.44	-	MISC.CRIMES	FR.
SCHERRER	266944	M	circa 09	Member, SD. L'isle s-Doubs Vichy, Clermont-Ferrand (Fr.) 2. 9. 44	-	MURDER	FR.
SCHERT	267487	M		Cpl., Feldgend. of Besancon, Bordeaux and vicinity (Fr.)44	-	MURDER	FR.
SCHEURINGER, Johann	308545	M		Member, Gestapo, Krakau (Pol.) 11.39-2.45	59/585	PILLAGE	POL.
SCHEWARTZ (see SCHWARTZ)	266596						
SCHICK, Franz	267332	M		Matrose, Navy, Senon (Fr.) 9.44	-	MURDER	FR.
SCHIEB, Simon	303920	M	26.12.19	SS-Mann, C.C. Majdanek (Pol.) 40-44	57/982	BRUTALITY	POL.
SCHIFFNER	265519	M		SS-Uschfhr., Warder, C.C. Treblinka (Pol.)	-	MURDER	POL.
SCHIHWERG, Arthur.	265518	M		Oberwachtmeister, Gend., Brzesko (Pol.)	-	MISC.CRIMES	POL.
SCHILD	308546	M		SS-Hptschfhr., Member, of the Jewish Departm. of the SD. and Sipo. Radom (Pol.) 41-43	59/586	MURDER	POL.
SCHILD, Otto	304400	M	23. 5.92	Gendarmeriewachtmeister, Duwehsee district Lauenburg (Ger.)42	58/583	MURDER	POL.
SCHILDING, Georg	308547	M		Member, Gestapo, Krakau (Pol.) 11.39-2.45	59/587	PILLAGE	POL.
SCHIIHAN, Josef	308548	M		Member, Gestapo, Krakau (Pol.) 11.39-2.45	59/588	PILLAGE	POL.
SCHILLER, Erich	265517	M		SS-Oschfhr., Gestapo, Krakau (Pol.)	-	MISC.CRIMES	POL.
SCHILLING	303921	M		Member, Gestapo, Warschau (Pol.) 39-45	57/986	RAPE	POL.
SCHILLINGER	265516	M		Member, Command C.C. Auschwitz,Brzezinka (Pol.)	-	MURDER	POL.
SCHILLINGS, M.	304401	M		Member,Schutzgruppen at "Laura Mine",Engelshoven (Neth.) 9.44	58/585	PILLAGE	NETH.
SCHIMMANN	303922	M		Member, Gestapo, Warschau (Pol.) 39-45	57/987	RAPE	POL.
SCHINDELHAUSER, Ewald	266594	M	00	Schfhr., SD. Auxerre, Region of Sens (Fr.) 6.44	-	MURDER	FR.
SCHINDLER, Friedrich	308550	M		Member, Gestapo, Krakau (Pol.) 11.39-2.45	59/591	PILLAGE	POL.
SCHINDOWSKI	303057	M		Member, Geh.Feldpol., Group 530, Bruessel (Bel.) 40-44	56/734	MURDER	BEL.
SCHINZ, Richard	308551	M		Member, Gestapo, Krakau (Pol.) 11.39-2.45	59/592	BRUTALITY	POL.
SCHIPPEL, Hans, Dr.	265617	M	22.10.80	See names listed under "Special Headings"			
SCHIPPERS	308552	M		Oschfhr., SS and Pol.Fuehrer, Radom (Pol.) 41-43	59/593	MURDER	POL.
SCHIPPLER, Wilhelm	308553	M		Oschfhr., Sipo.-School, Rabka (Pol.) 40-43	59/594	MURDER	POL.
SCHIRMER	265966	M		See names listed under "Special Headings"			
SCHIRMER, Adolf	264643	M		See names listed under "Special Headings"			
SCHIRMJAGER (see RAIMANN)	304366						
SCHITT, Paul	265539	M		SS-Hptschfhr., Extermination Camp; Sobibor (Pol.) 42-43	-	MURDER	POL.
SCHKOPEK (see SCHOPKA, Joseph)	266752						
SCHLAGER, Heinrich	265510	M	00	Secretary, Post-Office, Zamosc (Pol.)	-	BRUTALITY	POL.
SCHLAPP, Alfred	308554	M		Member, Gestapo, Krakau (Pol.) 11.39-2.45	59/596	PILLAGE	POL.
SCHLEIER, Paul	308555	M		Member, Gestapo, Krakau (Pol.) 11.39-2.45	59/597	PILLAGE	POL.
SCHLEIZNER, María	303059	F		Office-Employee, Staff of Gestapo, Kattowitz (Pol.) 39-42	56/736	PILLAGE	POL.
SCHLEIZNER, Max	303060	M		Krim.Assistent, Staff of Gestapo, Kattowitz (Pol.) 39-42	56/737	INTERR.	POL.
SCHLEMM	265939	M		SS-Osturmfhr., Ital.Freiw.Police Rgt. 2 Bn. 3 Coy. stationed at Ponte di Piave, near Treviso (It.) 2.45	-	SUSPECT	U.K.
SCHLENSAK, Paul	309078	M	28. 6.99	Uschfhr., Schutzgruppen, Brunssum (Neth.) 9.44	60/536	PILLAGE	NETH.
SCHLESSINGER	265509	M		Chief, Confidential agents and denunciators of the Gestapo Lublin (Pol.)	-	MISC.CRIMES	POL.
SCHLIESMANN	167238	M		Pvt., General Staff Kommandantur, Crest Drome La'Rochette (Fr.) 7.44-8.44	-	MURDER	FR.
SCHLINKER, Karl	303922	M	1. 4.06	SS-Mann, C.C. Majdanek (Pol.) 40-44	57/993	BRUTALITY	POL.
SCHLITTER, Max	266312	M	8. 7.11	See names listed under "Special Headings"			
SCHLOTTER, Albert	304402	M		Member, Gestapo at Chalons sur Marne, Dept. of Marne (Fr.)-44	-	MURDER	FR.
SCHLOTTERMULLER, Fritz	308556	M		Member, Gestapo, Krakau (Pol.) 11.39-2.45	59/598	PILLAGE	POL.
SCHLUDE, Hermann (or SCHLUTE)	197967	M	9. 3.96	Crim.Inspector, SS Osturmfhr., Strasbourg area (Fr.) 40-44	-	MURDER	U.K., FR
SCHLUNSS, Herbert	308557	M		Member, Gestapo, Krakau (Pol.) 11.39-2.45	59/599	PILLAGE	POL.
SCHLUTE, Hermann (see SCHLUDE)	197967						
SCHMACKPFEFFER	303924	M		Member, Gestapo, Warschau (Pol.) 39-45	57/995	BRUTALITY	POL.
SCHMALENBACH	303925	M		Member, Gestapo, Warschau (Pol.) 39-45	57/996	BRUTALITY	POL.
SCHMALT, Walter (or WALTER)	266816	M		Interpreter, SD, Brive, Correze (Fr.) 44	-	SUSPECT	FR.
SCHMEER, Hans	308558	M		Member, Gestapo, Krakau (Pol.) 11.39-2.45	59/600	PILLAGE	POL.
SCHMEIDE	309079	M		SS-Rottfhr., Krim.Employee, Radom (Pol.) 40-45	60/597	MURDER	POL.
SCHMERLER, Kurt	308559	M		Member, Gestapo, Krakau (Pol.) 11.39-2.45	59/601	PILLAGE	POL.
SCHMID, Max	304403	M		Doctor, near Marquise (Pas de Calais), (Fr.) 5.-6.44	58/587	MURDER	U.S.
SCHMIDHUBER	303926	M		Member, Gestapo, Warschau (Pol.) 39-45	57/1000	BRUTALITY	POL.
SCHMIDT	176330	M	circa 92	Capt., Bn. of "Georgian", NB. 799, Brive la Gaillarde (Fr.) 4.-6.44	38/267	MISC.CRIMES	FR.
SCHMIDT	265505	M		Vice sheriff, Brzesko (Pol.)	-	PILLAGE	POL.
SCHMIDT	265506	M		Member, Gestapo, Krasnik (Pol.)	-	MURDER	POL.
SCHMIDT	265547	M		Kapo, C.C. Auschwitz (Pol.)	-	MISC.CRIMES	POL.
SCHMIDT	265548	M		Member, Gendarmerie, Wlodawa (Pol.)	-	MURDER	POL.
SCHMIDT, Dr.	265549	M		Physician, SS Sturmbannfhr., C.C. Auschwitz (Pol.)	-	MURDER	POL.
SCHMIDT	266333	M		Lt., 34 Inf.Div. 107. Rgt. 1 Bn. 3 Coy., Breil (Fr.) 44	-	MURDER	FR.
SCHMIDT, Dr.	266334	M		See names listed under "Special Headings"			
SCHMIDT	267330	M		Hptsturmfhr., Gestapo, Marseille and vicinity (Fr.)	-	MURDER	FR.
SCHMIDT	267331	M	circa 95	Sgt.-Major, Navy, Le Trait (Fr.) 40-44	-	BRUTALITY	FR.
SCHMIDT	303062	M		Colonel, Lot et Garonne Gironde and Landes (Fr.) 3.-21.7.44	56/739	MURDER	FR.
SCHMIDT	303063	M		N.C.O., Kampfgruppe "Wilde" Lot et Garonne Gironde and Landes (Fr.) 3.-21.7.44	56/741	MURDER	FR.
SCHMIDT	303064	M	00	Lt., Department of Basses Pyrenees (Fr.) 8.44	56/741	MURDER	FR.
SCHMIDT (I)	303927	M		Member, Gestapo, Warschau (Pol.) 39-45	57/1001	BRUTALITY	POL.
SCHMIDT (II)	303928	M		Member, Gestapo, Warschau (Pol.) 39-45	57/1002	BRUTALITY	POL.

SCHM - SCHN

NAME	C.R.FILE NUMBER	SEX	DATE OF BIRTH	RANK	OCCUPATION	UNIT	PLACE AND DATE OF CRIME	UNWCC LIST/ SERIAL NO.	REASON WANTED	WANTED BY
SCHMIDT	308560	M			Inspector, Secr.Field-Police,HQ.G.F.P.Boulevard Piercot or the Avenue Rogier, Luettich (Bel.) 40-41			59/603	MURDER	BEL.
SCHMIDT	308561	M			Town Cmdt.,Deputy of Kreishauptmann,Dembica(Pol.)41-42			59/604	MURDER	POL.
SCHMIDT	308562	M			SS-Usturmfhr.,Cmdt.,Monte Lupi prison, Krakau (Pol.) 42			59/605	MURDER	POL.
SCHMIDT, Dr. (or SCHMIED)	308563	M			Town-Cmdt.,Krakau (Pol.) 40-41			59/606	MISC. CRIMES	POL.
SCHMIDT	309080	M			Feldpolizeikommissar,Antwerpen and Bruessel (Bel.)40-44			60/540	MURDER	BEL.
SCHMIDT	309081	M			Interpreter (?), Radom (Pol.) 40-45			60/541	MURDER	POL.
SCHMIDT called "ROEMER"	309082	M			SS-Sturmbannfhr., leader of the Aarhus Div.of terrorist group("Peter Group"), Aarhus (Den.) 7.44-24.10.44			60/542	MURDER	DEN.
SCHMIDT, A	303929	M	9. 7.97		SS-Oscharfhr., CC., Auschwitz (Pol.) 40-45			57/1003	MURDER	POL.
SCHMIDT, Adam	303930	M			Member, Gestapo, Warschau (Pol.) 39-45			57/1004	BRUTALITY	POL.
SCHMIDT, Alfred	265546	M			Secretary, Gestapo, Lodz (Pol.)			-	MISC.CRIMES	POL.
SCHMIDT, Alfred	267488	M			Chief Sgt.Major,Air-Force,71.Inf.Regt.5.Coy.2.Bn.Lds. Schtz.Regt.Air-Force Lisieux,Aude and Herault (Fr.)5.-8.44			-	MISC.CRIMES	FR.
SCHMIDT, Arthur	266943	M	7. 9.05		Rottfhr., Gestapo KDS IV S, Paris (Fr.) 43			-	SUSPECT	FR.
SCHMIDT, Benno	265324	M			Chief, Prison Monte-Lupich, Krakau (Pol.) 42			-	MURDER	POL.
SCHMIDT, Christian	265664	M			Lt.,Army, Paris (Fr.) 41-45			-	PILLAGE	FR.
SCHMIDT, Erwin	265507	M			Economic leader, SS-Hptscharfhr., C.C., Chelmno (Pol.)			-	MURDER	POL.
SCHMIDT, Erwin	265532	M			SS-Sturmscharfhr., Gestapo, Wielun-Lodz (Pol.)			-	MURDER	POL.
SCHMIDT, Franz	303931	M	27. 9.13		Guard,C.C., Majdanek (Pol.) 40-42			57/1006	BRUTALITY	POL.
SCHMIDT, Franz	308564	M			Member, Gestapo, Krakau (Pol.) 11.39- 2.45			59/607	PILLAGE	POL.
SCHMIDT, Friedrich, Dr.	266739	M	90		Commissary, Municipality, Parkocin (Pol.) 39			-	MISC.CRIMES	POL.
SCHMIDT, Georges	266336	M	circa 00		Sgt.,Feldgendarmerie 662 at Beaune,Manlay (Fr.)29.-31.7.44			-	MISC. CRIMES	FR.
SCHMIDT, Hans	265337	M			Gardener, Independent, Garmisch-Partenkirchen (Ger.) 5.41-4.45			-	BRUTALITY	POL.
SCHMIDT, Hans	265400	M			Driver, Bayonne and vicinity (Fr.) SD, 40-44			-	MURDER	FR.
SCHMIDT, Hans	265508	M			Extermination camp, Belzec (Pol.)			-	MURDER	POL.
SCHMIDT, Hans (Heinrich)	303067	M			SS-Uscharfhr.,Gestapo,Namestovo (Czech.)44 and 45			56/746	MISC.CRIMES	CZECH.
SCHMIDT, Hugo	267280	M			Uscharfhr., Gestapo, Bordeaux and vicinity (Fr.) 42-8.44			-	MURDER	FR.
SCHMIDT, Hugo	303068	M			Cpl.,Geh.Feldpol.Group 530, Bruessel (Bel.) 40-44			56/747	MURDER	BEL.
SCHMIDT, Johann	303069	M			Employee,Fischer, owner of Building enterprise,Mielec (Pol.) 42-44			56/748	MURDER	POL.
SCHMIDT, Karl	303932	M	28.12.04		SS-Mann, C.C., Majdanek (Pol.) 40-44			57/1007	BRUTALITY	POL.
SCHMIDT, Karl	308946	M			Member, Military Police, Czorkow nr.Lodz (pol.)39-42			60/545	MURDER	POL.
SCHMIDT, Kaspar	303933	M	21. 4.09		SS-Mann, C.C., Majdanek (Pol.) 40-44			57/1009	BRUTALITY	POL.
SCHMIDT, Kurt	303070	M			SS-Oscharfhr.,Staff of Gestapo, Kattowitz (Pol.) 39-42			56/749	MURDER	POL.
SCHMIDT, Oskar	308947	M	1. 6.01		Crim.secretary,Gestapo HQ at Kiel,various places (Ger. and Ger.occup.territory) between 25.3.44 and 13.4.44			60/546	MURDER	U.K.
SCHMIDT, Otto Karl	308948	M	7.11.08		Employee in the frontier and customs police at Kastrup, Denmark,Fire-station at Dragoer (Den.) 5.5.45			60/547	MURDER	DEN.
SCHMIDT, Philipp	303671	M			Employee, Factory, Mielec (Pol.) 41-44			56/750	MURDER	POL.
SCHMIDT, Rudolf	267583	M			Sgt.,G.F.P.|Groups 3, 738, 739, Charleroi,Mons,Namur, Tournai,Ath (Bel.)			-	BRUTALITY	BEL.
SCHMIDT, Wenzel	303934	M	2. 8.06		SS-Mann, C.C., Majdanek (Pol.) 40-44			57/1011	BRUTALITY	POL.
SCHMIDT, Wilhelm	304404	M			Cpl.,G.F.P., Bruessel (Bel.) 40-44			58/591	MURDER	BEL.
SCHMIDTCHEN, Hermann	308565	M			Member, Gestapo, Krakau (Pol.) 11.39- 2.45			59/610	PILLAGE	POL.
SCHMIED, Dr. (see SCHMIDT)	308563									
SCHMISCH, Arno	265534	M			SS-Sturmscharfhr., Gestapo, Krakau (Pol.)			-	MISC.CRIMES	POL.
SCHMIT, Armand	308949	M			Ger.prisoner,at Wolfenbuettel prison and at attached Commands, Wolfenbuettel (Ger.) between 42 and 45			60/549	MISC.CRIMES	BEL.
SCHMIT, Karl	265533	M			Owachtmstr.,Gendarmerie, Szczurowa (Pol.)			-	MISC.CRIMES	POL.
SCHMITT	266870	M			Member, SD, Pau (Fr.) 12.42-8.44			-	MISC.CRIMES	FR.
SCHMITT	267329	M	07		Lt.,Vienville (Fr.) 8.2.44			-	PILLAGE	FR.
SCHMITT	303072	M			Ex-Sgt.,Straflager, Siedenburg (Ger.)11.41- 7.42			56/751	MURDER	FR.
SCHMITT, Albert	266592	M			W.O., Feldgendarmerie 658,Paray le Monial and vicinity(Fr.)43-44			-	SUSPECT	FR.
SCHMITT, Arthur	265932	M			Capt.,Org.Todt Section Postal 40,260-II,Paris (Fr.)8.40-8.44			-	PILLAGE	FR.
SCHMITT,Hans-Joachim (see HOCHGRAEBE)	303253									
SCHMITT, Harry	303073	M			Member, Geh.Feldpolizei Group 530, Bruessel (Bel.) 40-44			56/752	MURDER	BEL.
SCHMITTS	266331	M			Lt.,Chief, SD of.Beauvais, Monceaux (Fr.) 8.8.44			-	MURDER	FR.
SCHMITZ	265491	M			Member, SS-Hptscharfhr., Gestapo, Sieradz (Pol.)			-	MISC.CRIMES	POL.
SCHMITZ	303074	M			SS-Hptscharfhr., Gestapo, Lodz (Pol.) 39-44			56/753	BRUTALITY	POL.
SCHMITZ, G.	304405	M			Member, Schutzgruppen at "Laura-mine", Eigelshoven(Neth.)9.44			58/594	PILLAGE	NETH.
SCHMITZ, Jakob	265492	M			Commissary, SS-Osturmfhr., Gestapo, Lodz (Pol.)			-	MISC.CRIMES	POL.
SCHMITZ, Paul	266712	M			Pvt., Army, Mont-sur-Marchienne nr.Charleroi (Bel.) 9.4.41			-	WITNESS	BEL.
SCHMOCK	266330	M	circa 00		Sgt., Feldgendarmerie 658,Paray le Monial and vicinity(Fr.)43-44			-	MISC.CRIMES	FR.
SCHMOELDER, Karl	265616	M	19.10.95		See names listed under "Special Headings"					
SCHMOLKE, Otto	303075	M			Office employee, Staff of Gestapo, Kattowitz (Pol.) 39-42			56/756	PILLAGE	POL.
SCHMOLL, Filip	303935	M	19. 4.21		SS-Mann, C.C., Majdanek (Pol.) 40-44			57/1012	BRUTALITY	POL.
SCHMUTZ, Karl	303936	M	16. 5.13		SS-Mann,Kriminal-Pol.Schreiber,C.C.,Majdanek (Pol.) 40-42			57/1013	PILLAGE	POL.
SCHNARTENDORF	303937	M			Member, Gestapo, Warschau (Pol.) 39-45			57/1014	BRUTALITY	POL.
SCHNEEMANN	308950	M			SS-Oscharfhr., Member of the SS,Radom (Pol.)1.40-1.45			60/551	TORTURE	POL.
SCHNEIDER	265527	M			SS-Usturmfhr., Gestapo, Lublin (Pol.)			-	BRUTALITY	POL.
SCHNEIDER	265550	M			Extermination camp, Belzec (Pol.)			-	MURDER	POL.
SCHNEIDER	265551	M			SS-Rottfhr., Block senior, C.C., Auschwitz (Pol.)			-	MURDER	POL.
SCHNEIDER	266020	M			Sen.W.O.,Sgt.Maj.,Feldgendarmerie, Quimperle (Fr.) 44			-	MURDER	FR.
SCHNEIDER	266332	M			Hptscharfhr.,Gestapo of Baccarat,Kdo.Wenger, Neufmaisons, Pexonne (Fr.) 9.44			-	MURDER	FR.
SCHNEIDER	266337	M			Pvt., Caen (Fr.) 6.44			-	MURDER	FR.
SCHNEIDER	303938	M			Member, Gestapo, Warschau (Pol.) 39-45			57/1015	PILLAGE	POL.
SCHNEIDER	304407	M			Cmdt.,Ordnungspolizei,Leeuwarden,Dronrijp (Neth.)4.45			58/597	MURDER	NETH.
SCHNEIDER (see SCHREIBER)	304417									
SCHNEIDER	308566	M			Official,German Labour Office,Radom (Pol.)41-43			59/611	MURDER	POL.
SCHNEIDER	308567	M			Wachtmstr.,Gendarmerie,Radom (Pol.) 40-43			59/612	MURDER	POL.
SCHNEIDER	308568	M			SS-Usturmfhr., SS, C.C. Birkenau (Pol.) 42-43			59/613	MURDER	POL.

SCHN-SCHR

NAME	C.R.FILE NUMBER	SEX	DATE OF BIRTH	RANK OCCUPATION UNIT PLACE AND DATE OF CRIME	UNWCC LIST/ SERIAL NO.	REASON WANTED	WANTED BY
SCHNEIDER	308951	M		Adjudant of the Commander,SS,SBF and Regierungsrat,Radom (Pol.) 1.40-1.45	60/552	MURDER	POL.
SCHNEIDER, Dr.	308958	M		Beauftragter d.Reichskommissars at Arnhem,Neth.,'s-Heerenberg (Neth.) 41-45	-	INTERR.	NETH.
SCHNEIDER,Alois	303939	M	19. 2.25	SS-Mann,C.C.Majdanek (Pol.) 40-44	57/1016	BRUTALITY	POL.
SCHNEIDER,August Adalbert	304408	M	2.11.10	Member,Welder,Eigelshoven Schutzgruppen,Coal mine "Adolf" on Netherlands-Limburg frontier,Eigelshoven (Neth.) 8.-13.9.44	58/598	PILLAGE	NETH.
SCHNEIDER,Berthold	303076	M		Office employee,Gestapo,Kattowitz (Pol.) 39-42	56/759	PILLAGE	POL.
SCHNEIDER,Erich	303077	M		Employee,Staff of Gestapo,Kattowitz (Pol.) 39-42	56/760	BRUTALITY	POL.
SCHNEIDER,Hermann	264644	M		See names listed under "Special Headings"			
SCHNEIDER,Johann	308952	M	20. 9.09	Driver,Gestapo,HQ at Munich,various places (Ger.) 25.3.-13.4.44	60/554	MURDER	U.K.
SCHNEIDER,Walter	265493	M	95	Member,Telegraph-Office,Post Office,Radom (Pol.)	-	BRUTALITY	POL.
SCHNEIDER,Willi	304410	M		Kapo,Labour Camps,Husum,Ladelund,Meppen,Dalum (Ger.) 40-45	58/600	MURDER	POL.
SCHNEIDER,Willy	308569	M		Member,Gestapo,Krakau (Pol.) 11.39-2.45	59/614	PILLAGE	POL.
SCHNEINERT	309078	M		SS-Oscharfhr.,Gestapo,Lodz, (Pol.) 39-44	56/761	BRUTALITY	POL.
SCHNELL	308570	M		Secretary,Secr.Field-Police,H.Q.G.F.P.Boulevard Piercot or the Avenue Rogier,Luettich (Bel.) 40-41	59/615	MURDER	BEL.
SCHNIDT,Otto	308571	M		Member,Gestapo,Krakau (Pol.) 11.39-2.45	59/617	PILLAGE	POL.
SCHNIJDER,Wilhelm	304411	M	circa 07	SS-Sturmscharfhr.,Member,SD-Aussenstelle Maastricht,Kripo Kleef,	58/601	MURDER	NETH.
SCHNITZ	265545	M		Manager of estate,Neple,Bohukaly (Pol.)	-	MISC.CRIMES	POL.
SCHNITZLER,Johann	308572	M		Member,Gestapo,Krakau (Pol.) 11.39-2.45	59/618	PILLAGE	POL.
SCHNITZLER,Josef	308953	M	circa 05	Crim.Secr.,Odense (Den.) 20.2.45 and 3.45	60/555	TORTURE	DEN.
SCHNOCK	304413	M		Sgt.,Feldgendarmerie at Paray-le-Monial and surroundings (Saone and Loire) (Fr.) 43-44	58/603	MURDER	FR.
SCHNORR,Wilhelm	267328	M	8. 4.14	Cpl.,Inf.Regt.487,Oignies and Courrieres (Fr.) 28.5.40	-	MURDER	FR.
SCHNUR	266644	M		Hptscharfhr.,Gestapo,St.Remy (Fr.) 30.9.44	-	MURDER	FR.
SCHNUR,Moritz	265544	M	01	SS-Usturmfr.,C.C.,SS magazines,Lublin-Majdanek (Pol.) 40-44	-	MURDER	POL.
SCHOCKL	303940	M		Member,Gestapo,Warschau (Pol.) 39-45	57/1022	PILLAGE	POL.
SCHOEDDER,Robert	308573	M		Member,Gestapo,Krakau (Pol.) 11.39-2.45	59/619	PILLAGE	POL.
SCHOEN,Michael	303941	M	6.12.14	SS-Mann,C.C.Auschwitz (Pol.) 40-45	57/1023	BRUTALITY	POL.
SCHOETBECK,Heinz	266753	M		Pol.-Wachtmeister,Schupo,Kulmhof (Pol.) 41-45	-	MURDER	POL.
SCHOENEMANN,Bruno	308954	M		Field-police-commissary,Field-Police,Antwerpen,Bruessel (Bel.) 40-44	60/556	MURDER	BEL.
SCHOENFELD	308955	M		Member,Waffen SS,Radom (Pol.) 1.40-1.45	60/557	TORTURE	POL.
SCHOENFELDER	308956	M		SS-Oscharfhr.,Verw.-Asst.,Radom (Pol.) 1.40-1.45	-	TORTURE	POL.
SCHOENHAUSEN,Albert	265323	M		Employee,Railway,Danzig-Prauss (Pol.) 39	-	MISC.CRIMES	POL.
SCHOERHOGGERN	265537	M		Chief,SS-Usturmfr.,Gestapo Section,Kalisz (Pol.)	-	MISC.CRIMES	POL.
SCHOENIG,Erich	303079	M	8. 9.00	Capt.,20 Corps Feldkommandantur,Poitiers (Fr.) 7.44	56/762	MURDER	U.K.
SCHOENNEMANN	308574	M		Commissioner,Secr.Field-Police,H.Q.G.F.P.Boulevard Piercot or the Avenue Rogier,Luettich (Bel.) 40-41	59/620	MURDER	BEL.
SCHOERNER	265536	M		Chief,SS-Obergruppenfhr.,Extermination Camp,Vernichtungskdo., Krakau,Plaszow (Pol.)	-	MURDER	POL.
SCHOLDEN (called "PLOUMS")	266335	M		Sgt.,3 Coy.,44 Section D.C.A.,Vern s/Seiche (Fr.) 14.7.44	-	MURDER	FR.
SCHOLTZ,Hermann	308575	M		Member,Gestapo,Krakau (Pol.) 11.39-2.45	59/621	BRUTALITY	POL.
SCHOLTZ,Walter	265385	M	29.10.99	Local Officer,SS-Standartenfhr.in Race and Settlement Problems in the South East District,Breslau (Ger.)	-	MISC.CRIMES	U.S.
SCHOLZ	265490	M		Member,Gendarmerie,Piaski (Pol.)	-	MURDER	POL.
SCHOLZ, Dr.	303080	M		Doctor of German Army,Benschop (Neth.) 44 or 45	56/764	MURDER	NETH.
SCHOLZ,Berthold	303081	M		Sgt.,Geh.Feldpolizei Group 530,Bruessel (Bel.) 40-44	56/765	MURDER	BEL.
SCHOMACKER,Otto	308577	M		Member,Gestapo,Krakau (Pol.) 11.39-2.45	59/623	BRUTALITY	POL.
SCHOMBURG,Wilhelm	308576	M		Member,Gestapo,Krakau (Pol.) 11.39-2.45	59/622	BRUTALITY	POL.
SCHOMBACH	265565	M		SS-Mann,SS Staff,Extermination Camp,Plaszow (Pol.)	-	MURDER	POL.
SCHOMBERGER,Anton	304088	M	1. 4.00	SS-Mann,C.C.Mauthausen (Aust.) 39-45	57/1025	BRUTALITY	BEL.
SCHONERBERG,Alfred	265577	M	22	Uscharfhr.,16 SS Pz.Div.,Massa Carrara (It.) 8.44	-	MURDER	U.K.
SCHONFELD,Ernst	303082	M		Hpt.Secr.,Gestapo-Staff,Kattowitz (Pol.) 39-42	56/768	PILLAGE	POL.
SCHONNAGEL,Albert	304415	M		Member,Terrorist unit of militarized railway-police,Pruszec (Pol.) 9.39	58/605	INTERR.	POL.
SCHONOGERN	303083	M		SS-Usturmfr.,Gestapo,Lodz (Pol.) 39-44	56/769	MURDER	POL.
SCHOPEK (see SCHOPKA,Joseph)	266752						
SCHOPKA,Joseph (or SCHOPEK or SCHKOPEK)	266752			Official,Electric railway,Krakau (Pol.) 39-45	-	MISC.CRIMES	POL.
SCHORN,Karl	267353	M	circa 15	Uscharfhr.,Gestapo,Marseille (Fr.)	-	MURDER	FR.
SCHORR (see SCHAAR)	782						
SCHOSSIG,Alfred	152114	M	10. 1.05	SS-Oscharfhr.,Gestapo,SD Einsatzkdo.z.b.V. 6,Gestapo Section IV A,Region D'Angers (Fr.) 42-44	27/872 45/528	MURDER	U.K.,FR.
SCHOTLER	304416	M		Chief of Section III of Gestapo,Bruessel (Bel.) 40-44	58/606	MURDER	BEL.
SCHOTT,Heinrich	308578	M		Member,Gestapo,Krakau (Pol.) 11.39-2.45	59/624	BRUTALITY	POL.
SCHOTT,Johan	266871	M		Member,Sipo,SD Perigueux Gestapo,Dordogne (Fr.) 43-44	-	SUSPECT	FR.
SCHOTT,Wilhelm	308957	M		Member,Army,Inf.-Unit,F.P.No.57727 B at L'lle a Bois,Larmor-Pleubian,Lighthouse at Creach-Maout (Fr.) 5.6.and 7.8.44	60/560	MURDER	FR.
SCHOTTSCHE	303942	M	23. 3.95	SS-Uscharfhr.,C.C.Auschwitz (Pol.) 40-45	57/1027	BRUTALITY	POL.
SCHRADER	266597	M		Lt.,Cmdt.,Inf.unit 42708,3 Coy.,205 Bn.,Biganos (Fr.) 20.1.44	-	MURDER	FR.
SCHRADER	266924	M		Sgt.,Flakmast 30/XII,Carcassonne (Fr.) 19.8.44	-	MURDER	FR.
SCHRADER	267327	M	circa 97	Feldkdt.,Feldkommandantur d'Auxerre,Licheres (Fr.) 28.7.44	-	MURDER	FR.
SCHRADER II	308959	M		Guard at prison and attached commands Wolfenbuettel (Ger.) 42-45	60/562	MISC.CRIMES	BEL.
SCHRADER,Gustav	308579	M		Member,Gestapo,Krakau (Pol.) 11.39-2.45	59/625	BRUTALITY	POL.
SCHRAMM	265535	M		Chief,Arbeitseinsatz,C.C.Dachau (Ger.)	-	MISC.CRIMES	POL.
SCHRAMM	303943	M		Member,Gestapo,Warschau (Pol.) 39-45	57/1029	PILLAGE	POL.
SCHRAMM,Hilde	308580	F		Member,Gestapo,Krakau (Pol.) 11.39-2.45	59/625	MURDER	POL.
SCHRAMM,Max	255570	M		See names listed under "Special Headings"			
SCHRAMM,Max	303084	M		Feldpol.Secr.,Geh.Feldpolizei Group 530,Bruessel (Bel.) 40-44	56/770	MURDER	BEL.
SCHRECKENSTEIN	303944	M		Member,Gestapo,Warschau (Pol.) 39-45	57/1031	PILLAGE	POL.

SCHR - SCHU

NAME	C.R.FILE NUMBER	SEX	DATE OF BIRTH	RANK OCCUPATION UNIT PLACE AND DATE OF CRIME	UNWCC LIST/ SERIAL NO.	REASON WANTED	WANTED BY
SCHREDER, Edwin	265531	M		SS-Rottfhr., C.C. Buchenwald, Dachau, Auschwitz, Lublin, Majdanek (Ger., Pol.) 40-45	-	MURDER	POL.
SCHREIBER (or SCHNEIDER)	304417	M		Pvt., G.F.P., Bruessel (Bel.) 40-44	-	MURDER	BEL.
SCHREIBER, Gustave	267514	M	circa 01	Chief Sgt.Major, Feldgendarmerie, Besancon and vicinity (Fr.) 44	-	MURDER	FR.
SCHREIBER, Helmuth	39896	M	25.3.17	Stubafhr., Coy.-Chief in the 3.Pz.Gren.Regt.SS "Deutschland", Div."Das Reich", F.P. No.34119 O.G., Marsoulas, Mazeres, Betchat, Justiniag (Fr.) 44	10/339	PILLAGE	FR.UNWCC.
SCHREIBER, Kurt	265965	M		Commander, Camp, Zwodau (Ger.) 44-45	-	MURDER	FR.
SCHREIBER, Rudolf	308581	M		Member, Gestapo, Krakau (Pol.) 11.39-2.45	59/626	MURDER	POL.
SCHRODER (called Wilhein)	303085	M		SS-Adjutant, SD and Sipo at St.Lo, Cherbourg and Dept. of La Manche (Fr.) 42-44	56/772	MURDER	FR.
SCHRODER, Dietrich	303086	M		Krim.Assist., Staff of Gestapo, Kattowitz (Pol.) 39-42	56/773	PILLAGE	POL.
SCHRODER, Erhard	308582	M		Member, Gestapo, Krakau (Pol.) 11.39-2.45	59/627	MURDER	POL.
SCHRODER, Hans	267326	M	97	Usturmfhr., Gestapo, Chief of Section IV A, Bordeaux and vicinity (Fr.) 42-8.44	-	MURDER	FR.
SCHRODER, Heinrich	267002	M	19.11.11	Uscharfhr., Gestapo BDS IV - E, Paris (Fr.) 43	-	SUSPECT	FR.
SCHRODER, Jakob	267525	M		Guard, SS, Camp Struthof-Natzweiler (Fr.) 41-45	-	MURDER	FR.
SCHRODER, Karl (or SCHROEDER)	265530	M		Member, SS-Unit, Szubin (Pol.) 39	-	MURDER	POL.
SCHRODER, Ludwig	308583	M		Member, Gestapo, Krakau (Pol.) 11.39-2.45	59/628	MURDER	POL.
SCHRODER, Walter	265495	M	14.8.21?	F.P. No. 57 727 B, Larmor-Pleubian (Fr.) 5., 6., 7.8.44	-	MURDER	FR.
SCHROEDER	308581	M		SS-Osturmfhr., Verwalt.Inspector, Radom (Pol.) 1.40-1.45	-	PILLAGE	POL.
SCHROEDER	308965	M		SS-Mann, Employee, Radom (Pol.) 1.40-1.45	60/566	PILLAGE	POL.
SCHROEDER, Else	308967	F		Wife of Farmer Heinrich Schroeder, Dakendorf (Ger.) 6.42	56/774	MISC.CRIMES	POL.
SCHROEDER, Fritz Hermann	308963	M		Crim.Assist., Szamotule nr.Posen (Pol.) 43-45	60/567	MISC.CRIMES	POL.
SCHROEDER, Heinrich	308966	M		Farmer, Dakendorf (Ger.) 6.42	56/775	MISC.CRIMES	POL.
SCHROEDER, Johann	308969	M		Pvt., Geh.Feldpolizei Group 530, Bruessel (Bel.) 40-44	56/776	MURDER	BEL.
SCHROEDER, Karl (see SCHRODER)	265530						
SCHROEDER, Wilhelm	308964	M		Pol.-Master, nr.Bremen (Ger.) on or about 28.5.44	60/568	BRUTALITY	U.S.
SCHROFF, Otto	308584	M		Member, Gestapo, Krakau (Pol.) 11.39-2.45	59/629	BRUTALITY	POL.
SCHROIFF, Werner	308965	M	20.1.90	Member, Surveyor, Schutzgruppe "Hendrik" State mine, Brunssum (Neth.) 9.44	60/569	PILLAGE	NETH.
SCHROLLER	308990	M		Member, Geh.Feldpolizei Group 530, Bruessel (Bel.) 40-44	56/779	MURDER	BEL.
SCHROTT	266627	M	circa 10	Cpl., Feldgendarmerie, Masleves, Coulanges and Blois (Fr.) 7.44 and 10.8.44	-	MURDER	FR.
SCHRUFF	304416	M		SS-Ufhr., Schutzgruppe at "Julia", State Coal Mine, Eigelshoven (Neth.) 8.-13.9.44	58/609	MISC.CRIMES	NETH.
SCHUBERT	266744	M		SS-Sturmfhr., Police Research-Office, Brzuchowice (Pol.) 39-45	-	PILLAGE	POL.
SCHUBERT	308945	M		Member, Gestapo, Warschau (Pol.) 39-45	57/1032	PILLAGE	POL.
SCHUBERT	308946	M		SS-Sturmfhr., Krakau (Pol.) 43	60/570	MISC.CRIMES	POL.
SCHUBERT (see SCHUGERT, Franz)	304419						
SCHUBERT, Kurt	265401	M	22.11.00	Member, SD, Gap, Hautes Alpes (Fr.) 43-44	-	SUSPECT	FR.
SCHUBERT, Kurt	267352	M	circa 10	Uscharfhr., Gestapo, Marseille (Fr.)	-	MURDER	FR.
SCHUBERTH, Hans	266338	M	91	Gen.Maj., Chief, Verbindungsstab of Digue (B.A.) Basses Alpes (Fr.) 44	-	MISC.CRIMES	FR.
SCHUCHOW (see SCHUKOFF, Ludwig)	266873						
SCHUETZ	266386	M		Physician, SS-Sturmbannfhr., C.C. Dachau (Ger.)	-	BRUTALITY	POL.
SCHUGERT, Franz (or SCHUBERT)	304419	M		Pvt., G.F.P., Bruessel (Bel.) 40-44	58/611	MURDER	BEL.
SCHUH, Franz	303091	M		Cpl., Geh.Feldpolizei, Group 530, Bruessel (Bel.) 40-44	56/781	MURDER	BEL.
SCHUHMACHER	265541	M		Gendarm, Gendarmerie, Teratin, Durienka (Pol.) 10.43	-	MURDER	POL.
SCHUHMACHER, Wilhelm	308585	M		Member, Gestapo, Krakau (Pol.) 11.39-2.45	59/631	BRUTALITY	POL.
SCHUMANN	308967	M		SS-Sturmscharfhr., Crim.secretary, Waffenwart, Radom (Pol.) 40-45	60/571	TORTURE	POL.
SCHUKOF, Ludwig (see SCHUKOFF)	266873						
SCHUKOFF (or SCHUKOF, Ludwig)	266873	M	6.10.96	Capt., Feldgendarmerie of Dijon, Lusigny (Fr.) 30.3.44	-	MURDER	FR.
SCHULE	265540	M		Member, Gestapo, Warschau (Pol.)	-	MISC.CRIMES	POL.
SCHULER, Gerhard	303947	M	9.12.20	SS-Rottfhr., C.C. Majdanek (Pol.) 40-44	57/1035	MURDER	POL.
SCHULL	267351	M		Agent, Gestapo, Marseille (Fr.)	-	MURDER	FR.
SCHULLER, Georg	303948	M	17.10.13	SS-Mann, C.C. Majdanek (Pol.) 40-44	57/1036	BRUTALITY	POL.
SCHULTE, Ewald	308586	M		Member, Gestapo, Krakau (Pol.) 11.39-2.45	59/632	BRUTALITY	POL.
SCHULTE, Wilhelm	308587	M		Member, Gestapo, Krakau (Pol.) 11.39-2.45	59/633	BRUTALITY	POL.
SCHULTE-OVERTRECH	303092	M		Lt.Col., Head of Administration, Dept. Basses-Pyrenees (Fr.) 8.6.- end of 8.44	56/782	MURDER	FR.
SCHULTZ	265568	M		Member SS, Lublin (Pol.) 42-43	-	MURDER	POL.
SCHULTZ	267494	M		Capt., Chief, Custom Post, Luchon and vicinity (Fr.) 1.43-7.44	-	MURDER	FR.
SCHULTZ, Alfred	308588	M		Member, Gestapo, Krakau (Pol.) 11.39-2.45	59/634	BRUTALITY	POL.
SCHULTZ, Anita	308589	F		Member, Gestapo, Krakau (Pol.) 11.39-2.45	59/635	MURDER	POL.
SCHULTZ, Bisbord?	267053	M		Agent, Gestapo, Arras (Fr.) 8.41	-	MURDER	FR.
SCHULTZ, Bruno Kurt, Prof.Dr.	264645	M		See names listed under "Special Headings"			
SCHULTZ, Colmuth	267350	M		Uscharfhr., Gestapo, Marseille and vicinity (Fr.)	-	MURDER	FR.
SCHULTZ, Edgar	308590	M		Member, Gestapo, Krakau (Pol.) 11.39-2.45	59/636	BRUTALITY	POL.
SCHULTZ, Hans	265542	M		Member, Selbstschutz, Lobrzenica nr.Wyrzysk (Pol.)	-	MURDER	POL.
SCHULTZ, Henri	266339	M		See names listed under "Special Headings"			
SCHULTZ, Johann	265543	M		Assessor, Post-Office, Lublin (Pol.)	-	MISC.CRIMES	POL.
SCHULTZ, Kurt	303093	M		Sgt. (Stabsfeldwebel), Feldgendarmerie, Angouleme (Fr.) 43-44, espec. 22.3.44	-	MURDER	FR.
SCHULTZE-LIPPERN	308968	M		General-Supervisor, "Hendrik" State mine, Brunssum (Neth.) 9.44	60/573	PILLAGE	NETH.
SCHULZ	265515	M		SS-Uscharfhr., Extermination Camp, Sobibor (Pol.) 42-43	-	MURDER	POL.
SCHULZ	266382	M		Commandant, Gendarmerie, Tyszowiec (Pol.) 42-43	-	MURDER	POL.
SCHULZ (or SZULC)	266420	M		Member, Gestapo, Lubartow, Stoczek (Pol.) 20.8.42	-	MURDER	POL.
SCHULZ	266552	M		Oberinsp., Unit No. L 38.440 - Airforce, Lesquin (Fr.) 1.9.44	-	SUSPECT	FR.
SCHULZ	267349	M	07	Oscharfhr., Gestapo, Marseille and vicinity (Fr.)	-	MURDER	FR.

SCHU-SCHW

NAME	C.R.FILE NUMBER	SEX	DATE OF BIRTH	RANK	OCCUPATION	UNIT	PLACE AND DATE OF CRIME	UNWCC LIST/ SERIAL NO.	REASON WANTED	WANTED BY
SCHULZ	303094	M			Member, Nachschub-Bn.623, Petit-Enghien (Bel.) 3.9.44			56/785	MURDER	BEL.
SCHULZ	308972	M			SS-Oschfhr., Driver, Radom (Pol.) 1.40-1.45			60/574	BRUTALITY	POL.
SCHULZ, Emil	308591	M			Member, Gestapo, Krakau (Pol.) 11.39-2.45			59/637	MURDER	POL.
SCHULZ, Erwin	265538	M			Member, Gestapo, SS-Uschfhr., Lodz (Pol.) 39-45				MISC.CRIMES	POL.
SCHULZ, Fritz, Dr.	264646	M	16. 6.01		See names listed under "Special Headings"					
SCHULZ, Fritz	267324	M	circa 10		Uschfhr., Gestapo, Bordeaux and vicinity (Fr.) 42-8.44			-	MURDER	FR.
SCHULZ, G.	303949	M			Member, Gestapo, Warschau (Pol.) 39-45			57/1038	PILLAGE	POL.
SCHULZ, Hans Heinrich	266959	M	23. 6.05		See names listed under "Special Headings"					
SCHULZ, Heinrich	264647	M	20. 7.93		See names listed under "Special Headings"					
SCHULZ, Herbert	303950	M			Member, Gestapo, Warschau (Pol.) 39-45			57/1040	BRUTALITY	POL.
SCHULZ, Hermann	266340	M			Sgt., Bn. Georgien, Coleyrac St.Cirq (Fr.) 14.-29.8.44			-	MURDER	FR.
SCHULZ, Karl	264599	M	· 7. 2.05		See names listed under "Special Headings"					
SCHULZ, Karl	265513	M			SS-Mann, C.C., Auschwitz (Pol.)			-	MURDER	POL.
SCHULZ, Oskar	308592	M			Member, Gestapo, Krakau (Pol.) 11.39-2.45			59/638	MURDER	POL.
SCHULZ, Otto	303951	M			Member, Gestapo, Warschau (Pol.) 39-45			57/1041	PILLAGE	POL.
SCHULZ, Werner	265512	M			Member, NSDAP, Debica (Pol.)			-	MURDER	POL.
SCHULZ, Wilhelm	308593	M			Member, Gestapo, Krakau (Pol.) 11.39-2.45			59/639	MURDER	POL.
SCHULZE	198031	M			Einsatzfhr.,SS-Oschfhr.,SS-Staff, C.C., Gusen (Aust.)			-	MURDER	POL.,BEL.
SCHULZE	265514	M			Prosecutor, Special Court SS, Nowogrodek (Pol.) 42			-	MURDER	POL.
SCHULZE	267348	M	08		Sturmschfhr., Gestapo, Marseille and environ (Fr.)			-	MURDER	FR.
SCHULZE	267495	M			Sgt.,36 Pz.Regt. S.P.58709-c, Revin (Fr.) 6.44			-	MURDER	FR.
SCHULZE, Dr.	303096	M			Staff of C.C., Breendonck (Bel.) 40-44			56/788	MURDER	BEL.
SCHULZE, Annem	303952	M			Member, Gestapo, Warschau (Pol.) 39-45			57/1042	BRUTALITY	POL.
SCHULZE, Frieda	303097	F			Woman Secretary, Gestapo, Lodz (Pol.) 39-44			56/789	MISC.CRIMES	POL.
SCHULZE, Fritz	309083	M			Policeman, Solingen (Ger.) 31.12.44			60/577	MURDER	U.K.
SCHULZE, Helmut	308594	M			Member, Gestapo, Krakau (Pol.) 11.39-2.45			59/640	RAPE	POL.
SCHULZE, Herbert	303099	M			Hpt.Sekr.,Gestapo-Staff, Kattowitz (Pol.) 39-42			56/791	PILLAGE	POL.
SCHULZE, M.	303953	M			Member, Gestapo, Warschau (Pol.) 39-45			57/1044	BRUTALITY	POL.
SCHULZE, Roland	264624	M	16.11.98		See names listed under "Special Headings"					
SCHULZE-KYOLING, Bernard	309084	M			Farmer, Distr.Hamm-Hessen (Ger.) 40-44			60/578	BRUTALITY	POL.
SCHULZER	265658	M			Inspector, Ruestungskommando Montbeliard or Belfort, Sochaux, Valentigney, Arbouans (Fr.) 41-45			-	PILLAGE	FR.
SCHUMACHER	266341	M			Cpl., Africa-Corps, Regt.Ruxleben, 6 Coy., 1 Section, Rte.Marne-Aube (Fr.) 25.-31.8.44			-	MURDER	FR.
SCHUMACHER	266385	M			Representative of Commandant,SS-Usturmfhr.,C.C.,Auschwitz (Pol.)			-	MURDER	POL.
SCHUMACHER	304421	M			Member, SD Aussenstelle at Maastricht, Limburg, Friesland (Neth.) 44-45			58/613	MURDER	NETH.
SCHUMACHER, Albert	267356	M			Uschfhr., Gestapo, Marseille (Fr.)			-	MURDER	FR.
SCHUMACHER, Emil	266384	M			SS-Osturmfhr., Extermination Camp, Sobibor (Pol.) 42-43			-	MURDER	POL.
SCHUMANN	265346	M			Capt., Army, 2 Bn., 369 Regt. "Teufels"-Div., Ljuti, Otok, Grabovac, District Sinj (Yugo.) 3. and 6.44			-	MISC.CRIMES	YUGO.
SCHUMANN	303954	M			Member, Gestapo, Warschau (Pol.) 39-45			57/1046	BRUTALITY	POL.
SCHUMERA, Max	303955	M	28. 4.90		SS-Uschfhr., C.C., Majdanek (Pol.) 40-44			57/1047	BRUTALITY	POL.
SCHUPETTA	267323	M	circa 15		Oschfhr., Gestapo, Bordeaux and vicinity (Fr.) 42-8.44			-	MURDER	FR.
SCHURZ, Johann	259428	M	28.12.13		SS-Hptsturmfhr., Chief of Political Bureau,C.C.,Auschwitz (Pol.) escaped from 6 C.I.C.Neuengamme on 7.12.46			45/539	MURDER	FR.,POL.
SCHUSTER	303101	M			Major, Commd of Nachschub-Bn.623, Petit-Enghien (Bel.) 3.9.44			56/794	MURDER	BEL.
SCHUSTER, Adolf	308595	M			Member, Gestapo, Krakau (Pol.) 11.39-2.45			59/641	RAPE	POL.
SCHUSTER, Franz	303102	M			Crim.Secretary, Staff of Gestapo, Kattowitz (Pol.) 39-42			56/795	BRUTALITY	POL.
SCHUSTER, Helmuth	142035	M	01		Hptsturmfhr.,SA, Chief, Organ.Todt, St.Helier, Channel-Islands, 8.42-4.44			-	TORTURE	U.K.
SCHWERNER (see SCHWERNER)	266342									
SCHWAB, Karol	266451	M			Member, Gestapo, Kazimierz Dolny (Pol.)			-	MURDER	POL.
SCHWABE	266450	M			Member, Gestapo, Wlodawa (Pol.) 41-43			-	MURDER	POL.
SCHWAES, Willi	266088	M			Bn.Cmdt., Army, Warschau (Pol.) 39			-	PILLAGE	POL.
SCHWALBE, Alexander	308596	M			Member, Gestapo, Krakau (Pol.) 11.39-2.45			59/642	RAPE	POL.
SCHWARTZ (or SCHWARTZ)	266596	M			Pvt.,Inf.unit: 42708, 205 Bn., 3 Coy., Biganos (Fr.) 20.1.44			-	MURDER	FR.
SCHWARTZ	266860	M			Sgt., Section Ia, Feldkommandantur 641 of Blois, Seillac (Fr.) 22.6.44			-	MISC.CRIMES	FR.
SCHWARTZ	267321	M			Schutzpolizei, Blamont (Fr.) 9.44			-	MURDER	FR.
SCHWARTZ, Anton	266874	M	16. 6.08		Shepherd, Civilian, Brieulles sur Meuse (Fr.) 40-43			-	BRUTALITY	FR.
SCHWARTZ, Kurt	308597	M			Member, Gestapo, Krakau (Pol.) 11.39-2.45			59/643	RAPE	POL.
SCHWARTZMEIER, Frany	266593	M			Oschfhr., SD Rennes,retreated to Meurthe, Moselle, Pettonville (Fr.) 6.10.44			-	MISC.CRIMES	FR.
SCHWARZ	266452	M			SS-Oschfhr., Gestapo, Lodz (Pol.) 39-44			56/799	MISC.CRIMES	POL.
SCHWARZ	266468	M			SS-Schfhr., Extermination Camp, Sobibor (Pol.) 42-43			-	MURDER	POL.
SCHWARZ	266469	M			SS-Uschfhr., Warder, Extermination Camp, Treblinka (Pol.) 42-43			-	BRUTALITY	POL.
SCHWARZ	303967	M			Member, Gestapo, Warschau (Pol.) 39-45			57/1050	BRUTALITY	POL.
SCHWARZ (see SCHARZ)	304396									
SCHWARZ, Albin	266449	M			Lagerfuehrer, Commandant, Penal Camp, Dretz near Neuruppin (Ger.)			-	BRUTALITY	POL.
SCHWARZ, Filipp	303957	M	20.10.09		SS-Mann, C.C., Majdanek (Pol.) 40-44			57/1052	BRUTALITY	POL.
SCHWARZ, Jakob	303956	M	22. 7.22		SS-Mann, C.C., Plaszow (Pol.) 39-45			57/1051	BRUTALITY	POL.
SCHWARZ, Johann	266470	M			Cmdt. substitute, Death Camp, Belzec (Pol.)			-	MURDER	POL.
SCHWARZ, Rudolf	309085	M			Civ., in charge of a stud.farm Lublin Distr.,Sarny (Pol.) 15.5.41-15.10.43			60/581	BRUTALITY	POL.
SCHWARZ, Wilhelm	128906	M	9. 1.98		Kriminal-Sekretaer, IV Ic of Gestapo H.Q., Lodz, Posen, Rzew, Koeln (Pol., Ger.) 40-45			-	MURDER	POL.
SCHWARZBACH	265963	M			Uschfhr., Div."Das Reich", Region de Rouen (Fr.) 8.44			-	MURDER	FR.
SCHWARZE	303958	M			Member, Gestapo, Warschau (Pol.)			57/1055	BRUTALITY	POL.
SCHWARZE, Erich	266471	M			SS-Hptsturmfhr.,C.C.,Sachsenhausen,Oranienburg (Ger.)			-	BRUTALITY	POL.
SCHWARZER	264409	M			SS-Oschfhr., C.C., Dachau (Ger.)			-	BRUTALITY	POL.
SCHWARZLOH, Karl	303104	M			Member, Geh.Feldpol. Group 530, Bruessel (Bel.) 40-44			56/801	MURDER	BEL.

SCHW - SIM

NAME	C.R.FILE NUMBER	SEX	DATE OF BIRTH	RANK OCCUPATION UNIT PLACE AND DATE OF CRIME	UNWCC LIST/ SERIAL NO.	REASON WANTED	WANTED BY
SCHWARZWALD	303959	M		Member, Gestapo, Warschau (Pol.) 39-45	57/1056	BRUTALITY	POL.
SCHWEBEL	267457	M		Member, Gestapo, Limoges and vicinity (Fr.) 44	-	SUSPECT	FR.
SCHWEEN	303960	M		Member, Gestapo, Warschau (Pol.) 39-45	57/1058	BRUTALITY	POL.
SCHWEERS, Heinz	304422	M	28. 8.11	SS-Uscharfhr., Gestapo, Hendaye, Basses Pyrenees (Fr.) 43-44	58/616	MURDER	FR.
SCHWEIGER, Josef	257810	M	10	Sturmscharfhr., Gestapo, escaped on 1.7.47 from W.C.Reutlingen, Chaumont (Fr.) 23.9.43	-	MISC.CRIMES	FR.
SCHWEINBACH	267367	M		Lt., 704 Ldschtz.Bn., Camp Ruchard near Tours (Fr.) 42	-	SUSPECT	FR.
SCHWEINITZER	57747	M		Hptsturmfhr., Gestapo, Koenigstein a.d.Elbe (Ger.) 19.1.45	-	MURDER	FR.
SCHWEINPACKER	266407	M		SS-Oscharfhr., C.C. Lublin-Majdanek (Pol.)	-	BRUTALITY	POL.
SCHWEINSBERG	267366	M		Agent, Gestapo, Marseille and vicinity (Fr.)	-	MURDER	FR.
SCHWEISS, Erich	304423	M	3.10.94	SS-Hptsturmfhr., Gestapo, Liberec (Czech.) 44-45	58/618	MURDER	CZECH.
SCHWEITZER, Franz	303105	M		Sgt., Feldgendarmerie at Angouleme, Chasseneuil, Charente (Fr.) 43-44, 22.3.44	56/802	MURDER	FR.
SCHWEIZER	266408	M		SS-Officer, C.C. Auschwitz (Pol.)	-	MURDER	POL.
SCHWEIZER	303961	M		Member, Gestapo, Warschau (Pol.) 39-45	57/1059	RAPE	POL
SCHWELA (see SCHWELLA), Dr.	4688						
SCHWELLA, Dr. (or SCHWELA)	4688	M		SS-Hptsturmfhr., C.C., Chief, Medical Service, Auschwitz (Pol.) 42-45	-	MURDER	POL.,YUGO.
SCHWENK, Karl	303106	M		Stabsfeldwebel, Feldgendarmerie at Angouleme, Chasseneuil (Fr.) 43-44, 22.3.44	56/803	MURDER	FR.
SCHWERNER (or SCHVERNER)	266342	M		Chief-Cpl., H.V.Stelle Laon 609, Collecting Center Soissons Administration-Coy.609, S.P.26300 N, Soissons (Fr.) 28.8.44	-	INCENDIARISM	FR.
SCHWESTER ANNI	266487	F		Chief, C.C., drug-store, hospital block No.6, Ravensbrueck (Ger.)	-	MISC.CRIMES	POL
SCHWITZKI, Hans	266343	M	circa 07	Uscharfhr., driver, Gestapo, Nantes and region (Fr.) 43-44	-	MURDER	FR.
SCIAK, Marian	308598	M		Member, Gestapo, Krakau (Pol.) 11.39-2.45	59/644	RAPE	POL.
SCTORASS (or STORASS)	266520	M		Guard, Buchloe Fort, Buchloe (Ger.)	-	MISC.CRIMES	FR.
SEBATS	267383	M		Sgt.-Major, 350 Regt. "Hindou", Department Indre (Fr.) 8.44	-	MURDER	FR.
SEEBRECHT, Rodolph	266944	M	circa 92	Lt., Chief, C.C., Merignac (Fr.) 43-44	-	BRUTALITY	FR.
SEEFELDT, Willy	308599	M		Member, Gestapo, Krakau (Pol.) 11.39-2.45	59/645	RAPE	POL
SEER, Rudolf	303962	M	3. 1.11	SS-Rottenfhr., C.C. Majdanek (Pol.) 40-44	57/1061	MURDER	POL.
SEGGER, Karl, Otto	304424	M	4. 9.05	Member, Verwaltungsinspektor, Ordnungspolizei, BDS at Den Haag, Zeist, Oldenzaal (Neth.) 44-45	58/620	PILLAGE	NETH.
SEIB	309086	M		Instructor, employee, G.F.P., Antwerpen, Bruessel (Bel.) 40-44	60/583	MURDER	BEL.
SEIBERT, Karl, Valentin	303963	M	12. 6.08	Oscharfhr., SS, Bde. "Dirlewanger", Warschau (Pol.) 40-44	57/1064	MURDER	POL.
SEIDEL	304425	M		Pvt., Custom, Harlingen, Dongjum, Friesland (Neth.) 8.3.45	58/621	MURDER	NETH.
SEIDEL, Hans, Otto	304426	M		Bezirks-Lt. of Gendarmerie, near Kemel (Ger.) 10.2.45	58/622	MURDER	U.S.
SEIDEL, Karl	303137	M		Crim.asst., Staff of Gestapo, Kattowitz (Pol.) 39-42	56/806	PILLAGE	POL
SEIDELMANN	267381	M		Interpreter, Gestapo, Bordeaux and vicinity (Fr.) 42-8.44	-	MURDER	FR.
SEIDER	265443	M	87	W.O., SD, Gestapo, Bayonne and vicinity (Fr.) 40-44	58/623	MURDER	FR.
SEIFRITZ	267055	M		Lt., 350 Regt. "Hindou", Lureuyl, Linge, St.Michelen Brenne, Vendosuvres, St.Maur, Ambrault, Ardentes, Neuillay-les-Blois (Fr.) 8.44	-	MURDER	FR.
SEIKLER (see SIGLER)	126812						
SEIRAUCH, Helmut	267365	M		Oscharfhr., Gestapo, Marseille and vicinity (Fr.)	-	MURDER	FR.
SEITZ, Erich	303138	M		Crim.asst., Gestapo-Staff, Kattowitz (Pol.) 39-42	56/807	BRUTALITY	POL
SELENT, Siegmunt	308600	M		Member, Gestapo, Krakau (Pol.) 11.39-2.45	59/647	BRUTALITY	POL.
SELIGER	267456	M		Member, Gestapo, Luchon and vicinity (Fr.) 1.43, 7.44	-	MURDER	FR.
SEMBAC	267458	M		Member, Gestapo, Limoges and vicinity (Fr.) 44	-	SUSPECT	FR.
SENGUPTA, Gustave	266553	M		Chief of Culture, Montigny les Vaucouleurs (Fr.) 6.8.44	-	BRUTALITY	FR.
SENNER, Hans	267364	M		Osturmfhr., Gestapo, Marseille and vicinity (Fr.)	-	MURDER	FR.
SERTEL, Richard	303964	M	20. 4.00	SS-Mann, C.C. Majdanek (Pol.) 40-44	57/1068	BRUTALITY	POL.
SESSELKAMPF, Bernard (or KESSELKAMPF)	267459	M	circa 95	Lt., Feldgendarmerie 509 of Auxerre, Toucy (Fr.) 9.44	-	MURDER	FR.
SETTING, Walter	303140	M		Krim.Beamter, Staff of Gestapo, Kattowitz (Pol.) 39-42	56/809	MURDER	POL.
SEUFERT	266923	M		Chief-Cpl., Flakmast 30-XII, Carcassonne (Fr.) 19.8.44	-	MURDER	FR.
SEYFRIED, Karl	308601	M		Member, Gestapo, Krakau (Pol.) 11.39-2.45	59/648	BRUTALITY	POL.
SHANT	265218	M	circa 06	General, 114 Inf.Div., Gubbio (It.) 22.6.44	-	SUSPECT	U.K.
SHIMENDA	266345	M		N.C.O., Unit No.12988 A, Lamotte-Bauvron (Fr.) 23.-24.8.44	-	WITNESS	FR.
SHOENBECK, Heinz	303142	M		Pol.Wachtmeister, Sonderkdo., Kulmhof (Pol.) 41-45	56/811	MURDER	POL
SICHELSCHMIDT, Hans Dr.	264649	M	13. 9.11	See names listed under "Special Headings"			
SIDORUK, Jan	303965	M	28. 4.16	Teacher, Civilian, Warschau, Krakau (Pol.) 39-45	57/1071	INTERR.	POL.
SIEBACH	303143	M		Oberfeldwebel, Feldgendarmerie at Angouleme, Chasseneuil, Charente (Fr.) 43-44, 22.3.44	56/812	MURDER	FR.
SIEBENEICHLER, Alfred	309088	M		Interpreter, Gestapo, Radom, Konskie (Pol.) 43-45	60/586	MURDER	POL.
SIEBERT	265437	M		SS-Hptscharfhr., chief, Gestapo, Registers, BDS IV, Paris (Fr.) 41-44	-	SUSPECT	FR.
SIEBERT, Klaus Dr.	264650	M	25. 1.04	See names listed under "Special Headings"			
SIEBMAN, Erich	267056	M		See names listed under "Special Headings"			
SIEDEL	303144	M		Lt., Feldgendarmerie, Les Ayvelles, Ardennen (Fr.) 26.6.44	56/813	MURDER	FR.
SIEFERT	39785	M		Capt., German Army, Leitungszahl L 54146, Cerisot, St.Emiland (Fr.) 4.8.44-12.8.44	-	MURDER	FR., UNWCC
SIEG	309145	M		Capt., Cmdt., German and Polish Unit, Luijksgestel (Neth.)8.9.44	56/814	MURDER	NETH.
SIEGEL	309089	M		Cpl., Secr. Field Police, Antwerpen, Bruessel (Bel.) 40-44	60/587	MURDER	BEL
SIEGERT	266554	M	circa 10	Ob.Lt., Feldgendarmerie 658, Paray le Monial and vicinity (Fr.) 43-44	-	MISC.CRIMES	FR.
SIEMSZEN	303146	M		Member, Geh. Feldpolizei, Group 530, Bruessel (Bel.) 40-44	56/815	MURDER	BEL
SIESKOWSKI	309090	M		Secretary, Secr.Field Police, Antwerpen, Bruessel (Bel.) 40-44	60/588	MURDER	BEL
SIEVERS (see SIEWERS)	129885						
SIEWERS (or SIEVERS)	129885	M	circa 09	SS-Usturmfhr., Crim.secretary, Gestapo, Lodz (Pol.)	-	INTERR.	POL.
SIEWERS, Johann	303147	M		SS-Hptscharfhr., Gestapo, Lodz (Pol.) 39-44	56/816	BRUTALITY	POL.
SIGLER (or SEIKLER)	126812	M	circa 10	Member, SD, Gestapo, Chalons sur Marne (Fr.) 43-44	-	SUSPECT	FR.
SIKUCZYNSKI	303966	M		Member, Gestapo, Warschau (Pol.) 39-45	57/1072	INTERR.	POL.
SIMECK, Rudolf	267461	M	circa 00	Chief Sgt.-Major, Feldgendarmerie, Besancon and vicinity (Fr.) 44	-	MURDER	FR.
SIMMS, Heinz	304428	M	3.10.09	SS-Oscharfhr., Gestapo, Liberec (Czech.) 44-45	58/629	MURDER	CZECH.
SIMOLEIT (or SIMULEIT)	309091	M		Secretary, Secr.Field Police, Antwerpen, Bruessel (Bel.) 40-44	60/589	MURDER	BEL
SIMON, Franz	265341	M	circa 15	SS-Uscharfhr., SS, agent, Gestapo, Belgrad (Yugo.) 28.4.42	-	MURDER	YUGO.

NAME	C.R.FILE NUMBER	SEX	DATE OF BIRTH	RANK OCCUPATION UNIT PLACE AND DATE OF CRIME	UNWCC LIST/ SERIAL NO.	REASON WANTED	WANTED BY
SIMON, Herbert	303148	M		Member,Selbstschutz, SA and NSDAP,Kolonia Ostrowicka (Pol.) 9.39- 40	56/817	BRUTALITY	POL.
SIMONS,	304429	M		Member,Schutzgruppen,"Laura-mine",Eigelshoven (Neth.) 9.44	58/691	PILLAGE	NETH.
SIMOTENKO, Johann	308602	M		Member,Gestapo,Krakau (Pol.) 11.39- 2.45	59/650	BRUTALITY	POL.
SIMULEIT (see SIMOLEIT)	309091						
SINGER	309092	M		Cpl.,Secr.Field-police,Antwerpen,Bruessel (Bel.) 40-44	60/591	MURDER	BEL.
SJAMKEN	197863	M		SS-Rottfhr.,C.C. Mauthausen,Gusen (Aust.)	-	MURDER	POL.,BEL.
SKIBBE	303968	M		Member,Gestapo,Warschau (Pol.) 39-45	57/1076	INTERR.	POL.
SKOCKENBERGER	267460	M		Member,Gestapo,Limoges and vicinity (Fr.) 44	-	SUSPECT	FR.
SKOCZOWSKI, Anna	308603	F		Member,Gestapo,Krakau (Pol.) 11.39- 2.45	59/652	MURDER	POL.
SKOWRANEK, Franz	309093	M	17. 9.99	Member,Schutzgruppen,Brunssum (Neth.) 9.44	60/593	PILLAGE	NETH.
SKRETOWICZ, Zenon	308604	M		Member,Gestapo,Krakau (Pol.) 11.39- 2.45	59/653	MURDER	POL.
SKRZEPINSKI, Leon	308605	M		Member,Gestapo,Krakau (Pol.) 11.39- 2.45	59/654	MURDER	POL.
SLLEIBACH	304431	M		Member,Schutzgruppen,"Laura-mine",Eigelshoven (Neth.)8.-13.9.44	58/633	PILLAGE	NETH.
SMOTER	303969	M		Member,Gestapo, Warschau (Pol.) 39-45	57/1080	PILLAGE	POL.
SOBERLITHS, Paul	266564	M		Chief,Sgt.,Major,Feldgendarmerie Unit No.658,Paray le Monial and environ (Fr.) 43-44	-	SUSPECT	FR.
SOBISCH	303970	M		Member,Gestapo,Warschau (Pol.) 39-45	57/1081	PILLAGE	POL.
SOBOTA, Frenz	308606	M		Member,Gestapo,Krakau (Pol.) 11.39- 2.45	59/655	MURDER	POL.
SOBOTKA, Hildegard	308607	F		Member,Gestapo,Krakau (Pol.) 11.39- 2.45	59/656	MURDER	POL.
SODER, Bartholomae	265964	M		Hptscharfhr.,SD,Chalons s.Marne (Fr.) 43-44	-	MISC.CRIMES	FR.
SOECK (or BOECK)	309094	M		Hptsturmfhr.,Crim.-Director,in charge of the Crim.Invest.Dep. Radom (Pol.) 1.40- 1.45	60/594	MURDER	POL.
SOELDER, Albert	265298	M		Member,Regt."Brandenburg",(It.)	-	SUSPECT	U.K.
SOENNICHSEN, Guenther	261175	M	11. 5.13	Fieldpolice-Secretary,G.F.P.Group 619 and 738,was detained in British custody - escaped on 11.4.47 (Bel.)	-	SUSPECT	BEL.
SOFFING	303150	M		Gefr.,Feldgend.at Angouleme,Chasseneuill (Charents)(Fr.) 43-44 (22. 3.44)	56/820	MURDER	FR.
SOHN, Hans	267041	M		Uscharfhr.,Gestapo Beziers,Hereult (Fr.) 43-44	-	SUSPECT	FR.
SOLEN, Hans	303971	M		SS-Guard,C.C. Auschwitz (Pol.) 40-45	57/1083	BRUTALITY	POL.
SOLLICH	309095	M		Crim.-employee,Interpreter ?, Radom (Pol.) 1.40- 1.45	60/595	MURDER	POL.
SOLMS, Arkadius	303151	M		Krim.Sekr.,Staff of Gestapo,Kattowitz (Pol.) 39-42	56/822	BRUTALITY	POL.
SOLTAU, Johann	303152	M		Hpt.Krim.Sekr.,Staff of Gestapo,Kattowitz (Pol.) 39-42	56/823	INTERR.	POL.
SOMMER	304432	M		Lt.,Arta,Epiros u.Western (Grc.) 43	58/696	MURDER	GRC.
SOMMER	267384	F	97	Secretary,Gestapo,Bordeaux and vicinity (Fr.) 42- 8.44	-	MURDER	FR.
SOMMER, Hermann	267057	M		Employee,Elektro- und Radio-Grosshandlung,Paris (Fr.) 12.-19.8.44	-	PILLAGE	FR.
SOMMER, Kurt	265439	M	10. 3.00	SS-Oscharfhr.,Member,Gestapo,KDS IV E 2,Paris (Fr.) 43-44	-	SUSPECT	FR.
SOMMER, Willy	308608	M		Member,Gestapo,Krakau (Pol.) 11.39- 2.45	59/658	MURDER	POL.
SONNEFELD	303972	M		Member,Gestapo,Warschau (Pol.) 39-45	57/1085	PILLAGE	POL.
SONNHOF	303973	M		Member,Gestapo,Warschau (Pol.) 39-45	57/1086	PILLAGE	POL.
SONNTAG	265511	M	circa 10	Employee,Post Office,Zamosc (Pol.)	-	MURDER	POL.
SONNTAG, Kurt	308609	M		Member,Secr.Field-police,H.Q.G.F.P. Boulevard Piercot or the Avenue Rogier,Luettich (Bel.) 40-41	59/659	MURDER	BEL.
SOPTA, Josef	303153	M		Pol.Asst.,Staff of Gestapo,Kattowitz (Pol.) 39-42	56/824	INTERR.	POL.
SORDA	267363	M		Oscharfhr.,Gestapo of Baccarat,Pexonne (Fr.) 27. 8.44	-	MISC.CRIMES	FR.
SORGE, Herbert	265501	M	22. 1.20	Official,Police,Chelmno (Pol.)	-	MISC.CRIMES	POL.
SOSNER	265500	M		Member,Gestapo,Krasny Staw (Pol.)	-	MURDER	POL.
SOTECK, Bernhard	265442	M		Member,Sturmscharfhr.,Gestapo,SS:KDS IV A 3,Paris (Fr.) 43-44	-	SUSPECT	FR.
SOUWARL, Paul	267016	M		Agent,Gestapo,Arras (Fr.) 8.41	-	MURDER	FR.
SOWALD (see ZOWALT)	267082						
SOWONJA, Josef	303974	M	20. 1.22	SS-Mann,C.C. Majdanek (Pol.) 40-44	57/1088	PILLAGE	POL.
SOYKA, Charles	267447	M		Lt.,Feldgend,Besancon and vicinity (Fr.) 44	-	MURDER	FR.
SPAETER, Kurt	308611	M		Secretary,Custom-official,Zwartsluis (Neth.) 8.10.44	59/661	MURDER	NETH.
SPANIER, Wilhelm	308610	M		Member,Gestapo,Krakau (Pol.) 11.39- 2.45	59/660	MURDER	POL.
SPECHT, Heinrich	266346	M	7.10.05	Sgt.,163.Gren.Res.Bn.,Clermont Ferrand (Fr.) 13.11.43	-	MURDER	FR.
SPECHT, Oskar	265322	M	17. 1.90	Mechanic,Railway,Ostrow (Pol.) 41-45	-	MURDER	POL.
SPECK, Erich	303154	M		Feldwebel,Geh.Field-police,Group 530,Bruessel (Bel.) 40-44	56/825	MURDER	BEL.
SPEER	266236	M	circa 95	Lt.,Feldgend., Dole (Fr.) 44	-	MISC.CRIMES	FR.
SPEETZEN	309096	M		SS-Sturmscharfhr.,Crim.-secretary,Radom (Pol.) 1.40- 1.45	60/597	BRUTALITY	POL.
SPERLING	308612	M		Member,Secr.Field-police,H.Q.G.F.P. Boulevard Piercot or the Avenue Rogier, Luettich (Bel.) 40-41	59/662	MURDER	BEL.
SPIEGEL, Helene	308613	F		Member,Gestapo,Krakau (Pol.) 11.39- 2.45	59/663	MURDER	POL.
SPIEHS	303975	M		Member,Gestapo,Warschau (Pol.) 39-45	57/1089	MURDER	POL.
SPIELHAGEN, Adolf	309097	M		Works inspector,prison,Hagen and the attached Commands (Ger.) Between 42-45	60/598	MISC.CRIMES	BEL.
SPIENMAN	265502			Gendarme,Gendarmerie,Brzesko (Pol.)	-	BRUTALITY	POL.
SPIES, Heinrich	308614	M		Member,Gestapo,Krakau (Pol.) 11.39- 2.45	59/664	MURDER	POL.
SPIESS, Mathias	266861	M		Chief-Cpl.,Army,Groslezac,Carsac,Peyrillac,Calviac,Carlux (Fr.) 8. 6.44	-	MISC.CRIMES	FR.
SPINGLER	266618			See names listed under "Special Headings"			
SPIROCH	267382	M	circa 00	Sturmscharfhr.,Gestapo,Bordeaux and vicinity (Fr.) 42-8.44	-	MURDER	FR.
SPITZ	266862	M	circa 10	Lt.,Feldgend.,Chaussin,Saint-Didier (Fr.) 25. 4.44	-	MISC.CRIMES	FR.
SPOEHER	309098	M		SS-Sturmscharfhr.,Crim.-Secretary,Radom (Pol.) 1.40- 1.45	60/599	TORTURE	POL.
SPROSS	265503	M		SS-Oberscharfhr.,Asst.,Gestapo,Lodz (Pol.)	-	MURDER	POL.
SRADNICK, Max	308615	M		Member,Gestapo,Krakau (Pol.) 11.39- 2.45	59/666	MURDER	POL.
STABENOW	303976	M		Member,Gestapo,Warschau (Pol.) 39-45	57/1095	BRUTALITY	POL.
STABSFELD-PATELONG	266402	M		Member,Criminal-police,Debica (Pol.)	-	MISC.CRIMES	POL.
STACHE, Paul	303977	M		SS-Uscharfhr.,C.C. Majdanek (Pol.) 40-44	57/1096	BRUTALITY	POL.
STADLER, Fritz	267121	M		Sgt.,Deputy Chief,Gestapo,Sinj (Yugo.) 8.9.43- 10.44	-	MURDER	YUGO.
STAEDELE, called Bado	266572	M		Guard,Treasurer,Camp Buchloe; NSDAP of Buchloe	-	BRUTALITY	FR.
STAENDER	309099	M		Member,Selbstschutz,Grudziadz (Pol.) 39	60/600	MURDER	POL.
STAERKER	265441	M		SS-Uscharfhr.,Member,Gestapo,KDS IV A 2,Paris (Fr.) 7.44	-	SUSPECT	FR.
STAEVES, Max	308616	M		Member,Gestapo,Krakau (Pol.) 11.39- 2.45	59/667	MURDER	POL.

STA - STE

NAME	C.R.FILE NUMBER	SEX	DATE OF BIRTH	RANK OCCUPATION UNIT PLACE AND DATE OF CRIME	UNWCC LIST/ SERIAL NO.	REASON WANTED	WANTED BY
STAFANI	266394	M		Member, Staff, C.C. Lublin-Majdanek (Pol.)	-	BRUTALITY	POL.
STAGINUS	309100	M		SS-Oscharfhr., Crim.-Employee, Radom (Pol.) 1.40-1.45	60/601	TORTURE	POL.
STAHL, Wilhelm (or STAHR)	265444	M	4. 6.15	Member, Crim.-Asst., Usturmfhr., Gestapo, SS Kds.IV E 4 Paris (Fr.) 44	-	SUSPECT	FR.
STAHR, Wilhelm (see STAHL)	265444						
STAHR, Wilhelm	267396	M	27. 3.01	Usturmfhr., Gestapo, F.D.S.II E 4, Paris and environ (Fr.)44	-	SUSPECT	FR.
STAL	266403	M		Member, Gend., Dubinsko (Pol.) 42-44	-	MURDER	POL.
STALINSKI	303157	M		SS-Usturmfhr., Gestapo, Lodz(Pol.) 39-44	56/830	MURDER	POL.
STALP, Heinz	266404	M		Kapo, C.C. Lublin-Majdanek (Pol.)	-	BRUTALITY	POL.
STALTER	266573	M		Civ.occupier, Gueblange les Dieuze (Fr.) 41-44	-	PILLAGE	FR.
STAMM	303978	M		Member, Gestapo, Warschau (Pol.) 39-45	57/1099	PILLAGE	POL.
STANDERMEIER, Otto	266405	M		Gendarm, Gend., Tomaszow Lubelski (Pol.) 40-44	-	MURDER	POL.
STANGEL	266406	F		Overseer, SS-Frau, Stockchamber, C.C. (Pol.)	-	BRUTALITY	POL.
STANGL, Heinrich	309979	M	22. 6.06	SS-Mann, C.C. Majdanek (Pol.) 40-44	57/1100	BRUTALITY	POL.
STANKENWITZ	265960	M		Oberkriegsgerichtsrat, Garnison, Brest (Fr.) 8.9.44	-	MURDER	FR.
STANKEVICIUS, Stasys	303980	M		SS-Mann, C.C. Majdanek (Pol.) 40-42	57/1101	BRUTALITY	POL.
STANKO, Mari	308617	F		Member, Gestapo, Krakau (Pol.) 11.39-2.45	59/668	MURDER	POL.
STANZIG Johann	266395	M		SS-Osturmfhr., Gestapo, Lublin (Pol.) 40-44	-	BRUTALITY	POL.
STAPEL, Erich	308618	M		Member, Polit.Ltr., SA, NSDAP, Osiek (Pol.) 39-44	59/669	MISC.CRIMES	POL.
STARCH	267017	M		Lt., 350 Regt. Hindou, Lureuil, Linge, St.Michel, Brenne, Vendoeuvrés, St.Maur, Ambrault, Ardentes and Neuillay-les Blois, Indre (Fr.) 8.44	-	MURDER	FR.
STASCH, N.	266396	M		Hptwachtmstr., Gend., Brzesko (Pol.)	-	MISC.CRIMES	POL.
STASSKIWITCH, Stefenia (STRASSKEWITZCH)	265440	F		Employee, Gestapo, KDS IV-E, Paris (Fr.) 43-44	-	SUSPECT	FR.
STATSENENGER	265529	M		Guard, SS-Uscharfhr., C.C. Mauthausen (Aust.)	-	MURDER	POL.
STAUB, Georg	303981	M	9. 5.24	SS-Sturmmann, C.C. Auschwitz (Pol.) 40-45	57/1104	BRUTALITY	POL.
STAUDINGER, Wilhelm	264651	M	4.12.02	See names listed under "Special Headings"			
STAWITZKI, Willi	139704	M	96	Chief, Cmdt., SS-Stubafhr., Gestapo, Sanok, Lwow (Pol.) 39-44	-	MURDER	POL.
STAWSKI	303982	M		Member, Gestapo, Warschau (Pol.) 39-45	57/1106	PILLAGE	POL.
STEBANOW (see STEBNOW), Dr.	266397						
STEBEL, Vincent	303158	M		Employee, staff of Gestapo, Kattowitz (Pol.) 39-42	56/831	INTERR.	POL.
STEBNOW, Dr.(or STEBANOW)	266397	M		Leader, Ghetto, Gestapo, Warschau (Pol.)	-	MURDER	POL.
STECAY, Johann	303983	M	15. 6.25	SS-Guard, C.C.Auschwitz (Pol.) 40-45	57/1107	BRUTALITY	POL.
STECHER	266260	M		Lt., Air Force Staff 91, Saint Christophe en Bezelle (Fr.) 11.-14.6.44	-	MURDER	FR.
STEENKEN	303160	M		SS-Scharfhr., Guard at Oldenburg Gaol (Ger.) 43-45	56/833	MURDER	POL.
STEFAINSKI, Karl	308619	M		Member, Gestapo, Krakau (Pol.) 11.39-2.45	59/670	MURDER	POL.
STEFFENS	266261	M		Pvt., Africa-Corps, Regt.Ruxleben, 6 Coy., 1 Sect., Hte.Marne-Aube (Fr.) 25.-31.8.44	-	MURDER	FR.
STEGEMANN	266398	M		Member, Gestapo, "Nursing Home for Children", Przemysl(Pol.)	-	MURDER	POL.
STEGEMANN, Walter	308620	M		Member, Gestapo, Krakau (Pol.) 11.39-2.45	-	MURDER	POL.
STEGER, Alfred	303161	M		Employee, staff of Gestapo, Kattowitz (Pol.) 39-42	56/834	BRUTALITY	POL.
STEDMULLER, Mathias	303984	M	13. 2.06	Orderly, C.C. Majdanek (Pol.) 40-42	57/1108	BRUTALITY	POL.
STEHR	303985	M		Gestapo, Warschau (Pol.) 39-45	57/1109	MURDER	POL.
STEIDLE	266262	M		Pvt., Africa-Corps, Unit 57502 B, Hte.Marne-Aube (Fr.)25.-31.8.44	-	MURDER	FR.
STEIGER	309106	M		Crim.-Employee, Interpreter, Radom (Pol.) 1.40-1.45	-	BRUTALITY	POL.
STEIGLER	267385	M		Capt., 2 Paratrooper Div., Brest and vicinity (Fr.) 7.-8.44	-	MURDER	FR.
STEIRMANN	266922	M		SS-Uscharfhr., 18 SS Pz.Gren.Div. "Horst Wessel", Oradour sur Glane (Fr.) 10.6.44	-	MURDER	FR.
STEIN	265366	M		Lt., Police Bn., Ladorudz New Kolo (Pol.) 23.12.39	-	MURDER	POL.
STEIN	304433	M		Member, Gestapo at Chalons sur Marne (Fr.) 43-44	58/640	MURDER	FR.
STEIN, Hans Dr.	266399	M		Physician, C.C. Auschwitz (Pol.)	-	BRUTALITY	POL.
STEIN, Herbert	304434	M	26. 3.12	Sgt., Div.Brehmer, Dordogne Correze Haute-Vienne (Fr.) 44	58/641	MURDER	FR.
STEINBACH	267018	M		Sgt., 148 Art.Regt., 1 Btty, Chalautre la Petite (Fr.) 27.8.44	-	MURDER	FR.
STEINBAUER, Josef	266400	M	23. 3.20	Official, Police, Chelmno (Pol.)	-	MISC.CRIMES	POL.
STEINBECK	265556	M	97	Stand.-Fhr., 16 SS Pz.Div., Massa Carrara (It.) 8.44	-	MURDER	U.K.
STEINBERG, Karl Erich Fritz	266491	M	24. 8.11	Amtskommissar, Radkowo (Pol.) 39-43	-	MURDER	POL.
STEINBRINCK	304435	M		Capt., German Res. "Beauftragte d.Reiches f.d.Kohlen in den besetzten u.angegliederten Westgebieten", Eigelshoven (Neth.) 8.-13.9.44	58/643	PILLAGE	NETH.
STEINER	266492	M		SS-Scharfhr., C.C. Janow (Pol.)	-	MURDER	POL.
STEINER	303986	M		Member, Gestapo, Warschau (Pol.) 39-45	57/1111	PILLAGE	POL.
STEINER	309102	M		Employee, Radom (Pol.) 1.40-1.45	60/604	PILLAGE	POL.
STEINER, Erich	266745	M		Member, Chief, NSDAP, Industrial-Section at the Municipality, Krakau (Pol.) 39-45	-	MISC.CRIMES	POL.
STEINER, Georg	308621	M		Member, Gestapo, Krakau (Pol.) 11.39-2.45	59/672	TORTURE	POL.
STEINERT	309103	M		Pvt., Army, 1 Coy., 1, 2 Schwaben-Bn., near Billingsbach (Ger.) 17.4.45	60/606	MURDER	U.S.
STEINGRIST (see STELGRIMM, Heinrich)	266527						
STEINHAUER, Kurt	266087	M		Marine-Bekleidungsamt, Gdynia (Pol.) 40-45	-	BRUTALITY	POL.
STEINHAUSER, Joseph	266851	M	2. 1.00	See names listed "Special Headings"			
STEINKAMP, Hermann Julius	266528	M	2. 3.23	See names listed "Special Headings"			
STEINKE	303213	M		SS-Oscharfhr., Gestapo, Lodz (Pol.) 39-44	56/840	BRUTALITY	POL.
STEINMANN	303987	M		Gestapo, Warschau (Pol.) 39-45	57/1115	PILLAGE	POL.
STEINMETZ	303988	M		Member, Gestapo, Warschau (Pol.) 39-45	57/1116	PILLAGE	POL.
STEINMEYER, Willy	308622	M		Gestapo, Krakau (Pol.) 11.39-2.45	59/673	TORTURE	POL.
STEINSEIFER	266824	M	ca. 96	Chief Sgt.Major, Ld.Schtz.No.772, 2 Coy., Marles les Mines (Fr.) 25.8.44	-	MURDER	FR.
STELGRIMM, Heinrich (or STELGRINN or STEINGRIST)	266527	M	ca. 05	Sgt., Kdo.coming from Lyon, Saint Die (Fr.) 11.44	-	MURDER	FR.
STELGRINN (see STELGRIMM, Heinrich)	266527						

NAME	C.R.FILE NUMBER	SEX	DATE OF BIRTH	RANK	OCCUPATION	UNIT	PLACE AND DATE OF CRIME	UNWCC LIST/ SERIAL NO.	REASON WANTED	WANTED BY
STELMACHOW, Leo Dr.	308623	M			Member,Gestapo,Krakau (Pol.) 11.39- 2.45			59/674	TORTURE	POL.
STELZER, Joseph	266921	M			Chief-Cpl.,Unit No.36 753 A,St.Livrade,Cazeneuve Casseneuil,Fougeres (Fr.) 28. 8.44			-	PILLAGE	FR.
STELZLE, Walter	308624	M			Member,Gestapo,Krakau (Pol.) 11.39- 2.45			59/675	MURDER	POL.
STENGL, Rosa	308625	F			Member,Gestapo,Krakau (Pol.) 11.39- 2.45			59/676	MURDER	POL.
STENGLIN	266488	M			SS-Uscharfhr., Extermination Camp,Sobibor (Pol.) 42-43			-	MURDER	POL.
STENZEL, Paul	266490	M			SS-Oscharfhr.,Gestapo,Krosno (Pol.) 40-44			-	MURDER	POL.
STENZEL, Paul	308626	M			Member,Gestapo,Krakau (Pol.) 11.39- 2.45			59/677	MURDER	POL.
STEPHAN	265450	M			Member,Gestapo,BDS.IV,Paris (Fr.) 42			-	SUSPECT	FR.
STEPHAN	266263	M			Usturmfhr.,SS-Div."Das Reich",2.Art.Btty.,1.Sect.,Selles sur Cher (Fr.) 14.,15.8.47			-	MURDER	FR.
STEPHAN	266353	M			Chief Cpl.,Africa-Corps,Regt.Ruxleben,6.Coy.,1.Sect.,Hte.Marne Aube (Fr.) 25.-31.8.44			-	MURDER	FR.
STEPHAN (or STEPHEN)	266423	M			Lt.,Cmdt.,Garrison,Wawer (Pol.) 12.39			-	MURDER	POL.
STEPHAN, Ernst	265451	M			Member,Uscharfhr.,Gestapo,KDS IV C,Paris (Fr.) 43-44			-	SUSPECT	FR.
STEPHAN	267020	M	circa 95		High Officer ranking,Parachute troops 9.Regt.,Carhaix (Fr.) 6.44			-	SUSPECT	FR.
STEPHANSKY	303214	M			Feldpol.Direktor,Geh.Feldpol.Group 530,Bruessel (Bel.) 40-44			56/841	MURDER	BEL.
STEPHEN (see STEPHAN)	266423									
STERGRISCH, Mathias	265961	M			Chief-Cpl.,Army,Feche-l'Eglise (Fr.) 1.10.44			-	MISC.CRIMES	FR.
STERK	303989	M			Member,Gestapo,Warschau (Pol.) 39-45			57/1122	MURDER	POL.
STERN	265959	M			Osturmfhr., SD,Chalons s.Marne (Fr.) 43-44			-	MISC.CRIMES	FR.
STERN	303990	M			Member,Gestapo,Warschau (Pol.) 39-45			57/1123	MURDER	POL.
STERN, Josef	304436	M			Pvt.,Ludenhausen (Ger.) 11. 7.44			58/647	MURDER	U.S.
STERN, Karl	304437	M			Civilian, nr.Ludenhausen (Ger.) 11. 7.44			58/648	MURDER	U.S.
STERN, Samuel	266489	M			Medical-man,C.C.,Block 28,Auschwitz (Pol.)			-	MURDER	POL.
STERNER, Heinrich	303991	M	20. 2.12		SS-Mann,C.C. Majdanek (Pol.) 40-44			57/1124	TORTURE	POL.
STERNFELD nee MULLER	267360	F			Gestapo,Marseille (Fr.) 43-44			-	MURDER	FR.
STERNFELD, Hans (or FISCHER)	267361	M			Gestapo,Marseille and environ (Fr.) 43-44			-	MURDER	FR.
STEUDLE, Alwin or Albin	265452	M	7. 2.13		Member,Hptscharfhr.,Gestapo,KDS IV E 3,Paris (Fr.) 43-44			-	SUSPECT	FR.
STEUER, Walter	303992	M	1. 6.08		Kapo,C.C. Bunzlau (Ger.) 39-45			57/1125	MURDER	POL.
STIBNER	266472	M			Chief,Gestapo,Chrubieszow (Pol.) 42-44			-	MURDER	POL.
STICH	266453	M			Manager,SS-Obersturmfhr., Magazin, C.C., Sobibor (Pol.) 42-43			-	MURDER	POL.
STIEF	309104	M			Oscharfhr.,Crim.Asst.,Radom (Pol.) 1.40- 1.45			60/609	RAPE	POL.
STIEFEL (or STIFEL)	266454	M			SS-Unterscharfhr., Extermination Camp,Sobibor (Pol.) 42-43			-	MURDER	POL.
STIELBAUER (or STILBAUER)	266354	M	circa 00		Capt.,Army, Plancher-Bas (Fr.) 1.9.-10.11.44			-	PILLAGE	FR.
STIER, Karl	266455	M			Interpreter,Clerk,Rottenfhr.,Gestapo,SS,Lodz (Pol.) 39-45			-	BRUTALITY	POL.
STIEWE	267021	M			Lt.,19.Pol.Regt., 3.Bn.,9.Coy., Limoges, Brive and environ (Fr.) 9. 7.44-25. 7.44			-	MURDER	FR.
STIFEL (see STIEFEL)	266454									
STILBAUER (see STIELBAUER), Fritz	266354									
STILLER	266456	M			SS-Oberscharfhr.,Bauleitung C.C. Auschwitz (Pol.)			-	BRUTALITY	POL.
STILLER	304438	M			SS-Hauptsturmfhr.,Cmdt.,SD,Vledder near Steenwijk (Neth.) 15. 9.1944			58/652	MURDER	NETH.
STIMPF	267380	M			Chief Physician, 2.Div. Paratrooper, Brest and vicinity (Fr.) 7.44 - 8.44			-	MURDER	FR.
STINGLE, Hans	266457	M			Prisoner (room-senior), C.C. Dachau (Ger.) 40			-	BRUTALITY	POL.
STIMER	266526	M			Sturmbannfhr.,SA,Bad Kreuznach,Sierk les.Bains (Fr.) 9.9.44			-	MURDER	FR.
STOCKE, Edmund	308627	M			Member,Gestapo,Krakau (Pol.) 11.39- 2.45			59/678	BRUTALITY	POL.
STOFFEL	265528	M			Member,Gestapo,Chelm (Pol.) 43-45			-	MISC.CRIMES	POL.
STOJBEL, Karl	266458	M			SS-Scharfhr., Extermination Camp,Sobibor (Pol.) 42-43			-	MURDER	POL.
STOLBA	266355	M			Lt.,Army,Ecuisses (Fr.) 7. 3.44			-	MISC.CRIMES	FR.
STOLL	303993	M			Member,Gestapo,Warschau (Pol.) 39-45			57/1127	MURDER	POL.
STOLTENBERG	303215	M			SS-Usturmfhr.,Gestapo,Lodz (Pol.) 39-44			56/844	BRUTALITY	POL.
STOLZ	267022	M			Agent,Gestapo,Arras (Fr.) 8.41			-	MURDER	FR.
STOLZ, Fritz	303217	M			Krim.Rat,Staff of Gestapo,Kattowitz (Pol.) 39-42			56/846	INTERR.	POL.
STOLZ, Johann	303994	M	14.12.21		SS-Mann,C.C. Majdanek (Pol.) 40-44			57/1129	BRUTALITY	POL.
STOLZMANN, Karl	266401	M	22. 9.97		See names listed under "Special Headings"					
STOPSACK	303218	M			Uffz.,Geh.Feldpolizei,Group 530,Bruessel (Bel.) 40-44			56/848	MURDER	BEL.
STORASS (see SCTORASS)	266520									
STORCH	303995	M			SS-Guard,C.C. Auschwitz (Pol.) 40-45			57/1130	MURDER	POL.
STORCH, Wilfried	304439	M			Cadet officer,Unit L.18.009 (Airforce),Marignane Bouches du Rhone (Fr.) 16. 8.44			58/653	MURDER	FR.
STOSCH, Otto	266993	M			Cmdt., Oberwachtmeister,Gend.,Szczurowa,Brzesko (Pol.)			-	MISC.CRIMES	POL.
STOSCH, Paul	266392	M			Meister der Schupo, Schutzpolizei, Brzesko (Pol.)			-	MISC.CRIMES	POL.
STOSZ	267023	M			Korvettenkapitaen,Lt.,Commander,Navy,Marseille (Fr.)			-	MURDER	FR.
STOUCHT (or STUCHT)	267024	M			Capt.,unit stationed at Jussey,Bateaucourt (Fr.) 10. 9.44			-	MURDER	FR.
STRACH	304440	M			Member of Schutzgruppen at: "Laura-mine", Eigelshoven (Neth.) 8.-13. 9.44			58/654	PILLAGE	NETH.
STRASSKEWITZCH, Stefenia (see STASSKIWITCH)	265440									
STRAUB (see STRAUP)	304441	M								
STRAUBE	265446	M			Capt.,8.Coy., 2.Bn., 36.Mot.Gren.Regt., 90.Pz.Gren.Div., Briancon (Fr.) 29. 8.44			-	MURDER	FR.
STRAUP (or STRAUB)	304441	M			Member,Gestapo at: Chalons sur Marne (Fr.) 43-44			58/655	MURDER	FR.
STRAUS	303996	M			Member,Gestapo,Warschau (Pol.) 39-45			57/1134	MURDER	POL.
STRAUSS	303219	M			Agent and Member,"Selbstschutz",Torun (Pol.) 9.39			-	MURDER	POL.
STRAUSS, Anton	266538	M			SD,Nancy,Bussang,St.Maurice s.Moselle (Fr.) 9.-11.44			-	MURDER	FR.
STREHLAU, Helmut Walter (see STRELAU)	266048									

STR - TAU

NAME	C.R.FILE NUMBER	SEX	DATE OF BIRTH	RANK OCCUPATION UNIT PLACE AND DATE OF CRIME	UNWCC LIST/ SERIAL NO.	REASON WANTED	WANTED BY
STREIB, Olek	266387	M		Gendarm, Gendarmerie, Rynek Tarnogrod (Pol.) 2.11.42	-	MURDER	POL.
STREIDT, Erich	308628	M		Member, Gestapo, Krakau (Pol.) 11.39-2.45	59/679	BRUTALITY	POL.
STREIT, Hermann	308629	M		Member, Gestapo, Krakau (Pol.) 11.39-2.45	59/680	BRUTALITY	POL.
STRELAU, Helmut Walter (or STREHLAU)	266048	M	3. 7.00	Foreman and Asst.Policeman, Airplane factory VDM, Marburg, Hamburg (Ger.) 44	-	MURDER	FR.
STROBEL	303220	M		Member, Geh.Feldpol. Group 530, Bruessel (Bel.) 40-44	56/852	MURDER	BEL.
STROBEL, Herbert	303997	M	24. 8.09	SS-Sturmmann, C.C., Majdanek (Pol.) 40-44	57/1136	MURDER	POL.
STROBEL, Max	304442	M		Commandant of SD at Sneem, Dongjum,Friesland (Neth.) 8.3.45	58/656	MURDER	NETH.
STROBERT	304443	M		Member, SD, Vledder nr. Steenwijk (Neth.) 15.9.44	58/657	MURDER	NETH.
STROEBEL	923	M		Official of Nazi Prison, Gestapo, Maastricht (Neth.) 1.-3.44	1/180	TORTURE	NETH.
STROEMER	309105	M	circa 95	Oberwachtmstr., Guards unit forming part of the crew of the V-weapon based at Hook van Holland, Wassenaar (Neth.) 11.44	60/612	MISC.CRIMES	NETH.
STROFF	266389	M		Officer, SS-Osturmfhr., Gestapo, Lublin (Pol.)	-	BRUTALITY	POL.
STROHMEIER, Johann	266390	M	16. 8.20	Oberwachtmstr., Gend., Extermination Camp, Chelmno (Pol.)	-	MURDER	POL.
STROJEWSKI	266391	M		SS-Mann, Extermination Camp, Plaszow (Pol.)	-	BRUTALITY	POL.
STROMBERG	303998	M		Member, Gestapo, Warschau (Pol.) 39-45	57/1137	MURDER	POL.
STROMHOF, Werner	267358	M		Agent, Gestapo, Marseille (Fr.)	-	MURDER	FR.
STRONSKI	266422	M		Kapo, C.C., Gusen (Aust.)	-	BRUTALITY	POL.
STROT, Johann	266720	M		Overseer, Strafgefangenenlager, Harsewinkel (Ger.) 43-45	-	BRUTALITY	BEL.
STRUMBERGER, Josef	303999	M		SS-Guard, C.C., Auschwitz (Pol.) 40-45	57/1138	BRUTALITY	POL.
STRUPP, Fritz	265225	M	circa 22	Sgt., Police, Albenga (It.) 12.44-45	-	MURDER	U.K.
STRUVE, Wilhelm	309107	M	10.12.07	Driver, Gestapo H.Q. at Kiel, various places (Ger.) 25.3.44-13.4.44	60/613	MURDER	U.K.
STUCHT (see STOUCHT)	267024						
STUCK, Irma	265448	F		Employee, Gestapo, Typist in the Records Section BDS IV, Paris (Fr.) 41-44	-	SUSPECT	FR.
STUESSBERG, Paul	304444	M	24. 8.01	SS-Oschfhr., Gestapo, Hendaye, Basses-Pyrenees (Fr.) 43-44	58/659	MURDER	FR.
STUHR, Adolf	304000	M		Guard of a P.O.W. working Party, Wingst (Ger.) 20.4.45	57/1142	MURDER	POL.
STUMPF, Johann	308631	M		Member, Gestapo, Krakau (Pol.) 11.39-2.45	59/682	BRUTALITY	POL.
STUMPF, Werner	303221	M		SS-Oschfhr., Feldpost-No.22 500, Gisors,Eure (Fr.) 14.8.44	56/857	MURDER	FR.
STUMPFE	266421	M		Member of SS-Staff, Chief of Guard, Extermination-Camp, Treblinka (Pol.) 42-44	-	MURDER	POL.
STUNDER, Hermann	304002	M	31. 5.09	SS-Mann, C.C., Majdanek (Pol.) 40-44	57/1143	TORTURE	POL.
STURM	180886	M		SS-Sgt., C.C. Linz II, Mauthausen (Aust.) 44	25/1195	TORTURE	POL., FR.
STURM, Dr.	266476	M		Commissary, Police, Lublin (Pol.) 42	-	MURDER	POL.
STURMANN	266474	M		Member, C.C. Staff, Janow (Pol.)	-	MURDER	POL.
STURNER	265447	M		Member, Gestapo, Osturmfhr., SS KDS IV E 4, Paris (Fr.) 44	-	SUSPECT	FR.
STURNER, Richard	265436	M	14.12.00	Member, Gestapo (M.S.D.), SS-Oschfhr., KDS IV E 4, Paris (Fr.) 43-44	-	SUSPECT	FR.
STURZ	266473	M		SS-Usturmfhr., C.C., Auschwitz (Pol.)	-	MURDER	POL.
SUCHOMIL	266475	M		SS-Uschfhr., Extermination Camp, Treblinka (Pol.) 42-43	-	MISC.CRIMES	POL.
SUESSDORF	266460	M		Wachtmeister, Gendarmerie, Debica (Pol.) 39-44	-	MURDER	POL.
SULZIER, Franz	308632	M		Member, Gestapo, Krakau (Pol.) 11.39-2.45	59/689	BRUTALITY	POL.
SUNKEL (or ZUNKEL)	266259	M		Major, 34 Inf.Div., 107 Regt., Breil (Fr.) 44	-	MURDER	FR.
SUREN	266459	M		Member, SS-Staff, SS-Hptsfhr., C.C., Sachsenhausen-Oranienburg (Ger.)	-	MURDER	POL.
SURICK	267448	M		Sgt., 350 Hindou-Regt., Departm.Indre (Fr.) 8.44	-	MURDER	FR.
SUSS, Hermann	303223	M		Lt., Feldgendarmerie, Marignac, Charente-Maritime (Fr.) 21.8.44	56/860	MURDER	FR.
SUSZE	303224	M		Feldpol.Komm., Geh.Feldpol. Group 530, Bruessel (Bel.) 40-44	56/861	MURDER	BEL.
SUTHER, Erwin	304003	M	6. 1.08	SS-Mann, C.C., Majdanek (Pol.) 40-44	57/1146	BRUTALITY	POL.
SUTORIS, Michael	304004	M	15. 1.09	SS-Mann, C.C., Majdanek (Pol.) 40-44	57/1147	MURDER	POL.
SUTROPP	266461	M		Member, SS-Osturmfhr., Commend, C.C., Dachau (Ger.)	-	MURDER	POL.
SUTTER, Pierre (Petrus or Paulus)	266807	M		Member, Sipo, SD, Perigueux Gestapo, Dordogne (Fr.) 43-44	-	SUSPECT	FR.
SUTZ (or GUTZ)	267169	M		Sgt.-Major, 242 Inf.Div., Ampus (Fr.) 7.44	-	MURDER	FR.
SWARAT, Herta	308633	F		Member, Gestapo, Krakau (Pol.) 11.39-2.45	59/684	BRUTALITY	POL.
SWATON	266746	M		Kapo, C.C., Barth nr.Ravensbrueck (Ger.) 43-45	-	MURDER	POL.
SWETGUER	265457	M		Capt., 99 Alpen-Jaeger-Bn. F.P.N.09346, 157 Jaeger-Div., Lemonstier Les Bains (Fr.) 11.,12.8.44	-	MURDER	FR.
SWIERCZYNSKI, Georg	303225	M		Crim.Official, Staff of Gestapo, Kattowitz (Pol.) 39-42	56/862	BRUTALITY	POL.
SYL	266920	M		Sgt.-Major, Feldgendarmerie, Sisteron (Fr.) 44	-	MISC.CRIMES	FR.
SYP, Albert	309108	M		Prisoner, Prison, attached Commands, Wolfenbuettel (Ger.) 42-45	60/614	MISC.CRIMES	BEL.
SZALKE (see SCHALKE, Johann)	265524						
SZATKOWSKI, Henryk, Dr.	303226	M		Member, SS-Goralen-Legion, Agent, Gestapo, Zakopane (Pol.) 39-44	56/863	MISC.CRIMES	POL.
SZCZEPANSKI, Rudolf	304005	M	19. 7.24	SS-Rottfhr., C.C., Oranienburg (Ger.) 39-45	57/1148	BRUTALITY	POL.
SZIDZIK	303227	M		Cpl., Feldgendarmerie at Angouleme, Chasseneuil-Charente (Fr.) 43-44	56/864	MURDER	FR.
SZULC (see SCHULZ)	266420						
SZWEDO	266446	M		Substitute, Sonderdienst-Commandant, Debica (Pol.) 40-44	-	MURDER	POL.
SZYMANSKI	266434	M		Interpreter, Gestapo, Biala Podlaska (Pol.)	-	BRUTALITY	POL.
TABAS, Antoni (or LANDA, Franciszek)	304006	M	13. 1.19	Kapo, C.C., Dachau (Ger.) 39-45	57/1152	BRUTALITY	POL.
TADER, Gerhard	304007	M	19. 6.20	SS-Rottfhr., C.C., Auschwitz (Pol.) 40-45	57/1153	BRUTALITY	POL.
TAEBENS (see TOEBBENS,W.C.)	266477						
TAL	266447	M		SS-Sturmfhr., Penal Camp, Lublin (Pol.)	-	BRUTALITY	POL.
TAMM	303228	M		SS-Oschfhr., Gestapo, Lodz (Pol.) 39-44	56/865	MURDER	POL.
TAMULIS, Stasys	304008	M		SS-Mann, C.C., Majdanek (Pol.) 40-42	57/1154	BRUTALITY	POL.
TANSCHER	266448	M		Member, SS, Schupo, C.C., Budzyn (Pol.) 42-44	-	MURDER	POL.
TASCHNER	309109	M		Sgt., Secr.Field-Police, Antwerpen, Bruessel (Bel.) 40-44	60/615	MURDER	BEL.
TAUBENSEE, Fritz	266809	M		Chief of culture, Brevilly (Fr.) 42-44	-	TORTURE	FR.
TAUER	267203	M		Capt., Organ.Todt, Marseille (Fr.) 9.43	-	PILLAGE	FR.

NAME	C.R.FILE NUMBER	SEX	DATE OF BIRTH	RANK OCCUPATION UNIT PLACE AND DATE OF CRIME	UNWCC LIST/ SERIAL NO.	REASON WANTED	WANTED BY
TAUSCHER, Walter	308634	M		Member, Gestapo, Krakau (Pol.) 11.39-2.45	59/ 686	BRUTALITY	POL.
TECH (see TESCH,Anne-Marie)	267019	F					
TECHNER (or TESCHNER)	265458	M		Member,SS Sturmscharfhr.,Gestapo, BDS IV E under Cmdt.Keller (M.S.D.), Paris (Fr.) 43-44	-	SUSPECT	FR.
TEEGE, Wilhelm	308635	M		Member, Gestapo, Krakau (Pol.) 11.39-2.45	59/ 687	MURDER	POL.
TEGEN, Paul	267209	M	12	Uscharfhr., Gestapo, Marseille and vicinity (Fr.)	-	MURDER	FR.
TEGTMEIER, Wilhelm	309112	M		Owachtmstr.,Hagen prison and the attached commands, Hagen (Ger.) 42-45	60/618	MISC.CRIMES	B'L.
TEICHERT, Ruth	308636	F		Member, Gestapo, Krakau (Pol.) 11.39-2.45	59/ 688	MURDER	POL.
TEICHERT, Walter	308637	M		Member, Gestapo, Krakau (Pol.) 11.39-2.45	59/ 689	MURDER	POL.
TEIFEL	266418	M		Member, Schupo, C.C. Budzyn (Pol.) 11.42-14.2.44	-	MURDER	POL.
TELLER, Helmut	266254	M	circa 04	Oscharfhr., Gestapo, Nantes and region (Fr.) 43-44	-	MURDER	FR.
TEMPLIN, Ewald	304009	M	20. 5.04	SS-Sturmmann, C.C. Majdanek (Pol.) 40-44	57/1158	BRUTALITY	POL.
TENDD	267449	M		Lt., 350 Hindou-Regt., Departm.Indre (Fr.) 8.44	-	MURDER	FR.
TEPE, Wilhelm (called: Guillaume)	267208	M	07	Scharfhr., Gestapo, Marseille and vicinity (Fr.)	-	MURDER	FR.
TERRAKOWSKI	304446	M		Member,Schutzgruppen "Laura-mine",Eigelshoven(Neth.)8.-13.9.44	58/ 664	PILLAGE	NETH.
TESCH (or TECH),Anne-Marie	267019	F	ca. 15	Secretary and Interpreter,Gestapo, Blois & Maves (Fr.)43-44	-	MURDER	FR.
TESCHNER (see TECHNER)	265458						
TESCHNER, Walter	267168	M		Hptsturmfhr.,Gestapo, Bordeaux and vicinity (Fr.) 42-8.44	-	MURDER	FR.
TESSERAUX, Ernst	264652	M	28. 9.00	See names listed under "Special Headings"			
TESSINGER	265591	M		Oberinspektor, Civ.C.C. Blechhammer (Pol.) 45	-	MURDER	POL.
THABUS	266926	M		Physician, Unit No. 17126, Le Videlaire (Fr.) 23.,27.7.40	-	WITNESS	FR.
THALER	267462	M	ca. 05	Capt., Feldgendarmerie,Besancon and vicinity (Fr.) 44	-	MURDER	FR.
THEDE, Theodor	308638	M		Member, Gestapo, Krakau (Pol.) 11.39-2.45	59/ 691	MURDER	POL.
THEIL	304447	M		Member,Schutzgruppen "Laura-mine",Eigelshoven(Neth.)8.-13.9.44	58/ 666	PILLAGE	NETH.
THEIL, Andreas	304011	M	12. 7.12	SS-Mann, C.C. Majdanek (Pol.) 40-44	57/1162	MURDER	POL.
THEISEN, Johannes	308639	M	13.10.05	Werkmstr., Member,Werkzeugbau Firm Henschel & Sohn,Kassel (Ger.) 16.1.44	59/ 692	MURDER	NETH.
THELEN, Kathe	303291	F		Typist, Staff of Gestapo, Kattowitz (Pol.) 39-42	56/ 870	PILLAGE	POL.
THESENFITZ	309113	M		Field-Police-Director,Field-Police,Antwerpen,Bruessel(Bel.)40-44	60/ 619	MURDER	BEL.
THEURER, Eugene	266808	M		Member, Sipo, SD Perigueux Gestapo, Dordogne(Fr.) 43-44	-	SUSPECT	FR.
THEUS, Karl	267170	M		Rottenfuehrer, Gestapo, Kitchen, Marseille and environ (Fr.)	-	MURDER	FR.
THEVES, Peter	303232	M		Cpl., Geh.Feldpol.Group 530,Bruessel(Bel.) 40-44	56/ 871	MURDER	BEL.
THIEL, Rudolf	265459	M		Member,SS-Sturmscharfhr.,Gestapo,SS KDS.IV A 2, Paris(Fr.) 7.44	-	SUSPECT	FR.
THIELE	304012	M		Member, Gestapo, Warschau (Pol.) 39-45	57/1165	MURDER	POL.
THIELE	309115	M		Lt., Army, 1 Coy.,1,2 Schwaben-Bn.,near Billingsbach(Ger.)17.4.45	60/ 622	MURDER	U.S.
THIELECKE, Hans	308641	M		Member, Gestapo, Krakau (Pol.) 11.39-2.45	59/ 694	MURDER	POL.
THIELEMANN	309116	M		Instructor, Employee, G.F.P.,Antwerpen,Bruessel (Bel.) 40-44	60/ 623	MURDER	BEL.
THIELL	266410	M		Dressing supervisor,SS-Uscharfhr.,C.C.,Lublin-Majdanek(Pol.)40-44	-	BRUTALITY	POL.
THIEME, Wilhelm	308642	M		Member, Gestapo, Krakau (Pol.) 11.39-2.45	59/695	MURDER	POL.
THIESING, August	303233	M		Member,Geh.Feldpol.Group 530, Bruessel (Bel.) 40-44	56/ 872	MURDER	BEL.
THIJSSEN, Pim	303234	M		Pol.Inspektor, Police at Utrecht, Benschop (Neth.) 12.44-1.45	56/ 873	MURDER	NETH.
THOESE, Max	304013	M	28. 5.08	SS-Sturmmann, C.C. Majdanek (Pol.) 40-44	57/1170	MURDER	POL.
THOMAS, Alfons	303235	M		Crim.-Official, Staff of Gestapo, Kattowitz (Pol.) 39-42	56/ 874	MISC.CRIMES	POL.
THOMAS, Florian	265672	M		Pvt., Army, Vatan (Fr.) 10.8.44	-	MURDER	FR.
THOMAS, Wolfgang	267171	M		Chief of culture, Civilian,Parfondrupt (Fr.) 23.7.-31.8.44	-	MISC.CRIMES	FR.
THOMER, Antoni Bonifacius	309117	M	14. 5.07	Crim.-Secretary; Kopenhagen (Den.) 5.44-5.45	60/ 624	MURDER	DEN.
THOMETZKY, Josef	308643	M		Member, Gestapo, Krakau (Pol.) 11.39-2.45	59/ 696	MURDER	POL.
THOMKE, Fritz	265336	M		Policeman, Gendarmerie, Niedrzwica-Duza (Pol.) 41-7.44	-	MURDER	POL.
THOMSEN, Rudolf	308644	M		Member, Gestapo, Krakau (Pol.) 11.39-2.45	59/ 697	MURDER	POL.
THORMAN, Walter	308640	M		Member, Customs Official, Zwartsluis (Neth.) 8.10.44	59/ 693	MURDER	NETH.
THOSS, Alfred Dr.	264692	M	12. 3.08	See names listed under "Special Headings"			
THOUM	266539	M		W.O. Sgt.-Major,Feldgendarmerie No.658,Paray Le Monial and environ (Fr.) 43-44	-	SUSPECT	FR.
THUMMLER, Josef Dr.	303236	M		Oberstaatsrat, Staff of Gestapo, Kattowitz (Pol.) 39-42	56/ 875	INTERR.	POL.
THUNAK, Werner	308645	M		Member, Gestapo, Krakau (Pol.) 11.39-2.45	59/ 698	MURDER	POL.
TIDOW, August	309118	M		Civilian, near Bremen (Ger.) 28.5.44	60/ 625	BRUTALITY	U.S.
TIEDEMAN, Wilhelm	309119	M		Civilian, near Bergdorf (Ger.) 6.11.44	60/ 626	BRUTALITY	U.S.
TIEFANGRUBER	266818	M		Officer, Div.SS "Adolf Hitler",Saint Germain-Langet.(Fr.)5,7,44	-	MURDER	FR.
TIEFEL, Karl	264634	M	14. 9.10	See names listed under "Special Headings"			
TIERAUCH	266925	M		Chief Sgt.-Major,Feldgendarmerie, Sisteron (Fr.) 44	-	MISC.CRIMES	FR.
TIERCK	266646	M		Lt., Army,29 Pz.Gren.Regt.,Mamey,Martincourt (Fr.) 1.,2.9.44	-	MURDER	FR.
TIESOLER, Maria Dr.	304448	F		Frauenklinik Luebeck"Ost"Hospital, Luebeck (Ger.) 43-45	58/ 668	BRUTALITY	POL.
TIFEK	266479	M		Extermination camp, Sobibor (Pol.) 42-43	-	MURDER	POL.
TIMMER I	28754	M		Oscharfhr.,Block-Leader,Waffen-SS,C.C.Sachsenhausen(Ger.)41-43	25/ 789	MURDER	CZECH.
TIPPNER, Adolf	265460	M	3.12.01	Member,Crim.-Secr.,SS-Sturmscharfhr.,Gestapo,M.S.D.,SS B.D.S. IV E, Paris (Fr.) 41-44	-	SUSPECT	FR.
TISCHBIERK, Josef	308646	M		Member, Gestapo, Krakau (Pol.) 11.39-2.45	59/ 699	MURDER	POL.
TITZ	266478	M		SS-Sturmann,C.C.,I Schutzhaftlager,Lublin-Majdansk(Pol.)40-44	-	MURDER	POL.
TJATJARE, Mario	304449	M		Italian Soldier from Naples,Italy, Leucas(Grc.) 42	58/ 670	TORTURE	GRC.
TOBLES, Heinrich	265670	M		Hptscharfhr.,Member,SD, Chalons s.Marne (Fr.) 43-44	-	MISC.CRIMES	FR.
TOBOLLA	304450	M		NCO,Nachtjagd Group No.4,vicinity of Charleroi (Bel.) 44	58/ 671	MURDER	BEL.
TOEBBENS,W.C.(or TAEBENS)	266477	M		SA-Mann, Ghetto, Warschau (Pol.)	-	MISC.CRIMES	POL.
TOEDT	265962	M		Sturmscharfhr., Gestapo De Pau,Basses Pyrennes (Fr.)	-	MURDER	FR.
TOENSHOFF, Paul Dr.	303240	M		Doctor,80 Feldkdtr., (Prison) Poitiers (Fr.) 7.44	56/ 881	MURDER	U.K.
TOMASCHEWSKI, Maria	308647	F		Member, Gestapo, Krakau (Pol.) 11.39-2.45	59/ 700	MURDER	POL.
TONCZYK	303239	M		NCO, Geh.Feldpol.Group 530, Bruessel (Bel.) 40-44	56/ 880	MURDER	BEL.
TOPFL, Friedrich	308648	M		Member, Gestapo, Krakau (Pol.) 11.39-2.45	59/ 701	MURDER	POL.
TOPPER, Szyja	304453	M		Foreman,later Kapo, Grotkow and C.C.Jaworzno(Pol.) 40-44	58/ 675	MURDER	POL.
TORMANN, Franz	128895	M	05	SS-Hptsturmfhr.,Crim.-Commissar,Gestapo,Lodz (Pol.) 39-42	-	MURDER	POL.
TOTTIMBERG	267013	M		See names listed under "Special Headings"			
TRAPPE, Albert	265648	M		Pvt.,Farmer,Civilian(Muehlhausen), Vatan (Fr.) 10.8.44	-	MURDER	FR.
TRAUP	264427	M		Gebietskommissar, Nowo Grodek (Pol.) 42-43	-	MURDER	POL.
TRAUTMANN, Hermann	264605	M		See names listed under "Special Headings"			

TRA - VAN

NAME	C.R.FILE NUMBER	SEX	DATE OF BIRTH	RANK OCCUPATION UNIT PLACE AND DATE OF CRIME	UNWCC LIST/ SERIAL NO.	REASON WANTED	WANTED BY
TRAUTNER, Konrad	267556	M		Custom Official, Frontier-Defence, Deputy of "Zollkommandant" Hans Nienkerpe, Harlingen (Neth.) 1.45	-	WITNESS	NETH.
TRAWNY	265649	M		Cpl., 558.Inf.Regt., 13.Coy.,Bruay en Artois (Fr.) 1.9.44	-	SUSPECT	FR.
TREBINO, Georg	265461	M		Member, SS-Sturmscharfhr., Gestapo, SS: BDS IV E, Connection Dr.Knochen, Paris (Fr.) 41-44	-	SUSPECT	FR.
TREIBER	265462	F		Typist, Gestapo, Record-Section BDS IV, Paris (Fr.)	-	SUSPECT	FR.
TREMME (or TREMMEL)	266428	M		Chief-Doctor, Hospital, C.C. Ravensbrueck (Ger.)	-	MURDER	POL.
TREMMEL (see TREMME)	266428						
TRENSCH, Cirno	265476	M		Member, Uscharfhr., Gestapo, SS: KDS A i, Paris (Fr.) 7.44	-	SUSPECT	FR.
TRESSEL, Mathias	308649	M		Member, Gestapo, Krakau (Pol.) 11.39-2.45	59/702	MURDER	POL.
TREUSCH, Wilhelm	264604	M		See names listed under "Special Headings"			
TREY (see KURTH, Hans Josef)	267149						
TRIEMER	304014	M		Member, Gestapo, Warschau (Pol.) 39-45	57/1180	MURDER	POL.
TROEHLER, Emil	304454	M	1. 8.06	Sub-Director, Trench-Work in the region of Belfort-St.Die, Guewenheim Haut Rhin (Ger.) 4.10.44	58/678	MURDER	FR.
TROMNAM, Heinrich	265416	M		Member, SS-Oscharfhr., Gestapo, SS: KDS IV A 2, Paris (Fr.)41-44	-	SUSPECT	FR.
TROSSMANN, Hans	267131	M		Coy.-Commander, Army, 264.Div.,893.Gren.Regt. 3.Bn.,Sinj (Yugo.) 8.9.43-10.44	-	MURDER	YUGO.
TRUBSCHER, Karl	265417	M	14. 2.03	Member,SS-Sturmscharfhr.,Gestapo MDS, SS:BDS or VI, Paris (Fr.) 42	-	SUSPECT	FR.
TRUEBLHER	265412	M		Member,Sturmscharfhr.,Interpreter, Gestapo, BDS or KDS IV/E 4, Paris (Fr.) 44	-	SUSPECT	FR.
TRUSCHINSKY (or TUSCHINSKY)	267014	M		Sonderfuehrer, XI Pz.Div.,3.Regt.10.Coy.,Jouquevieil (Fr.) 6.8.44	-	MURDER	FR.
TSCHAKERT	267450	M		Sgt.Major, Interpreter, Feldgendarmerie,Besancon and vicinity (Fr.) 44	-	MURDER	FR.
TSCHAMPEL	308650	M		Secretary,Secr.Field-Police,H.Q.Boulevard,Piercot or the Avenue Rogier, Luettich (Bel.) 40-41	59/703	MURDER	BEL.
TSCHOCHE	266817	M	circa 95	Usturmfhr., SD of Dijon, Essarois (Fr.) 11.6.44	-	MURDER	FR.
TULKA	308651	M		Member, Secr.Fiel-Police, H.Q. Boulevard Piercot or the Avenue Rogier, Luettich (Bel.) 40-41	59/704	MURDER	BEL.
TULUWEIT	265647	M		Cpl., 558.Inf.Regt.,13 Coy.,Bruay (Fr.) 1.9.44	-	SUSPECT	FR.
TUORRA	308652	M		Member, Secr.Fiel-Police, H.Q. Boulevard Piercot or the Avenue Rogier, Luettich (Bel.) 40-41	59/705	MURDER	BEL.
TUROWITSCH, Martin	266424	M	01	Asst., Post-Office, Chelm (Pol.)	-	BRUTALITY	POL.
TUSCHINSKY (see TRUSCHINSKY)	267014						
TUST	266416	M		Member, Gestapo, Ghetto, Lodz (Pol.) 39-45	-	MURDER	POL.
TYTZ	266417	M		Member, Gestapo, Krasnik (Pol.)	-	MURDER	POL.
UEBEL	304015	M		Member, Gestapo, Warschau (Pol.) 39-45	57/1188	MURDER	POL.
UEBELHOR, Friedrich, Dr.	961	M	25. 9.93	Regierungspraesident (Poland Governor General) Bde.-Fuehrer, Public Official (Member of Reichstag) Kreisleiter, SS, Lodz, Naumburg,Merseburg (Pol.,Ger.) 39-43	1/450	MURDER	POL.
UELMANN	266778	M		Pvt., Div."B",Dordogne,Correze,Haute Vienne (Fr.)	-	SUSPECT	FR.
UHIMANN	309122	M		Cpl., Secr.Field-Police, Antwerpen,Bruessel (Bel.) 40-44	60/629	MURDER	BEL.
UHL	267113	M		Capt., Army, 3.Bn., Rijeka,Susak and Hreljin (Yugo.) 15.9.43-7.10.43	-	MURDER	YUGO.
UHLENBROCK, Kurt, Dr.	8358	M		SS-Hptsturmfhr., C.C. Sachsenhausen, Oranienburg, Auschwitz (Ger.,Pol.)	6/718 13/243	MURDER	POL., CZECH.
UHLIG	304016	M		Member, Gestapo, Warschau (Pol.) 39-45	57/1189	MURDER	POL.
UHLIG, Albert Wilhelm, Dr.jur.	264606	M		See names listed under "Special Headings"			
UHLRICH	309123	M		Cpl.,Member of Guards unit forming part of Crew of V-weapon based at Hook van Holland,Wassenaar (Neth.) 44	60/630	PILLAGE	NETH.
UHMANN, Hubert	266779	M		SS-Uscharfhr., Agent, SD, Nice (Fr.) 44	-	SUSPECT	FR.
UJRIM	265957	M		Capt., 3.Bn. 200.Mot.Gren.Regt.,La Condamine,Chatelard Basses-Alpes (Fr.) 25.-29.8.44	56/887	MISC.CRIMES	FR.
UKA, Robert Otto	304457	M	4.11.04	General superintendent,"Laura mine",Member of German Schutz-gruppen,Eigelshoven (Neth.) 8.-13.9.44	58/682	PILLAGE	NETH.
ULBRICHT	304017	M		Member, Gestapo, Warschau (Pol.) 39-45	57/1191	MURDER	POL.
ULHEMANN, Eduard	267172	M		Uscharfhr., Gestapo, Marseille and vicinity (Fr.)	-	MURDER	FR.
ULIRIUH, Hans	267166	M		Oscharfhr., Gestapo, Marseille and vicinity (Fr.)	-	MURDER	FR.
ULLENTROP, Karl	303270	M		Uffz., Secr.Field-Police, Group 530, Bruessel (Bel.) 40-44	56/888	MURDER	BEL.
ULLRICH	303271	M		SS-Uscharfhr., Gestapo, Lodz (Pol.) 39-44	56/889	BRUTALITY	POL.
ULF`CH, Johannes	308653	M		Member, Gestapo, Krakau (Pol.) 11.39-2.45	59/706	BRUTALITY	POL.
ULMER, Karl	266411	M		SS-Oscharfhr., Gestapo, Lwow (Pol.)	-	BRUTALITY	POL.
UMSING	308654	M		Member, Gestapo, Krakau (Pol.) 11.39-2.45	59/707	MURDER	POL.
UNDA	265576	M	07?	SS-Hptfhr., 16.SS-Pz.Div.,Massa Carrara (It.) 8.44	-	MURDER	U.K.
UMFERHAU	266412	M		SS-Uscharfhr., Extermination Camp, Sobibor (Pol.) 42-43	-	MURDER	POL.
UNGER	265956	F	circa 06	Chief of Guardess, Camp, Zwodau (Ger.) 44-45	-	MURDER	FR.
UNGER	309124	M		Pvt.,Secr.Fiel-Police, Antwerpen,Bruessel (Bel.) 40-44	60/631	MURDER	BEL.
UNGER	309125	M		Kommissar, Field-Police, Antwerpen, Bruessel (Bel.) 40-44	60/632	MURDER	BEL.
UNGER, Richard	304458	M	circa 07	SS-Hptscharfhr., SD Aussenstelle Maastricht, Crim.Police, Limburg,Friesland (Neth.) 44-45	58/684	MURDER	NETH.
UNTCH, Johann	304018	M	18. 3.23	SS-Mann, C.C.Majdanek (Pol.) 40-44	57/1193	BRUTALITY	POL.
UNTERHUBERT	266413	M		SS-Hptsturmfhr.,Officer, Camp, Szebnie (Pol.)	-	BRUTALITY	POL.
URBAN, Johann	266414	M		Hptwachtmeister, Gendarmerie, Debica (Pol.)	-	MURDER	POL.
URBAN, Robert	266415	M		Chief of Gendarmerie, Debica (Pol.) 39-44	-	MURDER	POL.
URBAN, Werner	265350	M	1.10.10	Politischer Secretaer, Sipo and SD,Maribor,Trbovlje and other parts of Slovenia (Yugo.) 43-44	-	MURDER	YUGO.
URBANN, Leopold	265410	M		Member, SS-Scharfhr., Gestapo, SS: BDS IV A 1, Paris (Fr.)41-44	-	SUSPECT	FR.
UTIKAL, Margaretta	308655	M		Member, Gestapo, Krakau (Pol.) 11.39-2.45	59/708	MURDER	POL.
VALLERO	265411	M		Lt., Repression Unit "Edelweiss", Barcelonnette (Fr.) 11.-16.8.44	-	MISC.CRIMES	FR.
VAN ALMKERK, Nico	302876	M		Member, Either Feldgend. or Army, Breda (Neth.) 43-44	56/4	MURDER	NETH.
VAN CAMP	254270	F		Interpreter, Sipo, Abt. IV A, Bruessel (Bel.) 6.40-9.44	28/30	MURDER	BEL.
VANCKEL, Karl	266255	M	circa 07	Lt., Army, Unit No. 43.800, Tourcoing (Fr.) 1.9.44	-	MURDER	FR.
VAN DE BERG, Joop	308701	M		Member, Sonderkommando Feldmeier, Apeldoorn,Arnhem,Wageningen (Neth.) 16.10.43, 6.7.44, 28.10.44	45/37	MURDER	NETH.
VANDEL, Karl	265413	M		Member, Gestapo, BDS IV, Paris (Fr.) 44	-	SUSPECT	FR.
VAN DEN BERG	304522	M		Member, SD at Maastricht, Limburg and Friesland (Neth.) 44-45	59/35	MURDER	NETH.

VAN - VON

NAME	C.R.FILE NUMBER	SEX	DATE OF BIRTH	RANK OCCUPATION UNIT PLACE AND DATE OF CRIME	UNWCC LIST/ SERIAL NO.	REASON WANTED	WANTED BY
VAN DEN BOOM	197243	M		Capt.,Army,Sicherungs-Regt.No.1,Villeneuve,St.Denis (Fr.) 25.8.44	31/74	MURDER	FR.
VAN DER WAL	304480	M		Presumably a member,SD,collaborator of Dr.Schoengarth Bdefhr, SD,Zeist,Oldenzaal,Den Haag (Neth.) 44-45	58/697	PILLAGE	NETH.
VAN DETZEN	183	M		Uscharfhr.,C.C.,brother of Oscharfhr.Van Detzen same charge, Dachau (Ger.) 40-45	3/63	MURDER	FR.,BEL.
VAN EUPEN,Theodor	195792	M		Commandant,Penal-Labour,C.C.Treblinka (Pol.)	-	MURDER	POL.
VAN GAGELDONK	303124	M		Member,Either of the Feldgendarmerie Breda or Army,Breda (Neth.) 43-44	56/225	MURDER	NETH.
VASSAUT	266256	M		Lt.,Airforce-staff 91,Saint Christophe en pazelle (Fr.) 11.-14.6.44	-	MURDER	FR.
VAUER (see PAUER,Frans)	267574						
V.D.BOS	267558	M		Dienststelle Hengelo,Section of Abwehrstelle Wilhelmshaven, Hengelo (Neth.) 31.3.45	-	SUSPECT	NETH.
VEESER	309126	M		SS-Oscharfhr.,Crim.Asst.,Radom (Pol.) 40-45	60/634	TORTURE	POL.
VELTING,Hans Dr.	267436	M		Member,Staff of the Eckart Werke Plant,Velden near Hersbruck (Ger.)	-	MURDER	FR.
VELTJENS	266645	M		See names listed under "Special Headings"			
VENZLAFF	304019	M		Member,Gestapo,Warschau (Pol.) 39-45	57/1196	MURDER	POL.
VERBRUGEN,O. Wilhelm	308656	M		Member,Gestapo,Krakau (Pol.) 11.39-2.45	59/709	MURDER	POL.
VERCH	304020	M		Member,Gestapo,Warschau (Pol.) 39-45	57/1197	MURDER	POL.
VERHEGEN,Edward	265414	M	2.11.06	Member,Gestapo (MSD),SS-Hptscharfhr.,SS,KDS IV A 2,Nancy,Paris (Fr.) 7.44	-	SUSPECT	FR.
VETTER, Dr.	266463	M		SS-Osturmfhr.,C.C.Auschwitz (Pol.)	-	MURDER	POL.
VETTER,Friedrich	308657	M		Member,Gestapo,Krakau (Pol.) 11.39-2.45	59/711	MURDER	POL.
VETTER,Piotr	266482	M	9. 2.98	Commissary,Police,Raszkow (Pol.) 39-41	-	MURDER	POL.
VEURLAY	265415	M		Member,Crim.Comm.,Gestapo,BDS IV,Paris (Fr.) 6.44	-	SUSPECT	FR.
VEY,Kurt	266481	M		SS-Uscharfhr.,Extermination Camp,Sobibor (Pol.) 42-43	-	MURDER	POL.
VIEDMANN	266562	M		Chief Guard,C.C.Buchloe	-	MISC.CRIMES	FR.
VIETZ,Franz	264601	M	19. 2.08	See names listed under "Special Headings"			
VIEWEG	303272	M		Uffz.,Geh.Feldpol.Group 530,Bruessel (Bel.) 40-44	56/893	MURDER	BEL.
VIFTOR	266464	M		Kapo,C.C.Auschwitz (Pol.)	-	MURDER	POL.
VILLEIN	266467	M		SS-Uscharfhr.,Feldfhr.IV,C.C.Lublin-Majdanek (Pol.) 40-44	-	MURDER	POL.
VILLNOW	304021	M		Member,Gestapo,Warschau (Pol.) 39-45	57/1198	MURDER	POL.
VINKEN,Arthur	266465	M	29.11.09	Member of Staff,Extermination Camp Chelmno (Pol.) 42-43	-	MURDER	POL.
VISSER	265379	M		Member,SS-Hptscharfhr.,Gestapo,SS,BDS IV,Paris (Fr.) 41-44	-	SUSPECT	FR.
VITZER,Joseph	267167	M	21. 2.08	Oscharfhr.,Secondary school-master,Gestapo,BDS IV B,Paris and vicinity (Fr.) 43-44	-	SUSPECT	FR.
VOELKER	267114	M		Colonel,Army,Susak and Hreljin (Yugo.) 15.9.43-7.10.43	-	MURDER	YUGO.
VOGEL	266466	M		Member,Gestapo,Borek,Chelmno (Pol.) 42-45	-	MURDER	POL.
VOGEL	266561	M		Capt.,Asst.of Dr.Paul Bosse (Fr.) 42-44	-	PILLAGE	FR.
VOGEL	266780	M		Major,Airforce,Unit No.5867 E 18003,Eguilles (Fr.) 19.8.44	-	MURDER	FR.
VOGEL	304022	M		Member,Gestapo,Warschau (Pol.) 39-45	57/1200	MURDER	POL.
VOGEL	309129	M		SS-Hptscharfhr.,Crim.Oberasst.,later SS-Usturmfhr.and Crim.Comm., Radom (Pol.) 40-45	60/639	TORTURE	POL.
VOGEL,Georg	266419	M		Member,Security Unit,Chelm (Pol.) 39-44	-	BRUTALITY	POL.
VOGEL,Heinrich	303273	M		Leitender Feldpol.Director,Feldpol. (Bel.) 40-41	56/895	MURDER	BEL.
VOGEL,Hermann	972	M		Rottfhr.,SS,C.C.Majdanek (Pol.) 40-4.44	-	MURDER	BEL.,POL.
VOGEL,Kurt	266726	M		Block senior,Commandant,Strafkdo.,C.C.Gross Rosen (Ger.) 39-45	-	MURDER	POL.
VOGEL,Max	266775	M		Sgt.Chief of Detachment of six men,Unit No.26153,St.Michel de Fronsac (Fr.) 12.41	-	PILLAGE	FR.
VOGEL,Willy	266557	M		Senior W.O.,Feldgendarmerie 658,Paray le Monial and vicinity (Fr.) 43-44	-	SUSPECT	FR.
VOGLER	266820	M		Sonderfhr.,Section I a. Feldkommandantur 641 of Blois, Seillac (Fr.) 22.6.44	-	MISC.CRIMES	FR.
VOGT (see VOIGT)	265378						
VOGT	304023	M		Member,Gestapo,Warschau (Pol.) 39-45	57/1206	MURDER	POL.
VOGT,Eduard	303274	M		Uffz.,Geh.Feldpol.Group 530,Bruessel (Bel.) 40-44	56/897	MURDER	BEL.
VOGT,Erich	265372	M	circa 05	Sturmscharfhr.,SD,Chalons sur Marne (Fr.) 43-44	-	MISC.CRIMES	FR.
VOGT,Hans	266483	M	23. 5.20	Official Police,Chelmno (Pol.) 42-43	-	MURDER	POL.
VOGT,Hans	267015	M		Sturmmann,12 SS Pz.Div."Hitler Jugend",Aufklaerungs Abt.12, 4 Coy.,Ascq North (Fr.) 1.-2.4.44	-	MURDER	FR.
VOGT,Josef	265373	M		Member,Hptsturmfhr.,Gestapo,BDS IV F,Paris (Fr.) 44	-	SUSPECT	FR.
VOGT,Karl Dr.	264602	M	5. 9.07	See names listed under "Special Headings"			
VOGT,Werner	309130	M		Cpl.,German Army and deputy Orts-Cmdt.at Medemblick,Werversholf (Neth.) 44	60/641	MURDER	NETH.
VOHL,Otto	266801	M	circa 90	Capt.,Unit stationed at Lons le Saunier,Tassenieres (Fr.) 26.8.44	-	MISC.CRIMES	FR.
VOIGT (or VOGT)	265378	M		Member,Gestapo,Chief of personal,Osturmfhr.,SS,Interpreter, BDS IV 2-3,Paris (Fr.) 41-44	-	SUSPECT	FR.
VOIGT (or WOIGT)	265955	M	circa 18	N.C.O.,SD de Montpellier,Tournant (Fr.) 9.44	-	MISC.CRIMES	FR.
VOLGT	265377	M		Member,Interpreter,Gestapo,BDS IV,Paris (Fr.) 43-44	-	SUSPECT	FR.
VOLKERATH,Elisabeth nee MILAND	173552	F	12	Warder,C.C.,Brzezinka Oswiecim,Bergen-Belsen (Pol.,Ger.) 10.39-4.45	-	MURDER	POL.
VOLFMER	266485	M		Member,Staff,C.C.Lublin-Majdanek (Pol.) 40-44	-	BRUTALITY	POL.
VOLLBRICHT	266484	M		SS-Mann,official,Gestapo,Krakau (Pol.) 42	-	MISC.CRIMES	POL.
VOLLOSTER I	266486	M		SS-Uscharfhr.,Extermination Camp,Sobibor (Pol.) 42-43	-	MURDER	POL.
VON ALICH (see VON ALISH, Ernest)	31579						
VON ALISH,Ernest (or VON ALICH)	31579	M		Member,Gestapo,Paris (Fr.) 44	-	SUSPECT	FR.
VONALT (see VON ALT)	141448						
VON ALT (or VONALT)	141448	M		Col.of Infantry,Army,S.P.40675,Chenebier-Etobon (Fr.) 9.44	16/188	MURDER	FR.
VON ALVENSLEBEN	267570	M		Lt.,Island Commandant of Goeree in Overflakkee,Renesse (Neth.) 10.,12.44	-	MURDER	NETH.
VONAU,Helene	265376	F		Employee,Gestapo,KDS IV-E,Paris (Fr.) 43	-	SUSPECT	FR.

VON - WAG

NAME	C.R.FILE NUMBER	SEX	DATE OF BIRTH	RANK OCCUPATION UNIT PLACE AND DATE OF CRIME	UNWCC LIST/ SERIAL NO.	REASON WANTED	WANTED BY
VON BAEHREN, Paul	265690	M	1. 4.93	Lt.Col., Commander, Schutzpolizei, 20 Regt., Prag-Kobylisky (Czech.) 39-44	-	MURDER	CZECH.
VON BEHREN	304290	M		Col., Commander, Gendarmerie, Radom district (Pol.) 40-43	58/48	MURDER	POL.
VON BRUCK	126892	M	98	Owner, "Von Bruck & Co. Ltd.", West Saxony Granite Works, Distendorf (Ger.) 10.43-4.45	27/764	BRUTALITY	U.K.
VON BUELOW, Friedrich	264635	M	29.11.89	See names listed under "Special Headings"			
VON CHOLITZ (or VON CHOLTITZ)	267557	M	93	Lt.Col., 3 Bn., 16 Inf.Regt., 7 Flieger-Div., Rotterdam (Neth.) 14.5.40	-	WITNESS	NETH.
VON DEGOL	267526	M		Lt., 350 Regt. "Hindou", Departm. Indre (Fr.) 8.44	-	MURDER	FR.
VON DER MOSEL, Hans	304762	M		Gen.Major, 3 Coy. Paratroops, Relecq, Karhuon, Finistere (Fr.) 23.7. and 27.8.44	59/471	MISC.CRIMES	FR.
VON DORPOWSKI	308878	M		SS-Sturmbannfhr., Kriminalrat, previously to Boeck in charge of the Criminal-Direction, Radom (Pol.) 1.40-1.45	60/130	RAPE	POL.
VON DRYGALSKI, Erich Dr.	221417	M	19.12.01	Capt. Comd.III-307, Gren.Regt.163, Inf.Div., 20 Army, Finmark (Nor.) 11.44	8/247	MURDER	NOR.
VON DUEREN, Hans	302963	M		Feldpolizeikommissar, Group 530, Geh. Feldpolizei, Bruessel (Bel.) 40-44	56/154	MURDER	BEL.
VON EBERSTEIN, Ernst	266841	M		Osturmfhr., Div. "Das Reich", Dordogne, Correze, Creuse, Hte. Vienne (Fr.) 5., 6.44	-	SUSPECT	FR.
VON EHERSTEIN	267089	M		SS-Div. "Das Reich", (Fr.) 44	-	MURDER	FR.
VON FUCHS	161669	M		Cmdt., Camp X-A, Itzehoe, Luebeck (Ger.)	-	MISC.CRIMES	PCL.,FR.
VON GREUZ (or ADNER)	144541	M		Sonderfhr., Gestapo, Paris (Fr.)	-	SUSPECT	FR.
VON GROG	144524	M		Member, Gestapo, Nancy (Fr.)	-	SUSPECT	FR.
VON HATZ	31915	M		Capt., Army, Perigueux (Fr.) 6.-8.44	8/101	MURDER	FR.
VON HECHT	265780	M	65	Foreman, Amunition-factory, Skarzysko-Kamienna (Pol.) 41-45	-	TORTURE	POL.
VON HEIMBURG	308859	M		Vice-Admiral, Naval HQ. at Berlin, member, Volksgerichtshof, Saarbruecken (Ger.) 10. and 11.43	60/251	MURDER	FR.
VON HUBBENET	303696	M		Member, Gestapo, Warschau (Pol.) 39-45	57/486	MURDER	POL.
VON KDGARD (or KOGARDT)	165246	M		Lt.Col., Army, 343 Div., Bn. la, Brest, Kraljewo (Fr., Serb.) 41-9.44	-	MURDER	FR.
VON KORF, Graf	304256	M		SS-Hptsturmfhr., Commander, Gestapo, Chalons sur Marne (Fr.) 43-44	58/384	MURDER	FR.
VON KUEHT	265301	M	circa 05	Sonderfhr., Regt."Brandenburg", (It.)	-	SUSPECT	U.K.
VON LOEBEN	266647	M		Lt.Col., Army, 226 Inf.Div., Bergues (Fr.) 16.9.44	-	MURDER	FR.
VON MAUDGE	266107	M		SS-Osturmfhr., C.C. Plaszow (Pol.)	-	MURDER	POL.
VON MORNSDORF, Theodor	304761	M		Member, Gestapo, Krakau (Pol.) 11.39-2.45	59/470	MURDER	POL.
VON OSTERROTH, Helmut	267322	M	19. 1.94	Lt.Col., 2 Bn., 487 Inf.Regt., Oignies, Courrieres (Fr.) 28.5.40	-	MURDER	FR.
VON PAPEN, Gerard	265394	M		Lt., SS-Unit 59230, Acquigny (Fr.) 8.44	-	SUSPECT	FR.
VON SAMMERN-FRANKENEGG, Ferdinand Dr.	17017	M	7. 3.97	SS-Oberfhr., Police-leader, SS- und Polizeifuehrer, District Warschau, Warszawa (Pol.) 40-44	-	MURDER	POL.
VON SCHNEIDER	266595	M		Sturmbannfhr., SS, Luzoir (Fr.) 22.-31.8.44	-	MISC.CRIMES	FR.
VON SCHUBERT	266872	M	circa 10	Lt., Unit quartered in the Iron-Works, Magny-Vernois (Fr.) 9.44	-	MURDER	FR.
VON SIEMENS, Hermann	5587	M	9. 8.85	Chief, Siemens & Halske A.G. Berlin	-	MISC.CRIMES	U.S.
VON TESMAR (see VON TESSMAR), Juergen	128894						
VON TESSMAR, Juergen (or VON TESMAR)	128894	M	07	SS-Hptsturmfhr., Kriminalrat, Gestapo, Chief of Abwehr-Kommissariat, Sect.IV 2, IV 3, Lodz (Pol.) 40-45	-	MISC.CRIMES	POL.
VON TROSCHKE, Asmus	266429	M		Historian of Art, Chief Admin. over Museums in Gen.Gov., Krakau (Pol.)	-	PILLAGE	POL.
VON TSCHIRSCHNITZ, Horst (or VON TSCHIRSZHNITZ)	266425	M		Owner of the Firm "Photo Record", Krakau (Pol.)	-	MURDER	POL.
VON TSCHIRSZHNITZ, Horst (see VON TSCHIRSCHNITZ)	266425						
VON USLAR, Hans	264603	M		See names listed under "Special Headings"			
VON WODAK, Wenzel	131608	M		Hptscharfhr., SS, C.C., Flossenburg (Ger.)	25/1255 40/361	MURDER	U.S.,FR.
VOSBERG	304024	M		Member, Gestapo, Warschau (Pol.) 39-45	57/1212	MURDER	POL.
VOSS, Josef	308658	M		Member, Gestapo, Krakau (Pol.) 11.39-2.45	59/713	MURDER	POL.
VOSS, Otto	265375	M		Hptsturmfhr., Gestapo, BDS IV E, Paris (Fr.) 41-44	-	SUSPECT	FR.
VOUTTA, Max	267378	M	circa 07-09	Chief Sgt.-Major, 2 Div. Paratrooper, Brest and vicinity (Fr.) 7.-8.44	-	MURDER	FR.
WABNER, Toni	303276	M		SS-Hptscharfhr., Gestapo, Lodz (Pol.) 39-44	56/901	MURDER	POL.
WACHE	304025	M		Member, Gestapo, Warschau (Pol.) 39-45	57/1214	PILLAGE	POL.
WACHOLZ, Theo	303277	M		Feldgendarmerie, Dinan (Cotes du Nord) (Fr.) 8. and 11.44	56/902	MURDER	FR.
WACKERAM	267165	M		Chief of culture, Civilian, Parfondrupt, Darmont (Fr.) 23.7.-31.8.44	-	MISC.CRIMES	FR.
WAECHTER	266683	M		Member of Staff, SS-Uscharfhr., guard, C.C. Auschwitz (Pol.)	-	MURDER	POL.
WAFFENMEISTER	304460	M		Regt. "Deutschland", Div. "Das Reich", Aachen (Ger.) 7.9.44	58/692	MURDER	BEL.
WAGENER, Heinrich	309134	M	8.12.97	Member, Gendarmerie, Holzheim, 42-45	60/645	MURDER	POL.
WAGENKNECHT	265736	M	95 or 00	Capt., Volunteers Bn. of Turkestans, Villefranche de Panat, Salles-Curan (Fr.) 18.6.44	-	MISC.CRIMES	FR.
WAGNER	265419	M		SS-Oscharfhr., Gestapo, BDS IV, Paris (Fr.) 42	-	SUSPECT	FR.
WAGNER	266640	M		Member, Gestapo, Chrubieszow (Pol.)	-	MURDER	POL.
WAGNER	266641	M		Member, Zollfahndungstelle, Krakau (Pol.)	-	MISC.CRIMES	POL.
WAGNER	267379	M		Lt., Unit Sector Post - Nr.15483 B & S, La Reole (Fr.) 7.-9.6.44	-	MISC.CRIMES	FR.
WAGNER	304461	M	circa 03	SS-Uscharfhr., Hendaye-Gestapo, Hendaye, Basses-Pyrenees (Fr.) 43-44	58/693	MURDER	FR.
WAGNER, Gustav	266693	M		SS-Osturmfhr., Cmdt., Extermination Camp, Sobibor (Pol.) 42-43	-	MURDER	POL.
WAGNER, Heinrich, R.	304462	M		Gauleiter, NSDAP, Gau Baden, near Weisenbach, Gernsbach, Oberstrot (Ger.) 9.8.44	58/695	MURDER	U.S.
WAGNER, Johann	304026	M	14. 2.00	SS-Mann, C.C. Majdanek (Pol.) 40-44	57/1219	BRUTALITY	POL.
WAGNER, Josef	267214	M		Oscharfhr., Gestapo, Marseille and vicinity (Fr.)	-	MURDER	FR.
WAGNER, Michael	304027	M	26. 5.09	SS-Mann, C.C. Majdanek (Pol.) 40-44	57/1220	BRUTALITY	POL.
WAGNER, N.	266694	M		Wachtmeister, Gendarmerie, Brzesko (Pol.) 40-44	-	MURDER	POL.
WAGNER, Paul	266677	M		SS-Hptscharfhr., Gestapo, Lodz (Pol.)	-	BRUTALITY	POL.

NAME	C.R.FILE NUMBER	SEX	DATE OF BIRTH	RANK OCCUPATION UNIT PLACE AND DATE OF CRIME	UNWCC LIST/ SERIAL NO.	REASON WANTED	WANTED BY
WAGNER, Sigurd	265213	M	circa 14	Capt.,Cmdt.,SS-Police,Unit at Rocca di Mezzo from March 44, Goriano, Valli (It.) 10.1.44	-	SUSPECT	U.K.
WAGNER, Toni	266678	M		Member,SS-Hptscharfhr., Gestapo, Lodz (Pol.)	-	MISC.CRIMES	POL.
WAHL, Konrad	128938	M	05	Hptscharfhr.,Krim.Kommissar,Gestapo,Office,Lodz (Pol.)40-44	-	SUSPECT	POL.
WAIBAUM	267451	M		Member, Gestapo, Limoges and vicinity (Fr.) 44	-	SUSPECT	FR.
WAJS	266679	M		Member of Staff, Extermination camp, Sobibor (Pol.) 42-43	-	MURDER	POL.
WAKE	304028	M		Member, Gestapo, Warschau (Pol.) 39-45	57/1222	PILLAGE	POL.
WALASTER	266685	M		Member of Staff, Extermination camp, Sobibor (Pol.) 42-43	-	MURDER	POL.
WALDE, Eugen	308659	M		Member, Gestapo, Krakau (Pol.) 11.39- 2.45	59/714	MURDER	POL.
WALDEN	128937	M	95	SS-Usturmfhr.,Obersekretaer, Gestapo,Office, Lodz (Pol.)39-45	-	MISC.CRIMES	POL.
WALDENFELS, Georg	304464	M	28.10.04	SS-Hptsturmfhr.,bailiff, estate in Gora district of Srem (Pol.) 39-14.5.43	58/698	MURDER	POL.
WALDOWSKI	266697	M		Guard, Gestapo prison, Lublin (Pol.) 40-44	-	MURDER	POL.
WALIA, Erich	303278	M		Krim.Beamter, Staff of Gestapo, Kattowitz (Pol.) 39-42	56/907	BRUTALITY	POL.
WALKE, Karl	308660	M		Member, Gestapo, Krakau (Pol.) 11.39- 2.45	59/715	MURDER	POL.
WALLAS	309135	M		Member of Ger.Military Police,Ozorkow nr.Lodz (Pol.) 39-42	60/649	MURDER	POL.
WALLMEN, Thomas	304030	M	14.5.16	SS-Mann, C.C., Majdanek (Pol.) 40-44	57/1224	BRUTALITY	POL.
WALLOCH	266257	M		Cpl.,Africa-Corps,Regt.Ruxleben,6.Coy.,1.Sect.,Hte.Marne-Aube (Fr.) 25.-31.8.44	-	MURDER	FR.
WALLSCHIETZ, Hermann	266695	M	2.4.20	Member of Staff, Extermination camp, Chelmno (Pol.) 42-44	-	MURDER	POL.
WALTER	266617	M		Pvt., Feldgendarmerie, Paray le Monial and vicinity(Fr.)43-44	-	SUSPECT	FR.
WALTER (see BITNER)	266840						
WALTER	308661	M		Member,Secr.Field-Police,HQ.,Boulevard Piercot or the Avenue Rogier,Luettich (Bel.) 40-41	59/716	MURDER	BEL.
WALTER	309136	M		SS-Hptscharfhr. and Krim.Asst., Radom (Pol.) 40-45	60/650	TORTURE	POL.
WALTER, Alex, Dr.	264555	M	17.1.88	See names listed under "Special Headings"			
WALTER, Erich	303279	M		Hptpol.Sekr.,Staff of Gestapo, Kattowitz (Pol.) 39-42	56/908	INTERR.	POL.
WALTER, Ernst	309137	M		SS-Oscharfhr. and Krim.Asst.,Radom (Pol.) 40-45	60/651	TORTURE	POL.
WALTER, Helmut	267372	M	circa 09	Lt.,SD Rennes, Blamont (Fr.) 9.44	-	MURDER	FR.
WALTER, Kurt	266696	M		Commandant, Gestapo-prison "Pawiak",Warschau (Pol.) 43-44	-	MURDER	POL.
WALTER (see SCHMALT,Walter)	266816						
WALTHER	265420	M		SS-Hptsturmfhr.,leader, Gestapo - IV-E, Paris (Fr.) 44	-	SUSPECT	FR.
WALTHER, Karl	308662	M		Member, Gestapo, Krakau (Pol.) 11.39- 2.45	59/717	MURDER	POL.
WALZEL (called "Mimi")	266258	F		Agent, Gestapo, Nantes and region (Fr.) 43-44	-	MURDER	FR.
WANCZURA	266684	M		Confidential agent, C.C., Dachau (Ger.)	-	MURDER	POL.
WANDEL	309138	M		Krim.-Rat,Sturmbannfhr., Radom (Pol.) 40-45	60/652	RAPE	POL.
WANDEL, Karl	265421	M		SS-Uscharfhr.,employee, Gestapo, BDS IV, Paris (Fr.) 44	-	SUSPECT	FR.
WANDER, Karl	264627	M		See names listed under "Special Headings"			
WARMBIER	304031	M		Member, Gestapo, Warschau (Pol.) 39-45	57/1230	PILLAGE	POL.
WARNCKE, Willy	267585	M	circa 11	Rottfhr., SS, C.C., Neuengamme (Ger.)	-	MISC.CRIMES	U.K.
WARNECKE	265221	M	circa 95	Major, San Giacomo (It.) 3.1.44	-	SUSPECT	U.K.
WARNECKE, Fritz	303280	M		Medical orderly,"Georgschacht" pit, nr.Sulbeck, 39-45	56/909	MURDER	POL.
WARUTJES, Dirk	304032	M	24.5.00	Cook, C.C., Oldenburg (Ger.) 39-45.	57/1231	BRUTALITY	POL.
WARZECHA, Erich	308663	M		Member, Gestapo, Krakau (Pol.) 11.39- 2.45	59/718	MURDER	POL.
WARZOG	266686	M		Cmdt.,SS-Hptsturmfhr., Extermination camp,Sasy,Janow (Pol.)40-44	-	MURDER	POL.
WARZOK, Johann	308664	M		Member, Gestapo, Krakau (Pol.) 11.39- 2.45	59/719	MURDER	POL.
WASCHITZEK, Thomas	303282	M		Krim.Beamter, Staff of Gestapo, Kattowitz (Pol.) 39-42	56/911	PILLAGE	POL.
WASSERMANN, Mathias	265353	M	circa 95	Lt.,Gendarmerie, Litija (Yugo.) 44-45	-	MURDER	YUGO.
WATTERROTH, Francois	267452	M		Interpreter, Grenzpolizeipost, Gestapo,Luchon and vicinity (Fr.) 1.43- 7.44	-	MURDER	FR.
WATZAL	309139	M		Member, SS-Mann (?), of Waffen-SS, Radom (Pol.) 40-45	60/656	MURDER	POL.
WATZLAWIK, Rosa	308665	F		Member, Gestapo, Krakau (Pol.) 11.39- 2.45	59/720	MURDER	POL.
WAWOTZNY, Theodor	304033	M	4.11.91	SS-Uscharfhr., C.C., Majdanek (Pol.) 40-44	57/1233	BRUTALITY	POL.
WEBEL, Fritz	267135	M		Usturmfhr., SS, Sinj (Yugo.) 8.9.43-10.44	-	MURDER	YUGO.
WEBER	265660	M	circa 00	N.C.O., SD, Chalons Sur Marne (Fr.) 43-44	-	MISC.CRIMES	FR.
WEBER	266293	M		N.C.O., Air-Force, Staff,St.Christophe en Bazelle (Fr.)11.-14.6.44	-	MURDER	FR.
WEBER	266558	M		Farmer, Civilian, Gueblange les Dieuze (Fr.) 41-44	-	PILLAGE	FR.
WEBER	303283	M		N.C.O., C.C., Breendonck (Bel.) 40-44	56/913	MURDER	BEL.
WEBER (II)	304034	M		Member, Gestapo, Warschau (Pol.) 39-45	57/1235	PILLAGE	POL.
WEBER	309140	M		SS-Oscharfhr. and Krim.Asst., Radom (Pol.) 40-45	60/657	BRUTALITY	POL.
WEBER, Alfred	266754	M	21.10.01	Driver, Inspector, Electric Railway,Krakau (Pol.)	-	MISC.CRIMES	POL.
WEBER, Andreas	304035	M	5.4.11	SS-Mann, C.C., Majdanek (Pol.) 40-44	57/1236	TORTURE	POL.
WEBER, Ernst	308666	M		Farmer at Udemerfeld,Kleve district (Ger.) 39-45	59/721	BRUTALITY	POL.
WEBER, Hubert	308667	M		Member, Gestapo, Krakau (Pol.) 11.39- 2.45	59/722	MURDER	POL.
WEBER, Liessel	265422	F		Employee, Gestapo, KDS IV B, Paris (Fr.) 42-43	-	SUSPECT	FR.
WEBER, Richard	265423	M		SS-Hptscharfhr., Agent, SD, Briancon (Fr.) 43-44	-	SUSPECT	FR.
WEBER, Rudolf	303284	M		Pvt., Geh.Feldpolizei Group 530, Bruessel (Bel.) 40-44	56/914	MURDER	BEL.
WEBER, Walter, Dr.	303285	M	5.11.89	Medical Officer,Spec.Employment z.b.V.No.31 with 80th Corps HQ at Biarritz (Fr.),Poitiers (Fr.) 7.44	56/915	MURDER	FR.
WEBER, Wilhelm	265426	M		SS-Usturmfhr.,member,Gestapo (M.D.S.) KDS IV E 4,Paris (Fr.) 44	-	SUSPECT	FR.
WEBERPALS	304036	M		Member, Gestapo, Warschau (Pol.) 39-45	57/1241	PILLAGE	POL.
WECKE	266704	M		Member, Gestapo, Warschau (Pol.)	-	MISC.CRIMES	POL.
WEDERKA, Peter	266705	M		Kapo, C.C., Lublin-Majdanek (Pol.) 40-44	-	BRUTALITY	POL.
WEG, Heinrich	266643	M	circa 10	Member, Gestapo, Radzyn (Pol.)	-	MISC.CRIMES	POL.
WEGENER	1561	M	circa 05	Standartenfhr.,SS, execution officer,C.C.,Sachsenhausen-Berlin (Ger.) 5.43	25/792	SUSPECT	CZECH.
WEGENER, Dr.	266630	M		SS-Osturmfhr.,Upper-sector of Wartheland (Pol.)	-	MURDER	POL.
WEGHALY, Franz	303286	M		Krim.Asst., Gestapo-staff, Kattowitz (Pol.) 39-42.	56/916	BRUTALITY	POL.
WEGNER, Paul	303287	M		SS-Hptscharfhr., Gestapo, Lodz (Pol.) 39-45	56/917	BRUTALITY	POL.
WEGSCHEIDEN	266559	M		Pvt., SS-Mann, Unit SS-No. 20,188, Longwy (Fr.) 1.9.44	-	MURDER	FR.
WEGWERTH, Walter	308668	M		Member, Gestapo, Krakau (Pol.) 11.39- 2.45	59/723	BRUTALITY	POL.
WEHMEIER, Reinhold	308669	M		Member, Gestapo, Krakau (Pol.) 11.39- 2.45	59/724	INTERR.	POL.
WEHOFSICH, Franz, Dr.	264625	M		See names listed under "Special Headings"			
WEHRMANN, Alois (or WILDE, Kurt)	265424	M		Member, Gestapo (M.S.D.) KDS IV E, Paris (Fr.) 43	-	SUSPECT	FR.

WEI - WEN

NAME	C.R.FILE NUMBER	SEX	DATE OF BIRTH	RANK OCCUPATION UNIT PLACE AND DATE OF CRIME	UNWCC LIST/ SERIAL NO.	REASON WANTED	WANTED BY
WEICHELT	266691	M		SS-Hptsturmfhr.,chief,SD,Sanok,Przemysl (Pol.) 40-44	-	TORTURE	POL.
WEICHT, Walter	303288	M		Krim.Beamter,Staff of Gestapo at Kattowitz (Pol.) 39-42	56/918	BRUTALITY	POL.
WEIDE	266294	M		Chief-Cpl.,Africa-Corps,Regt.Ruxleben,6.Ccy.,1.Section Hte.Marne-Aube (Fr.) 25.-31.8.44	-	MURDER	FR.
WEIDEMANN, Heinrich	266692	M	03	Asst.,Post-office,Lublin (Pol.) 40-44	-	BRUTALITY	POL.
WEIDIG, Hans	308670	M		Member,Gestapo,Krakau (Pol.) 11.39- 2.45	59/725	BRUTALITY	POL.
WEIGAND, Karl	266714	M		Sgt.,G.F.P.,Gant and environ (Bel.) 40-45	-	TORTURE	BEL.
WEIGEL	304037	M		Member,Gestapo,Warschau (Pol.) 39-45	57/1244	PILLAGE	POL.
WEIGEL, Herbert	265425	M	circa 10	Hptkolonnenfhr.,NSKK,Brignoles,Caroes (Fr.) 25. 7.44	-	MURDER	FR.
WEIGERSTORFER	266693	M		Member,C.C. Lublin-Majdanek (Pol.) 40-44	-	BRUTALITY	POL.
WEIKHARDT	304038	M		SS-Hptscharfhr.,C.C. Majdanek (Pol.) 40-44	57/1246	MURDER	POL.
WEIL, Emil	309142	M	1. 1.10	Krim.Sekretaer,Gestapo,H.Q.,Muenchen (Ger.) (and German occupied territory) 1944	60/663	MURDER	U.K.
WEILAND, Dora	304465	F		Owner,Farm,village of Bojendorf,distr.of Oldenburg (Ger.) 42	58/705	MURDER	POL.
WEILAND, Franz	304466	M		Ortsgr.Ltr.,NSDAP,area of Weisenbach,Gernsbach,Oberstrot and Hilpertsau (Ger.) 9.8.44	58/706	MURDER	U.S.
WEILER	304039	M		Member,Gestapo,Warschau (Pol.) 39-45	57/1247	PILLAGE	POL.
WEINDEL	304040	M		Member,Gestapo,Warschau (Pol.) 39-45	57/1250	PILLAGE	POL.
WEINGARTE, Ewald	267453	M		Chief Sgt.-Major,Feldgend.,Besancon and vicinity (Fr.) 44	-	MURDER	FR.
WEINGARTNER,	303289	M		NCO,Guard,Gaol at Oldenburg (Ger.) 43-45	56/919	BRUTALITY	POL.
WEINGARTNER,	304041	M		Member,Gestapo,Warschau (Pol.) 39-45	57/1251	PILLAGE	POL.
WEINHOLD, Irmgard	308671	F		Member,Gestapo,Krakau (Pol.) 11.39- 2.45	59/726	MURDER	POL.
WEINHOLD, Walter	308672	M		Member,Gestapo,Krakau (Pol.) 11.39- 2.45	59/727	MURDER	POL.
WEINHOFF (see WIENLOOF)	265653						
WEINZIERL, Hans	303290	M		Uffz.,Geh.Feldpol. at Belgium 1940-44	56/920	MURDER	BEL.
WEIRAUCH	62443	M		Head of Bureau of population and relief of dept.of internal admin.of GG. (Pol.)	7	TORTURE	POL.,UNWCC
WEIRICH, Adam	267215	M	09	Oberwachtmstr., Schupo Ludwigshafen,Ban-St-Martin (Fr.) 41	-	PILLAGE	FR.
WEISBROT	267371	M		Lt.,Hitler-Jugend,Blamont (Fr.) 9.44	-	MURDER	FR.
WEISE	266560	M		Pvt.,SS-Mann,2.Pz.Ausbildung und Ersatz-Abt.,No. 1 "Rastenburg" (Ostpreussen),Cmey (Fr.) 28. 8.44	-	MURDER	FR.
WEISE	304042	M		Member,Gestapo,Warschau (Pol.) 39-45	57/1254	PILLAGE	POL.
WEISEL	142715	M		Oscharfhr.,SS,C.C. Drancy (Fr.)	-	SUSPECT	FR.
WEISKIRCH, Josef	304468	M		Cscharfhr.,SS,Member,Group 648 of the Secr.Field-police,H.Q. G.F.P.,Boulevard Piercot,Liege (Bel.) Between 40-44	58/709	TORTURE	BEL.
WEISMANN, Fritz	266703	M	circa 03	Chief,SS-Sturmbannfhr.,Kdtr.,Gestapo,Krakau, Zakopane (Pol.) 41 - 45	-	MURDER	POL.
WEISS	26227	M		Hptsturmfhr.,German Army,SS,C.C.,Neuengamme,Dachau (Ger.)	16/156	TORTURE	BEL.,U.K.
WEISS	265661	M		Sgt., Army, Montcontour (Fr.) 5. 8.44	-	MISC.CRIMES	FR.
WEISS	266616	M		See names listed under "Special Headings"			
WEISS	266699	M		Block senior,SS-Sturmmann,C.C. Auschwitz (Pol.)	-	MURDER	POL.
WEISS	267373	M		Sturmmann,Gestapo,Bordeaux and environ (Fr.) 42- 8.44	-	MURDER	FR.
WEISS	304043	M		Member,Gestapo,Warschau (Pol.) 39-45	57/1255	PILLAGE	POL.
WEISS	309143	M		SS-Usturmfhr., Krim.Obersekretaer,Radom (Pol.) 40-45	60/664	TORTURE	POL.
WEISS, Bruno	266629	M		SS-Oberscharfhr., Extermination camp,Sobibor (Pol.) 42-43	-	MURDER	POL.
WEISS, Hans	197449	M		SS-Standartenfhr.,Totenkopfstanderte, C.C. Sachsenhausen (Ger.) 40-45	-	MURDER	POL.
WEISS, Walter	303291	M		Oberpol.Inspektor,Staff of Gestapo,Kattowitz (Pol.) 39-42	56/921	BRUTALITY	POL.
WEISSAH, Hermann	265662	M	14. 8.21	Custom-Official,Unit No. 57727 B,Lermor-Pleubian (Fr.) 5.-7.8.44	-	MURDER	FR.
WEISSHART	266698	M		SS-Rottfhr., Extermination camp, Treblinka (Pol.) 42-43	-	BRUTALITY	POL.
WEISSINGER	266919	M		Engineer,Lt.,Car-service,Unit No.36 753 A,Casseneuil,Fougeres, St.Livrade,Cazeneuve (Fr.) 28. 8.1944	-	PILLAGE	FR.
WEISSMANN, Robert	308673	M		Member,Gestapo,Krakau (Pol.) 11.39- 2.45	59/730	INTERR.	POL.
WEISZENBORN, Willi	304045	M	22. 6.02	SS-Mann,C.C. Majdanek (Pol.) 40-44	57/1257	BRUTALITY	POL.
WEITH	267374	M		Oscharfhr., Gestapo, Bordeaux and environ (Fr.) 42- 8.44	-	MURDER	FR.
WEITZ	266803	M		Pvt., Div. "B", Dordogne,Correze,Haute Vienne (Fr.)	-	SUSPECT	FR.
WEITZ	309144	M		Lt., "Brehmer Div.",Dpt.Dordogne,Correze and Haute Vienne (Fr.) 1944	60/666	MURDER	FR.
WEITZE	304046	M		Member,Gestapo,Warschau (Pol.) 39-45	57/1258	PILLAGE	POL.
WEIZE	266008	M		Sgt., Field-police, Quimperle (Fr.) 44	-	MURDER	FR.
WEIZENEGGER, Dr.	266642	M	circa 93	Director,Hospital,Lublin (Pol.)	-	MISC.CRIMES	POL.
WEIZENMULLER	304469	M		SS-Sturmscharfhr.,Gestapo at Chalons s.Marne (Fr.) 43-44	58/712	MURDER	FR.
WELLEY	309145	M		Pvt.,Member,Guards unit forming part of the V-weapon based at Hook van Holland,Wessenaar,(Neth.) 44	60/668	PILLAGE	NETH.
WELLIAM, Ewald	308674	M		Member,Gestapo,Krakau (Pol.) 11.39- 2.45	59/731	INTERR.	POL.
WELLMAN, Georg	304047	M	2.10.10	SS-Mann,C.C. Majdanek (Pol.) 40-44	57/1260	MURDER	POL.
WELLMEYER, Karl	304048	M	12. 1.94	SS-Uscharfhr.,C.C. Majdanek (Pol.) 40-44	57/1261	BRUTALITY	POL.
WELTERS I	266766	M		Member of staff,C.C. Dachau (Ger.)	-	TORTURE	POL.
WELTERS II	266767	M		Member of staff,Block-senior,C.C. Dachau (Ger.)	-	MURDER	POL.
WELZ, Matthaeus	264626	M		See names listed under "Special Headings"			
WENDE	1006	M		Usturmfhr., SS, Crematorium C.C. Majdanek (Pol.) 40-4.44	-	MURDER	BEL.,FR.,POL.
WENDLAND, Valentin	303293	M		Oberkrim.Sekr.,Staff of Gestapo,Kattowitz (Pol.) 39-42	56/924	INTERR.	POL.
WENDLINGER, Johann	304049	M		SS-Rottfhr., Dirlewanger-Bde., Warschau,Lublin (Pol.) 40-45	57/1263	MURDER	POL.
WENDT	304050	M		Member,Gestapo,Warschau (Pol.) 39-45	57/1264	PILLAGE	POL.
WENDT, Rudolf	303294	M		Krim.Sekr.,Staff of Gestapo,Kattowitz (Pol.) 39-42	56/925	INTERR.	POL.
WENIGER, Gertrude	138150	F	circa 16	SS-Rapportfhr.,C.C. Auschwitz (Pol.)	-	MURDER	POL.,FR.
WENSCHE, Albert Karl	267059	M		Agent,Gestapo,Arras (Fr.) 8.41	-	MURDER	FR.
WENSZKY	304481	M		Kommissar,head,Abt.V of the B.D.S. (Krim.Pol.) at Den Haag Zeist,Oldenzaal and Den Haag (Neth.) 44-45	58/713	PILLAGE	NETH.
WENTLA	266710			SS-Unterscharfhr.,C.C.,penal camp,Lublin,Majdanek,Althammer (Pol.) 41-45	-	MURDER	POL.
WENZEL	266682	M		Commander,6.Bn., Berliner Polizei, Wawer nr. Warschau (Pol.) 27.12.1939	-	MURDER	POL.

NAME	C.R.FILE NUMBER	SEX	DATE OF BIRTH	RANK OCCUPATION UNIT PLACE AND DATE OF CRIME	UNWCC LIST/ SERIAL NO.	REASON WANTED	WANTED BY
WENZEL	267454	M		Hptsturmfhr., Gestapo, Paris (Fr.)	-	MURDER	FR.
WENZEL, Willi	303296	M		Employee, Staff of Gestapo, Kattowitz (Pol.) 39-42	56/927	MURDER	POL.
WERENER, Horst	308675	M		Member, Gestapo, Krakau (Pol.) 2.39-2.45	59/732	MURDER	POL.
WERFINGER	304052	M		SS-Mann, C.C.Majdanek (Pol.) 40-44	57/269	BRUTALITY	POL.
WERFINGER, Paul	304053	M	6. 5.13	Guard, C.C. Majdanek (Pol.) 40-42	57/1270	TORTURE	POL.
WERMETH, Josef	304054	M	28. 9.11	SS-Mann,Crim.Pol.-Schreiber, C.C.Majdanek (Pol.) 40-42	57/1272	BRUTALITY	POL.
WERNER	266681	M		Member of Staff, C.C. Dachau (Ger.)	-	MURDER	POL.
WERNER	267375	M		Interpreter, 2.Paratrooper-Div.,Brest and vicinity (Fr.) 7.and 8.44	-	MURDER	FR.
WERNER	303297	M		SS-Usturmfhr., Gestapo, Lodz (Pol.) 39/44	56/928	MURDER	POL.
WERNER	304055	M		Member, Gestapo, Warschau (Pol.) 39-45	57/1273	PILLAGE	POL.
WERNER, Albert	267144	M	13. 6.01	Gendarmerie-Master, Luxembourg (Lux.) 5.45	-	MURDER	LUX.
WERNER, Otto	309146	M		Cpl., Member of Guards Unit forming part of V-weapon based at Hook van Holland, Wassenaar (Neth.) 44	60/670	PILLAGE	NETH.
WERNIKE	266700	M		Confidental Agent, C.C. Dachau (Ger.)	-	SUSPECT	POL.
WERTLEINT	266701	M		Member, Staff, C.C. Lublin, Majdanek, Buchenwald (Pol.,Ger.)	-	BRUTALITY	POL.
WERTOW	266665	M		Substitute commissary, Gestapo, Lublin (Pol.) 40-44	-	MURDER	POL.
WERZEL	304471	M		Adjutant, Feldgendarmerie, Arlon and vicinity (Bel.) 24.,25.8. and 1.-3.9.44	58/716	MURDER	BEL.
WESSELS	304472	M		SS-Scharfhr.,Hendaye Gestapo, Hendaye, Basses-Pyrenees (Fr.) 43-44	58/717	MURDER	FR.
WESTFALL, Harry	304473	M		Cpl.,Geh.Feldpolizei, Bruessel (Bel.) 40-44	58/718	MURDER	BEL.
WESTHAGEN, Gerhard	303298	M		Pol.Insp.,Staff of Gestapo, Kattowitz (Pol.) 39-42	56/930	PILLAGE	POL.
WESTMAL	304056	M		Member, Gestapo, Warschau (Pol.) 39-45	57/1276	MURDER	POL.
WESTPHAL, Diether	266295	M		Chief, Gestapo, St.Quentin and region (Fr.) 40-44	-	MURDER	FR.
WESTPHAL, Helmut	303299	M		Krim.Beamter, Staff of Gestapo, Kattowitz (Pol.) 39-42	56/931	PILLAGE	POL.
WETLAND, Franz	267602	M		SS-Uscharfhr., Extermination Camp, Sobibor (Pol.) 42-43	-	MURDER	POL.
WEYGAN	266802	M		Capt., Division "Bode",Dordogne,Bergerac,St.Pierre,d'Eyraud and Beaumont (Fr.) 19.6.44-22.7.44	-	MISC.CRIMES	FR.
WEYGAND	128931	M	10	Sturmbannfhr. (Regierungsrat),Chief of Gestapo,Lodz and Duesseldorf (Pol.,Ger.) 39-43	-	MURDER	POL.
WICHA	266967	M	circa 94	Lt.,Unit 62011 E or F and L.63989 L.G.P.A. Bruessel,Troissereux (Fr.) 15.-18.8.44	-	MURDER	FR.
WICHARY, Luiza	308676	F		Member, Gestapo, Krakau (Pol.) 11.39-2.45	59/733	MURDER	POL.
WICHT, Wilhelm	309147	M		Member of Gostapo, Grudziadz (Pol.) 40-45	60/671	INTERR.	POL.
WIDANI, R.	265464	M		SS-Mann, Member, Gestapo, BDS or KDS IV E, Paris (Fr.) 41-44	-	SUSPECT	FR.
WIDAUER, Joseph (Sep)	267058	M		Member, Gestapo of Blois (charged with questions of attentats and sabotage), Blois, Maves and vicinity (Fr.) 43-44	-	MURDER	FR.
WIDEMANN, Dr.	266670	M		Prof. of medicine, University, C.C. Ravensbrueck (Ger.)	-	MISC.CRIMES	POL.
WIECHMANN, Ilse	308677	F		Member, Gestapo, Krakau (Pol.) 11.39-2.45	59/734	MURDER	POL.
WIECZORECK, Klaus	266296	M		Pvt.,Africa Corps,Regt.Unit-No. L 62564 A, Airforce, Hte.Marne-Aube (Fr.) 25.-31.8.44	-	MURDER	FR.
WIECZOREK	309148	M		SS-Uscharfhr., Crim.-Employee and Interpreter, Radom (Pol.)40-45	60/672	MURDER	POL.
WIEDE	267443	M		C.C. Leonberg (Ger.) 44-45	-	BRUTALITY	FR.
WIEDEMANN, Toni	266960	M		Sgt., Flakmast 30/XII, Baudrigues,nr.Carcassonne (Fr.) 19.8.44	-	MURDER	FR.
WIEDEMANN, Willibald	303300	M		Pol.Insp.,Staff of Gestapo, Kattowitz (Pol.) 39-42	56/933	PILLAGE	POL.
WIEDENHAMMER, Ludwig	304057	M		SS-Uscharfhr., C.C. Dachau (Ger.) 39-45	57/1280	BRUTALITY	POL.
WIEDMANN, Victor	265465	M	circa 05	Lt., SD Bayonne and vicinity (Fr.) 40-44	-	MURDER	FR.
WIEGAND, Hans Adelbert Ferdinand	303301	M		Feldwebel,Feldgendarmerie, Breda (Neth.) 43-44	56-934	MURDER	NETH.
WIEGAND, Konrad	138175	M		SS-Hptsturmfhr., C.C. Auschwitz (Pol.)	-	MURDER	POL.
WIEGAND, Temann	265463	M		Member, Hptsturmfhr., Gestapo, SS, BDS IV, Paris (Fr.) 43	-	SUSPECT	FR.
WIEGMANN	1021	M		Uscharfhr., SS, C.C. Scheveningen (Neth.) 41-42	1/182	MURDER	NETH
WIEHL, Emil	16823	M		Director, economic branch of German Foreign Office (Fr.) 41-44	-	PILLAGE	FR.
WIELAND	266307	M		Lt., Feldgendarmerie, Dole (Fr.) 44	-	MURDER	FR.
WIELANT	266667	M		SS-Usturmfhr., C.C. Lublin-Majdanek (Pol.)	-	BRUTALITY	POL.
WIENKOP (see WIENLOOP)	265653						
WIENLOOP (or WEINHOPF) (or WIENKOP or WIENROVE)	265653	M		Lt.Col., Kommandantur, Dordogne,Perigueux,Clermont-Ferrand (Fr.) circa 4.44	-	SUSPECT	FR.
WIENROVE (see WIENLOOP)	265653						
WIERZBICA, Stephan	266666	M		Functionary, Block No. 5, C.C. Auschwitz (Pol.)	-	BRUTALITY	POL.
WIESE, Willy	266308	M	4. 6.97	Lt.,Chief, Feldgendarmerie of Blois, Coulanges (Fr.) 23.7.44	-	MURDER	FR.
WIESNER, Richard	265466	M		SS-Hptscharfhr.,Member, Gestapo, BDS IV A 1, Paris (Fr.) 41-44	-	SUSPECT	FR.
WIEST, Hans	266309	M		Lt. or Osturmfhr., SS-Leibstandarte "Adolf Hitler",Metz (Fr.) 9.40-4.41	-	PILLAGE	FR.
WIETH	267377	M		Chief Sgt.Major, 242.Inf.Div.,Ampus (Fr.) 7.44	-	MURDER	FR.
WIGHARDT, Fritz	304058	M	18. 1.91	Guard, C.C. Majdanek (Pol.) 40-44	57/1282	BRUTALITY	POL.
WILBERTH, Heinrich	267217	M		Oscharfhr., Gestapo, Marseille and vicinity (Fr.)	-	MURDER	FR.
WILCZEK (see WILDCZEK,Heinr.)	308.678						
WILD (I)	304059	M		Member, Gestapo, Warschau (Pol.) 39-45	57/1283	BRUTALITY	POL.
WILD (II)	304060	M		Member, Gestapo, Warschau (Pol.) 39-45	57/1284	BRUTALITY	POL.
WILD (III)	304061	M		Member, Gestapo, Warschau (Pol.) 39-45	57/1285	BRUTALITY	POL.
WILDCZEK (or WILCZEK),Heinr.	308678	M		Member, Gestapo, Krakau (Pol.) 11.39-2.45	59/735	MURDER	POL.
WILDE, Kurt (see WEHRMANN, Alois)	265424						
WILDERMUTH, Jakob	266669	M	19. 9.20	Member, Staff, Extermination Camp, Chelmno (Pol.) 42-44	-	MURDER	POL.
WILDMANN, Peter	304062	M	18. 5.13	SS-Mann, C.C. Majdanek (Pol.) 40-44	57/1287	BRUTALITY	POL.
WILTERT	303302	M		SS-Usturmfhr.,Member, Sipo at Haaren, C.C.,Haaren,Udenhout heath,Helfert and Vught (Neth.) summer 44	56/936	MURDER	NETH.
WILHEWSKI, Gerhard	308679	M		Commissar, Secr.Field-Police, H.Q. Boulevard Piercot or the Avenue Rogier, Luettich (Bel.) 40-41	59/736	MURDER	BEL.
WILIY or OCZKO	266709	M		SS-Mann, Extermination Camp, Plaszow (Pol.)	-	MURDER	POL.
WILKE	266310	M	25. 2.93	Chief engineer, Mines of Joeuf region, Bassin de Briey (Fr.) 40-45	-	BRUTALITY	FR.

WIL - WOL

NAME	C.R.FILE NUMBER	SEX	DATE OF BIRTH	RANK OCCUPATION UNIT PLACE AND DATE OF CRIME	UNWCC LIST/ SERIAL NO.	REASON WANTED	WANTED BY
WILKE	303303	M		Uffz.,Geh.Feldpol.Group 530, Bruessel (Bel.) 40-44	56/ 937	MURDER	BEL.
WILKE	308680	M		Field-Pol.-commiss.,Secr.Field-Police,H.Q., Boulevard Piercot or the avenue Rogier,Luettich (Bel.) 40-41	59/ 737	MURDER	BEL.
WILKEN, Richard	303304	M		NCO, Guard, Gaol at Oldenburg (Ger.) 43-45	56/ 938	BRUTALITY	POL.
WILKOMM, Mathias	267143	M	ca. 05	Servant, Civilian, Luxemburg (Lux.) 5.45		MISC.CRIMES	LUX.
WILKOWSKA, Jeanine	264525	F		Wife of Bruno Becker, German Officer,Paris (Fr.)7.44	56/ 939	PILLAGE	FR.
WILL	303343	M		SS-Usturmfhr.,Gestapo, Lodz (Pol.) 39-44	56/940	MURDER	POL.
WILL, Adam	303344	M		Crim.-Secr.,Staff of Gestapo, Kattowitz (Pol.) 39-42	56/ 941	BRUTALITY	POL.
WILLCKIE	303346	M		Feldgendarmerie, Dinan (Fr.) 8.u.11.44	56/ 944	MURDER	FR.
WILLEBRINCK	267455	M		Sgt.Major, 350 Hindou-Regt.,Departm.Indre (Fr.) 8.44	-	MURDER	FR.
WILLENBRUCK	266311	M	14	Uscharfhr., SD of Vichy, Planchez-les-Mines,Chaux(Fr.)21.-22.9.44	-	MURDER	FR.
WILLHAUS, Gustav	266671	M		SS-Osturmfhr., Extermination Camp, Janow(Pol.)	-	MURDER	POL.
WILLISCH, Hans	308681	M		Member, Gestapo, Krakau (Pol.) 11.39-2.45	59/ 739	BRUTALITY	POL.
WILLMS, H.	304475	M		Member,Schutzgruppen"Laura-mine",Eigelshoven(Neth.)8.-13.9.44	58/ 723	PILLAGE	NETH.
WILSK	303347	M		Staff-Manager,Firm of Deschimag Seebeck,Wesermuendes-Camp (Ger.) 44-45	56/ 945	BRUTALITY	FR.
WIMMER, Georg	168238	M		Treuhaender Firm "Unitas", Krakau (Pol.) 9.39-44	10/ 186	PILLAGE	POL.,FR.
WINCKLER	265427	M		Lt.,6 Coy.,2 Bn.,36 Mot.Gren.Regt.,90 Pz.Gren.Div., Briancon (Fr.) 29.8.44	-	MURDER	FR.
WINDELSCHMIDT, Karl	303348	M		Uffz.,Geh.Feldpol.Group 530, Bruessel (Bel.) 40-44	56/946	MURDER	BEL.
WINDERNIAIL (see NIEDERMEIR)	265211						
WINDING	266795	M		Officer, 950 "Free India" 15 Coy.,Lacanau-Ocean(Fr.)28.5.44	-	MURDER	FR.
WINDISCH, August	308682	M		Member, Gestapo, Krakau (Pol.) 11.39-2.45	59/ 740	BRUTALITY	POL.
WINGAT	265429	F		Secretary, Gestapo, BDS IV, Paris (Fr.) 44	-	SUSPECT	FR.
WINGERT	304063	M		Member, Gestapo, Warschau (Pol.) 39-45	57/1289	BRUTALITY	POL.
WINKEL	266011	M		Member, Feldgendarmerie, Region of Cholet (Fr.) 7.,8.8.44	56/ 947	MURDER	FR.
WINKELMANN, Erich	267216	M	15	Uscharfhr., Gestapo, Marseille and vicinity (Fr.)	-	MURDER	FR.
WINKLER	191911	M		Lt.,9 Inf.Div.,361 th.Regt.,Lus La Croix Haute (Fr.) 7.44	-	MURDER	FR.
WINKLER	265342	M	ca. 05	Agent and Interrogating Officer, Gestapo, Belgrad(Yugo.)4.42	-	MISC.CRIMES	YUGO.
WINKLER	265654	M		Cpl.,558 Inf.Regt.,13 Coy.,Bruay en Artois (Fr.) 1.9.44	-	SUSPECT	FR.
WINKLER	266722	M		Arbeitsfhr., C.C. Linz (Aust.)	-	BRUTALITY	POL.
WINKLER	303350	M		Employee, Staff of Gestapo, Kattowitz (Pol.) 39-42	56/ 948	PILLAGE	POL.
WINKLER	304064	M		Member, Gestapo, Warschau (Pol.) 39-45	57/1290	BRUTALITY	POL.
WINKLER, Arnim	264554	M	9.4.05	See names listed under "Special Headings"	-		
WINOGRADOW, Peter	263517	M		See names listed under "Special Headings"	-		
WINPLINGER	267173	M		Major, Bn.Commander,704 Ld.Schtz.Bn.,Camp Ruchard nr.Tours(Fr.)42	-	SUSPECT	FR.
WINTER, Friedrich	303351	M		Sonderfhr.,Geh.Feldpol.Group 530, Bruessel (Bel.) 41-44	56/ 950	MISC.CRIMES	BEL.
WINTER, Heinrich	308683	M		Member, Gestapo, Krakau (Pol.) 11.39-2.45	59/ 741	BRUTALITY	POL.
WINTER, Oskar	266668	M	4.5.88	Doctor, Extermination Camp,Chelmno,Ragogoszcza (Pol.) 42-44	-	MURDER	POL.
WINTER, Richard	309149	M		Uscharfhr., Guard, Camp Missburg (Bel.) 44-45	60/ 678	MURDER	BEL.
WINTERHOF	267376	M		Commanding a School for Non.Com.Officers at Blamont, Viombois (Fr.) 9.44	-	MURDER	FR.
WIRSCHKE	267496	M		Sgt., Air-Force,71 Inf.Regt.,10 Coy., Aude & Herault (Fr.)5.-8.44	-	MISC.CRIMES	FR.
WIRTH (see GOEBEL)	144600						
WITWICH	267128	M		Capt., Army, 264 Div.,893 Regt., 3 Bn., Sinj (Yugo.)8.9.43-10.44	-	MURDER	YUGO.
WISCHMANN, Guenther	265571	M		Member, Abwehr (Southern Fr.) 40-45	-	BRUTALITY	FR.
WISNIEWSKI, Paul	266706	M		Member, Gestapo, Lublin (Pol.) 44	-	BRUTALITY	POL.
WITASEK	266707	M		SS-Gruppenfhr., SS-Unit, Warschau (Pol.)	-	MURDER	POL.
WITAUBT	266669	M		Sgt., 29 Pz.Gren.Regt.,Mamey and Martincourt (Fr.) 1.,2.9.44	-	MURDER	FR.
WITSCHONKE	304065	M		Member, Gestapo, Warschau (Pol.) 39-45	57/1297	PILLAGE	POL.
WITT	265431	M		Employee, Gestapo, BDS or KDS IV (Fr.) 41-44	-	SUSPECT	FR.
WITT	266687	F	19	Wardress, C.C. Auschwitz (Pol.)	-	BRUTALITY	POL.
WITTEK, Hans	266708	M		SS-Sturmscharfhr., Member, Gestapo, Jaslo (Pol.) 43-44	-	MURDER	POL.
WITTKER	267497	M		Cpl., Air-Force, Buxy-Montagny (Fr.) 20.7.44	-	MURDER	FR.
WITTOBORN	267080	M		Member, Gestapo, Arras (Fr.) 8.41	-	MURDER	FR.
WITZKE	304066	M		Member, Gestapo, Warschau (Pol.) 39-45	57/1301	BRUTALITY	POL.
WLACH	304067	M		Member, Gestapo, Warschau (Pol.) 39-45	57/1303	MURDER	POL.
WIOBARSKI, Hildegard	303352	F		Employee, Office of Gestapo Staff, Kattowitz(Pol.) 39-42	56/955	PILLAGE	POL.
WOCFECK, Paul	303353	M		SS-Rottfhr., SD, Rodez(Aveyron) 1.43-8.44	56/ 956	MURDER	FR.
WODEL	304068	M		Member, Gestapo, Warschau (Pol.) 39-45	57/1304	MURDER	POL.
WOELBING, Fritz	264568	M	30.10.06	See names listed under "Special Headings"	-		
WOHLERS	308684	M		Member, Secr.Field-Police,H.Q., Boulevard Piercot or the Avenue Rogier, Luettich (Bel.) 40-41	59/ 742	MURDER	BEL.
WOIGT (see VOIGT)	265955						
WOLF	265572	M	17	SS-Osturmfhr.,16 SS Pz.Div., Masso Carrara (It.) 8.44	-	MURDER	U.K.
WOLF	266023	M		Lt.,90 Pz.Gren.Div.,200 Mot.Gren.Regt.,7 Coy., La Condamine-Chatelard (Fr.) 27.,28.,29.8.44	-	INCENDIARISM	FR.
WOLF	266591	M	ca. 10	Kommando special Gestapo Dr.Berger, St. Die (Fr.) 11.44	-	MURDER	FR.
WOLF	266627	M		SS-Uscharfhr.,Rapportfhr.,C.C.Auschwitz (Pol.)	-	MURDER	POL.
WOLF	266664	M		See names listed under "Special Headings"	-		
WOLF	266793	M		Col., Inf.,Neigne and Champigny (Fr.) 14.and 26.8.44	-	MURDER	FR.
WOLF	267006	M		Kriminalrat, Halfweg near Amsterdam (Neth.) 21.3.41	-	MURDER	NETH.
WOLF	309150	M		German Prisoner, Wolfenbuettel Prison (Ger.) 42-45	60/ 681	MISC.CRIMES	BEL.
WOLF (or WOLFF) Charlotte Adelfine Ida Gotthardt	304478	F	9.2.09	Employed,Ein-and Ausreisestelle in The Hague,transferred to BDS Kasse,Zeist,Oldenzaal, Den Haag (Neth.) 44-45	58/ 730	PILLAGE	NETH.
WOLF, Friedrich	303437	M		Employee, Staff of Gestapo, Kattowitz (Pol.) 39-42	56/ 959	BRUTALITY	POL.
WOLF, Fritz	267174	M	29.4.08	Hptsturmfhr.,Gestapo, Paris and environ (Fr.) 44	-	SUSPECT	FR.
WOLF, Georg	304069	M	16.4.14	SS-Mann,Staff of C.C.Auschwitz (Pol.) 40-45	57/1307	BRUTALITY	POL.
WOLF, Hans	266625	M		SS-Uscharfhr.,Extermination Camp, Sobibor (Pol.) 42-43	-	MURDER	POL.
WOLF, Josef	266626	M		SS-Uscharfhr., Extermination Camp, Sobibor (Pol.) 42-43	-	MURDER	POL.
WOLF, Otto	304070	M		SS-Mann, C.C. Majdanek (Pol.) 40-44	57/1308	BRUTALITY	POL.
WOLFF	266628	M		SS-Ogruppenfhr.; C.C. Auschwitz (Pol.)	-	MISC.CRIMES	POL.
WOLFF	304071	M		Member, Gestapo, Warschau (Pol.) 39-45	57/1309	MURDER	POL.

WOL - ZIC

NAME	C.R.FILE NUMBER	SEX	DATE OF BIRTH	RANK OCCUPATION UNIT PLACE AND DATE OF CRIME	UNWCC LIST/ SERIAL NO.	REASON WANTED	WANTED BY
WOLFF (see WOLF, Charlotte Adelfine Ida Gotthardt)	304478						
WOLFF, Ludwig	264569	M	4. 8.08	See names listed under "Special Headings"			
WOLFRAM, Josef	303438	M		Krim.Asst.,Staff of Gestapo, Kattowitz (Pol.) 39-42	56/960	INTERR.	POL.
WOLKESDORFER (see WOLKESTORFER,Sepp)	264566						
WOLKESTORFER,Sepp (or WOLKERSDORFER)	264566	M	1. 9.05	See names listed under "Special Headings"			
WOLLANG, Helmut	264567	M	26. 9.01	See names listed under "Special Headings"			
WOLLENBERG, Hans	267175	M	circa 15	Scharfhr., Gestapo, Marseille and vicinity (Fr.)	-	MURDER	FR.
WOLLENSCHLAEGER	266086	M		SS-Member, C.C., Giebow near Halle (Ger.) 42	-	MURDER	POL.
WOLLHAUS (or CTYLLA)	266622	M		Chief, Extermination camp, Janow (Pol.)	-	MURDER	POL.
WOLLMANN, Karal	309151	M		Member of "Selbstschutz" and SS,Grudziadz, district (Pol.) 39-41	60/685	MURDER	POL.
WOLTER, Adolf	265306	M		Cpl., "Brandenburg" Regt. (It.)	-	SUSPECT	U.K.
WOLTERSDORFF	304479	M		SS-Sturmbannfhr.,commander,SS Art.Ers.Abt.,Amersfoort(Neth.)5.43	58/732	MURDER	NETH.
WONDRACK	265655	M	circa 00	Senior W.O., Prison, Vesoul (Fr.) 43-44	-	MISC.CRIMES	FR.
WONDROWITZ, Eugen	303440	M		Hpt.Krim.Asst.,Staff of Gestapo, Kattowitz (Pol.) 39-42	56/962	BRUTALITY	POL.
WOMLE, Ludwig	265430	M		Usturmfhr.,member,Gestapo BDS IV E SS-Fuehrer Schule before:St.Avola, Paris (Fr.) 42-44	-	SUSPECT	FR.
WORM (or WORMS)	309152	M		Feldpolizei-Inspector,Antwerpen and Bruessel (Bel.)40-45	60/686	MURDER	BEL.
WORMS (see WORM)	309152						
WORMS, Walter	267516	M		Chief Sgt.Major,Feldgendarmerie,Besancon and vicinity(Fr.)44	-	MURDER	FR.
WORTZON	266624	M		SS-Osturmfhr.,Chief,Gestapo,Political section,Lublin(Pol.)	-	MURDER	POL.
WOSNICZKA, Franz	308685	M		Member, Gestapo, Krakau (Pol.) 11.39- 2.45	59/743	INTERR.	POL.
WOSNITZKA, Erich	303441	M		Hpt.Krim.Asst., Staff of Gestapo, Kattowitz (Pol.) 39-42	56/963	PILLAGE	POL.
WOZNY, Jan	304482	M	circa 05	Member, employed, Gestapo, Krakau (Pol.) 41-42	58/735	BRUTALITY	POL.
WPOBE	265432	M		Usturmfhr.,member,Gestapo,BDS IV, Paris (Fr.) 1.8.43-44	-	SUSPECT	FR.
WROBEL, Gertrud	265433	F		Employee, Gestapo, KDS IV E, Paris (Fr.) 43	-	SUSPECT	FR.
WUERFER, Albert	266085	M		Member, German Police, Ostrowo (Pol.) 40-45	-	MISC.CRIMES	POL.
WULF	266010	M		Sgt.Maj.W.O., Feldgendarmerie, Quimperle (Fr.) 44	-	MURDER	FR.
WULFF, Ernst	264571	M		See names listed under "Special Headings"			
WULPES, Heinrich	267176	M		Oscharfhr., Gestapo,Marseille and vicinity (Fr.)	-	MURDER	FR.
WUNDER	266672	M		Repres., Chief of Gendarmerie, Tarnow (Pol.)	-	MURDER	POL.
WUNDER, Josef	304073	M	5. 3.21	SS-Scharfhr.,C.C., Majdanek (Pol.) 40-44	57/1314	BRUTALITY	POL.
WUNDERLICH, Rudolf	309153	M		Capt.and deputy commander to the commanding officer of SD Bn., Sochaczew (Pol.) 43-44	60/687	MURDER	POL.
WUNSCH, Emil	267498	M		Rottfhr., Gestapo,St.Etienne and vicinity (Fr.) 43-44	-	MISC.CRIMES	FR.
WUPACH	266794	M		Hptsturmfhr.,SS Div. "Das Reich",Terrasson (Fr.),10.6.44	-	MURDER	FR.
WURM	265434	M		SS-Oscharfhr.,member,Gestapo,BDS IV-A-I B IV 1-2,Paris(Fr.)43-44	-	SUSPECT	FR.
WURMI, Philippe	267333	M	21.12.07	Oscharfhr.,Paris and vicinity (Fr.)	-	SUSPECT	FR.
WURST	303442	M		Lt.,Insp.,Transport Service,Basses-Pyrenees.(Fr.)8.6.-8.44	56/965	MURDER	FR.
WURTH	267515	M		Member, Gestapo, Limoges and vicinity (Fr.) 44	-	SUSPECT	FR.
WUSTINGER	266688	M		See names listed under "Special Headings"			
WUTKE	266589	M		Chief manager for purchases (Fr.) 42-43	-	PILLAGE	FR.
WUTTIG	265659	M	circa 09	Oscharfhr., SD Mann, Sarthe,Mayenne (Fr.) 42-44	-	SUSPECT	FR.
WUTZKE	303444	M		SS-Scharfhr., Gestapo, Lodz (Pol.) 39-44	56/967	BRUTALITY	POL.
WYCISLIK, Johann	303445	M		Employee, Office of Gestapo-Staff, Kattowitz (Pol.) 39-42	56/968	PILLAGE	POL.
WYPEKOHL (see WYPUKOL)	309154						
WYPUKOL (or WYPEKOHL)	309154	M		Cpl., Geheime Feldpolizei,Antwerpen and Bruessel (Bel.)40-44	60/688	MURDER	BEL.
YABLONSKI	267081	M		Div. "Das Reich", South West France (Fr.) 44	-	MURDER	FR.
YUSS	266655	M	circa 08	Sgt., Army, Saint-Die (Fr.) 11.44	-	MURDER	FR.
ZACHARIAS, Erich	308702	M		Asst., Gestapo at Zlin,Hrabuvka nr.Moravska Ostrava (Czech.)3.44	32/141	MURDER	CZECH.
ZACZYK	266689	M	00	Official, County Office, Lublin (Pol.)	-	BRUTALITY	POL.
ZAILINGER	304074	M		Member, Gestapo, Warschau (Pol.) 39-45	57/1317	BRUTALITY	POL.
ZAJFMAN, Abram	304485	M		On the staff of Ostrowiec camp,Ostrowiec (Pol.) 40-45	58/739	MURDER	POL.
ZAJFMAN, Lajbue	304486	M		On the staff of Ostrowiec camp,Ostrowiec (Pol.) 40-45	58/740	MURDER	POL.
ZANDER, Otto	308686	M		Member, Gestapo, Krakau (Pol.) 11.39- 2.45	59/745	INTERR.	POL.
ZANKE	304075	M		Member, Gestapo, Warschau (Pol.) 39-45	57/1318	MURDER	POL.
ZAREMBI	304076	M	19. 3.10	SS-Guard, C.C., Auschwitz (Pol.) 40-45	57/1319	BRUTALITY	POL.
ZARITSAY (see ZARZITSAY)	303446						
ZARZITSAY (or ZARITSAY)	303446	M		Member,Feldgend.Unit 740,Marignac,Charente-Maritime(Fr.)21.8.44	56/969	MURDER	FR.
ZAWIERUCHA, Jan	304077	M	11. 4.95	Stellv.Block leader,C.C., Gross-Rosen (Ger.) 39-45	57/1320	MURDER	POL.
ZEBEL (or ZOBEL)	265555	M	15	Oscharfhr.,SS-Regt.,San Pancrazio,Civitella,Cornia(It.) 7.44	-	MURDER	U.K.
ZECHENTER, Paul	309156	M		SS-Sturmbannfhr., Head of Dpt.V (Crim.Pol.) of Ger.Sec.Pol., Kopenhagen (Den.) 43-45	60/693	MURDER	DEN.
ZEHENDER, Peter	266797	M		N.C.O., Feldgend.,624 Avallon region (Fr.) 44	-	MISC.CRIMES	FR.
ZEIDLER, Karol	266690	M		See names listed under "Special Headings"			
ZEIDLER	304078	M		Member, Gestapo, Warschau (Pol.) 39-45	57/1324	BRUTALITY	POL.
ZEIDLER, Robert	303447	M		Hpt.Krim.Sekr., Staff of Gestapo, Kattowitz (Pol.) 39-42	56/970	BRUTALITY	POL.
ZEISS	266725	M		SS-Hptscharfhr.,Cmdt., C.C., Barth nr.Ravensbrueck (Ger.)42-45	-	MURDER	POL.
ZELENKO	266776	M		Guard, C.C., Ravensbrueck (Ger.) 43-45	-	BRUTALITY	FR.
ZELLER	304079	M	21. 6.04	SS-Mann, stellv.Polizeifhr.,C.C., Majdanek (Pol.) 40-42	57/1326	MURDER	POL.
ZEMPEL, Hans	308687	M		Ortsbauernfhr.,member,NSDAP, Osiek (Pol.) 39-44	59/746	MISC.CRIMES	POL.
ZEMKE, Berthold (see ZUMKE)	303452						
ZEMRE, Berthold (see ZUMKE)	303452						
ZERTH, Erbert (?)	267177	M	circa 10	Osturmfhr., Gestapo, Marseille and vicinity (Fr.)	-	MURDER	FR.
ZERVEK, Hugo	266009	M		Member, Feldgend., Cholet (Fr.) 7.and 8.8.44	56/972	MURDER	FR.
ZESSIN, Hans	266691	M	12. 2.11	Member of Staff, Extermination camp, Chelmno (Pol.) 42-44	-	MURDER	POL.
ZEUNER	304080	M		Member, Gestapo, Warschau (Pol.) 39-45	57/1328	BRUTALITY	POL.
ZEUS I	266692	M		Investigation officer, C.C., Dachau (Ger.)	-	BRUTALITY	POL.
ZEUS II	266623	M		Investigation officer, C.C., Dachau (Ger.)	-	BRUTALITY	POL.
ZEUTARA	266635	M		SS-Mann, Sonderdienst, Szczurowa,Brzesko (Pol.)	-	MURDER	POL.
ZICKEL, Dr.	266673	M		Chief Doctor, SS, Lublin (Pol.)	-	BRUTALITY	POL.

ZIC - ZWI

NAME	C.R.FILE NUMBER	SEX	DATE OF BIRTH	RANK OCCUPATION UNIT PLACE AND DATE OF CRIME	UNWCC LIST/ SERIAL NO.	REASON WANTED	WANTED BY
ZICKER	266942	M		Sgt.,Feldgendarmerie,Sisteron (Fr.) 44	-	MISC.CRIMES	FR.
ZIEG,Wilhelm	251469	M		SS-Oscharfhr.,C.C.Auschwitz (Pol.)		MURDER	POL.,YUGO.
ZIEGLER	266652	M	circa 03	Sgt.,Army,275 Sichr.Regt.,2 Coy.,La Chapelle de Guinchay (Fr.) 26.7.44-27.8.44	-	MISC.CRIMES	FR.
ZIEGLER	309157	M		Instructor and Employee of G.F.P.,Antwerpen,Bruessel (Bel.) 40-44	60/695	MURDER	BEL.
ZIEGLER,Karl	304488	M		SS-Osturmfhr.,Gestapo at Chalons-sur-Marne,Department of Marne (Fr.) 42-44	58/743	MURDER	FR.
ZIELINSKI,Alois	308688	M		Member,Gestapo,Frakau (Pol.) 11.39-2.45	59/747	BRUTALITY	POL.
ZIELKE	266674	M		Interpreter,Gestapo,Radzyn (Pol.)	-	BRUTALITY	POL.
ZIELMANN,Walter	265589	M	circa 95	Guard of the prison,SA,Grossbeeren (Ger.) 43	-	MURDER	FR.
ZIEMER,Hubert	304489	M	21. 1.09	SS-Hptsturmfhr.,Gestapo,Liberec (Czech.) 44-45	58/744	MURDER	CZECH.
ZIER	266675	M		Kapo,C.C.Dachau (Ger.)	-	MURDER	POL.
ZIERHUT,Mattias	304490	M		SS-Osturmbannfhr.,Mayor,SS,Volkssturm,nr.Muhldorf (Ger.) 15.4.45	58/745	BRUTALITY	U.S.
ZIESEMER,Willy	264572	M		See names listed under "Special Headings"			
ZIESER	267178	M		Scharfhr.,Gestapo,Marseille and vicinity (Fr.)	-	MURDER	FR.
ZIESER	267334	M		Scharfhr.,Gestapo,Bordeaux and vicinity (Fr.) 42 u.8.44	-	MURDER	FR.
ZIGLOWSKI,Max	267179	M	10	Uscharfhr.,Gestapo,Marseille and vicinity (Fr.)	-	MURDER	FR.
ZIHR,Ferdinand	308689	M		Member,Gestapo,Krakau (Pol.) 11.39-2.45	59/748	BRUTALITY	POL.
ZILLMANN,Alfred	308690	M		Hptwachtmeister,Polizei,Blechhammer,Wielkie,Strzelce,Slask (Pol.) 1.-2.45	59/749	MURDER	POL.
ZIMMELSBACH, Dr.	308691	M		Member,Gestapo,Krakau (Pol.) 11.39-2.45	59/750	BRUTALITY	POL.
ZIMMER,Georg	308692	M		Member,Gestapo,Krakau (Pol.) 11.39-2.45	59/751	BRUTALITY	POL.
ZIMMERMANN	266651	M		Chief,Purchase office,Rare Metals Organisation of the Black Market (Fr.) 42-44	-	MISC.CRIMES	FR.
ZIMMERMANN	266656	M		Oscharfhr.,SS-school,Lordon (Fr.) 6.9.44	-	MURDER	FR.
ZIMMERMANN	266676	M		Kapo,C.C.Dachau (Ger.)	-	BRUTALITY	POL.
ZIMMERMANN	267180	M	03 or 05	Customs-officer,Arnaucourt (Fr.) 7.9.44	-	MURDER	FR.
ZIMMERMANN	309450	M		Lt.,Dept.Basses Pyrenees (Fr.) 8.6.-8.44	56/974	MURDER	FR.
ZIMMERMANN	309159	M		SS-Sturmscharfhr.,Crim.Obersecr.,Radom (Pol.) 40-45	60/697	TORTURE	POL.
ZIMMERMANN	309160	M		Feldpolizei-Kommissar,Antwerpen,Bruessel (Bel.) 40-44	60/698	MURDER	BEL.
ZIMMERMANN	309161	M		Oberinspector of Gruene Polizei of Guard unit forming part of crew of V-weapon based at Hook van Holland,Wassenaar (Neth.) 44	60/699	PILLAGE	NETH.
ZIMMERMANN,Fritz	304491	M	circa 15	Pvt.,member,Pionieren-Abt.I A-P I F.P.No.45696,Fort Hoek van Holland,Honselersdijk nr.Naaldwijk (Neth.) 28.4.45	58/746	MURDER	NETH.
ZIMMERMANN,Heinrich	266590	M	9. 9.10	See names listed under "Special Headings"			
ZIMMERMANN,Johann	304489	M	15. 4.13	SS-Mann,C.C.Majdanek (Pol.) 40-44	57/1330	BRUTALITY	POL.
ZIMMERMANN,Joseph	152043	M		Interpreter of Feldgendarmerie 958,Sisteron (Fr.) 6.44	14/180	MURDER	FR.
ZIMMERMANN,Peter	304492	M		"Deutschland" Regt.,Div. "Das Reich",Achene (Ger.) 7.9.44	58/747	MURDER	BEL.
ZIMMERMANN,Rudolf	266636	M		Member,Gestapo,Mielac (Pol.) 39-45	-	MURDER	POL.
ZIMMERMANN,Wilhelm	266637	M		Bezirks-Hptwachtmeister,Gendarmerie,Dabrowa (Pol.)	-	MURDER	POL.
ZINHOFF	265428	M		SS-Usturmfhr.,Member,Gestapo,BDS IV E-IV E-5 KDS,Paris (Fr.) 44	-	SUSPECT	FR.
ZINK	304081	M	21. 6.11	SS-Mann,C.C.Majdanek,Warschau (Pol.) 40-44	57/1332	BRUTALITY	POL.
ZINN,Arthur	251477	M		On Duty at SS,C.C.Auschwitz-Birkenau (Pol.) 1.43	16/764 40/579	MURDER	YUGO. POL.
ZINSSIUS,Hermann	267181	M		Agent,Gestapo,Marseille and vicinity (Fr.)	-	MURDER	FR.
ZOBEL (see ZEBEL)	265555	M					
ZOBEL,Hermann	303451	M		Employee,Office of Gestapo-Staff,Kattowitz (Pol.) 39-42	56/976	PILLAGE	POL.
ZOCKBAUM	304493	M		Town-Major of Jannina,Epiros and Western,Thessalia (Grc.) 10.43	58/748	MURDER	GRC.
ZOFHEL,Helmut	267079	M		Div. "Das Reich",(South West France) 44	-	MURDER	FR.
ZOWALT (or SOWALD,Paul)	267082	M		Agent,Gestapo,Arras (Fr.) 8.41	-	MURDER	FR.
ZUBER	267335	M		Usturmfhr.,Chief der Abt.V,Gestapo,Bordeaux and vicinity (Fr.) 42 u.8.44	-	MURDER	FR.
ZUELCH,Karl	266638	M		Member,SS,Szubin (Pol.) 39	-	MURDER	POL.
ZUGSBERGER	266654	M		SS-Mann,SS,Member,Screening column (Pol.)	-	MURDER	POL.
ZULCH	266639	M		Chief administrator,Hauptverwaltung der Museen im Gen.Gouvernement,Krakau (Pol.)	-	PILLAGE	POL.
ZULEGER	266680	M		Kapo,C.C.Dachau (Ger.)	-	MURDER	POL.
ZUMKE,Berthold (or ZEMKKE or ZEMPRE)	303452	M		SS-Scharfhr.,Secretary,Gestapo,Amiens and district (Fr.) 43-44	56/977	MURDER	FR.
ZUNKEL (see SUNKEL)	266259						
ZUPONIK,Gertrud	303453	F		Typist,Staff of Gestapo,Kattowitz (Pol.) 39-42	56/978	BRUTALITY	POL.
ZURZURTZI	267336	M		Gestapo,Limoges and vicinity (Fr.) 44	-	SUSPECT	FR.
ZWALLA	266501	M		See names listed under "Special Headings"			
ZWALLA	303454	M		Lt.,Deputy to General Hahne,Basses-Pyrénées (Fr.) 8.6.-8.44	56/979	MURDER	FR.
ZWER	309162	M		Sgt.,Geh.Feldpolizei,Antwerpen,Bruessel (Bel.) 40-44	60/700	MURDER	BEL.
ZWICKLER,Walter	265980	M	30.12.04	Officer,in Race and Settlements Problems,SS-Sturmbannfhr. in France with the seat in Paris (Fr.)	-	MISC.CRIMES	U.S.

ARL - GOE

NAME	C.R. FILE NUMBER	SEX	NATIONALITY	DATE OF BIRTH	ALL AVAILABLE INFORMATION AS TO THE RANK, OCCUPATION (CIVIL, PARTY OR MILITARY), PARTICULARS OF CRIME AND PHYSICAL DESCRIPTION - IF KNOWN.	WANTED BY
ARLT, Fritz Dr.	264661	M	Ger.	12. 4.12	Osturmfhr., Anthropologist. Defendant and-or witness in cases involving crimes against humanity and-or war crimes as defined in Control Council Law No.10, Article 2. Height: 1.74 cm.	U.S.
ARTMANN (see CONRAD)	266269					
BAATZ, Louis	264662	M	Ger.	15. 8.10	SS-Hptsturmfhr., Physician. Defendant and-or witness in cases involving crimes against humanity and-or war crimes as defined in Control Council Law No.10, Article 2.	U.S.
BAIER, Walter	265307	M	Ger.		Mistreatment, beating and sending of French slave laborers working in the plant to C.C. Address: Baier, plant, Stockdorf near Muenchen (Ger.)	FR.
BAUSBACH, Ferdinand	267445	M	Ger.	18.11.84	Director of the Wuerttembergische Metallwarenfabrik. Violation of the internial convention for the laws of war. Deportation, tortures and murders of French nationals. Contact Capt. Haris, Public safety officer - Tel. 3741 Ext. 395 Gopingen. Addr. Geislingen.	FR.
BENDER, Fritz	266792	M	Ger.	circa 15	Illegal confinement and deportation at Miellin and Haut-du-Them (Haute Saone) on 20.10. and 20.11.44. Height: 1.78. Hair: brown waved. Complexion: small build. Speaks French.	FR.
BERGER, Franz	264563	M	Ger.	16. 1.10	SS-Sturmbannfhr. Defendant an-or witness in cases involving crimes against humanity and-or war crimes as defined in Control Council Law No.10, Article 2.	U.S.
BILGERI, Georg Dr.	264562	M	Ger.	13. 2.98	SS-Oberfhr., Lawyer. Defendant and-or witness in cases involving crimes against humanity and-or war crimes as defined in Control Council Law No.10, Article 2. Height: 1.85 cm.	U.S.
BIRKMAN (see BRENSKMAN)	263313					
BODZUM, Peter	265309	M	Ger.	95	Farmer. Mistreatment and hanging of a French P.W. working in his farm in autumn 1941. Address: Brucken, District Alzenau.	FR.
BOSSE, Paul Dr.	266565	M	Ger.		Participated in the organisation of the Black Market in France, to the profit of Germany, this proceding to the looting of the French economy. (Fr.) 42-44.	FR.
BRANDT, Heinrich	264561	M	Ger.	3. 5.01	SS-Osturmfhr., truck-driver. Defendant and-or witness in cases involving crimes against humanity and-or war crimes as defined in Control Council Law No.10, Article 2. Height: 1.74 ½ cm.	U.S.
BRENSKMAN (or BIRKMAN)	263313	M			Guilty of murder at Hatry at Belfort in 1944. Height: 1.72 cm. Hair: brown. Complexion: pale.	FR.
BUCKER	266522	M	Ger.		Looting, rapes committed on nine persons, Unit No. 01664, Treasurer.	FR.
BUM	265308	M	Ger.		Chief foreman. Mistreatment, beating and sending of French slave laborer's working in the plant to C.C. Address: Baier, plant, Stockdorf near Muenchen (Ger.)	FR.
BURKHARDT, Arthur	267446	M	Ger.	10. 3.05	Violation of the internial convention for the laws of war. Deportation, tortures and murders of French nationals. Contact Capt. Haris, Public safety officer - Tel. 3741 Ext. 395 Gopingen. Address: Geislingen, Eberardstr.59.	FR.
BUSCH, Alfred	265608	M	Ger.	3.12.93	Bank Official, Dresdner Bank. Crimes against peace, war crimes and crimes against humanity as defined in Control Council Law No.10, Article 2.	U.S.
CONRAD (or ARTMANN)	266269	M	Ger.	circa 10	Hairdresser at Nuernberg. Guilty of looting at Allery (Saone et Loire) in 1940. Hair: brown. Height: 1.70 cm. Complexion: corpulence moyenne, middle build.	FR.
CZERNIN, Felix	265609	M	Ger.		Bank Official, Dresdner Bank. Crimes against peace, war crimes and crimes against humanity as defined in Control Council Law No.10, Article 2.	U.S.
DEKHEN	267229	M	Ger.		Member of Marseille Gestapo. Accused of murders, massacres and tortures committed in Bouches-du-Rhone department.	FR.
DENNER (or RENNER)	267232	M	Ger.		Telephone operator. Member of Marseille Gestapo. Accused of murders, massacres and tortures committed in Bouches-du-Rhone department.	FR.
DEUSSEN, August	264559	M	Ger.	24.10.84	SS-Sturmbannfhr., electrician. Defendant and-or witness in cases involving crimes against humanity and-or war crimes as defined in Control Council Law No.10, Article 2. Height: 172 cm. Hair: grey. Eyes: brown.	U.S.
DICKESCHEID, Heinrich	264558	M	Ger.	14.11.97	SS-Sturmbannfhr., owner or employed in agriculture. Defendant and-or witness in cases involving crimes against humanity and-or war crimes as defined in Control Council Law No.10, Article 2. Height: 168 cm.	U.S.
ECKSTEIN	266603	M	Ger.		Artl.Regt. Guilty of having tortured and executed thirteen inhabitants on Sept.4, 1944 at Hesmond (P.d.C.)	FR.
EICHENAUER, Konrad Dr.	264557	M	Ger.	13. 7.90	SS-Staf., commercial manager. Defendant and-or witness in cases involving crimes against humanity and-or war crimes as defined in Control Council Law No.10, Article 2. Height: 187 cm.	U.S.
ENGERER	266245	M	Ger.		Detached to Marchal Goering personnally. Looting of considerable quantities of precious objects belonging to M. Maurice de Rothschild and being in this town house, 41 Rue Faubourg St. Honore, on 19 and 23 September 1940.	FR.
ENTZIAN, Joachim Dr.	265610	M	Ger.	9. 7.91	Bank Official. War crimes, crimes vs. peace, crimes vs. humanity, as defined in Control Council Law No.10, Article 2.	U.S.
ERTL, Otto	263491	M	Ger.		Wanted for alleged murder. Suspect participated in shooting of prisoners during march of death at Choustnikovo Hradiste, county of Dvur Kralove (Czech.) on 18. and 19. February 1945, where about eighty prisoners, physically unable to continue the march, were shot to death.	CZECH.
EXNER, Gustav Dr.	264556	M	Ger.	9.10.08	SS-Osturmfhr. Defendant and-or witness in cases involving crimes against humanity and-or war crimes as defined in Control Council Law No.10, Article 2.	U.S.
FAEHNDRICH, Ernst Dr.	264565	M	Ger.	7. 1.08	SS-Osturmbannfhr., Oberregierungsrat, Volks- u. Betriebswirt (Economist ?). Defendant and-or witness in cases involving crimes against humanity and-or war crimes as defined in Control Council Law No.10, Article 2. Height: 185 cm.	U.S.
FISCHER, Johann, S.	265618	M			Auditor. Crimes against peace, war crimes and crimes against humanity as defined in Control Council Law No.10, Article 2.	U.S.
FRIEDEL, Paul, Gerhard	266916	M	Ger.	21. 4.09	Murder. Participated in the hanging affaire of Tulle (Correze) (Fr.)	FR.
FRIEDRICH, Herbert	264607	M	Ger.	31. 3.98	Sturmbannfhr., merchant or commercial employee. Defendant and-or witness in cases against humanity and-or war crimes as defined in Control Council Law No.10, Article 2. Height: 178 cm.	U.S.
GEHL, Friedrich	266131	M	Ger.		Illtreated Polish workers.	POL.
GERHER (see GERNER)	263321					
GERNER (or GERHER)	263321	M	Ger.		Guilty of murder committed in 1944 at Fort Hatry at Belfort (Fr.). Brown hair.	FR.
GLINZER, Josef	262512	M	Ger.	94	Murder of French P.W., near Konstanz (Ger.) autumn 1944.	FR.
GOETZ, Karl	264598	M	Ger.	11. 3.03	SS-Sturmbannfhr., high-school-teacher. Defendant and-or witness in cases involving crimes against humanity and-or war crimes as defined in Control Council Law No.10, Article 2. Height: 174 cm. Hair: brown.	U.S.

GUR - KOC

NAME	C.R.FILE NUMBER	SEX	NATIO-NALITY	DATE OF BIRTH	ALL AVAILABLE INFORMATION AS TO THE RANK, OCCUPATION (CIVIL, PARTY OR MILITARY), PARTICULARS OF CRIME AND PHYSICAL DESCRIPTION - IF KNOWN.	WANTED BY
GURKE, Oskar (or OGOREK)	266134	M	Ger.-Pol.		As Gestapo member he took part in tortures, mass arrestings and shootings of Poles.	POL
HALLENBERGER, Friedrich	264669	M	Ger.	7. 6.11	Sturmbannfhr., store salesman. Defendant and-or witness in cases involving crimes against humanity and-or war crimes as defined in Control Council Law No.10, Article 2. Height: 180 cm. Hair: dark blond. Eyes: brown.	U.S.
HAMMER, Max	264664	M	Ger.	27. 1.03	SS-Standartenfhr., mechanician. Defendant and-or witness in cases involving crimes against humanity and-or war crimes as defined in Control Council Law No.10, Article 2. Height: 181 cm.	U.S.
HAIM, Fritz (see HAUM)	266380					
HART, Otto	262593	M	Ger.		Wanted as witness to give precise information: the responsibles for the executions of Bonne Nouvelle prison at Rouen, the places where the victims have been buried. Rouen (Fr.) 1941-1944.	FR.
HAUM, Fritz (or HAIM)	266380	M	Ger.		Guilty of theft committed at Plancher Bas (Haute-Saone) between September 1st and November 20, 1944. Is said to have lived at following address: Schwabhause Thueringen.	FR.
HEIDER, Otto	264663	M	Ger.	26. 5.96	SS-Bdefhr. and General-Major of the Police, formerly electrical engineer. Defendant and-or witness in cases involving crimes against humanity and-or war crimes as defined in Control Council Law No.10, Article 2. Height: 178 cm.	U.S.
HEINRICHSBAUER, August	265636	M		15. 6.90	Chief-manager. Crimes against peace, war crimes and crimes against humanity as defined in Control Council Law No.10, Article 2.	U.S.
HELM, Leon	263192	M	Ger.	8. 6.96	Butcher. Subject has been condemned by the Polish Tribunal at Lublin to five years imprisonment for miscellaneous war crimes. Subject left Poland by a repatriation train on the 22.12.45. Subject's whereabouts unknown.	POL
HENCKEL VON DONNERSMARK, Graf	263325	M	Ger.		Subject is responsible for looting of Polish property. He is furthermore responsible for extermination of Polish population. Subject is identical with Crowcass List, File No. 79828. Subject is presently living at Tegernsee, Bavaria (Ger.). Kattowitz and other towns, 1940-1944.	POL
HERFURTH, Friedrich, Karl	264670	M	Ger.	30. 4.01	Hptsturmfhr., skilled worker in building trade, official. Defendant and-or witness in cases involving crimes against humanity and-or war crimes as defined in Control Council Law No.10, Article 2. Height: 172 cm.	U.S.
HERMANN, Walter	264671	M	Ger.	29. 5.95	SS-Obergruppenfhr., bank employee. Defendant and-or witness in cases involving crimes against humanity and-or war crimes as defined in Control Council Law No.10, Article 2. Height: 175 cm.	U.S.
HEUCKENKAMP, Rudolf Dr.	264668	M	Ger.	16.11.00	SS-Oberfhr., dentist. Defendant and-or witness in cases involving crimes against humanity and-or war crimes as defined in Control Council Law No.10, Article 2. Height: 173 cm.	U.S.
HINZEN, Heinz	254535	M	Ger.		Subject of att. W.R.254535 is not definitely identical with subject of same name on D.R.1119745 and W.Rs.254556-261449 (D.M.) and should be published (not published so far). Haut-Rhin, Urbes, Fr., 24.9.44 and 4. and 5.10.44. Murder. Address: Juchen near Duesseldorf, Bahnstr.37.	FR.
HOELLING, Alfred	265633	M	Ger.	6.11.88	Bank Official, Dresdner Bank. Crimes against peace, war crimes and crimes against humanity as defined in Control Council Law No.10, Article 2.	U.S.
HOERINGER, Josef	263010	M	Ger.	16. 6.06	Alleged participation in indiscriminate mass arrests. Subject collaborated with Gestapo. One of his victims whom he denounced, Antonin Kyos, was mistreated and tortured by Gestapo so that he died after three weeks imprisonment. Leitmeritz (Czech.) 1942-1944. Height: 174 cm. Hair: brown. Eyes: blue. Complexion: scars on chin. Teeth: decayed.	CZECH.
HOETTOPEIS	266908	M	Ger.		Belonged to action "B". Div. "B", Dordogne-Correze, Haute-Vienne (Fr.). Suspect.	FR.
HOFFEN, Alberts	266253	M	Ger.		Brutality. Guard of Camp Buchloe, demanded an undue labour from the prisoners, even the sick.	FR.
HOFFMEYER, Horst	264636	M	Ger.	29. 5.03	SS-Bdefhr., bank employee. Defendant and-or witness in cases involving crimes against humanity and-or war crimes as defined in Control Council Law No.10, Article 2. Height: 189 cm. Eyes: brown. Hair: grey.	U.S.
HOFLING, Fridrich	266543	M	Ger.		Arrest of an inhabitant, killed some hours later. Complicity of murder. Departm. Hte.Vienne (Fr.) 6.8.44.	FR.
HORN, Max Dr.	265625	M			Business manager, Ostindustrie G.m.b.H. Crimes against peace, war crimes and crimes against humanity as defined in Control Council Law No.10, Article 2.	U.S.
HUBER, Alfred	264638	M	Ger.	18. 1.22	Usturmfhr., draftsman in building trade. Defendant and-or witness in cases involving crimes against humanity and-or war crimes as defined in Control Council Law No.10, Article 2. Height: 174 cm.	U.S.
KALKHOFEN, Fritz	264637	M	Ger.	11. 1.04	SS-Standartenfhr. technician. Defendant and-or witness in cases involving crimes against humanity and-or war crimes as defined in Control Council Law No.10, Article 2. Height: 170 cm.	U.S.
KERLING, Hans	264564	M	Ger.	5. 2.04	SS-Osturmbannfhr., businessman or business employee. Defendant and-or witness in cases involving crimes against humanity and-or war crimes as defined in Control Council Law No.10, Article 2. Height: 170 cm.	U.S.
KEUSEN, Hellmuth	264616	M	Ger.	11. 9.09	Hptsturmfhr., Government Official. Defendant and-or witness in cases involving crimes against humanity and-or war crimes as defined in Control Council Law No.10, Article 2. Height: 176 cm.	U.S.
KIEFERT, Rudolf	264628	M	Ger.	6. 1.88	SS-Sturmbannfhr., Flyer. Defendant and-or witness in cases involving crimes against humanity and-or war crimes as defined in Control Council Law No.10, Article 2.	U.S.
KISSKALT, Wilhelm	265624	M	Ger.	21. 8.73	Bank Official, Aufsichtsrat d. Dresdner Bank. Crimes against peace, war crimes and crimes against humanity as defined in Control Council Law No.10, Article 2.	U.S.
KLEMENS, Gustav	264629	M	Ger.	15. 1.08	SS-Sturmbannfhr., technician. Defendant and-or witness in cases involving crimes against humanity and-or war crimes as defined in Control Council Law No.10, Article 2. Height: 172 cm. Hair: darkbrown. Eyes: green.	U.S.
KLINKERT, Hugo	266212	M	Ger.		Guilty of loot at Plancher-Bas (Haute Saone) between September 1, and November 20, 1944.	FR.
KLOSE, Julius	264617	M	Ger.	3. 1.93	SS-Sturmbannfhr., bank clerk. Defendant and-or witness in cases involving crimes against humanity and-or war crimes as defined in Control Council Law No.10, Article 2. Height: 172 cm.	U.S.
KOCH, Alfred	265868	M	Ger.		Illtreatment of Poles in district Poznan. File of Supervising Prosecution: Nr. III 540-45	POL

KOR - OVE

NAME	C.R. FILE NUMBER	SEX	NATIO-NALITY	DATE OF BIRTH	ALL AVAILABLE INFORMATION AS TO THE RANK, OCCUPATION (CIVIL, PARTY OR MILITARY), PARTICULARS OF CRIME AND PHYSICAL DESCRIPTION - IF KNOWN.	WANTED BY
KORSCHAN, Heinrich, L.	264600	M	Ger.	24.10.95	Civilian, official at Friedr. Krupp A.G. and Friedr. Krupp, Private Firm at Essen. Chargeable as defendant for the commission of crimes against peace, war crimes and crimes against humanity, under Article 2 of Control Council Law No. 10.	U.S.
KUBELKE, Heinz	264630	M	Ger.	29. 6.09	SS-Sturmbannfhr., iron dealer. Defendant and-or witness in cases involving crimes against humanity and-or war crimes as defined in Control Council Law No.10, Article 2. Height: 174 cm.	U.S.
KUBITZ, Hansjochen	264631	M	Ger.	6. 9.10	SS-Sturmbannfhr., junior-judge. Defendant and-or witness in cases involving crimes against humanity and-or war crimes as defined in Control Council Law No.10, Article 2. Height: 172 cm.	U.S.
KUEHNEL, Rudolf	264667	M	Ger.	8. 2.06	Sturmbannfhr., truck-driver. Defendant and-or witness in cases involving crimes against humanity and-or war crimes as defined in Control Council Law No.10, Article 2. Height: 176 cm.	U.S.
KUHN	266233	M	Ger.		Guilty of loot at Plancher-Bas (Ht.Saone) between September 1 and November 20, 1944. Is said to have following address: Bei Lisbeth Kauffingen, 16 Oberhausen Hessen Heisfeld.	FR.
KULEMANN, Alfred Dr.	264666	M	Ger.	5. 9.97	Staf., lawyer, bank manager. Defendant and-or witness in cases involving crimes against humanity and-or war crimes as defined in Control Council Law No.10, Article 2. Height: 177 cm.	U.S.
KUSTCHER, Fritz	266878	M	Ger.		Misc.Crimes. Belonged to unit having committed war crimes at Groslezac, Carsac, Peyrillac, Calviac and Carlux (Dordogne) (Fr.) 6.44.	FR.
KYLLMANN, Hans	264659	M	Ger.		Civilian, official of Friedr. Krupp A.G. Essen. Chargeable as witness to the commission of crimes against peace, war crimes and crimes against humanity, under Article 2 of Control Council Law No.10.	U.S.
LANGEN, Paul	266939	M		8.10.10	Zentralersatzlager, Paris (Fr.). Address of wife: Anna Langen, Iserlohn, Mengenerstr.126. Suspect.	FR.
LARCHE, Erich	264621	M	Ger.	19. 2.04	Osturmfhr., commercial employee. Defendant and-or witness in cases involving crimes against humanity and-or war crimes as defined in Control Council Law No.10, Article 2. Height: 174 cm.	U.S.
LENNER, Franz	264620	M	Ger.	27. 8.03	Sturmbannfhr., commercial clerk. Defendant and-or witness in cases involving crimes against humanity and-or war crimes as defined in Control Council Law No.10, Article 2. Height: 172 cm.	U.S.
LIEBL, Hermann	264622	M	Ger.	30. 3.12	Usturmfhr., catholic priest. Defendant and-or witness in cases involving crimes against humanity and-or war crimes as defined in Control Council Law No.10, Article 2. Height: 182 cm.	U.S.
LINDAU, Karl	265903	M	Ger.		Illtreated the Polish worker Miszynski Josef, his home address is: Hochstadt ueber Nordhausen.	POL.
LINHARDT, Julius	264618	M	Ger.	4. 3.05	Sturmbannfhr., commercial-employee. Defendant and-or witness in cases involving crimes against humanity and-or war crimes as defined in Control Council Law No.10, Article 2. Height: 177 cm.	U.S.
LINNEMANN, Hermann	265554	M	Ger.	15	Wanted in connection with the killings of Italian civilians. Civitella area (It.) 7.44.	U.K.
LOBA, Ernst	264619	M	Ger.	12.11.99	Sturmbannfhr., commercial-employee. Defendant and-or witness in cases involving crimes against humanity and-or war crimes as defined in Control Council Law No.10, Article 2. Height: 178 cm.	U.S.
LOESCH	265969	M	Ger.		Complicity of murder, looting and arsons at Brest in August and September 1944.	FR.
LORENZ, Josef	264665	M	Ger.	29.11.01	SS-Sturmbannfhr., merchant. Defendant and-or witness in cases involving crimes against humanity and-or war crimes as defined in Control Council Law No.10, Article 2. Height: 178 cm.	U.S.
LUIG, Wilhelm Dr.	264613	M	Ger.	30. 9.00	SS-Staf., editor. Defendant and-or witness in cases involving crimes against humanity and-or war crimes as defined in Control Council Law No.10, Article 2. Height: 181 cm.	U.S.
MACKENSEN	267044	M	Ger.		Wanted for illegal confinements, tortures, deportation committed in 1944 at Lavandou (Var.).	FR.
MAIER-KAIBITSCH, Alois	264611	M	Ger.	20. 5.91	SS-Staf., official in the department of woods and forests. Defendant and-or witness in cases involving crimes against humanity and-or war crimes as defined in Control Council Law No.10, Article 2. Height: 174 cm.	U.S.
MANNHEIM	267578	M	Ger.		Pillage at the Twentsche Bank at Wageningen. 3.45.	NETH.
MAYER, Kurt Dr.	264612	M	Ger.	27. 6.03	SS-Standartenfhr. Defendant and-or witness in cases involving crimes against humanity and-or war crimes as defined in Control Council Law No.10, Article 2.	U.S.
METZNER, Erwin	264610	M	Ger.	17. 7.90	SS-Oberfhr. Defendant and-or witness in cases involving crimes against humanity and-or war crimes as defined in Control Council Law No.10, Article 2.	U.S.
MEYER, Karl	264609	M	Ger.	7. 7.09	Sturmbannfhr. Defendant and-or witness in cases involving crimes against humanity and-or war crimes as defined in Control Council Law No.10, Article 2.	U.S.
MICHALSKI, Georg	263119	M	Ger.		Subject is responsible for atrocities committed at C.C. Paszow near Krakau (Pol.) Subject whereabout unknown.	POL.
MUELLER, Ernst	264608	M	Ger.	17. 9.93	SS-Staf. Defendant and-or witness in cases involving crimes against humanity and-or war crimes as defined in Control Council Law No.10, Article 2. Height: 178 cm. Hair: dark blond. Eyes: blue.	U.S.
MUELLER, Fritz	264656	M	Ger.	5. 3.94	Civilian, official of Friedr. Krupp A.G. and Friedr. Krupp private firm at Essen. Chargeable as defendant for commission of crimes against peace, war crimes and crimes against humanity, under Article 2, Control Council Law No.10.	U.S.
MUNDT, Heinrich	264623	M	Ger.	19. 3.00	SS-Osturmbannfhr. Defendant and-or witness in cases involving crimes against humanity and-or war crimes as defined in Control Council Law No.10, Article 2. Height: 186 cm.	U.S.
OGOREK, Oskar (see GURKE)	266134					
OHLE, Hugo	264633	M	Ger.	8. 3.91	SS-Osturmbannfhr., grain-dealer. Defendant and-or witness in cases involving crimes against humanity and-or war crimes as defined in Control Council Law No.10, Article 2.	U.S.
OSIANDER, Friedrich, Wilhelm	264615	M	Ger.	14. 9.03	Osturmbannfhr., active in agriculture. Defendant and-or witness in cases involving crimes against humanity and-or war crimes as defined in Control Council Law No.10, Article 2. Height: 187 cm.	U.S.
OVERBECK, August	265623	M	Ger.		Dresdner Bank. Crimes against peace, war crimes and crimes against humanity as defined in Control Council Law No.10, Article 2.	U.S.

PART II
(NON-GERMANS)

PAU - SCHU

NAME	C.R. FILE NUMBER	SEX	NATIO-NALITY	DATE OF BIRTH	ALL AVAILABLE INFORMATION AS TO THE RANK, OCCUPATION (CIVIL, PARTY OR MILITARY), PARTICULARS OF CRIME AND PHYSICAL DESCRIPTION - IF KNOWN.	WANTED BY
PAUL, Wilhelm	266284	M	Ger.	11. 6.05	Suspect. Identity disc No. 329 1-Inf. Regt.656. Address of family: Berlin N.18, Am Friedrichshain 19b. Last known assignment: From Gruppe Geheime Feldpolizei 736 striked off the list of control of Wehrmacht and put on 22.11.42 to the Sipo under the military Befehlshaber in France.	FR.
PERTHEN, Karl	264614	M	Ger.	8.12.11	SS-Osturmbannfhr., commercial employee. Defendant and-or witness in cases involving crimes against humanity and-or war crimes as defined in Control Council Law No.10, Article 2. Hair: brown. Eyes: grey-green. Height: 173 cm.	U.S.
PETER, Otto, Georg	266945	M	Ger.	26. 4.92	Pillage. Some kind of Economic Branch (Occ.) France. Address of wife: Else Peter, Hamburg-Bergedorf, Vierlaenderstr.14. Economic looting in France.	FR.
PUHL, Emil	265631	M	Ger.	28. 8.89	Bank Official. Crimes against peace, war crimes and crimes against humanity as defined in Control Council Law No.10, Article 2.	U.S.
PULS, Willi-Walter Dr.	264655	M	Ger.	9. 1.08	SS-Sturmbannfhr., university-teacher. Defendant and-or witness in cases involving crimes against humanity and-or war crimes as defined in Control Council Law No.10, Article 2. Height: 172 cm.	U.S.
RAGALLER, Ernst	264657	M	Ger.	10. 6.95	SS-Sturmbannfhr. Defendant and-or witness in cases involving crimes against humanity and-or war crimes as defined in Control Council Law No.10, Article 2. Height: 176 cm.	U.S.
REIDSCHELL	266204	M	Ger.		Med.Officer (Capt.). Doctor-Captain. Guilty of having, towards the end of 1944 and the beginning of 1945 at Rosendael (Nord) given to the men under his command the order for the sustematic destruction of the church and living houses of that place. Arrest Warrant No. 1245 from June 20, 1946.	FR.
REINHARDT, Fritz	264660	M	Ger.	27. 9.98	SS-Sturmbannfhr. Defendant and-or witness in cases involving crimes against humanity and-or war crimes as defined in Control Council Law No.10, Article 2.	U.S.
REINICKE	266859	M	Ger.		Misc.Crimes. Illegal confinements and deportation at Miellin and Haut-du-Them (Hte.Saone) on October and November 20, 1944. Is said to live at: Schilda ueber Kirchheim N.L.	FR.
REINKE, Helmut	264654	M	Ger.	23. 3.97	SS-Standartenfhr. Defendant and-or witness in cases involving crimes against humanity and-or war crimes as defined in Control Council Law No.10, Article 2.	U.S.
REMMERS, Hans, Hermann	264653	M	Ger.	13. 7.06	SS-Osturmbannfhr., merchant. Defendant and-or witness in cases involving crimes against humanity and-or war crimes as defined in Control Council Law No.10, Article 2. Height: 176 cm.	U.S.
RENNER (see DENNER)	267232					
RIEDIGER, Guenter	264658	M	Ger.	1.10.09	SS-Sturmbannfhr., theologian. Defendant and-or witness in cases involving crimes against humanity and-or war crimes as defined in Control Council Law No.10, Article 2. Height: 174 cm.	U.S.
RINN, Hans	265634	M	Ger.	4. 3.99	Bank Official, Chief Security Depot Dresdner Bank. Crimes against peace, war crimes and crimes against humanity as defined in Control Council Law No.10, Article 2.	U.S.
ROEHRICH, Dr.	264639	M	Ger.	12.10.07	Sturmbannfhr., Jurist. Defendant and-or witness in cases involving crimes against humanity and-or war crimes as defined in Control Council Law No.10, Article 2. Height: 172 cm.	U.S.
ROSA, Adolf, Theodor	267444	M	Ger.	15.10.93	Denunciations to the Gestapo and deportations of French nationals. Address: Nuernberg, 50 Johannstr.	FR.
RUEDEBUSCH, Hermann	266052	M	Ger.		Former manager of same Dairy - fanatic nazi and tyrannical task-master. Mistreatment of French forced laborers. Responsible for the death of a Frenchman in July 1943. Address: Frauenbergstr.2, Marburg, Dairy-Marburg-Lahn (Hessen-Ger.)	FR.
RUNGE, Friedrich	264640	M	Ger.	30. 7.07	Sturmbannfhr. Defendant and-or witness in cases involving crimes against humanity and-or war crimes as defined in Control Council Law No.10, Article 2. Height: 1.84	U.S.
SACK, Gerhard	264641	M	Ger.	2. 3.09	Sturmbannfhr., engineer. Defendant and-or witness in cases involving crimes against humanity and-or war crimes as defined in Control Council Law No.10, Article 2.	U.S.
SALZMANN	267282	M	Ger.		Guilty of participation in murders committed at Fort de Seclin (Nord) in August 1944.	FR.
SCHAFNER, Hans	265525	M	Ger.	23. 4.20	Misc.Crimes. Chelmno (Pol.)	POL.
SCHALLEMEYER, Luitpold	264642	M	Ger.	12. 3.11	Sturmbannfhr., businessman or commercial employee. Defendant and-or witness in cases involving crimes against humanity and-or war crimes as defined in Control Council Law No.10, Article 2. Height: 180 cm.	U.S.
SCHATNER, Hermann	265526	M	Ger.	2. 9.20	Misc.Crimes. Chelmno (Pol.)	POL.
SCHAUB	265567	M	Ger.		In Wlodawa he shot Polish and Jewish population. Wlodawa (Pol.)	POL.
SCHIPPEL, Hans Dr.	265617	M	Ger.	22.10.80	Bank Official, Dresdner Bank. Crimes against peace, war crimes and crimes against humanity as defined in Control Council Law No.10, Article 2.	U.S.
SCHIRMER	265966	M	Ger.		Engineer, Oberwerftdirektor. Complicity of murder, looting and arsons at Brest in August and September 1944.	FR.
SCHIRMER, Adolf	264643	M	Ger.	10. 1.14	Osturmfhr., merchant or commercial employee. Defendant and-or witness in cases involving crimes against humanity and-or war crimes as defined in Control Council Law No.10, Article 2. Height: 183 cm.	U.S
SCHLITTER, Max	266312	M	Ger.	8. 7.11	Chief of Hitler-Jugend. Witness.	LUX.
SCHMIDT, Dr.	266334	M	Ger.		Detached to Goering personnally. Looting of considerable quantities of precious objects, belonging to M. Maurice Rothschild and being in his town-house at 41 Fbg St.Honore, on September 19 and 23, 1940.	FR.
SCHMOELDER, Karl	265616	M	Ger.	19.10.95	Banker, Dresdner Bank, Landesausschuss. Crimes against peace, war crimes and crimes against humanity as defined in Control Council Law No.10, Article 2.	U.S.
SCHNEIDER, Hermann	264644	M	Ger.	29. 1.72	SS-Oberfhr. Defendant and-or witness in cases involving crimes against humanity and-or war crimes as defined in Control Council Law No.10, Article 2.	U.S.
SCHRAMM, Max	265570	M	Ger.		Murders of French nationals at St.Menehould (Fr.) from 25.8.44 to 1.9.44. Address: Hexenbruch near Wuerzburg.	FR.
SCHULTZ, Bruno, Kurt Prof. Dr.	264645	M	Ger.	3. 8.01	SS-Standartenfhr., university-professor. Defendant and-or witness in cases involving crimes against humanity and-or war crimes as defined in Control Council Law No.10, Article 2. Height: 1.75 cm.	U.S.
SCHULTZ, Henri	266339	M	Ger.		Guilty of loot committed at Plancher Bas (Hte.Saone) between Sept.1 and Nov.20, 1944. Is said to have lived at: Rolnberg 103, Kreis Salzwedel (Altmark)	FR.
SCHULZ, Fritz Dr.	264646	M	Ger.	16. 6.01	Hptsturmfhr. Defendant and-or witness in cases involving crimes against humanity and-or war crimes as defined in Control Council Law No.10, Article 2.	U.S.

NAME	C.R. FILE NUMBER	SEX	NATIO- NALITY	DATE OF BIRTH	ALL AVAILABLE INFORMATION AS TO THE RANK, OCCUPATION (CIVIL, PARTY OR MILITARY), PARTICULARS OF CRIME AND PHYSICAL DESCRIPTION - IF KNOWN.	WANTED BY
SCHULZ, Hans, Heinrich	266959	M	Ger.	23. 6.05	Pillage. Militaerverwaltung Frankreich. Economic looting in France. Address: Liselotte Schulz, Nikolassee, Teutonenstr.27.	FR.
SCHULZ, Heinrich	264647	M	Ger.	20. 7.93	SS-Osturmfhr. Defendant and-or witness in cases involving crimes against humanity and-or war crimes as defined in Control Council Law No.10, Article 2.	U.S.
SCHULZ, Karl	264599	M	Ger.	7. 2.05	SS-Osturmbannfhr., merchant. Defendant and-or witness in cases involving crimes against humanity and-or war crimes as defined in Control Council Law No.10, Article 2. Height: 172 cm.	U.S.
SCHULZE, Roland	264624	M		16.11.98	Scientific farmer and press chief for the Reich, peasant leader. As early as 1.1.1932 subject was chief of the agricultural political press department in the Reich directorate of the NSDAP and chief editor of the NS-Landpost. In 1933 he was Reich commissioner of the agricultural economic press in the Reich-ministry of food and agriculture. Head of department "D" (Press) in the staff office of the Reich peasant leader, and head of the district party office of the Reich office for agricultural politics, and the Reich directorate of the NSDAP in Muenchen. Schulze organized the press system in the Reich food estate. Schulze is an old party member and a close associate of Backe's since the days before 1933. Subject is a definite authority on the party policy, the public appeal of the Nazis, and suppressed news items. He was a wealth of general knowledge on the ministry personnel and due to his position can in form us of the many details required in the preparation of the case against Darre and Backe.	U.S.
SCHWARZENBERGER, Otto	264648	M	Ger.	22. 1.00	SS-Oberfhr., bank clerk, commercial employee. Defendant and-or witness in cases involving crimes against humanity and-or war crimes as defined in Control Council Law No.10, article 2. Height: 169 cm.	U.S.
SICHELSCHMIDT, Hans, Dr.	264649	M	Ger.	13. 9.11	SS-Hptsturmfhr., highschool-teacher. Defendant and-or witness in cases involving crimes against humanity and-or war crimes as defined in Control Council Law No. 10, article 2. Height: 177 cm.	U.S.
SIEBERT, Klaus, Dr.	264650	M	Ger.	25. 1.04	Staff, studied agriculture. Defendant and-or witness in cases involving crimes against humanity and-or war crimes as defined in Control Council Law No. 10, article 2. Height: 175 cm. Hair: fair. Eyes: blue. Characteristics: scar (chin).	U.S.
SIEBMANN, Erich	267056	M	Ger.		Wanted for illegal confinements, tortures, deportations committed in 1944 at Lavandou (Var.)	FR.
SPINGLER	266618	M	Ger.		Took an activ part in the massacres at Tulle (Correze) on June 6, 1944.	FR.
STAUDINGER, Wilhelm	264651	M	Ger.	4.12.02	SS-Standfhr. Defendant and-or witness in cases involving crimes against humanity and-or war crimes as defined in Control Council Law No. 10, article 2.	U.S.
STEINHAUSER, Joseph	266851	M	Ger.	2. 1.00	Complementary W.R. Identy disc: 222. Address of wife: Steinhauser Zenta, Eggen-Algaeu, Lindauerstr. 88. Cpl., 1 Schtz.Coy., Luftw.Inf.Regt.316.	FR.
STEINKAMP, Hermann Julius	266528	M	Ger.	2. 3.23	Student, lived before the war in Spain, Alicante. Guilty of murder, rape and arson committed at Autun (Saone et Loire). Arrest warrant delivered by Dijon Permanent Military Tribunal on March 27, 1947. - Autun (France) 8.9.44. Height: 185 cm. Hair: brown. Eyes: grey. Slim, oval face.	FR.
STOLZMANN, Karl	266401	M	Ger.	22. 9.97	Locksmith, Truppfhr. He sadistically ill-treated Poles. He Resides: Herford, Luebbestr. 15.	POL.
TESSERAUX, Ernst	264652	M	Ger.	28. 9.00	SS-Obersturmfhr. Defendant and-or witness in cases involving crimes against humanity and-or war crimes as defined in Control Council Law No. 10, article 2.	U.S.
THOSS, Alfred, Dr.	264632	M	Ger.	13. 3.08	SS-Obersturmbannfhr., highschool-teacher. Defendant and-or witness in cases involving crimes against humanity and-or war crimes as defined in Control Council Law No. 10, article 2. Height: 185 cm.	U.S.
TIEFEL, Karl	264634	M	Ger.	14. 9.10	SS-Obersturmfhr., stone-cutter. Defendant and-or witness in cases involving crimes against humanity and-or war crimes as defined in Control Council Law No. 10, article 2. Height: 185 cm.	U.S.
TOTTIMBERG	267013	M	Ger.		Wanted for illegal confinements, tortures, deportations committed in 1944 at Lavandou (Var.)	FR.
TRAUTMANN, Hermann	264605	M	Ger.	9. 5.99	Usturmfhr., merchant or commercial employee. Defendant and-or witness in cases involving crimes against humanity and-or war crimes as defined in Control Council Law No. 10, article 2. Height: 181 cm.	U.S.
TREUSCH, Wilhelm	264604	M	Ger.	24. 1.05	Sturmbannfhr., businessman or commercial clerk. Defendant and-or witness in cases involving crimes against humanity and-or war crimes as defined in Control Council Law No. 10, article 2. Height: 177 cm.	U.S.
UHLIG, Albert Wilhelm, Dr.jur.	264606	M	Ger.	9. 9.91	SS-Sturmbannfhr., high government official. Defendant and-or witness in cases involving crimes against humanity and-or war crimes as defined in Control Council Law No. 10, article 2. Height: 174 cm.	U.S.
VEITJENS	266645	M	Ger.		Col., Air-Force, proxi for Marchal Goering. Fr. 42-44. Created and developed, during the occupation, the Black Market for the profit of Germany by destructing and looting the French Economy. Is said to have been killed in an accident by aircraft in Italy. Address: Berlin W.8., Behrenstr. 43.	FR.
VIETZ, Franz	264601	M	Ger.	19. 2.08	SS-Obersturmbannfhr. Defendant and-or witness in cases involving crimes against humanity and-or war crimes as defined in Control Council Law No. 10, article 2.	U.S.
VOGT, Karl, Dr.	264602	M	Ger.	5. 9.07	SS-Sturmbannfhr. Defendant and- or witness in cases involving crimes against humanity and-or war crimes as defined in Control Council Law No. 10, article 2.	U.S.
VON BUELOW, Friedrich	264635	M	Ger.	29.11.89	Civ. Official of Friedr. Krupp A.G., and Friedr. Krupp, private firm at Essen. Chargeable as defendant for the commission of crimes against peace, war crimes and crimes against humanity, under Article 2 of Control Council Law No. 10.	U.S.
VON USLAR, Hans	264603	M	Ger.	1. 2.91	SS-Sturmfhr., professional officer. Defendant and-or witness in cases involving crimes against humanity and-or war crimes as defined in Control Council Law No. 10, article 2. Height: 176 cm.	U.S.
WALTER, Alex, Dr.	264555	M	Ger.	17. 1.88	SS-Sturmbannfhr. Defendant and-or witness in cases involving crimes against humanity and-or war crimes as defined in Control Council Law No. 10, article 2.	U.S.
WANDER, Karl	264627	M	Ger.	1.11.01	Staff. Medical student. Defendant and-or witness in cases involving crimes against humanity and-or war crimes as defined in Control Council Law No. 10, article 2. Height: 175 cm.	U.S.
WEHOFSICH, Franz, Dr.	264625	M	Ger.	13. 3.01	SS-Staff. Professor. Defendant and-or witness in cases involving crimes against humanity and-or war crimes as defined in Control Council Law No. 10, article 2. Height: 191 cm.	U.S.
WEISS	266616	M	Ger.		Participated in the organisation of the Black Market in France, to the profit of Germany, thus proceeding to the looting of the French economy. Purchases Paris - France 42-44.	FR.

WEL - ZWA

NAME	C.R. FILE NUMBER	SEX	NATIO-NALITY	DATE OF BIRTH	ALL AVAILABLE INFORMATION AS TO THE RANK, OCCUPATION (CIVIL, PARTY OR MILITARY), PARTICULARS OF CRIME AND PHYSICAL DESCRIPTION - IF KNOWN.	WANTED BY
WELZ, Matthaeus	264626	M	Ger.	4. 6.00	SS-Sturmbannfhr., manager of a land estate. Defendant and-or witness in cases involving crimes against humanity and-or war crimes as defined in Control Council Law No. 10, article 2. Height: 171 cm.	U.S.
WINKLER, Arnim	264554	M	Ger.	9. 4.05	Sturmbannfhr., commercial employee. Defendant and-or witness in cases involving crimes against humanity and-or war crimes as defined in Control Council No. 10, article 2.	U.S.
WINOGRADOW, Peter	263517	M	Ger.		Suspected of having, on September 4. and 5.,1944, at Nieppe (Nord) killed wounded persons and participated in the murder of 17 persons. Probably Co.No. 301 SS. Nieppe Nord-France. D.O.C. 5.9.44.	FR.
WOEIBING, Fritz	264568	M	Ger.	30.10.06	SS-Sturmbannfhr., engaged in agriculture. Defendant and-or witness in cases involving crimes against humanity and-or war crimes as defined in Control Council Law No. 10, article 2. Height: 183 cm.	U.S.
WOLF	266664	M	Ger.		Guilty of having tortured and executed 13 inhabitants on Sept.4, 1944 at Hesmond (P.d.C.) Artl.Regt.	FR.
WOLFF, Ludwig	264569	M	Ger.	4. 8.08	SS-Staf., theologian. Defendant and-or witness in cases involving crimes against humanity and-or war crimes as defined in Control Council Law No. 10, Article 2. Height: 176 cm.	U.S.
WOLKERSDORFER, Sepp (see WOLKESTORFER)	264566					
WOLKESTORFER, Sepp (or WOLKERSDORFER)	264566	M	Ger.	1. 9.05	SS-Sturmbannfhr., hatter. Defendant and-or witness in cases involving crimes against humanity and-or war crimes as defined in Control Council Law No. 10, Article 2. Height: 170 cm. Hair: fair. Eyes: brown.	U.S.
WOLLANG, Helmut	264567	M	Ger.	26. 9.01	SS-Sturmbannfhr., commercial employee. Defendant and-or witness in cases involving crimes against humanity and-or war crimes as defined in Control Council Law No. 10, Article 2. Height: 182 cm.	U.S.
WULFF, Ernst	264571	M	Ger.	1. 3.00	SS-Staf., merchant. Defendant and-or witness in cases involving crimes against humanity and-or war crimes as defined in Control Council Law No. 10, Article 2. Height: 175 cm.	U.S.
WUSTINGER	266688	M	Ger.		As Policeman he illtreated Polish population.	POL
ZEIDLER, Karol	266690	M	Ger.		Misc.Crimes at C.C., Extermination Camp, Chelmno (Pol.)	POL
ZIESEMER, Willy	264572	M	Ger.	5. 7.10	SS-Sturmbannfhr., interior decorator, commercial artist. Defendant and-or witness in cases involving crimes against humanity and-or war crimes as defined in Control Council Law No. 10, Article 2. Height: 182 cm.	U.S.
ZIMMERMANN, Heinrich	266590	M	Ger.	9. 9.10	Suspect. Identity disc No 335- 2 Inf.Ers.Bn.15. Last known assignment: Gruppe Geheime Feldpolizei 649 (11.1941). Address of wife: Emmi Zimmermann, Kassel, Albrechtstr.30.	FR.
ZWALIA	266501	M	Ger.		Looting, rapes committed on nine persons. Unit No. 02286.	FR.

ALB - DUK

NAME	C.R.FILE NUMBER	SEX	NATIO-NALITY	DATE OF BIRTH	RANK OCCUPATION UNIT PLACE AND DATE OF CRIME	UNWCC LIST/ SERIAL NO.	REASON WANTED	WANTED BY
ALBRECHT,Franz	265347	M	Aust.	28.11.89	Member,Gestapo,Maribor,Trbovlje and other districts in that part of Slovenia (Yugo.) 41-45	-	MURDER	YUGO.
AMORI	308705	M	Ital.		Pvt.,Carabinieri section of the "Cremona" Div.,Petreto-Biccisano,Ajaccio (Corsica) (Fr.) 43	60/3	MURDER	FR.
ANGERER,Karl	265332	M	Aust.-Ger.	circa 07	Chief,Gendarmerie Station,Pisece (Yugo.) 11.7.43	-	MURDER	YUGO.
ARTIS	308760	M	Ital.		Lt.,Bn."Nizza",Menton (Alpes Maritimes) (Fr.) 29.8.44	60/8	MURDER	FR.
ATZBERGER,Hans	265362	M	Aust.-Ger.	circa 10	Cpl.,German Army,Strzisce (Yugo.) 22.2.45	-	MURDER	YUGO.
BACHER,Konstantin	265363	M	Aust.-Ger.		Chief,Gendarmerie,Medvode (Yugo.) 21.10.43	-	MISC.CRIMES	YUGO.
BACHINGER,Johann	267136	M	Aust.-Ger.	17.10.06	Chief and SS-Mann,Gestapo and SS in the village of Radovljica (Yugo.) 42-44	-	MURDER	YUGO.
BAEUMANN,Eduard	265345	M	Aust.	16. 3.16	Member,Gestapo,Maribor,Trbovlje and other parts of Slovenia (Yugo.) 41-45	-	MURDER	YUGO.
BARTOLI	308720	M	Ital.		Attached to "Nizza" Bn.,Menton (Alpes Maritimes) (Fr.) 29.8.44	-	MURDER	FR.
BAUER,Gottfried	267115	M	Aust.-Ger.	09	Hptwachtmeister,Gendarmerie,St.Jurij on the river Scavnica (Yugo.) 7.42-5.45	-	MURDER	YUGO.
BAUER,Hans Dr.	265343	M	Aust.	5. 6.10	Expositursleiter,Stellvertreter,Politischen Kommissaers at Slovenjfradec.,Landrats fuer Maribor,Trbovlje and other district in that part of Slovenia (Yugo.) 41-45	-	MURDER	YUGO.
BAYER,Gottfried	308725	M	Aust.		Head of the II Dept."Dienststelle des Beauftragten des Reichskommissars f.d.Festigung des Deutschtums in Marburg" the occupied parts of Yugoslavia 41-45	60/25	MISC.CRIMES	YUGO.
BELANI,Peter	304292	M	Ital.		Pvt.,Art.Cuneo Div.from Milan (It.),Kaminia Platanou (Samos) (Grc.) 6.4.43	58/51	MURDER	GRC.
BILOVITZKI,Otto	265338	M	Aust.-Ger.	9. 9. 99	Manager,Secret Agent,Steel works,Gestapo,Ravne (Yugo.) 41-45	-	MISC.CRIMES	YUGO.
BISELLA,Francesco	304304	M	Ital.		Sgt.,Faschist Provincial Republican Army,2 Coy.,42 Bn.,Cortile (Province of Modena) (It.) 1.12.44	-	MURDER	FR.
BLISS	308747	M	Aust.		SS-Usturmfhr.,Head of the V Dept.of the "Dienststelle des Beauftragten des Reichskommissars fuer die Festigung des Deutschtums in Marburg",the occupied parts of Yugoslavian 41-45	60/53	MISC.CRIMES	YUGO.
BOCHINSKI,Pierre	266839	M	Pol.		Sgt.-Major,Army,Liesse (Fr.) 43	-	MISC.CRIMES	FR.
BOEHNISCH,Siegismund	265344	M	Aust.	8.11.09	SS-Oscharfhr.,Sipo and SD,Maribor,Trbovlje and other parts of Slovenia (Yugo.) 43	-	MURDER	YUGO.
BOHM,Josef	267185	M	Aust.	circa 05	Waffenwerkstatt,Chateaumeillant (Fr.) 27.6.44	-	MURDER	FR.
BONINI,Silvio	189907	M	Ital.		Generale-Commandant,Div."Venezia",Berane,Montenegro 41-43	5/71	SUSPECT	YUGO.
BORNEFELD,Wilhelm	265359	M	Aust.-Ger.		Chief,Lt.Col.,Recruiting Commission I,German Army,Kranj (Yugo.) 42-44	-	MISC.CRIMES	YUGO.
BRANDECKER	265331	M	Aust.-Ger.		Capt.,German Army "Nachrichten Coy.",District of Slovenjgrad-l (Yugo.) 8.-11.44	-	MISC.CRIMES	YUGO.
BRANDT,Karl Ludwig	308760	M	Aust.	23. 1.93	SS-Hptsturmfhr.,Head of the 1 Dept.of the "Dienststelle des Beauftragten des Reichskommissars fuer die Festigung des Deutschtums in Marburg",Member of NSDAP,the occupied parts of Yugoslavia 41-45	60/75	MISC.CRIMES	YUGO.
BRANDT,Ludwig	265357	M	Aust.	21. 8.08	Kriminalrat,Sipo and SD,Maribor,Trbovlje and other parts of Slovenia (Yugo.) 43	-	MURDER	YUGO.
BRANDTNER,Franz	265352	M	Aust.-Ger.	28. 9.06	SS-Mann and Crim.Secr.,Sipo and SD,Gestapo,Carinthia and Carniola (Yugo.) 7.42-5.45	-	MURDER	YUGO.
BRAUN,Rudolf	265356	M	Aust.	7. 4.11	Chauffeur of the Kommandant of Sipo and SD,Maribor,Trbovlje and other parts of Slovenia (Yugo.) 43-44	-	MURDER	YUGO.
BRODAR,Aribert Dr.	265361	M	Aust.-Ger.		Wine merchant,Civilian,Ormoz (Yugo.) 41	-	MISC.CRIMES	YUGO.
CARLO,Mario	308773	M	Ital.		Agent,O.V.R.A.,Petreto-Biccisano and Ajaccio,Corsica (Fr.) 43	60/98	MURDER	FR.
CASSABURI,Max	190922	M	Ital.		Commander,Tank Unit,Krstinje,near Vojnic (Yugo.) 9.41	15/246	PILLAGE	YUGO.
CASTILLIONE	308778	M	Ital.		Lt.,21 Regt.of the 3 Inf.Bn.,107 Coy.,Petreto-Biccisano and Ajaccio,Corsica (Fr.) 43	60/103	MURDER	FR.
CAVINO,Satto	304125	M	Ital.		Brigadiere,Chief,Isthmia Carabinieri (Corinth) 10.41	58/125	MURDER	GRC.
CECCARINI,Alfredo	304126	M	Ital.		Carabiniere,Samos Carabinieri from Milan (It.),Maratho-Kambos 8.42-8.43	58/126	MURDER	GRC.
CERMAK,Mirko (or TSCHERMACK)	265354	M	Aust.	12. 1.97	Member,Gestapo at Ljutomer,Maribor,Trbovlje and other parts of Slovenia (Yugo.) 41-45	-	MURDER	YUGO.
CHIACHI (see TCHACHI)	309111							
CICHETTI	190928	M	Ital.		Director,C.C.Montalbano (Rovezzano-Firenze) 41-43	15/252	TORTURE	YUGO.
COCCO,Giuseppe	308522	M	Ital.	18 or 19	Pvt.,sentry at P.G.166,Capua 19.4.43	26/14	MURDER	U.Y.
CONCEV,N.	190761	M	Bulg.		Assistant of Police Director at Babusnica,Pirot district (Yugo.) 41-44	15/47	MURDER	YUGO.
CONCINI,Alberto	304128	M	Ital.		Lt.Col.from Lecce-Italy,Leucas 10.-11.42	58/131	TORTURE	GRC.
COREL,Emilio	145691	M	Ital.		Carabiniere,Bde.at Split,Isle of Vis (Yugo.) 43	12/63	MURDER	YUGO.
COSTA,George Petrov	304130	M	Bulg.		Bulgarian Army of occupation,Aesymi-Hevros (Grc.) 41-44	58/134	MURDER	GRC.
DEHAN,Lucien	125024	M	Belg.	9. 3.07	Indicateur,Gestapo,SD,Poitiers-Chateau de Porteau (Fr.) 23.-24.8.44	13/377	MURDER	FR.
DEKA (see DUKA)	62066							
DE LORENZIS (see DE LORENZO)	304143							
DE LORENZO (or DE LORENZIS)	304143	M	Ital.		General,command of the Italian troops stationed at Pietralba Corsica (Fr.) 10.9.43	58/148	MURDER	FR.
DEUTSCHMANN,Josef	267137	M	Aust.or Ger.	9. 2.95	Agent,Gestapo,St.Vid near Ljubljana (Yugo.) 43-45	-	MURDER	YUGO.
DONAV,Willy	265355	M	Aust.	10. 6.19	Member,Gestapo at Brezice,Maribor,Trbovlje and other parts of Slovenia (Yugo.) 41-45	-	MURDER	YUGO.
DROESSEMEIER	308880	M	Aust.		Reichsoberinspector,Head of the Hauptkanzlei,chief of the Dienststelle d.Beauftragten d.Reichskommissars f.Festigung d.Deutschtums in Marburg,occupied parts Yugoslavia 41-45	60/132	MISC.CRIMES	YUGO.
DUKA (or DEKA)	62066	M	Rum.		Agent,Gestapo,Marseille (Fr.)	-	SUSPECT	FR.

DUN - LUJ

NAME	C.R.FILE NUMBER	SEX	NATIO-NALITY	DATE OF BIRTH	RANK OCCUPATION UNIT PLACE AND DATE OF CRIME	UNWCC LIST/ SERIAL NO.	REASON WANTED	WANTED BY
DUNKEL, Hermann	265358	M	Aust.	23. 6.06	Chief,Enlistment Department, Deputy of the Landrat,Maribor, Trbovlje and other parts of Slovenia (Yugo.) 41-45	-	MURDER	YUGO.
ERNESTO	308889	M	Ital.		Cpl., Bn.Nizza, Menton-Alpes Maritimes (Fr.) 29.8.44	60/146	MURDER	FR.
FABRI	198164	M	Ital.		Capt.,Coy.-Commander of the 63.Tagliamento-Bn., Varallo Prov.Vercelli, 15.4.44	39/2	MURDER	YUGO.
FALCONE, Emilio	197817	M	Ital.		Col.,Praesident, Military, Tribunal Military di Guerra, Susak (Yugo.) 41-43	26/56	MURDER	YUGO.
FELL, Johann	267138	M	Aust.or Ger.		Hptwachtmeister, Gendarmerie, in the village of Smartno ob Dreti,Smartno ob Paki,Velog and Bocna and Gornji Grad (Yugo.) 10.10.44, 12.12.44	-	MURDER	YUGO.
FERRUCCI, Nicola	308696	M	Ital.		Sgt.,stationed at P.G.66,Capua (Ital.) 19.4.43	26/1	MURDER	U.K.
FLUCH, Ulrich	267125	M	Aust.or Ger.	23. 6.07	Gendarmeriepostenfuehrer, Gendarmerie,St.Marjeta on the river Pesnica (Yugo.) 7.44-2.45	-	MISC.CRIMES	YUGO.
FRANZEK	267411	M	Pol.or Czech.		SS-Guard, C.C. Struthof-Natzweiler (Fr.) 40-45	-	MURDER	FR.
FREISINGER, I	267117	M	Aust.or Ger.	circa 00	Gendarmeriepostenfuehren, Gendarmerie, Velenje (Yugo.) 43-44	-	MISC.CRIMES	YUGO.
FREISINGER, Leopold	267410	M	Aust.	circa 07	Cpl., Feldgendarmerie, d'Avallon (Fr.) 44	-	MISC.CRIMES	FR.
FREY, Fritz	185125	M	Aust.or Ger.		Chief of block, C.C. Oranienburg, Sachsenhausen (Ger.)	32/207	PILLAGE	FR.
GAM	265334	M	Aust.or Ger.		Major, German Army, Sumetldica nr.Nova Gradiska (Yugo.) 28.7.43	-	INTERR.	YUGO.
GAMBARA, Gastone	149473	M	Ital.		General, took over command of XI.Army Corps from General Robotti, Prov.of Ljubljana, 41-43	5/88	MURDER	YUGO.
GASPARRE	266849	M	Aust.	circa 00	Capt., Airforce, Courier section, Avallon (Fr.) 8.7.40	-	PILLAGE	FR.
GIOLA	308834	M	Ital.		Pvt., Carabinieri section of the "Cremona"-Div.,Petreto-Biccisano and Ajaccio,Corsica (Fr.) 43	60/208	MURDER	FR.
GIUNTA, Francesco	193551	M	Ital.		Governor, Dalmatia (Yugo.) 2.-7.43	2/34	MURDER	YUGO.
GODOVEZE, Henny (see GOODVEZE)	266306							
GOODVEZE, Henny (or GODOVEZE)	266306	F	Dut.	circa 23	Chief, Block, Neubrandenburg (Ger.) 44	-	MURDER	FR.
GORCILOV	189968	M	Bulg.		Capt.,O.C. the Bulg.troops in Pirot, Chief of Intelligence Service Pirot, Liaison-Officer with Gestapo, Pirot (Yugo.) 41-12.3.43, 8.43	5/8	MISC.CRIMES	YUGO.
GOUSGOUNOV, Mavri	304200	M	Bulg.		Bulgarian Army, Aesymi-Hevros (Grc.) 41-44	58/245	MURDER	GRC.
GRAZIOLI, Emilio	147290	M	Ital.		Alto Commissario, Prov.of Ljubljana (Yugo.)	2/35.	MURDER	YUGO.
GRILLO, Marcel	144536	M	Ital.	21. 9.04	Agent, Gestapo, Chalons s.Saone (Fr.)	-	SUSPECT	FR.
HADJISKI	190766	M	Bulg.		Lt.Col., Cdr.of Garrison,Surdulica Jelasnica (Yugo.) 21.10.43	15/52	MURDER	YUGO.
HADZI-ILIJEV, Boja	189967	M	Bulg.		Lt.,Bulg.Army Res., Golo Selo,Trsteno (Yugo.)	5/9	MURDER	YUGO.
HAJNAL, Vitez	189937	M	Hung.		Officer, O.C. Hung.Unit,Senta (Yugo.)	5/39	MURDER	YUGO.UNWCC
HALASCHA	185110	M	Czech.		Political prisoner, C.C. Dachau (Ger.)	25/922	MURDER	FR.
HANKIS	304698	M	Hung.		Wachtmann, Member, Sipo Einsatz-Kdo.,SD-Wachtzug,Steenwijk, Steenwijkerwold,Kallenkote (Neth.) 2.,13.10.44	59/230	MURDER	NETH.
HASSBIMGER, Andre	266774	M	Rum.		Member, Sipo, SD Perigueux Gestapo, Dordogne (Fr.) 43-44	-	SUSPECT	FR.
HEEGER	266535	M	Aust.	circa 87	Capt., Paris, au chateau de Vincennes (Fr.) 8.44	-	MURDER	FR.
HOLZHAUSER, Arnold	267476	M	Lux.		Oscharfhr., Gestapo, St.Etienne and Departm.Loire and Adreche (Fr.) 43-44	-	MURDER	FR.
HORRATH	265754	M	Hung.		Chief,Col.Group XXI Ministry of the Honveds,Hungarian Army, Command of POW Camp, Famosmikola (Hung.) 41-44	-	MISC.CRIMES	POL.
HUBERT, Josef	265335	M	Aust.or Ger.		Commandant, Gendarmerie, Praprotno nr.Skofja Loka (Yugo.) 1.43-5.45	-	MISC.CRIMES	YUGO.
IWANIENKO	265717	M	Ukr.		SS-Mann, Guard, Amunition Factory, Skarzysk (Pol.)	-	BRUTALITY	POL.
JACOBS (or JAKOBS)	304756	M	Bel.		Guard, Member, Sipo Einsatz-Kdo. Steenwijk,Steenwijkerwold nr.Steenwijk,Kallenkote (Neth.) 2.and 13.10.44	59/295	MURDER	NETH.
JAKOBS (see JACOBS)	304756							
JANES	265725	M	Latv.		Zugwachtmeister, C.C. Plaszow (Pol.)	-	MURDER	POL.
JAROSCH	267119	M	Aust.or Ger.		Cpl.,Chief, Gestapo, Sinj (Yugo.) 8.9.43-10.44	-	MURDER	YUGO.
JEGER, Sascha	265712	M	Ukr.		Zugwachmann, Guard, Extermination Camp,Treblinka (Pol.) 42-43	-	MISC.CRIMES	POL.
KAJSER, Alex	265857	M	Russ.or Ger.	22	Interpreter, Chief, Extermination Camp, Sobibor (Pol.) 42-43	-	BRUTALITY	POL.
KALOVIANEV, George	304244	M	Bulg.		Asst. to the Mayor of Aesymi-Hevros, 41-44	58/345	MURDER	GRC.
KAMARADOWSKI, Joseph, Jos	265407	M	Pol.		Interpreter, Gestapo, SD Bayonne and vicinity (Fr.) 40-44	-	MURDER	FR.
KARAVICH, Ornik or Danes	304160	M	Bulg.		Pvt.,Bulgarian Army of Occupation, Aesymi-Hevros (Grc.) 41-44	58/349	MURDER	GRC.
KAREL, Augustin Ing.	267140	M	Aust.or Ger.		Councillor, Coal-Mining Establishment Civ.,Trbovlje (Yugo.) 41-45	-	MURDER	YUGO.
KIRTCHEV, Kostas	304167	M	Bulg.		Bulgarian Army of Occupation, Aesymi-Hevros (Grc.) 41-44	58/359	MURDER	GRC.
KOLINKA	266515	M	Pol.		Interpreter, C.C. Buchloe (Ger.)	-	BRUTALITY	FR.
KOMARNICKI, Bogdan	265850	M	Ukr.	13	Informer,Prisoner,Chief of the political section Grabner, C.C. Auschwitz (Pol.)	-	MISC.CRIMES	POL.
KOSTEIN, Stephen	266282	M	Rum.	08	SS-Mann, Gestapo, Nantes and region, (Fr.) 43-44	-	MURDER	FR.
KOUVATCHEV, Stephen	304260	M	Bulg.		Lt.,Town-Major of Aesymi-Hevros (Grc.) 41-44	58/389	MURDER	GRC.
KUPPER, Hermann	267150	M	Swiss		Interpreter, Gestapo, Marseille and vicinity (Fr.)	-	MURDER	FR.
KUTSCHERA, Alois	266886	M	Czech.		Chief of culture,Herbenval (Fr.) 41-44	-	MISC.CRIMES	FR.
LAZIO	308934	M	Ital.		Pvt. attached to 2.Alpine Regt. 30.Bn. 128.Coy,Digne-Basses Alpes (Fr.) 13.1.43	60/364	MURDER	FR.
LEINZE	304892	M	Bel.		Guard, Member, Secr.Police,Einsatzkommando Steenwijk,Steen- wijkerwold nr.Steenwijk,Kallenkote (Neth.) 2.and 13.10.44	59/387	MURDER	NETH.
LENHOFF, Alexandre	266219	M	Yugo.	circa 15	SS-Mann, Gestapo, Nantes and region (Fr.) 43-44	-	MURDER	FR.
LICATA, Giannantonio	304277	M	Ital.		Lt.,National Republican Guard, Reggio Emilia (It.) 10.11.44	58/422	MURDER	U.S.
LICATA	308940	M	Ital.		attached to "Nizza" Bn., Menton-Alpes Maritimes (Fr.) 29.8.44	60/373	MURDER	FR.
LINDNER, Otto	266218	M	Lux.		Manager of Culture, Poix-Terron (Fr.) 43-44	-	MISC.CRIMES	FR.
LOCH	265842	M	Ukr.		Zugwachmann, C.C. Treblinka (Pol.)	-	MURDER	POL.
LUJANOVITS, Gyorgelm	265888	M	Hung.		Capt.,Hungarian Army,Command-POW Camp,Femoskimowa (Hung.)	-	BRUTALITY	POL.

NAME	C.R.FILE NUMBER	SEX	NATIO-NALITY	DATE OF BIRTH	RANK OCCUPATION UNIT PLACE AND DATE OF CRIME	UNWCC LIST/ SERIAL NO.	REASON WANTED	WANTED BY
MAGLI, Guido (or MALDI)	308993	M	Ital.		Commandant of the Blackshirt-Bn."Nizza",Menton, Alpes-Maritimes (Fr.) 29.8.44	60/389	MURDER	FR.
MAJORIS	304929	M	Serb.		Guard,Wachtzug of the Sipo,Einsatzkommando Steenwijk, Zwartsluis,Steenwijker-wold-Kallenkote (Neth.)2.6.8.13.10.44	59/423	MURDER	NETH.
MALDI, Guido (see MAGLI)	308993							
MARANCHI	267219	M	Ital.		Pvt., Army, 4.Coy.,Bn.St.Marc,Toulon (Fr.) 7.5.43	-	MURDER	FR.
MARIANI	308996	M	Ital.		Pvt.,2.Alpine Regt.,30 Bn.,128.Coy., Digne-Basses-Alpes (Fr.) 13.1.43	60/394	MURDER	FR.
MARIANI, Umberto (see MARIONDO)	308997							
MARIONDO, Umberto (or MARIANI)	308997	M	Ital.		Capt., Petreto-Biccisano,Ajaccio,Corsica (Fr.) 43	60/395	MURDER	FR.
MARTZ, Josef	266098	M	Hung.		Capt.,Hung.Army, Member, P.O.W.Camp-Command,Siklos(Hung.)	-	MISC.CRIMES	POL.
MEERHEIN, Jone	266109	M	Hung.		Lt., Cmdt., Hung.Army, Int. Camp,Paski,Mosenmogyarowar (Hung.)	-	MISC.CRIMES	POL.
MEGAY, Laszlo, Dr.	265383	M	Hung.	11. 3.02	City Mayor, Civilian, Komarno (Czech.) 44-45	-	MISC.CRIMES	CZECH.
MIRKU	304964	M	Rum.or Hung.		Guard,member,Sipo, Einsatzkommando Steenwijk,Steenwijker-wold, Kallenkote (Neth.) 2.and 13.10.44	59/463	MURDER	NETH.
MOSER	266137	M	Fr.		Kapo, Extermination Camp, C.C.,Lublin-Majdanek (Pol.)	-	MURDER	POL.
MAII, Lorenzo	265302	M	Ital.		Pvt.(Guard),842.Frontier Guard Btty.1.Repatriation Coy., P.W.Camp 153, Suani Ben Adem (It.) 7.42	-	SUSPECT	U.K.
MUBER, Ludwig	309028	M	Aust.		Head of the F.Department (Landed Property and Economical Statistics), Reichsinspektor of the Dienststelle d.Beauftragten d.Reichskommissars fuer die Festigung des Deutschtums in Marburg,Occupied parts of Yugoslavia, 41-45	60/445	MISC.CRIMES	YUGO.
PACKERNIETH (or PATCHNEK or PATCHNECK)	37972	M	Aust.or Ger.	15	Sgt., Army, Staff of Working Party at Groppenstein of Wolfsberg Prison Camp, Groppenstein (Aust.) 42	-	BRUTALITY	U.K.
PATCHNECK (see PACKERNIETH)	37972							
PATCHNEK (see PACKERNIETH)	37972							
PERTL, Johann	265351	M	Aust.or Ger.	circa 10	Oberwachtmeister, Gendarmerie, Litija (Yugo.) 44-45	-	MURDER	YUGO.
PILLASCH, Willy	267163	M	Pol.		Member, Oscharfhr., Sonder-Kdo. A.S.,Gestapo,Marseille and vicinity (Fr.)	-	MURDER	FR.
PINIA	309036	M	Ital.		Pvt.,Petreto-Biccisano and Ajaccio,Corsica (Fr.) 43	60/463	MURDER	FR.
PIVA	304359	M	Ital.		Cpl.,2.Coy.42.Bn.of the Provincial Fascist Republican Army,Cortile,Province of Modena (It.) 1.12.44	58/519	MURDER	FR.
PRIANTSOV, Alexis	304361	M	Bulg.		Asst. to the mayor at Aesymi. Aesymi-Hevros (Grc.)41-44	58/526	MURDER	GRC.
PULLARAJO	303021	M	Russ.		Private serving, German-Polish-Unit,Luijksgestel (Neth.)8.9.44	56/660	MURDER	NETH.
PUSCEDO	309044	M	Ital.		Cpl., "Nizza" Bn., Menton,Alpes-Maritimes (Fr.)29.8.44	60/473	MURDER	FR.
RASVANIKOF, Vladimir	304369	M	Bulg.		President of the Community of Neon Kavakli-Rhodope (Bulg.)44	58/535	MURDER	GRC.
RICO, Ernesto	309052	M	Ital.		Lt. belonged to a "Black Shirt" unit,stationed in Folelle, commune of Penta-di-Casinca,Castellare-di-Casinca,Korsika (Fr.) 26.3.43	60/492	BRUTALITY	FR.
RIFA	309055	M	Ital.		Pvt.,telephonist,"Black Shirt" unit stationed in Folelle,commune of Penta-di-Casinca (Corsica),Castellare-di-Casinca (Fr.)26.3.43	60/495	BRUTALITY	FR.
RIVA, Antonio	309056-	M	Ital.		Pvt., Royal carabinieri, 29 th Bn.,Petreto-Biccisano and at Ajaccio,Corsica (Fr.) 43	60/496	MURDER	FR.
RIZZO	309057	M	Ital.		Pvt.,2.Alpine Regt. 30.Bn.128.Coy.,Digne,Basses-Alpes (Fr.)13.1.43	60/497	MURDER	FR.
ROSSI, Romeo	309063	M	Ital.		Pvt.,carabinieri section of the "Gremona" Div., Petreto-Biccisano and at Ajaccio (Corsica) (Fr.) 43	60/505	MURDER	FR.
RUFFINI	309067	M	Ital.		Brigadier, agent of carabinieri,O.V.R.A. 2.Coy. of the 29.Bn. of the carabiners,Petreto-Biccisano,Ajaccio(Corsica)(Fr.)43	60/512	MURDER	FR.
RUZZI, Vincenzo	265236	M	Ital.	12	Capt.,Italian Republican Army,Monte Rosa Div.,Carasco(It.)10.44	-	SUSPECT	U.K.
SANTANTONIC	304391	M	Ital.		Carabiniere attached to 1.Bde.stationed at Levie (Fr.)6.43	58/569	BRUTALITY	FR.
SCHABO, Janos (or SZABO)	266462	M	Hung.		Member, Sgt.,Staff, Hung.Army,POW Camp-Command,Komarom (Hung.) 41-44	-	BRUTALITY	PCL.
SCHNEIDER	265550	M	Russ.or Ger.		Extermination camp, Belzec (Pol.)	-	MURDER	POL.
SCHULZ	266383	M	Ukr.		Zugwachmann,Guard,Extermination camp,Treblinka (Pol.) 42-43	-	BRUTALITY	POL.
SCHULZ, Hermann	266340	M	Russ.or Ger.		Sgt., Bn.Georgian,Coleyrac St.Cirq (Fr.) 14.-23.8.44	-	MURDER	FR.
SCHUMCHUT, Servais	265958	M	Lux.		Chief of Culture, Chalandry (Fr.) 40-44	-	MISC.CRIMES	FR.
SEVI	309087	M	Ital.		Member, attached to the "Nizza" Bn.,Menton,Alpes-Marit.(Fr.)44	60/585	MURDER	FR.
SLATEF, Stephan	304430	M	Bulg.		S-Major of Gendarmerie,Neon Kavakli-Rhodope (Grc.)42-44	58/632	MURDER	GRC.
SMITH, Louis	266863	M	Pol.		Feldgendarmerie,Feldgendarmerie,Nord,Pas de Calais (Fr.)41-44	-	MURDER	FR.
STEFANI	309101	M	Ital.		Member,attached to "Nizza"-Bn,Menton, Alpes-Marit.(Fr.)29.8.44	60/602	MURDER	FR.
STEINER	267362	M	Aust.		Cpl.,Waffenwerkstatt 812,Chateaumeillant (Fr.) 27.6.44	-	MURDER	FR.
STOEFFEL (or STOFFEL)	267359	M	Bel.	circa 92	Interpreter, Gestapo, Marseille (Fr.)	-	MURDER	FR.
STOFFEL (see STOEFFEL)	267359							
STALLA, Alojzy	266388	M	Czech.		Member, Kripo, Trzebinia (Pol.) 43-45	-	MISC.CRIMES	POL.
SWACK	304445	M	Pol.	90	Brigadier of customs Zollsturm 6.Bn.3.Coy,Alpes-Maritimes (Fr.) 12.8.44	58/660	MURDER	FR.
SZABO, Janos (see SCHABO)	266462							
TCHACHI (or CHIACHI)	309111	M	Ital.		Pvt.,Army,Inf.Regt.21.,3.Bn.,107.Coy.of Machine Gunners, Petreto-Biccisano and Ajaccio,Corsica (Fr.) 43	60/617	MURDER	FR.
THURANSZKY, Arno	266480	M	Hung.		Capt.,Commandant, Hung.Army, P.O.W.Camp,Vamoskimola(Hung.)41-44	-	MISC.CRIMES	POL.
TROMI	309129	M	Ital.		Member, attached to "Nizza" Bn.,Menton(Alpes-Marit.)(Fr.)29.8.44	60/627	MURDER	FR.
TROTTA	309121	M	Ital.		Lt., "Nizza-Bn"., Menton (Alpes-Marit.) (Fr.) 29.8.44	60/628	MURDER	FR.
TSATSEF, Tsutso	304435	M	Bulg.		Mayor at Kavakli-Comotini (Bulg.)41-42	-	MISC.CRIMES	GRC.
TCCHURNACK,Marko (see CERNAK)	265354							
TURCHI, Ido	304456	M	Ital.		Member,38.Fire Bde.,Grosseto (It.) 26.4.43	58/681	MURDER	U.S.
VAN WEZZEL, Arrens	266711	M	Dutch	circa 03	Chief, Chamber of Trade, Lublin (Pol.)	-	MISC.CRIMES	POL.
VELIMI	309127	M	Ital.		Attached to "Nizza" Bn.,Menton Alpes-Maritimes (Fr.)29.8.44	60/635	MURDER	FR.
VERONESE, Luigi	265393	M	Ital.	24. 8.01	Officer in P.O.W.Camp,Cesano Moderno (It.)10.7.43	-	MURDER	FR.

VLA - ZIG

NAME	C.R.FILE NUMBER	SEX	NATIONALITY	DATE OF BIRTH	RANK	OCCUPATION	UNIT	PLACE AND DATE OF CRIME	UNWCC LIST/ SERIAL NO.	REASON WANTED	WANTED BY
VLATOWSKI, Paul (see WILATOWSKI)	266796										
VON ANHEIM, Baron (see VON ARNHEIM)	265333										
VON ARNHEIM, Baron (or VON ANHEIM)	265333	M	Dan.			Commandant, Army, 4 Coy., SS-Div."Hermann Goering", Landeck (Ger.) 2.45			-	MURDER	YUGO.
VOTTA	309131	M	Ital.			Attached to "Nizza-Bn.", Menton, Alpes-Maritimes (Fr.) 29.8.44			60/642	MURDER	FR.
VRECKO, Rudolf	309132	M	Yugo.			Hospital-attendant, Prison-Hospital, Kraisheim (Ger.) 44-45			60/643	TORTURE	BEL.
WASSERMANN, Mathias	265353	M	Aust.or Ger.	circa 95		Lt., Gendarmerie, Litija (Yugo.) 44-45			-	MURDER	YUGO.
WILATOWSKI, Paul (or VLATOWSKI)	266796	M	Pol.			Agent, Gestapo, Valenciennes (Fr.) 9.7.44			-	MURDER	FR.
ZAHAROF, Andreas	304484	M	Bulg.			President, Community, Nea Kallisti-Rhodope (Bulg.) 44			58/738	BRUTALITY	GRC.
ZECCHINA	309155	M	Ital.			Attached to "Nizza-Bn.", Menton, Alpes-Maritimes (Fr.) 44			60/692	MURDER	FR.
ZIGRAND, Carl	309158	M	Lux.			Guard, Heerenveen and Doniaga (Neth.) 45			60/696	MURDER	NETH.

www.ingramcontent.com/pod-product-compliance
Lightning Source LLC
Chambersburg PA
CBHW081436300426
44108CB00017BA/2386